ENCYCLOPÆDIA
BRITANNICA

MACROPÆDIA

Encyclopædia Britannica
published with the editorial advice
of the faculties of the University of Chicago;
a committee of persons holding
academic appointments at the universities
of Oxford, Cambridge, London, and Edinburgh;
a committee at the University of Toronto;
and committees drawn from members of the faculties
of the University of Tokyo
and the Australian National University.

THE UNIVERSITY OF CHICAGO

"Let knowledge grow from more to more
and thus be human life enriched."

The New Encyclopædia Britannica

in 30 Volumes

MACROPÆDIA
Volume 9

Knowledge in Depth

FOUNDED 1768
15 TH EDITION

Encyclopædia Britannica, Inc.
William Benton, Publisher, 1943–1973
Helen Hemingway Benton, Publisher, 1973–1974

Chicago
Auckland/Geneva/London/Manila/Paris/Rome
Seoul/Sydney/Tokyo/Toronto

First Edition	1768-1771
Second Edition	1777-1784
Third Edition	1788-1797
Supplement	1801
Fourth Edition	1801-1809
Fifth Edition	1815
Sixth Edition	1820-1823
Supplement	1815-1824
Seventh Edition	1830-1842
Eighth Edition	1852-1860
Ninth Edition	1875-1889
Tenth Edition	1902-1903

Printed in U.S.A.

Library of Congress Catalog Card Number: 82-84048
International Standard Book Number: 0-85229-413-1

Humidity, Atmospheric

Atmospheric humidity is the amount of water vapour, or moisture, in the air. On a weather chart it is related to the source of an air mass and its potential for storms; in a newspaper it is related to the comfort of the reader. Humidity is usually combined with temperature and ventilation to state the condition of the air because it is the most variable factor in the atmosphere, and it is important in both weather and biology.

At 30° C (86° F) 4 percent of the volume of the air may be occupied by water molecules. But where the air is colder than −40° C (−40° F), less than one-fifth of 1 percent of the air molecules can be water. Although the water vapour content may vary from one air parcel to another, these limits can be set because vapour capacity is determined by temperature. Temperature has profound effects upon some of the indices of humidity regardless of the presence or absence of vapour.

The connection between an effect of humidity and an index of humidity requires simultaneous introduction of effects and indices. Vapour in the air is a determinant of weather because it first absorbs the thermal radiation that leaves and cools the Earth and then emits thermal radiation that warms the Earth. Calculation of absorption and emission requires an index of the mass of water in a volume of air. Vapour also affects the weather because it condenses into clouds, and falls as rain or snow. Tracing the moisture-bearing air masses requires a humidity index that changes only when water is removed or added. Finally, the cooling effect of perspiration, the transpiration of water by vegetation, and evaporation from reservoirs is proportional to humidity differences.

For these reasons there are many means of expressing the water vapour content of the atmosphere. This article treats these indices and the relevance of humidity in climate and human affairs. For further information on these latter aspects see CLOUDS; PRECIPITATION; and CLIMATE.

HUMIDITY INDICES

Absolute humidity. Absolute humidity is the vapour concentration or density in the air. If m_v is the mass of vapour in a volume of air, then absolute humidity d_v is simply $d_v = m_v/V$, in which V is the volume and d_v is expressed in grams per cubic metre (g/m³). This index indicates how much vapour a beam of radiation must pass through. It also indicates the amount of water that can be extracted from the constant volume of air passing over a refrigerator coil or a cold carburetor. The ultimate standard in humidity measurement is made by weighing the amount of water gained by an absorber when a known volume of air passes through it, and this measures absolute humidity, which may vary from 0 g/m³ in dry air to 30 g/m³ when the vapour is saturated at 30° C. The d_v of a parcel of air changes, however, with temperature or pressure even though no water is added or removed because, as the gas equation states, the volume V increases with the absolute or Kelvin temperature and decreases with the pressure.

Specific humidity. The meteorologist requires an index of humidity that does not change with pressure or temperature. A property of this sort will identify an air mass when it is cooled or when it rises to lower pressures aloft without losing or gaining water vapour. Because all the gases will expand equally, the ratios of the weight of water to the weight of dry air, or the dry air plus vapour, will be conserved during such changes and will continue identifying the air mass.

The mixing ratio r is the dimensionless ratio $r = m_v/m_a$, where m_a is the mass of dry air, and the specific humidity q is another dimensionless ratio $q = m_v/(m_a + m_v)$. Because m_v is less than 3 percent of m_a at normal pressure and temperatures cooler than 30° C, r and q are practically equal. These indices are usually expressed in grams per kilogram (g/kg) because they are so small; the values range from 0 in dry air to 28 g/kg in saturated air at 30° C. Absolute and specific humidity indices have specialized uses, and so they are not familiar to most people.

Relative humidity. Relative humidity (U) is so commonly used that a statement of humidity, without a qualifying adjective, can be assumed to be relative humidity. U can be defined, then, in terms of the mixing ratio r that was introduced above. $U = 100r/r_w$, which is a dimensionless percentage. The divisor r_w is the saturation mixing ratio, or the vapour capacity. Relative humidity is, therefore, the water vapour content of the air relative to its content at saturation. Because the saturation mixing ratio is a function of pressure, and especially of temperature, the relative humidity is a combined index of the environment that reflects more than water content. In many climates the relative humidity rises to about 100 percent at dawn and falls to 50 percent by noon. A relative humidity of 50 percent may reflect many different quantities of vapour per volume of air or gram of air, and it will not likely be proportional to evaporation.

An understanding of relative humidity therefore requires a knowledge of saturated vapour, which will be discussed later in the section on the relation between temperature and humidity. But at this point the relation between U and the absorption and retention of water from the air must be considered. Small pores retain water more strongly than large pores; thus, when a porous material is set out in the air, all pores larger than a certain size (which can be calculated from the relative humidity of the air) are dried out.

The water content of a porous material at air temperature is fairly well indicated by the relative humidity. The complexity of actual pore sizes and the viscosity of the water passing through them makes the relation between U and moisture in the porous material imperfect and slowly achieved. The great suction also strains the walls of the capillaries, and the consequent shrinkage is used to measure relative humidity.

Development of the hygrometer

Leonardo da Vinci used a porous hygrometer, a ball of wool that became moister and heavier as the relative humidity rose. The commonest hygrometer of porous material, however, is the hair hygrometer introduced in 1783 by Horace B. de Saussure. When a hair is moved from an atmosphere of 100 percent to one of zero percent relative humidity, it shrinks about 2.5 percent of its length. The change in length per change of relative humidity U is proportional to $1/U$. This decreasing response at high humidity is compensated by cams that make the needle change regularly with humidity, and the hair hygrometer is eminently practical, even if somewhat inaccurate.

The absorption of water by salt solutions is also related to relative humidity without much effect of temperature. The air above water saturated with sodium chloride is maintained at 75 to 76 percent relative humidity, at a temperature between 0° and 40° C (32° and 100° F).

The absorption of water by lithium chloride is the principle of an electrical hygrometer of relative humidity.

Thus, relative humidity is a widely used environmental indicator, but U does respond drastically to changes in temperatures as well as moisture, a response caused by the effect of temperature upon the divisor r_w in U.

RELATION BETWEEN TEMPERATURE AND HUMIDITY

Tables that show the effect of temperature upon the saturation mixing ratio r_w are readily available. Humidity of the air at saturation is expressed more commonly, however, as vapour pressure. Thus, it is necessary to understand vapour pressure and in particular the gaseous nature of water vapour.

The pressure of the water vapour, which contributes to the pressure of the atmosphere, can be calculated from the absolute humidity d_v by the gas equation:

$$e = \frac{m_v}{V}\frac{RT}{M_w} = d_v\frac{RT}{M_w},$$

in which R is the gas constant, T the absolute temperature, M_w the molecular weight of water, and e is water vapour pressure in millibars.

Relative humidity can be defined as the ratio of the vapour pressure of a sample of air to the saturation pressure at the existing temperature. Further, the capacity for vapour and the effect of temperature can now be presented in the usual terms of saturation vapour pressure.

Within a pool of liquid water some molecules are continually escaping from the liquid into the space above, while more and more vapour molecules return to the liquid as the concentration of vapour rises. Finally, equal numbers are escaping and returning, the vapour is then saturated and its pressure is known as the saturation vapour pressure e_w. If the liquid and vapour are warmed, relatively more molecules escape than return, and e_w rises. There is also a saturation pressure with respect to ice. The vapour pressure curve of water has the same form as the curves for many other substances. Its location is fixed, however, by the boiling point of 100° C (212° F), where the saturation vapour pressure of water vapour is 1,013 millibars (mb), the standard pressure of the atmosphere at sea level. The decrease of the boiling point with altitude can be calculated. For example, the saturation vapour pressure at 40° C is 74 mb, standard atmospheric pressure near 18,000 metres (58,860 feet) above sea level is also 74 mb, and that is where water boils at 40° C.

The everyday response of relative humidity to temperature can be easily explained. On a summer morning the temperature might be 15° C (59° F) and the relative humidity 100 percent. The vapour pressure would be 17 mb and the mixing ratio about 11 g/kg. During the day the air could warm to 25° C (77° F), while evaporation added little water. At 25° C the saturation pressure is fully 32 mb. If, however, little water has been added to the air, its vapour pressure will still be about 17 mb. Thus with no change in vapour content, the relative humidity of the air has fallen from 100 to only 53 percent, illustrating why relative humidity does not identify air masses.

On the other hand, porous materials such as cloth will dry between morning and noon, seeking a water content that is in equilibrium with the new relative humidity. Thus the behaviour of porous materials is better indicated by the varying relative humidity than the invariant vapour pressure or mixing ratio; this again illustrates the different utilities of the different indices.

Dew-point temperature. The meaning of dew-point temperature can be illustrated by a sample of air with a vapour pressure of 17 mb. If an object at 15° C is brought into the air, dew will form on the object. Hence, 15° C is the dew-point temperature of the air; that is, the temperature at which the vapour present in a sample of air would just cause saturation, or the temperature whose saturation vapour pressure equals the present vapour pressure in a sample of air, is the dew point. Below freezing, this index is called the frost point. There is a one-to-one correspondence between vapour pressure and dew point, and one serves as well as the other. The dew point has the virtue of being easily interpreted because it is the temperature at which a blade of grass or a pane of glass will become wet with dew from the air. Ideally, it is also the temperature of fog or cloud formation.

The clear meaning of dew point suggests a means of measuring humidity. In 1751 J.B. LeRoy invented a dew-point hygrometer. He added cold water to water in a vessel until dew formed on the vessel, and the temperature of the vessel, the dew point, was a direct index of humidity. The greatest use of the condensation hygrometer has been to measure humidity in the upper atmosphere where a vapour pressure of less than a thousandth millibar makes other means impractical.

The saturation deficit

Another index of humidity, the saturation deficit, can also be understood by considering air with a vapour pressure of 17 mb. At 25° C the air has (31 − 17) or 14 mb less vapour pressure than saturated vapour at the same temperature. Or the saturation deficit is 14 mb.

The saturation deficit has the particular utility of being proportional to the evaporation capability of the air. The saturation deficit can be expressed as

$$e_w - e = e_w\left(1 - \frac{U}{100}\right),$$

and because the saturation vapour pressure e_w rises with rising temperature, the same relative humidity will correspond to a greater saturation deficit and evaporation at warm temperatures.

HUMIDITY AND CLIMATE

The small amount of water in atmospheric vapour, relative to water on the earth, belies its importance. Compared to one unit of water in the air, the seas contain at least 100,000 units, the great glaciers 1,500, the porous earth nearly 200, and rivers and lakes 4 or 5 units. The effectiveness of the vapour in the air is magnified, however, by its role in transferring water from sea to land by the media of clouds and precipitation, and that of absorbing radiation.

The vapour in the air is the invisible conductor that carries water from sea to land, making terrestrial life possible. Fresh water is distilled from the salt seas and carried over land by the wind. Water evaporates from vegetation, and rain falls on the sea, too, but the sea is the bigger source and rain that falls on land is most important to man. The invisible vapour becomes visible near the surface as fog when the air cools to the dew point. The usual nocturnal cooling will produce fog patches in cool valleys. Or the vapour may move as a tropical air mass over cold land or sea, causing widespread and persistent fog, such as occurs over the Grand Banks off Newfoundland. The delivery of water by means of fog or dew is slight, however, and condensation in clouds yields a far greater amount.

When air is lifted it is carried to a region of lower pressure where it will expand and cool as described by the gas equation. It may rise up a mountain slope or over the front of a cooler, denser air mass. If condensation nuclei are absent, the dew point may be exceeded by the cooling air, and the water vapour becomes supersaturated. If nuclei are present or if the temperature is very low, however, cloud droplets or ice crystals form, and the vapour is no longer in the invisible guise of atmospheric humidity.

The invisible vapour has another climatic role, namely, absorbing and emitting radiation. The temperature of the earth and its daily variation is determined by the balance between incoming and outgoing radiation. The wavelength of the incoming radiation from the sun is mostly shorter than three micrometres. It is scarcely absorbed by water vapour and its receipt depends largely upon cloud cover. The radiation exchanged between the atmosphere and earth and the eventual loss to space is in the form of long waves. These long waves are strongly absorbed in the 3 to 8.5 micrometre band and in the greater than

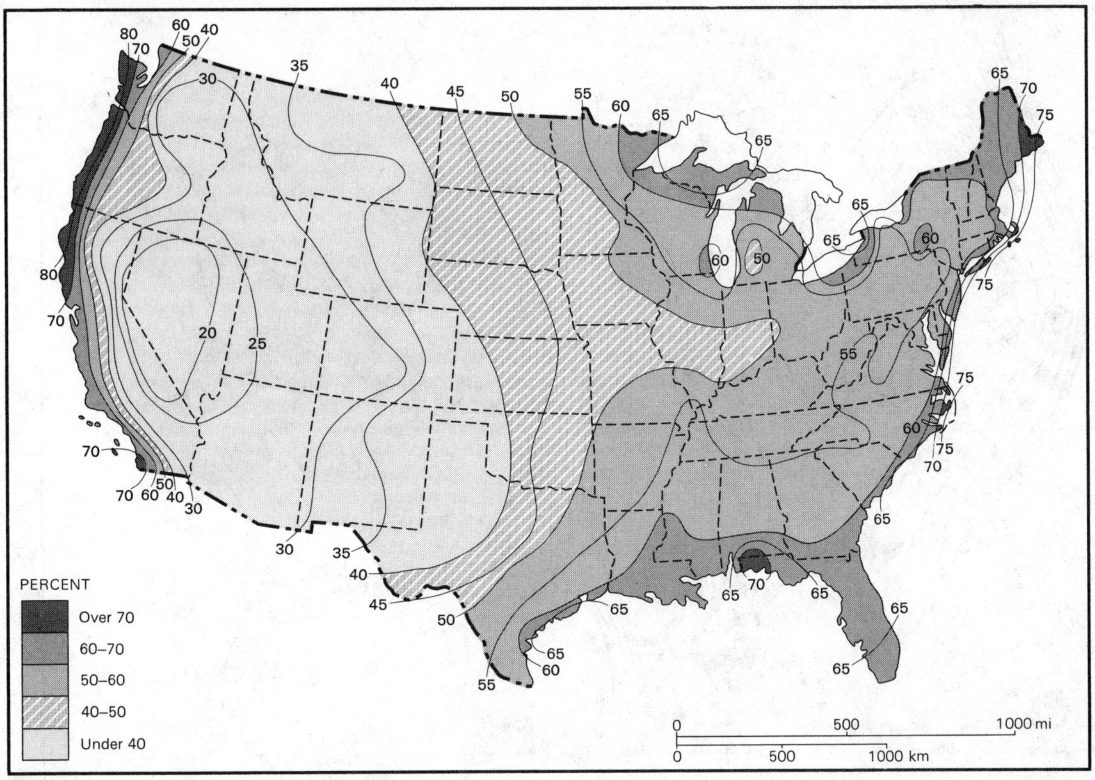

Figure 1: Average relative humidity, local noon, July.

11-micrometre range, where vapour is either partly or wholly opaque. Much of the radiation that is absorbed in the atmosphere is emitted back to earth, and the surface receipt of long waves, primarily from water vapour and carbon dioxide in the atmosphere, is slightly more than twice the direct receipt of solar radiation at the surface. Thus the invisible vapour in the atmosphere combines with clouds and the advection (horizontal movement) of air from different regions to control the surface temperature.

World distribution of humidity

The world distribution of humidity can be portrayed for different uses by different indices. To appraise the quantity of water carried by the entire atmosphere, the moisture in an air column above a given point on earth is expressed as a depth of liquid water. It varies from 0.5 millimetre over the Himalayas and 2 mm over the poles in winter, to 8 mm over the Sahara, 54 mm in the Amazon region, and 64 mm over India during the wet season. During summer, the air over the United States transports 16 mm of water vapour over the Great Basin and 45 mm over Florida.

The humidity of the surface air may be mapped as vapour pressure, but a map of this variable looks much like that of temperature. Warm places are moist and cool ones are dry; even in deserts, the vapour pressure is normally 13 millibars, whereas over the northern seas it is only about 4 millibars. Certainly the moisture in materials in two such areas will be just the opposite, and relative humidity is a more widely useful index.

The average relative humidity for July reveals the humidity provinces of the Northern Hemisphere when aridity is at a maximum. At other times the relative humidity generally will be higher. The humidities over the Southern Hemisphere in July indicate the humidities that comparable regions in the Northern Hemisphere will attain in January, just as July in the Northern Hemisphere suggests the humidities in the Southern Hemisphere during January. A contrast is provided by comparing a humid cool coast to a desert. The midday humidity on the Oregon coast, for example, falls only to 80 percent at midday, whereas in the Nevada desert it falls to 20 percent. At night the contrast is less, with averages being over 90 and about 50 percent in these two places.

Although the dramatic regular decrease of relative humidity from dawn to midday has been attributed largely to warming rather than declining vapour content, the content does vary regularly. In humid environments, daytime evaporation increases the vapour content of the air and the mixing ratio, which may be about 12 grams per kilogram, rises 1 or 2 g/kg in temperate places and may attain 16 g/kg in a tropical rain forest. In arid environments, however, little evaporation moistens the air and daytime turbulence tends to bring down dry air; this decreases the mixing ratio by as much as 2 g /kg.

Humidity also varies regularly with altitude. On the average, fully half the water in the atmosphere lies below .25 kilometres (820 feet), and satellite observations over the United States in April revealed one millimetre or less of water in all the air above 6 km (19,680 ft). A cross section of the atmosphere along 75° W longitude shows a decrease in humidity with height and toward the poles. The mixing ratio is 16 g/kg just north of the Equator, but it decreases to 1 g/kg at 50° N latitude or 8 km above the Equator. The transparent air surrounding mountains in fair weather is very dry indeed.

Nearer the ground, the vapour content also changes with height in a regular pattern. When vapour is condensing on the earth at night, the content is greater aloft than at the ground; during the day the content is usually less aloft than at the ground because of evaporation.

Evaporation and humidity

Evaporation, mostly from the sea and from vegetation, replenishes the humidity of the air. It is the change of liquid water into gaseous state, but it may be analyzed as diffusion. The rate of diffusion, or evaporation, will be proportional to the difference between the pressure of the vapour in the free air and the vapour that is next to, and saturated by, the evaporating liquid. If the liquid and air have the same temperature, evaporation is proportional to the saturation deficit. It is also proportional to the conductivity of the medium between the evaporator and the free air. If the evaporator is open water, the conductivity will increase with ventilation. But if the evaporator is a leaf, the diffusing water must pass through the still air within the minute pores between the water within and the dry air outside. In this case, the porosity may modify the conductivity more than ventilation.

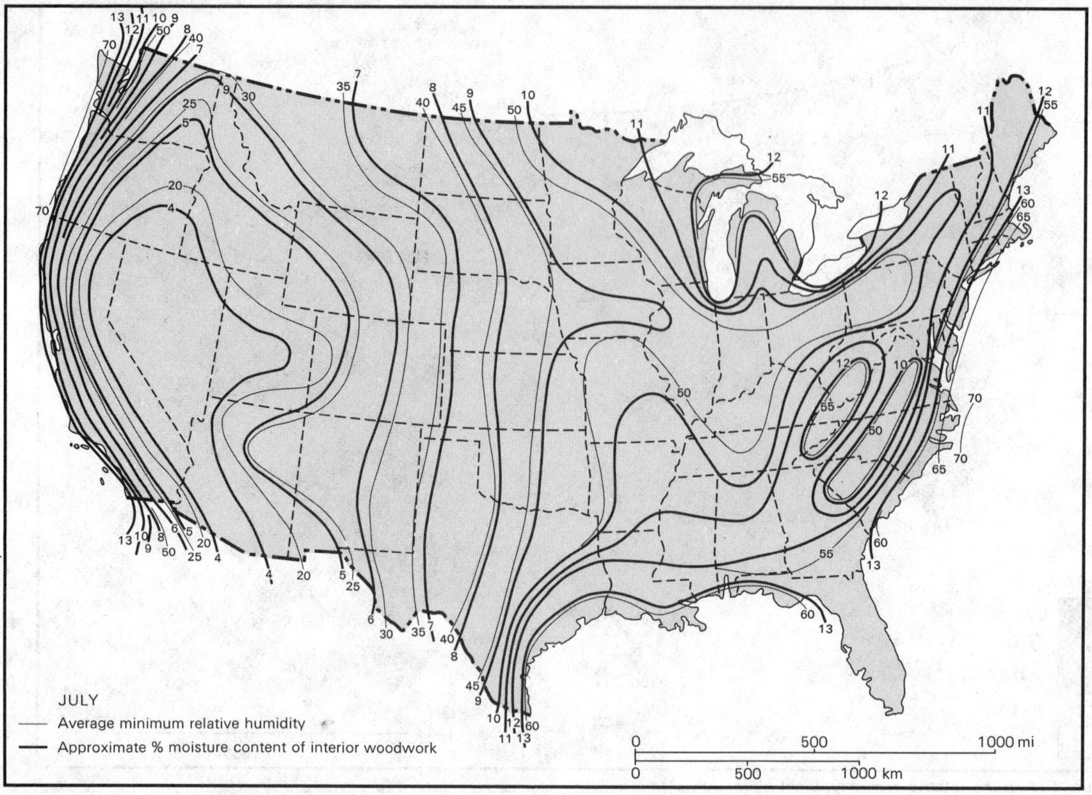

Figure 2: Relation of the moisture content of interior woodwork to outdoor relative humidity of various areas of the United States in July.

From *Humidity and Moisture: Measurement and Control in Science and Industry* by A. Wexler, © 1965 by Litton Educational Publishing, Inc.; reprinted by permission of Van Nostrand Reinhold Company

The temperature of the evaporator is rarely the same as the air temperature, however, because each gram of evaporation consumes about 600 calories and thus cools the evaporator. The availability of energy to heat the evaporator, therefore, is as important as the saturation deficit and conductivity of the air. Outdoors, some of this heat may be transferred from the surrounding air by convection, but much of it must be furnished by radiation. Evaporation is faster on sunny than cloudy days not only because the sunny day may have drier air but also because the sun warms the evaporator, thus raising the vapour pressure at the evaporator. In fact, according to the well-known Penman calculation of evaporation, this loss of water is essentially determined by the net radiation balance during the day.

The relation of humidity and evaporation also is illustrated by the wet-bulb hygrometer. A wet wick wrapped around a thermometer and ventilated rapidly in the shade will lose heat by vaporization and gain from convection until its temperature reaches an equilibrium at the wet-bulb temperature; this lies between the air and dew-point temperatures. The cooling of the wet bulb and the air temperature are indicators of the humidity, and wet-bulb psychrometers (a wet-bulb and a dry-bulb thermometer) are used as secondary standards for the calibration of other hygrometers.

HUMIDITY AND HUMAN AFFAIRS

The invisible water vapour in the air can harm man or the animals and plants around him by upsetting normal heat and water budgets or encouraging disease in these organisms.

The connection between humidity and some human diseases is clear. Malarial mosquitoes, for example, clearly thrive in moist places. But the connection between many diseases and humidity is too tenuous to discuss.

Most animals must maintain a stable internal temperature to function normally. This stability is accomplished by balancing gains and losses through radiation, convection, evaporation, and metabolism. The most striking effect of humidity is that of controlling the evaporation of perspiration that pours through the skin of a man labouring in a hot place. The cooling increases with the wetted area and as the square root of the measured ventilation. It also increases with the difference in vapour pressure between the wet skin and the air. Thus in warm weather, the ease of balancing the energy budget, and hence comfort, are determined by humidity in addition to temperature, ventilation, and radiation.

Indices of environmental stress

Numerous indices have been devised to indicate the stress or discomfort of an environment. The "effective temperature" employed by air-conditioning engineers integrates the effects of humidity, temperature, and ventilation and is linearly related to the heart rate of working men. Ventilation is often omitted, and then the comfortable "effective temperature" of 20 is obtained with an air temperature of 26° C (79° F) and a relative humidity of 10 percent or a combination of 20° C (68° F) and 100 percent. The discomfort, or temperature–humidity, index, employed by the U.S. Weather Bureau is also calculated from air temperature and humidity and it disregards ventilation and radiation. Hygienists have attempted to set sultriness limits on room conditions, although the variation in people and clothing makes the setting difficult. A sultriness limit for resting people has been tabulated by H.E. Landsberg:

Temperature, ° C.	40	35	30	25	20
Relative humidity, percent	20	33	44	60	85

Wilted leaves are a familiar manifestation of drought. Humidity modifies the evaporation that desiccates and kills them. Because leaves have a relatively impermeable epidermis but must assimilate carbon dioxide from the air for photosynthesis and growth, most leaves have pores, or stomata, that admit carbon dioxide. These same pores, however, let water evaporate, and the evaporation from a succulent field or forest is nearly as great as from a lake. This loss, which is equivalent to about 25 millimetres of rain per week, must be replaced by water drawn from the soil by roots. By modifying evaporation, humidity can prolong the time until soil water must be replenished by rain or irrigation.

While humidity is affecting the plants by changing evaporation, the plants can affect microclimates (*q.v.*) by modifying the humidity of the air within the canopy of leaves. For example, the relative humidity above a barren field fell to 20 percent at midday, but above a nearby irrigated sugarcane field the humidity decreased only to 40 percent.

Humidity has a distinct effect upon many plant diseases. The fungi that mildew shoes prosper in humid air, and many plant pathogens are other fungi that require humid air before they can bear spores on infected leaves or germinate and infect new leaves. Thus the Irish Famine in the mid-19th century was caused by a potato mildew encouraged by humid weather, and modern weather forecasts employ humidity observations to predict epidemics in crops.

Many other man-made objects also are affected by humidity. The corrosion of metal is related to relative humidity, not to rainfall or temperature, and things made of porous materials respond most dramatically to humidity. Their behaviour is exemplified by woodwork. The moisture content of wood at air temperature is about 30 percent when it has set (aged) in saturated vapour that is 100 percent relative humidity. At high humidities the content of wood declines considerably with a decrease in humidity, reaching 15 percent at 75 percent relative humidity. To attain 5 percent content, the wood must equilibrate with air at 20 percent relative humidity. In the United States in July (Figure 2), as elsewhere, the moisture content of interior woodwork is remarkably well predicted by the average minimum relative humidity. In the winter, the relative humidity of a heated building is determined largely by the drying of air outdoors in the cold, and the winter moisture content of woodwork is related to average temperature outdoors.

The shrinkage of drying wood is well-known and has even been employed in a sluggish hygrometer. Typically wood shrinks about 5 percent across the grain when the relative humidity changes from 100 to 20 percent.

The probability of ignition of wood decreases sharply to near zero when the moisture content of wood, in a house or on a forest floor, attains 30 percent as it does in saturated air. Thus forest fire danger ratings employ observations of relative humidity, and most great forest fires have burst forth in dry air.

BIBLIOGRAPHY. R.J. LIST, *Smithsonian Meteorological Tables* (1966), includes a full set of hygrometric tables and definitions of the indices of humidity; H.L. PENMAN, *Humidity* (1955), a booklet providing basic information on the problems of atmospheric and soil humidity; A. WEXLER (ed.), *Humidity and Moisture: Measurement and Control in Science and Industry*, 4 vol. (1965), symposium proceedings with extensive references to research on this subject; O.G. SUTTON, *The Challenge of the Atmosphere* (1961), gives an authoritative but readable account of how water works in the atmosphere, including rainmaking; D.I. BLUMENSTOCK, *The Ocean of Air* (1959), a popular book that relates meteorology to archaeology, medicine, and nuclear physics; P.E. WAGGONER (ed.), *Agricultural Meteorology* (1965), a technical book examining the full range of the effects of humidity upon animals and plants and evaporation.

(P.E.W.)

Humour and Wit

In all its many-splendoured varieties, humour can be simply defined as a type of stimulation that tends to elicit the laughter reflex. Spontaneous laughter is a motor reflex produced by the coordinated contraction of 15 facial muscles in a stereotyped pattern and accompanied by altered breathing. Electrical stimulation of the main lifting muscle of the upper lip, the zygomatic major, with currents of varying intensity produces facial expressions ranging from the faint smile through the broad grin to the contortions typical of explosive laughter.

The laughter and smile of civilized man is, of course, often of a conventional kind, in which voluntary intent substitutes for, or interferes with, spontaneous reflex activity; this article is concerned, however, only with the latter. Once laughter is realized to be a humble reflex, several paradoxes must be faced. Motor reflexes, such as the contraction of the pupil of the eye in dazzling light, are simple responses to simple stimuli whose value to survival is obvious. But the involuntary contraction of 15 facial muscles, associated with certain irrepressible noises, strikes one as an activity without any utilitarian value, quite unrelated to the struggle for survival. Laughter is a reflex but unique in that it has no apparent biological purpose. One might call it a luxury reflex. Its only function seems to be to provide relief from tension.

Paradoxes of laughter

The second related paradox is a striking discrepancy between the nature of the stimulus and that of the response in humorous transactions. When a blow beneath the kneecap causes an automatic upward kick, both "stimulus" and "response" function on the same primitive physiological level, without requiring the intervention of the higher mental functions. But that such a complex mental activity as reading a comic story should cause a specific reflex contraction of the facial muscles is a phenomenon that has puzzled philosophers since Plato. There is no clear-cut, predictable response that would tell a lecturer whether he has succeeded in convincing his listeners; but when he is telling a joke, laughter serves as an experimental test. *Humour is the only form of communication in which a stimulus on a high level of complexity produces a stereotyped, predictable response on the physiological reflex level.* Thus the response can be used as an indicator for the presence of the elusive quality that is called humour—as the click of the Geiger counter is used to indicate the presence of radioactivity. Such a procedure is not possible in any other form of art; and since the step from the sublime to the ridiculous is reversible, the study of humour provides the psychologist with clues for the study of creativity in general.

THE LOGIC OF LAUGHTER

The range of laughter-provoking experiences is enormous, from physical tickling to mental titillations of the most varied kinds. There is unity in this variety, however, a common denominator of a specific and specifiable pattern that reflects the "logic" or "grammar" of humour, as it were. A few examples will help to unravel that pattern.

1. A masochist is a person who likes a cold shower in the morning so he takes a hot one.

2. An English lady, on being asked by a friend what she thought of her departed husband's whereabouts: "Well, I suppose the poor soul is enjoying eternal bliss, but I wish you wouldn't talk about such unpleasant subjects."

3. A doctor comforts his patient: "You have a very serious disease. Of ten persons who catch it, only one survives. It is lucky you came to me, for I have recently had nine patients with this disease and they all died of it."

4. Dialogue in a French film:

"Sir, I would like to ask for your daughter's hand."

"Why not? You have already had the rest."

5. A marquis of the court of Louis XV unexpectedly returned from a journey and, on entering his wife's boudoir, found her in the arms of a bishop. After a moment's hesitation, the marquis walked calmly to the window, leaned out, and began going through the motions of blessing the people in the street.

"What are you doing?" cried the anguished wife.

"Monseigneur is performing my functions, so I am performing his."

Is there a common pattern underlying these five stories? Starting with the last, a little reflection reveals that the marquis's behaviour is both unexpected and perfectly logical—but of a logic not usually applied to this type of situation. It is the logic of the division of labour, governed by rules as old as human civilization. But his reactions would have been expected to be governed by a different set of rules—the code of sexual morality. It is the sudden clash between these two mutually exclusive codes of rules—or associative contexts—that produces the comic effect. It compels the listener to perceive the situation in two self-consistent but incompatible frames of reference at the same time; his mind has to operate simultaneously on two different wavelengths. While this unusual condition lasts, the event is not only, as is normally the case, associated with a single frame of reference, but "bisociated" with two. The term bisociation was coined by the present writer to make a distinction between the routines of disciplined thinking within a single universe of discourse—on a single plane, as it were—and the creative types of mental activity that always operate on more than one plane. In humour, both the *creation* of a subtle joke and the *re-creative* act of perceiving the joke involve the delightful mental jolt of a sudden leap from one plane or associative context to another.

Bisociation

Turning to the other examples, in the French film dialogue, the daughter's "hand" is perceived first in a metaphorical frame of reference, then suddenly in a literal, bodily context. The doctor thinks in terms of abstract, statistical probabilities, the rules of which are inapplicable to individual cases; and there is an added twist because, in contrast to what common sense suggests, the patient's odds of survival are unaffected by whatever happened before; they are still one against ten. This is one of the profound paradoxes of the theory of probability, and the joke in fact implies a riddle; it pinpoints an absurdity that tends to be taken for granted. As for the lady who looks upon death as "eternal bliss" and at the same time "an unpleasant subject," she epitomizes the common human predicament of living in the divided house of faith and reason. Here again the simple joke carries unconscious overtones and undertones, audible to the inner ear alone.

The masochist who punishes himself by depriving himself of his daily punishment is governed by rules that are a *reversal* of those of normal logic. (A pattern can be constructed in which *both* frames of reference are reversed: "A sadist is a person who is kind to a masochist.") But there is again an added twist. The joker does not really believe that the masochist takes his hot shower as a punishment; he only pretends to believe it. *Irony* is the satirist's most effective weapon; it pretends to adopt the opponent's ways of reasoning in order to expose their implicit absurdity or viciousness.

Thus the common pattern underlying these stories is *the perceiving of a situation in two self-consistent but mutually incompatible frames of reference or associative contexts.* This formula can be shown to have a general validity for all forms of humour and wit, some of which will be discussed below. But it covers only one aspect of humour—its *intellectual structure*. Another fundamental aspect must be examined—the *emotional dynamics* that breathe life into that structure and make a person laugh, giggle, or smile.

LAUGHTER AND EMOTION

When a comedian tells a story, he deliberately sets out to create a certain tension in his listeners, which mounts as the narrative progresses. But it never reaches its expected climax. The punch line, or point, acts as a verbal guillotine that cuts across the logical development of the story; it debunks the audience's dramatic expectations. The tension that was felt becomes suddenly redundant and is exploded in laughter. To put it differently, laughter disposes of emotive excitations that have become pointless and must somehow be worked off along physiological channels of least resistance; and the function of the "luxury reflex" is to provide these channels.

A glance at the caricatures of the 18th-century English artists William Hogarth or Thomas Rowlandson, showing the brutal merriment of people in a tavern, makes one realize at once that they are working off their surplus of adrenalin by contracting their face muscles into grimaces, slapping their thighs, and breathing in puffs through the half-closed glottis. Their flushed faces reveal that the emotions disposed of through these safety valves are brutality, envy, sexual gloating. In cartoons by the 20th-century American James Thurber, however, coarse laughter yields to an amused and rarefied smile: the flow of adrenalin has been distilled and crystallized into a grain of Attic salt—a sophisticated joke. The word witticism is derived from "wit" in its original sense of intelligence and acumen (as is *Witz* in German). The domains of humour and of ingenuity are continuous, without a sharp boundary: the jester is brother to the sage. Across the spectrum of humour, from its coarse to its subtle forms, from practical joke to brainteaser, from jibe to irony, from anecdote to epigram, the emotional climate shows a gradual transformation. The emotion discharged in coarse laughter is aggression robbed of its purpose. The jokes small children enjoy are mostly scatological; adolescents of all ages gloat on vicarious sex. The sick joke trades on repressed sadism, satire on righteous indignation. There is a bewildering variety of moods involved in different forms of humour, including mixed or contradictory feelings; but whatever the mixture, it must contain a basic ingredient that is indispensable: an impulse, however faint, of aggression or apprehension. It may appear in the guise of malice, contempt, the veiled cruelty of condescension, or merely an absence of sympathy with the victim of the joke—a momentary anesthesia of the heart, as the French philosopher Henri Bergson put it.

The aggressive element

In the subtler types of humour, the aggressive tendency may be so faint that only careful analysis will detect it, like the presence of salt in a well-prepared dish—which, however, would be tasteless without it. Replace aggression by sympathy and the same situation—a drunk falling on his face, for example—will be no longer comic but pathetic and will evoke not laughter but pity. It is the aggressive element, the detached malice of the comic impersonator, that turns pathos into bathos, tragedy into travesty. Malice may be combined with affection in friendly teasing; and the aggressive component in civilized humour may be sublimated or no longer conscious. But in jokes that appeal to children and primitive people, cruelty and boastful self-assertiveness are much in evidence. In 1961 a survey carried out among American children aged 8 to 15 made the researchers conclude that the mortification, discomfort, or hoaxing of others readily caused laughter, but witty or funny remarks often passed unnoticed.

Similar considerations apply to the historically earlier forms and theories of the comic. In Aristotle's view, laughter was intimately related to ugliness and debasement. Cicero held that the province of the ridiculous lay in a certain baseness and deformity. Descartes believed that laughter was a manifestation of joy mixed with surprise or hatred or both. In Francis Bacon's list of what causes laughter, the first place is again given to deformity. One of the most frequently quoted utterances on the subject is this definition in Thomas Hobbes's *Leviathan* (1651):

Theories of laughter

> The passion of laughter is nothing else but sudden glory arising from a sudden conception of some eminency in ourselves by comparison with the infirmity of others, or with our own formerly.

In the 19th century, the Scot Alexander Bain, one of the pioneers of experimental psychology, thought along the same lines:

> Not in physical effects alone, but in everything where a man can achieve a stroke of superiority, in surpassing or discomforting a rival, is the disposition of laughter apparent.

In Bergson's view, laughter is the corrective punishment inflicted by society upon the unsocial individual: "In laughter we always find an unavowed intention to humiliate and consequently to correct our neighbour." Sir Max Beerbohm, the 20th-century English wit, found "two elements in the public's humour: delight in suffering, contempt for the unfamiliar." The American psychologist William McDougall believed that "laughter has been evolved in the human race as an antidote to sympathy, a protective reaction shielding us from the depressive influence of the shortcomings of our fellow men."

However much the opinions of the theorists differ, on this one point nearly all of them agree: that the emotions discharged in laughter always contain an element of aggressiveness. It must be borne in mind, however, that aggression and apprehension are twin phenomena, so much so that psychologists are used to talking of "aggressive–defensive impulses." Accordingly, one of the typical situations in which laughter occurs is the moment of sudden cessation of fear caused by some imaginary danger. Rarely is the nature of laughter as an overflow of redundant tensions more strikingly manifested than in the sudden change of expression on a small child's face from anxious apprehension to the happy laughter of relief. This seems to be unrelated to humour; yet a closer look reveals in it the same logical structure as in the joke: the wildly barking little dog was first perceived by the child in a context of danger, then discovered to be a harmless pup; the tension has suddenly become redundant and is spilled.

Laughter as the release of tension

Immanuel Kant realized that what causes laughter is "the sudden transformation of a tense expectation into nothing." Herbert Spencer, the 19th-century English philosopher, took up the idea and attempted to formulate it in physiological terms: "Emotions and sensations tend to generate bodily movements. . . . When consciousness is unawares transferred from great things to small," the "liberated nerve force" will expend itself along channels of least resistance—the bodily movements of laughter. Freud incorporated Spencer's theory of humour into his own, with special emphasis on the release of repressed emotions in laughing; he also attempted to explain why the excess energy should be worked off in that particular way:

> According to the best of my knowledge, the grimaces and contortions of the corners of the mouth that characterise laughter appear first in the satisfied and over-satiated nursling when he drowsily quits the breast. . . . They are physical expressions of the determination to take no more nourishment, an "enough" so to speak, or rather a "more than enough" . . . This primal sense of pleasurable saturation may have provided the link between the smile—that basic phenomenon underlying laughter—and its subsequent connection with other pleasurable processes of de-tension.

In other words, the muscle contractions of the smile, as the earliest expressions of relief from tension, would thereafter serve as channels of least resistance. Similarly, the explosive exhalations of laughter seem designed to "puff away" surplus tension in a kind of respiratory gymnastics, and agitated gestures obviously serve the same function.

It may be objected that such massive reactions often seem quite out of proportion to the slight stimulations that provoke them. But it must be borne in mind that laughter is a phenomenon of the trigger-releaser type, where a sudden turn of the tap may release vast amounts of stored emotions, derived from various, often unconscious, sources: repressed sadism, sexual tumescence, unavowed fear, even boredom. The explosive laughter of a class of schoolboys at some trivial incident is a measure of their pent-up resentment during a boring lecture. Another factor that may amplify the reaction out of all proportion to the comic stimulus is the social infectiousness that laughter shares with other emotive manifestations of group behaviour.

Patterns of association

Laughter or smiling may also be caused by stimulations that are not in themselves comic but signs or symbols deputizing for well-established comic patterns—such as Charlie Chaplin's oversized shoes or Groucho Marx's cigar—or catchphrases, or allusions to family jokes. To discover why people laugh requires, on some occasions, tracing back a long, involved thread of associations to its source. This task is further complicated by the fact that the effect of such comic symbols—in a cartoon or on the stage—appears to be instantaneous, without allowing time for the accumulation and subsequent discharge of "expectations" and "emotive tensions." But here memory comes into play, having already accumulated the required emotions in past experiences, acting as a storage battery whose charge can be sparked off at any time: the smile that greets Falstaff's appearance on the scene is derived from a mixture of memories and expectations. Besides, even if a reaction to a cartoon appears to be instantaneous, there is always a process in time until the reader "sees the joke"; the cartoon has to tell a story even if it is telescoped into a few seconds. All of this shows that to analyze humour is a task as delicate as analyzing the composition of a perfume with its multiple ingredients, some of which are never consciously perceived while others, when sniffed in isolation, would make one wince.

In this article there has been a discussion first of the logical structure of humour and then of its emotional dynamics. Putting the two together, the result may be summarized as follows: the "bisociation" of a situation or idea with two mutually incompatible contexts in a person's mind and the resulting abrupt transfer of his train of thought from one context to another put a sudden end to his "tense expectations"; the accumulated emotion, deprived of its object, is left hanging in the air and is discharged in laughter. Upon hearing that the marquis in the story told earlier walks to the window and starts blessing the people in the street, the intellect turns a somersault and enters with gusto into the new game. The malicious and erotic feelings aroused by the start of the story, however, cannot be fitted into the new context; deserted by the nimble intellect, these feelings gush out in laughter like air from a punctured tire.

Separation of thought and emotion

To put it differently: people laugh because their emotions have a greater inertia and persistence than their thoughts. Affects are incapable of keeping step with reasoning; unlike reasoning, they cannot "change direction" at a moment's notice. To the physiologist, this is self-evident since emotions operate through the genetically old, massive sympathetic nervous system and its allied hormones, acting on the whole body, while the processes of conceptual thinking are confined to the neocortex at the roof of the brain. Common experience provides daily confirmation of this dichotomy. People are literally "poisoned" by their adrenal humours; it takes time to talk a person out of a mood; fear and anger show physical aftereffects long after their causes have been removed. If man were able to change his moods as quickly as his thoughts, he would be an acrobat of emotion; but since he is not, his thoughts and emotions frequently become dissociated. It is emotion deserted by thought that is discharged in laughter. For emotion, owing to its greater mass momentum, is, as has been shown, unable to follow the sudden switch of ideas to a different type of logic; it tends to persist in a straight line. Aldous Huxley once wrote:

> We carry around with us a glandular system which was admirably well adapted to life in the Paleolithic times but is not very well adapted to life now. Thus we tend to produce more adrenalin than is good for us, and we either suppress ourselves and turn destructive energies inwards or else we do not suppress ourselves and we start hitting people. (From *Man and Civilization: Control of the Mind*, ed. Seymour M. Farber and Roger H.L. Wilson. Copyright 1961. Used with permission of McGraw-Hill Book Company.)

A third alternative is to laugh at people. There are other outlets for tame aggression, such as competitive sports or literary criticism; but they are acquired skills, whereas laughter is a gift of nature, included in man's native equipment. The glands that control his emotions reflect conditions at a stage of evolution when the struggle for existence was more deadly than at present—and when the reaction to any strange sight or sound consisted in jumping, bristling, fighting, or running. As security and comfort increased in the species, new outlets were needed for emotions that could no longer be worked off through their original channels, and laughter is obviously one of them. But it could only emerge when reasoning had gained a degree of independence from the urges of emotion. Below the human level, thinking and feeling appear to form an indivisible unity. Not before thinking became gradually detached from feeling could man perceive his own emotion as redundant and make the smiling admission, "I have been fooled."

VERBAL HUMOUR

The foregoing discussion was intended to provide the tools for dissecting and analyzing any specimen of humour. The procedure is to determine the nature of the two (or more) frames of reference whose collision gives rise to the comic effect—to discover the type of logic or "rules of the game" that govern each. In the more sophisticated type of joke, the logic is implied and hidden, and the moment it is stated in explicit form, the joke is dead. Unavoidably, the section that follows will be strewn with cadavers.

Puns

Max Eastman, in *The Enjoyment of Laughter* (1936), remarked of a laboured pun by Ogden Nash: "It is not a pun but a punitive expedition." That applies to most puns, including Milton's famous lines about the Prophet Elijah's ravens, which were "though ravenous taught to abstain from what they brought," or the character mentioned by Freud, who calls the Christmas season the "alcoholidays." Most puns strike one as atrocious, perhaps because they represent the most primitive form of humour; two disparate strings of thought tied together by an acoustic knot. But the very primitiveness of such association based on pure sound ("hol") may account for the pun's immense popularity with children and its prevalence in certain types of mental disorder ("punning mania").

From the play on sounds—puns and Spoonerisms—an ascending series leads to the play on words and so to the play on ideas. When Groucho Marx says of a safari in Africa, "We shot two bucks, but that was all the money we had," the joke hinges on the two meanings of the word buck. It would be less funny without the reference to Groucho, which evokes a visual image instantly arousing high expectations. The story about the marquis above may be considered of a superior type of humour because it plays not on mere words but on ideas.

It would be quite easy—and equally boring—to draw up a list in which jokes and witticisms are classified according to the nature of the frames of reference whose collision creates the comic effect. A few have already been mentioned: metaphorical versus literal meaning (the daughter's "hand"); professional versus common sense logic (the doctor); incompatible codes of behaviour (the marquis); confrontations of the trivial and the exalted ("eternal bliss"); trains of reasoning travelling, happily joined together, in opposite directions (the sadist who is kind to the masochist). The list could be extended indefinitely; in fact *any* two frames of reference can be made to yield a comic effect of sorts by hooking them together and infusing a drop of malice into the concoction. The frames may even be defined by such abstract concepts as "time" and "weather": the absent-minded professor who tries to read the temperature from his watch or to tell the time from the thermometer is comic in the same way as a game of table tennis played with a soccer ball or a game of rugby played with a table tennis ball. The variations are infinite, the formula remains the same.

Jokes and anecdotes have a single point of culmination. The literary forms of *sustained humour*, such as the picaresque novel, do not rely on a single effect but on a series of minor climaxes. The narrative moves along the line of intersection of contrasted planes, such as the fantasy world of Don Quixote and the cunning horse sense of Sancho Panza, or is made to oscillate between them. As a result, tension is continuously generated and discharged in mild amusement.

Comic verse

Comic verse thrives on the melodious union of incongruities, such as the "cabbages and kings" in Lewis Carroll's "The Walrus and the Carpenter," and particularly on the contrast between lofty form and flat-footed content. Certain metric forms associated with heroic poetry, such as the hexameter or Alexandrine, arouse expectations of pathos, of the exalted; to pour into these epic molds some homely, trivial content—"beautiful soup, so rich and green / waiting in a hot tureen"—is an almost infallible comic device. The rolling rhythms of the first lines of a limerick that carry, instead of a mythical hero such as Hector or Achilles, a young lady from Ohio for a ride make her ridiculous even before the expected calamities befall her. Instead of a heroic mold, a soft lyrical one may also pay off:

. . . And what could be moister
Than tears of an oyster?

Another type of incongruity between form and content yields the bogus proverb: "The rule is: jam tomorrow and jam yesterday—but never jam today." Two contradictory statements have been telescoped into a line whose homely, admonitory sound conveys the impression of a popular adage. In a similar way, nonsense verse achieves its effect by pretending to make sense, by forcing the reader to project meaning into the phonetic pattern of the jabberwocky, as one interprets the ink blots in a Rorschach test.

Satire and allegory

The *satire* is a verbal caricature that shows a deliberately distorted image of a person, institution, or society. The traditional method of the caricaturist is to exaggerate those features he considers to be characteristic of his victim's personality and to simplify by leaving out everything that is not relevant for his purpose. The satirist uses the same technique, and the features of society he selects for magnification are, of course, those of which he disapproves. The result is a juxtaposition, in the reader's mind, of his habitual image of the world in which he moves and its absurd reflection in the satirist's distorting mirror. He is made to recognize familiar features in the absurd and absurdity in the familiar. Without this double vision the satire would be humourless. If the human Yahoos were really such evil-smelling monsters as Gulliver's Houyhnhnm hosts claim, then Jonathan Swift's *Gulliver's Travels* (1726) would not be a satire but the statement of a deplorable truth. Straight invective is not satire; satire must deliberately overshoot its mark.

A similar effect is achieved if, instead of exaggerating the objectionable features, the satirist projects them by means of the *allegory* onto a different background, such as an animal society. A succession of writers, from the ancient Greek dramatist Aristophanes through Swift to such 20th-century satirists as Anatole France and George Orwell, have used this technique to focus attention on deformities of society that, blunted by habit, are taken for granted.

SITUATIONAL HUMOUR

The coarsest type of humour is the practical joke: pulling away the chair from under the dignitary's lowered bottom. The victim is perceived first as a person of consequence, then suddenly as an inert body subject to the laws of physics: authority is debunked by gravity, mind by matter; man is degraded to a mechanism. Goose-stepping soldiers acting like automatons, the pedant behaving like a mechanical robot, the Sergeant Major attacked by diarrhea, or Hamlet getting the hiccups—all show man's lofty aspirations deflated by his all-too-solid flesh. A similar effect is produced by artifacts that masquerade as humans: Punch and Judy, jack-in-the-box, gadgets playing tricks on their masters as if with calculated malice.

In Henri Bergson's theory of laughter, this dualism of subtle mind and inert matter—he calls it "the mechanical encrusted on the living"—is made to serve as an explanation of *all* varieties of the comic. In the light of what has been said, however, it would seem to apply only to *one* type of comic situation among many others.

From the "bisociation" of man and machine, there is only a step to the man–animal hybrid. Walt Disney's creations behave as if they were human without losing their animal appearance. The caricaturist follows the reverse procedure by discovering horsey, mousy, or piggish features in the human face.

This leads to the comic devices of imitation, impersonation, and disguise. The impersonator is perceived as himself and somebody else at the same time. If the result is slightly degrading—but only in that case—the spectator will laugh. The comedian impersonating a public personality, two pairs of trousers serving as the legs of the pantomime horse, men disguised as women and women as men—in each case the paired patterns reduce each other to absurdity.

The most aggressive form of impersonation is the *parody*, designed to deflate hollow pretense, to destroy illusion, and to undermine pathos by harping on the weaknesses of the victim. Wigs falling off, speakers forgetting their lines, gestures remaining suspended in the air: the parodist's favourite points of attack are again situated on the line of intersection between the sublime and the trivial.

Playful behaviour in young animals and children is amusing because it is an unintentional parody of adult behaviour, which it imitates or anticipates. Young puppies are droll because their helplessness, affection, and puzzled expression make them appear more "human" than full-grown dogs; because their growls strike one as impersonations of adult behaviour—like a child in a bowler hat; because the puppy's waddling, uncertain gait makes it a choice victim of nature's practical jokes; because its bodily disproportions—the huge padded paws, Falstaffian belly, and wrinkled brow—give it the appearance of a caricature; and lastly because the observer feels so very superior to a puppy. A fleeting smile can contain many logical ingredients and emotional spices.

Both Cicero and Francis Bacon regarded *deformity* as the most frequent cause of laughter. Renaissance princes collected dwarfs and hunchbacks for their merriment. It obviously requires a certain amount of imagination and empathy to recognize in a midget a fellow human, who, though different in appearance, thinks and feels much as oneself does. In children, this projective faculty is still rudimentary: they tend to mock people with a stammer or a limp and laugh at the foreigner with an odd pronunciation. Similar attitudes are shown by tribal or parochial societies to any form of appearance or behaviour that deviates from their strict norms: the stranger is not really human; he only pretends to be "like us." The Greeks used the same word, barbarous, for the foreigner and the stutterer: the uncouth barking sounds the stranger uttered were considered a parody of human speech. Vestiges of this primitive attitude are still found in the curious fact that civilized people accept a foreign accent with tolerance, whereas imitation of a foreign accent strikes them as comic. The imitator's mispronunciations are recognized as mere pretense; this knowledge makes sympathy unnecessary and enables the audience to be childishly cruel with a clean conscience.

Other sources of innocent laughter are situations in which *the part and the whole* change roles, and attention becomes focussed on a detail torn out of the functional context on which its meaning depended. When the phonograph needle gets stuck, the soprano's voice keeps repeating the same word on the same quaver, which suddenly assumes a grotesquely independent life. The same happens when faulty orthography displaces attention from meaning to spelling, or whenever consciousness is directed at functions that otherwise are performed automatically. The latter situation is well illustrated by the story of the centipede who, when asked in which order he moved his hundred legs, became paralyzed and could walk no more. The self-conscious, awkward youth, who does not know what to do with his hands, is a victim of the paradox of the centipede.

Comedies have been classified according to their reliance on situations, manners, or characters. The logic of the last two needs no further discussion; in the first, comic effects are contrived by making a situation participate simultaneously in two independent chains of events with different associative contexts, which intersect through coincidence, mistaken identity, or confusions of time and occasion.

Tickling

Why tickling should produce laughter remained an enigma in all earlier theories of the comic. As Darwin was the first to point out, the innate response to tickling is squirming and straining to withdraw the tickled part—a defense reaction designed to escape attacks on vulnerable areas such as the soles of the feet, armpits, belly, and flank. If a fly settles on the belly of a horse, it causes a ripple of muscle contractions across the skin—the equivalent of squirming in the tickled child. But the horse does not laugh when tickled, and the child not always. The child will laugh only—and this is the crux of the matter —when it perceives tickling as a *mock attack*, a caress in mildly aggressive disguise. For the same reason, people laugh only when tickled by others, not when they tickle themselves.

Experiments at Yale University on babies under one year revealed the not very surprising fact that they laughed 15 times more often when tickled by their mothers than by strangers; and when tickled by strangers, they mostly cried. For the mock attack must be recognized as being only pretense, and with strangers one cannot be sure. Even with its own mother, there is an ever-so-slight feeling of uncertainty and apprehension, the expression of which will alternate with laughter in the baby's behaviour. It is precisely this element of tension between the tickles that is relieved in the laughter accompanying the squirm. The rule of the game is "let me be just a little frightened so that I can enjoy the relief."

Thus the tickler is impersonating an aggressor but is simultaneously known not to be one. This is probably the first situation in life that makes the infant live on two planes at once, a delectable foretaste of being tickled by the horror comic.

Humour in the visual arts and music

Humour in the visual arts reflects the same logical structures as discussed before. Its most primitive form is the distorting mirror at the fun fair, which reflects the human frame elongated into a column or compressed into the shape of a toad. It plays a practical joke on the victim, who sees the image in the mirror both as his familiar self and as a lump of plasticine that can be stretched and squeezed into any absurd form. The mirror distorts mechanically while the caricaturist does so selectively, employing the same method as the satirist—exaggerating characteristic features and simplifying the rest. Like the satirist, the caricaturist reveals the absurd in the familiar; and, like the satirist, he must overshoot his mark. His malice is rendered harmless by the knowledge that the monstrous potbellies and bowlegs he draws are not real; real deformities are not comic but arouse pity.

The artist, painting a stylized portrait, also uses the technique of selection, exaggeration, and simplification; but his attitude toward the model is usually dominated by positive empathy instead of negative malice, and the features he selects for emphasis differ accordingly. In some character studies by Leonardo da Vinci, Hogarth, or Honoré Daumier, the passions reflected are so violent, the grimaces so ferocious, that it is impossible to tell whether the works were meant as portraits or caricatures. If one feels that such distortions of the human face are not really possible, that Daumier merely *pretended* that they exist, then one is absolved from horror and pity and can laugh at his grotesques. But if one feels that this is indeed what Daumier saw in those dehumanized faces, then they are not comic but tragic.

Humour in *music* is a subject to be approached with diffidence because the language of music ultimately eludes translation into verbal concepts. All one can do is to point out some analogies: a "rude" noise, such as the blast of a trumpet inserted into a passage where it does not belong, has the effect of a practical joke; a singer or an instrument out of tune produces a similar reaction; the imitation of animal sounds, vocally or instrumentally, exploits the technique of impersonation; a nocturne by Chopin transposed into hot jazz or a simple street song performed with Wagnerian pathos is a marriage of incompatibles. These are primitive devices corresponding to the lowest levels of humour; more sophisticated are the techniques employed by Maurice Ravel in *La Valse*, a parody of the sentimental Viennese waltz, or by Zoltán Kodály in the mock-heroics of his Hungarian folk opera, *Háry János*. But in comic operas it is almost impossible to sort out how much of the comic effect is derived from the book and how much from the music; and the highest forms of musical humour, the unexpected delights of a lighthearted scherzo by Mozart, defy verbal analysis, unless it is so specialized and technical as to defeat its purpose. Although a "witty" musical passage that springs a surprise on the audience and cheats it of its expectations certainly has the emotion-relieving effect that tends to produce laughter, a concert audience may occasionally smile but will hardly ever laugh: the emotions evoked by musical humour are of a subtler kind than those of the verbal and visual variety.

STYLES AND TECHNIQUES IN HUMOUR

The criteria that determine whether a humorous offering will be judged good, bad, or indifferent are partly a matter of period taste and personal preference and partly dependent on the style and technique of the humorist. It would seem that these criteria can be summed up under three main headings: (1) originality, (2) emphasis, and (3) economy.

Originality, emphasis, and economy

The merits of originality are self-evident; it provides the essential element of surprise, which cuts across our expectations. But true originality is not very often met either in humour or in other forms of art. One common substitute for it is to increase the tension of the audience by various techniques of suggestive emphasis. The clown's domain is the rich, coarse type of humour: he piles it on; he appeals to sadistic, sexual, scatological impulses. One of his favourite tricks is repetition of the same situation, the same key phrase. This diminishes the effect of surprise, but it has a tension-accumulating effect: emotion is easily drawn into the familiar channel—more and more liquid is being pumped into the punctured pipeline.

Emphasis on local colour and ethnic peculiarities, such as Scottish or Cockney stories, for example, is a further means to channel emotion into familiar tracks. The Scotsman or Cockney must, of course, be a caricature if the comic purpose is to be achieved. In other words, exaggeration and simplification once more appear as indispensable tools to provide emphasis.

In the higher forms of humour, however, emphasis tends to yield to the opposite kind of virtue—economy. Economy, in humour and art, does not mean mechanical brevity but implicit hints instead of explicit statements—the oblique allusion in lieu of the frontal attack. Old-fashioned cartoons, such as those featuring the British lion and the Russian bear, hammered their message in; the modern cartoon usually poses a riddle that the reader must solve by an imaginative effort in order to see the joke.

In humour, as in other forms of art, emphasis and economy are complementary techniques. The first forces the offering down the consumer's throat; the second tantalizes to whet his appetite.

RELATIONS TO ART AND SCIENCE

Earlier theories of humour, including even those of Bergson and Freud, treated it as an isolated phenomenon, without attempting to throw light on the intimate connections between the comic and the tragic, between laughter and crying, between artistic inspiration, comic inventiveness, and scientific discovery. Yet these three domains of creative activity form a continuum with no sharp boundaries between wit and ingenuity, nor between discovery and art.

It has been said that scientific discovery consists in seeing an analogy where nobody has seen one before. When, in the Song of Solomon, Solomon compared the Shulamite's neck to a tower of ivory, he saw an analogy that nobody had seen before; when William Harvey compared the heart of a fish to a mechanical pump, he did the same; and when the caricaturist draws a nose like a cucumber, he again does just that. In fact, all the logical patterns discussed above, which constitute a "grammar" of humour, can also enter the service of art or discovery, as the case may be. The pun has structural equivalents in the rhyme and in word games, which range from crossword puzzles to the deciphering of the Rosetta Stone, the key to Egyptian hieroglyphic. The confrontation between diverse codes of behaviour may yield comedy, tragedy, or new psychological insights. The dualism of mind and inert matter is exploited by the practical joker but also provides one of the eternal themes of literature: man as a marionette on strings, manipulated by gods or chromosomes. The man–beast dichotomy is reflected by Walt Disney's cartoon character Donald Duck but also in Franz Kafka's macabre tale *The Metamorphosis* (1915) and in the psychologist's experiments with rats. The caricature corresponds not only to the artist's character portrait but also to the scientist's diagrams and charts, which emphasize the relevant features and leave out the rest.

Synthesis, juxtaposition, and collision

Contemporary psychology regards the conscious and unconscious processes underlying creativity in all domains as an essentially combinative activity—the bringing together of previously separate areas of knowledge and experience. The scientist's purpose is to achieve *synthesis;* the artist aims at a *juxtaposition* of the familiar and the eternal; the humorist's game is to contrive a *collision*. And as their motivations differ, so do the emotional responses evoked by each type of creativity: discovery satisfies the exploratory drive; art induces emotional catharsis; humour arouses malice and provides a harmless outlet for it. Laughter has been described as the "Haha reaction"; the discoverer's Eureka cry as the "Aha! reaction"; and the delight of the aesthetic experience as the "Ah . . . reaction." But the transitions from one to the other are continuous: witticism blends into epigram, caricature into portrait; and whether one considers architecture, medicine, chess, or cookery, there is no clear frontier where the realm of science ends and that of art begins: the creative person is a citizen of both. Comedy and tragedy, laughter and weeping, mark the extremes of a continuous spectrum, and a comparison of the physiology of laughter and weeping yields further clues to this challenging problem, which lies, however, beyond the terms of reference of the present article.

THE HUMANIZATION OF HUMOUR

The Bushmen of the Kalahari desert of South West Africa are among the oldest and most primitive inhabitants of the earth. An anthropologist who made an exhaustive study of them provided a rare glimpse of prehistoric humour:

> On the way home we saw and shot a springbok, as there was no meat left in camp. The bullet hit the springbok in the stomach and partly eviscerated him, causing him to jump and kick before he finally died. The Bushmen thought that this was terribly funny and they laughed, slapping their thighs and kicking their heels to imitate the springbok, showing no pity at all, but then they regard animals with great detachment.

But the Bushmen remained "in good spirits, pleased with the amusement the springbok had given them." (From Elizabeth Marshall Thomas, *The Harmless People;* Alfred A. Knopf, New York, 1959.)

Obviously the Bushmen, like most primitive people, do not regard animals as sentient beings; the springbok's kicking in his agony appears to them funny because in their view the animal *pretends* to suffer pain like a human being, though it is incapable of such feelings. The ancient Greeks' attitude toward the stammering barbarian was similarly inspired by the conviction that he is not really human but only pretends to be. The ancient Hebrews' sense of humour seems to have been no less harsh: it has been pointed out that in the Old Testament there are 29 references to laughter, out of which 13 are linked with scorn, derision, mocking, and contempt and only two are born of joy.

As laughter emerged from antiquity, it was so aggressive that it has been likened to a dagger. It was in ancient Greece that the dagger was transformed into a quill, dripping with poison at first, then diluted and infused with delightfully lyrical and fanciful ingredients. The 5th century BC saw the first rise of humour into art, starting with parodies of Olympian heroics and soon reaching a peak, in some respects unsurpassed to this day, in the comedies of Aristophanes. From here onward, the evolution of humour in the Western world merges with the history of literature and art (see also COMEDY; SATIRE; and CARICATURE, CARTOON, AND COMIC STRIP).

If the overall trend was toward the humanization of

humour from primitive to sophisticated forms, there also have been ups and downs reflecting changes in political and cultural climate. George Orwell's satire of the 20th century, for example, is much more savage than that of Jonathan Swift in 18th-century England or of Voltaire in 18th-century France. If the Dark Ages produced works of humorous art, little of it has survived. And under the tyrannies of Hitler in Germany and of Stalin in the Soviet Union, humour was driven underground. Dictators fear laughter more than bombs.

Non-Western styles. About non-Western varieties of humour, the Westerner is tempted to repeat the middle-aged British matron's remark on watching Cleopatra rave and die on the stage: "How different, how very different from the home life of our dear Queen." Humour thrives only in its native climate, embedded in its native logic; when one does not know what to expect, one cannot be cheated of his expectations. Hindu humour, for instance, as exemplified by the savage pranks played on humans by the monkey-god Hanuman, strikes the Westerner as particularly cruel, perhaps because the Hindu's approach to his mythology is fundamentally alien to the Western mind. The humour of the Japanese, on the other hand, is astonishingly mild and poetical, like weak, mint-flavoured tea:

> The boss of the monkeys ordered his thousands of henchmen to get the moon reflected in the water. They all tried various means but failed and were much troubled. One of the monkeys at last got the moon in the water and respectfully offered it to the boss, saying "This is what you asked for." The boss was delighted and praised him, saying, "What an exploit! You have distinguished yourself!" The monkey then asked, "By the way, master, what are you going to do with this?" "Well, yes . . . I didn't think of that." (From *Karukuchi Ukibyotan*, 1751; in R.H. Blyth, *Japanese Humour*, 1957.)

The next dates from about a century later:

> There was once a man who was always bewailing his lack of money to buy saké (rice wine) with. His wife, feeling sorry for him, dutifully cut off some of her hair and sold it to the hairdresser's for twenty-four mon, and bought her husband some saké. "Where on earth did you get this from?" "I sold my hair and bought it." "You did such a thing for me?" The wretched man shed tears, and fondling his wife's remaining hair said, "Yes, and there's another good half-bottle of saké here!" (From *Chanoko-mochi*, 1856; in Blyth.)

The combination of maudlin tears and brazen selfishness, and the crazy logic of equating the wife's coiffure with a liquid measure of saké, show the familiar Western pattern of the clash of incompatibles, even though transplanted into another culture.

Humour in the contemporary world. Humour today seems to be dominated by two main factors: the influence of the mass media and the crisis of values affecting a culture in rapid and violent transition. The former tends toward the commercialized manufacture of laughter by popular comedians and gags produced by conveyor-belt methods; the latter toward a sophisticated form of black humour larded with sick jokes, sadism, and sex.

Fashions, however, always run their course; perhaps the next one will delight in variations on the theme of the monkey boss who, having gained possession of the moon, does not know what to do with it. The only certainty regarding the humour of the future is contained in Dr. Samuel Johnson's dictum: "Sir, men have been wise in many different modes, but they have always laughed in the same way."

BIBLIOGRAPHY. GUILLAUME DUCHENNE (DE BOULOGNE), *Le Mécanisme de la physionomie humaine* (1862); and J.M. RAULIN, *Étude anatomique, psycho-physiologique et pathologique sur le rire et les exhilarants* (1899), contain valuable source material on the much neglected study of the physiology of laughter, including experiments by the pioneer neurologist Jean Martin Charcot and the Nobel laureate Charles Richet. HERBERT SPENCER, the English philosopher, in his "The Physiology of Laughter," *Essays on Education and Kindred Subjects* (1910), outlined the tension-relieving function of humour, on which FREUD elaborated in his *Der Witz und seine Beziehung zum Unbewussten* (1905; Eng. trans., *Wit and Its Relations to the Unconscious*, 1916), with special emphasis on infantile and repressed elements in the comic. HENRI BERGSON, *Le Rire* (1900; Eng. trans., *Laughter*, 1911), is a classic work attempting to derive all types of humour from the contrast between mind and matter. M.F. EASTMAN, *Enjoyment of Laughter* (1936), is unique among theoreticians of humour in that he denies the malicious element in laughter. R.H. BLYTH, *Japanese Humor*, 2nd ed. (1957), throws a delightful sidelight on a different culture. D.H. MUNRO, *Argument of Laughter* (1951), contains a valuable summary of earlier theories. A. KOESTLER, *Insight and Outlook* (1949) and *The Act of Creation* (1964), attempt to present a synthetic theory of humour and its interrelations with art and discovery.

(A.Ko.)

Hunan

Hunan (Hu-nan in Pin-yin romanization) is one of the 21 provinces, or *sheng*, of the People's Republic of China. It is a landlocked province covering an area of 81,274 square miles (210,500 square kilometres). A major rice-producing area, Hunan is situated to the south of the Yangtze River Basin. It is bounded by the provinces of Hupeh to the north, Kiangsi to the east, and Kwangtung to the southeast, by the Kwangsi Chuang Autonomous Region to the southwest, and by the provinces of Kweichow and Szechwan to the west. The name Hunan is formed from the Chinese words *hu* ("lake") and *nan* ("south"), meaning the land to the south of the lakes from Sha-shih, Hupeh, to Chiu-chiang, Kiangsi. Hunan's population is estimated at 38,000,000. The capital and most important city of the province is Ch'ang-sha, situated in the northeast, on the banks of the Hsiang Chiang (Siang Kiang).

Although mining and industry have been developed since 1949, Hunan's economy remains basically agricultural. It ranks third among China's provinces in rice production; two crops a year are planted in the south. From the earlier decades of the 20th century, Hunan was a centre of revolutionary activity; it was the birthplace of many Chinese Communist leaders, including Mao Tse-tung, revolutionist and founder of the Chinese Communist state, and Liu Shao-ch'i, theoretician and former chairman of the People's Republic. (For an associated physical feature, see YANGTZE RIVER; for historical background, see CHINA, HISTORY OF.)

History. From 350 to 221 BC, Hunan formed the southernmost extension of the state of Ch'u, which nominally was ruled by the Chou dynasty. From 221 to 206 BC, Hunan was ruled by the Ch'in dynasty, which subdued contending feudal states and joined them into the first unified state of China, of which Hunan formed part of the central area. Most of Hunan at this time was covered with dense primeval forest that was sparsely inhabited by tribes who engaged in hunting, fishing, and clearing land by burning or cutting for temporary cultivation. These tribes also supplied the copper and tin that was used in the north for making bronze.

After the downfall of the Ch'in dynasty, the area became quickly incorporated into the Chinese Empire ruled by the Han dynasty from 206 BC to AD 220. During this period persistent waves of migrant Han-jen (northern Chinese) occupied the land, and the indigenous tribesmen (Miao, T'uchia, T'ung, and Yao) were pushed west and southwest into the hills, which they still occupy. By the end of the Chin dynasty in AD 317, the Tung-t'ing flood plain to the north and the Hsiang Chiang (Hsiang River) Valley in the east were relatively well populated. Chinese migration from the north continued under subsequent dynasties, with migrants fleeing first from Mongol and then from Manchu invasions. Those who went further south, crossing the Nan Ling (Nan Mountains) in the southern part of the province to enter Kwangtung, have since considered themselves T'ang Jen, or southern Chinese, but the Hunanese have remained Han-jen in both culture and speech.

Early migrations

Population pressures on the land increased markedly in the 19th century during the latter part of the Ch'ing dynasty (1644 to 1911), leading to peasant unrest, particularly among the non-Chinese tribes. When the Taiping Rebellion broke out in Kwangsi in 1850, it spread northward into Hunan along the Hsiang Chiang Valley. Hunan, together with other provinces on the lower Yangtze River Basin, was desolated in the subsequent fighting, although the city of Ch'ang-sha withstood a Taiping siege in the 1850s. It was a Hunanese, Tseng Kuo-fan, who ultimately crushed the rebellion.

Hunan was not opened to foreign trade until 1904, following the conclusion of the Treaty of Shanghai between China and Japan. A foreign settlement was established at Ch'ang-sha; British and Japanese firms built warehouses there. The first uprisings against Yüan Shih-k'ai's attempted regency over the Chinese Empire occurred in the province in 1910, although the more widespread revolution that finally overthrew the tottering Manchu dynasty and established the Republic of China did not occur until the following year. Thereafter, Hunan remained in a state of unrest from which it had little respite until 1949, when the People's Republic of China was established. Mao Tse-tung, who was born in Shao-shan-ch'ung, near the border with Kiangsi, was largely responsible for encouraging the peasants and miners to make the abortive Autumn Harvest Uprising of 1927. He subsequently held the Communist forces together in Chin-kang Shan, where they withstood repeated attacks by the forces of Chiang Kai-shek, the Chinese Nationalist leader. In 1934 Mao set out from the Hunan-Kiangsi border region, leading his forces westward on what later came to be known as the Long March.

The years of unrest (1910–49)

During the Sino-Japanese War (1937 to 1945), Hunan was the scene of bitter fighting between 1939 and 1941, when, after the fall of Hunan to the Japanese, the Chinese general Hsueh Yueh successfully defended Ch'angsha against the Japanese invaders until 1944. Between 1946 and 1949 the province was relatively peaceful. In 1949, despite damage to bridges and communications, the province experienced comparatively little destruction when the Chinese Nationalist forces retreated rapidly southward before the Chinese Communist forces.

The landscape. *Relief.* More than one-quarter of the terrain lies at a height of more than 1,650 feet, and much of it is well over 3,000 feet above sea level. The highlands in the west run from northeast to southwest, forming the eastward edge of the Kweichow Plateau, whose extension, the Hsüeh-feng Shan (Hsüeh-feng Mountains) lie in the heart of the province. These mountains are composed mainly of hard, metamorphic rocks (*i.e.*, rocks that have been structurally changed as a result of heat and pressure) consisting of slate, quartzite, and sandstone; they are deeply incised by river valleys.

The Nan Ling in the south run from east to west at altitudes of between 500 and 1,650 feet, forming a broad mountain border between Hunan, Kwangtung Province, and Kwangsi Chuang Autonomous Region. They are largely dome shaped and granitic; although in lower-lying areas, limestone and red clay are found. In the east, the mountain ranges of Chu-kuang Shan and Wukung Shan form the border with Kiangsi; they generally run from northeast to southwest. The Chukuang Shan, in the extreme southeast of the province, rise to a height of 6,600 feet.

The uplands of the west, south, and east fall steadily in altitude toward the plain of the Tung-t'ing Hu (Tung-t'ing Lake) in the north, which is contiguous to the Hupeh plain and forms part of the flood plain of the Yangtze River. The part of the plain that lies within the borders of Hunan has an area of 3,800 square miles; it has been formed by the silt carried down from the mountains by the Yangtze and its right-bank tributaries. The Tung-t'ing Hu is a broad and shallow lake, consisting of the remnants of a former inland sea, which once filled the entire Yangtze Basin. Its area varies considerably between summer and winter; it acts as a filter and regulator for waters draining into the Yangtze.

Tung-t'ing Lake

Drainage. Hunan's entire river system drains into the Tung-t'ing Hu, with the exception of the Lin Shui (Lin Stream), which divides into two parts, with one distributary draining directly into the Yangtze River, and the other draining into the Tung-t'ing Hu. The western highlands are drained by the Yüan, the Tzu, and the Li rivers. The Yüan and the Tzu in their upper courses are torrents, fast-flowing in summer, that run through deep gorges, broadening out to wider valleys in their lower courses. Hunan's largest river, the Hsiang Chiang, rises in the heart of the Nan Ling, as do its tributaries the Ch'un-ling Shui and the Lei Shui. Many smaller rivers that rise in the mountains along the eastern border flow westward to join the Hsiang in its northward course.

Climate. The north generally experiences more extreme weather conditions, both in summer and in winter, than does the south. In winter, occasional waves of cold air from a high-pressure zone centred over Mongolia sweep southward, injuring tea bushes and fruit trees in northern Hunan. The average minimum temperature for December and January is 43° F (6° C). Summers are long and humid, and temperatures are slightly higher in the north. The average maximum temperature in July and August is 86° F (30° C). The north has an average of 260 frostless days a year, while in the south the average is 300 days. Rainfall is ample, with the maximum precipitation occurring between spring and summer, at which season the humidity is highest. The total annual rainfall of 56 inches (1,602 millimetres) decreases from south to north. Hunan lies in the path of cyclones that pass from west to east along the Yangtze Basin in summer, bringing with them at times long periods of heavy rain, resulting in extensive flooding of low-lying lands around the Tung-t'ing Hu.

Soils. The soils of the province are largely pedalferic (rich in alumina and iron), and are mainly lateritic (leached, iron-bearing) yellow earths or Quaternary red clays (*i.e.*, formed within the past 2,500,000 years). In the hilly regions of central and southern Hunan, the soils are for the most part lateritic heavy clays that are strongly acidic and poor in organic material. These regions are subject to soil erosion, especially when deforestation has occurred and plant cover is poor. The alluvial soils of the northern plains are less acidic and form a neutral zone between the pedalfers (iron and alumina-rich soils) of the south and the pedocals (arid or semiarid soils, enriched with lime) that occur further north; they are used for growing rice.

Vegetation and animal life. The natural vegetation of Hunan was originally dense deciduous and coniferous forest. Over the centuries, as the population has increased, all the lowlands and much of the highlands have been cleared to make way for cultivation. Despite this vast deforestation, however, large stands of pine, cedar, bamboo, and camphor are found in the western highlands. Other important trees and shrubs include tung (from which tung oil is obtained), tea (from which tea seed oil is obtained), and the liquidambar. Bamboo groves planted along the roadsides are characteristic of Hunan and provide a source of supply for the province's craft industries. As elsewhere in central and southern China, groves of bamboo, camphor, and cedar are usually found around villages, contributing greatly to the charm of the countryside.

Tree species

During the early decades of the 20th century, heavy and wasteful cutting of Hunan's timber reserves occurred. In 1954 attention was focussed on the problem of deforestation in the province, and at that time it was estimated that commercially accessible timber reserves amounted to some 350,000,000 cubic feet. Since then, stricter control of cutting has been enforced, and some reforestation carried out. Experiments in sowing pine seed by air, as well as in spraying insecticide from the air, were tried over wide areas in the 1960s.

Wild life on the densely settled plains has largely disappeared. Rodents, such as rats, rabbits, and hares, abound, as also do snakes, scorpions, and centipedes. There is abundant bird life, including pheasant, wild ducks, blue jays, and golden orioles. Some deer are found in the wooded hills of the plains. The mountains to the west abound in gibbons and deer. There are also some tigers and wild pigs.

Population. Hunan covers 2 percent of China's land area, and contains about 5 percent of its population. In

China's first scientific census in 1953, the province's inhabitants numbered about 33,000,000, and in 1970 they were estimated to total 38,000,000. The average population density is 469 persons per square mile, but in some of the more fertile districts it rises to between 1,000 and 1,600 persons per square mile. In the more remote mountain regions density drops to between 130 and 260 persons per square mile. The demarcation between rural and urban population is not clear. Agricultural communities of 2,000 people or less are classed as rural, but mining communities of the same size are classed as urban. There is no doubt, however, that the overwhelming majority of the population is rural.

Ethnic composition and distribution. The population is primarily concentrated on the Tung-t'ing Plain and in the main river valleys. Over 97 percent of it is Han-jen (northern Chinese).

The minority tribes

In addition, there are some 900,000 members of tribes living in the western highlands. These minority peoples consist mainly of four tribes, the Miao, numbering about 370,000; the T'uchia, 390,000; the T'ung, 124,000; and the Yao, 70,000. The way of life and economy of the Miao and the T'uchia are similar, and much intermarriage has occurred between them. The two tribes were not differentiated in the 1953 census, when they were officially referred to as the Miao and reported to number about 750,000. They live in the southwest, where their economy is based on the cultivation of terraced fields in the foothills and narrow valleys. They grow corn on mountain slopes and elsewhere cultivate tung, tea, and galla nuts, from each of which they express oil. Each tribe has its own distinctive handicrafts, notably embroidery and cross-stitch work; they engage little in trade.

The T'ung inhabit their own autonomous counties (*hsien*) in the extreme southwest, with their centres at T'ung-tao and Hsin-huang. Their language, economy, and way of life are similar to those of the Han-jen; their cultural standards are higher than those of the other minority peoples. The Yao are widely scattered over the mountainous regions of the south and west. They practice dry farming (a mode of farming depending largely upon methods of tillage that render the soil more receptive to moisture and reduce evaporation) and are known for their expertise in cedar-tree culture. Much of their livelihood comes from forestry; the lumber they cut is floated down the tributaries of the Tzu Shui and the Lien Shui.

Linguistic patterns. The Han-jen of the province speak a dialect—Hunanese—that approximates quite closely to Mandarin. Radio broadcasting has had the effect of slowly reducing differences in local dialects, which can be considerable. The written language is the same in Hunan as in Peking. The minority languages were unwritten until missionaries devised scripts for some of them, such as the Samuel Pollard script for the Miao language. Since 1949 these scripts have been revised, extended, or replaced by a phonetic script, based on the Latin alphabet, that is akin to the Pin-yin script adopted for the Chinese (Han) language. There is growing literacy among both the Miao and T'ung peoples.

Religious affiliations. The interweaving of Confucianism, Buddhism, and Taoism, as well as Islām and Christianity, are most complicated. Since 1949, the growth of Maoism has infiltrated and directed life in all its aspects. The extent of de facto religious freedom and the number of open temples and churches varies from district to district.

Patterns of urban and rural settlement. Villages are usually small, and it is not unusual for an entire village to belong to one extended family, from which the settlement takes its name. Most of the farms on the plain south of the Tung-t'ing Hu are built on islands of Yangtze alluvium, protected by dikes from summer flooding.

The cities

Urban population was estimated at only 2,600,000 in 1957. There are 30 cities with populations of between 10,000 and 30,000; these are located mainly on the plains and function as marketing centres for local produce. In addition, there are ten cities with populations between 30,000 and 100,000 and five cities of 100,000 or more. Ch'ang-sha (population 700,000), Hsiang-t'an (250,000), and Chu-chou (190,000) lie close together at the intersection of road, rail, and river communications along the Hsiang Chiang. They are growing rapidly and are already coming to form a single vast conurbation. Other large cities include Heng-yang, the economic and communications centre of southern Hunan, and Ch'ang-te, the marketing centre for the Yüan Chiang Basin.

Administration. From 1949 to 1954 Hunan was part of the South Central Administrative Area, which extended from Hupeh in the north to Kwangtung and Kwangsi in the south. In 1954 provincial (*sheng*) government was re-established throughout the country. Since then the province's administrative structure has gone through several changes. In 1968 the administrative divisions were two municipalities (*shih*), nine special districts (*chuan-ch'ü*), and one autonomous district (*tzu-chih-chou*). These were further divided into five municipalities, 84 counties (*hsien*), and four autonomous counties (*tzu-chih-hsien*).

In 1958 the establishment of communes led to considerable change in the pattern of local government. Each commune, grouping together a number of cooperatives into a single unit, assumed the functions of *ch'ü*, rural districts, and towns, and became responsible for the political, economic, and cultural life of its enlarged area, including such matters as ideology, agriculture, industry, education, public health, local militia, and recreation. There was much variation in practice from commune to commune. The outbreak of the Cultural Revolution in 1966, when so much of the Chinese Communist Party authority was challenged, once again threw local government into confusion. It was not until 1970 that the position became clear, by which time Revolutionary Committees had been established for all provinces. One of the earliest of these was Hunan's, appointed in 1968. It consists of 14 members who are appointed by provincial groups and approved by Peking; eight are members of the People's Liberation Army (PLA), four are revolutionary cadres (members of the party élite) and two are representatives of the revolutionary masses (those who are politically correct, not only party members). From this it will be seen that there is a decided military predominance in Hunan. The communes have lost many of their former functions.

The Revolutionary Committee

Social conditions. *Education.* Before the revolution, Western learning was largely acquired through Christian missionary schools, and some 90 percent of the population remained illiterate. Since the establishment of the People's Republic in 1949, a countrywide literacy drive has been pursued with vigour and enthusiasm and a large measure of success. In formal education, political (ideological) correctness is given pre-eminence at all levels. Since the formation in 1958 of the communes, which were made responsible for primary and middle education, and particularly since the Cultural Revolution and the formation of part-work–part-study schools, great emphasis has been placed on the teaching of self-reliance and technical skills. In the mid-1960s, 30,000 commune members in Hunan were trained as pump operators, electricians, and mechanics, capable of working in the fields and tending machines. Ch'ang-sha has retained its historic role as the province's cultural and educational centre and is the focus of higher education in the province. It is the location of technical institutes, teacher-training colleges, and institutes for minorities.

Health. Emphasis is laid on preventive medicine. After 1949, doctors' training was reduced from six to three years and public health teams were sent into the country to vaccinate and inoculate and to advise on and supervise public hygiene. Debilitating diseases such as malaria and schistosomiasis—a disease of the blood and tissues that is spread by larvae in the droppings of animals in the rice fields—have been attacked. Dermatitis of the hands and feet, common among rice farmers, is receiving special attention. While these teams of "barefoot" doctors are increasing, doctors are once more receiving the full six years' training; full use is made of traditional Chinese medicine. By 1964 it was claimed that every county (*hsien*) in Hunan had at least one fully staffed hospital as well as a training school for assistant physicians and medical teams. Since 1949 there has been a marked fall in infant mortality and an increase in life expectancy.

The economy. *Agriculture.* Hunan has some 58,000,000 *mow* (one *mow* equals an acre) of cultivated land, representing 18 percent of the total area of the province. An estimated 22 percent of the land is covered with forest, 24 percent is barren hills considered suitable for reforestation, and 5 percent consists of water. The remaining land is regarded as unsuitable for development. Of Hunan's cultivable land, more than 30 percent lies in the plain around Tung-t'ing Hu that stretches south to Hsiang-t'an and Chu-chou.

Rice production

One of China's great rice-producing regions, Hunan exports a large surplus to other provinces. It is estimated that 85 percent of the cultivable land is devoted to paddies (rice fields), a great many of which produce two crops of rice and demand careful cultivation. The first crop is planted at the end of April, transplanted in June, and harvested at the end of July. One week of hectic plowing and puddling is followed by the planting of the second crop, which is harvested in November. The autumn period is the most difficult, as decreasing rainfall and increasing evaporation necessitate continuous irrigation over a 180-day period. About one-third of the paddy field lies fallow in the winter. With improved irrigation, a decreasing amount of rice is grown on *t'ien shui t'ien* ("heaven water fields"), in which the crop relies totally on rainfall. Other food crops include sweet potatoes, corn (maize), barley, potatoes, kaoliang (tall, drought-resistant sorghum), buckwheat, garden peas, millet, and horse beans.

Industrial crops occupy almost 6 percent of the cultivable area. Rape—an herb grown for its seeds—is cultivated mainly in the upper valleys of the Hsüeh-feng Shan, while cotton, ramie (a shrub that yields a fibre used in textile manufacture), and jute are produced in the northern plains around the Tung-t'ing Hu. Red and black tea are grown on the foothills of the Hsüeh-feng Shan around An-hua and on Mu-fou Shan and Chiu-ling Shan on the eastern border. Peanut cultivation is widespread, and tung trees and tea seed shrubs are grown and their oils expressed in the western and southern highlands. There is a marked zoning of fruit growing. Oranges, mandarin oranges, and grapefruit are grown in the south; tangerines, pears, and peaches are raised in the central region; and chestnuts, pears, and peaches are grown in the north.

Cultivation has been much improved by the use of fertilizer. By 1965 in Hunan an estimated 2,550,000 acres were under green-manure crops (green crops ploughed in as fertilizer); the use of chemical fertilizer had also increased six times within the decade. Seed selection has helped to increase production, and new strains of rice have been developed. Most farms are small, and mechanization is confined to the use of simple machines and tools, such as the rice transplanters, foot-operated rice threshing machines, rubber-tired carts and wheelbarrows, and a tube water raiser that is replacing the old wooden trough and paddles.

Fisheries. Fish are taken in large quantities from lakes, rivers, and village ponds. The most common varieties are carp, silver carp, and "silver fish." The full exploitation of fishpond culture was attempted only in the early 1970s.

Stock raising. In 1957 there were an estimated 3,000,000 head of cattle in Hunan, of which more than one-third were water buffalo. Cattle are used almost exclusively for draft purposes. In the same year there were nearly 9,000,000 hogs, concentrated mainly in the central and eastern areas, where the population is most dense.

Water control. Much of the low-lying land around the Tung-t'ing Hu is subject to flooding when the rivers come down in spate during the summer months. The system of dikes built to contain the flood waters is supplemented by a vast network of electric pumping stations that serve an area of 1,000,000 acres in 13 counties (*hsien*). These pumps have the double function of draining the fields when waterlogged and irrigating them in time of drought.

In the dry hill lands more than 100 medium-sized water-control projects have been built since the formation of the communes in 1958. In these projects, valleys are dammed and "mountain pools" formed, from which channels are led to the thirsty land. One of these schemes—the Shaoshan Irrigation System—has been built in Mao Tse-tung's own county. It diverts some of the upper waters of the Lien Shui, thus irrigating the dry hill land and also controls flooding in the river's lower reaches; it has two main canals of 89 miles combined length that irrigate 150,000 acres—thus converting them from single-crop to double-crop rice land. The main canals are navigable by 30-ton boats.

The Shaoshan Irrigation System

Mining and industry. The province's considerable mineral wealth includes ample coal reserves, adequate iron-ore and manganese deposits, and rich deposits of antimony, lead, zinc, and tungsten. The main coal measures are located in the south. Little developed before 1949, total coal production had risen in the 1950s to 3,000,000 tons annually as a result of the opening of large mines at San-tu (Tzu-hsing county), north of Ch'en-hsien in the extreme south. The Tzu-hsing mine serves the Wu-han Iron and Steel Corporation and the Wu-han–Canton Railway.

Iron ore is widely distributed, and there is a long established local industry that produces iron pots. The main iron mines are located in the hills east and south of Ch'ang-sha and Hsiang-t'an. Development of the iron and steel industry is centred in the triangle formed by the three large cities of Ch'ang-sha, Hsiang-t'an, and Chu-chou. Antimony production is centred on Hsin-hua, northwest of Shao-yang. Some antimony is shipped to Ch'ang-sha for refining. Hunan is China's third largest producer of tungsten, a gray-white metallic element used for electrical purposes. It is chiefly mined in the hills between the Tzu and Yüan rivers around Yüan-ling. Tungsten mines have also been opened near Heng-yang.

Plants producing both iron and steel are located in Hsiang-t'an, while Chu-chou is the centre of large-scale heavy industry and also specializes in electrical machinery and equipment. There is also a large chemical fertilizer plant and a rolling-stock repair plant in Chu-chou. Ch'ang-sha is Hunan's centre for light industry, which includes rice milling, food processing, and textile manufacture. It is also famous for its handicrafts, which include *hsiang* (border) embroideries, duck-down quilts, umbrellas, and leather goods. Mining and processing equipment for nonferrous metals is manufactured at Heng-yang.

I-yang—the "Bamboo Town"

I-yang—known as "the Bamboo Town"—on the Tzu Shui is typical of many of the smaller towns specializing in one particular handicraft. Nearly everything required in domestic life—from beds and cupboards to mats and scrubbing brushes—is made from bamboo. Based on the raw material from the thick bamboo groves on the surrounding hills, the industry was established several hundred years ago, and by the 1970s employed about 700 workers and 17 producer cooperatives.

There are several famous pottery kilns that date back to the T'ang dynasty (618–907). Situated at Yüeh-yang (Yoyang), Hsiang-yin, and near Ch'ang-sha, they have at different epochs produced all sorts of wares, according to the market of the period. Their fortunes have fluctuated through the centuries. In recent years they have increased their output, especially in the Hsiang-yin kilns, which produce large quantities of crockery for the general market.

Transport. Hunan stands at the crossroads of China's historical lines of communication—the great waterway of the Yangtze River, which flows from Szechwan Province to the sea, and the Imperial Highway, running from Canton northward to Peking.

Railways. Railway construction began in 1912 when track was laid between Wu-han in Hupeh Province and Chu-chou, with an extension to P'ing-hsiang in Kiangsi for the transport of coking coal. The line was eventually extended to Canton in Kwangtung Province in 1936, where it connected with the line to Kowloon in Hong Kong, which had been built in 1911. Since 1949 the whole length of the railway has been double-tracked, and bridges and rolling stock, damaged during years of warfare, repaired. The line is now in heavy use for passenger and freight transport. There is a junction at Heng-yang leading to Kueilin, Liu-chou, and Nan-ning, in the Kwangsi Chuang Autonomous Region, from where the line continues to Hanoi in North Vietnam. From Chu-chou, the Che–Kan Railway runs via Nan-ch'ang to Chiu-chiang on the Yangtze, both in Kiangsi Province, and also to Hangchow in Chekiang Province and Foochow in Fukien Province on the east coast. Another railway is that running from Hsiang-t'an westward via the Lien Shui and Tzu Shui valleys on to Kuei-yang on the Kweichow Plateau in Kweichow Province. This line opens up the hitherto remote western lands.

Shipping. Shipping is the most important means of transportation. An estimated 80 percent of Hunan's goods are moved by water, mainly by sailing junks using the rivers and their tributaries. Traffic on the Hsiang Chiang is the most important; cargoes consist mainly of food grains, timber, salt, and mining construction equipment. The Tung-t'ing Hu has innumerable shallow waterways connecting four main rivers. Yüeh-yang in the northeast corner of the lake is the collecting centre for the timber rafts that sail the Yangtze River to Wuhan.

Roads. Road building is largely the work of the communes. There is one main trunk road running from north to south, following the railway through Yüeh-yang, Ch'ang-sha, Hsiang-t'an, and Heng-yang to Ch'en-hsien and Kuei-lin, both of which are in the Kwangsi Chuang Autonomous Region. Three other main routes run from east to west and are of growing importance because they open up areas not served by the railways. They originate at Hsiang-t'an or Ch'ang-sha and reach to the upper Tzu Shui and to Yüan-ling and to Kuei-yang. These western roads carry passengers and light goods.

Air service. Air transport is entirely in the hands of the national government. It is used mainly for official purposes and for transporting urgently needed engineering goods. Ch'ang-sha is Hunan's main airport.

Cultural life and institutions. Although the aim of the government is to promote linguistic uniformity, Hunanese—which is Mao Tse-tung's own dialect and which is fairly akin to Mandarin—persists.

Since 1949 and especially since the formation of the communes, there has been a marked development in village life. Every village of any size has its civic centre and library, however humble. Being better lighted than the homesteads, these centres provide attractive places for meetings and social gatherings with their radios and Ping-Pong tables. The old art of story telling, using contemporary themes, has been considerably developed, and villages are visited by travelling players. There is no television. Local newspapers are published only in the largest cities but "wall newspapers"—akin to village notice boards—in civic centres and factories are popular.

BIBLIOGRAPHY. SUN CHING-CHIH (ed.), *Economic Geography of Central China (Hupeh, Hunan, Kiangsi) Communist China* (1960; orig. pub. in Chinese, 1958), one of many volumes by Chinese geographers covering the whole country; NAVAL INTELLIGENCE DIVISION OF THE BRITISH ADMIRALTY, *Geographical Handbook Series: China Proper*, 3 vol. (1944–45); K.M. BUCHANAN, *The Transformation of the Chinese Earth* (1970), a general geography by a writer committed to the present regime; A. DONNITHORNE, *China's Economic System* (1967), a standard work, drawing extensively on Chinese sources; S. CHANDRASEKHAR, *China's Population* (1959), an analysis of the census of 1953–54; T.R. TREGEAR, *A Geography of China* (1965), a general geography to serve university undergraduates; *Economic Geography of China* (1970), more advanced than the above, amplifying the economic and social section; *China Quarterly* (1960–), a scholarly journal; A. HERRMANN, *An Historical Atlas of China*, new ed. (1966).

(T.R.T.)

Hundred Years' War

The Hundred Years' War is the name usually given by historians, not quite accurately, to the long struggle between France and England that, interrupted by two treaties and by numerous truces, continued intermittently from 1337 to 1453. The confiscation (May 24, 1337) of the English-held duchy of Guyenne by the French king Philip VI is generally accepted as marking its outbreak. This confiscation, however, had been preceded by others and was but one episode in a series of disputes that had long exacerbated relations between the two countries (see also FRANCE, HISTORY OF; BRITAIN AND IRELAND, HISTORY OF).

In the first half of the 14th century, France was without doubt the richest, largest, and most populous kingdom of Western Christendom; it had, moreover, derived immense prestige from the fame and exploits of its monarchs, especially of Louis IX (St. Louis), and it had grown powerful through the loyal service given by its administrators and officials. But England was the best-organized and most closely integrated Western state and the most likely to rival France, since the Holy Roman Empire was paralyzed by deep divisions. In these circumstances serious conflict between the two countries was perhaps inevitable, but its extreme bitterness and long duration are more surprising. The length of the conflict can be explained, however, by the fact that a basic struggle for supremacy was exacerbated by complicated problems such as that of the English territorial possessions in France and the disputed succession to the French throne; it was also prolonged by bitter litigation, commercial rivalry, and greed for plunder.

REMOTE AND PROXIMATE CAUSES

The problem of the English lands in France. The complicated political relationship existing between France and England in the first half of the 14th century derived ultimately from the position of William the Conqueror (d. 1087), the first sovereign ruler of England who also held fiefs on the continent of Europe as a vassal of the French king. The natural alarm caused to the Capetian kings by their overmighty vassals, the dukes of Normandy, who were also kings of England, was greatly increased by events involving Henry Plantagenet. Already duke of Normandy (1150) and count of Anjou (1151), Henry became not only duke of Aquitaine in 1152, by right of his wife, Eleanor of Aquitaine, recently divorced from Louis VII of France, but also king of England as Henry II in 1154. A long conflict inevitably ensued, in which the French kings steadily reduced and weakened the Angevin empire. This struggle, which could well be termed the First Hundred Years' War, was ended by the Treaty of Paris between Henry III of England and Louis IX of France, which was finally ratified in December 1259. By this treaty Henry III was to retain the duchy of Guyenne (a much-reduced vestige of Aquitaine, with Gascony), doing homage for it to the French king, but had to resign his claim to Normandy, Anjou, Poitou, and most of the other lands of Henry II's original empire that the English had in any case already lost. In return Louis pledged himself in due course to hand over to the English certain territory that protected the border of Guyenne; *i.e.*, lower Saintonge, Agenais, and some lands in Quercy. This treaty stood a fair chance of being respected by two rulers such as Henry and Louis, who admired each other and were closely related (they had married sisters), but it posed many problems for the future. It had been agreed, for instance, that the lands in Saintonge, Agenais, and Quercy that were held at the time of the treaty by Louis IX's brother Alphonse, count of Poitiers and Toulouse, should go to the English at his death if he had no heir. When Alphonse died without issue in 1271, the new king of France, Philip III, tried to evade the agreement; and the question was not settled until Edward I of England received the lands in Agenais by the Treaty of Amiens (1279) and those in Saintonge by the Treaty of Paris (1286). Edward surrendered his treaty rights to the Quercy lands. By the Treaty of Amiens, moreover, Philip acknowledged the rights of Edward's consort, Eleanor of Castile, to the countship of Ponthieu.

Treaty of Paris, 1259

Meanwhile, the French kings' suzerainty over Guyenne

gave their officials an excuse for frequent intervention in the duchy's affairs. The result was that French royal seneschals and their subordinates encouraged malcontents in the duchy to appeal against their duke to the French king and to the *parlement* of Paris. Such appeals strained relations between the French and English courts on more than one occasion, and the homage that had to be done again whenever a new ruler ascended either throne was given only grudgingly.

The first serious crisis after the conclusion of the Treaty of Paris came in 1293 when ships from England and Bayonne were engaged in a series of skirmishes with a Norman fleet. Demanding compensation, Philip IV of France announced the confiscation of Guyenne (May 19, 1294). By 1296, as a result of the successful campaigns there of his brother Charles, count of Valois, and his cousin Robert II of Artois, Philip had become the effective master of almost the whole duchy; but Edward I then allied himself in 1297 with Guy of Dampierre, count of Flanders, another rebellious vassal of France. A truce (October 1297), confirmed a year later through the arbitration of Pope Boniface VIII, ended this phase of hostilities.

The question of Edward's homage

Shortly after his succession to the English throne Edward II did homage for his French lands to Philip IV in 1308. But Edward was reluctant to repeat the ceremony on the accessions of Philip's three sons, Louis X (1314), Philip V (1316), and Charles IV (1322). Louis X died before Edward proffered homage; Philip V did not receive it until 1320; and Edward's delay in paying homage to Charles IV, combined with the destruction (November 1323) by the Gascons of the newly built French fortress at Saint-Sardos in Agenais, led the French king to declare Guyenne forfeit (July 1324). The duchy was overrun again (1324–25) by the forces of Charles of Valois. Even so, both sides had intermittently been seeking a solution to this troublesome problem. Edward II and Philip V had tried to solve it by the nomination of seneschals or governors for Guyenne who were acceptable to them both, and the appointment of the Genoese Antonio Pessagno and later of Amaury de Craon to this post had proved successful for a time. A similar expedient was adopted by the appointment (1325) of Henri de Sully, who held the office of butler in the French royal household and was a friend of Edward II. In the same year Edward renounced the duchy in favour of his son the future Edward III. But this solution, which avoided the awkwardness of requiring one king to do homage to another, proved unfortunately of short duration, since the new duke of Guyenne returned almost immediately to England (September 1326) to dethrone his father (1327).

The problem of the French succession. A fresh complication was introduced when Charles IV died on Feb. 1, 1328, while his wife was pregnant. Since there existed at that time no definite rule about the succession to the French crown in such circumstances, it was left to an assembly of magnates to decide who ought to be regent. The two principal claimants were Edward III of England, who derived his claim through his mother, Isabella, sister of Charles IV, and Philip, count of Valois, son of Philip IV's brother Charles.

Preparations for war

The assembly decided in favour of the count of Valois, who became king as Philip VI. Edward III protested vigorously, threatening to defend his rights by every possible means; but after his rival had defeated some Flemish rebels at the Battle of Cassel (August 1328), he withdrew his claim and did simple homage for Guyenne at Amiens in June 1329. But Philip required liege homage and was, moreover, determined not to restore certain lands for which Edward asked; war nearly broke out and Edward was ultimately obliged to renew his homage, in private, on the French king's terms (March–April 1331). Anglo-French relations remained cordial for more than two years; but from 1334 onward, encouraged by Robert III of Artois (grandson of Philip IV's cousin), who quarrelled with Philip and took refuge in England, Edward seems to have regretted his weakness, seeking to recover the Gascon lands lost to Charles IV and demanding an end of the alliance between France and Scotland. He intrigued against Philip in the Low Countries and in Germany, while Philip, for his part, organized a small expedition to help the Scots (1336) and formed an alliance with Castile (December 1336). Both parties were preparing for war; Philip declared Guyenne confiscate on May 24, 1337, and in October, Edward began to declare that the kingdom of France was rightfully his.

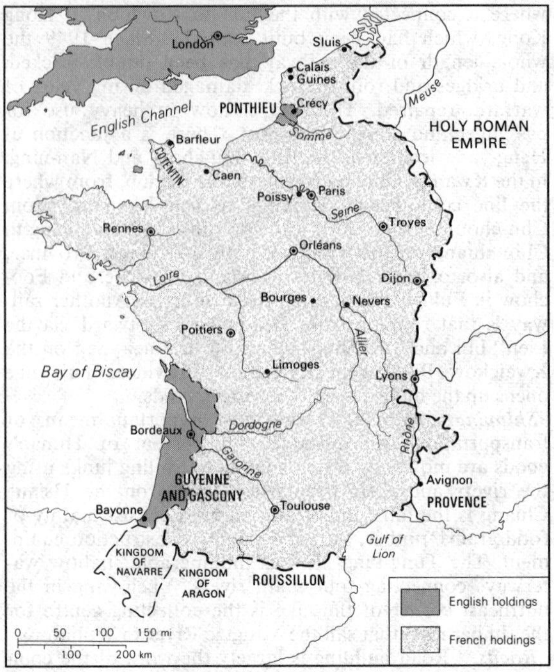

France at the beginning of the Hundred Years' War.
Adapted from *Atlas of European History;* Oxford University Press

FROM THE OUTBREAK OF WAR TO THE PEACE OF BRETIGNY, 1337–60

Hostilities in the Hundred Years' War began at sea with battles between privateers. Edward III did not disembark on the continent until 1338. He settled at Antwerp and made an alliance (1339) with Jacob van Artevelde, a citizen of Ghent, who had become the leader of the Flemish towns; in their anxiety to ensure the continued supply of English wool for their textile industries, the Flemish towns had rebelled against Count Louis of Nevers, who supported Philip. Edward also won the support of several rulers in the Low Countries, such as his brother-in-law William II, count of Hainaut, and John III, duke of Brabant. He also made an alliance (1338) with the emperor Louis IV the Bavarian. He besieged Cambrai in 1339; and on October 22 of that year a French and an English army came within a few miles of each other at Buironfosse, without, however, daring to join battle. A similar encounter occurred near Bouvines in 1340, after an English army supported by Flemish militia had failed to take Tournai. Meanwhile at sea Edward's ships defeated the French fleet, supported by Castilian and Genoese squadrons, in the Battle of Sluis on June 24, 1340, thus making it possible for him to move troops and provisions to the continent. After this victory the Truce of Esplechin (Sept. 25, 1340), brought about by the mediation of Philip VI's sister, Margaret, and of Pope Benedict XII, temporarily suspended hostilities.

The scene of operations shifted in 1341 to Brittany, where, after the death of Duke John III in April, the help of the French and English kings was invoked respectively by Charles of Blois and by John of Montfort (d. 1345), rival claimants for the succession. The troops of both kings invaded the duchy and their armies were confronting each other near Vannes by December 1342 when the legates of the new pope, Clement VI, intervened and managed to negotiate the Truce of Malestroit (Jan. 19, 1343).

The Capetian Succession in the Hundred Years' War

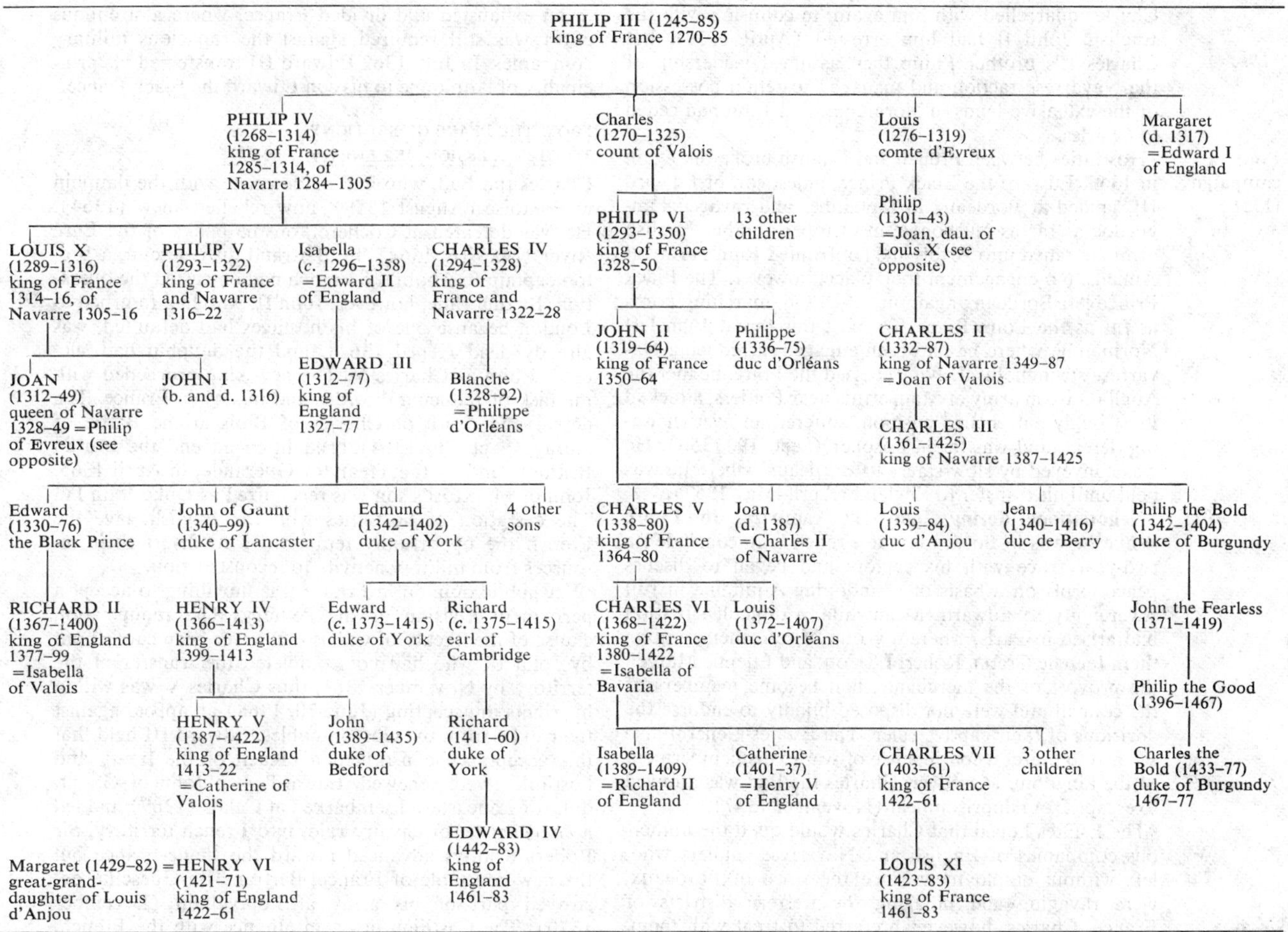

At this stage neither king was anxious to press the conflict to the issue of a decisive battle; each hoped to achieve his purpose by other means. They embarked on an intensive war of propaganda, Edward trying to enlist French support for his claims by means of proclamations nailed on church doors, and Philip cleverly exploiting to his own advantage all the traditions of the French kingship and losing no opportunity of stressing his claim to be the lawful successor of his Capetian ancestors. Edward's propaganda and promises were partly successful in fomenting rebellions in the west of France (1343 and 1344); these, however, Philip crushed with severity. Edward resumed the offensive in 1345, this time in Guyenne, since the murder of Jacob van Artevelde (July 1345) made it no longer easy for the English to use Flanders as a base for operations. Henry, earl (later duke) of Lancaster (d. 1361), defeated the French under Bertrand de l'Isle-Jourdain at Auberoche (October 1345) and took La Réole; in 1346 he repelled at Aiguillon an army led by John, duke of Normandy, Philip's eldest son.

Crécy campaign and its aftermath (1346–54). Meanwhile, Edward III himself landed in the Cotentin (July 1346), penetrated into Normandy, took Caen, and marched on Paris. Without attempting to take the capital he crossed the Seine River by the bridge at Poissy and set out toward Picardy and his fief of Ponthieu. Philip pursued him, catching up near Crécy in Ponthieu and immediately giving battle. The French army was crushed and many of the highest nobility were slain (Aug. 26, 1346). Edward made no attempt to exploit his victory and marched straight to Calais, which he besieged from September 1346 to August 1347. Under the leadership of Jean de Vienne, the garrison there put up a stubborn defense but was finally forced to yield through shortage of provisions. Then followed the celebrated episode of the surrender of the burghers of Calais, who gave themselves up at Edward's order, wearing only their shirts and with ropes round their necks. Their lives were saved by the intercession of Edward's queen, Philippa of Hainaut.

Siege of Calais

During the siege of Calais, the Scots, led by King David II, invaded England. They were beaten, however, at Neville's Cross (Oct. 17, 1346) and David was captured. The English were also fortunate in Brittany, where Charles of Blois was defeated and captured near La Roche-Derrien. In France the political situation became very confused after Crécy; there were changes in the king's council, and John of Normandy lost influence for a while. The possibility of Philip's adopting as his heir Edward instead of John, as part of a peace plan devised by the papacy and St. Bridget of Sweden, came to nothing. During these years the incidence of the Black Death and the financial straits of both governments combined to bring the war to a standstill; the truce signed (September 1347) after the fall of Calais was twice renewed (1348 and 1349) during the last years of Philip VI's reign and again (September 1351) after the accession of the duke of Normandy to the French crown as John II. John considered it his duty to bring about peace even at the cost of allowing the English king to enjoy free possession of his continental fiefs without having to do homage for them. But this suggestion so outraged public opinion in France that John was unable to conclude peace on such terms at the conferences held at Guînes (July 1353 and March 1354). Edward III then refused to prolong the truce.

The political situation in France at this time was further complicated by the intervention of Charles II the Bad, king of Navarre, who had married John II's daughter Joan in 1352. As a grandson of Louis X on his mother's side, Charles could maintain that his claim to the Capetian inheritance was better than Edward III's and that he was accordingly entitled to profit from any concessions that John II might be willing to make. After a first dispute with his father-in-law had apparently been settled by the treaties of Mantes (1354) and Valognes (1355), Charles quarrelled with him again, in collusion with the English. John II had him arrested (April 1356), but Charles II's brother Philip then assumed leadership of the Navarrese faction and managed to retain possession of the extensive lands in Normandy that John had ceded to Charles.

Poitiers campaign (1356)

Hostilities between French and English broke out again in 1355. Edward the Black Prince, eldest son of Edward III, landed at Bordeaux in September and ravaged Languedoc as far as Narbonne; in October another English army marched into Artois and confronted John's army at Amiens. No engagement took place, however. The Black Prince left Bordeaux again in July 1356, marching north as far as the Loire River. To meet this threat John left Normandy, where he had been engaged in reducing Navarrese strongholds. Having crossed the Loire, he met the Anglo-Gascon army at Maupertuis near Poitiers, attacked its strongly entrenched position, suffered an overwhelming defeat, and was taken prisoner (Sept. 19, 1356). He was conveyed by slow stages to Bordeaux, where he was held until his transfer to England (April–May 1357).

Negotiations during John II's captivity (to 1360). While he was in Bordeaux, the French king concluded a two-year truce with his captors and began to discuss peace terms on a basis of abandoning Aquitaine in full sovereignty to Edward. Meanwhile, a difficult situation had arisen in Paris, where a group of reformers, among them Jean de Craon, Robert Le Coq, and Étienne Marcel, the provost of the merchants, had become members of the council and were not disposed blindly to endorse the decisions of their captive ruler. The Estates-General also seemed to prefer a continuance of war to dismemberment of the kingdom. Moreover, Charles the Bad was allowed to escape from imprisonment (November 1357).

The Estates hoped that Charles would quell the numerous companies of English and Navarrese soldiers who, left without employment since the truce of Bordeaux, were ravaging and pillaging the western districts of France. Charles, however, preferred to treat with them. Though officially hostilities between France and England were suspended, the devastation became at this period more serious than ever. Disorder and misery were much increased by the Jacquerie, a revolt of the peasants, north of the Seine, which was brutally repressed by the nobility.

After the death of Étienne Marcel (July 31, 1358), the dauphin Charles, son of John II, was able to reenter Paris, from which he had been forced some months earlier to withdraw. King John, following up the peace talks begun at Bordeaux, concluded with Edward III the first Treaty of London (January 1358). This provided for the cession of the old duchy of Aquitaine to the English in full sovereignty and for the payment of 4,000,000 gold *écus* as John's ransom, while Edward in return would abandon his claim to the French crown. But delays in collecting and paying early installments of the ransom invalidated this treaty, and in March 1359 Edward imposed on his prisoner the harsher terms of the second Treaty of London, by which hostages were to be held until part of the ransom was paid; additional territory, the old Angevin lands lying between the Loire and the Channel, were also to be ceded to the English. The French estates, however, refused to ratify this second treaty, and Edward III landed once more at Calais (October 1359) and marched across Artois and Champagne. He failed to take Reims, however, and instead ravaged the district of Beauce. At Brétigny near Chartres, peace talks were held with the dauphin, and agreement was reached (May 8, 1360) on terms subsequently ratified by the treaties of Calais (July–October 1360). By these treaties France ceded the whole of the old Aquitaine and, in northern France, Ponthieu, Calais, and Guînes in full sovereignty to the English; the ransom was reduced to 3,000,000 gold *écus*, for payment of which hostages were taken, but John was to be released after a first installment of 600,000 *écus* had been received; and the French king was to make a formal resignation of all sovereignty and jurisdiction over the ceded territories by Nov. 30, 1361. Set free in October 1360, John went back to an exhausted and divided France, where a strenuous effort was still required against the rapacious military companies. In July 1362 Edward III transferred his principality of Aquitaine to his son Edward the Black Prince.

Treaty of Brétigny

FROM THE PEACE OF BRETIGNY TO THE ACCESSION OF HENRY V, 1360–1413

Charles the Bad, who had made peace with the dauphin at Pontoise (August 1359), now rebelled anew (1364). He was defeated at Cocherel, on the banks of the Eure River (May 16, 1364), by Bertrand du Guesclin, a Breton captain to whom the French had entrusted the operation. By that time, however, John II, who had returned to London because one of his hostages had defaulted, was already dead (April 1364), and the dauphin had succeeded him as Charles V. The new king proceeded with the task of reducing disorder and misery in France. The defeat and death of Charles of Blois at the Battle of Auray (Sept. 29, 1364) brought to an end the war in Brittany; and by the Treaty of Guérande, in April 1365, John of Montfort's son was recognized as Duke John IV. The cessation of hostilities with the English gave the French the opportunity temporarily to divert their resources from military activity to reconstruction.

Yet public opinion in France was unwilling to accept a permanent division of the country. The renunciation clause of the Treaty of Calais had never been carried out by John II, who had not completed the transfer of the territory by November 1361; thus Charles V was within his rights in accepting (June 30, 1368) an appeal against their duke from the Gascon nobles. Edward III held that this acceptance constituted a breach of the treaty and hostilities were renewed. Edward's son John of Gaunt, duke of Lancaster, disembarked at Calais (1369) and led a *chevauchée*, or cavalry raid, into French territory; Sir Robert Knollys advanced toward the Île-de-France but the new constable of France, Bertrand du Guesclin, destroyed part of his army at Pontvallain (December 1370). The Castilian navy, in alliance with the French, defeated an English fleet off La Rochelle (1372), and John of Gaunt conducted a more ambitious *chevauchée* (1373) across France from Calais to Bordeaux. In the intervals between these expeditions, the French king's younger brother, Louis I of Anjou, and du Guesclin were carrying out, partly by warfare but mainly by diplomacy and by bribing local lords, a patient reconquest of the territories ceded in 1360.

A truce was effected at Bruges in 1375, which lasted until 1377. The Black Prince died on June 8, 1376, and when King Edward III died (June 21, 1377), his heir, the Black Prince's son Richard II, was only ten years old. The war dragged on in a desultory fashion, and Charles V found himself once again the target of the ambitious designs of Charles the Bad and of John of Montfort. Thus when Charles V and du Guesclin died in 1380, the English had still not been completely driven out of France.

For the next few years both the English and the French thrones were occupied by children, Richard II and Charles V's son Charles VI. England was divided and weakened by the Peasants' Revolt of 1381 and by the political and constitutional struggles between Richard and his opponents; there was no surplus energy for active campaigning in France. In France, on the other hand, Charles VI's uncles were too busy jostling for power and dividing the spoils to complete the expulsion of the English. The most serious source of dispute between the two countries was now the problem of Flanders. Henry le Despenser, bishop of Norwich, led an expedition (nominally a crusade against the Avignon papacy) to Dunkerque and Ypres (1383), but it proved a total fiasco; and after the death without male heirs (January 1384) of the count of Flanders, Louis of Male, Flanders came into the possession of his son-in-law Philip the Bold, duke of Burgundy, the French king's uncle. The French made considerable preparation to invade England between 1385 and 1387, but for reasons not known the project was abandoned. Shortly afterward, the acquisition of political power by groups in both countries who favoured peace led to the inauguration of truce talks.

"Marmousets" and "Appellants"

In France the princes had been ousted (1388) from control of the royal council in favour of the "Marmousets," who represented its traditional membership as in Charles V's time; and in England the magnate group known as the "Appellants" had achieved temporary ascendancy. Discussions began (November 1388) in the small town of Leulinghen in Picardy, and a three-year truce was signed on June 18, 1389; the English were to evacuate certain places, such as Brest and Cherbourg, and agreed that Richard II should do homage for Aquitaine, thus ignoring the terms of the Treaty of Calais. But the conclusion of a firm peace was prevented by disputes over the duchy's boundaries. At this point, however, Richard II rid himself of the tutelage of the Appellants and entered into direct negotiation with Charles VI. As he was now a widower, he asked for the hand of Charles's daughter Isabella, and a marriage by proxy took place in Paris on March 12, 1396. At the same time the kings agreed that the Truce of Leulinghen, already previously renewed, should be extended for 28 years. Subsequently the two kings met (October 1396) between Calais and Ardres; this encounter was the occasion both for magnificent festivities and keen diplomatic bargaining. Though it proved impossible then to conclude a final peace treaty, the two kingdoms seemed at any rate to be developing a relationship perhaps sufficiently cordial for the remaining problems ultimately to be settled.

Unfortunately few of his subjects shared Richard II's desire for peace. The nobility and the knights had acquired a taste for profitable *chevauchées* through France, while the rest of the population had absorbed the war propaganda issued in Edward III's reign and regarded the French as responsible for all their ills. In any case it was not long before sharp opposition to Richard II again developed; and when John of Gaunt's heir, Henry Bolingbroke, earl of Derby, returned from banishment in June 1399 to wrest his inheritance from Richard, all the discontented rallied round him. Richard was deposed and imprisoned (he died in prison in February 1400), and Bolingbroke was proclaimed king of England as Henry IV in his stead. Though Henry legitimately sought to discredit the claims of Edward I's descendants to the English crown, he did not scruple to adopt Edward III's claim to the French and decisively reversed the pacific policy of his predecessor.

Henry's primary task, however, was the consolidation of his power in England, and he allowed Richard's widow, Isabella, to return to France (August 1400), though he kept her jewelry. Since the French king was only intermittently sane, his brother Louis, duc d'Orléans, presided over the royal council. Louis tried to make trouble for Henry of England by renewing the traditional support given by France to Scotland and by supporting the rebellion of the Welsh leader Owen Glendower (Owain Glyndŵr); and, profiting from Henry's preoccupations, he began the reconquest of Aquitaine. In 1405 the constable of France, Charles d'Albret, took many towns in Saintonge and Périgord, while Bernard VII d'Armagnac was threatening Bordeaux. But in 1406 the French suffered two reverses: Orléans failed to take Blaye on the Gironde River, while John the Fearless, duke of Burgundy, was repulsed before Calais.

Armagnacs and Burgundians

These reverses in the French fortunes were due primarily to the rivalry that had arisen between the duc d'Orléans and John the Fearless (*q.v.*), which was seriously dividing France. Orléans was anxious to attack the English positions with energy and dispatch; John the Fearless, on the other hand, seemed inclined to seek a settlement with Henry IV. Charles VI was not sane for sufficiently long intervals to impose his will on his quarrelsome kinsmen, so had to leave many decisions to his consort, Isabella of Bavaria. The personal rivalry of the two princes culminated in the assassination of the duc d'Orléans (November 1407) at the instigation of John the Fearless; but this murder set off a bitter civil war in which France was divided between the Burgundian faction and the Armagnac, the latter taking its name from Bernard VII, comte d'Armagnac, leader of the movement to avenge the murder. Under these circumstances, both sides in the civil war in turn sounded Henry IV in an attempt to obtain his assistance. Henry gave a little help to John the Fearless in 1411, by sending through Calais a small contingent that relieved Paris from siege by other princes of the House of Valois. The Armagnacs sought Henry's help in 1412, offering him the restitution of Aquitaine, but Henry died in March 1413. In 1413, likewise, the Burgundians in Paris issued the series of reforms known as the Ordonnance Cabochienne after Simon Caboche, the Paris butcher and demagogic leader, but this was promptly annulled by their opponents.

FROM THE ACCESSION OF HENRY V TO THE SIEGE OF ORLEANS, 1413–28

Battle of Agincourt

From the moment of his accession, it was clear that the new English king, Henry V, intended to act decisively on the continent. Conversations with the emissaries of Charles VI proved fruitless because of the intransigence of Henry's demands, and he embarked his troops on Aug. 10, 1415, landing at Le Chef-de-Caux on the estuary of the Seine. He took Harfleur (September), moved toward Picardy, and awaited the arrival of the French army at Agincourt in Artois, where, on Oct. 25, 1415, he utterly routed it. But he failed to follow up his advantage, retiring thereafter to Calais, whence he sailed for England. Though in no way strategically decisive, this victory won for Henry V the alliance of the German king Sigismund, who in August 1416 recognized his claim to the title and attributes of king of France. John the Fearless was equally impressed and, at an interview with Henry at Calais, offered not only alliance but homage.

Henry V did not return to France until 1417, and then it was to effect the methodical subjugation of Normandy town by town and district by district; Caen, Alençon, and Evreux successively opened their gates to him. Meanwhile Isabella of Bavaria, who had been for a while imprisoned by the Armagnacs, and John the Fearless joined forces at Troyes in November 1417 and there set up a rival government to that of Isabella's own son, the dauphin Charles. After a Parisian revolt (May 1418), as a result of which the dauphin retired to Berry, John the Fearless was able to enter the capital; but he and Isabella could oppose Henry V no more effectively than could the Armagnacs, and Henry seized Rouen (January 1419), the Pays de Caux, and the Vexin. John the Fearless now became so alarmed at the English progress that he made overtures of peace to the Armagnacs and the dauphin; but John himself was assassinated on the bridge of Montereau by the dauphin's emissary (Sept. 10, 1419). Thereupon his heir, Philip the Good (*q.v.*), wishing to avenge him, allied himself (December 1419) with Henry V against the dauphin. By the Treaty of Troyes (May 21, 1420), concluded between Queen Isabella and Philip the Good (both acting for Charles VI), and King Henry, the dauphin was disinherited in favour of Henry V, who was, on June 2, 1420, to marry Catherine, one of Charles VI's daughters. This arrangement was intended to set up a dual monarchy, based on a personal union of the French and English crowns, under which, however, each of the kingdoms would retain its separate institutions and character. The dual monarchy was never achieved. In practice, France fell into three parts, controlled respectively by Henry V, by the duke of Burgundy, and by the dauphin. Henry's authority was firm enough in Normandy and in Guyenne and was acknowledged in Paris and in the surrounding district; but Philip the Good retained considerable power in fact in the Paris area and was naturally supreme in Burgundy; and from his court at Bourges or at Poitiers the dauphin ruled over central France and Languedoc. The frontiers between these rival territories were never clearly delineated, being constantly altered by intermittent warfare, and allegiances did not necessarily follow the boundaries.

Treaty of Troyes

When the Treaty of Troyes had been signed, Henry V set about capturing the Armagnac fortresses that menaced his conquests. He seized Melun (1420) and his subordinates overran Maine and Perche. After a visit to England (January–July 1421), he returned to rout the army with which the dauphin was marching toward Paris. Subsequently he took Meaux and Compiègne (May and June 1422) but died on Aug. 31, 1422. Thereafter the French territories of his infant successor Henry VI were governed by Henry V's brother John, duke of Bedford. Charles VI died seven weeks after his son-in-law, on Oct. 22, 1422; his long reign ended in disorder and shame.

The dauphin immediately proclaimed himself king as Charles VII. The next few years saw a series of ineffective and tortuous diplomatic negotiations, conducted severally between Bedford, Burgundy, John V of Brittany, and Charles VII, whose policy was much influenced by his mother-in-law, Yolande of Aragon. An understanding that might have changed the civil war into a war against the English was nearly achieved between Burgundy and Charles at the time (March 1425) when Arthur of Richemont became constable of France (see RICHEMONT, CONSTABLE DE); but nothing came of the rapprochement, and in 1427 Bedford's army invaded the Loire Valley. Bedford decided in 1428 to besiege Orléans, which could provide a good base for an attack on Charles VII's stronghold south of the Loire. The siege began on October 1428, all attempts to relieve the city failed, and by the beginning of 1429 its surrender seemed imminent.

Adapted from R. Treharne and H. Fullard (eds.), *Muir's Historical Atlas: Ancient, Medieval and Modern*, 9th edition (1965); George Philip & Son Ltd., London

France in 1429.

EXPULSION OF THE ENGLISH, 1428–53

Joan of Arc

The siege of Orléans proved the turning point of the war, the event that enabled Joan of Arc (*q.v.*) to fulfill her mission and save France. A peasant girl from Domrémy in the borderland between Champagne and Lorraine, she managed to persuade Robert de Baudricourt, Charles VII's captain at Vaucouleurs, to send her to Charles's court at Chinon. She gained the confidence of the king and his advisers and went with a small force to try to relieve Orléans. A few days after their arrival the English raised the siege. The psychological effect of this was considerable. The morale of the French army soared, and in June 1429 the constable de Richemont defeated the English in the Battle of Patay. Charles, persuaded by Joan, then went to Reims for his coronation; the city made no show of resistance and opened its gates to him. Once crowned and anointed (July 17, 1429), his position as legitimate king was unassailable and the terms of the Treaty of Troyes became of no significance. Laon, Soissons, and Compiègne now acknowledged his sovereignty, but his attempt on Paris (September 8) was repulsed.

After several other expeditions Joan entered Compiègne (1430) in order to strengthen its defense against Philip the Good, who had just renewed (March 1430) his alliance with the duke of Bedford. During a sortie she fell into the hands of the Burgundians (May 23). She was sold to the English, imprisoned at Rouen, tried before an ecclesiastical tribunal according to the procedure of the Holy Office, and adjudged a heretic. Though she signed a recantation, she quickly revoked it and was burned to death at Rouen on May 30, 1431.

Joan's death in no way checked the French recovery that she had inaugurated. Seeing which way the wind was now blowing, Philip the Good opened negotiations (1432) with Charles VII. The Treaty of Arras, which they signed on Sept. 21, 1435, terminated the civil war, and Paris submitted to Charles on April 13, 1436.

Bedford died in September 1435 and was replaced as Henry VI's lieutenant general and governor of France and Normandy by Richard, duke of York (from 1436 to 1437 and from 1440 to 1447), and by Richard Beauchamp, earl of Warwick (from 1437 to 1439). Military operations continued sporadically for several years in Bordelais and on the borders of Normandy. Charles VII was faced with the immense task of restoring order to his kingdom; and in France, no less than in England, royal authority was severely weakened by faction within the royal councils. General exhaustion on both sides of the Channel created an atmosphere favourable to negotiation; and after Henry VI had sent William de la Pole, earl of Suffolk, to France a first local truce was signed in April 1444. More comprehensive talks were then begun at Tours; and when it proved impossible to agree on terms for a final treaty, it was decided to sign a renewable truce at Tours (May 28, 1444) and to strengthen it by the marriage (April 1445) of Henry VI with Margaret of Anjou, niece of the French king's consort Mary of Anjou. This truce legalized the status quo, the English retaining Maine, Bordelais, parts of Artois and Picardy and most of Normandy.

Truce of Tours

Reconquest of Maine and Normandy. The need to renew the truce and the prospect of attaining a firm peace treaty encouraged the exchange of diplomatic envoys. Jean Jouvenel, archbishop of Reims, crossed to England in July 1445 to discuss a proposed meeting between the two kings; he obtained a promise that Henry VI would give up Maine to his father-in-law René of Anjou. But the English were slow in honouring this promise, and not until Charles VII's army had surrounded it was Le Mans surrendered (1448).

No longer respecting the truce, the French took several towns from the English. With assistance from Francis I of Brittany, they began the reconquest of Normandy; and Charles VII made a solemn entry into Rouen, the capital, in November 1449. The following spring a small English army landed at Cherbourg, recovered several fortresses in the Cotentin, but was then defeated in the Battle of Formigny on April 15, 1450. The French subsequently took Caen and brought the whole of Normandy under their control. The English reverses had considerable domestic repercussions; they were partly the cause of Suffolk's fall from power (1450) and led to the revolt of Jack Cade and to the increase of Yorkist influence in opposition to the Lancastrian dynasty.

Conquest of Guyenne (1453). Charles VII and his advisers took advantage of the confused political situation in England to attack what remained of English-held Guyenne. There, however, they encountered a population that, unlike that of Normandy, had a long tradition of loyalty to the English crown. The campaign, begun in 1449, continued into 1450 with the capture of Bergerac (October 1450) and of Bazas. Jean, comte de Dunois, began to encircle Bordeaux (1451), taking most of the towns on which its strategic defense depended. Bordeaux capitulated in June and Bayonne in August 1451. But the people of Bordelais were in no way resigned to the ending of English rule; when the veteran general John Talbot, earl of Shrewsbury, landed an army on the Gironde estuary (October 1452), they rose against the French, enabling Shrewsbury to make a triumphant entry into Bordeaux. Charles VII waited long enough to raise a considerable army, which then marched into Guyenne in the early months of 1453. The English suffered a severe defeat in the Battle of Castillon, near Libourne, on July 17; and Bordeaux, once more besieged, finally capitulated on October 19, 1453. This time English rule in Aquitaine was really at an end.

Battle of Castillon

Peace, however, seemed no nearer, for even if the English had lost all their continental possessions except Calais and the countship of Guînes, they would in no way admit defeat, mainly because neither of the contending Yorkist and Beaufort factions dared incur the odium of treating with the French. On the other hand, Charles VII was prevented from attacking Calais or the English coast by the uncertain attitude of Philip of Burgundy. After Charles VII's death (1461), his son and successor, Louis XI, managed to make the Truce of Saint-Omer (1463) with the Yorkist king of England Edward IV; it was renewed, after some difficulties, in 1466 and again in 1471. But after 1474 Edward IV allied with his brother-in-law Charles the Bold, duke of Burgundy, and prepared for a fresh invasion of France. In 1475 a powerful English army landed at Calais; French and English forces faced each other across the Somme River, but neither side dared to cross and join battle. Edward IV and Louis XI then met at Picquigny (August 29, 1475) and decided upon a seven years' truce, agreeing in future to settle their differences by negotiation rather than by force of arms. Edward was to withdraw from France, receiving in compensation a payment of 75,000 gold *écus* and an annual payment of 50,000 while both kings lived. This truce, seemingly fragile, survived various stresses and can be held to mark the end of the Hundred Years' War, but no peace treaty was ever signed. Calais was retained by the English until 1558, and English kings continued to bear the title king of France until 1801.

SIGNIFICANCE OF THE WAR

The Hundred Years' War, begun on the pretext of an English claim to the French throne, was later renewed and perpetuated in an attempt to establish in reality Henry V's grandiose conception of a dual monarchy by which the English king should rule two kingdoms on either side of the Channel. It demonstrated, however, that English authority could not become effective in a hostile France; nor, on the other hand, were the French strong enough to make the English kings recognize the utter folly and impracticability of their pretensions. In fact, during the 14th and 15th centuries, behind the facade of claims and counterclaims, behind the battles and political manoeuvres, two nations were being forged whose natural development and juxtaposition were bound to lead to warfare.

The initial claim to the French throne can be explained only by Edward III's strong ties with France and by a feeling for his Capetian ancestry as strong as his manifest pride in his English kingdom. By the 15th century, however, this feeling was virtually dead in the Lancastrian and Yorkist kings who challenged Charles VII and Louis XI. But during the previous three or four generations the English had acquired a taste for profitable expeditions to the Continent, from which they always hoped to return laden with spoil and with prisoners for ransom, so that France was ravaged and wasted as it had been when the Vikings and Northmen raided the Carolingian Empire. Apparently unable to remedy this state of affairs, the French sought instead to alleviate their sufferings by reforming the monarchy—a reform that took effect, after the Paris revolution of 1356–58, in the reigns of John II and of Charles V. But the weakening of the monarchy by the minority and the insanity of Charles VI left the greed of the princes and of favourite ministers unbridled and the country a prey to extortion. Public disgust at these abuses was expressed more and more frequently with ever-increasing violence but with less and less effect.

Ultimately the fact that the malcontents compromised themselves by adhering to the English and to the Burgundians gave the French monarchy the chance of asserting itself; and the royal power that emerged was not only freed from former constitutional restraints but also capable of settling definitively, to its own advantage, the perennial problem of the English continental fiefs.

The 14th and 15th centuries marked, both in France and in England, a prolonged struggle for power between the crown, the nobility, and various reforming elements. Similarities in political and constitutional development and the common experience of social upheaval might well have resulted in alliances between parallel parties on either side of the Channel. But, as it happened, when one group was in the ascendant in France, the other was frequently ruling in England so that, far from bringing the two countries closer together, their similar experiences divided them more bitterly. National consciousness, born and nurtured in the long struggle, grew in the end so strong that any project of union—even a merely personal union of the crowns as envisaged by Henry V—was doomed to failure. The most obvious result of the Hundred Years' War was to make both France and England determined to avoid the revival of such a struggle, in which both sides had squandered their manpower and resources, utterly without profit. In both countries, rulers and populace alike gladly turned their energies to other projects.

Growth of national consciousness

BIBLIOGRAPHY. E. LAVISSE (ed.), *Histoire de France depuis les origines jusqu'à la Révolution*, vol. 4 (1902); E. PERROY, *La Guerre de cent ans* (1945; *The Hundred Years' War*, Eng. trans. by W.B. WELLS, 1951); M. MCKISACK, *The Fourteenth Century* (1959); PHILIPPE CONTAMINE, *La Guerre de cent ans* (1968). For the preliminaries of the Hundred Years' War, see E. DEPREZ, *Les Préliminaires de la guerre de cent ans* (1902); H.S. LUCAS, *The Low Countries and the Hundred Years' War, 1326–1347* (1929); G.P. CUTTINO, *English Diplomatic Administration 1259–1339* (1940); and G. TEMPLEMAN, "Edward III and the Beginnings of the Hundred Years War," *Transactions of the Royal Historical Society*, 5th series, 2:69–88 (1952). For particular periods and aspects of the war, see R. DELACHENAL, *Histoire de Charles V*, 5 vol. (1909–31); A.H. BURNE, *The Crécy War: A Military History of the Hundred Years War from 1337 to the Peace of Brétigny, 1360* (1955) and *The Agincourt War: A Military History of the Latter Part of the Hundred Years War from 1369 to 1453* (1956); P.E. RUSSELL, *The English Intervention in Spain and Portugal in the Time of Edward III and Richard II* (1955); E.F. JACOB, *Henry V and the Invasion of France* (1947); E.C. LODGE, *Gascony Under English Rule* (1926); and H. DENIFLE, *La Désolation des églises, monastères et hôpitaux en France pendant la guerre de cent ans*, 2 vol. (1897–99).

(Ra.C.)

Hungary

Located in the heart of Europe and occupying part of the oval Carpathian Basin, Hungary has ethnic and linguistic roots that reach far back into the past of the Continent. Hungary (or the Hungarian People's Republic) is closely connected politically, economically, and culturally with its Socialist neighbours. It is a member of both the Warsaw Pact and the Council for Mutual Economic Assistance (Comecon), which promotes economic, scientific, and technical cooperation among the Socialist nations. Its area is 35,920 square miles (93,032 square kilometres) and its population less than 11,000,000.

Hungary is bordered by Czechoslovakia in the north, Romania and the Soviet Union in the east, Austria in the west, and Yugoslavia in the south. Lying mostly within the Danube drainage basin, it is of lowland character, and the frontiers generally follow the foothills of the mountain chains surrounding it. Budapest, the capital city, which dominates much of national life, is situated a few miles downstream from the Danube Bend, where the Danube (Hungarian Duna) abruptly changes course from an easterly to a southerly direction. (For information on related subjects, see HUNGARY, HISTORY OF; BALATON, LAKE; DANUBE RIVER; and BUDAPEST.)

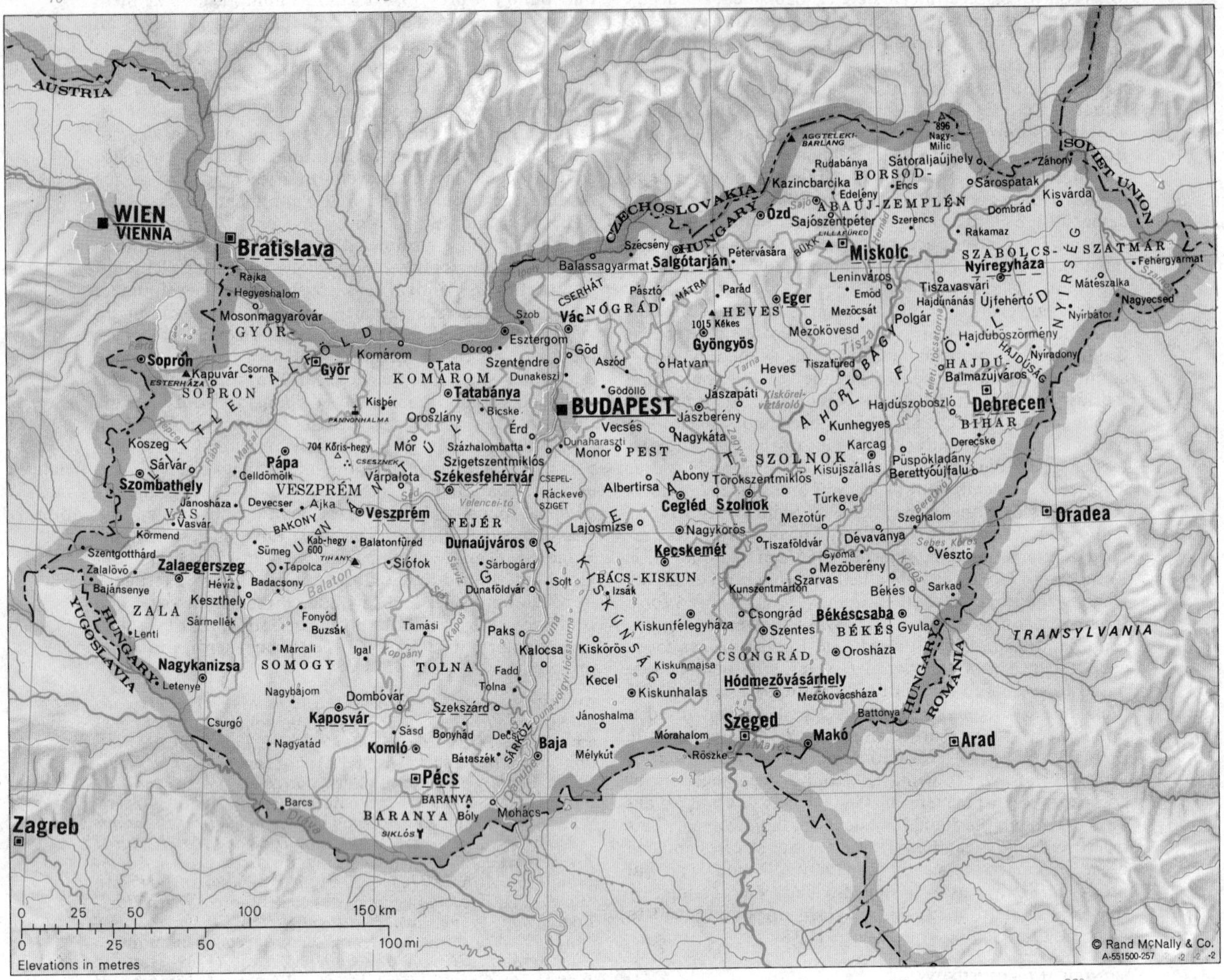

HUNGARY

MAP INDEX

Political subdivisions

Bács-Kiskun.....46·30n 19·25e
Baranya.........46·05n 18·15e
Békés...........46·45n 21·00e
Borsod-Abaúj-Zemplén.......48·15n 21·00e
Budapest.........47·30n 19·05e
Csongrád........46·25n 20·15e
Debrecen........47·32n 21·38e
Fejér............47·10n 18·35e
Győr.............47·42n 17·38e
Győr-Sopron.....47·40n 17·15e
Hajdú-Bihar.....47·25n 21·30e
Heves............47·50n 20·15e
Komárom.........47·35n 18·20e
Miskolc..........48·06n 20·47e
Nógrád...........48·00n 19·35e
Pécs.............46·05n 18·13e
Pest.............47·25n 19·20e
Somogy..........46·25n 17·35e
Szabolcs-Szatmár........48·00n 22·10e
Szolnok..........47·15n 20·30e
Tolna............46·30n 18·35e
Vas..............47·10n 16·45e
Veszprém........47·10n 17·40e
Zala.............46·40n 16·50e

The name of a political subdivision if not shown on the map is the same as that of its capital city.

Cities and towns

Abony...........47·11n 20·01e
Ajka............47·06n 17·34e
Albertirsa.......47·15n 19·38e
Aszód...........47·39n 19·31e
Badacsony.......46·47n 17·30e
Baja............46·11n 18·57e
Bajánsenye......46·48n 16·23e
Balassagyarmat .48·05n 19·18e
Balatonfüred....46·57n 17·53e
Balmazújváros...47·37n 21·21e
Barcs...........45·58n 17·28e
Bátaszék.........46·12n 18·44e
Battonya.........46·17n 21·01e
Békés...........46·46n 21·08e
Békéscsaba......46·41n 21·06e
Berettyóújfalu....47·14n 21·32e
Bicske...........47·29n 18·37e
Bóly.............45·58n 18·32e
Bonyhád.........46·19n 18·32e
Budapest.........47·30n 19·05e
Buzsák...........46·39n 17·35e
Cegléd...........47·10n 19·48e
Celldömölk.......47·16n 17·09e
Csongrád........46·43n 20·09e
Csorna...........47·37n 17·16e
Csurgó...........46·16n 17·06e
Debrecen.........47·32n 21·38e
Decs.............46·17n 18·46e
Derecske.........47·21n 21·34e
Dévaványa.......47·02n 20·58e
Devecser.........47·06n 17·26e
Dombóvár........46·23n 18·08e
Dombrád.........48·14n 21·56e
Dorog............47·43n 18·44e
Dunaföldvár......46·48n 18·55e
Dunaharaszti.....47·21n 19·05e
Dunakeszi........47·38n 19·08e
Dunaújváros......46·58n 18·57e
Edelény..........48·18n 20·49e
Eger.............47·54n 20·23e
Emőd............47·56n 20·49e
Encs.............48·20n 21·08e
Érd..............47·23n 18·56e
Esztergom.......47·48n 18·45e
Fadd.............46·28n 18·50e
Fehérgyarmat....47·58n 22·32e
Fonyód..........46·44n 17·34e
Göd.............47·42n 19·08e
Gödöllő..........47·36n 19·22e
Gyoma...........46·56n 20·50e
Gyöngyös........47·47n 19·56e
Győr.............47·42n 17·38e
Gyula............46·39n 21·17e
Hajdúböszörmény..........47·40n 21·31e
Hajdúnánás......47·51n 21·26e
Hajdúszoboszló...47·27n 21·24e
Hatvan...........47·40n 19·41e
Hegyeshalom.....47·55n 17·10e
Heves............47·36n 20·17e
Hévíz............46·47n 17·11e
Hódmezővásárhely..........46·25n 20·20e
Igal.............46·31n 17·55e
Izsák............46·48n 19·22e
Jánoshalma......46·18n 19·20e
Jánosháza.......47·08n 17·10e
Jászapáti........47·22n 20·09e
Jászberény......47·30n 19·55e
Kalocsa..........46·32n 18·59e
Kaposvár........46·22n 17·47e
Kapuvár..........47·36n 17·02e
Karcag...........47·19n 20·56e
Kazincbarcika....48·16n 20·37e
Kecel............46·32n 19·16e
Kecskemét.......46·54n 19·42e
Keszthely........46·46n 17·15e
Kisbér...........47·30n 18·02e
Kiskőrös.........46·38n 19·17e
Kiskunfélegyháza.........46·43n 19·52e
Kiskunhalas......46·26n 19·30e
Kiskunmajsa.....46·30n 19·45e
Kisújszállás......47·13n 20·46e
Kisvárda.........48·13n 22·05e
Komárom.........47·44n 18·08e
Komló............46·12n 18·16e
Körmend.........47·01n 16·37e
Kőszeg...........47·23n 16·33e
Kunhegyes.......47·22n 20·38e
Kunszentmárton.46·51n 20·18e
Lajosmizse.......47·02n 19·34e
Leninváros.......47·56n 21·05e
Lenti............46·37n 16·33e
Letenye..........46·26n 16·43e
Makó............46·13n 20·29e
Marcali..........46·35n 17·25e
Mátészalka......47·57n 22·19e
Mélykút..........46·13n 19·24e
Mezőberény......46·50n 21·02e
Mezőcsát........47·49n 20·55e
Mezőkovácsháza.46·25n 20·46e
Mezőkövesd.....47·50n 20·34e
Mezőtúr.........47·00n 20·38e
Miskolc..........48·06n 20·47e
Mohács...........45·59n 18·42e
Monor............47·21n 19·27e
Mór..............47·23n 18·12e
Mórahalom.......46·13n 19·53e
Mosonmagyaróvár..........47·51n 17·17e
Nagyatád.........46·14n 17·22e
Nagybajom.......46·23n 17·31e
Nagykanizsa.....46·27n 17·00e
Nagykáta.........47·25n 19·45e
Nagykőrös........47·02n 19·43e
Nyíradony........47·41n 21·55e
Nyírbátor.........47·50n 22·08e
Nyíregyháza.....47·59n 21·43e
Orosháza.........46·34n 20·40e
Oroszlany........47·30n 18·19e
Ózd..............48·14n 20·18e
Paks.............46·39n 18·53e
Pápa.............47·19n 17·28e
Parád............47·55n 20·02e
Pásztó...........47·55n 19·42e
Pécs.............46·05n 18·13e
Pétervására......48·01n 20·06e
Polgár...........47·52n 21·08e
Püspökladány....47·19n 21·07e
Ráckeve.........47·10n 18·56e
Rajka............48·02n 17·11e
Rakamaz.........48·08n 21·30e
Röszke..........46·11n 20·03e
Rudabánya......48·23n 20·38e
Sajószentpéter...48·13n 20·44e
Salgótarján......48·07n 19·48e
Sárbogárd.......46·53n 18·38e
Sarkad...........46·44n 21·23e
Sármellék........46·44n 17·10e
Sárospatak.......48·19n 21·34e
Sárvár...........47·15n 16·57e
Sásd.............46·15n 18·06e
Sátoraljaújhely...48·24n 21·39e
Siófok...........46·54n 18·04e
Solt.............46·48n 19·00e

MAP INDEX (continued)

Sopron..........47·41n 16·36e
Sümeg..........46·59n 17·17e
Szarvas.........46·52n 20·34e
Százhalombatta .47·20n 18·56e
Szécsény........48·06n 19·31e
Szeged..........46·15n 20·09e
Szeghalom......47·01n 21·11e
Székesfehérvár...47·12n 18·25e
Szekszárd.......46·21n 18·42e
Szentendre......47·40n 19·05e
Szentes.........46·39n 20·16e
Szentgotthárd...46·57n 16·17e
Szerencs........48·09n 21·13e
Szigetszentmiklós..........47·21n 19·03e
Szob............47·50n 18·52e
Szolnok.........47·10n 20·12e
Szombathely.....47·14n 16·38e
Tamási..........46·38n 18·18e
Tapolca.........46·53n 17·27e
Tata.............47·39n 18·18e
Tatabánya.......47·34n 18·26e
Tiszavasvári.....47·58n 21·22e
Tiszaföldvár.....46·59n 20·15e
Tiszafüred.......47·27n 20·46e
Tolna............46·26n 18·46e
Törökszentmiklós..........47·11n 20·25e
Túrkeve.........47·06n 20·45e
Újfehértó........47·48n 21·41e
Vác..............47·47n 19·08e
Várpalota........47·12n 18·09e
Vasvár..........47·03n 16·49e
Vecsés..........47·25n 19·16e
Veszprém........47·06n 17·55e
Vésztő..........46·55n 21·16e
Záhony..........48·25n 22·11e
Zalaegerszeg....46·51n 16·51e
Zalalövő.........46·51n 16·35e

Physical features and points of interest

Aggteleki-barlang, *caves*...48·30n 20·32e
Bakony, *mountains*......47·15n 17·50e
Balaton, *lake*.....46·50n 17·45e
Baranya, *physical region*..46·00n 18·30e
Berettyó, *river*....46·59n 21·07e
Bükk, *mountains*.48·05n 20·30e
Csepel-sziget, *island*..........47·15n 18·57e
Cserhát, *mountains*......47·55n 19·30e
Csesznek, *ruins*..47·16n 17·53e
Danube (Duna), *river*............45·54n 18·48e
Dráva, *river*......45·33n 18·55e
Duna, see Danube
Dunántúl, *physical region*..47·00n 18·00e
Duna-völgyi-főcsatorna, *canal*............46 12n 18·56e
Esterháza, *castle*.47·37n 16·53e
Fertő, *lake*.......47·40n 16·40e
Great Alföld, *physical region*..47·11n 20·01e
Hajdúság, *physical region*..47·35n 21·30e
Hernád, *river*....47·56n 21·08e
Hortobágy, *historic region*...47·35n 21·00e
Ipoly, *river*.......47·49n 18·52e
Kab-hegy, *mountain*.......46·58n 17·30e
Kapos, *river*.....46·44n 18·30e
Kékes, *mountain*.47·55n 20·02e
Keleti-főcsatorna, *canal*...........48·01n 21·20e
Kiskúnsag, *physical region*..46·35n 19·15e
Koppány, *river*...46·35n 18·26e
Kőris-hegy, *mountain*.......47·18n 17·45e
Körös, *river*......46·43n 20·12e
Lillafüred, *scenic area*............48·07n 20·38e
Little Alföld, *plain*............47·30n 17·00e
Marcal, *river*.....47·41n 17·32e
Maros, *river*......46·15n 20·13e
Mátra, *mountains*......47·55n 20·00e
Nagy-Milic, *mountain*.......48·35n 21·28e
Nyirség, *physical region*...........47·50n 21·55e
Pannonhalma, *monastery*......47·28n 17·50e
Rába, *river*.......47·42n 17·38e
Répce, *river*......47·41n 17·03e
Sajó, *river*.......47·56n 21·08e
Sárköz, *physical region*...........46·15n 18·48e
Sárvíz, *river*......46·24n 18·41e
Sebes Körös, *river*............46·55n 20·59e
Séd, *river*........47·08n 18·11e
Siklós, *castle*.....45·52n 18·28e
Sió, *river*.........46·22n 18·48e
Szamos, *river*....48·07n 22·22e
Tarna, *river*......47·31n 19·59e
Tihany, *historic site*............46·54n 17·53e
Tisza, *river*......46·10n 20·05e
Velencei-to, *lake*............47·12n 18·35e
Zagyva, *river*.....47·10n 20·13e

THE LANDSCAPE

The Great and Little Alfölds

Relief. Dominating the relief are the great lowland expanses that make up the core of Hungary. The Little Alföld (Kis Alföld, or Little Plain) lies in the northwest, fringed on the west by the easternmost extension of the sub-Alps along the border with Austria and bounded on the north by the Danube. The Little Alföld is separated from the Great Alföld (Nagy Magyar Alföld, or Great Hungarian Plain) by a low mountain system extending across the country from southwest to northeast for a distance of 250 miles (400 kilometres). This system, which forms the backbone of the country, is made up of the Transdanubian (Dunántúl) and Northern mountains. The former lie to the southwest of the gorge of the Danube at Visegrád and are dominated by the Bakony Mountains, which consist of dolomite and limestone plateaus at heights of between 1,300 and 2,300 feet (400 and 700 metres) above sea level interspersed with volcanic peaks. Regions of hills reaching altitudes of 800 to 1,000 feet lie on either side of the mountain backbone, while to the south and west of Lake Balaton is an independent upland region of more subdued, loess-covered topography. The Great Alföld covers most of central and southeastern Hungary. Like its northern counterpart, it is a basinlike structure filled with fluvial and windblown deposits. Four types of surface may be distinguished: floodplains, composed of river alluvium; alluvial fans, wedge-shaped features deposited at the breaks of slopes where the rivers emerge from the mountain rim; alluvial fans overlain by sand dunes; and plains buried under loess, a windblown deposit derived from the continental interior. These lowlands range in height from 260 to 660 feet (80 to 200 metres) above sea level.

Temperatures

Climate. Because of its situation within the Carpathian Basin, Hungary has a moderately dry continental climate. The mean annual temperature is around 50° F (10° C), ranging from a chilly 32°–25° F (0° to –4° C) in January to July temperatures of 64°–73° F (18°–23° C). A summer temperature as high as 106° F (41° C) has been recorded, while the absolute winter minimum is –29° F (–34° C). In the lowlands, precipitation generally ranges from 20 to 24 inches (500 to 600 millimetres), rising to 24 to 31 inches (800 millimetres) over higher areas. The Great Alföld is the driest and the southwest uplands the wettest part of the country. Up to two-thirds of annual precipitation falls during the growing season.

Drainage. Hungary lies within the drainage basin of the Danube. The Danube and its two most important Hungarian tributaries, the Rába and the Drava, are of Alpine origin, while the Tisza and its tributaries, which drain much of eastern Hungary, rise in the Carpathians.

The Danube floods regularly twice a year, the first occurring in early spring and the second in early summer. During these phases, discharge is up to 10 times greater (212,000 to 282,000 cubic feet [6,000 to 8,000 cubic metres] per second) than that recorded during the low-water periods of autumn and winter. Where it flows through Hungary, the Tisza is of floodplain character, and large meanders and oxbow lakes marking former channels are typical features. At Szolnok, peak discharges 50 times greater than average have been recorded. Approximately once a decade, floods of catastrophic dimensions occur on the Danube, the Tisza, and their tributaries; a system of dams has diminished the risk for 15,000 square miles (39,000 square kilometres) of the Great and Little Alfölds.

Surface water covers about 1 percent of the area of Hungary, and there are only three natural lakes: Lake Balaton, the largest, and Velence Lake (Velencei-tó) and Lake Fertő (Austrian Neusiedlersee), on the Austrian border.

Natural vegetation, soils, and animal life. The activities of man over the ages have largely destroyed the natural vegetation of Hungary. Nearly two-thirds of the land is regularly cultivated, the remainder comprising meadows and rough pasture (14 percent of the total area) and forest and woodland (16 percent), while about 10 percent is in nonagricultural uses. No part of the country is of sufficient altitude to support natural coniferous forest, beech being the climax species at the highest elevations and oak woodland alternating with scrubby grassland being the climax at lower altitudes in the upland regions.

Soils

In the forest zones, gray-brown podzolic (leached) and brown forest soils predominate, while under the forest-steppe has evolved rich black-earth, or chernozem, soil, although sand dunes and dispersed alkali soils are also characteristic.

Deer and wild pig are abundant in the higher forested areas, while the lowlands have an animal population of rodents, hares, partridges, and pheasants. The once numerous varieties of marsh waterfowl survive only in nature reserves. Significant water and air pollution occurs in some of the industrial regions of the country, but the state has instituted strict measures of environmental control.

Traditional regions. The Great Alföld is the largest region of the country. Traditionally it is divided into two parts: the area lying between the Danube and Tisza rivers, and Trans-Tisza (Tiszántúl), the region east of the Tisza. The former consists primarily of a mosaic of small landscape elements—sand dunes, loess plains, and floodplains—in the Kiskunság. Kecskemét is the market centre for the region, which is also noted for its isolated farmsteads, known as *tanyák*. Several interesting ethnographic groups live here, including the people of the Kalocsa-Sárköz, who are noted for their hand-embroidered costumes and folklore. The Matyó, who live in the northern part of the plain around the town of Mezőkövesd, are also noted for hand embroidery and multicoloured costumes. In the generally homogeneous flat plain of the Trans-Tisza region, only the Nyírség presents any form of topographical contrast. Closely connected with this latter area are the Hajdúság and the Hortobágy, and all three areas look to Debrecen, the largest city of the plain. The Hortobágy presents an interesting survival of the steppe life of earlier times, since the original Hungarian cattle (and cowboys), horse, and sheep breeds have been preserved there as part of the national heritage.

The Little Alföld, the second major natural region, is situated in the northwest and is traversed by the Danube and Rába rivers and their tributaries. It is more favourably endowed naturally than the Great Alföld; the settlement hierarchy is better developed, and both agriculture and industry are more advanced.

Transdanubia

The third major region is Transdanubia (Dunántúl), which embraces all of the country west of the Danube except the Little Alföld. It includes the Transdanubian Mountains and, strictly speaking, the Little Alföld also. To the south of Lake Balaton are the hills of Somogy, Tolna, and Baranya, where the people view Pécs, a mining and industrial city, as the economic and cultural centre. The Transdanubian Mountains include the Bakony mountains, whose isolation, densely forested ridges, small closed basins, and medieval fortresses and monasteries have afforded protection to the local inhabitants over the course of many stormy centuries. Although modern industrial towns, drawing on the bauxite, manganese, and brown coal resources of the area, have recently sprung up, the cultural centre of the area is the historic city of Veszprém. Along the southern boundary of the Transdanubian Mountains are ranged a number of health resorts and centres of wine production, notably Keszthely, Hévíz, Badacsony, and Balatonfüred.

The Northern Mountains, the fourth major geographical region of the country, contain two important industrial areas, the Nógrád and Borsod basins. Miskolc, the second largest city of the country and a major industrial centre, is situated in the latter. Budapest is located where all four regions meet, to the south of the gorge of the Danube.

Patterns of settlement. There are 83 towns and cities in Hungary and another 60 or so settlements that provide urban-type functions. Since the town is a legal-administrative concept rather than one based on function, the proportion of the population living in towns and cities (50.2 percent of the total in 1976) is an underestimate of the actual percentage of the population living in urban-like surroundings.

Urban Hungary is dominated by Budapest (an estimated 2,065,000 inhabitants in 1976), which is more than 10 times the size of the second city, Miskolc. Within its bounds live some two-fifths of all urban residents and almost half of the industrial working force of the country. The major provincial centres are Miskolc, Debrecen, Szeged, Pécs, and Győr, each of which has a population exceeding 100,000, an economic, cultural, and administrative hinterland that reaches deep into the surrounding countryside, and a rapidly expanding industrial capacity. Below the provincial centres in the hierarchy are the traditional market towns, such as Kecskemét, Székesfehérvár, Nyíregyháza, Szombathely, and Szolnok, with new suburbs added to medieval or Baroque town centres and having populations in the range of 50,000 to 90,000. Also worthy of note are the predominantly industrial towns located close to the mineral resources of the Northern Mountains, which, from small beginnings in the early 20th century, have developed into major industrial centres since 1950. They include Ajka, Tatabánya, Salgótarján, and Ózd. In addition, a number of entirely new industrial towns (new Socialist towns) have been created on green-field sites as part of deliberate planning policy.

The vast majority of towns in Hungary have populations of less than 40,000. Thus the range of services they offer is limited and indeed is below that normally expected of places of similar size in western Europe and North America, because they were functionally, until very recently, vastly overgrown villages rather than towns. An important aspect of regional policy is to remedy this deficiency and thus improve the services available to the rural population. A hierarchical structure of settlements is being deliberately created, and the range of services that each settlement offers is strictly planned.

Rural population distribution

The distribution of rural population varies widely from one part of the country to another. For historical reasons connected with resettlement following the Turkish occupation in the 16th century, the compact villages of the Great Alföld are comparatively small in number but large in size. By comparison, rural settlement in Transdanubia and in the Northern Mountains takes the form of many small nucleated and linear villages. The isolated farmsteads known as *tanyák* tend to be concentrated in the Great Alföld. This form of agrarian settlement is regarded as incompatible with large-scale cooperative and state farming, and attempts are being made to concentrate the *tanya* population in new, compact *tanya* villages.

THE PEOPLE

Nationality and language. According to the estimate of January 1, 1976, the population of Hungary was 10,572,000, giving an overall density of 295 persons per square mile (114 per square kilometre), which is around the median value for the continent of Europe. The mother tongue of 98.5 percent of the population is Hungarian, which belongs to the Finno-Ugric linguistic group of the Uralic family and is related only to Finnish and Estonian among the major languages of Europe.

The Hungarian people, known ethnically as Magyars, migrated from the steppes of eastern Europe and settled in the Carpathian Basin during the 9th century AD. They are a homogeneous people, and subgroups within them are difficult to distinguish. Germans make up the largest ethnic minority, some 0.5 percent of the population, followed by small numbers of Southern Slavs (mainly Croatians and Serbians), Slovaks, and Romanians. The Gypsy population forms a distinctive group, numbering in the early 1970s some 180,000 to 185,000, of whom about 35,000 speak Romany as their mother tongue.

Emigration

After World War I some two-thirds of the former territory of Hungary was annexed by neighbouring states, and as a consequence upwards of 3,000,000 Hungarians now live in Romania, Czechoslovakia, Yugoslavia, and the Soviet Union. In addition, the possibility of improved living standards abroad led to the emigration up to 1939 of 1,500,000 Hungarians, the majority of whom went to North America. Since 1945 emigration has been insignificant because of restrictions placed on freedom of movement, except during the aftermath of the uprising of 1956 (the Hungarian Revolution), when 200,000 sought homes in other countries; of these, approximately 20,000 later returned to Hungary. Though the religious affiliation of the population has not been enumerated since the census of 1949, it is estimated that 90 percent of the people have some kind of religious affiliation at the present time. Of these, approximately 60 percent are Roman Catholics and 25 percent Lutherans and Calvinists; Unitarians, Baptists, and a small Jewish community (much reduced in size following the deportations toward the end of World War II) represent the most significant of the minor religious groups.

Demographic trends. Paralleling the trends exhibited by most countries of western and central Europe, the rate of population growth in Hungary during the 20th century has been comparatively low. During the interwar period the annual rate of increase fluctuated between 0.7 and 0.8 percent, and, ignoring the period of the war, it remained at that general level until the mid-1950s. During the subsequent 10 years a marked deceleration in the pace of growth set in, but since the mid-1960s the rate has stabilized at around 0.35 percent per year, although a slight upswing has been observed in the 1970s.

The low rate of increase can be ascribed to the declining birth rate, in 1962 to what was until then the lowest figure observed for any country in Europe, only 12.9 per 1,000 population. In 1974 and 1975, however, a strong upsurge was observed in the birth rate, to around 20 per 1,000, and, although caution must be exercised over interpretation, it is reasonably clear that this development is a consequence of the new population policy that makes abortion more difficult to obtain, gives preference in housing allocation and house-building grants to families with children, safeguards the employment rights of mothers, and provides generous child allowances.

The crude death rate of the population is around 11.5 per 1,000 and, because of the aging of the population, has shown a tendency to rise. Life tables suggest that male life expectancy at birth is now virtually static at 66.9 years, while female longevity continues to increase (at an increasingly lower rate), life expectancy at birth being 72.6 years. The long-term implications of the birth and death rates of the 1960s and early '70s are for eventual population decline, but the upsurge in births in the mid-1970s meant that the net reproduction ratio rose above unity for the first time since 1957.

The proportion of the population over the age of 60 years has been rising steadily, from 11.6 percent in 1949 to almost 19 percent in 1976, primarily because of the falling birth rate. In addition, the migration of young people from the countryside to the towns has meant that population aging has been more accentuated in rural than in urban areas. Every Hungarian census since 1869 has recorded a female surplus. The heavy male mortality during World War II strengthened the imbalance, and in 1949 a sex ratio of 1,081 females per 1,000 males was recorded; this has since fallen to 1,062 females per 1,000 males. An overall female surplus is to be expected within a country such as Hungary because of the strong sex differential in mortality. It should, however, be mentioned that among the younger population males outnumber females and that the female preponderance becomes evident only among people over the age of 40. Migration again produces geographical disparities in the sex ratio; although the female surplus is greater in rural than in urban areas because more men than women migrate to the towns, it is most pronounced among the resident population of Budapest, females outnumbering males by four to three among permanent migrants to the capital.

A surplus of women

Active wage earners constitute about half the total population. Of these, industry and the tertiary sector each employ some 35 percent, agriculture around one quarter of the total. Since the 1950s there has been an enormous restructuring of occupations in the country, the agricultural sector suffering great depletion because of the rapid growth of industry and the associated process of urbanization. The consequence has been a marked shift in population distribution through the process of internal migration. Between 1960 and 1973 Budapest experienced a net influx of approximately 280,000 migrants, and almost as many people moved into the neighbouring settlements that go to make up the Budapest metropolitan area.

Some 28 percent of the total population of the country lives within the Budapest metropolitan area, and sizable concentrations of population also occur within the industrial and mining regions of the Northern Mountains. Rural population density is greatest in the northeastern part of the Great Alföld, where the rate of natural increase has remained comparatively high. Nevertheless, the major part of the plain is sparsely settled because of large-scale out-migration, low natural increase, and a lack of urban centres. It is expected that the number of rural inhabitants will continue to decline, but increasingly it will be local urban centres rather than the large cities that are the recipients of population through this process.

Great Alföld population

THE NATIONAL ECONOMY

In terms of per capita gross national income, Hungary has achieved a medium level of development. In overall economic performance it ranks immediately after Italy and Austria but ahead of Spain, the Balkan countries, and Poland. Since approximately 15 percent of the Gross National Product is derived from agriculture, Hungary can be classed as an industrial–agrarian country.

Natural resources. The major natural endowments of Hungary are fertile soils and a climate favourable for agriculture. The power resources are modest, and the only significant mineral wealth is bauxite and the manganese deposits associated with it in the Bakony mountains. The one iron mine, at Rudabánya near Miskolc, produces low-grade ore of 24 to 27 percent metal content and can satisfy only one-tenth of national demand. The basic materials for the construction industry are mostly found within the country. Coal output is mainly of low-grade brown coal from mines in the Northern Mountains; black coal of good quality is mined only at Komló near Pécs, and most coal mining is slowly being phased out. Uranium-containing sands are found at Kővágószőllős, also close to Pécs. Electricity is generated by thermal power stations burning coal and to a lesser extent oil, but they will be supplemented by a nuclear station under construction on the Danube south of Budapest. The lowland nature of the country and the consequent absence of fast rivers rules out the generation of hydroelectricity.

Hungary, Area and Population

	area		population	
	sq mi	sq km	1970 census	1974 estimate
Regions				
Alföld (lowland region)				
Megyék (counties)				
Bács-Kiskun	3,229	8,362	574,000	564,000
Békés	2,175	5,632	447,000	431,000
Csongrád	1,517	3,928	323,000	288,000
Hajdú-Bihar	2,226	5,765	375,000	354,000
Pest	2,468	6,393	875,000	921,000
Szabolcs-Szatmár	2,292	5,937	590,000	562,000
Szolnok	2,165	5,608	449,000	437,000
Megyei jogú városok (county-ranked cities)				
Debrecen	172	446	157,000	177,000
Szeged	129	335	119,000	165,000
Dunántúl (Danube region)				
Megyék (counties)				
Baranya	1,694	4,388	280,000	271,000
Fejér	1,689	4,374	391,000	402,000
Győr-Sopron	1,482	3,837	304,000	302,000
Komárom	869	2,250	302,000	310,000
Somogy	2,348	6,082	363,000	360,000
Tolna	1,393	3,609	259,000	251,000
Vas	1,288	3,337	280,000	278,000
Veszprém	2,003	5,187	412,000	419,000
Zala	1,270	3,288	267,000	261,000
Megyei jogú város (county-ranked city)				
Győr	67	175	100,000	113,000
Pécs	57	145	145,000	159,000
Észak (northern region)				
Főváros (capital city)				
Budapest	203	525	1,945,000	2,047,000
Megyék (counties)				
Borsod-Abaúj-Zemplén	2,712	7,024	607,000	588,000
Heves	1,404	3,638	347,000	340,000
Nógrád	982	2,544	240,000	233,000
Megyei jogú város (county-ranked city)				
Miskolc	86	224	172,000	193,000
Total Hungary	35,920*	93,032*	10,322,000	10,428,000*

*Figures do not add to total because of rounding.
Source: Official government figures.

Sources of national income. Before World War II the economy of Hungary was based primarily on agriculture, but the industrialization drive since 1950 has fundamentally altered the balance. Whereas agriculture accounted for almost half the national income in 1938, this proportion had fallen to about one-seventh by the mid-1970s. The contribution of industry, construction, and mining rose correspondingly.

Hungary is virtually self-sufficient in food production, and agriculture also provides valuable commodities for export. Maize (corn), wheat, sugar beets, and potatoes are the principal crops, but beef, pork, and poultry production are also important. Slightly more than half the total area of the country is under arable cultivation, and a further 6 percent is planted to orchards, vegetables, and vineyards.

Agriculture is organized into cooperative and state farms. Initially collectivization was forced, and many units disbanded spontaneously in 1956. The cooperative sector was subsequently expanded again along largely voluntary lines, and by the mid-1970s more than 94 percent of agricultural land was farmed within the Socialist sector (cooperative and state farms combined). The private plots of cooperative labourers, however, also make a significant contribution to total output. Paralleling reorganization has been the modernization and mechanization of agriculture.

Cooperative and state farms

Between 50 and 55 percent of all imports consist of raw materials and semifinished products. The only sizable export of this type is bauxite, which is sent to Czechoslovakia, Poland, and the Soviet Union. In the past, Hungary depended very heavily on coal as a source of energy, but production has been decreasing rapidly as use of oil and natural gas has expanded. Much of the crude oil supply comes by pipeline from the Soviet Union, although an increasing quantity is being imported from the Middle East. Natural gas is produced in Hungary in the vicinity of Szeged, and more is imported from Romania. A small quantity of crude oil is also produced at home. Gas is being increasingly utilized in the chemical industry as well as for heating and household purposes, while the consumption of electricity is also rising rapidly.

By the mid-1970s approximately 1,816,000 persons were employed in industry, and production was some six times higher than in 1950. During the early 1950s industry concentrated on the production of capital goods, but from the late 1950s greater emphasis has been placed on consumer goods. Engineering accounts for just under half the total industrial output; textiles, clothing, and paper products combined contribute a further third, and food and chemicals are other significant sectors.

Financial services and foreign trade. The financial system is centralized and owned by the state. The Hungarian National Bank (Magyar Nemzeti Bank) is concerned with money supply and the granting of credits to companies, cooperative farms, state farms, and similar bodies. The State Development Bank (Allami Fejlesztési Bank) finances major investment projects and oversees national investment trends, while the Hungarian Foreign Trade Bank (Magyar Külkereskedelmi Bank) is concerned with foreign currency transactions.

Foreign trade

Before World War II, food products were the main exports. Postwar industrialization, however, has meant a restructuring of foreign trade, and the import of capital equipment and raw materials and the export of industrial articles have become dominant.The orientation of foreign trade has also undergone change, and the countries of the Communist bloc now account for some 60–65 percent of the total. The Soviet Union remains by far the largest trading partner; among the capitalist countries, West Germany is the most important trading partner, ranking, indeed, ahead of Bulgaria and Romania.

Management of the economy. The national economy of Hungary is based on public ownership of the fundamental means of production. The economy is divided into three sectors: state, cooperative, and private. Large industrial and agricultural enterprises and the banks are owned by the state and supervised by ministries or local authorities. The cooperative sector is made up of farming cooperatives (cultivating some 80 percent of agricultural land), manufacturing and artisans' cooperatives, and a number of marketing and consumption cooperatives. The insignificant private sector of the economy comprises artisans, retail tradesmen, and small farmers. Some three quarters of national income is generated by the state sector, one-fifth by cooperatives, and only 2–3 percent by private initiative.

Fourth and Fifth Five-Year Plans. The aims and implementation of economic policy are set out in the five-year plans of the national economy. The goals of the 1971–75 plan, for example, called for a 30 to 32 percent increase in national income; a similar increase in industrial production; a 15 to 16 percent increase in agricultural output; and growth of 25 to 27 percent in the real income of the population. The targets seem generally to have been fulfilled, but domestic consumption and investment rose in line with the original target but at the expense of the balance of trade. Under the Fifth Five-Year Plan, covering 1976 to 1980, similar increases are again projected for national income and industrial and agricultural production. Since the Hungarian economy faces severe manpower constraints, the achievement of output targets is contingent upon substantial improvements in labour productivity. The effect of imported inflation from the West and a further worsening of the terms of trade could adversely affect the plan targets.

The New Economic Mechanism. At the beginning of 1968 a reformed system of economic management (the New Economic Mechanism, or Új Gazdasági Mechanizmus) was introduced, replacing the previous rigid system of central planning—the direction of the economy by means of centrally determined, obligatory targets for individual enterprises. The basic aim of the New Economic Mechanism is to improve economic efficiency, both in domestic production and in foreign trade activities. Achieving this has involved the abolition of directive planning and an increase in the importance of prices in determining decisions about enterprises. Producers' prices have been reformed to bring them more into line with production costs, and a system of taxation has been devised to allow the payment of bonuses to workers and management in accordance with profits achieved rather than plan norms. Economic regulators—prices, taxation, credits, export and import licenses, and income regulators—are now the main elements of plan fulfillment. Enterprises are allowed a wide degree of autonomy about future investment. They can also handle their own foreign trade relations, set up companies abroad, and participate in foreign companies. Joint ventures with Western companies holding up to 49 percent of the equity have been permitted since 1972, although by mid-1974 only two Western concerns had forged such links.

Improving economic efficiency

The reform is generally considered to have been successful. More balanced growth has been maintained than in the earlier period, although controls on prices and profits had to be tightened to prevent the development of excessive income disparities and to maintain a low rate of inflation. Problems have also arisen regarding the profitability of some enterprise investment programs, and after January 1976 enterprises were required to repay state investment credits in full (previously 80 percent) over 10 years. In addition, unscheduled increases in costs now have to be covered by the enterprises themselves.

Taxation. The main sources of state finance are the taxes and other payments collected from nationalized and cooperative enterprises. Since the bulk of consumer prices are fixed by the state, it can be argued that a hidden tax is also levied on many articles and services, although others are heavily subsidized. Taxes paid directly by the population include an annual property tax, a progressive income tax (although only the higher wage earners and those in the private sector are seriously affected), a gift tax, and death duties.

Organizations. A number of organizations represent the interests of industrial enterprises, cooperatives, and employees. The common interests of state-owned companies are safeguarded by the appropriate ministry. The specialist companies and other enterprises participating in foreign trade can voice their common view through the Hungarian Chamber of Commerce (Magyar Kereskedelmi Kamara). Nonagricultural cooperatives also have their joint organizations, as does the private sector. Agrarian cooperatives are organized territorially and are coordinated by the National Council of Producer Cooperatives (Termelőszövetkezetek Országos Tanácsa).

Nineteen trade unions, all affiliated to the National Council of Hungarian Trade Unions (Magyar Szakszervezetek Országos Tanácsa), represent the interests of the working population. Trade union membership is voluntary, the closed shop is illegal, and some 4,000,000 persons possess union membership. Each union represents the interests of workers in a given branch of the economy or profession, and in most instances one union only is active at a particular workplace. Union officials are elected once every four years.

Trade unions

The functions of trade unions in Hungary differ considerably from those in the West. On the one hand, they are concerned with such economic matters as wage levels and job protection. This role has been increased within the framework of the New Economic Mechanism and the introduction of a modified labour code in which many of the restrictions on termination of employment and the obligation of the state to fix wages were abolished. Collective agreements between the enterprise management and the union have thus taken on greater significance. By contrast with usual practice in the West, unions are obliged to further agreed government policy. Disputes with management over collective agreements are settled through the courts, and the strike is not used. Additionally, enterprise managements are compelled by law to consult the unions about the living and working conditions of employees. Hungarian unions also serve an important social and cultural role. Union holiday homes are to be found in the principal resort areas of the country, providing inexpensive vacations for members. Unions also control the social and cultural funds accumulated by enterprises.

TRANSPORTATION

The industrialization and urbanization of Hungary have increased the importance of transport. The population is more mobile than previously, while the demands of industry for the movement of raw materials and finished articles have significantly risen. The growing tourist traffic between East and West also places greater burdens on the transport system.

Transport in Hungary is strongly centralized, and every main rail link and principal road converges on Budapest. Roads have already overtaken railways in terms of volume of freight transported, although when expressed in ton-kilometres rail still has the edge by virtue of the considerable movement of raw materials from the Soviet Union. More people also now use roads for personal transport since the upsurge in car ownership. In addition, transport by pipeline is rapidly developing.

Railways. The main elements of the Hungarian railway system were constructed in the second half of the 19th century to connect the principal provincial cities with Budapest, and, taking frontier changes into account, traffic is still concentrated in these few important lines. Domestically, the most important links are between Budapest and northern industrial areas; internationally, the main lines to the Soviet Union, Czechoslovakia, the German Democratic Republic, and Poland carry the most traffic.

Modernization of railways

The railways are undergoing extensive modernization. Steam has virtually been eliminated in favour of diesel traction, and the main east–west link from the Austrian to the Soviet frontier is electrified. Improvements to track and rolling stock and the automation of signalling equipment will increase capacity by allowing higher speeds. Unimportant branch lines (a total of 1,300 miles, or 2,100 kilometres, will eventually be dismantled) are being closed and traffic transferred to the roads. It is also planned to eliminate some 1,000 little used stations on the lines that will be retained and to reorganize the network around modernized district stations.

Roads. Approximately half the 18,600 miles (30,000 kilometres) of roads in the country have modern asphalt or concrete surfaces. The main roads, all of which radiate from Budapest, have been modernized since the 1950s but are still inadequate for the rapidly rising volume of traffic. Although the bulk of road passenger transport is still by bus, car ownership is expanding dramatically; the growth of domestic and international road haulage is also placing severe pressure on parts of the system. The London–Damascus and Hamburg–Bucharest international highways cross the country. A four-lane expressway, from Budapest to Lake Balaton, is largely complete, and the next phase of the program is the linkup with the European international road network.

Water transport. The Danube is the only waterway in the country transporting a significant amount of freight, much of it international and in transit. The principal port is Csepel free port in Budapest. Tourism provides the bulk of a highly seasonal traffic on other waterways, Lake Balaton deserving special mention in this connection.

Air transport. The small size of the country means that operation of domestic air services is not economically feasible, and the last internal route was discontinued in 1969. International air traffic centred on Ferihegy Airport, Budapest, is rapidly expanding. Malév, the national airline, operates to almost every country of Europe as well as to the Middle East. Ferihegy is also used by a number of major Western airlines.

ADMINISTRATION AND SOCIAL CONDITIONS

Government structure. Hungary is a people's republic whose structure of government and laws are set out in the constitution of 1949 as revised in 1972. The supreme organ of state is Parliament which possesses "all the rights emanating from popular sovereignty." Parliament elects the members of the collective sovereign body, the Presidential Council of the Hungarian People's Republic, as well as the members of the Council of Ministers, the president of the Supreme Court, and the chief public prosecutor.

When Parliament is not in session its functions are executed by the Presidential Council. The council calls Parliament into session according to need, generally several times a year, and promulgates legal decrees that must be presented for approval at the next parliamentary session. It also supervises state administration and appoints the more important state officials.

The main organ of state administration is the Council of Ministers, whose president and individual ministers have the authority to issue orders. To ensure the effective management of the economy, the Council of Ministers delegates authority to an economic commission, which promulgates compulsory decrees. In addition, commissions concerned with specialist spheres, such as scientific policy and international economic relations, operate within the framework of the Council of Ministers.

Local government. Local administration is based on a hierarchical structure of local councils. At the base of the hierarchy are village councils, which are directly responsible to rural district authorities. Fulfilling the same administrative role as the latter are the urban district councils. Both rural and urban district authorities are subordinate to the county council within whose geographical sphere they lie, there being 19 such authorities. Of equal rank to the latter are the five municipal councils (subdivided into subordinate municipal district councils) of Debrecen, Győr, Miskolc, Pécs, and Szeged. The administration of the capital is the responsibility of the Metropolitan Council of Budapest and the 22 subordinate metropolitan district authorities. At the head of the hierarchy is the City Council of Budapest, which transmits its authority through the Office of Councils. As a reform measure, village councils of villages with small populations have been amalgamated into joint village councils, which makes possible the extension of services (such as health centres, libraries, and primary schools) to rural communities where previously there was no economic justification. The county and municipal authorities together with the Budapest metropolitan and metropolitan district councils represent the most important tier of local government. Their specialist executive committees deal with fiscal matters, economic administration (including the running of some industry and many retail functions), planning and control of education, and the supervision of public health. Since 1971 the rural and municipal district councils have not been elected and are in effect executive committees of the corresponding county or municipal authorities.

County and municipal councils

Elections and political organizations. Parliamentary and council elections are held every four years on a franchise extended to all Hungarian citizens over the age of 18. Members of Parliament and of village, urban district, municipal, and metropolitan district councils are elected directly by secret ballot. Because the county and Budapest metropolitan councillors represent the interests of a whole city or county, they are elected by the members of the subordinate village, urban, and metropolitan district councils rather than by direct franchise. Candidates are chosen at nomination meetings, and more than one candidate can stand for election in a given constituency. Independents have the right to stand, but candidates are usually proposed by the Patriotic People's Front (Hazafias Népfront) or the Hungarian Socialist Workers' Party (Magyar Szocialista Munkáspárt; *i.e.*, the Communist Party). When several candidates contest a constituency, the winner is the one who obtains an absolute majority of the votes cast. Elected members of Parliament and of councils are accountable to their constituents, who have the right to remove them in the case of incapacity or lack of confidence. In such a case, and when a member dies, a special election is held.

The Hungarian Socialist Workers' Party

The Hungarian Socialist Workers' Party (the only political party), whose members number some 760,000, plays the leading political and ideological role in the Hungarian People's Republic, and many members of its Political Committee are or have in the past been members of the government. The directives of the party are implemented through the educational and organizational work of its members and its support groups. The latter include the Hungarian Communist Youth Association (Magyar Kommunista Ifjúsági Szövetség; with some 800,000 members), the trade unions (with some 4,000,000 members), the National Council of Hungarian Women (Magyar Nők Országos Tanácsa), and the Patriotic People's Front, a mass organization based on collective, in contrast to individual, membership.

Through these organizations the citizen has the opportunity to voice opinions on public affairs and to submit comments, complaints, and suggestions to the administrative authorities of the state. The citizen also has the right to be heard in local or central political organs and has freedom of expression through the mass media, provided the social, economic, and political order of the country, as defined by the constitution, is respected. This freedom does not, therefore, extend to the expression of views that are contrary to the ideology and fundamental aims of the state.

Justice. The administration of justice is the responsibility of the chief public prosecutor, who is elected for a six-year term by Parliament. Civil and criminal proceedings come under the jurisdiction of district and county courts and of the Supreme Court. District courts deal with first instances, county courts with more serious crimes, civil actions of first instance, and cases on appeal, and the Supreme Court normally with appeals, although first instances may be referred by the chief public prosecutor. The Supreme Court also passes judgment on matters of principle, which are then binding on the other courts. Although special courts are possible under the constitution, military courts are the only such courts presently in existence. In addition, local government executive committees may try petty offenses, and the police have power to deal summarily with minor traffic infringements and other misdemeanours. District and county court judges and lay assessors are elected by the respective district and county councils and members of the Supreme Court by Parliament, on the recommendation of the Presidential Council.

Armed forces and the police. The armed forces of the Hungarian People's Republic consist of the People's Army, which includes the air force, the frontier guards, the police, the workers' militia (a voluntary paramilitary group), and the customs police. All males over the age of 18 are liable for compulsory military training, the length of which varies according to the branch of the services entered. The police safeguard social property, public order, and the personal and material security of citizens and are responsible for traffic control. The police force, which is also supported by voluntary groups, comes under the jurisdiction of the National Police Board. The Internal Security Forces (Belső Karhatalom, or BKH) are under the Ministry of the Interior. Four Soviet divisions are stationed in the country.

Education. In Hungary schooling is free (financed out of general exchequer funds, with parental contribution toward cost of books and stationery) and compulsory between the ages of six and 16, although many children attend crèches and kindergartens before reaching the age of six. Elementary education extends over eight years and embraces the six to 14 age group. At the age of 14 children embark upon their secondary education in grammar schools, technical schools, or schools specializing in the fine arts or music. Entrance into secondary school is based upon elementary school reports and parental choice, and most pupils stay on until the age of 18. The curricula followed in the various types of school are laid down by the Ministry of Education and are standardized throughout the country. Technical schools have become increasingly popular because in addition to teaching traditional subjects they also provide pupils with a vocational background. All schools, with the exception of a handful of secondary establishments run by religious denominations, are controlled by the state.

Higher education

Institutions of higher education, of which there are more than 80, range from the traditional university to the very specialized college, such as the College of Chemical Engineering at Kazincbarcika. Acceptance into university is dependent upon the results of an entrance examination, although social background is also taken into account and, as elsewhere in eastern Communist Europe, children of workers and peasants may be given preference. While higher education is not free, the number of students paying fees is small, and most can also expect to receive a maintenance grant.

Health and welfare services. In 1972 the national health plan was extended to the entire population of the country. Under the plan, medical treatment is available free of charge (except nontherapeutic abortions and hospitalization because of drunkenness). Also free of charge are drugs provided in hospitals, vaccine serums and lifesaving drugs, and drugs prescribed for minors. Otherwise a charge amounting to 15 percent of the cost is made for medicaments and medical appliances. The health service is administered by local councils under the supervision of the Ministry of Health. Medical care is generally of a high standard, and the number of doctors and hospital beds per capita is well up to international levels. Care is provided not only by hospitals but also by the district general practitioner, by medical centres at places of work, and by outpatient clinics containing departments of general medicine, pediatrics, surgery, gynecology, etc. Great attention is paid to disease prevention through the screening of the population for tuberculosis and cancer and through mass immunization against smallpox, infantile paralysis, and tuberculosis.

Social insurance, which is paid for by the contributions of employers, provides for sickness, maternity, and death benefits. Sick pay is usually fixed at 75 percent of wages and is available for one year without restriction. In addition to 20 weeks of paid maternity leave, mothers can receive a monthly child-nursing grant for a period of three years after birth. Both employers and employees contribute to the pension fund, from which are drawn retirement (at 60 years of age for men and 55 for women) and disability pensions. The social and pension funds are administered by the Trade Union Social Insurance Centre (Szakszervezeti Társadalombiztosítási Központ), under the supervision of the Council of Ministers. Retired persons who are not entitled to a pension, together with those whose pensions are too low, receive social care from the appropriate council. Councils also provide homes for the aged who have no immediate family and, in conjunction with employers, maintain nurseries and kindergartens as well as day homes for children of school age. Family allowances are paid on a progressive scale to married couples with two or more children and to single-parent families with one or more children. Children in need of care are looked after in homes maintained by the state.

Housing. Housing remains a severe problem despite the completion in 1975 of a 15-year building program that went a long way toward ameliorating the housing shortage. The basic premise of housing policy is that every family is entitled to its own home at reasonable cost and each family member to a separate room. Overcrowding, shared tenancies, sublettings, and the involuntary sharing of accommodation with parents are nevertheless common. While the state is very active in the housing field, some 72 percent of dwellings are privately owned. Public sector housing is controlled by local authorities and is generally allocated according to need. There is a multiplicity of home types. The state in the form of the local authority is the largest landlord, yet it builds homes for sale (*öröklakás*) as well as for rent. The state and private sectors are bridged by the cooperative housing sector (*szövetkezeti lakás*), although the cooperative

Housing shortage

scene also includes groups of individuals who voluntarily form themselves into a "private" cooperative to build a modest apartment house of not more than 10 flats (*társasház*). The privately owned single-family dwelling is commonest in small towns and villages.

Deficiencies in housing policy regarding availability, upkeep, and social distribution of homes led to a major reform of the system in 1971. While committing more funds from the central exchequer, the reform has also increased the financial involvement of individual households in home construction and maintenance. Rents, which contain a capital cost as well as an upkeep element, were raised, and a uniform structure was introduced. Rents are still low by most Western standards, however. To reduce the burden on the state, private ownership is encouraged through the provision of subsidies and 30–35-year mortgages at low rates of interest. Housing policy and population policy are interconnected in that housing subsidies go to families with young children or to married couples who agree to have children within five years.

Wages and the cost of living. Since 1950 unemployment in Hungary has been rare, and indeed there exists an overall shortage of manpower. The work week has been progressively reduced over the years and by the mid-1970s was 44 hours or less.

The extremes of income disparity among the various groups in society have been reduced, and the average incomes of rural and urban dwellers are very similar. Between 1970 and 1975, consumer prices rose at an annual average of around 2.5 to 3 percent, showing a tendency to increase at a faster rate toward the end of the period as the country adjusted itself to higher energy and food prices, while real per capita income grew at 4 to 5 percent per year.

CULTURAL LIFE AND INSTITUTIONS

The cultural milieu. A large number of Hungarians have made substantial contributions to the arts and sciences. The achievements of the Hungarian-born scientists Albert Szent-Györgyi, Georg von Békésy, Eugene Wigner, Edward Teller, Leo Szilard, and John von Neumann have gained world recognition and many Nobel prizes. The music of Franz (Ferenc) Liszt, Béla Bartók, and Zoltán Kodály is also known throughout the world, and many contemporary Hungarian musical artists and conductors have become eminent internationally. In addition, the works of the poets János Arany, Sándor Petőfi, and Endre Ady as well as those of the writers Kálmán Mikszáth, Zsigmond Móricz, and Ferenc Molnár have been translated into many languages.

Before World War II Hungary had a well-developed cultural life, but one largely confined to the upper classes. The working class was regarded as uncultured, and illiteracy was widespread. Since 1945 the government has made great efforts to promote mass culture, and large sums have been and continue to be spent by the state in this respect. Cultural opportunities have been greatly expanded, and prices are kept low through state support of literature, music, the visual arts, and the popular arts.

Mass culture

Hungary in general and Budapest in particular are noted for their vigorous cultural life. Hungarian performers often appear abroad and have achieved many successes in international competitions, while in the capital and other cities celebrated foreign artists often perform. Foreign exhibitions are also frequently put on for the benefit of the Hungarian public. The Hungarian cinema has received numerous awards at international film festivals, and films produced in some 20 countries are regularly shown to Hungarian audiences.

Amateur groups—numbering more than 10,000 and with about 200,000 members—are also active, and some preserve the Hungarian traditions of pottery making, carving, weaving, and embroidery. These crafts are also supported by the activities of art cooperatives, whose embroidery and lace are appreciated both inside and outside the country. Also well known are the handicrafts of Matyó-land, Sárköz, and Buszák, the lace of Kalocsa, and the folk murals decorating peasant homes in Tolna and Bács-Kiskun counties. Other folk products include the pottery of Békés county, and the glass of Nógrád.

Cultural institutions. Free public libraries are found in almost every town and village of Hungary, comprising some 8,300 general and 1,700 specialized technical libraries. An important role in the spread of culture in the village is also played by the cultural centre (*kultúrház*) and in the population at large by the 207 national museums. A dozen or so scientific societies exist, and the Hungarian Academy of Sciences maintains 38 research institutes. The country has 3,600 or so motion-picture houses. Travelling theatres perform in the villages, and the theatre companies of the large cities also go on tour. The price of both cinema and theatre tickets is kept low by government subsidy. As in other countries, the spread of television has caused a drop in theatre and cinema audiences and in attendance at cultural programs in general. This has generated a wide-ranging debate regarding the relative claims for state help of the different cultural forms.

A large range of daily and weekly newspapers and periodicals is published. Radio remains popular but since the mid-1960s has been displaced from its former prominent position by television. There are some 4,200 sports clubs in the country. Football (soccer) remains the most popular sport, but the country is also strong in swimming, rowing, boxing, pentathlon, wrestling, and weight lifting. Tennis has been gaining in popularity.

Sports

PROSPECTS AND PROBLEMS

Hungary now stands on the threshold of becoming a fully fledged industrial nation. Most industry has been established since 1950, and according to long-range plans the country should reach the current industrial level of western Europe by the late 1980s. Despite industrial expansion, agriculture still plays an important role in the national economy. Economic cooperation and integration within the Communist bloc continue to be important factors in economic development. Just over two-thirds of foreign trade is conducted with the member countries of Comecon, which provide an important outlet for Hungarian engineering exports and remain a valuable source of raw material imports.

Economic trends indicate that future industrial growth will be capital intensive, drawing on a body of increasingly skilled manpower. Major emphasis will be placed on the engineering, electronic, telecommunications, and pharmaceutical industries. The decline in agricultural population is expected to continue, although agriculture is likely to retain its importance in domestic and export markets. The rate of natural increase has climbed above the low levels of the 1960s and early '70s, and it is no longer certain that Hungary is heading for a stationary population in the medium term. Despite these impending changes, Hungarian traditions, especially the cultural traditions, are firmly grounded, and future stability seems fairly well assured.

BIBLIOGRAPHY. FERENC ERDEI (ed.), *Information Hungary* (1968), gives a detailed picture of the history, geography, people, and social, economic, and cultural life of the country; *Hungary Today* (issued irregularly), compiled by the HUNGARIAN CENTRAL STATISTICAL OFFICE, offers a survey of the economic and cultural life, utilizing statistical data; the same agency also issues the *Statistical Pocket-Book of Hungary* and the more comprehensive *Statistical Yearbook* (both annual), the latter appearing somewhat later but containing more complete coverage; MÁRTON PÉCSI and BÉLA SÁRFALVI, *The Geography of Hungary* (1964; orig. pub. in Hungarian 1960), gives a detailed picture of the physical and economic geography; MÁRTON PÉCSI, *Geomorphological Regions of Hungary* (1970), is a description of individual regions; ISTVÁN FRISS (ed.), *Reform of Economic Mechanism in Hungary* (1969), gives information on theoretical and practical questions relating to the new methods of economic management; *Hungary* (annually, 1966–), published by the PANNONIA PRESS, contains a wide range of articles by various authors and a statistical digest. Non-Hungarian published sources include ELMER BAKO, *Guide to Hungarian Studies*, 2 vol. (1973); I.T. BEREND and G. RANKI, *Hungary: A Century of Economic Development* (1974); and P. IGNOTUS, *Hungary* (1972).

(Ed.)

Hungary, History of

Hungary came into existence when the Magyars occupied the middle basin of the Danube in the late 9th century. Parts of its territory had formed the ancient Roman provinces of Pannonia and Dacia. When Rome lost control of Pannonia at the end of the 4th century, it was occupied, first by Germanic tribes, then by Slavs. The subsequent history of Dacia is unrecorded. The central plains had formed the bases of nomadic immigrant peoples from the steppes north of the Black Sea—Huns, Bulgars, Avars—some of whom extended their domination further afield. The Avars, who dominated the basin in the 7th and 8th centuries, were crushed *c.* 800 by Charlemagne, whose successors organized the western half of the area in a chain of Slavonic vassal "dukedoms." One of these, Croatia, which extended as far north as the Sava, made itself fully independent in 869, while another, Moravia, which then extended as far as the Gran, had openly defied its Carolingian overlord for as long. The Byzantine Empire and Bulgaria exercised loose authority over the south and east of the area.

This article is divided into the following sections:

I. The kingdom to 1526

THE ARPADS

History of the Magyars

In 892 the Carolingian emperor Arnulf, attempting to assert his authority over the Moravian duke Sviatopluk, called in the help of the Magyars, a Finno-Ugric people, whose early homes had been on the upper waters of the Volga and Kama rivers in the present Soviet Union; unrecorded causes had driven them, at an uncertain date, southward into the steppes, where they had adopted the life, appropriate to their environment, of peripatetic herdsmen. In the 9th century they were based on the lower Don, ranging over the steppes to the west of that river. They then comprised a federation of hordes, or tribes, each under a hereditary chieftain, and each composed of a varying number of clans, the members of which owned a real or imagined blood kinship. The clansmen were all free men, but the community included slaves taken in battle or in raids. There were seven "Magyar" hordes, but other elements were included in the federation, including three hordes of Turki Khazars (the "Kavars"). Either from this fact, or perhaps from a memory of earlier conditions, this federation was known to its neighbours as the On-Ogur (*i.e.*, literally, the "Ten Arrows"), from the Slavonic pronunciation of which the name "Hungarian" is derived.

In 889 attacks by the newly arrived Pechenegs had driven the Magyars and their confederates to the western extremities of the steppes, where they were living when Arnulf's invitation arrived. The band sent to Arnulf reported back that the plains across the Carpathians would form a suitable new homeland that could be easily conquered and defended from the rear. Having elected as their chief Árpád, the leader of their most powerful tribe, the Magyars crossed the Carpathians en masse, probably in 896, and easily subjugated the peoples of the sparsely inhabited central plain, their first place of settlement. They destroyed the Moravian Empire in 906 and in the next year occupied Pannonia, having defeated a German force sent against them. They were then firmly established in the whole centre of the basin, over which their tribes and their associates distributed themselves, Árpád taking the central area west of the Danube for his own tribe. The periphery was guarded by outposts, which were gradually pushed forward, chiefly to the north.

The Christian kingdom. During the next half-century the Magyars were chiefly known to Europe for the forays they made across it, either as mercenaries in the service of warring princes, or in search of booty for themselves—treasure or slaves for domestic use or sale. But terrifying to others, their mode of life was not always profitable to themselves. Their raiding forces suffered several severe reverses, culminating in a disastrous defeat at the hands of the emperor Otto I, in 955, on the Lechfeld, outside Augsburg. By this time the wild blood of the first invaders was thinning out and new influences, in particular that of Christianity, were beginning to operate. Both the Eastern and the Western churches strove to draw them, with the other peoples of east central Europe, into their orbits. They had established pacific, almost friendly relations with Bavaria. The decisive step was taken by Árpád's great-grandson, Géza, who succeeded to the hereditary chief leadership in 972 and re-established its authority over the tribal chiefs. In 973 he sent an embassy to Otto II at Quedlinburg, and in 975 he and his family were received into the Western Church. In 996 his son, Stephen (István), married Gisella, a Bavarian princess.

Magyar defeat at Lechfeld

Stephen I (997–1038) carried on his father's work. With the help of heavily armed Bavarian knights, he crushed his rivals for the headship. Applying to the Holy See, he received the insignia of royalty from it and, according to tradition, was crowned king on Christmas Day, 1000. The event was of immeasurable importance, for not only did Hungary now enter the spiritual community of the Western world but Pope Sylvester's personal relationship with his former pupil, Otto III, enabled it to do so without admitting the political suzerainty of the empire. Stephen then carried through the conversion of his people to Christianity, establishing a network of archiepiscopal and episcopal sees, which he reinforced with lavishly endowed monastic foundations. Later, he crushed the surviving disputants of his authority—notably the Kavars—and, carrying on his father's work, organized his state on a system which was to remain for many centuries the essentially unaltered basis of Hungary's political and social structure. The tribes, as units, disappeared, but the fundamental social stratification was not altered. The descendants in the male line of the old conquerors, and elements later equated with them, remained a privileged class, personally free, answerable in judgment only to the king or his representative, and entitled to appear in general assemblage. Their lands—which at this time, since the economy was mainly pastoral, were held by clans or subclans, in semicommunal ownership—were inalienable, except for proved delinquency, and free of any obligation. The only duty required by the state of members of this class was that of military service, on call. They were allowed to retain their slaves, although Stephen freed his own. All land outside that held by this class—then more than half the whole, for it included the areas in the interior not settled by the original invaders, all land lying beyond the original frontiers, and also any confiscated for rebellion—belonged to the crown, which could, indeed, donate at will. The nonservile inhabitants of these lands—descendants of the pre-Magyar population, manumitted slaves, invited colonists, etc.—were subjects of the crown or of the local landholder.

Conversion to Christianity

The whole of this land was divided into counties (*megyék*) each under a royal official, an *ispán* (later *fő* [head] *ispán*) who represented the king's authority in it, administered its unfree population, and collected the taxes that formed the national revenue, central and local. Each *ispán* maintained at his headquarters, or *vár* (fortress), an armed force composed of freemen who took service under him, or of persons freed by the king. In Stephen's day there were about 45 such counties.

The early kings. Once St. Stephen (he was canonized in 1083) established his rule, his authority was rarely questioned. He fought few foreign wars and made his long reign a period of peaceful consolidation. But his death in 1038 was followed by many years of discord, for his only son, Imre (Emeric), had predeceased him, and the nation rebelled against his designated successor, Peter, and expelled him in 1041. Peter returned in 1044, with the help of Emperor Henry III. The "national" king, Samuel Aba, who had taken his place, was murdered, but Peter himself was killed in another rebellion in 1046. Andrew (András) I, of a collateral branch of the House of Árpád, was killed in 1060 fleeing from his brother, Béla I, and after Béla's death there was a further conflict between his sons, Géza and Ladislas (László), and Andrew's son, Salamon. Peace returned only when, after Géza's short rule (1074–77), the throne passed to Ladislas I, who occupied it until 1095; and even then, the curse of dynastic jealousy proved to have been exorcised only temporarily. Ladislas' successor, Coloman (Kálmán; 1095–1116), who was Géza I's elder son, had his own brother, Álmos, and Álmos' infant son, Béla, blinded to secure the throne for his own son Stephen II (1116–31), perhaps Hungary's worst king. Béla II (1131–41; the blinded boy, whom his father's friends had brought up in secrecy) and Béla's eldest son, Géza II (1141–61), ruled thereafter unchallenged, but the succession of Géza's son, Stephen III (1161–73) was disputed by two of his uncles, Ladislas II (1162–63) and Stephen IV (1163–65). Happily, the death of Stephen IV exhausted the supply of uncles, and Stephen III's brother, Béla III (1173–96), had no domestic rivals to the throne, but the short reign of Béla's elder son, Emeric (Imre) (1196–1204), was spent largely in disputes with his younger brother, Andrew II, who on Emeric's death expelled his infant son, Ladislas III (who died the next year), before beginning his own long reign (1205–35).

Period of disputed succession

Consolidation and expansion. These royal disputes caused Hungary much harm. Claimants to the throne often invoked foreign help, for which they paid in political degradation or temporary or permanent loss of territory: both Peter and Salamon did homage to the Holy Roman emperor for their thrones; and Aba's war against Peter's protectors cost Hungary its previous territories west of the Leitha, while the wars of the 12th century cost it areas in the south. The uncertainty delayed political consolidation, and even Christianity did not take root easily: there was a widespread pagan revolt in 1047, and another in 1063.

Yet the political unity of the country and the new faith somehow survived the earlier troubles, and both were firmly established by Ladislas I, one of Hungary's greatest kings, and by Coloman, who, in spite of his atrocious crime, was a competent and enlightened ruler.

Meanwhile, many factors worked for Hungary. The international situation was favourable. After Austria had grown big at the expense of the imperial authority, most of Hungary's neighbours were states of approximately the same size and strength as itself, and the Hungarians lived with them on terms of mutual tolerance and even friendship. The steppes were quiet: the Kuman (Latin Cumani; Hungarian Kunok), after destroying the Pechenegs there, did not try to go further, and after two big raids had been successfully repelled by Ladislas, they left Hungary in peace. The breathing space thus provided allowed Hungary to extend its effective frontiers to the Carpathian crest in the north, and over Transylvania. Magyar advance guards pushed up the valleys of both areas, and these were reinforced in the Szepes area and central Transylvania by imported colonies of Germans (usually called "Saxons"), while colonies of Szekels, a people akin to the Magyars who had preceded the latter into the central plains, were settled behind its eastern passes. The county system was extended to both areas, although with modifications in Transylvania, where the "Saxons" and Szekels constituted free communities and the whole was placed under a voivode, or governor. In the south, Ladislas occupied (or reoccupied after an interval) the area between the Sava and Drava rivers; Coloman assumed the crown of Croatia, which then included Bosnia and Northern Dalmatia, although this remained a separate "Land of the Hungarian Crown," over which a governor (ban) acted as deputy for the king.

Imported colonists

In the interior, too, natural growth and continued immigration swelled the population, which by 1200 had risen to the large figure, for the age, of some 2,000,000. The rulers of this big and populous state were now important men. After Ladislas' day, nothing more was heard of German claims to suzerainty over it. In the 12th century Hungary was intervening in its neighbours' affairs as often as they in Hungary's. Béla III, who married a French princess, had the largest revenues of any European monarch, after the two emperors.

Social and political developments. Meanwhile, the pattern of Hungarian society had been changing. The numbers of the free class, or "nobles" as they were coming to be called, although frequently reinforced by new admissions to its ranks, probably hardly increased in absolute terms, and certainly far less than those of the unfree population: from perhaps half the total in 896, they had been reduced by 1200 to about one-eighth. Further, as the economy became agricultural, the old clan lands dwindled until only pockets remained. Where the rest had been, and in large parts of the old crown lands, which improvident donations had greatly reduced, the land was held in the form of individual estates, the owner of each of which was master of the unfree population on it: the "nobles" had, to a large extent, become a landed oligarchy. Some individual estates were very large, and their owners had come to constitute a "magnate" class, not yet institutionalized or legally differentiated from their poorer co-nobles but far above them in wealth and influence. The nonnobles, although slavery had practically disappeared, were still a "subject" class; and although many of them, including the burghers of the towns (most of which were German foundations) and such communities as the Saxons and Szekels, were protected by special charters and personally free, even they stood, politically, outside the magic ring of the "natio Hungarica."

Throughout these developments, the political form of the country had remained that of the absolutist patrimonial kingship. The king maintained a council of *optimates*, but his prerogatives were not restricted and his authority on matters falling within it remained absolute. A strong king, such as Béla III, could always curb a recalcitrant magnate by simply confiscating his estate. Only the follies and extravagances of the feckless Andrew II evoked a revolt culminating, in 1222, in the issue of the famous "Golden Bull," to which every Hungarian king thereafter had to swear, as the basic charter of national liberties. Its purpose was twofold: to reaffirm the rights of the smaller nobles, old and new (*servientes regis*), against both the crown and the magnates, and to defend those of the whole nation against the crown by restricting the powers of the latter in certain fields, and legalizing refusal to obey its unlawful commands. But Andrew had done much harm, by dissipating the royal revenues through his extravagances and by huge grants of land to his partisans.

Issuance of the "Golden Bull"

The Mongol invasion: the last Árpád kings. Andrew's successor, Béla IV (1235–70), began his reign with a series of measures designed to re-establish the royal authority, but his work was soon interrupted by the frightful disaster of the Mongol invasion. In the spring of 1241 the Mongols quickly overran the country and before they left it, a year later, had inflicted ghastly devastation. Only a few (but not all) fortified places and the impenetrable swamps and forests escaped their ravages. The country lost about half its population, the incidence ranging from 60 percent in the Alföld or central plain (100 percent in parts of it) to 20 percent in Transdanubia; only parts of Transylvania and of the northwest came off fairly lightly. Returned from Dalmatia, where he had taken somewhat inglorious refuge, Béla, whom his country not unjustly dubbed its second founder, reorganized the army, built a chain of fortresses, and called in new settlers to repopulate the country. He paid special attention to the towns. But he was forced to give some of the magnates practically a free hand on their own estates, and a few families rose to near-sovereign local status. Further, one group of

Rebuilding under Béla IV

immigrants, a body of Kumans who had fled into Hungary before the Mongols, proved so powerful and so turbulent that to ensure their loyalty Béla had to marry his son, Stephen V, to a Kuman princess. Stephen survived his father only two years, after which the country passed under the regency of his widow, the "Kumanian woman," whom the Hungarians detested. Her son Ladislas IV "the Kumanian" (1272–90) grew up into a wild, undisciplined youth, who took pleasure only in Kuman mistresses, and who came so near to paganism that Pope Nicholas IV preached a crusade against him. He was assassinated (by a Kuman) and left no legitimate heir. Such of Hungary's neighbours as could pretend to the succession by descent from an Árpád through the female line prepared to put in their claims. One male of the Árpád line was, however, discovered in Italy. His legitimacy was impugned, but his supporters got him into the country, and the young man, Andrew III, proved a wise and capable king. Unhappily, he died in 1301, without male issue, and with him the national dynasty became extinct.

HUNGARY UNDER FOREIGN KINGS

The extinction of the old dynasty created a new situation for Hungary. The nation was now entitled to choose its successor; but the principle of the blood tie was still generally regarded as determinant, and all of the candidates for the throne—Wenceslaus of Bohemia, Otto of Bavaria, and Charles Robert of the Angevin House of Naples—based their claims on descent from an Árpád in the female line. But the old Árpáds had always regarded themselves, and had been regarded by their subjects, as essentially embodiments of their nation's aspirations and defenders of its interests. All the three claimants now were foreigners; one of them and the father of another were actually seated on a foreign throne. From that time until its extinction, the kingship of Hungary was in fact invariably—with two exceptions, one of them disputed—held by a foreigner, nearly always by one occupying simultaneously at least one foreign throne. This could be to the advantage of Hungary if he used the resources of those thrones in its service; and he could also fructify its life with beneficial imported innovations. But he could, alternatively, neglect and exploit Hungary in his other interests and use his power to crush its national freedoms and institutions. Securing the advantages of foreign rule while escaping its dangers was the abiding dilemma—seldom successfully resolved—of Hungarian history.

The Angevin kings. The problem did not pose itself at first, for Charles Robert of Anjou (1308–42), still a child when his supporters won out, had no foreign throne and grew up a true Hungarian. He was also a capable man. After growing to manhood, he crushed the most rebellious of the "kinglets" and won over the rest; after this his rule was unquestioned and peaceful at home. The international situation, with Germany distraught by the power struggle between empire and papacy, the Mongolian Tatars grown passive, and the power of Byzantium in full decay, was again favourable to the states of the "middle zone" of eastern Europe and the Balkans; it is no accident that Poland, Hungary, Bohemia, and Serbia all look on the 14th century as their golden age. As this situation favoured Hungary's neighbours, as well as itself, Charles Robert's attempts at expansion were only moderately successful. In the Balkans, he made Bosnia his friend and client but lost Dalmatia to Venice and other territories to Serbia and the newly emerged "Voivody" of Walachia. But he drove Czech and Austrian marauders out of the land and on the whole preserved friendly relations with Austria, Bohemia, and Poland.

Charles' son, Louis (Lajos) I (1342–82), the only Hungarian king on whom his country has bestowed the name "Great"—a name given in love as well as fear—built on his father's foundations. Keeping peace with the West, he repaired his father's losses in the south, and surrounded his kingdom with a ring of dependencies over which Hungary presided as *archiregnum* in the Balkans, on the lower Danube, and in Galicia. The climax of his dynastic glory came when, in 1370, he also ascended the throne of Poland, in virtue of an earlier family compact.

Hungary in 1360.

Adapted from R. Treharne and H. Fullard (eds.), *Muir's Historical Atlas: Ancient, Medieval and Modern*, 9th ed. (1962); George Philip & Son Ltd., London

Angevin prosperity

Both Angevin kings owed much to the wealth they derived from the gold mines of Transylvania and north Hungary, the yield of which eventually reached the remarkable figure of 3,000 lb. annually—five times that of any other European state. Some 35 to 40 percent of this went to the king, enabling him to maintain a splendid court. Spared for two generations from serious invasion or civil war, the rest of the country blossomed materially as never before. The population rose to 3,000,000 and the country contained 49 Royal Free Boroughs, over 500 smaller towns, and some 26,000 villages. The economy was still mainly rural, but the crafts prospered, trade expanded, and the arts flourished: a university, one of the oldest in Europe, was founded at Pécs in 1367 (it is true that it proved short-lived).

The rule of the two Angevin kings was essentially despotic, although enlightened. Themselves no bureaucrats, they introduced elements of feudalism into the political, and especially the military, system: each lord was responsible for maintaining his own armed contingent (*banderium*). But the magnates were held firmly in check, and Louis reaffirmed the rights and privileges of the common nobles and carried further a process, begun in the previous century, under which the counties were developing from "royal" into "noble" institutions, each still under a royal official but administered with a wide measure of autonomy by elected representatives of the local nobility. He also standardized the obligations of the peasants at the figure of one-ninth of their produce to the lord, a tithe to the church, and a house tax (*porta*) that went direct to the state.

Sigismund of Luxembourg. The benefits of Louis' rule would have been far greater still had he not wasted enormous sums of money and many lives on endeavours to secure the throne of Naples for his nephew; and it is also true that his foreign acquisitions served his personal glory more than they did the real interests of his country; much of the imposing edifice collapsed when he died, leaving as issue only two daughters. Louis had destined the elder, Maria, to succeed him on both his thrones, but the Poles refused to continue the union. They accepted the younger daughter Hedwig (Jadwiga) as queen but married her to Jagiełło of Lithuania, and the ways of Poland and Hungary for a time parted. The Hungarians crowned Maria, whose husband, Sigismund of Luxembourg, had himself crowned as her consort in 1387 and after her death eight years later ruled alone until his own death in 1437. Under him, matters took a sharp turn for the worse. Sigismund was no fool. He did much for arts, commerce, and, above all, for the towns. Also, like Andrew II, he promoted Hungarian political institutions by creating the need for them. The principle that the consent of representatives of the privileged classes, assembled in Diet, was necessary for the grant of any subsidy or additional taxation, and even, later, for any legislation, dates from his reign, being made necessary by his extravagance and arbitrariness. His frequent and prolonged absences called into being the peculiar Hungarian institution of the Palatine, an officer elected jointly by the king and the nation, who represented the king during his absences and also acted as intermediary between him and the nation. But these were only palliatives against abuses that were bitterly felt. The nation, besides hating him for the cruelty he showed at the outset of his reign against the supporters of a rival, resented bitterly the absenteeism of his later years, when he occupied himself chiefly with imperial and Bohemian affairs (he was elected German king in 1411 and became titular king of Bohemia in 1419), neglecting—it felt—the numerous problems of Hungary. There was much discontent among the peasants, who were subjected to heavy exactions both by the crown and by their masters, the unrest being aggravated by the spread of radical Hussite religious doctrines from Bohemia; there were serious revolts in north Hungary and Transylvania. Above all, there was the growing danger from the Ottoman Turks, who, though they had already taken Bosnia from Louis, could not threaten Hungary proper while Serbia still stood. But in 1389 the power of Serbia was broken at the Battle of Kossovo, and the danger became urgent. Sigismund recognized the threat and organized a crusade, but this was disastrously defeated at Nicopolis in 1396. Timur gave Europe a respite by his attack on the Turkish rear, but the advance was resumed in 1415. Walachia submitted in 1417; thereafter Transylvania and south Hungary suffered repeated raids.

The growing Ottoman threat

János Hunyadi and Matthias Corvinus. The Ottoman sultan Murad II was preparing a grand assault on Hungary, when Sigismund died in 1437, leaving as issue a daughter, married to Albrecht V of Austria. The country accepted Albrecht as Sigismund's successor, but only on condition that he should not become Holy Roman emperor and should not reside outside the country without permission of the estates. Albrecht set about organizing the country's defenses but, disastrously, died in 1439, leaving his widow big with child. To avoid an interregnum and a minority, perhaps with a girl queen, the country elected Wladyslaw III Jagiełło of Poland as king; when he fell in battle against the Turks in 1444, they accepted Albrecht's son, Ladislas V ("Posthumus"), appointing as his guardian and governor of Hungary the great general János Hunyadi (*q.v.*), who had been successfully repelling the renewed Turkish attacks. Hunyadi kept up the defense under increasing difficulties, constantly thwarted by jealous magnates and harassed by the Czech condottiere Jan Jiskra, while the emperor Frederick III encroached on the western provinces.

Hunyadi died in 1456 of a fever contracted during his crowning achievement, long celebrated throughout Christendom, the recapture of Belgrade from the Turks. Ladislas' maternal uncle, Ulrich of Cilli, aware of the country's devotion to Hunyadi, had the latter's elder son assassinated and his younger son Matthias (Mátyás) Corvinus (*q.v.*) imprisoned in Prague. Ladislas Posthumus himself died suddenly, still unmarried, a year later. The country was tired of foreign rule and its agents, and on January 24, 1458, a great concourse of nobles acclaimed Matthias king. Extracted from Prague with some difficulty, he was brought to Buda and crowned amid nationwide rejoicing.

The only national king to reign over all Hungary after the Árpáds, Matthias Corvinus (so called from his crest of a raven) has been seen through something of a golden haze by his country's historians. He was, indeed, a remarkable figure. A true Renaissance prince, he was a fine natural soldier, a first-class administrator, an outstanding linguist, a learned astrologer, an enlightened patron of the arts and learning. His collections of illuminated manuscripts, pictures, statues, and jewels were famous throughout Europe. Artists and scholars of European repute were welcomed at his court, which could vie in magnificence with any on the continent. Sumptuous buildings sprang up in his capital and other centres.

Politically, too, he represented the ideas of the Renaissance. He listened to his council, convoked the Diet regularly and actually enlarged the autonomous powers of the counties. But at heart he was a despot; his real instruments of government were his secretaries, men picked by himself, usually young and often of humble origin. His rule was in practice a despotism, and in the main an efficient and, on balance, a benevolent one. He simplified and improved the administration, and, above all, the laws, enforcing justice with an even hand. The debit side of his rule was the increased taxation imposed by him for his administrative innovations, his collections (which cost his subjects vast sums), and above all, the mercenary standing army, 30,000 strong (largely composed of the defeated Hussites and known after its commander, "Black John" Haugwitz, as the "Black army"), which he kept as part of the royal *banderium* for use against enemies, at home and abroad.

Matthias' despotism

At first he had much need for such a force, for although the Turks were quiescent for a decade, there were discontented magnates, and both the Czechs and the Austrians were unquiet neighbours. But after Matthias had crushed, expelled, or bought off these enemies, had built a chain of fortresses along the southern frontier, and had even re-established a nominal and, in practice, worthless suzerainty over Bosnia, Serbia, Walachia, and Moldavia, he let himself be drawn into an everwidening circle of campaigns against Bohemia and Austria. In 1469 he made himself master of Moravia, Silesia, and Lusatia, with the title (although this was also borne simultaneously by Podiebrad) of king of Bohemia, and in 1478 he forced Frederick to cede him Lower Austria and Styria. He argued to his subjects that his neighbours were untrustworthy and that he could not organize the great crusade against the Turks without the resources of the imperial and Bohemian crowns. But they were unconvinced, and in 1470 a party actually conspired to depose him in favour of a Polish prince. This enterprise collapsed, and Matthias next entered on a complex transaction with the new emperor, Maximilian I, under which his illegitimate son John (he had no legitimate issue) was to marry Maximilian's daughter in return for re-cession of the Austrian provinces and Maximilian's recognition of John. But on May 6, 1490, when on his way to the meeting that should have sealed the bargain, Matthias died suddenly, and the whole enterprise collapsed.

The Jagiellonian kings: national decay. The magnates, who did not want another heavy-handed king, procured the accession of Vladislav Jagiełło of Bohemia (Ulászló II in Hungarian history) precisely because of his notorious weakness—he was known as King "Dobre" ("OK") from his habit of accepting with that word every paper laid before him. The Emperor Maximilian contented himself with reoccupying his lost provinces and establishing a sort of paternal patronage over Hungary. This was consolidated in 1515 by an agreement under which Vladislav's son, Louis, married Maximilian's granddaughter, Mary, while Louis' sister, Anne, married Maximilian's grandson, Ferdinand, who was to succeed to Louis' thrones if Louis died without issue. The agreement was made over the heads of the Hungarians, and the Diet in 1505 passed a resolution never again to accept a foreign king. The candidate of the "national party" was János Zápolya, voivode of Transylvania.

Meanwhile the magnates had disbanded the Black army (without replacing it) and allowed the country's fortresses to fall into disrepair. Vladislav was their helpless prisoner; he could take no decision without their consent and his revenues were looted so ruthlessly that for very subsistence he was reduced to selling Matthias' collections. Nearly all of Matthias' reforms were cancelled, and the peasants were oppressed grievously (as they were, indeed, throughout central Europe). In 1514 a great mass of peasants, led by a Szekel soldier, György Dózsa, rose against their lords. The revolt was put down with ghastly barbarity. The Diet of 1514 sentenced the peasants to "real and perpetual servitude" and bound them irrevocably to the soil (it is true, and not so well known, that this sentence was repealed only a few years later), and increased their dues and obligations.

When Vladislav died in 1516, his nine-year-old son was

Renewed Ottoman threat

proclaimed king as Louis II. The defenses of the kingdom went from bad to worse, and in 1521 the new Ottoman sultan, Süleyman the Magnificent, sent Louis a demand for tribute; when this was rejected, Süleyman marched on Belgrade and took it. Suddenly alive to the Turkish danger, the magnates voted the re-establishment of a standing army, but nothing was done to raise it, since each rival faction tried to put the burden of its upkeep on the others. Appeals for help from abroad met with little response. In the summer of 1526 the Sultan advanced into Hungary. The general call to arms was proclaimed, but the most important forces—those from Transylvania and Croatia—were late in obeying it. Louis, with a force of 16,000 men, moved down the Danube, made contact with the Turks at Mohács on August 28, and attacked the next day. The Hungarian Army, heavily outnumbered, was almost annihilated. Louis himself was drowned in his flight. Unable to believe that the pitiful array that had met him was Hungary's national army, the Sultan advanced with extreme caution. He occupied Buda on September 10, but returned across the Danube by the end of October, taking with him over 100,000 captives.

II. The period of partition

Since the Sultan had not meant to remain in Hungary, the disaster of Mohács would not have been irreparable had the king not perished; but as it was, both Zápolya and Ferdinand of Habsburg (later Holy Roman emperor as Ferdinand I) claimed the throne, and each had his supporters in the country. After each had failed to drive his rival out, Zápolya appealed to the Sultan, who installed him in Buda, confining Ferdinand's effective rule to the western third of the country. A secret agreement was mediated in 1538 by Zápolya's adviser, György Martinuzzi ("Friar George"), that Ferdinand should succeed to the whole heritage when Zápolya, the older man, died. The agreement was upset when, just before Zápolya died, his wife bore him a son whom the national party recognized as king. The Sultan then decided to act for himself. He recognized the infant as king, but as his own vassal, and further occupied Buda himself and incorporated a great wedge of central and southern Hungary in his own dominions. Ferdinand had to conclude a truce and to pay a tribute in return for recognition of his de facto rule over the territory then held by him. The transaction was completed when, in 1566, the Sultan formally declared Transylvania an autonomous principality under his own suzerainty; two years later Ferdinand's successor, Maximilian II, was forced to recognize this arrangement and to accept the reduction of "Royal Hungary" (that part of Hungary under Habsburg rule) to the western fringe of the country, the northwestern mountains, and Croatia.

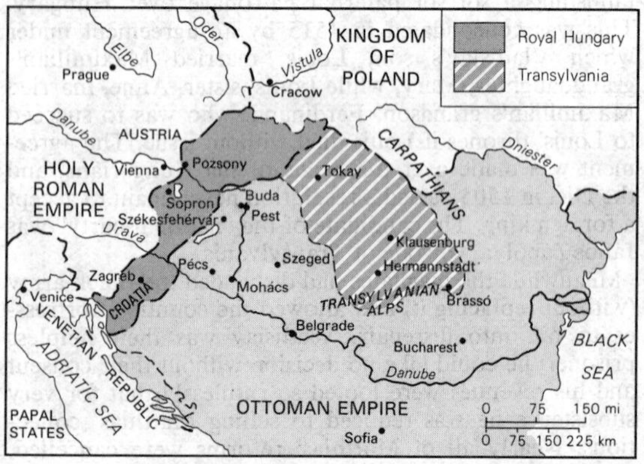

The partition of Hungary in 1564.

Adapted from C.A. Macartney, *Hungary: A Short History* (1962); Aldine Publishing Company

The "age of trisection" was the blackest in all Hungarian history. The advances of the Turkish army in each campaign were marked by swaths of smoking hamlets and ruined towns; its withdrawals were followed by long trains of captives destined for the slave markets of Anatolia, unless they were slaughtered on the way as too much trouble to transport. The fighting and slave raiding, which went on even in times of nominal peace, reduced the whole south of the country to a wasteland occupied by only a few seminomadic Vlach herdsmen; villages disappeared and fields reverted to swamp and forest. Behind the new frontier the population was partially preserved to supply the garrisons, but the old landholders were replaced by Turkish officials and soldiers who, since their fiefs were not hereditable nor even always long-term, exploited the wretched cultivators to the maximum. Conditions were relatively tolerable only in those *kazalar* (districts) managed directly by the Ottoman government. In these districts, most of which lay along the two banks of the Tisza, the people flocked into the great "village towns" that are still a feature of the area. Here they enjoyed a measure of protection; but the country between these towns was left empty except for scattered huts (*tanyas*) in which the men-folk spent the summer scratching a precarious living from the soil.

Religious toleration

The Turks left Transylvania relatively unmolested. Martinuzzi devised a constitution based on earlier institutions, and consisting, under the Prince, of representatives of the three "nations," the Hungarian nobles of the counties, the Saxons, and the Szekels. Transylvania was also spared internecine religious strife, when the representatives of the Roman Catholic, Calvinist, Lutheran, and Unitarian churches agreed on a regime under which these four confessions ranked as "established" on a basis of equal freedom and mutual toleration. The Greek Orthodox faith of the Romanians, who constituted the rest of the population, was only "tolerated," since the Romanians as such, or even their nobles, did not constitute a "nation."

ROYAL HUNGARY AND THE RISE OF TRANSYLVANIA

In the first years after his accession, when he was still hoping to bring the whole kingdom under his rule (when it would have been by far his largest possession), Ferdinand I handled Royal Hungary with kid gloves. He respected its constitution and its institutions and convoked the Diet regularly. But his hopes faded, and after his succession to the imperial crown in 1558, Royal Hungary became no more than a small outlying annex of his mighty dominions. As it was also an exposed one, without the resources to defend itself, Ferdinand and his successor, Maximilian II, organized a chain of fortresses, mostly garrisoned by German troops, and a defensive "military frontier," inhabited by Serb and Walach refugees from the Balkans and administered from Vienna. The Hungarians were soon complaining that they were being ruled and exploited as a subject people, by foreigners, while Vienna looked on them as truculent rebels. Matters grew worse when Maximilian was succeeded by the unbalanced Rudolph, whose advisers hated Hungary and its traditions; and now a religious conflict supervened on the constitutional dispute, for in the preceding half-century the Reformation had swept over Hungary, its Magyars adopting the Calvinist form of faith and its Germans, the Lutheran, and the attempts of Vienna to reintroduce Catholicism were fiercely resented and resisted.

Religious antagonism played an important part when war between the empire and the Turks broke out again in 1591. In the so-called Fifteen Years' War imperial troops entered Transylvania and their commander, George Basta, behaved there (and in north Hungary) with such insane cruelty toward the Hungarian Protestants that one of the Transylvanian generals, István Bocskay, formerly a Habsburg supporter, revolted. He improvised an army out of the wild herdsmen (*hajduks*), drove out Basta, and on June 23, 1606, concluded with Rudolph the Peace of Vienna, which left him prince of an enlarged Transylvania and also guaranteed the rights of the Protestants of Royal Hungary. He then mediated the Peace of Zsitvatorok (November 11, 1606) between the Emperor and the Sultan, which kept the territorial status quo, but relieved the Emperor of his tribute to the Sultan.

These two treaties ushered in a new era. The power of the Turks had begun to wane and in central Hungary their rule became almost benevolent, or at any rate, slack.

Their place in the power-equation was taken by Transylvania, which entered a half century of prosperity. Bocskay died suddenly, in 1606, and the usual scramble for power followed; but in 1613 the Porte imposed the election of the man who proved the most famous of all the princes of Transylvania, Gabriel (Gábor) Bethlen (1613–29). At home, Bethlen's rule was thoroughly despotic: through his monopoly of foreign trade and through his development of the principality's internal resources, he almost doubled his revenues, devoting the proceeds partly to the upkeep of a sumptuous court, partly to the maintenance of a standing army. But he was also an enlightened patron of the arts and a strong defender of Calvinism in central Europe. Keeping peace with the Porte, he often intervened against the emperor in the Thirty Years' War (*q.v.*) and safeguarded the rights of the Protestants in Royal Hungary. Under the Treaty of Nikolsburg (December 31, 1621) he retained the title of Prince of Transylvania and Hungary (the Porte vetoed his acceptance of the Hungarian crown), and a big extension of the principality, and a duchy in Silesia, besides further guarantees for the Protestants of Royal Hungary. When he died suddenly in 1629 his subjects abolished most of his internal reforms, but his successor, György Rákóczi I, maintained the international position of Transylvania, which figured as a sovereign state in the Peace of Westphalia of 1648 ending the Thirty Years' War. This support from Transylvania and also the divisions prevailing between their own members prevented the Habsburgs from enforcing the Counter-Reformation in Hungary as early and as fully as they did in Austria and Bohemia, and up to the middle of the 17th century Royal Hungary retained a considerable measure of political and religious liberty and was spared the ravages of the Thirty Years' War. Nevertheless, the genius of the cardinal-primate Péter Pázmány won over for Catholicism the majority of the local magnates, who came to form a party attached to the Habsburg cause, which was the more influential because they now formed a separate "Table" of the Diet. The nation was thus divided, not only vertically (Transylvania versus the West) but also horizontally, between the Catholic magnates and their subjects, and the smaller landowners, most of whom remained Protestants. In religious matters, the Hungarian Catholic nobles were no more tolerant toward their Protestant fellow countrymen than were the Emperor's own German and Czech advisers, although they were not willing to acquiesce in the political centralization championed by the latter.

Reign of Gabriel Bethlen

WAR AND LIBERATION

The running sore remained the Turkish occupation of central Hungary, for every Hungarian resented the policy of the dynasty of leaving the Turks unmolested while promising ambitious policies in the west. It erupted in 1657 when György Rákóczi II of Transylvania, who had succeeded his father in 1648, allowed the prospect of obtaining the crown of Poland to seduce him into sending across the Carpathians an expeditionary force which was annihilated by Tatars. The great Grand Vizier Mehmed Köprülü, the architect of the Porte's renaissance, led a force against Transylvania, detached it from the western adjuncts that had been its strength, and installed a new puppet prince. Emperor Leopold sent a force against the Turks; but although the Austrian general Raimondo Montecuccoli defeated the Turks at Szentgotthárd on August 1, 1664, the subsequent Peace of Vasvár recognized all the Sultan's gains.

Reassertion of Turkish power

Now even the highest magnates of Royal Hungary plotted to expel the Habsburgs with Turkish and French help, but the conspiracy was betrayed and Vienna took its revenge. Nobles were executed or lost their estates, Protestant pastors were sentenced to be galley slaves. In 1673 the constitution was suspended and Hungary placed under a "Directorate." But the wheel had been set in motion. A young Transylvanian, Imre Thököly, led a revolt that forced Leopold, in 1681, to restore the constitution and revoke many of his harshest measures. The Porte, encouraged by Thököly's successes against the empire, now sent into Hungary a vast army that in 1683 reached the walls of Vienna itself. Then the tide ebbed as swiftly as it had advanced. Vienna was relieved, the Turks routed, and the great imperial general Prince Eugene of Savoy led a series of campaigns in which all western and central Hungary, with Buda, were cleared of the Turks in 1686. Transylvania was liberated in the years following. By the Peace of Karlowitz (Karlovci; January 26, 1699), the Sultan relinquished all of Hungary except the corner between the Maros and the Tisza rivers. (This was ceded in 1718 but kept until 1779 under Austrian administration as the Bánát of Temesvár.) The military frontier (progressively extended) was kept under a similar regime, and Transylvania organized as a separate "principality."

III. Habsburg rule, 1699–1918

HABSBURG RULE TO 1867

The emperor, not Hungary, was the victor, for the retreating Turks and the advancing armies of the "liberators" ravaged the country as cruelly as had the Turks in the previous century, and although in 1687 Leopold reconfirmed the constitution subject to Hungary's acceptance of his dynasty in the male line and to the abolition of the *jus resistendi* conceded under Andrew's Golden Bull of 1222, what followed was in fact another cruel centralist dictatorship. In 1703 this provoked another rebellion, led by the young Ferenc (Francis) Rákóczi II; it took eight years of indecisive and fruitless fighting, until peace was established by the Treaty of Szatmár (April 30, 1711). On paper, this did little more than confirm what had been agreed in 1687, but the new king Charles III (Emperor Charles VI) genuinely wanted peace with Hungary, and the worst abuses were now ended.

Charles III and Maria Theresa. Charles' chief concern was simply to secure the acceptance in Hungary of the Pragmatic Sanction, the imperial decree by which his daughter Maria Theresa should inherit his dominions. After the Diet accepted the Pragmatic Sanction in 1723, Charles convoked it only once again, and Maria Theresa, after her coronation in 1740, only twice more—each time to ask for money. Her rule, like her father's, was essentially autocratic and gave Hungary just cause for complaint in several fields. She was severe toward the Protestants, and she allowed her advisers to exclude Hungary, by discriminatory devices, from the subsidized industrialization that was bringing wealth to other parts of her dominions. But her rule was not more than severe, even toward the Protestants. Toward the magnates, on whom she lavished many favours, it was positively benign, and she respected the most cherished liberty of the lesser nobles, their exemption from taxation. Exhausted by so many wars and rebellions, the country during her reign asked for nothing more, contenting itself with the supreme blessing that her rule brought it an uninterrupted peace that enabled the population to grow once again and the material ravages to be repaired. These were blessings indeed: the reverse side of the picture was the lethargy that descended on the country. Political life sank to the parish-pump level, and the towns stagnated. The peasants, into whose conditions the Queen introduced some improvements without touching the root evil of their subject condition, followed their masters in aspiring to nothing more than as much material comfort as could be obtained with a minimum of effort. The national language itself was becoming little more than a peasant dialect, since the language of public administration and the Diet was Latin, and of business life, German: and with the language, the national spirit seemed near moribund.

The Pragmatic Sanction

Joseph II and Leopold II. The nation was shocked out of its lethargy by the accession of Maria Theresa's son, Joseph, on her death in 1780. Evading the obligation of a king on coronation to swear to the constitution by not submitting himself to coronation at all (he had the Holy Crown conveyed to Vienna), Joseph pressed Hungary into his great machine. The counties were transformed into local branches of the State service, taking all their orders from above, and were required to conduct their business in German, which was also made the language of all education above the elementary level. The land was surveyed in preparation for taxing all estates in it equally. That the position of the peasants was improved pleased them, but not their lords. When Joseph fell mortally sick in the course of conducting an ill-conceived, expensive, and mismanaged campaign against the Porte, the country was on the brink of open revolt; and although on his deathbed he retracted his administrative reforms, his successor, Leopold II (1790–92) was obliged to restore the ancient constitution and to swear to treat Hungary as a wholly independent kingdom, to be ruled only in accordance with its own laws and customs.

Francis I: the "Reform Generation." When Leopold died with tragic suddenness in 1792, his young son, Francis, at first made the motions of conforming with his coronation oath, but he soon slipped back into the old ways. The Diet was convoked simply to extort its consent to supply men and money for Francis' wars and, after 1811, was left unconvoked for 13 years. Social reaction accompanied the political absolutism, and the stranglehold on the country's economic development was not relaxed.

For many years the Diet, composed either of magnates who identified their interests with those of the court, or of lesser but still substantial landowners who had prospered during the Napoleonic Wars, was as nonprogressive as Francis himself; but in wider circles the spirit of the age, stimulated by Joseph's over haste, had given birth to a great cultural revival that was now bringing forth its first literary fruits, and the new national pride that it at once embodied and enhanced was demanding fulfillment of Leopold's promises and an end to the veiled but oppressive dictatorship of Vienna. And now it was going further than this. A great reform movement was set on foot by Count István Széchenyi, himself a great magnate, who boldly proclaimed that the ancient privileges of the nobility, the defense of which against Vienna had preoccupied earlier generations, were no bastion, but a prison. He argued that the servile state of the peasants was humanly degrading and a source of weakness to the nation, and also that the system of forced field labour, grudgingly and inefficiently rendered as it was, as well as the nobles' exemption from taxation, was economically harmful even to its supposed beneficiaries. After financial stringency had forced Francis to reconvoke the Diet in 1825, and thereafter to convoke it regularly, these doctrines were taken up, with variations, by a whole "reform generation," the most prominent figures of which were the legal expert Ferenc Deák, Baron József Eötvös, leader of a little group of "Centralists," and above all, Lajos Kossuth, who largely changed the current of the reform movement by his insistence that social and economic reform could be fully realized only after the achievement of the political independence promised by Leopold. After Francis had been followed on the throne in 1835 by the luckless Ferdinand—in practice by the government of Metternich and Kolowrat—"Vienna" was driven increasingly onto the defensive and forced to make repeated concessions, especially in respect of the replacement of Latin and German by Magyar as the language of the Diet, administration, and education—a demand pressed with especial insistence by many of the reformers.

Leaders of the reform movement

The nationalities. This raised a new and painful issue. The population of Hungary, even excluding Croatia, had never from the first been purely Magyar, but the pre-Magyar inhabitants of the plains and the newcomers to them (outside the towns) had quite quickly become magyarized; and while this was not true of the peripheral areas, their populations were relatively sparse. By the end of the 15th century, the Slovaks and Ruthenes of the north; the Germans of the free boroughs, the Szepes, and Transylvania; and the Romanians numbered hardly more than 20 to 25 percent of the total; the rest were Magyar in speech and sentiment. This majority included almost the entire politically active "noble" class, the non-Magyar recruits to which assimilated most readily. The surviving non-Magyar peasants had neither the wish nor the ability to question the "Magyar" character of the state, which for its part was uninterested in what languages were spoken by the politically disregarded, unfree men.

But between 1500 and 1800 the ethnic composition of the country changed. It was the most purely Magyar areas that were most heavily depopulated during the Turkish wars and their sequels, and these losses were accompanied, or followed, by mass immigrations of Serbs, Croats, and Romanians from the Balkans, and then by the introduction by the Austrian government of large numbers of German and other colonists to fill the open spaces. By 1720 the Magyars numbered only some 35 percent of the total population of the Hungarian lands. By 1780 the figure had risen to nearly 40 percent, but the periphery, although it contained islands of Magyar population, was still preponderantly non-Magyar.

Further, ethnic conditions were no longer politically irrelevant. The Serb immigrants, who enjoyed cultural self-government under their patriarch, were from the moment of their arrival bitterly anti-Magyar and anti-Hungarian. The resentment of the Romanians against their social grievances expressed itself in national terms. The other nationalities were slower to awaken, but among some of them, too, especially the Slovaks, there were nationalist stirrings similar to those among the Magyars. The nationally minded among them (by no means all were so minded) regarded the campaign to substitute Magyar for the neutral Latin as a threat to their national existence, while their resistance was interpreted by Magyar chauvinists as a threat to the security of Hungary, which, in their view, had to be politically unitary and Magyar in its superstructure. Some extremists felt that the safety of the state lay in eliminating the aspirations of the nationalities by actually magyarizing them. They pressed these demands with an intemperate impatience that at once justified and fed the very disaffection that it hoped to stifle in the womb.

Resentment of magyarization

From 1790 the Croats, too, were in conflict with Hungary. The first issue was a constitutional one: was Croatia in any way subordinate to Hungary, or was it Hungary's full equal? Then, when the linguistic campaign gained ground, the Croats consistently denounced as intolerable the suggestion that their representatives in the central services or in parliament should be required to use Magyar instead of Latin. Around 1830 a Croat national movement of the modern type emerged, fully as intemperate as the Magyar, and with a political program that in its more extreme form demanded the reconstitution of Croatia, enlarged with other southern Slav areas, as an entirely separate unit within the Habsburg monarchy.

Revolution, reaction, and "Compromise." The Hungarian reformers' opportunity came in the spring of 1848, when revolution, caused by breakdown of central authority in Vienna, enabled them to rush through a body of laws (the "April Laws"), which—besides enacting important internal reforms such as the generalizing of taxes, the abolition of villein status and the transfer of villein holdings to their cultivators, and the reorganizing of the lower "Table" of Parliament on a representative basis—provided for the restoration of the territorial integrity of the lands of the Hungarian crown (subject, in the case of Transylvania, to the agreement of its Diet), and the appointment of a "responsible independent Hungarian Ministry." This was to include ministries of defense, finance, and external relations. A ministry of all the talents, headed by a progressive magnate, Count Lajos Batthyány, and including Kossuth (finance), Széchenyi (communications), Deák (justice), and Eötvös (education) took office. But the new government had enemies: the conservatives resented the land reform, and the Centralists in Vienna regarded the independent ministry, particularly its three "common" portfolios, as dangerous to the integrity of the monarchy. They found allies among the disaffected "nationalities," notably the Serbs and Romanians, and in the Croats, whose ban or governor, Josip Jelačić, a nominee of Vienna's, refused to recognize the authority of Buda-Pest. Tension between Vienna and Pest mounted steadily, and in September, when the rest of the monarchy had been reduced, Jelačić, on Vienna's orders and with its support, invaded Hungary. Batthyány and other ministers resigned, leaving

Revolution of 1848

Kossuth in charge. An improvised national army drove Jelačić out of the country, but in December Ferdinand (who had sanctioned the April Laws and whose coronation oath bound him to observe them) was made to abdicate in favour of his young nephew, Francis Joseph. The invasion was now renewed. A panmonarchic constitution had already abolished the concessions of the April Laws, in reply to which a rump Diet, inspired by Kossuth, proclaimed the full independence of Hungary and the deposition of the Habsburg dynasty (April 14). The Hungarian forces, led by a young soldier of genius, Artúr Görgey, held their own until in May the Austrian court appealed for help to the Russian tsar, who sent an army across the Carpathians. Bitter fighting went on for some weeks more, but the odds were too heavy. On August 12, Kossuth fled the country, transferring his authority to Görgey, who the next day surrendered at Világos to the Russian commander.

Reprisals from Vienna

Savage reprisals followed, and the country was again dismembered and subjected to an absolutist and extortionate rule exercised from Vienna through a foreign bureaucracy. This "Bach regime" (after Alexander Bach, Austrian minister of the interior) was maintained, unrelaxed in principle, although with some alterations in practice, until Austria's defeat in Italy in 1859 forced Francis Joseph to begin his retreat from absolutism. The followers of the exiled Kossuth were irreconcilable, but a large part of opinion inside Hungary wanted a compromise and rallied behind Deák, who held that the April Laws were legally valid and that Hungary's right to complete internal independence was inalienable, but that under the Pragmatic Sanction, which he accepted, foreign affairs and defense were subjects "common" to the two halves of the monarchy and that a machinery could be devised for handling these affairs constitutionally, on that basis. A Diet convoked in 1861 was dissolved after a few weeks, since the gap between the Hungarians' views and those of Francis Joseph and his Centralist ministry in Vienna proved to be still too wide to be bridged. Absolutism was reimposed; but the pressure of international and internal economic difficulties gradually drove Francis Joseph to see the necessity of further concessions. In July 1865 he dismissed his Centralist ministry; in December a new Diet was convoked and the negotiations reopened. Interrupted by the outbreak of the Seven Weeks' War, they were resumed after Austria's defeat by Prussia in 1866 had further convinced both parties of the necessity of agreement.

THE DUAL MONARCHY, 1867–1918

A new Transylvanian Diet had already revoted the union with Hungary. In February 1867 Francis Joseph, having admitted the validity of the April Laws conditionally on the revision of those dealing with "common" affairs, appointed a responsible Hungarian ministry under Count Gyula Andrássy. A committee of the Diet then elaborated a law that, while laying down Hungary's full internal independence, provided for common ministries for foreign affairs and defense, each under a joint minister; a third common minister was in charge of the finance for these portfolios; these rendered account to delegations from the Austrian and Hungarian parliaments; the respective quotas to be paid for these services by each half of the monarchy were reconsidered every ten years, as were commercial and customs agreements. At first, the two countries formed a customs union. The Diet voted this into law on May 29 (Law XII of 1867). On June 8 Francis Joseph was crowned, and on July 28 he gave his assent to the law.

Treatment of minorities

Francis Joseph had stipulated that the settlement should include a revised Hungaro-Croat agreement and provisions guaranteeing adequate rights for the non-Magyars of Hungary. The Croat settlement (Law XXX of 1868) left Croatia including Slavonia a part of the lands of the Hungarian crown, under a ban appointed on the proposal of the Hungarian prime minister. Croatia was to enjoy full internal autonomy, but certain questions (including long-distance communications) were designated as "common" to Croatia and Hungary. When these were under discussion, Croat deputies attended the central parliament, in which they could speak in Croat. The sole language of internal official usage in Croatia was Croat.

The Nationalities Law (Law XLIV of 1868) laid down that all citizens of Hungary, whatever their nationality, constituted politically "a single nation, the indivisible, unitary Hungarian nation," and there could be no differentiation between them except in respect of the official usage of the current languages, and then only in so far as necessitated by practical considerations. The language of the central administrative and judicial services, and of the university, was Magyar, but there were to be adequate provisions for the use of non-Magyar languages on lower levels. The use of them in private life was to be entirely free. The consolidation was completed by the incorporation of the military frontier (in stages lasting several years) and of Transylvania, the latter process involving the abolition of the old "Three Nations," except that the Saxon "university" was allowed to survive as a purely cultural institution.

Hungary under dualism. The "Compromise" (*Ausgleich*) of 1867 restored its territorial integrity to Hungary, and gave it more real internal independence than it had enjoyed since 1526; the monarch's powers in internal affairs were strictly limited, and no other factor outside Hungary had any voice in them whatever. It was true that Hungary was not autonomous in the conduct of foreign affairs or defense; in these respects Hungary still formed only part of the monarchy, and its interests in these fields had to be coordinated with those of its other components. But Hungary had a large voice in the monarchy's policy in these fields and enjoyed the great advantage—which weighed heavily with soberer men, including Deák, when negotiating the Compromise—that the resources of the great power of which it formed a part stood behind the country. To some, however, the price still seemed too high, and the parliamentary life of Hungary from 1867 to 1918 was dominated by the conflict between the supporters and the opponents of the Compromise, the latter ranging from complete separatists to those who accepted the Compromise in theory but wanted details of it altered.

The supporters of the Compromise, then known as the Deák Party, were in office first but soon got into such financial and personal difficulties that complete chaos threatened. It was averted when, in 1875, Kálmán Tisza, the leader of the moderate nationalist Left Centre, carried through a fusion between his party and the remnants of the Deákists on a program that amounted to putting his party's main demands into cold storage until the political and financial situation was stabilized. This new Liberal Party then held office nearly 30 years, up to 1890 under Tisza's personal leadership, and from 1890 to 1904 under a succession of politically short-lived premiers. During these years the Compromise stood intact, but there was mounting friction with Vienna over the army, which the Hungarians regarded, with some reason, as imbued with a spirit hostile to themselves, over the economic provisions of the Compromise, and over the question of Hungarian participation in control of the National Bank. An army question in 1889 marked something of a turning-point, after which relations between the supporters of the Compromise, behind whom stood the crown, and its nationalist opponents were permanently strained. The tension reached a climax in 1903, when the obstruction of the "national opposition" made parliamentary government practically impossible. The premier, Count István Tisza (Kálmán Tisza's son), dissolved parliament. Elections in January 1905 gave a coalition of "national" parties a parliamentary majority, but Francis Joseph refused to entrust the government to them on their program, which included "national" concessions over the army, and a period of nonparliamentary government followed until, in April 1906, the coalition leaders, under threat of an extension of the suffrage if they proved recalcitrant, gave the King a secret undertaking that if appointed, they would not press the essentials of their program. On this basis he appointed a coalition government, but under a Liberal, Sándor Wekerle.

Rise of the Liberal Party

With their hands thus tied, the coalition made a wretched showing. Tisza reorganized the Liberal Party as the "Party of Work" and in the elections of 1910 this secured a large majority. After Count Károly Khuen-Héderváry (1910–12) and László Lukács (1912–13), Tisza himself again became prime minister, and Francis Joseph ceased to press his demand for effective franchise reform, to which Tisza was inexorably opposed.

Social and economic developments. Hungary underwent much change after 1867. The achievements of the Deákist and Liberal governments were not inconsiderable. The political consolidation included, besides the assimilation of the former outlying areas of Transylvania and the military frontier, a reform (somewhat halfhearted, owing to nationalist opposition) of the relations between the central government and the counties, and a general reorganization of the administration. The judicial system was modernized. Relations between the state and the churches were, after a long struggle (a by-product of which was the reorganization of the chief stronghold of the old order, the upper house of parliament) restated in 1894–95 on terms satisfactory to the liberal philosophy of the day, which brought with them full emancipation for Hungary's large Jewish population. In 1868 Eötvös carried through an admirable elementary education act and much headway was afterward made in raising the educational and cultural level of the country. After long difficulties, the national finances were put in order and the public debt reduced. There was considerable economic progress in many fields. Agriculture remained the mainstay of the economy. The medium and small landowners had been hard hit by the land reform of 1848, but the survivors were helped by the high agricultural prices and the secure Austrian market. Afterward, the general European agricultural depression plunged even the big landowners into difficulties, but these diminished near the turn of the century, when prices rose again, while the quality and quantity of production improved. Many branches of industry failed to survive the customs union with Austria, but the agricultural industries prospered, and later, as domestic capital accumulated (the earlier developments were nearly all effected with the help of foreign, chiefly Austrian, capital), a process of industrialization, helped by state legislation, set in which became extremely rapid after 1890. As late as 1910 agriculture was still the most important branch of the economy, and 70 percent of the population still derived its livelihood from the soil, but over 16 percent now did so from industry and mining.

Economic progress

Urbanization proceeded apace. The growth of Budapest was meteoric—its population before World War I topped 800,000, and two other cities had populations of over 75,000, and a dozen around 50,000. Communications were largely modernized.

For all this, Hungary was still a relatively poor country. The extremely rapid growth of the population (from 13,000,000 in 1850 to 19,000,000 in 1910) had far outstripped that of the means of production. The growth of industry was still too slow to absorb the surplus rural population, and in spite of high emigration, which in the last years averaged a full 100,000 annually, acute rural congestion had developed. While 35 percent of the land was held in 4,000 large estates, some of them enormous, there were something like 2,000,000 small, or dwarf, holdings, and a further 1,700,000 persons (wage earners) were totally landless. A large proportion of this rural proletariat was forced to live in conditions of extreme misery, near starvation. The living standards and conditions of the industrial workers, especially the unskilled, were also very low.

The political structure was still highly unmodern. The unreformed franchise excluded the masses from political influence, and even the vocational organization that they were able to achieve was primitive. The industrial and financial development had been largely the work of Jews (who also held a iarge part in the professions) or of magyarized Germans. Its own quasi-alien character as well as its small numbers prevented the Hungarian bourgeoisie from developing into a positive factor in the political life, which continued to be dominated, at least on the surface, by a landowning class whose social and political ideas failed to move with the times.

The nationalities. The "nationalities problem" remained intractable. After 1868 Hungarian political philosophy insisted more strongly than ever that the Hungarian state must be Magyar in spirit, in its institutions, and as far as possible, linguistically. Suggestions to the contrary, or appeals to the Nationalities Law, met with derision or abuse. In spite of the law, the use of minority languages was banished almost entirely from administration and even justice. While the autonomy of the church schools was hardly attacked until the 20th century, the higher direction of the Roman and Greek Catholic churches and the Lutheran outside Transylvania, not to mention the Calvinist (in any case, purely Magyar), saw to it that all secondary education in their schools, with trivial exceptions, should be in Magyar, which was also represented far above its due in the primary schools, as was practically all instruction in the state schools founded from 1870 onward.

This was not all waste labour. By the end of the century the state apparatus was entirely Magyar in language, as were business and social life above the lowest levels. The proportion of the population with Magyar as its mother-tongue rose from 46.6 percent in 1880 to 51.4 percent in 1900. The magyarization of the towns had proceeded at an astounding rate. Nearly all middle-class Jews and Germans, and many middle-class Slovaks (on whom there was great pressure) and Ruthenes had magyarized.

Magyarization of the middle classes

Most of the magyarization, however, had been in the centre of Hungary and among the middle classes. It had hardly touched the rural populations of the periphery, and the linguistic frontiers had hardly shifted from the line on which they had been stabilized in the 18th century. In these areas, moreover, a hard core of national feeling had survived. This had weakened during the first decades after the Compromise but was reviving again at the turn of the century, especially among the Romanians, and was now being encouraged from across the frontiers of Romania and Serbia, and (in the case of the Slovaks) from Bohemia. Hungaro-Croatian relations, too, deteriorated, after a period of quiescence, when the Serbian government began propagating a theory of "Yugoslav" unity designed to detach the Croats from the monarchy.

Many of these developments threatened the very basis of the Compromise, and to this another uncertainty was added. Francis Joseph could be trusted, so long as he lived, to support and to accept the policies of any Hungarian government that on its side maintained the Compromise loyally; but he was an old man, and his heir presumptive, the Archduke Francis Ferdinand, was notoriously hostile to the Hungarian regime. In touch with many of its opponents, the Archduke was credited with designs of overthrowing the Compromise to the benefit not, of course, of its traditional opponents, the Hungarian "Independents," but of its enemies in the opposite camps, especially the nationalities.

World War I. The assassination of the Archduke on June 28, 1914, removed this danger and plunged Austria-Hungary into World War I. For the first two years of the war, Tisza upheld the internal system and held the country to its international course; and when Francis Joseph died, he persuaded the new king, Charles IV, to accept coronation (December 30, 1916), thus binding himself to uphold the integrity and constitution of Hungary. Charles, however, insisted on electoral reform, and Tisza resigned (May 1917). While short-lived minority governments struggled with increasing difficulties, the threefold agitation grew; of the Hungarian nationalists, against a war into which, they maintained, Hungary had been drawn in the interest of Germany and Austria; of the political left, growing daily more radical under the stimuli of privation and the Russian Revolution; and of the nationalities, encouraged by the favour that their kinsfolk were finding with the Entente. The country began to listen to Count Mihály Károlyi, leader of a fraction of the Party of Independence, who proclaimed that a program of independence from Austria, repudiation of the alliance with Germany, and peace with the Entente, combined with social and internal political reform and concessions to the nationalities, would safeguard Hungary against all dangers at once.

IV. Revolution, counter-revolution, and the Regency, 1918–45

On October 31, 1918, when the defeat of the monarchy was imminent, Charles appointed Károlyi prime minister at the head of an improvised administration based on a left-wing National Council, and after the monarchy had signed an armistice on November 3, and Charles had "renounced participation" in public affairs on the 13th, the National Council, on the 16th, dissolved parliament and proclaimed Hungary an independent republic, with Károlyi as provisional president. The separation from Austria was popular, but all Károlyi's supposed friends disappointed him, and all his premises proved mistaken. Serb, Czech, and Romanian troops installed themselves in two-thirds of the helpless country, and in the confusion ordered social reform was impossible. The government steadily moved left and on March 21, 1919, Károlyi's government was replaced by a "soviet republic," controlled by Béla Kun, who had promised Hungary Russian support against the Romanians. The help never arrived, and Kun's doctrinaire Bolshevism, resting on a "red terror," antagonized almost the entire population. On August 4 Kun and his associates fled, and two days later Romanian troops entered Budapest. Shadow counter-revolutionary governments had already formed themselves in Szeged (then occupied by French troops) and Vienna and pressed the Allies to entrust them with the new government. The Allies insisted on the formation of a provisional regime including democratic elements that must hold elections on a wide, secret suffrage. The Romanians were, with difficulty, induced to retire across the Tisza, and a government, under the presidency of Károly Huszár, was formed in November 1919, and the elections (for a single House) held in January 1920. The new parliament began by declaring all measures enacted by the Károlyi and Kun regimes, and also the legislation embodying the 1867 Compromise, null and void. The institution of the monarchy was thus restored, but pending a settlement, on which feelings were deeply divided, of the relationship between the nation and the dynasty, Admiral Miklós Horthy, who had organized the counter-revolutionary armed forces, was elected regent as provisional head of state (March 1, 1920). The Huszár government then resigned, and on March 14 a coalition government, composed of the two main parties in the parliament (the Christian National Union and the Smallholders) took office under Sándor Simonyi-Semadam.

The "soviet republic" of Béla Kun

THE REGENCY, 1920–45

The Treaty of Trianon. The Allies had long had their peace terms for Hungary ready, but had been unwilling to present them to an earlier regime. It was thus the Simonyi-Semadam government that was forced to sign the Treaty of Trianon (June 4, 1920). This was hard indeed, for the Allies not only assumed without question that Hungary's non-Magyar populations should be deemed to be wishing to leave Hungary but also allowed the successor states, especially Czechoslovakia, to annex large areas of Magyar population, on economic and strategic grounds. The final result was to leave Hungary with only 92,963 square kilometres (35,893 square miles) of the 325,411 square kilometres (125,641 square miles) that had comprised the area of the lands of the Hungarian crown. Romania, Czechoslovakia, and Yugoslavia all took large fragments, while others went to Austria, and even to Poland and Italy. Of the population of 20,866,447 (1910 census), Hungary was left with 7,615,117. Romania received 5,257,467, Czechoslovakia, 3,517,568, Yugoslavia, 4,131,249, and Austria, 291,618. Of the 10,050,575 persons of Magyar mother tongue, no fewer than 3,219,579 were allotted to the successor states: 1,704,851 to Romania, 1,063,020 to Czechoslovakia, 105,948 + 441,787 to Yugoslavia, and 26,183 to Austria. While the homes of some of these—*e.g.*, the Szekels—had been in the remotest corners of historic Hungary, many were living in compact blocs immediately across the frontiers.

In addition, the treaty required Hungary to pay in reparations an unspecified sum, which was to be "the first charge upon all its assets and revenues," and limited its armed forces to a long-service force of 35,000, to be used exclusively for the maintenance of internal order and on frontier defense.

Postwar confusion and reconstruction. Conditions in Hungary in 1920 were exceedingly difficult in every respect. The prolonged war, the Bolshevik regime, before which mobile capital had fled headlong, and the rapacious Romanian occupation had exhausted its resources, and the economy had been further disrupted by the new frontiers, which cut the factories off from both their accustomed supply sources and their markets. Industrial unemployment had reached unprecedented heights and the surviving national resources were being strained to support nearly 400,000 refugees from the successor states.

There was extreme social cleavage and unrest. Both the industrial and the agrarian proletariats were embittered by the failure of their revolutionary hopes. Even more dangerous were the armies of the "new poor," the homeless refugees above all, but also a large part of the middle classes in general, reduced to penury by the galloping inflation. They formed another radical army, but its radicalism was one of the right: they ascribed their misery precisely to the revolutions, on which they put the blame for all Hungary's misfortunes. Feeling ran particularly high against the Jews, who had played a disproportionately large part in both revolutions, especially Kun's, but the resentment extended also to the Social Democrats and even to Liberal democracy. "White terrorists" wreaked indiscriminate vengeance on persons whom they associated with the revolutions. Huszár's government itself had turned so sharply on the Social Democrats and the trade unions that the former withdrew their representatives from the government and boycotted the elections, in protest against the widespread arrests and internments.

Formation of the "Right Radicals"

Finally, the country was split from top to bottom on the dynastic question—whether Charles was still the lawful king of Hungary, or whether his declaration of November 13, 1918, entitled the nation to fill the throne by "free election."

The government of Pál Teleki, who succeeded Simonyi-Semadam in July 1920, blunted the edge of the agrarian unrest by a modest reform—promised, indeed, only as a first installment—that took 1,700,000 acres (7.5 percent of the total area of the country) from the biggest estates for distribution in smallholdings, but it had hardly touched any other social problem when in March 1921 the Legitimist question was raised in acute form by King Charles' sudden return to Hungary. He was forced to withdraw, the command coming from the Allies, but too willingly obeyed by the "Right Radicals," toward whom Horthy was then leaning. The government, several of whose members were Legitimists, resigned, and the succession was assumed by the conservative Count István Bethlen, who had been waiting behind the scenes for his cue. Bethlen devised a formula that, while not legally excluding the king's return (under Entente pressure, parliament had voted a law dethroning the Habsburgs, but even Hungary's own anti-Legitimists never took it as morally binding), excluded it in practice. In return for this, the Smallholders agreed with the anti-Legitimists of the Christian Nationals to form a new "Party of Unity" under Bethlen's leadership. He persuaded parliament to accept as still legally in force the franchise enacted in 1918, which reduced the number of voters and reintroduced open voting in rural districts. Elections in May 1922 gave this party a large majority.

The end of Legitimism

Meanwhile, a second attempt by the King (in October 1921) to recover his throne again ended in failure, and soon after, the Legitimist question lost its acuteness with Charles' death. In December 1921 Bethlen concluded a secret pact with the Social Democrats, under which the latter promised to abstain from agitation on the land and to support the government's foreign policy in return for the cessation of persecution, the release of political prisoners, and the restoration of the sequestrated trade union funds. The peasant leaders were persuaded to accept the indefinite postponement of the second installment of the land reform. The "white terror" was liquidated, quietly but effectively, chiefly by finding government employment for the "Right Radical" leaders.

Bethlen's domestic program was made possible by his cautious international policy. Almost all Hungarians were passionately convinced of the injustice of the Treaty of Trianon, revision of which was the all-dominant motive of Hungary's foreign policy throughout the interwar period, and the key to the hostile relations between Hungary and those states that had chiefly profited by it (which also enjoyed the support of France). Bethlen was as revisionist at heart as any of his countrymen, but he was convinced that Hungary could not act effectively in this field until it had acquired friends abroad, and had achieved political and economic consolidation at home. This, as he saw it, depended on financial reconstruction; and to achieve this, he applied for Hungary's admission to the League of Nations, which was granted (not without difficulty) in September 1922. In March 1924, in return for an undertaking to carry out loyally the obligations of the treaty, he obtained a League loan, which had almost magical effects. The inflation stopped immediately; the League loan was followed by a flood of private lending; and the expatriated domestic capital returned. With this help, Hungary enjoyed some years of prosperity, during which agriculture revived and industrialization made progress.

Abroad, Bethlen's only other important move was the conclusion, in 1927, of a treaty of friendship with Italy. At home, his regime, which was conservative but not tyrannical, rested on what came to be called Hungary's "Conservative-Liberal" forces, to the exclusion of extremism from left or right.

FINANCIAL CRISIS: THE RISE OF "RIGHT RADICALISM"

Bethlen's command of parliament was complete and was not even shaken by the disastrous fall in world wheat prices in 1929. In June 1931 he had just held elections that returned his party with the conventional large majority when the supervention of a world financial crisis on the economic one shattered the foundations of his structure. The foreign creditors called in their money, and Hungary, its trade balance annihilated by the collapse of the wheat market, could not meet their demands and had to apply for help from the League of Nations, which imposed a regime of rigid orthodox deflation. Industrial unemployment soared again, the agricultural population was rendered almost literally penniless, the government services were forced to carry through large-scale dismissals and salary deductions in the interests of a balanced budget.

In August Bethlen resigned. His successor, Count Gyula Károlyi, was unable to cope with the situation. Political agitation mounted, and on October 1, 1932, Horthy appointed as prime minister the leader of the "Right Radicals," Captain (as he then was) Gyula Gömbös.

Gömbös' failure at home

At home Gömbös in the event found the leading strings of financial forces, international and domestic, as invincible as had his predecessors. Previously a violent anti-Semite, he had to make a public recantation of his views on this point and was unable to carry through any other points of his neofascist program, particularly as Horthy at first refused to allow him to hold elections; neither was he able to realize his foreign political ideal of an "Axis" composed of Hungary, Italy, and Germany, since his two proposed partners were then at loggerheads over Austria, and Gömbös, one of whose first acts had been to dash to Rome and breathe new life into Hungary's friendship with Italy, found himself drawn into the "Rome Triangle" (Italy, Austria, and Hungary) that was directed precisely against Germany. Finally, Hitler upset another of his calculations by telling him that while Germany would help Hungary against Czechoslovakia, it would not do so against Romania or Yugoslavia.

Nevertheless, when Gömbös died prematurely in October 1936, he could feel that his years of office had not been entirely wasted. Shortly before, Horthy had at last allowed him to hold elections, and these had brought into parliament a strong Right Radical contingent from which it could never thereafter free itself. Abroad, when Mussolini surrendered to Hitler, Hungary found itself after all in a sort of Axis camp, membership of which might help it at least to partial revision of the treaty. On the other hand, if Germany chose to put economic or political pressure on her, she would be practically defenseless, but for such shadow help as Italy could give her.

This threat was already looming large, and thenceforward it became inextricably involved with Hungary's own internal politics, by reason of the ideological character of the Nazi regime and in particular its anti-Semitism. Anti-Semitism at that stage was running high in Hungary itself, and those infected by it—the Right Radicals of various brands, but even other members of the middle classes—welcomed Germany's support for their own ideas, while making light of its dangers. They even argued, not without reason, that the danger lay in affronting Germany, which could easily crush unarmed little Hungary but would not wish to attack a friend and ideological partner. They further believed (nearly all the army officers held this view) that should Hitler's policies lead to war, Germany would emerge the victor; and that Hungary's salvation thus lay in joining forces with Germany. On the other side there came into being a curious shadow front, composed of all elements antagonistic to Nazism—above all Hungary's Jews, but also the Legitimists, the traditionalist "Liberal Conservatives," right down to the Social Democrats. Many of these were not convinced that Germany was invincible, and they held that if war came only disaster could follow for Hungary if it became too closely involved with Germany. Even they, however, were unwilling to draw the ultimate conclusion that Hungary should abandon all its revisionist claims and join hands with the Little Entente, which, for its part, indicated that it would accept nothing short of total renunciation. It was of the highest importance that by this time Horthy had shed his earlier Right Radical leanings and sympathized with this shadow front.

The question of support for Germany

How to secure Germany's help without paying Germany's price was the painful problem with which successive Hungarian governments struggled thenceforward. To succeed Gömbös, Horthy appointed Kálmán Darányi, who was more of a conservative than a Right Radical; the appointment was ill received in Germany, which grew even more hostile the next year, when Darányi's foreign minister, Kálmán Kánya, obtained the tacit consent of the Little Entente for Hungary to rearm, although Hungary was still sadly short of armaments, for which, again, Germany was her only source of supply. On a visit to Berlin, Darányi and Kánya smoothed over the difficulties; but when Darányi tried to placate the extremists at home, Horthy replaced him (in May 1938) by Béla Imrédy, who introduced a largely token "Jewish Law" but nevertheless pinned his hopes on the West. When the Munich crisis broke in September, Imrédy and Kánya, while presenting Hungary's claims on Czechoslovakia, limited the claims to what they hoped would be acceptable to the Western powers, whose endorsement they made every effort to obtain. The West ignored them, however, and the Hungarian leaders had, after all, to turn to Germany and Italy, which, under the "First Vienna Award" of November 2, gave Hungary the Magyar-inhabited fringe of southern Slovakia. Imrédy, disillusioned with the West, dismissed Kánya for the pro-Axis Count István Csáky and sought to recover Hitler's favour by introducing a more far-reaching Jewish Law. Imrédy's enemies secured his resignation in February 1939 by unearthing documents purporting to show a Jewish strain in his own ancestry. Pál Teleki, who succeeded him, was a most convinced Westerner; but Hungary's recovery of Carpatho-Ruthenia (March 1939) was, again, sanctioned by Hitler.

WAR AND RENEWED DEFEAT

When Germany attacked Poland (September 1, 1939), Hungary refused to allow German troops to cross Hungarian territory. In the first months of World War II none of the belligerents wanted the war extended to southeastern Europe, and so Teleki and Horthy were able to keep Hungary "nonbelligerent" and, after the Soviet Union had occupied Bessarabia in June 1940, to force a reluctant Germany (but a willing Italy) to recede to northern Transylvania under the "Second Vienna Award" of August 30. But they then allowed German troops to cross Hungarian territory into southern Romania, and in November they signed the Tripartite Pact.

German troops in Hungary

The next step was more fatal still. In his search for cautious reinsurance, Teleki concluded with the like-minded government of Yugoslavia a treaty (December 12), unluckily named one of "Eternal Friendship." On March 26, 1941, that Yugoslav government was overthrown by a pronouncedly pro-Western one. Hitler prepared to invade Yugoslavia and called on Hungary to help him. Hungary, caught in an unanticipated situation, refused to join in the attack but again allowed German troops to cross its territory. Great Britain threatened to declare war; and Teleki, blaming himself for having allowed to come into being a situation that it had been his life's aim to avoid, took his own life on April 2. His successor, László Bárdossy, waited until Croatia had declared its independence (April 10); then, arguing that Yugoslavia had already disintegrated, he occupied the ex-Hungarian areas of inner Hungary.

Bárdossy, although no Fascist, believed that the Axis would win the war and that Hungary's salvation lay in placating it; otherwise, he believed, Romania (now demonstratively pro-Axis) would persuade Hitler to reverse the Second Vienna Award. Accordingly, when Germany attacked the U.S.S.R. (June 22), Bárdossy sent a token force to assist in what everyone expected to be a brief operation. The strength of the Soviet resistance upset the calculation, and in January 1942 the Germans forced Hungary to mobilize practically all its available manpower and send it to the U.S.S.R. Meanwhile, Britain had identified the Western cause with that of the Soviet Union. In December 1941 Britain declared war on Hungary, which in its turn declared war on the United States. Further, Britain recognized the Czechoslovak government in exile and withdrew recognition of the First Vienna Award, and the U.S.S.R. recognized Czechoslovakia's 1937 frontiers. The re-creation in shadow form of the Little Entente was nearly complete.

Hungary in the war

Many Hungarians by then agreed with Bárdossy that Hungary's only course was to fight on until the Axis won the war—the more so because all Hungarians except those of the extreme left regarded Bolshevism as the embodiment of evil. Horthy, however, while sharing the latter view, still believed in a Western victory and thought it possible for Hungary, while continuing the struggle in the East, to regain the favour of the West. In March 1942 he replaced Bárdossy by Miklós Kállay, who shared these hopes. For two years Kállay conducted a remarkable balancing act—protecting Hungary's Jews and allowing the left (except for the Communists) almost untrammelled freedom, while putting out innumerable feelers to the West, to which he actually promised to surrender unconditionally when its troops reached Hungary's frontiers. The active prosecution of the campaign in the East had meanwhile been brought to an end in January 1943, when the Hungarian expeditionary force suffered a crushing defeat at Voronezh that cost it much of its manpower and nearly all its equipment.

But the Western forces did not approach the Danube Valley; and as the Soviet Army neared the Carpathians, Hitler, from whom few of Kállay's activities were hidden, decided that he could not leave his vital communications at the mercy of an untrustworthy regime. In March 1944 he summoned Horthy and offered him the choice between full cooperation under German supervision or undisguised German occupation with the treatment accorded to an enemy country. Horthy chose the former course and appointed a collaborationist government under Gen. Döme Sztójay. For a while the Germans did much as they wished—they suppressed parties and organizations of the left and arrested their leaders (also the leading Legitimists), and they rounded up Hungary's Jews, except those in the capital, and sent them to forced labour camps or to gas chambers.

In the summer the pressure relaxed; and in August, after Romania's surrender to the Allies, Horthy appointed a new government under the loyal general Géza Lakatos and reopened the peace feelers. A mission was sent to Moscow, where it duly concluded a "preliminary armistice"; but when, on October 15, Horthy announced this on the wireless, he was abducted by the Germans, who forced him to recant and to abdicate. The Germans put Ferencz Szálasi, the leader of the right-wing extremist "Arrow Cross" movement, in charge. By then, however, Soviet troops were far inside the country. The Germans and their Hungarian allies were driven slowly back, while numerous refugees fled with them. The last armed forces crossed the Austrian frontier on April 4, 1945.

Soviet troops in Hungary

The defeat was sealed in a new peace treaty, signed in Paris on February 10, 1947, which restored the Trianon frontiers, with a rectification in favour of Czechoslovakia; it imposed on Hungary a reparations bill of $300,000,000 and limited its armed forces. The implementation of the treaty's provisions was to be supervised by a Soviet occupation force, a large contingent of which remained in the country.

V. The People's Republic

As in 1920, it was a new regime that recognized the defeat of its predecessor. As early as December 31, 1944, a makeshift "Provisional National Assembly" had accepted a government list and program presented to it by Communist agents following in the train of the Soviet armies. The Communists began cautiously. They announced that the new Hungary was to rest on "all its democratic elements." The government contained only two Communists; its other members were representatives of four non-Communist left-wing parties—the Smallholders, the Social Democrats, the "National Peasants," and the "Progressive Bourgeoisie"—and four men associated with the Horthy regime, including two generals who had been in Moscow in connection with the armistice talks. The program provided for the expropriation of the large estates and the nationalization of the banks and heavy industry; but it promised guarantees of democratic rights and liberties, respect for private property as such, and encouragement of private initiative in trade and small industry.

THE COMMUNIST REGIME

The full political takeover, however, proceeded systematically, although not according to timetable, for the Communists, misjudging feeling in the country, allowed the first elections (November 1945) to be relatively free. Only the parties of the coalition were allowed to contest them; but the adherents of the proscribed parties voted for the Smallholders, who received an absolute majority. The head of the Soviet mission, however, insisted that the coalition must be maintained; a Smallholder was allowed to be prime minister, but the Ministry of the Interior, with the control of the police, was given to the Communists. Pressure and intimidation were then applied to the Smallholders to expel their more courageous elements as "Fascists"; and in the next elections (August 1947), the Smallholders polled only 15 percent of the votes cast. The Communists had meanwhile forced the Social Democrats to form a "workers' bloc" with them. Although the pressure this time was considerable, the bloc still polled only 45 percent of the votes (other parties were allowed to stand this time); but the Communists then forced the Social Democrats to fuse with them in a single "Workers' Party," from which the recalcitrants were expelled.

Communist takeover

In the next elections (May 1949) voting was open, and the voters were presented with a single list, on which Smallholders and "National Peasants" still figured, but the persons using these descriptions were mere tools of the Communists. In August a new constitution was enacted—a copy of that of the Soviet Union. Hungary, a republic since February 1, 1946, now became a "people's republic," and, although its president (Zoltán Tildy) and for a while its prime ministers (Ferenc Nagy, then Lajos Dinnyés) were Smallholders, all real power rested with the Workers' Party, which was controlled by its first secretary, Mátyás Rákosi, by then the real power in the country. Finally, the party's "Muscovite wing" turned on its "national wing." The leader of this latter group, László Rajk, was executed on questionable charges in October 1949, and his chief adherents were similarly executed or imprisoned. Meanwhile, hundreds of persons had been executed or imprisoned as war criminals, many of them for no other offense than loyalty to the Horthy regime. Many thousands more were interned. The State Security Department (AVO) was omnipotent. The judiciary, civil service, and army were purged, and party orthodoxy became the criterion for positions in them. The trade unions were made into mere executants of party orders. After the dissolution of the parties, the chief ideological opposition to the Communist regime came from the churches; but their estates were expropriated, making it impossible for them to maintain their schools, and in July 1948 the entire educational system was nationalized. The Calvinist and Lutheran churches accepted arrangements under which the state made good their remaining expenditure. The head of the Roman Catholic Church, József Mindszenty, who refused to follow their example, was arrested on transparent charges in December 1948 and condemned to life imprisonment. The monastic orders were dissolved. After this the Roman Catholic Church accepted financial terms similar to those of the other churches; and eventually the bishops, with visible repugnance, took the oath of loyalty to the state.

The Communists' economic program, like their political program, could not be realized immediately, because in 1945 the country was in a state of economic chaos worse even than that of 1918. This time the country had been a theatre of war. Many cities, notably Buda, were in ruins, and communications were wrecked; the retreating Germans had destroyed the bridges between Buda and Pest and had taken with them all they could of the country's portable wealth. The Soviet armies lived off the land, and the Soviet Union took its share of reparations in kind, placing its own values on the objects seized.

Economic programs

A three-year plan introduced in August 1947 was devoted chiefly to the repair of immediate damage. This was declared completed, ahead of schedule, on December 31, 1949. By then the Communists were in full political control, and measures nationalizing banking, most industry, and most internal and all foreign trade had been enacted. The land, outside the big estates, was not touched at first, but in 1948 Rákosi announced a policy of collectivization of agriculture. Three forms were envisaged: state farms and two types of cooperative. Peasants were forced by various pressures into the cooperatives, the character of which approached ever more closely that of the state farms.

The three-year plan was succeeded by a five-year plan, the aim of which was to turn Hungary into a predominantly industrial country, with heavy industry taking first place. Huge sums were devoted to the construction of foundries and factories, many of them planned with little regard for Hungary's real resources and less still for its needs. In fact, the plan was concerned with the needs of the Soviet Union, for which Hungary was to serve as a workshop. Hungary's newly discovered deposits of uranium went straight out of the country. Industrial production rose steeply, but the standard of living did not; the production of consumer goods was throttled, and that of agriculture stagnated.

THE REVOLUTION OF 1956

Rákosi—who in 1952 came to preside over the government as well as the party—was, under Moscow, all-powerful until the death of Stalin in 1953, when a period of fluctuations set in. In July 1953 Rákosi was deposed from the prime ministership in favour of Imre Nagy—a "Muscovite" but a Hungarian in his attitudes and not unpopular in the country. Nagy promised a new course—end of the forced development of heavy industry, more consumer goods, no more forcing of peasants into the collectives, release of political prisoners, and closing of internment camps. He introduced some of these reforms, but Moscow hesitated to support him. In the spring of 1955 Nagy was dismissed from office and expelled from the party. Rákosi, reinstated, put the country back on its previous course but was dismissed again in July 1956, this time from all his offices and in disgrace. The new Soviet leader, Nikita S. Khrushchev, had sacrificed Rákosi as a gesture to President Tito of Yugoslavia, whom he wished to placate and whom Rákosi had offended personally. The new man in charge was Ernő Gerő, Rákosi's deputy and almost as detested as Rákosi himself. Gerő promptly announced that there would be no concessions on matters of principle to Nagy and his group.

Revolution and change

The relaxation of pressure under Nagy, however (though transitory), Khrushchev's "secret speech" denouncing Stalin's cult of personality delivered at the 20th Congress of the Communist Party of the Soviet Union (February 1956), and the Polish challenge to the Soviet Union in the spring and summer of 1956 emboldened Hungarians. On October 23, students in Budapest staged a great procession, which was to end with the presentation of a petition asking for redress of the nation's grievances. People flocked into the streets to join them. Gerő answered with an unwise and truculent speech, and police fired into the crowds. The shots turned a peaceful demonstration into a revolutionary one. The army joined the revolutionaries, and army depots and munitions factories handed out arms. Outside Budapest local councils sprang up in every centre; the peasants reoccupied their confiscated fields. The Communist bureaucracy melted away. Prison doors were opened. The members of the AVO fled if they could. A cheering crowd escorted Cardinal Mindszenty back to the palace.

In kaleidoscopic political changes, Nagy resumed power but was driven from one concession to the next, until he found himself at the head of a genuine coalition government composed of Smallholders, the Social Democrats, and the National Peasant parties, which, with a "Catholic Association," had reconstituted themselves.

The Soviet troops had withdrawn and Nagy was negotiating for the complete evacuation of Hungary. On November 1 he announced Hungary's withdrawal from the Warsaw Pact (to which it had adhered since 1955) and asked the United Nations to recognize Hungary as a neutral state, under the joint protection of the Great Powers. High officials from Moscow flew to Budapest and were in two minds whether to let matters take their course. But Nagy's denunciation of the Warsaw Pact seemed too dangerous to them, and their tanks, which had halted just across the frontier, began to return, reinforced by other units. By November 3, the tanks were in position around the main centres of Hungary; at 4 AM on the 4th they entered Budapest. Nagy took refuge in the Yugoslav Embassy, Cardinal Mindszenty in the U.S. Legation. Gen. Pál Maléter, head of the Hungarian national forces, who had been invited by the Soviet commanders to negotiate, was imprisoned.

A Communist leader, Ferencz Münnich, speaking from a radio station behind the Soviet lines, announced the formation of a new "revolutionary peasant-worker government." János Kádár, a "National Communist" who had been imprisoned under Rákosi and had actually joined the revolutionaries on October 24, formed a new government, consisting entirely of Communists, with himself as prime minister. Kádár promised that when the "counter-revolution" had been suppressed and order restored he would negotiate on the withdrawal of the Soviet garrison (although the denunciation of the Warsaw Pact was retracted); he dissociated himself from the "Rákosi-Gerő clique" and promised internal reforms.

The country was not convinced, and fighting broke out. But the odds were too heavy, and the major hostilities were over within a fortnight. The workers, however, proclaimed a general strike, and it was many weeks before they were brought to heel.

Meanwhile, Nagy, who had left his place of refuge under safe conduct, had been abducted to Romania. After a secret trial, he, Maléter, and a few close associates were executed in 1958. Many lesser figures were seized and transported to the Soviet Union, some never to return. More than 150,000 refugees escaped to the West. Thus, a substantial proportion of Hungary's educated classes was lost to the country. Material damage was also heavy.

End of the revolution

THE KADAR REGIME

In the first uncertain weeks of his regime Kádár made many promises. Workers' councils were to be given a large amount of control in the factories and mines. Compulsory deliveries of farm produce were to be abolished, and no compulsion, direct or indirect, was to be put on the peasants to enter the collectives. The five-year plan was to be revised to permit more production of consumer goods. The exchange rate of the ruble and forint was to be adjusted and the uranium contract revised. For a time there was even talk of a coalition government.

The larger hopes were dashed after representatives of the Soviet Union, East Germany, Czechoslovakia, Romania, and Bulgaria conferred with those of Hungary in Budapest in January 1957. A new program was soon issued stating that Hungary was a dictatorship of the proletariat, which in foreign policy relied on the Soviet Union and the Soviet bloc. Further, it was asserted that the Soviet garrison was in Hungary to protect the nation from imperialist aggression. Internal reforms were again promised, however, and foreign trade agreements were to be based on complete equality and mutual advantage.

Subsequently, Kádár was at great pains to give the Soviet Union no cause for uneasiness over Hungary's loyalty. Whenever any international issue arose, he invariably supported Moscow's policy with meticulous orthodoxy, even sending a contingent into Czechoslovakia in 1968. At home he ignored some of his promises and honoured others only superficially. The peasants were put under such pressure to enter cooperatives that within a few years practically no private farms survived. The workers' councils were dissolved, but trade unions were later granted rights to query decisions by management. Parliament remained a rubber stamp, and a "Patriotic People's Front," on which non-Communists were represented, was a mere facade.

Improvements under Kádár

Nevertheless, conditions changed very much for the better. Kádár enunciated the principle that "he who is not against us is with us," which for the ordinary people meant that they could go about their business without fear of molestation or even much surveillance and could speak, read, and even write with reasonable freedom. Technical competence replaced party orthodoxy as a criterion for posts of responsibility. More scope was allowed to private small-scale enterprise in trade and industry, and the New Economic Mechanism (NEM), initiated in 1968, even introduced the profit motive into state-directed enterprises. Agricultural cooperatives were allowed to produce industrial goods for their own use or to sell on demand, while the private plots of their members supplied a large proportion of fruits and vegetables for the rest of the population. Contacts with the West were encouraged. A *modus vivendi* was found with the Vatican and with Protestant churches. The standard of living began to rise substantially. In 1978 almost 10,000,000 tourists, 1,100,000 of them from western Europe, the U.S., and Canada, visited Hungary. Hungarians travelling abroad surpassed 5,000,000, including 350,000 visitors to the West.

The decade of the NEM, which went beyond the liberalization that took place in the Soviet Union itself, was only partially successful. Productivity failed to rise according to expectations. Government regulations persisted in many areas, and the economy remained geared to the Soviet-led Comecon. A burdensome system of subventions aimed at keeping down the price of basic necessities and services and at promoting the production of state-preferred goods made realistic cost accounting impossible. The price rise of oil and other industrial raw materials on the world market also aggravated the situation of a country that was dependent on the Soviet Union for oil, produced about 80 percent of its needed coal and lignite and negligible hydroelectric power, and imported 70 percent of the nonferrous metals for its rapidly developing industries. The gap between the price of energy, sophisticated industrial hardware, and raw materials on the one hand, and the price of agricultural products, a main item in Hungary's foreign trade, on the other, grew.

To prevent the deterioration of a stagnating economy, the government in the summer of 1979 increased rather considerably the price of consumer goods, including food and fuel as well as basic services in many walks of life, as a first step in the direction of adjusting the price of commodities to the cost of their production. Hungarians, who had hardly recovered from the monstrosities of the first Five-Year Plan, were again adjured not to live beyond their means and to tighten the belt. The question was whether this could be done without forfeiting that relative measure of sunshine in which this talented and hardworking people had for some time been basking.

BIBLIOGRAPHY. There are three major histories of Hungary: S.A. SZILAGYI (ed.), *A Magyar nemzet története*, 10 vol. (1895–98); B. HOMAN and G. SZEKFU, *Magyar történet*, 2nd ed., 5 vol. (1936; the first two vol. trans. into German, *Geschichte des ungarischen Mittelalters*, 1940–43); three of an intended 10-vol. history, *Magyarország története*, vol. 6, ENDRE KOVACS (ed.), vol 7, PETER HANAK (ed.), and vol. 8, GYORGY RANKI (ed.), covering the period 1848–1945, appeared in 1976–79. Major sections dealing with Hungary in the Austrian Academy's multivolume *Die Habsburgermonarchie 1848–1918*, ed. by ADAM WANDRUSZKA and PETER URBANITSCH, appeared in 1973 and 1975. All these, with the exceptions noted, are in Hungarian. In English there are short histories, such as D. KOSARY, *A History of Hungary* (1941); D. SINOR, *A Short History of Hungary* (1959); and C.A. MACARTNEY, *Hungary, a Short History*, 2nd ed. (1962).

Works on special periods and questions (in English, French, and German only) include: (*Origins and early settlement*): C.A. MACARTNEY, *The Magyars in the Ninth Century* (1930, reprinted 1968). (*Medieval period*): B. HOMAN (*op.cit.*). (*Eighteenth century*): H. MARCZALI, *Hungary in the Eighteenth Century* (Eng. trans. 1910); E. WANGERMANN, *From Joseph II to the Jacobin Trials*, 2nd ed. (1969); D. SILAGI, *Ungarn und der Geheime Mitarbeiterkreis Kaiser Leopold II* (1966). (*1790–1918*): C.A. MACARTNEY, *The Hapsburg Empire*, 2nd ed. (1971), a general survey. (*19th century*): G. BARANY, *Stephen Széchenyi and the Awakening of Hungarian Nationalism, 1791–1841* (1968); GYORGY SPIRA, *A Hungarian Count in the Revolution of 1848* (1974, Hung. ed. 1964); B.K. KIRALY, *Ferenc Deák* (1975); ISTVAN DEAK, *The Lawful Revolution: Louis Kossuth and the Hungarians, 1848–1849* (1979); L. EISENMANN, *Le Compromis Austro-Hongrois de 1867* (1904); E. WERTHEIMER, *Graf Julius Andrássy*, 3 vol. (1910–13). (*The nationalities question*): R.W. SETON-WATSON, *Racial Problems in Hungary* (1908); C.A. MACARTNEY, *Hungary and Her Successors* (1937, reprinted 1965). (*1918–19*): M. KAROLYI, *Fighting the World* (Eng. trans. 1923) and *Faith Without Illusion* (Eng. trans. 1956); R.L. TOKES, *Béla Kun and the Hungarian Soviet Republic* (1967). (*Treaty of Trianon*): *The Hungarian Peace Negotiations*, published by the PEACE CONFERENCE DELEGATION, 3 vol. (1921–22); F. DEAK, *Hungary at the Paris Peace Conference* (1942). (*1920–45*): C.A. MACARTNEY, *October 15th: A History of Modern Hungary, 1929–1945*, 2nd ed., 2 vol. (1960); (*Hungary under Communism*): E.C. HELMREICH (ed.), *Hungary* (1957); MIKOS MOLNAR, *A Short History of the Hungarian Communist Party* (1978). (*Revolution of 1956*): F. VALI, *Rift and Revolt in Hungary* (1961); P.E. ZINNER, *Revolution in Hungary* (1962). Current information may be found in the *Austrian History Yearbook* (annual).

(C.A.M./G.Ba.)

Hung Hsiu-ch'üan

Inspired by Christianity and believing himself to be the second son of God, Hung Hsiu-ch'üan (in Pinyin romanization Hong Xiuquan) led the Taiping Rebellion (1850–64). This great upheaval, in which more than 20,000,000 people are said to have been killed, drastically altered the course of modern Chinese history.

Hung was born January 1, 1814, in the small village of Fu-yüan-shui in the South China province of Kwangtung. He was the youngest son of four children in a poor but proud Hakka family. The Hakkas were an industrious people who had migrated into South China from the north several centuries earlier and still retained their original customs. At an early age, Hung showed signs of great intelligence; his entire village sponsored him in his studies, hoping that he would eventually pass the Confucian civil service examination, enter the government bureaucracy, and bring wealth and honour to his family and friends.

Hung took the government examination for the first time in 1827 and failed to obtain even the lowest official degree, an outcome not surprising in view of the great number of candidates competing. He took the test several times, each time travelling to the provincial capital in Canton, which was also the centre for trade with the West. When he failed the exam for the third time in 1837, the strain was more than he could bear. He suffered an emotional collapse. During a delirium that lasted several days, he imagined himself to be in the presence of a venerable old man with a golden beard. The old man complained that the world was overrun by evil demons, and he gave Hung a sword and seal to use in eradicating the bad spirits. Hung also believed himself to have encountered a middle-aged man who aided and instructed him in the exterminations of demons.

When Hung recovered he returned to his occupation as a village schoolteacher. In 1843 he took the examination for the fourth and last time, but again he failed. Shortly after this, Li Ching-fang, a cousin, noticed on Hung's bookshelves an unusual work entitled *Ch'üan-shih liang-yen* ("Good Words for Exhorting the Age"). Written by a Chinese missionary, the work, which explained the basic elements of Christianity, had been given Hung on his visit to Canton in 1837. Apparently, Hung had briefly glanced at the book's contents and then forgotten about it. When Li brought it to his attention, Hung re-examined the work and suddenly discovered the explanation for his visions. He realized that during his illness he had been transported to heaven. The old man he had spoken with was God, and the middle-aged man was Jesus Christ. Hung further understood that he was the second son of God, sent to save China. In reading the portions of the Bible contained in the *Ch'üan-shih liang-yen,* Hung often translated the pronouns I, we, you, and he as referring to himself, as if the book had been written for him. He baptized himself, prayed to God, and from then on considered himself a Christian.

Factors in Hung's conversion to Christianity

Hung began to propagate the new doctrine among his friends and relatives. One of his most important converts was his schoolmate Feng Yün-shan. In 1844 Hung lost his job because he had destroyed the tablets to Confucius in the village school where he was teaching, and Feng accompanied him on a preaching trip to neighbouring Kwangsi Province. Hung returned from Kwangsi after a few months, but Feng remained, establishing the Pai Shang-ti Hui (God Worshippers' Society), a religious group devoted to Hung's new doctrines.

In 1847 Hung went to Canton to study Christianity with the Rev. I.J. Roberts, an American missionary. The two months he spent with Roberts marked his sole formal training in the doctrines of Christianity; his writings show little understanding of concepts alien to Chinese culture. New Testament ideas of humility and kindness are ignored, as are the Christian ideas of original sin and redemption. Rather Hung stressed a wrathful Old Testament God, one who was to be worshipped and obeyed. He demanded the abolition of evil practices such as opium smoking, gambling, and prostitution and promised an ultimate reward to those who followed the teachings of the Lord.

Hung's contacts with Western Christianity did, however, teach him that there were other nations in the world. Rather than the traditional Chinese ethnocentrism, he postulated a world of many nations, all of them equal under God. Moreover, he was iconoclastic in his attitude toward the Chinese culture of his day, labelling it the work of evil demons and insisting that all symbols of it be destroyed.

After leaving Roberts, Hung joined Feng and the God Worshippers and was immediately accepted as the new leader of the group. Conditions in the countryside were deplorable, and sentiment ran high against the foreign Manchu rulers of China. As a result, Hung and Feng began to plot the rebellion that finally began in July 1850. Hung's rebels expanded into neighbouring districts, and on January 1, 1851, Hung's 37th birthday, he proclaimed his new dynasty, the T'ai-p'ing T'ien-kuo (Heavenly Kingdom of Great Peace) and assumed the title of T'ien Wang, or Heavenly King. The Taipings pressed north through the fertile Yangtze River Valley. As the rebels passed through the countryside, whole towns and villages joined them. They grew from a ragged band of a few thousand to a fanatical but highly disciplined army of over a million, divided into separate divisions of men and women soldiers. Men and women were considered equal by the Taipings but were allowed no contact with one another—even married couples were forbidden sexual intercourse.

The Taiping Rebellion

After Hung's army captured the great central China city of Nanking on March 10, 1853, he decided to halt his troops and make the city his permanent capital, renaming it T'ien-ching (Heavenly Capital). A northern expedition to capture the Manchu capital at Peking failed, but Taiping troops scored great victories in other places.

Meanwhile, Hung's friend Feng had died en route to Nanking, and Hung had placed much power in the hands of his minister of state, Yang Hsiu-ch'ing. It was Yang who organized the new Taiping state and mapped the strategy of the Taiping armies. Eventually Yang began to chastise Hung and to usurp his prerogatives as supreme leader. To legitimize his authority, Yang occasionally lapsed into trances in which his voice supposedly became that of the Lord's. In one of his trances, Yang claimed that the Lord demanded Hung be whipped for kicking one of his concubines (although Taiping followers were allowed no sexual relations with members of the opposite sex, Taiping leaders maintained enormous harems). On September 2, 1856, Hung had Yang murdered by Wei Ch'ang-hui, another Taiping general. Wei in turn became haughty, and Hung had him slain as well.

After this, Hung ignored his ablest followers and entrusted affairs of state to his incompetent elder brothers. He withdrew from all government matters for long periods, spending his time with his harem or in religious speculation. By 1862 Hung's generals were telling him that the situation at Nanking was desperate and that he ought to abandon the city. He refused, stating that he trusted in divine guidance. He even declined to lay in supplies in a case of a siege because he was sure that God would provide. On June 1, 1864, Hung, despairing after a lingering illness, committed suicide. His young son succeeded him on the throne. The city finally fell on July 19, 1864, and government troops initiated a terrible slaughter in which over 100,000 people were said to have been killed. Sporadic Taiping resistance continued in other parts of the country until 1866.

BIBLIOGRAPHY. THEODORE HAMBERG, *The Visions of Hung-Siu-Tshuen and the Origin of the Kwang-si Insurrection* (1854, reprinted 1935), is the best account of Hung and the early development of the Taipings. Two more recent studies of the Taipings that also deal with Hung are: SSU-YU TENG, *New Light on the History of the Taiping Rebellion* (1950, reprinted 1966); and FRANZ MICHAEL, *The Taiping Rebellion* (1966).

(L.N.F.)

Hung-wu

In 1368 the Chinese emperor known by the reign title Hung-wu (in Pin-yin romanization Hong-wu) founded the Ming dynasty, which was to reign in China for nearly three centuries. In his progress from a mendicant monastery to the Imperial palace, the Hung-wu emperor illustrates the chaos into which China had fallen under the preceding late Yüan dynasty. The Yüans were alien Mongol conquerors who had nevertheless absorbed many Chinese features during their reign. Their administration was faltering by the Hung-wu emperor's time, and a combination of famine, drought, and anarchy killed more than 7,000,000 people. The Hung-wu emperor's achievement, first as rebel leader and then as emperor, was to focus national resentment against the foreign rulers and to resuscitate a more truly Chinese way of government. This he did so forcefully that his reign has been seen as a culmination of the despotic trends that had been in evidence since the Sung dynasty (960–1279). He considered certain groups (for instance, maternal relatives; court eunuchs, who were often entrusted with power; and the military) as having been peculiarly prone to intrigue in the past, and vigorously stamped out such tendencies. He prohibited eunuchs, for instance, from participating in government, forbade the empress to meddle with court politics, and appointed civilian officials to control military affairs. Of lowly peasant origins, he always was aware of the popular misery that administrative corruption could engender, and he savagely punished malpractices.

By courtesy of the National Palace Museum, Taipei, Taiwan, Republic of China

The Hung-wu emperor, portrait by an unknown artist. In the National Palace Museum, Taipei, Taiwan.

Background and rebel career. The Hung-wu emperor was born in 1328 as Chu Yüan-chang, a poor peasant of Hao-chou (about 100 miles northwest of Nanking, near China's east coast). Orphaned at 16, he became a monk at the Huang-chüeh monastery near Feng-yang to avoid starvation—a common practice for sons of poor peasants to the present day. As a wandering mendicant, he often begged for food at Ho-fei (some 80 miles west of Nanking) and surrounding areas, where no constituted authority existed. Indeed, all Central and North China was suffering from drought and famine, and more than 7,000,000 persons starved, a situation that encouraged the popular rebellions that started from around 1325. Led by plebeian bandits, the rebels attacked the rich, distributing their wealth and goods among the people.

Life as a mendicant

Emergence as general. One such rebel was Kuo Tzu-hsing, who in 1352 led a large force to attack and take Hao-chou. Chu Yüan-chang joined the rebel forces, rising from the ranks to become second-in-command. Kuo Tzu-hsing, a mere bandit leader, became jealous of Chu Yüan-chang, who distinguished himself as a military leader. These problems were later mitigated when Chu Yüan-chang married Kuo's adopted daughter, the princess Ma, who was influential in reconciling the two men.

In 1353 Chu Yüan-chang captured Ch'u-chou (now Ch'u district in Anhwei Province, an area west of Nanking). Subsequently he received important commissions, gaining a following of outstanding men, some of whom later became officials under the early Ming dynasty. In 1355 Kuo Tzu-hsing died, and Chu Yüan-chang took over the leadership of the rebel army.

Chu Yüan-chang attacked and captured towns and cities in eastern China and, on reaching the Yangtze Delta, encountered educated men of the gentry class. Some decided to join his movement, and Chu had the foresight to seek their guidance. From them he learned the rudiments of the Chinese language and studied Chinese history and the Confucian Classics. More significantly, he learned the principles of government and built up an effective administration in local areas alongside the military structure. Moreover, he was persuaded by his scholars to present himself as a national leader against the Mongols rather than as a popular rebel. His choice of advisers and his shrewd ability to adopt sound governmental measures ultimately made him the most formidable leader against the Mongols.

Now determined to overthrow the Yüan dynasty (1279–1368), Chu Yüan-chang marched toward Nanking and captured it in 1356. Nanking was a strategic point, close to the rich lands of the Yangtze Delta. Proclaiming himself duke of Wu, Chu established an effective administration over the Nanking area with the help of the scholars and on their advice refrained from roaming aimlessly from place to place to plunder. He also encouraged agriculture by granting unused land to the landless peasants, but, in spite of his successes, he was still reluctant to proclaim himself king (*wang*). At that time he acknowledged the Sung dynasty pretender, Han Lin-erh, as his superior, even though Han was ineffectual.

Capture of Nanking

Meanwhile, the northern provinces were as restless as the south, and, when various rebels defied the Mongols, the capable Mongol minister T'o-t'o personally led troops to subdue them. The north, thus, had a semblance of peace, whereas the south could not be controlled by the Mongol authorities.

National military leadership. Chu Yüan-chang now emerged as the national leader against the Mongols, though he had other rivals for power. Chief among them were Ch'en Yu-liang and Chang Shih-ch'eng. Ch'en Yu-liang was the self-proclaimed emperor of the Han dynasty and was based on Wu-ch'ang (in Hupeh Province, about 400 miles west of Shanghai), controlling a large portion of western China. Chang Shih-ch'eng, the self-proclaimed Prince Ch'eng of the Chou dynasty, operated at P'ing-chiang (in Kiangsu Province adjoining the east coast and including Nanking) in the east.

In 1363 a decisive naval battle at the Po-yang Lake (south of the Yangtze in the north of Kiangsi Province) was fought between Ch'en Yu-liang's huge fleet of war junks and Chu's small but swift barges. The three-day battle ended with Ch'en's death and the destruction of his fleet. Wu-ch'ang, Ch'en's stronghold, was captured in 1364, followed by the capture of Hupeh, Hunan (a large province west of Kiangsi Province), and Kiangsi provinces. In the same year Chu proclaimed himself prince of Wu.

With the death of Ch'en Yu-liang, events moved quickly to a climax. In 1367 the Sung pretender Han Lin-erh felt so threatened by the Mongols at his headquarters at Ch'u-chou that he decided to flee to Nanking for protection. Escorted by one of Chu Yüan-chang's men during the trip, Han died by drowning when his boat capsized—an event perhaps contrived by Chu. In the same year Chang Shih-ch'eng was captured and brought to Nanking, where he committed suicide. Other rebels decided to submit or were eliminated. One such was Fang Kuo-chen, one of the first to rebel against the Mongols, who had operated as a pirate along the coast; when he surrendered to Chu Yüan-chang, he was given honours and a stipend but no real power. On the other hand, Ch'en Yu-ting, a Yüan loyalist who protected Fukien Province (on the southeast coast, opposite Taiwan), was captured and brought to Nanking for execution.

Reign as Emperor. With the south pacified, Chu Yüan-chang sent his generals Hsü Ta and Ch'ang Yü-ch'un to lead troops against the north. At the beginning of 1368 Chu Yüan-chang finally proclaimed himself emperor of the Ming dynasty, establishing his capital at Nanking. "Hung-wu" ("vastly martial") was adopted as his reigning title, and he is usually referred to as the Hung-wu emperor, though T'ai Tsu is more strictly correct.

The troops sent to conquer the north were highly successful. Shantung and Honan provinces (south of Peking) submitted to Ming authority. By August 1368, Ming troops had entered Peking. The Mongol emperor Shun Ti fled to Inner Mongolia, and, although Mongol power was not immediately destroyed, historically the Yüan dynasty now came to an end. The rest of the country fell easily as Ming troops subdued first the northwest, then the southwest (Szechwan and Yünnan). Unification was completed by 1382.

The Hung-wu emperor was cruel, suspicious, and irrational, especially as he grew older. Instead of eliminating Mongol influence, he made his court resemble the Mongol court, and the despotic power of the emperor was institutionalized for the rest of the dynasty.

One of his political acts was to grant principalities to all his sons, ostensibly from fear of another Mongol invasion, so that the imperial princes could be given military powers to aid the regular armies. A contributing factor was his interest in maintaining personal control over the empire through his sons' principalities.

Despotic tendencies. The trend toward political despotism can be seen in the Hung-wu emperor's various other actions. In 1380 the prime minister Hu Wei-yung was implicated in a widespread plot to overthrow the throne and was executed along with 30,000 members of his clique. The Emperor consequently abolished the prime ministership in perpetuity as well as the central chancellery. Thus, the next highest level of administration, the six ministries, became merely advisory to the Emperor himself, who now exercised direct control. This change had serious defects, the most important being the inability of even the most vigorous emperor to attend to all the affairs of state. In an attempt to overcome this difficulty, the Emperor made use of six or more grand secretaries, who were responsible for routine administration. The institution of the grand secretaries evolved from that of the Hanlin Academy, the original function of which was to assist in the education of the heir designate. Although superior in practice to the six ministries, the grand secretaries (later institutionalized as the grand secretariat) were mere servants of the despotic emperor.

Rehabilitation of the scholar class

The Sung emperors, learning from the T'ang dynasty's experience, had felt that the militarists were the most dangerous group in the country and had purposely encouraged the scholar class, but the Hung-wu emperor felt that, after the Mongol expulsion, the scholars formed the most dangerous group. Nevertheless, his interest in restoring traditional Chinese values involved rehabilitating the Confucian scholar class, and from experience he knew that effective government depended upon the scholars. He therefore encouraged education and purposely trained scholars for the bureaucracy. At the same time he used methods to deprive them of power and position and introduced the use of heavy bamboo as a punishment at court, often beating to death scholar–officials for the slightest offense. He felt that scholars should be mere servants of the state, working on behalf of the emperor. Because of the Emperor's attitude, a great many members of the gentry were discouraged from embarking on official careers.

Administration. To train scholars for the bureaucracy, the Hung-wu emperor in 1369 ordered the establishment of schools at each local level. Students were subsidized and were privileged to apply for admission to the Hanlin Academy, which presumably formulated policy and supervised the local schools. As a result of this edict, more schools developed during the Ming than in previous periods of Chinese history, and education became inseparable from civil-service recruitment by examination, the realization of which had been an ideal during the T'ang and Sung dynasties. Imperial authorities controlled the system of examination as far down as the provincial examinations that provided candidates for the metropolitan and palace examinations at the capital. The examination system made it possible to recruit the best minds for governmental service, though examinations stressed only the Sung Neo-Confucian interpretation of the Classics and forced candidates to write in an artificial literary style, discouraging the development of originality.

The Hung-wu emperor's military system, the *wei-so* ("guard-post") system, was of earlier origin. The practice of granting land to soldiers for cultivation in peace realized his ideal of having the troops support themselves so as not to burden the people.

Influence abroad

Foreign affairs. In foreign relations the Hung-wu emperor extended the Ming empire's prestige to outlying regions: southern Manchuria was brought into the empire; outlying states, such as Korea, the Liu-ch'iu (now Ryukyu) Islands, Annam, and other states, sent tribute missions to acknowledge the suzerainty of the Ming emperor; and, not satisfied with the expulsion of the Mongols, he sent two military expeditions into Mongolia, reaching the Mongol capital of Karakorum itself. Ming forces even penetrated Central Asia, taking Hami (in the Gobi desert) and accepting the submission of several states in the Chinese Turkistan region. When Ming emissaries traversed the mountains to Samarkand, however, they were met with a different reception. Timur (one of history's greatest conquerors) was building a new Mongol empire in that region, and the Chinese envoys were imprisoned. Eventually, they were released, and Timur and the Ming exchanged several embassies, which the Chinese regarded as tributary missions. Timur was preparing an invasion of China when he died in 1405.

The Hung-wu emperor was less successful with Japan, the buccaneers of which ravaged the Chinese coast. Three missions went to Japan, armed with inducements and threats, but were unable to curb piracy, because the Japanese authorities were themselves helpless.

The succession. A great problem for the Hung-wu emperor was the succession. His first choice, made when he was prince of Wu, was Piao, his eldest son, later known as the heir designate I-wen. As the Hung-wu emperor's reign progressed there were indications that he favoured his fourth son, Ti, the prince of Yen, whose principality was at Peking and whose personal qualities and military ability were more impressive. In 1392, when the heir designate I-wen died, the Hung-wu emperor was persuaded to appoint I-wen's eldest son as his successor, rather than the Prince of Yen, who was angered by this decision. After the Hung-wu emperor's death in June 1398, he was succeeded by his grandson Yün-wen, known in history as the emperor Hui, who reigned until 1402, when the throne was usurped by the Prince of Yen.

BIBLIOGRAPHY. No biography or definitive works dealing with the Hung-wu emperor and his period exist in English. CHARLES HUCKER (ed.), *Chinese Government in Ming Times: Seven Studies* (1969), contains articles based on recent research covering the political, military, and educational aspects of the Ming.

(D.B.C.)

Hunting, Sport

The sport of hunting involves seeking, pursuing, and taking game and wild animals in their natural habitat, primarily for the pleasure and challenge of the stalk or chase and the joy of being out of doors, often added to which are the satisfaction of riding horseback or working with dogs and the comradeship of association with other hunters. In Great Britain and western Europe, hunting is defined as the taking of wild animals by the aid of hounds that hunt by scent, and the sport of taking small game and game birds with a gun is known as shooting; in the United States and elsewhere the term hunting encompasses not only hunting with hounds but also the shooting of both large and small game. For records of North American big-game animals, see SPORTING RECORD in the *Ready Reference and Index*.

Definitions of hunting and shooting

HISTORY

Primitive hunters. To early man, hunting was a necessity. Not alone a means of obtaining food, it also provided clothing and tools. Both archaeological evidence from the past and observations of the simpler societies of the present reveal a widespread preoccupation with, and ingenuity in, methods of hunting. These varied with the nature of the country and of the animal hunted, the ingenuity and inventiveness of the hunters, and the materials and technologies at their disposal. Weapons included sticks or stones to knock over birds and small game; specially shaped clubs and throwing sticks such as the African knobkerry, the more specialized trombash of the Upper Nile, and the Australian boomerang; and spears ranging from simple sticks with one end pointed and hardened in the fire to spears having a separate foreshaft, usually barbed, and heads of sharpened stone, bone, or metal. In some areas, as in Australia and Arctic America, for example, spear throwers were used to give greater range. Except in Australia, bows and arrows were universal among primitive hunters. Stone arrowheads were widely used at an early date; examples of great antiquity have been found in many countries. The blowpipe or blowgun with its poisoned darts was one of the most deadly weapons in the hands of the primitive hunter.

Patience and cunning of a high order are seen in the camouflages and disguises used to conceal the hunter as he approached his quarry and, also, in the various nooses, traps, nets, snares, game pits, decoys, baits, and poisons found almost universally among primitive hunters. It is probable that dogs have been trained to track and kill game at least from Neolithic times.

With the development of agriculture, hunting became an accessory activity—principally to provide variety in the diet or to protect crops, flocks, or herds from wild animals—and then survived as a sport or recreation. But even before that time hunting had contained elements of sport. One of the basic functions of sports, as of games, is to let man develop and display his physical skills and accomplishments (see GAMES, HISTORY OF). This hunting does, not only in the hunt but in the continual training and practice in throwing stones, sticks, clubs, and spears, in shooting bows and arrows and blowguns, and in the arts of trailing and stalking that are a part of the primitive hunter's way of life. Such practice gave the young hunter especially the satisfaction of measuring his own improvement and the pleasures of demonstrating his skills to others in competing with his peers. Hunting also fulfilled important social functions including participation in group activities, the assignment and attainment of status within the group, and the maintenance of tribal traditions.

Elements of sport in early hunting

Among the ancients. In more advanced civilizations, hunting for sport early became an employment of the rulers, those having the most leisure and wealth. In ancient Egypt the huntsmen constituted a social class; they hunted on their own or acted as attendants of the nobles, taking charge of the dogs and securing and bringing home the game. Game was sought in open deserts bordering both sides of the valley of the Nile, but sometimes the animals were driven into enclosed spaces or preserves. The animals hunted included gazelle, antelopes (ibex, oryx), stag, wild ox, Barbary sheep, and hare; ostrich for its plumes; and fox, jackal, wolf, hyena, and leopard for their skins or because they were enemies of the farmyard. The hunters used the net, noose, arrow, and dart. The lion was occasionally trained to hunt. In the later periods the sportsman appears, occasionally, to have ridden in a chariot or on horseback.

The Egyptians' partiality to the chase was shared by the Assyrians and Babylonians, as is shown by the frequency with which hunting scenes are depicted on the walls of their temples and palaces; for example, Ashurbanipal, the Hunting King, had his own image as a huntsman immortalized in bas-relief on the walls of ancient Nineveh along with his proud boast, "I killed the lion." One of many indications that the chase was also held in high esteem in Lydia and in Persia is the portrayal, on a 5th-century silver dish, of the Sāsānian king Kavadh I galloping at full tilt after wild sheep. The first known use of hawks or falcons in hunting was in Assyria (before 700 BC); the art of falconry was widely known in the East—in India and China, for example—at an early date (see also FALCONRY). Biblical indications that game was plentiful and that it was much sought after and duly appreciated by the Jews in Old Testament times are numerous.

The interest of the ancient Greeks in hunting developed at a very early period. It first found adequate literary expression in Xenophon's *Cynegeticus*, which expounded his principles and embodied his experiences in his favourite sport. The treatise dealt chiefly with the capture of the hare, but boar and stag hunting were also described; and lions, leopards, lynxes, panthers, and bears were mentioned, the latter taken in pitfalls or speared by mounted horsemen. Among the Romans hunting seems to have been viewed with less favour as an occupation for gentlemen and to have been left to inferiors and professionals.

Europe. For centuries, the European hunter has pursued his quarry with a fanatical zeal unrivalled by hunters of other lands. The addiction of the Franks and other Teutonic people to falconry and the chase became so intense in later centuries that not only the laity but also the clergy were warned by provincial councils against spending so much of their time and money on hounds, hawks, and falcons. Originally, among the northern nations the sport was open to everyone except slaves, who were not permitted to bear arms; the growth of the idea of game preserving accompanied the development of feudalism. The right to hunt became generally attached to the ownership of land. Because of their ancient and hereditary claim to the title of "Lord High Masters of the Chase for the Holy Roman Empire," the old electors of Saxony enjoyed exceptional opportunities to hunt. During his 24-year reign (1656–80), Elector John George II of Saxony shot an astonishing total of 42,649 red deer. He refused the crown of Bohemia, not for political reasons but because Bohemian stags were inferior in size. To make certain that nobody shot any of his prized stags, he built a high and very expensive fence along the boundary between Saxony and Bohemia. So eager were the Europeans for the chase that an early landgrave of Hesse had a codicil added to the Lord's Prayer: "Give us this day our daily hart in the pride of grease," meaning a stag taken in fat condition during the month preceding the rut. In 11th-century England Edward the Confessor delighted in riding after stag hounds, and in 18th-century France Louis XV was so fond of hunting that he stopped on the way home from his coronation to chase stag in the Villars-Cotterets forest. In 1726 he somehow managed, affairs of state to the contrary notwithstanding, to spend 276 days hunting. In Russia the tsars had superb hunting in the imperial forest of Belovezh, and one remarkable 12-day shoot ended up with a tally of 36 elk, 53 stags, 325 roebuck, 42 bison (wisent), and 138 wild boars.

And it was not only European men. Princess Frederika of Eisenach was famous for her skill at deer-stalking; while Maria, governess of the Netherlands, could track her stag, shoot it neatly with a crossbow, and then proceed to remove the entrails from her trophy. In France, Diane de Poitiers, with her paramour Henry II (ruled 1547–59), hunted stag, roe deer, and boar from the saddle out of Chenonceaux, Europe's most magnificent hunting box; and in England, Elizabeth I was fond of both hunting and hawking.

Codes of behaviour. For 1,000 years Europeans have preserved a distinction between hunting for sport and hunting for food. For the Normans, for instance, the chase was the principal source of meat, and for that purpose it was organized in whatever way would provide the most kills with the least effort. But where hunting was a pastime a strict code of behaviour developed, based on standards enjoined by kings and noblemen. These turned on the contrast between pleasure and necessity. A gentleman taking winged game for recreation did so by falconry, but a fowler, who earned his livelihood by serving the market, was regarded as doing the natural thing in netting all the birds he could catch.

Hunting for sport and hunting for food

From this distinction has grown up the complex, often mystifying, and seemingly contradictory European canon of respect and fair play for the hunted. The essence of it is that those who are preying on wild creatures in any measure for their own amusement must limit their means so as to give the quarry a fair chance of escape and to avoid unnecessary suffering of wounded game. Thus, for example, shooting a sitting duck, one that is on the water instead of flying in the air, is frowned upon, and hiding out in wait for a big-game animal to come to a water hole or a block of salt is considered unsportsmanlike. As for avoiding unnecessary suffering, a hunter's behaviour in following up any wounded game is regarded by most as a measure of his sportsmanship: the code demands that he track down and kill an animal he has wounded.

The principles of the code are upheld everywhere by hunters who regard themselves as sportsmen. So strict have been the European game laws that hunting is still excellent in many areas. It is notable that even Slav hunters whose nations are now Communist continue to observe the outward pomp of the aristocratic past. This protocol has given sport with the gun a residual prestige, amounting at times to snob appeal, long after social changes have removed its origins. The spread of income now permits participation at some level in some form of it by virtually all who wish for it in nearly every country. Inclination, not social standing, has become the definitive factor. As real property, the right to shoot vested in the ownership of land always could be sold or let. In western Europe there has been an increase in the acquisition of such rights by shooting clubs, generally with large memberships, on a cooperative basis. In most of the Communist countries of eastern Europe shooting rights theoretically passed into the hands of the communes; in practice, however, the rights also are often let to clubs or syndicates, sometimes from other countries.

The impact of gunpowder. It is not known how soon after the introduction of gunpowder guns were first used for hunting, but there are records of the shooting of game with firearms in the 16th century. The gun greatly increased the hunters' ability to kill game at greater distances and in larger numbers; moreover, with each improvement in the range, accuracy, and rapidity of fire of firearms, the hunters' kill was further increased. These improvements eventually led sportsmen to adopt additional conventions (generally unwritten but sometimes included in game laws) to limit their means of destruction. In Great Britain and many other countries, for example, the pump gun, or repeater, is not accepted as a sporting weapon. Nothing more lethal than a double-barrelled shotgun is used because this compels a pause after a maximum of two shots, either to reload or to change guns, during which the quarry has opportunity to get out of range. Thus, although the hunter's ability to kill was increased, his actual kill was kept under control by such codes of behaviour (see below *Game management*).

Exploration and colonization. *North America.* When European explorers and settlers first arrived in North America, game was abundant from coast to coast. Moose were fairly common in the eastern forests and New England woodlands; deer roamed freely over large areas along the coast and inland; and there was a profusion of game birds (including the wild turkey), waterfowl, and small game animals. To the west, the American buffalo (bison) blackened the plains, and passenger pigeons blackened the skies. Elk (wapiti), mountain goat, sheep, and pronghorns were numerous, as were predators such as the puma, cougar, lynx, bobcat, wolf, and coyote.

Attitudes of the North American pioneers

To the pioneers, freed from an aristocracy of large landowners holding rights to all game, the European distinction between hunting for sport and hunting for food was less clear. They hunted for sport, but they also hunted to put meat on the table. Pioneering attitudes did not tend toward conservation; they focussed rather on complete self-reliance. The pioneer farm family, depending entirely on what it could win from the land, harvested the game of the swamps and forests as naturally as it harvested the produce of the fields. Besides, the supply of game seemed limitless.

That the sporting aspects of hunting also appealed strongly to the pioneers is suggested by the fact that the one sporting event most likely to be found at any gathering and the one that would attract the most participants and spectators was the shooting match.

The pioneer mystique of every man a hunter has persisted for long in much of the American culture.

Africa. When Europeans began to settle Africa in the late 19th century, the colonists shot game for the sake of meat and hides, and hunting became a principal means of survival—as it had been for the native populations. As in the pioneer days of North America there seemed to be an unlimited game supply, and there was much unnecessary waste. Again as in North America, as populations increased so did the amount of hunting, and wild animal populations were reduced at a correspondingly quicker rate. When hunting was no longer necessary, it was continued as a sport, and some species have been hunted to extinction.

Asia. In Asia, in contrast to North America and Africa, colonization by Europeans led to the conservation of wildlife and ended the over-exploitation of game. The successful introduction of European game management practices stopped the indiscriminate slaughter of migratory birds, for example, and conserved the stock of animal life. In the second half of the 20th century, however, several species (*e.g.*, the tiger and the Asiatic rhinoceros), which were not previously in danger, became threatened by extinction. These species and others have been placed under protection (with special licenses required) in most areas and, with the assistance and encouragement of the International Union for Conservation of Nature and Natural Resources, improved wildlife conservation and protection programs have been inaugurated.

South America and Australasia. The European settlers of South America and Australasia found little in the way of big game to hunt. South America has only three indigenous animals that qualify as big game: the jaguar of Brazil and Paraguay, the spectacled bear of the high Andes, and a puma. With only three big-game animals, hunting tended to be for meat and hides, and the quarry was usually game birds and small animals. Later, wild game animals were imported with considerable success. In 1906 a shipment of red deer and wild boar of the Carpathians was imported, followed by fallow deer from England, blackbuck and axis deer from India, and, still later, Indian buffalo. These imports form the basis of modern hunting for sport in South America.

Australia has no basic big game at all. New Zealand, however, is well supplied with big-game animals, but all of them are exotic (*i.e.*, transplanted imports). New Zealand game now includes red and fallow deer and chamois from Europe; sambar, axis, and Japanese deer and tahr from Asia; and moose, wapiti, and whitetail deer from North America. All species have done well, and some have grown better horns than in their homelands. Commercial meat hunting has made heavy inroads into big game in recent years.

The impact of technology. The ease and speed of international communication brought about by the airplane in the second half of the 20th century has represented perhaps the biggest impact of modern technology on the sport of hunting since the invention of gunpowder. Whereas formerly the exotic big game fields of East Africa, Central and southeastern Asia, and northern Canada and Alaska were virtually inaccessible to all but the wealthiest hunters of Europe and North America—to those who could afford the time and money for expeditions lasting weeks or months—air transport brought Nairobi, Karāchi, and Nome to within a few hours of Chicago, London, or Paris. By the 1960s and 1970s airlines were offering packaged 10-day safaris from London or New York to East Africa, for example, with air flights between base camps. On a smaller scale, a hunter in Cleveland, Ohio, could fly to Nebraska or North Dakota for a week or a weekend of pheasant shooting or to Montana for pronghorn (American antelope).

Accessibility of game fields

Hunters' weapons and equipment have also benefitted from advances in technology. Shotguns, rifles, and ammunition, and hunting bows and arrows and crossbows have all undergone improvement and refinement. Clothing and camp equipment have been perfected to provide protection and even comfort in Arctic cold or tropic heat. And field transport has been revolutionized by motorized two-wheel drive, four-wheel drive, and all-terrain vehicles, snowmobiles, and helicopters and light planes.

HUNTING AND ECOLOGY: THE NEED FOR CONSERVATION AND CONTROLS

Disappearing game. Of 4,000 species of mammals and more than 8,500 species of birds, 120 kinds of mammals and 150 varieties of birds had ceased to exist by the 1970s, according to the World Wildlife Fund: more than 900 other species were endangered and nearing extinction. In addition, large areas of the world, formerly well supplied with game, had been so denuded of wildlife that hunting was no longer feasible.

Well-known examples from the past include the extinction by market hunters of the passenger pigeon of North America that formerly numbered in the billions. In South Africa, Dutch settlers were responsible for the extinction of the quagga, a kind of zebra formerly found in great herds on the plains of South Africa, and the general extermination of game from the greater part of the country. An example of near-extinction is the bison, once innumerable in North America, which still exist only because a few survivors were formed into a breeding herd and carefully preserved.

In North America the elimination of big-game animals started in the northeastern sector of the United States and spread gradually across the Allegheny Mountains and westward. As the country developed, the encroachments of civilization and widespread population growth marked the end of big-game hunting in many parts of the United States and Canada. In Africa, although the game fields there were the last to be discovered, they have suffered from the attacks of hunters more than those of any other parts of the world except some parts of North America.

The defenders of hunting as a sport argue that such attacks have not been delivered by the man who shot for sport and that, if sport alone had been the object of pursuit, it is doubtful whether the number of game would have decreased materially. But wherever commercialism entered the picture, the fate of wild game was sealed. The bison, passenger pigeon, and quagga all fell before the onslaught of commercial hunters, who have also decimated and threatened the extinction of many other species: selected examples include the African elephant, slaughtered for its ivory tusks, and the African rhinoceros, which—because of the magical and aphrodisiacal properties attributed to its horn—has been hunted down since the Middle Ages until it is now a threatened species.

Commercial hunting and the encroachment of civilization

Overhunting alone, however, has not been entirely responsible for the elimination of big game in many areas. The encroachment of civilization in North America has been mentioned above. In Africa, too, colonization by European settlers drove the wild animals into country that was unsuitable for them. The spread of industry and agriculture, accelerated by modern methods of forest clearance, opened up Africa at unexpected speed; and a further element was the presence of a native population newly possessed of weapons, which gave them the ability to destroy animals on a large scale in places where it was profitable.

In addition to the extinct passenger pigeon, small game, too, has been threatened by commercial hunting (*e.g.*, wild ducks and, in some areas, rabbits, pheasants, and other game shot for market) and by the growth of population and the spread of civilization. In industrially advanced countries, housing developments, urban sprawl, and superhighway construction have filled in swamps and valleys, levelled hills, and denuded forests, brush, and grasslands, eliminating wildlife habitat over large areas. Even in areas that are still rural, improved agricultural techniques and the mechanization of farming have resulted in the elimination of hedgerows and such practices as the early plowing of stubble, removing the cover, nesting places, and food supplies of partridges, for example, and other small game. Along with the growth of civilization and technology has come increasing pollution—by industrial wastes and discharges, insecticides, oil spills and slicks, and the introduction of detergents and other non-biodegradeable products into the environment.

Controls and game management. *Controls.* Because of the indiscriminate slaughter of animals by market hunters and sportsmen, laws have been passed in nearly every country to protect wild game. Limits were put on the number of animals that each hunter was entitled to kill, and licenses, which bring in a substantial revenue, became part of modern game management. In the United States, for example, the federal government controls migratory game birds within the nation's borders because these migrate not only from state to state but also between Canada and Mexico. Other game comes under the jurisdiction of the individual states, all of which have highly developed programs and trained staffs to enforce regulations covering hunting seasons and game-in-season bag and possession limits. Similar game conservation schemes began to be implemented in India in 1860, in Africa at the end of the 19th century, and in eastern Europe in the years after World War II. In Great Britain, Scandinavia, and the rest of western Europe, because the right to hunt is generally attached to the ownership of land, the preservation of wildlife is a function exercised or delegated by landowners.

Although legal codes have been drawn up for the protection of wildlife in Africa, these are more easily devised than enforced. Several factors, apart from the vast distances common to most African countries, combine to make enforcement difficult. There are, for instance, different game codes in different territories and, except in those places where major rivers or mountain ranges separate one national territory from another, migrating game herds crossing the frontier may be in double peril because of conflicting regulations on either side of it. These regulations define hunting areas, closed seasons, and numbers which sportsmen are permitted to kill, but they necessarily vary from year to year. In spite of attempts at regulation, the lion, for example, which traditionally has been the hunter's most desired quarry, is diminishing. Some ecologists believe that in the Africa of the future the lion may be in danger of extinction as a wild animal. The spread of farming communities has meant that lions, though they seldom become man-eating, have nevertheless become regarded as a menace to human life, and they are hunted down over ever-widening areas. Elsewhere, tribesmen have freely employed their newly acquired means of destruction. Simultaneously, the general contraction of game areas has reduced the number of beasts on which lions prey, also restricting their habitat. The consequence is that few heavy-maned lions remain outside the Masai tribal areas (where, it is worth noting, the spearing of lions is a tribal custom and test of manhood). Lions remaining elsewhere are generally of inferior type and of less interest to the sporting hunter. Licenses to shoot lions have been issued on a reduced scale by several African administrations. Regulations in other parts of the world also have had to be strengthened: in Asia the position of the magnificent Bengal tiger of India had become so critical that it was placed under complete protection from hunting in 1970, and in Arctic America and Siberia the polar bear, threatened with extinction by hunting, is now protected by international treaty.

Difficulties of enforcement

Game management. Game management has long been carried on in Europe by gamekeepers, employed by the lords or landowners to protect the game from poachers and from natural enemies. These practices were reinforced by the elaborate hunter's codes that prohibited the hunting of stags, for example, during the breeding season and limited the quarry to only warrantable (five years old or older) stags. In later years gamekeepers developed or adopted practices to increase the stock—for example, systematically burning old heather off of grouse moors to stimulate new and vigorous growth of the birds' chief food supply, a method, incidentally, known to primitive hunters including North American Indians—as well as other measures to maintain or replenish the stock, such as raising pheasants and other game birds artificially.

In North America, by the middle 1800s, there were those who felt that the end of big-game hunting was in sight. Surprisingly, increasingly effective game management resulted in a continuation of this form of sport to the present time. The picture would have been bleak indeed had it not been for the amazing comeback of the deer, principally the Virginia whitetail; mule deer and Columbia blacktail deer have also done well. Experts aver that there are more deer in the United States now than when Europeans first arrived on the continent. Sound game-management practices not only saved the

Some examples of successful management

remnants of these and other popular big-game animals but also enabled them to thrive and multiply.

Game-management practices have also been employed in the United States for the preservation and propagation of small game. A voluntary organization of sportsmen and conservationists has spearheaded one outstanding program to preserve and restore the wetland breeding, hatching, and rearing grounds of ducks and other waterfowl in the northern United States and, especially, on the Canadian prairies. This program of habitat management has strongly supplemented federal government programs of shooting controls, carried out under international treaties with Canada and Mexico, and of maintaining sanctuaries as winter resting places for wildfowl. In Europe each country makes its own regulations concerning migratory birds. The artificial raising of upland game birds, especially quail and pheasant but also chukar, Hungarian, and red-legged partridges, is widely practiced in the United States. Markedly successful has been the live-trapping and subsequent re-establishment of wild turkey: in areas where the turkey had all but disappeared there has been a strong resurgence, and, even in areas where turkeys had been unknown for years, the introduction of wild birds has enabled the establishment of good-sized flocks with open hunting seasons. A hopeful and growing trend is seen in conservation, land-bank, and similar programs to withdraw previously cropped land from production, permitting it to grow wild again so that it provides cover for small game birds and animals.

Game-management programs in Africa have been focussed primarily on the establishment of adequate game preserves and wildlife sanctuaries. International programs are conducted by the International Union for Conservation of Nature and Natural Resources (IUCN), in cooperation with the United Nations Educational, Scientific and Cultural Organization (UNESCO) and the independent World Wildlife Fund (see also CONSERVATION OF NATURAL RESOURCES and COMMUNITY, BIOLOGICAL).

THE SPORT OF HUNTING

The sport of hunting continues to thrive and in some places to grow. Though it is no longer a requirement for survival and the inculcation of its art and skills is no longer a major concern in the education of the young, it still provides a link with nature and, some say, with life as it used to be or is imagined to have been.

Equipment. The hunter's equipment includes his clothing, camping equipment, and weapons. His clothing must be suitable for the climate and terrain in which he intends to hunt. As in all outdoor activities, his footgear especially must be appropriate. Camping equipment and supplies may be provided by private or commercial hunting lodges, by professional guides, or by safaris. If on his own, the hunter (or party) must provide for a tent or other shelter; all the equipment and provisions needed for cooking, eating, sleeping, and all other necessary or desired activities; and for first aid or other emergencies for the duration of the trip—all in relation to the transport that will be available.

Choice of weapons

Weapons are selected according to the particular game being sought. For big game, rifles are used (an exception being that in some areas regulations for deer require the use of a shotgun firing a slug). Shotguns are used for shooting waterfowl, game birds, and most small animals, although squirrel hunters prefer a small (.22 calibre) rifle. Bows and arrows and crossbows are used chiefly for small game, but bow hunting for deer has become so popular in some areas of the United States, for example, that special seasons have been set aside for it. Other large game has successfully been taken with a bow, including grizzly and Kodiak bear, moose, and most of the other big-game animals of North America, Africa, and India (see also SHOOTING and ARCHERY).

Instead of weapons, more and more sportsmen, increasingly aware of the need to preserve surviving stocks of game, go into the field equipped with cameras to stalk and photograph animals in their native habitats.

Methods. There are many methods of hunting, the method used depending on the type of country in which the game is found, the climate and weather, the size and habits of the game being sought, and the preferences of the hunter.

Basic methods. The basic methods of hunting for sport are stalking, still-hunting, tracking, driving, sitting up, and calling.

In open country free from trees, game can be viewed from afar; in these conditions a slow and stealthy approach is necessary, use being made of every tuft of grass, rock, or hollow as a means of concealment, with careful attention being paid to the direction of the wind. This is known as stalking.

In dense forest, undergrowth, brush, or scrub, it is impossible to see more than a few yards. Game in these conditions is come upon suddenly, and the best chance of getting a shot is to walk slowly and cautiously, ever on the alert. This form of hunting has been known by different names—as "jumping" a deer, for example—but it is thought that the North American still-hunting is more descriptive of the general method.

Some animals cannot be stalked or still-hunted, particularly elephants and other large animals that herd together. They leave well-defined tracks, or spoor, in soft ground, and a skillful hunter can follow their trail even on hard ground. This method is called tracking.

Other animals inhabit, or retire to, patches of dense jungle so thick that it is impossible for a man to advance silently within shooting distance. Tracking and still-hunting are out of the question, and there the best chance of success is to drive the animal out into the open or along some path where the hunter is waiting. This is done with the help of a number of men or dogs, or, in certain parts of India, with a line of elephants—methods universally known as driving or beating. If, however, no form of help is available in circumstances such as these, the only course for the sportsman is to wait in hiding over some spot where the animal will probably pass or return. Such a place may be a water hole, game trail, crossing point (such as a saddle between two mountains, for example), or a salt block; in the case of beasts of prey, it may be a half-eaten kill (as noted above, however, sitting up over water or a block of salt is not generally considered a sportsmanlike procedure, and it is prohibited by law in some localities). This waiting method is known as sitting up, or sitting. In the German *Hochstand* version of sitting up, which has also been adopted by the British, the hunter waits on a shooting platform erected in a tree to ambush animals passing below.

Another form of hunting, commonly practiced in pursuit of deer, is known as calling. It consists of waiting in hiding and making noises in imitation of the call of a female during the rutting season or of the male making a challenge. In either case the caller hopes a male will answer and gradually approach, believing the caller to be a possible mate or a probable antagonist. Calling deer is one of the oldest European hunting techniques, dating back long before the introduction of firearms. Much used by hunters of roebuck in Germany and Austria, it has been successfully adopted by moose hunters in North America.

Small game variants. The basic methods of hunting are used in hunting small game. But their application in some instances represents differences of substantial magnitude. A team of beaters driving grouse, partridges, or pheasants over a party of shooters waiting in camouflaged butts, or shooting stands, is an activity of an order different from that of the large band of beaters (or a line of elephants) trying to drive a tiger out of a jungle swamp.

A form of another basic method, sitting up, is the most popular method of hunting waterfowl. But instead of sitting in a tree or on a *Hochstand*, the shooter crouches in a blind in a lake or pond, along a shore line, in shallow water, or, especially on the Canadian prairies, in stooks (stubble fields). Before the blind are placed decoys made of wood or other materials. Wild birds, passing over, notice the flock of "feeding ducks" (or geese) and swing in to alight. When the decoyed birds come within shotgun range, the hunters fire. In Great Britain this method is known as flighting. Sitting up by waiting in

Table 1: Selected List of Big Game Animals

	where found
Antelope	plains, savannas, deserts; some forests; some jungles and swamps
Addox	North Africa (Sahara); oryx-like
Antelope, roan	southeast Africa
Antelope, sable	northern Transvaal, Angola; one of the top ten trophies, strictly preserved
Antelope, Tibetan	Tibet (Ch'iang-T'ang)
Black buck	Asia (India); small, 85 lbs; spiral horns; protected (successfully transplanted in South America and Texas)
Bongo	West Africa (Kenya, Congo, Sierra Leone), one of the top ten trophies; a forest dweller; 500 lbs
Bushbuck	East Africa (Kenya)
Chamois	central and southern Europe
Dikdik	East Africa (Kenya)
Eland, common	east to southern Africa
Eland, Derby's, or giant	northwest Africa (The Sudan); world's largest antelope; weighs one ton
Gazelle	Mongolia and Tibet through southwestern Asia; north, east, and central Africa
Gazelle, Grant's	East Africa (Kenya)
Gazelle, Somering's	East Africa (Somalia)
Gazelle, Thompson's	East Africa
Gemsbok	southeast Africa (Kalahari and surrounding desert)
Goat, Rocky Mountain	northwestern North America
Koodoo (Kudu)	southeast Africa (Zambia, Mozambique)
Lechwe, Mrs. Gray's	North Africa (swamps along the White Nile); 200 lbs; Turkish-slipper hoofs
Nilgai	India
Nyala, or inyala	southeast Africa (Mozambique, Zululand); a cousin of the koodoo
Nyala, mountain	Southeast Asia
Oryx	northeast and East Africa
Oryx, Arabian	western Asia
Oryx, Scimitar	North Africa (southeast of the Sahara); magnificent curving horns
Pronghorn, pronghorned, or American antelope	western North America
Sitatunga, or water antelope	west central Africa (Uganda)
Springbok	Africa
Bears	mountains; forests; the far north; some jungles and swamps
Alaskan brown bear	Pacific slope of Alaska and islands (Kodiak Island)
American black bear	northern North America (Canada, Alaska)
European brown bear	central and southern Europe, northern U.S.S.R.
Grizzly bear	northwestern North America
Himalayan, or Asian, black bear	Himalayas, India; 250 lbs
Himalayan brown bear (related to European brown)	Himalayas
Polar bear	circumpolar; protected by international treaty
Sloth, or honey bear	India, Sri Lanka, Burma
Buffalo	plains, savannas, deserts; jungles and swamps
Cape, or African, buffalo	East and southeast Africa; one of the most dangerous to hunt; requires special license
Indian buffalo	India to Indonesia; 5 ft horns; extinct in Bihār and Bengal; requires special license elsewhere
Indian, or water, buffalo	India, Sri Lanka; Southeast Asia
West African buffalo, or bush cow	western Africa
Cats	forests; plains, savannas, deserts; jungles and swamps; some in the far north
Jaguar	South America to southern North America
Leopard	western Asia, Southeast Asia, India, Sri Lanka, Burma
Leopard, snow, or ounce	Tibet, Himalayas
Lion	East Africa (Kenya, Tanzania, Botswana); black-maned males among the most prized trophies; one of the most dangerous to hunt; requires special license
Lynx, Tibetan	Tibet and Himalayas
Mountain lion, cougar, or puma	western North and South America
Tiger	western through southern and southeastern Asia; prized trophy, now protected in India and some other areas

	where found
Deer	mountains; forests; the far north; some jungles and swamps
Barasingh	India; 400 lbs; near extinction, now protected
Caribou	northern North America (Canada, Alaska)
Chital	Asia; spotted coat; huge antlers; abundant
Deer, fallow	Europe
Deer, mule, blacktail, or Columbia black-tailed	western North America
Deer, red	Europe
Deer, sika	eastern Asia including Japan
Deer, Schomburgh's	Thailand
Deer, swamp	India
Deer, Thorold's	Tibet and Himalayas
Deer, Virginia white-tail	eastern North America
Elk	northern Europe, Asia (Scandinavia; European, Siberian U.S.S.R.)
Maral	western Asia
Moose	northwestern North America (Canada, Alaska)
Reindeer	northern Europe, Asia (Scandinavia; European, Siberian U.S.S.R.)
Roebuck	Europe, western Asia
Sambar, or Ceylon elk	India, Southeast Asia; 600 lbs
Shou	Himalayas
Stag, Kashmir	Himalayas
Wapiti, or American elk	North America (Rocky Mountains)
Yarkand stag	Turkestan
Elephant	jungles and swamps
African elephant	East Africa, western and west central Africa; one of the most dangerous to hunt; requires special license
Indian elephant	Southeast Asia, India, Sri Lanka, Burma
Rhinoceros	jungles and swamps
Black rhinoceros	East Africa (Kenya); 3 tons (1,360 kg); one of the most dangerous to hunt; requires special license
Indian rhinoceros	India
Javan rhinoceros	Southeast Asia
Sumatran rhinoceros	Southeast Asia
White rhinoceros	East Africa (reserves in southern Sudan, northern Congo, Uganda)
Wild ox	tropical jungles
Gaur, Indian bison, or seledang	Southeast Asia, India, Burma, Malay peninsula; up to 2,700 lbs; requires special license
Tsine, or banteng	Burma
Wild sheep and goats	mountains; plains, savannas, and deserts
Ammon	central Asia
Argali	central Asia
Argali, Tibetan, or nayaur	central Asia, Tibet
Bharal, or wild blue sheep	Himalayas and Tibet
Ibex	northeast Africa and western Asia (the Red Sea littoral), Central Asia, Himalayas, Europe
Markhor	Himalayas westward to Afghanistan
Mouflon	western Asia, Sardinia
Pasan, or Persian wild goat	western Asia
Sheep, Ammor	Asia (Altaic Mountains)
Sheep, Barbary, or aoudad	North Africa
Sheep, Dall	North America (Alaska)
Sheep, Karelin	Asia (Tien Shan)
Sheep, Marco Polo's	Asia (Pamir Plateau); greatest of wild sheep
Sheep, Rocky Mountain, or bighorn	western North America (Mexico to Arctic)
Sheep, Stone	northwestern North America (British Columbia to Yukon)
Tahr	western Asia, Himalayas, India
Takin	India-Burma border at 10,000 ft; 500 lbs
Urial	Himalayas
Others	
Boar, wild	central Europe (West Germany)
Goral (goatlike Bovidae)	Himalayas
Okapi (allied to giraffe)	Africa (Congo)
Serow (goatlike Bovidae)	Himalayas
Wolf	Tibet, Himalayas, northwestern North America, northern U.S.S.R.
Zebra	Africa (Kenya)

concealment on the line of the birds' migration is also used by hunters of waterfowl and other migrating game birds—*e.g.*, snipe and woodcock. Waiting along known routes to and from feeding grounds also is used.

The method of calling is also used in hunting wildfowl. Some hunters are extraordinarily skillful in using a duck or goose call to entice the wild birds into range; but the calls are flock or feeding calls, not enticements or challenges to the male.

When the ground is covered with snow, tracking is a favourite method of small game hunters, especially for rabbits. The general method of hunting game birds in dense cover is still-hunting. Some small game animals such as the North American woodchuck and prairie dog and the European marmot are hunted by stalking.

Extended hunting expeditions

Safaris. Safari hunting implies an expedition into remote country to reach the selected hunting grounds, a hunt lasting from several days to a number of weeks. The term is from the Arabic *safarīyah*, of a trip or journey, and originally was applied to such expeditions in East

Africa. The safari itself is the caravan consisting of all the equipment, supplies, and necessary personnel. The safari is led by one or more professional hunters (in former years known as "white hunters"). Until recently the caravan would require large numbers of porters to carry the necessary equipment and supplies; they have been largely replaced by trucks and smaller four-wheel-drive vehicles.

A safari usually includes cooks, gun bearers, trackers, skinners, and other service personnel.

Hunting with hounds and gun. Throughout the history of hunting, hounds have been used to track and kill game. Early evidence includes remains found in Neolithic and earlier deposits, and ancient Egyptian wall paintings show greyhounds hunting gazelles.

Use of hounds and gun dogs

One of the principal types of hunting with hounds is coursing, the pursuit of game by hounds hunting by sight and not by scent. The dogs used are of the greyhound, deerhound, wolfhound, and Afghan type, collectively known as gazehounds, and the quarry are gazelle and other game of the plains, as well as deer and wolves. In Great Britain the sport of stag hunting with hounds, once the most fashionable of noble sports, was called hunting at force. The coursing of greyhounds after hare developed in the Near East and later was taken to Great Britain and thence to the United States. In it, two hounds at a time pursue one hare and are judged on points of performance. Out of it developed the sport of greyhound racing with a mechanical lure.

Another principal type of hunting with hounds is the pursuit of game by hounds hunting by scent, including fox hunting. Other small game hunted by scent include hare, rabbit, and, popular in some areas of the central and southern United States, raccoon. Hounds that hunt by scent also are used to track and tree or bring to bay many species of large game including, for example, bear and mountain lion (cougar). They are also used instead of beaters to drive big game from cover.

One aspect of hunting with hounds, whether by sight or scent, that has been of special appeal to many sportsmen has been following the chase on horseback, as has been associated specifically with the British forms of stag and fox hunting.

Spaniels, setters, and pointers, which hunt by sight as well as scent, now are known as gun dogs, but their history long antedates the appearance of the gun. Certainly in Roman times, perhaps much earlier, such dogs were used for driving game birds and waterfowl into nets and for finding game to which falcons could be flown.

Retrieval of game

The growing use of fowling pieces and sporting guns in the 17th century called for a new skill on the part of dogs: finding and retrieving shot birds falling at a distance (sometimes beyond obstacles such as rivers) or, if merely winged, running to cover. The adaptable setters, spaniels, and pointers learned to perform this function, as they still do, though the retrieving instinct has faded in some strains of pointers and setters through disuse. When the muzzle-loading gun was superseded by the breech-loader, the pattern and tempo of shooting changed. More frequent shots meant more game to be brought in. Instant reloading meant less time for retrieval. The need for the specialist retriever had arrived. Hence, modern retriever breeds have evolved only since the later 19th century, unlike the pointers, setters, and spaniels with their millennium and more of selective, purposeful breeding.

All retrievers are composite, their genetic composition heavily influenced by the necessity of producing a dog that can retrieve over water.

The functions of the three groups are now distinct. Pointers and setters work only prior to the shot, retrievers only after it, and spaniels all the time. So pointers and setters range freely, covering a beat about a quarter of a mile wide. On locating game it is essential that it not be flushed until the shooter arrives, and the dogs indicate it by the characteristic pose—motionless, gaze directed at the source of game scent, one forepaw raised, tail extended stiff and straight—until the command is given to put the birds into the air. Spaniels hunt only within gunshot and flush their game instantly. They then halt, to avoid distracting the shooter, and remain still until ordered to bring in whatever is shot or to continue hunting. Retrievers work on colder lines of scent and at much greater distance from the shooter than spaniels do, being especially useful to duck hunters to retrieve birds downed in the water.

PRINCIPAL GAME HABITATS

Big-game habitats. *Mountains.* The principal game animals sought in the high mountains include wild sheep and goat in the mountains of western North America from Mexico to the Arctic Circle, of Asia Minor and the Russian Caucasus, of Central Asia and the Himalayas, of North and South China, and of central and southern Europe. Bears are found in the Himalayas and in the mountains of western North America, northern Europe, and, more rarely, central and southern Europe. In Scandinavia, reindeer are found above the timberline.

Forests. Below the mountain peaks and on the forested slopes are found bear, deer (including, in North America, the wapiti, or American elk), wolf, and, more rarely, mountain lion (cougar), leopard, and lynx. The forests of mountain slopes, hills, and lowlands are the principal habitat of deer in North America, Europe, and Asia and of bear, wolf (in some areas), and forest-dwelling antelope, which also are found in Africa. The largest member of the deer family, known as the moose in America and the elk in Europe, is found in the northern forests of those continents. Other forest dwellers in Asia include leopards and tigers.

Plains, savannas, and deserts. Antelope, gazelle, and sheep and goat are characteristic of the plains, savannas, and deserts of the world. North America also has the pronghorn (a distant relative of the antelope also known as the pronghorned, or American, antelope) and, until its near-extinction in the late 1800s, the bison. In Africa, in addition to the more than 60 different species of antelope and gazelle, there are zebra, giraffe, and okapi; and the lion, often thought of as a jungle dweller, subsists off the animals of the plains. In Tibet the range of the Tibetan antelope is the northern desert at an altitude of 15,000 feet (about 5,000 metres), where also are found herds of wild yak. Some wild cattle (buffalo) are also found on the plains and deserts of Asia and Africa, and the only big-game animal of Australia is the buffalo, descended from domesticated cattle that escaped to the wild, and is now found on the bushland plains of the Northern Territory.

Rain forests and swamps. The most sought-after big-game animals of the African swamps and rain forest include the lion, leopard, rhinoceros, elephant, buffalo, and water antelope (sitatunga). The tropical rain forests of Asia harbour tiger, wild ox (gaur), buffalo, deer, bear, elephant, and rhinoceros. Jaguars are found in the jungles of South America.

The far north. The animals of the far north include the polar bear (now internationally protected), reindeer and elk (from northern Europe across Asia), caribou and moore (North America), lynx, bear, and wolf. The North American musk-ox is now protected. It is thought that some of the best hunting grounds of the future may lie in the far north of the Soviet Union.

Small-game habitats. Although small-game hunting, or "shooting," as it is known in Great Britain and western Europe, is practiced in most countries of the world, it is most popular as a sport in Europe and North America. Small game exists where big game exists and often is shot to supplement provisions or as an incidental sport for safaris or other extended expeditions. But in Europe and North America it usually is sought closer to home—in wooded, open, or hilly countryside; on farmlands, prairies, moors, and wetlands; around lakes and ponds; and along watercourses. Small game found in these habitats include upland game birds—grouse, partridge, pheasant, quail, and, in North America, wild turkey—and small animals including fox, hare, rabbit, and, again in North America, squirrel; in some areas other small animals (*e.g.,* raccoon, opossum, woodchuck [groundhog],

Game birds

Table 2: Selected List of Small Game Birds and Animals

	where found
Upland game birds and shore birds	
Grouse	
Capercaillie	Europe, Asia
Grouse, black	Europe, Asia
Grouse, blue	North America
Grouse, pinnated, or prairie chicken (sharp-tailed grouse and sage hen)	north central North America
Grouse, red	British Isles (Scotland and Ireland)
Grouse, ruffed	north central North America
Grouse, spruce, or Canada spruce	northern North America
Grouse, willow	Europe excepting British Isles
Ptarmigan	British Isles, Scandinavia
Ptarmigan, white-tailed	northwestern North America
Partridge	
Chukar or chukor	southeastern Europe to India, arid regions of North America
Gray, or Hungarian partridge	central Europe, western North America
Red-legged partridge	Europe (Spain, Portugal, France)
Woodcock	
American woodcock	North America
European woodcock	Europe
Others	
Dove, mourning (pigeon)	North America, British Isles, Europe
Pheasant	Europe, north central North America, Asia, Australia, New Zealand
Quail (many species)	North America, Europe, Africa, Asia
Snipe, common	Europe, North America
Turkey, wild	North America
Waterfowl	
Duck	
Duck, ring-necked	North America
Duck, wood	North America
Mallard	North America, Europe, Asia, North Africa, Australia
Garganey	England, Asia
Pintail	North America, Europe, Asia
Pochard (canvasback)	North America, Europe, Asia
Scaup	North America, Europe, Asia
Sheldrake (shelduck)	North America, Europe, Asia, North Africa, Australia, South America
Shovler	North America, Europe, Asia
Teal	North America
Widgeon (baldpate)	North America, Europe
Goose	
Barnacle	Europe, Asia
Brant (brent)	North America, Europe, Asia
Goose, bean	Asia, Africa
Goose, blue	North America
Goose, Canadian	North America
Goose, snow	North America
Goose, white-fronted	Europe, Asia, North America
Grayleg	Europe, Asia
Small animals	
Fox	
Red fox	Europe and North America north of Mexico
Gray fox	North America except western plains
Hare	
Hare, arctic	northern North America
Hare, common	British Isles, central and southern Europe
Rabbit, European	Europe
Rabbit, jack	western North America
Rabbit, marsh	southeastern North America
Rabbit, North American, or cottontail	North America east of Rocky Mountains
Rabbit, snowshoe	northern North America
Rabbit, swamp	southeastern North America
Others	
Opossum	North America
Raccoon	North America except western plains
Squirrel	North America, Europe, Asia

marmots, and prairie dogs) may be hunted as small game or as predators. Migratory birds (*e.g.*, snipe and woodcock) and waterfowl, or wildfowl, especially ducks and geese, usually are shot along the well-defined north–south flyways over which they migrate.

BIBLIOGRAPHY. There are many authoritative works on the history of hunting and the practice of the sport. Some books treat the game itself and some the art of hunting it. Many titles could be listed here, but representative are NASH BUCKINGHAM's excellent works, *De Shootinest Gent'man, and Other Tales* (1943), *Mark Right!* (1944), *Tattered Coat* (1944), *Ole Miss'* (1946), and *Hallowed Years* (1953), incomparable tales of shooting game, upland game birds, and waterfowl. CLYDE ORMOND has covered a wide range with his *Hunting Our Biggest Game* (1956), *Hunting Our Medium Size Game* (1958), *Small Game Hunting* (1967), and *Complete Book of Hunting*, 2nd ed. rev. (1972). RAY CAMP did a superlative job of editing *The Hunter's Encyclopedia* (1951), a source of invaluable information by authoritative contributors. BYRON W. DALRYMPLE, *Complete Guide to Hunting Across North America* (1970), is a reliable source of up-to-date information. Big-game hunters will be fascinated by RUSSELL B. AITKEN's highly regarded *Great Game Animals of the World* (1969); LOREN D. STARK, *Big Game Hunting on Three Continents* (1971), intimate, first-person stories by a dedicated sportsman relating rewarding experiences of a score of safaris; ER M. SHELLEY, *Hunting Big Game with Dogs in Africa* (1940); W.D.M. BELL, *Karamojo Safari* (1949), whose exploits hunting elephants gained him distinction; and JIM CORBETT, *Man-Eaters of India* (1957), on tigers. CHARLES ASKINS, *The African Hunt* (1958), is an intriguing work by a recognized authority. The deer hunter is referred to ARTHUR H. CARHART, *Hunting North American Deer* (1946); and RUSSELL TINSLEY, *Hunting the Whitetail Deer* (1965), not to overlook GEORGE MATTIS, *Whitetail: Fundamentals and Fine Points for the Hunter* (1969). ALBERT M. DAY contributed a classic work with his NORTH AMERICAN WATERFOWL, 2nd ed. (1959). Nimrods questing upland game birds will find recommended reading in RAY P. HOLLAND, *My Gun Dogs* (1929); WILLIAM H. FOSTER, *New England Grouse Shooting* (1942); DURWARD L. ALLEN (ed.), *Pheasants in North America* (1956); and EUGENE V. CONNETT (ed.), *Upland Game Bird Shooting in America* (1930). Turkey hunters are referred confidently to ROGER LATHAM, *Complete Book of the Wild Turkey* (1956).

Big game: ROWLAND WARD, *Records of Big Game*, 13th ed. (1969), the definitive list of trophies, according to international points standards; JAMES E. CORBETT, *Jungle Lore* (1953), a standard work on Indian big game; JOHN H. TAYLOR, *Big Game and Big Game Rifles* (1953); ANTHONY CULLEN and SYDNEY DOWNEY, *Saving the Game* (1960); T.R.H. OWEN, *Hunting Big Game, with Gun and Camera in Africa* (1960); JOHN PEARSON, *Wildlife and Safari in Kenya* (1967); *The South and East African Year Book and Guide* and *The Year Book and Guide to Southern Africa* (both annual), directories to local conditions, facilities, and legislation.

Small game: J.E.M. RUFFER, *The Art of Good Shooting* (1972); and CHARLES LANCASTER, *The Art of Shooting*, 13th ed. (1962), two standard works on the use and etiquette of the shotgun; P.R.A. MOXON, *Gundogs: Training and Field Trials* (1952); JAMES WENTWORTH-DAY, *The Dog in Sport* (1938); MICHAEL BRANDER, *The International Encyclopedia of Shooting* (1972); CHARLES COLES, *The Complete Book of Game Conservation* (1971); NOEL SEDGWICK, PETER WHITAKER, and JEFFREY HARRISON, *The New Wildfowler in the 1970's* (1970).

Hunting to hounds (fox hunting): PETER BECKFORD, *Thoughts on Hunting* (1781); WILLOUGHBY DE BROKE, *Hunting the Fox* (1920); A. HENRY HIGGINSON, *Letters from an Old Sportsman to a Young One* (1929); J. IVESTER LLOYD, *Beagling* (1954); DAVID JAMES and WILSON STEPHENS, *In Praise of Hunting* (1960); MICHAEL CLAYTON, *A Hunting We Will Go* (1967); GUY WHEELER, *The Year 'Round: A Perennial Miscellany for Fox-Hunters* (1972); SIEGFRIED SASSOON, *The Memoirs of a Foxhunting Man* (1930, reprinted 1967); DALESMAN, *Here Lies My Story* (1964); HAROLD P. HEWETT, *The Fairest Hunting* (1963); H.B.C. POLLARD, *The Mystery of Scent* (1937).

(Wi.S./W.F.B./G.P.L.)

Hunyadi, János

Hungarian general and governor of the Kingdom of Hungary from 1446 to 1452, János Hunyadi (Latin Johannes de Hunyad) was the most successful military leader against the Turks in the 15th century.

Hunyadi's date of birth is unknown; he is first mentioned, probably as a small child, in the diplomas by which King Sigismund transferred possessions of Hunyad castle (now at Hunedoara, Romania) to one of his knights, Woyk (or Vajk), who was Hunyadi's father. János may have been born a few years before the issuance of these diplomas, perhaps in 1407. He was of Wallachian (a region now in Romania) ancestry.

According to the usage of Hungarian noblemen of the time, János took his family name after his landed estate. The royal donation had elevated the Hunyadi family to the top ranks of the lesser (nonbaronial) group of Hungarian nobility. Proprietors of a domain containing 40 villages, they were considered as well-to-do but ranked far below the great magnates who formed the king's council and exercised the real power in the country.

Early career

Young János followed the normal career of his class. As a knight leading troops of up to 12 mounted warriors, he offered his services to more influential members of the ruling class. Through the influence of Stephan Lazarević, prince of the northern Serbs, and Philippo Scolari, one of Sigismund's best soldiers, Hunyadi found his way to the royal court. Soon after, he married Erzsébet Szilágyi, daughter of a nobleman who had distinguished himself in military actions along the borders. The young knight accompanied the King to Italy and other foreign countries. In Milan he made the acqaintance of the *condottiere* (mercenary captain) Francesco Sforza and studied the new military art of Italy; he later studied the techniques of warfare developed by the Hussite insurgents in Bohemia.

On his return home, Hunyadi was considered the best warrior in southern Hungary. He was still without high office, but he commanded 50 to 100 armed men against the increasing wave of Turkish attacks. His victories, though of local importance, attracted wide notice. With Ottoman troops occupying Serbia in 1439, the peril of a direct invasion of Hungary became imminent. Thus, Hunyadi was appointed *bán* (military governor) of Severin (now in Romania), a district exposed to continual attacks. His success in this command brought him rapid advancement and higher honours, including gifts of landed properties and other income. He was made *voivode* (governor) of Transylvania, count of Temes (now Timiş, Romania), captain of Belgrade, and military leader of the whole defense system on the southern borders. He soon reached and surpassed the level of the wealthiest old baronial families. In the years that followed, he was able to repel the Turks not only from the borderlands of Hungary but from neighbouring Walachia as well.

After the death of the Habsburg German king Albert II, who, as Sigismund's son-in-law, also was the king of Hungary, Hunyadi supported the election of the young Polish king Władysław III (Ulászló I in Hungary) in the hope of active and powerful support for a crusade against the Turks.

The "Long Campaign"

The famous "Long Campaign" took place in the autumn and winter of 1443–44. The preparations needed time. Internal troubles in Hungary and the hostility of the Habsburgs were mollified with papal help. Venice and the papacy supported Hunyadi's army financially and diplomatically. Poland and other neighbouring countries sent troops, and in Hungary the King levied an "extraordinary" tax for the crusade. Hunyadi himself recruited some 10,000 to 12,000 well-trained soldiers, including Czech veterans of the Hussite wars. Hunyadi recognized the inefficiency and unreliability of feudal levies and was one of the first European commanders to employ a regular army on a large scale. The whole army, after having penetrated into Serbian territories under Turkish occupation, reached a total in excess of 30,000 men. The combined forces crossed the Danube in October and occupied Niš (now in Yugolsavia), Sofia (now in Bulgaria), and some fortified Turkish garrisons. Hunyadi's troops, advancing ahead of the rest of the army, prevented the Turks from unifying their forces and dispersed them in a series of battles. The crusader force reached the Balkan Mountains in December, but frost and difficulties of supply forced its retreat. They returned to Buda at the beginning of February, having broken the Sultan's power in Bosnia, Hercegovina, Serbia, Bulgaria, and Albania.

By courtesy of the trustees of the British Museum; photograph, J.R. Freeman & Co., Ltd.

Hunyadi, engraving by André Thevet (1504–1592).

The success of the campaign was unprecedented in the history of Turkish wars in Europe and evoked great enthusiasm in the Christian world. Sultan Murad II sued for peace. A 10-year truce was concluded but was broken when it was learned that a Venetian fleet was sailing to the Dardanelles to prevent the Sultan from recrossing into Europe. In July the Hungarian army went on the offensive to drive the remaining Ottoman forces from Europe. When the Venetian fleet failed to reach the Dardanelles, however, the Sultan crossed over with a large army and overwhelmed the outnumbered Christian forces at Varna on November 10, 1444. Although Hunyadi's troops were able to disperse the Turkish cavalry, King Ulászló's attack on the Sultan's camp miscarried. The King was killed, and Hunyadi narrowly escaped.

Governor of Hungary

The renewal of feudal anarchy in Hungary after the death of Ulászló demanded exceptional measures, and in 1446 Hunyadi was elected to rule the country as a governor during the minority of the young King Ladislas Posthumus (László V in Hungary). Hampered internally by the jealousy of the magnates and harassed externally by Emperor Frederick III, Hunyadi nevertheless restored order and tried to reorganize the economic, political, and military base of the country for a counterattack against the Turks. In 1448, before he could make contact with his Albanian allies, he met the Turkish army at Kosovo, where he lost a hard-fought battle. After that defeat his influence in Hungary waned, though he remained captain general of the kingdom with the right to administer royal incomes. He was unable to launch a counterattack against the Turks and could not go to the aid of Constantinople during the Turkish onslaught in 1453. A few years later, Sultan Mehmed II, conqueror of Constantinople, mounted a new offensive and in 1456 laid siege to Belgrade. Hunyadi provisioned and armed the fortress of Belgrade. He collected a considerable army of mercenaries and was joined by a poorly equipped and ragged army of peasants. This untrained army, with the aid of Hunyadi's troops, won one of the most remarkable victories in the history of Turkish wars, on July 22, 1456. Not only was the siege raised, but the relieving forces actually made sorties into the enemy camp. A few days later, on August 11, Hunyadi died of an epidemic that had broken out among the troops. The military success remained unexploited, though not without consequences; Hungary was saved from Ottoman conquest for 70 years.

Though he never realized the dream of contemporary humanists of driving the Turks from Europe, Hunyadi earned a glorious name by his considerable successes and by the mere fact that he succeeded in stopping the supposedly invincible Turkish armies: hence, his characterization in contemporary sources, "the only fear of Turks" or—with an expression of Turkish origin—"war's lightning and thunderbolt"—an appraisal rarely granted by Turkish warriors even to their own leaders.

BIBLIOGRAPHY. There is no modern biography of Hunyadi in English. LAJOS ELEKES, *Hunyadi* (1952), is an analysis (in Hungarian) of contemporary sources concerning the family, personality, and political and military activities of Hunyadi, with bibliographical notes.

(L.El.)

Hupeh

Hupeh (Hu-bei in Pin-yin romanization), one of the 21 provinces of the People's Republic of China, lies in the heart of the country and forms a part of the middle basin of the Yangtze River. Until the reign of the great Ch'ing emperor K'ang Hsi (1661–1722), Hupeh and its neighbour Hunan formed a single province, Hu-kuang. They were then divided and given their present names, Hupeh (*hu*, "lake," *peh*, "north"; *i.e.*, north of the lakes of the Yangtze River) and Hunan (*nan*, "south"; south of the lakes). Hupeh has an area of 72,400 square miles (187,500 square kilometres). Its capital is Wu-han, the composite name of the three cities of Hankow, Han-yang, and Wu-ch'ang, which lie at the confluence of the Han Shui (Han River) and the Yangtze at a point approximately 600 miles from the sea and halfway between Shanghai and Chungking.

Historical background. When China was slowly evolving in the Honan–Shansi region during the Shang and Chou dynasties (18th to 3rd centuries BC), Hupeh formed part of the kingdom of Ch'u. It was subjugated by Ch'in Shih Huang Ti (221 to 210 BC), who created the first united empire of China; it was finally assimilated into the Chinese state under the Han dynasty (206 BC–AD 220). Hupeh at that time was described by the ancient Chinese historian Ssu-ma Ch'ien as:

> a large territory, sparsely populated, where people eat rice and drink fish soup; where land is tilled with fire and hoed with water; where people collect fruits and shellfish for food; where people enjoy self-sufficiency without commerce. The place is fertile and suffers no famine and hunger. Hence the people are lazy and poor and do not bother to accumulate wealth.

From this time on, the facility of communications afforded by its river system has caused Hupeh to figure prominently in Chinese history.

Since the mid-19th century it has been the centre of many momentous events, sometimes to its sorrow. The Taiping Rebellion, led by the Hakka, Hung Hsiu-ch'üan, broke out in Kwangsi in 1850, after which the rebel armies moved north, taking Wu-ch'ang in 1853. During the succeeding ten years the central plains of Hupeh and Hunan were terribly devastated by fighting and banditry. After China's defeat in the "Arrow" War of 1856–60, the Hupeh cities of Hankow, I-ch'ang, and Sha-shih were opened to Western nations as commercial ports. From this time on, European influence in central China steadily increased. Hankow became the head of international oceangoing traffic. In the first 20 years (*i.e.*, until 1880) trade was based almost exclusively on tea, but, with increasing Indian and Ceylonese competition, Hankow became the centre for the collection and processing of other central Chinese raw materials, notably vegetable oils, egg products, and tobacco.

Early role as a trade and industrial centre

Hupeh's industrialization began with the establishment of the Han-Yeh-P'ing ironworks in Han-yang by Chang Chih-tung, the governor of the province, who also established a cotton mill in Wu-ch'ang opposite Hankow. The ironworks had a checkered career. At first it enjoyed some government protection and tax exemption but later suffered from internal political unrest and instability, lack of capital, and poor management. Subsequently, a Japanese concern gained financial control with a view to securing ore from Hupeh for its ironworks in Japan. The Han-yang works were allowed, even induced, to fall into decay. They were destroyed by bombing during the Sino-Japanese War of 1937–45 and were restored only after the advent of the Communist government in 1949.

The Revolution of 1911, which established the Chinese republic, began in Hupeh. The army in Hankow mutinied; the soldiers, led by their commander, Li Yuan-hung, took the cities of Hankow, Han-yang, and Wu-ch'ang. Yüan Shih-k'ai led his northern troops, on behalf of the Emperor, against them and retook Hankow but was unable to cross the Yangtze and eventually retired. This was the only fighting of any significance during the revolution. When Nanking was taken by the Japanese in 1937, Hankow served as a temporary headquarters for the Nationalists, until their retreat to Chungking.

The landscape. *Physiography.* Almost all of Hupeh Province lies immediately north of the Yangtze River. Western Hupeh has highlands that lie at an altitude of over 6,000 feet and consist of the eastern extension of two ranges, the Ta Pa Shan and Fang Tou Shan (Chinese *shan*, "mountain range"), marking the boundary between Hupeh and Szechwan. The Shih Pao Shan range forms the boundary between southwest Hupeh and northwest Hunan. The level of the land falls rapidly, from west to east, to a lake-studded alluvial plain, much of which is no more than 200 feet above sea level. This flat or gently undulating country is often suddenly interrupted by steeply rising isolated hills or ranges. The plain is the remnant of a former depression or old lake basin formed in the Pliocene Epoch (from 2,500,000 to 7,000,000 years ago), which has largely been filled with eroded red sandstone from Szechwan and which covers beds of limestone, micaceous sandstone, quartzites, and conglomerates (rounded fragments of rock cemented together by another mineral substance). The process of filling in is not yet complete; in consequence, large areas adjoining the Yangtze and Han rivers are covered by innumerable shallow lakes.

Hupeh is bounded on the north by the eastern extension of the axis of the Tsinling Shan, T'ung-pai Shan, and Ta-pieh Shan ranges. In the southeast the Mu-fou Shan divides the province from Kiangsi. Along its central southern border there is no clear physical divide apart from the Yangtze itself; the lake plain continues uninterruptedly southward to the Tung-t'ing Hu (*hu*, "lake") in Hunan.

Rivers

The Yangtze, or Ch'ang—as it is known in Hupeh—cuts its way from the Szechwan Basin through the Ta-pa Shan in a series of magnificent gorges and descends rapidly to the Hupeh Plain in I-ch'ang. The bed of the river at I-ch'ang is only 130 feet above sea level and is 960 miles from the sea. From this point onward its velocity decreases and its bed widens as it winds its way across the province from west to east. Finally, it forces a passage between the Mu-fou Shan and Ta-pieh Shan into Anhwei and Kiangsi provinces. Here the river again narrows to less than half a mile in width. In its course through Hupeh the Yangtze receives the waters of two tributaries, the Han and the Ch'ing. It also receives, through the Tung-t'ing Hu, the entire drainage of Hunan. The Han, itself a considerable river even by Chinese standards, rises in the Tsinling Shan and flows eastward in Shensi Province for about 200 miles. On entering Hupeh, it turns south in a much broader valley, or floodplain, and widens its bed, which varies from half a mile to a mile in width over much of this stretch. About 100 miles from its confluence with the Yangtze at Hankow (*kow*, "mouth"), it turns east, threads its way through a maze of lakes, and, in the last few miles, narrows its bed to a mere 250 yards—a factor that is responsible for much flooding in summer.

The variation in the regime of the Yangtze between summer and winter is striking. At Hankow, where the river is nearly a mile wide, the average difference between summer and winter levels is 45 feet. In winter the river is sluggish, with many shallows, and is navigable up to Hankow only by specially built flat-bottomed river steamers of six feet draft. With the coming of the spring and summer rains the change is dramatic; the river comes down as a mighty flood. In times of exceptional flood, as in 1931 and 1954, the flow reaches astronomical figures. In 1954 the flow was measured at more than 2,500,000 cubic feet per second (*cf.* the London Thames, which has a flow of 2,300 cubic feet per second). In summer Hankow is an ocean port, capable of receiving vessels of 10,000 to 15,000 tons. There are, however, navigational hazards at this time. Flooding of large areas of the surrounding low-lying land is normal each summer, when river and lakes combine. Marco Polo, who visited the area in the 13th century, reported that in places the river was more than ten miles wide; his report was discredited as a gross exaggeration, but he had seen the Yangtze in the summer flood. At that season the danger to shipping is twofold. Great care has to be taken that a vessel does not stray from the true river course and become grounded in more shallow water. If this happens, refloating is an urgent matter as the river is liable to quite rapid falls in level, and the vessel may be left high and dry for a year. Navigation lights, in the form of lightships and light buoys, have been maintained fairly efficiently over the last 50 years; these have been greatly improved since the establishment of stable government in 1949, so that in recent years the passage has become much safer.

Hupeh lies in a neutral soil zone between the pedocals (soils of arid or semi-arid regions, enriched in lime) of North China and the pedalfers (soils of humid regions, enriched in alumina and iron) of the south. The uplands are mainly brown mountain earth, the lower hilly lands yellow-brown soil, and the lowlands alluvium and red earth.

Climate. Hupeh's rainfall follows the general Chinese seasonal pattern, governed by the rainbearing monsoon winds. Hankow, 118 feet above sea level, has an average minimum rainfall of about an inch in December and a maximum of almost ten inches in June, with a total annual fall of about 50 inches. Rainfall throughout the province decreases from southeast to northwest. Much of this rainfall is caused by cyclones, which pass down the Yangtze Valley from west to east. In July 1931 a series of seven cyclones passed in rapid succession, bringing phenomenal rainfall. The river rose to the record height of 53.6 feet, topping the bund (embankment) in Hankow by six feet. Disastrous floods, covering about 35,000 square miles, much of which was under crops, resulted.

Flood control measures

A similar rise occurred in 1954, but big cities, such as Wu-han, were saved because local dikes had been raised and strengthened under the new regime. Apart from the doubtful remedy of dike raising, the main short-term attempt at flood control has been the construction of two large artificial retention basins, one at Sha-shih (covering 355 square miles, with a capacity of 7,000,000,000 cubic yards), between the Yangtze and the Tung-t'ing Hu, and the other at Tachiatai, between the Han and the Yangtze rivers. These basins form reservoirs into which the waters can be deflected and held, if necessary, while the rivers are in spate. The long-term scheme to meet the flood menace is to build great dams across the river in and above the gorges, but this is still in the planning stage.

Hupeh winters, although usually short, are often rigorous, with heavy and glazed frost and some snow brought by bitter north winds in January and February, when the average temperatures are 40° F (4° C) and 43° F (6° C), respectively. Summers are hot, with July temperatures averaging 85° F (29° C), and are long and oppressive because of the high relative humidity. Any light breeze by day tends to die out in the evening, leading to intolerable nights when mothers bring their bamboo beds into the streets and sit fanning their children through the weary hours. There are about 270 frostless days in the south and 250 in the north.

Vegetation. The natural vegetation of Hupeh is dense forest, but this was cleared from the lowlands and hills many centuries ago, leaving only the western highlands densely wooded. The forests and woodlands are mainly of *ma wei* (pine), *shu mu* (cedar), camphor, yellow sandalwood, maple, and poplar. As a result of deforestation, soil erosion has been serious. Despite sporadic efforts to plant the hillsides with trees on "Arbor Day" during the earlier decades of the 20th century, the poverty of the people and the demand for fuel has led to the trees being continually stripped. Since the advent of the People's Republic there has been a determined effort at afforestation and its maintenance.

Animal life. There is a sparsity of large wild animals. Some small barking deer are found in the scant cover on the hills rising from the plain. Deer and wild pig are plentiful in the wooded mountains in the west. There is abundant birdlife, including wild duck, pheasants, blue jays, and golden orioles. Snakes, centipedes, and scorpions abound.

Population. Hupeh's population in 1970 was estimated at 33,700,000 which was nearly 4,300,000 less than that of Hunan. It has an average density of 440 people per square mile. Its ethnic composition is homogeneous, being overwhelmingly Han-jen (*i.e.*, Chinese with affinities rather to the north than south). Their dialect is Hupehese, which is closely akin to pure Mandarin. In 1953–54 there were about 40,000 minority peoples, of whom about two-thirds were Muslim, widely scattered throughout north Hupeh and the Han plain. There are some T'uchia and Miao people in the highlands of the southwest.

Population centres

Population distribution, as in the rest of China, is predominantly rural, only about 11 percent being classed as urban. The main concentrations of rural population are found in the lake plain around the Yangtze and lower Han, notably from Wu-han downriver to Huang-shih; the lower Han Basin below Chung-hsiang (former An-lu) to Wu-han; and between I-ch'ang and Sha-shih. There is a smaller concentration at Hsiang-fan at the confluence of the Han and Tang rivers. Density in these lake plains is over 520 people per square mile; in some specially favoured areas it is as high as 1,000 per square mile. Here the villages are often strung along high, mud riverbanks, which give safety in time of flood. Away from the lake plain, in the low hill regions to the north and south, the density is usually 260 persons per square mile. Villages are small, usually ten families or less that very often comprise a production team. Villages are usually only a few *li* apart (*li* = one-third mile). In the mountainous west, density is less than 130 per square mile.

Urban population is concentrated in a few large towns and a large number of small ones. Wu-han (3,000,000 in 1970), the second largest industrial and commercial city in the Yangtze Basin, is a conurbation of the three cities of Hankow, the commercial and industrial centre; Han-yang, formerly residential but now largely industrialized; and Wu-ch'ang, the administrative, educational, and cultural hub of the province. Other large towns (with 1957–58 population estimates) are Huang-shih (200,000), 60 miles below Wu-han, an industrial and mining centre; Sha-shih (120,000); I-ch'ang (110,000); and Hsiang-fan (90,000). There are about 30 towns of 10,000 to 20,000 inhabitants and 180 small market towns. Formerly, many of the larger towns were walled; many of these walls have been demolished recently and the stone used for building and road construction.

Administration. Administration of the province, in common with the rest of China, has undergone revolutionary changes during the 20th century. It passed from rule of a viceroy under the Imperial Ch'ing dynasty (1900–11) to rule of a *tu-chün*, or warlord (1916–27). From 1928 to 1938 there was some attempt at local government of a democratic Western pattern, followed by the rule of the Japanese invader between 1938 and 1945. Then came several years of near chaos until the establishment of the People's Republic in 1949. From 1949 to 1954 Hupeh was part of the Central South Administrative Area, one of six such areas formed for ad hoc government during the period of recovery and rehabilitation. In 1954 provincial (*sheng*) government was re-established directly under the central government. This followed a common pattern throughout the country, with many local variations.

Provincial divisions

The province was divided into counties (*hsien*), which were subdivided into rural districts or villages (*hsiang*) and market towns (*chen*). Municipalities (*shih*) and autonomous regions (*chou*) for the government of minority peoples within the province were separately and directly responsible to the province. In 1958 this pattern of local government was further greatly modified by the formation of communes, which took over the duties of the rural districts and market towns (*hsiang* and *chen*) and were made responsible for the functioning of all local life at this level—for agriculture, industry, education, public health, local militia, recreation, etc. Much of the work and functions of the different bodies was loose and ill-defined, leaving room for adaptation to local circumstances. With the Cultural Revolution (1966–69), local administration underwent further upheaval and change and only in 1970 did it take definite shape. Hupeh, in company with other provinces, is now governed by a Revolutionary Committee composed of party cadres (CCP), army (PLA), and the revolutionary masses organization. The communes have lost many of their former powers.

The economy. *Agriculture.* Hupeh lies in the agricultural transition zone between the wheat-growing north and the rice-growing south. In south and southeast Hupeh, where rainfall is greater and irrigation more easily practiced, 40 to 60 percent of the cultivated land is devoted to rice growing and less than 15 percent to wheat. In northern parts, where rainfall is less and variability greater, rice occupies only 30 to 40 percent of the cultivated area and wheat over 30 percent. Over 70 percent of paddy area is planted with a single crop—middle-season rice (rice planted in the middle of the season after winter wheat or barley has been harvested)—new strains of which have a basic field-growing period (*i.e.*, from transplanting to harvesting) of only 90 days. Winter crops on paddy fields are usually wheat, barley, rape (a herb of the mustard family), broad beans, and green fertilizer (clover vetches, etc., which are ploughed back in). Irrigation in the hilly lands is mainly by gravity from ponds dammed higher up in the valleys. On the plains, where water has to be raised, wooden paddle pumps operated by hand are still used, but mechanized irrigation made much progress between 1960 and 1970, and electrical pumping stations are rapidly replacing human labour. Food production decreases rapidly westward, where cultivation is confined mainly to deep valleys in the highlands.

In 1957 the major food crops were rice and wheat; almost 20,000 acres were planted with rice and 10,000 acres with wheat. Other crops grown included barley, corn (maize), sweet potatoes, millet, beans, and peas. Hupeh ranks fourth—after Szechwan, Hunan, and Kwangtung—among China's rice-producing provinces.

Cotton and oil and fibre crops

Hupeh ranks high among the Chinese provinces as a producer of economic crops, of which cotton is the most important. In 1957 more than 300,000 tons of raw cotton were produced. Most of the cotton is short staple. The main growing area lies north of the Yangtze in a belt stretching from Sha-shih eastward along the lower Han to Wu-han. Most of the raw cotton is processed in the large modern textile mills of Han-yang and Wu-ch'ang. Other important economic crops are vegetable oils (sesame, peanut, and rapeseed) and fibres (ramie and hemp). Ramie is the fibre from which grass cloth or Chinese linen is made. Some tea is grown on the hills in the southeast. Tung oil, a valuable forest product used in paints and varnishes, comes mainly from the western regions and the upper reaches of the Han and Yüan rivers. It is pressed locally and sent down the rivers in bamboo crates lined with oiled paper.

Industry. Hupeh's mineral wealth consists chiefly of iron, copper, phosphorus ores, coal, and gypsum. Some of China's richest and best iron ore is found at Ta-yeh in southeastern Hupeh. It was on the exploitation of this ore, and of the coking coal of P'ing-hsiang in Hunan, that the Han-Yeh-P'ing ironworks in Han-yang were founded; it is also largely on the use of ore from Ta-yeh and from four newly opened mines that the Wu-han Iron and Steel Corporation, China's second largest integrated ironworks, is based. Completed in 1961, these works, some five miles below Hankow on the right bank of the Yangtze, cover about four square miles, have an annual output capacity of 3,000,000 tons of steel, and contain the largest blast furnaces in China. These and the blooming mills (which roll ingot steel into rails, bars, or girders) are entirely automatically controlled. Huang-shih on the right bank of the Yangtze near Ta-yeh has also developed as a large iron and steel centre.

Copper is found at Yang-hsin in the east and also at Ta-yeh. Reserves are large as compared with other provinces, and production has increased considerably in recent years. Bituminous coal is found in the west and anthracite (hard coal), generally in thin seams, in the south and east. There are large reserves of gypsum and salt in the northeast.

Transportation and communications. For more than 2,000 years waterways have been the main means of communication in Hupeh. The Yangtze and Han rivers, with their tributaries, are used by all manner of craft. Large ocean freighters reach Hankow, and small steam launches penetrate much farther inland. Huge coaster junks from Chekiang and Fukien provinces sail to Sha-shih and I-ch'ang, and the little stern-oared *hua tzu* (small boats each rowed from the stern by one man) ply the smaller streams. Steam and oil-fired craft carry only about one-tenth of the total waterborne freight. After 1950 much blasting work was done in the rocky rapids of the three gorges between I-ch'ang and Feng-chieh (Szechwan), making them navigable for 500- to 600-ton river steamers. By 1970 the navigational channel of this dangerous stretch was clearly shown by modern markers. In addition to the rivers, the lake plain is a network of drainage channels that are used for intercommunication by the local people. The main upstream traffic to Wu-han consists of vessels carrying coal, petroleum, iron and steel, machinery, ores, building material, cement, and cloth. Downstream traffic consists of timber in great rafts and craft carrying tung oil, crude varnish, medicinal herbs, raw cotton, ramie, tea, and egg products.

Railways

Until 1958, Hupeh had only 290 miles of railway. This consisted entirely of the single-track Peking to Hankow and Wu-ch'ang to Canton line, which ran from north to south across the province. Almost from the day of completion of the Peking–Hankow sector in 1905 it fell steadily into decay from neglect—caused by political unrest, corruption, or lack of funds. By 1949 the track, bridges, and culverts were in so parlous a state that speeds of over ten miles an hour in some stretches were dangerous. Rapid repair work was carried out by the Communist government; by 1951 the line was in good running order. In 1959 the completion of the bridge over the Yangtze between Han-yang and Wu-ch'ang—the first bridging of the river over a length of 3,400 miles—wrought a revolution in the system. Formerly, both Hankow and Wu-ch'ang were linked only by a ferry across the river. The bridge itself, which is about 5,430 feet long, was built by Russian and Chinese engineers. It carries a double-track rail on its lower level and a six-lane highway on its higher level. The building of the bridge greatly increased the value and efficiency of the whole north–south line from Peking to Canton, which had already been double-tracked. A new electrified line, serving the steelworks of Wu-han and Huang-shih, runs via Ta-yeh to Chiu-chiang in Kiangsi Province.

Before 1949, about 4,000 miles of roadway had been constructed in the province; owing to the Sino-Japanese War and to subsequent unrest, however, more than half was unusable. Since 1949, much reconstruction and repair work has been done, mainly by local (commune) labour; by 1957 there were about 4,500 miles of paved highway in use. The major new road constructed runs from Wu-han, via the Han Valley, to Hsiang-yang and thence to Nan-yang, Honan, and the north; a branch runs westward to I-ch'ang, Tzu-kuli, En-shih, and so to Chungking.

Wu-ch'ang has become an important centre for air traffic, second only to Peking. Air services are entirely under central government control.

In addition to the national dailies, Wuhan has its own local newspapers. Every factory and institution of any size has its own wall newspaper. Central government authorities rely heavily on the radio for dissemination of national news and for maintaining communication with all parts of the country. No village is without its central radio receiving set. It is stated that on average there is one receiving set per three households.

Education and health. The eductional pattern in Hupeh is similar to that in the rest of the country. From 1949 onward determined efforts have been made to overcome illiteracy. By 1970 it was estimated that over 60 percent of the people were literate. Universal primary education has not yet been achieved and therefore part-time schools, run largely by the communes, have been opened. Wu-ch'ang, which was the early capital of the ancient province of Hu-kuang, has remained the educational and cultural heart of Hupeh. Under the Nationalist (Kuomintang) government (1928–49), a national university was built beside the beautiful Tung Hu (East Lake—one of the three large lakes outside the old walled city), and a Christian university, Hua Chung Ta Hsioh, was established inside the city itself. After 1949 both these institutions were incorporated into the new educational system; many institutes—specializing in such subjects as engineering, science, and teacher training—were built around the lakes. The Central Southern Institute of Minorities, similar to that in Peking and situated by South Lake, trains representatives from the tribal people of the western highlands—such as the Miao, Tai, Lolo, and T'uchia—for leadership in their own autonomous regions and districts (*chou*).

Medical service

Before the People's government of the Republic of China came to power in 1949, there were large, efficient modern hospitals, run by Christian missions and secular bodies in both Hankow and Wu-ch'ang; good though most of them were, however, they were inadequate to meet the needs of the people in the countryside. Insofar as rural needs were met at all, they were served by medical missionaries and nurses, scattered sparsely throughout the province, as well as by Chinese doctors, herbalists, and acupuncturists (practitioners of an ancient Chinese system of medicine in which specific diseases are treated by puncturing certain areas of the skin with needles). In the 1950s and 1960s the city hospital services were greatly enlarged, offering a choice of Western or Chinese medicine; most attention has, however, been paid to public health and to preventative medicine. Doctors' training was reduced to three years, after which graduates were sent out into the countryside to practice among the villages; debilitating diseases such as schistosomiasis (a parasitic disease) and malaria were attacked; drinking water and the proper disposal of sewage were supervised; standards of personal hygiene and of the cleanliness of streets and public places were raised to an impressive level. In Wu-han, in 1965, two new textbooks on village hygiene and modern child delivery were published especially for volunteer peasant health workers, and 170,000 copies of the first printing were sold. These measures, and the equitable distribution of food, have served to improve health and increase production. The death rate in Hupeh, as in all provinces, has fallen, and in 1958 the national life expectancy had risen to an average of 54 years.

Cultural life and institutions. In common with all other provinces, Hupeh has experienced considerable change in its cultural life since 1949. The great extension of education and the increase in literacy have had a far-reaching effect. In the cities, museums and libraries have been opened and are much patronized. Large stadia, sports halls, and swimming pools have been built. Games and athletics have reached a high international standard. These halls are also often used for ideological assemblies. Trade unions and factories have clubs and social activities.

The theatre still retains great popularity. The old Chinese operas are still produced, but more common today are modern themes aimed at promoting social consciousness and social revolution.

The rural districts, no less than the towns, have undergone great cultural change. Electricity has been extended to villages and hamlets. The growth of the advanced cooperative, and later the commune, has had the effect of developing a much greater community consciousness. Every village of any size now has its own stores, its library, and its hall, in which the production teams or brigades meet to discuss their affairs, in which the health clinics are held, and where the table tennis tables are erected. Being probably better lighted than individual homesteads, the hall has become the place where villagers assemble to chat or listen to the radio. Story-telling—an age-long profession, which is still very popular—is serving to preserve folklore. Country life is enlivened by occasional visits of professional players, entertainers, and acrobats.

BIBLIOGRAPHY. K. BUCHANAN, *The Transformation of the Chinese Earth* (1970), a good general geography; A. DONNITHORNE, *China's Economic System* (1967), a standard work, drawing extensively on Chinese sources; A. FEUERWERKER, "China's Nineteenth Century Industrialization," in C.D. COWAN (ed.), *The Economic Development of China* (1964), a historical analysis of industrial development; SUN CHING-CHIH, *Economic Geography of Central China* (Eng. trans. 1960), one of many volumes by Chinese geographers covering the whole country; T.R. TREGEAR, *A Geography of China* (1966), a general, college-level text; *Economic Geography of China* (1970), more advanced, amplifying the economic and social section; and "Shih Hui Yao: A Chinese River Port with a Future," *Geography*, vol. 39, pt. 2 (1954). LI SHAO-CHEN, "Wu-han: Metropolis on the Middle Yangtze," *China Reconstructs*, vol. 14, no. 11 (1965).

(T.R.T.)

Hurricanes and Typhoons

Hurricanes and typhoons are severe tropical storms characterized by winds of hurricane force (64 knots [32.7 metres per second] or more). The winds spiral inward toward the storm centre (which characterizes cyclonic flow), clockwise in the Southern Hemisphere, and counterclockwise in the Northern Hemisphere. At the centre of the storm there are light breezes, even calm. Barometric pressure decreases rapidly toward the centre, where record low pressures have been recorded. Wind speed, humidity, and rainfall increase toward the central zone, termed the eye, where they suddenly decrease. If there is a strong downdraft in the eye, temperatures there may be some 8° to 10° C higher than in the storm's main body.

Tropical cyclones (the general term for hurricanes and typhoons) are not common. Their total number in a given year may vary from 30 to 100, with about one-quarter occurring near Southeast Asia, one-seventh in the Caribbean and adjacent waters, and one-tenth in the southwest Pacific and Australian waters. They play a noticeable, if spasmodic, role in the general circulation of the atmosphere, transporting large amounts of warm, moist air from very low to middle latitudes. It is estimated that a mature hurricane may export more than 3,500,000,000 tons of air per hour, thus contributing greatly to redistribution within the troposphere. The development of a hurricane entails the release of large amounts of energy and the transfer of substantial quantities of water over several degrees of latitude.

CATASTROPHIC STORMS

Tropical cyclones have caused many deaths and incalculable losses of property. In terms of human life, one of the most catastrophic cyclones known hit near Calcutta on October 7, 1737, causing a 12-metre storm surge ("wall" of water) and killing about 300,000 people. In December 1789 at Coringa, farther south on the Bay of Bengal, three successive storm surges destroyed the town, killing 20,000 persons. In the same region a 12-metre storm surge killed some 50,000 persons and 100,000 cattle at Contai, in 1864, and disease following the flood caused some 30,000 more fatalities. During an 1876 cyclone the storm surge blocked the ebbing tide and the Megna estuary near Chittagong, flooding 7,800 square kilometres, drowning 100,000 persons and causing diseases that killed another 100,000. About 40,000 died in a 1942 cyclone, and several thousands were drowned in 1960. The fatalities caused by the cyclone that swept all low-lying islands in the same area in November 1970 will never be known; estimates of the death toll were as great as 500,000.

Asian disasters

In 1881 at Haiphong, Vietnam, about 300,000 people were killed by a typhoon, mostly by drowning. In 1904 a typhoon drowned nearly 5,000 in the Mekong delta.

The Muroto typhoon of September 21, 1934, was the most powerful storm to hit Japan in the last 40 years. Its power was calculated to be approximately 3×10^{25} ergs per second, its pressure sank to 912 millibars, and its diameter was about 1,800 km. It destroyed 45,600 houses and 11,594 stream control works and killed 3,066 persons. Tide waters entered 183,740 houses in the Osaka region alone. The Makurazaki typhoon of September

1945 attained a power of 2×10^{25} ergs per second; it wrecked 60,978 houses, killing 3,122 persons. The Ise Bay typhoon of September 1959 killed 5,378 persons. But destructiveness is in part only a matter of whether vulnerable targets are available and, thus, is only partly proportional to power: in 30 years, Hurricane "Jane" in 1950 ranked about 18th among typhoons in order of power, 5th in terms of houses destroyed, and 9th in loss of life.

Loss of life and property in the Western Hemisphere

A most disastrous hurricane hit Galveston, Texas, on September 8, 1900, killing 6,000 people and causing some $20,000,000 worth of damages. A seawall was built, and when Galveston was hit by a 1915 hurricane, which caused damages of $50,000,000, there were only 275 fatalities. Miami had its worst hurricane on September 17–18, 1926, when 114 persons were killed and 25,000 were made homeless; damages were estimated at well over $50,000,000. At Moore Haven, where Lake Okeechobee overflowed, over 300 people were drowned, and total damages reached $165,000,000. A hurricane in September 1928 killed over 600 persons in Guadeloupe, about 300 in Puerto Rico, leaving 200,000 homeless, and between 1,800 and 2,500 from West Palm Beach to the Everglades. On September 3, 1930, a hurricane destroyed Santo Domingo (Dominican Republic), killing 8,000, injuring 12,000, and causing property losses of $20,000,000. On November 9, 1932, at Santa Cruz del Sur, Cuba, 2,500 persons out of 4,000 were drowned by a hurricane's storm surge. On September 2–3, 1935, a small but intense storm killed 408 out of about 760 persons living on the Florida Keys and destroyed a stone causeway that supported the Overseas Railroad. On September 21, 1938, a hurricane that had departed from the more normal storm track produced catastrophic winds, storm surge, and river floods in New England. It killed 682 persons, injured more than 1,500, and caused property losses for 93,122 and damages amounting to more than $400,000,000. At one stage the whole hurricane was advancing at nearly 50 knots.

In 1954 three major hurricanes hit North America: in October, one of these alone caused $136,000,000 damages in coastal North Carolina and over $100,000,000 near Toronto, bringing record high winds to Washington and New York. Total hurricane damage in that year reached about $1,000,000,000, but there were only 150 fatalities. In August 1955 two hurricanes followed each other within a few days. Since the ground was saturated by rains from the first, which caused floods from North Carolina to New York, the exceptionally heavy rain from the second ran off in torrents causing flash floods. In Connecticut 100 persons died and damage amounted to $200,000,000. Six states were declared disaster areas, total damage reached $1,500,000,000, and 310 persons died. A hurricane killed 390 people in Louisiana in 1957, when warnings went unheeded because the storm appeared to be a weak one until it crossed the coastline. In 1963 "Flora" killed 7,193 persons (5,000 of them in Haiti where over 100,000 were left homeless) and caused damages of $528,000,000. Even with continuous tracking by radar, satellite, and aircraft, a hurricane in September 1965 knocked out New Orleans' power, communications, and water purification systems and caused $1,420,000,000 worth of damages.

The central Pacific may also be hit: on January 13, 1903, a cyclone caused waves that swept over the Society Islands, killing some 1,000 persons.

The first American hurricane watch service was established and maintained from Havana by Father Benito Viñes, S.J., from 1875 to 1893. The first hurricane report by wireless from a ship at sea came in 1909. From then on, the chances of early detection and warning of approaching hurricanes became much greater. Weather balloons and radiosondes (atmospheric probes) helped from the 1930s onward. In the 1940s regular aircraft reconnaissance of hurricanes became feasible. Radar and satellite observations followed. All these methods are now used most effectively (see WEATHER FORECASTING).

Improved methods of forecasting hurricanes and their probable paths have resulted in a considerable saving of human life: in the United States the ratio changed from 166 fatalities per $10,000,000 of property damage in 1926–30 to fewer than two in 1961–65.

ORIGINS

A tropical cyclone is likely to occur whenever several of the following prerequisites occur simultaneously: (1) latitude sufficiently high (5–6°) for the Coriolis effect (effect of the earth's rotation on moving bodies, including air currents) to be appreciable; (2) a warm-water surface (at least 27° C) of sufficient area to supply the overlying air with large amounts of vapour; in some cases a cyclone may form over water at 23° or 24° C, if much colder air is present at higher altitude; (3) pronounced instability in the air column or relatively low pressure at the surface and often an anticyclone aloft; (4) little or no vertical wind shear (shearing effect produced by the movement of one air mass past another). These conditions are most likely to occur over the oceanic areas where the intertropical convergence zone moves 10° or more away from the Equator (see also ATMOSPHERE; WINDS AND STORMS; CYCLONES AND ANTICYCLONES).

Wind flow and cyclonic triggering

The Coriolis effect is proportional to both the latitude and the angular velocity (rotational speed) of the earth. At these low latitudes, the value of the Coriolis effect is minimal; this is why, in large and shallow tropical depressions with very weak winds, the pattern of air flow is indistinct. The general instability and enormous vapour load make the air most susceptible to any triggering factor and especially to convergence due to external wind flow. Convection may rapidly become tumultuous. With a strengthening of convection, the centripetal wind flow gains speed; soon the angular velocity component of the Coriolis effect becomes sufficient to impart a definite cyclonic curvature to the air flow, and a cyclone becomes established. The input of warm, very moist air continues. Large-scale condensation of moisture occurs during the ascent, and enormous amounts of previously latent energy are released. This energy results in stronger winds, which in turn lead to the intake and uplift of larger amounts of humid air, with a further release of energy. The evolution from tranquil tropical depression to violent tropical cyclone takes four to eight days. Strong vertical wind shear (*e.g.*, by a jet stream (*q.v.*) overhead) would impede convection and prevent the development of the cyclone. Latent heat is the main source of energy in a tropical cyclone. Thus, a rapid inflow of dry air can reduce the cyclone to a much slower tropical depression.

Development and classification. The life span of a tropical cyclone may vary from a few hours to nearly three weeks; most cyclones last five to ten days. All of them begin as tropical depressions over warm oceanic waters over an area 200 to 400 kilometres (km) across. They may remain in this formative, rather shapeless stage, with bulging but not closed isobars (lines of equal pressure) and pressure above 1,000 millibars (mb) for many days; many tropical depressions never evolve to a cyclonic stage.

The immature stage of a tropical storm begins when the wind gains strength (weak storm 35–47 knots, cyclonic storm with gale-force winds 48–64 knots) and follows a spiralling path toward a distinct centre. The eye usually measures 5–15 km across. Wind and pressure gradients are extremely steep around it. Some isobars are closed, and pressure falls somewhat below 1,000 mb. The diameter decreases to 80–200 km. Many storms remain at this stage throughout their life span. In some there may be occasional gusts of hurricane force.

The term tropical cyclone (hurricane, typhoon) should be reserved for the mature stage of intense tropical storms, those in which wind speed exceeds 64 knots (hurricane force) usually over an area of at least 100 km in diameter. A great hurricane of 1944 had hurricane force winds within a diameter of 320 km and gale-force winds within nearly 1,000 km. Isobars are very nearly circular at first, and pressure falls well below 1,000 mb at the centre, but gradients become less steep. The size of the cyclone as shown by the closed isobars may vary con-

Table 1: Lowest Pressure at Centre of Typhoons
(millibars)

month	Jan.	Feb.	March	April	May	June	July	Aug.	Sept.	Oct.	Nov.	Dec.
Pressure	940	...	...	930	920	950	925	910	900*	915	910	920

*Lowest on record.
Source: V.S. Samoilenko *et al.*, *Meteor Usloviya nad Tikhim Okeanom*, 1966.

siderably from just over 100 to over 2,000 km in diameter at the surface, with a 20-to-100-km eye.

The cyclone may reach a decaying stage, in which the pressure rises and the wind slows down, while the eye becomes wider and less distinct, and a revitalized stage, in which the inflow of cold, moist air brings new energy, and a frontal structure arises.

Classification of storms

The international classification, in use since the 1950s, is based on wind speed. Tropical cyclones are evaluated according to several objective criteria, namely: (1) minimum pressure; (2) wind speed that may be measured over 5, 3, or 1 minutes or in single gusts; (3) wind direction; (4) rainfall quantity and intensity; (5) area or diameter of the widest closed isobar or the isobar of 1,000 mb, or area or diameter with winds more than 47 or 64 knots; and (6) point of origin and characteristics of the track.

Core structure. A record low pressure of 877 mb at 2,400 metres (m) was measured in the eye of a typhoon in the Guam area in September 1958. The lowest pressure on land, 892 mb, occurred in a 1935 Florida hurricane. The pressure gradient may reach 3 millimetres per kilometre (mm/km); pressure has been observed to fall 38 mb in 30 minutes and 16 mb in 5 minutes.

Radar observations show the dynamic core of the cyclone as a near-circular, echoless area, also revealed by the inward spiralling rainbands, 10–20 km wide and 100–150 km long, which converge to form a central ring. The core (eye) is quite distinct from the barometric centre, which may be up to 80 km away from it on the poleward side while the cyclone travels westward and later on to the equatorward side when the cyclone heads eastward. The position of the core near the ground also differs from its position as shown by radar, because the rain that causes the radar echoes occurs at about the 700-mb level.

Travel and modification. A tropical cyclone travelling over a land surface loses much energy because of increased friction, and wind speeds are reduced. Most of the cyclones that reach the high Vietnamese and Malagasy escarpments die out immediately. On the other hand, the low Western Australian plateau is no obstacle, and cyclones have been known to travel 1,500 to 1,800 km over it. Hurricane "Camille" (1969) travelled 1,800 km along a broad arc from Louisiana to Virginia, losing much strength but preserving its structure. The intake of much dry air, as occurs in high-pressure situations on the west coasts of Asia, North America, and Australia, fails to supply any further latent energy and may lead to the rapid decay and dissipation of the cyclone, especially if it travels over cool water. Similar developments occur on the east coasts of these continents but are less frequent because coastal waters are usually warmer and lasting high-pressure situations are less common in the hurricane season.

A most significant development occurs when a tropical cyclone happens to enter a long north–south pressure trough. The cyclone may then reach the middle latitudes without too much change or loss of energy. The intake of moist air is still possible, especially on east coasts, where warm currents (Gulf Stream, Kuro Shio) are present.

Middle latitude occurrences

When a stream of midlatitude air is drawn into the cyclone, frontogenesis (formation of frontal structure) occurs, generally with the appearance of an extraordinarily active warm front due to the high speed of the original cyclonic circulation. This results in the new extratropical frontal structure of the revitalized cyclone becoming apparent on surface maps, while at altitude (500-mb level and higher) the nonfrontal tropical features remain almost unchanged. At this stage three possibilities arise, namely: (1) the cyclone meets a large anticyclone and is rapidly filled, eliminating its centre; (2) the cyclone continues on its course for some distance and disappears gradually by infilling without much further change; or (3) the cyclone continues on its course until it enters a westerly stream where wind speed exceeds the wave velocity, in which case the transformation to full-scale midlatitude depression rapidly extends upward and becomes total. For some time, however, the cyclone may remain distinctly warm and humid and relatively homogeneous, and the inner end of the frontal surface still remains eccentric. In the meantime a cold front is likely to arise on the equatorward side, usually also eccentrically. Considerable amounts of moisture will condense and fall as rain. The additional energy thus released, combined with the more pronounced Coriolis effect due to the higher latitude, causes the cyclone to travel at greatly increased speed. During this phase much damage may occur in coastal areas of Japan and the Atlantic United States.

PHYSICAL PROPERTIES

The shape of the streamlines in a tropical cyclone is not a simple spiral, as it would be if there were no zonal (horizontal belt) easterly winds around it. Because of the greater speed around the core, the zonal easterlies are slightly deflected outward before they begin their inward spiralling course toward the centre of cyclonic indraft. Also, downwind of the cyclonic spiral there is a hyperbolic (saddle-shaped) divide between the airstreams that flow into the cyclone and those that rejoin the zonal, easterly flow after having been deflected around the edge of the cyclone. Winds are weakest near this hyperbolic divide: there is no wind at all at the point where the air may equally likely flow into the cyclonic indraft or away from it. This is the stagnation point, and it is a necessary element of the cyclonic structure. The corridors of convergence that cross the stagnation point may be marked by a line of clouds, which are only small cumulus on either side of the stagnation point and build up to towering cumulonimbus both eastward and westward where the air streams crowd together.

Table 2: Speed of Travel of Typhoons by Month and Latitude
(knots)

latitude	Jan.	Feb.	March	April	May	June	July	Aug.	Sept.	Oct.	Nov.	Dec.	year
0°–10°	...	9	8	...	12*	10	6	8	8	6	16*	11	9
10°–20°	13	10	6	9	9	10*	10*	9	9	10	11*	9	10
20°–30°	...	21	22*	19	12	13*	11	9	10	11	14	17	15
30°–40°	...	22	17	19	27*	22	13	11	18	18	22*	19	19
40°–50°	...	17	16	19	20*	...	15	22	25	30*	23	...	21
Mean	13	16*	14	13	16*	14	11	11	14	15	17*	14	14

*Highest values.
Source: V.S. Samoilenko *et al.*, *Meteor Usloviya nad Tikhim Okeanom*, 1966.

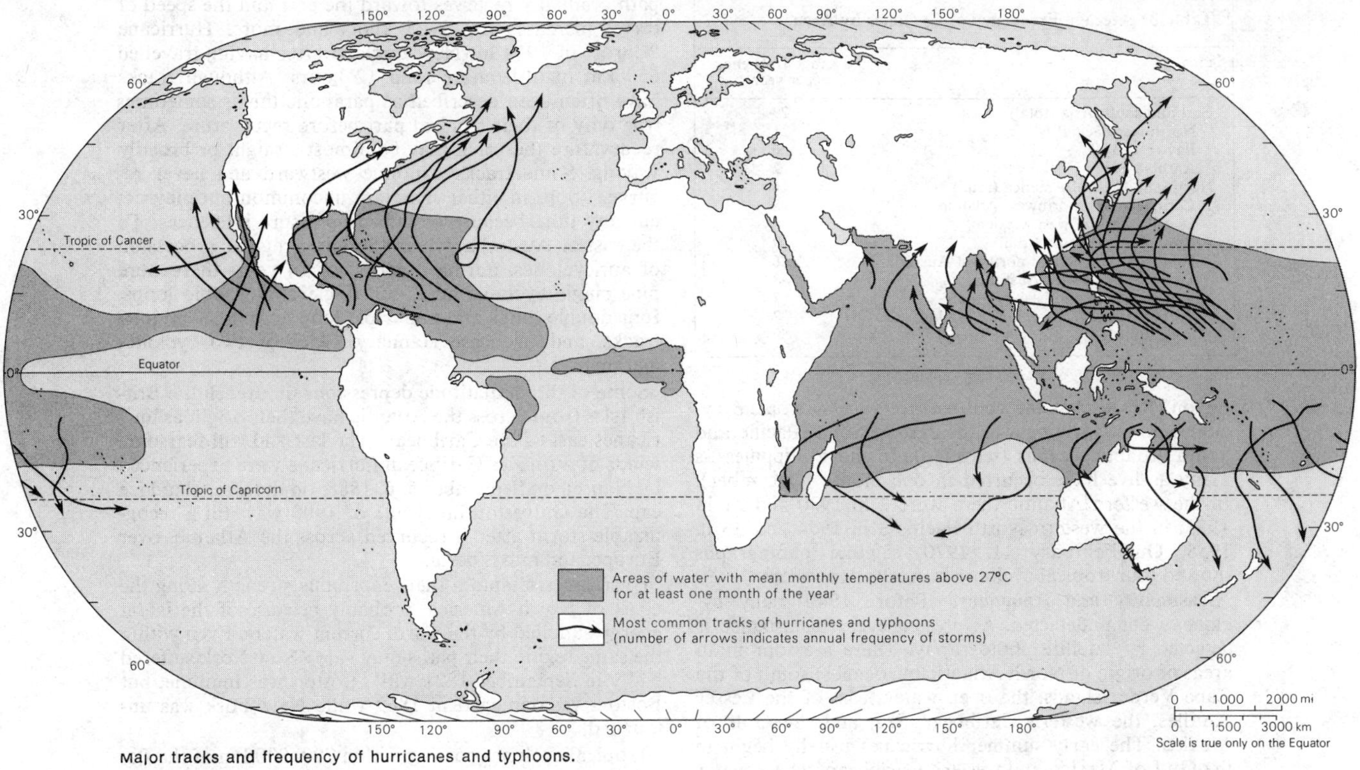

Major tracks and frequency of hurricanes and typhoons.

A tropical cyclone is often preceded 1,000 km ahead of itself by a short spell of fine weather due to divergence and subsidence in the prevailing (and preceding) easterly air flow. Pressure then begins to fall, but cloudiness does not appear until the cyclone is fewer than 300 to 500 km away.

Wind velocity. Wind gusts fluctuate rapidly from 20 or 30 to over 100 knots, even within two or three minutes, but there is no rhythm or regularity. Strong winds often are associated with rain bands. The highest gust velocities, recorded around the eye, may be close to 140 knots (uncorrected instrument readings to 160 knots have been obtained). The strongest gust recorded (1966) reached 171 knots. Within the eye, calms or light breezes prevail. Beyond the eye, the strongest gusts resume from the opposite direction.

The actual wind velocity is the result of two distinct movements, namely the inward spiralling of the air streams and the progress of the cyclone as a whole along its path. The zonal wind strengthens or weakens the wind field, thereby extending or reducing the area of strong winds and making it asymmetrical. Before its recurvature, a cyclone lies in the trade-wind belt (zonal easterlies); its poleward side may already have hurricane winds 100 to 130 km from the centre because the trade winds add momentum to that side of the spiralling flow. Conversely, the storm area is greatly reduced on the equatorward side. The speed and direction of travel of the cyclone and the strength and direction of the trade winds are, however, always minor elements in cyclonic wind patterns, the spiralling winds being paramount.

Onset of a tropical storm

Clouds and precipitation. The usual herald of a tropical storm is a broad trail of cirrus. Heavy showers of rain may fall on a coastline 500 to 600 km ahead of the oncoming storm. Cirri depart in all directions at high altitude. A thin watery veil may pervade the air. Within a day or two the storm appears as a distant wall of cumulonimbus. The middle and high clouds travel along divergent paths. The lower the clouds, the less direct the exit. Altocumulus may diverge by 20° from the tangents to the isobars. Low clouds, which may travel 50 m above the ground, tend to follow a converging course. The wind freshens and rain begins to fall. Cloudiness suddenly becomes overwhelming. The wind becomes much more violent and rain showers much heavier. The heaviest rainfall occurs patchily just before the eye, in a radius of 20–50 km, until one side of the wall passes over. There follows a 10–45-minute rainless interval with calm or light breezes while the eye passes overhead. Then follow the heaviest downpours and strongest gusts from the opposite direction, which occur beneath the steepest towering portion of the cloud wall. In coastal locations much sea spray is added to the rain. This second rainy spell is also likely to last longer, extending radially over a further 20–30 km. The rain gradually decreases but may still last two or three days if enough moist air is available. The increase or decrease of rainfall intensity is normally decided by streamline convergence (confluence of air flow) or divergence, hence the spiralling bands of intense rain. Rain gauges may miss up to 50 percent of the falling rain because of the driving wind, and they may overflow before readings are taken. In some cases all instruments have been blown away. It is certain, however, that cyclones have brought the majority of the heaviest rainfalls recorded (*e.g.,* 1,583 millimetres (mm) in 24 hours in April 1958 to Aurère, located on a mountain slope on Réunion Island, and 1,067 mm on a hillside at Baguio, Philippines, in 1911).

When the hurricane's structure becomes revitalized a renewal of precipitation takes place. The new rainfall zone is more distinctly asymmetrical with respect to the hurricane's track. The rain may reach 150 or even 200 mm in 24 hours at the most active point of the front, but in general it is 50–60 mm over some 20,000–30,000 square kilometres, enough to cause local flooding in some situations.

Energy of storms. The power of a typhoon K in ergs per second may be derived from the empirical formula relating power to the lowest pressure of the storm and the radius of the largest circular isobar, namely:

$$K = 0.71 \times 10^{22} (1010 - P_{min}) (R/111)^2,$$

in which P_{min} is the lowest pressure in the typhoon and R is the radius of the largest near-circular isobar in km. The energy that is associated with very severe storms is about 10^{25} ergs/sec by this formulation.

WORLD DISTRIBUTION

The average distribution and frequency of hurricanes and typhoons in the world is shown in the map. More details appear in Table 3, which gives the frequency by area or

Table 3: Average Frequency of Cyclones by Area

area	average frequency per year
East and south Asia (total)	29
Northwest Pacific	21
Bay of Bengal	6
Arabian Sea	2
North and Central America (total)	14
Caribbean and northwest Atlantic	8
East Pacific and west Mexico	6
Australia and Oceania (total)	9
Southwest Pacific and northeast Australia	6
Timor Sea and west Australia	3
Southeast Africa and islands (total)	7
Southwest Indian Ocean and Madagascar	7
World (total)	59

region. Because of the cool surface waters, tropical cyclones do not originate in the eastern South Pacific and South Atlantic oceans (see map). In the Philippines as many as five have occurred in one month (December). In the western Atlantic there were 2 in 1930 and 21 in 1933; in the western North Pacific 3 in 1954 and 36 in 1958. On February 11, 1970, satellite photographs showed four tropical cyclones in Australian waters.

Seasonality and frequency. Before 1940 many cyclones went undetected. At present every disturbance is detected by satellite photography. There are four main areas of origin of North Atlantic hurricanes: south of the Cape Verde Islands, the open waters east of the Lesser Antilles, the western Caribbean Sea, and the Gulf of Mexico. The early summer hurricanes usually begin in the Gulf of Mexico and western Caribbean, where water temperatures rise early because of the shallows and the nearby heated land. Low pressure farther north often allows the hurricane to enter the Gulf area. As the broad expanses of Atlantic surface waters warm to 28° C or more in late July and August, more hurricanes form much farther east, as far as the Cape Verde Islands. They gather more energy as they travel west before recurving over the West Indies. By mid-September, surface waters are cooler, but outbursts of cold air aloft are likely; the area of origin moves west again to the Caribbean and to the Gulf of Mexico. The high-pressure outflow of continental air often pushes the recurving hurricane along a more easterly path so that it may sweep over Florida or the Atlantic seaboard.

Migration of tropical storms

Table 4 shows the monthly occurrence of tropical cyclones as percent of the total. The frequency is bimodal (two dominant occurrences) in the peripheral seas; *e.g.*, Arabian Sea, South China Sea, and Caribbean Sea.

Cyclonic tracks. Whereas a tropical depression may remain almost stationary, a cyclone becomes smaller and more intense and begins to travel along a westward path, slowly at first, then at 4 to 15 knots. The path gradually recurves toward the tropic, and the speed of travel decreases, in some cases practically to a standstill. The westernmost point is reached at latitude 15–30° when the path gradually recurves toward the east and the speed of travel increases to 15–25 knots and more. Hurricane "Carol" of 1954 hit New England after having travelled 650 km in little more than 12 hours. Although tracks have often been described as parabolic this is sometimes true only of their tropical part before recurvature. After recurvature the track may be almost straight or broadly waving. Some tracks continue westward and never recurve. Loops in either sense are uncommon but may occur any time because of outside pressure influences. To the east of Australia, where there is a regular procession of anticyclones, during a period of 14 years there were nine single cyclonic and four single anticyclonic loops, four double loops and one triple loop among 93 cyclone tracks, and one case (January 1956) of two cyclones merging.

Some of the midlatitude depressions that reach the British Isles from across the Atlantic have their origin as hurricanes east of the Caribbean. The last and still fearsome winds of a former Caribbean hurricane were experienced by Nansen on September 5–6, 1888, on the Greenland ice cap. The Galveston hurricane of 1900 was still a recognizable storm after it recurved across the Atlantic, over Europe, and into Siberia.

Hurricanes maintain their enormous strength along the coast of North America, probably because of the latent energy supplied by the warm current waters. Even within the same region their paths may vary: New York suffered badly in September 1821 while Boston was immune, but Boston was damaged in 1869 while New York was untouched.

Tropical cyclones passing within 700–800 km of the Pacific coast of Mexico send violent southerly winds against the shore, where they are known as cordonazos. On the average there are six such cyclones a year, mainly in the summer and early autumn, with a peak of two in September. The average duration recorded is one to eight days per storm. Most of these cyclones travel parallel to the coast for some distance and then recurve onshore before reaching the tropic. A few (fewer than one a year) continue northward without recurving and may then affect Baja California or, very rarely, southern California north of San Diego. Their travelling speed varies from nearly seven knots in June to over 11 in August and falls rapidly by September. A high-pressure situation over the western United States tends to hold a cyclone further offshore, and the resulting greater pressure gradient causes strong hot winds. A pressure trough over the western United States induces a more rapid recurvature.

An index of relative cyclonicity has been devised, based on the formula relating cyclonicity to the numbers of closed isobars and numbers of cyclones, namely:

$$j = \frac{1}{n}\Sigma a_i^2$$

in which a_i is the number of closed isobars in the cyclone, and n the number of cyclones in a given latitudinal zone. The index for latitudes 0° to 40° is given in Table 6.

Table 4: Monthly Percentage Occurrence of Tropical Cyclones

Northern Hemisphere	Jan.	Feb.	March	April	May	June	July	Aug.	Sept.	Oct.	Nov.	Dec.	period	total
Eastern North Pacific Ocean	4.4	2.9	2.9	0	2.9	4.4	4.4	19.2	41.3*	11.8	2.9	2.9	1903–40; 1953–60	68
Western North Pacific Ocean	0.8	0.2	0.5	1.1	4.5	6.5	18.9	20.6	20.7*	13.9	8.8	3.2	1884–1955	1,428
Origin in South China Sea	3.6	0	0	1.8	10.7*	8.9	23.2	28.6*	14.3	7.1	1.8	0	1903–40; 1953–60	56
Bay of Bengal	1.3	0	1.6	4.3	6.9	10.9	14.6*	10.7	12.0	16.7*	14.9	6.1	1891–1950	376
Arabian Sea	4.3	0.7	1.4	2.9	11.4	17.9*	2.9	1.4	6.4	24.3*	19.3	7.1	1890–1950	140
Western North Atlantic Ocean	0	0	0.3	0	0.6	4.8	7.0	27.9	36.8*	18.7	3.3	0.6	1886–1961	358
Origin E of 70° W	...	...	...	...	...	1.3	7.0	28.2	41.2*	18.8	3.2	...	1887–1932	155
Origin W of 70° W	...	...	...	...	...	15.8*	4.3	1.4	20.0*	44.1*	14.3	...	1887–1932	70
Southern Hemisphere	**July**	**Aug.**	**Sept.**	**Oct.**	**Nov.**	**Dec.**	**Jan.**	**Feb.**	**March**	**April**	**May**	**June**	**period**	**tota**
Western South Pacific Ocean	6.2	1.6	4.6	1.6	1.6	3.1	10.7	13.8	35.2*	7.7	7.7	6.2	1903–40; 1953–60	65
E of 160° E	0.4	0.4	0.8	1.6	2.9	13.9	26.9*	19.6	25.3*	6.9	0.8	0.8	1789–1924	245
W of 160° E	4.0	0	2.5	3.0	2.0	8.0	22.0*	17.5	20.5*	8.5	6.5	5.5	1867–1923	200
Eastern South Indian Ocean														
Western Australia	0.4	0.4	0.4	2.5	11.0	25.6*	24.5	25.8*	7.7	1.3	0	0.4	1870–1969	236
Western South Indian Ocean	0	0	0.5	0	2.8	8.9	29.4	31.3*	17.7	7.0	1.9	0.5	1912–1961	214

*Highest values.

Table 5: Frequency of Cyclonic Centres by Month and Latitude
(western North Pacific, 1953–1960)

latitude	Jan.	Feb.	March	April	May	June	July	Aug.	Sept.	Oct.	Nov.	Dec.	year
0°–10°	5*	0	1	3	5*	0	1	2	1	5*	4	4	31
10°–20°	8	5	1	5	9	19	29	39	48	72*	21	27	283
20°–30°	0	2	2	0	0	12	25	58*	48	20	13	9	189
30°–40°	0	0	0	0	0	6	5	16*	15	6	3	0	51
Total	13	7	4	8	14	37	60	115*	112	103	41	40	554

*Highest values.
Source: V.S. Samoilenko *et al.*, *Meteor Usloviya nad Tikhim Okeanom*, 1966.

DAMAGE AND PREVENTION

Tropical cyclones can cause immense damage, both directly (by wind, pressure, and rain) and indirectly (mainly through storm surges and floods).

Wind and pressure damage

The wind causes damage that generally increases in proportion to the square of its velocity, according to the basic formula $P = KV^2$, in which P is the pressure exerted by the wind against vertical surfaces, V is the wind velocity, and K is a factor depending on air density and drag. A wind of 40–50 knots strips leaves and small branches off trees; at 60–70 knots it can topple over shallow rooted trees or snap weaker trees outright, blow down thin walls, shift roofing materials, and occasionally lift a whole roof. A wind of this force may blow in large glass windows. At about 70 knots, lifting of roofs and snapping of trees is general. Hurricane winds may exert a pressure of more than 400 kg/m² on tall structures and can flatten weak buildings at first impact. Gusty winds, combined with a suitable period of vibration of a given structure, have a dynamic effect because they may produce resonance (vibrations in phase and, hence, reinforcing) leading to breaking point. Damage is also caused to roofs and windows by the suction produced by strong winds on the downwind side, amounting to 0.5–1 times the windward pressure. As with tornadoes, whirlwinds, and waterspouts (*q.v.*), much direct damage is caused by the rapid fall of external pressures. The pressure differential could amount to 300–400 kg/m² for a sealed structure. Damage may be increased by the fact that the strongest gusts, in excess of 100 knots, occur immediately after the transit of the eye and blow in the contrary direction to the preceding gusts, thus adding a considerable stress to any structures exposed to them. Loose objects lifted by the wind become missiles that shatter glass, batter walls, and flatten roofs. Wind causes injuries and deaths by toppling over structures and hurling loose or torn objects about with enormous force. Since the eye may take from a few minutes to an hour or more to pass over a given point, depending on (1) the central or eccentric position of that point, (2) the size of the eye itself, and (3) the travelling speed of the cyclone, many victims are struck after they have left their shelters in the belief that the storm was over. The kinetic energy of the whole cyclonic system is nearly proportional to its power, but the amount of damage and loss of life depends on many other factors, among which lack of warning and insufficient preparedness can be extremely significant. In Japan loss of life from typhoons had over many years been roughly proportional to the cube and the number of totally destroyed houses to the fifth power of the maximum wind speed. The torrential rain may also cause damage by eroding the soil, causing landslides in mountain country and making streams and reservoirs overflow. Nearly half the floods in Japan are due to typhoon downpours, and the damage alone reaches some 50,000,000,000 yen per year. Much damage is caused by mud and debris carried by the water.

Storm surges

Indirect damages are mostly due to the storm surge. This is a complex surface deformation of the sea induced by the cyclonic winds on coastal waters, which surge as a sudden tide against the coast, flooding the countryside and impeding the flow of rivers. The level of the sea is raised by up to three metres for a period that may last several hours, depending on the characteristics and relative position of the cyclone and of the coastline affected. The level of the sea is raised a further 0.5–1 m by the low atmospheric pressure. Extreme tides (*q.v.*) recorded on the Gulf Coast were all due to hurricanes. Hurricane "Hazel" (1954) brought a 3.5-m tide to North Carolina. The worst storm surge in Tokyo Bay (October 1917) rose 2.3 m above normal. Osaka Bay had nine storm surges in half a century, one of them (Sept. 21, 1934) reaching 3.1 m above normal. Most coastal cities are less than 3 m above sea level and may thus be extensively flooded. Industrial plants in coastal areas may be badly damaged by salt spray and seawater. Pounding waves are an additional cause of damage to coastal installations and structures. Coastal erosion may reach catastrophic proportions. Most significant may be the cumulative effect of a close succession of two or three cyclones, as happened in North America in 1954 and 1955. Lakes are affected in the same way as the sea but over shorter periods. Because of their smaller dimensions they may develop storm-surge seiches (oscillations) of remarkable amplitude; *e.g.*, the disastrous 5.5-m swelling of the southern end of Lake Okeechobee in 1926.

Cyclone warning

Because of the small diurnal pressure changes common in the low latitudes, it is difficult to single out changes due to approaching cyclones in time for a useful warning. A local drop in pressure of more than 3–4 mb in 24 hours (or over a distance of 500 km or less) may be considered a danger sign. The development of markedly curved isobars moving toward the observer is a much more definite indication of an approaching cyclone, and the roughly circular shape of the isobars soon reveals the position of the cyclone's centre. A rapid increase in the height of any thermal inversion, as revealed by misty or hazy layers aloft, is often a sign of an approaching cyclone, as is a reversal of the wind direction in altitude. Humidity is normally high and is no useful indicator, but cloud types and movements—*e.g.*, a sheet of cirrus or bright red sunsets—may provide a belated warning.

Clearer advance warning may be given by a long ocean swell with a slower frequency (two to four times the usual interval) than that of normal waves. This swell travels outward from the centre for hundreds of miles.

Table 6: Index of Cyclonicity by Month and Latitude
(western North Pacific, 1953–1960)

latitude	Jan.	Feb.	March	April	May	June	July	Aug.	Sept.	Oct.	Nov.	Dec.	year
0°–10°	45	...	...	85*	...	...	...	...	...	4	...	81*	54
10°–20°	74	...	...	192*	77	19	34	29	46	54	110*	87	72
20°–30°	11	...	...	...	144*	26	123*	60	103	134*	78	62	79
30°–40°	...	...	...	...	10	...	36	37	59*	33	...	12	31

*Highest values.
Source: V.S. Samoilenko *et al.*, *Meteor Usloviya nad Tikhim Okeanom*, 1966.

In Australia a cyclone warning station was set up on Willis Island, off the Queensland coast, in 1921. Special hurricane forecast centres have been maintained by the United States Weather Bureau since 1935.

If a ship reports strong winds or rapidly falling pressure, unusual squall activity, or even a wind flow unusual for the season, special observations at three-hour intervals are requested from all ships in the area, and warnings are issued. Because the shape of the cyclone's path mainly depends on the pressure pattern of the time (the cyclone tends to travel toward any locus of lower pressure and around or away from any locus of high pressure), a synoptic barometric map may allow a gross forecast of a cyclone's track. Pioneer flights into a hurricane took place in 1943. Regular aerial hurricane patrols began in 1945, reporting location, characteristics, and movements of any likely disturbance. Flights may be made into, through, and above the storm. The easiest access to the eye of a cyclone is from the side of the stagnation point, where the hyperbolic divide is located. Because this is essentially an area of very light winds, exact location is very difficult without the use of drift smoke signals. The smoke plumes soon reveal the direction of the air flow. The plume extending toward the lower pressure will follow the indraft-accosting spiral, which leads in the shortest time (but not as the shortest route) to the centre of indraft. A distinct, clear break along a line of growing cumulus to cumulonimbus clouds is likely to be due to the prevailing stillness at the stagnation point and may be taken as an indicator.

Tracking activities

Radar units are installed at suitable points to give warning of any storm within range. The characteristic spiral banding of dense clouds and rain makes cyclonic storms easy to identify. A great expansion of hurricane study and warning services has taken place since 1955, when the National Hurricane Research Project was started.

Satellites transmit photographs of any part of the earth and its cloud systems. They give the most reliable and comprehensive coverage of cloud patterns and reveal storm systems from remote areas, where other methods of detection may not always penetrate.

After the 1900 hurricane, Galveston built a seawall 13 km long, 5 m thick at the base, and 1.3 m higher than the highest storm wave, or 5 m above the lowest city ground. All buildings were lifted accordingly. Granite filling added 7.5 m to the thickness. The total cost was over $9,000,000. It is almost certain that this first seawall, completed in 1904, saved over 5,000 lives during the 1915 hurricane. After that, it was strengthened even further. In the 1930s a rock levee 137 km long and 10–11 m high was built around the southern part of Lake Okeechobee to protect the surrounding low-lying country from any repetition of the 1928 hurricane floods. Greater safety in hurricanes is ensured by suitable building rules.

BIBLIOGRAPHY. Research sponsorship by the World Meteorological Organization and the U.S. Weather Bureau has enabled many experts to undertake a thorough study of this field, with a considerable output of learned papers in specialist periodicals. Many hurricanes have been fully described in recent issues of the *Bulletin of the American Meteorological Society* (monthly), and *Weatherwise* (bi-monthly). A popular, absorbingly written book is M.S. DOUGLAS, *Hurricane* (1958). An excellent coverage of Atlantic hurricanes may be found in I.R. TANNEHILL, *Hurricanes*, 9th ed. (1956), and G.E. DUNN and B.I. MILLER, *Atlantic Hurricanes*, rev. ed. (1964). Full accounts of modern observations and research will be found in the volumes of proceedings or reports on symposia held at Tokyo (1954), Ciudad Trujillo (1956), Brisbane (1956), Tokyo (1962), Rotorua (1963), and Houston (1966).

(J.G.)

Hus, Jan

The most important Czech religious Reformer of his age was Jan Hus. His work was transitional between the medieval and the Reformation periods and anticipated the developed Lutheran Reformation by a full century.

Early life and career. Hus was born in 1372 or 1373 of poor parents in Husinec in southern Bohemia. At the age of 13 he entered the elementary Latin school in nearby Prachatice. Five years later he enrolled in the University of Prague, earning his living as a choirboy. Hus's life was hard, and although he looked back on these years with some humour, he frankly admitted that the reason he wanted to become a priest was "to secure a good livelihood and dress and be held in esteem by men." Two years after his graduation in 1394 he received his master's degree and began teaching at the university.

Hus as teacher

As a teacher, Hus lectured for two years on Aristotle and on the Realist philosophy of the radical English reformer John Wycliffe, whose views were enthusiastically received by the nationalistic Czech university masters. As a young master, Hus lived a gay life—of which he later genuinely repented, but which in reality consisted chiefly in being proud of his academic costume, in the love of fine apparel, in playing chess, and in sharing in the feasts and the other pastimes of his colleagues. His "conversion" into a rather stern religious reformer remains a mystery, one that he never explicitly explained, except to state that "when the Lord gave me knowledge of the Scriptures, I discarded from my foolish mind that kind of stupid fun-making."

Because the university did not pay a salary to masters—only to a few full professors—Hus had to seek some other means of livelihood. Thus, after he was ordained a priest, he received an appointment (1402) as rector and preacher of the large Bethlehem Chapel in Prague, the centre of the growing national reform movement where sermons were preached in Czech rather than in Latin. In his 12 years of preaching he became the popular leader of the reform movement. Hus also had become the adviser to the young nobleman Zbyněk Zajíc of Hazmburk when Zbyněk was named archbishop of Prague in 1403, a move that helped to give the reform movement a firmer foundation.

Despite his extensive duties at the Bethlehem Chapel, Hus continued to teach in the university faculty of arts, and became a candidate for the doctor's degree in theology. It had not been until 1401, when the theological works of Wycliffe had been brought to Prague, that Hus had become acquainted with them; earlier, he had known only Wycliffe's philosophical realism. Of these books, Jerome of Prague, a disciple of Hus, brought in Wycliffe's *Dialogus*, *Trialogus*, and perhaps *De eucharistia*. He stoutly supported Hus when other former friends dared not do so. He even intended to come to his aid at the trial in Constance, but was taken prisoner, condemned to death, and burned at the stake a year later than Hus. In 1403 a German university master, Johann Hübner, drew up a list of 45 articles, presumably selected from Wycliffe's writings, and had them condemned as heretical. Because the German masters had three votes as against only one vote for the Czech masters, the Germans easily outvoted the Czechs and the 45 articles were henceforth regarded as a test of orthodoxy. The principal charge against Wycliffe's teaching was his tenet of remanence; *i.e.*, that the bread and wine in the Eucharist retain their material substance. Wycliffe also declared the Scriptures to be the sole source of Christian doctrine and denounced the Pope as Antichrist. Hus did not share all of Wycliffe's radical views, such as that on remanence, but several members of the reform party did, among them Hus's teacher, Stanislav of Znojmo, and his fellow student, Štěpán Páleč.

Influence of Wycliffe's ideas

During the first five years of Zbyněk's reign as archbishop Hus's attitude toward the "evangelical party" radically changed. The opponents of reform won him over to their side and, in 1407, succeeded in charging Stanislav and Páleč with heresy, and they were cited to the Roman Curia for examination. They returned completely changed in their theological views and became the principal opponents of the Reformers. Thus, Hus was brought into the forefront of the party and into conflict with his former friends.

Hus and the Great Schism. Ever since 1378 the church had been split by the Great Schism, during which the papal jurisdiction was divided between two popes. The French king, with the aid of King Wenceslas (Václav IV) of Bohemia, sought to terminate this division by calling a council to Pisa in 1409. Wenceslas had the support of the Czech university masters, Hus among them, whereas the Archbishop and the German masters were opposed. This so enraged the King that in January 1409 he subverted the university constitution by granting the Czechs three votes and the Germans only one; the result was a mass emigration of the Germans from Prague to several German universities. In the fall of 1409 Hus was elected rector of the then Czech-dominated university.

The final break with the Archbishop

The final break between the Archbishop and Hus occurred when the Council of Pisa deposed both Pope Gregory XII, whose authority was recognized in Bohemia, and the antipope Benedict XIII and in their place elected Alexander V. The deposed popes, however, retained jurisdiction over portions of western Europe; thus, instead of two, there were three popes.

The Archbishop and the higher clergy remained faithful to Gregory, whereas Hus and the reform party acknowledged the new pope. After being forced by the King's punitive measures to recognize Alexander V as the legitimate Pope, the Archbishop, through a large bribe, induced Alexander to prohibit preaching in chapels, including the Bethlehem Chapel. Nevertheless, Hus refused to obey the Pope's order, whereupon he was excommunicated and denounced at the Curia before which he was ordered to appear. Instead, Hus sent three procurators to represent his case, and even Wenceslas and the Queen sent letters urging that Hus be absolved. There were two reasons that Hus did not go to Rome: his enemies were plotting to kill him on his journey to Rome, and he believed there was "but little of God's truth at the papal court." The Archbishop, however, sent rich gifts to be distributed among the cardinals and even to the Pope, and Hus was excommunicated for failing to appear (1411), although not for heresy. Despite his condemnation, Hus continued to preach at the Bethlehem Chapel and to teach at the university.

The Archbishop's faction thereupon accused Hus of the heresy of remanence, a move that incensed King Wenceslas for the aspersion of heresy that it cast upon his country and led him to take punitive measures against the higher clergy and pastors. The Archbishop fled from Prague and excommunicated the royal officials who carried out the King's order; he even imposed an interdict on Prague. Wenceslas ordered that the interdict be ignored and appointed an arbitration commission to judge between him and the Archbishop. The commission directed that the Archbishop submit to the King, lift the interdict, and annul Hus's excommunication. He was even to write to the Pope to stop all the proceedings against Hus and to declare that there was no heresy in the land. The Archbishop submitted, but then, without fulfilling his promise, fled to the country to seek protection of King Sigismund of Hungary. At Bratislava, however, he died suddenly under mysterious circumstances.

Conflict over the "crusading" bull

An even greater conflict arose in the same year (1411) when Pope John XXIII issued his "crusading" bull against King Ladislas of Naples, who was a supporter of the deposed Gregory XII and had driven John out of Rome. The bull ordered all the secular rulers to seize the sword "in defense of the Church and us." All who obeyed the summons were promised "remission of their sins of which they were heartily contrite." Pope John also ordered a sale of indulgences to finance his campaign against Gregory XII.

Unable to remain silent in the face of John's call to a fratricidal war and "trafficking in sacred things," Hus vigorously denounced the bull as un-Christian and blasphemous. But in this struggle he lost the support of King Wenceslas, who shared in the proceeds of the sale of indulgences. The Prague populace rose in revolt against the sales and conducted a mock burning of the papal bulls. The King then called the representatives of the warring camps to his castle, and the royal council ruled that no one was to oppose the sale of indulgences. About the same time three young opponents of indulgences were seized and beheaded; thus the reform movement gained its first martyrs.

Hus's enemies then renewed his trial at the Curia, where he was declared under major excommunication for refusing to appear and an interdict was pronounced over Prague or any other place where Hus might reside, thereby denying certain sacraments of the church to communicants in the interdicted area. In order to spare the city the consequences, Hus voluntarily left Prague in October 1412. He found refuge mostly in southern Bohemia in the castles of his friends, and during the next two years engaged in feverish literary activity. His enemies, particularly Stanislav and Páleč, wrote a large number of polemical treatises against him, which he answered in an equally vigorous manner. The most important of his treatises was *De ecclesia.* He also wrote a large number of treatises in Czech, among them, "The Exposition of the Faith," "The Exposition of the Decalogue," and "The Exposition of the Lord's Prayer," and a collection of sermons entitled *Postilla.*

Period of literary activity

Hus's final trial. With the Schism continuing unabated, King Sigismund of Hungary, as the newly elected (1411) King of Germany, saw an opportunity to gain prestige as the restorer of the church's unity. He forced Pope John to call a council to Constance to find a final solution of the Schism and to put an end to all the heresies. Sigismund, therefore, sent an emissary to invite Hus to attend the council—an invitation Hus naturally was reluctant to accept. But when the Pope threatened King Wenceslas for noncompliance with the interdict, and after Sigismund had assured Hus of safe-conduct for the journey to Constance and back (no matter what the decision might be), Hus finally consented to go.

He left for Constance on October 11, 1414, but did not receive the safe-conduct until two days after his arrival in Constance, on November 3. He could move freely in the city, for the Pope had suspended the interdict. Nevertheless, in less than a month he was lured into the papal residence and imprisoned in the dungeon of the Dominican monastery, and his enemies, particularly Michael de Causis, the papal procurator, and Štěpán Páleč, succeeded in having him put on trial as a Wycliffite heretic. A panel of judges—all Hus enemies—was appointed by the council and subjected him to an examination, which was illegal because he had come to Constance freely under a safe-conduct and not under an accusation. He had been promised an opportunity to present his faith to the whole council. The trial is described in great detail by the eyewitness, Hus's former pupil, Petr of Mladoňovice who was in the service of one of the Czech nobles appointed to guard Hus.

At first the judges had hoped to convict him of heresy on the grounds of 45 articles ostensibly summarizing Wycliffe's teachings, but distorting them in the Hussite view. Hus successfully refuted most of the charges. Thereupon, Páleč selected 42 articles, presumably from Hus's *De ecclesia,* to which 20 other articles were added.

In the meantime, the sentiment of the council turned against all three popes; John fled from Constance on March 21, 1415, hoping thereby to render the council illegitimate. The council, however, declared itself supreme over the whole church, including the popes, and reorganized itself. Hus's trial then was entrusted to a new commission headed by Cardinal Pierre d'Ailly. In January Sigismund had repudiated his safe-conduct to Hus in exchange for the promise that Hus be given a free hearing before the council, which was finally permitted on June 5. The session became so disorderly, however, that it was adjourned until June 7, when the trial resumed.

Trial under a new commission

Hus was accused of many serious offenses through the testimonies of witnesses from Prague and Constance. Hus again resolutely denied the charge of the Wycliffite heresy of remanence. When Cardinal d'Ailly demanded that Hus abjure the articles, in vain Hus insisted that he did not then and never had held such beliefs and that he would be committing perjury if he recanted them. He begged only that the council prove to him from Scripture where he was wrong. This the council refused to do.

The final session was held on July 6 in the cathedral before the general congregation of the whole council.

The final 30 articles—none of which correctly stated Hus's teachings—were read to him. When Hus still refused to recant on the ground that such teachings had been falsely ascribed to him, he was declared a Wycliffite heretic, deposed from priesthood and ignominiously divested of his priestly garments and functions with appropriate ritualistic anathemas, and his soul was consigned to the devil. He himself committed his soul to God. Thereupon, Hus was turned over to the secular arm for execution and on the same day was burned at the stake on the outskirts of the city. He prayed loudly until the flames choked him.

BIBLIOGRAPHY. MATTHEW SPINKA, *John Hus: A Biography* (1968), a comprehensive account of his life and thought, with emphasis upon the concept of the church; *John Hus at the Council of Constance* (1965), contains a translation of Petr of Mladoňovice's *Relatio* and Hus's letters from Constance; *John Hus' Concept of the Church* (1966), a fairly comprehensive account of his theological system, stressing his differences from such scholars as John Wycliffe; and *John Hus and the Czech Reform* (1941, reprinted 1966), a brief treatment of his life, with emphasis on his trial at Constance; PAUL DE VOOGHT, *L'Hérésie de Jean Huss* (1960), the most important French account of his life and work from the Roman Catholic point of view; F.M. BARTOS, *Čechy v době Husově, 1378–1415* (1947), an account of Bohemia in the time of Hus, written by the acknowledged Czech authority on the subject; V. NOVOTNY and V. KYBAL, *M. Jan Hus*, 5 vol. (1919–31), a basic critical study still indispensable for the subject, but poorly arranged and without an index.

(M.Sp.)

Hu Shih

Hu Shih was one of the influential leaders of the May Fourth Movement (named for a mass demonstration of students at Peking on May 4, 1919), in which the authority of China's ancient cultural heritage—language, history, classics, ethics, customs, politics—was challenged in the light of modern Western ways of thinking. Hu Shih's role as a moving force in the establishment of the vernacular (*pai-hua*) as the written language earned him the title father of the Literary Revolution. He was also an influential propagator of American pragmatic methodology as well as the foremost political liberal in Republican China, advocating building a new country not through political revolution but through mass education.

By courtesy of the Academia Sinica, Nankang, Taipei

Hu Shih, 1958.

Early life and education

Hu Shih was born on December 17, 1891, in Shanghai, where his father, a scholar-official from Chi-ch'i county in Anhwei Province, was serving at the time. When Hu Shih was three years old, his father died. His mother, though uneducated herself, laid great emphasis on the education of her son, which alone would enable him to pass competitive civil service examinations that led to a career as an official.

Since passing the examinations was the aim of education, the content of the examinations became almost exclusively the content of education. By the time Hu Shih began his schooling, traditional education had solidified into a rigid orthodoxy, remote from contemporary life and learning. It was based on the Confucian classics—and on a narrow interpretation of them introduced by the reigning Manchu dynasty to justify monarchical rule. Moreover, the emphasis had shifted from the study of the content of the classics to the study—almost the worship—of their literary form. It became so important that a scholar's writing conform to the orthodox literary style that, if his ideas could not be adapted to the style, they were often changed. The language itself hampered the development of new ideas, as well as the dissemination of those ideas to the masses. Although some writers had used the vernacular, the respected books were those written in the classical Chinese language. As remote from the living, spoken language as Latin from English, it was so difficult to learn that it was largely responsible for the very widespread illiteracy in China.

Although the pressure for the modernization was forcing educational orthodoxy to compromise with Western learning (and in 1905 was to force the Manchus to abolish the civil service examinations), the compromise was not very great in 1895 when Hu Shih began his schooling at the age of four. Taught in Chi-ch'i by his uncle and cousin, the manifestly gifted child studied the classics and the old vernacular stories and novels.

In 1904 Hu went to Shanghai for a "modern education." In 1910, having won a scholarship, he went to the United States to study agriculture, and then philosophy, at Cornell University, Ithaca, New York. After receiving his B.A. degree in 1914, he became a student of the philosopher John Dewey at Columbia University. Dewey's philosophy discouraged the quest for absolute truths and recommended instead the acceptance as true what works in any given set of circumstances; man should believe nothing, Dewey maintained, except that which has been subjected to the "test of consequences." This philosophy had a profound influence on Hu Shih. It gave expression and direction to his rational, skeptical, liberal cast of mind and was to him a means of helping his country free itself from blind submission to ancient tradition.

Dewey's influence

Hu returned to China in 1917, after completion of his doctoral dissertation under Dewey. Despite the high hopes engendered by the Revolution of 1911, which abolished the monarchy and established a Western style republic, Hu found a China not radically changed from the nation he had left seven years earlier. Only nominally a republic, the country was overrun by warlords (provincial military rulers) fighting for dominance; there had been two attempts to restore the monarchy; the old conservative intellectual bureaucracy was still powerful; China's political and economic sovereignty were still threatened by foreign powers; and the masses were still 90 percent illiterate and still obedient to ancient traditions.

The intellectuals who had returned from study abroad concluded that for Western style government to work there must first be a thorough re-examination and total regeneration—after the Western model—of traditional Chinese culture. The centre of this cultural reform movement was Peking National University, the faculty of which Hu joined in 1917. Although some Peking intellectuals were more politically minded than others, in 1917 they all agreed, as Hu explains,

> to keep away from politics for twenty years and to be devoted only to educational, intellectual, and cultural activities, to build a political foundation by way of non-political factors.

Reforms of language and education

Early in 1917, Hu's "Tentative Proposal for Literary Reform" ("Wen-hsüeh kai-liang ch'u-i") was published in *Hsin ch'ing-nien* ("New Youth"), an influential magazine established by Ch'en Tu-hsiu, Hu's colleague at Peking University, who was to become the founder of the Chinese Communist Party. In this article Hu made himself the champion of the *pai-hua* movement. He proposed a new, living literature, liberated from the tyranny of the "dead" language and style, accessible to the people, and flexible enough to express all kinds of new ideas. The poems Hu wrote in 1918 (which were published in 1920 as *A Book of Experiments* [*Ch'ang-shih chi*]) were just the beginning of a flood of new literature in the vernacular, resulting in new short-story and essay forms, new drama, and translations of modern European literature. Despite severe attacks from the traditionalists, "vernacular literature," as Hu said, "spread as though it wore seven-league boots." By 1922 the government had proclaimed the vernacular as the national language.

The literary revolution was, however, a single aspect of a broader campaign directed against the deadweight of the traditional values. To reappraise China's cultural heritage, Hu emphasized the need to use the new Deweyan pragmatic methodology. The slogan he propounded in 1919 generated much enthusiasm among intellectuals: "Boldness in suggesting hypotheses coupled with a most solicitous regard for control and verification" ("Ta-tan chia-she, hsiao-hsin ch'iu-cheng") Hu's *Outline of the History of Chinese Philosophy* (*Chung-kuo che-hsüeh shih ta-kang*, published 1919), which examined the logic of the ancient philosophers, and his later studies of the old vernacular literature, which verified authorship and authenticity, demonstrated how the scientific method could be applied in the study of traditional Chinese literature. So effective was Hu's advocacy of pragmatic methodology that it led to the examination and destruction of many of the accepted—and invalid—versions of ancient Chinese history.

Escape from politics was not long-lived. The agreement made by Hu and his colleagues began to disintegrate in 1919 after the May Fourth incident, when patriotic, anti-Japanese sentiment exploded into a student demonstration against the decision of the Versailles Peace Conference to support Japan's claims to Shantung Province. The demonstration hastened the inevitable split between the leftist intellectuals, who had been incipient political activists all along, and the liberal intellectuals, who tended to avoid political activism.

The split became overt on July 20, 1919, when Hu challenged the leftists in an article entitled "More Study of Problems, Less Talk of 'Isms'." Deeply convinced of the feasibility of the experimentalist approach, with its reliance on coolness and reflective deliberation, he counselled gradualism and the individual solution of individual problems. In his view, the invocation of such abstract formulas as Marxism and anarchism, in the hope that one specific Western doctrine would solve all of China's problems, was futile; in coping with real issues he felt they would most likely lead to disastrous consequences. By appealing to cool reason at a time when the whole nation was ringing with sentimental battle cries, however, Hu Shih and his fellow liberals were bound to face frustration. Moreover, by urging the acceptance of pragmatism, which dismisses isms as unproven fabrications yet is itself an ism, Hu's position seemed to be untenable and unconvincing.

Because of this position, Hu not only made himself the declared antagonist of the Chinese Communists but also found himself frequently in uneasy relationships with the Nationalists. It was not until war with Japan broke out in 1937 that a modus vivendi was reached between Hu and the Nationalist government. He served as its ambassador to Washington from 1938 to 1942 and in 1945 was appointed chancellor of the government-sponsored Peking National University. After the establishment of the Communist government in 1949, Hu lived in New York, where in 1957 he served as Nationalist China's representative to the United Nations. In 1958 he went to Taiwan to assume the presidency of the Academia Sinica, China's leading scholarly organization. He died on Taiwan on February 24, 1962.

BIBLIOGRAPHY. HU SHIH, *The Chinese Renaissance* (1934), a collection of lectures presenting Hu Shih's views on the cultural changes of modern China through disintegration and readjustment; BERTRAND RUSSELL *et al., Living Philosophies: A Series of Intimate Credos* (1931), includes an English adaptation of Hu Shih's autobiography; JEROME B. GRIEDER, *Hu Shih and the Chinese Renaissance: Liberalism in the Chinese Revolution 1917–1937* (1970), an historical account of the roots and developments of Hu Shih's liberal ideas between 1917 and 1937; CHOW TSE-TSUNG, *The May Fourth Movement: Intellectual Revolution in Modern China* (1960), a definitive study of the intellectual revolution in modern China in which the leading role played by Hu Shih is thoroughly examined; CHAN WING-TSIT, "Hu Shih and Chinese Philosophy," *Philosophy, East and West*, 6:3–12 (1956–57), a summary of Hu Shih's contribution to Chinese philosophy; CHAN LIEN, "Chinese Communism vs. Pragmatism: The Criticism of Hu Shih's Philosophy, 1950–1958," *Journal of Asian Studies*, 27:551–570 (1968), an interpretation of the meaning of the criticisms launched by the Chinese Communists against Hu Shih during the 1950s.

(C.Li.)

Husserl, Edmund

A philosopher, Edmund Husserl, in Germany, was the founder of Phenomenology, a new method for the description and analysis of consciousness through which philosophy gains the character of a strict science. The method reflects an effort to resolve the opposition between Empiricism, which stresses observation, and Rationalism, which stresses reason and theory, by indicating the origin of all philosophical and scientific systems and developments of theory in the interests and structures of the experiential life. Though Husserl did not publish many works during his lifetime, the influence that he exerted from the beginning of the 20th century through his teaching and his students, who came from many lands, was considerable. Phenomenology stands today beside Analytical philosophy as one of the most widespread philosophical orientations. Its influence extends to logic and the philosophy of science, to the philosophy of language and psychology, and to the social sciences and the philosophy of religion.

The Phenomenological method

Archiv fur Kunst und Geschichte

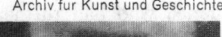

Husserl, *c.* 1930.

Education and early life. Husserl, the son of Jewish parents, was born on April 8, 1859, in Prossnitz (Prostějov), a small city in Moravia. He completed his qualifying examinations on June 30, 1876, at the German public gymnasium in the neighbouring bishop city of Olmütz (Olomouc) and then studied physics, mathematics, astronomy, and philosophy at the universities of Leipzig, Berlin, and Vienna. In Vienna he received his doctor of philosophy degree on November 22, 1882, with a dissertation entitled *Beiträge zur Theorie der Variationsrechnung* ("Contributions to the Theory of the Calculus of Variations"). After working in Berlin as the assistant to his teacher, the mathematician Karl Weierstrass, famous for arithmetizing analysis, Husserl, in the autumn of 1883, moved to Vienna to study with a philosopher (and psychologist), Franz Brentano, an influential teacher.

Brentano had been a Catholic priest, but on the occasion of the publication of the dogma of the infallibility of the pope, he had left the church and worked as professor of philosophy at the University of Vienna. His fundamental work, *Psychologie vom empirischen Standpunkte*, had already appeared in 1874. Brentano's critique of any psychology oriented purely along scientific and psychophysical lines and his claim that he had grounded philosophy on his new descriptive psychology had a widespread influence. Husserl received a decisive impetus from Brentano and from his circle of students (to which Tomáš Masaryk, later the first president of Czechoslovakia, also belonged). The spirit of the Enlightenment of Joseph II (who near the close of the 18th century had been the Holy Roman emperor), with its religious tolerance and its quest for a rational philosophy, was very much alive in this circle. Husserl's striving for a more strictly rational foundation found its corroboration here. From the very outset, such a foundation meant for him not only a theoretical act but, at the same time, the moral meaning of responsibility in the sense of ethical autonomy. Later, Husserl depicted himself as a man who was sick as long as his ideas did not come to clarity; already he had impressed his friends as one who was possessed by his thoughts.

Influence of Brentano and Stumpf

In Vienna Husserl converted to the Evangelical Lutheran faith, and one year later, in 1887, he married Malvine Steinschneider, the daughter of a secondary-school professor from Prossnitz. As his energetic and skilled wife, she was his indispensable support, until his death, in all of the things of their daily life, in which the scholar had been virtually helpless. From their marriage came three children: Elisabeth, who married Jacob Rosenberg, a famous expert of Dutch art who was curator of the Kaiser-Friedrich Museum and then a professor at Harvard University; Gerhart, a lawyer and professor of law; and Wolfgang, a gifted mathematician.

Lecturer at Halle. In 1886 Husserl went—with a recommendation from Brentano—to Carl Stumpf, the oldest of Brentano's students, who had further developed his psychology and who was professor of philosophy and psychology at Halle. On July 26, 1887, Husserl qualified as a lecturer in the university (*Habilitation*). He was indebted to Stumpf for many suggestions in the formation of his own descriptive concepts and was a close friend of Stumpf until his death. The theme of Husserl's *Habilitation* thesis, *Über den Begriff der Zahl: Psychologische Analysen* ("On the Concept of Number: Psychological Analyses"), already showed Husserl in the transition from his mathematical research to a reflection upon the psychological source of the basic concepts of mathematics. These investigations were an earlier draft of his *Philosophie der Arithmetik: Psychologische und logische Untersuchungen*, the first volume of which appeared in 1891. The title of his inaugural lecture in Halle was "Über die Ziele und Aufgaben der Metaphysik" ("On the Goals and Problems of Metaphysics"). In the traditional sense metaphysics is the study of Being or ultimate reality. Though the text cannot be found, it is clear that Husserl already understood his method of the analysis of consciousness to be the way to a new universal philosophy and metaphysics, which would lay all previous schemes of metaphysics to rest.

Discouragement

The years of his teaching in Halle, from 1887 to 1901, were later seen by Husserl to have been his most difficult. He often doubted his ability as a philosopher and believed he would have to give up his occupation. The problem of uniting a psychological analysis of consciousness with a philosophical grounding of formal mathematics and logic seemed insoluble. But from this crisis there emerged the insight that the philosophical grounding of logic and mathematics must commence with an analysis of that experience which lies before all formal thinking. It demanded an intensive study of the British Empiricists (such as Locke, Berkeley, Hume, and Mill) and a coming to terms with the logic and semantics stemming from this tradition—especially the logic of John Stuart Mill—and with the attempts at a "psycho-logic" grounding of logic then being made in Germany. The fruits of this interaction were presented in the *Logische Untersuchungen* (1900–01; "Logical Investigations"), which employed a method of analysis that Husserl now designated as "phenomenological." The revolutionary significance of this work was only gradually recognized, for its method could not be subsumed under any of the philosophical orientations well-known at that time. Bertrand Russell, in a retrospective glance at the *Logische Untersuchungen*, spoke of them as comprising one of the monumental works of the present philosophical epoch.

Ausserordentlicher Professor at Göttingen. After the publication of the *Logische Untersuchungen*, Husserl was called, at the instigation of David Hilbert, a Formalist mathematician, to the position of *ausserordentlicher Professor* by the University of Göttingen. Husserl's time of teaching in Göttingen, from 1901 to 1916, was important as the source of the Phenomenological movement—*i.e.*, as marking the formation of a school reaching out to many lands and branching out in numerous directions. The phenomenological analysis of experienced reality—*i.e.*, of reality as it immediately presents itself to consciousness—not only drew the German students who were unsatisfied with the Neo-Kantianism that then prevailed in Germany but also many young foreign philosophers who came from the traditions of Empiricism and Pragmatism. At times, Husserl's seminar brought together students from 12 nations. From about 1905 on, Husserl's students formed themselves into a group with a common style of life and work. Standing in close personal contact with their teacher, they always spoke of him as the "master" and often accompanied him, philosophizing, on his daily walks. They understood Phenomenology as the way to the reform of the spiritual life. In their rejection of the superficial life of the Wilhelmene Era (around the turn of the century), this group shared many of the traits of the German youth movement. It was not a school, however, in any sense of swearing by every word of the master; Husserl gave each of his students the freedom to pursue the master's suggestions in an independent way. He wanted his teaching to be not a transmission of finished results but rather the preparation for a responsible setting of the problem. Thus, he understood Phenomenology as a field to be worked over by the coming generations of philosophers and claimed for himself only the role of the "beginner." In view of this freedom of his teaching, the fact that Phenomenology soon branched off in many directions is understandable, and it explains its rapid international expansion.

His influence as a teacher

Husserl himself had developed an individual style of working: all of his thoughts were conceived in writing—the minutes, so to speak, of the movement of his thought. During his life he produced more than 40,000 pages written in Gabelberger stenographic script.

Husserl was still at Göttingen when Max Scheler, who was at that time a *Privatdozent* in Jena and who later became an important Phenomenologist, came in contact with Husserl (1910–11). Scheler was influenced methodologically by Husserl but soon elaborated in an entirely different direction a speculative metaphysics. Because of these facts, as well as for personal reasons, there later ensued an estrangement between them.

Husserl's friendship with Wilhelm Dilthey, a pioneering theoretician of the human sciences, also falls within the Göttingen period. Dilthey saw the publication of the *Logische Untersuchungen* as a new encouragement to the further development of his own philosophical theory of the human sciences; and Husserl himself later acknowledged that his encounter with Dilthey had turned his attention to the historical life out of which all of the sciences originated and that, in so doing, it had opened for him the dimension of history as the foundation of every theory of knowledge.

Phenomenology as the universal science

In the Göttingen years, Husserl drafted the outline of Phenomenology as the universal philosophical science. Its fundamental methodological principle was what Husserl called the phenomenological reduction. It focusses the philosopher's attention on uninterpreted basic experience and the quest, thereby, for the essences of things. In this sense, it is "eidetic" reduction. On the other hand, it is also the reflection on the functions by which essences become conscious. As such, the reduction reveals the ego for which everything has meaning. Hence, Phenomenology took on the character of a new style of transcendental philosophy, which repeats and improves Kant's mediation between Empiricism and Rationalism in a modern way. Husserl presented its program and its systematic outline in the *Ideen zu einer reinen Phänomenologie und phänomenologischen Philosophie* (1913; Eng. trans., "Ideas; General Introduction to Pure Phenomenology," 1931), of which, however, only the first part was completed. (Completion of the second part was hindered through the outbreak of World War I.) With this work, Husserl wanted to give his students a manual. The result, however, was just the opposite: most of his students took Husserl's turn to transcendental philosophy as a lapse back into the old system of thought and therefore rejected it. Because of this turn, as well as the war, the Phenomenological school fell apart.

In contrast to the esteem that Husserl enjoyed from his students, his position among his colleagues in Göttingen was always difficult. His appointment to *Personlichen Ordinarius* in 1906 had resulted from the decision of the minister of education against the will of the faculty. The representatives of the humanities faculty had predominantly philological and historical interests and had little appreciation for philosophy, whereas the natural scientists were disappointed that, with the division of the philosophical faculty, Husserl did not go over to the new faculty of natural sciences.

Ordentlicher Professor at Freiburg. Thus Husserl's call in 1916 to the position of *ordentlicher Professor* at the University of Freiburg meant a new beginning for Husserl in every respect. His inaugural lecture on "Die reine Phänomenologie, ihr Forschungsgebiet und ihre Methode" ("Pure Phenomenology, its Area of Research and its Method") circumscribed his program of work. He had understood World War I as the collapse of the old European world, in which spiritual culture, science, and philosophy had held an incontestable position. In this situation, the epistemological grounding that he had previously provided for Phenomenology no longer satisfied him; after this, his reflections were directed with special emphasis upon philosophy's task in the renewal of life. In this sense he had set forth in his lectures on *Erste Philosophie* (1923–24; "First Philosophy") the thesis that Phenomenology, with its method of reduction, is the way to the absolute vindication of life—*i.e.*, to the realization of the ethical autonomy of man. Upon this basis, he continued his clarification of the relation between a psychological and a phenomenological analysis of consciousness and his research into the grounding of logic, which he published as the *Formale und transzendentale Logik: Versuch einer Kritik der logischen Vernunft* (1929; *Formal and Transcendental Logic*, 1969).

Phenomenology and the renewal of spiritual life

Husserl's teaching, in this last period of his life, assumed a different style from that at Göttingen. It did not lead to the founding of a new school. Husserl was so intent upon completing his work that his thinking and teaching assumed more the character of a monologue. At the same time, however, his influence upon his listeners and the members of his seminar was not diminished, and he placed his intellectual stamp upon many of them. Numerous foreign guests usually took part in his seminar. For a period, Rudolf Carnap, a leading figure in the Vienna Circle, where Logical Positivism was born, also studied under Husserl.

Broadening influence and recognition

Recognition from without was not wanting. In 1919 the law faculty of the University of Bonn bestowed upon Husserl the title of *Dr. jur. honoris causa.* He was the first German scholar after the war to be invited to lecture at the University of London (1922). He turned down a prestigious call to the University of Berlin as the successor to Ernst Troeltsch in order to devote his energies to Phenomenology without interruption. An invitation followed to give some lectures at the University of Amsterdam and later, in 1930, at the Sorbonne—lectures that furnished the occasion for preparing a new systematic presentation of Phenomenology, which then appeared in a French translation under the title of *Méditations cartésiennes* (1931). When he retired in 1928, Martin Heidegger, who was destined to become a leading Existentialist and one of Germany's foremost philosophers, became his successor. Husserl had looked upon him as his legitimate heir. Only later did he see that Heidegger's chief work, *Sein und Zeit* (1927; *Being and Time*, 1962), had given Phenomenology a turn that would lead down an entirely different path. Husserl's disappointment led to a cooling of their relationship after 1930.

Later years. Hitler's seizure of power in 1933 did not break Husserl's ability to work. Rather, the experience of this upheaval was, for him, the occasion for concentrating more than ever upon Phenomenology's task of preserving the freedom of the mind. He was excluded from the university; but the loneliness of his study was broken through his daily philosophical walks with his research assistant, Eugen Fink, through his friendships with a few colleagues who belonged to the circles of the resistance and the "Denominational Church," and through numerous visits by foreign philosophers and scholars. Condemned to silence in Germany, he received, in the spring of 1935, an invitation to address the Cultural Society in Vienna. There he spoke freely for two and one-half hours on "Die Philosophie in der Krisis der europäischen Menschheit" ("Philosophy in the Crisis of European Mankind"). The impression made by this lecture was so great that he had to repeat it two days later.

During this time, the Cercle Philosophique de Prague made it possible through a Rockefeller grant for Ludwig Landgrebe, a *Dozent* (lecturer) at the German University in Prague and Husserl's former assistant, to begin the classification and transcription of Husserl's unpublished manuscripts. Through the Cercle, Husserl received an invitation to address the German and Czechoslovakian University in Prague in the fall of 1935, after which many discussions took place in the smaller circles. Thus, in a place which already stood under the threat of Hitler, the voice of free philosophy was once again audible through Husserl. The impression of his absolute sovereignty over all of the confusions of this time was overpowering for his listeners.

Last work

Out of these lectures came Husserl's last work, *Die Krisis der europäischen Wissenschaften und die transzendentale Phänomenologie: Eine Einleitung in die phänomenologische Philosophie* (1936; *The Crisis of European Sciences and Transcendental Phenomenology*, 1970), of which only the first part could appear, in a periodical for emigrants. The following period until the summer of 1937 was entirely devoted to the continuation of this work, in which Husserl developed for the first time his concept of the *Lebenswelt* ("life-world"). In the summer of 1937, the illness that made it impossible for him to continue his work set in. From the beginning of 1938 he saw only one remaining task: to be able to die in a way worthy of a philosopher. Not committed to a particular church creed, he had respect for all authentic religious belief, just as his philosophy demanded the recognition of each authentic experience as such. His concept of absolute philosophical self-responsibility stood close to the Protestant concept of the freedom of man in his immediate relationship to God. Thus, it is evident that Husserl characterized the maintenance of the phenomenological reduction not only as a method but also as a kind of religious conversion. Thus, on the one hand, he could refuse spiritual help at his death—"I have lived as a philosopher," he said, "and I want to die as a philosopher"—and yet, on the other hand, he could explain a few days before his death: "God has in grace received me and allowed me to die." He died on April 21, 1938, and his ashes were buried in the cemetery in Günterstal near Freiburg.

Shortly before the beginning of the massive persecution of the Jews in Germany, a young Franciscan, H.L. van Breda, who had written his doctoral dissertation on Phenomenology, saved Husserl's literary remains and placed them in the Institut Supérieur de Philosophie at the University of Louvain in Belgium; and after the war, the Husserl Archives, which holds the publication rights of Husserl's literary remains, was founded under his direction.

BIBLIOGRAPHY. Husserl's *Logische Untersuchungen*, 2nd ed., 2 vol. (1913–21; Eng. trans. *Logical Investigations*, 2 vol., 1970), are ably reported on in J.N. FINDLAY's article "Phenomenology" in the 1956 through 1966 printings of the *Encyclopædia Britannica* and more fully paraphrased in MARVIN FARBER, *The Foundation of Phenomenology* (1943). The first book of Husserl's *Ideen zu einer reinen Phänomenologie und phänomenologischen Philosophie* is available in a not always reliable translation (1931, reissued 1952); the *Cartesianische Meditationen* in a faithful rendering (1960). The *Husserliana* edition of the Husserl Archives (1950 *ff.*) in its early volumes emphasized previously unpublished materials but will eventually include all of Husserl's works. Husserl's article "Phenomenology" in the 1929 edition of *Encyclopædia Britannica* (retained until 1956) appears in the light of the German original (*Husserliana* IX) as an over-condensation by the translator, which cannot claim to be an authentic text.

References to the major works of the Phenomenological movement may be found in H. SPIEGELBERG, *The Phenomenological Movement*, 2nd ed. (1965). Most of the original German studies on Phenomenology appeared in the *Jahrbuch für Philosophie und phänomenologische Forschung* (1913–30). There is not yet a definitive biography of Husserl. A short biography is given in the "Husserl" article in the *Neve deutsche Biographie* (forthcoming). Reflections on his personality may be found in *Edmund Husserl zum Gedächtnis: Zwei Reden gehalten von Ludwig Landgrebe und Jan Patočka* (1938); and *Edmund Husserl, 1859–1959*, "Phaenomenologica," vol. 4 (1959), containing a bibliography of Husserl's works and translations of his works.

(L.M.L.)

Hutton, James

The originator of one of the most fundamental principles in geology, the Scottish geologist James Hutton formulated the uniformitarian principle, which states that natural processes now at work on and within the earth have been operating in the same general manner throughout many geological ages.

By courtesy of Lord Bruntisfield

Hutton, oil painting by Sir Henry Raeburn (1756–1823). In the collection of Lord Bruntisfield.

James Hutton was born in Edinburgh on June 3, 1726. His father, William, a merchant and city officeholder, died when his son was quite young, but the boy obtained an education in the local grammar school and at the University of Edinburgh. Although already interested in chemistry, he entered the legal profession. But as a lawyer's apprentice, he is said to have devoted more time amusing his fellow clerks with chemical experiments than to copying legal documents. He, along with his friend James Davie, was also deeply interested in investigating the manufacture of sal ammoniac from coal soot. As a result, he was released from law apprenticeship before his first year was out, and he turned to the study of medicine as most closely related to chemistry. He spent three years at the University of Edinburgh, then two in Paris, and finally was granted his M.D. degree in Holland in September 1749.

But medicine as a career apparently held small appeal for him. His association with Davie in developing an inexpensive method for the manufacture of sal ammoniac was proving financially rewarding. With money in his pocket, Hutton decided to take up farming in England. His inheritance included a small farm in Berwickshire. During the years that Hutton devoted to agriculture, he also became interested in studying rocks and the action of running water on soils and rocks. He made occasional trips to the Continent, primarily to learn more about farming but also to examine rocks and minerals.

By 1765 both the farm and the company producing sal ammoniac were prospering, and Hutton became a partner in the firm with Davie. With a good income available, he gave up farming in 1768 to establish himself in Edinburgh, where he could pursue his scientific interests. In the flourishing intellectual community of his day he soon became closely associated with Joseph Black, the chemist who discovered carbonic acid; John Clerk of Eldin, the naval tactician; John Playfair, the physicist and mathematician; and Adam Smith, the economist-philosopher.

Hutton devoted his time to extensive reading, particularly on scientific subjects, and to scientific meetings. He travelled widely to inspect rocks and observe the actions of natural processes. Manuscripts and a few published works indicate that Hutton was knowledgeable in many subjects. But his chief contribution to scientific knowledge is the uniformitarian principle put forward in his papers presented to the Royal Society of Edinburgh in 1785. At the March 7 meeting of the Society, Joseph Black delivered a paper for his friend James Hutton that synthesized the results of many years of reading about, observing, and discussing the effects of such natural processes as rain, running water, tides, and volcanoes on the development of the earth. That paper and a second delivered a month later by Hutton himself were published in 1788 in the *Transactions of the Royal Society of Edinburgh* under the title "Theory of the Earth; or an Investigation of the Laws Observable in the Composition, Dissolution, and Restoration of Land Upon the Globe."

Uniformitarian principle

Until this time, Hutton's view that geologic phenomena can be explained in terms of observable geologic processes—though contrary to prevailing theories—had gained little notice. His friends were not particularly aroused by his ideas; they were used to hearing him speak of them or had been with him on excursions to see evidences in the rocks on which his conclusions were founded. Probably none of them realized that the two papers marked a turning point for geology. But from that time on, geology became a science founded upon the principle of uniformitarianism. His principle assumed an enormously long span of time during which the natural processes he described had been active on and within the earth, and that the different kinds of rocks that compose the earth had been formed by diverse processes.

Hutton's ideas were astonishing, however, when viewed in the context of the opinion of his day. It was not until five years later (1793), however, that his views were vigorously attacked in a speech by Richard Kirwan, a prominent Irish chemist and mineralogist. Kirwan dismissed much of Hutton's evidence in favour of the prevailing precipitation theory, which held that all rocks of which the earth is composed were formed by mineral deposits from the oceans—each type of rock in its turn.

In the face of Kirwan's attack, Hutton, although recuperating from a serious illness, pushed himself to complete a manuscript in which he amply documented the evidence on which his conclusions were based. His work was published in two volumes, *Theory of the Earth*, in 1795. A third volume was partly finished at the time of Hutton's death on March 26, 1797. A portion of the unfinished manuscript was published years later.

Theory of the Earth

Because Hutton's ideas were opposed to acceptable opinions of earth history, and because his writing style was difficult to understand, a stormy controversy broke out over his conclusions. Happily for scientific knowledge, John Playfair, his close friend and frequent companion on geological excursions, wrote a concise exposition of Hutton's principle. Playfair's remarkably precise condensation of Hutton's work, embellished with additional observations of his own, was published in 1802, entitled *Illustrations of the Huttonian Theory of the Earth.* It went far toward establishing the correctness of uniformitarianism, the cornerstone on which the science of geology is erected.

BIBLIOGRAPHY. JOHN PLAYFAIR, "Biographical Account of the Late Dr. James Hutton, F.R.S., Edin.," *Transactions of the Royal Society of Edinburgh*, 5:39–99 (1805), an authoritative biographical account written by a close friend; E.B. BAILEY, *James Hutton: The Founder of Modern Geology* (1967), a biographical account by a distinguished geologist with a detailed commentary on Hutton's geological work.

(W.B.N.B.)

Huxley Family

In modern times there has perhaps been no family so distinguished in so many fields of action and thought as that of Thomas Henry Huxley, the brilliant son of an unsuccessful schoolmaster in 19th-century England. Through two succeeding generations, his descendants have achieved prominence in biology, anthropology, engineering, physical science, literature, commerce, art, diplomacy, pedagogy, physical activity, and international administration. The success of individual members of the family throws into sharp relief the genius and multivalent character of T.H. Huxley himself. Of the more recent members of the family, Julian Huxley and Aldous Huxley seem, in a sense, to polarize the two most important aspects of their grandfather: in the one there reappeared the scientist, humanist, and educator; in the other was seen again the man of letters and the mystic. But T.H. Huxley's other qualities have also shown themselves in his descendants. His artistic skills and sensitivity were handed on through the female line, notably to his ill-fated daughter Marian; his disregard for purely formal convention without real social value was followed by his daughters Ethel and Henrietta; the explorer cropped out again in several grandchildren; the statesman and man of affairs came again through Ethel's marriage to John Collier; and his unfulfilled childhood ambition to become an engineer was satisfied in grandchild surrogate by the remarkable trio of Eckersley brothers, sons of his daughter Rachel.

Early promise. The Huxley genius flowered suddenly, with no hint from earlier generations of what was to come. Thomas Henry Huxley was born on May 4, 1825, in Ealing, Middlesex, the seventh of eight children of George Huxley, a schoolmaster, and Rachel Huxley (née Withers). Although the family was not actually poor, there was never money to spare. In 1833 Thomas began attending Ealing school (at which his father taught mathematics until 1835, when his post terminated for some obscure reason). Thomas thus had only two years' schooling, between the ages of eight and ten. Perhaps this was as well, for later he wrote, "the society I fell into at school was the worst I have ever known . . . the people who were set over us cared about as much for our intellectual and moral welfare as if they were baby-farmers."

By courtesy of the Gernsheim, Collection, The University of Texas at Austin

Thomas Henry Huxley.

Apart from the admirable mother, whom T.H. Huxley resembled both physically and temperamentally, the family was not auspicious. The father became "sunk in worse than childish imbecility of mind" and died in an asylum. Of the eight children, only Thomas and his favourite sister, Eliza, seem to have led fairly normal lives, and even she became involved in an odd affair about a legacy and emigrated to Tennessee with her husband.

Little is recorded of T.H. Huxley's life for a few years after 1835, but it is known that he taught himself German; that at the age of 12 he was reading advanced works on geology and logic; and that during early adolescence he was recording the results of simple, self-conducted scientific experiments. Huxley wanted to become an engineer but never had the chance. At the age of 15 he was apprenticed to a medical practitioner in London's poverty-stricken East End but soon secured a free scholarship at Charing Cross Hospital Medical School in central London. Despite a tendency to follow his own intellectual inclinations instead of the prescribed courses, he carried off several prizes at the medical school, and had his first research paper published while he was still a student.

T.H. Huxley's exploration of the southern seas

In his 21st year, Huxley's scholarship came to an end, and, though still unqualified, he secured a posting as assistant surgeon with HMS "Rattlesnake," a cockroach-ridden frigate being fitted out for exploration in the southern seas. For the next four years, wherever the ship sailed, Huxley—with his microscope lashed down against the ship's pitching and tossing and with such primitive aids as a wire-mesh meat safe adapted as dredge—studied marine specimens. From each port he packeted his observations back home, where they were accepted by such journals as those of the Royal Society and the Royal Institution. When eventually he returned to England in October 1850, the leading biologists of the day were all anxious to make the acquaintance of this brilliant young newcomer to their ranks.

T.H. Huxley immediately and effectively manoeuvred to ensure special treatment from the Royal Navy. He managed to secure three years' leave, on pay, for research on specimens collected during his voyage. He had hoped that one day he might be able to study for a degree, but, after being elected fellow of the Royal Society within a year of his return, at the early age of 26, he naturally enough did not bother to do so. His only degree "qualifications" thus were honorary doctorates—from Breslau, Edinburgh, Dublin, Cambridge, Würzburg, Oxford, Bologna, and Erlangen.

During the 1850s Huxley established his reputation by publishing important papers on animal individuality, the cephalous mollusks (*e.g.*, squids), the methods of paleontology, the methods and principles of science and science education, the structure and functions of nerves, and the theory of the vertebrate skull. In 1854, however, he was struck off the Navy List for rejecting a thrice-repeated Admiralty order to return to active service—blandly insisting that not all his researches were as yet published! He was by now extremely anxious to marry, for, while ashore in Sydney from the "Rattlesnake," he had met Henrietta Anne Heathorn and immediately fallen in love with her. At this time there were very few paid scientific posts, and he once contemplated settling in Australia, where a job in brewing would have enabled him to get married. But he managed to secure a part-time (later full-time) lectureship at the tiny government School of Mines in London and began to make additional earnings by his prolific pen; in 1855, his fiancée came to England for almost immediate marriage. For the rest of his life—despite extremely attractive offers from Edinburgh, Oxford, Harvard, and other universities—Huxley stayed with his original institution, gradually transforming it, first into the Normal School of Science and then into the great Royal College of Science.

The second generation. T.H. Huxley's marriage was singularly happy. His wife bore him eight children, and their family life was unusually warm and relaxed. Noel, their first-born, died in infancy, but the other seven all survived to display some sort of real ability, predominantly in arts and letters.

Their daughter Jessie Oriana, an occasional author, married Frederick William Waller, a cathedral architect, in 1877. Marian, probably the most brilliant of the children, studied in London at the Slade School of Art, and several of her works were hung in the Royal Academy. In 1879 she married a portraitist, John Collier, but, tragically, died young, following an attack of deepest melancholia with eventual loss of sanity. Leonard had considerable natural ability and became a reputable biographer and man of letters, but his development seems to have been in some way inhibited, probably by his father's massive reputation. In 1885, after studying at Oxford and lecturing in Greek at St. Andrews University, he married Julia Frances Arnold (niece of the poet and critic Matthew Arnold) and settled down to schoolmastering at Charterhouse, a well-known English school at Godalming, in Surrey. (After the death of his first wife, he married, in 1912, Rosalind Bruce, whose father had played an important part in the clearance of London's worst slums.) Meanwhile, Rachel, a resourceful and adventurous young woman, had, in 1884, married William Alfred Eckersley, a distinguished railroad engineer. She travelled widely with him, bearing her children in places as far apart as Algeria and Mexico, until her husband died, in San Salvador, in 1895. She then married Harold Shawcross, a Lancashire cotton manufacturer.

In 1889 Henrietta married John Harold Roller, a young picture restorer to whom she had—without any objection—become engaged before her parents had even met him (highly unusual in an English Victorian family). She moved in artistic circles (her friends included Oscar Wilde) and evidently found a settled domestic life too restrictive. She left her husband, and for many years supported herself and her young daughter by touring Europe, as a concert singer. Henry, in 1890, married Sophy Wilde Stobart, a nurse whom he had met during medical training. He became engaged to her before she had met his parents. ("By the way," his father wrote upon hearing of the engagement, "you might mention her name; it is a miserable detail, I know, but would be interesting.")

The youngest Huxley child, Ethel Gladys, was a prizewinner in modelling at the Slade School of Art. She fell in love with John Collier, Marian's widower, but could not marry him in England because of the law's "deceased wife's sister" prohibition. Her father, however, advised her to ignore that and in 1889 accompanied the young couple to a marriage ceremony in Norway, whence they soon returned to reside in England.

Widening spheres of influence. In 1859 Charles Darwin's *Origin of Species* burst like a bombshell on the 19th-century scene. Huxley, despite his youth, was one of three scientists (the others being Sir Joseph Dalton Hooker and Sir Charles Lyell) whose blessing Darwin sought before publication. A very close attachment developed between the two men, and, while Darwin kept as far as possible out of the fray, Huxley became his "bulldog" for the next tumultuous decade, acting as his chief public supporter.

Relationship with Darwin

The most famous occasion of the Darwinian debate came in 1860 at the meeting at Oxford University of the British Association for the Advancement of Science. Bishop Samuel Wilberforce had decided that this gathering presented an opportunity to squash the "dangerous" new evolutionary theory, and the assembly room was crowded. Huxley sat quietly while the bishop spoke "with inimitable spirit, emptiness and unfairness." Wilberforce made the fatal error of voicing an offensive personal inquiry about Huxley's simian ancestry, whereupon Huxley murmured to his neighbour, "The Lord hath delivered him into mine hands." Soon the meeting was calling out for him to reply, which he did with devastating effect:

> If . . . the question is put to me, would I rather have a miserable ape for a grandfather or a man highly endowed by nature and possessed of great means of influence, and yet who employs these faculties and that influence for the mere purpose of introducing ridicule into a grave scientific discussion —I unhesitatingly affirm my preference for the ape.

The significance of this occasion was not merely that it secured something like a fair hearing for Darwin's theory but that science had made its declaration of independence from theology.

During the 1860s Huxley did valuable work in paleontology, taxonomy (especially the classification of birds), and ethnology. He served as secretary and later as president of the Geological Society, was Hunterian professor at the Royal College of Surgeons, president of the Ethnological Society, and acted on several royal commissions. He became honorary principal of the South London Working Men's College, was an active member of the Metaphysical Society, and served on the Jamaica committee set up (though unsuccessfully) to secure the murder trial of Gov. Edward John Eyre, who had suppressed a colonial uprising with some brutality. He also lectured up and down the country—not only to scientific societies but also to semipopular audiences and to the artisans whom he always held in such high esteem.

Role in educational reform

The 1870s saw a decisive development of Huxley's influence on educational reform. He was the dominant member of the first London School Board, on which he did much to set the organizational pattern of English popular elementary education for the next 75 years. Partly by his essays and public addresses but much more by his influence along the tortuous corridors of power—which he knew intimately—he also played a major part in the reorganization of British and many other institutions of higher education. Even during the current scientific and technological revolution, his views on education have retained a remarkable relevance.

During this period he contributed authoritative articles to the 9th edition of *Encyclopædia Britannica*, published several seminal textbooks of science, and began the first courses of effective practical training for science teachers. He became secretary (and later president) of the Royal Society and a senator of London University. He visited the United States to speak at the opening of Johns Hopkins University in Baltimore, served as reforming rector of the Aberdeen University in Scotland, and gave notable help to the Working Men's Club and Institute Union. As a governor of Eton College (Buckinghamshire), he provided the chief motivating force for the development of science teaching at that famous boarding school, and he cajoled the wealthy guilds and livery companies of the City of London into putting some of their vast funds into the promotion of technical education.

All this time he carried on his full-time teaching work at the School of Mines, under its successive titles, and continued his own researches. Not surprisingly, his health kept breaking down. But he always managed to recover sufficiently to alarm his friends once more by his activities. "The great secret," he once told an inquirer (as if it was the simplest thing in the world), "is to retain the capacity for working 18 hours a day."

In 1878, wishing to study the philosophy of Aristotle in the original Greek, he began teaching himself that language (he had long spoken French and German, had been reasonably competent in Italian, and was a fair translator of Latin). His interest in philosophy deepened, and—although never technically a philosopher—some of his writings on David Hume, George Berkeley, and René Descartes are still illuminating. Deeply interested in theology and coining the word agnostic—now a common term—to indicate his own intellectual position, he equipped himself with those powerful armaments of disputation that, during the 1880s, he brilliantly discharged at the bishops and their allies.

In 1885 Huxley resigned his professorship at what was by then the Normal School of Science but continued as its honorary (though by no means inactive) dean. He thought he had only a short time to live; but in fact his health permitted his engaging in many exciting disputations—from which he usually emerged the victor—with theologians, politicians, and, indeed, anyone he considered either intellectually dishonest or inclined to suppress intellectual freedom. He finally left London in 1889, moving to Eastbourne, a quiet resort on the south coast of England. From there he continued to conduct sparkling controversy by writing, and, most fittingly, it was in the middle of debate—with one half of an essay in print, the rest in proof—that he died, of influenza and bronchitis, on June 29, 1895. On July 4 he was buried, without religious ceremony, at Finchley, now part of north London.

Recognition of Huxley's significance

Huxley's eminence won worldwide recognition. Leaving quite aside his dominant position at home, he was honoured by at least 53 scientific societies overseas, in Egypt, Russia, Sweden, Italy, New Zealand, the United States, Austria, Prussia, Belgium, The Netherlands, and many other countries. Although there have been greater scientists than he, there have been few so influential over so wide a field of scientific development and perhaps no other so effective in the total movement of thought and action within his own generation. And, certainly, it is difficult to think of one whose views on a wide range of matters remain as relevant as Huxley's in the second half of the 20th century.

The third generation. Somewhat surprisingly, the most distinguished descendants of T.H. Huxley have been those of his son Leonard, who, although much more than capable, did not display anything that could properly be called brilliance. By his first wife, Julia Arnold—a granddaughter of Thomas Arnold of Rugby School, niece of the poet Matthew Arnold, and sister of the novelist Mrs. Humphry Ward—he had four children, Julian, Noel Trevenen (1889–1914), Aldous, and Margaret Arnold. The second son, "Trev," had outstanding ability in mathematics and mountaineering. Tragically, he became desperately melancholic and eventually committed suicide. Leonard's daughter, Margaret, did not marry; she conducted a very successful girls' school at Bexhill, Sussex. By his second wife, Rosalind Bruce, Leonard was the father of David Bruce (born 1915) and Andrew Fielding. David Huxley became attorney general of Bermuda, and in 1964 his daughter Angela married George Pember Darwin, great grandson of T.H. Huxley's contemporary, making the first direct relationship between the two families.

Sir Julian Huxley. Leonard's oldest child, Julian Sorell Huxley (later Sir Julian), who was born on June 22, 1887, at London, became a figure of world fame as biologist, scientific administrator, rationalist, philosopher of science, and "international civil servant." His scientific researches included important work on hormones, developmental processes, ornithology, and ecology. He worked for some years at the Rice Institute in Houston, Texas; became professor of zoology at King's College, London University; served for seven years as secretary to the Zoological Society of London, transforming the zoo at Regent's Park and being actively involved in the development of that at Whipsnade in Bedfordshire; and became the first director general of the United Nations Educational, Scientific and Cultural Organization (UNESCO). In 1919 he had married Marie Juliette Baillot, daughter of a Swiss lawyer, by whom he had two sons. The elder, Anthony Julian Huxley, conducted valuable operational research on aircraft, became an authority on exotic garden plants, and produced the standard encyclopaedia on mountains. The younger, Francis Huxley, moved from zoology to social anthropology, becoming a lecturer at Oxford. Sir Julian died in London on February 14, 1975.

Julian's scientific research

Horst Tappe—EB Inc.

Sir Julian Huxley, 1967.

Aldous Huxley. Leonard's third child, Aldous Leonard Huxley, born July 26, 1894, at Godalming, Surrey, overcame early near-blindness to become as famous as Julian but in the fields of literature and mysticism. He had written an 80,000-word novel (unpublished) by the age of 17, and he established himself as a major author in his first few published novels (including *Antic Hay* and *Point Counter Point*), which displayed not only literary elegance and wit but also a preoccupation with interpersonal relationships. After settling in the United States in 1937, his works exhibited an increasing interest in mysticism, one that led to experiments with hallucinogenic drugs. In 1919 he had married Maria Nys, daughter of a Belgian industrialist, who bore him one child, Matthew (who became an anthropologist). In 1956, following Maria's death, he married Laura Aschera, an Italian violinist. Aldous Huxley's death, on November 22, 1963, at Los Angeles, followed a long period of recurrent illness.

Walter Bird

Andrew Fielding Huxley.

Andrew Fielding Huxley. Leonard's son Andrew Fielding became the family's first Nobel laureate. He was born in London on November 22, 1917, and was associated with Cambridge University from 1941 to 1960, as a fellow and later director of studies at Trinity College and as demonstrator, then assistant director of research, and finally reader in experimental biophysics in the Department of Physiology. In 1960 he went to University College, London, first as Jodrell professor and then, from 1969, as Royal Society Research Professor, in the Department of Physiology. With Alan Hodgkin and Sir John Eccles he received the Nobel prize for physiology or medicine in 1963, for researches in nerve conduction. Huxley and Hodgkin's researches were concerned largely with the physicochemical analysis of the fundamental phenomena involved in the excitation in a peripheral nerve fibre and in conduction of excitation along it. Apart from the researches directly mentioned in the Nobel citation, Andrew Huxley made contributions of fundamental importance to knowledge of the process of contraction by a muscle fibre.

Andrew's Nobel Prize

Other descendants. Thomas Henry Huxley's seventh child, Henry, had five offspring, and this line also produced some extremely capable descendants, though of lesser distinction. Marjorie Huxley married Edward J. Harding (later Sir Edward) of the Dominions Office. Gervas Huxley went into the shipping business and eventually became a high-level advertising initiator. He was married twice, his second wife being Elspeth Josceline Grant, who became a well-known writer as Elspeth Huxley. Henry's third child, Michael Heathorn Huxley, entered the Foreign Office, became an adventurous traveller, and in 1934 founded and edited *The Geographical Magazine*. The fourth child, Christopher Huxley, entered Sandhurst and became a regular army officer. Henry's youngest child, Anne Huxley, married Geoffrey Cooke.

It is easy to overlook the fact that hereditary factors may equally well be passed through daughters—whose descendants lose the family name—as through name-continuing sons. T.H. Huxley's daughters Jessie, Marian, and Henrietta all had capable offspring. Ethel gave birth to Laurence Collier (later Sir Laurence), who became a distinguished diplomat. His daughter Rachel bore a remarkable trio of brothers, Roger, Thomas, and Peter Eckersley.

Roger Huxley Eckersley was among the earliest enthusiasts for radio as education and as entertainment and in 1925 became the British Broadcasting Corporation's first organizer of programs. He later served as chief censor to the BBC during World War II—and showed typical Huxley versatility by composing the theme song "Here's to the Next Time," for a popular radio show. Thomas Lydwell Eckersley became a distinguished radio research scientist, was awarded the Faraday Medal for his work on the mathematical theory of wave propagation, and by a happy coincidence was, in 1938, elected fellow of the Royal Society at the same meeting as his cousin Julian Huxley. Peter Pendleton Eckersley was also a pioneer radio enthusiast and became the first chief engineer of the BBC.

Despite this record of brilliance by individual members of the Huxleys in so many fields of endeavour, it is perhaps the way in which they have, taken as a group, come close to realizing the full potential of Thomas Henry Huxley himself that is their most remarkable corporate family achievement.

MAJOR WORKS

THOMAS HENRY HUXLEY: *Evidence as to Man's Place in Nature* (1863); *An Introduction to the Classification of Animals* (1869); *Lessons in Elementary Physiology* (1866); *Protoplasm: The Physical Basis of Life* (1869); *Lay Sermons, Addresses and Reviews* (1870; 3rd enl. ed., 1895); *A Manual of the Anatomy of Vertebrated Animals* (1871); *More Criticisms on Darwin, and Administrative Nihilism* (1872); *Critiques and Addresses* (1873); *A Manual of the Anatomy of Invertebrated Animals* (1877); *Physiography* (1877); *American Addresses* (1877); *Hume* (1878); *The Crayfish: An Introduction to the Study of Zoology* (1880); *Science and Culture* (1881); *Essays upon Some Controverted Questions* (1892); *Evolution and Ethics* (1893); *T.H. Huxley's Diary of the Voyage of H.M.S. Rattlesnake*, ed. by Julian Huxley (1935). Many of Thomas Huxley's more general writings were republished in his *Collected Essays*, 9 vol. (1894–1908). Most of his research papers were republished after his death in his *Scientific Memoirs*, 5 vol. (1898–1903).

LEONARD HUXLEY: *Life and Letters of Thomas Henry Huxley*, 2 vol. (1900); *Life and Letters of Sir Joseph Dalton Hooker*, 2 vol. (1918); *Anniversaries* (1920); *Thomas Henry Huxley* (1920); *Charles Darwin* (1921); *The House of Smith Elder* (1923), printed for private circulation; *Progress and the Unfit* (1926).

JULIAN HUXLEY: *The Individual in the Animal Kingdom* (1912); *Essays of a Biologist* (1923); *Religion Without Revelation* (1927); with H.G. and G.P. Wells, *The Science of Life*, 3 vol. (1929–30); *Ants* (1930); *Bird-Watching and Bird Behaviour* (1930); *What Dare I Think?* (1931); *A Scientist Among the Soviets* (1932); *Problems of Relative Growth* (1932); *The Captive Shrew* (poems, 1932); with Sir Gavin de Beer, *The Elements of Experimental Embryology* (1934); *The Beginnings of Life* (1938); *The Uniqueness of Man* (1941); *Evolution: The Modern Synthesis* (1942); *On Living in a Revolution* (1944); *Soviet Genetics and World Science* (1949); *Evolution in Action* (1953); *New Bottles for New Wine* (1953); *From an Antique Land* (1954); *The Human Crisis* (1963); *Essays of a Humanist* (1964); *Memories* (1970).

ALDOUS HUXLEY: *The Defeat of Youth* (1918); *Limbo* (1920); *Crome Yellow* (1921); *Antic Hay* (1923); *Jesting Pilate* (1926); *Point Counter Point* (1928); *Brave New World* (1932); *Eyeless in Gaza* (1936); *Grey Eminence* (1941); *The Perennial Philosophy* (1946); *Ape and Essence* (1949); *The Doors of Perception* (1954); *Collected Essays* (1958); *Literature and Science* (1963).

ANDREW FIELDING HUXLEY: Has published many important papers in journals, particularly the *Journal of Physiology*, and in other scientific periodicals.

ANTHONY JULIAN HUXLEY: *Cacti and Succulents* (1953); *House Plants* (1954); *Standard Encyclopedia of the World's Mountains* (1962); *Flowers in Greece: An Outline of the Flora* (1964); with Oleg Polunin, *Flowers of the Mediterranean* (1965); *Standard Encyclopedia of the World's Rivers and Lakes*, ed. with R.K. Gresswell (1965); *Mountain Flowers in Colour* (1967).

BIBLIOGRAPHY. The standard filial biography—LEONARD HUXLEY, *Life and Letters of Thomas Henry Huxley* (1900)—is still valuable as a framework, but it contains some strange errors and omissions, especially relating to family matters and its subject's more radical views. There have been many later biographies, few of them containing anything new. Of some value are EDWARD CLODD, *Thomas Henry Huxley* (1902); CLARENCE E. AYRES, *Huxley* (1932); ERNEST W. MACBRIDE, *Huxley* (1934); and HOUSTON PETERSON, *Huxley: Prophet of Science* (1932). The first really fresh full study is CYRIL BIBBY, *T.H. Huxley: Scientist, Humanist, and Educator* (1959). Bibby has also produced three other substantial studies: *The Essence of T.H. Huxley* (1967), *T.H. Huxley on Education* (1971), and *Scientist-Extraordinary: The Life and Scientific Work of T.H. Huxley* (1972). These four volumes give bibliographic references to a considerable number of research papers on various aspects of Huxley's life and work. There is additional material of interest in JULIAN HUXLEY (ed.), *T.H. Huxley's Diary of the Voyage of H.M.S. Rattlesnake* (1935). For detailed reference to scientific researches, see MICHAEL FOSTER and E. RAY LANKESTER (eds.), *The Scientific Memoirs of T.H. Huxley*, 5 vol. (1898–1903). For information about other members of the family, see RONALD W. CLARK, *The Huxleys* (1968).

(C.Bi.)

Huygens, Christiaan

Christiaan Huygens, 17th-century Dutch mathematician, astronomer, and physicist, who is recognized as the founder of the wave theory of light, also discovered the true shape of the rings of Saturn and made original contributions to dynamics—the study of the action of forces on bodies—including the mathematics of circular motion, which he applied successfully to the oscillation of the compound pendulum.

Huygens was born at The Hague on April 14, 1629, into a wealthy and distinguished middle class family. His father, Constantijn Huygens, a diplomat, Latinist, and poet, was the friend and correspondent of many outstanding intellectual figures of the day, including the scientist and philosopher René Descartes. From an early age, Huygens showed a marked mechanical bent and a talent for drawing and mathematics. Some of his early efforts in geometry impressed Descartes, who was an occasional visitor to the Huygens' household. In 1645 Huygens entered the University of Leiden, where he studied mathematics and law. Two years later he entered the College of Breda, in the midst of a furious controversy over the philosophy of Descartes. Although Huygens later rejected certain of the Cartesian tenets including the identification of extension and body, he always affirmed that mechanical explanations were essential in science, a fact that later was to have an important influence on his mathematical interpretation of both light and gravitation.

Influence of Descartes and Pascal

In 1655 Huygens for the first time visited Paris, where his distinguished parentage, wealth, and affable disposition gave him entry to the highest intellectual and social circles. During his next visit to Paris in 1660, he met Blaise Pascal, with whom he had already been in correspondence on mathematical problems. Huygens had already acquired a European reputation by his publications in mathematics, especially his *De Circuli Magnitudine Inventa* of 1654, and by his discovery in 1659 of the true shape of the rings of Saturn—made possible by the improvements he had introduced in the construction of the

Huygens, portrait by C. Netscher, 1671. In the Collection Haags Gemeentemuseum, The Hague, The Netherlands.
By courtesy of the Collection Haags Gemeentemuseum, The Hague, The Netherlands

telescope with his new method of grinding and polishing lenses. Using his improved telescope, he discovered a satellite of Saturn in March 1655 and distinguished the stellar components of the Orion nebula in 1656. His interest, as an astronomer, in the accurate measurement of time then led him to his discovery of the pendulum as a regulator of clocks, as described in his *Horologium* (1658).

In 1666 Huygens became one of the founding members of the French Academy of Sciences, which granted him a pension larger than that of any other member and an apartment in its building. Apart from occasional visits to Holland, he lived from 1666 to 1681 in Paris, where he made the acquaintance of the German mathematician and philosopher Gottfried Wilhelm Leibniz, with whom he remained on friendly terms for the rest of his life. The major event of Huygens' years in Paris was the publication in 1673 of his *Horologium Oscillatorium*. That brilliant work contained a theory on the mathematics of curvatures, as well as complete solutions to such problems of dynamics as the derivation of the formula for the time of oscillation of the simple pendulum, the oscillation of a body about a stationary axis, and the laws of centrifugal force for uniform circular motion. Some of the results were given without proof in an appendix, and Huygens' complete proofs were not published until after his death.

Theorem on centrifugal force and nature of light

The treatment of rotating bodies was partly based on an ingenious application of the principle that in any system of bodies the centre of gravity could never rise of its own accord above its initial position. Earlier Huygens had applied the same principle to the treatment of the problem of collisions, for which he had obtained a definitive solution in the case of perfectly elastic bodies as early as 1656, although his results remained unpublished until 1669.

The somewhat eulogistic dedication of the *Horologium Oscillatorium* to Louis XIV brought to a head murmurs against Huygens at a time when France was at war with Holland, but in spite of this he continued to reside in Paris. Huygens' health was never good, and he suffered from recurrent illnesses, including one in 1670 which was so serious that for a time he despaired of his own life.

A serious illness in 1681 prompted him to return to Holland, where he intended to stay only temporarily. But the death in 1683 of his patron, Jean-Baptiste Colbert, who had been Louis XIV's chief adviser, and Louis' increasingly reactionary policy, which culminated in the revocation (1685) of the Edict of Nantes, which had granted certain liberties to Protestants, militated against his ever returning to Paris.

Huygens visited London in 1689 and met Sir Isaac Newton and lectured on his own theory of gravitation before the Royal Society. Although he did not engage in public controversy with Newton directly, it is evident from Huygens' correspondence, especially that with Leibniz, that in spite of his generous admiration for the mathematical ingenuity of the *Principia*, he regarded a theory of gravity that was devoid of any mechanical explanation as fundamentally unacceptable. His own theory, published in 1690 in his *Discours de la cause de la pesanteur* ("Discourse on the Cause of Gravity"), though dating at least to 1669, included a mechanical explanation of gravity based on Cartesian vortices. Huygens' *Traité de la lumière* (*Treatise on Light*), already largely completed by 1678, was also published in 1690. In it he again showed his need for ultimate mechanical explanations in his discussion of the nature of light. But his beautiful explanations of reflection and refraction—far superior to those of Newton—were entirely independent of mechanical explanations, being based solely on the so-called Huygens' principle of secondary wave fronts.

As a mathematician Huygens had great talent rather than genius of the first order. He sometimes found difficulty in following the innovations of Leibniz and others, but he was admired by Newton because of his love for the old synthetic methods. For almost the whole of the 18th century his work in both dynamics and light was overshadowed by that of Newton. In gravitation his theory was never taken seriously and remains today of historical interest only. But his work on rotating bodies and his contributions to the theory of light were of lasting importance. Forgotten until the early 19th century, these latter appear today as one of the most brilliant and original contributions to modern science and will always be remembered by the principle bearing his name.

The last five years of Huygens' life were marked by continued ill health and increasing feelings of loneliness and melancholy. He made the final corrections to his will in March 1695 and died after much suffering on July 8 of the same year.

BIBLIOGRAPHY. CHRISTIAAN HUYGENS, *Traité de la lumière: avec, un discours de la pesanteur* (1690; Eng. trans., *Treatise on Light*, 1912), in which are explained the causes of that which occurs in reflexion and in refraction and particularly in the strange refraction of Iceland crystals; *Oeuvres complètes* (1888–1950), vol. 1–10 contains correspondence, vol. 22 biography and portraits; A.E. BELL, *Christiaan Huygens and the Development of Science in the Seventeenth Century* (1947); H.L. BRUGMANS, *Le Séjour de Christian Huygens à Paris et ses relations avec les milieux scientifiques français* (1935).

(J.He.)

Hyderābād

The capital of the state of Andhra Pradesh in southern India, Hyderābād was founded in about 1591 by a Muslim ruler and served until 1948 as the capital of the fabled Niẓāms, the Muslim rulers of the princely state of Hyderābād. The city not only symbolizes the synthesis of Hindu and Muslim cultures but also is a complex mosaic exhibiting other widely diverse linguistic and cultural patterns.

History. Hyderābād was built by the Quṭb Shāhī sultans of Golconda, under whom the kingdom of Golconda attained a position of importance next only to that of the Mughal Empire in the north, attracting many foreigners as residents. The old fortress town of Golconda proved inadequate and unhealthy, and Muḥammad Qulī Quṭb Shāh, the fifth of the Quṭb Shāhīs and an amateur architect, decided to build a new city. Thus, on an expanse of level ground on the eastern bank of the Mūsi River a few miles from Golconda, the foundation for the new city Hyderābād was laid. With many magnificent monuments, broad and straight avenues, public utilities such as hospitals and waterworks, royal palaces, shopping centres, residential areas, and scores of gardens and parks, it was a marvel of planning and an architectural wonder.

The Chārmīnār, a grand architectural composition in Indo-Saracenic style with open arches and with four minarets, each about 180 feet high, springing from their

Architectural attractions of the city

abutments, is regarded as the supreme achievement of the Quṭb Shāhī period. It formed the centrepiece around which the city was planned. The Mecca Masjid, a mosque, was built later. It can accommodate 10,000 people. It features lofty pillars and engraved arches and is decorated in stucco style with Indian polished plaster.

Ewing Galloway

The Chārmīnār in the centre of Hyderābād's old city. At right is the Osmania University.

Popularly known as the "city of gardens," Hyderābād's beauty and affluence elicited praise from many a foreign traveller. A Mughal chronicler called it "a resort of heavenly peace and worldly comfort." But the glory of the city lasted only as long as the Quṭb Shāhīs, for the Mughals were anxious to annex the Deccan, and Emperor Aurangzeb occupied and annexed Hyderābād in 1685. The Mughal occupation resulted in plunder and destruction, and for two centuries the city lay neglected. Succeeding decades saw the decline of the Mughals and the intervention of European powers in Indian affairs. In 1724, Āṣaf Jāh Niẓām-ul-Mulk, the Mughal viceroy in the Deccan, declared independence. His successors, in order to consolidate their hold, obtained support first from the French and later from the British. This Deccan kingdom, with Hyderābād as its capital, came to be known as Hyderābād. With the establishment of British paramountcy, the state became the largest princely domain and Hyderābād the fifth largest city in India. The Āṣaf Jāhīs, during the 19th century, started to rebuild, expanding to the north of the old city across the Mūsi. Farther north, Secunderābād grew as a British cantonment, connected to Hyderābād by a mile-long bund (embankment) on the Husain Sāgar Lake. This serves as a promenade and is the pride of the city. Under the Niẓāms and their nobles many new structures, reflecting a beautiful blend of Hindu and Muslim styles, were added. Secunderābād also contains a number of houses of European styles.

Under the Niẓāms the Hindu and Muslim populations lived in amity, although immediately after Indian independence a fanatical Muslim faction, the Raẓākārs, fomented tensions in the state and the city. The Indian government intervened, and the Niẓām, Mīr Usmān ʿAlī Khān, mindful of the desires of the people, four-fifths of whom were Hindus (in the state as a whole), acceded to India, the state of Hyderābād becoming a unit in the Indian federation. In 1956 it was split up, its Telugu-speaking areas being combined with the erstwhile Andhra state to form the state of Andhra Pradesh with Hyderābād as capital.

The modern city. The present area of the city is 75 square miles (194 square kilometres); the city's master plan proposes to extend this to 120 square miles and to add an additional area of 300 square miles as a metropolitan area. Business localities are in the city centre, which is circled by residential areas. Industry is located in the northern and the eastern outskirts.

Climate. Hyderābād enjoys a salubrious climate, with average maximum and minimum temperatures of 110° F (43° C) and 50° F (10° C). The annual rainfall is about 29 inches, occurring mostly during the period May to October. The climate being hot and dry, vegetation is rather sparse, exhibiting xerophytic adaptations. Toddy, palm, mango, guava, tamarind, and banyan are common. A wide range of nonindigenous plants abound in parks and gardens. Fauna is confined to domesticated types.

Population and housing. According to the 1971 census, the city's population was 1,361,335. At the 1961 census the city's population was 1,251,119, and of this total, 61 percent were Hindu, 32 percent Muslim, and 3 percent Christian. Telugu was spoken by 48 percent of the population; Urdu by 37 percent; Hindi by 6 percent; Tamil by 3.5 percent; and Marathi by 2.5 percent. The integration of coastal districts into Andhra Pradesh led to an influx of population from these districts into the city. Regional diversities were accentuated by economic and social problems, and new tensions arose.

As regards housing, a survey estimated that about 153,000 additional units were needed in addition to the 175,000 existing ones to relieve congestion and to achieve the desirable standard densities. To this end it was decided to set apart 25,000 acres for the construction of houses for various income groups.

Transportation. The city has ideal transport facilities. A major railway and airway junction, it has direct rail and air services to Delhi, Calcutta, Bombay, Madras, and Bangalore, as well as to historical places such as Ajantā and Ellora. Two main national highways connecting north, south, east, and west pass through it, while many state highways converge on the city. Taxis, autorickshas, cycle rickshas, private vehicles, and suburban bus and rail services provide local transport.

Economic development. Hyderābād made a considerable industrial advance even during the rule of the Niẓāms. After 1950, under India's drive for industrialization, the central and the state governments located large engineering and manufacturing industries in the city area. The private sector also expanded in Hyderābād, notably in cigarette and textile manufacture and service industries, so that there are more than 600 industrial establishments employing over 200,000 people. The rapid development of industry and commerce has buoyed the city's economy and made possible a higher standard of living than is to be found in many other Indian cities.

Health facilities. The city has two government general hospitals with medical colleges attached and a number of special hospitals for treatment of women and children as well as facilities for treating leprosy, tuberculosis, cancer, and eye diseases. Private bodies run a few large medical institutions. Service is free for low-income groups in state hospitals.

Administration. As the state capital, the city contains the legislature, the governor's residence, the secretariat, and the high court, as well as the local offices of political parties. The twin cities of Hyderābād and Secunderābād are administered by a corporation with an elected council of 94 members, a mayor elected by the council, and a state-appointed commissioner assisted by a large permanent staff. The corporation provides the normal municipal services. It derives its revenues from taxes.

Education. Primary and secondary education were originally under private patronage, Christian missions in particular taking the initiative. The government had by 1916 assumed the main responsibility over primary education, which since 1961 has been free and compulsory. By 1967 all boys of school age and 90 percent of the girls were enrolled in nearly 400 primary schools. The government also stepped into the area of middle-school and secondary education by opening many free institutions. Privately managed schools receiving government aid have also increased in number. The city also has a few English-type "public" (*i.e.*, private) schools. There are more than 250 middle and secondary schools.

Universities and colleges

Initially, Hyderābād was the location of two colleges of the University of Madras. In 1918, however, the Niẓām established the Osmania University, which in a short time introduced professional courses in medicine, law, and engineering. It is now one of the best universities in India. An agricultural university has also been established. The central government located a number of advanced research and training institutes in Hyderābād. Non-governmental institutions, such as the American Studies Research Centre and the German Institute of Oriental Research, are also to be found in the city.

Cultural life and recreation. Abounding in public and private cultural organizations, such as state-sponsored dramatic, literary, and fine arts academies, and in the societies of diverse linguistic and cultural communities, the city is culturally most active. The public auditorium, Ravindra Bharati, provides an ideal venue for frequent dance and music festivals. Of the several museums, the Salar Jung is the best known. Started as a private collection by a former prime minister, it contains more than 40,000 rare pieces, including jade, jewelry, paintings, and furniture. The collection is unique in the East and perhaps in the world. The city has a number of public and private libraries.

A large number of daily newspapers and numerous periodicals, many devoted to news and current affairs, are published in various languages. The city contains a powerful broadcasting station of the All-India Radio.

The public gardens provide the main recreational facilities. Many parks and the large parade grounds in Secunderābād offer scope for play and relaxation. The zoological gardens and the university's botanical gardens are popular picnic spots. Hyderābād is reputed for its soccer and cricket. There is also a racecourse.

BIBLIOGRAPHY. ABDUL MAJEED SIDDIQUI, *History of Golconda* (1956), traces the origins, developments, and decline of the city of Hyderābād as the capital of the kingdom of Golconda and its revival as the capital of the Nizām's Dominion of Hyderābād. JADUNATH SARKAR, *A Short History of Aurangzib, 1618–1707* (1930), is a monumental study of the last of the powerful Mughal Emperors who conquered and annexed the kingdom of Golconda leading to the decline of Hyderābād; contains much evidence about the beauty, wealth, and strength of the city during these times. The GOVERNMENT OF ANDHRA PRADESH, *Hyderabad City Guide* (1963), includes general information about the city and its municipal corporation. See also SHAH MANZOOR ALLAM, *Hyderabad-Secunderabad (Twin Cities): A Study in Urban Geography* (1965).

(R.V.R.C.R.)

Hydraulics, Applications of

Liquids in motion or under pressure did useful work for man for many centuries before French scientist-philosopher Blaise Pascal and Swiss physicist Daniel Bernoulli formulated the laws on which modern fluid-power technology is based.

Pascal's law

Pascal's law, formulated *c.* 1650, states that pressure in a liquid is transmitted equally in all directions; *i.e.*, when water is made to fill a closed container, the application of pressure at any point will be transmitted to all sides of the container. In the hydraulic press, Pascal's law is used to gain an increase in force; a small force applied to a small piston in a small cylinder is transmitted through a tube to a large cylinder, where it presses equally against all sides of the cylinder, including the large piston.

Bernoulli's law, formulated about a century later, states that energy in a fluid is due to elevation, motion, and pressure, and if there are no losses due to friction and no work done, the sum of the energies remains constant. Thus velocity energy, deriving from motion, can be partly converted to pressure energy by enlarging the cross section of a pipe, which slows down the flow but increases the area against which the fluid is pressing.

Until the 19th century it was not possible to develop velocities and pressures much greater than those provided by nature, but the invention of pumps brought a vast potential for application of the discoveries of Pascal and Bernoulli. In 1882 the city of London built a hydraulic system that delivered pressurized water through street mains to drive machinery in factories; the system is still used to operate hoists, cranes, lift bridges, and fire curtains in theatres. In 1906 an important advance in hydraulic techniques was made when an oil hydraulic system was installed to raise and control the guns of the USS "Virginia." In the 1920s self-contained hydraulic units consisting of a pump, controls, and motor were developed, opening the way to applications in machine tools, automobiles, farm and earth-moving machinery, locomotives, ships, airplanes, and spacecraft.

In fluid-power systems there are five elements: the driver, the pump, the control valves, the motor, and the load. The driver may be an electric motor or an engine of any type. The pump acts mainly to increase pressure. The motor may be a counterpart of the pump, transforming hydraulic input into mechanical output. Motors may produce either rotary or reciprocating motion in the load.

Modern applications

The growth of fluid-power technology since World War II has been phenomenal. In the operation and control of machine tools, farm machinery, construction machinery, and mining machinery, fluid power can compete successfully with mechanical and electrical systems. Its chief advantages are flexibility and the ability to multiply forces efficiently; it also provides fast and accurate response to controls. Fluid power can provide a force of a few ounces or one of thousands of tons.

Hydraulic power systems have become one of the major energy-transmission technologies utilized by all phases of industrial, agricultural, and defense activity.

Modern aircraft use hydraulic systems to activate their controls and to operate landing gear and brakes. Virtually all missiles, as well as their ground-support equipment, utilize fluid power. The Apollo space exploration missions depended on fluid power. Automobiles use hydraulic-power systems in their transmissions, brakes, and steering mechanisms. Mass production and its offspring, automation, in many industries have their foundations in the utilization of fluid-power systems.

Pumps. Of the many types of pumping devices, hydraulic-power systems use four: gear, vane, piston, and screw (see PUMP). All are mechanical devices that characteristically work by entrapping a fixed volume of fluid during the suction part of the pumping cycle, isolating this volume momentarily within the mechanism during the transfer operation, and forcibly ejecting the fluid into the system against whatever resistance the system offers. The name of the pump is indicative of the kind of mechanism used to achieve the pumping action.

Modern gear pumps, of the type used in hydraulic power systems, can deliver fluid at pressures up to 2,500 pounds per square inch (psi) and at rates up to 200 gallons per minute (gpm). Thus they are capable of delivering about 250–300 horsepower to the system, which was the maximum capability in the early 1970s. The norm would fall closer to 1,500–1,800 psi and a flow rate of 40–50 gpm, corresponding to about 40–50 horsepower. Vane pump capabilities fall very close to those for gear pumps. Maximum pressures of about 3,000 psi are attainable, with the norm closer to 1,000–1,500 psi. Flow rates are in the 150–200 gpm range.

While gear pumps are of the fixed displacement type—that is, they cannot be adjusted for varying flow rates—vane pumps can be of either fixed or variable displacement design. A variable displacement pump can deliver an infinitely adjustable flow of fluid from zero to maximum capability of the pump. This range provides a flexible speed control technique for fluid-power systems.

Screw pumps can best be thought of as helical gears. Because of the screw action between displacement elements, this is the quietest running pump. Some screw pumps can operate to 3,000 psi pressure level. Others are capable of delivering hundreds of gallons per minute.

Piston pumps

Piston pumps for hydraulic power systems are of two types, namely: radial piston pumps, in which the axes of the multiple pistons in the pump extend radially outward from the centre of the pump shaft; and axial piston pumps, in which the axes of the pistons are parallel to the centre line of the pump shaft. Both designs are available in either fixed or variable displacement types with a wide variety of controls to adapt them to specific functions, such as hydrostatic transmissions, constant horsepower output, and constant speed output. Piston pumps carry the highest pressure ratings of all the pump types. A pressure of 3,000 psi is quite common, while several designs are rated at 5,000–6,000 psi. A few pumps are rated up to 10,000 psi and some have been run at levels as high as 15,000–20,000 psi. A particular design known as the "in-line" piston pump is available in pressure ratings up to 50,000 and 100,000 psi. These are not generally used on power transmission systems but, rather, in installations in which very high pressure at relatively low flow rates is needed. There are many variations of these four basic designs.

Motors. Motors have the reverse function of the pump in a hydraulic-power system; that is, they accept the energy-charged fluid delivered by the pump, transfer the energy across the motor mechanism, convert it to a mechanical output, and deliver the mechanical output to the load. The form this output takes depends upon the type and design of the hydraulic motor involved.

There are two basic types of hydraulic motors and several subclasses: (1) linear motors (hydraulic cylinders), either single acting or double acting; (2) rotational motors, either with limited rotation (sometimes called rotary cylinders) or continuous rotation.

Hydraulic cylinders consist of a cylindrical outer casing with a fixed closure at one end and at the other end a removable closure with a hole in it through which the piston rod projects (see Figure 1). The piston rod is con-

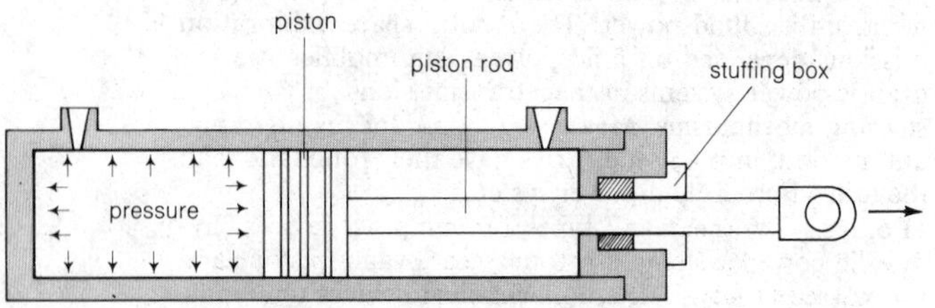

Figure 1: Hydraulic cylinder.

nected to the piston, inside the cylinder. The piston is the mechanical interface across which the energy transfer takes place. Hydrostatic pressure acts on one side of the piston. A force is produced that is equal to the product of the pressure and the total area of the piston face on which it is acting. This force is transmitted to the piston rod. The piston rod is the element that couples the mechanical force generated inside the cylinder to the external load.

A single-acting cylinder can deliver a force in only one direction. The opposite action must come from the load itself, or from a return spring built into the cylinder. A double-acting cylinder can produce a force in both directions. Hydraulic cylinders are used as brake cylinders on automobiles, hoist cylinders on grease racks in garages, control actuators on aircraft, cylinders to raise and lower the blade on bulldozers, to adjust the depth of a plow on a farm tractor, and in the handling of logs at a sawmill. Cylinders operate presses to form parts for automobiles, inject molten metal into die-casting machines, and plastics in injection-molding machines. The hydraulic cylinder is useful in any place where there is a

Hydraulic cylinders

need for a high-force-level, straight-line motion on a machine or in a production process.

Hydraulic cylinders can easily generate forces that would be difficult to achieve by any other means. It is possible, for example, to obtain ready-made cylinders rated at 1,000,000 pounds of force. And special cylinders can be designed to produce even higher forces.

The limited rotation motor illustrated in Figure 2 can be thought of as a rotary cylinder. Instead of producing a straight-line motion like the cylinder, the rotary actuator produces a rotation of its shaft—generally limited to about 300 degrees in a single-vane design and 150 degrees in a double-vane type. As with cylinders, rotary actuators can be either single or double acting.

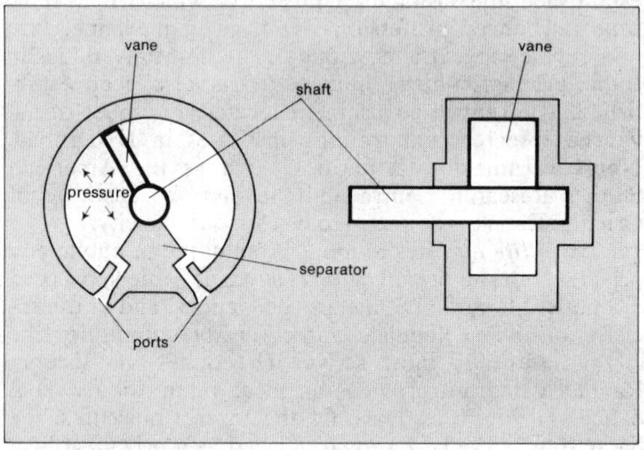

Figure 2: Vane type limited rotation actuator.

Rotary actuators are available in almost any torque rating (turning force). In addition to the vane type rotary actuator, other designs provide several revolutions of motion.

Applications include machines in which a limited rotational motion is needed and space is restricted, such as with swinging booms and crane arms, some types of ditch-digging equipment, raceway gates, materials-holding jigs, and other fixtures in production processes.

Continuous rotation hydraulic motors are the inverse—or the "mirror image"—of their pump counterparts. Motors are available in gear, vane, and piston designs, as well as many of the variations discussed under PUMP. In many cases the same component can be used as either a pump or a motor, depending on the source of energy. If a gear unit is driven by a prime mover and the piping is properly connected to it, the unit functions as a pump. If, on the other hand, the gear unit is connected to a load and is piped so as to receive pressurized fluid, it functions as a motor. The same is essentially true of the other designs.

The characteristic output from a continuous rotation hydraulic motor is a torque or turning force that is a function of pressure differential across the motor and its displacement. The torque is delivered at a speed that is determined by the input flow rate and motor displacement.

Hydraulic motors are used in all kinds of applications requiring this performance characteristic, such as: power drives on vehicles, winches, spindle drives on machine tools, table drives for machine tools, earth augers, steering gear on ships, roll stand drives for paper-making machines, printing presses, plastic laminating machines, and power take-off drives for agricultural equipment.

Hydrostatic transmissions. The combination of a hydraulic pump and a hydraulic motor along with the necessary control devices is called a hydrostatic transmission. Hydrostatic transmissions range from the simplest, using a fixed-displacement pump and a similar motor, which must be controlled by throttling flow across a valve, to very complex systems utilizing variable displacement units and servo control, *i.e.*, related mechanical control devices. A hydrostatic transmission using a variable-displacement pump and fixed-displacement motor is called a constant-torque transmission because, assuming a fixed-pressure differential across the motor, the torque will be constant because the motor's displacement will remain so. The speed of the motor and the power transmitted, however, will vary as a function of pump displacement. Conversely, a hydrostatic transmission with a fixed pump and a variable motor is called a constant-power transmission. Motor torque and speed vary inversely in a variable motor. As the displacement is reduced, the output torque is also reduced proportionately and the speed increases. Power remains essentially constant.

Hydromechanical transmission

Transmissions that combine a hydrostatic drive with supplementary mechanical elements are called hydromechanical transmissions. Their operating characteristics are very complex. In general, hydromechanical transmissions combine the infinite speed variation of the hydrostatic drive with the higher efficiency of the gear drive over a wide range of speed ratios.

Controls. Means must be provided in all hydrostatic fluid-power systems for controlling the pressure and the rate and direction of fluid flow. The control function is accomplished by valves, classified appropriately as pressure-control, flow-control, and direction-control valves.

Pressure-control valves are used in several ways. To avoid structural failure of the components in a system, relief or safety valves, which open at a predetermined pressure, are used; the safety valve on a steam boiler, for example, "lets off steam" when the steam pressure reaches a value still below that which would cause catastrophic failure. When two branches of the same circuit must operate simultaneously at different pressures, reducing valves are used. If fluid in a primary circuit is to be switched to a secondary circuit when pressure in the primary circuit exceeds a certain level, sequence valves are used.

The operation of a typical pressure-control valve is illustrated in Figure 3. The fluid pressure creates a force on one end of the control spool that is opposed by the spring

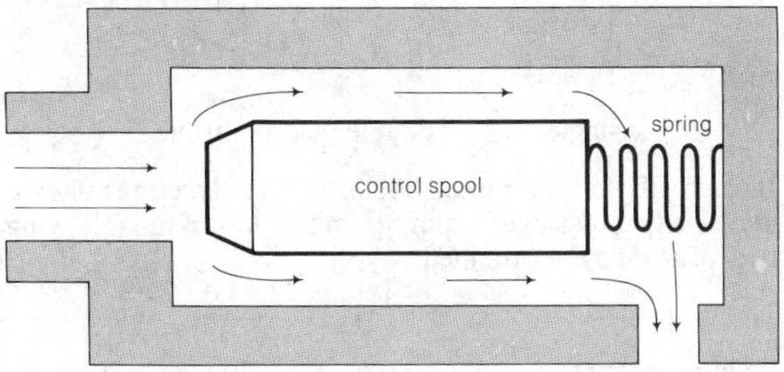

Figure 3: Force-balance principle in control valve.

force. In the closed position, the fluid force is less than the spring force. When the fluid force exceeds the spring force, the valve will open and permit fluid to pass through the annular opening around the spool.

Flow-control valves are similar in design and construction to those used for pressure control.

A direction-control valve is basically a fluid switching device. It contains flow passages and one or more movable elements designed to switch the fluid stream between these passages and direct it from an inlet port to appropriate outlet ports. Provision must also be made for the return of the hydraulic fluid to the reservoir, which is the storage place for unused fluid in a system.

An active port in a valve is called a "way." Thus a valve with one inlet port and one outlet port is called a "two-way" valve. A three-way valve has an inlet (pump) port, a return (reservoir) port, and a motor or actuator port. When a second motor port is added it becomes a four-way valve.

A two-way valve is a simple on-off fluid switch; a three-way valve permits the fluid stream to be switched from the inlet port to the motor port, or from the motor port to the return port, thus providing control for a single-acting motor or actuator. A four-way valve has two motor ports that can be connected successively to the inlet port while the other is connected to the return port. Valves of this type are necessary for the control of double-acting or reversible motors or actuators.

If the valves in a hydrostatic fluid power system are controlled by the operator, the system is said to be open-loop. If the control system uses a form of feedback and is self-regulating, it is said to be closed-loop. Feedback as defined here consists of sampling any output variable—speed, torque, force, position, acceleration—comparing its actual state with the required state, and when there is a difference (called the "error"), making the necessary adjustments in the control element so that the desired state is maintained.

Hydraulic fluids. Water and oil are the main liquids used in hydraulic systems. On account of its higher specific gravity and lower viscosity, water is more effective than oil in hydrokinetic systems; in a fluid coupling, for example, a gallon of water will generate more torque or turning moment than a gallon of oil. Water corrodes and evaporates, however, and consequently oil is the most commonly used liquid in both hydrokinetic and hydrostatic fluid-power systems.

In an attempt to overcome the fire hazard in oil-hydraulic systems, fire resistant fluids have been developed. These fluids include water-soluble oils, water-glycol mixtures, and synthetic fluids such as phosphate esters.

Special fluids have been developed for aerospace and military applications; these fluids, requiring fire resistance, lubricity, and chemical stability, must perform satisfactorily under a wide range of climatic conditions.

BIBLIOGRAPHY. C.V. DAVIS and K.E. SORENSEN (eds.), *Handbook of Applied Hydraulics*, 3rd ed. (1969), a comprehensive handbook including dissertations on many facets of hydraulics technology; R.W. HENKE, *Introduction to Fluid Mechanics* (1966), a basic text on fluid mechanics with an orientation toward fluid-power technology and industrial applications; *Introduction to Fluid Power* (1971), an introductory-level text on fluid-power technology, with emphasis on its energy transmission characteristics; and *Introduction to Fluid Power Circuits and Systems* (1970), a non-mathematical treatise on the design and analysis of fluid-power circuits, including a treatment of open-loop, logic design, and closed-loop systems; H. ROUSE and S. IWCE, *History of Hydraulics* (1957), a chronology of the art and science of hydraulics, with biographical sketches of some of the outstanding contributors to it; V.L. STREETER, *Handbook of Fluid Dynamics* (1961), an advanced engineering-level handbook, mathematically oriented, to which authorities in the field of fluid mechanics have contributed articles on their specialty.

(R.W.H.)

Hydrocarbons

Chemical substances containing only the elements hydrogen (H) and carbon (C) generally are called hydrocarbons. In hydrocarbon molecules the carbon atoms make up the skeleton or framework that gives the molecules their general shape, and the hydrogen atoms are attached to the carbon atoms, completing the molecular structure. The carbon atoms may be arranged in chains that are consecutive or branched, in rings, or in more complex three-dimensional frameworks. The number of carbon atoms per molecule has no apparent upper limit:

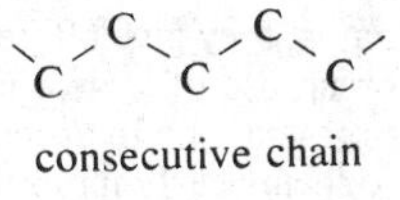

consecutive chain

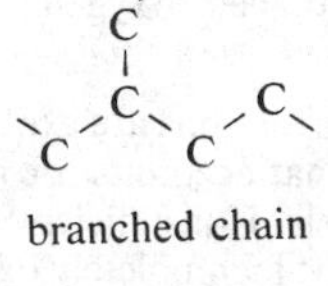

branched chain

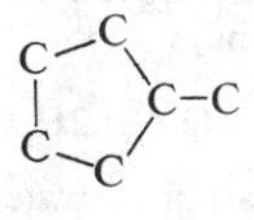

ring with one branch

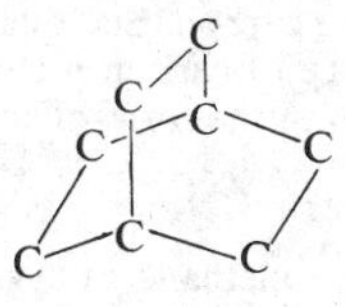

a three-dimensional framework

Hydrocarbons with as many as 110 carbon atoms in a consecutive chain have been synthesized.

Occurrence. Many hydrocarbons occur in nature. As constituents of petroleum and natural gas, they are important energy sources. Because petroleum and natural gas are available in large supply, these hydrocarbons also serve as raw materials for the manufacture of plastics, synthetic rubber, solvents, explosives, lubricants, alcohols, synthetic fabrics, and many other useful products.

Certain hydrocarbons are present in trees and other plants. A hydrocarbon known as α-pinene (alpha-pinene), for example, with the empirical formula $C_{10}H_{16}$ (that is, with molecules each composed of ten carbon atoms and 16 hydrogen atoms), is the major component of turpentine, which is obtained from pine trees; and *n*-heptane, with the formula C_7H_{16}, can be obtained in pure form and in large quantities from the Jeffrey pine. Hydrocarbons also are present in plant and insect waxes: beeswax contains 10–14 percent hydrocarbons (mainly $C_{31}H_{64}$). Hydrocarbons with fairly long carbon chains (up to C_{29}) have been isolated from cabbage and tobacco leaves, and from the cuticle (waxy film) of apples. Lycopene ($C_{40}H_{56}$) is the red pigment in ripe tomatoes and watermelon, and the carotenes (also with the formula $C_{40}H_{56}$ but with different arrangements of the atoms in the molecule) are important pigments in carrots and green leaves. Over 98 percent of crude plantation rubber is a hydrocarbon polymer, a chainlike molecule made of many small units joined together, with the formula $(C_5H_8)_n$, with *n* being a number averaging approximately 20,000.

Hydrocarbons in foods, tobacco, and rubber

Chemical and physical properties. Regardless of their diverse molecular structures, all hydrocarbons have a number of properties in common. They are virtually insoluble in water and, being less dense, float on its surface. Hydrocarbons are, however, usually soluble in one another as well as in certain organic solvents such as ether. Hydrocarbons may be gases, liquids, or solids at room temperature, their physical state depending mainly on their molecular weight. Those with four carbon atoms or fewer are gases. It is more difficult, however, to generalize about the demarcation between liquids and solids because crystallinity depends on molecular shape as well as on molecular weight. Some hydrocarbons, despite comparatively low molecular weights, are crystalline because their structures are highly symmetrical or compact. An example is hexamethylethane, the only hydrocarbon out of a total of 18, all of which have the formula C_8H_{18}, that is a solid at room temperature. It has the remarkably high melting point of 104° C, only 3° below its boiling point.

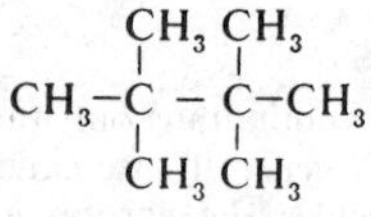

hexamethylethane

Combustibility

All hydrocarbons are combustible. If burned completely with sufficient oxygen, they produce carbon dioxide (CO_2) and water (H_2O). For example, the combustion of methane, the main component of natural gas, can be expressed:

$$\underset{\text{methane}}{CH_4} + \underset{\text{oxygen}}{2O_2} \longrightarrow \underset{\text{carbon dioxide}}{CO_2} + \underset{\text{water}}{2H_2O} + \text{heat}.$$

Such reactions are exothermic (that is, they give off heat), a fact that accounts for the widespread use of hydrocarbons as fuels. If insufficient oxygen is present, the hydrocarbon may be incompletely oxidized, producing carbon monoxide or pure carbon. Such incomplete combustion explains the presence of carbon monoxide in automobile exhaust, and carbon in the form of soot in chimneys.

$$\underset{\text{methane}}{CH_4} + \underset{\text{oxygen}}{\tfrac{3}{2}O_2} \longrightarrow \underset{\text{carbon monoxide}}{CO} + \underset{\text{water}}{2H_2O}$$

$$\underset{\text{methane}}{CH_4} + \underset{\text{oxygen}}{O_2} \longrightarrow \underset{\text{carbon}}{C} + \underset{\text{water}}{2H_2O}$$

Varieties of carbon–carbon bonds

Classification. Hydrocarbons are in a sense the parent compounds from which can be derived all other organic compounds, as the large class of compounds containing carbon is called. In addition, the hydrocarbons illustrate several types of chemical bonding between carbon atoms, and their nomenclature forms the basis for the names of other organic compounds. More complicated molecules can be related structurally in a systematic way to hydrocarbons by the replacement of one or more of the hydrogens by other atoms or groups of atoms. Some examples are:

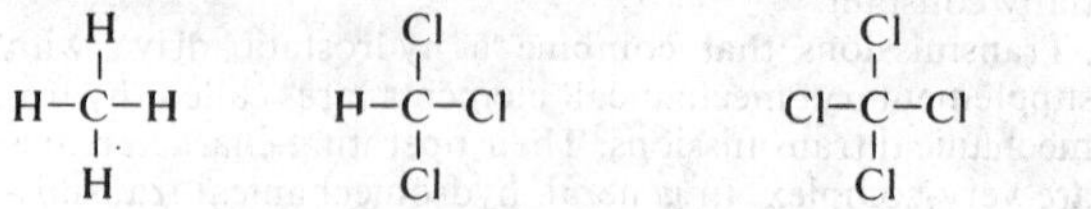

methane — chloroform or trichloromethane — carbon tetrachloride or tetrachloromethane

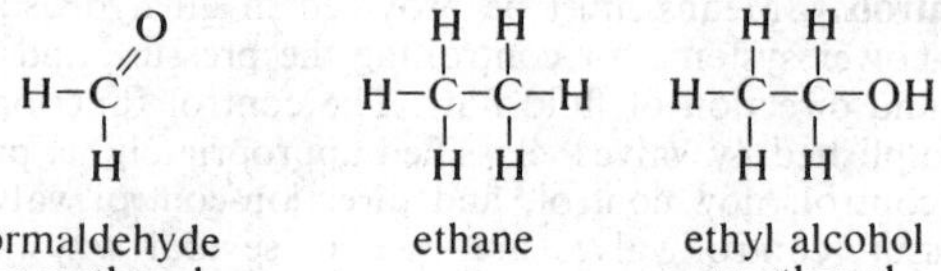

formaldehyde or methanal — ethane — ethyl alcohol or ethanol

The structures of particular hydrocarbons and their chemistry depend in large measure upon the types of chemical bonds that the carbon atoms of the hydrocarbon molecules form with one another. Carbon atoms have a maximum valence, or chemical binding power, of four; this is a consequence of the fact that each carbon atom has four valence electrons, which it can share with other atoms including, of course, other carbon atoms. A single carbon atom, however, can share more than one of these electrons with another atom, again including carbon, thereby forming double or triple bonds, as shown in the following diagram. Thus, carbon atoms may be attached to four, three, or two other atoms.

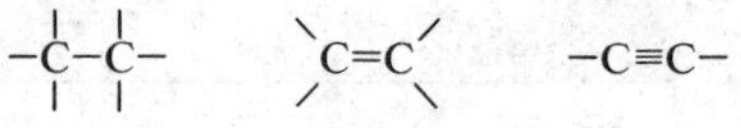

single — double — triple

If each of the remaining bonds in the structures shown above is to a hydrogen atom, the structures of the following hydrocarbons are obtained:

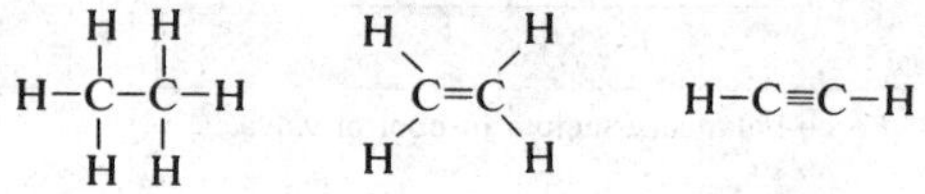

ethane — ethylene — acetylene

In each case there are four bonds to each carbon atom and one bond to each hydrogen atom, hydrogen atoms always having a valence of one. The type of bonding present, whether single or multiple, affects the molecular structure and chemical behaviour of the hydrocarbon in characteristic ways, which will be discussed as each class of hydrocarbons is considered below.

In order to group together compounds with similar chemical behaviour, hydrocarbons are divided into several major classes according to their structure:

- Aliphatic hydrocarbons
  - Saturated (alkanes, cycloalkanes)
  - Unsaturated
    - Alkenes, dienes, polyenes; related cycloalkenes, etc.
    - Alkynes, cycloalkynes
- Aromatic hydrocarbons
  - Benzenoid (mono-, di-, and polycyclic)
  - Nonbenzenoid

The two major categories are aliphatic (Greek *aleiphar*, "fat") and aromatic (Greek *arōmatikos*, "aromatic"). The aliphatic hydrocarbons can be defined most simply as all those hydrocarbons that are not aromatic. The chemical sense of the word aromatic no longer has any relation to the term aroma from which it was originally derived. Rather, aromatic compounds are now loosely defined as those substances the molecules of which have closed rings of atoms joined by a type of bond regarded as a hybrid of the single bond and the double bond. (For further treatment of this special bond, see *Aromatic hydrocarbons* below.) Aliphatic substances include all hydrocarbons of which the molecules contain chains but no rings of carbon atoms, called acyclic, as well as those with carbon rings, called alicyclic, or carbocyclic, except for those classed as aromatic. Aliphatic hydrocarbons may be further categorized according to the types of carbon–carbon bonds present. If all the bonds are single, the compound is said to be saturated. The systematic names for such classes of compounds are alkanes and cycloalkanes. If a multiple bond connects any two carbon atoms, the hydrocarbon is referred to as unsaturated; the bonds may be double, as in alkenes or alkadienes, or triple, as in alkynes; some substances contain both types of multiple bonds in the same molecule. Aromatic compounds are classed as benzenoid if they contain six-membered aromatic rings, as in the parent compound benzene, or nonbenzenoid if they do not. They are further classified according to the number of rings they contain.

Saturated and unsaturated hydrocarbons

The nomenclature, structure, physical properties, synthesis, and chemical reactions of each of these classes of hydrocarbons are discussed below.

Aliphatic hydrocarbons

ALKANES

Alkanes have the general formula C_nH_{2n+2}, n being an integer and signifying the number of carbon atoms; each member of the class differs from the next higher and lower member, called homologues, by one carbon and two hydrogens. Formulas for the first two members of the series, methane, CH_4, and ethane, C_2H_6, have been given above. Only one structure is possible for each of these, and for the compound propane, C_3H_8, in which $n = 3$, but when $n = 4$, giving butane, C_4H_{10}, two structural formulas consistent with the valence rules can be written, depending on whether the carbon chain is consecutive or branched. In fact, substances corresponding to each butane structure can be prepared, as shown below. (The prefix "*n*-" refers to a normal, or consecutive, chain of atoms; "iso-" in this case implies a branched structure.)

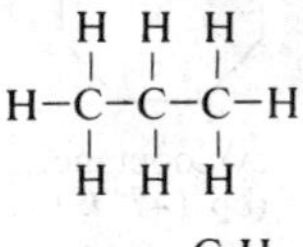

propane, C_3H_8

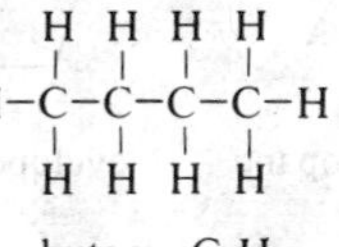

n-butane, C_4H_{10}

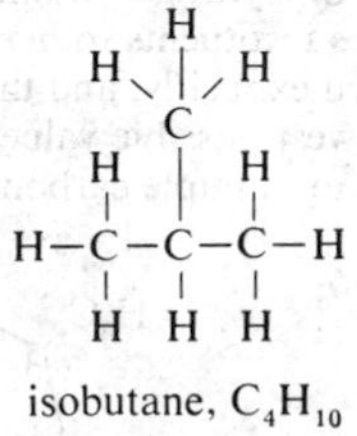

isobutane, C_4H_{10}

This phenomenon—called isomerism—is a general one, perhaps one of the most important in organic chemistry. Molecules are said to be isomers if they have the same molecular formula, as in the case of the butanes, C_4H_{10}, but different structural formulas (*i.e.*, different arrangements of the atoms in the molecule, as in *n*-butane and isobutane). Isomers usually have similar but not identical properties; both butanes, for example, are colourless gases, but *n*-butane boils at a slightly higher temperature (−0.5° C) than does isobutane (−12° C).

The number of possible isomers rises sharply with increasing *n*, as shown in Table 1. All alkanes up to and including the 35 isomers corresponding to formula C_9H_{20} have been synthesized, and in each case the number of isomers found corresponded with that predicted. Of the groups containing more than nine carbons, only a few isomers have been prepared, chiefly because there has been no practical incentive for chemists to synthesize them.

Table 1: Number of Possible Isomeric Alkanes

n	number of isomers	*n*	number of isomers
5	3	10	75
6	5	15	4,347
7	9	20	366,319
8	18	30	4,111,846,763
9	35	40	6.25×10^{13}

Nomenclature. Because of the existence of numerous isomers corresponding to each formula, the need for a systematic way of naming hydrocarbons quickly became apparent to chemists. A system originally devised by an international congress of chemists held in 1892 in Geneva, Switzerland, and later revised by the International Union of Pure and Applied Chemistry (IUPAC), is now used universally by organic chemists. In this system the saturated hydrocarbons are known as alkanes, the "*-ane*" ending being reserved for saturated compounds. After the first four members of the series, whose names have already been given, the normal (straight or consecutive chain) alkanes are named using Greek or Latin prefixes to indicate the number of carbon atoms in the chain:

IUPAC nomenclature

C_5 *pent*ane	C_9 *non*ane	C_{13} *tridec*ane
C_6 *hex*ane	C_{10} *dec*ane	C_{14} *tetradec*ane
C_7 *hept*ane	C_{11} *undec*ane	C_{15} *pentadec*ane
C_8 *oct*ane	C_{12} *dodec*ane	C_{20} *eicos*ane

Branched-chain hydrocarbons are regarded as derivatives of normal hydrocarbons, the longest consecutive chain being considered the parent. The carbon atoms of this longest chain are then numbered from the end that gives the branches the lowest possible numbers. The names of the branches are attached as prefixes to the parent name, and their position is indicated by giving the number of the atom to which they are attached. If there are two branches on the same carbon, the number is repeated. The numbers precede the groups and are separated from them by hyphens. Finally, groups are named by changing the "-ane" ending to "-yl." For example:

CH_4	CH_3-	CH_3CH_3	CH_3CH_2-
methane	methyl group	ethane	ethyl group

The system is illustrated by the following examples:

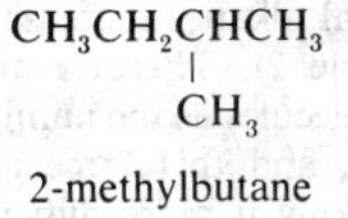

2-methylbutane

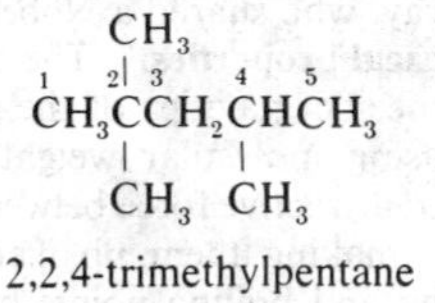

2,2,4-trimethylpentane

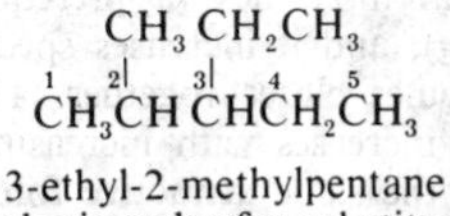

3-ethyl-2-methylpentane
(alphabetic order for substituents)

Special rules have been provided to handle unusually complex structures.

Three-dimensional structures. Although flat, or two-dimensional, formulas are customarily used to represent the structures of organic compounds, the molecules themselves are in fact three-dimensional. The electron pairs making up chemical bonds usually adopt positions that keep them as far from one another as possible, since electrons carry like charges and repel one another. When the carbon atom has four groups attached to it (all with single bonds), the most stable arrangement is for the atom itself to be at the centre of a regular tetrahedron with the bonds extending toward its corners. Thus in methane, all H–C–H bond angles are equal to 109.5° (if the methane molecule were flat, the average angle between bonds would be only 90°). The

Tetrahedral structure of the carbon atom

tetrahedral structure, with slight angle variations (106–112°) if the tetrahedron is not entirely symmetric, is common to all alkanes.

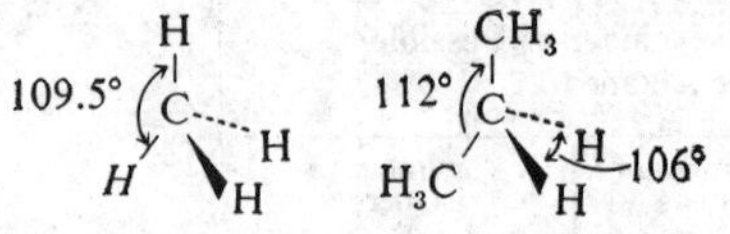

methane propane

The carbon–carbon bond distance in alkanes is almost always 1.54 angstroms (Å) (one angstrom = 10^{-8} centimetre), and the carbon–hydrogen bond distance is 1.09 Å. The distance between hydrogens on adjacent carbons varies, however, because of rotation of the atoms about the carbon–carbon single bond. This phenomenon can be observed in the structure of ethane, in which the hydrogen–hydrogen distances are greatest in the so-called staggered conformation—that is, the shape the molecule assumes by rotation about the carbon–carbon bond; conversely, the hydrogen–hydrogen distances are smallest in another con-

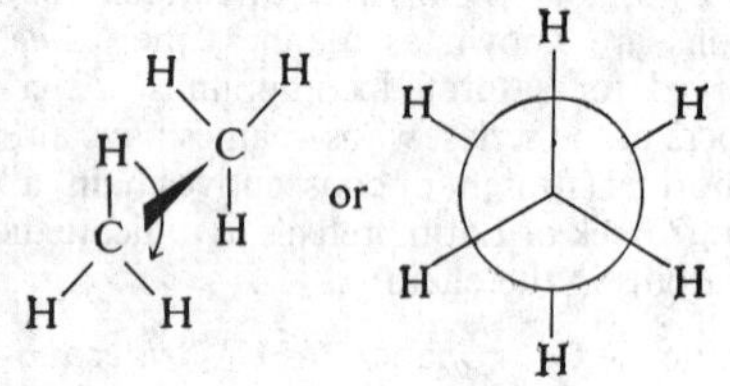

ethane
(staggered conformation)

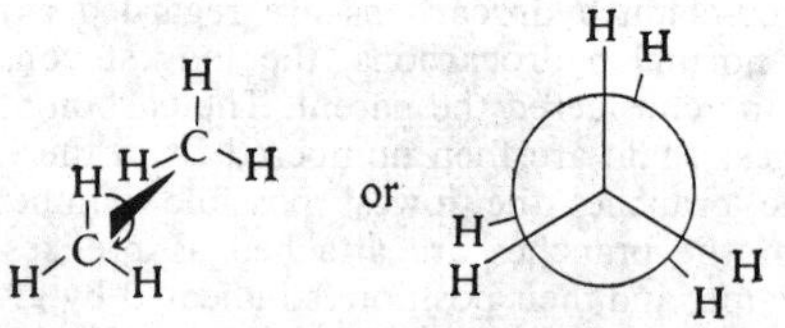

ethane
(eclipsed conformation)

formation, called the eclipsed conformation. Because of energy considerations, the staggered arrangement is more stable, and at room temperature most ethane molecules have this conformation. Conformational analysis, the analysis of physical properties and chemical reactions as a function of molecular shape, was first developed during the 1950s by D.H.R. Barton of England and Odd Hassel of Norway, who shared a Nobel Prize in 1969 for their work.

Conformational analysis

Physical properties. The boiling points, melting points, and specific gravities of the normal alkanes increase with increasing molecular weight (Table 2). There is an enhanced attractive force between molecules as the number of atoms making them up increases, and this force affects melting and boiling points by making it more difficult to separate individual molecules (a prerequisite for either melting or boiling), and it increases specific gravities by pulling the molecules closer together. The viscosity, or "stickiness," also increases with increasing chain length, partly because of the same attractive force, and also because the greater lengths of the larger molecules increases the possibilities for entanglement and decreases the ability of the molecules to slip past one another. Branched-chain isomers almost always have lower boiling points than do the straight-chain isomers of the same compounds. This is clearly demonstrated by the three isomers of the hydrocarbon C_5H_{12} as shown below:

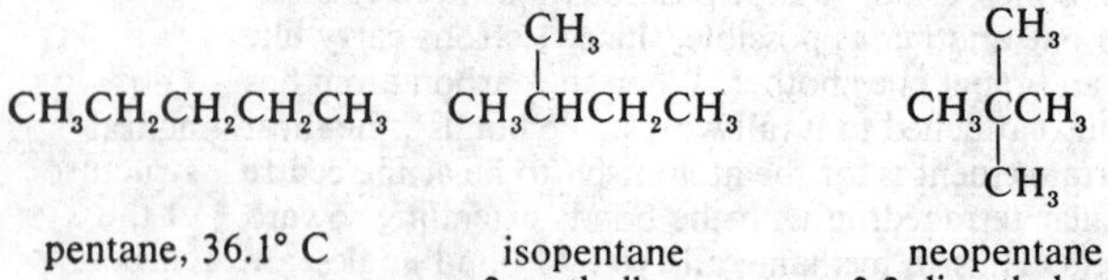

pentane, 36.1° C — isopentane or 2-methylbutane, 28° C — neopentane or 2,2-dimethylpropane, 9.5° C

This effect stems from the fact that branching forces the molecules to remain farther apart and consequently decreases their mutual attraction.

Table 2: Physical Properties of *n*-Alkanes

name	formula	boiling point (°C)	melting point (°C)	specific gravity
Methane	CH_4	−164	−182.5	.466
Ethane	C_2H_6	−88.6	−183.3	.572
Propane	C_3H_8	−42	−189.7	.501
Butane	C_4H_{10}	−0.5	−138.35	.601
Pentane	C_5H_{12}	+36.1	−129.7	.626
Hexane	C_6H_{14}	+68.9	−95.0	.660
Heptane	C_7H_{16}	+98.4	−90.6	.684
Octane	C_8H_{18}	+125.6	−56.8	.703
Nonane	C_9H_{20}	+150.8	−51.0	.718
Decane	$C_{10}H_{22}$	+174.1	−29.7	.730
Pentadecane	$C_{15}H_{32}$	+270	+10	.769
Octadecane	$C_{18}H_{38}$	+316.1	+28.2	.777
Eicosane	$C_{20}H_{42}$	+343	+36.8	.778
Triacontane	$C_{30}H_{62}$	+449.7	+65.8	.775
Tetracontane	$C_{40}H_{82}$	—	+81	—
Pentacontane	$C_{50}H_{102}$	—	+92	.794

Cycloalkanes. The general formula for cycloalkanes with one ring is C_nH_{2n}, where n is an integer equal to or greater than three. Thus, there are two fewer hydrogen atoms in the molecule of a cycloalkane than there are in the molecule of the corresponding alkane.

This condition exists because a valence bond from each of two carbon atoms is used in forming the ring. Rings are classified generally as small (n = 3 or 4), ordinary (n = 5 or 6), medium (n = 7 to 10), and large (n greater than 10). They are named with the same roots as alkanes, but with the prefix "cyclo-":

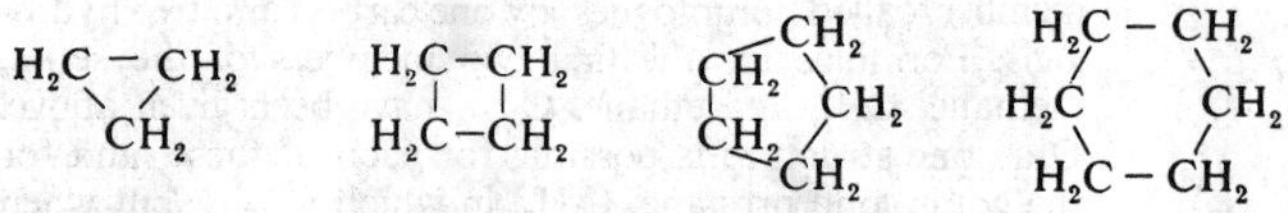

cyclopropane (bp −33° C) — cyclobutane (bp +12° C) — cyclopentane (bp+49.3° C) — cyclohexane (bp +80.7° C)

Frequently the formulas for cycloalkanes are represented by geometric figures that correspond to the rings. Each

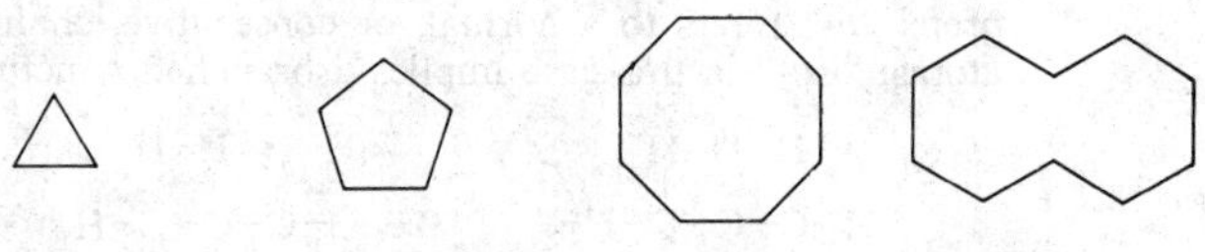

cyclopropane — cyclopentane — cyclooctane (bp 147° C) — cyclodecane (bp 201° C)

corner of the figure stands for a carbon atom with the appropriate number of hydrogen atoms to complete the valence of four. If substituents other than carbon are present they are shown explicitly, and the ring is numbered to assign them the lowest possible values. The "-ane" ending is retained when no multiple carbon–carbon bonds are present.

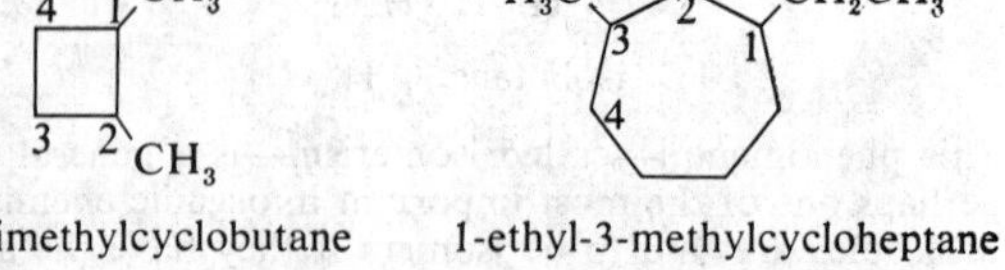

1,2-dimethylcyclobutane — 1-ethyl-3-methylcycloheptane

The three carbon atoms of cyclopropane necessarily define a plane, and the six hydr ogen atoms are oriented above and below this plane. Since the carbons are at the corners of an

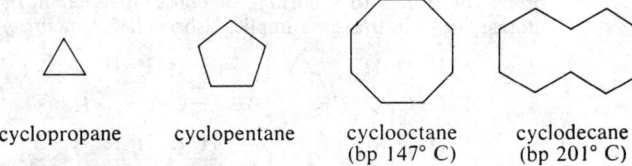

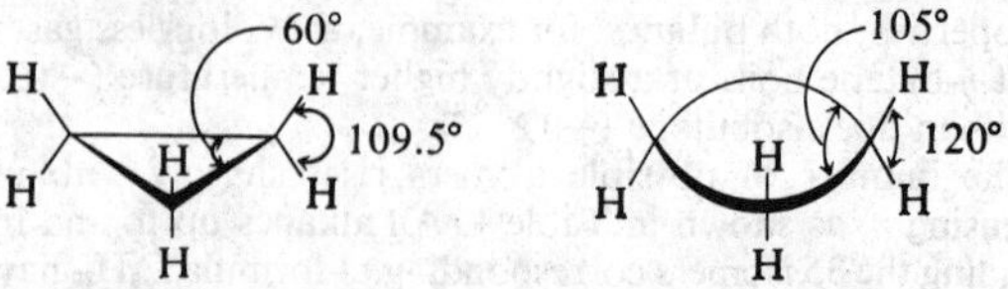

equilateral triangle structure for cyclopropane — bent bond structure for cyclopropane equilateral triangle, the angles between the carbon–carbon bonds should be 60°. This small angle imposes considerable strain on the molecule, however, because the normal angle between carbon–carbon bonds (with the tetrahedral structure) is 109.5°. The molecule accommodates to this situation in two ways: (1) the angles between carbon–hydrogen bonds spread to 120° (larger than usual), allowing the angles between carbon–carbon bonds to contract, and (2) the electrons that constitute the carbon–carbon bonds do not lie along the direct lines between the centres of the carbon atoms, but rather they bulge outward in the plane of the ring, so that the actual bond angle becomes 105°. The chemical consequence of this "bending" of the bonds is that the electrons of the bond are more accessible than usual to attacking reagents. The cyclopropane ring, therefore, can be broken more easily than can larger rings.

Cyclobutane molecules also are strained. If the molecule were planar, each angle between carbon–carbon bonds would be 90°, and all hydrogens on adjacent carbons would

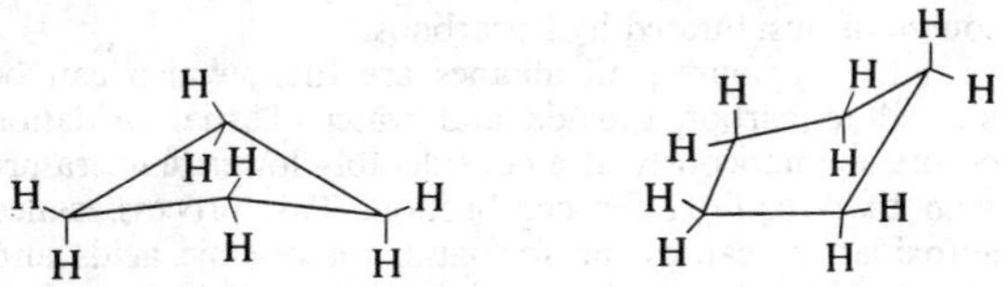

cyclobutane cyclopentane

be eclipsed. The ring puckers to decrease the interaction between hydrogens, even at the expense of some further decrease in the carbon–carbon bond angles. A puckered conformation is also adopted by cyclopentane, even though the internal angles of a regular pentagon are very close (108°) to the tetrahedral angle preferred by saturated carbon atoms. The puckered conformation in this case is assumed almost solely to avoid eclipsing of hydrogens.

Cyclohexane conformations

The conformations of cyclohexane, in particular, have been carefully studied because of the common occurrence of six-membered rings in many natural products, especially the steroids (*e.g.*, cholesterol). Three distinct conformations can be defined, the two rigid forms, chair and boat, and the

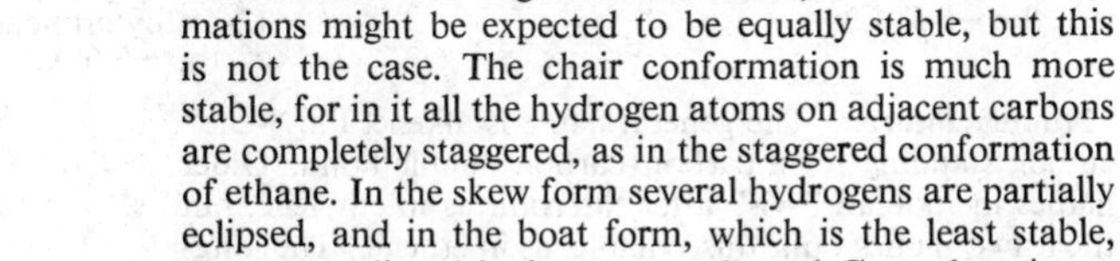

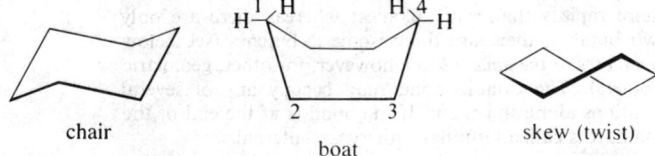

chair boat skew (twist)

flexible skew, or twist, form. In each, the angle between carbon–carbon bonds is 109.5° and strainless, and the forms are interconvertible by simple rotations about the C–C bonds. Since the angles are identical, the three conformations might be expected to be equally stable, but this is not the case. The chair conformation is much more stable, for in it all the hydrogen atoms on adjacent carbons are completely staggered, as in the staggered conformation of ethane. In the skew form several hydrogens are partially eclipsed, and in the boat form, which is the least stable, there are eclipsed hydrogens on C_2 and C_3, and again on C_5 and C_6, and in addition two of the hydrogens on C_1 and C_4 point in toward one another and are badly crowded. Because of these interactions, 999 of every 1,000 cyclohexane molecules will be in the chair form (the other being skew) at room temperature.

There are two types of carbon–hydrogen bonds in the chair conformation of cyclohexane; these are called axial (*a*) or equatorial (*e*), depending on whether they are perpendicular or parallel to the mean molecular plane. The three axial hydrogens on each side of the molecule come close to one another in space. The two types (axial and equatorial) are interchangeable if the ring "flips" (this cannot be done directly; the skew forms are intermediates in the process). Any substituent other than hydrogen, the smallest atom, prefers an equatorial position since it avoids interaction with the axial hydrogens, and where "flipping" is possible this is the conformation observed. Conformational effects are important in explaining subtle differences in the chemical behaviour of cyclic molecules.

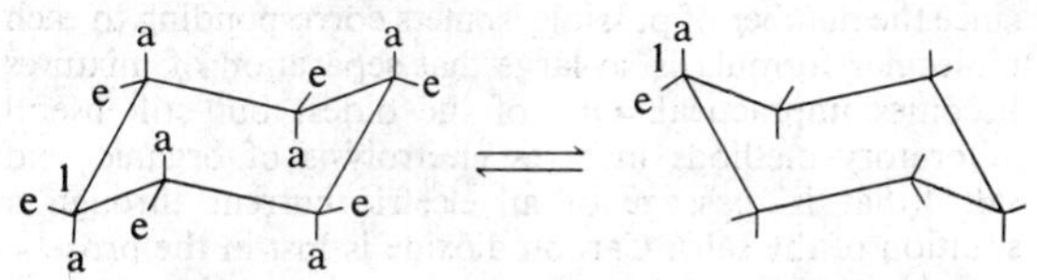

All larger rings also are puckered and free of angle strain, but those with seven to 12 carbons suffer unfavourable interactions between nonbonded hydrogens (hydrogens on different carbon atoms). The molecules adopt conformations that minimize these strains. Rings with more than 12 carbons are sufficiently flexible to adopt essentially strain-free conformations, analogous to those of the open-chain alkanes.

Many hydrocarbons with more than one ring are known. Among these are *trans*-decalin and adamantane, both hav-

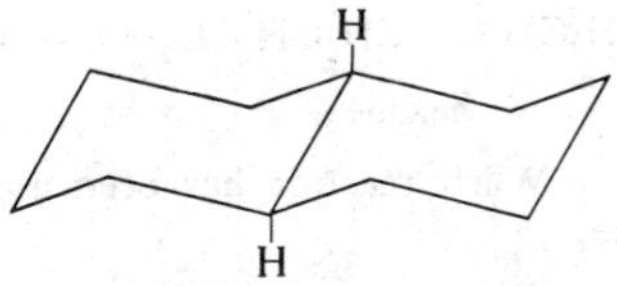

trans-decalin, $C_{10}H_{18}$

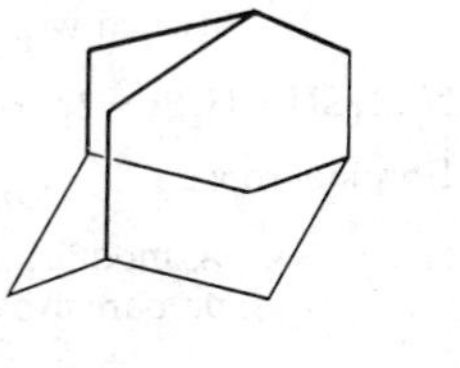

adamantane, $C_{10}H_{16}$

bicyclobutane, C_4H_6

spiropentane, C_5H_8

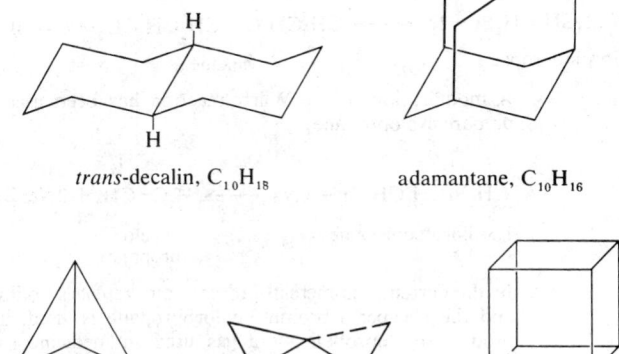

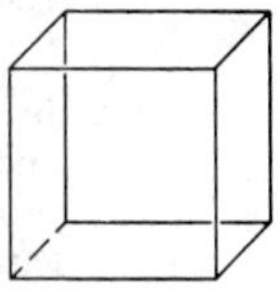

cubane, C_8H_8

ing essentially strain-free molecules and both being substances found in petroleum. Three highly strained small-ring structures, bicyclobutane, spiropentane, and cubane, are examples of the unusual cyclic hydrocarbon molecules created by organic chemists in their laboratories.

Geometric isomerism

Certain cyclic structures show a type of isomerism in which two molecules differ only in the arrangement of substituent groups in space. For example, in 1,2-dimethylcyclopropane, the methyl groups may be on the same (*cis*) or on opposite (*trans*) sides of the ring plane. The resulting

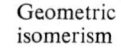

cis-1,2-dimethylcyclopropane (bp 37° C) *trans*-1,2-dimethylcyclopropane (bp 29° C)

two substances are different, each having its own properties. *Cis–trans* isomers normally cannot be interconverted at room temperature, because to do so requires the breaking and remaking of chemical bonds. Alkenes, incidentally, also exhibit *cis–trans* isomerism (see below *Alkenes*). Biological reactions, controlled by enzymes, frequently are so sensitive to molecular structure that they can readily distinguish between a pair of geometric (*cis–trans*) isomers.

Sources and synthesis. The main commercial sources of alkanes are petroleum and natural gas. The latter contains 60–80% methane, 5–9% ethane, 3–18% propane, and 2–14% higher hydrocarbons. Over 150 pure hydrocarbons have been isolated from petroleum; about half are alkanes or cycloalkanes (the latter with C_5 or C_6 rings). Thermal and catalytic cracking (see below *Chemical reactions*) of petroleum and hydrogenation of coal are other alkane sources. Lower members of the series (through C_4) can be obtained in pure form by distillation. Annual production of each lower alkane is in the billion-pound range, and each sells for around one cent per pound.

Individual higher alkanes and cycloalkanes usually are synthesized by reactions designed to give a unique product, since the number of possible isomers corresponding to each molecular formula is so large that separation of mixtures becomes impractical. One of the oldest but still useful laboratory methods involves electrolysis of organic acid salts (that is, passage of an electric current through a solution of the salt). Carbon dioxide is lost in the process, and the resulting organic radicals combine in pairs to form an alkane. For example,

$$2CH_3CH_2CH_2CO_2^-Na^+ - 2e$$

sodium butanoate

$$\xrightarrow[H_2O]{\text{electrolysis}} CH_3CH_2CH_2CH_2CH_2CH_3 + 2CO_2 + 2Na^+.$$

hexane

The reaction is quite general, the structure of the product depending upon the particular acid salt used. In a formally related reaction, the French chemist Charles-Adolphe Wurtz found in 1855 that organic halides couple when treated with sodium:

$$2CH_3CH_2CH_2Br + 2Na \longrightarrow CH_3CH_2CH_2CH_2CH_2CH_3 + 2Na^+Br^- .$$

1-bromopropane — hexane

A modification of the Wurtz reaction has been used to prepare cyclopropane:

$$CH_2BrCH_2CH_2Br + 2Na \longrightarrow H_2C\overset{CH_2}{\diagup\diagdown}CH_2 + 2Na^+Br^-.$$

1,3-dibromopropane — cyclopropane

In the current commercial process, zinc replaces sodium, and the cheaper 1-bromo–3-chloropropane is used. The product, cyclopropane, is a gas used in medicine as a general anesthetic.

Saturated hydrocarbons are also synthesized from corresponding unsaturated molecules, by the process of hydrogenation (see below *Alkenes; physical and chemical properties*).

Chemical reactions. Saturated hydrocarbons are unaffected at room temperature by most acids, alkalies, or oxidizing or reducing agents. This relative inertness gave rise to the name paraffins (Latin *parum*, "little"; *affinitas*, "affinity") sometimes applied to these substances, but it is now known that alkanes and cycloalkanes are more reactive than was once supposed. Methane, for example, will exchange its hydrogens for deuterium (a heavy isotope of hydrogen with chemical symbol, D) when placed in the extremely strong acid, deuterofluorosulfuric acid–antimony pentafluoride, $FSO_3D–SbF_5$, at 80° C. Also, certain alkanes can be isomerized to highly branched structures. This isomerization reaction, carried out with the aid of an aluminum chloride catalyst, is used commercially to convert *n*-butane to isobutane, which is an important raw material for high-octane fuels.

Isomerization reactions

$$CH_3CH_2CH_2CH_3 \xrightarrow{AlCl_3} CH_3\underset{\displaystyle CH_3}{\underset{|}{C}}HCH_3$$

n-butane — isobutane

The most common reactions of saturated hydrocarbons involve replacement of one or more of the hydrogens by other atoms or groups of atoms. The reaction was discovered in a curious way. At a ball in France in 1830 guests were driven from the ballroom by choking fumes given off by the burning candles. It was found that the candles had been bleached by a process using chlorine; some hydrogen atoms in the hydrocarbon molecules of the wax were replaced by chlorine atoms and, on heating gave off hydrogen chloride fumes. The reaction was investigated systematically and found to be useful synthetically. When an alkane, or cycloalkane, is treated with chlorine or bromine at elevated temperature or in the presence of ultraviolet light, substitution occurs in the following manner:

$$RH + Cl_2 \xrightarrow[\text{light}]{\text{heat or}} RCl + HCl.$$

(R = an organic radical or group of atoms.) More than one hydrogen on a given carbon can be replaced, as in the sequence:

$$CH_4 \xrightarrow[-HCl]{Cl_2} CH_3Cl \xrightarrow[-HCl]{Cl_2} CH_2Cl_2 \xrightarrow[-HCl]{Cl_2} CHCl_3 \xrightarrow[-HCl]{Cl_2} CCl_4 .$$

methane — methyl chloride — dichloromethane — chloroform — carbon tetrachloride

The reaction conditions can be modified to give predominant mono- or poly- substitution, as desired.

Cracking

At high temperatures (500–700° C) higher alkanes undergo rupture, or cracking, to give a mixture of smaller organic molecules and hydrogen gas. It is clear that if a given alkane, such as $C_{20}H_{42}$, is cracked to furnish another acyclic alkane, perhaps $C_{10}H_{22}$, along with a molecule of hydrogen (H_2), some of the remaining fragments must be unsaturated since, in the example chosen, only 18 hydrogen atoms are available to be distributed among the remaining ten carbon atoms. Cracking is therefore an important commercial source of unsaturated hydrocarbons.

Finally, of course, all alkanes are fuels, which can be burned to carbon dioxide and water. Partial oxidation occurs spontaneously at a considerably lower temperature than that required for combustion. This process, called autoxidation, causes the formation of organic acids and other corrosive materials during the use of hydrocarbon lubricating oils. Various antioxidants and inhibitors are added to automotive oils to slow down this undesirable reaction.

ALKENES

Alkenes, also called olefins, have two fewer hydrogens per molecule than do alkanes. They are unsaturated, with the general formula C_nH_{2n}, and their most characteristic structural feature is a carbon–carbon double bond. The first two members of the series are ethylene, C_2H_4, and

$$CH_2{=}CH_2 \qquad CH_3CH{=}CH_2$$

ethylene (ethene) (bp −102.4° C) — propylene (propene) (bp −47.7° C)

propylene, C_3H_6. The number of possible isomers increases more rapidly than with alkanes; whereas there are only two butanes, there are three isomeric butenes (see below *Geometry of the double bond*, however, for other, geometric isomers). The double bond may occupy any of several positions along the chain. If the bond is at the end of the chain, it is called terminal; otherwise, internal.

$$\overset{1}{C}H_2{=}\overset{2}{C}H\overset{3}{C}H_2\overset{4}{C}H_3 \qquad \overset{1}{C}H_3\overset{2}{C}H{=}\overset{3}{C}H\overset{4}{C}H_3 \qquad \overset{3}{C}H_3\overset{\overset{\displaystyle CH_3}{2|}}{C}{=}\overset{1}{C}H_2$$

1-butene (bp −6.5° C) — 2-butene — isobutylene (2-methylpropene) (bp −6.6° C)

Nomenclature. The general name is alkene, the "-ene" ending standing for a carbon–carbon double bond. (Older names include an "-yl-" after the root, as in ethylene, but the IUPAC names omit this syllable, as in ethene.) The longest chain incorporating the double bond determines the root of the name, which is the same as that of the alkane with the same number of carbon atoms. The position of the double bond is designated by the lower number of the two carbons involved in the bond, and the chain is numbered so as to give the double bond the lowest possible number (as in the formulas of 1- and 2-butene, above). The number that refers to the position of the double bond is sometimes omitted if this causes no ambiguity, as is often the case with cycloalkenes. Substituents are named in the same way as with alkanes, the numbering being determined, however, by the position of the double bond. These rules are illustrated by the examples at the end of this section.

Vinyl and allyl groups

Two unsaturated groups have useful common names, the vinyl and allyl groups. The vinyl group is $CH_2{=}CH–$, forming, *e.g.*, $CH_2{=}CHCl$, vinyl chloride, or chloroethene. The allyl group is $CH_2{=}CH—CH_2—$, forming $CH_2{=}CHCH_2Br$, allyl bromide, or 3-bromopropene.

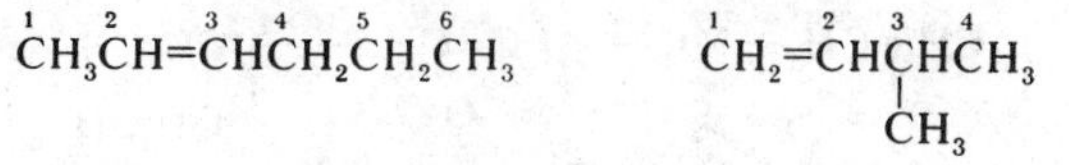

$\overset{1}{C}H_3\overset{2}{C}H=\overset{3}{C}H\overset{4}{C}H_2\overset{5}{C}H_2\overset{6}{C}H_3$ — 2-hexene

$\overset{1}{C}H_2=\overset{2}{C}H\underset{CH_3}{\overset{3}{C}H}\overset{4}{C}H_3$ — 3-methyl-1-butene

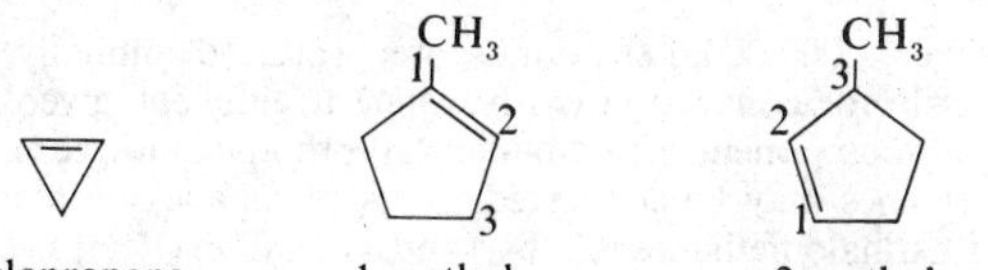

cyclopropene — 1-methylcyclopentene — 3-methylcyclopentene

Geometry of the double bond. Each of the carbon atoms involved in a double bond is attached to only two other atoms or groups, because the total number of bonds to carbon can be no greater than its normal valence of four. In principle, the best geometric arrangement, which minimizes the repulsion between the electrons in the bonds, has all four atoms (carbon and the three atoms attached to it) in a single plane, with three equal bond angles of 120°. In practice the planar geometry is observed but the angles vary slightly from 120°, as shown for ethylene.

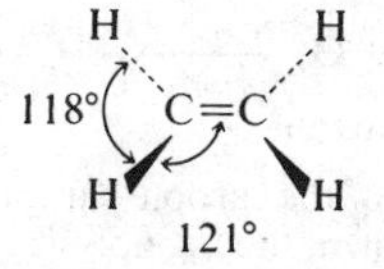

The average carbon–carbon double-bond distance is 1.34 Å, appreciably shorter (by 0.2 Å) than that of the carbon–carbon single bond. This decrease results from the fact that two electron pairs, rather than only one, bind the two carbon nuclei to one another.

The position of the two electron pairs is of some significance in explaining the reactions of alkenes. One pair, as in a single bond, occupies the space directly between the two carbon nuclei, in an orbital (region of space within which the electrons are localized) that is symmetric about an axis drawn between the two nuclei. Bonds with this symmetry are referred to as σ (sigma) bonds. The second electron pair, in order that it not occupy the same space as the first, cannot lie directly between the nuclei that it binds together. It lies instead in an orbital that is both immediately above and immediately below the plane formed by the two carbons and the atoms attached to them; this is called a π (pi) bond. The π bond is somewhat weaker and more easily broken than the σ bond. The π electrons, not being buried between

Sigma and pi bonds

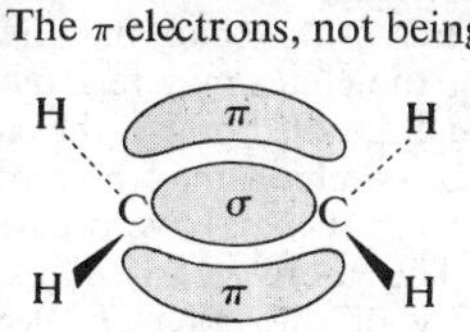

two atomic nuclei, are quite accessible to chemical reagents. For this reason, alkenes and cycloalkenes are much more reactive than alkanes, and most of the reactions involve breaking the π bond or adding to it.

The presence of two bonds between adjacent carbon atoms imposes some geometric restrictions on the molecule. Sigma bonds, being centrosymmetric about the C–C axis, permit relatively free rotation of one carbon with respect to another, as in ethane. But the π bond has no such symmetry; to rotate one carbon of a double bond 180° with respect to the other carbon would require that the π bond be broken and eventually reformed. This process usually requires considerably more energy than is available at room temperature. Consequently, rotation about double bonds is ordinarily not possible except at high temperatures, or in the presence of other energy sources, or during chemical reactions in which the π bond is temporarily broken anyway. Restricted rotation around double bonds leads to geometric, or *cis–trans*, isomers, like those found in cycloalkanes (see above *Cycloalkanes*), when the two groups attached to each carbon of the double bond are different. Thus there are two 2-butenes, *cis* and *trans*. In all small and ordinary sized ring compounds with a double bond (cycloalkenes), the geometry is necessarily *cis*; the smallest stable ring structure with a *trans* double bond has eight carbon atoms.

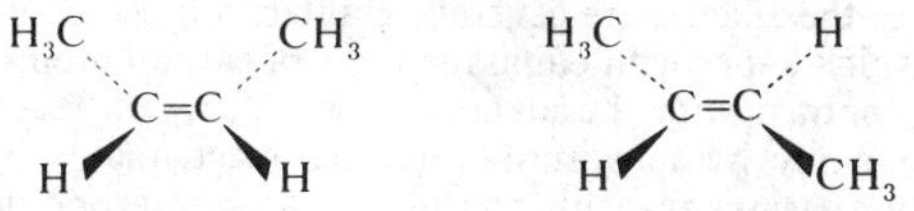

Cis and *trans* isomers

cis-2-butene (bp +3.7° C) — *trans*-2-butene (bp +0.88° C)

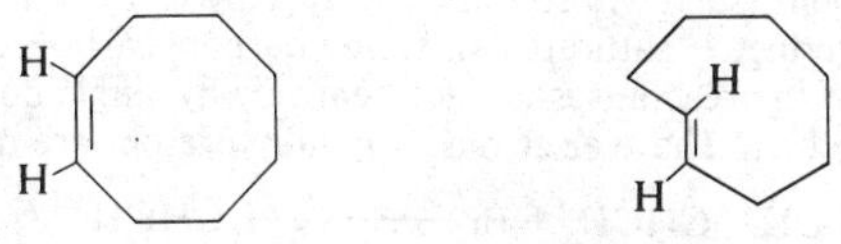

cis-cyclooctene — *trans*-cyclooctene

Geometric isomers may differ rather drastically in molecular shape. The carbon chain in *cis*-2-butene, for example, is appr oximately U-shaped, whereas that of the *trans* isomer is Z-shaped. In biological systems such drastic structural changes can be very significant, because they affect the way in which an unsaturated molecule interacts with enzymes. The chemistry of vision constitutes a particularly important example. A visual pigment called retinene contains a number of double bonds, and the conversion of one of these from the *cis* to the *trans* form occurs when the pigment is exposed to light. This isomerization alters the degree of attachment of retinene to a protein molecule and brings ab out other changes in the chemicals of the retina.

Sources and synthesis. The lower alkenes (through C_4) are produced commercially by cracking natural gas or petroleum or mixtures of hydrocarbons derived from them. Annual production of ethylene, by far the most important alkene industrially, is over 10,000,000,000 pounds. About 35 percent is used as a raw material for making the plastic polyethylene, 25 percent goes to make ethylene oxide (used in turn to make glycol antifreeze and other products), 20 percent is converted to ethyl alcohol, 10 percent is consumed in the production of the plastic polystyrene, and the remaining 10 percent is for various miscellaneous uses. Propylene and the butenes, also manufactured on a large scale, are sources of other chemicals that are used as solvents or as starting materials for the manufacture of plastics, detergents, synthetic rubber, food preservatives, and numerous other products.

Individual higher alkenes and cycloalkenes may be synthesized by reactions in which a double bond is introduced into a saturated precursor. The principle behind most of these methods is expressed by the equation:

$$-\underset{X}{\overset{|}{C}}-\underset{Y}{\overset{|}{C}}- \longrightarrow -\overset{|}{C}=\overset{|}{C}- + X{-}Y$$

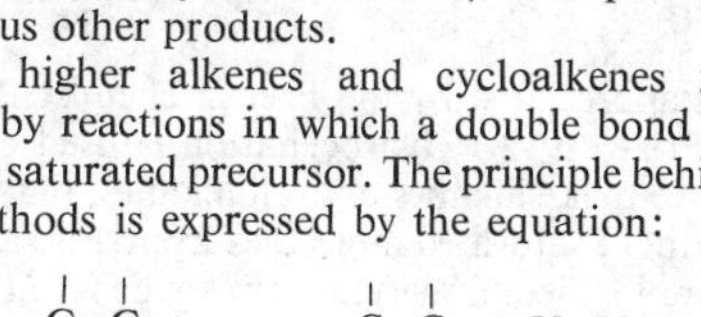

in which X and Y are two atoms or groups attached to adjacent carbon atoms and capable of forming some small molecule X–Y. The process is called an elimination reaction (X and Y being eliminated from the starting compound). Examples include the dehydration of alcohols and the removal of a halogen acid from an alkyl halide.

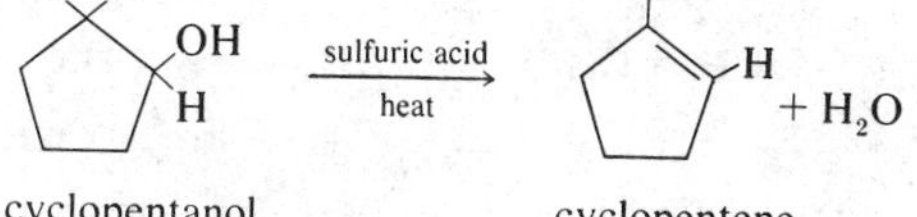

cyclopentanol, an alcohol — cyclopentene

$$CH_3CH_2CH_2\underset{H}{\overset{H}{\overset{|}{C}}}-\underset{H}{\overset{Cl}{\overset{|}{C}}}-H \xrightarrow[\text{heat}]{\text{alkali}} CH_3CH_2CH_2CH=CH_2 + HCl$$

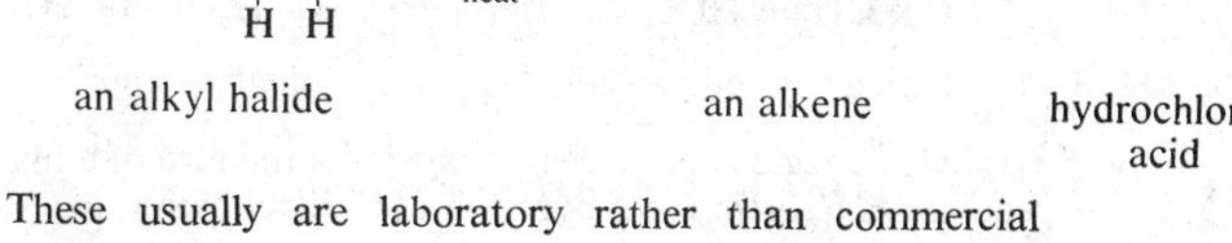

an alkyl halide — an alkene — hydrochloric acid

These usually are laboratory rather than commercial

methods. Alkenes also can be prepared by partial hydrogenation of alkynes (see below *Alkynes; reactions*).

Physical and chemical properties. The physical properties of the alkenes are generally similar to those of alkanes or cycloalkanes with equal numbers of carbon atoms.

Addition reactions

In contrast with the alkanes, however, which react predominantly by substitution, alkenes react mainly by addition; various reagents add to the carbon–carbon double bond by reactions that are the reverse of elimination. These reactions are frequently very rapid, even at room temperature.

Halogens, such as bromine, add rapidly to most alkenes. The product is saturated since the carbon–carbon double bond in the reactant is replaced entirely by single bonds in the product. The π electrons originally present are used to

$$CH_2{=}CHCH_3 + Br_2 \longrightarrow \underset{Br\ \ Br}{CH_2CHCH_3}$$

propene 1,2-dibromopropane

form single (σ) bonds to the bromine atoms. One bromine adds to each carbon of the double bond (note that the only product from propene is 1,2-dibromopropane; no 1,1- or 1,3- or 2,2-isomer is formed).

The reaction with bromine is frequently used as a test for unsaturation in a molecule. Alkenes are colourless, bromine is a reddish-brown liquid, and the product, an organic dibromide, is colourless. When a reddish-brown solution of bromine in some inert solvent (*e.g.*, carbon tetrachloride) is added to an alkene, the bromine reacts instantly to form the colourless product. The bromine solution is "decolourized." If the substance being tested has no carbon–carbon double bonds, the bromine does not react, or reacts only slowly by substitution, and the colour of the bromine solution remains essentially unchanged. The reaction can be modified and used to determine the percentage of alkenes present in an unknown mixture; bromine is added until it is no longer decolourized, and the amount required for a given sample weight is measured.

Alkenes can be converted to alkanes by hydrogen, usually under pressure and in the presence of a finely divided metal catalyst, such as platinum, palladium, or nickel. The generality of this reaction, called catalytic hydrogenation,

$$\gt C{=}C\lt + H_2 \xrightarrow[\text{or Ni}]{\text{Pt, Pd}} -\underset{H}{\overset{|}{C}}-\underset{H}{\overset{|}{C}}-$$

was first appreciated by the French chemist Paul Sabatier (Nobel Prize, 1912). Hydrogenation is used commercially not only to make alkanes or cycloalkanes, but in general to produce more saturated molecules from less saturated ones (for example, oleomargarine from soybean oil).

Alkenes are converted to alcohols by hydration; the reaction requires an acid catalyst. Most of the ethanol produced for industrial use is obtained from ethylene.

$$CH_2{=}CH_2 + HOH \xrightarrow[\text{acid}]{\text{sulfuric}} CH_3CH_2OH$$

ethyl alcohol (ethanol)

The following similar reaction gives isopropyl alcohol from propylene.

$$CH_2 = CHCH_3 + HOH \xrightarrow{\text{acid}} \underset{OH}{CH_3CHCH_3}$$

propylene isopropyl alcohol

Alcohols also add to alkenes in the presence of acid. Ether (more correctly, diethyl ether), the widely used solvent and anesthetic, is made from ethylene in this way.

$$CH_2{=}CH_2 + HOCH_2CH_3 \xrightarrow{\text{acid}} CH_3CH_2OCH_2CH_3$$

ethylene ethyl alcohol diethyl ether

Ethylene oxide is produced by passing a mixture of ethylene and air (or oxygen) over a heated silver catalyst:

$$CH_2{=}CH_2 + \tfrac{1}{2}O_2 \xrightarrow{Ag} H_2C\underset{O}{-}CH_2 \xrightarrow[200°]{HOH} \underset{OH\ OH}{CH_2CH_2}.$$

ethylene oxide (oxirane) ethylene glycol

Over 2,000,000,000 pounds are produced annually, primarily for conversion (with water) to ethylene glycol, the main component of permanent automotive antifreeze.

Alkenes may be converted to cyclopropanes by reaction with dihalomethanes (CH_2X_2) and a metal; in effect, a $-CH_2-$ group is added to the double bond, as for example:

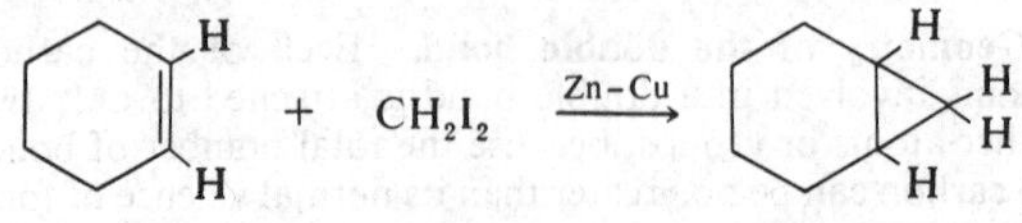

diiodomethane norcarane

Alkenes and cycloalkenes react rapidly with ozone. Although ozone first adds to the double bond, the net reaction is cleavage of the molecule, a process called ozonolysis; two fragments with C=O (carbonyl) groups are produced.

$$\gt C{=}C\lt + O_3 \longrightarrow \gt C{=}O + O{=}C\lt$$

ozone

When the position of the carbon–carbon double bond in the molecule is unknown, the ozonolysis reaction can be used to locate it, if the carbonyl products can be identified. For example, on ozonolysis 2-butene gives a single product, acetaldehyde, $CH_3CH{=}O$, whereas 1-butene gives two products, formaldehyde, $CH_2{=}O$, and propionaldehyde, $O{=}CHCH_2CH_3$.

Polymerization

One alkene molecule can add to the double bond of another; each is said to be a monomer, and the product is a dimer. If the process is repeated, trimers, and eventually polymers, substances composed of a great many monomer units, are obtained. Polymerization is one of the most important reactions used by the chemical industry.

Ethylene can be converted to polyethylene by several processes:

$$nCH_2{=}CH_2 \xrightarrow{\text{catalyst}} -CH_2CH_2-(CH_2CH_2)_{n-2}-CH_2CH_2-$$

polyethylene

the product is essentially an alkane and therefore is chemically inert. The ends of the chain may have catalyst molecules attached, or the chain may terminate by loss of one hydrogen, leaving a double bond at the end. Depending on the catalyst used, the chain may be almost entirely consecutive as shown, or it may have occasional branches of smaller chains. The more nearly linear the chain, the greater the density of the polymer. Because of its high molecular weight (n often is over 1,000), polyethylene is insoluble in most solvents. But it is thermoplastic (softens and flows on heating), and it can be extruded into sheets or films and molded into various shapes that are retained on cooling.

Substituted ethylenes also form polymers according to the reaction

$$nCH_2{=}CHX \xrightarrow{\text{catalyst}} -CH_2\underset{X}{CH}-(CH_2\underset{X}{CH})_{n-2}-CH_2-\underset{X}{CH}-$$

a vinyl compound a vinyl polymer

If X = Cl the product is polyvinyl chloride, over a billion pounds of which are used annually to make floor tiles, shoe soles, raincoats, phonograph records, and textile fibres. If X = C_6H_5 (a phenyl group, derived from benzene: see below *Aromatic hydrocarbons*), the product is polystyrene, often foamed and used as a lightweight structural and insulating material. If X = CH_3, the product is polypropylene, used to make films, molded articles, and fibres.

Some alkenes form useful dimers or other lower polymers.

For example, if isobutylene is treated with aqueous sulfuric acid, the products are mainly the two dimers shown in the equation

$$2CH_3\underset{\underset{CH_3}{|}}{C}{=}CH_2 \xrightarrow{60\% \; H_2SO_4} CH_3\underset{\underset{CH_3}{|}}{\overset{\overset{CH_3}{|}}{C}}CH_2\overset{CH_3}{\underset{}{C}}{=}CH_2$$

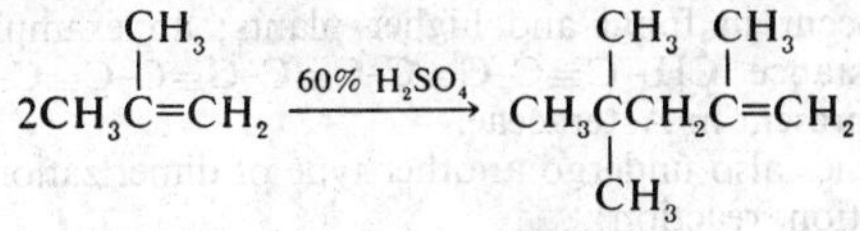

2,4,4-trimethyl-1-pentene
(80%)

$$+ \; CH_3\underset{\underset{CH_3}{|}}{\overset{\overset{CH_3}{|}}{C}}CH{=}C\overset{CH_3}{\underset{}{C}}CH_3 \; .$$

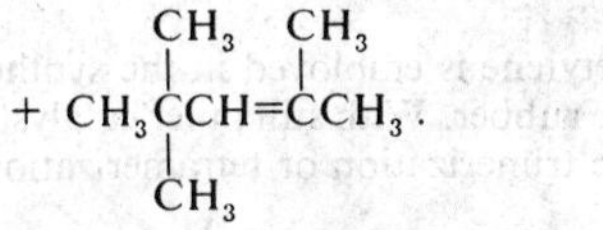

2,4,4-trimethyl-2-pentene
(20%)

Although isobutylene is a gas, with too low a boiling point for effective use as gasoline, the dimers fall nicely within the gasoline boiling range, and their highly branched structures are particularly desirable in preventing engine knock. Hydrogenation of the dimer mixture produces 2,2,4-trimethylpentane, the hydrocarbon used as a standard for 100 octane number. Both reactions, dimerization and hydrogenation, are carried out in most petroleum refineries to produce high-octane gasolines.

In the presence of ultraviolet light and a sensitizer, alkenes may dimerize in another way:

$$\underset{\underset{CH_2}{\|}}{CH_2} \; + \; \underset{\underset{CH_2}{\|}}{CH_2} \xrightarrow[mercury]{UV \; light} \underset{\underset{H_2C{-}CH_2}{|}}{H_2C{-}CH_2} \; .$$

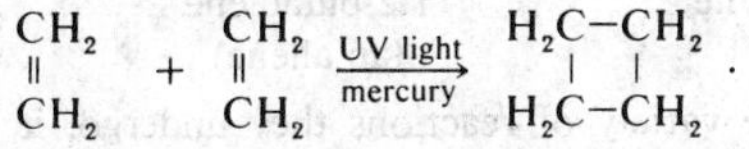

The reaction, called a cycloaddition, is useful for laboratory synthesis of cyclobutanes.

ALKYNES

A carbon–carbon triple bond is the characteristic structural feature of alkynes, or acetylenes. The simplest and commercially most important of the series, acetylene itself, was first prepared as long ago as 1836, though its name was coined some 25 years later. The general formula for the class is C_nH_{2n-2}.

Nomenclature and structure. Alkynes are named in the same way as alkenes, except that the ending that designates the triple bond is "-yne." Acetylene is almost always called by that name, though its IUPAC name is ethyne:

$$HC{\equiv}CH \qquad CH_3C{\equiv}CH \qquad \overset{1}{C}H_3\overset{2}{C}{\equiv}\overset{3}{C}\overset{4}{C}H_3 \; .$$

ethyne   propyne   2-butyne
(acetylene) (methylacetylene) (dimethylacetylene)

Other alkynes usually are named systematically, but they also may be named as derivatives of acetylene (examples of these names are given above in parentheses).

Only one other atom or group can be attached to a carbon atom of a triple bond. The molecule is linear:

$$\overset{180°}{H{-}C{\equiv}C{-}H} \; .$$

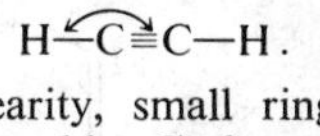

Because of this linearity, small rings incorporating a triple bond are not stable. Cyclooctyne is the smallest cyclic acetylene of which synthesis has been reported, though evidence has been obtained for smaller cycloalkynes as reaction intermediates (which are not actually isolated).

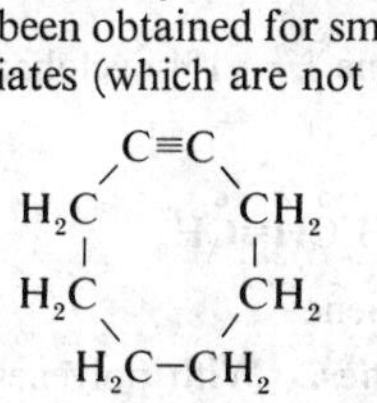

$$\begin{array}{c} C{\equiv}C \\ H_2C \qquad CH_2 \\ | \qquad\qquad | \\ H_2C \qquad CH_2 \\ H_2C{-}CH_2 \end{array}$$

cyclooctyne

The $C{\equiv}C$ distance is 1.20 Å, appreciably shorter than both the $C{=}C$ and $C{-}C$ distances (see above *Geometry of the double bond*), because three electron pairs bind the two

carbon atoms in the first case. The triple bond consists of one sigma (σ) bond along the C–C internuclear axis, and two pi (π) bonds lying in mutually perpendicular planes. A view down the carbon–carbon axis (the z axis) shows only the π bonds, the σ bond being symmetric along the z axis. The two groups attached to the triple bond also lie along the z axis, so that no geometric (*cis–trans*) isomerism is possible.

The carbon–carbon triple bond

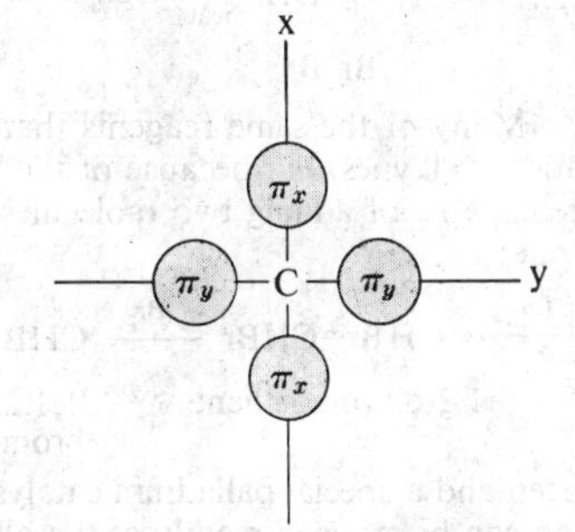

Physical properties. In general, alkynes boil 10°–20° C higher than do the corresponding alkenes and alkanes. They are slightly more dense than alkenes, and more soluble in water. Owing to its symmetric structure, acetylene has an unusually high melting point, within 2° of its boiling point ($-83.4°$ C). When liquefied, acetylene is sensitive to shock and may explode, forming its elements: $C_2H_2 \rightarrow 2C + 2H_2$ + heat. For this reason the gas cannot be liquefied safely under pressure for shipping. Acetylene gas, however, is remarkably soluble in acetone, and at a pressure of 180 pounds per square inch one volume of acetone will dissolve 300 volumes of acetylene. Since this solution is stable, acetylene usually is transported under pressure in tanks filled with porous material, such as asbestos, that is saturated with acetone.

Other alkynes, especially those with an internal triple bond, are less sensitive than is acetylene itself. Internal alkynes generally boil higher than the isomeric terminal alkynes, as shown by the last two pairs of entries in Table 3.

Table 3: Boiling Points of Alkynes

name	carbon skeleton	boiling point (°C)
Acetylene	C≡C	−84.0
Propyne	C≡C—C	−23.2
1-Butyne	C≡C—C—C	+8.1
2-Butyne	C—C≡C—C	+27.0
1-Pentyne	C≡C—C—C—C	+40.2
2-Pentyne	C—C≡C—C—C	+56.1

Sources and synthesis. Acetylene is the only alkyne produced commercially in large amounts. It is made by the reaction of water with calcium carbide, which, in turn, comes from coke and lime, as represented in the following reactions:

Commercial production of acetylene

$$3C \; + \; CaO \xrightarrow{2,500°} CaC_2 \; + \; CO$$

coke   lime   calcium   carbon
carbide   monoxide

$$CaC_2 + 2H_2O \xrightarrow[temperature]{room} HC{\equiv}CH + Ca(OH)_2 \; .$$

acetylene   calcium
hydroxide

Acetylene also is a major product from high-temperature cracking of methane:

$$2CH_4 \xrightarrow{1,600°} C_2H_2 + 3H_2 \; ;$$

a considerable fraction of commercial acetylene comes from this source.

Before the era of electricity, acetylene was used as a component of illuminating gas, for it burns with a white flame. Now about half the acetylene produced is consumed in oxyacetylene torches for welding and cutting metals; the oxyacetylene flame is intensely hot (about 2,800° C). The remaining acetylene produced is used as a raw material for other organic chemicals (see below *Reactions*).

Other alkynes can be made from acetylene (see below *Reactions*) or by extensions of the methods used for introducing double bonds, as, for example:

$$CH_3CH=CH_2 \xrightarrow{Br_2} CH_3\underset{\underset{Br}{|}}{\overset{\overset{H}{|}}{C}}-\underset{\underset{Br}{|}}{\overset{\overset{H}{|}}{C}}H \xrightarrow[heat]{alkali} CH_3C\equiv CH(+2HBr).$$

Reactions. Many of the same reagents that add to alkenes also add to alkynes, but because of the triple bond the latter are capable of adding two molecules of reagent rather than one:

$$\underset{\text{acetylene}}{HC\equiv CH} \xrightarrow{Br_2} \underset{\text{1,2-dibromoethene}}{CHBr=CHBr} \xrightarrow{Br_2} \underset{\substack{\text{1,1,2,2-tetra-}\\\text{bromoethane}}}{CHBr_2CHBr_2}.$$

When hydrogen and a special palladium catalyst are used, hydrogenation can be stopped readily at the alkene stage. Since both of the hydrogen atoms are delivered to the same side of the triple bond from the catalyst surface, this reaction provides a good method for obtaining *cis*-alkenes:

$$CH_3C\equiv CCH_3 + H_2 \xrightarrow[catalyst]{Pd} \underset{\text{cis-2-butene}}{\overset{\overset{CH_3\quad CH_3}{\diagup}}{\underset{H\qquad H}{C=C}}}.$$

Perhaps the most important commercial reaction of acetylene is its hydration. The initial product (vinyl alcohol) is unstable and rearranges to the carbonyl compound acetaldehyde, an important precursor of many other industrial organic chemicals.

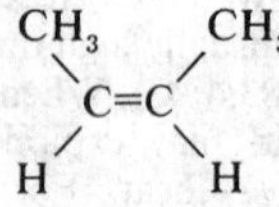

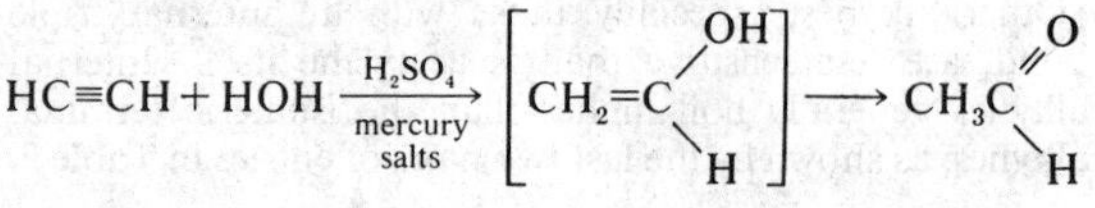

$$HC\equiv CH + HOH \xrightarrow[\substack{\text{mercury}\\\text{salts}}]{H_2SO_4} \left[\underset{\text{vinyl alcohol}}{CH_2=C\overset{OH}{\underset{H}{\diagdown}}}\right] \longrightarrow \underset{\substack{\text{acetal-}\\\text{dehyde}}}{CH_3C\overset{O}{\underset{H}{\diagup}}}$$

Hydrogen cyanide also adds to acetylene. The product, acrylonitrile, is a valuable monomer used to make synthetic fibres (Acrilan, Orlon, Dynel).

$$HC\equiv CH + HC\equiv N \xrightarrow[heat]{catalyst} \underset{\text{acrylonitrile}}{CH_2=CHC\equiv N}$$

Terminal alkynes are very weak acids, and the hydrogen attached to the triple bond may be replaced by metals, producing salts called acetylides, although the calcium salt is almost always called the carbide. This process is accomplished most commonly by reaction in liquid ammonia with sodium amide, a very strong base:

$$RC\equiv CH + Na^+NH_2^- \xrightarrow[\text{ammonia}]{\text{liquid}} \underset{\substack{\text{a sodium}\\\text{acetylide}}}{RC\equiv C^-Na^+} + NH_3.$$

Acetylides are reactive, and can be used to introduce triple bonds into other molecules. Sodium acetylide, for example, reacts with ethyl bromide, to produce 1-butyne, in a reaction somewhat reminiscent of the Wurtz reaction (see above *Alkanes*; *Sources and Synthesis*):

$$HC\equiv C^-Na^+ + CH_2BrCH_3 \longrightarrow \underset{\text{1-butyne}}{HC\equiv CCH_2CH_3} + Na^+Br^-$$

In principle any higher alkyne can be made from acetylene itself by judicious use of this reaction.

Silver, copper, and other heavy metal acetylides, when dry, explode under the influence of heat or shock, and hence they are used in detonators. In suspension, however, copper acetylides are useful in synthesis as, for example, in oxidative coupling of two alkynes to produce a product having two triple bonds:

$$2RC\equiv CH + \tfrac{1}{2}O_2 \xrightarrow[\text{salt}]{\text{cuprous}} RC\equiv C-C\equiv CR + H_2O.$$

Some hydrocarbons with triple bonds separated by single bonds occur in fungi and higher plants; an example is the substance $CH_3-C\equiv C-C\equiv C-C\equiv C-C\equiv C-CH=CH_2$, present in Asteraceae.

Acetylenes also undergo another type of dimerization, or self-addition, reaction:

$$HC\equiv CH + HC\equiv CH \xrightarrow[\substack{\text{ammonium chloride}\\\text{hydrochloric acid}}]{\text{cuprous chloride}} \underset{\text{vinylacetylene}}{CH_2=CHC\equiv CH}.$$

Vinylacetylene is employed in the synthesis of neoprene, a synthetic rubber. With still other catalysts acetylenes undergo cyclic trimerization or tetramerization:

$$3 \text{ or } 4HC\equiv CH \xrightarrow{\text{catalyst}}$$

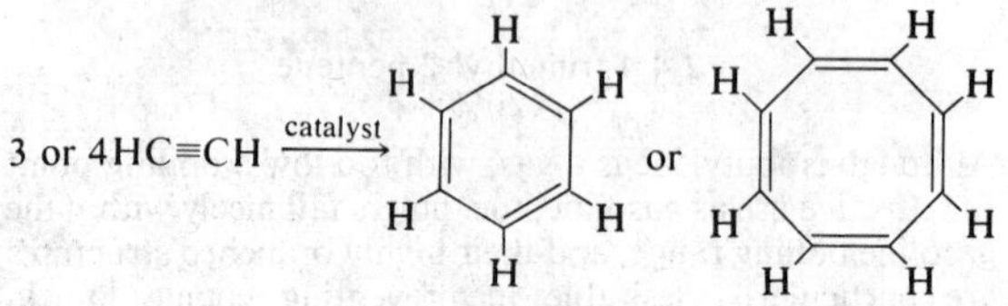

benzene cyclooctatetraene

In a strong base they may be isomerized to other alkynes or to compounds with two double bonds on the same carbon atom, allenes:

$$\underset{\substack{\text{1-butyne}}}{CH_3CH_2C\equiv CH} \underset{\text{base}}{\overset{\text{strong}}{\rightleftharpoons}} \underset{\substack{\text{1,2-butadiene}\\\text{(an allene)}}}{CH_3CH=C=CH_2} \underset{\text{base}}{\overset{\text{strong}}{\rightleftharpoons}} \underset{\substack{\text{2-butyne}}}{CH_3C\equiv CCH_3}.$$

From the variety of reactions they undergo, it is understandable that alkynes are particularly useful synthetic intermediates in organic chemistry.

DIENES AND POLYENES

Compounds with more than one carbon–carbon double bond occur widely in nature and are commercially important. The chemical properties of dienes, compounds with two C=C bonds, depend on the relative positions of the double bonds. The most important class, having alternate double and single bonds, are called conjugated dienes. Other classes have isolated double bonds (separated by two or more single bonds) or cumulative double bonds as in allenes.

$$\underset{\text{conjugated}}{C=C-C=C} \qquad \underset{\text{isolated}}{C=C-C-C=C} \qquad \underset{\text{cumulative}}{C=C=C}$$

Nomenclature. The system for naming polyenes is the same as for alkenes, except that the positions of all double bonds must be designated by appropriate numbers. The following examples are illustrative:

$$\underset{\substack{\text{propadiene}\\\text{(allene)}}}{CH_2=C=CH_2} \qquad \underset{\text{1,3-butadiene}}{\overset{1}{C}H_2=\overset{2}{C}H\overset{3}{C}H=\overset{4}{C}H_2} \qquad \underset{\text{1,2-butadiene}}{\overset{1}{C}H_2=\overset{2}{C}=\overset{3}{C}H\overset{4}{C}H_3}$$

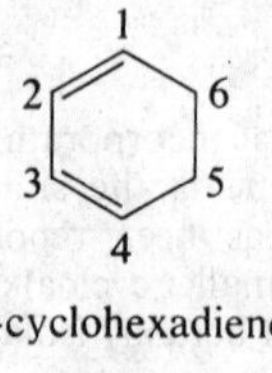

1,3-cyclohexadiene 1,4-cyclohexadiene $\underset{\substack{\text{2-methyl-1,3-butadiene}\\\text{(isoprene)}}}{\overset{1}{C}H_2=\overset{2}{\underset{\underset{CH_3}{|}}{C}}\overset{3}{C}H=\overset{4}{C}H_2}$

$$\underset{\text{1,5-hexadiene}}{\overset{1}{C}H_2=\overset{2}{C}H\overset{3}{C}H_2\overset{4}{C}H_2\overset{5}{C}H=\overset{6}{C}H_2} \qquad \underset{\text{1,3,5-hexatriene}}{\overset{1}{C}H_2=\overset{2}{C}H\overset{3}{C}H=\overset{4}{C}H\overset{5}{C}H=\overset{6}{C}H_2}$$

Physical properties. With polyenes, the physical properties commonly determined, such as boiling point and density, are similar to those of alkanes or alkenes with an equal number of carbon atoms. The most exceptional characteristic of polyenes is the intense colour often associated with those in which the double bonds are

Dimerization of acetylenes

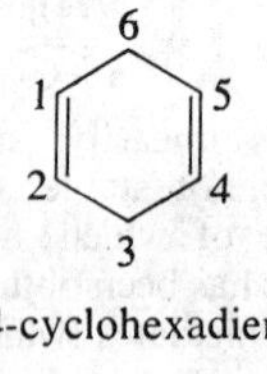

conjugated. Some examples (with only the skeletons shown) are:

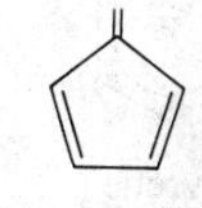

fulvene, C_6H_6 (bright yellow)

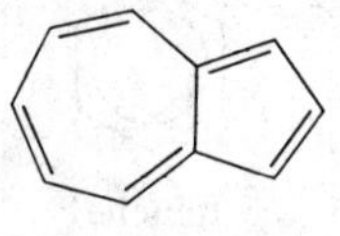

azulene, $C_{10}H_8$ (deep blue)

The colour depends both on the number of double bonds and on their arrangement in the molecule.

Occurrence and synthesis. A rather large number of hydrocarbons with more than one double bond occur in nature. Many of them belong to a class of compounds called terpenes. These substances have ten carbons or more (in multiples of five) with structures based on the linking together of isoprene units, fragments with the carbon atoms arranged as in isoprene (2-methyl-1,3-butadiene).

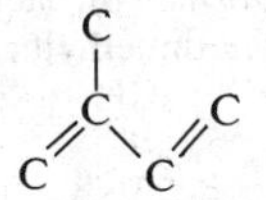

isoprene unit

Examples of these structures, together with their common names and sources, are given below, showing only the skeleton.

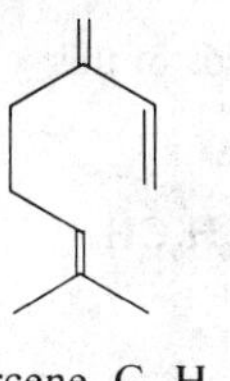

myrcene, $C_{10}H_{16}$ (bayberry)

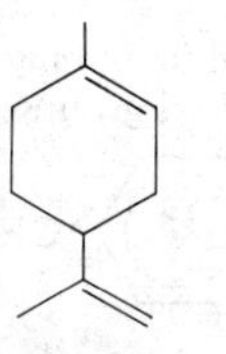

limonene, $C_{10}H_{16}$ (lemon, orange)

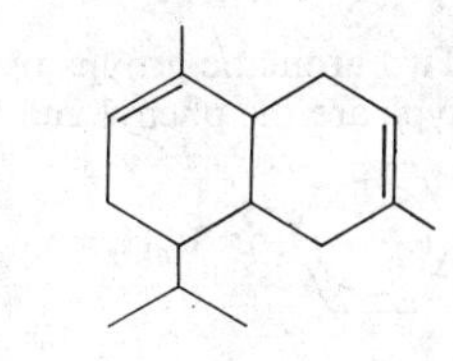

cadinene, $C_{15}H_{24}$ (oil of cade and of cubebs)

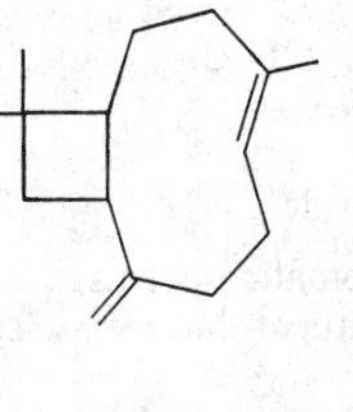

caryophyllene, $C_{15}H_{24}$ (oil of cloves)

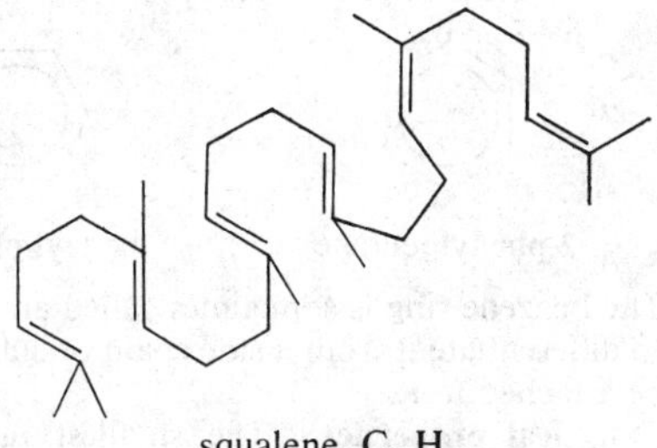

squalene, $C_{30}H_{50}$ (whale oil)

The most important commercial diene is 1,3-butadiene. It is manufactured by dehydrogenation of butenes:

$$\left.\begin{array}{l}CH_2{=}CHCH_2CH_3\\ \text{and/or}\\ CH_3CH{=}CHCH_3\end{array}\right\} \xrightarrow{\text{calcium nickel phosphate, 650°}} CH_2{=}CHCH{=}CH_2 + H_2.$$

Isoprene is a product of hydrocarbon cracking, and it also can be obtained synthetically from propene, or from acetone and acetylene. Butadiene and, more recently, isoprene are used to manufacture synthetic rubber. Cyclopentadiene, a coproduct of butadiene and isoprene from cracking reactions, is the most readily available cyclic diene. Its chlorinated derivatives are used as insecticides (aldrin, dieldrin). Other dienes and polyenes can be synthesized by extensions of the reactions used to make simple alkenes.

Reactions. Dienes and polyenes undergo many of the reactions of simple alkenes. They add bromine, hydrogen, and acids; they can be converted to epoxides; and they undergo ozonolysis and polymerization. Conjugated dienes show certain special properties. In particular they show a propensity to add reagents to the ends of the conjugated system. The majpr product from the addition of one molecule of bromine to 1,3-butadiene, for example, is 1,4-dibromo-2-butene. The process is called 1,4-addition, in

$$\overset{1}{C}H_2{=}CHCH{=}\overset{4}{C}H_2 \xrightarrow[\text{1,4-addition}]{Br_2} \underset{\displaystyle Br}{\underset{|}{CH_2}}CH{=}CH\underset{\displaystyle Br}{\underset{|}{CH_2}}$$

1,4-dibromo-2-butene

contrast to the usual addition to ordinary alkenes which is called 1,2-addition. A double bond appears between carbons 2 and 3 in the addition product.

Conjugated dienes undergo 1,4-cycloaddition with alkenes. For example, 1,3-butadiene and ethylene give cyclohexene:

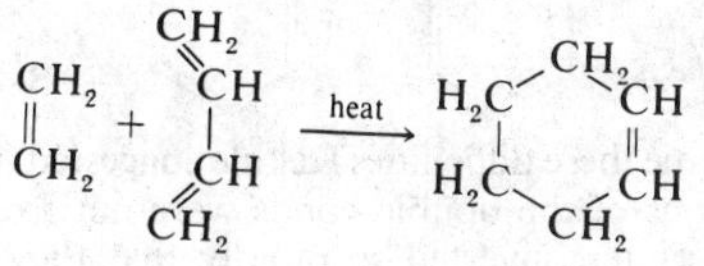

cyclohexene

The reaction is general and constitutes the most important method for making 6-membered rings. It was discovered by, and is named after, the German chemists Otto Diels and Kurt Alder (Diels–Alder reaction), who received a Nobel Prize in 1950. In the presence of certain catalysts, isoprene undergoes 1,4-polymerization to form a product indistinguishable from natural rubber, in which the isolated double bonds have the *cis* geometry.

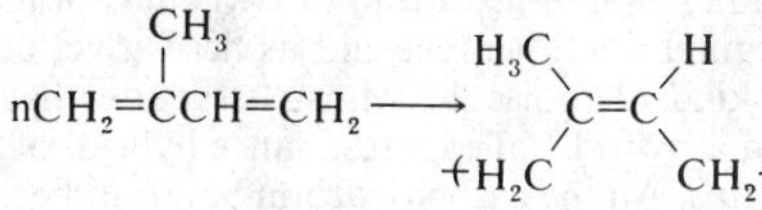

isoprene rubber

Aromatic hydrocarbons

It was recognized during the first half of the 19th century that there exists a fairly large class of organic substances with distinctly different properties from the aliphatic compounds. The hydrogen–carbon ratio in the formulas of these compounds suggests unsaturation—it is often less than one, whereas in alkenes it is two, and it is even higher in alkanes. Nonetheless, these substances do not react as if they were unsaturated: they do not readily add bromine, are not easily oxidized, and mainly undergo substitution rather than addition reactions. Frequently these substances have pleasant aromas; for example, they can be obtained from the volatile oils of cloves, cinnamon, anise, wintergreen, vanilla, etc., and hence they were often called aromatic compounds. Joseph Loschmidt, an Austrian chemist, recognized in 1861 that most aromatic substances have formulas that can be derived from that of the hydrocarbon benzene, C_6H_6, by replacing one or more of the hydrogens of that substance by other atoms or groups. Following this observation the term aromatic lost its original, nontechnical meaning, and to the chemist came to mean any compound structurally derived from benzene. In the 1930s the concept of aromaticity was broadened considerably, and now both benzenoid and nonbenzenoid aromatic compounds are recognized. The former constitute the larger, and technically more important, class.

Origin of the term aromatic compound

BENZENOID

Structure of benzene. Friedrich August Kekule, the German chemist, suggested in 1865 that each carbon atom in benzene was at the corner of a regular hexagon, with one hydrogen atom attached to each carbon. To give each carbon a valence of four, Kekule inserted a conjugated system of double bonds into the ring. This formula satis-

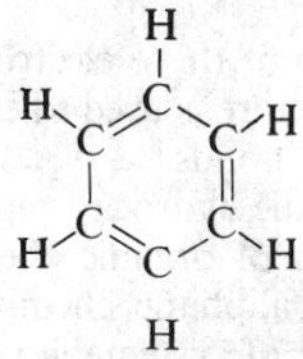

or, by convention

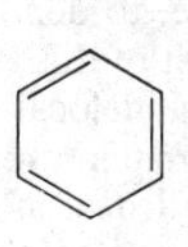

factorily explained the observation that benzene forms only one mono-substitution product (*e.g.*, one C_6H_5Cl,

I
tic
rea

…d one C_6H_5OH). All six hydrogens occupy …ions in the Kekule formula. But it does not … other observations; for example, benzene …olourize bromine rapidly at room temperature …nsaturated molecules do. Nor does it explain …en two adjacent hydrogens are replaced by other …(say X), only one compound is obtained. Kekule's …ula predicts two isomers, depending on whether a …uble or a single bond separates the substituted carbons:

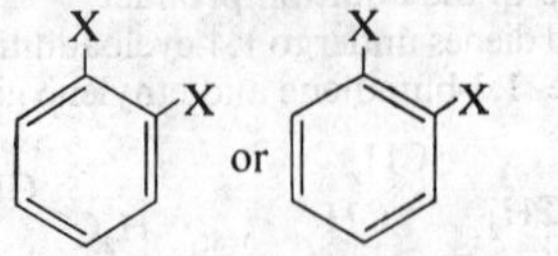

To overcome these difficulties Kekule suggested in 1872 that the positions of the double bonds were not fixed, but the two forms interconverted so rapidly that they could not be separated.

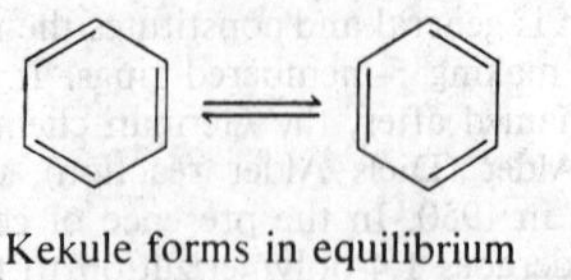

Kekule forms in equilibrium

The current view of the benzene structure differs from that of Kekule in an important conceptual way, though his formulas are still useful. Instead of two kinds of molecules in rapid equilibrium, benzene and its derivatives consist of only one kind of molecule, with a structure that can be considered a hybrid, called a resonance hybrid, of the two Kekule forms. All the carbon–carbon bonds in benzene are identical; they are neither single nor double, but of a new, hybrid type (superficially, one-and-a-half bonds). The most direct evidence for this structure comes from the molecular geometry. It has been shown that the carbon atoms in benzene are in fact at the corners of a regular hexagon, and the carbon–carbon bond distances are all identical at 1.39 Å, a value intermediate between those of the normal C–C and C=C distances (see above *Geometry of the double bond*). The hydrogen atoms of the molecule lie in the same plane as the carbons, and all angles (between carbon–hydrogens as well as between carbon–carbon bonds) are 120°. Looked at in another way, the six carbons in a benzene ring are joined by six σ bonds (six electron pairs that lie in the plane of the ring, one pair between each adjacent pair of carbon atoms); in addition, there are six π electrons (one pair for each of the three double bonds in a Kekule structure), and these lie in three π orbitals, occupying the space above and below the molecular plane. The π electrons are said to be delocalized, or spread over all six carbons.

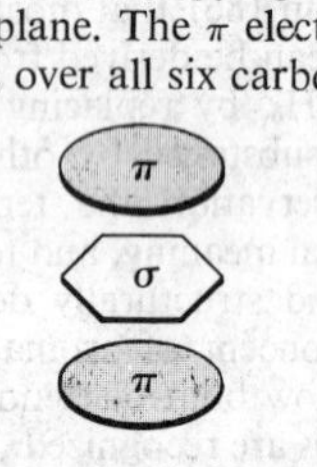

Space occupied by the σ and π electrons in benzene

The hybrid structure of benzene is represented in various ways: one is to show a double-headed arrow between Kekule structures; another is a hexagon with a circle in the

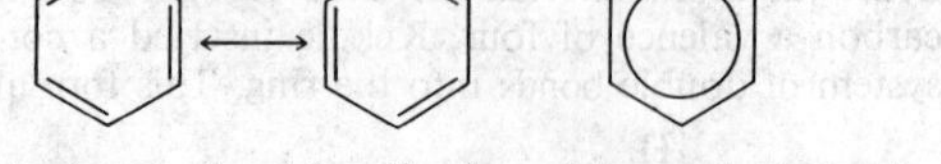

middle, to denote the delocalization of the π electrons. In the rest of this article, the latter structure is used to emphasize the delocalization of the double bonds.

Nomenclature. Benzenoid aromatic hydrocarbons often are called arenes. Since this branch of organic chemistry developed at an early date, before aliphatic chemistry in general and before the development of systematic nomenclature, common names are used more frequently here than they are with aliphatic compounds. Some examples are:

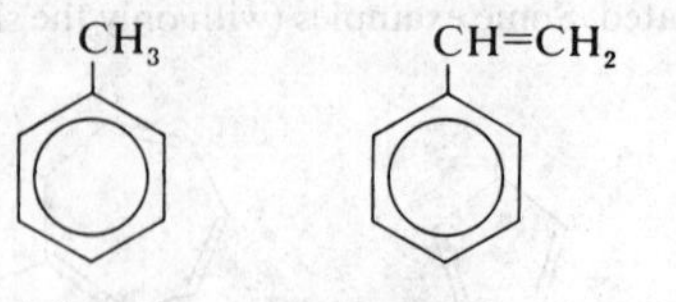

toluene (methylbenzene) — styrene (vinylbenzene)

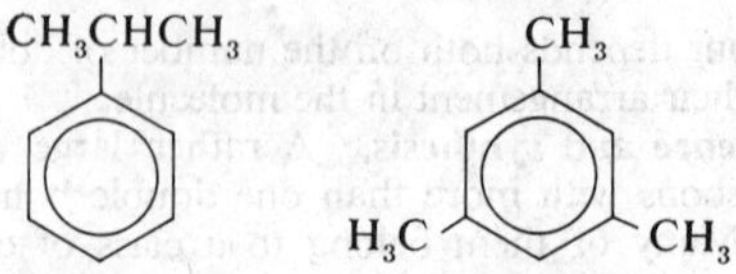

cumene (isopropylbenzene) — mesitylene (1,3,5-trimethylbenzene)

Two substituents may have three possible orientations on a benzene ring, called *ortho* (*o*), *meta* (*m*), or *para* (*p*), as illustrated with the three dimethylbenzenes, or xylenes:

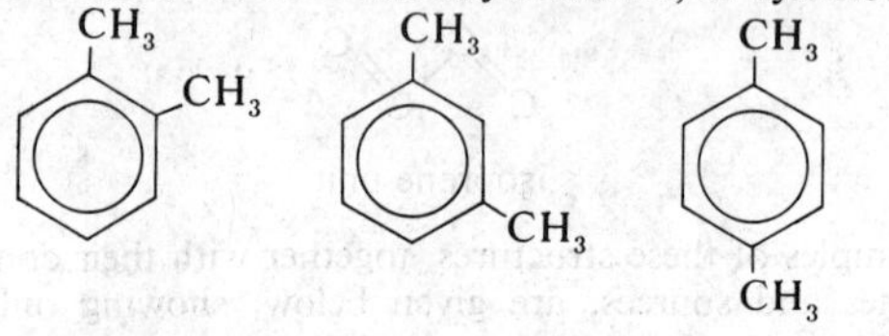

o-xylene — *m*-xylene — *p*-xylene

Phenyl and benzyl groups

Two aromatic groups useful in naming compounds of this type are the phenyl and benzyl groups:

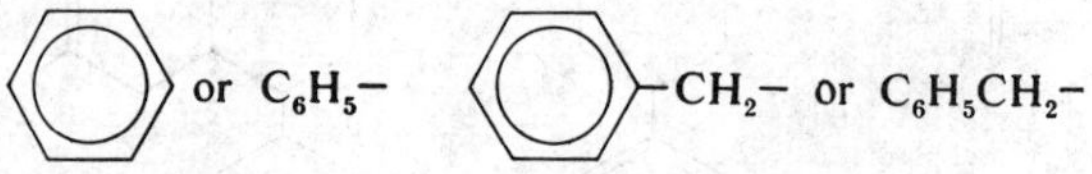

phenyl group — benzyl group

as in

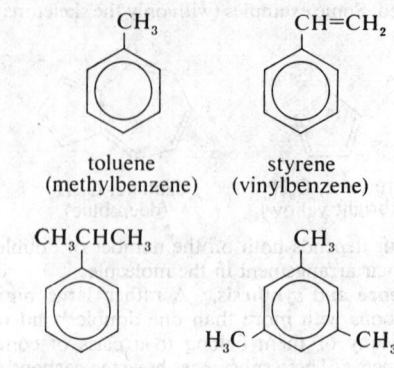

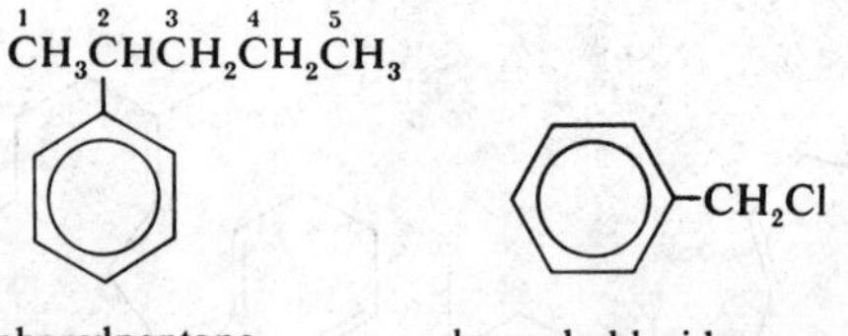

2-phenylpentane — benzyl chloride

The benzene ring is sometimes called an aromatic nucleus, to differentiate it from a side chain or substituent that may be attached to it.

Physical properties. The smallest number of carbon atoms that an aromatic hydrocarbon can contain is six; hence none of these substances can have molecules small enough to be gases at room temperature (Table 4). Because

Table 4: Physical Constants of Benzene and the Methylbenzenes

name	formula	boiling point (°C)	melting point (°C)
Benzene	C_6H_6	80.1	+5.5
Toluene	$C_6H_5CH_3$	110.6	−95
o-Xylene	1,2-$(CH_3)_2C_6H_4$	144.4	−25
m-Xylene	1,3-$(CH_3)_2C_6H_4$	139.1	−48
p-Xylene	1,4-$(CH_3)_2C_6H_4$	138.4	+13
Hemimellitene	1,2,3-$(CH_3)_3C_6H_3$	176.1	−25
Pseudocumene	1,2,4-$(CH_3)_3C_6H_3$	169.4	−44
Mesitylene	1,3,5-$(CH_3)_3C_6H_3$	164.7	−45
Prehnitene	1,2,3,4-$(CH_3)_4C_6H_2$	205	−6
Isodurene	1,2,3,5-$(CH_3)_4C_6H_2$	198	−24
Durene	1,2,4,5-$(CH_3)_4C_6H_2$	197	+80
Pentamethylbenzene	$C_6H(CH_3)_5$	232	+54
Hexamethylbenzene	$C_6(CH_3)_6$	265	+166

of their symmetrical structures, benzene, *p*-xylene, durene, and hexamethylbenzene have relatively high melting points compared to those of closely related compounds that are more unsymmetrical. Toluene is used in place of mercury, which has a melting point of −38.9° C, in low-temperature thermometers because of its low freezing point (−95° C) and its large coefficient of expansion (which means that large volume changes accompany small temperature changes). Aromatic hydrocarbons are better solvents for certain substances, such as lacquers, paints, and synthetic enamels, than are alkanes. Aromatic solvents need adequate ventilation, however, because even low concentrations are toxic, and prolonged exposure, especially to benzene vapours, can damage red blood cells.

Source and synthesis. The chemistry of aromatic compounds was initially investigated during the last half of the 19th century, mainly in Germany and England, where illuminating gas and coke were produced by the large-scale carbonization of coal. Coal tar, a by-product of the process, contains about 25 percent by weight of aromatic hydrocarbons, together with other useful components.

Aromatic hydrocarbons from petroleum

Currently, however, over 80 percent of aromatic hydrocarbon production is based on petroleum. Some aromatic hydrocarbons are present in crude petroleum and can be obtained directly, but most are produced by catalytic dehydrogenation of alkanes, a process called reforming:

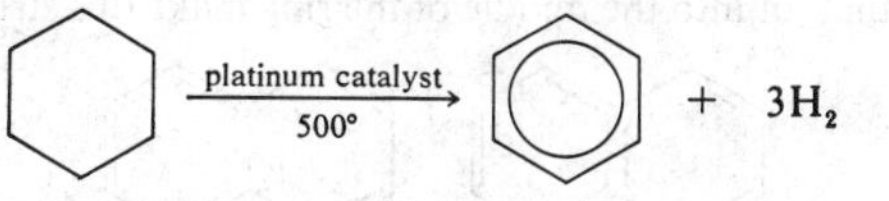

cyclohexane benzene hydrogen

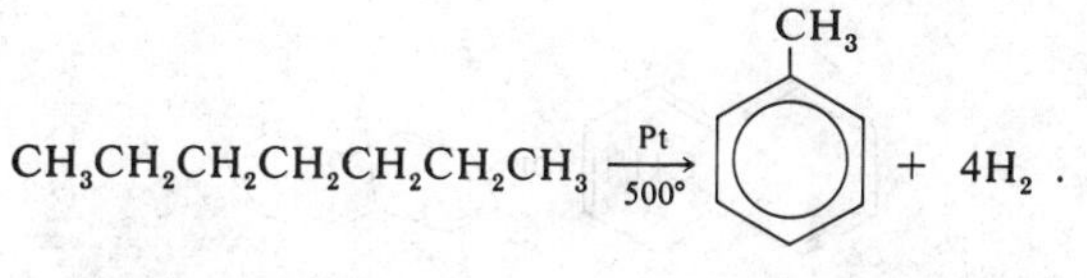

heptane toluene hydrogen

Other aromatic hydrocarbons can be obtained through synthesis, *e.g.*, ethylbenzene and styrene from benzene:

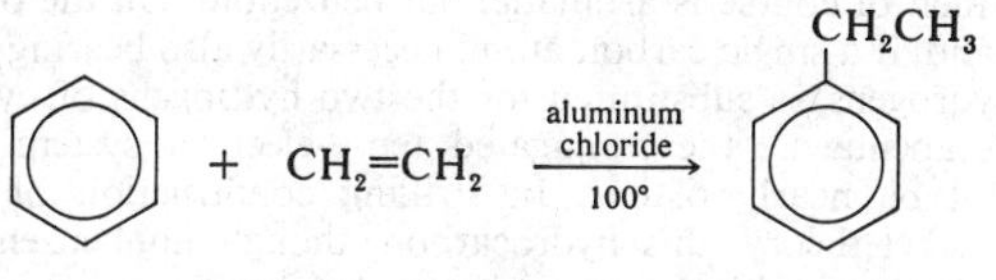

benzene ethylbenzene

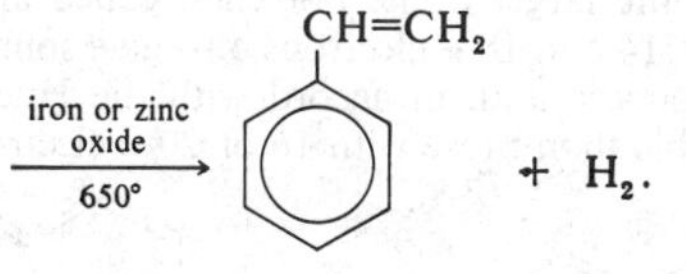

styrene

Reactions. The most characteristic reaction of aromatic hydrocarbons is substitution; *i.e.*, replacement of the aromatic hydrogens by other atoms or groups. Some of the more important substitution reactions are illustrated below:

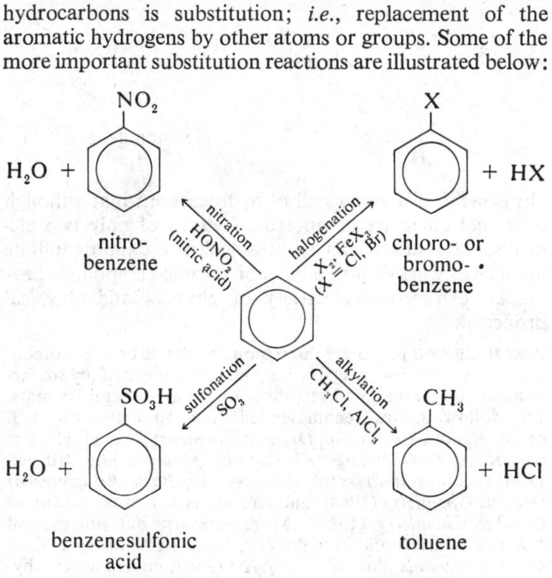

The reaction may be repeated to replace additional hydrogens, producing di- or polysubstituted compounds, as in the chlorination of chlorobenzene and the nitration of toluene.

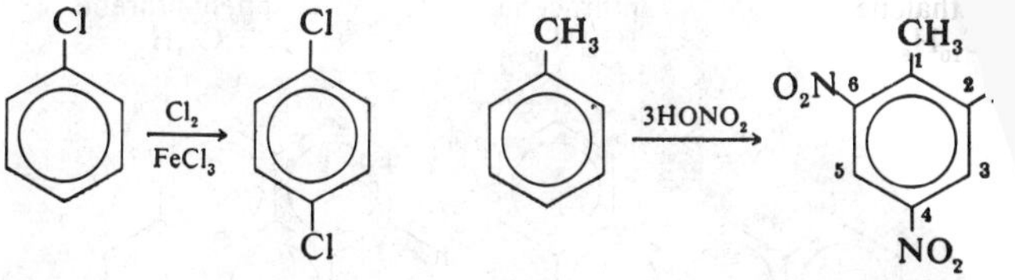

chloro-benzene *p*-dichloro-benzene toluene 2,4,6-trinitro-toluene or TNT

The products of these substitution reactions may be useful in their own right or as precursors of other useful materials, such as synthetic dyes, plastics, fabrics, and medicinals.

Under special conditions, aromatic hydrocarbons undergo addition reactions like those of unsaturated compounds. Thus benzene compounds can be catalytically hydrogenated to cyclohexanes, although higher temperatures and pressures are required than is the case with hydrogenation of simple alkenes. In the presence of light, benzene adds six atoms of halogens; the product from chlorine (1,2,3,4,5,6-hexachlorocyclohexane) is a widely used insecticide (Lindane).

Polycyclic aromatic hydrocarbons. Many aromatic hydrocarbons with more than one benzene ring are known. Two or more rings may be joined to one another directly through a single carbon–carbon bond, as in biphenyl, or with one or more carbon atoms between the rings, as in

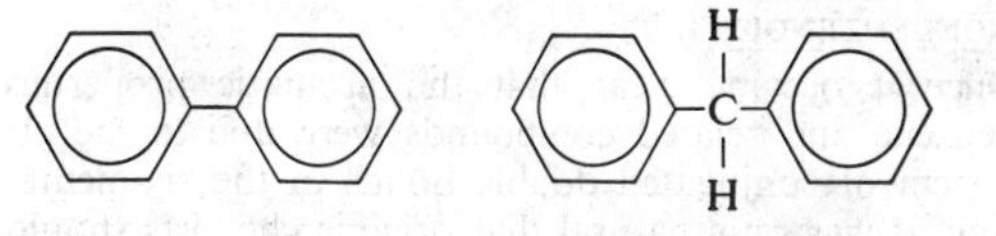

biphenyl diphenylmethane

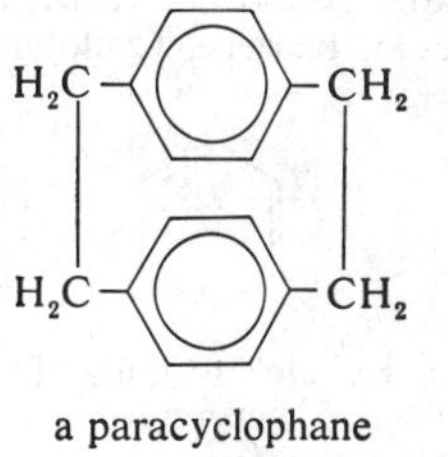

a paracyclophane

Fused ring compounds

diphenylmethane or paracyclophanes. More important commercially are the aromatic hydrocarbons with fused or condensed rings, in which two or more carbon atoms are shared in common by several aromatic rings. Naphthalene, anthracene, phenanthrene, dibenzanthracene, and coronene are well-studied examples. As the number of fused rings increases, the carbon–hydrogen ratio also increases—from 1.0 in benzene to 2.0 in coronene. If the hexagonal network in coronene is extended indefinitely in all directions, the flat, cellular structure of graphitic carbon is obtained.

Most condensed aromatic hydrocarbons are beautifully crystalline solids. Many are present in coal tar; naphthalene is the most abundant, constituting about 10 percent of the tar, or 40 percent of the available aromatic hydrocarbons. Over 50,000,000 pounds are produced annually from that source, and another 300,000,000 pounds are obtained from petroleum reforming. Although most naphthalene is used to make polymeric resins and plasticizers employed in the manufacture of products made of plastics, appreciable quantities are consumed in the manufacture of dyes, insecticides, and medicinals. Anthracene, also present in

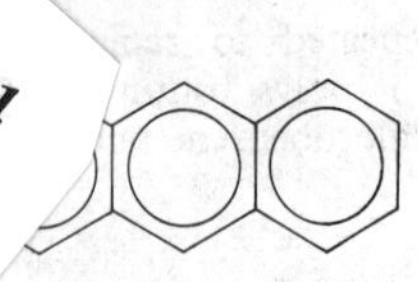

anthracene
$C_{14}H_{10}$

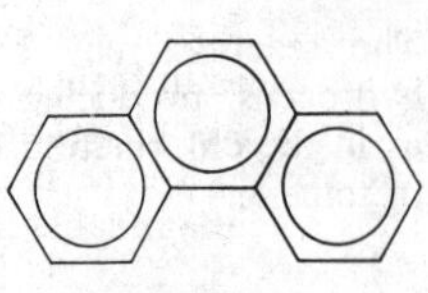

phenanthrene
$C_{14}H_{10}$

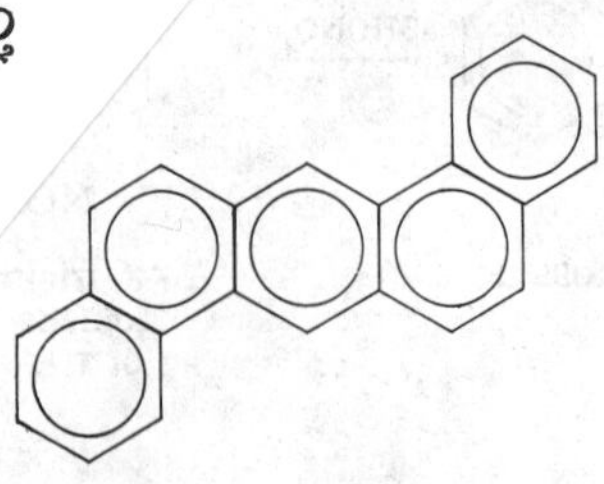

dibenzanthracene
$C_{22}H_{14}$

coronene
$C_{24}H_{12}$

coal tar, is colourless when pure; it exhibits a strong, pale-blue fluorescence when exposed to ultraviolet light. Many synthetic dyes contain the anthracene ring system. The phenanthrene ring system, especially in partially or fully hydrogenated form, is present in many natural products, such as the steroid hormones. Some fused polynuclear aromatic hydrocarbons, such as the dibenzanthracene shown, are carcinogenic—they produce skin cancers when applied locally to the skin and sarcomas (cancers of muscle, bone, or connective tissue) when injected subcutaneously in mice.

The same types of substitution reactions common with benzene also can be carried out with polynuclear compounds. Condensed ring hydrocarbons, such as naphthalene, usually react more readily than benzene does.

NONBENZENOID

Once it became clear that the aromatic properties of benzene and related compounds were due to the closed system of conjugated double bonds in the six-membered ring, it was only natural that organic chemists should attempt to synthesize both larger and smaller rings with conjugated systems of double bonds. The first targets were cyclobutadiene and cyclooctatetraene, the next lower and higher analogues of benzene. Cyclobutadiene has proved

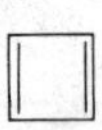

cyclobutadiene
C_4H_4

Kekule's formula of benzene
C_6H_6

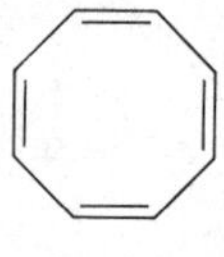

cyclooctatetraene
C_8H_8

particularly elusive; most attempts to prepare it or its derivatives have failed. Cyclooctatetraene was first synthesized by Richard Willstätter, a German chemist, winner of a Nobel Prize in 1915. Although this substance is fairly stable, it does not have a planar conformation like that of benzene; rather, the molecule is tub-shaped. Cyclooctatetraene readily decolourizes bromine, undergoes addition

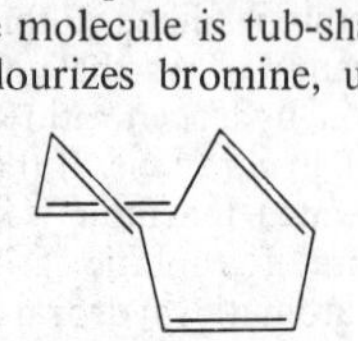

cyclooctatetraene

rather than substitution reactions, and, in short, behaves like a polyene rather than an aromatic compound.

Some nonbenzenoid hydrocarbons with definitely aromatic properties are known, however. Erich Hückel, a German chemist, deduced theoretical reasons why cyclic, planar, conjugated systems must have $4n + 2$ π electrons (*i.e.*, 2, 6, 10, 14...) and not $4n$ π electrons (*i.e.*, 4, 8, 12...), or any other number, if they are to be aromatic. Thus cyclobutadiene, with four π electrons, and cyclooctatetraene, with eight, are not aromatic; whereas benzene, a planar molecule with six electrons, is aromatic. Other examples that conform to the Hückel rule are:

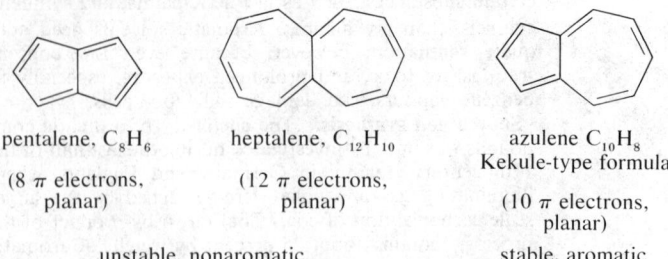

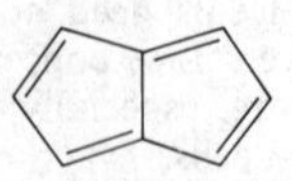

pentalene, C_8H_6
(8 π electrons, planar)

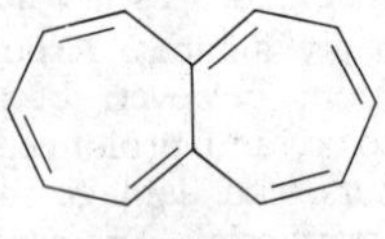

heptalene, $C_{12}H_{10}$
(12 π electrons, planar)

unstable, nonaromatic

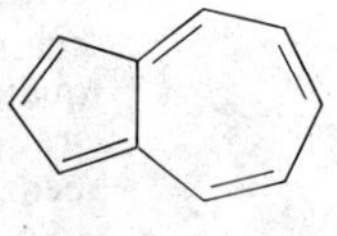

azulene $C_{10}H_8$
Kekule-type formula
(10 π electrons, planar)
stable, aromatic

Thus, azulene, a nonbenzenoid compound, isomeric with naphthalene, readily undergoes substitution reactions, a property of aromatic rather than unsaturated systems.

Cyclodecapentaene, with ten π electrons, also should be aromatic according to the Hückel rule. But the two hydrogens that jut into the middle of the ring make this structure

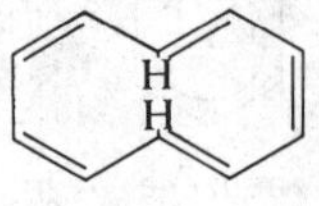

cyclodecapentaene

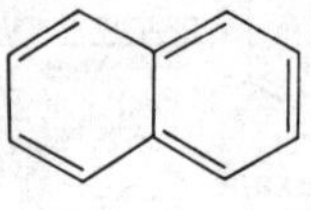

naphthalene

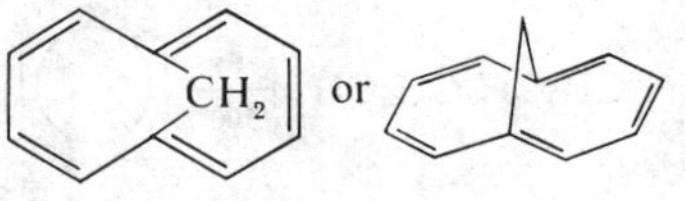

aromatic

difficult to synthesize. If the two hydrogens are replaced with a bond, the resulting compound is naphthalene, which of course is aromatic, but benzenoid. On the other hand, if a single carbon atom, necessarily also bearing two hydrogens, is substituted for the two hydrogens of cyclodecapentaene, the conjugated ten-π-electron system can still be nearly planar. In striking confirmation of the Hückel theory, this hydrocarbon, though nonbenzenoid, undergoes substitution reactions and has other aromatic properties.

Among the larger cyclic polyenes, called annulenes, the ones with 14 and 18 π electrons also give some evidence of being aromatic and, in accord with the Hückel rule, are more stable than those with 16 or 20 π electrons.

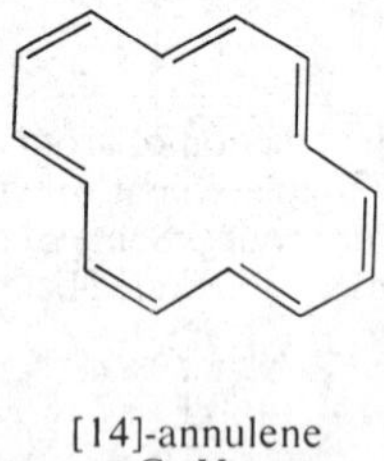

[14]-annulene
$C_{14}H_{14}$

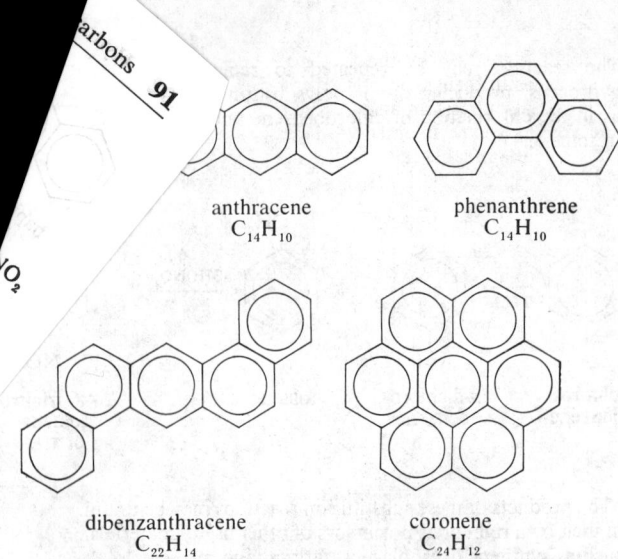

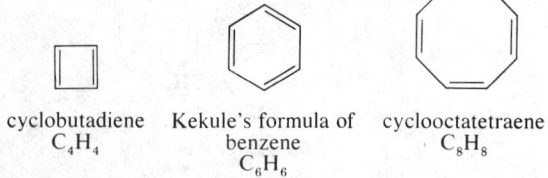

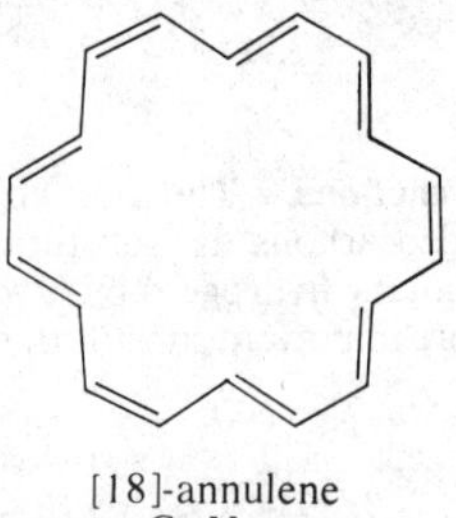

[18]-annulene
$C_{18}H_{18}$

In general, it may be said of hydrocarbons that although their molecules are composed of atoms of only two elements, these atoms can be arranged in an almost infinite number of ways to give a class of organic compounds having an extraordinary variety of physical and chemical properties.

BIBLIOGRAPHY. Brief discussions of the structure, nomenclature, properties, preparation, and reactions of hydrocarbons are presented in all introductory organic chemistry texts. The following are recommended: J.B. HENDRICKSON, D.J. CRAM, and G.S. HAMMOND, *Organic Chemistry*, 3rd ed. (1970); C.R. NOLLER, *Chemistry of Organic Compounds*, 3rd ed. (1965); J.D. ROBERTS and M.C. CASERIO, *Basic Principles of Organic Chemistry* (1964); and L.F. and M.A. FIESER, *Advanced Organic Chemistry* (1961). More extensive but still general discussions are found in S. COFFEY, *Rodd's Chemistry of Carbon Compounds*, 2nd ed., vol. 1A (1964), covers acyclic hydrocarbons, vol. 2 (1967–69), cyclic, but not aromatic, hydrocarbons. For the latter, see vol. 3 (1955–56) of the first edition.

Special classes of hydrocarbons are discussed in these more advanced treatises: F.D. ROSSINI, B.J. MAIR, and A.J. STREIFF, *Hydrocarbons from Petroleum* (1953), a classic work that describes the isolation of pure hydrocarbons from petroleum; B.T. BROOKS *et al.* (eds.), *The Chemistry of Petroleum Hydrocarbons*, 3 vol. (1954–55); S. PATAI (ed.), *The Chemistry of Alkenes* (1964); H.G. VIEHE (ed.), *Chemistry of Acetylenes* (1969); E.J. CLAR, *Polycyclic Hydrocarbons*, 2 vol. (1964), mainly on compounds with fused six-membered rings (vol. 1 includes a chapter by R. SCHOENTAL on the cancer-producing properties of certain hydrocarbons); D. GINSBURG (ed.), *Non-benzenoid Aromatic Compounds* (1959); J.L. SIMONSEN, *The Terpenes*, 2nd ed., 5 vol. (1947–57), the standard work in this field; P. DE MAYO, *Mono- and Sesquiterpenoids*, and *The Higher Terpenoids* (both 1959), briefer but more up-to-date than Simonsen.

(H.Ha.)

Hydrogen and Its Compounds

The most abundant element in the galaxy (ten times as abundant as helium, the next most widely occurring element), hydrogen makes up only about 0.14 percent of the Earth's crust by weight but is present in vast quantities as part of the water in oceans, ice packs, rivers, lakes, and the atmosphere. As part of innumerable carbon compounds, hydrogen is present in all animal and vegetable tissue and in petroleum. Though it is often said that there are more known compounds of carbon than of any other element, the fact is that since hydrogen is contained in almost all carbon compounds and also forms a multitude of compounds with all other elements (except some of the noble gases), it is possible that hydrogen compounds are more numerous. Hydrogen is an odourless, tasteless, colourless gas; the lightest and simplest chemical element. A hydrogen atom, represented by the symbol H, has, for its nucleus, a single proton (*i.e.*, a particle of matter with a positive charge equal to the opposite, negative charge of an electron) surrounded by one orbiting electron. Under ordinary conditions, hydrogen gas is a loose aggregation of hydrogen molecules, each consisting of a pair of atoms, a diatomic molecule, H_2. The earliest known important chemical property of hydrogen is that it burns with oxygen to form water, H_2O; indeed, the name hydrogen is derived from Greek words meaning "maker of water." Because hydrogen can lose an electron to become the positive ion, H^+, it is usually placed in Group Ia of the periodic table of the elements, the group containing the powerfully electropositive (tending to lose electrons) alkali metals. Because hydrogen can also acquire an electron to become a negative ion, H^-, it is sometimes placed in Group VIIa as well, with the powerfully electronegative (tending to acquire electrons) nonmetals, the halogens. No other element can be placed in two groups in the periodic table.

Elementary hydrogen finds its principal industrial application in the manufacture of ammonia (a compound of hydrogen and nitrogen, NH_3) and in the hydrogenation of carbon monoxide and organic compounds.

Hydrogen has three known isotopes; *i.e.*, there are three species of hydrogen atom, identical in atomic number but not in atomic mass. The atomic mass of an element is essentially the sum of the masses of the neutrons and protons in the nucleus, the masses of the electrons orbiting the nucleus being very small. All atoms of an element have the same number of protons, called the atomic number; the number of neutrons varies, and the different species produced by this variation are called the isotopes of that element. The mass numbers of hydrogen's isotopes are 1, 2, and 3, the most abundant being the mass 1 isotope generally called hydrogen (symbol H, or ^1H) but also known as protium. The mass 2 isotope, which has a nucleus of one proton and one neutron and has been named deuterium, or heavy hydrogen (symbol D, or ^2H), constitutes 0.0156 percent of the ordinary mixture of hydrogen. Tritium (symbol T, or ^3H), with one proton and two neutrons in each nucleus, is the mass 3 isotope and constitutes about 10^{-15} to 10^{-16} percent of hydrogen. The practice of giving distinct names to the hydrogen isotopes is justified by the fact that there are significant differences in their properties.

Early experimentation with hydrogen

Paracelsus, physician and alchemist, in the 16th century unknowingly experimented with hydrogen when he found that an inflammable gas was evolved when a metal was dissolved in acid. The gas, however, was confused with other inflammable gases, such as hydrocarbons and carbon monoxide. In 1766 Henry Cavendish, English chemist and physicist, showed that hydrogen, then called inflammable air, phlogiston, or the inflammable principle, was distinct from other combustible gases because of its density and the amount of it that evolved from a given amount of acid and metal. In 1781 Cavendish confirmed previous observations that water was formed when hydrogen was burned, and Antoine-Laurent Lavoisier, the father of modern chemistry, coined the French word *hydrogène* from which the English form is derived. In 1929 Karl Friedrich Bonhoeffer, a German physical chemist, and Paul Harteck, an Austrian chemist, on the basis of earlier theoretical work, showed that ordinary hydrogen is a mixture of two kinds of molecules, *ortho*-hydrogen and *para*-hydrogen. Because of the simple structure of hydrogen, its properties can be theoretically calculated relatively easily. Hence hydrogen is often used as a theoretical model for more complex atoms, and the results are applied qualitatively to other atoms.

PROPERTIES AND COMPOUNDS OF HYDROGEN

Table 1 lists the important properties of molecular hydrogen, H_2. The extremely low melting and boiling points result from weak forces of attraction between the molecules. The existence of these weak intermolecular forces is also revealed by the fact that, when hydrogen gas expands from high to low pressure at room temperature, its temperature rises, whereas the temperature of most other gases falls. According to thermodynamic principles, this implies that repulsive forces exceed attractive forces between hydrogen molecules at room temperature, otherwise the expansion would cool hydrogen. In fact, at −68.6° C (−91.5° F) attractive forces predominate, and hydrogen, therefore, cools upon being allowed to expand below that temperature. The cooling effect becomes so pronounced at temperatures below that of liquid nitrogen (−196° C or −321° F) that the effect is utilized to achieve the liquefaction temperature of hydrogen gas itself.

Table 1: Some Properties of Normal Hydrogen and Deuterium

	normal hydrogen	deuterium
Atomic hydrogen		
Atomic number	1	1
Atomic weight	1.0080	2.0141
Ionization potential	13.595 eV	13.600 eV
Electron affinity	0.754 eV	—
Nuclear spin	½	1
Nuclear magnetic moment (nuclear magnetons)	2.7927	0.8574
Nuclear quadrupole moment	0	2.77 × 10^{-27} cm²
Electronegativity (Pauling)	2.1	~2.1
Molecular hydrogen		
Bond distance	0.7416 Å	0.7416 Å
Dissociation energy (25° C)	104.19 kcal/mole	105.97 kcal/mole
Ionization potential	15.427 eV	15.457 eV
Density of solid	0.08671 g/cm³	0.1967 g/cm³
Melting point	−259.20° C	−254.43° C
Heat of fusion	28 cal/mole	47 cal/mole
Density of liquid	0.07099 (−252.78°)	0.1630 (−249.75°)
Boiling point	−252.77° C	−249.49° C
Heat of vaporization	216 cal/mole	293 cal/mole
Critical temperature	−240.0° C	−234.8° C
Critical pressure	13.0 atm	16.4 atm
Critical density	0.0310 g/cm³	0.0668 g/cm³
Heat of combustion to H_2O(g)	−57.796 kcal/mole	−59.564 kcal/mole

Hydrogen is transparent to visible light, to infrared light, and to ultraviolet light to wavelengths below 1800 angstroms. (An angstrom is the unit used for measuring wavelengths of light, equal to 10^{-10} metre.) Because its molecular weight is lower than that of any other gas, its molecules have a velocity higher than those of any other gas at a given temperature and it diffuses faster than any other gas. Consequently, kinetic energy is distributed faster through hydrogen than through any other gas; it has, for example, the greatest heat conductivity.

The hydrogen molecule

A molecule of hydrogen is the simplest possible molecule. It consists of two protons and two electrons held together by electrostatic forces. Like atomic hydrogen, the assemblage can exist in a number of energy levels.

Ortho-hydrogen and para-hydrogen. Two types of molecular hydrogen (*ortho* and *para*) are known. These differ in the magnetic interactions of the protons due to the spinning motions of the protons. In *ortho*-hydrogen, the spins of both protons are aligned in the same direction—that is, they are parallel. In *para*-hydrogen, the spins are aligned in opposite directions and are therefore antiparallel. The relationship of spin alignments determines the magnetic properties of the atoms. Normally, transformations of one type into the other (*i.e.*, conversions between *ortho* and *para* molecules) do not occur and *ortho*-hydrogen and *para*-hydrogen can be regarded as two distinct modifications of hydrogen. The two forms may, however, interconvert under certain conditions. Equilibrium between the two forms can be established in several ways. One of these is by the introduction of catalysts (such as activated charcoal or various paramagnetic substances); another method is to apply an electrical discharge to the gas or to heat it to a high temperature.

The concentration of *para*-hydrogen in a mixture that has achieved equilibrium between the two forms depends on the temperature as shown by the following figures:

−253.1° C	99.82%	−153.1° C	32.87%
−223.1° C	76.89%	0° C	25.13%
−193.1° C	48.39%	200° C	25.00%

Isolation of *para*-hydrogen

Essentially pure *para*-hydrogen can be produced by bringing the mixture into contact with charcoal at the temperature of liquid hydrogen; this converts all the *ortho* into *para*. The *ortho*-hydrogen, on the other hand, cannot be prepared directly from the mixture because the concentration of *para*-hydrogen is never less than 25 percent.

The two forms of hydrogen have slightly different physical properties. The melting point of *para*-hydrogen is 0.10° lower than that of a 3:1 mixture of *ortho*-hydrogen and *para*-hydrogen. At −252.77° C (−422.99° F) the pressure exerted by the vapour over liquid *para*-hydrogen is 1.035 atmospheres (one atmosphere is the pressure of the atmosphere at sea level under standard conditions, equal to about 14.69 pounds per square inch), compared with 1.000 atmosphere for the vapour pressure of the 3:1 *ortho–para* mixture. As a result of the different vapour pressures of *para*-hydrogen and *ortho*-hydrogen, these forms of hydrogen can be separated by low-temperature gas chromatography, an analytical process that separates different atomic and molecular species on the basis of their differing volatilities.

Reactivity of hydrogen. One molecule of hydrogen dissociates into two atoms ($H_2 \rightarrow 2H$) when an energy equal to or greater than the dissociation energy (*i.e.*, the amount of energy required to break the bond that holds together the atoms in the molecule) is supplied. The dissociation energy of molecular hydrogen is 104,000 calories per mole—written 104 kcal/mole (mole: the molecular weight expressed in grams, which is two grams in the case of hydrogen). Sufficient energy is obtained, for example, when the gas is brought into contact with a white-hot tungsten filament or when an electric discharge is established in the gas. If atomic hydrogen is generated in a system at low pressure, the atoms will have a significant lifetime—*e.g.*, 0.3 second at a pressure of 0.5 millimetre of mercury. Atomic hydrogen is very reactive. It combines with most elements to form hydrides (*e.g.*, sodium hydride, NaH), and it reduces metallic oxides, a reaction that produces the metal in its elemental state. The surfaces of metals that do not combine with hydrogen to form stable hydrides (*e.g.*, platinum) catalyze the recombination of hydrogen atoms to form hydrogen molecules and are thereby heated to incandescence by the energy that this reaction releases.

Molecular hydrogen can react with many elements and compounds, but at room temperature the reaction rates are usually so low as to be negligible. This apparent inertness is in part related to the very high dissociation energy of the molecule. At elevated temperatures, however, the reaction rates are high.

Explosive mixtures

Sparks or certain radiations can cause a mixture of hydrogen and chlorine to react explosively to yield hydrogen chloride, as represented by the equation $H_2 + Cl_2 \rightarrow 2HCl$. Mixtures of hydrogen and oxygen react at a measurable rate only above 300° C (570° F), according to the equation $2H_2 + O_2 \rightarrow 2H_2O$. Such mixtures containing 4 to 94 percent hydrogen ignite when heated to 550°–600° C (1,000°–1,100° F) or when brought into contact with a catalyst, spark, or flame. The explosion of a 2:1 mixture of hydrogen and oxygen is especially violent. Almost all metals and nonmetals react with hydrogen at high temperatures. At elevated temperatures and pressures hydrogen reduces the oxides of most metals and many metallic salts to the metals. For example, hydrogen gas and ferrous oxide react, yielding metallic iron and water, $H_2 + FeO \rightarrow Fe + H_2O$; hydrogen gas reduces palladium chloride to form palladium metal and hydrogen chloride, $H_2 + PdCl_2 \rightarrow Pd + 2HCl$.

Hydrogen reacts with bromine vapour at a negligible rate in the absence of light, which is a catalyst for the reaction, unless the temperature is raised to 200°–300° C (400°–600° F). In the initial step of the reaction, bromine molecules dissociate into bromine atoms (because this reaction is reversible—*i.e.*, some bromine atoms react to reform the molecules—double arrows are used in the equation): $Br_2 \rightleftharpoons 2Br$. The bromine atoms react with hydrogen molecules to give hydrogen bromide molecules and hydrogen atoms: $Br + H_2 \rightleftharpoons HBr + H$. Hydrogen atoms next react with bromine molecules to form hydrogen bromide molecules and more bromine atoms: $H + Br_2 \rightarrow HBr + Br$. As long as both hydrogen and bromine atoms or molecules are present, the latter two reactions can continue indefinitely in a chain reaction and their sum will correspond to the overall reaction of hydrogen with bromine: $H_2 + Br_2 \rightarrow 2HBr$. A uniform (steady state) concentration of atoms is maintained during the reaction, and, although these atom concentrations are very low, they are adequate to permit the chain reaction to proceed at a measurable rate. Many reactions of molecular hydrogen with other gases (*e.g.*, those with oxygen, chlorine, and fluorine) proceed by similar chain mechanisms involving atomic hydrogen.

Chain reactions

Saltlike hydrides. Hydrogen can either lose or gain an electron to form either a positive ion (proton, H^+) or a negative ion (hydride ion, H^-). At high temperatures, hydrogen reacts with the alkali metals (main group I of the periodic table) and the alkaline-earth metals (main group II of the periodic table), except beryllium, to form salts, such as sodium hydride (NaH) and calcium hydride (CaH_2), which contain the hydride ion, H^-. The electrolysis of molten lithium hydride (LiH), for example, liberates lithium metal at the negative electrode and hydrogen gas at the positive electrode: $Li^+ + e^- \rightarrow Li$; $H^- \rightarrow \frac{1}{2}H_2 + e^-$. These hydrides have physical properties similar to corresponding fluorides, partly because the ions F^- and H^- have nearly the same radii (1.36 and 1.40 angstroms [Å], respectively). Lithium hydride, like lithium fluoride of the fluorides, is the most stable of the alkali-metal hydrides.

These hydrides react vigorously with solvents that ionize to give protons, such as water (H_2O), alcohol (C_2H_5OH), and liquid ammonia (NH_3), to form a base (a base can be defined as a substance that accepts—*i.e.*, bonds to itself—protons) and hydrogen. Thus, in the case of potassium hydride: $KH + H_2O \rightarrow K^+ + OH^- + H_2$; $KH + C_2H_5OH \rightarrow K^+ + C_2H_5O^- + H_2$; $KH + NH_3 \rightarrow K^+ + NH_2^- + H_2$. Sodium hydride finds considerable use as a reducing agent in synthetic chemistry. It reacts with methyl borate at elevated temperatures to form sodium borohydride (sodium hydroborate), $NaBH_4$, which in turn is a useful reducing agent. Similarly, lithium hydride is an intermediate in the preparation of lithium aluminum hydride (lithium tetrahydridoaluminate), $LiAlH_4$, which is an important reagent in synthetic chemistry.

Metallike hydrides. Hydrogen is absorbed at high temperatures by many transition metals (scandium, 21, through copper, 29; yttrium, 39, through silver, 47; hafnium, 72, through gold, 79; and metals of the actinide (actinium, 89, through lawrencium, 103) and lanthanide series (lanthanum, 57, through lutetium, 71) to form hard, alloy-like hydrides. These are often called interstitial hydrides because, in many cases, the metallic crystal lattice merely expands to accommodate the dissolved hydrogen without any other change. Metallike hydrides usually have a rather large range of composition without marked change in structure. In palladium hydride, for example, the H:Pd ratio may vary from 0.4 to 0.7 without any major change in the arrangement of the palladium atoms. These hydrides are also electrical conductors. Hydrogen dissolved in wires of palladium, tantalum, titanium, and other transition metals migrates to the negative end when an electrical current is flowing, a behaviour that can be interpreted as evidence that hydrogen exists as protons, H^+, in these hydrides.

Transition-metal hydride complexes. Until the late 1950s, very few compounds were known in which hydrogen atoms were bonded directly to transition-metal atoms. Since then, numerous compounds of this type have been discovered. Most of them have the general formula MH_xL_y, in which M is a transition metal and L is a ligand (*i.e.*, an atom or molecule capable of direct chemical bonding to a metal atom). Examples are: $K_3[CoH(CN)_5]$, a homogeneous hydrogenation catalyst for the conversion of alkynes to alkenes; *trans*-$PtHCl[P(C_2H_5)_3]_2$, a compound so stable that it can be vaporized without decomposition in a vacuum; $OsHCl_2[P(C_4H_9)_2C_6H_5]_3$, a complex with an odd number of electrons and therefore paramagnetic; and K_2ReH_9, remarkable because the transition metal is bonded to an unusually large number of hydrogen atoms and to no other ligands.

Ligands

Many transition-metal ions and complexes catalyze certain reactions of molecular hydrogen. In each case the H_2 molecule is split, with the formation of a reactive transition-metal hydride complex as an intermediate.

Volatile hydrides. Hydrogen atoms can form bonds with other atoms by a process in which each atom donates an electron to the bond, the pair then being associated with both atoms. Such bonds are called covalent, and hydrogen can be covalently bonded to elements such as boron, of Group IIIa of the periodic table, and the elements of main Groups IVa, Va, VIa, and VIIa (hydrogen molecules are also covalently bonded atoms of hydrogen). The hydrides of boron, which is the most electropositive of these elements, react as if their hydrogen atoms had "hydridic" character; that is, were somewhat like H^- ions. Volatile hydrides, such as diborane (B_2H_6), and water react to form hydrogen: $B_2H_6 + 6H_2O \rightarrow 6H_2 + 2H_3BO_3$. Hydrides of the more electronegative elements, such as those of Groups VIa and VIIa, react as if their hydrogen had protonic (H^+) character, and they form salts or adducts (*i.e.*, mixtures in which some of the molecules of one component are trapped within the lattice arrangement of the atoms of the other) with bases (H^+ acceptors, like NH_3): $HCl + NH_3 \rightarrow NH_4Cl$. Hydrides of the elements of intermediate electronegativity, such as those of Group IVa, have neither marked hydridic nor protonic character and may show either character, depending on the reagent. Germane, GeH_4, is hydridic in its reaction with hydrogen bromide, $GeH_4 + HBr \rightarrow GeH_3Br + H_2$, protonic in its reaction with sodium amide, $GeH_4 + NaNH_2 \rightarrow NaGeH_3 + NH_3$.

The study of hydrides of carbon and their derivatives constitutes the enormous field of organic chemistry. Carbon atoms are remarkable for their ability to catenate; that is, to bond to each other to form molecular chains, as in the open-chain hydrocarbons (alkanes) that are found in petroleum. Other elements have this ability to a much lesser extent. Silicon hydrides (silanes) analogous to the organic alkanes have silicon chain lengths of up to ten—*i.e.*, $Si_{10}H_{22}$. The longest molecular chain hy-

drides that have been characterized for other elements (germanium [Ge], tin [Sn], nitrogen [N], phosphorus [P], arsenic [As], antimony [Sb], oxygen [O], and sulfur [S]) are $Ge_{10}H_{22}$, Sn_2H_6, N_3H, P_3H_5, As_5H_5, Sb_2H_4, H_2O_3, and H_2S_6.

Hydrogen bond. Some covalently bonded hydrides have a hydrogen atom bound simultaneously to two separate electronegative atoms, which are then said to be hydrogen bonded. The strongest hydrogen bonds exist between the small, highly electronegative atoms of fluorine (F), oxygen, and nitrogen. In the bifluoride ion, HF_2^-, the hydrogen atom links two fluorine atoms. In the crystal structure of ice, each oxygen atom is surrounded by four other oxygen atoms, with hydrogen atoms between them. Some of the hydrogen bonds are broken when ice melts, and the structure collapses with an increase in density. Hydrogen bonding is important in biology because of its major role in determining the configurations of molecules. The helical (spiral) configurations of certain enormous molecular chains, as in proteins, are held together by hydrogen bonds. Extensive hydrogen bonding in the liquid state explains why hydrogen fluoride (HF), water (H_2O), and ammonia (NH_3) have boiling points much higher than those of their heavier analogues, hydrogen chloride (HCl), hydrogen sulfide (H_2S), and phosphine (PH_3). At the higher boiling temperatures, thermal energy is available to break up the hydrogen bonds and to permit vaporization.

Acids. The hydrogen in a strong acid, such as hydrochloric (HCl) or nitric (HNO_3), behaves quite differently. When these acids dissolve in water, hydrogen in the form of a proton, H^+, separates completely from the negatively charged ion, the anion (Cl^- or NO_3^-), and interacts with the water molecules. The proton is strongly attached to one water molecule (hydrated) to form the oxonium ion (H_3O^+), which in turn is hydrogen-bonded to other water molecules, forming species with formulas such as $H(H_2O)_n^+$ (the subscript n indicates the number of H_2O molecules involved). The oxidation of hydrogen (oxidation is the chemical change in which an atom loses one or more electrons) can be represented as the half reaction: $\frac{1}{2}H_2 \rightarrow H^+ + e^-$. The energy needed to bring about this reaction can be expressed as an oxidation potential. The oxidation potential for hydrogen is taken by convention to be zero, and all metals with positive oxidation potentials—*i.e.*, metals that are more easily oxidized (*e.g.*, zinc; $Zn \rightarrow Zn^{2+} + 2e^-$, 0.763 volt)—can, in principle, displace hydrogen from a strong acid solution: $Zn + 2H^+ \rightarrow Zn^{2+} + H_2$. Metals with negative oxidation potentials (*e.g.*, silver; $Ag \rightarrow Ag^+ + e^-$, −0.7995 volt) are inert toward the aqueous hydrogen ion.

Oxidation potential

Boron hydrides. The hydrides of boron (boranes) have always fascinated chemists because their structures cannot be explained by classical bonding theory. The simplest boron hydride, diborane, B_2H_6, has only 12 valence electrons to hold its eight atoms together, whereas the hydrocarbon ethane (C_2H_6) has 14 valence electrons. Fourteen valence electrons provide seven two-atom electron-pair bonds for its molecular structure. If each covalent bond—*i.e.*, each electron-pair—is represented by a single line between the bonded atoms, the structure may be shown as:

$$\begin{array}{ccc} H & & H \\ | & & | \\ H-C&-&C-H. \\ | & & | \\ H & & H \end{array}$$

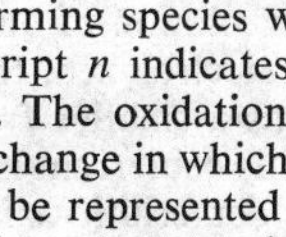

Only six such bonds could be formed for the structure of the diborane molecule, B_2H_6. In fact, B_2H_6 does not have a structure like ethane but rather a structure in which two of the hydrogen atoms act as bridges between the boron atoms:

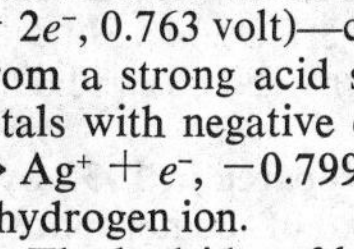

By assigning a pair of electrons to each of the three-atom, B — H — B, bridge bonds, and a pair to each of the two-atom, B — H, bonds, the structure can be explained in terms of only 12 valence electrons. By using similar combinations of two-atom and three-atom bonds, it is possible to explain the structures of the other hydrides as, for example, B_4H_{10}, B_5H_9, B_5H_{11}, B_6H_{10}, $B_{10}H_{14}$, etc.

Carboranes are electron-deficient hydrides containing both boron and carbon atoms, usually in a polyhedral framework. They have generally been prepared by reactions of acetylene or substituted acetylenes with boron hydrides. The most thoroughly studied carborane is $B_{10}C_2H_{12}$, in which the boron and carbon atoms form the 12 corners of an icosahedron. It is an extremely stable molecule, with the framework resisting attack by strong acids, alkalies, and oxidizing agents.

ISOTOPES OF HYDROGEN

Discovery of deuterium, ^2H, or D

By means of the mass spectrograph he had invented, Francis William Aston in 1927 observed that the line for hydrogen corresponded to an atomic weight on the chemical scale of 1.00756. This value differed by more than the probable experimental error from the value based on the combining weights of hydrogen compounds, 1.00777. Other workers showed that the discrepancy could be removed by postulating the existence of a hydrogen isotope of mass 2 in the proportion of one atom of ^2H to 4,500 atoms of ^1H. The problem interested the U.S. physicist Harold C. Urey, who from theoretical principles predicted a difference in the vapour pressures of hydrogen (H_2) and hydrogen deuteride (HD) and thus the possibility of separating these substances by distillation of liquid hydrogen. In 1931 Urey and two collaborators detected deuterium by its atomic spectrum in the residue of a distillation of liquid hydrogen. Deuterium was first prepared in pure form by the electrolytic method of concentration: when a water solution of an electrolyte, such as sodium hydroxide, is electrolyzed, the hydrogen formed at the cathode contains a smaller fraction of deuterium than the water, and thus deuterium is concentrated in the residue. Almost pure deuterium oxide (D_2O, heavy water) is obtained when the solution is reduced to 0.00001 of its original volume. Deuterium can be concentrated also by the fractional distillation of water and by various chemical exchange reactions such as the following (g and l indicate gaseous and liquid states, respectively): $H_2O(g) + HD(g) \rightleftharpoons HDO(g) + H_2(g)$; $HDO(g) + H_2S(g) \rightleftharpoons HDS(g) + H_2O(g)$; $NH_3(l) + HD(g) \rightleftharpoons NH_2D(l) + H_2(g)$.

Creation of tritium, ^3H, or T

Tritium was first prepared in 1935 by bombarding deuterium (in the form of deuterophosphoric acid) with high-energy deuterons (deuterium nuclei):

$$^2D + ^2D \longrightarrow ^1H + ^3T.$$

Tritium is present in minute concentrations in natural water. It is formed continuously in the upper atmosphere by cosmic-ray-induced nuclear reactions. Cosmic rays, consisting mainly of high-energy protons, react with nitrogen atoms to form neutrons, which in turn react with more nitrogen atoms to form tritium:

$$^{14}N + ^1H \longrightarrow ^{14}O + ^1n \qquad ^{14}N + ^1n \longrightarrow ^{12}C + ^3T.$$

This naturally formed tritium ends up in the form of water and reaches the surface of the Earth in rain. Tritium is radioactive; it has a half-life of 12.5 years, decaying to a very soft (low energy) negative beta particle (electron; the positive beta particle is called a positron) and a helium-3 nucleus. When a sample of water is stored, it gradually loses its tritium because of radioactive decay. Thus by analyzing water for its tritium content, it is possible to elucidate details of water circulation among oceans, the atmosphere, rivers, and lakes. Tritium is made artificially in nuclear reactors by the reaction of thermal neutrons with lithium:

$$^6Li + ^1n \longrightarrow ^3T + ^4He.$$

Corresponding compounds of the hydrogen isotopes differ slightly in their physical properties. This difference is shown by the properties of the waters, listed in Table 2, and of the elements, listed in Table 1. The same is true of their chemical properties, both thermodynamic and kinetic. Both deuterium and tritium are useful as isotopic tracers for the investigation of chemical structures and of reaction mechanisms. Generally the value of a tracer arises from the fact that, although its difference in mass or its radioactivity permits its detection, it is essentially active in the same way that the ordinary atoms of the element are. For most elements, a change of one or of a few mass units is such a small percentage of the total mass that the chemical differences between isotopes are negligible. For hydrogen, however, chemical reactions involving the different isotopes proceed at measurably different rates. These kinetic-isotope effects can be utilized in detailed studies of reaction mechanisms. The rates of reactions of compounds containing deuterium or tritium are usually less than those of the corresponding compounds of ordinary hydrogen.

Table 2: Physical Properties of the Waters

	H_2O	D_2O	T_2O
Density at 25° C in g/ml	0.99707	1.10451	—
Melting point, °C	0	3.81	4.49
Boiling point, °C	100	101.41	—
Temperature of maximum density, °C	3.98	11.21	13.4
Maximum density in g/ml	1.00000	1.10589	1.21502

The replacement of hydrogen by deuterium in biological systems can markedly alter the delicately balanced processes. It has been established that neither plants nor animals continue to live and thrive in water containing deuterium oxide in high concentrations.

Energy from deuterium and tritium

Deuterium and tritium are of interest in connection with thermonuclear (fusion) reactions. The explosion of a hydrogen bomb involves the collision and fusion of light nuclei, including deuterium and tritium. Should a method be found for controlling such fusion processes, as was done with the fission process of the earlier atomic bomb, the raw material for a practically unlimited supply of energy would be available in the deuterium content of water.

Deuterium oxide is useful in nuclear reactors as a moderator to slow down but not appreciably capture neutrons. It has the advantage of being a liquid that absorbs neutrons only slightly.

PRODUCTION AND APPLICATIONS OF HYDROGEN

The most important industrial method for the production of hydrogen is the catalytic steam–hydrocarbon process, in which gaseous or vaporized hydrocarbons are treated with steam at high pressure over a nickel catalyst at 650°–950° C (1,200°–1,750° F) to produce carbon oxides and hydrogen: $C_nH_{2n+2} + nH_2O \rightarrow nCO + (2n + 1)H_2$; $C_nH_{2n+2} + 2nH_2O \rightarrow nCO_2 + (3n + 1)H_2$. The primary reaction products are processed further in various ways, depending on the desired application of the hydrogen.

Another important process for hydrogen production is the noncatalytic partial oxidation of hydrocarbons under elevated pressures: $C_nH_{2n+2} + (n/2)O_2 \rightarrow nCO + (n + 1)H_2$. This process requires a feed system for delivering precise rates of fuel and oxygen, burners of special design to give rapid mixing of the reactants, a refractory-lined reactor, and a cooling system to recover heat from the effluent gases. The latter process is exothermic (heat producing), in contrast to the endothermic (heat-absorbing) steam–hydrocarbon process.

In a third process, called the pressure catalytic partial oxidation method, the two preceding processes are combined to maintain the required reaction temperature without external heating of the catalyst bed. Superheated steam and hydrocarbons are mixed, preheated, and blended with heated oxygen in a diffuser at the top of the catalytic reactor. The oxygen reacts with the hydrocarbons in a space above the catalyst. The reactants then pass through a bed of nickel catalyst in which the steam–hydrocarbon reactions proceed almost to equilibrium.

Before 1940 most of the world production of hydrogen was made by processes based on coal or coke, the principal one being a water–gas reaction between steam and red-hot coke: $H_2O + C \rightarrow CO + H_2$. By 1970, however, relatively little hydrogen was being produced by such processes. For many years relatively small amounts of hydrogen had been produced by the electrolysis of aqueous solutions of salt or sodium hydroxide, the electrode reaction being $H_2O + e^- \rightarrow \frac{1}{2}H_2 + OH^-$. The reaction between sulfuric or hydrochloric acid and an active metal like zinc is utilized to liberate hydrogen in the laboratory, but such hydrogen usually contains trace quantities of volatile hydrides, such as arsine (AsH_3) and phosphine (PH_3), produced by impurities in the metal. These volatile impurities may be removed by bubbling the mixture of gases through a solution of a strong oxidizing agent, such as potassium permanganate.

A commercial method was developed for separating hydrogen from carbon monoxide synthesis gas by diffusion. The gas flows under pressure through bundles of tiny hollow polyester fibres through whose walls the hydrogen passes.

The largest single use of hydrogen in the world is in ammonia manufacture, which consumes about two-thirds of the world's hydrogen production. Ammonia is manufactured by the so-called Haber process, in which hydrogen and nitrogen react in the presence of a catalyst at pressures around 1,000 atmospheres and temperatures around 500° C (900° F): $N_2 + 3H_2 \rightarrow 2NH_3$. Large amounts of hydrogen are used in the preparation of methanol by the reaction $CO + 2H_2 \rightarrow CH_3OH$. This process is carried out in the presence of certain mixed catalysts containing zinc oxide and chromium oxide at temperatures between 300° and 375° C (575° and 700° F) and at pressures between 275 and 350 atmospheres.

Another major application of hydrogen is in the catalytic hydrogenation of organic compounds. Unsaturated vegetable and animal oils and fats are hydrogenated to make margarine and vegetable shortening. Hydrogen is used to reduce aldehydes, fatty acids, and esters to the corresponding alcohols. Aromatic compounds can be reduced to the corresponding saturated compounds, as in the conversion of benzene to cyclohexane and of phenol to cyclohexanol. Nitro compounds can be reduced easily to amines.

Use of hydrogen as rocket fuel

Hydrogen has been used as a primary rocket fuel for combustion with oxygen or fluorine and is favoured as a propellant for nuclear-powered rockets and space vehicles. Another increasing use of hydrogen is in the direct reduction of iron ores to metallic iron and in the reduction of the oxides of tungsten and molybdenum to the metals. A hydrogen (reducing) atmosphere is employed in the pouring of special castings, in the manufacture of magnesium, in the annealing of metals, and for the cooling of large electric motors. Hydrogen was once used for inflating lighter-than-air vessels, such as dirigibles and balloons, but now helium is generally used because it is nonflammable. The barrage balloons used in England during World War II, however, were filled with hydrogen. Liquid hydrogen is used in the laboratory to produce low temperatures.

ANALYSIS

When atoms are excited, as in an electric discharge, they radiate light at discrete wavelengths that appear as lines in the spectrum. Inasmuch as the wavelengths of atomic spectral lines are characteristic of the element, the atomic spectrum may be used for identifying the element. The simplest of all such spectra is that of hydrogen. Johann Jakob Balmer, a Swiss mathematician and secondary school teacher, in 1885 discovered an equation for representing the wavelengths of hydrogen spectral lines, of which nine had been observed in the laboratory and of which five more were photographed in the spectrum of the star Sirius. The wavelengths, lambda (λ), in angstroms, were represented by the formula: $\lambda = 3645.6\,[m^2/(m^2 - 4)]$, m taking the successive values 3, 4, 5, etc. It was not until 1913 that a theoretical basis for this empirical relation was given by the Danish physicist Niels Bohr in his theory of atomic radiation.

The spinning motion of the proton gives it magnetic properties and causes it to precess in an applied magnetic field, much as a spinning top precesses in a gravitational field. The frequency at which a particular proton precesses is determined by its local electrical environment and by the strength of the applied magnetic field. When hydrogen compounds are irradiated with electromagnetic waves of a particular frequency, the phenomenon of resonance absorption occurs at magnetic field strengths that are different for each structurally (magnetically) distinguishable proton in the compound. Thus, proton magnetic resonance makes it possible to distinguish the structural types of hydrogen atoms present; furthermore, the absorption peak intensities are proportional to the number of hydrogen atoms of each kind. The absorption peaks are often split, however, because of the magnetic interaction of the proton magnetic moments among themselves. Proton-magnetic-resonance measurements provide data for the investigation of chemical structure.

One method for determining the total hydrogen content of a substance is to oxidize the substance completely in a stream of pure oxygen, which reacts with the hydrogen to produce water vapour. The resulting vapours are passed through a powerful dehydrating agent, such as magnesium perchlorate, which absorbs the water. From the increase in weight of the absorption tube containing the desiccant, the amount of hydrogen oxidized can be calculated. Gaseous hydrogen or hydrogen compounds may be oxidized by passing them over hot copper oxide, and the resulting water can then be collected and weighed and the amount of hydrogen calculated; to measure the hydrogen gas itself, the water vapour from the oxidation may be reduced to hydrogen gas by passing it over hot uranium metal—the hydrogen then being measured in a simple device called a gas buret.

Strongly acidic hydrogen atoms (as in compounds such as HCl, HNO_3, H_2SO_4, etc.) can be determined in solution by adding measured amounts of a strong base, such as sodium hydroxide, $NaOH$, until the acid is neutralized, using an indicator to determine the end point. The net reaction is $H^+ + OH^- \rightarrow H_2O$. Weakly acidic hydrogen atoms (such as that attached to the oxygen in ethanol, C_2H_5OH, and those attached to the nitrogen in acetamide, CH_3CONH_2) can be converted to methane (measured in a gas buret) by reaction with the methyl Grignard reagent, CH_3MgI. Hydridic hydrogen atoms (as in $NaBH_4$, LiH, etc.) can be converted to molecular hydrogen (measured in a gas buret) by reaction with an aqueous acid.

BIBLIOGRAPHY

General: F.A. COTTON and G. WILKINSON, *Advanced Inorganic Chemistry*, 2nd rev. ed. (1966); and W.L. JOLLY, *The Chemistry of the Non-Metals* (1966), give brief accounts of the chemistry of hydrogen and its compounds.

Ortho- and para-hydrogen: A. FARKAS, *Orthohydrogen, Parahydrogen and Heavy Hydrogen* (1935), is a classic monograph by an early researcher in this area.

Hydrides: K.M. MACKAY, *Hydrogen Compounds of the Metallic Elements* (1966); and G.G. LIBOWITZ, *Solid-State Chemistry of Binary Metal Hydrides* (1965), are short, but contain many experimental data. J. CHATT, "Hydride Complexes," *Science*, 160:723–729 (1968), is a brief modern review of this important topic. E.L. MUETTERTIES (comp.), *The Chemistry of Boron and Its Compounds* (1967), gives a good survey of the boron hydrides and their derivatives.

Deuterium and tritium: I. KIRSHENBAUM, *Physical Properties and Analysis of Heavy Water* (1951), is a comprehensive treatise. S. KAUFMAN and W.F. LIBBY, "The Natural Distribution of Tritium," *Phys. Rev.*, 93:1337–1344 (1954), is the classic article on tritium dating. E.A. EVANS, *Tritium and Its Compounds* (1966), is a compact source of information.

Production and application: R.M. REED, "Hydrogen," in *Kirk-Othmer Encyclopedia of Chemical Technology*, 2nd ed., vol. 11, pp. 338–379 (1966).

Proton magnetic resonance: J.D. ROBERTS, *Nuclear Magnetic Resonance: Applications to Organic Chemistry* (1959), is a relatively simple introductory text for a technique that is of major importance to chemists.

(W.L.J.)

Hydrographic Charting

Hydrographic charting is the art and science of compiling and producing charts of water-covered areas of the earth's surface. The word chart is derived from the Latin *carta* ("paper") and has been used in English in the sense of a map since the 16th century. The present form is an abbreviation of sea chart.

HISTORY OF NAUTICAL CHARTING

The earliest navigators coasted from headland to headland; they did not require charts until adoption of the magnetic compass made it possible to proceed directly from one port to another. The earliest record of the magnetic compass in Europe (1187) is followed within a century by the earliest record of a sea chart. This was shown to Louis IX, king of France, on the occasion of his participation in the Eighth Crusade in 1270. The earliest surviving chart dates from within a few years of this event. Found in Pisa and known as the Carta Pisana, it is now in the Bibliothèque Nationale, Paris. Thought to have been made about 1275, it is hand drawn on a sheepskin and depicts the entire Mediterranean Sea. Such charts are often known as portolans (from the Italian *portolano*, derived from late Latin *portulanus*, "pertaining to ports"). Later terms are rutter or ruttier, dating from about 1500 (French *routier*), and wagoner (from Lucas Janssen·Waghenaer, a Hollander who published an atlas in 1584). The first portolans were hand drawn and very expensive. They were based entirely on magnetic directions and map projections that assumed a degree of longitude equal to a degree of latitude. The assumption did little harm in the Mediterranean but caused serious distortions in maps of higher latitudes. Development of line engraving and the availability, in the 16th century, of large sheets of smooth-surfaced paper facilitated mass production of charts, which soon replaced the manuscript portolans. Probably the first chart showing soundings was one made by Juan de la Cosa, a companion of Columbus, in 1504. The theory of trigonometrical surveying was disclosed in 1533 by Gemma Frisius, a Flemish mathematician. In 1569, Gerhard Kremer, known as Gerardus Mercator, solved the projection problem by producing his famous world map with the meridians vertical and parallels having increased spacing in proportion to the secant (a trigonometric function) of the latitude. Edward Wright published (1599) mathematical tables giving the basis of Mercator's projection.

Portolans

The terms hydrography and hydrographer date from the middle-16th century and are based on French coinages, formed on the analogy of geography and geographer. The British East India Company employed hydrographers in the 18th century, and the first hydrographer of the British Navy, Alexander Dalrymple (1737–1808), was appointed in 1795. A naval observatory and hydrographical office was established administratively in the United States Navy in 1854; in 1866 a hydrographic office was established by statute, and in 1962 it was renamed the U.S. Naval Oceanographic Office.

Interest in the charting of oceanic areas away from seacoasts developed in the second half of the 19th century, concurrently with the perfection of submarine cables. As knowledge of the configuration of the ocean basins increased, the attention of scientists was drawn to this field of study. A feature of marine science since the 1950s has been increasingly detailed bathymetric (water-depth measurement) surveys of selected portions of the sea floor. Together with collection of associated geophysical data and sampling of sediments, these studies assist in interpreting the geological history of the ocean-covered portion of the earth's crust.

Bathymetric surveys

CHARTING AGENCIES

Hydrographic offices. Hydrographic offices are governmental organizations established by most maritime nations to furnish their mariners with nautical charts and other publications necessary for navigation of their territorial waters and the oceans of the world. Activities of these offices thus comprise surveys at sea and along the coasts as well as publication and distribution of nautical documents. In many countries hydrography is carried out under the ministry of defense; especially trained naval officers supervise field work. This is the case, for example, in Great Britain, Australia, New Zealand, and France. In other countries the hydrographic office is under a civil branch of the government: the Department of Energy, Mines, and Resources in Canada; the Department of Communications in Norway; or the Department of Transport in the Federal Republic of Germany. The U.S. has a unique combination of these two, the Oceanographic Office of the Navy being responsible for foreign waters and the Coast and Geodetic Survey (founded in 1807) of the Department of Commerce, for waters of the U.S. and possessions. The U.S. Coast and Geodetic Survey became a part of the Environmental Science Services Administration in 1965; this component in turn became part of the National Oceanic and Atmospheric Administration in 1970.

International hydrographic organizations. The International Hydrographic Bureau (IHB) was formally founded in June 1921. At the invitation of Prince Albert of Monaco, who was intensely interested in nautical and oceanographic matters, it had its seat in Monaco and has continued to be based there in quarters provided by the Princely Government. The purposes of the Bureau were to establish close association between hydrographic offices, to encourage adoption of the best hydrographic survey methods, to coordinate hydrographic work, to make navigation easier and safer, and to obtain maximum uniformity in hydrographic documents so mariners can use publications issued by other countries. Member countries paid annual dues on the basis of their total tonnage of naval and merchant ships. An International Hydrographic Conference, composed of delegates of the member states, was held every five years to review the work of the Bureau. During the life of the League of Nations, the Bureau was recognized by and functioned officially under that organization.

At the 9th International Hydrographic Conference, held in 1967, steps were taken to reconstitute the IHB on a more regular basis. By this time it had grown from the original membership of 18 countries, in 1921, to 41. A new draft convention, adopted in May 1967, provided for creation of an International Hydrographic Organization (IHO) to consist of the International Hydrographic Bureau and the International Hydrographic Conference. With the ratification of 28 members, this convention went into force in 1970 and was registered with the United Nations Secretariat under Article 102 of the United Nations Charter.

A major operation of the International Hydrographic Bureau has been compilation of the *Carte générale bathymétrique des océans* (*General Bathymetric Chart of the Oceans*), commonly known by contraction of its English title as GEBCO. It consists of 16 sheets on Mercator projection at the scale of 1:10,000,000 at the Equator and 8 polar sheets on stereographic projections (see MAPS AND MAPPING) on the scale 1:3,100,000 (as measured at latitude 72°). In 1965, the French Institut Geógraphique National was assigned the task of preparing, publishing, and issuing the new editions of the GEBCO sheets. For most, the fourth edition was compiled from plotting sheets prepared at 1:1,000,000 scale by the hydrographic offices of 16 cooperating IHO member countries.

MODERN SURVEY TECHNIQUES

Regardless of the scale on which it is carried out, a hydrographic survey consists essentially of two operations: determination of the horizontal coordinates of points on the sea surface (position fixing) and determination of the depth of water at these points. Modern aerial photogrammetry makes possible the simultaneous determination of horizontal coordinates and ground elevations in a single operation from stereoscopic aerial photographs. The relative opacity of seawater, however, necessitates the time-consuming task of obtaining soundings from a vessel or boat moving across the sea surface.

Position fixing. In hydrographic surveying, position fixing must be accomplished both on land and at sea. The shape of the coastline is an essential feature of any chart. Nowadays it is determined with aerial photographs, although in the early days of hydrography it had to be derived through the laborious processes of triangulation and later, by trilateration. In *triangulation*, an imaginary network of triangles (triangulation net) is established with corners (vertices) at selected points (stations) in the area to be surveyed. A *base line* of known length and position forms one side of one of the triangles. Stations are usually located on prominent landmarks, such as lighthouses or hilltops. By careful measurement of the angles at the vertices of each triangle and use of them together with the base line, the position of any point within the triangulation net can be computed by large-scale plotting of angles and distances. *Trilateration* is a similar process that involves measurement of the *length* of each line in the net rather than the angles between lines. This process, although difficult with tape measures, became practical when electronic distance-measuring devices were invented.

Triangulation and trilateration

The Geodimeter, introduced in 1946, measures the time required for a pulse of visible light to pass from the observer to a distant mirror and return; calculation based on the speed of light gives the distance. An improvement is the Tellurometer, introduced in 1956, which uses 3 GHz (3 gigahertz = 3,000,000,000 cycles per second) microwaves and hence is less sensitive to atmospheric conditions. A more recent microwave distance-measuring system, the Electrotape, operates on a carrier frequency of 10 to 10.5 GHz.

Having established the base line, the surveyor then "cuts in" the other points of the triangulation net, visiting each point in turn and measuring all the angles to other points. If visibility is impaired, the surveyor now has the option of trilateration, employing one of the distance-measuring devices to establish the distances between survey stations. Several such stations along a coast, marked with signals visible from both the air and the sea, become basic control points for both aerial photography and a hydrographic survey. The difficulty in erecting survey beacons on headlands along a coast was greatly reduced after 1950 by the introduction of helicopters for transporting survey parties and materials.

Once the control signals have been erected ashore and their positions fixed, the work of sounding can commence. Where visibility is adequate, the position of a sounding boat is usually determined with a sextant, whose readings are converted to geographical position by use of a three-arm protractor.

Where the shore is no longer visible, other methods of measurement are used. In 1921 the British Admiralty developed a method of trilateration at sea through use of taut-wire traverses. In this method, buoys are anchored on the continental shelf; their distances from inshore points located by visual methods are determined by measuring the amount of fine piano wire paid out as the ship steams from buoy to buoy. Another method, developed by the U.S. Coast and Geodetic Survey in 1924, is radio acoustic-ranging. This method employs buoys equipped with underwater hydrophones and radio transmitters, planted at known locations. As the sounding ship steams along, small explosive charges are detonated at intervals in her wake. The explosive sound travels underwater to the sono-buoys and is then transmitted by radio signal back to the ship. Provided the speed of sound through the water can be established accurately, the elapsed time between explosion and receipt of return signal can be used to calculate the distance from the buoy.

Taut-wire traverses

Both taut-wire traverses and radio acoustic-ranging were supplanted after 1945 by a number of systems that involve only electromagnetic transmissions; some of these have high precision but short range; others possess much greater range but are suitable only for small-scale surveys. One of these systems is electronic position indicator (EPI), developed by the U.S. Coast and Geodetic Survey, which has a range of 10 to 500 nautical miles (18.5–926 kilometres) using a frequency of 1,850 or 1,950 kilohertz (1 kilohertz = 1000 hertz = 1000 cycles per second). It measures the distance to each of two fixed ground stations with a radial accuracy of about 100 metres (330 feet), or a ship length.

A somewhat similar system, called shoran, operates in the range of 230 to 310 megahertz (1 megahertz = 1,000,000 cycles per second) and has line-of-sight range, depending on the height of ground station and ship antennas. This range can be calculated from the equation $D = K(\sqrt{H} + \sqrt{h})$, in which D is the range in miles or kilometres, H and h the elevation of ground station and shipboard antennas in feet or metres, and K is a constant expressing the curvature of the earth in miles per foot or kilometres per metre. Shoran has a distance accuracy of about 20 metres (65 feet); a more accurate version called hiran has been developed.

A third widely used system is Raydist, which employs frequencies of 1.6 to 3.2 megahertz and has ranges over 200 miles (323 kilometres). In the late 1960s a system called Autotape was developed, operating at 2.9 to 3.1 gigahertz with ranges of 100 kilometres (62 miles). Coupled to a digital depth sounder and clock, it produces a magnetic or punched tape output of two ranges—sounding depth and time. By 1970 systems were under development to reduce the labour of compilation of survey results by feeding the output of both the position-finding system and the sounding system into a computer whose output would be a drafted chart ready for reproduction.

Sounding. Virtually every method of sounding employed by the navigator is also used by the hydrographic surveyor. For large-scale operation in shallow water, sounding poles are still used. In water deeper than 12 feet (3.7 metres), echo sounders are universally employed; yet they must be supplemented by the leadline or sounding line to verify the least depth on shoals and sunken rocks, to confirm echo sounding in kelp or grass, and to obtain bottom samples.

The adoption of echo sounding has greatly diminished the labour of conducting a hydrographic survey. In inshore waters, most sounding lines are run by hydrographic launches. Typically, these are power craft 26 to 30 feet (8–9 metres) in length, equipped with portable echo sounders and either electronic or visual navigation devices. Following a prescribed plan, the surveyors aboard the sounding launch maintain a logbook of depth indications and record also the data by which the sounding launch's position is controlled. At the end of each day's operation, the soundings, corrected for tide, are plotted on boat sheets (special paper designed to receive hydrographic survey information).

Boat sheets

Depth contours are drawn on the boat sheets, which are used as guides for determining the spacing of sounding lines and for the special examination of undersea features as work develops. Boat sheets, in turn, are used as the basis for compiling smooth sheets or fair charts, which are manuscript charts prepared to high cartographic standards. In this form, the season's surveying results are submitted to the hydrographic office for eventual publication.

Wire dragging. In regions of volcanic, coral, or glaciated topography, the possibility is high that the conventional survey may fail to detect pinnacles or coral heads. In such waters, it is necessary to verify that depths safe for navigation exist by carrying out a wire-drag survey. Two vessels carry out the operation, sinking a horizontal wire between them to the desired depth from floating buoys and towing it through the water. Accurate position control is as necessary in wire dragging as in conventional hydrography.

Echo sounding from larger vessels. The ordinary echo sounder projects a fairly wide beam (15° on each side). Since the ship may be rolling, this beam width is necessary to ensure that the return echo will be received by the ship. Over a rough bottom, echoes may be received from different points; there may be no clear indication of the actual physical features at sea bottom. A less ambiguous record can be obtained by making use of narrow-beam echo sounding, in which the beam width is reduced to 3° and the transducer (sound source and echo detector) is stabilized vertically by mechanical or electrical means. A further application of this principle, multibeam-array survey sonar, was developed in the 1960s for the U.S. Navy. It projects a fan of sound with an angle of 90° across the ship's track and processes the incoming signals to yield 30 to 60 discrete depths across this distance. The system has as output a contoured strip chart of a seabed covering a width of bottom about twice the depth of water. Thus, the effective number of soundings obtained by a single pass of the ship is increased at least 30-fold.

Survey scales and sounding-line spacing. Surveys are always carried out at a scale larger than that of the largest scale chart to be produced from them, preferably at a scale twice as large. Since the maximum number of soundings that can be recorded legibly is about 100 to the square inch (645 square millimetres) there is no practical reason to space lines more closely than 10 to the inch (25 millimetres).

In harbours, bays, rivers, and channels, sounding lines are spaced at a maximum distance of 100 metres (330 feet) in depths less than 11 fathoms (one fathom is six feet, or 1.8 metres), 200 metres (656 feet) in depths from 11 to 30 fathoms, and 400 metres (1,310 feet) in greater depths. Over smooth bottom, along an open coast, sounding lines are spaced 200 metres in depths less than 11 fathoms, 400 metres in depths from 11 to 20 fathoms, and 800 metres (2,620 feet) in greater depths. Where bottom contours are irregular, line spacing is decreased to 200 metres in less than 20 fathoms (100 metres around rocky points and in channel entrances), 400 metres in 20 to 30 fathoms, and 800 metres in 30 to 50 fathoms.

In water deeper than 50 fathoms, lines are spaced 1,600 metres (one statute mile) in 50 to 100 fathoms, 3,200 metres (two miles) in 100 to 500 fathoms, and 8,000 metres (five miles) in greater depths.

Tidal and magnetic observations. Both for safety and efficiency in boat handling during the course of a survey and for ensuring the quality of the finished chart, it is necessary to know the characteristics of the tide along the coast that is being surveyed. An important part of the preparation for a hydrographic survey is, therefore, the establishment of a tide gage (an instrument that records tide height and time) at an appropriate location in the area to be surveyed and the processing of records from it. At least two weeks of daily recordings are required to establish the datum plane below which all the soundings are to be referred. Longer series of records are required for accurate tide prediction data.

Observations of local magnetic declination are also required as part of the information that will appear on the published chart, and any local anomalies that are detected need to be investigated to determine their extent.

Other data. The products of hydrographic surveying are both charts and sailing directions. The latter (called Coast Pilots by the U.S. Coast and Geodetic Survey, and until 1968 called Admiralty Pilots by the British Admiralty) are printed books of information giving detailed facts that cannot readily be reduced to chart form such as descriptions of routes, weather conditions, harbour installations, and repair facilities. An important part of nautical charting, therefore, is the collection of data for the preparation and revision of sailing directions.

Coast Pilots

Names are another important consideration in nautical charting. Names for capes, reefs, shoals, and bays are the primary means of cross-referencing between charts and sailing directions. Survey specifications therefore require the field parties to observe and record names for all such features. Disputed names are referred to an appropriate authority for resolution (in the U.S. to the Board of Geographic Names, under the Secretary of the Interior). There is no international authority for geographic names; each government publishes its own gazetteer.

CHART CONSTRUCTION

When the field notes and smooth sheets have been transferred from the survey party in the field to the hydrographic office, the work of chart construction commences. The first considerations are scale and projection.

Chart scale. The scale of a chart is the relationship between a given distance on the chart and the actual distance that it represents on the earth's surface, usually expressed as a ratio. Thus 1:100,000 means that one inch (or centimetre) on the chart corresponds to 100,000 inches (or centimetres) on the earth. In metric units such comparisons are simple; in English units they can be assisted by noting that one nautical mile (6,076 feet or exactly 1,852 metres), which is one minute of latitude, is 72,912 inches. Also, one degree of latitude is 111.1 kilometres or 60 nautical miles.

By courtesy of the U.S. Department of Commerce, Environmental Science Services Administration

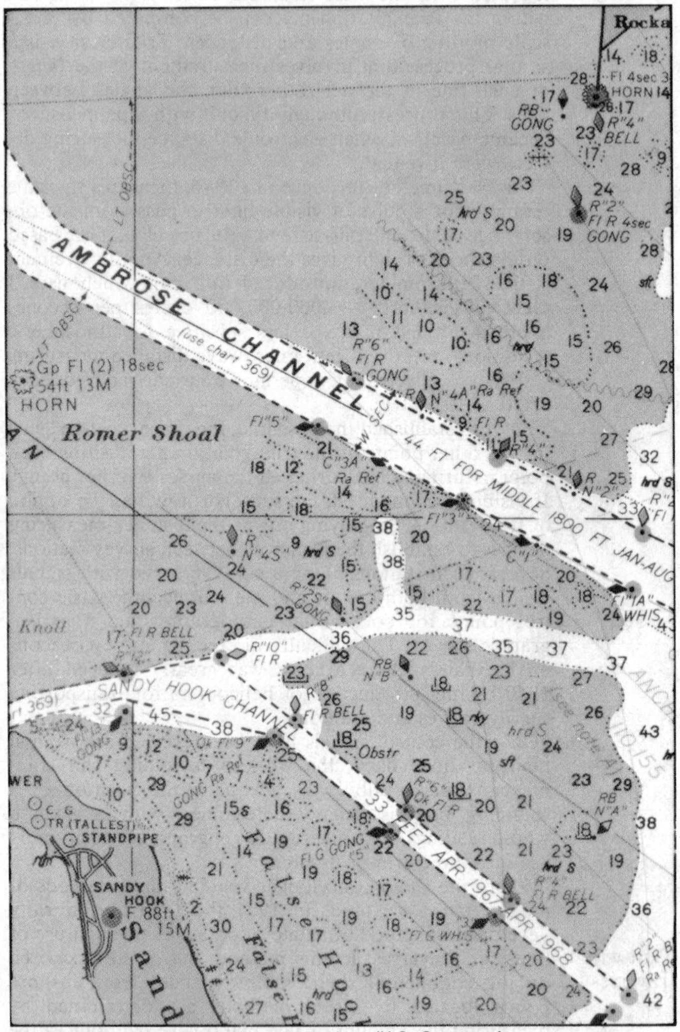

Small section of a large hydrographic chart (U.S. Coast and Geodetic Survey No. 1215) of the approaches to New York harbour. The scale is 1:80,000.

Charts are constructed on widely different scales and can be generally classified as follows: ocean sailing charts are small-scale charts, 1:5,000,000 or smaller, used for planning long voyages or marking the daily progress of a ship. Sailing charts, used for offshore navigation, show a generalized shoreline, only offshore soundings, and are at a scale between 1:600,000 and 1:5,000,000. As an illustration of chart use, a ten-knot ship covers about 29 inches at 1:600,000 scale in a day.

General charts are used for coastwise navigation outside outlying reefs and shoals and are at a scale between 1:100,000 and 1:600,000.

Coast charts are intended for use in leaving and entering port or navigating inside outlying reefs or shoals and are at a scale between 1:50,000 and 1:100,000.

Harbour charts are for use in harbours and small waterways, with a scale usually larger than 1:50.000.

Chart size. Charts are commonly rather large sheets of paper, 28 x 40 inches (70 centimetres x 1 metre) being an internationally accepted maximum size. In order that a navigator may work with them efficiently, charts must be kept with a minimum of folding in drawers in a large chart table in a compartment of the ship having ready access to the navigating bridge, known as the chart room, or chart house. Such structures are not possible in small craft, which therefore require charts of a more convenient size. With the recognition that there are many more small boats in the world, particularly recreational craft, than there are ships, and that they are navigated primarily by piloting rather than by celestial or electronic means, many hydrographic offices have given attention to the production of special chart series in a small format for yacht navigators. A typical series is that produced by the U.S. Coast and Geodetic Survey with the designation SC (for small craft). Such charts are only 15 inches (38.1 centimetres) in the vertical dimension and thus need to be folded only in the vertical direction. Printed on both sides of the sheet, they are oriented along the most probable route rather than by parallels and meridians. Several are stapled together into a stiff cardboard folder for protection. Along with the ordinary chart information, they contain a year of tide tables and information on small-craft facilities in the area. New editions are produced annually.

SC charts

Chart projections. Virtually all navigational charts are constructed on the ordinary Mercator projection, in which a compass course always appears as a straight line and the meridians and parallels form a rectangular grid. Survey smooth sheets, on the other hand, are commonly plotted on gnomonic or polyconic projections, so that compass bearings (which are great circles) appear as straight lines. The only navigational charts not on ordinary Mercator projections are great-circle charts and charts of the polar regions. Great-circle charts, which are maps of large areas, such as the entire Pacific Ocean, are ordinarily on very small scales with gnomonic projection. The navigator uses them to lay out a track between ports perhaps thousands of miles apart and then transfers the latitudes corresponding, for example, to each 5° of longitude, to his ocean sailing chart. He thus arrives at a series of short rhumb-line courses, each of which makes the same angle with all meridians, that closely approximate the shortest distance between the two ports.

Charts of the polar regions cannot be drawn on the ordinary Mercator projection. Such charts are commonly constructed on stereographic projections, modified Lambert conformal projections, or on a transverse Mercator projection where the projecting cylinder is tangent to a meridian.

Chart compilation. The aim of the chart maker is to render survey results in the form of a permanent though alterable and reproducible form. In the 19th century, this was accomplished by hand engraving on copper plates. These, however, had to be executed as negatives (in reverse) and lacked durability when used for long press runs. The disadvantages of copper plates were overcome by the introduction of offset printing. In this technique, a positive original has its ink impression transferred as a negative to a soft rubber roller, from which it is transferred as a positive to a sheet of paper. Photolithographic procedures supplanted the engraver's stylus with the draftsman's pen and facilitated preparation of multiple matching plates, one for each colour. Photolithography in several colours greatly increased the information content of a single chart and at the same time simplified production of revised editions, since features most likely to change, such as buoys and lights, could be confined to a single colour plate. To make the colour plates, a number of dimensionally exact copies of the original base plate are prepared in blue. The features desired on each colour plate are then traced by the draftsman with black ink. The photographic emulsions used in photolithography are not sensitive to blue, and only the added information will appear on the plate after it is rephotographed.

The 1960s witnessed a return to the stylus, employing an opaque plastic sheet for such features as depth contours and scribing the curves on it for direct use as a negative in sensitizing the printing plate. There was also increasing use of computer-programmed digital plotters for constructing the basic projection and navigational grid and in drawing the families of hyperbolic curves required for use with loran and similar navigation systems. Charts are drafted at the same scale at which they are to be reproduced; a high order of accuracy is required in their compilation. For this reason the use of hand lettering has been abandoned in favour of words and figures printed by type or by a photographic process onto transparent material that is "floated" onto the compilation and anchored by an adhesive wax backing in the proper place. Compass roses and graphic scales are added in the same manner.

In transferring soundings from the smooth sheets to the finished charts, only a representative selection of the actual observed soundings is shown; depth contours and colour tones indicate the shape and extent of shoal areas. The modern tendency is to include more depth contours and to suppress the actual sounding numbers, since the possession of echo sounders enables the mariner to use his own sounding record as a means of assisting him in locating his position.

Transfer to finished charts

Indications of bottom composition, whether sand, shell, stone, or otherwise, and of its colour are placed on the charts for the use of the mariner equipped with a hand lead. Conventional symbols for rocks, shoals, buoys, wrecks, and the like are standardized by the International Hydrographic Bureau and are added to the compilation in the appropriate locations.

Chart colours. Practical uses of charts impose some constraints on the selection of colour. Red, for example, would logically be chosen as the color in which to print warnings of navigational hazards. But navigators, who must work at night, prefer to retain the darkness adaptation of their eyes by viewing their charts under red light. Under such illumination, red, orange, and buff are invisible. Hence these colours have been superseded on modern charts by magenta, purple, and gray.

Chart paper. Charts are working instruments, and, since ships often voyage far from where replacement charts are readily obtainable, hydrographic offices give attention to the quality of the paper on which charts are printed. A ship's reckoning is kept in pencil and erased after each voyage. Thus, printing stock that permits multiple erasures is chosen. In view of the environment where charts are used, another quality commonly sought is high wet strength.

Depth units and data. The traditional depth unit used for centuries in navigation was the fathom, derived from the amount of line a man could encompass between his two outstretched hands. In English units, the fathom is 6 feet (1.8 metres). The equivalent in other countries (French *brasse*, Norwegian *favn*, etc.) was generally close to the English value. To complicate matters, depths on large-scale charts in English-speaking countries are usually shown in feet. In the 20th century, however, except in English-speaking countries, the metre has become the universal nautical depth unit. The British Admiralty issued its first metric chart in 1969.

The fathom

In the choice of a datum plane below which sounding depths are expressed, hydrography becomes an art rather than a science. Clearly, charts should show the worst condition that is likely to occur, leaving the navigator with a margin of safety at other times. In the U.S., chart datum for soundings is taken as mean low water on the Atlantic coast and mean lower low water on the Pacific coast. Canada uses lowest normal low water. In Great Britain, where tide ranges tend to be greater, a datum below mean low water springs, referred to as lowest astronomical tide, is used. Elevations, on the other hand, are measured from a mean high water datum. Besides these vertical datums the title of a chart generally contains a reference to the geodetic survey on which its latitude and longitude values are based. This is referred to as the horizontal datum.

Practices vary in the conversion of sonic depths as shown on the charts. Echo sounders actually measure time, not depth. Their readings are converted to depth by applying an assumed value for the average speed of sound in seawater. In the United States, this value is usually 4,800 feet (1,463 metres) per second; other countries use 1,500 metres per second (4,921 feet). Some hydrographic offices make a practice of measuring the actual average speed of sound and applying a correction to give a true geometrical distance. This procedure had been recommended by the International Hydrographic Bureau. In 1969, however, a commission of the IHB recommended the plotting of uncorrected soundings, based on 1,500 metres per second, as being of more utility to the navigator.

CHART CORRECTION AND DISTRIBUTION

The work of a hydrographic office does not end with printing a chart. The chart must be placed in the hands of the user, who in turn must be provided with up-to-date information as to its correctness. Hydrographic offices therefore maintain branch offices or sales agents in the principal seaports where mariners can purchase charts. Corrections are listed in weekly *Notices to Mariners*, which were first promulgated by the British Admiralty in 1857 and are now issued in every maritime country. Hydrographic offices themselves put the corrections on their undistributed inventory of charts. This work is carried out by hand using electric erasers, rubber stamps, silk-screen printing, and even attaching "pasters" with reprinted versions of small areas. Such charts are stamped "Corrected by *Notices to Mariners* up to . . .", and it is the purchaser's responsibility to refer to the *Notices* issued after the date indicated and to keep his charts current. Since in effecting a policy of marine insurance, a shipowner represents to the underwriters that his ship is seaworthy; and since courts hold that a ship not provided with up-to-date navigational information is not seaworthy, large capital amounts may be at stake if charts are not correct.

CHARTING THE WORLD'S WATERS

Only four countries, France, U.K., U.S., and U.S.S.R., attempt to provide their mariners with world chart coverage. To accomplish this, each maintains on issue between 4,000 and 5,000 separate charts. In many cases each of these countries has compiled its chart from an original survey carried out by a fifth country, which has then been redrawn and reproduced according to national standards. It is estimated that in the first seven decades of the 20th century the major hydrographic offices spent several hundred man-centuries in nonfacsimile copying of each other's charts. Yet the rapid increase in draft of ships that occurred after the closing of the Suez Canal in 1967 made it necessary to repeat much of the existing charting. Older surveys designed to ensure that no obstructions to navigation existed in depths less than 50 feet (15 metres) were useless for loaded supertankers drawing 65 and 70 feet (19.8–21 metres).

To reduce the work involved in producing these new charts, the International Hydrographic Bureau in 1967 took action to design a truly international series of charts, initially at 1:1,000,000 or smaller, which could be reproduced in facsimile by all IHB members through the interchange of reproduction materials.

BIBLIOGRAPHY

Historical: M. BLEWITT, *Surveys of the Seas: A Brief History of British Hydrography* (1957), a useful, concise text with plates showing the chronological development of smooth sheets; SIR ARCHIBALD DAY, *The Admiralty Hydrographic Service 1795–1919* (1967); G.S. RITCHIE, *The Admiralty Chart: British Naval Hydrography in the 19th Century* (1967), *Challenger: The Life of a Survey Ship* (1957); A.H.W. ROBINSON, *Marine Cartography in Britain: A History of the Sea Chart to 1855* (1962).

Technical: K.T. ADAMS, *Hydrographic Manual* (1942), a standard authority for U.S. Coast and Geodetic Survey procedures; K.B. JEFFERS, *Hydrographic Manual* (1960), primarily a revision of Adams; *Admiralty Manual of Hydrographic Surveying* (1938); A.L. ALLAN, J.R. HOLLWEY, and J.H.B. MAYNES, *Practical Field Surveying and Computations* (1968), an up-to-date book covering the shore side of hydrographic surveying; INTERNATIONAL HYDROGRAPHIC BUREAU, *Radio Aids to Maritime Navigation and Hydrography*, 2nd ed. (1956).

Practical: American Practical Navigator, rev. ed. (1958); B.W. LUCKE, *A Course on the Chart* (1966); M. CHRISS and G.R. HAYES, *An Introduction to Charts and Their Use*, 3rd ed. (1964); D.A. MOORE, *Marine Chartwork and Navaids* (1967); *Hydrographic Dictionary*, 3rd ed. (1970); *International Hydrographic Review* (semi-annual).

(J.Ly.)

Hydrologic Cycle

The hydrologic cycle is the central focus of the science of hydrology, which is concerned with the waters of the earth, their occurrence, circulation, distribution, and chemical and physical properties. The hydrologic cycle is not a simple link but rather a group of paths through which the water in nature circulates and is transformed from one state to another. These paths penetrate through the entire hydrosphere that surrounds the earth; they extend upward to about 15 kilometres (nine miles) in the atmosphere and downward to an average depth of one kilometre (0.62 mile) in the earth's crust.

The cycle has no beginning or end, and many processes are involved. As water evaporates from the oceans and the land, it becomes a part of the atmosphere (the evaporation process). The evaporated moisture is lifted and carried in the atmosphere until it finally precipitates to the earth, either on land or in the oceans (the precipitation process). The precipitated water may be intercepted or transpired (emitted as vapour from the surface of plant parts) by plants (the interception and transpiration processes), may flow over the ground surface (the overland-flow process) or down the ground slope within the soil layers (the throughflow process) and into streams (the runoff process), or may infiltrate into the ground (the infiltration process). The water remaining on the ground fills in depressions, where it is stored for later evaporation (the retention process) or later runoff (the detention process). Much of the intercepted and transpired water and the surface runoff returns to the atmosphere through evaporation. The infiltrated water may percolate to deeper zones (the percolation process) to be stored as groundwater. It may later flow out as springs or may seep into streams, finally flowing to the sea and evaporating into the atmosphere to complete the hydrologic cycle. Thus, the hydrologic cycle consists of various complicated processes of precipitation, evaporation, interception, transpiration, infiltration, percolation, retention, detention, overland flow, throughflow, and runoff. Figure 1 shows a schematic illustration of the hydrologic cycle in which the several processes are indicated.

The hydrologic cycle is composed of numerous cycles of continental, regional, and local magnitude—all of which are interrelated components of the global system. Although the total amount of water in the global hydrologic cycle remains essentially constant, the distribution of this water is continually changing on continents, in regions, and within local drainage basins. The hydrologic behaviour of water in an area is fundamentally determined by the climate of the region, which varies in time and space. The distribution of the water in an area is further affected by the natural physiographic factors, including topographical features, geological formations, and types of vegetation. These physiographic factors, in turn, may modify the climatic factors, such as the magnitude, distribution, and frequency of rainfall; the occurrence of snow and ice; and the effects of wind, temperature, humidity, and solar radiation on evapotranspiration (the loss of water from the soil by both evaporation and transpiration). As civilization develops, additional effects on water regimen—caused by man's works and activities—gradually encroach upon the natural water environment, disturbing the dynamic equilibrium of the natural hydrologic cycle and initiating new hydrologic processes and events.

From ancient times to about AD 1400, the concept of the hydrologic cycle was speculated upon by many, in-

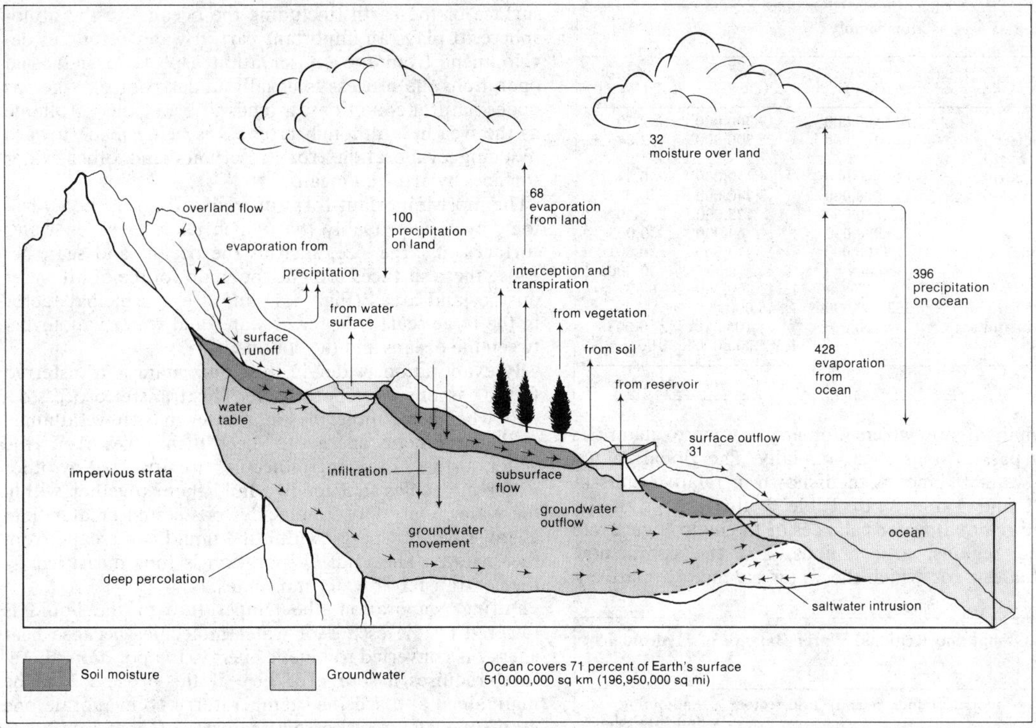

Figure 1: Hydrologic cycle with global annual average water balance shown in relative numerical units.

History of investigations and concepts

cluding the poet Homer (about 1000 BC), and the philosophers Thales, Plato, and Aristotle in Greece; Lucretius, Seneca, and Pliny in Rome; and many biblical scholars during that time. Whereas most of these philosophical concepts were erroneous from a scientific point of view, the Greek philosopher Anaxagoras of Clazomenae (500–428 BC) formed a primitive concept of the gross hydrological cycle. He believed that the sun lifts water from the sea into the atmosphere, from which it falls as rain, and rainwater is then collected in underground reservoirs that feed the river flows. Further improvement of this concept was made by the Greek philosopher Theophrastus (*c.* 372–*c.* 287 BC), who correctly described at least part of the hydrologic cycle that operates in the atmosphere; he gave a sound explanation of the formation of precipitation by condensation and freezing. After studying the works of Theophrastus carefully, the Roman architect and engineer Marcus Vitruvius, who lived about the time of Christ, conceived a theory that is now generally accepted. He extended Theophrastus' explanation and stated that groundwater is largely derived from rain and snow, through infiltration from the ground surface. Thus, Vitruvius' theory may be considered a forerunner of modern concepts of the hydrologic cycle.

During the Renaissance, a gradual change from the pure philosophical concepts of hydrology toward observational science occurred. Based on observations, for example, the Florentine artist and scientist Leonardo da Vinci and the French Huguenot potter and scientist Bernard Palissy, as well as the French naturalist Pierre Perrault, achieved a correct understanding of the concept of the hydrologic cycle, especially the infiltration of rain and the return of the water through springs.

Next to air, water is the most vital substance for human existence. To cope with his daily problems and to satisfy his curiosity, man has always sought a clearer knowledge of his water environment. Since the scientific concept of the hydrologic cycle was first conceived by such men as Vitruvius, Leonardo da Vinci, and Palissy, scientists have been ceaselessly trying to understand the hydrologic cycle, but their progress has been slow because of the complexity and intricacy of the phenomena and the lack of sufficient and adequately observed hydrologic data. Now, in the atomic and space age, new scientific concepts and knowledge are emerging, and new methods and tools for scientific investigation, such as electronic computers and nuclear techniques, are becoming available. The most important recent advance in hydrologic knowledge is a better understanding of the hydrologic cycle on a more sophisticated level. The new concept of the hydrologic cycle is to treat it as a dynamic sequential system, which consists of an input, an output, and some working medium, which is water (known as throughput) passing through the system. The study of either a hydrologic cycle or a part of it can be considered either as a system or a subsystem problem. For example, a drainage basin or watershed can be considered as a system. For this system, the input is the rainfall and groundwater inflow; the output is the evapotranspiration, infiltration, and runoff; and the throughput is the water moving through the watershed. By the systems concept, the hydrologic cycle can be readily interpreted physically by modern system-analysis techniques, and then it can be simulated by mathematical models and electronic computers. Consequences of significance to man, such as the flooding effects of record precipitation, can be predicted by such analyses.

The world water supply. The total amount of water and its partition, movement, and balance, or equilibrium, in the global hydrologic cycle have been the topics of speculation and investigation since the second half of the 19th century; but quantitative data are scarce and the complete global hydrologic cycle is not well known. Only approximate values or estimates can be assigned most components of the world hydrologic system.

Table 1 shows the estimated world water supply. Of all the water in the world, about 97 percent, or about 1,350,000,000 cubic kilometres (325,000,000 cubic miles), is contained in the oceans. If the world were a uniform sphere, this quantity would be sufficient to cover it to a depth of about 2,650 metres (8,000 feet). The total amount of fresh water is estimated at about 37,300,000 cubic kilometres (9,000,000 cubic miles). It is distributed roughly as follows: 76 percent in polar ice and glaciers; 13 percent in groundwater between depths of 800 and 4,000 metres (2,600 and 13,000 feet); 10 percent in groundwater at depths less than 800 metres; 0.33 percent in lakes; 0.18 percent as soil moisture; 0.036 percent in atmosphere; and a negligible 0.004 percent in rivers.

The estimated values of world water supply are, however, stationary estimates of distribution. Although the water contents of the atmosphere and rivers are rela-

Table 1: Estimated World Water Supply

item	area (km²)	volume (km³)	percent of total water
Fresh water	147,900,000	37,300,000	2.70
Polar ice and glaciers	15,100,000	28,200,000	2.04
Groundwater			
800 to 4,000 m deep	130,900,000	4,710,000	0.34
Less than 800 m deep	130,900,000	3,740,000	0.27
Lakes	830,000	125,000	0.009
Soil moisture	130,900,000	69,000	0.005
Atmospheric vapour	510,100,000*	13,500	0.001
Rivers	—	1,500	0.0001
Salty water		1,348,000,000	97.3
Oceans	362,200,000	1,348,000,000	97.3
Saline lakes and inland seas	700,000	105,000	0.008
Total supply		1,385,000,000	100

*Area of earth's surface.

tively small at any given moment, immense quantities of water pass through them annually. The global annual average water balance is then shown in relative units in Figure 1 and Table 2. In Table 2 also are given the estimated regional water balances of the hydrologic cycle in humid regions, arid regions, and the continental United States—for which the water balance is relatively

Table 2: Estimated Global and Regional Water Balance of Hydrologic Cycle*

item	global	humid region	arid region	adjoining continental U.S.
Precipitation				
On land	100	100	100	100
On ocean	396	—	—	—
Total	496	100	100	100
Evaporation				
From land	68	59	100	73
From ocean	428	—	—	—
Total	496	59	100	73
Runoff to sea				
From land surface	31	40	—	26
From groundwater	1	1	—	1
Total	32	41	—	27

*Numbers are in relative units. For annual average 100 units = 25,500 mi³ (106,000 km³) of water for the global balance and 1,410 mi³ (5,870 km³) for the adjoining continental U.S.

well documented. It can be seen that the global average annual precipitation is about 39 times as much as the moisture contained in the entire atmosphere at any one time, while the average annual precipitation on land surface is about 27 times as great as the moisture in the air over the land. Thus, the cycling time of the atmospheric moisture is about nine days in the global hydrological cycle and 13.5 days over the land. Furthermore, it can be calculated that the mean annual precipitation for the entire earth is about 104 centimetres (41 inches) per year, which under stationary conditions is balanced by an equally large evaporation amount. Thus, the average evaporation for the whole earth amounts to 2.84 millimetres (0.1 inch) of water per day.

This article covers the several components of the hydrologic cycle—evaporation, water vapour in the atmosphere, precipitation, surface runoff, groundwater, and ice—and presents a summary of the operative processes and influencing factors in each case. Hence, it is intended as a hydrologic overview; for further details on the several parts of the world hydrologic system see the separate articles: ATMOSPHERE; OCEANS AND SEAS; HUMIDITY, ATMOSPHERIC; PRECIPITATION; RIVERS AND RIVER SYSTEMS; LAKES AND LAKE SYSTEMS; GROUNDWATER; and ICE SHEETS AND GLACIERS. See also WATER RESOURCES for additional information on the world water supply; and the article HYDROLOGIC SCIENCE for an account of hydrology and its relationship to allied subjects.

Role of evaporation in the hydrologic cycle

EVAPORATION FROM WATER SURFACES

Nature of the process. Evaporation in the hydrologic cycle is the process of transferring moisture from the surface of the earth (including the oceans) to the atmosphere. It plays an important part in water-resources development from the conservation aspect. In industrial operations the process is usually under control, whereas under natural conditions, it tends to be as uncontrollable as the weather, although progress is being made toward reducing evaporation from reservoirs and other water surfaces by artificial means.

The most important form of evaporation in the hydrologic cycle is probably that which takes place on water surfaces of large size, such as the oceans and seas, because these surfaces provide the main source of all water on the land areas (Figure 1) and are a principal factor in the large-scale transfer of water and water vapour between the oceans and the continents.

By evaporation, water in the liquid state is transferred to the gaseous, or vapour, state. This transfer process occurs when some molecules in a water mass have attained sufficient kinetic energy to eject themselves from the water surface. Escaping molecules are attracted by other water molecules that tend to hold them together within the water. Only those molecules possessing greater than average kinetic energy within the liquid can escape from the surface. The total evaporation is thus measured by the net transfer of water molecules.

Conversion of heat to kinetic energy

During evaporation, the temperature of the liquid is lowered by the escape of water molecules because heat energy is converted to kinetic energy. Evaporation, therefore, requires a source of heat if the process is to be maintained at a specified temperature. To evaporate one gram of water requires 540 calories of heat at 100° C (212° F); 600 calories are required at 0° C (32° F). An external heat supply must, therefore, be available, which may be solar radiation, heat from the atmosphere or from the ground. The heat supply also may be drawn from the kinetic energy of the water molecules, cooling the water until equilibrium with the atmosphere is established and evaporation stops. In general, solar radiation is the major energy supply for evaporation.

The motion of the molecules forming the water vapour through the water surface produces a pressure, known as vapour pressure. Actually, it is only the partial pressure of the water vapour in the atmosphere, because in a mixture of gases each gas exerts a partial pressure that is independent of the presence of other gases in the mixture. Escaping molecules collide with those in the air, and some of the former will drop back into the water. Net transfer of water molecules into the air occurs only when there is a vapour-pressure difference between the evaporating surface and the air. Evaporation essentially becomes zero when the relative humidity of the air is 100 percent, because the vapour in the air is completely saturated. When this occurs, the number of molecules that escape equals the number of those that fall back into the water, and the vapour pressure difference is zero. Meanwhile, some of the molecules in the air having sufficient kinetic energy will penetrate the water surface and others will condense from vapour to liquid because of a lowering of temperature. Thus, evaporation from a water surface and condensation into a water surface are continuous processes. Evaporation is faster than condensation if the air is not saturated.

The rate of evaporation depends upon the difference between the vapour pressure of the water and that of the air above the water surface. Under a given set of conditions, evaporation is proportional to the difference between the pressure of saturated vapour at the temperature of the water and the actual vapour pressure of the air. This fact is known as Dalton's law because the English scientist John Dalton first recognized it, in 1802.

Factors that influence evaporation. In nature, however, Dalton's law is greatly influenced by the environmental condition, and evaporation is affected by many meteorological and physiographic factors. Major meteorological factors include temperature, humidity, wind, barometric pressure, and precipitation; and major physiographic factors include water quality, depth of water body, and composition and extent of water surface. Although the combined effect of all the influencing factors can be determined, it is difficult to assess the relative importance of the complicated relationships among them.

Because the change of water to vapour requires heat energy, it is evident that radiation is of considerable importance in the process of evaporation. There is no doubt that solar radiation is a major source of heat energy for natural evaporation. It has been suggested that the term solar radiation is basically applicable to the water losses from a free water surface. In fact, there is a very close relationship between the monthly totals of solar radiation and evaporation. Because solar radiation is an important factor, evaporation varies with time of day, the season, latitude, and sky condition.

Dalton's law and evaporation rates

Dalton's law indicates that the rate of evaporation depends on the difference between the saturated vapour pressure and the vapour pressure of the air. These pressures are influenced by air and water temperatures. Because the temperatures are largely dependent on solar radiation, it would be expected that they should be closely correlated to the rate of evaporation. Observed data generally fail to show such a close correlation between, for example, the mean monthly totals of evaporation and air temperature. It is obvious that evaporation does not depend as closely on temperature as it does on solar radiation. The temperature of the water surface is important because it governs the rate at which water molecules leave the surface and enter the overlying air. It may have a profound short-term effect upon evaporation, but it is the net movement of water molecules and the distribution of the escaping molecules near the water surface that mainly condition the evaporation process. Consequently, wind speed and other environmental factors also play a significant role, jointly with the temperature.

As humidity of the air is mainly governed by the air temperature, it has indirect effects upon evaporation. Because the actual humidity and the saturated humidity at given temperatures determine the actual and saturated vapour pressures, it follows from Dalton's law that they affect the rate of evaporation. Accordingly, the relative humidity, which is the ratio between the actual and saturated humidities, controls the evaporation. Because relative humidity increases as the air temperature decreases, a fall in temperature will result in a decrease in evaporation. Thus, in cold weather, evaporation is usually low.

Effect of wind and pressure

Wind or air movement will remove escaping water molecules from the water surface and affects evaporation. The effect of wind or air movement is modified by wind speed and surface roughness, which also share a significant role in the evaporation process. Wind speed affects evaporation only to a certain limit, however, beyond which water molecules are clearly removed as soon as they emerge from the surface, and evaporation will continue under that condition and not be affected further. If the incoming air is preheated, for example by flowing over heated ground, it will supply additional energy for evaporation. Conversely, a cool-air mass may reduce evaporation and cause condensation. This phenomenon is called advection.

In theory the barometric pressure, as well as latitude and air-mass movement, affects evaporation because water molecules can escape more easily from the free water surface as the density of the overlying air decreases. In nature, however, the individual effect of barometric change is masked by other interrelated meteorological factors. For example, the barometric effect may be somewhat compensated for by the change in vapour pressure with change in latitude. The quantity, intensity, and distribution of precipitation will affect evaporation as a result of their disturbance of the escaping water molecules and the composition of the water surface.

The presence of dissolved material in water will reduce the vapour pressure. Water quality, therefore, affects the process of evaporation. For example, evaporation decreases by about 1 percent for every 1 percent increase in salinity, so that evaporation from seawater with an average salinity of about 3.5 percent is some 2 to 3 percent less than evaporation from freshwater. The turbidity (sediment content) of the water affects the reflectivity and, consequently, the balance of heat and the temperature of the water; turbidity may have an indirect effect on the evaporative process.

The water depth may have a considerable effect upon evaporation. In shallow waters, the water temperature alone may lag behind the air temperature in short periods, but the lag may not be too great for long periods such as months. In deep waters, the lag may be great and heat may be stored to considerable depth. As the surface water is cooled or heated, a vertical thermal current will be set up, which will affect the surface temperature and consequently the evaporation.

A body of water with a flat surface has greater vapour pressure than one with a concave surface, but less than one with a convex surface under the same condition. It is evident that more water molecules are exposed to the air over the convex surface than over the concave surface. Also, small surfaces generate less evaporation than large surfaces because escaping molecules are more confined than on large surfaces, where wind and other meteorological influences become much more effective.

Measurement of evaporation. The important role played by evaporation in the hydrologic cycle results in efforts continually being made to improve the accuracy of its measurement and estimation. The measurement of evaporation from water surfaces can be made only at point locations. The instruments commonly used are evaporation pans and atmometers. Direct measurement over large water bodies is not possible, although attempts are being made to make such measurements possible someday by remote sensing techniques.

Use of evaporation pans

The evaporation pan is the most widely used instrument for evaporation measurement on lakes and reservoirs. The instrument is not everywhere identical, but, in general, it is constructed in accord with the same concept. The Class A pan of the U.S. Weather Bureau, adopted by the World Meteorological Organization and the International Association of Scientific Hydrology—renamed the International Association of Hydrological Sciences (IAHS) in 1972—for the International Geophysical Year, is a cylindrical tank made of unpainted galvanized iron, 122 centimetres (four feet) in diameter and 25 centimetres (ten inches) deep. The bottom is supported on a wooden frame and is raised from the ground surface to permit circulation of air below the pan. The pan may also float on water in lakes and reservoirs or be sunken into the ground. Water-surface level is measured daily, and evaporation is computed as the difference between observed levels, adjusted for any precipitation recorded in a nearby standard rain gauge. Because the rate of evaporation from small areas is greater than that from large areas, it is recommended that the observed evaporation be multiplied by a pan coefficient of 0.6 to 0.8 for its conversion to an estimated value of evaporation.

Another device in use is the atmometer, a water-filled glass tube with an open end through which water evaporates from a filter paper or porous plate. The tube supplying water is graduated to read evaporation in millimetres. The registered evaporation may bear little or no direct relation to evaporation from any surface, because it only reflects the saturation deficit of the air and can only be calibrated by comparison with readings from a standard instrument in a similar exposure. The instrument is more responsive to wind speed than radiant energy and is often used in confined quarters.

In the absence of direct measurement, estimation of evaporation often is required. For the estimation of evaporation, several approaches are commonly used; namely, empirical equations, the water-balance method, the energy-balance method, and the mass-transfer method.

Because evaporation in the hydrologic cycle depends on many environmental factors, many empirical and semi-empirical equations have been developed to express the evaporation from water surfaces in terms of these factors. Most of them are based on Dalton's law, with modifications for factors affecting evaporation. These equations are useful in making a fast estimation, but few have any value outside their own limited regions.

Methods of estimation

The water-balance method is based on measurement of the continuity of water flow—essentially, the budget comprised by the various items of input, output, and water storage of the hydrologic system. This method holds true for any time interval and applies to any drainage basin and to the earth as a whole. Theoretically it is possible to use this method to determine the evaporation from any water body. Practically, however, it is difficult to do so accurately because of the effects of errors in measuring various items involved in the water balance. Evaporation determined by this method is subject to considerable error if it is small compared with other items.

The energy-balance method is similar to the water-balance method except that it deals with the continuity of energy flow instead of water flow. This method has been applied to estimate annual evaporation from the oceans and lakes. The method also is subject to error because several necessary items are difficult to evaluate. Solution of the energy-balance equation, for example, requires evaluation of such items as atmospheric radiation, long-wave radiation from the water body, the conduction of heat and energy to or from the body of water, and energy storage by the water body. If the requisite observational data are available, then the method is practical for estimating evaporation over periods as short as an hour. From studies conducted on Lake Hefner, Oklahoma, it was concluded that the method is probably adequate when applied to periods of less than a week. For greater periods, the estimated evaporation was found to approach 5 percent of the actual mean evaporation.

The mass-transfer method is based on discontinuous and continuous mixing, or mass transfer, in the boundary layer of air above the water surface. The method involves computation of the evaporation from knowledge of the physical factors controlling the removal of water vapour from the evaporating surface. These factors are mainly the vertical humidity gradient and the turbulence of airflow. The method has been applied principally to ocean surfaces, but only for monthly averages. Elaborate mathematical expressions have been developed for various conditions, but their value is limited mainly to providing independent estimates of evaporation for research purposes. A number of methods also have been developed to combine this method with the energy-budget method, thereby eliminating certain measurement difficulties that each possesses.

On the basis of an estimation, the total amount of water that is evaporated from all oceans in the global hydrologic cycle is about 45,368,000 cubic kilometres (10,411,000 cubic miles) per year.

Evaporation reduction. Because the water stored in lakes and reservoirs may become an important source of supply for various purposes, many methods of evaporation suppression have been developed to conserve available water. The most common practice is to spread a monomolecular film or layer over the water surface so that evaporation is retarded; escape of water molecules through the film is difficult. Although chemical research on this method was initiated in laboratories in the United States around 1920, it was not until 1952 that the idea was first applied in the field to reservoirs in Australia. Several kinds of chemical compounds can form a film one molecule thick on the surface of water. The most effective organic compounds are the long-chain fatty alcohols called octadecanol and hexadecanol. The molecules of these compounds have a hydroxyl, or OH, group at one end that is attractive to water, whereas the hydrocarbon chain at the other end is repelled by water. The molecules therefore are oriented vertically with respect to the water surface to form a watertight film, but one that is penetrable by oxygen and carbon dioxide molecules. Because the monomolecular film can be broken easily by disturbances of the water surface, particularly by strong winds, the method becomes less effective on large water surfaces. Theoretically, one kilogram (2.2 pounds) of hexadecanol forms a compact film on 4,500 square metres (about 5,400 square yards) of water surface. In practice, considerably more chemical is required because of its removal by wind, birds, insects, and aquatic life. The chemical compound also is subject to biologic attrition and needs to be replenished from time to time, in any case. The evaporation reduction achieved by this method varies approximately from 10 to 40 percent or more, depending largely on the field condition.

Use of monomolecular films

EVAPORATION FROM SOILS, SNOW, AND ICE

Nature of the process and influencing factors. Evaporation from soil surfaces is governed by the same meteorological environmental conditions as is evaporation from water surfaces. The difference, however, is in the nature of the surface from which evaporation takes place. Water molecules have to overcome greater resistance to escape from soils than from a water surface because of the greater attraction of soil particles for water. In other words, in the case of a free water surface, the supply of moisture is so plentiful that it exerts no limiting influence on the rate of water loss, whereas evaporation from soils is often less than evaporation from a free water surface for the same given environmental conditions because there is an insufficient supply of water in the soil to be evaporated. When the moisture content of the surface soil becomes relatively low, the loss of moisture by surface evaporation practically ceases.

In addition to the factors that govern evaporation from water surfaces, evaporation from soils is affected by such additional factors as the soil characteristics and conditions, namely soil moisture, soil texture and colour, depth of water table, and presence of vegetation.

Soil moisture and its effect

The actual moisture content of the soil surface exerts the most direct influence on evaporation from soils. Saturated soils provide greater evaporation opportunity than a free water surface of the same covering surface area because the irregular soil particles comprise a larger total evaporation surface. As the surface-moisture content falls from a saturated or near-saturated condition, however, the rate of evaporation will be kept practically constant at a certain range of moisture content until a low moisture content is reached and then will fall rapidly to zero when the soil becomes completely dry. The moisture content of the upper three to five centimetres (1.2 to two inches) of surface soil plays a decisive role in evaporation. The subsoil may be saturated, but because of slow upward movement of soil moisture, it may have a negligible effect on evaporation from the surface. If other conditions remain constant, evaporation will be greater from a soil surface wetted by frequent intermittent showers than from one thoroughly soaked by the same amount of rain falling in a single storm.

In areas in which soil moisture is not frequently replenished by rainfall, soil evaporation tends to vary closely with those factors that effect the capillary rise of moisture stored immediately beneath the surface. This condition occurs because the upward movement of soil water from capillary action will replenish the diminishing moisture on the soil surface. Thus, when other conditions are constant, evaporation will be greater in coarse-textured soil than in fine-textured soil because capillary movement is more effective in coarse material. Soil colour modifies the reflectivity of the soil surface, which in turn influences evaporation.

Soil evaporation is at a maximum when the water table is at the surface, because soil moisture is 100 percent. As the water table lowers, the evaporation decreases rapidly. After the water table reaches a critical depth, and below this level, the decrease in the rate of evaporation will be very slight. The critical depth depends on the capillary characteristics or texture of the soil; in general, it is about 35 centimetres (14 inches) in coarse sand, 70 centimetres (28 inches) in fine sand, and 85 centimetres (33 inches) in heavy loam soil.

The presence of vegetation offers a shelter that will reduce the soil evaporation because it shades the soil surface from solar radiation, reduces wind speed, and increases the humidity of the overlying air. A litter layer, composed of straw, leaf, coniferous needles, and the like, will have the same effect as vegetation.

The change of water from a solid state, as in ice, to a gaseous state without passing through the usual intermediate liquid state is called sublimation. Evaporation from snow or ice is actually a process of sublimation.

Because snow or ice melts at 0° C (32° F), and because evaporation is possible only when the vapour pressure of the overlying air is less than that of the surface of snow or ice, evaporation from the snow or ice will cease when the dew point (the temperature at which condensation begins when air is cooled at a constant pressure and vapour content) rises to 0° C, although some evaporation of meltwater may take place. As temperatures rise above freezing, the rate of snowmelt or icemelt must exceed the rate of evaporation. Evaporation from snow or ice under such conditions is, therefore, limited, although reliable data are insufficient to verify this conclusion.

Measurement and control. The measurement of soil evaporation is complicated by the fact that the evaporation rate rarely reaches that which would occur over a free water surface, unless the soil is saturated with water. In most cases the depletion of soil-moisture storage reduces the total evaporation from a soil surface. The soil evaporation must be measured from confined moist soil or from soil exposed only to natural precipitation and not affected by capillary rise from below. In order to maintain a high soil-moisture content, soil-filled tanks may be artificially watered from above or moistened by a fixed water table from below. The soil tank is then weighed continuously or at specified intervals, and the evaporation is determined by the change in weight adjusted for the amount of any added water. Another technique to measure soil moisture is to use drain gauges or percolation gauges exposed to the prevailing environmental conditions. These gauges are simply tubes driven into the ground. Measurement is made of the quantity of water percolating through the gauges, and then evaporation is equal to rainfall minus percolation. This method must be used with care, or the soil in the guage will fail to represent that under the natural undisturbed condition.

Soil tanks, drain gauges, and percolation gauges

There are various methods of controlling evaporation losses from soil. A commonly used method in agricultural practice is mulching (adding a protective cover) by dust, ash, paper, or even pebbles. It is believed that loosening the soil surface by mulching will allow rapid drying and the development of a dry surface that will act as a blanket to suppress evaporation. The actual result of mulching, however, may not be as satisfactory as is supposed. Another method of decreasing evaporation involves the chemical alteration of soil-moisture characteristics, as by addition of polyelectrolytes (large molecules carrying a number of ionizable groups).

TRANSPIRATION BY PLANTS

Nature of transpiration. Transpiration is essentially the evaporation of water from the leaf cells of plants. By this process, water in the soil is first absorbed by the root system of a plant and then discharged to the atmosphere as vapour through the leaves. In the process, only a minute fraction of 1 percent of the water is retained for use in building the tissues for plant growth and development.

Role of leaf stomata

Leaves are composed mainly of thin-walled spongy cells, and a surface layer of epidermis cells covers the entire leaf. This layer is largely impervious to moisture and gases, but it contains numerous stomata, or pores, through which moisture and gases may be transmitted. An individual stoma is a small pore enclosed by a pair of crescent-shaped, chlorophyll-containing guard cells. Water vapour from the intercellular spaces of the leaf moves through the pores into the atmosphere whenever the internal pressure is greater than the external pressure. By this process, the intercellular water is evaporated.

The opening and closing of the stoma is governed by the condition of the guard cells. As water moves into the guard cells, causing them to swell, the stoma opens. When the moisture content becomes reduced in the guard cells they shrink, and the stoma closes. This operation is caused by a change in water pressure, known as turgor pressure, exerted by the cell contents against the cell walls. It is affected by such factors as light intensity, moisture supply of leaves, air temperature, humidity, and chemical changes. Stomata usually open in the light and close in the dark; but in certain species, such as cactus and pineapple, the opposite is true. Stomata close with reduced moisture, causing the guard cells to lose turgor. Temperature affects the speed with which the stomata open and close, and high humidity allows them to open wider and to remain open longer.

Stomata also permit carbon dioxide in the air to enter the leaf and to combine with water in the leaf tissues in the presence of chlorophyll and sunlight to produce sugars for use by the plant during growth and development. The sugar may change to starch, which is usually found in the protoplasm of guard cells. When the sugar content of the guard cells increases, as usually occurs in daylight, the osmotic pressure of the cell sap increases, water is drawn in from nearby cells, turgor pressure increases, and the stomata open. When the sugar content of the guard cells decreases, changing to starch, as usually occurs in darkness, the osmotic and the turgor pressures decrease, and the stomata close.

The supply of water to the leaves is attained by the flow of water from the soil to the root systems of the plant, and thence through the stem to the leaves. This flow is initiated in the leaf. When solar radiation is available, the leaf absorbs it, thereby increasing its temperature and causing evaporation and loss of water from the intercellular spaces through the stomata. While the water is removed in this way, a pressure deficit develops and water flows from the internal regions of higher pressure towards the evaporating surface. This pressure deficit is relayed continuously by capillary action, all the way down to the plant roots and the reservoir of soil moisture. The flow for transpiration is thus initiated.

Plants with a supply of water good enough, that are not losing water more rapidly by transpiration than they can absorb it, are normally turgid. On the other hand, if water is in short supply, or if the rate of transpiration from the leaves exceeds the rate of absorption by the roots, the plant will lose its turgidity. As a result the guard cells collapse inward and, by closing the stomata pores, limit further loss of water. Chiefly through its effect on the turgor of guard cells, the water supply of plants influences growth rates and the ultimate size attained by various tissues and organs of the plant.

Stomata actually have only a very limited control over the transpiration rate. They close after darkness or wilting begins, but not ahead of it. When the stomata are open, the transpiration rate is controlled by the same factors that control evaporation alone. The stomata exercise a slight regulatory influence only when they are nearly closed. This phenomenon tends to verify some experiments that have shown that a decrease in soil-moisture supply had initially no effect on transpiration, but after the soil moisture decreased to the permanent wilting content, stomata began to close and a progressive decline in transpiration occurred. This stage was reached even at higher soil-moisture contents than the permanent wilting point as the potential rate of transpiration increased. This fact agrees with findings that the growth of corn and other plants was reduced more often by atmospheric demand of moisture than by low soil-moisture content.

Effect of environmental factors

Transpiration is essentially the evaporation from plants. It differs from evaporation from a water surface in that it is subject to biological functions of the plant and thus is strongly influenced by light. The factors affecting evaporation also affect transpiration. The factors affecting transpiration may be physiological or environmental. Important physiological factors are density and behaviour of stomata, extent and character of protective coverings, leaf structure, and plant diseases. Environmental factors include temperature, solar radiation, wind, and soil moisture when permanent wilting content is reached.

Regarding temperature, it is the temperature of the leaf rather than that of the air that is of direct importance to transpiration. The leaf temperature is usually higher than the surrounding air temperature. When the air temperature increases, the leaf temperature also will increase in order to attain a greater vapour pressure than that of the air. Transpiration will usually result from an increase in air temperature for this reason.

Solar radiation is, of course, directly related to temperature that affects transpiration. It has an additional function, however, because it governs photosynthesis of the plant, which requires flow of water initiated by transpiration. In fact, there is a good correlation between radiation and transpiration. Shading leaves from radiation by spraying them with blackening chemicals has been found to be one way to reduce transpiration.

Wind will remove water vapour near the leaf surface and thus increase transpiration. A gentle wind may be just as effective as a strong wind in increasing the transpiration rate. The former will stimulate transpiration whereas the latter may have a tendency to check it.

Evapotranspiration. Evaporation and transpiration over land areas are closely interrelated. Seldom is a serious attempt made to separate them and to assess their respective contributions to total water losses in the hydrologic cycle. In fact, transpiration loss from an appreciably large area under natural conditions is practically impossible to measure. Measurements by small samples under laboratory conditions are possible but very unreliable and often bear little more than an indication of water use in the field. Evaporation and transpiration are of utmost importance in determining irrigation water requirements, but engineers and planners are only interested in their combined evaluation rather than their individual effects. For practical purposes, the evaporation from all water, soils, snow, ice, vegetation, and other surfaces and transpiration are lumped together and called evapotranspiration, or sometimes total evaporation.

Estimation and measurement of evapotranspiration

Estimation of the actual evapotranspiration is difficult because it involves the consideration of too many interrelated factors that affect both evaporation and transpiration. Usually, potential rather than actual evapotranspiration is estimated. The potential evapotranspiration is the evapotranspiration that would occur if there were an adequate moisture supply at all times. In this way many of the complicating plant and soil factors can be ignored, and effort can be focussed on the meteorological factors. Numerous formulas containing such factors have been developed, but most of them give only approximate results, and no formula, except through chance, gives a correct result.

Like estimation by formulas the actual measurement of evapotranspiration also is inaccurate, although several methods are widely used for field measurement in research and engineering investigations. Actual evapotranspiration usually is measured by lysimeters of various designs. A lysimeter is a soil-filled tank in which plants are grown. The losses of water necessary to maintain satisfactory growth can be measured and can be considered the amount of evapotranspiration. This method is suitable for individual crops and natural vegetation. For potential evapotranspiration, evapotranspirometers are often used. The evapotranspirometer consists of three or more watertight tanks. At least two of the tanks are filled with soil that supports a vegetation cover, such as grass, and they receive either natural or artificial precipitation. These tanks are connected by piping to the third tank, where water percolated from the other two or more tanks can be collected and then measured. The difference between the amount of water that enters and leaves the tanks will represent the water loss by evapotranspiration, if allowance is made for changes of moisture storage within the soil tanks and if the soil moisture is maintained at or just above the field capacity; *i.e.*, the maximum amount of soil moisture that can be held by the soil under gravity.

There are also indirect methods of estimation or measurement of evapotranspiration, including the application of the water-balance and energy-balance principles to large land areas, the summation of the products of evapotranspiration for each vegetation times its covering areas, and the measurement of the groundwater fluctuations as an indication of the water loss in soil caused by evapotranspiration.

Role of water vapour in the hydrologic cycle

DISTRIBUTION IN THE ATMOSPHERE

Water existing in the atmosphere occurs largely in gaseous form, or vapour; its liquid form, such as rainfall and water droplets in clouds, and its solid form, such as snowfall, hail, and ice crystals in clouds, occur only momentarily and locally. As shown in Table 1, the total amount of water vapour in the atmosphere is comparatively small. If it condensed on the earth's surface, it would form a layer about 2½ centimetres (about one inch) thick on the average. At any given instant, the amount of water vapour in the atmosphere contains only a hundred-thousandth of all the waters in the cycle.

Quantity and importance of water vapour

Although the total quantity of water vapour in the atmosphere is relatively small, it is of prime importance because it constitutes the ascending phase of the hydrologic cycle. That is, the water vapour forms largely by evaporation from liquid water on the earth's surface. It is then lifted thousands of metres by rising currents of air and is carried to the highest mountain peaks and to the centres of the continents. When water vapour condenses, it forms precipitation that falls upon the earth's surface, providing the major part of the descending phase of the hydrologic cycle. Without water vapour, the hydrologic cycle could not be made complete.

Water vapour fulfills another important function, though considerably less conspicuous. Although water vapour permits penetration by most of the incoming solar radiation, it retains and absorbs the radiation from the earth, which is reflected skyward; this reflected radiation cannot escape into outer space. This phenomenon keeps the temperature of the earth's surface at a much higher level than would otherwise be the case. Without water vapour to maintain a normal temperature on earth, neither liquid water nor life could be maintained.

The atmospheric water vapour content is determined by local evaporation, air temperature, and the horizontal atmospheric transportation of moisture. The distribution of water vapour depends on the process of diffusion, or transfer, of the vapour and varies with such factors as altitude, latitude, seasons, and topographic features. Because of the lower temperature at higher elevations, the water vapour content in the atmosphere decreases rapidly with height; it is practically nil at about ten kilometres (6.2 miles). Vapour content is higher in summer than in winter, because the average temperature is greater during that season. The moisture in the atmosphere results from evaporation from water surfaces, from vegetation, and from other moist surfaces. It usually produces greater absolute and relative humidity near the sources from which the moisture may be derived. (The absolute humidity specifies the mass of water vapour in a unit volume of air; the relative expresses the amount of water vapour in a volume of air as a percent of the maximum possible amount.) Over most of the warm oceanic regions the air is always near saturation, because the winds that flow over the warm ocean surface gradually increase in temperature as they travel and are continually supplied with vapour to maintain an almost saturated condition. Over the deserts, where the supply of moisture is very limited, the vapour content of the air is far below saturation values. In general, the amount of vapour decreases inland over continents, but this decrease is modified by rainfall conditions, the presence of high mountains, large lakes, extensive forests and swamps, and by prevailing wind movements. It also is a general rule that the amount of water vapour diminishes from the Equator toward the poles. Absolute humidity, therefore, declines with increasing latitude, but relative humidity, which is inversely related to temperature, rises with increasing latitude. In reality, it changes in direction according to diverse wind, pressure, and temperature gradients and meteorological factors in general.

Movement from oceanic to land areas

It is necessary to distinguish between vertical and horizontal movements of the air, because vertical movements generally cause condensation of water vapour whereas horizontal movements seldom do. Horizontal winds or air-mass movements transport vapour from the ocean to land. The horizontal and vertical movements of the air cannot be separated, because it is not uncommon for the air to ascend or descend along a slope, and the two components of the movement are then merged to become a single phenomenon.

Winds primarily result from differential solar heating. When the sun rises and day begins, the land becomes warmer than the surrounding sea, and the air near the ground is heated and then rises. A sea breeze then begins to blow moist air towards the land. At night, the process is reversed. The same process takes place on a much larger scale and in "slow motion" when a whole continent becomes warm in summer and the moisture-laden winds blow in from the ocean. In the cold season, the air currents go in the opposite direction towards the sea. The net exchange of water vapour between the oceans and the continental areas consists of about 3,400,000 cubic kilometres (800,000 cubic miles) of moisture; this quantity enters the land annually to compensate for the total annual runoff into the sea.

VAPOUR RELEASE BY CONDENSATION

The transition process from the vapour state to the liquid state is called condensation. By condensation, water vapour in the atmosphere is released to form precipitation. During this process, water droplets are formed if the temperature is above 0° C; otherwise ice crystals are produced. When first formed the ice crystals or water droplets are so minute (0.005 to 0.05 millimetres [0.0002 to 0.002 inches] in diameter) that they continue to float freely. These water droplets and ice crystals in large quantities create a cloud. When the droplets or crystals coalesce to produce larger drops, 0.1 to 0.5 millimetres (0.004 to 0.02 inches) in diameter, the drops may become so heavy that they will eventually fall as precipitation.

Condensation may take place as soon as the air contains more water vapour than it can receive from a free water surface through evaporation at the prevailing temperature. This condition occurs as the consequence of either cooling or mixing. If a mass of warm saturated air mingles with a mass of cold saturated air, the vapour pressure of the mixture may exceed the maximum pressure permitted by the resultant. This mingling, however, seldom causes more than a tenuous cloud or mist on the surface of the earth.

Condensation in clouds and fogs

All clouds are formed as the result of cooling to below the dew point, the temperature at which condensation commences when air is cooled at constant pressure and vapour content. If the cooling air contains no water droplets, however, condensation may not take place even if the temperature is at the dew point or slightly below it. This process creates a condition of supersaturation without actual condensation of vapour into water droplets.

The condition of supersaturation is very unstable and a slight disturbance may bring a few water molecules together to form a nucleus and thus initiate condensation. The nucleus of condensation also may be served by any small floating particle, such as dust, in the air. Normal dust seems to be relatively inactive, but particles of salt, derived from evaporated spatters of seawater, are most apt to start condensation because the salt particle attracts water. Condensation often takes place to form fog near the cold ground or sea surface where hydroscopic, or water-attracting, particles are present.

In contrast to the formation of fog, clouds are created by the lifting and cooling of moist air, but not by release of heat to the surroundings. As air is lifted, it is exposed to decreasing atmospheric pressure, expands, and consequently cools. This type of cooling causes precipitation. If the lifting is due to the convergence of air into a low-pressure area, or cyclone, then cyclonic precipitation will result. This condition occurs principally in plains regions. If the lifting is caused by the natural rising of warm, light air in cold, dense surroundings, convective precipitation is produced, as in thunderstorms. If lifting of air results from the presence of a topographic barrier, such as a mountain, orographic precipitation will occur on the windward side of the barrier. In nature, the effects of these various types of cooling are often interrelated and the resulting precipitation may be of several types.

PRECIPITATION AND ITS DISTRIBUTION

Precipitation in the hydrologic cycle may be disposed of in four main ways. It may be evaporated during its fall or after it reaches the ground surface. It may be intercepted by vegetation and then evaporated from the surfaces of leaves. It may infiltrate into the ground to become part of the soil moisture that ultimately joins groundwater or afterwards emerges from the ground to be evaporated from the ground surface or to become part of surface water runoff. It may directly fall on streams, rivers, lakes, or any surface-water body and then evaporate or become part of surface-water runoff. Of these various ways of distributing precipitation, evaporation has been discussed, interception and infiltration are discussed immediately below, and surface runoff will be described at length later.

Interception by vegetation. When precipitation falls on vegetation, three paths may be taken. It may drip through and from the leaves to the ground surface, a process that is called throughfall. It may trickle along twigs and branches and finally down the main trunk to the ground surface, a process called stemflow. It also may be held by the leaves and later evaporated from their exposed surfaces, a process called interception. By this process, water is prevented from reaching the ground surface, and the hydrologic cycle is completed without its land-borne part.

Views about the hydrologic significance of interception are conflicting. Many hydrologists consider interception as a primary loss of precipitation that would otherwise have been available at the ground surface for direct evaporation, for infiltration into the soil moisture reserves, or for overland flow to runoff. Other authorities believe that interception is essentially evaporative. Because there is only a certain amount of energy available for evaporation at any time, this energy will be used either to transpire water from within the plant or to evaporate water from surfaces of the leaves, that is, intercepted water. In this sense, interception is an alternative and not an addition to evapotranspiration, and it will have little effect upon the water balance of a drainage basin area. This view may be true at a given time, but over a certain length of time the available energy changes and the evapotranspiration with and without interception would be different. From still another viewpoint, leaves not only intercept precipitation but may also collect dew or water from condensation of water vapour in the air. This phenomenon also has been considered as interception by some hydrologists. Consequently, they believe that the total interception may result in a net gain of water in a drainage basin, particularly in forested areas where fogs or low clouds are prevalent and will enhance dew collection.

Interception is affected by many factors. The most important is the type and density of vegetation. High interception obviously occurs in forested areas. Although leaf density is greater in deciduous (leaf dropping) than in coniferous forests, the latter shows greater interception, probably because the needlelike leaves of coniferous trees will hold water droplets longer for evaporation and also because their open texture allows freer circulation of air and consequently more rapid evaporation of the retained water. As the total leaf area of a continuous cover of mature grass or shrub closely resembles that of a closed canopy forest, the interceptions of the two types of vegetation are similar. The grass or shrub cover does not have the secondary interception capacity of the undergrowth of the forest, however, which may constitute an appreciable portion of the total interception when the precipitation is heavy and long.

Meteorological factors

Among all meteorological factors, wind speed is of real significance to interception because evaporation increases with increasing wind speed, thus increasing loss of water by interception. High wind speed may have adverse effects when the rainfall duration is short, however, because wind force may dislodge water collected on leaf surfaces and intercepted water cannot be replaced later for further evaporation. Because interception is greatest at the beginning of a rainstorm, when the leaves are dry and interception capacity is large, it is apparent that the frequency of rainfall is a more important factor affecting interception than the duration and magnitude of rainfall.

Frequent rainfalls usually result in high interception loss of water.

Experimental data on interception have been extensively collected by many investigators. Because of varied experimental conditions and techniques used, such information cannot be easily evaluated or summarized for general application. The direct measurement of interception usually involves a random placing of containers or interceptometers under the vegetation canopy. A comparison is then made between the collected throughfall plus measured stemflow and the precipitation measured above the vegetation. Interception is equal to the difference between the amounts of water measured above and below the canopy.

Interception is apparently greatest in forested areas. For well-developed forest canopies, it has been found to exceed 40 percent of the summer precipitation in some cases and to range between 10 and 20 percent of the annual rainfall. For cut or burned areas or heavily grazed range, it may approach zero.

Infiltration. After reaching the ground surface, some part of precipitation will be absorbed by, or will soak into, the surface layers of the soil. This phase of the hydrologic cycle is known as infiltration. The infiltrated water may move downwards through the soil, subsoil, and rock layers, eventually becoming part of one or more of the several existing moisture zones. As shown in Figure 2, the infiltrated water adds to the soil moisture by first

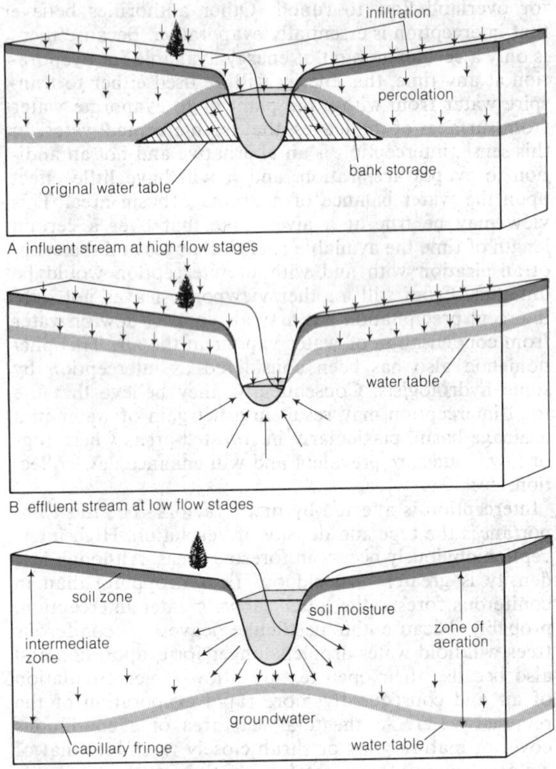

Figure 2: Interaction of streamflow, groundwater, and soil moisture (see text).

entering the soil zone, which is a relatively thin layer of soil near the ground surface. The soil moisture may then leave the soil zone by surface evaporation, by evapotranspiration, or by means of downward percolation towards the water table. Immediately above the water table is the capillary fringe, where water is held by capillary action against the force of gravity. Between the soil zone and the capillary fringe is the intermediate zone, where water moves generally downwards and also laterally downstream whenever a hydraulic gradient develops in that direction. The soil layers above the water table, containing soil moisture but unsaturated, constitute the zone of aeration. This zone is a zone of transition in which water is absorbed, held, or transmitted downward towards the water table, upward towards the soil surface, or laterally in a downstream direction.

The rate at which precipitation is absorbed by a soil is known as the infiltration rate. The maximum infiltration rate is called infiltration capacity, which provides a limit to the infiltration of the precipitation falling upon a drainage basin. Both the infiltration rate and the infiltration capacity normally vary widely over a drainage basin in response to a number of closely related influencing factors. After the falling rain has filled the surface storage of the ground, the infiltration rate has a direct relationship to the intensity of rainfall. This relationship holds only up to a certain limit; that is, when the infiltration rate reaches the infiltration capacity of the soil and no rainfall can be further absorbed by the soil. In nature, further increase in rainfall intensity may be accompanied by an increase in the size of raindrops and an increase in their compacting force, thus modifying the surface conditions of the soil and changing the infiltration capacity.

Importance of soil conditions

The surface conditions of the soil obviously exert an important influence on infiltration. In the absence of a vegetation cover, falling raindrops may so compact the surface of the soil that infiltration is rapidly and greatly reduced. This effect is more noticeable on clay soils, which can be made virtually impermeable in this way, than on clear sandy soils, which are less susceptible to raindrop compaction. Similar effects will result from any other forms of compaction, such as by animal or human activities. Fine particles carried in suspension by infiltrating water may clog pores in the soil surface and will have an effect similar to compaction on infiltration. Frozen ground also will limit or even stop infiltration completely. Also, gentle or flat slopes and a large amount of surface storage will each have a tendency to reduce the infiltration rate because the flow of water will be retarded, allowing more time for the intake of water.

Some other surface conditions will definitely increase infiltration. Cracks or openings on the soil surface developed by sun baking or evapotranspiration will provide opportunities for large amounts of infiltration. Terracing and contour plowing tend to increase the total infiltration by retarding surface flow, but plowing of natural vegetation surfaces usually results in a reduction of infiltration capacity because the soil structure will be somewhat more compacted than under its natural condition.

Cover of the ground surface is also one of the main factors governing the amount of infiltration. A vegetation cover tends to increase infiltration because it retards surface flow, allowing more time for the water to enter the soil; shields the soil surface from the direct impact of raindrops; and increases permeability of the soil by its root systems. The density of vegetation cover seems to be more important than the differences in vegetation type. A layer of ground litter normally has a more pronounced effect to increase infiltration rates than the main vegetation. A snow cover seems to have the same effect, provided the ground is not frozen. Urbanization increases the percentage of impervious areas and reduces total infiltration, resulting in high surface runoff rates.

It should be noted that water cannot continue to infiltrate the soil surface faster than it can be accepted by the underlying soil mass. The available storage capacity in the soil, therefore, is another important factor affecting the infiltration, being largely controlled by the transmissibility of the zone of aeration and the pre-existing amount of soil moisture. The transmissibility further depends on the thickness of the zone of aeration, and also on texture, particle size and shape, organic matter content, biotic activities, root penetration, swelling of colloidal matter, and other characteristics of soil structure and stability that affect the noncapillary porosity of the soil. The noncapillary porosity is the porosity that is higher than that which can be taken up by capillary water. As soil moisture content increases, more of the available pore spaces in the soil become filled. This filling diminishes the available space for storing infiltrated water and reduces the infiltration capacity of the soil. This increase in soil moisture will also indirectly affect infiltration because of consequent colloidal swelling.

Another group of factors that affect infiltration include the temperature, chemical content, and viscosity of the water. Most of these factors have usually a lesser degree of importance, however, although some of them, such as salt content, will not only affect the viscosity of the water but also the rate of swelling of colloids.

If the soil is initially dry, strong capillary forces during the initial stage of the infiltration process will pull in water to fill up the capillary pores much faster than would occur by the action of gravity. Although the initial infiltration capacity is always high, it is much higher in dry soils. The moisture condition before the onset of precipitation, therefore, will greatly affect the initial infiltration capacity of the soil. Normally, the infiltration capacity falls very rapidly during the early stages of rainfall as a result of the combined effects of such factors as surface compaction, in-washing of fine particles, colloid swelling, the closing up of cracks in soil, increasing soil-moisture content, and the marked reduction in capillary forces. From a mathematical viewpoint, the infiltration capacity decreases almost exponentially with time—usually the infiltration capacity decreases rapidly for only a few to ten minutes and then gradually approaches an ultimate infiltration capacity within an hour. The ultimate infiltration capacity can be further lowered if transmissibility of the subsoils is suddenly reduced by an impervious layer at some depth below the surface.

Determination of infiltration

Because the infiltration rate and the infiltration capacity vary with time and space, their determination over a large drainage basin can only be very roughly estimated. In practice, a direct measurement by infiltrometers is commonly applied to small, clearly defined areas. The infiltrometer is a tube, or other boundary, designed to isolate a vertical column of soil that extends downward from the ground surface. The soil surface area confined by the tube or boundary varies from one-tenth of a square metre (about one square foot) to several hundred square metres. The area is flooded with water or sprinkled with simulated rainfalls. The infiltration rate is equal to the amount of water applied to maintain a constant head (depth of water) over the area by flooding or equal to the difference between the amount of water applied by sprinkling and the measured surface runoff. Because the natural soil condition may be disturbed by driving a tube into the soil or by installing a boundary, and because the natural rainfall cannot be simulated exactly, the infiltration capacity measured in this way is likely to differ from the true infiltration. Experiments have indicated that infiltrometers usually give higher infiltration rates in tests than occur under natural conditions.

An extension of the sprinkler-type infiltrometer technique is the analysis of the hyetograph and its corresponding hydrograph for a drainage basin. The hyetograph is a time recording of the rainfall, which is equivalent to the measure of water applied to an infiltrometer throughout the period of the application. The hydrograph is the time recording of the surface runoff. The difference between the hyetograph and the hydrograph at different intervals during the period of rainfall can be calculated to yield the infiltration rates at these time intervals. On natural basins, allowance for subsurface flow and surface storage must be made in the analysis. Because subsurface flow and surface storage cannot be estimated accurately by any methods available, it is extremely difficult to obtain reliable infiltration data from natural drainage basins by such techniques.

Runoff and subsurface water

Water on the ground surface is mainly derived from precipitation through a direct or an indirect path. As precipitation begins, much of it falling during the first part of a storm is stored in surface depressions as surface storage and the remaining part either infiltrates into the soil or flows downslope as overland flow, which upon entering a channel will form a part of streamflow. As precipitation continues, surface storage also will be built up if the rate of rainfall exceeds the infiltration capacity of the soil. A large portion of the water in surface storage will be eventually evaporated and will not appear either as infiltration or as surface runoff in the form of overland flow. This portion is known as retention storage or surface retention. The remaining portion of the surface storage, which is detained temporarily and later becomes either infiltration or overland flow, is called detention storage. Large bodies of water on the earth's surface are but combinations of retention and detention storages. In general, surface water consists of the water in surface storage, overland flow, and streamflow.

Kinds of runoff and their distribution

A very important role of the surface water in the hydrologic cycle is played by the runoff. Runoff is that part of the precipitation eventually appearing in surface streams of either perennial or intermittent form. Runoff is the flow collected largely within a drainage basin that subsequently appears at the outlet of a basin. According to the source from which the flow is derived, runoff may consist of surface runoff, subsurface runoff, and groundwater runoff. The surface runoff is that part of the runoff travelling over the ground surface and through channels to reach the basin outlet. The portion of the surface runoff that flows over the land surface toward stream channels is the overland flow. After the flow enters a stream, it joins with other components of flow to form the total runoff or the streamflow in the stream channel. Precipitation falling directly on the channel is of relatively small amount and is usually considered as part of the surface runoff.

Overland flow occurs when rainfall intensity is so great that not all the water can infiltrate. This type of flow is fairly common in semi-arid or arid lands, where vegetation is sparse and raindrops are not impeded; their impact tends to cause an almost impermeable skin on the soil surface. In humid and semihumid areas, where vegetation increases the infiltration and shields the soil from the impact of raindrops, overland flow is rare except on paved surfaces.

The subsurface runoff, also known as throughflow, is the runoff component caused by that part of the precipitation that infiltrates the surface soil and moves laterally through the upper soil layers toward the streams. A part of the subsurface runoff may enter the stream promptly, but the remaining part may take a long time before joining the streamflow or may reappear on the soil surface to evaporate without reaching the stream channel.

The groundwater runoff is that part of the infiltrated water joining the groundwater by percolation and then discharging into a stream.

Average runoff from the landmasses of the world can be estimated from precipitation, evaporation, and evapotranspiration data if allowance is made for areas of inland drainage. For all continents the average annual runoff is 26.7 centimetres (10.5 inches). The distribution of this total global runoff has been estimated by M.I. Lvovich, a Soviet hydrologist (see Table 3).

Table 3: Distribution of Total Global Runoff

	land area		percent of total global runoff
	sq mi	sq km	
Africa	11,500,000	29,800,000	17
Asia	16,000,000	42,000,000	20
Australia and New Zealand	3,000,000	8,000,000	2
Europe	3,700,000	9,600,000	7
Greenland	1,500,000	3,800,000	2
Malay Archipelago	1,000,000	2,600,000	12
North and Central Americas and the Caribbeans	7,900,000	20,500,000	18
South America	6,900,000	17,900,000	22

SURFACE RUNOFF CYCLE

The phenomenon of runoff may be considered as a cycle corresponding to that portion of the hydrologic cycle between precipitation over land areas and later discharge of this water through river channels or evapotranspiration. This runoff cycle can be described in five phases with respect to an idealized cross section of a drainage basin at selected times. The following discussion of the five phases should also be referred to the channel cross-sectional profiles shown in Figure 2.

Onset and continuation of rainfall

The first phase covers rainless periods just before the beginning of rainfall and after an extended dry period. During this phase, the groundwater table is low and its elevation continues to decrease gradually. In mountainous areas or where steep slopes occur, there may be no continuous water table and the streamflow is maintained by draining areas containing water in perched layers or in rock interstices. In arid regions, where there may be no water table or perched groundwater contributing flow to streams, the channels are dry. In addition to disposal of water by streamflow, water also is lost on land and water surfaces through evaporation and by transpiration from plants. If snow, ice, or frost is present and temperatures are below freezing, the phenomena described remain almost unchanged. If temperatures are above freezing, the snow, ice, or frost will melt as runoff, thus entering the second phase of the cycle.

The second phase of the runoff cycle covers the initial period of rain (Figure 2A). As the rain starts, its amount is divided among channel precipitation, interception by vegetation, infiltration into the soil, and detention and retention in surface depressions. The infiltrated water results in a gradual increase of water in the zone of aeration after the natural storage or field moisture capacity is satisfied. During this phase there is little overland flow except on impervious surfaces, and evaporation and transpiration are slight. Groundwater runoff to the stream channels may or may not continue, depending on whether the first phase continued until streamflow ceased. If snow is present, it will absorb part of the falling rain and its storage effect will lengthen the period of this phase. If frost is present, infiltration will be reduced when moisture content is high, but increased when moisture content is low and the ground is frozen. The runoff will be augmented only when thawing releases stored water in the snow, ice, and frost.

The third phase of the runoff cycle covers a continuing period of rain at variable intensity (Figure 2B). As rain continues, the capacities of vegetation interception and retention of surface depressions are reached, and the excess rain becomes a source of runoff and detention storage on land surfaces and in channels. Overland flow occurs when the net rate of rain exceeds the infiltration rate; but it may or may not reach the stream channels, depending on retention and detention capacities of the land surface over which it travels. The infiltrated water will saturate the upper part of the zone of aeration, which has been depleted in the previous phases, and it will then move downward to the water table. If rain continues, the water table will rise and the groundwater contribution to streamflow will increase. As the zone of aeration is saturated, subsurface runoff may contribute also to the streamflow. If the stage of flow in the channels rises rapidly and becomes higher than the relatively slowly rising groundwater table, the streams will change from effluent streams to influent streams—they will contribute to the groundwater and developing bank storage of water. During this phase, evaporation and transpiration are slow. If snow, ice, and frost are present, their effects will be about the same as in the previous phase. When frost is gone, the groundwater recharge will momentarily increase rapidly and the overland flow and subsurface runoff will diminish accordingly. Through groundwater recharge, the subsurface runoff will increase in later periods.

The fourth phase of the runoff cycle covers the continuing period of rainfall until all natural storage has been satisfied. The infiltration rate will approach the rate of water transmission through the zone of aeration to both groundwater table and subsurface runoff. The amount of subsurface runoff, which will join the streamflow almost as promptly as the overland runoff, apparently depends on the porosity of the material through which it is transmitted. As the rain continues, the water table rises constantly until the groundwater runoff balances the maximum rate of recharge possible, and all additional rain results in direct increment to runoff. Although this ultimate condition may rarely be reached, it is approximately attained in flat swampy areas after periods of heavy and prolonged rainfall. The effects of snow, ice, and frost are similar to those in the third phase.

The fifth phase of the runoff cycle covers the period between the termination of rain and the time when the first stage is to be reached (Figure 2C). This period usually involves a relatively long time for channel storage and surface retention to become depleted. Evaporation and transpiration are active and infiltration continues. Water in the zone of aeration is reaching the water table or the stream channels. Streamflow is sustained by releasing stored water from stream channels, subsurface flow, and groundwater flow. The water table is rising and then falling when its peak stage is over and the stored water is diminishing. When the temperature is below freezing, the presence of snow and ice has little effect on runoff; if the temperature rises above freezing, their presence will prolong this phase.

FACTORS AFFECTING RUNOFF

Runoff from a drainage basin is influenced by two major groups of factors: meteorological factors and physiographic factors. Meteorological factors include mainly the effects of various forms and types of precipitation, interception, evaporation, and transpiration, all of which exhibit seasonal variations in accordance with the climatic environment. Physiographic factors may be classified into two kinds: basin characteristics and channel characteristics. Basin characteristics include such factors as size, shape, and slope of drainage area; permeability and capacity of groundwater-bearing formations; presence of lakes and swamps; land use; and antecedent basin condition. Channel characteristics are related mostly to hydraulic properties of the channel that govern the movement of streamflow and determine channel storage capacity. It should be noted, however, that this classification of factors is by no means exact, because many factors are mutually dependent to a significant extent.

Basin and channel characteristics

The factors affecting runoff generally tend to cause large drainage areas to show different hydrologic behaviour than that shown by most small drainage areas. As a result, drainage basins may be classified as large and small, not on the basis of the size alone but because of the effects of certain dominating factors. Two drainage basins of nearly the same size, for example, may exhibit quite different runoff phenomena. One basin may show prominent channel storage effects, like most large basins, whereas the other may manifest strong influence of the land use, like most small basins. A distinct characteristic of small basins is that the effect of overland flow, rather than the effect of channel flow, is a dominating factor affecting the peak runoff. Also, small basins are very sensitive to high-intensity rainfalls of short duration and to land use. On large basins, however, the effect of channel storage is so pronounced that such sensitivities are greatly suppressed. There is no clear demarcation of size between small and large basins. In general, a small basin may have a size from a few to 400 hectares (1,000 acres), or even up to 260 square kilometres (100 square miles). The upper limit depends on the condition at which the above mentioned sensitivities become minimized because of an overwhelming channel-storage effect.

ANALYSIS OF RUNOFF

Measurement and time distribution. Determination and prediction of runoff is of fundamental importance in water-resources planning and development. Direct measurement of runoff in stream channels is usually made by stream gauges. A commonly used stream gauge consists of a float measuring the water level, or stage, in the channel and a clock mechanism that registers the measured stage to produce a time–stage chart. The relationship between the stage and the discharge of runoff in the channel can be established by field measurements at various flow conditions. The field measurement involves the measurement of the channel cross-sectional area at a given stage of flow and the measurement of the average velocity of flow through the area by means of a current meter.

The discharge of runoff is then equal to the product of the area and the velocity. By means of the stage and discharge relationship, the time–stage chart can be converted to a graph known as a hydrograph, describing the time variation of the runoff. Figure 3 shows a typical

The hydrograph and hyetograph

From Ven Te Chow (ed.), *Handbook of Applied Hydrology*, Copyright 1964; by permission of McGraw-Hill Book Company

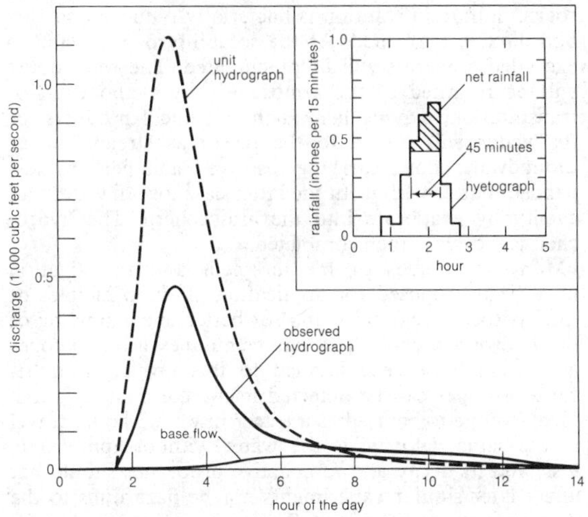

Figure 3: An example of unit hydrograph analysis (see text).

single-peaked hydrograph, which consists of a rapidly rising limb and a rapidly lowering and then gradually receding limb. The time distribution of the rainfall that caused the rise of runoff is shown by a hyetograph in the figure. The shape of the hydrograph is evidently governed by various meteorological and physiographical factors affecting runoff as mentioned previously. The peak of a hydrograph represents the highest concentration of the runoff from a drainage basin for a given storm. The gradually lowering limb represents the withdrawal of water from the channel storage after inflow to the channel has suddenly diminished because the rainfall has ended. The gradually receding segment shows that the channel storage is so much reduced that withdrawal has to be furnished slowly from the groundwater contribution to the subsurface flow.

For the purpose of runoff analysis, storm runoff may be more or less arbitrarily divided into storm runoff and base flow, although in practice this division procedure varies and in reality such a division cannot be exact because of the complexity of runoff phenomena. The storm runoff is that part of the runoff entering the stream promptly after the rainfall started, consisting mainly of the surface and subsurface runoff. Entirely because of the contribution of the net rainfall, it constitutes the large peak portion of the hydrograph. The net rainfall is the gross storm rainfall minus the water losses caused by interception, direct evaporation, evapotranspiration, and infiltration. The shaded area represents net rainfall.

The base flow is the sustained, or fair-weather, runoff, which would be equal to the streamflow under normal conditions if there were no storms. It is entirely the contribution of the groundwater runoff. In Figure 3, a dashed line, usually drawn by judgment, is shown to separate the observed hydrograph into the storm runoff portion and the base flow portion.

The unit hydrograph method. In 1932, Leroy K. Sherman, U.S. hydrologist, proposed the unit hydrograph method. The storm runoff is assumed to vary directly with the net rainfall, and by Sherman's definition, the unit hydrograph of a drainage basin is a hydrograph of the storm runoff resulting from one inch of net rainfall that falls uniformly over the basin area at a uniform intensity for a specified duration. Sherman originally used the word unit to denote the specified duration of the net rainfall. Later, however, this word has been often interpreted as an indication of one inch or any other assigned unit depth of the net rainfall.

For a given observed hydrograph as shown in Figure 3, the equivalent uniform depth of the net rainfall, or the same for the storm runoff, is 1.09 centimetres (0.42 inch), covering a drainage basin of 1,150 hectares (2,850 acres). The duration of the net rainfall is 45 minutes. The unit hydrograph can be computed by dividing the storm runoff part of the observed hydrograph by 0.42. Thus, the resulting unit hydrograph shown in the figure has an area below it equal to one inch. This unit hydrograph is apparently the storm runoff hydrograph resulting from one inch of net rainfall of uniform intensity and uniform distribution over the basin area for a duration of 45 minutes. For net-rainfall durations other than 45 minutes, corresponding unit hydrographs can also be derived by additional analysis based on the same principle of the method. Once the unit hydrograph is computed, it can be used in the hydrologic design of water-resources projects, such as for the prediction of a flood caused by a given storm rainfall.

Underlying assumptions of the method

The unit hydrograph method apparently involves many assumptions that are only approximations of the real condition. The major assumptions are the uniform net-rainfall intensity, the uniform net-rainfall distribution over the basin area, the direct proportionality between storm runoff and net rainfall, the constant duration of storm runoff, and the invariability of the unit hydrograph with respect to basin conditions. Through the years the original unit hydrograph method has been modified so that it can be applied to cases of variable rainfall intensity and distribution and variable basin conditions, but the assumption of direct proportionality between net rainfall and storm runoff and the assumption of constant storm runoff duration remain the essential features of the method. From the modern systems viewpoint, the assumption of proportionality is essentially the concept of a linear system. For a linear hydrologic system, the output storm runoff of the system should vary linearly with the input net rainfall to the system. Because the hydrologic behaviour of natural drainage basins is so complex that it does not follow the assumptions exactly, the results obtained by the unit hydrograph method can only be considered approximate. The method is popular among practicing hydrologists and engineers because it is relatively simple to use. For a refined analysis, more elaborate methods based on the concept of nonlinear systems have been developed.

GROUNDWATER

After the precipitated water soaks into the soil, a part of it may percolate downward to reach the water table, becoming groundwater in the zone of aeration (see Figure 2). Because this percolated water is derived originally from precipitation, it is termed meteoric water. In many arid areas with underground drainage, the major source of meteoric water is seepage from stream runoff and lakes. Besides the meteoric water, groundwater is also contributed in small quantities by some minor sources of water located in the earth's crust. These sources include the connate water, which was trapped in some sedimentary rocks at the time of their formation, and the juvenile water, which was formed chemically within the earth and brought to the surface for the first time as a result of volcanic activity. Because of their origin, connate and juvenile waters often contain undesirable minerals.

Groundwater boundaries

Groundwater is distinguished from other types of subsurface water, such as soil moisture in the form of soil water or capillary water, because it occurs within saturation zones where the hydrostatic pressure is equal to or greater than atmospheric pressure. The upper boundary of the saturation zone varies, depending on whether the groundwater is free or confined. In the case of free groundwater, this boundary is the water table, where the pore-water pressure is equal to atmospheric pressure. In the case of confined groundwater, the upper boundary of the water body is formed by an overlying stratum that is so dense in texture that it is practically impermeable. Confined groundwater is usually confined under high pore-water pressure that is much greater than atmospheric pressure. By drilling a well through the overlying confining stratum into the confined groundwater formation, water may flow out of the well under such artesian pressures without pumping. In both cases, the lower boundary of groundwater is a geologic formation where the interstices are so sparse and so small that further downward movement is practically impossible. This boundary is frequently formed by a stratum of impervious bedrocks. If the underlying confining stratum is not continuous over a very large area but situated at some height above the bedrock and separated from it by previous strata where groundwater occurs, the groundwater is then described as perched.

Groundwater may be distributed in various natural ways. When a lake or stream intersects the water table, groundwater may directly communicate with the surface water. If the prevailing water table is higher than the surface-water level, as in the case of the effluent stream in Figure 2B, a hydraulic-pressure gradient slopes toward the surface water and it will receive groundwater augmentation. On the other hand, if the water table is lower than the level of the surface water, surface water will seep into the ground to join groundwater, as in the case of the influent stream in Figure 2A. Where confined groundwater intersects the ground surface, water will flow out at the surface to form a spring. Where the water table of free groundwater is close to the ground surface, groundwater may be lost through soil evaporation and evapotranspiration. Most groundwater, however, ultimately will enter stream channels and flow to the sea as surface water. In the global hydrologic cycle, it contributes on the average approximately 30 percent of total runoff, although within different geographical regions this proportion varies considerably.

The groundwater cycle. Groundwater is constantly in motion. Compared to surface water in general, it moves very slowly and variably. It may move only a few thousandths of a centimetre per day in soil and some fine-grained pervious rocks, to as much as several thousands of metres in fissured geologic formation. When the velocity is low, the flow is laminar (nonturbulent) and the velocity depends on the permeability of the material through which the water flows and on the hydraulic pressure gradient, which is the slope of the water table in case of free groundwater or the slope of the pressure head line, known also as the piezometric level, in the case of confined artesian groundwater. This phenomenon of groundwater movement through porous media is described as Darcy's law because it was originally proposed by Henri Darcy, French hydraulic engineer, in 1856, for flow through sand.

Movement of groundwater is necessary as a part of the hydrologic cycle. Groundwater not only changes environment to become other parts of the hydrologic cycle, but it also exhibits internal circulation. Near the water table, the average cycling time of water may be a year or less, but in deep aquifers (water-bearing strata), it may be as long as thousands of years. Also, in deep-seated connate water having high concentrations of salt, any circulation may have a time scale of geological epochs, thus isolating it from the currently active hydrologic cycle.

Tracer techniques and remote sensing. Because groundwater lies below the ground surface, its movement cannot be observed or measured easily. Consequently, its exact role in the hydrologic cycle has not been well understood. Since the 1960s, hydrologists have been studying the movement of certain foreign substances that are carried by water as tracers. Because such tracers can be detected more easily than the water itself, knowledge of their movement will give a better indication about the movement of groundwater.

Using natural chemical substances in water as tracers, the portion of the hydrologic cycle that relates the chemical character of water to its natural environment can be studied. This concept is called the hydrochemical cycle of water. Its principal processes can be briefly summarized as follows: Wind blowing over the ocean carries sodium chloride and other substances landward. As water vapour condenses, nitrogen, oxygen, and carbon dioxide of the atmosphere dissolve and together with substances carried from the ocean are transported to the ground in precipitation. Although soil is rich in organic matter, additional carbon dioxide will dissolve as water percolates through the soil. Furthermore, minerals in the soil will dissolve and release many chemical constituents. Sulfide minerals will oxidize to provide sulfate and some other constituents. Some ions (charged atoms) in the solution will be exchanged for those in the soil and rocks. Sulfate in solution is bacterially reduced and carbon dioxide is formed. As the solubility of the water is exceeded, minerals will be precipitated. The water itself will be returned to the atmosphere by evaporation or transpiration, leaving behind the chemical products, or the water will return to the ocean as streamflow or groundwater flow, carrying dissolved and perhaps suspended matter with it. In the latter case, ocean water will eventually evaporate into the atmosphere. The hydrochemical cycle is then completed.

The hydrochemical water cycle

Many techniques of measurement and investigation have been proposed for application of the principles of the hydrochemical cycle and for better understanding of the hydrologic cycle. Nuclear techniques using isotopes as tracers have been applied to this investigation because isotopes can be detected in minute quantities. An ideal isotope to be used as a tracer in water should travel at the same velocity as the water without appreciable loss, and its decay and radioactive properties should not affect later similar experiments nor be hazardous to the user or to the environment. The adequate use of isotopes depends more or less on the nature of the problems being investigated. Some typical problems in connection with the hydrologic cycle are the study of movement of groundwater by radioactive iodine-132 or cobalt-60 and the evaluation of the interaction between surface and groundwaters by tritium.

Another modern approach to the study of the movement of groundwater is by remote sensing. The essence of this technique is to acquire information about an object without keeping the measuring device in physical contact with the object. Commonly used devices for groundwater studies are infrared photography and infrared imagery techniques. For example, infrared photography has been used to locate groundwater outflow such as geysers and springs, and infrared imagery has been found successful in discovering fresh groundwater leakage into the sea. Infrared photography and imagery can detect very slight temperature differences. Because groundwater is usually cooler than surface water, it can be easily identified by such techniques.

Role of ice in the hydrologic cycle

DISTRIBUTION, ACCUMULATION, AND ABLATION

Ice crystals in the atmosphere

Ice exists in various forms in the hydrologic cycle. In the atmosphere, ice crystals of snow are formed in clouds by the solidification of water vapour below freezing temperatures. Depending on the temperature at which they form and the type and thickness of the cloud through which they fall, the size of ice crystals varies from half of a millimetre (0.02 inch) to a centimetre or more (about 0.4 inch) in diameter. In general, large snowflake formation occurs at warmer temperatures, and the smaller, more solid grains of snow are produced at colder temperatures. When temperature is above freezing and raindrops form instead of snow crystals, rising convective air currents may carry the raindrops into supersaturated cooling air and result in frozen water drops, or hail. The hailstones may increase in size by additional coating with ice layers as they descend through one or several regions of supercooled and supersaturated cloud. Thus, their size may vary from one-half to five or more centimetres (0.2 to two or more inches) in diameter. The existence of ice in the atmosphere is largely temporary. Such ice is of relatively very small amount, but it participates actively in the hydrologic cycle.

During the winter, soil moisture may freeze to form ice particles. In perennially frozen ground, or permafrost (*q.v.*), ground ice often occurs in the form of grains, small irregularly shaped masses, or even large masses and layers several feet thick. Because the permafrost regions in the world occupy about 22 percent of the world's land surface, a considerable quantity of ground ice is embedded in these regions. The ground ice is immobile, however, and little of the water contained in permafrost participates in the hydrologic cycle.

On the ground, falling snow may accumulate to form a cover. The fresh snow cover has a density varying from about 0.06 to 0.16; it is filled with air and transmits water readily. Whereas the surface snow may evaporate after melting or sublimate (pass directly from the solid to vapour state) a little, the lower part ultimately will be transformed into compact, coarsely crystalline, glassy ice. This ice sheet is impervious to water, having a density close to 0.9 and containing practically no air spaces between its tightly interlocked crystals. Also, surface water can freeze to form solid ice sheets in rivers, ponds and lakes. Any large mass of snow or ice on the land that persists for many years constitutes stationary ice sheets or moving glaciers. Perennial ice masses range in size from the Antarctic Ice Sheet to small pockets of ice less than a square kilometre in size. In the sea, seawater may freeze to produce sea ice, and glaciers may break off into the sea to form icebergs.

In recent geological time, some 10,000 to 20,000 years ago, glaciers and ice caps covered about one-third of the earth's land surface. Today, some 12 percent of the land surface remains covered by them. Although these ice masses contain about 2 percent of the total global water (see Table 1), they represent the largest share, about 76 percent, of the world's fresh water. Table 4 shows the

Table 4: Distribution of World's Ice Caps and Glaciers

regions	area (km^2)	volume (km^3)
The Antarctic		
East Antarctica	12,100,000	26,600,000
West Antarctica	200,000	400,000*
Other ice masses	700,000	1,400,000*
The Arctic		
Greenland	1,730,000	2,600,000
Other ice masses	140,000	280,000*
Asiatic continent	112,000	224,000*
American continent		
North America	80,000	160,000*
South America	25,000	50,000*
European continent	10,000	20,000*
New Zealand	1,000	2,000*
Africa	20	40*
New Guinea	15	30*
Total	15,100,000	31,700,000

*Assuming an average depth of 2 metres.

estimated distribution of ice caps and glaciers in the world; the total volume of ice is about 31,700,000 cubic kilometres (7,600,000 cubic miles). Assuming an average density of 0.89 for ice masses, the water equivalent of all the ice masses on earth is about 28,200,000 cubic kilometres (6,800,000 cubic miles). It can be seen that a large quantity of the ice masses, about 94 percent, is locked up in the ice of Antarctica and Greenland.

Addition to the earth's ice reservoir

When ice accumulates, water is added to the earth's ice reservoir constantly. Accumulation is predominantly due to snowfall; other processes also exist but they do not contribute so greatly to the accumulation of ice masses in the hydrologic cycle. In some environments, condensation of vapour on the ground surface in the form of frost and hoar is an important process, and hail and rime may add small amounts of ice to the surface. When the temperature of a surface layer of an ice mass is below freezing, rain falling upon the surface will melt some ice, then refreeze, adding to the accumulation.

In mountainous areas, the accumulation from snowfall is often found to be greater in depressions and low areas than on ridges or neighbouring slopes because snow is moved in by wind and avalanches. This accumulation can happen at the time of snowfall or at a later time. Some small glaciers owe their existence to the concentration of accumulation by these two processes.

During the winter season, the temperature in some regions of the world may drop below freezing, and surface water will freeze to form ice sheets. Freezing temperature may extend below the ground surface to the frost line, thus causing soil moisture to freeze and produce ice particles in the soil. In the permafrost zone, the top layer of the ground freezes in winter and thaws in summer; its thickness varies from a few centimetres to a metre or more.

Ablation of ice is a process by which water is removed from ice masses. In glaciers and ice caps this process often takes place by melting, evaporation, and calving and drifting. In temperate glaciers the temperature of the ice is close to the melting point of ice and melting is the major process of ablation. Evaporation is in general insignificant quantitatively in such regions. Glaciers that terminate in lakes or oceans lose mass by the calving of icebergs. In some high Arctic environments, substantial snow and ice are blown off by wind erosion. In some unusual cases, glaciers lose mass by the breaking off of avalanches.

Most ablation takes place on the surface of ice masses. In many temperate glaciers, melting at the surface exceeds several metres per year. Melting may also take place internally or at the base because of heat produced by friction. The heat released from the earth cannot be conducted through the ice mass, and normally it melts a small amount of ice at the base.

THE ICE CYCLE

From the modern viewpoint, snow and ice that occur in the hydrosphere may be viewed as a simple input and output subsystem, or as an ice cycle, within the much larger system of the hydrologic cycle. In the ice cycle, the growth or diminution of ice masses is a response to net differences between the input represented by accumulation and the output that occurs through ablation.

Hydrologic balance of a glacier

The hydrologic balance of an ice mass is the net quantity of water gain or loss occurring in the ice mass over a balance year, the time interval between two consecutive summer surfaces. The summer surface occurs at the time when minimum ice mass occurs at the site. Summer surface marks the beginning of the winter season of a balance year. It begins when the rate of accumulation exceeds the rate of ablation. The winter season is then followed by the summer season of the balance year when the ablation rate exceeds the accumulation rate. In a glacier, accumulation caused by snowfall may largely occur in the upstream portion, resulting in net water gain, while ablation caused by melting and evaporation occurs in the downstream portion, resulting in net water loss. The upstream accumulation zone and the downstream ablation zone are separated on the surface by the firn (névé line, the line formed by partially compacted snow forming the surface). The glacier will retain its original shape and volume if the total accumulation is equal to total ablation, or the water equivalent of ice flowing across the cross section under the firn line will equal total accumulation or total ablation. Thus, the ice cycle is said to be in equilibrium.

The ice cycle of a temperate glacier may be further examined. Starting with late spring, the glacier is covered entirely by a thick snow blanket at the melting temperature. Melted water and liquid precipitation will move through the snow blanket by slow percolation until reaching well-developed drainage channels in the solid ice below. In summer the snow blanket becomes thinner and drainage passages in the snow become well defined. Some bare ice is exposed and bears surface drainage. Thus, melted water and liquid precipitation can move through the glacier more easily than during the spring. During the fall, a thin, dense snow layer covers only part of the glacier and the remaining part is exposed, with bare ice. Water will travel very quickly from the surface to the outflow stream. When winter comes, snow accumulates and the surface layer freezes. The movement of the melted water and precipitation at the surface stops entirely. Any rain falling on the glacier will freeze and add to the accumulation. Deep within the glacier, a small amount of water drains out slowly. Finally, spring comes and the surface begins to thaw.

Melted water and rain will quickly thaw holes in the winter-chilled layer. The area between the holes will also be thawed gradually and the snow cover reaches a uniform temperature at the melting point. This condition occurs first at the lower elevations of the glacier, and the thawed zone slowly moves to higher altitudes as spring proceeds. The entire seasonal ice cycle is thus completed. During the ice cycle, the physical characteristics of the glacier change; these changes are summarized in Table 5.

Table 5: Seasonal Changes in Glacier Characteristics

season	snow-cover thickness	albedo	diurnal fluctuation in streamflow	amount of runoff	runoff due to direct precipitation
Winter	moderate to high	very high	nil	slight	all stored
Spring	highest	high	slight	moderate	delayed
Summer	moderate	moderate to low	high	high	slightly delayed
Fall*	low	low	moderate	moderate	immediate

*Before a snow blanket is formed.

The ice cycle, therefore, may be viewed as an open-ended system that constitutes a relatively long term storage element in the hydrologic cycle. Minor fluctuations of ice mass systems occur continuously in short seasonal ice cycles, but large changes are cumulative over decades and centuries. Climatic variation is mainly responsible for the ice balance, but its exact interaction with the ice masses is extremely complex and poorly understood. It is difficult to comprehend fully the magnitude of the water contained in the world's ice sheets and glaciers. If the water could feed all the rivers of the world at their present rates of discharge, it would take nearly 900 years to run off.

The actual discharges during an ice cycle, however, vary with seasonal changes as shown in Table 5. The total amount of all water discharges from the ice masses can be estimated to be roughly 3,000 cubic kilometres per year (700 cubic miles). The average cycling time of water in Alpine, piedmont, and valley glaciers varies from a few decades to centuries. Today's snowfall at the edge of an ice sheet may return to the sea tomorrow, but ice and snow in the mass of great ice sheets may remain in residence for hundreds of thousands, and perhaps millions, of years.

BIBLIOGRAPHY. VEN TE CHOW (ed.), *Handbook of Applied Hydrology: A Compendium of Water-Resources Technology* (1964), contains a wealth of useful information on virtually all areas of hydrology. It presents complete, authoritative coverage of the basic theories, principles, and required data for the study and management of water resources. O.E. MEINZER (ed.), *Hydrology: Physics of the Earth*, vol. 9 (1942), is a classic book on hydrology, containing a great deal of technical information mainly developed by U.S. hydrologists prior to 1942. Although it does not cover the latest development, the book summarizes the basic scientific principles upon which modern hydrology is based. KAZIMIERZ DEBSKI, *Continental Hydrology*, vol. 2, *Physics of Water, Atmospheric Precipitation, and Evaporation* (1966; orig. pub. in Polish, 1956), covers the following topics: physical characteristics and moving forces of water circulation; water in the atmosphere; atmospheric precipitation; variability of precipitation; evaporation from free water surfaces; and total evaporation. O.A. DROZDOV and A.S. GRIGOR'EVA, *The Hydrologic Cycle in the Atmosphere* (1965; orig. pub. in Russian, 1963); describes the results of investigations of the hydrologic cycle carried out in the Soviet Union during the 15 years prior to its publication, and various other Soviet and non-Soviet studies of the moisture balance in the atmosphere. J.L. DYSON, *The World of Ice* (1962), provides a descriptive account of the ice in the hydrologic cycle. It serves as interesting reading material for laymen as well as for scientists. D.K. TODD (ed.), *The Water Encyclopedia* (1970), is a compilation of useful factual data on water resources, including the following items: climate and precipitation; hydrologic elements; surface water; groundwater; water use; water quality and pollution control; water-resources management; agencies and organizations; and constants and conversion factors.

(V.T.C.)

Hydrologic Sciences

Scope of the hydrologic sciences

The several hydrologic sciences deal with the waters of the Earth. Hydrology is the study of the occurrence, circulation, and distribution of the waters, their chemical and physical properties, and their interaction with the environment. It embraces the hydrologic cycle that operates in the hydrosphere of the Earth, but in practice hydrology is usually confined to the waters on land and does not include the oceans and seas. Study of the latter is the principal domain of oceanography.

In the atmosphere, the study of the distribution and transportation of water is dealt with by another hydrologic science, namely, meteorology. The study of climate or the long-term meteorological effects over a region is the main concern of climatology. Topical specialization may develop sufficiently to warrant the creation of new hydrologic sciences. Hydraulics and fluid mechanics, for example, are disciplines concerned with the mechanics of water motion and transport, and cryology is often proposed as a hydrological science that treats snow and ice. In most countries the study of ice in all its aspects is termed glaciology.

Surface-water hydrology is the study of waters having a free surface. The measurement of waters on the Earth, particularly streamflow, is called hydrometry, and the description and mapping of the surface waters is the subject of hydrography.

New hydrologic sciences are proposed from time to time. In recent years, the term hydrobiology has been proposed to deal with the biological aspects of water and the term hydro-ecology to deal with the ecological and environmental aspects of the waters on the Earth. The more commonly cited hydrologic sciences and their special subjects of study may be summarized as follows:

hydrologic sciences	subject of study
hydrology	hydrologic cycle
hydraulics	mechanics of liquid water
hydrometeorology	meteorologic water
cryology	snow and ice
surface-water hydrology	surface waters
hydrography	description and mapping of surface waters with usual application to navigation
hydrometry	measurement of water, particularly streamflow
potamology	surface streams
limnology	large bodies of freshwater, such as lakes and ponds
glaciology	large bodies of solid waters, mainly glaciers, in American practice; ice, in European practice
oceanography	large bodies of salt water, such as oceans and seas
groundwater hydrology	groundwater
geohydrology	geologic aspects of hydrology
hydrogeology	hydrologic aspects of geology

Water is the most abundant substance on Earth and is the principal constituent of all living things. Water is a key factor in air-conditioning the Earth for human existence and in influencing the development of civilization. Today, water is often considered as a commodity that has economic value and as a right that is subject to legal, social, and political entanglement. The hydrologic sciences, which treat all phases of the waters on Earth, have tremendous importance to man. As the world population expands and the standard of living rises, the demand for water use and control grows sharply and becomes increasingly complex. Man must manage his water resources wisely, and the hydrologic sciences that provide a scientific understanding of water are concerned with the basic knowledge required to meet this important challenge.

Environmental and economic importance of the hydrologic sciences

Hydrologic sciences are of basic importance in the development, management, and control of water resources and thus are influential in agriculture, forestry, geography, watershed management, political science (water law and policy), economics (hydro-economics), and sociology. Practical applications include the design of hydraulic structures, water supply, waste-water disposal and treatment, irrigation, drainage, hydropower generation, flood control, navigation, land erosion and sediment control, salinity control, pollution abatement, recreational use of water, fish and wildlife preservation, insect control, and coastal works.

Moreover, changes in the distribution, circulation, temperature, or optical properties of the Earth's waters can have far-reaching effects. The ice ages, for example, are a manifestation of such effects, even though the exact cause-and-effect relationship is still uncertain. There is some cause for concern, therefore, because many unplanned modifications of the water environment are now occurring as a result of human activities. The increase of chemical fertilization with a release of nitrogen compounds into rivers and oceans is one such modification. Such activities are leading to gradual pollution of the rivers, lakes, and even coastal waters and may have detrimental effects on human welfare. The role of the hydrologic sciences is to provide solutions to such problems and guidance for wise planning and management of water resources.

A vast amount of information is available on the hydrologic sciences, but this article covers only the nature, scope, and methods of a few major hydrologic sciences, namely, hydrology, limnology, glaciology, and oceanography. Basic hydrologic knowledge per se is principally treated in related articles: RIVERS AND RIVER SYSTEMS; LAKES AND LAKE SYSTEMS; ESTUARIES; HYDROLOGIC CYCLE; WATER RESOURCES; GROUNDWATER; FRESHWATER, GEOCHEMICAL PROPERTIES OF; ICE SHEETS AND GLACIERS; OCEANS AND SEAS; WINDS AND STORMS; and CLIMATE. For further information see EARTH SCIENCES for coverage of the interaction of the hydrologic, geologic, and atmospheric sciences.

This article is divided into the following sections:

I. Hydrology
  Study of water quantity
  Study of water quality
  Studies of hydrologic interrelationships
  Hydrology as a discipline
II. Limnology
  Study of limnologic interrelationships
  Limnology as a discipline
III. Glaciology
  Methods of investigation
  Glaciology as a discipline
IV. Oceanography
  Oceanographic studies
  Oceanography as a discipline

I. Hydrology

STUDY OF WATER QUANTITY

Hydrology is concerned with the quantities of water in the hydrosphere that are distributed in several hydrologic environments. Precipitation, evapotranspiration, runoff, soil moisture, and groundwater, each of which is a component of the hydrologic cycle, will be discussed in turn in the article.

Precipitation. Precipitation is produced as a result of condensation that occurs when air is cooled to its dew-point temperature and suitable nuclei are present to initiate the process of droplet formation. A decrease in temperature to the dew point is usually accomplished by the uplift of the air.

The kinds of precipitation may be classified as follows:

type	*description*
dew	deposition on cold ground surface or vegetation canopy, typically amounting to 0.1 to 1 mm per night
hoarfrost	dew in frozen form
fog drip	deposition on vegetation and other objects from fog at rates of up to 4 mm per hour
rime	fog drip in frozen form
drizzle	liquid water droplets less than 0.5 mm in diameter at rates of 0.2 to 0.5 mm per hour
freezing drizzle	drizzle when surface temperature is below freezing
rain	liquid water droplets greater than 0.5 mm in diameter, normally 1 to 2 mm in diameter, occurring at rates of less than 2 mm per hour for light rain and more than 7 mm per hour for heavy rain
snow	precipitation of solid water in the form of branched hexagonal crystals or stars
snowflakes	aggregations of ice crystals as large as several centimetres in diameter
snow grains (granular snow)	very small, flat opaque grains of ice, or drizzle in solid form
snow pellets (groupel, or soft hail)	opaque pellets of ice 2 to 5 mm in diameter that fall in showers
sleet	melting snow or a mixture of snow and rain; in U.S. usage it is rain that freezes to pellets of ice when falling through a layer of cold air
ice pellets (small hail)	clear ice encasing a snowflake or snow pellet; equivalent to sleet in U.S. usage
hail	roughly spherical lumps of ice, 5 to 50 mm or more in diameter, showing a layered structure of opaque and clear ice in cross section

Aspects of storm rainfall

In the study of precipitation, basic information is supplied by rain gauges and climatological stations. From these data, usually on a daily basis, statistics of the average monthly and annual precipitation, the degree of seasonal and annual variability, and the number of rainy days are compiled. Invaluable as such records are, it is essential in hydrologic studies to know more about the characteristics of individual rainstorms. Four important parameters of storm rainfall are intensity, duration, frequency, and areal extent.

Rainfall intensity and duration are of vital interest to hydrologists, engineers, and conservationists in dealing with flood control, land drainage, and soil erosion. As a rule, the mean rainfall intensity decreases with the increase of duration. In many water-resources studies it is necessary to know the average period of time within which a rainfall of specified amount or intensity can be expected to occur once in a given duration. This is known as the rainfall frequency, or, technically, as the "recurrence interval." The determination of the rainfall frequency is based on statistical methods and probability theories. Rainfall frequencies varying from two to 50 years are commonly selected as criteria for the designs of urban and highway drainage structures. For very important drainage structures, higher frequencies (of 50 to 100 years) are used.

The total amount of rainfall in a storm depends on the type and scale of the precipitation and its velocity of movement. The distribution of rainfall over the area covered by a particular storm will not be uniform. The average total depth of rainfall over a storm area usually decreases with the increase of the size of the area but its intensity increases with the decrease of the duration of the rainfall.

Distribution of rainfall

Precipitation varies not only within the storm area but also over the entire world. Consequently, certain parts of the world are considered to be wet, whereas other parts are dry. Although the average annual rainfall amount for the land areas has been estimated to be 28.3 inches (71.9 centimetres), there is in fact an extreme contrast between some of the driest desert areas, such as Arica, Chile, which receives 0.02 inch (0.5 millimetre), the world's lowest average annual rainfall (the lowest recorded; there may be desert areas elsewhere that actually receive less annual rainfall, however), and Mt. Waialeale, Hawaii, which receives 460 inches (1,168 centimetres) the world's greatest average annual rainfall. Consideration of the mass transfer phenomenon within the atmosphere leads initially to a simple concept of the zonal distribution of precipitation over the Earth. Thus, in polar and subtropical regions, the general tendency is for the gradual subsidence of air from higher altitudes in the atmosphere leading to its warming and relative desiccation. The midlatitude and intertropical regions are areas of convergence disturbance and uplift at the polar and intertropical fronts, respectively. In these two zones precipitation is most likely to occur. This general concept suggests the cause of the Earth's precipitation distribution, but other factors modify it. Because evaporation from the oceans provides the major source of precipitable moisture, precipitation tends to decrease with increasing distance from the sea. Wind plays an important role as it moves the atmospheric moisture, thus increasing precipitation in the prevailing direction of air movement. Orographic conditions (*i.e.*, topographic barriers that cause uplift of air masses) and urbanization also produce noticeable effects but on a local (smaller) scale.

The study of precipitation may include investigation of cyclic, secular, seasonal, and diurnal variations and trends of precipitation. Many attempts have been made to determine the cyclic variations of precipitation from studies of annual totals. Accurate information on such variations would be extremely useful in the planning and management of water-resources projects, such as in forecasting floods, droughts, and the availability of water supply in future years. At present no generally applicable cycles of long-term precipitation have been found, but secular variations caused directly by a combination of geographical and climatological factors are believed to exist in certain parts of the world. The seasonal or diurnal pattern of precipitation regime has provided an undisputed example of a short-term cyclic variation in some areas.

The statistical probability of precipitation is often studied by assuming rainfall amounts to be random variables. In many parts of the world, there seems to be a tendency for dry weather or wet weather to occur in spells. This phenomenon is described as hydrologic persistence, and its study has been attempted by a special branch of probability theory known as the theory of stochastic processes; this will be discussed later in this article.

The potential evapotranspiration concept

Evapotranspiration. In hydrologic studies the potential evapotranspiration (PE) is a fundamentally significant concept, defined as the evapotranspiration that would occur if there were an adequate moisture supply at all times. The PE reflects the combined effects of a number of climatic factors, and information on its seasonal and annual variations can therefore provide a useful guide to the major climatic characteristics (excluding precipitation) of a given area. In areas where moisture supplies are abundant, PE can also serve as an accurate guide to detect natural water losses over the area.

Of greatest importance is the relationship between precipitation and the PE. On a global scale the relationship is commonly used by hydrologists, climatologists, and geographers to define drought and to delimit deserts.

Evapotranspiration is important, of course, in the planning of irrigation projects. The purpose of irrigation is the control of soil moisture between a lower limit that will not restrict plant growth and an upper limit that avoids waterlogging. One calculation of irrigation need is based on the concept of PE in order to determine the consumptive use of water by plants. One simplified calculation for crop water use or consumptive use has been devised by the American hydrologists H.F. Blaney and W.D. Criddle. In their scheme, the monthly consumptive use is equal to the product of a consumptive-use coefficient that depends upon (1) mean monthly temperature and (2) crop stage of growth, and a monthly consumptive-use factor that equals the product of the mean temperature in degrees Fahrenheit and the fraction of daytime hours occurring during the month. More elaborate formulas also have been proposed.

Soil moisture. Soil moisture exists in the zone of aeration below the ground surface. Depending on its concentration in the zone, soil moisture occurs in three categories. Hygroscopic water absorbed from the air forms thin films of moisture on soil-particle surfaces. The adhesive forces are very strong, and thus this water is unavailable to plants. Capillary water exists as a continuous film around the soil particles. It is held by surface tension, moved by capillary action, and is available to plants. The third type of occurrence, gravitational water, is excess soil water that drains through the soil under the action of gravity. The study of soil moisture in hydrology is extensive, and the separate disciplines of soil chemistry and soil physics have gradually evolved. Soil moisture plays a vital role in planning and design of irrigation and drainage engineering projects. It is also important in the erosion and denudation of the landscape and in the stability of earth dams and other structures made of the soil mantle. The weathering of solid rock masses into loose debris and the direct transport of material out of the soil mantle in the form of soil particles, solutes, and colloids are affected by the soil moisture present. The stability of a soil mantle on a hillside or on the slope of an earth dam depends on the shear stresses that exist within the soil mass and the shear strength to withstand these stresses. The shear stress depends on the slope, the depth, and the density of the soil mass, and the last of the three varies with the soil moisture. The shearing strength of the soil mass is derived from a cohesive element and a frictional component that depends on the soil-moisture pressure in the pores of the soil (see further EARTH MOVEMENTS ON SLOPES).

Effects on rock weathering and soil stability

Groundwater. The subsurface water that exists in the zone of saturation is called groundwater; the top of this zone is the water table. Sometimes groundwater is trapped under pressure because it is confined between layers of impervious geologic formations. Thus, the groundwater is said to be under artesian condition. When a water table exists, the groundwater pressure reacts directly to the outside atmospheric pressure, and the groundwater is said to be under water-table, or gravity, condition. (For details on the nature of groundwater and its movement, see HYDROLOGIC CYCLE; GROUNDWATER.)

In hydrologic studies a major purpose is to delineate and develop the groundwater resources. Groundwater exists in geologic formations known as aquifers and groundwater reservoirs. The aquifer may be a layer of gravel or sand, a layer of sandstone or of cavernous limestone, or even a large body of nonlayered rock that has sizable openings. It may be only a few feet thick or tens or hundreds of feet. When under artesian condition, an artesian aquifer exists. If a well is drilled into the artesian aquifer, groundwater will flow out of the well under artesian pressure, thus creating an artesian well. If the pressure is insufficient, then pumping will be necessary to bring the water to the ground surface.

Groundwater recharge

Practically all groundwater originates as surface water. When depleted by wells it is necessary to replenish or recharge the groundwater. Principal sources of natural recharge include precipitation, streamflow, lakes, and surface reservoirs. Other contributions made artificially (artificial recharge) result from excess irrigation, seepage from canals, and water purposely applied to augment groundwater supplies. Other reclaimable waters potentially useful for artificial recharge are floodwaters, industrial wastes, and domestic sewage. Several methods have been developed to recharge these waters, including water spreading; recharging through pits, excavations, wells, and shafts; and pumping to induce recharge from surface water bodies at higher elevations. The choice of a particular method is governed by local topographic, geologic, hydrologic, and soil conditions; the quantity of water to be recharged; and the ultimate water use. In special circumstances, land values, water quality, and even climate may become important factors.

Runoff. The movement of water over the surface of the Earth under the influence of gravity, in channels ranging from tiny streams to large rivers, is called runoff. Considering the hydrologic cycle over a drainage basin or watershed, runoff is a residual of the hydrologic process, because it represents the excess of precipitation over evapotranspiration when allowance is made for storage on and under the ground surface. When precipitation is spasmodic and irregular in space, time, and amount, runoff from the land surface is usually low and becomes a comparatively constant factor. This contrast between runoff and precipitation, from which the former is derived, results mainly from the storage capacity of the surface layers of the Earth, by which much of the excess precipitation is held back and released only gradually into the streams. It has been estimated that one foot of soil normally holds more water than that in the entire overlying atmospheric column. (For details on the role of runoff in the hydrologic cycle, see HYDROLOGIC CYCLE; RIVERS AND RIVER SYSTEMS.)

The rate or discharge of runoff is usually expressed as a volume per unit time. When the water discharge is plotted against the time, the plot is called a hydrograph. Analysis of the hydrograph can reveal much about the watershed characteristics that affect the disposal of precipitation and, consequently, the apportioning of surface and groundwater runoff. Hydrologic studies of runoff are important in various respects. The study of runoff over the land and in the channel is necessary for the development of land drainage and river-engineering works. A study of the short-term runoff patterns involves the analysis of flood hydrographs, flood frequencies, flood forecasting, and routing floods through the river channels. These are basic in flood-control engineering and floodplain regulation. A study of the annual runoff characteristics and long-term trends of runoff involves the analysis of river regimes; basin geomorphology and theoretical probability analyses are required for the planning and development of irrigation, waterpower, water supply, and other water-resources projects. Modern engineers and planners of such projects require a thorough understanding of the quantitative as well as qualitative nature of the runoff.

Hydrograph analyses and studies of flooding

STUDY OF WATER QUALITY

Water chemistry. Natural water is a dilute electrolytic solution of elements dissolved from the Earth's crust or washed from the atmosphere. Its ionic concentration varies from much less than 100 milligrams (one milligram equals 0.001 gram) per litre in rain, snow, hail, some bog lakes, and many mountain and tropical streams to as high as 400,000 milligrams per litre in saline lakes of closed basin and "fossil" waters associated with marine sediments.

In the chemical analysis of natural waters, constituents commonly considered are silica, iron, calcium, magnesium, sodium, potassium, bicarbonate, carbonate, sulfate, chloride, fluoride, nitrate, boron, and dissolved solids. Certain properties such as hardness, alkalinity, acidity, specific conductance (a measure of ionic concentration), and colour are also regularly investigated and reported. If there is reason to believe that other substances are present in significant quantities, they are frequently included in the chemical analysis. These may consist of aluminum, arsenic, barium, bromide, chromium, copper, iodide, lead, manganese, phosphate, selenium, strontium, and zinc. Dissolved gases, including oxygen, carbon dioxide, ammonia, and hydrogen sulfide, are measured in many waters. In studies of waters contaminated by industrial and domestic wastes, measurements may include biochemical oxygen demand (BOD, the amount of oxygen required to remove organic matter), phenol, alkyl benzene sulfonate, chlorinated hydrocarbons, and bacteria and viruses (see further FRESHWATER, GEOCHEMICAL PROPERTIES OF).

Controls of water quality. Water quality is influenced by natural factors and by the activities of man; both causes are the subject of much hydrologic study. Since the beginning of geologic time, natural processes have affected the chemical, physical, and biological characteristics of water. Winds blowing across the oceans and land surfaces transport tons of minerals to lakes and rivers over a given area and time and also introduce small quantities of dissolved solids into rainwater; these solids are later washed into rivers and lakes. Natural quality of water varies from place to place with the season of the year, with climate, and with the kinds of rocks and soils through which the water moves. After precipitation reaches the ground, water dissolves minerals from the Earth's crust, percolates through organic materials such as roots and leaves, and reacts with living things such as microscopic organisms (*e.g.*, plankton or algae). It is modified by water temperature, by soil bacteria, by evaporation, and by flora, fauna, soils, geology, and other environmental factors.

Natural influences on water quality

Living organisms control the natural water quality both in freshwater and salt water. Studies have shown that algae and moss help to separate the mineral calcite from creek water. In the early history of a lake, the water is clear and contains abundant oxygen. After a certain time, dissolved minerals, such as plant nutrients, nitrates, and phosphates, may increase. The water becomes turbid and commonly contains abundant plant growths that give off an unpleasant odour and appearance upon decay. Thus, oxygen levels decline and decomposition products accumulate. Organic matter at the lake bottom, lacking oxygen, is attacked by bacteria that release a foul-smelling gas of hydrogen sulfide. A process known as eutrophication is said to take place, indicating the forthcoming death of the lake. In some coastal areas, certain algae secrete poisons that destroy marine life. The algae contain pigment cells that change from yellow to red in such large quantities that the result is called the "red tide."

Geology, involving the kinds of rocks and their distribution, definitely affects water quality. Many springwaters are world renowned because of their distinctive geologic origin. Because of geologic differences, some streams are clear at their source but become muddy a certain distance downstream. Wells a short distance apart may yield water that differs in quality. For the same reason, lake water may be fresh or salty, may have a characteristic odour or taste, and may even have an unusual feel, as, for example, the alkaline water of Soap Lake in Washington.

To degrade the natural quality of water through man's activities is commonly described as pollution. Examples of such activities are the disposal to natural waters of industrial wastes, irrigation return flows containing salts and fertilizers, and silting of man-made reservoirs.

STUDIES OF HYDROLOGIC INTERRELATIONSHIPS

Modern advances in scientific instrumentation provide the hydrologist with better tools for studying hydrologic interrelationships or for measuring hydrologic data, determining parameters in the hydrologic cycle, and solving difficult and complicated hydrologic problems. The most important are hydrologic modelling, remote-sensing methods, nuclear techniques, and electronic computers.

Hydrologic modelling. Whereas conventional hydrologic studies are based largely on experience, judgment, empiricism, and crude assumptions, modern hydrologic investigations depend more and more on mathematical modelling. The natural hydrologic phenomena are often so complex that no exact laws have yet been discovered that can explain these phenomena completely and precisely. Before such laws can ever be found, complicated hydrologic phenomena can only be approximated essentially by simulation through the procedure of modelling.

In hydrologic modelling, the hydrologic phenomena are treated as hydrologic systems: a physical system is a system in the real world; a sequential system is a physical system that consists of input, output, and some working medium (matter, energy, or information) known as "throughput" passing through the system; and a dynamic system is a physical system that receives certain quantitative inputs and acts under given constraints to produce certain quantitative outputs. The hydrologic system can therefore be considered as a physical, sequential, dynamic system.

Hydrologic systems and mathematical simulation

Mathematical simulation of natural hydrologic systems may be achieved by means of either a lumped-system model or a distributed-system model. When the system is simulated by a lumped-system model, it is treated as a "black box." A gross representation of the black box is determined from the input and output data pertaining to the box, but no interest or concern is given to the process going on inside the box. In such models, space coordinates (position) are not important, and all parts of the system being simulated are regarded as being located at a single point in space. On the other hand, if the internal process of the model is analyzed, the system is not regarded as being considered at a single point in space, and various distributed points or areas within the internal space of the system must be simulated, thus constituting a distributed-system model.

The simulation of rainfall and runoff relationships, for example, is conventionally achieved through the use of a unit hydrograph, which is essentially a black-box model determined from historical rainfall and streamflow data.

Many mathematical models of such black-box models have been developed in recent years. Such models are all of the lumped-system type. The fundamental principles involved in this approach have not been extensively investigated theoretically or experimentally as far as the internal process of the black box is concerned. In other words, the use of a lumped-system model does not explain the basic mechanism of the hydrologic process, because it is only a simulation of the black box as a whole and offers in effect only a mechanical aid to data fitting.

By distributed-system models, the simulation of rainfall and runoff relationships as exemplified above has resort to hydrodynamic laws and principles. The distributed-system model involves more than one independent variable—that is, the space coordinates—in addition to the usual time variable. Mathematically, therefore, it can be represented by, for example, a set of partial differential equations as against ordinary differential equations for a lumped-system model.

When the mathematical equation representing the hydrologic model is nonlinear, the hydrologic system and its model are nonlinear. Otherwise, they are linear. For a linear model, such as the unit hydrograph, the output is directly proportional to the input.

Probabilistic systems and stochastic models

Furthermore, hydrology and its model are said to be deterministic if the system response at any time due to a given input is uniquely determined. The unit hydrograph is again a good example. If, on the contrary, the system response is subject to uncertain influences, the hydrologic system and its model are said to be probabilistic. In a probabilistic hydrologic system, the uncertain influence may vary according to unknown causes that are assumed to follow a probabilistic law, thus resulting in a probabilistic hydrologic model. If there is a probabilistic sequential relationship between the occurrences of the uncertain influence, the hydrologic system and its model are called stochastic. The natural hydrologic phenomena are mostly stochastic in the sense that they change with time in accordance with the law of probability, as well as with the sequential relationship between their occurrences. Because of the profoundness of the stochastic theory, research to develop mathematical stochastic models has developed only in recent years. Stochastic modelling represents the most advanced stage in hydrologic modelling.

Remote sensing. The essence of remote sensing is to acquire information about an object without keeping the measuring device in physical contact with the object. Man's eyes, ears, and nose are types of natural remote sensors, but their capabilities are surprisingly limited. Today, remote-sensing techniques of scientific invention are beginning to yield information about the world around us that would otherwise be unobtainable by our natural sensors. These techniques are developed to measure the emitted radiation or force fields of an object by means of suitable detectors sensitive to the radiation or force. In hydrology, for example, it is possible to spot diseased crops, polluted water, or the flow of hot springs with infrared cameras, to survey ice thickness and distribution with microwave detectors, and to measure soil moisture and rainfall intensity and distribution in thunderstorms by radar. These and many other potential applications have aroused great interest among hydrologists. Many remote-sensing techniques are considered extremely promising for hydrologic investigation. The most important ones involve the use of radar, special photography, and artificial satellites.

Applications of remote-sensing techniques

Radar was first introduced into hydrology to ascertain the rainfall characteristics of thunderstorms, as noted. A very short-pulse VHF radar, mounted in a ground vehicle, has been used for analyzing soil moisture, whereas high-definition radar, operating at a height of about 41,000 feet, has been investigated as a means of studying large hydrological regions and identifying drainage patterns. Its main advantages are the very wide area of coverage and the almost all-weather capability.

Special aerial photography can provide various kinds of unusual hydrological measurement. Time-lapse stereo photography has been used to determine river-flow velocities based on measurements of a floating object in the river. Coloured aerial photography permits superior interpretation for water-depth mapping as compared with black and white pictures. Infrared photography is vastly superior to standard photography in delineating a shoreline or water-course. It is also useful for the hydrothermal mapping of large bodies of water and for locating hydrothermal features such as geysers and hot springs. Infrared sensing has been used to study lake ice, and 8–14-μm infrared imagery, depicting temperature variation, has been used to locate freshwater seeps and also to study the water and energy balance by detecting areas cooled by evaporation. An airborne multispectral camera, operating in the 0.35- to 5-μm band of the visible and infrared spectrum, permits interpretative study of the vegetation, moisture content, and geological conditions of a watershed.

With rapid advances in space technology, artificial satellites can now be used as communication devices for collecting and disseminating hydrologic information. Remote sensors can be mounted on artificial satellites to detect many hydrologic phenomena and to make certain hydrologic measurements with a much broader coverage than the conventional methods of collecting point data at isolated hydrologic gauging stations.

Nuclear techniques. Because of their unique characteristics, nuclear techniques are invaluable tools for certain scientific measurements and research. Recently, the potential value of their use in hydrology has been recognized; isotopes in particular are being introduced into hydrologic research and field investigations.

Three unique properties that make radioactive isotopes particularly useful in hydrology are: penetrability of radiation, radioactive decay with time, and detectability in minute quantities. The radiation from radioactive isotopes can penetrate material in a fashion that can be correlated in some way with certain external and internal properties of the material, such as thickness, density, and composition, thereby determining these properties. Several applications of radioactive isotopes in hydrology that result from their radiation penetrability include the following: (1) measuring the thickness of snow cover; (2) measuring the variation of elevation of a riverbed during floods; (3) measuring the concentration of suspended sediment or bed load in rivers and reservoirs; (4) determining the amount and distribution of soil moisture; and (5) determining the infiltration rate of water above a root zone.

Utilization of radioactive isotopes

By radioactive decay, radioactive isotopes will produce different kinds of particles (alpha, beta, and gamma rays) at a rate that varies as an exponential function of time. This property provides a unique means for dating the age of water. Several interesting applications of this property may be mentioned, namely: (1) determination of the isotopic exchange, storage times, stratification, recent recharge, and amounts of old waters in an aquifer; (2) determination of the transient state of groundwater; and (3) study of the pattern of water balance between precipitation and river runoff.

The ability to detect minute quantities makes the radioisotope tracer excellent for application. An ideal isotope to be used as a tracer in water should travel at the same velocity as the water without any loss, and its decay and radiation properties should not affect later similar experiments nor be hazardous to the user or the environment. The adequate use of certain radioactive isotopes as tracers depends more or less on the nature of the problems being investigated. Several interesting applications that are based on this detectability property include: (1) flow measurement in canals, streams, and rivers; (2) study of the velocity and direction of movement of groundwater or hot springs; (3) determination of sediment transport and littoral (alongshore) drift; (4) study of flow processes in karst (cavernous) or fractured terrains; (5) estimation of the direct contribution of meteoric water (precipitation) to river waters; (6) study of the vertical movement of water in unsaturated soil; and (7) study of the recharge or leakage in groundwater reservoirs.

Computer technology. Modern electronic computers are noted for their high computing speed and simplified programming of solutions. Their major applications in hydrology include routine data processing, solution of equations for mathematical models that describe hydrologic systems, and control of hydrologic instrumentation and experimentation. Complicated mathematical models that cannot be analyzed by manual calculation can now be solved quickly by electronic computers. Many such hydrologic models are being solved by digital computers, but analog computers that offer the additional advantage of a quick visual response of the simulated system are particularly useful for the evaluation of groundwater resources by practicing hydrologists. The computer is built as a scale model of the aquifer and is composed of a network of electrical resistors and capacitors that simulate the hydrodynamic characteristics of the aquifer (see further GROUNDWATER).

HYDROLOGY AS A DISCIPLINE

Hydrology has as its objective the study of the interrelationship and reaction between water and its environment in the hydrologic cycle and thus embraces the investigation, analysis, and interpretation of the occurrence, circulation, distribution, and quality of water in the Earth's atmosphere, on the Earth's surface, and in the soil and rock strata. Hydrologic studies require application of mathematics, physics, and chemistry and involve principles drawn from such other disciplines as meteorology, geology, soil science, plant physiology, and hydraulics.

World organizations and global study

In recognizing that a full understanding of the hydrologic cycle requires an investigation on a global scale and that water itself is a universal problem that is common to all nations, the International Association of Scientific Hydrology (IASH) was organized in 1922. In 1972 it was renamed the International Association of Hydrological Sciences (IAHS). Beginning in 1965, more than 100 nations and many organizations, including particularly the IASH, the World Meteorological Organization, the World Health Organization, the Food and Agricultural Organization, the International Council of Scientific Unions, and the International Atomic Energy Agency, have been cooperating in the most important international program on hydrology in history—the International Hydrological Decade (IHD) under the auspices and coordination of the United Nations Educational, Scientific and Cultural Organization.

The general objective of the IHD is to benefit all of mankind by strengthening the science of hydrology through international cooperation. To implement this general objective, three basic goals have been agreed upon, namely: (1) to strengthen the scientific and technological base for water development, use, and conservation; (2) to stimulate education and training in water science and technology; and (3) to improve the ability of developing countries to cope with their own problems.

Hydrologic activities and programs can be classified into five broad categories:

1. Basic data. This category includes hydrologic benchmark basins and stations and the planning, design, and establishment of hydrologic data networks.

2. Inventories and water balances. This category includes study of the global water balance; preparation of hydrologic and hydrogeologic maps; world inventory of perennial and annual ice and snow masses; measurements of glacier variations on a worldwide basis; combined water-, ice-, and heat-balance measurements at selected representative glacier basins; gross sediment transport into the oceans; the discharge of tritium to the oceans by major rivers; and the hydrology of fractured limestones or karst terrain.

Hydrologic research topics

3. Research. This category includes study of the water balance of the Earth and its variations in time; chronological hydrology; incidence and spread of continental drought; hydrology of deltaic and coastal areas, estuaries, and coastal marine waters; relations between soil moisture and runoff; relations between excess of soil moisture, drainage, and the behaviour and yield of various plant species; genesis and physical chemistry of natural waters; effect of land use on water quality in forested, agricultural, and urban drainage basins; effects of physiographical features on precipitation; depth–duration–frequency relations of precipitation in various geographic regions; the study of water balance in connection with the evaluation of the water-regulating and water-conserving roles of forests; relations between sediment transport, streamflow, and channel morphology; prediction of sediment distribution in reservoirs; dispersion in moving groundwater; investigations on artificial recharge of groundwater; effects of variations in piezometric head (the height to which groundwater will freely rise in a well) on land subsidence; hydrology and hydrodynamics of the zone of vadose water (subsurface water that occurs above the saturated zone); evapotranspiration processes; maximum runoff from rainfall and melting snow; hydrologic consequences of irrigation and drainage projects; hydrology of forest, grassland, and arable land; ecology of water-loving vegetation; a world program for research on methods of geophysical exploration of groundwater; evaporation reduction from open surfaces; dynamics of lakes and reservoirs; applications of stable isotopes in hydrology; and water–soil relations and the degree of aridity. Many subjects of research that are meteorological in nature also could be cited.

4. Exchange of information and standardization of information. This category includes the dissemination and availability of results and data and the improvement, comparison, and standardization of hydrologic instruments and techniques.

5. Education and training of hydrologists.

In general, the IHD will promote worldwide assembly and analysis of scientific information about water, its quantity, its quality, its distribution, and its behaviour. It will achieve worldwide realization that a science of hydrology exists; that teaching, training, and research must be greatly expanded; and that many varied career opportunities are open for hydrologists and other scientists concerned with water.

II. Limnology

Limnology is the study of lakes in all their aspects. For information on the physical and chemical properties of lake waters and their circulation, biota, and basin morphology, see LAKES AND LAKE SYSTEMS. See also SWAMPS, MARSHES, AND BOGS for coverage of the basic properties and characteristics of lakes that are affected by vegetation. Discussion in this article will focus upon methods of study of some aspects of lakes and on limnology as a discipline. The study of former lakes is the science of paleolimnology. Paleolimnologic studies have been made on the basis of the analysis of sediments, pollen deposits, and fossil remains on former lake bottoms (see further POLLEN STRATIGRAPHY; VARVED DEPOSITS).

STUDY OF LIMNOLOGIC INTERRELATIONSHIPS

Lake modelling. Because of the complex nature of the numerous elements involved in a lake system, studies of the water quantity, the water quality, energy, and hydrodynamics of a lake have been made by hydrologic modelling techniques. The principle of water balance, or water budget, is the basis for modelling water quantity interrelationships in a lake. One simple water-quantity model of a lake, relating change in quantity to water inputs and outputs, may be formulated by the following mass balance equation:

Water budget of lakes

$$S = I - O + R + P - E - L \pm D,$$

in which S is the change in lake storage, I is the inflow from upstream, O is the outflow to downstream, R is the runoff from the drainage area that contributes water to the lake, P is the precipitation on the lake surface, E is the evaporation from the lake, L is the leakage, and D is the water diversion in or out of the lake. A modification of such models can serve as a tool for evaluating the response of lake level to the various parameters and for the forecasting of future lake levels. An ideal case is that of rain falling on the drainage basin and reaching the lake in a short time. If the area of the lake is small compared with the area of the drainage basin including the lake, the following model equation, relating precipitation and evaporation over the lake and its drainage basin to water level, may be written:

$$Ad = A(P - E) + (A' - A)(P' - E') - AO',$$

in which A is the area of lake, A' is the area of drainage basin including the lake, d is the mean rate of change of water level, P is the mean precipitation rate over lake surface, P' is the mean precipitation rate over rest of drainage basin, E is the mean evaporation rate over lake surface, E' is the mean evaporation rate from rest of drainage basin, and O' is the mean discharge of outflow in any channel per unit of lake area.

In a similar manner, energy- or heat-budget models of various kinds have been devised to express aspects of the thermal regimes of lakes. Analysis of the heat budget is essentially an attempt to assess the internal distribution of the annual heat input received by the lake. A classic model is one primarily concerned with the division of annual heat input between winter and summer. A more informative but more elaborate and more difficult model is the analytical heat-budget model, which is employed to determine the amounts of heat received from the sun, sky, atmosphere, environment, and influent waters and also to follow the attrition of this heat by several sources of heat loss until it is possible to determine the heat storage in the water and sediments of the lake.

Use of hydrodynamic models

Hydrodynamic models have been proposed to study surface waves, seiches, currents, and the circulation or movement of water in the lake. The development of a water-quality model is much more difficult because it would involve considerations not only of the mass and energy balances and the hydrodynamic principles but also of other physical, chemical, and biological factors. Attempts are being made, for example, to model water quality of a subregion of the Great Lakes of North America. Considerations involved in such a model include pollution inputs of various locations, types, and amounts; present and past water-use demands and water-quality standards; the physical nature of lake currents; physical, chemical, and biological transformations; transfer functions applicable to the exchange of water and material between subregions; the biological or chemical transformations, or both, describing water quality; and the mean water quality at the outlet.

Remote-sensing and sampling methods. Aerial photography and infrared and multispectral scanning are the remote-sensing techniques that have been proposed for hydrobiological investigations. They are now being considered for the studies of the Great Lakes, the Everglades (in Florida), and other lakes and swamps. Such techniques are extremely useful in detecting some hydrobiological features and identifying thermal pollution and sediment movement in shallow lakes.

Many techniques used for oceanographic studies are applicable to or can be modified for limnologic studies. Ships have been employed for the hydrographic and hydrologic investigations of the Great Lakes, for example, and nearly all the samplers designed for oceanographic purposes can be used either directly or with some modifications for limnologic sampling.

LIMNOLOGY AS A DISCIPLINE

Limnology deals with the study of more or less enclosed bodies of inland waters, such as lakes and swamps. Traditionally, it has been closely related to hydrobiology, which is concerned with the application of physics, chemistry, geology, and geography to solution of ecological problems and knowledge of the environmental conditions of living things in water. Both limnology and oceanography deal with large bodies of water, but they have definite differences. Oceanography studies the oceans and seas that cover seven-tenths of the Earth's surface, invariably contain salty water, and represent the longest continuum in both space and time.

Limnology and oceanography compared

Limnology, on the other hand, studies the inland waters that make up scarcely one-fiftieth of the Earth's surface, contain mostly freshwater except in some salt lakes, and are ephemeral bodies measured by the standards of geologic time. Because of the difference in water quality and the relatively continual change in lake environment during short intervals of geologic time, the inland waters have very restricted and special biotic communities in comparison with the sea. Hydrologically, the sea has a dominating influence on the global hydrologic cycle, but it is less affected by the land mass. The role of the inland waters in this respect is the reverse.

Limnology was recognized as one of four divisions of hydrology during the meeting of the executive committee of the International Association of Scientific Hydrology in Zürich in 1938. In the United States there is an American Society of Limnology and Oceanography, and several organizations in the United States and Canada are devoted to study of the Great Lakes, the largest body (as a whole) of freshwater in the world. Much research also has been undertaken elsewhere—for example, in the Alpine lakes, Lake Baikal, and Lake Chad, among others. Current and future limnologic studies are directed to a better understanding of lakes as systems, of the interrelationships among all factors involved, and to the relationships of lakes and swamps to man and the environment.

III. Glaciology

Glaciology is the study of ice in all its forms and modes of occurrence. It is concerned, therefore, with the physical properties, general characteristics, and formation and distribution of ice; with glacier flow and the mechanics of flow; and with the hydrologic interrelations of ice and climate. For details on these subjects, see ICE SHEETS AND GLACIERS; ICEBERGS AND PACK ICE; ICE IN RIVERS AND LAKES; PLEISTOCENE EPOCH; CLIMATE; CLIMATIC CHANGE; and HYDROLOGIC CYCLE. Discussion here will be limited to a brief exposition of some of the methods of glaciology and the nature of the discipline.

METHODS OF INVESTIGATION

Various methods of investigation have been employed in the study of glaciology. To verify the validity of the many proposed flow laws for complex stress systems of glacier flow, a borehole test applied to a real glacier provides the best approach. The satisfactory agreement between borehole measurements and laboratory results has given considerable confidence to the theory of conditions in real glaciers.

Nuclear techniques in glacier studies

Nuclear techniques also have been found useful in glaciological studies. Artificial and naturally occurring isotopes have been used to study snowpack and snowmelt runoff. The isotope data also provided insight to the mechanism of snowmelt processes. Deuterium and oxygen-18 have more depleted values in winter precipitation than in summer. These seasonal differences are marked at higher latitudes and form the basis of an important method for studying flow patterns of glaciers, as well as determining past rates of accumulation in the upper layers.

It was believed that stable isotope measurements of glacier ice could serve as an indicator of past climates. An elegant substantiation of this belief was attempted in a detailed study of an ice core 1,390 metres (4,560 feet) deep from Camp Century on the Greenland Ice Sheet. Seasonal oscillations of isotope content become difficult to identify with increase in depth of the core, however, because of diminution of the isotope gradients. This gradual obliteration of the oscillations is caused by molecular diffusion in the firn and solid ice and by progressive thinning of the deeper layers. For these reasons, dating of glaciers and ice sheets is limited to a few thousand years. Any long-term variations, however, will be preserved and will therefore reflect the average climatic conditions that obtained when that part of the core was deposited. Thus, a gradual increase of oxygen-18 concentration will correspond to a climatic warming and a decreasing isotope concentration to a climatic cooling.

In the case of the Camp Century core, the approximate ages of different core sections were obtained from a consideration of the generally accepted flow pattern in a glacier and certain assumptions concerning the controlling parameters. Long-term variations in isotope composition were related to climatic changes of the past

100,000 years. The main features of this oxygen-18 profile agreed with chronologies established on the basis of carbon-14 dated pollen, the advances and retreats of the Laurentian Ice Sheet in the Ontario–Ohio region, and part of a generalized temperature variation for surface waters of the central Caribbean.

GLACIOLOGY AS A DISCIPLINE

Modern concerns of glaciology

Glaciers have been studied scientifically for more than a century. The years since 1950, however, have seen a major advance in glaciology. Today it is a broad interdisciplinary science that includes such distinct subjects as the geographical distribution of snow, glaciers, sea ice, and permafrost; glacial and preglacial morphology of land areas; snow and glacier hydrology; ground-air exchanges of energy and mass; the physics of precipitation in the form of snow and ice; studies of rare isotopes, fallout, and micrometeorites in ice caps; and the dynamics of glaciers and ice sheets.

Glaciology, particularly the study of glacier theory, is still a confused and controversial subject because the active workers in this field are few and isolated. Furthermore, field data are very scarce. Collection of field information and measurement of real glaciers are perhaps the most important future need in this discipline. Organizations devoted to glaciological investigations are also few but usually have outstanding reputations, such as Laboratoire de Glaciologie in Grenoble, France; the U.S. Army Terrestrial Sciences Center (particularly the Cold Regions Research and Engineering Laboratory) in Hanover, New Hampshire; and the International Commission of Snow and Ice, established by the International Association of Scientific Hydrology. Much first-rate research on snow and ice has been accomplished in various institutions and laboratories in Japan and the Soviet Union.

IV. Oceanography

Scope of oceanography

Oceanography, the last of the hydrologic sciences to be discussed, is divided into four separate but related branches—physical oceanography, chemical oceanography, biological oceanography, and geologic oceanography. The latter is sometimes called marine geology. Physical oceanography is concerned with the physical properties of seawater, including the formation of sea ice, and with physical oceanic processes, particularly ocean currents and circulation, waves and tides, and ocean–atmosphere interactions. Chemical oceanography deals with the composition of seawater, the distribution of constituents, and the processes (various types of chemical reactions) that influence and control the composition of seawater. Biological oceanography deals with all aspects of plant and animal life in the sea, including food production and life cycles; and geologic oceanography treats the geologic structure, processes, and history of the ocean basins of the world.

For details on the subject matter of relevance to these several concerns, see OCEANS AND SEAS; OCEANS, DEVELOPMENT OF; OCEAN CURRENTS; WATER WAVES; TIDES; OCEAN BASINS; OCEANIC RIDGES; and MARINE SEDIMENTS. See also EARTH, PHYSIOGRAPHY OF; HYDROGRAPHIC CHARTING; and HYDROLOGIC CYCLE. Discussion in this article will be restricted largely to some of the topics and methods of oceanographic study.

OCEANOGRAPHIC STUDIES

Utilization of temperature-salinity diagrams

Salinity and temperature. When the salinity of a seawater sample is plotted against the corresponding temperature on rectangular coordinates, a temperature-salinity diagram, or TS-diagram, can be constructed. When water in a certain region of the sea possesses a definite temperature and salinity for a wide variety of conditions, it forms a continuous water mass. If the water mass is homogeneous, then the oceanographic factors in it are constant, and it is plotted as a single point on the TS-diagram. The position of the single point will not change if this homogeneous water mass is moved in any direction. Due to certain processes such as mixing, radiation, or evaporation, however, the water mass may lose its homogeneity, and its position on the diagram will change. Such changes usually occur in the surface layer down to about 150 metres (500 feet), where the water is subject to climatic influence. On the TS-diagram, lines of equal density (or any other property) can be added to supply certain instructive information about the water mass. One practical application of TS-diagrams is to enable the oceanographer to delete errors and correct them in the preparation of oceanographic data. If the data do not plot consistently on the diagram, an observational error or a faulty computation usually is indicated. Corrections can be made by comparison with similar plots for neighbouring stations.

Because the specific heat of seawater (about 0.95) is much higher than that of the land (about 0.50, on the average), the temperature variation in seawater is much less than that of the land. The temperature in the open ocean varies between about 32° C (90° F) and the freezing point −2° C (28° F), and more than half the ocean surface is warmer than 20° C (68° F). About 93 percent of the ocean volume is colder than 10° C (50° F) and 76 percent colder than 4° C (39° F).

Study of temperature variations

The horizontal variation of the surface temperature of seawater depends on many factors, including solar radiation, ocean currents, flow from rivers, evaporation, wind, and precipitation. The vertical variation in temperature may divide the ocean into several layers. The shallow surface layer usually maintains a high close-to-surface temperature that decreases very gradually with increase in depth. This layer is followed by a thermocline layer in which temperature decreases rapidly with depth. Below the thermocline layer is the deepwater layer, in which the temperature decreases gradually again with depth; at its lower end the temperature scale becomes asymptotic to the constant low temperature of the bottom-water layer—that is, it very closely approaches this low temperature without actually reaching it. The thermocline layer has a mean thickness of 200 metres (650 feet). It may be permanent and extend to more than a mile deep. It may also be shallow and vary with the seasons, thus becoming known as seasonal thermocline. The distribution of these several temperature layers is one of the principal concerns of physical oceanography.

Ocean currents. The average surface ocean currents result from heating at the tropics and cooling at the poles, which induces a general surface motion toward the poles and a depth motion toward the Equator. The motions are further modified by the effect of Earth rotation, gravity, the irregular solid boundaries of the sea, and by wind effects. In contrast to other small-scale, more or less local currents, the large-scale circulating currents transport great amounts of water.

Theory and measurement of ocean currents

The hydrodynamics of ocean currents can be described by the dynamic equation of incompressible fluid. Because of the effect of the Coriolis force (an apparent force due to the Earth's rotation; moving bodies in the Northern Hemisphere are deflected to the right and those in the Southern Hemisphere to the left) and the eddy viscosity (stresses generated by turbulence of fluid flow), the drift current in deep water decreases in velocity and changes in direction as depth increases. This phenomenon can be best illustrated by the mathematical model developed by the British oceanographer Vagn Walfrid Ekman. The average deflection of the drift current from the direction of the wind has been observed to be about 45° to the right of the wind direction, independent of latitude, as predicted by Ekman's theory.

There are numerous methods to measure ocean currents. Commonly used are two direct methods, the Eulerian and Lagrangian methods, and two indirect methods, geostrophic and electromagnetic methods.

The Eulerian method consists of mechanical or dynamical measurements of the flow past a geographically fixed point, such as an anchored ship, seabed, or any fixed man-made structures in shallow waters. The velocity of flow is determined as a function of depth and time. The flow of water can be measured by current meters or counting the rate of rotation of a free-turning propeller; by measuring the torque of an arrested propeller or rotor; by measuring the ram pressure on a plate, membrane, sphere, or Pitot orifice (an L-shaped, hollow tube); measuring the deflection of a suspended cable supporting a known drag; by measuring the change of the velocity of sound between two points a known distance apart; or by measuring the electromotive force generated by flow through a known magnetic field.

In the Lagrangian method, the trajectories of water parcels are tracked and plotted in space and time with the aid of tracers. The tracers may consist of drift bottles, radio buoys, contaminants or dye stuffs, current poles, deep drogues (devices having a large drag at the level of measurement and hanging on a small floating buoy with a fine wire), neutrally buoyant floats, and ship drift.

When fluid flow is both unaccelerated and frictionless, its motions are known as "geostrophic," and the pressure gradient, Coriolis force, and force of gravity balance one another. The currents thus developed are known as geostrophic currents, and these can be computed by mathematical theory. In oceanic regions remote from solid boundaries and the free surface of the sea, such geostrophic currents have been found to be good approximations to the actual currents.

In the electromagnetic method, ocean currents are determined from measurements of the electromagnetic effects by means of electrodes being towed by a ship. Seawater contains an abundance of highly ionized salts and is an electrolyte of relatively high conductivity. The motion of this electrolyte through the Earth's magnetic field produces electromagnetic effects that can be measured. The modern instrument used for such purposes is known as a geomagnetic electrokinetograph (usually abbreviated as GEK).

Measurements of sea level, tides, and waves

The sea surface. The position of the sea surface is represented by sea level, which is the height of the boundary between sea and air. Sea level is measured relative to a fixed reference point on land and hence is susceptible to changes in time for the following reasons: changes in the distribution of oceanographical factors, such as temperature and salinity of seawater; changes in the distribution of climatological factors, such as wind and barometric pressure; changes in the distance of the reference point from the centre of the Earth because of sudden movements in the Earth's crust, glaciation, and tide-generating forces; and changes in the long-period astronomical and pole tides.

Mean sea level is the plane about which the tide oscillates. It is determined from tidal observations by averaging the recorded hourly heights of the tide over a period of several years. Mean sea level varies with locality of observation and method of computation, and hence it has no absolute constant value. In order to simplify the computation, mean tide level is sometimes used as a substitute for mean sea level. Mean tide level is simply equal to the average of the observed high and low waters, and it is considered a poor substitute in many cases because of the appreciable influence of short-period tides. Fluctuations of sea level range from short-period oscillations of surface waves and tides to long-period secular variations.

Early theoretical studies of surface waves resulted in classic theories that deal with periodic motions of waves by assigning average values of wavelengths and directions. In recent years the randomness of sea waves has been studied by statistical analysis and measured by modern recording instruments. In such modern approaches, the variables are treated not as analytical functions but as stochastic processes, definable only in terms of probabilities. The modern approaches not only have explained some observed features, such as tidal waves, that cannot be analyzed satisfactorily by classic theories but also have been successfully applied to important engineering problems connected with the sea, such as the motions of ships and beach erosion.

Study of ocean–atmosphere interaction

Heat transport. Important thermal processes involved in the interactions between ocean and atmosphere are advective and convective processes. The advective process is the transference of heat by horizontal currents of air. The convective process is the transmission of heat by the mass movement of air or water.

In the atmosphere the heat supply is mainly from the sea surface and land, and thus atmospheric circulations depend on heating from below. In the oceans, on the other hand, heat supply is mainly from above. Because heating and cooling take place at nearly the same level, these processes cannot maintain large-scale circulations in the oceans, but they are of importance to the development of convection currents in the surface layer, to the local exchange of energy with the atmosphere, and to the slow deepwater circulation. Large-scale circulations in the oceans are mainly due to the distribution of mass in the sea and the superimposing effect of the prevailing winds.

Although some new theories have been advanced in recent years, the convective circulations in the oceans are not yet as well understood as those in the atmosphere. It is known, however, that the heat exchange between the ocean and the atmosphere follows a pattern similar to evaporation. Where the sea surface is warmer, heat is transferred from the sea to the air and is transported to great heights by eddy conductivity and by convection currents in the air. Such heat transfer is small, however, in the tropics, where radiation surplus is mainly used for evaporation.

As an ocean has an enormous heat-storage capacity, it tends to stabilize the atmospheric circulations and characteristics and thus to reduce the range of weather extremes closer to the mean than is the case on land. In general, thermal processes control oceanic climate greatly. Ocean climates are largely determined by the response of the ocean to atmospheric circulation. In turn, both ocean climate and atmospheric circulation respond to the distribution of solar heat over the Earth's surface.

Composition of seawater. The composition of seawater is not accurately known. One reason is that many parts of the ocean have not yet been sampled and analyzed. Many factors control or influence the chemical composition of seawater, including interactions with the atmosphere, runoff from the land, solubility of different materials, bacterial action, freezing and melting of sea ice, chemical reactions, and biological processes.

Residence time of elements in the sea

Chemical reactions. Different chemical elements in seawater react differently with the marine environment. Assuming the continuity of transport of the material and rapid, uniform mixing, the chemical reactions involved depend essentially on residence time—the time that is required for an element entering the ocean to be deposited in sediments on the ocean floor. It has been found that the elements with long residence times generally have very low reactivities and therefore remain in the ocean for considerable periods of time. Silicon, manganese, iron, and aluminum have low residence times and high chemical reactivities but are involved in biological activity. Their high reactivities are mainly due to their quick settlement in view of their usual volcanic origin and their oxidation and their tendency to form mineral deposits covering large portions of the ocean floor. The relative reactivities of the elements in seawater are also related to the degree of saturation of the different compounds that an element forms. The elements become less reactive when saturation is approached.

Biochemical reactions. Photosynthesis and respiration constitute the biochemical cycle that largely influences the biochemical reactions in seawater. By photosynthesis the surface waters become saturated with oxygen, while waters of intermediate depth are depleted of it due to respiration and oxidation. Oxidation is independent of light and may take place at any depth. During the growth of sea plants, nitrogen, carbon, phosphorus, and some trace elements are taken in by the plants and later released into the sea as wastes and organic decomposed products. Because of decomposition and digestion by organisms, organic materials usually do not accumulate. The nutrients in seawater can be provided by plankton. Oxidation of the plankton by anaerobic bacteria depletes oxygen in water and releases nutrients at intermediate depths. The nutrients can return to the surface photosynthetic zone only by physical circulation of the water in order to complete the biochemical cycle. The nutrient concentration also varies with the depth and is subject to seasonal changes. Study of the biochemical cycle is one of the principal concerns of chemical and biological oceanography.

Conti-nental drift and sea-floor spreading

Origin of the ocean basins. The origin of the oceanic platform has been explained by many theories. One theory is that the Earth is expanding, and thus the oceanic platform is formed by large cracks on the Earth's crust. Currently popular is the theory of continental drift, which was first proposed by the German geographer Alexander von Humboldt in the early 1800s and later modified by others. This theory explains that the continents are floating on subcrustal material and are drifting apart to create oceans by deep-seated convection currents operating within the Earth's mantle. A new theory, called sea-floor spreading, assumes that the sea floor itself is moving and that the cracks are filled with basaltic material originating within the mantle. Incorporating the old theories with earthquake studies and the broader structural features of the Earth, a more recent interpretation is termed the new global tectonics. This theory assumes that the earth's crust is composed of about 20 plates that move to create oceans and continents as rigid blocks, having oceanic ridges, deep-sea trenches, and faults as boundaries. Information obtained by deep drilling and study of magnetic anomaly patterns on the ocean floors has thus far favourably supported the sea-floor spreading theory (see further CONTINENTAL DRIFT; SEA-FLOOR SPREADING; ROCK MAGNETISM; and OCEANIC RIDGES).

Use of submersibles in oceanographic research

Modern research methods. The most important instrument for oceanographic research is the research vessel, which provides a working platform and the necessary crew and instruments at the site of investigation. Deep submergence research vessels, known as submersibles, have become popular in recent years. A submersible has many advantages over a surface vessel. The important advantages are the possibility of direct and detailed observation at various depths; independence from the sea surface, wave action, and drifting; and ease of navigation compared to surface vessels. The major disadvantage, however, is dependence on surface ships to tow or carry submersibles to the dive site. This may involve the difficulties of launching and retrieving it. Two well-known submersibles are "Aluminaut," owned by the Reynolds Metal Company of the United States, and "Alvin," owned by the U.S. Office of Naval Research and operated by Woods Hole Oceanographic Institution. Both were built in 1965.

Drilling ships, platforms, and electronic devices

The use of drilling ships in the deep sea began successfully in the early stages of the Mohole Project, an attempt to drill through the Earth's crust in the ocean. More extensive deep-sea drilling projects drilled numerous deep holes for research on major geological features in the oceans. Fixed and floating platforms are also used for research; platforms "Maud" and "Fram," for example, were frozen into the polar ice and allowed to drift with it for several years.

Other important instruments for oceanographic research include airplanes, expendable bathythermographs (instruments that record water depth and temperature; they can be towed by ships and retrieved or are automated for dropping by airplanes), various electronic devices for navigation and sounding, pingers that emit sound-pulses to position instruments, underwater cameras, underwater television, and side-looking sonar. Also, there are new types of samplers for chemical, biological, and geological oceanographic research and new bathythermograph and telemetering devices for physical oceanographic investigations.

Theoretical stochastic models are being developed to simulate oceanic processes and circulations, and remote-sensing techniques are applied to determine oceanographic information. Research methods in oceanography can therefore be said to range from the most simple (*e.g.*, drift bottles) to the most sophisticated.

OCEANOGRAPHY AS A DISCIPLINE

Oceanography is an assemblage of many sciences oriented toward a study of the Earth's oceans. Traditionally, it is subdivided into the main branches of physical, chemical, and biological oceanography, but this classification is restrictive. Today it may appropriately include marine meteorology, marine geology and geophysics, and certain branches of engineering.

Scientific inquiry about the oceans can be traced back to the ancient Greeks, and use of the ocean and its resources is of even more ancient origin. In recent decades, however, oceanographic studies have been rapidly growing, and there are many universities and research institutes where good training in oceanography is available. Among the foremost of such institutes are Scripps Institution of Oceanography in La Jolla, California; Woods Hole Oceanographic Institution in Woods Hole, Massachusetts; Lamont Geological Observatory in Palisades, New York; and Musée Océanographique de Monaco, Monte Carlo.

The scope of oceanographic research is as broad as the ocean itself. Interest in the seas and exploration of the oceans may be said to have barely begun in view of the tremendous potentials for research and development that exist. The continental shelves of the world have yet to be thoroughly and systematically explored; protein deficiencies plague millions in developing countries located near abundant fishery resources; pollution of the oceans and estuaries will increase manyfold by the year 2000; and much oil and mineral wealth has yet to be extracted from the sea. Current research is directed principally to such problems, as well as to enhancement of scientific knowledge on oceans, the exploration for ocean resources, and the betterment of oceanic environment. The next decade will be undoubtedly one of increased and more intelligent use of the ocean, and future needs should therefore include training of more oceanographers and the development of new instruments, techniques, and analytical methods for ocean exploration.

BIBLIOGRAPHY

On hydrology: V.T. CHOW (ed.), *Handbook of Applied Hydrology* (1964).

On limnology: G.E. HUTCHINSON, *A Treatise on Limnology*, 2 vol. (1957–66), the most comprehensive and authoritative work on all aspects of the subject.

On glaciology: L. LLIBOUTRY, *Traité de glaciologie*, vol. 1, *Glace, neige, hydrologie nivale* (1964), vol. 2, *Glaciers, variations du climat, sols gelés* (1965), two volumes (in French) that constitute one of the few available comprehensive, authoritative, and recent treatises on glaciology. See also works by B. KAMB, "Glaciers Geophysics," *Science*, 146:353–365 (1964), an excellent and up-to-date review article; W.S.B. PATERSON, *The Physics of Glaciers* (1969), which attempts to explain the physical principles underlying the behaviour of glaciers and ice sheets, and discusses the transformation of snow and ice, the mass balance of a glacier, energy exchange at a glacier surface, measurements relating to glacier flow, glacier flow theories of ice deformation and basal sliding, the flow of ice sheets, distribution of temperature in glaciers and ice sheets, the response of a glacier to changes in mass balance, and glaciers and climate; and R.P. SHARP, *Glaciers* (1960), an excellent account of glacier structures, flow, and mass budget, made easily understandable for the nonspecialist.

On oceanography: P.K. WEYL, *Oceanography: An Introduction to the Marine Environment* (1970); a popular textbook on oceanography including subjects on the Earth as a heat engine, the earth beneath the sea, the salt of the sea, life in the sea, and the marine environment; M. SEARS (ed.), *Oceanography* (1961), many papers relating to oceans; H.U. SVERDRUP, M.W. JOHNSON, and R.H. FLEMING, *The Oceans: Their Physics, Chemistry, and General Biology* (1942), a classic textbook on oceanography of advanced level; D.A. ROSS, *Introduction to Oceanography* (1970), an up-to-date elementary textbook on the subject that contains a treatment of the origin of the Earth, the ocean, and life, a history of oceanography, instruments and techniques, chemical oceanography, biological oceanography, physical oceanography, marine geology and geophysics, and resources of the ocean; J.J. MYERS, C.H. HOLM, and R.F. MCALLISTER (eds.), *Handbook of Ocean and Underwater Engineering* (1969), a volume containing one section on basic oceanography, one section on the basic hydrodynamics of oceans, one section on wind and wave loads, and nine other sections on ocean engineering; A. DEFANT, *Physical Oceanography*, 2 vol. (1961), the most comprehensive treatise on the subject.

(V.T.C.)

Hymenoptera

The members of the order Hymenoptera comprise the third largest and perhaps the most beneficial to man of all insect groups. More than 110,000 species have been described, including ants, bees, ichneumons, chalcids, sawflies, wasps, and lesser known types. Except in the polar regions, they are abundant in most habitats, particularly in tropical and subtropical regions.

Collectively, the Hymenoptera are most important to man as pollinators of wild and cultivated flowering plants, as parasites of destructive insects, and as makers of honey. The Hymenoptera are divided into two suborders: Symphyta (mainly sawflies and horntails) and Apocrita (wasps, ants, bees, and most parasitic forms).

The order includes the best known of the social insects —bees and ants. Most species, however, are solitary in habit. Hymenopterans may be parasitic or nonparasitic; carnivorous, phytophagous, or omnivorous.

By courtesy of (elm sawfly, wheat stem sawfly) U.S. Department of Agriculture; (fig wasp) California Agricultural Experiment Station; (braconid) Connecticut Agricultural Experiment Station; from (horntail) *Invertebrate Identification Manual* by Richard A. Pimentel, © 1967 by Litton Educational Publishing, Inc., reprinted by permission of Van Nostrand Reinhold Company; (others) *An Introduction to the Study of Insects*, revised edition, by Donald J. Borror and Dwight M. DeLong, © 1964 by Holt, Rinehart and Winston, Inc., © 1954 by Donald J. Borror and Dwight M. DeLong, reprinted by permission of Holt, Rinehart and Winston, Inc.

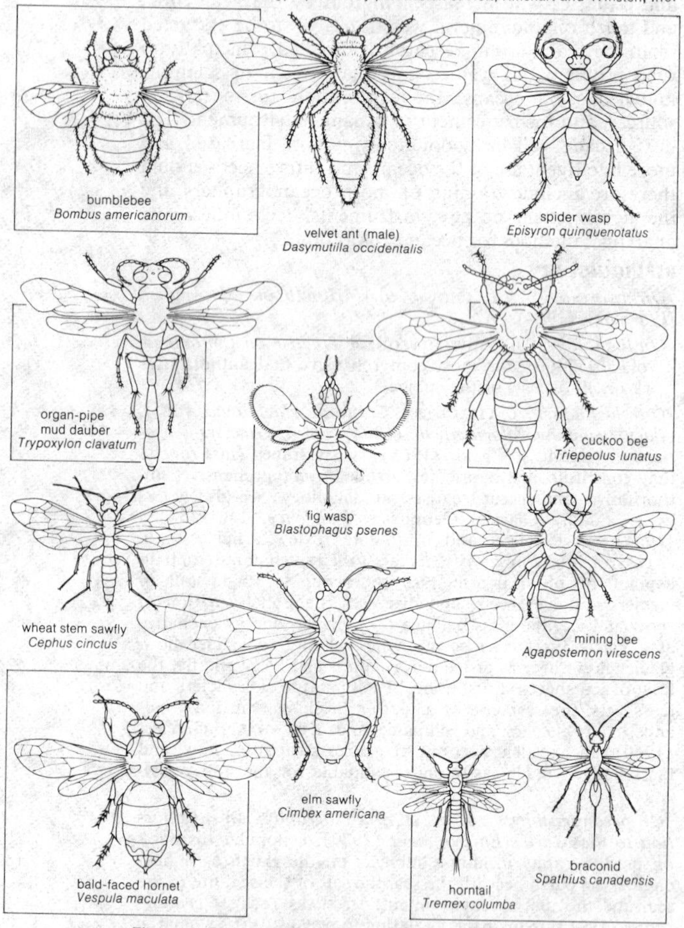

Figure 1: Representative Hymenoptera.

GENERAL FEATURES

Hymenopterans are chiefly small to medium-sized insects, usually with four membranous wings and a narrow waist that sets off the abdomen from the thorax, or body midregion. The mouthparts are of the biting type or of the biting–sucking type. In the higher evolutionary forms —bees, for example—mouthparts are modified into a sucking apparatus. The ovipositor, or egg-laying organ in the female, is often very long and may be modified for piercing, sawing, or stinging. Metamorphosis is complete —*i.e.*, the insect develops through four distinct stages: egg, larva, pupa, and adult. Sex is usually determined by whether or not an egg is fertilized; fertilized eggs develop into females; unfertilized ones become males.

Hymenoptera display an array of interesting behavioral characteristics, particularly in social species. The dancelike movements of honeybees communicate information from one individual to another about the location, distance, quantity, and quality of a particular food source; such movements have been carefully studied by the German entomologist Karl von Frisch. Trophallaxis, or the mutual exchange of food between larvae and adults of bees, ants, and wasps, has been of special interest to hymenopterists. Hyperparasitism—the parasitic habit of one species upon another parasitic species—has also attracted attention. Polyembryony, the development of many individuals (as many as 1,000) from a single egg, is an unusual phenomenon occurring in some members of the families Chalcididae and Proctotrupidae. Parthenogenesis (production of young by females that are not fertilized by males) also occurs in some forms.

Honeydew

Certain ants are remarkable for their relationship with insects that provide so-called honeydew or other sweet fluids. Among these cooperating insects are scale insects, aphids, leafhoppers, rove beetles, and the caterpillars (larvae) of many butterflies (Lepidoptera). The so-called honey ant (*Myrmecocystus* in the United States, *Plagiolepis* in Africa) has in the nest a division of worker ants known as repletes, which are fed sugary secretions; as a consequence of high food intake, the abdomens of repletes swell into globules up to one centimetre (about 0.4 inch) in diameter. Ants that obtain sweet fluids from the caterpillars of blue butterflies (Lycaenidae) reciprocate by allowing the caterpillars to devour ant larvae.

Hymenoptera, even those equipped with a sting, are sought as food by other animals. Skunks, badgers, field mice, shrews, and other animals attack bee nests for the insects as well as for the honey. The larvae of the wax moth (*Galleria mellonella*) live in bee nests, where they eat beeswax, thus damaging the nest. The cuckoo bee (Anthophorinae), a close relative of the bumblebee, lays its eggs in bumblebee nests, where the larvae are cared for and nourished by bumblebee workers.

Size range and diversity of structure. Hymenopterans range in size from the smallest fairyflies (Mymaridae), which are about 0.21 millimetre (about 0.008 inch) in length, to the largest of the Pelecinidae, which may exceed five centimetres (about two inches) in length. Most members of the order, however, are less than 2.5 centimetres (1 inch) long.

Principal differences in structure within the order include the presence or absence of wings (when present, there are two pairs); the presence or absence of a "waist"; modifications of the ovipositor; and adaptations of mouthparts for specific eating habits. Polymorphism—*i.e.*, the occurrence of two or more forms of a species—is highly developed in some of the social Hymenoptera. A honeybee colony, for example, contains at least one queen, plus workers and drones; each form is structurally and physiologically different from the others.

Distribution and abundance. Bees and wasps, as the most significant agents for the pollination of flowers, are found virtually everywhere that flowering plants occur. Social species may live in colonies of as many as 1,000,000 individuals. Ants are mostly heat-loving insects and are consequently most numerous in tropical and subtropical regions, both in numbers and in species. The number of ant species in arctic or Alpine regions is extremely small. The group appears to be absent over great areas north of the Arctic Circle.

Importance. The honeybee has been valued since pre-Christian times for its honey and beeswax. Beekeeping in modern times has become a lucrative and highly developed enterprise (see BEEKEEPING). Royal jelly, produced by honeybee workers, has enjoyed some popularity as a cosmetic, although its beneficial properties in this respect have not been satisfactorily demonstrated.

Beneficial parasites

Certain parasitic forms are valuable control agents against insect pests. Notable among these are the parasitic wood wasps, parasitic on wood-boring beetles; braconids, parasitic on the European corn borer, other Lepidoptera, and wood-boring beetles; ichneumons, parasitic on various Lepidoptera and wood-boring beetles; eulophids, parasitic on scale insects; pteromalids, parasitic on several crop pests; chalcids and trichogrammatids, parasitic on a variety of orchard pests; and tiphiids, parasitic on the Japanese beetle. Fig insects (Agaonidae) are valuable as the only pollinators of the Smyrna fig, an important crop in the Western United States.

Relatively few Hymenoptera species are serious economic pests. Chief among these, however, are the wheat-stem sawfly (Cephidae); some seed chalcids, also pests of wheat; the larch sawfly (*Pristiphora erichsonii*), which destroyed much of the larch forests in Britain and North America late in the 19th century; and the European spruce sawfly (*Gilphinia*), once a serious pest in North America. In order to control the European spruce sawfly, parasitic wasps were introduced from Europe.

The fire ant (*Solenopsis saevissima*), introduced into the United States from South America, feeds on young plants and seeds and is known to attack young mammals. The destructive habit of legionary ants, or army ants (Dorylinae), is of particular importance in South America. Armies of as many as 1,500,000 such insects destroy almost all animal life they encounter. Leaf-cutting ants (*Atta*) are serious pests, especially in Brazil, where they may ravage extensive plantings of cultivated plants overnight. These insects are eaten locally in South America.

NATURAL HISTORY

Reproduction. The ovary of the queen bee is composed of several hundred ovarioles, each of which contains about 60 eggs and so-called nutrition cells. The so-called spermatheca, a sperm reservoir that collects sperm from the male in the course of several matings, connects with the oviduct, through which eggs are carried to the outside. The sperm can remain alive and viable in the fluid medium of the spermatheca for several years.

Facultative sex determination

When an egg passes down the oviduct, it may or may not be fertilized by emerging sperm, according to the "discretion" of the female. Fertilization occurs if the female relaxes a muscular ring around the sperm duct, thus allowing the duct to open and sperm to pass through. Since unfertilized eggs result in males and fertilized eggs result in females, the queen determines the sex of the offspring by relaxing or closing the muscular ring.

In addition to this so-called facultative sex determination, hymenopteran reproduction is often remarkable in other respects. An extreme and pronounced dimorphism, for example, often exists between the two sexes. Some male and female hymenopterans once, in fact, were thought to represent different species. The consequence of such extreme difference is that the two sexes, with markedly different ways of life, also have different tasks in the insect community. As a rule, only the female cares for the brood; the male lives only briefly, just long enough to mate. This dimorphism also involves the senses. Female bees, for instance, are sensitive to yellow, blue-green, blue, and ultraviolet light. The drones (males), however, are blind to yellow but are particularly sensitive to ultraviolet light. The yellow colour of many flowers is of no significance to the drones since they cannot feed themselves. Sunlight, however, which contains much ultraviolet light, is important in orienting the insect during the mating flight.

Parthenogenesis

Parthenogenesis, which occurs in many insect orders, is particularly common in the Hymenoptera; it occurs in three forms: arrhenotoky, thelytoky, and deuterotoky. In arrhenotoky, male honeybees are produced from unfertilized eggs laid by mated (impregnated) females or by so-called second, or supplementary, queen bees, which have not been impregnated. In thelytoky, which occurs in many species of the suborder Symphyta, unimpregnated females produce males. In deuterotoky, unimpregnated females of some Symphyta species produce females as well as males. The occurrence of these forms is not always mutually exclusive; it has been found in *Apis*, for example, that about 1 percent of the eggs laid by second queen bees may be female.

Parthenogenetic reproduction in Hymenoptera often occurs in a cycle of alternate generations. In chalcids, the first generation, consisting of males and females, produces a second generation of females, which lay unfertilized eggs; from these are produced both males and females, thus repeating the first generation. In some gall wasps (Cynipidae) no males have yet been observed. The females of these wasps invariably produce thelytokous females.

The first generation of the braconid *Microtonus brevicollis* is parthenogenetic and parasitizes the adult form of the beetle *Haltica amphelophaga*. The second generation, however, lives in the larvae of the same beetle, and the females are impregnated by males. The occurrence of parthenogenesis is determined by a nutritional or hormonal factor in the larva of the host. The mode of reproduction is also determined by the number of chromosomes (*i.e.*, cell structures that contain hereditary information) in the egg.

Polyembryony

Polyembryony, the development of more than one individual from a single egg, occurs in numerous parasitic Hymenoptera, including chalcids, encyrtids, proctotrupoids, braconids, and dryinids. In this type of reproduction, the embryo divides into several separate, identical parts at an early stage; each part then develops into an individual insect. In *Litomatix truncatellus*, which is parasitic on the larvae of the noctuid moth *Plusia gamma*, about 1,000 embryos develop from one egg. The offspring from one egg are all male or all female; as a rule, several eggs are laid at one time, so that both sexes will occur in one brood. It is believed that polyembryony is controlled by internal factors, either genetic or chemical, a view supported by the fact that in some species (Platygasteridae) only part of a brood may occur polyembryonically.

Life cycle. *Solitary forms.* The solitary wasps, of which there are about 20,000 species, usually build nests or cells, which they provision with permanently paralyzed insects or spiders. One egg is laid in each cell and the body of the paralyzed host provides all the nutriment needed by the developing larva. Some solitary wasps nest in woody or pithy stems; others dig tunnels in the soil; still others, the mason or potter wasps, construct nests of mud, which are sometimes vaselike or juglike and may be found attached to twigs or other objects.

Sawflies, which are phytophagous, lay their eggs in incisions in plants, cut by the sawlike blades of the ovipositor. Species of several genera, notably *Pontania*, induce the growth of galls on willows. In many species of sawflies in which males are unknown, parthenogenesis occurs.

The spider wasps (Pompilidae) usually construct single cells in the ground, in rotten wood, or in rock crevices and provision them with paralyzed spiders. The thread-waisted wasps (Sphecidae) have diverse nesting habits. Most of them nest in the ground and use leafhoppers, treehoppers, cicadas, stinkbugs, bees, winged ants, beetles, or caterpillars as food for the young, each species or group confining itself to one type of prey. Mud daubers (*Sceliphron*, *Chalybion*) build small nests of mud, often in attics, outbuildings, or eaves, and store them with the bodies of paralyzed spiders.

The females of the superfamily Ichneumonoidea deposit their eggs in or on the larvae or pupae (rarely eggs or adults) of the host species; the legless, maggot-like larvae that hatch from these eggs feed on the body fats and fluids of the host until fully grown. At this time, the larvae usually spin silken cocoons, within which they pupate and from which the adult parasites eventually emerge. Those species parasitizing exposed hosts usually develop as internal parasites; those attacking hosts concealed in wood burrows, plant stems, cocoons, or leaf mines feed externally. In the case of internal parasites, the hosts feed and behave normally until shortly before the parasitic larvae have completed their development; the hosts of the external feeders are paralyzed by the female parasites. In most cases, one parasitic larva completes its development within or upon its host; in some species, however, many larvae develop in one host.

Adults of ichneumon flies feed principally on honeydew secreted by aphids and related insects or on host juices that exude from punctures made by the ovipositor. Most cuckoo wasps (Chrysididae) lay their eggs in the nests of solitary wasps or bees. Among the exceptions is an African species that is parasitic on the tsetse fly. Tiphiidae and Scoliidae are mostly parasites of beetle grubs that live in the soil. The female wasp digs into the soil to locate the grub, stings and paralyzes it, and deposits an egg on it. The wasp larva lives on the outside of the grub.

Solitary bees

Most species of the superfamily Apoidea are solitary bees; that is, each female makes her own nest (usually a burrow in the ground) and provisions it. Among such bees there are no castes (worker, queen). The mother bee constructs cells, each of which is an enclosed space provided with a supply of pollen and honey, lays an egg in each cell, then closes it, and goes on to build and provision another.

Most solitary bees are short-lived as adults. Some species may be in flight only a few weeks, having spent the rest of the year in their cells as eggs, larvae, pupae, and young adults. Other species have several generations yearly, so that adults may be found more or less continually. In temperate climates, solitary bees usually pass the winter in their cells, either as mature larvae (prepupae) or as young adults.

Several families of bees have evolved species that are called parasitic because they lay their eggs in cells of various working bees. The young larva, which usually has a large head and large jaws, destroys the egg or young larva of the host, then eats the provisions of the host. Such bees not only lack the scopa (*i.e.*, pollen-collecting apparatus) and other structures associated with collecting and carrying pollen but also lack the various structures of the jaws and legs that other species use for making nests.

Social forms. In several families of Hymenoptera the larvae are completely dependent upon the continuous care of the adults. The colony is a family community of which every insect is an integral unit. Apart from the community he cannot properly function or survive. The essential work in the society—namely, nest building, feeding and tending the brood, and defense of the nest—is performed by the female workers. The fertile female, the queen, performs only one task: egg laying. The workers can be differentiated morphologically and physiologically as soldiers, outside workers, inside workers, and nest builders. The males play no part in everyday nest activities. They live only for a short time at a specific time of year, occur in limited numbers, and are virtual parasites of the colony that must feed them.

Conditions of social behaviour

The activities of certain solitary bees of the subfamily Halictinae are helpful in understanding certain aspects of the evolution of the highly organized hymenopteran societies. The females of *Halictus quadricinctus* survive the hatching of their own offspring. Mother and daughter stay together in the same nest, which consists of single brood cells; thus, although each female takes care of her own cells, they build and defend the nest together. In *Augochloropsis sparsalis* there is a further development: the females of one nest stay together for one summer, and a division of labour occurs. Some of the young females return, still unmated, from the nuptial flight; they then take charge of the gathering of pollen and nectar and further building of the nest and are called worker bees. The mated females merely deposit eggs.

From an illustration by James Gordon Irving from *Zoology*, a Golden Science Guide; Copyright 1958 by Western Publishing Company, Inc.

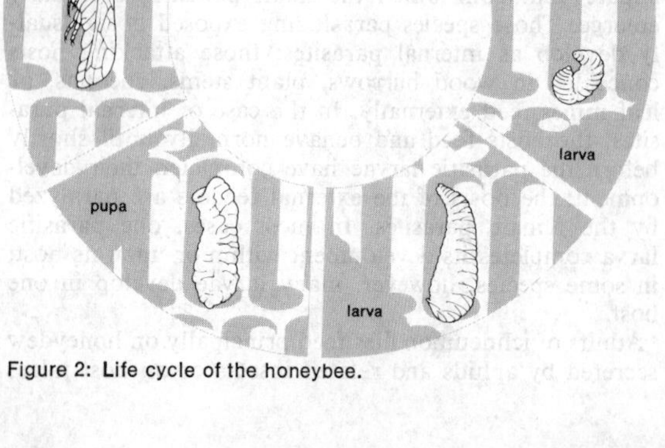

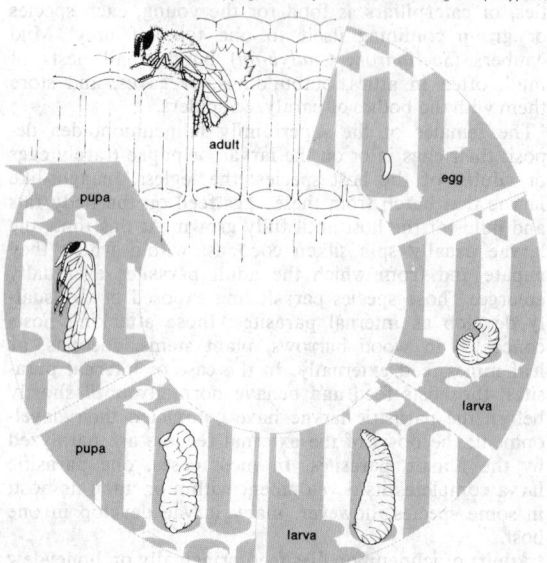

Figure 2: Life cycle of the honeybee.

The social behaviour of *Halictus* (*Evylaeus*) *malachurus* has advanced another step; morphological differences are apparent between the ovipositing female and the assisting females. The latter are poorly fed as larvae; they are, as a result, smaller and their sexual organs are poorly developed. In the bumblebee colony, different castes are clearly established. Social companionship and division of labour have become "obligatory": although the mated queen can build a nest independently and raise the first worker bees herself, she needs the assistance of workers to help rear sexually mature bees.

Similar preliminary stages to a social organization are found in the Vespidae. The female *Stenogaster depressigaster* passes several generations in the communal nest, and the daughters build their own cells and care for their own offspring. In the case of *Belenogaster*, however, whose nests include about 60 cells, the females not only feed their own brood but also indiscriminately feed all larvae present. Trophallaxis, or exchange of food between workers and larvae, is a further development.

The first evolutionary step toward a division of labour occurs in *Polybia*. Some female *Polybia* only lay eggs; the gonads of the assisting females are poorly developed. These females take charge of repair and construction, larvae care, and food gathering. They thus are useful in the society, even though they produce no offspring. This society lasts at least one summer and possibly as long as several years before it dissolves, and young sexually mature insects establish a new nest in spring.

"Immortality" of colony

The life of the honeybee colony is potentially endless. Because the queen's honey-collecting apparatus and her pharyngeal glands and wax glands are degenerated, she is incapable of building a nest or feeding and tending the brood. The continued survival of the colony results from the fact that young queens replace the old. After their nuptial flight young queens return to the home nest. If, during the spring, many offspring develop, the colony population greatly increases, and the number of cells in the comb for developing young is no longer adequate. The colony then divides by swarming, during which the old queen leaves the nest with about half of the worker bees, and the old nest is relinquished to a newly hatched queen. The swarm finds a new nesting place and builds new combs. To make the task easier, all the departing workers are provided with honey.

For nest building the Polistinae (paper wasps) and Vespinae (*e.g.*, yellow jackets) use paperlike coverings, which they construct by gnawing wood particles from structures—such as fences, telephone poles, and barn doors—then kneading them together with saliva to form a little ball. After returning to the nest, insects roll the balls into layers of paper-thin cell walls. Vespinae also build the outer nest covering in several layers to help modulate the interior temperature, the air between the layers of paper serving as insulation. Interior warmth is produced by the body heat of the larvae and by the constant contraction of the muscles of the adults. This agitation, like human shivering, generates heat; as a result, the temperature of the hive is raised. If the nest becomes overheated, drops of water are carried in. Temperature regulation of the nest is so precise that on warm days a constant temperature of 35° C (95° F) can be maintained. An equally precise temperature regulation occurs in the hive of the honeybee.

All ant species are social in habit. The virgin queen ant, who is usually winged, mates in flight with only one male. During the flight he transfers to her seminal receptacle all the sperm she will require for the rest of her life—

which may be as long as 15 years. Each fertilized queen is immediately capable of establishing or taking over a nest. After the mating flight has ended, she first seeks a place to raise her brood; then her wings drop off, and the bulky wing muscles degenerate. The substances composing the muscle tissue are processed into nutritive materials.

As soon as the wings have fallen the ovaries become functional, and egg laying begins. In primitive species the queen leaves the nest and forages for food for the larvae. In more advanced forms, the queen rarely leaves the nest. She feeds so-called nutrition eggs or other food stores within her own body to the first brood. The larvae that survive in the nest develop into dwarf workers, which forage outside the nest for food to nourish additional larvae.

A few ant species (*e.g.*, *Atta*) have developed colonies that live for long periods, one queen succeeding another. In *Eciton* the young queens, which are wingless, mate in the nest and are dependent upon the help of the workers as the nest is being built.

Division of labour. The degree of social organization in a Hymenoptera colony is most evident in the division of labour. In honeybee colonies the division of labour is achieved in an especially interesting manner. Tasks are assigned according to age. The first day after the bee's emergence as an adult, the first tasks of the female worker are to carry out wastes, to clean the cells, and to line them with a disinfectant secretion preparatory to deposition of the egg. About three days later, this young bee advances to brood nursing—*i.e.*, she provides the older larvae with honey and pollen. On the sixth day she also nurses the young larvae with specific larval food from her pharyngeal glands. After about ten days more the bee becomes active in building, secreting wax and using it to make the comb. Soon afterward, she makes her first orientation flight outside the hive. About the twentieth day she begins serving as an entrance guard; finally she becomes a collector bee, remaining at this job until her death. This activity sequence parallels certain physiological changes in the bee. The pharyngeal glands start to secrete about the third or fourth day. The wax glands become active about the tenth day. By the time the bee moves to service outside the hive, the pharyngeal glands as well as the wax glands have degenerated.

The life of a worker bee

In the division of labour among some ant forms highly specialized types of polymorphism have been developed. The *Cryptocercus* ants, for example, make nests in hollow stems of plants, then bore a circular entrance that remains under constant surveillance by special guards whose heads are modified into pluglike structures that fit the entrance. Each guard is relieved after several hours and another guard takes its place. Nest members who wish to enter indicate that they are members by means of a special movement of the antenna. Entrance guards are useless for other tasks. Repletes (see above *General features*) are a special worker caste of the honey ant. When food is plentiful, these workers are fed so much that the size of the abdomen is greatly increased. Unable to walk, they hang as living honey jugs from the ceiling of the nest, to be used as a food source when fresh food is scarce.

Social parasitism. The very close relationship between insects that are social parasites of the Hymenoptera and their hosts is made possible by their highly differentiated behaviour and by a special secretion of the parasite. The beetles *Lomechusa* and *Atemeles* (Staphylinidae) enter unmolested into the nests of ants, such as *Formica* and *Myrmica*, and are fed by the hosts. The beetle larvae are adopted and reared together with the ant brood. The adults and larvae of the beetle pacify their hosts by means of the secretion, which induces the ants to care for them.

Communication. The highly integrated activities of the Hymenoptera colony require sophisticated methods of passing information among its members. The so-called dance of the honeybee is perhaps the most remarkable demonstration of methods of communication in insects.

After a bee has discovered a new source of food, she returns fully loaded to the comb, delivers nectar and pollen, and notifies the other bees about the new food source before returning to the field, communicating information about the location and quality of the food source by means of various dancelike movements. Information about the plant species is conveyed by the odour of the flower, which adheres to the bee's body. The other bees sense this information through their antennae. But information about the quality and quantity of the food source is conveyed by the liveliness and duration of the dance movements of the bee. If the food source is unusually rich and of high quality, certain sounds are also made to convey this information. The location of the food source is indicated by the rhythm of the dance and by the orientation of the axis of the tail with respect to gravity. If the food source is near the hive, a "round" dance is performed. A "tail-wagging" dance indicates that

The bee dance

From K. Von Frisch, *Bienenfibel*

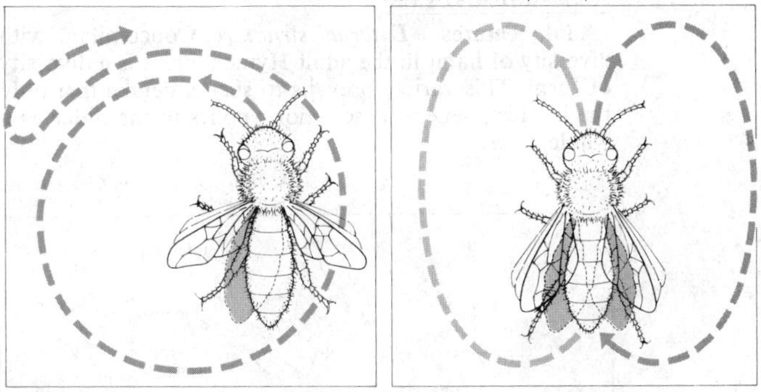

Figure 3: *Dance movements of the honeybee.*
(Left) round dance and (Right) tail-wagging dance of the honeybee.

the food source is more than 80 metres (260 feet) away. This dance transmits precise information about direction as well as distance. The number of dance cycles performed by the bee in a certain length of time is inversely related to the distance of the food source. Thus, about 10 cycles are performed every 15 seconds for a food source 100 metres (330 feet) away, but only one cycle is made in that period if the food source is 10,000 metres (33,000 feet) away. The bee measures the distance in terms of how much energy she expends in travelling to the food source. The sun and gravity are used in conveying directional information. During the flight to the food source the bee determines the angle between the line of flight and the sun. The angle to the vertical at which she then dances on the vertical face of the honeycomb describes the angle between the line of flight to the food source and a line drawn in the direction of the sun. An upward tail-wagging run means: "The flight is toward the sun." A downward run means: "The flight is away from the sun." A run 45° to the left indicates that the source is 45° to the left of the sun. Because the position of the sun changes during the day, the dance angle must also change in the course of the day; and this actually occurs. If the sun is concealed behind the clouds or behind some obstruction such as a mountain or a group of trees, the bee analyzes the pattern of polarized light coming from the sky. If only a small opening of sky appears between the clouds, it reveals to the bee's eye a typical pattern that travels along with the sun. A particular intensity of polarized light is generated toward the earth's surface from every point in the sky. The sun's position is determined by virtue of the bee's sensitivity to polarization differences.

The tail-wagging dance is also performed when the swarm is searching for a new dwelling. When a swarm accompanies its queen from the hive, it gathers first in the immediate neighbourhood of the mother hive. Scouts fly out in all directions looking for a suitable nesting place. When a suitable site is found, the scouts return to the cluster and announce the site by means of the dance, and the swarm then moves en masse.

Ecology. As the principal insect pollinators of flowering plants, the Hymenoptera have played a vital ecological role ever since the two groups evolved. The mutual dependency of many species of bees and wasps, on the one hand, and flowering plants, on the other, is firmly established. Indeed, many plants cannot reproduce without the helpful intervention of a particular insect species, most often a hymenopteran (see POLLINATION).

Parasitic control of insect populations

Parasitism, which occurs among most families of Hymenoptera, is usually apparent to none but the interested student; yet, the ecological significance of parasitism within the order might well overshadow that of pollination. Hymenoptera, the most prevalent and successful of insect parasites, exert a profound, if subtle, control over populations of other insects and certain other arthropods—groups that might otherwise overpopulate and thus upset their particular ecosystem. Man has utilized this control mechanism to his own advantage by importing, breeding, and maintaining many species of Hymenoptera parasites that prey upon insect pests.

FORM AND FUNCTION

Adult features. *External structure.* Concomitant with diversity of habit in the adult Hymenoptera is a diversity of form. This variety prevails to such a degree that only the briefest, general description applies to the order as a whole.

From H. Weber, *Grundriss der Insektenkunde*, 4th ed.; Gustav Fischer Verlag, Stuttgart

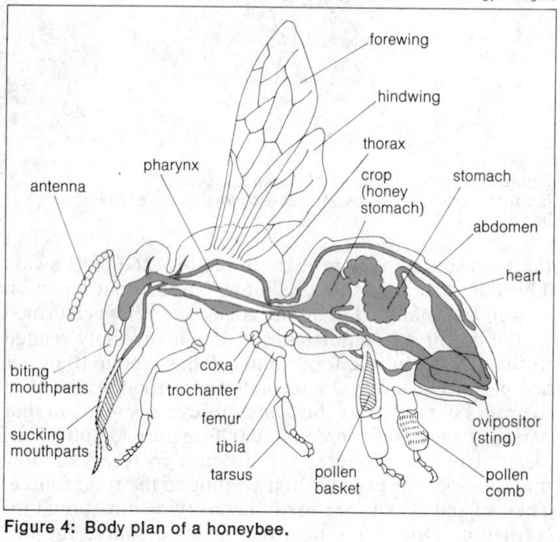

Figure 4: Body plan of a honeybee.

As in all adult insects, the segmented body consists of three primary body regions: head, thorax, and abdomen. In most forms a narrow constriction at the anterior (front) end of the abdomen separates that section markedly from the thorax. Two pairs of membranous wings are usually present. The vein pattern in the wings is usually reduced, and, in some forms, veins are entirely absent. The hindwings, noticeably smaller than the forewings, are interlocked with the latter by tiny hooklets on the anterior margin. In certain solitary wasps, particularly the wasp family called velvet ants (Mutillidae), the females are wingless, and worker ants lack wings. Winglessness also occurs in scattered genera of ichneumons and chalcids—usually only in females, sometimes in both sexes, but rarely in the males alone.

The mouthparts are usually modified for biting or for biting and sucking. The compound eyes (*i.e.*, consisting of many mosaic-like facets) are large. There are usually three ocelli, or simple eyes, arranged in a triangle on the top of the head. The antennae vary greatly in form. Rarely are they shorter than the head is wide. Usually they are moderately long, sometimes longer than the body, and composed of many segments. Often the basal segment, or scape, is greatly elongated; sometimes the segments near the tip are modified into a club. Sometimes the segments are branched. The leg is nearly always characterized by five segments, of which the fifth is the tarsus, or "foot." The abdomen of the female has an ovipositor at the tip. In the sawflies, the ovipositor is modified into a sawlike tool used for making slits in the leaves or stems of plants in which the eggs are deposited, but in all other Hymenoptera it is modified for stinging or piercing.

Internal structure. The form of the digestive system in Hymenoptera is relatively uniform throughout the order. In ants, an infrabuccal chamber located under the mouth has as its apparent purpose the trapping of indigestible particles that have been ingested along with food. The solid residue is regurgitated as a pellet.

The crop, or honey stomach

In stinging forms the esophagus enlarges near the stomach into a crop, or honey stomach, which serves as a reservoir for liquids to be later regurgitated. In honey ant repletes, the crop may be greatly distended. In honeybees, it may contain as much as 75 milligrams (0.003 ounce) of nectar—about one-third the insect's total weight. In bees and wasps, the stomach, or ventriculus, is the largest part of the digestive system; in most ants, solitary wasps, and other forms, however, it is quite small.

The two pairs of salivary glands are well developed, particularly in bees. One pair is found in the head, the other in the thorax; the ducts leading from them unite to form a single canal that passes into the pharynx. Drones and queen bees also have a mass of salivary gland cells in the head near the ocelli. Worker bees have one pair of pharyngeal glands that produce food, especially royal jelly, for the young larvae. Larvae that develop into workers are fed secretion from the pharyngeal glands only during the first three days after hatching from the egg. Afterward this food is mixed with pollen and honey. The pharyngeal glands are rudimentary in drones and absent in queens.

The function of the mandibular glands, opening near the inner angle of the mandible, is not fully understood. In gall wasps, however, their secretion is known to cause an abnormal growth of cells in leaves. Among social forms, this gland in the queen produces the substance that inhibits ovary development in workers and another that attracts males during her mating flight.

The so-called Nassonow gland, opening on the dorsal side of the abdomen, produces a substance that is used to mark the entrance to the bee hive as well as food sources away from the hive. Honeybees, bumblebees, stingless bees, and many solitary bees have wax glands on the sternites (ventral body plates). The wax is used in the construction of combs—*i.e.*, of brood cells and cells for the storage of pollen and honey.

Features of immature stages. *Egg and larva.* The eggs of parasitic forms are often attached to a surface by means of a pedicel, or stalk. In some forms, the pedicel may be five or six times the length of the egg itself.

The larva typically has a distinct head region, three thoracic segments, and usually nine or ten abdominal segments. In the suborder Symphyta, the larvae are usually caterpillar-like. The head covering is especially tough and the mouthparts powerfully developed. There are usually three pairs of legs on the thorax and six or eight on the abdomen. Symphyta larvae that are wood borers or stem borers have no abdominal legs and the thoracic legs are smaller than those of nonborers.

With rare exceptions larvae of the suborder Apocrita have no legs and are maggot-like in form. The head covering is softer and thinner than in the Symphyta. In parasitic forms, the head is often greatly reduced and partially withdrawn into the prothorax, or anterior part of the thorax. Sense organs appear to be poorly developed. There are no ocelli. Antennae are absent or very small. The mandibles are toothlike, sickle-like, or spine-like. In most Apocrita larvae the stomach is a blind sac until the final larval stage, when it opens into the intestine. The larvae of stinging forms (Aculeata) generally have ten pairs of spiracles, or breathing pores; in parasitic forms nine pairs are usually present.

Pupa. In the Apocrita, the final stage, the prepupa, begins to show certain adult features—*e.g.*, adult wings and legs. The prothoracic segment has begun to distend because of the growing head. The first abdominal segment, or propodium, becomes part of the thorax. The pupa is exarate; *i.e.*, the developing adult appendages (legs and wings) are separate from the body rather than molded into its surface.

The cocoon

A cocoon is usually formed. It may be parchment-like in texture or made of soil particles. In stinging forms, it is usually a thin, silken lining within the larval cell. Certain ants form no cocoon whatever.

Special adaptations. A great variety of structural adaptations have evolved in hymenopterans. Several are of particular interest. In worker bees hairs on the tarsi of the forelegs are used to brush pollen from flowers. The tarsi of the forelegs and middle legs are used to brush pollen from the hairs of the body of the bee. During the flight from one blossom to another, the collected pollen is passed to the pollen-carrying organs, which vary among different kinds of bees.

Some primitive bees (*e.g.*, in the families Colletidae and Halictidae) have masses of long hairs on the basal segments (coxae, trochanters, femurs) of the hind legs and on the undersurface of the abdomen. These hairs constitute the scopa, or pollen-bearing structure. In many colletids and halictids, the scopa is limited to the hind legs. In two subfamilies, Panurginae and Anthophorinae, the scopa is enlarged on the fourth segment (tibiae) of the hind legs and reduced or absent on the abdomen and on the basal leg segments. In the social bees, the scopa is limited to the outer sides of the hind tibiae, where it consists of long hairs surrounding a smooth area, the entire structure being called a pollen basket, or corbicula. In leaf-cutting bees (Megachilidae), the scopa is limited to the underside of the abdomen. In some colletids (Hyaleinae), the scopa is absent, and the pollen, mixed with nectar, is carried to the nest in the crop (anterior end of the digestive tract).

Special senses. Reproduction, the search for food, and, in the case of social species, coordinated group activity require highly developed sensory and orientative capability. In these respects the Hymenoptera are the most advanced of the insects.

Optical. It has been demonstrated that the eye of the bee is sensitive to ultraviolet radiation. It is blind to red light, however. White flowers, which only partially reflect ultraviolet as a rule, appear coloured to a bee. Certain colour combinations, while invisible to the human eye, are not only visible but also may be of special interest to bees. In response to certain colour combinations, they instinctively extend the proboscis (feeding organ) into the flower for nectar.

Some flowers that appear entirely yellow to the human eye reflect ultraviolet from the outer ends of the petals. Only the inner part, then, appears yellow to the bee, directing it to the nectar source.

The facetted compound eye of the insect is apparently unable to perceive forms in sharp outline, and it seems to be the patterns of flowers that attract bees rather than their geometric shapes. In addition, striking landmarks serve for orientation from the hive to the food source.

Chemical. Recognition of a member of the same species and society and discovery of a mate and of the nest are largely determined by smell. Guards at the beehive entrance test every bee who seeks to enter to determine, by smell, if she belongs to the colony. Each colony has its specific odour.

Scent marks

Ants use scent marks, which they place on their pathways. They are thus able to find their way back to the nest and direct other colony members to a food source. When danger threatens, ants, wasps, and bees secrete an alarm substance. This marks the place of danger and notifies other colony members to be on the alert.

During the nuptial flight of the bees, the queen announces her presence to the drones by releasing a substance from her mandibular gland. If this secretion is obtained experimentally and sent aloft by means of a balloon, a swarm of drones will gather around it. A queen bee constantly identifies herself in the hive by means of the so-called queen substance, which also originates from the mandibular gland. This secretion, passed by certain workers in minute portions to all hive inmates, inhibits ovary development. It is also perceived by smelling and controls certain types of behaviour. As long as the odour is present in the hive, the bees are unable to produce new queen cells. As soon as the queen disappears or is ill, with the consequence that the substance is no longer produced, substitute queens are immediately bred from young larvae. The sense of smell is also essential to many parasitic forms in their search for a host. Some parasites can detect, chemically, whether another parasite has already laid an egg in an intended host. If such is the case, no egg will be deposited by the second visitor.

Mechanical. Nest building and mutual communication are aided in numerous ways by mechanical means of orientation. Wasp and bee nests, which have horizontal and vertical combs, as well as ant nests are designed with respect to gravity. Highly developed gravity organs have been found in bees and ants. Hair tufts on the neck and in the leg joints sense the response of the various body parts to gravity. In this way the individual parts of the body assist the organs of balance, and the brain is informed of each change in position. In ants the hair tufts on the basal antennae segment also are used for the perception of gravity.

PALEONTOLOGY AND CLASSIFICATION

Evolution. According to S.I. Malyshev, a Soviet entomologist, the first hymenopterans appeared early in the Mesozoic Era (about 225,000,000 years ago)—about the same time as the first butterflies, moths, and flies. It is his thesis that the Hymenoptera derived from the so-called Eumecoptera—ancestors of the modern scorpion fly (order Mecoptera), the first insects to undergo complete metamorphosis. Another expert fixes the appearance of the first Hymenoptera in the middle of the Jurassic Period (150,000,000 years ago). So-called protohymenopterans, found in Permian beds (250,000,000 years old) in Kansas, have been regarded by some paleoentomologists as ancestral to the modern order. These resembled modern sawflies in having forewings and hindwings of about equal size and in lacking marginal hooklets for joining the two pairs.

True sawflies (Tenthredinoidea) are also extant from the Jurassic Period. Because of the many longitudinal veins in the wings of these forms, they were believed to share a common origin with cockroaches, which have wings that exhibit a similar vein pattern.

Many fossil ants are known from the Early Tertiary Period (60,000,000 years ago), both from Europe and North America. Some of them have been assigned to living genera. Males, females, and workers were already clearly differentiated in ants at that time.

Appearance of stinging forms

The aculeates, or stinging Hymenoptera, were one of the most recent large groups of insects to evolve. By the Tertiary Period both parasitic forms and aculeates had become abundant. The first bees, according to the fossil record, appeared in the Miocene Epoch (26,000,000 years ago). These were leaf-cutting bees (*Lithargus*). Since many of the flowering plants depend upon bees for pollination, it is believed that such plants and bees evolved at about the same time.

Classification. *Annotated classification.* Some disagreement on the taxonomic structure of the order Hymenoptera exists among systematists. For many years it was customary to separate the suborder Apocrita into two subdivisions: the stinging forms (Aculeata) and the parasitic forms (Parasitica). So many exceptions to such a dichotomy were encountered, however, that it has been generally discredited. Biologically, the basis for such a separation is slim. Many forms assigned to the Parasitica are phytophagous, and a number of the Aculeata are parasites. In the generic, or nontaxonomic, sense the term aculeate still applies to the stinging forms.

The classification given below is based on that of Borror and DeLong (1964), which, in turn, is essentially that of Muesebeck *et al.* (1951) and Krombein *et al.* (1958). It covers 71 families, of which 28 are relatively scarce.

ORDER HYMENOPTERA (chalcids, ichneumons, sawflies, ants, wasps, and bees)

One of the largest insect orders; over 110,000 described species; size range from about 0.21 mm (0.008 in.) to about 5 cm (2 in.) in length; usually 4 membranous wings, hind pair smaller than front pair; wings with relatively few veins; mouthparts modified for chewing or for chewing and sucking;

in some forms, especially bees, certain mouthparts (labium and maxillae) form a structure for sucking liquid food; antennae usually with 10 or more segments; in higher forms the ovipositor is modified into a sting; complete metamorphosis; larvae usually maggot-like (*i.e.*, legless); compound eyes large, usually 3 simple eyes (ocelli) present; worldwide in many types of habitat; many beneficial to man, including those that pollinate flowers, make honey and beeswax, or parasitize insect pests; many forms have a complex social organization.

Suborder Symphyta (sawflies and horntails)

The oldest hymenopterans, Jurassic to present; all fliers. Larvae mostly plant eaters, usually caterpillar-like, with variable number of legs; some serious pests of trees and shrubs; in adults, thorax joined broadly to abdomen; ovipositor well-developed.

Superfamily Megalodontoidea (primitive sawflies)

A rather scarce group.

Family Xyelidae (xyelid sawflies). Mostly less than 10 mm long; ovipositor long to very long; larvae feed on hickory, on elm, and on pine flowers.

Family Pamphiliidae (web-spinning and leaf-rolling sawflies). Stout-bodied; usually shorter than 15 mm; ovipositor short. Larvae sometimes gregarious (living in groups) in rolled leaves or webs.

Superfamily Tenthredinoidea (sawflies)

Ovipositor sawlike in shape and function.

Family Pergidae (pergid sawflies). Antennae six-segmented; larvae eat oak and hickory leaves.

Family Argidae (argid sawflies). Stout-bodied; more than 400 species, distributed worldwide; mostly black or dark; larvae feed on various trees and herbs.

Family Cimbicidae (cimbicid sawflies). Stout, often large and bumblebee-like; antennae clubbed; larvae often partly curled and covered with waxy powder.

Family Diprionidae (conifer sawflies). Includes serious pests of conifers; 13 or more antennal segments.

Family Tenthredinidae (typical sawflies). About 4,000 known species; adults wasplike, often brightly coloured; usually shorter than 20 mm; larvae feed chiefly on leaves of trees and shrubs, some highly destructive.

Superfamily Siricoidea (horntails and wood wasps)

Mostly medium to large insects.

Family Syntexidae (cedar-wood wasps). In United States represented by 1 California species; larvae eat wood of incense cedar.

Family Siricidae (horntails). Usually 2.5 cm or more in length; often black and yellow or metallic blue; female with long ovipositor; larvae wood borers, usually in trees past their prime.

Family Xiphydriidae (wood wasps). About 12–20 mm long; larvae are borers in dead and decaying deciduous trees (those that annually lose leaves).

Family Orussidae (parasitic wood wasps). A small, rare group; larvae parasitic on metallic wood-boring beetles (Buprestidae).

Superfamily Cephoidea (stem sawflies)

Contains one family, Cephidae.

Family Cephidae (stem sawflies). Slender insects; larvae live in stems of grasses (including commercial grains) and berry plants; sometimes highly destructive; wheat-stem sawfly (*Cephus cinctus*) important wheat pest in Western U.S.

Suborder Apocrita

Abdomen and thorax separated by narrow "waist"; ovipositor adapted for piercing or stinging; many species with complex social organization; many forms carnivorous; larvae usually without legs, often parasitic; some species parthenogenetic.

Superfamily Ichneumonoidea (parasitic hymenopterans)

Wasplike in appearance but seldom sting.

Family Stephanidae (stephanids). Rare insects parasitic on wood-boring beetles; about 100 species.

Family Braconidae (braconids). A large group; some forms highly beneficial to man by being parasitic on insect pests; mostly less than 15 mm long; many pupate in silk cocoons outside host's body.

Family Ichneumonidae (ichneumons). One of the largest of all insect families, about 4,000–5,000 species; hosts of these parasites include other insects, spiders, false scorpions; adults vary in size, colour, shape; many resemble slender wasps; largest about 3.7 cm (about 1.5 in.) long; ovipositor may be twice as long as body and used to penetrate host's tunnel in wood.

Superfamily Chalcoidea (chalcids)

A large, important group; chiefly found on flowers and foliage.

Family Mymaridae (fairyflies). Mostly less than 1 mm long; smallest about 0.21 mm; all are parasites of eggs.

Family Trichogrammatidae (trichogrammatids). About 0.3–1 mm long; egg parasites.

Family Eulophidae (eulophids). A large group; adults 1–3 mm long; often with brilliant metallic colours; parasites on many crop pests.

Family Elasmidae (elasmids). A small but widely distributed group; small and black; parasites on moths, butterflies, or on parasites of Lepidoptera.

Family Thysanidae (thysanids). Small, robust insects parasitic on scale insects, whiteflies (Homoptera), or other chalcids.

Family Eutrichosomatidae (eutrichosomatids). A small group parasitic on snout beetles (Curculionidae).

Family Tanaostigmatidae (tanaostigmatids). Snout-beetle parasites.

Family Encyrtidae (encyrtids). A large, widespread group, mostly 1–2 mm long; mostly parasitic on aphids, scale insects, whiteflies.

Family Eupelmidae (eupelmids). A large group of parasites with wide host range, including Lepidoptera, beetles, spiders.

Family Eucharitidae (eucharitids). Rather uncommon, medium-sized insects, usually black or metallic blue or green; mostly parasitic on ant pupae.

Family Perilampidae (perilampids). Stout-bodied insects, often green or black; mostly hyperparasitic on Diptera and Hymenoptera that parasitize caterpillars.

Family Agaonidae (fig insects). The Smyrna fig is pollinated only by fig insects; includes species with a remarkable degree of sexual dimorphism.

Family Torymidae (torymids). Rather slender, metallic green. Length 2–4 mm; ovipositor long; includes parasites as well as plant-eating species.

Family Ormyridae (ormyrids). A small group similar to torymids, but with short ovipositor.

Family Pteromalidae (pteromalids). Largest group in superfamily; mostly black, metallic green, or bronze; parasitic, with wide range of hosts including crop pests.

Family Eurytomidae (eurytomids, seed chalcids). Some parasitic, some phytophagous forms; some produce gall on grain stems; some live in bee or wasp nests; others parasitize Orthoptera eggs.

Family Chalcidectidae (chalcidectids). Mostly 2–7 mm long; parasitic on Lepidoptera, Diptera, Coleoptera, Hymenoptera.

Family Chalcididae (chalcidids). Two to 7 mm long; parasitic on various Lepidoptera, Diptera, Coleoptera.

Family Leucospidae (leucospids). Rather rare; usually black and yellow; parasites of wasps and bees.

Superfamily Cynipoidea (gall wasps and relatives)

Mostly small or minute gall-forming insects; usually black; some parasitic.

Family Ibaliidae (ibaliids). Mostly 7–16 mm long; uncommon; parasites on horntails.

Family Liopteridae (liopterids). Few species; rather large; rare.

Family Figitidae (figitids). Parasitic on pupae of Diptera and lacewings (Neuroptera).

Family Cynipidae (mostly gall wasps). The gall wasps proper comprise a single subfamily, Cynipinae, which includes most of the family; gall wasps are gall makers or inquilines (*i.e.*, living in a gall but not feeding on it).

Superfamily Proctotrupoidea (parasitic hymenopterans)

All species parasitic on immature forms of other insects.

Family Evaniidae (ensign wasps). A widely distributed group; all parasites of cockroach egg capsules; mostly 10–15 mm long; abdomen held high, thus the name ensign.

Family Gasteruptiidae (gasteruptids). Slender insects with ovipositor about same length as body; black, sometimes with red abdomen; rather scarce; parasites of solitary wasps and bees.

Family Pelecinidae (pelecinids). Only 1 species in North America, *Pelecinus polyturator*, the female of which is about 5 cm long or more; parasitic on June-beetle larvae.

Family Vanhorniidae (vanhorniids). In North America only 1 species, parasitic on larvae of false click beetles.

Family Roproniidae (roproniids). Includes 3 North American species, all rare.

Family Heloridae (helorids). In North America only 1 species, *Helorus paradoxus*, about 4 mm long, black; parasitic on lacewing larvae.

Family Proctotrupidae (proctotrupids). Mostly 3–6 mm long; parasitic on beetle larvae.

Family Ceraphronidae (ceraphronids). A rather large group; parasitic on braconids or chalcids that are parasitic on aphids or scale insects.

Family Diapriidae (diapriids). Small black insects mostly parasitic on Diptera.

Family Scelionidae (scelionids). Small insects parasitic on insect or spider eggs; some used to combat crop pests.

Family Platygasteridae (platygasterids). Minute black insects; largest group in the superfamily; parasitic on gall midges, including the Hessian fly, a serious wheat pest.

Superfamily Bethyloidea (parasitic hymenopterans)

All rare except cuckoo wasps (Chrysididae).

Family Chrysididae (cuckoo wasps). Brilliant metallic colour, green, red, or blue; widely distributed; mostly less than 12 mm long; mostly parasites of wasp or bee larvae.

Family Bethylidae (bethylids). Rare.

Family Sclerogibbidae (sclerogibbids). Rare.

Family Dryinidae (dryinids). Rare; most species exhibit marked sexual dimorphism.

Family Trigonalidae (trigonalids). Rare.

Superfamily Scolioidea (parasitic wasps and ants)

Some families very similar to those of superfamily Vespoidea and are placed there by some authorities.

Family Tiphiidae (tiphiid wasps). Medium-sized, black, hairy wasps; many parasitic on scarab beetles, including the destructive Japanese beetle.

Family Sierolomorphidae (sierolomorphid wasps). Rare.

Family Mutillidae (velvet ants). So called because the females are wingless, antlike, and covered with short, dense hairs; mostly brightly coloured; mostly parasitic on larvae and pupae of wasps and bees.

Family Rhopalosomatidae (rhopalosomatid wasps). Rare; parasitic on crickets.

Family Scoliidae (scoliid wasps). Large, hairy, black wasps often with a yellow band or bands on abdomen; parasites of scarab-beetle larvae.

Family Sapygidae (sapygid wasps). Rare; parasitic on leaf-cutting bees.

Family Formicidae (ants). A large familiar group; worldwide distribution, but most common in tropics and subtropics; more than 5,000 species known; all social in habit; a few parasitic; some extreme polymorphism.

Superfamily Vespoidea (vespoid wasps)

Adults usually feed on nectar or sap; larvae eat spiders, other insects; antennae usually 12- or 13-segmented.

Family Vespidae (paper wasps, potter wasps, and relatives). Solitary as well as social; includes the well-known yellow jackets and hornets; a widespread group including some large species; the queen of *Vespula ducalis* of Himalaya region reaches 4 cm in length and more than 8 cm in wingspread.

Family Pompilidae (spider wasps). Distribution nearly worldwide; mostly dark-coloured, with dusky wings; usually 12–25 mm long; some 75 mm long; larvae of most species feed on spiders.

Superfamily Sphecoidea (sphecoid wasps)

All species solitary.

Family Ampulicidae (ampulicids). Small, black, rather rare.

Family Sphecidae (sphecid wasps). A large group; adults most often found in flowers; most nest in wood, earth burrows, or in cells of mud.

Superfamily Apoidea (bees)

Distribution nearly worldwide; differ from most wasps in that larvae are usually fed pollen and honey rather than animal food; maxillae and labium form a "tongue" through which nectar is sucked.

Family Colletidae (plasterer bees, yellow-faced bees). A primitive group; plasterer bees are earth burrowers; hairy, moderate in size; yellow-faced bees are small, nearly hairless, nest in crevices, plant stems, or in the earth.

Family Adrenidae (mining bees). Nest in the ground; a large, widely distributed group.

Family Halictidae (mining bees). Usually nest in the ground; often important in plant pollination; small to medium in size; often metallic in colour.

Family Melittidae (melittids). Rare; similar in habit to Andrenidae.

Family Megachilidae (leaf-cutting bees). Medium-sized, stout insects; cut pieces from leaves to line cells in nest; some parasitic; includes so-called sweat bees that are attracted by human perspiration.

Family Apidae (mining bees, digger bees, cuckoo bees, carpenter bees, bumblebees, honeybees). Social as well as solitary; important in flower pollination; the honeybee, *Apis mellifera* in particular, is one of the few domesticated insects.

Critical appraisal. Among systematists in the United States the number of families assigned to the Hymenoptera is relatively moderate. European authorities tend to assign few families to the group (less than 20 according to some), while those of South America tend to assign more. As further information is gained about the behaviour, physiology, and biochemistry of the Hymenoptera, it is probable that comparative studies will reveal unsuspected relationships within the order. As the fossil record also reveals new facts, it is inevitable that additional refinements to the present taxonomic scheme will occur.

BIBLIOGRAPHY

Insects, general: D.J. BORROR and D.M. DELONG, *An Introduction to the Study of Insects*, rev. ed., pp. 517–605 (1964); A.D. IMMS, *A General Textbook of Entomology*, 9th ed. entirely rev. by O.W. RICHARDS and R.G. DAVIES, pp. 674–750 (1957).

Hymenoptera, general: K.V. KROMBEIN *et al.*, *Hymenoptera of America North of Mexico* (1958).

Hymenoptera, evolution: S.I. MALYSHEV, *Genesis of the Hymenoptera and the Phases of Their Evolution* (1968; orig. pub. in Russian, 1966).

Social insects, general: C.D. and M.H. MICHENER, *American Social Insects* (1951); D.W. MORLEY, *The Evolution of an Insect Society* (1954); W.M. WHEELER, *The Social Insects: Their Origin and Evolution* (1928).

Hymenoptera, specific taxonomic groups: C.H. ANDREWES, *The Lives of Wasps and Bees* (1969); W.S. CREIGHTON, *The Ants of North America* (1950); H.E. EVANS, *The Comparative Ethology and Evolution of the Sand Wasps* (1966) and *Wasp Farm* (1963); M. LINDAUER, *Communication Among Social Bees*, 3rd ed. (1971); T.B. MITCHELL, *Bees of the Eastern United States*, 2 vol. (1960–62); C.R. RIBBANDS, *The Behaviour and Social Life of Honeybees* (1953); K. VON FRISCH, *The Dance Language and Orientation of Bees* (1967); W.M. WHEELER, *Ants: Their Structure, Development and Behaviour* (1910).

(M.Li.)

Hypnosis

The term hypnosis was coined in the 1840s by James Braid, a Scottish surgeon; it stems from the Greek *hypnos* ("sleep") and refers to a sleeplike state that nevertheless permits a wide range of behavioral responses to stimulation. The hypnotized individual appears to heed only the communications of the hypnotist. He seems to respond in an uncritical, automatic fashion, ignoring all aspects of the environment other than those made relevant by the hypnotist. Apparently with no will of his own, he sees, feels, smells, and tastes in accordance with the suggestions in apparent contradiction to the stimuli that impinge upon him. Even memory and awareness of self may be altered by suggestion, and the effects of the suggestions may be extended (posthypnotically) into subsequent waking activity.

Induction

The following descriptive account indicates what typically occurs in a hypnotic encounter. The person to be hypnotized (subject) is invited to relax in comfort and to fix his gaze on some object. The hypnotist continues to suggest, usually in a quiet, low voice, that relaxation will increase and that the subject's eyes will grow tired. Soon the eyes do show the normal signs of fatigue, and it is suggested that they will close. The subject will probably allow his eyes to close and then begin to show signs of profound relaxation such as limpness and regular breathing. The hypnotist now makes suggestions, typically in vivid, concrete terms; thus the subject may be told that his hand is so heavy that he cannot lift it but that he should try. The subject responds, often seeming quite puzzled by his inability to raise the arm. The hypnotist then tells him that it really does not matter, and he need not try any longer, that he is relaxing untroubled except for a mosquito buzzing around and landing on his forehead. The subject probably will grimace and may attempt to brush away or swat the imaginary insect. Relaxation is restored by the suggestion that the mosquito is flying away. It next may be suggested that as the insect departs the subject will totally forget what has happened this year, and last year, and the year before, back to (say) ten years ago. Shortly thereafter, the subject is invited to open his eyes, to walk about, and to engage in conversation. Asked the date, he may give some day a decade past;

questioned about the recent news, he probably will describe political or social events of that time.

The session might be concluded by telling the subject that he is returning to the present time and that, on

Awakening

awakening at the count of ten, he will remember nothing of what has just happened until he is asked to relax and to recall everything. It is also suggested that, after the subject wakes, he will remove his wristwatch when he sees the hypnotist signal (*e.g.*, by folding his arms). When he opens his eyes, the subject may act as if he suddenly finds himself in a strange place but seems to feel comfortable. Asked what has just occurred, he may say that he must have just dozed off; he cannot account for the period of hypnosis. If events which occurred during that time are described, he may deny that they did. Yet, when he sees the hypnotist fold his arms, he absent-mindedly takes off his watch. Asked why, he may rationalize by winding it and return it to his wrist. When the hypnotist later folds his arms, the subject again slips off his watch but may seem embarrassed by his own behaviour; he may begin to suspect that his actions have something to do with the hypnosis. Finally the subject may be asked to relax and, as the hypnotist counts to five, to recall everything that went on since he first was hypnotized. At the count the subject's expression usually will reveal a dawning awareness of the forgotten events. He may now describe his puzzling inability to lift his arm and his annoyance at the mosquito. He may also mention the awakening of memory as if part had been dissociated from awareness and then had suddenly become accessible and, further, his disappointment at knowing where he was and what he was doing.

In general, when a subject is hypnotized, he seems to accept as real the distortions of perception and memory suggested by the hypnotist, even though they surprise him. Activities such as grimacing at an invisible mosquito, quite unremarkable in themselves, strike the observer as strange because they imply the occurrence of perceptual experiences that are not usually brought about by simple assertion. Since, however, subjects characteristically report their experiences to others in much the same way as to the hypnotist, their behaviour cannot be explained as conscious playacting. In addition to responses explicitly suggested, subjects tend to show deep relaxation, regular breathing, passivity, and relative immunity to distractions.

HISTORY

Hypnotic techniques have been used since antiquity; healing practices by priests of ancient Egypt and Greece are striking examples. Trancelike behaviour attributed to "spirit possession" has played a role in Christianity, Judaism, and in many primitive religions. Miraculous powers ascribed to witches and the arts of faith healing throughout the ages are probably related to hypnosis.

Mesmer

The "discovery" of hypnosis in Europe is generally credited to Franz Anton Mesmer (1734–1815), an Austrian physician working in France at the time of the American Revolution. He found that some ailing people were benefitted by passing magnets over their bodies. Participants in his group séances sat around an open tub from which magnetized metal bars protruded; some would develop a "crisis" (a kind of convulsive fit), lapse into apparent sleep, and awaken cured or much improved. Mesmer later found that magnets were not crucial; it often seemed sufficient to touch the person or even to touch (or "magnetize") water before the sufferer drank it. Mesmer concluded that he was gifted with "animal magnetism," a kind of "fluid" that he could store and transfer to others to heal them. A follower of Mesmer, the nobleman Chastenet de Puységur, "magnetized" a tree on his estate, at which his peasants would obtain relief from their ailments. By 1780 he had found that the "mesmeric crisis" was unnecessary and that he could influence a mesmerized person just by talking to him. He, in short, used hypnosis much as it is used today.

The notoriety that followed Mesmer's spectacular therapeutic claims led to the appointment in Paris of an investigating commission that included the American diplomat Benjamin Franklin and the French chemist Antoine-Laurent Lavoisier. In 1784 it concluded that no magnetic "fluid" exists; striking recoveries from illness were not denied but attributed to "mere imagination." Thus discredited, hypnosis as a topic of objective investigation was neglected and tended to be linked with mysticism and quackery.

Anesthesia

About 1840, physicians John Elliotson in London and James Esdaile in Calcutta made extensive use of mesmeric trance to carry out painless major surgery, including leg amputations. Elliotson endorsed belief in Mesmer's invisible "fluid" and held the metal nickel to be particularly useful in trance induction. The editor of the British medical journal *Lancet* surreptitiously exchanged nickel with lead; since the lead seemed to work just as well, he denounced such belief as "mesmeric humbug."

Braid agreed that no magnetic "fluid" was involved but observed that people being treated with mesmerism seemed profoundly influenced. He introduced the term hypnotism to divorce the phenomenon from theories about animal magnetism and held that concentration on a single focus of attention (monoideism) was a major factor in the situation.

Hysteria

Hypnosis attracted widespread scientific interest in the 1880s as a result of a controversy in France. Ambroise-Auguste Liébeault, an obscure country physician at Nancy who used mesmeric techniques, drew the support of Hippolyte Bernheim, professor of medicine at Strasbourg. Independently they wrote that the phenomenon involved no physical forces and no physiological processes but were psychologically mediated responses to suggestions. In disagreement, Jean-Martin Charcot, professor of neurology at the Sorbonne in Paris, held that hypnosis occurs only in sufferers of hysteria, is therefore pathological, and does involve the influences of magnets and metals. (Charcot had become interested in the possible transfer of symptoms by magnets and in the effects of drugs at a distance.) History has shown that the effects of magnets and similar physical factors are really brought about by implicit psychological suggestions.

At about the same time, the Austrian physician Sigmund Freud visited France and was impressed by the therapeutic potential of hypnosis for neurotic disorders. On his return to Vienna he used hypnosis to help neurotics recall forgotten disturbing events. As he began to develop his system of psychoanalysis, theoretical considerations, as well as the difficulty he encountered in hypnotizing some patients, led Freud to discard hypnosis in favour of free association. Generally psychoanalysts have tended to view hypnosis as a somewhat masked intimate personal relationship.

Despite Freud's influential rejection of hypnosis, some use was made of the technique in treating combat neuroses during World Wars I and II. Pierre Janet in France and Morton Prince in the United States suggested that "dissociation of mental systems" is common both to the neurotic disorder called multiple personality and to the phenomenon of hypnosis. Prince showed that a hypnotized person seems to be able to carry on two or more independent streams of mental activity simultaneously.

Hypnosis as sleep

Ivan Pavlov, the Russian physiologist, came to view sleep as reflecting widespread inhibitory processes in the brain and concluded that hypnosis is a similar inhibitory state in which there remain a few centres of neural excitation. His views enjoy wide acceptance among Soviet and eastern European workers who also tend to use prolonged periods of sleep in psychiatric therapy.

In America, experimental psychologist Clark Hull, applying controlled quantitative methods to the laboratory study of this complex and elusive phenomenon, concluded in 1933 that, as Bernheim had argued, hypnosis is best understood as a form of hypersuggestibility. Important basic research has continued in Hull's tradition with normal volunteer subjects. A combined clinical-experimental approach, inspired by Milton Erickson's pioneering work in the 1940s, has been effective as a research strategy and has led to novel therapeutic applications which have helped spark renewed widespread interest in hypnosis.

Scientific journals devoted exclusively to hypnosis are published in England, Japan, South America, the U.S., and Sweden. National societies in many countries hold annual scientific meetings, and international congresses on hypnosis have been held in France (1965), Japan (1967), Germany (1970), and Sweden (1973).

MODERN THEORIES

Despite active empirical study of hypnotic phenomena, there is no single generally accepted explanatory theory. Some theorists influenced by Pavlov think of hypnosis as a state of altered consciousness or partial sleep in which a person tends to respond to suggestions automatically and uncritically. While this view does not ignore increased suggestibility, it still holds that a subject not at the moment responding to a suggestion may nevertheless be in a trance state. There may be neurophysiological components of such a state. Such a position would be consistent with the notion, not generally accepted, that some animals can be hypnotized, as when a chick, suddenly placed on its back, tends to remain immobile in that position (see DORMANCY).

Social interaction

Other theorists stress the social or interpersonal interactions that hypnotic behaviour involves. They emphasize how an actor willingly and wittingly permits a director to guide him into living a part; how a patient may be relieved of a headache if given a pill that is actually pharmacologically inert (a placebo); how an uncommitted person becomes an enthusiastic supporter of crowd feeling at a demonstration; how a spectator flinches and jabs along with his favourite fighter; and how a student changes his views to those of an admired teacher. Hypnosis is held to consist of nothing more than events like these, there being no need to assume additional special states such as the inhibition of parts of the brain. Hypnotic events are results of interpersonal influences in which various abilities, skills, and response propensities are brought into play.

Evidence can be found to support both major theoretical approaches. Neural changes indeed do occur in hypnosis, but a unique physiological basis for the phenomenon remains to be established. Perhaps this reflects incomplete understanding of physiological alterations that may produce psychological change. Social-interaction theorists find it difficult to explain why posthypnotic suggestions are carried out even when the hypnotist neither knows nor apparently cares about the subject's behaviour. While most current investigators tend to work within one or the other explanatory framework, most feel free to use propositions from both if they seem consistent with experimental or clinical observations.

INDUCTION OF HYPNOSIS

Techniques to induce hypnosis share common features. Responsiveness is maximized when the subject seems to believe that he can be hypnotized, that the hypnotist is competent and trustworthy, and that the undertaking is safe, appropriate, and congruent with his wishes. Therefore induction is generally preceded by the establishment of suitable rapport between subject and hypnotist. After this the hypnotist proceeds to try to focus attention on the procedure proper.

Establishing rapport

Ordinary inductions begin with simple suggestions that will almost inevitably be accepted by all subjects. At this stage neither subject nor hypnotist can readily tell whether the subject's behaviour constitutes a hypnotic response or mere cooperation. Then, gradually, suggestions are given that demand increasing distortion of perception or memory. In the eye-closure method described above, for example, the suggestions of visual fatigue are consistent with and take advantage of normal strain during fixation and thus serve to heighten expectations of positive response. It is difficult for hypnotist, subject, or outside observer to be sure whether eye closure indicates hypnosis or mere voluntary compliance. But the hypnotist gradually moves on to suggest that it will be difficult or impossible to open the now-shut eyes. Although not all subjects respond positively, those who do seem to have gone beyond the point of simple compliance. By linking any successful responses with ensuing suggestions, the hypnotist often can elicit increasingly marked distortions of perception, belief, memory, and attitude. The success or failure of any suggestion is considerably influenced by how well the hypnotist observes and uses the subject's natural talents.

While induction is usually carried out in a quiet, dimly lit room, it may be done in normal illumination. The subject may be asked to attend to any of a wide variety of stimuli—his own hand, his breathing, an imaginary visual image, or a tone. He need not be seated and relaxed; indeed, in some methods the subject is asked to tense his muscles. Even carefully selected distractions can be used to facilitate progress.

Expectations

Induction of hypnosis may take considerable time but sometimes requires only a few seconds. Hypnotists in theatres and night clubs capitalize on developing appropriate expectations and selecting individuals ready and willing to enter deep hypnosis. Much of the effort in clinical settings is directed toward establishing appropriate attitudes in the subject. The advertising and publicity given the stage hypnotist before he faces the audience likewise facilitate response; with such preparation, he sometimes can induce hypnosis all but instantaneously, merely by shaking a particularly susceptible subject's hand or by saying in a commanding voice, "Sleep!" Given suitable preparation, tape-recorded induction procedures may be as effective as an experienced hypnotist.

With suitable subjects hypnosis also can be induced by a series of suggestions without any reference to sleep or eye closure. Some waking individuals go directly into the same state produced by telling a deeply hypnotized subject that he will open his eyes while in the trance.

Resistance to hypnosis

In general, hypnosis cannot be induced against an individual's will. Occasionally experiments have been reported in which individuals were asked to resist but nonetheless were hypnotized. In all such examples the hypnotist solicited the subject's cooperation in an experiment; only then did he ask for resistance. Assuming the subject is capable of hypnosis, his response seems to depend on whether he wishes to help in solving the experimental problem or whether he wants to follow the specific instruction to resist. It is unwarranted to assume that under these circumstances the subject truly does not wish to enter hypnosis; it has not been convincingly shown that hypnosis can be induced in someone independently motivated to resist. This does not mean, however, that a willing person cannot be hypnotized without his formal consent. It is unusual, but in some therapeutic or religious contexts, for example, people have been observed to exhibit trancelike or hypnotic behaviour without evidence of intention on their part or even on the part of a hypnotist.

Hypnotic suggestions. A peculiar quality of speech seems helpful in making hypnotic suggestions. Most people can identify the voice quality, traditionally described as monotonous and repetitious but probably more accurately as intense, insistent, and simple. Suggestions seem most effective when the hypnotist paints a vivid word picture of concrete images that are easily imagined.

Suggestions also are best given in indicative rather than imperative form. Instead of saying, "Lift your hand," for example, the hypnotist encourages a passive attitude in which the subject neither strives to help nor to hinder the arm and says, "It is becoming light . . . the fingers are beginning to rise . . . they feel like balloons as they float into the air . . . ."

As the subject begins to respond, the hypnotist often behaves as if he shares the subject's unusual experiences. When, for example, the person seems to be hallucinating a familiar friend in response to suggestion, the hypnotist may ask to be introduced. He will begin to talk to the subject's hallucination as if he too were seeing the imaginary person.

The popular impression of the hypnotist as authoritarian and dominating fits the behaviour of many stage hypnotists and of psychiatrists using hypnosis in the last century. Just as the authoritarian bedside manner of medical practitioners is no longer the norm, however, so has the approach of the medical hypnotist changed with the times. Under most circumstances, therapeutic hypnosis is now carried out in an atmosphere of cooperation, the hypnotist assuming the role of a teacher who can help his student achieve a mutually sought goal.

Technical aids. A wide variety of devices has been employed to facilitate fixation. A rotating picture of a spiral has been popular, its movement tending to focus attention on the centre. Arrangements of mirrors and fixation points also have been used, just as the subject may focus attention on his own breath sounds. Particular theoretical interest has been shown in the use of a flashing light, especially when adjusted to the subject's own electrical brain rhythms (typically nine or ten pulses per second).

Use of drugs

Drugs also have been used, especially sedatives (*e.g.*, barbiturates) for relaxation prior to hypnotic induction. (Paradoxically, injections of such stimulants as amphetamines also have been reported to help.) Any procedure that produces momentary clouding of consciousness can be used to activate responses to suggestions. Hypnotic efforts are enhanced when a person is drowsy or about to fall asleep (with or without drugs). Similarly, dulled awareness readily can be achieved by pressure on blood vessels in the neck to deprive the brain of oxygen. This potentially injurious technique most often is employed by medically untrained hypnotists. There also is some indication that people under sensory deprivation (conditions of silence, darkness, and isolation) become unusually suggestible.

These procedures appear effective primarily in heightening expectations; it has never been shown that persons who are not susceptible to ordinary induction procedures abruptly become hypnotizable with these aids.

HYPNOTIC PHENOMENA

Appropriate suggestions can induce a remarkably wide range of psychological responses among deeply hypnotized persons.

Ideomotor responses. When one vividly imagines moving his body, he has a marked tendency to do what he is thinking. If the responsive subject stands with his back to the hypnotist, for example, and it is suggested that he is falling backward farther and farther, as he concentrates he will begin gradually to sway in that direction. Similarly it may be suggested that his hand will grow lighter and float upward or that it will become heavy and be pulled down. Waking individuals also respond to suggestions of movement, and there is some question whether hypnotic induction increases the probability of such behaviour. Since the tendency of subjects to respond to suggested movement is related to their general suggestibility, such ideomotor phenomena are widely considered to be a kind of hypnotic response.

Challenge suggestions. Challenge suggestions are those in which the subject is told he is unable to implement his own will; for example, "Your eyelids are shutting tight . . . tighter . . . tighter. You cannot open them even if you try. . . . Try to open them. . . . You cannot. . . . They are stuck together." Similarly, a hypnotized subject may be informed that his eyelids will force themselves open despite his effort to keep them shut. Challenge suggestions are of theoretical interest in that they seem to prevent voluntary action, striking observer and subject as dramatic demonstrations of external control over the individual. Such experiments have little therapeutic application; they also can be carried out with some people without formal hypnotic induction procedure, although response to challenge tends to be augmented during trance states. Response among waking individuals can serve as a test of hypnotic susceptibility; generally, those who respond very positively to challenge subsequently are found to be deeply hypnotizable. Challenge items emphasize the compelling character of hypnotic suggestion.

It has been observed that challenge suggestions may impose a logical "double bind"; *e.g.*, that the instruction to try actually means to attempt and fail to open one's eyes. Some theorists suggest that it is not possible to comply with the instruction to try to open one's eyes and at the same time to cooperate with the generic instruction to be hypnotized. Whatever the validity of this theoretical formulation, many subjects say they feel genuinely unable to overcome such a challenge.

Perceptual distortions. With appropriate suggestion, the hypnotic subject may perceive stimuli not actually present or fail to perceive stimuli that are present. In response, for example, to the suggestion that an absent person is present, the subject may report that he sees, hears, and feels the hallucinated person and even spontaneously carry on a conversation with the hallucinated image.

Other perceptual distortions, such as feeling warm or cold or having a sweet or acid taste, may readily be suggested. It is typically easier to induce illusory experience —for example, that a lemon is a peach of which one can enjoy the delicate flavour—than to produce a positive hallucination in the absence of external objects. The most difficult to elicit are negative hallucinations in which the subject seems unable to perceive objects actually present.

Painless surgery

Hypnotic analgesia and anesthesia may involve both the reduction of fear, relatively easily achieved by hypnosis, and the more difficult negative hallucination of pain. Since anticipation of pain tends to heighten discomfort substantially in the dentist's chair, some dentists report that more than 90 percent of their patients show a greatly increased pain threshold and a marked reduction in the need for local anesthesia even under light hypnosis. Such results largely stem from the effect of hypnosis on the reduction of fear; on the other hand, major surgical operations can be performed without anesthetic drugs but require deep hypnosis. This seems feasible with a much smaller number of individuals, and such anesthesia is likely to involve a negative hallucination of the pain experience.

Negative hallucination also seems to be a major part of hypnotic rapport. Once hypnosis is induced, subjects typically ignore all stimuli but the hypnotist. This appears to be a response to the suggestion to ignore the environment (*e.g.*, "You will pay attention only to my voice."), a kind of negative hallucination for everything outside the hypnotic context. Nevertheless, once hypnotic rapport has been established, it can readily be transferred by suggestion from the hypnotist to someone else.

Alterations of memory. Among the most dramatic experiences of the hypnotized individual are distortions of recall. If it is suggested that fictitious events really have occurred, the subject may not only seem to remember them, he may also elaborate on them. Suggestions may be given to forget what happened yesterday or one's own name. Told to forget the number 6, for example, a subject will count his fingers as . . . 5, 7, 8 . . ., ending with what he seems to perceive as an 11th finger. Encouraged to explore this peculiarity, he may note that he can count five fingers twice with no difficulty and correctly conclude that there must be a problem with his ability to count between five and ten. Yet this inference does not necessarily help him to recall the missing number.

Age regression

A special case of memory distortion is hypnotic age regression; an adult, for example, appears to relive events that occurred when he was a child—his speech, writing, and general motor behaviour becoming childlike. He appears to recall events and skills long since lost or forgotten, such as playing a musical instrument or speaking a foreign language learned in childhood. Some investigators have taken the phenomenon of age regression as evidence for total storage of all sensory impressions, but carefully controlled studies generally have failed to find support for this assumption. When verifiable details of memory are checked, there seems to be little recall of factual information beyond what was available in the adult waking state.

Hypnotic age regression does seem to make the subject less concerned about the accuracy of his memory, and he fills in memory gaps with vivid imagination. This in turn may promote recall of repressed, emotionally charged actual experiences; however, even then it is often difficult to distinguish fact from fiction. The individual may be both convinced and convincing despite a tendency to elaborate, embroider, and distort what actually occurred.

Hypnotic age regression has been advocated and used in legal cases. Great care should be taken in evaluating the accuracy of testimony even if the witness seems to be totally convinced of the honesty of his report. Hypnosis is no guarantee against falsification.

It remains controversial whether hypnotic suggestions can improve memory effectively. The effect, if any, is small for the kinds of information ordinarily employed in laboratory studies of learning and forgetting. The popular opinion that hypnosis facilitates recollection has not been supported by adequately controlled subsequent research. The common belief of the student who has neglected his studies that through hypnosis he may recall enough to pass his examinations, sadly, lacks reliable foundation.

Posthypnotic amnesia. Many subjects seem unable to recall what happened while they were in deep hypnosis. It is unclear whether this posthypnotic amnesia is a spontaneous consequence of deep hypnosis or whether it results entirely from suggestion. While suggestions made during hypnosis do have substantial effects on what the subject subsequently recalls, it remains to be shown that they account for all posthypnotic remembering or forgetting. Posthypnotic amnesia may be successfully removed by appropriate hypnotic suggestions.

Other kinds of hypnotic suggestions. *Delusions.* Appropriate hypnotic suggestions also can prompt the subject to embrace false beliefs (delusions). Told that he is a famous actor on his way to a television interview, the hypnotized person will show through his posture, mannerisms, attitudes, and speech clear alterations that are consistent with the delusion. Deluded behaviour also may be elicited through age progressions, in which it is suggested to a young adult, for example, that he is now an old man. The ease with which subjects respond to suggestions of age progression indicates that age regression, including regression to previous "incarnations," may be equally delusional.

Time distortion. Suggestions may be given that the passing of time will speed up or slow down. In the latter case, for example, a hypnotized subject may seem to experience a full-length motion-picture film in only a few seconds. It is quite unlikely, however, that such hypnotic time distortion can in reality accelerate the learning of new information.

Attitude change. Of special therapeutic potential is the effect of hypnotically suggesting altered attitudes. It may be suggested to someone who feels unattractive, for instance, that he will find that people like him and are drawn to his company. When used judiciously, suggestions such as these may result in enduring therapeutic changes by modifying the person's behaviour toward others. To the degree that his new optimism leads to friendlier, more confident approaches to people, their typically reciprocal responses will reinforce the changes initiated by hypnotic suggestion.

Physiological alterations. A broad variety of bodily changes have been produced by suggestion in hypnotized individuals. These usually are elicited indirectly by mentioning appropriate circumstances; for example, viral cold sores (herpes) have been induced, not by directly suggesting their appearance but rather by suggesting emotional distress of the sort that previously was associated with their eruption. Similarly, suggestions that they feel cold lead some subjects to show such bodily signs as shivering and circulatory alterations. Suggested sudden pain, discomfort, or stress can change the electrical resistance of the subject's skin and alter his respiration and heart rate. On the other hand, successful suggestions of diminished pain do not seem to abolish such bodily responses to the stress.

Blisters

There is controversy about the hypnotic induction of blisters. Told that a cool coin touching him is red hot, a subject shows intense discomfort; sometimes there may be redness and blistering skin. Generally not reproducible under controlled laboratory conditions with normal volunteer subjects, psychologically induced blisters seem most likely to appear only in those prone to convert emotional disturbances into symptoms of skin disease.

Although some surgeons and many dentists report hypnotic control of bleeding after such procedures as tooth extraction, this remains to be verified by controlled experiment.

Posthypnotic suggestion. A deeply hypnotized individual can be induced to carry out an action in response to a specific cue some time after trance termination. With adequate amnesia, he will not be aware of the source of his impulse to act and may rationalize his behaviour. Even with awareness, he may still feel compelled to carry out the action and, if he attempts to resist doing so, evidence of conflict can usually be observed.

Posthypnotic suggestion, however, is not a particularly powerful means of controlling behaviour. Simple requests to a cooperative individual are responded to more consistently and over longer periods than posthypnotic suggestions. A group of subjects in deep hypnosis, for example, given postcards and instructed to mail one every day, sent fewer cards than others merely asked to carry out this action. This holds for trivial tasks, easily carried out, but the situation is reversed when the suggestion concerns behaviours the individual has difficulty in controlling himself.

A treatment for smoking

Thus, posthypnotic suggestions have been quite effective in the treatment of habits such as smoking. In these instances, the posthypnotic suggestion is congruent with the individual's desires and reinforces them. Efforts to use posthypnotic suggestion as a means to force an individual to behave in a manner undesirable to him are usually doomed to failure, though such suggestions may occasionally lead to troublesome mental conflict.

In contrast to a simple request, posthypnotic responses are carried out not simply to please the hypnotist, but rather they may persist even in private when the hypnotist apparently could not know or care about the execution of the action.

All phenomena that can be elicited during hypnosis can, in suitable subjects, be elicited posthypnotically. This raises serious theoretical issues and has led some theorists to argue that the posthypnotic cue reinstates hypnosis.

LIMITATIONS AND POTENTIALITIES OF HYPNOSIS

The objectively observable phenomena of hypnosis are not so different from those of voluntary waking cooperation as once was supposed. It has been shown that during a lecture a student asked by his teacher to take off his shoe, to exchange neckties with a neighbour, or engage in other slightly embarrassing, ludicrous actions will do so. Had hypnosis first been induced, observers might have wrongly concluded that the subject was in the "power" of the hypnotist.

When unhypnotizable subjects are asked to simulate hypnosis, their performance can deceive experienced hypnotists. Simulating subjects convincingly perform extraordinary feats of strength and memory; for example, tolerating a needle through the arm without flinching. Such feats have mistakenly been taken as proof that hypnosis confers abilities that transcend those of waking activity.

Investigators once were inclined to conclude that deeply hypnotized subjects can be compelled against their "will" to carry out self-damaging and antisocial behaviour. They cited independent studies demonstrating that such individuals will attempt to pick up a poisonous snake, to pick up with their bare fingers a coin dissolving in a beaker of fuming nitric acid, and to throw the acid at a research assistant. Asked in the waking state whether they would obey such suggestions, the same subjects were quick to deny the possibility. In subsequent work, however, deeply hypnotized people were mingled with simulating subjects without the experimenter's knowledge, which ensured that he treated all subjects in the same persuasive way. Instructed to carry out these perilous, undesirable acts, five out of six hypnotized subjects did so, but all of six simulators did likewise. The experiment demonstrates that different answers emerge when waking subjects are asked whether they will carry out an action and when they are instructed to do so in a way that clearly communicates expectation of compliance. Under the latter circumstances waking subjects correctly seem to surmise that safety precautions have been taken; indeed, no responsible investigator permits subjects or assistants to be hurt. The further implication is that the genuine hypnotic subjects also may have surmised that the situation was safe; it thus remains undemonstrated that they were under the hypnotist's "power."

This experiment is typical of a number of controlled studies that call many earlier extravagant claims about hypnosis into serious question. It now seems quite unlikely that the hypnotized person can transcend his waking potentials in physical strength, perceptiveness, learning ability, and productivity. Similarly, it seems most improbable that hypnotized people can be compelled to do what they would be most unwilling to do in the waking state. But hypnosis may be used, as various other methods may also be used, to induce a person to alter his usual behaviour.

The inability of the hypnotized subject to transcend his waking potential does not call into question the reality of hypnosis. When a hypnotized person reports a hallucination, all the evidence indicates that it is real to him. The significant aspects of hypnosis are found in the quality or characteristics of the subject's induced experiences. The statements of people after trance indicate that hypnotic experiences are qualitatively distinct from those reported by simulators. Genuinely hypnotized subjects, for example, tolerate the discrepancy of actually seeing a person and of simultaneously hallucinating that person at another location without being especially cued; this does not hold for the simulator. Hypnotized people tend to carry out suggestions during or after trance whether the hypnotist is present or not; simulators cease to respond when they are quite sure they have no audience.

Altogether then, hypnosis should not be considered as a technique for achieving supernormal performance or control. Rather it is a collaborative enterprise in which the inner experience of the subject can be dramatically altered.

Hypnotic responsiveness. Some suggestions, such as those of eye closure and feelings of heaviness, warmth, and relaxation, are effective with most individuals. Other suggestions, including those of analgesia to a pinprick or difficulty in opening one's eyes when challenged, elicit positive responses from a lesser number. Hallucinations, general posthypnotic amnesia, and other memory distortions are achieved only in approximately one-quarter of the population; negative visual hallucinations, profound surgical anesthesia, and response to bizarre posthypnotic suggestions are feasible with only a few people. On this evidence, items of suggestion can be graded roughly in terms of difficulty. Occasionally a subject may respond to a generally difficult item and not to one that is rated easy, but this is not the usually observed pattern.

Such data have led to the development of a number of standardized scales for assessing hypnotic susceptibility.

Tests of susceptibility

Designed for research with normal subjects, they avoid highly personal or emotionally upsetting items. *The Stanford Hypnotic Susceptibility Scales* are widely used. Some, consisting of easier items, are used for preliminary screening. Others contain more difficult items, and some are designed to reveal the particular kinds of suggestion to which the subject best responds. Variations of the Stanford scales include the *Children's Hypnotic Susceptibility Scale* and the *Harvard Group Scale*, the latter also employing tape-recorded procedure.

Scales of this sort are fairly reliable in that most subjects' responses are reasonably stable from one time to another and from one form of the scale to another. (If a person chooses to resist the hypnotic procedure, however, he will score low even though he may be quite capable of responding. Susceptibility scales, like intelligence tests, can be misleading unless the individual tries his best.) The Table summarizes typical variations in depth of hypnosis induced among normal college students with a graded series of items from the Stanford scales.

Any individual's overt responses to a standardized scale may be objectively scored and evaluated against such a table of norms. The investigator also may ask the individual how strongly he felt affected by the procedure. Results from objective scoring and from the person's subjective report tend to yield similar estimates of depth of hypnosis, but concordance is far from perfect. One subject may give marked overt responses but later say that he merely was trying to be helpful; another more lethargic person may not emphatically respond but subsequently may report profound awareness of hypnotic change. Such verbal reports are of particular interest in clinical, therapeutic settings.

Level of Hypnosis at Initial Induction with Stanford Scale

level achieved	items passed (max = 12)	percentage of cases
Complete trance	12	4
Very high	11	7
High	8–10	19
Moderate	5–7	28
Low	2–4	32
No response	0–1	10

Source: E.R. Hilgard, *Hypnotic Susceptibility* (1965).

Depth of hypnosis

Some subjects manifest very deep hypnosis in responding to even the most difficult items yet later say their experiences differed little from the fantasy of ordinary daydreaming. Others who fail to respond to all of the more difficult suggestions nonetheless seem deeply affected by the discovery that they have responded at all. They may say that having their eyes grow heavy was vastly different from, and more impressive than, any other experience they can recall. In therapeutic contexts this latter evidence of hypnotic depth often seems closely related to the individual's attitude toward his therapist. Probable therapeutic response, however, has not been shown to be adequately predictable from any of these criteria of depth of hypnosis. Sufferers have been deeply hypnotized in terms of all such criteria and have failed to be relieved of their psychiatric symptoms; others who seem barely affected during hypnotic efforts nevertheless show substantial improvement under hypnotic treatment.

Effect of repeated hypnosis. Initial anxiety or conflict about entering hypnosis generally interferes with an individual's responsiveness. Subsequent improvement of rapport with the hypnotist and growing familiarity with the procedure help many subjects to produce more profound experiences, but each soon reaches a particular plateau at which the kind of phenomena elicited seems to stabilize. Practice beyond this point, however, does tend to increase the speed of response, which may account for the widely held belief that depth of hypnosis continues to improve with practice.

The posthypnotic suggestion often is given that a subject in future will immediately enter a trance on a specified cue. The ease and rapidity with which this can occur in a trained subject should not be taken to mean that he is becoming more susceptible, nor that he cannot resist if he truly wishes to do so.

Undue dependence on the hypnotist does not ordinarily occur in experimental work but has been reported for some therapeutic relationships. Such a response may complicate all forms of therapy but is most likely to occur with lay hypnotists and other individuals who ineptly attempt psychotherapeutic interventions without appropriate training and experience.

Hypnotizability. The stability of one's hypnotic responsiveness seems as great as that of other abilities such as mechanical or verbal skills, and much research has been devoted to the search for personal attributes related to hypnotizability. Early investigators assumed that women enter hypnosis more readily than men, but this has not been borne out in most studies; similarly, hypnotizability is not especially related to intelligence nor to education. There does appear to be a significant relationship with age, ability to respond reaching a peak before puberty, stabilizing in the early adult years, and declining in very old age. Traits popularly characterized as evidence of gullibility are not related to hypnotizability. There is some indication that a history of parentally approved daydreaming, fantasizing, and imaginative play during childhood is associated with increased ability to respond. The extent to which an individual spontaneously becomes absorbed in a play to the point of feeling the emotions portrayed also has some predictive value. There is evidence that hypnotizability is greater among individuals who seem generally well adjusted. Among those with psychiatric disorders, hysterics respond better than others. Most individuals with obsessive-compulsive or schizophrenic symptoms are unresponsive, but even with these difficulties some can enter deep hypnosis.

EVALUATION OF THE APPLICATIONS OF HYPNOSIS

By the 1970s hypnosis had been officially endorsed as a therapeutic method by medical, psychiatric, dental, and psychological associations throughout the world.

Because of the availability of safe and effective anesthetic drugs, hypnosis is used in major surgery only rarely. On the other hand, it has been found most useful in preparing people for anesthesia, enhancing the drug response, and reducing the required dosage. In childbirth it is particularly helpful, since it is effective in alleviating the mother's discomfort while avoiding drug-induced impairment of the child's physiological function. The technique also has been helpful in painful, relatively minor procedures such as changing dressings over severe burns. Hypnosis is highly regarded in the management of otherwise intractable pain, including that of terminal cancer. It is valuable in reducing the widespread fear of dental procedures; the very people whom dentists find most difficult to treat frequently respond best to suggestions. It has also proven useful in such aspects of dentistry as suppressing undesirable gagging reflexes and in helping people adapt to new dentures.

In the area of psychosomatic medicine hypnosis has been used in a variety of ways. Patients have been trained to relax and to carry out, in the absence of the hypnotist, exercises that have had salutary effects on some forms of high blood pressure, headaches, and functional disorders. Specific suggestions have also been used in some of these contexts but tend to have limited applicability compared with more general procedures designed to reduce the patient's tension. Many fascinating isolated case reports of dramatic therapeutic changes induced by hypnosis, especially in dermatology, are in the literature, but overall effectiveness in dermatology has not yet been adequately evaluated. In many instances, the appropriate treatment for psychosomatic difficulties is psychotherapy, in which hypnosis may or may not be included.

The use of hypnosis in psychotherapy. In psychotherapy, hypnosis has been used in a variety of ways. Specific suggestions to relieve troublesome symptoms have limited utility. Those symptoms that may be suppressed with confidence and safety are the ones least likely to be central problems to the patient, and considerable care should be taken in evaluating the nature of the problem before such treatment is undertaken. The use of hypnotic suggestions to change psychological attitudes has been mentioned. The technique of revivifying traumatic events, leading to a cathartic emotional release, was originally employed by Freud and continues to be a useful treatment in relieving neuroses with traumatic onset (see PSYCHONEUROSES), such as those that develop in combat, among individuals with relatively stable prior adjustments. There are a variety of other, more specialized ways in which hypnosis has been employed to help patients understand their own reactions and to become aware of their own feelings. Hypnosis itself is never the treatment, however; rather, it is a technique used in the context of an overall treatment approach. It has been used in modern behaviour therapy, for example, as well as in psychoanalytically oriented approaches. In countries where the Pavlovian school is particularly important, there has been a tendency to employ prolonged hypnotically induced sleep as a way of bringing about curative rest.

General comments about the use of hypnosis in treatment. The induction of hypnosis requires little training and no particular skill, a tape recording often being sufficient. Though the technique and skill of the hypnotist are not totally irrelevant, the personality and motivation of the subject and his interaction with the situation are of paramount importance. Nevertheless, there is an erroneous though widely held belief that individuals capable of inducing hypnosis have some special power or skill that makes them equipped to treat. Congruent with this belief is the view that there is a science of hypnosis.

While an appropriate topic of scientific inquiry, hypnosis is not a science in its own right. On the contrary, it is the task of psychological science to discover how hypnosis can be accounted for by its general laws. While little skill is required to induce hypnosis, considerable training is needed to evaluate whether it is the appropriate treatment technique and, if so, how it should properly be employed.

Abuse of hypnosis

When used in the treatment context, hypnosis should never be employed by individuals who do not have the competence and skill to treat such problems *without the use of hypnosis.* For this reason hypnosis "schools" or "institutes" cannot provide the needed training for individuals lacking the more general scientific and technical qualifications of the healing professions. In most major cities individuals advertise in the classified sections of telephone books as professional hypnotists, offering to treat a wide range of medical and psychological problems. Since the ethical codes of the professions would prevent any physician, psychologist, or dentist from advertising in such a fashion, individuals who consult someone who holds himself out to be a hypnotist should be aware that such a person is extremely unlikely to have the necessary training or skill to treat medical or psychological problems. Improperly used, hypnosis may add to the patient's psychiatric or medical difficulties. Thus, a sufferer of an undiscovered brain tumor may sacrifice his life in the hands of a practitioner who successfully relieves his headache by hypnotic suggestion, thereby delaying needed surgery. Broad diagnostic training and therapeutic skill are indispensable in avoiding the inappropriate and potentially dangerous use of hypnosis.

Interrogation and discovery of truth. Hypnosis has not been found reliable in obtaining truth from a reluctant witness. Even if it were possible to induce hypnosis against one's will, it is well documented that the hypnotized individual still can willfully lie. It is of even greater concern that cooperative hypnotized subjects remember distorted versions of actual events and are themselves deceived. When recalled in hypnosis, such false memories are accompanied by strong subjective conviction and outward signs of conviction that are most compelling to almost any observer. Caution and independent verification are essential in such circumstances.

Augmenting performance. Hypnosis used in attempts to increase athletic prowess usually yields equivocal results. Psychological factors clearly affect performance, and under some circumstances one might expect that hypnosis could be effective; nevertheless, it is seriously questioned whether it ought to be employed in competitive athletics. The widespread belief that hypnosis facilitates total recall is an irresistible idea, especially to students about to be examined. As noted earlier, objective evidence unfortunately fails to support this belief; hypnosis has not been particularly effective as an adjunct to memory or recall. Equal or better performance can be obtained by motivating individuals in other ways.

Antisocial uses of hypnosis. Despite many fictional stories about the use of hypnosis to persuade victims to help in criminal acts, no authenticated instance has come to light where hypnosis was successfully employed to force a person to act criminally to the advantage of the hypnotist, in the absence of an intense personal (but nonhypnotic) relationship with the hypnotist, or a pre-existing willingness to behave criminally. The dangers of antisocial use have been greatly exaggerated.

Future directions in hypnosis. The story of hypnosis illustrates errors not infrequent in the history of science in general. As Mesmer was, other theorists are over-ready to extend a concept beyond the limits of its applicability. Critics, with due regard for evidence, expose the error, but, overdoing skepticism, often fail to discern the real grain of truth in the original material. In the long run, progress is achieved by dint of a succession of nearer approximations. At any time, the way new data are handled depends markedly on the state of science at that time.

Full understanding of hypnosis depends on the state of psychological and psychiatric science. There can be no separate science of hypnosis. More particularly, when there are improved techniques of describing and quantifying mental states and subjective experiences, and greater knowledge of the physiology underlying attention and reality-testing, then a more adequate explanatory account of hypnosis will become possible. However, progress in hypnotic research will not await those achievements, but rather will contribute to them, just as hypnotic studies have already contributed insights about unconscious mental processes, about psychological influences in somatic illnesses, and about the powerful effects of expectations on behaviour.

BIBLIOGRAPHY. A classic of historical interest in its emphasis on the psychological character of hypnosis is H. BERNHEIM, *Hypnosis and Suggestion in Psychotherapy* (Eng. trans. 1888, reprinted 1964). Also of historical interest is C.L. HULL, *Hypnotism and Suggestibility: An Experimental Approach* (1933), the first major systematic effort to study hypnosis in the psychological laboratory. On techniques, a comprehensive treatment of induction and therapeutic application, supported by detailed illustrations, is L.R. WOLBERG, *Medical Hypnosis*, vol. 1, *The Principles of Hypnotherapy*, vol. 2, *The Practice of Hypnotherapy* (1948). A current account of experimental studies of hypnosis, including a substantial amount of original research, is E.R. HILGARD, *Hypnotic Susceptibility* (1965). M.T. ORNE, "Hypnosis, Motivation and the Ecological Validity of the Psychological Experiment," a paper in the *Nebraska Symposium on Motivation* (1970), summarizes empirical work, documenting both the limitations of hypnosis and some of its unique attributes. No single volume adequately covers theorizing about hypnosis. M.M. GILL and M. BRENMAN, *Hypnosis and Related States* (1959), presents a psychoanalytically oriented theory of hypnosis; T.X. BARBER, *Hypnosis: A Scientific Approach* (1969), a skeptical view. Contributions of other theorists, especially those of White, Kubie, Sarbin, and Erickson are included in the collection of basic readings: R.E. SHOR and M.T. ORNE (eds.), *The Nature of Hypnosis* (1965).

(M.T.O./A.G.H.)

Ibadan

Ibadan, the capital of Western State, Nigeria, is a city conscious of its past. A traditional Yoruba town whose origins are rooted in legend, its importance was well established before the arrival of colonial powers. Because of its location near the boundary between rain forest and savanna, the original town was ideally situated as a trade centre. The importance of the site is reflected in its Yoruba name, Eba Odan, which literally means "near the savanna." The city's commercial development gathered momentum with the arrival of the railway from the Atlantic coast in 1901. Ibadan—now the largest sub-Saharan city ever to have been a colonial administrative centre—has a metropolitan population of about 1,500,000. Virtually without industry, it has retained its rural character. The University of Ibadan, however, has contributed a modern flavour to the city's life style. As the capital of the Western State of Nigeria, Ibadan houses the state government administrative agencies, as well as several branches of Nigeria's federal ministries, including the army, police, and the Central Bank. The Ibadan City Council consists of 66 members, four of whom are nominated female members. The majority are elected from the city's 46 wards.

History. Ibadan's beginnings are shrouded in mystery; they were recorded only in oral tradition. It is said that the earliest group of settlers at Ibadan were fugitives from justice who were expelled from nearby villages. This small group later swelled with the arrival of immigrants from all over Yorubaland (now western Nigeria).

The town's origins

Recorded history begins in 1829, after the region had been convulsed by extended intertribal wars. In that year, the victorious armies of the Ife, Ijebu, and Oyo kingdoms camped at Ibadan and formed the nucleus of the modern city. Its population was drawn from every part of Yorubaland. Ibadan consequently evolved a social system and government in which title and rank depended upon a man's strength or wealth rather than on heredity. The city never had a crowned head or hereditary chief, nor a formal palace. By 1851 the city had evolved a dual system of government. Military authority was divided between the Balogun, or general of the army, and the Seriki, leader of the young soldiers. The civilian jurisdiction was represented by a male and a female head.

The British colonial government assumed control of the city in 1893, administering it in consultation with the council of traditional chiefs. After the railway arrived from Lagos (1901), the line was extended northward to Kano (1912), thus ensuring the city's continuing economic importance.

Physical character. Ibadan is located almost directly north of Lagos, about 100 miles (160 kilometres) inland from the coast at a general elevation of 700 feet (200 metres) above sea level. It is a city of hills and valleys interspersed by gently rolling plains. A central ridge running north to south roughly bisects the city and constitutes its most prominent feature. Numerous streams flow through the city; among these, the Ogunpa and the Kudeti dominate the drainage, uniting at Ibadan's southern limit. Flooding and erosion occur during the rainy season.

Ibadan covers about 50 square miles (130 square kilometres) of built up area within the municipality. The metropolitan area, however, extends much farther to include rapidly developing residential suburbs, such as Akpata to the southwest. Development to the north of the city is attracted by the University of Ibadan and by the International Institute of Tropical Agriculture.

Environment. *Climate.* The climate is hot and humid. It is characterized by a wet season occurring from mid-March to October, and by a dry season that lasts from November to late March. The annual average rainfall is about 45 inches (115 centimetres), over 90 percent of which falls during the rainy season. The mean daily temperature is generally over 85° F (30° C), while the daily range is about 20° F (11° C). Extreme day temperatures of over 95° F (35° C) are often recorded in the dry season months, the hottest period being from February to April. The relative humidity varies from about 65 percent in the dry season to well over 90 percent in the rainy season.

Vegetation. The original vegetation was tropical low rain forest, merging into wooded grassland toward the north. Along the river courses relatively thicker gallery forests existed, while most of the hilltops were very thickly forested. Today, however, the vegetation cover has been reduced to bush and grassland. Some of the hilltops and slopes on the outskirts have been established as teak forest reserves.

Pollution. Air pollution is as yet not a cause for concern because of low industrial development. Water shortage and water pollution are more acute problems. Because of the rate of population increase the demand for water is outstripping the supply; during the dry season some sections may receive no water for weeks at a time. Poor sewage and refuse disposal methods have resulted in badly polluted streams that are generally infested with bilharzia, a tropical parasitic worm harmful to man.

The city plan. Old Ibadan forms the approximate geographical centre of the city. At its centre stand Iba Market and Mapo Hall (housing the local administration offices), which are surrounded by residential slums that constitute about 60 percent of the city's residential area and contain over 70 percent of its population.

The new city

The functional centre of the new city is Gbagi, the central business district, which developed after the rail link to Lagos was built. Covering about 350 acres, the area consists of leasehold plots allocated by the Ibadan City Council. In recent years, because of the great demand for land in the area, multistory commercial build-

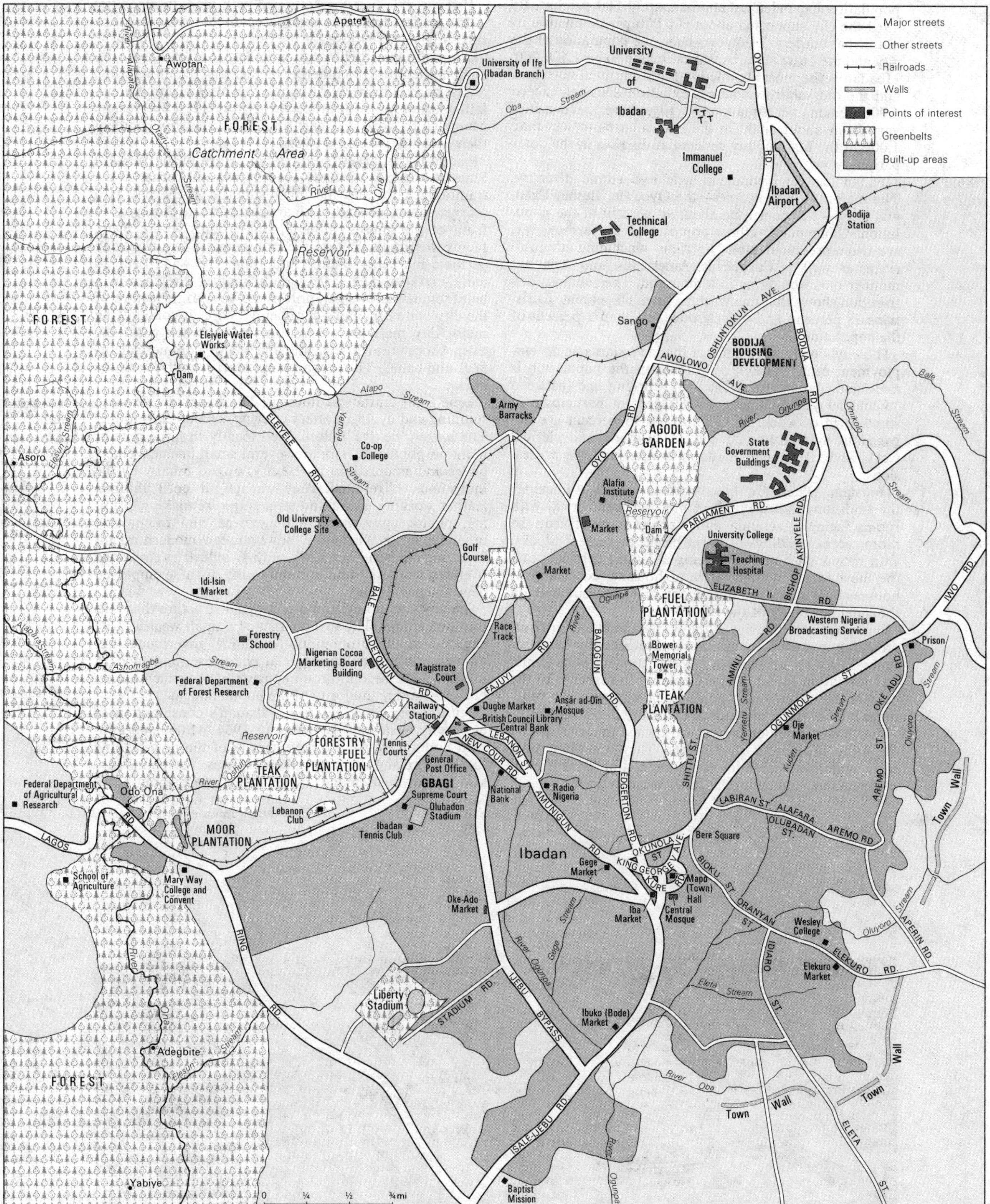

Ibadan and its environs.

ings have been constructed. Gbagi itself is surrounded by both old and new suburbs. In general, the new city consists of three types of residential region—firstly, older, low-quality, unplanned districts in the old suburbs; secondly, newer, low- to medium-quality buildings in areas with irregular street plans lying to the east and west; and thirdly, well-built districts with rectangular street plans and ring roads, consisting of government-planned housing estates and reservations, as well as privately developed zones.

Population. Ibadan has experienced a rapid population growth. In the century between 1851 and 1952 the population expanded by approximately 500 percent. By 1963 the city supported about 600,000 persons within its municipal borders. Two years later, the population of the city and the outer suburbs was estimated to be 1,500,000.

Ibadan is the most crowded in the traditional core area and the old suburbs, where population densities exceed 4,000 persons per square mile. Elsewhere the densities vary from about 2,000 in the new suburbs to less than 1,000 in the high-quality residential districts in the outer periphery.

Ethnic groups

Ibadan has retained its historic and ethnic diversity. The major Yoruba peoples—the Oyo, Ife, Ilesha, Egba, and Ijebu—still constitute about 90 percent of the population. Other major ethnic groups of Nigeria, however, are also represented. Non-Nigerians—including other Africans as well as Europeans, Americans, and Asians—number only about one in a thousand. The religious distribution shows that the Muslims form 60 percent, Christians 38 percent, and other groups less than 1 percent of the population.

The city's population reflects Ibadan's status as an employment centre. About 57 percent of the population is male and about 70 percent is of working age (between 15 and 59 years of age), but 80 percent participate in some form of work; of these, about 35 percent are engaged in agriculture, 20 percent in trade and clerical work, and 10 percent in administration and the professions.

Housing. There are three broad categories of housing: the traditional houses built of mud or burnt brick, with rooms facing a veranda built around a courtyard; the more recent buildings of burnt bricks or cement blocks, with rooms on both sides facing a central corridor; and the most recent Western style of housing, consisting of houses, bungalows, or apartment buildings situated on the outer periphery of the city.

The traditional housing is the poorest in the city; overcrowding is extreme, with four or five generations sometimes living under one roof. Ventilation is inadequate, and sanitation facilities often lacking. In response to the demand for improved conditions, new rooms are sometimes built in the courtyards or two-story houses erected.

The central-corridor houses are owned or occupied by the more prosperous immigrants. They are often two-story buildings whose lower floors, equipped with electricity, water, and bathroom facilities, are rented.

Western style housing equipped with modern amenities is the most expensive; rents are, on the average, nine times higher than those for the central-corridor houses.

Economic life. The economic activities of Ibadan include agriculture, commerce, handcrafts, manufacturing, and service industries. Although the city's farming population is still large for an urban area, it is fast decreasing. Many cultivators are part-time farmers who augment their earnings with other work.

Ibadan is the largest commercial centre in the Western State of Nigeria. Virtually every street and corner in the traditional core and the inner suburbs of the city is a market square or stall, with articles of trade displayed in front of the houses or in separate rooms within them, facing the streets. Within the city there are two eight-day periodic markets—Ibuko (Bode) and Oje—and over 30 daily markets. The largest daily market stretches in a belt from the railway station in the west to the centre of the city and is Ibadan's commercial core. It contains the major day markets, the central motor truck park, the main shopping districts, and the major commercial offices and banks. The second main market centre is to the north.

Crafts and small businesses

Some local crafts still flourish. These include weaving, spinning and dyeing, pottery making, and blacksmithing. The *adire* ("tie-dye") cloth dyed locally in large pots of indigo is popular. There are several small business enterprises and associations in the city, owned usually by the indigenous Nigerians. They engage in corn milling, leather working, wood and steel furniture making, printing, photography, hotel management, and motor and other repairing. There are, however, few modern manufacturing industries. In 1963, only 47 industries employed over ten workers each, and only nine of these employed over 100 people each.

The city's economy supports a social structure that falls into two groups. The first consists of a small wealthy elite engaged in the professions (including government administration), large commercial enterprise, and modern industry. The second group consists of the much larger, but low-earning, majority of the population.

Utilities and other services. Ibadan's consumption of electricity is steadily growing. In 1964, 41,000,000 kilowatt-hours were sold, three-quarters of the power going to commercial and industrial enterprises. Telephones are also in growing demand. In 1971 there were about 8,150

Marc and Evelyne Bernheim—Rapho Guillumette

New and old sections of Ibadan, Nigeria. Commercial buildings among a vast area of houses.

subscribers; there were over 6,000 subscribers to a radio-telephone system in 1968.

The city's health services are extensive. There are several government, mission, and private hospitals; maternity centres; and health centres. The University College Teaching Hospital is the largest and best equipped in the country. The city also houses the administrative headquarters of the Western State fire and police services.

Transportation. Ibadan is well served by roads. These are generally tarred, except for a few obscure streets that are still earth-surfaced or undeveloped. The city has a large fleet of privately owned taxi cabs and minibuses, and regular bus services are operated within the city and its suburbs by the Ibadan City Council and by private individuals. In general, traffic is heavy; the roads are overcrowded, and traffic jams and accidents are frequent.

Education and recreation. About 77 percent of the population is illiterate. The city's educational institutions include, however, over 200 primary schools, about 70 secondary modern and grammar schools, eight teacher-training colleges, the University of Ibadan and a technical institute. Specialized institutions include the Federal and Western State Departments of Agricultural Research, the Federal Department of Forest Research, the Nigerian Institute of Social and Economic Research, and the International Institute of Tropical Agriculture. Libraries include those of the Western State, The British Council, the United States Information Service, and the University of Ibadan. The university library maintains the largest collection of books in the country. There is also a branch of the National Archives on the university campus.

Research institutions

Ibadan has several cinemas, and there is a university theatre. Several national and local newspapers are published in both English and Yoruba. Both the Western Nigeria Broadcasting Service and a branch station of Radio Nigeria are established in the city. There is also a television service.

Of the city's six parks, the most important is Agodi Garden, which occupies about 130 acres of which only about 30 acres have been developed for public use. There are also four major semipublic zoological and botanical gardens, three picnic grounds, and about ten swimming pools.

Ibadan has two main stadiums, the Olubadan and the Liberty. The Liberty Stadium, with a capacity of about 35,000 spectators, is the best in the country, and is used for international games. In addition, the city has 74 playing fields, four gymnasiums, and five boxing arenas.

BIBLIOGRAPHY. S.O. BIOBAKU, I.O. DINA, and P.C. LLOYD (eds.), *Ibadan*, published for the Third International West African Conference (1949), useful information on history and conditions through the 1940s; C.H. ELGEE, *The Evolution of Ibadan* (1914), an old but still useful account; A.L. EPSTEIN, *Politics in an Urban African Community* (1958), a study in politics and city administration in Ibadan; IBADAN TOWN PLANNING AUTHORITY, *Industrial Survey (of Ibadan)* (1963); ROBERT LEVINE, NANCY H. KLEIN, and CONSTANCE R. OWEN, "Father-Child Relationships and Changing Life-Styles in Ibadan, Nigeria," in HORACE M. MINER (ed.), *The City in Modern Africa*, pp. 215–255 (1967), a sociological study of the effect of urbanization on family life; P.C. LLOYD, A.L. MABOGUNJE, and B. AWE (eds.), *The City of Ibadan: A Symposium on Its Structure and Development* (1967), scholarly chapters on the history, morphology, and social character of the city; A.L. MABOGUNJE, "Ibadan: Black Metropolis," *Nigeria Mag.*, 68:12–26 (1961); *Yoruba Towns* (1962); "The Growth of Residential Districts in Ibadan," *Geogrl. Rev.*, 52:56–77 (1962); *Urbanization in Nigeria*, ch. 8–9 (1968), a description of the growth and organization of the city and its suburbs; GEOFFREY PARRINDER, *Religion in an African City* (1953), a study of churches and religious attitudes in Ibadan; ENYINNAYA NNOCHIRI, *Parasitic Disease and Urbanization in a Developing Community* (1968).

(H.I.A.)

Ibn al-ʿArabī

Ibn al-ʿArabī (in full, Muḥyi ad-Dīn Abū ʿAbd Allāh Muḥammad ibn ʿAlī ibn Muḥammad ibn al-ʿArabī al-Ḥātimī aṭ-Ṭāʾī ibn al-ʿArabī) was a celebrated Muslim mystic–philosopher or theosopher who as ash-Shaykh al-Akbar (Doctor Maximus), the honorary title by which he is known in the Islāmic world, was one of the colossal figures in the history of Muslim thought. Besides being a master of profound mystic experiences including visions, he was a first-rate intellectual who could work his visions and insights into a major theosophical system. Moreover, all the important mystical doctrines that had appeared in Islām in a fragmentary and nonsystematic fashion before him were incorporated into his system and given an explicit theoretic formulation. Through him, the esoteric dimension of Islāmic thought for the first time found a full-fledged philosophic expression.

Early life

Ibn al-ʿArabī was born at Murcia in the southeast of Spain on July 28, 1165 (17th Ramaḍān AH 560), a man of pure Arab blood whose ancestry went back to the prominent Arabian tribe of Ṭāʾī. It was in Seville, then an outstanding centre of Islāmic culture and learning, that he received his early education. He stayed there for 30 years, studying traditional Islāmic sciences; he studied with a number of mystic masters who found in him a young man of marked spiritual inclination and unusually keen intelligence. During those years he travelled a great deal and visited various cities of Spain and North Africa in search of masters of the Ṣūfī (mystical) Path who had achieved great spiritual progress and thus renown.

It was during one of these trips that Ibn al-ʿArabī had a dramatic encounter with the great Aristotelian philosopher Ibn Rushd (Averroës; 1126 [AH 520]–1198 [AH 595]) in the city of Córdoba. Averroës, a close friend of the boy's father, had asked that the interview be arranged because he had heard of the extraordinary nature of the young, still beardless lad. After the early exchange of only a few words, it is said, the mystical depth of the boy so overwhelmed the old philosopher that he became pale and, dumfounded, began trembling. In the light of the subsequent course of Islāmic philosophy the event is seen as symbolic; even more symbolic is the sequel of the episode, which has it that when Averroës died in 1198 (AH 595), his remains were returned to Córdoba; the coffin that contained his remains was loaded on one side of a beast of burden, while the books written by him were placed on the other side in order to counterbalance it. It was a good theme of meditation and recollection for the young Ibn al-ʿArabī, who said: "On one side the Master, on the other his books! Ah, how I wish I knew whether his hopes had been fulfilled!"

Travels and works

In 1198 (AH 595), while in Murcia, he had a vision in which he felt he had been ordered to leave Spain and set out for the East. Thus began his pilgrimage to the Orient, from which he never was to return to his homeland. The first notable place he visited on this journey was Mecca (1201 [AH 598]), where he "received a divine commandment" to begin his major work *al-Futūḥāt al-Makkīyah* ("The Meccan Revelations"), which was to be completed much later in Damascus. In 560 chapters, it is a work of tremendous size, a personal encyclopaedia extending over all the esoteric sciences in Islām as Ibn al-ʿArabī understood and had experienced them, together with valuable information about his own inner life.

It was also in Mecca that he became acquainted with a young girl of great beauty who, as a living embodiment of the eternal *sophia* (wisdom), was to play in his life a role much like that Beatrice played for Dante. Her memories were eternalized by Ibn al-ʿArabī in a collection of love poems (*Tarjumān al-ashwāq;* "The Interpreter of Desires"), upon which he himself composed a mystical commentary. His daring "pantheistic" expressions drew down on him the wrath of Muslim orthodoxy, some of whom prohibited the reading of his works at the same time that others were elevating him to the rank of the prophets and saints.

After Mecca, he visited Egypt (1201 [AH 598]), and then Anatolia, where, in Qunya, he met Ṣadr ad-Dīn al-Qūnawī who was to become his most important follower and successor in the East. From Qunya he went on to Bagdad and Aleppo. By the time his long pilgrimage had come to an end at Damascus (1223 [AH 620]), his fame had spread all over the Islāmic world. Venerated as the greatest spiritual master, he spent the rest of his life in Damascus in peaceful contemplation, teaching, and writing. It was during his Damascus days that one of the most important works in mystical philosophy in Islām, *Fuṣūṣ al-ḥikam* ("The Bezels of Wisdom") was composed in 1229 (AH 627), about ten years before his death. Consisting only of 27 chapters, the book is incomparably smaller than *al-Futūḥāt al-Makkīyah*, but its importance as an expression of Ibn al-ʿArabī's mystical thought in its most mature form cannot be overemphasized. He died on November 16, 1240 (AH 638).

BIBLIOGRAPHY. A.M. PALACIOS, *El Islam cristianizado; estudio del "sufismo" a través de las obras de Abenarabi de Murcia* (1931); R.A. NICHOLSON, *Studies in Islamic Mysticism* (1921); A.E. AFFIFI, *The Mystical Philosophy of Muhyid-Din Ibnul ʿArabi* (1939); S.H. NASR, *Three Muslim Sages* (1963); M.M. SHARIF (ed.), *A History of Muslim Philosophy*, vol. 2 (1963); HENRY CORBIN, *Creative Imagination in the Sūfism of Ibn ʿArabī* (Eng. trans. 1969); OSMAN YAHYA, *Histoire et classification de l'oeuvre d'Ibn ʿArabī*, 2 vol. (1964); T. IZUTSU, *A Comparative Study of the Key Philosophical Concepts in Sufism and Taoism: Ibn ʿArabî and Lao Tzû, Chuang Tzû*, 2 *vol.* (1966–67). See especially the works of Palacios, Nasr, and Corbin for biographical information.

(T.I.)

Ibn Baṭṭūṭah

Abū ʿAbd Allāh Muḥammad ibn ʿAbd Allāh al-Lawātī aṭ-Ṭanjī, known as Ibn Baṭṭūṭah, was the greatest medieval Arab traveller and the author of one of the most famous travel books in history.

Early life and travels

Born at Tangier, Morocco, on February 24, 1304, into a family that produced a number of Muslim judges (*qāḍīs*), he received the traditional juristic and literary education in his native town. In 1325, at the age of 21, he started his travels by undertaking the pilgrimage to Mecca. At first his purpose was to fulfill this religious duty and to broaden his education by studying under famous scholars in the Near East (Egypt, Syria, and Hejaz). That he achieved his objectives is corroborated by long enumerations of scholars and Ṣūfī (Islāmic mystic) saints whom he met and also by a list of diplomas conferred upon him (mainly in Damascus). These studies qualified him for judicial office, whereas the claim of being a former pupil of the then-outstanding authorities in traditional Islāmic sciences greatly enhanced his chances and made him thereafter a respected guest at many courts.

But this was to follow later. In Egypt, where he arrived by the land route via Tunis and Tripoli, an irresistible passion for travel was born in his soul, and he decided to visit as many parts of the world as possible, setting as a rule "never to travel any road a second time." His contemporaries travelled for practical reasons (such as trade, pilgrimage, and education), but Ibn Baṭṭūṭah did it for its own sake, for the joy of learning about new countries and new peoples. He made a living of it, benefitting at the beginning from his scholarly status and later from his increasing fame as a traveller. He enjoyed the generosity and benevolence of numerous sultans, rulers, governors, and high dignitaries in the countries he visited, thus securing an income that enabled him to continue his wanderings.

From Cairo, Ibn Baṭṭūṭah set out via Upper Egypt to the Red Sea but then returned and visited Syria, there joining a caravan for Mecca. Having finished the pilgrimage in 1326, he crossed the Arabian Desert to Iraq, southern Iran, Azerbaijan, and Baghdad. There he met the last of the Mongol khans of Iran, Abū Saʿīd (1316–36), and some lesser rulers. Ibn Baṭṭūṭah spent the years between 1327 and 1330 in Mecca and Medina leading the quiet life of a devotee, but such a long stay did not suit his temperament.

Embarking on a boat in Jidda, he sailed with a retinue of followers down both shores of the Red Sea to Yemen, crossed it by land, and set sail again from Aden. This time he navigated along the eastern African coast, visiting the trading city-states as far as Kilwa (modern Tanzania). His return journey took him to southern Arabia, Oman, Hormuz, southern Persia, and across the Persian Gulf back to Mecca in 1332.

There a new, ambitious plan matured in his mind. Hearing of the sultan of Delhi, Muḥammad ibn Tughluq (1325–51), and his fabulous generosity to Muslim scholars, he decided to try his luck at his court. Forced by lack of communications to choose a more indirect route, Ibn Baṭṭūṭah turned northward, again passed Egypt and Syria, and boarded ship for Asia Minor in Latakia. He crisscrossed this "land of the Turks" in many directions at a time when Anatolia was divided into numerous petty sultanates. Thus, his narrative provides a valuable source for the history of this country between the end of the Seljuk power and the rise of the house of Ottoman. Ibn Baṭṭūṭah was received cordially and generously by all the local rulers and heads of religious brotherhoods (*ākhīs*).

His journey continued across the Black Sea to the Crimea, then to the northern Caucasus and to Saray on the lower Volga, capital of the khan of the Golden Horde, Muḥammad Özbeg (1312–41). According to his narrative, he undertook an excursion from Saray to Bulgary on the upper Volga and Kama, but there are reasons to doubt his veracity on this point. On the other hand, the narrative of his visit to Constantinople in the retinue of the khan's wife, a Byzantine princess, seems to be an eyewitness record, although there are some minor chronological discrepancies. Ibn Baṭṭūṭah's description of the Byzantine capital is vivid and, in general, accurate. Although he shared the strong opinions of his fellow Muslims toward unbelievers, his account of the "second Rome" shows him as a rather tolerant man with a lively curiosity. Nevertheless, he always felt happier in the realm of Islām than in non-Muslim lands, whether Christian, Hindu, or pagan.

After his return from Constantinople through the Russian steppes, he continued his journey in the general direction of India. From Saray he travelled with a caravan to Central Asia, visiting the ancient towns of Bukhara, Samarkand, and Balkh, all of these still showing the scars left by the Mongol invasion. He took rather complicated routes through Khorāsān and Afghanistan, and, after crossing the Hindu Kush ("mountains"), he arrived at the frontiers of India on the Indus River on September 12, 1333, by his own dating. The accuracy of this date is doubtful, as it would have been impossible to cover such enormous distances (from Mecca) in the course of only one year. Because of this discrepancy, his subsequent dating until 1348 is highly uncertain.

Sojourn in India

At this time he was already a man of some importance and fame, with a large train of attendants and followers and also with his own harem of legal wives and concubines. India and its ruler, Muḥammad ibn Tughluq, lived up to Ibn Baṭṭūṭah's expectations of wealth and generosity, and the traveller was received with honours and gifts and later appointed grand *qāḍī* ("judge") of Delhi, a sinecure that he held for several years.

Though he had apparently attained an easy life, it soon became clear that his new position was not without danger. Sultan Muḥammad, an extraordinary mixture of generosity and cruelty, held sway over the greater part of India with an iron hand that fell indiscriminately upon high and low, Muslim and Hindu alike. Ibn Baṭṭūṭah witnessed all the glories and setbacks of the Sultan and his rule, fearing daily for his life as he saw many friends fall victim to the suspicious despot. His portrait of Muḥammad is an unusually fine piece of psychological insight and mirrors faithfully the author's mixed feelings of terror and sympathy. Notwithstanding all his precautions, Ibn Baṭṭūṭah at last fell into disgrace, and only good fortune saved his life; gaining favour again, he was appointed the Sultan's envoy to the Chinese emperor in 1342.

He left Delhi without regrets, but his journey was full of other dangers: not far away from Delhi his party was waylaid by Hindu insurgents, and the traveller barely escaped with his life. On the Malabar Coast he became involved in local wars and was finally shipwrecked near Calicut, losing all his property and the presents for the Chinese emperor. Fearing the wrath of the Sultan, Ibn Baṭṭūṭah chose to go to the Maldive Islands, where he spent nearly two years; as a *qāḍī*, he was soon active in politics, married into the ruling family, and apparently even aspired to become sultan.

Finding the situation too dangerous, he set out for Ceylon, where he visited the ruler as well as the famous Adams Peak. After a new shipwreck on the Coromandel Coast of eastern India, he took part in a war led by his brother-in-law and went again to the Maldives and then to Bengal and Assam. At this time he decided to resume his mission to China and sailed for Sumatra. There he was given a new ship by the Muslim sultan and started for China; his description of his intinerary contains some discrepancies.

He landed at the great Chinese port Zaytūn (identified as Ch'üan-chou near Amoy) and then travelled on inland waterways as far as Peking and back. This part of his narrative is rather brief, and the itinerary, as well as the chronology, presents many problems and difficulties, not yet surmounted, that cast shadows of doubt on his veracity.

Equally brief is his account of the return voyage via Sumatra, Malabar, and the Persian Gulf to Baghdad and Syria. In Syria he witnessed the ravages of the Black Death of 1348, visited again many towns there and in Egypt, and in the same year performed his final pilgrimage to Mecca. At last he decided to return home, sailing from Alexandria to Tunisia, then to Sardinia and Algiers, finally reaching Fès, the capital of the Mārinid sultan, Abū ʿInān, in November 1349.

But there still remained two Muslim countries not yet known to him. Shortly after his return he went to the kingdom of Granada, the last remnant of Moorish Spain, and two years later (in 1352) he set out on a journey to the western Sudan. His last journey (across the Sahara to West Africa) was taken unwillingly at the command of the Sultan. Crossing the Sahara, he spent a year in the Empire of Mali, then at the height of its power under Mansa Sulaymān; his account represents one of the most important sources of that period for the history of that part of Africa.

Toward the end of 1353 Ibn Baṭṭūṭah returned to Morocco and, at the Sultan's request, dictated his reminiscences to a writer, Ibn Juzayy, who embellished the simple prose of Ibn Baṭṭūṭah with an ornate style and numerous fragments of poetry. After that he passes from sight, and it is known only that he died in 1368 or 1369, holding the office of *qāḍī* in some town in Morocco, and that he was buried in his native town, Tangier.

The claim of Ibn Baṭṭūṭah to be "the traveller of Islām" is well founded: it is estimated that the extent of his wanderings was 75,000 miles, a figure hardly surpassed by anyone before the age of steam. He visited, with few exceptions (central Persia, Armenia, and Georgia), all Muslim countries, as well as many adjacent non-Muslim lands. While he did not discover new or unknown lands, and his contribution to scientific geography was minimal, the documentary value of his work has given it lasting historical and geographical significance. He met at least 60 rulers and a much greater number of viziers, governors, and other dignitaries; in his book he mentioned more than 2,000 persons who were known to him personally or whose tombs he visited. The majority of these persons are identifiable by independent sources, and there are surprisingly few errors in names or dates in Baṭṭūṭah's material.

The *Riḥlah*

His *Riḥlah* (*Travels*), as his book is commonly known, is an important document shedding light on many aspects of the social, cultural, and political history of a great part of the Muslim world. A curious observer interested in the ways of life in various countries, he describes his experiences with a human approach rarely encountered in official historiography. His accounts of his travels in Asia Minor, East and West Africa, the Maldives, and India form a major source for the histories of these areas, whereas the parts dealing with the Arab and Persian Near East are valuable for their wealth of detail on various aspects of social and cultural life.

On the whole, Ibn Baṭṭūṭah is reliable; only his alleged journey to Bulgary was proved to be invented, and there are some doubts concerning the Far Eastern part of his travels. A few grave and several minor discrepancies in the chronology of his travels are due more to lapses in his memory than to intentional fabrication. A number of formerly uncertain points (*e.g.*, travels in Asia Minor and the visit to Constantinople) have been cleared away by recent research and the discovery of new corroborative sources.

Another interesting aspect of the *Travels* is the gradual revealing of the character of Ibn Baṭṭūṭah himself; in the course of the narrative the reader may learn the opinions and reactions of an average middle-class Muslim of the 14th century. He was deeply rooted in orthodox Islām but, like many of his contemporaries, oscillated between the pursuit of its legalistic formalism and an adherence to the mystic path and succeeded in combining both. He did not offer any profound philosophy but accepted life as it came to him, leaving to posterity a true picture of himself and his times.

BIBLIOGRAPHY. C. DEFREMERY and B.R. SANGUINETTI (eds.), *Voyages d'Ibn Batoutah*, 4 vol. (1853–58), remains still the standard Arabic edition and French translation; the reprint of 1969 is useful for a new introduction and commentary by VINCENT MONTEIL. SIR HAMILTON GIBB, *The Travels of Ibn Battuta*, vol. 1 (1958), vol. 2 (1962), vol. 3 (1971), no. 110, 117, and 144, 2nd ser. of the Hakluyt Society, is an unabridged translation of high literary merit with excellent footnotes (the remaining volume not yet published). An abridged version by the same author, *Ibn Battuta, Travels in Asia and Africa* (1929), is more popular. HERMAN F. JANSSENS, *Ibn Batoutah: Le Voyageur de l'Islam* (1948), is the best account of the traveller and his travels, short and precise but without scholarly claims. IVAN HRBEK, "The Chronology of Ibn Battuta's Travels," *Archiv Orientalní*, 30:409–486 (1962), attempts to solve the chronological problems and to reconstruct the true itinerary. MAHDI HUSAIN, *The Rehla* (*India, Maldive Islands and Ceylon*) (1953), comments exhaustively but not always objectively on Ibn Baṭṭūṭah's travels in India; the West African part of the travels is dealt with in R. MAUNY *et al.*, *Textes et documents relatifs à l'histoire de l'Afrique: Extraits tirés des voyages d'Ibn Battuta* (1966).

(I.Hr.)

Ibn Gabirol

Solomon ben Yehuda ibn Gabirol was one of the outstanding literary and intellectual figures of the Jewish Golden Age in Moorish Spain. He represents the acme of the Hebrew school of religious and secular poetry in Moorish Spain and was also an important Neoplatonic philosopher. He has been called the first Spanish philosopher.

Early life and career. Born in Málaga, Spain, about 1022—apparently his parents had emigrated from Córdoba when the Berbers seized the town—Ibn Gabirol received his higher education in Saragossa, where he joined the learned circle of other Córdoban refugees established there around famed scholars and the influential courtier Yekutiel ibn Ḥasan. Protected by this patron, whom Ibn Gabirol immortalized in poems of loving praise, the 16-year-old poet became famous for his religious hymns in masterly Hebrew. The customary language of Andalusian literature had been Arabic, and Hebrew had only recently been revived as a means of expression for Jewish poets. At 16 he could rightly boast of being world famous:

The young prodigy

. . . My song is a crown for kings
  and mitres on the heads of governors.
My body walks upon the earth,
  while my spirit ascends to the clouds.
Behold me: at sixteen my heart
  like that of a man of eighty is wise.

He made, however, the mistake of lampooning Samuel ha-Nagid, a rising Jewish statesman and vizier in the Berber kingdom of Granada, who was also a talented poet, Talmudist, strategist, and model writer of letters. After making poetical amends, Ibn Gabirol seems to have been admitted to the favour of this vizier, whose main court encomiast he subsequently became.

This happened while the poet was involved (on the Saragossan side) in the disproportionate strife between the grammarians of Saragossa and those of Granada concerning Hebrew linguistics. Being an emancipated Córdoban, he offended the orthodox with heresies such as recommending childlessness, denunciation of the "world," Neoplatonism, and an almost insane self-aggrandizement (coupled with the use of animal epithets for his opponents). He apparently had to flee from Saragossa; the circumstances leading to his departure are described in his "Song of Strife":

Sitting among everybody crooked and foolish
his [the poet's] heart only was wise.
The one slakes you with adder's poison,
the other, flattering, tries to confuse your head.
One, setting you a trap in his design
will address you: "Please, my lord."
A people whose fathers I would despise
to be dogs for my sheep. . . .

His "Song of Strife" and other poems show that his being a synagogal poet did not protect him against the hatred of his co-religionists in Saragossa, who called him a Greek because of his secular leanings.

Against all warnings by his patron Yekutiel, Ibn Gabirol concentrated on Neoplatonic philosophy, after having composed a non-offensive collection of proverbs in Arabic, *Mukhtār al-jawāhir* (*Choice of Pearls*), and a more original, though dated, ethical treatise (based on contemporary theories of the human temperaments), also in Arabic, *Kitāb iṣlāḥ al-akhlāq* (*The Improvement of the Moral Qualities*). The latter contains chapters on pride, meekness, modesty, and impudence, which are linked with the sense of sight; and on love, hate, compassion, and cruelty, linked with hearing and other senses.

In need of a new patron after the execution of Yekutiel in 1039 by those who had murdered his king and taken over power, Ibn Gabirol secured a position as a court poet with Samuel ha-Nagid, who, becoming the leading statesman of Granada, was in need of the poet's prestige. Ibn Gabirol composed widely resounding poems with a messianic tinge for Samuel and for Jehoseph (Yūsuf), his son and later successor in the vizierate of Granada. All other biographical data about Ibn Gabirol except his place of death, Valencia, must be extrapolated from his poetry. He probably died about 1070.

Poetry. The Jewish subculture of Moorish Andalusia (southern Spain) was engendered by the cultural "pressure" of the Arab peers. Ibn Gabirol's dual education, typical for the Jewish intelligentsia in the larger cities, must have encompassed both the entire Hebrew literary heritage—the Bible, Talmud, and other rabbinic writings and, in particular, Hebrew linguistics—and the Arabic, including the Qur'ān, Arabic secular and religious poetry and poetics, and the philosophical, philological, and possibly medical literature.

His poetry, like that of the entire contemporary Hebrew school, is modelled after the Arabic. Metrics, rhyme systems, and most of the highly developed imagery follow the Arabic school, but the biblical language adds a particular tinge. Many of Ibn Gabirol's poems show the influence of the knightly Arab bard al-Mutanabbī and the pessimistic Abū al-ʿAlāʾ al-Maʿarrī.

Poetic subject matter

His secular topics included exaggerated, Arab-inspired self-praise, justified by the fame of the child prodigy; love poems (renouncing yet keenly articulate); praise of his noble and learned protectors, together with scathingly satirical reproach of others; dirges (the most moving of which are linked with the execution of the innocent Yekutiel); wine songs (sometimes libertine); spring and rain poems; flower portraits; the agonizingly realistic description of a skin ailment; and a long didactic poem on Hebrew grammar. Ibn Gabirol's long poetic description of a castle led to the discovery of the origins of the first Alhambra palace, built by the above-mentioned Jehoseph. Of a very rich production, about 200 secular poems and even more religious ones were preserved, though no collection of his poems survived. Many manuscript fragments of the former came to light only recently, preserved in synagogue attics by his co-religionists' respect for the Hebrew letter. Many of his religious poems were included in Jewish prayer books throughout the world.

His religious poems, in particular the poignant short prayers composed for the individual, presuppose the high degree of literacy typical of Moorish Spain, and they, too, show Arabic incentive. His famed rhymed prose poem "Keter malkhut" ("The Crown of the Kingdom"), a meditation stating the measurements of the spheres of the universe, jolts the reader into the abject feeling of his smallness but, subsequently, builds him up by a proclamation of the divine grace.

The following morning meditation exemplifies his religious poetry:

See me at dawn, my Rock;
my Shelter, when my plight
I state before Thy face
likewise again at night,
Outpouring anguished thought—
that Thou behold'st my heart
and what it contemplates
I realise in fright.
Low though the value be
of mind's and lip's tribute
to Thee (accomplishes aught
my spirit with its might?).
Most cherish'st Thou the hymn
we sing before Thee. Thus,
while Thou support'st my breath,
I praise Thee in Thine height.
Amen.

Philosophy. His *Fountain of Life*, in five treatises, is preserved in toto only in the Latin translation, *Fons vitae*, with the author's name appearing as Avicebron or Avencebrol; it was re-identified as Ibn Gabirol's work by Salomon Munk in 1846. It had little influence upon Jewish philosophy other than on León Hebreo (Judah Abrabanel) and Benedict de Spinoza, but it inspired the Kabbalists, the adherents of Jewish esoteric mysticism. Its influence upon Christian Scholasticism was marked, although it was attacked by St. Thomas Aquinas for equating concepts with realities. Grounded in Plotinus and other Neoplatonic writers yet also in Aristotelian logic and metaphysics, Ibn Gabirol developed a system in which he introduced the conception of a divine will, like the Logos (or divine "word") of Philo. It is an essential unity of creativity of and with God, mutually related like sun and sunlight, which mediates actively between the transcendent deity and the cosmos that God created out of nothingness (to be understood as the potentiality for creation). Matter emanates directly from the deity as a prime matter that supports all substances and even the "intelligent" substances, the sphere-moving powers and angels. This concept was accepted by the Franciscan school of Scholastics but rejected by the Dominicans, including St. Thomas, for whom form (and only one, not many) and not matter is the creative principle. Since matter, according to Aristotle and Plotinus, "yearns for formation" and, thus, moving toward the nearness of God, causes the rotation of the spheres, the finest matter of the highest spheres is propelled by the strongest "yearning," which issues from God and returns to him and is active in man (akin to the last line of Dante's *Divine Comedy:* "The love which moves the sun and the other stars").

Philosophical system

Yet, the dry treatise does not betray the passionate quest of the Neoplatonist author. A philosophical poem, beginning "That man's love," reveals the human intent. Therein, a disciple asks the poet-philosopher what importance the world could have for the deity (to be understood in Aristotelian terms as a deity that only contemplates its own perfection). The poet answers that all of existence is permeated, though to different degrees, by the yearning of matter toward formation, and he declares that this yearning may give God the "glory" that the heavens proclaim, as the Bible teaches.

BIBLIOGRAPHY. A brief biography may be found in ISRAEL DAVIDSON and ISRAEL ZANGWILL, *Selected Religious Poems of Solomon ibn Gabirol* (1923). Other biographical treatments are in H. GRAETZ, *History of the Jews,* vol. 3 (1956); S.W. BARON, *A Social and Religious History of the Jews,* vol. 7–8 (1958), which also gives a characterization of the poet's works; and F.P. BARGEBUHR, *El Palacio de la Alhambra en el siglo XI* (1966; Eng. trans., *The Alhambra: A Cycle of Studies* *on the Eleventh Century in Moorish Spain*, 1968), with translations of secular poems—biographical information is contained in the preface to the English edition. See also ERMENEGILDO BERTOLA, *Salomon ibn Gabirol (Avicebron): vita, opere e pensiero* (1953).

Religious poems: Translated in Davidson and Zangwill (see above); and BERNARD LEWIS, *The Kingly Crown* (1961).

Ethical treatise: STEPHEN S. WISE (ed. and trans.), *The Improvement of the Moral Qualities* (1902).

Philosophy: CLEMENS BAEUMKER, *Fount of Life* (1892); JOHN GOHEEN, *The Problem of Matter and Form in the "De Ente et Essentia" of Thomas Aquinas* (1940); H.E. WEDECK (trans.), *The Fountain of Life* (1963).

(F.P.B.)

Ibn Ḥazm

Abū Muḥammad ʿAlī ibn Aḥmad ibn Saʿīd ibn Ḥazm was an erudite literary and political gadfly of 11th-century Islāmic Spain. Prolific literary activity, extraordinary breadth of learning, and mastery of the Arabic language secured for him an enviable place in Islāmic history as litterateur, historian, jurist, and theologian.

Family and political involvement

Ibn Ḥazm was born in Córdoba on the 30th day of Ramaḍān, AH 384 (November 7, AD 994) into a notable family that claimed descent from a Persian client of Yazīd, the brother of Muʿāwiyah, the first of the Umayyad dynasty rulers in Syria. Muslim families of Iberian (Spanish) background commonly adopted genealogies that identified them with the Arabs; scholars therefore tend to favour evidence suggesting that Ibn Ḥazm was a member of a family of Iberian, Christian background from Manta Līsham (west of Seville). Ḥazm, his great-grandfather, probably converted to the Islāmic faith, and his grandfather Saʿīd moved to Córdoba, the capital of the caliphate. Aḥmad, his father, a devout and learned man, held a high position under al-Manṣūr and his successor, al-Muẓaffar, a father and son who ruled efficiently in the name of the caliph Hishām II.

Living in the circles of the ruling hierarchy provided Ibn Ḥazm, an eager and observant student, with excellent educational opportunities. Experiences in the surroundings of the harem made an indelible impression upon him.

Circumstances for Ibn Ḥazm changed drastically upon the death of al-Muẓaffar in AD 1008, when the stability that the Umayyads had provided for over two and one-half centuries collapsed. A bloody civil war ensued and continued until 1031, when the caliphate was abolished and a large number of petty states replaced any semblance of a centralized political structure. The family was uprooted and Aḥmad died in 1012; Ibn Ḥazm continued to boldly and persistently support Umayyad claimants to the office of caliph, for which he was frequently imprisoned.

By 1031 he began to express his convictions and activistic inclinations through literary activity, becoming a very controversial figure. With the exception of a short stay on the island of Majorca, he apparently spent most of his time on the family estate in Manta Līsham. According to one of his sons, he produced some 80,000 pages of writing, comprising about 400 works. Less than 40 of these works are still extant.

Literary activities

The varied character of his literary activity covers an impressive range of jurisprudence, logic, history, ethics, comparative religion, and theology. His appreciation of the resources of the Arabic language and his skillful use of poetry and prose are evident in all his works. One delightful example is *The Ring of the Dove* (*Ṭawq al-ḥamāmah*), on the art of love. Probably best known for his work in jurisprudence and theology, for which the basic qualification was a thorough knowledge of the Qurʾān (the Islāmic scripture) and Ḥadīth (Tradition), he became one of the leading exponents of the Ẓāhirī school of jurisprudence. The Ẓāhirī principle of legal theory relies exclusively on the literal (*ẓāhir*) meaning of the Qurʾān and Tradition. Though his legal theories never won him many followers, he creatively extended the Ẓāhirī principle to the field of theology. He made a comparative study on the religious pluralism of his day, which is among the earliest of such studies and is highly regarded for its careful historical detail.

An activist by nature with a deep sense of the reality of God, Ibn Ḥazm lived very much in the political and intellectual world of his times; in spite of his activism, however, he was very much a nonconformist and a loner. He conversed and debated with the leading contemporaries of his area, to whom he exhibited an insatiable thirst for knowledge as well as uncompromising convictions. Most observant, careful in analysis, meticulous in detail, and devoted to the clarity of his positions, he demanded the same of others. According to a saying of the period, the tongue of Ibn Ḥazm was a twin brother to the sword of al-Ḥajjaj, a famous 7th-century general and governor of Iraq. He attacked, in his writings, deceit, distortion, and inconsistency; but at the same time Ibn Ḥazm exhibited a sensitive spirit and expressed profound insights about the dimensions of human relationships. He was shunned and defamed for his political and theological views. When some of his writings were burned in public, he said that no such act could deprive him of their content.

Ibn Ḥazm died at the family estate in Manta Līsham on the 28th of Shaʿbān, AH 456 (August 15, 1064). Although attacks against him continued after his death, various influential defenders appeared. Though he apparently was easy to despise, Ibn Ḥazm could hardly be ignored. He was frequently and effectively quoted, so much so that the phrase "Ibn Ḥazm said" became proverbial.

BIBLIOGRAPHY. IBN HAZM, *Ṭawq al-hamāma*, trans. by A.R. NYKL, *The Dove's Neck-Ring* (1931), also by A.J. ARBERRY, *The Ring of the Dove* (1953), contains many references to Ibn Ḥazm's experiences. Arberry's English translation is recommended. E. GARCIA GOMEZ's translation in Spanish, *El Collar de la Paloma* (1952), contains a good introduction to Ibn Ḥazm's life and also an extensive biobibliography. The article by R. ARNALDEZ in the *Encyclopaedia of Islam*, new ed. (1968), is one of the few up-to-date comprehensive surveys of Ibn Ḥazm's life, works, and thought. IGNAZ GOLDZIHER, *Die Ẓāhiriten, ihr Lehrsystem und ihre Geschichte* (1884; Eng. trans., *The Ẓāhirīs: Their Doctrine and Their History*, trans. and ed. by WOLFGANG BEHN, 1971), is a basic work on the Ẓāhirī school of law and Ibn Ḥazm's application of the system to theology. See the biography of Ibn Ḥazm in IBN KHALLIKAN, *Wafayāt al-A'yān wa-Anbā' al-Zamām*, Eng. trans. by BARON MACGUCKIN DE SLANE, 4 vol. (1842–71, reprinted 1961), a translation of a famous biographical dictionary of the 13th century.

(J.W.F.)

Ibn Khaldūn

Abū Zayd ʿAbd ar-Raḥmān ibn Khaldūn, an Arab philosopher of history, historian, and sociologist, was the greatest social scientist of Islām and indeed the outstanding figure in the social sciences between Aristotle and Machiavelli. He developed one of the world's most significant philosophies of history and wrote a definitive history of Muslim North Africa.

Background and early life. Ibn Khaldūn was born in Tunis on May 27, 1332; the Khaldūnīyah quarter in Tunis still stands almost unchanged and, in it, the house where he is believed to have been born.

As Ibn Khaldūn relates in his autobiography (*at-Taʿrīf bi-Ibn Khaldūn*), the family claimed descent from Khaldūn, who was of South Arabian stock, came to Spain in the early years of the Arab conquest, and settled in Carmona. The family subsequently moved to Seville, played an important part in the civil wars of the 9th century, and was long reckoned among the three leading houses of that city. In the course of the next four centuries, the Ibn Khaldūns successively held high administrative and political posts under the Umayyad, Almoravid, and Almohad dynasties; other members of the family served in the army, and several were killed at the Battle of az-Zallāqah (1086), which temporarily halted the Christian reconquest of Spain. But the respite thus won proved short, and in 1248, just before the fall of Seville and Córdoba, the Ibn Khaldūns and many of their countrymen judged it prudent to cross the Straits of Gibraltar and landed at Sabtah (now Ceuta, a Spanish exclave), on the northern coast of Morocco.

There the refugees from Spain were on a much higher level than the local North Africans, and the family was soon called to occupy the leading administrative posts in Tunis. The historian's father also became an administrator and soldier but soon abandoned his career to devote himself to the study of theology, law, and letters. In Ibn Khaldūn's words:

> He was outstanding in his knowledge of Arabic and had an understanding of poetry in its different forms and I can well remember how the men of letters sought his opinion in matters of dispute and submitted their works to him.

In 1349, however, the Black Death struck Tunis and took away both his father and his mother.

Education

Ibn Khaldūn gives a detailed account of his education, listing the main books he read and describing the life and works of his teachers. He memorized the Qur'ān, studied its principal commentaries, gained a good grounding in Muslim law, familiarized himself with the masterpieces of Arabic literature, and acquired a clear and forceful style and a capacity for writing fluent verse that was to serve him well in later life when addressing eulogistic or supplicatory poems to various rulers. Striking by their absence are books on philosophy, history, geography, or other social sciences; this does not mean that he did not study these subjects—scholars know that he wrote summaries of several books by the 12th-century Arab philosopher Averroës—but it is to be presumed that Ibn Khaldūn acquired most of his very impressive knowledge in these fields after he had completed his formal education.

This came at the age of 20, when he was given a post at the court of Tunis, followed three years later by a secretaryship to the Sultan of Morocco in Fez. By then he was married. After two years of service, however, he was suspected of participation in a rebellion and was imprisoned. Released after nearly two years and promoted by a new ruler, he again fell into disfavour, decided to leave Morocco, and crossed over to Granada, for whose Muslim ruler he had done some service in Fez and whose prime minister, the brilliant writer Ibn al-Khaṭīb, was a good friend. Ibn Khaldūn was then 32 years old.

The following year he was sent to Seville to conclude a peace treaty with Pedro I the Cruel of Castile. There he saw "the monuments of my ancestors." Pedro "treated me with the utmost generosity, expressed his satisfaction at my presence and showed awareness of the pre-eminence of our ancestors in Seville." Pedro even offered him a post in his service, promising to restore his ancestral estates, but Ibn Khaldūn politely declined. He gladly accepted the village that the Sultan of Granada bestowed on him, however, and, feeling once more secure, brought over his family, which he had left in safety in Qunsṭanṭinah (Constantine). But, to quote him once more, "enemies and intriguers" turned the all-powerful prime minister, Ibn al-Khaṭīb, against him and raised suspicions regarding his loyalty; it can be conjectured that the task of these enemies must have been greatly facilitated by the apparent jealousy between the two most brilliant Arab intellectuals of the age. Once more, Ibn Khaldūn found it necessary to take his leave, and he returned to Africa. The following ten years saw him change employers and employment with disconcerting rapidity and move from Bejaïa (Bougie) to Tilimsān (Tlemcen), Biskra, Fez, and once more to Granada, where he made an unsuccessful effort to save his old rival and friend, Ibn al-Khaṭīb, from being killed by order of its ruler. During this period Ibn Khaldūn served as prime minister and in several other administrative capacities, led a punitive expedition, was robbed and stripped by nomads, and spent some time "studying and teaching." This extreme mobility is partly explained by the instability of the times. The Almohad Empire, which had embraced the whole of North Africa and Muslim Spain, had broken down in the middle of the 13th century, and the convulsive process from which Morocco, Algeria, and Tunisia were subsequently to emerge was under way; wars, rebellions, and intrigues were endemic, and no man's life or employment was secure. But in Ibn Khaldūn's case two additional factors might be suspected—a certain restlessness and a capacity to make enemies, which may account for his constant complaints about the "intriguers" who turned his employers against him.

Refuge at Qalʿat ibn Salāmah. In 1375, craving solitude and withdrawal from the exhausting business of politics, Ibn Khaldūn took the most momentous step of his life: he sought refuge with the tribe of Awlād ʿArīf, who lodged him and his family in the safety of a castle, Qalʿat ibn Salāmah, near what is now the town of Frenda, Algeria. There he spent four years, "free from all preoccupations," and wrote his massive masterpiece, *The Muqaddimah* (an introduction to history). His original intention, which he subsequently achieved, was to write a universal history of the Arabs and Berbers, but before doing so he judged it necessary to discuss historical method, with the aim of providing the criteria necessary for distinguishing historical truth from error. This led him to formulate what the 20th-century English historian Arnold Toynbee has described as "a philosophy of history which is undoubtedly the greatest work of its kind that has ever yet been created by any mind in any time or place," a statement that goes even beyond the earlier eulogy by Robert Flint:

Philosophy of history

> As a theorist on history he had no equal in any age or country until Vico appeared, more than three hundred years later. Plato, Aristotle and Augustine were not his peers. . . .

But Ibn Khaldūn went even further. His study of the nature of society and social change led him to evolve what he clearly saw was a new science, which he called *ʿilm al-ʿumrān* ("the science of culture") and which he defined thus:

> This science . . . has its own subject, viz., human society, and its own problems, viz., the social transformations that succeed each other in the nature of society.

Indeed it is not too much to claim, as did a contemporary Arab scholar, Sāṭiʿ al-Ḥuṣrī, that in Book I of *The Muqaddimah*, Ibn Khaldūn sketches a general sociology; in Books II and III, a sociology of politics; in Book IV, a sociology of urban life; in Book V, a sociology of economics; and in Book VI, a sociology of knowledge. The work is studded with brilliant observations on historiography, economics, politics, and education. It is held together by his central concept of *ʿaṣabīyah*, or "social cohesion." It is this cohesion, which arises spontaneously in tribes and other small kinship groups, but which can be intensified and enlarged by a religious ideology, that provides the motive force that carries ruling groups to power. Its inevitable weakening, due to a complex combination of psychological, sociological, economic, and political factors, which Ibn Khaldūn analyzes with consummate skill, heralds the decline of a dynasty or empire and prepares the way for a new one, based on a group bound by a stronger cohesive force.

It is difficult to overstress Ibn Khaldūn's amazing originality. Muhsin Mahdi, a contemporary Iraqi-American scholar, has shown how much his approach and fundamental concepts owe to classical Islāmic theology and philosophy, especially Averroism. And, of course, he drew liberally on the historical information accumulated by his predecessors and was doubtless influenced by their judgments. But nothing in these sources or, indeed, in any known Greek or Latin author can explain his deep insight into social phenomena, his firm grasp of the links binding the innumerable and apparently unrelated events that constitute the process of historical and social change.

One last point should be made regarding his basic philosophy of history. Clearly, for Ibn Khaldūn, history was an endless cycle of flowering and decay, with no evolution or progress except for that from primitive to civilized society. But, in brief descriptions of his own age, which have not received as much attention as they deserve, he showed that he could both visualize the existence of sharp turning points in history and recognize that he was witnessing one of them: "When there is a general change of conditions . . . as if it were a new and repeated creation, a world brought into existence anew." The main cause he gives for this great change is the Black Death, with its profound effect on Muslim society, but he was fully aware of the impact of the Mongol invasions, and he may also have been impressed by the development of Europe, the merchants and ships of which thronged the seaports of North Africa and some of the soldiers of which served as mercenaries in the Muslim armies.

Journey to Egypt. During his stay in Qalʿat ibn Salāmah, Ibn Khaldūn not only completed the first draft of *The Muqaddimah*, but he also wrote part of his massive history, *Kitab al-ʿibar*, a work that is not of such universal significance but which does constitute the best single source on the history of Muslim North Africa. Such a task, however, required frequent reference to other books and archives; this, together perhaps with nostalgia for the more active world of politics, drew him back to city life. A severe illness finally convinced him to leave his refuge; he secured permission to return to Tunis, where he "engaged exclusively in scholarly work," completing much of his history. But once more he aroused both the jealousy of a prominent scholar and the suspicion of the ruler, and in 1382, at the age of 50, he received permission to sail to Egypt, ostensibly for the purpose of performing the pilgrimage to Mecca. After 40 days he landed in Alexandria and shortly afterward was in Cairo, then, as now, by far the largest and most opulent city in the Arab world. Its impact on him was profound: "I saw the metropolis of the earth, the garden of the world, the gathering place of the nations . . . the palace of Islām, the seat of dominion . . . ." His curiosity about Cairo was evidently of long duration, for he quotes the replies several eminent North Africans had made to his enquiries on their return from that city, including: "He who has not seen it does not know the power of Islām."

Return to city life

Within a few days "scholars thronged on me, seeking profit in spite of the scarcity of merchandise [!] and would not accept my excuses, so I started teaching at al-Azhar," the famous Islāmic university. Shortly afterward, the new Mamlūk ruler of Egypt, Barqūq, with whom he was to remain on good terms except for one or two brief periods of misunderstanding, appointed him to a professorship of jurisprudence at the Qamḥīyah college and, within five months, made him chief judge of the Mālikī rite, one of the four recognized rites of Sunnī Islām. Barqūq also successfully interceded with the ruler of Tunis to allow Ibn Khaldūn's family to rejoin him, but the ship carrying them foundered in the port of Alexandria, drowning all on board.

Later years. Ibn Khaldūn took his judicial duties quite seriously; he claimed to have been guided in his judgments solely by the merits of each case and attempted to reform the numerous abuses that had developed in the administration of justice. He must have struck the tolerant and easy-going Egyptians as somewhat dour and puritanical, and his own opinion is recorded by one of his students: "These Egyptians behave as though the Day of Judgement would never come!" At any rate, "trouble gathered against me from every quarter and darkened the atmosphere between me and the rulers"; he was dismissed and served again as chief judge only for one year, toward the end of his life. But he was given another professorship—he pointed out that endowed chairs were plentiful in Cairo—and spent his time teaching, writing, and revising his *Muqaddimah*. He was also able to perform the pilgrimage to Mecca, sailing from aṭ-Ṭawr, near Suez, and returning by way of Upper Egypt. Some years later he went to Damascus and the Holy Cities of Palestine, thus further widening his knowledge of the eastern Arab world. It is interesting to note that he visited the tomb of Abraham in Hebron and the Church of the Nativity in Bethlehem, both Abraham and Jesus being honoured prophets, but he refused to enter the Holy Sepulchre, "the site of what they claim to be the Crucifixion," an event that Muslims deny occurred.

Ibn Khaldūn was forced to play a minor part in the palace revolt of 1389, but he apparently did so under duress, and Barqūq seems to have borne him no grudge. Otherwise, one gets the impression of a ripe, wise, and respected scholar, surrounded by admirers, sought out by visitors, peacefully enjoying the calm pleasures of old age. He had every reason to expect this state of affairs to continue, but fate had reserved for him one more encounter, the most dramatic of all. In 1400 Timur and his victorious Tatar horde invaded Syria, and the new sultan of Egypt, Faraj, went out to meet them, taking Ibn Khaldūn and other notables with him. Shortly thereafter, the Mamlūk army returned to Egypt, leaving Ibn Khaldūn in besieged Damascus. The situation soon becoming hopeless, the civilian notables of the city started negotiations with Timur, during the course of which he asked to meet Ibn Khaldūn. The latter was thereupon lowered over the city wall by ropes and spent some seven weeks in the Tatar camp, of which he has given a detailed description in his autobiography. Timur treated him with respect, and the historian used all his accumulated worldly wisdom and courtly flattery to charm the ferocious world conqueror. Probably dreaming of further conquests, Timur asked for a detailed description of North Africa and got not only a short lecture on that subject, on the caliphate, and on *ʿasabīyah* but also an extensive written report. Ibn Khaldūn took advantage of Timur's good mood to secure a safe-conduct for the civilian employees left in Damascus and permission for himself to return to Egypt but not before he witnessed the sack of the city and the burning of its great mosque.

Meeting with Timur

After an exchange of gifts with Timur, he headed southward but was robbed and stripped by a band of bedouins and only with difficulty made his way to the coast. There a "ship belonging to Ibn Osman, the sultan of Rum, stopped, carrying an ambassador to the sultan of Egypt" and took him to Gaza, establishing his only contact with what was soon to become the dominant power in the Middle East—the Ottoman dynasty. The rest of his journey to Cairo was uneventful, as indeed were the remaining years of his life. He died on March 17, 1406, and was buried in the cemetery outside Bāb an-Naṣr, one of Cairo's main gates.

Significance. Just as Ibn Khaldūn had no known predecessors in the history of Muslim thought, so he had no worthy successors. But he did make an impact on his students in Cairo, one of whom, al-Maqrīzī, showed an insight worthy of his master in analyzing the inflation that was rampant in his time and was the author of several voluminous works that cast much light on contemporary social conditions. Indeed, it is perhaps not too fanciful to attribute to Ibn Khaldūn's influence the remarkable revival of historical writing in 15th-century Egypt. Later, several distinguished 16th- and 17th-century Ottoman scholars and statesmen took a keen interest in Ibn Khaldūn's work, and a partial translation of *The Muqaddimah* into Turkish was made in the 18th century. But it was only after the 1860s, when a complete French translation of *The Muqaddimah* appeared, that Ibn Khaldūn found the worldwide audience his incomparable genius deserved.

BIBLIOGRAPHY. The autobiography was published by MUHAMMAD AL-TANJI, *At-taʿrîf bi-Ibn Khaldûn* (1951); an excellent translation of the introduction is FRANZ ROSENTHAL, *Ibn Khaldun: The Muqaddimah*, 3 vol. (1958); a translation of passages dealing with the social sciences is provided by CHARLES ISSAWI in *An Arab Philosophy of History* (1950). The best comprehensive study is MUHSIN MAHDI, *Ibn Khaldun's Philosophy of History* (1957); the encounter with Timur is described in WALTER FISCHEL, *Ibn Khaldun and Tamerlane* (1952).

(C.I.)

Ibn Saʿūd

Ibn Saʿūd (in full, ʿAbd al-ʿAzīz ibn ʿAbd ar-Raḥmān ibn Fayṣal ibn Turkī ibn ʿAbd Allāh ibn Muḥammad Al Saʿūd) is remembered as the man who united central Arabia, formed it into the modern state of Saudi Arabia, and initiated the exploitation of its oil. He was born around 1880 (the year is uncertain) in the Saudi capital of Riyadh.

The Saʿūds ruled much of Arabia from 1780 to 1880, but while Ibn Saʿūd was still an infant his family, driven out by their rivals, the Rashīds, became penniless exiles in Kuwait. In 1901 Ibn Saʿūd, then 21, set out from

Ibn Sa'ūd.
Camera Press—Pix

Kuwait with 40 camelmen in a bold attempt to regain his family's lands.

Reaching their old family capital, Riyadh, the little group slipped into the town by night (January 1902). The Rashīdī governor slept in the castle but came out every morning after dawn. Ibn Sa'ūd lay hidden until the governor emerged. Then, rushing forward with his men, he killed him and seized the castle.

This exploit roused the former supporters of his dynasty. They rallied to so magnetic a leader, and in two years of raids and skirmishes Ibn Sa'ūd reconquered half of central Arabia. Tall and powerfully built, his personal magnetism led men to love and obey him.

Ibn Rashīd, however, appealed for help to the Turks, who sent troops; Ibn Sa'ūd suffered a defeat at their hands on June 15, 1904. But he was not driven from central Arabia and soon reconstituted his forces, the years 1907 to 1912 being passed in desultory fighting. The Turks eventually vanished, unable to supply their troops.

Role of religion in Ibn Sa'ūd's policy

Ibn Sa'ūd decided, in the years before World War I, to revive his dynasty's support for Wahhābism, an extremist Muslim puritan revival. Ibn Sa'ūd was in fact a devoted puritan Muslim—to him the Qur'ān was literally the word of God, and his life was regulated by it. Yet he was also aware that religious fanaticism could serve his ambition, and he deliberately fostered it, founding a militantly religious tribal organization known as the Ikhwān (Brethren). This fanatical brotherhood encouraged his followers to fight and to massacre their Arab rivals, and it helped him to bring many nomadic tribesmen under more immediate control. He was able to persuade the religious leaders to declare it a religious duty of all Wahhābīs to abandon nomadism and to build houses at the desert wells. Thus settled, they could more easily be levied into his army. But the scheme was unrealistic: nomads who sold their flocks were often unable to cultivate and were reduced to penury. The destitution of the more fanatical tribes, however, made them more eager to raid, and Ibn Sa'ūd was not slow to suggest that they plunder the subjects of Ibn Rashīd.

During World War I Ibn Sa'ūd entered into a treaty with the British (December 1915), accepting protectorate status and agreeing to make war against Ibn Rashīd, who was being supported by the Turks. But despite British arms and a subsidy of £5,000 a month from the British government (which continued until 1924) he was inactive until 1920, arguing that his subsidy was insufficient. During 1920–22, however, he marched against Ibn Rashīd and extinguished Rashīdī rule, doubling his own territory but without much increasing his meagre revenue.

Ibn Sa'ūd now ruled central Arabia except for the Hejaz region along the Red Sea. This was the territory of Sharīf Ḥusayn of Mecca, who had become king of the Hejaz during the war and who declared himself caliph (head of the Muslim community) in 1924. Sharīf Ḥusayn's son 'Abd Allāh had become ruler of Transjordan in 1921, and another son, Fayṣal, king of Iraq. Ibn Sa'ūd, fearing encirclement by this rival dynasty, decided to invade the Hejaz. He was then at the height of his powers; his strong personality and extraordinary charm had won the devotion of all his subjects. A skillful politician, he worked closely with the religious leaders, who always supported him. Relying on the Ikhwān to eliminate his Arab rivals, he sent them to raid his neighbours, then cabled the British, whose imperial interests were involved, that the raid was against his orders. In 1924 the Ikhwān took Mecca, and the Hejaz was added to his dominions.

At this point, there were no more rivals whom Ibn Sa'ūd could conquer, for those remaining had treaties with Britain. But the Ikhwān had been taught that all non-Wahhābī Muslims were infidels. When Ibn Sa'ūd forbade further raiding, they charged him with treachery, quoting his own words against him. In 1927 they invaded Iraq against his wishes. They were repulsed by British aircraft, but Ibn Sa'ūd's authority over them had vanished, and on March 29, 1929, the Ikhwān, the fanatics whom he himself had trained, were crushed by Ibn Sa'ūd himself at the Battle of Sibilla.

Foundation of Saudi Arabia

This battle opened a new era; thereafter Ibn Sa'ūd's task was government, not conquest. In 1932 he formally unified his domains into the Kingdom of Saudi Arabia. An absolute monarch, he had no regular civil service or professional administrators. All decisions were made by him or by those he personally delegated for a particular task. There was little money, and he himself was not interested in finance. In May 1933 Ibn Sa'ūd signed his first agreement with an American oil company. Not until March 1938 did the company strike oil, and work virtually ceased during World War II, so that Ibn Sa'ūd was again nearly penniless.

Saudi Arabia took no part in the war, but toward its end the exploitation of oil was resumed. By 1950 he had received a total of about $200,000. Three years later, he was getting some $2,500,000 a week. The effect was disastrous on the country and on Ibn Sa'ūd. He had no idea of what to do with all the money, and he watched helplessly the triumph of everything he hated. His austere religious views were offended. The secluded, penurious, hard, but idealistic, life of Arabia was vanishing. Such vast sums of money drew half the swindlers in the Middle East to this puritan religious sanctum. Ibn Sa'ūd was unable to cope with financial adventurers. Bewildered, unhappy, crippled by arthritis and nearly blind, in his last years he was a pathetic sight. He died in his sleep at aṭ-Ṭā'if on November 9, 1953, at the age of 73.

BIBLIOGRAPHY. DAVID A. HOWARTH, *The Desert King* (1964), is the best biography; J.B. GLUBB, *War in the Desert* (1960), describes Ikhwān raids and meetings with Ibn Sa'ūd. See also H.ST.J. PHILBY, *Arabia of the Wahhabis* (1930). Philby knew Ibn Sa'ūd intimately, but was strongly prejudiced in his favour. AMEEN F. RIHANI, *Ibn Sa'oud of Arabia* (1928), is an account of a visit to Idn Sa'ūd in 1923.

(J.B.Gl.)

Ibn Taymīyah

Ibn Taymīyah, who was born in Harran, Mesopotamia, in 1263, was one of Islām's most forceful theologians. Educated in Damascus, where he had been taken in 1268 as a refugee from the Mongol invasion, he later steeped himself in the teachings of the Pietist school founded by Ibn Ḥanbal (died 855). Though he remained faithful throughout his life to that school, of whose doctrines he had an unrivalled mastery, he also acquired an extensive knowledge of contemporary Islāmic sources and disciplines: the Qur'ān (Islāmic scripture), the Ḥadīth (sayings attributed to the Prophet Muḥammad), jurisprudence (*fiqh*), dogmatic theology (*kalām*), philosophy, and Ṣūfī (Islāmic mystical) theology.

His life was marked by persecutions. As early as 1293 Ibn Taymīyah came into conflict with local authorities for protesting a sentence, pronounced under religious law, against a Christian accused of having insulted the Prophet. In 1298 he was accused of anthropomorphism (ascribing human characteristics to God) and for having criticized, contemptuously, the legitimacy of dogmatic theology.

During the great Mongol crisis of the years 1299 to 1303, and especially during the occupation of Damascus, he led the resistance party and denounced the suspect faith of the invaders and their accomplices. During the ensuing years Ibn Taymīyah was engaged in intensive polemic activity: either against the Kasrawān Shīʿites in the Lebanon; the Rifāʿīyah, a Ṣūfī religious brotherhood; or the *ittiḥādīyah* school, which taught that the Creator and the created become one, a school that grew out of the teaching of Ibn al-ʿArabī (died 1240), whose monism he denounced.

Leadership of the resistance party

In 1306 he was summoned to explain his beliefs to the governor's council, which, although it did not condemn him, sent him to Cairo; there he appeared before a new council on the charge of anthropomorphism and was imprisoned in the citadel for 18 months. Soon after gaining his freedom, he was confined again in 1308 for several months in the prison of the *qāḍīs* (Muslim judges who exercise both civil and religious functions) for having denounced the worship of saints as being against religious law (Sharīʿah).

He was sent to Alexandria under house arrest in 1309, the day after the abdication of the sultan Muḥammad ibn Qalāwūn and the advent of Baybars II al-Jāshnikīr, whom he regarded as a usurper and whose immanent end he predicted. Seven months later, on Ibn Qalāwūn's return, he was able to return to Cairo. But in 1313 he left Cairo once more with the sultan, on a campaign to recover Damascus, which was again being threatened by the Mongols.

Ibn Taymīyah spent his last 15 years in Damascus. Promoted to the rank of schoolmaster, he gathered around him a circle of disciples from every social class. The most famous of these, Ibn Qayyim al-Jawzīyah (died 1350), was to share in Ibn Taymīyah's renewed persecutions. Accused of supporting a doctrine that would curtail the ease with which a Muslim could traditionally repudiate a wife and thus ease the ill effects of the practice, Ibn Taymīyah was incarcerated on orders from Cairo in the citadel of Damascus from August 1320 to February 1321.

In July 1326 Cairo again ordered him confined to the citadel for having continued his condemnation of saint worship, in spite of the prohibition forbidding him to do so. He died in prison, deprived of his books and writing materials, on September 26, 1328, and was buried in the Ṣūfī cemetery amid a great public gathering. His tomb still exists and is widely venerated.

Works and ideas

Ibn Taymīyah left a considerable body of work—often republished in Syria, Egypt, Arabia, and India—that extended and justified his religious and political involvements and was characterized by its rich documentation, sober style, and brilliant polemic. In addition to innumerable *fatwā*s (legal opinions based on religious law) and several professions of faith, the most beautiful of which is the *Wāsiṭīyah*, two works merit particular attention. One is his *As-Siyā-sat ash-sharʿīyah* ("Treatise on Juridical Politics"), available in French and English translations. The other, *Minhāj as-sunnah* ("The Way of Tradition"), is the richest work of comparative theology surviving from medieval Islām.

Ibn Taymīyah desired a return to the sources of the Muslim religion, which he felt had been altered too often, to one extent or another, by the different religious sects or schools. The sources were the Qur'ān and the *sunnah*: revealed writing and the prophetic tradition. The *ijmāʿ*, or community consensus, had no value in itself, he insisted, unless it rested on those two sources. His traditionalism, however, did not prevent Ibn Taymīyah from allowing analogical reasoning (*qiyās*) and the argument of utility (*maṣlaḥah*) a large place in his thought, on the condition that both rested on the objective givens of revelation and tradition. Only such a return to sources, he felt, would permit the divided and disunited Muslim community to refind its unity.

In theodicy (the justification of God as good when evil is observable in the world), Ibn Taymīyah wished to describe God as he is described in the Qur'ān and as the Prophet did in the *sunnah*, which led him to side with theological schools in disagreement with contemporary opinion. This position was the point of departure for a critique, often conducted with very subtle argument, of the ideas of such dogmatic theologians as al-Ashʿarī or Fakhr ad-Dīn ar-Rāzī, such philosophers as Avicenna and Averroës, or such mystics as Ibn al-ʿArabī.

Concerning praxes (practices), Ibn Taymīyah believed that one could only require, in worship, those practices inaugurated by God and his Prophet and that one could only forbid, in social relations, those things forbidden by the Qur'ān and the *sunnah*. Thus, on the one hand, he favoured a revision of the system of religious obligations and a brushing aside of condemnable innovations (*bidʿah*); and, on the other, he constructed an economic ethic that was more flexible on many points than that espoused by the contemporary schools.

In politics Ibn Taymīyah recognized the legitimacy of the first four caliphs, but he rejected the necessity of having a single caliphate and allowed for the existence of many emirates. Within each emirate he demanded that the prince apply the religious law strictly and rely on it for his legal opinion; and Ibn Taymīyah demanded from those under the prince's jurisdiction that they obey the established authority except where it required disobedience to God, every Muslim being required to "will the good and forbid the bad" for the benefit of the common welfare.

Significance and influence on Islām

Though Ibn Taymīyah had numerous religious and political adversaries in his own time, he has strongly influenced modern Islām for the last two centuries. He is the source of the Wahhābīyah, a strictly traditionist movement founded by Muḥammad ibn ʿAbd al-Wahhāb (died 1792), who took his ideas from Ibn Taymīyah's writings. Ibn Taymīyah also influenced various reform movements that have posed the problem of reformulating traditional ideologies by a return to sources.

BIBLIOGRAPHY. HENRI LAOUST, *Essai sur les doctrines sociales et politiques de Takī-d-Dīn Aḥmad b. Taimīya* (1939), a study of the religious and political thought of Ibn Taymīyah in the framework of history and an analysis of his influence on Wahhābism and contemporary Muslim reformism; *Contribution à une étude de la méthodologie canonique de Takī-d-Dīn Aḥmad b. Taimīya* (1939), an annotated French translation of two of Ibn Taymīyah's dissertations on the foundation of law, particularly on the analogic reasoning in Muslim law; "*La Biographie d' Ibn Taimīya d'après Ibn Kathīr*" *Bulletin d'Études Orientales*, 9:115–162 (1943), complementary notes provided by the historian Ibn Kathīr in the *al-Bidāyah*, on the subject of Ibn Taymīyah's disagreements with his contemporaries; *Les Schismes dans l'Islam* (1965), places Ibn Taymīyah in the general development of Islām. The following two translations of Ibn Taymīyah's juridical political treatise, the *Kitāb al-Siyāsah al-sharʿīyah*, should also be noted: one in French by HENRI LAOUST, *Le Traité de droit public d'Ibn Taimīya* (1948); and the other in English by OMAR A. FARRUKH, *Ibn Taimiyya on Public and Private Law in Islam* (1966).

(H.L.)

Ibsen, Henrik

Norwegian dramatist and poet, Henrik Ibsen is widely acknowledged as one of the pioneers of modern European drama. Although honoured (and in some quarters vilified) during his own lifetime as the source of what G.B. Shaw termed "Ibsenism" (*i.e.*, a critique in dramatic form of contemporary morality), he first achieved recognition as the creator of modern, realistic prose drama. More recent criticism esteems other qualities in his work: his supreme technical mastery, his penetrating psychological insight, his symbolism, and the bleak poetry of his dramatic prose. The span of his creative career, from the publication of his first play *Catilina* in 1850 to his last work and "epilogue" *When We Dead Awaken* in December 1899, fits almost exactly the second half of the 19th century. Early experimentation in a range of different styles led to the more controversial dramas of his later years—works that, by their exploration of the nature of reality and illusion, of what is genuine and what spurious in the individual and in society, contributed much to the development and enrichment of prose drama in general.

Ibsen, lithograph by Edvard Munch, 1902. In the Munch-museet, Oslo.
By courtesy of the Oslo Kommunes Kunstsamlinger, Munch-museet, Oslo

Early years. Henrik Johan Ibsen was born on March 20, 1828, in Skien, a small timber port about 100 miles southwest of Christiania (now Oslo). He was the second child of a prosperous businessman. In an unfinished autobiographical fragment written in 1881, Ibsen described how as a boy he saw from his window "only buildings, nothing green"—he remembered particularly the church, the pillory, the jail, and the madhouse—and remarked how the many sawmills filled the air all day with a sound like the noise of whining, moaning, shrieking women. When, in the mid-1830s, his father went bankrupt, the Ibsens moved to nearby Venstøp, where they remained for the next eight years. This move away from familiar surroundings, together with the disgrace attached to it, led the already introverted young Ibsen to find comfort in daydreams, in reading, and in his puppet theatre. Impressions and memories from these early years are found in many of his later plays: Skien provided the small-town background of *The League of Youth*; the attic at Venstøp suggested the Ekdals' attic in *The Wild Duck* (published in 1884); and members of his family often served as models for his characters.

Childhood impressions

Progressive separation and alienation from "home"—his childhood home, his hometown, and his home country—is an obvious pattern in Ibsen's life. At the age of 15, he left Skien behind with the same feelings of release, the same sense of escape, that filled him 20 or so years later when he left Norway to live abroad. Even as an old man nearing 70 and recently returned to Norway, he could still write to a friend: "Up here by the fjords is my native land, but . . . where do I find my homeland?" In 1844 he went to Grimstad—later to form the background of *The Pillars of Society*—where he was apprenticed to a chemist. When he was no more than 18, one of the servant girls in the house where he lived, who was a good ten years older, bore him an illegitimate child; for 14 years he supported his son, but the incident was kept as one of the darker secrets of his life. In spare hours he studied for his matriculation examination and also found time for writing. His first drama, *Catilina,* was in part inspired by the revolution throughout Europe in 1848 and in part by the Latin texts set for his examination. It created little sensation when it was published; but, as Ibsen himself explained in the preface to the second edition of 1875, it treated a theme he would return to frequently: "the clash of ability and aspiration, of will and possibility, at once the tragedy and the comedy of mankind and of the individual."

In April 1850 he moved to Christiania, the capital, stopping on the way at Skien to take final leave of his family; in Christiania, he lived for 18 rather frugal months. He studied at a crammer's, but he was not wholly successful at his examination in August (he failed in arithmetic, Greek, and oral Latin) so that he never became a fully matriculated student, although he participated in a number of ways in student life. In particular, he contributed to and helped to edit a periodical called *Andhrimner*. On September 26, 1850, the first performance of an Ibsen play took place: *The Burial Mound*, a historical play, strongly nationalistic in style. It was unsuccessful, and for the rest of the year he earned a meagre living by journalism.

Failure of first play

Association with the Norwegian Theatre. In 1851 he was offered a job with the recently established Norwegian Theatre in Bergen, primarily as "dramatic author," in which capacity he had to write one new play a year to be performed on January 2, the anniversary of the founding of the theatre. Almost immediately, however, he was also drawn into the production of the plays. He was too reserved by temperament ever to be a good producer. A contemporary described him as a quiet, taciturn, withdrawn, and not particularly prepossessing young man who suffered acute embarrassment whenever he had to rebuke or even correct the players:

> A man who found difficulty or reluctance in forming close or intimate or confidential relations with anybody, preferring to walk alone. . . . As he "padded about" back-stage in his peculiar, shapeless and shabby greatcoat, he was respected but he aroused little fellow-feeling.

Ibsen later described his life in the theatre as "a daily abortion." Nevertheless, the experience of these early years—including the study tour he undertook in 1852 of theatres in Denmark and Germany—greatly enriched his later writing. In these years, he had some part in the production of no fewer than 145 different plays. Between 1851 and 1857, five of his own plays were produced in Bergen; some were disasters, none achieved any significant success. In 1856 he became engaged to Suzannah Thoresen, but it was another two years before they could afford to marry; their son and only child, Sigurd, was born on December 23, 1859.

In September 1857 he returned to Christiania to become artistic director of the Norwegian Theatre there. The theatre, never very sound financially, was forced by economic circumstances to include a great deal of farce and vaudeville in its repertory, which gave little scope to an ambitious artist. When, in 1862, it finally went bankrupt, Ibsen found a temporary, abysmally paid job as literary adviser to another theatre, the Christiania Theatre. To these disappointments were added many other frustrations—mounting debts, attacks of depression, public indifference, and even hostility—which brought him almost to the point of despair. Admittedly, the three dramas he completed in Christiania between 1857 and 1864—*The Vikings at Helgeland*, *Love's Comedy*, and *The Pretenders*—are on an altogether higher level than anything he had written previously, but when, in 1863, he was awarded a small state grant, he paid what he could of his debts, and in April 1864 he left Norway for Italy. For the next 27 years he lived abroad, mainly in Rome, Dresden, and Munich; and only twice during this time, in 1874 and 1885, did he return to Norway for short visits.

Years in Italy and Germany

Mature drama. The next few years saw a breakthrough in his career. *Brand* (first performed 1885), first conceived as a narrative poem and then recast as a verse drama, was completed near Rome in the summer of 1865 and published in Copenhagen the following year. It was an immediate artistic and commercial success in Scandinavia. Thereafter he astonished his friends in Rome by the new elegance of his dress, the new cut of his beard, the new dignity of his manner, and even the new firmness of his handwriting. *Brand* was followed in 1867 by *Peer Gynt* (first performed 1876). Both plays are in a sense polemic pieces directed against what Ibsen felt was the narrowness of Norwegian life and the complacency of this Norwegian character.

After nearly four years in Rome, he moved in 1868 to Dresden, where he remained until 1875. After the publication in 1871 of his *Digte* ("Poems"), Ibsen went on to complete his enormous "double" drama in ten acts, *Emperor and Galilean* (published 1873; first performed 1896), a work based on the career of Julian the Apostate; in following the conflict between paganism and Christianity, the play puts forward the concept of "the third realm," that realm where man may bridge the gap between his passions and his spirit. Although it was generally regarded as one of his weakest plays, Ibsen seems to have considered it his greatest achievement.

In 1875 he moved to Munich; but by the late autumn of 1878 he was back in Rome where—apart from a short period of residence in Munich in 1879–80—he made his home until 1885; between 1885 and 1891 he was again living in Munich. The *Pillars of Society*, which appeared in 1877, marks the end of his poetic period and the first of the so-called social satires for which Ibsen became generally known. The play properly established his wider fame in Germany; within two months of its original publication, by February 1878, it was being played at five different theatres in Berlin alone, in three quite different translations. It was followed by *A Doll's House* in 1879, a play that created a major scandal. In it Ibsen exposes the individual's loss of freedom and expression as he conforms to society's conventions by observing how a husband brings about, although unwittingly, his wife's intellectual and financial enslavement. At its London production in 1889, *A Doll's House* touched off the vehement debates about "Ibsenism" that characterized literary controversy in the 1890s.

Moralistic social satires

Ghosts (published 1881), on its author's admission a more "extreme" play than its two predecessors—although they acted as a kind of introduction or preparation—came to be linked with the establishment of Europe's "independent" theatres—the Freie Bühne in Berlin (1889), the Théâtre-Libre in Paris (1877), and the Independent Theatre in London (1891), each of which selected *Ghosts* for its opening production. The play uses the problem of hereditary venereal disease as a symbol for the moral diseases inherited from the past that kill the living. The hostile reception given to this play by the Norwegian public and critics (though mild in comparison with the vitriolic comments of the majority of the London press in 1891) can be seen as an inspiration for Ibsen's next three plays: *An Enemy of the People* (1882), *The Wild Duck*, and *Rosmersholm* (1886). All these plays deal with the varying destinies of those who dare, or who cannot forbear, or who fear, to tell the truth.

Last years. It was Ibsen's habit in the years before his return to Norway in 1891 to spend the summer months away from his residence, usually at his favourite spot of Gossensass (Colle Isarco) in the Tirol. It was there in 1889 that he met both the young Helene Raff from Munich, who became a frequent guest in the Ibsen household much to the jealous irritation of his wife, and also Emilie Bardach, an 18-year-old Viennese girl, whom he later described as his "May sun in a September life." These relationships with younger, attentive women, the precise significance of which for Ibsen is difficult to define, left their mark both on *Hedda Gabler*, one of his greatest plays, and on *The Master Builder*. In 1891, by now a world-famous author, Ibsen returned to Norway and took up residence in Christiania. In the years that followed, the person probably closest to him was the daughter of one of his friends, Hildur Andersen, who was studying to be a concert pianist; it was with her that he seemed able to discuss his literary plans most freely.

On October 11, 1892, Ibsen's son married Bergliot Bjørnson, daughter of Norway's other great realistic poet and playwright of these years, Bjørnstjerne Bjørnson. Ibsen's attitude toward Bjørnson had for nearly 40 years been a mixture of admiration, envy, contempt, and affection; when the two young people married, Ibsen had a diplomatic illness and did not attend the ceremony.

Last plays

The shift of emphasis in Ibsen's last plays from *The Lady from the Sea* (1888) onward is clear. *Hedda Gabler* (1890), *The Master Builder* (1892), *Little Eyolf* (1894), and *John Gabriel Borkman* (1896) mark a development away from an expressly social, moralist, or problematical mode of drama to a more psychological, a more visionary, and more symbolic style. Finally, *When We Dead Awaken*, "a dramatic epilogue" as its author subtitled it, incorporated in the figure of Rubek a final and merciless piece of self-analysis and brought Ibsen's creative career to a close. A stroke in 1900 and another a year later left him an almost helpless invalid; he died in Christiania on May 23, 1906.

Ibsen was a most meticulous artist; his usual practice in later life was to allot two years to each play, working it out by way of preliminary notes, scenarios, and repeatedly revised draft versions until it reached its final form; these drafts, many of which have survived, not only provide a fascinating account of the genesis of the plays but also uniquely document the nature of dramatic composition in general.

MAJOR WORKS

PLAYS: *Catilina* (1850; *Catiline*); *Kjaempehøjen* (first version 1850, second version 1854; *The Burial Mound*); *Norma, eller en politikers kjaerlighed* (1851; *Norma, or a Politician's Love*); *Sankthansnatten* (1853; *St. John's Night*); *Fru Inger til Østeraad* (1855; *Lady Inger*); *Gildet paa Solhoug* (1856; *The Feast at Solhoug*); *Olaf Liljekrans* (1857); *Haermaendene paa Helgeland* (1858; *The Vikings at Helgeland*); *Kjaerlighedens komedie* (1862; *Love's Comedy*); *Kongsemnerne* (1863; *The Pretenders*); *Brand* (1866); *Peer Gynt* (1867); *De unges forbund* (1869; *The League of Youth*); *Kejser og Galilaeer* (1873; *Emperor and Galilean*); *Samfundets støtter* (1877; *Pillars of Society*); *Et dukkehjem* (1879; *A Doll's House*); *Gengangere* (1881; *Ghosts*); *En folkefiende* (1882; *An Enemy of the People*); *Vildanden* (1884; *The Wild Duck*); *Rosmersholm* (1886); *Fruen fra havet* (1888; *The Lady from the Sea*); *Hedda Gabler* (1890); *Bygmester Solness* (1892; *The Master Builder*); *Lille Eyolf* (1894; *Little Eyolf*); *John Gabriel Borkman* (1896); *Naar vi døde vaagner* (1899; *When We Dead Awaken*).

POETRY: "Paa vidderne" (1859; "On the Heights"); "Terje Vigen" (1862); *Episke Brand* (written 1864–65, pub. 1907, ed. by K. Larsen; *Epic Brand*); *Digte* (1871).

OTHER WORKS: The letters were collected in *Breve fra Henrik Ibsen*, 2 vol., ed. by H. Koht and J. Elias (1904); the unpublished papers in *Efterladte skrifter*, 3 vol., ed. by H. Koht and J. Elias (1909).

TRANSLATIONS: William Archer's influential edition of *The Collected Works of Henrik Ibsen*, 12 vol. (1906–12), contains all but five of the plays listed above, along with a selection from the unpublished papers. *The Oxford Ibsen*, ed. by James McFarlane (to be completed in 8 vol., 1960–), is a scholarly edition that takes in all the plays, the *Episke Brand*, a full selection from the unpublished papers, a number of Ibsen's critical essays, and has critical commentaries. Modern translations of many individual plays by Ibsen have also been prepared in English, notably for the "Everyman Library," the "Penguin Classics," the "Bantam Classics," and the "Signet Classics" series. Michael Meyer has translated 15 of the plays specifically for modern stage performance. A full selection of the poems has been translated by F.E. Garrett in *Lyrics and Poems from Ibsen* (1912). *The Correspondence of Henrik Ibsen*, trans. and ed. by Mary Morison (1905), offers a selection of the letters; Evert Sprinchorn included also some of the speeches in his *Ibsen: Letters and Speeches* (1964). The standard German and French translations of the works are: *Sämtliche Werke*, ed. by G. Brandes, J. Elias, and P. Schlenther, 10 vol. (1898–1902); and *Oeuvres complètes*, trans. by P.G. La Chesnais, 16 vol. (1914–45).

BIBLIOGRAPHY. The two standard bibliographical works are H. PETTERSEN, *Henrik Ibsen bedømt af samtid og eftertid . . .* (1928); and I. TEDFORD, *Ibsen Bibliography 1928–57* (1961); these may be supplemented for subsequent years by the annual bibliographies in the *Ibsen Årbok* (1952–). The main Ibsen manuscript collection is in the University Library, Oslo, though several important manuscripts are in the Royal Library, Copenhagen. The scholarly *Samlede verker*, ed. by F. BULL, H. KOHT, and D.A. SEIP, 21 vol. (1928–57), includes the dramas, prose works, poems, and letters, together with drafts of the author's working papers. In 1954 H. KOHT revised and expanded his earlier (1928) edition of *Henrik Ibsen: eit diktarliv* (Eng. trans., *Life of Ibsen*, 1971); this standard biography may be supplemented by M. MEYER, *Henrik Ibsen*, 3 vol. (1967–71), which collates much scattered information. BERGLIOT IBSEN, *De Tre* (1949; Eng. trans., *The Three Ibsens*, 1951), gives a family (and sometimes partial) view. G.B. SHAW, *The Quintessence of Ibsenism* (1891; 2nd augmented ed., 1913), valued the plays primarily as social criticism; this pattern of evaluation yielded in time to a more literary assessment in H.J. WEIGAND, *The Modern Ibsen* (1925); B.W. DOWNS, *Ibsen: The Intellectual Background* (1946), and *A Study of Six Plays by Ibsen* (1950); J.R. NORTHAM, *Ibsen's Dramatic Method* (1953); and M.J. VALENCY, *The Flower and the Castle* (1964). JAMES MCFARLANE'S anthology of critical pieces, *Henrik Ibsen: Penguin Critical Anthology* (1970), gives a selection of 20th-century critical opinion.

(J.W.McF.)

Icebergs and Pack Ice

Ice in the waters of the earth's polar regions occurs in two forms, namely, pack ice and icebergs. Pack ice forms from seawater and is generally only one to two years old, whereas icebergs are fragments of ice sheets and glaciers that formed on land areas during intervals of thousands of years. Pack ice expands during winter to cover large areas of the oceans in both hemispheres. Melting occurs in spring and summer and the margins of the pack ice retreat. This warmer weather aids calving (separation) of icebergs at the boundaries of ice sheets and glaciers, however, and many icebergs start their transit toward the Equator at this time.

Importance of ice at sea

This ice at sea is of substantial importance to man. Major shipping routes around the world could be shortened by as much as 30 percent if regular navigation through the Arctic Ocean became feasible, for example. The economics of freshwater extraction from icebergs also is instructive. A ten-mile-long iceberg could be hauled into the Peru (Humboldt) Current, which flows from the south along South America, and ultimately to Los Angeles where it could supply freshwater to that city for three weeks at less than the 1970 rates. Factors of wind effect, breakup, grounding, accessible supply, and controlled melting on delivery argue against this venture, however. In the Northern Hemisphere about 10,000 icebergs are produced each year from the West Greenland glaciers and an average of 375 flow south of Newfoundland into the North Atlantic shipping lanes.

Because ice reflects four to five times more sunlight than does the ocean, the change in areal coverage of sea ice between winter and summer is climatically important. There is a change in areal coverage of 20 percent from winter to summer in Arctic pack ice extent, and 80 percent in Antarctic pack ice maximum to minimum coverage. This winter to summer change in area of pack ice coverage is equivalent to twice the area of the United States.

This article treats the formation, distribution, and characteristics of icebergs and pack ice. For similar treatment of ice in freshwater, see ICE IN RIVERS AND LAKES, and for coverage of ice on land see ICE SHEETS AND GLACIERS; the latter article includes the physical properties of ice in general. See also OCEANS AND SEAS; CLIMATE; and articles on the polar regions of the earth for relevant effects of icebergs and pack ice. A treatment of ice disasters and navigation in ice areas also is presented here.

World ice distribution. A summary of the volumes and areas of water and ice is shown in Table 1. The majority of the earth's freshwater is tied up in the Greenland and Antarctic ice sheets. Although the total amount of ice is less than 2 percent of the world's freshwater and seawater, the water equivalent of this ice is equal to 46,000 years of Mississippi River discharge, or a world sea level rise of more than 39 metres (130 feet). The ice sheet that covers Antarctica comprises 90 percent of the world's ice. The volume of this ice, some of which is below sea level, is 5,750,000 cubic miles (24,000,000 cubic kilometres).

Table 1: World Distribution of Icebergs and Pack Ice*

	area (× 10⁶)		volume (× 10⁶)		thickness	
	sq mi	sq km	cu mi	cu km	ft	m
Antarctic Ice Sheet	5.2	13.5	5.8	24.1	7,200	2,195
Greenland Ice Sheet	.67	1.7	.62	2.58	4,900	1,494
Greenland glaciers	.023	.060	.012	.050		
Antarctic pack ice						
Winter	7.7	19.9				
Summer	1.5	3.9	5.5×10^{-3}	22.9×10^{-3}	6–10	1.8–3.0
Arctic pack ice						
Winter	4.6	11.9				
Summer	3.5	9.1	2.2×10^{-3}	9.2×10^{-3}	10–13	3–4
Western North Atlantic annual melting	.467	1.210				
Arctic icebergs	.003	.008	1.82×10^{-3}	7.57×10^{-3}		

*The area and volume of the world ocean, from which the ice is principally derived, are 361 × 10^6 square kilometres and 1,370 × 10^6 cubic kilometres.

Icebergs are produced at a rate of approximately 280 cubic kilometres per year (67 cubic miles per year) in the Arctic and 1,800 cubic kilometres (430 cubic miles) per year in the Antarctic. They spread over nearly 19 percent of the world ocean, and 93 percent of their mass is in the Antarctic region.

ICEBERGS

Formation and distribution. Probably the first mention of icebergs was that of St. Brendan, an Irish monk whose partly fictional writings suggest that he encountered a "floating crystal castle" on the high seas. After calving (breaking off) from the Greenland and Antarctic ice sheets and smaller outlying glaciers, icebergs can move thousands of miles in a few years; those in the Arctic can slip down along the eastern North American coast to be caught up in the Gulf Stream and, while melting, be carried in a few weeks to within a few hundred miles of England and Ireland, or by a combination of wind and current to Bermuda, as happened in 1907 and 1926. These and other rare sightings are shown in Figure 1.

When snow and freezing rain continue to precipitate over a continent in excess of evaporation, glaciers will form and icebergs will break off their ends and appear in the surrounding ocean. At the point where glaciers or large, extensive ice shelves meet the sea, water pressure beneath the ice shelf or glacier tongue interacts with the outward creeping glacier. The tides, which have ranges up to 20 feet in the Arctic, along with small sea level changes associated with wind and swells, result in an intermittent increase and decrease in force on the protruding end of the glacier or ice shelf resulting in the birth of a large monolith of drifting ice. There are other ways in which an iceberg is formed. One, which is characteristic of southern Greenland glaciers, consists of a melting or evaporation of the surface portions of the glacier near its terminus at a greater rate than the water erosion on its underside. This results in an underwater shelf and eventually, through the erosion of water and periodic tidal and other hydraulic forces, this is broken off and an iceberg floats to the surface. Icebergs of varying shapes are produced in this way. A third mechanism by which icebergs are formed is through gradual break off from a hanging glacier or ice shelf. The type of iceberg mechanism is related to the surrounding topography, the climate, and the rate of flow of associated glaciers.

Movement of glaciers producing icebergs

The speed of the ice sheet spread, or creep, over Greenland and the Antarctic varies from zero near their centres to as much as six miles per year in the ice streams that make up glaciers. For the same inclination relative to gravity, ice moves ¹⁄₁₀,₀₀₀ as fast as water. The average movement in the Antarctic is 360 metres per year (1,200 feet per year), with most of the measurements between extremes of 110 and 1,100 metres per year (360 and 3,600 feet per year). These measurements are obtained from glaciers near the coast and thus are much higher than the average flow rate over the entire Greenland or Antarctic ice sheets. The fastest flowing glaciers have been measured along the western shore of Greenland. The one known as the Quarayaq Glacier flows at a velocity between 20 and 24 metres per day (65 and 80 feet per day), greater than the velocity of most alpine glaciers. Jakobshavn Glacier at latitude 70° N, approximately, produces 10 percent of all the Greenland icebergs (approximately 1,350 annually), and flows at about 20 metres (65 feet) per day. The icebergs accumulate in a fjord, and periodically spill from this fjord in groups accompanied by noise that can be heard for several miles. This greatest iceberg-producing glacier measures only 7.0 kilometres (4.4 miles) along its front and is 90 metres (300 feet) above sea level. In contrast to the rapidly moving glaciers, the very wide glaciers that move slowly produce only very small icebergs. Some glaciers, such as the Frederikshåb, Greenland, with a 33-kilometre front, have rates of flow equal to the rate of melting, and thus

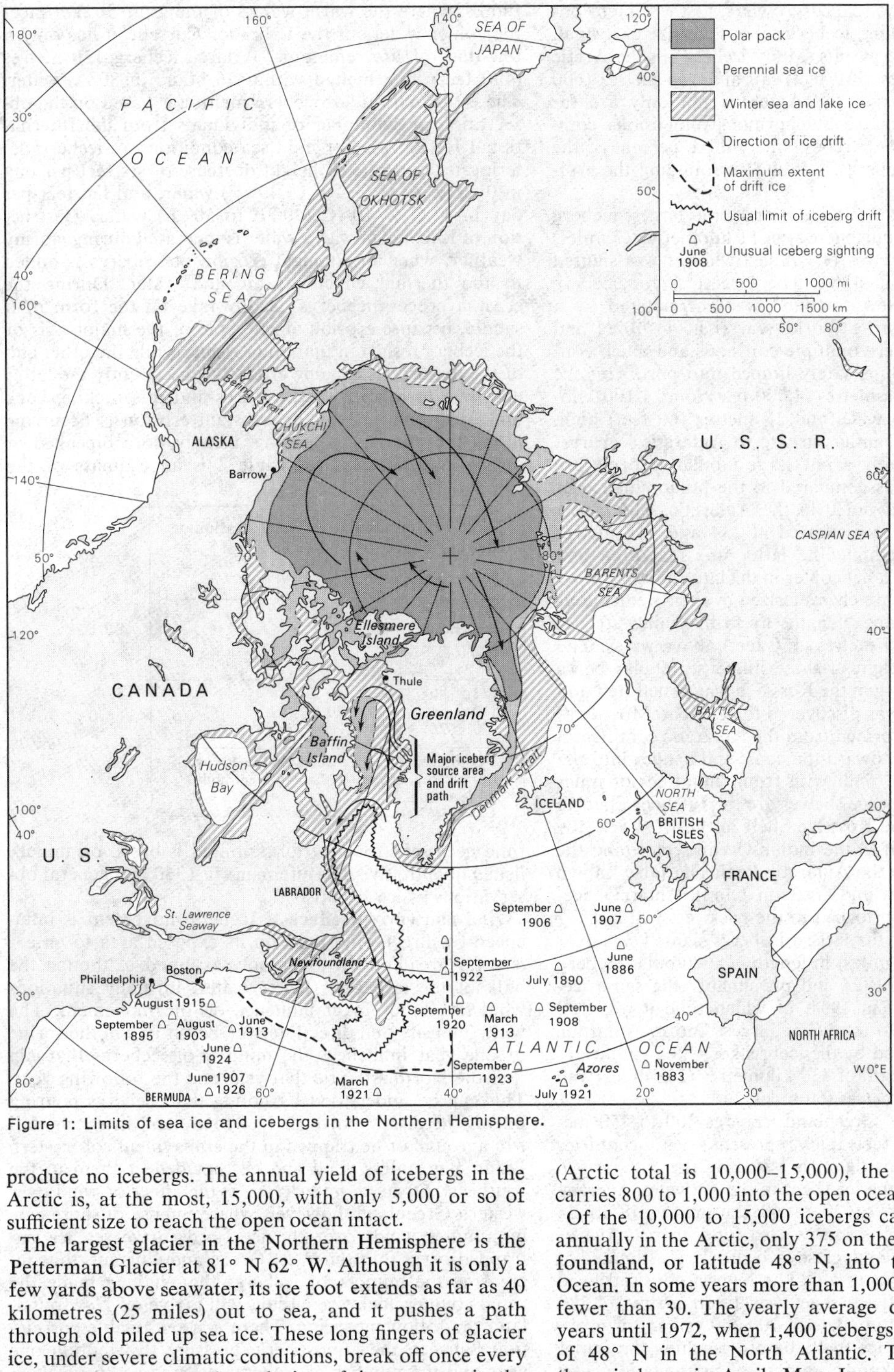

Figure 1: Limits of sea ice and icebergs in the Northern Hemisphere.

produce no icebergs. The annual yield of icebergs in the Arctic is, at the most, 15,000, with only 5,000 or so of sufficient size to reach the open ocean intact.

The largest glacier in the Northern Hemisphere is the Petterman Glacier at 81° N 62° W. Although it is only a few yards above seawater, its ice foot extends as far as 40 kilometres (25 miles) out to sea, and it pushes a path through old piled up sea ice. These long fingers of glacier ice, under severe climatic conditions, break off once every 10 to 20 years. Another glacier of importance is the Jungersen Glacier in northern Greenland. This glacier and the Petterman Glacier produce very large tabular icebergs, known in the Arctic as "ice islands." They are similar in shape and mode of formation to the large tabular icebergs of the Antarctic, but are much smaller.

East Greenland icebergs tend to move northward; they are small and few in number. The icebergs that do leave the fjord and the coast area enter the East Greenland Current, and some join the West Greenland icebergs. The icebergs that reach the North Atlantic Ocean from northern Greenland, Siberia, and the Northwest Territories constitute less than 10 percent of the total icebergs produced in the Northern Hemisphere. They do not affect the sea routes and, other than their formation of ice islands, have no importance to man. Most icebergs originating from western Greenland are of great importance; of an annual production of about 7,500 bergs (Arctic total is 10,000–15,000), the Labrador Current carries 800 to 1,000 into the open ocean.

Sightings in the North Atlantic

Of the 10,000 to 15,000 icebergs calved from glaciers annually in the Arctic, only 375 on the average pass Newfoundland, or latitude 48° N, into the North Atlantic Ocean. In some years more than 1,000 are seen, in others fewer than 30. The yearly average diminished over 20 years until 1972, when 1,400 icebergs were sighted south of 48° N in the North Atlantic. The distribution of these icebergs in April, May, June, and July is shown in Figure 1.

There are few icebergs in the Arctic Basin proper. The major source area for icebergs in the Barents Sea is Franz Josef Land. Icebergs are not found in the North Pacific except in sounds along the Alaskan-Canadian coast between 55° N and 60° N latitudes.

In the Southern Hemisphere the maximum limit of iceberg drift is 1,600 kilometres (1,000 miles) farther north than the northern extent of sea ice in the Antarctic (Figure 2). Most icebergs are concentrated south of the Antarctic current convergence at about 60° S. Some icebergs from the ice shelves of Antarctica drift north of 42° S latitude in the Atlantic Ocean, but only to latitude 56° S in the South Pacific Ocean. One Antarctic iceberg was sighted only 30 miles south of the Cape of Good Hope (Africa) in 1850. The northern limit of ice sighted in the Southern Hemisphere was 26°30′ S.

Size of icebergs. Arctic icebergs vary in size from the size of a large piano, called growlers, to the dimensions of a ten-story building. Icebergs about the size of a small house are called bergy bits. Many icebergs in the Arctic are about 45 metres (150 feet) tall and 180 metres (600 feet) long. Icebergs of the Antarctic not only are far more abundant but are of enormous dimensions compared to those in the Arctic. Ninety-three percent of the world's mass of icebergs is found surrounding the Antarctic.

Other than Arctic Basin ice islands, the largest iceberg in the Northern Hemisphere was 11 kilometres (7 miles) long and 5.9 kilometres (3.7 miles) wide; it was sighted near Baffin Land in 1882. The largest Arctic iceberg sighted south of Newfoundland was encountered by a convoy of ships during World War II at 43°10′ N and 49°33′ W. There were multiple collisions and much confusion before all ships safely limped into port. This ice island was 1,350 kilometres (4,500 feet) long, 1,100 kilometres (3,600 feet) wide, and 18 metres (60 feet) high. These icebergs are similar in size to Antarctic icebergs, but by and large only a few large tabular icebergs are seen in the Arctic as compared to the predominance of the tabular icebergs noted in the Antarctic. The tallest icebergs known were measured at 134 and 158 metres (447 and 527 feet) high; the latter was measured and photographed from a helicopter in the late 1950s.

Antarctic icebergs are characterized by their tremendous size and tabular shape. Lengths up to five miles are not unusual, with ice 45 metres (150 feet) above water. The discovery of the origin of these immense tabular bergs was made in 1841 when the Ross Sea was penetrated and the Ross Ice Shelf was discovered to be afloat. Most Antarctic icebergs are formed from the Antarctic continental ice sheet as it thins toward the coast and exudes into the ocean as a great ice shelf with fronts hundreds of miles long. The four major ice shelves are the Filchner Shelf in the Weddell Sea, the Ross Ice Shelf in the Ross Sea, the Shackleton Ice Shelf in the Indian Ocean sector, and the Larsen Ice Shelf on the Antarctic Peninsula (also known as Palmer Peninsula and Graham Land). Antarctic icebergs, if they remain locked in the pack ice, will last for many years. One of the largest icebergs sighted was over 140 kilometres (90 miles) in length. This tabular iceberg was first sighted in 1927 and presumably the same iceberg was later seen in 1931, at which time it was 100 kilometres (60 miles) long. The largest known Antarctic iceberg was measured by the icebreaker U.S.S. "Glacier" in 1956; it had a length of 333 kilometres (208 miles) and a width of 100 kilometres (60 miles).

Age and melting. Greenland icebergs 300 to 450 metres (1,000 to 1,500 feet) thick represent several centuries of precipitation. This figure is based on the comparison of the thickness of the ice sheet to the known or average annual precipitation of 20 to 60 centimetres (8 to 24 inches) per year in the source area for icebergs. Age of ice in central Greenland, close to bedrock, is estimated at 30,000 to 150,000 years old. The longest core retrieved from the Greenland ice sheet was 1,370 metres (4,580 feet) long with a bottom date of 100,000 years. It is probable that the oldest ice melts before reaching the outlet glaciers. From the known amount of precipitation over Greenland, and the assumption that the ice volume and precipitation rate now are approximately the same as they were many centuries ago, it can be estimated that the mean age of icebergs is 5,000 years. Measurements by carbon-14 dating of entrapped air show that icebergs are hundreds to thousands of years old—the oldest actual measurement being 3,000 years. Arctic ice islands and giant Antarctic bergs last as long as ten years at high latitude. Most icebergs from western Greenland melt within two years of calving from the parent glacier.

Deterioration of icebergs at sea

Once an Arctic iceberg has been calved and moves out to the open sea, it sojourns in Baffin Bay for three months to two years, during which time it undergoes some disintegration through melting and calving of small chunks of ice from its perimeter. This results in a decrease in mass of about 90 percent by the time it reaches the coast of Newfoundland and the Grand Banks in the North Atlantic. When the iceberg enters the region of the Grand Banks, where the warm waters of the Gulf Stream meet the colder waters of the Labrador Current, it has only a few days of life remaining. A large iceberg 120 metres (400 feet) long melted within 36 hours in 80° F water. The estimated rate of iceberg melting is based on the observation of a number of individuals from the International Ice Patrol. For mild sea conditions an iceberg deteriorates at a rate of height decrease of six feet per day in 0° C to 4° C (32° F to 40° F) water, and ten feet per day in 4° C to 10° C (40° F to 50° F) water. Destruction of icebergs in warm water is increased during stormy weather, when mechanical erosion of icebergs is added to the thermal effects of air and water. During the erosion process icebergs usually take on the form of a saddle, because erosion at one pole of the major axis of the iceberg results in that point rising, while the other end of the major axis is being eroded. Subsequently the latter end, due to loss in weight, arises and this rocking back and forth continues while constant erosion is occurring along the minor axis leading, usually, to a bipeaked or saddle-shaped structure. Table 2 is an estimate of the time necessary for deterioration and is based on unpublished quantitative measurements in 1960 and general observations by ice scientists.

Table 2: Representative Deterioration or Melting Times for Icebergs
(at 45° N; estimated)

seawater temperature		melting time (in days)	
°F	°C	*	†
32	0	40	80
40	4	10	20
70	21	4	8

*For an iceberg 80 feet high, 300 feet long.
†For an iceberg greater than 150 feet high, 500 feet long.

Wind and current effects. Iceberg movement is influenced by direct wind push on its exposed area to an extent far greater than commonly assumed. Although the bulk of the iceberg is below water, in many situations wind has a dominant influence on the movement. The wind intensity and direction over Baffin Bay in the spring of one year influences the number of icebergs that slip into the North Atlantic that year and the following year. This can be understood by noting that icebergs pouring out of the Arctic north of Newfoundland in spring will run aground or be trapped in the embayments of western Baffin Bay unless wind and current deflect them to the southeast. Of more importance is the effect of wind over western Greenland, however, where intense offshore early summer winds over the ice fjords drive sea ice entrapped bergs into the West Greenland Current, thus increasing the number of icebergs that, having made the usual counterclockwise circuit, will arrive off Newfoundland the following spring. There is a reasonable correlation between the atmospheric pressure distribution one year and the number of icebergs drifting south of Newfoundland in the following year.

The day-to-day movement of an iceberg is controlled by the size and shape of the iceberg, previous and present wind, surface wind current, and general ocean current. The most important factor in assessing wind drift of icebergs is size and shape. Although most icebergs have a specific gravity of 0.9, and thus six-sevenths of the mass is below the sea surface, it is not true that this means that a 30-metre- (100-foot-) high iceberg is 180 metres (600 feet) deep in all cases. This is true only for the rectangular, blocky, or flat-topped icebergs common to the Antarctic. Table 3 gives the relation between exposed and underwater areas for various shapes of icebergs.

Winged icebergs, those with sail-like pinnacles around the central mass, are very much influenced by the winds and move at speeds of one knot, or 24 nautical miles, per day under the influence of steady winds of 30 knots.

Table 3: Exposed-to-Submerged Proportions, and Wind Factors, for Icebergs

iceberg description	proportions (exposed : underwater)	wind factor
Flat-topped or blocky	1 : 6	.004
Rounded or domed	1 : 4	.005
Usual Greenland iceberg	1 : 3	.01
Pinnacled or drydock	1 : 2	.03
Winged	1 : 1	.04

Windage and drift

The wind force on an iceberg does not result in movement directly downwind, but because of the rotation of the earth (Coriolis effect), windage on an iceberg is 30 to 50 degrees to the right in the Northern Hemisphere and to the left in the Southern Hemisphere.

The momentum of icebergs is so great that once in motion they continue for hours after the wind has abated. It is possible for an iceberg to be driven before a 30-knot wind at one knot in a direction 30 degrees to the right of the wind, and after the wind stops the iceberg will slow and circle in what is known as an inertial circle, associated with the rotation of the earth. An iceberg near the Grand Banks will be moving in a direction opposite to that toward which the wind was blowing about eight hours after the wind stops; however, the speed would be low and such anomalous movement would not be observed unless the initial speed and momentum were great. A careful accounting of berg underbody dimensions, and the relationship of wind-current forces and iceberg mass, will lead to explanations of anomalous iceberg movements. To emphasize the importance of wind effect and its prediction, one potentially disastrous case will be cited. In 1960, a 60-metre- (200-foot-) high, 300-metre- (1,000-foot-) long iceberg was driven off the tail of the Grand Banks into the shipping lanes by northwesterly winds averaging 80 kilometres (50 miles) per hour. This iceberg moved 140 kilometres (90 miles) at as much as 3 knots across the Labrador Current and resulted in an emergency move of the North Atlantic shipping lanes to the south.

The drift of icebergs and pack ice is the result of the ocean current and the wind. When the winds are variable or less than 32 kilometres (20 miles) per hour, and the current greater than 0.5 knot, the current predominates, but when steady 30-knot winds blow for more than 12 hours, the wind effect becomes important even in areas where the ocean current is one to two knots. In addition to windage on the iceberg and the ocean gradient current, the wind induced surface current has the effect of increasing drift speed by about 10 percent for small icebergs and increasing the angle of drift direction.

Sea ice drift is better understood, but in some respects it is more complicated than iceberg drift. In addition to size, inertia, and exposed-to-underwater dimensions, important additional information on surface roughness, water drag, and internal resistance due to ice-field concentration is needed to describe the motion. The observations of American and Soviet scientists drifting on ice islands in the Arctic Basin, Baffin Bay, and Gulf of St. Lawrence, along with Japanese and Soviet long-term ice-field observations, are summarized in Table 4. As noted from the table, ice fields consisting of 10 percent ice and 90 percent open water will move at 1 to 8 percent of the surface wind velocity. The angle of drift is from 20 to 40 degrees to the right of the wind in the Northern Hemisphere. The speed will be reduced by a factor of four as the ice becomes packed to 90 percent coverage of the ocean. Smooth ice drifts with less speed than rough ice because the wind has greater effect on a rough surface. Rough or hummocked ice usually is thicker and thus has greater inertia; ice of great inertia takes longer to reach the wind factor speed, but after the wind stops the ice continues to move longer than light ice. This phenomenon results in strings of ice floes aligned perpendicular to the wind with small floes packed to windward against larger floes. This wind sorting of ice is a phenomenon of great importance in navigating pack ice, and the strips of open water aligned in a direction approximately perpendicular to the direction of wind explain the successful navigation in ice performed by sailing vessels in the past.

Table 4: Wind Factor for Speed of Sea-Ice Drift

sea covered by ice (percent)	wind factor	
	rough hummocky surface	smooth floes
10	.08	.01
50	.05	.005
90	.02	.003

Sediment transport. Both icebergs and pack ice transport sediment in the form of pebbles, cobbles, boulders, and finer material, and even plant and animal life, thousands of miles from their source area. The distribution of icebergs 10,000 years ago, for example, can be inferred from sediments that are widely disseminated on the ocean floor of the North Pacific Ocean as far south as 48° N latitude and in the South Atlantic Ocean as far north as the latitude of the Cape of Good Hope in the Southern Hemisphere. Ice rafting competes with kelp rafting as an explanation for the occurrence of pebbles and boulders on the sea floor as far south as Baja California and other areas of the world ocean.

Bottom freezing of ice shelves and reduction of the ice surface results in migration of sediments and organisms upward. Layering of sediment can be seen in sea-ice floes and icebergs from ice shelves. Fossil penguin bones have been found as far north as 30° S and massive banks of boulders have been noted on the sea floor off South Africa. Thicknesses of as much as 130 centimetres (50 inches) of glacial till have been noted on the ocean floor from discharge by icebergs, apparently during the last 1,000,000 years.

Icebergs are coloured brown, black, and green by a combination of sediment, plankton deposits under the source area ice shelf, and glacial blue ice.

Reliability of radar detection

Iceberg detection and destruction. In the open ocean most ice is seen by radar at ranges depending upon fragment size, but smaller icebergs or growlers can only be detected when the sea surface is calm, and then only at ranges of about one mile. During slight wind conditions, in particular in heavy seas, the echoes from the waves, known as sea return, may completely mask the echoes of large, potentially very hazardous chunks of ice. In addition, radar return from rain and snow obscures the return from ice in either rain, snow, or fog conditions. Neither radar nor sonar can be relied upon for detection of icebergs and pack ice in choppy seas. The reflectivity of ice and snow to light is great, but reflectivity to radar or short radiowaves is very poor. An iceberg seven metres (22 feet) high cannot be detected with modern equipment if the waves are over four feet high. Various innovations since the inception of radar during World War II have not improved significantly the capabilities of radar to detect icebergs, thus ships are still bound by international agreement to proceed at slow speed in fog.

Sonar is effective in detecting icebergs; however, the range of detection is frequently limited by the water conditions and speed of commercial vessels. The likelihood of insufficient warning for high-speed passenger and cargo ships leaves this mode of detection inadequate. Other suggestions of dropping radio transducers or metal reflectors onto icebergs have the common fault that they are subject to icebergs rolling over and calving, which are frequent occurrences as a dying iceberg melts its way deep into the warmer waters of the shipping lanes.

The problem of iceberg protection, therefore, is one of tracking icebergs as they come down the Labrador Current, and reporting the whereabouts of these floating menaces to all North Atlantic shipping as often as twice daily. This sometimes involves 300 icebergs and requires a team of iceberg experts, oceanographers, aviators, and seamen. During heavy ice conditions two U.S. Coast

Guard planes fly six- to eight-hour reconnaissance missions from Argentia, Newfoundland, over the Grand Banks off Newfoundland and contiguous areas. Positions of icebergs are plotted and are correlated with previous positions of the same icebergs or groups of icebergs. When dangerous icebergs approach the shipping lanes, a ship departs for the scene to stand by near the iceberg and warn approaching ships.

Once an iceberg is spotted in a position of threat to ships, it should be of no harm if destroyed. Destroying a 200,000 ton block of ice is, however, a task whose difficulties leave it impractical in most situations. The first successful results on breaking up icebergs by explosives were reported in 1929, when a few hundred pounds of thermite cracked an iceberg into smaller pieces through thermal stress; these then melted more rapidly due to the greater surface area exposed. Similar thermite experiments on two icebergs in 1959 did not corroborate the original findings, however. Attempts at bombing, torpedoing, shelling, and even ramming have been unsuccessful. With twenty 450-kilogram (1,000-pound) bombs acting as direct hits, or as depth charges, it is possible to chip away about 20 percent of a 250,000-ton iceberg. The International Ice Patrol has even tried painting half of an iceberg with lampblack or charcoal to induce thermal stress by heat aborption but, like other experiments, these attempts were inconclusive.

PACK ICE

Formation and characteristics. On superficial examination, frozen ocean or salt water appears similar to freshwater ice; there are two principal differences, however. First, because the maximum density of seawater occurs below the freezing point, even after freezing the water below the ice will continue to turn over or circulate. As the surface water near the ice becomes colder, it becomes heavier and sinks, resulting in a continuous turnover or vertical circulation of the water beneath the ice. This is a different situation from that which occurs in lakes where, because the maximum density of freshwater is above the freezing point, once ice forms the colder water is lighter than the deeper, somewhat warmer water, and mixing does not occur. A second characteristic is the fact that as seawater freezes, minute pools of salty water called brine pockets are entrapped. The final form and the macroscopic physical properties of the ice are very much dependent upon the concentration of the brine pockets within the ice block. Once an ice field has formed, the physical and chemical properties are not locked in a frozen coffin, but vary as brine pockets migrate through the ice block in response to gravity and thermal gradients.

In the Northern Hemisphere during September and October, the air temperature lowers sufficiently to form a thin sheet of ice. Freezing temperature for average northern ocean salt water of about 3.5 percent salt composition by weight (usually designated 35 parts per thousand) is -1.8° C (28.7° F). The first signs of freezing are changes in the colour and texture of the sea surface as thin, gray-coloured needles and crystal plates form a surface thin sludge. If quiet sea conditions prevail, sheets of crystalline aggregates plate the ocean surface. Initially the ice film is entirely fresh, but as more ice crystals form, pockets of salt water (brine pockets) become entrapped between lamellae (very fine layers) of tiny ice plates. The amount of brine entrapped depends on the temperature of formation and the age of the ice. The shape of the initial ice crystals varies from square discoids to hexagonal dendritic forms. The average width is one inch and the thickness up to about 0.15 centimetres (0.06 inches). During the surface veneer formation stage each grain is free to grow both laterally and vertically until the sheet consolidates. As the ice sheet thickens, the orientation of these grains will change. Due to slight breezes and water motion, the thin sheets of ice jostle about and, after but a few hours, form a field of ice paddies. The appearance is very much similar to a lily pond completely covered with large gray lily leaves with slightly raised white fringes around their periphery. These disks of ice are known as pancake ice. If the temperature remains below freezing, the pancake ice coalesces as more ice forms, and within a few days the ice cover can be three to four inches thick with a slightly corrugated surface, unless snow prevails, in which case the entire sea area appears as a smooth white plain. As seawater continues to freeze at the bottom edge and sides of ice floes and fields, snow cover increases and the pressures associated with the stresses and strains caused by water and wind movement result in a hummocking and ridge development in some places and open water in other places.

The freezing process

The rate at which the ice forms and thickens depends on the air temperature, ocean turbulent heat flux (mixing conditions), and amount of snow acting as a heat or cold insulator. An empirical formula has been developed and used extensively by the U.S.S.R. and the U.S. to predict ice appearance and growth rate. The equations are based on the simple concept that ice growth is directly related to the length of time during which the air temperature is below the freezing point for seawater. By adding the number of Fahrenheit degrees below the freezing point for each day, a measure of the severity of cold and time of exposure is obtained. This measure is known as the freezing degree days. In north polar regions there are about 8,000 freezing degree days, which is equivalent to four months of -18° C (0° F) air temperature or a mean annual Arctic air temperature of -12° C (10° F; 22° F below freezing).

During ice growth there is surface evaporation and sublimation and bottom ablation when upward heat conduction in the ice is less than ocean upward heat conduction. The balance between ablation (losses of all sorts), and freezing or accumulation, results in an equilibrium thickness of about 3.5 metres (11.6 feet) of ice in the Arctic and probably about the same in the Antarctic. The lifetime of this North Polar sea ice is five to eight years, and the lifetime of Antarctic polar class ice found only in the Bellingshausen and Weddell seas is about three years. These lifetime values are related to the rate with which the whole Arctic or Antarctic pack in certain areas moves toward the Equator.

Sometimes early in the season there is sufficient warming and wind induced surface motion to completely disintegrate the ice field. Oftentimes after four or five inches of ice and snow have been formed in a more-or-less uniform manner, a large crack develops, which, through wind and stress, opens into a wide canal commonly known as a lead. This phenomenon is seen frequently in older ice and during the spring breakup. Leads are frequently followed by ships navigating in ice fields, but unfortunately the leads sometimes have a dead end with a very large iceberg blocking the way. With alternating freezing, partial melting, snow, and wind and swell, the ice field develops over a matter of a few weeks to a month into a six-inch- to two-foot-deep ocean cover. At this point the ice field is still navigable by most large vessels; however, if a vessel finds itself in the far north two weeks after the commencement of active surface freezing (*e.g.*, in late October), it is in peril of being locked in for the remainder of the winter.

Saltiness of sea ice

The salt content of seawater as it freezes is always less than that of normal seawater. The amount of salt in the seawater during its first moment in the solid state is dependent upon the rapidity with which the seawater freezes, but in general the salt content is about one-tenth that of seawater. The slower the freezing process, the less the salt content. The most rapid freezing is that which occurs during the first day, and this ice is saltier than underlying ice which forms at the ice water interface. The salt that remains in the ice is located in tiny pockets of fluid surrounded by normal crystals. These pockets of fluid migrate, mainly by gravity, through the matrix of ice crystals and, after a few weeks to a few months, the surface of the ice becomes lower in salt content than the deeper layers. It had once been thought that the difference in temperature, or thermal gradient, was the principal driving force for brine pocket migration; careful experiments indicate, however, that although the thermal gradients are a factor, it is principally gravity that accounts for the movement of these brine pockets.

In the summer, when the ice temperature rises, there is a rapid increase in the migration of salt out of the ice. The sea ice surface becomes potable and, in fact, is used by Eskimos as a source of freshwater. Salinity reaches a value of less than 0.01 percent. In summary, when first formed the surface layer may have a salinity of 2 to 4 percent, but by April the salinity has dropped to between 0.4 and 0.7 percent, while sea ice that has been through at least one melt season has a salt content below 0.1 percent.

Arctic pack ice. The pack ice of the Northern Hemisphere covers an average area of 4,100,000 square miles (see Figure 1), filling the Arctic Ocean Basin and adjacent North Atlantic Ocean. The polar ice field consists of 4,700,000 square kilometres (1,800,000 square miles, of 3- to 6-metre- (10- to 20-foot-) thick polar ice that never melts. Infrared imagery from aircraft, however, shows that 10 percent of the polar pack is open water even during winter. Along with Arctic Basin seasonal sea ice, this Arctic pack exudes into the northern Atlantic through two ice streams. The major exit of drifting pack ice from the Arctic Basin is along the eastern side of Greenland, mostly west of Spitsbergen. This ice tongue stretches 2,400 kilometres (1,500 miles) out of the Arctic Ocean and empties a stream of sea ice at a drift rate of eight miles per day. The second icy arm of the north consists of a discharge through the Arctic-Canadian Archipelago and along the eastern American shore. This outpouring of ice is the principal deterrent to easy Northwest Passage ship transit and northern American migration and exploration. During winter, fast ice and local sea ice form along the Siberian coast, Barents and Kara seas, East Greenland, and Labrador coasts down to Newfoundland. The maximum extent of drifting sea ice is about 42° N latitude (about the same latitude as Boston); however, this represents the limit of floating ice pieces and not the hazardous ice-pack edge, which seldom reaches south of Newfoundland. During the summer, the 240-kilometre (150-mile) belt of ice lying along the Labrador coast from Newfoundland northward melts to leave the approaches into Hudson Bay and the Canadian Northwest Territories clear. The motion of the polar ice follows a giant clockwise eddy with a centre 85° N 170° W.

Ice streams into the North Atlantic

In the North Pacific Ocean comparatively little pack ice and icebergs are encountered. The Bering Sea is clear of pack ice during the northern summer, but commencing in September pack ice forms in bays and is carried through the Bering Strait. In winter and spring pack ice is found as far south as 40° N. This is drifting ice from northern latitudes and the Sea of Okhotsk. During winter, pack ice forms in the northern part of the Sea of Japan.

Antarctic pack ice. Approximately twice as much pack ice forms in the oceans surrounding Antarctica as is found in the Arctic. There are, however, only limited regions in the Bellingshausen and Weddell seas where true polar perennial ice similar to the polar ice cap of the Arctic occurs. The maximum area of Antarctic pack ice is 20,000,000 square kilometres (7,700,000 square miles), or about 8 percent of the Southern Hemisphere.

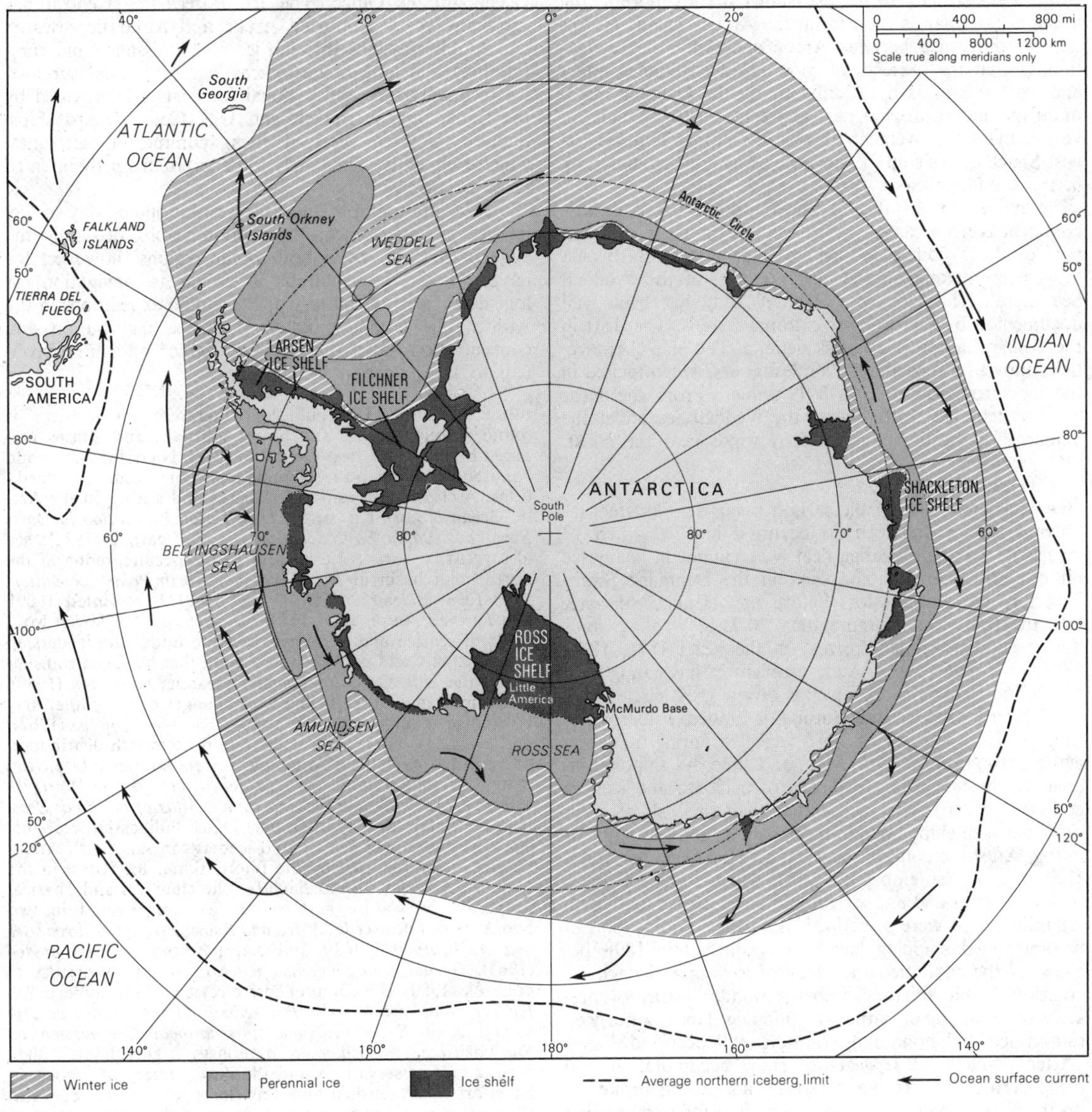

Figure 2: Limits of sea ice and icebergs in the Southern Hemisphere.

Figure 2 indicates the extent of Antarctic pack ice. It forms a fairly constant band of drifting sea ice around the continent, with the farthest northern extent occurring at the end of the austral (southern) winter in October. The greatest extension of pack ice in the South Pacific sector is found in about latitude 62° S, and in the South Atlantic pack ice extends to 52° S. The average northern boundary for icebergs is 56° S in the Pacific and 42° S in the South Atlantic. The minimum ice coverage occurs in March, when most of the Antarctic coast is free of ice, except for the Weddell and Bellingshausen seas. The eastern and western coasts of the Weddell Sea are ice free, but the Weddell itself is covered by a slowly (clockwise) revolving pack that seems to have a two-year cycle. The west coast of the Ross Sea is the most predictably open area during the Antarctic summer, and it is here at the approaches to McMurdo Base that most of the Antarctic expeditions have worked their way to the continent. Much of the sea ice encountered in November and December on approaching the continent hundreds of miles from landfall represents ice that formed near the coast from the previous austral winter. In January and February there usually is clear water adjacent to the coast in all sectors around the continent, but this navigable water might be blocked by hundreds of miles of pack ice barrier farther out to sea.

Movement of Antarctic ice

The Antarctic freeze-up commences with pack ice formation in the southerly parts of the Weddell Sea followed by pack ice appearance in the Bellingshausen and Ross seas. Beginning in March, ice is formed in sheltered bays, and it extends northward as the sea surface temperature drops. From late February to August, snowfall adds more to the ice thickness than is the case in the Arctic. This is an important difference between Arctic and Antarctic navigation, in that the presence of snow has a cushioning effect and ice breaking is more difficult. By the October maximum the action of wind, sea, and some melting results in very active ice movement. It was in October that Sir Ernest Shackleton's ship "Endurance" was crushed and sank in the Weddell Sea in 1915.

The movement of the ice sheet around the Antarctic continent is from east to west except in the most northern part of the Weddell Sea, where there is a west to east movement making up the northern arm of the Weddell Sea Gyral. This clockwise Weddell eddy has been well documented by the drifts of entrapped ships. The drift in the Bellingshausen Sea is less definite. The ship "Antarctic" followed a meandering, aimless course when locked in the ice throughout the 1898–99 winter. From the Ross Sea, ice definitely drifts toward the Weddell Sea under the influence of the prevailing easterly winds near the coast.

NAVIGATION IN ICY REGIONS

Ice disasters. One of the earliest major sea disasters involving sea ice and icebergs occurred in 1777 when 12 vessels of a Dutch whaling fleet were caught in heavy ice off eastern Greenland and sank in the Denmark Strait. Probably the greatest loss before the "Titanic" disaster was the total loss of more than 50 U.S. whaling ships during sudden Arctic "freezes" in the years 1871, 1876, 1888, and 1896. The greatest problem in navigating past the Grand Banks region, which is on the great circle route from North America and Europe, is limited visibility due to a low-lying fog; this is most persistent during the worst ice threat period of April, May, and June. As shipping increased, the increasing frequency of pack ice and iceberg collisions became less of a threat than the risk of collisions between ships bound on opposite courses at night or in fog. After the collision between a French steamer and a U.S. ship on September 27, 1854, which took 300 lives, separate eastbound and westbound lanes across the North Atlantic Ocean were prescribed. A further modification of recommended shipping lanes was instituted in 1898 because of the continued frequency of iceberg and pack ice collisions. Unfortunately, icebergs wander astray of prescribed limits, and, although shipping lanes were well established and honoured, collisions still occurred.

After perhaps 3,000 years of snow accumulation and creep across the Greenland terrain, an iceberg broke off on the West Greenland coast and drifted for perhaps two years, until April 1912. In the Labrador Current, sailing at one to two knots toward the North Atlantic shipping routes, this iceberg had a ram (underwater projection), as most icebergs do by the time they enter the warmer waters near the Gulf Stream. Under control of wind and current, this iceberg drifted into the path of the "Titanic" on April 14, 1912, and they collided in latitude 41°46′ N, longitude 50°14′ W with the loss of 1,513 lives. This tragedy led to the establishment of the International Ice Patrol in 1913 to patrol and guard by ship, plane, or other means the eastern, southern, and western limits of drifting Arctic ice during the most dangerous part of the year. Ships are warned twice daily by detailed messages broadcast to all North Atlantic shipping concerning the boundaries of ice and position of dangerous icebergs. The U.S. Coast Guard has operated the ice patrol since 1913.

The sinking of the "Titanic"

The most recent major iceberg tragedy occurred near the tip of Greenland out of the patrol area of the International Ice Patrol, but ironically just after the U.S. Coast Guard initiated an intensive reevaluation of the known poor ability of radar to detect icebergs. In January 1959 the Danish ice-breaking passenger cargo ship "Hans Hedtoft" sank after colliding with an iceberg in heavy seas. Ninety-five passengers and valuable historical documents were lost.

Ice forecasting and reconnaissance. Sea ice reconnaissance and forecasts in the Arctic and Antarctic are conducted by a number of nations, but the principal work is done by the U.S. Navy, either through the Fleet Weather Office or the Ice Forecasting Central of the U.S. Naval Oceanographic Office. The Ice Forecasting Central has for many years supported Arctic and Antarctic research and supply missions through ice reconnaissance and careful short and long range forecasting. Additional supportive reconnaissance and regional forecasts are provided by the Canadian government and U.S. Coast Guard ships. Support is even received from commercial airplanes, which frequently spot lonely icebergs far from the area of usual occurrence.

Satellite photographs lack the resolution for day-to-day iceberg reconnaissance; these photographs do show the edge of the sea ice in both polar regions, however. Ice navigation in the Antarctic is similar to navigation for logistic support of military and scientific expeditions in the Arctic. The emphasis is on pack ice distribution and concentration rather than icebergs, which offer little problem to ships once in the ice pack.

BIBLIOGRAPHY. The published literature on icebergs is found mainly in U.S. and Soviet journals, and atlases prepared by the U.S. Coast Guard and U.S. Navy for Arctic and Antarctic military and scientific maritime resupply expeditions. A classic discussion of icebergs and sea ice in the Arctic Ocean is ADM. E.H. SMITH, *The Marion Expedition to Davis Strait and Baffin Bay: Scientific Results*, part. 3 (1931); see also FRIDTJOF NANSEN's treatment of the oceanography of the north polar basin in *The Norwegian North Polar Expedition, 1893–1896: Scientific Results*, vol. 3 (1902, reprinted 1969), and *Farthest North*, 2 vol. (1898). A great deal of Soviet work on both sea ice and icebergs was done under the leadership of N.N. ZUBOV and published in a book that has been translated by the U.S. Office of Naval Research, *Arctic Ice* (1948). The importance of ice in the water budget of the planet may be studied by consulting J.L. DYSON, *The World of Ice* (1962); and two atlases that present the month-to-month distribution of ice in the Arctic and Antarctic: U.S. NAVAL OCEANOGRAPHIC OFFICE (HYDROGRAPHIC OFFICE), *Ice Atlas of the Northern Hemisphere* (1946), and *Oceanographic Atlas of the Polar Seas*, part 1, "Antarctic," Hydrographic Office Publication No. 705. The distributions of sea ice and icebergs in the North Atlantic Ocean are reported by the International Ice Patrol in the annual U.S. COAST GUARD *Bulletin*. The chemical and physical properties of sea ice and iceberg ice are covered in two books: W.D. KINGERY (ed.), *Ice and Snow: Properties, Processes and Applications* (1963); and E.R. POUNDER, *Physics of Ice* (1965). *Dynamics of Snow and Ice Masses*, ed. by SAMUEL C. COLBECK (1980), is a comprehensive review of the subject. *Sea Ice Processes and Models: Proceedings of the Arctic Ice Dynamics Joint Experiment and International Commission on Snow and Ice Symposium*, ed. by ROBERT S. PRITCHARD (1980), reports field observations and the development of models in an effort to establish usable flow laws for sea ice. See also U.S. NAVAL OCEANOGRAPHIC OFFICE (HYDROGRAPHIC OFFICE), *A*

Functional Glossary of Ice Terminology, H.O. Pub. No. 609 (1952); and WORLD METEOROLOGICAL ORGANIZATION, *Sea-Ice Nomenclature* (1970).

The age of icebergs can be understood from consulting W. DANSGAARD *et al.,* "One Thousand Centuries of Climatic Record from Camp Century on Greenland Ice Sheet, *Science,* 166:377–381 (1969); and P.F. SCHOLANDER *et al.,* "Composition of Gas Bubbles in Greenland Icebergs," *J. Glaciol.,* 3: 813–822 (1961). A major reference work on the proposed use of icebergs as a freshwater source is *Iceberg Utilization: Proceedings of the First International Conference and Workshops on Iceberg Utilization,* ed. by A.A. HUSSEINY (1978).

Ice navigation is discussed in U.S. NAVAL OCEANOGRAPHIC OFFICE (HYDROGRAPHIC OFFICE), *Manual of Ice Seamanship,* H.O. Pub. No. 551 (1950); see also TREVOR HATHERTON (ed.), *Antarctica* (1965); and M.K. PETROV, *Sailing in Ice* (Eng. trans. 1955).

(T.F.B.)

Ice Hockey

With its speed, its violence and brutality, and, sometimes, its ballet-like movements, ice hockey has become one of the most popular of international sports. Even countries normally not associated with ice-skating—such as Spain and Australia—have international teams. The game is an Olympic sport, and in the Soviet Union there are more than 1,000,000 registered players performing regularly in leagues. It is perhaps Canada's most popular game and is ingrained so deeply into that country's consciousness that it is not unusual for boys of 14 or 15 years of age to be assigned to clubs hundreds of miles from home. For good reason ice hockey is called the world's fastest team game. In no other contact sport do the competitors reach speeds of 30 miles per hour, and the puck they hit has been clocked at speeds of more than 100 miles per hour.

The game's basic simplicity

Although ice hockey has many rules, its basic simplicity has helped elevate it to worldwide prominence. The game requires two teams, each with six players wearing ice skates. The object is to propel a vulcanized rubber disk, the puck, past a goal line and into a net guarded by a goalkeeper. Because of its speed and excitement, the game is appreciated and watched in countries that do not have many ice hockey participants. Fans of several National Hockey League teams in the United States, for example, regularly fill their arenas to near capacity, even though the vast majority of the league's players are Canadian.

This articles traces the history of ice hockey and outlines its present status. For information on the specific rules or on how to play the reader should consult the works listed in the *Bibliography.* For modern records, see under SPORTING RECORD in the *Ready Reference and Index.* See also *Olympic Games* tables in ATHLETIC GAMES AND CONTESTS.

History. Many countries claim credit for the beginnings of the stick and ball games that were the forerunners of the two modern hockey games, field hockey and ice hockey. For a brief account of these beginnings, see the article HOCKEY (FIELD). The beginnings of ice-skating were similarly ancient (see WINTER SPORTS).

In any event, it seems apparent that British soldiers stationed in eastern Canada in the 1850s and 1860s brought with them a hockey-type game (shinty, or shinny), as well as rudimentary skates. Because many of the lakes and the grounds around their camps were frozen for most of the winter, the soldiers adapted their game of shinty to their new environment, strapping on skates and taking to the ponds. It is impossible to determine whether they played a game on ice before American Indians did. Certainly, by this time, many Canadians also were playing shinty on ice. The soldiers had flexible rules, and as many as 15 or 20 players would compete for each side. As their assignments shifted across Canada, they took the game with them.

Several cities in Canada lay claim to being the cradle of the sport. The first record of a puck being used instead of a ball was at Kingston Harbour, Ontario, in 1860. The first game with rules, many borrowed from field hockey, is believed to have been played in Montreal in December 1879. It was held between two teams of students from McGill University, 30 to a side, and led to the formation of the first recognized team, the McGill University Hockey Club, in 1880. The McGill students eventually codified the rules and permitted a maximum of only nine players. The sport's popularity soon mushroomed, but games were played on natural ice and thus were confined to the winter months. The game continued to borrow from other sports. Wooden barriers, a foot or so high, were placed around the playing area, which came to be known as a "rink," a Scottish word that means a "course." The word had been used previously to describe the marked-off area on the ice on which the game of curling was played.

By the 1880s hockey sticks were being manufactured in Montreal to meet the demand of ice hockey players. Manufacturers also produced skates. But most of the players' equipment still was borrowed from other sports. Goaltenders, for example, used the same type of chest protector as that worn by a baseball catcher.

By the 1880s and 1890s the game was vying with lacrosse as Canada's national pastime. It still was unorganized, and rules followed by one team were not observed by the next. In 1885 a group of hockey men met in Montreal to further codify the game. They formed the Amateur Hockey Association (AHA) of Canada, the first national hockey organization. One of their key rulings, reducing the number of players on a side from nine to seven, helped stop the helter-skelter nature of the game. Also in 1885 the first league was formed in Kingston, Ontario. It was composed of four teams: Queens University, the Royal Military College, the Kingstons, and the Athletics. The first championship game was won by Queens University, which scored a 3–1 victory over the Athletics.

Spurred on by the formation of a governing association and by the league, cities began to build arenas all over eastern Canada. The arenas, built around natural ice surfaces, were dimly lit by oil lamps, and the spectators were colder than the players. This did not deter construction or interest, and dozens of small cities built arenas to house their local teams. Other leagues also were formed, but the AHA was the strongest, and most of the interest remained centred in the east. In 1892, however, national attention was focussed on the game, perhaps giving it its strongest impetus. That year the Canadian governor general, Frederick Arthur, Lord Stanley of Preston, donated a cup to be given annually to the top Canadian team, which was to be determined by a play-off. The three-foot-high silver cup, which cost 10 pounds, became known as the Stanley Cup. It was first played for in 1893–94, and the first winner was the Montreal Amateur Athletic Association team; since 1917 it has gone to the winner of the National Hockey League play-offs.

The AHA, although the strongest league in Canada, was plagued by dissension, and in 1899 a splinter group, the Canadian Amateur Hockey League, was formed. All hockey in Canada at the time was "amateur." Even though it was common practice for players to be paid, the leagues insisted on the term amateur since it was considered, in those years, "ungentlemanly" to accept pay for athletic services. Thus it was that the first acknowledged professional hockey team in the world was formed in the United States, in 1903, in Houghton, Michigan. The team, the Portage Lakes, was owned by a dentist named J.L. Gibson, who imported Canadian players. In 1904 Gibson formed the first acknowledged professional league, the International Pro Hockey League. The idea of professionalism was not well received by the Canadian leagues, even though many of their players took money to play for Gibson and then became "amateurs" again by playing in Canada. Finally, Canada had to accept professional hockey, but it did not do so until 1908, when the Ontario Professional Hockey League was formed. By that time Canada had become the world's hockey centre.

Emergence of professional hockey

The National Hockey Association (NHA), the forerunner of the National Hockey League, was organized in 1910 and became the strongest association in North America. The rising tide of interest in the game created problems, however, for at the time there were only eight artificial ice rinks in the world, and none in Canada. A boom in construction was soon under way. In 1911 the Pacific Coast Hockey Association was formed by the Patrick family—Joseph and his sons Lester and Frank—who believed that hockey would prove successful on Canada's west coast and who built two enclosed, artificial-ice arenas in British Columbia, one in Vancouver and the other in Victoria.

The Patricks' league became involved in a money and player war with the NHA. Although the NHA ultimately emerged as the stronger league, it was the Patricks' league that introduced many of the changes that speeded up the game and gave it worldwide acceptance. The only radical rule change adopted by the NHA was to reduce the number of players on a side to six, and that move was made to save money. The western league retained seven-man hockey, but it allowed the goalie to leave his feet to stop the puck. Under the previous rules, a goalie had had to remain stationary and could not leap or dive. The western league also changed the offside rule. Under the old rules a player had been deemed offside if he was ahead of the puck carrier when he received a pass. The Patricks' league divided the ice into three zones by painting two blue lines across the surface and allowed forward passing in the centre zone between the blue lines. This opened up the game and made it more exciting. Another innovation in the western league was the idea of the assist. Previously, only the goal scorer had been credited with a point in his personal scoring statistics. In the Patricks' league the player or players who set up his goal were credited with an assist. The first numbered uniforms also appeared in their league. This helped give the game an intimacy for spectators who did not know the players by sight and attracted many new fans.

Like some of its predecessors the NHA had its dissenters. In a move to eject one of the league members, the NHA decided to disband and form a new league. The result was the creation of the National Hockey League (NHL) on November 22, 1917. It has become the world's most famous hockey league, and its players, all professionals, are among the best in the world.

International ice hockey

On the international level, however, amateur hockey has remained supreme. League competition among amateurs in England began in 1903. The International Ice Hockey Federation was formed in Europe in 1908, the same year the first game was held in Scotland, at Glasgow, and the first professional league was formed in Canada. Its five original members were Great Britain, Bohemia, Switzerland, France, and Belgium. Its players were amateurs and have remained so. The first European championship was held at Avants, Switzerland, in 1910, with Great Britain the winner. Since then the federation has broadened its membership, taking applicants from the world over. The overwhelming number of Canada's players also remained amateur. They were so good that Canada captured the first Olympic Games title, in 1920, and concurrently the first International Ice Hockey Federation world championship. Canada also won the ice hockey competition at the first Winter Olympic Games in 1924, retaining both Olympic and world championships until 1936, when Great Britain triumphed. In 1963 the Soviet Union began a long sequence of international successes.

Except for the inclusion of an ever-increasing number of new teams, there has been no dramatic change in the organization of European ice hockey. The organization of North American professional ice hockey, however, has undergone several important changes since the 1920s. One of the National Hockey League's most far-reaching decisions came in 1924, when it took in for the first time a team from the United States—the Boston Bruins. In 1925 the New York Americans and Pittsburgh Pirates were admitted, followed by three more teams in 1926—the New York Rangers, the Chicago Black Hawks, and the Detroit Cougars (later to be known as the Red Wings). To stock the new teams, the NHL bought out the Patricks' league in 1926 for $250,000. Among the players who shifted to Boston was Eddie Shore, a defenseman who eventually was elected to the Hockey Hall of Fame. Shore was known as a "rushing" defenseman, then a rarity, and his style helped change the game. He was one of the sport's most ferocious players and best fighters, and, many experts say, its most skilled player. Pittsburgh and the New York Americans eventually dropped out of the league, and for nearly 30 years, until the expansion of 1967, the NHL was composed of six teams—the Rangers, the Bruins, the Black Hawks, the Red Wings, the Toronto Maple Leafs, and the Montreal Canadiens.

In 1967 the NHL undertook one of the most dramatic expansions ever of any professional sports league when it doubled in size to 12 teams. Six more teams were added from 1970 to 1974. A new 12-team league, the World Hockey Association (WHA), was formed in 1972, and the ensuing rivalry caused a substantial rise in players' salaries. The WHA failed in 1979, and four of its teams were absorbed by the NHL. By 1980 the NHL had 21 teams (seven in Canada and 14 in the United States), divided into two conferences, with two divisions in each conference.

The modern game. The modern game on every level—amateur, collegiate, international, and professional—has been influenced largely by the National Hockey League. There is small difference in style today between, for example, a Soviet player and a player at a U.S. university. Virtually all hockey is played on a standard-sized rink, shaped like a round-cornered rectangle 200 feet long and 85 feet wide (see diagram), although competition is also permitted on rinks of slightly different dimensions. The object is to put the puck past a goaltender and into the goal cage, which is four feet high and six feet wide. Any shot that completely clears the goal line, a two-inch-wide stripe in front of the cage, is considered a goal.

The blue lines that divide the ice into three zones are 60 feet out from the goal line and are painted across the width of the ice. The area between the blue lines is called the neutral zone. United States college rules call for checking—body contact to take an opponent out of the play—only in a team's defending and neutral zones. A team may not check inside its opposition's blue-line zone. In other hockey competition checking is permitted at any place on the ice. In professional and Canadian hockey the ice is further divided by a red line running the width of the center of the ice. Players in such games may not make or take a pass that has travelled over a red line and a

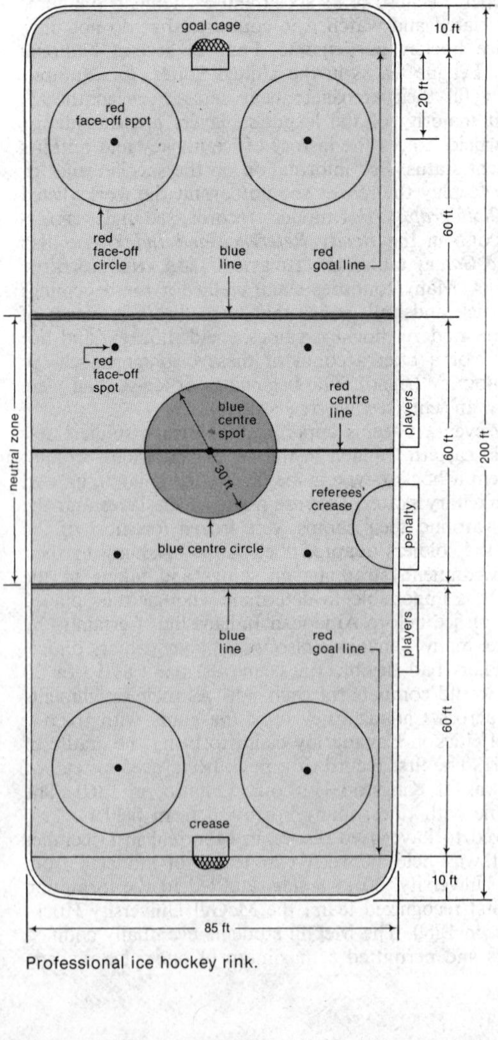

Professional ice hockey rink.

Referee about to drop the puck as players for Harvard and Boston College prepare for a face-off in the neutral zone.
Clif Garboden—Stock, Boston, Inc.

blue line. If they do, they are ruled offside. A face-off, in which an official drops the puck between opposing players, follows the infraction. In hockey competition that has no red line an offside infraction involves a pass that has travelled across the two blue lines. Face-offs are held at the point of the infraction. Players who precede the puck into the attacking zone also are ruled offside, and a face-off is held at a "face-off spot" near the attacking blue line. A face-off also begins each period and is used as well after a goal and after any stoppage of play.

Players and principles of play

The least mobile of the six players on a squad is the goalie, who rarely leaves his goal area. The usual alignments of the other five players are three forwards—the centre, a left wing, and a right wing—and two defensemen—a left defenseman and a right defenseman.

Ideally, the attacking team moves as a unit, led by the forwards. The centre generally is the most adroit stickhandler of the attackers and must be able to get by onrushing defenders. When he cannot, he passes off to one of his wings or drops the puck behind him for one of his defensemen. If he is able to get over the other team's blue line, he attempts to set up his men. He tries to do this by drawing the opposition toward him and then passing to one of his wings or defensemen.

A player may handle the puck as often or as long as he likes, so long as he does not close his glove on the puck. A player may not pass the puck with his open hand. The goalie, however, is generally not subject to either restriction.

The game is divided into three periods of 20 minutes playing time each. As many as 30 percent of all games end in ties because of the low-scoring nature of the sport. In the case of a tie in U.S. college games an overtime, period is played to determine the winner. The only situation in which an overtime period is used in other hockey competition is to determine a winner in championship play. In organized ice hockey a victory is worth two points in the standings; a tie is worth one. No points are awarded for a loss. A goal counts as a point for the team, but points may be awarded to as many as three players for one goal. One point goes to the player who scored the goal, and a point each is awarded for an assist to the last two of the scorer's teammates who touched the puck, providing that the opposition did not handle the puck in the interim.

Of the major sports ice hockey is the only one in which substitutions are permitted while the game is in play. The game is so fast and so demanding that forwards generally skate only 90 seconds at a time. This means that there are at least 10 "line changes" a period, and if play were stopped each time a line change is made the tempo would be markedly decreased. Defensemen usually stay on the ice for a slightly longer period of time, since they do not generally have to make rink-length rushes.

Infractions and penalties

Because of the speed and contact there are many infractions, not all of them having to do with "hitting" penalties. Play is stopped for an offside and for the infraction called icing. The latter occurs when a team shoots the puck out of its zone past the other team's goal line. Icing is a manoeuvre favoured by a team when it is shorthanded and wants to stall or is being pressured; a face-off follows an icing. No player, however, may delay the game by intentionally shooting the puck out of the rink or by shifting the goalposts. Both are minor infractions.

Minor penalties are most commonly assessed for excessive use of the body or equipment to impede the opposition. For a minor infraction the offending player must remain in the penalty box at the side of the rink for two minutes while his team plays shorthanded. If the opponents score at any time during that span, the penalized player may return to the ice. Penalties incurred by the goalie are served by a teammate. A major penalty for violent play or a misconduct penalty for abusing an official results in the loss of a player for five or 10 minutes or for the remainder of the game. Unless there is deliberate injury, the offender's team makes a substitution and is not shorthanded when play resumes. Violent play in modern professional hockey has drawn much criticism.

Equipment

Virtually all equipment—for children, amateurs, or professionals—is the same. Goalies generally wear face masks, which became popular among professionals in the 1960s. Before then amateur goaltenders wore masks resembling those of baseball catchers. Forwards and defensemen wear the same type of skates, but the goaltender's blades are flatter, because they need more balance and are stationary for longer periods. The shoes of goaltenders' skates are fitted with rubber protection for the toes. Under their uniforms goaltenders wear a chest protector, shoulder pads, quilting from wrist to shoulder, and pads to protect the kidneys, thighs, and knees. Except for the chest protector, forwards and defensemen wear the same protective gear under their uniforms. Players in international and amateur competition must wear helmets, but the rule is waived in the professional ranks.

Over his uniform a goalie wears extra equipment. Pads up to ten inches in width protect him from the tip of his skates to above his knees. They aid him not only in protection but also in blocking and kicking away shots. On his free hand the goalie wears a glove similar to a first-baseman's baseball mitt, with a wide webbing that enables him to catch the puck. The stick hand is encased in a five-finger glove with a wide backing that protects his arm. Gauntlets of both gloves extend well up the arms. The goalie's stick has a wider shaft and blade than those of the other players. Fully dressed, goaltenders carry 30 pounds of equipment, five pounds more than the others.

The protection is essential. The slap shot of Bobby Hull, one of the National Hockey League's top scorers, was timed at more than 100 miles an hour. The slap shot has become an increasingly popular offensive weapon, adopted in recent years by European players. It differs from the wrist shot in that the player winds up, bringing his stick back so far that it is nearly perpendicular with the ice, and then brings the stick down in an arc, swatting the puck as he goes into his follow-through. It is not as accurate as the wrist shot, in which the player puts his stick on the ice near the puck and without a windup snaps his wrist to fire off a shot.

The other most common shot is the backhander, taken when the puck goes to the other side of the stick from which the player normally shoots. If he is a right-handed shooter, for example, he takes the backhander from his left side. It is taken when there is not enough time to shift the puck to his normal shooting position. The backhander generally is not as hard or as accurate as the wrist shot, but it has the advantage of being taken quickly. Many experts agree the hardest backhander in the professional game belonged to Maurice ("the Rocket") Richard of the Montreal Canadiens. A natural left-handed shooter, he played right wing. He was hockey's first 50-goal player, and many of his goals were scored off his backhand.

Offensive and defensive play and strategy

Speed is an essential requirement of the game. In the sport's early days a team could get away with having a few slow-footed defensemen. But contests at all levels have become so quick that offensive and defensive roles often are reversed, and defensemen may wind up in the forefront of the action. Slower players must have other attributes to make a team; they must, for example, be able to check well, to prevent the other players from getting past them. But, since everyone on the team handles the puck at some point during a game, a premium is placed on puck-carrying ability. The man with the puck at any given moment is in control, and the play can go only so fast as he is able to direct the disk.

If a forward has the puck, the defensemen trail the play. If a defenseman is leading an offensive thrust, called a "rush," one of the forwards backs him up. The opposition, meanwhile, attempts to gain control of the puck or to dislodge it. The most common way is for the defending player to poke his stick at the puck. A defender may also block, check, or hit the player with his body, as long as it falls within the rules defining allowable contact. Ideally, the defending team's defensemen lay back, straddling their blue line, away from the boards. They then can move to the centre to halt a breakthrough or can drive a man into the boards if he attempts to go along the sides. If the attacking players find that they have difficulty in stickhandling past the opposition, they may try a long shot "on goal." They may also shoot the puck into the other team's zone and chase it, two attacking players going after the puck—one to handle the opponent who is sure to go after it as well, and the other to try to wrest the puck away. The third forward, meanwhile, takes up a position about 20 feet in front of the goal, in the centre of the ice, in a spot known as the "slot." In the slot he is in good position to shoot if his men can get the puck to him. The defensemen on the attacking team take up positions on the blue line to prevent the defending team from getting a breakaway. Often the puck is passed to the defensemen, who shoot from the blue line, 60 feet out, from their position known as the "point." Long shots rarely go in, so defensemen try to keep long shots low, which gives the attackers a chance at a rebound attempt.

Many fans do not see goals scored in hockey because so many go in on rebounds or deflections. While a shot is taken, no attacking player may be in the goalie's crease, a rectangle eight feet across and four feet out from the goal line; but there is much physical contact in front of the net, and the puck may ricochet off a skate, a stick, or any part of the body. Any kind of shot that puts in a goal is allowable, except if the shooter has raised his stick above his elbow; but the puck may not be deliberately kicked in, and it cannot be thrown in with the hand.

One of the most unusual spectacles in hockey occurs when a team that is trailing by one goal takes its goaltender out of the net in the final seconds of the game. The goalie is replaced by a forward in the hope that the extra man on offense will give the team a chance for a tie. Another rare and exciting play is the penalty shot, which is called when a stick is thrown to deflect a shot or when a player with an open path to the goal is pulled down from behind. The team against which the infraction was committed selects a player to skate unopposed to the opponent's goal and take one shot to beat the goalie.

The officials

Under international rules games are controlled by two referees. The professional game is under the complete control of one referee, who is responsible for calling all penalties and is the final arbiter of whether a goal has been scored. He is assisted by two linesmen, who call offsides and icing infractions, and by two goal judges, who are stationed behind each cage, in a raised booth behind the boards. The goal judges' function is to signal a goal when the puck has crossed the goal line. They are not concerned with whether the goal is legal, merely whether it was scored. To indicate a goal, they flip a switch that stops the clock and triggers a red light. The other officials are the penalty timekeeper, who must not let a player out of the penalty box until the infraction is over or a goal scored; the game timekeeper, who is in charge of running the official clock and who stops the clock during play stoppages; and the official scorer, who decides who gets credit for the goals and assists and also keeps track of the goalie's saves, or stops.

Through effective checking and alert goalkeeping the defense for Merrimack College prevents the Air Force Academy from scoring.

Horst Schafer—Peter Arnold, Inc.

Play-offs and championships. In the National Hockey League, the ultimate prize is the Stanley Cup. The winner is determined after a series of play-offs. Before 1967 the teams that finished first and third and second and fourth played best-of-seven series to determine which would play for the Stanley Cup. The winners then met in another best-of-seven series for the cup. When the league formed two divisions, each division held a similar series. The finalists from each then met. Beginning in 1980, an expanded play-off system involved 16 of the league's 21 teams.

NHL individual awards are the Vezina Trophy, for the goalie or goalies with the team permitting the fewest goals; the Calder Trophy, for the rookie of the year; the Hart Trophy, for the most valuable player; the Norris Trophy, for the outstanding defenseman; the Art Ross Trophy, for the top point scorer; the Lady Byng Trophy, for the player best combining clean play with a high degree of skill; the Conn Smythe Trophy, for the play-offs' outstanding performer; the Frank J. Selke Trophy, for the best defensive forward; the Jack Adams Award, for the coach of the year; the Bill Masterton Memorial Trophy, for the player who best exemplifies perseverance, sportsmanship, and dedication to hockey; and the Lester Patrick Trophy, for outstanding service to hockey in the United States. NHL players receive cash awards if they are voted onto the first or second teams of the all-stars.

Few non-Canadians have played in the NHL. The growth of collegiate hockey in the United States, however, has led to a greater proportion (about 10 percent by 1980) of NHL players born in the United States. The level of hockey in Europe—especially in the Soviet Union, Czechoslovakia, and Sweden—increased greatly in the years following World War II. One of Sweden's most famous athletes following the war was a player who legally changed his name to "Tumba" because his nickname (actually, the name of his hometown) was more famous in his country than his real name. To take advantage of their speed, endurance, and passing skills, the NHL had signed several European players by the early 1980s. The Soviet Union's national team has become one of the strongest in international competition and in 1972 almost beat Team Canada, made up of selected Canadian-born NHL stars. The Canadian team, however, came from behind to win a special eight-game series (four in Canada and four in the Soviet Union) by four games to three, with one tie. Soviet teams continued their outstanding play in subsequent competition with North American professionals.

Amateur hockey

The Amateur Hockey Association of the United States has more than 3,800 teams and 50,000 skaters. The AHA, in conjunction with the United States Olympic Committee, chooses players for the Olympics, which are held every four years; and it chooses the national team for world championships, which are held annually. Most of its players are collegians. The major college championship in the United States is the National Collegiate Athletic Association tournament. In Canada the Canadian Amateur Hockey Association has about 550,000 registered players. Its decline in international competition has been blamed on the fact that many of its men were turning professional while teenagers. A ruling now forbids any boy from turning professional until he reaches his 20th birthday. Canadian senior amateur hockey—which has no age limit—has as its top prize the Allan Cup, determined after eliminations. The junior players—up to 20 years of age—meet in a similar series for the Memorial Cup.

To determine which teams meet for the world amateur championship, the International Ice Hockey Federation has set up three classes. Six countries are in Class A, eight in Class B, and the rest in Class C. The six teams in Class A automatically are eligible for the world championship and the Olympics. The team that does the worst in that division moves down the next year to Class B. The team with the best record in Class B automatically moves up to Class A. The same procedure is followed in Group C.

BIBLIOGRAPHY

History: GERALD ESKENAZI, *Hockey*, rev. ed. (1971), a history of the game from its precedents in Europe through its development in Canada and up to the formation of the National Hockey League; FOSTER HEWITT, *Hockey Night in Canada: The Maple Leaf's Story* (1953), reminiscences of the game's early days by a well-known hockey broadcaster; DICK BEDDOES, STAN FISCHLER, and IRA GITLER, *Hockey! The Story of the World's Fastest Sport*, rev. ed. (1973), histories of NHL clubs, great players, great events in the game, and the history of the league; ANATOLY TARASOV, *Road to Olympus* (1969), details of European hockey, the world amateur championships, and the Olympics by the coach of the Soviet Union's national team; HENRY ROXBOROUGH, *The Stanley Cup Story*, 3rd rev. ed. (1966), great moments in the National Hockey League play-offs that started in 1893; C.L. COLEMAN, *The Trail of the Stanley Cup*, 2 vol. (1966), the year-by-year events of the NHL from 1893 to 1946 with statistics for each year for every team and every player; BRIAN MCFARLANE, *60 Years of Hockey* (1976), a history of the National Hockey League and of the Stanley Cup that includes statistics and records from 1917 to the mid-1970s; TIM WENDEL, *Going for the Gold* (1980), an account of the U.S. victory at Lake Placid in the 1980 Olympics.

Additional titles may be found in DOUGLAS J. THOM and TOM WATT, *The Hockey Bibliography: Ice Hockey Worldwide* (1978).

General Works: GERALD ESKENAZI, *A Thinking Man's Guide to Pro Hockey*, rev. ed. (1976); STAN FISCHLER and SHIRLEY FISCHLER, *Ice Hockey Encyclopedia*, rev. ed. (1979).

Rules: ROBERT SCHARFF, *Ice Hockey Rules in Pictures*, rev. ed. (1974), easy-to-follow diagrams of infractions and rules, including mandatory equipment; *National Hockey League Official Rule Book*, the official rules for National Hockey League play, which is virtually the same for all professional leagues; *Official Collegiate Scholastic Ice Hockey Guide*, official handbook for U.S. colleges.

How to play: LLOYD PERCIVAL, *Hockey Handbook*, rev. ed. (1961), the definitive book on how to play the game, by position, and its science, strategy, and techniques; JOE TAYLOR (ed.), *Lloyd Percival's Total Conditioning for Hockey* (1978); FRED SHERO and ANDRE BEAULIEU, *Hockey for the Coach, the Player and the Fan* (1979), a well-illustrated hockey instruction book.

Statistics: The National Hockey League Guide (annual), records for all phases of the game and year-by-year performances of current skaters.

(G.Es.)

Ice in Rivers and Lakes

Over much of the world ice forms on rivers and lakes every year and remains on these surface-water bodies for varying lengths of time. About 80 percent of the conterminous United States experiences freezing or near-freezing water temperatures in an average year; freezing surface-water temperatures persist for more than 100 days in an average year over about 25 percent of the same area (see map). The surface waters of 48 percent of the Northern Hemisphere (19,000,000 square miles, or 49,000,000 square kilometres) freeze annually. Data are less complete for the Southern Hemisphere, but with the exception of southern South America and Antarctica, the landmasses there do not extend above 40° latitude, and surface-water freezing is uncommon except at high altitudes. Lakes in Antarctica are completely ice covered perennially; and in Greenland, Canada, Siberia, and other high-Arctic lands, lakes may have a partial ice cover throughout the year. In some areas where freezing is general, certain lakes and river reaches may avoid freezing because of thermal springs, significant influxes of above-freezing groundwater (which is usually at a temperature close to the mean annual temperature of a region), unusually high salt content, or inputs of water artificially heated in industrial cooling processes. Extreme turbulence also may prevent ice-cover formation, particularly in certain reaches of rivers or at inlets or outlets of lakes. Very deep lakes may not freeze because winter cooling does not sufficiently lower the temperatures of their large water volumes.

By courtesy of the U.S. Army Cold Regions Research and Engineering Lab

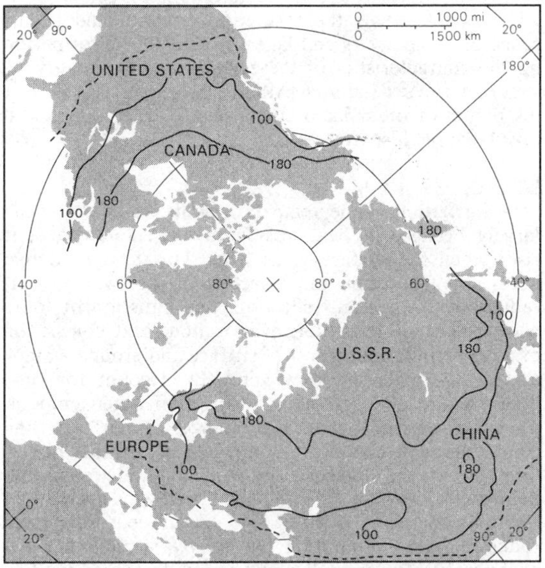

—— Average annual days with ice cover
------ Approximate southern boundary of the occurrence of annual lake and river freezing

Distribution of ice cover in the Northern Hemisphere.

Economic and practical importance

River and lake ice is of great practical and economic importance. Until the development of mechanical refrigeration, ice was annually cut from lakes and rivers and used to refrigerate food; the practice persists in some regions. The greatest economic impact of freshwater ice is doubtless in preventing navigation on inland waterways, however. In North America the annual loss attributed to inability to navigate frozen waterways approaches $200,000,000 on the Mississippi River and the Great Lakes–St. Lawrence Seaway combined. In Siberia, where other forms of transportation are less well developed, the losses due to the short shipping season are of even greater relative importance. Losses of life and severe economic losses are associated with flooding due to ice jams and river icings, which are annual occurrences in many mid- and high-latitude regions.

River ice also greatly reduces the exchange of oxygen between the air and the water, markedly slowing natural re-oxidation of water transporting biochemically degradable wastes. Freezing also reduces stream-flow quantities available for water supply, waste dilution, and power generation; the ice cover represents water in storage and, hence, water that is temporarily unavailable. On a 30-metre- (100-foot-) wide river with an ice cover one foot thick, about 15,000 cubic metres (528,000 cubic feet, or 12 acre-feet) of water is in storage for each mile of river.

The thermal expansion and contraction of both river ice and lake ice generates significant stresses against dams, piers, and other structures, which must be accounted for in engineering designs. During breakup ice jams are often major causes of damaging floods; floating ice cakes associated with high river flows have been known to dislodge bridge superstructures from their piers. Hydroelectric power plants may cease generation because of the accumulation of ice on intake trash racks or screens, completely blocking river flow through the turbines. Frozen lakes and rivers provide some positive economic benefits: recreational resources for skaters, ice fishermen, and iceboaters. In remote areas with significant freezing, lake ice generally provides the most suitable landing sites for aircraft.

Effects on flora and fauna

Lake and river flora and fauna are affected by freezing in several ways. Surface feeding by fish is prevented, and waterfowl can no longer rest and feed when an ice cover forms. Light penetration is restricted and photosynthesis virtually ceases. Shore vegetation may be injured or destroyed by ice formation and subsequent vertical and horizontal movement of the ice cover. Several studies have shown that ice formation on river bottoms dislodges and disperses bottom organisms; however, the ecological effects of this are apparently not great.

This article treats the formation, growth, and occurrence of ice in rivers and lakes. For further information on the characteristics of these water bodies, see RIVERS AND RIVER SYSTEMS; and LAKES AND LAKE SYSTEMS. For discussion of other ice occurrences, see ICE SHEETS AND GLACIERS; see also CLIMATE.

ICE IN LAKES

Ice formation. The temperature of most lakes falls largely because of heat loss from the lake surface; it rises when the surface gains heat. This heat exchange occurs by absorption and reflection of shortwave (solar) radiation; absorption, reflection, and emission of longwave (thermal) radiation; evaporation; and convection of air. Precipitation, inflow of surface and ground waters, and geothermal heat flow generally account for only minor heat exchanges. Thus, for a given water temperature, the rates of radiation exchange, evaporation, and conduction-convection are controlled by weather conditions. When the difference between air and water temperature is less than 5° C (9° F) at high wind speeds and less than 20° C (36° F) at low wind speeds, longwave radiation and evaporation principally account for the heat loss. With larger temperature differences, conductive-convective heat exchange dominates.

As a lake cools from a temperature exceeding 4° C (39° F), the water at the surface loses heat, becomes denser than the water below it, and sinks. This process continues until all water in the lake is at 4° C, which is the temperature of maximum density for water. Wind not only accelerates surface heat loss but promotes cooling by increasing internal circulation. Further cooling at the surface produces a less dense layer, which tends to remain at the surface. Cooling of the surface layer proceeds until a temperature a few tenths of a degree below the freezing point, 0° C (32° F), is reached.

Super-cooling and ice-crystal formation

Supercooling is required so that the latent heat of freezing can be carried away. In water at exactly 0° C, any freezing will liberate heat (80 calories per gram, or 144 British Thermal Units [BTU] per pound, of water freezing), thus warming the unfrozen water above 0° C and inhibiting further freezing. The degree of supercooling required depends on the character of nuclei present. Nuclei generally are existing ice crystals or dissolved or suspended minerals that have crystal structures like that of ice; such impurities are virtually always present in natural water. If nuclei are not present, small ice crystals eventually form, but at greater degrees of supercooling.

In a small isolated body of still water, spontaneously forming ice crystals initially occur in the form of disks a few millimetres in diameter. The disk shape is dictated by the condition of minimum surface energy and by the crystallographic structure of ice. As the disk enlarges, the curvature of the circumference decreases, and the heat of freezing cannot be efficiently disposed of. At this point, minor irregularities in the disk begin to enlarge and grow into a system of branching needles, called dendrites.

Crystal growth is fastest in the direction in which the heat of freezing is most readily dissipated. For a floating crystal, this direction is parallel to the surface (Figure 1). On still water, the surface can be completely covered with a thin skim of ice, called sheet ice, very quickly.

From Ven Te Chow (ed.), *Handbook of Applied Hydrology*, Copyright 1964; used with permission of McGraw Hill Book Company

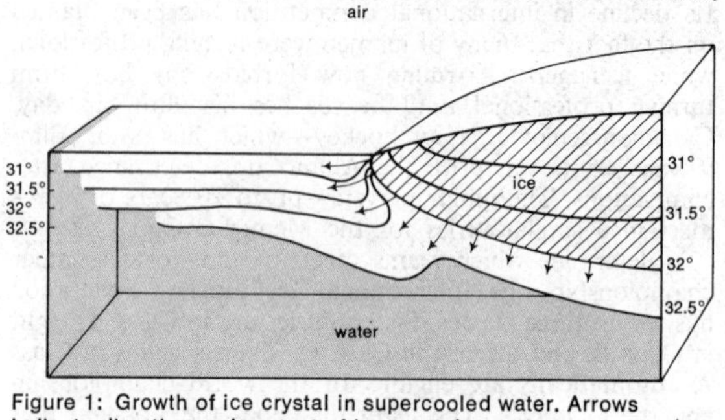

Figure 1: Growth of ice crystal in supercooled water. Arrows indicate direction and amount of ice-crystal growth.

Where there is some agitation of the surface by wind, a thin skim may be broken by wave action. Individual pieces are then subject to abrasion before finally fusing together to form one type of agglomeratic ice. A second type of agglomeratic ice forms when snow falls on a water surface that is very near the freezing point. The resulting irregular masses of slush will subsequently freeze together if cooling continues. On large water bodies, agglomeratic ice generally forms the first complete ice cover. On most lakes, a skim of ice, or thin agglomeratic ice, forms and dissipates up to several times before the "permanent" seasonal ice cover is established.

Ice growth. After a complete ice cover is established, it thickens largely by freezing on the underside. This growth occurs in the form of downward-growing columns. Dissolved impurities and air bubbles, which are largely rejected from the ice during the freezing process, tend to be trapped and concentrated along the boundaries of the columns. The faster this downward freezing occurs, the greater the incorporation of impurities along these crystal boundaries. Additional thickening can occur when an ice cover cracks from the weight of snow, allowing water to flow over the surface. When this mixture freezes, a condition called snow ice is produced.

Equilibrium thickness of ice

The rate of accretion of ice on the underside is controlled by the rate of heat flow, and, hence, the temperature gradient through the ice (and perhaps snow on the surface). The equilibrium thickness of an ice sheet, in the absence of snow cover, depends on the air temperature and time as shown by the following formula:

$$x = \sqrt{\frac{2k_i\,(T_o - T_a)t}{Q_L\,\rho_i}},$$

in which x is the equilibrium thickness, k_i is the thermal conductivity of ice (.00535 cal/cm • sec • ° C, or .000358 BTU/ft • sec • ° F), T_o is the freezing temperature of ice, T_a is the air temperature, t is time, Q_L is the latent heat of freezing, or heat emitted by crystallization of a unit amount (80 calories per gram or 144 BTU per pound), and ρ_i is the density of ice (0.92 grams per cubic centimetre or 57.4 pounds per cubic foot).

Time Required for Ice-Sheet Formation

thickness (cm)	air temperature −1° C	−5° C	−10° C	−20° C
1	1.9 hours	0.38 hour	0.19 hour	0.10 hour
2	7.6 hours	1.5 hours	0.76 hour	0.38 hour
5	2.0 days	9.5 hours	4.8 hours	2.4 hours
10	7.9 days	1.6 days	19.0 hours	9.5 hours
20	32 days	6.3 days	3.2 days	1.6 days
50	198 days	40 days	20 days	9.9 days

The effect of snow on an ice layer is to increase the time required for the ice to reach a given thickness, because snow is an efficient insulator. This effect is taken into account in an empirical equation for ice-thickness prediction:

$$x = \beta(1.06\sqrt{D}),$$

in which x is ice thickness in inches; β is a coefficient ranging from 0.65 to 1.00, depending upon the effects of snow cover, winds, and other environmental factors; and D is accumulated degree-days below 0° C since freeze-up. Hence, the ice thickness varies with time and temperature but also with snow cover and other factors whose effects are assigned numerical values between 0.65 and 1.00.

Several studies have indicated that there is a gradual increase in water temperature at depth after ice-cover formation. This has been attributed to five possible causes: (1) solar radiation transmitted through the ice cover and absorbed by the water; (2) transfer of heat stored in lake-bottom sediments to bottom water; (3) inflow of warm groundwater or surface water; (4) oxidation of organic material in bottom sediments; and (5) geothermal heat flow. The few studies to date suggest that release of heat stored in bottom sediments is the principal cause for at-depth temperature increase.

Ice decay. The presence of water at above-freezing temperatures beneath the ice indicates an upward flow of heat. The net heat flow to the ice–water interface, however, remains negative (*i.e.*, heat is removed and freezing occurs as indicated above) until air temperatures rise to approximately the freezing point. At such time melting occurs at both upper and lower surfaces, but is much more intense on the upper surface. Solar radiation, conduction from the air, and heat derived from rain are the principal energy sources leading to decay and dissipation of the ice cover. Melting is most rapid along crystal boundaries, due to the concentration of impurities (which lowers the freezing point of a solution) and to the presence of imperfections in the crystal lattice that are concentrated at such boundaries. If the crystals are columnar, so-called candle ice forms as a result. Thus, an ice cover may weaken significantly during the early melt season without a corresponding decrease in thickness. As surface melting proceeds, the presence of water on and in the snow or ice cover rapidly reduces the albedo (reflectivity) of the surface. This increases the rate at which solar radiation is absorbed (from perhaps 10 percent absorbed for dry snow to 70 percent for slush) and thus hastens melting.

Factors influencing surficial melting

Melting generally accelerates along the lakeshore and near an inlet or outlet stream. Near-shore melting is a response to conduction and long-wave radiation from shoreline materials and vegetation, which absorb more solar radiation than does ice or snow. An ice cover may thaw completely around the shore and become completely freed; wind and wave action at the edges may then contribute to dissipation. Flowing water at inlets or outlets is a constant source of heat transport to the underside of the ice cover, and ice is generally thinner in such places.

It has been observed that water temperatures begin to fall as melting progresses, particularly if there are open zones along the lake shore. Any of three processes (or a combination of them) may account for this: (1) near-freezing water released at the water–ice interface as the ice melts; (2) inflow of meltwater down through cracks in the ice cover; and (3) inflow of meltwater from streams and lake shore. The relative importance of these processes probably varies from lake to lake, but few data are available on which to base quantitative statements. Once the ice cover is gone, water temperatures again begin to increase by solar heating.

Forecasts of ice breakup are based on air-temperature indices established for particular locations.

Dates of freeze-up

Geographic distribution. In Canada, the average date of the first appearance of ice in lakes (freeze-up) ranges from September 1 in the extreme north to December 20 in the Great Lakes region. Complete freeze-over of lakes generally occurs about ten days after first ice. Although freeze-over and freeze-up times are generally correlative with latitude, both are strongly modified by altitude and distance from the ocean. In general, areas with continental climates experience freeze-over and freeze-up considerably earlier than do areas with maritime-influenced climates at the same latitude. At latitude 60° N, for example, average freeze-over dates range from January 1 near the Pacific coast to November 1 in the area around Hudson Bay. Because the moderating influence of the ocean is less pronounced along Canada's east coast (because of the cold Labrador Current), average freeze-over date is approximately November 15 at the same latitude there.

In the United States east of the Rockies, freeze-up dates range from November 15 in the north central states to about January 1 at latitude 40° N and have a fairly consistent relationship to latitude. West of the Rockies, however, patterns are more complicated because of topography and the influence of strong maritime climates in the Pacific Northwest, and data are insufficient to reveal consistent patterns. In much of the area, freezing does not occur every year.

Mean dates of lake freezing in the Soviet Union range from about October 1 at or above latitude 72° N to mid-January at latitude 45° N. East of the Urals, freeze-over dates are generally correlated with latitude, with minor modifications in areas of strong continentality—*i.e.*, where climate is governed principally by the presence of large land areas. In the western portion of the U.S.S.R., dates of freeze-over become later as one progresses westward; at 60° N, they range from November 1 at the Urals to mid-December at the Baltic Sea.

Data on the relation between lake-freezing dates and altitude are scarce throughout the world. In general, temperatures decrease about 6° C for each 1,000 metres of increase in elevation (about 3.5° F per 1,000 feet), but quite significant variations should be expected, depending on local climatic factors (the microclimate).

Dates of breakup

In Canada, the first distinct signs of breakup on lakes (surface melting or open water) appear on the average as early as March 10 in the extreme southern Great Lakes area to mid-July in the Arctic archipelago. Breakup may occur from ten days to a month after the day on which average air temperature first rises to 0° C (32° F). Dates on which ice completely disappears from lakes occur usually from five to 30 days after the initial signs of breakup: April 1 in the far south to August 1 in the extreme north. As with freezing dates, the pattern of average breakup and clearing dates is strongly modified by continentality. The total ice-free season on Canadian lakes lasts for as few as 30 days in the extreme northern islands to as many as 270 days in the Great Lakes.

Breakup in lakes in the United States begins in early March near the southern limit of annual freezing (about 40° N, east of the Rockies) and in late April in northern Minnesota and Maine. Again, because freezing is not an annual occurrence in much of the area west of the Rockies and because irregular patterns result from topographic effects, no generalizations can be made.

Alberta Government Photograph

Figure 2: Shell ice flow on the Athabasca River, Alberta.

In the Soviet Union, average breakup dates extend from late June in the Arctic Ocean islands to mid-February near latitude 42° N.

ICE IN RIVERS

Formation and growth. Temperature changes in rivers, as in lakes, are caused principally by heat exchange across the surface, and the same cooling processes are important. The important difference between freezing processes in rivers and lakes is that, unlike lakes, virtually all natural streams are turbulent. This means that the flow is well mixed—*i.e.*, that any parcel of water is continually changing its vertical, as well as its horizontal, position in the flow. Because of that turbulence, temperature stratifications cannot arise, and sheet ice cannot form in streams, except along the edges where velocities are at or close to zero. Even in deep rivers, water temperatures are usually at or very close to the freezing point throughout the vertical profile from surface to river bottom during the ice season.

Frazil ice and anchor ice

In rivers, only small degrees of supercooling are needed to form ice, as turbulence quickly carries away the heat of freezing, losing it to the atmosphere at the river surface. If cooling is rapid and turbulent water is supercooled a few hundredths to a tenth of a degree Celsius, small disks of ice, called frazil ice, begin to form. If ice is already present as sheet ice near the edges of the flow, these disks form at the water–ice interface at temperatures of −0.01° to −0.03° C (31.98° to 31.95° F) and quickly break off and become suspended in the water. If no ice is present, the frazil disks form throughout the flow, apparently at greater degrees of supercooling (−0.04° to −0.08° C [31.93° to 31.86° F]).

Although the frazil ice has the same density as normal ice (0.917 grams per cubic centimetre), turbulence is commonly sufficient to keep it in suspension, so that it does not collect at the surface. The frazil disks have a high degree of adhesiveness for each other and for certain surfaces. Consequently, they form large, slushy, irregular masses that may subsequently adhere to the bottom as anchor ice. As frazil ice collects on a rock on a stream bottom, the buoyancy of the adhering ice may be sufficient to lift the rock and carry it downstream. That adhesive property of frazil ice causes the trouble at hydroelectric plants; frazil ice collects on the trash racks of intakes to the turbines, where it may quickly accumulate to block the flow and cause the plant to shut down.

The sequence of events leading to establishment of a complete ice cover on a river varies from area to area and from year to year, depending principally on channel configuration and hydrologic and meteorologic conditions. Generally, the process begins with the formation of sheet ice or agglomeratic ice or both where velocities are low—*e.g.*, along the banks and in backwaters. Sheet ice may continue to form over the entire river width if velocities are everywhere less than about 0.5 metres per second (1.6 feet per second).

In faster flowing reaches, where turbulence prevents sheet-ice formation, frazil ice forms instead. As the frazil-ice particles are carried downstream and encounter stretches of lesser turbulence, they may float to the surface and collect in slushy masses one foot to a few feet across, forming shell ice. Along with pieces of sheet ice that have been broken from the shore by buoyancy forces as velocities change and river levels vary, such slushy masses generally collect at a channel constriction or where border sheet ice extends across the surface, forming an ice bridge.

Effects of an ice bridge or channel constriction

If upstream of the ice bridge the river's flow slows to less than a critical value—depending on the thickness of the bridge and the flow depth—the ice cover will progress upstream. This critical velocity, V_c, is given by the formula

$$V_c = \left(1 - \frac{h}{H}\right)\sqrt{2g\left(\frac{\rho - \rho_i}{\rho}\right)h}$$

in which g is acceleration of gravity, ρ and ρ_i are the densities of water and ice, respectively, h is thickness of the ice bridge, and H is flow depth just upstream of the ice bridge. If flow velocity exceeds V_c, the ice floes arriving at the upstream edge of the bridge will be carried under it, along with frazil disks and needles, if present. Some of this ice may adhere to the underside of the ice bridge, causing it to thicken. This thickening increases the value of h in the above equation and also reduces the flow velocity upstream, so that eventually the critical velocity for upstream growth is reached and the ice cover can progress. The rate of thickening depends upon the amount of ice carried by the flow per unit time, the flow velocity under the ice, and the roughness of the underside of the ice bridge. Thickening of an existing ice bridge can also occur by plastic deformation or by breaking and refreezing if stresses, due mainly to hydraulic forces at the edge of the ice, are sufficient.

As an ice bridge extends upstream by accumulation of floes, turbulence is reduced in the surface layers of water among the floes and freezing proceeds by cooling at the surface, so that the ice cover becomes complete. Further, river discharge is generally decreased as more water goes into storage as ice, or is stored in backwaters caused by local ice formation. This reduces flow velocities and thereby makes conditions for upstream ice growth more favourable.

In some cases, shell-ice and sheet-ice floes may accumulate at a natural constriction or at such an artificial obstacle as bridge piers to such an extent that an ice dam may form. Such a dam may extend all the way to the river bottom and may cause backwaters extending great distances upstream, perhaps giving rise to flooding.

On streams large enough to provide a depth of flow greater than the ice thickness, a complete ice cover is suspended from the channel banks and floats on the river surface. The ice generally is flexible enough to rise and fall with changes in river level. If a change in level is rapid, or if the weight of snow accumulating on the ice is sufficient, cracks may develop, allowing water to spill over the surface where it subsequently freezes and adds to the thickness of the ice cover.

Even in the absence of cracking, the ice thickness changes during the course of a winter in response to weather and flow conditions. Thinning occurs if water discharge increases, if atmospheric and radiational processes supply heat to the ice sufficient to cause surface melting and evaporation, or if sufficient snow is deposited. The snow acts as an insulator and decreases the flow of heat from the water through the ice–snow layer to the air; consequently, melting occurs at the interface of ice and water.

The underside of a river-ice cover is generally rough, especially where ice dams have formed. Even where the ice surface is relatively smooth, however, observations indicate that streamlined forms closely resembling the ripples and dunes of alluvial streambeds are present, at least where velocities are greater than 0.5 metres per second (1.6 feet per second). Contrary to earlier speculations, the roughness of these forms shows a tendency to increase through the winter.

Groundwater and surface water discharges

Many arctic and subarctic streams experience freezing that arises differently from the more general sequence of events in temperate zone areas. In those extremely cold regions, winter freezing of the ground is profound, and groundwater flow is reduced to insignificant amounts. This is particularly true where permafrost is present and freezing from the surface eventually reaches to or nearly to the permafrost table. Groundwater flow, which maintains streamflow during periods of snow cover, therefore, is impeded; and stream discharges dwindle or halt altogether. Under these conditions, and especially in the typically wide, shallow rivers of glacial areas, rivers may freeze solid early in the winter. When drainage is thus blocked, pressures in the flowing groundwater or surface water may increase to such an extent that the water breaks through to the surface near the upstream end of a solidly frozen reach. This water spreads out over the surface and freezes. Successive sheets of overflow ice build up icings (German *aufeis*; Russian *naled*) as much as three metres (ten feet) thick and of great extent. Such river icings may persist well into the summer, and even through several years in high arctic areas, and may block roads at bridges or culverts. They can also give rise to ice jams and flooding during breakup.

Decay and ice jams. Breakup of river ice occurs as a result of increased solar radiation, which melts and weakens the ice cover as it does in lakes, and of the increased discharge accompanying snowmelt and spring rains. As river levels rise and flow velocities increase, the weakened ice is broken loose and begins to move downstream. As the ice cover is thus diminished, an additional increase in flow occurs when the water held in storage by the retarding effect of the ice cover is released. In most cases, river breakup is a sudden and dramatic event, and only a few hours may be required to clear large reaches.

Ice jams, or gorges, of greater or lesser magnitude almost invariably accompany breakup. They occur at natural or artificial channel constrictions, as during ice-cover formation, or at an ice bridge or icing where breakup has not occurred. Ice jams during breakup usually cause much more serious problems than during freeze-up, as much greater amounts and thicknesses of ice are present and river discharges are typically near their annual peaks.

When the collected ice floes form dams, the flowing water may spread widely over the upstream flood plain. The damming action will continue until sufficient pressure builds up to free the jam or until the water finds another channel and bypasses the obstruction. Either result generally releases a sudden surge of water and ice downstream of the jam, possibly doing serious damage to bridges and flood plain structures (Figure 3) and causing severe bank and channel erosion. The water and ice released at one jam may accumulate at another downstream or may be of sufficient force to dislodge a downstream jam, causing a chain reaction that results in serious flooding.

Water surges and ice floe damage

By courtesy of the Soil Conservation Service—United States Department of Agriculture

Figure 3: Damaged railroad track caused by ice cakes and high water from the Ammonoosuc River, New Hampshire.

The ice floes themselves can do tremendous damage in eroding banks and in dislodging large structures—a ten-foot-square ice floe one foot thick weighs about three tons (2,700 kilograms). High, ice-laden flows have been known to remove bridge superstructures completely from their piers.

River stretches that have low slopes, broad channels, and numerous bends, islands, and constrictions are most susceptible to ice-jam formation. Large rivers with northerly courses are subject to jams because breakup occurs in the headwater areas to the south before it occurs in the lower reaches. Ice jams commonly form at the same places year after year, but it is very difficult to predict their severity. In a given river reach, the following conditions contribute to severe jamming: (1) low water levels at freeze-up, resulting in a restricted flow section; (2) a cold, prolonged winter, resulting in thick ice; and (3) a rapid thaw, resulting in the production of large amounts of snowmelt runoff in a short period of time.

Forecasting spring ice jams and related flooding is an inexact science. Prediction schemes have been based on such data as the severity of ice-jam formation during the preceding freeze-up season; observations of river level in the early stages of breakup; and observations and forecasts of air temperature, ice thickness, amount of water in the snow pack, and the intensity of solar heating. Some degree of success has been reported with these methods, and predictions will undoubtedly improve as observational networks improve and experience accumulates.

Ice modification. Because of the great human and economic losses associated with ice-jam flooding and restrictions on navigation during the ice season, operations have been undertaken to alleviate ice jams and maintain navigation routes, particularly in the northern United States, Canada, northern Europe, and the Soviet Union. The use of icebreaking ships and tugs is widespread in the U.S.S.R., northern Europe, and the Great Lakes–St. Lawrence Seaway, both to delay freeze-up and to accelerate and assure a jam-free breakup.

Dusting ice with carbon black or other material that increases the absorption of solar radiation by the ice surface (or decreases its albedo [reflectivity]) accelerates melting. In this increasingly popular procedure, the material generally is applied as a powder from an airplane. The method is effective only during the normal melt season; if applied too early, the resulting melt water may refreeze, or the black material may be covered by snow, rendering it ineffective. The application is usually made on river ice and not specifically on ice jams.

Explosives, diversion structures, and thermal pollution

Explosives, such as dynamite, are used extensively in ice-jam removal. An ice-free channel below the jam and a sufficient flow velocity to carry away the loosened ice are required for success in removing an ice jam by explosives. Blasting operations are most effective when begun soon after the jam forms; underwater charges are more effective than surface charges. Aerial bombing and rocketry have also proved of some success in destroying ice jams.

Ice retention and diversion structures, including especially designed dams and ice booms, are also used to prevent ice jams. Basically, these structures are designed to retain ice so that it will melt where it has formed or to collect it so that it will melt where damaging floods will not occur, while allowing the water to flow past. In 1964 a three-kilometre- (two-mile-) long ice boom was installed on Lake Erie between Buffalo, New York, and Fort Erie, Ontario, at the head of the Niagara River. The boom successfully prevented large quantities of ice from moving from the lake to the river, particularly during periods of high westerly winds.

Changes in water level achieved by opening and closing sluice gates of dams or other flow-control structures have been used to break up an ice cover or to float away ice that would otherwise accumulate in a jam. River modification, including channel dredging, widening, and straightening, are sometimes used to eliminate places where jams frequently form.

Steam-electric power plants, many industrial processes, and sewage-treatment plants release water that has been artificially heated. It has been suggested that this warm effluent ("thermal pollution") could be used to keep river reaches free of ice and thereby extend navigation seasons and reduce ice-jam flooding hazards. Although no conscious efforts have been made to manage water temperatures deliberately by proper positioning of thermal pollution sources, changes in river temperature regimes and ice conditions that have resulted from such sources have been widely noted.

A recent study has investigated the feasibility of extending the navigation season of the Great Lakes–St. Lawrence Seaway by judicious location of nuclear electrical generating plants. Economic gains amounting to $100 million annually would accrue if year-round navigation could be maintained there.

Calculations predict that a nuclear reactor of the size typically constructed in the early 1970s could maintain between one-half and all of the 32-kilometre- (20-mile-)

long South Shore Canal (above Montreal) in an ice-free condition, depending on severity of winters. In later years, when reactors two to three times as big become available, correspondingly longer reaches of the seaway could be kept ice-free. Those figures indicate the definite feasibility of using nuclear-reactor power-plant cooling effluent to keep at least selected portions of the St. Lawrence Seaway ice-free for much of the winter.

Geographic distribution. The general pattern and dates of river freezing are similar to those for lakes. Complete freeze-over in Canada usually begins in late September in the extreme north, and on the average about December 20 in the Great Lakes region and January 10 in western British Columbia. There is a general correlation with latitude, but the pattern is less regular than for lakes because of the many local factors that affect the freezing of rivers. Over most of Canada, rivers freeze over from zero to 40 days after lakes.

In the United States and the Soviet Union, the dates and patterns of river freeze-up and breakup are essentially the same as previously cited for lakes. Again, local variations are to be expected.

The initial breakup of ice in Canadian rivers begins on the average as early as March 1 in western British Columbia and about March 20 in the Great Lakes and averages about June 10 north of Hudson Bay. Clearing of ice from rivers occurs 10 to 20 days later.

BIBLIOGRAPHY

General: H.T. BARNES, *Ice Engineering* (1928), is old and largely outdated but is still useful. Many interesting observations of ice phenomena are presented, and it provides a good introduction to the subject if supplemented with more contemporary works. A modern and complete treatment of freshwater ice is by B. MICHEL, "Winter Regime of Rivers and Lakes," *United States Army Cold Regions Research and Engineering Laboratory Science and Engineering Monograph III-Bla* (1971).

Ice formation, growth and decay: M.F. MEIER, "Ice and Glaciers," in V.T. CHOW (ed.), *Handbook of Applied Hydrology,* (1964), gives a brief but accurate treatment of ice structure and physical properties and the growth, formation, and decay of river and lake ice. R.K. LINSLEY *et al., Applied Hydrology* (1949), provides a short engineering-oriented discussion of the same topics, J.H. ZUMBERGE and J.C. AYERS, "Hydrology of Lakes and Swamps," also in *Handbook of Applied Hydrology,* summarizes adequately the formation, growth, and decay of lake ice and gives some useful references. S.J. BOLSENGA, "River Ice Jams," *United States Lake Survey Research Report 5–5* (1968), is a thorough compilation of all aspects of ice jams, with extensive extracts from the pertinent literature. K.L. CAREY, "Icings," *United States Army Cold Regions Research and Engineering Laboratory Science and Engineering Monograph III-D3* (1970), is a comprehensive review of the causes, problems, and engineering aspects of river icings, with many references.

Geographic Distribution: The UNITED STATES HYDROGRAPHIC OFFICE, *Ice Atlas of the Northern Hemisphere* (1946), gives maps showing dates of opening and closing of navigable waters due to ice. The *Fiziko-Geograficheskiy Atlas Mira,* published by the ACADEMY OF SCIENCES OF THE U.S.S.R. (1964), provides similar but more contemporary information for the Soviet Union. W.T.R. ALLEN, "Break-Up and Freeze-Up Dates in Canada," *Canada Department of Transport, Meteorological Branch Circular 4116* (1964), summarizes the data for rivers and lakes in the form of maps for that country.

(S.L.D.)

Iceland

An island country in the North Atlantic, Iceland is a land of vivid contrasts. It has sparkling glaciers lying across ruggedly beautiful mountain ranges, and the island's vast subterranean thermal activity makes it one of the most active volcanic regions of the globe. Glaciers and beds of cooled lava each cover about a tenth of the country; the glaciers are a reminder of the Arctic Circle, which nearly touches an upper peninsula of the island, and the volcanoes reflect Iceland's position atop the Mid-Atlantic Ridge, reaching deep into the unstable interior of the Earth. The largest glacier, Vatnajökull, is equal in area to all the glaciers on the European continent. It is estimated that the volcanoes of Iceland have poured out a third of the total lava flow from the Earth since 1500.

Iceland (Ísland in the Icelandic language) is also a country that was founded more than 1,000 years ago during the Viking Age of exploration. The capital, Reykjavík (Bay of Smokes), is near the site of the island's first farmstead. A settlement primarily of Norwegian seafarers and adventurers, it fostered further excursions to Greenland and the coasts of North America, or Vinland. In spite of its physical isolation nearly 500 miles (800 kilometres) from Scotland, the nearest European neighbour, it has remained very much a part of European civilization throughout its history and is a Scandinavian country, modern in nearly every respect. The Icelandic sagas, most of which relate heroic episodes in the island's founding and settling, are regarded as among the finest literary achievements of the Middle Ages. Viking heritage

THE LANDSCAPE

The land itself. Geologically young, Iceland contains about 200 volcanoes of various types. A new volcano erupting on the bottom of the sea between November 1963 and June 1967 created the island of Surtsey, off the southwestern coast. The new island was nearly ⅘ square mile (2.1 square kilometres) in area and rose more than 560 feet (170 metres) above sea level, a total of 950 feet from the ocean floor.

Volcanic activity has been particularly frequent since the 1970s. A major eruption took place in 1973, when a volcano on the island of Heimaey spilled lava into the town of Vestmannaeyjar, an important fishing centre. Most of the 5,300 residents had to be evacuated, and there was considerable property damage, although the harbour remained intact. A number of eruptions have damaged geothermal projects and grazing land, but many have occurred outside of populated areas.

Iceland is largely a tableland broken up by structural faults. Its average height is 1,640 feet above sea level. The highest point is at an altitude of 6,952 feet. A quarter of the country lies below 1,000 feet. The glaciers range in size from small ones in mountain recesses to enormous glacial caps topping extensive mountain ranges. The maximum thickness of Vatnajökull is more than 3,000 feet, its area 3,240 square miles.

Much of Iceland is underlain by basalt, a dark rock of thermal origin. None is older than the Tertiary Period, which began about 65,000,000 years ago. The landscape in basaltic areas is one of plateau and fjord, characteristic of which are successive layers of lava visible one above the other on the valley sides. The basalt sheets tend to tilt somewhat toward the centre of the country. Glacial erosion played an important part in giving the valleys their present shape. The depressed zones between the basalt areas have extensive plateaus above which rise single volcanoes, table mountains, or other mountain masses with steep sides.

Iceland is richer in hot springs and solfataras—vents emitting only hot gases or vapours—than any other country in the world. Alkaline hot springs are found in some 250 locations throughout the country. The largest, Deildartunguhver, emits 53 gallons (200 litres) of boiling water per second. The total power output of the largest of the 14 high-temperature solfatara regions, the Torfajökull area, is estimated to be equal to 1,500,000,000 watts. Earthquakes, frequent in Iceland, rarely result in serious damage. Most of the buildings erected since the mid-20th century have been designed and built of reinforced concrete to withstand severe earthquake shocks. Hot springs

Heavy rainfalls feed the numerous rivers and lakes in the glaciated landscape. Many of the lakes are dammed by lava flows or glacial ice. The presence of many waterfalls is typical of the young, geologically faulted landscape. The rivers are mainly debris-laden streams of glacial origin or clear streams formed by springs from underground water. The coasts are irregular in outline, rocky, and incised with numerous fjords and smaller inlets in the regions not drained by glacier rivers. There are many fine natural harbours, since the innermost parts of the fjords often have been deepened by glacial erosion. Elsewhere the coasts are sandy and smooth in outline, with extensive offshore sandbars that form lagoons to the landward.

The soils of the country are both mineral and organic in composition. The mineral soils are basically a yellow-brown loam known as loess, formed by deposits of wind-transported matter. The soils are suitable for agriculture except that, because of the slow rate of biological activity in the northern climate, they require heavy fertilization.

The climate. The climate of Iceland may be characterized as cold-tempered oceanic. It is influenced by the location of the country on the boundary between two air currents, one of polar and one of tropical origin. It is affected also by the confluence of two ocean currents, the Gulf Stream, from near the Equator, and the East Greenland Polar Current. The latter sometimes carries Arctic drift ice to Iceland's northern and eastern shores.

Seasonal fluctuations in temperature and precipitation depend chiefly on the weather fronts crossing the North Atlantic. The passage of a low-pressure front south of Iceland brings relatively cold weather, especially in northern districts; one moving northeastward between Iceland and Greenland brings mild, rainy weather. Although its northernmost tips nearly touch the Arctic Circle, Iceland is much warmer than might be expected.

Mean annual temperatures for Reykjavík, on the west coast, for Akureyri, in the north, and for Vík, in the south are, respectively, 41° F (5.0° C), 39° F (3.9° C), and 42° F (5.7° C). Mean January and July temperatures for the same locations are 31° F (−0.6° C) and 52° F (11.2° C), 29° F (−1.5° C) and 52° F (10.9° C), and 34° F (1.2° C) and 52° F (11.3° C). In the northwest snow falls on about 100 days a year, in the southeast on about 40. Precipitation ranges from more than 80 inches annually in the south, more than twice that on the southern slopes of some ice-capped mountains, to only 16 inches in some higher northern plateaus. Gales are frequent, especially in winter, but thunderstorms are rare and fogs uncommon. Reykjavík averages a bit more than 1,300 hours of bright sunshine a year. Northern lights often appear, especially in fall and early winter.

Vegetation and animal life. Iceland also lies on the border between a tundra vegetation zone of treeless plains and one of coniferous forests. Only about a quarter of the country is covered by a continuous carpet of vegetation. Bogs and moors are extensive, and sparse grasslands are often overgrazed. The remains of larger

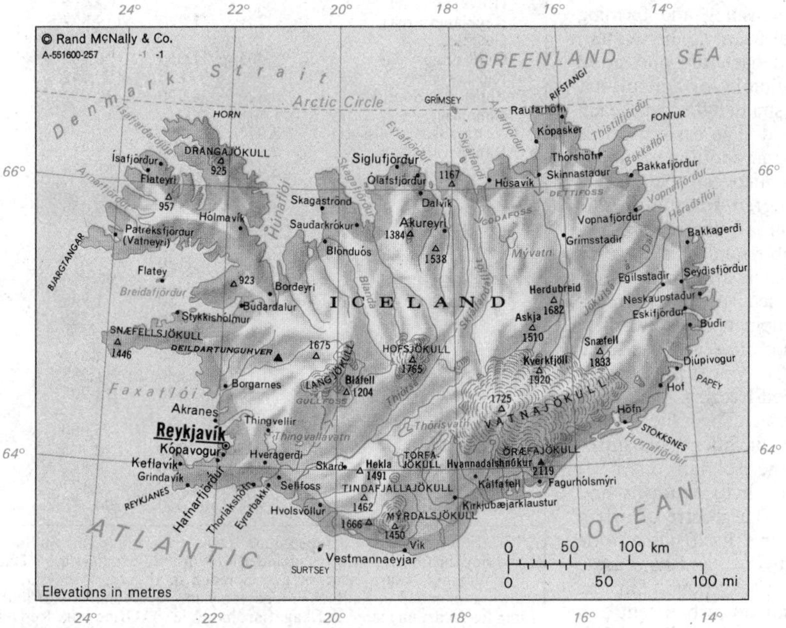

ICELAND

MAP INDEX

Cities and towns

Akranes..........64·18n 22·02w
Akureyri.........65·44n 18·08w
Bakkafjördur.....66·04n 14·45w
Bakkagerdi.......65·32n 13·48w
Blönduós.........65·39n 20·15w
Bordeyri.........65·15n 21·10w
Borgarnes........64·35n 21·53w
Búdardalur.......65·10n 21·42w
Búdir............64·56n 13·58w
Dalvík...........65·59n 18·32w
Djúpivogur.......64·40n 14·10w
Egilsstadir......65·16n 14·18w
Eskifjordur......65·04n 13·59w
Eyrarbakki.......63·53n 21·05w
Fagurhólsmýri....63·54n 16·38w
Flatey...........65·19n 23·07w
Flateyri.........65·59n 23·42w
Grímsstadir......65·40n 16·01w
Grindavík........63·52n 22·27w
Hafnarfjördur....64·03n 21·56w
Hof..............64·34n 14·39w
Höfn.............64·17n 15·10w
Hólmavík.........65·43n 21·43w
Húsavík..........66·04n 17·18w
Hveragerdi.......64·03n 21·10w
Hvolsvöllur......63·45n 20·10w
Ísafjördur.......66·08n 23·13w
Kálfafell........63·58n 17·40w
Keflavík.........64·02n 22·36w
Kirkjubæjark-
laustur..........63·47n 18·04w
Kópasker.........66·20n 16·24w
Kópavogur........64·06n 21·50w
Neskaupstadur....65·10n 13·43w
Ólafsfjördur.....66·06n 18·38w
Patreksfjördur
(Vatneyri).......65·38n 23·57w
Raufarhöfn.......66·30n 15·57w
Reykjavík........64·09n 21·51w
Saudarkrókur.....65·46n 19·41w
Sellfoss.........63·56n 20·57w
Seydisfjördur....65·16n 14·00w
Siglufjördur.....66·10n 18·56w
Skagaströnd......65·53n 20·17w
Skard............64·03n 19·50w
Skinnastadur.....66·07n 16·24w
Stykkishólmur....65·06n 22·48w
Thingvellir......64·17n 21·07w
Thorlákshöfn.....63·53n 21·18w
Thórshöfn........66·13n 15·17w
Vatneyri, see
Patreksfjördur
Vestmannaeyjar...63·26n 20·12w
Vík..............63·25n 19·01w
Vopnafjördur.....65·47n 14·44w

Physical features and points of interest

Arnarfjördur,
fjord..........66·15n 16·45w
Askja, *volcano*....65·00n 16·48w
Atlantic Ocean...63·15n 18·45w
Axarfjördur,
river..........66·15n 16·45w
Bakkaflói, *river*...66·10n 14·45w
Bjargtangar,
point..........65·31n 24·32w
Bláfell, *mountain*.64·32n 19·53w
Blanda, *river*.....65·39n 20·18w
Breidafjördur,
bay............65·15n 23·15w
Deildartunguhver,
hot springs......64·40n 21·25w
Denmark Strait...67·00n 23·00w
Dettifoss,
waterfall........65·50n 16·20w
Drangajökull,
glacier..........66·11n 22·15w
Eyjafjördur, *fjord*.65·54n 18·15w
Faxaflói, *river*....64·25n 23·00w
Fontur, *point*.....66·23n 14·30w
Godafoss,
waterfall........65·40n 17·30w
Greenland Sea...67·00n 15·00w
Grímsey, *island*..66·34n 18·00w
Gullfoss,
waterfall........64·24n 20·08w
Hekla, *volcano*....64·00n 19·39w
Heradsflói, *bay*...65·45n 14·10w
Herdubreid,
mountain.........65·13n 16·18w
Hofsjokull,
glacier..........64·48n 18·50w
Horn, *cape*........66·28n 22·28w
Hornafjördur,
lagoon...........64·17n 15·16w
Húnaflói, *bay*.....65·50n 20·50w
Hvannadalshnúkur,
mountain.........64·01n 16·41w
Ísafjardardjúp,
fjord............66·10n 23·00w
Jökulsá á Brú,
river............65·41n 14·13w
Kverkfjöll,
mountain.........64·43n 16·38w
Langjökull,
glacier..........64·42n 20·12w
Mýrdalsjökull,
glacier..........64·03n 16·38w
Mývatn, *lake*......65·37n 16·58w
Öræfajökull,
glacier..........64·03n 16·38w
Papey, *island*.....64·37n 14·11w
Reykjanes,
peninsula........63·49n 22·43w
Rifstangi, *point*...66·35n 16·10w
Skagafjördur, *bay*.65·55n 19·35w
Skjálfandafljót,
river............65·57n 17·38w
Skjálfandi, *bay*...66·08n 17·38w
Snæfell,
mountain.........64·48n 15·32w
Snæfellsjökull,
glacier..........64·50n 23·49w
Stokksnes, *point*..64·17n 14·54w
Surtsey, *island*...63·16n 20·32w
Thingvallavatn,
lake.............64·12n 21·10w
Thistilfjördur,
bay..............66·20n 15·25w
Thjórsé, *river*....63·47n 20·48w
Thórisvatn, *lake*..64·50n 19·26w
Tindafjallajökull,
glacier..........63·47n 19·35w
Torfajökull,
glacier..........63·54n 19·00w
Vatnajökull,
glacier..........64·25n 16·50w
Vopnafjördur,
bay..............65·52n 14·40w

birch forests are found in many places. A spruce reforestation program has had some success.

Introduction of animal life

Foxes were the only land mammals in Iceland at the time of its settlement. Humans brought house and farm animals and accidentally introduced mice and rats. Later, reindeer were introduced, and some them remain in the central highlands. After 1930 the mink also became wild in the country. Birdlife in Iceland is varied. Many nesting cliffs are densely inhabited, and the colony of ducks at Lake Mývatn, in the north, is the largest and most varied in the world. Salmon and trout abound in the lakes, brooks, and rivers. The fishing banks off the Icelandic shores formerly were abundantly endowed with fish, although their resources were considerably eroded by overexploitation by various nations following World War II. There are no reptiles or amphibians in Iceland.

Regional characteristics. Iceland traditionally has been divided according to the four points of the compass. The centre of the country is uninhabited. In the southwest several good natural harbours have directed interest toward the sea, and the country's best fishing grounds lie off its shores. There is little farmland there because of the extensive lava fields and heaths with sparse vegetation. The middle west is divided between fishing and farming and has many places of great natural beauty. The western fjords have numerous well-sheltered harbours and good fishing grounds but little lowland suitable for agriculture.

The north is divided into several smaller districts, each of which has relatively good farmland. The eastern fjords resemble the western fjords but have in addition an innerlying lowland. The southeast, locked between the glaciers and the sea, has a landscape of rugged splendour. The southern lowland comprises the main farming region. Soil and climatic conditions are favourable, and it is close to the country's largest market, Reykjavík and environs.

Human settlement. The development of communities was primarily a 20th-century phenomenon. Previously, farms were not clustered together, nor did seasonal fishing lead to the formation of villages. The typical present-day village has a fishing fleet and a food-freezing plant, but some have other trades and industries. Their life is monotonous, but travel and recreation facilities have introduced a degree of modernity into the isolation.

Major urban centres

About 87 percent of the population lives in towns and villages with 200 residents and more. The centre of urban life is Reykjavík, the capital. The town itself has a wide variety of economic and cultural activities, and its seaside location has a colourful mountain background. On the whole, Reykjavík and vicinity is a modern urban centre in appearance, though its downtown nucleus has been slow to develop. Iceland's second town in importance is Akureyri, at the head of Eyjafjördhur on the north coast. With about 13,100 residents, it is a trade and tourist centre with historical links situated alongside modern factories.

Keflavík is a fishing port next to the major international airport bearing its name. The Vestmannaeyjar (Westman Islands) off the south coast, with a population of only 4,700, have the most important fishing and fish-processing industry in Iceland. Akranes, located across the bay from Reykjavík, is a service town for its region and has some industry, including Iceland's only cement plant. Ísafjördhur is a service town for the western fjord area. Siglufjördhur in the north was once the centre of the herring industry, but both fishing and town have declined in size and importance. There are several very small towns along the eastern fjords, but because of the mountainous landscape none has acquired a dominant status. Selfoss in the southern lowlands, serving the farming region, is the largest rural community in Iceland away from the coast.

Iceland, Area and Population

	area		population	
	sq mi	sq km	1970 census	1980 estimate
Regions *(landsvaedun)*				
Austurland (East)	8,683	22,490	11,315	12,856
Counties *(sýslur)*				
Nordhur-Múlasýsla*	4,799	12,430	3,130	3,294
Sudhur-Múlasýsla*	1,537	3,980	6,610	7,385
Austur-Skaftafellssýsla	2,347	6,080	1,575	2,177
Nordhurland eystra (Northeast)	8,370	21,680	22,225	25,700
Counties				
Sudhur-Thingeyjarsýsla†	4,691	12,150	4,825	5,387
Nordhur-Thingeyjarsýsla	2,077	5,380	1,761	1,768
Eyjafjardharsýsla†	1,602	4,150	15,639	18,545
Nordhurland vestra (Northwest)	4,973	12,880	9,909	10,631
Counties				
Vestur-Húnavatnssýsla	996	2,580	1,389	1,571
Austur-Húnavatnssýsla	1,900	4,920	2,324	2,571
Skagafjardharsýsla‡	2,077	5,380	6,196	6,489
Rekjavíkursvaedhiog Reykjanessvaedhi (Reykjavík and Reykjanes area)	741	1,920	119,822	135,000
Counties				
Gullbringusýsla§	405	1,050	20,280	30,416
Kjósarsýsla§	336	870	99,542	104,584
Sudhurland (South)	9,649	24,990	18,052	19,637
Counties				
Vestur-Skaftafellssýsla	3,050	7,900	1,393	1,344
Rangárvallasýsla‖	3,197	8,280	8,385	8,220
Árnessýsla‖	3,401	8,810	8,274	10,073
Vestfirdhir (West Peninsula)	3,676	9,520	10,050	10,479
Counties				
Austur-Bardhastrandarsýsla	444	1,150	475	416
Vestur-Bardhastrandarsýsla	598	1,550	1,948	2,045
Vestur-Ísafjardharsýsla	436	1,130	1,725	1,710
Nordhur-Isafjardharsýsla¶	1,181	3,060	4,614	5,124
Strandasýsla	1,015	2,630	1,288	1,184
Vesturland (West)	3,676	9,520	13,205	14,884
Counties				
Borgarfjardharsýsla♀	753	1,950	5,660	6,648
Mýrasýsla	1,262	3,270	2,145	2,537
Snaefellsnessýsla	846	2,190	4,223	4,597
Dalasýsla	815	2,110	1,177	1,102
Total Iceland	39,768	103,000	204,578	229,187

*Eskifjördhur and Neskaupstadhur towns are included in Sudhur-Múlasýsla, and Seydhisfjördhur town is included in Nordhur-Múlasýsla. †Dalvik, Ólafsfjördhur, and Akureyri towns are included in Eyjafjardharsýsla, and Húsavík town is included in Sudhur-Thingeyjarsýsla. ‡Saudhárkrókur and Siglufjördhur towns are included in Skagafjardharsýsla. §Grindavík, Keflavík, Gardhabaer, Njardhvík, and Hafnarfjördhur towns are included in Gullbringusýsla, and Kópavogur, Seltjarnarnes, and Rekjarík towns are included in Kjósarsýsla. ‖Vestmannaeyjar town is included in Rangárvallasýsla, and Selfoss town is included in Arnessýsla. ¶Bolungarvík and Ísafjördhur towns are included in Nordhur-Ísafjardharsýsla. ♀Akranes town is included in Borgarfjardharsýsla.
Source: Official government figures.

THE PEOPLE OF ICELAND

Makeup. The people of Iceland are an extremely homogeneous population in almost every way. They are descendants of settlers that began arriving in AD 874 and continued in heavy influx for about the next 50 years. Historians differ as to their exact origin and ethnic composition but agree that between 60 and 80 percent were of Nordic stock from Norway. The remainder, from Scotland and Ireland, was largely of Celtic stock. The dominant language in the period of settlement was Old Norse, the language spoken throughout Scandinavia at that time. Through the centuries it has evolved into modern Icelandic, which is spoken throughout the country. There are no racial or ethnic distinctions. The early Nordic and Celtic stocks have long since merged, and the small number of subsequent immigrants had no major effect on the population structure. The Lutheran faith has been the dominant religion since the mid-16th century. About 93 percent of the population belongs to the state-supported Evangelical Lutheran Church, and 4 percent to independent Lutheran denominations. There is freedom of religion.

Homogeneity of people

Numbers and trends. The first comprehensive census in Iceland was taken in 1703, at which time 50,358 were reported. The 18th century was marked by great economic hardship, and by 1801 the population had declined to 47,240. In the 19th century there had been a slow increase, and in 1901 the count rose to 78,470. An accelerated economic growth during the early decades of the 20th century was paralleled by a rapid growth in population, which in 1940 reached 121,474. During World War II and the postwar period there was rapid improvement in the standard of living and a new acceleration in the rate of population growth. The annual growth rate of 1.1 percent between 1930 and 1940 rose to 1.7 percent during the 1940s and to 2.1 percent during the 1950s. The annual growth rate declined after 1960, however, primarily because of a sharply reduced birth rate and increased emigration. It amounted to 1.6 percent during the 1960s and was 1.2 percent during the 1970s.

In the century prior to World War II the birth rate declined steadily. In 1831–40 it was 38.9 per 1,000 population, declining to 29.1 in 1896–1905 and to 20.9 in 1935–39. During and after World War II a sharp increase took place, to 23.5 in 1940–44 and to 28.3 in 1955–59. In 1961–65 it declined to 25.4 and in 1974–78 to 19.2. The number of illegitimate children increased sharply during the postwar period, and by 1980 Iceland had the highest proportion in Europe. From 1886 to 1905 illegitimate children constituted about 15 percent of all births, live and stillborn, but the proportion rose to 23 percent between 1936 and 1940 and was 33 percent by 1971–74.

Death rates steadily declined from 17.4 per 1,000 population in 1897–1906 to 12.7 in 1921–30 and 6.5 during 1974–78. Infant mortality similarly was reduced from 23.8 percent of live births during the first year of life, in 1851–60, to 11.9 percent in 1891–1900, and to 0.9 percent in 1976–78. Life expectancy at birth for males and females was 73.4 and 79.3 years, respectively, in 1977–78. By comparison it was only 31.9 and 37.9 years in 1850–60, and 44.4 and 51.4 years in 1890–1901.

Migration. Between 1870 and 1901 there was a large-scale emigration to Canada and the United States because of unfavourable conditions in Iceland. More than 12,000 Icelanders emigrated in excess of immigration, the equivalent of about one-fifth of the 1901 population. Between 1901 and 1960 the net emigration was 2,900, most of it in the first two decades. In 1961–66 there was a net emigration of 1,028, and in 1970–74 a net of 1,282.

Like other Western countries, Iceland has had a considerable country-to-city migration throughout its development. The urbanized population rose from less than 11 percent in 1900 to more than 86 percent by 1980. The largest urban concentration is in Reykjavík and its environs, where about 121,000 residents, slightly more than half of the nation's population, lived in 1980. The city of Reykjavík itself had a population of more than 80,000.

THE NATIONAL ECONOMY

The Icelandic economy is based heavily on fishing and a broad variety of fish products, but it incorporates manufacturing and services as well. More than 45 percent of the gross national product is exported, the principal trading partners being the United States and the United Kingdom. Despite the small population, the economy is modern, and the standard of living is on a par with that of Denmark, Norway, and the United Kingdom.

Potential of natural heat and hydro-energy

Energy resources. Iceland's energy resources are vast. Only about 10 percent of the potential hydroelectric power of the rivers had been tapped by the beginning of the 1970s, and the cost per kilowatt hour of harnessing the remainder is estimated to be low. Geothermal heat from the waters of the hot springs heats more than 90 percent of Reykjavík and about 70 percent of the nation; it is used as steam for industrial energy and in commercial vegetable farming in greenhouses.

Fishing and related industry. A steady improvement in fishing technology has increased catches despite the gradual erosion of the once enormously rich fish populations off the coasts. The concern over declining fish stocks brought about several extensions of the fishing limit by the Icelandic government. In 1952 the limit was four nautical miles, but it was extended to 12 miles in 1958, to 50 miles in 1972, and to 200 miles in 1975. These measures, however, were protested by several nations and led to the dispute over fishing rights that became known as the "cod war." There have been a number of confrontations between Icelandic and foreign fishing vessels, notably those of the United Kingdom and West Germany, in the disputed area, but temporary agreements have been reached.

Cod and capelin make up two-thirds of the total catch, and such white fish as cod and haddock are exported fresh, frozen, or in salted or dried form. Capelin and herring are usually reduced to oil and meal but also are salted. More than 74 percent of Iceland's exports in 1980 were fish products. Such fishing-related industries as boat yards, repair docks, and net factories are also important.

Manufacturing and mining. In the early 1960s the government initiated a policy of encouraging foreign investment for the exploitation of the country's resources. A Swiss-owned aluminum smelter of imported ore began operation in 1969 with plans for rapidly increasing production. In 1967 a plant operating with geothermal steam began the refining of diatomaceous earth mined from Lake Mývatn into pure diatomite for use in industrial filtration. Shell sand is mined for use in the cement industry, and perlite and pumice (volcanic cinders) are among the mineral resources. There are possibilities for the extraction of salt and minerals from seawater and the processing of seaweed for commercial purposes. There are also small industries for fertilizer, appliances, food and clothing, and books.

Agriculture. In 1930, 36 percent of Iceland's population lived on farms or were engaged in agriculture, but by 1980 the proportion had fallen to less than 9 percent. The raising of livestock, mostly sheep, and dairy farming are the main occupations. About 20 percent of the land is arable, most of it used for grazing. The cultivation of grains is not commercially feasible, although greenhouses are profitable businesses, especially in southern Iceland. Important agricultural products are livestock, hay, and grass. Iceland is virtually self-sufficient in fresh foods and dairy items, but it imports most other foodstuffs.

Tourism. Icelandair (Flugleidir) is a major international carrier that has helped make the tourist trade increasingly important in the national economic picture. In 1950 only 4,000 tourists visited the island, but by the late 1970s the figure had risen to almost 77,000. International conventions have been held in Reykjavík, and in Akureyri facilities for spring and summer skiing have been developed.

Financial services. Banking and other financial services are well developed. There are several commercial banks with branches throughout the country, and more than 40 savings banks. Other financial institutions include the government-owned investment credit funds, private pension funds, insurance companies, and the social insurance system. The national unit of currency is the krona (plural, kronur), divided into 100 aurar.

Management and taxation. Although most of Iceland's production is in private hands, ownership by the government has increased gradually, especially in the fishing industry. The central government also owns most of the banking and finance and, with local governments, most of the electrical systems. Since World War II the government has aimed for full employment, a high rate of economic growth, protection of the balance of payments, price stability, and income equalization. The central government receives a major portion of its income from such indirect taxes as import duties and sales levies, whereas local governments derive most of their money from corporate and personal income taxes. The total tax revenues of central and local governments amount to about a third of the gross national product.

Economic planning

Workers' associations. More than 90 percent of Iceland's labour force belong to trade unions or employer organizations. The Icelandic Federation of Labour, a loose organization of almost all blue-collar and some white-collar workers, is the largest labour group and had a membership of 47,000 by the early 1980s. Farmers have a separate union, as do state and local government employees. Private employers are organized into the Employers' Federation. Wage agreements are generally negotiated first between the Employers' Federation and the Icelandic Federation of Labour. Only governmental employees do not have the right to strike.

Economic problems. In the postwar period fluctuations in fish catches and in prices abroad for fish products produced rapidly changing cycles in domestic income. Along with domestic pressures for higher wages and prices, this led to persistent inflation and frequent currency devaluations. The productivity of the fishing industry, better than that of other export sources, prevented any major diversification of exports and of manufacturing. Fishing resources are diminishing, however.

TRANSPORTATION

The historic isolation of Iceland by the rough seas of the North Atlantic and by the country's small market and industry was broken when steam vessels began to visit Icelandic shores late in the 19th century, when the first telegraph cable to Iceland was laid in 1906, and when the Icelandic Steamship Company was founded in 1914. Roads had been practically unknown, the horse being the means of transportation throughout the island. Iceland never built railroads, and in several places the Icelanders jumped straight from horseback to airplane.

Iceland has more than 7,000 miles of roads. Most of these are dirt, some mere tracks on the ground. Much of the system is impassable in winter. During the summer, however, driving is possible on the extensive sandy plains in the uninhabited interior, permitting expeditions between the glaciers. By the mid-1970s there were only about 90 miles of paved concrete roads in Iceland. The Ringroad, which stretches for 900 miles and forms a circle around the island, was completed in 1974.

Iceland has more than 90,000 motor vehicles, including about 82,000 private automobiles, trucks, and buses. The merchant-marine fleet carries from a third to a half of Iceland's imports and from a half to two-thirds of its exports. Icelandair and local service carriers are important internally in compensating for the limited road system.

ADMINISTRATION AND SOCIAL CONDITIONS

Governmental framework and process. Iceland is a parliamentary democracy with an elected president as head of state. In 1980 Vigdís Finnbogadóttir became the first woman elected a head of state. The powers of the presidential office are very similar to those of other heads of state in western European democracies. A 60-member parliament, the Althing (Althingi), one of the oldest legislative assemblies in the world, is divided into upper and lower houses with equal power, serving for four years or until dissolved. The executive branch is headed by a cabinet consisting of a prime minister and six other ministers. The cabinet must have majority support in parliament or at least be able to avoid censure. Alternatively, it must resign. The judiciary consists of a supreme court and a system of lower courts, most of which hear both civil and criminal cases. Cases are heard and judged by appointed judges; there is no jury system. All lower court verdicts, except for those involving certain misdemeanours, can be appealed to the supreme court. The constitution provides all citizens with the civil rights and liberties customarily accorded in Western democracies.

Iceland is divided into more than 20 independent towns, *kaupstadhir*, and 23 counties, *sýslur*. The latter are divided into more than 200 rural communes, *hreppar*. Each town, county, and district administers local affairs through an elected council. Local government responsibilities are chiefly in the areas of education, municipal services, social affairs, and health services. Towns and counties have the power to levy income taxes, property taxes, and a business turnover tax, the first being their most important source of income.

The president, Althing, and local councils are elected every four years, but not necessarily all at once. All citizens 20 years of age and older may vote. There are four main political parties. The Independence Party, centre-to-conservative in political outlook, has commanded up to 40 percent of the popular vote. The agrarian Progressive Party, with about 25 to 30 percent of the popular vote, draws its strength from rural areas. The Social Democrats and the People's Alliance each have taken 15 to 20 percent of the vote. Both are slightly left of the political centre and appeal to the urban labour vote. Several parliamentary seats are awarded to parties who did not gain seats in proportion to the total voting strength they showed in elections.

Political parties

Iceland is a charter member of the United Nations and the North Atlantic Treaty Organization (NATO). In the postwar period it centred its foreign policy around international cooperation and participated in joint Western defense efforts. It does not maintain an army or a navy, and the United States, having assumed responsibility for its defenses, maintains a naval air station at Keflavík International Airport under NATO auspices.

Health and education. Iceland, with compulsory health insurance that finances many medical services, has one of the highest standards of public health in the world. Hospital services are provided entirely without charge, and other medical services are offered at very low cost. Dental care is free for the 6–15 age-group; the elderly and children 3 to 5 years of age receive a 50 percent discount. All contagious diseases that were major causes of death in the 19th century have been virtually eradicated. Mortality due to such epidemic diseases as influenza and measles has been minimized. Heart disease and cancer, each accounting for about a quarter of all deaths, are the major causes of death. Welfare services include unemployment insurance, old-age and disability pensions, family allowances, childbearing cash grants, and sickness benefits. The medical and welfare systems are financed by central and local government.

Almost all schools from the primary level through the university are free. Education is compulsory through age 16, and secondary and higher education is widely available. Students can enroll in five four-year academic colleges at the age of 15 or 16. Graduation entitles the student to admission to the University of Iceland, founded in 1911, in Reykjavík. It offers a rounded curriculum in the liberal arts, sciences, law, medicine, and theology and has an enrollment of more than 3,000 students. There are also a number of technical, vocational, and specialized schools.

Living conditions. Icelandic housing standards are high compared with those of other parts of northern Europe. The postwar population boom has led to emphasis on construction, accounting for a large percentage of the gross national product. About 55 percent of the more than 55,000 housing units are less than 30 years old. About 75 percent of all housing is owner occupied, and more than 97 percent of the people live in electrified homes. The level of wages and salaries generally has been on a par with those of Norway and Denmark. The cost of living is somewhat higher than in neighbouring countries, mostly because of the cost of importing a large part of all resources used and the relatively steep import duties. Iceland is relatively devoid of social divisions based on social class or economic status. One reason for this is the absence of long-established family wealth, since most private wealth has been generated in the postwar period. Another important reason may be the absence of ethnic groups or of any differences in language and educational status between the regions of the country. The system of free education for everyone also facilitates social mobility.

Housing

CULTURAL LIFE

The arts. Icelanders are proof that a rich cultural life can be developed despite a small population. For centuries Iceland's writers concentrated on rewriting the great sagas of the Middle Ages. Other arts included weaving, silver crafting, and wood carving. In the 20th century poetry declined in popularity, but writing was pursued with eagerness, as were painting and theatre, both relatively new traditions in the country. The government heavily subsidizes museums and the National Theatre in Reykjavík and provides annual stipends to writers and other artists on a nonpolitical basis.

The Reykjavík area, which supports two professional theatres, a symphony orchestra, and several art galleries, bookstores, cinemas, and museums, has a cultural activity that compares favourably with many towns or cities several times its size. The town's situation between Europe and North America brings many celebrities, especially in music, to the island, and various exhibitions stop there for a day or a week on their way between continents. The first biennial international art festival in Reykjavík was held in 1970.

Formerly, art in Iceland was often connected with the

church, first the Catholic and later Lutheran. The first professional secular painters appeared in Iceland about 1800. Gradually increasing in number, the painters seemed eager to portray the character and beauty of their country. The best known was Jóhannes Kjarval. There is much painting activity in Iceland, but it is of mixed quality. A number of painters show strong foreign influences. The old traditions in silver working have been retained, the most characteristic of which is the use of silver thread for ornamentation. Newer trends also have flourished.

The old literary tradition of the saga writers was revived in the mid-19th century, and the tales were increasingly elaborated. The writers used Icelandic settings almost exclusively. Several writers became well known abroad, including Halldór Laxness, who received the Nobel Prize for Literature in 1955. Some have written for the theatre, which was more international in character and writing.

Music also has been cultivated in Iceland. The Icelandic Symphony Orchestra plays programs from an international repertoire, and one or more operas or musicals are performed every year in the National Theatre. Few Icelandic composers are known outside the country. On the lighter side, popular music is enjoyed in all its rapidly changing styles as it is throughout the West. The Music Society operates a college of music.

Traditional folk crafts

National folk traditions in applied art have been given a new strength by a lively trade in art and souvenir shops. Many people in the country take part in this industry, producing high-quality goods. For most residents, it is a hobby producing extra income. Old designs and forms have been revived, some modified to please modern tastes. Wool, knitted or woven, is the most used material.

In sports, a special old form of wrestling is maintained, but much more popular is pony trekking. Swimming, in naturally heated swimming pools, and various ball games are popular. Seasonal sports include fishing and hiking in summer and skiing in the winter.

Cultural institutions. The National Library of Iceland was founded in 1818, and the University Library in 1940. Plans have been made to combine these two research libraries. The National Archives were founded in 1882. The National Museum of Iceland, dating from 1863, has collections representing native Icelandic culture dating from the Viking Age. Many old houses and ruins throughout the country are preserved under its auspices.

The Art Gallery of Iceland was founded in 1885. The great majority of its works are by modern Icelandic artists. The Natural History Museum, founded in 1889, has always been small as a museum, but its sections of geology and geography, of botany, and of zoology have been active in various areas of research.

The National Theatre began operation in 1950. It performs Icelandic as well as foreign plays, operas, ballets, and musicals. It sponsors some activities outside the theatre in Reykjavík. Some book clubs are active, the oldest one being the Icelandic Literary Society, founded in 1816.

Communications. The six daily papers published in Reykjavík had a total circulation of about 129,000 by 1980 and are read throughout the country. Small local papers are published in many towns, most regularly in Akureyri. One illustrated weekly has a wide circulation. The state radio, started in 1930, has been the most important medium of entertainment and education in the sparsely populated country. State-owned television began in 1966. Both radio and television are neutral in political affairs, and their budget is paid in part by advertising.

BIBLIOGRAPHY. J. NORDAL and V. KRISTINSSON (eds.), *Iceland 874–1974* (1975), provides a comprehensive survey of Iceland, with emphasis on contemporary socioeconomic and cultural standards. Briefer accounts of similar nature are: O. HANSSON, *Facts About Iceland* (1967); H. LEAF, *Iceland Yesterday and Today* (1949); B. THORDARDSON, *Iceland Past and Present*, 3rd ed. (1945); and H.P. BRIEM, *Iceland and the Icelanders* (1945).

Factual material on the Icelandic economy may be found in the *Statistical Bulletin* (quarterly), published by the STATISTICAL BUREAU OF ICELAND; and *Economic Surveys: Iceland* (annual), published by the OECD.

Publications of geographical interest include: S. THORARINSSON, *The Thousand Years Struggle Against Ice and Fire* (1956); V. STEFANSSON, *Iceland: The First American Republic* (1939); A.C.Z. SOMME (ed.), *A Geography of Norden: Denmark-Finland-Iceland-Norway-Sweden*, new ed. (1968); S. RIST, *Islenzk vötn-Icelandic Fresh Waters* (1956); and H. PREUSSER, *The Landscape of Iceland: Types and Regions* (1976). O. HALFDANARSON (ed.), *Iceland Road Guide* (1975), covers the national network, with a brief description of all interesting places en route.

A vivid description of Icelandic art is found in K. ELDJARN, *Ancient Icelandic Art* (1957).

The beauty of the Icelandic landscape is captured in many picture books, such as S. THORARINSSON, *Hekla* (1970), *Surtsey: The New Island in the North Atlantic* (1967); H. BARDARSON, *Island* (1965; English, French, and German texts); and K. DROST, *Iceland* (1963).

(Va.K./B.M.)

Ice Sheets and Glaciers

A glacier may be defined as a large mass of perennial ice that originates on land by the recrystallization of snow or other forms of solid precipitation and that shows evidence of past or present flow. The definition is not precise, because exact limits for the terms large, perennial, and flow cannot be set. Except in terms of size, a small snow patch that persists for more than one season is hydrologically indistinguishable from a true glacier. One international group has recommended that all persisting snow and ice masses larger than 0.1 square kilometre (about four-hundredths square mile) be counted as glaciers. Hence, in the absence of an agreed-upon upper size limit for glaciers, a body of ice as large as the Antarctic Ice Sheet (slightly smaller than the conterminous United States and Europe combined) could properly be considered a glacier.

GENERAL CONSIDERATIONS

Main types of glaciers

Glaciers are classifiable in three main groups: (1) glaciers that extend in continuous sheets, moving outward in all directions, are called ice sheets or continental glaciers if they are the size of Antarctica or Greenland and ice caps or ice fields if they are smaller; (2) glaciers confined within a path that directs the ice movement are called mountain glaciers; and (3) glaciers that spread out in cakelike sheets on level ground or on the ocean at the foot of glaciated regions are called piedmont glaciers or shelf ice, respectively. Glaciers in the third group are not independent and are treated in terms of their sources: ice shelves with ice sheets and piedmont glaciers with mountain glaciers.

Distribution of glaciers. A most distinctive aspect of the last ice age, the Pleistocene Epoch (from 2,500,000 to 10,000 years ago), was the recurrent expansion and contraction of the world's ice cover. These glacial fluctuations influenced geological, climatological, and biological environments and affected the evolution and development of early humans. Pleistocene chronology is based primarily on ice-sheet fluctuations. Most of Canada, the northern third of the United States, much of Europe, all of Scandinavia, and large parts of eastern Siberia were engulfed by ice during the major glacial stages. At times during the Pleistocene Epoch, glacial ice covered 30 percent of the world's land area; at other times the ice sheets may have shrunk to less than their present size. It may not be improper, then, to state that the world is still in an ice age. Because the term glacial implies ice-age events or Pleistocene time, in this article "glacier" is used as an adjective whenever reference is to present ice or present events.

Glacier ice stores about three-fourths of all the freshwater in the world, covers about 11 percent of the world's land area, and would cause a world sea-level rise of about 90 metres (300 feet) if all ice melted. Glaciers occur in all parts of the world and at almost all latitudes. In Ecuador, Kenya, Uganda, Congo, and Irian Jaya (New Guinea), glaciers even occur at the Equator.

Cause of glacier fluctuations

Development of glaciers. The cause of the development and fluctuation of the world's glacier cover is still not completely understood. There is evidence that periodic fluctuations in the heat received from the Sun caused changes in ocean-surface temperature and that these also correlate with major fluctuations of glacier advance and retreat. Large ice sheets themselves, however, contain several "instability mechanisms" that may have contributed to the larger changes in world climate. One of these mechanisms, and certainly a most important one, is the very high reflectivity (albedo) of dry snow to solar radiation. No other material of widespread distribution on the Earth even approaches the albedo of snow. Thus, as an ice sheet expands it causes an ever larger share of the sun's radiation to be reflected back into space, less is absorbed on the Earth, and presumably the world's climate then cools. It has been calculated that, if the Earth's surface were covered with dry snow, the radiation balance would be changed so much that the average surface temperature would drop to −88.6° C (−128° F). Another instability mechanism is implied by the fact that the thicker and more extensive an ice sheet is, the more snowfall it will receive, due to orographic precipitation (precipitation resulting from highland effects), and the less melting will occur, due to the higher altitude of its surface and attendant lower temperature. A third possible instability mechanism has been suggested: the Antarctic Ice Sheet may periodically surge outward and grossly extend its boundaries, thus causing a worldwide cooling and the development of ice sheets elsewhere. Although the causes of ice ages are not known with certainty, the world's ice cover is in a state of delicate balance, and slight external or internal changes could cause a slow but inexorable change to a new ice age or to a climate warmer and drier than now.

Importance of glacier ice. Glaciers are important to man in many other ways. In the Alps, Scandinavia, Central Asia, western Canada, and the Pacific Northwest of the United States, glacier runoff is an important source of water during dry periods and naturally regulates the flow of large rivers, thus compensating for extremes of precipitation. In the state of Washington, for instance, there is as much water temporarily stored as glacier ice as there is stored in all of the state's surface water reservoirs and lakes, and as much water is released from glaciers in July and August (the driest months) as is pumped out of the ground for a whole year.

Physical action of glacier ice

Glacier ice is an important geological agent. Mountain glacier erosion produces the spectacular U-shaped valleys, serrated ridges, and Matterhorn-like peaks that are the basis of the great beauty of Alpine scenery. The products of this erosion are deposited as moraines (ridges or sheets of glacier-derived sediment) that form a rich but rocky agricultural soil that can be dated to obtain records of past climatic events.

Glacier ice is a crystalline solid so weak that it flows because of its own weight. Because of this, the flow of glaciers has long attracted the attention of scientists concerned with solid-flow phenomena. The study of ice sheets and glaciers is part of the broader field of glaciology—the study of ice and snow in all its aspects. This discipline is discussed in the article HYDROLOGIC SCIENCES. For further information on the role of precipitation in the formation of ice sheets and glaciers, see PRECIPITATION; SNOW AND SNOWFLAKES. See also CLIMATIC CHANGE for treatment of the changes associated with partial glaciation of the Earth, and PLEISTOCENE EPOCH and HOLOCENE EPOCH for the glacial events and chronology of the last 2,000,000 to 3,000,000 years of Earth history. The direct effect of glacier ice is treated in the article GLACIATION, LANDFORMS PRODUCED BY; the formation and nature of river ice and lake ice is the subject of ICE IN RIVERS AND LAKES; and the forms of sea ice are covered in ICEBERGS AND PACK ICE.

FORMATION AND CHARACTERISTICS OF GLACIER ICE

Transformation of snow to ice. Snow that falls on a glacier is eventually transformed to glacier ice. Many processes are involved, and the speed of transformation depends on wetness and temperature. Snow crystals are tiny hexagonal plates, needles, stars, or other intricate shapes. In a deposited snowpack these intricate shapes are usually unstable, and ice molecules evaporate off the points of crystals and are deposited in hollows or re-entrants. This causes a general rounding of the tiny ice grains so that they fit more closely together. In addition, the wind may break off the points of the intricate crystals and thus pack them more tightly. Thus, the density of the snowpack begins to increase, from its low initial value of 0.25 megagram per cubic metre (equal numerically to grams per cubic centimetre) or less, and further changes take place. Ice grains may rotate to fit more tightly together, or touching ice grains may develop necks of ice that connect them (sintering) and that grow at the expense of other parts of the ice grain. All of these processes proceed more rapidly at temperatures near the melting point and more slowly at colder temperatures.

The process of densification

If liquid water is present, the rate of change is many times more rapid because of the lubrication qualities of the water, the melting of ice from ice-grain extremities with refreezing elsewhere, the compacting force of surface tension, refreezing after pressure melting (regulation), and the freezing of water in air spaces.

This densification of the snow proceeds more slowly after reaching a density of 0.5–0.6 megagram per cubic metre, and many of the processes mentioned above become less and less efficient. Recrystallization becomes predominant, and grains change in size and shape in order to minimize the stress on them. This change usually means that certain favourably oriented grains grow at the expense of smaller ones. Stresses due to glacier flow may cause individual crystals to deform, and recrystallization, proceeding hand in hand with this deformation, causes an increase in the density and size of the average grain.

When the density of the aggregate reaches about 0.84

By courtesy of the U.S. Army; photographs, A.J. Gow

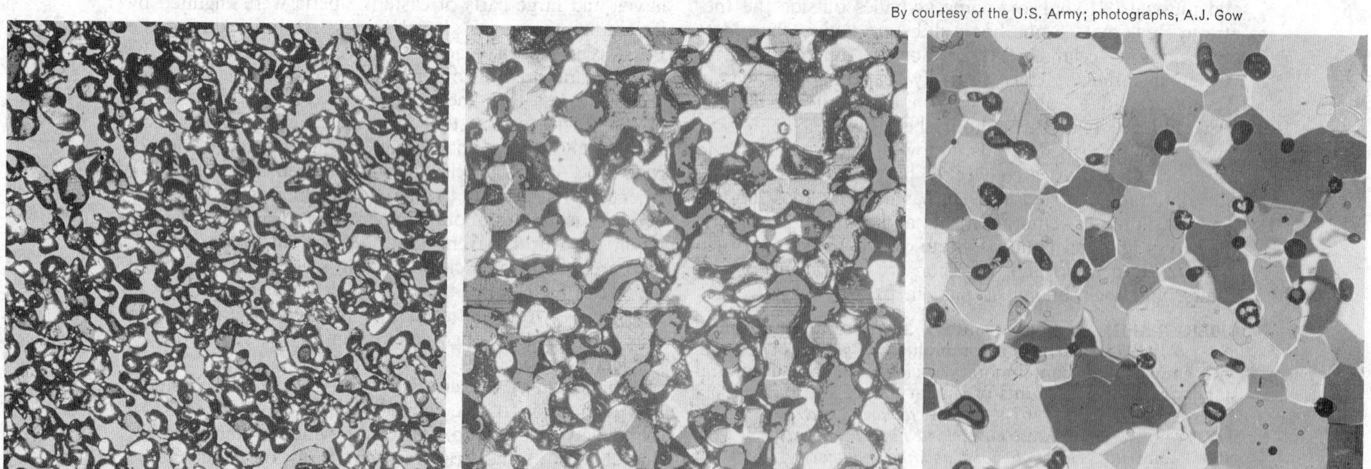

Figure 1: Thin-section photographs illustrating snow-to-ice transformation at depths of (left) 1 metre, (centre) 22 metres, and (right) 100 metres (magnified about 4.6 ×). At 1 metre and 22 metres the uniformly gray areas between grains of snow represent pore spaces. At 100 metres the snow has become ice and the bubbles become rounded and smaller because of compression of the entrapped gas. Photographs from Camp Century, Greenland, were taken between crossed polaroids to reveal crystal structure.

megagram per cubic metre (Mg/m³), the air spaces between grains are sealed off, and the material becomes impermeable. Density then rises largely by the compression of air bubbles. Only rarely in mountain glaciers does the density exceed 0.90 Mg/m³, but at great depths in ice sheets the density may approach that of pure ice (0.917 Mg/m³ at 0° C and atmospheric pressure).

Firn (névé)

Snow that has survived one melting season is called firn (or névé); its density usually is greater than 0.5 Mg/m³ in temperate regions but can be as low as 0.3 Mg/m³ in polar regions. The permeability change at a density of about 0.84 Mg/m³ marks the transition from firn to glacier ice. The transformation may take only three or four years and less than ten metres (33 feet) of burial at South Cascade Glacier in the warm and wet environment of Washington state, but high on the plateau of Antarctica the same process takes several thousand years and burial to depths of about 150 metres (442 feet).

Glacier ice is an aggregate of irregularly shaped, interlocking single crystals that range in size from a few millimetres to several tens of centimetres. A small amount of air is present as tiny bubbles; at great depths in ice sheets the air may be dissolved in the crystals. During recrystallization, impurities migrate ahead of the grain boundary so that the interiors of large crystals are chemically very pure, especially if meltwater is involved in the process.

Structure and properties of ice. Ice, the solid form of water, has an interesting crystalline structure. The crystal lattice is made up of water molecules joined to one another by comparatively weak hydrogen bonds. The oxygen atoms are situated in puckered or dimpled layers, and the atoms within each layer are arranged in a hexagonal fashion. The hexagonal structure can be seen in the symmetry of a snow crystal and also by focussing the sun's radiation into the centre of a large single crystal to cause internal melting, which may produce striking melt figures called Tyndall figures, or Tyndall flowers. The crystal lattice of ice has an open structure in which each oxygen atom has only four close neighbours. Thus ice has a low density, and the density rises upon melting.

From *Proceedings of the Royal Society* (1958)

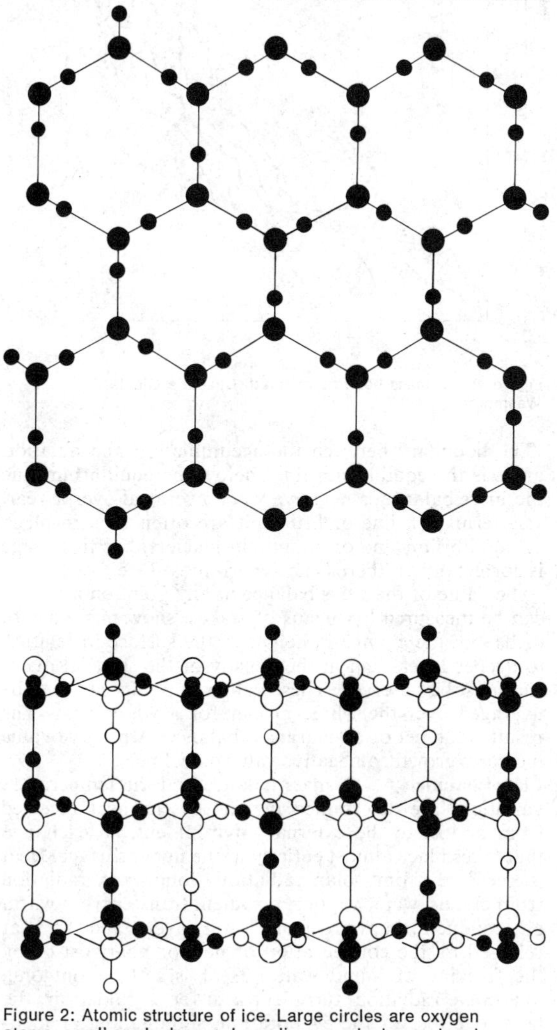

Figure 2: Atomic structure of ice. Large circles are oxygen atoms, small are hydrogen. Long lines are hydrogen bonds, short are covalent bonds. The top figure is viewed parallel to the hexagonal axis, the bottom figure perpendicular to it.

Although the oxygen atoms are arranged in a regular crystallographic lattice, the hydrogen atoms are arranged randomly, their positions governed only by the fact that there must be two hydrogen atoms connected by covalent bonds (in which electrons are shared by the bonded atoms) to each oxygen atom, and there must not be more than one hydrogen atom between any pair of neighbouring oxygen atoms (one covalent and one hydrogen bond). Because of its laminar structure, the ice crystal can deform by gliding, like a deck of cards. When this deformation occurs, however, the bonds between layers all break, and the hydrogen atoms involved in those bonds must become attached to different oxygen atoms. In doing so, they migrate within the lattice, more rapidly at higher temperatures. Sometimes not all the hydrogen atoms can reach positions in which the rules stated above are satisfied, so that a few oxygen atoms remain covalently bound to one or to three hydrogen atoms. Such oxygen atoms are the sites of electric charge. The speed of crystal deformation depends on these readjustments, which in turn are very sensitive to temperature. Thus the mechanical, thermal, and electrical properties of ice are interrelated.

Deformation of ice and the Glen flow law

Mechanical properties. Like any other crystalline solid, ice subject to stress undergoes elastic deformation, returning to its original shape when the stress ceases. The resistance of ice to elastic elongation is about two-thirds that of lead and about 1/20 that of steel. Of far greater importance to the study of glaciers is the susceptibility of ice to plastic deformation, or creep, which permanently alters the shape of the specimen. If a shear stress or force is applied to a sample of ice

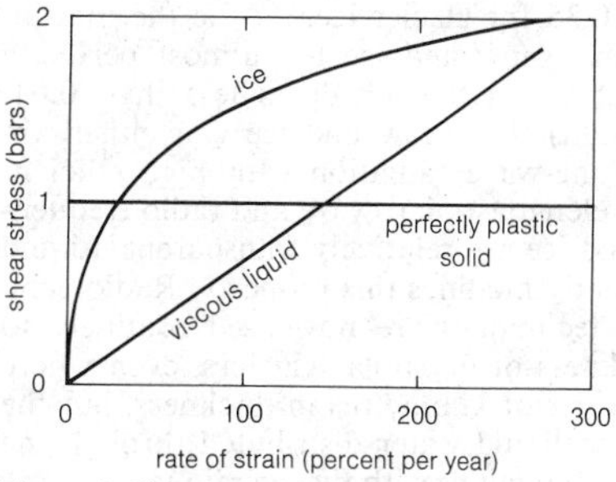

Figure 3: Flow law of ice.

for a long time, the sample will first deform elastically and will then continue to deform plastically. This latter deformation, or flow, involves two processes: intracrystalline gliding, in which the layers within an ice crystal shear parallel to each other without destroying the continuity of the crystal lattice; and recrystallization, in which crystal boundaries change in size or shape depending on the orientation of the adjacent crystals and the stresses exerted on them.

The rate of plastic deformation under constant shearing stress is initially high but tapers off to a steady value. If this steady value, the shear-strain rate, is plotted against the stress for many different values of applied stress, a curved graph results. The rate of shearing strain is approximately proportional to the cube of the shear stress: this is the flow law for ice. Often called the Glen flow law, it is the basis for all analyses of the flow of ice sheets and glaciers. For ice at the melting temperature, a stress of one bar causes ice to deform about 30 percent per year. If the temperature is −15° C (+5° F) the creep rate for the same stress drops to only 3 percent per year. Only shear stress is considered here; hydrostatic (equal in all directions) pressure has no effect whatever, provided the temperature is held constant relative to the freezing point. This flow law implies that ice does not flow like a very viscous liquid. The strain rate of viscous liquids is directly proportional to the stress, rather than to the cube of the stress. Sometimes a "perfectly plastic" approximation is used for glacier flow in which deformation does not occur until a certain critical stress of about one bar is reached, and then the stress cannot rise above that value.

The strength of ice, which depends on many factors, is difficult to measure. If ice is stressed for a long time it deforms by plastic flow and has no yield point (at which permanent deformation begins) or ultimate strength. For short-term experiments with conventional testing machines, typical strength values in bars are 38 for crushing, 14 for bending, 9 for tensile, and 7 for shear.

Thermal properties. The heat of fusion (heat absorbed on melting of a solid) of water is 334 kilojoules per kilogram, or 79.8 calories per gram. The specific heat of ice at the freezing point is 2.04 kilojoules per kilogram per degree Celsius (0.506 calorie per degree Celsius per gram). The thermal conductivity at this temperature is 0.0226 joule per degree Celsius per second (54×10^{-4} calories per degree Celsius per second). Another property of importance to the study of glaciers is the lowering of the melting point due to hydrostatic pressure, 0.0074 degree Celsius per bar. Thus for a glacier 300 metres (984 feet) thick, everywhere at the melting temperature, the ice at the base is 0.25 degree Celsius (0.45 degree Fahrenheit) colder than at the surface.

Optical properties. Pure ice is transparent, but the air bubbles in snow and firn render it somewhat opaque. The absorption coefficient, or rate at which incident radiation decreases with depth, is about 0.1 cm^{-1} for snow and only 0.001 cm^{-1} or less for clear ice. Ice is weakly birefringent, or doubly refracting, which means that light is transmitted at different speeds in different crystallographic directions. Thin sections of snow or ice therefore can be conveniently studied under polarized light in much the same way that rocks are studied.

Albedo and radiative properties of ice

Electrical properties. The albedo, or reflectivity (an albedo of 0 means that there is no reflectivity), to solar radiation ranges from 0.5 to 0.9 for snow, 0.3 to 0.65 for firn, and 0.15 to 0.35 for glacier ice. At the thermal infrared wavelengths, snow and ice are almost perfectly "black" (absorbent), and the albedo is less than 0.01. This property means that snow and ice can either absorb or radiate long-wave radiation with high efficiency. At longer wavelengths (microwave and radio frequencies), dry snow and ice are relatively transparent. Liquid water in them greatly modifies this property. Radio echo sounding (radar) techniques are now used routinely to measure the thickness of dry polar glaciers, even where they are on the order of kilometres in thickness, but the slightest amount of liquid water distributed through the mass creates great difficulties with the technique.

INTERACTION OF GLACIERS WITH THE ENVIRONMENT

Mass balance. Glaciers are nourished by snowfall, and they waste away by melting or marginal breaking (calving). In order for a glacier to remain at a constant size, there must be a balance between income (accumulation) and outgo (ablation). If this mass balance is positive (more gain than loss) the glacier grows; if it is negative the glacier shrinks.

Processes of accumulation and ablation

Accumulation refers to all processes that contribute mass to a glacier. Snowfall is the predominant process, but additional contributions may be made by hoarfrost (direct condensation of ice from water vapour), rime (freezing of supercooled water droplets on striking a surface), hail, the freezing of rain or meltwater, or avalanching of snow from adjacent slopes.

Ablation refers to all processes that remove mass from a glacier. In temperate regions, melting at the surface normally predominates. Calving (the breaking off of icebergs into the ocean or a lake) is usually the most important process on large glaciers in polar regions and on some temperate glaciers as well. Evaporation and loss by ice avalanches are important in certain special environments; floating ice may lose mass by melting from below.

Because the processes of accumulation, ablation, and the transformation of snow to ice proceed so differently, depending upon temperature and the presence or absence of liquid water, it is customary to classify glaciers in terms of various thermal conditions. Thus, a polar glacier is defined as one below the freezing temperature throughout its mass for the entire year; a subpolar glacier is mostly below the freezing temperature throughout its mass, except for surface melting in the summer; and a temperate glacier is at the melting temperature throughout its mass, but surface freezing occurs in winter.

A newer classification distinguishes the surface zones, or facies (lateral aspects), of a glacier (few single glaciers will show the full sequence). In the dry-snow zone no surface melting occurs even in summer; in the percolation zone some surface melting may occur, but the meltwater refreezes at a shallow depth so that the whole thickness of the winter snow layer is not affected; in the soaked zone sufficient melting and refreezing take place to raise the whole winter snow layer to the melting temperature; and, in the superimposed-ice zone, refrozen meltwater at the base of the snowpack (superimposed ice) forms a continuous layer that is exposed at the surface by the loss of overlying snow. These zones are all parts of the accumulation area, in which the mass balance is always positive. Below the superimposed-ice zone is the ablation zone, or ablation area, in which annual loss exceeds the gain by snowfall.

From *Journal of Glaciology*, vol. 5, No. 41 (1965) by permission of the Glaciological Societ

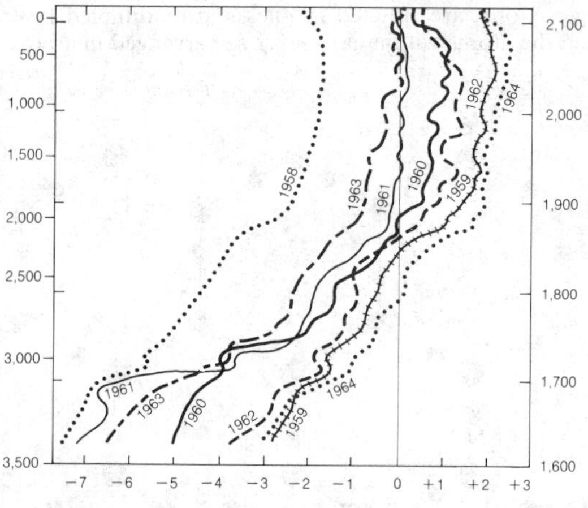

Figure 4: Net mass balance of South Cascade Glacier, Washington, 1958–64.

The boundary between the accumulation and ablation areas is the equilibrium line. Below the equilibrium line the mass balance is negative when averaged over a year. The terms firn line or firn limit are often used in place of equilibrium line on mountain glaciers, but this usage is correct only if there is no superimposed ice.

The value of the mass balance at any point on a glacier can be measured by means of stakes, snow pits, or core drills, but the change in height of the surface in relation to deeper layers and to the density of the surficial material must be observed. These values at points can then be averaged over the whole glacier for a whole year. The result is the net or annual mass balance. A positive value indicates growth, a negative value a decline.

Heat balance. The mass balance and the temperature variations are determined in part by the heat received from or lost to the external environment, an exchange that takes place almost entirely at the upper surface. Heat is received from solar radiation, long-wave radiation from clouds, water vapour, turbulent transfer from warm air, conduction upward from lower layers, and the heat released by the condensation of dew or hoarfrost or by the freezing of liquid water. Heat is lost by outgoing long-wave radiation, turbulent transfer to colder air, the heat required for the evaporation, sublimation, or melting of ice, and conduction downward to lower layers.

Heat income and heat loss

In temperate regions, solar radiation is normally the

greatest heat source (although 55 to 90 percent of the incoming radiation is reflected from a snow surface), and most of the heat loss goes to the melting of ice. It is incorrect to think of snow or ice melt as directly related to air temperature; even in those situations in which heat from the air is an important factor, it is the wind structure near the surface that determines the heat transfer. This is because ordinary molecular heat conduction through the air is extremely inefficient, and the heat can be moved to a surface only by turbulent eddies.

In polar regions, heat is gained primarily from incoming solar radiation and lost by outgoing long-wave radiation, but other processes, such as heat conduction from lower layers, turbulent transfer, and the heat of evaporation, are also involved.

Glacier flow. In the accumulation area the mass balance is positive year after year. Here the glacier would become thicker and thicker were it not for the compensating flow of ice away from the glacier. This flow also supplies mass to the ablation area to compensate for the continual loss of ice there. Glacier flow is a simple consequence of the weight and creep properties of ice. As ice tends to build up in the accumulation area, a surface slope toward the ablation area is developed. This slope and the ice's own weight induce a shearing stress throughout the mass. Each element of ice deforms according to the magnitude and direction of the shear stress and the flow law of ice. The net effect of adding up, or integrating, the sheer deformation of each increment is a velocity profile. In the simplest case, velocity decreases from the surface downward, at a rate approximately proportional to the fourth power of the depth.

Deformation and velocity distribution

When the ice temperature is entirely below freezing, it cannot slide on the underlying bedrock. If the ice is at the melting temperature in the lower layers, two mechanisms operate to permit sliding. First, small protuberances on the bed cause stress concentrations in the ice, increased plastic flow, and the ice streams around the protuberances. Second, ice on the upstream side of protuberances is subjected to higher pressure, which lowers the melting temperature and causes some of the ice to melt; on the downstream side the converse is true, and meltwater freezes. The latent heat of melting must flow upstream from the freezing side to the melting side of each bump, and the rate of heat flow partly determines the speed with which this process, termed regelation, can take place. The first process is most efficient with large knobs, and the second process is most efficient with small bedrock irregularities. Together they produce bed slip; in some situations cavities may form in the lee of bedrock knobs. Although the process of glacier sliding over bedrock is understood in a general way, none of several detailed theories has been confirmed by field observation. This problem is perhaps the most important unsolved one in glacier physics.

An area in which the velocity increases in a downglacier direction is called an area of extending flow (the separation between two stakes driven into the surface will increase with time). An area in which the velocity decreases as one moves downglacier is an area of compressing flow (the separation between stakes decreases with time). The ice itself does not actually compress or expand; the ice only deforms, and new ice is added from above or the sides, or the glacier thins in extending flow; conversely, ice is lost to the surface or goes into lateral expansion or longitudinal thickening in compressing flow.

From J.F. Nye, "A Numerical Method of Inferring Budget History of a Glacier from Its Advance and Retreat," *Journal of Glaciology*, vol. 5, no. 41 (1965); by permission of the Glaciological Society

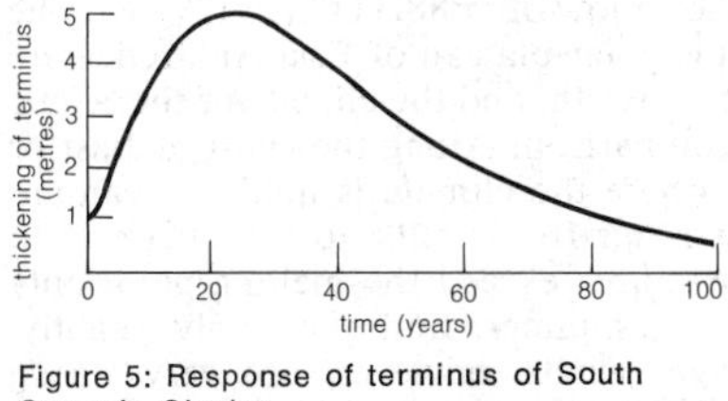

Figure 5: Response of terminus of South Cascade Glacier.

Climatic changes and glacier fluctuations. The relationship of glaciers to changes in climate is sequential. The general climatic or meteorological environment determines the local mass and heat-exchange processes at the glacier surface, and these in turn determine the net mass balance of the glacier. Changes in the net mass balance produce a dynamic response; that is, changes in the speed of ice flow. The dynamic response causes an advance or retreat of the terminus, which may produce lasting evidence of the change in the glacier margin. If the climate changes toward increased winter snowfall rates, this change makes the net mass balance more positive, which is equivalent to an increase in ice thickness. The rate of glacier flow depends on thickness in a sensitive way, so that a slight increase in thickness produces a larger increase in ice flow. This increase causes the lower margin of the glacier to push out farther before all ice is removed by melting or calving. The result is known as a glacier advance.

Glacier advance and retreat

The process, however, cannot be traced backward with assurance. A glacier advance can, perhaps, be related to a period of positive mass balances, but to ascertain the meteorological cause is difficult because either increased snowfall or decreased melting can produce a positive mass balance. As an additional complication, widespread glacier advances will add more area of high albedo to the land surface and thus tend to cause a general cooling of the atmosphere, which will, of course, promote glacier growth.

By courtesy of the U.S. Geological Survey

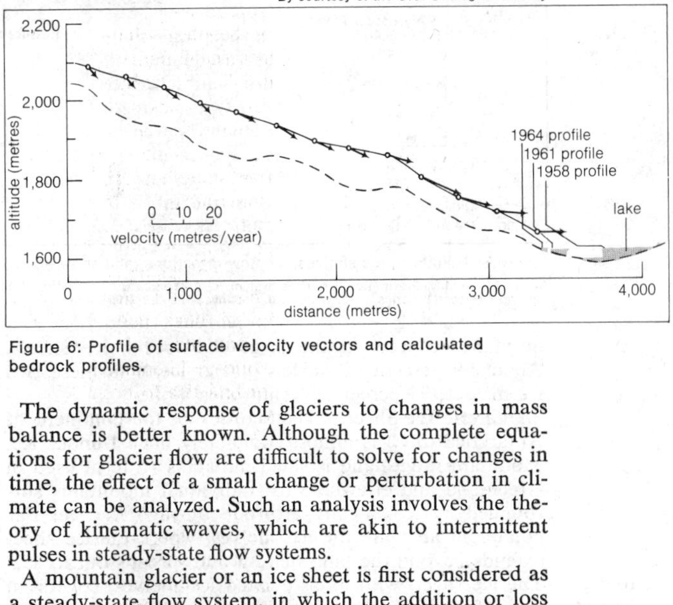

Figure 6: Profile of surface velocity vectors and calculated bedrock profiles.

The dynamic response of glaciers to changes in mass balance is better known. Although the complete equations for glacier flow are difficult to solve for changes in time, the effect of a small change or perturbation in climate can be analyzed. Such an analysis involves the theory of kinematic waves, which are akin to intermittent pulses in steady-state flow systems.

A mountain glacier or an ice sheet is first considered as a steady-state flow system, in which the addition or loss of material at any point is exactly balanced by changes in flow, so that the overall dimensions of the glacier do not change with time. Then the effect of a small or slowly varying change on the mass balance of the system is considered. A complex differential equation, which must be solved numerically, describes the effect of this perturbation on the glacier's longitudinal profile and its subsequent advance or retreat. In this way a history of mass-balance changes can be used to predict the subsequent advance or retreat of a glacier. The converse problem (determining past mass-balance changes from a known history of advance or retreat) is of more practical importance and is in actual fact far easier to do. The main problem with these analyses is the long and complex response times inherent in glaciers: even though there may be some immediate response at the terminus to change in climate, the complete response cycle may take hundreds, thousands, or even (in the case of major ice sheets) tens of thousands of years.

THE GREAT ICE SHEETS

Two great ice masses, the Antarctic and Greenland ice sheets, stand out in the world today and may be similar

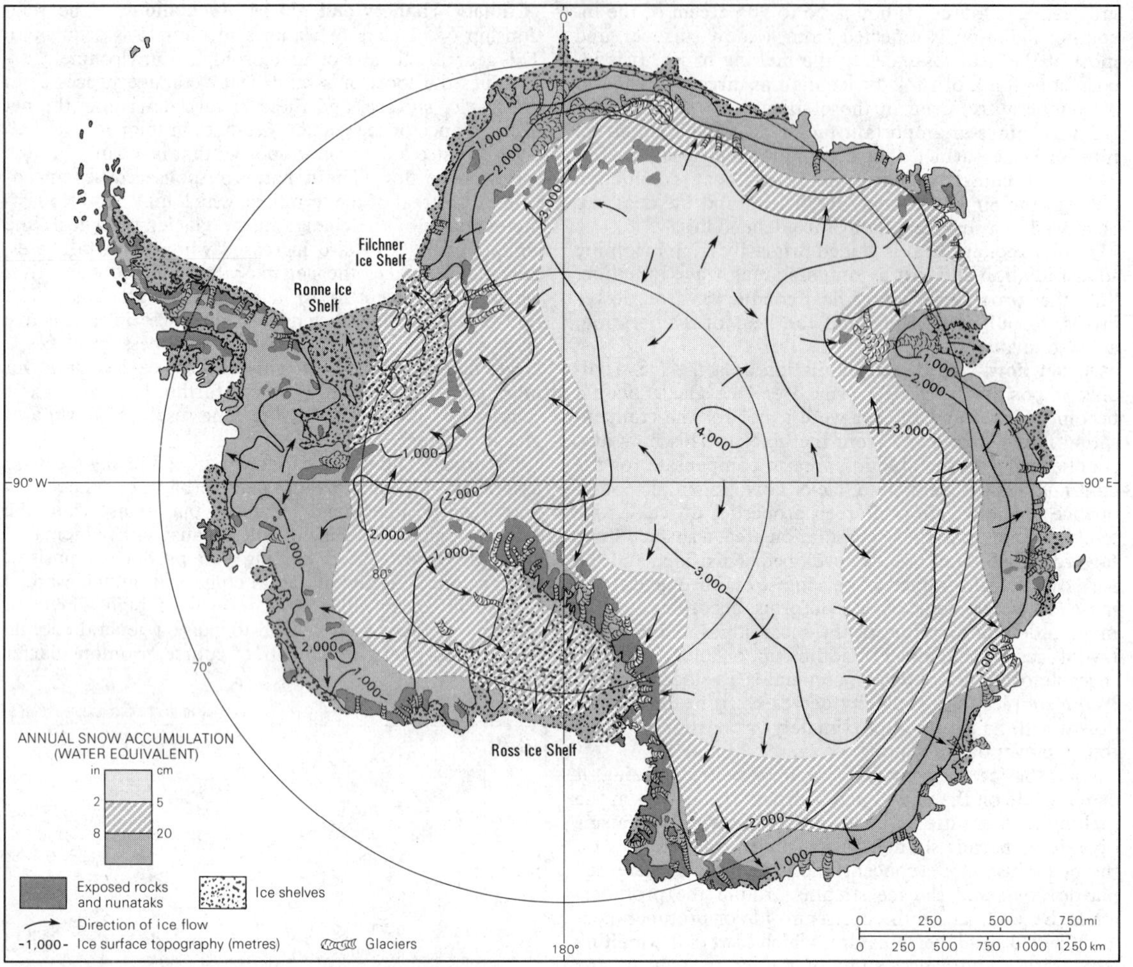

Figure 7: Nunataks, ice shelves, ice flow directions, and snow accumulation in Antarctica.
Adapted from M.B. Giovinetto, "Drainage Systems of Antarctica: Accumulation," *Antarctic Snow and Ice Studies*, Antarctic Research Series, vol. 2; American Geophysical Union (1964)

in many respects to the large Pleistocene ice sheets. About 99 percent of world's glacier ice is in these two ice masses, 91 percent in Antarctica alone.

Antarctic Ice Sheet. The bedrock of the continent of Antarctica (*q.v.*) is almost completely buried under ice. Mountain ranges and isolated nunataks (a term used in Greenland and elsewhere for individual mountains surrounded by ice) locally protrude through the ice. Far greater in area are the ice shelves, where the ice sheet extends beyond the land margin and spreads out to sea.

Ice topography and physical characteristics

The ice sheet, with its associated ice shelves, covers an area of 13,800,000 square kilometres (5,330,000 square miles); exposed rock areas total less than 200,000 square kilometres (77,000 square miles). The mean thickness of the ice is between 1,720 and 2,200 metres (5,600 and 7,200 feet) and the volume of ice between 25 and 30 million cubic kilometres, according to different estimates. The land surface beneath the ice is below sea level in many places, but this surface is depressed due to the weight of the ice. If the ice sheet were melted, uplift of the land surface would eventually leave only a few deep troughs and basins at or below sea level—even though the sea level itself would also rise about 80 metres (260 feet) from the addition of such a large amount of water. Because of the thick ice cover, Antarctica has by far the highest mean altitude of the continents (2.2 kilometres [1.3 miles]); all other continents have mean altitudes less than one kilometre (0.6 mile).

Antarctic Peninsula. Antarctica can be divided into three main parts: the smallest and the mildest in climate is the Antarctic Peninsula, extending from latitude 63° S off the tip of South America to a juncture with West Antarctica at a latitude of about 74° S. The ice cover of the Antarctic Peninsula is a complex of ice caps, piedmont and mountain glaciers, and small ice shelves.

West Antarctica. The part of the main continent lying south of the Americas, between 45° west longitude and 165° east longitude, is characterized by irregular bedrock and ice-surface topography and numerous nunataks and deep troughs. Two large ice shelves occur in West Antarctica: the Filchner Ice Shelf, south of the Weddell Sea, has an area of about 390,000 square kilometers (150,000 square miles), and the Ross Ice Shelf, south of the Ross Sea, has an area of about 496,000 square kilometres (191,000 square miles).

East Antarctica. A huge single ice dome of about 10,200,000 square kilometres (3,900,000 square miles), separated from West Antarctica by the Transantarctic Mountains, occurs in East Antarctica. This major mountain range extends from the eastern margin of the Ross Ice Shelf almost to the Filchner Ice Shelf. The bedrock of East Antarctica is approximately at sea level, but the ice surface locally exceeds 4,000 metres (13,000 feet) above sea level on the highest parts of the polar plateau.

Antarctic climatic conditions

At the South Pole the snow surface is 2,800 metres (9,200 feet) in altitude, and the mean annual temperature is about −50° C (−58° F), but at the Soviet Vostok Station (78°27′ S, 106°52′ E), 3,500 metres (11,500 feet) above sea level, the mean annual temperature is −58° C (−73° F), and in August 1960 (the winter season) the temperature reached a low of −88.3° C (−127° F). The temperatures on the polar plateau of East Antarctica are by far the coldest on Earth, and the climate of the Arctic is quite mild by comparison. Along the coast of East or West Antarctica, where the climate is milder, mean annual temperatures range from −20° to −9° C (−4° to 16° F), but temperatures exceed the melting point only for brief periods in summer, and then only slightly. Katabatic (drainage) winds, however, are very strong along the coast; the mean annual wind speed at Commonwealth Bay is 20 metres per second (45 miles per hour).

Greenland Ice Sheet. The Greenland Ice Sheet, though subcontinental in size, is huge compared with all the other glaciers in the world except that of Antarctica. Greenland (2,190,000 square kilometres [846,000 square miles]) is mostly covered by this single large ice sheet (1,730,000 square kilometres [668,000 square miles]), but isolated glaciers and small ice caps totalling 76,000 square kilometres (29,300 square miles) occur around the periphery. The ice sheet is almost 2,400 kilometres (1,500 miles) long in a north–south direction, and its greatest width is 1,100 kilometres (680 miles) at a latitude of 77° N, near its northern margin. The mean altitude of the ice surface is 2,135 metres (7,004 feet). Often the term Inland Ice, or, in Danish, Indlandsis, is used for this ice sheet.

The bedrock surface is near sea level over most of the interior of Greenland, but mountains occur around the periphery. Thus, this ice sheet, in contrast to the Antarctic Ice Sheet, is confined along most of its margin. The ice surface reaches its greatest altitude on two north–south elongated domes, or ridges. The southern dome reaches altitudes of just under 3,000 metres (9,800 feet) at latitudes 63–65° N; the northern dome reaches about 3,290 metres (10,790 feet) at about the latitude 72° N. The crests of both domes are displaced to the east of the centre line of Greenland.

The unconfined ice sheet does not reach the sea along a broad front anywhere in Greenland, so that no large ice shelves occur. The ice margin just reaches the sea, however, in a region of many nunataks and irregular topography in the area of Melville Bay southeast of Thule. Large outlet glaciers, which are restricted tongues of the ice sheet, move through the bordering valleys to calve off into the ocean, producing the numerous icebergs that often penetrate the North Atlantic shipping lanes.

The climate of the Greenland Ice Sheet, though cold, is not as extreme as that of central Antarctica. The lowest mean annual temperatures, about −31° C (−24° F), occur on the north central part of the north dome, and temperatures at the crest of the south dome are about −20° C (−4° F).

Mass balance of the ice sheets. *Accumulation.* The rate of precipitation on the Antarctic Ice Sheet is so low that it may be called a cold desert. Snow accumulation over much of the vast polar plateau is less than five centimetres (two inches) water equivalent per year. Only around the margin of the continent, where cyclonic storms penetrate frequently, does the accumulation rise to values of more than 30 centimetres (13 inches). The mean for Antarctica is 15 centimetres or less. In Greenland values are higher: less than 15 centimetres (six inches) in a comparatively small area of north central Greenland, 30 centimetres (13 inches) along the crests of the domes, and values over 80 centimetres (31 inches) along the southeast and southwest margins. The mean annual snow accumulation in Greenland is about 37 centimetres (16 inches) of water equivalent.

Snow accumulation occurs mainly as direct snowfall when cyclonic storms move inland. At high altitudes on the Antarctic polar plateau, ice crystals form in the cold air during clear periods and slowly settle out as fine "diamond dust." Hoarfrost and rime deposition are generally minor items in the snow-accumulation totals. It is almost impossible to measure the precipitation directly in these climates; precipitation gauges are almost useless for the measurement of blowing snow, and the snow is blown about almost constantly in some areas. Thus, the thickness and density of snow deposited on the ground is measured, and this figure actually equals the precipitation at the place of measurement, plus the hoarfrost and rime deposition, less evaporation, less the snow blown away, and plus the snow blown in from somewhere else. The last two phenomena are thought to approximately cancel each other, except in the coastal areas, where fierce drainage, or katabatic, winds move appreciable quantities of snow and sometimes sweep it out to sea.

Difficulty of measuring precipitation

The snow surface may be smooth, as in the polar areas where soft powder snow is deposited with no wind, or very hard packed and rough when high winds occur during or after snowfall. Two features are prominent: snow dunes are depositional features resembling sand dunes in their several shapes; and sastrugi are jagged erosional features (often cut into snow dunes) caused by strong prevailing winds after snowfall. Sharp, rugged sastrugi up to two metres high have been observed in high-wind areas; these make travel by vehicle or on foot very difficult. The annual snow layers exposed in the side of a snow pit can usually be distinguished by a very low density layer (depth hoar) that forms by metamorphism of the snow deposited in the fall at a time when the temperature is changing rapidly.

Most of the Antarctic Ice Sheet lies within the dry-snow zone. The percolation, soaked, and superimposed ice zones occur only in a very narrow strip in a small area along the coast. In Greenland only the central part of the northern half of the ice sheet, or about 30 percent of the total area, is within the dry-snow zone. Almost half of the area of the Greenland ice sheet is considered to be in the percolation zone. In flat areas near the equilibrium line, especially in west central Greenland, there are notorious snow swamps, or slush fields, in summer; some of this water runs off, but much of it refreezes to form ice crusts or superimposed ice.

Ablation. The ice sheets lose material by several processes, including surface melting, evaporation, wind erosion (deflation), calving, and the melting of the bottom surfaces of floating ice shelves by warmer seawater.

In Antarctica, calving of ice shelves and outlet glacier tongues clearly predominates among all of the processes of ice loss, but the rate of calving cannot be measured accurately at the present time. The amount of surface melt and evaporation is small, amounting to about 22 centimetres (nine inches) of ice lost from a five-kilometre (three-mile) ring around half the continent. Wind erosion is difficult to evaluate but probably accounts for only a very small loss in the mass balance. The undersides of ice shelves near their outer margins are subject to melting by the ocean water, but the rate of melting decreases inland. At some point far back under the ice shelves, freezing of seawater rather than melting must occur, but there is no agreement at the present time as to exactly where the dividing line is.

In Greenland, surface melt is more important, calving is less so, and under-shelf melting is nonexistent. Most of the calving is from the termini of a relatively few very large outlet glaciers in the middle latitudes, such as the Jakobshavn and Grand Qarajaq glaciers. In Greenland and in other areas, vertical-walled melt pits in the ice are a feature of the ablation zone. Ranging from a few millimetres to a metre in diameter, these pits are floored with a dark, silty material called cryoconite, once thought to be of cosmic origin but now known to be terrestrial dust. The vertical melting of the holes is due to the absorption of solar radiation by the dark silt, possibly augmented by biological activity.

Net mass balance. Because two great ice sheets contain 99 percent of the world's ice, it might be thought that scientists would have conclusively determined whether this ice is growing or shrinking under present climatic conditions. Such is not the case. The task is simply too difficult. Because of the concentrated study of these ice sheets during and since the International Geophysical Year (1957–58), much more is known about accumulation and ablation, but some terms (such as calving) still cannot be defined satisfactorily.

Whether the ice sheets are growing or shrinking

It appears that the Antarctic Ice Sheet is growing. An important summary in 1967 listed values, in cubic kilometres of water equivalent, per year, as follows:

Accumulation	
Snow accumulation	+1,900
Ablation	
Melting and evaporation	−10
Calving of ice sheet	−50
Calving of glaciers	−520
Calving of ice shelves	−880
Bottom melting, ice shelves	−200
Total ablation	−1,660

The net difference (240 cubic kilometres), however, is of the same order of magnitude as the probable errors in estimation of the various quantities, so that a positive net balance is not a certainty. The value for accumulation is relatively lower then most, and the ablation values are relatively higher, so that the budget is a conservative one; most other modern calculations show a positive balance at least as great.

In the case of Greenland, the net balance appears to be closer to zero, but the errors are again too large for definite conclusions. The estimated balance is as follows, again in cubic kilometres of water equivalent:

accumulation		ablation	
Snow accumulation	+630	Melting	−120 to −270
		Calving	−240
			−360 to −510

Earlier investigators had calculated an annual loss of mass, but the earlier values of melting now seem to have been grossly overestimated. Thus, the Greenland ice sheet may be growing or shrinking.

The fact that the amount of ice in the world appears to be increasing is difficult to reconcile with the observation that the sea level is also rising. Insufficient ice is lost from retreating mountain glaciers to make up the difference, and the rise in sea level must be due to other causes, such as a warming of the ocean or uplift of part of the ocean floor.

Flow of the ice sheets. In general, the flow in ice sheets is from central high points radially outward to the sea. In areas of subdued subglacial relief, a dome-shaped form of dynamic equilibrium is clearly apparent; from the margin the ice surface rises inland as an elliptic or parabolic curve. Wherever subglacial features are large compared with ice thickness, the ice flow is distorted and the ice surface topography is complicated. The ice of much of East Antarctica has a rather simple domal shape. Greenland resembles an elongated dome, or ridge with two summits. West Antarctica is a complex of converging and diverging flow because of the jumble of ridges and troughs in the subglacial bedrock.

Flow rates

Flow rates in the interior of an ice sheet are very low, being measured in centimetres or metres per year because the surface slope is miniscule. As the ice moves outward the rate of flow increases to a few tens to hundreds of metres per year, and this rate of flow increases still further if the flow is channeled into outlet glaciers or narrow ice shelves. Ice shelves continue the flow but in a somewhat different way—ice spreads out in ever thinner layers. This spreading, coupled with the influx of new ice from the landward side, causes the velocities to increase still more. At the edge of the Ross Ice Shelf, ice is moving out about 900 metres (3,000 feet) per year toward the ocean.

This simple picture of ice flow is made more complicated by the dependence of the flow law of ice on temperature. Because a temperature increase of about 15° C (27° F) causes a tenfold increase in the deformation rate of ice, the temperature distribution of an ice sheet partly determines its flow structure. The cold ice of the central part of an ice sheet is carried down into warmer zones. This shift modifies the static temperature distribution, and the shearing deformation is concentrated in a thin zone of warmer ice at the base. The forward velocity may be almost uniform throughout the depth to within a few tens or hundreds of metres from the bedrock.

Another important effect on ice flow is the heat produced by friction, caused by the sliding of the ice on bedrock or by internal shearing within the ice. If a portion of the ice sheet deforms more rapidly than its surroundings, the slight amount of extra heat production raises the temperature of this portion, causing it to deform even more readily. This increased deformation may explain the phenomena of ice streams—currents of ice moving several times faster than the ice on either side of them. These are very effective in moving ice from large drainage areas of Greenland out to the sea. Such ice streams have been discovered also in Antarctica, where they may be of similar importance.

Information from deep cores. Most of the Antarctic Ice Sheet is classified as polar because it is below freezing throughout its mass. It is so thick, however, that the normal gradient of temperature might be expected to increase with depth to produce melting temperatures at the base. A hole bored through 2,164 metres (7,098 feet) of ice at Byrd Station did in fact show this, and liquid water entered the hole at the base. Melting temperatures at the base probably occur in much of central Antarctica,

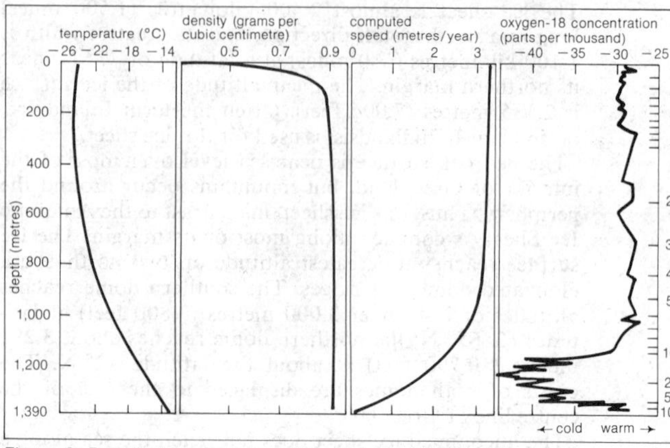

Figure 8: Data from a deep bore hole to bedrock at Camp Century, northwest Greenland.

but the thinner marginal areas are below freezing at the bed. A similar situation probably occurs in Greenland, most of which is classified as subpolar. A drill hole in northwest Greenland, where the ice is 1,390 metres (4,559 feet) thick, revealed a temperature of −13° C (+9° F) at the base.

The availability of such continuous cores through ice sheets represents one of the most exciting of modern developments. Because there is no melting, the layered structure in the ice preserves a continuous record of snow accumulation, air temperature, air composition, and artificial and natural fallout. This record extends back into the Pleistocene Epoch and is uniquely valuable for reconstructing past climates.

Near the surface it is possible to pick out the annual layers by visual inspection and quickly to detect changes in the yearly accumulations of snow. Radioactivity measurements also provide a close check on the recent layers by locating atomic- and hydrogen-bomb fallout. Interesting data have been obtained on the history of fallout of products of industrialization, such as tetraethyl lead and DDT, as well as of tiny black spherules identified as cosmic fallout.

Oxygen isotopes and paleotemperatures

A very useful technique for measuring past temperatures involves the use of oxygen isotopes, namely, oxygen-18 and oxygen-16 and their ratio. The concentration of oxygen-18 in precipitation, particularly at high latitudes, depends on the temperature. Winter snow has a more negative O^{18}–O^{16} ratio with respect to mean ocean water than summer snow. Closely spaced core samples from depths of 300 metres (1,000 feet), for example, show variations that can be clearly identified with summer and winter snows. Unfortunately, these seasonal patterns are difficult to find at great depths, because molecular diffusion tends to homogenize the isotopic variations, and the layers are progressively thinned at depth because of plastic flow.

Other techniques must be used to reconstruct a chronology from very deep cores. The most useful so far involves theoretical analysis of the flow. If the vertical profile of ice flow is known, and if it can be assumed that the rate of accumulation has been approximately constant through time, then an expression for the age of the ice as a function of depth can be developed.

This technique has been used to analyze the 1,390-metre (4,559-foot) core to bedrock from Camp Century in northwest Greenland. A plot of oxygen-18 concentration against time shows temperature variations as far back as 100,000 years, before the Wisconsin glacial period. Although these oxygen-18 changes in north Greenland cannot yet be directly converted to temperature changes, the curve agrees with known climatic variations in other parts of the world and provides far more detailed information than is available by other means. Unlike other terrestrial deposits, ice cores from the dry-snow zones of ice sheets can provide continuous sedimentary records spanning perhaps several hundred millennia.

MOUNTAIN GLACIERS

Classification of mountain glaciers. Mountain glaciers are, by definition, confined to a more or less marked path directing their movement. The shape of the channel and the degree to which the glacier fills it determine the type of glacier. Valley glaciers are of classic type; they flow at least in part down a valley and are longer than they are wide. Cirque glaciers, short and wide, are confined to cirques, or amphitheatres, cut in the mountain landscape. Other types include transection glaciers, which fill systems of valleys, and glaciers in special situations, such as summit glaciers, hanging glaciers, ice aprons, crater glaciers, and regenerated or reconstituted glaciers. Many glaciers are irregular shapes situated on mountainsides; these are often lumped into the category of wall-sided glaciers or ice patches. Included in the discussion here are glaciers that spread out at the foot of the mountain ranges (the large, composite piedmont glaciers and the smaller expanded foot glaciers) and outlet glaciers from ice sheets, ice caps, and ice fields.

Types of mountain glaciers

As the amount of glacier cover in a region increases with time, there is a gradual change from predominately cirque glaciers to valley glaciers to transection glaciers to an ice field (almost burying the topography), with large piedmont glaciers, to an ice cap (completely covering the mountains). Thus, it is not surprising that clear distinctions among the various types of glaciers are difficult to draw. The broad spectrum of glacier types, except for the ice-cap stage, can be seen today in the St. Elias Mountains of Alaska and Yukon Territory.

Mountain glaciers are also classified as polar, subpolar, or temperate and their surfaces by the occurrence of dry-snow, percolation, saturation, and superimposed ice zones, as for ice sheets.

Surface features. The snow surface of the accumulation area of mountain glaciers displays the same snow dune and sastrugi features found on ice sheets, especially in winter, but normally these features are not as large or as well developed. Where appreciable melting of the snow occurs, several additional features may be produced. During periods of clear, sunny weather, sun cups (cup-shaped hollows usually between five and 50 centimetres [two and 20 inches] in depth) may develop. On very high-altitude, low-latitude snow and firn fields these may grow into spectacular narrow blades of ice, up to several metres high, called penitentes, or nieve penitentes. Rain falling on the snow surface (or very high rates of melt) may cause meltwater runnels (shallow grooves trending downslope).

Other features are characteristic of the ablation zone. Below icefalls (steep reaches of a valley glacier), several types of curved bands can be seen. The surface of the glacier may rise and fall in a periodic manner, with the spacing between wave crests approximately equal to the amount of ice flow in a year. Called wave ogives (pointed arches), these arcs result from the great stretching of the ice in the rapidly flowing icefall. The ice that moves through the icefall in summer has more of its surface exposed to melting and is greatly reduced in volume compared with the ice moving through in winter. The alternating thick and thin portions of the glacier appear as waves in the slower moving ice below the icefall. Dirt-band ogives also occur below icefalls. These are alternating layers of dark- and light-coloured ice, which may be caused by seasonal differences in the amount of dust or by snow trapped in the icefall. Frequently these two types of ogives occur together. In plan view, the ogives are invariably distorted into arcs or curves convex down-glacier; hence the name ogive.

Ogives and ice stratification

The ice of the ablation zone normally shows a distinctive layered structure. This can be relic stratification developed by the alternation of dense and light or clean and dirty snow accumulations higher on the glacier. This stratification is later subdued by recrystallization accompanying plastic flow. A new layering called foliation is developed by the flow. Foliation is expressed by alternating layers of clear and bubbly or coarse-grained and fine-grained ice. This structure has also been produced experimentally by shearing ice specimens. Although the origin of this structure is not fully understood, it is analogous to the process that produces foliated structures in metamorphic rocks (*q.v.*).

The ice crystals in strongly deformed, foliated ice invariably have a preferred orientation, relative to the stress directions. In some situations, more often in polar than in temperate ice, the hexagonal axes are aligned perpendicularly to the plane of foliation. This alignment is easy to explain, because it places the crystal glide planes parallel to the planes of (presumed) greatest shearing. In most other locations the hexagonal crystal axes are preferentially aligned in four different directions, none perpendicular to the foliation. This enigmatic pattern has resisted explanation so far, in spite of much intensive experimental and theoretical study.

Crevasses are common to both the accumulation and ablation zones of mountain glaciers, as well as ice sheets and all other types of glaciers. Transverse crevasses, perpendicular to the flow direction along the centre line of valley glaciers, are caused by extending flow. Splaying crevasses, parallel to the flow in midchannel, are caused by a transverse expansion of the flow. The drag of the valley walls produces marginal crevasses, which intersect the margin at 45°. Transverse and splaying crevasses curve around to become marginal crevasses near the edge of a valley glacier. Other, less common situations produce sigmoidal (S-shaped), en echelon (overlapping), and radial crevasse patterns. Splaying and transverse crevasses may occur together, chopping the glacier surface into discrete blocks or towers, called seracs.

Crevasses deepen until the rate of surface stretching is counterbalanced by the rate of plastic flow tending to close the crevasses at depth. Thus, crevasse depths are a function of the rate of stretching and the temperature of the ice. Crevasses deeper than 50 metres (160 feet) are rare in temperate mountains, but crevasses to 100 metres (330 feet) or more in depth may occur in polar regions. Often the crevasses are concealed by a snow bridge, built by accumulations of windblown snow.

Mass balance of mountain glaciers. The rate of accumulation and ablation on mountain glaciers depends on latitude, altitude, and distance downwind from sources of abundant moisture, such as the oceans. The glaciers along the Pacific coast of Washington, British Columbia, and southeastern Alaska, as well as coastal glaciers on the South Island of New Zealand, Iceland, and southwestern Norway, receive prodigious snowfall. Snow accumulation of three to five metres (ten to 16 feet) of water equivalent in a single season is not uncommon. With this large income, glaciers can exist at low altitudes in spite of very high melt rates. The rate of snowfall increases rapidly with increasing altitude; thus, the gradient of net mass balance with altitude is steep. This gradient also expresses the rate of transfer of mass by glacier flow from high to low altitudes. The gradient of net balance at the equilibrium line is called the activity index.

Accumulation and ablation on mountain glaciers

Typical of the temperate, maritime glaciers is South Cascade Glacier, in western Washington. Its activity index is high, normally about 17 millimetres per metre (0.017 foot per foot; the net balance is 17 millimetres more positive for each metre gain in altitude), the yearly snow accumulation averages about 3.1 metres (10.2 feet; water-equivalent), and the equilibrium line is at the low altitude of 1,900 metres (6,200 feet). This glacier contains only ablation and saturation zones; the winter chill is so slight that no superimposed ice is formed.

In the maritime environment of southeastern Alaska are many very large glaciers; Bering and Seward-Malaspina glaciers (piedmont glaciers) cover 5,800 and 5,200 square

Figure 9: South Cascade Glacier, Washington.
By courtesy of the U.S. Geological Survey; photograph, Austin Post

kilometres (2,240 and 2,000 square miles) in area, respectively. Equilibrium lines are lower than those in Washington state, but the rates of accumulation and ablation and the activity indices are about the same. Because these mountains are high, and some glaciers extend over a great range of altitude, all surface zones except the dry-snow zone are represented.

Ural-type glaciers

In more continental (inland) environments, the rate of snowfall is much less, and the summer climate is generally warmer. Thus, glaciers can exist only at high altitudes. High winds may concentrate the meagre snowfall in deep, protected basins, however, allowing glaciers to form even in areas of low precipitation and high melt rates. Glaciers formed almost entirely of drift snow occur at high altitudes in Colorado and are often referred to as Ural-type glaciers because of the prevalence of this type of glacier in the polar Ural Mountains. Superimposed ice and soaked zones are found in the accumulation area. Because of the decrease in melt rates, continental glaciers in high latitudes occur at lower altitudes and have lower accumulation totals and activity indices. McCall Glacier, in the northwestern part of the Brooks Range in Arctic Alaska, has the lowest activity index (two millimetres per metre [0.002 foot per foot] measured in western North America. None of these glaciers is high enough to extend into the dry-snow zone. Glaciers in intermediate climates have intermediate equilibrium-line altitudes, accumulation or ablation totals, and activity indices.

Flow of mountain glaciers. Ice flow in valley glaciers has been studied extensively. The first measurements date from the mid-18th century, and the first theoretical analyses date from the middle of the 19th century. In general, these glaciers flow at rates of 0.1 to two metres (0.3 to six feet) per day, faster at the surface than at depth, faster in midchannel than along the margins, and usually faster at or just below the equilibrium line than at the head or the terminus. The flow is due, at least partly, to internal deformation, which depends primarily on the surface slope and the thickness. Glaciers that are at the melting temperature may also slide on the bed.

A common formula used to compute the speed of flow equates the speed of flow to products of ice thickness and sine of slope angle, namely,

$$u = k_1 \sin^3 \alpha\, h^4 + k_2 \sin^2 \alpha\, h^2,$$

in which u is the speed of flow at the surface, α is the surface slope, h is ice thickness, k_1 is a constant involving the shape of the channel, ice density, and other factors, and k_2 is another constant, involving a measure of the roughness of the bed. The first term on the right-hand side expresses the flow caused by internal deformation, and the second term expresses the rate of sliding on the bed. This formula is an approximation, because it ignores longitudinal changes in velocity and thickness and other complicating influences, but it has proved to be useful in simple field situations and shows that the rate of movement is very sensitive to slight changes in ice thickness.

When the thickness of a glacier is altered by changes in the net mass balance, the glacier adjusts its rate of flow to develop a different longitudinal profile. This process is normally a slow one and can be illustrated by South Cascade Glacier, Washington. It may be asked, for instance, how long it would take the glacier to overcome a minor perturbation and return to its steady state if the glacier were in complete harmony with a constant, unvarying climate, and one metre of excess thickness were added to the whole glacier for only one year. One analysis has produced the following results in terms of the behaviour of the terminus: After the initial thickening of one metre, the terminus would continue to thicken as the increased thickness propagated down from higher reaches of the glacier, and some 23 years later the glacier would be almost five metres thicker at the terminus, and then it would begin to thin. The process is so slow, however, that even after 100 years the glacier would still be 0.6 metre thicker than at the outset. Steep, rapidly flowing glaciers should respond more rapidly and reach equilibrium more quickly, but none has been completely analyzed yet.

Glacier surges. Most glaciers follow a regular and nonspectacular pattern of advance and retreat in response to a slowly varying climate. A very different behaviour pattern has been reported for certain glaciers in several parts of the Soviet Union, Nordaustlandet (North-eastland; an island in the Arctic Ocean off the coast of Norway), Iceland, and in the Alaska Range and St. Elias Mountains of Alaska and Yukon Territory. These glaciers may, after a period of stagnation, or quiescence, lasting ten to 100 years, suddenly begin to flow very rapidly, to up to five metres (16 feet) per hour. This rapid flow, lasting only a year or two, causes a sudden depletion of the upper part of the glacier, accompanied by a swelling and advance of the lower part, although these usually do not reach positions beyond the limits of previous surges. Advances of several kilometres in as many months have been recorded. Even more interesting is the fact that these glaciers periodically repeat cycles of quiescence and activity, irrespective of climate. These unusual glaciers are called surging glaciers, pulsatory glaciers, catastrophically advancing glaciers, or galloping glaciers by various authorities.

Although surging glaciers are not rare in some areas (*e.g.*, Alaska Range and St. Elias Mountains), they are

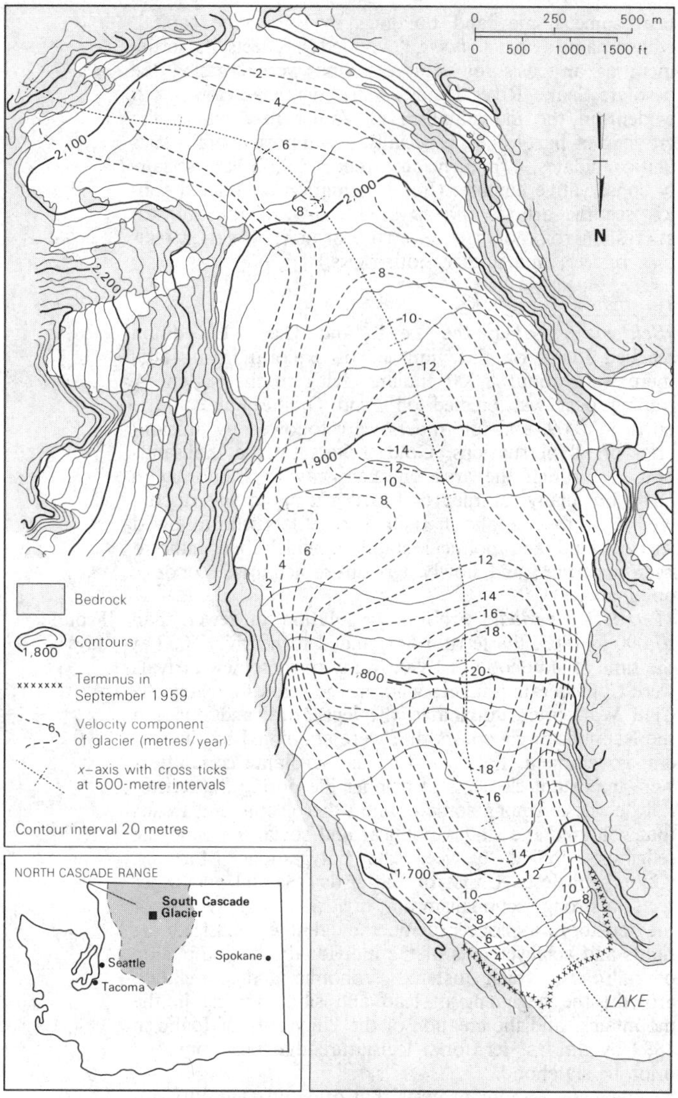

Figure 10: Topography and flow velocity of South Cascade Glacier.

Adapted from Meier and Tangborn, "Net Budget and Flow of South Cascade Glacier, Washington"; *Journal of Glaciology*, vol. 5 no. 41 (1965); by permission of the Glaciological Society

Difficulty of explaining surging glaciers

totally absent in other areas of similar topography, bedrock, climate, etc. (*e.g.*, western Chugach Mountains and Coast Mountains). Furthermore, glaciers of all shapes and sizes, from tiny cirque glaciers to major portions of a large ice cap, have been known to surge. Surging glaciers can be recognized readily during the active phase. Wildly shattered surfaces, sheer cliffs of ice where the main glacier has separated from tributary ice in the upper parts, and bulging masses of broken ice riding over older moraines and stagnant ice in the lower parts are characteristic. Usually they are easy to identify during the quiescent phase also, because medial moraines (central ridges of rock debris) on the surface are looped and zigzagged in a distinctive way. The flow instability that permits glacier surges has something to do with an abrupt decoupling of the glacier from its bed, but beyond that statement it is still impossible to explain glacier surges. Surging glaciers represent one of the most interesting enigmas in present-day glaciology.

Glacier hydrology. A temperate glacier is essentially a reservoir that gains precipitation in both liquid and solid form, stores a large share of this precipitation, and then releases it with little loss at a later date. The hydrologic characteristics of this reservoir, however, are complex, because its physical attributes change during a year.

In late spring the glacier is covered entirely by a thick snowpack at the melting temperature. Meltwater and liquid precipitation must travel through the snowpack by slow percolation until reaching well-defined meltwater channels in the solid ice below. In summer the snowpack becomes thinner, and drainage paths within the snow are more defined. Bare ice is exposed, and on this there may be surface drainage. Thus, meltwater and liquid precipitation are transmitted through the glacier rapidly. In winter, snow accumulates, and the surface layer freezes. This condition completely stops the movement of surface meltwater and precipitation, and rain that falls on the frozen surface can only refreeze to join the ice reservoir.

Runoff from glacier ice

The runoff from a typical Northern Hemisphere temperate glacier reaches a peak in late July or early August. Solar radiation, the chief source of heat to promote melt, reaches a peak in June. The delay in the peak melt rates is primarily because of the changing albedo (surface reflectivity) during the summer; initially the snow is very reflective and covers the whole glacier, but as the summer wears on the snow becomes wet (less reflective), and in addition more and more of the ice of much lower albedo is exposed. Thus, even though the incoming radiation decreases during midsummer, the proportion of it that is absorbed to cause melt is greatly increased. Other heat-exchange processes, such as turbulent transfer from warm air, also become more important in midsummer and late summer.

This albedo variation produces a runoff "buffering effect" against unusually wet or dry years. An unusually heavy winter snowpack causes high-albedo snow to persist longer over the glacier in summer; thus, less meltwater is produced. Conversely, an unusually light winter snowfall causes older firn and ice of lower albedo to be exposed earlier in the summer, producing increased melt and runoff. This variation can be shown by comparing data from two different years at South Cascade Glacier. During 1957–58 the spring snowpack was abnormally low (2.31 metres [eight feet] of water, 77 percent of average), and the summer runoff was therefore high (5.76 metres [18.9 feet], 158 percent of average). By way of contrast, during 1963–64, the spring snowpack was high (3.53 metres [11.6 feet], 117 percent of average), and the runoff was low (2.31 metres, 68 percent of average).

Thus, glaciers naturally regulate the runoff, seasonally and from year to year. When glacier runoff is combined with nonglacier runoff in roughly equal amounts, the result is very stable and even streamflow. This condition is part of the basis for the extensive hydrologic development of regions such as western Washington.

Glacier streams are characterized by high sediment concentrations. The sediment ranges from boulders to the distinctive fine-grained material called rock flour, glacier flour, or glacier milk, which is colloidal in size (often less than one micron in diameter). The suspended sediment concentration is a function of distance from the glacier, but the rock-flour component may persist for great distances and remain suspended in lakes for many years; it is rock flour that is responsible for the green colour of Alpine lakes. Glacier erosion has had little direct observational study, and so not much can be said about how much sediment is produced from a glacier of a given size or activity. Glacier streams vary in discharge with the time of day, and this variation causes a continual readjustment of the stream channel and the transportation of reworked debris, adding to the sediment load.

Glacier floods. Glacier outburst floods, or *jøkulhlaups*, can be spectacular or even catastrophic. These happen when drainage within a glacier is blocked by internal plastic flow and water is stored in or behind the glacier. The water eventually finds a narrow path to trickle out. If any excess heat is available in the water, this movement will cause the path to be enlarged by melting, causing faster flow, more melting, a larger conduit, and so on until all of the water is released quite suddenly. The word *jøkulhlaup* is Icelandic in origin, and Iceland has experienced some of the world's most spectacular outburst floods. The 1922 Grimsvötn outburst released about 7.1 cubic kilometres (1.7 cubic miles) of water in a flood that was estimated to have reached almost 57,000 cubic metres per second (2,000,000 cubic feet per second). Lake George (Knik Glacier), near Anchorage, and Tulsequah

Glacier, near Juneau, Alaska; Summit Lake (Salmon Glacier), near Prince Rupert, British Columbia; and Kautz and Nisqually glaciers, at Mt. Rainier, Washington, are sites of outburst floods. Many outburst floods occur regularly each year, some at intervals of two or more years, and some are completely irregular and impossible to predict.

BIBLIOGRAPHY. L. LLIBOUTRY, *Traité de glaciologie,* 2 vol. (1965), an authoritative work on the subject of glaciology, with an especially thorough treatment of glaciers and ice sheets with emphasis given to the geophysical, quantitative approach; W.S.B. PATERSON, *The Physics of Glaciers,* 2nd ed. (1981), an excellent, clearly written text on glaciers and ice sheets emphasizing the mechanics of flow; D.E. SUGDEN and B.S. JOHN, *Glaciers and Landscape* (1976), a well-illustrated text on the process of glaciation and the resulting modifications to landforms; P.A. SHUMSKIY, *Principles of Structural Glaciology* (1964; originally published in Russian, 1955), a reference work mainly on the petrography of ice, including sections on ice physics and chemistry, ice formation, ice metamorphism, and methods of study; C.R. BENTLEY, "The Structure of Antarctica and Its Ice Cover," H.C. HOINKES, "Glacial Meteorology," P.A. SHUMSKIY, A.N. KRENKE, and I.A. ZOTIKOV, "Ice and Its Changes," and M.J. RUBIN, "Antarctic Weather and Climate," in H. ODISHAW (ed.), *Research in Geophysics,* vol. 2, ch. 14–17 (1964), excellent reviews of the state of knowledge of glacier meteorology and the Antarctic Ice Sheet as of the end of the International Geophysical Year, by leading authorities; M.F. MEIER, "Ice and Glaciers," in V.T. CHOW (ed.), *Handbook of Applied Hydrology,* sect. 16 (1964), a discussion of ice and its properties, ice formation, and glaciers at an intermediate technical level, with some emphasis on glacier hydrology; R.P. SHARP, *Glaciers* (1960), an excellent, well-illustrated introduction to the subject of glacier study.

(M.F.M.)

Idaho

After many years of having been shifted from one frontier territory to another and of having had its own area sharply reduced, Idaho finally was admitted as the 43rd state of the United States in 1890. Part of the original Oregon country that was ceded to the United States by Great Britain in 1846, the present-day state was first split between the Oregon and Washington territories from 1853 to 1859. It was entirely in Washington until 1863, when it was organized separately to include present-day Montana (until 1864) and the greater part of Wyoming (until 1868). Along with Oregon, Washington, and the northwestern counties of Montana, Idaho is classified as part of the Pacific Northwest region, a region unified by the Continental Divide as an eastern boundary and by the Columbia River drainage basin, which covers virtually the entire area.

With 83,557 square miles (216,412 square kilometres), including 880 square miles of inland water, Idaho has twice the combined area of the six New England states. Its boundaries are both geographical and historical in derivation. The boundary with the Canadian province of British Columbia on the north follows the 49th parallel of latitude, while the southern border with Utah and Nevada follows the 42nd parallel—a line that was established between the United States and Spain in 1819. The state's eastern border with Wyoming follows the Continental Divide and incorporates a small slice of Yellowstone National Park before twisting northwestward atop the Beaverhead Mountains and the Bitterroot Range of the Rockies bordering Montana. On the west, Idaho's border with Washington and Oregon is a 480-mile (770-kilometre) straight stretch except between Weiser and Lewiston, where Hells Canyon of the Snake River serves as a natural boundary.

Geographical and historical borders

Idaho appropriately is shaped much like a logger's boot, thereby accidentally reflecting the state's rugged forest and mountain terrain in which logging and mining play major roles. The more than 943,000 residents of Idaho enjoy some of the largest unspoiled natural areas in the United States, including about 2,500,000 acres (1,012,000 hectares) of wilderness and primitive land in which roads and vehicles are seldom to be found. Since its development in 1936 Sun Valley has become an internationally known area for winter sports. The state also has large supplies of underground water. Artesian wells are used to heat some homes and buildings in Boise, the capital, whose name (French *boisé,* "wooded") reflects its settlement as an oasis for explorers who were crossing the desolate Snake River Plains. A frontier character is still evident in the individualism of voting that makes the crossing of party lines, especially to support liberal issues and candidates, a frequent occurrence in an otherwise fairly conservative climate. (For information on related topics, see the articles UNITED STATES OF AMERICA; UNITED STATES, HISTORY OF THE; NORTH AMERICA; NORTH AMERICAN DESERT; and ROCKY MOUNTAINS.)

THE HISTORY OF IDAHO

Settlement. When the Lewis and Clark Expedition reached Idaho on their journey of exploration in 1805, there were about 8,000 Indians living in the region. A trading post was erected on Pend Oreille Lake in the north in 1809, and fur traders were followed by missionaries of all persuasions. Gold seekers by the thousands poured through the area on their way to California in 1848, but many returned eastward after gold was discovered in northern Idaho in 1860. The settlers who followed wanted land and political stability, which had hitherto been uncertain; and slowly agriculture acquired economic dominance.

Frontier days

Territorial period. From a population of fewer than 17,000 in 1863, the territory expanded to nearly 90,000 at the time of statehood in 1890. Many of these new arrivals were Confederate refugees who, in the years following the Civil War, often dominated the legislature and opposed the Republican governors that were appointed by the federal government. Political strife and vigilante committees were important elements in frontier life during the territorial decades. Among some of the other events and trends that coloured the state's political and social life were the religious conflicts between the polygamous Mormons (Church of Jesus Christ of Latter-day Saints) and other sects; a strong sectionalism that divided various regions of the territory; a pioneer democracy that emphasized the rights and achievements of the individual; the completion of railroads, which fostered economic and population growth; the beginning of lead and silver mining in the mountains; and the creation of the University of Idaho in 1889 by the last territorial legislature that was convened prior to statehood.

Statehood. Labour protests that often erupted into violence were features of the 1890s era in Idaho. Through his unsuccessful prosecution in 1907 of William D. Haywood, an organizer of the Industrial Workers of the World (IWW), Sen. William Borah became Idaho's major national figure until his death in 1940. During the 20th century Idaho has been engaged in developing its agriculture, forestry, and industry, while maintaining the more satisfying aspects of modern life at the doorstep of a natural wilderness.

THE NATURAL AND HUMAN LANDSCAPE

Diversity of the natural environment is the most common characteristic of Idaho's landscape, creating a sectionalism that is reflected in its community life, politics, economy, and cultural development, as well as in the varieties of its soils and animal and plant life. Altitude is often a more important factor in controlling Idaho's climate than is latitude. The northern areas of the state are lower in elevation on the average than are much of the central and southern areas. Prevailing westerly winds from the Pacific Ocean blanket most of the state, especially the northern and southwestern regions. A drier, colder, continental climate is more noticeable in the southeastern counties, but Idaho has a milder climate than most of the states located in the same latitudes east of the Continental Divide.

The natural environments. The controlling physiographic features of Idaho are the Northern Rocky Mountains and the drainage patterns that they produce. These mountains dominate the characteristics of the state's rivers, landscapes, vegetation, animal life, and climate. The geographical regions of the Northern Rockies are the Lost Rivers, Sawtooth, Seven Devils, Bitterroot, and Cut Over.

Mountain ranges and rivers

These regions cover most of the state that lies to the north of the Snake River Plains, with the exception of the Palouse and Camas Prairie region in the northwest. The other regions are the Caribou, a part of the Middle Rockies in the southeast, the Owyhee Plateau in the southwest, and the Basin and Range region following the Snake through the south.

From these geographical regions flow 10 major rivers. The Kootenai and St. Joe flow into the Columbia drainage area. The Clearwater, Salmon, Weiser, Payette, Boise, and Wood flow into the Snake River drainage area, which joins the Columbia in eastern Washington. The Bear River flows into Utah's Great Salt Lake, and the five Lost rivers disappear into the earth on the northern edge of the Snake River Plains.

The Snake River, next to the Northern Rocky Mountains, is the major natural feature of the state. It rises in the southeastern part of the state, with tributaries in Yellowstone National Park, and flows from east to west through "sagebrush Idaho." With huge reclamation projects, the valley contains the greatest amount of Idaho's irrigated land, and three-fourths of Idahoans depend upon it for support. The course of the Snake includes Hells Canyon, North America's deepest (7,900 feet [2,400 metres]) gorge, and 212-foot-high Shoshone Falls, while its valley is a geologically complex sequence of lakes, lava beds, and desertscape symbolized by the barren craters and cones of the Craters of the Moon National Monument.

Idaho has 81 distinct mountain ranges and more than 2,000 lakes, with water its greatest single resource. A major portion of the industry, agriculture, and population follows the Snake, which furnishes an abundance of water for one of the nation's largest irrigated areas and developed hydroelectric-power sources. Crop production is favoured by both precipitation and temperature. Average rainfall in the northern part of the state is 20 inches (510 millimetres) annually, and 12 inches in the southern portion, but most of it falls outside the growing season. The average mean temperature ranges from 52° F (11.1° C) at Lewiston, at 1,413 feet in elevation, to 41° F (5° C) at Montpelier, at 6,000 feet. The average for the middle Snake is 55° F (12.8° C). The growing season varies between 120 and 300 days. The topography and climate provide a haven for big-game animals, game birds, fur animals, and migratory birds, and the rivers and lakes yield about 120,000 pounds (54,430 kilograms) of fish annually.

Patterns of human settlement. Many influential factors—religion, agriculture, transportation, topography, industry, cultural ties, and sectional pride—have contributed to Idaho's diverse regional characteristics. For many years writers and politicians consistently referred to the division of Idaho as northern Idaho—the 10 northern counties—and southern Idaho—the rest of the state. Studies of voting behaviour, however, indicate that four sections with distinct voting patterns have emerged: the 10 northern counties and three separate areas in the south, roughly the southwestern, the south central, and the southeastern sections. A more realistic regionalism has developed around trading and marketing centres, sometimes crossing the state boundaries. It consists of the following areas: Lewiston and Spokane, Washington, in the north; Boise, Twin Falls, Pocatello, and Idaho Falls in the south; and the Logan–Ogden–Salt Lake City axis in northern Utah.

Sectional characteristics

With the exceptions of mining and lumbering settlements, most of the settlements in southern Idaho tend to follow the course of the Snake River. In a narrow strip running from Pocatello northeast, agriculture is the economic base except in Pocatello itself, where manufacturing predominates. Agriculture continues its dominance to the west as far as the Boise Valley, where the state's largest population is located. Agriculture, service industries, and public employment are the most important factors in this area's economy. The Palouse and Camas Prairie are primarily agricultural, while Nez Perce County (Lewiston) is industrial and service oriented. Mining, lumbering, and agriculture are important throughout the north, while rural villages centre around a community life that includes churches, schools, commercial trading, banking, and service businesses to support the region's population. The only city in the state with more than 50,000 residents is Boise, with a population of more than 100,000.

THE PEOPLE OF IDAHO

The original inhabitants. Before the 1840s, when the buffalo herds disappeared and the wagon trains of settlers who were bound for California began to arrive, Indians had lived in the Idaho region for at least 10,000 years. The internal political structures of the five linguistic and cultural groups were weak, as were the ties between them. In the north were the Kutenai, the linguistically identical Salish (Kalispel), the Coeur d'Alene, and the Nez Percé. Northern Paiute lived in the west central region, while the western Shoshoni and the northern Shoshoni occupied most of the southern lands. Most of these groups lived in small villages, consisting largely of family groups that moved according to the fishing, hunting, and wild-plant gathering seasons. The tribes still live in approximately the same areas, some on the several reservations that are located within the state.

Indian groups

Religious life. In addition to fur trading, missionary activity among the Indians provided a major impetus to early settlement. The Methodist Jason Lee conducted services at Ft. Hall in 1834, and the Presbyterian Henry Spalding and his wife founded a mission at Lapwai in 1836. Roman Catholics under the leadership of the Jesuit Father Pierre-Jean de Smet supervised the establishment of missions at St. Joe, de Smet, and Cataldo in the northern Rockies between 1842 and 1863. The Mormons established a colony at Ft. Lemhi in 1855. The conflicts of these competing Christian sects were most severe between the Mormons and other Protestant groups. The religious, economic, and social differences, notably polygamy, became so acute that Congress passed an antipolygamy act in 1882. The Idaho legislature prevented Mormons from holding county office and tried to enforce a "test oath" against Mormons, and the state constitution still has a clause against celestial marriage, the Mormons' marriage for eternity. Mormonism continued as a major political issue for many years, and though anti-Mormonism has declined, it is still a noticeable factor in Idaho's social climate.

Mormon conflicts

There are about 400,000 church members in the state and about half of them are Mormons. The next largest denominational groups are Roman Catholic, Methodist, Presbyterian, Church of the Nazarene, Lutheran, Episcopalian, Church of Christ, and Baptist. The proximity to Mormon headquarters in Salt Lake City has resulted in strong religious ties to Utah, and the populations of some of the cities in the southeastern part of the state are 95 percent Mormon.

Demography. Idaho's population increased by one-third between 1970 and 1980. The state has one of the lowest mortality rates in the nation, and its birth rate exceeds the national average. Although the state is sparsely populated—fewer than 12 persons per square mile—more than half of the residents are urban dwellers, and about two-thirds live in nine counties, seven on the Snake River or nearby.

The rural counties of Idaho continue to lose people to the cities, although farms and ranches continue to get larger. With few exceptions, even the villages continue to lose population to the cities. Two counties had fewer than 850 residents by 1980. Most of the immigration comes from the Western, North Central, and Southern states, whereas the bulk of emigration goes to the West. The population is more than 95 percent white, with only about 3,000 blacks and 39,600 members of other races, including Indians. Almost one-third of the European stock comes from the United Kingdom, Germany, Norway, Sweden, and Denmark, some by way of Canada.

THE STATE'S ECONOMY

In its economic development, Idaho occupies a position between the highly developed and the underdeveloped states. Industrial expansion has been a feature of the 20th century, replacing traditional dependence on agriculture, lumbering, and mining, and by the early 1970s the state had emerged among the top dozen states in tourist income. Government furnishes the second largest portion of Idaho's income. Labour, except in agriculture and small business, is heavily organized.

Agriculture, lumbering, mining, and industry

Traditional economic bases. Huge herds of beef cattle and sheep graze not only in the prairie regions but also among the plateaus of the mountain regions. Of the farm crops, potatoes have become almost synonymous with Idaho, though wheat and other grains, sugar beets, peas, beans, and alfalfa seed are important sources of farm income. More than one-third of the state's area is in forests, and about 1,800,000,000 board feet (4,250,000 cubic metres) of lumber are cut from commercial timber lands each year. Although the discovery of gold and the subsequent gold rush created Idaho's mining industry, gold is no longer important to the state's economy. Idaho, however, ranks among the three leading states in silver, lead, and zinc production. Phosphate mining and processing is important in the southeast.

Power. Hydroelectric power, much of it provided by power stations on the Snake River, is the main source of energy for both business and private users in Idaho. Natural gas and oil have been used increasingly, while waste wood products have declined in importance. The Idaho National Engineering Laboratory near Arco, operated primarily as a research and testing site for nuclear reactors by the federal government, also is used for energy production.

Manufacturing. Value added by, and personal income from, manufacturing exceeds the contributions of agriculture to the economy. Much of it is related to the processing of foods and forest and mining products, however, indicating how dependent the economy remains on primary products.

Transportation. The primitive area in central Idaho and the mountains have made transportation difficult. Idaho has 67,500 miles of roads, but only one major highway connects southern and northern Idaho. Almost all interstate highways that pass through the state run from east to west. Three transcontinental railroads cross the Panhandle, and one railroad serves the southern portion. Geographical conditions influence air travel as well, with many small airfields providing service to remote areas. These airfields are used largely by private and contract fliers. Three scheduled airlines serve a number of commercial airports. Idaho has a water route to the ocean, from Lewiston by way of the Snake and Columbia rivers. Due to slack water that permits oceangoing barges to dock at Lewiston, the city is an important industrial and shipping centre.

ADMINISTRATION AND SOCIAL CONDITIONS

Structure of government. Typical of states admitted to the Union after the Civil War, Idaho has a constitution establishing the usual separation of executive, legislative, and judicial powers but limiting the governor's strength. The constitution is detailed and includes many provisions that rightly belong in the statutes, and though it has been amended more than 90 times and is outdated, the voters rejected a new constitution in 1970.

Executive, legislature, and judiciary

The only change in the government between 1890 and 1914 was the creation of numerous service and regulatory commissions and boards largely independent of the governor. Administrative reorganization after World War I consolidated these agencies in an effort to make them democratically responsive. The Depression of the 1930s brought on dozens of new commissions and boards, however, and the growth has continued. In 1974 the state government was again reorganized. The executive branch consists of six elected officers, independent of the governor, and 19 departments, under which more than 100 boards, commissions, councils, and committees are placed. The legislature meets annually and comprises 35 senators and 70 representatives. Justice is administered by the Supreme Court and seven district courts, and county magistrate's courts. The district courts may originate cases and hear appeals. Civil and criminal cases generally are tried within a short time. This factor may result from the state's relatively low rates of crime against persons or property, which may reflect inadequate reporting or low rates of apprehension.

Voter independence

Politics. Few voters in the nation are as independent as those of Idaho, and party cohesiveness is difficult to maintain. National, state, and local officials elected at one time often show a startling diversity of party and ideological stances. This independence usually is issue oriented in state and national elections and personality oriented in local elections.

In 1892 the Populist Party dominated the state, and in 1918 members of the Nonpartisan League successfully filed as candidates for all major state posts on the Democratic Party ticket and, with one exception, were nominated. Aside from these events, the two major parties have dominated Idaho's political life. The voters have chosen Republican candidates slightly more than half the time, but the crossover vote, usually issue oriented, can swing the outcome of any statewide election. The major crossover vote has historically been a liberal vote, which, when added to either party's normal support, swings an election. The pre-primary party convention has been replaced by open primaries.

Finances. Of Idaho's more than 1,700 units of government, less than one-half have taxing power, and state debt is limited constitutionally to $2,000,000. The difficulty of achieving an equitable base for a sound system of public finance is further increased by federal and state ownership of about 70 percent of Idaho's land area. The state's major revenue comes from personal and corporate income taxes and a sales tax, most of which is returned to public school districts. The state controls virtually no businesses or utilities except liquor sales, and among conditions made favourable to business development is the state's stance as a service rather than as a regulatory agency.

Education. Indian mission schools were supplemented by classes for whites when settlement began during the 1860s, and by the time of statehood the land-grant university had been chartered. The state Department of Education, dating from 1912, supervises appropriated funds, teacher certification, and related functions. The junior college system, begun on a district basis in 1939, became a state function in 1965. The publicly supported University of Idaho (created in 1889 at Moscow), Idaho State University (1901, in Pocatello), and Boise State College (1932), as well as the private College of Idaho (1891, in Caldwell), offer advanced degrees. The University of Idaho is both a college of agriculture and the state's major educational institution, offering bachelor's and advanced degrees in areas that are related to the state's economy—engineering, mining, forestry, and wildlife-and-range science—and in other areas of business, education, and arts and letters.

Living conditions. The electorate of Idaho is generally conservative on economic matters, but the allocations in the social and educational areas are liberal and are endorsed by both parties. In addition, notable achievements have been based on a sense of social ethics, including a superior civil rights law.

Health and welfare

Living standards are relatively high because labour contracts follow national patterns, and living costs are below those of many states. Nearly one-fifth of the state tax revenues goes into public health and public assistance programs.

Although the relative level of health conditions of the state is high, the number of doctors and dentists per 100,000 people is relatively low. Most of the more than 50 hospitals are located in larger cities, but some are in remote areas.

CULTURAL LIFE AND THE FUTURE

The arts. The opera houses in the mining camps, with various types of musical shows and serious drama, were Idaho's first "culture." The missionaries and the churches set the patterns of cultural development for a long period. The University of Idaho has taken a leading role in developing programs in music, art, architecture, creative writing, and theatre. Students who return to small towns—many as teachers, farmers, or foresters—are, in many instances, the only college-educated people in the community, with the exception of the local attorney and physician. Such other institutions of higher learning as Ricks College, Northwest Nazarene College, College of Idaho, Lewis-Clark Normal School (now Lewis-Clark State College), Boise State University, and Idaho State University have developed strong fine arts programs. Although public education leans toward practical subjects and university education toward agriculture, mining, engineering, and forestry, the fine arts are still a major feature of educational curricula.

Although a young state in terms of culture, Idaho has contributed artists with wide reputations, including Vardis Fisher, a novelist whose writing decried dogma and tyranny; and Carol Ryrie Brink, who wrote books for adults and children. Ernest Hemingway wrote many of his books while living in Idaho, which he enjoyed for its wilderness aspects.

All of the colleges and universities have symphony orchestras, choral groups, and theatre programs, and a number of cities—including Boise, Pocatello, and Lewiston—have orchestras. The University of Idaho and the cities of Coeur d'Alene, Lewiston, McCall, and Caldwell have summer theatres. The Idaho Commission on the Arts and Humanities has sponsored and promoted the developments of art exhibits, lectures, literature, films, theatres, and music throughout the state.

Communications. By 1980 Idaho had 14 daily newspapers, 56 weekly papers, 72 radio stations, and 8 commercial television stations, though out-of-state papers and television stations from Spokane, Washington; Salt Lake City, Utah; and Portland, Oregon, furnish strong competition. The *Idaho Statesman*, covering the Boise Valley, is the oldest and largest of the newspapers. Educational television stations broadcast regularly from Moscow, Boise, and Pocatello.

PROSPECTS

Idaho has largely avoided the slums, the increasing crime, and the alarming delinquency that so often characterize urbanization and cultural conflicts, but it increasingly has become a part of the larger national culture. Manufacturing and tourism have risen in importance, and as a result, people seeking jobs, land, and a more leisurely way of life have immigrated to the state. These groups tend, however, to accentuate the sectionalism between geographical regions and between rural and urban Idaho. As new industries continue to move into the state, environmental issues are likely to become major concerns, although much legislation has been passed to restrict both water and air pollution. Creativity in public affairs is needed to accommodate the increasing demands for health, educational, and public-assistance services that require funding far beyond the capacity of the tax structure.

BIBLIOGRAPHY. MERRILL D. BEAL and MERLE W. WELLS, *History of Idaho*, 3 vol. (1960), the most complete history of Idaho; JAMES H. HAWLEY, *History of Idaho*, 4 vol. (1920), a detailed account of Idaho politics from 1890 to 1919, written by a former governor; BOYD A. MARTIN, RAY C. JOLLY, and GLENN W. NICHOLS (eds.), *State and Local Government in Idaho: A Reader* (1970), thorough coverage of state and local government; *Idaho Blue Book* (annual), an expanded report on the secretary of state, including some history, election returns, and the names of all public officers of state and local governments; *The Idaho Almanac: Territorial Centennial Edition, 1863–1963* (n.d.), a special edition providing encyclopaedic coverage for these 100 years; ROBERT I. VEXLER, *Chronology and Documentary Handbook of Idaho* (1978), a concise reference of basic data on the state; M.S. GHAZANFAR, *Idaho Statistical Abstract*, 3rd ed. (1980), a ready reference to state statistics.

(B.A.M.)

Idealism

As a philosophical term, Idealism refers to any view that stresses the central role of the ideal or the spiritual in human interpretation of experience. It may hold that the world or reality is essentially a spirit or consciousness, that abstractions and laws are more fundamental in reality than sensory things, or, at least, that whatever exists is known in dimensions that are chiefly mental—through and as ideas. Thus its two basic forms are metaphysical Idealism, which asserts the ideality of reality, and epistemological Idealism, which holds that in the knowledge process the mind can grasp only the psychic or that its objects are conditioned by their perceptibility. In its metaphysics, Idealism is thus directly opposed to Materialism, which retains the view that the basic substance of the world is matter and that it is known primarily through and as material forms and processes; and in its epistemology, it is opposed to Realism, which holds that in human knowledge all objects are grasped and seen as they really are—in their existence outside and independently of the mind. As a philosophy often expressed in bold and expansive syntheses, Idealism is also opposed to various restrictive forms of thought: to Skepticism, with occasional exceptions as in the British Hegelian F.H. Bradley (1846–1924); to Positivism, which stresses observable facts and relations rather than ultimates and therefore spurns the speculative "pretensions" of every metaphysic; and often to atheism, since the Idealist commonly extrapolates the concept of mind to embrace an infinite Mind. The essential orientation of Idealism can be sensed through some of its typical tenets: "Truth is the whole, or the Absolute"; "to be is to be perceived"; "reality reveals its ultimate nature more faithfully in its highest qualities (mental) than in its lowest (material)"; "the Ego is both subject and object."

Contrasts with opposing schools

APPROACHES TO UNDERSTANDING IDEALISM

Idealism may be clarified by approaching it in three ways: through its basic doctrines and principles, through its central questions and answers, and through its major arguments.

Basic doctrines and principles. Six common, basic conceptions distinguish Idealistic philosophy:

The union of individuality and universality. Abstract universals, such as "canineness," which express the common nature or essence that the members of a class (*i.e.*, individual dogs or wolves) share with one another, are acknowledged by all philosophers. Many Idealists, however, emphasize the concept of a concrete universal, one that is also a concrete reality, such as "mankind" or "literature," which can be imagined as gatherable into one specific thing. As opposed to the fixed, formal, abstract universal, the concrete universal is essentially dynamic, organic, and developing. Thus universality and individuality merge.

Six core concepts

The contrast between contemporaneity and eternity. While most philosophers tend to centre on matters of contemporary concern, Idealists always seek a much wider perspective that includes epochs and eras in the broad sweep of history. In the words of the 17th-century Rationalist Spinoza, they strive to view the contemporary world "under the aspect of eternity." Thus, in spite of the extensive formative influence of culture, Idealists claim that their philosophy transcends the parochialism of a particular culture; and Idealisms are found in all of the major cultures of the world.

The doctrine of internal relations and the coherence theory of truth. It seems natural to suppose, as non-Idealists usually do, that the consideration of two things in their relatedness to one another can have no effect on the things themselves—*i.e.*, that a relation is something in addition to the things or terms related and is thus external. On this basis truth would be defined as a relation of correspondence between a proposition and a state of affairs. The Idealist believes, however, that reality is more subtle than this. The relationship between a mineral deposit and the business cycle, for example, is an internal one: the deposit changes to an ore when prices render it profitable to mine the mineral. Similarly, it is part of the essence of a brick that it is related to a wall or pavement. Thus terms and relations logically determine one another. Ultimate reality is therefore a system of judgments or propositions, and truth is defined in terms of the coherence of these propositions with one another to form a harmonious whole. Thus a successful spy is judged either a hero or a villain only in relation to a total system of international relations, an accepted philosophy of history, and the moral judgments involved. There are therefore degrees of reality and degrees of truth within a system of truth cohering by internal relations, and the truth of a judgment reflects its place in this system.

The dialectical method. Idealism seeks to overcome contradictions by penetrating into the overall coherent system of truth and continually creating new knowledge to be integrated with earlier discoveries. Idealism is thus friendly to all quests for truth, whether in the natural or behavioral sciences or in art, religion, and philosophy. It seeks the truth in every positive judgment and in its contradictory as well. Thus it uses the dialectical method of reasoning to remove the contradictions characteristic of human knowledge. Such removal leads to a new synthetic judgment that incorporates in a higher truth the degree of truth that was present in each of the two lower judgments.

The centrality of mind in knowledge and being. Idealism is not reductive, as are opposing philosophies that identify mind with matter and reduce the higher level of reality to the protons and electrons of mathematical physics. On the contrary, Idealism defends the principle that the lower is explained by the higher—specifically, that matter can be explained by mind but that mind cannot be explained by matter. The word spirit can be substituted for "mind" or even placed above it; and "Spiritualism" is often used, especially in Europe, as a synonym for Idealism.

The transmutation of evil into good. Nearly all Idealists accept the principle that the evils with which man has to deal may become ingredients in a larger whole that overcomes them. The eminent American Hegelian Josiah Royce (1855–1916) held that the larger whole is the Absolute Mind, which keeps evils under control as a man might hold a viper under the sole of his boot. Along with this doctrine of the sublimation or transmutation of evil, Royce incorporated into his metaphysics a point from the 19th-century irrationalism of Schopenhauer, itself a voluntaristic form of Idealism, viz., that "the world is my idea." Schopenhauer, however, was probably the only Idealist who defended the converse principle that good is transmuted into evil.

Basic questions and answers. In defining philosophical Idealism in its historical development as a technical metaphysical doctrine, three most difficult and irreducible questions arise. From the efforts to answer these questions there has been created an extensive literature that is the corpus of philosophical Idealism.

Metaphysical and logical issues

Ultimate reality. The first of the three questions is metaphysical: What is the ultimate reality that is given in human experience? Historically, answers to this question have fallen between two extremes. On the one hand is the Skepticism of the 18th-century Empiricist David Hume, who held that the ultimate reality given in experience is the moment by moment flow of events in the consciousness of each individual. This concept compresses all of reality into a solipsistic specious present—the momentary sense experience of one isolated percipient. At the other extreme, followers of the 17th-century Rationalist Spinoza adopted his definition of ultimate substance as that which can exist and can be conceived only by itself. According to the first principle of his system of pantheistic Idealism, God, or Nature, or Substance is the ultimate reality given in human experience. Hegel said that this dogmatic absolutism was the lion's den into which all tracks enter and from which none ever returns. In answering the first question, most philosophical Idealists steer between Hume and Spinoza and in so doing create a number of types of Idealism, which will be discussed below.

The given. The second question to arise in defining Idealism is: What is given? What results can be obtained from a logical interpretation and elaboration of the given? According to Idealists the result, though it is frequently something external to individual experience, is, nevertheless, a concrete universal, an order system (like the invisible lattice structure of a crystal), or an ideality in the sense explained earlier. In Hegel's words: "What is real is rational, and what is rational is real." Idealists believe that the collective human spirit of intellectual inquiry has discovered innumerable order systems that are present in external, nonhuman reality, or nature, and that this collective creative intelligence has produced the various sciences and disciplines. This production has required a long period of time called history. But history was antedated by the achievements of ancestors who created languages and religions and other primitive institutions. Consequently, the logical interpretation and elaboration of the given is actually the complete transformation of the earth by its various inhabitants; so that the moon flights portend a similar transformation of the planetary system. An inherent part of the collective intelligence is the spiritual force that Idealists call the spirit of philosophy.

Change. The third question is: What position or attitude is a thinker to take toward temporal becoming and change, and toward the presence of ends and values within the given? According to Idealists, reason not only discovers a coherent order in nature but also creates the state and other cultural institutions, which together constitute the cultural order of a civilized society. Idealistic political philosophers recognize the primacy of this cultural order over the private order or family and over the public order—the governing agencies and economic institutions. The conservation and enhancement of the values of all three orders is the basic moral objective of every civilized people. A useful distinction drawn by the German philosopher Ernst Cassirer (1874–1946), a member of the late 19th- and 20th-century Marburg school of Neo-Kantianism (see below), between the efficient energies and the formative energies of a people emphasizes the way in which these moral forces function: the efficient energies are the conserving, and the formative are the creative forces in society. It is on the basis of this distinction that Idealists have made a contribution to international ethics, which charges that no nation has a right to use its efficient energies to exercise power over another civilized people except to further the formative energies of that people, to enrich their cultural order. Ethically, then, there can be no power over without power for; economic exploitation is wrong.

Order and value in nature and society

Modern Idealists have also created an Idealistic philosophy of history. An eminent early 20th-century Italian Idealist, Benedetto Croce (1866–1952), expressed it in the formula "every true history is contemporary history"; and at the same time in France a subjective Idealist, Léon Brunschvicg (1869–1944), agreed. There are close relations between the philosophy of history and the philosophy of values.

Basic arguments. Idealists delight in arguments. They agree with Socrates and Plato in thinking that every philosopher should follow the argument wherever it leads, and like them, they believe that it will eventually lead to some type of Idealism. Four basic arguments found in the literature of Idealism may be briefly summarized.

Epistemological issues

The esse est percipi (to be is to be perceived) argument of Berkeley. According to this argument all of the qualities attributed to objects are sense qualities. Thus hardness is the sensing of a resistance to a striking action, and heaviness is a sensation of muscular effort when holding the object in one's hand, just as blueness is a quality of visual experience. But these qualities exist only while they are being perceived by some subject or spirit equipped with sense organs. A classical 18th-century British Empiricist, George Berkeley (1685–1753), rejected the idea that sense perceptions are caused by material substance, the existence of which he denied. Intuitively he grasped the truth that "to be is to be perceived." The argument is a simple one, but it has provoked an extensive and complicated literature, and to some contemporary Idealists it seems irrefutable.

The reciprocity argument. Closely related to the *esse est percipi* argument is the contention that subject and object are reciprocally dependent upon each other. It is impossible to conceive of a subject without an object, since the essential meaning of being a subject is being aware of an object and that of being an object is being an object to a subject, this relation being absolutely and universally reciprocal. Consequently, every complete reality is always a unity of subject and object—*i.e.*, an immaterial ideality, a concrete universal.

The mystical argument. In the third argument, the Idealist holds that in man's most immediate experience, that of his own subjective awareness, the intuitive self can achieve a direct apprehension of ultimate reality, which reveals it to be spiritual. Thus the mystic bypasses normal cognition, feeling that, for metaphysical probings, the elaborate processes of mediation interposed between sense objects and their perceptions reduces its reliability as compared to the direct grasp of intuition.

It is significant that the claims of this argument have been made by numerous thinkers, in varying degrees Idealistic and mystical, living in different periods and in different cultures. In ancient Greece, for example, it was made by Plato, to whom the final leap to the Idea of the Good was mystical in nature. In Indian Hindu Vedānta philosophy it was made by the 9th-century monistic theologian Śánkara, by the 12th-century dualistic Brahmin theist Rāmānuja, and by the recent philosopher-president of India Sarvepalli Radhakrishnan. In Buddhism the claims were made by the sometimes mystical, extreme subjectivism of the Vijñānavāda school of Mahāyāna (represented by Aśvaghoṣa in the 1st and Asaṅga in the 4th century) and in China by the Ch'an school and by the 7th-century scholar Hui-neng, author of its basic classic *The Platform Scripture.* In Islāmic lands it was made by Ṣūfīs (mystics)—in particular, by the 13th-century Persian writer Jalāl ad-Dīn ar-Rūmī. And in the recent West it was made by several distinguished Idealists: in Germany, by the seminal modern theologian Friedrich Schleiermacher (1768–1834); in France, by the evolutionary intuitionist Henri Bergson (1859-1941), by the philosopher of action Maurice Blondel (1861–1949), and by the Jewish religious Existentialist Martin Buber (1878–1965); and in English-speaking countries, by the Scottish metaphysician James Frederick Ferrier (1808–64) and the American Hegelian William E. Hocking (1873–1966).

The ontological argument. This famous argument originated as a proof of the existence of God. It came to the 11th-century Augustinian, St. Anselm of Canterbury, as an intuitive insight from his personal religious experience that a being conceived to be perfect must necessarily exist, for otherwise he would lack one of the essentials of perfection. God's perfection requires his existence. Some Idealist philosophers have generalized the argument to prove Idealism. They distinguish conceptual essences that exist only in the intellect from categorial essences that actually exist *in re* (in the thing). Every actual reality, therefore, is a unity of one or more categorial essences and existence; and again, this means that it is an immaterial ideality or concrete universal. According to Hegel "the ideality of the finite" is "the main principle of philosophy."

TYPES OF PHILOSOPHICAL IDEALISM

Several types of Idealism have already been distinguished. Some modern types should now be mentioned, classified first by cultures and then by branches of philosophy.

Types classed by culture. Cultural differences suggest a division into Western and Oriental Idealisms.

Subjective, transcendental, objective, and absolute Idealisms

Western types. Berkeley's Idealism is called subjective Idealism because he reduced reality to spirits (his name for subjects) and the ideas entertained by spirits. In Berkeley's philosophy the apparent objectivity of the world outside the self was accommodated to his subjectivism by claiming that its objects are ideas in the mind of God. The foundation for a series of more objective Idealisms was laid in the late 18th century by Immanuel Kant, whose epochal work *Kritik der reinen Vernunft* (2nd ed., 1787; Eng. trans., *Critique of Pure Reason,* 1929) presented a formalistic or transcendental Idealism, so named because Kant thought that the human self, or "transcendental ego," constructs knowledge out of sense impressions, upon which are imposed certain universal concepts that he called categories. Three systems constructed in the early 19th century by, respectively, the moral Idealist J.G. Fichte, the aesthetic Idealist F.W.J. Schelling, and the dialectical Idealist G.W.F. Hegel, all on a foundation laid by Kant, are called objective Idealisms in contrast to Berkeley's subjective Idealism. The designations, however, are not consistent; and when the contrast with Berkeley is not at issue, Fichte himself is often called a subjective Idealist, inasmuch as he exalted the subject above the object, employing the term Ego to mean God in the two memorable propositions: "The Ego posits itself" and "The Ego posits the non-Ego (or nature)." And in contrast now to the subjective Idealism of Fichte, Schelling's is called an objective Idealism and Hegel's an absolute Idealism.

All of these terms form backgrounds for contemporary Western Idealisms, most of which are based either on Kant's transcendental Idealism or on those of Fichte, Schelling, and Hegel. Exceptions are those based on other great Idealists of the past—Plato, Plotinus, Spinoza, Leibniz, and others. A revised form of Spinoza's spiritual monism, for example, which held that reality is one Substance to be identified with God, has been formulated by the Idealist logician H.H. Joachim (1868–1938), a follower of the British Hegelian F.H. Bradley.

Kantian and theistic Idealisms

Unwilling to accept any of the above titles, one school of modern Idealists adopted the motto "Back to Kant" and are thus called Kantian Idealists. Edward Caird (1835–1908), who imported German Idealism into England, and the German philosopher of "As If," Hans Vaihinger (1852–1933), who held that much of man's so-called knowledge reduces to pragmatic fictions, were Kantian Idealists or transcendentalists. On this tradition are based the Idealism of the austerely religious essayist Thomas Carlyle (1795–1881) in *Sartor Resartus* (1833–34) and the New England transcendentalism of Ralph Waldo Emerson (1803–82). It must be stated, however, that Kant preferred the name critical Idealism to that of transcendental Idealism.

Another group of Idealists, adopting the motto "From Kant forward," founded the so-called Marburg school of Neo-Kantian, or scientific, Idealism. They rejected the Idealisms of Fichte, Schelling, and Hegel and the classical Newtonian dynamics presupposed by Kant and built instead upon the new quantum and relativity theories of modern physics. Founded by Hermann Cohen (1842–1918), champion of a new interpretation of Kant, and his colleague, the Platonic scholar Paul Natorp (1854–1924), who applied Kant's critical method to humanistic as well as to scientific studies, this school underwent a remarkable development, especially under the leadership of Ernst Cassirer, noted for his profound analyses of man defined as that animal that creates culture through a unique capacity for symbolic representation. The Russian novelist Boris Pasternak, in his *Autobiography,* tells of enrolling in Cohen's graduate seminar on Kant at the University of Marburg. Undoubtedly this type of Idealism continues to wield considerable influence on intellectuals in Soviet Russia.

Theistic Idealism was founded by the medical instructor R.H. Lotze (1817–81), who became a broadly learned metaphysician and whose theory of the world ground, in which all things find their unity, has been widely accepted by theistic philosophers and Protestant theologians. To Lotze, the world ground is the transcendent synthesis of an evolutionary world process, which is both mechanical and teleological (purposive); it is an infinite spiritual being, or God. In England, the absolute Idealism of T.H. Green (1836–82), a philosopher influenced chiefly by Plato and Kant, was shared by his disciple, the more Hegelian thinker Bernard Bosanquet (1848–1923), whose views are based upon Lotze's Idealism, and by the somewhat skeptical metaphysician of the movement, F.H. Bradley (1846–1924).

Theistic absolutism is represented by a pioneer of contemporary philosophical theology, F.R. Tennant (1866–

1957), and by the eminent German-American theologian Paul Tillich (1886–1956). It differs from the personalistic form of absolute Idealism in accepting the traditional theological monotheism that is essential to the Jewish, Christian, and Islāmic religions. It revives classic arguments for the existence of God that were rejected by Kant and uses recent advances in the physical, biological, and behavioral sciences to support these revisions. The cosmological argument, for example, is restated as the continuing relation of the cosmos to a world ground that is spiritual in essence; thus the concept of God as a first cause is rejected. The concept of the fitness of the environment to life and to human history and other recent scientific concepts are used to modernize the teleological argument. Nevertheless, all of this revision is kept within the framework of Idealistic metaphysics and epistemology. A theistic spiritual pluralism, which interprets reality in terms of a multitude of interacting psychic monads (elementary units), was developed by the English philosopher James Ward (1843–1925). On the other hand, an atheistic spiritual pluralism, which holds that reality consists entirely of individual minds and their contents, was espoused by the Cambridge Hegelian J.M. Ellis McTaggert (1866–1925).

Hegelian Idealism, Personalism, and other Idealisms

During the late 19th century a movement known as American Hegelian Idealism (see HEGELIANISM: *Development and diffusion of Hegelianism in the later 19th century*) arose in the United States. The movement found vigorous early expression in the work of W.T. Harris (1835–1909), central figure in a midwestern group of scholars known as the St. Louis school and editor of its *Journal of Speculative Philosophy*, and finds current expression in the recently organized Hegel Society of America. In its later development, American Idealism split into two branches: one, of the aforementioned Bradley–Bosanquet type, and a second, of the Royce–Hocking type, so-called because it was founded by one of America's most distinguished philosophers, the absolute Idealist and personal pantheist Josiah Royce (1855–1916) and developed by his disciple W.E. Hocking (1873–1966). The American philosopher of religion Borden Parker Bowne (1847–1910) founded another important American school, that of Personalism, a Kantian- and Lotzean-based variety of theistic Idealism similar to the spiritual pluralism of Ward. Whereas most previous Idealisms had stressed the rational as the highest category of reality and hence as its paradigm, Personalism saw in the centred structures of personhood, both finite and infinite, an even higher category, displaying dimensions richer than the rational alone. Personalism has had an influential development in America, most notably through the Methodist philosopher E.S. Brightman (1884–1953), known for his defense of the doctrine of a finite God, and through *The Personalist*, edited by one of Bowne's disciples, R.T. Flewelling (1871–1960). Personalism is also found in the French philosopher C.B. Renouvier (1815–1903) and in several Latin American philosophers.

To the above types should be added the vitalism or creative evolutionism of the French anti-intellectualist Henri Bergson (1859–1941), which first found in the apprehension of subjective time a more valid insight into reality than in that of an objective space-time order and then, extending this metaphysics to the cosmic level, discerned there an Idealistic *élan vital* (or vital impetus) that is more fundamental than matter, which subsequently appeared in the role of a husk born of the mechanization of the *élan*. In this same tradition, the voluntarism of Maurice Blondel (1861–1949), a unique theory of belief in God as a live option that must be deliberately willed by the self before it can be found to be true in experience, is an important contribution to Idealistic philosophy. Miguel de Unamuno y Jugo (1864–1936), a Spanish philosopher, developed a unique type of Idealism, more literary than philosophical. He stressed the significance of each individual and argued for personal immortality (see EXISTENTIALISM; PHENOMENOLOGY).

Eastern types. For centuries, philosophical Idealism has dominated the philosophy of India. An Idealism that is quite influential in Japan is that of Nishida Kitarō, a distinguished Berlin-trained philosopher. Prior to World War II, Kitarō created a system of absolute Idealism that employed the dialectical method of Hegel to clarify the Zen Buddhist doctrine of nothingness, which, in his view, is that of which all phenomenal existences are determinations and in which they all appear.

Some classical types of Indian and Chinese Idealism were considered above (see *The mystical argument*). A number of gifted Indian and Chinese scholars have restated and revitalized the principles and arguments of classic Oriental Idealisms in an extensive literature.

Indian Idealism

Probably the major recent proponent of Indian Idealism has been Radhakrishnan, who has spent a long lifetime expounding and defending its mystical types and has presented authoritative analyses of all of its classical systems. He saw his modernized Idealism as destined to save civilization from exploitation by Western commercial technology. Surendranath Dasgupta, an outstanding Sanskrit and Pāli scholar, in a monumental work, has revived the classic systems of Indian Idealism, concluding that "Idealism has not only been one of the most dominant phases of Indian thought in metaphysics, epistemology, and dialectics, but it has also very largely influenced the growth of the Indian ideal as a whole." Ghose Aurobindo, reinterpreting the Indian Idealistic heritage in the light of his own Western education, rejected the *māyā* doctrine of illusion, replacing it with the concept of evolution. Arguing that the "illumination of individuals will lead to the emergence of a divine community," Aurobindo founded the influential Pondicherry Ashram, a religious and philosophical community, and headed it until his death. Late in the 19th century, Swami Vivekananda, a spiritual monist, promulgated the Idealistic philosophy of mystical Brahmanism in lectures on the Vedānta delivered and published widely.

The inwardness of subjectivity of Indian Idealism has been contrasted with the outwardness of Western objective Idealism, and a synthesis of the two has been advocated in comparative studies made by P.T. Raju, an Indian philosopher who has taught both in Indian universities and in the U.S.

Prior to World War II, Sir Rabindranath Tagore, a distinguished Hindu Idealist poet and Nobel laureate, contributed to what Dasgupta has called the "Indian ideal as a whole." A selection from Tagore's aphorisms will convey its spirit:

> Let your life lightly dance on the edges of Time like dew on the tip of a leaf.
> Our little heaven, where dwell only two immortals, is too absurdly narrow.
> Is it then true that the mystery of the Infinite is written on this little forehead of mine?
> Where is this hope for union except in thee my God?
> Raise my veil and look at my face proudly, O Death, my Death.
> All is done and finished in the eternal Heaven. But Earth's flowers of illusion are kept externally fresh by death.
> If my claims to immortal fame after death are shattered, make me immortal while I live.
> This I know that the moment my God has created me he has made himself mine.

Chinese Idealism

In addition to the Ch'an and Hui-neng schools mentioned above (see *The mystical argument*), three other notable Idealistic schools have flourished in China. Representing one wing of the Neo-Confucian movement of the 11th and 12th centuries, Ch'eng Hao and his disciple, the rationalist Chu Hsi, developed a dualistic philosophy that has been compared to Cartesianism. In this view, however, reason takes precedence over matter and the two together are the primary cause of the universe or the absolute; thus this view is essentially Idealistic. At the turn of the 15th century, a more purely Idealistic school arose—forming the other wing of Neo-Confucianism—under the leadership of Wang Yang-ming, who, having had an inner experience of enlightenment, sought to understand the cosmos within his own mind and heart. The third school is that of the 20th-century Idealist Hsung Shih-li, who, borrowing to some extent from Wang Yang-ming, proclaimed a "new doctrine of consciousness only," of which the basic ideas are the unity of substance and function and the primacy of the original Mind. To Hsung Shih-li, reality and all of its manifestations are one, and the original Mind is will and consciousness as well as reason.

Types classed by branches of philosophy. Another way of classifying Idealisms is to use branches of philosophy to distinguish the various types. Such types, however, overlap those given above.

Metaphysical, epistemological, and axiological Idealisms

A term that covers several of the above types (the spiritual, theistic, and Hegelian; Personalism; vitalism) is metaphysical Idealism. A.N. Whitehead (1861–1947), noted for his collaboration with Bertrand Russell in mathematical logic and for his process metaphysics, who was profoundly influenced by Bradley, created an original Idealistic philosophy of science, a highly complicated form of metaphysical Idealism; and the leading metaphysician Charles A. Hartshorne (1897–   ) may be regarded as a representative of Whiteheadian Idealism, although rightly claiming originality. Epistemological Idealism, of which the Kantian scholar N.K. Smith's (1872–1958) *Prolegomena to an Idealist Theory of Knowledge* is an excellent example, covers all Idealistic theories of epistemology, or knowledge. Aesthetic Idealism is devoted to philosophical theories of beauty in nature and in all forms of art. Because Schelling claimed that art is the best approach to an understanding of philosophy, his system is designated aesthetic Idealism. Axiological Idealism is a name referring to such philosophies as those of Wilbur M. Urban (1873–1952) and others who have developed Idealistic theories of value and valuation. Ethical Idealism deals with moral values, rights, and obligations. Several of the above-mentioned philosophers, such as Fichte and Green, as well as the Plato scholar A.E. Taylor (1864–1945), the theistic pluralist Hastings Rashdall (1858–1924), and the absolutist W.R. Sorley (1855–1935), could be called ethical Idealists in the sense that they have produced well-thought-out systems of ethics. The writings of the German philosopher of life and action Rudolf Eucken (1846–1926) provide an excellent example of ethical Idealism.

These classifications are not exhaustive. The actual existence of so many types of philosophical Idealism, however, proves its fertility and ubiquity.

CRITICISM AND APPRAISAL

Obviously, some of the types of Idealism in the above classifications conflict with one another. For example, spiritual monism and spiritual pluralism are opposite types; Personalism rejects absolute Idealism; and atheistic spiritual pluralism is in sharp conflict with theistic spiritual pluralism. These and other debatable issues keep Idealists in dialogue with each other, but each type tends to preserve itself.

Perry, Moore, Positivism, Marxism

Over against these internal disputes stand the criticisms of the anti-Idealists. The wide-ranging Realist Ralph Barton Perry's (1876–1957) article "The Ego-Centric Predicament" (1910), is a widely discussed criticism. Perry admitted that the primary approach of every philosopher to the problem of ultimate reality must be through his own thought, using his own ideas; but this is a human predicament that has been unjustifiably exploited by the Idealists, according to Perry, and turned into the "fallacious" *esse est percipi* argument.

The famous "Refutation of Idealism" prepared by the meticulous Cambridge philosopher G.E. Moore (1873–1958) and a similar refutation by the Realist Bertrand Russell (1872–1970) rest upon the distinction between a subject's act of perceiving and the perceptual object of this act, which they both called a "sense datum." They claimed that Berkeley's *esse est percipi* argument is vitiated by his failure to make this distinction.

Logical Positivism claims that a basic weakness in Idealism is its rejection of the doctrine of empirical verifiability, according to which every proposition that claims to be true must be verified by searching out the sense experience in which its terms originated. Linguistic philosophy attacks Idealism by making a detailed analysis of its more technical terms in an effort to prove that they are full of ambiguities and double meanings. Critics have also severely attacked the ontological and the mystical arguments for Idealism. Karl Marx (1818–83) and his followers borrowed and adapted the dialectical argument of Hegel and used it effectively to develop dialectical Materialism, an archenemy of all Idealisms. Buttressed by the political endorsements of various Communist regimes, Marxism (*q.v.*) poses a formidable opposition to Idealism; and even in the non-Communist countries of Europe it presents a significant cultural alternative to spiritualism and Thomism.

Idealists consider all of the foregoing criticisms to be external. Instead of answering them in detail, some Idealists prefer to challenge the critics to make really constructive efforts to build an adequate substitute for Idealism—a system to be reached by seriously working at the problems from within philosophy. So far a satisfactory substitute has not been achieved. To produce such a substitute would require careful reconsideration of the arguments of at least some of the above Idealistic systems.

Prognosis

In evaluating the effects of these criticisms and attacks, the question remains: Will they succeed in eradicating philosophical Idealism? Although it is now on the wane, at least in Western culture, the great Idealist tradition has survived many other historic periods of turmoil and has often been reborn in prolonged periods of settled and peaceful social conditions. Will it rise again? Only the future holds the answer. But Idealism shows evidence of being, perhaps, a reflection of some permanent aspect of the human spirit, and it may then be a perennial philosophy. In any case, it seems highly unlikely that such a rich heritage of philosophical thought will vanish entirely.

BIBLIOGRAPHY. The two best books on Idealism in English are A.C. EWING, *Idealism: A Critical Survey* (1933); and R.F.A. HOERNLE, *Idealism as a Philosophy* (1927). A.C. EWING (ed.), *The Idealist Tradition from Berkeley to Blanshard* (1957), is a useful volume containing selections from the texts of the major Idealists and selected criticisms of Idealism. Other important collections are C. BARRETT (ed.), *Contemporary Idealism in America* (1932); J.H. MUIRHEAD (ed.), *Contemporary British Philosophy: Personal Statements*, First–Second Series, 2 vol. each (1924); and G.P. ADAMS and W.P. MONTAGUE (eds.), *Contemporary American Philosophy*, 2 vol. (1930). Works on the history and theory of the subject include: B. BLANSHARD, *Reason and Analysis* (1962), a careful critical examination of schools of philosophy opposed to Idealism; G.W. CUNNINGHAM, *The Idealistic Argument in Recent British and American Philosophy* (1933), a thorough and dependable treatise; S.N. DASGUPTA, *Indian Idealism* (1933); NICOLAI HARTMANN, *Die Philosophie des Deutsches Idealismus*, vol. 1, *Fichte, Schelling, und die Romantik* (1923), vol. 2, *Hegel* (1929), 2nd ed. (1 vol., 1960); A.J.M. MILNE, *The Social Philosophy of English Idealism* (1962); J.H. MUIRHEAD, *The Platonic Tradition in Anglo-Saxon Philosophy: Studies in the History of Idealism in England and America* (1931); P.T. RAJU, *Idealistic Thought of India* (1953); L.S. ROUNER (ed.), *Philosophy, Religion, and the Coming World Civilization: Essays in Honor of William Ernest Hocking* (1966); and A. STERN, *Philosophy of History and the Problem of Values* (1962), a good secondary source.

On the classical systems of Indian philosophy, see S. RADHAKRISHNAN, *Indian Philosophy*, 2 vol. (1923–27), an authoritative exposition; S.N. DASGUPTA, *A History of Indian Philosophy*, 5 vol. (1922–55), an erudite examination of the Sanskrit and Pāli texts; *Indian Idealism* (1933); SRI AUROBINDO, *The Life Divine* (1949), a reinterpretation of the heritage; and SWAMI VIVEKANANDA, *The Yogas and Other Works* (1953), a collection with biography. In *Pragmatism* (1907) and in *The Varieties of Religious Experience* (1902), WILLIAM JAMES quoted Vivekananda at length as a typical representative of spiritual monism. In the *Sacred Books of the East*, 50 vol., ed. by F. MAX MULLER (1879–1910), see especially vol. 1 and 15, *The Upanishads* and vol. 8, *The Bhagavadgîtâ*. In the *Harvard Oriental Series*, 47 vol., ed. by CHARLES ROCKWELL LANMAN (1890–1968), see especially vol. 3, *Buddhism in Translations*, and vol. 17, *The Yoga-System of Patañjali.*

Writings of Idealists are listed in their biographies. P.A. SCHILPP, editor of "The Library of Living Philosophers Series," has issued four important volumes on Idealists: *The Philosophy of Alfred North Whitehead*, 2nd ed. (1951); *The Philosophy of Ernst Cassirer* (1949); *The Philosophy of*

Sarvepalli Radhakrishnan (1962); and *The Philosophy of Martin Buber* (1967); and a volume on Brand Blanshard is in preparation. Other works on Idealists include: J.H. COTTON, *Royce on the Human Self* (1954), one of the best books on Royce; D.S. ROBINSON, *Royce and Hocking: American Idealists* (1968); and GABRIEL MARCEL, *La Métaphysique de Royce* (1945; Eng. trans., 1956), which shows the relation of Marcel to Royce and Hocking. H.T. KIM, "Nishida and Royce," *Philosophy East and West*, 1:18–29 (1952), and "The Logic of the Illogical: Zen and Hegel," *ibid.*, 5:19–29 (1955), are informative accounts of Nishida's contributions to Idealism. The following volumes of the *Revue Internationale de Philosophie* contain valuable bibliographies: *Henri Bergson*, vol. 3 (1948); *Léon Brunschvicg*, vol. 5 (1951); *Hegel*, vol. 6 (1952); *George Berkeley*, vol. 7 (1953); *Benedetto Croce*, vol. 7 (1953); *Kant*, vol. 8 (1954); *Whitehead*, vol. 15 (1961); *Leibniz*, vol. 20 (1966); and *Josiah Royce*, vol. 21 (1967).

(D.S.R.)

Ideology

An ideology is a form of social or political philosophy in which practical elements are as prominent as theoretical ones; it is a system of ideas that aspires both to explain the world and to change it.

ORIGINS AND CHARACTERISTICS OF IDEOLOGY

Ideology in the era of the French Revolution. The word first made its appearance in French as *idéologie* at the time of the French Revolution, when it was introduced by a philosopher, A.L.C. Destutt de Tracy, as a short name for what he called his science of ideas, which he claimed to have adapted from the epistemology of the philosophers John Locke and Étienne Bonnot de Condillac, for whom all human knowledge was knowledge of ideas. The fact is, however, that he owed rather more to the English philosopher Francis Bacon, whom he revered no less than did the earlier French philosophers of the Enlightenment. It was Bacon who had proclaimed that the destiny of science was not only to enlarge men's knowledge but also to "improve the life of men on earth," and it was this same union of the programmatic with the intellectual that distinguished Destutt de Tracy's *idéologie* from those theories, systems, or philosophies that were essentially explanatory. The "science of ideas" was a science with a mission; it aimed at serving men, even saving them, by ridding their minds of prejudice and preparing them for the sovereignty of reason.

Destutt de Tracy and his fellow *idéologues* devised a system of national education that they believed would transform France into a rational and scientific society. Their teaching combined a fervent belief in individual liberty with an elaborate program of state planning, and for a short time under the Directory (1795–99) it became the official doctrine of the French Republic. Napoleon at first supported Destutt de Tracy and his friends, but he soon turned against them, and in December 1812 he even went so far as to attribute blame for France's military defeats to the influence of the *idéologues*, of whom he spoke with scorn.

Thus "ideology" has been from its inception a word with a marked emotive content, though Destutt de Tracy presumably had intended it to be a dry, technical term. Such was his own passionate attachment to the "science of ideas," and such was the high moral worth and purpose he assigned to it, that the word *idéologie* was bound to possess for him a strongly laudatory character. And equally, when Napoleon linked the name of *idéologie* with what he had come to regard as the most detestable elements in Revolutionary thought, he invested the same word with all of his feelings of disapprobation and mistrust. Ideology was, from this time on, to play this double role of a term both laudatory and abusive not only in French but in German, English, Italian, and all the other languages of the world into which it was either translated or transliterated.

Nature of modern ideologies. Some historians of philosophy have called the 19th century the age of ideology, not because the word itself was then so widely used, but because so much of the thought of the time can be distinguished from that prevailing in the previous centuries by features that would now be called ideological. Even so, there is a limit to the extent to which one can speak today of an agreed use of the word. The subject of ideology is a controversial one, and it is arguable that at least some part of this controversy derives from disagreement as to the definition of the word "ideology." One can, however, discern both a strict and a loose way of using it. In the loose sense of the word, ideology may mean any kind of action-oriented theory or any attempt to approach politics in the light of a system of ideas. Ideology in the stricter sense stays fairly close to Destutt de Tracy's original conception, and may be identified by five characteristics: (1) it contains an explanatory theory of a more or less comprehensive kind about human experience and the external world; (2) it sets out a program, in generalized and abstract terms, of social and political organization; (3) it conceives the realization of this program as entailing a struggle; (4) it seeks not merely to persuade but to recruit loyal adherents, demanding what is sometimes called commitment; (5) it addresses a wide public, but may tend to confer some special role of leadership on intellectuals. In this article the noun ideology is used only in its strict sense; the adjective ideological is used to refer to ideology as loosely defined.

Ideology loosely and strictly defined

On the basis of the five features above, then, one can recognize as ideologies systems as diverse as Destutt de Tracy's own science of ideas, the Positivism of the French philosopher August Comte, Communism and several other types of Socialism, Fascism, Nazism, and certain kinds of nationalism. That all these "-isms" belong to the 19th or 20th century may suggest that ideologies are no older than the word itself—that they belong essentially to a period in which secular faith has increasingly replaced traditional religious faith.

Ideology and religion. Ideologies, in fact, are sometimes spoken of as if they belonged to the same logical category as religions. Both are assuredly in a certain sense "total" systems, concerned at the same time with questions of truth and questions of conduct; but the differences between ideologies and religions are perhaps more important than the similarities. A religious theory of reality is constructed in terms of a divine order and is seldom, like that of the ideologist, centred on this world alone. A religion may present a vision of a just society, but it cannot easily have a practical political program. The emphasis of religion is on faith and worship; its appeal is to inwardness and its aim the redemption or purification of the human spirit. An ideology speaks to the group, the nation, or the class. Some religions acknowledge their debt to revelation, whereas ideology always believes, however mistakenly, that it lives by reason alone. Both, it may be said, demand commitment, but it may be doubted whether commitment has ever been a marked feature of those religions into which a believer is inducted in infancy.

Even so, it is in certain religious movements that the first ideological elements in the modern world can be seen. The city of Florence, which in so many fields witnessed the birth of modernity, produced perhaps the first "ideological" Christian. The attempt of Girolamo Savonarola to construct a puritan utopia was marked by several of the qualities by which one recognizes a modern ideology: Savonarola treated the vision of a Christian community as a model that men should actually seek to realize in the here and now. His method was to dominate the state through an appeal to the populace, and then to use the powers of the state to control both the economy and the private lives of the citizens. The enterprise was given a militant spirit; it was presented by Savonarola as being at one and the same time an outward struggle against papal corruption, the commercial ethos, and Renaissance Humanism, and an inward struggle against worldly ambitions and carnal desires.

Savonarola as an ideologist

Savonarola had numerous followers in his attempt to give Christianity an ideological dimension: he inspired Calvin's Geneva and the Puritan communities of the New World. Indeed, in both the Reformation and the Counter-Reformation, when Christianity was invested with a new militancy and a new intolerance, when a new emphasis was placed on creeds and conversion, religion itself moved that much nearer to ideology.

Ideology in early political thought. The Italian political philosopher Niccolò Machiavelli was one of Savonarola's sharpest critics, but he was also, like him, a precursor of modern ideologists. Historians who speak of him only as an immoralist overlook the extent to which Machiavelli was a man with an ideal—a republican ideal. Rousseau recognized this when he spoke of *The Prince* as a "handbook for republicans." Machiavelli's dream was to see revived in modern Italy a republic as glorious as that of ancient Rome, and he suggested that it could be achieved only by means of a revolution that had the strength of will to liquidate its enemies. Machiavelli was the first to link ideology with terror but he was too much of a political scientist to enact the role of the ideologue.

Ideology in 17th-century England

Seventeenth-century England occupies an important place in the history of ideology. Although there were then no fully fledged ideologies in the strict sense of the term, political theory, like politics itself, began to acquire certain ideological characteristics. The swift movement of revolutionary forces throughout the 17th century created a demand for theories to explain and justify the radical action which was often taken. John Locke's *Two Treatises of Government* (1690) is an outstanding example of literature written to justify the rights of man against absolutism. This growth of abstract theory in the 17th century, this increasing tendency to construct systems and discuss politics in terms of principles, marks the emergence of the ideological style. In political conversation generally it was accompanied by a growing use of concepts such as right and liberty—ideals in terms of which actual policies were judged.

IDEOLOGY AND DETERMINIST PHILOSOPHY

Hegel and Marx. Although the word ideology in the sense derived from Destutt de Tracy's understanding has passed into modern usage, it is important to notice the particular sense that ideology is given in Hegelian and Marxist philosophy, where it is used in a pejorative way. Ideology there becomes a word for what these philosophers also call "false consciousness." Hegel argued that people were instruments of history; they enacted roles which were assigned to them by forces they did not understand; the meaning of history was hidden from them. Only the philosopher could expect to understand things as they were. This Hegelian enterprise of interpreting reality and reconciling the world to itself was condemned by certain critics as an attempt to provide an ideology of the status quo, in that if individuals were indeed mere ciphers whose actions were determined by external forces, then there was little point in trying to change or improve political and other circumstances. This is a criticism Marx took up, and it is the argument he developed in *The German Ideology* and other earlier writings. Ideology in this sense is a set of beliefs with which people deceive themselves; it is theory that expresses what they are led to think, as opposed to that which is true; it is false consciousness.

Marx, however, was not consistent in his use of the word ideology, for he did not always use the term pejoratively, and some of his references to it clearly imply the possibility of an ideology being true. Twentieth-century Marxists, who have generally discarded the pejorative sense of ideology altogether, have been content to speak of Marxism as being itself an ideology. In certain Communist countries "ideological institutes" have been established, and party philosophers are commonly spoken of as party ideologists. Marxism is an excellent example, a paradigm, of an ideology.

The sociology of knowledge. The use of the word ideology in the pejorative sense of false consciousness is found not only in Marx himself but in other exponents of what has come to be known as the sociology of knowledge, including the German sociologists Max Weber and Karl Mannheim, and numerous lesser figures. Few such writers are wholly consistent in their use of the term, but what is characteristic of their approach is their method of regarding idea systems as the outcome or expression of certain interests. In calling such idea systems ideologies, they are treating them as things whose true nature is concealed; they consider the task of sociological research to be the unveiling of what Mannheim called the "life conditions which produce ideologies."

From this perspective, the economic science of Adam Smith, for example, is not to be understood as an independent intellectual construction or to be judged in terms of its truth, consistency, or clarity; rather, it is to be seen as the expression of bourgeois interests, as part of the ideology of capitalism.

The sociology of knowledge in its more recent formulations has sought support in Freudian psychology (notably in borrowing from Freud the concepts of the unconscious and of rationalization), in order to suggest that ideologies are the unconscious rationalizations of class interests. This refinement has enabled sociologists of knowledge to rid their theory of the disagreeable and unscientific element of bald accusation; they no longer have to brand Adam Smith as a deliberate champion of the bourgeois ethos but can see him now as simply the unconscious spokesman of capitalism. At the same time, these same sociologists of knowledge have argued that Freudian psychology is itself no less a form of ideology than is Adam Smith's economics, for Freud's method of psychoanalysis is essentially a technique for adjusting rebellious minds to the demands and constraints of bourgeois society.

Critics of the sociology of knowledge have argued that if all philosophy is ideology, then the sociology of knowledge must itself be an ideology like any other idea system and equally devoid of independent validity; that if all seeming truth is veiled rationalization of interest, then the sociology of knowledge cannot be true. It has been suggested that although Weber and Mannheim inspired most of the work that has been done by sociologists of knowledge, their own writings may perhaps be exempted from this criticism, if only on the ground that neither of them put forward a consistent or unambiguous theory of ideology. Both used the word ideology in different ways at different times. Weber was in part concerned to reverse Marx's theory that all idea systems are products of economic structures, by demonstrating conversely that some economic structures are the product of idea systems (that Protestantism, for example, generated capitalism and not capitalism Protestantism). Mannheim, on the other hand, tried to restore in a more elaborate form Marx's suggestion that ideologies are the product of the social structure. But Mannheim's analysis may have been obscured by his proposal that the word ideology should be reserved for idea systems that are more or less conservative, and the word utopia for idea systems of a more revolutionary or millennarian nature. Mannheim did not, however, remain faithful to this stipulative definition, even in his one book entitled *Ideology and Utopia.*

On the other hand, Mannheim was well aware of the implication of the doctrine that all idea systems have a class basis and a class bias. As a way out of the dilemma he envisaged the possibility of a classless class of intellectuals, a "socially unattached intelligentsia," as he put it, capable of thinking independently by virtue of its independence from any class interest or affiliation. Such a detached group might hope to acquire knowledge that was *not* ideology. This vision of a small elite of superior minds rising above the myths of ordinary society seemed to some readers to put Mannheim closer to Plato than to Marx and to cast new doubts on the claim of the sociology of knowledge to be a science.

IDEOLOGICAL POLITICS AND CIVIL POLITICS

Mannheim's suggestion that intellectuals as a class might be able to rise above ideology is a striking inversion of Napoleon's view that ideology is *par excellence* the work of intellectuals. And Napoleon's view is by no means outdated. A number of modern critics of ideology has sought to defend a conception of politics understood as a practical activity and to defend it against those enthusiastic theorizers whom they speak of as ideologists. There is, of course, a difference in the use of language; whereas Mannheim spoke of ideology in the technical sense belonging to the sociology of knowledge, these critics use the word in the more ordinary sense outlined in the first paragraphs of this article.

Antipathy of ideology and pluralism

Some political theorists see the growth of ideology as a danger to the continued existence of politics itself and have suggested that a civil (nonideological) society is one containing a plurality of groups and individuals who have severally their own interests and aims. The diversity of ends is, then, a defining characteristic of civil society, and although a civil society must have the loyalty of its citizens, such loyalty, according to these theorists, should be instinctive rather than impassioned. A civil society also requires a fair measure of shared adhesion to the same social and moral values; but this is properly a matter of habit, custom, and tradition rather than of the conscious and reasoned adoption of formulated creeds. An equally important feature of civil society is civility, a willingness to tolerate with a decent grace the fact that others have opinions and objectives different from one's own.

Ideology is clearly inimical to such a conception of civil society, for ideologists typically conceive of society as an enterprise with distinctive aims and make the achievement of the aims a dominating enterprise. Ideology, moreover, is not content with habitual and instinctive loyalty; it tries to recruit zealous devotion. It has been argued that ideologists distort the true nature of civil society by trying to remodel it on the lines of an altogether different type of society—namely the religious sect or militant clan.

Ideology, rationalism, and romanticism. If some theorists emphasize the kinship between ideology and various forms of religious enthusiasm, others stress the connection between ideology and what they call rationalism, or the attempt to understand politics in terms of abstract ideas rather than of lived experience. Like Napoleon, some theorists are suspicious of those who think they know about politics because they have read many books; they believe that politics can be learned only by an apprenticeship to politics itself.

Such people are not unsympathetic to political theories, such as Locke's, but they argue that their value resides in the facts that are derived from experience. One of them, Michael Oakeshott in England, has described Locke's theory of political liberty as an "abridgement" of the Englishman's traditional understanding of liberty, and has suggested that once such a conception is uprooted from the tradition that has given it meaning it becomes a rationalistic doctrine or metaphysical abstraction, like the Rights of Man, which were so much talked about after the French Revolution but rarely actually enjoyed, in France or elsewhere.

Whereas Oakeshott has seen ideology as a form of rationalism, an American, Edward Shils, has seen it more as a product of, among other things, romanticism with an extremist character. His argument is that romanticism has fed into and swelled the seas of ideological politics by its cult of the ideal and by its scorn for the actual, especially its scorn for what is mediated by calculation and compromise. Since civil politics demands both compromise and contrivance and calls for a prudent self-restraint and responsible caution, he suggests that civil politics is bound to be repugnant to romanticism. Hence Shils concludes that the romantic spirit is naturally driven towards ideological politics.

Ideology and terror. The "total" character of ideology, its extremism and violence, have been analyzed by other critics, among whom the French philosopher-writer Albert Camus and the Austrian-born British philosopher Sir Karl Popper merit particular attention. Beginning as an Existentialist who subscribed to the view that "the universe is absurd," Camus passed to a personal affirmation of justice and human decency as compelling values to be realized in conduct. An Algerian by birth, Camus also appealed to what he believed to be the "Mediterranean" tradition of moderation and human warmth and joy in living as opposed to the "northern" Germanic tradition of fanatical, puritan devotion to metaphysical abstractions. In his book *L'Homme révolté* (*The Rebel*), he argued that the true rebel is not the man who conforms to the orthodoxy of some revolutionary ideology, but a man who could say "no" to injustice. He suggested that the true rebel would prefer the politics of reform, such as that of modern trade-union socialism, to the totalitarian politics of Marxism or similar movements. The systematic violence of ideology—the *crimes de logique* that were committed in its name—appeared to Camus to be wholly unjustifiable. Hating cruelty, he believed that the rise of ideology in the modern world had added enormously to human suffering. Though he was willing to admit that the ultimate aim of most ideologies was to diminish human suffering, he argued that good ends did not authorize the use of evil means.

Existential critique of ideology

A somewhat similar plea for what he called "piecemeal social engineering" was put forward by Sir Karl Popper, who argued that ideology rests on a logical mistake: namely the notion that history can be transformed into science. In his *Logik der Forschung* (*The Logic of Scientific Discovery*), Popper suggested that the true method of science was not one of observation, hypothesis, and confirmation, but one of conjecture and experiment, in which the concept of falsification played a crucial role. By this concept he meant that in science, there is a continuing process of trial and error; conjectures are put to the test of experiment, and those that are not falsified are provisionally accepted; thus there is no definitive knowledge but only provisional knowledge that is constantly being corrected. Popper saw in the enterprise of ideology an attempt to find certainty in history and to produce predictions on the model of what were supposed to be scientific predictions. Ideologists, he argued, since they have a false notion of what science is, can produce only prophecies, which are quite distinct from scientific predictions and which have no scientific validity whatever. Though Popper was well disposed toward the idea of a "scientific" approach to politics and ethics, he suggested that a full awareness of the importance of trial and error in science would prompt one to look for similar forms of "negative judgment" elsewhere.

By no means are all ideologists explicit champions of violence, but it is characteristic of ideology both to exalt action and to regard action in terms of a military analogy. Some observers have pointed out that one has only to consider the prose style of the founders of most ideologies to be struck by the military and warlike language that they habitually use, including words like struggle, resist, march, victory, and overcome; the literature of ideology is replete with martial expressions. In such a view, commitment to an ideology becomes a form of enlistment so that to become the adherent of an ideology is to become a combatant or partisan.

In the years that followed World War II, a number of ideological writers went beyond the mere use of military language and made frank avowals of their desire for violence. Not that it was a new thing to praise violence. The French political philosopher Georges Sorel, for example, had done so before World War I in his book called *Réflexions sur la violence*. Sorel was usually regarded as being more a Fascist than a Socialist. Sorel also used the word violence in his own special way; by violence he meant passion, not the throwing of bombs and the burning of buildings.

Sartrian ideology

Violence found eloquent champions in several black militant writers of the 1960s, notably the Martinican theorist Frantz Fanon. Moreover, several of the French philosopher Jean-Paul Sartre's dramatic writings turn on the theme that "dirty hands" are necessary in politics and that a man with so-called bourgeois inhibitions about bloodshed cannot usefully serve a revolutionary cause. Sartre's attachment to the ideal of revolution tended to increase as he grew older, and in some of his later writings he suggested that violence might even be a good thing in itself.

In considering Sartre's views on the subject of ideology it must be noted that Sartre sometimes uses the word ideology in a sense peculiarly his own. In an early section of his *Critique de la raison dialectique* (1960), Sartre drew a distinction between philosophies and ideologies in which he reserves the term philosophy for those major systems of thought, such as the Rationalism of Descartes or the Idealism of Hegel, which dominate men's minds at a certain moment in history. He defined an ideology as a minor system of ideas, living on the margin of the genuine philosophy and exploiting the domain of the greater system. What Sartre proposed in his *Critique de la raison dialectique* was a revitalization and modernization of the "major philosophy" of Marxism through the integration of elements drawn from the "ideology," or minor system of Existentialism. What emerged from the book was a theory in which the Existentialist elements are more conspicuous than the Marxist.

Ideology and pragmatism. A distinction is often drawn between the ideological and the pragmatic approach to politics, the latter being understood as the approach that treats particular issues and problems purely on their merits and does not attempt to apply doctrinal, preconceived remedies. Theorists have debated whether or not politics has become less ideological and whether a pragmatic approach is better than an ideological one.

On the first question, there seemed to be good reason for thinking that after the death of Stalin and the repudiation of Stalinism by the Communist Party, the Soviet Union, at least, was becoming more interested in the "pragmatic" concerns of national security and the balance of power and less interested in the ideological aim of fostering universal Communism. This in turn seemed to many to have resulted—in both the U.S. and the Soviet Union—in a shift toward a pragmatic policy of coexistence and a peaceful division of spheres of influence. There were indications in many countries that the old antagonisms between capitalist and socialist ideologies were giving way to a search for techniques for making a mixed economy work more effectively for the good of all.

But while many observers believed that there was much evidence of a decline of ideology in the latter 1950s, others believed that there were equally manifest signs in the following decade of a revival of ideology, if not within the major political parties, then at least among the public generally. Throughout the world various left-wing movements emerged to challenge the whole ethos on which pragmatic politics was based. Not all these ideologies were coherent, and none possessed the elaborate intellectual structure of the 19th-century ideologies; but together they served to demonstrate that the end of ideology was not yet at hand.

As suggested earlier, certain controversies about ideology have to some extent been rooted in the ambiguity of the word itself, and this is perhaps especially relevant to the confrontation between ideology and pragmatism, since the word pragmatism raises problems no less intractable than those involved in connection with the word ideology. In the senses outlined at the beginning of this article, ideology is manifestly not the only alternative to pragmatism in politics, and to reject ideology would not necessarily be to adopt pragmatism. Ordinary language does not yet yield as many words as political science needs to clarify the question, and it becomes necessary to introduce such expressions as belief system, or to name the relevant distinctions, to further the analysis.

Almost any approach to politics constitutes a belief system of one kind or another. Some such belief systems are more structured, more ordered, and generally systematic than others. Though an ideology is a type of belief system, not all belief systems are ideologies. One man's belief system may consist of a congeries of ill-assorted prejudices and inarticulate assumptions. Another's may be the result of deep reflection and careful study. It is sometimes felt to be convenient to speak of a belief system of this latter type as a philosophy or, better, to distinguish it from philosophy in the technical or academic sense, as a *Weltanschauung* (literally, a "view of the world").

The confrontation between ideology and pragmatism may be more instructive if it is translated into a distinction between the ideological and the pragmatic, taking these two adjectives as extremes on a sliding scale. From this perspective, it becomes possible to speak of differences of degree, to speak of an approach to politics as being more or less ideological, more or less pragmatic. At the same time it becomes possible to speak of a belief system such as liberalism as lending itself to a variety of forms, tending at the one extreme toward the ideological, and at the other toward the pragmatic.

IDEOLOGY AND INTERNATIONAL RELATIONS

It has been said that ideology has transformed international relationships in the 20th century—in appearance at least. Earlier centuries experienced dynastic wars, national, civil, and imperial wars, and diplomacy designed to further national security or national expansion or to promote mutual advantages and general peace. Such factors, indeed, appeared to govern international relations until recent times. International relations today are seemingly dominated more often than not by the exigencies of "-isms": wars are fought, alliances are made, and treaties are signed because of ideological considerations. The balance of power in the contemporary world is a balance weighted by ideological commitment. "The Communist bloc" confronts "the Free peoples"; and in the "Third World," emergent nations cultivate a nationalist, anticolonialist ideology in their search for identity and their efforts to achieve modernity.

Dominance of contemporary international relations by ideology

But this is not to assert that ideological wars, or ideological diplomacy, are entirely new. What has become the most conspicuous element in contemporary international relations—so conspicuous that other elements are often entirely ignored—was present, to a lesser degree, in earlier international relations. It is necessary here to distinguish between the actual events of history and the interpretations that are put on history, for some events lend themselves more readily than others to an ideological interpretation. The ideological perspective has become increasingly significant as the general public has come to play a role in considering questions of war and peace. When questions of defense and diplomacy were settled by kings and their ministers and wars were fought by professional soldiers and sailors, the public was not expected to have any opinion about international relations, and in such a situation there was little place for ideology.

Ideology in the World Wars. In the course of World War I, however, a new element appeared to have been introduced. The war was seen by those who experienced it as being in its early stages a national war of the traditional kind, and as such it was not at first expected to assume any profoundly disturbing form. Each combatant people viewed itself as fighting for king and country in a just war. But by 1916 the Allies were being urged to think of their endeavour as a war "to make the world safe for democracy," and the Germans, on their side, were correspondingly encouraged to visualize the war as a struggle of "culture" against "barbarism." On both sides, the casualties were far more terrible than anyone had foreseen, and the need to sustain the will to war by an appeal to ideology was plainly felt by all the nations involved. Whether such "war aims" were really the main objectives of the governments concerned is another question; what is important is that as the need was increasingly felt for a justification of war, the justification took an ideological form. Whether or not World War I changed its real nature between 1914 and 1918, the prevailing conception of it underwent significant alteration. This became more marked after the Russian Revolution of 1917, when the Bolsheviks submitted to harsh German peace terms for reasons that were not only practical but ideological—namely, the preservation and promotion of Communism. Pres. Woodrow Wilson brought the Americans into the war on the Allied side with an alternative ideological vision—that of ensuring permanent peace through the League of Nations and of establishing democratic governments in all the conquered countries.

The rise of Communism clearly marked a corresponding increase in the role of ideology in international relations. Fascism helped to speed the process. The Spanish Civil War of the 1930s was an almost clear-cut confrontation between the ideologies of left and right (not entirely clear-cut because of the ambiguous relationship between Communism and anarchism).

The precise extent of ideological commitment in World War II is a matter of some controversy. At one level, the 1939 war is seen as a continuation of the war of 1914. Two of the leading protagonists—Great Britain and the U.S. agreed more in their anti-ideological stance, and their hostility to Nazism than in promoting an alternative ideology. Pres. Franklin D. Roosevelt, suspicious of British and French imperialism and eager to cultivate a progressive ideological outlook, was critical of Prime Minister Winston Churchill's politics, hostile toward Charles de Gaulle's, but surprisingly tolerant of Joseph Stalin's. The revival of Wilson's idealistic war aims in the Atlantic Charter provided a basis for a kind of general ideological union of the Allies. But such formulations proved to be of small significance compared to the profound ideological commitment of the Soviet Union to Communism, and that of the U.S. to an international position more ideologically anti-Communist than pro anything.

Ideology of the Cold War. What came to be called the Cold War in the 1950s must be understood, to a large extent, as an ideological confrontation, and whereas Communism is manifestly an ideology, the "non-Communism," or even the "anti-Communism" of the West is negatively ideological. To oppose one ideology is not necessarily to subscribe to another, although there is a strong body of opinion in the West that feels that the free world needs a coherent ideology if it is to successfully resist an opposing ideology.

The connection between international wars and ideology can be better expressed in terms of a difference of degree rather than of kind: some wars are more ideological than others, although there is no clear boundary between an ideological and nonideological war. An analogy with the religious wars of the past is evident, and there is indeed some historical continuity between the two types of war. The Christian Crusades against the Turks and the wars between Catholics and Protestants in early modern Europe have much in common with the ideological conflicts of the contemporary period. Religious wars are often communal wars, as witness those between Hindus and Muslims in India; but an "ideological" element of a kind can be discovered in many religious wars, even those narrated in the Old Testament, in which the people of Israel are described as fighting for the cause of righteousness—fighting, in other words, for a universal abstraction as distinct from a local and practical aim. In the past this "ideological" element has in the main been subsidiary; what is characteristic of the modern period is that the ideological element has become increasingly dominant, first in the religious wars (and the related diplomacy) which followed the Reformation, and then in the political wars and diplomacy of recent times.

BIBLIOGRAPHY. Only a small proportion of the writings of the early French *idéologues* is available in English. The most important of these works are DESTUTT DE TRACY, *Élémens d'Idéologie*, 2nd ed. (1817); and the expository study by F.J. PICAVET, *Les Idéologues* (1891). For an analysis in French of the nature of ideology, written from a 20th-century standpoint, see JEANNE HERSCH, *Idéologies et Réalité* (1956).

JOHN PLAMENATZ, *Ideology* (1970), is a useful introductory essay by a political philosopher. R.H. COX (ed.), *Ideology, Politics and Political Theory* (1969), contains excerpts from central works in ideological theory from Destutt de Tracy to recent times; the commentary is of exceptional interest. GEORGE LICHTHEIM, *The Concept of Ideology* (1967), is an unbiassed study of the place of ideology in Hegelian and Marxist thought. KARL MARX, *Die deutsche Ideologie* (1932; Eng. trans., *The German Ideology*, ed. by R. PASCAL, 1939), is the key text in this field. KARL MANNHEIM's attempt to formulate a neo-Marxist theory of ideology may be found in his *Ideology and Utopia* (1963). For SARTRE's conception of ideology as a "marginal system of ideas," see his *Critique de la raison dialectique* (1960).

Sociological aspects of ideology are explored in DONALD MACRAE, *Ideology and Society* (1961); and NORMAN BIRNBAUM, *The Sociological Study of Ideology, 1940–1960* (1962). Historical studies which take a view of ideology include: F.M. WATKINS, *The Age of Ideology: Political Thought, 1750 to the Present* (1964); and PATRICK CORBETT, *Ideologies* (1966). Historical studies written from a standpoint hostile to ideology include: KARL POPPER, *The Poverty of Historicism* (1957); and ALBERT CAMUS, *L'Homme Révolté* (1951; Eng. trans., *The Rebel*, 1953). RAYMOND ARON, *L'Opium des intellectuals* (1955; Eng. trans. *The Opium of the Intellectuals*, 1957), and *The Industrial Society* (1967), predict a decline in ideological politics; as does DANIEL BELL in *The End of Ideology* (1960). An even more elaborate attack on the whole notion of ideological politics may be found in MICHAEL OAKESHOTT, *Rationalism in Politics* (1962).

ARNE NAESS, *Democracy, Ideology and Objectivity* (1956), provides a sophisticated logical analysis of the concept of ideology. Subsequent works on the subject by political philosophers include: Z.A. JORDAN, *Philosophy and Ideology* (1963); JUDITH N. SHKLAR (ed.), *Political Theory and Ideology* (1966); and ROBERT DERATHE (ed.), *Idéologie* (1970). Notable among the books written from the perspective of political science are: ROBERT LANE, *Political Ideology* (1962); WILLIAM E. CONNOLLY, *Political Science and Ideology* (1967); and DANTE GERMINO, *Beyond Ideology* (1967). ANDREW GYORGY and GEORGE D. BLACKWOOD, *Ideologies in World Affairs* (1967), studies the emergence of ideology as a dominant factor in international relations.

(M.C.)

Idrīsī, al-

Al-Idrīsī (in full Abū ʿAbd Allāh Muḥammad ibn Muḥammad ibn ʿAbd Allāh ibn Idrīs al-Ḥammūdī al-Ḥasanī al-Idrīsī; usually known as ash-Sharīf al-Idrīsī) was a 12th-century Arab geographer and scientist who wrote one of the greatest medieval works of descriptive geography. He was a close friend and adviser to Roger II, the Norman king of Sicily, at whose court he served as official geographer.

Idrīsī traced his descent through a long line of princes, caliphs, and holy men to the Prophet Muḥammad. His immediate forebears, the Ḥammūdids of the short-lived caliphate (1016–58) in Spain and North Africa, were an offshoot of the Idrīsids of Morocco (789–985), a dynasty descended from Muḥammad's eldest grandson, al-Ḥasan ibn ʿAlī. Family ancestry

Few facts are known about al-Idrīsī's life. He was born in 1100 in Sabtah (now Ceuta, a Spanish exclave in Morocco), where his Ḥammūdī ancestors had fled after the fall of Málaga, their last foothold in Spain, in 1057. He spent much of his early life travelling in North Africa and Spain and seems to have acquired detailed and accurate information on both regions. He is known to have studied in Córdoba for a number of years and also to have lived in Marrakesh, Morocco, and Qusṭanṭinah (Constantine), Algeria. Apparently his travels took him to many parts of western Europe, including Portugal, northern Spain, the French Atlantic coast, and southern England. He is also known to have visited Asia Minor when he was barely 16 years old.

In about 1145, while still at the peak of his powers, al-Idrīsī entered the service of Roger II of Sicily—a step that marked a turning point in his career. Henceforward, all his great achievements were to be indissolubly linked to the Norman court at Palermo, where he lived and worked for the rest of his life. Some Western scholars have suggested that al-Idrīsī may have been regarded as a renegade by other Muslims for entering the service of a Christian king and praising him lavishly in his writings. Moreover, some writers have attributed the paucity of biographical information on al-Idrīsī in Muslim sources to these circumstances.

There has always been uncertainty about al-Idrīsī's reasons for going to Sicily. It has been suggested that he may have been induced to do so by some of his Ḥammūdī kinsmen, who are known to have settled there and who, according to the Spanish–Arab traveller Ibn Jubayr (1145–1217), enjoyed great power and prestige among Sicilian Muslims. According to the 14th-century Arab scholar aṣ-Ṣafadī, Roger II invited al-Idrīsī to Sicily to make a map of the world for him, telling him:

> You are a member of the caliphal family. For that reason, when you happen to be among Muslims, their kings will seek to kill you, whereas when you are with me you are assured of the safety of your person.

Al-Idrīsī agreed to stay, and Roger settled upon him a king's pension.

Al-Idrīsī's service in Sicily resulted in the completion of three major geographical works: (1) a silver planisphere on which was depicted a map of the world; (2) a world map consisting of 70 sections formed by dividing the Earth north of the Equator into seven climatic zones of equal width, each of which was subdivided into ten equal parts by lines of longitude; and (3) a geographical text intended as a key to the planisphere. This was his great work of descriptive geography, known as *Kitāb nuzhat al-mushtāq fī ikhtirāq al-āfāq* ("The Pleasure Excursion of One Who is Eager to Traverse the Regions of the World") and which also is known as *Kitāb Rujār* or *al-Kitāb ar-Rujārī* ("The Book of Roger"). In compiling it, al-Idrīsī combined material from Arabic and Greek geographical works with information obtained through first-hand observation and eyewitness reports. The King and his Arab geographer chose a number of persons, including men skilled in drawing, and dispatched them to various countries to observe and record what they saw. Al-Idrīsī completed the book in January 1154, shortly before Roger's death.

Al-Idrīsī's major works

The silver planisphere has been lost, but the maps and book have survived. A German scholar, Konrad Miller, published the maps in his *Mappe Arabicae* (Stuttgart, 1926–31), and later an emended world map, based upon Miller's work, was published by the Iraq Academy (Baghdad, 1951). The first loose sections of a critical edition of Idrīsī's *Kitāb nuzhat al-mushtāq*, undertaken by a committee of Italian scholars in cooperation with a group of international experts, had begun to appear in the early 1970s.

Kitāb nuzhat al-mushtāq represents a serious attempt to combine descriptive and astronomical geography. That this effort was not an unqualified success apparently stems from the author's inadequate mastery of the physical and mathematical aspects of geography. He has been criticized not only for failing to make use of the important geographical contributions of other scientists of his times, such as the 11th-century Arab scholar al-Bīrūnī, but also for his uncritical use of earlier Greek and Arab sources. Nevertheless, al-Idrīsī's book is a geographical monument of vast proportions. It is particularly valuable for its data on such regions as the Mediterranean basin and the Balkans.

A number of other geographical works are attributed to al-Idrīsī, including one (now lost) written for William I (William the Bad), Roger's son and successor who reigned from 1154 to 1166, as well as several critical revisions and abridgments. The Medici press in Rome published an abridgment of *Kitāb nuzhat al-mushtāq* in 1592; a Latin translation was erroneously published under the title *Geographia Nubiensis*. The only complete translation of the work in any language is P.A. Jaubert's two volume *Géographie d'Édrisi* (Paris, 1836–40); it is unreliable, however, because it was based on faulty manuscripts. Al-Idrīsī's scientific interests embraced medical matters as well, and his *Kitāb al-adwiya al-mufradah* ("Book of Simple Drugs"), in which he lists the names of drugs in as many as 12 languages, shows the range of his linguistic abilities. Al-Idrīsī seems to have had a good knowledge of Arabic literature, and—judging by some of his verse that has survived—he was also an accomplished poet. No details are known about the last years of his life. He is believed to have died in 1165 or 1166, but it is not known whether he died in Sicily or in his birthplace, Sabtah.

BIBLIOGRAPHY. G. OMAN, "Al-Idrīsī," *Encyclopaedia of Islam*, new ed., vol. 3, pp. 1032–35 (1971), provides compact coverage of Idrīsī and his work. IGNATII I. KRACHKOVSKII's comprehensive survey in Russian (1957) has been translated into French by M. CANARD under the title "Les Géographes arabes des XIe et XIIe siècles en Occident," in the *Annales de l'Institut d'Études Orientales de l'Université d'Alger*, 18–19:24–54 (1960–61). TADEUSZ LEWICKI, *Polska i kraje sąsiednie w świetle "Księgi Rogera," geografa arabskiego z XII w. al-Idrīsī'ego*, 2 pt. (1945–54), is a good study of Idrīsī in which the author speculates about the nature of his relationship with King Roger. A summary of Lewicki's hypothesis, together with much interesting information on Idrīsī, is given by S. MAQBUL AHMAD in the introduction to his English translation of Idrīsī, *India and the Neighbouring Territories in the Kitāb Nuzhat al-Mushtāq fi'Khtirāq al-'Afāq*, pt. 2, pp. 1–19 (1960). The most scholarly study of Idrīsī in Arabic appears in HUSAYN MUNIS, *Tā'rīkh al-Jughrāfīyah wa al-Jughrāfiyīn fi al-Andalus*, pp. 165–280 (1967).

(W.Jw.)

Ignatius of Antioch, Saint

St. Ignatius, bishop of Antioch in Syria, was an influential church leader and theologian whose seven letters, written during a journey from Antioch to Rome as a prisoner condemned to die for his faith, form an important source of knowledge of the Christian Church at the beginning of the 2nd century. There is no record of his life prior to his arrest, but his letters reveal his personality and his impact on the Christianity of his time. Ignatius represented the Christian religion in transition from its Jewish origins to its assimilation in the Greco-Roman world. He laid the foundation for dogmas that would be formulated in succeeding generations. His advocacy of a hierarchical structure of the church with emphasis on episcopal authority, his insistence on the real humanity of Christ, and his ardent desire for martyrdom are subjects that have generated much discussion. He has also been an important witness to the life of Christian communities of his day and their mutual contacts.

Journey from Antioch to Rome. Eusebius of Caesarea, whose *Ecclesiastical History* is the chief primary source for the history of the church up to 324, reported that Ignatius' arrest and his condemnation to the wild beasts in the Roman arena occurred during the reign of the Roman emperor Trajan (98–117). Eusebius, on unknown grounds, dates the event to 107 or 108. Ignatius' letters contain the only reliable information about him, but only one of them—that to the church in Rome—is dated (August 24), and even then no year is given.

Ignatius, surnamed Theophoros (God Bearer), was bishop of Antioch at the time of his arrest. Whether he was a native of the city is uncertain; his Greek prose, however, does have an Oriental flavour characteristic of that part of the Hellenistic world. His thought is strongly influenced by the letters of St. Paul and also by the tradition connected with the Apostle John. It is possible that he knew John personally.

Ignatius was taken prisoner during a persecution of the Antioch church; he was put in chains and escorted, along with others, by a unit of soldiers to Troas in northwestern Asia Minor for embarkation to Rome. By that time he must have been a well-known figure among Christians. All along his way delegations of churches, even from places off his route, accompanied him from town to town. For unknown reasons, the journey was interrupted at Smyrna (modern Izmir, Turkey), where he was warmly received by the local Christians and their bishop, Polycarp, who was to become his beloved friend. There he was also met by representatives—the bishop, some elders, or presbyters, and some deacons—of the nearby churches of Ephesus, Magnesia on the Maeander, and Tralles, who as far as possible looked after his needs. After these delegations left Smyrna, he wrote letters to their respective communities thanking them for their attentions and offering them guidelines for their lives as Christians. At his request the deacon Burrus of Ephesus was allowed to stay with him. Ignatius also wrote to Rome, urging his fellow Christians there not to prevent his martyrdom by intercession on his behalf and commending to their charity Syrian Christians who had arrived there ahead of him.

Arrival in Smyrna

From Smyrna his journey continued to the district of Troas, where a shorter stay was made pending embarkation. This stopover was not long enough for Ignatius to write to all the churches he wished to address. He did, however, write to the congregations at Philadelphia and Smyrna (these letters were delivered by Burrus, who had accompanied him to Troas) and to Bishop Polycarp, asking him in a personal letter to write to other churches in his name. At Troas he had been joined by the deacons Philo of Cilicia and Agathopus from Syria; they gave him the consoling news that Antioch was again "at peace." It is not certain whether this meant a lull in the persecution of Christians or perhaps—to judge from Ignatius' use of the word peace elsewhere—a return of the community to concord after some religious dissension. In his letter to Polycarp, Ignatius asked to have a deacon appointed to bring the people of Antioch the congratulations of the church of Smyrna and to encourage other churches to follow Smyrna's example. Some time later Polycarp wrote to the church of Philippi in Macedonia for news about Ignatius and his companions, who had recently passed through their city. His death in the Roman arena is recorded by Polycarp's disciple Irenaeus, who died about 200/203. Documentation ends here; the rest is inference.

Warnings to the churches on doctrine and teachers

Contents of the letters. The letters of Ignatius abound in warnings against false doctrines and false teachers and in admonitions to preserve peace and concord by willing subordination in all religious matters to the clergy and above all to the bishop. Nevertheless, he frequently assures his readers that their own church gives no cause for concern and that his words are prompted merely by pastoral solicitude. Only in his letter to the church of Philadelphia does he intimate that at least some of the community tended to segregate, and, in a passage in the letter to the Smyrnaeans, he seems to imply that there had been dissenters. Smyrna is the only place along his journey where Ignatius stayed for a sufficiently long time to have firsthand knowledge of the state of their church; he knew of the others from informants, who gave him little grounds for worry. Ignatius' anxiety, perhaps, had its roots in his experiences as a bishop at Antioch. If the peace that returned to Antioch after he left is to be understood as the restoration of concord within the Christian community, then the church of Antioch might have been divided on the very same issues about which Ignatius writes to the other churches.

Ignatius apparently fought two groups of heretics: Judaizers, who did not accept the authority of the New Testament and clung to such Jewish practices as observing the sabbath; and Docetists (from the Greek *dokein*, "to seem"), who held that Christ had suffered and died only in appearance. Ignatius untiringly affirmed that the New Testament was the fulfillment of the Old Testament and insisted upon the reality of Christ's human nature. For him, Christ's Passion, death, and Resurrection were a vital guarantee of "life everlasting" in the risen Christ. Ignatius believed that, had Christ died only in appearance, his own suffering and his readiness to sacrifice his life for Christ would have no meaning.

Such sentiments are a strong argument against the proposition that Ignatius had come under the influence of some early form of Gnosticism—a dualistic religion that stressed salvation by esoteric knowledge, or *gnōsis*, rather than by faith. Some of Ignatius' formulations possibly echo Gnostic language, and he seems to have made an impression on certain Gnostic sects. Nevertheless, there is no trace in his letters of the basic Gnostic equation of good and evil with spirit and matter. He does not even take up St. Paul's antinomy of flesh and spirit. For him, the spirit is above the flesh rather than against it; even what the "spiritual man" does "according to the flesh" is spiritual.

Structure of the church and desire for martyrdom

Concern for the doctrine that Christ is man as well as God is the main reason that Ignatius insisted so emphatically on "siding with the bishop." On this earth the bishop represents to his church the true bishop, Christ. Union with the bishop in belief and worship means union with Christ. Those who in a spirit of pride break away from the bishop destroy that union. The unity of the church with its monarchical structure is for Ignatius a concrete realization already on earth of the future life in Christ; authority within the church has not yet become for him a principle of institutional discipline. Ignatius used, for the first time in Christian literature, the expression catholic church, meaning the whole church that is one and the same wherever there is a Christian congregation.

Ignatius' letter to the church of Rome is by far the longest and the richest in laudatory epithets. Throughout his letter he speaks of the Roman Christians in terms of special distinction. But even when he states that their church holds the first place in the whole Christian "community of love [*agapē*]," he acknowledges a position of pre-eminence rather than of jurisdiction.

Ignatius' desire to become a martyr is also linked with his understanding of union with Christ. To be a perfect disciple of Christ means to imitate Christ in his Passion, to share in it, to be united with Christ in suffering. Many times in his letters Ignatius accuses himself of being imperfect because he has not yet been put to this test. Now, on his journey to Rome, he at last "begins to be a disciple," and his great fear is that his friends in Rome might obtain for him a pardon and so deprive him of his way to perfection. This longing for martyrdom has sometimes been interpreted as a neurotic obsession. Although the language used by Ignatius in voicing this desire does often sound exaggerated, his attitude was shared by many Christians of his time. For Ignatius, love of martyrdom ultimately springs from a deep conviction that only by union with Christ's Passion will he participate in Christ's glory. Even this belief does not free him from the fear that he might recoil in the face of death, and he asks the churches to pray for his strength and constancy.

Personal relationships

Only rare glimpses of Ignatius' personal relations are possible from the letters. His greetings, in the manner of St. Paul, to individuals at the end of his letters seldom have a personal ring. In his letter to the church of Smyrna he singles out Tavia for special mention, but his reason seems to be pastoral. Another woman of that town, Alke, is remembered twice as "a name dear to me," and a certain Attalus as "my beloved." Among the clergy Ignatius finds words of special warmth for the deacons. They are "most dear" to him, and he likes to speak of them as his "fellow-slaves." By his time deacons apparently were no longer mere dispensers of the church's charities, as they are depicted in the Acts of the Apostles. If the bishop represents Christ as shepherd, the deacons are images of Christ as "the servant of all." In emphasizing his fellowship with them, Ignatius insists on the common bond among all Christians in the service of God.

Among all the persons known from Ignatius' correspondence, Polycarp, bishop of Smyrna, stands out as his personal friend. Ignatius made the acquaintance of his younger colleague during his stay at Smyrna. He addresses him and generally speaks of him with an affection that is absent in his praise of other bishops. Polycarp received the only personal letter from Ignatius; it is a letter of advice from an experienced older man to a younger one who, for all the promise he shows for the future, still has to find his way. Polycarp, in turn, when writing to the Philippians, praises Ignatius as an example of patience and of willingness to suffer for Christ. Some 40 years later (perhaps in 155) Polycarp himself was to follow in his friend's footsteps to a martyr's death.

History of the letters. Polycarp made a collection of Ignatius' letters and sent them to the church of Philippi, as he had been requested by the Philippians. The collection apparently contained some, if not all, of the seven letters that were known to Eusebius and are now commonly held to be genuine. The letter to the Romans was quoted as early as the 2nd century by Irenaeus, then bishop of Lugdunum (modern Lyon, France). In the 4th century these letters were corrupted by the heavy insertions of an interpolator, and the collection was augmented by six letters forged under Ignatius' name. This enlarged collection was commonly known in the Middle Ages. A single Latin version based on the original text of the seven genuine letters was, however, made in England in the 13th century, perhaps by the great scholar and translator Robert Grosseteste. The genuine collection, freed from interpolations and forgeries, was restored by 17th-century scholarship. In the period after the Protestant Reformation, Ignatius' notion of the church, as found in the enlarged collection, was greatly emphasized by Roman Catholics and harshly criticized by Protestants; the rediscovery of the letters in their original form, however, has led to a just and objective assessment of his personality and his views against their historical background.

BIBLIOGRAPHY. J.B. LIGHTFOOT, *The Apostolic Fathers . . .*, 3 vol., part 2 (1885), is a fundamental work. Good English translations of the genuine letters are found in J.A. KLEIST, *The Epistles of St. Clement of Rome and St. Ignatius of Antioch* (1946); and R.M. GRANT, *The Apostolic Fathers*, vol. 4, *Ignatius of Antioch* (1966). See also C.C. RICHARDSON, *The Christianity of Ignatius of Antioch* (1935), a good presentation of the material; J. QUASTEN, *Patrology*, vol. 1, pp. 63–76 (1950), a concise general assessment; and V. CORWIN, *St. Ignatius and Christianity in Antioch* (1960), a reconstruction of the background of Ignatius' letters, the last two with bibliography.

(L.G.J.B.)

Igneous Rocks

Igneous rocks are the predominant solid constituents of the Earth, formed through the cooling of molten or partly molten material at or beneath the Earth's surface. As the products of natural melts or magmas, igneous rocks are distinguished from sedimentary rocks, which in general represent either surface accumulations of fragmental materials or mineral precipitates from surface waters. They are also distinguished from metamorphic rocks, which result from the transformation of preexisting solid rocks at depth beneath the surface of the Earth.

The molten materials that congeal to form igneous rocks are known as magmas (from a Greek word meaning "a paste of solid and liquid matter"); where magmas reach the Earth's surface, they are called lavas. Lavas yield many kinds of extrusive, or volcanic, rocks, whereas the magmas that cool at depth form an even greater variety of intrusive, or plutonic, rocks. Nearly all magmas are complex silicate solutions; as such, they can exist only at high temperatures. Some of them are wholly liquid, but most contain suspended crystals or other solid matter, often in considerable abundance. Although dissolved water and other volatile substances generally are present only as minor constituents, their influence on the behaviour of magmas can be very great.

The study of igneous rocks involves their origin and history, their mineral and chemical composition, their texture and fabric, and their structural relationships and mode of occurrence. Insight to the mineralogical and textural properties of igneous rocks can be gained from their microscopic examination in polarized light, whereas certain aspects of rock structure and origin can be deduced from field study. Experimental work also is of great importance, however. Serious efforts to apply the results of experimental investigation toward an understanding of igneous processes date from nearly two centuries ago, when a Swiss physician, Horace de Saussure, fused several kinds of granitic rocks in his laboratory. In 1798 the English scientist Sir James Hall demonstrated that basaltic rock could be melted and then resolidified to yield either dark-coloured glasses or crystalline mineral aggregates like those in the parent rocks, depending upon the rate of cooling. Half a century later, two French investigators, Élie de Beaumont and Gabriel-Auguste Daubrée, successfully synthesized numerous minerals and rocks. Then, beginning in 1878, more systematic work by two other French scientists, Ferdinand Fouqué and Auguste Michel-Lévy, yielded valuable data on the melting and crystallization of rocks and rock-forming minerals. In several of their syntheses, Fouqué and Michel-Lévy demonstrated the important effects of steam and other fluxing agents (substances used as an aid in fusing and in melting other substances) in promoting crystallization. That the laws of solutions can be applied to magmatic liquids, as first suggested in 1861 by the German chemist Robert Bunsen, was confirmed during the period from 1884 to 1906 by Johan Vogt, a Norwegian geologist and petrologist, who studied the behaviour of silicate slags and drew many parallels with crystallization processes in magmas.

Early experimental work

More rigorous application of the laws of physical chemistry to igneous petrology began at about the turn of the present century, most notably with establishment in 1904 of the Geophysical Laboratory of the Carnegie Institution in Washington, D.C. As techniques were improved and refined in this and in a growing number of other especially equipped laboratories, the experimental approach became increasingly valuable as a controlled simulation of magmatic and allied processes. Perhaps most important, it was combined with theoretical principles to provide a sound basis for determining what can happen and what should not happen in the formation of igneous rocks.

Petrology in the present century has been progressively extended beyond description and classification to include detailed studies of igneous rock masses, their internal structure and compositional variations, and their relationships with other rocks. The generation, emplacement, and consolidation of magmas as chemical systems have been considered in terms of the Earth's thermal budget, compositional inhomogeneities, and structural history; and the timing of many significant crustal events has been established in more recent years through the age dating of igneous rocks by radiometric methods.

This article treats the nature, classification, and formation of igneous rocks, as well as their occurrence in nature. For greater detail on the principal groups of igneous rocks, see the articles IGNEOUS ROCKS, EXTRUSIVE; IGNEOUS ROCKS, INTRUSIVE; and IGNEOUS ROCKS, PYROCLASTIC. See also ELEMENTS, GEOCHEMICAL DISTRIBUTION OF; EARTH, STRUCTURE AND COMPOSITION OF; MOUNTAIN-BUILDING PROCESSES; and MINERALS for further information on the distribution of igneous rocks in nature and of their chemical and mineralogical constituents. The basis of experimental study of rocks is covered in the article GEOCHEMICAL EQUILIBRIA AT HIGH TEMPERATURES AND PRESSURES.

PROPERTIES OF IGNEOUS ROCKS

Igneous rocks form about four-fifths of the Earth's crust; thus, the crust is mainly a complex product of volcanic and plutonic processes. The geologic record indicates that igneous activity has been widely distributed in space and time and that it has varied considerably in both environment and scale. Its expressions at the Earth's surface have ranged from isolated small eruptions of volcanic ash to vast outpourings of basaltic lava; and at depth, from injection of thin stringers of magma to the emplacement of enormous igneous cores in developing mountain ranges. Magmatic activity has played a vital part in the spreading of ocean basins and has made the principal contributions to the oceanic crust; it also has been closely related to repeated thrusting of oceanic crust beneath the continents. Quite apart from their leading roles in the Earth's history, igneous rocks define much of the present landscape and have directly yielded a variety of materials for man's use. Further, many kinds of valuable mineral deposits are genetically related to them.

Nearly 1,500 different names have been suggested for various igneous rocks, of which about 900 are valid expressions of distinctive rock types. The number is so large because these rocks represent a wide variety of chemical systems and conditions of formation, and because there are so many different physical and chemical bases for description and characterization. The more important of these variations and bases are described below.

Chemical composition. Analyses of thousands of igneous rocks indicate that only nine elements—oxygen, silicon, aluminum, iron,, calcium, sodium, potassium, magnesium, and titanium—account for more than 99 percent of their total composition. Oxygen and silicon together constitute nearly 75 percent by weight and 93 percent by volume of this total, and aluminum and iron are dominant among the remaining elements. It is interesting to note that many elements of considerable economic value, such as carbon, nickel, copper, lead, zinc, and uranium, are present in igneous rocks at very low levels of average concentration.

The nine principal elements of igneous rocks

Because oxygen is the overwhelmingly preponderant constituent, it is common practice to indicate the chemical composition of igneous rocks in terms of oxides. Table 1 shows the ordinary ranges in levels for the major oxides, and Table 2 shows the percentage of contained silica (SiO_2) in igneous rocks, a useful basis for making

Table 1: Major Oxide Constituents of Igneous Rocks

constituent	common range (weight percent)	approximate average value (weight percent)
Silica (SiO_2)	35–78	59.1
Alumina (Al_2O_3)	10–21	15.4
Ferric oxide (Fe_2O_3)	0–7	3.1
Ferrous oxide (FeO)	0–10	3.8
Calcium oxide (CaO)	0–12	5.1
Magnesium oxide (MgO)	0–20	3.5
Sodium oxide (Na_2O)	1–7	3.8
Potassium oxide (K_2O)	0–7	3.1
Water (H_2O)	0–2	1.2

Source: Based on approximately 6,000 analyses of fresh rocks and in part adapted from W.A. Richardson and G. Sneesby, "The Frequency Distribution of Igneous Rocks: I. Frequency Distribution of the Major Oxides in Analyses of Igneous Rocks," *Mineralog Mag.*, (1922).

the broad distinctions listed. Rocks that are relatively rich in silica and alumina also are referred to as sialic (from the chemical symbols for silicon and aluminum); those relatively rich in iron, magnesium, or certain other constituents are referred to as femic (from the symbols for iron and magnesium). All acid and a few intermediate rocks are called oversaturated because they contain SiO_2 in sufficient abundance to form quartz or other silica minerals in addition to the amounts of silica required to form all other mineral constituents that are present. Correspondingly, in this context undersaturated rocks, which include all ultrabasic as well as some basic and intermediate types, are characterized by a deficiency of SiO_2. Such rocks commonly contain minerals that cannot exist in equilibrium with free silica. Other igneous rocks generally are regarded as essentially saturated in terms of silica.

Alumina tends to be most abundant in the intermediate rocks; CaO in intermediate to basic rocks; and Fe_2O_3, FeO, and MgO in basic and ultrabasic rocks. The alkalies Na_2O and K_2O are much less abundant in such rocks; instead, they are generally concentrated in intermediate to silicic types. Rocks that are relatively rich in the alkalies are known as alkalic or alkaline, the latter term sometimes being restricted to an important group of alkali-rich rocks that contain relatively low percentages of silica and, hence, are undersaturated. Abundance relationships between SiO_2 and the other major oxides of igneous rocks are shown graphically in Figure 1.

The rock-forming minerals

Mineral composition. Only seven groups of minerals—feldspars, feldspathoids, quartz and other silica minerals, olivines, pyroxenes, amphiboles, and micas—are abundantly represented among the common igneous rocks. All are silicates or aluminosilicates, and together they include all of the essential (definitive) minerals and most of the varietal minerals in the major rock types that have been named. By far the most abundant are feldspars, which probably constitute as much as 60 percent of the igneous minerals in the Earth's crust. Quartz, pyroxenes, amphiboles, and micas follow in that order. The most widespread accessory constituents, ordinarily present in minor amounts, are silicates, oxides, and phosphates, represented mainly by allanite, apatite, garnets, ilmenite, iron oxides, sphene, spinel, and zircon. Most prominent among the solid products developed through alteration of earlier formed minerals are chlorites, clay minerals, epidote, serpentine, and iron oxides.

As shown in Table 3, the felsic minerals of igneous rocks are the feldspars, feldspathoids, silica minerals, and

Table 2: Silica Content in Igneous Rocks

general designation of rock	percentage of silica (SiO_2)*
Acid or silicic	>66
Intermediate	55–66
Subsilicic	
Basic	45–55
Ultrabasic	<45

* >—greater than; <—less than.

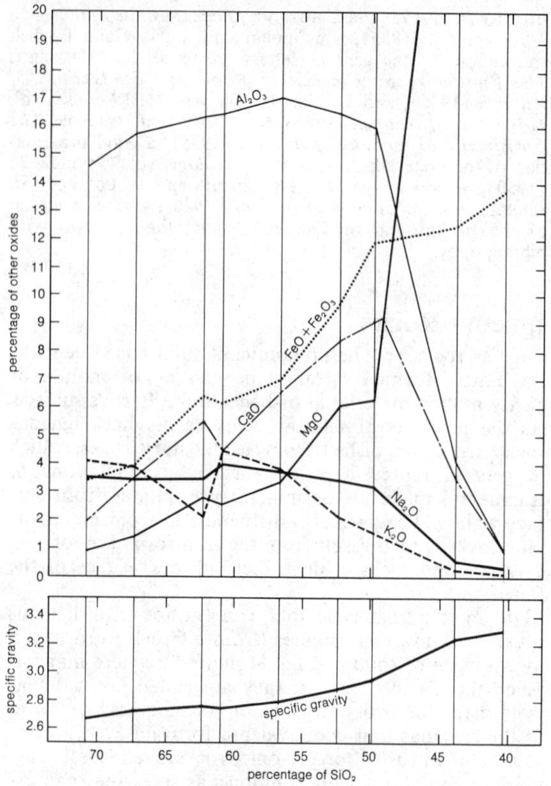

Figure 1: Silica variation diagram, showing trends in chemical composition and specific gravity among the most important groups of igneous rocks.

muscovite. The mafic minerals are the principal ferromagnesian silicates, which contain magnesium or iron (Fe), or both. Similar designations are given to rocks in which one or the other kind of minerals is prominent. Felsic rocks are relatively light coloured, and most of them are chemically salic or silicic. Mafic rocks, which

Table 3: The Common Minerals of Igneous Rocks

mineral groupings	generalized composition*
Essential and varietal	
Felsic	
Quartz, tridymite, cristobalite	SiO_2
Feldspars	
Plagioclases	(Ca, Na)(Al, Si)$_4$O$_8$
Alkali feldspars	(K, Na)AlSi$_3$O$_8$
Feldspathoids	
Nepheline	(Na, K)AlSiO$_4$
Leucite	(K, Na)AlSi$_2$O$_6$
Muscovites	(K, Na)Al$_2$(OH)$_2$ AlSi$_3$O$_{10}$
Mafic	
Olivines	(Mg, Fe)$_2$SiO$_4$
Pyroxenes	(Ca, Na)(Mg, Fe, Al) (Si, Al)$_2$O$_6$
Amphiboles	(Ca, Na)$_2$(Mg, Fe, Al)$_5$ (OH)$_2$(Al, Si)$_2$Si$_6$O$_{22}$
Biotites	K(Fe, Mg)$_3$(OH)$_2$ AlSi$_3$O$_{10}$
Accessory	
Allanite	(Ca, Fe)$_2$(Al, Ce, Fe)$_3$ (OH)(SiO$_4$)$_3$
Apatite	Ca$_5$(F, OH, Cl)(PO$_4$)$_3$
Garnets	(Ca, Fe, Mg)$_3$(Al, Fe)$_2$ (SiO$_4$)$_3$
Ilmenite	FeTiO$_3$
Spinels	
Magnetite	Fe$_3$O$_4$
Others	(Mg, Fe)(Al, Fe)$_2$O$_4$
Hematite	Fe$_2$O$_3$
Sphene	CaTiSiO$_5$
Zircon	ZrSiO$_4$

*Formulas, even though generalized, represent only the most common members of the mineral groups.

tend to be much darker, include most of the chemically femic or basic and ultrabasic types. Both felsic and mafic minerals are abundant in many other rocks, which thus are intermediate or uneven in colour.

Within the general limits imposed by the bulk composition of a rock, the relative abundances of major minerals are further limited by their own compositional requirements (Table 3). The high atomic ratio (3:1) of Si to Al and Si to K + Na in alkali feldspars, for example, demands so much silica that the relatively sialic and alkali-rich rocks in which these feldspars are abundant must also be very rich in total SiO_2 if significant amounts of quartz are present. But in the plagioclase feldspars the Si to Al ratio ranges downward to 1:1, and the Si to Na + Ca ratio ranges downward to 2:1. Therefore, these rocks require smaller percentages of silica. This explains why many relatively sialic rocks with high ratios of plagioclase to alkali feldspar contain quartz even though they are not extremely rich in total SiO_2. The effects of these differences in silica requirements can be large because the feldspars are so abundant. This abundance is the main reason why the oversaturated rocks span a fairly broad range in SiO_2 content.

Because the ratio of Ca + Na + K to Al is slightly greater than unity in the average igneous rock, all aluminum in such a rock could be fixed in the form of felsic minerals unless there were substantial amounts of calcium in one or more of the mafic minerals (Table 3). This is in reasonable accord with the 1:1 ratio of Na + K to Al in the alkali feldspars and the feldspathoids and with the somewhat smaller average ratio of Ca + Na to Al in the plagioclases. Where aluminum is present in greater than average abundance, the excess over that required to form feldspars or feldspathoids ordinarily appears in the form of muscovite, biotite, aluminous pyroxenes or amphiboles, accessory minerals, or some combination of these. On the other hand, an excess of alkalies over aluminum commonly results in the development of alkali-bearing pyroxenes, amphiboles, or accessory minerals.

These and other examples can be useful, up to a point, in relating mineral composition to rock chemistry. The compositional constraints that must be involved in the distribution of constituents within igneous rocks explain why certain mineral pairs such as quartz–leucite, quartz-nepheline, quartz–magnesian olivine, and muscovite-pyroxene are not found as products of magmatic crystallization. Such knowledge of compositional constraints permits remarkably accurate predictions concerning the mineralogy of some rocks with known bulk composition, but it is possible for widely different mineral assemblages to exist among rocks of almost identical composition.

Textural features. The texture of an igneous rock normally is defined by the size and form of its constituent mineral grains and by the spatial relationships of individual grains with one another and with any glass that may be present. Texture can be described independently of the entire rock mass, and its geometric characteristics provide valuable insights into the conditions under which the rock was formed.

Degree of crystallinity

Among the most fundamental properties of igneous rocks are crystallinity and granularity, two terms that closely reflect differences in magma composition and the differences between volcanic and various plutonic environments of formation. Crystallinity generally is described in terms of the four categories shown in Table 4.

Those holocrystalline rocks in which mineral grains can be recognized with the unaided eye are called phanerites, and their texture is called phaneritic; some examples are shown in Figure 2. Those with mineral grains so small that their outlines cannot be resolved without the aid of a hand lens or microscope are termed aphanites, and their texture is termed aphanitic; some examples are shown in Figure 3. Aphanitic rocks are further described as either microcrystalline or cryptocrystalline, according to whether or not their individual constituents can be resolved under the microscope. The sub-aphanitic, or hyaline, rocks are referred to as glassy in terms of granularity.

Table 4: Crystallinity Categories of Igneous Rocks

crystallinity	rock term
Entirely crystalline	holocrystalline
Crystalline material and subordinate glass	hemicrystalline or hypocrystalline
Glass and subordinate crystalline material	hemihyaline or hypohyaline
Entirely glassy	holohyaline or hyaline

Richard H. Jahns

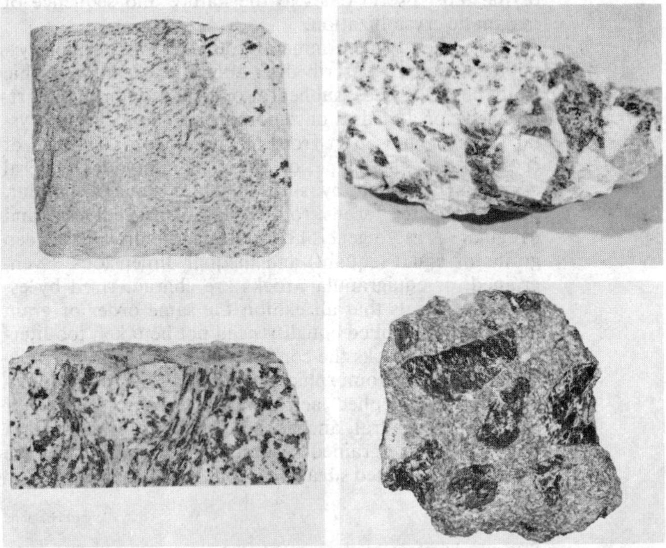

Figure 2: *Textural and structural features of typical phaneritic intrusive rocks.*
(Top left) Fine-grained quartz monzonite in contact with coarse-grained leucocratic granite, Milford, Massachusetts. (Top right) Coarse-grained quartz monzonite grading downward into coarser grained pegmatite, Milford, New Hampshire. (Bottom left) Coarse-grained granite showing flow structure formed by movements in the magma during late-stage crystallization, Conway, New Hampshire. (Bottom right) Very coarsely porphyritic lamprophyre (camptonite) with anhedral phenocrysts of hornblende, near Hoover Dam, Arizona-Nevada border. The specimens range from four to six inches in maximum dimension.

Aphanitic and glassy textures represent relatively rapid cooling of magma and, hence, are found mainly among the volcanic rocks. Slower cooling, either beneath the Earth's surface or within very thick masses of lava, promotes the formation of crystals and, under favourable circumstances of magma composition and other factors, their growth to relatively large sizes. The resulting phaneritic rocks are so widespread and so varied that it is convenient to specify their grain size as shown in Table 5.

Table 5: Categories of Rock Grain Size

terms in common use	general grain size	
	igneous rocks in general	pegmatites
Fine grained	<1 mm	<1 in.
Medium grained	1–5 mm	1 in.–4 in.
Coarse grained	5 mm–2 cm	4 in.–12 in.
Very coarse grained	>2 cm	>12 in.

The general grain size ordinarily is taken as the average diameter of dominant grains in the rock; for the pegmatites, which are special rocks with extremely large crystals, it can refer to the maximum exposed dimensions of dominant grains. Most aphanitic rocks are characterized by mineral grains less than 0.3 millimetre in diameter, and those in which the average grain size is less than 0.1 mm commonly are described as dense.

A major part of rock texture is fabric or pattern, which is a function of the form and outline of its constituent grains, their relative sizes, and their mutual relationships in space. Many specific terms have been employed to shorten the description of rock fabrics, and even the sampling offered here may seem alarmingly extensive. It should be noted, however, that fabric provides some of the most useful clues to the nature and sequence of magmatic crystallization.

The degree to which mineral grains show external crystal faces can be described as euhedral or automorphic (fully crystal faced), subhedral or hypautomorphic (partly faced), or anhedral or xenomorphic (no external crystal faces). Quite apart from the presence or absence of crystal faces, the shape, or habit, of individual mineral grains is described by such terms as equant, tabular, platy, elongate, fibrous, rodlike, lathlike, needlelike, and irregular. A more general contrast can be drawn between grains of equal (equant) and inequal dimensions. Even-grained, or equigranular, rocks are characterized by essential minerals that all exhibit the same order of grain size, but this implied equality need not be taken too literally. For such rocks the combination terms automorphic-granular, hypautomorphic-granular, and xenomorphic-granular are applied according to the occurrence of euhedral, subhedral, and anhedral mineral grains within them. Many fine-grained xenomorphic-granular rocks are more simply termed sugary, saccharoidal, or aplitic.

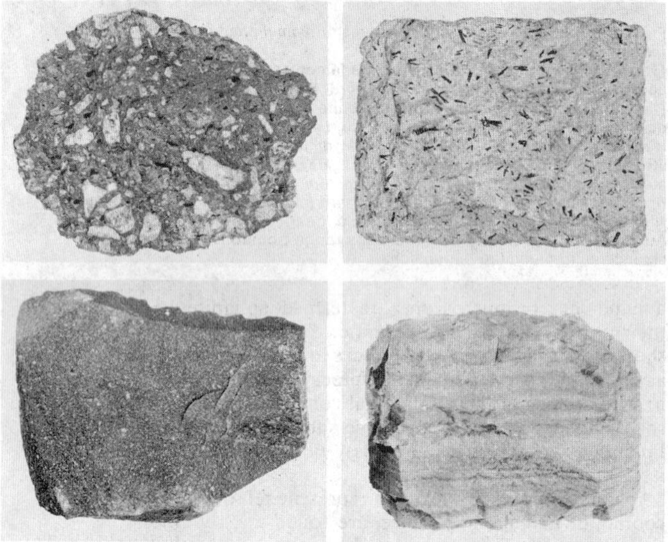

Richard H. Jahns

Figure 3: *Textural and structural features of typical aphanitic and glassy volcanic rocks.*
(Top left) Vesicular basalt with large crystals of plagioclase (labradorite), Sonora, Mexico. (Top right) Porphyritic andesite with bladelike phenocrysts of hornblende in aphanitic matrix, Mount Shasta, California. (Bottom left) Aphanitic basalt except for scattered white crystals of plagioclase, Lassen Peak, California. (Bottom right) Felsite with taffy-like flow layering, Iron Mountain, New Mexico. The specimens are from four to five inches in maximum dimension.

Porphyritic texture

Rocks that are uneven grained, or inequigranular, are generally characterized either by a seriate fabric, in which the variation in grain size is gradual and essentially continuous, or by a porphyritic fabric, involving more than one distinct range of grain sizes. Both of these kinds of texture are common. The relatively large crystals in a porphyritic rock ordinarily occur as separate entities, known as phenocrysts, set in a groundmass or matrix of much finer grained crystalline material or glass (see Figure 3). The size of phenocrysts is essentially independent of their abundance relative to the groundmass, and they range in external form from euhedral to anhedral. Most of them are best described as subhedral. Because the groundmass constituents span almost the full ranges of crystallinity and granularity, porphyritic fabric is abundantly represented among the phaneritic, aphanitic, and glassy rocks.

The sharp break in grain size between phenocrysts and groundmass reflects a corresponding change in the conditions that affected the crystallizing magma. Thus, the phenocrysts of many rocks probably grew slowly at depth, following which the nourishing magma rose to the Earth's surface as lava, cooled much more rapidly, and congealed to form a finer grained or glassy groundmass. Other porphyritic rocks may well reflect less drastic shifts in position and perhaps more subtle and complex changes in conditions of temperature, pressure, or crystallization rates. Many phenocrysts could have developed at the points where they now occur, and some may represent systems with two fluid phases, magma and coexisting gas. Appraisals of the composition of phenocrysts, their distribution, and their periods of growth relative to the accompanying groundmass constituents are important to an understanding of many igneous processes.

The articulation of mineral grains is described in terms of planar, smoothly curved, sinuous, sutured, interlocked, or irregular surfaces of mutual boundary. The distribution and orientation of mineral grains and of mineral grains and glass are other elements of fabric that can be useful in estimating the conditions and sequence of mineral formation in igneous rocks. The following are only a few of the most important examples:

Directive textures are produced by the preferred orientation of platy, tabular, or elongate mineral grains to yield grossly planar or linear arrangements; generally a result of magmatic flowage.

Graphic texture refers to the regular intergrowth of two minerals, one of them generally serving as a host and the other appearing on surfaces of the host as striplike or cuneiform units with grossly consistent orientation; the graphic intergrowth of quartz in alkali feldspar is a good example.

Ophitic texture is the association of lath-shaped euhedral crystals of plagioclase, grouped radially or in an irregular mesh, with surrounding or interstitial large anhedral crystals of pyroxene; it is characteristic of the common rock type known as diabase.

Poikilitic texture describes the occurrence of one mineral that is irregularly scattered as diversely oriented crystals within much larger host crystals of another mineral.

Reaction textures occur at the corroded margins of crystals, from the corrosive rimming of crystals of one mineral by finer grained aggregates of another, or as a result of other features that indicate partial removal of crystalline material by reaction with magma or other fluid.

Replacement textures occur where a mineral or mineral aggregate has the external crystal form of a pre-existing different mineral (pseudomorphism) or where the juxtaposition of two minerals indicates that one was formed at the expense of the other.

Finally, crystal zoning describes faintly to very well defined geometric arrangements of portions within individual crystals that differ significantly in composition (or some other property) from adjacent portions; most common are successive shells grouped concentrically about the centres of crystals, presumably reflecting shifts in conditions during crystal growth.

Structural features. The structure of an igneous rock is normally taken to comprise the mutual relationships of mineral or mineral–glass aggregates that have contrasting textures, along with layering, fractures, and other larger scale features that transect or bound such aggregates. Structure often can be described only in relation to masses of rock larger than a hand specimen, and most of its individual expressions can be closely correlated with physical conditions that existed when the rock was formed.

Vesicles and amygdules

Among the most widespread structural features of volcanic rocks are the porelike openings left by the escape of gas from the congealing lava. Such openings are called vesicles, and the rocks in which they occur are said to be vesicular. Where the openings lie close together and form a large part of the containing rock, they impart to it a slaglike, or scoriaceous, structure. Their relative abundance is even greater in the type of sialic glassy rock known as pumice, which is essentially a congealed volcanic froth. Most vesicles can be likened to peas or nuts in their ranges of size and shape; those that were formed when the lava was still moving tend to be flattened and drawn out in the direction of flow. Others are cylindrical, pearlike, or more irregular in shape, depending in part on the manner of escape of the gas from the cooling lava;

most of the elongate ones occur in subparallel arrangements.

Many vesicles have been partly or completely filled with quartz, chalcedony, opal, calcite, epidote, zeolites, or other minerals. These fillings are known as amygdules, and the rock in which they are present is amygdaloidal. Some are concentrically layered, others also include centrally disposed series of horizontal layers, and still others are featured by central cavities into which well-formed crystals project.

Features of glassy rocks

Spherulites are light-coloured subspherical masses that commonly consist of tiny fibres and plates of alkali feldspar radiating outward from a centre. Most range from pinpoint to nut size, but some are as much as several feet in diameter. The relatively large ones tend to be internally complex and to contain concentric shells of feldspar fibres with or without accompanying quartz, tridymite, or glass. Spherulites occur mainly in glassy volcanic rocks; they also are present in some partly or wholly crystalline rocks that include shallow-seated intrusive types. Many evidently are products of rapid crystallization, perhaps at points of gas concentration in the freezing magmas. Others, in contrast, were formed more slowly, by devitrification (formation of minute crystals) of volcanic glasses, presumably not long after they congealed and while they were still relatively hot.

Lithophysae, also known as stone bubbles, consist of concentric shells of finely crystalline alkali feldspar separated by empty spaces; thus, they resemble an onion or a newly blooming rose. Commonly associated with spherulites in glassy and partly crystalline volcanic rocks of salic composition, many lithophysae are about the size of walnuts. They have been ascribed to short episodes of rapid crystallization, alternating with periods of gas escape when the open spaces were developed by thrusting the feldspathic shells apart or by contraction associated with cooling. The curving cavities commonly are lined with tiny crystals of quartz, tridymite, feldspar, topaz, or other minerals deposited from the gases. Lithophysae are developed early in the consolidation history of the enclosing volcanic rocks and, like early-formed spherulites, many of them show the effects of subsequent magmatic flowage.

Some glassy rocks of silicic composition are marked by domains of strongly curved, concentrically disposed fractures that promote breakage into rounded masses of pinhead to walnut size. Because their surfaces often have a pearly or shiny lustre, the name perlite is applied to such rocks. The manner in which they fracture has been ascribed to contraction during rapid cooling of relatively homogeneous glass.

Numerous structural features of comparably small scale occur among the intrusive rocks; these include miarolitic, orbicular, plumose, and radial structures. Miarolitic rocks are salic phanerites distinguished by scattered pods or layers, ordinarily a few inches in maximum thickness, within which their essential minerals are coarser grained, subhedral to euhedral, and otherwise pegmatitic in texture. Many of these small interior bodies, called miaroles, contain centrally disposed crystal-lined cavities that are known as druses or miarolitic cavities. An internal zonal disposition of minerals also is common, and the most characteristic sequence is alkali feldspar with graphically intergrown quartz, alkali feldspar, and a central filling of quartz. Miarolitic structure probably represents local concentration of gases during very late stages in consolidation of the host rocks.

The term orbicular is applied to rounded, onion-like masses with distinct concentric layering that are distributed in various ways through otherwise normal-appearing phaneritic rocks of silicic to basic composition. The layers within individual masses are typically thin, irregular, and sharply defined, and each differs from its immediate neighbours in composition or texture. Some layers contain tabular or prismatic mineral grains that are oriented radially with respect to the containing orbicule and, hence, are analogous to spherulitic layers in volcanic rocks. The minerals of most orbicules are the same as those of the enclosing rock, but they are not necessarily present in the same proportions. The concentric structure appears to reflect rhythmic crystallization about specific centres, commonly at early stages in consolidation of the general rock mass.

The normal fabric of some relatively coarse-grained plutonic rocks is interrupted by clusters of crystals with radial grouping but without concentric layering. A characteristic plumelike, spraylike, or rosette-like structure is imparted by the markedly elongate form of the participating crystals or crystal aggregates, which seem to have developed outward from common centres by direct crystallization from magma or by replacement of pre-existing solid material.

Large-scale structural features

Many kinds of larger scale features occur among both the intrusive and the extrusive rocks (see Figure 4). Most of these are mentioned later in connection with rock occurrence or are discussed in other articles, but several are properly introduced here:

Richard H. Jahns

Figure 4: Irregular branching dikes and tongues of medium-grained quartz–diorite in darker coloured gabbro and metamorphic rocks, near Escondido, California. The boundaries are sharply defined, and very thin, straight stringers of light-coloured aplite transect all the other rocks.

Clastic structures. Various features that express the accumulation of fragments or the rupturing and dislocation of solid material. In volcanic environments they generally result from explosive activity or the incorporation of solid fragments by moving lava; as such, they characterize the pyroclastic rocks. Among the plutonic rocks, they appear chiefly as local to very extensive zones of pervasive shearing, dislocation, and granulation, commonly best recognized under the microscope. Those developed prior to final consolidation of the rock are termed protoclastic; those developed after final consolidation, cataclastic.

Flow structures. Planar or linear features that result from flowage of magma with or without contained crystals. Various forms of faintly to sharply defined layering and lining typically reflect compositional or textural inhomogeneities, and they commonly are accentuated by concentrations or preferred orientation of crystals, inclusions, vesicles, spherulites, and other features.

Fractures. Straight or curving surfaces of rupture directly associated with the formation of a rock or later superimposed upon it. Primary fractures, distributed on various scales and in various patterns, generally can be related to emplacement or to subsequent cooling of the host rock mass. The columnar jointing found in many basic volcanic rocks is a typical result of contraction upon cooling.

Inclusions. Rounded to angular masses of solid material enclosed within a rock of recognizably different composition or texture. Those consisting of older material not directly related to that of their host are known as xenoliths, and those representing broken-up and detached older parts of the same igneous body that encloses them are termed cognate xenoliths or autoliths.

Pillow structures. Aggregates of ovoid masses, resembling pillows or grain-filled sacks in size and shape, that occur in many basic volcanic rocks. The masses are separated or interconnected, and each has a thick vesicular crust or a thinner and more dense glassy rind. The interiors ordinarily are coarser grained and less vesicular. Pillow structure is formed by rapid chilling of highly fluid lava in contact with water or water-saturated sediments, accompanied by the development of budlike projections with tough, elastic crusts. As additional lava is fed into each bud, it grows into a pillow and continues to enlarge until rupture of the skin permits escape of fresh lava to form a new bud and a new pillow.

Segregations. Special types of inclusions that are intimately related to their host rocks and in general are relatively rich in one or more of the host-rock minerals. They range from small pods to extensive layers and from early-stage crystal accumulations formed by gravitational settling in magma to very late-stage concentrations of coarse-grained material developed in place.

Zonal structures. Arrangement of rock units with contrasting composition, or texture, in an igneous body, commonly in a broadly concentric pattern. Chilled margins, the fine-grained or glassy edges along the borders of many extrusive and shallow-seated intrusive bodies, represent quick freezing, or quenching, of magma along contacts with cooler country rock. Other kinds of zones generally reflect fractional crystallization of magma and are very useful in tracing courses of magmatic differentiation, as will be noted later.

The colour index: felsic and mafic minerals

Colour and specific gravity. Differences between the inherently light colours of the felsic minerals and the darker colours of most mafic minerals can be useful indications of general rock composition. Colour index, which is either employed directly or is implied in nearly all classifications of igneous rocks, is simply the sum of the mafic minerals expressed as a volume percentage of the entire rock. It is correlated with the common descriptive terms shown in Table 6.

Table 6: Terminology Based on Colour Index

rock term	colour index
Leucocratic	<30
Mesocratic	30–60
Melanocratic	60–90
Hypermelanic	>90

The colour index may or may not correspond to the actual gross colour of a rock in terms of lightness or darkness. Many of the iron-poor mafic minerals, for example, are pale green, gray, or otherwise not dark coloured. Thus, a rock rich in a magnesian olivine may be lighter coloured than one rich in a dark-gray plagioclase, despite its much higher colour index. Colour itself also can be misleading if taken as a guide to the composition of individual minerals or of very fine-grained or glassy rocks. Thus, crystals of alkali feldspar in many coarse-grained leucocratic rocks are dark reddish brown, and many highly silicic volcanic glasses appear dark gray or black. Unfortunately the more meaningful colour index, dependent on recognition of component minerals, is readily determinable only among the phanerites.

Most light-coloured rocks also are light in weight, and hence there is a fairly consistent relationship between colour index and specific gravity (the ratio of the weight of a substance to the weight of an equal volume of water, the specific gravity of which is expressed as 1). Specific gravity ranges between extremes of 2.6 and 3.4 among the more common igneous rocks (Figure 1) and between 2.7 and 2.9 for most leucocratic and mesocratic rocks without vesicles or other large voids. Both specific gravity and colour index tend to increase with increasing percentages of iron and magnesium and with increasing ratios of iron to magnesium and calcium to alkalies.

CLASSIFICATION OF IGNEOUS ROCKS

According to mineralogy and texture. An ideal classification would clearly relate origin and mode of occurrence, mineral and chemical composition, and all major physical properties for the many known kinds of igneous rocks. These features are interrelated in such complex ways, however, that the ideal cannot even be approached without introducing cumbersome qualifications and details. Thus, most practical classifications are based primarily upon elements of composition and texture, and they represent various compromises among such factors as adequate coverage of the most common rock types, simplicity and consistency, adaptability for work without a microscope, and retention of long-established concepts and terms.

One kind of useful compromise is illustrated in Table 7. The lines in this chart are drawn solely for convenience in recognizing general positions of the indicated properties and names; they are not intended to suggest that clear-cut breaks exist between adjoining categories, as the actual situation in nature ordinarily is one of transition. The igneous rocks are divided into clans on the basis of mineral composition and implied chemical composition, and the arrangement of the clans reflects progressive increases in colour index and specific gravity from left to right. A general shift from acid rocks to basic and ultrabasic rocks occurs in the same direction, although between the granite and diorite clans there are alternations among clans of oversaturated rocks and ones of saturated or undersaturated rocks. Salic alkaline rocks, such as nepheline syenite and phonolite—here included with the syenite clan—are sometimes treated as members of a separate clan. Another alkaline clan of basic rocks, such as leucite basalt and the alkali gabbros, could be similarly distinguished from the normal gabbro clan.

Classification by rock clans

Quartz, alkali feldspar, and plagioclase are the essential minerals used to define nearly all of the clans in Table 7. Those clans in the left-hand and central parts of the chart are characterized by high percentages of total feldspars; those in the right-hand part, by percentages of feldspars decreasing to a minimum in the ultrabasic clan. Comparison with Figure 5 will indicate how the ratio of alkali feldspar to plagioclase, an important element of this classification, decreases progressively from left to right in the chart and how plagioclase composition shifts from sodic to calcic in the same direction. The crystalline rocks in four of the clans contain quartz to the extent of 10 percent or more in the granite clan and five percent or more in the others. Rocks of the remaining clans contain lesser amounts or are quartz free, as jointly indicated by "without quartz" in Table 7 (see also Figure 5). The megascopic distinction between the diorite and gabbro clans can be drawn from the relative abundances of felsic and mafic minerals or, alternatively, on the basis of the principal mafic minerals, amphibole in the dioritic rocks and pyroxene or olivine in the gabbroic ones.

The chemical trends among common representatives of the major clans are shown in the silica variation diagram of Figure 1. Here the rocks are arranged from left to right in order of decreasing SiO_2 content, from acid to ultrabasic types. Minor differences between this order and that of clans in the classification chart, which is based mainly upon feldspar ratios and colour index, correspond to reversed trends in the plots for Na_2O and K_2O in the variation diagram. The reversals are attributable chiefly to differences in the ratio of alkali feldspar to plagioclase, as already noted in connection with rock composition. On this score, the abundance of quartz in rocks of the quartz diorite to granite range, with SiO_2 contents of 62 percent to more than 70 percent, correlates with the range in which the general trend in CaO content is opposite from those of Na_2O and K_2O.

Major elements of texture provide a means for dividing the various clans into rock families that are represented among the phanerite, aphanite, glass, and fragmental categories. Three of these four textural groups include porphyritic rock types, but an additional category of porphyries is commonly employed to distinguish rocks with more than 20 percent of phenocrysts in groundmasses that are fine-grained, aphanitic, or glassy. The individual rock names noted in the chart are those in most general use, and several other common names that

Table 7: General Megascopic Classification of Igneous Rocks

		granite	syenite	quartz monzonite (adamellite)	monzonite	granodiorite	quartz diorite (tonalite)	diorite	gabbro	ultrabasic rocks
rock clan		granite	syenite	quartz monzonite (adamellite)	monzonite	granodiorite	quartz diorite (tonalite)	diorite	gabbro	ultrabasic rocks
general trends	colour	light					intermediate			dark
	colour designation	leucocratic				mesocratic		melanocratic		hypermelanic
	specific gravity	low					intermediate			high
	major constituents	felsic minerals								mafic minerals
principal felsic essential minerals	ratio of alkali feldspar to plagioclase	2:1 or greater		2:1 to 1:2		1:2 to 1:7	1:7 or less	1:2 or less	alkali feldspar rare or absent	feldspars rare or absent
	quartz	with quartz	without quartz	with quartz	without quartz	with quartz		without quartz		
textural categories: plutonic—occurrence—intrusive	*phanerites* even- or uneven-grained, porphyritic or nonporphyritic	granite	syenite nepheline syenite*	quartz monzonite (adamellite)	monzonite (syenodiorite)	granodiorite	quartz diorite (tonalite)	diorite	gabbro alkali gabbro* anorthosite† diabase	peridotite pyroxenite hornblendite dunite magmatic ores
		aplites								
		pegmatites								
textural categories: volcanic—occurrence—extrusive	*aphanites* porphyritic or nonporphyritic	rhyolite	trachyte phonolite*	quartz latite (rhyodacite)	latite (trachyandesite)	quartz latite	dacite (rhyodacite)	andesite	lamprophyres; basalt scoria	‡
		felsites								
	glasses porphyritic	vitrophyres			‡	‡	‡		tachylyte (sideromelane)	‡
	glasses nonporphyritic	obsidian pitchstone pumice perlite			‡	‡	‡		palagonite	‡
					‡	‡	‡	‡	‡	‡
	fragmental rocks clastic	tuffs, volcanic breccias, and agglomerates								§

*Sometimes considered to represent a separate alkali-rich clan characterized by essential alkali feldspars or feldspathoids or both. †Unusually felsic member of gabbro clan with predominant plagioclase. ‡Representatives of clan unknown or extremely rare. §Represented mainly by special kinds of intrusive breccias.

are synonymous or nearly so are shown in parentheses. Typical rock types can be designated texturally and related to geological occurrence, as indicated by the examples from the granite and gabbro clans shown in Table 8.

Exceptions to the classification scheme

Some common rock types are exceptional relative to some aspect of the scheme of classification, others do not fit readily into a single category, and many others are so fine-grained (or glassy) that they must be grouped on the basis of chemical composition rather than essential mineralogy. Thus, anorthosite, though a felsic rock, is a legitimate member of the gabbro clan because of its close genetic associations with more typically basic rocks; and diabase, a more mafic rock distinguished by ophitic texture, is found in both plutonic and volcanic environments. Wide ranges in composition characterize the aplites, which are felsic rocks with fine-grained, sugary texture, and the pegmatites, generally felsic rocks that are in part extremely coarse-grained. Individual occurrences are identified by such combination terms as granodiorite aplite and granite pegmatite, and most can be variously assigned to the granite, syenite, and quartz monzonite clans. The lamprophyres—in effect extending across the diorite, gabbro, and ultrabasic clans—are special mesocratic to hypermelanic porphyritic rocks with alkaline groundmasses. They ordinarily are classified according to their dominant mafic minerals; like other and more abundant types of alkaline rocks, they have been subdivided into a host of specifically named varieties.

Light-coloured aphanites with relatively few phenocrysts or none at all are simply termed felsites, and those

From *Internal Constitution of the Earth* by G. Gutenberg, Dover Publications, Inc., New York—fig. 3, p. 84

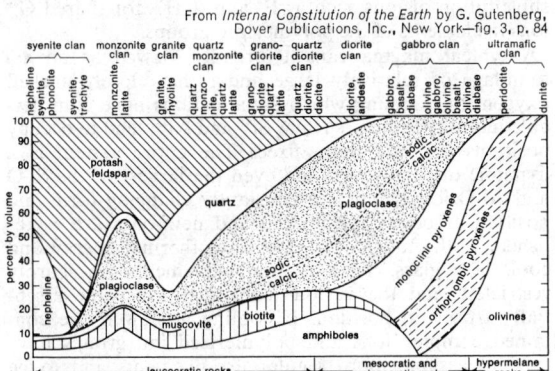

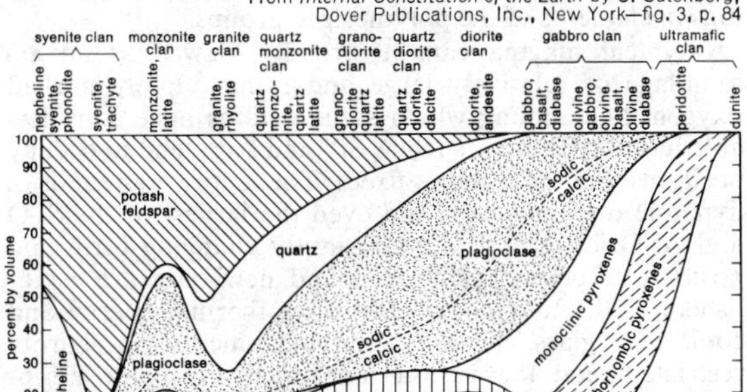

Figure 5: Semi-quantitative representation of mineral composition among the major igneous rock clans and families. The alkali feldspars are represented by the potash feldspar field plus the upper part of the sodic plagioclase field.

Table 8: Geologic Occurrence and Textural Designation of Typical Rock Types

typical geologic occurrence	general textural designation	rock family*
Plutonic, intrusive		
Abyssal	phanerite	granite (hornblende-biotite granite); gabbro (olivine gabbro)
Hypabyssal	porphyry	rhyolite porphyry (biotite rhyolite porphyry); basalt porphyry (augite basalt porphyry)
Volcanic, extrusive		
	aphanite	rhyolite (spherulitic rhyolite); basalt (scoriaceous basalt)
	glass	rhyolite (obsidian); basalt (tachylite)
	pyroclastic rock	rhyolite (crystal tuff); basalt (basalt agglomerate)

*Example of specific rock type is given in parentheses.

light-coloured porphyries in which the phenocrysts cannot be readily identified are referred to as felsite porphyries. Obsidian is relatively massive volcanic glass with vitreous lustre. Pitchstone also is massive but generally contains more water, has a resinous or pitchy lustre, and is more extensively cracked. Both these natural glasses tend to be dark coloured, mainly because of finely divided mafic accessory constituents, but they are compositional correlatives of only the most leucocratic types among the holocrystalline rocks. A similarly restricted range characterizes their porphyritic equivalents, the vitrophyres. Pumice and perlite, distinguished, respectively, by froth and fracture structures, have a compositional range that extends little beyond that of the granite clan. The basic part of the rock spectrum is represented among the glasses by tachylite, which generally is dark coloured and crowded with tiny crystals, and by palagonite, which contains substantial amounts of water and has a duller lustre. The name palagonite also is applied to yellowish and brownish rocks consisting of altered basaltic glass with or without grains or fragments of plagioclase and mafic minerals.

Pyroclastic rocks

The pyroclastic rocks are those formed partly or wholly of solid fragments accumulated during volcanic eruptions. Agglomerates are coarse accumulations of lava clots and bombs that were erupted in a liquid or plastic state, and breccias consist mainly of angular blocks that were solid when accumulated from volcanic vents or incorporated within moving lava. Both blocks and bombs are greater than 32 millimetres in diameter. Fragments with diameters in the range 4–32 millimetres comprise lapilli (rounded) and cinders (rough, angular); smaller fragments include volcanic ash, sand, and dust. Various combinations of these finer grained materials constitute volcanic tuffs and the matrices of tuff breccias. Tuffs can be subdivided into lithic, crystal, and vitric types according to whether they consist principally of crystalline rock fragments, separate crystals and crystal fragments, or bits of glass, respectively. Welded tuffs, which often have been mistaken for congealed lava, are composed primarily of particles that were sufficiently hot and plastic to be fused together at the time of deposition or emplacement.

According to chemical composition. Classifications based upon chemical composition have fundamental advantages over all other schemes. They directly and quantitatively relate rocks to one another as products of natural chemical systems; they also permit useful comparisons of rock types with the results of experimental investigations on synthetic systems of known composition. Such schemes, which begin with compositional information that can be no more than inferred in classifications like that shown in Table 7, are of special value in dealing with very fine grained or glassy rocks. The required data, however, can be obtained only from chemical analyses or, less satisfactorily, from calculations based upon mineral composition. And, when such data are available, they apply more to magmas than to rocks unless the data are combined with knowledge of texture, mineral content and sequence, and geologic occurrence of the rocks involved.

Most chemically based classifications express certain definite combinations of constituents that are well-known among the principal rock-forming minerals. In the widely used CIPW system (the letters refer to the last names of the four men who devised the system), for example, a given rock analysis is recast in the form of "standard mineral molecules" to yield the norm, an assemblage of specifically selected minerals that theoretically could have developed from a magma of the indicated bulk composition. The rock is then classified according to the proportions of calculated normative minerals. All minerals of the norm actually are present in many rocks, but in most rocks some are not. Also, the assemblage of minerals actually present, known as the mode, commonly includes some that are not considered in the "standard" normative suite. Nonetheless, major constituents such as quartz and the feldspars generally appear in both the norm and mode of a given rock.

FORMATION OF IGNEOUS ROCKS

Nature of magmas. Magmas are chemically complex fluid systems that differ in many ways from ordinary solutions, in which water is the solvent and the dominant constituent. They can be thought of as mutual solutions, or melts, of rock-forming components that are variously present as simple ions (atoms that carry positive or negative electric charges), as complex ions and ionic groups, and as molecules. The most abundant of the simple ions in common magmas are such singly and doubly charged cations (positive ions) as Na^+, K^+, Ca^{2+}, Mg^{2+}, and Fe^{2+}. Because these ions can move about rather freely in the system, they occupy no fixed positions with respect to other ions that are present. In contrast, the smaller and more highly charged cations, notably Si^{4+}, Al^{3+}, and (to a lesser degree) Fe^{3+}, are surrounded or screened by O^{2-} ions and other anions (negative ions) to form parts of relatively stable complex ions such as $(SiO_4)^{4-}$, $(AlO_4)^{5-}$, and $(FeO_6)^{9-}$. Simple anions, including F^-, Cl^-, O^{2-}, and $(OH)^-$, ordinarily are present in much smaller amounts. Water, hydrochloric acid (HCl), hydrogen fluoride (HF), carbon dioxide (CO_2), and other volatile molecular substances occur as well, generally in equilibrium with ionic forms such as $(OH)^-$, Cl^-, F^-, and $(CO_3)^{2-}$.

Ionic constituents

Because the bond that unites silicon and oxygen is a remarkably strong one, $(SiO_4)^{4-}$ ions are stable in magmas even at very high temperatures. They also tend to join with one another, or polymerize, to form more complex anionic groups, a tendency that is especially great in the more silicic magmas. The joining is accomplished by a sharing of oxygen ions between adjacent silicon ions to form Si-O-Si bridges like those in many silicate and aluminosilicate minerals; in the simplest such case, $(Si_2O_7)^{6-}$ ions are the result. Because the $(AlO_4)^{5-}$ ions also have a strong tendency to polymerize, most of the large ionic groups in magmas probably contain both silicon and aluminum ions. These groups, which resemble the frameworks of many rock-forming minerals but are geometrically less regular, significantly affect the viscosity and crystallization of magmas.

Viscosity of magmas

The viscosity of magmas, which spans an enormous range of values, affects their flow behaviour, the movements of crystals and inclusions of foreign matter within them, the diffusion of materials through them, and the growth of crystals from them. It increases greatly with decreasing temperature and less markedly with increasing pressure. Viscosity also can be governed in part by the amount and distribution of any solid materials or bubbles of gas that may be present. Finally, it varies considerably among magmas of differing gross composition, mainly because of the differences in the degree of Si-O and Al-O polymerization. Thus, highly silicic magmas generally are more viscous than basic ones by several orders of magnitude, a difference reflected by contrasts in the eruptive behaviour of rhyolitic and basaltic lavas. The presence of certain volatile constituents can markedly increase the fluidity of magmas, even those that are rich in SiO_2. This effect has been attributed to the breaking of Si-O-Si bridges (depolymerization) through substitution of ions such as F^- and $(OH)^-$ for shared O^{2-} ions in elements of the polymerized groups.

A typical magma can be broadly viewed as an assemblage of relatively large and rather closely packed oxygen ions, among which some cations have considerable mobility; others, such as Si^{4+} and Al^{3+}, tend to occupy positions that are more fixed. The entire system is a dynamic one, however, and even the largest of the Si-O and Al-O ion groups are constantly changing form and position as bonds are broken and new ones are established. If the magma quickly loses thermal energy and cools to a glass, these internal movements are sharply restricted, and the various constituents become essentially frozen in position. If cooling is slower, the contained complex ions and polymerized ion groups have time to assume more regular arrangements and to be stabilized by cations of appropriate size, charge, and other properties. Crystalline solids are thereby formed. Their regular internal structure is relatively conserving of space, and hence they have somewhat higher specific gravities than the magma from which they were nourished.

Crystallization from magmas. Regardless of their cooling rates, magmas consolidate over ranges of temperature that vary with composition and generally amount to hundreds of degrees. Completely fluid basaltic lavas generally have temperatures in the range of 1,000° to 1,150° C (1,800° to 2,100° F), and during the course of their solidification they may retain some capacity for flowage at temperatures as low as 700° C (1,300° F). Rhyolitic lavas have lower initial temperatures, generally in the range of 850° to 950° C (1,550° to 1,750° F), and most lavas of intermediate composition seem to have correspondingly intermediate temperatures between this and the basaltic range. Plutonic magmas of basic composition probably are emplaced chiefly in a temperature range similar to that of basic lavas, and those of more silicic composition in the range of 800° to 950° C (1,475° to 1,750° F). There is little reason to believe that magmatic temperatures on or within the Earth's crust are significantly higher than about 1,150° C (2,100° F), except for some plutonic magmas of ultrabasic composition and possibly some basic lavas under special conditions of gas discharge.

Magmatic temperatures

Crystallization of most intrusive magmas probably begins at temperatures between 800° and 1,100° C (1,475° and 2,000° F) and continues through ranges of a few tens of degrees to as much as 300°. The levels and lengths of these ranges depend mainly upon compositional factors, including any volatile fluxing agents that may be present. Thus, many granitic magmas containing dissolved water, for example, may not be completely solidified until they cool to points within the 600°–700° C (1,100°–1,300° F) range. Special types of volatile-rich magmas, such as those that form pegmatites and lamprophyres, can remain partly fluid at temperatures below 600° C (1,100° F).

The melting points of all important rock-forming substances except ice are raised by increasing pressure, a significant factor in the generation and emplacement of magmas. Because pressure also affects, in contrasting degrees, the respective solubilities of different minerals in magmas, it exercises some control on the sequence of crystallization. More importantly, it strongly controls the amounts of water and other substances that a magma can hold in solution. And, where such substances are present as a separate dense gas phase at high pressures, they can exercise a significant solvent action on silicate minerals.

Prevailing pressures

The confining pressure exerted upon a lava flow at the Earth's surface is essentially one atmosphere (about one kilogram per square centimetre); that upon a body of intrusive magma is related mainly to the weight of the overlying column of rocks. Where pressure is equivalent to this weight, it is termed lithostatic pressure. This pressure increases at a rate of about 100 atmospheres for every 375 metres (1,200 feet) of depth beneath a cover of silicic igneous rocks or the lighter coloured sedimentary rocks and their metamorphic counterparts. It increases at higher rates in the more basic, denser parts of the Earth's crust. The rates of increase are by no means uniform in detail, however, because the crust is far from homogeneous.

Most large bodies of intrusive magma probably crystallize under confining pressures ranging from about 1,000 to 10,000 atmospheres. A notable range in pressure also must be expected for any single body with a large vertical extent, the result of progressive changes, with increasing depth, in the lithostatic load, the mass of overlying magma, and the Earth's gravitational field. A directed pressure also is present where the magma is under stress other than that due to load, as in regions of crustal compression. Magmas that reach points high in the Earth's crust also can be under confining pressures that are less than the prevailing lithostatic pressures if water-filled fissures or other interconnected openings traverse the column of overlying rocks. The term hydrostatic pressure is applied in such situations, as its effective value relates to the water rather than to the denser rocks.

Phase equilibria in silicate melts. The apportioning of constituents among the mineral phases in a crystallizing magma is a complicated process that is governed primarily by temperature, pressure, and composition of the system. Many textural and structural features in igneous rocks indicate that the contained minerals were formed in part simultaneously and in part sequentially, and this is confirmed by phase-equilibrium studies in the laboratory.

Diopside–anorthite equilibria

Under a pressure of one atmosphere, the pyroxene diopside ($CaMgSi_2O_6$) melts at a temperature of 1,391° C (2,536° F), and the plagioclase anorthite ($CaAl_2Si_2O_8$) melts at 1,553° C (2,874° F). When a mixture of these two substances is heated, however, melting begins at only 1,274° C (2,293° F) and yields a liquid with a composition corresponding to 57 percent diopside and 43 percent anorthite (see Figure 6). Continued melting under

From *American Journal of Science*, vol. 240 (1942)

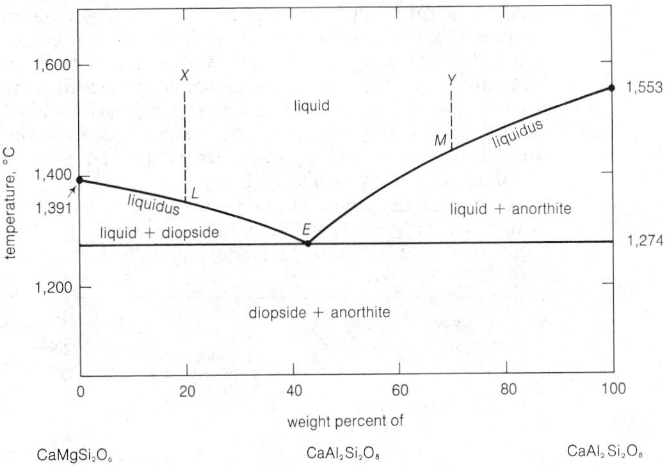

Figure 6: Equilibrium diagram showing melting and crystallization relationships of diopside and anorthite in the system $CaMgSi_2O_6$–$CaAl_2Si_2O_8$ at a pressure of one atmosphere.

equilibrium conditions generates increasing amounts of this same liquid at a constant temperature of 1,274° C until all of one substance melts. The remainder of the other substance then melts as the temperature rises. Viewing the process in reverse (and referring to Figure 6), the cooling of a melt with composition *X* begins to yield crystals of diopside at a temperature near 1,350° C (2,460° F; point *L*). With further cooling, additional diopside forms at steadily decreasing temperature, and the liquid becomes progressively enriched in $CaAl_2Si_2O_8$ until, at 1,274° C, anorthite begins to crystallize at what is termed the eutectic point (*E* in the diagram). The path of diopside crystallization thus far completed is represented by the line *LE*, a part of the liquidus for the system. The liquidus is the line along which liquid and solid phases are in equilibrium and above which no solid phase can exist in equilibrium.

Once the eutectic point is reached, the remaining liquid is used up in simultaneous crystallization of diopside and anorthite in a constant ratio and at a constant temperature to form a eutectic mixture of composition *E*. Because of the presence of earlier formed diopside, the overall ratio of the two minerals in the final solid product corresponds to the initial composition *X*. Similar relationships obtain if the composition of the initial melt is richer in the $CaAl_2Si_2O_8$ component, as represented by *Y* in the diagram, except that anorthite now begins to crystallize at the liquidus (point *M*). It continues to form until the eutectic point *E* is reached, when diopside also begins to appear. In the special case of an initial liquid with eutectic composition, crystallization begins and ends with a eutectic mixture at a constant temperature of 1,274° C.

Eutectic melting relationships characterize many pairs of minerals, among them diopside–albite, diopside–leucite, enstatite–quartz, quartz–albite, albite–olivine, and albite–nepheline. Other pairs, in marked contrast, form solid solutions; these include such important rock-forming constituents as the olivines, plagioclases, and alkali feldspars. (See the articles OLIVINES; PYROXENES; FELDSPARS; and GEOCHEMICAL EQUILIBRIA AT HIGH TEMPERATURES AND PRESSURES for coverage of several relevant solid-solution relationships.)

The continuous and dis-continuous series

Bowen's reaction series. By correlating observations of mineral relationships in igneous rocks with data obtained from experimental studies, the American petrologist Norman L. Bowen identified the principal reactions that can take place during crystallization of ordinary magmas. He ordered the most common mineral products into two reaction series, one continuous and the other discontinuous. The continuous series comprises the plagioclase feldspars and represents a general solid–solution relationship; *i.e.*, one in which the rocks exist within a range of continuously varying chemical composition. The discontinuous series, which comprises reaction pairs of mafic mineral groups, indicates that under many circumstances olivines react with residual liquid to form pyroxenes, that pyroxenes react with residual liquid to form amphiboles, and that amphiboles similarly react to form biotites. Within each of these groups are various solid solutions that bespeak continuous reaction; the discontinuous reactions occur only between groups and series of compounds in a crystalline melt.

The two series generally are shown in a Y-shaped arrangement (Figure 7) in order to suggest their gradual convergence toward a single series, and a third series can

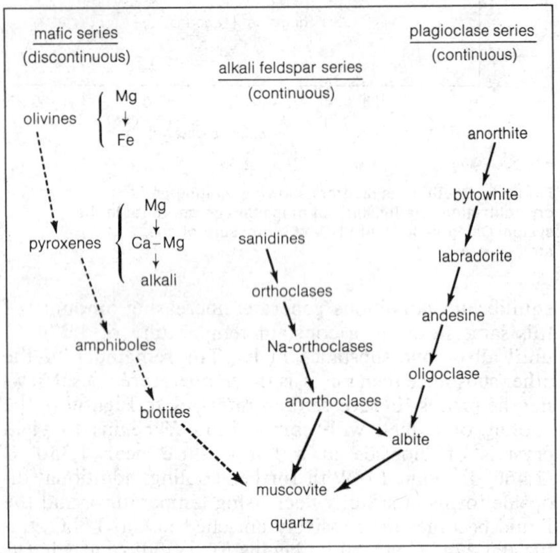

Figure 7: Trends in the major reaction series that occur among the crystalline igneous rocks.

be added to represent continuous reaction among the alkali feldspars and their merging with sodic members of the plagioclase series. The diagram indicates the progression of events to be expected as magmas cool, and relative temperatures are implied in the vertical distribution of its various parts. Minerals in the relatively low temperature region of convergence, chiefly the stem of the Y, are not included on the general basis of reaction relationships. Instead, these minerals with adjacent members of the feldspar series reflect various approaches to eutectic crystallization.

The mineral groups of the mafic series differ markedly from one another in terms of crystal structure. As shown in Figure 8, the discontinuous reactions involve changes in structural arrangements from isolated SiO_4 groups (olivines) to single chains (pyroxenes) to double chains (amphiboles) to sheets (micas). This is in contrast to the consistent presence of three-dimensional framework structures in the other series. A noteworthy chemical convergence of all three series results from the compositional shifts within each of them. Thus, initially different atomic ratios of Si to Al converge to a common value of three, and the ratios of Na + K to Al to a common value of one. Muscovite and quartz do not reflect these trends, which is compatible with their positions farther down on the diagram and outside the region of reaction relationships.

The reaction series not only express broad compositional trends between liquid and crystals during the cooling of a magma, but they also suggest what can happen when it is in contact with foreign solid materials. If a foreign mineral belongs to one of the reaction series but represents an earlier stage of that series than the minerals being crystallized from the magma, it can be converted by reaction to later stage minerals, just as if it had been formed earlier from the magma. If it represents a later stage, it can be dissolved by the magma. A foreign mineral that does not belong to one of the series also will tend to react with the magma, thereby causing shifts in composition of both the liquid and the crystalline phases being formed from it. In addition, a magma might also react to some extent with the surrounding wall rock, affecting its composition. Consequently, new mineral assemblages could form.

Adapted from J. Von Eckerman, *Some Notes on the Reaction Series*

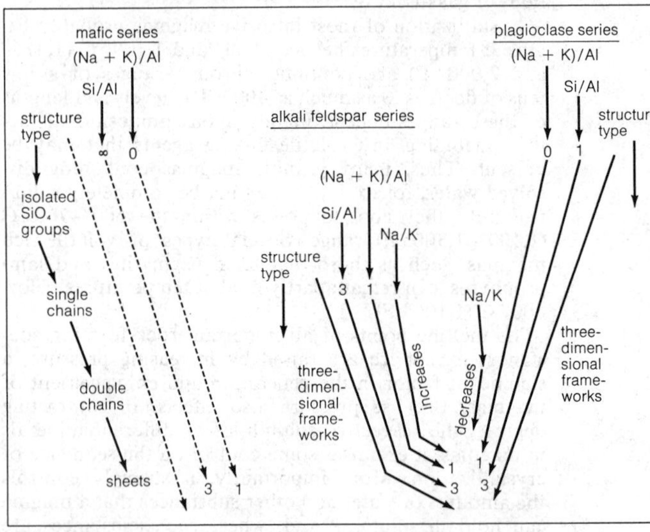

Figure 8: Principal trends in composition and structure type among minerals of the reaction series shown in Figure 7.

The presence of a certain mineral in an igneous rock does not necessarily indicate that it was developed by reaction from another mineral higher in its series, because the overall composition of the system dictates whether or not certain minerals can form. A calcium-free magma, for example, can yield no diopside or intermediate plagioclase, and a potassium-free magma can yield no orthoclase or leucite. Some magmas, in effect, encompass the entire span of the reaction series; whereas others complete their crystallization in the upper parts, and still others begin theirs in the lower parts. Finally, the specific courses of crystallization can vary considerably with respect to the timing of events within and between the reaction series, in part because of the fractionation of different elements among the many solid phases forming in a typical system. Despite these and other complexities of detailed application, the reaction principle is an extremely valuable indicator of general sequence and compositional trends in magmatic processes.

Effects of water and other fluid phases

Volatile constituents and late magmatic processes. Water and most other volatile substances profoundly influence the properties and behaviour of magmas in which they are dissolved. They reduce viscosity, lower temperatures of crystallization by tens to hundreds of degrees, and participate directly in the formation of minerals that contain essential hydroxyl (OH) or elements such as the halogens. They also increase rates of crystallization and reaction, especially when they are present as a fluid phase distinct from the magma. In general, however, they have only a limited influence on the sequence of magmatic crystallization, except in the latest stages of the reaction series.

The relatively low confining pressures in volcanic environments permit ready escape of volatile constituents, which nonetheless leave their imprint in the form of special mineral assemblages and a variety of textural and structural features among the volcanic rocks. Under the higher pressures of plutonic environments, these constituents tend to be maintained in magmatic solution and to be increasingly concentrated as crystallization progresses with falling temperature. Few members of the reaction series require them as compositional contributors; water, for example, is not thus used until amphiboles or micas begin to form, and even then the amounts removed from the melt rarely are large. Escape of volatiles from the system can occur "osmotically" if the enclosing rocks are pervious to them but not to the magma, but in general they are fractionated in favour of the residual melt until their concentration reaches the limit of solubility under the prevailing conditions of temperature and effective confining pressure. When this happens, normally at a very late stage of magmatic crystallization, they are exsolved from the melt as a separate fluid phase that under most circumstances is a supercritical gas. This process has been referred to as resurgent boiling, a somewhat misleading term because the exsolved fluid is not necessarily expelled from the system.

Pegmatites and late-stage mineralization

Coexistence of residual magma and a volatile-rich fluid (generally aqueous) promotes the partitioning and segregation of constituents, as well as the growth of very large crystals. The exsolved fluid, with its very low viscosity, not only can move readily through open spaces in the nearly solid igneous rock and in adjacent rocks but also serves as a medium through which various substances can diffuse rapidly in response to concentration gradients. Thus, it plays an important role in the formation of such special rock types as the pegmatites (Figure 9) and lamprophyres, special features such as miaroles and plumose mineral aggregates, and many kinds of ore deposits whose constituents are derived from the original magma.

Most plutonic systems remain at elevated temperatures for long periods of time after all magma has been used up, and during these periods hydrothermal conditions normally obtain. These depend upon the continued presence of a typically aqueous fluid that further facilitates crystallization and exchanges of materials. It speeds up exsolution within homogeneous solid phases and devitrification of any glass that may be present, and it is a potent agent in the alteration, leaching, and replacement of minerals. Rock textures thereby are modified, especially along boundaries between original mineral grains, and details of composition also can be much changed.

Richard H. Jahns

Figure 9: Giant lathlike crystals of spodumene in very coarse-grained pegmatite, Harding mine, Dixon, New Mexico. These crystals, four to 10 feet long, have been warped, cross fractured, and "healed" with quartz (dark). Spodumene, a lithium pyroxene, forms the largest crystals known among the igneous rocks.

In some instances the bulk chemistry of the rock is markedly affected.

Among the constituents commonly added during hydrothermal alteration are water, hydroxyl, carbon dioxide, boron, fluorine, chlorine, and sulfur. Calcium and magnesium ordinarily are subtracted, silicon is either added or subtracted, and aluminum and the major alkalies are shifted about in complex ways. The alterations favour development of phases such as albite, carbonates, chlorites, clay minerals, epidotes, iron oxides, micas, silica minerals, talc, and zeolites, and many of them are accompanied by gross changes in volume.

OCCURRENCE OF IGNEOUS ROCKS

The behaviour of magma at the Earth's surface is governed by an interplay of factors that include scale and rate of extrusion, timing of extrusive episodes, shape and distribution of vents, nature of the surrounding rocks, configuration of the surface that is occupied, and the temperature, composition, and gas content of the magma itself. The natural result is a great variety of volcanic bodies with considerable ranges in form and size. Some of them express relatively quiet effusions of lava, and others express explosive production of pyroclastic debris. These are described in the articles VOLCANOES; IGNEOUS ROCKS, EXTRUSIVE; and IGNEOUS ROCKS, PYROCLASTIC.

Any intrusive body of igneous rock is generally called a pluton. Many plutons are almost entirely enclosed by the invaded rocks and are termed injected bodies. Others, generally of larger size, extend to great depths and have no known or inferred floors; they are termed subjacent bodies. Concordant plutons are essentially parallel, or conformable, with the principal structural features of the flanking or enclosing rocks, whereas discordant ones are transgressive with respect to the host-rock structure. Classification also is made in terms of general shape (see Figure 10). The more common plutons are described in the article IGNEOUS ROCKS, INTRUSIVE.

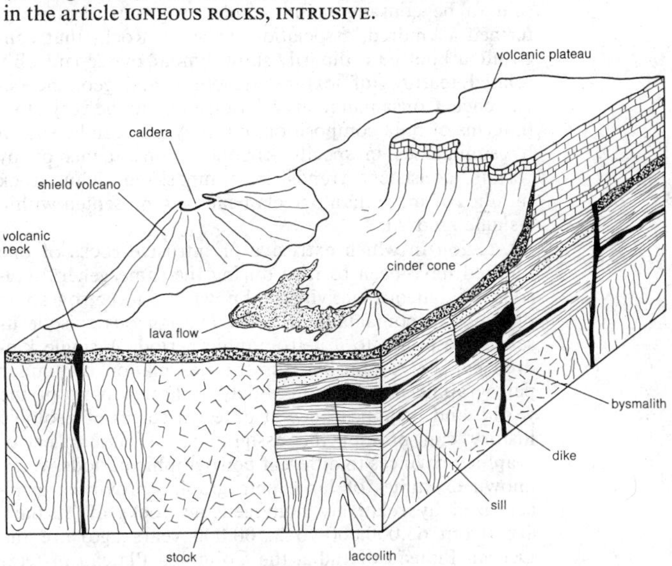

Figure 10: Block diagram showing general forms and relationships among various igneous bodies.

Rock distribution and abundance. The plutonic igneous rocks are by far most abundantly exposed in the great mountain chains and ancient shield areas of the Earth's continental masses. The volcanic rocks also are widely represented in these environments of former strong crustal deformation, as well as in many relatively undeformed parts of the continents. Basic volcanic rocks are dominant in the ocean basins. Within the Earth's crust as a whole, deep-seated plutonic rocks are much more abundant than volcanic and hypabyssal types.

Plutonic and extrusive rocks

Among the exposed intrusive rocks, the granites, quartz–monzonites, granodiorites, and quartz–diorites together are more than 20 times as abundant as the members of all other families combined. The saturated and undersaturated alkalic rocks such as syenites, monzonites, and nepheline syenites represent less than 1 percent of the total volume of all intrusive rocks, and the diorites, gabbros, and ultrabasic rocks are not much more abundant. Among the extrusive rocks, however, the situation is quite different. Basalts are at least five times more abundant than members of all other extrusive families combined, and andesites and basalts taken together are much more than 50 times as abundant as the remainder of the extrusive rocks. This contrast reflects the facts that members of the four oversaturated clans form most of the very large intrusive bodies in the Earth's crust and that members of the basalt and andesite clans form all of the Earth's great volcanic sheets and piles.

Nearly all of the common rock types are represented throughout the geologic column, the granitic and basaltic rocks most consistently and abundantly so. The general diversity of magmas may have changed little with time, but some significant shifts are suggested by the following relationships: (1) the granites and rhyolites are far more abundant in Precambrian terranes (*i.e.*, rocks that are older than 570,000,000 years) than in those of lesser age; (2) the other quartz-bearing igneous rocks are most abundant in post-Precambrian terranes, especially so in those of post-Paleozoic age (younger than 225,000,000 years); (3) members of the monzonite and syenite clans show a similar but less well-defined trend toward relative abundance in younger parts of the geologic column; (4) anorthosites seem to have been essentially restricted in their development to Precambrian time; and (5) emplacement of great sill-like and lopolithic masses of basic magma was far more characteristic of the Precambrian than of any subsequent part of geologic history.

Consanguineous association

Rock kindreds and petrographic provinces. Many igneous rocks that are closely associated in space and time also resemble one another so closely in major aspects of mineral and chemical composition that an intimate genetic relationship is strongly suggested. Such rocks are said to be consanguineous, and any group of them is termed a kindred, association, or suite. Rocks that constitute a kindred ordinarily show similar or recognizably related features of texture, structure, and geologic occurrence. Consanguineous relationships can be very close in terms of bulk composition, but they also can be shown by similarities in specific chemical constituents or by certain consistent trends in composition. Thus rock families of more than one clan can be represented within a single kindred.

A region in which extrusive or intrusive rocks of one kindred have been formed during the same general episode of igneous activity is known as a petrographic province or comagmatic region. The igneous episode itself corresponds to a petrographic period. A single kindred can be responsible for the designation of similar petrographic provinces in widely separated parts of the world, and its appearance at different stages of geologic history can prompt the assignment of similar petrographic provinces to different petrographic periods. Well-known examples of large petrographic provinces characterized by relatively homogeneous rocks of Tertiary age (from 65,000,000 to 2,500,000 years ago) are the Deccan Plateau of India, the Columbia Plateau of Oregon, and parts of Western Australia, where enormous volumes of tholeiitic basalts are present. These rocks are richer in SiO_2 and somewhat poorer in MgO, Na_2O, and K_2O than the alkaline olivine basalts.

The common basalt–andesite–dacite–rhyolite kindred forms the Cenozoic Cascade Province of California, Oregon, and Washington, the San Juan Province of southwestern Colorado, the Yellowstone Province of northwestern Wyoming, and the Black Range Province of southwestern New Mexico. The plutonic gabbro–quartz diorite–granodiorite–granite kindred is well represented by the great Mesozoic (from 225,000,000 to 65,000,000 years ago) batholiths of western North America. A broad kindred in which the granites are dominant characterizes the world's Precambrian shield areas. Olivine basalts that contain leucite and potassium feldspar constitute a distinctive and remarkably uniform kindred that appears in widely separated provinces, among them the Leucite Hills of Wyoming, the Roman Province of Western Italy, at least two major volcanic fields in Uganda, and the West Kimberley area of Western Australia.

The volcanic chain fringing the shore from Tierra del Fuego to Alaska and on to Japan to Java and Sumatra represents a large province. The rocks within have many similar characteristics and are believed to be of allied origin. They are subalkalic and calcic in composition and show an abundancy of lime, magnesia, and iron oxides. They range from Tertiary to Recent in age, covering the last 65,000,000 years.

These and many other examples illustrate correlations between certain kindreds and broad elements of crustal structure. Thus, the tectonic environment of the basalt–andesite–dacite–rhyolite, the peridotite–serpentinite, and the gabbro–quartz diorite–granodiorite–granite associations is typically continental and involves large-scale deformation of the mountain-building type. The alkalic kindreds are much less common in such settings and, instead, occur mainly in the ocean basins and in parts of the continental crust that either have been fairly stable or have been dislocated by faulting. Some genetic connection between structural behaviour of the Earth's crust and the diversification of magmas (*i.e.*, the derivation of numerous magmas of diverse composition from a relatively small number of initial types) seems inescapable, but it remains to be fully deciphered.

The question of one or more magmas

Diversification of magmas. Only two general magma types, granitic and basaltic, have had wide distribution throughout geologic time. A primary basaltic magma might have yielded all other known magma types by various processes of differentiation based upon crystal fractionation, but this seems unlikely. The quantitative relationships among the exposed igneous rocks are difficult to reconcile with this simple model, and in particular the existing volumes of granitic rocks are much too large relative to those of rocks that represent intermediate stages in the differentiation process. The concept of a parent basalt remains sound in principle, but an alternative general mechanism of magma generation also is required. By far the most satisfactory among several possibilities that have been considered is partial or complete melting of the crustal and subcrustal igneous materials.

Partial melting is essentially the reverse of fractional crystallization, and the trend in composition of the liquid being produced is the reverse of that indicated by the reaction series for a crystallizing liquid. If water and other volatile substances are present in the rocks, melting can begin at relatively low temperatures, as these volatiles are incorporated in the initial fractions of liquid being formed. This is the reverse operation relative to exsolution of volatiles during late stages in a crystallizing magma. When the volatiles are completely dissolved in the liquid, generally at an early stage in the fusion process, further melting occurs with temperatures that can be expected to rise more sharply. The composition of the newly formed magma depends upon the point at which insufficient heat is present for further melting or upon the point at which this liquid is drawn off from the residuum of materials that belong higher in the reaction series. Given sufficient thermal energy, the melting process can go to completion and yield a magma equivalent in composition to the initial rocks.

The abundant granitic rocks of the Earth's crust can be correlated with low-melting fractions of deeper crustal and subcrustal materials. Such fractions must be very large in many parts of the crust but small in the underlying relatively basic mantle. Magmas of intermediate composition could be similarly derived through partial fusion of basic rocks. For the fusion process in general, a balance can be expected among four factors—the amount and composition of partial melt and the amount and composition of unfused residue. As in late stages of the crystallization process, the less the amount of melt that is present, the greater is its compositional contrast with the coexisting solid materials.

Large bodies of granitic magmas evidently have been developed in belts where upper parts of the Earth's

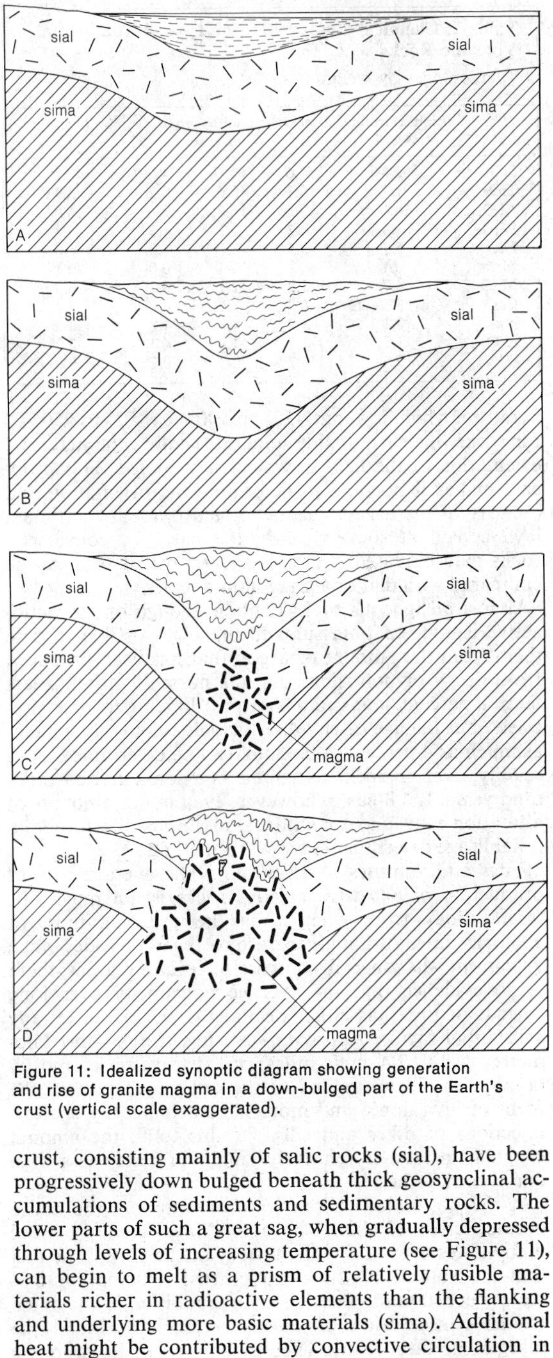

Figure 11: Idealized synoptic diagram showing generation and rise of granite magma in a down-bulged part of the Earth's crust (vertical scale exaggerated).

Granitic magmas and geosynclines

crust, consisting mainly of salic rocks (sial), have been progressively down bulged beneath thick geosynclinal accumulations of sediments and sedimentary rocks. The lower parts of such a great sag, when gradually depressed through levels of increasing temperature (see Figure 11), can begin to melt as a prism of relatively fusible materials richer in radioactive elements than the flanking and underlying more basic materials (sima). Additional heat might be contributed by convective circulation in the underlying mantle, and the thick cover of overlying strata, much deformed and in part metamorphosed during the later stages of downbuckling (Figure 11, C), would slow the rate of heat escape and hence serve as a thermal blanket over the sag. These conditions would favour the generation of magmas by partial or complete fusion and attendant volume increase of the salic materials, with or without accompanying fusion of the underlying more basic rocks. These magmas then could rise through the denser overlying solid materials (Figure 11, D) to form the intrusive rocks of intermediate to silicic composition that are so abundant in the cores of many continental mountain ranges.

Deeper origins are plainly indicated for the basaltic rocks of the ocean basins, which probably represent partial melting of mantle materials beneath oceanic crust. Such rocks presumably are being formed today along axes of sea-floor spreading (*q.v.*), and they also appear in volcanoes that locally rise to points above present sea level. Other volcanic activities mark the zones along which oceanic crust is being thrust beneath masses of continental crust. Correlation of these activities with intrusive processes in adjacent parts of the continents is a fascinating and challenging problem that awaits complete solution.

BIBLIOGRAPHY. Textbooks treating the igneous rocks are quite numerous and only a sample of the available works can be given here. General treatments include ALFRED HARKER, *Petrology for Students*, 8th ed. rev. (1954); K.C. JACKSON, *Textbook of Lithology* (1970); J.F. KEMP, *A Handbook of Rocks*, 6th ed. rev. and ed. by F.F. GROUT (1940); L.V. PIRSSON, *Rocks and Rock Minerals*, 3rd ed. rev. by ADOLPH KNOPF, (1947); S.J. SHAND, *The Study of Rocks*, 3rd ed. rev. (1951); and G.W. TYRRELL, *The Principles of Petrology: An Introduction to the Science of Rocks*, 2nd ed. (1929, reprinted 1963). Among the more advanced textbooks available that treat nomenclature, classification, and theoretical igneous petrology, the following works are recommended to the interested reader: T.F.W. BARTH, *Theoretical Petrology*, 2nd ed. (1962); BRIAN BAYLY, *Introduction to Petrology* (1968); N.L. BOWEN, *The Evolution of the Igneous Rocks* (1928; republished with new introduction by J.F. SCHAIRER, 1956); C.W. CROSS *et al.*, *Quantitative Classification of Igneous Rocks, Based on Chemical and Mineral Characters, with a Systematic Nomenclature* (1903); R.A. DALY, *Igneous Rocks and the Depths of the Earth* (1933, reprinted 1968); ARTHUR HOLMES, *The Nomenclature of Petrology* (1920, reprinted 1971); ALBERT JOHANNSEN, *A Descriptive Petrography of the Igneous Rocks:* vol. 1, *Introduction, Textures, Classifications and Glossary*, 2nd ed. (1939); vol. 2, *The Quartz-Bearing Rocks* (1932); vol. 3, *The Intermediate Rocks* (1937); and vol. 4, pt. 1, *The Feldspathoidal Rocks*, pt. 2, *The Peridotites and Perknites* (1938); S. J. SHAND, *Eruptive Rocks*, 3rd. ed. (1947); F.J. TURNER and JOHN VERHOOGEN, *Igneous and Metamorphic Petrology*, 2nd ed. (1960); E.E. WAHLSTROM, *Introduction to Theoretical Igneous Petrology* (1950); and HOWEL WILLIAMS, F.J. TURNER, and C.M. GILBERT, *Petrography* (1954).

Other references of interest include ROBERT BALK, "Structural Behavior of Igneous Rocks," *Mem. Geol. Soc. Am. 5* (1937); N.L. BOWEN, "Magmas," *Bull. Geol. Soc. Am.*, 58: 263–279 (1947); JAMES GILULLY (ed.), "Origin of Granite," *Mem. Geol. Soc. Am. 28* (1948); H.H. HESS and ARIE POLDERVAART, (eds.), *Basalts*, 2 vol. (1967–68); ARIE POLDERVAART, (ed.), "Crust of the Earth," *Spec. Pap. Geol. Soc. Am. 62* (1955); J.J. SEDERHOLM, *Selected Works: Granites and Migmatites* (1967); O.F. TUTTLE and N.L. BOWEN, "Origin of Granite in the Light of Experimental Studies in the System $NaAlSi_3O_8$–$KAlSi_3O_8$–SiO_2–H_2O," *Mem. Geol. Soc. Am. 74* (1958); L.R. WAGER and G.M. BROWN, *Layered Igneous Rocks* (1967); P.J. WYLLIE, *The Dynamic Earth: Textbook in Geosciences* (1971); and (ed.), *Ultramafic and Related Rocks* (1967). A host of additional treatments of descriptive and analytical nature can be found in geological journals such as the *American Journal of Science* (monthly), *Bulletin of The Geological Society of America* (monthly), *Economic Geology* (8/year), *Journal of Geology* (bimonthly), *Journal of Geophysical Research* (3/month), *Journal of Petrology* (3/year), and *Quarterly Journal of The Geological Society* (London).

(R.H.J.)

Igneous Rocks, Extrusive

Extrusive igneous rocks are formed from molten silicate liquids (magmas) that rise from the earth's interior and then erupt at the surface through volcanic vents. They constitute a major fraction of the earth's crust, and, in the course of geologic time, the process by which they are generated at depth and rise to the surface has been responsible for most of the evolution of the Earth's crust and upper mantle (the zone separating the crust and the core). Volcanic rocks form the major part of at least the upper kilometre or so (about 3,300 feet or more) of the oceanic crust; although they cover less than a quarter of the land surface of the earth, they were the primary source for the constituents of most of the sedimentary and metamorphic rocks that derived from them by weathering, erosion, and chemical and mineralogical alteration.

Extrusive igneous rocks occur on all continents and are most prominent in areas such as India and the northwestern United States, where the Deccan Traps and Columbia River basalts, respectively, can be termed flood basalts because of their great lateral extent. Other occurrences of note include, of course, areas of active volcanism today, such as the circum-Pacific island-arc zone—the ring of fire. Throughout geological time there have been similar extrusions of magma, and many of the world's present and former mountain systems contain extrusive igneous rocks that were deposited in submerged geosynclines, major depositional troughs and loci of subsequent mountain building.

This article treats the properties of extrusive igneous rocks and their occurrence, distribution, classification, and origin. For coverage of associated intrusive rocks and their relationship to extrusive varieties, see IGNEOUS ROCKS; and IGNEOUS ROCKS, INTRUSIVE. The special characteristics of extrusive rocks that are formed by the accumulation of violently ejected volcanic particles are covered in the separate article IGNEOUS ROCKS, PYROCLASTIC. See also the articles VOLCANOES; ISLAND ARCS; RIFT VALLEYS; and MOUNTAIN-BUILDING PROCESSES for further information on the present and former occurrence and significance of extrusive igneous rocks.

GENERAL CHARACTERISTICS

Physical and chemical properties. With the exception of certain very rare types of extrusive rocks, the vast majority are composed of silicate minerals and fall within the range of compositions illustrated in Tables 1 and 2. Their physical properties are a reflection of their chemical and mineralogic composition.

Table 1: Chemical Composition of Typical Oceanic Volcanic Rocks
(percentages by weight)

	tholeiitic basalt	alkali basalt	nepheline basanite	icelandite	mugearite	trachyte	phonolite
SiO_2	49.5	46.5	44.3	59.3	51.9	65.3	55.8
TiO_2	2.0	3.0	2.6	1.1	2.6	0.7	0.3
Al_2O_3	14.5	14.6	12.8	14.5	16.0	14.8	19.2
Fe_2O_3	3.0	3.3	3.4	3.4	4.2	3.2	2.3
FeO	8.5	9.1	9.2	4.6	6.3	1.5	0.9
MnO	0.2	0.1	0.2	0.1	0.2	0.1	0.1
MgO	6.6	8.2	11.0	2.0	3.7	0.6	0.2
CaO	10.6	10.3	10.5	4.8	6.3	1.2	0.9
Na_2O	2.1	2.9	3.6	4.4	5.2	6.1	9.8
K_2O	0.4	0.8	1.0	2.1	2.0	3.0	5.7
P_2O_5	0.3	0.4	0.4	0.5	0.8	0.2	0.1

The density of solid lavas free of bubbles varies inversely with silica content and ranges from about 2.3 grams per cubic centimetre (1.3 ounces per cubic inch) for rhyolite to 2.4 or 2.5 (1.4 to 1.45 ounces per cubic inch) for andesite and 2.7 to 2.8 (1.55 to 1.6 ounces per cubic inch) for basalt. Rocks are about 5 to 10 percent less dense in the liquid state than in the crystalline state. The number of bubbles, or vesicles, in a rock may decrease its density until, as in the case of pumice, it may be less than one, and thus the rock will float on water.

Melting temperatures at atmospheric pressure are also a function of composition and decrease from about 1,200° C (2,200° F) for basalt to 950° C (1,750° F) for rhyolite. Load pressure increases the melting temperature of most rocks by about 3° or 4° for each kilometre of burial, but elevated water pressure decreases the melting temperature, so that rhyolite melts at about 600° C (1,100° F) at pressures equivalent to a depth of 30 kilometres (about 100,000 feet). All extrusive rocks are erupted at temperatures close to, or somewhat below, the crystallization temperature of their constituent minerals. There is no record of a lava reaching the surface at a temperature significantly above its melting temperature at atmospheric pressure.

The viscosity of lavas ranges from values as low as 10^2 poises (dyne-seconds per square centimetre; the force required to overcome internal friction and thus produce flow at a unit rate) for certain alkali basalts to 10^8 or higher for rhyolite. The former value is about equivalent to the viscosity of heavy motor oil, whereas the latter is comparable to cold asphalt. The viscosity of lavas increases sharply when water or other gases are exsolved, and cooling has a similar effect.

Table 2: Chemical Composition of Typical Continental Volcanic Rocks
(percentages by weight)

	high-alumina basalt	andesite	dacite	rhyolite	lamprophyre
SiO_2	52.8	58.6	63.6	74.6	40.7
TiO_2	1.1	0.8	0.6	0.2	3.9
Al_2O_3	18.0	17.5	16.7	12.6	16.0
Fe_2O_3	3.4	3.2	2.2	1.3	5.4
FeO	5.7	3.5	3.0	1.0	7.8
Mn	0.1	0.1	0.1	0.0	0.1
MgO	4.7	3.2	2.1	0.1	5.8
CaO	9.3	6.3	5.3	0.6	9.2
Na_2O	3.1	3.8	4.0	4.2	3.5
K_2O	1.3	1.7	1.8	4.7	2.0
P_2O_5	0.5	0.2	0.2	0.2	0.6

Most lavas that contain at least a few percent of magnetite have a high magnetic susceptibility and thermoremnant magnetism. As they cool through the Curie temperature, which is about 450° to 500° C (850° to 950° F) for rocks, their iron oxide minerals acquire the magnetic orientation of the field in which they cooled. This property makes it possible to determine the orientation and polarity of the earth's magnetic field (*q.v.*) at the time a lava cooled at some time in the past, or, conversely, rocks may be dated if their magnetic orientation can be compared with that of a known time scale.

Magnetic properties and age dating

Almost all igneous rocks contain enough of the radioactive isotope of potassium to make it possible to date them from the amount of argon that has been produced from decay of potassium. Basalts normally contain less than 1 percent potassium and are difficult to date precisely, but the age of rhyolites, which commonly contain as much as 4 percent potassium, can be determined more readily, even in rocks as young as a few hundred thousand years. In all cases, however, even minor amounts of alteration may make it difficult or impossible to obtain reliable age determinations by this method.

Rates and volumes of eruption. The average rate of production of extrusive igneous rocks is not much different today from what it has been during most of geologic time. Although there have been episodes when volcanism was especially intense in certain regions, there is no evidence that the average volcanicity over long periods of time has either declined or increased by any substantial factor. Approximately five to ten cubic kilometres (1.2 to 2.4 cubic miles) of extrusive rocks, mostly oceanic basalt, are added to the crust each year in the form of lava flows, and more is contributed by shallow injections of dikes and sills. Of this total, the amount erupted on land is relatively small, probably less than one cubic kilometre.

At the postulated current rate of eruption, the entire oceanic crust of the globe could have been produced many times over during the history of the earth. The fact that the volume of the oceanic crust remains approximately constant despite this annual addition is attributed to the consumption of crust in trenches around the margins of the oceans. The volcanic rocks thrust down into the mantle must be recycled in some manner over extended periods of geologic time. In contrast, material erupted on the continents is preserved in one form or another as a permanent addition to the crust.

OCCURRENCE AND DISTRIBUTION

Despite the generally constant rate of volcanism for the earth as a whole over long periods of time, activity has been especially intense in certain regions during restricted intervals of the past. Throughout the geological record, volcanism has shifted from one region to another. During Permian time (225,000,000 to 280,000,000 years ago) volcanism was intense throughout the western part of North America and much of northwestern Europe. A large proportion of the volcanic rocks of Great Britain and western Germany were laid down during this period, and great piles of lava of the same age are found in parts of California, Oregon, Nevada, and British Columbia. Similarly, the Triassic Period (190,000,000 to 225,000,000 years ago) witnessed eruptions of great sheets of basaltic lava in South Africa and similar lavas and shallow intrusions in the eastern United States. Comparable activity marked the early part of the Tertiary Period (about 60,000,000 years ago) in the British–Arctic province and large areas of India. Miocene time (7,000,000 to 26,000,000 years ago) was a period of intense volcanic activity throughout most of the circum-Pacific region, especially in the northwestern United States, where the lavas of the Columbia Plateau were erupted in great sheets that at one time covered almost 500,000 square kilometres (190,000 square miles).

The circum-Pacific chain of fire

At present, most of the recently active land volcanoes of the earth are concentrated in a narrow belt around the margins of the Pacific Ocean. Sometimes called the Pacific chain of fire, this belt follows the Andes through Chile, Peru, and Ecuador, misses Colombia and Panama, but appears again in Costa Rica, Nicaragua, El Salvador, and Guatemala. A separate link of the chain crosses central Mexico, and small cones are scattered throughout northwestern Mexico and the southwestern United States. The Cascade Range between northern California and southern British Columbia displayed little activity during historic times but has been the scene of numerous eruptions in the very recent past. There are few volcanoes in northern British Columbia, but an almost unbroken chain crosses Alaska and the Aleutian Islands to Kamchatka and Asia. The western Pacific is fringed with a series of volcanic-island arcs extending from the Kurile Islands through Japan, the Mariana Islands, and the Ryukyu Islands, the Philippines and Melanesia, the Tonga–Kermadec Arc, and New Zealand. Most of these belts are characterized by large composite andesitic volcanoes that have attained their present size through intermittent activity during most of Quaternary time (the last 2,500,000 years, approximately).

The remaining volcanic activity on land is concentrated in a few areas, mainly in Indonesia, East Africa, the Mediterranean, the Antilles, and Iceland. Elsewhere, even in regions of strong mountain building, such as the Alps and Himalayas, there are few if any young volcanoes, and those that have been recently active have had only small sporadic eruptions. In certain very ancient regions of the continents, such as the Canadian Shield, South Africa, the eastern part of South America, and large areas of Asia, there has been no significant volcanism for hundreds of millions of years.

Submarine volcanoes

Volcanism is also unevenly distributed in the deep ocean basins. Most of the emergent volcanoes are situated close to oceanic ridges, such as the East Pacific Rise and Mid-Atlantic Ridge. They are especially common where these ridges are intersected by transverse fracture zones. The Galápagos Islands, one of the most active volcanic regions on earth, lie near the junction of the East Pacific Rise, the Cocos Ridge, and the Galápagos Fracture Zone. The Hawaiian Islands are somewhat anomalous in that they are far removed from the East Pacific Rise. They are aligned along a northwest-tending fracture that extends for 2,500 kilometres (1,550 miles) across the central northern Pacific. Activity has migrated with time toward the southeast, and all recent activity has been concentrated in the islands at the southeastern extremity.

If the thousands of submarine volcanoes that form seamounts and guyots (flat-topped forms) on the ocean floor could be observed, large concentrations of activity would be noted in certain regions, such as the western Pacific and the Gulf of Alaska, whereas other regions, such as the abyssal plain of the Atlantic Ocean east of Argentina, would indicate only sparse volcanic activity during the last 100,000,000 years.

Oceanic volcanic rocks. The major volume of submarine lava is extruded from fissures along the crests of oceanic ridges. There is no way of observing such eruptions directly; the nature and origin of the rocks can only be deduced from bottom photographs, dredge hauls, geophysical measurements, and other indirect methods. Much of what is known about submarine volcanism has been learned in places where the ancient sea floor has been uplifted and exposed, so that the nature of the rocks can be observed.

The morphology of subaqueous lavas is quite distinct. They are characterized by "pillow" structures, in which the basalt forms globular masses roughly the size and shape of pillows. Each pillow has a dark, glassy shell of quickly chilled lava encasing a crystalline interior that cooled more slowly. Under the pressure of several thousand metres of water, there is little exsolution of the water vapour and other gases that are dissolved in fluid basalt, so that gas bubbles (vesicles) are small or totally absent. At shallower levels and lower water pressures, the size and number of vesicles increase. On the submarine slopes of Hawaii, for example, there is a progressive increase in the proportion of gas cavities in the lavas from the base of the volcano up to sea level. At shallow depths, where bubbles expand to a large volume and expose a wider surface area to the quenching action of water, the glass may shatter into myriads of small, angular fragments. Masses of this material, sometimes referred to as hyaloclastites, may accumulate in deposits several hundreds of metres thick in which the lavas have disintegrated to the point where they are unrecognizable as distinct flow units. Alteration and hydration of this fragmental glass advance rapidly and convert it to palagonite, a yellowish-brown mixture of clay and other secondary minerals. Chemical alteration of basalt in seawater results in a steady loss of sodium, calcium, manganese, and magnesium and a gain of potassium, titanium, iron, and water.

Interaction of submarine lavas and seawater

Prolonged activity at a centralized submarine vent produces broad symmetrical cones, or "shield volcanoes," that may reach enormous size. According to recent estimates, there are more than 20,000 submarine volcanoes with a relief of more than 1,000 metres (3,300 feet). Although only a small number of these volcanoes grow large enough to reach the surface and emerge as islands, there are hundreds, if not thousands, of submarine volcanoes that exceed the height and volume of Mt. Etna, in Sicily, the largest volcano on land.

On approaching the surface of the sea, the extruded lava vaporizes the seawater with which it comes in contact and causes a sudden volumetric expansion of steam with attendant explosive eruptions, often of great violence. Under such conditions, lavas are unable to form, and, instead, the eruption produces only fragmental debris. Not until the volcano passes through this stage and the vent is high enough to be protected from the inrush of seawater will lava flows be restored. An excellent example of a young volcano that passed through this stage is the recently formed island of Surtsey off the southern coast of Iceland.

Subsequent growth of oceanic volcanoes above sea level results from accumulation of thin lava flows with relatively little interlayered ash and scoria. The elevation to which volcanic islands rise is normally less than 2,000 metres (6,600 feet) above sea level, but Mauna Kea in Hawaii, the highest volcano in the oceans, rises 4,200 metres (13,800 feet) above sea level, and, if measured from its base on the ocean floor, it has a height that approximates that of Mt. Everest.

Oceanic basalts, such as those of Hawaii or the Galápagos Islands, are erupted at temperatures between 1,050° and 1,200° C (1,920° and 2,200° F). Their viscosity is unusually low (about 2,000 to 4,000 poises), so that the flows move rapidly down gentle slopes toward the sea. Lava with a smooth or ropelike surface texture, called pahoehoe by the Hawaiians, is common, especially near the source, but a clinkery scoriaceous type of lava, called aa, is also abundant. Many of the lava eruptions come from radial or concentric fissure vents around the summit. Eruptions from fissures on the flanks of Hawaiian volcanoes produce especially voluminous flows, commonly at rates as high as 10,000 to 20,000 cubic metres (353,000 to 706,000 cubic feet) per day. The average rate of outpouring during historic time for the island of Hawaii is approximately 0.025 cubic kilometres (0.006 cubic miles) per year.

Rocks of the orogenic system. The igneous rocks that are erupted in the course of development of mountain-building systems have a character and a geologic association that are distinct from those of the igneous rocks of the oceans. Modern examples are closely related to the linear volcanic belts, trenches, and zones of earthquake activity that follow the boundaries between some of the oceanic and continental regions, and it seems likely that similar relations prevailed in the past.

In the early geosynclinal stages—when large volumes of clastic sediments such as sandstones are accumulating in a subsiding trough—volcanic rocks are normally erupted from vents near the landward margin of the deepest part of the geosyncline. These vents may not necessarily be large composite cones; many are probably fissures. Basaltic and andesitic pyroclastic material and detritus from subaerial erosion contribute a large volume to the sedimentary material poured into the trough. At the same time, submarine lavas or shallow intrusions of dikes and sills are interlayered with the sediments. Many submarine lavas from this environment have unusually high sodium contents and distinctive mineral assemblages. Basalts of this type are called spilites, and the more siliceous rocks, keratophyres. Both contain a sodic plagioclase—albite or oligoclase—and abundant chlorite, greenish pyroxene, epidote, and calcite. To a large degree, these rocks owe their present compositional features to low-grade metamorphism under submarine conditions. Not all submarine lavas of this environment are spilites; nor are all spilites confined to the orogenic association—they have also been reported from modern oceanic ridges. It is believed, therefore, that many of the basaltic lavas found in geosynclinal sediments were erupted much earlier on the floor of the deep ocean basin far from their present site, were subjected to various degrees of alteration, and were then carried into the trench as part of the oceanic crust. In this sense, they belong to the true oceanic series considered in the preceding section.

Spilites and keratophyres

The great majority of orogenic volcanic rocks are erupted from large andesitic cones, much like those that are seen today in the island arcs and continental margins of the circum-Pacific. They normally form a belt parallel to an oceanic trench, about 100 to 150 kilometres (60 to 90 miles) away from the trench on the continental side. Strong negative-gravity anomalies are found near the axis of the trench, and positive ones are common, though less distinct, along the volcanic axis. Large numbers of earthquakes are localized along a plane, commonly referred to as the Benioff zone, that extends from the trench downward at angles of about 45° to 60° beneath the volcanoes. In areas of active volcanism, these earthquakes occur down to depths as deep as 700 kilometres (450 miles), but the main axis of volcanism lies above a portion of the zone in which earthquakes are fewer in number and have a depth of 100 to 200 kilometres (60 to 120 miles; see further EARTHQUAKES).

Andesitic volcanoes

The lavas of even the largest andesitic cones are much less voluminous than those of oceanic volcanoes. Individual eruptions seldom produce more than a few thousand cubic metres of lava, and there are usually long intervals between events, especially in older volcanoes. The proportion of explosive pyroclastic ejecta is higher than that of oceanic volcanoes and in some regions may account for a larger volume than lava.

The life-span of an individual andesitic volcano is seldom long. Many of the large volcanoes of the Cascade Range of the western United States attained their full size in less than 1,000,000 years and are already on the decline. Growth is usually most rapid in the early stages; some of the moderately large volcanoes of Central America and Japan have grown to their present size within historic time. But, as they advance in age, eruptions become less frequent and more erratic. Many mature volcanoes go through violent eruptions of pumice that drain their magma reservoir and cause the summit region to collapse and form a caldera, such as that of Crater Lake in Oregon. In others, such as the famous puys of the Auvergne in central France or Mt. Pelée in Martinique, a spine or steep-sided dome of viscous lava may be protruded from the summit or from satellite vents around the flanks and base.

Volcanism often continues for periods of several million years and then gives way to an episode of plutonic intrusion. Surface eruptions may later be renewed, normally along a new axis slightly offset from the first, and continue through a second or even a third sequence of volcanic and plutonic activity before large-scale deformation causes folding, faulting, and uplift of the entire region. The detailed histories of no two regions are the same, but broadly similar sequences are found in most of the orogenic systems that have evolved during past geological periods.

Continental flood lavas. The most voluminous extrusions of lava in the geological record are the vast sheets of basalt that have poured out in several regions at widely spaced intervals of time. The lava flows of Iceland are the only modern example, and these are relatively small compared with prehistoric flows in other regions. The 1783 eruption of the Icelandic volcano Laki spread 12.3 cubic kilometres (three cubic miles) of basalt over an area of 565 square kilometres (220 square miles). During the first 50 days of the eruption, the lava was extruded from a 25-kilometre-long (15-mile-long) fissure at an average rate of 2,200 cubic metres (77,600 cubic feet) per second. This is a relatively small flow compared with some of the lavas that were erupted on the Columbia River plateau some 10,000,000 to 15,000,000 years ago and covered an area of about 500,000 square kilometres (193,000 square miles). Some of the Columbia River lavas have been traced as far as 150 kilometres (93 miles) and have volumes as great as 300 cubic kilometres (72 cubic miles). Despite the great volume of individual eruptions, however, the average rate of production of lava over long periods of time was only about 0.03 cubic kilometres (0.007 cubic miles) per year, because there were long periods of quiet between individual eruptions. Other examples of flood lavas are the Late Cretaceous and Early Tertiary (about 65,000,000 years ago) Deccan basalts of India, which still cover an area of 650,000 square kilometres (251,000 square miles), and the Jurassic (136,000,000 to 190,000,000 years ago) Paraná basalts of Paraguay and Brazil, which cover more than 750,000 square kilometres (290,000 square miles).

The Icelandic flows of 1783

In all of these regions, the source vents were long fissures rather than cones with central vents. The high fluidity of the lavas produced wide areas of low relief that never rose much above sea level, despite the great thickness of accumulated lavas. Subsidence of the base of the volcanic pile seems to have kept pace with the outpouring of lavas on the surface.

Some of the lavas flowed into shallow bodies of water, probably lakes and streams, and produced pillow lavas and hyaloclastites similar to those from marine environments. Others, such as those in Iceland, erupted under ice sheets. The melting of glaciers during the 1783 eruption of the Laki Fissure produced great floods of meltwater that devastated much of southern Iceland. Subglacial eruptions commonly cause fragmentation of the quenched lava, which accumulates around the vent and forms a steep-sided ridge or mound as it rises into space produced by melting of ice. When the cover of ice and water is breached, lava may emerge as coherent flows that form a flat, resistant cap and protect the weaker, underlying fragmental material from erosion long after the ice has disappeared. The result is a table mountain, which is a common feature of the Icelandic landscape.

Siliceous ignimbrite sheets

The only other igneous extrusive rocks that approach the extent of flood basalts are the silica-rich ignimbrite sheets that have been erupted from fissure vents to spread over wide areas of the continents. These rocks differ from basalt not only in composition but also in their mode of eruption. They must have contained large amounts of gas, which exsolved and disrupted the liquid as it emerged from the vent, but, instead of being ejected vertically as in normal pyroclastic eruptions, the hot fluidized mixture of gas, magma, and crystals flowed with great mobility as a turbulent cloud across the surface. Few eruptions of this type have been observed during historic times, and those few examples that have been described by eyewitnesses were all small, but there is plentiful evidence that very large eruptions of this type covered wide areas in the past. Much of Nevada, Utah, and adjacent parts of the Great Basin of the western United States were once covered by ignimbrites to depths of several hundred metres. Similar deposits are found in western Mexico, central Honduras, and along the western slope of the Chilean Andes. Most of these examples were erupted during Tertiary time (from 2,500,000 to 65,000,000 years ago), but some of the ignimbrites of North Island, New Zealand, have been erupted within the last few thousand years.

CLASSIFICATION AND ORIGIN

Extrusive volcanic rocks are logically divided into three major groups according to the geologic setting in which they are found; namely, the oceans, the orogenic systems at continental margins, and the relatively stable regions of the continental interior. Rocks of each of these regions are characterized by distinctive chemical and mineralogic features that reflect the conditions under which they were produced.

Oceanic lavas. Basalts are by far the dominant rocks of the oceanic environment. They account for all but a minute fraction of submarine lavas and at least 90 percent of the volume of most oceanic islands. The basalts, though superficially uniform, vary significantly within certain broad compositional limits. Most common are the tholeiitic basalts, which normally contain about 50 percent silica (Table 1) and crystallized labradorite, augite, titaniferous magnetite, and in some cases a calcium-poor pyroxene. Olivine may be abundant as large crystals (phenocrysts), but it is not found as a stable mineral in the fine-grained matrix. The dark iron–magnesium minerals account for more than 40 percent of the volume. Basalts of this type are by far the most abundant submarine lavas, and they make up a major portion of many volcanic islands, such as Hawaii and Iceland.

Tholeiitic and alkali basalts

With decreasing silica content and a corresponding increase in sodium, potassium, magnesium, and titanium, tholeiitic basalts grade into the somewhat less common group of alkali basalts (Table 1). Olivine is an important constituent of the fine-grained matrix of these rocks; the augite is richer in titanium; and calcium-poor pyroxenes are absent. Basalts of this type appear in the late stages of activity in Hawaii; but elsewhere in the oceans, especially on islands far removed from the oceanic ridges, they may be the only type of basalt in the emergent part of the volcano. Extreme varieties of alkali basalt grade into basanites, which, in addition to the other minerals just named, contain a silica-deficient aluminous mineral, such as nepheline.

The significance of the subtle differences between varieties of basalt was recognized during the first part of this century by geologists working in the ancient volcanic centres of western Scotland, where it was found that the tholeiitic type is associated with a distinctive series of increasingly siliceous differentiated rocks terminating in rhyolites and granites with large amounts of excess silica in the form of quartz, whereas the alkali basalts appear to be the parent magma of a less siliceous group of rocks trending toward trachytes and syenites with little or no quartz. Thus, the small differences in the basalts were found to be magnified in divergent series of derivative liquids, one becoming increasingly oversaturated with silica and the other less so.

The workers in the Scottish districts viewed the alkali basalt as the single, primary parent of all other rocks, including the tholeiitic type, mainly because it was the first to be erupted and is the most voluminous rock in the province. The tholeiitic basalt was thought to result from contamination of the more primitive earlier magma by quartz-rich metamorphic and plutonic rocks of the continental crust. The logic of this explanation seemed all the more compelling when it was pointed out that alkali basalts seemed to be characteristic of oceanic volcanoes, while tholeiitic lavas seemed to be confined to continental regions where silica-rich crustal rocks are available.

This interpretation was widely accepted as a general model for basalts but was soon to be questioned by N.L. Bowen, a United States experimental petrologist whose interest in igneous rocks was that of a physical chemist. Bowen pointed out certain difficulties in balancing some of the chemical constituents involved in the contamination scheme and proposed an alternative relationship based on precipitation and removal of early-crystallizing minerals, mainly olivine, from the primary basalt to leave a residual liquid depleted in magnesium and relatively enriched in silica. Based as it was on modern laboratory studies of the crystallization of silicate liquids that provided a simplified analogue of natural rocks, Bowen's scheme offered a tangible demonstration of the mechanism of differentiation of igneous rocks and attracted immediate and widespread attention, especially in America. Within a short time, an imposing array of experimental evidence was compiled, by which it became possible to explain the composition of almost any igneous rock in terms of demonstrable physicochemical processes involving the precipitation of crystals from a melt and separation of successive liquids.

Bowen reaction series and rock differentiation

The problem of oceanic basalts arose again, however, when subsequent studies of the lavas of Hawaii and other volcanic islands showed that tholeiitic basalts were not restricted to the continents, as had been supposed, but made up a major part of the main mass of certain very large volcanoes. Obviously, they could not have resulted from the assimilation of continental material in alkali basalt, because such rocks are absent from the oceans. Bowen's mechanism of crystal fractionation, by which the tholeiitic basalts were produced by removal of olivine and other early-crystallizing minerals from a cooling alkali basalt, was equally inadequate; the alkali basalts appear late in the evolution of Hawaiian volcanoes and constitute a minor proportion of the total volume. If tholeiitic basalt were produced by partial crystallization of an alkali basalt and separation of the differentiated liquid, the order of eruption and relative volumes of the two types of lavas should be the reverse of what is actually observed.

R.A. Daly, a United States geologist, offered a possible solution of this dilemma when he suggested that alkali basalts resulted from assimilation of coral from old reefs buried within the interior of the volcano and caught up in the rising magma. The effect of contamination of the tholeiitic basalt with calcium carbonate from the corals would be to precipitate large amounts of calcium-rich plagioclase and pyroxene and thereby deplete the magma in alumina and silica, while residually enriching it in sodium, iron, and titanium. The special conditions and implausible volume relations that this mechanism required prevented it from being accepted as a general theory, although it may still hold for certain special cases.

A more satisfactory solution began to emerge only when experimental techniques were perfected that permitted studies of silicate melts at pressures and temperatures equivalent to those prevailing in the earth's mantle, at depths where basalts are thought to be derived. The results of this work, though still incomplete, have already demonstrated the important role of pressure in determining the composition of basaltic magmas. With increasing depth, partial melting of the mantle yields liquids that decrease in silica content as they become richer in alkalies and magnesium. Thus, it is now evident that no single basalt is the parent of all other igneous rocks, but that there is an entire spectrum from the tholeiitic basalts produced at relatively shallow depths (15 to 25 kilometres [9 to 16 miles]) to increasingly silica-deficient alkali basalts from greater depths, possibly down to 100 kilometres (60 miles) or more.

Importance of depth and pressure

Other lines of evidence support the experimental data on the depth of origin of basaltic lavas. It has been observed that earthquakes beneath the oceanic ridges seldom exceed a few tens of kilometres in depth and are concentrated at levels that are consistent with the generation of magma at shallow depths in the mantle. The earthquakes in overlying horizons may reflect the rise of magma as it passes through more brittle rocks on its way to the surface. In other parts of the oceans, earthquake focuses tend to be deeper, and the composition of the lavas indicates that they come from correspondingly greater depths. Similarly, precise measurements of the amount of heat reaching the surface of the sea floor from the earth's interior have been made in many regions of recent oceanic volcanism and are found to be extraordinarily high near the oceanic ridges and relatively lower at increasing distances down the flanks. High surface heat flow implies a steep thermal gradient and, hence, a shallow depth of melting consistent with the tholeiitic nature of the rocks in these regions. Low heat flow, which characterizes regions in which the lavas are more alkaline, indicates a low thermal gradient and deep levels of melting.

Many of the lavas of Hawaii and other oceanic islands contain inclusions of coarse-grained rocks composed almost entirely of olivine and pyroxene and little if any feldspar. The mineralogical character of the inclusions indicates that they have been carried up from the earth's mantle, possibly from the levels at which their host lava was formed. At the surface, some of the minerals of the inclusions are out of equilibrium with the lava in which they are found, but at high pressures the equilibrium conditions change, so that the minerals may be compatible with the liquid. Experimental studies of these relations show that the pressures at which the inclusions and lavas are compatible are consistent with the depths of melting deduced from experimental and geophysical evidence.

Most depth-dependent variations in lavas are confined to basaltic rocks, and it appears that the processes that lead to differentiation of basalt to various derivative rocks through increase of feldspar and loss of iron–magnesium minerals take place at relatively shallow depths, possibly within the conduit or in a shallow reservoir within the volcanic edifice. Deep erosion of volcanoes has exposed bodies of slowly cooled rock that appear to have crystallized at depths of only a few kilometres and produced a wide range of compositional variations as the liquid cooled and differentiated. In Tahiti, for example, very coarse grained rocks, ranging from gabbro to syenite, are now exposed by erosion in the cores of the large volcanoes. The process of differentiation of these levels is poorly understood, but it seems to be one that exaggerates the original chemical character of the parent basaltic magmas. Tholeiitic basalts, such as those of Iceland or the Galápagos Islands, yield first a group of intermediate lavas, sometimes called "icelandites," that are enriched in silica, iron, and sodium and depleted in calcium and magnesium. With further differentiation, iron begins to fall off rapidly, and the end product is a quartz trachyte or sodic rhyolite with as much as 70 percent silica and very few of the dark minerals (*e.g.*, pyroxene, olivine, or magnetite).

Mildly alkaline lavas, such as those of Hawaii or Réunion, yield a similar series with somewhat less silica enrichment. Intermediate rocks, called hawaiite and mugearite, resemble basalts, but their feldspars are more sodic (andesine and oligoclase, respectively), and the most differentiated rocks are trachytes that contain abundant alkali feldspars but little if any quartz.

The most silica deficient alkaline magmas, such as the nepheline basanites of Tahiti or Kerguelen Island, give rise to a series of derivative lavas that are characterized by increasingly high sodium contents and silica-poor minerals, such as nepheline, hauyne, and analcite, crystallizing in place of plagioclase. Their pyroxenes are also deficient in silica and contain instead relatively high proportions of aluminum, titanium, and sodium. The end-member of this series is normally phonolite, which consists almost entirely of alkali feldspar and a feldspathoid, such as nepheline.

Rocks in continental tectonic zones. In contrast with the great diversity of oceanic rocks, the extrusive rocks of tectonically active zones are relatively similar wherever they occur. They belong to what is commonly called the calc-alkaline series because of their relatively high proportion of plagioclase components. Andesite is by far the most voluminous and characteristic rock of this suite.

The calc-alkaline suite

Although there are minor variations that distinguish the andesites of island arcs, continental margins, or interior regions of continents, almost all of them share several principal features in common. They contain between 53 and 60 percent silica and have very abundant plagioclase; dark minerals, such as pyroxene, hornblende, and magnetite, make up less than 40 percent of their volume. Although the rocks are rich in silica and rarely have olivine, few contain quartz. Almost all of the calc-alkaline rocks are markedly porphyritic; that is, they have an important fraction of crystals, mainly plagioclase, that are much larger than the minerals of the matrix in which they are set.

Basalt, normally rich in alumina, commonly appears early in an episode of orogenic volcanism and may form the broad base upon which the large andesite cones are subsequently built. Basalt may also be erupted at late stages as small flows from scattered subsidiary vents around the flanks of the main cones, but in some regions, such as parts of the Cascade Range of the Pacific Northwest, it is absent or trivial in volume.

Differentiated rocks, such as dacite and rhyolite, differ from andesite in that they have fewer iron–magnesium minerals and more alkali feldspar and quartz. Typical chemical compositions of members of the calc-alkaline suite are given in Table 2. Dacite and rhyolite are often erupted from mature andesitic volcanoes as viscous flows or, more often, as pumiceous pyroclastic ejecta. They rarely constitute a large part of andesitic cones in orogenic belts, but they have been erupted in great volumes from linear or arcuate fissures that may be unrelated to older andesitic volcanoes. This latter type of occurrence is discussed more fully below.

Evidence from experimental studies

Andesites have been ascribed to at least three major genetic processes—differentiation of basaltic magma by crystal fractionation, contamination of basaltic magma with granitic material of the continental crust, and generation of a primary magma by partial melting of the mantle. Experimental studies have shown that basaltic liquids can differentiate to andesitic compositions under conditions where olivine, pyroxene, and abundant magnetite crystallize and settle out of the magma. A condition essential to this process is a high oxidation state of the liquid; this may be induced by the water-bearing sedimentary and metamorphic rocks through which andesites must rise to reach the surface.

Despite its theoretical validity, the derivation of natural andesites by crystal fractionation has been questioned. Minerals that are found to have separated from such magmas in nature commonly differ in composition and proportion from those that must be postulated to produce the observed changes in the liquid. Moreover, the high oxidation state required for large-scale crystallization of magnetite does not seem to prevail in natural rocks. The fact that andesites occur only in orogenic and continental regions where the underlying crust consists of thick series of sedimentary, metamorphic, and plutonic (intrusive) rocks and never where the crust is thin and of oceanic composition has suggested the possibility that assimilation of these crustal rocks by basaltic magma could produce a mixed rock with the composition of andesite. This hypothesis has lost favour in recent years, partly because of the scarcity of well-documented examples of andesites contaminated with vestiges of partially assimilated material. The rarity of foreign inclusions in andesite does not seem consistent with the massive amount of assimilation that would be required if this process were an important one. Trace-element concentrations and the isotopic composition of strontium and lead in andesites are similar to those of basalts and other rocks that are the direct result of melting of the mantle and are quite unlike the composition of rocks of the continental crust or a mixture of continental rocks in a mantle-derived magma.

It has recently been found, through experimental studies of the melting behaviour of mantle assemblages under high pressures of water vapour, that partial melting would yield liquids that are richer in silica and plagioclase than the corresponding liquids produced by melting at equally high pressure under dry conditions. The liquids produced have most of the essential characteristics of calc-alkaline rocks, but the mechanism that generates these magmas in nature is still uncertain.

The close spatial relationship between andesitic volcanoes, deep trenches, and zones of earthquakes where it appears that the oceanic crust and lithosphere are being thrust beneath the continental margins was previously noted. The generation of andesitic magma is clearly related to this process, but the mechanism is still not understood. Frictional heating along zones of shearing may cause melting; or water driven out of the descending slab of oceanic rocks as they undergo compression may rise into hotter regions, where it acts as a flux and causes melting. These problems are still very speculative and are far from being resolved.

The origin of the voluminous silica-rich magmas erupted as ignimbrites must be closely related to that of other members of the calc-alkaline suite, but the great volume of these effusions severely limits the mechanisms that may plausibly be considered. Differentiation of basaltic magma, for example, can be dismissed as a serious possibility, simply because of the immense amount of basalt that would have to crystallize to produce such large volumes of differentiated magmas. Large-scale partial melting of continental crustal rocks provides the only convenient way of producing liquids that are very rich in silica, alumina, and alkalies. Studies of the melting behaviour of common metamorphic rocks, such as schist and gneiss, have demonstrated that the first stages of melting yield compositions close to those of natural rhyolite. The melting temperatures are in the range of 700° to 850° C (1,300° to 1,550° F), depending on depth and the amount of water available. Temperatures in this range are probably reached within the continental crust during periods of deep burial and metamorphism. It has been pointed out, however, that certain trace-element characteristics of rhyolites, notably the isotopic ratios of strontium and lead, are similar to those of magmas derived from the mantle and unlike the crustal rocks from which these magmas are thought to be derived.

Rocks in continental interiors. Extrusive igneous rocks are not abundant in the interior of stable continental regions, but those that erupt there have quite distinctive compositions. Most are rich in alkalies, especially potassium, and low in silica. Leucite or nepheline basanites are found in scattered localities in all the continents, normally as small lava flows or pyroclastic ejecta; but in certain regions, such as Italy and East Africa, these rocks have been erupted in substantial volumes, even during historic times. The lavas of Vesuvius, for example, are exceptionally rich in potash and contain abundant leucite.

Lamprophyres, carbonatites, and kimberlites

The lamprophyres also must be included in this category of continental rocks. These form a particularly heterogeneous group of rocks, most of which are very rich in iron–magnesium minerals, such as olivine, amphibole, and magnesian mica, and contain little or no feldspar. Some of these rocks have been erupted as lavas, but more often they are found as small, shallow intrusions. Closely associated with them in certain localities are carbonatites, consisting almost entirely of calcite. Carbonatites are exceptionally rare, and the only historic eruption of carbonatite lavas occurred during 1960 from the volcano Ol Doinyo Lengai, in Tanzania.

The unusual compositions of these rocks of the continental interior regions have been attributed to reactions with mica or carbonate-rich rocks of the deep continental crust, but in recent years it has become apparent that most of the chemical and mineralogic character of the rocks is imparted to them at very deep levels. Of all the extrusive rocks of the world, these contain the most convincing evidence of having risen from great depth. They commonly contain inclusions of coarse-grained, garnet-bearing rocks, such as eclogite, and, in the case of kimberlite, a variety of lamprophyre, they contain diamonds, which have been brought up from depths approaching 100 kilometres (60 miles). Their high content of carbonates, alkalies, and other relatively volatile components may be attributable to the fact that they are the first magmas to be drawn from the mantle and consequently are abnormally rich in those elements that are most readily driven out of high-pressure mineral assemblages.

BIBLIOGRAPHY. F.H. HATCH, A.K. and M.K. WELLS, *Petrology of the Igneous Rocks*, 12th ed. (1961), a basic modern text on the composition and occurrence of most common igneous rocks; C.A. COTTON, *Volcanoes as Landscape Forms* (1969), an excellent descriptive account of the morphology of volcanic features; ARTHUR HOLMES, *Principles of Physical Geology*, ch. 5 and 12, rev. ed. (1965), a simple introductory text with emphasis on the role of igneous phenomena in physical geology; H.H. HESS and A. POLDERVAART, *Basalts*, 2 vol. (1967–68), a detailed treatment of almost all physical, chemical, and geological aspects of basalts; A.R. MCBIRNEY, "Some Current Aspects of Volcanology," *Earth Sci. Rev.*, 6:337–352 (1970), a review of recent research and theoretical problems related to the origin and behaviour of extrusive igneous rocks.

(A.R.McB.)

Igneous Rocks, Intrusive

General occurrence and distribution

Magma (from a Greek word meaning "paste") is mobile, molten rock that may contain suspended crystals and dissolved gases; the term was first applied in geology in 1872. Intrusive (injected) igneous rocks result when magma cools and solidifies below the surface of the Earth. These rocks may come to light only if erosion later removes the overlying rock, exposing intrusive rocks long after they have ceased to be hot and mobile.

The term intrusive implies that magma forced its way into the space where it solidified (and which it now occupies) but that the magma was generated elsewhere, perhaps far below. During intrusion, magma must either displace or dissolve the surrounding rock (called country rock) to make room for itself. The intrusive contact (the surface along which intrusive rock touches the country rock) commonly cuts across the structures of the pre-existing rock, suggesting a vertical rise of magma under pressure.

When magma breaks through the Earth's surface, it may flow out as lava, forming extrusive igneous rocks such as basalt, or may erupt explosively as the dissolved gases are expelled, forming hot fragments that accumulate as pyroclastic rocks.

Intrusive igneous rocks make up the deeply eroded portions of some mountain ranges (*e.g.*, the Sierra Nevada of California and large parts of the Andes), but in others (including the Appalachians, Pyrenees, Himalayas, and the Atlas Mountains) these rocks are subordinate to metamorphic (altered) rocks and deformed sedimentary rocks.

On a smaller scale, individual volcanic mountains, when deeply dissected by erosion, reveal intrusive cores formed by magma that froze in the throats of the volcanoes. Mt. Kenya, Tahiti Nui, and Mt. Pelée are examples of volcanic cones reinforced against erosion by resistant intrusive spines and ribs (see Figure 1). The "swelling" of volcanoes shortly before eruption and studies of old, deeply eroded volcanoes indicate that a large portion of a volcanic cone may be intrusive rock, rather than extrusive or pyroclastic material.

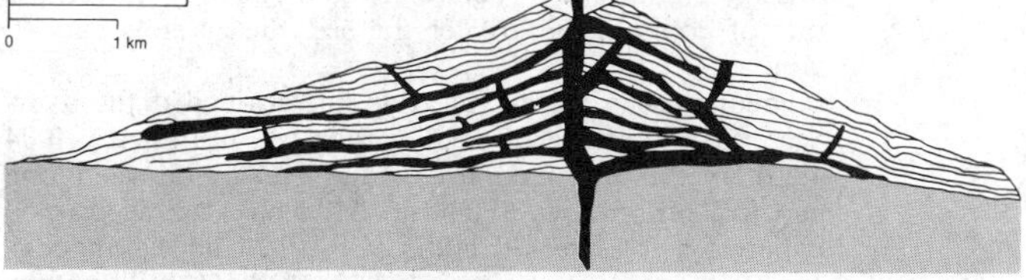

Figure 1: Cross section of a volcano showing intrusive rock in the form of a central neck or spine giving rise to ribs.

In all of the continents, intrusive igneous rocks make up approximately half of the ancient shield areas, or so-called basements, forming a rigid, stable foundation beneath veneers of younger extrusive, pyroclastic, and sedimentary rocks.

Importance to man

Igneous rocks in general influence human economy in several ways; most essential is the production of rich agricultural soils by weathering of these rocks. Extrusive rocks, particularly basalt lavas, are most important in this regard, by virtue of their great areal extent, great susceptibility to weathering, and high content of trace elements essential to plant growth. In local or restricted areas some intrusive igneous rocks also underlie rich soils and are intensively cultivated in many regions. From an economic standpoint, however, intrusive rocks are the principal associates of ore deposits. Magmas have brought such metals as iron, nickel, chromium, platinum, uranium, titanium, tin, tungsten, molybdenum, copper, zinc, lead, gold, silver, mercury, and beryllium from inaccessible depths to the upper levels of the Earth's crust and have concentrated them into relatively small volumes from which they can profitably be extracted.

Throughout history, intrusive igneous rocks also have provided raw materials for ceramics and stone for buildings and monuments.

This article treats the description, classification, and origin of intrusive igneous rocks and provides summaries of several intrusive bodies that are well-known because they have been the subjects of intensive studies. For parallel treatment of the other kinds of igneous rocks, see IGNEOUS ROCKS, EXTRUSIVE; and IGNEOUS ROCKS, PYROCLASTIC. See also IGNEOUS ROCKS for a general overview of all types of igneous rocks and their interrelationships; see also VOLCANOES for description of closely related processes. The articles ROCKS, PHYSICAL PROPERTIES OF; EARTH, STRUCTURE AND COMPOSITION OF; GEOCHEMICAL EQUILIBRIA AT HIGH TEMPERATURES AND PRESSURES; ROCK DEFORMATION; and MOUNTAIN RANGES AND MOUNTAIN BELTS should be consulted for further information on the properties, origin, and general occurrence of intrusive rocks.

CLASSIFICATION OF INTRUSIVE ROCKS

In 1785 the St. Petersburg Academy of Sciences offered a prize for the best essay on rock classification. The award was won jointly, but the classificatory schemes of the winners were never adopted. To this day, the difficulty of classification has remained one of the greatest obstacles to an understanding of the origin of igneous rocks. The difficulties arise because many variable properties are significant and must be considered in classification and because it is difficult to classify any rocks without introducing genetic implications and assumptions that may or may not be warranted.

A descriptive classification of intrusive igneous rocks must take into account texture and mineralogy. Texture (the size, shape, and arrangement of mineral grains) is a record of the history or sequence of crystallization involved in the formation of an igneous rock. The important textural aspect for classification is grain size, which is governed by the rates of nucleation and growth of crystals. Glasses form when molten silicates (natural or synthetic) are cooled so rapidly that interatomic forces do not have time to arrange the constituent atoms in an orderly crystalline structure. In general, the slower the rate of cooling, the greater the size the crystals can attain.

Igneous rocks are classified as fine-grained if the average crystal diameter is smaller than one millimetre (0.04 inch), medium-grained if the diameter is between one and five millimetres (0.04 and 0.2 inch), coarse-grained if between five and 30 millimetres (0.2 and 1.2 inches), and very coarse if the grain size exceeds 30 millimetres. Fine-grained igneous rocks are more likely to be extrusive (because extrusive rocks cool more rapidly than do those that form at depth within the Earth), and medium- and coarse-grained igneous rocks tend to be intrusive, but there are exceptions.

The texture of many igneous rocks records a two-stage history of crystallization. Large crystals (formed by slow crystallization at greater depth) are enclosed by a groundmass of finer grained or glassy material indicative of more rapid cooling on or near the Earth's surface. Such a texture is called porphyritic.

After texture, the mineral content of an igneous rock is the most significant factor in classification. Of more than 2,000 minerals, only about 30 are important in igneous rocks. Mineralogical classification can be based upon two criteria. One is simply the presence or absence of certain minerals, and the other is the relative proportions of the minerals present.

Mineralogical classification

The most practical mineralogical classification of intrusive igneous rocks utilizes the following data: presence or absence of quartz or feldspathoids; proportions of quartz, feldspathoids (silicate minerals containing aluminum, sodium, calcium, or potassium but with less silica present than in feldspars), alkali feldspar, plagioclase feldspar, and mafic minerals.

The presence or absence of quartz (SiO_2) or of the feldspathoids (*q.v.*), the commonest of which is nepheline, is significant because quartz and feldspathoids cannot coexist in the same igneous rock. Such chemical reactions as the combination of nepheline and quartz to yield albite, namely,

$$\underset{\text{(nepheline)}}{NaAlSiO_4} + \underset{\text{(quartz)}}{2SiO_2} = \underset{\text{(albite, sodium feldspar)}}{NaAlSi_3O_8},$$

produce feldspar until all the quartz or all the feldspathoid is consumed. The presence or absence of quartz or feldspathoids therefore provides an absolute criterion based upon the degree of silica saturation. If a rock contains sufficient silica to make quartz, the rock is silica oversaturated, and, if the rock contains so little silica that feldspathoids are stable, it is silica undersaturated. Magnesium-rich olivine is another mineral that is stable only in silica-undersaturated rocks. Some rocks have ratios of silica to sodium, potassium, and aluminum such that alkali feldspar but neither quartz nor feldspathoids is stable; such rocks are called silica saturated.

Aside from quartz and feldspathoids, which make up less than 50 percent of most rocks and may be entirely absent in some, the other important mineral groups are feldspars and mafic minerals.

Feldspars (*q.v.*) are divided into two groups; plagioclase is a solid solution (a single crystalline phase of variable composition) of albite and $CaAl_2Si_2O_8$ (anorthite) in varying proportions. Alkali feldspar is a solid solution of albite and $KAlSi_3O_8$ (potassium feldspar). The ratio of plagioclase to total feldspar (plagioclase plus alkali feldspar) is universally accepted by petrologists as a variable important in igneous-rock classification. Some significant rock types must be further distinguished according to the percentage of anorthite in the plagioclase.

Mafic minerals include all minerals except quartz, feldspathoids, and feldspars. The term mafic is in allusion to the common presence of magnesium and iron (Fe) in most of these minerals, which include olivines, pyroxenes, garnets, amphiboles, micas, melilites, oxides, phosphates, carbonates, and sulfides. The total percentage of mafic minerals in a rock is the remaining variable of significance in igneous-rock classification (see the Table).

The terms acid, basic, and alkaline, once applied to igneous rocks, are remnants of erroneous concepts of rock chemistry and should be abandoned. Acid referred to salic rocks (those rich in silicon and aluminum), basic to mafic, and alkaline to rocks with high proportions of sodium and potassium relative to silicon and aluminum.

The chemical compositions and the conditions of crystallization of igneous rocks determine their mineralogy. Chemical composition is therefore a fundamental property, but, since it cannot be determined conveniently in the field, it does not enter directly into the classification. Other, more easily observable attributes of rocks, such as colour, density, and strength, are determined by the texture and mineralogy and do not serve as basic criteria for a workable classification. The rock types listed in the Table may be characterized as follows.

Ultramafic rocks. These rocks, characterized by a content of at least 90 percent mafic minerals, are further classified on the basis of the percentage of olivine, pyroxene, or carbonate minerals present (see the Table).

Laboratory experiments show that ultramafic rocks become molten at very high temperatures. On the other hand, field relations indicate that many such rocks were intruded as solid masses (no molten material was pres-

Classification of Intrusive Igneous Rocks*
(in percentage)

	olivine	pyroxenes	carbonates	
Ultramafic rocks (mafic minerals 90–100% of total rock)				
Dunite	90–100	—	—	
Peridotite	30–90	—	—	
Pyroxenite	—	70–100	—	
Carbonatite	—	—	70–100	
	mafic minerals	quartz	plagioclase / total feldspar	anorthite in plagioclase
Gabbroic rocks				
Gabbro (diabase, basalt)	10–90	0–10	90–100	50–100
Diorite (andesite)	10–90	0–10	90–100	0–50
Anorthosite	0–10	0–10	90–100	—
Quartz diorite (quartz andesite)	0–90	10–50	90–100	—
Granitic rocks				
Granite (rhyolite)	0–90	10–50	0–65	—
Granodiorite (dacite)	0–90	10–50	65–90	—
Monzonite (latite)	0–90	0–10	35–90	—
Syenite (trachyte)	0–90	0–10	0–35	—
Feldspathoidal rocks (phonolite)	0–90	†	0–100	—

*Names of fine-grained equivalents, either intrusive or extrusive, are given in parentheses. †Feldspathoids present.

ent) and therefore are not strictly igneous. Country rock near the intrusive contacts with ultramafic rocks rarely shows any effect of strong heating, which is in conflict with the laboratory investigations. Regardless of the degree of care with which such experiments are performed, however, it must be asked whether they imitate the actual processes taking place in nature. As a solution to the conflict between field and laboratory evidence, some recent experiments suggest that addition of small amounts of potassium will lower the melting temperatures of ultramafic rocks by several hundred degrees. These results indicate that ultramafic rocks could be intruded as relatively cool magma and thus be incapable of intensely baking the adjacent rocks. Upon solidification of the magma, the potassium would likely be released and carried away in solution. The existence of ultramafic magmas is demonstrated by the recent recognition of ultramafic lava flows in South Africa, Western Australia, Cyprus, and Siberia.

Peridotites, serpentinites, kimberlites, and carbonatites

The Earth's mantle (the zone beneath the crust) is thought to be made up of ultramafic rock, specifically peridotite. One line of evidence leading to this conclusion is the presence of ultramafic fragments within some intrusive and extrusive rocks that have been carried upward by magma and frozen within the igneous rock. Some such fragments contain assemblages of minerals that should have formed, according to experiments, at depths exceeding 100 kilometres (60 miles).

Ultramafic rocks are highly susceptible to mineralogical changes produced by reaction with water at low temperatures. The olivine and pyroxene originally present may be completely replaced by the mineral serpentine, a hydrous magnesium silicate. Serpentinites, altered ultramafic rocks, occur in belts outlining the trends of ancient eroded mountain ranges and, according to one current hypothesis, represent slices of mantle pushed into the crust during collision of migrating oceanic and continental crustal plates (see further MOUNTAIN-BUILDING PROCESSES). Serpentinites are commercially important as sources of talc and asbestos. Unaltered and serpentinized ultramafic rocks are the major sources of chromium and platinum.

Kimberlite is a mica-bearing peridotite that contains large crystal fragments of olivine, pyroxene, garnet, chromite, and phlogopite in a fine-grained groundmass of serpentine and carbonates. Most kimberlites were intruded explosively at shallow depths, but apparently the rock was derived from great depth. Ultramafic fragments, presumed to be from the Earth's mantle, make up nearly half the volume of most kimberlites. The great economic importance of some of these rare but widespread rocks is due to the presence of diamonds, which apparently formed at depths of 150 to 200 kilometres (90 to 120 miles) in the mantle and were carried up with kimberlite and ultramafic fragments. Transport was so rapid that diamond did not have time to revert to graphite (the form of carbon that is stable at lower pressures and temperatures).

Carbonatites are ultramafic rocks composed largely of carbonate minerals. For many years petrologists thought that carbonatites were not igneous but, rather, that they were deposited from hot dilute solutions or were metamorphosed limestone fragments that had been engulfed by magma. Early experiments had shown that calcium carbonate does not melt until an extremely high temperature is reached, but, in 1960, experiments indicated that a carbonate melt can form at geologically reasonable temperatures if water is present. In the same year the volcano Ol Doinyo Lengai, in Tanzania, erupted flows of carbonate lava.

Carbonatites are widely distributed on the continents in the form of small intrusive bodies and in nearly all known instances are associated with feldspathoidal rocks. Prospecting since 1960 has revealed many more carbonatite intrusions than were previously suspected to exist. Carbonatite is mined for niobium and rare-earth elements and locally for copper and other metals. In regions lacking limestone, carbonatite has provided lime for fertilizer and cement manufacture.

Gabbroic rocks. The major minerals of gabbro are plagioclase and pyroxene; other common constituents are olivine, amphibole, and biotite. Quartz, or feldspathoids, and alkali feldspar may be present in minor amounts. Gabbro is medium- to coarse-grained and consists of plagioclase crystals partly surrounded by pyroxene (see Figure 2). Other minerals may be enclosed by individual

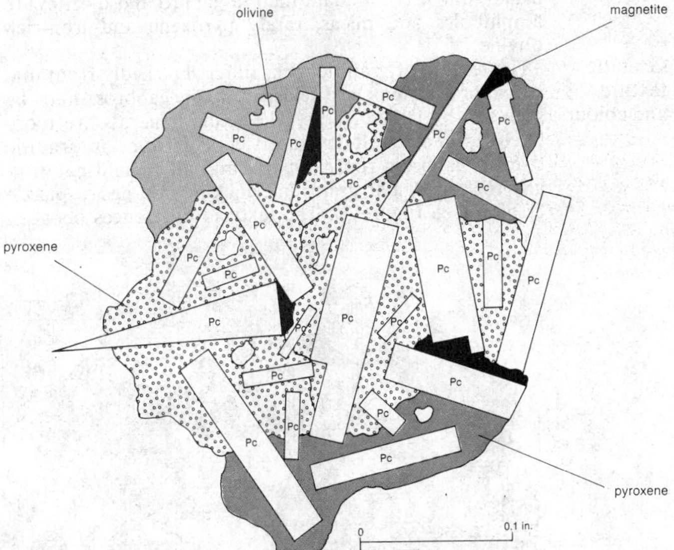

Figure 2: Typical texture of gabbro. Pc = plagioclase; irregular grains of olivine and magnetite, and pyroxenes of differing texture, are distributed as shown.

Gabbro ("black granite"), diorite, and anorthosite

pyroxene grains or may fill spaces between plagioclase and pyroxene. Textural relations between plagioclase and pyroxene are easily seen in polished slabs of gabbro that is marketed as "black granite" for decorative and memorial purposes. If gabbro contains olivine and sulfides, these minerals may break down, staining the polished surface with rust.

Small to very large intrusive bodies of gabbro (up to hundreds of cubic kilometres) are widespread in the continents and probably in the oceanic crust as well.

The rock name diorite, from the Greek word meaning "to distinguish," refers to the necessity and difficulty of setting this type apart from gabbro. Arbitrarily but on sound chemical grounds, this distinction is made according to the composition of the plagioclase. In many examples of diorite, amphibole takes the place of pyroxene, and the texture, even if the major minerals are plagioclase and pyroxene, is not the same as the typical texture of gabbro. In diorite, the feldspar and the mafic minerals tend to form irregular, interlocking grains, and there is no strong tendency for one mineral consistently to be surrounded by another.

Diorite occurs in many small intrusive bodies that commonly are unrelated to and older than other intrusive rocks in the same area. The equivalent extrusive rock, andesite, is much more abundant than diorite. The reason for this disparity may be a tendency for geologists to apply the term andesite to rocks that are really fine-grained equivalents of rocks other than diorite.

Anorthosite is relatively rare and has two distinct modes of occurrence; one is in small and usually layered bodies within gabbroic and ultramafic rocks, and the other is in large masses that cover several hundred square kilometres, associated with granite and syenite. The large masses, all ranging from 1,100,000,000 to 1,700,000,000 years old, are found in southern Africa, India, North America, and Scandinavia. The restriction of these massive anorthosite bodies in space and time remains a puzzle. Extrusive equivalents of anorthosites are unknown.

Quartz diorite. As implied by the name, this rock contains more quartz (is more strongly silica oversaturated) than diorite, but it differs from diorite in its field relations. Quartz diorite occurs as large intrusive bodies that formed approximately at the same time as neighbouring granitic rocks. It grades into the granites through a decrease in the ratio of plagioclase to total feldspar.

Granitic rocks. Intrusive rocks of this group are abundant, forming large portions of some mountain ranges as well as smaller isolated intrusions. Petrologists distinguish several rock types within this group, according to the ratio of plagioclase to total feldspar. Mafic minerals, usually far less abundant than in gabbro and diorite, are amphiboles and micas, rarely pyroxene and iron-rich olivine.

Granitic texture and colour

The texture of granitic rocks differs markedly from that of gabbro. Plagioclase feldspar, as in gabbros, may be bounded by crystal faces. The mafic minerals are more likely to show well-developed crystal forms in granitic than in gabbroic rocks. Quartz and alkali feldspar usually form irregular grains interlocking in a jigsaw-puzzle fashion (see Figure 3). The textural differences between

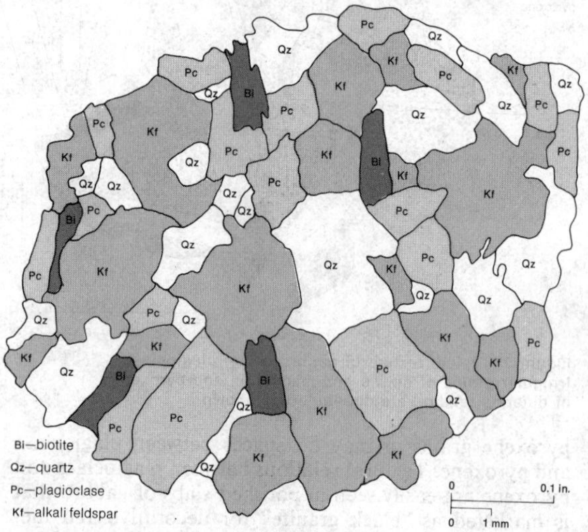

Figure 3: Typical texture of granite.

gabbro and granite are partly due to the tendency of minerals of gabbro to crystallize one after another through a wide interval of temperature, whereas in granites the minerals tend to crystallize simultaneously over a narrow temperature range.

The lower content of dark mafic minerals produces the characteristic (but not diagnostic) light colours of granites: pink, white, gray, or green shades are governed by the colours of the feldspars.

Granitic rocks are strong (because of the interlocking texture) and are more resistant to weathering than more mafic rocks (because of the smaller amounts of the more easily decomposed mafic minerals and plagioclase and the higher content of quartz, which is extremely stable). These intrusive igneous rocks are therefore most commonly used in construction and ornamentation.

Many ore deposits of copper, lead, zinc, molybdenum, tin, and tungsten are located in or near granitic intrusions.

Monzonite. Rocks of this group are not abundant, and the group itself is somewhat a miscellany. It has been said that the term monzonite is a generously hospitable category for many a stray rock of dubious pedigree. In general appearance and in field relations monzonites resemble granitic rocks; they differ from granites by reason of their lower quartz content (see the Table).

Syenite. This rock type, subordinate in abundance to granitic and gabbroic rocks, occurs only in relatively small intrusive bodies. It commonly grades into granitic or feldspathoidal rocks by changes in the amount of quartz or feldspathoid. Syenites, by definition, are silica saturated, containing neither a great excess nor deficiency of silica. The relative rarity of syenite is perhaps testimony to the soundness of the classification scheme; any good classification should minimize the number of "fence straddlers."

Feldspathoidal rocks. These silica-undersaturated rocks form small but widespread intrusive bodies. Although these rocks make up no more than 1 or 2 percent of the mass of all intrusive igneous rocks, nearly half the names applied to igneous rocks have been coined for members of this group. Feldspathoidal rocks have received attention that is disproportionate to their abundance because of their contrast with normal igneous rocks. As in other scientific endeavours, study of the abnormalities has led to greater understanding of more common rock-forming processes. Thus, the scientific significance of these rocks far outweighs both their abundance and their economic importance (largely as sources of rare-earth elements, niobium, and raw materials for ceramics).

The absolute amounts of any rock types in the Earth's crust can be estimated only when the geology of the Earth is more completely known, on the surface and in depth. Some responsible attempts have been made to estimate amounts of intrusive and corresponding extrusive igneous rocks (Figure 4). The reasons for the contrasts in abundance between intrusive and extrusive types are not known, but the problem may be traceable to inconsistent use of the classification scheme.

MODES OF FORMATION

Magma generation. The sources of most magmas are now believed to be in the Earth's upper mantle rather than in the crust. Until the early 1960s most petrologists thought that granite magma was generated by melting crustal rocks. Granite becomes molten at lower temperatures than do other abundant rocks, and, according to the results of experiments, it could not remain solid within the deeper parts of the crust. By this hypothesis, granite magma would form by partial melting of metamorphic or more mafic igneous rock, to produce a small proportion of granitic liquid within otherwise solid rock.

The liquid could, in theory, migrate upward from its parent rock. If sufficient heat were available, the liquid might increase in amount by dissolving more anorthite-rich plagioclase and mafic minerals, thus changing composition from that of granite to granodiorite.

Another hypothesis held that gabbroic magma could dissolve (assimilate) sufficient granite as it moved upward in the crust to change the composition of the liquid to that of rocks intermediate between gabbro and granite, namely, to granodiorite, quartz diorite, monzonite, and diorite.

From 1963 on, evidence has been accumulating that contradicts these hypotheses of partial melting and of

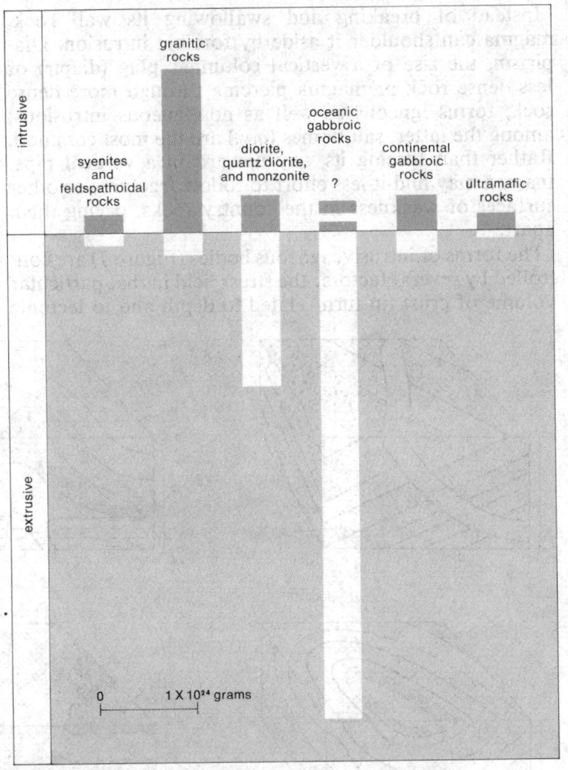

Figure 4: Estimated abundances of igneous rocks in the Earth's crust. The amount of intrusive rock in oceanic crust is least certain.

Evidence of origin in the mantle

assimilation. One line of evidence is based on the radioactive decay of the isotope rubidium-87 to strontium-87. There is strong documentation that rubidium has been progressively removed from the mantle and concentrated in the crust through geological time. Magmas formed from crustal material should therefore be richer in strontium-87 produced by decay of rubidium-87, whereas magmas generated in the mantle (where the rubidium content has long been low) should show perceptibly smaller abundances of strontium-87. Not only do gabbroic and ultramafic rocks have strontium isotope contents consistent with origin in the mantle, but so do many granites and intermediate rocks. Such magmas, according to isotopic and experimental evidence, must form by partial melting of ultramafic rocks in the mantle.

The low-velocity zone at a depth of 100 to 400 kilometres (60 to 250 miles) in the mantle (defined by a decrease in seismic-wave velocities) is probably caused by partial melting and seems a likely source for magmas. Such liquids in the mantle are probably distributed as thin films and small puddles that may coalesce into larger bodies as they migrate upward into the crust. There is no world-encircling reservoir of almost completely liquid magma but only small "pustules" that are relatively near the Earth's surface. These local infections form at many times and places, are active for brief periods of time, geologically speaking, and then disappear.

The locations of magmatic intrusion are varied. Gabbroic magma approaches the Earth's surface under the ocean floor and along the crests of mid-oceanic ridges, as well as on the continents. Granitic magma, in contrast, seems confined to continental crust. Continental margins, where the major plates that comprise the continents and ocean basins are colliding, are sites of ultramafic and intermediate (quartz-diorite and granodiorite) magma injection, whereas stable continental interiors seem more susceptible to intrusion by granite, kimberlite, carbonatite, and feldspathoidal magmas. Much more field and laboratory work is needed before a unifying theory can be erected to explain the segregation of different magma types in different crustal environments. At present, petrologists are not certain of the degree to which such segregation has occurred.

Magmatic evolution. The high viscosity of most magmas is caused partly by the suspended solids and partly by linking together of silicon–oxygen and aluminum–oxygen tetrahedra in the liquid. The viscosity varies from that of hot oil in gabbroic melts to that of cold molasses or asphalt in granitic melts.

The temperature of magma where it is erupted on the surface as lava varies from 650° C (1,200° F; granitic) to 1,250° C (2,300° F; gabbroic). The density of magma is slightly less than that of the corresponding crystalline rock. Drill-hole observations of slowly crystallizing lava lakes in Hawaii indicate that magma undergoes an abrupt transition from behaviour as a viscous liquid to behaviour as a brittle solid. The change occurs when the lava is about half crystallized.

Mechanisms of magmatic differentiation

Several varieties of igneous rocks apparently formed from the same magma at nearly the same time. Magmatic differentiation is the set of processes by which more than one kind of igneous rock is derived from one magma. The chief mechanisms by which magmas differentiate are crystal settling, or flotation, flow differentiation, and filter pressing. All involve the separation of liquid from crystals. As a mineral grows it subtracts material from the melt, which therefore changes composition, becoming less rich in those elements that make up the mineral. If, after crystallization has proceeded for some time, the crystals settle out or the liquid is drained off, the solid crystals will form a rock with a composition different from that of the remaining liquid. The liquid will continue to crystallize, its composition changing still more, and the process may be repeated.

Crystal settling (or flotation) is a common means of separation of a liquid from minerals that have already crystallized from it. Charles Darwin was one of the first to recognize the importance of this process. He observed a lava flow in the Galápagos Islands with a higher proportion of feldspar crystals in its bottom part. The mineralogical composition of the flow varies so much from bottom to top that different rock names must be applied at different levels.

Settling of crystals of one mineral, followed by precipitation of another, can produce layering in igneous rocks that resembles the stratification seen in sedimentary rocks. One spectacular layer of mafic minerals accumulated in the Bushveld Complex, a large gabbro intrusion in South Africa, to form the Merensky Reef, only a metre or two thick but continuous for at least 240 kilometres (150 miles). The layer consists of olivine, pyroxene, iron oxides, and various sulfides and native metals and contains an enormous reserve of platinum.

As magma flows through a conduit, suspended crystals and rock fragments tend to concentrate in the centre, away from the walls, and tend to lag behind the liquid portion of the magma. Flow differentiation can thus effectively separate the crystals from melt and thereby change the composition of the magma.

Filter pressing, the squeezing of liquid out of a crystal-rich mush, is still another mechanism of magmatic differentiation.

Bowen's reaction series and magmatic composition

The textural relations of minerals, particularly the tendency of certain minerals to grow around others, suggest a sequence in which minerals crystallize from magma. Laboratory experiments with synthetic magmas have confirmed and amplified this textural evidence and have given rise to a mineral reaction series called Bowen's reaction series, named for the Canadian-born U.S. experimental petrologist N.L. Bowen. Minerals essential to ultramafic and gabbroic rocks occur at the high-temperature ends of the series, and those essential to granite occur at the low-temperature ends of the series. The sequence outlined by Bowen's reaction series (Figure 5) is not obeyed by all magmas, however.

Applying Bowen's sequence to a magma of normal gabbroic composition, it is possible to calculate the chemical composition of the remaining liquid after certain proportions of early-formed minerals have been removed. Geologists have concluded from such calculations, if separation of crystals from liquid is highly efficient, that 100 parts of magma should differentiate to

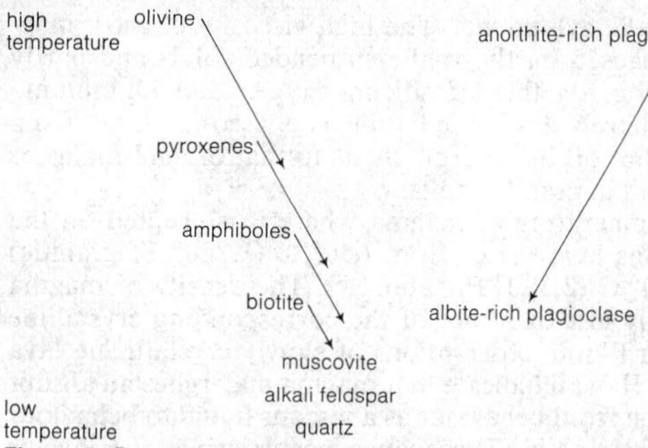

Figure 5: Reaction series of igneous materials, showing the sequence of crystallization with falling temperature. The mafic mineral series (left) and the plagioclase series (right) converge at low temperature.

yield 80 parts of gabbro, ten parts of diorite, five parts of granodiorite, and five parts of granite. These proportions may hold in some differentiated intrusions, but crustal abundances of the rock types on a global scale do not support the hypothesis that most igneous rocks evolve by differentiation of "primary" gabbroic magma.

At depth, magma is hot and highly charged with chemically reactive volatile constituents (*e.g.*, water, hydrogen fluoride, hydrochloric acid, carbon dioxide, hydrogen sulfide) that can react with and dissolve country rock. Assimilation of country rock can change the composition of magma, the degree of change depending on the relative amount of country rock that the magma assimilates and on the compositional contrasts between magma and country rock. To dissolve rock requires heat from the magma; to liberate this heat, the magma must partly crystallize. The amount of material assimilated is therefore limited by the temperature and composition of the magma compared with those of the country rock. Under ordinary conditions, no more than about ten parts of country rock can be assimilated into 100 parts of magma, and the change in magmatic composition is correspondingly small.

Emplacement of magma. Magma can make room for itself in several ways as it invades the crust. By means of the process called stoping, magma can detach fragments of country rock, which may sink or become assimilated. Piecemeal stoping is an inefficient mechanism of intrusion and usually occurs on a minor scale, serving only to modify contacts of intrusions that were emplaced in other ways.

On a much larger scale, magma can break loose portions of the overlying crust, extending all the way to the Earth's surface. Such blocks may founder in a pool of magma (Figure 6), resulting in large-scale subsidence

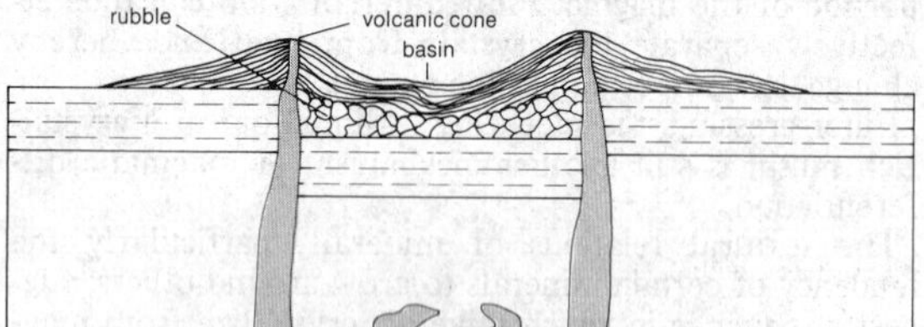

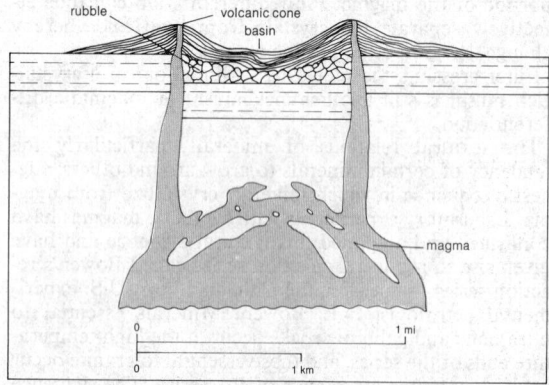

Figure 6: Caldron subsidence in cross-section. A central block of crust has sunk into magma. The surface expression is a basin (caldera) floored by rubble (breccia) and ringed by volcanic cones. The subsidence may be repeated.

(called caldron subsidence) at the surface and catastrophic eruption of volcanic rocks. Shallow intrusive bodies thus formed have the outlines of crude rings. Successive intrusions, generally younger toward the centre, build up forms that are termed ring complexes.

Instead of breaking and swallowing its wall rock, magma can shoulder it aside by forcible intrusion. Diapirism, the rise of a vertical columnar plug (diapir) of less dense rock or magma piercing through more dense rock, forms igneous as well as non-igneous intrusions; among the latter, salt domes (*q.v.*) are the most common. Rather than forcing its way upward in a vertical pipe, magma may find it less effort to follow fractures or other surfaces of weakness in the country rocks, prying them apart.

Forms of intrusive bodies

The forms of intrusive igneous bodies (Figure 7) are controlled by several factors: the stress field in that particular volume of crust (in turn related to depth and to tectonic

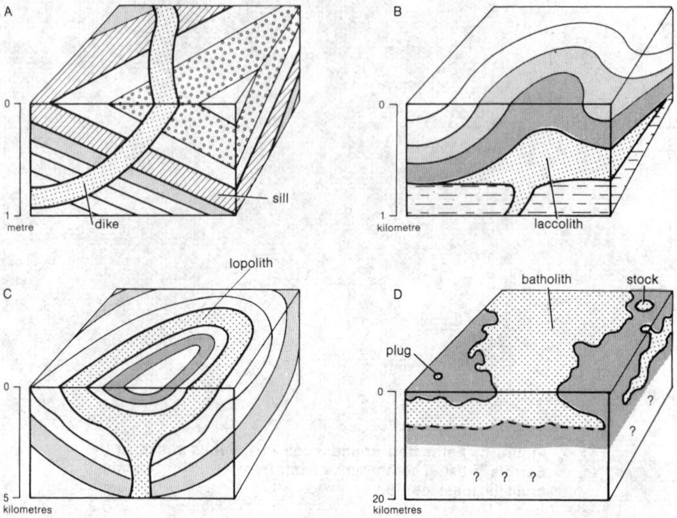

Figure 7: Forms of intrusive igneous rock bodies in hypothetical sections of Earth strata. Note the change of scale from A through D.

setting); the behaviour of the country rock (whether it is homogeneous or layered, brittle or plastic); the viscosity and density of the magma; and the rate of intrusion.

Volcanic necks, such as Devil's Tower, Wyoming, and Ship Rock, New Mexico, are the intrusive fillings of the central conduits of volcanoes (Figure 1).

Dikes are magma-filled fractures that cut across the structure of the country rock. Sills form when magma congeals in fractures that are parallel to layering of the country rock. Horizontal or gently dipping sills, such as the Palisades Sill along the west bank of the Hudson River, must have formed at shallow depths in order to have permitted the magma to lift its roof of overlying rocks.

Laccoliths are sills with updomed roofs; lopoliths sag in the centre. Lopoliths are considerably larger than laccoliths and, as a general rule, are composed of more mafic rocks. Lopoliths are apparently fed by dikes that form narrow keels at the bases of the intrusions.

Larger intrusive bodies are usually irregular in form and are classified arbitrarily according to the size of their area presently exposed. Plugs, stocks, and batholiths, in increasing order of size, complete the roster of intrusive forms. Batholiths are defined as intrusive bodies that crop out over areas greater than 100 square kilometres (40 square miles), were not intruded as one pulse of magma but grew by successive intrusions, and consist of more than one rock type (usually ranging from quartz diorite to granite). Intrusive bodies of unknown or unspecified shape are called plutons, a general term for all such bodies except dikes, sills, and volcanic necks.

Post-orthomagmatic processes. The orthomagmatic stage embraces the process of crystallization of minerals from a melt. Because most abundant igneous minerals are anhydrous (that is, they contain no water in their chemical formulas), water becomes progressively concentrated in the liquid as crystallization proceeds. The increasing water content may cause the liquid to boil—

i.e., liberate a vapour from the liquid; this is considered to be an important mechanism in explosive volcanic eruptions. Vapour or gas at high temperature and pressure is a powerful solvent able to hold much dissolved material. As temperature or pressure eventually decreases, minerals crystallize from the vapour as well as from the liquid.

Formation of pegmatites

When minerals begin to precipitate from a vapour associated with magmatic liquid, the orthomagmatic stage ends, and the pegmatitic stage begins. Pegmatites are very coarse-grained rocks having the compositions of gabbro, anorthosite, syenite, or feldspathoidal rocks but most commonly of granite. Crystals grown from water-rich vapour may attain enormous size in pegmatites; single feldspar crystals may reach 2 by 3½ by 9 metres (7 by 12 by 30 feet), and crystals of mica four metres (14 feet) thick and ten metres (33 feet) across have been found. Many pegmatites of granitic composition are concentrically zoned, each zone having distinctive texture or mineralogy. The central core may consist almost entirely of quartz.

During the orthomagmatic stage, certain elements could not be accommodated within the crystal structures of minerals precipitating from the melt; they became concentrated in the remaining liquid and eventually in the vapour. During the pegmatitic stage, these elements, highly concentrated in the small quantity of fluid remaining, were precipitated to form rare and economically important minerals. Among the elements thus concentrated are lithium, cesium, beryllium, tin, niobium, zirconium, uranium, thorium, boron, phosphorus, and fluorine. Pegmatites thus supply enriched concentrations of valuable materials that are ordinarily so dispersed and diluted in orthomagmatic rocks that these rocks are not profitable to mine.

The hydrothermal and deuteric stages

As the temperature of a magmatic body continues to drop, a residual water-rich hydrothermal fluid may remain active inside the intrusion, eventually invading the country rock. The hydrothermal stage grades imperceptibly from the pegmatitic stage, from which it is distinguished mainly by the lack of large crystals.

If an igneous intrusion cannot retain its volatile constituents but continually loses them to the surrounding rock, then the pegmatitic stage is omitted, and the hydrothermal stage directly follows the orthomagmatic stage.

Hydrothermal veins are fractures filled with minerals deposited from hot solutions or gases. The most abundant veins contain quartz or calcite, but sulfides of iron, copper, lead, and zinc commonly crystallize in this late stage of mineral deposition, as do such native metals as gold, silver, arsenic, bismuth, antimony, and mercury (see further ORE DEPOSITS).

If the hydrothermal fluid permeates the country rock surrounding the intrusive body, it may deposit minerals, either by filling cavities or by replacing certain of the original minerals. The poorly understood process of replacement involves metasomatism, the addition or subtraction of elements in solid rock. Apparently, hydrothermal fluids can selectively dissolve out one mineral while precipitating another in its place, so that the crystal form of the original mineral is inherited by the newly precipitated mineral.

Hydrothermal effects above still-cooling igneous bodies are visible in many parts of the world as geysers and fumaroles (*q.v.*). Most of the water erupted in geysers and hot springs is rainwater that percolated into the country rock and was heated and driven back to the surface. Only a very small proportion may be water actually released from the magma.

As igneous rock cools, fluids and minerals react, and the rock can be said to "simmer in its own juice"; this is the stage of deuteric alteration. Like the pegmatitic and hydrothermal stages, the deuteric stage is defined by its products, not by conditions of temperature or pressure. The original minerals that crystallized from magma react with the residual fluid, partly or completely, to form calcite, chlorite, epidote, micas, and albite, and the rock commonly acquires a bleached appearance. Deuteric breakdown of mafic minerals may liberate metals that are carried out into the surrounding rocks, where they concentrate as ore deposits.

Even after deuteric alteration has ended and the igneous rock has cooled to the temperature of the surrounding rock, the active history of the intrusive body may not be ended. Igneous rocks can be rejuvenated to flow and deform as plastic solids. Granite is particularly susceptible to such remobilization if temperature and stresses again increase. A granitic body, long after its emplacement as magma, may become mobile and intrude upward as a diapir into rocks that did not even exist at the time the granite was initially emplaced.

FIELD EXAMPLES

Black Jack Sill. A horizontal sill of gabbro, 150 metres (500 feet) thick, intruded flat-lying Permian and Triassic sedimentary rocks (from 190,000,000 to 280,000,000 years old) in New South Wales, Australia, and now forms the resistant cap of a hill 1½ kilometres (one mile) in diameter; unfortunately, the top contact has been eroded away, and the original extent of the sill is unknown. Below the sill, the Permian sedimentary rocks contain two layers of coal. Coal mines penetrate dikes that supplied magma to the sill.

Vertical differentiation of minerals

Most of the sill was emplaced as one pulse of magma that had already undergone differentiation within a temporary storage chamber at unknown depth below the sill; the magma carried crystals of olivine and plagioclase in suspension as it intruded. This pulse of magma crystallized from the bottom of the sill upward. At progressively higher elevations, olivine becomes less abundant and becomes richer in iron; plagioclase increases in amount and becomes richer in sodium. The changes in both minerals indicate progressively cooler crystallization temperatures of more highly differentiated magma at higher levels in the sill. Pyroxene and iron–titanium oxides, the other abundant minerals, also show changes indicating solidification from the bottom up. Residual liquid, displaced by the crystals, migrated upward. This liquid, trapped in pores within the gabbro, especially at higher levels within the sill, crystallized to form syenite.

The gabbro becomes coarser upward, indicating slower crystallization in the presence of residual, more water-rich liquid. Differentiation is also indicated by enrichment of chromium, nickel, cobalt, and vanadium in the early-formed minerals; these metals were absent in the residual syenitic liquid, but zirconium, barium, and rubidium were concentrated in this melt. Deuteric alteration increases upward in the sill.

Skaergaard Intrusion. This intensively studied, well-exposed intrusion in eastern Greenland shows some of the same features as the Black Jack Sill but on a much larger scale. Approximately 500 cubic kilometres (100 cubic miles) of gabbroic magma were intruded rapidly, pushing out a downward-tapering plug of country rock (one block of metamorphic rock as large as one kilometre [½ mile] long and one-half kilometre [¼ mile] thick, was lifted at least two kilometres [one mile] above its original level).

Magma streamed upward along the surface of the funnel-shaped cavity, carrying fragments of country rock. This marginal sheath of magma congealed relatively rapidly along the walls and roof of the intrusion, forming the Border Group (see Figure 8). Within this great body of liquid, now effectively sealed by the Border Group, magma crystallized slowly. Crystals settled in magma that was stirred by convection currents as hotter liquid rose and cooler, denser magma sank. Crystal settling and current action produced the Layered Series, a succession of sheets resembling saucers stacked one above the other.

Stratification, like that in sedimentary rocks, resulted from the gravitative settling of particles in the moving liquid. As in the Black Jack Sill, iron and sodium increase upward in the Layered Series, at the expense of magnesium and calcium.

Magnet Cove Complex. A series of concentric rings totalling five kilometres (three miles) in diameter near Magnet Cove, Arkansas, was formed by successive in-

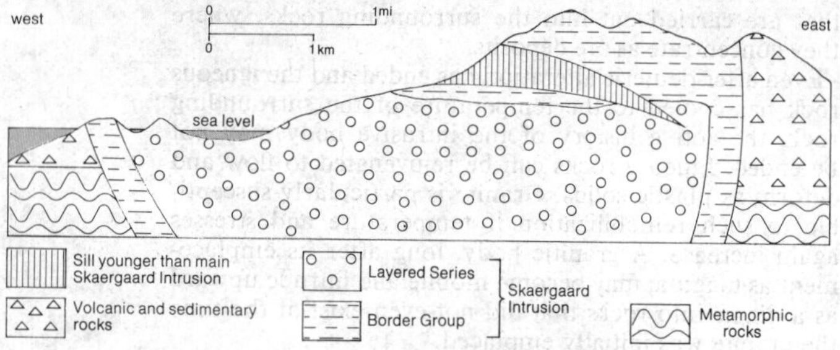

Figure 8: Cross-section of the Skaergaard Complex, eastern Greenland.

From L.R. Wagner and G.M. Brown, *Layered Igneous Rocks* (1968); Oliver and Boyd, Edinburgh

trusion of mafic rocks followed by fine- and coarse-grained salic feldspathoidal rocks and finally by irregular bodies of carbonatite. The surrounding Paleozoic sedimentary rocks had been folded and faulted long before magma was intruded, and they were not further deformed by intrusion but were thermally metamorphosed over distances as great as 800 metres (2,500 feet) from the intrusive contact.

The Magnet Cove Complex apparently formed by cauldron subsidence, although there is no direct evidence that magma breached the surface to form a volcanic field in this locality. On the other hand, pyroclastic rocks of the same distinctive compositions as the Magnet Cove intrusive rocks and of the same age are interbedded with Cretaceous sedimentary rocks (65,000,000 to 136,000,000 years old) in the Gulf Coastal Plain.

Boulder Batholith. Igneous rocks in southwestern Montana that now cover an area of 6,000 square kilometres (2,000 square miles) were injected into a pile of pyroclastic rocks three to five kilometres (two to three miles) thick that had accumulated a short time (geologically speaking) before intrusion. Magma was emplaced as a succession of pulses, from mafic to generally more salic. Small masses of diorite are the oldest intrusions, followed by dark granodiorite. Many small bodies of granitic rocks, making up 75 percent of the area of the batholith, were then intruded. These were emplaced and crystallized within about 8,000,000 years. Deuteric alteration of the granites produced the large copper-ore deposits at Butte, Montana. The batholithic rocks are overlain by presumably unrelated volcanic rocks that were erupted 20,000,000 years after the intrusive episode.

Variation among granitic intrusives

Donegal Granites. Ordovician granites, emplaced by a variety of mechanisms, are well exposed on the Donegal coast (see Figure 9). The Thorr and Fanad granodiorites contain abundant inclusions of country rock. Distinctive layers within the surrounding rock continue as "ghostly" trains of fragments within the granodiorites, preserving the structure of rocks that had previously occupied the space. Locally, the granodiorite flowed, disrupting the continuity of these lines of inclusions over short distances. Transitional contact zones suggest that the granodiorite quietly soaked into the surrounding rock. These oldest of the Donegal intrusions show abundant evidence that assimilation and metasomatic replacement were effective mechanisms of reaction between magma and country rock.

In contrast, the Ardara Pluton is a diapir that forcibly shouldered its country rock aside. Outer contacts are sharp, smooth, and nearly vertical.

The Rosses Ring Complex contains slightly different granitic rocks filling concentric rings, each younger than the one outside it. The adjacent country rock was neither deformed nor metamorphosed by the intrusion. Outlines of the granites are polygons exhibiting straight contacts, some segments of which are two kilometres (one mile) long. The Rosses Complex formed by the sinking of successively smaller central blocks.

The Barnesmore Pluton is made up of sheets of granite filling archlike fissures produced by the partial collapse of the roof. Intrusive contacts dip outward and cut across the structure of the country rock.

In the Main Donegal Granite, 58 kilometres (36 miles) long and six or eight kilometres (four or five miles) wide, a nearly horizontal flow of crystal–liquid mush wedged its way into the country rocks. Long trains of inclusions are parallel to the long axis of the granite body and to fine vertical layering (alternations of light and dark, coarse and fine granite) produced by compression of the mush from the sides as it was intruding. The marginal portions of the granite are intensely sheared, and the neighbouring country rocks exhibit high grades of thermal metamorphism. In the southwest, where residual fluid apparently was trapped, the roof of the intrusion is pegmatite.

The Trawenagh Bay Pluton, the youngest intrusive body, is a lobe of the Main Donegal Granite, though emplaced in a different manner. The granite is not layered and shows irregular contacts with country rock, which was not deformed by the intrusion. This body is probably a flat-topped stock modified by piecemeal stoping of the roof during the later stages of emplacement.

Origins of granite. The Donegal granites illustrate the problems that generated a controversy over the magmatic versus metasomatic origins of granite. In theory, granite can be intruded or formed in place. Either way, a melt may or may not be present. During slow cooling of an igneous intrusion, after the final drop of liquid has crystallized, textural and mineralogical changes continue to occur. Since these hydrothermal and deuteric changes may be regarded as aspects of metamorphism (of which metasomatism is a specific type involving change in chemical composition), some features of an igneous rock may be magmatic, whereas others are metamorphic.

In the granite controversy, some partisans on each side sought to attribute all features, whether dating from time of emplacement or long after, to an igneous or to a metamorphic origin exclusively. Petrologists now generally recognize that both magmatic and metasomatic granites exist, and the healthy controversy has now focussed on deciding the origin of each particular granite body, rather than generalizing to all granites. The old

Adapted from M. Naggar and M. Atherton, *Journal of Petrology* (1970)

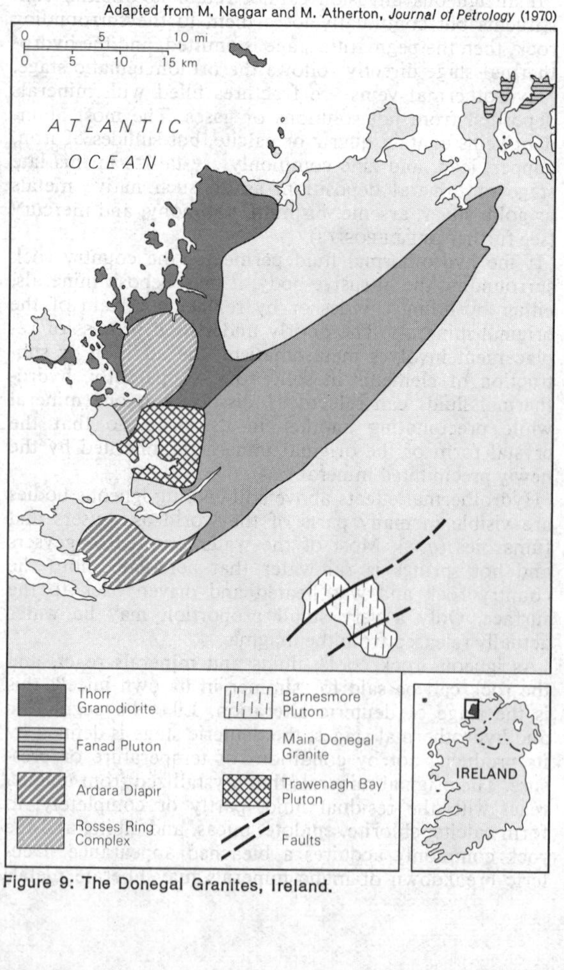

Figure 9: The Donegal Granites, Ireland.

doctrine of "one rock, one origin" is being rejected, but understanding the origin of any specific rock remains difficult because of the complicated history of rocks that cool slowly within the Earth's crust.

BIBLIOGRAPHY. N.L. BOWEN, *The Evolution of the Igneous Rocks* (1928, reprinted 1956), the classic exposition of the physical chemistry of magmatic crystallization—although later experimental investigations have modified some of the details, the basic principles remain correct and are nowhere more clearly expressed; R.A. DALY, *Igneous Rocks and the Depths of the Earth* (1933, reprinted 1968), partly out of date, but comprehensive—some chapters are so boldly imaginative that they are less controversial now than they were a decade ago; H.H. READ, *The Granite Controversy* (1957), collected papers by an emphatic but open-minded protagonist in the granite controversy, championing metasomatism and emphasizing field relations rather than chemistry; A.B. RONOV and A.A. YAROSHEVSKY, "Chemical Composition of the Earth's Crust," in P.J. HART (ed.), *The Earth's Crust and Upper Mantle*, pp. 37–57 (1969), a carefully documented estimate of the abundances of elements, minerals, and rocks in the crust—other chapters in this volume are also valuable, up-to-date reviews covering a wide range of petrological and geophysical topics, with excellent bibliographies; A.L. STRECKEISEN, "Classification and Nomenclature of Igneous Rocks," *Neues Jb. Miner. Abh.*, 107:144–240 (1967), the most successful attempt yet to establish an internationally accepted classification scheme; the classification in the table of this article is based upon Streckeisen's proposal.

(D.S.B.)

Igneous Rocks, Pyroclastic

Pyroclastic materials (Greek *pyr*, "fire"; *klastos*, "broken in pieces") are the fragmental products of explosive volcanic eruptions; their lithified deposits are pyroclastic rocks. Pyroclastic accumulations commonly have textures, structures, and dimensions comparable to other kinds of clastic sedimentary deposits, but they are classified as igneous because they originate from the activity of magma—molten silicate material—within the Earth. Another term in use for aerially dispersed pyroclastic fragments is *tephra* (Greek "ashes"). Vertically ejected pyroclastic materials form deposits that usually are distinct from those deposited by turbulent pyroclastic flows moving along the ground (glowing clouds; base surges). Subaqueous pyroclastic accumulations, modified by their interaction with water, form by falls of ash into water following eruptions on land, or from volcanic eruptions under the water.

Magma, a completely or partially molten mass of silicates containing molecularly dissolved gases, is generated within the upper mantle or deep within the crust of the Earth. If it rises to the surface, pressures decrease and the contained gases begin to expand. Whether pyroclastic fragments or lava flows are produced during an eruption depends largely upon the condition of the magma just prior to eruption. If the volume of water and other volatile substances is relatively high, and the rate of pressure release is rapid, gas bubbles will quickly grow, coalesce, and cause the magma to fly apart explosively during eruption. The viscosity of a magma is determined by water content, the ratio of alkalies (soda and potash) to aluminum, and the silica content. At equivalent temperatures, silicic magmas tend to be more viscous than mafic magmas—*e.g.*, those rich in iron and magnesium. Thus, during extrusion and rapid cooling, gases escape from silicic magmas with greater difficulty than from mafic magmas and this gives rise to a greater tendency for explosive disruption and the production of pyroclastic fragments. If the water content and vapour pressures are sufficiently high, however, basaltic (mafic) eruptions may produce abundant pyroclastic debris. In many volcanic episodes the initial eruptions may be explosive but, with a progressive loss of volatile substances, explosions may be followed by quieter outflows of lava.

Hazards and benefits to man

Since about AD 1500 volcanic activity has caused an estimated 200,000 deaths, although nearly one-half of the total were lost from just three eruptions—Tambora (1815), Krakatoa (1883), and Mt. Pelée (1902; Table 1). This total, though large, is small compared to the fatalities that have been caused by earthquakes during the same span of time and is much less than automobile fatalities on modern highways in the United States alone. Though explosive eruptions are to be given a healthy respect, death by direct volcanic action is rare, even in densely populated regions. Thus, in areas of active volcanism, predetermined plans to prevent panic, disruption of communications, or damage by floods, mudflows, and landslides that may occur during an eruption or following heavy falls of ash are the best protection against volcanic hazards. It should be noted that the largest number of fatalities from direct volcanic action occurred during the 1902 Mt. Pelée eruption, which produced a glowing avalanche that swept over the town of Saint-Pierre on the isle of Martinique and instantly destroyed all but two of its nearly 30,000 inhabitants. Two men escaped death; one was a prisoner at the time of the event.

Table 1: Comparative List of the World's Most Destructive 19th- and 20th-Century Eruptions

volcano	date	estimated volume of tephra (km³)	estimated number of deaths and primary cause
Tambora; Indonesia	1815	40, (150)*	12,000; sea waves, burial
Novarupta (Mt. Katmai); Alaska†	1912	20*	few or none
Krakatoa; Indonesia	1883	18	36,000; sea waves
Cosigüina; Nicaragua	1835	10, (50)*	few or none
Bezmianny; Kamchatka	1956	3	few or none
Bandaisan; Japan	1888	1	460; mudflow from crater collapse during eruption
Taal; Philippines	1911	0.5	1,300; base surge
Hekla; Iceland	1947–48	0.4	few or none
Pelée; Martinique	1902	<0.1	30,000; nuée ardente
Kelud; Java	1919	<0.1	5,100; mudflow from eruption through crater lake

*Old estimates of volume were based upon belief that top of volcano was blown off. Top probably collapsed into vent emptied by eruption. †Recent work proves that the eruption centred around Novarupta rather than Katmai Volcano.

Despite the potential for harm, the long-range benefits to agriculture from pyroclastic volcanism far outweigh the destructive aspects. If ash fall is moderate or light, say less than five to ten centimetres (two to four inches), the fragments become readily worked into the ground by farmers or by natural soil-forming processes. Chemical weathering of the ash—in particular, the easily decomposed glass particles that are commonly present—releases potassium, calcium, and other elements essential for plant growth, besides forming secondary clays essential for good soil. A striking testimonial to the fertilizing effects of ash is given by the volcanic lands of Java, which support about 1,200 people per square mile, compared with the nonvolcanic soils of Borneo, which support only about 15 people per square mile.

This article treats the nature of pyroclastic materials, their dispersal in air, on the ground, and beneath the sea, and the general stratigraphy of pyroclastic deposits. Further detail on the origin of igneous rocks in general and on the several kinds and forms of lava that may accompany the ejection of pyroclastic material is covered in IGNEOUS ROCKS; IGNEOUS ROCKS, EXTRUSIVE; and VOLCANOES. The articles SEDIMENTARY ROCKS and CONGLOMERATES AND BRECCIAS carry additional coverage of the many sedimentary textures and structures that may occur in pyroclastic deposits as well as a discussion of the other ways in which clastic rocks can form.

THE NATURE OF PYROCLASTIC MATERIALS

Classification of fragments

Pyroclastic ejecta. The classification and nomenclature of pyroclastic fragments and rocks is based on size, origin, and composition of the particles. Blocks and bombs exceed 64 millimetres (2.5 inches) in their largest dimension, lapilli lie between two and 64 millimetres, and ash particles are less than two millimetres (.08 inch) in size. Many volcanologists, however, prefer the size limits of four and 32 millimetres (.16 and 1.25 inches) instead of two and 64 millimetres for the size subdivisions. According to origin, fragments are juvenile (essential) if derived from fresh fluid magma, accessory (cognate) if derived from rocks of earlier related eruptions of the same volcano, and accidental if derived from basement rocks penetrated by the vent (see Table 2).

Table 2: Size Classification of Pyroclastic Fragments and Their Consolidated Rock Equivalents

fragment name	size (mm)	pyroclastic rock name*	origin of fragment
Bombs and blocks	>64	pyroclastic breccia; agglomerate	*Juvenile:* from fresh magma
Lapilli	2–64	lapillistone	*accessory:* from co-magmatic rocks in vent or cone
Ash†	<2	tuff	*accidental:* from basement rocks penetrated by vent

*Rocks composed of mixtures are named according to predominating sizes, such as tuff-breccia and lapilli-tuff. †Fine ash is also called volcanic dust, or dust, and the corresponding rock is called fine tuff. The size boundary is 1/16 mm.

Scoria, cinders, and pumice, which have vesicular structures, are named without reference to size. Scoria and cinders, nearly synonymous terms, are irregular fragments usually with rough or spiny surfaces formed by gas-rich basaltic to andesitic eruptions. Pumice is a lightweight glass foam; common varieties readily float in water.

Bombs solidify from clots of fresh lava during ejection and flight, their final shapes determined by flight velocity, viscosity, and initial size. Fresh lava may be shaped by frictional air resistance into oval-shaped spindle bombs: some have twisted ends caused by in-flight differential rotation between a rigid exterior and fluid centre. Highly fluid basalt may eject large filaments that freeze as ribbon bombs; spheroidal globs may be flattened into cow-dung or pancake bombs. Partially solidified outer surfaces may crack from internal expansion of vesicles and produce bread-crust bombs. A deposit composed primarily of bombs is known as agglomerate. Agglutinate forms by accumulations of liquid or slightly tacky bombs that stick together upon impact.

Blocks may be essential or accidental in origin, and therefore vary widely in shape and composition, depending upon type of rock beneath the volcano. Broken angular shapes are common, but vents may penetrate and eject water-worn gravels, as at Menan Buttes, Idaho.

Breccias, composed mainly of blocks in a matrix of finer grained debris, originate in diverse ways: aerial ejection, eruptions through crater lakes, crumbling of volcanic spines, flows of cooling lava, and others. If fine-grained debris is abundant in the matrix, the rock is called tuff-breccia.

Lapilli include fragments of juvenile, accessory, or accidental origin. Lapillistone is the rock equivalent; lapilli-tuff is a mixture of ash and lapilli-size ejecta. Accretionary lapilli are volcanic hailstones that form in eruption clouds by the accretion of ash around moist particles. Recurring turbulent updrafts may repeat the accretionary process many times, resulting in lapilli that show concentric, onion-ring structures, and with diameters of up to ten centimetres (four inches). If they are present in sufficient quantity, the rock is called accretionary-lapilli tuff, and suggests an origin by airborne dispersal; although it is suspected that accretionary lapilli also form within horizontally moving steam-rich base surges derived from phreatic volcanic eruptions. Phreatic eruptions also give rise to armoured lapilli whereby solid particles become coated with moist, sticky, fine-grained ash.

"Fire fountains" and Pele's tears

The rapid evolution and streaming of gases through highly fluid basalt produces spectacular "fire fountains" typical of Hawaiian eruptions. The fountaining magma produces drops of spray that rapidly freeze in a wide variety of shapes. Some are drawn into fine glass threads known as Pele's hair that may drift downwind like strands from spider webs. Others form glass beads called Pele's tears, variously shaped as spheres, ovoids, pendants, or dumbbells.

Ash refers to unconsolidated pyroclastic accumulations consisting of juvenile, accessory, or accidential particles less than two millimetres in diameter; tuff is consolidated ash. Coarse ash particles are 1/16 to 2 millimetres in size; particles of fine ash (volcanic dust) have diameters less than 1/16 millimetre. According to the relative abundance of rock (lithic) particles, crystals, or glass (vitric) fragments, such names as crystal ash, vitric ash, or lithic ash, or equivalent rock terms may be applied.

Glass particles and pyrogenic minerals. Bombs, lapilli, glass fragments, and crystals derived from fresh magma reflect the pre-eruptive chemical composition of magma. The composition of bombs and juvenile lapilli is closest to that of the original magma, whereas glass is the rapidly cooled product of the liquid phase; crystals represent the solid phase prior to disruption.

Gas-rich magmas, rapidly expanding, may produce pumice—a highly inflated foam with bubbles enclosed by thin glass walls—as well as glass shards formed by shattering of bubble walls (Figure 1). Glassy particles include mafic (iron-magnesium) as well as silicic varieties, but silicic glass is most common.

By courtesy of R.V. Fisher

Figure 1: Photomicrograph of silicic glass shards formed from broken bubbles. White zones within some shards are microvesicular frothy areas (magnified 60 x).

In its greatest expanded state, the porosity values of silicic pumice may attain 90 percent or more; density values are less than water. Vesicles, ranging in size from less than .003 millimetre (.0001 inch) to cavities larger than 10 centimetres (4 inches), are typically distorted by impinging bubbles, but because viscosity values of silicic magma increase very rapidly as it cools, cavities are rarely connected (Figure 2).

Varieties of pumice and scoria

The shapes of vesicles in some varieties of pumice are roughly circular, whereas in others they are tubular and impart a strong fibrous structure to the pumice. During an initial gas-rich eruptive phase, rapid expansion and extrusion may produce pumice characterized by roughly circular vesicles, but, with a progressive loss of volatile gases, vesicles may be drawn out into tubular shapes during flowage up the vent. Thus, within pumice accumulations produced by different eruptive phases, a progressive loss of volatiles for each phase may be recorded: basal layers containing relatively high amounts of nonfibrous pumice will be succeeded upward by layers containing abundant fibrous pumice. This has been noted for each of ten eruptive cycles in New Zealand that produced a relatively thick accumulation of pumice layers (the Younger Taupo Pumice).

Scoria, another highly vesicular rock, commonly develops in the early gas-rich phases of basaltic eruptions. In some instances, such as at Kilauea Iki, Hawaii, during the 1959–60 eruption, highly vesicular glassy lapilli and bombs are produced that may properly be called mafic

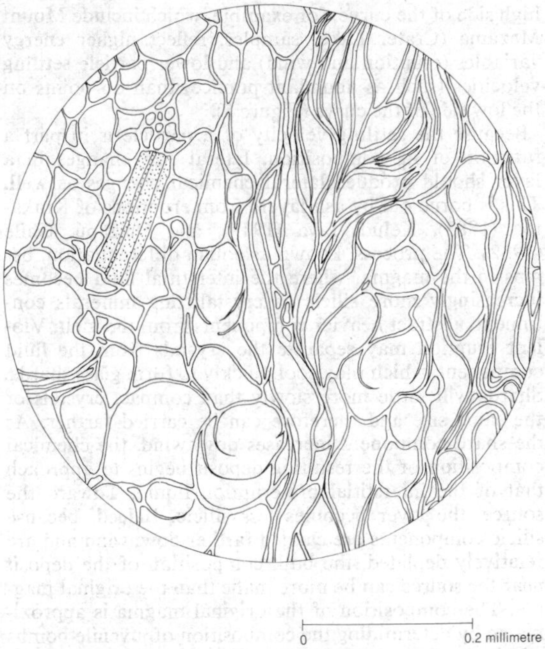

Figure 2: Vesicular structure of silicic pumice as seen under microscope.

pumice. Unlike silicic pumice, vesicles in mafic varieties (Figure 3) are usually undistorted spheres. Those that touch readily coalesce with smooth openings into one another. The striking differences between mafic and silicic pumice illustrate the effects of viscosity on bubble growth, gas migration, and pumice structures.

A less common form of mafic pumice is reticulite ("thread lace scoria"), a highly unusual rock that attains maximum porosity values between 98 and 99 percent. It consists of an open three-dimensional framework of triangular glass rods connected in regular, somewhat rounded, polygons. Unlike silicic pumice, it quickly sinks in water because the voids are interconnected. The rods occupy quickly chilled bubble junctions that solidified after the bubbles broke and surface tension drew the fluid into each junction. Glassy outer surfaces of reticulite samples have the appearance of partially melted cotton candy; they probably formed as breaking bubbles ran together during breakdown of the foam from the surface

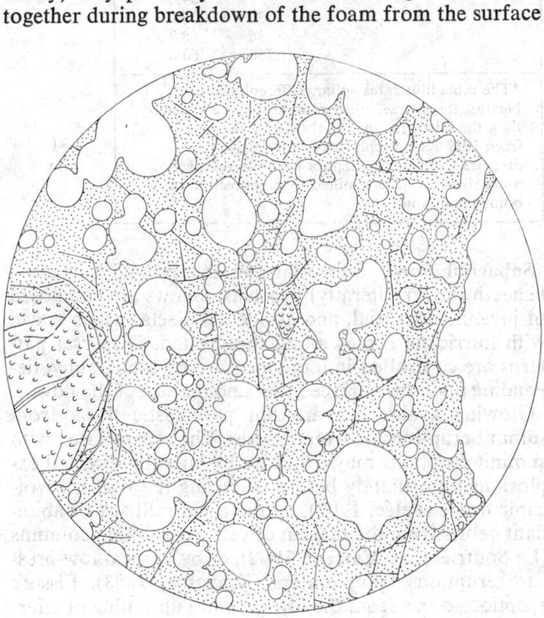

Figure 3: Vesicular structure of mafic pumice as seen under a microscope.

inward. Reticulite is an almost perfect natural replica of a Kelvin minimum area tetrakaidecahedron, which is the best model for a foam with a stable configuration. The tetrakaidecahedron is defined as a body that can be filled with neighbours of the same shape and size in such a way as to fill all available space.

The most common variety of glass shard forms during rapid vesiculation and gaseous disruption or mechanical abrasion of silicic pumice. As governed by structures of the original bubbly foam, they occur in curved plates, pieces with angular prongs where two or more bubbles once joined, or small fragments of microvesicular pumice. Mafic glass shards are produced from finely divided basalt spray formed during fire-fountaining from mechanical abrasion of mafic pumice or from steam explosions as ascending basalt contacts water. Steam explosions caused by basalt flows entering water also produce typical mafic shards.

The pyrogenic minerals that have crystallized in a magma prior to extrusion occur in deposits as phenocrysts (larger, visible crystals in a fine-grained rock groundmass, or matrix) within bombs or glass fragments, and as isolated, whole, or broken crystals. Mineral suites indicative of rhyolitic (silicic) magmas include alkalic feldspar (sanidine, anorthoclase), sodic plagioclase (albite, oligoclase), and dipyramidal quartz crystals; they may be associated with iron-rich clinopyroxene, brown hornblende, and biotite. Andesite magmas (intermediate between silicic and mafic varieties) are characterized by andesine and labradorite in associations with clinopyroxene and hypersthene. Basaltic magmas (mafic—rich in iron and magnesium) may produce calcium-rich plagioclase (labradorite, bytownite), augite, and olivine. Mineral ratios vary considerably, however, and a full suite of minerals may not necessarily occur within a single deposit.

Mineral suites and magma types

Pyrogenic minerals are typically sharply formed crystals unless broken during ejection or dispersal. Feldspar commonly breaks along cleavage planes; quartz dipyramids are more likely to be preserved intact or to splinter along conchoidal fractures, which are curved fractures typical of ordinary glass. Pre-eruptive corrosive action (resorption) by magma, caused by changing equilibrium conditions, produces embayments, or wormy indentations, on well-formed crystal faces and rounds off sharp crystal terminations. In some deposits, crystals are typically jacketed with a rind of bubble-ridden glass.

DISPERSAL OF PYROCLASTIC MATERIALS

Aerial dispersal. The distribution patterns and geometry of tephra deposits depend largely upon wind directions at various altitudes and upon magmatic factors that determine the volume of ejected debris, the size, shape, and density of individual fragments, and the altitude attained by the particles. Fragments with the highest settling velocities tend to accumulate nearest the source; those of progressively lower settling velocities are carried increasingly farther away, although progressive changes are not regular in detail.

According to the kinetic energy imparted to the ejected debris, a size limit exists above which fragments follow ballistic trajectories and below which they are suspended by turbulence in the eruption cloud. As turbulent energy within the cloud progressively decreases, the maximum size at which particles can be suspended become less, and increasingly smaller particles drop back to Earth unless they are small enough for turbulent suspension by atmospheric wind. Strong winds, however, modify the paths of all but the largest particles; ballistic paths may become elongate downwind, and eruption clouds are pushed en masse in the same direction.

The ground pattern of tephra deposits reflects wind velocity and direction. At any given moment in time, however, velocities and directions may differ at different altitudes, and can change during the course of eruption. Above about 9,000 metres (29,500 feet) frictional interaction with the ground is negligible and winds are regular, but irregularities and variations are more pronounced nearer the surface. Thus, tephra may be dispersed in dif-

Ground patterns of deposits

ferent directions at different altitudes, providing that ejecta is delivered to that height, as determined by eruption energy. An example is the 1919 eruption of Kelud, Java: ash below 3,200 metres (10,500 feet) was carried eastward; above 3,200 metres it was carried to the west (Figure 4). If winds are undirectional, the largest volume of tephra is distributed in an elongate, symmetrical, oval pattern, with an axis of maximum thickness coinciding with the geometric axis. Thickness tends to decrease downwind exponentially. Decrease in fragment sizes tends to follow the same patterns. If low-level winds distribute the bulkier coarse-grained ejecta in directions different than high-level winds (which spread the fine-grained ejecta and therefore determine the outer limits of distribution), the two axes will not coincide. This also may happen if inclined and strongly directed eruptions, like that at Bezmianny, Kamchatka, in 1956, carry most of the coarsest ejecta at an angle to wind directions.

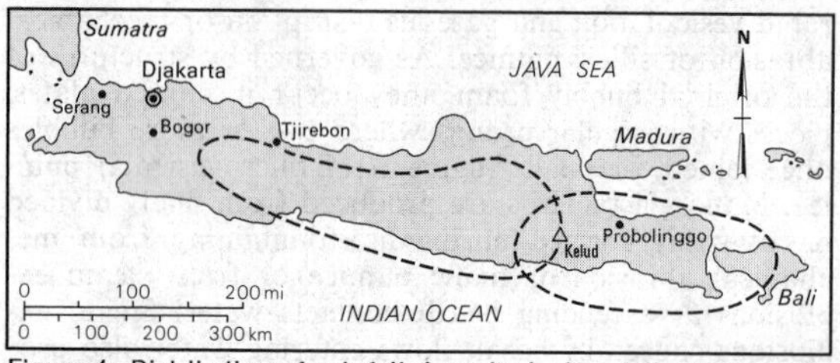

Figure 4: Distribution of ash fall deposits in Java following the eruption of Kelud in 1919.

Size-distribution parameters, such as median size and sorting within a single ejecta blanket, commonly show progressive lateral variations. Such variations are rarely completely systematic because of pulsations in eruptive energy (controlling fragment sizes and their ejected height), shifting wind directions, irregularities of turbulent cell energy in the eruption cloud, associated rainfall, and topographic irregularities.

Subject to the many variables, median diameters of particles from samples from a single ash fall layer tend to decrease exponentially with distance, as shown by tephra from the 1947 eruption of Hekla, Iceland. The slope of the median diameter–distance curve depends upon a combination of eruption energy, wind strength, and particle settling velocity. Plots of data compiled from several different volcanoes, therefore, show wide variations in median grain sizes at a given distance. Points on the high side of the curve, for example, which include Mount Mazama (Crater Lake) samples, reflect higher energy variables (eruption and wind) and lower particle settling velocities (such as abundant pumice) than do points on the low side of the curve (Figure 5).

From R.V. Fisher, *Journal of Geophysical Research* (1964)

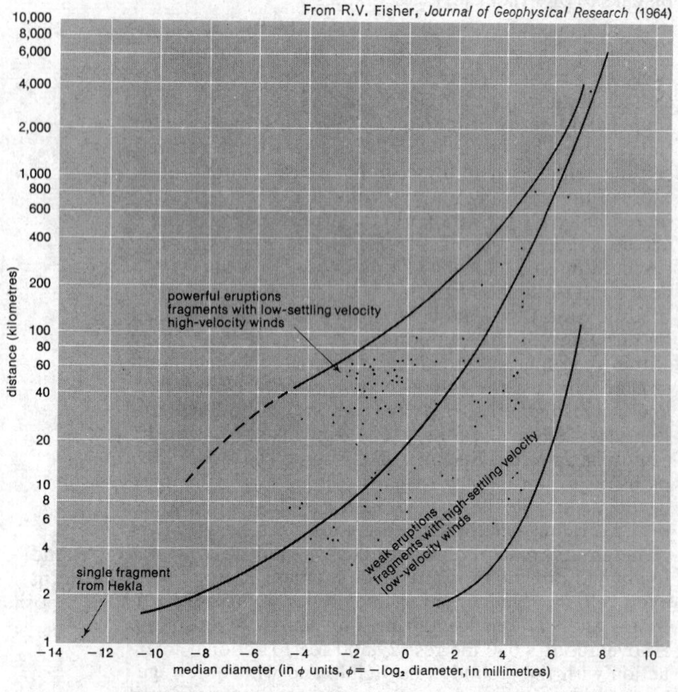

Figure 5: Relation of median size of ash particles to distance from source.

Because the settling velocity of a particle is in part a function of its composition, lateral size changes in a layer should produce lateral chemical changes as well. This is borne out by ash layers from eruptions of Krakatoa (1883), Kelud, Java (1919), and Quizapú, Chile (1932). The process, known as eolian differentiation, begins in the magma, where the interstitial fluid becomes increasingly more silicic as crystallizing minerals continue to abstract heavier components from the melt. Violent eruption may separate the crystals from the fluid component, which may cool quickly to form glass shards. Shards will settle more slowly than compact crystals of the same size and therefore can be carried farther. As the shard component increases downwind, the chemical composition of the resulting deposit begins to approach that of the interstitial pre-eruption liquid. Toward the source, the layer becomes less silicic. Indeed, because silicic components are carried farther downwind and are relatively depleted, the bulk composition of the deposit near the source can be more mafic than the original magma. The composition of the original magma is approximated by determining the composition of juvenile bombs within the deposits (Table 3).

Table 3: Variations in Silica Content of Tephra With Distance From Source, Two Examples*

eruption	SiO_2 content of original magma (percent)†	SiO_2 content at varying distances: distance (km)	SiO_2 content at varying distances: SiO_2 content (percent)
Quizapú, Chile (1932)		230	67.5
	63.8	780	70.2
	64.6	1,120	69.8
		downwind	
Kelud, Java (1919)	57.6	36	54.3
		36	55.0
		54	57.0
		166	60.0
		upwind	
		5	56.1
		9	54.5
		9	54.8
		36	58.0
		36	58.7
		360	60.8

*The table illustrates eolian differentiation. Nearest the source, silica content may be lower than the initial magma as shown by samples from 1919 Kelud tephra. With increasing distance from source, tephra becomes relatively more silicic. †Determined by composition of bombs and lapilli.

Subaerial flow. Subaerial (on the ground surface—beneath the air, literally) pyroclastic flows are composed of juvenile, essential, and accidental ejecta, which travel with hurricane forces along the ground. Dispersal patterns are controlled in large measure by topography, depending upon the surface relief and the size of the flow.

Glowing avalanches and ignimbrite deposits

Glowing avalanches are hot pyroclastic flows from summit eruptions or from fissures. Those associated with summit eruptions may originate by laterally directed explosions immediately before or during the rise of a volcanic dome (Pelée, 1902), by the rapid fallback of abundant debris from the margin of vertical eruption columns (La Soufrière, St. Vincent, 1902), or by vertical low-pressure eruptions from craters (Krakatoa, 1883). Fissure eruptions occur from the low-pressure upwelling of effervescing magma (Valley of Ten Thousand Smokes, 1912). The world's largest deposits, however, are of Quaternary age (the last 2,500,000 years) or older and have vented from fissures associated with subsidence structures, either calderas or volcanic-tectonic depressions.

Table 4: Dimensions of Some Large Ignimbrite Fields of the World

location	age	aerial extent (km²)	volume (km³)	comment
Nevada; western Utah	early Oligocene to late Pliocene	200,000	50,000	one known sheet covers 12,800 km² with a volume of about 2,000 km³
North Island, New Zealand	Plio-Pleistocene	25,000	8,000	many sheets with several sources
Lake Toba, Sumatra	Pleistocene	25,000	1,200	probably erupted over a short period of time
Yellowstone, Wyoming	Pleistocene	10,000	1,700	probably emplaced in rapid sequence; 300 metres maximum thickness

Glowing avalanches are derived mainly from silicic to intermediate magmas: their deposits may be termed ignimbrite. Many geologists, however, prefer the term ash-flow for the process of flowage, and ash-flow tuff for the deposits. Glowing avalanches produced from summit eruptions are comparatively small in lateral extent and volume. Their deposits are usually unconsolidated mixtures of lithic (rock), crystal (mineral), or vitric (glass) particles in various proportions that form the matrix within a chaotic mixture of blocks, bombs, and lapilli of pumice, or accessory and accidental debris.

Ignimbrite sheets that are derived from fissures associated with subsidence structures cover vast areas in parts of the western United States, New Zealand, Sumatra, and other countries (Table 4). One of the largest known ignimbrite fields extends across the state of Nevada and into western Utah. The field, which contains many individual ignimbrite sheets, totals about 50,000 cubic kilometres (12,000 cubic miles) in volume and covers about 200,000 square kilometres (77,000 square miles) in area. One sheet alone is about 2,000 cubic kilometres (500 cubic miles) in volume and covers an area of 12,800 square kilometres (4,950 square miles). Some estimates suggest that large flows are capable of travelling up to 160 kilometres (about 100 miles) in one direction.

Glowing avalanches issue forth at temperatures estimated to be 550° to 900° C (1,020° to 1,650° F) or more. Thick deposits at rest (in place) take many months or years to cool, and the fragmental deposit undergoes considerable modification because of the high temperatures. Near the base, for example, glass shards and pumice fragments become typically flattened and fused together to form a zone of welded tuff. Vapours escaping upward may deposit hematite (iron oxide), tridymite (high-temperature quartz), and other minerals within cavities to produce a vapour-phase zone above the welded zone. Ignimbrite above the vapour-phase zone may remain essentially unaltered and unwelded during the cooling period.

Fragments within extensive ignimbrite sheets exhibit a great size range, from large pumice and lithic blocks near the source to the size of lapilli toward their edges, thus reflecting decreasing flow energy during emplacement. Deposits at any single locality, however, typically are poorly sorted and commonly lack features of bedding or stratification. Pumice, glass shards, and pyrogenic minerals indicative of rhyolitic (silicic) to dacitic (intermediate) magma are usually the dominant constituents.

Role of steam explosions

Base surge flow. Base surges of volcanic origin are turbulent pyroclastic flows that form at the base of vertically rising eruption columns and expand outward along the ground at velocities of 20 to 50 metres per second (65 to 165 feet per second). The flows, composed of water vapour or steam, solid ejecta, and rapidly cooling fluid volcanic particles, develop from steam explosions where rising magma encounters large amounts of water at a shallow depth. The 1965 phreatic eruption of Taal Volcano in the Philippines gave rise to a destructive base surge that moved as far as six kilometres (four miles) from the source, and left dune-shaped deposits composed of lithic (rock) and vitric (glass) fragments as large as a metre (three feet) in diameter scattered in a poorly sorted matrix of ash and lapilli. Cross-bedded deposits, somewhat similar in appearance to wind- or stream-deposited sediments, were produced by dune migration. The fact that trees were not charred and deposits stuck to vertical objects as does cohesive mud shows that initial temperatures were not much greater than that of steam, and that water vapour or steam was the dominant gaseous component within the cloud.

Base surge deposits, identified chiefly by low-angle cross-bedded structures, occur most frequently within nearly horizontal rim sequences of low-standing volcanoes with wide bowl-shaped craters known as tuff rings, a variety of maar, or explosion, volcano. Zuni Salt Lake and Kilbourne Hole in New Mexico, and Salt Lake Crater, Oahu, are three outstanding examples of tuff rings with well-exposed cross-bedded deposits. Base surge deposits derived from the formation of the Laacher See volcanic structure in the Eifel district of West Germany exhibit some of the finest examples of cross-bedded dune-like structures in the world. Current directions determined from the orientation of the cross-bedding show that the base surges flowed radially outward from the source.

The remarkable distances to which large volumes of coarse- and fine-grained debris can flow is little understood, but initial mobility is supplied by the kinetic energy of expanding gases. Additional aid to the turbulent suspension of particles during flow may be from fragments emitting gases, or by the engulfment, heating, and expansion of air by the flow as it moves along the ground. Both of these processes require initial high temperatures and may be important in the emplacement of large, widespread ignimbrite layers. The external similarities in style of flow, velocity, and mobility of the relatively cool base surge flows and hot glowing avalanches, however, suggest that some other cause for suspension may be equally or more important. Calculations indicate that a relatively high concentration of fine-grained ash, with close spacing within a turbulent flow, would inhibit the diffusion of gas through the mass and greatly retard settling rates. By retarding deflation and therefore sedimentation from the flow, the distance travelled would be considerably lengthened.

Subaqueous deposits. Eruptions on land have contributed large volumes of silicic and intermediate ash to the sea. Depending upon the volume, settling rates, and bottom currents, the fragments are variously mixed with nonvolcanic particles. Considerable mixing by marine organisms may occur in some layers. Undisturbed layers commonly have sharp bottom contacts and diffuse upper contacts, and grade upward according to decreasing particle-settling rates. The slow rate at which pumice fragments become waterlogged inhibits their sinking; they eventually settle on top of the smaller crystals and shards unless ocean currents carry them away.

Correlation and distribution of submarine ash deposits

The correlating of widespread submarine ash layers, using the refractive index (measure of light transmission) of glass shards without detailed knowledge of associated pyrogenic minerals, is a rather dubious practice. Eruptions from several sources may widely disperse shards with similar physical and chemical characteristics in the sea over a large span of time. Several volcanoes along the length of the Cascade Range, for example, have produced shards with nearly identical refractive indices despite the multiple source involved.

Layers of silicic to intermediate ash have been identified in the North Atlantic, the Gulf of Mexico, off the coast of Central and South America, the Gulf of Alaska and the north Pacific, the Tyrrhenian Sea and eastern Mediterranean Sea, east of New Zealand, and Indonesia. Mafic ash with brown glass fragments occurs in the South Atlantic between the mid-Atlantic Ridge and South Sandwich Islands; the debris was derived from basaltic eruptions in the islands.

The distribution of submarine ash deposits, despite reduced settling rates in water and the consequent increase in the influence of water currents, is controlled in large measure (before deposition in the sea) by the direction of high-level winds, as indicated by the 1815 Tambora ash found on the sea floor north and east of Java. Lack of systematic thickening of 1912 Novarupta (Katmai) ash in the Gulf of Alaska, however, suggests that the ash was redistributed by bottom currents. Both factors probably are operative.

Tertiary volcanic rocks derived from underwater eruptions that produced flows of pyroclastic debris have been described from Japan and Mount Rainier National Park, Washington. The process involved eruptions that flooded the submarine environment with large volumes of ejecta. The smaller density differences between fragments and water than between fragments and air, and the greater drag resistance of the water on particles, results in more efficient sorting processes: dense lapilli settle rapidly to form subaqueous flows; slower settling sand-size ash forms repeated small surges and turbidity currents; slow-settling shards are transported in suspension by slowly moving currents of water; and pumice floats to the surface of the sea. An important criterion of subaqueous pyroclastic deposits is the presence of pumice near the tops of the layers—recognizable even in ancient low-grade metamorphic rocks.

STRATIGRAPHY OF PYROCLASTIC SEQUENCES

Factors that complicate the stratigraphy

The stratigraphic (sequence of strata, or layers) relationships of thick pyroclastic accumulations are extremely complex. Near the source, deposits are typically thick and lenticular (lens-shaped) and consist of coarse-grained breccias of many kinds, agglomerate, and interbedded tuff and lapilli-tuff. Layering may be absent, and deposits are, as a rule, extremely poorly sorted. Individual layers are difficult to trace (follow laterally) because of numerous erosional unconformities (missing strata) and because of their massive and undistinguished features. Lava flows may be common but may terminate abruptly with pyroclastic beds at their margins. Another complicating factor is that subaerial volcanic centres are generally hilly or mountainous, and pyroclastic flows or mud and lava flows are confined to canyons. Thus, individual units in ancient deposits appear to have no continuity, and thick deposits may disappear over very short distances. If the volcanic accumulations build up steep slopes, high initial dips complicate attempts to unravel tectonic trends and modifications.

Air fall layers that extend far beyond the source, however, provide excellent stratigraphic markers. Unlike most sedimentary deposits, topographic relief is no barrier to transport, and ash may fall simultaneously in many widely separated depositional basins. The precision in correlation afforded by single ash layers from dated eruptions with well-described mineralogical characteristics provides a powerful tool for archaeologists, palynologists, soil scientists, and geologists working on Pleistocene and Recent problems.

Stratigraphic nomenclature. The pyroclastic sequences may be subdivided into members, formations, and groups, as with nonpyroclastic rocks. Their explosive igneous origin, however, places particular importance on individual beds and sequences that provide information about magmatic conditions and type of eruption. Consequently, "member, formation, and group" are not used in the formal stratigraphic sense as they are with other sedimentary formations. The classification shown in Table 5 is useful for stratigraphic work on or near volcanic fields associated with Pliocene–Pleistocene, Recent or modern volcanoes (those active during the last 7,000,000 years, inclusively), rather than older areas of volcanism, where conventional stratigraphic nomenclature can be used. It is based on work at Oshima Volcano, Japan, and in North Island, New Zealand.

Table 5: Stratigraphic Terms for Pyroclastic Sequences

descriptive term	corresponding genetic term
Group	eruptive period
Formation	eruptive interval
Member	eruptive episode
Multiple fall unit	eruptive phase
Fall unit	individual explosion

A fall unit is deposited from an individual explosion or a short and nearly continuous eruption. Layers may have lateral continuity and show distinctive textures, compositions, and progressive lateral gradations in grain size and thickness. Individual units are rarely traceable in areas of thick volcanic accumulations, unless they have diagnostic mineral or textural features. The stratigraphic utility of the fall unit in interbasin correlation, however, increases at long distances from the source.

A multiple fall unit, composed of several petrogenetically related fall units, is deposited from prolonged eruptions or several closely spaced eruptions that may be termed an eruptive phase. Minor erosional breaks or layers with minor differences in texture and composition may be produced by variation in eruptive behaviour and the wind; although close to the source, coarse-grained and poorly sorted thick units may appear to be a single fall unit. Bedding planes are either transitional (in colour or texture) without marked physical breaks or else are relatively sharp. As thickness and grain size of individual fall units decrease with increasing distance from source, distinctive features between them may become marked; but at great distances these features are lost and multiple units may become indistinguishable from single fall units. Thus, close to the source, or in places where multiple units are very thin, they may not be distinguishable. Because of the possible lateral variations, the multiple fall unit is the most useful basic and mappable stratigraphic unit.

A member comprises the petrogenetically related deposits of an eruptive episode, and includes two or more multiple fall units. Parts of the sequence may be reworked pyroclastic debris, and lava flows may occur within it. Members may be separated from each other by minor erosional or weathering breaks, with or without marked changes in composition. At Oshima Volcano, Japan, members occur in genetically related cycles, but at other localities cycles do not necessarily occur.

A formation, deposited during an eruptive interval, includes two or more petrogenetically related members. The members may be separated by unconformities, or compositional changes. Formations may thin away from the source with their members separated by sedimentary layers, lava flows, or pyroclastics from other sources, or by weathering profiles. Variations in thickness within isolated closed basins with an outside source are controlled by the shape of the basin, although fragments tend to be larger in the source direction.

A group consists of more than one formation formed during an eruptive period. The formations may interfinger with nonvolcanic formations, and may be separated by unconformities. Whereas formations are usually derived from single volcanoes or several closely related vents, a group can include formations derived from petrogenetically unrelated sources.

Primary structures. Complex geometric relationships between layers close to pyroclastic sources and on volcanic slopes are created by rapid deposition of coarse debris, landslides on oversteepened slopes, heavy rainfall on loose material and resulting debris flows, and complexities produced by lava flows. Unconformities may quickly form by the development of a landslide scar on one day and its subsequent burial by tephra on the next. Deposits may rapidly fill a topographic low to considerable thickness but abruptly thin or die out over an adjacent high.

Bedding planes between pyroclastic layers are typically

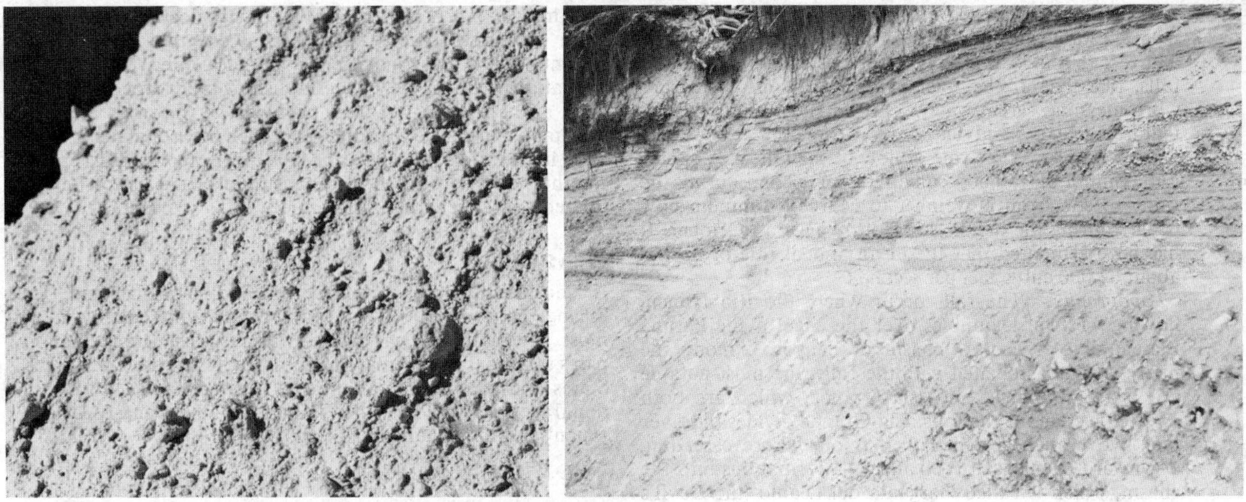

Tuff and lapilli-tuff, contrasting depositional features. (Left) Pyroclastic flow deposits, unbedded, coarse-lapilli and ash-size particles in poorly sorted arrangement (reduced about one fourth). (Right) Well-bedded air-fall deposits; the sequence is five feet thick.
By courtesy of R.V. Fisher

Bedding planes and graded bedding

gradational, depending upon the fluctuations of eruptions and factors of dispersal. Layering is commonly manifested by gradual or sudden textural or colour changes, or by poorly defined lateral zones containing lapilli or larger fragments, which lie in a matrix of nearly uniform ash. Sharp bedding planes are caused (in addition to erosional or weathering processes) by drastic and sudden changes in the type or rate of dispersal, as when pyroclastic flows occur over ash falls, or when a sudden rapid fall of coarse ash covers fine ash that has been slowly accumulating over a period of years.

Well-defined graded bedding with an upward decrease in size is not especially common in coarse pyroclastic deposits close to the source because size variation is controlled in large measure by pulsations in eruption strength as well as by wind and settling velocity. Layers may coarsen from bottom to top, top to bottom, or toward the middle and commonly show no systematic grading. At greater distances, however, where wind factors control dispersal, tuff beds are more likely to be graded according to particle-settling velocity. At great distances, where most of the large particles have dropped out, grain-size differences are small and grading or layering may not be evident (see photograph).

Maar volcanoes (those with wide bowl-shaped craters that may or may not contain lakes) produce deposits with rather distinct features, particularly base surge deposits. Tuff tends to be in thin, even layers, or may show well-defined cross beds. Accretionary lapilli are common. Quickly chilled glass shards are characteristic of the deposits. Ballistic ejecta, such as blocks and bombs that fall into the originally wet cohesive ash, plastically bend the layers downward by the force of impact to produce beddings sags ("bomb sags"), a characteristic feature of many maars.

BIBLIOGRAPHY. Articles that contain reviews on various aspects of pyroclastics fragments, deposits, or rocks include: C.K. WENTWORTH and HOWELL WILLIAMS, "The Classification and Terminology of the Pyroclastic Rocks," *Bull. Natn. Res. Coun.*, 89:19–53 (1932); R.V. FISHER, "Rocks Composed of Volcanic Fragments and their Classification," *Earth Sci. Rev.*, 1:287–298 (1966); R.E. WILCOX, "Some Effects of Recent Volcanic Ashfalls, with Especial Reference to Alaska," *Bull. U.S. Geol. Surv. 1028–N*, pp. 409–476 (1959), and "Volcanic-Ash Chronology," in H.E. WRIGHT, JR. and D.G. FREY (eds.), *The Quaternary of the United States*, pp. 807–816 (1965); R.L. SMITH, "Ash Flows," *Bull. Geol. Soc. Am.*, 71:795–841 (1960); W.H. PARSONS, "Criteria for the Recognition of Volcanic Breccias: Review," *Mem. Geol. Soc. Am. 115*, pp. 263–304 (1969); G.P. EATON, "Windborne Volcanic Ash: A Possible Index to Polar Wandering," *J. Geol.*, 72:1–35 (1964).

Significant works that wholly or in part treat tephra deposits from specific regions or from particular volcanoes include: SIGURDUR THORARINSSON, "The Tephra Fall from Hekla on March 29, 1947," in *The Eruption of Hekla 1947–48*, pp. 1–68 (1954); HOWELL WILLIAMS, *The Geology of Crater Lake National Park, Oregon* (1942); SHIGEO ARAMAKI, "Geology of Asama Volcano," *J. Fac. Sci. Tokyo Univ.*, sect. 2, 14: 229–443 (1963); ANTHONY EWART, "Petrology and Petrogenesis of the Quaternary Pumice Ash in the Taupo Area, New Zealand," *J. Petrology*, 4:392–431 (1963); JAMES HEALY, "Stratigraphy and Chronology of Late Quaternary Volcanic Ash in Taupo, Rotorua, and Gisborne Districts," *Bull. N.Z. Geol. Surv. 73*, pt. 1, pp. 1–42 (1964); KAZUAKI NAKAMURA, "Volcano-Stratigraphic Study of Oshima Volcano, Izu," *Bull. Earthq. Res. Inst.*, 42:649–728 (1964).

Articles dealing with the origin of fragmental volcanic debris or mechanisms of their emplacement include: JEAN VERHOOGEN, "Mechanics of Ash Formation," *Am. J. Sci.*, 249: 729–739 (1951); C.N. FENNER, "The Origin and Mode of Emplacement of the Great Tuff Deposit of the Valley of Ten Thousand Smokes," *Tech. Pap. Natn. Geogr. Soc.*, Katmai series, vol. 1, no. 1 (1923); R.S. FISKE and T. MATSUDA, "Submarine Equivalents of Ash Flows in the Tokiwa Formation, Japan," *Am. J. Sci.*, 262:76–106 (1964); R.V. FISHER, "Mechanism of Deposition from Pyroclastic Flows," *Am. J. Sci.*, 264:350–363 (1966); R.L. HAY, "Formation of the Crystal-Rich Glowing Avalanche Deposits of St. Vincent, B.W.I.," *J. Geol.*, 67:540–562 (1959); J.G. MOORE, "Base Surge in Recent Volcanic Eruptions," *Bull. Volcan.*, 30:337–363 (1967); R.V. FISHER and A.C. WATERS, "Base Surge Bedforms in Maar Volcanoes," *Am. J. Sci.*, 268:157–180 (1970); A.R. MCBIRNEY, "Factors Governing the Nature of Submarine Volcanism," *Bull. Volcan.*, 25:455–469 (1963), and "Factors Governing Emplacement of Volcanic Necks," *Am. J. Sci.*, 257:431–448 (1959).

A classic treatment of erosional processes on an active volcano is KENNETH SEGERSTROM, "Erosion Studies at Parícutin, State of Michoacán, Mexico," *Bull. U.S. Geol. Surv. 965-A* (1950).

Important papers that discuss submarine pyroclastic accumulations include: M.N. BRAMLETTE and W.H. BRADLEY, "Geology and Biology of North Atlantic Deep-Sea Cores Between Newfoundland and Ireland," *Prof. Pap. U.S. Geol. Surv. 196-A*, pt. 1, pp. 1-34 (1940); D. NINKOVICH *et al.*, "South Sandwich Tephra in Deep-Sea Sediments," *Deep Sea Res.*, 11:605–619 (1964).

A particularly useful dictionary, giving names in English, Dutch, French, and German, with a 58-page section on vulcanology (including pyroclastics), is A.A.G. SCHIEFERDECKER (ed.), *Geological Nomenclature* (1959).

(R.V.F.)

Iguaçu Falls

Iguaçu Falls (Saltos do Iguaçu in Portuguese, and Cataratas del Iguazú in Spanish) are the most spectacular waterfalls in South America. They are located on a stretch of the Rio Iguaçu that forms the boundary between Brazil and Argentina, about 14 miles (23 kilometres) above the confluence of the Iguaçu and Paraná rivers. The falls are horseshoe shaped and are nearly two-and-a-half miles wide—four times the width of Niagara Falls in North America. Numerous rocky and wooded islands on the edge of the escarpment over which the Rio Iguaçu plunges divide the falls into some 275 separate waterfalls or cataracts, varying between 200 and 269 feet (60 and 82 metres) in height. The name of the falls, like that of the river, is derived from a Guaraní word meaning "great water." (For an associated physical feature, see PARANA RIVER.)

Hydrography. The rate of flow of the falls may rise to a maximum of 450,000 cubic feet per second during the rainy season from November to March. Minimum flow occurs during the dry season from August to October. It has been estimated that the mean annual rate of flow is about 62,000 cubic feet per second.

Rate of flow

Topography. The falls occur where the Rio Iguaçu, flowing westward, tumbles over the edge of the Paraná Plateau into a narrow chasm or canyon. Among the many islands associated with the falls, the most notable are Isla San Martin and Isla Grande, which are both situated just above the falls. Isla Grande divides the river into two branches, which then rejoin before cascading downward over basalt rock and lava formations into the chasm, which is called Garganta del Diablo (the Devil's Throat); the effect has been described as that of "an ocean plunging into an abyss." (The Rio Iguaçu then continues its course through the canyon to its junction with the Paraná River.)

Many of the individual falls are broken midway by protruding ledges; the resultant deflection of the water, as well as the spray that arises, creates what appears to be a barrage of rainbows. From the foot of the falls, a curtain of mist rises nearly 500 feet into the air, adding to the spectacular rainbow effect.

From Isla San Martin, which is situated in the Argentinian half of the river, a fine view of the Argentine sector of the falls may be obtained; individual falls to be seen from this vantage point include those known as San Martin, Bossetti, the Two Sisters, Mitré, and the Three Musketeers. Tourists visiting the falls on the Argentine side are permitted complete freedom of movement and can climb in and out of the falls as they wish. From the Brazilian shore, the falls can be seen in their entirety; among individual Brazilian falls are those known as Benjamin Constant, Deodoro, and Floriano.

Exploration. The first Spanish explorer to discover the falls was Alvar Núñez Cabeza de Vaca, who in 1541 named them Salto de Santa María; the falls, however, retained their original name, Iguaçu. Jesuit missionaries began to investigate the falls in the 18th century, but these explorations were cut short by the expulsion of the Jesuits from South America in 1767. The first topographic maps of the falls were not completed until 1892.

Nature reserves. In 1897 Edmundo de Barros, a Brazilian army officer, envisaged the establishment of a national park at Iguaçu Falls, comparable in many respects to the Yellowstone National Park in the United States. Following boundary rectifications between Brazil and Argentina, two separate national parks were established, one by each state. Both parks were created for the preservation of the vegetation, wildlife, and scenic beauty associated with the falls; both also have government-owned hotels for the accommodation of tourists, who numbered 2,000,000 in 1969 alone. The Argentine park also maintains a natural-history museum. Each park prohibits hunting but permits fishing.

The vegetation of the region is rich and varied, ranging from semideciduous to tropical, and has been a focus of botanical interest. Water plants include a family (Podostemaceae) that grows only in rushing water and is found on the ledges of the falls. Contrasts are also abundant, with orchids growing next to pines, bamboos next to palm trees, and mosses next to lianas and colourful begonias.

Animal life is equally varied and abundant but has been much less studied. Mammals include several members of the cat family (ocelots and jaguars), deer, tapir, and innumerable smaller animals. Birds of many varieties are also to be found. Fish include the dorado (golden salmon), mandi, and cascudo.

Future prospects. In addition to continuing to form a major tourist attraction, a possibility also exists that the falls may be harnessed to provide hydroelectric power. Since 1967 negotiations have been in progress between Argentina and Brazil, with the aid of United Nations mediation, with a view to establishing a hydroelectric plant at the falls. Apart from problems of the two states in establishing a cooperative approach, seasonal variations in the rate of flow and the lack of a potential market for the power produced also constitute obstacles to the immediate realization of the project. (E.G.My.)

The hydroelectric potential

Ii Naosuke

Ii Naosuke, a Japanese feudal lord and statesman and, during the two years from 1858 to 1860, his country's most powerful political figure, was responsible for Japan's signing the first treaty of commerce with the United States and for the last attempt at reasserting the traditional political role of the Tokugawa—the dynasty of Japan's military rulers—before its fall in 1867.

By courtesy of the International Society for Educational Information, Tokyo, Inc.

Ii Naosuke, portrait by his second son, Naoyasu, second quarter of the 19th century. In the collection of Gotoku-ji, Setagaya, Tokyo.

Ii and his family

The Ii family, from which he was descended, ruled the fief of Hikone and played an important part in the administration of the shoguns; *i.e.*, the military dictators who had in effect ruled Japan since the 12th century. The family owed its prominent position to its standing among the *fudai* daimyo, the barons who had helped the Tokugawa become shoguns in the early 17th century. When Ii Naosuke was born on November 30, 1815, the 14th son of Ii Naonaka, his father had already turned over power to his eldest son. After the father's death, all sons except the heir had by family custom to be adopted into other baronial families or else be reduced to the status of family retainer with a small stipend. The only son for whom an adoptive family could not be found, Ii devoted himself to his studies at an academy established by his family. As a samurai, a member of the warrior class, he was schooled in the arts of warfare, as well as in Japan's cultural traditions, and he developed into a strong-willed and independent individual.

At 31, Ii's fortunes suddenly brightened when his brother's son died, and, ironically, as he was the only brother who had not been adopted, he was made heir apparent. When his brother died in 1850, Ii, then 35 years old, became lord of Hikone and thus acquired a base from which to project himself into national politics.

Arrival of Perry

The arrival of a U.S. flotilla under Commo. Matthew Perry in 1853 produced a major crisis for the shogunate. Perry had been sent by his government to demand that the country abandon its traditional isolation and enter into relations with the outside world. The Tokugawa authorities, confronted with the display of superior U.S. power, broke with precedent and sought the advice of the feudal nobles. Ii Naosuke was among those who favoured developing relations with the West. He argued that, while Japan was not yet strong enough to defend itself against foreign aggression, foreign contact would eventually provide Japan with the strength necessary to reimpose a policy of isolation. Others, however, urged that the intruders should be repelled by force if necessary. Since the Tokugawa government did not have the military capability to repulse the Americans, it signed the Perry Convention of 1854, which opened two Japanese ports to U.S. ships needing supplies and repairs. The task of arranging for trade, not covered in the Perry Convention, fell to Townsend Harris, who became the first U.S. consul to Japan.

Trade proved to be a controversial issue because the proponents of continued isolation would not be silenced. The problem was compounded by a crisis in domestic politics centring on the choice of an heir apparent to the reigning shogun, Iesada, who was childless.

There were two candidates with strong support. One was the Shogun's first cousin, who was still a child. The other was a grown man of demonstrated ability, the son of Tokugawa Nariaki, who was only collaterally related to the Shogun and not a member of the ruling group but who assiduously promoted the candidacy of his son. The Shogun's cousin, on the other hand, was supported by the senior councillors (*rōjū*), a small group of *fudai* daimyo who had acquired policy-making power in the shogunate. This group, anxious to preserve its power position, preferred to have a child as shogun. The stage was thus set for a great political struggle.

Ii entered the conflict in 1858, when he assumed direct control of the government as honorary chief councillor (*tairō*), a position filled only intermittently, usually in crisis situations. Before he took office, the shogunate had sought the imperial court's permission to sign the U.S. treaty, but antitreaty forces had succeeded in blocking approval. Ii authorized his negotiators to sign the treaty without waiting for imperial permission. He had learned that, if it were delayed, Japan might have to make even greater concessions, since it appeared that Britain and France were likely to seek even more far-reaching treaties.

Succession to the shogunate

On the succession issue Ii took a much more conservative position than on foreign affairs. He ignored pressure from Nariaki and others to bring new groups into the policy-making machinery and acted in favour of the *fudai* daimyo, who had appointed him, by promoting the Shogun's cousin as heir apparent.

In response, an angry delegation of barons led by Nariaki criticized the Chief Councillor for having signed the treaty without the Emperor's consent and demanded that Nariaki's son be made heir apparent to the Shogun. Ii rejected these complaints and demands and purged the opposition. He placed Nariaki under house arrest, stripped other barons of their rank, and arrested and even executed some officials.

Ii's victory proved short-lived. On March 25, 1860, Ii, accompanied by his retainers and bodyguards, was on his way to the Shogun's castle when a band of armed followers of Nariaki waylaid them. Ii's bodyguards were unable to defend him, and the attackers cut off his head, ending his meteoric rise to power when he was only 45 years old. His bold leadership as *tairō* secured for a time the stability of the shogunate and the continuity of Tokugawa rule; neither was to survive him for long.

BIBLIOGRAPHY. Two older books, SHUNKICHI AKIMOTO (trans.), *Lord Ii Naosuké and the New Japan* (1909); and H. SATOH, *Agitated Japan: The Life of Baron II Kamon-nokami Naosuké* (1896), both based on Japanese accounts, have not been superseded by more recent studies. GEORGE WILSON, "The Bakumatsu Intellectual in Action: Hashimoto Sanai in the Political Crisis of 1858," in ALBERT CRAIG and DONALD SHIVELY (eds.), *Personality in Japanese History* (1970), brings out the importance of the shogunal succession issue; while W.G. BEASLEY (ed. and trans.), *Selected Documents on Japanese Foreign Policy, 1853–1868* (1955), provides documentation on the treaty issue. CONRAD D. TOTMAN, *Politics in the Tokugawa Bakufu, 1600–1843* (1967), describes the institutional setting in which Lord Ii worked.

(N.I.)

Illinois

An east-north central state of the United States admitted as the 21st member of the Union in 1818, Illinois is a state that long has been profoundly divided within itself. The growth of Chicago in the 19th century into a great world centre of population, industry, transportation, and finance created the first and most basic division that was to have deep social, economic, and political consequences for the state and its people. Illinois continues to be essentially two states, with more than 7,100,000 of the more than 11,400,000 Illinoisans living in the Chicago metropolitan area and maintaining a minimum of common interests and sympathies with people "Downstate." A downstater visiting Chicago for sight-seeing or shopping travels in and out of the city by train or expressway, rarely seeing deeply into the city and the problems behind its swift-paced, modern facade. A Chicagoan seeking relaxation is most likely to drive to Wisconsin or Michigan, thus never developing a feeling for "the other Illinois."

Overview of the state

The divisions go even deeper, with large pockets of poverty existing in a state that is one of the most affluent in the nation by many economic indexes. Illinois's divisions, however, are far more social than economic. Internal distrust is probably the most serious symptom: distrust between races, between the nationality groups, and between urban and rural populations. To compound difficulties, Illinois is both a Northern and a Southern state in attitudes. It encompasses 56,400 square miles (146,075 square kilometres) and stretches 400 miles (644 kilometres) from Wisconsin in the north to the area known as "Little Egypt," which lies farther south than Richmond, Virginia. These divisions among the people of Illinois manifest themselves at the administrative and legislative levels of the state and are carried over into organizations, institutions, and political parties.

These problems, not unique to Illinois, perhaps became magnified through the state's critical role in the economic and political life of the nation. Rich in coal and oil reserves and ideally located for the acquisition of raw materials and distribution of finished goods, Illinois ranked second among states in exports in the late 1970s, and was third in agricultural income and fourth in manufacturing. Chicago, America's second largest city, has one of the busiest railroad systems in the country; its O'Hare International Airport is the world's most heavily trafficked, and Illinois highways and waterways are thick with commercial traffic. Politically, Illinois has continued to be a "swing state," its votes often mirroring fluctuating social tensions that underlie the growing, but unevenly distributed, economic prosperity. (For information on related topics, see the articles UNITED STATES OF AMERICA; UNITED STATES, HISTORY OF THE; NORTH AMERICA; and CHICAGO.)

THE HISTORY OF ILLINOIS

Archaeologists have found evidence dating from around 8000 BC of a paleo-Indian culture in southern Illinois. The Mississippian people, whose religious centre was Cahokia in southwestern Illinois, constituted probably the largest pre-Columbian (around AD 1300) community north of Mexico in the Mississippi River Valley floodplain. Indian tribes in Illinois were all of the Algonkian stock. In the north, the Kickapoo, Sac, and Fox roamed; the Potawatomie, Ottawa, and Ojibwa (Chippewa) dominated the Lake Michigan area; the Kaskaska, Illinois, and Peoria stalked the central prairies; and the Cahokia and Tamaroa roamed the south.

Settlement. The first Europeans to visit Illinois were the French explorers Louis Jolliet and Jacques Marquette, in 1673, when they explored the Mississippi and Illinois rivers. Near present-day Peoria, Lasalle established the first French foothold, Ft. Crévecoeur, and built Ft.-Saint-Louis near Ottawa. After the French and Indian War in the 1760s, France ceded to Britain its claim to lands east of the Mississippi. The following years were uneasy—British policy was unfavourable to the area's economic development, Indians resented the British, and settlements were without civil government. By 1773 the number of settlers had declined to about 1,000 plus a few hundred slaves.

In 1778 the American capture of Kaskaskia, the British seat of government, made Illinois a county of Virginia. The first settlement on the site of Chicago was made in 1779 by the black pioneer Jean Baptiste Point Sable (or Pointe du Sable), and in 1809 Congress made Illinois a territory.

Early years of statehood. At the time of statehood, in 1818, two-thirds of the population lived along the eastern and western edges of southern Illinois, primarily engaged in the fur trade. By 1830 the population had risen to nearly 160,000. The final conflict with the Indians was the Black Hawk War in 1832.

Southern and central Illinois remained the more heavily settled areas of the state during the early 19th century. In 1848 the Illinois and Michigan Canal was completed, linking points on the Illinois River on opposite sides of the Mississippi–Lake Michigan watersheds. With rail expansion many towns became prosperous. The National Road, leading westward from Maryland and terminating at Vandalia, brought many settlers to Illinois.

Slavery as a constitutional issue

The Illinois Constitution of 1818 gave blacks the status of indentured servants, and slavery would have been legalized except for fear that such a move would prevent admission. In 1824 Illinois voters rejected a proposal for a constitutional convention whose implicit if unstated purpose was to legalize slavery. Following the heavy influx of Yankees into northern Illinois during the 1830s and 1840s, which offset the southern attitudes, abolitionist sentiment translated itself into the Constitution of 1848, which abolished slavery and forbade the importing of slaves.

When the Civil War broke out, northern Illinois remained loyal to the Union and to the Illinoisan in the White House, Abraham Lincoln. A movement to ally southern Illinois with the Confederacy failed. Some 250,000 Illinoisans fought for the Union; among them was its most able general and future president, Ulysses S. Grant.

Economic and social maturation. Chicago's great fire of 1871 proved only a temporary deterrent in its progress toward becoming an industrial colossus among American cities. Its mills, railyards, and slaughterhouses were filled with workers recruited from the waves of Irish, Poles, Bohemians, and other Europeans who joined the many freed black immigrants who came to Illinois beginning in the 1860s. Until well into the 20th century, Illinois was a main focus of the American labour movement. Two events in Chicago, the Haymarket Square Riot of 1886 and the Pullman strike of 1894, became landmarks in the militant rise of the unions.

At the same time, Illinois was becoming a pioneer in social legislation, with a state board of health created in 1877; a compulsory school-attendance law in 1883; a "sweatshop act" providing for factory inspections and restrictions on child labour; and an eight-hour-day, 48-hour-week work limit for children, both enacted in 1893. The World's Columbian Exposition of 1893, missing by one year the 400th anniversary of Columbus' landing in the New World, was America's first international exhibition of the nation's vast technological and scientific strides during the 19th century.

Scenes of violence. During the decades up to and including the 1920s and 1930s, the name Chicago became an international byword for bootleg liquor, gangsterism, and syndicate crime. Downstate Illinois at the same time was gaining its share of notoriety as a region of violence.

"Bloody Williamson" county

Williamson County first gained the epithet "Bloody Williamson" for a feud, beginning in 1868, among five families of Tennessee and Kentucky origin. A dispute over a card game in a tavern near Carbondale grew into an eight-year vendetta fought by ambush or nighttime murder in barnyards, bars, and country stores. This violent tradition continued into the 1920s with the antiblack crusades of the Ku Klux Klan, the coal strikes, and the wars among the Shelton, Birger, and other bootleg gangs.

Positive growth. Amid the violence and the scandals that periodically rocked both state and municipal governments in Illinois, the state underwent tremendous growth economically and culturally. A reorganization of state government in 1917 brought more than 100 independent agencies and commissions under the governor and became a managerial model for many other states. Chicago became America's second largest city in the 1880s, and in 1933–34 its Century of Progress Exposition drew attention again to further industrial achievement. In 1942 the world's first controlled atomic chain reaction was set off at the University of Chicago, ushering in the atomic age.

THE NATURAL AND HUMAN LANDSCAPE

Illinois is drained by more than 500 streams emptying into either the Mississippi or the St. Lawrence River systems, the latter through Lake Michigan. The state is bounded on the north by Wisconsin, on the northeast by Lake Michigan, on the east by Indiana, on the southeast by Kentucky, and on the west by Missouri and Iowa.

The natural environment. *Surface features and waters.* Flat prairies cover much of Illinois, with irregular plains in the western, northern, and southern sections. The southernmost part of the state is in many ways out of character with the rest of Illinois. Shawnee National Forest, the only federal forest or park area in Illinois, covers a great part of this region. Southern Illinois consists of open hills, gently sloping with crests, which have Ozarkian or Appalachian characteristics. Gently rolling hills in the northwest include the state's highest point, 1,241 feet (378 metres) above sea level. The statewide average elevation is about 600 feet. Most of the 368 lakes of 40 acres (16 hectares) or more are man-made. Water lies under all of Illinois in natural underground reservoirs. Except for Chicago and the lakefront communities, which draw their water from Lake Michigan, most of northern Illinois's public water is pumped from underground wells. Some of these regions face a dwindling water supply; around Joliet, the water table has been lowered more than 700 feet in the past 100 years.

Water consumption and resources

The deep black soil of much of northern and central Illinois has unusual richness, and its quality for agriculture is among the finest in the world. The soils of the southern third of the state are far less suited for farming.

Climate. As is true in most temperate zones, Illinois experiences typically cold, snowy winters and hot summers although extremes are somewhat ameliorated around Lake Michigan. Mean winter temperatures are about 22° F (−6° C) in the north, and 37° F (3° C) in the south; summer equivalents are 70° F (21° C) and 77° F (25° C). Mean annual precipitation in the north ranges from 32 to 48 inches (810 to 1,220 millimetres) and in the south from 48 to 64 inches. The growing season varies from 210 days in the south to 160 days in northernmost counties.

Vegetation and animal life. Illinois vegetation is traditionally separated into the Fayette prairie of northern and central Illinois and the oak-hickory forest of the western and southern regions. Before white settlers moved in, oak-hickory forests prevailed also in the north. The settlers' needs for fuel and construction material and the lumbering industry stripped most of the trees, leaving only 10 percent of the forests in northern and central Illinois. Some 4,000,000 acres of forests remain in the west and south, more than 700,000 of them in the Shawnee National Forest. The state's great length—the equivalent of from New England to Virginia—gives it an unusual variety of northern and southern plant life. Both northern and southern wild flowers grow in Illinois, as well as a great variety of trees such as white pine, tamarack, walnut, cypress, and tupelo gum.

Before 1800 wildlife in abundance roamed the prairies and forests, but the bison, bear, wolf, mountain lion, and elk have disappeared entirely. Wild deer became extinct in 1910, but in 1933 the Department of Conservation placed small herds that resulted in a growing deer population. Game birds such as quail and pheasant are still in abundance, as are waterfowl during spring and fall migration. Pollution has nearly wiped out many fish that once were plentiful, but bullheads, carp, and catfish still abound.

Human imprints. Aside from the aforementioned distinction between the Chicago area and Downstate derived from population patterns, Illinois can be separated into three broad regions that differ markedly in their economic and social characteristics. A highly urbanized band—with extensive farming areas in between—reaches across the state in the north from Chicago to the Rock Island–Moline complex on the Mississippi and includes Kankakee, Joliet, and Rockford. Most of the farmland, although decidedly rural, has easy access to a sizable urban centre. The region is characterized by heavy industry around Chicago and the other large centres with a sprawl of large suburban developments of shopping centres, single-family dwellings, and apartment-house complexes.

Economic and social regions

The central third of the state includes such cities as Springfield, Bloomington, Peoria, Champaign, Danville, Galesburg, Quincy, and Decatur. The economic base of the region is its highly developed agriculture. Some cities (such as Peoria) support such large industries as farm machinery and construction equipment; others are centred on institutions—the state government complex in Springfield and the University of Illinois in Champaign–Urbana. The focus of communications and transportation is scattered among four or five metropolitan areas. The character of the people tends to remain rural or small-town, with a highly developed sense of tradition and history. The 1970 census showed a large influx of people into the Bloomington–Normal area, the home of two large universities, and the area's population continued to increase from 1970 to 1980, although at a slower rate. The more rural counties, however, have experienced only slight population increases, if any.

St. Louis, Missouri, tends to dominate southern Illinois. East St. Louis, Belleville, Alton, and Granite City are medium-sized cities, but they are located in only two counties, leaving the rest rural. Since it was the region of Illinois that was settled earliest, most of its communities have longer historical traditions than do their northern neighbours. The unique features of southern Illinois are its coal mines, oil wells, and the Shawnee National Forest, which covers parts of 10 counties. The region is Southern-mountain in character, and the pace of living is slightly slower because of fewer cities and a depressed economy. The rapidly growing Southern Illinois University in Carbondale has provided considerable economic and cultural stimulation to the region.

THE PEOPLE OF ILLINOIS

Waves of immigration. After most of the French had left Illinois following the French and Indian War, English settlers and colonists of Anglo-Saxon stock from Virginia, Tennessee, and Kentucky moved in. New Englanders and New Yorkers arrived by way of the Great Lakes or the National Road. When the United States experienced the great waves of European immigrants beginning in the 1840s, large numbers of Germans and Irish went to northern Illinois; and from the 1880s until World War I, immigrants streamed in from such countries as Poland, Hungary, Italy, Norway, Sweden, Austria, and Russia. In 1910 Germans ranked first in number among the foreign-born, Austrians and Hungarians ranked second, about 200,000 each, followed by Russians, Scandinavians, Irish, and Italians. Among the immigrants were the Jews. Culturally an urban-oriented group, they settled heavily on Chicago's south and west sides.

The great ethnic mix

Recent immigrants have tended to come from origins different and more diverse than in the 19th century. In Chicago, particularly, it is common to hear Greek, Persian, Polish, Spanish, and Czech spoken. Small, stable communities of Japanese, Chinese, Filipino, Puerto Rican, and Mexican peoples also make Chicago their home.

Blacks have lived in Illinois since the first slaves were imported in 1719, but their numbers remained low until the Civil War. By 1870 the Negroes numbered 28,000, and by 1910 migrant blacks had settled in the southern counties and totalled 110,000. With World War I, a steady flow of blacks began to the major industrial centres, and by 1970 the more than 1,400,000 blacks in Illinois made up nearly 13 percent of the state's population, almost all of them in Chicago. The 1980 census reported more than 1,600,000 blacks living in Illinois, almost 1,200,000 of them in Chicago. In addition, whites from poverty-stricken Appalachia, American Indians, and Puerto Ricans searching for higher paying employment opportunities have joined the migration to Chicago.

The religious diversity in Illinois is reflected in the different origins of the people themselves. In the early 1800s Methodist circuit riders nourished tiny congregations throughout downstate Illinois, and the Methodists remain strong today in the small towns. The Irish, some of the Germans, and later the southern and eastern Europeans brought the Roman Catholic faith to the larger cities, and the Roman Catholic archdiocese of Chicago continues to be the nation's largest in membership. Also serving the city are scores of Eastern Orthodox and Protestant churches and Jewish synagogues.

Contemporary demography. Illinois has population characteristics similar to those of the nation as a whole: the state grew by about 3 percent from 1970 to 1980; cities continued to lose whites to suburban areas, while both the number and percentage of blacks within city limits increased. The flight of young people from rural areas and small towns, however, has slowed. In the 1960s, 49 of the 102 counties lost population, while during the 1970s only 15 counties had a decrease.

In 1978 birth and mortality rates in Illinois were similar to national averages, though the rate of natural increase—surplus of births over deaths—for blacks was almost twice that of the state as a whole. Illinois was about 83 percent urban compared to the national figure of about 74 percent.

Patterns of migration

During the 1970s Chicago lost more than 10 percent of its population, but its six-county metropolitan area grew rapidly. The black population in the suburbs grew by more than 55 percent from 1970 to 1980 but still made up only 5.6 percent of the total. More than 80 percent of the whites left East St. Louis in the decade, symptomatic of the racial tensions and frequent confrontations that continued to grip some parts of southern Illinois.

On a statewide basis, more whites have left Illinois since 1960 than have moved in, and the immigration of blacks, though on a large scale, has not offset the trend toward net loss of population by migration. The state's growth, therefore, has been the result of natural increase, the rate of which demographers expect will decrease in coming years. A state population of about 11,900,000 was forecast for 1990.

THE STATE'S ECONOMY

The diversified nature of its economy—strength in manufacturing, agriculture, finance, mining, transportation, government, and services—makes Illinois a microcosm of the national economic scene as a whole. This diversity generally provides greater stability at times when other states with more narrowly based industries suffer—as, for example, when military contracts are cut, with a resulting increase in unemployment. In the late 1970s more than 19,500 manufacturing companies were located in Illinois.

Major components of the economy. *Manufacturing*. Illinois has the second highest number of factories producing fabricated metals in the nation, and the third highest number of electrical machinery and printing and publishing establishments. It ranks fourth as a centre for establishments producing nonelectrical machinery, which accounts for a large share of its foreign exports. Illinois is a major automotive centre as well, with more than 160,000 persons employed in the manufacture and use of motor vehicles in the late 1970s. Some 250 industrial parks are scattered throughout the state, the greatest concentration being in the Chicago metropolitan area.

Natural resources and power. The 40 or more coal seams in Illinois are relatively thin, but the underground mines in the south have among the highest production per man-day in the country. In 1980 the state's total coal production ranked fourth in the nation. Peak petroleum production was reached in 1940 and has declined since; nevertheless, output remains fairly high. In the late 1970s Illinois ranked fifteenth nationally in petroleum production. Illinois also leads in mining of lead, zinc, limestone, and silica sand used in the glass and steel industries.

Developments in nuclear power

The resources of coal and oil contribute heavily to the production of electrical power, although atomic-energy stations are beginning to assume increasing shares of the state's industrial and consumer needs. The Argonne National Laboratory, near Lemont, is a major research and development installation of the U.S. Department of Energy, and the Dresden Nuclear Power Station, near Joliet, produces electricity for eight companies in and around Chicago. A facility located in Zion on Lake Michigan began commercial operation in 1973.

Agriculture. Illinois's greatest natural resource, however, is its rich, black soil. In 1979 some 108,000 farms covered more than 80 percent of the state's area. For years Illinois has been the nation's major soybean producer, and from year to year it trades places with Iowa for first-place rank in corn. In 1980 Illinois was second in pork production, while other grains, dairy products, and meat animals held high positions. Government payments to Illinois farmers in 1980 were the 12th highest in the nation. The average size of an Illinois farm was about 270 acres. In spite of a growing national trend toward large corporate-farm operations, family-owned farms account for more than 85 percent of farms in Illinois.

Finance. In 1980 Illinois ranked second only to Texas in number of independent banks, attributable to the state's prohibition against branch banking. This issue long has produced complex political battles in Springfield, with frequent charges and occasional exposures of political graft connected with it. Observers see opposition to change coming primarily from small banks downstate that fear elimination by the huge Chicago banks and from the currency exchanges that operate with high service charges, especially in inner-city areas that cannot support an independent banking institution.

In addition to its banking strength, Illinois is a major insurance centre, headquartering the two largest automobile insurers in the world. Chicago is the seat of the seventh district of the Federal Reserve Bank as well as of the Midwest Stock Exchange and the Chicago Board of Trade. Although well below the New York and American exchanges in volume, the Midwest Stock Exchange had nearly 1,700 issues available for trade in the early 1980s. The Board of Trade is the nation's oldest and largest commodity market, dealing in contracts for grains, soybeans and their products, silver, plywood and lumber, livestock, and dairy products.

Economic management and labour. The state and private business organizations give considerable attention to expanding Illinois's balanced economy. The Illinois Department of Business and Economic Development has an office in Brussels to stimulate the importation into Europe of Illinois products. The department also aggressively seeks to attract new industries to Illinois and to provide advice to communities that wish to do the same. This department and the Department of Labor also provide data on economic trends, wages, local taxes, and marketing. The state offers services relating to the development of business enterprises by blacks and other ethnic minorities and disseminates information to private enterprises that wish to benefit from new technological developments. Private organizations, local and regional in nature, traditionally have played a significant part in attracting industry, in the development or rehabilitation of downtown areas, and in technological advancement.

Strong union-political ties

Trade unions are strong in Illinois, both politically and economically, but neither they nor the employer groups are strong enough to impose their will on the other. Mediation in labour-management disputes by politicians is a frequent occurrence, notably in Chicago, where union ties to political parties and leaders are accepted facts of life.

In recent years Illinois has found itself more and more deeply involved with the dual needs of maintaining its economic stability and of improving the environment. Politicians found themselves involved with the demands of the public and of conservationists, the uncertainty of federal pollution (and related) standards, and the self-defenses of industry. The increasing pollution of Lake Michigan, of the skies of the industrial centres, and of streams throughout the state by industry, by public utilities, and by municipalities themselves posed one of the most perplexing questions for the state's economic future.

Transportation. Illinois is recognized as the transportation centre of the United States. Few comparable areas are served by so many different means of transportation. Before the Amtrak (federal) passenger train merger in 1971, 30 passenger railroads and 37 industrial lines served the state. By the early 1980s the number of passenger trains was reduced to 21 inbound and 21 outbound trains. Chicago remains the country's rail capital, and the state's more than 11,000 miles of track rank it second highest in the nation. Eight commuter railroads continue to serve the Chicago area, carrying an average of 250,000 passengers every weekday. Proposals to create an agency for overall operation of public transportation in northeastern Illinois have not yet been successful.

Railways, waterways, and airways

Water transportation became more efficient when Lake Michigan was connected to the Mississippi River in 1848 by means of the Illinois and Michigan Canal, linking the Chicago and Illinois rivers. With other later canals, barge traffic linking Chicago, the Mississippi, and Gulf Coast ports has become extensive. The St. Lawrence Seaway stimulated the commercial expansion of the Port of Chicago. Harbours for oceangoing freighters have been developed at Navy Pier near the downtown area and at Calumet Harbor in South Chicago. The dollar value and the tonnage of maritime exports handled through the Port of Chicago have increased more than 800 percent since 1958.

Chicago has two major airports, O'Hare International and Midway, and a third on the lakefront, Meigs Field, which serves small planes. In 1979 Illinois had a total of 96 public and 796 private airports.

ADMINISTRATION AND SOCIAL CONDITIONS

Structure of government. *The state level.* The first state constitution was adopted in 1818, a second in 1848, and in 1870 a third that was to remain in effect for 100 years.

Major provisions of the 1970 constitution

The constitution adopted by the people in December 1970 added new concepts to the Illinois Bill of Rights: no discrimination on the basis of race, creed, colour, national ancestry, or sex in employment or the sale or rental of property; no discrimination on the basis of sex; no discrimination against the physically or mentally handicapped; and the promotion of individual dignity.

Throughout the new document were examples of modernization in the structure and tone. A new article proclaimed a public policy of maintaining a healthful environment, to be enforced by state law; it provides that "Each person has the right to a healthful environment. Each person may enforce this right against any party, governmental or private, through appropriate legal proceedings. . . ."

The larger cities and counties were granted powers to tax, to license, and to incur debt without prior authorization of the state legislature. The governor was granted powers to reorganize state government, and his veto power was augmented by the authority to reduce appropriations and to object to certain portions of legislation without having to veto the entire act. The election of the judiciary was retained, as was the unique electoral framework of the House of Representatives, under which each district sent three representatives to Springfield, with the district's minority party virtually assured of one seat. In 1980 a referendum abolished this system in favour of single-member districts. Voters rejected separate constitutional proposals to abolish the death penalty and reduce the voting age to 18, though the latter issue was resolved by an amendment to the federal constitution in 1971.

Local government and taxation. Illinois recognizes three levels of local government—county, township, and municipality—plus innumerable special districts. Counties are classed as township and nontownship, with Cook County, containing Chicago and most of its major suburbs, in a class by itself. All counties elect a number of administrative officials. The 85 township counties are governed by boards of commissioners elected from districts, the 16 nontownship counties by three-member boards elected at large, and Cook County by a 15-member board, 10 from Chicago and five from the suburbs.

Townships act primarily as road-maintenance and general-assistance units. The annual town meeting, a gathering of all qualified voters, is still a feature of local government remaining from earlier centuries. Municipal government usually is of the mayor-council type, though other forms are permitted; villages utilize a president-trustee system.

Overall, Illinois has more than 6,300 units of local government and more than 36,000 elected officials, resulting in a crazy-quilt of overlapping administrative, educational, park, fire, sanitary, sewage, drainage, and other special districts. Most were formed to circumvent restrictions in the old constitution but have become self-perpetuating. Patterns of taxation are similarly chaotic. In addition to the usual taxes on personal and business income, cigarettes, liquor, and retail sales, Illinois formerly imposed a personal-property tax, which drew public and official complaints because of its uneven enforcement, few residents of Chicago even being billed for it. In 1979 the Illinois General Assembly passed tax legislation to replace revenue from the personal-property tax with increased corporate taxes. Real-estate taxes contribute the major local support for schools and other services, though the state supplies "no-strings-attached" grants to municipalities and counties from income-tax revenues.

The chaos of taxation

Political life. Since the Civil War Illinois has had intense competition between the Republican and Democratic parties. This factor and its large electoral vote make it a major battleground in presidential elections. The three distinguishable political regions are Chicago, which is heavily Democratic; Chicago's suburban metropolitan area and the rich farmlands of north and central Illinois, which are strongly Republican; and southern Illinois, which may swing one way or the other. In recent years both parties have had almost equal strength statewide.

The two parties are highly organized, from precinct to state levels. During the state's history both parties have been so frequently the target of corruption and fraud that Illinois politics has gained a checkered reputation on a nationwide scale. From 1955 until his death in 1976, Mayor Richard J. Daley of Chicago built up enormous statewide—and nationwide—power in the Democratic Party, largely through his administrative control of all city, and, effectively, Cook County departments and their patronage. If the governor is Republican, he almost always leads the party, but is ordinarily unable to command the huge bloc vote possible in Chicago.

With the proliferation of districts and officials, elections and referendums are held frequently throughout Illinois. Although widespread support has been voiced for adoption of the Missouri Plan, under which judicial candidates and incumbent judges at all levels are reviewed by qualified nonpartisan boards and then appointed, the partisan election of judges continues. Judges at all levels run for reelection on their record, the voter designating "yes" or "no" on retention. Until three-member districts were abolished by the voters in 1980, Illinois had a unique system for electing state representatives; a voter could cast 3 votes for 1 candidate, 1½ for each of 2, or 1 vote for each of 3.

The social milieu. Since World War II the profound social divisions within Illinois probably have been based most strongly on the issue of race. Chicago with its one-third or more black population, its heavy concentration of many white ethnic groups staunchly maintaining their identities as they move into the middle class, and its almost hereditary political control by an alliance of white ethnic, union, and business leaders, inevitably has been the focus. The appeals of Chicago to the state for funds to remedy its problems in education, housing, transportation, and welfare produced years of acrimonious debate in the legislature and between Chicago's city hall and the statehouse. Observers have seen this continuing contention as stemming both from a great lack of understanding of urban problems by downstate and urban legislators and from a basic unwillingness of the city administration to enforce laws designated to ameliorate and ultimately eliminate the effects of racial segregation and unequal opportunity.

Divisiveness of ethnic groups and geographic regions

Instances of violence and heated confrontations have not been limited to the Chicago area, however, and such southern Illinois cities as East St. Louis and Cairo have undergone prolonged sieges with overt racial overtones. In addition, sporadic student and other minority-group outbreaks have occurred, the best known of which were between police and youthful demonstrators during the 1968 Democratic National Convention in Chicago.

Social services. Health and welfare assistance and services are provided by both state and local government, most of which receive funds from diverse federal agencies, although representatives of the low-income groups most requiring the services have been in frequent conflict with local officials over the question of who is to administer the funds and the programs.

Chicago's public housing is primarily a municipal or county responsibility, often with federal aid. Both the Model Cities Program, public housing funded entirely by the federal government, and the Chicago Housing Authority (CHA) have met with strong opposition to proposals to locate public housing in predominantly white neighbourhoods. Throughout the 1960s public housing was built mainly in black neighbourhoods, and the few projects in white neighbourhoods used assignment policies to keep the number of black residents to a minimum. In 1969 the CHA was found guilty of discrimination against blacks and was ordered to promote integration, which it refused to do. All public housing construction in Chicago ceased from 1969 to 1974. In 1973 the CHA announced plans for a program of scattered public housing in the white northwest and southwest sides of the city, but progress has been slow and the opposition strong. Complaints of violations of the fair housing provisions of the 1968 Civil Rights Act for refusal to rent and to sell are among the highest in the nation. Needs for welfare assistance to poor families, dependent children, and other groups has met resistance in the legislature in Springfield, whereas independent attempts to establish free neighbourhood medical clinics in low-income black and Spanish-speaking areas of the city has encountered hostility from city administrators.

Thus, whereas medical facilities throughout most of Illinois are among the finest in the nation, and Chicago is a major centre for medical and psychiatric services and training, many Illinoisans continued to be served inadequately. And despite the fact that per capita income in Illinois is the highest of any state in the Midwest and among the highest in the nation, the increasing burdens of public assistance seemed far from solution or even agreement on goals. Illinois, in the social sphere as in the economic, might well be seen as a microcosm of the American nation as it approached the final decades of the 20th century.

Education. In the field of education as well, Illinois displays a startling juxtaposition of wealth and poverty. In many academic subjects the University of Chicago (founded 1891) is respected as among the finest institutions of higher learning in the nation, yet it is situated like an island on the south side amid one of the most deteriorated of the city's ghetto sections. Northwestern University (1851), in nearby Evanston, has a distinguished faculty in several areas, as do the Illinois Institute of Technology, in Chicago, and Southern Illinois University, in Carbondale and Edwardsville. In addition to the last-named institution, the state system includes four state universities as well as the University of Illinois, with campuses at Champaign–Urbana and Chicago, and two state colleges. Numerous sectarian and nonaffiliated private colleges are scattered throughout the state along with numerous community and junior colleges.

Institutions of higher learning

The Illinois Office of Education was created in 1975 after the new Illinois Constitution directed that responsibilities for public elementary and secondary education be transferred from an elected superintendent to a state Board of Education. The board consists of 17 members appointed by the governor with the consent of the state Senate. The Chicago system, as operated by the city's board, has been continuously controversial. Most schools in the system adhere to neighbourhood housing patterns, and critics long have charged deliberate gerrymandering of districts to keep racial integration minimal. The issue of funding of Chicago schools long has been among the most bitter points of city–state contention.

CULTURAL LIFE AND INSTITUTIONS

The arts. In spite of its reputation of being a brash industrial and commercial city, Chicago long has been one of the major centres of the arts in the United States. By 1900 Chicago architects were designing commercial and private buildings that became models for schools of modern architecture throughout the world. In the 1910s and 1920s it was a major centre for literary leaders, and today the holdings of its public and private institutional libraries are enormous. Its Art Institute, Museum of Science and Industry, Field Museum of Natural History, and other civic landmarks have collections and research facilities among the most complete in the world. Although it is no longer a major centre of the performing arts—before Hollywood was discovered about 1910, it was the centre of the American film industry—its downtown, suburban, and experimental theatres offer a broad spectrum of standard and avant-garde works. Dance is widely available, and its symphony orchestra is among the five major American musical organizations.

Communities outside the Chicago area have thriving artistic lives as well, often revolving around the theatre, music, art, or various science departments of the many colleges and universities in Illinois or around community theatre or musical organizations. Belleville boasts the second-oldest symphony orchestra in the nation, founded in 1867. The Eagle's Nest Art Colony, founded in Oregon in 1898 by the sculptor Lorado Taft, included many well-known Illinois artists; it was acquired by Northern Illinois University in 1950. The Illinois Arts Council was created by the state in 1965 as the primary agency to fund statewide or local programs in the several arts, including free street programs in the cities. It is supported by the state; the National Endowment for the Arts, a federal agency; and private donors.

Historic and recreational sites. Aside from Chicago's great number of historic memorabilia, recreational facilities, and tourist attractions, much of Illinois's full repertory remains relatively unknown, even to Illinoisans. Among old cities of interest on the Mississippi are Galena, which preserves the home of Pres. Ulysses S. Grant, and Nauvoo, founded in 1839 by the Mormons and their point of departure in 1846 on the trek that took them to Utah. New Salem, near Springfield, is a preservation of the community of log cabins in which Abraham Lincoln spent much of his young manhood. Throughout much of central Illinois the Lincoln Trail joins many places associated with the president, including his home in Springfield and the sites of his famous debates with Sen. Stephen A. Douglas. The Spoon River Trail in north central Illinois leads through the country made famous by the poet Edgar Lee Masters. Major scenic areas include the Mississippi Palisades State Park and Apple River Canyon State Park in the northwest, Starved Rock State Park in north central Illinois, and the forests of the south. The Chicago suburb of Oak Park, home of the pioneer modern architect Frank Lloyd Wright, contains many of the best examples of his early work.

Among Illinois's finest recreational offerings are the sandy beaches of Lake Michigan, from Chicago to the Wisconsin border, and the forest preserves that bring rustic retreats close to the state's urban areas. Although Illinois has virtually no wilderness areas, many camping sites are located throughout the state, and boating and fishing are avidly pursued on the state's many lakes and streams.

Communications. About 80 daily and 700 weekly newspapers are published throughout Illinois. In 1980 Chicago was served by five dailies, two of which had circulations of more than 650,000. The largest of these papers, the *Chicago Tribune*, became a nationally recognized symbol of the political and social conservatism of the Midwest under the long reign of publisher Robert R. McCormick, and it continues to have wide distribution throughout the Midwest. Its point of view is offset somewhat by the more moderate-to-liberal *Chicago Sun-Times*, the second largest daily in Chicago. The *Chicago Daily Defender*, with a circulation of more than 17,000, is published primarily for the black community.

Newspapers and the broadcast media

Southern Illinois is influenced also by newspapers and broadcasts from St. Louis. Across the state, 28 television channels and about 250 radio stations are in operation, with educational or "public" television available in Chicago, Champaign, and Carbondale and from St. Louis.

Chicago is the third largest publishing centre in the nation, exceeded only by New York City and San Francisco. Much of its publishing is specialized in the areas of education, encyclopaedias, medicine, and business.

PROBLEMS AND PROSPECTS

Although Illinois is faced with all the problems of a complex modern social system, it has the capacity to respond to the challenge. Perhaps the best example of this was the adoption by the electorate of a new state constitution in 1970, which had a number of innovative features. The electorate also has displayed a remarkable capacity to select their candidates for public office on a basis other than party label. The state Senate and the U.S. Congressional delegation are equally divided between parties, while the state House of Representatives is very closely divided. In spite of racial tensions, Illinois was the first state to have a black legislator as a leader of one of the houses. In spite of strong unionism and large corporate structures, there has been general industrial peace and high production.

Illinois continues to attract newcomers, some from other states, some from other countries. In their province may lie the possibility of effecting greater unity among the many diversities that characterize the state.

BIBLIOGRAPHY. RONALD E. NELSON (ed.), *Illinois: Land and Life in the Prairie State* (1978), a good general geography; JOHN CLAYTON, *The Illinois Fact Book and Historical Almanac, 1673–1968* (1970), a comprehensive compilation of political, geographical, and historical information about Illinois—includes data on primitive man in Illinois, local government, all municipalities and their populations from the year of incorporation to 1960, maps, and a short Illinois Who's Who; ILLINOIS SESQUICENTENNIAL COMMISSION, *Illinois Guide and Gazetteer* (1969), an interesting guide that describes many cities and towns, provides several excellent motor tours throughout the state, and includes an extensive description of the cultural aspects of Chicago emphasizing the architectural heritage of the city; BAKER BROWNELL, *The Other Illinois* (1958), a historical, colourful portrait of southern Illinois from the early 18th century to the present, with interesting details of a culture of a relatively obscure region; DAVID KENNEY, *Basic Illinois Government: A Systematic Explanation*, rev. ed. (1974), a scholarly, comprehensive review of Illinois government and political parties from the state's inception (particularly good in the detailed history of politics in Illinois), including an extensive bibliography and informative maps; L.E. AHLSWEDE, *Township Government Today* (1968), a short study on township government in Illinois, explaining the importance of the annual town meeting and the future of township government; ILLINOIS, SECRETARY OF STATE, *Illinois Blue Book* (biennial), a compilation of information on the functions of Illinois state government, including portraits and biographies of state officials.

(R.T.L./J.M.Ca.)

Illusions and Hallucinations

Illusion and hallucination are terms formulated to describe subjective (perceptual) experiences that contradict objective "reality" as it is defined by general agreement among people. Such experiences are not necessarily signs of psychiatric disturbances; they are or have been regularly and consistently reported by virtually everyone. Generally, illusions comprise misinterpretations of "real" sensory stimuli (*e.g.*, the child who perceives tree branches at night as if they are hobgoblins). Hallucinations are experiences that seem to originate when no external source of such stimulation appears (*e.g.*, one's name is called by a voice that no one else seems to hear).

Illusions

Illusions, then, are special perceptual experiences in which information arising from "real" external stimuli leads to an incorrect perception, or false impression, of the object or event from which the stimulation comes.

Some of these false impressions may arise from factors beyond an individual's control (such as the characteristic behaviour of light waves that makes a pencil in a glass of

Causes of illusions

water seem bent), from inadequate information (as under conditions of poor illumination), or from the functional and structural characteristics of the sensory apparatus (*e.g.*, distortions in the shape of the lens in the eye). Such visual illusions are experienced by every sighted person.

Another group of illusions results from misinterpretations one makes of seemingly adequate sensory cues. In such illusions, sensory impressions seem to contradict the "facts of reality" or fail to report their "true" character. (For more profound philosophical considerations, see EPISTEMOLOGY.) In these instances the perceiver seems to be making an error in processing sensory information. The error appears to arise within the central nervous system (brain and spinal cord); this may result from competing sensory information, psychologically meaningful distorting influences, or previous expectations (mental set). The driver who sees his own headlights reflected in the window of a store, for example, may experience the illusion that another vehicle is coming toward him even though he knows there is no road there.

TYPES OF ILLUSORY EXPERIENCE

Stimulus-distortion illusions. This type of illusory sense perception, common to mankind, arises when the environment changes or warps the stimulus energy on the way to the person, who efficiently receives it in its distorted pattern (as in the case of the "bent" pencil referred to above).

Auditory illusions. A common phenomenon is the auditory impression that a blowing automobile horn changes its pitch as it passes an observer on a highway. This is known as the Doppler effect, for C. Doppler, an Austrian physicist, who in 1842 noted that the pitch of a bell or whistle on a passing railroad train is heard to drop when the train and the perceiver are moving away from each other and to grow higher when they are approaching each other. The sound heard is also affected by such factors as a wind blowing toward or away from the person.

Uses of the pseudophone

Another auditory illusion was described in 1928 by P.T. Young, an American psychologist, who tested the process of sound localization (the direction from which sound seems to come). He constructed a pseudophone, an instrument made of two ear trumpets, one leading from the right side of the head to the left ear and the other vice versa. This created the illusory impression of reversed localization of sound. While walking along the street wearing the pseudophone he would hear footsteps to his right when they actually came from the left.

When two sources of sound in the same vicinity emit sound waves of slightly different frequencies (*i.e.*, vibrations per second), there will come intervals when waves from both sources arrive at the ear in phase (simultaneously) and produce the experience of a combined, louder sound. These intervals of combined sound will be perceived as "beats," or periodic alternations of sound intensity. When such auditory beats occur too rapidly to be discriminated, the resulting experience may be that of a harsh, continuous noise. These periodic alternations are of two kinds: summation tones (in which the waves reinforce each other), which are weaker and harder to observe, and difference tones (waves cancel each other), which are obvious, distinguishable, and which reinforce each other. Piano tuners depend in part upon their ability to employ these experiences in a reliable way in tightening and loosening the strings of the instruments.

Visual illusions. Numerous optical illusions are produced by the refraction (bending) of light as it passes through one substance to another. A ray of light passing from one transparent medium (air) to another (water) is bent as it emerges. Thus, the pencil standing in water seems broken at the surface where the air and water meet; in the same way, a partially submerged log in the water of a swamp gives the illusion of being bent.

Rainbows result from another characteristic of light waves, called diffraction. As the sun's rays pass through rain, the droplets separate (diffract) the white light into its component colours (see LIGHT). As rays of white light from any source pass through a prism, they are diffracted (broken up) to give the appearance of a spectrum of colour as in the rainbow of a summer morning. Another illusion that depends on atmospheric conditions is the mirage, in which, for example, the vision of a pool of water is created by light passing the layers of hot air above the heated surface of a highway. In effect, cooler layers of air refract the sun's rays at different angles than do less dense strata of heated air, giving the appearance of water where there is none; nearby objects (*e.g.*, barns, telephone poles) may even appear to be reflected in it. Under unusual conditions, more elaborate mirages may appear as cities, forests, "unidentified flying objects," oases, and even as the images of ships in a nearby body of water plying the sky of a desert.

Perceiver-distortion illusions. Some illusions are related to perceiver characteristics such as brain function. When an observer is confronted with a visual assortment of dots, for example, the brain may appear to group the dots that "belong together." These groupings are made on the basis of such things as observed similarity (*e.g.*, red versus black dots), proximity, common direction of movement, perceptual set (the way one is expecting to see things grouped), and extrapolation (one's estimate of what will happen based on an extension of what is now happening). A more detailed discussion of how the brain may function to form such perceptual configurations (called *Gestalten* in German) is to be found in the article PERCEPTION.

Time-induced error is an example of a Gestalt illusion that occurs over brief time intervals. Two images of the same line, for example, will appear to differ in length if they are flashed quickly one after the other.

Closure (another Gestalt term) is the illusion of seeing an incomplete stimulus as though it were whole. Thus, one unconsciously tends to complete (close) a triangle or a square with a gap in one of its sides. In watching movies, closure occurs to fill the intervals between what are really rapidly projected still pictures, giving the illusion of uninterrupted motion.

Visual illusion. The "figure and ground" illusion is commonly experienced when one gazes at the illustration of a white vase the outline of which is created by two black profiles (see Figure 1). At any moment one will be

Figure 1: Ambiguous figure seen as either white vase or two black profiles.

able to see either the white vase (in the centre area) as "figure" or the black profiles on each side (in which case the white is seen as "ground"). The fluctuations of figure and ground may occur even when one fails deliberately to shift attention, appearing without conscious effort. Seeing one aspect apparently excludes seeing the other.

Another example of ambiguity and object reversibility is the Necker cube (see Figure 2), which may seem to "flip-flop"; younger people tend to perceive these reversals more readily than do their elders.

The so-called Müller-Lyer illusion (also Figure 2) is based on the Gestalt principles of convergence and divergence: the lines at the sides seem to lead the eye either inward or outward to create a false impression of length. The Poggendorff illusion depends on the steepness of the intersecting lines. As obliqueness is decreased, the illusion becomes less compelling. In the Zöllner illusion, the cross-hatching disturbs the perception of parallel lines. A figure seen touching converging lines, as in the Ponzo illusion, creates the impression of size larger than does another figure placed between the lines where they are farther apart. In a related experience, linear perspective creates the illusion that parallel lines or contours (such as railroad tracks) converge as they recede from the viewer. If it were not for these converging lines, a figure in the distant background might appear smaller than would an identical figure in the foreground.

Colour in visual illusions

Visual illusions include contrast colour phenomena. A successive contrast occurs when, after one stares at a red surface, a green surface looks much brighter. As one enters a dark room from bright sunshine, the room at first seems quite dark by contrast. A simultaneous contrast occurs when an area of brightness is seen against a less intense or a more intense background. If a gray patch of paper is placed on a black background, it looks whiter than before; if placed on a white background, it looks darker.

In studies of visual verticality, experimenters investigated the conditions that determine perception of the "upright." A tilted chair that could be mechanically controlled by the subject was placed in a slanted room containing visual indicators of verticals and horizontals. When various persons were asked to sit in the chair and align themselves in a vertical position, some of the subjects aligned themselves with the "true vertical" determined by gravity, while others experienced the illusion of verticality by aligning themselves with the visual directions they saw in the slanted room. Closing the eyes made "true" alignment easier (see also SPACE PERCEPTION).

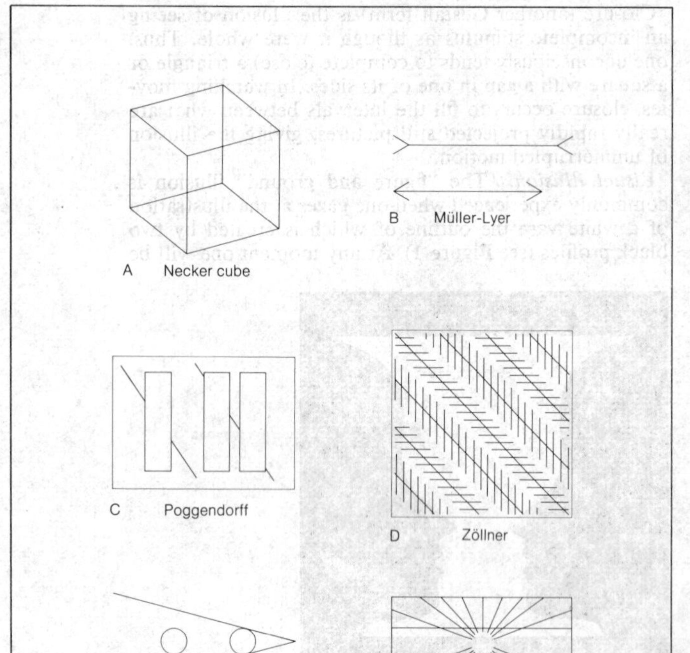

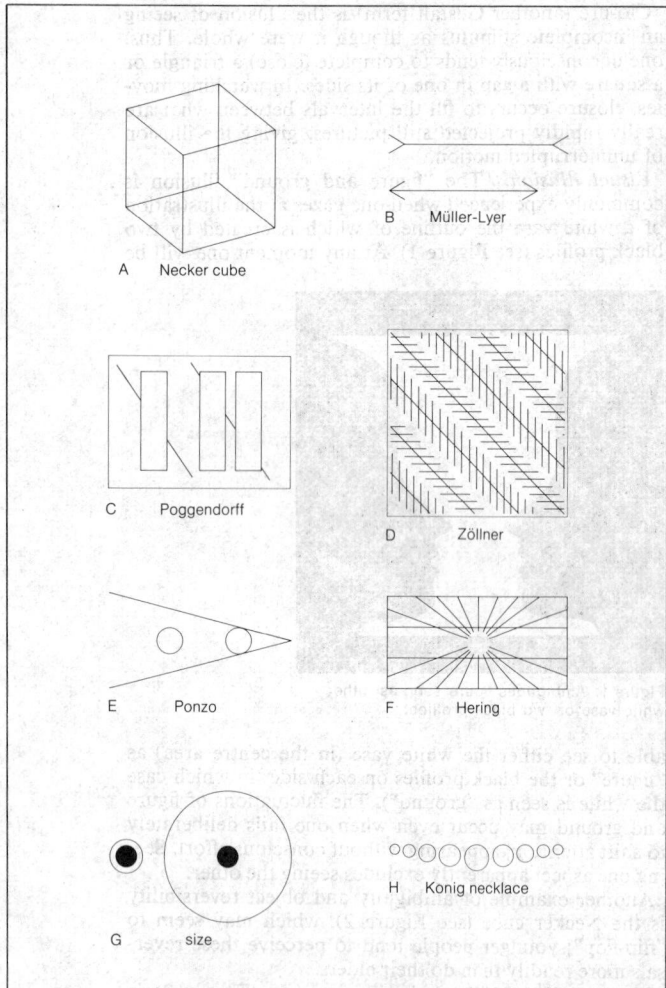

Figure 2: Examples of optical illusions.
(A) Cube changes orientation. (B) Lines are equal in length. (C) Lines covered by rectangles are straight. (D) All long lines are parallel. (E) Circles are equal size. (F) Horizontal lines are parallel. (G) Black dots are equal size. (H) Tops of circles are on a straight line.

Staring at a single bright spot in an otherwise darkened room creates the illusion that the stationary light is moving (autokinetic effect). One theory to account for this is that the impression is caused by minute eye movements of the observer (see also PERCEPTION OF MOVEMENT). The so-called phi phenomenon is an illusion of movement that arises when stationary objects, light bulbs for example, are placed side by side and illuminated rapidly one after another. The effect is frequently used on theatre marquees to give the impression of moving lights.

There is a well-known apparent difference in the size of the moon when it is at the horizon and when it is fully risen. The horizon moon, though it is actually farther away from the observer, looks much larger than it does when it is high in the sky and closer. This phenomenon was explained by English physicist S. Tolansky:

> . . . we are expecting, like all other objects, that its size should diminish as it nears the horizon. This does not happen. So, because it does not get smaller, as we expect, it therefore appears larger than it should be.

The illusion of the size of the moon

Other explanations have attributed the moon illusion to the fact that the fully risen moon cannot be readily compared to the terrain, as it can at the horizon; to atmospheric haze, which alters the impression of distance and size; to the change in the angle of elevation of the observer's eyes; and to the idea that the moon's increase in altitude (above the horizon) creates an expectation of decrease in size. (This last point seems to be at odds with Tolansky's ideas.) The moon illusion remains a paradox since, although the retinal images (in the eye) of the high moon and the horizon moon are about the same, the perceived size differs grossly.

Other illusory experiences. *Successive-contrast illusions.* Gestalt psychologists have proposed a "fading trace" theory to explain such illusions as occur in successive weight lifting (in which the same object seems to change in weight). It is suggested that, in such contrast illusions (in all the senses), a physical trace (in the form of temporarily excited nerve cells) of the original stimulus is left in the brain even after that stimulus stops; and that this trace influences the estimate or appreciation of a subsequent stimulus.

Recently, it has been suggested that not all people are equally receptive to optical illusions. The thesis is that an aftereffect is a surviving neural "trace" left by the imprint of a visually fixated (stared at) stimulus. The strength of the aftereffect or the speed of its disappearance varies greatly in individual cases. Persons who are field dependent (that is, who tend to observe a field in its totality) are said to show weaker aftereffect traces. Conversely, field-independent subjects (those who, by selective attention, are more likely to consider a specific stimulus apart from its context) show stronger perceptual aftereffects (see ATTENTION). When experimental subjects viewed a curved line and then the Hering figure (displayed elsewhere in this article), it was found that those who exhibit potent aftereffects (and are field independent) are able to counteract optical illusions, while those who have weaker aftereffects are more prone to experience visual illusions.

Tactual illusions. The skin contains numerous "spots" that respond selectively to either cold or warmth, but generally not to both. It can happen, however, that a very warm stimulus will produce a sensation of cold when placed on a spot that responds to cold. Thus, when a warm stimulus is perceived as cold, the illusion is called that of "paradoxical cold."

Illusions of hot and cold

"Paradoxical heat," a less frequent experience, results from stimulating warm and cold spots simultaneously. It appears to be a fusion of warm and paradoxical cold effects, producing a strange, somewhat unpleasant sensation of "heat" that seems to be attended by uneasiness resembling that of pain. The sensation is sometimes called "psychological heat."

Sudden temperature contrasts can play tricks on the senses. If hot water is run over one hand, and cold water over the other long enough for both to adjust to the temperatures and both are then plunged into lukewarm water, the resulting sensation will be that the cold hand will feel warm and the hot, cold. It would seem that in plunging the cold-adapted hand, nerve cells for perceiving cold were suddenly inhibited and those for perceiving hot were suddenly stimulated, while in the hot-adapted hand the reverse took place.

A single pencil may be felt as if it were two when it is held between crossed fingers in such a way that the skin is simultaneously stimulated at two points that would usually require two separate objects to produce such a sensation.

Anchor-effect phenomena. Sensitivity in any sense (sight, hearing, touch, and so on) may be measured as the just-perceptible intensity (threshold, or limen) of the appropriate stimulus. A light too dim to see is said to be subliminal (or below the visual threshold); a sound stimulus that is loud enough to hear is described as being above the auditory threshold (as being supraliminal). The smallest detectable stimulus is called the absolute threshold; the smallest detectable change in the intensity of a stimulus is called the difference threshold. Since such thresholds fluctuate within the same individual under different conditions, they are recognized as statistical (average) values rather than as fixed personal characteristics. At any rate, such thresholds can serve as points of reference, or anchors, against which subsequent stimuli are judged or perceived.

Other colour illusions. The normal human eye can function to detect about 130 gradations of colour in the visible spectrum (as in the rainbow), about 20 barely noticeable differences within a given colour, and about 500 of brightness. When two spots of equally bright light are observed in close succession, the first intensity may seem brighter. (This aftereffect is another example of time error.) The first light may be said to serve the function of brightness adaptation (or adjustment) in the eye, causing the second light to fall on a partly adapted and therefore less sensitive retina. In a brief time such excitement in the retina (or even in the brain) tends to subside, or fade. As a result of what theorists call "fading traces" of excitement (held to produce such aftereffect phenomena), various hues of a given colour may appear to be lighter or darker when looked at successively or in contrast to the background.

Weight illusions. The felt perception of differences in weights received experimental attention in 1899, which experiments indicated that a second weight is felt to be either heavier or lighter than an immediately preceding first one, partially as a result of the expectancy of the person doing the lifting. Having lifted the first weight, the subject is "set" for a certain effort on the next try. If the second weight is lifted quickly and easily, it will feel lighter than the first; if it comes up more slowly, it will feel heavier. Expectancy, or set, is often invoked in efforts to explain the size–weight illusion, in which a large cardboard box feels lighter than a smaller box even though both weigh the same.

Weight perception

Olfactory intensity. Smell (olfactory) discrimination is influenced by any odour to which the olfactory structures already have adapted. Receptors in the nose, however, adapt quickly and cease to respond to a particular stimulus producing so-called olfactory fatigue. Thus, an odour that is strong at first will gradually become imperceptible, as happens when one becomes unaware of the smell of his own body. There may also be present the phenomenon of masking; this is a decrease in sensitivity to one odour after exposure to another (for example, a strong-smelling disinfectant).

Loudness illusions. The human ear typically serves to distinguish between about 1,500 levels of pitch. For loudness, differential-threshold studies reveal about 325 separately perceived levels in the region of greatest auditory sensitivity (about 1,000 to 4,000 cycles per second). The number of discriminable tones is in the hundred thousands. When two sounds are heard in close succession (time error once more) the intensity or loudness of the second is judged by comparing it with the first. Thus, a murmur may sound loud when compared to a whisper, or a "deafening" noise may make all other sounds inaudible. The hum of an electric fan may help to diffuse the street noises of traffic and thus improve the discrimination of sounds in the room.

Intersensory effects. Normally, the senses combine to produce a kind of common, unitary, or integrated perceptual experience. In dining, for example, the visual array on the table, the conversational tones or background music, the tactile sensations, aromas, and taste of the food, all combine to enhance the gustatory experience with each sense (*e.g.*, sight, hearing) contributing to it. Physiologically, taste and smell appear to be particularly subject to intersensory effects (interdependent). In other situations, seeing, hearing, touching, and often smelling and tasting are all employed in an intersensory way in object identification or location.

Synesthesia. A "crossing" of the senses, analogous to a short circuit in a radio and called synesthesia, has been reported. "Colour-hearing," in which people say that specific sounds evoke in them the actual experience of certain colours, is relatively frequent. Some musicians and others report that they see particular colours whenever they hear given tones and musical passages; poets sometimes claim to hear sounds or musical tones when they see words, images, and colours. Synesthesia may be induced with drugs, and in rare psychiatric disorders the sufferer may not be able to tell whether he is seeing or hearing.

Sounds can evoke visual experiences

Intersensory rivalry and facilitation. Stimulation through one sense may enhance the function of another. Seeing a boat rocked by waves may activate the sense of balance in an observer on a pier to the point at which it causes seasickness. A painting of an Arctic scene of frost and snow may evoke the sensation of cold or a shiver that produces gooseflesh. An explosion or gunshots may give a bystander the illusion of being struck; and a picture of appetizing food may evoke sensations of taste and smell.

Sensory rivalry, in which one stimulus inhibits the perception of another, may result from a conflict of cues if sensory information is ambiguous or discrepant, as in the tilted-room experiment, during which the visual sense conflicts with cues from the sense of equilibrium. States of pain, panic, monotony, or fatigue may create conditions in which various senses mask or inhibit each other. A witness of a terrifying sight, for example, may become oblivious to all sounds around him. Distraction can elevate the pain threshold, as in the case of wounded soldiers whose injuries become painful only after the stress of combat subsides. In a similar way, some dentists use auditory analgesia (a "masking" of pain by sound).

Illusions of psychiatric significance. Illusions called pseudohallucinations occur at times when feelings of anxiety or fear are projected on external objects, as when a child perceives threatening faces or monsters in shadows at night or sees hobgoblins in trees. A soldier tense with apprehension may, in his fear, perceive inanimate objects as an attacking enemy or one of his own comrades as the foe. In literature, the character Don Quixote perceived windmills as enemy knights. Psychiatric patients have perceived other people as machines, or as teddy bears, or as devils.

The déjà vu phenomenon is a feeling that a past episode is repeating itself in the present; there is a fusion of past and present to create an illusion that one is reliving an experience and that he therefore knows its outcome. It might be called a "hallucination" of familiarity; some theorists interpret the experience as being based on reactivation of old memory traces by stimuli resembling those experienced in the past in the way that a pressed rose discovered in a long-forgotten dance program, for example, may trigger a flood of old memories.

Déjà vu

Emotions, compelling associations, or strong expectations frequently cause illusional misperceptions in everyday life. The hostile listener hears someone say "wire" and thinks he is being called a "liar"; the self-consciously obese girl misinterprets the word "fate" as "weight." There is also the mistaken identification of strangers as friends in the street. It is as if John thinks Tom is Dick because he is hoping to see Dick or because he definitely wants to avoid Tom.

Hallucinations

Traditional psychiatric sources define hallucinations as "perceptions without corresponding stimuli from without" (Swiss psychiatrist E. Bleuler), or as the "apparent perception of an external object when no such object is present" (L.E. Hinsie and J. Shatzky, *Psychiatric Dictionary*, 1940). A historical survey of the subject of hallucinations clearly reflects the development of scientific thought in psychiatry, psychology, and neurobiology. By 1838 the significant relationship between the content of dreams and of hallucinations had been pointed out. In the 1840s the occurrence of hallucinations under a wide variety of conditions (including psychological and physical stress) as well as their genesis through the effects of such drugs as stramonium and hashish had been described.

A.J.F. Brierre de Boismont, a French physician, in 1845 described many instances of hallucinations associated with intense concentration, or with musing, or simply occurring in the course of psychiatric disorder. In the last half of the 19th century, studies of hallucinations continued. Investigators in France were particularly oriented toward abnormal psychological function, and from this came descriptions of hallucinosis during sleepwalking and related reactions. Perhaps the most simple and yet enduring conceptions were those evolved by Sir Francis Galton in the 1880s, and English neurologist John Hughlings Jackson's formulation of the hallucination as being released or triggered by the nervous system was a milestone along the way.

During the first three decades of the 20th century, a spirited interest in hallucinations continued. Freud's concepts of conscious and unconscious activities added new significance to the content of dreams and hallucinations.

Infantile hallucinations

It was theorized that infants normally hallucinate the objects and processes that give them gratification. Although the notion has recently been disputed, the "regression" hypothesis (*i.e.*, that hallucinating is a regression, or return, to infantile ways) is still widely employed, especially by those who find it clinically useful. During the same period, others put forth theories that were more broadly biological than Freud's but that had more points in common with Freud than with each other.

The medical and scientific literature has continued to contain many references to hallucinatory phenomena, though for 20 years after 1932 there was a surprising decrease of interest. Attention has been revived by the recent upsurge of work on hallucinogenic drugs.

THE GENERAL THEORY OF HALLUCINATION

The general theory of hallucinations here delineated rests upon two fundamental assumptions. One is that life experiences influence the brain in such a way as to leave in that organ enduring physical changes that have variously been called neural traces, templates, or engrams. Ideas and images are held to derive from the incorporation and activation of these engrams in complex circuits involving nerve cells. Such circuits in the cortex (outer layers) of the brain appear to subserve the neurophysiology of memory, thought, imagination, and fantasy. The emotions associated with these intellectual and perceptual functions seem to be mediated through cortex connections with the deeper parts of the brain (the limbic system or "visceral brain," for example), thus permitting a dynamic interplay between perception and emotion through transactions that appear to take place largely at unconscious levels (*i.e.*, without the individual's awareness).

Insofar as conscious awareness can be interpreted neurophysiologically, it is found to be regulated through a general arousal process the influence of which is mediated by the ascending midbrain reticular activating system (a network of nerve cells in the brainstem). Analyses of hallucinations reported by sufferers of neurological disorders and by neurosurgical patients in whom the brain is stimulated electrically have shown the importance of the temporal lobes (at the sides of the brain) to auditory hallucinations, for example, and of other functionally relevant parts of the brain in this process.

Interaction of internal and external stimuli

A second basic assumption is that the total human personality is best understood in terms of the constant interplay of forces that continually emanate from inside (as internal physiological activity) and from outside the individual (as sensory stimuli). Such transactions between the environment and the individual may be said to exert an integrating and organizing influence upon memory traces stored in the nervous system and to affect the patterns in which sensory engrams are activated to produce experiences called images, fantasies, dreams, or hallucinations, as well as the emotions associated with these patterns. If such a constantly shifting balance exists between internal and external environmental forces, both physiological considerations (*e.g.*, brain function) and cultural, experiential factors emerge as major determinants of the content and meaning of hallucinations.

One's brain is bombarded constantly by sensory impulses, but most of these are excluded from consciousness in a dynamically shifting, selective fashion. The exclusion seems to be accomplished through the exercise of integrative inner mechanisms that permit the limited field of one's awareness to hold selected parts of potential experience in clear focus. (The sound of a ticking clock, for example, fades in and out of awareness.) These mechanisms somehow must simultaneously survey previously stored information within the brain, select tiny samples needed to give adaptive significance to the incoming flow of information from the environment, and bring forth only a few items for actual recall from the brain's enormous "memory banks."

Attention. Thus, the work of concentration or attention (*q.v.*) may be defined as a scanning and screening process, tending to keep out of consciousness what is not needed or wanted. Theoretically, this work principally involves an activity akin to information retrieval in digital computers (called "secondary process" thinking by Freud), which employs mainly the associative memory functions of the most recently evolved parts of the brain cortex. It may be contrasted with the way in which unconscious, instinctual, and emotional (analogue) information processing (Freud's "primary process" thinking) primarily involves functions of the parts of the brain that appeared much earlier in evolution. In conditions of psychological health, these primary and secondary functions seem highly integrated with each other. There is evidence that in dreams, delirium, or major psychiatric disorder (*e.g.*, schizophrenia), images, feelings, thoughts, and perceptions become disconnected (dissociated) from each other and that fragments of information arising within the brain itself are confused with new input (*i.e.*, information coming in from the external environment).

During normal wakefulness, the input of information through the sensory pathways serves a basic function in maintaining the organization of scanning and screening activity. As long as it is working well, the brain mechanism of scanning and screening seems to exclude from awareness not only information from the internal and external environments that is either undesired or has low priority for the individual but also the vast bulk of information already stored within the brain in the form of neural traces, their derivations, and interrelations. Some of this information can be brought deliberately into awareness in the service of memory. (One readily recalls his address when asked, for example.) Many children and a few adults can screen in and scan perceptual memory traces with great clarity, thereby permitting eidetic ("photographic") or near-eidetic imagery.

Reduced sensory activity. When, as in sleep (*q.v.*), sensory input is diminished, distorted, or impaired, its organizing effect upon the screening and scanning mechanism tends to decrease. Simultaneously, as a rule, there is a decrease in the stimulating effect of sensory input on the ascending midbrain reticular activating system (through connections from the major incoming sensory pathways, such as tactual structures, passing through the brainstem), and, as a result, arousal and awareness diminish. Under a variety of circumstances, however, great reduction or impairment of sensory input may be accompanied by a residual awareness of considerable degree. In such instances, when the usual information-input level no longer suffices completely to inhibit their emergence, ordinarily quiescent perceptual traces stored in the brain may be activated or "released" and re-experienced (sometimes with hallucinatory vividness) in familiar or new combinations. Some people are able to control this perceptual release to an astonishing degree. The English poet Samuel Taylor Coleridge described this quality in himself, writing, "My eyes make pictures, when they are shut" (presumably even without benefit of the opium he is said to have used).

Released perceptions of this sort do not ordinarily become conscious with hallucinatory vividness. Indeed, there appear to be two prerequisites for their emergence even into clear awareness. First, there must be a sufficient general level of arousal for awareness to occur; second, the particular perception-bearing brain circuits must trigger and reverberate sufficiently to command awareness.

A sustained level and variety of sensory input normally contributes to the process that inhibits the emergence of reactivated memory traces from within the brain itself. When effective (attention-commanding) sensory input decreases sufficiently, there may be a release into awareness of previously recorded perceptions through disinhibition (loss of inhibition) of the brain circuits that represent them. If a general level of cortical arousal persists to a sufficient degree or is stimulated in any one of several ways, these released perceptions can enter awareness and be experienced as fantasies, illusions, visions, dreams, or hallucinations. The greater the level of arousal, the more vivid the hallucinations will be.

INDUCTION OF HALLUCINATIONS

Direct brain stimulation. Under some circumstances these clearly hallucinatory experiences can be brought about through direct stimulation of the exposed brain, as in cases of local cortical arousal under the neurosurgeon's stimulating electrode. Under circumstances other than surgery or such situations as, for example, some forms of epilepsy, however, there must be a decrease in the forces that ordinarily dominate consciousness (and inhibit the release of recorded percepts) before hallucinations occur. These inhibiting forces require for their maintenance a relatively high level of sensory input of appropriate quality and frequency.

Sleep. The ways in which the reticular network of cells in the brainstem acts as a regulatory and integrating system for these relationships remain under intensive study. Since levels of brain arousal during sleep and wakefulness also are mediated via reticular formation activity, sleeping and dreaming merit consideration as hallucinatory activities. As a person falls asleep, he passes through a period of "partial sleep" in which awareness of the environment drops rapidly but in which the level of cortical arousal (which falls less rapidly) remains sufficiently high to permit some appreciation of external stimulation. Thus, the so-called hypnagogic phenomena occur.

Dreams and hallucinations

Hypnagogic hallucinations. Common hypnagogic hallucinations may be visual (*e.g.*, scenes from the previous few hours appear) or auditory (*e.g.*, one seems to hear his name called or a knock is heard as if at the door). A frequently occurring hypnagogic hallucination is the sensation of loss of support or balance, perhaps accompanied by a fragmentary "dream" of falling, missing a step, or stumbling, followed immediately by a jerking reflex recovery movement (the myoclonic jerk) that may even jolt the sleeper back into wakefulness.

Dreams. With progressive loss of contact with the environment, sleep begins and appears at first to be dream free, the sleeper producing large, slow brain waves that may be recorded with a device called the electroencephalograph (EEG.) Sensory stimuli from without (*e.g.*, noise, cold) or stimuli from within the body (*e.g.*, dyspepsia, anxiety), plus a somewhat regular spontaneous fluctuation in the depth of sleep, periodically (perhaps every 90 minutes or so) bring the sleeper into a state that favours perceptual release, in which case dreaming tends to take place. This state (with specific EEG signs and rapid movements of the closed eyes) probably occurs several times every night in all normal people, so that more than 20 percent of an average man's sleep is taken up with several dreams, each of about ten to 15 minutes' duration. At the time of awakening, the typical sleeper again passes through a period of perceptual release, often experiencing dreams that increase in intensity, and perhaps may have the hallucinations of "partial sleep," these now being called hypnopompic experiences.

A simplified but perhaps helpful way of characterizing these conditions might be to imagine a man standing at a closed glass window opposite his fireplace, looking out at his garden in the sunset. He is so absorbed by the view of the outside world that he fails to visualize the interior of the room at all. As it becomes darker outside, however, images of the objects in the room behind him can be seen reflected dimly in the window glass. For a time he may see either the garden (if he gazes into the distance) or the reflection of the room's interior (if he focusses on the glass a few inches from his face). Night falls, but the fire still burns brightly in the fireplace and illuminates the room. The watcher now sees in the glass a vivid reflection of the interior of the room behind him, which appears to be outside the window. This illusion becomes dimmer as the fire dies down, and, finally, when it is dark both outside and within, nothing more is seen. If the fire flares up from time to time, the visions in the glass reappear.

In an analogous way, hallucinatory experiences such as those of normal dreams (*q.v.*) occur when the "daylight" (sensory input) is reduced while the "interior illumination" (general level of brain arousal) remains "bright," and images originating within the "rooms" of our brains may be perceived (hallucinated) as though they came from outside the "windows" of our senses.

Another analogy might be that dreams, like the stars, are shining all the time. Though the stars are not often seen by day, since the sun shines too brightly, if, during the day, there is an eclipse of the sun, or if a viewer chooses to be watchful awhile after sunset or awhile before sunrise, or if he is awakened from time to time on a clear night to look at the sky, then the stars, like dreams, though often forgotten, may always be seen.

A more brain-related concept is that of a continuous information-processing activity (a kind of "preconscious stream") that is influenced continually by both conscious and unconscious forces and that constitutes the potential supply of dream content. The dream is an experience during which, for a few minutes, the individual has some awareness of the stream of data being processed. Hallucinations in the waking state also would involve the same phenomenon, produced by a somewhat different set of psychological or physiological circumstances.

Excessive excitation. It is valuable to consider the probable relationship between the level of physiological arousal in the brain and information processing during the waking state. The functions of consciousness apparently reach an optimal point in relation to level of arousal, beyond which they disorganize progressively as arousal increases excessively. The presence of marked arousal (produced, for example, by extreme anxiety or by chemical stimulation of the brain) is accompanied by marked disturbance of concentration. Again, contact with external stimuli is impaired, this time by excessive input that "jams the circuits," in which case spontaneous dissociative experiences may occur. Finally, as arousal reaches high proportions, the hallucinations of full-blown delirium or psychotic excitement may appear with frightening vividness, intensity, and emotional accompaniment. Greater brain arousal than this might result in generalized seizure phenomena as in epilepsy.

Sensory deprivation. When people are kept in isolation (sensory deprivation), information input via the senses (*e.g.*, hearing and sight) is depatterned or reduced. If such a person remains alert, he is likely to experience vivid fantasies and perhaps hallucinations. A slight amount of stimulation of the hallucinated sense may enhance the likelihood of the hallucination's appearance. If stimuli are markedly reduced and the level of arousal is high, the hallucinations can be especially vivid and emotionally charged.

Loss of sleep. In 1883 Galton wrote, "The cases of visions following protracted wakefulness are well-known, and I have collected a few of them myself." Progressive sleep loss appears to decrease one's capacity for integrating perceptions of the external environment. Hallucinations probably will occur in anyone if wakefulness is sufficiently prolonged; the presence of the excessive arousal of anxiety is likely to hasten or to enhance hallucinatory production. The disorganizing effect of excessive wakefulness has been exploited in extorting false confessions (*e.g.*, from prisoners, many of whom report that they experience hallucinations during prolonged sleep deprivation). Other observations suggest that fleeting hallucinations typically begin after two or three days without sleep, and that after 100 to 200 sleepless hours a progressive personality disorganization will develop gradually and be marked by periods of hallucinosis or, in some cases, by a reappearance of previously existing psychiatric disorder.

False confessions

Hypnosis and trance states. The mystic achieves hallucinations by gaining control of his own dissociative mechanisms; perhaps this is a form of self-hypnosis. Such individuals can accomplish an astonishing withdrawal from the environment by prolonged intense concentration (*e.g.*, by gazing at some object). The hallucinations occurring under such circumstances may be of the type in which the person perceives his "inner self" to leave his body to view himself (autoscopic hallucination) or to be transported to new surroundings. Or the hallucinations may take the form of unique visual imagery; for example, the so-called *yantra* is a special visual hallucination of a coloured, geometrical image that appears at a level of trance of the sort experienced by practitioners of Yoga. It has been called an expression of "ecstasy which cannot be translated into concepts" (H. Ahlenstiel and R. Kauffman, *Schweiz. Z. Psychol.*, 1952). The recurrence of certain designs and patterns in human hallucinatory experience is very likely related to structural aspects of the visual system.

Ordinary experimental hypnotic and posthypnotic suggestions of hallucinations are well-known (see HYPNOSIS). The hypnotic subject (who can be described as a person in a controlled dissociative state) may on occasion also experience spontaneous hallucinations in the absence of specific suggestions.

Prolonged monotony or fixation of attention may lead to diminished responsiveness to the environment with a general effect similar to that of absolute reduction of stimulation or of hypnotic trance. Under these conditions such dissociative phenomena as "highway hypnosis" among drivers of motor vehicles may occur. Similar phenomena that occur among aviators have been called fascination or fixation. During prolonged, monotonous flight, pilots may experience visual, auditory, and bodily (kinesthetic) hallucinations; for example, one may suddenly feel that his plane is in a spin or a dive or that it is upside down, even though it is flying level. A kinesthetic hallucination such as this can be so vivid that the pilot will attempt "corrective" manoeuvring of the aircraft, with potentially tragic results.

Sensory defects. Many other examples of hallucinations related to decrease or impairment of sensory input are known in clinical medicine. Visual hallucinations not infrequently occur in cases of cataract (opaque lens in the eye) and have been compared with phantom limb experiences (*e.g.*, "pain" in the toes of a missing foot), since there is an absence of normal stimuli from the environment in both cases. It is well-known that auditory hallucinations may occur in individuals who suffer a progressive loss of hearing, musical hallucinations being not uncommon. A case of combined visual and auditory hallucinations in a patient with progressive blindness (from cataracts) and with deafness from ear disease (otosclerosis) has been observed. Hallucinations of the phantom limb probably arise as the projection of an experientially established set of brain engrams in the absence of long-accustomed sensory input from the missing part. Differences in nerve impulses from those once produced by a missing limb may cause the phantom to be perceived as being distorted in proportion or in size.

Hallucination of a phantom limb

Psychological factors. Although the role of expectation (mental set) continues to be studied in relation to perception (*q.v.*), there can be no doubt of the significance of psychological factors in determining the nature of hallucinated objects. It may be that the psychophysiologic basis for recognition requires the unconscious preparation of a perceptual engram (the physically stored memory of a previously seen object, for example) against which to match incoming sensory information for identification, significance, and meaning in terms of past experience. If some external object is present but inadequately recognized, an incorrect perceptual engram may be activated to be experienced as an illusion; in the absence of an external stimulus, such an engram is perceived as a hallucination. This theoretically may account for the specificity of collective visions (*i.e.*, those shared by more than one person). Among lifeboat survivors at sea, for example, several people who share similar expectancies (mental sets) may see the same nonexistent ship projected against the blank screen of empty sea and sky. Such an experience may persist in some of the people for many minutes, even after a logical belief in its impossibility has been communicated to all.

Multiple factors undoubtedly combine in bringing about the psychiatric symptoms of the psychoses (*q.v.*); these symptoms often resemble the waking dreams in which hallucinations (usually auditory) may figure prominently. Such additive effects can also be demonstrated among "normal" people in the laboratory; for example, one may readily produce signs of hallucinations among sleep-deprived subjects or among subjects in a state of sensory isolation by administering otherwise subhallucinatory doses of drugs such as LSD or mescaline. In hospital cases of acute psychotic reactions with hallucinosis, combinations of factors clearly can be inferred to be at work: hereditary and cultural predispositions; excessive arousal in anxiety or panic; auto-intoxication (self-poisoning via deranged body physiology) through stress, exhaustion, sleep loss, and dehydration (water loss); and dissociative mechanisms that impair or distort the reception of information from a frightening or threatening social environment.

Chemical factors; drugs. Hallucinations may be produced by chemical changes that derive from internal metabolic disturbances, that are otherwise engendered inside of the body, or that originate from outside of the body. Some chemicals that produce hallucinatory experiences seem to act by reducing sensory input; for example, dramatic hallucinatory recall of intense experiences from the recent past can be brought about by injections of anesthetic drugs (narcosynthesis), such as sodium amybarbital, which favours the conditions for perceptual release. Hallucinations during induction of (and emergence from) general surgical anesthesia induced by a variety of other chemicals are well-known and can be explained on the same basis.

Thus, such hallucinogenic chemicals seem to impair sensory input specifically by decreasing the transmission of nerve impulses by raising the resistance of the nervous system to their passage. Other chemicals, however, just as easily produce markedly increasing nerve transmission, disrupting the orderly input of information and "jamming the circuits." Many botanically derived hallucinogens seem to function this way—*e.g.*, LSD (lysergic acid diethylamide) and the ergot (a fungus) that grows on rye, psilocybin from mushrooms, mescaline from the peyote cactus, and tetrahydrocannabinol (THC) from marijuana (see HALLUCINOGEN). Hallucinations also can be induced by jamming the circuits through input overload produced mechanically, bombarding several sensory systems with intense stimuli simultaneously (*e.g.*, with bright flashing lights and loud noises).

Hallucinogenic drugs are substances that, administered in pharmacological doses (not toxic overdoses), create gross distortions in perception without causing loss of consciousness. These distortions frequently include hallucinations. Such compounds also are likely to exert profound effects on mood, thought, and observable behaviour. These resemble (or mimic) the disturbances generated in spontaneously occurring psychoses; indeed some hallucinogens have been termed "psychotomimetic" or "psychotogenic" on this account.

Self-experimentation

Research scientists and clinicians such as psychiatrists have sometimes deliberately taken these compounds in efforts to understand how it feels to be a severely psychiatric patient. It has been hoped that the study of such chemically induced "model psychoses" would lead to improved methods of treatment. In addition, some psychiatric workers speak of "psychedelic" (mind-manifesting) substances, controversially held to expand perceptual horizons and insight among a variety of people under treatment for such disorders as alcoholism, rigid personality patterns, and sexual frigidity.

The potentially dangerous psychological changes produced by psychedelic chemicals have sometimes been interpreted as "loosening ego structures," "dissolving ego boundaries," or "disrupting ego defenses." Such changes may include the experiencing of thoughts, feelings, and perceptions that are usually outside the individual's awareness ("unconscious" or "repressed"). Persons who take such drugs (*e.g.*, LSD) may become hypersuggestible, emotionally labile (unstable), and unusually aware of their own reactions and those of others. Feelings of transcendence of ordinary experience, distortions in time perception (*e.g.*, time may seem to slow down), and hallucinations have also been reported.

An increasing number of people throughout the world are believed to be taking various hallucinogenic substances, frequently acquired through illegal channels and employed without medical supervision, in efforts to participate in special group experiences having cultlike characteristics. While these social druggings may be recalled by the participants with great enthusiasm, the unintoxicated (unpoisoned) observer often finds little in the way of verbal or nonverbal communication to account for the joyous sense of communion so often described. Not infrequently (especially with LSD) a severe emotional disturbance will result from taking the drug. This is referred to by psychedelic aficionados as a "bad trip." In addition to suicidal attempts, such bad trips may lead into persistent long-term psychotic behaviour (*e.g.*, prolonged delirious reactions, excitements, or stupors).

It appears that all human behaviour and experience (normal as well as abnormal) is well attended by illusory and hallucinatory phenomena. While the relationship of these phenomena to mental illness has been well documented, their role in everyday life has perhaps not been considered enough. Greater understanding of illusions and hallucinations among normal people may provide explanations for experiences otherwise relegated to the uncanny, "extrasensory," or supernatural. Such understanding may also illuminate the remarkable certainty that individuals express in their contrary interpretations of the same basic information. "Reality," like beauty, lies in the eye of the beholder.

BIBLIOGRAPHY. R. BRAIN, *The Nature of Experience* (1959), a discussion for the layman of theories of perception, finally applied to the meaning of symbols and images in life and art; A. BRIERRE DE BOISMONT, *Des hallucinations . . .*, 2nd ed. (1852; Eng. trans., *Hallucinations: Or, the Rational History of Apparitions, Dreams, Ecstacy, Magnetism, and Somnambulism*, 1853), an early classic; S. TOLANSKY, *Optical Illusions* (1964), most of the known visual illusions illustrated, in one of the few modern books on this subject; W. GREY WALTER, *The Neurophysiological Aspects of Hallucinations and Illusory Experience* (1960), visual phenomena viewed by a brain researcher; L.J. WEST (ed.), *Hallucinations* (1962), an analysis of the subject by contributors from several scientific disciplines.

(L.J.W.)

Immunity

The concept of immunity first evolved in medicine to describe the ability of man and other animals either to resist or to recover from invasion by microbes (*e.g.*, bacteria, viruses, protozoans) and larger parasites (*e.g.*, helminths). Thus a person said to be immune to a particular disease would not contract it although others might do so. In the course of searching for and trying to understand the mechanisms of resistance to infection, it has become clear that they are not only subtle and complex but that they represent the most important general means by which higher organisms actually distinguish between the materials of which they are constituted (that are peculiar to them) and those from which they differ (hence, that are treated as foreign). The distinction is, in other words, the difference between "self" and "not self." Further, it has been recognized that a mechanism that is protective in one situation may actually cause disease in another. The subject matter of this article includes both the immunity that protects an animal from the large number of potentially parasitic organisms in its environment and aspects of the subject that may appear to be unrelated to it but are, nevertheless, caused by and explained by the same processes.

The evolution of the immunological system probably conferred a selective advantage on animals that developed it by providing them with protection against microbial invasion. Among the several elements comprising such a system, the first are the external barriers against microbial invasion—*i.e.*, the skin and the mucous membranes. Although these barriers are, in general, effective because of their mechanical properties, their ability to renew and repair themselves, and their secretion of a variety of chemical antimicrobial agents—*e.g.*, oleic acid, a fatty acid, and lysozyme, an enzyme (biological catalyst) that destroys bacterial cell walls—they can be penetrated in numerous ways by microbes; for example, through a scratch or an insect bite. That tissue fluids and cells provide a suitable environment for the growth of microbes is evident from the speed with which putrefaction after death occurs in a warm environment; that microbes do not cause putrefaction in living things is one function of the mechanisms of immunity.

Definitions

Immunological mechanisms are either nonspecific or specific. Specific immunity usually increases after an animal has had contact with microbes and is often referred to as acquired immunity. The term antigen is used to describe any material, usually of a complex nature, that stimulates a specific bodily immunity because the body recognizes it as foreign. More than one component of the structural pattern of an antigen can be recognized by the immunological system as foreign; each component so recognized is known as an antigenic determinant. An antigen can be modified by the addition of a simple chemical group, which acts as an antigenic determinant and is called a hapten (Greek *haptein*, "to grasp").

An antibody is a specialized protein (called an immunoglobulin) that is able to combine specifically with an antigen. After antibodies are released from the cells in which they are synthesized, they enter body fluids and are responsible for specific protective properties, sometimes called humoral immunity, that are present, especially in blood. Antibodies also cause certain forms of hyperreactivity or hypersensitivity to antigens. Other hypersensitivity reactions are caused by the mechanisms of cell-mediated immunity—*i.e.*, a manifestation of specific immunity that is not attributable to antibodies circulating in the bloodstream but is the result of the action of certain cells (lymphocytes) reacting directly with an antigen and requiring the cooperation of scavenging cells called macrophages to exert some of their effects.

The terms immunization and sensitization describe the process of stimulating an immunological response in an animal by the administration of an antigen. When an antigen is reintroduced into an organism several weeks after the first introduction, the immunological response is usually greater and occurs more rapidly than did the initial response; the phenomenon is commonly known as immunological memory. An animal that fails to make the expected immunological response to an antigen is described as immunologically tolerant. The inability of an animal species to make immunological responses to its own constituents, although many of them would act as antigens in another animal species, is termed self-tolerance.

Immunosuppression describes the suppression (brought about by drugs and other treatments) of the development of an immunological response. Immunosuppressants act, in general, by interfering with the activities (especially proliferation) of lymphocytes.

This article is divided into the following sections:

I. General features of immunological mechanisms

TYPES OF IMMUNOLOGICAL MECHANISMS

Nonspecific immunity. Nonspecific immunity refers to general protective mechanisms that either kill or prevent the multiplication of microbes and other parasites. Because the effectiveness of a nonspecific immunological mechanism against a microbe does not increase after contact with it, in sharp contrast to the mechanism of specific (acquired) immunity, nonspecific mechanisms are sometimes referred to as innate mechanisms.

Protective substances. The blood and other tissue fluids contain various chemical agents that, when separated from other fluid constituents, are capable of killing a variety of microbes; their actual function in animals has not yet been established with certainty. Two of these substances are spermine, an organic compound similar to a protein, and properdin, a protein that can combine with a specific structural component found in several bacterial species. Other naturally occurring compounds combine with and neutralize the activity of certain enzymes that are released after the death of cells in an animal body and are also able to inactivate certain microbial enzymes. Another substance, a protein called transferrin, which binds iron atoms and conveys them in tissue fluids from the gut to organs where they are stored or used for making red blood cells, deprives bacteria of the iron necessary for their multiplication in an animal body.

Scavenging cells. In addition to protective substances that circulate in body fluids, all higher animals contain scavenging cells, which ingest and destroy foreign particles. Most vertebrates, including all mammals, possess two main kinds of scavenging cells. The importance of such cells was first recognized in 1884 by Russian biologist Élie Metchnikoff, who named them microphages and macrophages, after Greek words meaning "little eaters" and "large eaters."

Granulocytes

Microphages, now usually known as polymorphonuclear leucocytes, or granulocytes, contain granules that are, in fact, packets of powerful digestive enzymes and bactericidal (*i.e.*, bacteria-killing) agents. Granulocytes are continuously produced from cells in bone marrow (stem cells), from which they enter the bloodstream, circulate for a few days, and die. Granulocytes are motile cells that are attracted by and migrate to foreign materials, including bacteria, ingesting and, in many cases, digesting them. Bacteria deposited beneath the skin, for example, are attacked within a few minutes by granulocytes that move to the invasion site from nearby blood vessels. Various agents attract granulocytes; *e.g.*, some are produced by microbes and others are produced by the interaction of microbes with proteins in the blood plasma. One potent stimulus to the movement of granulocytes is the activation of "complement," an important part of the immunological system (see below *The interaction of antigens and antibodies*); granulocytes, however, are able to move to an invasion site without the participation of a specific mechanism. Although granulocytes may be regarded as the first line of defense in nonspecific immunity, some microbes produce toxins that poison granulocytes and thus prevent ingestion; other microbes resist digestion by the granulocytes and thus are not killed. The aspect of nonspecific immunity provided by granulocytes, therefore, is of limited effectiveness and is substantially reinforced by the mechanisms of specific immunity.

Macrophages, like granulocytes, circulate in the blood, though in smaller numbers; macrophages, however, also are present in practically every other body tissue and are especially abundant in lymphoid tissues (chiefly the spleen and lymph nodes), which serve as filters for the removal of microbes and other foreign particles from blood and lymph. Like granulocytes, macrophages originate from cells in the bone marrow (stem cells), but, unlike granulocytes, they are able to live for long periods and to multiply in the tissues. Macrophages move more sluggishly than do granulocytes and are attracted by different stimuli; they usually arrive at an invasion site after granulocytes. Macrophages, however, effectively ingest foreign particles and are able to digest bacteria. The way by which macrophages select foreign particles for ingestion, while leaving other cells such as red cells untouched, has not yet been established with certainty. Evidence suggests that a combination of foreign particles with immunoglobulins is important in many instances, in which case the immunity provided by macrophages is dependent on acquired mechanisms capable of recognizing foreign materials. The methods by which these materials are subsequently destroyed, however, are nonspecific ones. It is probably correct to regard macrophages as the second line of defense in nonspecific immunity, but their function is more effective as a result of the mechanisms of specific (acquired) immunity.

Specific immunity. Specific immunity refers to mechanisms that are activated individually after a microbe or some other foreign material invades an animal body; as mentioned above, the mechanisms may exert their effects by one or more routes, including the nonspecific mechanisms (granulocytes and macrophages) described in the preceding section. The essential distinction between specific and nonspecific immunity is that in the former an initial specific step involves the foreign material or some closely related substances. Specific immunity is usually undetectable in an animal not previously exposed to an invasion by a particular microbe; several days after the first invasion occurs, however, the animal acquires a greatly increased and lasting resistance to subsequent invasion by the same microbe, although its resistance to unrelated microbes remains unchanged. Specific immunity was once called specific acquired immunity, in contrast to specific natural immunity, which was used to describe a state of resistance to particular microbes prior to any known contact with them. In most instances, however, such natural immunity is attributable to unapparent stimulation by materials resembling the microbes and is, in this sense, also acquired. As knowledge of the immunological system has accumulated, it has become apparent that very low, often undetectably low, levels of specific immunity are present even in animals not previously exposed to any given foreign material; thus a specific stimulation by a foreign substance greatly increases a pre-existing low level of specific immunity.

Origin of specific immunity

It is worthwhile to consider briefly the way in which the need for specific immunity arises. Once microbes have penetrated the body, they become intimately associated with the body's cells, and any reactions by the body to destroy the microbes must be able to discriminate between invader and self; this implies that invading organisms and other foreign substances must be recognized by the body as foreign in some way. Since foreign substances differ chemically and share no common structural features, the body must be capable of recognizing a wide range of substances, practically any large molecule, in fact, whether of microbial or other origin. All organisms are constructed from essentially the same compounds (*e.g.*, amino acids, carbohydrates, nucleotides, lipids), which are, however, assembled in different ways into larger molecules; the differences between two organisms, therefore, depend largely upon the distinctive patterns into which the compounds comprising them are assembled. Recognition that materials are foreign thus is dependent upon the capacity of an organism to distinguish its molecular patterns from those of other materials. The ability to recognize a substance as foreign is useless unless the organism is able to initiate mechanisms that render foreign materials harmless and then remove them. A remarkable and economical feature of the immunological system is that both recognition and inactivation are achieved by the same means—*i.e.*, the action of white blood cells (lymphocytes) formed in lymphoid tissue and the specialized proteins they make, which are called immunoglobulins.

THE EVOLUTION OF THE IMMUNOLOGICAL SYSTEM

Primitive multicellular organisms possess scavenging cells with functions analogous to those of macrophages and are able effectively to distinguish (by some as yet unidentified mechanism) between foreign materials and their own cells. The circulating fluids (hemolymph) of insects and crustaceans contain protein molecules capable of combining nonspecifically with many foreign particles and of killing bacteria. Although the concentration of these proteins increases in response to antigens, they are not considered to be true antibodies.

Immunological responses in cyclostomes and other vertebrates. The most primitive vertebrates, the cyclostomes, are the most primitive animals in which a specific immunological response akin to that of mammals is detectable. The cyclostomes are divided into two main groups, the hagfishes (Myxinidae) and the lampreys (Petromyzonidae), of which the hagfishes are considered to be the more primitive. Members of both groups not only slowly reject grafts of tissue from other individuals of the same species but reject a second graft from the same individual more rapidly than the first—*i.e.*, cyclostomes show evidence of "immunological memory."

Cyclostomes can form antibodies against at least some foreign proteins; the hagfish, however, does so only very slowly. Although the hagfishes lack a thymus gland (a lymphoid tissue) and have no organs that correspond to lymph nodes, they possess a primitive spleen; the blood contains primitive granulocytes but lacks cells resembling lymphocytes. At sites of injury in hagfishes, granulocytes and what may be macrophages accumulate, and the overall inflammatory reaction is not unlike the one that occurs in higher animals. Lampreys, on the other hand, possess a rudimentary thymus gland, which contains a few lymphocytes; lymphocytes also are present in the blood and in both the bone marrow and the spleen. The one class of immunoglobulins detected thus far in hagfishes and lampreys appears to correspond to the immunoglobulin M class of higher animals (see below *Immunoglobulins* [*antibodies*]).

Immunological responses in fishes

Other primitive vertebrates whose immunological responses have been examined carefully include the elasmobranch fishes of the shark family. Elasmobranch fishes, which possess well-defined thymus glands and have numerous lymphocytes in the blood and in other tissues, readily make antibodies similar to the immunoglobulin M class. Teleost (bony) fishes, reptiles, birds, and mammals have thymus glands, lymphocytes, and lymphoid organs; in addition, these animal groups make various types of antibodies. Evidence indicates that lymphocytes evolved in conjunction with the development of the thymus gland; that the elaborate pattern of immunological responses in higher animals evolved at least 200,000,000 years ago when the bony fishes were evolving; and that the pattern of immunological responses has remained essentially stable since its evolution.

Amino-acid sequences in immunoglobulins. Evidence concerning the evolution of immunoglobulins has come from the analysis of the sequences of amino acids comprising immunoglobulin molecules. The immunoglobulins of mammals as different in appearance as mouse and man have very close structural resemblances, although they differ in many other details; furthermore, the structures of immunoglobulin molecules sufficiently resemble each other so that it can be concluded that they evolved by modification of a common ancestral protein. A widely accepted current hypothesis is that a gene controlling the synthesis of a protein with some properties of an antibody—*e.g.*, the capacity to combine with a variety of micro-organisms—appeared early in vertebrate evolution and that this ancestral gene evolved into the numerous genes that control the synthesis of the components comprising present-day vertebrate immunoglobulins.

II. The cellular basis of immunological response

GENERAL FEATURES

Important contributions have been made to the understanding of the nature of immunological responses since 1965; the most significant of these have involved the determination of the general structure of immunoglobulins and the realization that the many kinds of immunoglobulins now known to exist possess important biological properties in addition to their capacity to act as antibodies and to combine with antigens—*e.g.*, the activation of the complement system, whereby secondary effects are produced in the animal body. Other important advances in immunology include an appreciation of both the role of lymphocytes as the source of immunoglobulins and their complex life cycle. Sufficient agreement now exists among immunologists to permit a general explanation of the principal features of immunological responses in terms of the behaviour of lymphocytes, as first predicted in 1959 by an Australian biologist, Sir Macfarlane Burnet.

The majority of lymphocytes are small, rather featureless cells consisting of a nucleus and a minimum of the other necessary cellular components. Nevertheless, the nuclei of lymphocytes possess all the genetic information of the animal in which they are found. It is now known that, when suitably stimulated, they differentiate into active protein-secreting cells and multiply rapidly. An average adult human has about 10^{12} lymphocytes, which are undifferentiated cells—*i.e.*, have no obvious specialized activity—and, until their involvement in immunological responses was recognized, had no known function.

In adult animals lymphocytes are derived from stem cells, which are continuously formed in the bone marrow (Figure 1); stem cells pass in the bloodstream from the

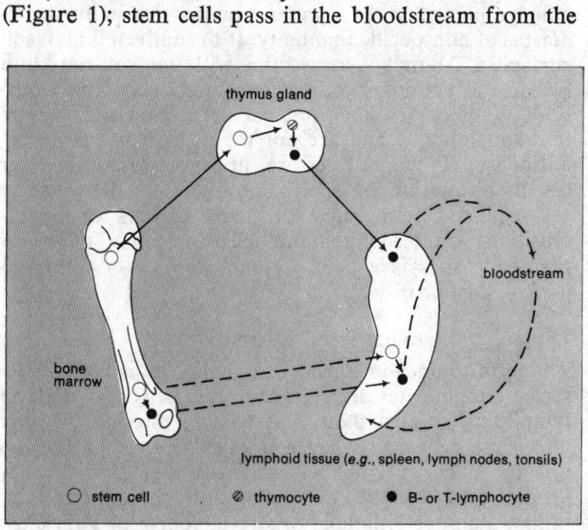

Figure 1: Circulation of lymphocytes (see text).

bone marrow to specialized tissues known as lymphoid organs—*e.g.*, spleen, lymph nodes, tonsils, appendix, and structures (called Peyer's patches) in the gut wall. The distinct and functionally important lymphoid tissue, the thymus gland, is situated in the chest.

The life cycle and behaviour of lymphocytes depend on the location of the stem cells from which they originate—*i.e.*, whether the stem cells migrate from the bone marrow into the thymus gland or into other lymphoid tissues. Although all lymphocytes are similar in appearance they acquire characteristic components in surface membranes and differences in behaviour, depending upon the lymphoid tissues to which they migrate.

THYMUS-DERIVED (T-) LYMPHOCYTES

Two kinds of cells found in the thymus gland include the lymphocytes and the thymus epithelium; the latter is thought to be responsible for the special properties of the lymphocytes that originate in the thymus. Stem cells entering the thymus from the bloodstream undergo rapid and continuous division—a process that gradually slows as an animal ages. Most of the daughter cells die within the thymus; those that survive, the thymus-derived, or T-, lymphocytes, leave the thymus, travel in the bloodstream to other lymphoid organs, and never return to the thymus. Once in the lymphoid organs, the T-lymphocytes normally do not multiply; rather, they persist in the body for many weeks, sometimes even years, passing from lymphoid tissues to circulate as components either of the lymph or of the blood, and returning again to the lymphoid tissues. When T-lymphocytes come into contact with an antigen, however, those that are able to interact with the antigen may be stimulated in one of two ways. First, they may—paradoxically—be inactivated, probably killed, and thus eliminated; if all of them are eliminated, the animal loses that part of its T-lymphocyte population able to recognize the antigen and no longer treats it as foreign. Alternatively, the T-lymphocytes may be stimulated to differentiate into large active cells, each of which divides to form two daughter lymphocytes the properties of which are the same as those of the parent. The lymphocytes may divide several times, resulting in a marked increase in the population of lymphocytes able to recognize and to react with the antigen. This process is partly responsible for the more rapid and greater immunological response that follows a second contact with the same antigen.

Results of T-lymphocyte stimulation

The factors involved in determining which of these alternatives occurs have not yet been established with certainty, but both probably occur simultaneously. T-lymphocytes that interact with the antigen may release agents that increase the activities of neighbouring macrophages; *i.e.*, the macrophages engulf particles more readily, manufacture more enzymes, and become more effective scavengers. The increase in scavenger activity is not confined to action on the antigen that stimulates specific lymphocytes, but represents an increase in the mechanisms of nonspecific immunity. If the antigen is on a cell surface, a T-lymphocyte reacting with that cell can kill it by some as yet unknown mechanism. As stated previously, T-lymphocytes have not yet been shown to secrete immunoglobulins and are not the source of circulating antibodies. T-lymphocytes are, however, responsible for the manifestation of specific immunity called specific cell-mediated immunity, for some aspects of hypersensitivity, and for immunological rejection of transplanted tissues (see below *Manifestations of immunological reactions*).

THYMUS-INDEPENDENT (B-) LYMPHOCYTES

The term thymus-independent lymphocyte is used to describe lymphocytes derived from stem cells that settle in lymphoid tissues without first passing through the thymus gland. Strong evidence implies that, in birds, thymus-independent lymphocytes acquire their special properties during early life by passing through, and multiplying in, a unique lymphoid organ (the bursa of Fabricius) in the hindgut. Although no similar organ exists in mammals, a similar function may be exerted by some as yet unidentified part of the lymphoid system, equivalent to the avian bursa. Because these lymphocytes originate in the avian bursa and because the cells from which they are formed (precursors) are found in bone marrow, thymus-independent lymphocytes often are called B-lymphocytes. The behaviour of B-lymphocytes differs from that of T-lymphocytes in several respects. First, B-lymphocytes are found in distinct sites in lymphoid tissues, notably in closely packed aggregations of cells called lymphoid follicles and germinal centres. The latter are sites of very active cell proliferation; *i.e.*, new lymphocytes are continuously being formed. Second, although B-lymphocytes can circulate from lymphoid tissues to the bloodstream and back as do T-lymphocytes, a substantial proportion appear to remain lodged in lymphoid tissues for long periods of time. Third, and most important, B-lymphocytes make and secrete the immunoglobulins that are present in blood and other body fluids and are, in fact, the potential antibody-producing cells.

The surfaces of B-lymphocytes, like those of T-lymphocytes, have antigen-combining receptors that, in the case of B-lymphocytes, represent the specific immunoglobulin molecules they can synthesize. Evidence suggests that each lymphocyte may synthesize a few, possibly only one, different kinds of immunoglobulin molecule and that each lymphocyte makes a specific immunoglobulin that differs slightly in molecular structure from that made by most other lymphocytes. As a consequence, only a small proportion of the total population of lymphocytes has receptors capable of combining with a particular antigen.

Contact between an antigen and a B-lymphocyte bearing appropriate antigen-combining receptors results in an interaction in which the B-lymphocyte is stimulated to change from a resting state to one of active cell division. The resulting daughter cells may be lymphocytes resembling their parents, thereby, as in the case of T-lymphocytes, increasing the extent to which these lymphocytes are represented in the total lymphocyte population. A proportion of the daughter cells, however, become capable of synthesizing and secreting the immunoglobulin characteristic of them at a high rate; these lymphocytes, which differ in appearance from other lymphocytes, are called plasma cells. A plasma cell may secrete more than 1,000 immunoglobulin molecules per second for several days. Since each plasma cell secretes many immunoglobulin molecules capable of combining with the antigen that stimulated them (*i.e.*, the plasma cells synthesize a specific antibody), a specific antibody enters the circulation in amounts much greater than the quantity of antigen that was required to initiate the process. Stimulation of B-lymphocytes by antigen results both in the production of circulating antibodies so long as (and possibly much longer than) antigen is present to provide a stimulus and in an increase in the number of B-lymphocytes able to be stimulated by the antigen to make more antibody in the future. Antibody production and B-lymphocyte synthesis usually are stimulated simultaneously by an antigen. Very large amounts of antigen can kill or exhaust the appropriate antigen-combining B-lymphocytes, so that they are no longer able to make antibodies —*i.e.*, they become immunologically tolerant of the antigen.

Plasma cells

The factors involved in determining whether or not an antigen stimulates or kills a B-lymphocyte have not yet been established, but one condition favouring stimulation of antibody synthesis is that the antigen should also stimulate T-lymphocytes.

T-lymphocytes, which can react with an antigen, release factors that are able to make the appropriate B-lymphocytes respond more effectively to relatively small amounts of that antigen. In animals from which T-lymphocytes have been removed, no antibody is made against many antigens that would evoke a marked antibody response in normal animals. Another condition favouring stimulation of antibody synthesis is that the antigen should be trapped and some part of it retained by macrophages at the surface of the cell, so as to increase the antigen concentration and to facilitate interaction between the trapped antigen and the appropriate lymphocytes as the latter migrate through the lymphoid tissues. T-lymphocytes help to concentrate the antigen at macrophage surfaces, presenting it more effectively to the B-lymphocytes; other types of interactions also may occur.

THE ORIGIN OF LYMPHOCYTE RECEPTORS

Evidence indicates that B-lymphocytes interact with antigens by virtue of immunoglobulin receptor molecules synthesized by the lymphocytes and present on their surfaces; in the case of T-lymphocytes, however, it has not yet been proved that the receptor molecules are immunoglobulins. The immunoglobulins synthesized by most lymphocytes differ slightly in molecular structure; as a result, only a small proportion of a total population of lymphocytes (*i.e.*, those with the appropriate receptors) can interact with and be stimulated by a particular antigen. This specificity implies that lymphocytes differ from other protein-secreting cells, of which each type forms a similar product. The composition of one region of the polypeptide chains (*i.e.*, sequences of amino acids) of which immunoglobulin molecules are composed is the same in all immunoglobulins; that of another region of each molecule is highly variable from one lymphocyte to another. Because the sequence of amino acids in any protein is specified by a gene in the cell nucleus, immunoglobulin chains containing different amino-acid sequences must be coded by different genes; this, in turn, means that the lymphocytes in an animal should contain many thousands of different genes, each of which controls the synthesis of one specific immunoglobulin. It is unlikely that each body cell inherits all of these genes, only one of which is expressed in any single lymphocyte. The most plausible alternative explanation is that a relatively small number of genes control immunoglobulin synthesis and that they can undergo somatic mutations—*i.e.*, mutations, or genetic changes, that occur during the growth of individual lymphocytes and are passed to daughter cells when the lymphocytes divide. If this explanation is correct, however, the rate of mutation must be much greater than that known to occur for any other genes studied thus far.

Control of immunoglobulin synthesis

III. Immunoglobulins (antibodies)

Immunoglobulin is the term accepted by international agreement in 1964 to describe the group of structurally related proteins that includes antibodies. Although immunoglobulins resemble one another in having a common basic structure and in being the products of plasma cells (transformed B-lymphocytes), they differ in both physical and chemical properties. As stated previously, each lymphocyte and its daughter cells have the capacity to make a limited number, possibly only one, of types of immunoglobulin molecule, and these differ from those made by other lymphocytes.

GENERAL STRUCTURE AND BIOLOGICAL PROPERTIES

Light and heavy chains

General structure. In 1960 it was proposed that immunoglobulin molecules are composed of two pairs of polypeptide chains. The size of one pair (the light, or L, chains) is about half that of the other (the heavy, or H, chains); and the two pairs of chains are joined together by disulfide linkages (chemical bonds between two sulfur atoms) shown as —S—S— in Figure 2. Arranged in this way, the molecule has two "arms," each of which carries both an antibody-combining site (present on the part of the L chain indicated by broken wavy lines in Figure 2B) and a region lacking specific antibody function (indicated by solid wavy lines in Figure 2B) but possessing the other properties attributed to immunoglobulins (see *General biological properties*). The proposed structure accounts for certain known features of antibodies—that each molecule has two identical combining sites; that treatment of an antibody with a protein-digesting enzyme (*e.g.*, pepsin or papain) splits the molecules into fragments; and that the disruption of disulfide bonds by mild chemical treatment liberates two types of polypeptide components, the so-called light (L) and heavy (H) chains. If papain is used to split the molecule, three fragments are obtained, one of which (called F_c) does not bind the antigen, while each of the other two (denoted F_{ab}) contains one antigen-binding site. Pepsin also yields three fragments: one is called

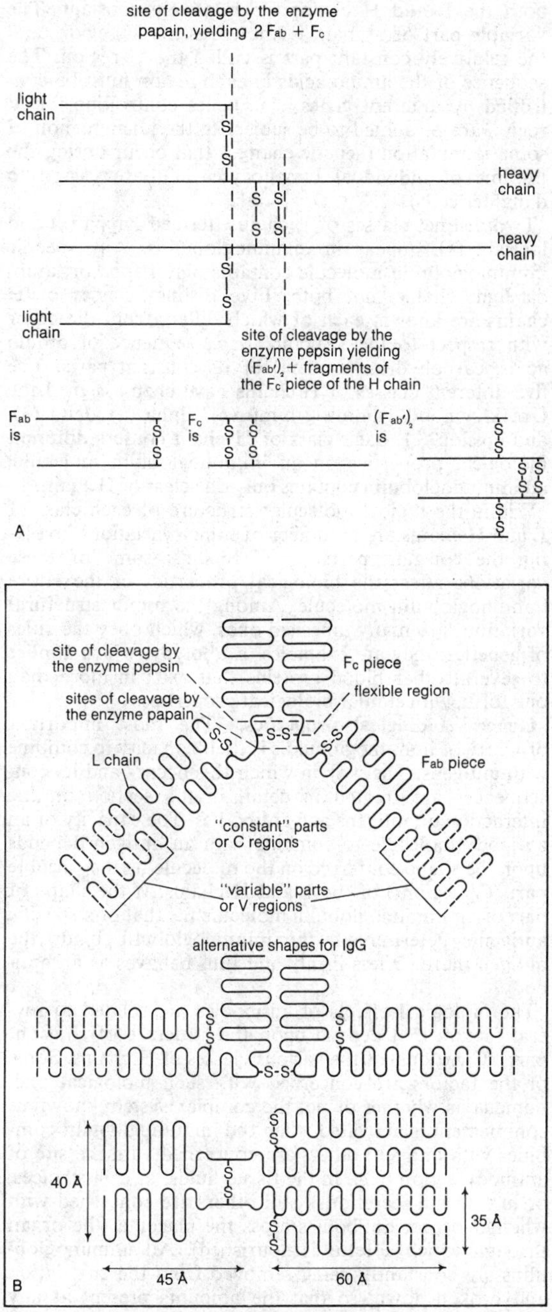

Figure 2: Diagrammatic representations of immunoglobulin molecules (see text). (A) The four polypeptide chains forming an antibody molecule. (B) Different shapes assumed by immunoglobulin molecules. One angstrom unit (Å) is 10^{-7} millimetre.

From J. Humphrey, *Immunology for Students of Medicine*

$(F_{ab'})_2$ because it contains two antigen-binding sites, and the other two are inactive pieces of the heavy chains.

Many persons have confirmed that this structure is essentially correct, but the molecule is better represented as a Y-shaped structure that is very flexible at the region where the arms branch, as illustrated in Figure 2B. Individual antibody molecules studied using the technique of electron microscopy appear to be remarkably similar to the model. Additional structural features exist in immunoglobulin molecules, not only in those of man but also in those from other animal species; some of them are enumerated in the following paragraphs.

The sequences of amino acids in the amino-terminal half of the L chains and in the amino-terminal quarter of the H chains are variable from one immunoglobulin molecule to another; the amino-acid terminals are the ends of the molecule with an uncombined amino ($-NH_2$) group. The amino acid sequences in the remainder of both the L and H chains are relatively constant. The variable part of a chain is known as the V region, and the relatively constant part is called the C region. The sequence of the amino acids in each region must be controlled by different genes. The genes controlling the V region are presumed to be subject to the phenomenon of somatic mutation (genetic changes that occur during the lifetime of individual lymphocytes and are passed to daughter cells).

Two distinct classes of L chains, termed kappa (κ) and lambda (λ), appear in immunoglobulins. Any specific immunoglobulin molecule contains only kappa or lambda light chains, not both. Five distinct classes of H chains are known, each of which differs from the other with respect to the structure (*e.g.*, sequence of amino acids, carbohydrate content) of its constant parts. The five different classes of H chains have been assigned the Greek symbols gamma (γ), mu (μ), alpha (α), delta (δ), and epsilon (ε). Each class of H chain confers different biological properties on an immunoglobulin molecule; an immunoglobulin contains only one class of H chain.

Within the typical molecular structure of each class of L and H chains are a number of minor variations involving the constant parts, or C regions; some of these variations affect the biological properties of the entire immunoglobulin molecule. Among the minor structural variations are many inherited ones, which obey the rules of genetics; they are examples of allotypy, which applies to several other blood proteins that exist in more than one form, with similar biological properties.

General biological properties. The most important property of immunoglobulins is their capacity to combine with antigens. The way in which this occurs and its consequences are treated in detail in the section on the interaction of antigens and antibodies. The capacity of an antibody molecule to combine with an antigen depends upon the shape conferred on the molecule by the variable parts (V regions) of the L and H chains. If the shape of part of an immunoglobulin molecule fits that of a specific antigenic determinant, the immunoglobulin binds the antigen more or less firmly and thus behaves as an antibody.

Importance of constant parts of H chains

The biological effects of antibodies are related to several factors that depend upon the structure of constant parts (C regions) of the various classes of H chains. Some of the factors are concerned with such biological phenomena as whether or not the complex system known as complement is activated when the immunoglobulin combines with antigen; others are concerned with the site of antibody action (*e.g.*, in the tissue fluids, at cell surfaces, or in external secretions); still others are concerned with whether or not antibodies cross the placenta (the organ through which a fetus is nourished). All immunoglobulins are constantly being removed from the circulation and broken down, so that the amounts present at any time represent a balance between the rates of formation and of disappearance. An average of four to 21 days is required for half the immunoglobulins present in the bloodstream at any time to be removed; this is also dependent on the class of H chain present in them.

IMMUNOGLOBULIN CLASSES

The several classes of immunoglobulins known to be present in man are designated IgG, IgM, IgA, IgD, and IgE. For convenience, the abbreviation Ig commonly is used to denote immunoglobulin. An immunoglobulin class is determined by the class of heavy (H) chains comprising it—*i.e.*, gamma in IgG, mu in IgM, alpha in IgA, delta in IgD, and epsilon in IgE. The two classes of L chains, as stated previously, are called kappa and lambda. Two members of either the kappa or lambda class combine with two members of one class of H chains (except mu) to form the four chains of an immunoglobulin molecule. The formula for an IgG molecule, for example, may be kappa$_2$ gamma$_2$ or lambda$_2$ gamma$_2$, depending on the class to which the L chains belong; the subscripts "2" represent the two L and the two H chains (see Figure 2). A single immunoglobulin molecule consisting of four chains, therefore, is symmetrical; that is, its L chains belong to one class and are identical in structure, and its H chains belong to one class and are identical.

Free light chains

Light chains (L) not joined to heavy ones are called free light chains; they occur in minute amounts in normal persons. Described as long ago as 1847, free light chains occur in large amounts in the urine in some disease states, in such cases, they are called Bence Jones proteins. Free light chains have no detectable antibody activity but provide valuable material for structural studies of immunoglobulins.

IgG antibodies. The IgG class of immunoglobulins (kappa$_2$ gamma$_2$, lambda$_2$ gamma$_2$) is the most abundant one in the blood of normal humans, in which about ten milligrams (one milligram = 0.001 gram) are found in one millilitre (one millilitre = about 1/32 ounce) of blood plasma. It has two combining sites per molecule; the structure is diagrammatically illustrated in Figure 2B. IgG can activate the complement system and passes from mother to fetus across the placenta. IgG antibodies apparently are general-purpose antibodies. Four distinct subclasses of IgG exist; their separate biological functions have not yet been defined.

IgM antibodies. IgM antibodies [(kappa$_2$, mu$_2$)5, (lambda$_2$, mu$_2$)5], are the first antibodies that form in response to antigens especially in primitive animals. Most natural antibodies (*i.e.*, those formed in response to stimulation by bacteria in the gut) belong to this class. Because IgM molecules are much larger in size than other immunoglobulins, they are sometimes known as macroglobulins. Each IgM molecule has ten L and ten H chains, a total of 20 chains instead of the four that comprise IgG antibodies. The L and H chains in IgM are arranged as shown in Figure 3. IgM antibodies have ten antigen-combining sites per molecule and are therefore able to combine firmly with large antigens (*e.g.*, bacteria, other cells), which have closely spaced repeating arrangements of antigenic determinants on them. The complement system is activated by IgM antibodies, which are very effective in killing microbes. Normal humans have 0.5 to 2 milligrams of IgM antibodies per millilitre of blood plasma. IgM does not cross the placenta.

From H. Metzger, *Advances in Immunology*, vol. 12 (1970); Academic Press

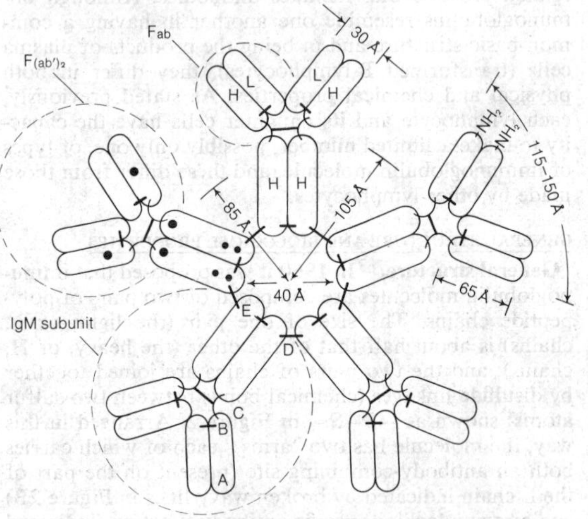

Figure 3: Schematic representation of IgM. Disulfide linkages are indicated by solid bars. The letters A–E refer to the peptides described in Figure 2. The circles, for clarity shown in only one subunit [$F_{(ab')_2}$], indicate possible areas for attachment of carbohydrate chains.

IgA antibodies. IgA antibodies (kappa$_2$ alpha$_2$, lambda$_2$ alpha$_2$, and multiples called polymers) are present in secretions such as saliva, tears, nasal mucus, and the mucus of the respiratory tract. Although IgA antibodies do not cross the placenta, they are present in the first milk (colostrum) secreted after birth and thus provide newborn animals with a source of antibodies against many of the microbes in the environment. IgA is normally present in blood plasma in large amounts (0.2 to 5 milligrams per millilitre), and it usually is in a form containing two combining sites per molecule, although some forms with four or more combining sites may also be present. IgA antibodies in the blood do not activate the complement system but can combine with and neutralize antigens such as bacterial toxins (poisons) and viruses.

Before IgA is secreted in, for example, saliva or tears, a protein, which is not an immunoglobulin, is added to it; the resulting complex molecule contains two IgA units linked by the protein. Secretions of this so-called polymeric IgA inactivate viruses and can kill bacteria, especially in conjunction with the enzyme lysozyme, which occurs in many animal secretions and attacks bacterial cell walls after they have been weakened by the antibody. IgA antibodies are important as mechanisms of local resistance to microbes inhabiting the gut and the respiratory tract.

IgD and IgE antibodies. IgD (kappa$_2$ delta$_2$, lambda$_2$ delta$_2$) is present only in the blood (from less than 0.01 to 0.14 milligram per millilitre of plasma), and knowledge of its properties derives solely from the study of their proteins when they are made in abnormally large amounts in the disease myelomatosis. Although antibodies occur in this immunoglobulin class, their biological properties are not yet known.

IgE (?kappa$_2$ epsilon$_2$, lambda$_2$ epsilon$_2$), the most recently discovered immunoglobulin class, is present in very small amounts in the blood of normal persons (about 0.0025 milligram per millilitre of plasma); in the blood of allergic persons, however, the concentration may be many times greater (see *Manifestations of immunological reactions*). IgE antibodies were first recognized because their activity is destroyed by moderate temperatures, which do not harm other kinds of antibodies. The characteristic property of IgE antibodies is that they are cytotropic—*i.e.*, they bind firmly to the surfaces of certain cells, especially mast cells (components of connective tissue) from which the interaction of IgE and an appropriate antigen triggers an explosive release of potent agents such as histamine. IgE antibodies do not activate the complement system or cross the placenta.

Important properties of IgE antibodies

The problem of establishing the relationships within a group of proteins such as the immunoglobulins, which have overlapping properties, is particularly difficult because many of the analytical procedures used to study other proteins cannot be applied to them; research involving immunoglobulins has utilized a pathological condition in man and mice named myelomatosis, which is characterized by the presence of tumours (myelomas) composed of large numbers of plasma cells and by the appearance in the blood (and sometimes in the urine) of large quantities of one kind of immunoglobulin. Myelomas result from a great proliferation of immunoglobulin-producing cells derived originally from a single cell that, for unknown reasons, escapes the control mechanisms that ensure orderly cell growth and acquires malignant properties without losing the capacity to make its characteristic immunoglobulin product. All myelomas studied thus far in different people or mice secrete different proteins; if the myeloma proteins from several hundred individuals are compared, however, they span the range of properties found in the immunoglobulins of normal persons, suggesting that myelomas may result from a more or less random change in the lymphocyte population. Indeed, some myeloma proteins have specific antibody properties (*i.e.*, they are able to combine with recognizable antigenic determinants), although there is no reason to suppose that myelomas arise as a result of intensive and prolonged stimulation of lymphocytes by antigens.

IV. Antigens

GENERAL PROPERTIES

Structure and size. Antigens must contain molecular patterns unlike those that are present in materials with which lymphocytes normally come into contact; *i.e.*, antigens must, in some way, be foreign to lymphocytes. Distinct molecular patterns may result from either a unique arrangement of the components from which organisms are constructed or from chemical structures not normally present in biological materials. Each recognizably unfamiliar molecular pattern constitutes an antigenic determinant. Most antigens have many different antigenic determinants, which constitute an "antigenic mosaic," any one or all of which may stimulate immunological responses from specific lymphocytes. The immunological response to an antigen, therefore, is the sum of the responses of the lymphocytes to each antigenic determinant. Some antigenic determinants are more effective than others in stimulating an immunological response, presumably because a larger number of responsive lymphocytes is present. When two different antigens have one common antigenic determinant, some of the antibodies made against one antigen are able to react with the other; such antigens are known as cross-reacting antigens.

Antigenic mosaic

In addition to being foreign to lymphocytes, antigens must be of a certain minimum size in order to stimulate an immunological response. Molecules with molecular weights below 1,000 (based on the weight of a hydrogen atom as one) have rarely been found to stimulate an immunological response unless they are attached to larger molecules. Antigens with molecular weights of 10,000 or more stimulate an immunological response. Materials with molecular weights exceeding 100,000 are usually potent antigens, in part because the larger the size of a molecule, the greater the variety of antigenic determinants it is likely to possess and the longer it is likely to be retained in the body; and in part because large molecules are taken up more readily by macrophages, which helps to stimulate antibody formation (see below *Adjuvants*). Many large antigens, such as a bacterium or some other foreign cell, contain a wide variety of molecules, any one of which may be antigenic. Such composite antigens elicit immunological responses largely against the components on their surfaces because this is the part with which responsive lymphocytes are likely to come into contact. An antigen with a variety of antigenic determinants generally elicits stronger immunological responses, as measured by antibody production, than one lacking a variety of determinants, probably because T-lymphocytes and B-lymphocytes cooperate—*i.e.*, T-lymphocytes that interact with one antigenic determinant can effectively concentrate the antigen so that other determinants on the same antigen are better able to stimulate responsive B-lymphocytes to make an antibody (see above *The cellular basis of immunological response*).

Immunization. Proteins generally are potent antigens, as are certain carbohydrates. Lipids are sometimes able to elicit immunological responses but do not do so readily, probably because they are broken down rapidly in the body and have few distinctly foreign molecular patterns. Nucleic acids are composed of a limited number of building blocks (the nucleotides), and are not antigenic unless modified chemically. Antibodies react only with altered or denatured nucleic acids; this means that antibodies are not normally formed against a body's own genetic material or against the genetic material of invading microbes.

The early-20th-century discovery that minor alterations in the structures of antigens, such as bacterial toxins, destroy poisonous properties without affecting the capacity to stimulate the formation of antibodies capable of reacting with untreated toxins was an extremely important one; minor structural alterations convert toxins to toxoids and provide the basis for prophylactic (protective) immunization against the toxic products of various diseases —*e.g.*, diphtheria, tetanus. In a similar manner, microbes killed by various means retain their surface antigens and thus are able to stimulate the formation of antibodies against living bacteria of the same species; this method is used in immunization against diseases such as typhoid, typhus, and plague. It is important and often difficult, however, to ensure that the antigens produced by bacteria after they invade the body are also found in the vaccines produced by these organisms when grown outside the body.

Whenever possible, immunization against a virus is achieved by the administration of an attenuated form; *i.e.*, the virus can multiply to a limited extent in the body without causing manifestations of disease and thus provides a strong antigenic stimulus. Attenuated strains of a virus are obtained by careful selection of variants that have been grown in abnormal hosts or under abnormal conditions. Attenuated strains must be able to stimulate immunity against the antigens of fully virulent strains and should not revert to virulent forms. Attenuated strains of microbes have been used to immunize man against smallpox since 1798, tuberculosis since 1927, and the 17D strain of yellow fever since about 1936.

Factors involved in antigenic efficiency

Adjuvants. The efficiency with which antigens evoke immunological responses and the kind and duration of the responses depend not only on the nature and quantity of the antigen but also on the way in which it is introduced; for example, antigens that remain in the body for a long period of time generally stimulate immunological responses more effectively than do those that are broken down or excreted quickly. In addition, antigens that form particles or aggregates are more effective than are those that dissolve in body fluids; one reason is that dissolved antigens are apparently more likely to kill or inactivate lymphocytes rather than to stimulate them to activity, thus causing tolerance instead of immunity. Antigens that form particles or aggregates are rapidly taken up by macrophages and, as a result, have less opportunity to cause tolerance. Many antigens are much more effective in stimulating immunity after they are taken up by macrophages. Evidence suggests that some antigens taken up by macrophages remain on their surfaces and, instead of being ingested and destroyed, are concentrated and are thus better able to stimulate the appropriate lymphocytes. Evidence also indicates that lymphocytes are stimulated to differentiate and divide when they are in contact (as occurs in lymphoid tissues) with macrophages previously activated by the ingestion of foreign material.

Before any of the evidence cited above was available, it was found empirically that nonliving antigens can often be made more effective either by mixing them with certain compounds (*e.g.*, aluminum hydroxide, aluminum phosphate) to which they became attached, or adsorbed, or by mixing them in certain oils. Such compounds, known as adjuvants, increase immunological responses in a nonspecific way and enable the responses to persist for longer periods of time, partly by retaining a reserve supply of the antigen, which is protected by (and slowly released from) the adjuvant, so that stimulation of lymphocytes is a repeated process, and partly by attracting and activating macrophages. Adjuvants thus make possible the achievement of prophylactic immunization with much smaller amounts of substances, bacterial toxoids, for example, than would otherwise be needed.

Other adjuvants affect lymphocytes directly, causing them to congregate at the sites in the body where antigens are deposited and, probably, thereby increasing the opportunity for stimulation; such adjuvants tend to have unacceptable toxic side effects, however, and thus far have not been used in man.

SOME IMPORTANT TYPES

Many foreign materials obviously are potential antigens and would evoke an immunological response if introduced into the body. Comparatively few foreign materials, however, normally enter the body, at least in significant quantities, because they are unable to pass the body's mechanical barriers—the skin and the mucous membranes. Both microbes and parasites, however, may penetrate mucous membranes or enter the body through cuts or bites; in addition, small quantities of foreign materials such as pollen and dust can enter the body through the respiratory tract, and large amounts of foreign materials may be introduced by medical procedures—*e.g.*, blood transfusions, serum injections, and surgical transplantations. Molecules such as chemical dyes or drugs, despite their small size, may also act as antigens under certain circumstances—*e.g.*, an aniline dye, the phenolic acid component of poison ivy, or an antibiotic such as penicillin may combine with proteins found in the body. As a result, the proteins acquire a new antigenic determinant (*i.e.*, the dye, the acid, or the antibiotic), which, since it can be recognized as foreign by lymphocytes, can evoke immunological response. Antibodies that may be produced in response to the determinant react with the determinant regardless of the attached proteins but not with the same proteins lacking the determinant.

Common antigens

Protein antigens. Protein antigens of practical importance for prophylactic immunization include bacterial toxins; *e.g.*, those produced by the causative agents of diphtheria, tetanus, botulism, or cholera. Protein antigens are purified and inactivated to form toxoids before they are used in immunization.

The infective part of a virus—*i.e.*, its nucleic acid—is enclosed in a protective coat of protein; effective immunity, therefore, is achieved by eliciting the formation of antibodies that react with the specific protein components of a virus. Some of the surface components of bacteria (*e.g.*, flagella) are also proteins. The outer walls of bacteria, however, are composed of small and simple protein-like molecules (polypeptides) combined with carbohydrates and a variable amount of lipids. Their antigen specificity is mainly determined by another type of antigen, carbohydrate.

Carbohydrate antigens. Carbohydrates are important surface constituents of many cells, and, because they project outward from the cell surface, carbohydrates often form the most important antigenic determinants of certain cell types—*e.g.*, many bacteria and mammalian cells such as red blood cells. The molecular structures of many complex carbohydrates are known, so that it is possible to compare molecular structures with antibody specificities. Antibody specificity is determined predominantly by the sugar unit at the end of the carbohydrate molecule; evidence suggests that as many as four adjacent sugar units (rarely six), however, may exert some effect on the combination of a carbohydrate antigen with its corresponding antibody. The antigen-combining site on the antibody, therefore, must be large enough to accommodate a structure comprised of four sugar units.

Site of antibody specificity

Antigenic specificity in the human blood-group substances (A, B, O, or H) is largely determined by the terminal sugar units. The molecular structure of the blood-group antigens consists of a polypeptide core with a long carbohydrate branch. The carbohydrate molecules of all the major blood groups have a common structure, except at the ends, where they differ from one another; the specificity of blood group A is determined by the carbohydrate alpha-N-acetylgalactosaminoyl-(1 $\rightarrow$ 3)-galactose, that of B by alpha-D-galactosyl-(1 $\rightarrow$ 3)-galactose, and that of H by L-fucose.

Histocompatibility antigens. Histocompatibility (or H) antigen is a term used to describe a membrane component found in all the cells of an animal. H antigen, when given to another animal of the same species, stimulates an immune response in the recipient; this means that grafts of tissue between the two are destroyed by the specific immunological reaction evoked by the H antigen of the donor. Such antigens, called iso-antigens, are completely identical only in genetically identical individuals.

H antigens are glycoproteins—*i.e.*, combinations of proteins and carbohydrates—and the antigenic determinants are usually found in the protein moiety. More than 20 different antigens of a group called HL antigens are now known, and the production of each is controlled by a separate gene. The strongest and most important, known as HL-A, include eight different varieties. An individual inherits from each parent the capacity to make one or two of them; thus the probability that any two individuals chosen at random have the same combination is very small (although there is a 25 percent chance that brothers or sisters will have the same combination). Successful transplantation of tissues depends upon selection of donor and recipient with the minimum number of HL-A differences.

Histocompatibility antigens are present on tumours, but many tumours, especially those caused by viruses, possess additional or altered antigens, called T antigens, at their surfaces. In the case of virus-induced animal tumours, the tumour antigen is characteristic of the virus that causes the malignant transformation of normal cells, even though the presence of the virus itself may no longer be detectable.

V. The interaction of antigens and antibodies

GENERAL AND PROTECTIVE EFFECTS

As stated previously, antibodies generally have two identical combining sites situated toward the end of flexible arms (see Figure 3); an antigen molecule may contain a number of different antigenic determinant groups, each of which may be present one or more times. The combination of an antigen and an antibody involves the specific interaction of the combining sites on the antibody with the appropriate antigenic determinant groups and results in a firm but reversible union between them. Although this union does not involve chemical (*i.e.,* covalent) bonds, it is sometimes convenient to use the term valency to denote the number of binding sites. The number of antibody binding sites on an antigen may vary from one or two to several hundred; the number of antigen-combining sites on most antibodies is two or ten (*e.g.,* IgM). Antigen and antibody combine according to the ratio in which they are present, rather than in fixed proportions. In this way, a three-dimensional lattice of antigen molecules linked by antibody molecules is built up; as the lattice increases in size, the antigen–antibody complex very often becomes insoluble in water, and a precipitate forms. After a certain ratio of antibody to antigen, known as the optimal proportion, occurs, both components may precipitate completely from solution. Figure 4 shows the way in which lattices with different ratios may occur.

Lattice hypothesis

Adapted from *American Chemical Society Journal* (1940)

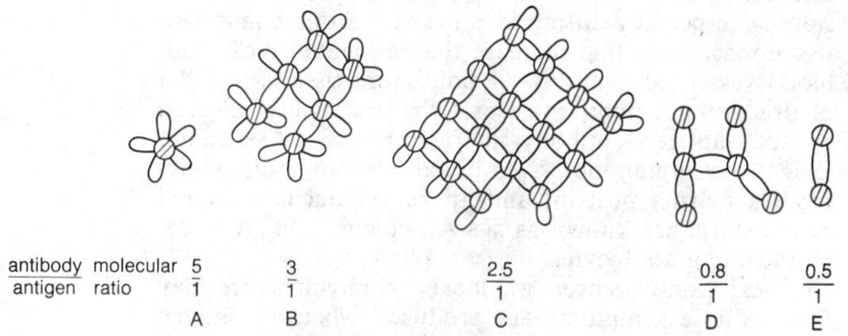

Figure 4: Hypothetical arrangement of antigen (shaded) and antibody molecules in antigen–antibody complex, according to lattice hypothesis. (A) Extreme antibody excess with all five valencies (binding sites) of antigen satisfied by excess antibody. (B) Moderate antibody excess. (C) "Optimal proportions." (D) Antigen excess. (E) Extreme antigen excess with both valencies of antibody satisfied.

The complex forces that bind the antigen and the antibody to each other include bonding between oppositely charged groups (ionic bonding), van der Waals forces (in which strength is inversely proportional to the sixth power of the distance between the groups involved), and, in some cases, bonds formed by a shared hydrogen atom. The strength of the forces that bind antigen and antibody is dependent on a close fit between the amino acids at the combining site on the antibody and the molecular pattern of the antigenic determinant.

The combination with antibody is sufficient to neutralize antigens such as toxins and to inactivate enzymes, because the antibody interferes with the groups required to make these molecules active. In a similar manner, the attachment of antibodies to the protein coat of viruses prevents them from penetrating and infecting cells.

Other properties of antibodies, in addition to their ability to bind to antigens, also are important in antigen–antibody interactions. As mentioned before, these properties depend upon the constant part (C region) of the H chains (see Figure 2). When antibody molecules form clumps, or aggregates, with antigens, their shapes are distorted as a result of the combination of the combining sites with the antigen; the distortion in shape exposes part of the H chain and confers two very important biological properties on the antigen–antibody complex—one is the capacity to activate complement, which is discussed below; the second is the capacity to attach to macrophages, which appear to have receptors at their surface that bind immunoglobulins regardless of the nature of the antigen component. The attachment of the complex to macrophages increases the rate at which antigens can become engulfed and digested. The importance of the attachment of antigen–antibody complexes to macrophages was recognized around 1900 and is termed opsonization.

ACTIVATION OF COMPLEMENT

Properties of complement

Complement is the term used to describe a property present in the freshly drawn blood of immunized animals and necessary, in addition to antibody, for killing bacteria or other cells. Shortly after this property was first observed in 1898, it was discovered that a similar property exists in the blood of normal nonimmunized animals and that it is very labile—*i.e.,* it disappears if blood serum is heated for 30 minutes at 56° C (133° F) or allowed to stand for several hours at room temperature. It gradually became clear that the property depends on not one but several factors in the blood, some of which are relatively stable and others of which are not. Much of the mystery of complement now has been solved, and its functions have been shown to be a very important adjunct to immunity, not only with respect to killing microbes but also for initiating the local inflammation that accompanies many antigen–antibody reactions.

Complement (C) comprises a system made up of nine distinct components, numbered C1 to C9, which are present in the blood and in the tissue fluids of normal animals of the mammalian species thus far carefully examined. Whether exactly analogous components are present in all vertebrates is not yet known, but birds, fishes, and amphibians possess complement systems generally similar to those of mammals, indicating that this elaborate system probably conferred important survival advantages in the course of evolution. All of the components of the complement system are proteins, which differ greatly in size and in other properties. Some components, such as C3, are present in relative abundance (one milligram per millilitre of blood serum); the concentration of others, such as C2, is 1,000-fold less. The sequence of the reaction of the components of complement is well established, and some of the early-acting ones (Cl, C2, and C4) are inactive forms of enzymes (called esterases), which are converted into active forms by the action of a previous component of the series. The mechanism by which the later members of the series act has not yet been established. The complement system constitutes a sequence of trigger mechanisms well suited to enlarge and diversify the effects of an antigen–antibody interaction, while simultaneously preventing the effects from becoming widespread; *i.e.,* some of the activated intermediates are unstable and thus break down quickly, and others are inactivated by pre-existing inhibitor molecules in the blood.

Only IgG and IgM classes of antibody are able to activate the complement system. Two adjacent molecules of IgG antibody are required; a single molecule of IgM is sufficient. The first stage in the sequence involves the combination of the C1 component with the region of H chains (near the L chain attachment site) exposed by the combination of an IgG or IgM antibody with antigen. The attachment to the antibody of C1, which is composed of three protein molecules linked together by calcium, results in the conversion of one of the protein molecules to an active enzyme, which, in turn, causes the attachment and activation of C4; this results in the attachment and activation of C2. The activated complex composed of C1, C2, and C4 attached to antibody now combines with the C3 component, and a number of biologically important events occur: the complex substance formed by antigen, antibody, and the C1 through C4 components of complement stick to cells and are readily ingested and digested by macrophages; a polypeptide molecule called anaphylatoxin, which splits from

Sequential activation of components

the third complement component, increases the permeability (*i.e.*, ability of substances to pass through) of small blood vessels (capillaries) and causes contraction of smooth muscle fibres; and the combination of antigen, antibody, and four complement components acts upon the next complement components (C5, C6, and C7), which generally attach together. From this material is liberated a second polypeptide molecule with activity similar to anaphylatoxin; in addition, a chemotactic factor is formed (*i.e.*, one that attracts granulocytes and causes them to migrate toward the combination of antigen, antibody, and the first seven complement components).

Finally, the C8 and C9 components act in the following way: when the initial antigen–antibody interaction occurs at the surface of a cell, such as a bacterium or a red blood cell, the effect of C8 and C9 is to disrupt the outer lipid layer of the cell membrane, so that it loses the capacity to control permeability, and the cell dies as its contents leak through the membrane.

Since the action of the complement system is independent of the antigenic specificity of the antibody, the system enables the body to bring into action, where needed, the common biological defense mechanisms involved in inflammation—increased local blood flow and immigration of granulocytes and macrophages. This is probably the most important function of the complement system. The fact that it enables a very small number of IgM antibody molecules (in theory a single molecule) to kill a susceptible bacterium is presumably also significant, especially since natural antibodies and the antibodies most rapidly synthesized are of this class.

VI. Manifestations of immunological reactions

CELL-MEDIATED IMMUNITY

It has been pointed out that thymus-derived (T-) lymphocytes do not secrete antibodies but may be stimulated by contact with an appropriate antigen to become large active cells that divide to form daughter cells able to interact with the antigen. In addition, T-lymphocytes enable the antibody-forming B-lymphocytes to respond more effectively to small amounts of antigen, play a role in the specific mechanisms involved in killing foreign cells (*e.g.*, the cells of a transplanted tissue, cells with foreign antigenic specificities acquired as a result of infection by viruses or by intracellular parasites), and are responsible for certain kinds of hypersensitivity and for stimulation of nonspecific immunity. T-lymphocytes that interact specifically with an antigen release factors with the following properties: the ability to stimulate macrophages to increase their enzyme content and the adhesiveness of their surface membranes; the ability to stimulate other lymphocytes to undergo cell division; and the ability to stimulate the migration of other lymphocytes toward them.

Delayed hyper-sensitivity reactions

Immunological reactions that are mediated by lymphocytes rather than by circulating antibody were once known as delayed hypersensitivity reactions, because they occur gradually over the course of many hours rather than in a few minutes as do antibody-mediated reactions. Cell-mediated immunity is a more accurate term, however, since the primary cause for the delay is that lymphocytes able to interact with a specific antigen must, as they circulate in the bloodstream, accumulate at the site of antigen deposition, and the accumulation process is a relatively slow one.

The reactions of cell-mediated immunity are most evident when a sufficient population of reactive lymphocytes (usually the result of previous stimulation by the same antigen) is present, and the antigen is at the surface of body cells, as occurs with antigens on grafted tissue cells; viral antigens on infected cells, in which a virus is multiplying; bacterial antigens on macrophages, in which certain microbes are able to grow; and chemical sensitizing agents that have penetrated the skin and reacted with body cells at the site of penetration. As reactive lymphocytes arrive at the site of antigen deposition, they trigger the mechanisms that cause an influx of lymphocytes and activated macrophages, which destroy the affected body cells; when these cells are infected and the infective agent is also destroyed, or when the target cell is part of a tumour, the consequences are beneficial. An important side effect of the reactions of cell-mediated immunity is that a large population of macrophages may become activated and thus be more effective at destroying not only the microbes that stimulated their activation but unrelated organisms as well. The resulting state of generally heightened resistance is known as cellular immunity (see also INFLAMMATION).

HYPERSENSITIVITY AND ALLERGY

It has been mentioned that the immunological system does not distinguish between antigens that are potentially harmful and those that are not; in addition, the reactions that occur during immunological responses are not always beneficial. This was recognized about 1905, and the term allergy was proposed to describe a specifically altered capacity to react that is caused by prior exposure to specific antigens. Hypersensitivity, which implies a specifically increased capacity to react, is often used interchangeably with the term allergy.

Types of hyper-sensitivity reactions

Hypersensitivity reactions do not differ from those resulting from the interactions between antigens and antibodies or antigens and reactive lymphocytes (cell-mediated immunity); but they have damaging, rather than potentially beneficial, consequences, usually because the reactions are intense and occur in response to the introduction of otherwise harmless materials. Hypersensitivity reactions may be conveniently classified into three main types: anaphylactic reactions, arthus-type reactions, and delayed-type hypsersensitivity; more than one may occur simultaneously.

Anaphylactic reactions are caused by the interaction of antigens with antibodies (usually of the IgE class); the interaction stimulates the very rapid release of substances, especially histamine, derived from connective tissue mast cells, that increase the permeability of small blood vessels, the outflow of fluid from tissues, and the contraction of smooth muscles. Other substances released by such antigen–antibody interaction include serotonin (5-hydroxytryptamine), from blood platelets; bradykinin, from a plasma protein; and an as yet uncharacterized acidic substance known as SRS-A, which probably is derived from granulocytes.

Typical consequences of local anaphylaxis are hay fever, whose symptoms are produced when an antigen (usually pollen) comes into contact with the mucous membranes, the nose, or the conjunctiva of the eyes; asthma, which occurs when antigens such as pollen, dander, or dust reach the bronchial tree of the lungs; and urticaria (nettle rash, hives), which occurs when antigens reach the skin, either directly or through the bloodstream. General anaphylaxis may follow the entry of small amounts (less than one milligram) of an antigen into the bloodstream of a suitably sensitized subject and may cause death (see also ALLERGY AND ANAPHYLACTIC SHOCK).

Arthus-type reactions, named after the man who first described them in 1903, result from the formation of antigen–antibody complexes in the circulation. The deposition of antigen–antibody combinations in the walls of blood vessels causes the activation of the complement system and may result in severe local inflammatory reactions. Diseases caused in this way are sometimes known as antigen–antibody-complex diseases. The less severe diseases include reactions to repeated insect bites, which result from sensitization against insect saliva; severe ones include serum sickness, certain forms of kidney disease, lung diseases such as farmer's lung syndrome, and the manifestations of various auto-immune diseases discussed below.

Delayed type hypersensitivity is the pathological manifestation of cell-mediated immunity. One common form is the chronic skin problems that recur when chemical substances such as aniline dyes or chromic salts combine with and alter skin proteins, causing them to act as antigens. Another form is the result of a cell-mediated immunological response to infective agents; when the extent of tissue destruction is excessive, as may occur in persons suffering from tuberculosis or syphilis, the damaging effects of the immunological response, rather than the infective agents, are the main cause of the disease. Delayed-type hypersensitivity is also a cause of auto-immune diseases.

AUTO-IMMUNITY (AUTO-ALLERGY)

For many years it was assumed that the body would not make an immunological response against components of its own tissues. In general, this assumption is correct, at least so far as components constantly in contact with lymphoid tissues are concerned. The way in which self-tolerance is achieved is presumably similar to the way by which tolerance to other potential antigens comes about (see below *Immunological tolerance*). Self-tolerance must be actively maintained, however, and if it breaks down, antibodies or the mechanisms of cell-mediated immunity may be directed against components of the body's own cells. This phenomenon is commonly called auto-immunity, although the term auto-allergy is more appropriate, since immunity in the ordinary sense of protection is not involved.

Self-tolerance

An immunological response of the body against components of itself can occur in several ways. One of these results from the acquisition of new antigens or the release of normally inaccessible antigens, to which the immunological system is not already tolerant. If such antigens come in contact with lymphocytes (as a result of trauma, for example), they may stimulate an immunological response. Examples of new antigens include spermatozoa, which are not formed before puberty, and antigens acquired as a result of viral infection or malignant transformation (*i.e.*, tumour antigens). Normally inaccessible antigens include those of specialized cells such as the lens of the eye, the pigment cells of the retina of the eye, nerve cells, or internal constituents of heart muscle.

An immunological response against self may also occur if the structure of normally occurring body constituents is altered so as to reveal new antigenic determinants; for example, antibodies whose shapes are distorted by combination with antigens expose amino-acid sequences (which can act as antigenic determinants) not revealed on the uncombined antibodies and thus may stimulate the formation of antibodies against themselves. Some of the components of the complement system may also act in this way. Antibodies so formed react exclusively with the determinants revealed in the distorted antibodies or in the complement components. The rheumatoid factor characteristic of rheumatoid arthritis is an antibody formed in response to altered immunoglobulins.

A third way in which an immunological response may be stimulated against self is by immunization with a cross-reacting antigen (*i.e.*, one that shares with another antigen some, but not all, of the same antigenic determinants). One example occurs after infections (*e.g.*, rheumatic fever) caused by certain strains of streptococcal bacteria; in this case, antibodies form against the membrane of heart muscle (sarcolemma).

Hereditary predisposition

None of the immunological responses to self mentioned thus far requires the breakdown of a pre-existing state of self-tolerance. A number of diseases occur, especially in elderly persons, in which antibodies appear against one or more body constituents; the history of such a person's family usually indicates a hereditary predisposition to make such antibodies, suggesting an instability of the normal mechanisms both for maintaining self-tolerance and for suppressing lymphocytes capable of making antibodies against self. Similar conditions produced in genetically predisposed mouse strains suggest that chronic infection with certain viruses may play a role in the breakdown of self-tolerance. No evidence that viruses play a similar part in affected humans has been found thus far, although instability of the immunological system in humans is suggested by the association of auto-immune diseases with tumours of the lymphoid tissues and with conditions of partial immunological deficiency.

Three types of auto-immune diseases appear to result from breakdown of self-tolerance. In one of them, called auto-immune hemolytic anemia, antibodies are made against the body's own red blood cells, often against antigenic determinants commonly found on the red cells; red blood cell destruction and anemia are manifestations of the disease. In a second type, antibodies are made against components of specialized tissues such as the thyroid gland or the gastric mucosa. Antibodies against more than one of these tissues may occur in the same person. Destructive diseases of these tissues are often, but not invariably, present, and it is not yet certain whether or not antibodies are the primary causes of the diseases. In the third type, antibodies are made against components (*e.g.*, nucleic acids) common to a variety of animal tissues. Disease results not so much from destructive lesions of tissues containing the components as from the fact that complex substances that form between antibodies and antigens released by normal wear and tear of cells become trapped in small blood vessels, especially in the kidney, where they cause chronic inflammation.

IMMUNOLOGICAL TOLERANCE

Immunological tolerance is a condition in which an animal fails to make an immunological response against one or more antigens (*i.e.*, the animal tolerates them) but retains a normal capacity to respond to other antigens. This broad definition includes not only tolerance of components of self but tolerance of other antigens.

Immunological tolerance results from the absence of lymphocytes able to interact with certain antigens, rather than from the presence of factors that might prevent such interaction. Lymphocytes arise by a random process and have immunoglobulin receptors capable of reacting with an enormous variety of antigenic determinants; included in a lymphocyte population may be certain cells capable of reacting with components of self. It is reasonable to infer that, during fetal life, many potentially self-reacting lymphocytes probably are prevented from reaching the bloodstream; hence, an effective means of specifically destroying self-reactive lymphocytes must exist.

Immunological tolerance has been achieved by foreign antigens introduced into an animal shortly after birth—*i.e.*, before its immunological system is mature. Similar tolerance can be achieved in adult animals, provided the antigen is administered in a form that is not readily taken up by macrophages, so that at least part of it persists in the circulation. Both the administration of very small amounts of antigen repeatedly over a period of weeks and the administration of very large amounts for a shorter period of time stimulate specific immunological tolerance (*i.e.*, the animal can no longer make an immunological response against the antigen). The likelihood of achieving tolerance rather than immunity is greatly increased if the number of potentially responsive lymphocytes is low (as is the case, for example, during fetal life). Different mechanisms may be involved when small amounts of antigen are in contact with lymphocytes for a long time than when large amounts are used for a shorter time. In the former case, lymphocytes that interact with the antigen and are not stimulated to differentiate and divide apparently become inactivated—probably by being killed. In the latter case, all potential antibody-producing lymphocytes probably develop into plasma cells that secrete a specific antibody, thus exhausting the supply of lymphocytes able to respond to a new antigen.

Maintenance of tolerance

The maintenance of tolerance, even to antigens of self, must be a continuous process, since new responsive lymphocytes may arise from stem cells, which, because they lack immunoglobulin receptors, cannot be affected by antigens. The proposal that lymphocytes are especially liable to inactivation by antigens within the thymus, where they first develop from stem cells, is supported by the observation that T-lymphocytes are more readily made tolerant than are B-lymphocytes. Apart from the importance of maintaining tolerance of self, the inducement of specific tolerance for medical purposes (*e.g.*, against transplantation antigens, against antigens that cause severe allergies) sometimes seems advantageous. Although specific tolerance has been achieved experimentally in animals, the procedures are generally too drastic to be applied in man.

IMMUNOSUPPRESSION

Although immunity is beneficial in most circumstances, it is occasionally necessary to prevent an immunological response or to suppress one that has already occurred. If the recipient of a kidney graft, for example, could be prevented from making an immunological response against it, most surgery involving kidney grafts would be successful; and if persons suffering from auto-immune diseases or disabling allergies could be prevented from making the immunological responses that harm them, the illnesses would be cured.

The practical difficulty in achieving immunosuppression is that it is difficult to suppress selectively an unwanted immunological response without impairing protective immunity against microbes in general. The most obvious method of selective immunosuppression would be to induce a lasting state of specific immunological tolerance, but this is still very difficult to do. An alternative method prevents immunization when the antigen is identified and will be present for only a limited period. The method involves providing an excess amount of antibodies against the antigen before the latter can take effect; the antibodies combine with the antigen (thus covering its combining sites, so as to prevent their interaction with lymphocytes) and accelerate destruction of the antigen. Immunization of a pregnant woman against the rhesus antigen of her child's red blood cells, for example, is suppressed by the injection of human anti-rhesus antibodies at the time the child is born.

Another example of the successful application of methods to alter the character of immunological responses is that of specific desensitization. The agent to which a person is allergic is carefully introduced in such a way as to encourage the production of sufficient amounts of harmless antibody (*e.g.*, IgG), which combine preferentially with the antigen, so that it is prevented from reacting with other forms of antibody (*e.g.*, IgE in acute allergies) or with circulating lymphocytes (in delayed-type hypersensitivity).

Methods used in tissue transplants

None of these methods can yet be applied for the purposes of tissue transplantation. The approach with tissue transplants is to suppress the immunological response in general, in the hope that unwanted responses will be weakened without totally obliterating protective immunity. The immunological response is depressed by killing lymphocytes or preventing the multiplication of stimulated ones. Lymphocytes are killed by agents such as ionizing radiation (X-rays) and certain drugs to which lymphocytes are especially susceptible. It is difficult, however, to choose a quantity of the agent used that does not damage other important cells in the body. The multiplication of stimulated lymphocytes may be prevented by drugs that interfere with the synthesis of the nucleic acids required for cell division. The difficulty again is confining the effects to lymphocytes and avoiding damage to other tissues (*e.g.*, bone marrow, intestine) in which cell division occurs constantly. T-lymphocytes may eventually be eliminated selectively by a method involving the use of a specific antiserum prepared against them (antilymphocyte serum).

Even when adequate suppression of immunological responses is not possible, certain methods are used to mitigate their effects or to change their character to something less harmful. Acute allergic reactions are alleviated by drugs that inhibit the effects of histamine and similar substances (*e.g.*, serotonin); anti-inflammation drugs, especially cortisone and similar compounds, can markedly lessen the damaging effects of inflammation and of cell-mediated immunity reactions.

IMMUNOLOGICAL DEFICIENCY

Immunological deficiency, which occurs rarely in man, may result from the failure of nonspecific or of specific immunity mechanisms and may be present at birth or acquired later in life. Following are some of the ways in which immunological deficiency may occur.

Failure of nonspecific immunity. Inherited deficiencies of granulocytes are known. These include infantile agranulocytosis, chronic granulomatous disease, and the so-called Chediak-Higashi syndrome, which is a rare disease of children characterized by a tendency to chronic infections and defective pigmentation of eyes, hair, and skin. Congenital (inherited) deficiencies of individual components of the complement system, which may occur in man and in experimental animals, may modify but usually do not nullify the effectiveness of specific immunological reactions. Failure of nonspecific immunity may be acquired after the bone marrow stem cells are poisoned either by drugs or by substances such as benzene. Excessive destruction of bone marrow or lymphoid tissues also may occur as a result of tumours, X-rays, or, occasionally, surgical removal of the spleen.

Hereditary defects in lymphocytes

Failure of specific immunity. Defects in specific immunity mechanisms may result from hereditary defects in the B-lymphocytes, the T-lymphocytes, or both. Congenital sex-linked immunoglobulin deficiency is a B-lymphocyte defect affecting male infants who lack plasma cells and all forms of immunoglobulin; the thymus is normal, however, as is the capacity to develop cell-mediated specific immunity. A reasonable state of health may be maintained in such males by regular transfusions of immunoglobulins obtained from normal adults. In another hereditary defect (thymic aplasia), the thymus fails to develop, and the immunity dependent on T-lymphocytes is absent; infants born with this defect have functioning B-lymphocytes and can make immunoglobulins, although the capacity to make antibodies is impaired because the cooperative effect provided by T-lymphocytes is unavailable. Survival of infants born with thymic aplasia is usually brief; in a less severe and later occurring disease accompanied by thymic deficiency (ataxia telangiectasia), survival may be prolonged. In the most extreme hereditary condition, alymphocytic agammaglobulinemia, both T- and B-lymphocytes fail to develop and only a rudimentary thymus is present. Both lymphocytes and immunoglobulins are lacking, and victims die within a short time. Intermediate forms of this type of hereditary disease also occur; some are characterized by the inability to make particular classes of immunoglobulin, presumably because of defects in the genes controlling the synthesis of H chains.

Failure to produce adequate numbers of lymphocytes can be caused in ways similar to those described above for acquired failure of nonspecific immunity. In addition, some viruses preferentially damage lymphocytes. Specific immunity is commonly depressed in subjects with advanced malignant disease, even when this does not involve the lymphoid tissues.

BIBLIOGRAPHY. W.C. BOYD, *Fundamentals of Immunology*, 4th ed. (1967), a good general account of immunology, mainly from the point of view of immunochemistry; F.M. BURNET, *Cellular Immunology* (1969), a clear and well-documented account of the development of current concepts concerning the cellular basis of the immunological response, written by the world-famous immunologist who first proposed them—the first half is for general reading, the second half for specialized reading; "Antibodies," *Cold Spring Harbour Symposia on Quantitative Biology No. 32* (1967), a collection of a large number of articles highlighting the problems of modern immunology (suitable for specialized reading); J.H. HUMPHREY and R.G. WHITE, *Immunology for Students of Medicine*, 3rd ed. (1970), a widely used and readable textbook, discussing immunology primarily with relation to medicine; H.J. PARISH, *Victory with Vaccines: The Story of Immunization* (1968), a well-documented nonspecialized account of the practical achievements of prophylactic immunization; M. SAMTER, and H.L. ALEXANDER (eds.) *Immunological Diseases* (1965), an authoritative reference work, mainly for specialists, concerned with the pathological consequences of immunological response; H. ZINSSER, *Rats, Lice and History* (1965), a paperback edition of Hans Zinsser's witty account, first published in 1935, of the effects of infectious diseases on man throughout history.

Concise accounts of current ideas and problems in various fields of immunology may be found in the following publications in the World Health Organization Technical Report Series: No. 448, *Factors Regulating the Immune Response* (1970); No. 423, *Cell-Mediated Immune Responses* (1969);

No. 402, *Genetics of the Immune Response* (1968); No. 396, *Immunology of Malaria* (1968); and No. 315, *Immunology and Parasite Diseases* (1965).

(J.H.Hy.)

Inca Religion

Inca religion, an admixture of complex ceremonies, practices, animistic beliefs, varied forms of fetishism (belief in objects having magical powers), and nature worship, culminated in the worship of the sun, which was presided over by the priests of the last native pre-Columbian conquerors of the Andean regions of South America. Though there was a state religion of the sun, presided over by the priests of the Incas, the substrata religious beliefs and practices of the pre-Inca peoples exerted an influence on the Andean region prior to and after the conquest of most of South America by the Spaniards in the 16th century.

Sources. Because of the absence of written records among the Incas—such as the various Mexican (*e.g.*, Aztec) cultures and the Maya possessed—there is no absolute date in the history of Peru until the arrival of the Spaniards in 1527. The knot-string records, the *quipu*, used by the Incas to record events and other important aspects of their culture are of little value since they impart no information without the official rememberers, the *khipo-kamayoq* (*quipu-camayoc*), who became extinct after the Spanish conquest.

Present knowledge of Inca and pre-Inca religious beliefs and practices is derived from archaeological studies and the written records of the Spanish conquerors and native writers who composed their works either in Spanish or in the native languages that had been reduced to alphabets, such as in the language of the people of the Incas (Quechua). The first grammar and lexicon in Quechua was published in 1595, though initial efforts in this direction had been made soon after the arrival of the Spaniards. The first known of the many Spanish accounts of Inca life and customs was that of the Anonymous Conqueror in 1532; it was followed by the reports and observations of many Spanish soldier-secretaries. The first extensive examination of the Incas, their organization and history, was given by Pedro de Cieza de León, a Spanish soldier, in 1553. By this time Westerners were made aware that the Inca Empire was composed of hundreds of distinct languages and tribes, some so recently conquered that their oral histories had survived. The Cholo chroniclers (part Inca, part Spanish), called the "new race," then began to relate the native ethnic histories. The Cholo Felipe Guamán Poma de Ayala (born 1534) wrote a 1,200-page letter, including 400 of his own drawings, addressed to the King of Spain. This document, which gave details of the various ethnic groups, Inca agricultural cycles, and Inca festivals, was unknown until the early part of the 20th century, when it was discovered in the Royal Library at Copenhagen. Another Cholo, Garcilaso de la Vega (the son of a Spanish knight and a royal Inca lady and thus called "El Inca"), published the *Royal Commentaries,* a history from the Inca's point of view, in 1609. This was followed by many other histories by inquiring native Roman Catholic priests, some of whom were of the "new race," who thus had an interest in the religious beliefs and practices of the pre-Spanish period. Because there are no known pre-Spanish, written records of Inca and pre-Inca religion, archaeological evidence alone, though significant, does not provide the kind of material that is as informative as that of other ancient civilizations (*e.g.*, the Aztec and Maya).

The Cholo chroniclers

History. Systematic archaeolgy, especially in the 20th century, confirmed that the Andean civilization centring in Peru preceded the Incas by thousands of years and that the Inca civilization was built upon and enriched by several pre-existing cultures. The religions of the pre-Inca peoples were polytheistic (believing in many gods); they involved the practice of ancestor worship and included various aspects of magic (*e.g.*, amulets, fertility figurines, and *apacheta*, or piles of stones). The peoples of the Chavín culture (1200–400 BC), named for the site (Chavín de Huánter) in the lower Andes where impressive buildings were discovered in the latter part of the 19th century, venerated a ferocious looking jaguar-god, which is depicted on pottery, stonework, and weavings. Among the coastal Paracas (*c.* 700 BC–*c.* AD 100) south of Lima (in Peru), the feline type of god has been found in weavings discovered in graves in 1925. Little else is revealed about their religious beliefs, though their advanced material culture is obvious. The peoples of the Nazca culture (*c.* AD 100–800) in southern Peru practiced a cult of the dead and, as among the Chavín and Paracas, venerated a feline-like god. The gods of the Nazcas, however, included a new element; they hold shrunken heads.

The Mochicas (*c.* 100 BC–*c.* AD 900) and the Chimú (*c.* 1000–1461) in the coastal areas and valleys north and south of Trujillo (in Peru) venerated the moon, called Si. Worship of the moon may have united these coastal peoples during the later Inca times (since the Incas were sun worshippers), both politically and religiously. Among the Mochicas and Chimú the sun was the lesser god. Temples and shrines built in honour of the moon (called Si-An, Houses of the Moon) were constructed near the coast, and the ruins and other evidence indicates that children were often sacrificed in these structures. Because of these cultures' proximity to the sea, there was also a cult dedicated to the waters (Ni) to which white maize and other things were offered. The sea rocks (called *alecpong*) also were worshipped. Among the Chimú and Mochicas every person was believed to have a guardian spirit (*hauqui*) who protected him. Since the dead were elaborately buried, there may have been a belief that the afterlife was similar to this life.

The dominant pre-Inca religion of the Andes was the Tiahuanaco (*c.* 1000–*c.* 1300) in the south highlands of Peru. The ruins of a gigantic Tiahuanaco site lie on the Bolivian side of Lake Titicaca at an altitude of 12,500 feet. The site was not metropolitan but rather religious, visited by pilgrims for several hundred years before the Spanish conquest. Though little is known about the religious rituals of the site, the ruins (with the famous Gateway of the Sun holding two staffs adorned with puma and condor heads) depict the motif of the weeping god, which is spread throughout the highlands and the coasts.

After 1200 the conquest by the Incas began, first south and north, then in all directions. The conquest was both imperialistic and religious. The religion of the sun god was imposed on all that the Incas conquered. The conquered were allowed to keep their respective dress, customs, and certain religious observances that did not conflict with the cult of the sun.

The religion of the sun

After the arrival of the Spaniards and Christianity, the cult of the sun was suppressed. Adaptations of the earlier native beliefs and practices occurred, however; Christian holidays were selected to be celebrated on the same days as pagan sacred times, and saints were carried from nearby villages to Cuzco in a manner similar to the practice of carrying royal mummies in pre-Christian days. Despite centuries of effort, Christianity has not succeeded in eradicating pagan elements. In popular belief, God is still identified with the sun, and prayers are still offered to the Earth Mother, who is now confused with the Virgin Mary. Santiago (St. James, in Spanish), whom the conquistadores evoked in their battles, is identified with Apu Illapu, the thunder god and giver of rain; and *huaca* (sacred, or divine) fetishes are still offered for sale. Since the Roman Catholic Church has been unable to root out the traditional beliefs of the Andean peoples, Christian holidays have been made to coincide with the Inca religious calendar. Thus, the Inca religion, albeit in a debased form, still continues among the 6,000,000 to 7,000,000 Quechua-speaking Indians.

The gods. The creator god of the Incas and pre-Inca peoples was Viracocha, who was also a culture hero. Creator of earth, man, and animals, Viracocha has a long list of titles: Lord Instructor of the World, the Ancient One, the Old Man of the Sky. Some would have him creator of the Tiahuanaco civilizations, of which the Incas were the cultural heirs. Viracocha went through several transmogrifications (alterations, often with grotesque or humorous effects). He made peoples, destroyed them, re-created them of stone; and when they were re-created, he dispersed mankind in four directions. As a culture hero he taught people various techniques and skills. He journeyed widely until he came to the shores of Manta (Ecuador), where he set off into the Pacific—some say in a boat made of his cloak, others that he walked on the water. This part of the myth was seized upon by present-day mythmakers, and, as Kon Tiki, Viracocha was said to have brought Inca culture to Polynesia.

Viracocha was the divine protector of the Sapa Inca (emperor) Pachacuti (died 1471); he appeared to Pachacuti in a dream when the Inca's forces were being besieged by the Chancas. Upon victory, Pachacuti raised a temple to Viracocha in Cuzco. He was represented by a gold figure "about the size of a ten-year-old child."

Inti, the sun god

Inti, the sun god, was the ranking deity in the Inca pantheon. His warmth embraced the Andean earth and matured crops; and as such he was beloved by farmers. Inti was represented with a human face on a ray-splayed disk. He was considered to be the Incas' divine ancestor: "my father" was a title given to Inti by one lord-Inca.

Apu Illapu, the rain giver, was an agricultural deity to whom the common man addressed his prayers for rain. Temples to Illapu were usually on high structures; in times of drought, pilgrimages were made to them and prayers were accompanied by sacrifices—often human, if the stress was sufficient. The people believed that Illapu's shadow was in the Milky Way from whence he drew the water that he poured down as rain.

Mama-Kilya, wife of the sun god, was the Moon Mother, and the regulator of woman's menstrual cycle. The waxing and waning of the moon was used to calculate monthly cycles from which the time periods for Inca festivals were set. Silver was considered to be tears of the moon. The stars had minor functions. The constellation of Lyra, which was believed to have the appearance of a llama, was entreated for protection. The constellation Scorpio was believed to have the shape of a cat; the Pleiades were called "little mothers" and festivals were celebrated on their reappearance in the sky. Earth was called Paca-Mama, Earth Mother. The sea, which was relatively remote to the Incas until after 1450, was called Mama Qoca, the Sea Mother.

Practices and institutions. *Temples and shrines.* Temples and shrines housing fetishes of the cult were occupied by priests, their attendants, and the Chosen Women (*aclla cuna*). In general, temples were not intended to shelter the celebrants, since most ceremonies were held outside the temple proper. The ruins of the Temple of Viracocha at San Pedro Cacha (Peru), however, had a ground plan that measured 330 by 87 feet, which indicates that it was designed for other than the storage of priestly regalia.

The Sun Temple in Cuzco is the best known of the Inca temples. Another, at Vilcashuman (regarded as the geographical centre of the empire), has a large temple still existing. Near Ancocagua, one of Peru's highest peaks, "there was a temple . . . an ancient oracle held in high regard where they made their sacrifices," and on Titicaca Island, one of the largest of several islands in Lake Titicaca, there was a temple of the sun.

As the Incas conquered new territories, temples were erected in the new lands. In Caranqui, Ecuador, one such temple was described by a chronicler as being filled with great vessels of gold and silver. At Latacunga (Llacta cunga) in Ecuador there was a sun temple where sacrifices were made; part of the temple was still visible when the German explorer Alexander von Humboldt sketched the ruins in 1801.

The Sun Temple in Cuzco built with stones "all matched and joined," had a circumference of over 1,200 feet (350 metres). A fragment of the wall still extant is testimony to the accuracy of the chronicler's description. Within the temple was an image of the sun "of great size," and in another precinct, the Corincancha (Golden Enclosure), were gold models of cornstalks, llamas, and lumps of earth. Portions of the land, which supported the temples,

Incas of the eastern part of the empire worshipping at their sacred places by burning the fat of snakes, coca, maize, and the feathers of birds; they sacrifice to the jaguar not because he is *huaca* (sacred) but because they fear him and hope to placate him. Drawing by Felipe Guamán Poma de Ayala, a 16th-century Inca. In the Royal Library of Copenhagen.

By courtesy of the Hamlyn Group

the priests, and the Chosen Women, were allotted to the sun and administered for the priests.

Along with the shrines and temples, *huacas* (sacred sites) were widespread. A *huaca* could be a man-made temple, mountain, hill, or bridge, such as the great *huacachaca* across the Apurímac River. A *huaca* also might be a mummy bundle, especially if it was that of a lord-Inca. On high points of passage in the Andes, propitiatory cairns (*apacheta*, piles of stones) were made, to which, in passing, each person would add a small stone and pray that his journey be lightened. The idea of *huaca* was intimately bound up with religion, combining the magical and the charm-bearing.

Functions of priests and Chosen Women

Priests and Chosen Women. Priests resided at all important shrines and temples. A chronicler suggests that a priest's title was *umu*, but in usage his title was geared to his functions as diviner of lungs, sorcerer, confessor, and curer. The title of the chief priest in Cuzco, who was of noble lineage, was *Villac umu.* He held his post for life, was married, and competed in authority with the Inca. He had power over all shrines and temples and could appoint and remove priests. Presumably, priests were chosen young, brought up by the more experienced, and acquired with practice the richly developed ceremonialism.

In the selection and training of the Chosen Women (*aclla cuna*), only the most comely and skillful girls were chosen from throughout the realm at an early age and nurtured in the sun "convents." (Those candidates not selected were known as the "leftout girls.") Under the superintendence of old women, the initiates were sworn to perpetual chastity—unless chosen by the Inca high caste for concubinage. Their time was spent weaving textiles used by the Inca (he discarded a new one each day) as well as those used by priests and sacrificial candidates. The high priestesses, always of noble lineage, had the title Coya Pacsa and were believed to be the wives of the sun.

Divination. Divination was, as with the Romans, the prerequisite to all action. Nothing of importance was undertaken without recourse to divination. It was used to diagnose illness, to predict the outcome of battles, and to ferret out crimes, thus giving it a judiciary function. Divination was also used to determine what sacrifice should be made to what god. Life was believed to be controlled by the all-pervading unseen powers, and to determine these portents, the priests had recourse to the supernatural. Oracles were considered to be the most important and direct means of access to the wayward gods. One oracle of a *huaca* close to the Huaca-Chaca Bridge across the Apurímac River near Cuzco was described by a chronicler as a wooden beam as thick as a fat man, with a girdle of gold about it with two large golden breasts like a woman. These and other idols were blood-spattered from sacrifices—animal and human. "Through this large idol," a chronicler wrote, "the demon of the river used to speak to them." Another famed oracle was housed in a temple in the large adobe complex of Pachacamac near Lima. The *huaca* was first seen by the Spanish conquistadore Hernando Pizzaro in 1530. Its oracle was in a darkened chamber, carved from a tree trunk and covered with sacrificial blood.

Divination also was accomplished by watching the meandering of spiders and the arrangement that coca leaves took in a shallow dish. Another method was to drink *ayahuasca*, a narcotic that has profound effects on the central nervous system. This was believed to enable one to communicate with the supernatural powers.

Fire also was believed to provide spiritual contact. The flames were blown to red heat through metal tubes, after which a practitioner (*yacarca*) who had narcotized himself by chewing coca leaves summoned the spirits with fiery conjuration to speak—"which they did," wrote a chronicler, by "ventriloquism." Divination by studying the lungs of a sacrificed white llama was considered to be efficacious. The lungs were inflated by blowing into the dissected trachea (there is an Inca ceramic showing this) and the future was foretold by priests who minutely observed the conformance of the veins. On the reading of this augury, political or military action was taken, similar to the Roman practice of consulting chicken livers for favourable auguries.

The role of confession

Confession was part of the priestly ritual of divination. Should rain not fall or a water conduit break without cause, it was believed that such an occurrence could arise from someone's failure to observe the strictly observed ceremonies. This was called *hocha*, a ritual error. The tribe, or here the *ayllu*, a basic social unit identified with communally held land, was wounded by individual misacts. Crimes had to be confessed and expiated by penitence so as not to call down the divine wrath.

Sacrifice. Sacrifice, human or animal, was offered on every important occasion; guinea pigs (more properly *cui*), llamas, certain foods, coca leaves, and *chica* (an intoxicant maize beverage) were all used in sacrifices. Many sacrifices were daily occurrences for the ritual of the sun's appearance. Fire was kindled, maize thrown on the coals, and then toasted. "Eat this, Lord Sun," officiating priests objured, "so that you will know that we are your children." On the first day of every lunar month 100 pure-white llamas were driven into the Great Square, Huayaca Pata in Cuzco; they were moved about to the various images of the gods and then assigned to 30 priestly attendants, each representing a day of the month. The llamas were then sacrificed; chunks of flesh were thrown onto the fire, and the bones were powdered for ritual use. Ponchos of excellent weave or miniature vestments were burned in the offering. The Sapa Inca wore his poncho only once: it was ceremoniously sacrificed in fire each day. Humans also were sacrificed; when the need was extreme, 200 children might be immolated, such as when a new Sapa Inca assumed the royal fringe. Defeats, famine, and pestilence all called for human blood. Even a Chosen Woman from the Sun Temple might be taken out for sacrifice. Children, before being sacrificed, were feasted "so that they would not enter the presence of the gods hungry and crying." It was important in human sacrifice that the sacrificed person be without blemish. Many were chosen from the conquered provinces as part of regular taxation; "blood money" was scarcely a speech metaphor. Garcilaso de la Vega, "The Inca," and other apologists for their social system have attempted to gloss over this aspect of Inca culture; but human sacrifice was very real.

Burial practices. The people of the Incas believed in a life after death. Those who obeyed the Inca dictum: *ama sua, ama llulla, ama chella*—"do not steal, do not lie, don't be lazy"—went to live in the sun's warmth. Those who did not conform to this dictum spent their eternal days in the cold earth. People were careful not to anger these undead, since they were in reality still living but had become invisible, implacable, and invulnerable; hence, there was a great preoccupation for comforts for the dead. "Indeed," writes a chronicler about the numerous burial *chulpas* (turret-like tombs) that were about Lake Titicaca, "the great tombs are so numerous that they occupy more space than the habitations for the living."

The moral dictum

Festivals. The 30-day calendar was religious, and each month had its own festival. First, there was ritual drunkenness (*taqui*), then mimetic dances of great variety and pageantry. Festivals gave the *puric* (the tax-paying Indian) a sense of belonging: the dance, the ritual, and the drink made him part of this collective form of hypnotism, and the various states of ecstasy transported him to a life beyond life. Hymns were sung. Though the Inca music has disappeared, the verses have remained.

The agricultural sequences coincided with the religious festivals. The months and celebrations of the calendar are shown in the Table.

Months and Celebrations of the Inca Calendar

Gregorian months	Peruvian months	translation
December	Capac Raimi	magnificent festival
January	Huchuy Pocoy	small ripening
February	Hatun Pocoy	great ripening
March	Paucar Warai	garment of flowers
April	Airiway	dance of the young maize
May	Aimuari	song of the harvest
June	Inti Raimi	festival of the sun
July	Anta Situwa	earthly purification
August	Capac Situwa	general purification sacrifice
September	Coya Raimi	festival of the queen
October	Uma Raimi	festival of the water
November	Ayamarca	procession of the dead

BIBLIOGRAPHY. PEDRO DE CIEZA DE LEON, *La Chrónica del Perú* (1553; Eng. trans., *The Incas*, ed. by V.W. VON HAGEN, 1959), is a well-balanced history based on 17 years of travel immediately after the conquest. GARCILASO DE LA VEGA, EL INCA, *Los commentarios Reales de los Incas* (1609, Eng. trans., *The Incas: The Royal Commentaries of the Inca*, by ALAIN GHEERBRANT, 1961), whose author was born of Spanish-Inca parentage, left Peru at 19, and in his old age wrote his commentaries, which must be taken with caution. FELIPE GUAMAN POMA DE AYALA, *Nueva Crónica y buen gobierno*, written by one of similar birth and born the same year (1534), was unknown until 1908; the drawings remain a primary source of information. The edition of ARTHUR POSNANSKY (1944) is the best; a new edition is planned by the Royal Library, Copenhagen. ANTONIO DE LA CALANCHA, *Coronica moralizada del Orden de San Augustin en el Perū*, 2 vol. (1638), was written out of his attempt to eradicate Inca paganism; he is most explicit on coastal religion. BERNABE COBO, *Historia del Nuevo Mundo*, 4 vol. (1890–95), written in the 17th century, is excellent for the author's judicious inquiries. JUAN POLO DE ONDEGARDO, *Los errores y los supersticiones de los Indios*, vol. 3, pp. 45–188 (1918), written by a lawyer who flourished about 1540, is both intelligent and compassionate. JOHN H. ROWE, "Inca Culture at the Time of the Spanish Conquest," in J.H. STEWARD (ed.), *Handbook of South American Indians*, vol. 2 (1946), is known for its succinct accuracy. B.C. BRUNDAGE, *Lords of Cuzco: A History and Description of the Inca People in Their Final Days* (1967), has an elaborate bibliography; and ALFRED METRAUX, *Les Incas* (1963; Eng. trans., *The History of the Incas*, 1969), gives an excellent summary. See also JOHN HEMMING, *The Conquest of the Incas* (1970).

(V.W.v.H.)

Income and Employment Theory

The theory of income and employment has as its central concern the problems of economic instability: fluctuations in output, employment, and prices. The ultimate objective of research in the field is to provide the foundation for stabilization policy—that is, for the systematic use of fiscal and monetary policies to improve the economy's performance. The main tasks, therefore, are to explain how levels of prices, output, and employment are determined and, on a more applied level, to furnish predictions of changes in these variables—predictions on which stabilization policy can be based.

The problems with which the theory of income and employment deals have, naturally, been of concern to economists for a very long time. As a field in itself, however, income and employment theory is fairly new. It emerged from the confluence of two developments of the depression decade of the 1930s. One was the development of national income statistics (see NATIONAL INCOME ACCOUNTING), the other, the re-orientation of theoretical thinking often referred to as the "Keynesian revolution" (named for the English economist John Maynard Keynes, 1883–1946).

STABILITY AND INSTABILITY

To understand why the theoretical contributions of Keynes are regarded as so important, one must examine the workings of a modern economy. Such an economy comprises millions of people engaged in millions of distinct activities; these activities include the production, distribution, use, and consumption of all of the different goods and services that a modern economy provides. Some of the economic units are large, with hierarchies of executives and other managerial specialists who coordinate the productive activities of thousands or tens of thousands of people. Aside from these relatively small islands of preplanned and coordinated activity, most of the population pursues its myriad economic tasks without any overall supervised direction. It resembles an immensely complicated, continuously changing puzzle that is continually being solved and solved again through the market system. A breakdown in the coordination of activities, such as occurred in the depression decade of the 1930s, is very rare—in fact, it happened on that scale only once—or this system of organization would not survive. The way in which the economic puzzle is solved without anyone thinking about it has been the broad main theme of economic theory since the time of the English economist Adam Smith (1723–90).

The problem of coordination. If one singles out a particular household from the millions of economic units and studies it over a period of time, one can draw up a budget of that household's transactions. The budget will come out as a long list of amounts sold and amounts bought. If at any time this economic unit had tried to do something different from what it actually did (cutting down, say, on meat purchases to buy another pair of shoes), the solution of the economic puzzle would have been correspondingly different. At the prevailing prices the supply of meat would have exceeded the demand, and the demand for shoes would have exceeded the supply.

The price system; role of incentives

The point is that, if the economy is to function as a coordinated system, the activities of each economic unit must be somehow controlled—and controlled quite precisely. This is done through price incentives. By raising the price of a good (relative to the prices of everything else), any economic unit can, generally speaking, be made to demand less of it or to supply more of it; by lowering the price, it can be made to demand more or to supply less. Through the conflux of prices, an individual unit is thus led to fit its activities into the overall puzzle of market demands and supplies. If economic units could not be controlled in this fashion, the market-organized system could not possibly function.

In any given situation there exists, theoretically, one and only one list of prices that will make the puzzle come out exactly right. But the amounts that economic units choose to supply or demand of various goods at any given price list depend on numerous factors, all of which change over time: the size of the population and labour force; the stock of material resources, technology, and labour skills; "tastes" for particular consumer goods; and attitudes toward consumption as against saving, toward leisure as against work, and so on. Government policies—tax rates, expenditures, welfare policies, money supply, the debt—also belong among the determinants of demand and supply. A change in any of these determinants will mean that the list of prices that previously would have equilibrated all of the different markets must be changed accordingly. If prices are "rigid," the system cannot adjust and coordination will break down.

Price flexibility. For coordination of activities to be preserved (or restored) when the economy is disturbed by changes in these determinants, something still more is required: each separate price must move in a direction that will restore equilibrium. This necessity for prices to adjust in certain directions may be expressed as a communications requirement. To put it in somewhat extreme form: for a given economic unit to plan its activities so that they will "mesh" with those of others, it must have information about the intentions of everyone else in the system. When one of the determinants underlying market supplies and demands changes so as to disequilibrate the system, ensuing price movements must communicate the requisite information to everyone concerned.

One may suppose, for example, that in some period of political crisis the supply of crude oil from the Middle East is cut off. The immediate result will be a worldwide excess demand for oil and oil products of large proportions—that is, supply will fall far short of demand at going prices. At the same time, those who derive their income from Middle East oil production will have their incomes reduced, and excess supplies will emerge in the markets for the goods on which those incomes previously were spent. For the system to adjust, orders will have to go out to all demanders to cut down on their consumption of oil and for all other suppliers of oil to increase their output so that the gap between demand and supply can be closed. This is, in effect, what a rise in the world price of oil and oil products will accomplish—millions of gasoline and heating oil users the world over will respond to the pinch of higher prices, and the higher prices will also create a profit incentive for supply to be increased. (Falling prices will, in an analogous manner, close the gaps in the markets in which the initial disturbance caused excess supplies to develop.)

Prices that are not rigid for some institutional reason will move in response to excess demands and excess supplies. When demand exceeds supply, disappointed buyers will bid up the price; when supply exceeds demand, unsuccessful suppliers will bid it down. This mechanism solved the excess demand for the oil problem in the illustration above. The question, however, is whether throughout the system as a whole it will always act so as to move each of the prices toward its general equilibrium value.

Causes of depression

Keynes said no. He maintained that there can be conditions under which excess demands (or supplies) will not be "effectively" communicated so that, although certain prices are at disequilibrium levels, no process of bidding them away from these inappropriate levels will get started. This is the flaw in the traditional conception of the operation of the price system that prompted Keynes to introduce the concept of "effective demand." To pre-Keynesian economists the implied distinction between "effective" and (presumably) "ineffective" demand would have had no analytical meaning. The logic of traditional economic theory suggested two possibilities that might make the price system inoperative: (1) that, in some markets, neither demanders nor suppliers respond to price incentives, so that a "gap" between demand and supply cannot be closed by price adjustments and (2) that, for various institutional reasons, prices in some markets are "rigid" and will not budge in response to the competitive pressures of excess demands or excess supplies. Keynes discovered a third possibility that, he argued, was responsible for the depth and duration of severe depressions:

under certain conditions, some prices may show no tendency to change even though desires to buy and to sell do not coincide in the respective markets and even though no institutional reasons exist for the prices to be rigid.

Say's Law. Many writers on economic issues before Keynes had, to be sure, raised the question whether a capitalist economic system, relying as it did on the profit incentive to keep production going and maintain employment, was not in danger of running into depressed states from which the automatic workings of the price mechanism could not extricate it. But they tended to formulate the question in ways that allowed traditional economics to provide a demonstrable, reassuring answer. The answer is known in the economic literature as Say's Law of Markets, after the early 19th-century French economist Jean-Baptiste Say.

For western Europe, the 19th century was a period of rapid economic growth interrupted by several sharp and deep depressions. The growth was made possible in large measure by new modes of organizing production and new technologies, such as the spreading use of steam power. Was it possible that output might grow so great that there would not be a market for it all? Say's Law denied the possibility. "Supply creates its own demand," ran the answer. More precisely, the law asserted that the sum of all excess supplies, evaluated at market prices, must be identically equal to the sum of the market values of all excess demands. It could be neither more nor less. In the theoretical system of traditional economics, any inequality between these sums would quickly work itself out.

An important special case should be noted. The good in excess demand might, for instance, be money. One possibility, then, is excess supply for all the other goods, matched by an excess demand for money. A situation with excess demand for money matched by an excess supply of everything else is one in which the level of all money prices is too high relative to the existing stock of money. If this is the only trouble, however, Say's Law suggests a relatively simple remedy: increase the money supply to whatever extent required to eliminate the excess demand. The alternative is to wait for the deflation to work itself out. As the general level of prices declines, the "real" value of the money stock increases; this too, will, in the end, eliminate the excess demand for money.

Involuntary unemployment. Another possible cause of a general depression was suggested by Keynes. It may be approached in a highly simplified way by lumping all occupations together into one labour market and all goods and services together into a single commodity market. The aggregative system would thus include simply three goods: labour, commodities, and money. The Table provides a rough outline (a full treatment would be both technical and lengthy) of the development of a "Keynesian" depression. One may begin by assuming (line 1) that the system is in full employment equilibrium—that is,

Model of a "Keynesian" Depression

	Excess Demand (ED) or Excess Supply (ES) for:			notes
	labour	commodities	money	
Initial state	0	0	0	Equilibrium
State 2	0	ES_C	ED_M	$pES_C = ED_M$
State 3	ES_L	0	ED_M	$wES_L = ED_M$
State 4	ES_L	ED_C	0	$wES_L = ED_C$

prices and wages are at their equilibrium levels and there is no excess demand. Next the model may be put on the path to disaster by postulating either (1) some disturbance causing a shift of demand away from commodities and into money or (2) a reduction in the money supply. Either event will result in the situation described in the Table as State 2, but the one assumed is a reduction in the money supply by, say, 10 percent. The result is shown in the right-hand column of the Table, where the quantity of commodities supplied minus the quantity demanded multiplied by the price level (p) is equal in value to the excess demand for money.

If money wages and money prices could immediately be reduced in the same proportion (10 percent), output and employment could be maintained, and profits and wages would be unchanged in "real" terms. If money wages are initially inflexible, however, business firms cannot be induced to lower prices by 10 percent and maintain output. In this example they maintain prices in the neighbourhood of the initial price level—prices, then, are also "inflexible"—and deal with the excess supply by cutting back output and laying off workers. Reducing supply eliminates the excess supply of commodities by throwing the burden of excess supply back on the labour market. Thus, output and employment (which are "quantities") give way before prices do. This brings us to State 3 where, as in the Table, the excess supply of labour times the money wage rate (w) equals the excess demand for money in value.

The lack of effective demand

If, with the system in this state, money wages do not give way and the money supply is not increased, the economy will remain at this level of unemployment indefinitely. One should recall that the only explanation for persistent unemployment that the pre-Keynesian economics had to offer was that money wages were "too high" relative to the money stock and tended to remain rigid at that level.

Money wages might, nevertheless, give way so that, gradually, both wages and prices go down by 10 percent —that is to say, a reduction of the size that would have solved the entire problem had it occurred immediately (*before* unemployment could develop). This is shown in the last line of the Table, which represents (albeit crudely) what Keynes described as a state of "involuntary unemployment" and explained in terms of a failure of "effective demand."

In State 4, it is assumed, the excess demand for money is zero. Hence there is, at least temporarily, no tendency for money income either to fall further or to rise. The prevailing level of money income is too low to provide full employment. The excess supply of labour and the corresponding excess demand for commodities (of the same market value) show State 4 to be a disequilibrium state. The question is why the state tends to persist. Why is there no tendency for income and output to increase and to absorb the unemployment? Specifically, why does not the excess demand for commodities induce this expansion of output and absorption of unemployment?

Basically, the answer is that the unemployed do not have the cash (or the credit) to make the excess demand for commodities *effective*. The traditional economic theory would postulate that, when actual output is kept at a level below that of demand, competition between unsuccessful potential buyers would tend to raise prices, thereby stimulating an expansion. But this does not occur. The unemployed lack the means to engage in such bidding for the limited volume of output. The excess demand for commodities is not effective. It fails to produce the market signals that would induce adjustments of activities in the right direction. Business firms, on their side of the market, remain unwilling to hire from the pool of unemployed—even at low wages—because there is nothing to indicate that the resulting increment of output can actually be sold at remunerative prices.

Keynes called this "involuntary unemployment." It was not a happy choice of phrase since the term is neither self-explanatory nor very descriptive. Some earlier analysts of the unemployment problem had, however, tended to stress the kind of deadlock that might develop if workers held out for wages exceeding the market value of the product attributable to labour or if business firms insisted on trying to "exploit" labour by refusing to pay a wage corresponding to the value of labour's product. With the term "involuntary unemployment," Keynes wanted to emphasize that a thoroughly intractable unemployment situation could develop for which neither party was to blame in this sense. His theory envisaged a situation in which both parties were willing to cooperate, yet failed to get together. An effective demand failure might be described as "a failure to communicate."

The failure of the market system to communicate the

necessary information arises because, in modern economies, money is the only means of payment. In offering their labour services, the unemployed will not demand payment in the form of the products of the individual firms. If they did, the excess demand for products would be effectively communicated to producers. The worker must have cash in order to exercise effective demand for goods. But to obtain the cash he must first succeed in selling his services.

When business begins to contract, the first manifestation is a decrease in investment that causes unemployment in the capital goods industries; the unemployed are deprived of the cash wage receipts required to make their consumption demands effective. Unemployment then spreads to consumer goods industries. In expansion, the opposite occurs: an increase in investment (or in government spending) leads to rehiring of workers out of the pool of unemployed. Re-employed workers will have the cash with which to exert effective demand. Hence business will pick up also in the consumer goods industries. Thus the theory suggests the use of fiscal policy (an increase in government spending or a decrease in taxes) to bring the economy out of an unemployment state that is due to a failure of effective demand.

Another observation may be made on Keynes's doctrine of effective demand. The fact that the persistence of unemployment will put pressure on wages also turns out to be a problem. The assumption in the foregoing discussion was that money wages were at the equilibrium level. Unemployment will tend to drive them down. Prices will tend to follow wages down, since declining money earnings for the employed will mean a declining volume of expenditures. In short, both wages and prices will tend to move away from, rather than toward, their "correct" equilibrium values. Once the economy has fallen into such a situation, Keynes pointed out, wage rigidity may actually be a blessing—a paradoxical conclusion from the standpoint of traditional economics.

THE CIRCULAR FLOW OF INCOME AND EXPENDITURE

A proper understanding of income and expenditure theory requires some acquaintance with the concepts used in national income accounting. These accounts provide quantitative data on national income and national product. Reliable information on these was, for the most part, not available to economists working on problems of economic instability before the 1930s. Modern economics differs from earlier work most markedly in its quantitative, empirical orientation. The development of national income accounting made this possible.

Economic sectors

The definitions of the major components of national income and product may, accordingly, be introduced in the course of explaining income and employment theory. The basic characteristic of the national income accounts is that they measure the level of economic activity in terms of both product supplied and of income generated. Correspondingly, national income analysis divides the economic system into distinct *sectors*. The simplest approach uses two sectors: a business sector and a household sector. All product is regarded as created by the business sector (thus, self-employed persons have to be treated as businesses in earning their income and as households in disposing of it). Final goods output is divided into two components: consumer goods produced for sale to households and investment goods for sale to firms. Similarly, all income is generated in the business sector and none of it in the household sector (nonmarket activities, such as the work of housewives or the home improvements of husbands, are simply not counted in national product and income). The level of income generated equals the market value of final goods output.

Next is the household sector. All resources in the economy ultimately belong to households. The households, therefore, have claim to all of the income generated through the utilization of these resources by firms in creating the national product. Not all of the income is, however, actually paid out to households, since corporations retain part of their earnings. In building a simple model of the economy, one can disregard the "gross business saving" item of the national income accounts and deal with income as if it were all paid out (which means adopting the fiction that retained earnings are first paid out to shareholders who then reinvest the same amount in the same firms). The households, finally, dispose of their income in two ways: as expenditure on consumption goods and as saving.

The foregoing discussion has made two accounting statements involving income. First, income *generated* (Y) equals the value of consumption goods output (C^s) plus the value of investment goods output (I): $Y \equiv C^s + I$. Second, consumption goods expenditures (C^d) plus savings (S) equal income *disposal:* $Y \equiv C^d + S$. Both equalities hold simply because of the way that the variables are defined in the national income accounts. They hold true, moreover, whatever the actual level of income happens to be. Such equalities, which are true simply by definition, are called *identities* (and are marked as such by using the sign $\equiv$ instead of the usual equality sign). Another accounting convention may be noted here. Investment (I) is defined to include any discrepancy between consumer goods produced and consumer goods sold. If production exceeds sales, the unsold goods are part of inventory investment; if sales exceed output, inventory investment is negative, and I is reduced by the corresponding amount. It follows that C^s and C^d must be identically equal, so that it becomes unnecessary to distinguish between them by superscript. Since income generated is identically equal to income disposal, finally, it is clear that actual investment must always equal actual saving: $I \equiv S$. Investment is the value of additions to the system's stock of capital. Saving is the increase in the value of the household sector's wealth. (For treatment of depreciation and of capital gains and losses in this connection, see NATIONAL INCOME ACCOUNTING.) For the system as a whole, the two must be equal.

Figure 1 shows the circular flow of income and expenditures connecting the two sectors. Investment and consumption expenditures add up to the *aggregate demand* for final goods output. The value of final goods output is paid out by the business sector as income to the household sector. The major part of income goes back to the business sector as expenditures on consumption goods; the remainder is allocated by households to saving. Corresponding to the counterclockwise money flow (but not shown) is the clockwise flow of the things that the money is paid for: labour and other resource services from households to firms in exchange for money income; consumer goods and services in exchange for consumption expenditures from firms to households; and equities, bonds, and other debt instruments issued by firms in return for the funds saved by households.

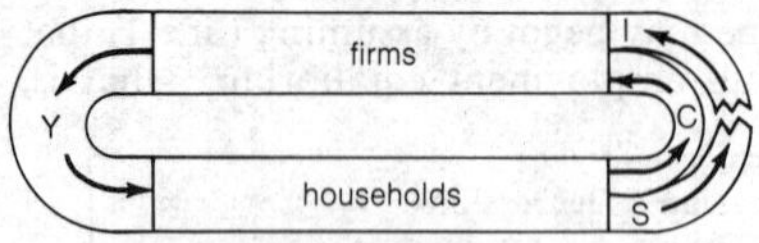

Figure 1: The circular flow of income expenditures (see text).

Figure 1 shows a break in the flow of saving as it passes into investment. From the accounting standpoint—where investment necessarily equals saving—there is no rationale for this. It has been done here to focus attention on the point in the circular flow that, in the income–expenditure theory, represents the causal nexus in the income-determining process. This theory, in its simplest form, is the next topic.

A SIMPLE INCOME–EXPENDITURE MODEL

The dynamics of income and expenditure

Because accounting identities—between gross national product and gross national income, between saving and investment, and so on—express relationships that must hold whatever the level of income, they cannot be used to explain what determines the particular level of income in a given period or what causes the level of income to change from one period to the next. The explanation of what happens must be based on statements about the behaviour of the participants in the economic system; in the present context, this means the behaviour of firms and households.

The following oversimplified model of an economy assumes that the business sector will be satisfied to maintain *any* given level of output as long as *aggregate demand* (that is, expenditures on final goods) exactly equals the volume of income generated at that level of output. If, in a given period, aggregate demand exceeds the income payments made by firms in producing that period's output, firms will be expanding in the next period; if aggregate demand falls short of the income payments made, firms will contract in the next period. The naïveté of this supply hypothesis is evident from the fact that the behaviour of firms is described without any reference to the costs of their inputs or to the price of their outputs; the business sector passively adapts output and income generated to the level of aggregate demand. In this model, the level of income is entirely determined by aggregate demand. Firms will act so as to maintain that income flow if, and only if, the exact same amount as they pay out as incomes "comes back to them" as spending on final goods output. If aggregate demand shrinks, production and employment will decline and there will be downward pressure on the price level; if aggregate demand swells, there will be an inflationary problem.

Leakages and injections. In the system of Figure 1, all of the income generated accrues to households. Households allocate their income to consumption and saving. With consumption there is no problem—it constitutes spending on final goods. Saving, however, does not constitute spending on final goods output. This part of the income generated by the business sector does not automatically come back to it in the form of revenue from sales. Saving, therefore, may be treated as a *leakage* from the circular flow.

Investment, which consists of spending of capital by the business sector on new plant and equipment and on desired additions to inventories, is, in the same terminology, an *injection* into the circular flow. If, for example, investment and saving each amount to $20,000,000 per year, the leakage and the injection will balance. But if saving is $20,000,000 per year and the injection of investment expenditures is only $10,000,000 per year, there will be a disequilibrium. Unsold goods will accumulate at an annual rate of $10,000,000. The business sector, however, will not rest content with this state of affairs but will act to reduce output, employment, and (perhaps) prices. Households will be forced to reduce their consumption spending. The reduction of income will go on until the planned (or desired) rates of saving and investment become equal. A similar argument will show that, if the leakage of planned saving were to fall short of the injection of planned investment, the level of income would rise.

When income is at a level such that there is no ongoing tendency for it to change in either direction, the system is in "income equilibrium." The simple system depicted in Figure 1 is in income equilibrium when the condition shown by this equation is fulfilled: I = S. This is not, however, the accounting identity discussed earlier. The symbols I and S now refer to planned, or desired, magnitudes, which may very well be unequal. When planned investment exceeds planned saving, income will be rising. When planned saving exceeds planned investment, income will be falling. An equivalent way of stating the above "equilibrium condition" is to write Y = C + I. In this equation the left-hand side is actual income and the right-hand side is planned aggregate demand.

This is the simplest class of income-determination model. It makes no allowance for international trade or government economic activity. Those may be treated in the same way that saving and investment were treated—as leakages or injections. Thus exports constitute spending by foreign nationals on domestic goods—an injection. Imports constitute spending out of domestic income on foreign goods—a leakage. Taxes are taken out of the circular flow—a leakage—whereas government expenditures are an injection. The effects of these leakages and injections on the level of income are analogous to those of saving and investment. If income is initially at an equilibrium level, an increase in a leakage (if not at the same time offset by a decrease in another leakage or an increase in an injection) will cause income to fall. An increase in an injection (not offset by a decrease in another injection or an increase in a leakage) will cause income to rise. An income equilibrium is reached when the sum of all leakages is balanced by the sum of all injections.

The multiplier. The simple income–expenditure model of the economy is not a complete model. It suffices to show only the *direction* of the change in income that would result from, say, a decline in planned investment (or a rise in taxes or a decline of exports). It does not show the *extent* of the income change.

The role of the consumer

To do this the model must be expanded to include a description of how consumers spend their incomes. For the sake of the exposition, one may assume that the spending of households varies according to the size of their incomes. A simple way of putting this is the following equation: $C = a + by$. In this equation the coefficient a is a constant indicating the amount that households will spend on consumption independently of the level of income received in the current period, and the coefficient b gives the fraction of each dollar of income that will be spent on consumption goods.

If one were able to obtain reliable quantitative information on the volume of investment spending being planned and on the coefficients a and b of the "consumption function" above, one could then calculate the value of aggregate demand (C + I) for every possible level of income Y. Only one of these alternative levels of income is an equilibrium one; that is, one for which aggregate demand will ensure that all of the income paid out by firms "comes back" to the business sector as spending on final goods. The equilibrium condition is: Y = C + I.

Figure 2 shows how the level of income in the system is determined, on the assumption that investment is $20,000,000, that the coefficient a is $20,000,000, and that the coefficient b (the fraction of each dollar of income that consumers will spend) is 0.6. The horizontal axis measures income, the vertical, aggregate demand (C + I). The line drawn at a 45° angle (from 0) contains all of the points at which *suppliers* might be in equilibrium; *i.e.*, the points in the space at which aggregate demand would have the same value as income. The investment schedule (marked $I = \bar{I}_0$) is drawn parallel to the income axis at height 20, showing that investment spending does not depend on income. The consumption function (marked $C = a + by$) starts at 20 on the vertical axis (the value of a) and rises 60 cents for each dollar of income (the value of b) to the right. The aggregate demand schedule (marked $C + \bar{I}_0$) is obtained by the vertical summation of the C and $\bar{I}_0$ schedules. It contains all of the points at which *demanders* would be in equilibrium, showing, for each level of income, the volume of spending on final goods that they would be satisfied to maintain.

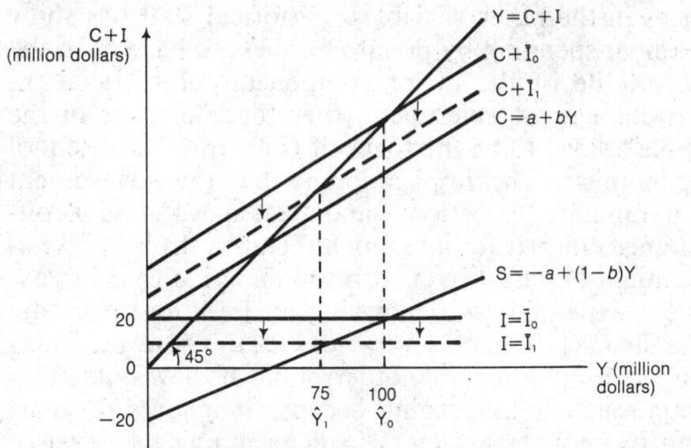

Figure 2: Relation between income and aggregate demand (see text).

The only position that demanders and suppliers will both be satisfied to maintain is given by the intersection of the aggregate demand schedule with the 45° line. In

Figure 2 this point ($\hat{Y}_0$) is found at an income level of \$100,000,000. For this simple system, which has but one leakage and one injection, the equilibrium level of income may equally well be regarded as determined by the condition that planned saving equals planned investment. Since saving is defined as household income not spent on consumption (*i.e.*, $Y - C \equiv S$), one obtains (by substituting $a + by$ for c) the saving schedules $S = -a + (1 - b) Y$, which in Figure 2 is shown to intersect the investment schedule at Y = \$100,000,000.

Figure 2 shows what will happen if this equilibrium is disturbed. Consider a (temporary) situation in which income is running at *more than* \$100,000,000 per year. At all levels of income to the right of $\hat{Y}_0$ aggregate demand ($C + \bar{I}_0$) is seen to fall below supply as given by the 45° line. (Also, saving exceeds investment.) The business sector will not be willing to maintain this state of affairs but will contract. *An excess supply of final goods is associated with falling income.* Similarly, at income levels to the left of $\hat{Y}_0$, where investment exceeds saving, aggregate demand will exceed supply. *An excess demand for final goods is associated with rising income.*

Finally, Figure 2 shows how much income would fall as a result of a decline in investment by \$10,000,000 per year (*cf.* the dotted lines). The decline in investment is shown by the shift of the investment schedule from $\bar{I}_0$ to $\bar{I}_1$, which results in a downward shift of the aggregate demand schedule from $C + \bar{I}_0$ to $C + \bar{I}_1$. The new income equilibrium ($\hat{Y}_1$) is found at Y = \$75,000,000.

Thus a change in investment spending (ΔI) of \$10,000,000 is found to lead to a change in income (ΔY) of a larger amount, here \$25,000,000, which is to say, by a multiple of 2.5. The reason is that, when the \$10,000,000 is transmitted to households as income, households will increase their consumption spending by \$6,000,000 ($b \times$ \$10,000,000). This rise in consumption spending again raises income, and of this additional income 60 percent is also spent on consumption—and so on. Each time, 40 percent of the increment to income "leaks" into saving. The relationship between the initial change in "autonomous spending" (ΔI) and the change in the level of income (ΔY), which will have taken place once this process has run its course, is given by:

$$\Delta Y = \left(\frac{1}{1 - b}\right) \Delta I$$

where, following Keynes, the expression $\left(\frac{1}{1 - b}\right)$ is called the "Multiplier."

Stabilization policy. The model of income determination presented above is exceedingly simple; it captures little of the complexity of a modern industrialized economy. It does, however, suggest one approach to the problem of stabilizing the economy at a high level of income and employment. Assuming that the consumption function is fairly stable (*i.e.*, that the level of consumption spending associated with any level of income can, with a fair degree of accuracy, be predicted on the basis of past experience), fluctuations in income may be attributed to changes in the other variables. Historical statistics show investment spending by private business to have been the most volatile of the major components of national income; changes in investment, therefore, tend (as in the example above) to be the focus of concern for one school of economists. The implication is that the government can manipulate "injections" and "leakages" so as to offset changes in private investment. Thus a drop in investment might be offset by a corresponding increase in government expenditures (increasing an injection) or a decrease in taxes (decreasing a leakage). These measures belong to fiscal policy. Another point of view holds that this approach is misleading because it ignores the part played by monetary factors in determining the level of economic activity. The following discussion presents an alternative model, which, though equally simplistic, suggests that primary reliance be put on monetary policy.

A SIMPLE QUANTITY THEORY MODEL

"Money" in what follows may be taken to refer to currency (coins and notes) plus the checking deposit liabilities of commercial banks. For the sake of brevity, the model developed in the preceding section will be referred to as the income model. The naïve quantity theory model that will be explained here may be labelled the money model.

The dynamics of income and money

The income model dealt with changes in money income in terms of the demand for and supply of output. The money model focusses on the supply of and demand for money. The income model explained the determination of the level of income in terms of relationships between its component flows. The money model emphasizes the relationship between money supply and income. The structure of the income model was based on the distinction between household and business (and government) sectors. In the money model, the distinction is between the banking sector (supplying the money) and the nonbanking sectors (the demanders). The concept of income is the same in both models.

In the money model, the supply of money is treated with the same simplicity that was accorded investment in the income model—as "autonomously" determined, which is to say that it is not affected by other factors: $M^s = \bar{M}$. This assumes that the central bank is able completely to control the stock of money, which is held at whatever level the bank desires.

The dynamic relationship in the income model was the consumption function. Here it is the money demand function. The amount of money demanded is assumed to vary with income (and, in this naïve version of quantity theory, with nothing else). The simplest relationship between income and the demand for money would be: $M^d = kY$. Here, k is a constant. Since Y is a flow (measured per year) and M^d a stock (the average stock of money over the year), k has the dimension of a "storage period." If $k = 1/4$, for example, the equation states that the nonbanking public desires on the average to hold a cash balance that is equal to the total of three months' income.

Since there is a determined amount of money in the system, it can be in equilibrium only when the nonbanking sector is satisfied to hold exactly the amount of money that exists, no more and no less: $M^d = M^s$. The system represented by these three equations is shown in Figure 3. The determination of income in the system is shown by assuming M^s = \$25,000,000 and $k = 1/4$. The amount of money demanded is equal to supply when income is \$100,000,000. A reduction of the money supply to \$20,000,000 will cause income to decline to a level of \$80,000,000 per year.

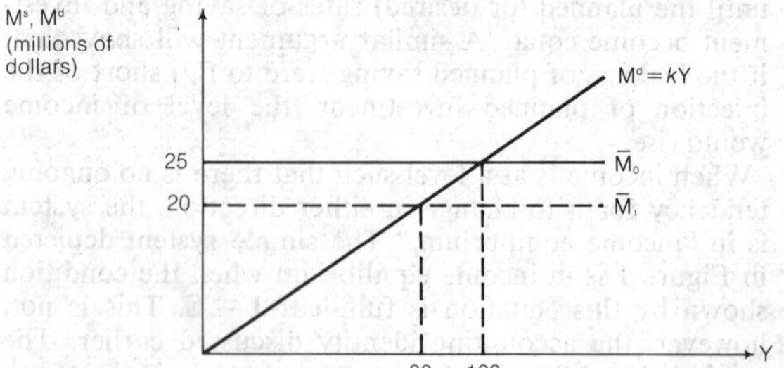

Figure 3: Relation between money demand and income (see text).

Changes in cash balances

Figure 3 shows what will happen if income temporarily exceeds the figure of \$100,000,000 per year. To the right of $\hat{Y}_0$, the amount of money demanded exceeds the existing stock of it. The way for an individual to build up his cash balance is to reduce his disbursements below his receipts. But his spending (to the extent that it is spending on final goods at least) is somebody else's income. A general attempt to build up cash balances cannot succeed—it does not induce an increase in the money supply in this model—because it will result in a decline of income throughout the system. This decline will continue to whatever level is required to make the nonbanking sector bring the amount of money it demands into line with the amount in existence. *An excess demand for money is associated with falling income.* Similarly, if the amount of money demanded falls short of the amount supplied, an individual may decide to reduce his cash balance by increasing his disbursements—but the money stays in the system; incomes will rise all around. *An excess supply of money is associated with rising income.*

The stabilization policy that this model suggests is obvious: if the relationship between income and the demand for money is stable, the system can be maintained in equilibrium by keeping the money supply constant or, in a growing economy, by allowing the money stock to grow at roughly the same rate as real output. If the relationship between income and the demand for money is found to shift about over time, the money stock should be made to grow more rapidly in periods of increasing demand for money and more slowly in periods of decreasing demand.

The two models compared. Although the two models seem to have nothing in common—the crucial variables of one do not even appear in the other—their descriptions of what happens during income level movements are not contradictory. Falling income is associated with an excess supply of goods and services in the income model, with an excess demand for money in the money model. Rising income is associated with an excess demand for goods in the first model, with an excess supply of money in the other. Evidently the two models give only *partial* descriptions of what is going on: one model looks at the process from the "real" side only and the other from the "monetary" side. But an excess demand for goods on one side will be associated with an excess supply of money on the other, and vice versa, so in this respect the two are consistent.

The controversy between the two schools of thought represented by the models has mainly to do with two issues. One issue is which set of policy instruments—fiscal or monetary—provides the best means of stabilizing the economy. The other, more fundamental, issue concerns the causes of income movements. As seen above, changes in investment were the main cause of income movements in the income model; changes in the money stock were the main cause in the money model. Simplistic as the two models are, they embody the conflicting hypotheses of the two contending schools. Income–expenditure theorists attribute the instability of income primarily to events that influence the business sector's expectations with regard to the profitability of new investment, thus influencing investment. The modern quantity theorists see the irregular time path of the money stock as the most important factor.

The gross features of economic history do not contradict either hypothesis. Private investment has indeed been the most volatile component of Gross National Product. Similarly, the movements of the money stock have conformed to those of money income: rapid inflation has been associated with a rapid growth of the money supply; severe recessions, with a decline in the money supply; and mild recessions, with a slowdown in the growth of the money supply. ("Mild" recessions may be thought of as recessions during which total employment stagnates, and the growth in unemployment, therefore, is largely due to the growth of the labour force.) The controversy has in large measure come to concern the *direction of causation:* one side maintains that shifts in investment cause income changes and infers that these in turn induce changes in the money stock which go in the same direction; the other side maintains that changes in the size or rate of growth of the money stock cause income changes that in turn will tend to fall most heavily on the investment component of income.

The problem of resolving this controversy is twofold. First, the theoretical issue is less clear-cut than implied above. Each side acknowledges that neither investment nor the money supply is autonomous and that each affects the other. The question has become, therefore, which model is "most nearly true" and which model, consequently, should be regarded as a "first approximation" in guiding stabilization policy.

Second, the empirical methods at the disposal of economists are not yet adequate for settling such issues. Attempts have been made to compare the performance of the two models by testing whether the best predictions of income are obtained by using actual data for "autonomous expenditures" and assuming that consumption will obey the consumption–income relation that has generally obtained in the past or by using actual money stock figures and assuming that money demand will obey the relation to income that has generally obtained in the past. These attempts have bogged down in disagreements on various statistical matters and must be judged inconclusive. They have shown, however, that even with consumption functions and money demand functions that are a good deal more "reasonable" than the naïve relationships above, the predictions of both models are too inaccurate for the purposes of stabilization policy.

Each model emphasizes one set of disturbances ("real" or "monetary," respectively) that will cause income to change. Each gives a partial view of the process of income-level movements. What is needed, therefore, is a third model explaining the linkages between "real" and "monetary" forces that these two simple models leave out.

A THIRD MODEL

The interest rate as the link between real and monetary phenomena

The new model brings a crucially important—but hitherto entirely neglected—element into the picture of the economic system; namely, financial markets. For simplicity, the model has only one financial market; there is only one class of financial instruments (referred to as "securities") and only one yield (a single interest rate). The standard security may be thought of as a bond promising to pay annually a fixed number of dollars. The interest rate is the value of the coupon expressed as a percentage of the market price of the bond. Consequently, if excess demand for bonds brings their price up, the interest rate falls; if excess supply sends the bond price down, the interest rate rises.

The interest nexus. The working of the financial market is depicted in the model as follows. Investment by the business sector is assumed to be financed through the issue of securities. The higher the interest rate that firms must pay on their securities, the smaller will be the investment program that they see as promising to be profitable. Thus investment will be discouraged by a rise and encouraged by a fall in the interest rate. Households, in deciding how to divide their income between consumption and saving, will consider the amount of future consumption that can be gained by abstaining from consumption now (*i.e.*, by saving). The higher the rate of interest, the larger the amount that can be spent on future consumption per dollar not spent in the present. Thus saving is encouraged by a rise and discouraged by a fall in the interest rate. Coins, notes, and checking deposits are assets on which interest is not paid. An individual who holds them has the alternative of converting some part of his money holdings into interest-bearing form. Thus the amount of money demanded will tend to diminish when the interest rate rises and to increase when it falls. The banking system creates money by buying assets from the public, paying for the assets through the issuance of additional monetary liabilities (*e.g.*, checking deposits). Banks must decide whether turning part of their cash reserves to an income-earning use is worth the risks of decreased "liquidity" entailed by lower bank reserves. Hence there is a tendency for the money supply to increase when the interest rate rises and to decrease when it falls.

In this model, then, the interest rate acts as a price in controlling the behaviour of the individual agents whose activities are to be coordinated. The interest rate itself is determined by the demand for and supply of money and securities. An increase in planned investment will be associated with the issuance of a large volume of securities. It will tend, therefore, to create an excess supply of securities, to lower securities prices, and to raise the rate of interest. Similarly, an increase in planned saving will tend to create an excess demand for securities, to raise their prices, and to lower the rate of interest. An increased demand for money will, in part, reduce the demand for and increase the supply of securities; it tends to create an excess supply of securities and to raise the interest rate. An increase in the supply of money will tend to reduce the rate of interest.

These qualitative propositions are the framework of the new model, integrating the two previous models as follows: (1) $I = I(r)$; (2) $C = C(Y,r)$; (3) $S = Y - C$; (4) $S = I$; (5) $M^d = M^d(Y,r)$; (6) $M^s = M^s(r)$; and (7) $M^d = M^s$. Here, Equations 1 through 4 restate the income model with the modification that investment is no longer simply "autonomous" but depends on the current level of the interest rate (r). Equations 5 through 7 restate the money model with the modification that the demand for money and the supply of money also depend on the interest rate. Two conditions now have to be simultaneously fulfilled for the system to be in equilibrium: desired saving must equal desired investment (Equation 4), and the amount of money that individuals and firms desire to hold must equal the amount that the banking sector desires to supply (Equation 7).

Illustrative examples. Only a partial account of the way this model works can be given here. The following illustrative examples begin with the system in equilibrium at full employment. The first illustration adopts the view of someone who has learned the income model and hence is thoroughly imbued with the idea that rising income results from an excess of planned investment over planned saving. Faced with the proposition, drawn from the money model, that an increase in the money supply will also cause income to rise, he will ask how such a change in the money supply can cause a discrepancy between saving and investment when there was none to begin with. The answer is that an increase in M^s will mean that there is an excess supply of money and a corresponding excess demand for commodities and securities, but the *immediate* impact of excess demand will be felt almost exclusively in the securities market. The excess demand for securities drives the rate of interest down—and this encourages investment and discourages saving. At that point, consequently, a "gap" opens up between desired saving and investment.

For the second illustration, consider instead someone who has learned the money model and who, consequently, knows that income falls when the amount of money demanded exceeds the supply. In Keynes's work the "disturbance" given the most play is some unspecified event that makes business firms take a darker view of the returns to be expected from new investment. Hence, the amount of investment that they will want to undertake at the prevailing interest rate declines. The question is how such a change in planned investment can cause a discrepancy between money demand and money supply when there was none to begin with. The simplest answer is that a decline in planned investment will be associated with a reduction in the amount of securities floated on the market and thus with the emergence of an excess demand for securities. This drives securities prices up, which is to say that the interest rate falls. At a lower rate of interest, individuals will desire larger money balances than before; in addition, the banks will tend to reduce the money stock somewhat. At that point, consequently, a gap will open between the amount of money demanded and the amount supplied.

Government fiscal policy

The analysis of the consequences of government fiscal action is somewhat more complicated. If the government tries to stimulate the economy through increased expenditures, the effects will be felt in at least two ways. First, the increased spending is an "injection" added to commodity demand and may be treated, therefore, from the Model A standpoint in the same way as an increase in private investment. Second, however, this spending may be financed through increased taxes, through government borrowing, through creation of new money, or through some combination of the three. The strongest effects are gained by following the third alternative, the creation of new money. The excess demand for goods and services created by the increase in spending will then be matched by an excess supply of money, which, as seen above, will drive down the interest rate and cause increased investment, etc. To the direct stimulus of the spending program, this method of paying for it adds the indirectly achieved stimulus of increased private investment. (Needless to say, the double effect on money income is not always desirable. The fact that this method of financing government spending has almost always been heavily resorted to in wartime accounts for the historical association of large inflations with wars.) The method of the second alternative, government borrowing, consists of financing the increase in spending through the issue of government bonds. This creates an excess supply of securities, driving up the interest rate. At the higher interest rate, money demand is lessened and money supply somewhat increased, but the consequent excess supply of money will be of smaller magnitude than that entailed by creating new money. The higher interest rate will also discourage private investment. Thus the indirect effects of government borrowing are seen to involve a decrease in private investment partially offsetting the initial increase in government spending. The size of this offset has become one of the major issues between "monetarist" and "income–expenditure" economists. The monetarists argue that the offset is so nearly complete that fiscal action will be largely ineffectual unless it is accompanied by an increase in the money supply, but an increase in the money supply will have almost as powerful effects without any simultaneous fiscal action. The other side concedes that fiscal action will be more powerful when financed through changes in the money supply but maintains that countercyclical variations in government spending financed through borrowing must still be regarded as an important stabilization method.

The "natural" rate of interest

The thought of Wicksell. Around the turn of the century, the Swedish economist Knut Wicksell contributed greatly to the understanding of the function of the rate of interest in the mechanism determining income and price-level movements. Assuming an economy initially in full-employment equilibrium, Wicksell analyzed the various ways in which the system might depart from that position because of discrepancies between the prevailing market rate of interest and what he termed the "natural rate." The latter rate, hypothetical rather than directly observable, may be thought of as the interest rate level that would have to prevail for the system to remain at full employment with stable prices. In illustrating the use made of this concept, one should distinguish between processes initiated by "real" disturbances (the first two examples below) and those initiated by "monetary" disturbances (the third example).

The first example is one in which business firms see increased opportunities for profitable investment. The system is already at full employment, and hence an increase in spending on investment without a corresponding decrease in spending for consumption would spell inflation. What kind of adjustment will maintain stable prices? A rise in the interest rate will (1) moderate the increase in investment spending and (2) cause households to divert some of their income from consumption into increased saving. The hypothetical level of the interest rate that will exactly match the net increase in investment with the decrease in consumption (increase in saving) is the new value of Wicksell's "natural rate." But the adjustment of the market rate may, for several reasons, come to a halt after going only part of the way to the new natural rate level. At some level of the market rate below natural rate, where planned investment still exceeds the savings that households provide for its financing, the banks may step in and finance the difference through expansion of the money supply. Thus inflation results. In Wicksell's theory there is inflationary pressure on the system associated with a market rate below the natural level and, in the version of it given here, with an increase in the money supply.

The second example involves a change in public behaviour in that households desire to save more and consume less, out of any given level of income. The decreased demand for consumption goods threatens to cause deflation (or unemployment). To prevent this it is necessary to switch resources over to investment goods production, which requires a lowering of the interest rate. Thus an increase in saving means that the natural rate of interest declines. The adjustment of the market rate of interest may again be incomplete if falling rates induce banks, say, to reduce their new lending below scheduled loan repayments, thus reducing the money supply. Part of the saving done by households then goes, directly or indirectly, into reducing the private sector's indebtedness to banks rather than into financing investment. Thus deflationary pressure on the system is, in Wicksell's theory, associated with a market rate of interest above the natural rate and, in this example, with a decreased supply of money.

The third example is one in which banks desire to expand their loans and, thereby, their monetary liabilities —creating a "monetary" disturbance. Since "real" incentives to save and to invest have not changed, the natural rate of interest has not changed. The increased supply of bank credit will, however, drive the market rate down. It goes below the natural rate, the money supply is increased in the process, and inflation is the result.

Keynes and Wicksell. Keynes first took up Wicksell's idea in his *Treatise on Money* (1930). In Wicksell's writings, discrepancies between the natural and market rates had invariably been associated with expansion or contraction of bank credit. Keynes emphasized that such discrepancies may develop and continue without expansion or contraction of the money supply, because of speculation in the securities markets. For example, if the natural rate has decreased and the market rate starts to edge down in response to an excess of the household savings offered in demand for securities over the supply of new securities marketed to finance investment, securities prices will rise. This, Keynes suggested, will cause some speculators in "old" securities to enter the market and supply savers with securities from their holdings. The excess demand pressure on the market is thus relieved and the rise in prices (fall of the market rate) halted. The motive for these transactions is the speculators' hope that they can buy back their securities at lower prices later. In the meantime, the speculators hold their funds in the form of ready money; there has been an increase in the amount of money demanded rather than, as Wicksell assumed, a decrease in the supply.

The Wicksell–Keynes theory was an important contribution to the theory of the income-determination process. Yet there is nothing in its main elements that should have startled a pre-Wicksellian traditional economist. The natural rate is essentially the interest rate that would prevail in general equilibrium, and a market rate different from the natural rate is a disequilibrium interest rate. Traditional economics was clear enough as to the consequences that will follow if one or more of the prices in the system "gets stuck" at a disequilibrium level. The Wicksell–Keynes theory, therefore, may be regarded as a particular application of previously familiar principles.

Keynes returned to the Wicksellian theme in *The General Theory of Employment, Interest and Money* (1936), but in that revolutionary work he gave the theory a genuinely novel twist: he argued that the system might be seriously out of equilibrium even though the prevailing interest rate was exactly at the Wicksellian natural level. This might happen because the interest rate mechanism cannot ensure that the plans of households and business firms with regard to future consumption and production will mesh with each other. There might, for example, be an increase in household saving—that is, a decrease in the demand for current consumption goods and an increase in the planned demand for future goods. Coordination of household and business activities requires that business firms respond by shifting resources out of the production of present consumption goods and into investment activities that lay the groundwork for increased output in the future. Households, in carrying out their saving decisions, do not place contractual orders with producers for future deliveries of particular goods and services. Thus, the future demands implicit in current saving decisions may not be effectively communicated to producers, as efficient coordination would require. If producers draw up their investment plans on the basis of forecasts of future demand that do not correspond to the spending that households are prepared to undertake in the future, there will be an excess demand (or excess supply) for future output.

Such effective demand failure is not the result of changes in interest rates or in the supply of money. The logical way of dealing with it—when it occurs—is through fiscal policy measures. The effective demand doctrine is the signal contribution of Keynesian economics to income and employment theory. It is thus no coincidence that Keynesian economics has become associated with an emphasis of the use of fiscal, rather than monetary, stabilization policies.

BIBLIOGRAPHY. The basic principles of the modern theory of income analysis, often called macroeconomics, may be found in any contemporary textbook of economics. The following works are more specialized or intensive treatments of the subject: GARDNER ACKLEY, *Macroeconomic Theory* (1961), an introductory text; JOHN MAYNARD KEYNES, *The General Theory of Employment, Interest and Money* (1936, reprinted 1965), the classic theoretical work in the field; and S.E. HARRIS (ed.), *The New Economics: Keynes' Influence on Theory and Public Policy* (1947), a collection of early essays on Keynes and his ideas, representing the thinking of its time. Later evaluations by leading economists of the significance and influence of Keynesian ideas may be found in ROBERT LEKACHMAN (ed.), *Keynes' General Theory: Reports of Three Decades* (1964). A retrospective survey from a "monetarist" point of view is H.G. JOHNSON, "The General Theory after Twenty-five Years," *American Economic Review*, 51:1–17 (1961). An interesting but difficult appraisal of the development of "Keynesian" ideas is AXEL LEIJONHUFUD, *On Keynesian Economics and the Economics of Keynes* (1968). HERBERT STEIN, *The Fiscal Revolution in America* (1969), examines the relationship between Keynesian thinking and governmental policies in the United States. ROY F. HARROD, *The Life of John Maynard Keynes* (1951), offers insight into the genesis of Keynes's ideas.

Income Tax, Corporation

Nearly all countries assess income taxes on corporations as well as on individuals. Corporation income taxes apply to net profits, computed as the excess of receipts over allowable costs, but differ widely in detailed provisions and rates. Since industrialized countries generally have larger corporate sectors than less developed countries, corporation income taxes tend to be greater in relation to national income and total government revenue in the former than in the latter countries except in major mineral-producing areas. The corporation income tax is an especially productive revenue source in New Zealand, the Republic of South Africa, the United States, Canada, Australia, and Japan. Less developed countries such as Kuwait, Iraq, Venezuela, Trinidad and Tobago, Guyana, Chile, and Zambia obtain substantial funds from taxing the net income of oil and other mining corporations.

Rationale of the corporation tax. In the United States the federal corporation income tax, adopted in 1909, predates the modern individual income tax (authorized by constitutional amendment in 1913). Until World War II the corporation tax usually yielded more revenue than the individual income tax, but with wartime changes the individual tax quickly surpassed the corporation tax and by the 1960s produced more than twice as much revenue. Three-fourths of the states also levy corporation income taxes. The United Kingdom for a long time applied the income tax on corporations (companies) purely as a supplement to the taxation of individuals. Shareholders had to pay tax on dividend income only to the extent that the rate of individual tax applicable to such income exceeded the corporate rate and received refunds if that rate was less than the corporate rate. This system was modified in 1937 and replaced in 1965 by a separate corporation tax. In 1972 the United Kingdom adopted an "imputation system," which resembles in some respects that in effect up to 1965. The earlier British system continues in several Commonwealth countries.

The separate taxation of the incomes of corporations and their shareholders follows the legal principle that they are distinct entities. Some scholars argue that it also accords with economic reality, particularly for large corporations having many shareholders who do not participate actively in controlling the enterprise. They consider a corporation income tax justified as a charge for the privilege of doing business in the corporate form, as a means of covering the costs of public services that especially benefit business and as a way of capturing part of the profits of large enterprises.

Other scholars maintain that corporations act on behalf of shareholders and should be taxed only to the extent that their profits are not reached by the individual income tax. Most of them concede that a tax may have to be assessed on corporations to prevent shareholders from escaping current taxation on undistributed profits and, as their shares appreciate in value, converting this income into capital gains, which in most countries either are taxed at lower rates than ordinary income or are free of income tax. A corporation income tax also enables a country or state to tax profits earned within its borders by corporations whose shareholders reside elsewhere.

The problem of rates

Corporation income taxes are mainly flat-rate levies, rather than extensively graduated taxes with rates rising according to income as in the typical individual income tax. An acceptable schedule of progressive rates could hardly be devised for corporations because they differ greatly in scale of operations and numbers of shareholders. In the late 1960s a number of industrialized countries had corporation income tax rates on the order of 50 percent, sometimes with reduced rates for small corporations. Where the latter feature exists, safeguards may be instituted to prevent its abuse by enterprises that split into nominally independent corporations without giving up unified control. More spectacular and significant are mergers or acquisitions of corporations motivated or facilitated by the possibility of saving taxes through offsetting the losses of some against the profits of others.

Corporation taxes may be graduated according to the rate of return on invested capital rather than the absolute size of profits. This is accomplished by an excess-profits tax on profits above a certain "normal" rate of return, sometimes further graduated according to the degree to which actual profits exceed the exempt level. The excess-profits tax has been used widely during wars and other national emergencies and to a much lesser extent under other conditions. There are serious difficulties involved in determining accurately the value of invested capital and in selecting an appropriate normal rate of return.

Economic effects. Sharp differences of opinion exist concerning the economic effects of the corporation income tax, partly because it is difficult to determine who actually bears it. The traditional conclusion of economic theory is that the tax is not reflected in prices in the short run and hence must be paid out of profits. If firms try to maximize their profits, the tax will give them no reason to change their prices. The price and output that yield maximum profits before tax will yield maximum profits after tax. Although the tax must be covered by sales receipts, it is not a cost of production in the same sense as, for example, wages but is a share of profits that can be computed only after gross receipts and production costs are known. This reasoning applies equally to competitive and to less competitive or wholly monopolized industries. Certain qualifications have always been made, but they are fairly minor in nature. More important, the theory relates only to the determination of prices and output given the existing stock of capital. (The technical definition of "short run" in economics is a period of time over which the capital stock does not change.) The theory does not tell us what the long-run effects of the tax will be, although it indicates that they will be those of a tax that rests in the first instance on profit recipients rather than on consumers.

Tax shifting

This view of the incidence of the corporation income tax has been increasingly challenged. Its opponents argue that in many industries prices are decisively influenced by the actions of a few leading firms, which have as their objective not maximum profits in the short run but a target rate of return over a period of years. When the rate of corporate income tax is increased, they say, the leading firms will raise their selling prices in order to maintain the target return, and other firms will follow. According to this hypothesis, prices are not competitively determined and are generally at levels lower than those that would yield maximum profits in the short run.

The debate among economists and businessmen over the question has not been resolved by empirical research. Studies indicating that in the United States, Canada, and Germany the corporate income tax is largely shifted forward to consumers by short-run price rises have been vigorously criticized; other studies have supported a contrary conclusion.

If the tax is not shifted forward by increases in prices, it must tend to reduce the return on corporate-equity capital. (Since interest payments are nearly always deductible in determining taxable profits, the return on borrowed capital is not subject to the corporation tax.) The returns on capital in unincorporated enterprises and on bonds and mortgages will tend over time to fall as investors try to avoid the corporate tax by moving to untaxed fields. A general reduction in rates of return may curtail investment by cutting the reward for success and by reducing the amount of resources available in the form of retained corporate profits and personal savings. This will tend to reduce the rate of growth of national product; however, the effect may not be dramatic. Capital investment is only one factor influencing growth rates, and some analyses indicate that it is less important than influences such as technological innovation and education.

If the corporation income tax falls on the returns on capital, it will be broadly progressive in the aggregate; that is, it will reduce disposable income proportionately more for high-income persons than for low-income persons. This is because the fraction of total income represented by returns from ownership of corporate stock and other capital assets rises with income. This holds, however, only in the aggregate. Some low-income people, including many retired persons, depend heavily on investment income.

On the other hand, to the extent that the tax is shifted through higher prices, it will fall mainly on consumers and, like a sales tax, be regressive with respect to income. A shifted corporation tax will not be especially harmful to investment but it may have an adverse effect on industrial efficiency and the competitive position of exports in foreign markets.

Depreciation allowances

The adverse effect of the corporate income tax on investment can be lessened by accelerating the rate at which the cost of new machinery and buildings is written off against taxable income through depreciation allowances. Accelerated depreciation may take the form of an additional deduction in the first year—an "initial allowance"—or may be spread over several years. Although the increase in early years in depreciation allowances for any one asset will be matched by a reduction in allowances for this asset in future years—the total being limited to 100 percent of cost—the acceleration is advantageous to the taxpayer. It facilitates financing of investment out of internal funds, saves interest costs, and reduces risk. Another form of incentive, the investment allowance, permits investors to deduct from taxable income a certain percentage of the cost of eligible assets in addition to depreciation allowances. The total deductions thus may exceed the cost of an eligible asset over its lifetime. A related scheme, the tax credit, reduces the income tax payable by a certain percentage of the cost of eligible forms of new investment. Alternatively, an investment grant, in the form of a payment from the government to those making certain kinds of new investment, may be provided. Investment allowances, tax credits, and investment grants reduce the cost of new equipment and plant and thus make investment more attractive. Many industrialized countries, including the United States, Canada, and the United Kingdom, have used accelerated depreciation and the other special incentives. These incentives reduce tax revenues but may be considered preferable to an outright cut in tax rates, because they are selective, being extended to firms that make new investments but not to other firms. The less developed countries, in an effort to attract investment by both foreign and domestic companies, sometimes offer accelerated depreciation or investment allowances and more often "tax holidays" that provide full exemption from income tax for new firms for the first several years of operation.

Outlays for research and development, like purchases of plant and equipment, are intended to yield returns over a period of years and are frequently given special tax treatment. In the United States, corporations and individual taxpayers may choose between deducting research and development expenditures in full when made or capitalizing them and writing them off over their useful life—or over five years if the useful life is indeterminable. Canada allows corporations to deduct, immediately, current and capital expenditures for scientific research related to the business and exempts from tax government grants to corporations for research and development.

Accelerated depreciation allowances and current deductions of research and development outlays will result in accounting losses when they exceed net income computed without regard to these deductions. The incentive effects of the provisions can be enhanced (and the discouragement of risky investment resulting from the corporation tax reduced) by permitting net operating losses suffered in one year to be offset against taxable income of other years. Tax laws commonly allow such losses to be carried back against income of prior years (thus giving rise to refunds of income taxes previously paid) or carried forward to future years. In the United States the carry-back period is three years, the carry-forward five years.

Policy issues. A major policy issue is whether income taxes on corporations and shareholders should be integrated. Partial integration may be attained by lessening or eliminating the so-called double taxation of distributed profits resulting from separate income taxes on corporations and shareholders. Full integration could be achieved only by overlooking the existence of the corporation for income tax purposes and taxing shareholders on undistributed profits as well as on dividends. This approach may be suitable for corporations having few shareholders. It is allowed on an optional basis in the United States for certain corporations having only one class of stock and no more than ten shareholders. Full integration, however, is generally conceded to be impracticable and undesirable for corporations with large numbers of shareholders.

Reducing double taxation

One method of partial integration is to apply a reduced rate of corporation tax to the distributed part of profits, as in the split-rate system of the Federal Republic of Germany. With a zero rate on distributed profits, the corporate tax would become an undistributed profits tax. The split-rate system offers a tax incentive for distribution of profits and sometimes has been advocated as an instrument for curtailing internal financing of corporations. In support of such a policy, it has been argued that liberal payouts of dividends will strengthen the capital market, improve the allocation of investment funds, and lessen the concentration of industry. Critics have questioned whether these objectives will be attained and have pointed out that larger dividend distributions would tend to reduce savings and investment because shareholders would consume part of the additional income received.

Another approach to integration is to allow shareholders a credit (offset against their individual tax liability) for the corporate tax allocable to dividends received. The system formerly employed in the United Kingdom allowed a credit equal to the full corporate tax, whereas France currently provides resident shareholders a credit for one-half of the corporate tax. A Canadian credit, like a small credit previously granted in the United States, lacked two refinements present in the French and former British systems—the inclusion in dividends of the credit and refunds for shareholders whose individual tax rate is less than the corporate rate. The omission of these features favours high-income shareholders who are subject to high individual tax rates compared with those having lower incomes. Effective in 1972 Canada adopted an extensive tax reform including, for resident shareholders, a modified dividend tax credit.

Opinions on the desirability of tax integration differ widely, as do judgments about the economic effects of the corporation tax and the nature of the relationship between corporations and their shareholders. A key question is whether the revenue that is foregone when distributed profits are relieved of so-called double taxation can be replaced by other taxes that are preferable from the standpoint of equity and economic effects.

The extent to which investment incentives in the form of accelerated depreciation, investment allowances, tax credits, and investment grants should be offered is another major policy issue. It is related to the large question of how much emphasis should be placed on present consumption, private and public, rather than future consumption that would result from increased investment. This raises philosophical and political questions as well as technical economic ones. If special investment incentives are offered, should they be varied in order to afford a greater stimulus in recession years than in boom years? This could be a useful means of cyclical stabilization, but there are obvious difficulties in deciding exactly when the changes should be made and, moreover, the variations complicate the planning of private investors.

Depletion allowances

A problem that has attracted much attention in the United States is that of depletion allowances for mineral producers. Depletion allowances are an issue for the individual income tax as well as for the corporation tax, but, like depreciation allowances, they have their chief significance in the corporate area. In order to define net income correctly, investors in exhaustible mineral deposits should be allowed deductions from gross income for depletion of these deposits for the same reason that investors in machinery and equipment are granted depreciation allowances. In the United States depletion allowances may be based on "cost depletion" or on "percentage depletion." Cost depletion spreads the cost of acquisition and development of the mineral deposit over its life. Percentage depletion is a stated percentage of annual gross income from mineral extraction (subject to a limit equal to a certain fraction of net income computed without regard to the allowance) and is not restricted to the actual costs incurred in acquiring and developing the minerals. In addition, certain capital costs of development and exploration may be written off immediately when incurred. Percentage depletion has been attacked as an unfair special privilege to mineral producers—particularly the petroleum industry, which accounts for three-fourths of the total allowances. Another criticism is that the provision results in economic inefficiency because it encourages excessive production of minerals by attracting capital and labour that could produce more in other uses. The defense offered for percentage depletion is that it is necessary to encourage sufficient exploration and production, considering the especially risky character of these activities and the strategic importance of minerals.

International double taxation. Increasing attention has been given to the prevention of double taxation between countries, since many corporations operate in more than one country, and the stockholders of a corporation often reside outside the country in which it operates. A country may tax income produced within its borders and also income received within its jurisdiction. To illustrate how double taxation may come about, consider a corporation A that has its headquarters in country X and a manufacturing plant in country Y. Country X may tax the profits earned in Y and so may Y. Further complications may arise if some of the shareholders of A live in country Z and are subject to income tax there on dividends received from A, which may also be subject to a withholding tax in X. Relief from double taxation can be provided unilaterally or by treaty. Country X may allow A a foreign tax credit for income tax paid in Y; this is done by, for example, the United States, the United Kingdom, Canada, and the Federal Republic of Germany. Alternatively, country X might unilaterally give up its right to tax certain profits earned abroad; this approach is followed by, for example, France and The Netherlands. Countries X and Z might enter into a tax treaty relieving dividends paid by corporations in X to shareholders residing in Z from withholding tax and providing some compensating advantages for X. A network of tax treaties exists among the industrialized countries, but they apply only sketchily to the less developed countries. There are doubts as to whether the standard provisions found in agreements between rich countries are suitable for agreements between industrialized countries and those at earlier stages of economic development.

BIBLIOGRAPHY. R.B. GOODE, *The Corporation Income Tax* (1951), an economic analysis and appraisal of policy implications; J.A. PECHMAN, *Federal Tax Policy*, ch. 5 (1966), a concise treatment of major issues, including statistical material; A.R. PREST, *Public Finance in Theory and Practice*, ch. 16–18 (1960), a well-known British textbook; A.J. RADLER, *Corporate Taxation in the Common Market*, vol. 2, *Guides to European Taxation* (1964), gives details for members of the European Common Market, loose-leaf volume kept up-to-date by revisions and supplements; E.R. ROLPH and G.F. BREAK, *Public Finance*, ch. 10 (1961), a leading textbook for college and university courses; D.T. SMITH, *Federal Tax Reform*, ch. 6–10 (1961), covers broad policy aspects and introduces technical issues.

(R.B.G.)

Income Tax, Personal

A personal income tax is a tax that is levied on individuals or family units and that is computed on the basis of income received. It is usually classified as a direct tax because the burden of the tax is presumably on the individuals who pay it, as distinguished from indirect taxes (such as sales taxes), which are passed on to others. Before World War II, the personal income tax was usually a class tax in the sense that most wage earners, salaried employees, and self-employed individuals were, in effect, exempted from it. Since that time exemptions have been sharply reduced in those countries that use the tax as a major fiscal instrument, so it has become a mass tax.

The income tax as an instrument of policy

As an instrument of national policy, the personal income tax has played different roles in different countries at different times. In Great Britain, where the income tax first made its appearance at the close of the 18th century, it was accepted without enthusiasm as a temporary means of raising badly needed revenue in a war emergency. It was revived in 1842 as a peacetime levy to help finance civil expenditures during a period of tariff reform. By 1914 the personal income tax had come to be regarded in a number of countries not only as an important revenue instrument but also as an instrument for achieving social reform through income redistribution. Finally, in most economically advanced countries, it has been found capable of serving as an important stabilizer against economic fluctuations because its effect on purchasing power varies inversely with changes in income and employment.

THE RATIONALE OF INCOME TAXATION

The present widespread acceptance of income taxation as the fairest kind of tax is based on the premise that an individual's income is the best single index of his ability to contribute to the support of government. Moreover, to the extent that a person's ability to pay taxes is affected by other circumstances, such as the number of dependents he has to support or the philanthropic obligations to which he is committed, it is easier to make adjustments for such circumstances by changes in the personal income tax than by changes in sales or property taxes.

The meaning of income. Still, whether or not income is an accurate measure of taxpaying ability depends on how it is defined. The only definition that has been found to be completely consistent and free from anomalies and capricious results is "accrued income," which is the money value of the goods and services consumed by the taxpayer plus or minus any change in his net worth during a given period of time. But this is not a definition that can be applied without important modifications. In the first place, it is generally recognized that changes in net worth resulting from gifts, bequests, and other gratuitous transfers cannot be included in the taxable income of the individual. Secondly, because of the difficulties of estimation, accretions to wealth are ordinarily not included in an individual's taxable income until they are "realized"; that is, converted into cash or some easily valued form. Finally, and for much the same reason, most countries have chosen not to include in taxable income such forms of imputed income as the rental value of owner-occupied homes.

In some countries the personal income tax is imposed on the total income of an individual or family unit, whereas in others income from different sources is taxed under separate rules and often at somewhat different rates. Countries with multiple schedules do, however, frequently supplement them with a progressive rate scale applicable to total income. These schedular income taxes are today found in many South American and African countries and in a few European countries, including Italy. In other industrialized nations, such as Great Britain, personal income has to be reported on one of a number of separate schedules, but assessable income is then lumped and only one tax is imposed. This kind of personal income tax is not usually regarded as a schedular tax.

The tests of equity. Before a tax on personal income can be considered to be a completely fair tax, it has to meet the two tests of horizontal and vertical equity. Horizontal equity is achieved when it can be said that persons with the same income will, under like circumstances, pay the same amount of tax. The important issue here is, of course, what is meant by "like circumstances." Clearly, two families with the same income would not be equally able to pay taxes if one consisted of husband and wife and the other of husband, wife, and four dependent children. But suppose neither family had any children but in one the entire income was earned by the husband whereas in the other both husband and wife worked. Would horizontal equity require that they pay the same or different taxes? Similar questions have been raised concerning families whose equal incomes take the form of wages and salaries in one case and dividends and interest in another or whose income has to be used to pay interest on personal indebtedness or to pay state and local taxes to a greater extent in one case than in the other. In order to compensate for those differences in the sources and uses of income that are thought to affect an individual's ability to pay income tax, most countries allow a wide variety of deductions from statutory personal income before the tax is imposed.

The concept of vertical equity relates to the taxes paid by individuals at different income levels. Clearly, they should not be the same if income is a good index of ability to pay; but how different should they be at different income levels? If a single rate of tax is applied to all personal income in excess of the allowed exclusions, exemptions, and deductions, the tax will be proportionate to taxable income. If, however, different tax rates are applicable to different blocks or brackets of income, and if these rates rise as one moves from the lowest bracket to successively higher ones, the tax will be progressive. Those countries that tax total personal income today almost always use graduated or progressive rates; those with schedular income taxes may or may not do so. The question of vertical equity relates to how much graduation there should be and over what range of personal incomes it should extend.

Many attempts have been made to develop a theory that would not only justify the principle of progression but would also result in a mathematically exact scale of equitable taxation. Some theorists, accepting the notion that the taxes a man pays ought to bear some close relation to the benefits he enjoys from the operation of government, have tried to show that, at some levels of income, benefits increase more rapidly than income. But their efforts have served to do little more than reveal the shortcomings of "benefit theory." Others, starting with the premise that an equitable tax is one that imposes equal sacrifices on individuals at different income levels and accepting the view that the utility of any given unit of money becomes less the more money one has, have tried to demonstrate that progression is needed if the sacrifices imposed on the wealthy are not to be less than those imposed on the less well off. But it is debatable whether a dollar has less utility for a very rich man than for a moderately rich man or whether it is scientifically possible to make the sort of interpersonal comparisons that the "sacrifice theories" call for.

Its merits as compared with other taxes

Another argument for income taxation proceeds from its effects on the national economy. The yield from the personal income tax tends to move up in booms and down in recessions more than do the yields of sales or wealth taxes. This is partly because personal income itself is quite sensitive to changes in the level of economic activity and partly because, under the usual progressive rate structure, when individual incomes rise the additional income received by some taxpayers is taxable at higher bracket rates. Consequently, their tax liabilities fluctuate more than their incomes. Thus the tax serves to offset the effects of expansionary and contractionary forces during business cycles.

The personal income tax reduces the amount of income individuals have available to spend on consumer goods and services or to save and invest. But this is, of course, what any tax is supposed to do. The question is whether other taxes may achieve the same end more efficiently or with fewer undesirable side effects. It has been argued that an income tax is less favourable to economic growth than a tax on expenditures (such as a sales tax) because an income tax does, and an expenditure tax does not, fall on income that is saved and made available for investment. On the other hand, an income tax does not have the distorting effect on consumer expenditures that selective excise taxes have (causing buyers to shift from taxed to untaxed items). Whether an income tax reduces the incentive to work, as some have argued, is difficult to say. To the extent that the tax reduces total income after taxes, it may lead some persons to work longer in an effort to maintain an established standard of living. To the extent that the tax reduces the reward for an extra hour's work, it may make the taxpayer decide to work less and to indulge in more leisure; presumably, the larger his income and the more steeply progressive the tax, the greater this effect will be. Finally, a progressive income tax is sometimes said to have an adverse effect on investment, especially in the case of risky ventures, but this has been shown to depend on the adequacy of the loss-offset provisions in the tax law.

Ease of administration. So long as the tax is basically a tax on realized income, and does not require an assessment to be made of accrued but unrealized capital gains and losses, it is generally held to be an easier tax to administer than either an expenditures tax or a wealth tax. A tax on consumer expenditures would require the subtraction of net saving from realized income, and balance sheets would be needed to make certain that saving was correctly reported. The administration of a wealth tax would obviously require a complete accounting for assets and liabilities.

The enforcement of the income tax in many countries, such as the United States, has been made easier by the practice of withholding the tax from wages and salaries. Although compliance is undoubtedly incomplete, this tax is still believed to raise revenue more efficiently and at a lower out-of-pocket cost to the government than any alternative tax. Finally, because its yield is so sensitive to changes in the level of national income and so responsive to slight changes in rates and exemptions, the future revenue potential of the income tax is doubtless greater than that of other taxes.

TYPES OF PREFERENTIAL TREATMENT

A corollary of the proposition that taxes should bear similarly on persons similarly situated is the proposition that when persons are not similarly situated their tax liabilities should differ. To accomplish this, the income tax statutes usually provide for (1) personal allowances or exemptions, which differentiate between large and small family units, and (2) deductions that give preferential treatment to taxpayers reporting expenditures that are thought to justify some lightening of their burden.

Treatment of the family. There are several ways of allowing for differences in family units. One is to give an exemption for each dependent, either on a flat per capita basis or in accordance with a schedule such as the one used in West Germany, where in 1970 the allowance for one child was DM 900, for two children DM 1,680, and for three or more children DM 1,800. When income is taxed at graduated rates, exemptions are worth more to high-income than to low-income families. In order to give equal tax allowances for dependents to families of the same size at different income levels, each exemption can be multiplied by the standard or basic rate of tax, and so be converted into a uniform tax credit. In India, in lieu of exemptions, the basic income tax is reduced by a stated number of rupees for each of the first two children.

But it is not only with respect to the number of dependents that families may differ in taxpaying capacity. In some families only the husband earns income, whereas in others the wife too may work. If, in a family of the latter type, husband and wife are allowed to file separate returns, their combined tax liabilities under a progressive income tax may be less than those of a family similarly situated but with a single income recipient. On the other hand, if husband and wife are required to file a joint return in which their earnings are pooled, the two families will pay the same tax; many would argue that this discriminates against the family with the working wife. The issue between joint and separate returns is further complicated by the fact that if separate returns are permitted, and are subject to the same rate structure as joint returns, families with investment income can reduce their tax liabilities by splitting up their holdings.

Various ways of dealing with this problem have been adopted in different countries. In the United States full income splitting has, in effect, been allowed since 1948 when taxpayers were given the option of filing joint returns using a rate schedule with brackets twice as wide as those in the schedule for married persons electing to file separate returns. This means that the tax on joint returns is twice the tax that would be imposed if there were only one income receiver and his income were half as large as the joint income. In Great Britain, husband and wife are treated as a single unit; their incomes are summed and taxed as one, but an adjustment is made with respect to the wife's earned income. In France, the family is the tax unit; there is only one rate schedule, but relief for family commitments is achieved by what is known as the family-quotient system. This is a form of income splitting in which the single graduated rate schedule is applied to a figure arrived at by dividing total family income by the number of "units" represented, with each child counting as half a unit. The tax, as so determined on a fraction of the family's income, is then multiplied by the number of family "units" to arrive at the family's tax liability. In West Germany, husband and wife are assessed jointly, but income splitting is allowed in the same way that it is in the United States. Sweden also has a dual rate structure, but in that country the difference between the rates applicable to married couples and to single persons varies with the level of income: in the middle income brackets, couples are more heavily taxed; in the high brackets burdens are much the same. Finally, in a number of countries, including India, Japan, Argentina, and Israel, separate returns are mandatory.

Personal deductions. Practice with respect to personal deductions also varies widely. In the United States, for example, where personal deductions represent roughly 15 percent of the adjusted gross income reported on individual income tax returns, such deductions include interest paid on personal debt, abnormal medical expenses, philanthropic contributions, and most state and local taxes. In Great Britain, on the other hand, virtually no deductions are granted that do not in some measure bear a direct relation to the production of earned income. In South America, where multischedule income taxes are the rule, some countries allow virtually no deductions, whereas in others the latitude permitted in the deduction of personal expenses is very great.

The varied treatment of medical, charitable, and other expenses

In those countries that allow the deduction of extraordinary medical expenses, a stated percentage of the taxpayer's income has to be used for this purpose before any deduction can be taken. In the United States, only those expenses that exceed 3 percent of adjusted gross income are deductible, and a similar rule is found in West Germany. On the other hand, in The Netherlands, where the minimum is set at 6 percent of income for a single individual, and, for a married man, at 6 percent less one-half of 1 percent for each dependent child, the whole expense becomes deductible once the minimum is exceeded. The justification for a deduction of this type is that medical expenses are not generally controllable and, when incurred above a certain normal level, reduce an individual's ability to pay taxes relative to others at the same income level.

The justification for deduction of contributions to religious, charitable, educational, and cultural organizations is usually found in the encouragement of socially desirable activities rather than in any allowance for differences in taxable capacity. The contributions that qualify for this deduction vary from country to country, and total contributions are usually limited to some percentage of the taxpayer's income. In the United States, the limit on the deductibility of "charitable contributions" has been 50 percent of adjusted gross income, whereas in Germany, where there is a separate allowance for church tax, charitable contributions are limited to 5 percent of income. In Japan, contributions made to government, to local authorities, or to institutions for scientific experiment or research are deductible up to 15 percent of taxable income but only to the extent that such payments exceed the lesser of either 3 percent of income or 100,000 yen. This, of course, denies any deductions to taxpayers whose contributions amount to only a small fraction of their incomes.

A third type of deduction—one that serves neither to relieve hardship nor to encourage voluntary support of socially desirable activities—is the deduction that is allowed in some countries for certain kinds and limited amounts of personal saving. These have included: (1) social security contributions and compulsory contributions to private pension funds, for which deductions are allowed in Japan, France, The Netherlands, and Belgium and (2) limited amounts of life insurance premiums, which are deductible in Great Britain, Japan, France, and West Germany. Deductions have also included limited amounts of savings earmarked for the construction of dwellings or placed in savings deposits. One justification for these allowances has been that they encourage low-income taxpayers to seek the protection afforded by life insurance, pension plans, and savings deposits. Another is that they channel the personal savings of such individuals into banks and other financial institutions where they can be used to support capital expansion. Special tax-privileged savings plans were introduced in Japan, West Germany, and Sweden during the late 1950s and early 1960s. In none of these countries, however, were they found to be particularly effective in increasing total personal saving.

Another frequently permitted deduction, the justification for which is not entirely clear, is that allowed for interest paid on personal indebtedness. In some situations this can be viewed as a cost of obtaining nonbusiness income, but in the case of interest paid on home mortgages, it is generally regarded as one of several special tax concessions granted to home owners. In the United States, there are few limitations on the interest deduction other than the denial of any deduction in the case of debt incurred for the purpose of acquiring tax-exempt securities. In Canada, on the other hand, the interest deduction is denied in the cases of consumer debt and of most home mortgages. Loan interest is deductible in West Germany as a "special expense," as it is in France on monies borrowed from third parties.

Still another deduction that does not appear to have much to do with the determination of true income is the deduction for taxes paid. In the United States this means state and local taxes on property, income, and motor fuels, as well as state and local general sales taxes. Foreign taxes on real property and income are also deductible, although most taxpayers elect instead to credit their foreign income taxes against their U.S. tax. Japan and Germany also allow deductions for local taxes, although Japan specifically excludes the income taxes of prefectural and municipal inhabitants from the exemption allowed for other taxes. Ordinarily, the tax paid with respect to income in one year is not allowed as a deduction in determining the same tax the following year, but an exception to this rule is found in Belgium in the cases of both the multischedule tax on wages and salaries and the progressive surtax on total income. Among the justifications offered for the deduction of taxes paid, the most widely accepted is that it contributes to fiscal coordination in a federal system and avoids extremely high rates in the case of overlapping income taxes.

One way of limiting the use of itemized personal deductions for taxpayers whose total deductions are small is to provide an optional standard deduction. Examples of this practice are found in the United States, where a standard deduction of 10 percent of adjusted gross income, but not exceeding $1,000, was allowed in the early 1970s, and in West Germany, where a standard deduction of DM 564 ($152) was allowed against wage and salary income to cover the expenses of employment.

Capital gains. The taxation of capital gains and losses presents a special set of problems to which different countries have found different answers. Although capital gains can result from a number of different causes, they invariably take the form of an increase in the value of a capital asset—a share of stock, a corporate or government bond, or perhaps a piece of real estate. Since an increase in the market value of any such asset increases the net worth of its owner, it may also be said to increase his income. But this is where the difficulty begins. First, there is the problem of valuing all of the capital assets a taxpayer may own so as to be able to determine how much his net worth has increased or decreased during the taxable year. In practice, this difficulty has usually been avoided by taking into account only those gains and losses that have been realized in the form of cash or its equivalent.

Second, there is the problem of deciding upon the appropriate rate at which realized gains should be taxed. One answer to this is that they should be treated no differently than other forms of income. The difficulty with this answer is that under many circumstances this would be unfair to the taxpayer and might also have undesirable economic effects. If capital gains that have been accruing over a number of years are taxed at regular progressive income tax rates in the year of their realization, the tax on them may be much higher than it would have been if the unrealized gains had been taxed annually as they accrued. The knowledge that capital gains are subject to very heavy taxes upon realization can deter individuals subject to high-bracket rates from making investment decisions that are socially desirable. This difficulty is usually handled by taxing such gains at a relatively low rate or by excluding a stated percentage of the gain from taxable income. In either case, this special treatment applies only to long-term gains involving a sold asset that had been held for a minimum length of time.

Some countries, including Canada, France, and West Germany, do not tax capital gains unless they arise out of a business, although the line between a business transaction and a personal one is not easy to draw. Countries that do not, in principle, tax individuals on their capital gains also do not allow capital losses to enter into the determination of taxable income. Those that do tax capital gains ordinarily take capital losses into account only as offsets to capital gains.

The negative income tax. The idea of a negative income tax has been considered in the United States as a method of providing very low income families with a stable subsistence level of income in the form of government payments geared into the personal income tax structure. It is viewed as a possible substitute for public assistance or as an alternative to family allowances. The basic elements of this and other so-called transfer-by-taxation plans are (1) a guaranteed minimum level of income adjusted to the size and composition of the family unit, (2) a tax rate to be applied to the difference between the family's income and some specified amount, and (3) a break-even level of income at the point at which the tax liability equals the guaranteed allowance. According to one plan, a negative 50 percent tax rate would be applied to the unused tax exemptions and deductions of families with little or no taxable income. For example, if the family was entitled to total exemptions and deductions of $3,000 and had an adjusted gross income of $1,000, it would receive "negative taxes" amounting to $1,000 (50 percent of $3,000 minus $1,000). In this case the guaranteed minimum—for a family with no adjusted gross income—would be $1,500, and the break-even level would be $3,000. Above the break-even level the family would receive no negative tax.

HISTORY OF PERSONAL INCOME TAXATION

Great Britain. The first country to enact a general income tax was Great Britain, in 1799. To finance the Napoleonic Wars the tax was imposed at a rate of two shillings in the pound (10 percent) on all incomes in excess of £200, with lower rates applying to income between £60 and £200 and income below £60 being exempt. When the war ended in 1815, the tax was allowed to lapse until 1842, when it was revived at seven pence in the pound by the prime minister, Sir Robert Peel. It was again adopted as a temporary measure, this time to enable the government to avoid budget deficits while carrying out major tariff reforms. But succeeding governments, confronted with steadily rising expenditures, were unable to dispense with a tax that was so flexible and elastic, and by the 1880s it was generally accepted as a permanent levy.

At about this time taxation began to be regarded as a social instrument; but it was not until 1910 that graduated rates were introduced and an abatement was granted of £10 per child to taxpayers whose income did not exceed £500. Then came World War I, during which time the standard rate was raised to six shillings with a supertax on top of that.

Europe. In Europe, a number of German states began experimenting with income taxes in the 1840s. But it was not until the Prussian reforms of 1891 that the income tax became an effective fiscal instrument in any of these states. Thereafter the reform movement spread to other states, and by 1913 the share of the income tax in all state tax collections had risen to about 60 percent. Until 1920, German income taxes were exclusively state taxes; from 1920 to 1945, they were federal taxes. At the close of World War II, they again became state taxes and are now regulated by federal law.

Efforts to enact an income tax in France were begun in the 1870s, but it was not until 1909 that an income tax bill finally passed the Chamber of Deputies only to be held up by opposition in the Senate. The bill was finally enacted as an emergency measure two weeks before war began in 1914, but it was another three years before a permanent income tax system was adopted.

Italy adopted an income tax in 1864 as one of the first products of its unification. The system introduced at that time was one of "objective" taxes that attempted to tax the "productive sources" of income—*i.e.*, land, buildings, and movable wealth. It was not until 1925 that a nationwide tax on total family income was imposed with graduated rates.

Among the Scandinavian countries, Norway introduced an income tax in 1892 and made its rates progressive in 1896; not until 1910 did Sweden adopt a modern income tax on a permanent basis.

The United States. During the Civil War the U.S. enacted an income tax that remained in effect from 1862 to 1872. The minimum rate in the 1862 law was 3 percent on income above a personal exemption of $600; the maximum rate was 5 percent on income above $10,000. Subsequent amendments raised the maximum rate to 10 percent on incomes over $5,000. An income tax was again enacted in 1894, after President Grover Cleveland had been elected on a platform that promised lower tariffs and other reforms sought by the farmers in the West and South. This law was, however, held to be unconstitutional by the Supreme Court, which forced its backers to seek an amendment to the Constitution that would give Congress the right to impose income taxes without apportionment among the states. In 1913 the Sixteenth Amendment was ratified, and a new personal income tax with rates ranging from 1 to 7 percent on income in excess of $3,000 for a single individual was voted by Congress shortly thereafter. At the end of World War II the minimum rate was 23 percent and the maximum rate was 94 percent; the exemption for a single individual was only $500. By 1970, 39 of the 50 states also had personal income taxes.

INTERNATIONAL VARIATIONS IN RATE STRUCTURES

Attention has already been called to several types of variations found in the income tax practices of different countries, mainly those having to do with the determination of taxable income. Something should now be said about variations in rate structures. The important variants in these structures are (1) the starting of first bracket rates, (2) the top bracket or maximum marginal rates, and (3) the income range within which rates rise from the lowest to the highest levels.

Tax brackets

In some countries, such as France and Italy, starting rates as low as 4 or 5 percent are found. In 1970, the starting rate was 14 percent in the United States, 19 percent in West Germany, and 30 percent in the United Kingdom. The lower the starting rate and the narrower the lowest income brackets, the more progressive an income tax is likely to be at low and medium income levels. Most top-bracket rates are found ranging between 55 and 75 percent, although in 1970 India had an 85 percent top rate, and the combination of the United Kingdom's 41.25 percent standard rate and its 50 percent top surtax rate amounted to a maximum marginal rate of 91.25 percent at £15,000 ($36,000). In the United States, the maximum marginal 70 percent rate in 1970 applied to income over $100,000 for single individuals and to $200,000 for married couples; in West Germany, a 53 percent maximum rate applied correspondingly to income in excess of DM 110,039 ($30,062) and DM 220,079 ($58,136). In France, where the marginal maximum rate of 65 percent in 1970 applied to income in excess of 74,000 francs ($12,960), the rate structure—as it applied to wage earners and families—was not nearly so progressive as it appeared. In the first place, a 20 percent earned income credit on top of at least a 10 percent normal standard deduction made it certain that no French worker need be taxed on more than 72 percent of his gross employment income. Second, account must be taken of a family's income-splitting opportunities. This illustrates the difficulty of making meaningful comparisons of the rate structures of different countries.

An example of steep middle-income progression is found in India, where in 1970 income in excess of 20,000 rupees ($2,666) was taxed at a 30 percent marginal rate, and income in excess of only twice that figure was subject to a 60 percent rate.

During war emergencies, high marginal tax rates on personal income are viewed as a necessary complement to wage and price controls, but their value in a peacetime tax structure has been questioned. To the extent that they cannot be avoided, such high rates weaken work and risk-taking incentives, and they yield little revenue. There are many people who believe that a personal income tax with fewer exclusions and deductions, and with generally lower rates, would make a good tax a still better one.

BIBLIOGRAPHY. RICHARD MUSGRAVE, *Theory of Public Finance* (1959), the best general treatise for persons with a good foundation in economic theory; CARL SHOUP, *Public Finance* (1969), a treatise on the theory and practice of public finance; R.B. GOODE, *The Individual Income Tax* (1964), the best guide to an understanding of the strengths and weaknesses of the U.S. individual income tax; NICHOLAS KALDOR, *An Expenditure Tax* (1955), a discussion of the theoretical and practical advantages of an expenditure tax over a personal income tax; H.C. SIMONS, *Personal Income Taxation* (1938), a classic but still timely discussion of the concepts of personal income as a basis for taxation; W.S. VICKREY, *Agenda for Progressive Taxation* (1947), an excellent analysis of many of the problems of income taxation; B.E.V. SABINE, *A History of Income Tax* (1966), a history of the income tax in the United Kingdom from 1799 to the present; E.R.A. SELIGMAN, *The Income Tax*, 2nd rev. ed. (1914), a history of pre-World War I income taxation both in the U.S. and elsewhere; U.S. CONGRESS, HOUSE COMMITTEE ON WAYS AND MEANS, *Tax Revision Compendium* (1959), a collection of papers dealing with many aspects of federal income tax reform; WILFRED LEWIS, *Federal Fiscal Policy in the Postwar Recessions* (1962), an analysis of the fiscal stabilizers and their operation during the recessions starting in 1948, 1953, 1957, and 1960; W.J. BLUM and H. KALVEN, *The Uneasy Case of Progressive Taxation* (1953), a critical analysis of the arguments for and against progressive taxation; CHRISTOPHER GREEN, *Negative Income Taxes and the Poverty Problem* (1967), on the major proposals for dealing with the problem of poverty by using the income tax system rather than welfare agencies; L.H. SELTZER, *The Nature and Tax Treatment of Capital Gains and Losses* (1951), a comprehensive discussion of the theory and practice of capital gains taxation; E.R.A. SELIGMAN, "Income Tax," in *Encylopedia of the Social Sciences*, 7:626–638 (1932); J.A. PECHMAN, "Personal Income Taxes," in *International Encyclopedia of the Social Sciences*, 15:529–537 (1968).

(E.G.K.)

India

India, also known as Bhārat, a republic in southern Asia formed of a union of states and territories, is the seventh largest and the second most populous country in the world. It covers an area of 1,261,810 square miles (3,268,090 square kilometres), with a land frontier of 9,425 miles and a coastline of 3,535 miles. At the time of the 1971 census its population was approximately 550,000,000. It has an annual population-growth rate of 2.3 percent—representing an increase of around 13,000,000 a year; the birth bulge consequently constitutes one of the country's most serious problems.

Physically, India is cut off from the greater part of Asia. The mountain ranges of the Himalayas to the north have virtually isolated the country from two of the mainstreams of Asian history—the civilization of China and the Islāmic world of the Middle East. India can claim to represent a third distinct stream of Asian history, going back to the Indus Valley civilization of Mohenjo-daro, which dates to around 2,500 BC. Ancient artifacts recovered at the site of Mohenjo-daro (located in the Lārkāna district of the Pakistan province of Sind) suggest that the religion of the Indus people was the lineal progenitor of the Hindu religion. This would make the origins of Hinduism almost coincidental with the beginnings of Indian civilization.

India's boundaries

India's neighbours to the north are the Chinese Tibetan Autonomous Region, the independent states of Nepal, Bhutan, and Sikkim, and the Sinkiang Uighur Autonomous Region of China. To the northwest, India shares a boundary with Pakistan. To the east, India is bounded by Burma, while the territory of Bangladesh forms an enclave, within India, bounded by the Indian states of West Bengal, Assam, Meghalaya, and Tripura, and the Indian union territory of Mizoram. To the south, India tapers like a triangle, with its apex pointing downward. At the Tropic of Cancer the landmass of the country thins between the Bay of Bengal on the east and the Arabian Sea on the west. The southern tip of India, Cape Comorin, is washed by the Indian Ocean. Off the cape, the Gulf of Mannar and Palk Strait separate India from Sri Lanka (Ceylon). The Andaman and Nicobar Islands in the Bay of Bengal and the Laccadive, Minicoy, and Amīndīvi Islands in the Arabian Sea are parts of Indian territory.

India is more a subcontinent than a country. Its regional diversities are reflected in the mosaic of its myriad races, languages, and religions, in the differing dress, manners, ways of life and thought, and in its wide disparities in education and illiteracy, in poverty and wealth. India's people range from the primitive to the most sophisticated. The overall literacy rate at the start of the present decade averaged barely 30 percent of the population, and the average per capita income was less than U.S. $80 a year. Since 1960, per capita real income has tended to slow down, though the net national income has increased—a paradox that is largely explained by the intimidating rate of population growth.

Within the country's socio-religious framework, strong divisive influences such as caste, the status of untouchability, and linguistic chauvinism operate. The wonder is that, despite these limitations, India still functions as the world's largest working democracy.

The paradox of India lies in its political survival, despite the age-old maze of social and economic contradictions that it has inherited. Well over 80 percent of the country's total population are Hindus, and of the Hindu population some 60 percent comprise orthodox Hindu society. Despite divisive internal pulls and urges, Hinduism is the one unifying factor that has kept the large mass of the peoples of India together. The only common link between the Dravidian Hindus of southern India and the Aryan Hindus of the north is, in fact, Hinduism.

Two great Indian nationalists—Mahatma Gandhi (*q.v.*) and Jawaharlal Nehru (*q.v.*)—exerted an immense influence on contemporary India. By encouraging women to participate actively in his nonviolent civil-disobedience movements, Mahatma Gandhi helped to emancipate them and to draw them into the mainstream of political and public life; one consequence has been that India has been able to accept a woman prime minister, Indira Gandhi. (See city articles on BOMBAY; CALCUTTA; MADRAS; and DELHI; see also articles on individual Indian states; for associated physical features, see ARABIAN SEA; BENGAL, BAY OF; BRAHMAPUTRA RIVER; EVEREST, MOUNT; GANGES RIVER; HIMALAYAN MOUNTAIN RANGES; INDIAN OCEAN; INDUS RIVER; and THAR DESERT; for historical aspects, see INDIAN SUBCONTINENT, HISTORY OF THE.)

This article contains the following sections:

The land

THE NATURAL ENVIRONMENT

The three mainland regions

Relief features. The Indian mainland comprises three broad well-defined regions. These are, first, the mountain wall of the Himalayas and associated mountains, which stretch across northern India from west to east in an irregular crescent; second, the Indo-Gangetic Plain,

1,500 miles long and 150 to 200 miles wide, which is formed by the basins of the Indian subcontinent's three great rivers—the Indus, the Ganges, and the Brahmaputra; and, third, the peninsula, or Deccan Plateau, separated from the Indo-Gangetic Plain by a mass of mountain and hill ranges varying from 1,500 to 4,000 feet in height.

While three major landforms—mountains, plains, and plateaus—are thus represented in India by distinct tracts of country, there are many topographical variations. Within the Himalayas, for example, is the Vale of Kashmir (divided between India and Pakistan), which has a plains topography.

While the geological placement of India was for long one of the puzzles of geology, it had become increasingly accepted by the early 1970s that the explanation might lie in the drifting of continental masses over the surface of the world after the breakup of the ancient continent of Gondwanaland (see CONTINENTAL DRIFT). One of these masses—peninsular India—would, according to this theory, have collided with the southern shore of the Asian landmass, causing the uplifting of the Himalayan mountain ranges. The erosive action of rivers flowing down from the Himalayas would then, in subsequent eras, have resulted in the creation of the Indo-Gangetic Plain, which today is one of the world's longest stretches of alluvium and also one of the most densely populated areas in the world.

The Himalayas. The Himalayas consitute the highest mountain system of the world, containing most of the world's highest peaks, some ten of which rise above 25,000 feet. Mount Everest (29,028 feet [8,848 metres]), which dominates the Himalayas, also extends into Nepal and Tibet. Geologically, the Himalayas constitute the world's youngest and longest east–west mountain system, extending almost without interruption for about 1,500 miles.

The Himalayas have variegated landscapes, consisting of snow-clad peaks, sprawling ice fields above the heads of large valley glaciers, waterfalls tumbling over high precipices, deep river gorges, and wide valleys. Such scenes are well represented in Jammu and Kashmir and in Himachal Pradesh, as well as in the northern regions of Uttar Pradesh, West Bengal, and Assam. The valleys of Kulu and Kangra in Himachal Pradesh are popular holiday resorts. In Uttar Pradesh is the celebrated Nanda Devi group of mountains.

Glaciers and snowfields

Except for the polar regions, India has the world's largest area under snows and glaciers. The world's largest mountain glaciers are to be found in the Himalayas, where the snowfields cover about 15,500 square miles, extending from Kashmir in the west to Assam in the east. The two highest ranges of the Himalayan system, the Great Himalaya and the Karakoram Himalaya, have a number of large ice streams that have no parallel in any other mountain system of the world.

Plains. The plains of India cover more than 400,000 square miles, the greater part of which consists of the Indo-Gangetic Plain in the north. There is also an extensive slice of plains land in the south, mainly deltaic in character. From the standpoint of human use, the plains of India are the most important type of landform in the country. They represent the most extensively cultivated and densely populated areas, particularly where water is available. The alluvial plains covering the greater part of West Bengal, Bihār, Uttar Pradesh, Haryana, and Punjab, are most extensive in North India. They are also to be found in Assam and Rājasthān. In the east coast region, from Cape Comorin in the south to the Mahānadi Delta, the alluvial plains stretch across the deltas of India's southern rivers.

Plateaus. Geologically, the peninsular plateau is the oldest part of India's land surface. It consists largely of ancient crystalline rocks in various stages of change and deformation. The rocks generally range in age from 300,000,000 to 500,000,000 years. Until the Koyna Mahārāshtra earthquake in 1967, the peninsula was believed to be a region of relative stability that was rarely subject to seismic disturbances. Some geologists hold that the Koyna earthquake originated from the so-called Malabar fault, which extends from Kutch on the west coast to Cape Comorin in the south and with which is associated a series of parallel fractures; not all geologists, however, agree with this explanation.

The Deccan Plateau

The peninsula, or Deccan Plateau, is bordered to the north by the Vindhya Mountains, which separate it from the Indo-Gangetic Plain; other prominent mountain and hill ranges associated with it are the Aravālli, Sātpura, Maikala, and Ajanta ranges. The plateau is flanked on the east by the Eastern Ghāts, which have an average elevation of about 2,000 feet. A narrow coastal strip separates the Western Ghāts from the Arabian Sea. Between the Eastern Ghāts and the Bay of Bengal is a broader coastal area. At the southern tip of the plateau, the Eastern and Western Ghāts meet at a point formed by the Nīlgiri Hills.

Plateaus occur in other parts of India as well. Among the most notable, the Ladākh Plateau has an average elevation of almost 17,400 feet and is situated in the northeast part of the Kashmir Himalayas. It is the highest plateau in India and one of the most inaccessible; it has all the landform characteristics of a steppe (treeless plain). North of the Chāng Chenmo Range, which runs from west to east and divides Ladākh, the Chāng Chenmo River flows westward into a flat-floored valley. Farther north is a typical interior drainage basin, carved out of limestone and shale, containing some salt lakes with centripetal drainage.

Drainage. *Groundwater basins.* India contains at least three major groundwater basins. These are the Ganges Basin, which is the largest; the Punjab alluvial basin in the northwest, which runs from Ludhiāna to Amritsar; and the western basin, covering a portion of Rājasthān and curving southward toward the Gujarāt plains as far as Ahmadābād (Ahmedabad). Because of the flat terrain, the flow of groundwater in these basins is not substantial. The underlying structure of the greater part of India is not favourable for storing up a substantial portion of the rains precipitated during the monsoon months.

Conditions for artesian water are most favourable among the porous sandstones of the Himalayan foothills. Another favourable artesian area occurs along the edge of the Narmada Valley to the north of the Sātpura Range in the northwest part of the peninsula; here, water-bearing conglomerate beds (formed of agglomerated fragments of sedimentary rock) are overlain by low ridges of impervious crystalline rocks. Aquifers (water-bearing beds of rock) also occur in such areas as the Mahārāshtra lava plateau on the west of the peninsula and in some artesian zones in Gujarāt in the westernmost part of India.

Groundwater, like the surface streams, also flows in hilly areas where the rocks are pervious. Such underground streams occur near Cherrapunji in the Khāsi Hills in Meghalaya and near Dehra Dūn in Uttar Pradesh. In the Rāmgarh Hills in Madhya Pradesh there are natural caves carved out of sandstone. Sinkholes and short, blind valleys are common along the southern fringe of Meghalaya in the east, where the rock is limestone.

Springs and streams appearing on the surface from the groundwater below are to be found mainly in three regions—the Kumaun Himalaya, in Uttar Pradesh; the low hills and uplands of southern Bihār; and the foot of the Western Ghāts, in the Konkan region. The majority of these are cold springs, but a few are hot springs, either with or without sulfur.

India's lakes

For such a large country, India has very few lakes. Most of the lakes in the Himalayas are basins scooped out by glaciers or dammed by moraines and subsequently filled with water. The Wular Lake, with an area varying from 12 to 100 square miles, is the largest lake in the Kashmir Valley. An example of a crater lake of volcanic origin is the Lonar Lake, in the Buldāna district of Mahārāshtra, in the Deccan. There are a number of long lakes between sand dunes in western Rājasthān.

On the coastal plains a totally different type of landscape occurs, typified by the backwaters of Bombay harbour, on the Konkan Coast; farther south is Asthamudi Lake.

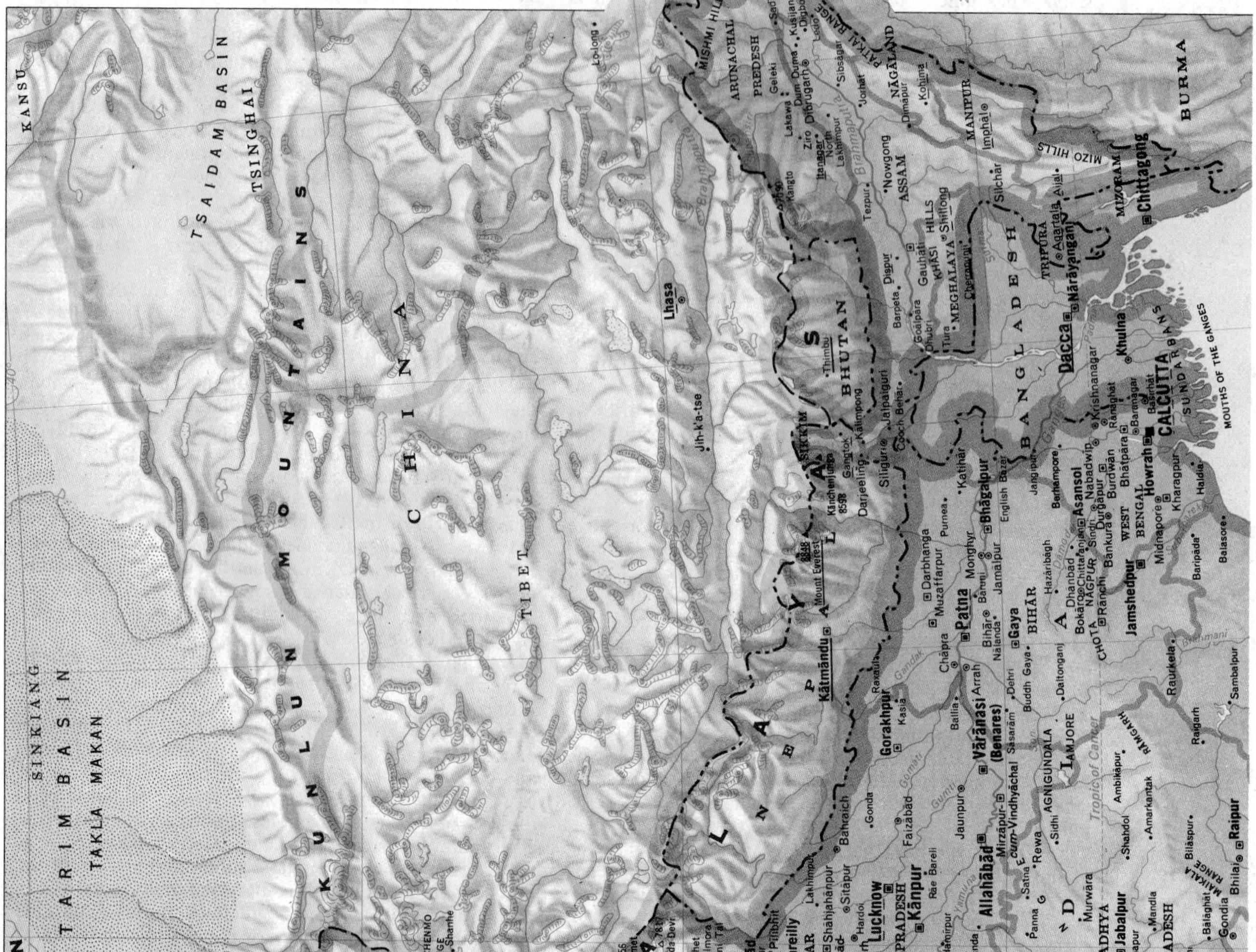
SOVIET UNION
AFGHANISTAN
CHINA
TIBET
KUNLUN MOUNTAINS
HIMALAYA
TIEN SHAN
TARIM BASIN
TAKLA MAKAN
TSAIDAM BASIN
TSINGHAI
SINKIANG
KANSU
HINDU KUSH
PAMIRS
KARAKORAM RANGE
NEPAL
BHUTAN
SIKKIM
BANGLADESH
BURMA
PAKISTAN
THAR DESERT
(GREAT INDIAN DESERT)
RAJASTHAN
KASHMIR
Kābul
Dushanbe
Samarkand
Kashgar
Lhasa
Islāmābād
Rāwalpindi
Lahore
Lyallpur
Multān
Sukkur
Hyderābād
KARĀCHI
Srīnagar
Amritsar
DELHI
New Delhi
Jaipur
Ajmer
Jodhpur
Bīkaner
Ahmadābād
Vadodara (Baroda)
Surat
Indore
Bhopāl
Gwalior
Agra
Kānpur
Lucknow
Allahābād
Vārānasi (Benares)
Patna
Kātmāndu
Mount Everest
CALCUTTA
Howrah
Dacca
Chittagong
Khulna
Jamshedpur
Jabalpur
Raipur
Shillong
Imphāl
ASSAM
MANIPUR
NĀGĀLAND
MIZORAM
TRIPURA
MEGHALAYA
ARUNACHAL PRADESH
UTTAR PRADESH
MADHYA PRADESH
HARYANA
PUNJAB
HIMACHAL PRADESH
BIHAR
WEST BENGAL
GUJARĀT
KĀTHIĀWĀR
RANN OF KUTCH
SULAIMAN RANGE
KĪRTHAR RANGE
ARAVALLI RANGE
SĀTPURA RANGE
MOUTHS OF THE GANGES
SUNDARBANS
Indus
Brahmaputra
Tropic of Cancer

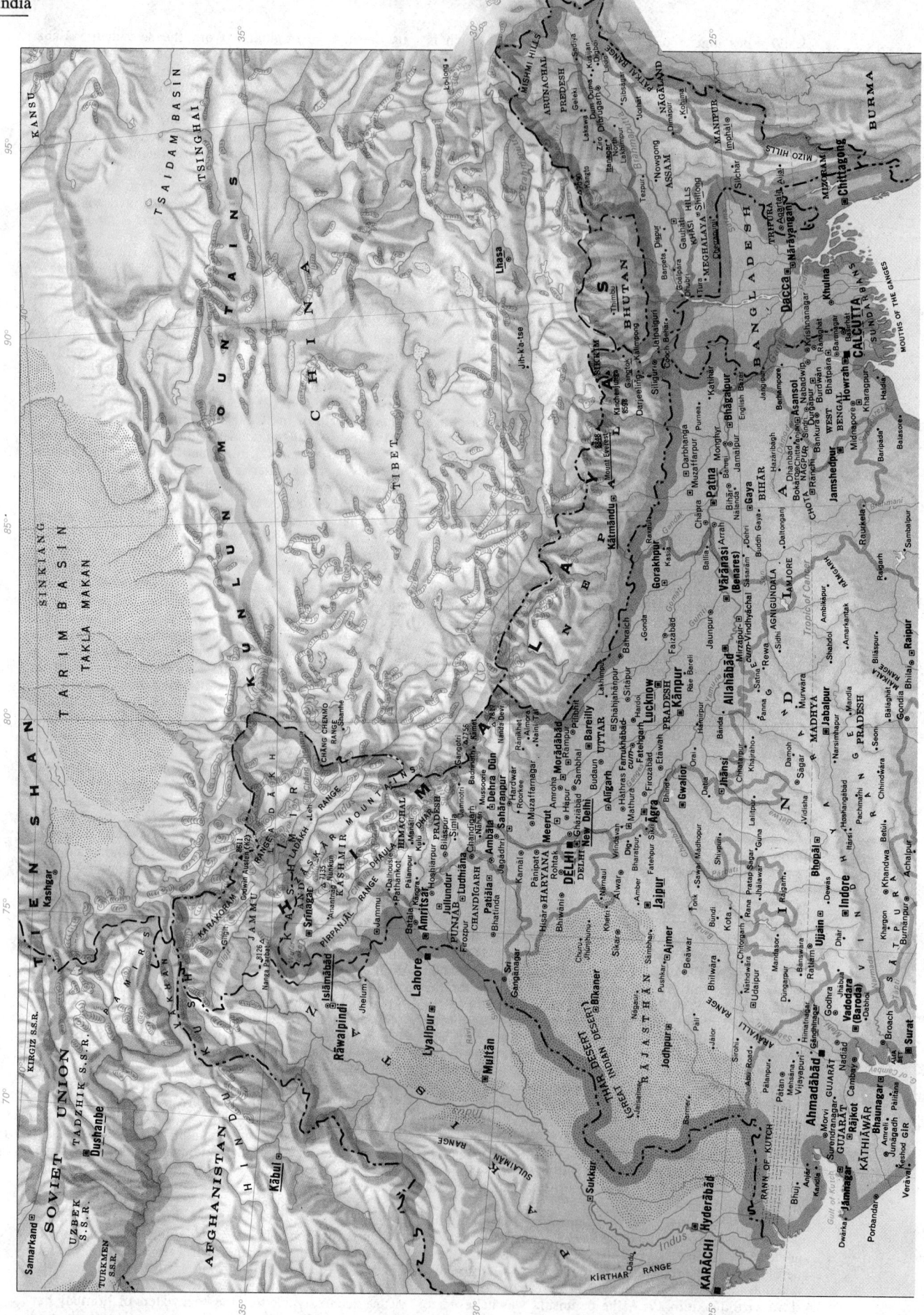

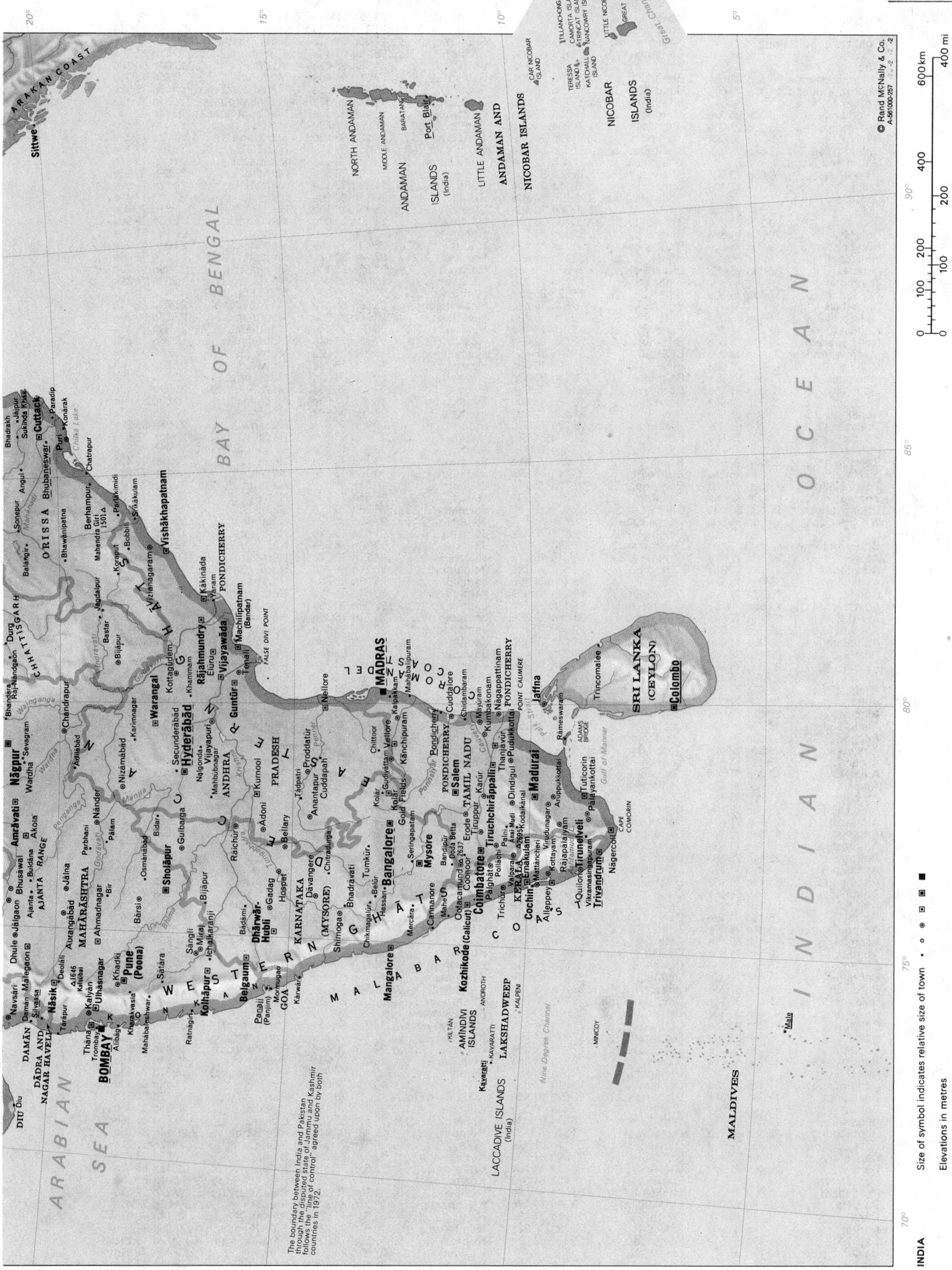
INDIA
ARABIAN SEA
BAY OF BENGAL
INDIAN OCEAN
ARAKAN COAST
Sittwe
ANDAMAN AND NICOBAR ISLANDS
NORTH ANDAMAN
MIDDLE ANDAMAN
BARATANG
Port Blair
LITTLE ANDAMAN
ANDAMAN ISLANDS (India)
NICOBAR ISLANDS (India)
CAR NICOBAR ISLAND
GREAT NICOBAR
LITTLE NICOBAR
Great Channel
DIU
DAMĀN
DĀDRA AND NAGAR HAVELI
BOMBAY
Thāna
Pune (Poona)
Nāsik
MAHĀRĀSHTRA
AJANTA RANGE
Aurangābād
Nāgpur
Amrāvati
ORISSA
Cuttack
Bhubaneswar
Puri
Chilka Lake
CHHATTISGARH
Vishākhapatnam
Rājahmundry
Vijayawāda
Machilipatnam (Bandar)
FALSE DIVI POINT
Hyderābād
Secunderābād
Warangal
ANDHRA PRADESH
Guntūr
Nellore
MADRAS
Kurnool
Sholāpur
Gulbarga
Belgaum
GOA
Panaji (Panjim)
Dhārwār-Hubli
KARNATAKA (MYSORE)
Bangalore
Mysore
Mangalore
Kozhikode (Calicut)
Coimbatore
Cochin
Ernākulam
Alleppey
KERALA
Trivandrum
TAMIL NADU
Salem
Tiruchchirāppalli
Madurai
Tirunelveli
Nāgercoil
CAPE COMORIN
Pondicherry
PONDICHERRY
POINT CALIMERE
Palk Strait
ADAMS BRIDGE
Gulf of Mannar
Jaffna
Trincomalee
SRI LANKA (CEYLON)
Colombo
WESTERN GHĀTS
EASTERN GHĀTS
MALABAR COAST
COROMANDEL COAST
LACCADIVE ISLANDS (India)
LAKSHADWEEP
AMINDIVI ISLANDS
Kavaratti
MINICOY
Nine Degree Channel
MALDIVES
Male
The boundary between India and Pakistan through the disputed state of Jammu and Kashmir follows the "line of control" agreed upon by both countries in 1972.
Size of symbol indicates relative size of town
Elevations in metres
© Rand McNally & Co.
A-561000-257
0 100 200 400 600 km
0 100 200 400 mi

MAP INDEX

Political subdivisions

Andaman and Nicobar Islands 10·30n 93·00e
Andhra Pradesh 16·00n 79·00e
Arunachal Pradesh 28·30n 95·00e
Assam 26·00n 92·00e
Bihār 25·00n 86·00e
Chandīgarh 30·45n 76·45e
Dādra and Nagar Haveli 20·05n 73·00e
Delhi 28·37n 77·10e
Goa, Daman and Diu 15·35n 74·00e
20·25n 72·50e
Gujarāt 22·30n 71·30e
Haryana 29·20n 76·20e
Himachal Pradesh 32·00n 77·00e
Jammu and Kashmir 34·00n 76·00e
Karnataka (Mysore) 14·00n 76·00e
Kerala 10·00n 76·30e
Lakshadweep 10·00n 73·00e
Madhya Pradesh 23·00n 79·00e
Mahārāshtra 19·00n 76·00e
Manipur 25·00n 94·00e
Meghalaya 25·30n 91·15e
Mizoram 23·30n 93·00e
Nāgāland 26·00n 95·00e
Orissa 20·00n 84·00e
Pondicherry 11·56n 79·50e
Punjab 31·00n 72·30e
Rājasthān 27·00n 74·00e
Sikkim 27·35n 88·35e
Tamil Nadu 11·00n 78·15e
Tripura 27·00n 92·00e
Uttar Pradesh 27·00n 80·00e
West Bengal 24·00n 88·00e

Cities and towns

Abu Road 24·29n 72·47e
Achalpur 21·16n 77·31e
Ādilābād 19·40n 78·32e
Ādoni 15·38n 77·17e
Agartala 23·50n 91·16e
Āgra 27·12n 77·59e
Ahmadābād 23·02n 72·35e
Ahmadnagar 19·05n 74·45e
Aijal 23·44n 92·43e
Ajanta 20·30n 75·48e
Ajmer 26·27n 74·40e
Akola 20·42n 77·00e
Alībāg 18·39n 72·53e
Alīgarh 23·59n 87·20e
Allahābād 25·27n 81·50e
Alleppey 9·30n 76·20e
Almora 29·36n 79·41e
Alwar 27·46n 76·37e
Amarkantak 22·40n 81·45e
Ambāla 30·23n 76·46e
Amber 27·00n 75·51e
Ambikāpur 23·08n 83·11e
Amrāvati 20·56n 77·47e
Amreli 21·36n 71·12e
Amritsar 31·38n 74·53e
Amroha 28·54n 78·38e
Anantapur 14·41n 77·37e
Anantnāg 33·44n 75·10e
Angul 20·51n 85·06e
Anjār 23·07n 70·02e
Arrah 25·33n 84·40e
Aruppukkottai 9·31n 78·07e
Asansol 23·41n 86·59e
Aurangābād 19·53n 75·20e
Bādāmi 15·52n 75·46e
Badrīnāth 30·44n 79·30e
Bahraich 27·36n 81·36e
Bālāghāt 21·49n 80·11e
Balāngīr 20·43n 83·30e
Balasore 21·29n 86·56e
Ballia 25·45n 84·20e
Bānda 25·29n 80·21e
Bandar, see Machilīpatnam
Bandipūr 11·40n 76·38e
Bangalore 12·58n 77·36e
Bānkura 23·14n 87·04e
Bānswāra 23·32n 74·26e
Baranagar 22·38n 88·22e
Bareilly 28·20n 79·25e
Baripāda 21·56n 86·44e
Barmer 25·45n 71·23e
Baroda, see Vadodara
Barpeta 26·19n 91·00e
Bārsi 18·15n 75·42e
Bāruni 25·29n 85·59e
Basīrhāt 22·39n 88·52e
Bastar 19·12n 81·56e
Batāla 31·48n 75·13e
Beāwar 26·06n 74·20e
Belgaum 15·52n 74·31e
Bellary 15·09n 76·56e
Belūr 22·38n 88·20e
Benares, see Vārānasi
Berhampore 24·06n 88·15e
Berhampur 19·19n 84·48e
Betūl 21·54n 77·54e
Bhadrakh 21·03n 86·30e
Bhadrāvati 13·52n 75·43e
Bhāgalpur 25·15n 86·58e
Bhandāra 21·10n 79·39e
Bharatpur 27·26n 77·30e
Bhatinda 30·13n 74·56e
Bhātpāra 22·52n 88·24e
Bhaunagar 21·47n 72·09e
Bhawānipatna 19·55n 83·10e
Bhilai 21·11n 81·20e
Bhīlwāra 25·21n 74·40e
Bhind 26·35n 78·48e
Bhiwāni 28·48n 76·08e
Bhopāl 23·15n 77·25e
Bhubaneswar 20·15n 85·50e
Bhuj 23·17n 69·41e
Bhusāwal 21·03n 75·46e
Bīdar 17·55n 77·33e
Bihār 25·12n 85·33e
Bijāpur 16·50n 75·42e
Bījāpur 18·47n 80·49e
Bīkaner 28·01n 73·18e
Bilāspur 22·05n 82·08e
Bilāspur 31·19n 76·45e
Bīr 18·59n 75·46e
Bobbili 18·35n 83·22e
Bokāro 23·51n 86·02e
Bombay 18·58n 72·50e
Broach 21·42n 72·58e
Budaun 28·03n 79·07e
Buddh Gaya 24·35n 84·58e
Buldāna 20·32n 76·11e
Būndi 25·26n 75·41e
Burdwān 23·14n 87·52e
Burhānpur 21·19n 76·14e
Calcutta 22·34n 88·20e
Calicut, see Kozhikode
Cambay 22·19n 72·37e
Cannanore 11·58n 75·21e
Chandīgarh 30·44n 76·47e
Chandrapur 19·57n 79·18e
Chāpra 25·46n 84·45e
Chatrapur 19·21n 85·00e
Cherrapunji 25·17n 91·44e
Chhatarpur 24·55n 79·36e
Chhindwāra 22·04n 78·56e
Chidambaram 11·24n 79·42e
Chikmagalūr 13·20n 75·47e
Chitorgarh 24·54n 74·39e
Chitradurga 14·14n 76·24e
Chittaranjan 23·52n 86·52e
Chittoor 13·14n 79·07e
Churu 28·18n 74·58e
Cochin 9·58n 76·15e
Coimbatore 11·00n 76·57e
Cooch Behār 26·20n 89·27e
Coonoor 11·21n 76·49e
Cuddalore 11·45n 79·46e
Cuddapah 14·29n 78·50e
Cuttack 20·26n 85·53e
Dabhoi 22·08n 73·26e
Dalhousie 32·32n 75·59e
Daltonganj 24·03n 84·04e
Damān 20·25n 72·50e
Damoh 23·50n 79·27e
Darbhanga 26·10n 85·56e
Darjeeling 27·02n 88·16e
Datia 25·41n 78·28e
Dāvangere 14·28n 75·56e
Dehra Dūn 30·20n 78·02e
Dehri 24·53n 84·14e
Delhi 28·37n 77·12e
Deolāli 19·56n 73·50e
Dewās 22·57n 76·04e
Dhānbād 23·47n 86·26e
Dhār 22·36n 75·18e
Dhārwār-Hubli 15·20n 75·08e
Dhubri 26·01n 89·59e
Dhule 20·54n 74·47e
Dibrugarh 27·29n 94·55e
Dīg 27·28n 77·20e
Digboi 27·23n 95·38e
Dimāpur 25·54n 93·45e
Dindigul 10·21n 77·58e
Dispur 26·09n 91·46e
Diu 20·43n 70·59e
Dum Duma 27·33n 95·33e
Dūngarpur 23·50n 73·43e
Durg 21·11n 81·17e
Durgāpur 23·29n 87·20e
Dwārka 22·15n 68·58e
Elūru 16·42n 81·07e
English Bāzār 25·00n 88·09e
Ernākulam 9·59n 76·17e
Erode 11·21n 77·43e
Etāwah 25·33n 76·22e
Faizābād 26·47n 82·08e
Farrukhābād-*cum*-Fatehgarh 27·24n 79·35e
Fatehpur Sīkri 27·06n 77·40e
Fīrozābād 27·09n 78·24e
Fīrozpur 30·55n 74·38e
Gadag 15·25n 75·38e
Gāndhīnagar 23·13n 72·41e
Gangotri 30·56n 79·02e
Gangtok 27·20n 88·37e
Gauhāti 26·10n 91·45e
Gaya 24·48n 85·03e
Geleki 27·51n 94·40e
Ghāziābād 28·40n 77·26e
Goālpāra 26·11n 90·37e
Godhra 22·46n 73·36e
Gonda 27·08n 81·58e
Gondia 21·27n 80·12e
Gorakhpur 26·45n 83·22e
Gudiyāttam 12·57n 78·53e
Gulbarga 17·20n 76·50e
Guna 24·39n 77·19e
Guntūr 16·17n 80·28e
Gwalior 26·13n 78·10e
Haldia 22·00n 88·00e
Hamīrpur 25·57n 80·09e
Hāpur 28·44n 77·46e
Hardoi 27·24n 80·07e
Hardwār 29·52n 78·10e
Hassan 13·01n 76·06e
Hāthras 27·36n 78·03e
Hazāribāgh 23·59n 85·21e
Himatnagar 23·36n 72·58e
Hisār 29·09n 75·44e
Hoshangābād 22·45n 77·44e
Hoshiārpur 28·35n 77·22e
Hospet 15·16n 76·24e
Howrah 22·35n 88·20e
Hyderābād 17·23n 78·29e
Ichalkaranji 16·41n 74·28e
Imphāl 24·48n 93·56e
Indore 22·43n 75·52e
Itanagar 27·20n 93·50e
Itārsi 22·37n 77·46e
Jabalpur 23·10n 79·57e
Jagādhri 30·10n 77·18e
Jagdalpur 19·04n 82·02e
Jaipur 26·56n 75·50e
Jaisalmer 26·55n 70·55e
Jajpur 20·49n 86·37e
Jālgaon 21·03n 76·32e
Jālna 19·50n 75·53e
Jālor 25·21n 72·37e
Jalpaiguri 26·32n 88·44e
Jamālpur 25·25n 86·40e
Jammu 32·44n 74·52e
Jāmnagar 22·28n 70·05e
Jamnotri 30·57n 78·30e
Jamshedpur 22·48n 86·11e
Jangipur 24·28n 88·03e
Jaunpur 25·45n 82·42e
Jhābua 22·46n 74·35e
Jhālawār 24·36n 76·11e
Jhānsi 25·27n 78·35e
Jhūnjhunu 28·08n 75·24e
Jodhpur 26·17n 73·01e
Jorhāt 26·46n 94·13e
Jullundur 31·20n 75·35e
Junāgadh 21·31n 70·27e
Kākināda 16·57n 82·14e
Kālimpong 27·05n 88·29e
Kalpakkam 12·50n 80·15e
Kalyān 19·15n 73·08e
Kānchipuram 12·50n 79·43e
Kandla 23·02n 70·14e
Kāngra 32·06n 76·16e
Kānpur 26·28n 80·20e
Karīmnagar 18·26n 79·08e
Karnāl 29·41n 76·59e
Karūr 10·57n 78·05e
Kārwār 14·48n 74·08e
Kasia 26·44n 83·54e
Katihār 25·32n 87·35e
Kavaratti 10·33n 72·38e
Keshod 21·20n 70·19e
Khadki 18·34n 73·52e
Khajrāho 24·50n 79·58e
Khammam 17·15n 80·09e
Khandwa 21·50n 76·20e
Kharagpur 22·20n 87·19e
Kharakvasla (Khadakvasla) 18·26n 73·46e
Khargon 21·50n 75·37e
Khetri 27·59n 75·48e
Kodaikānal 10·14n 77·29e
Kohīma 25·40n 94·06e
Kolār 13·08n 78·08e
Kolār Gold Fields 12·55n 78·17e
Kolhāpur 16·42n 74·13e
Konārak 19·53n 86·10e
Koraput 18·48n 82·41e
Kota 25·11n 75·50e
Kottagūdem 17·33n 80·39e
Kottayam 9·35n 76·31e
Kozhikode (Calicut) 11·16n 75·48e
Krishnanagar 23·24n 88·30e
Kulu 31·58n 77·06e
Kumbakonam 10·57n 79·23e
Kurnool 15·50n 78·03e
Kusijan 27·33n 95·35e
Lakawa 27·50n 94·40e
Lakhīmpur 27·57n 80·47e
Lalitpur 24·42n 78·25e
Ledo 27·18n 95·44e
Leh 34·10n 77·36e
Lucknow 26·50n 80·52e
Ludhiāna 30·55n 75·51e
Machilīpatnam (Bandar) 16·11n 81·08e
Madras 13·04n 80·16e
Madurai 9·56n 78·08e
Mahābaleshwar 17·56n 73·42e
Mahābalipuram 12·37n 80·13e
Mahbūbnagar 16·44n 77·59e
Mahe 11·42n 75·32e
Mālegaon 20·33n 74·32e
Manāli 32·15n 77·10e
Mandasor 24·04n 75·04e
Mandla 22·36n 80·23e
Mangalore 12·52n 74·52e
Mathura 27·30n 77·41e
Mattāncheri 9·57n 76·16e
Māyūram 11·06n 79·39e
Meerut 29·00n 77·43e
Mehsāna 23·36n 72·24e
Mercāra 12·26n 75·45e
Midnapore 22·25n 87·20e
Mīraj 16·50n 74·39e
Mirzāpur-*cum*-Vindhyāchal 25·09n 82·35e
Monghyr 25·23n 86·29e
Morādābād 28·50n 78·47e
Mormugao 15·26n 73·50e
Morvi 22·50n 70·50e
Murwāra 23·50n 80·24e
Mussoorie 30·27n 78·05e
Muzaffarnagar 29·28n 77·42e
Muzaffarpur 26·08n 85·24e
Mysore 12·18n 76·39e
Nabadwīp 23·25n 88·22e
Nadiād 22·42n 72·52e
Nāgappattinam 10·46n 79·50e
Nāgaur 27·12n 73·45e
Nāgercoil 8·11n 77·26e
Nāgpur 21·08n 79·04e
Nāhan 30·33n 77·13e
Naini Tāl 29·23n 79·28e
Nālanda 25·07n 85·25e
Nalgonda 17·03n 79·16e
Nānder 19·10n 77·21e
Nārnaul 28·03n 76·07e
Narsimhapur 23·00n 79·10e
Nāsik 19·59n 73·47e
Nāthdwāra 24·56n 73·51e
Navsāri 20·57n 42·56e
Nellore 14·26n 79·59e
New Delhi 28·36n 77·15e
Nizāmābād 18·40n 78·06e
North Lakhimpur 27·14n 94·07e
Nowgong 25·04n 79·27e
Ootacamund 11·25n 76·43e
Orai 25·59n 79·32e
Osmānābād 18·10n 76·02e
Pachmarhi 22·28n 78·26e
Pālam 19·01n 76·57e
Pālampur 32·07n 76·32e
Pālanpur 24·10n 72·26e
Pālayankottai 8·43n 77·44e
Pālghāt 10·46n 76·40e
Pāli 25·46n 73·20e
Pālitāna 21·31n 71·49e
Palni 10·27n 77·31e
Panaji (Panjim) 15·29n 73·50e
Pānīpat 29·25n 76·59e
Panjim, see Panaji
Panna 24·43n 80·12e
Paradip 20·15n 86·41e
Parbhani 19·16n 76·47e
Parlākimidi 18·47n 84·06e
Pātan 23·51n 72·06e
Pathānkot 32·17n 75·40e
Patiāla 30·19n 76·23e
Patna 25·36n 85·06e
Pīlībhīt 28·37n 79·48e
Pollāchi 10·40n 77·01e
Pondicherry 11·56n 79·50e
Poona, see Pune
Porbandar 21·38n 69·36e
Port Blair 11·39n 92·45e
Proddatūr 14·45n 78·33e
Pudukkottai 10·24n 78·49e
Pune (Poona) 18·31n 73·54e
Puri 19·48n 85·50e
Purnea 25·47n 87·31e
Pushkar 26·28n 74·36e
Quilon 8·53n 76·36e
Rāe Bareli 26·14n 81·15e
Rāichūr 16·12n 77·21e
Raigarh 21·55n 83·24e
Raipur 22·48n 86·57e
Rājahmundry 17·01n 81·48e
Rājapālaiyam 9·27n 77·33e
Rājgarh 24·02n 76·43e
Rājkot 22·18n 70·47e
Rāj-Nāndgaon 21·06n 81·03e
Rāmeswaram 9·17n 79·19e
Rāmpur 29·48n 77·27e
Rānāghāt 23·11n 88·35e
Rana Pratap Sagar 25·00n 76·00e
Rānchī 23·22n 85·19e
Rānīkhet 29·38n 79·26e

MAP INDEX (continued)

Ratlām 23·28n 75·00e
Ratnāgiri 16·59n 73·17e
Raurkela 22·14n 84·54e
Raxaul 26·59n 84·51e
Rewa 24·32n 81·17e
Rohtak 28·54n 76·35e
Roorkee 29·53n 77·52e
Sadiya 27·50n 95·40e
Sāgar 14·10n 75·02e
Sahāranpur 29·57n 77·48e
Salem 11·39n 78·10e
Sambalpur 21·28n 83·59e
Sambhal 28·35n 78·34e
Sāmbhar 26·55n 75·12e
Sāngli 16·52n 74·34e
Sasarām 24·57n 84·02e
Sātāra 17·41n 73·59e
Satna 24·35n 80·51e
Sawai Mādhopur 26·00n 76·39e
Secunderābād 17·27n 78·29e
Seoni 22·06n 79·32e
Seringapatam 12·25n 76·42e
Sevagram 20·45n 78·30e
Shahdol 23·20n 81·21e
Shāhjahānpur 27·53n 79·55e
Shillong 25·35n 91·53e
Shimoga 13·56n 75·35e
Shivpuri 25·25n 77·40e
Sholāpur 17·40n 75·55e
Sibsāgar 26·59n 94·39e
Sidhi 24·24n 81·53e
Sīkar 27·36n 75·08e
Silchar 24·49n 92·48e
Silīguri 26·43n 88·27e
Silvassa 20·17n 73·00e
Simla 31·06n 77·09e
Sindri 23·45n 86·42e
Sirohi 24·54n 72·51e
Sītāpur 27·35n 80·40e
Sonepur 20·50n 83·54e
Sri Gangānagar 29·55n 73·52e
Srīkākulam 18·18n 83·55e
Srīnagar 34·05n 74·49e
Sukinda Khās 20·58n 85·55e
Surat 21·12n 72·50e
Surendranagar 22·43n 71·38e
Tādpatri 14·55n 78·01e
Tārāpur 19·51n 72·42e
Tenāli 16·14n 80·40e
Tezpur 26·37n 92·48e
Thāna 19·12n 72·59e
Thanjāvūr 10·47n 79·09e
Tiruchchirāppalli 10·48n 78·41e
Tirunelveli 8·44n 77·41e
Tiruppur 11·06n 77·21e
Tonk 26·11n 75·47e
Trichūr 10·31n 76·13e
Trivandrum 8·28n 76·57e
Trombay 19·02n 72·54e
Tumkūr 13·21n 77·06e
Tura 25·31n 90·13e
Tuticorin 8·50n 78·09e
Udaipur 24·35n 73·41e
Ujjain 23·12n 75·46e
Ulhāsnagar 19·13n 73·07e
Vadodara (Baroda) 22·18n 73·12e
Valparai 10·19n 76·58e
Vārānasi (Benares) 25·20n 83·00e
Vellore 12·56n 79·09e
Verāval 20·54n 70·20e
Vidisha 23·32n 77·49e
Vijayapuri 16·52n 79·35e
Vijayawāda 16·31n 80·37e
Vikramasingapuram 8·43n 77·24e
Virudunagar 9·35n 77·57e
Vishākhapatnam 17·43n 83·19e
Vizianagaram 18·07n 83·25e
Vrindāvan 27·35n 77·42e
Warangal 18·00n 79·33e
Wardha 20·45n 78·36e
Yanam 16·35n 82·10e
Ziro 27·40n 92·40e

Physical features and points of interest

Adams Bridge, *shoal* 9·04n 79·37e
Agnigundala, *physical region* 24·00n 83·50e
Ajanta Range, *mountain range* 20·30n 76·00e
Alia Bet, *island* 21·36n 72·40e
Amīndīvi Islands 11·23n 72·23e
Amjore, *physical region* 24·00n 83·30e
Anai Mudi, *mountain* 10·10n 77·04e
Andaman Islands 12·00n 93·00e
Androth, *island* 10·49n 73·40e
Arabian Sea 19·00n 69·00e
Arāvalli Range, *mountain range* 25·00n 73·30e
Ashtamudi Lake 8·59n 76·36e
Banās, *river* 25·55n 76·45e
Baratang, *island* 12·15n 92·45e
Bengal, Bay of 15·00n 88·00e
Betwa, *river* 25·55n 80·12e
Bhīma, *river* 16·24n 77·18e
Brāhmani, *river* 20·45n 87·00e
Brahmaputra, *river* 26·00n 89·55e
Calimere, Point 10·20n 79·52e
Cambay, Gulf of 21·30n 72·30e
Camorta Island 8·10n 93·30e
Car Nicobar Island 9·10n 92·45e
Cauvery, *river* 11·10n 79·51e
Chambal, *river* 26·30n 79·15e
Chenāb, *river* 33·00n 74·30e
Chhattīsgarh, *plain* 21·15n 82·00e
Chilka Lake 19·45n 85·25e
Chota Nāgpur *plateau* 23·30n 84·30e
Comorin, Cape 8·06n 77·33e
Coromandel Coast 13·30n 80·30e
Dāmodar, *river* 23·14n 87·39e
Deccan, *plateau* 17·00n 78·00e
Dhaula Dhār, *mountains* 32·12n 76·33e
Doda Betta, *mountain* 11·26n 76·44e
Eastern Ghāts, *mountains* 16·00n 79·00e
False Divi Point 15·45n 80·50e
Gandak, *river* 25·35n 85·12e
Ganges (Ganga), *river* 24·00n 88·45e
Gīr, *forest* 21·00n 70·40e
Godāvari, *river* 16·37n 82·18e
Gomati, *river* 25·32n 83·11e
Great Channel 6·25n 92·40e
Great Indian Desert, see Thar Desert
Great Nicobar, *island* 7·00n 93·50e
Gujarāt, *physical region* 22·51n 71·30e
Gumti, *river* 25·31n 83·10e
Himalayas, *mountains* 32·30n 77·30e
Indrāvati, *river* 18·43n 80·17e
Indus, *river* 34·30n 76·30e
Kalpeni *island* 10·05n 73·38e
Kalsūbai, *mountain* 19·35n 73·42e
Kāmet, *mountain* 30·54n 79·37e
Kānchenjunga, *mountain* 27·42n 88·09e
Kangto, *mountain* 27·50n 92·25e
Kashmir, *physical region* 34·30n 76·30e
Katchall Island 7·55n 93·25e
Kāthiāwār, *peninsula* 22·00n 71·00e
Kavaratti, *island* 10·34n 72·39e
Khāsi Hills 25·45n 91·30e
Kiltān, *island* 11·30n 73·00e
Konkan, *physical region* 17·00n 73·00e
Krishna, *river* 15·43n 80·55e
Kutch, Gulf of 22·30n 69·30e
Laccadive Islands 10·00n 73·00e
Ladākh, *physical region* 35·00n 78·00e
Ladākh Range, *mountain range* 34·00n 77·30e
Little Andaman, *island* 10·40n 92·30e
Little Nicobar, *island* 7·20n 93·40e
Lūni, *river* 24·40n 71·15e
Mahānadi, *river* 20·00n 86·25e
Mahendra Giri, *mountain* 18·58n 84·25e
Mahi, *river* 22·15n 73·00e
Maikala Range, *mountains* 22·30n 81·30e
Malabar Coast 11·00n 75·00e
Mānjra, *river* 18·49n 77·52e
Mannar, Gulf of 8·30n 79·00e
Middle Andaman, *island* 12·30n 92·53e
Minicoy, *island* 8·17n 73·04e
Mishmi Hills 29·00n 96·00e
Mizo Hills 23·30n 93·00e
Nancowry Island 7·58n 93·33e
Nanda Devi, *mountain* 30·22n 79·59e
Narmada, *river* 21·32n 72·35e
Nicobar Islands 8·00n 93·50e
Nine Degree Channel 9·00n 73·00e
North Andaman, *island* 13·20n 93·00e
Nunkun, *mountain* 33·59n 76·02e
Palk Strait 9·30n 79·30e
Pārbati, *river* 25·51n 76·34e
Pātkai Range, *mountain range* 27·00n 96·00e
Penganga, *river* 19·53n 79·09e
Penner, *river* 14·35n 80·11e
Pīr Panjāl Range, *mountain range* 32·37n 74·32e
Ponnaiyār, *river* 11·46n 79·48e
Rāmgarh, *hill* 22·57n 82·52e
Rann of Kutch, *salt flat* 24·00n 70·00e
Sābarmati, *river* 22·25n 73·20e
Sātpura Range, *mountain range* 22·00n 78·00e
Shyok, *river* 35·13n 75·53e
Son, *river* 25·40n 84·51e
Subansiri, *river* 26·48n 93·50e
Subarnarekha, *river* 21·33n 87·12e
Sundarbans, *physical region* 22·00n 88·45e
Surma, *river* 24·42n 91·24e
Sutlej, *river* 31·30n 74·30e
Tāpti, *river* 21·05n 72·40e
Teressa Island 8·15n 93·10e
Thar Desert, (Great Indian Desert) 27·30n 72·00e
Tillanchong Island 8·30n 93·38e
Trincat Island 8·05n 93·35e
Tungabhadra, *river* 15·57n 78·15e
Vindhya Range, *mountain range* 23·00n 77·00e
Wainganga, *river* 18·50n 79·55e
Wardha, *river* 19·36n 79·48e
Western Ghāts, *mountains* 14·00n 75·00e
Wular Lake 34·30n 74·30e
Yamuna, *river* 25·25n 81·50e
Zāskār Mountains 33·00n 77·30e

River systems. India's rivers may be grouped into the Himalayan rivers, the Deccan rivers, the coastal rivers, and the rivers of the inland drainage basin.

The total available volume of flow from India's rivers is assessed at 2,200,000,000,000 cubic yards per year. The Indo-Gangetic Plain is formed from deposits made by the eastern tributaries of the Indus, by the Ganges and its affluents, and by the Brahmaputra. The east coast deltas are formed from deposits made by the Mahānadi, Godāvari, Krishna, and Cauvery rivers.

The three principal watersheds are the Great Himalaya, with its Karakoram branch, in the north; the Vindhya Range, with the Sātpura–Maikala ranges, in central India; and the Western Ghāts, directing the courses of most of the Deccan rivers. The Himalayan rivers are generally snow fed, as well as rain fed, and therefore have an almost continuous flow. The Deccan rivers are subject to great fluctuations in volume; many of them shrink into streamlets in the hot season. The coastal rivers are short and have limited catchment areas. The few rivers of western Rājasthān mostly drain toward basins or salt lakes or are lost in the sands.

The Ganges Basin receives waters from about a quarter of India's total area, the Godāvari Basin, from about 10 percent. The basins of the Brahmaputra, in the east, and of the Indus within Indian territory are nearly equal in area. The Krishna Basin is the second-largest in peninsular India, with the Mahānadi Basin ranking third. The basins of the Narmada and the Cauvery are about equal in area but of different character and shape. India has practically all types of soils, ranging from alluvial soils to arid desert soil, mountain and hill soils, black and red soils, laterite, and swampy lowland soil.

With the exception of Himachal Pradesh, Delhi, and Jammu and Kashmir, alluvial soil is found in almost every state in India. It is most frequently found on the coastal fringes of states like Kerala, Andhra Pradesh, Mysore (Karnataka), Gujarāt, West Bengal, and Tamil Nadu. It is also found in Assam and Madhya Pradesh. Andhra Pradesh is rich in black soil, on which the farmers depend, and in red soil, which is spread throughout the state. Mahārāshtra is another reservoir of black soil, as also is Manipur. Tamil Nadu has much red soil.

Laterite soil exists in certain parts of Kerala, Tamil Nadu, Mahārāshtra, and West Bengal. Rājasthān is one of few areas in India in which arid desert soil covers the greater part of the state. The eastern strip of Kerala has mountain and hill soils, as also has the central part of Bihār. *Terai* soil is associated with the lowland belt of India, including such areas as the region which dips between plain and hills in Uttar Pradesh. Soil charged with peaty, carbonized, and other organic matter exists in some parts of Kerala and Bihār.

Climate. Broadly speaking, the climate of India is governed by the tropical monsoon (rain-bearing winds) regime. The Indian Meteorological Department recognizes four seasons. These are the cold-weather season, from December to March; the hot-weather season, in

April and May; the rainy (monsoon) season, from June to September; and the season of the retreating southwest monsoon, from October to November. In effect, however, there are only three noticeable seasons—the cold season, from about November to the end of February; the hot season (when it can be intensely warm, particularly in central and northern India), from about March to June; and the rainy season, from about June until October, by which time the southwest monsoon expends itself.

Three seasons

Rainfall and temperature show wide variations in India, which experiences two rain-bearing winds, the northeast monsoon, which blows from December to February, and the southwest monsoon.

There are four broad climatic regions based on rainfall. Practically the whole of Assam and the west coast of India lying at the foot of the Western Ghāts and extending from the north of Bombay to Trivandrum are areas of very heavy rainfall. Cherrapunji, in Assam, averages 425 inches annually—the largest amount in India. In contrast to these tracts, the Rājasthān desert, extending to Kutch, as well as the high Ladākh Plateau of Kashmir, extending westward to Gilgit, are regions of low precipitation, receiving only nominal amounts of rainfall; the Thar Desert, in Rājasthān, for example, receives a mere four inches of rain annually.

In between these regions at the extreme end of the rainfall range are two areas, one of moderately high and one of low rainfall. The former consists of a broad belt in the eastern part of the peninsular plateau, which seasonally moves northward to the Indo-Gangetic Plains and then southward toward the coastal plains; in this belt the annual rainfall averages around 60 inches. The latter constitutes an area extending from the Punjab plains across the Vindhya Mountains into the western part of the Deccan and fanning out into the Mysore Plateau; this belt receives about 30 inches of rainfall a year.

Temperature varies as much as rainfall in different parts of India. Hill stations in the Himalayan region, such as Darjeeling and Simla, have the lowest temperatures, with annual averages of between 54° and 57° F (about 12° and 14° C). In the Indo-Gangetic Plain, Delhi registers an average of 79° F (about 26° C) and Allahābād about 79° F (26° C). In the foothills of the Himalayas, Dehra Dūn has an average of about 71° F (22° C), while Palayamhottai, Madras, records 85° F (29.5° C), the highest average for all India. In the coastal area, Bombay, on the west coast, has an average temperature of about 82° F (28° C), while Madras, on the east coast, records 83.5° F (29° C). Because of India's great climatic diversity, it is practicable to talk only in terms of local temperature averages, rather than of national averages.

Vegetation. With its great latitudinal spread, encompassing a wide range of temperature conditions, its varied humidity and rainfall, and its altitudinal extremes, India produces a rich and varied vegetation, which differs according to region.

Palms of different kinds are endemic to the dry, elevated tableland of the Deccan region. The Malabar area, covering the west coast and the mountains of the Western Ghāts, is rich in tropical vegetation. Commercial crops such as coconuts, betel nuts, pepper, ginger, rubber, and bananas of all varieties thrive in the midlands and coastal areas of this region. At a higher elevation are plantations of coffee, tea, and cardamom. The forest areas abound in such hardwoods as rosewood, ironwood, and teak. Numerous varieties of softwood and bamboos of different kinds also grow here.

River valley vegetation

The Indus region, covering the plains of Punjab, Rājasthān, Kutch, and northern Gujarāt, is very poor in endemic plants; in the Ganges region, however, which spreads from the Yamuna River to West Bengal and Orissa, forests of widely differing types occur, with forests of sal (a tree with light-brown, close-grained hardwood) predominating. The vegetation in the Brahmaputra and Surma valleys of the Assam region and of the intervening hill ranges is particularly luxuriant and is characterized by tall grass, broad-leaved forests, and thick clumps of bamboo.

About 4,000 species of flowering plants along with 20 variants of palms flourish in the eastern Himalayan region, which stretches eastward from Sikkim. Many laurels, maples, alder, birch, conifers, and junipers grow here. Rhododendrons, dwarf willows, and bamboos abound. The western Himalayan region, which extends from the Kumaun hills to Kashmir, consists of three zones—alpine, temperate, and lower—whose vegetation differs. Characteristic trees in the alpine zone are the high-level silver fir, the silver birch, and junipers. Forests of conifers are to be found in the temperate zone, which also contains deodar (an East Indian cedar), spruce, and silver fir. A belt of sal forest stretches across the lower zone, where a few species of palms also grow. In the outlying islands of Andaman and Nicobar are a variety of forests—mangrove, beech, evergreen, semi-evergreen, and deciduous.

India's main cultivated plants include rice, wheat, pulses (leguminous plants with edible seeds, such as peas and beans), and grains. Castor, sesamum, and peanuts (groundnuts) are among other important seeds grown. The chief fruit trees include mango, coconut, areca nut (from the betel palm) and certain citrus fruit. The Himalayan valleys produce apples, peaches, pears, apricots, and walnuts. Apart from tea, coffee, cardamom, pepper, and rubber, which are grown extensively in the south, cinchona (a tree whose bark contains alkaloids, such as quinine, used as a specific in malaria) is cultivated in some of the damper regions.

Animal life. India has a large variety of wild animals, some of which are classified within the "big game" category.

Among the big game are three large cats—the tiger, panther, and cheetah. The tiger, the monarch of almost all Indian forests, is found in various parts of India, principally in grassy plains and swamps but also in forests. A popular hunting ground for tigers is the long forest tract that runs for 1,000 miles along the foothills of the Himalayas. Indian tigers live principally on cattle, goats, deer, and wild hog; when old they may become man-eaters. There are four species of panther—the common leopard found all over India, the all-black and albino leopards, and the snow leopard, which is seen only in the Himalayas. The cheetah, or hunting leopard, renowned for its swiftness in the chase, has practically disappeared from India. So has the Asiatic lion, once widespread in North India but now found only in the Gīr forest in Saurāshtra, a region of Gujarāt, where it is strictly protected. In 1880 there were barely a dozen head left in the Gīr forest, but the lion population is now estimated to number about 300.

Indian elephants

Elephants roam the forests of peninsular India. They are numerous in Orissa and are also found in fair numbers in the jungles of the Western Ghāts and in north Coimbatore in Tamil Nadu. Apart from being used for hauling logs from inaccessible forests, elephants also figure in ceremonial processions, although to a lesser degree in the 1970s, with the passing of the princely order of society. A favourite haunt of the elephant is Assam, where only proclaimed rogue elephants may be shot. The great Indian one-horned rhinoceros was also once threatened with extinction, but is now a protected species; over 400 roam the sanctuaries provided for them in Assam state.

There are various kinds of bear, deer, antelope, gazelle, goat, and sheep. The sloth bear, or common black bear, is found all over India. The snow, red, or brown bear, as well as the Asiatic black bear, roam the western Himalayas. There is only a single species of panda, but there are 18 species of martens, weasels, and otters. Civets and mongooses are found throughout India. The Indian, or striped, hyena is the only extant species of this family in the country but is to be seen in many forests. There are two types of wolf—the woolly wolf of the western Himalayas and the small Indian wolf, which is common throughout the country. The jackal is common, and there are at least four species of fox, as well as several strains of Indian wild dog. India has different varieties of wildcats—the Indian desert cat, the common jungle cat, the leopard cat, and the fishing cat. The lynx's main habitat is in Kashmir; the karakul (a breed of Asian sheep) lives in northwestern India.

Two species of wild pig survive, the wild boar and the pygmy hog. The deer family is represented by the mouse deer, spotted deer, barking deer, and sambar (a kind of deer having three-pointed antlers), which are spread over various parts of India. The musk deer is confined to Kashmir, and the Sikkim stag has become rare. A disappearing species is the Kashmir stag, or hangul, now a protected animal. The Indian gazelle, the four-horned antelope, and the Indian black buck roam wide areas of the country.

To the wild buffalo family belong the gaur, also known as the Indian bison; one of the most handsome specimens of wild bull, it is preserved in the southern sanctuaries of Bandipur in Mysore, and Mudumalai in Tamil Nadu. The nilgai, or blue bull, ranges all over India except West Bengal and Malabar. The markhor (a kind of wild goat, having spiral horns and long, shaggy hair) is found in the Himalayas, which is also the home of the ibex (another kind of wild goat). The wild yak inhabits the uplands of Ladākh.

Domestic animals include cattle, buffalo, sheep, goats, horse, ponies, mules, donkeys, and camels. The cobra is the best known among the Indian reptiles. There are two varieties of cobra, the common cobra and the king cobra (also known as the hamadryad), which both grow up to lengths of more than 14 feet. One of the most deadly poisonous snakes is the krait, of which there are 11 species. Vipers are represented by more than 20 species, the commonest among them being Russell's viper, the pit viper, and the saw-scaled viper. Common snakes include the rat snake, the grass snake, and the wolf snake. Three species of crocodile are found in India, but there are no alligators. There are about 50 species of turtles, tortoises, and terrapins (a kind of edible turtle).

Birdlife

About 1,200 species of birds inhabit India; together with subspecies, the total number is about 2,000. Of these, about 1,750 are resident in India, and the rest are migratory. Birds of prey include vultures, falcons, hawks, and osprey (fish hawks). Among fish eaters are pelicans, cormorants, frigate birds, and darters. Perching birds or songbirds comprise more than half of India's birdlife. The various kinds of parrots are remarkable for their beauty. Kingfishers of various kinds, as well as herons, are notable for their plumage. The myna bird, a member of the starling family, is a familiar feature of the country's ornithological landscape and like the parrot can imitate speech. Feathered game includes duck, goose, snipe, pheasant, and both gray and black partridge. The desert areas of Rājasthān are the home of the sand grouse, including the much-prized imperial sand grouse. Jungle fowl are plentiful, and the bustard, florican (smaller species of bustard), quail, green pigeon, and several other varieties of game bird are also found. The Indian peacock, with its showy, resplendent blue plumage, has been declared the national bird and is now a protected species.

India offers generous opportunities to the angler, since many of its rivers and lakes are well stocked with a large variety of indigenous fish. Trout is available in hill streams, particularly in Kashmir, the Kulu Valley, and Ootacamund, in Tamil Nadu. The mahseer, or Indian salmon, is found in most of the large rivers of India. Other varieties of edible fish include members of the carp family and catfishes; the hilsa, a type of herring, is popular on the east coast and the pomfret (a kind of East Indian fish) in Bombay.

Notorious among Indian insects are mosquitoes, which abound everywhere. Locust invasions also occur, although only infrequently. Among the more useful insects are the bee, silkworm, and coceus laca, which yields lac, from which shellac is made. There are many beautiful species of butterflies.

THE HUMAN IMPRINT

Traditional regions. From the Himalayas southward, India consists of a mosaic of traditional regions, reflecting variegated and sometimes confusing patterns of race and language. Since Indian independence, there has been a marked tendency to make state boundaries coextensive with those of linguistic or traditional regions. Further information on many of the traditional regions mentioned below may be found in the appropriate state articles.

The Himalayan region. The Himalayan region stretches between the arm of the Indus River, which curves in a great bend near Gilgit, in Kashmir, and a similar sharp turn of the Brahmaputra in Upper Assam. Traditionally the abode of the gods, the Himalayas are the meeting ground of two cultures and civilizations, Aryan and Mongolian. The Kulu and Kangra valleys of Himachal Pradesh, at the foot of the Dhaula Dhār Range of the Himalayas, are also a meeting ground of Hindu and Buddhist religions. In the union territory of Arunachal Pradesh (formerly the North East Frontier Agency; NEFA), Buddhism and Hinduism again meet, but animism is also represented.

At the northernmost tip of India is the trans-Himalayan region of Ladākh, which spreads over a plateau that has an average elevation of 19,000 feet and occupies the northeastern part of the Kashmir Himalaya. Below the snow line, its terrain consists of rugged barren landmasses interspersed with deep vertical valleys with sparse green belts of vegetation and occasional rivulets and streams. Ladākh is a dry arid region which might be described as a high altitude desert. Its population, barely 88,000, is Tibetan, and is Buddhist by religion. It covers an area of about 38,000 square miles; its terrain is dotted with villages of mud huts, multistoried monasteries, and stone and brick houses.

Ladākh is part of the state of Jammu and Kashmir (*q.v.*). The state, which is claimed by both India and Pakistan, who each occupy part of it, is divided by geography, race, and religion into three areas. In the north are the Tibetan and semi-Tibetan tracts, which include Ladākh and Gilgit; the latter, since 1948, has been part of Pakistan. In the south are the large, level areas of Jammu, inhabited mainly by the Hindu Dogras. In between is the Vale of Kashmir, in which the population is well over 80 percent Muslim. As a traditional region, Jammu and Kashmir represents a microcosm of the in-between world wedged between the Himalayas and the Indo-Gangetic Plain. The relics of three civilizations and religions—Buddhist, Hindu, and Muslim—survive in this area. The Buddhist monasteries are located almost exclusively in the eastern district of Ladākh.

Another traditional region in the Himalayan area is Arunachal Pradesh, or the North East Frontier Agency (NEFA), peopled by a variety of Indo-Mongoloid tribes, including the Monpas, Abors, Khambas, Mishmis, Tangsas, and Wanchos. They occupy more than 31,440 square miles of mountainous country bounded by Bhutan to the west, the Tibetan and Sinkiang regions of China to the north and east, and Burma to the southeast.

Only about 450,000 singularly hardy people live in this region, crisscrossed by countless streams and rivers, which become raging torrents during rainy periods. Almost all these tribal peoples live in pile dwellings, raised well above the ground to avoid the damp. Though the tribes differ, they have a common affinity in their way of life. Each tribe is broadly endogamous (practicing marriage within the group) and is divided into clans, which are exogamous (practicing marriage outside the clan). A breach of the clan rules is a major social calamity. Society is patrilineal. Polygamy is common. There are traces of polyandry among some tribes, such as the Gallongs and the Tibetan-influenced border tribes of the far north.

Environment for many centuries has been the real ruler of the tribal peoples; among some of them, gods are identified with the elements. Christianity and Hinduism have had little influence on the tribes, and even Tibetan or Burmese Buddhism has had little effect. On the whole, the tribal people are more prosperous than the Indian peasantry; they are also more hardy.

Indo-Gangetic region. Like the Himalayan belt regions, the Indo-Gangetic Plain contains some traditional regions, characterized by distinctive racial, religious, or regional factors.

The Punjab region

Before independence in 1947, the Punjab (Pañjāb) region, in the heart of the Indo-Gangetic Plain, existed as a composite mosaic of Sikhs living beside Hindu and Muslim Punjabis. After independence the Punjab was divided into east and west Punjab, the former, predominantly Sikh and Hindu, becoming a part of India, the latter, exclusively Muslim, becoming part of Pakistan. Since 1966, east Punjab has been further divided into Punjab—a predominantly Sikh region—and the largely Hindu-populated state of Haryana.

Sikh-dominated Punjab is the traditional homeland of the Sikhs, a sect that became a people. The Sikhs are physically vigorous and provide India with some of its best farmers and soldiers. The area of Punjab they now control is some 19,450 square miles. They number about 13,700,000.

West of Punjab stretches Rājasthān, notable for the Rājput clans who inhabit this sprawling, largely desert region. Rājasthān is famed in Indian history as the cradle of Hindu chivalry and culture; it was the Rājputs who offered the main Hindu resistance to the early Muslim invaders. Their principles of conduct were then founded upon the heroes of the ancient Hindu epics; today, however, their social structure is innately conservative. Their princely rulers seem to belong to past ages, rather than to present-day India.

Rājasthān is largely an amalgam of the old princely states of Rājputana. Among the more prominent of these medieval domains are Udaipur, Jaipur, Jodhpur, Bīkaner, and Jaisalmer. The principal languages of this region, which covers more than 132,000 square miles and has a population of more than 25,000,000, are the Rajasthani dialects and Hindi.

India's post-independence political leaders come principally from the huge state of Uttar Pradesh, which extends over 113,000 square miles. The country's three prime ministers—Jawaharlal Nehru, Lal Bahadur Shastri, and Indira Gandhi—have all come from Uttar Pradesh, a region that stretches from the Yamuna to Bihār, in which is the heartland of modern Hinduism and the ancient centre of legendary Hinduism. It contains the holy cities of Mathurā and Banaras—the latter renowned for its temples and for its Brahmin priesthood, which is the most conservative in the country. Hindi, the principal language of this state, has also been declared the national language.

The Bengal region

East of Uttar Pradesh, beyond Bihār, is Bengal, a traditional region peopled by the Bengalis. The Bengalis have produced a great number of literary, artistic, philosophic, religious, and political figures; these have included the poet and mystic Rabindranath Tagore, Swami (a title meaning "religious teacher") Vivekananda, and Aurobindo Ghose. The Bengalis, whether Hindu or Muslim, speak the same language and wear the same dress, except in the towns. Bengal has been described as the land of the dhoti, a flowing white-cotton loincloth tucked up in front and fastened behind. Politically, Bengal is one of the chief centres of Maoist Communism and its Indian offshoot, the Naxalite movement, which seeks to destroy society by violence before restructuring it.

Nāgāland, Manipur, and Tripura. Nāgāland, further to the east, between the Brahmaputra Valley and Upper Burma, is another traditional region. The Nāgas, though constituting tribes of mixed origins and varied cultures and often differing in physical appearance, have a composite character and are identifiable. They were once notorious as headhunters, but a considerable number of them have been converted to Christianity. They speak diverse languages, but all belong to the Tibeto-Burman family. The mountainous borderland they occupy covers nearly 6,400 square miles. They number more than 500,000.

Manipur, south of Nāgāland, and Tripura, west of Assam, are other traditional regions in the east that possess their own distinctive languages and cultures. Both the Manipuris and Tripuris show physical traces of a Mongolian origin. The language of the Manipuris is a branch of the Kuki-Chin family; their women enjoy a high social position and are active in trade; the dominant religion is Hindu. The region is noted for its popular Manipuri dances. Some hold that polo was introduced to the British from Manipur. Tripura is said to have once extended as far as to Arakan, in Burma.

Gujarāt and Mahārāshtra. These two distinctive traditional regions lie in the west, grouped around the Gujarati and Marāthā peoples. The mainland of Gujarāt extends from the Rann of Kutch and the Arāvali Hills to the Damanganga River and includes Saurāshtra and Kutch and the hilly tracts to the northeast of the state. Gujarāt's area is a little more than 72,000 square miles. The Gujaratis number over 25,000,000; the prevalent language is Gujarati, spoken by the Hindus, Muslims, and Jains of the region. Until 1960 Gujarāt formed part of Bombay state (now Mahārāshtra), from which it was separated on linguistic grounds. The Gujaratis are noted for their enterprise and business acumen, both at home and abroad. They are much influenced by Jain philosophy, which includes belief in the inviolability of all life; Mahatma Gandhi was himself a Gujarati, and his doctrine of nonviolence had an instinctive appeal to his regional kinsmen.

The language of Mahārāshtra is Marathi. Mahārāshtra forms a major part of peninsular India, having its coastline on the Arabian Sea, to the west. It extends over 118,000 square miles and has a population of over 50,000,000.

The Marāthās, a physically small people, inhabit the western hills, from where, in the 17th century, they resisted the armies of the Mughal invaders. Later, the Marāthās disputed the domination of the British and—with the Sikhs—were the last to offer military resistance to British rule. The Marāthās are noted for their intense local patriotism and pride; for nearly 300 years they have dominated the life of western India. The Brahmins among them have produced many scholars, historians, jurists, and lawyers, although it is the non-Brahmins who today are paramount in political life.

Goa. Another traditional region is Goa (capital Panaji), on the Konkan coast of Mahārāshtra, which until 1961 was a Portuguese possession. Goa is the heartland of Catholicism in India. The Goan Catholics—who number about 250,000—form a distinctive community strongly influenced by Portuguese culture, largely because of the link of religion. Though Hindus constitute the majority in Goa, which has a total population of more than 850,000, the Goan Catholics, because of the political patronage of the Portuguese, acquired a special place in this region.

The Dravidian region. In the southern part of India are the Dravidian lands of the Tamil, Andhra, Kannada, and Malayali peoples. Many customs, such as polyandry and matriarchy, unknown in northern India survive in the south. The caste system exists there but only in a modified form; the Kṣatriya (warrior) and Vaiśya (trader) castes are practically nonexistent.

The Tamils

The Tamils have the longest cultural tradition of these groups; Tamil is the oldest and principal Dravidian tongue—"Dravida" and "Tamil" being two forms of the same word. They inhabit the region and state known as Tamil Nadu, at the southeastern extremity of the Indian peninsula.

The Malayalis who inhabit the picturesque state of Kerala comprise two distinct communities, the Hindu Nāyars and the Syrian Christians. Kerala state—formerly known as Malabar—emerged from the integration of two former princely states, Travancore and Cochin, united by the common tie of language, which is Malayalam. Of its varied communities, two are of especial interest in the context of traditional regions—the Syrian Christians and the white and black Jews. The latter live in the Cochin region, while the former are spread throughout Malabar along the west coast. Another distinctive community is formed by the Muslim Moplahs, who also inhabit the west coast and are descendants of Arab traders.

As a traditional region, Kerala is notable for some distinct social features. Matriarchal and matrilineal influences are pronounced, and the women of Malabar probably enjoy greater freedom than women in any other part of India.

Pondicherry. Pondicherry, in the east, represents an enclave somewhat different from the rest of India because of its long association with the French. Founded by the French in 1674 on the site of a village, it was later also held at different times by the Dutch and the British before being finally restored to the French in 1816; it was held by them until 1954, when it was transferred to India, becoming a legal part of India in 1962.

Pondicherry to some extent bears the impress of its past confused history, but in the early 1970s the impress of France seemed as strong in this territory as the impress of Portugal in Goa.

Patterns of urban and rural settlement. Some 80 percent of India's 550,000,000 people live in villages. Growing industrialization in the cities and towns has, however, led to an increasing drift toward urban areas.

There are more than 2,900 towns and more than 567,000 inhabited villages in India. Nearly 150 towns have a population of over 100,000 each. Nine cities have a population of over 1,000,000. Greater Bombay ranks second, with about 6,000,000; Calcutta first, with 7,000,000; and greater Delhi third, with nearly 3,600,000; Madras comes fourth, with around 3,100,000; Hyderābād fifth, with 1,800,000; Ahmadābād sixth, with 1,700,000; Bangalore seventh, with 1,650,000; Kanpur eighth with 1,300,000, and Poona ninth with 1,100,000.

People and population

GROUPS HISTORICALLY ASSOCIATED WITH CONTEMPORARY INDIA

Ethnic groups. The peoples of India are largely the product of successive invasions that, from immemorial times, have swept into the country. Historically, the Indian subcontinent has formed a cul-de-sac; successive migratory waves of peoples have been largely halted here—although a part of some of the migratory waves also spread into Southeast Asia—and have consequently intermingled to such an extent that racially distinct categories of peoples are hard to establish on a definitive basis. Language, rather than ethnic origin, is the primary distinction between India's peoples. It may nevertheless be said that the main ethnic strains that have mingled in various combinations are the Caucasoid, Mongoloid, Australoid, and Negroid.

Linguistic groups. A British authority, Sir George Grierson, who compiled a monumental *Linguistic Survey of India* (1903–28), listed 225 main languages and dialects. (This list, however, included dialects that vary almost from valley to valley in the Himalayan region, as well as languages that are spoken by only a very few people; Sanskrit, for example, although it is recognized by the government of India as one of the national languages, was spoken by fewer than 3,000 people in the early 1970s.) Officially, 15 national languages are recognized by the Indian government. These are: (1) Assamese, (2) Bengali, (3) Gujarati, (4) Hindi, (5) Kannada, (6) Kashmiri, (7) Malayalam, (8) Marathi, (9) Oriya (the language in Orissa), (10) Punjabi, (11) Sanskrit, (12) Sindhi, (13) Tamil, (14) Telegu, and (15) Urdu.

The national languages

Broadly, the languages of India can be reduced to four families, two of which—Dravidian and Indo-Iranian (Aryan)—are spoken by the great majority of the people. The remaining two families are Austro-Asiatic and Sino-Tibetan. The Austro-Asiatic language family is limited principally to the Munda subgroup of languages, spoken in the hills and forests of central and eastern India. The Sino-Tibetan tongues are confined to the northeastern frontier area. In the course of centuries, there have been mutual borrowings by each of the four language families, but the individual character of each remains distinct and easily identifiable. Some language scholars maintain that certain Indian languages reveal no affinity to any of the four families. An example is the Nahali dialect, spoken in Bihār, which seems to be a survival of a fifth language group, as yet unidentifiable.

The Dravidian languages are spoken primarily in southern India. They do not extend outside India and Pakistan, as the Indo-Iranian, Austro-Asiatic, and Sino-Tibetan language families do. Of the four major languages of the Dravidian group—Tamil, Telegu, Malayalam, and Kannada (or Kanarese)—Tamil is the oldest. In recent years Malayalam, the smallest and the youngest of the Dravidian languages, has shown signs of a more rapid growth than the other three; as a medium, it lends itself to the production of novels, poetry, drama, and journalism.

The Dravidian languages spread from the borders of Orissa to Cape Comorin through eastern and southern India. Tamil is spoken principally in Tamil Nadu. Telegu is spoken mainly in Andhra Pradesh. Malayalam is the language of Kerala, and Kannada the language of Kanara (Mysore state).

The Indo-Iranian languages, of which the Indo-Aryan subgroup is found in India, belong to the larger Indo-European language family, to which Latin, Greek, the Germanic, Slavic, Romance, and other European languages belong. (The other Indo-Iranian subgroup is Iranian, spoken in Iran, Afghanistan, and parts of the Soviet Union.) According to some scholars, an easterly group of Indo-Iranian dialects was carried to India by invaders during the 2nd millennium BC. The root of the Indo-Iranian (*i.e.*, Indo-Aryan) languages of India is to be found in Sanskrit, the classical language of India, which ceased to be a generally spoken language many centuries ago. The various spoken dialects that evolved from Sanskrit are known as Prākrits.

Roots in Sanskrit

One of the oldest Prākrits, which like Sanskrit itself is no longer a generally spoken language but is still extant as a static and sacred literary language, is Pāli; the Buddha used Pāli to convey his teachings to the general populace so that they could understand him without the intervention of the Brahmin caste, whose sacred language was Sanskrit.

Various new spoken dialects emerged as everyday use of Sanskrit and Pāli lapsed. Indian languages were then strongly affected by the great population movements that occurred in northern and western India in the 6th and 7th centuries AD; the pattern stabilized somewhat, however, around the year 1000, as the country's population became more settled. The basic ingredients of these Indo-Aryan languages were Sanskrit and *desh* (local dialect words absorbed largely from the languages of the invaders or from local Dravidian dialects).

Hindi, the most prominent of these languages, developed from the Prākrit that was prevalent from the Yamuna River to Bihār; Rajasthani, Gujarati, and Punjabi also derive from the same Prākrit. Sindhi, Kashmiri, and Marathi, however, stem from other Prākrits.

With the coming of the Muslims, Persian, an Iranian language, became the language publicly used in northern India from the 13th century onward. The Muslim influx promoted the rise of a hybrid tongue, Hindustani (a dialect originating in the area between Delhi, Meerut, and Sahāranpur); it is spoken today in various parts of India outside the north. From colloquial Hindustani, two literary languages—Hindi (showing a strong Sanskrit influence) and Urdu (with a Persianized vocabulary)—emerged.

The present-day Indo-Aryan languages of northern India are nevertheless all related, though with varying degrees of kinship, with Sanskrit. The chief of these Indo-Aryan languages are Hindi, Bengali, Punjabi, Gujarati, Marathi, Sindhi, and the Rājput dialects.

Hindi is spread over the greater part of the northern plain—east of Punjab, north of Gujarāt and Mahārāshtra, west of Orissa, and south of Nepal. It includes several languages and dialects, although strictly Hindi covers only the so-called Western Hindi dialects; these are Kanauji, Bundeli, Braj Bhasa, vernacular Hindustani, Jatu, and Hindustani proper (the speech of Delhi).

Both Urdu and High Hindi (a refined form of Hindi, used in literature and by the educated) have rich literatures. Urdu, which dates to the 13th century, used the Perso-Arabic script and developed as a literary language in the 18th century under the patronage of the Mughal emperors. Hindi literature in High Hindi dates to the 18th century; the Hindi script is known as Devanāgarī.

Among other forms of Hindi are Kosali, or Eastern Hindi, which differs from Western Hindi. It has three dialects: Awadhi (or Baiswari), the language of medieval India, Bagheli, and Chattisgarhi.

The Magadhan language group

Yet other forms are included in the Magadhan group. The western Magadhan languages comprise Bhojpuri and Sadani (or Chota Nagpuri), which is a dialect of Bhojpuri. Its speakers number more than 20,000,000, but they have adopted High Hindi as their language for education, public life, and literature. Central Magadhan consists of two tongues—Maithili, current in northern Bihār, and Magadhi, current in southern Bihār. Maithili has a remarkable literature, although the officially recognized language in both these regions is Hindi and, to some extent, Urdu. To the eastern Magadhan family belong Bengali, Assamese, and Oriya—the language of Orissa. Bengali is spoken by more than 44,000,000 people in West Bengal in India (1971 census) and has a highly developed literature. Assamese is current in the Brahmaputra Valley of Assam and is spoken by about 14,000,000 people. Oriya is current among 20,000,000 people; although it is an archaic language, it has quite an extensive literature.

Punjabi is divided into two linguistic areas—western Punjabi, which is spoken in the western districts of Punjab, and eastern Punjabi, spoken in and near Lahore and Amritsar. The former has no noteworthy literature. Eastern Punjabi might be regarded as the standard form; it is written mostly in the Gurmukhi script, but Muslims show a preference for the Persian script, and Hindus for the Devanāgarī script. Differences of script were one of the major factors that led to the division in 1966 of the old Punjab state into the new Punjab (Sikh) state and Haryana (a Hindu state). Eastern Punjabi is a rich language and has developed a vigorous literature.

Rajasthani is not a single language but a group of dialects. There are two important types, known as Dundhari (or Jaipur Rajasthani) and Marwari, which is spoken at Jodhpur. Dundhari has not developed a literature, but Marwari (which closely resembles Rajasthani) has. Subsidiary, in a certain sense, to these languages are Gujarati and—more distantly—Marathi. Gujarati was akin to Rajasthani until about AD 1500, when Rajasthani became influenced by Western Hindi and thence passed into the Hindi orbit; after this, Gujarati developed independently. Marathi is spoken by more than 25,000,000 people and claims a literature that goes back to the 12th century. It has two speeches—Konkani, spoken in and around Goa, and Haldi, current in the Bastar district of Madhya Pradesh.

In the Indo-Aryan language group may also be included the Himalayan dialects, such as Pahari and Himali, which again are divided into various groups. These languages have little literature. Eastern Himalayan includes Nepali, a developing language going back to the 17th century. Kashmiri also belongs to this group and is essentially a Dardic dialect, belonging to the complex of Indic languages spoken in the upper valley of the Indus. There are two major dialects in Kashmir—Kashmiri and Shina; both are essentially branches of the Indo-Aryan group.

The Austro-Asiatic languages

The Austro-Asiatic languages are spoken by a substratum of the Indian population and are today a reminder of a largely forgotten past. These languages are spoken mainly by the tribal people and belong to the Munda, or Kolari, group. They are still current in eastern and central India and to some extent in North Bengal and Assam. This group comprises a number of allied dialects, the most important of which are Kherwari, current in eastern India; Santali, spoken by 3,000,000 people, largely the Santāl group of aborigines; and Mundari.

The Austro-Asiatic languages have virtually no script, although European missionaries tried to reduce some of its languages and dialects to a form of script in the 19th century with indifferent success. One of the Austro-Asiatic languages is Khasi, which is spoken by about 300,000 people and has a Roman script introduced by European missionaries. The University of Calcutta recognizes three Santali scripts—Devanāgarī, Bengali, and Roman.

The Sino-Tibetan languages are represented in India today by various offshoots of the Tai and Chinese language groups. Thus, for example, Khamti is spoken by a small tribe in the extreme northeastern frontier of India. There also exist some Tibeto-Burman dialects, such as Manipuri, or Meithei, which are spoken or understood today by about 500,000 people. These dialects were originally written in an alphabet of their own, but about the middle of the 18th century, they adopted the Bengali script. Beyond the Indian frontier, but to some extent seeping over the frontier, are Newari, or Nepali, the language current in Nepal and adjacent areas. Newari uses the Devanāgarī Hindi script and has a literature that goes back to the 14th century AD. Another Tibeto-Burman language is Lepcha, spoken in eastern Nepal and Sikkim but also in Darjeeling, in India. It has a script of its own and is believed to be a branch of the Nāga group of the Tibeto-Burman family.

There are various minor languages that exist in India. Among these are Andamanese, spoken by the original inhabitants of the Andaman Islands; this seems to be a survival of an early Negroid language. Nicobarese is spoken by people of the Nicobar group of islands adjoining the Andaman group and seems to be a form of the Mon-Khmer speech of the Austro-Asiatic family of languages; perhaps about 10,000 people use it today.

Various immigrant communities have adopted Indian languages as their mother tongue. Among these are the Parsis of Bombay, who speak Gujarati, and the Bene-Israeli Jews of Mahārāshtra, who speak Marathi.

Although it is not classified as one of the 15 national languages, English—which was introduced in the wake of the British conquest in the 18th and 19th centuries—is the only lingua franca shared by the Dravidian south and the Hindi north. The 1950 constitution of India stipulated that Hindi (in the Devanāgrī script) should be the common language of India and that Arabic numerals should be used as common numerals. It was also agreed that English should be retained as an official language until 1965, after which it was to be replaced by Hindi. In the event, however, opposition from the Dravidian south to the abandonment of English in favour of Hindi compelled another adjustment. English retained the status of an additional official language, with no definite date being set for its abandonment. The Official Languages Amendment Act of 1967 further provided that either Hindi or English should be compulsory languages for recruitment to the central government service. Correspondence in English was obligatory, however, only between the Union government and a non-Hindi-speaking state. Hindi states dealing with non-Hindi states could send their communications in Hindi provided that English translations were also supplied.

Religious groups. India is the birthplace of many religions and has become the home of many others. Through the ages Indians have shown strong proclivities toward a religious outlook, resulting in the development of indigenous religions, chief among which are Hinduism, Jainism, Buddhism, and Sikhism. This religious bent has also encouraged the growth of such extraneous religions as Islām, Christianity, Judaism, and Zoroastrianism.

The oldest of all Indian religions is animism, which is still practiced by the more remote tribes, such as the Santāls, Bhīls, and Gonds.

Hinduism

Hinduism is, however, above all the traditional religion of India; some date its origin back to the Vedas of the Aryans, between 2000 and 1500 BC. There is evidence, however, that Hinduism, as it later emerged, is not the religion preached in the Aryan Vedas but contains Dravidian elements going back to a pre-Aryan age, thus representing a fusion of two cultures. About 83 percent of the population of India is Hindu.

While Hinduism has been a great unifying force, its association with the caste system has also made for division and a sense of separateness. Whatever its origin—whether induced by race, colour, occupation, or the mere fact of conquest—caste has constituted a major divisive force throughout Indian history and has even permeated non-Hindu groups.

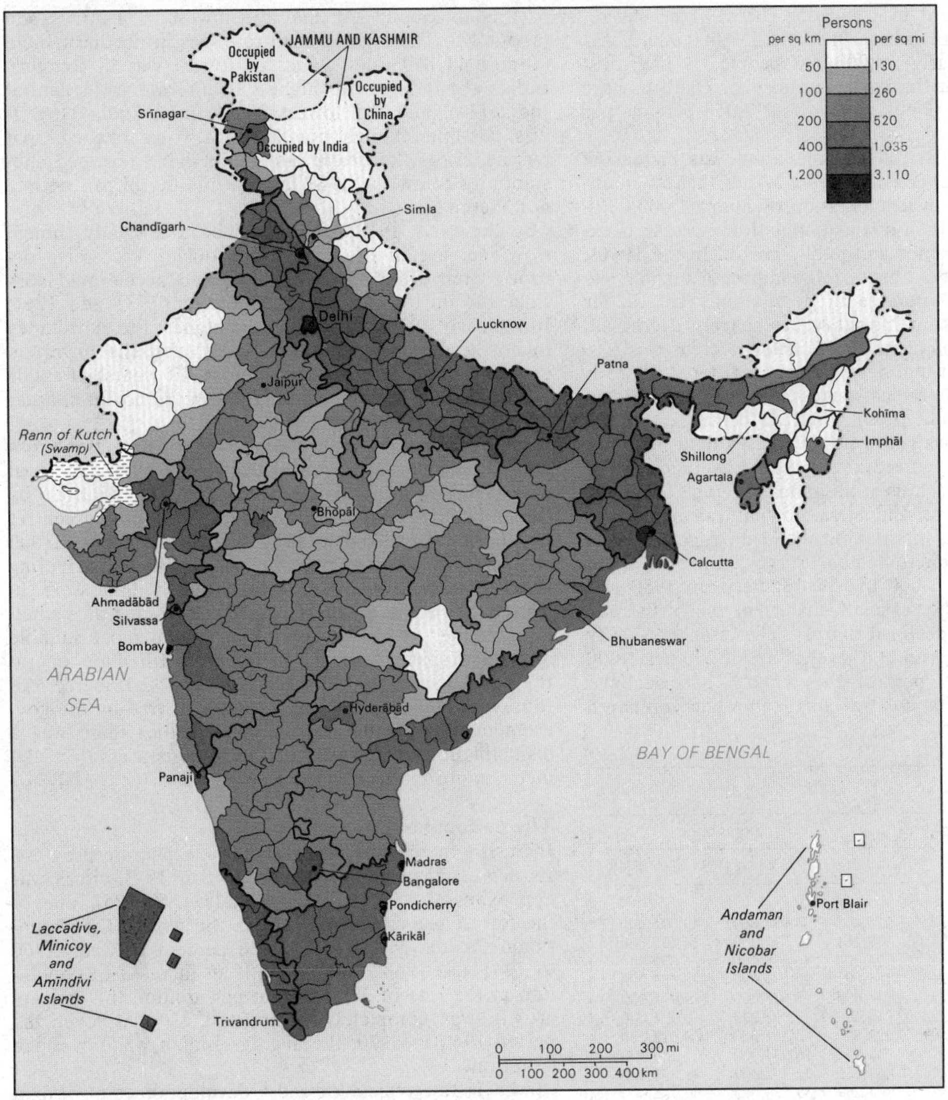

Population density of India.

Jainism and Buddhism were the first offshoots of Hinduism, coming into being in the 6th and 5th centuries BC, respectively. Jainism survives today largely in Gujarāt and Rājasthān, where it has about 2,000,000 followers. Its principles of nonviolence and asceticism have left their imprint on Hindu thought; Mahatma Gandhi (*q.v.*) was deeply influenced by these two principles.

Buddhism, a younger rival of Jainism, spread over India largely as a result of the example of Áśoka, the great Mauryan emperor of India who embraced this religion. After his death, the influence of Buddhism steadily declined, being superseded by a resurgent Hinduism. Buddhism, however, spread to Tibet, China, Japan, Korea, Mongolia, and other lands, thus becoming a world religion; Jainism remains confined to India.

Of the religions that are extraneous to India, Islām, primarily introduced by conquest, has struck the deepest roots. Originally brought into India by foreign traders, it gained strength in the wake of the Muslim invasions; after the establishment of the Mughal Empire in the 16th century, the greater part of India became Muslim dominated. Muslims today constitute more than 11 percent of India's total population.

The other foreign religions are Christianity, Judaism, and Zoroastrianism. Judaism was introduced by early Jewish traders who established settlements in the coastal towns, one of their principal centres being Cochin; Jews today form a microscopic proportion of India's population. Zoroastrianism entered India between AD 700 and 800 with the influx of Persian refugees fleeing from Muslim persecution; the descendants of these refugees, the Parsis, are today concentrated largely in Bombay. Christianity claims to date back to AD 52, when St. Thomas, one of the Apostles of Christ, is said to have landed on the west coast of India, where he established a few churches; according to tradition, he then travelled from the west coast to the east coast, where he was martyred at Mylapore, in Madras. The descendants of the Christians he converted are known today as Syrian Christians. A new era of Christian proselytization began with the advent of the Europeans in India; however, the Christians form only about 2.5 percent of India's population and are concentrated mostly on the west coast.

According to the 1971 census figures, Hindus constitute nearly 83 percent of the population, Muslims more than 11 percent, Christians around 3 percent, Sikhs about 2 percent, Buddhists about 0.75 percent, and Jains less than 0.5 percent. Other religions count for less than 0.5 percent of the population. In the states and territories, Hindus have their greatest majority in Himachal Pradesh, where they number nearly 97 percent. The Muslims constitute nearly 94 percent of the population in the Laccadive, Minicoy and Amīndīvi Islands, and 66 percent in Jammu and Kashmir. The highest percentage of Christians occurs in Nagaland, where it amounts to almost 67 percent; Meghalaya has the second largest proportion—nearly 47 percent. The Sikhs represent nearly 60 percent in Punjab and 7 percent in Delhi.

DEMOGRAPHY

In 1951 India's population was about 361,000,000; in 1961 it amounted to nearly 440,000,000—an increase of nearly 22 percent in a decade. The 1971 census reported India's population to be about 550,000,000. Uttar Pradesh, with nearly 90,000,000 people, is the most populous state, but the union territory of Delhi has the highest density of population—about 7,058 persons per square mile.

Population trends in 1970s

In the early 1970s, India's population was increasing at the rate of 2.5 percent a year, a rate that, if maintained, will result in a population of about 1,000,000,000 by AD 2000. Much of this population increase is explained by improvements in public health. In the 1940s, infant mortality took a heavy toll and proportionately reduced the rate of increase in population. With better health services, infant mortality has sharply decreased, while the population has proportionately increased.

Since many births and deaths are unregistered, there is an evident difference between the figures based on registration data and those based on census estimates. According to studies based on the census data for 1951 and 1961, births occurred at an annual average rate of 42 per 1,000, and deaths at an annual average of 23 per 1,000, resulting in an annual rate of natural increase of 19 per 1,000. The infant mortality rate reported as a result of the National Sample Survey made in about 1958 was 146 per 1,000 live births. Between 1950 and 1970 there was only a small change in the birth rate, but the death rate declined sharply. The infant mortality rate, which used to run at a level of about 250 per 1,000 births in the early part of the century, had declined greatly by the 1970s but was still high when compared with other countries.

India, Area and Population

	area		population	
	sq mi	sq km	1961 census	1971 census*
States				
Andhra Pradesh	106,272	275,244	35,983,000	43,395,000
Assam	30,294	78,461	10,837,000	14,630,000
Bihār	67,184	174,008	46,456,000	56,332,000
Gujarāt	72,236	187,091	20,634,000	26,687,000
Haryana	17,010	44,056	7,591,000	9,971,000
Himachal Pradesh	21,490	55,658	2,812,000	3,424,000
Jammu and Kashmir‖	86,050	222,870	3,561,000	4,615,000
Kerala	15,007	38,869	16,904,000	21,280,000
Madhya Pradesh	171,220	443,459	32,372,000	41,651,000
Mahārāshtra	118,637	307,269	39,554,000	50,335,000
Manipur	8,628	22,346	780,000	1,070,000
Meghalaya	8,666	22,445	769,000	983,000
Mysore	74,037	191,757	23,587,000	29,263,000
Nāgāland	6,366	16,488	369,000	516,000
Orissa	60,178	155,860	17,549,000	21,935,000
Punjab	19,495	50,491	11,255,000	13,730,000
Rājasthān	132,149	342,267	20,156,000	25,724,000
Tamil Nadu	50,180	129,966	33,687,000	41,103,000
Tripura	4,035	10,451	1,142,000	1,557,000
Uttar Pradesh	113,655	294,366	73,746,000	88,365,000
West Bengal	33,852	87,676	34,926,000	44,440,000
Union territories				
Andaman and Nicobar Islands	3,202	8,293	64,000	115,000
Arunachal Pradesh (North East Frontier Agency)	31,439	81,426	337,000	445,000
Dādra and Nagar Haveli	189	489	58,000	74,000
Delhi	573	1,483	2,659,000	4,044,000
Goa, Daman, and Diu	1,441	3,733	627,000	857,000
Laccadive, Minicoy, and Amīndīvi Islands	11	28	24,000	32,000
Mizoram	8,134	21,067	266,000	322,000
Pondicherry	183	473	369,000	471,000
Total India	1,261,810†	3,268,090	439,073,000‡	547,368,000‡

*Provisional. †Converted area figures do not add to total given because of rounding. ‡Figures do not add to total given because of rounding. ‖Total includes the 32,358 sq mi (83,806 sq km) area of the Pakistani-occupied Jammu and Kashmir, and the census population figures refer to Indian-occupied portion of Jammu and Kashmir only. The estimated population (1971) for Pakistani-occupied Jammu and Kashmir is 1,300,000.
Source: Official government figures.

Among the states, the highest birth rate during the 1950s and 1960s was in Assam (about 49 per 1,000), and the lowest in Tamil Nadu (about 35); the highest death rate was also in Assam (about 27), and the lowest in Kerala (about 16). The highest natural-increase rate was in Punjab (about 26), and the lowest in Tamil Nadu (about 12). The highest birth rate was in northern India (almost 44 per 1,000), and the lowest was in southern India (about 38). The highest death rate is in central India (24), and the lowest in northern India (19). It was possible, though not statistically established, that by the 1970s the death rate might have declined substantially below the 1961 level, while the birth rate had not altered greatly.

By the early 1970s, there had been a steady though slow increase in life expectancy during successive decades from 1891 onward, but it had accelerated considerably during the 30 years between 1931 and 1961. In the early 1970s, males had the highest life expectancy in northern India (almost 50 years) and the lowest in central and eastern India (almost 40 years). Female expectation of life was also highest in the northern areas and lowest in the central.

One of India's major problems—if not its major problem—is population control. In the early 1970s, the goal was to reduce the birth rate from 41 to 25 per 1,000 by the end of 1976. A network of family-planning centres had been set up, and in 1971 there were about 30,000 centres giving family-planning advice and distributing free contraceptives; of these, about 25,000 were in rural areas. After extensive trials, the placing of a small loop in the uterus was found to be the most suitable method of birth control for India. Sterilization operations had increased, but not to any marked degree. All family-planning services were provided free by the government, but among various communities there was a disinclination on the part of the more conservative elements to utilize these services. (F.R.M.)

The national economy

India is experiencing relatively slow economic progress. Its per capita net domestic product at 1971 prices was approximately 552 rupees (roughly U.S. $75), one of the lowest per capita incomes in the world. India's national income rose by about 26 percent between 1960 to 1961 and 1968 to 1969. With an increase in population at the rate of 2.25 percent per annum, this meagre growth was completely neutralized, so that, over the period 1960 to 1970, the average Indian was not much better off.

India's economic structure

India is not typical of most developing countries, in that it has a sophisticated administrative and political structure, a well-equipped bureaucracy, a large supply of educated manpower, and a considerable transport and communications network. Between independence in 1947 and the early 1970s, it had made great progress and undertaken large investments: the major gains in agriculture were, however, very recent. India had acquired a sophisticated industrial base that placed it among the top 20 industrial nations of the world. This had yet to be reflected in its foreign trade—its exports at the beginning of the 1970s accounted for less than 1 percent of total world exports, and in aggregate they were below those of Hong Kong. The country suffered enormous disparities in incomes, with the rich being very rich and the poor very poor. A small elite enjoyed very high standards of living, while the bulk of the population had incomes below the subsistence level. The top 30 percent of the population accounted for over 60 percent of total consumption.

THE EXTENT AND DISTRIBUTION OF RESOURCES

Mineral resources. India is fairly endowed with mineral resources. It has vast reserves of coal and one-seventh of the total iron-ore reserves of the world. It also has reserves of manganese ore. But reserves of nonferrous metals, with the exception of aluminum, are not enough to meet domestic needs. India completely lacks elemental sulfur and phosphorus.

Despite some of these serious gaps in resources, mineral production and export earnings have moved upward. Mineral production between 1950 and 1970 rose by nearly 500 percent, while the total foreign-exchange earnings from mineral exports increased from about

U.S. $49,000,000 in 1951 to $216,000,000 during 1968 to 1969. The main mineral commodities that India exports are iron ore, manganese ore, mica, and kyanite (aluminum silicate).

It has been inferred that India has about 116,000,000,000 metric tons of coal reserves, out of which 96,000,000,000 metric tons have been proved. The estimate of reserves is expected to increase if seams deeper than 2,000 feet are considered.

In the early 1970s it was clear that coal would be the country's primary fuel for years. Fears expressed that India would use up her coal reserves within a few decades are unfounded. The country has enough noncoking coal to meet its requirements, unless, of course, the initial rate of exploitation increases substantially—for example to the United States level of consumption—or the growth rate of the economy becomes increasingly rapid. Coking-coal resources were, however, in 1971 estimated at 4,000,000,000 tons—insufficient to match India's iron-ore resources.

In 1970 to 1971 the country produced more than 75,000,000 tons, which fully met its needs. The slow pace of the industrial economy and the rapid change to the use of diesel engines by the railways, with a resulting drop in the demand for coal, were expected to prevent the aggregate annual production of coal from reaching 100,000,000 tons by 1973 to 1974.

The country's coal reserves are not evenly distributed all over the country. The 56 workable or potential coal mines are concentrated in Bihār, West Bengal, Madhya Pradesh, and Andhra Pradesh. Coal required in southern and western India has consequently had to be carried for several hundred miles.

Apart from coal, India has lignite reserves of more than 2,000,000,000 tons. Sizable deposits have been located in Tamil Nadu, Rājasthān, and Gujarāt. But, with the exception of Tamil Nadu, the reserves had yet to be exploited in the early 1970s; the Tamil Nadu reserves were being systematically exploited by means of an industrial complex that produced power, fertilizers, and briquettes (small bricks made of compressed coal dust, which are used for fuel).

Iron-ore reserves

Iron-ore reserves totalled 22,000,000,000 tons in the early 1970s. In 1970 to 1971, India produced almost 28,000,000 tons and exported 21,000,000 tons, thus earning foreign exchange worth U.S. $156,000,000. In the early 1970s, India was one of the world's leading iron-ore exporters. The country's most extensive iron-ore deposits are found in Bihār, Orissa, Madhya Pradesh, Mysore, Goa, Andhra Pradesh, and Tamil Nadu; quality is generally very good.

India has vast manganese-ore deposits, concentrated mainly in Madhya Pradesh and Mahārāshtra; some are also scattered in Bihār, Orissa, Mysore, Andhra Pradesh, and Goa. Total reserves amount to 187,000,000 tons. Exports in 1970 to 1971 totalled about 1,636,000 tons, accounting for the bulk of all output. There is a considerable amount of chromite in the country, but, by the early 1970s, there had been no systematic exploitation of it; similarly, India had yet to produce titanium (a very hard metallic element used to toughen steel), in spite of ample reserves of rutile and ilmenite—both of which are sources of titanium.

Nonferrous metals

India is desperately short of nonferrous metals, excluding aluminum. Copper output in the early 1970s was about 9,600 tons per annum, while the requirement was calculated at more than 100,000 tons; to make up the difference, copper worth U.S. $63,000,000 had to be imported in 1969 to 1970. The situation regarding zinc was no better—output was about 25,000 tons, while the demand was about 117,000 tons. Only 2,000 tons of lead is produced per year, against a need for about 80,000 tons.

The scarcity in the supply of nonferrous metals is not because of a deficiency in resources. Investigations by the Geological Survey of India have revealed important deposits in the Agnigundala region, in Andhra Pradesh; in the Khetri region, in Rājasthān; in Gujarāt, Mahārāshtra, and Madhya Pradesh; and at Sukinda Khās, in Orissa. But, until the estimates of these reserves are known and exploitation begins, India will have to depend entirely on imports to meet her needs. In 1970 to 1971, the country imported almost U.S. $120,000,000 worth of nonferrous metals annually, and this was likely to nearly double by the end of 1973 to 1974. India has plenty of bauxite—the ore for aluminum—concentrated in Bihār, Madhya Pradesh, Mahārāshtra, Mysore, Tamil Nadu, Gujarāt, and Orissa. The reserves are estimated to amount to 165,000,000 tons, out of which 95,000,000 tons are classed as high-grade reserves.

Since India lacks access to the other nonferrous metals, scientists at the National Metallurgical Laboratory are experimenting with the possibility of substituting aluminum for copper in the electrical industry, for zinc in galvanization, and for nickel and copper in coinage.

India does not have deposits of elemental sulfur, but plans have been made to extract sulfur from pyrites found at Amjore, Bihār. Phosphorus has been found in the form of rock-phosphate deposits in a long belt near Udaipur, in Rājasthān, and near Mussoorie, in Uttar Pradesh. In the early 1970s, preliminary investigations indicated that each of these reserves may have about 10,000,000 tons of phosphorus, which was sufficient to meet a part of India's requirements.

India has few known petroleum resources, and such known resources as exist will be exhausted within a generation. The oil fields in Gujarāt, for example, are being worked out very rapidly; their output will start declining by the end of the 1970s and, by the early 1980s, may fall to very low levels. In the early 1970s, the country had high hopes for further discoveries of oil as a result of shallow offshore drilling in progress near Aliabet in the Gulf of Cambay and deep offshore drilling due to begin in 1973 over a geological structure named "Bombay High," off the Gujarāt coast. Some new deposits of oil had also been discovered in Lokawa, Galeki, and Kusijan, in Upper Assam—the only state besides Gujarāt that produces oil and natural gas. Prospective oil-bearing areas are also believed to exist in Tripura and in offshore areas of the east coast.

Because of low oil output, the country has to import more than 60 percent of its crude-oil requirements. Of the 18,000,000 tons of crude oil refined by Indian refineries in 1970 to 1971, 11,000,000 tons had to be imported; with the decline in the output of the Ankleshwar field, India's oil imports doubled between 1965 and 1970, and the value of crude oil and petroleum products imports in 1970 to 1971 rose substantially. With demand growing rapidly, an attempt is being made to shift the emphasis back to indigenous sources of energy, particularly coal.

Biological resources. About 50 percent of India is cultivated, and 19 percent is forested, while the rest is uncultivated. The quality of the soil is generally poor, and soil erosion is common in some parts of the country. Efforts at soil conservation and improvement have been woefully inadequate to meet the need that exists. Out of the 185,000,000 acres of the total land area under forests, 140,000,000 acres are "reserved" or "protected." The remaining area consists of unclassified forests not generally under systematic management. The forest area is unevenly distributed; forests are most scarce in areas where most needed—for instance, in the densely populated and intensively cultivated Gangetic Basin. Only the Himalayan belt and a few mountainous areas have thick forests. The fact that most of the plains are bereft of any worthwhile forest cover has led to some desiccation of the climate and vegetation; this in turn has had an adverse effect on precipitation from the monsoon clouds.

Forest land acreage

Among the economically important species of trees are teak (20,000,000 acres), sal (25,000,000 acres), and the coniferous group (10,000,000 acres). A total of about 95 percent of the forests are owned by the state, about 3 percent belong to *pañcāyat*s, while only about 2 percent are in private hands.

Although India has the largest livestock population in the world—344,000,000 head—milk yields are extremely low. The total milk production is estimated at about

22,000,000 tons per annum against a demand for about 56,000,000 tons. The average milk yield of a cow is about 50 gallons, while that of a buffalo is 130 gallons per annum. The buffalo, in fact, is the main milk producer; it produces at least 55 percent of the marketed milk. Cows yield 43 percent, while the remaining 2 percent is produced by goats, sheep, asses, and camels.

The low yield of milk is due to the poor quality of the stock, highly inadequate fodder resources, the limited grassland area, and old-fashioned methods of livestock management. It has been estimated that the present feed and fodder resources are sufficient only for about 60 percent of India's livestock strength, which is widely distributed throughout the country.

Despite these handicaps, it has been demonstrated by competent Indian dairy farmers that good crossbred cows can easily produce 700 gallons of milk a year. About 22,000,000 such cows could meet the total milk requirements of the country, while 54,000,000 cows and 26,000,000 buffalo were, in the early 1970s, unable to meet half the requirement.

India produces 76,000,000 pounds of wool every year from about 40,000,000 sheep, but the country's sheep are poor wool yielders. The average annual yield of greased (uncleaned) wool from a sheep is about two pounds, with the range extending between 0.75 and five pounds. This output is very poor compared with that in Australia and New Zealand, where the annual yield per sheep is from eight to 12 pounds. The bulk of Indian wool is coarse, containing a high proportion of hair and kempy (short, coarse, and brittle) fibres that are mainly suitable for making carpets. Most wool-yielding sheep are in the arid region of the plains of Rājasthān, Gujarāt, and Haryana and the Himalayan region. The sheep of peninsular India have a low yield of wool that is of poor quality.

Hydroelectric and other power resources. India has made considerable progress in the development of power since 1950. The installed generating capacity increased from 2,300,000 kilowatts in 1950 to 16,429,000 kilowatts in 1971. Electricity generation increased from 6,574,000,000 to 55,800,000,000 kilowatt-hours during the same period, and the per capita consumption rose from 18 to 83 kilowatt-hours. The Fourth Five-Year Plan (1969 to 1974) envisages increasing the generating capacity to 23,000,000 kilowatts.

Hydroelectric power constitutes the most economic source of electricity production in the country. The capital outlay on hydroelectric stations is comparable with (and in some cases lower than) that on thermal power stations and is very much lower than that on nuclear stations. The cost of energy from hydroelectric stations is significantly lower than the cost of energy from other sources.

By courtesy of the United Nations

Sheep farm in Mālpura, Rājasthān, India, 1965.

SOURCES OF NATIONAL INCOME

Agriculture, forestry, and fishing. Agriculture, forestry, and fishing account for roughly one-half of India's gross domestic product at current prices and are a source of livelihood for four-fifths of the entire population. Agricultural production increased steadily during the 1950s, but its course was more erratic in the 1960s. After relative stagnation in the early 1960s, there was a marked increase in output from 1964 to 1965, followed by two very bad years when production fell sharply because of adverse weather conditions. In 1967 to 1968 production once again reached a record level, and progress since then has been impressive. In the 20 years from 1949–50 to 1968–69, agricultural production rose by 2.9 percent per annum, due both to an increase in acreage (1.4 percent per annum) and an increase in production (1.5 percent per annum). Food-grains output, which represented two-thirds of the total value of agricultural production, grew by almost 2.8 percent per annum in this period, while output of other grains grew by almost 3.2 percent. India's potential arable area is 407,200,000 acres. Of this, about 83 percent was already under cultivation by the early 1970s, and it was widely recognized that further gains in production would have to come largely from an increase in productivity.

Rice is India's most important food-grain crop, and, at the beginning of the 1970s, rice production was estimated at a little less than 42,000,000 tons, compared with 26,000,000 tons in 1949 to 1950. The area under rice was roughly 91,000,000 acres, or approximately one-third of all the area under food grains. Rice production was not rising very rapidly, largely because of the slow rate of acceptance of new high-yielding varieties that were grown only in a small part of the total area under rice. Wheat, India's second food-grain crop, however, showed a remarkable increase in production. Between 1964–65 and 1968–69, the acreage under wheat increased by 19 percent, and productivity by 28 percent, resulting in a total increase in production of 52 percent. Wheat, however, accounted for less than 15 percent of the total acreage under food grains, and hence—despite this dramatic increase in production—India was still not quite self-sufficient in food. The increase in wheat output was largely because of the successful evolution of new wheat varieties, both foreign and domestic strains, and because of the rapid expansion of minor irrigation in the form of tube (driven) wells in the major wheat-growing areas. In the northwestern state of Punjab, the number of tube wells rose from 7,000 to 120,000 within a single decade, largely reducing the dependence on the monsoon. Other food-grain crops include *jowār* (sorghum), *bājrā* (a type of millet), *ragi* (a cereal grass), barley, and small millets. Of these, *jowār* and *bājrā* are by far the most important. Total food-grain production in India in 1971 was estimated at 107,800,000 tons—twice the level of output at the end of the 1940s.

Rice production

In the 1950s, non-food-grain production had been rising faster than food-grain production, but, in subsequent years, it began to lag behind. The most important non-food-grain crop is oilseed, the production of which has been erratic in the late 1960s and early 1970s. The area under oilseeds was approximately 54,000,000 acres in the early 1970s, and the 3 percent per annum increase in output registered by this crop in the 20 years up to 1968–69 was largely because of an increase in acreage rather than an increase in yield. Other major non-food-grain crops are sugar, raw cotton, jute, tea, coffee, rubber, and tobacco. India, together with Bangladesh, accounts for the bulk of the world's jute production and, with Sri Lanka (Ceylon), accounts for the bulk of the world's tea production. Livestock and dairying account for about 5 percent of the national income. The output of milk and milk products is estimated to be increasing by 3 percent per annum, but demand greatly exceeds supply.

"Bucket-chain" system irrigation wells near Najafgarh, Delhi union territory.

By courtesy of World Health Organization

Indian agriculture is still largely traditional; it is dependent on the vagaries of the weather, and the land under cultivation is extremely unevenly distributed. Only one-fourth of the net sown area is irrigated, and less than two-thirds of the potential arable area can be irrigated from potential surface and ground-water resources. A very large percentage of farmers are concentrated on a very small percentage of the total area under cultivation; agriculture typically suffers from lack of water and credit, lack of incentives because of the land-tenure system, and fragmentation of holdings. Smallholders, defined as those with less than five acres, account for 52 percent of rural households and 19 percent of landholdings. The Green Revolution (a slogan referring to spectacular increases in agricultural production) is largely confined to land with assured water supply and to farmers with large holdings. This is, in fact, a direct consequence of the government's intensive Agricultural District Programme started in 1960, in which districts adjudged the most responsive to development programs were chosen for concentrated development. By the early 1970s, this strategy had, in fact, worked in terms of production. But, since the beneficiaries are a small number of large farmers, it has also accentuated disparities in rural incomes, resulting in new social and economic problems that have begun to produce new political responses. To quote the Indian Planning Commission, there is danger of a "sharp polarisation between the more privileged and less privileged classes in the rural sector, the privilege in this instance relating to the resources and tools of development."

With a long coastline and many major river systems, there is an enormous potential for the development of fisheries, which remains largely untapped. Fish production in 1960 was estimated at 960,000 tons; at the end of the 1960s, it was estimated to have increased to 1,500,000 tons. Exports of seafood and other sea products have also increased dramatically and, at the end of the 1960s, were worth about U.S. $44,000,000 a year. Considerable progress has been made in mechanizing the fishing industry. About 6,000 mechanized boats were purchased, and several small harbours were developed in the 1960s. Little has been done so far to develop either inland fishery or deep-sea fishing in the Indian Ocean (*q.v.*).

Fisheries

Despite the fact that forests occupy 19 percent of the land surface of the country, the contribution of forestry and logging to net domestic production in the early 1970s was only a little more than 1 percent at current prices. The average per acre production of forests in India is estimated at 7.6 cubic feet per annum, or one-fourth of the world average. India's forest wealth is rapidly being exhausted. Consumption of industrial wood in 1968 to 1969 was estimated at 390,000,000 cubic feet and was expected to increase to 600,000,000 cubic feet by the end of the 1970s.

Mining and quarrying. India is an important producer of iron ore and coal, but, in the early 1970s, its mineral development had yet to reach a level that would meet domestic and export demand. As a consequence, the mining sector still contributed very little to gross national product. Imports of petroleum, nonferrous metals, and nonmetallic minerals such as rock phosphate and sulfur were costing India about U.S. $300,000,000 a year in the late 1960s. With some exceptions, the mineral industry was in the public sector. Responsibility for exploration rested with the Geological Survey of India and—in the case of petroleum—with the Oil and Natural Gas Commission. A little over one-third of the output of India's refineries was from indigenous crude oil, the rest being imported. The demand for oil products at the end of the 1960s was estimated at around 16,000,000 tons and was expected to increase to 27,000,000 tons by the mid-1970s. India is exploring for oil in the shallow coastal waters of the Gulf of Cambay and was planning exploration, in the mid-1970s, with Japanese collaboration, in the deep waters of the gulf.

The demand for oil

There is a well-developed aluminum industry, which was formerly entirely in the private sector, although two public-sector plants were under construction in the early 1970s. Attempts to develop India's copper and zinc resources were also being made, but progress was slow. It was expected that iron ore might become India's most promising metal. Exports in the early 1970s exceeded $156,000,000, and production was expected to double during the years of the Fourth Five-Year Plan, ending March 1974.

Manufacturing. In the 1950s and 1960s—the first two decades of economic planning—India succeeded in acquiring a sizable and diversified industrial base. In the year 1969 the industrial structure was still dominated by consumer-goods industries; in this sector the most important industries were cotton weaving, tea, sugar, and pharmaceuticals, and cotton spinning was also significant. Capital-goods industries accounted for just over one-tenth of production by weight, and, of these, railroad equipment and motor vehicles were the most important.

In the early 1970s, India had a relatively sophisticated industrial structure, with major investment in steel, machine tools, fertilizers, cement, aluminum manufacturing, industrial machinery and components, and electrical and transport equipment. Progress in industries making intermediate goods (such as tires and synthetic fibres) and consumer goods had been slower, but India's requirements for consumer goods were met almost totally by domestic production, and the government's policy was to encourage self-sufficiency in as many areas as possible. Consumer-goods industries were almost entirely privately owned, but most of the investment in the capital-goods and basic-industries sector was the responsibility of the state. More than four-fifths of investment in public-sector enterprises at the end of the 1960s was in steel, engineering, chemicals, petroleum, mines, and minerals.

Industrial production during the 1960s was rather erratic. In the early 1960s the index of production increased by about 8 percent per year. Agricultural setbacks in 1966 and 1967 caused production to decline. Production increased toward the end of the 1960s and was increasing at the rate of 6 to 7 percent in the late 1960s. The level of public investment fell sharply in the second half of the 1960s, but attempts to revive it began in the early 1970s. Private investment at this time also tended to fall off because of political uncertainties and an excess of capacity over demand. Demand, nevertheless, was rising faster than the rate of expansion in capacity would suggest.

The Fourth Five-Year Plan (1969 to 1974) envisaged an investment of approximately U.S. $7,000,000,000 in organized industry and mining, of which about $4,000,000,000 was to be in the public sector and $3,000,000,000 in the private sector. Of the public-sector outlay, over one-third was for steel and heavy engineering, of which the largest was for a 4,000,000-ton steel plant being built in Bokaro, Bihār, with Russian assistance. The existing

The Fourth Five-Year Plan

public-sector steel plants at Raurkela (Orissa), Durgāpur (West Bengal), and Bhilai (Madhya Pradesh) were being expanded, and new plants were proposed at Vishākhapatnam (Andhra Pradesh), Hospet (Mysore), and Salem (Tamil Nadu). Steel capacity was expected to increase from 9,000,000 tons in 1968–69 to 12,000,000 tons in 1973–74.

The plan also envisaged significant expansion in the aluminum, copper, and zinc industry. India's shipbuilding capacity at Vishākhapatnam shipyard was to increase from 12,500 to 80,000 deadweight tons. A second shipyard was being built at Cochin. Fertilizer capacity was expected to rise to 3,000,000 tons of nitrogen by 1974 from more than 1,000,000 tons at the end of the 1960s. A giant public-sector petrochemical complex was planned in Gujarāt. To meet the increased demand for refinery capacity, a refinery was under construction in Haldia, West Bengal; others were proposed in the northwestern region and in Assam.

Industrial production in the public sector was approximately one-tenth of the total production of organized industry. Although the Indian government is committed to the concept of a mixed economy, private industry is viewed with some suspicion, and relations between government and industry are not always smooth. In the late 1950s and the early 1960s, the private sector was given considerable encouragement, but as a result of the operation of the industrial licensing system and prevailing tax laws and import controls, considerable distortions have been introduced into the ownership pattern of Indian industry. Private industry is still largely in the hands of a few family business houses, the most notable of which are the Birlas and Tatas. These business houses formerly dominated Indian industry through a system of managing agencies that have now been closed down by the government. But the pace of introduction of professional standards of management is slow, and there is considerable inefficiency in production. Excessive concern over concentration of industry has led to disregard for the benefits offered by a mass-production economy. High tariff walls also protect considerable inefficiencies in production. The vast expansion of industry has meant relying on a first-generation labour force that is extremely vulnerable to political influence, so that labour unrest and low productivity are often manifest. Despite these teething troubles characteristic of a predominantly agricultural society that is trying to industrialize, there has been considerable progress; this is because of the availability of a plentiful supply of educated manpower, the existence of a highly developed administrative system, and large investments in transport and power.

Energy. India's energy resources are adequate but not abundant. The Himalayas and smaller mountain ranges in other parts of the country have an estimated potential of between 80,000,000 and 100,000,000 kilowatts of commercially exploitable hydroelectric power. Coal is abundantly available, but most of it is located in Bihār and West Bengal, and its high ash content makes it difficult to use. Known indigenous crude-oil resources are insignificant, and the rising oil prices on the world market add to the foreign-exchange constraint inhibiting imports. Consumption of hydroelectric power increased by 13 percent a year between 1960–61 and 1968–69. Oil consumption in the same period rose by 8 percent a year, while coal consumption rose by more than 5 percent a year. The growth of road transport and the electrification policy of the railways, as well as the introduction of diesel engines, are partly responsible for the decrease in coal consumption in the transport sector, which altogether accounts for one-fourth of India's total energy consumption. In rural India, cow dung is still the basic domestic fuel, closely followed by wood—a fast-depleting source. Kerosene and electric power are gaining wide acceptance. In cities kerosene, domestic gas, and electric power are the major sources of domestic fuel.

India has a well-organized system of generating, transmitting, and distributing power. The national power supply was growing rapidly in the early 1970s and, except in certain areas, at a pace sufficient to cope with demand. Electrical energy requirements had been increasing since 1950 at the rate of 12 percent a year. Per capita consumption of electricity at the end of the year 1960–61 was 38 kilowatt-hours, and, at the end of the 1960s, it was 80 kilowatt-hours. Industry accounted for three-fourths of total consumption. The sources of electrical power are coal, oil, natural gas, atomic fuel, and water. The most important source was low-grade coal. Thermal-production capacity was a little more than half the total power capacity and was followed closely by hydroelectrical power.

The government was to spend more than U.S. $3,260,000,000 on power generation and distribution and rural electrification during the Fourth Five-Year Plan in order to increase the net installed capacity from about 14,000,000 kilowatts in 1969 to 23,000,000 kilowatts. Thus it was expected that by 1974 about 9,400,000 kilowatts of power would be generated from hydroelectric plants, about 12,500,000 kilowatts from thermal stations, and 980,000 kilowatts from nuclear stations. India's first atomic-power station went into operation at Tārāpur (Mahārāshtra) in 1969. The second station at Rana Pratap Sagar (Rājasthān) was to be commissioned in the early 1970s. A third station at Kalpakkam (Tamil Nadu) was expected to go into operation in the mid-1970s. The bulk of the equipment required for the power-expansion program was to be supplied by Indian factories. In the early 1970s a major problem with the power system was that regional grids were not well developed, and there was as yet no national grid. As a consequence, there were shortages in some regions and surpluses in others.

Financial services. India has a relatively highly developed banking and financial system. The Reserve Bank of India, as the central bank, strictly regulates all banking activities through both general and selective control measures. The important commercial banks in India were until recently owned by the large industrial houses and supplied all the short-term credit needs of trade and industry to the neglect of agriculture and small-scale industry. It was with a view to diversifying and enlarging the scope of banking operations that the government nationalized the 14 largest banks in the country in 1969. Foreign banks and banks with deposits of less than $66,700,000 were not nationalized. This brought 80 percent of the banking industry into the public sector. Ever since nationalization, credit to agriculture and small-scale industry has grown rapidly, but industry and trade have faced tight credit conditions. Bank branches expanded rapidly after nationalization; by 1971, all commercial bank offices numbered about 13,000.

Banking

Apart from bank credit, industry depends for its short-term requirements on public deposits at high rates of interest. For medium- and long-term capital investment, industry draws on several public industrial financial institutions, at both the central governmental and state level, and the Life Insurance Corporation. For their credit requirements, agriculturists still largely rely on the village moneylender, who, although he charges exorbitant interest rates, demands no security and is easy about repayments. To combat him, the government has encouraged the growth of cooperative credit societies. But, in the early 1970s, these societies were poorly run, with 35 percent of loans overdue. They were dominated by large farmers and, in most states, were of little help to the small farmer or tenant.

Membership of the 168,000 societies, covering 94 percent of the country's 500,000 villages, amounted to 29,000,000 in 1969. Supplementary credit is available from central and state cooperative banks, and long-term credit from land-development banks. Commercial banks are now becoming an important source of credit, which is also available from the Agricultural Refinance Corporation and the Rural Electrification Corporation.

India has a relatively underdeveloped capital market. Although there are several stock exchanges in the major cities (of which Bombay, Calcutta, Madras, and Ahmadābād [Ahmedabad] are the most important), companies have been reluctant to come forth to raise money. Tax laws encourage reinvestment and discourage declaration of dividends. The existence of high tax rates, which is responsible for the large black money market, deprives the capital market of adequate funds. The excess of demand far over the supply of reliable stocks accounts for the considerable capital appreciation enjoyed by some major stocks.

A few reliable companies are over-subscribed several times, while the majority of issues are under-subscribed. Institutional buyers such as the Life Insurance Corporation dominate the market. Both central and state governments rely heavily on market borrowing for their budgetary needs. The central government meets its public debt through market loans and the sale of treasury bills and long-term securities. Small savings are also an important source of funds, obtained through national savings certificates and post-office deposits.

The growth of savings and banking operations has been checked by the pursuance of a low-interest-rate policy that is designed to encourage investment but that is handicapped because it ignores the scarcity of capital and discourages the movement of funds from the larger unorganized money market to the organized money market.

Foreign trade. Foreign trade constitutes a very small proportion of India's gross national product: India's share in world exports is less than 1 percent. In the 1950s, traditional items such as jute manufactures, tea, and cotton textiles dominated India's exports. These three items accounted for just under one-half of the total value of exports in 1960 and 1961. The pattern of Indian exports changed rapidly during the 1960s. While jute and textile exports remained stagnant, iron ore, iron and steel, and engineering goods became major export items. Cooperation between government and industry is more noticeable where exports are concerned than it is in other fields.

Exports

In the early 1970s, the Indian Planning Commission expected that exports of traditional products such as tea, jute, and cotton textiles would continue to grow slowly and that the major expansion in Indian exports that was expected to take place during the 1970s at the rate of 7 percent per annum would come from increased trade in metals and metal manufactures, iron ore, chemicals, and allied products. By 1971 a few Indian export firms had secured some important footholds in world markets, assisted by export incentives and rebates, cheap bank credit, and the devaluation of the rupee in 1966.

India's imports consist largely of raw materials, intermediate manufactures, and capital goods. Throughout the 1960s, India imported large quantities of cereals and cereal preparations, but, with growing domestic production, these began to decline. Of the raw-material and intermediate imports, the most important are raw cotton, petroleum, oils and lubricants, fertilizers and fertilizer materials, iron and steel, and nonferrous metals. In the capital-goods sector, the biggest imports are of nonelectrical machinery, apparatus, and appliances.

The Indian Planning Commission expected that during the 1980s it would have to depend on imports for fertilizer materials (rock phosphate and sulphur), nonferrous metals, aluminum, and crude oil, for which India had neither adequate resources nor economic substitutes. Nonfood imports in the 1970s were expected to grow at the rate of 5.5 percent per annum. In 1971 India's trade balance was in deficit by a mere U.S. $130,000,000, a remarkable improvement on previous years, when imports exceeded exports by between $660,000,000 and $800,000,000. India's major trading partners are the United States, the United Kingdom, West Germany, the Soviet Union, and Japan.

Throughout the 1960s, India's balance of payments was in deficit because of the slow growth of exports and the large imports necessitated by domestic agricultural failures and the defense requirements resulting from two wars—with Pakistan and China. As a consequence, throughout the 1960s the government was following a policy of strict import controls, relying on foreign aid to keep its payments position in equilibrium. But net foreign aid had declined sharply from previous years, partly because less aid was available and partly because of the growing debt burden ($600,000,000 in 1971 to 1972). Imports had also fallen sharply, however, owing to growing domestic self-sufficiency in food, capital, and intermediate goods. With increasing exports, India's foreign-exchange reserves amounted to more than U.S. $1,000,000,000 at the end of the 1960s.

The largest amount of aid—much of it for food—has been received from the United States. The United Kingdom, West Germany, the Soviet Union, and Japan are other important donors.

MANAGEMENT OF THE ECONOMY

The private sector. The government regulates and controls large-scale industry by means of specific price and allocation controls and general capital issues, its industrial licensing policy, and the Monopolies and Restrictive Practices Act. Thus government, in effect, affects the private decision-making process at every level, determining such matters as the salaries paid to a company's directors, the nature of the company's imports, the location of its plant, and the amount of capital it can raise. These controls are reinforced by elaborate taxation laws that discriminate against companies with very few shareholders as well as against intercorporate investment. All this has not succeeded in checking the growth in the concentration of economic power in the hands of a few large business families.

Relations between government and private industry

The compulsions of populist politics have forced the government to take a strict line with private industry and to discourage its growth in key and basic industries. Government policy broadly encourages small- and medium-sized industry and confines the commanding heights of the economy to the public sector. Large private industry, which grew remarkably in the 1950s and 1960s, found the avenues for further growth narrowly laid down by the early 1970s. Relations between government and industry deteriorated greatly in the late 1960s. This was partly because of an excessive concern with profits in the private sector and because of a failure on the part of government to recognize the importance of the profit motive and of the economic benefits resulting from large-scale enterprises. The reality is that government regulations have worked to the advantage of a certain breed of industrialists who thrived in a regime of controls that they soon learned to manipulate to their advantage. In the early 1970s, these industrialists dominated the private sector; they disliked competition and fought against any measures of import liberalization or the removal of licensing controls that would introduce an element of competitiveness. Since the bureaucracy also thrives on controls, there is now a strong vested interest in favour of controls.

The public sector. In the early 1970s, the public sector was expected eventually to emerge as a dominant area of the economy. Rail, air, and sea transport, power generation, banking, insurance, petroleum, steel, mines, minerals, and heavy engineering were predominantly in the public sector, which had been increasing at the rate of 30 percent per annum. This vast increase in state investment in industry had not been without its problems. The rate of return on capital employed was about 3 percent—well below a reasonable economic return under Indian conditions. Considerable public-sector capacity was under-utilized. Expectations of a significant contribution to planned resources from the initial resources of these enterprises were being disappointed. In fact, several enterprises were relying on budgetary support to meet cost losses. There were several reasons for this poor performance. First, since much of the investment was in heavy industry, returns were necessarily slow to come. Second, public-sector companies were highly prone to political interference. This led to location decisions geared to political rather than economic considerations, to huge investments in worker's welfare amenities, to an inflated labour force, and to unhappy labour relations. Third, management of public enterprises was in the hands of bureaucrats seeking sinecures, rather than of professional managers. Fourth, these enterprises were subjected to close parliamentary supervision, which grossly violated their autonomy. The position, however, was improving by 1971. There was increasing realization of the need for professional management and modern management practices, but progress was uneven.

Taxation. In the early 1970s, tax revenue produced 14 percent of national income. This low burden of taxation was largely due to the fact that the agricultural sector bore no direct taxation, and that commodities that entered into agricultural consumption were only lightly taxed, if at all.

Direct taxation of nonagricultural incomes was in the hands of the central government. Indirect taxes were at both central and state levels. A formula laid down by the Finance Commission laid down the state's share in central taxation. Tax revenue accounted for more than four-fifths of revenue of all central and state governments.

The tax revenue of the central government was roughly three-fourths of total revenue. Only one-fourth of this came from direct taxes, of which income and corporation taxes accounted for the bulk. In the field of indirect taxation, union excise duties accounted for more than three-fourths of all indirect tax revenue and more than 60 percent of all tax revenue. Of these, the excise duties on petroleum products, tobacco, and sugar accounted for half the revenue from excise duties.

The burden of direct taxation in the early 1970s bore somewhat heavily on individuals and, with the combination of wealth and other taxes, could exceed 100 percent. Marginal income tax rates rose to as high as 97 percent. There was consequently considerable tax evasion. Since agricultural incomes were not taxed, there were only about 2,500,000 income-tax payers. The burden of taxation on corporations was very high, and rates varied from 55 to 80 percent. The effective burden was lower—because of various incentives or rebates—but could rise to 97 percent in certain cases.

Trade unions and employer associations. The labour force in public- and private-sector nonagricultural establishments (other than defense services) employing more than ten persons totalled more than 16,600,000 in 1969. Workers in organized industry were protected under elaborate labour laws that conform closely to International Labour Organisation (ILO) models, and, in both the public and private sectors, comprehensive labour-welfare measures were becoming the rule rather than the exception. The principle of collective bargaining is widely accepted. In the early 1970s, disputes between employers and workers were increasingly being settled through adjudication by tribunals and courts and by recourse to the legal machinery—thus greatly delaying settlements. The existence of a large small-industry sector has resulted in unfair labour practices by employers, who take advantage of the vast amount of unemployment in the country and the inability of workers to organize themselves into unions.

Relations between management and labour

In 1970 about 19,000,000 man-days were lost on account of work stoppages. These were largely the result of the lack of professionalization in management, the total absence of trained supervisory staff, and the politicization and multiplicity of unions.

The All-India Trade Union Congress was founded as far back as 1920, and a Trade Unions Act was passed in 1926 to give formal recognition to the right of workers to be recognized. The unions increased rapidly after independence as political parties sought to organize labour for their own ends. The percentage of union membership varies enormously from industry to industry. Unionization is highest in the coal, tobacco, cotton textiles, and iron and steel industries and in banks. Since any seven persons can constitute a union, and since the prescribed membership fee is small, there are over 7,500 unions with an average membership of over 500. In the early 1970s, three-fourths of the unions had fewer than 300 members, while, at the other end of the scale, about 130 unions had a membership of over 5,000, accounting for half the unionized labour force. Approximately one in every four industrial workers is unionized.

In the early 1970s, there were five major central trade-union organizations, of which the two most important were the Indian National Trade Union Congress, affiliated to the ruling Congress Party (accounting for 60 percent of membership in 1966), and the All-India Trade Union Congress, dominated by the pro-Moscow Communist Party of India (accounting for 18 percent of membership in 1966). A third growing force was the Confederation of Indian Trade Unions allied to the pro-Peking Communist Party of India (Marxist). Political rivalry prevented a united labour position on national issues. Unions generally cover all workers without distinction of craft or category. There were all-India unions covering several important industries. Some craft unions existed in air transport, ports, and docks. Interunion rivalry, the primary cause of most industrial disputes, generally revolved around the issue of recognition of the union as the official and sole bargaining agent.

Employers are generally organized through industrial associations at regional and national levels. The regional bodies are affiliated to the Central Industrial Organisation. The development of these organizations has been encouraged by the government in order to help policy makers consult industry on various issues. The three major employers' organizations are the Employers' Federation of India, the All-India Organisation of Industrial Employers, and the All-India Manufacturers' Organisation. Multiplicity of organizations has not been a problem for employers, and the three employers' organizations coordinate their activities through the Council of Indian Employers.

The government in India has always played an interventionist role in industrial relations by enacting both procedural and substantial laws and by setting up conciliation, arbitration, and adjudication machinery.

Problems and prospects. Although India has made some economic gains in the post-independence period, the development of the economy has been rather unsteady. In the Second and Third Five-Year plans (1956–61 and 1961–66), the emphasis was on industrialization, with a great deal of investment being put into heavy industries such as steel and heavy-machinery plants. The gestation periods of such investments were long, and the gains not immediately obvious.

The consequent relative neglect of the agricultural sector was brought home sharply to the government by two years of acute food scarcity, from 1965 to 1967, and the enforced dependence on food aid from the United States. The crisis years produced a disenchantment with the planning process and a move in favour of agricultural investment. This change of emphasis resulted in improvements in agricultural production, especially in food grains. But there was premature talk of a "green revolution" following the success of high-yielding varieties of wheat. Experts recognize that, if India is to make a major breakthrough, it must be in the form of increased production of rice and cash crops and in the evolution of a technology that is suited to the large tracts of land that are deficient in water resources.

Industrial growth has been inhibited by shortages of essential raw materials and of foreign exchange. The low level of public and private investment has contributed to the slackening in the pace of industrial development. A fall in public investment was a direct result of the agricultural failures, which led to an industrial recession and a fall in government revenues. Attempts to raise public investments have not been very successful because of poor administrative organization and the encroachment on public savings of public consumption expenditure. Private investment (which has been discouraged by political and economic uncertainties) usually takes its cue from government investment, and, since this has not been forthcoming at the required rate, the revival had not occurred by the early 1970s, although there were encouraging signs that it might be coming. There was an acute lack of data on private investment, and, as time lags in obtaining data are enormous, government policy could only react to certain indicators that were not always reliable.

Investment problems

The growth in national income has been largely eroded by the rapid increase in population. India has a major family-planning program—probably the largest in the world. The government is spending U.S. $420,000,000 on family planning in the Fourth Five-Year Plan—almost 15 times the amount spent under the third plan. By the early 1970s, the program had met with little success, but there was evidence that family planning was gaining ground. The fourth plan assumed that the birth rate would drop from the present level of 39 per 1,000 to about 25 per 1,000 in 1980. Even so, there would then be nearly 700,000,000 Indians by 1980.

The inadequate rate of economic development in the early 1970s was accompanied by widening disparities in incomes. Dissatisfaction with rising prices and the failure to improve living standards among the vast multitudes who live in abject poverty had its impact on government policies. The debacle suffered by the ruling Congress Party in the 1967 general elections resulted in a shift in policies toward a more populist and radical approach. The theme was one of economic growth combined with social justice. The term social justice covered a wide range of concerns, including income disparities, unemployment, and concentration of economic power. Economic policies reflected these new concerns. There was much emphasis on land reforms and on the imposition of a limit on the amount of agricultural land an individual could own. Although little action had been taken about this, there was increasing realization that insecurity of tenure and large rural income differentials would aggravate social tensions and prevent the spread of the new technology to the tenant cultivator or small farmer. The budget for 1971–72 provided U.S. $100,000,000 for programs to relieve unemployment, with special emphasis being placed on the educated unemployed. On the industrial side, there was considerable concern about the growth in the concentration of economic power in the hands of a few large business houses. As a consequence, the government revised its industrial licensing policy with a view to restricting the growth of these large houses in the field of consumer goods and medium-sized investments. At the same time, the Monopolies and Restrictive Practices Act (1970) placed a further obstacle to the growth of these industries. Large businesses as well as large profits are regarded with suspicion.

In the early 1970s, this populism was also reflected in the heavy taxation of private, industrial, and corporate incomes and in the discouragement built into the tax structure for savings and investments. India was probably one of the highest taxed countries in the world, but the tax burden fell largely on a narrow urban base. The government was also committed to enlarging the sphere of public-sector activity. Life insurance was nationalized in 1956. As already mentioned, all Indian banks with deposits exceeding U.S. $66,700,000 were nationalized in 1969, and general insurance was nationalized in 1971. The government was also progressively taking over the country's foreign trade. Seventy percent of imports were canalized through the public sector. This attitude of suspicion of private industry and the progressive increase in the economic power of the state meant that the mixed economy to which the government stands committed was not functioning effectively. As a consequence, both growth and distribution suffered.

In sum, India's fundamental economic problem remained one of ever-growing millions of people to feed, clothe, shelter, and educate and of ever-growing numbers of men and women who join the ranks of the unemployed. The rate of economic growth will have to be increased if India is to begin to overcome this problem. But it was apparent to most that growth alone will not help, unless investments are specifically directed to the task of creating more jobs through an emphasis on sectors making intensive use of labour, such as agriculture, and by applying technologies that make use of India's natural resources. (E.I.U.)

Transportation

NATIONAL PATTERNS

Little attention was paid to road development until the 1920s, mainly because the government had previously focussed its attention on railways. In 1927 it was decided that road development was beyond the capacity of the provincial governments and that the central government should consequently bear a substantial part of the cost. In the British era, roads were developed largely for strategic or commercial reasons. In 1943, the road mileage in India totalled roughly 220,000 miles, and it was then decided that this total should be increased to 331,000 miles, of which 123,000 miles would be paved. This project, known as the Nagpur Plan, formed the basis for future road-development plans.

Since independence there has been considerable road-building activity. Following the Nagpur Plan, roads have been classified as (1) national highways, (2) state highways, (3) major district roads, and (4) minor district roads and village roads. The national highways connect capitals, ports, and important towns and constitute the main lines of communication; strategic roads for defense are also included in this category. State highways are major roads, connecting each state capital with major towns in the state, as well as with national highways. District roads connect district headquarters with important areas within the region and link up with the national and state highways or the railways that pass through the district. Minor district roads and village roads connect various villages to one another.

The Indian railway system, with a total length of a little more than 37,000 miles is the fourth largest railway network in the world, ranking after the United States, the Soviet Union, and Canada. It is also the largest state undertaking in the country. Employing more than 1,400,000 people, it has a fleet of about 12,000 locomotives and operates about 10,000 trains, which carry nearly 6,000,000 passengers a day and more than 500,000 tons of freight a day.

Water transport

Transport by road and rail is largely integrated, as also is transport by inland waterway (until recently the cheapest form of transport in the country). The expansion of the railway system and the development of road transport have, however, reduced the importance of water transport. Even so, in some parts of India, notably West Bengal and Kerala, water transport is still important. Today there are about 8,700 miles of navigable waterways, of which the most important include the Ganges and the Brahmaputra in West Bengal, the Godāvari and the Kistna in Andra Pradesh, the Cauvery in Tamil Nadu, and the backwaters and canals of Kerala and Orissa.

Airmail service in India was started on an experimental basis in 1920, after which interest in aviation increased considerably. Between 1930 and 1945, Indian civil aviation expanded rapidly; by 1945 there were as many as 11 air companies in operation, carrying passengers and freight. In 1953 the government nationalized air services, establishing two corporations—Indian Airlines and Air India.

Shipping supplements these national transport facilities. As a step towards securing a major share of the Indian shipping trade for Indian ships, the coastal trade of India was reserved for Indian vessels by two acts—the Control of Shipping Act (1947) and the Merchant Shipping Act (1958). In the early 1970s the Indian merchant fleet consisted of more than 250 ships, which carried more than 7,000,000 tons of overseas cargo. There are several prominent Indian shipping lines; since independence, shipbuilding has been increased, both for commercial and for military reasons.

COMPONENT SYSTEMS

Road networks. The national highways are solely the responsibility of the central government, while the state highways and district and village roads are constructed and maintained by the states. The central government, however, participates in the construction of state highways and district roads when they constitute major arterial links or are of strategic significance. The present national highway system has a total length of about 15,000 miles of roads; there are also 215 major bridges.

The national highways include the following roads—

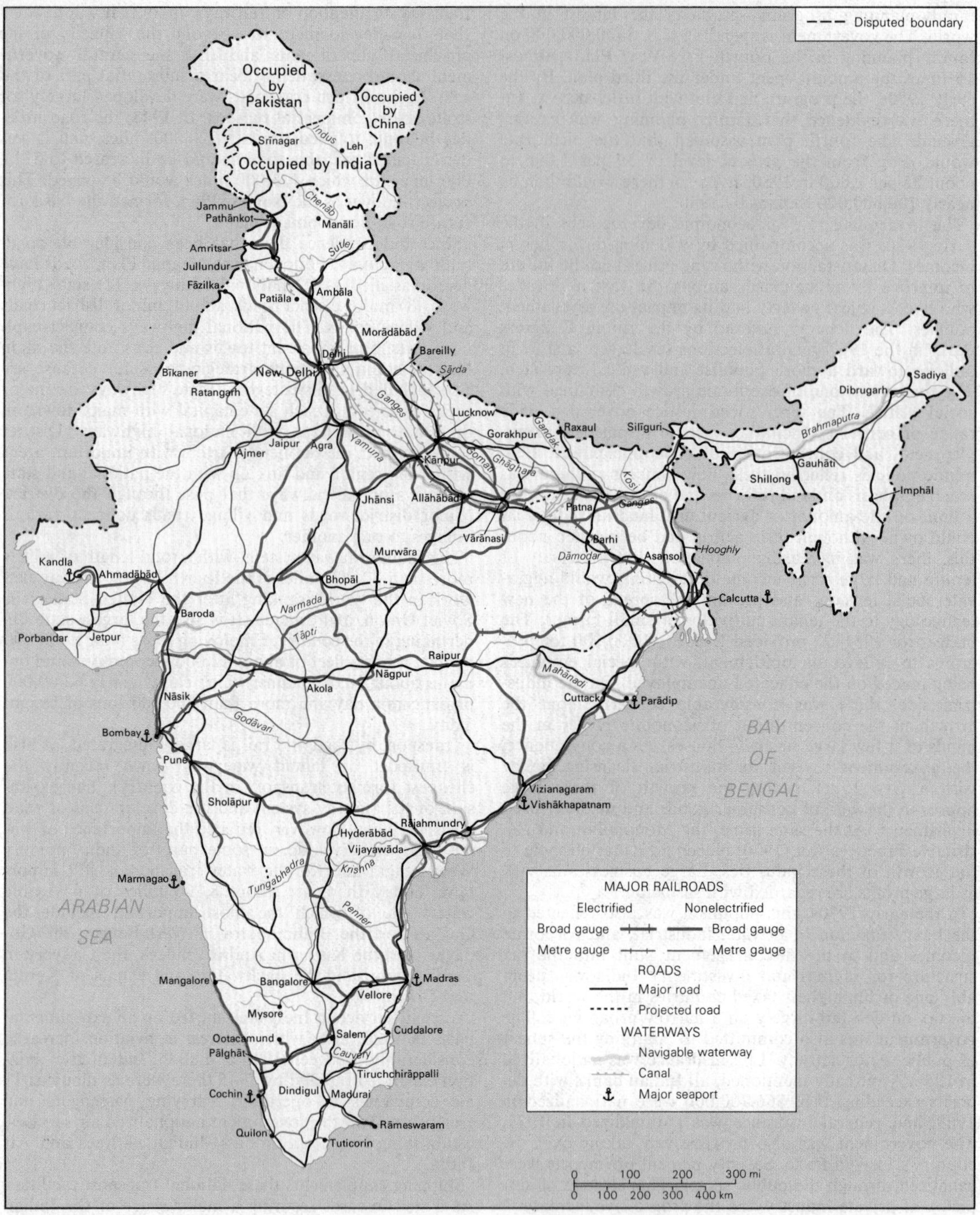

Surface transportation system of India.

the Grand Trunk Road from Calcutta to Amritsar (Punjab), via Vārānasi, Kānpur, and Āgra (all in Uttar Pradesh), and Delhi; the Āgra to Bombay road; the Bombay to Bangalore (Mysore) to Madras road; the Madras to Calcutta road; and the Calcutta to Nāgpur (Mahārāshtra) to Bombay road. Various other roads are also classified as national highways, totalling 13 major roads altogether.

In addition to the national highways there are five express highways designed for fast motor traffic. Two of these are on the northern outskirts of Bombay and are known as the western and express highways. One of the other three is an express highway joining the city of Calcutta to Dum Dum International Airport.

During the 1960s and early 1970s there was considerable road development for communications, trade, touristic, and military reasons. India has the largest national highway network in Asia. There was also encouraging improvement in some of the low-grade surfaced sections of the existing highways.

A major development anticipated in the future is the linking up of India's national highways to an international highway network, as proposed by the United Nations Economic Commission for Asia and the Far East (ECAFE). The main international highway is designed to link India with Lahore, Pakistan, to the west and Mandalay, Burma, to the east; the highway, running westward from Lahore to Turkey, would link Asian highways to the European highways system in the west, while in the east it would run from Mandalay to Rangoon, continuing via Bangkok and Saigon to Singapore.

The border roads

In 1960, a Border Roads Development Board was formed to accelerate the economic development of India's north and northeastern border areas, where difficult terrain and high altitudes are frequently encountered, especially near parts of the frontier. One such border road is the Pathānkot-Jammu-Srīnagar-Uri National Highway.

India claims to have the world's highest road, which is the one running from Manāli in the Kulu Valley in

Himachal Pradesh to Leh in Ladākh (part of Jammu and Kashmir). The average altitude of the terrain is 14,000 feet, and the road traverses four very high passes at altitudes varying from 16,000 to 18,000 feet. This road has substantially reduced the distance between Chandīgarh (Punjab) and Ladākh.

Railways. India's railway network is grouped into six main administrative zones; these are the central, eastern, northern, northeastern, western, and southern railway zones. Since 1956 three smaller zones have also been formed—the southeastern, northeast frontier, and south central railway zones.

India's railways are the direct responsibility of the minister of railways: he is assisted by the Railway Board, which is responsible for day-to-day administration. India is self-sufficient in the production of steam locomotives and rolling stock. In 1971 electric and diesel locomotives were produced at the rate of about 150 each per year. There are three production plants—the Chittaranjan Locomotive Works (Chittaranjan, West Bengal), the Integral Coach Factory at Madras, and The Diesel Locomotive Works at Vārānasi. In the early 1970s, India was exporting steam locomotives, passenger coaches, freight wagons, and other equipment; orders for wagons, coaches, and components had come from African, Asian, and European countries.

Port facilities. Though shipping is mainly the responsibility of the Ministry of Shipping and Transport, it is also the concern of various other ministries, including those of commerce, industry, and defense. In order to coordinate the policies of these various ministries, a Directorate General of Shipping was established in Bombay in 1949. A statutory body known as the National Shipping Board has also been constituted to advise the government on policy matters relating to shipping. The publicly owned Shipping Corporation is the largest maritime company in India and owns more than 60 ships, as well as a number of tankers. In the private sector, Scindia is the largest shipping company, owning about 45 vessels. India has two publicly owned shipbuilding yards, the Hindustan Shipyard at Vishākhapatnam (Andhra Pradesh) and the Mazagon Dock at Bombay; a third yard is under construction at Cochin (Kerala).

The major ports

India has eight major ports—Calcutta, Paradip (Orissa), Vishākhapatnam, and Madras on the east coast, and Kandla (Gujarāt), Bombay, Mormugao (Goa), and Cochin on the west coast. These ports are administered by statutory autonomous port trusts. The construction of major all-weather ports at Mangalore (Mysore) and Tuticorin (Tamil Nadu) is in progress, and a new dock system is being built at Haldia, 40 miles downstream from Calcutta on the Hooghly River. Traffic handled by the major ports amounts to nearly 60,000,000 tons a year. The Indian coastline is also served by about 225 intermediate and minor ports, of which 150 are in active use; these together handle a coastal and overseas traffic of about 9,000,000 tons a year. The administration of these ports is the responsibility of the state governments. The National Harbour Board advises the central and state governments on the coordination of port development with special emphasis on that of minor ports.

Another body, the Merchant Navy Training Board, advises the government on the training of merchant-navy personnel for which there are six training establishments. The Maritime Freight Commission advises the government on matters relating to freight rates. There is also a Freight Investigation Bureau, whose function is to assist shippers and shipping lines in overcoming shipping space and freight problems.

Air transport. In addition to the two government controlled corporations—Indian Airlines and Air India—there are about 20 flying clubs and ten air transport companies holding permits for nonscheduled services. The Indian Airlines, which operates domestic services, also maintains services over the entire subcontinent, extending to Afghanistan, Nepal, Burma, and Ceylon.

Air India, in the early 1970s, operated service to and from New York, London, Moscow, the Middle East, and Europe. In addition it flew to Kuwait, Nairobi (Kenya), Singapore, Djakarta (Indonesia), Sydney (Australia), and Fiji.

The flying clubs are subsidized. There are also three government gliding centres at Bangalore, Lucknow (Uttar Pradesh), and Pune (Poona; Mahārāshtra), and 13 subsidized gliding clubs at other places including Delhi, Ahmadābād (Gujarāt), Amritsar, Jaipur, and Kānpur.

India's 85 aerodromes are controlled and operated by the Civil Aviation Department. There are four categories of aerodromes—international, major, intermediate, and minor. In the international category are Bombay, Calcutta, Delhi, and Madras. The category of major aerodromes include those at Ahmadābād (Gujarāt), Nāgpur (Mahārāshtra), Agartala (Tripura), and Gauhāti (Assam), among other centres.

Research and development for civil aviation is undertaken by the Research and Development Organization of the Civil Aviation Department in New Delhi.

Administration, social conditions, and cultural life

STRUCTURE OF GOVERNMENT

The constitutional framework. India is a sovereign democratic republic. It is variously called the Republic of India, the Union of India, and the Indian Union. The constitution of India, which came into force on January 26, 1950, is the lengthiest written constitution in the world, containing much that in other countries is to be found in statutory rather than in constitutional law. It was promulgated on the day that India was proclaimed a republic—the first republic to achieve membership in the Commonwealth and to acknowledge the British monarch as head of that organization. By the early 1970s this arrangement had undergone several revisions, the amendments generally following certain decisions of India's Supreme Court. The constitution has been described as a quasi-federal document providing for a unitary state and having subsidiary federal features rather than a federal constitution with subsidiary unitary features.

Form of government

India's constitution derives from several sources, but was mainly influenced by the British concept of parliamentary government and—in its definition of certain presidential powers and in its adoption of the constitution of the federal Supreme Court—by United States government. The Indian president, however, is more a constitutional sovereign than a chief executive. Other sources were the Canadian constitution, upon which India based its quasi-federal structure, and the Irish constitution, to which its directing principles owe much.

The broad framework on which the Indian constitution is largely based is the Government of India Act (1935; enacted by the British government), which contains no constitutional principles but a great number of administrative details. Broadly, the distribution of powers between the centre and the states follows the accepted principle that those matters which, for convenience and efficiency, ought to be administered on an all-India basis are vested in the union governments, while other matters—mainly those which fall within the nation-building category—can conveniently be administered by the state governments. Thus, defense, foreign affairs, transport and communication, currency and coinage, and the administration of justice at the higher level are all central subjects. State powers include powers over the police, public health, education, forests, and similar matters of primarily local concern.

Certain fundamental rights are guaranteed to citizens, although those relating to property have recently been whittled down. Freedom of speech and expression is guaranteed, and preventive detention is forbidden except in certain cases (primarily concerned with attempts to overthrow the government by armed force). India is a secular state and, as such, upholds freedom of conscience. Untouchability (the state of belonging to the hereditary "untouchable" group, having in traditional Hindu belief and practice the quality of defiling members of a higher caste by contact) is constitutionally abolished, although in practice it still prevails.

The 21 states with the capital towns in parentheses are (1) Andhra Pradesh (Hyderābād); (2) Assam (Shillong);

(3) Bihār (Patna); (4) Gujarāt (Ahmadābād); (5) Haryana (Chandīgarh, which is the capital of both Punjab and Haryana); (6) Himachal Pradesh (Simla); (7) Kerala (Trivandrum); (8) Madhya Pradesh (Bhopāl); (9) Tamil Nadu (Madras); (10) Mahārāshtra (Bombay); (11) Manipur (Imphāl); (12) Meghalaya (Shillong); (13) Mysore (Bangalore); (14) Nāgāland (Kohīma); (15) Orissa (Bhubaneswar); (16) Punjab (Chandīgarh); (17) Rājasthān (Jaipur); (18) Tripura (Agartala); (19) Uttar Pradesh (Lucknow); (20) West Bengal (Calcutta); and (21) Jammu and Kashmir (Srīnagar). Control over the disputed state of Jammu and Kashmir is divided between India and Pakistan on either side of a "line of control" agreed upon by both countries in 1972.

The eight union territories, with capital towns in parentheses, are (1) the Andaman and Nicobar islands (Port Blair); (2) the Laccadive, Minicoy, and Amīndīvi islands (administrative headquarters on Kavaratti Island); (3) Delhi (Delhi); (4) Dādra and Nagar Haveli (Silvassa); (5) Goa, Daman, and Diu (Panaji); (6) Pondicherry (Pondicherry); (7) Arunachal Pradesh (Ziro); and (8) Mizoram (Aijal).

The union executive

The centre. The centre, or union executive, consists of the president, vice president, and the council of ministers, headed by the prime minister. The president is elected by an electoral college, consisting of elected members of both houses of parliament and of the legislative assemblies of the states. The president must be a citizen of India, not less than 35 years old, and eligible for election as a member of the lower house of parliament. The president, whose term of office is five years, is eligible for reelection. The vice president is also elected by an electoral college, consisting of both houses of parliament. The Council of Ministers, responsible to the House of the People, is headed by the prime minister; it comprises ministers who are members of the cabinet, ministers of state who are not members, and deputy ministers.

The political process. *Elections.* Since India attained independence in August 1947, five general elections have been held, the most recent being in 1971. India has a parliamentary form of government based on universal adult franchise. Citizens of India aged 18 and above are eligible to vote. Members of parliament must be at least 30 years of age and must be citizens of India. The legislature of the union government, which is called Parliament, consists of two houses—the Council of States (Rajya Sabha) and the House of the People (Lok Sabha).

The House of the People consists of not more than 500 members directly elected from territorial constituencies in the states and of not more than 25 members representing the union territories, who are chosen in such manner as parliament by law provides. The president may nominate two members to the House of the People to represent the Anglo-Indian community, if in his opinion it is not adequately represented. The term of the house is five years from the date of its first meeting.

The Council of States consists of not more than 250 members, of whom 12 are nominated by the president and the rest indirectly elected. The Council of States is not subject to dissolution; one-third of its members retire at the end of every second year. Elections to the Council are indirect, the allotted quota of representatives from each state, as provided by the constitution, being elected by the elected legislators of that state through a system of proportional representation.

The total number of members in the Council of States, as constituted in 1971, was 240, of whom 228 were elected representatives of the states and union territories and 12 were nominated by the president. The strength of the House of the People was 523, with 496 members from the 21 states and 24 members from the eight union territories, all directly elected. The president also nominated two members to represent Anglo-Indians.

State government

In the states, the system of government closely resembles that of the union. The state executive consists of the governor—appointed by the president for a term of five years—and the council of ministers, with a chief minister at its head. Every state has a legislature, which normally consists of two houses, except in the case of Assam, Gujarāt, Kerala, Orissa, Rājasthān, and Nāgāland, which each have only one house, known as the Legislative Assembly. The other states have a Legislative Council in addition to the Legislative Assembly. Each state has a high court at the head of its judicial administration.

By courtesy of the United Nations

High Court building, Chandīgarh, Punjab, India, 1959.

Elections are held under the supervision of the chief election commissioner of the central government. Article 324 of the constitution empowers this official with the superintendence, direction and control of the preparation of the electoral rolls for, and the conduct of, all elections to Parliament and to the Legislature of every State." The commissioner is an independent officer who cannot be removed from office "except in like manner and on the like grounds as a Judge of the Supreme Court."

Parties. A political party that contests in more than one state and, in a general election, secures more than 4 percent of the votes cast in the country as a whole, is classified as a recognized multistate party for the next general election. Each recognized party is allotted a reserved (or specific) symbol, and the candidates it sponsors in different states are allotted the same symbol. In 1971 there were eight recognized multistate parties: (1) the Indian National Congress (which split into two in 1970); (2) the Communist Party of India; (3) the Swatantra Party (a right-wing party); (4) the Communist Party of India (Marxist); (5) the Bharatiya Jan Sangh (an extreme Hindu party); (6) the Praja Socialist Party; (7) the Samyukta Socialist Party; (8) the Republican Party of India.

In addition to the recognized multistate parties, in the early 1970s there were also recognized parties in different states; these numbered nearly 20. The more important among them were the Dravida Munnetra Kazhagam of Tamil Nadu, which in 1972 constituted the government of that state; the Muslim League of Kerala, which was one of the constituents in Kerala's coalition government; the Kerala Congress party; the Shiromani Akali Dal, a Sikh group in Punjab; the Forward Block in West Bengal; the United Goans in Goa, Daman and Diu; the All-Party Hill Leaders' Conference in Assam; and the Naga National Organisation in Nāgāland.

De facto political developments. The Indian electorate as a whole comprises about 250,000,000 voters, of whom more than 60 percent usually record their vote. In the 1971 general election, the voters included a large number of women and of individuals under 30—who contributed to the landslide victory of Mrs. Indira Gandhi as prime minister after her Congress Party won 350 seats in the House of the People out of a membership of 523.

Justice. At the head of the judicial establishment—which consists of the federal high court, the state high court, and local and district courts—is the Supreme Court, which consists of the chief justice of India and seven other judges. Every state has a high court. The judges of the high court are appointed by the president after consultation with the chief justice, the governor of the state, and the chief justice of the state high court. Each judge of the Supreme Court is appointed by the president after consultation with the chief justice of the Supreme Court. A judge of the Supreme Court holds office until the age of 65 and is not liable to be removed from his office except by an order by the president issued after an address to each house of parliament that is supported by the majority of the total membership of that house and by not less than two-thirds of the members present and voting.

Armed forces. Supreme command of all armed forces is vested in the president. Responsibility for their administrative and operational control lies with the Ministry of Defence and with the army, navy, and air force headquarters. The main functions of the ministry are to ensure that the development and the activities of the three services are coordinated; that decisions on policy matters are obtained from the government, transmitted to the three service headquarters, and implemented; and that financial sanction for defense expenditure is obtained from parliament. Although the overall control of the three services is vested in the Ministry of Defence, each service functions under its respective chief of staff.

Role of the Ministry of Defence

In coordinating the activities of the three services, the Ministry of Defence has established a network of committees at different levels. At the highest level is the defense committee of the cabinet; all important policy matters relating to defense are decided by this committee, which is presided over by the prime minister.

The army. The army is organized into four commands—western, eastern, southern, and central. The commands are subdivided into areas, each of which is further subdivided into subareas. The authorized strength of the regular Indian army is 860,000 men. It has 25 divisions (two tank, ten mountain, and 13 infantry) and nine independent brigades (one tank, two parachute, and six infantry).

Supplementing the regular army is the Territorial Army, which is an auxiliary force and constitutes the second line of defense; it has an authorized strength of 50,000 men, consisting of citizens who receive military training in their spare time.

A number of training institutions service the army. Recruitment for the permanent cadre of commissioned ranks in the army is the responsibility of the National Defence Academy, Kharakvasla (Mahārāshtra), and the Indian Military Academy, Dehra Dūn (Uttar Pradesh).

The air force. The air force is divided into three main branches—the air branch, which deals with operations, training, policy, the reserve, and intelligence; the administration branch; and the maintenance branch. The air force has three operational commands, with headquarters at Pālam, Mahārāshtra; Allāhābād, Uttar Pradesh; and Shillong, Meghalaya. These are known, respectively, as western, central, and eastern air commands. The maintenance command is at Nāgpur, while the training command is located at Bangalore.

The air force fleet consists of a variety of fighter, bomber, transport, and maritime reconnaissance aircraft. There is also a helicopter fleet. In 1971–72, the strength of the Indian air force was reported as 45 squadrons, with about 100,000 personnel. The air force had some 650 combat planes and a limited but unspecified number of surface-to-air missiles.

The navy. The Indian navy is administratively and operationally controlled from naval headquarters in New Delhi. Naval personnel in early 1970 numbered 40,000 officers and men. The three main naval commands are the western naval command, with its base in Bombay; eastern naval command, with its base in Vishākhapatnam; and the southern naval area, with its base in Cochin.

Besides the 16,000-ton aircraft carrier the "Vikrant," which is the flagship of the navy, the Indian fleet consists of two cruisers, two destroyer squadrons, a number of frigate squadrons (including some anti-submarine and anti-aircraft frigates), four submarines, a submarine depot ship, and some patrol boats. In addition, the fleet has some survey ships, a tanker, and some auxiliary craft. A naval base and dockyard are under construction at Vishākhapatnam, and it has also been decided to develop Mormugao, in Goa, as a naval base. The first Indian-built frigate should be available in 1972, after which it is planned to construct one each year.

Naval strength

The naval air arm was established in 1948 for training air crews; there is a naval air station at Cochin.

Auxiliary units. Besides the three regular branches of the armed services, there are supplementary semi-military bodies, such as the National Cadet Corps, which consists of three divisions—senior, junior, and girls. The senior and junior divisions are each divided into army, navy, and air force branches. Gliding has been introduced as part of the training of air cadets. The strength of the NCC is about 1,350,000, including about 200,000 girls.

ADMINISTRATIVE SERVICES

Educational services. Education is primarily the responsibility of the state governments; the union government, for its part, is primarily concerned with the coordination of educational facilities, with the determination of standards for higher education, and with research, as well as with scientific and technical education. Coordination in other sectors is the responsibility of a standing committee of the Central Advisory Board of Education. The union government is also responsible for the running of five universities—the universities of Aligarh (Benares) and Delhi, Visva-Bharati University, and the Nehru University in Delhi. A Central Advisory Board of Education lays down general educational policy; it is assisted by four standing committees which deal with elementary, secondary, university, and social education.

About 30 percent of India's population can read and write—nearly twice as many as in 1947 when the country attained independence. The number of children going to school in the early 1970s had more than trebled since independence, totalling about 80,000,000; eight out of ten children in the age group six to 11 were attending school. For nine out of ten children there is a primary school within walking distance (*i.e.*, less than a mile from home).

Primary education up to the fourth standard (ages 7 to 9) is free throughout the country. Education up to the eighth standard (15 to 17) is free in all union territories and in nine states. In the early 1970s, the total number of schools, primary and secondary, was slightly more than 500,000, and there were nearly 2,000,000 teachers, of whom about 500,000 were women. An important secondary education program was concerned with the establishment of multipurpose schools, which numbered about 4,000, compared with less than 400 in 1956. Enrollment in colleges nearly trebled during the 1960s and in 1971 amounted to almost 2,000,000. The number of colleges, general and professional, had doubled, to about 4,000, and the number of universities, which in 1960 amounted to 45, had risen to 81. In the early 1970s, engineering colleges and technical institutes numbered about 140. An autonomous university-grants commission promotes university education and maintains standards in teaching and research. A sixth of all students attending colleges obtain scholarships. About 100,000 skilled craftsmen are trained annually at various centres.

It is doubtful that quality has kept pace with the quantitative increases in educational facilities. Standards of education have generally declined, not only in the academic but also in the scientific and technological spheres. Apart from difficulties arising from the growing pressure of numbers, difficulty is also encountered in imparting high standards of education in the various languages. Progress has, however, been encouraging in some spheres, notably in women's education, social education, and rural higher education. Some impressive advances have also been made in the fields of science and technology. For a country in which bullock carts outnumber automobiles by 12 to one, it is a notable achievement that India is able to build jet engines, construct a plutonium plant, design computers, develop a new rocket fuel, and manufacture transformers, steel-mill machinery, oil rigs, electronic equipment, and television receivers.

Since 1951, the five-year plans have been designed to reduce dependence on imported machinery and to build up India's strength in technological experience and research. In the early 1970s there were more than 12 scientific research centres in India. The research centre at Trombay, near Bombay, was producing enough radio isotopes and radioactive compounds not only to meet domestic needs but also to permit some exports to countries in Asia, Africa, and Europe. The plant genetics centre in New Delhi was evolving new varieties of seeds, while the hydrological research station in Pune had carried out studies on which the designs of most of India's dams had been based. Progress had also been achieved in research in tropical medicine and in the manufacture of drugs and pharmaceuticals. Some 600 scientific periodicals are published annually in India, and a considerable number of scientific and technical books are published.

Health and welfare services. Public health is primarily a state responsibility, although the union government plays a vital role in health programs and provides substantial financial grants to the union territories of Delhi, Andaman and the Nicobar islands, and Minicoy and the Amīndīvi islands.

The union government has shown particular interest in sponsoring and supporting major national schemes for the prevention and control of disease. These include programs to combat malaria, tuberculosis, leprosy, venereal diseases, smallpox, trachoma (a contagious inflammation of parts of the eyes), and cancer. The union government is also concerned with schemes relating to sanitation, water supply, and nutrition.

In the early 1970s there were nearly 5,000 primary health centres, 109,000 doctors, 66,000 nurses, and 48,000 pharmacists in the country. Medical education is a state responsibility but the Central Health Education Bureau also plays a coordinating role.

Family planning

Family planning, on the other hand, is centrally sponsored but locally implemented. The broad aim of the family-planning program is to reduce the birth rate and to stabilize the population at a level consistent with the requirements of national economy. This involves planning on a vast scale, since it has to cover at least 90,000,000 couples in the reproductive age group. The program is voluntary.

It was calculated that, in the early 1970s, a child born in India could expect to live to the age of 50, whereas in the mid-1950s life expectation was about 32. The death rate in the same period had dropped from 27 per 1000 to 14 and infant mortality from 183 to 109. As a result of the drive against preventable disease, some diseases have been successfully brought under control. Plague, for instance, has been almost completely wiped out. Deaths from cholera had fallen from 87,000 to 8,300 per year; though the disease was still endemic in a few scattered areas, epidemics were rare. Deaths from smallpox had fallen from more than 40,000 to less than 9,000 per year. Malaria cases had dropped from 75,000,000 to 110,000 per year.

There were nearly twice as many hospitals and dispensaries in the country in the early 1970s as there were in the whole of India before partition in 1947. In the same period, the number of doctors had more than doubled, while the number of nurses had risen sevenfold.

The improvement of water supplies and of sanitation also form part of the public-health program. Thousands of children and nursing mothers are given free milk by citizens committees with the help of international organizations. Children also obtain free meals during school hours in a few states, but the system is not prevalent throughout most of india.

Housing. Housing is one of India's major problems; in some 70,000,000 rural houses and 10,000,000 urban houses the average number of persons per room amounts to three in rural areas and nearly four in urban areas. In rural areas about 94 percent and in urban areas about 46 percent of the families own their homes. The bulk of the rural houses are made of mud. A large proportion of industrial workers in the city also live in substandard accommodations. The overall housing shortage is estimated to increase at the rate of more than 2,000,000 units annually.

In 1952 a separate portfolio for housing was created by the union government; organized efforts were then made to improve the housing situation in general and in particular to provide financial assistance for the construction of houses not only by individuals but also by cooperatives, industrial employers, planters, and local bodies. Most funds for these schemes are provided by the union government and by the Life Insurance Corporation of India, which is government controlled. While the central government exercises overall control, schemes are implemented by the various state governments and their executive agencies. In the union territories schemes are implemented by local administrative bodies.

About 400,000 housing units were constructed during the first three five-year plans; the likely target for the Fourth Five-Year Plan (1969–74) is about 600,000 housing units. Housing shortages, particularly in urban areas, largely result from a considerable increase in population, as well as the large-scale movement of population from the country to the towns and cities. Two major factors impeding the progress of housing schemes have been the scarcity of developed land at reasonable prices and the shortage of building material. Under the Land Acquisition and Development Scheme, state governments are acquiring and developing land for housing in urban areas on a large scale. In addition to this scheme, the National Building Organisation, established in 1954, is attempting to bring about a reduction in building costs by undertaking research into building materials and building techniques and designs. The findings are made available to construction agencies throughout the country.

Police services. The states control their own police forces through their home ministers. At the centre, the home minister of the union government exercises a coordinating role, controlling various all-India bodies, such as the Central Bureau of Investigation, the Central Detective Training School, the Central Forensic Laboratory, the Central Fingerprint Laboratory, and the National Police Academy at Mount Abu, Rājasthān, where the Indian police service is trained. The Indian police service, about 1,700 strong, recruits university graduates by competitive examination and provides all the senior officers of the state police forces. The cities of Calcutta, Madras, Bombay, and Hyderābād have separate police organizations. The total strength of all police services in India is about 700,000.

The wage boards. The government of India has appointed several central wage boards to supervise wage levels in various industries such as the cement, cotton textile, iron and steel, heavy chemical and fertilizer, jute, and leather and leather goods industries. In the early 1970s, a steering group consisting of representatives of government, employers, and workers was engaged in drawing up a wage map of India both by industry and by region, in order to provide a guide for those authorities responsible for fixing wages. Several adjudicators have also been appointed at various regional centres to grant extra allowances to offset the rise in the cost of living.

The cost of living

The cost of living was increasing rapidly in the early 1970s, but it was difficult to obtain any reliable statistics relating to the price index and the cost of living in various centres. The calendar year 1960 has been adopted as the base period for all the new series of cost-of-living index numbers, but these varied from state to state, and it was not practicable to attempt any enumeration on a national basis.

CULTURAL LIFE AND INSTITUTIONS

Indian art and culture has developed over many centuries and has many different manifestations, varying from folk art to modern painting and sculpture. Since independence, the union government and some state governments have attempted to promote artistic and cultural activities, as well as a heightened artistic consciousness, through various agencies. These include the Lalit Kala Akademi (academy of art), the Sangeet Natak Akademi (academy of dance, drama, and music), and the Sahitya Akademi (academy of letters). Some mass-communications facilities, such as the cinema, radio, and television, have also been utilized to make the Indian people more conscious of their cultural heritage. A number of institutions have collaborated in the task of popularizing traditional arts and culture.

Cultural institutions. The Lalit Kala Akademi, set up in 1954, promotes the development of fine arts and undertakes programs for promoting awareness and understanding of developments in painting, sculpture, and other graphic arts. It also coordinates the activities of the regional or state academies. The academy holds a national exhibition of art every year and also organizes exhibitions of arts and crafts of eastern and western countries in India, as well as of Indian arts and crafts abroad. In 1968 it began to hold an international exhibition of contemporary art once every three years. The academy also makes annual awards to outstanding artists who participate in the national exhibition; it is also engaged in making facsimiles of important frescoes in various parts of the country.

Drama, dance, and music are primarily encouraged through the medium of the Sangeet Natak Akademi, inaugurated in 1953; the academy promotes research, encourages the establishment of theatrical centres and training institutions, organizes seminars and festivals, awards prizes, and fosters cultural exchanges. It also maintains libraries of records, books, and films and maintains a museum of musical instruments, masks, and costumes, as well as a sound-recording studio. The academy also runs three training institutions—the National School of Drama and Asian Theatre Institute at New Delhi; Kathak Kendra (a school specializing in Indian dances) at New Delhi; and the Jawaharlal Nehru Manipuri Dance Academy at Imphāl.

The All-India Radio popularizes these activities and broadcasts programs of Indian drama and literature in Hindi and the regional languages. All-India Radio has also sponsored a national program of music in order to give young musicians and dramatists an opportunity to display their talents.

Indian literature is fostered by the Sahitya Akademi, inaugurated in 1954; it has published a bibliography of Indian literature published in the 20th century in the 15 major languages specified in the constitution, as well as of books in English published in India or written by Indian authors abroad. In addition, it has translated a number of Indian and foreign classics into various Indian languages; it has also published 90 translations of works by the poet Rabindranath Tagore. The academy publishes two journals, a quarterly in English called *Indian Literature* and a semi-annual in Sanskrit called *Sanskrita Pratibha.*

The National Book Trust

The National Book Trust, established in 1957, is designed mainly to encourage literary production and to make moderately priced literary works available to libraries, educational institutions, and the general public. The trust also publishes standard works on education, science, culture and the humanities, and classical Indian literature, as well as translations of foreign classics in Indian languages. It also organizes an annual national book fair and occasionally holds regional book exhibitions, seminars, writer's camps, and workshops. The trust has organized exhibitions of Indian books at major international book fairs abroad.

To promote cultural relations with foreign countries the Indian Council for Cultural Relations was established in 1950 as an autonomous organization with the object of establishing, reviving, and strengthening cultural relations between India and other countries. The council, which has its headquarters in New Delhi, has regional offices in Bombay, Calcutta, and Madras.

Press and broadcasting. During the era of British rule the press was subjected to fairly rigorous control. On the attainment of independence the right to freedom of speech and expression was guaranteed by Article 19 of the constitution, which is accepted as including the freedom of the press. In general, the Indian press enjoys a remarkable degree of freedom, respected by both the central and state governments.

In the early 1970s there were more than 10,000 Indian- or English-language periodicals—published as dailies, tri-weeklies, bi-weeklies, annuals, monthlies, and bimonthlies. The number of dailies was approximately 650. The largest number of newspapers were published in Hindi (186 dailies), followed by Urdu (98 dailies), after which English ranked third (about 70 dailies). The highly literate state of Kerala has 57 dailies in various languages, but a large number of these are no more than two- to four-page news sheets. The largest number of newspapers and periodicals are published in the state of Mahārāshtra (1,593), followed by Uttar Pradesh (1,460). In addition to the 15 principal languages, newspapers are also published in 37 other languages, including Manipuri, Maithili, Naga, Dogri, Santali, and Konkani. A number of foreign-language newspapers are also published in India, although their circulation is small; these include papers published in Arabic, Burmese, Chinese, Nepali, Portuguese, and Swahili. The overall daily newspaper circulation of English language and Indian language newspapers is about 7,000,000.

Radio and television

In a country in which barely 30 percent of the population are literate, the spoken word is more important than the written one. Because of this, audio-visual media, such as radio and television, reach out to a far bigger audience than does the press. All-India Radio, in its medium-wave broadcasts, is estimated to cover 70 percent, or 350,000,000, of the country's population; its short-wave broadcasts cover practically the whole of the country. Apart from about 10,000,000 licensed radio receivers, there are estimated to be another 500,000 unlicensed sets, as well as government-sponsored community listening schemes in rural areas, which have almost 140,000 additional radios.

Since radio and television are entirely operated under a government monopoly, controlled by the central government, they represent the most powerful media of publicity and propaganda in the country. Television is still in its infancy in India and is confined largely to Delhi and adjoining areas.

The cinema. India ranks with Japan and the United States among the largest producers of films in the world. The film industry occupies eighth place among Indian industries and provides employment for more than 100,000 persons. On an average about 70,000,000 people visit the cinema every year. In addition to those in the cities, movie theatres are found in all the towns, townships, and major villages of India.

The cinema, as well as radio and, to a smaller extent, television, has developed into a powerful medium of mass communication, and the government has appointed several committees to investigate the workings of the film industry. The production of Indian films increased from fewer than 30 in 1931 to about 450 in 1970. Films in the Dravidian languages of the south predominate, accounting for well over half of the total output. The national language, Hindi, comes next, followed by Bengali and Marathi.

A National Film Archive was established in 1954 in order to trace, acquire, and preserve the heritage of the national film industry, in addition to a selection of films produced in other countries. In the early 1970s the archive was housed in the premises of the film institute in Pune. In addition, a children's film society promotes the production and distribution of children's films. The Film Institute of India, established by the Ministry of Information and Broadcasting, provides technical training in film production and facilities for research into film techniques; training is given in film direction, screen writing, motion-picture photography, sound recording, film editing, and acting.

Indian film themes

Social themes dominate Indian films, though their presentation may often seem crude by Western standards; mythology and legend as well as devotional subjects also play some part in Indian films. Apart from commercial productions, the films division of the Ministry of Information and Broadcasting produces many documentaries and newsreels, some of which are of a high quality and have won international awards. Documentaries and newsreels are produced in India's 15 official languages; every cinema is required, under the terms of its license, to exhibit at each performance not less than 2,000 feet of films approved by the authorities that either are documentary films, have scientific and educational value, or deal with news and current events.

The government has established a film finance corporation with an authorized capital of 10,000,000 rupees (Rs. 7.50 = $1.00 U.S.; Rs. 18 = £1 sterling, on December 1, 1971), of which half is subscribed by the government. The corporation grants loans to producers of films of good quality, giving preference to those projecting national problems and dealing with subjects of social and cultural value.

The government is also interested in the export of Indian films abroad and for this purpose set up in 1963 the Indian Motion Pictures Export Corporation. Established markets in foreign countries are mainly confined to East Africa, Mauritius, the West Indies, Sri Lanka, Singapore, Malaysia, Burma, Thailand, Fiji, Indonesia, the Persian Gulf, and West Africa. Soviet and eastern European countries have evinced interest in Indian films. The major demand abroad is for Hindi films, with Tamil and Bengali films next in popularity. The Indian film maker with the greatest following in the West, Satyajit Ray, works in Bengali.

Films are subject to censorship, and for this purpose a central board of film censors was constituted in 1951 to certify films for public exhibition. All the members of the board, which has its headquarters in Bombay, are government appointed; on the average nearly 3,000 films are scrutinized by the board each year.

PROSPECTS FOR THE FUTURE

With its vast territory, enormous population, and rapid rate of population increase, it is remarkable that India, which is composed of so many diverse ethnic and linguistic elements and comprehends so many different geographical regions, should have been able to achieve the degree of unity that it has. The challenge posed by successive confrontations with Pakistan—first in 1948, again in 1965 in the Rann of Kutch and in Kashmir and, later, in 1971, in Bangladesh (formerly East Pakistan)—has increased the polarization between India and Pakistan, thus adding a further variable element to the factors affecting India's future prospects.

BIBLIOGRAPHY.

General works: Among the best known standard works on India are *The Cambridge History of India*, 6 vol. (1922–32); and VINCENT A. SMITH, *The Oxford History of India* (1919; 3rd ed. rev. by PERCIVAL SPEAR *et al.*, 1958). A controversial and provocative book is K.M. PANIKKAR, *A Survey of Indian History*, 3rd ed. (1960). A book representing Indo-British collaboration is *A Short History of India* by W.H. MORELAND and A.C. CHATTERJEE, 4th ed. (1957). See also PERCIVAL SPEAR, *India* (1961); and H.G. RAWLINSON, *India*, rev. ed. (1952). These publications represent a valuable and objective guide to a general reading of Indian history.

Land and people: The following titles, though produced largely by government sources, contain much useful information and statistical data: S.N. AGARWALA, *Population* (1967); M.R. CHAUDHURI, *Economic Geography* (1969); *The Wealth of India: A Dictionary of Indian Raw Materials and Industrial Products*, 8 vol. to date, issued by the INDIAN COUNCIL OF SCIENTIFIC AND INDUSTRIAL RESEARCH (1948–69); *India: A Physical Geography* (1968); and *The Gazetteer of India* (1965), both issued by the PUBLICATIONS DIVISION OF THE MINISTRY OF INFORMATION AND BROADCASTING of the Government of India; S.L. OGALE, *The Tragedy of Too Many* (1969); *The Census of India* (1951 and 1961) by the Census Commissioner for India. Two useful books are D.N. WADIA, *Geology of India*, 3rd ed. rev. (1957); and (ed.), *Minerals of India* (1966).

Government: There has been a spate of books on government since the constitution came into force in January 1950. The following are among the more informative and authoritative books: GRANVILLE AUSTIN, *The Indian Constitution: Cornerstone of a Nation* (1966); P.B. GAJENDRAGADKAR, *The Constitution of India* (1969); ALAN GLEDHILL, *Fundamental Rights of India* (1955); SIR MAURICE GWYER and ANGADIPURAM APPADORAI, *Speeches and Documents on the Indian Constitution, 1921–1947*, 2 vol. (1957); M. HIDAYATULLAH, *Parliamentary Privileges: The Press and the Judiciary* (1969); SIR BENEGAL NARSINGA RAU, *India's Constitution in the Making*, ed. by B. SHIVA RAO, rev. ed. (1963); B. SHIVA RAO, *Framing India's Constitution*, 5 vol. (Indian Institute of Public Administration, 1966–68); R.J. VENKATESWARAN, *Cabinet Government in India* (1967).

Legislature: Among the better known books on the legislature are the *Reports on the General Elections in India* published since 1955 (on the 1951–52 elections) by the Election Commission in India; RAJNI KOTHARI *et al.*, *Party System and Election Studies* (1967); W.H. MORRIS-JONES, *Parliament in India* (1957); K.C. RAY, *The Law of Elections in India* (1969); and MYRON WEINER and RAJNI KOTHARI (eds.), *Indian Voting Behaviour* (1965).

Executive and judiciary: Among the better known and more useful sources that may be consulted are PAUL H. APPLEBY, *Public Administration in India* (1953); ASOK CHANDA, *Indian Administration* (1958); A.D. GORWALA, *Report on Public Administration* (1953); N.C. ROY, *The Civil Service in India*, 2nd ed. (1960); GHOPAL DAS KHOSLA, *Our Judicial System* (1949); and R.G. CHATURGEDI, *Judiciary Under Constitution* (1967).

Defense: Authoritative works on this subject are few. These include *Defence and Security in the Indian Ocean Area* by the INDIAN COUNCIL OF WORLD AFFAIRS (1958); LORNE J. KAVIC, *India's Quest for Security* (1967); RAVI KAUL, *India's Strategic Spectrum* (1969); S.S. KHERA, *India's Defence Problem* (1968); H.M. PATEL, *The Defence of India* (1963); and K.M. PANIKKAR, *Problems of Indian Defence* (1960).

Education: Education is a popular topic that has been subjected to wide scrutiny. The official government publications cover an extensive field. A valuable report is one on *Indian Universities* by C.P. RAMASWAMY AIYAR (1964). The University Grants Commission, the Institute of Constitutional and Parliamentary Studies, and the Inter-University boards of India and Ceylon have produced various reports and pamphlets. The Ministry of Education has also issued several reports and reference books.

Cultural activities: Some of the best known books on India's cultural activities have been written by foreigners, mainly English and American. Those worth consulting include KAY AMBROSE, *Classical Dances and Customs of India* (1950, reprinted 1965); and the two volumes by PERCY BROWN, *Indian Painting*, 7th ed. (1960) and *Indian Architecture*, 5th ed., 2 vol. (1965–68). KAMALADEVI CHATTOPADHYAYA, *Carpets and Floor Coverings of India* (1969), is a standard work. A.K. COOMARASWAMY, *The History of Indian and Indonesian Art* (1927, reprinted 1965), is regarded as a classic. STELLA KRAMRISCH, *The Art of India* (1954), is also a standard work.

Scientific research: The most authoritative sources on this subject consist mainly of government reports published by the Council of Scientific and Industrial Research and the Department of Atomic Energy. A good book on agriculture, though somewhat outdated, is M.S. RANDHAWA, *Agricultural Research in India* (1958).

Health and social welfare: There are several informed books on family planning. One of these is SRIPATI CHANDRASEKHAR, *Population and Planned Parenthood in India*, rev. ed. (1961). There are several official publications by the Ministry of Health and Family Planning. A good book on social welfare is A.R. WADIA (ed.), *History and Philosophy of Social Work in India*, 2nd ed. (1968). There are also several works on rehabilitation and some books on the untouchables and underprivileged classes. The two best known books on this subject are MAHATMA GANDHI, *The Removal of Untouchability*, ed. by BHARATAN KUMARAPPA (1954); and B.R. AMBEDKAR, *The Untouchables*, 2nd ed. (1969), by the well-known Harijan leader. An informative book on tribal life is G.S. GHURYE, *The Scheduled Tribes*, 2nd ed. (1959).

Press, radio, and films: There are several reports by various governmental commissions and committees on the press, broadcasting, and information. See the annual governmental report *Film in India*. Several books are also available, both by Indian and foreign authors, on the freedom of the press in India. Among the best known is that of the Dutch author JOSEPH MINATTUR, *Freedom of the Press in India* (1961).

(F.R.M.)

Indiana

Indiana, though officially classified as an east north central state of the United States, is perhaps the most Southern in character of all Northern states. This is in large degree a reflection of the heavy early settlement of the region by immigrants from the Southern hills, who carried with them the institution of slavery and a hearty distrust of the federal government. Indiana's 36,291 square miles (93,993 square kilometres) make it, except for Hawaii, the smallest state west of the Appalachian Mountains. Its population of 5,490,000 in 1980, 8 percent of which was black, was 64 percent urban. The capital has been at Indianapolis since 1825, nine years after Indiana was admitted as the 19th state of the union.

An overview of the state

Indiana is basically a manufacturing state, and its northern half lies in the mainstream of the great industrial belt stretching from Pennsylvania and New York state westward to Illinois. Many of its people, nevertheless, continue to cherish an image derived from 19th-century America: largely white, dedicated to the Protestant ethic of sobriety and hard work, oriented to the small town and medium-sized city, and, especially, interested in maintaining the prerogatives of local self-determination. It is not by coincidence that Indiana's federal aid in the late 1970s was the lowest per capita of any American state, or that the Indianan's nickname, "the Hoosier," remains a symbol in the nation's lore for a kind of homespun wisdom, wit, and folksiness that harkens back to what is popularly regarded as a less hurried and sophisticated period of history.

Indiana is, as its motto states, "in the center of things." Its borders face Lake Michigan and the state of Michigan on the north, Ohio on the east, Kentucky on the south, and Illinois on the west, making it an integral part of the Midwest. The northwestern cities form an industrial, economic, and social continuum with neighbouring Chicago. Their heavy black populations and black political power aspirations contrast strikingly with life in the cities and towns on the Ohio River. The state is at once Northern and black, Southern and white-dominated, with all the problems attendant on both circumstances. Though generally considered a conservative and Republican stronghold, Indiana has voted into both state and national office an almost equal number of liberals and Democrats. (For information on related topics, see the articles UNITED STATES OF AMERICA; UNITED STATES, HISTORY OF THE; and NORTH AMERICA.)

THE HISTORY OF INDIANA

Exploration. Archaeologists have discovered remains of the earliest known inhabitants at Angel Mounds, an archaeological site on the Ohio River near Evansville. Early historical records show that Algonkin (Algonquin) Indians organized tribes of the area into the Miami Confederation, which fought to protect the lands from the unfriendly Iroquois. Other important Indian tribes were the Potawatomi and the Delaware. In the 17th century the French made treaties with the Iroquois allowing them to trade with the Miami Confederation.

In 1679 Robert Cavelier, sieur de La Salle, travelled by boat from Michigan down the St. Joseph River. To the south, traders from the Carolinas and from Pennsylvania settled on the Ohio and the Wabash river shores, threatening the French traders, to whom the region was a means of connecting Canada and Louisiana. To protect the route to the Mississippi, the French built Fort-Miami (1704); Fort-Ouiatanon (1719), near present-day Lafayette; and Fort-Vincennes (1732), one of the first permanent white settlements west of the Appalachians.

In 1763 the area, part of what came to be known as the Northwest Territory, was ceded to England, which forbade further white settlement. The prohibition was largely ignored, and in 1774 Parliament annexed the lands to Quebec. During the American Revolution, Virginia, Connecticut, and Massachusetts made claims on the land, and in 1779 George Rogers Clark secured the area for the rebelling colonies by leading his troops on a surprise march from Kaskaskia to Vincennes.

Territorial period. The Northwest Territory was ceded to the United States by the Treaty of Paris ending the Revolution in 1783, and the following year the first U.S. settlement was established at Clarkville, in the southern part of the state. Warfare between the Indians and the westward-moving whites continued until 1794, when Gen. Anthony Wayne defeated the Indians in a battle near Fallen Timbers, near the present-day Ohio–Indiana line, and the Indians were forced to make land concessions. Increasing numbers of white immigrants from Southern states entered the area after 1800, leading to renewed Indian resistance, and in 1811 the last major encounter, the Battle of Tippecanoe, was fought near Lafayette, with Gen. William Henry Harrison the victor. Between 1820 and 1840 the major Indian tribes abandoned the area. The Ordinance of 1787 creating the Northwest Territory prohibited slavery, but it did not abolish slavery already in existence, and in 1800 the territory had at least 175 slaves. With the end of Indian resistance came rapid settlement and in 1816 statehood. The territorial capital, Corydon, became the first state capital.

Indian warfare

Statehood. The patterns of rural life and local autonomy were established in the first half of the 19th century as settlement progressed from south to north. The utopian community of New Harmony, on the Wabash River in the southwest, was settled by George Rapp in 1815 and taken over by Robert Owen in 1825. In 1801 the first college was founded in Vincennes, and in 1820 Indiana University was chartered. A single-car, horse-drawn railroad arrived in Shelbyville in 1834. The new constitution of 1851, which remains the framework of state government, made it nearly impossible for the state to go into debt, reinforced local powers, and created a tax-supported public-school system. Article XIII of the constitution prohibited the entrance of blacks into the state, but this was struck down by the U.S. Supreme Court, in 1866, as being in conflict with the federal Civil Rights Act of that year.

The period from 1850 to 1900 was one of agricultural and then industrial growth. The Civil War gave impetus to industrialization, and the northern part of the state emerged as a major sector in its own right. With the founding of the steel-making city of Gary in 1906, midway between the iron ore of Minnesota's Mesabi Range and the coal of southern Indiana and Illinois, and with the subsequent development of automobile manufacturing in South Bend, Indiana moved from an agricultural to an industrial base. The isolation, independence, and spirit of Jeffersonian and Jacksonian democracy that underlay the constitution of 1851, however, continued to leave their mark upon the state. The document was written when towns and villages were days rather than minutes and hours apart. It was not until 1970 that annual rather than biennial meetings of the legislature were approved. Other features of the constitution remain impediments to effective management of 20th-century social and political problems, and the ideology of localism is still deeply ingrained.

Development of rural–industrial dichotomy

THE NATURAL AND HUMAN LANDSCAPE

Physical features. Indiana forms part of the east central lowlands that slope downward from the Appalachians to the Mississippi. Approximately five-sixths of its surface was modified by glacial action, leaving a vast quantity of excellent soil material and extensive deposits of sand gravel. The more eroded southern part of the state gives way to the central plain, an extremely fertile agricultural belt with large farms, and then to the flat and heavily glaciated northern regions. The highest elevation is along the Ohio border, at 1,257 feet (383 metres) above sea level, while its low point, 320 feet, is where the Wabash enters the Ohio. About 90 percent of the land lies between 500 and 1,000 feet, and Indianapolis, in the centre of the state, has an elevation of 793 feet.

Natural environment

The general slope and drainage pattern is toward the southwest, though an almost imperceptible groundswell in the northeast forms a St. Lawrence–Mississippi water divide. The Wabash, the Ohio, and the east and west forks of the White River follow this slope, forming part of the Mississippi Basin. In the north, the St. Joseph River meanders into Lake Michigan, while in the east the Maumee flows northeastward into Lake Erie. The northern half of the state is dotted with many small lakes, including several of the state's largest. Forest cover totalled 3,943,000 acres (1,596,000 hectares) in 1977, of which 97 percent was commercially owned. Among the dramatic features of the landscape are the sand dunes along Lake Michigan, most of which have been removed from the public domain by industry and private homes. This situation was remedied somewhat with the dedication in 1972 of Indiana Dunes National Lakeshore. The most scenic part of the state is the south-central region around Brown County, an area popular with tourists, and Indiana University.

Climate. Indiana has four distinct seasons and a temperate climate, usually escaping extremes of cold and heat. The mean temperature in January ranges from about 35° F (2° C) in Evansville on the Ohio River to 25° F (−4° C) in South Bend in the north. In July ranges are from about 78° F (26° C) to 73° F (23° C) in corresponding regions, and precipitation varies from 44 inches (1,118 millimetres) in the south central region to 35 inches in the north. Snow may fall over a six-month period and averages more than 20 inches annually, with the cities along the north central border often reporting more than 100 inches. Fall is perhaps the most delightful season, with colours provided by maples, oaks, tulips, and a wide variety of other trees, whereas the spring is generally erratic and unstable. Year-round weather systems moving over Lake Michigan tend to afflict the north central regions with extremes of rain or snow, and, in the spring and early summer, Indiana is part of the belt of states called Tornado Alley as a result of air currents from the Gulf of Mexico.

Vegetation and animal life. Indiana is typical of east north central America in its variety of trees, birds, and small game animals, and like its neighbours it has through the years thinned out the numbers of many of these, including the great variety of life once common to the sand dunes. The steady growth of agriculture, cities, and industry and the consequent varied forms of pollution have taken a steady toll of natural life. Pollution of both air and water is particularly severe along the southern tip of Lake Michigan.

Human imprints. The three major regions of Indiana, which generally follow physiographic divisions, are: the flat northern region of industry and truck gardening; the fertile central plains; and the large southern region, less fertile but forested, which is the site of caves and limestone quarries.

The nighttime skies of northwestern Indiana are alive with the belching volcanoes of its steel furnaces, and during the daytime such cities as Gary and Hammond are darkened by clouds of smoke and airborne industrial wastes. Because of this dramatically apparent air pollution, the contamination of inland and lake waters, and the steady encroachment of industry upon the dunes and other lakefront areas since the early years of the 20th century, the area has become a major national target of conservationists. Southward to the Wabash Valley are rich farmlands, obtained largely by draining and deforesting marshes. To the east, South Bend is an important manufacturing city and a noted educational centre. The northeastern part of the state is more forested and pastoral, although Elkhart and Fort Wayne are major industrial cities.

Indianapolis, a city designed after Versailles, France, and Washington, D.C., dominates the central plains. It is a strongly conservative city and a national symbol of superpatriotism; its growth has occurred largely through immigration from rural areas and annexation. A railway and highway hub, Indianapolis also serves the surrounding farming belt as packer and distributor, and it is a major industrial city as well.

The advent of industry and railroads ended southern Indiana's early dominance, which was based on the river traffic of the Ohio and Wabash. The region's major city, Evansville, also serves adjacent areas of Kentucky and Illinois, and between it and Terre Haute to the north lie most of the state's oil and coal deposits. Many handsome examples of pre-Civil War architecture are found in the river towns. An old buffalo trace used by pioneers moving from Kentucky to the western prairies leads from New Albany, across the Ohio from Louisville, Kentucky, to the Wabash at Vincennes. Southward from Bloomington is a vast limestone belt underlain by numerous caves, which makes the state a major limestone producer. Brown County remains largely a backwoods area where log cabins abound on hillside farms.

THE PEOPLE OF INDIANA

Ethnic composition. The people of Indiana are predominantly white, native-born Americans of native-born parents, most of whom trace their ancestry ultimately to England, Scotland, Ireland, and Germany. Notable exceptions occur in Indianapolis and such areas as South Bend and northwestern Lake County, which have black populations of more than 70 percent in Gary and about 30 percent in East Chicago. Citizens of Polish descent form the largest ethnic group in South Bend; and, along with Hungarian, Belgian, Italian, and Mexican groups, they are numerous throughout the north. The Amish people constitute a small group located in the northeast, in and around Middlebury, Nappanee, and Goshen. They conduct a model farm at Amish Acres in Nappanee. Mennonites, who also live in this area, have established a college in Goshen. The state's overall lack of ethnic and linguistic mix—common on the East and West coasts and in most large cities—helps to account for the continuing strength of Hoosier localism.

White Protestant domination

Religion. Almost one-third of the people of Indiana are Protestant, a figure considerably above the national average. Roman Catholics, who make up 15 percent of the population, are concentrated largely in the urban areas with large continental and Irish ethnic groups, particularly South Bend. Jews, comprising a very small percentage of the state's population, live almost exclusively in urban centres.

Contemporary demography. Indiana's 6 percent growth between 1970 and 1980 was accounted for entirely by an excess of births over deaths. The birth rates and death rates generally followed national patterns during the decade, the birth rate falling gradually and the death rate remaining stable. Marriage and divorce rates were well above the national average.

About one-half of the state's residents live in the 61 cities with populations of more than 10,000. More than one-fifth of the people are concentrated in the Indianapolis Standard Metropolitan Statistical Area, and another 12 percent are in the Gary–Hammond–East Chicago complex. The national pattern of deserting the central city for the suburbs has generally occurred throughout the state, with South Bend, for example, losing population during the 1960s and 1970s, while its surrounding county grew. Of the counties losing population, most were located in the south.

THE STATE'S ECONOMY

Overview. During the 1960s *Fortune* magazine found Indiana the state most preferred by companies planning to build or relocate industrial facilities. Other studies have suggested the availability of labour and essential materials to be major advantages, as well as the state's location within 800 miles of 40 of the nation's 50 largest consumer and industrial markets and its high rank in interstate-highway mileage. The legislature passed laws in 1965 providing financial incentive for industrial expansion, and the two areas consistently receiving the most federal grants in the state are highways and agriculture. Heavy industrialization, however, has made the state's economy particularly vulnerable to recession.

Sources of economic strength

The American Railway Union, America's first industrial (as distinct from craft) union, was founded in Terre Haute in 1893 by Eugene Debs, five-time Socialist candidate for president. The following year it was heavily involved in the Pullman Strike that brought the intervention of federal troops and Debs's imprisonment. Since that time Indiana has had its share of labour strife, especially in the steel industry, but, in general, the state Chamber of Commerce and the unions tend to work with the state government to help maintain an atmosphere attractive to industry.

Natural resources. Indiana is a major producer of U.S. building stone, quarried in the Bedford–Bloomington region. Bituminous coal from the southwest is the state's leading commodity for heating and generating electrical power. Natural gas must be brought in by pipelines, though during the 1880s Indiana's "Gas Belt" was the world's largest. Few attempts were made to conserve the gas, however, and by 1898 the supply was virtually exhausted. The Indiana and Michigan Electric Company's nuclear generating station in southwestern Michigan, with a capacity of more than 2,000,000 kilowatts, began operation in 1975.

Manufacturing. Since the 1850s manufacturing gradually has become the dominant source of income for the state, with the steel industry a major component. Features of interest include production of musical instruments, of which Indiana is a major manufacturer, and Fort Wayne's diamond-tool industry, producing a large proportion of the world's supply. Overall, Indiana ranks among the nation's top 10 states in manufacturing, which accounts for about 35 percent of the state's labour force.

Agriculture. The value of farm products more than tripled from the 1950s to the 1970s. Along with forestry and fisheries, agriculture employs about 3 percent of the labour force. Technological changes have resulted in startling increases in output per acre, per animal, and per worker, despite drops in total farm acreage and number of farms. Indiana ranks near the top nationally in cash receipts from farm marketing. Major crops include corn (maize), soybeans, and wheat, with tomatoes the principal vegetable crop. Hogs continue to be the most numerous livestock, with cattle, sheep, and poultry of increasing importance.

The highway system

Transportation. Signs on the Indiana Toll Road proclaim the state to be the "Main Street of the Midwest," perhaps a fair estimate of its position in interstate transportation, whether by highway, waterway, air, or rail. Indianapolis is served by more major highways than any other American city, some of the nation's largest moving companies have their headquarters there, and more than 30,000 persons are employed statewide in trucking.

Responsibility for road construction and maintenance rests with city, county, state, and federal governments. County and state highway departments are subject to a widely deplored spoils, or patronage, system under which changes in administration bring on political dismissal and employment, resulting in instability in management. Nonetheless, Indiana ranks high nationally in road mileage per square mile of area, and almost all of its rural roads are paved, as against a 75 percent national average. Though quantity may sometimes surpass quality of highway mileage, virtually all intrastate passengers and much commercial produce travel by road. Indiana has about 5,300 miles (8,500 kilometres) of mainline railroad track and about 2,800 miles of other trackage. All lines running east from Chicago and St. Louis pass through Indiana. As in other states, however, the Amtrak system that went into operation in 1971 has sharply reduced passenger service. Commercial air service is available in 11 Indiana cities, and there are more than 300 public and private airports in the state.

The Ohio River, linking Indiana with the Mississippi River system, carries more low-cost freight than does the Panama Canal. The Port of Indiana Harbour, on Lake Michigan about 10 miles east of Gary, created artificially and opened in 1970, connects Indiana with world commerce by way of the St. Lawrence Seaway.

ADMINISTRATION AND SOCIAL CONDITIONS

Structure of state government. Indiana's executive, legislative, and judicial structures are similar to those of other states, but they show some marked differences. The governor is elected for a four-year period and can serve no more than two consecutive terms. As a result, gubernatorial influence on the General Assembly is generally weak during the second half of an administration. The governor has veto power over legislation, but the veto can be overridden by a simple majority of the two houses. The governor's authority is wielded largely through statutory power to appoint and remove heads of nearly all departments, commissions, and governing boards of institutions. Several thousand jobs are subject to the spoils system.

The General Assembly

The bicameral General Assembly includes 50 senators, serving four-year terms, and 100 representatives, serving for two years. They may be reelected, but there is often a high turnover. In 1970 the voters approved annual sessions for the two bodies. The state constitution requires that the legislature reapportion itself according to population every six years. This law was ignored, however, from 1923 to 1963, during which time the rural areas exerted an influence far out of proportion to their declining population. Under pressure from the U.S. Supreme Court, the state eventually achieved a reapportionment based on the "one man, one vote" principle in 1965.

The Indiana constitution provided for the establishment of a Supreme Court, circuit courts, and other courts as the General Assembly deemed necessary. The Supreme Court is composed of five judges appointed by the governor and a judicial nominating commission after a rigorous screening procedure. A new judge serves for a period of two years and then, if retained, for a term of 10 years. The Court of Appeals consists of three regional divisions with three appellate judges each. Decisions are expected to be two to one, but cases are not referred automatically to the Supreme Court if there is a lack of consensus.

Overlapping of governmental units

Local government. The four principal types of local government are the county, township, town, and civil city. There are also school towns, townships, and cities concerned with the operation of the school system; these may be independent or may overlap other political units. Townships, greatly reduced in importance, function primarily in the area of welfare. The county, town, and city have many areas of overlapping activity. Boards of county commissioners have executive and legislative powers, while county councils are concerned almost exclusively with fiscal affairs. City voters elect a mayor and common council.

The political process. Indiana is a two-party state, the Republicans having a slight advantage since the last quarter of the 19th century, especially in control of the governor's office and the General Assembly and in presidential voting. Voting trends show about one-third of the counties to be Republican, one-third Democratic, and one-third doubtful. During the 1960s Indiana replaced a conservative Republican senator, and for several years (until 1976), it had two liberal Democratic senators in Washington. The state created a stir in 1964 by giving George Wallace of Alabama almost 30 percent of the Democratic vote in the primary, but in the elections of 1968 Wallace received only 12 percent of the vote. In 1967 Gary and Cleveland, Ohio, became the first major U.S. cities to elect black mayors.

At the national level, the state can claim one president, Benjamin Harrison, the grandson of William Henry Harrison, and four vice presidents. In 1940 the Indiana native son Wendell L. Willkie was the Republican candidate for president.

Taxation. Indiana's state and local governments rely largely on personal and corporate income taxes, retail sales taxes, and taxes on such items as motor fuels, tobacco products, and alcoholic beverages. Until the late 1970s, however, Hoosiers paid a lower per-capita state tax than the average U.S. citizen, and they continue to pay property taxes that are well below the national median. In keeping with its traditional distrust of the federal government, the state accepts only a minimal amount of federal aid (the lowest per-capita amount in the nation in the late 1970s). In addition, Indiana's revenue from corporate taxes is significantly below the national average. To ease local property taxes, legislation in 1967 provided for disbursement to local governments of 8 percent of revenues from income and sales taxes.

Attitudes toward public welfare. Hoosiers take their politics seriously and do not take well to the idea of supporting public welfare programs. Indiana is among the more prosperous states in the nation, but like many other states it fails to apply its wealth to public programs. For example, not until the 1970s did the average weekly unemployment benefit in Indiana exceed the national average.

In comparison with its neighbouring states, Indiana ranks lowest in per-capita allotments for public welfare. Approximately 70 percent of Indiana's public assistance funding comes from federal and state funds; few other states in the nation finance so large a proportion of their assistance programs from local levels. Partially for this reason, Indiana is well below the national average in the number of recipients of general assistance per 1,000 population. Distrust of federal programs has tended to militate against making maximum use of aid that could be available, thus necessitating continued taxes at the state and local level that are a greater burden on the aged, on those with fixed incomes, and on the working and lower middle classes. The problem that the state confronts in financing public welfare programs is as much ideological as it is financial.

The racial situation. Despite federal and state prohibitions, slavery continued to exist well into the first half of the 19th century. In 1831 blacks entering the state had to deposit $500 bonds as surety that they would not become burdens on the state, but the total exclusion of blacks in the constitution of 1851 was the high point of such sentiment.

Racial integration

Despite annulment of that provision, blacks continued to be the victims of vigilante and other less-open methods of repression; by the early 1900s the Ku Klux Klan was flourishing and for some years all but controlled state government. Only in 1943 were teams from black schools allowed to participate in the annual state high school basketball tournament. The "Jim Crow" ward of Indianapolis Marion County General Hospital was not abolished until 1949, and hospitals moved only gradually after that to admit black doctors to their staffs. All forms of segregation were officially declared illegal in 1949, and since the 1950s the state has slowly emerged as one of the most effective enforcers of civil rights legislation in the nation, although there are persisting pockets of school and housing segregation in some cities, such as Gary and East Chicago.

Education. The state's educational system is headed by a board of education and a superintendent of public instruction. Although the state was spending more than $2,000,000,000 annually on public schools in the early 1980s, Indiana ranks in the lower half of the states in per-pupil outlay. The state's elementary and secondary educational systems are good, but they are not considered to be innovative or outstanding.

In the realm of higher education, on the other hand, Indiana has made notable achievements. The three leading universities of the state are Indiana, in Bloomington; Purdue, in West Lafayette; and Notre Dame, in South Bend. Indiana University, founded in 1820, has become noted for its work in several fields, including English, foreign languages, biology, medicine, and law, and its university press rates among the nation's finest, especially in the arts. More than a dozen of its departments were rated among the nation's best in a study by the American Council on Education. The university's School of Music has become internationally known; among its performance series are works staged annually by the Opera Theater. Purdue, organized in 1869 as a land-grant college, is one of the nation's leading engineering and agricultural schools.

Notre Dame, dating from 1842, is widely regarded as the leading Roman Catholic university of the United States. Its faculty in a dozen graduate programs has become recognized at the national level, helping to overcome its image as an institution devoted solely to athletics. Notre Dame, originally a men's school, in 1972 began enrolling women from St. Mary's College, also located in South Bend.

CULTURAL LIFE AND INSTITUTIONS

The arts. The fine arts flourish in most of Indiana's major cities and even in some of the smaller towns. The Indianapolis Symphony has a respected place among the nation's fine orchestras, and the city also boasts the Indianapolis Museum of Art and the Civic Theater, the nation's oldest continuously operating theatrical organization. South Bend and Fort Wayne also have symphony orchestras, and one of the best known art colonies in the United States is located in Nashville, in the heart of Brown County.

The popular arts

Indiana has made a special contribution to the popular arts in the United States, with the prototypical Hoosier poet James Whitcomb Riley, novelists Booth Tarkington and Lew Wallace, satirist George Ade, and the World War II chronicler of the foot soldier, Ernie Pyle. Some of the country's most popular songs have been written by such Hoosiers as Hoagy Carmichael ("Star Dust"), Cole Porter ("Begin the Beguine"), J. Russel Robinson ("Margie"), Albert von Tilzer ("Take Me Out to the Ball Game," "In the Evening by the Moonlight"), and Paul Dresser ("On the Banks of the Wabash," "My Gal Sal"), brother of the novelist Theodore Dreiser. Among the most notable of Indiana comedians have been Herb Shriner and Red Skelton.

Sports and recreation. Almost every citizen seems to participate in "Hoosier Hysteria," the state's annual high school basketball tournament. Notre Dame, well known for its football talent, vies annually with Purdue and Indiana to provide Hoosiers with exceptional intercollegiate athletics. Indiana University has also become a mecca for basketball and for some of the world's greatest swimmers. At the professional level, Indianapolis is internationally known for the "Indy 500," the world's most spectacular auto race, which is held annually on Memorial Day. The first race was held in 1911, while the city was still an automobile-manufacturing centre. The entire month of May has become devoted to the race, with such attendant events as a major professional golf meet. Indianapolis is also the site of the annual U.S. Clay Court Championships, which attract top international tennis players.

Hoosiers fond of the outdoor world can find haven in walking or camping in its many state parks. Though they were among the leading state parks in the nation in the early part of the century, they have become badly in need of remodelling, expanding, and refurbishing.

PROSPECTS

The circumstances that once favoured Indiana's economy, a strong industrial base and a central geographic location, may play a diminished role in the future. The state, with much of its heavy industry vulnerable to recession, must contend with the relocation of many of its industries in the South and West. The state also faces many of the nation's most pressing problems: racial tension, dirty air and water, expensive transportation, and the need to rethink priorities in the allocation of wealth in private and public matters. Indiana's constitutional clause forbidding deficit spending has increased the strains on social services. The numbers of poor have grown, and the state's revenue base has declined. The state has been particularly slow in developing welfare programs that compare favourably with those of its neighbours; its prison system is in need of reform; and its educational system, though fundamentally sound, requires new approaches to financing so as to maintain and improve its quality.

BIBLIOGRAPHY. JACOB PIATT DUNN, *Indiana and Indianans,* 5 vol. (1919), one of the earliest documented studies of Indiana; HUBERT H. HAWKINS (comp.), *Indiana's Road to Statehood* (1964), a publication authorized by the Indiana Sesquicentennial Commission consisting of a selection of documents relating to the transition from territory to state; JAMES B. KESSLER (ed.), *Empirical Studies of Indiana Politics* (1970), a series of articles dealing with political behaviour in Indiana; IRVING LEIBOWITZ, *My Indiana* (1964), a highly readable view of the political and social events in Indiana, written by a journalist; THEODORE DREISER, *A Hoosier Holiday* (1916; reprinted 1974), an account by the native-son novelist; JULIA HENDERSON LEVERING, *Historic Indiana,* rev. ed. (1916), an interesting and detailed sociocultural history of Indiana, including a bibliography; CLIFTON J. PHILLIPS, *Indiana in Transition: The Emergence of an Industrial Commonwealth, 1880–1920* (1968), part of a five volume series discussing most of the significant political, economic, and social changes involved in Indiana's transition from a primarily rural-agricultural society to a predominantly urban-industrial commonwealth; MORTON M. ROSENBERG and DENNIS W. MCCLURG, *The Politics of Pro-Slavery Sentiment in Indiana, 1816–1861* (1968), a well-documented monograph on the immigration pattern in Indiana in relation to the rise and decline of proslavery sentiment; DAVE O. THOMPSON and WILLIAM L. MADIGAN, *One Hundred and Fifty Years of Indiana Agriculture* (1966), a description of the lives and activities of the pioneers, settlers, builders, experimenters, and agricultural scientists of early Indiana; EMMA LOU THORNBROUGH, *Since Emancipation: A Short History of Indiana Negroes 1863–1963* (1963), an historical survey, which includes a summary of trends and developments and a bibliography.

(W.V.D'A.)

Indian Ocean

The Indian Ocean is that part of the world ocean that lies south of Asia and between Africa and Australia, extending south to Antarctica. Although it stretches for more than 6,200 miles (10,000 kilometres) between the southern tips of Africa and Australia and although—after the Pacific and Atlantic—it is the third largest ocean of the world, it comprises only about 20 percent of the total ocean area. Including the Red Sea and the Persian Gulf, it is estimated to have a total area of about 28,400,000 square miles (73,600,000 square kilometres).

The ocean is bounded by India, Pakistan, and Iran to the north; the Arabian Peninsula and Africa to the west; Australia, the Sunda Islands of Indonesia, and the Malay Peninsula to the east; and Antarctica to the south. In the southwest it joins the Atlantic Ocean south of the southern tip of Africa, and to the east and southeast its waters mingle with those of the Pacific. For the most part, it lies in the Southern Hemisphere; for that reason and because its maritime trade routes cross through the tropical zone, it is often thought of as a tropical sea, despite the fact that it extends south to Wilkes Land in Antarctica. Its northernmost extensions—the Red Sea and the Persian Gulf—reach to 30° N.

The question of defining the oceanic limits of the Indian Ocean is complicated and remains unsettled. The clearest border and the one most generally agreed upon is that with the Atlantic Ocean, which runs from Cape Agulhas, at the southern tip of Africa, due south along the 20° E meridian to the shores of Antarctica. The border with the Pacific Ocean to the southeast is usually drawn from South East Cape on the island of Tasmania, south along the 147° E meridian to Antarctica. Bass Strait, between Tasmania and Australia, is considered by some researchers as part of the Indian Ocean, by others as part of the Pacific.

Boundaries with other oceans

The northeastern border is the most difficult to define. Some researchers believe that this border runs across the Torres Strait between Australia and the island of New Guinea, and then from the island of Adi, off the western New Guinea coast, along the southern shores of the Lesser Sunda Islands and the island of Java, thence across the Sunda Strait to the shores of Sumatra. Other researchers, however, consider the Arafura Sea and even the Timor Sea as parts of the Pacific and not the Indian Ocean. Between the island of Sumatra and the Malay Peninsula the boundary is sometimes drawn at Singapore, but it sometimes is drawn from Cape Pedro to the northeast, thus making the Strait of Malacca a part of the Pacific Ocean.

In comparison with the other oceans, the Indian Ocean has the fewest seas. To the north are the inland seas—the Red Sea and the Persian Gulf; the marginal seas are the Arabian Sea to the northwest, the Andaman Sea to the northeast, and the Timor and Arafura seas to the east. The large gulfs of Aden and Oman are to the northwest, the Bay of Bengal to the northeast, the Gulf of Carpentaria off the north coast of Australia, and the Great Australian Bight off the south coast of the continent; to the south is Antarctica—with the Rüser-Larsen Sea, Sea of the Cosmonauts, Commonwealth Bay, Davis Sea, Mouson Sea, d'Urville Sea—and bays such as Prydz Bay and others.

The average depth of the Indian Ocean is 12,760 feet (3,890 metres); and it contains an average of 70,086,000 cubic miles (292,131,000 cubic kilometres) of water.

PHYSIOGRAPHY AND GEOLOGY

Shores and islands. The shores of the Indian Ocean are multiform. Wave-eroded and sedimentary coastlines are widely represented; they are indented and levelled, with eroded cliffs. The sedimentary coasts are alluvial, lagoonal, and deltaic. Some are coral, some caused by faults, and some, in Antarctica, glacial. The shoreline is gently indented, with the exception of the northern part of the ocean, where the seas and bays have cut deeply into the land.

The Indian Ocean has few islands; the large ones, such as Madagascar, Socotra, and Sri Lanka (formerly Ceylon), are continental—as are the Seychelles. The volcanic islands of Kerguelen, Crozet, Prince Edward, Nouvelle (New) Amsterdam and Saint-Paul lie to the south. Coral atolls, which predominate in the tropical reaches, include the Laccadive, Maldive, Amirante, Farquhar, and Cocos islands and the Chagos Archipelago. There also are volcanic islands ringed by coral reefs, including the Mascarenes and the Comoro islands.

Bottom deposits. The floor of the Indian Ocean can be divided into four major topographical features: the continental margin, the island arc, the ocean basin floor, and the mid-ocean ridge.

Four major topographic features

The continental margin. The underwater parts of the continents include continental shelves and continental slopes; the continental rise—a relatively smooth wedge of sediments at the base of the continental slope—is located mainly on the ocean basin floor, and represents a marginal inclined accumulative plane. The Indian Ocean continental shelf essentially consists of a narrow, flat surface up to 60 miles wide, broadening to a width of between 120 and 180 miles in the Arabian and Andaman seas as well as in the Bay of Bengal, and, in the Great Australian Bight, spreading to a width of 600 miles between Australia and New Guinea. The outer edge of the shelf lies mainly at depths of 150 to 600 feet, but off northwestern Australia the depths reach 900 to 1,200 feet. The Antarctic shelf has acquired a more complex structure because of ice action. The shelf is divided into two parts, outer and inner, by an abrupt underwater cliff, or scarp, with a longitudinal depression at the base in some places; the levelled portion of the outer shelf is submerged to a depth of 1,200 to 1,500 feet, while the inner shelf lies from 450 to 600 feet deep. In addition, the Antarctic shelf is intersected by deep transverse depressions, which are glacial troughs. In the tropical zone, coral reefs are widespread—as fringing reefs, barrier reefs, and atolls. Channels, banks, shoals, sandwaves, and dunes also have been created by the flow of the currents in the straits of Malacca, Singapore, and Bass; in the gulfs of Cambay and Kutch; and near the mouths of the Ganges, Irrawaddy, and Shatt al-Arab rivers.

Beyond the shelf edge, the continental slope of the Indian Ocean is represented, for the most part, by steep scarps, with slopes of from 10° to 30°, which are complicated in places by marginal plateaus (Western Australia) or which are dissected by valleys and canyons (Indus, Ganges, Trincomalee, Perth, and others).

The Island arc. In the northeastern Indian Ocean the Sunda arc (most of Indonesia and other islands) extends for more than 3,200 miles from Burma to Australia. Along more than half of its length lies the Java (or Sunda Double) Trench, the deepest place in the Indian Ocean, reported at 24,442 feet (7,450 metres)—a figure, however, that has not been confirmed by Soviet investigations, which have established a flat bottom there at 23,392 feet. The Sunda arc is divided into two chains: (1) an inner ridge of islands consisting of the volcanic chain of the Greater and Lesser Sunda islands (Sumatra, Java, Timor, and others) and (2) an outer ridge, an uplift consisting of the Andaman, Nicobar, and Mentawai islands and the submerged Bali Ridge.

Asia
Africa
India
Arabian Sea
Persian Gulf
Gulf of Aden
RED SEA RIFT
Suqutra
3694
5143
INDUS CANYON
INDUS FAN
3858
ARABIAN BASIN
INDIA ABYSSAL PLAIN
5870
CARLSBERG RIDGE
1752
846
CHAIN RIDGE
SOMALI ABYSSAL PLAIN
SOMALI BASIN
5115
5340
Seychelles
Amirante Islands
AMIRANTE TRENCH
Coetivy Island
Agalega Islands
Farquhar Group
Cerf
Aldabra Islands
COMORO RIDGE
Comoro Islands
Mozambique Channel
Madagascar
MASCARENE BASIN
Tromelin
Cargados Carajos Shoals
NAZARETH BANK
SAYA DE MALHA BANK
18
SEYCHELLES-MAURITIUS PLATEAU
VEMA TRENCH
6237
Chagos Archipelago
CHAGOS-LACCADIVE PLATEAU
Laccadive Islands
Maldive Islands
5408
3244
Equator
Ceylon
5243
CEYLON ABYSSAL PLAIN
NIKITIN (AFANASIY) SEAMOUNT
1549
MID-INDIAN BASIN
6090
RIDGE
NINETY EAST RIDGE
Bay of Bengal
GANGES CANYON
GANGES FAN
2359
2095
Andaman Islands
ANDAMAN BASIN
Nicobar Islands
COCOS BASIN
6335
Cocos Islands
MENTAWEI RIDGE
MENTAWEI TROUGH
Sumatera
Malay Peninsula
Gulf of Siam
65
South China Sea
MACCLESFIELD BANK
Kalimantan (Borneo)
Java Sea
Djawa
JAVA TRENCH
7450
Christmas Island
KARMA RISE
CHRISTMAS RISE
ROO RISE
WHARTON BASIN
WEST
ARGO ABYSSAL PLAIN
CORONA SEAMOUNT
ROWLEY SHOALS
EXMOUTH
20°
10°
0°
30°
40°
50°
60°
70°
80°
90°
100°
110°

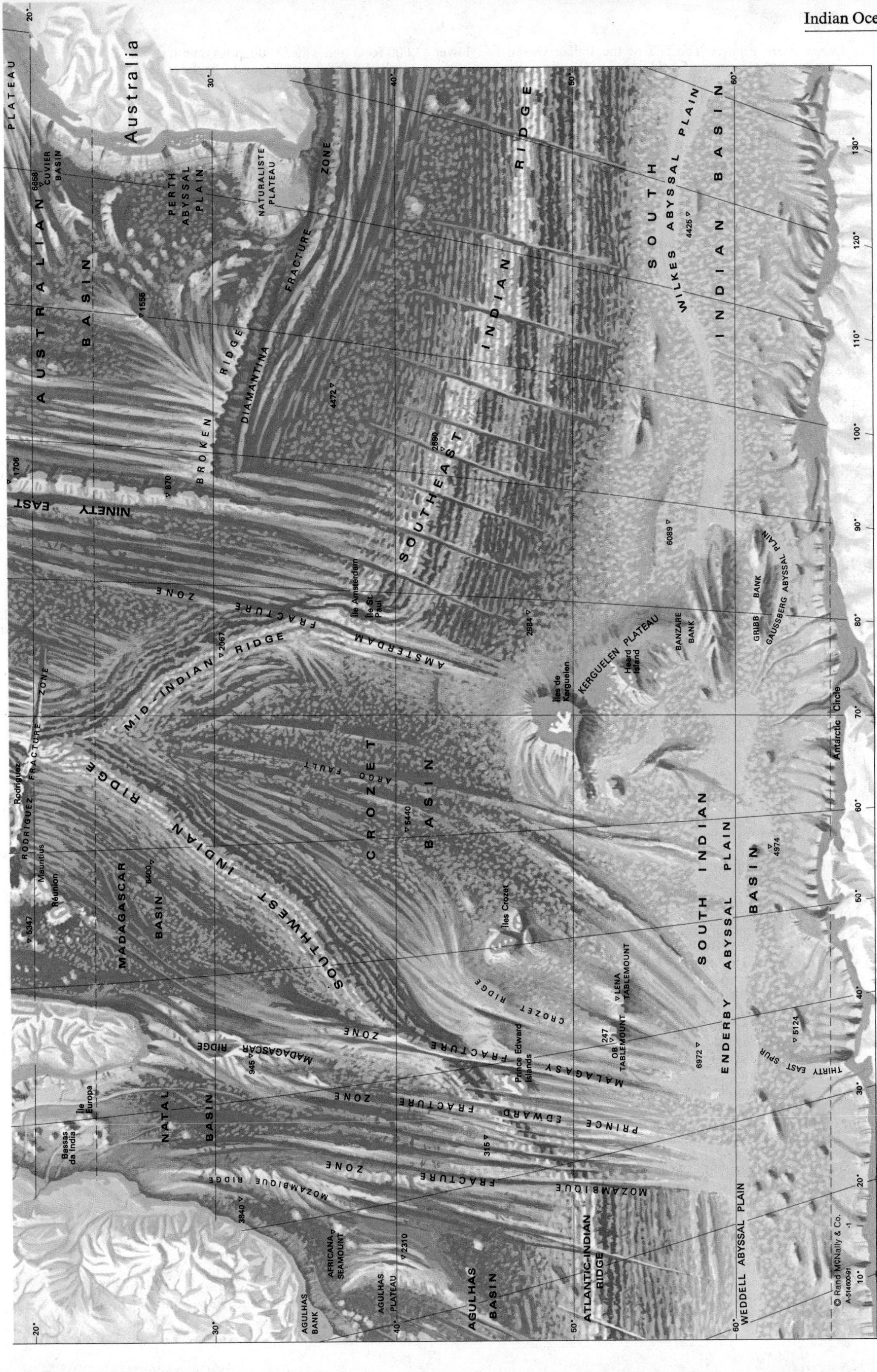

Colours used are thought to be those of the various rocks and sediments on the sea floors. Differences in relief are shown by relief shading.

Depths in metres

INDIAN OCEAN

Ocean Basin Floor. The bed of the Indian Ocean is separated by a system of mid-ocean ridges into three parts or segments—African, Australasian, and Antarctic—that in turn are subdivided by ridges, plateaus, rises, and chains of seamounts into basins extending from 200 miles (Comoro and North Australian basins) to 5,600 miles (South Indian, or Australian Antarctic, Basin).

Basins and plains

Some basins—the Arabian, for example—are surrounded by uninterrupted high ridges, and others, such as the Mid-Indian Basin, have in some places low barriers; a third type—the Crozet and Atlantic-Indian basins—are unobstructedly connected by wide, deep gaps.

Two types of topography dominate the bottoms of the oceanic basins; smooth topography (abyssal plains) occurring near the continents in areas where sediment is abundantly spread out, and rough or uneven topography (abyssal hills) occurring in the central part of the ocean where a very thin sedimentary layer is deposited. Deep-sea channels—elongated depressions a few miles across but up to 1,500 miles long with low rises (levees) along the banks and maximum wall heights of 600 feet—are one of the common features of the abyssal plains. As they approach the continents, the plains are transformed into abyssal fans (cones), such as the Indus and Ganges fans, or into marginal inclined planes (the lower continental rise), as occurs off the coast of Equatorial Africa. Along the periphery of the abyssal cones and inclined planes, the flattest surfaces of the bottom occur; they are called abyssal plains, such as the Ceylon and Somali plains. The rough topography of the basin is characterized by widespread development of hills and volcanic seamounts. The hills usually have conical profiles up to 1,500 feet in height (higher ones are considered low mountains), distributed individually or in groups over the whole basin bed. Flat-topped hills with steep sides are also encountered.

Among the ridges of the Indian Ocean, the Ninety East Ridge (the East Indian Ridge) is distinguished by its straightness and length (approximately 3,100 miles). It was discovered in 1962. It is connected on the south, at a right angle, to the Broken (or West Australian) Ridge.

Mountains and fracture zones

Large ridges stretch to the south from the Hindustān Peninsula, from the island of Madagascar, and from the eastern shore of South Africa. In the south the massive Kerguelen Plateau runs from northwest to southeast. Trenches occur at the foot of a number of the ridges; these include the East-Indian, Chagos, Ob', and Amirante trenches. The large aseismic (earthquake-resistant) ridges and plateaus (Madagascar, Seychelles, Mauritius, Agulhas, Kerguelen, and West Australian) represent a considerable thickness of the earth's crust; sometimes, when formed of a continental type of rock, they are called microcontinents.

Large fractures, called fracture zones, have been discovered on the ocean bottom. The Diamantina, Mascarene, and other fracture zones form narrow strips from about 30 to 90 miles wide and up to 1,800 miles long, with severely disrupted relief that consists of deep trenches, ridges, mountains, and scarps. Volcanoes with conical peaks are widely represented on the ocean basin floor, forming large groups with massive structures, such as that culminating in the Farquhar Islands, or ranges found here and there to the east of the Cocos (Keeling) Islands and to the north of Madagascar.

The mid-oceanic ridges. The mid-oceanic ridges form an enormous mountain system made up of three sections diverging from the centre of the ocean: one toward the north (the Carlsberg, or Arabian-Indian, Ridge), the second toward the southwest (the West-Indian and Atlantic-Indian, and Southwest Indian ridges), and the third toward the southeast (the Mid-Indian Ridge and the Southeast Indian Rise or Australian Antarctic Ridge). The first two branches represent a complex mountain structure 250 to 600 miles in width and from 6,000 to 10,000 feet in height, with the most rugged topography occurring along the crest, and characterized by the occurrence of a rift valley surrounded by rift mountains. The third, southeastern, branch of the mid-oceanic ridge to the east of New Amsterdam (Amsterdam) Island is lower (3,000 feet) and wider (900 miles), with a severely but not deeply dissected surface, and is usually devoid of rift valleys. The mid-oceanic ridges of the Indian Ocean are intersected by numerous fracture zones, some of which are large, such as the Owen Fracture Zone, which extends into the bottoms of the Arabian and Somali basins. Horizontal displacement of the bottom was found for 200 miles along the Owen Fracture Zone.

Bottom structures. Stable crustal structures are predominant in the Indian Ocean, both on the bed and on the periphery (continental platforms). The actively developing structures—recent geosynclines (depressions) such as the Sunda Islands arc and rift formations (the mid-oceanic ridges)—occupy a smaller area and are extensions of the corresponding land structures (the Alpine ranges of Burma and the rifts of East Africa). The volcanic mountain ranges on the ocean floor are usually crowned with coral islands (the Maldive and Amirante islands and the southern part of the Mascarene Ridge). Developing sea-bottom structures include trench fractures (Chagos, Ob'), fracture zones (Owens, Diamantina, Mauritius), rift zones and scarps, all formed by movements of the earth's crust. The microcontinents (small continental platforms) are stable aseismic features, such as ridges and plateaus (the Madagascar, Kerguelen, West Australian, Crozet, and other features).

Actively developing structures

Sediments and bottom rocks. The greatest thicknesses (up to 6,500 feet) of bottom sediments in the Indian Ocean are near the continents. In the centre the sediments are thin (approximately 300 feet), and in areas of rough topography their distribution is intermittent. Most widely represented are: calcareous remains of foraminifera (one-celled protozoans) found on the continental slopes, on the ridges, and in the majority of the basin bottoms to depths up to 14,000 feet; the siliceous shells of diatom algae (between the 50th parallel and Antarctica); the minute, opaline silica shells of radiolaria (another protozoan) near the Equator; and the coral sediments. Red clays are distributed south of the Equator at depths of from two to more than four miles; terrigenous (land-derived) sediments predominate on the continental shelves and upper parts of the continental slopes. Deposits formed by chemical action are represented by phosphorite and manganese nodules. In the rift zone of the mid-oceanic range a special type of sediment occurs; it is formed by the disintegration of the intrusive rock. Outcrops of bedrock—encountered most often on the continental slopes (sedimentary and metamorphic), on the mountains (basalt), and on the midoceanic ridges (basalt and also peridotite, cherzolite, and other rocks)—represent little changed substances from the upper mantle of the Earth.

Genesis. According to many scholars, the genesis of the Indian Ocean Basin appears to have occurred during the Mesozoic Era (225,000,000 to 65,000,000 years ago) with the breakup of an ancient continent in the Southern Hemisphere—Gondwanaland—into huge blocks (South America, Africa, Australia, Antarctica, Madagascar, and India) that subsequently drifted to their present positions. According to another hypothesis, the basin of the Indian Ocean was formed as the result of a subsidence and oceanization of the continental crust. Future submarine drilling in the Indian Ocean should permit a more exact answer to this question. (V.F.K.)

CLIMATE

The Indian Ocean can be roughly subdivided into four basic latitudinal climatic zones according to the special characteristics of atmospheric circulation.

Four basic climatic zones

The first zone, extending north from 10° S, has a monsoon climate (characterized by rain-bearing winds). Atmospheric circulation in summer (May to October) is determined by the counterclockwise movement of the South Asiatic cyclone (depression or low-pressure area), and in winter (October to April) by the clockwise circulation of the Asiatic anticyclone (high-pressure area). A seasonal alteration occurs in the direction of the prevailing winds, which in summer blow strongly from the southwest at speeds of up to 40 feet per second and in the winter gently from the north and northeast. The average annual precipitation in the eastern part of the Arabian Sea and in the Bay of Bengal exceeds 40 inches. Some western areas have less than ten inches, and the equatorial regions average approximately 70 inches. Air temperature in the summer is 77° to 82° F (25° to 28° C), but along the northeast coast of Africa it drops to 73° F (23° C) as a result of the upwelling of the cold, deep waters of the Somali Current. The winter air temperature drops to 72° F (22° C) in the northern ocean, remaining almost unchanged along and south of the Equator. Cloudiness is 60 to 70 percent in summer and 10 to 30 percent in winter in the monsoon region.

The second zone, that of the trade winds, lies between 10° and 30° S. Here very steady southeasterly trade winds prevail in the tropical and subtropical latitudes. The prevailing air mass is tropical sea air, which forms in the South Indian anticyclone. In the northern part of the zone the summer air temperature averages 77° F (25° C) and slightly higher in winter; along the 30th parallel it is 61° to 63° F (16° to 17° C) in summer and 68° to 72° F (20° to 22° C) in winter. Because of warm ocean currents the air temperature is 4° to 6° F (2 to 3° C) higher in the western trade-wind zone than in its eastern portion. Precipitation distribution is zonal. The annual precipitation decreases from eight inches in the north to four inches in the south. Hurricanes occur in the summer and autumn in the western trade-wind zone.

The third zone lies in the subtropical and temperate latitudes of the Southern Hemisphere, between 30° and 45° S. The dynamic system of the zone is shaped by the influence of the South Indian anticyclone situated at approximately 35° S. In the northern part of the zone the prevailing winds are light and variable; in the southern area, moderate to strong westerly winds prevail. Throughout the entire year the average air temperature decreases continuously with increasing south latitude: from 68° to 72° F (20° to 22° C) down to 50° F (10° C) in winter, and from 61° to 63° F (16° to 17° C) to 43° to 45° F (6° to 7° C) in summer. The uniformly distributed average precipitation is about 40 inches.

Antarctic influences

Finally, the fourth, or subantarctic and Antarctic, zone occupies the wide belt between 45° S and the continent of Antarctica. The atmospheric circulation over the ocean in this region is determined by the interaction of the Antarctic low-pressure belt and the subtropical belt of high atmospheric pressure. Steady westerly winds prevail, reaching gale force at times with their passage through the deep Antarctic cyclones. The influence of the continental ice upon the wind regime is evident in a narrow coastal belt where strong easterly winds prevail. The average summer (December, January, February) air temperature varies from 43° to 45° F (6° to 7° C) in the north to 3° F (−16° C) near the continent. The corresponding winter temperatures vary within the limits of 50° to 25° F (10° to −4° C). The precipitation varies from 40 to 20 inches southward. The annual range of air-temperature variations is not large, approximately 9° to 11° F (5° to 6° C), over most of the ocean waters, except in the south where it exceeds 27° F (15° C).

HYDROLOGY

The hydrological characteristics of the Indian Ocean depend not only on the atmospheric circulation described above but also on the complex interaction with and absorption of the waters of the Red Sea and of the Atlantic, Pacific, and Antarctic oceans.

Zonal and seasonal variations

Water temperatures. A zonal asymmetry is noted in the surface-water temperature distribution in summer, north of 20° S. Summer surface temperatures are higher in the eastern part of this region than in the western. In the Bay of Bengal the maximum temperature is around 82° F (28° C). The minimum temperature is about 72° F (22° C) in the area of Ra's Guardafui, and is associated with the upwelling of cold, deep water off the African coast north of the Equator. South of 20° S the temperature of the surface waters decreases at a uniform rate with increase of latitude, from 72° to 75° F (22° to 24° C) to 30° F (−1° C) near Antarctica.

Near the Equator, winter surface temperatures in excess of 82° F (28° C) are encountered in the eastern part of the ocean. Winter surface-water temperatures are around 72° to 73° F (22° to 23° C) in the northern portion of the Arabian Sea, and 77° F (25° C) in the Bay of Bengal. At 25° S the temperature is about 77° to 81° F (25° to 27° C); at the 40th parallel, 57° to 61° F (14° to 16° C); and at the coast of Antarctica, 32° to 30° F (0° to −1° C). The annual variation in surface-water temperatures over the major portion of the Indian Ocean is approximately 7° to 9° F (4° to 5° C). In the eastern equatorial region and south of 60° S, the annual variation is less than 4° F (2° C); in the south-Indian high-pressure region it may reach 18° F (10° C); and in the peripheral seas of the northern Indian Ocean it corresponds to that of the air temperature (in the Persian Gulf the annual variation exceeds 25° F [14° C]).

Salinity. The salinity of Indian Ocean surface waters varies within the limits of 32 to 37 parts per 1,000. The Red Sea and Persian Gulf are the sources of the high salinity in the northwestern part of the ocean. There, between the Equator and the Arabian Peninsula, maximum salinity exceeds 37 parts per 1,000, while in the northeast the salinity drops to 34 parts and even to 32 parts per 1,000 as the result of the considerable drainage from rivers and of greater precipitation. From 40° S to the shores of Antarctica the salinity gradually decreases from 35 to 33.5 parts per 1,000 as a result of the erosion and thawing of the Antarctic continental and pack ice. Surface salinity in the remaining waters of the ocean slightly exceeds 35 parts per 1,000 on the average.

Surface water density. Temperature has a decisive influence on water density in the open ocean; the surface-water density shows the same distribution characteristics as the temperature. The lowest density in the northern portion of the Indian Ocean is found on the surface of the Bay of Bengal, where it is 1.022 grams per cubic centimetre (0.591 ounces per cubic inch). The highest density, in the western Arabian Sea, is approximately 1.025 grams per cubic centimetre (0.593 ounces per cubic inch). Density distribution in the southern half of the ocean is zonal, increasing gradually from 1.023 grams per cubic centimetre (0.592 ounces per cubic inch) at the Equator to 1.027 grams per cubic centimetre (0.594 ounces per cubic inch) in the Antarctic region.

Vertical structure of the water. A usual characteristic of seawater is its decrease in temperature and salinity and increase in density with increased depth. In the Antarctic region of the Indian Ocean, from 45° to 50° S, the temperature does not follow this pattern. Instead, a layer of relatively warm water of subtropical origin is distributed at a depth of from 1,500 to 9,000 feet beneath the cold surface waters. North of 40° S a layer of lower salinity water of Antarctic origin is everywhere found at intermediate depths (1,500 to 3,000 feet).

North of 10° S the effect of the highly saline waters of the Red Sea and of the diluted waters from the Bay of Bengal cause local maximums and minimums of salinity to occur in the uppermost 1,500 feet of water. Fundamental changes in temperature, salinity, and density of the ocean are concentrated, as a rule, in the uppermost 3,600- to 4,500-foot layer of water. At this layer the average water temperature is 39° to 43° F (4° to 6° C), salinity is 34.6 to 34.7 parts per 1,000, and density is 1.027 to 1.028 grams per cubic centimetre (about 0.594 ounces per cubic inch). Water temperatures on the bottom are 34° to 36° F (1° to 2° C) and drop to 30° F (−1° C) in the Antarctic region. Below 4,500 feet the salinity and density do not vary materially.

Floating ice and icebergs

Ice. In the Indian Ocean, ice is formed in the south polar region during the Antarctic winter. The coastal ice is packed solid and reaches a thickness of six to 12 feet. The outer edge of the ice pack may extend for tens of miles from the shore. Between January and February the melting coastal ice is broken up by severe storms and, in the form of large blocks and broad floes, carried away by wind and currents to the open ocean. In some coastal areas the tongues of ice-shelf glaciers break off to form icebergs. West of the 90° E meridian in the Indian Ocean the northern limit for floating ice lies close to 65° S. To the east of that meridian, however, floating ice is commonly encountered to 60° S; large icebergs are sometimes carried as far north as 40° S.

Tidal range. In the open areas of the Indian Ocean the tidal range is small and is basically semidiurnal. Tides along the coasts average 1½ to 4½ feet. In certain areas, however, such as the bays of northern Australia, tides vary from 20 to 30 feet. Similarly, a large tidal range is found also in some coastal regions of the Arabian Sea and the Bay of Bengal.

Currents. Surface-water movement is determined by the prevailing winds. Under the influence of the monsoon winds the currents change from season to season north of 10° S. During the winter there is a counterclockwise circulation in the Arabian Sea, where the currents have an average velocity of 30–50 centimetres per second (12–20 inches per second). In summer the current reverses its direction. A counterclockwise rotation with average velocities of 20–30 centimetres per second (8–12 inches per second) is maintained throughout the year in the Bay of Bengal. Under the influence of southwesterly winds, blowing in summer, the Monsoon (North Equatorial) Current flows within a 10° zone along both sides of the Equator, the water moving from west to east at a speed of approximately 40 centimetres per second.

Reversing and shifting currents

In winter the Monsoon Current changes its direction to west-northwest and no longer flows to the east of the Maldive Ridge. During this period an equatorial countercurrent develops in the equatorial zone, flowing in the opposite direction to the prevailing wind.

Southward from the Equator the currents are virtually constant throughout the year. This system of currents is composed of the Tradewind (or South Equatorial) Current, the Cape Needle (or Agulhas) Current, the South Indian Ocean Current, and the West Australian Current. All these currents together form a southern tropical anticyclonic circulation pattern.

Between 40° S and 60° to 65° S the belt of the Antarctic Circumpolar Current moves eastward under the influence of the westerly winds, and near Antarctica there is a chain of local clockwise currents. Their southern portions are known as the East Wind Drift.

The characteristic pattern of the horizontal structure of the surface currents is maintained to a depth of about 1,500 feet in the northern part of the ocean. In the deeper layers, where the seasonal changes do not penetrate, a westerly movement with an average velocity of several inches a second prevails in the open ocean to the north of 30° S. The eastward movement of the Antarctic Circumpolar Current remains unchanged right to the very bottom of the ocean. On the edges of currents moving in opposite directions and in regions of abrupt changes in their velocities there are zones of maximum vertical movement of the water. An upwelling of the water occurs along 5° S in the area of the subequatorial divergence (division of the current); and downwellings occur both in the south-tropical and subtropical convergence (30° to 10° S) and by the cold waters in the area of the Antarctic Convergence Zone (50° to 55° S). The upwelling and downwelling of the water in these zones play an important role in the generation of water masses in the Indian Ocean. (V.G.N.)

NATURAL RESOURCES

Minerals. There are many minerals on the bottom of the Indian Ocean: petroleum and gas on the continental shelves (Persian Gulf, Red Sea, Bass Strait, Western Australia, and elsewhere); rutile and zircon (Northwestern Australia); the rare-earth mineral monazite in beach sands (India); diamonds, phosphorite nodules (Agulhas Bank); and coralline limestones. Sediments that contain enormous amounts of iron, copper, manganese, and other metals have been discovered in the Red Sea; and chrome ores have been found in the rift zone of the mid-oceanic ridge. Huge accumulations of manganese nodules containing numerous metals, some of them rare, lie on the ocean bed.

Vegetation and animal life. The greater part of the water area of the Indian Ocean lies within the tropical and temperate zones. The shallow waters of the tropical zone are characterized by numerous corals and other organisms capable of building, together with calcareous red algae, coral islands and atolls. These coralline structures shelter a thriving marine animal life consisting of sponges, worms, crabs, mollusks, sea urchins, brittle stars, starfish, and small but exceedingly brightly coloured coral fish. The major portion of the tropical coasts is covered with mangrove thickets with an animal life specific to that environment; the clearest representative adapted to it may be the mud-jumper, a fish that is capable of existing for long periods out of the water. Animal life in the tropical tidal zone of the beaches and rocks is not widespread because of the inhibiting effect of the sunlight. In the temperate zone, however, where the sun is less intense, are found dense growths of red and brown algae and a rich variety of invertebrates.

Abundant life is also a characteristic of the open expanses of the Indian Ocean, especially of the surface-water layer down to 300 feet (90 metres). Among the one-celled planktons, several types of algae predominate. In the Arabian Sea the blue-green algae occurs, which often produces a luxuriant fluorescent bloom.

Planktonic life

The small crustaceans, including more than 100 species of minute copepods, form the bulk of the animal life, followed by small mollusks, jellyfish, and polyps, and other invertebrate animals ranging from single-celled radiolaria to large Portuguese man-of-war jellyfish, which attain a size of several feet. The squid form large schools. Of the fishes, the most abundant are several species of flying fish, luminous anchovies, lantern fish, large and small tunnies, sailfish, and various types of sharks. Here and there are found sea turtles and large marine mammals, such as dugongs, or sea cows, toothed and baleen whales, dolphins, and seals. Among the birds the most common are the albatross and frigate birds, but there also are several species of penguins populating the Antarctic coast and the islands lying in the ocean's temperate zone.

NAVIGATION AND EXPLORATION

Study of the Indian Ocean began long ago. The Egyptians, Phoenicians, and Indians made long journeys in the northern portion of it during the 1st millennium BC, as did Chinese and Arabic seafarers from the middle of the 1st millennium AD onward. The writings of medieval Arab and Persian pilots from the 9th to the 15th centuries include detailed sailing instructions and information on navigation, winds, currents, coasts, islands, and ports from Sofala in East Africa to China. It was on an Indian trading vessel that the Russian voyager Afanasiy Nikitin sailed to India in 1469. Vasco da Gama, sailing around Africa in 1497, signed on an Arabian pilot at Malindi before he crossed the Indian Ocean to reach the western shores of India.

Early seafarers and explorers

The Dutch, English, and French followed the Portuguese to the Indian Ocean. In 1521 the Spanish navigator Juan Sebastián del Cano crossed the central part of the ocean, continuing the first voyage of circumnavigation of the globe after the death of the original commander, Ferdinand Magellan, in the Philippine Islands. The Dutch navigator Abel Tasman, pursuing voyages of discovery in the eastern Indian Ocean from 1642 to 1644, explored the northern coast of Australia and discovered the island of Tasmania. The southern waters of the Indian Ocean were explored by Captain James Cook in 1772. Beginning in 1806 the Indian Ocean was crossed repeatedly by Russian ships commanded by Adam Johann Krusenshtern, Otto von Kotzebue, and others.

Between 1819 and 1821 the expedition of the Russian explorer Fabian Gottlieb von Bellingshausen that circumnavigated Antarctica penetrated the Indian Ocean south of the 60th parallel. A number of important voyages to Antarctica followed, led by the explorers Lieut. Charles Wilkes (American), Jules Sébastien César Dumont d'Urville (French), James Ross (Scottish), Jean-Baptiste Charcot (French), and others.

Beginning of systematic investigations

The famous round-the-world expedition of the "Challenger," a British naval vessel, began in 1872 and marked the beginning of systematic investigation of the oceans, including the Indian Ocean. Thereafter, there were numerous expeditions.

Circumnavigational voyages following World War II were made by the Danish "Galathea," the Swedish "Albatross," and the English "Challenger II," which explored the northern portion of the Indian Ocean. During the preparation and execution of the International Geophysical Year (1957 to 1958) and in subsequent years systematic explorations of the southern Indian Ocean were carried out by Australian, New Zealand, Soviet, French, Japanese, and other expeditions. The International Indian Ocean Expedition, from 1960 to 1965, was a cooperative effort by more than 20 research ships of many countries. Similar studies of the ocean are continuing.

BIBLIOGRAPHY. P.L. BEZRUKOV and V.F. KANAEV, *Principal Features of the Structure of the Bottom of the North-Eastern Part of the Indian Ocean* (Eng. trans. from the Russian, 1963); M. EWING *et al.*, "Sediment Distribution in the Indian Ocean," *Deep Sea Res.*, 16:231–248 (1969); R.W. FAIRBRIDGE, "The Indian Ocean and the Status of Gondwanaland," *Prog. Oceanography*, 3:83–136 (1965); R.L. FISHER, G.L. JOHNSON, and B.C. HEEZEN, "Mascarene Plateau, Western Indian Ocean," *Bull. Geol. Soc. Am.*, 78:1247–1266 (1967); M.N. HILL (ed.), "A Discussion Concerning the Floor of the Northwest Indian Ocean," *Phil. Trans. R. Soc.*, Series A, 259:133–298 (1966); B.C. HEEZEN and M. THARP, *Physiographic Diagram of the Indian Ocean, the Red Sea, the South China Sea, the Sulu Sea and the Celebes Sea* (1964); V.G. NEYMAN, *The New Current Charts of the Indian Ocean* (Eng. trans. from the Russian, 1970); D.J. ROCHFORD, *Hydrology of the Indian Ocean*, 3 vol. (1961–64); H.U. SVERDRUP, M.W. JOHNSON, and R.H. FLEMING, *The Oceans* (1942).

(V.F.K.)

Indian Philosophy

Indian philosophy, which includes both orthodox (*āstika*) systems, namely, the Nyāya, Vaiśeṣika, Sāṃkhya, Yoga, Pūrva-mīmāṃsā, and Vedānta schools of philosophy, and unorthodox (*nāstika*) systems, such as Buddhism and Jainism, has been concerned with various philosophical problems. Significant among these concerns have been the nature of the world (cosmology), the nature of reality (metaphysics), logic, the nature of knowledge (epistemology), ethics, and religion.

This article is divided into the following sections:

I. General considerations

SIGNIFICANCE OF INDIAN PHILOSOPHIES IN THE HISTORY OF PHILOSOPHY

Relations to Western thought

In relation to Western philosophical thought, Indian philosophy, offers both surprising points of affinity and illuminating differences. The differences highlight certain fundamentally new questions that the Indian philosophers asked. The similarities reveal that even when philosophers in India and the West were grappling with the same problems and sometimes even suggesting similar theories, Indian thinkers were advancing novel formulations and argumentations. Problems that the Indian philosophers raised that their Western counterparts never did include such matters as the origin (*utpatti*) and apprehension (*jñapti*) of truth (*prāmāṇya*). Problems that the Indian philosophers ignored but that helped shape Western philosophy include the question of whether knowledge arises from experience or from reason and distinctions such as that between analytic and synthetic judgments or between contingent and necessary truths. Indian thought, therefore, provides the historian of Western philosophy with a point of view that may supplement that gained from Western thought, reveals certain inadequacies of Western thought, and makes clear that some concepts and distinctions may not be as inevitable as they may otherwise seem. Knowledge of Western thought gained by Indian philosophers has also been advantageous to them.

Vedic hymns, Hindu scriptures from the 2nd millennium BC, are the oldest extant record from India of the process by which the human mind makes its gods and of the deep psychological processes of mythmaking leading to profound cosmological concepts. The *Upaniṣads* (Hindu philosophical treatises) contain one of the first conceptions of a universal, all-pervading, spiritual reality leading to a radical monism (absolute nondualism, or the essential unity of matter and spirit); they also contain early Indian speculations about nature, life, mind, and the human body, not to speak of ethics and social philosophy. The classical, or orthodox, systems (*darśanas*) debate, sometimes with penetrating insight and often with tiresome repetition, such matters as the status of the finite individual; the distinction as well as the relation between the body, mind, and the self; the nature of knowledge and the types of valid knowledge; the nature and origin of truth; the types of entities that may be said to exist; the relation of realism to idealism; the problem of whether universals or relations are basic; and the very important problem of *mokṣa*, or salvation—its nature and the paths leading up to it.

GENERAL CHARACTERISTICS OF INDIAN PHILOSOPHY

Common concerns. Indian philosophies contain such a diversity of views, theories, and systems that it is almost impossible to single out characteristics shared by all. Acceptance of the authority of the Vedas characterizes all the orthodox (*āstika*) systems, but not the unorthodox (*nāstika*) systems, such as Cārvāka (radical materialism), Buddhism, and Jainism. Moreover, even when philosophers professed allegiance to the Vedas, their allegiance did little to fetter the freedom of their speculative ventures. On the contrary, the acceptance of the authority of the Vedas was a convenient way for one's views to become acceptable to the orthodox, even if a thinker introduced a wholly new idea. Thus, the Vedas could be cited to corroborate a wide diversity of views; they were used by the Vaiśeṣika thinkers (*i.e.*, those who believe in ultimate particulars, both individual souls and atoms) as much as by the Advaita (monist) philosophers.

Authority of the Vedas and the ideal of *mokṣa*

In most systems, the acceptance of the ideal of *mokṣa*, like allegiance to the authority of the scriptures, was only remotely connected with the systematic doctrines propounded. Many epistemological, logical, and even metaphysical doctrines were debated and decided on purely rational grounds that did not directly bear upon the ideal of *mokṣa*. Only the Vedānta ("end of the Vedas") and Sāṃkhya (a system that accepts a real matter and a plurality of the individual souls) philosophies may be said to have a close relationship to the ideal of *mokṣa*. The logical systems—Nyāya, Vaiśeṣika, and Pūrva-mīmāṃsā—are only very remotely related. Also, both the philosophies and other scientific treatises, including even the *Kāma-sūtra* ("Aphorisms on Love") and the *Artha-śāstra* ("Treatise on Material Gain"), recognized the same ideal and professed their efficacy for achieving it.

When Indian philosophers speak of intuitive knowledge, they are concerned with making room for it and demonstrating its possibility, with the help of logic—and there the task of philosophy ends. They do not seek to justify religious faith; philosophic wisdom itself is given the dignity of religious truth. Theory is not subordinated to practice, but theory itself, as theory, is regarded as being supremely efficacious.

Three basic concepts form the cornerstone of Indian philosophical thought: the self, or soul (*ātman*), works (*karma*), and salvation (*mokṣa*). Leaving the Cārvākas aside, all Indian philosophies concern themselves with these three concepts and their interrelations, though this is not to say that they accept the objective validity of these concepts in precisely the same manner. Of these, the concept of *karma*, signifying moral efficacy of human actions, seems to be the most typically Indian. The concept of *ātman*, not altogether absent in Western thought, corresponds, in a certain sense, to the Western concept of a transcendental or absolute spirit self—important differences notwithstanding. The concept of *mokṣa* as the concept of the highest ideal has likewise been one of the concerns of Western thought, especially during the Christian era, though it probably has never been as important as for the Hindu mind. Most Indian philosophies assume that *mokṣa* is possible, and the "impossibility of *mokṣa*" (*anirmokṣa*) is regarded as a material fallacy likely to vitiate a philosophical theory.

Indifference to mathematics and history as philosophical problems

In addition to *karma*, the lack of two other concerns further differentiates Indian philosophical thought from Western thought in general. Since the time of the Greeks, Western thought has been concerned with mathematics, and in the Christian era, with history. Neither mathematics nor history has ever raised philosophical problems for the Indian. In the lists of *pramāṇas*, or ways of knowing accepted by the different schools, there is none that includes mathematical knowledge or historical knowledge. Possibly connected with their indifference towards mathematics is the significant fact that Indian philosophers have not developed formal logic. The theory of the syllogism (a logical structure) is, however, developed, and much sophistication has been achieved in logical theory. Indian logic offers an instructive example of a logic of cognitions, or perceptual knowledge (*jñānāni*) rather than of abstract propositions—a logic not sundered from psychology and epistemology, because it is meant to be the logic of man's actual striving to know what is true of the world.

Forms of argument and presentation. There is, in relation to Western thought, a striking difference in the manner in which Indian philosophical thinking is presented as well as in the mode in which it historically develops. Except for the presystematic age of the Vedic hymns and the *Upaniṣads* and many diverse philosophical ideas current in the pre-Buddhistic era, there was with the rise of the age of the *sūtras* (aphoristic summaries of the main points of a system) a neat classification of systems (*darśanas*), a classification that was never to be contradicted and to which no further systems are added. No new school was founded, no new *darśana* came into existence. But this conformism, like conformism to the Vedas, did not check the rise of independent thinking, new innovations, or original insights. There is, apparently, an underlying assumption that no individual can claim to have seen the truth for the first time and, therefore, that an individual can only explicate, state, and defend in a new form a truth that had been seen, stated, and defended by countless others before him: hence the tradition of expounding one's thoughts by affiliating oneself to one of the *darśanas*. If one is to be counted as a great master (*ācārya*), one has to write a commentary (*bhāṣya*) on the *sūtras* of the *darśana* concerned or comment on one of the *bhāṣyas* and write a *ṭīkā* (subcommentary). The usual order is *sūtra–bhāṣya–vārttika* (collection of critical notes)–*ṭīkā*. At any stage, one may introduce a new and original point of view, but at no stage can one claim originality for oneself. Not even an author of the *sūtras* could do that, for he was only systematizing the thoughts and insights of countless predecessors. The development of Indian thought has thus been able to combine, in an almost unique manner, conformity to tradition and adventure in thinking.

ROLES OF SACRED TEXTS, MYTHOLOGY, AND THEISM

The role of the sacred texts in the growth of Indian philosophy is different in each of the different systems. In those systems that may be called *adhyātmavidyā*, or sciences of spirituality, the sacred texts play a much greater role than they do in the logical systems (*ānvīkṣikīvidyā*). In the case of the former, Śaṅkara, a leading Advaita Vedānta philosopher (*c.* 788–820), perhaps best laid down the principles: reasoning should be allowed freedom only as long as it does not conflict with the scriptures. In matters regarding supersensible reality, reasoning left to itself cannot deliver certainty, for, according to Śaṅkara, every thesis established by reasoning may be countered by an opposite thesis supported by equally strong, if not stronger, reasoning. The sacred scriptures, embodying as they do the results of intuitive experiences of seers, therefore, should be accepted as authoritative, and reasoning should be made subordinate to them.

Whereas the sacred texts thus continued to exercise some influence on philosophical thinking, the influence of mythology declined considerably with the rise of the systems. The myths of creation and dissolution of the universe persisted in the theistic systems but were transformed into metaphors and models. With the Nyāya (problem of knowledge)–Vaiśeṣika (analysis of nature) systems, for example, the model of a potter making pots determined much philosophical thinking, as did that of a magician conjuring up tricks in the Advaita (nondualist) Vedānta. The *nirukta* (etymology) of Yāska, a 5th-century-BC Sanskrit scholar, tells of various attempts to interpret difficult Vedic mythologies: the *adhidaivata* (pertaining to the deities), the *aitihāsika* (pertaining to the tradition), the *adhiyajña* (pertaining to the sacrifices), and the *ādhyātmika* (pertaining to the spirit). Such interpretations apparently prevailed in the *Upaniṣads;* the myths were turned into symbols, though some of them persisted as models and metaphors.

The issues of theism and atheism

The issue of theism vis-à-vis atheism, in the ordinary senses of the English words, played an important role in Indian thought. The ancient Indian tradition, however, classified the classical systems (*darśanas*) into orthodox (*āstika*) and unorthodox (*nāstika*). *Āstika* does not mean "theistic," nor does *nāstika* mean "atheistic." Pāṇini, a 5th-century-BC grammarian, stated that the former is one who believes in a transcendent world (*asti paralokah*) and the latter is one who does not believe in it (*nasti paralokah*). *Āstika* may also mean one who accepts the authority of the Vedas; *nāstika* then means one who does not accept that authority. Not all among the *āstika* philosophers, however, were theists, and even if they were, they did not all accord the same importance to the concept of God in their systems. The Sāṃkhya system did not involve belief in the existence of God, without ceasing to be *āstika*, and Yoga (a mental–psychological–physical meditation system) made room for God not on theoretical grounds but only on practical considerations. The Pūrva-Mīmāṃsā (Rational Conclusions) of Jaimini, the greatest philosopher of the Mīmāṃsā school, posits various deities to account for the significance of Vedic rituals but ignores, without denying, the question of the existence of God. The Advaita Vedānta of Śaṅkara rejects atheism in order to prove that the world had its origin in a conscious, spiritual being called Īśvara, or God, but in the long run regards the concept of Īśvara as a lower order concept negated by a metaphysical knowledge of Brahman, the absolute, nondual reality. Only the non-Advaita schools of Vedānta and the Nyāya-Vaiśeṣika remain zealous theists, and of these, the god of the Nyāya-Vaiśeṣika school does not create the eternal atoms, universals, or individual souls. For a truly theistic conception of God, one has to look to the non-Advaita schools of Vedānta, the Vaiṣṇava, and the Śaiva systems. Whereas Hindu religious life continues to be dominated by these last-mentioned theistic systems, the philosophies went their own ways, far removed from that religious demand.

A GENERAL HISTORY OF DEVELOPMENT AND CULTURAL BACKGROUND

The three periods of Indian philosophy

S.N. Dasgupta, a 20th-century Indian philosopher, has divided the history of Indian philosophy into three periods: the prelogical (up to the beginning of the Christian Era), the logical (up to the 11th century AD), and the ultralogical (from the 11th to the 18th century). What Dasgupta calls the prelogical stage covers the pre-Mauryan and the Mauryan periods (*c.* 321–185 BC) in Indian history. The logical period begins roughly with the Kuṣāṇas (1st–2nd centuries AD) and finds its highest development during the Gupta era (3rd–5th centuries AD) and the age of imperial Kanauj (7th century AD).

The prelogical period. In its early prelogical phase, Indian thought, freshly developing in the Indian subcontinent, actively confronted and assimilated the diverse currents of pre-Aryan and non-Aryan elements in the native culture that the Aryans sought to conquer and appropriate. The marks of this confrontation are to be noted in every facet of Indian religion and thought: in the Vedic hymns in the form of conflicts, with varying fortunes, between the Aryans and the non-Aryans; in the conflict between a positive attitude toward life that is interested in making life fuller and richer and a negative attitude emphasizing asceticism and renunciation; in the great variety of sceptics, naturalists, determinists, indeterminists, accidentalists, and no-soul theorists that filled the Ganges Plain; in the rise of the heretical, unorthodox schools of Jainism and Buddhism protesting against the Vedic religion and the Upaniṣadic theory of *ātman;* and in the continuing confrontation, mutually enriching and nourishing, that occurred between the Brahminic (Hindu priestly) and Buddhist logicians, epistemologists, and dialecticians. The Aryans, however, were soon followed by a host of foreign invaders, Greeks, Śakas and Hūṇas from Central Asia, Pushtans (Pathans), Mongols, and Mughals (Muslims). Both religious thought and philosophical discussion received continuous challenges. The resulting responses have a dialectical character: sometimes new ideas have been absorbed and orthodoxy modified; sometimes orthodoxy has been strengthened and codified in order to be preserved in the face of the dangers of such confrontation; sometimes, as in the religious life of the Christian Middle Ages, bold attempts at synthesis have been made. Nevertheless, through all the vicissitudes of social and cultural life, Brahminical thought has been able to maintain a fairly strong current of continuity.

In the chaotic intellectual climate of the pre-Mauryan era, there were skeptics (*ajñānikah*) who questioned the possibility of knowledge, materialists, the chief of which were the Ājīvikas (deterministic ascetics) and the Lokāyatas (the name by which Cārvāka doctrines—denying the authority of the Vedas and the soul—are generally known), and the two unorthodox schools of *yadṛchhāvāda* (accidentalists) and *svabhāvavāda* (naturalists), who rejected the supernatural. Kapila, the legendary founder of the Sāṃkhya school, supposedly flourished during the 7th century BC. Pre-Mahāvīra Jaina ideas were already in existence when Mahāvīra (flourished 6th century BC), the founder of Jainism, initiated his reform. Gautama the Buddha (flourished 6th–5th centuries BC) apparently was familiar with all of these intellectual ideas and was as dissatisfied with them as with the Vedic orthodoxy. He sought to forge a new path—though not new in all respects—that was to assure blessedness to man. Orthodoxy, however, sought to preserve itself in a vast *Kalpa-* (ritual) *sūtra* literature—with three parts: the *Śrauta-*, based on *śruti* (revelation); the *Gṛhya-*, based on *smṛti* (tradition); and the *Dharma-*, or rules of religious law, *sūtras*—whereas the philosophers tried to codify their doctrines in systematic form, leading to the rise of the philosophical *sūtras*. Though the writing of the *sūtras* continued over a long period, the *sūtras* of most of the various *darśanas* probably were completed between the 6th and 3rd centuries BC. Two of the *sūtras* appear to have been composed in the pre-Maurya period, but after the rise of Buddhism; these are the *Mīmāṃsā-sūtras* of Jaimini (*c.* 400 BC) and the *Vedānta-sūtras* of Bādarāyaṇa (*c.* 500–200 BC).

Development of philosophical–religious literature and philosophical systems

The Maurya period brought, for the first time, a strong centralized state. The Greeks had been ousted, and a new self-confidence characterized the beginning of the period. This seems to have been the period in which the epics *Mahābhārata* and *Rāmāyaṇa* were initiated, though their composition went on through several centuries before they took the forms they now have. Manu, a legendary lawgiver, codified the *Dharma-śāstra;* Kauṭilya, a minister of King Candragupta Maurya, systematized the science of political economy (*Arthaśāstra*); and Patañjali, an ancient author or authors, composed the *Yoga-sūtras*. Brahminism tried to adjust itself to the new communities and cultures that were admitted into its fold: new gods—or rather, old Vedic gods that had been rejuvenated—were worshipped; the Hindu trinity of Brahmā (the creator), Viṣṇu (the preserver), and Śiva (the destroyer) came into being; and the Pāśupata (Śaivite), Bhāgavata (Vaiṣṇavite), and the Tantra (esoteric meditative) systems were initiated. The *Bhagavadgītā*—the most famous epic of this period—symbolized the spirit of the creative synthesis of the age. A new ideal of *karma* as opposed to the more ancient one of renunciation was emphasized. Orthodox notions were reinterpreted and given a new symbolic meaning, as, for example, the *Gītā* does with the notion of *yajña* ("sacrifice"). Already in the pre-Christian era, Buddhism had split up into several major sects, and the foundations for the rise of Mahāyāna ("Greater Vehicle") Buddhism had been laid.

The logical period. The logical period of Indian thought began with the Kuṣāṇas (1st–2nd centuries). Gautama (a shadowy figure called Akṣapāda, the "foot-eyed") and his 5th-century commentator Vātsyayana established the foundations of the Nyāya as a school almost exclusively preoccupied with logical and epistemological issues. The Mādhyamika ("Middle Way"), or Śūnyavāda ("Voidist") school of Buddhism, arose and the thought of Nāgārjuna (*c.* 200), the great propounder of Śūnyavāda (dialectical thinking), reached great heights. Though Buddhist logic in the strict sense of the term had not yet come into being, a logical style of philosophizing was in existence in such schools of thought.

During the reign of the Guptas, there was a revival of Brahminism of a gentler and more refined form. Vaiṣṇavism of the Vāsudeva cult, centred on a prince-god and advocating renunciation by action, and Śaivism prospered, along with Buddhism and Jainism. Both the Mahāyāna and the Hinayāna ("Lesser Vehicle"), or Theravāda ("Way of the Elders"), schools flourished. The most notable feature, however, was the rise of the Buddhist Yogācāra school, of which Asaṅga (4th century AD) and his brother Vasubandhu were the great pioneers. Toward the end of the 5th century, Dignāga, a Buddhist logician, wrote the *Pramāṇasamuccaya* ("Compenduim of the Means of True Knowledge"), which laid the foundations of Buddhist logic.

The greatest names of Indian philosophy belong to the post-Gupta period from the 7th to 10th centuries. Buddhism was on the decline and the Tantric cults were rising, which led to the development of the tantric forms of Buddhism. Śaivism was thriving in Kashmir, and Vaiṣṇavism in the south. The great philosophers Mīmāṃṣakas Kumārila (7th century), Prabhākara (7th–8th century), Maṇḍana Miśra (8th century), Śālikanātha (9th century), and Pārthasārathi Miśra (10th century) belong to this age. The greatest philosopher of the period, however, was Śaṅkara. All defended Brahminism against the "unorthodox" schools, especially against the criticisms of Buddhism. The debate with Buddhism was continued, on a logical level, by philosophers of the Nyāya school—Uddyotakara, Vācaspati Miśra, and Udayana.

The ultralogical period. Muslim rule in India had consolidated itself by the 11th century, by which time Buddhism, for all practical purposes, had disappeared from the country. Hinduism had absorbed Buddhist ideas and practices and reasserted itself, with the Buddha appearing in Hindu writings as an incarnation of Viṣṇu. The Muslim conquest created a need for orthodoxy to readjust itself to a new situation. In this period the great works on Hindu law were written. Jainism, of all the "unorthodox" schools, retained its purity, and great Jaina works, such as Devasūri's *Pramāṇanayatattvālokālaṃkāra* ("The Ornament of the Light of Truth of the Different Points of View Regarding the Means of True Knowledge," 12th century AD) and Prabhācandra's *Prameyakamalamārtaṇḍa* ("The Sun of the Lotus of the Objects of True Knowledge," 11th century AD). Under the Cōla (Chola) kings (*c.* 850–1279) and later in the Vijayanagara kingdom (which, along with Mithilā in the north, remained strongholds of Hinduism until the middle of the 16th century), Vaiṣṇavism flourished. Yamunācārya (flourished AD 1050) taught the path of *prapatti*, or complete surrender to God. The philosophers Rāmānuja (11th century), Madhva, and Nimbārka (*c.* 12th century) developed theistic systems of Vedānta and severely criticized Śaṅkara's Advaita Vedānta.

Creativity in logic, epistemology, and religious life

Toward the end of the 12th century, creative work of the highest order began to take place in the fields of logic and epistemology in Mithilā and Bengal. The 12th–13th-century philosopher Gaṅgeśa's *Tattvacintāmaṇi* ("The Jewel of Thought on the Nature of Things") laid the foundations of the school of Navya-Nyāya ("New-Nyāya"). Five great members of this school were Pakṣadhara Miśra of Mithilā, Vāsudeva Sārvabhauma (16th century), his disciple Raghunātha Śiromaṇi (both of Bengal), Gadādhara Bhaṭṭācāryya, and, especially, the great Raghunātha.

Religious life was marked by the rise of great mystic saints, chief of which are Rāmānanda, Kabīr, Caitanya, and Gurū Nānak, who emphasized the path of *bhakti*, or devotion, a wide sense of humanity, freedom of thought, and a sense of unity of all religions. Somewhat earlier than these were the great Muslim Ṣūfī (mystic) saints, including Khwāja Muʿin-ud-Din Ḥasan, who emphasized asceticism and taught a philosophy that included both love of God and love of humanity.

The British period in Indian history was primarily a period of discovery of the ancient tradition (*e.g.*, the two histories by Radhakrishnan, scholar and president of India from 1962 to 1967, and S.N. Dasgupta) and of comparison and synthesis with the philosophical ideas from the West. Among modern creative thinkers have been Mahatma Gandhi, who espoused new ideas in the fields of social, political, and educational philosophy; Sri Aurobindo, an exponent of a new school of Vedānta that he calls Integral Advaita, and K.C. Bhattacharyya, who developed a phenomenologically oriented philosophy of subjectivity conceived as freedom from object.

II. Historical development of Indian philosophy

PRESYSTEMATIC PHILOSOPHY

Śruti and the nature of authority. All "orthodox" philosophies can trace their basic principles back to some statement or other in the Vedas. The Vedānta schools, especially, had an affiliation with the authority of *śruti*, and the school of Mīmāṃsā concerned itself chiefly with the questions of interpreting the sacred texts. The Hindu tradition regards the Vedas as being *apauruṣeya*—*i.e.*, as not composed by any person. Sāyana, a famous Vedic commentator, said that this means an absence of a human author. For Sāyana, the eternality of the Vedas is like that of space and time; man does not experience their beginning or end. But they are, in fact, created by Brahmā, the supreme creator. For the Advaita Vedānta, because no author of the Vedas is mentioned, an unbroken chain of Vedic teachers is quite conceivable, so that the scriptures bear testimony to their own eternality. The authoritative character of *śruti* may then be deduced from the fact that it is free from any fault (*doṣa*), or limitation, which characterizes human words. Furthermore, the Vedas give knowledge about things—whether *dharma* (what ought to be done) or Brahman (the absolute reality)—which cannot be known by any other empirical means of knowledge. The authority of the Vedas cannot, therefore, be contradicted by any empirical evidence. Later logicians of the "orthodox" schools sought to give these arguments precision and logical rigour.

Significance of the Vedic hymns

The Vedic hymns (*mantras*) seem to be addressed to gods and goddesses (*deva*, one who gives knowledge or light), who are personifications of natural forces and phenomena (Agni, the fire god; Indra, the rain god; Vāyu, the wind god). But there are gods not identifiable with such phenomena (*e.g.*, Aditi, the infinite mother of all gods; Mitra, the friend; Varuṇa, the guardian of truth and righteousness; Viśvakarman, the all-maker; *śraddhā*, faith). Also, the hymns show an awareness of the unity of these deities, of the fact that it is one God who is called by different names. The famed conception of *ṛta*—meaning at once natural law, cosmic order, moral law, and the law of truth—made the transition to a monistic view of the universe as being but a manifestation of one reality about which the later hymns continue to raise fundamental questions in a poignant manner, without, however, suggesting any dogmatic answer.

Development of the notion of transmigration. The hymns may, in general, be said to express a positive attitude toward human life and to show interest in the full enjoyment of life here and hereafter rather than an anxiety to escape from it. The idea of transmigration and the conception of the different paths and worlds traversed by good men and those who are not good—*i.e.*, the world of Viṣṇu and the realm of Yama—are found in the Vedas. The chain of rebirth as a product of ignorance and the conception of release from this chain as the greatest good of the spiritual life is markedly absent in the hymns.

Meanings of Brahman–*ātman*

Origin of the concept of Brahman and ātman. The *Upaniṣads* answer the question "Who is that one Being?" by establishing the equation Brahman = *ātman*. Brahman—meaning now that which is the greatest, than which there is nothing greater, and also that which bursts forth into the manifested world, the one Being of which the hymn of creation spoke—is viewed as nothing but *ātman*, identifiable as the innermost self in man but also, in reality, the innermost self in all beings. Both the words gain a new, extended, and spiritual significance through this identification. *Ātman* was originally used to mean breath, the vital essence, and even the body. Later etymologizing brought out several strands in its meaning: that which pervades (*yad āpnoti*), that which gives (*yad ādatte*), that which eats (*yad atti*), and that which constantly accompanies (*yacca asya santato bhavam*). Distinctions were made between the bodily self, the vital self, the thinking self, and the innermost self, whose nature is bliss (*ānanda*), the earlier ones being sheaths (*kośas*) covering the innermost being. Distinctions were sometimes drawn between the waking (*jāgrat*), dreaming (*svapna*), and dreamless-sleep (*suṣupti*) states of the self, and these three are contrasted with the fourth, or transcendent (*turīya*), state that both transcends and includes them all. The identification of the absolute reality underlying the universe with the innermost being within the human person resulted in a spiritualization of the former concept and a universalization of the latter. This final conception of Brahman or *ātman* received many different explications from different teachers in the *Upaniṣads*, some of which were negative in character (*neti* = *neti*, "not this, not this") while others positively affirmed the all-pervasiveness of Brahman. But there were still others who insisted on both the transcendence and immanence of Brahman in the universe. Brahman is also characterized as infinite, truth, and knowledge and as existence, consciousness, and bliss.

The principles underlying macrocosm and microcosm. Though the objective and the subjective, the macrocosm (universal) and the microcosm (individual), came to be identified according to their true essences, attempts were made to correlate different macrocosmic principles with corresponding microcosmic principles. The manifested cosmos was correlated with the bodily self; the soul of the world, or Hiraṇyagarbha, with the vital self; and Īśvara, or God as a self-conscious being, with the thinking self. The transcendent self and the Brahman as bliss are not correlates but rather are identical (see also HINDU SACRED LITERATURE).

EARLY BUDDHIST DEVELOPMENTS

Background. Buddhism was not a completely new phenomenon in the religious history of India; it was built upon the basis of ideas that were already current, both Brahminic and non-Aryan. Protests against the Brahminic doctrines of *ātman*, *karma*, and *mokṣa* were being voiced in the 6th century BC, prior to the Buddha, by various schools of thought: by naturalists, such as Pūraṇa ("The Old One") Kassapa, who denied both virtue and vice (*dharma* and *adharma*) and thus all moral efficacy of human deeds; by determinists, such as the Ājīvika Makkhali Gosāla, who denied sin and freedom of will; and by materialists, such as Ajita Keśakambalin, who, besides denying virtue, vice, and afterlife, resolved man's being into material elements, Nigantha Nātaputta, who believed in salvation by an ascetic life of self-discipline and hence in the efficacy of deeds and the possibility of omniscience, and, finally, Sanjaya Belathiputta, the skeptic, who, in reply to the question "Is there an afterlife?" would not say "It is so" or "It is otherwise," nor would he say "It is not so" or "It is not not so."

Of these six, the Jaina tradition identifies Nigantha with Mahāvīra; the designation "Ājīvika" is applied, in a narrow sense, to the followers of Makkhali and in a loose sense to all nonorthodox sects other than the Jainas—the skeptics and the Lokāyatas.

Buddhism, Jainism, and the Ājīvikas rejected, in common, the sacrificial polytheism of the *Brāhmaṇas* and the monistic mysticism of the *Upaniṣads*. All recognized the rule of natural law in the universe. Buddhism, however, retained the Vedic notions of *karma* and *mokṣa*, though they rejected the other fundamental concept of *ātman*.

The four noble truths and the nature of suffering. In such an intellectual climate Gautama the Buddha taught his four noble truths: (1) *duḥkha* (generally but misleadingly translated as "suffering"); (2) the origination of *duḥkha* (*duḥkhasamudāya*); (3) the cessation of *duḥkha;* and finally, (4) the way leading to the cessation.

The concept of *duḥkha*

Though the word *duḥkha* in common parlance means suffering, its use by Gautama was meant to include both pleasure and pain, both happiness and suffering. There are three aspects of this conception: *duḥkha* as suffering in the ordinary sense; *duḥkha* arising out of the impermanence of things, even of a state of pleasure; and *duḥkha* in the sense of five aggregates meaning that the "I" is nothing but a totality of five aggregates—*i.e.*, form, feeling, conception, disposition, and consciousness. In brief, whatever is noneternal—*i.e.*, subject to the law of causality—is characterized by *duḥkha;* for Gautama, this is the human situation. One who recognizes the nature of *duḥkha* also knows its causes. *Duḥkha* arises out of craving (*tṛṣṇā*), craving arises out of sensation (*vedanā*), *vedanā* out of contact (*sparśa*), so that man is faced with a series of conditions leading back to ignorance (*avidyā*)—a series in which the rise of each succeeding member depends upon the preceding one (*pratītyasamutpāda*).

The path of liberation: methods of eightfold path. The four noble truths follow the golden mean between the two extremes of sensual indulgence and ascetic self-torture, both of which Gautama rejected as spiritually useless. Only the middle path consisting in the eight steps—the eightfold path—leads to enlightenment and Nirvāṇa ("Bliss"). The eight steps are (1) right views, (2) right intention, (3) right speech, (4) right action, (5) right livelihood, (6) right effort, (7) right mindfulness, and (8) right concentration. Of these eight, 3, 4, and 5 are grouped under right morality (*śīla*); 6, 7, and 8 under right concentration (*samādhi*); and 1 and 2 under right wisdom (*prajñā*).

The concepts of selflessness and Nirvāṇa. Two key notions, even in early Buddhism, are those of *anātman* (no-self) and Nirvāṇa. The Buddha apparently wanted his famed doctrine of *anātman* to be a phenomenological account of how things are rather than a theory. In his discourse to the wandering monk Vacchagotta, he rejected the theories of both eternalism (*śāsvatavāda*) and annihilationism (*ucchedavāda*). The former, he stated, would be incompatible with his thesis that all laws (*dharmas*) are selfless (*sabbe dhammā anattā*); the latter would be significant only if one had a self that is no more in existence. Thus, by not taking sides with the metaphysicians, the Buddha described how the consciousness "I am" comes to constitute itself in the stream of consciousness out of the five aggregates of form, feeling, conception, disposition, and consciousness. The doctrine of "no-self" actually has two aspects: as applied to *pudgala*, or the individual person, and as applied to the *dhammas*, or the elements of being. In its former aspect, it asserts the fact that an individual is constituted out of five aggregates; in its latter aspect it means the utter insubstantiality of all elements. Intuitive realization of the former truth leads to the disappearance of passions and desires, realization of the latter removes all misconceptions about the nature of things in general. The former removes the "covering of the passions" (*kleśāvaraṇa*); the latter removes "the concealment of things" (*jñeyāvaraṇa*). Together, they result in Nirvāṇa.

The concept of Nirvāṇa

Both negative and positive accounts of Nirvāṇa are to be found in the Buddha's teachings and in early Buddhist writings. Nirvāṇa is a state of utter extinction, not of existence, but of passions and suffering; it is a state beyond the chain of causation, a state of freedom and spontaneity. It is also a state of bliss. Nirvāṇa is not the result of a process; were it so, it would be but another perishing state. It is the truth—not, however, an eternal, everlasting substance like the *ātman* of the *Upaniṣads*, but the truth of utter selflessness and insubstantiality of things, of the emptiness of the ego, and of the impermanence of all things. With the realization of this truth, ignorance is destroyed, and, consequently, craving, suffering, and hatred (see also BUDDHISM; BUDDHISM, HISTORY OF; and BUDDHIST PHILOSOPHY).

THE PHILOSOPHICAL PORTIONS OF THE "MAHABHARATA"

The great epic *Mahābhārata* represents the attempt of Vedic Brahminism to adjust itself to the new circumstances reflected in the process of the aryanization (integration of Aryan beliefs, practices, and institutions) of the various non-Aryan communities. Many diverse trends of religious and philosophical thought have thus been synthesized in this work (see also HINDUISM, HISTORY OF).

"Mokṣadharma." *Proto-Sāṃkhyan texts.* In its philosophical views, the epic contains an early version of Sāṃkhya (a belief in real matter and the plurality of individual souls), which is prior to the classical Sāṃkhya of Īśvarakṛṣṇa, a 3rd-century philosopher. The chapter on "Mokṣadharma" in Book 12 of the *Mahābhārata* is full of such proto-Sāṃkhya texts. Mention is made of four main philosophical schools: Sāṃkhya-Yoga, taught by Kapila (a sage living before the 6th century BC); Pāñcarātra, taught by Viṣṇu; the Vedas; and Pāśupata ("Lord of Creatures"), taught by Śiva. Belonging to the Pāñcarātra school, the epic basically attempts to accommodate certain presystematic Sāṃkhya ideas into the Bhāgavata faith. Sāṃkhya and Yoga are sometimes put together, sometimes distinguished. Several different schemata of the 25 principles (*tattvas*) of the Sāṃkhya are recorded. One common arrangement is that of eight productive forms of *prakṛti* (the unmanifest, intellect, egoism and five fine elements: sound, smell, form or colour, taste, and touch) and 16 modifications (five organs of perception, five organs of action, mind, and five gross elements: ether, earth, fire, water, and air), and *puruṣa* (man). An un-Sāṃkhyan element is the 26th principle:

Iśvara, or the supreme Lord. One notable result is the identification of the four living forms (*vyūhas*) of the Pāñcarātra school with four Sāṃkhya principles: Vāsudeva with spirit, Saṃkarṣaṇa with individual soul, Pradyumna with mind, and Aniruddha with the ego-sense.

Non-Sāṃkhyan texts. Besides the Sāṃkhya-Yoga, which is in the foreground of the epic's philosophical portions, there are Vedānta texts emphasizing the unity of spirits and theistic texts emphasizing not only a personal deity but also the doctrine of *avatāra*, or incarnation. The Vāsudeva-Kṛṣṇa cult characterizes the theistic part of the epic.

Early theories of kingship and state. In the *Śānti Parvan* ("Book of Consolation," 12th book) of the *Mahābhārata*, there is also a notable account of the origin of kingship and of *rājadharma*, or the *dharma* (law) of the king as king. Bhīṣma, who is discoursing, refers with approval to two different theories of the origin of kingship, both of which speak of a prior period in which there were no kings. According to one account, this age was a time characterized by insecurity for the weak and unlimited power for the strong; the other regards it as an age of peace and tranquility. The latter account contains a theory of the fall of mankind from this ideal state, which led to a need for kingship; the former account leads directly from the insecurity of the prekingship era to the installation of king by the divine ruler for the protection and the security of mankind. Kingship is thus recognized as having an historical origin. The primary function of the king is that of protection, and *daṇḍanīti*, or the art of punishment, is subordinated to *rājadharma*, or *dharma* of the king. Though it recognizes a quasi-divinity of the king, the *Mahābhārata* makes the *dharma*, the moral law, superior to the king (see also SACRED KINGSHIP).

The "Bhagavadgītā." The *Bhagavadgītā* ("Divine Song" or "Song of the Lord") forms a part of *Mahābhārata* and deserves separate consideration by virtue of its great importance in the religious life and thought of the Hindus. Not itself a *śruti*, it has, however, been accorded the status of an authoritative text and is regarded as one of the sources of the Vedānta philosophy. At a theoretical level, it brings together Sāṃkhya metaphysics, Upaniṣadic monism, and a devotional theism of the Kṛṣṇa-Vāsudeva cult. In its practical teaching, it steers a middle course between the "path of action" of the Vedic ritualism and the "path of renunciation" of the Upaniṣadic mysticism, and it accommodates all the three major "paths" to *mokṣa:* the paths of action (*karma*), devotion (*bhakti*) and knowledge (*jñāna*). This synthetic character of the work accounts for its great hold on the Hindu mind. The Hindu tradition treats it as one homogenous work, having the status of a *Upaniṣad*.

The paths of *mokṣa*

Neither performance of the duties prescribed in the scriptures nor renunciation of all action is conducive to the attainment of *mokṣa*. If the goal is freedom, then the best path to the goal is to perform one's duties with a spirit of nonattachment without caring for the fruits of one's actions and without the thought of pleasure or pain, profit or loss, or victory or failure, with a sense of equanimity and equality. The Kantian ethic of "duty for duty's sake" seems to be the nearest Western parallel to Kṛṣṇa's teaching at this stage. But Kṛṣṇa soon went beyond it, by pointing out that performance of action with complete nonattachment requires knowledge (*jñāna*) of the true nature of the self, its distinction from *prakṛti*, or Matter (the primeval stuff, not the world of matter perceived by the senses), with its three component elements (*sattva—i.e.*, tension or harmony; *rajas—i.e.*, activity; and *tamas—i.e.*, inertia), and of the highest self (*puruṣottama*), whose higher and lower aspects are Matter and finite individuals, respectively. This knowledge of the highest self or the supreme lord, however, would only require a devotional attitude of complete self-surrender and performance of one's duties in the spirit of offering to him. Thus, *karma-yoga* (yoga of works) is made to depend on *jñāna-yoga* (yoga of knowledge), and the latter is shown to lead to *bhakti-yoga* (yoga of devotion). Instead of looking upon Kṛṣṇa's teaching as laying down alternative ways for different persons in accordance with their aptitudes, it would seem more logical to suppose that he taught the essential unity and interdependence of these ways. How one should begin is left to one's aptitude and spiritual makeup.

DOCTRINES AND IDEAS OF THE BUDDHIST "TRIPITAKA"

In the *Tripiṭaka* ("The Three Baskets"), collected and compiled 300 years after the Buddha's *mahāparinirvāṇa* (attainment of Buddhahood), at the council at Pāṭaliputra (3rd century BC), both the canonical and philosophical doctrines of early Buddhism were codified. *Abhidamma piṭaka*, the last of the *piṭakas*, has seven parts: *Dhammasaṅgaṇi*, which gives an enumeration of *dhammas*, or elements of existence; *Vibhaṅga*, which gives further analysis of the *dhammas*; *Dhatukathā*, which is a detailed classification, following many different principles, of the elements; *Puggalapaññatti*, which gives descriptions of individual persons according to stages of their development; *Kathāvatthu*, which contains discussions and refutation of other schools (of Buddhism); *Yamaka*, which derives its name from the fact that it deals with pairs of questions; and *Paṭṭhāna*, which gives an analysis of relations among the elements.

The notion of *dhamma*

The key notion in all this is that of *dhamma*. Because Buddhist philosophers denied any permanence, whether in outer nature or in inner life, they felt compelled to undertake a detailed, systematic, and complete listing and classification of the different elements that constitute both the external world and the mental, inner life. Each of these elements, except for the three elements that are not composed of parts (*i.e.*, space, or *ākāśa*, and the two cessations, Nirvāṇa and a temporary stoppage, in states of meditation, of the flow of passions, or *apratisamkhyānivodha*), is momentary. The primary interest of these thinkers was not so much an analysis of outer nature as it was the human person (*pudgala*). The human person, however, consists in material (*rūpa*) and mental (*nāma*) factors, which led to an account of the various elements of matter. The primary interest, nevertheless, is in man, who is regarded as an aggregate of various elements. Such an analysis, together with the underlying denial of an eternal self, was supposed to provide the theoretical basis for the possibility of a good life conducive to the attainment of Nirvāṇa.

The individual person was analyzed into five aggregates (*skandhas*): material form (*rūpa*); feeling (*vedanā*); conception (*saṃjñā*); disposition (*saṃskāra*); and consciousness (*vijñāna*). Of these, the last four constitute the mental; the first alone is the material factor. The material is further analyzed into 28 states, the *saṃskāra* into 50 (falling into three groups: intellectual, affectional, and volitional), and the *vijñāna* into 89 kinds of states of consciousness. Another principle of classification leads to a list of 18 elements (*dhātus*): five sense organs, five objects of those senses, mind, the specific object of mind, and six kinds of consciousness (visual, auditory, olfactory, gustatory, tactual, and purely mental). A third classification is into 12 bases (*āyatanas*), which is a list of six cognitive faculties and their objects. The Buddhist analysis of matter was in terms of sensations and sense data, to which the sense organs were also added. The analysis of mind was also in terms of corresponding modes of consciousness and their objects.

EARLY SYSTEM BUILDING

History of the sūtra style. A unique feature of the development of Indian thought was the systematization of each school of thought in the form of *sūtras*, or extremely concise expressions, intended to reduce the doctrines of a science or of a philosophy into a number of memorizable aphorisms, formulas, or rules. The word *sūtra*, originally meaning "thread," came to mean such concise expressions. A larger work containing such *sūtras* also came to be called a *sūtra*. The aid of commentaries becomes indispensable for the understanding of the *sūtras*, and it is not surprising that philosophical composition took the form of commentaries and subcommentaries. The earliest *sūtras*, the *Kalpa-sūtras*, however, are not

Rise of the *sūtra* form of philosophical and ritualistic works philosophical but ritualistic. These *Kalpa-sūtras* fell into three major parts: the *Śrauta-sūtras*, dealing with Vedic sacrifices; the *Gṛhya-sūtras*, dealing with the ideal life of a householder; and the *Dharma-sūtras*, dealing with moral injunctions and prohibitions. In the works of Pāṇini, a Hindu grammarian, the *sūtra* style reached a perfection never attained before and only imperfectly approximated by the later practitioners. The *sūtra* literature began before the rise of Buddhism, though the philosophical *sūtra*s all seem to have been composed afterward. The Buddhist *sutta*s, though called *sūtra*s, are of very different style. They are rather didactic texts, discourses, or sermons, possibly called *sutta* to the extent that they carry the thread of the tradition of the Buddha's teachings.

The "Pūrva-mīmāṃsā-sūtras" and Śabara's commentary. The Pūrva-mīmāṃsā ("First Reflection"), or Karma-mīmāṃsā ("Study of [Ritual] Action"), is the system that investigates the nature of Vedic injunctions. Though this is the primary purpose of the system, this task also led to the development of principles of scriptural interpretation and, therefore, to theories of meaning and hermeneutics (critical interpretations). Jaimini, who composed *sūtra*s about the 4th century BC, was critical of earlier Mīmāṃsā authors, particularly of one Bādari, to whom is attributed the view that the Vedic injunctions are meant to be obeyed without the expectation of benefits for oneself. According to Jaimini, Vedic injunctions do not merely prescribe actions but also recommend these actions as means to the attainment of desirable goals. For both Jaimini and Śabara (3rd century), his chief commentator, performance of the Vedic sacrifices is conducive to the attainment of heaven; both emphasize that nothing is a duty unless it is instrumental to happiness in the long run.

Hermeneutical principles of Jaimini

Jaimini's central concern is *dharma*, which is defined as the desired object (*artha*), whose desirability is testified only by the injunctive statements of the scriptures (*codanā-lakṣaṇo*). In order to substantiate the implied thesis that what ought to be done—*i.e.*, *dharma*—cannot be decided by either perception or reasoning, Jaimini proceeds to a discussion of the nature of ways of knowing. Because perceptual knowledge arises from contact of the sense organs with reality that is present, *dharma* that is not an existent reality but a future course of action cannot possibly be known by sense-experience. Reasoning based on such sense experience is for the same reason useless. Only injunctive statements can state what ought to be done. Commands made by finite individuals are not reliable, because the validity of what they say depends upon the presumption that the persons concerned are free from those defects that render one's words dependable. Therefore, only the injunctions contained in the scriptures—which, according to Mīmāṃsā and the Hindu tradition, are not composed by any finite individual (*apauruṣeya*)—are the sources of all valid knowledge of *dharma*. The Mīmāṃsā rejects the belief that the scriptures are utterances of God. The words themselves are authoritative. In accordance with this thesis, Jaimini developed the theory that the relation between words and their meanings is natural (*autpattikastu śabdasyārthena sambandhah*, or "the relation of word to its meaning is eternal") and not conventional, that the primary meaning of a word is a universal (which is also eternal), that in a sentence the principal element is the verb, and that the principal force of the verb is that which specifically belongs to the verb with an optative ending and which instigates a person to take a certain course of action in order to effect the desired end.

Though this provided the Mīmāṃsā with a psychological and semantic technique for interpreting the sentences of the scriptures that are clearly in the injunctive form, there are also other kinds of sentences: prayers, glorifications, those referring to a thing by a name, and prohibitions. Attempts were therefore made to show how each one of these types of sentences bears, directly or indirectly, on the central, injunctive texts. Furthermore, a systematic classification of the various forms of injunctions is undertaken: those that indicate the general nature of an action, those that show the connection of a subsidiary rite to the main course of action, those that suggest promptness in performance, and those that indicate the right to enjoy the results to be produced by the course of action enjoined.

The commentary of Śabara elaborated the epistemological themes of the *sūtras*; in particular, Śabara established the intrinsic validity of experiences and traced the possibility of error to the presence of defects in the ways of knowing. He also critically examined Buddhist subjective idealism and the theory of utter emptiness of things and proved the existence of soul as a separate entity that enjoys the results of one's actions in this or next life.

The "Vedānta-sūtras." *Relation to the "Mīmāṃsā-sūtras."* Along with Bādari and Jaimini, Bādarāyaṇa, a contemporary of Jaimini, was the other major interpreter of Vedic thought. Just as the *Mīmāṃsā-sūtra* traditions of Bādari's tradition were revived by Prabhākara, a 7th–8th-century scholar, and Jaimini's defended by Śabara and Kumārila, a 7th–8th-century scholar, Bādarāyaṇa's *sūtra*s laid the basis for the development of Vedānta philosophy. The relation of the *Vedānta-sūtras* to the *Mīmāṃsā-sūtras*, however, is difficult to ascertain. Bādarāyaṇa approves of the Mīmāṃsā view that the relation between words and their significations is eternal. There are, however, clear statements of difference: according to Jaimini, for example, the dispenser of the "fruits" of one's actions is *dharma*, the law of righteousness itself, but for Bādarāyaṇa it is the supreme lord, Īśvara. Often, Jaimini's interpretation is contrasted with that of Bādari; in such cases, Bādarāyaṇa sometimes supports Bādari's view and sometimes regards both as defensible.

Hermeneutical principles of Bādarāyaṇa

The overall difference that emerges is that whereas Jaimini lays stress on the ritualistic parts of the Vedas, Bādarāyaṇa lays stress on the philosophical portions—*i.e.*, the *Upaniṣads*. The former recommends the path of Vedic injunctions, hence the ideal of *karma;* the latter recommends the path of knowledge. The central concept of Jaimini's investigation is *dharma*—*i.e.*, what ought to be done; the central theme of Bādarāyaṇa's investigations is Brahman—*i.e.*, the absolute reality. The relationship between these two treatises remains a matter of controversy between later commentators—Rāmānuja, a great South Indian philosopher of the 11th–12th centuries, defending the thesis that they jointly constitute a single work with Jaimini's coming first and Bādarāyaṇa's coming after it in logical order, and Śaṅkara, an earlier great South Indian philosopher of the 8th–9th centuries, in favour of the view that the two are independent of each other and possibly also inconsistent in their central theses.

Contents and organization of the four books. Bādarāyaṇa's *sūtra*s have four books (*adhyāyas*), each book having four chapters (*pādas*). The first book is concerned with the theme of *samanvaya* ("reconciliation"). The many conflicting statements of the scriptures are all said to agree in converging on one central theme: the concept of Brahman, the one absolute being from whom all beings arise, in whom they are maintained, and into whom they return. The second book establishes *avirodha* ("consistency") by showing the following: (1) that dualism and Vaiśeṣika atomism are neither sustainable interpretations of the scriptures nor defensible rationally; (2) that though consciousness cannot conceivably arise out of a nonconscious nature, the material world could arise out of spirit; (3) that the effect in its essence is not different from the cause; and (4) that though Brahman is all-perfect and has no want, creation is an entirely unmotivated free act of delight (*līlā*). The Buddhist (Vijñānavāda) view that there are no external objects but only minds and their conceptions is refuted, as also the Buddhist doctrine of the momentariness of all that is. The Jaina pluralism and the theism of the Pāśupatas and the Bhāgavatas are also rejected. Because, according to Vedānta, only Brahman is external, the third and the fourth chapters of the second book undertake to show that nothing else is eternal. The third book concerns the spiritual discipline and the various stages by which the finite individual (*jīva*) may realize his essential identity with Brahman. The fourth and last book deals with the final result of the modes of discipline outlined in the preceding book and distinguishes between the results achieved by worshipping a personal Godhead and those achieved by knowing the one Brahman. Included is some discussion of the possible "worlds" through which the spirits travel after death, but all this discussion is subordinate to the one dominant goal of liberation and consequent escape from the chain of rebirth.

Variations in views. Bādarāyaṇa's *sūtras* refer to interpreters of Vedānta before him who were concerned with such central issues as the relation between the finite individual (*jīva*) and the absolute spirit (Brahman) and the possible bodily existence of a liberated individual. To Āśmarthya, an early Vedānta interpreter, is ascribed the view that the finite individual and the absolute are both identical and different (as causes and their effects are different—a view that seems to have been the ancestor of the later theory of Bhedābheda). Auḍulomi, another pre-Bādarāyana Vedānta philosopher, is said to have held the view that the finite individual becomes identical with Brahman after going through a process of purification. Another interpreter, Kāśakṛtsna, holds that the two are identical—a view that anticipates the later "unqualified monism" of Śaṅkara. Bādarāyaṇa's own views on this issue are difficult to ascertain: the *sūtras* are so concise that they are capable of various interpretations, though there are reasons to believe that Rāmānuja's is closer to their intentions than Śaṅkara's.

The relation between the finite individual and the absolute spirit

The "Sāṃkhya-kārikās." *Relation to orthodoxy.* Īśvarakṛṣṇa's *Sāṃkhya-kārikā* (or "Verses on Sāmkhya," *c.* 2nd century AD) is the oldest available Sāṃkhya work. Īśvarakṛṣṇa describes himself as laying down the essential teachings of Kapila as taught to Āsuri and by Āsuri to Pañcaśikha. He refers also to *Ṣaṣṭitantra* ("Doctrine of 60 Conceptions"), the main doctrines of which he claims to have expounded in the *kārikās*. The Sāṃkhya of Caraka, which is substantially the same as is attributed to Pañcaśikha in the *Mahābhārata*, is theistic and regards the unmanifested (*avyakta*) as being the same as the *puruṣa* (the self). The *Mahābhārata* refers to three kinds of Sāṃkhya doctrines: those that accept 24, 25, or 26 principles, the last of which are theistic. The later *Sāṃkhya-sūtra* is more sympathetic toward theism, but the *kārikās* are atheistic, and the traditional expositions of the Sāṃkhya are based on this work.

The nature of the self (puruṣa). According to the *kārikās*, there are many selves, each being of the nature of pure consciousness. The self is neither the original matter (*prakṛti*) nor an evolute of it. Though matter is composed of the three *guṇas* (qualities), the self is not; though matter, being nonintelligent, cannot discriminate, the self is discriminating; though matter is object (*viṣaya*), the self is not; though matter is common, the self is an individual (*asāmānya*); unlike matter, the self is not creative (*aprasavadharmin*). The existence of selves is proved on the ground that nature exhibits an ordered arrangement the like of which is known to be meant for another (*parārthatva*). This other must be a conscious spirit. That there are many such selves is proved on the grounds that different persons are born and die at different times, that they do not always act simultaneously, and that they show different qualities, aptitudes, and propensities. All selves are, however, passive witnesses (*sākṣin*), essentially alone (*kevala*), neutral (*madhyastha*), and not agents (*akartā*).

The nature, origin, and structure of the world (prakṛti). Phenomenal nature, with its distinctions of things and persons (taken as psychophysical organisms), is regarded as an evolution out of a primitive state of matter. This conception is based on a theory of causality known as the *satkāryavāda*, according to which an effect is implicitly pre-existent in its cause prior to its production. This latter doctrine is established on the ground that if the effect were not already existent in its cause, then something would have to come out of nothing. The original *prakṛti* (primeval stuff) is the primary matrix out of which all differentiations arose and within which they all were contained in an undistinguished manner. Original Matter is uncaused, eternal, all-pervading, one, independent, self-complete, and has no distinguishable parts; the things that emerge out of this primitive matrix are, on the other hand, caused, noneternal, limited, many, dependent, wholes composed of parts, and manifested. But Matter, whether in its original unmanifested state or in its manifested forms, is composed of three *guṇas*, nondiscriminating (*avivekin*), object (*viṣaya*), general, nonconscious, and yet creative.

The evolution of original matter

The order in which Matter evolves is laid down as follows: *prakṛti* → *mahat* or *buddhi* (Intelligence) → *ahaṃkāra* (ego-sense) → *manas* (mind) → five *tanmātras* (the sense data: colour, sound, smell, touch, and taste) → five sense organs → five organs of action (tongue, hands, feet, organs of evacuation and of reproduction) → five gross elements (ether, air, light, water, and earth). This emanation schema may be understood either as an account of cosmic evolution or as a logical–transcendental analysis of the various factors involved in experience or as an analysis of the concrete human personality.

The concept of the three qualities (guṇas). A striking feature of this account is the conception of guṇa: nature is said to consist of three *guṇas*—originally in a state of equilibrium and subsequently in varying states of mutual preponderance. The *kārikās* do not say much about whether the *guṇas* are to be regarded as qualities or as component elements. Of the three, harmony or tension (*sattva*) is light (*laghu*), is pleasing, and is capable of manifesting others. Activity (*rajas*) is dynamic, exciting, and capable of hurting. Inertia (*tamas*) is characterized by heaviness, conceals, is static, and causes sadness. Man's varying psychological responses are thus hypostatized and made into component properties or elements of nature—an argument whose fallacy was exposed, among others, by Śaṅkara.

Epistemology. The *Sāṃkhya-kārikā* delineates three ways of knowing (*pramāṇa*): perception, inference, and verbal testimony. Perception is defined as the application of the sense organs to their respective objects (*prativiṣayādhyavasāya*). Inference, which is not defined, is divided first into three kinds, and then into two. According to the former classification, an inference is called *pūrvavat* if it is based on past experience (such as when one, on seeing a dark cloud, infers that it will rain); it is called *śeṣavat* when from the presence of a certain property in one part of a thing the presence of the same property is inferred in the rest (such as when, on finding a drop of sea water to be saline, one infers the rest to be so); it is called *sāmānyato-dṛṣṭa* when it is used to infer what is not perceivable (such as when one infers the movement of a star on seeing it occupy two different positions in the firmament at different times). According to the other classification, an inference may be either from the mark to that of which it is the mark or in the reverse direction. Verbal testimony, in order to be valid, must be the word of one who has authoritative knowledge.

Perception and inference

There is, in addition to the three ways of knowing, consideration of the modes of functioning of the sense organs. The outer senses apprehend only the present objects, the inner senses (*manas*, *antaḥkaraṇa*, and *buddhi*) have the ability to apprehend all objects—past, present, and future. The sense organs, on apprehending their objects, are said to offer them to *buddhi*, or intelligence, which both makes judgments and enjoys the objects of the senses. *Buddhi* is also credited with the ability to perceive the distinction between the self and the natural components of the person.

Ethics. In its ethics, the *kārikās* manifest an intellectualism that is characteristic of the Sāṃkhya system. Suffering is due to ignorance of the true nature of the self, and freedom, the highest good, can be reached through knowledge of the distinction between the self and nature. In this state of freedom, the self becomes indifferent to nature; it ceases to be an agent and an enjoyer. It becomes what it in fact is, a pure witness consciousness.

The "Yoga-sūtras." *Relation to Sāṃkhya.* The *Yoga-sūtras* of Patañjali (2nd century BC) are the earliest extant textbook on Yoga. Scholars now generally agree that the author of the *Yoga-sūtras* is not the grammarian Patañjali. In any case, the *Yoga-sūtras* stand in close relation to the Sāṃkhya system, so much so that tradition regards the two systems as one. Yoga adds a 26th principle to the Sāṃkhya list of 25—*i.e.*, the supreme lord, or Īśvara—and has thus earned the name of Seśvara-Sāṃkhya, or theistic Sāṃkhya. Furthermore, there is a difference in their attitudes: Sāṃkhya is intellectualistic and emphasizes metaphysical knowledge as the means to liberation; Yoga is voluntaristic and emphasizes the need of going through severe self-control as the means of realizing intuitively the same principles.

God, self, and body. In the *Yoga-sūtras,* God is defined as a distinct self (*puruṣa*), untouched by sufferings, actions, and their effects; his existence is proved on the ground that the degrees of knowledge found in finite beings, in an ascending order, has an upper limit—*i.e.*, omniscience, which is what characterizes God. He is said to be the source of all secular and scriptural traditions; he both revealed the Vedas and taught the first fathers of mankind. Surrender of the effects of action to God is regarded as a recommended observance.

Distinction between the self and the mind

As in Sāṃkhya, the self is distinguished from the mind (*citta*): the mind is viewed as an object, an aggregate. This argument is used to prove the existence of a self other than the mind. The mental state is not self-intimating; it is known in introspection. It cannot know both itself and its object. It rather is known by the self, whose essence is pure, undefiled consciousness. That the self is not changeable is proved by the fact that were it changeable the mental states would be sometimes known and sometimes unknown—which, however, is not the case, because a mental state is always known. To say that the self knows means that the self is reflected in the mental state and makes the latter manifested. The aim of Yoga is to arrest mental modifications (*citta-vṛtti*) so that the self remains in its true, undefiled essence and is, thus, not subject to suffering.

The attitude of the *Yoga-sūtras* to the human body is ambivalent. The body is said to be filthy and unclean. Thus, the ascetic cultivates a disgust for it. Yet, much of the discipline laid down in the *Yoga-sūtras* concerns perfection of the body, with the intent to make it a fit instrument for spiritual perfection. Steadiness in bodily posture and control of the breathing process are accorded a high place. The perfection of body is said to consist in "beauty, grace, strength and adamantine hardness."

Theories and techniques of self-control and meditation. Patañjali lays down an eightfold path consisting of aids to Yoga: restraint (*yama*), observance (*niyama*), posture (*āsana*), regulation of breathing (*prāṇāyama*), abstraction of the senses (*pratyāhāra*), concentration (*dhyāna*), meditation (*dhāraṇā*), and trance (*samādhi*). The first two constitute the ethical core of the discipline: the restraints are abstinence from injury, veracity, abstinence from stealing, continence, and abstinence from greed. The observances are cleanliness, contentment, purificatory actions, study, and surrender of the fruits of one's actions to God. *Ahiṃsā* (nonviolence) also is glorified, as an ethics of detachment.

Various stages of *samādhi* are distinguished: the conscious and the superconscious, which are subdivided into achievements with different shades of perfection. In the final stage, all mental modifications cease to be and the self is left in its pure, undefiled state of utter isolation. This is freedom (*kaivalya*), or absolute independence.

The "Vaiśeṣika-sūtras." The *Vaiśeṣika-sūtras* were written by Kaṇāda, a philosopher who flourished *c.* 2nd–4th centuries. The system owes its name to the fact that it admits ultimate particularities (*viśeṣa*). The metaphysics is, therefore, pluralistic.

Organization and contents. The *Vaiśeṣika-sūtras* are divided into ten chapters, each with two sections. Chapter 1 states the purpose of the work: to explain *dharma*, defined as that which confers prosperity and ultimate good on man. This is followed by an enumeration of the categories of being recognized in the system: substance, quality (*guṇa*), action, universality, particularly, and inherence (*samavāya*). Later authors add a seventh category: negation (*abhāva*). This enumeration is followed by an account of the common features as well as dissimilarities among these categories: the categories of "universal" and "particularity" and the concepts of being and existence. Chapter 2 classifies substances into nine kinds: earth, water, fire, air, ether, space, time, self, and mind. There next follows a discussion of the question of whether sound is eternal or noneternal. Chapter 3 is an attempt to prove the existence of self by an inference. Chapter 4 explains the words "eternal" and "noneternal," the noneternal being identified with *avidyā*, and distinguishes between three different forms of the substances earth, water, fire, and air—each of these is either a body, a sense organ, or an object. Chapter 5 deals with the notion of action and the connected concept of effort, and the next traces various special phenomena of nature to the supersensible force, called *adṛṣṭa.* Chapter 6 argues that performance of Vedic injunctions generates this supersensible force and that the merits and demerits accumulated lead to *mokṣa.* Chapter 7 argues that qualities of eternal things are eternal and those of noneternal things are noneternal. Chapter 8 argues that the self and mind are not perceptible. Chapter 9 argues that neither action nor qualities may be ascribed to what is nonexistent and, further, that negation may be directly perceived. Chapter 9 also deals with the nature of *hetu*, or the "middle term" in syllogism, and argues that the knowledge derived from hearing words is not inferential. Chapter 10 argues that pleasure and pain are not cognitions because they do not leave room for either doubt or certainty.

The categories of being in the Vaiśeṣika system

Structure of the world. This account of the contents of the *sūtra*s shows that the Vaiśeṣika advocates an atomistic cosmology (theory of order) and a pluralistic ontology (theory of being). The material universe arises out of the conjunction of four kinds of atoms: the earth atom, water atom, fire atom, and air atom. There also are the eternal substances: ether, in which sound inheres as a quality; space, which accounts for man's sense of direction and distinctions between far and near; and time, which accounts for the notions of simultaneity and nonsimultaneity and which, like space, is eternal and is the general cause of all that has origin.

Atomistic cosmology and pluralistic ontology

Naturalism. The overall naturalism of the Vaiśeṣika, its great interest in physics, and its atomism are all counterbalanced by the appeal to *adṛṣṭa* (a supersensible force), to account for whatever the other recognized entities cannot explain. Among things ascribed to this supersensible force are movements of needles toward a magnet, circulation of water in plant bodies, upward motion of fire, movement of mind, and movements of soul after death. These limit the naturalism of the system.

Epistemology. Knowledge belongs to the self; it appears or disappears with the contact of the self with the senses and of the senses with the objects. Perception of the self results from the conjunction of the self with the mind. Perception of objects results from proximity of the self, the senses, and the objects. Error exists because of defects of the senses. Inference is of three kinds: inference of the nonexistence of something from the existence of some other things, inference of the existence of something from nonexistence of some other, and inference of existence of something from the existence of some other thing.

Ethics. *Mokṣa* is a state in which there is no body and no rebirth. It is achieved by knowledge. Works in accordance with the Vedic injunction may help in its attainment.

The "Nyāya-sūtras." The *Nyāya-sūtras* probably were composed by Gautama or Akṣapāda about the 2nd century BC, though there is ample evidence that many *sūtra*s were subsequently interpolated.

Content and organization. The *sūtra*s are divided into five chapters, each with two sections. The work begins with a statement of the subject matter, purpose, and relation of the subject matter to the attainment of that purpose. The ultimate purpose is salvation—*i.e.*, complete freedom from pain—and salvation is attained by knowledge of the 16 categories: hence the concern with these categories, which are means of valid knowledge (*pramāṇa*); objects of valid knowledge (*prameya*); doubt (*saṃśaya*); purpose (*prayojana*); example (*dṛṣṭānta*); conclusion (*siddhānta*); the constituents of a syllogism (*avayava*); argumentation (*tarka*); ascertainment (*nirṇaya*); debate (*vāda*); disputations (*jalpa*); destructive criticism (*vitaṇḍā*); fallacy (*hetvābhāsa*); quibble (*chala*); refutations (*jāti*); and points of the opponent's defeat (*nigrahasthāna*).

The categories of the *Nyāya* system

Epistemology. The words "knowledge," *buddhi*, and "consciousness" are used synonymously. Four means of valid knowledge are admitted: perception, inference, comparison, and verbal testimony. Perception is defined as the knowledge that arises from the contact of the senses with the object, which is nonjudgmental, or unerring or judgmental. Inference is defined as the knowledge that is preceded by perception (of the mark) and classified into three kinds: that from the perception of cause to its effect; that from perception of the effect to its cause; and that in which knowledge of one thing is derived from the perception of another with which it is commonly seen together. Comparison is the knowledge of a thing through its similarity to another thing previously well-known.

The validity of the means of knowing is established as against Buddhist skepticism, the main argument being that if no means of knowledge is valid then the demonstration of their invalidity cannot itself claim validity. Perception is shown to be irreducible to inference, inference is shown to yield certain knowledge, and errors in inference are viewed as being faults in the person, not in the method itself. Knowledge derived from verbal testimony is viewed as noninferential.

Theory of causation and metaphysics. Although the *sūtras* do not explicitly develop a detailed theory of causation, the later Nyāya theory is sufficiently delineated in Chapter 4. No event is uncaused. No positive entity could arise out of mere absence—a thesis that is pressed against what seems to be a Buddhist view that in a series of momentary events every member is caused by the destruction of the preceding member. Cause and effect should be homogeneous in nature, and yet the effect is a new beginning and was not already contained in the cause. The Buddhist thesis that all things are negative in nature (inasmuch as a thing's nature is constituted by its differences from others) is rejected, as is the view that all things are eternal or that all things are noneternal. Both these latter views are untrue to experience. Thus, the resulting metaphysics admits two kinds of entities: eternal and noneternal. The whole is a new entity over and above the parts that constitute it. Also, the idea that God is the material cause of the universe is rejected. God is viewed as the efficient cause, and human deeds produce their results under the control and cooperation of God.

The syllogism and its predecessors. Of the four main topics of the *Nyāya-sūtras* (art of debate, means of valid knowledge, syllogism, and examination of opposed views) there is a long history. There is no direct evidence for the theory that though inference (*anumāna*) is of Indian origin, the syllogism (*avayava*) is of Greek origin. Vātsāyana, the commentator on the *sūtras*, referred to some logicians who held a theory of a ten-membered syllogism (the Greeks had three). The *Vaiśeṣika-sūtras* give five propositions as constituting a syllogism but give them different names. Gautama also supports a five-membered syllogism with the following structure:

The propositions of the *Nyāya* syllogism

1. This hill is fiery (*pratijñā:* a statement of that which is to be proved).
2. Because it is smoky (*hetu:* statement of reason).
3. Whatever is smoky is fiery, as is a kitchen (*udāharaṇa:* statement of a general rule supported by an example).
4. So is this hill (*upanaya:* application of the rule of this case).
5. Therefore this hill is fiery (*nigamana:* drawing the conclusion).

The most characteristic feature of the Nyāya syllogism is its insistence on the example—which seems to suggest that the Nyāya logician wanted to be assured not only of formal validity but also of material truth. Five kinds of fallacious "middle" (*hetu*) are distinguished: the inconclusive (*savyabhicāra*), which leads to more conclusions than one; the contradictory (*viruddha*), which opposes that which is to be established; the controversial (*prakaraṇasama*), which provokes the very question that it is meant to settle; the counterquestioned (*sādhyasama*), which itself is unproved; and the mistimed (*kālātīta*), which is adduced "when the time in which it might hold good does not apply."

Other characteristic philosophic matters. Other philosophical theses stated in the *sūtras* are as follows: the relation of words to their meanings is not natural but conventional; a word means neither the bare individual nor the universal by itself but all three—the individual, the universal, and structure (*ākṛti*); desire, aversion, volition, pleasure, pain, and cognition are the marks of the self; body is defined as the locus of gestures, senses, and sentiments; and the existence and atomicity of mind are inferred from the fact that there do not arise in the self more acts of knowledge than one at a time.

The beginnings of Mahāyāna Buddhist philosophy. *Contributions of the Mahāsaṅgikas.* When the Mahāsaṅgikas ("School of the Great Assembly") seceded from the Elders (Theravādins) about 400 BC, the germs were laid for the rise of the Mahāyāna Buddhism. The Mahāsaṅgikas admitted non-*arhat* monks and worshippers (*i.e.*, those who had not attained perfection), deified the Buddha, taught the doctrine of the emptiness of the elements of being (and not merely the emptiness of the individual person), distinguished between the mundane and the supramundane reality, and considered consciousness (*vijñāna*) to be intrinsically free from all impurities. These ideas found varied expression among the various groups into which the Mahāsaṅgikas later divided (see also BUDDHIST PHILOSOPHY).

Contributions of the Sarvāstivādins. The Sarvāstivādins ("realists" who believe that all things, mental and material, exist or also that all *dharma*s—past, present, and future—exist) seceded from the Elders about the middle of the 3rd century BC. They rejected, in common with all other sects, *pudgalātmā*, or a self of the individual, but admitted *dharmātman*—*i.e.*, self-existence of the *dharma*s (categories), or the elements of being. Each *dharma* is a self-being; the law of causality applies to the formation of aggregates, not to the elements themselves. *Dharma*s, whether they are past or are in future, exist all the same. Of these, three are said to be unconditioned: space (*ākāśa*) and the two cessations (*nirodha*)—the cessation that arises from knowledge and the cessation that arises prior to the attainment of knowledge, the former being Nirvāṇa, the latter being an arrest of the flow of passions through meditation prior to the achievement of Nirvāṇa. By *śūnyatā* the Sarvāstivādins mean only the truth that there is no eternal substance called "I." Because all elements—past, present, or future—exist, the Sarvāstivādins are obliged to account for these temporal predicates, and several different theories are advanced. Of these, the theory advanced by Vasumitra, a 1st–2nd-century-AD Sarvāstivādin, viz., that temporal predicates are determined by the function of a *dharma*, is accepted by the Vaibhāṣikas—*i.e.*, those among the Sarvāstivādins who follow the authority of the texts known as the *Vibhāṣā*. To this latter sect belonged the great Vasubandhu before he was converted to the Yogācāra by his brother Asaṅga.

The concept of the existence of all things and all *dharma*s

Contributions of the Sautrāntikas. The Vaibhāṣika doctrine of eternal elements is believed to be inconsistent with the fundamental teachings of the Buddha. The Sautrāntikas (so-called because they rest their case on the *sūtras*) insist on the noneternality of the *dharma* as well. The past and the future *dharma*s do not exist, only the present ones do. The so-called unconditioned *dharma*s are mere absences, not positive entities. Thus, the Sautrāntikas seem to be the only major school of Buddhist philosophy that comes near to regarding Nirvāṇa as entirely negative. In epistemology, whereas the Vaibhāṣikas are direct realists, the Sautrāntikas hold a sort of representationism, according to which the external world is only inferred from the mental conceptions that alone are directly apprehended.

The world view of the "Arthaśāstra." Kauṭilya's *Arthaśāstra* (c. 321–296 BC) is the science of *artha*, or material prosperity, which is one of the four goals of human life. By *artha*, Kauṭilya meant "the means of subsistence of man," which is, primarily, wealth and, secondarily, earth. The work is concerned with the means of fruitfully maintaining and using the latter—*i.e.*, land. It is a work on politics and diplomacy.

Political philosophical ideas

Theories of kingship and statecraft. Though Kauṭilya recognized that sovereignty may belong to a clan (*kula*), he was himself concerned with monarchies. He advocated the idea of the king's divine nature, or divine sanction of the king's office, but he also attempted to reconcile it with a theory of the elective origin of the king. He referred to a state of nature, without king, as an anarchy in which the stronger devours the weaker. The four functions of the king are to acquire what is not gained, to protect what is gained, to increase what is protected, and to bestow the surplus upon the deserving. The political organization is held to have seven elements: the king, the minister, the territory, the fort, the treasury, the army, and the ally. These are viewed as being organically related. The three "powers" of the king are power of good counsel, the majesty of the king himself, and the power to inspire. The priest is not made an element of the state organization. The king, however, is not exempt from the laws of *dharma*. Being the "promulgator of *dharma*," the king should himself be free from the six passions of sex, anger, greed, vanity, haughtiness, and overjoy. What Kauṭilya advocated was an enlightened monarchical paternalism.

Concepts of the public good. In the happiness of the subjects lies the king's happiness. The main task of the king is to offer protection. Monarchy is viewed as the only guarantee against anarchy. Thus, the king's duty is to avert providential visitations such as famine, flood, and pestilence; he ought also to protect agriculture, industry, and mining, the orphan, the aged, the sick, and the poor, to control crime with the help of spies, and to settle legal disputes.

Relations between states. Regarding relations with other states, Kauṭilya's thoughts were based not so much on high moral idealism as on the needs of self-interest. He wrote of six types of foreign policy: treaty (*sandhi*), war (*vigraha*), marching against the enemy (*yāna*), neutrality (*āsana*), seeking protection from a powerful king (*saṃśraya*), and dual policy (*dvaidhībhāva*). The rules concerning these are: he who is losing strength in comparison to the other shall make peace; he who is gaining strength shall make war; he who thinks neither he nor the enemy can win shall be neutral; he who has an excess of advantage shall march; he who is wanting in strength shall seek protection; he who undertakes work requiring assistance shall adopt a dual policy.

The formation and implementation of policy. Kauṭilya's views about the formation and implementation of policy were as follows: a treaty based on truth and oath is binding for temporal and spiritual consequences; a treaty based on security is binding only as long as the party is strong. He who inflicts severe punishments becomes oppressive; he who inflicts mild punishments is overpowered; and he who inflicts just punishments is respected. Kauṭilya advocated an elaborate system of espionage for domestic as well as foreign affairs.

Fragments from the Ajīvikas and the Cārvākas. *The Ājīvikas.* About the time of the rise of Buddhism, there was a sect of religious mendicants, the Ājīvikas, who held unorthodox views. In the strict sense, this name is applied to the followers of one Makkhali Gosāla, but in a wide sense it is also applied to those who taught many different shades of heretical teachings. Primary sources of knowledge about these are the *Dīgha Nikāya*, *Aṅguttara Nikāya*, *Saṃyutta Nikāya*, the *Sūtrakṛtanga-sūtra*, Śilāṅka's commentary on the *Sutrakṛtanga-sūtra*, the *Bhagavatī-sūtra*, the *Nandī-sūtra*, and Abhayadeva's commentary on *Samavayanga-sūtra*.

Makkhali's views may be thus summarized. There is no cause of the depravity of things; they become depraved without any reason or cause. There is also no cause of the purity of beings; they become pure without any reason or cause. Nothing depends either on one's own efforts or on the efforts of others. All things are destitute of power, force, or energy. Their changing states are due to destiny, environment, and their own nature. Thus, Makkhali denies sin, or *dharma*, and denies freedom of man in shaping his own future. He is thus a determinist, although scholars have held the view that he might leave room for chance, if not for freedom of will. He is supposed to have held an atomistic cosmology and that all beings, in the course of time, are destined to culminate in a state of final salvation. He believes not only in rebirth but also in a special doctrine of reanimation according to which it is possible for one person's soul to be reanimated in the dead bodies of others. Thus, the Ājīvikas are far from being materialists.

The Cārvākas. Another pre-Buddhistic system of philosophy, the Cārvāka, or the Lokāyata, is one of the earliest materialistic schools of philosophy. The name Cārvāka is traced back to one Cārvāka, supposed to have been one of the great teachers of the school. The other name, Lokāyata, means "the view held by the common people," "the system which has its base in the common, profane world," "the art of sophistry," and also "the philosophy that denies that there is any world other than this one." Bṛhaspati probably was the founder of this school. Much knowledge of the Cārvākas, however, is derived from the expositions of the later Hindu writings, particularly from Mādhava's *Sarva-darśana-saṃgraha* ("Compendium of All Philosophies," 14th century). Haribhadra in his *Ṣaḍdarśanasamuccaya* ("Compendium of the Six Philosophies," 5th century AD) attributes to the Cārvākas the view that this world extends only to the limits of possible sense experience.

Materialistic views of the Cārvākas

The Cārvākas apparently sought to establish their materialism on an epistemological basis. In their epistemology, they viewed sense perception alone as a means of valid knowledge. The validity of inferential knowledge was challenged on the ground that all inference requires a universal major premise ("All that possesses smoke possesses fire") whereas there is no means of arriving at a certainty about such a proposition. No amount of finite observations could possibly yield the required universal premise. The supposed "invariable connection" may be vitiated by some unknown "condition," and there is no means of knowing that such a vitiating factor does not exist. Since inference is not a means of valid knowledge, all such supersensible objects as "afterlife," "destiny," or "soul" do not exist. To say that such entities exist though there is no means of knowing them is regarded as absurd, for no assertion of existence is meaningful unless there is, in principle, some way of verifying it.

The authority of the scriptures also is denied. First, knowledge based on verbal testimony is inferential and therefore vitiated by all the defects of inference. The Cārvākas regard the scriptures as characterized by the three faults: falsity, self-contradiction, and tautology. On the basis of such a theory of knowledge, the Cārvākas defended a complete reductive materialism according to which the four elements of earth, water, fire, and air are the only original components of being and all other forms are products of their composition. Consciousness thus is viewed as a product of the material structure of the body and characterizes the body itself—rather than a soul—and perishes with the body. In their ethics, the Cārvākas upheld a hedonistic theory according to which enjoyment of the maximum amount of sensual pleasure here in this life and avoidance of pain that is likely to accompany such enjoyment are the only two goals that men ought to pursue.

FURTHER DEVELOPMENTS OF THE SYSTEM

Developments in Mahāyāna. *Nāgārjuna and Śūnyavāda.* Though the beginnings of Mahāyāna are to be found in the Mahāsaṅgikas and many of their early sects, Nāgārjuna gave it a philosophical basis. Not only is the individual person empty and lacking an eternal self, according to Nāgārjuna, but the *dharmas* also are empty. He extended the concept of *śūnyatā* to cover all concepts and all entities. "Emptiness" thus means subjection to the law of causality or "dependent origination" and lack of an immutable essence and an invariant mark (*niḥsvabhāvatā*). It also entails a repudiation of dualities between the conditioned and the unconditioned, between subject and object, relative and absolute, and between *saṃsāra* and Nirvāṇa. Thus, Nāgārjuna arrived at an ontological monism; but he carried through an epistemological dualism (*i.e.*, a theory of knowledge based on two sets of criteria) between two orders of truth: the conventional (*samvṛtti*) and the transcendental (*paramārtha*). The one reality is ineffable. Nāgārjuna undertook a critical examination of all the major categories with which philosophers had sought to understand reality and showed them all to involve self-contradictions. The world is viewed as a network of relations, but relations are unintelligible. If two terms, A and B, are related by the relation R, then either A and B are different or they are identical. If they are identical, they cannot be related; if they are altogether different then they cannot also be related, for they would have no common ground. The notion of "partial identity and partial difference" is also rejected as unintelligible. The notion of causality is rejected on the basis of similar reasonings. The concepts of change, substance, self, knowledge, and universals do not fare any better. Nāgārjuna also directed criticism against the concept of *pramāṇa*, or the means of valid knowledge.

Ontological monism and epistemological dualism

Nāgārjuna's philosophy is also called Mādhyamika, because it claims to tread the middle path, which consists not in synthesizing opposed views such as "The real is permanent" and "The real is changing" but in showing the hollowness of both the claims. To say that reality is both permanent and changing is to make another metaphysical assertion, another viewpoint, whose opposite is "Reality is neither permanent nor changing." In relation to the former, the latter is a higher truth, but the latter is still a point of view, a *dṛṣṭi*, expressed in a metaphysical statement, though Nāgārjuna condemned all metaphysical statements as false.

Nāgārjuna used reason to condemn reason. Those of his disciples who continued to limit the use of logic to this negative and indirect method, known as *prasaṅga*, are called the *prāsaṅgikas*: of these, Āryadeva, Buddhapālita, and Candrakīrti are the most important. Bhāvaviveka, however, followed the method of direct reasoning and thus founded what is called the *svatantra* (independent) school of Mādhyamika philosophy. With him Buddhist logic comes to its own, and during his time the Yogācāras split away from the Śūnyavādins.

Contributions of Vasubandhu and Asaṅga. Converted by his brother Asaṅga to the Yogācāra, Vasubandhu wrote the *Vijñapti-mātratā-siddhi* ("Establishment of the Thesis of Cognitions—Only"), in which he defended the thesis that the supposedly external objects are merely mental conceptions. Yogācāra idealism is a logical development of Sautrāntika representationism: the conception of a merely inferred external world is not satisfying. If consciousness is self-intimating (*svaprakāśa*) and if consciousness can assume forms (*sākāravijñāna*), it seems more logical to hold that the forms ascribed to alleged external objects are really forms of consciousness. One only needs another conception: a beginningless power that would account for this tendency of consciousness to take up forms and to externalize them. This is the power of *kalpanā*, or imagination. Yogācāra added two other modes of consciousness to the traditional six: ego consciousness (*manovijñāna*) and storehouse consciousness (*ālaya-vijñāna*). The *ālaya-vijñāna* contains stored traces of past experiences, both pure and defiled seeds. Early anticipations of the notions of the subconscious or the unconscious, they are theoretical constructs to account for the order of individual experience. It still remained, however, to account for a common world—which in fact remains the main difficulty of Yogācāra. The state of Nirvāṇa becomes a state in which the *ālaya* with its stored "seeds" would wither away (*ālayaparāvṛtti*). Though the individual ideas are in the last resort mere imaginations, in its essential nature consciousness is without distinctions of subject and object. This ineffable consciousness is the "suchness" (*tathatā*) underlying all things. Neither the *ālaya* nor the *tathatā*, however, is to be construed as being substantial.

Ego consciousness and stored consciousness

Vasubandhu and Asaṅga are also responsible for the growth of Buddhist logic. Vasubandhu defined "perception" as the knowledge that is caused by the object, but this was rejected by Dignāga, a 5th-century logician, as a definition belonging to his earlier realistic phase. Vasubandhu defined "inference" as a knowledge of an object through its mark, but Dharmottara, an 8th-century commentator pointed out that this is not a definition of the essence of inference but only of its origin.

Contributions of Dignāga and Dharmakīrti. Dignāga's *Pramāṇasamuccaya* ("Compendium of the Means of True Knowledge") is one of the greatest works on Buddhist logic. Dignāga gave a new definition of "perception": a knowledge that is free from all conceptual constructions, including name and class concepts. In effect, he regarded only the pure sensation as perception. In his theory of inference, he distinguished between inference for oneself and inference for the other and laid down three criteria of a valid middle term (*hetu*), viz., that it should "cover" the minor premise (*pakṣa*), be present in the similar instances (*sapakṣa*), and be absent in dissimilar instances (*vipakṣa*). In his *Hetucakra* ("The Wheel of 'Reason' "), Dignāga set up a matrix of nine types of middle terms, of which two yield valid conclusions, two contradictory, and the rest uncertain conclusions. Dignāga's tradition is further developed in the 7th century by Dharmakīrti, who modified his definition of perception to include the condition "unerring" and distinguished, in his *Nyāyabindu*, between four kinds of perception: that by the five senses, that by the mind, self-consciousness, and perception of the *yogins*. He also introduced a threefold distinction of valid middle terms: the middle must be related to the major either by identity ("This is a tree, because this is an oak") or as cause and effect ("This is fiery, because it is smoky"), or the *hetu* is a nonperception from which the absence of the major could be inferred. Dharmakīrti consolidated the central epistemological thesis of the Buddhists that perception and inference have their own exclusive objects. The object of the former is the pure particular (*svalakṣaṇa*), and the object of the latter (he regarded judgments as containing elements of inference) is the universal (*sāmānya-lakṣaṇa*). In their metaphysical positions, Dignāga and Dharmakīrti represent a moderate form of idealism.

Pure sensation as perception

Pūrva-mīmāṃsā: the Bhāṭṭa and Prābhākara schools. *Principal texts and relation to Śabara.* Kumārila commented on Jaimini's *sūtra* as well as on Śabara's *bhāṣya*. The *Vārttika* (critical gloss) that he wrote was commented upon by Sucarita Miśra in his *Kāśikā* ("The Shining"), by Someśvara Bhaṭṭa in his *Nyāyasudhā* ("The Nectar of Logic"), and Pārthasārathi Miśra in *Nyāyaratnākara* ("The Abode of Jewels of Logic"). Pārthasārathi's *Śāstradīpikā* ("Light on the Scripture") is a famous independent Mīmāṃsā treatise belonging to Kumārila's school.

Prabhākara, who most likely lived after Kumārila, was the author of the commentary *Bṛhatī* ("The Large Commentary"), on Śabara's *bhāṣya*. On many essential matters, Prabhākara differs radically from the views of Kumārila. Prabhākara's *Bṛhatī* has been commented upon by Śālikanātha in his *Ṛjuvimalā* ("The Straight and Free from Blemishes"), whereas the same author's *Prakaraṇapañcikā* ("Commentary of Five Topics") is a very useful exposition of the Prābhākara system. Other works belonging to this school are Mādhava's *Jaiminīyā-nyāya-mālā-vistara* ("Expansion of the String of Reasonings by Jaimini"), Appaya Dīkṣita's *Vidhirasāyana* ("The Elixir of Duty"), Āpadeva's *Mīmāṃsā-nyāya-prakāśa* (Illumination of the Reasonings of *Mīmāṃsā*) and Laugākṣi Bhāskara's *Artha-saṃgraha* ("Collection of Treasures").

Where Kumārila and Prabhākara differed, Kumārila remained closer to both Jaimini and Śabara. Kumārila, like Jaimini and Śabara, restricted Mīmāṃsā to an investigation into *dharma*, whereas Prabhākara assigned to it the wider task of enquiring into the meaning of the Vedic texts. Kumārila understood the Vedic injunction to include a statement of the results to be attained; Prabhākara—following Bādari—excluded all consideration of the result from the injunction itself and suggested that the sense of duty alone should instigate a person to act.

Metaphysics and epistemology. Both the Bhāṭṭa (the name for Kumārila's school) and the Prabhākara schools, in their metaphysics, were realists; both undertook to refute Buddhist idealism and nihilism. The Bhāṭṭa ontology recognized five types of entities: substance (*dravya*), quality (*guṇa*), action (*karma*), universals (*sāmānya*), and negation (*abhāva*). Of these, substance was held to be of ten kinds: the nine substances recognized by the Vaiśeṣikas and the additional substance "darkness." The Prābhākara ontology recognized eight types of entities; from the Bhāṭṭa list, negation was rejected, and four more were added: power (*śakti*), resemblance (*sadṛsa*), inherence-relation (*samavāya*), and number (*sāṃkhyā*). Under the type "substance," the claim of "darkness" was rejected on the ground that it is nothing but absence of perception of colour; the resulting list of nine substances is the same as that of the Vaiśeṣikas. Though both the schools admitted the reality of the universals, their views on this point differed considerably. The Prābhākaras admitted only such universals as inhere in perceptible instances and insisted that true universals themselves must be perceivable. Thus, they rejected abstract universals, such as "existence," and merely postulated universals, such as "Brahminhood" (which cannot be perceptually recognized in a person).

Refutation of Buddhist idealism and nihilism

The epistemologies of the two schools differ as much as their ontologies. As ways of valid knowing, the Bhāṭṭas recognized perception, inference, verbal testimony (*śabda*), comparison (*upamāna*), postulation (*arthāpatti*), and nonperception (*anupalabdhi*). The last is regarded as the way men validly, and directly, apprehend an absence: this was in conformity with Śabara's statement that *abhāva* (nonexistence) itself is a *pramāṇa* (way of true knowledge). Postulation is viewed as the sort of process by which one may come to know for certain the truth of a certain proposition, and yet the Bhāṭṭas refused to include such cases under inference on the grounds that in such cases one does not say to himself "I am inferring" but rather says "I am postulating." "Comparison" is the name given to the perception of resemblance with a perceived thing of another thing that is not present at that moment. It is supposed that because the latter thing is not itself being perceived, the resemblance belonging to it could not have been perceived; thus, it is not a case of perception when one says "My cow at home is similar to this animal."

The Prābhākaras rejected nonperception as a way of knowing and were left with a list of five concerning definitions of perception. The Bhāṭṭas, following the *sūtra*, define perception in terms of sensory contact with the object, whereas the Prābhākaras define it in terms of immediacy of the apprehension.

Ethics. As pointed out earlier, Kumārila supported the thesis that all moral injunctions are meant to bring about a desired benefit and that knowledge of such benefit and of the efficacy of the recommended course of action to bring it about is necessary for instigating a person to act. Prābhākara defended the ethical theory of duty for its own sake, the sense of duty alone being the proper incentive. The Bhāṭṭas recognize *apūrva* (supersensible efficacy of actions to produce remote effects) as a supersensible link connecting the moral action performed in this life and the supersensible effect (such as going to heaven) to be realized afterward. Prābhākara understood by *apūrva* only the action that ought to be done.

Hermeneutics and semantics. In their principles of interpretation of the scriptures, and consequently in their theories of meaning (of words and of sentences), the two schools differ radically. Prābhākara defended the thesis that words primarily mean either some course of action (*kārya*) or things connected with action. Connected with this is the further Prābhākara thesis that the sentence forms the unit of meaningful discourse, that a word is never used by itself to express a single unrelated idea, and that a sentence signifies a relational complex that is not a mere juxtaposition of word meanings. Prābhākara's theory of language learning follows these contentions: the child learns the meanings of sentences by observing the elders issuing orders like "Bring the cow" and the juniors obeying them, and he learns the meaning of words subsequently by a close observation of the insertion (*āvāpa*) and extraction (*uddhāra*) of words in sentences and the resulting variations in the meaning of those sentences. From this semantic approach follows Prābhākara's principle of Vedic interpretation: all Vedic texts are to be interpreted as bearing on courses of action prescribed, and there are no merely descriptive statements in the scriptures. Furthermore, only the Vedic injunctions yield the authoritative verbal testimony that may be regarded as a unique way of knowing, whereas all other verbal knowledge is really inferential in character. In matters concerning what ought to be done, Prābhākara therefore regarded only the Vedas as authoritative.

Language and learning

Kumārila's theory is very different. In his view, words convey their own meanings, not relatedness to something else. He therefore was more willing to accommodate purely descriptive sentences as significant. Furthermore, he regarded sentence meaning as composed of separate word meanings held together in a relational structure; the word meaning formed, for him, the simplest unit of sense. Persons thus learn the meaning of words by seeing others talking as well as from advice of the elders.

Religious consequences. The Mīmāṃsā views the universe as being eternal and does not admit the need of tracing it back to a creator. It also does not admit the need of admitting a being who is to distribute moral rewards and inflict punishments—this function being taken over by the notion of *apūrva*, or supersensible power generated by each action. Theoretically not requiring a God, the system, however, posits a number of deities as entailed by various ritualistic procedures, with no ontological status assigned to the gods.

The linguistic philosophies: Bhartṛhari and Maṇḍana-Miśra. The linguistic philosophers considered here are the grammarians led by Bhartṛhari (7th century AD) and Maṇḍana-Miśra (8th century AD); the latter, reputed to be a disciple of Kumārila, held views widely different from the Mīmāṃsākas. The grammarians share with the Mīmāṃsākas their interest in the problems of language and meaning. But their own theories are so different that they cut at the roots of the Mīmāṃsā realism. The chief text of this school is Bhartṛhari's *Vākyapadīya.* Maṇḍana's chief works are *Brahma-siddhi* ("Establishment of Brahman"), *Sphoṭa-siddhi* ("Establishment of Word Essence"), and *Vidhiviveka* ("Inquiry into the Nature of Injunctions").

As his first principle, Bhartṛhari rejects one of the doctrines on which the realism of Mīmāṃsā and Nyāya had been built up—the view that there is a kind of perception that is nonconceptualized and that places persons in direct contact with things as they are. For Bhartṛhari this is not possible, for all knowledge is "penetrated" by words and "illuminated" by words. Thus, all knowledge is linguistic, and the distinctions of objects are traceable to distinctions among words. The metaphysical monism of word (*śabdādvaita*) is not far from this—*i.e.*, the view that the one word essence appears as this world of "names and forms" because of man's imaginative construction (*kalpanā*). Metaphysically, Bhartṛhari comes close both to Śaṅkara's Advaita and the Buddhist philosophers, such as Dharmakīrti. This metaphysical theory, however, makes use of another doctrine—the doctrine of *sphoṭa* ("that from which the meaning bursts forth"). Most Indian philosophical schools were concerned with the problem of what precisely is the bearer of the meaning of a word or a sentence. If the letters are evanescent

All knowledge as linguistic

and if, as one hears the sounds produced by the letters of a word, each sound is replaced by another, one never comes to perceive the word as a whole, and the question is how one grasps the meaning of the word. The same problem could be stated with regard to a sentence. The Mīmāṃsākas postulated an eternity of sounds and distinguished between the eternal sounds and sound complexes (words, sentences) from their manifestations. The grammarians, instead, distinguished between the word and sound and made the word itself the bearer of meaning. As bearer of meaning, the word is the *sphoṭa*.

Sounds have spatial and temporal relations; they are produced differently by different speakers. But the word as meaning bearer has to be regarded as having no size or temporal dimension. It is indivisible and eternal. Distinguished from the *sphoṭa* are the abstract sound pattern (*prākṛtadhvani*) and the utterances (*vikṛtadhvani*). Furthermore, Bhartṛhari held that the sentence is not a collection of words or an ordered series of them. A word is rather an abstraction from a sentence; thus, the sentence-*sphoṭa* is the primary unit of meaning. A word is also grasped as a unity by an instantaneous flash of insight (*pratibhā*). This theory of *sphoṭa*, itself a linguistic theory required by the problems arising from the theory of meaning, was used by the grammarians to support their word monism.

Maṇḍana-Miśra, in his *Vidhiviveka*, referred to three varieties of this monism: *śabdapratyāsavāda* (the doctrine of superimposition on word; which is the same as *śabdāhyāsavāda*), *śabda-parināmavāda* (the doctrine of transformation of word), and *śabdavivartavāda* (the doctrine of unreal appearance of the word). According to the first two, the phenomenal world is still real, though either falsely super-imposed on words or a real transformation of the word essence. The last, perhaps more consistent than the other two, is the view that the phenomenal distinctions are unreal appearances of an immutable word essence.

Maṇḍana attempted to integrate this linguistic philosophy into his own form of *advaitavāda*, though later followers of Saṅkara did not accept the doctrine of *sphoṭa*. Even Vācaspati, who accepted many of Maṇḍana's theories, rejected the theory of *sphoṭa* and in general conformed to the Śaṅkarite's acceptance of the Bhāṭṭa epistemology.

Nyāya-Vaiśeṣika. *The old school.* Although as early as the commentators Praśastapāda (5th century AD) and Uddyotakara (7th century AD) the authors of the Nyāya-Vaiśeṣika schools freely used each other's doctrines and the fusion of the two schools was well on its way, the two schools continued to have different authors and lines of commentators. About the 10th century AD, however, there arose a number of texts that sought to combine the two philosophies more successfully. Well-known among these syncretist texts are the following: Bhāsarvajña's *Nyāyasāra* ("The Essence of Nyāya"; written *c.* 950), Varadarāja's *Tārkikarakṣā* ("In Defense of the Logician"; *c.* 1150), Vallabha's *Nyāyalīlāvatī* ("The Charm of Nyāya"; 12th century), Keśava Miśra's *Tarkabhāṣā* ("The Language of Reasoning"; *c.* 1275), Annam Bhāṭṭa's *Tarkasaṃgraha* ("Compendium of Logic"; *c.* 1623) and Viśvanātha's *Bhāṣāpariccheda* ("Determination of the Meaning of the Verses"; 1634). The scheme of Viśvanātha, as an example of how this amalgamation was effected, is given in Table 1.

Table 1: Visvanatha's Scheme of Amalgamation

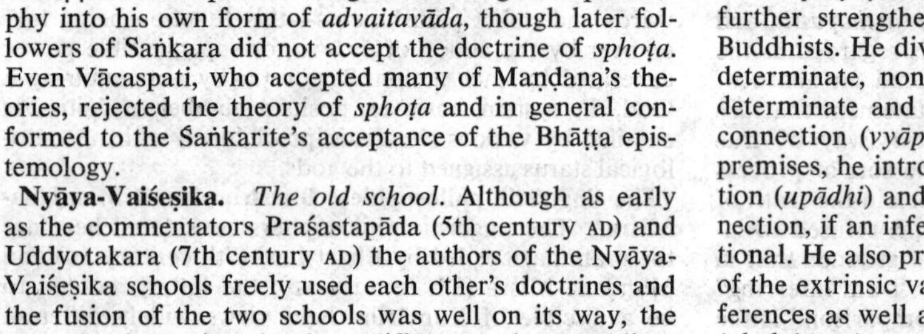
padārthas (categories of being)
dravya (substance)
7 Vaiśeṣika categories
9 substances (as in Vaiśeṣika)
ātman (self)
buddhi (knowledge)
anubhuti (knowledge other than memory)
smṛti (memory)
pratyakṣa (perception)
anumāna (inference)
śabda (verbal testimony)
upamāna (comparison)
pramāṇa (ways of knowing)

Both the schools are realistic with regard to things, properties, relations, and universals. Both are pluralistic (also with regard to individual selves) and theistic. They admit external relations (the relation of inherence being only partly internal), atomistic cosmology, new production, and the concept of existence (*sattā*) as the most comprehensive universal. They all regard knowledge as a quality of the self, and they subscribe to a correspondence theory regarding the nature of truth and a pragmatic-cum-coherence theory regarding the test of truth. The points that divide the schools are of minor nature: they concern, for example, their theories of number, and some doctrines in their physical and chemical theories.

The Nyāya and Vaiśeṣika commentary tradition

Gautama's *sūtras* were commented upon about AD 400 by Vātsāyana, who replied to the Buddhist doctrines, especially to some varieties of Śūnyavāda scepticism. Uddyotakara's *Vārttika* (*c.* 635) was written after a period during which major Buddhist works, but no major Hindu work, on logic were written. Uddyotakara undertook to refute Nāgārjuna and Dignāga. He criticized and refuted Dignāga's theory of perception, the Buddhist denial of soul, and the *anyāpoha* (exclusion of the other) theory of meaning. Positively, he introduced, for the first time, the doctrine of six modes of contact (*saṃnikarsa*) of the senses with their objects, which has remained a part of Nyāya-Vaiśeṣika epistemology. He divided inferences into those whose major premise (*sādhya*) is universally present, those in which one has to depend only upon the rule "Wherever there is absence of the major, there is absence of the middle (*hetu*)," and those in which both the positive and the negative rules are at one's disposal. He rejected the *sphoṭa* theory and argued that the meaning of a word is apprehended by hearing the last letter of the word together with recollection of the preceding ones. Vācaspati Miśra in the 9th century wrote his *Tātparyaṭīkā* (*c.* 840) on Uddyotakara's *Vārttika* and further strengthened the Nyāya viewpoint against the Buddhists. He divided perception into two kinds: the indeterminate, nonlinguistic, and nonjudgmental and the determinate and judgmental. In defining the invariable connection (*vyāpti*) between the middle and the major premises, he introduced the concept of a vitiating condition (*upādhi*) and stressed that the required sort of connection, if an inference is to be valid, should be unconditional. He also proposed a modified version of the theory of the extrinsic validity of knowledge by holding that inferences as well as knowledges that are the last verifiers (*phalajñāna*) are self-validating.

Praśastapāda's Vaiśeṣika commentary (6th century) does not closely follow the *sūtras* but is rather an independent explanation. Praśastapāda added seven more qualities to Kaṇāda's list: heaviness (*gurutva*), fluidity (*dravatva*), viscidity (*sneha*), traces (*saṃskara*), virtue (*dharma*), vice (*adharma*), and sound. The last one was regarded by Kaṇāda only as a mark of ether, whereas Praśastapāda made it a quality of the latter. He also made the Vaiśeṣika fully theistic by introducing doctrines of creation and dissolution.

The Nyāya-Vaiśeṣika general metaphysical standpoint allows for both particulars and universals, both change and permanence. There are ultimate differences as well as a hierarchy of universals, the highest universal being existence. Substance is defined as the substrate of qualities and in terms of what alone can be an inherent cause. A quality may be defined as what is neither substance nor action and yet is the substratum of universals (for universals are supposed to inhere only in substances, qualities, and actions). Universal is defined as that which is eternal and inheres in many. Ultimate particularities belong to eternal substances, such as atoms and souls, and these account for all differences among particulars that cannot be accounted for otherwise. Inherence (*samavāya*) is the relation that is maintained between a universal and its instances, a substance and its qualities or actions, a whole and its parts, and an eternal substance and its particularity. This relation is such that one of the relations cannot exist without the other (*e.g.*, a whole cannot exist without the parts). Negation (*abhāva*), the seventh category, is initially classified into difference ("A is not B") and absence ("A is not in B"), absence being further divided into absence of a thing before its origin, its absence after its destruction, and its absence in places other than where it is present. For these schools, all that is is knowable and also nameable.

Meta-physics and episte-mology

Knowledge is regarded as a distinguishing but not essential property of a self. It arises when the appropriate conditions are present. Consciousness is defined as a manifestation of object but is not itself self-manifesting; it is known by an act of inner perception (*anuvyavasāya*). Knowledge either is memory or is not; knowledge other than memory is either true or false; and knowledge that is not true is either doubt or error. In its theory of error, these philosophers maintained an uncompromising realism by holding that the object of error is still real but is only not here and now. True knowledge (*pramā*) apprehends its object as it is; false knowledge apprehends the object as what it is not. True knowledge is either perception, inference, or knowledge derived from verbal testimony or comparison. Perception is defined as knowledge that arises from the contact of the senses with their objects, and is viewed as either indeterminate and nonlinguistic or as determinate and judgmental. Both aspects of the definition of perception are viewed as valid—a point that is made against both the Buddhists and grammarians. Furthermore, perception is either ordinary (*laukika*) or extraordinary (*alaukika*). The former takes place through any of the six modes of sense-object contact recognized in the system. The latter takes place when one perceives the proper object of one sense through another sense ("The cushion looks soft") or when, on recognizing universal in a particular, one perceives all instances of the universal as its instances. Also extraordinary are the perceptions of the *yogin*s, who are supposed to be free from the ordinary spatiotemporal limitations.

Four conditions must be satisfied in order that a combination of words may form a meaningful sentence: a word should generate an intention or expectancy for the words to follow ("Bring"—"What?"—"A jar"); there should be mutual fitness ("Sprinkle"—"With what?"—"Water, not fire"); there should be proximity in space and time; and the proper intention of the speaker must be ascertained, otherwise there would be equivocation.

Among theistic proofs offered in the system, the most important are the causal argument ("The world is produced by an agent, since it is an effect, as is a jar"); the argument from a world order to a lawgiver; and the moral argument from the law of *karma* to a moral governor. Besides adducing these and other arguments, Udayana in his *Nyāya-kusumāñjali* stressed the point that the nonexistence of God could not be proved by means of valid knowledge.

The new school. The founder of the school of Navya-(New) Nyāya, with an exclusive emphasis on the *pramāṇas*, was Gaṅgeśa Upādhyāya (13th century), whose *Tattvacintāmaṇi* ("The Jewel of Thought on the Nature of Things") is the basic text for all later developments. The logicians of this school were primarily interested in defining their terms and concepts and for this purpose developed an elaborate technical vocabulary and logical apparatus that came to be used by, other than philosophers, writers on law, poetics, aesthetics, and ritualistic liturgy. The school may broadly be divided into two subschools: the Mithilā school represented by Vardhamāna (Gaṅgeśa's son), Pakṣadhara or Jayadeva (author of *Āloka* gloss), and Śaṅkara Miśra (author of *Upaskāra*); and the Navadvīpa school, whose chief representatives were Vāsudeva Sārvabhauma (1450–1525), Raghunātha Śiromaṇi (*c.* 1475–*c.* 1550), Mathurānātha Tarkavāgīśa (fl. *c.* 1570), Jagadīśa Tarkālaṅkāra (fl. *c.* 1625), and Gadādhara Bhaṭṭacārya (fl. *c.* 1650).

By means of a new technique of analysing knowledge, judgmental knowledge can be analyzed into three kinds of epistemological entities in their interrelations: "qualifiers" (*prakāra*); "qualificandum," or that which must be qualified (*viśeṣya*); and "relatedness" (*saṃsarga*). There also are corresponding abstract entities: qualifierness, qualificandumness, and relatedness. The knowledge expressed by the judgment "This is a blue pot" may then be analyzed into the following form: "The knowledge that has a qualificandumness in what is denoted by 'this' is conditioned by a qualifierness in blue and also conditioned by another qualifierness in potness."

Navya-Nyāya meta-physics and episte-mology

A central concept in the Navya-Nyāya logical apparatus is that of "limitorness" (*avacchedakatā*), which has many different uses. If a mountain possesses fire in one region and not in another, it can be said, in the Navya-Nyāya language, "The mountain, as limited by the region *r*, possesses fire, but as limited by the region *r′* possesses the absence of fire." The same mode of speech may be extended to limitations of time, property, and relation, particularly when one is in need of constructing a description that is intended to suit exactly some specific situation and none other.

Inference is defined by Vātsāyana as the "posterior" knowledge of an object (*e.g.*, fire) with the help of knowledge of its mark (*e.g.*, smoke). For Navya-Nyāya, inference is definable as the knowledge caused by the knowledge that the minor term (*pakṣa*, "the hill") "possesses" the middle term (*hetu*, "smoke"), which is recognized as "pervaded by" the major (*sādhya*, "fire"). The relation of invariable connection, or "pervasion," between the middle (smoke) and the major (fire)—"Wherever there is smoke, there is fire"—is called *vyāpti*.

The logicians developed the notion of negation to a great degree of sophistication. Apart from the efforts to specify a negation with references to its limiting counterpositive (*pratiyogi*), limiting relation, and limiting locus, they were constrained to discuss and debate such typical issues as the following: Is one to recognize, as a significant negation, the absence of a thing *x* so that the limiter of the counterpositive *x* is not *x*-ness but *y*-ness? In other words, can one say that a jar is absent as a cloth even in a locus in which it is present as a jar? Also, is the absence of an absence itself a new absence or something positive? Furthermore, is the absence of colour in general nothing but the sum total of the absences of the particular colours, or is it a new kind of absence, a generic absence? Gaṅgeśa argued for the latter alternative, though he answers the first of the above three questions in the negative.

Though the philosophers of this school did not directly write on metaphysics, they nevertheless did tend to introduce many new kinds of abstract entities into their discourse. These entities are generally epistemological, though sometimes they are relational. Chief of these are entities called "qualifierness," "qualificandumness," and "limiterness." Various relations were introduced, such as direct and indirect temporal relations, *paryāpti* relation (in which a number reside, in sets rather than in individual members of those sets), *svarūpa* relation (which holds, for example, between an absence and its locus), and relation between a knowledge and its object.

Introduction of new abstract entities

Among the Navya-Nyāya philosophers, Raghunātha Śiromaṇi in *Padārthatattvanirūpaṇa* undertook a bold revision of the traditional categorial scheme by (1) identifying "time," "space," and "ether" with God; (2) eliminating the category of mind by reducing it to matter;

(3) denying atoms (*paramāṇu*) and dyadic (paired) combinations of them (*dvyaṇuka*), (4) eliminating "number," "separateness," "remoteness," and "proximity" from the list of qualities; and (5) rejecting ultimate particularities (*viśeṣa*) on the grounds that it is more rational to suppose that the eternal substances are by nature distinct. He added some new categories, however, such as causal power (*śakti*) and the moment (*kṣaṇa*), and recognized that there are as many instances of the relation of inherence as there are cases of it (as contrasted with the older view that there is only one inherence that is itself present in all cases of inherence).

Sāṃkhya and Yoga. *Texts and commentaries until Vācaspati and the "Sāṃkhya-sūtras."* There are three commentaries on the *Sāṃkhya-kārikā:* that by Raja, much referred to but not extant; that by Gauḍapāda (7th century), on which there is a subcommentary *Candrikā* by Nārāyaṇatīrtha; and the *Tattva-kaumudī* by Vācaspati (9th century). The *Sāṃkhya-sūtras* is a much later work (*c.* 14th century) on which Aniruddha (15th century) wrote a *vṛtti* and Vijñānabhikṣu (16th century) wrote the *Sāṃkhya-pravacana-bhāṣya* ("Commentary on the Sāṃkhya Doctrine"). Among independent works, mention may be made of *Tattvasamāsa* ("Collection of Truths"; *c.* 11th century).

The *Yoga-sūtras* were commented upon by Vyāsa in his *Vyāsa-bhāṣya* (5th century), which again has two excellent subcommentaries: Vācaspati's *Tattvavaiśāradī* and Vijñānabhikṣu's *Yogavārttika*, besides the *vṛtti* by Bhoja (*c.* 1000).

Metaphysics and epistemology. For Vācaspati, creation was viewed in terms of the mere presence of the selves and the mere presentation to them of Matter (the undifferentiated primeval stuff). Such a view has obvious difficulties, for it would make creation eternal, because the selves and Matter are eternally copresent. Vijñānabhikṣu considered the relation between the selves and Matter to be a real relation that affects Matter but leaves the selves unaffected. Creation, in accordance with Bhikṣu's theism, is due to the influence of the chief self—*i.e.*, God. Furthermore, whereas the earlier Sāṃkhya authors, including Vācaspati, did not consider the question about the ontological status of the *guṇas*, Bhikṣu regards them as real, as extremely subtle substances—so that each *guṇa* is held to be infinite in number. In general, the *Sāṃkhya-sūtras* show a greater Brahminical influence, and there is a clear tendency to explain away the points of difference between the Sāṃkhya and the Vedānta. The author of the sutras tried to show that the Sāṃkhya doctrines are consistent with theism or even with the Upaniṣadic conception of Brahman. Vijñānabhikṣu made use of such contexts to emphasize that the atheism of Sāṃkhya is taught only to discourage men to try to be God, that originally the Sāṃkhya was theistic, and that the original Vedānta also was theistic. The Upaniṣadic doctrine of the unity of selves is interpreted by him to mean an absence of difference of kind among selves, which is consistent with the Sāṃkhya. *Māyā* (illusion) for Bhikṣu means nothing but the *prakṛti* (Matter) of the Sāṃkhya. Furthermore, the *sūtras* give a cosmic significance to *mahat*, the first aspect to evolve from Matter, which then means a cosmic Intelligence: this sense is not found in the *kārikās*.

The tendency to de-emphasize the difference between Sāṃkhya and Vedānta

In epistemology the idea of reflection of the spirit in the organs of knowing, particularly in the *buddhi*, or intelligence, comes to the forefront. Every cognition (jñāna) is a modification of the *buddhi*, with consciousness reflected in it. Though this is Vācaspati's account, it does not suffice according to Bhikṣu. If there is the mere reflection of the self in the state of the *buddhi*, this can only account for the fact that the state of cognition seems to be a conscious state; it cannot account for the fact that the self considers itself to be the owner and experiencer of that state. Accounting for this latter fact, Bhikṣu postulated a real contact between the self and *buddhi* as a reflection of the *buddhi* state back in the self.

Vācaspati, taking over a notion emphasized in Indian epistemology for the first time by Kumārila, introduced into the Sāṃkhya theory of knowledge a distinction between two stages of perceptual knowledge: a first stage of nonconceptualized (*nirvikalpaka*) perception that apprehends its object vaguely and in a most general manner. This vague knowledge (*ālocanamātram*) is then interpreted and conceptualized by the mind. The interpretation is not so much synthesis as analysis of the vaguely presented totality into its parts. Bhikṣu, however, ascribed to the senses the ability to apprehend determinate properties, even independently of the aid of *manas*. For Sāṃkhya, in general, error is partial truth; there is no negation of error, only supplementation, though later Sāṃkhya authors tended to ascribe error to wrong interpretation.

An important contribution to epistemology was made by the writers on the Yoga: this concerns the key notion of *vikalpa*, which stands for mental states referring to pseudo-objects posited only by words. Such mental states are neither "valid" nor "invalid" and are said to be unavoidable accompaniments of one's use of language.

Ethics. Because the self is not truly an agent, neither merit nor demerit, arising from one's actions, attaches to the self. Morality has empirical significance. In the long run, what really matters is knowledge. Nonattached performance of one's duties is an aid toward purifying intelligence so that it may be conducive to the attainment of knowledge: hence the importance of the restraints and observances laid down in the *Yoga-sūtras*. The greatest good is freedom—*i.e.*, aloofness (*kaivalya*) from matter.

Rāja Yoga and Haṭha Yoga. Though Patañjali's yoga is known as Rāja Yoga (that in which one attains to self-rule), Haṭha Yoga (*haṭha* = "violence," "violent effort": *ha* = "sun," *ṭha* = "moon," *haṭha* = "sun and moon," breaths, or breaths travelling through the right and left nostrils) emphasizes bodily postures, regulation of breathing, and cleansing processes as means to spiritual perfection. A basic text on Haṭha Yoga is the *Haṭha-yoga-pradīpikā* ("Light on the Haṭha Yoga"; *c.* 15th century). As to the relation between the two yogas, a well-known maxim lays down that "No *rāja* without *haṭha*, and no *haṭha* without *rāja*."

Religious consequences. The one religious consequence of the Sāṃkhya-Yoga is an emphasis on austere asceticism and a turning away from the ritualistic elements of Hinduism deriving from the Brāhminical sources. Though they continue to remain as an integral part of the Hindu faith, no major religious order thrived on the basis of these philosophies.

Vedānta. *Fragments from the Māṇḍukya-kārikā until Śaṅkara.* No commentary on the *Vedānta-sūtras* survives from the period before Śaṅkara, though both Śaṅkara and Rāmānuja referred to the *vṛttis* by Bodhāyana and Upavarṣa (the two may indeed be the same person). There are, however, pre-Śaṅkara monistic interpreters of the scriptures, three of whom are important: Bhartṛhari, Maṇḍana (both mentioned earlier), and Gauḍapāda. Śaṅkara referred to Gauḍapāda, as the teacher of his own teacher Govinda, complimented him for having recovered the *advaita* (nondualism) doctrine from the Vedas, and also wrote a *bhāṣya* on Gauḍapāda's main work: the *kārikās* on *Māṇḍukya Upaniṣad*.

The revival of nondualism

Gauḍapāda's *kārikās* is divided into four parts: the first part is an explanation of the *Upaniṣad* itself, the second part established the unreality of the world, the third part defends the oneness of reality, and the fourth part, called *Alātaśānti* ("Extinction of the Burning Coal"), deals with the state of release from suffering. It is not accidental that Gauḍapāda used as the title of the fourth part of his work a phrase in common usage among Buddhist authors. His philosophical views show a considerable influence of Mādhyamika Buddhism, particularly of the Yogācāra school, and one of his main purposes probably was to show that the teachings of the *Upaniṣads* are compatible with the main doctrines of the Buddhist idealists. Among his principal philosophical theses were the following: All things are as unreal as those seen in a dream, for waking experience and dream are on a par in this regard. In reality, there is no production and no destruction. His criticisms of the categories of change and causality are reminiscent of Nāgārjuna's. Duality is imposed on this one reality by *māyā*, or the power of illusion-producing ignorance. Because there is no real coming into being, Gauḍapāda's philosophy is often called *ajātivāda*. Though thus far agreeing with the Buddhist Yoga cārās, Gauḍapāda rejected their thesis that *citta*, or mind, is real and that there is a real flow of mental conception.

Śaṅkara greatly moderated Gauḍapāda's extreme illusionistic theory. Though he regarded the phenomenal world as a false appearance, he never made use of the analogy of dream. Rather, he contrasted the objectivity of the world with the subjectivity of dreams and hallucinations. The distinction between the empirical and the illusory—both being opposed to the transcendental—is central to his way of thinking.

Varieties of Vedānta schools. Though Vedānta is frequently referred to as one *darśana* (viewpoint), there are, in fact, radically different schools of Vedānta; what binds them together is common adherence to a common set of texts. These texts are the *Upaniṣads*, the *Vedānta-sūtras*, and the *Bhagavadgītā*—known as the three *prasthānas* (the basic scriptures, or texts) of the Vedānta. The founders of the various schools of Vedānta have all substantiated their positions by commenting on these three source books. The problems and issues around which their differences centre are the nature of Brahman; the status of the phenomenal world; the relation of finite individuals to the Brahman; and the nature and the means to *mokṣa*, or liberation. The main schools are: Śaṅkara's unqualified nondualism (*śuddhādvaita*); Rāmānuja's qualified nondualism (*viśiṣṭādvaita*), Madhva's dualism (*dvaita*); Bhāskara's doctrine of identity and difference (*bhedābheda*); and the schools of Nimbārka and Vallabha, which assert both identity and difference though with different emphasis on either of the two aspects. From the religious point of view, Śaṅkara extolled metaphysical knowledge as the sole means to liberation and regarded even the concept of God as false; Rāmānuja recommended the path of *bhakti* combined with knowledge, and showed a more tolerant attitude toward the tradition of Vedic ritualism; and Madhva, Nimbārka, and Vallabha all propounded a personalistic theism in which love and devotion to a personal God are rated highest. Although Śaṅkara's influence on Indian philosophy could not be matched by these other schools of Vedānta, in actual religious life the theistic Vedānta schools have exercised a much greater influence than the abstract metaphysics of Śaṅkara.

The concepts of Advaita (nondualism)

Śaṅkara's philosophy is one among a number of other nondualistic philosophies: Bhartṛhari's *śabdādvaita*, the Buddhist's *vijñānadvaita*, and Gauḍapāda's *ajātivada*. Śaṅkara's system may then be called *ātmādvaita*—the thesis that the one, universal, eternal, and self-illuminating self whose essence is pure consciousness without a subject (*āśraya*) and without an object (*viṣaya*) from a transcendental point of view alone is real. The phenomenal world and finite individuals, though empirically real, are—from the higher point of view—merely false appearances. In substantiating this thesis Śaṅkara relied as much on the interpretation of scriptural texts as on reasoning. He set down a methodological principle that reason should be used only to justify truths revealed in the scriptures. His own use of reasoning was primarily negative; he showed great logical skill in refuting his opponents' theories. Śaṅkara's followers, however, supplied what is missed in his works—*i.e.*, a positive rational support for his thesis.

Śaṅkara's metaphysics is based on a criterion of reality, which may be briefly formulated as follows: the real is that whose negation is not possible. It is then argued that the only thing that satisfies this criterion is consciousness, because denial of consciousness presupposes the consciousness that denies. It is conceivable that any object is not existent, but the absence of consciousness is not conceivable. Negation may be either mutual negation (of difference) or absence. The latter is either absence of a thing prior to its origination or after its destruction or absence of a thing in a place other than where it is present. If the negation of consciousness is not conceivable, then none of these various kinds of negations can be predicated of consciousness. If difference cannot be predicated of it, then consciousness is the only reality and anything different from it would be unreal. If the other three kinds of absence are not predicable of it, then consciousness should be beginningless, without end, and ubiquitous. Consequently, it would be without change. Furthermore, consciousness is self-intimating; all objects depend upon consciousness for their manifestation. Difference may be either among members of the same class or of one individual from another of a different class or among parts of one entity. None of these is true of consciousness. In other words, there are not many consciousnesses; the plurality of many centres of consciousness should be viewed as an appearance. There is no reality other than consciousness—*i.e.*, no real *prakṛti;* such a thing would only be an unreal other. Also, consciousness does not have internal parts; there are not many conscious states. The distinction between consciousness of blue and consciousness of yellow is not a distinction within consciousness but one superimposed on it by a distinction among its objects, blue and yellow. With this, the Sāṃkhya, Vijñānavādin Buddhist, and Nyāya-Veiśeṣika pluralism are refuted. Reality is one, infinite, eternal, and self-shining spirit; it is without any determination, for all determination is negation.

Śaṅkara's theory of error

The basic problem of Śaṅkara's philosophy is how such pure consciousness appears, in ordinary experience, to be individualized ("my consciousness") and to be of an object ("consciousness *of* blue"). As he stated it, subject and object are as opposed to each other as light and darkness, yet the properties of one are superimposed on the other. If something is a fact of experience and yet ought not to be so—*i.e.*, is rationally unintelligible—then this must be false. According to Śaṅkara's theory of error, the false appearance is a positive, presented entity that is characterized neither as existent (because it is sublated when the illusion is corrected) nor as nonexistent (because it is presented, given as much as the real is). The false, therefore, is indescribable either as being or as nonbeing, it is not a fiction, such as a round square. Śaṅkara thus introduced a new category of the "false" apart from the usual categories of the existent and the nonexistent. The world and finite individuals are false in this sense: they are rationally unintelligible, their reality is not logically deducible from Brahman, and their experience is cancelled with the knowledge of Brahman. The world and finite selves are not creations of Brahman; they are not real emanations or transformations of it. Brahman is not capable of such transformation or emanation. They are appearances that are superimposed on Brahman because of man's ignorance. This superimposition was sometimes called *adhyāsa* by Śaṅkara and was often identified with *avidyā*. Later writers referred to *avidyā* as the cause of the error. Thus, ignorance came to be regarded as a beginningless, positive something that conceals the nature of reality and projects the false appearances on it. Śaṅkara, however, did distinguish between three senses of being: the merely illusory (*prātibhāsika*), the empirical (*vyāvahārika;* which has unperceived existence and pragmatic efficacy), and transcendental being of one, indeterminate Brahman.

In his epistemology, Śaṅkara's followers in general accepted the point of view of the Mīmāṃsā of Kumārila's school. Like Kumārila, they accepted six ways of knowing: perception, inference, verbal testimony, comparison, nonperception, and postulation. In general, cognitions are regarded as modifications of the inner sense in which the pure spirit is reflected or as the pure spirit limited by respective mental modifications. The truth of cognitions is regarded as intrinsic to them, and a knowable fact is accepted as true so long as it is not rejected as false. In perception a sort of identity is achieved between the form of the object and the form of the inner sense; in fact, the inner sense is said to assume the form of the object. In their theory of inference, the Nyāya five-membered syllogism is rejected in favour of a three-membered one. Furthermore, the sort of inference admitted by the

Nyāya, in which the major term is universally present, is rejected, because nothing save Brahman has this property according to the system.

Śaṅkara's ethical and religious concerns

Śaṅkara regarded moral life as a necessary preliminary to metaphysical knowledge and thus laid down strict ethical conditions to be fulfilled by one who wants to study Vedānta. For him, however, the highest goal of life is to know the essential identity of his own self with Brahman, and though moral life may indirectly help in purifying the mind and intellect, over an extended period of time knowledge comes from following the long and arduous process whose three major stages are study of the scriptures under appropriate conditions, reflection aimed at removing all possible intellectual doubts about the nondualistic thesis, and meditation on the identity of *ātman* and Brahman. *Mokṣa* is not, according to Śaṅkara, a perfection to be achieved; it is rather the essential reality of one's own self to be realized through destruction of the ignorance that conceals it. God is how Brahman appears to an ignorant mind that regards the world as real and looks for its creator and ruler. Religious life is sustained by dualistic concepts: the dualism between man and God, between virtue and vice, and between this life and the next. In the state of *mokṣa*, these dualisms are transcended. An important part of Śaṅkara's faith was that *mokṣa* was possible in bodily existence. Because what brings this supreme state is the destruction of ignorance, nothing need happen to the body; it is merely seen for what it really is—an illusory limitation on the spirit.

Śaṅkara's chief direct pupils were Sureśvara, the author of *Vārttika* ("Gloss") on his *bhāṣya* and of *Naiṣkarmya-siddhi* ("Establishment of the State of Non-Action"), and Padmapāda, author of *Pañcapādika*, a commentary on the first five *pādas*, or sections, of the *bhāṣya*. These early pupils raised and settled issues that were not systematically discussed by Śaṅkara himself—issues that later divided his followers into two large groups: those who followed the *Vivaraṇa* (a work written on Padmapāda's *Pañcapādika* by one Prakāṣātman in the 12th century) and those who followed Vācaspati's commentary (known as *Bhāmatī*) on Śaṅkara's *bhāṣya*. Among the chief issues that divided Śaṅkara's followers was the question about the locus and object of ignorance. The *Bhāmatī* school regarded the individual self as the locus of ignorance and sought to avoid the consequent circularity (arising from the fact that the individual self is itself a product of ignorance) by postulating a beginningless series of such selves and their ignorances. The *Vivarana* school regarded both the locus and the object of ignorance to be Brahman and sought to avoid the contradiction (arising from the fact that Brahman is said to be of the nature of knowledge) by distinguishing between pure consciousness and valid knowledge (*pramājñāna*). The latter, a mental modification, destroys ignorance, and the former, far from being opposed to ignorance, manifests ignorance itself, as evidenced by the judgment "I am ignorant." The two schools also differed in their explanations of the finite individual. The *Bhāmati* school regarded the individual as a limitation of Brahman just as the space within the four walls of a room is a limitation of the big space. The *vivaraṇa* school preferred to regard the finite individual as a reflection of Brahman in the inner sense. As the moon is one, but its reflections are many, so also Brahman is one, but its reflections are many. Later followers of Śaṅkara, such as Śrīharṣa in his *Khaṇḍanakhaṇḍakhādya* and his commentator Citsukha, used a destructive, negative dialectic in the manner of Nāgārjuna to criticize man's basic concepts about the world.

Concepts of *bhedābheda*

The philosophies of transcendence and immanence (*bhedābheda*) assert both identity and difference between the world and finite individuals, on the one hand, and Brahman, on the other. The world and finite individuals are real and yet both different and not different from the Brahman.

Among pre-Śaṅkara commentators on the *Vedānta-sūtras*, Bhartṛprapañca defended the thesis of *bhedābheda*, and Bhāskara (*c.* 9th century) closely followed him. Bhartṛprapañca's commentary is not extant; the only known source of knowledge is Śaṅkara's reference to him in his commentary on the *Bṛhādaraṇyaka Upaniṣad*, in which Bhartṛprapañca is said to have held that though Brahman as cause is different from Brahman as effect, the two are identical inasmuch as the effect dissolves into the cause, as the waves return into the sea. Bhāskara viewed Brahman as both the material and the efficient cause of the world. The doctrine of *māyā* was totally rejected. Brahman undergoes the modifications by his own power. As waves are both different from and identical with the sea, so are the world and the finite individuals in relation to Brahman. The finite selves are parts of Brahman, as sparks of fire are parts of fire. But the finite soul exists, since beginningless time, under the influence of ignorance. It is atomic in extension and yet animates the whole body. Corresponding to the material world and the finite selves, Bhāṣkara ascribed to God two powers of self-modification. Bhāṣkara, in his theory of knowledge, distinguished between self-consciousness that is ever-present and objective knowledge that passively arises out of appropriate causal conditions but is not an activity. Mind, thus, is a sense organ. Bhāṣkara subscribed to the general Vedānta thesis that knowledge is intrinsically true, though falsity is extrinsic to it. In his ethical views, Bhāṣkara regarded religious duties as binding at all stages of life. He upheld a theory known as *jñāna-karma-samuccaya-vāda:* performance of duties together with knowledge of Brahman leads to liberation. In religious life, Bhāskara was an advocate of *bhakti*, but *bhakti* is not a mere feeling of love or affection for God, but rather is *dhyāna*, or meditation, directed toward the transcendent Brahman who is not exhausted in his manifestations. Bhāṣkara denied the possibility of liberation in bodily existence.

The *bhedābheda* point of view had various other adherents: Vijñānabhikṣu, Nimbārka, Vallabha, and Caitanya.

Concepts of the Viśistādvaita

Rāmānuja (11th century) sought to synthesize a long tradition of theistic religion with the absolutistic monism of the *Upaniṣads*, a task in which he had been preceded by no less an authority than the *Bhagavadgītā*. In his general philosophical position, he followed the *vṛttikāra* Bodhāyana, the Vākyakāra (to whom he referred but whose identity is not established except that he advocated a theory of real modification of Brahman), Nāthamuni (*c.* 1000), and his own teachers' teacher Yāmunācārya (*c.* 1050).

The main religious inspirations are from the theistic tradition of the Ālvār poet-saints and their commentators known as the Ācāryas, who sought to combine knowledge with action (*karma*) as the right means to liberation. There is also, besides the Vedic tradition, the religious tradition of *Āgamas*, particularly of the Pāñcarātra literature. It is within this old tradition that Rāmānuja's philosophical and religious thought developed.

Rāmānuja rejected Śaṅkara's conception of Brahman as an indeterminate, qualityless, and differenceless reality on the ground that such a reality cannot be perceived, known, thought of, or even spoken about, in which case it is nothing short of a fiction. In substantiating this contention, Rāmānuja undertook, in his *Śrī-bhāṣya* on the *Vedānta-sūtras*, a detailed examination of the different ways of knowing. Perception, either nonconceptualized or conceptualized, always apprehends its object as being something; the only difference between the two modes of perception being that the former takes place when one perceives an individual of a certain class for the first time and thus does not subsume it under the same class as some other individuals. Nor can inference provide one with knowledge of an indeterminate reality, because in inference one always knows something as coming under a general rule. The same holds true of verbal testimony. This kind of knowledge arises from understanding sentences. For Rāmānuja there is nothing like a pure consciousness without subject and without object. All consciousness is of something and belongs to someone. He also held that it is not true that consciousness cannot be the object of another consciousness. In fact, one's own past consciousness becomes the object of present consciousness. Consciousness is self-shining only when it reveals an object to its own owner—*i.e.*, the self.

Rāmānuja's views of Brahman

Rejecting Śaṅkara's conception of reality, Rāmānuja defended the thesis that Brahman is a being with infinitely perfect excellent virtues, a being whose perfection cannot be exceeded. The world and finite individuals are real, and together they constitute the body of Brahman. The category of body and soul is central to his way of thinking. Body is that which can be controlled and moved for the purpose of the spirit. The material world and the conscious spirits, though substantive realities, are yet inseparable from Brahman and thus qualify him in the same sense in which body qualifies the soul. Brahman is spiritual–material–qualified. Rāmānuja and his followers undertook criticisms of Śaṅkara's illusionism, particularly of his doctrine of *avidyā* (ignorance) and the falsity of the world. For Rāmānuja, such a beginningless, positive *avidyā* could not have any locus or any object, and if it does conceal the self-shining Brahman, then there would be no way of escaping from its clutches.

A most striking feature of Rāmānuja's epistemology is his uncompromising realism. Whatever is known is real, and only the real can be known. This led him to advocate the thesis that even the object of error is real—error is really incomplete knowledge—and correction of error is really completion of incomplete knowledge.

The state of *mokṣa* is not a state in which the individuality is negated. In fact, the sense of "I" persists even after liberation, for the self is truly the object of the notion of "I." What is destroyed is egoism, the false sense of independence. The means thereto is *bhakti*, leading to God's grace. But by *bhakti*, Rāmānuja means *dhyāna*, or intense meditation with love. Obligation to perform one's scriptural duties is never transcended. The state of liberation is a state of blessedness in the company of God. A path emphasized by Rāmānuja for all persons is complete self-surrender (*prapatti*) to God's will and making oneself worthy of his grace. In his social outlook, Rāmānuja was liberal; he believed that *bhakti* does not recognize barriers of caste and classes.

The doctrinal differences among the followers of Rāmānuja is not so great as among Śaṅkara's. Writers such as Sudarśana Sūri and Veṅkatanātha continued to elaborate and defend the theses of the master, and much of their writing is polemical. Some differences are to be found regarding the nature of emancipation, the nature of devotion, and other ritual matters. The followers are divided into two schools: the Uttara-kalārya, led by Veṅkatanātha, and the Dakṣiṇa-kalārya, led by Lokācārya. One of the points at issue is whether or not emancipation is destructible; another, whether there is a difference between liberation attained by mere self-knowledge and that attained by knowledge of God. There also were differences in interpreting the exact nature of self-surrender to God and the degree of passivity or activity required of the worshipper.

Madhva (born 1199?) belonged to the tradition of Vaiṣṇava religious faith and showed a great polemical spirit in refuting Śaṅkara's philosophy and in converting people to his own fold. An uncompromising dualist, he traced back dualistic thought even to some of the *Upaniṣads*. His main works are his commentaries on the *Upaniṣads*, the *Gītā*, and the *Vedānta-sūtras*. He also wrote a commentary on the *Mahābhārata* and several logical and polemical treatises.

Concepts of *Dvaita* (dualism)

He glorified difference. Five types of differences are central to Madhva's system: difference between soul and God, between soul and soul, between soul and matter, between God and matter, and that between matter and matter. His ontological framework may be stated as in Table 2. Brahman is the fullness of qualities, and by his own intrinsic nature, Brahman produces the world. The individual, otherwise free, is dependent only upon God. The Advaita concepts of falsity and indescribability of the world were severely criticized and rejected. In his epistemology, Madhva admitted three ways of knowing: perception, inference, and verbal testimony. God's existence cannot be proved; it can be learned only from the scriptures.

Bondage and release both are real and devotion is the only way to release, but ultimately it is God's grace that saves. Scriptural duties, when performed without any ulterior motive, purify the mind and help one to receive God's grace.

Among the other theistic schools of Vedānta, brief mention may be made of the schools of Nimbārka (*c.* 12th century), Vallabha (15th century), and Caitanya (16th century).

Nimbarka's philosophy is known as Bhedābheda because he emphasized both identity and difference of the world and finite souls with Brahman. His religious sect is known as the Sanaka-sampradāya of Vaiṣṇavism. Nimbārka's commentary on the *Vedānta-sūtras* is known as *Vedānta-pārijāta-saurabha* and is commented on by Śrīnivāsa in his *Vedānta-kaustubha.* Of the three realities admitted—God, souls, and matter—God is the independent reality, self-conscious, controller of the other two, free from all defects, abode of all good qualities, and both the material and efficient cause of the world. The souls are dependent, self-conscious, capable of enjoyment, controlled, atomic in size, many in number, and eternal but seemingly subject to birth and death because of ignorance and *karma.* Matter is of three kinds: nonnatural matter, which constitutes divine body; natural matter constituted by the three *guṇas*; and time. Both souls and matter are pervaded by God. Their relation is one of difference-with-nondifference. Liberation is because of a knowledge that makes God's grace possible. There is no need for Vedic duties after knowledge is attained, nor is performance of such duties necessary for acquiring knowledge.

Vallabha's commentary on the *Vedānta-sūtras* is known as *Aṇubhāṣya* ("The Brief Commentary"), which is commented upon by Puruṣottama in his *Bhāṣya-prakāśa* ("Lights on the Commentary"). His philosophy is called pure nondualism—"pure" meaning "undefiled by *māyā*."

Table 2: Madhva's Ontological Framework

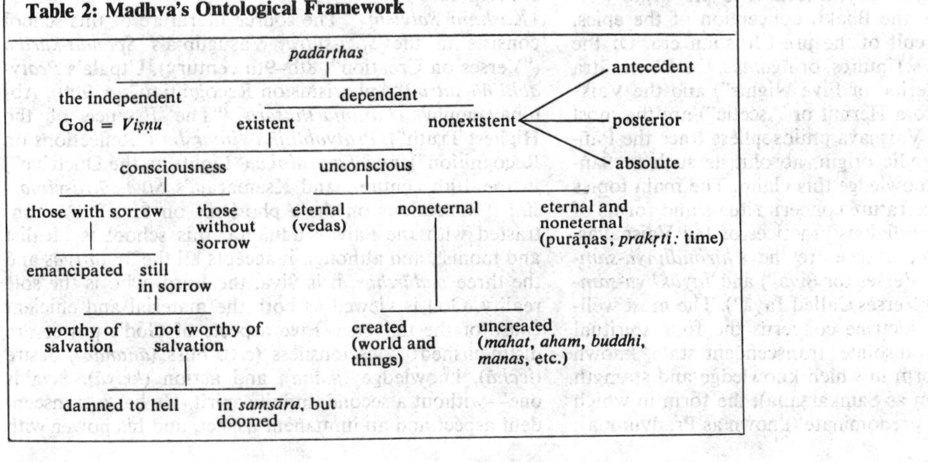

His religious sect is known as the Rudra-sampradāya of Vaiṣṇavism and also Puṣṭimārga, or the path of grace. Brahman, or Śrī Kṛṣṇa, is viewed as the only independent reality; in his essence he is existence, consciousness, and bliss, and souls and matter are his real manifestations. *Māyā* is but his power of self-manifestation. Vallabha admitted neither *pariṇāma* (of Sāṃkhya) nor *vivarta* (of Śaṅkara). According to him, the modifications are such that they leave Brahman unaffected. From his aspect of "existence" spring life, senses, and body. From "consciousness" spring the finite, atomic souls. From "bliss" spring the presiding deities, or *antaryāmins*, for whom Vallabha finds place on his ontology. This threefold nature of God pervades all beings. World is real; but *saṃsāra*, the cycle of birth and death, is unreal, and time is regarded as God's power of action. Like all other Vedāntins, Vallabha rejected the Vaiśeṣika relation of *samavaya* and replaced it by *tādātmya*, or identity. The means to liberation is *bhakti*, which is defined as firm affection for God and also loving service (*sevā*). *Bhakti* does not lead to knowledge, but knowledge is regarded as a part of *bhakti*. The notion of "grace" plays an important role in Vallabha's religious thought. He is also opposed to renunciation.

The influence of Caitanya

Caitanya (1485–1533) was one of the most influential and remarkable of the medieval saints of India. His life is characterized by almost unique emotional fervour, hovering on the pathological, which was directed toward Śrī Kṛṣṇa (the incarnation of Viṣṇu). He has not written anything, but the discourses recorded by contemporaries give an idea of his philosophical thought that was later developed by his followers, particularly by Rūpa Gosvāmin and Jīva Gosvāmin. Rūpa is the author of two great works: *Bhakti-rasāmṛta-sindhu* ("The Ocean of the Nectar of the Essence of Bhakti") and *Ujjvalanīlamani* ("The Shining Blue Jewel"). Jīva's main work is the great and voluminous *Ṣaṭsaṃdarbha*. These are the main sources of the philosophy of Bengal Vaiṣṇavism. Caitanya rejected the conception of an intermediate Brahman. Brahman, according to him, has three powers: the transcendent power that is threefold (the power of bliss, the power of being, and the power of consciousness) and the two immanent powers, namely, the powers of creating souls and the material world. Jīva Gosvāmin regarded bliss to be the very substance of Brahman who, with the totality of all his powers, is called God. Jīva distinguished between God's essential power, his peripheral power that creates the souls, and the external power (called *māyā*) that creates cosmic forms. The relation between God and his powers is neither identity nor difference, nor identity-with-difference. This relation, unthinkable and suprarational is central to Caitanya's philosophy. For Jiva, the relation between any whole and its parts is unthinkable. *Bhakti* is the means to emancipation. *Bhakti* is conceived as a reciprocal relation between man and God, a manifestation of God's power in man. The works of Jīva and Rūpa delineated a detailed and fairly exhaustive classification of the types and gradations of *bhakti*.

Vaiṣṇava schools. The main philosophers of the medieval Vaiṣṇavism have been noted above. Vaiṣṇavism, however, has a long history, traceable to the Viṣṇu worship of the Ṛgveda, the Bhakti conception of the epics, and the Vāsudeva cult of the pre-Christian era. Of the two main Vaiṣṇava scriptures, or *āgamas*, the Pāñcarātra ("Relating to the Period of Five Nights") and the Vaikhānasa ("Relating to a Hermit or Ascetic") are the most important. Though Vaiṣṇava philosophers trace the Pāñcarātra works to Vedic origin, absolutists such as Śaṅkara refused to acknowledge this claim. The main topics of the Pāñcarātra literature concern rituals and forms of image worship and religious practices of the Vaiṣṇavas. Of philosophical importance are the *Ahirbudhnya-saṃhitā* ("Collection of Verses for Śiva") and *Jayākhya-saṃhitā* ("Collection of Verses Called Jayā"). The most well-known Pāñcarātra doctrine concerns the four spiritual forms of God: the absolute, transcendent state, known as Vāsudeva; the form in which knowledge and strength predominate (known as Saṃkarṣana); the form in which wealth and courage predominate (known as Pradyumna); and the form in which power and energy predominate (known as Aniruddha). Śaṅkara identified Saṃkarṣana with the individual soul, Pradyumna with mind, and Aniruddha with the ego sense. Furthermore, five powers of God are distinguished: creation, maintenance, destruction, favour, and disfavour. *Bhakti* is regarded as affection for God and associated with a sense of his majesty. The doctrine of *prapatti*, or complete self-surrender, is emphasized.

Śaiva schools. The Śaiva schools are the philosophical systems within the fold of Śaivism, a religious sect that worships Śiva as the highest deity. There is a long tradition of Śiva worship going back to the Rudra hymns of the Ṛgveda, the Śiva-Rudra of the Vājasaneyi-Saṃhitā, the Atharvaveda, and the *Brāhmaṇas*. Mādhava in his *Sarva-darśana-saṃgraha* referred to three Śaiva systems: the Nakulīśa-Pāśupata, the Śaiva, and the Pratyabhijñā systems. The Śaiva system of Mādhava's classification probably corresponds to Śaiva-siddhānta of Tamil country, and the Pratyabhijñā is known as Kashmir Śaivism. The Śaiva-siddhānta is realistic and dualistic; the Kashmir system is idealistic and monistic.

Śaiva-siddhānta. The source literature of the Śaiva-siddhānta school consists of the *Āgamas*, Tamil devotional hymns written by Śaiva saints but collected by Nambi (*c.* 1000 AD) in a volume known as *Tirumurai*, *Śiva-jñāna-bodham* ("Understanding of the Knowledge of Śiva") by Meykaṇḍadevar (13th century), Śivācārya's *Śiva-jñāna-siddhiyār* ("Attainment of the Knowledge of Śiva"), Umāpati's *Śivaprakāśam* ("Lights on Śiva") in the 14th century, Śrīkaṇṭha's commentary on the *Vedānta-sūtras* (14th century), and Appaya Dīkṣita's commentary thereon. This school admits three categories (*padārthas*): God (Śiva or Pati, Lord), soul (*paśu*), and the bonds (*pāśa*), and the 36 principles (*tattvas*). These 36 are divided into three groups: at the top, in order of manifestation from Śiva, are the five pure principles—*śivatattva* (the essence of Śiva), *śakti* (power), *sadā-śiva* (the eternal good), *īśvara* (lord), and *śuddha-vidyā* (true knowledge); seven mixed principles—pure *māyā*, five envelopes (destiny, time, interest, knowledge, and power), and *puruṣa*, or self; and 24 impure principles beginning with *prakṛti* (this list is broadly the same as that of Sāṃkhya). Śiva is the first cause: his *śakti*, or power is the instrumental cause, *māyā* the material cause. This *māyā-śakti* is not God's essential power but is assumed by him; it is *parigraha-śakti* ("Assumed Power"). The relation of Śiva to his essential power is one of identity. Bonds are of three kinds: *karma*, *māyā*, and *avidyā*. The world and souls are real, and emancipation requires the grace of Śiva. The Śaiva-siddhānta always insisted on the preservation of the individuality of the finite soul, even in the state of emancipation, and rejected Śaṅkara's nondualism. Appaya Dīkṣita's commentary shows the tendency to attempt a reconciliation between the *Āgama* tradition of realism and pluralism with the Advaita tradition. The soul is eternal and all-pervasive, but, owing to original ignorance, it is reduced to the condition of *āṇava*, which consists in regarding oneself as finite and atomic. Knowledge of its own nature as well as God's is possible only by God's grace.

Śaivite categories and principles

Kashmir Śaivism. The source literature of this school consists in the *Śiva-sūtra*, Vasugupta's *Spanda-kārikā* ("Verses on Creation"; 8th–9th century), Utpala's *Pratyabhijñā-sūtra* ("Aphorisms on Recognition"; *c.* 900), Abhinavagupta's *Paramārthasāra* ("The Essence of the Highest Truth"), *Pratyabhijñā-vimarśini* ("Reflections on Recognition"), and *Tantrāloka* ("Lights on the Doctrine") in the 10th century, and Kṣemarāja's *Śiva-sūtra-vimarśini* ("Reflections on the Aphorisms on Śiva"). As contrasted with the Śaiva-siddhānta, this school is idealist and monist, and although it accepts all the 36 *tattvas* and the three *padārthas*, it is Śiva, the Lord, who is the sole reality. God is viewed as both the material and efficient cause of the universe. Five aspects of God's power are distinguished: consciousness (*cit*), bliss (*ānanda*), desire (*icchā*), knowledge (*jñāna*), and action (*kriyā*). Śiva is one—without a second, infinite spirit. He has a transcendent aspect and an immanent aspect, and his power with its fivefold functions constitutes his immanent aspect. The individual soul of a person is identical with Śiva; recognition of this identity is essential to liberation.

MUGHAL PHILOSOPHY

Reference has been made earlier to the Ṣūfī (Islāmic mystics), who found a resemblance between the ontological monism of Ibn al-ʿArabi and that of Vedānta. The Shaṭṭārī order among the Indian Ṣūfīs practiced Yogic austerities and even physical postures. Various minor syncretistic religious sects attempted to harmonize Hindu and Muslim religious traditions at different levels and with varying degrees of success. Of these, the most famous are Rāmānanda, Kabīr, and Gurū Nānak. Kabīr harmonized the two religions in such a manner that, to an enquiry about whether he was a Hindu or a Muslim, the answer given by a contemporary was "It is a secret difficult to comprehend. One should try to understand." Gurū Nānak rejected the authority of both Hindu and Muslim scriptures alike and founded his religion (Sikhism) on a rigorously moralistic, monotheistic basis.

Among the great Mughals, Akbar attempted, in 1581, to promulgate a new religion, Dīn-i Ilāhī, which was to be based on reason and ethical teachings common to all religions and which was to be free from priestcraft. This effort, however, was short-lived, and a reaction of Muslim orthodoxy was led by Shaykh Aḥmed Sirhindī, who rejected ontological monism in favour of orthodox unitarianism and sought to channel mystical enthusiasm along Qurʾānic (Islāmic scriptural) lines. By the middle of the 17th century, the tragic figure of Dārā Shikōh, the Mughal emperor Shāh Jahān's son and disciple of the Qādirī sufis, translated Hindu scriptures, such as the *Bhagavadgītā* and the *Upaniṣads*, into Persian and in his translation of the latter closely followed Śaṅkara's commentaries. In his *Majmaʿ al-baḥrayn* he worked out correlations between Ṣūfī and Upaniṣadic cosmologies, beliefs, and practices. During this time, the Muslim elite of India virtually identified Vedānta with Ṣūfīsm. Later, Shāh Walī Allāh's son, Shāh ʿAbd-ul-ʿAzīz, regarded Kṛṣṇa among the *awliyāʾ* (saints).

19TH- AND 20TH-CENTURY PHILOSOPHY IN INDIA AND PAKISTAN

Influence of Western philosophies

In the 19th century, India was not marked by any noteworthy philosophical achievements, but the period was one of great social and religious reform movements. The newly founded universities introduced Indian intellectuals to Western thought, particularly to the empiricistic, utilitarian, and agnostic philosophies in England, and John Stuart Mill, Jeremy Bentham, and Herbert Spencer had become the most influential thinkers in the Indian universities by the end of the century. These Western-oriented ideas served to generate a secular and rational point of view and stimulated social and religious movements, most noteworthy among them being the Brahmo (Brahma) Samaj movement founded by Rammohan Ray. Toward the later decades of the century, the great saint Ramakrishna Paramahamsa of Calcutta renewed interest in mysticism, and many young rationalists and sceptics were converted into the faith exemplified in his person. Ramakrishna taught, among other things, an essential diversity of religious paths leading to the same goal, and this teaching was given an intellectual form by Swami Vivekananda, his famed disciple.

The first Indian graduate school in philosophy was founded in the University of Calcutta during the first decades of the 20th century, and the first incumbent of the chair of philosophy was Sir Brajendranath Seal, a versatile scholar in many branches of learning, both scientific and humanistic. Seal's major published work is *The Positive Sciences of the Ancient Hindus*, which, besides being a work on the history of science, shows interrelations among the ancient Hindu philosophical concepts and their scientific theories. Soon, however, the German philosophers Kant and Hegel came to be the most studied philosophers in the Indian universities. The ancient systems of philosophy came to be interpreted in the light of German idealism. The Hegelian notion of Absolute Spirit found a resonance in the age-old Vedānta notion of Brahman. The most eminent Indian Hegelian scholar is Hiralal Haldar, who was concerned with the problem of the relation of the human personality with the Absolute, as is evidenced by his book *Neo-Hegelianism*. The most eminent Kantian scholar is K.C. Bhattacharyya.

Contributions of modern Indian philosophers

Among those who deserve mention for their original contributions to philosophical thinking are Sri Aurobindo (died 1950), Mahatma Gandhi (died 1948), Rabindranath Tagore (died 1941), Sir Muḥammed Iqbāl (died 1938), K.C. Bhattacharyya (died 1949), and Sarvepalli Radhakrishnan (1888–). Of these, Sri Aurobindo was first a political activist and then a *yogin*, Tagore and Iqbāl poets, Gandhi a political and social leader, and only Radhakrishnan and Bhattacharya university professors. This fact throws some light on the state of Indian philosophy in this century.

In his major work, *The Life Divine*, Sri Aurobindo starts from the fact of human aspiration for a kingdom of heaven on earth and proceeds to give a theoretical framework in which such an aspiration would be not a figment of imagination but a drive in nature, working through man toward a higher stage of perfection. Both the denial of the materialist and that of the ascetic are rejected as being one-sided. The gulf between unconscious matter and fully self-conscious spirit is sought to be bridged by exhibiting them as two poles of a series in which spirit continuously manifests itself. The Vedāntic concept of a transcendent and all-inclusive Brahman is sought to be harmonized with a theory of emergent evolution. Illusionism is totally rejected. The purpose of man is to go beyond his present form of consciousness. Yoga is interpreted as a technique not for personal liberation but for cooperating with the cosmic evolutionary urge that is destined to take mankind ahead from the present mental stage to a higher, supramental stage of consciousness. A theory of history, in accordance with this point of view, is worked out in his *The Human Cycle*.

Rabindranath Tagore's philosophical thinking is no less based on the *Upaniṣads*, but his interpretation of the *Upaniṣads* is closer to Vaiṣṇava theism and the Bhakti cults than to traditional monism. He characterized the absolute as supreme person and placed love higher than knowledge. In his *Religion of Man*, Tagore sought to give a philosophy of man in which human nature is characterized by a concept of surplus energy that finds expression in creative art. In his lectures on *Nationalism*, Tagore placed the concept of society above that of the modern nation state.

Mahatma Gandhi preferred to say that the truth is God rather than God is the truth, because the former proposition expresses a belief that even the atheists share. The belief in the presence of an all-pervading spirit in the universe led Gandhi to a strict formulation of the ethics of nonviolence (*ahiṃsā*). But he gave this age-old ethical principle a wealth of meaning so that *ahiṃsā* for him became at once a potent means of collective struggle against social and economic injustice, the basis of a decentralized economy and decentralized power structure, and the guiding principle of one's individual life in relation both to nature and to other persons. The unity of existence, which he called the truth, can be realized through the practice of *ahiṃsā*, which requires reducing oneself to zero and reaching the furthest limit of humility.

Influenced by the British philosopher J.M.E. MacTaggart's form of Hegelian idealism and the French philosopher Henri Bergson's philosophy of change, Muḥammed Iqbāl conceived reality as creative and essentially spiritual, consisting of egos. "The truth however is that matter is spirit," he wrote,

> in space-time reference. The unity called man is body when we look at it as acting in regard to what we call external world; it is mind or soul when we look at it as acting in regard to the ultimate aim and ideal of such acting.

Influenced by British Neo-Hegelianism in his interpretation of the Vedāntic tradition, Sarvepalli Radhakrishnan is primarily an interpreter of Indian thought to the Western world. He defends a realistic interpretation of the concept of *māyā*—thereby playing down its illusionistic connotation, a theory of intuition as the means of knowing reality, and a theory of emergent evolution of spirit (not unlike Sri Aurobindo, but without his doctrine of supermind) in nature and history. The most original among modern Indian thinkers, however, is K.C. Bhattacharya, who rejects the conception of philosophy as a construction of a worldview and undertakes a phenomenological description of the various grades of subjectivity: (1) the bodily, (2) the psychic, and (3) the spiritual. With regard to 1, he distinguishes between the objective body and the felt body and regards the latter as the most primitive level of the subjective sense of freedom from the objective world. The stage 2 includes the range of mental life from image to free thought. In introspection, the level 2 is transcended, but various levels of introspection are distinguished, all leading to greater freedom from objectivity. It would seem, however, that for Bhattacharyya absolute freedom from objectivity is a spiritual demand. According to his theory of value, value is not an adjective of the object but a feeling absolute, of which the object evaluated appears as an adjective, and his logic of alternation is a modern working out of the Jaina theories of *anekānta* (non-absolutism) and *syādvāda* (doctrine of "may be").

Both the major trends of Western thought—the analytical and the phenomenological—have exercised considerable influence in varying degrees and manners, but there has been an interest in the less doctrinaire, more logical, analytical, and phenomenological contents of the classical systems.

BIBLIOGRAPHY

General histories: S.N. DASGUPTA, *A History of Indian Philosophy*, 5 vol. (1922–55), the most comprehensive account of Indian philosophy in English, though its scholarship tends to outweigh philosophical insight; M. HIRIYANNA, *Outlines of Indian Philosophy* (1932), lucidly written, based on reliable acquaintance with original source material, but leaves out many minor, though important, schools of thought; S. RADHAKRISHNAN, *Indian Philosophy*, 2 vol. (1923–27), a very readable account written from an idealistic point of view—may often mislead; S.C. VIDYABHUSAN, *A History of the Mediaeval School of Indian Logic* (1909), still indispensable, though outdated and containing many inaccuracies; U.N. GHOSHAL, *A History of Indian Political Ideas: The Ancient Period and the Period of Transition to the Middle Ages* (1959).

Critical studies from the point of view of modern western thought: K.H. POTTER, *Presuppositions of India's Philosophies* (1963); N. SMART, *Doctrine and Argument in Indian Philosophy* (1964); and B.K. MATILAL, *Epistemology, Logic and Grammar in Indian Philosophical Analysis* (1971), three books that attempt to look at Indian philosophy from the point of view of contemporary philosophical problems, though they differ in their approaches—together they form a good introduction to the logical, dialectical, and analytical aspects of Indian philosophy.

English translations of Sanskrit sources: S. RADHAKRISHNAN and C.A. MOORE (eds.), *A Source Book in Indian Philosophy* (1957), the best one-volume collection of source materials (does not include many masterpieces of medieval works on logic and epistemology); *The Thirteen Principal Upanishads*, 2nd ed., trans. by R.E. HUME (1931); *The Bhagavadgītā*, trans. by S. RADHAKRISHNAN (1948).

Selected readings on the systems and texts: (*Upaniṣads*) R.D. RANADE, *A Constructive Survey of Upanishadic Philosophy* (1926). (*Bhagavadgītā*): SRI AUROBINDO, *Essays on the Gita* (1950). (*Mahābhārata*): E.W. HOPKINS, *The Great Epic of India* (1901). (*Cārvākas and Ājīvikas*): D. SASTRI, *A Short History of Indian Materialism, Sensationism and Hedonism* (1930); DALE RIEPE *Early Indian Philosophical Naturalism* (1954); A.L. BASHAM, *The History and Doctrines of the Ājīvikas* (1951). (*Buddhism*): B.M. BARUA *Prolegomena to a History of Buddhist Philosophy* (1918); T. STCHERBATSKY, *Buddhist Logic*, 2 vol. (Eng. trans. 1932–30; paperback edition, 1955), a work of great scholarship, marred by too hasty comparisons with 19th-century European philosophers, contains an English translation of Dharmakīrti's *Nyayavindu;* T.R.V. MURTY, *The Central Philosophy of Buddhism* (1955); M. HATTORI, *Dignāga, on Perception* (1968). (*Mīmāṃsā*): F. EDGERTON, "Some Linguistic Notes on the Mimamsa System," *Language*, 4:171–177 (1928); A.B. KEITH, *Karma-mīmāṃsā* (1921); P. SHASTRI, *Introduction to the Purva Mimamsa* (1923). (*Vedānta*): T.M.P. MAHADEVAN, *Gaudapāda: A Study in Early Vedanta* (1952); SAROJ K. DAS, *Towards a Systematic Study of the Vedānta* (1931); E. DEUTSCH, *Advaita Vedānta: A Philosophical Reconstruction* (1969); P.N. SRINIVASACHARI, *The Philosophy of Viśiṣṭādvaita* (1943). (*Vaiṣṇavism and Śaivism*): R.G. BHANDARKAR, *Vaiṣṇavism, Śaivism and Minor Religious Systems* (1913). (*Nyāya-Vaiśeṣika*): H. UI, *The Vaiśeṣika Philosophy* (1917); S.C. CHATTERJEE, *Nyāya Theory of Knowledge* (1939); K. SASTRI, *Essentials of Indian Logic* (1931); D.H. INGALLS, *Materials for the Study of Navya-Nyāya Logic* (1951). (*Sāṃkhya-Yoga*): S.N. DASGUPTA, *The Study of Patanjali* (1920); MIRCEA ELIADE, *Le Yoga: immortalité et liberté* (1954; Eng. trans., *Yoga: Immortality and Freedom*, 1958). (*Mogul philosophy*): AZIZ AHMAD, *Studies in Islamic Culture in the Indian Environment* (1964).

Contemporary Indian philosophy: R.N. TAGORE, *Religion of Man* (1931); SRI AUROBINDO, *The Life Divine* (1947); K.C. BHATTACHARYA, *Studies in Philosophy*, 2 vol. (1955–57); S. RADHAKRISHNAN, *The Reign of Religion in Contemporary Philosophy* (1920) and *Eastern Religion and Western Thought* (1939); S. RADHAKRISHNAN and J.H. MUIRHEAD (eds.), *Contemporary Indian Philosophy*, 2nd ed. (1952); P.T. RAJU, *Idealistic Thought of India* (1953).

(J.N.M.)

Indian Subcontinent, History of the

The Indian subcontinent, the great landmass of South Asia, is the home of one of the world's oldest and most influential civilizations. In this article, the subcontinent (which for historical purposes is usually called simply "India") is understood to comprise the areas of the present states of Bharat (the republic of India), Pakistan, and Bangladesh.

The earliest periods (before 1750 BC) of the history of India are known only through historical reconstructions from archaeological evidence. These early phases are conveniently divided into two periods: (1) the prehistoric period (before 2300 BC) and (2) the period of the Indus civilization (2300–1750 BC). The Indus civilization, an early urban culture in the Indus River Basin, is also known as Harappan culture or civilization after the name of one of the most important archaeological sites (Harappā) of the period. Consequently, the prehistoric period is often termed pre-Harappan to indicate that it predates the development of urban civilization in the Indus Valley.

Since early times the Indian subcontinent appears to have provided an attractive habitat for man. Toward the south it is effectively sheltered by wide expanses of ocean, which tended in ancient times to isolate it culturally, while to the north it is protected by the massive Himalayan ranges, which also sheltered it from the arctic winds and the air currents of Central Asia. Only in the northwest and northeast is there an easier access by land, and through these two sectors most of the early contacts with the outside world took place. Within the framework of hills and mountains represented by the Indo-Iranian borderlands on the west, the Indo-Burmese borderlands in the east, and the Himalayas to the north, the subcontinent may in broadest terms be divided into two major divisions: in the north are the basins of the Indus and Ganges rivers, and to the south is the block of Archaean rocks that forms the Indian Peninsula. The expansive alluvial plains of the river basins provided the environment and focus for the rise of two great phases of city life: at the end of the 3rd millennium BC the civilization of the Indus (Sindhu) Valley and during the first millennium BC that of the Ganges (Ganga). To the south of this zone, and separating it from the peninsula proper, is a belt of hills and forests, running generally from west to east and to this day largely inhabited by "tribal" people. This belt has played mainly a negative role throughout Indian history, but it is traversed by various routes linking the more attractive areas north and south of it. Toward the west through this belt flows the Narmada (Narbada) River, which has long been regarded as the symbolic boundary of North and South India.

Moving from west to east, the northern parts of India represent a series of contrasting regions, each with its own distinctive cultural history and with its own distinctive modern population. In the west, the valleys of the

Baluchistan uplands are a low-rainfall area, producing mainly wheat and barley and to this day having a low density of population. These mainly tribal people are in many respects closely akin to their Iranian neighbours. The adjacent Indus plains are also an area of extremely low rainfall, but the annual flooding of the river in ancient times, and the exploitation of its waters by canal irrigation in modern times, have given greater agricultural productivity, and the population is correspondingly denser than that of Baluchistan. The Indus Valley may be divided into three parts: In the north are the plains of the five tributary rivers of the Punjab (Panjāb). In the centre the consolidated waters of the Indus and its tributaries flow through the alluvial plains of Sind, and in the south pass naturally into the Indus Delta. East of the latter is the Thar, or Great Indian Desert, which is in turn bounded on the east by the Arāvalli Hills, the northernmost extent of the peninsular block. Beyond them is the hilly country of Rājasthān and the Mālwa Plateau. To the south is the Kāthiāwār Peninsula, forming both geographically and culturally an extension of Rājasthān. All these regions have a relatively denser population than the preceding group, but for topographical reasons they have tended to be somewhat isolated, at least during historical times.

Geography of the Indus Valley

East of the Punjab and Rājasthān, North India develops in a series of belts running broadly east to west and following the line of the foothills of the Himalayan ranges in the north. The southern belt consists of a hilly, forested area broken by the numerous escarpments of the edge of the peninsular block and comprising the Vindhya, Bhānrer, and Kaimur mountain ranges. Between the hills of central India and the Himalayas lies the Ganges Valley proper, constituting an area of high-density population, moderate rainfall, and high agricultural productivity. Archaeology suggests that, from the beginning of the 1st millennium BC, rice cultivation has played a large part in supporting this population. The Gangetic Plains divide into three major parts: to the west is the *doab*, or "mesopotamia," of the Yamuna (Jumna) and Ganges rivers; east of the confluence of these rivers lies the Middle Ganges Valley, in which population tends to increase and cultivation of rice predominates; to the southeast lies the extensive delta of the combined Ganges and Brahmaputra rivers. The Brahmaputra flows from the northeast, rising beyond the Himalayas and emerging from the mountains into the Assam plain, being bounded on the south and east by the hills of the Burmese borders. These hills are an area of extremely high rainfall, largely inhabited by tribal people, but they present no absolute barrier to communication with China and Southeast Asia, and there is plenty of evidence that influences reached India from this direction in ancient times, even if they are less prominent than those that arrived from the west.

The materials available for a reconstruction of the history of India prior to the 3rd century BC are almost entirely the products of archaeological research. Traditional and textual sources, transmitted orally for many centuries, are available from the closing centuries of the 2nd millennium BC; but their use must depend largely upon the extent to which any passage can be dated or associated with archaeological evidence. For the rise of civilization in the Indus Valley and for contemporary events in other parts of the subcontinent, the evidence of archaeology is still the principal source of information. Even when it becomes possible to read the short inscriptions of the Harappan seals, it is unlikely that they will provide much information to supplement other sources. In these circumstances it is necessary to approach the early history of India largely through the eyes of the archaeologists, and it will be wise to retain a balance between an objective assessment of archaeological data and its synthetic interpretation.

Importance of archaeological evidence

In the following pages certain terms have been used that have not always gained universal currency even among archaeologists writing about India. The Stone Age will be treated in terms of Early, Middle, and Late, because since 1961 there has been fairly general acceptance of these terms to denote the three major stages of the Indian Stone Age. The first and second appear to correspond in general typological terms with the Early and Middle Palaeolithic stages in Europe, while the third might be said to correspond with the Mesolithic. The terms Neolithic and Chalcolithic have been used very sparingly, preferring in general to name cultures broadly in terms of their methods of subsistence (when known). In India-Pakistan the two terms are used in a broadly overlapping sense. The terms pre-Harappan and Harappan are used primarily in a chronological way, but also loosely in a cultural sense, relating respectively to periods or cultures that precede the Indus civilization, and thus the appearance of city life in the Indus Valley, and to the Indus, or Harappan, civilization itself.

This account of the history of the Indian subcontinent is divided into the following sections:

I. India from the Late Stone Age to the decline of the Indus civilization (1750 BC)

THE EARLY PREHISTORIC PERIOD

Late Stone Age hunters. The oldest traces of human activity discovered so far in India-Pakistan belong to the Late Stone Age. Evidence then begins to have a direct bearing upon the later history of the subcontinent, since there are clear indications that groups of Late Stone Age hunters long continued to flourish and had contact with later settled communities of agriculturalists. Late Stone Age sites, identified by assemblages of microliths, have been discovered in large numbers in many parts of the subcontinent, from Baluchistan in the west to Bengal in the east, and from the North-West Frontier Province in the north to Sri Lanka in the south. But, as the vast majority of the finds were from surface sites, they long remained without precise dates or cultural contexts. Only in recent years have a number of cave and dune sites been excavated from which radiocarbon samples and animal remains have been obtained. These excavations are as yet incompletely published, but they have already added a new dimension to the scholarly view of the origins of Indian civilization. Three sites are particularly notable, Lānghnaj in Gujarāt, Bāgor near Udaipur in Rājasthān, and Adamgarh on the Narmada River. Bāgor has produced evidence of long occupation of a sand dune, with radiocarbon dates ranging between the 6th and 3rd millennia BC, while Adamgarh produced a date from the 6th millennium. From later phases at Bāgor and Lānghnaj copper objects were discovered as well as pottery and, in the latest level, objects of iron. It is likely that excavations in other regions will reveal equally early, if not even older, settlements of this type. The animal remains, as far as they have been analyzed, suggest that these communities subsisted mainly by hunting and collecting, but remains of domesticated species, including cattle, buffalo, sheep, and goats, are also present, at any rate in the later stages. It will be interesting to learn, as research progresses, at what dates and in what order these species appear in the sections. The equipment of these people must have included the bow and arrow, and their arrows and harpoons may be inferred to have been barbed with composite points using stone microliths. Burials have been excavated at a number of Late Stone Age sites, but only those from Lānghnaj have been studied and published. The skeletons were considerably deformed, and it is difficult to draw conclusions regarding their ethnic type, but it has been stated that they indicate traits characteristic of Mediterranoids and Veddoids.

Important sites

Thus, it is now evident that, for an as yet indefinite period before agricultural and pastoral communities appeared upon the scene in India-Pakistan, there were communities of stone-using and hunting and collecting—and perhaps fishing—peoples spread widely throughout the country; many of these communities continued to exist as recognizably separate entities for long after the appearance of the first agriculturalists, or users of copper, bronze, and even iron. The relations of these groups of hunters and agriculturalists thus present a most interesting field of research.

First settlements in Baluchistan. The Indo-Iranian borderlands form the eastern extension of the Iranian Plateau and, from many points of view, mirror the environment of the Fertile Crescent (an arc of agricultural lands extending from the Tigris–Euphrates to the Nile Basin) in the Middle East. Across the plateau, lines of communication existed from very early times, and throughout the whole area it is to be expected that settled life with agriculture and domestication of animals would have spread, once developed, without undue delay. But for whatever reason, the eastern portions are still less well known than their western counterparts, and up till now the earliest radiocarbon date for a settlement in Baluchistan is not much older than 3500 BC. It is evident, however, that settlements of some kind had existed for a considerable period prior to that date, and it may be expected that further research will reveal sites of considerably greater antiquity.

The stages of development leading to the appearance of city life in the Indus Valley may be classified as three. The first stage, at present known from southeastern Afghanistan (Mundigak), the Quetta Valley (Kili Ghul Mohammad), Kalāt (Anjira), and northern Baluchistan (Rana Ghundai), appears to have consisted of seminomadic pastoralism with some limited cultivation. All of these sites lie at relatively high levels in the valleys of Baluchi-

Stages of development before the appearance of urban life

stan or in the more open valleys of the Helmand River in southern Afghanistan. At some sites there are no traces of permanent habitations, while at others the first houses of mud brick or with pressed-earth walls occur. Stone blades and grinding stones are found, along with bone points and crude pottery, some made by pressing wet clay into baskets. The indications are that metal in the form of copper was present from the first at Mundigak, but at other sites it is not attested in this period. The people kept cattle and apparently sheep and goats (materials for study are still very limited), and cultivated club wheat and perhaps barley. The picture is of semipermanent camp sites at which a greater or lesser part of the year was spent, probably much like those of the semi-nomadic tribes of northwest Pakistan down to the present day. The first stage appears to have ended *c.* 3500 BC.

After this in Baluchistan there followed the second stage, a period of consolidation, with the development of cultivation and of pastoralism. This second stage corresponds with a time when the settlements grew in size and the houses became larger, probably indicating an increasing density of population. Copper tools became more common, and the traditions of fine painted pottery for which Baluchistan is renowned came into their own. This period also saw a marked regional diversification in the styles of pottery painting, though what, if any, wider cultural implications this may have is not yet known. One scholar suggests that this stage continued until around 2500 BC when, according to him, it passed into a third stage—one of fully developed sedentary village life, with regionalization but with growing evidence of interregional contacts. This latter third stage coincides with the transition to urbanization in the Indus Valley, or at Mundigak.

The climate and geography of the valleys of Baluchistan make large-scale cultivation impossible, and hence it is probable that pressure was felt to expand to adjacent regions as the density of population increased. It appears that a movement of this sort eastward toward the Indus plains took place around the end of the 4th millennium. This movement is as yet not well documented, but the evidence is sufficient to testify that in the south, on the northern flank of the Indus Delta and in the hills adjoining the plains, a group of sites were settled at this time. Of these Amrī has been recently excavated by J.M. Casal, and it has been shown that during the first period a long development took place, with features of culture recalling those of Baluchistan. Several of the sites of this period appear to have been surrounded by massive defensive walls, in some cases perhaps as defense from floods but in others clearly as defense against men or animals. Two radiocarbon dates and other indications suggest that the pre-Harappan occupation at Amrī lasted from *c.* 3000 to *c.* 2300 BC.

Early settlements in the Indus Valley. It must have been at some such site as Amrī that the enormous agricultural potentials of the Indus floodplains were first appreciated. Rejuvenated by an annual deposit of silt, these plains offer the prospect of food production employing a minimum of skill, labour, and implements. It would seem that the pattern was repeated over a wide area in the succeeding centuries. At Kot Diji to the north of Amrī a similar settlement was established around 2600 BC, situated on a small outcrop of rocks near one of the flood channels east of the Indus. It is probable that Mohenjo-daro, some 30 miles away across the river, was also the site of a similar settlement; and it is now known that there was another situated beneath the later city of Harappā some 300 miles to the northeast in the Punjab. Another pre-Harappan settlement, dating from around 2450 BC, was established at Kalibangan on the banks of the now dry Sarasvatī River in north Rājasthān, over 100 miles southeast of Harappā. This site recently has been carefully excavated by the Archaeological Survey of India. Here, too, the mud-brick houses were contained within a broad surrounding wall of brick, but the houses lack the regular alignment of those of the later Indus civilization, and the bricks are of a different size. Perhaps the most exciting find of this period at Kalibangan is part of

Kalibangan

the plowed surface of a field, with furrows running in two directions, just as in the modern plowing of the region. It is too soon to piece together a coherent account of the life of these people. Objects of copper are present from the beginning at Amrī, but they are reportedly very rare at Kot Diji and rare also at Kalibangan. A stone-blade industry was a regular feature, and at Kot Diji leaf-shaped arrowheads of stone, recalling those of contemporary Baluchistan, are reported. Other objects include querns (hand mills for grinding grain), steatite beads and shell bangles, and (from Kot Diji) a fragment of a terra-cotta bull anticipating a Harappan type. Some of the painted pottery recalls that of northern Baluchistan; some at Amrī has a tendency to geometric patterns, again recalling Baluchistan; while the pottery from Kalibangan in particular has a strongly individual character that distinguishes it from the rest and that appears to represent the beginnings of a process of Indianization. In spite of these differences there are many common traits —some direct anticipations of the mature Harappan, or urban, culture—at all the sites, and they give the impression of an overriding uniformity throughout the considerable area they cover.

Some idea of the extent of this pre-Harappan phase of settlement can be gauged when recently reported discoveries from the vicinity of Dera Ismāīl Khān and Taxila (Sarai Khola) are included. These indicate that there were sites almost from the mouth of the Indus to the foothills of the Himalayas and from west of the Indus to well beyond the modern borders of India. Indeed, by this time such a distribution begins to approximate that of the Harappan civilization itself. Thus, this pre-Harappan phase in the Indus Valley and the Punjab must now be discussed as much because of its extent as because of the suggestions of cultural homogeneity, and because it can be seen to be antecedent to the urban stage that succeeds it in all these areas.

First settlements east of the Indus system. It is still not at all clear at what date settlements of agriculturalists or pastoralists first appeared east of the Indus system, but available evidence suggests that this development took place in pre-Harappan or pre-urban times. Nor is it clear whether the highly individual character of the remains indicates movements from the west, via the Iranian Plateau; movements from the east, from the area of South China or Southeast Asia; or a primarily local and spontaneous development. Probably the truth includes elements of all three of these possibilities. As indicated above, there were groups of Late Stone Age hunters spread throughout India-Pakistan, and some evidence points to their having made a major contribution to the cultures that developed in peninsular India; other traits strongly suggest the movement of peoples from the direction of Iran; and still others appear to favour the arrival of influences from the east. A further complicating factor is that in not all of these regions is there definite evidence to associate the "Neolithic" ground or polished stone axes found there with actual settlements from which the date and other aspects of the culture (including details of economy and subsistence) may be gauged. Yet when evidence has become available, it has in each case tended to support the hypothesis that this development began in pre-Harappan times, even if it continued in some instances long after the Indus civilization had disappeared. The coexistence of groups of different cultural levels in neighbouring areas has always been a special feature of India.

Stone axes

Four main areas have attracted attention through the discovery of very large numbers of stone axes. The first is the Vale of Kashmir, where at Burzahom a settlement has been excavated revealing a people who dug deep pits, apparently as dwellings for protection from the cold, and who made a burnished gray pottery. Radiocarbon samples indicate that this settlement was already in existence by *c.* 2375 BC and was continued down to the arrival of iron (that is, the opening of the 1st millennium BC). A series of bone and antler harpoons and needles was also discovered. The ground-stone axes are of an unspecialized type and do not throw much light upon the cultural affinities of the group. There is as yet no clear evidence of what (if any) grains were cultivated or of what animals were domesticated, but evidently the hunt played a large part in the economy. It is strange that there is so far no direct evidence of cultural contact with the Indus civilization, even though the Kashmir Neolithic culture flourished at the same time. There are also a number of curious traits, including some stone tools and the custom of burying dogs or animals of the hunt in ritual fashion, that appear to indicate contacts with regions far to the north of the Himalayas rather than with any other parts of India or Pakistan.

The second main area in which stone axes have been discovered is located in Mysore. In the northern parts of Mysore the nucleus from which stone-ax-using pastoralists spread to many parts of the southern peninsula has been located. The earliest radiocarbon dates obtained in this area are from ash mounds formed by the burning on these sites of great masses of cow dung inside cattle pens. These indicate that the first settlers were semi-nomadic and that they had large herds of zebu cattle. The earliest dates go back to *c.* 2400 BC. A number of settlements have been excavated in recent years in this region, but so far they have produced only dates from the 2nd millennium, suggesting that the culture continued with little change for many centuries. The early sites produced distinctive burnished gray pottery, smaller quantities of black-on-red painted pottery, stone axes, and bone points, and in some instances evidence of a stone-blade industry. The axes have a generally oval section and triangular form with pointed butts. Cattle bones are in the majority; those of sheep or goats are less common but are also certainly present. There is as yet no report of metal from the earliest period, probably because of its extreme scarcity rather than because of a total absence.

Stone axes of a generally similar form have been found widely throughout the southern peninsula and may be taken as indications of the spread of pastoralists throughout the region during the 2nd millennium BC.

A third concentration of ground-stone tools has been found in the hills of Assam. These have as yet barely been located in actual settlements, but in the few excavations of cultural deposits that have been made so far they are found to be associated with a crude cord-impressed pottery, suggestive of the fabric of Chinese Neolithic wares. A number of the axes have been ground to a rectangular section, again suggestive of Chinese forms. But this culture is still undated, and little more can be said of its age or affinities.

Finally, in a fourth area—throughout the hills and forests of central India—ground-stone axes are found to be widely distributed. In these areas the major finds are from the surface and no early sites have been excavated as yet. These finds must be treated with caution, since stone axes occur in settlements throughout the area down to the 1st millennium BC. But there is reason to expect that further research may reveal sites of the early period in this area also.

These developments have been discussed at some length because, problematic though much of the evidence may be, they may be inferred to provide (at least in some regions) a major element of the population and culture of succeeding periods. Also, if the relations between the Indus cities and adjacent regions are to be understood, it is necessary to know something of the cultural levels of the peoples they encountered. The technical equipment of these "Neolithic" cultures may have had certain common features, but both the technical equipment and the economies show profound differences. Thus, there is no evidence of cattle or domestication in Kashmir, while cattle seem to have been the mainstay in Mysore. A microlithic blade industry developed as one element in the south, while in Kashmir there was none. The burnished gray pottery of these two areas stands in complete contrast to the cord-impressed pottery of Assam and other localities. Much more work needs to be done before the questions raised can be dealt with and the origins, relationships, and later histories of these Neolithic cultures properly understood.

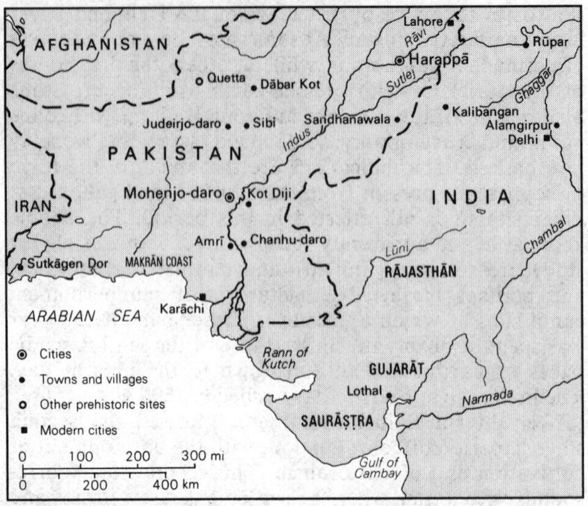

Principal sites of the Indus civilization.

Adapted from Sir Mortimer Wheeler, *Civilizations of the Indus Valley and Beyond* (1966), Thames and Hudson, Ltd., London, and McGraw-Hill Book Company, New York; original map by Shalom Schotten

THE INDUS CIVILIZATION

Origins. It has been seen above how the oldest settlements of agriculturalists in India-Pakistan appear to have been in the upland valleys of Baluchistan. Throughout this area settlements occur during the 4th millennium, perhaps earlier. By the beginning of the 3rd millennium there is evidence of a fairly dramatic extension of settlements of agriculturalists onto the floodplains of the Indus, where there were almost unlimited possibilities for agriculture. This appears to have developed first in the south, in the vicinity of the modern Indus Delta region (which was considerably smaller at that time than it is today), and to have spread north and east during succeeding centuries, reaching Kalibangan only around the middle of the millennium. The size of Kalibangan, the only settlement for which there is any reasonable estimate, was considerable—roughly 240 by 180 metres (800 by 600 feet). It may be inferred that by the middle of the 3rd millennium the population was expanding rapidly, and the number of settlements and probably the area settled grew in the same manner. Thus, these centuries may be taken as a time of incipient urbanization.

Agriculture and the rise of cities

It is striking that when Sir John Marshall and his colleagues completed the first round of excavations at Mohenjo-daro, Harappā, and Chanhu-daro (before World War II), scarcely any traces of this pre-Harappan stage had been uncovered or recognized, and hence even Stuart Piggott in 1948 could still write of the Indus civilization as having "no known beginnings, no tentative early phases." Hence some writers also tried to explain its origins in terms of immigration from outside, for example from the cities of Mesopotamia. These views must be reconsidered in the light of more recent discoveries, which reveal a widespread local culture as the direct antecedent, even if there are also indications that some sort of external influence contributed to the rise of the Indus cities. Suffice it to say that somewhere around or after 2300 BC a combination of causes led to the fairly profound changes that mark the end of the pre-Harappan stage at all the sites so far known and the appearance of the mature Harappan or urban phase. At two sites, there is evidence that the transformation may have been a violent one. At Kot Diji and at Amrī thick layers of ash suggestive of a major conflagration were revealed. At other sites, particularly Kalibangan, the evidence is less clear and the transformation may well have been peaceful. This need not imply that the Harappan culture did not owe an important debt to stimuli, probably in the form of trade arriving from Mesopotamia, where the empire of Sargon of Akkad (2334–2279 BC) heralded a period of unprecendented foreign contacts; nor that the particular events that initiated the urbanization may not have coincided with some sort of incursions of people, perhaps from southern Baluchistan or beyond, where the Kulli culture had flourished for some time, or even simultaneously from northern Baluchistan. Rather it may indicate that the economic potentials and expanding population on which the civilization were based were already present within the Indus valley itself.

The nature and significance. The Indus civilization marks the culmination of a period of rapid development. Seen in this light it appears as an indigenous response to the challenge of the environment. The direct contact with the civilization of Mesopotamia must have provided a strong incentive to this development, but the process itself must be seen as indigenous. Nearly all the earlier writers have sensed the Indianness of the civilization, even when they have been largely unable to describe or explain it. Thus, V. Gordon Childe wrote that:

The unique character of the new civilization

> India confronts Egypt and Babylonia by the 3rd millennium with a thoroughly individual and independent civilization of her own, technically the peer of the rest. And plainly it is deeply rooted in Indian soil. The Indus civilization represents a very perfect adjustment of human life to a specific environment. And it has endured; it is already specifically Indian and forms the basis of modern Indian culture.

Even before the Indus Valley script (found on seals) is read, the force of Childe's words can be appreciated: the attention paid to domestic bathrooms, the drains, and the Great Bath at Mohenjo-daro can all be compared with elements in the later Indian civilization. The bullock carts with a framed canopy, called *ikkā*s, and boats are little changed to this day. The absence of pins, the love of bangles and of elaborate nose ornaments are all peculiarly Indian. The religion of the Indus also is replete with suggestions of traits known from later India. The significance of the bull, the tiger, and the elephant; the composite animals; the seated yogi god of the seals; the tree spirits and the objects resembling the Śiva *liṅga* (a device, symbolic of the god Śiva, that has a phallic shape) of later times—all these are suggestive of enduring forms in later Indian civilization.

It is still impossible to do more than guess at the social organization or the political and administrative control implied by this vast area of cultural uniformity. The evidence of widespread trade in many commodities, the apparent uniformity of weights and measures, the common script, the uniformity—almost common currency—of the seals, all indicate some measure of political and economic control and point to the great cities Mohenjo-daro and Harappā as their centres. The presence of the great granaries on the citadel mounds in these cities and of the "citadels" themselves suggests, partly on the analogies of the cities of Mesopotamia, the existence of priest-kings, or at least of a priestly oligarchy, that controlled the economy and civil government. The intellectual mechanism of this government and the striking degree of control implicit in it are still matters of speculation. Nor can scholars yet speak with any certainty regarding relations between the cities and surrounding villages. Much more research needs to be done, on many such topics, before the full character of the Indus civilization can be revealed.

Chronology. Until radiocarbon dating became available, the chronolgy of these events, and indeed of the whole life of the Indus civilization, was dependent upon often tenuous cross-dating with Mesopotamia for objects of Indian origin discovered in the excavations there. These indicated a central period of 2300 to 2000 BC, with probable extensions at either end, and led the British archaeologist Sir Mortimer Wheeler to propose the generally accepted overall span of 2500 to 1700 BC. Radiocarbon dating has, in general, tended to confirm the correctness of this view. On the basis of some 30 samples, mainly from Kalibangan, it would appear that at both that site and Kot Diji the beginning of the urban phase—that is to say, the mature Harappan—was as late as 2150 to 2100 BC. Even if, as appears probable, it was somewhat earlier at Mohenjo-daro (which may be regarded as the epicentre of the whole civilization), it is not likely that the crucial transformation took place much before 2300 BC. The end of the civilization is even more unclear, but it appears likely that the mature Harappan culture came to a close around 1750 BC, to be succeeded at Harappā, Chanhu-daro, and other sites by late or post-Harappan phases. Thus, the present indications are that the mature Harappan civilization had a time span of not more than five centuries, rather than the 1,000 years it was formerly allotted.

Extent. All the earlier writers have stressed the remarkable uniformity of the products of the Harappan civilization, and for this reason they provide a definite hallmark for its settlements. The present evidence suggests that, if the outermost sites are joined by lines, the area enclosed will be a little less than 500,000 square miles—considerably larger than modern Pakistan—and if, as is generally inferred, this cultural uniformity coincided with some sort of political and administrative unity, the size of the resulting "empire" is truly vast. Within this area over 70 sites have been identified, the great majority of which are on the plains of the Indus or its tributaries or on the now dry course of the ancient Sarasvatī River (now Ghaggar or Hakra), which flowed south of the Sutlej and then southward to the Indian Ocean, east of the main course of the Indus itself. Outside the Indus system a few sites occur on the Makrān Coast, the westernmost of which is at Sutkāgen Dor, near the modern frontier with Iran. These sites were probably ports or trading posts, supporting the sea trade with the Persian Gulf, and were established in what otherwise remained a largely separate cultural region. The uplands of Baluchistan, while showing clear evidence of trade and contact with the Indus civilization, appear to have remained outside the direct Harappan rule.

To the east of the Indus Delta other coastal sites are found beyond the marshes of Kutch (Kacch) and in the interior of the Kāthiāwār Peninsula (Saurāṣṭra). The most important thus far is the estuarine trading post at Lothal on the Gulf of Cambay. Other coastal sites have been claimed on the mainland in Gujarāt, but it is doubtful if any were actually established during Harappan times. West of the Indus River a number of important sites are situated on the alluvial Kacchi plain toward Sibi and Quetta. This area may have been one of the routes by which cultural influence from Baluchistan reached the Indus Valley. East of the Indus system, toward the north, a number of sites occur right up to the edge of the Himalayan foothills, where at Alamgirpur, east of Delhi, the easternmost Harappan (or perhaps, more properly, Late Harappan) settlement has been discovered and partly excavated. If the area covered by these sites is compared with that of the pre-Harappan settlements, it will be seen that there is an expansion in several directions, along the coast to both the west and east, and eastward through the Punjab toward the Ganges-Yamuna *doab*.

Planning and architecture. The Harappan sites range from extensive cities to small villages or outposts. The two largest are Mohenjo-daro and Harappā, each perhaps originally about a mile square in overall dimensions. Each shares a characteristic layout, oriented roughly north–south with a great fortified "citadel" mound to the west and a larger "lower city" to the east. A similar layout is also discernible in the somewhat smaller town of Kalibangan (originally perhaps about 400 metres, or 1,300 feet, square), and several other major settlements appear to have shared this scheme. Other large sites are Dābar Kot in the Loralai Valley of northern Baluchistan; Amrī, Chanhu-daro, and Judeirjo-daro in Sind; Sandhanawala in Bahāwalpur; and Rūpar in the Punjab. Among the smaller sites, special interest attaches to Lothal, where a number of unique and problematic features were discovered in excavations. Of all the sites, Harappā, Mohenjo-daro, Kalibangan, and Lothal have been most extensively excavated, and more can be said of their original layout and planning. Thus, they are considered in greater detail below.

Layout of cities

The layout of the cities commands respect. At the three major sites, the citadel mound is on a north–south axis and about twice as long as it is broad. The lower city is laid out in a grid pattern of streets; at Kalibangan these were of regularly controlled widths, the major streets running through, while the minor lanes were sometimes offset, creating different sizes of blocks. At all three sites the citadel was protected by a massive, defensive wall of brick, which at Kalibangan was strengthened at intervals by square or rectangular bastions. At Kalibangan traces of a somewhat less substantial wall around the lower town have also been discovered. In all three cases the city was situated close by a river, although in modern times the rivers have deserted their former courses.

The most common building material at every site was brick, but the proportions of burnt brick to unburnt mud brick vary. Mohenjo-daro employs burnt brick, perhaps because timber was more readily available, while mud brick was reserved for fillings and mass work. Kalibangan, on the other hand, reserved burnt brick for bathrooms, wells, and drains. Most of the domestic architecture at Kalibangan was in mud brick. Brick was generally bonded in courses of alternate headers and stretchers, the so-called English bond. Stone was rarely, if ever, employed structurally. Timber was occasionally used as a lacing for brickwork, particularly in large-scale work such as the defenses or the granary at Mohenjo-daro. The common bricks were made in an open mold, but for special purposes sawn bricks were also employed. Timber was used for the universal flat roofs, and in some instances the sockets indicate square cut beams with spans of as much as 14 feet (four metres).

Shops, workshops, and houses

The houses were invariably entered from the side lanes, the walls to the main streets presenting a blank brick facade, broken only by the drainage chutes. Apart from domestic structures, a wide range of shops and craft workshops have been encountered, including potters' kilns, dyers' vats, and the shops of metalworkers, shellworkers, and bead makers. There is surprisingly little evidence of places of worship, although at Mohenjo-daro a number of possible temples were unearthed in the lower city, and other buildings of a ritual character were reported in the citadel. The size of houses varies very considerably. At the one extreme are single-roomed barracks, with cooking and bathing areas formed within by partition walls, and at the other are large houses around a central courtyard or sometimes with a set of intersecting courtyards, each with its own adjoining rooms. Nearly all the larger houses had private wells. In many cases brick stairways led to what must have been upper stories or flat roofs. Almost every house had at least one bathroom, and there is also evidence of bathrooms or privies. The wastes from these bathrooms were carried by a drainage channel to a chute built in the thickness of the wall, in turn emptying into the main street drains. A number of pottery drainpipes also have been discovered. The bathrooms were usually indicated by the fine quality of the brickwork in the floor and by these drains. Some of the smaller examples were probably used as privies. The flooring of common rooms was of either beaten earth or brick, and for certain special purposes floors were made of sawn brick.

Important sites. *Mohenjo-daro.* The mounds of Mohenjo-daro lie near the right bank of the Indus in the Lārkāna district of Sind. The excavations revealed that occupation continued to a depth of about 30 feet below the modern level of the plain, because of the annual deposition of alluvial silt during the floods. The lowest levels are thus below the modern water table and are still largely unexcavated. The main features of the layout of Mohenjo-daro, with a citadel to the west and a lower city and grid of streets to the east, have already been alluded to above. Enough has been said of the general features of the lower city to make it unnecessary to say more of the considerable areas excavated in that part. The citadel, however, demands further attention. In the citadel Sir John Marshall discovered a massive platform of mud brick and clay approximately 20 feet in depth, above which were six main building levels. Under this platform lay the remains of the early period. The upper strata he designated as the intermediate and late periods. It appears that the mature Indus culture embraces all three of these periods and thus that any pre-Harappan remains must lie still lower. It is probable, but by no means certain, that the platform was raised as protection against floods. Both it and the great brick defensive wall around the perimeter were built at the beginning of the intermediate period.

The Great Bath

The main buildings of the citadel apparently belong to the same period. The most striking of these is the Great Bath, which occupies a central position in the better preserved northern half of the citadel. It is built of fine brickwork, measures 39 by 23 feet (12 by seven metres), and is eight feet (two metres) lower than the surrounding pavement. The floor of the bath consists of two skins of sawn brick set on edge in gypsum mortar, with a layer of bitumen sealer sandwiched between the skins. Water was evidently supplied by a large well in an adjacent room, and an outlet in one corner of the bath led to a high corbelled drain disgorging on the west side of the mound. The bath was reached by flights of steps at either end, originally finished with timbered treads set in bitumen. The significance of this extraordinary structure can only be guessed at, but it has generally been thought that it is linked with some sort of ritual bathing. To the north and east of the bath were groups of rooms that evidently were also designed for some special function, probably associated with the group of administrators or priests who controlled not only the city but the great state which it dominated. To the west of the bath a complex of brick platforms about five feet high and separated from each other by narrow passages formed a podium of some 150 by 75 feet (50 by 25 metres), which has been identified by Sir Mortimer Wheeler as the base of a great granary similar to that known at Harappā. Below the granary were brick loading bays. In the southern part of the mound an oblong "assembly hall" was discovered, having four rows of fine brick plinths, presumably to take wooden columns. In a room adjacent to this hall a stone sculpture of a seated male figure was discovered and nearby a number of large worked-stone rings, possibly of some architectural significance. In view of the scarcity of all kinds of stone or sculpture at Mohenjo-daro, it seems certain that this area was invested with some special significance and may well have been a temple or connected with some religious cult.

Harappā. The vast mounds at Harappā stand on the left bank of the now dry course of the Rāvi River in the Punjab. The ruins attracted the attention of travellers early in the 19th century and were visited by General Cunningham in 1853 and 1873. Between these years they provided a source of ballast for local railway construction, and irreparable damage appears to have been done. They were excavated between 1920 and 1934 by the Archaeological Survey of India, in 1946 by Sir Mortimer Wheeler, and more recently by the Pakistan Archaeological Department. When first discovered, the extensive surviving brick ramparts led to the site's being described as a ruined brick castle. The lower city is partly occupied by a modern village, and it has been seriously disturbed by erosion and brick robbers. The citadel, to the west, is roughly a parallelogram on plan, measuring approximately 400 by 200 metres (1,300 by 650 feet). Excavation here revealed a great platform of mud brick about 20 feet in thickness, with a massive brick wall around the perimeter. Below the defenses were discovered traces of the pre-Harappan period, and in the uppermost levels an intrusive pottery named after its presence in the nearby site known as cemetery H was found alongside the normal Harappan pottery. The excavations were not extensive enough to reveal the layout of the interior, but about six building periods were discovered above the platform. The most interesting remains were discovered immediately north of the citadel, close to the bed of the river. Here there were a series of circular platforms evidently intended to hold mortars for pounding grain; a remarkable series of brick plinths, which are inferred to have formed the podium for two rows of six granary buildings, each of 50 by 20 feet and of a different design from those at Mohenjo-daro; a series of pear-shaped furnaces, apparently used for metallurgy; and two rows of single-roomed barracks, which have generally been assigned to a coolie or "slave" community. Two other dis-

Granary buildings

coveries at Harappā were made to the south of the citadel. Here two cemeteries were found—"R. 37," belonging to the Harappan period, and "H," dating from the late or even post-Harappan period. These contained different styles of burial and will be discussed below.

Kalibangan. Third place in magnitude and importance among excavated Harappan sites must now be accorded Kalibangan. Excavations by the Archaeological Survey of India have only recently been completed and the results are still largely unpublished. Kalibangan stands on the left bank of the dry bed of the Ghaggar River in northern Rājasthān. As mentioned above, a pre-Harappan settlement lies beneath the later remains, and the main Harappan township has a layout strikingly similar to that of Mohenjo-daro and Harappā. In the lower town excavation has revealed as many as nine building phases. The citadel mound is a parallelogram on a plan of about 130 metres (430 feet) on the east–west axis and 260 metres (850 feet) on the north–south. The whole site has been drastically reduced by brick robbers, but careful excavation revealed the foundation courses of an accurately laid rhomboid central section with oblong bastions at each corner and smaller bastions on the north and south walls. The principal access was from the south via a flight of steps. Access from the north was via a narrow postern reached by a stairway, beyond which was a further rhomboid section, having an inset gateway in the northwest corner, near the riverbank. Traces of a brick wall around the lower town were also encountered. The central sector of the citadel contained a series of high brick platforms divided by narrow passages. The upper parts of these platforms had been very seriously damaged, and their function is at present mysterious, but they do not appear to have been the foundation for a granary. The northern sector contained normal domestic housing. A cemetery was discovered a short distance to the west of the town. It may be expected that when the excavation of this site is published, it will add greatly to knowledge of the Indus civilization.

Lothal. One other among the excavated sites deserves special attention; this is Lothal, a small settlement built on low-lying ground near a tributary of the Sābarmatī River on the west side of the Gulf of Cambay. It appears to have served as a port or trading station. Its layout is distinctive: the site is roughly rectangular, measuring about 360 metres (1,180 feet) on the long north–south axis and 210 metres (690 feet) on the east–west. It was surrounded by a massive brick wall, probably used for flood protection. The southeastern quadrant takes the form of a great platform of brick with earth filling, rising to a height of about four metres. On this were built a series of further smaller platforms with intersecting air channels, reminiscent of the granary at Mohenjo-daro, with overall dimensions of about 48.5 by 42.5 metres (159 by 139 feet). Behind this block were other buildings including a row of 12 bathrooms with connected drains, also strongly reminiscent of those found on the citadel at Mohenjo-daro. The remaining enclosed area was evidently taken up by houses and shops. Among the significant finds were a bead maker's factory and the shops of goldsmiths and coppersmiths. The main street ran from north to south.

The Lothal dock

The most unexpected discovery at Lothal, however, was a great brick basin measuring some 219 by 37 metres with extant brick walls of 4.5 metres in height. This lay east of the settlement, alongside the platform on which the granary block stood. At one end of the basin was a small sluice or spillway with a locking device.

The excavator has inferred that the basin was a dock to which ships could be brought from the nearby estuary via an artificial channel that would have been kept clear of silt by the controlled flow of water from the spillway. This view has not been universally accepted, but no other explanation of the function of the basin appears to be so satisfactory. A cemetery was found outside the perimeter of the wall, west of the site. The final report on this excavation also is not yet published.

Other important sites. Mention has been made above of the pre-Harappan settlements at Amrī and Kot Diji in Sind. Each of these lies beneath a Harappan settlement, but neither compares in size with the major cities. Moreover, the area hitherto excavated is comparatively small, and therefore little can be said regarding the later period except that in each case there are the same indications of the cultural uniformity that dominates all aspects of the civilization. The excavator at Amrī divides the period into four phases, the last being equivalent to the post-Harappan phase named after the type-site of Jhukar. Chanhu-daro is another site in Sind, some 20 miles east of Amrī, excavated in 1935–36, and showing three phases of Harappan culture followed by the distinctive Jhukar phase and a subsequent phase with coarse gray pottery, probably dating to *c.* 1000 BC and named after the type-site of Jhangar. The Harappan remains were characteristic, and a remarkable bead maker's factory was also discovered. Another excavated site is at Rūpar northwest of Chandīgarh in the Punjab, but the report on this work is not yet published.

Population. There have been two independent estimates of the population of Mohenjo-daro. Both are based on an estimation of the original area covered and the density of the people living there, using traditional settlements in the region in recent times for comparison. H.T. Lambrick proposed a figure of 35,000 for Mohenjo-daro and a roughly similar figure for Harappā; while W.A. Fairservis estimated the former at around 41,250 and the latter around 23,500. These figures are probably conservative. It would be possible to produce estimates of the population for other sites along similar lines—notably for Kalibangan, of which the lower city has an area about one-fifth that of Mohenjo-daro.

Recently the physical type of skeletons recovered from Harappan sites has been studied in much greater detail than hitherto. The results have shown that the earlier classifications of very small samples that included a variety of racial types—Mongoloid, Proto-Australoid, Mediterranean, and Alpine—are largely meaningless and that the Harappan population was far more homogeneous than has so far been supposed. The people of Mohenjo-daro and Harappā appear to have been tall, long-headed, and high-domed; they were markedly broad-nosed. The population of Lothal seems to have had a more notably brachycephalic (broad-skulled) element. To postulate the presence of several distinct races thus appears to be erroneous on the basis of this evidence.

Agriculture and animal husbandry. It is certain that such great concentrations of population had never been seen in India-Pakistan before that date. Nor could the hunting–fishing and collecting economy of the Late Stone Age groups, nor the small-scale agriculture of the dry valleys of Baluchistan and of the settlements east of the Indus, have sustained such numbers. Clearly the exploitation of the Indus floodplains and the use of the plow attested in pre-Harappan times by finds in Kalibangan were matters of supreme importance. Lambrick has shown how the traditional exploitation of the floods could provide a simple means of growing the principal crops without even plowing, manuring, or using major irrigation. The main cereals would be sown at the end of the inundation on land that had recently emerged from the floods, and the crop would be harvested in March or April. Other crops might be sown in embanked fields at the beginning of the floods so that they could receive necessary water while growing and be harvested in the autumn. Wheat samples from the Indus cities have been identified as of two subspecies of *Triticum sativum*, *vulgare* and *compactum*, and of *Triticum sphaerococcum*. Barley is also found, of the species *Hordeum vulgare*, variety *nudum* and variety *hexastichum*. Rice is recorded in Harappan times at Lothal in Gujarāt, but whether wild or cultivated is not yet clear. Other crops include dates, melon, sessamum, and varieties of leguminous plants, such as field peas. From Chanhu-daro seeds of mustard (most probably *Brassica juncea*) were obtained. Finally, there is evidence that cotton was cultivated and used for textiles.

Principal crops and domesticated animal species

A number of domesticated animal species have been found in excavations at the Harappan cities. The Indian humped cattle (*Bos indicus*) were most frequently encountered, though whether along with a humpless variety, such as that shown on the seals, is not clearly established. The buffalo (*Bos bubalis*) is less common and may have been wild. Sheep and goats occur, as does the Indian pig (*Sus cristatus*). The camel is present as well as the ass (*Equus asinus*). Bones of domestic fowl are not uncommon; these fowl were domesticated from the indigenous jungle fowl. Finally, the cat and dog were both evidently domesticated. Present, but not necessarily as a domesticated species, is the elephant. The horse is possibly present but extremely rare and apparently only present in the last stages of the Harappan period.

Communications. It is clear that to achieve the degree of uniformity of material culture evidenced in the excavations, considerable contact must have been maintained between the towns and cities of the Indus state. Such contact may have been by both land and river, just as the foreign trade must have employed both overland and sea routes. For land travel the predominant means was probably the pack bullock, camel, or ass. All of these animals are still, or were until recently, used for pack transport in the more remote country districts of India-Pakistan. For travel on the flat alluvial plains, the bullock cart was probably the main vehicle. Terra-cotta models of such carts, apparently very little different from the modern Indian cart, are frequently encountered. For the transport of persons, smaller carts, with a body raised above the level of the axle and a framed canopy (much like the modern *ikkā*), are known from small bronze models. Several representations of boats also occur. They are mostly of simple design without masts or sails, and would be more suitable for river travel than for sea travel. A terra-cotta model of another type of boat with a socket for mast and eye holes for rigging was discovered at Lothal. This appears to be a somewhat more seaworthy vessel. The dock basin at Lothal could provide berth for ships of the size of the country craft that still ply between India and the Persian Gulf. Heavy pierced stones discovered in the vicinity of the dock basin at Lothal were assumed by the excavator to be similar to stones still used by the local boatmen as anchors.

Craft and technology. The Indus civilization reveals a wide range of crafts and technical skills. It may be remarked that while these skills ultimately depended upon the same discoveries as were exploited by the Egyptians or the Sumerians, their employment in India is often distinctive and gives to each craft a character of its own.

Use of copper and bronze

Throughout the period copper and bronze were the principal metals used for making tools and implements. These include flat oblong axes, chisels, knives, spears, arrowheads (of a kind that was evidently exported to neighbouring hunting tribes), small saws, and razors. All these could be made by simple casting, chiselling, and hammering. Throughout the sites, bronze is less common than copper, and it is notably rarer in the lower levels. Four main varieties of metal have been found: crude copper lumps in the state in which they left the smelting furnace; refined copper, containing trace elements of arsenic and antimony; an alloy of copper with 2 to 5 percent of arsenic; and bronze with a tin alloy, often of as much as 11 to 13 percent. (A copper arsenic alloy is also found in Egypt.) The copper and bronze vessels of the Harappans are among their finest products, formed by hammering sheets of metal. Casting of copper and bronze was understood, and figurines of men and animals were made by the cire-perdue (lost-wax) technique. These, too, are technically outstanding.

Other metals used were gold, silver, and lead. The latter was employed occasionally for making small vases and such objects as plumb bobs. Silver is relatively more common than gold, and more than a few vessels are known, generally in forms similar to copper and bronze examples. Gold is by no means common and was generally reserved for such small objects as beads, pendants, and brooches. Much of the Indus gold is light in colour, indicating a high silver content.

Other special crafts include the manufacture of faience (earthenware decorated with coloured glazes)—for making beads, amulets, and sealings, and for making small vessels—and the working of stone for bead manufacture and for seals. The seals were generally cut from steatite and were carved in intaglio or incised with a copper burin (cutting tool). Beads were made from a variety of substances, but the carnelians are particularly noteworthy. They include several varieties of etched carnelian and long barrel beads made with extraordinary skill and accuracy. Shell and ivory were also worked and were used for beads, inlays, combs, bracelets, and the like.

After copper and bronze, stone probably played a major role in the life of the Harappans. Blocks of chert were dressed at the quarries at Sukkur (Sakhar) on the Indus, some 50 miles northeast of Mohenjo-daro, and cores were prepared from which stone blades of great regularity and size were struck. These blades are a common find at almost all of the Harappan sites. Other special uses for stone were in making bowls and small vessels of alabaster (probably imported); while hammer-dressed blocks of limestone were imported from the nearby hills for occasional use, for example, as covers for brick drains.

Pottery

The pottery of the Indus cities has all the marks of mass production. A substantial proportion is thrown on the wheel (probably the same kind of footwheel that is still found in the Indus provinces and to the west to this day, as distinguished from the Indian spun wheel common throughout the remaining parts of the subcontinent). The majority of the pottery is competent plain ware, well formed and fired but lacking in aesthetic appeal. A substantial portion of the pottery has a red slip and is painted with black decoration. Larger pots were probably built up on a turntable. Among the painted designs, conventionalized vegetable patterns are common, and the elaborate geometric designs of the painted pottery of Baluchistan give way to simpler motifs, such as intersecting circles or a scale pattern. Birds, animals, fish, and more interesting scenes are comparatively rare. Of the vessel forms, a shallow platter on a tall stand (the so-called offering stand) is noteworthy, as is also a tall cylindrical vessel perforated with small holes over its entire length and often open at top and bottom. The function of this latter vessel remains a mystery.

Although little has survived, very great interest attaches to the fragments of cotton textiles recovered at Mohenjo-daro. These provide the earliest evidence of a crop and industry for which India has long been famous. It is assumed that the raw cotton must have been brought in bales to the cities to be spun, woven, and perhaps dyed, as the presence of dyers' vats would seem to indicate.

Trade and external contacts. It has been seen above that the area covered by the Indus civilization had a remarkably uniform level of material culture. Such uniformity suggests a closely knit and integrated administration and implies internal trade within the state. Evidence of the actual exportation of objects is not always easy to find, but the wide diffusion of chert blades made of the characteristic Sukkur stone and the enormous scale of the factory at the Sukkur site strongly suggest trade. Other items also appear to indicate trade, such as the almost identical bronze carts discovered at Chanhu-daro and Harappā, for which a common origin must be postulated.

The wide range of crafts and special materials employed must also have caused the establishment of economic relations with peoples living outside the Harappan state. Such trade may be considered to be of two kinds: first, the obtaining of raw materials and other goods from the village communities or forest tribes in regions adjoining the Indus culture area; and second, trade with the cities of Mesopotamia. There is ample indication of the former type, even if the regions from which specific materials were derived are not easy to pinpoint. Gold was almost certainly imported from the group of settlements that sprang up in the vicinity of the gold fields of northern Mysore; silver probably came from Afghanistan or Iran; and copper could have come from several sources—some certainly from Rājasthān, some perhaps from East or South India on the one side, and some from Baluchistan or farther afield on the other. Lead may have come from Rājasthān or elsewhere in India. Lapis lazuli was probably imported from Iran rather than directly from the mines at Badakhshan, for the recent discovery of a large depot in Seistan seems to indicate the centre from which this material was traded throughout the ancient East. Turquoise probably came from Iran; fuchsite from Mysore; alabaster from Iran; amethyst from Mahārāshtra; and jade from Central Asia. There is unfortunately little evidence of what the Harappans gave in exchange for these materials—possibly nondurable goods such as cotton textiles and probably various types of beads. They may have also bartered tools or weapons of copper.

Trade with Mesopotamia

For the trade with Mesopotamia there are literary evidences as well as archaeological. The Harappan seals were evidently used to seal bundles of merchandise, as clay seal impressions with cord or sack marks on the reverse side testify. The presence of a number of Indus seals at Ur and other Mesopotamian cities and the discovery of a "Persian Gulf" type of seal at Lothal—otherwise known from the Persian Gulf ports of Bahrain and Failaka, and from Mesopotamia—provide convincing corroboration of the sea trade suggested by the Lothal dock. Once again it is difficult to pin down the actual goods imported or exported. Probably carnelian and etched carnelian beads, shell and bone inlays, including the distinctly Indian kidney shape, were among the goods sent to Mesopotamia. Also ivory combs, pearls, and precious timbers may have been among items of export. Copper ingots appear to have been imported to Lothal from the Persian Gulf. The trade documents for Mesopotamia provide valuable corroboration, and the lists of goods imported from Meluhha, which has often been supposed to be the ancient name for the Indus Valley region, are highly suggestive. These references date particularly from the 3rd dynasty of Ur and the Larsa period (*i.e.*, *c.* 2100–1770 BC).

Language and scripts, weights and measures. The maintenance of so extensive a set of relations as those implicit in the size and uniformity of the Harappan state and the extent of trade contacts must have called for a well-developed means of communication. The Harappan script has long defied attempts to read it, and therefore the language remains unknown. Recent analyses of the order of the signs on the inscriptions have led several scholars to the view that the language is not of the Indo-European family; nor is it close to Sumerian, Hurrian, or Elamite; nor can it be related to the structure of the Munda languages of modern India. If it is related to any modern language family it appears to be the Dravidian, presently spoken throughout the southern part of the Indian Peninsula. The script, which was written from right to left, is known from the 2,000-odd short inscriptions so far recovered, ranging from single characters to inscriptions of around 20 characters. There are more than 500 signs, many appearing to be compounds of two or more other signs; but it not yet clear whether these signs are ideographic, logographic, or other. Numerous attempts to read the script have been made during the past decades, most recently by a Russian team under Y. Knorozov and a Scandinavian group led by A. Parpola. The Scandinavian group claims to have read many of the inscriptions, taking the language to be Dravidian, akin to Old Tamil, but few scholars are as yet prepared to accept their results.

The Harappans also employed regular systems of weights and measures. An analysis of a fair number of the well-formed chert weights indicates that they follow a binary system for lower denominations and a decimal system for higher; that is, a series of 1, 2, 4, 8, 16, 32, 64, and then 320, 640, 1,600, 3,200, 8,000. Several scales of measurement were found in the excavations, one a decimal scale of 1.32 inches rising probably to 13.2 inches, apparently corresponding with the "foot" that was widespread in western Asia; another is a bronze rod marked in lengths of 0.367 inches, apparently half a digit of a "cubit" of 20.7 inches, also widespread in western Asia. Measurements from some of the structures show that these units were accurately applied in practice.

It has also been suggested that certain curious objects may have been accurately made optical squares with which surveyors might offset right angles, and in view of the accuracy of so much of the architectural work this appears quite plausible.

Art. The excavations of the Indus cities have produced much evidence of artistic activity. Such finds are important because they provide an insight into the minds, lives, and religious beliefs of their creators. Stone sculpture is extremely rare, and much of it is very crude. The total repertory cannot compare with the work done in Mesopotamia during the same periods. The figures are apparently all intended as images for worship. Such figures include seated men, recumbent composite animals, or in unique instances (from Harappā) a standing nude male and a dancing figure. The finest pieces are of excellent quality. There is also a small but impressive repertory of cast-bronze figures, including several fragments and complete examples of dancing girls, small chariots, carts, and animals. The technical excellence of the bronzes suggests a highly developed art, but the number of examples is still very small. Nevertheless, they appear to be Indian workmanship rather than imports.

Sculpture

The popular art of the Harappans was in the form of terra-cotta figurines. The majority are of standing females, often heavily laden with jewelry, but standing males—some with beard and horns—are also present. It has been generally agreed that these figures are largely deities (perhaps a Great Mother and a Great God); but some small figures of mothers with children or of domestic activities are probably toys. There are varieties of terra-cotta animals, carts, and toys—such as monkeys pierced to climb a string and cattle that nod their heads. Painted pottery is the only evidence that there was a tradition of painting. Much of the work is executed with boldness and delicacy of feeling, but the restrictions of the art do not leave much scope for creativity. The steatite seals, to whose manufacture reference was made above, form the most extensive series of objects of art in the civilization. The great majority show a humpless "unicorn" or bull in profile, while others show the Indian humped bull, the elephant, bison, rhinoceros, or tiger. The animal frequently stands before a ritual object, variously identified as a standard, manger, or even incense burner. A considerable number of the seals contain scenes of obvious mythological or religious significance. The interpretation of these seals is, however, often highly problematic. The seals were certainly more widely diffused than other artifacts and show a much higher level of workmanship. Probably they functioned as amulets as well as more practical devices to identify merchandise.

Religion and burial customs. In spite of the unread inscriptions, there is a considerable body of evidence that allows for conjecture concerning the religious beliefs of the Harappans. First, there are the buildings identified as temples or as possessing a ritual function, such as the Great Bath. Then there are the stone sculptures found to a large extent associated with these buildings. Next, there are the terra-cotta figures, and finally, the seals and amulets that depict scenes with evident mythological or religious contents. The interpretation of such data necessarily involves a largely subjective element, but most commentators have felt that they indicate a religious system that was already distinctly Indian. It is assumed that there was a Great God—who had many of the attributes later associated with the Hindu god Śiva—and a Great Mother who was the Great God's spouse and shared the attributes of Śiva's wife Durgā-Pārvatī. Evidence also exists of some sort of animal cult, related particularly to the bull, the buffalo, and the tiger. Mythological animals include a composite bull–elephant. Some seals suggest influence from or at least traits held in common with Mesopotamia; among these are the Gilgamesh (Mesopotamian epic) motif of a man grappling with a pair of tigers and the bull-man Enkidu (a human with horns, tail, and rear hooves of a bull). Among the most interesting of the seals are those that depict cult scenes or symbols: a god, seated in a yogic (meditative) posture and surrounded by beasts, with a horned headdress and erect phallus; the tree spirit with a tiger standing before it; the horned tree spirit confronted by a worshipper; a composite beast with a line of seven figures standing before it; the pipal leaf motif; and the swastika.

Form of burial

Many burials have been discovered, giving clear indication of belief in an afterlife. The cemeteries excavated at Harappā, Lothal, and Kalibangan are clearly separated from the settlement and show that the predominant rite was extended inhumation, with the body lying on its back and the head generally positioned to the north. Quantities of pottery were placed in the graves, and sometimes personal ornaments adorned the bodies. Some graves took the form of brick chambers within which the body was placed. At Lothal several pairs of skeletons were found in the same grave, and it has been suggested that this is an indication of some form of *satī* (a later Hindu custom in which the wife ends her life after the death of her husband).

The end of the Indus civilization. Around 1750 BC the uniform culture of this great area broke up, apparently with different results in the various provinces. The cause or causes of the end of the Indus civilization are not easy to determine. At Mohenjo-daro the latest levels show a marked decline in civic standards, and groups of sprawling skeletons in this period suggest some sort of massacre, perhaps an invasion. At Harappā in the top strata of the citadel there was a similar decline and a new pottery style occurs alongside the Harappan. Such pottery is found also in the cemetery H, where it is associated with two periods of burial, the earlier inhumations and the later fractional burials in urns. At Chanhu-daro and Amrī there is no evidence of a major break in the occupation, but a distinct pottery and material culture seems to have taken over (the so-called Jhukar culture). At Lothal, too, in the late period, a somewhat similar material culture follows directly on the Harappan.

How is this evidence to be interpreted, and where in all this, if at all, are traces of the arrival of early groups of Indo-European-speaking tribes, or of the Aryans to be found? It has recently been suggested that the end of Mohenjo-daro was associated with a vast and calamitous flood brought on by tectonic (structural) change farther down the Indus, but several serious objections to this view have been raised. More plausible is the suggestion that the Indus suffered one of its periodic major alterations of course, cutting off the floodwaters from economically vital agricultural land and resulting either in desiccation around Mohenjo-daro or in an influx of refugees to that city from elsewhere. Another somewhat similar and equally plausible explanation sees the growth of population leading to a wearing out of the countryside and hence drying up of necessary food supplies for men or cattle. Whatever the causes, they must have led to a growing strain within the system and must have made the city an easy prey for invaders. It should be remembered that there is likely to have been more than one wave of Indo-Iranian-speaking peoples into India-Pakistan, and archaeology can supply evidence of several influxes between 1750 and 1000 BC. Such evidence, however, is still extremely difficult to interpret and may largely reflect a period long after the breakdown of the Harappan civilization. The period succeeding this event used to be called a dark age, and in terms of scholarly knowledge this was once justified; but archaeology is steadily throwing more light upon the hiatuses, and in many parts of India the period is becoming quite well-known. What emerges is that, during and after the downfall of the Harappan civilization, a whole series of regional cultures appear in India-Pakistan, in some cases as direct descendants of the old Neolithic cultures, in others as new developments. These cultures appear to have shared in some ways the legacy of the Harappans and in their turn provide the framework for the integration of Indian and Aryan elements that contributed to the rise of civilization in the Ganges Valley. Most scholars have concluded that later Indian civilization owes an incalculable debt to the Harappans and that an as yet indefinable part of later Indian tradition and ideology must derive from them. Thus, it is probable that, by analogy with such tangible evidence of survival as the types of carts or ornaments, one may legitimately infer the Harappan origin of less tangible aspects of Indian life and institutions, such as the caste system or certain patterns of thought. (F.R.Al.)

II. The development of Indian civilization from c. 1500 BC to c. AD 1200

Though the Indian people have been concerned with both material and spiritual aspects of life, Indian history has in general been thought of as static and concerned only with things spiritual. Indologists, pre-eminently a 19th-century German, Max Müller, relied heavily on the Sanskritic tradition and saw Indian society as an idyllic village culture emphasizing qualities of passivity, meditation, and otherworldliness. In sharp contrast was the approach of the British historian James Mill and the Utilitarians, who condemned Indian culture as irrational and inimical to human progress. Mill first formulated a periodization of Indian history into Hindu, Muslim, and British periods. Direct contact with Indian institutions through administration in the 19th century, together with the utilization of new evidence from recently deciphered inscriptions, numismatics, and local archives, has provided fresh insights. Nationalist Indian historians of the early 20th century have tended to exaggerate the glory of the past but nevertheless, introduced controversy into historical interpretation, which in turn resulted in more precise studies of Indian institutions of the past.

The change in the orientation of Indian historical studies

A major change in the orientation of Indian history has been a questioning of an older notion of Oriental despotism as the key to Indian history. Arising out of a traditional European perspective on Asia, this image of despotism grew to enormous proportions in the 19th century and provided an intellectual justification for both colonialism and imperialism. Its deterministic assumptions clouded the precise understanding of early Indian interrelationships between political forms, economic patterns, and social structure.

In a study of political forms during this period, a considerable change is noticeable in the role of the institutions. Tribal societies had assemblies, whose political role changed with the transformation of tribe into state and with republican and monarchical governments. Centralized imperialism, which emerged in the Mauryan period, gave way gradually to decentralized administration and to what has been called a type of feudalism in the post-Gupta period. Although the village as an administrative and social unit remained constant, its relationship with the mainstream of history varied. Divinity in kingship was known but rarely taken seriously, the claim to the status of the caste of royalty becoming more important. Because conformity to the social order had precedence over allegiance to the state, the idea of representation found expression not so much in political institutions as in caste and village assemblies. The pendulum of politics swung from large to small kingdoms, with the former attempting to establish empires—the single, totally successful attempt being that of the Mauryan. Thus, true centralization was rare because local forces were often the determinants of historical events. Though imperial or near-imperial periods were marked by attempts at the evolution of uniform cultures, the periods of smaller kingdoms (often referred to as the Dark Ages by earlier historians) were more creative at the local level and witnessed significant changes in society and religion. It was also these small kingdoms that boasted of the most elaborate and impressive monuments.

The major economic patterns were those relating to land and to commerce. The transition from tribal to peasant society was a continuing process, with the gradual clearing of wasteland and the expansion of the village economy based on plow agriculture. Recognition of the importance of land revenue coincided with the emergence of the imperial system in the 4th century BC; and from this period, although the imperial structure did not last long, land revenue became central to the administration and income of the state. Frequent mentions of individual ownership, references to crown lands, numerous land grants to religious and secular grantees in the post-Gupta period, and detailed discussion in legal sources of the rights of purchase, bequest, and sale of land all clearly indicate that there was private property in land. Much emphasis has been laid on the state control of the irrigation system; yet a systematic study of irrigation in India reveals that it was generally privately controlled and that it serviced small areas of land. When the state built canals, they were mainly in the areas of the winter and summer monsoons and where village assemblies played a dominant part in revenue and general administration, as for example in the Cōḷa kingdom of South India.

The urban economy was crucial to the rise of the Indus Valley civilization (*c.* 2300–*c.* 1750 BC). Later, the 1st millennium BC saw an urban civilization in the Ganges Valley and in coastal South India. The emergence of towns was based on the needs and requirements of trade. In the 1st millennium AD, when commerce expanded to include trade with western Asia, the eastern Mediterranean, and Central and Southeast Asia, revenue from trade contributed substantially to the economies of the participating kingdoms, as indeed Indian religion and culture played a significant part in the cultural evolution of Central and Southeast Asia. Gold coins were issued for the first time by the Kuṣāṇas and in large quantity by the Guptas, both of which kingdoms were active in foreign trade. Gold was imported from Central Asia and Rome and later perhaps from eastern Africa because, in spite of the country's recurring association with gold, its sources were limited. Expanding trade encouraged the opening up of new routes, and this coupled with the expanding village economy led to a marked increase of knowledge about the geography of the subcontinent during the post-Maurya period. With increasing trade, guilds became more powerful in the towns. Members of the guilds participated in the administration, were associated with politics, and controlled the development of trade through merchant embassies sent to places as far afield as Rome and China. Not least, guilds and merchant associations held envied and respectable positions as donors of religious institutions.

Emergence of urban civilization

The structure of Indian society was unique in being characterized by caste, which largely accounts for the survival of that structure to the present day. The constant features of a caste society were endogamous kinship groups (*jāti*) arranged in a hierarchy of ritual ranking, based on notions of pollution and purity, with an intermeshing of service relationships. Although ritual hierarchy was unchanging, there appears to have been considerable mobility within the framework. Migrations of peoples both within the subcontinent and from outside encouraged social mobility and change. The nucleus of the social structure was the family, with the pattern of kinship relations varying from region to region. The family related to the village, and the village in turn to the region. The urban structure was a more complex one in which the guilds occasionally took on *jāti* functions, and there was a continual emergence of new social and professional groups.

Religion in early Indian history did not act as a monolithic force. Even when attempts were made by royalty to encourage certain religions, there was no idea of a state religion. In the main, there were three levels of religious expression. The most widespread was the worship of local cult deities with vague associations of a major deity, as seen in fertility cults, in the worship of mother-goddesses, in the so-called Śākta-Śakti cult, and in Tantrism. Less widespread but popular, particularly in the urban areas, were the more puritanical sects of Buddhism, Jainism, and the *bhakti* tradition of Hinduism. A third level included classical Hinduism and more abstract levels of Buddhism and Jainism, with an emphasis on the major deities in the case of the former and on the teachings of the founders in the case of the latter. It was this level, endorsed by affluent patronage, that provided the base for the institutionalization of religion. But the three levels were not isolated; the shadow of the third fell over the first two, whose more homely rituals and beliefs often crept into the third. This was the case particularly with Hinduism, the very flexibility of which was largely responsible for its survival. Forms of Buddhism, ranging from an emphasis on the constant clarification and refinement of its doctrine, on the one hand, to an incorporation of magical fertility cults in its beliefs, on the other, faded out toward the end of this period.

Sanskrit literature and the building of Hindu and Buddhist temples and sculpture both reached apogees in this period. Although literary works in Sanskrit continued to be written and temples were built in later periods, the achievement was never again as inspiring.

C. 1500–C. 600 BC

By about 1500 BC an important change began to occur in the northern half of the Indian subcontinent. The Harappā culture in the Indus Valley had declined by about 1750 BC, and the stage was being set for a second and more continuous urbanization in the Ganges Valley. The Harappā decline resulted in the collapse of city civilization and marked the end of the Indus region as a centre of civilization. The new areas of occupation were contiguous with, but seldom identical to, the Harappan area. There was continuity of occupation in the Punjab (Pañjāb) and Gujarāt. Geological and ecological factors, such as changing river courses, the encroachment of the desert, and repeated flooding, may well have made the area physically inhospitable, ultimately resulting in the decline of the cities.

Decline of the Harappā culture

Urbanization in the Ganges Valley. A new thrust toward urbanization came from the migration of peoples from the Punjab into the Ganges Valley.

Early Ganges cultures. Coterminous with the Harappā culture was a series of Neolithic cultures with their nuclei in Kashmir, eastern India, and the Deccan. In the immediate post-Harappan phase, the Ganges Valley sheltered two cultures, which scholars have so far been unable to connect. The Doab was dotted with small settlements using a crude ochre-colour pottery, rolled, and heavily weather-beaten through wind or water effects; its origin is uncertain, and the suggestion that it was a degenerate pottery produced by migrants from the Harappā culture moving eastward generally has not been accepted. The Ganges Valley to the east of the Doab has produced isolated hoards of copper objects—harpoons, spearheads, celts, swords, anthropomorphic figures—often discovered in fields rather than in excavations. Both the Ochre Colour Pottery people and the Copper Hoard people date to approximately 1800–1200 BC.

Substantial remains in the Doab show that, subsequent to the Ochre Colour Pottery culture, there was a so-called Painted Gray Ware culture, which formed the substratum to the urbanization of the region, with its upper limit in about the 5th century BC. Remains suggest communities of pastoralists and agriculturalists who used a distinctive gray pottery decorated generally in black with floral and geometrical patterns.

The Painted Gray Ware culture was strikingly different from the Harappā culture. Apart from the fact that it was not an urban culture, it introduced a new metal technology of iron, which facilitated the transition to urbanization in the Ganges Valley. It also introduced the horse, the domestication of which had been unknown to the country. A gradual change in food habits from wheat and barley in the Doab to rice in the east resulted in changing pottery shapes. To the east of the Doab, the appearance of what has come to be called the Northern Black Polished Ware coincided with urbanization.

The earliest literary evidence in India is the Vedic literature. The Vedas, an orally transmitted tradition during the early period, consist of four major texts—the Ṛg, Sāma, Yajur, and Atharva Veda. Of these, the Ṛg is believed to be the earliest. The language of the texts is Vedic Sanskrit, and the contents relate to hymns, charms, spells, and ritual observations of the Aryan-speaking peoples in India. ("Aryan" is used here only as a linguistic term, referring to the people who spoke Indo-Aryan, and does not carry any ethnic connotation.)

Theories of the origin of the Aryans in India relate to the question of what has been called the Indo-European homeland. In the 17th and 18th centuries AD, European scholars who first studied Sanskrit were struck by the similarity in its syntax and vocabulary to Greek and Latin. This resulted in the theory that there had been a common ancestry for these and other related languages, which came to be called the Indo-European group of languages. This, in turn, resulted in the notion that the Indo-European speaking people had had a common homeland from which they had migrated to various parts of Asia and Europe. The theory led to unlimited speculation, which continues today, regarding the original homeland and the date of the dispersal from it. The early history of India is still beset by "the Aryan Problem," which often clouds a genuine search for historical insight into this period.

Origin of the Aryans in India

That there was a migration of Indo-European speakers, possibly in waves, which can be dated to the 2nd millennium BC, is clear from archaeological and epigraphic evidence in western Asia. Mesopotamia witnessed the arrival, in about 1760 BC, of the Kassites, who introduced the horse and the chariot and bore such obviously Indo-European names as Surias, Indas, and Maruttas (Sūrya, Indra, and Marutaḥ in Sanskrit). A treaty *c.* 1400 BC between the Hittites, who were recent arrivals to Anatolia, and the Mittannis invoked four deities—Indara, Uruvna, Mitira, and Našatiya (names that occur in the Ṛgveda as Indra, Varuṇa, Mitra, and Nakṣatras). An inscription at Boğazköy of about the same date refers to certain Indo-European technical terms in the training of horses. Clay tablets dating to about 1400 BC, written at Tell el-Armarna in Babylonian cuneiform, mention the names of princes, such as Biridashva and Artamanya, which are also Indo-European. The association of the horse with these peoples would point to Central Asia or the southern Russian steppes as their place of origin.

Nearer India, the Iranian Plateau was subject to a similar migration. The literature of the Iranian Aryans, the Avesta, when compared with Vedic literature indicates that there had once been a close relationship between the two. It would appear that a branch of the Iranian Aryans migrated to northern India and settled in the Sapta Sindhu region, the area extending from the Kābul River in the north to the Sarasvatī and upper Doab in the south. The Sarasvatī, the sacred river at the time, flowed through northern Rājasthān but soon after disappeared into the desert. It was in the Sapta Sindhu that the majority of the hymns of the Ṛgveda were composed.

The Ṛgveda is divided into ten *maṇḍala*s (books), of which the tenth is believed to be somewhat later than the others. Each *maṇḍala* consists of a number of hymns, and most *maṇḍalas* are ascribed to a priestly family, such as Kaṇva, Gautama, Viśvāmitra, Vāmedeva, Atri, Bhāradvāja, and Vasiṣṭha. The ninth *maṇḍala* is a collection of all the hymns dedicated to *soma*, the sacred and intoxicating juice that was drunk on ritual occasions. The hymns include invocations to the gods, ritual hymns, battle hymns, narrative dialogues, and satirical observations. They provide incidental information on geographical location, social and political organization, tribal names and incidents connected with them, and, to a much greater degree, the evolution of Vedic religion.

Few events of political importance are related to the hymns. Perhaps the most impressive of those that are is a description of the battle of the ten kings in the Dasarājanya hymn: when Sudās, the king of the pre-eminent Bharata tribe of southern Punjab, replaced his chief priest Viśvāmitra with Vasiṣṭha, Viśvāmitra organized a confederacy of ten tribes, including the five famous tribes of the Pūru, Yadu, Turvaśas, Anu, and Druhyu, which went to war against Sudās. The Bharata tribe survived and continued to play an important role in historical tradition. Among the tribes there is little distinction between Aryan and non-Aryan, but the hymns refer to a local people, the Dāsas, who are said to have had an alien language and a dark complexion and to worship strange gods. Some Dāsas were rich in cattle and lived in fortified places (*pur*) often attacked by the god Indra. In addition to the Dāsas, there were the wealthy Paṇis, who were hostile and stole cattle.

This was the period of transition from nomadic pastoralism to settled village communities (*grāma*) with an intermixture of pastoral and agrarian economies. That the notion of cattle remained the dominant factor is indicated by the use of such words as *gotra* ("cowpen") for the endogamous kinship group and *gaviṣṭi* ("searching for cows") for war. That the family structure was patriarchal and the extended family constituted the unit is seen in the practice of *niyoga* ("levirate"), which permitted a widow to marry her husband's brother. A group of families constituted a *grāma*. The tribal unit was the *viś*. Tribal assemblies appear to have been frequent in the early stages, with meetings for both secular and religious purposes. Various categories of assemblies are referred to, such as the *vidatha*, *pariṣad*, *sabhā*, and *samiti*, the latter two being more common, although the precise distinction between them is not clear. The king, whose powers were checked by the *sabhā* and *samiti*, was primarily a war leader with the responsibility for protecting the tribe. He received a *bali* (tribute) for performing this function, which included the maintenance of civil order. Punishment was based on the system of wergild, in which a slain man's family was compensated according to the value of his life. The chief priest, or *purohita*, was largely a magic man whose rituals ensured prosperity and valour for the king. The other occasion for the tribal assembly was the *yajña* (religious sacrifice), which was the central ritual of Vedic religion and involved a large hierarchy of priests. The ceremonies lasted many days and entailed the conspicuous consumption of wealth in kind.

Settled village communities

Later Vedic period (c. 1000–500 BC*).* The sources for this period are both archaeological and literary. In the Ganges Valley the Painted Gray Ware culture continues to provide the major archaeological evidence. The literary sources are primarily the Sāmaveda, Yajurveda, and Atharvaveda, mainly ritual texts that include the *Brāhmaṇas* as well as the *Upaniṣads* and the *Āraṇyakas*—collections of philosophical and metaphysical discourses. Associated with these Vedas are the *sūtra* texts, largely explanatory aids to the other sections, being manuals on sacrifices and ceremonies, domestic observances, and social and legal relations. Because the texts were continually revised, they cannot be dated accurately to the early period. The *Dharma-sūtra* texts of this period became the nuclei of the sociolegal *Dharma-śāstras* of later centuries.

Some historians date the two epics, the *Mahābhārata* and the *Rāmāyaṇa*, to this period, though the date of each is a subject of considerable controversy. Both are mixtures of the historical and the legendary: both were rewritten and edited, and both suffered from frequent interpolations even as late as the early centuries AD. Consequently, important as they are to the literary and religious tradition (both epics were later accepted as sacred literature, and their heroes were deified), it is difficult to identify them as historical source material. The central event of the *Mahābhārata*, whose geographical background is the upper Doab and adjoining areas, was a war between two groups of cousins—the Kauravas and the Pāṇḍavas. Though the traditional date for the war is 3102 BC, most historians would prefer a date between 1400 and 900 BC, and a few attempts to correlate the archaeological evidence with the epic actually point to *c.* 800 BC as more likely. The events of the *Rāmāyaṇa* relate to Ayodhyā, the middle Ganges Valley, and central India, with later interpolations extending the area as far southward as Ceylon.

Another group of texts that are taken as reference material for this period, although they were composed much later, are the *Purāṇas*. The major *Purāṇas* contain a section on royal genealogies, which, initially preserved as part of the oral tradition, claim to trace the descent of the two important royal lineages, the Sūryavaṃśa (Solar lineage) and the Candravaṃśa (Lunar lineage), and dynasties from the period of the Flood in the 4th millennium BC to the middle of the 1st millennium AD. Much of the material appears to be mythological, but the dynasties listed for the historical period (*c.* 600 BC–AD 500) do refer to known dynasties.

The geographical focus of the later Vedic period moves

from the Sapta Sindhu region into the Ganges-Yamuna Doab and the territories on its fringe, the Ganges by then being the sacred river. The people beyond these areas were the *mlecchas*, the impure barbarians, unfamiliar with the speech and customs of the *ārya*, the noble ones. The land to the south of the Vindhyas, *dakṣināpatha* (literally, the "route to the south"), is referred to, but in a rather vague way.

Tribes of the regions

The literature is replete with the names of tribes occupying these regions. The most powerful tribe, commanding the greatest respect, was the Kuru-Pañcāla, which incorporated the two families of Kuru and Pūru (and the earlier Bharata tribe) and of which the Pañcāla was a confederation of lesser known tribes. This tribe occupied the upper Doab and the Kurukṣetra region. In the north the Kāmboja, Gandhāri, and Madra tribes were the dominant people. In the middle Ganges Valley the neighbours of the Kuru-Pañcālas were the Kāśī, Kosala, and Videha, who worked in close cooperation with each other and were rivals of the Kuru-Pañcālas. The Magadha, Aṅga, and Vaṅga peoples in the lower Ganges Valley and Delta were outside the Aryan pale and regarded as *mlecchas*. Magadha (Patna and Gayā districts of Bihār) is also associated with the *vrātya* people, who occupied an ambiguous position between the *ārya* and *mleccha*. Other tribes frequently mentioned are the Sātvants of the Chambal Valley and such tribes of the Vindhyan and northern Deccan region as the Andhras, Vidarbhas, Niṣadha, Pulinda, and Śabara. These were all *mleccha* tribes, and none was yet Aryanized. Because there was a consciousness of *mleccha* peoples and *mleccha* lands, there was an equally strong awareness of the pure land of the *āryas*, called the Āryāvarta. This was virtually the Ganges-Yamuna Doab and the encircling areas. The location of all these tribes is of considerable historical interest because they gave their names to the geographical area. By the end of the period, tribal identity had changed gradually to territorial identity, and the areas of settlement were now regarded as states, each with a recognized political system.

Political institutions

The *sabhā* and *pariṣad* (referring to an assembly, generally of a few persons of expertise) continued in general use and as political institutions into later periods. The larger assemblies declined. Rudimentary notions of taxation were the genesis of administration as also were the *ratnin*s (jewel bearers), consisting of officials and of representatives of various professions advising the king. A major transformation occurred in the notion of kingship, which ceased to be merely an office of a war leader; territorial identity provided it with power and status, symbolized by a series of lengthy and elaborate ceremonies—the *abhiṣekha*, *rājasūya*, *vājapeya*, and *aśvamedha*. The latter ceremony was a famous horse sacrifice, in which a specially selected horse was permitted to wander at will and was followed by a body of soldiers; the area through which the horse wandered unchallenged was claimed by the king conducting the sacrifice. Thus, theoretically at least, only kings of considerable power could perform this sacrifice. The assumption of these sacrifices was a permanent settling of a tribe in a particular area, marking the end of large-scale nomadism. This in turn led to the idea of the king owning the land, because he was permitted to give away portions of it as part of his charitable activities (*dāna*). The new trends emphasized the importance of the priests and the aristocracy (Brahmins and Kṣatriyas), who were the mainstay of kingship. The introduction, through royal sacrifices, of notions of divinity in kingship further strengthened the role of the priests. This was also the period in which kingship became hereditary.

Iron technology, or the use of *kṛṣṇa ayas* (dark metal), as it was apparently referred to in the later Vedic literature, and the migration into the Ganges Valley had resulted in the stabilization of agriculture and the formation of settlements of a permanent nature. Some of these settlements along the rivers evolved into towns, essentially as craft and commercial centres. By the middle of the 1st millennium BC, the second urbanization, this time in the Ganges Valley, had begun.

The development of caste

The factor with the most far-reaching consequences on Indian culture, and frequently referred to in literature, is the structure of society that has come to be called caste. In a late section of the Ṛgveda, a famous "Puruṣa-sūkta" hymn, containing a description of the primeval sacrifice, refers to the emergence of four groups from the body of the god Prajāpati—the Brahmins (Brāhmaṇs) from his mouth, the Kṣatriyas from his arms, the Vaiśyas from his thighs, and the Śūdras from his feet. This is clearly a mythologized attempt to describe the origin of the four *varṇa*s, which came to be regarded as the four major castes of Indian society. *Brahma*, meaning magical or divine knowledge, is the base of *Brāhmaṇ*—one who possesses such knowledge; *kṣatra*, he who is endowed with power or sovereignty, became the Kṣatriya; Vaiśya derived from *viś*, a settlement, and was thus a person settled on the land or a member of the *viś* or tribe; the derivation of Śūdra is not clear, which may suggest that it was a non-Aryan word. The texts continually repeat that it is the business of the Śūdra to serve the three higher castes. In addition to *varṇa* there are references to the term *jāti* (birth), which gradually came to acquire a closer connotation to caste and appears to mean the endogamous kinship group. In course of time the Brahmins became the pre-eminent priestly group, the intermediaries with the gods at the sacrificial rituals, and the recipients of large donations for priestly functions; and in the process they acquired a number of privileges, such as exemption from taxes and inviolability. Claims to purity of birth added to their prestige and were only occasionally challenged by the theory that learning is the primary criterion of being a Brahmin. The Kṣatriyas, which appear to have been the landowning families, assumed the role of military leaders and of the natural aristocracy having connections with royalty. In the early sections of the texts, *rājanya* is sometimes used as an alternative term for the Kṣatriya. The Vaiśyas were more subservient, and, although their status was not as inferior as that of the Śūdras, they appear to have been crucial to the economy. The traditional view of the Śūdras is that they were non-Aryan cultivators, who came under the domination of the Aryans and in many cases were enslaved and therefore had to serve the upper three castes. But not all references to the Śūdras are to slaves. Sometimes rich Śūdras are mentioned, and in later centuries some of them even became kings. The traditional view that *varṇa* reflected the organization of Indian society has recently been questioned; it has been suggested that perhaps there is a distinction between the model of such a social structure and the actual manner of its functioning and that the concept of *jāti* is more central to caste functioning than *varṇa*, which may be the theoretical rationalization. The ingredients of caste may be listed as conformity to the rules of endogamy, rigid concepts of purity and pollution, the hierarchical ordering of occupations and an emphasis on their being hereditary, and an adherence to a geographical location. Because not all of the *jāti*s could have been discussed in the legal codes, *varṇa* may have been used as a kind of model largely to indicate the process of social relationships. This view is strengthened by the fact that the non-Brahmanical literature of later periods does not always conform to the picture of caste society depicted in the *Dharma-śāstras*.

Neolithic–Chalcolithic and Megalithic cultures

Other cultures of the period. This was broadly the picture in the Ganges Valley. In other parts of the subcontinent, there had evolved a series of cultures of the general Neolithic–Chalcolithic variety, concentrated mainly in the east and the south. Limited excavations in Assam suggest connections with parts of China and Southeast Asia. Sites in West Bengal, such as Pandu-rajar-dhibi and Mahisdal (in the Bīrbhūm district), cover a range from pre-Iron Age into Iron Age and reveal black and red ware in the early stages, with the arrival of iron dating to about the 7th century BC. Traces of such cultures continued along the eastern coast, as at Patpad and Kesarpalli (Andhra Pradesh) and as far south as Pondicherry. A more concentrated group of southern sites around the Raichūr Doab, such as Sangankallu, Piklihal, Maski, Tekkalkota, and Hallur, marked the transition to metal technology, and late phases at these sites suggest a cattle-rearing people with gram and millet as their staple diet (unlike the eastern sites, which cultivated rice). Noticeable is the association with the northwestern Deccan and central India—the Jorwe-type sites, which suggest Harappan affinities. Perhaps the most interesting of these Neolithic–Chalcolithic sites are the ones (*c.* 1600–1200 BC) that carry traces of post-Harappan connections evident in the pottery and artifacts of such sites in Kāthiāwār as Rojdi, Rangpur, and Somnāth. The Banās Valley sites of Ahār and Gilund (Udaipur district), although less influenced by Harappan types, show evidence of contact with the western coastal sites as well as with those of Mālwa (Nāgda and Navdatoli). The Mālwa sites in turn have connections with those of the northern Deccan, such as the Jorwe-culture sites at Jorwe, Prakāsh, Bāhāl, Nevāsa, Daimabad, etc. Mālwa and the northwestern Deccan have traditionally been on the route from the Ganges Valley to the western coast and to the south; thus the presence of spouted vessels of the Jorwe kind in the sites of the Raichūr Doab is not surprising. It has also been suggested that the central Indian sites were in contact with Iran. Most of the sites provide evidence of iron in the period 1000–500 BC, which can therefore be regarded as a period of change. There is no conclusive evidence, however, to prove the hypothesis that the arrival of iron in these areas coincided with the arrival of the Indo-Aryan language.

A more mature display of Iron Age culture during and subsequent to this period comes from the southern half of the peninsula—what has frequently been termed the Megalithic culture. The Megalithic culture remains problematical because neither its origin nor its evolution are yet clear. Some scholars have linked it with the megaliths of western India, others with those of central India, and many have suggested maritime connections with the eastern Mediterranean. Carbon-14 dates point to *c.* 1000 BC as the earliest level, and the discovery of Roman pottery in the upper levels at some sites provide a terminal date of the 1st century AD. Burial methods vary in type from urn burials to menhirs and dolmens (stone monuments) and burial chambers marked off by a circle of stones, some of which are referred to in early Tamil sources. Some of the northern sites of this culture bear traces of contact with the Jorwe type. The Megalithic sites indicate a fairly sophisticated industry in iron artifacts and pottery, and the frequency of horse bits in the graves points to the use of horses. Curiously, however, it is precisely in the regions that used iron and were associated with the horse that the Indo-Aryan languages did not spread. Even today these are the regions of the Dravidian language group.

Native Indian Dynasties

dynasty	location	dates (in centuries)
Haihaya	Magadha	6–4 BC
Nanda	Magadha	4
Maurya	India, barring the area south of Mysore	4–2
Indo-Greeks	north India	2–1
Śuṇga	Ganges valley and parts of central India	2–1
Sātavāhana	north Deccan	1 BC–3 AD
Śaka	western India	1 BC–4 AD
Kuṣāṇa	N India and C Asia	1–3 AD
Gupta	N India	4–6
Harṣa	N India	7
Pallava	Tamil Nadu	4–9
Cālukya	western and central Deccan	6–8
Pāla	Bengal	8–12
Pratihāra	W India and Upper Ganges Valley	9–11
Rāṣṭrakūṭa	western and central Deccan	8–10
Cōla	Tamil Nadu	9–13
Candella	Bundelkhand	10–12
Cauhān	Rājasthān	10–12
Caulukya	Gujarāt	10–13
Paramāra	western and central India	10–11
Later Cālukyas	western and central Deccan	10–12
Hoysaḷa	central and southern Deccan	12–14
Yādava	N Deccan	12–13
Pāṇḍya	Tamil Nadu	13–14

THE BEGINNING OF THE HISTORICAL PERIOD, C. 600–150 BC

For this phase of Indian history a variety of historical sources are available. The Buddhist canon, pertaining to the period of the Buddha (6th century BC) and later, is invaluable as a cross reference for the Brahmanical sources. This is also true, though to a more limited extent, of Jaina sources. In the 4th century BC there are secular writings on political economy and accounts of foreign travellers. The most important sources, however, are inscriptions of the 3rd century BC.

Buddhist writings on eastern India

Pre-Mauryan states. Buddhist writings referring to the 6th and 5th centuries BC with a perspective on politics in eastern India mention 16 major states (*mahājanapada*) dominating the northern part of the subcontinent. A few of these, such as Gandhāra, Kāmboja, Kuru-Pañcāla, Matsya, Kāśī, and Kosala, continued from the earlier period and are mentioned in Vedic literature. The rest were new states, either freshly created from declining older ones or new areas coming into importance, such as Avanti, Aśvaka, Śūrasena, Vatsa, Cedi, Malla, Vṛjji, Magadha, and Aṅga. The mention of so many new states in the area of the eastern Ganges Valley was due in part to the eastern focus of the sources and was partly the antecedent to the increasing pre-eminence of the eastern regions.

Location. Gandhāra lay astride the Indus and included the districts of Peshāwar and the lower Swāt and Kābul valleys. For a while its independence was terminated by its inclusion as one of the 22 satrapies of the Achaemenid Empire of Persia (*c.* 519 BC). Its major role as the channel of communication with Iran and Central Asia continued, as did its trade in woollen goods. Kāmboja adjoined Gandhāra. Originally regarded as a land of Aryan speakers, Kāmboja soon lost its important status, ostensibly because its people did not follow the sacred Brahmanical rites—a situation that was to prevail extensively in the north as the result of the introduction of new peoples and cultures through the processes of invasion, migration, and trade. Kāmboja was noted for its horses, which came from Central Asia and were traded to other parts of India.

The Kekayas had settled in the region between Gandhāra and the Beās River; they and the Madras and Uśīnaras were described as descendants of the Anu tribe. The Matsyas were located to the southwest of Delhi; but the Kuru-Pañcāla, still dominant in the Doab, were extending their control southward and eastward. The Kuru capital was reportedly moved from Hastināpura to Kauśāmbī when the former was devastated by a great flood, the evidence for which is clear in the excavations at Hastināpura and dates to about the 9th century BC. The Mallas were located in eastern Uttar Pradesh. Avanti arose in the Ujjain-Narmada Valley region, with its capital at Mahiṣmatī; during the reign of King Pradyota, there was a matrimonial alliance with the royal family at Kauśāmbī. Śūrasena had its capital at Mathurā, and the tribe claimed descent from the Yadu clan. A reference to the Sourasenoi in later Greek writings is often identified with the Śūrasena, and the city of Methora, with Mathurā. The Vatsa state was based on Kauśāmbī. The Cedi state (in Bundelkhand) lay on the route to the northwestern Deccan. South of the Vindhyas, on the Godāvari River, Aśvaka continued to thrive.

The mid-Ganges Valley was dominated by Kāśī and Kosala. Kāśī maintained close affiliations with its eastern neighbours, and its capital was later to acquire renown as the sacred city of Vārānasi (Benares). Kāśī and Kosala were continually at war over the control of the Ganges; in the course of the conflict, Kosala extended its frontiers to the north and the south, and ultimately it was constituted into Uttar and Dakṣina (northern and southern) Kosala. The new states of Magadha (Patna and Gayā districts) and Aṅga (north of the delta) were also interested in controlling the river and soon made their presence felt. The conflict was joined by the Vṛjji state (Besar and Muzaffarpur district). For a while, Videha (modern Tirhut), with its capital at Mithilā, also remained powerful. References to the states of the northern Deccan appear to repeat statements from sources of the earlier period, suggesting that there was little further knowledge of the region.

Political systems. The political system in these states was either monarchical or a type of representative government that variously has been called republican or oligarchical. Sometimes within the state itself there was a gradual change from one system to the other, as in the case of Vaiśālī, the nucleus of the Vṛjji state. Apart from the major states there also were many smaller republican states, such as those of the Koliyas, Moriyas, Jñātṛkas, Śākyas, and Licchavis. The Jñātṛkas and Śākyas are especially remembered because they were the tribes to which Mahāvīra and Gautama Buddha belonged; the Licchavis were eventually to become extremely powerful.

The republics

The republics were constituted by either a single tribe or a confederacy of tribes. The elected chief or the president (*gaṇapati, gaṇarāja*) functioned with the assistance of a council of elders probably selected from the Kṣatriya families. The most important institution was the general assembly, or *pariṣad*, to the meetings of which members were summoned by kettledrum. There was a prescribed seating arrangement for the members, an agenda, and an order of speaking and debate that terminated in a decision. A distinction was maintained between the families represented and the others. Sovereignty was vested in the *pariṣad*, which included in its powers the election of important functionaries. An occasional lapse into hereditary office on the part of the chief may account for the tendency toward monarchy. The danger of factions destroying the system was realized and was warned against.

The political system of these republics suggests a stabilized agrarian economy. There is frequent mention of the wealthy Kṣatriyas (*khhattiya-gahapati*) employing slaves and hired labourers to work on their lands. That there was an increase in urban settlements and trade is clear not only from references in the literary sources but also from the introduction of two characteristics of urban civilization—a script and coinage. Evidence for the script comes from references to letters of the alphabet in the literary sources and, in the 3rd century, from inscriptions, the latter indicating a considerable period of familiarity with a script. The most widely used script was Brāhmī, which is germane to most Indian scripts used subsequently. A variant during this period was Kharoṣṭī, used only in northwestern India and indicating an association with Aramaic from Iran. The most commonly spoken languages were Prākrit, which had its local variations in Śaurasenī (from which Pālī evolved), and Māgadhī, in which the Buddha preached. Sanskrit, the more cultured language as compared to Prākrit, was the language of the educated few and of the Vedic religion. Pāṇini's grammar, the *Aṣṭādhyāyī*, and Yāska's etymological work, the *Nirukta*, suggest considerable sophistication in the development of Sanskrit.

Economy. Silver bent bar coins and silver and copper punch-marked coins came into use in the 5th century BC. It is not clear whether the coins were issued by a government authority or were the legal tender of moneyers. The gradual spread in the same period of a characteristic type of luxury ware, the northern black polished ware, is an indicator of expanding trade. The main trade routes were along the Ganges River and across the Indo-Gangetic watershed and the Punjab to Taxila and beyond, and alternatively from the Ganges Valley via Ujjain and the Narmada Valley to the western coast or southward to northwestern Deccan. The route to the Ganges Delta became more popular, and this permitted maritime contact with ports on the eastern coast of India. The expansion of trade and consequently of towns resulted in an increase in the number of artisans and merchants; they were organized in guilds (*śreṇi*), each of which tended to inhabit a particular part of a town. The guild system encouraged specialization of labour and the hereditary principle in professions, which became characteristic of caste functioning. Gradually some of the guilds acquired caste status. The practice of usury encouraged the activity of financiers, some of whom formed their own guilds and found that investment in trade proved increasingly lucrative.

Religion. These changing features of social and economic life were linked to religious and intellectual changes. Orthodox traditions maintained in certain sections of Vedic literature were questioned by teachers referred to in the *Upaniṣads* and *Āraṇyakas* and by others whose speculations and philosophy are recorded in other texts. There was a sizable heterodox tradition current in the 6th century BC, and speculation ranged from idealism to materialism. The Ājīvikas and the Cārvākas, among the smaller sects, were popular for a time as were the materialist theories of the Buddha's contemporary, Ajita Keśakambalin. Even though such sects did not sustain an independent religious tradition, the undercurrent of their teachings cropped up time and again in later religious trends.

Jainism and Buddhism

Of all these sects the only two that acquired the status of major religions were Jainism and Buddhism; the former remained within the Indian subcontinent; the latter spread to Central Asia, China, Japan, and Southeast Asia and, for a substantial period, was the dominant religion of Asia. Both religions were founded in the 6th century BC; Mahāvīra gave shape to earlier Nirgrantha ideas and formulated Jainism (the teachings of the Jina, or Conqueror, Mahāvīra), and the Buddha (the Enlightened One) preached a new doctrine.

There were many similarities among these two sects. Religious rituals, though few, were essentially congregational. Monastic orders (the *saṅgha*) were introduced with monasteries organized on democratic lines and initially accepting persons from all strata of life. Some of the monasteries developed into important centres of education. The functioning of monks in society was greater, however, among the Buddhist orders. Wandering monks, preaching and seeking alms, gave the religions a missionary flavour. The recruitment of nuns signified a special concern for the status of women. Both religions questioned Brahmanical orthodoxy and the authority of the Vedas. Both were opposed to the sacrifice of animals, and both preached nonviolence. Both derived support in the main from the wealthy Kṣatriya landowners and the mercantile community; because trade and commerce did not involve killing, the principle of *ahiṃsā* (nonviolence) could be observed in these activities. The Jainas participated widely as the middlemen in financial transactions and in later centuries became the great financiers of western India. Both religions disapproved of the inequality of castes and, although not directly attacking the assumptions of a caste society, generally projected themselves as non-caste movements, thereby securing the support of low-caste groups. Because Buddhism borrowed its rituals and practices from popular local cults, women of the royal families became its supporters.

Struggle over the Ganges Valley

Magadhan ascendancy. The political focus in the 6th century BC centred on the control of the Ganges Valley. The states of Kāśī, Kośala, Magadha, and the Vṛjjis battled for this control for a century until Magadha emerged victorious. Magadha's success was due in part to the political ambition of its king, Bimbisāra, who came to the throne in *c.* 543 BC. According to some sources he was of the Śaśunāga dynasty, though others maintain that the Śaśunāgas came later. At any rate, Bimbisāra conquered Aṅga, which gave him access to the Ganges Delta—a valuable asset in terms of the nascent maritime trade. Bimbisāra's son Ajātaśatru came to the throne in *c.* 491 BC and fully implemented his father's intentions within about 30 years. Ajātaśatru strengthened the defenses of the Magadhan capital, Rājagṛha, and built a small fort on the Ganges at Pāṭaligrāma, which was to become the famous capital of Pāṭaliputra (Patna). He then attacked and annexed Kāśī and Kośala. He still had to subdue the confederacy of the Vṛjji state, and this turned out to be a protracted affair lasting 16 years. Ultimately the Vṛjjis were overthrown, having been weakened by Ajātaśatru, who was able to sow dissension in the confederacy. The most important tribe in the confederacy was the Licchavi, which became historically quiescent for many centuries and then came to the fore again in the 4th century AD.

The success of Magadha was due not alone to the ambition of Bimbisāra and Ajātaśatru. Magadha had an excellent geographical location controlling the lower Ganges and thus drew revenue both from the fertile plain and the river trade. Access to the delta also brought in lucrative profits from the eastern coastal trade. Neighbouring forests provided timber for building and elephants for the army. Above all, rich deposits of iron ore gave Magadha a lead in technology.

Bimbisāra had been one of the earliest Indian kings to emphasize efficient administration, and the beginnings of an administrative system took root. Rudimentary notions of land revenue developed. Each village had a headman who was responsible for collecting taxes and another set of officials who supervised the collection and conveyed the revenue to the royal treasury. But the full understanding of the utilization of land revenue as a major source of state income was yet to come. The clearing of land continued apace, but the agrarian settlements were probably small because literary references to journeys from one town to another mention long stretches of forest paths.

Ajātaśatru died in *c.* 459 BC, and, after a series of ineffective rulers, a new dynasty was founded by Śiśunāga and lasted for about half a century until ousted by Mahāpadma Nanda. The Nandas are universally described as being of low origin, perhaps Śūdras. Despite these rapid dynastic changes, Magadha retained its position of strength. The Nandas continued the earlier policy of expansion. They are proverbially connected with wealth, probably because they realized the importance of regular collections of land revenue.

Invasions of Alexander the Great. The northwestern part of India had seen the campaign of Alexander of Macedon, who, in 327 BC, in pursuing his campaign to the eastern extremities of the Achaemenid Empire of Darius, entered Gandhāra. He campaigned successfully across the Punjab as far as the Beās River, where his troops refused to continue fighting. The vast army of the Nandas is referred to in Greek sources, and some historians have suggested that Alexander's Greek soldiers may have mutinied out of fear of this army. The campaign of Alexander made no impression, historically or politically, on India, nor are there any references to it in Indian sources. The most significant outcome of his campaign was that some of his Greek companions, such as Onesicritus, Aristobulus, and his admiral Nearchus, recorded their impressions of India. Strabo and Arrian, as well as Pliny and Plutarch, incorporated much of this material into their writings. But some of the accounts are fanciful and make for better fiction than history. Alexander established a number of Greek settlements, which provided an impetus for the development of trade and communication with western Asia. Most valuable to historians was a reference to Alexander meeting the young prince Sandrocottos, a name identified in the 18th century as Candragupta, thus providing a chronological landmark in early Indian history.

The Mauryan Empire. The accession (dated to *c.* 325–*c.* 321 BC) of Candragupta Maurya is significant in Indian history because it inaugurated the first Indian empire. The Mauryan dynasty was to rule the entire subcontinent, except the area south of Mysore, and substantial parts of present-day Afghanistan under a centralized, imperial system.

Candragupta Maurya. Candragupta overthrew the Nanda power in Magadha and then campaigned in central and northern India. Greek sources report that he engaged in a conflict in 305 BC in the trans-Indus region with Seleucus I Nicator, one of Alexander's generals who, on the death of Alexander, had founded the Seleucid dynasty in Iran. The campaign terminated with a treaty by which Seleucus ceded the trans-Indus provinces to the Maurya and the latter presented him with 500 elephants. A marriage alliance is mentioned, but no details are recorded.

Mauryan–Seleucid friendship

The treaty ushered in an era of friendly relations between the Mauryas and the Seleucids, with exchanges of envoys and gifts throughout the 3rd century BC. The most important of the envoys of Seleucus was Megasthenes, who left his observations in the form of a book, the *Indica.* Though the original has been lost, extensive quotations from it survive in the works of such later Greek writers as Strabo, Diodorus, and Arrian. A work of major importance in Sanskrit is the *Artha-śāstra* of Kauṭilya (or Cāṇakya, as he is sometimes called). Kauṭilya was prime minister to Candragupta Maurya, to whom this book, a treatise on political economy, is as-

Adapted from C.C. Davies, *An Historical Atlas of the Indian Peninsula* (1959); Oxford University Press

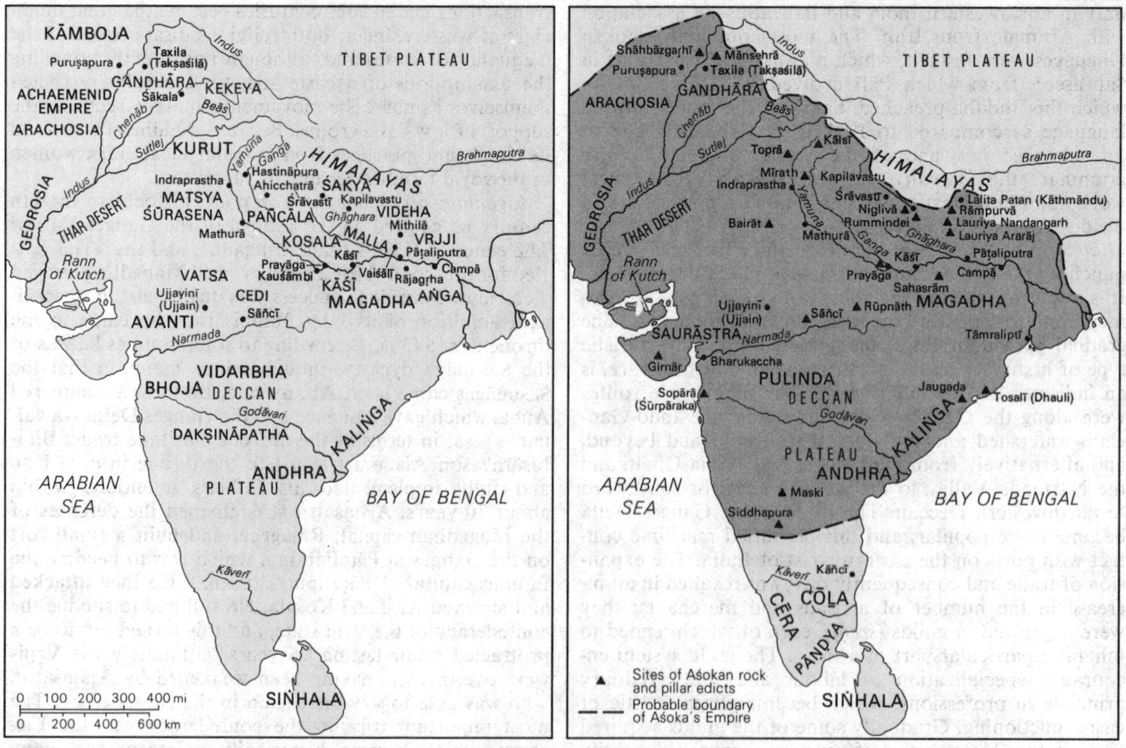

(Left) India *c.* 500 BC and (right) Aśoka's empire at its greatest extent, *c.* 250 BC.

cribed. In describing an ideal government, Kauṭilya indicates contemporary assumptions of political and economic theory, and the description of the functioning of government occasionally tallies with present-day knowledge of actual conditions derived from other sources. The date of origin of the *Artha-śāstra* remains problematical, with suggested dates ranging from the 4th century BC to the 4th century AD. Most authorities now agree that the kernel of the book was originally written during the early Mauryan period, but interpolations continued to be compiled perhaps until the Gupta period.

According to Jaina literary sources Candragupta became a Jaina toward the end of his reign. He abdicated in favour of his son Bindusāra, became an ascetic, and travelled with a group of Jaina monks to South India, where he died in the orthodox Jaina manner by deliberate slow starvation.

Bindusāra. The second Mauryan emperor was Bindusāra, who came to the throne in *c.* 297 BC. Greek sources refer to him as Amitrochates, the Greek for the Sanskrit *amitraghāta*, the "destroyer of foes." This name perhaps reflects a successful campaign in the Deccan, Candragupta having already conquered northern India. Bindusāra's campaign stopped at Mysore, probably because the kingdoms of the extreme south, such as the Cōlas, Pāṇḍyas, and Cēras, were well-disposed in their relations toward the Mauryas.

Aśoka and his successors. Bindusāra was succeeded by his son Aśoka, either directly in 272 BC or, after an interregnum of four years, in 268 BC (some historians say *c.* 265 BC). Aśoka's reign is comparatively well documented, particularly by epigraphical evidence. He issued a large number of edicts, which were inscribed in many parts of the empire and were composed in Prākrit, Greek, and Aramaic, depending on the language current in a particular region. The inscriptions composed in Greek and Aramaic are limited to Afghanistan and the trans-Indus region.

The first major event in Aśoka's reign, which he describes in one of his edicts, was a campaign against Kaliṅga in 260 BC. The suffering that resulted caused him to reevaluate the notion of conquest by violence, and gradually he was drawn to the Buddhist religion. About 12 years after his accession, he began issuing edicts at regular intervals. In one of them he referred to five Greek kings who were his neighbours and contemporaries—these were Antiochus II Theos of Syria, the grandson of Seleucus I Nicator; Ptolemy Philadelphus of Egypt; Antigonus Gonatas of Macedonia; Magas of Cyrene; and Alexander (either of Epirus or Corinth). He had sent envoys to all these kingdoms, and local tradition asserts that he had contacts with Khotān and Nepal. Close relations with Tissa, the king of Ceylon, were furthered by the fact that Mihinda, Aśoka's son (or his younger brother according to some sources), was the first Buddhist missionary in Ceylon.

Aśoka ruled for 37 years. After his death a political decline set in, and half a century later the empire was reduced to a part of the Ganges Valley alone. Tradition asserts that his son Kunāla ruled in Gandhāra. Epigraphic evidence indicates that his grandson Daśaratha ruled in Magadha. Some historians have suggested that his empire was bifurcated. In 185 BC the last of the Mauryas, Bṛhadratha, was assassinated by his Brahmin commander in chief Puṣyamitra, who founded the Śuṅga dynasty.

The Mauryan achievement

Financial base for the empire. The Mauryan achievement was its ability to weld the diverse parts of the subcontinent into a single political unit and to maintain an imperial system for almost 100 years. The financial base for an imperial system was provided by the income from land revenue and, to a lesser extent, from trade. The gradual expansion of the agrarian economy and improvements in the administrative machinery for collecting revenue increased the income from land revenue. This is confirmed by both the theories of Kauṭilya and the account of Megasthenes; Kauṭilya maintained that the state should organize the clearing of wasteland and settle it with villages of Śūdra cultivators. It is likely that some 150,000 persons deported from Kaliṅga by Aśoka after the campaign were settled in this manner. Megasthenes writes that there were no slaves in India, yet Indian sources speak of various categories of slaves, the most commonly used term being *dāsa-bhṛtaka* (slaves and hired labourers). It is likely that there was no large-scale slavery for production, although slaves were used on the land, in the mines, and in the guilds, along with the hired labour.

The nature of land revenue has been a subject of controversy—some scholars maintaining that the state was the sole owner of the land, and others contending that there was private and individual ownership as well. References to private ownership would seem to be too frequent to be ignored. There are also references to the crown lands (*sītā*), the personal property of the king. The problem relates to the rest of the land, where a clear distinction was not always maintained between ownership by the king and by the state. It may be argued that, because the distinction between the king as a symbol of the state and the state per se was rather blurred in political theory, the king collected revenue from the land, on behalf of the state rather than in his personal capacity. Two types of taxes were levied—one on the amount of land cultivated and the other on the produce of the land. State-controlled irrigation was known in limited periods and in limited areas. By and large irrigation systems were privately controlled by cultivators and landowners. There is no support for a thesis that control of the hydraulic machinery was crucial to the political control of the country.

Another source of income, which acquired increasing importance, was revenue from taxes levied on both internal and foreign trade. The attempt at uniform political administration helped to break the economic isolation of various regions. Roads built to ensure quick communication with the local administration inevitably became arteries of trade.

Mauryan society. According to Megasthenes, Mauryan society was divided into seven castes: philosophers, farmers, soldiers, herdsmen, artisans, magistrates, and councillors. He defined caste as endogamous and the professions as hereditary. The philosophers included a variety of priests, monks, and religious teachers; they formed the smallest caste in number but were the most respected and were exempt from taxation. The farmers were the largest in number. The soldiers were very well paid, and, if Pliny's figures for the army are correct—9,000 elephants, 30,000 cavalry, and 600,000 infantry—it must have required a considerable financial outlay. The mention of herdsmen as a socio-economic group suggests that, although the agrarian economy was expanding and had become central to the state income, pastoralism still continued to play an important economic role.

The artisans probably represented a major section of the urban population. The listing of magistrates and councillors as distinct and separate groups suggests that the personnel involved in administration was large and recognizable.

Mauryan government. The Mauryan government was a centralized bureaucracy, organized around the king. Aśoka saw his role as essentially paternal: "All men are my children." He was anxious to be in constant touch with public opinion, and to this end he travelled extensively throughout his empire and appointed a special category of officers to gauge public opinion. His edicts indicate frequent consultations with his ministers, the ministerial council being a largely advisory body. The offices of the *sannidhātṛ* (treasurer), who kept the account, and the *samāhartṛ* (chief collector), who was responsible for revenue records, formed the hub of the revenue administration. Each administrative department, with its superintendents and subordinate officials, acted as a link between local administration and the central government. Kauṭilya believed that a quarter of the total income should be reserved for the salaries of the officers. That the higher officials expected to be handsomely paid is clear from the salaries suggested by Kauṭilya and from the clerk's salary of 500 *paṇas* and the minister's of 48,000 *paṇas*. Public works and grants absorbed another large percentage of state income.

Divisions of the empire

The empire was divided into four provinces, and at the head of each was generally placed a prince of the royal family. Local officials were probably selected from among the local people because no method of impersonal recruitment to administrative office is mentioned. The emperor sent officers on inspection once every five years for an additional audit and check on provincial administration. Some categories of officers in the rural areas, such as the *rājjūkas*, combined judicial functions with assessment duties. Fines were the most general form of punishment, although capital punishment was imposed in extreme cases. Provinces were subdivided into districts and these again into smaller units. The village was the basic unit of administration and has remained so throughout the centuries. The headman continued to be an important official, as did the accountant and the tax collector (*sthānika* and *gopa*). For the larger units Kauṭilya suggests the maintenance of a census of the population as well. Megasthenes reports that there was a committee of 30 officials, divided into six subcommittees, who catered to the administration of Pāṭaliputra. The most important single official was the city superintendent (*nāgaraka*), who had virtual control of all aspects of city administration.

Aśoka's edicts. It was against this background of imperial administration and a changing socio-economic framework that Aśoka issued edicts that carried his message concerning the idea and practice of *dhamma*, the Prākrit form of the Sanskrit *dharma*, which is virtually impossible to translate. It carries a variety of meanings depending on the context, such as the universal law, the social order, piety, or righteousness; the Buddhists frequently used it with reference to the teachings of the Buddha. This, in part, coloured the earlier interpretation of Aśoka's use of the word to mean that he was propagating Buddhism. Until his inscriptions were deciphered in 1837, Aśoka was practically unknown except in the Buddhist chronicles of Ceylon—the *Mahāvaṃsa*, *Dīpavaṃsa*, and the *Vaṃsattapakāsinī*—and the works of the northern Buddhist tradition—the *Divyāvadāna* and the *Aśokāvadāna*—where he is extolled as a Buddhist emperor *par excellence* whose sole ambition was the expansion of Buddhism. Most of these traditions were preserved outside India in Ceylon, Central Asia, and China. Even after the edicts were deciphered, it was believed that they corroborated the theory of the Buddhist sources because in some of the edicts Aśoka avowed his personal support of Buddhism. More recent analyses suggest, however, that, although he was personally a Buddhist, as his edicts addressed to the Buddhist *saṅgha* (order) attest, the majority of the edicts in which he attempted to define *dhamma* do not suggest that he was merely preaching Buddhism. These edicts addressed to the people were inscribed on rock surfaces or on especially erected and finely polished sandstone pillars, in places where people were likely to congregate.

It has been suggested that the idea of issuing edicts was borrowed from the Achaemenid emperors, especially from Darius; but the tone and content of Aśoka's edicts are quite different. The pillars with their animal capitals have also been described as imitations of Achaemenid pillars, but there are substantial differences in style. The animal capitals are fine examples of imperial Mauryan art and contrast with numerous small, gray terra-cotta figures found at urban sites, which were clearly expressions of popular art (the official emblem of India since 1947 is based on the four-lion capital of the pillar at Sārnāth near Vārānasi).

Aśoka's ethic of behaviour

In his edicts Aśoka defines the main principles of *dhamma* as nonviolence, tolerance of all sects and opinions, obedience to parents, respect for the Brahmins and other religious teachers and priests, liberality toward friends, humane treatment of servants, and generosity toward all. It suggests a general ethic of behaviour to which no religious or social group could object. It could also act as a focus of loyalty to weld together the diverse strands that made up the empire. Interestingly, the Greek versions of these edicts translate *dhamma* as *eusebeia* (piety), and no mention is made anywhere of the teachings of the Buddha, which would be expected if Aśoka had been propagating Buddhism. His own activities under the impact of *dhamma* included attention to the welfare of his subjects, the building of roads and rest houses, the planting of medicinal herbs, the setting up of centres to cater to the sick, a ban on animal sacrifices, and the curtailing of killing animals for food. He also instituted a body of officials known as the *dhamma-mahāmattas*, who served the dual function of propagating the *dhamma* and keeping him in touch with public opinion. Some of these *dhamma-mahāmattas* were sent on missions to the neighbouring kingdoms.

Mauryan decline. Some historians maintain that the disintegration of the Mauryan Empire was an aftermath of Aśoka's policies and actions and that his pro-Buddhist policy caused a revolt among the Brahmins. The edicts do not support such a contention. It has also been said that his insistence on nonviolence resulted in the emasculation of the army, which was consequently unable to meet the threat of invaders from the northwest. There is, however, no indication in any source that Aśoka deliberately ignored the military wing of his administration despite his emphasis on nonviolence.

Other explanations for the decline of the empire appear more plausible. Among these is the idea that there may have been an economic pressure on the empire. It has been thought that the silver currency of the Mauryas was debased as a result of this pressure. The expense required for the army and the bureaucracy must have tied up a substantial part of the income. It is equally possible that the expansion of agriculture did not keep pace with the expansion of the empire, and, because many parts of the empire were nonagricultural, the revenue from the agrarian economy may not have been sufficient for the maintenance of the empire. It is extremely difficult to compute the population of the empire, but, on a purely impressionistic basis, approximately 50,000,000 can be suggested. For such a population of mixed agriculturalists and others to support an empire of this size would have been extremely difficult. Recent excavations at urban sites show economic standards distinctly higher than the Mauryan levels of these sites, probably based on a sudden increase in trade; but the income from trade was unlikely to have been sufficient to supplement fully the land revenue in financing the empire.

It has been argued that the Mauryan bureaucracy at the higher levels tended to be oppressive. This may have been true during the reigns of the first two emperors, from which the evidence is cited, but oppression is unlikely during Aśoka's reign because he was responsible for a considerable decentralization at the upper levels and for continual checks and inspections. A more fundamental weakness lay in the process of recruitment, which was probably arbitrary, with the hierarchy of officials locally recruited.

The concept of the state. Allegiance presupposes the existence of the concept of the state. A number of varying notions had evolved to explain the evolution of the state. Some theorists pursued the thread of the Vedic monarchies, in which the tribal chief became the king and was gradually invested with divinity. An alternative set of theories arising out of Buddhist and Jaina thought ignored the idea of divinity and assumed instead that, in the original state of nature, all needs were effortlessly provided but that slowly a decline set in and man became evil, developing desires, which led to the notions of private property and of family and finally to immoral behaviour. In this state of chaos, the people gathered together and decided to elect one among them (the *mahāsammata*, or "great elect") in whom they would invest authority to maintain law and order. Thus the state came into being. Post-Buddhist theorists retained the notion of a contract between a ruler and the people (most Brahmanical theorists held that the gods appointed the ruler and a contract of dues was concluded between the ruler and the people). Prevalent was the theory of *mātsya-nyāya*—that in periods of chaos, when there is no ruler, the strong devour the weak, just as in periods of drought big fish eat little fish. The legitimacy of the need for a ruler was made absolute. The existence of the state was primarily dependent on two factors: *daṇḍa* (authority) and *dharma* (the social order; *i.e.*, the preservation of the caste structure).

But the importance of the political notion of the state gradually began to fade, partly because of a decline of the political tradition of the republics and the proportional dominance of the monarchical system, in which loyalty was directed to the king. The emergence of the Mauryan Empire strengthened the political notion of monarchy. The second factor was that the *dharma*, in the sense of the social order, demanded a far greater loyalty than did the rather blurred idea of the state. The king's duty was to protect *dharma*, and, as long as the social order remained intact, anarchy would not prevail. Loyalty to the social order, which was a fundamental aspect of Indian civilization, largely accounts for the impressive continuity of the major social institutions over many centuries. But it also deflected loyalty from the political notion of the state, which might otherwise have permitted more frequent empires and a greater political consciousness. The re-emergence of an empire was to take many centuries.

Loyalty toward the social order

150 BC–AD 300

The disintegration of the Mauryan Empire gave rise to a number of small kingdoms, whose regional pattern was often to be repeated in subsequent centuries. The Punjab and Kashmir were drawn into the orbit of Central Asian politics. The lower Indus Valley became a passage for movements from the north to the west. The Ganges Valley played a largely passive role except when faced with campaigns from the northwest. In the northern Deccan there arose the first of many important kingdoms that were to play a key role as the bridge between the north and the south. Kaliṅga was once more independent. In the extreme south, the prestige and influence of the Cēra, Cōla, and Pāṇḍya kingdoms continued unabated. Yet in spite of political fragmentation, this was a period of economic prosperity, resulting partly from a new source of income—foreign trade. Indian trading interests were established in Central Asia, China, the eastern Mediterranean and Southeast Asia.

Rise of small kingdoms in the north. The Seleucids, involved in the politics of the eastern Mediterranean, allowed their control over northeastern Iran to relax, and Bactria and Parthia thus broke away. Diodotus, the Greek governor of Bactria, rose in rebellion against the Seleucid king Antiochus and declared his independence, which was recognized by Antiochus in 250 BC.

Indo-Greek rulers. A later Bactrian king, Demetrius II (ruled *c.* 180–165 BC), took his armies into the Punjab and finally down the Indus Valley and gained control of northwestern India. This introduced what has come to be called Indo-Greek rule. The chronology of the Indo-Greek rulers is based largely on numismatic evidence. Their coins were, at the start, imitations of Greek issues, but by the 2nd century BC they had acquired a style of their own and were particularly noted for excellent portraiture. The legend was generally inscribed in Greek and Brāhmī, the latter being the script used for Prākrit in this case.

The best known of the Indo-Greek kings was Menander, known to Indian sources as Milinda. He is featured in the Buddhist text, the *Milinda-pañha* ("Questions of Milinda"), written in the form of a dialogue between the King and the Buddhist philosopher Nāgasena, as a result of which the King is converted to Buddhism. Menander is known to have ruled during the years 155–130 BC. He controlled Gandhāra and Punjab, although his coins have been found farther south. According to one theory, he may have attacked the Śuṅgas in the Yamuna region and attempted to extend his control into the Ganges Valley, but, if he did so, he failed to annex it. Incidental references are made to the Yavanas in Madhyadeśa in the grammar *Mahābhāṣya* of Patañjali (*c.* 2nd century BC). Meanwhile, in Bactria itself, the descendants of the line of Eucratides, who had branched off from the original Bactrian line, now began to take an interest in Gandhāra and finally annexed Kābul and the kingdom of Takṣaśilā (Taxila). An important Prākrit inscription at Besnagar (Bhilsā district) of the late 2nd century BC, inscribed at the instance of a Greek, Heliodorus, records his devotion to the Vaiṣṇava Vāsudeva sect; he describes himself as the envoy of King Antialcidas of Taxila.

Asian rulers. The Bactrian control of Taxila was disturbed by an intrusion of the Scythians, known to Indian sources as the Śakas. They had attacked the kingdom of Bactria and now moved into India. The determination of the Han (rulers of China) to keep the Central Asian nomadic tribes (the Hsiung-nu, Wu-sun, and Yüeh-chih) out of China forced these nomadic tribes in their search for fresh pastures to migrate southward and westward; a branch of the Yüeh-chih, the Ta Yüeh-chih, moved farthest west to the Aral Sea, and this displaced the existing Śakas, who poured into Bactria and Parthia. The Parthian king Mithridates II tried to hold them back, but after his death (88 BC) they swept through Parthia and continued into the Indus Valley; among the early Śaka kings was Maues, or Moga (1st century BC), who ruled over Gandhāra. The Śakas moved southward under pressure from the Pahlavas, who ruled briefly in northwestern India toward the end of the 1st century BC. At Mathurā the Śaka rulers of note were Rājuvala and Śoḍāsa. Ultimately the Śakas settled in western India and Mālava and came into conflict with the kingdoms of the northern Deccan and the Ganges Valley, particularly during the reigns of Nahapāna, Caṣṭana, and Rudradāman in the first two centuries AD. Rudradāman's fame is recorded in a lengthy Sanskrit inscription at Junāgadh, dating to 150.

Intrusion of the Śakas

Kujūla Kadphises, the Yüeh-chih chief, conquered northern India in the 1st century AD. He was succeeded by his son Vīma, and after him came Kaniṣka, the most powerful among the Kuṣāṇa (Kushan) kings, as they came to be called. The date of Kaniṣka is controversial, ranging from 78 to 248. The generally accepted view is 78, based largely on literary and epigraphical evidence from Indian sources and archaeological evidence and carbon-14 dating of finds from Soviet Central Asia. More recent numismatic evidence, however (particularly the similarity between Roman and Kuṣāṇa coins), as well as evidence from Chinese and Iranian sources, points to a date as late as the 2nd century AD. The era based on 78, which is used in addition to the Gregorian calendar by the present Indian government and presumably was started by the Śakas, is sometimes explained by the assumed date of Kaniṣka's accession; the era was widely used in Mālava, Ujjain, Nepal, and Central Asia. The Kuṣāṇa kingdom was essentially oriented to the north, with its capital at Puruṣapura (near modern Peshāwar), although it extended southward as far as Sāñcī and into the Ganges Valley as far as Vārānasi. Mathurā was the most important city in the southern part of the kingdom. Kaniṣka's ambitions included control of Central Asia, which if not directly under the Kuṣāṇas did come under their influence. Kaniṣka's successors failed to maintain Kuṣāṇa power. The southern areas were the first to break away, and, by the middle of the 3rd century, the Kuṣāṇas were left virtually with only Gandhāra and Kashmir. By the end of the century, they were reduced to vassalage by the Sasanian king of Persia.

Not surprisingly there were administrative and political terms in northern India at this time commonly found in western and Central Asia. The Persian term for the governor of a province, *khshathrapavan*, as used by the Achaemenids, was Hellenized into "satrap" and widely used by these dynasties. Its Sanskrit form was *kṣatrapa.* The governors of higher status came to be called *mahākṣatrapa;* they frequently issued inscriptions in whatever era they chose to follow, and they minted their own coins, indicating a more independent status than is generally associated with governors. Imperial titles were also taken by the Indo-Greeks, such as *basileus basileōn* ("king of kings"), similar to the Persian *shāhanshāh*, of which the later Sanskrit form was *mahārājādhirāja*. A title of Central Asian derivation was the *daivaputra* of the Kuṣāṇas, which is believed to have come originally from the "son of heaven" current in China.

Local tribal republics and kingdoms. The watershed between the Indus and Ganges valleys was the nucleus of a number of tribal republics whose local importance rose and fell in inverse proportion to the rise and fall of larger kingdoms. According to numismatic evidence, the most important politically were the Ārjunāyanas, Mālavas, Yaudheyas, Śibis, and the Ābhīra. The Ārjunāyanas had their base in the present Bharatpur-Alwar region. The Mālavas appear to have migrated from the Punjab to Jaipur (Rājasthān), perhaps after the Indo-Greek invasions; they are associated with the Mālava era, which has been identified with the Vikrama era, also known as the Kṛta era and dating to 58 BC. It is likely that southern Rājasthān as far as the Narmada River and the Ujjain district was named after the Mālavas. Yaudheya evidence is scattered over many parts of the Punjab and the adjoining areas of Rājasthān and Uttar Pradesh, but during this period their stronghold appears to have been the Rohtak district, north of Delhi; the frequent use of the term *gaṇa* in Yaudheya coins points to an adherence to the tribal tradition. References to Śaivite deities, especially Kārttikeya or Skanda, the legendary son of Śiva, are striking. The Śibis also migrated from the Punjab to Rājasthān and settled at Mādhyamika (near Chittor). The Ābhīras lived in scattered settlements in various parts of western and central India as far as the Deccan. Most of these tribes claimed descent from the ancient lineages of the *Purāṇas*, and some of them were later connected with the rise of Rājput dynasties.

In addition to the tribal republics, there were small monarchical states, such as Ayodhyā, Kauśāmbī, and the scattered Nāga kingdoms, the most important of which was the one at Padmāvatī (Gwalior). Ahicchatrā (the Bareilly district of Uttar Pradesh) was ruled by kings who bore names ending in the suffix *-mitra*.

Successors to the Maurya

The Śuṅga kingdom. Magadha was the nucleus of the Śuṅga kingdom, which succeeded the Mauryan. The kingdom extended westward to include Ujjain and Vidiśā. The Śuṅgas came into conflict with Vidarbha and with the Yavanas, probably Bactrian Greeks attempting to move into the Ganges Valley. (The word *yavana* is derived from the Prākrit *yonā*, suggesting that the Ionians were the first Greeks to come into contact with Persia and India, presumably during the Achaemenid period. In later centuries Yavana was used for all peoples coming from western Asia and the Mediterranean, and it then included the Romans, Persians, and Arabs). The Śuṅga dynasty lasted for about one century and was then overthrown by the Brahmin minister Vāsudeva, who founded the Kāṇva dynasty, which lasted 45 years and was in turn overthrown by the Andhras, the ruling power of the Deccan. But the Andhras are not known to have ruled in Magadha, which area faded out of history until the 4th century AD.

Kaliṅga. Kaliṅga rose to importance in the 1st century BC under its king Khāravela. His date is controversial, but an earlier identification of the 3rd century BC would conflict with the fact that Kaliṅga was then a part of the Mauryan Empire. Khāravela claimed, perhaps exaggeratedly for a pious Jaina, successful campaigns in the western Deccan and against the Yavanas and Magadha and a triumphal victory over the Pāṇḍyas of South India.

The Andhras and their successors. The Andhras are listed among the tribal peoples in the Mauryan Empire. Possibly they rose to being local officials and then, on the disintegration of the empire, gradually became independent rulers of the northwestern Deccan. It cannot be ascertained for certain whether they arose in the Andhra region (*i.e.*, the Krishna–Godāvari deltas) and moved up to the northwestern Deccan or whether their settling in the delta gave it their name. There is also controversy as to whether the dynasty became independent at the end of the 3rd century BC or at the end of the 1st century BC. Their alternative name, Sātavāhana, is presumed to be the family name, whereas Andhra was probably that of the tribe. It is likely that Sātavāhana power was established during the reign of Śātarkarṇi I, with the borders of the kingdom reaching across the northern Deccan; subsequent to this the Sātavāhanas suffered an eclipse when they were forced out of the northwestern Deccan by the Śakas in the 1st century AD, and they settled in Andhra. In the 2nd century AD the Sātavāhanas re-established their power in the northwestern Deccan; among other things, coins of the Śaka Nahapāna found in this region are often overstruck by the name Gautamīputra Śātakarṇi. That he did not control Mālava and Ujjain is clear from the claim of the Śaka king Rudradāman to these regions. The last of the important Andhra kings was Yajñaśrī Śātakarṇi, who ruled at the end of the 2nd century AD and asserted his authority over the Śakas. The 3rd century saw the decline of Sātavāhana power as the kingdom broke into small pockets of control under various branches of the family.

The Sātavāhana feudatories then rose to power. The Ābhīras were the successors in the Nāsik area and were associated with the Kalacuri-Cedi era of 248–249; their inscriptions, like those of other successors to the Sātavāhanas, bear the strong imprint of the Sātavāhana style. The Ikṣvākus succeeded in the Krishna–Guntūr region. The Cūtū dynasty in Kuntala (southern Mahārāshtra) had had close connections with the Sātavāhanas. The Bodhis ruled briefly in the northwestern Deccan. The Bṛhatphalāyanas came to power at the end of the 3rd century in the Masulipatnam area. In these regions the Sātavāhana pattern of administration continued; most of the rulers had matronymics, which have been interpreted as a possible derivation from earlier matriarchal societies. Many of the royal inscriptions record donations made to Buddhist monks and monasteries, often by princesses, and also land grants to Brahmins and the performance of Vedic sacrifices by the rulers.

Southern Indian civilizations. According to legend the sage Agastya travelled southward and introduced both the Sanskrit language and Aryan culture to the far south early in the 1st millennium BC. His disciple composed the first Tamil grammar, the *Tolkāppiyam*. Significant historically attested contact between the north and the Tamil regions can be reasonably dated to the Mauryan period. The third Buddhist council, held in about 250 BC, resulted in Buddhist missionary activities in these regions. Expansion in trade brought in the markets of the southern kingdoms. An inscription of Khāravela refers to the powerful confederacy of the Tamil countries; the most important evidence, however, on the early history of the south are the epigraphs of the region, the Tamil *caṅgam* literature, and archaeological evidence.

Inscriptions in Brāhmī (recently read as Tamil Brāhmī) date to between the 2nd century BC and the 4th century AD. Most of the inscriptions record donations made by royalty or by merchants and artisans to Buddhist and Jaina monks. They are useful to check the evidence from the *caṅgam* literature, a collection of a large number of poems in classical Tamil, which, according to tradition, were recited at three assemblies of poets held at Madurai. Included in this literature are the so-called Eight Anthologies (*Ettutogai*) and Ten Idylls (*Pattuppāṭṭu*). It is said that the *Tolkāppiyam* is also of the same period. Though some scholars regard the *Śilappadikaram* (*Śilappadigāram*) and the *Maṇimekhalai* as of this period, most maintain that they were written some centuries later. The literature probably belongs to the same period as the inscriptions, although some scholars suggest a much earlier date. The historical authenticity of sections of the *caṅgam* literature has recently been confirmed by archaeological evidence

The *caṅgam* literature

Tamilākam, the abode of the Tamils, was defined in *caṅgam* literature as the area from Kanyā Kāmārī to the Tirupati Hill and from the east coast to the west. North of the Tirupati Hill the language changed. Tamilākam was divided into 13 *nāḍus* (districts), of which the region of Madurai was the most important as the core of the Tamil speakers. The three major kingdoms of Tamilākam were those of the Pāṇḍyas (Madurai), the Cēras (Malabar Coast and the hinterland), and the Cōlas

(Thanjāvūr and the Kāverī Valley). The inscriptions of the Pāṇḍyas, recording royal grants and other grants made by local citizens, go back to the 2nd century BC. The king Neduñjeliyaṉ (early 3rd century AD) is celebrated by the poets of the *caṅgam* as the victor in campaigns against the Cēras and the Cōlas. Cēra inscriptions of the 2nd century AD referring to the Irrumporai dynasty have been found near Karūr (Tiruchchirāpalli district), which has been identified with Korura, the inland capital of the Cēra kingdom according to Ptolemy. *Śaṅgam* literature mentions the names of Cēra kings who have been dated to the 1st century AD. Among them Nedunjēral Ādan is said to have attacked the Yavana ships and held the Yavana traders to ransom. His son Śenguṭṭuvan, much eulogized in the poems, is also mentioned in the context of King Gajabāhu of Ceylon, who can be dated to either the first or last quarter of the 2nd century AD, depending on whether he was the earlier or the later Gajabāhu. Among the Irrumporai kings was Perunjēral, who is said to have annexed the neighbouring northern area (Salem district). Karikālaṉ (late 2nd century AD) is the best known of the early Cōla kings and was to become almost a kind of eponymous ancestor to many families of the south claiming Cōla descent. The early capital was at Uraiyūr, the nucleus of the Cōla kingdom, which stretched from the Vaigai River in the south to Toṇḍaimaṇḍalam in the north. The three major kingdoms were frequently at war; in addition there were often hostilities with Ceylon. Mention is also made of the ruler of Toṇḍaimaṇḍalam with its capital at Kāñchīpuram, which was to be the heart of Pallava power. There are also references to the minor chieftains, the Vel, who ruled small areas in many parts of the Tamil country. Some of them claimed ancestry from a person who sprang out of the sacrificial fire of a northern sage, a story which was to be repeated in connection with the ancestry of a group of later northern Indian dynasties. Ultimately all the kingdoms suffered at the hands of the Kalvār, or Kalabras, who came from the border to the north of Tamilākam and were described as evil rulers; but they were overthrown in the 5th century AD, with the rise of the Cālukyas and Pallavas.

Caṅgam literature reflects the indigenous cultural tradition as well as elements of the intrusion of the northern Aryan tradition, which by now was beginning to come into contact with these areas, many of which changed from tribal chieftainships to kingdoms. The predominant economy remained a pastoral-cum-agrarian economy, with an increasing emphasis on agriculture. In one of the poems in which reference is made to the different castes, the word *kudi*, literally meaning a "group," is used for caste. Each village had its *sabhā*, or council, which conducted local affairs and attended to the problems of the village. This tradition was to continue for centuries and became the base for the village councils of the later Cōla period. Religion concentrated in the main on worshipping a number of deities, pre-eminently Murugaṉ, and the ritual of worship in this case was sacrifice.

Trade between northern and southern India

The main economic momentum for the South Indian kingdoms was provided by trade with the Yavanas and with the northern parts of the subcontinent. Given the terrain of the peninsula and the agricultural technology of the time, large agrarian-based kingdoms like those of northern India were not feasible. Inevitably trade played more than a marginal role, and overseas trade became a major economic activity. Almost as soon as the Roman trade began to decline, the Southeast Asian trade was initiated; in subsequent centuries this became the focus of maritime interest.

Contacts with the West. Trade between western Asia and the western coast of India is often mentioned in sources referring to the 1st millennium BC. Hebrew texts refer to the port of Ophir—identified with Sopārā, the Śūrpāraka of the west coast of India near Bombay, described as a market for gold, spices, precious stones, ivory, apes, and peacocks. Indian teak and cedar were used in Babylonian buildings in the 7th and 6th centuries BC. The Buddhist *Jātaka* literature mentions trade with Baveru, the Indian name for Babylon. After the decline of Babylon, Arab merchants from southern Arabia apparently continued the trade, probably supplying goods to Egypt and the eastern Mediterranean. The trade was then taken up by Greek and, to a larger extent, Roman traders. The discovery of the regular seasonal monsoon winds, enabling ships to drive a straight course across the Arabian Sea, made a considerable difference to shipping and navigation on the route from western Asia to India. Unification of the Mediterranean and western Asian world at the turn of the Christian Era under the Roman Empire brought Roman trade into close contact with India—overland with northern India and by sea with southern India. The emperor Augustus received two embassies from India in 25–21 BC, and these almost certainly were trade missions.

Trade with the Romans

The *Periplus Maris Erythraei*, written in the 1st century AD, lists a series of ports along the Indian coast including Muziris (Cranganore), Colchi (Korkai), Poduca, and Sopatma. Even more impressive is the evidence from archaeology and numismatics. An excavation at Arikamedu (near Pondicherry), believed to be the Poduca of the *Periplus* and Ptolemy, revealed a Roman trading settlement of the 1st and 2nd centuries AD; quantities of Roman pottery, beads, intaglios, lamps, glass, and coins point to a continuous occupation. It would seem that textiles were prepared to Roman specification and exported from such settlements. Pottery and graffiti in Brāhmī provide the local evidence.

Large hoards of Roman coins substantiate other evidence. Coins of the 1st century AD are found mainly around Coimbatore (Tamil Nadu), suggesting that initially the ships berthed along the western coast and that goods were transported overland to the eastern coast. The coins are mainly of the emperors Augustus (ruled 27 BC–AD 14), Tiberius (ruled 14–37), and Nero (ruled 54–68). Their frequency suggests that the Romans paid for the trade in gold coins, and the fact that many are overstruck with a bar may indicate that they were used as bullion in India; certainly, Pliny complained that the Indian luxury trade was depleting the Roman treasury. The coins are found most often in trading centres or near the sources of semiprecious stones, especially quartz and beryl. *Caṅgam* literature attests the prosperity of Yavana merchants trading in towns such as Kāvēripaṭṭinam (in the Kāverī Delta). The *Periplus* lists the major exports of India as pepper, pearls, ivory, silk, spikenard (an aromatic plant), precious stones, malabathrum, tortoiseshells, and textiles. For these the Romans traded glass, copper, tin, lead, realgar, orpiment, antimony, and wine, or else they paid in gold coins. The balance of trade appears to have been in favour of India.

Legend has it that St. Thomas travelled from western Asia to Malabar in AD 52. He is believed to have established a number of Syrian churches, which would perhaps account for Syrian Christianity being the major form of Christianity until the arrival of the Portuguese in India in the 15th century. Historical evidence of the Christian community in India cannot be found, however, earlier than the 7th century AD.

Maritime trade routes

The maritime trade routes from the Indian ports were primarily to the Persian Gulf and southern Arabia, from where they went overland to the eastern Mediterranean and to Egypt. Indian merchants also ventured out to Southeast Asia seeking spices and semiprecious stones. Initially merchants from western India, Kaliṅga, and South India settled in small trading communities in Burma, Malaya, Cambodia, Sumatra, Java, and Bali; gradually merchants from other coastal areas also began to participate in this trade. The river valleys and the Mauryan roads were the chief routes within India. Greek sources refer to a royal highway built by the Mauryas, connecting Taxila with Pāṭaliputra and terminating at Tāmraliptī, the main port in the Ganges Delta. On the western coast the major port of Bhṛgukaccha (modern Broach) was connected with the Ganges Valley via Rājasthān or, alternatively, Ujjain. From the Narmada Valley there were routes going into the northwestern Deccan and continuing along rivers flowing eastward to various parts of the peninsula. Goods were transported mainly in caravans of oxen and donkeys, but only in the hot and cool seasons, the rains creating an impossible time for travel. Coastal and river shipping, used where possible, was clearly cheaper than land routes. In the north the route from Taxila went to Kābul and Qandahār and from there branched off in various directions, mainly linking up with routes across Persia to the Black Sea ports and the eastern Mediterranean. The route connecting China with Bactria via Central Asia, soon to become famous as the Old Silk Route, linked the oases of Kashgar, Yarkand, Khotan, Miran, Kucha, Karashahr, and Turfan, in all of which Indian merchants were to establish trading stations. The Central Asian route brought Chinese goods in large quantities into the Indian and west Asian markets.

Society and culture. The commercial economy played a central role during this period. Agrarian expansion was not arrested, and land revenue continued to be a major source of income, but profit from trade made a substantial difference to the economy. Not surprisingly there was a marked improvement in the urban standard of living.

Guilds. Related to commercial activity was the development of the social institution most closely connected with it—the *śreṇi* (guild), through which trade was channelled at various levels. The guilds were registered with the town authority, and the behaviour of guild members was regulated by the *śreṇi-dharma* (rules of conduct of the guild). The more wealthy guilds employed slaves and hired labourers in addition to their own artisans, though the percentage of such slaves appears to have been small. Guilds had their own seals and insignia. They often made lavish donations to Buddhist and Jaina monasteries, and some of the finest Buddhist monuments of the period were the result of such donations. In some areas, such as the Deccan, members of the royal family invested money with a particular guild, and the accruing interest became a regular donation to the Buddhist *saṅgha.* This must also incidentally have increased the political importance of the guild.

Finance. With the development of the money economy, the role of the financier and banker became extremely important. Sometimes this role was performed by the richer guilds, but the more regular source of money was the merchant financier (*śreṣṭhin*). There was a large variety of coins, minted with a high degree of professional skill in the various kingdoms. The most commonly used were the gold *dīnāras* and *suvarṇas*, based on the Roman denarius (124 grains); a range of silver coins, such as the earlier *kārṣāpaṇa* or *paṇa* (57.8 grains) and the *śatamāna;* an even wider range of copper coins, such as the *kārṣāpaṇa* (144 grains), *māṣa* (nine grains), *kākiṇī* (2.25 grains), and a variety of unspecified standards; and other coins, issued in lead and potin, particularly in western India. Usury was a regular part of the banker's trade, with 15 percent being the generally accepted interest rate, although this varied according to the enterprise for which the money was borrowed. Increasing trade also led to the use of a great variety of weights and measures.

Impact of trade. The economic impact of foreign trade was probably greatest in the south, but the interchange of ideas appears to have been more substantial in the north. This may have been due to a longer association with western Asia and the colonial Hellenic culture exported from these lands. Greek together with Aramaic was widely spoken in Afghanistan and was doubtless understood in Taxila. The spurt of geographical studies in the Mediterranean resulted in works with extensive descriptions of the trade with India; these included Strabo's *Geography*, Ptolemy's *Geography*, the *Periplus Maris Erythraei*, and Pliny's *Natural History*. The most obvious and visible impact was in Gandhāra art, which depicted Indian themes in the Greco-Roman style of Alexandrian art—an attractive hybrid that accelerated the frequency of the icon in Buddhist art.

Religious patronage

Religion. If art remains are an index to patronage, then Buddhism seems to have been the most favoured religion. Buddhist centres generally had a complex of three structures—the monastery (*vihāra*), the hall of worship (*caitya*), and the sacred tumulus (*stūpa*)—all of which were freestanding structures in the north but were initially rock-cut monuments in the Deccan. The Jainas found more patrons in the Deccan. Hindu temples are referred to in literature, but none has been actually found dating to this period. Apart from the Gandhāra style of sculpture, a number of indigenous centres in other parts of India, such as Mathurā, Kārlī, Nāgārjunakoṇḍa, and Amarāvatī, portrayed Buddhist legends in a variety of local stone. The more popular medium was terra-cotta, by then changed from gray to red, depicting not only men and women in the ordinary walks of life and animal figures but also large numbers of mother-goddesses, indicating the continued and popular worship of these deities.

The practice of Buddhism was itself undergoing change. Affluent patronage provided the big monasteries with endowments of land and slaves to work the land. Association with royalty gave Buddhism access to power. The proselytizing consciousness that had gradually evolved now saw Buddhist monks as missionaries travelling to Central Asia and China, western Asia, and Southeast Asia. New situations inevitably led to the need for new ideas, as is most clearly seen in the contact of Buddhism with Christianity and Zoroastrianism in Central Asia. Certain aspects of the legend of the lives of the Buddha and Christ are strikingly similar (*e.g.*, a miraculous birth, the fasting in the wilderness, the temptation by the devil). The practices of the Essenes also reflect some knowledge of Indian belief and life. Arguments over the original teaching of the Buddha had already resulted in a series of councils called to clarify the doctrine. The two main sects were the Theravāda, with its centre at Kauśāmbī, which compiled the Pāli canon on Buddhist teachings, and the Sarvāstivāda, which arose at Mathurā, spread northward, and finally established itself in Central Asia, using Sanskrit as the language for preserving the Buddhist tradition. A fourth council, held in Kashmir during the reign of Kaniṣka, ratified the separation of the two main schools of Buddhism—the Mahāyāna (Greater Vehicle) and the Hīnayāna (Lesser Vehicle).

Jainism had by now also split into two groups—the Digambara (Sky-Clad; *i.e.*, naked), the more orthodox, and the Śvetāmbara (White-Clad), the more liberal. The Jainas were not as widespread as the Buddhists, their main centres being in western India, Kaliṅga for a brief period, and the Mysore and Tamil country.

Brahmanism also underwent changes with the gradual fading out of some of the Vedic deities. The two major gods were Viṣṇu and Śiva, around whom there emerged a monotheistic trend perhaps best expressed in the *Bhagavadgītā*, which most authorities would date to the 1st century BC. The doctrine of *karma* and rebirth, emphasizing the influence of actions performed either in this life or in former births on the present and future lives, became central to Hindu belief and influenced both religious and social notions. Vedic sacrifices were not discontinued but gradually became symbols of such ceremonial occasions as royal consecrations. Sacrificial ritual was beginning to be replaced by the practice of *bhakti* (personal devotion), positing a personal relationship between the individual and the deity.

Literature. Popular epics, such as the *Mahābhārata* and the *Rāmāyaṇa*, were injected with didactic sections on religion and morality and given the status of sacred literature. Their heroes Kṛṣṇa and Rāma were incorporated into Vaiṣṇavism as *avatāras* (incarnations) of Viṣṇu. The concept of incarnations was useful in incorporating local deities and cults.

Sacred literature

The epics were also used as a treasury of stories, which were converted into poems and plays. The dramas of Bhāsa were among these. His two best known plays, *Svapnavāsavadatta* and *Pratijñāyaugandharāyaṇa*, formed parts of the foundation of Sanskrit drama. Aśvaghoṣa, another major Sanskrit dramatist, based his works on Buddhist themes. The popularity of drama necessitated the writing of a work on dramaturgy, the *Nāṭya-śāstra* ("Treatise on Dramatic Art") of Bharata. The composition of *Dharma-śāstras* (law books), among which the most often quoted is ascribed to Manu, became important in a period of social flux in which traditional social law and usage were important as precedent. A new grammar of Sanskrit had been provided by the *Mahābhāṣya* of Patañjali, timely because even the non-Indian dynasties of the north and west made extensive use of Sanskrit. The two sciences that received attention were astronomy and medicine, both of which indicate an interchange of ideas with western Asia. Doubtless, the new navigation along midocean routes was a considerable incentive to improved knowledge in astronomy. Two basic medical treatises, composed by Caraka and Suśruta, date to this period.

Assimilation of foreigners. The presence of foreigners, most of whom settled in Indian cities and took on Indian habits and behaviour in addition to religion, became a problem for social theorists because the newcomers had to be fitted into caste society. It was easier to accommodate a group rather than an individual into the social hierarchy, because the group could be given a *jāti* status. Technically, conversion to Hinduism was difficult because one had to be born into a particular caste, and it was *karma* that determined one's caste. The theoretical definition of caste society continued as before, and the four *varṇa*s were referred to as the units of society. The problem of including new groups was more acute in the two upper castes. The assimilation of local cults, for instance, demanded the assimilation of cult priests, who had to be accommodated within the Brahmanical hierarchy. The Greeks and the Śakas, clearly of non-Indian origin, who were initially the ruling group were referred to as "fallen Kṣatriyas." The Vaiśya and Śūdra groups did not pose such a serious problem because they were vaguely defined and consequently socially more mobile. It is likely that in such periods of social change some lower caste groups may have moved up the ladder of social hierarchy.

Adapted from C.C. Davies, *An Historical Atlas of the Indian Peninsula* (1959); Oxford University Press

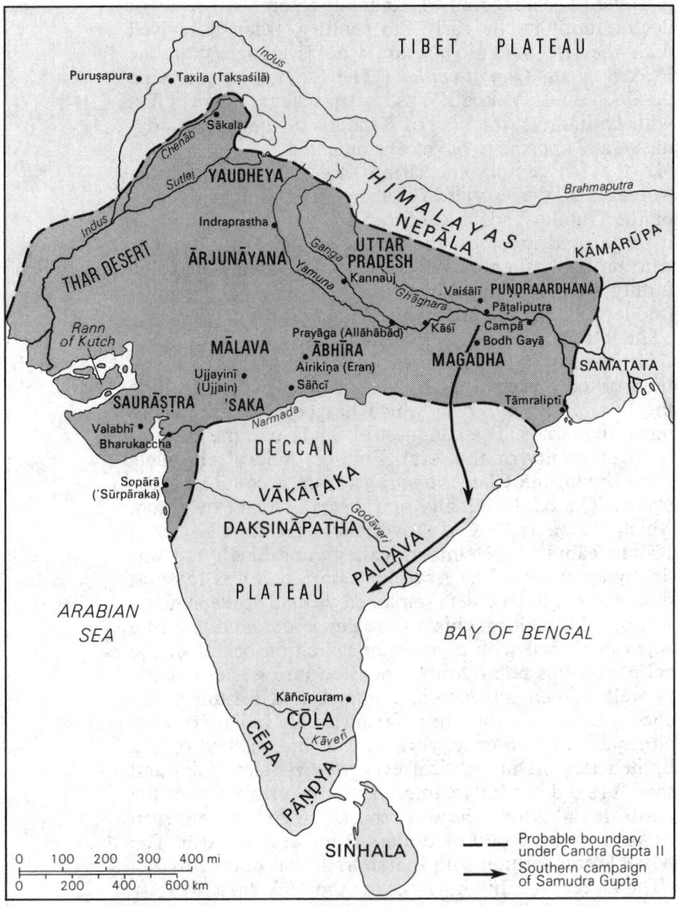

The Gupta Empire at the end of the 4th century.

AD 300–750

Northern India. *The Guptas.* The Gupta period (*c.* 320–540) has often been called the Classical Age of India. It was a period during which the norms of Indian literature, art, architecture, and philosophy were established, at least in some parts of India, in the form that came to be regarded as standard. It was an age of material prosperity in most areas, particularly among the urban elite, and it was a period of renascent Hinduism. The Gupta period has also been called an imperial age, but with less justification, since administrative centralization so characteristic of an imperial system is less apparent than during the Mauryan period.

The Guptas, a comparatively unknown family, came from either Magadha or eastern Uttar Pradesh. The third king, Candra Gupta I, took the title of *mahārājādhirāja*. He married a Licchavi princess—an event celebrated in a series of gold coins. It has been suggested that, if the Guptas ruled in Prayāga (modern Allāhābād in eastern Uttar Pradesh), the marriage alliance may have added Magadha to their domain, assuming that the Licchavis had no heir. The Gupta Era began in 320, but it is not clear whether this date commemorated the accession of Candra Gupta or the assumption of the title of independence.

Campaigns of Samudra Gupta

Candra Gupta appointed his son Samudra Gupta to succeed him *c.* 330, according to a long eulogy (*praśasti*) to Samudra Gupta inscribed on a pillar at Allāhābād. The coins of an obscure prince, Kācha, suggest that there may have been contenders for the throne but that it was Samudra Gupta who was successful. Samudra Gupta's campaigns took him in various directions and resulted in many conquests. Not all the conquered regions were annexed, but the range of operations established the military prowess of the Guptas. According to the Allāhābād inscription, eight rulers of Āryāvarta in northern India were "violently uprooted." Samudra Gupta also conquered the states of Dakṣināpatha but reinstated the conquered rulers. The route of this campaign was along the east coast as far south as Kāñcīpuram (near Madras). Mention is also made of forest chiefs who were reduced to servitude. Five border states in the east, in addition to Nepal and the north, acknowledged the Gupta king. Nine tribal republics including the Mālavas, Ārjunāyanas, Yaudheyas, and Ābhīras are listed as having become subservient. Another category included more distant rulers who were regarded as subordinate: the Daivaputra-shāhi-shāhanushāhi of the northwest, Śaka, Muruṇḍa, and the inhabitants of "all the other islands," including Siṅhala (Ceylon). It would seem that the campaign extended Gupta power in northern and eastern India and virtually eliminated the republics and the minor kings of central India and the Ganges Valley. The more distant regions may not have been subordinate, but they were included largely because the composition was a eulogy. The islands remain problematical, since they could have been the ones close to India or else those of Southeast Asia with which communication was now close. It would appear that the conquest of the Ganges Valley and central India was the extension of the kingdom and remained the area under direct administrative control. The campaign in the eastern coastal areas may have been prompted by the desire to acquire the trading wealth of these regions. The grim image of Samudra Gupta as a military conqueror is ameliorated, however, by references to his love of poetry and music. That this portrait was not mere flattery is indicated by coins on which he is depicted playing the lute (*vīṇā*).

Samudra Gupta was succeeded *c.* 380 by his son Candra Gupta II, though there is some evidence that there may have been an intermediate ruler. Candra Gupta II's major campaign was against the Śaka rulers of Ujjain, the success of which was celebrated in a series of silver coins. Gupta interest lay not merely in the political control of the west but in the wealth the area derived from trade with western and southeastern Asia. Gupta territory adjoining the northern Deccan was secured through a marriage alliance with the Vākāṭaka dynasty, the successors of the Sātavāhanas in the area. Though Candra Gupta II took the title of Vikramāditya (Sun of Valour), his reign is associated more with cultural and intellectual achievements than it is with campaigns. It was also during his reign that Fa-hsien, a Chinese Buddhist, travelled to India and left an account of his impressions.

There is considerable epigraphic evidence relating to the administration of the Gupta kingdom. The kingdom was divided into provinces called *deśa* or *bhukti*, and these in turn into smaller units, the *pradeśa* or *viṣaya*. The provinces were governed by *kumārāmātyas*, high imperial officers or members of the royal family. That there was decentralization is clear from the composition of the municipal board (*adhiṣṭhāna-adhikaraṇa*), which consisted of the guild president (*nagara-śreṣṭhin*), the chief merchant (*sārthavāha*), and representatives of the artisans and of the scribes. During this period the term *sāmanta*, which originally meant neighbour, was beginning to be applied to landed intermediaries who had been given grants of land or to conquered feudatory rulers. There was also a noticeable tendency for some of the higher administrative offices to become hereditary.

The Hūṇas invasion

The first hint of a fresh invasion from the northwest comes in the reign of Candra Gupta's son and successor, Kumāra Gupta (*c.* 415–455). The threat was that of the Huns, or Hūṇas as they are called in Indian sources. Skanda Gupta (*c.* 455–467), who succeeded Kumāra Gupta, and his successors all had to face the full-fledged invasion of the Hūṇas. Skanda Gupta managed to rally Gupta strength for a while, but after his death the situation deteriorated. Dissensions within the royal family added to the problem. Gupta genealogies of this period show considerable variance in their succession lists. By the mid-6th century, when the dynasty apparently came to an end, the kingdom had dwindled to a small size. Northern India and parts of central India were in the hands of the Hūṇas.

The Hūṇas were a branch of the Ephthalites, or White Huns, one section of which migrated to the Volga Valley and another to the Oxus. The latter invaded Persia and Afghanistan, and from there a group swept into northern India. The first Hūṇa king in India was Toramāṇa (early 6th century), whose inscriptions have been found as far south as Eran (Madhya Pradesh). His son Mihirakula, a patron of Śaivism, is recorded in Buddhist tradition as uncouth and extremely cruel. The Gupta rulers, together with Yaśodharman of Mālava, seem to have confronted Mihirakula and forced him back to the north. Ultimately his kingdom was limited to Kashmir and Punjab with the capital at Śākala (Siālkot). Hūṇa power declined after his reign.

The coming of the Hūṇas brought northern India once more into close contact with Central Asia, and a number of Central Asian tribes migrated into India. It has been suggested that the Gurjaras, who gradually spread to Kashmir, Punjab, Rājasthān, Gujarāt, and northern Mahārāshtra, may be identified with the Khazars of Central Asia. The Hūṇa invasion challenged the stability of the Gupta kingdom, even though the ultimate decline may have been caused by internal factors. A severe blow to the Gupta kingdom was the disruption of the Central Asian trade caused by the Hun movement and the consequent disruption of the income that northern India had derived from it. Some of the tribes of northern India migrated to other regions, and this movement of peoples affected changes in the social structure of the post-Gupta period. The rise of Rājput families and "Kṣatriya" dynasties (see below *The Rājputs*) are associated by some scholars with tribal chiefs in these new areas.

Successor states. Of the kingdoms that arose as inheritors of the Gupta territory, the most important were those of Valabhī (Saurāṣṭra and Kāthiāwār); Gujarāta (originally the area near Jodhpur), believed to be the nucleus of the later Pratihāra kingdom; Nandipurī (near Broach); Maukhari (Magadha); the kingdom of the later Guptas (in the area between Mālava and Magadha) and those of Bengal, Nepal, and Kāmarūpa. In Nepal, effective political power passed into the hands of Aṃśuvarman, an erstwhile feudatory chief—a pattern by no means peculiar to Nepal. In the Assam valley the royal family of Kāmarūpa became independent of Gupta sovereignty. Orissa was under the Māṇa and Śailodbhava dynasties before being conquered by Śaśāṅka, king of Gauḍa (lower Bengal), who in the early 7th century annexed a substantial part of the Ganges Valley, where he came into conflict with the Maukharis and the rising Puṣpabhūti dynasty of Thānesar (north of Delhi).

The reign of Harṣa

The Puṣpabhūti dynasty aspired to imperial status during the reign of Harṣa (Harṣavardhana). Sthāṇvīśvara (Thānesar) appears to have been a small principality, probably under the suzerainty of the Guptas. Harṣa came to the throne, in Thānesar, in 606 and ruled there for 41 years. The first of the major historical biographies in Sanskrit, the *Harṣacarita* ("Deeds of Harṣa"), was written by Bāṇa, a celebrated author attached to his court, and contains information on Harṣa's early life. A full account of the period also survives, written by the Chinese Buddhist pilgrim Hsüan-tsang, who travelled through India and stayed for some time at a monastery at Nālandā. Harṣa (Farrukhābād district) acquired Kannauj and thereafter a large kingdom. A major but unsuccessful campaign was fought against Pulakeśin II, the Cālukya king of the northern Deccan, and Harṣa was confined to the northern half of the subcontinent. Nor was his success spectacular in western India against Valabhī, Nandipurī, and Sindh (lower Indus Valley). But in his eastern campaign, Harṣa met with little resistance (Śaśāṅka having died in 636) and acquired Magadha, Vaṅga, and Koṅgoda (Orissa). Although Harṣa failed to build an empire, his kingdom was of no mean size, and he earned the reputation of being the pre-eminent ruler of the north. Harṣa is remembered as the author of three Sanskrit plays—the *Ratnāvalī* and *Priyadarśikā* and the *Nāgānanda*—the theme of the last indicating his interest in Buddhist thought. The T'ang emperor of China, T'ai Tsung, sent a series of embassies to Harṣa. One of these arrived after Harṣa's death and found that the throne had been usurped. Finally the allies of Harṣa defeated the usurper, who, it is claimed, was taken to China as a prisoner. The kingdom of Kannauj entered a period of decline until in the early 8th century, when it revived with the rise of Yaśovarman, who is eulogized in the Prākrit poem *Gauḍa-vadha* ("The Slaying of the King of Gauḍa") of Vākpati. Yaśovarman came into conflict with Lalitāditya, the king of Kashmir of the Karkoṭa dynasty, and appears to have been defeated.

In the 8th century the rising power in western India was that of the Gurjara-Pratihāra. The Rājput dynasty of the Guhilla had its centre in Mēwar (with Chitor as its base) and arose on the defeat of the Mori Rājputs, who probably then moved to the Kotah area. The Cāpa family were associated with the city of Aṇahilapāṭaka (modern Pātan) and are involved in early Rājput history.

The Arab invasion

The late 7th and early 8th centuries saw a new threat—this time in Sindh—the invasion of the Arabs. Inscriptions of the western Indian dynasties speak of controlling the tide of the *mleccha*, which has been interpreted to mean the Arabs. The conquest of Sindh was the easternmost extremity of the Arab Empire. A local chronicle from Sindh, the *Chach-nāma*, gives an account of these events. The Arabs initially sent a small naval expedition, which was a failure. An overland expedition attacked Kābul, Zābul (the Helmand Valley), and Sindh and was finally successful. The Arab hold on Sindh was loose at first, and the local chiefs remained virtually independent. But by 724 the local chiefs were deposed, and direct rule was established with a governor ruling on behalf of the caliph. At this point Arab expansion into western India, as well as their advance into Punjab and Kashmir, was checked. The Arabs are referred to in Indian records either as *mleccha* or as *yavana*. The Indians had only a limited interest in political events in western Asia, and therefore did not fully comprehend the seriousness of the Arab threat. Along the west coast, the Arabs were seen as yet another group of traders from western Asia. The possible competition with Indian trade was not realized.

The Deccan. In the Deccan, the Vākāṭaka dynasty was closely tied to the Guptas. With a nucleus in Vidarbha, the founder of the dynasty, Vindhyaśakti, extended his power northward as far as Vidiśā (near Ujjain). At the end of the 4th century, a collateral line of the Vākāṭakas was established by Sarvasena in Vatsagulma (Bāsim, in Akola district), and the northern line helped the southern to conquer Kuntala (southern Mahārāshtra). That the main Vākāṭaka line dominated the northern Deccan during this period is clearly established by the matrimonial alliances not only with the Guptas but also with other peninsular dynasties such as the Viṣṇukuṇḍins and the Kadambas. The Vākāṭakas were weakened by attacks from Mālava and Kosala in the 5th century. Ultimately, the Cālukyas of Vātāpi (Bādāmi) ended their rule.

Inscriptions issued by the Nala kings show that part of the territory in Vidarbha was ruled by them in the 6th century. Nala territory extended through Bastar as far as Koraput (in Orissa). The Bhojas were also powerful in Vidarbha, probably in the Amraoti region. The Traikūṭakas were ruling in the northern coastal areas from approximately Bombay to Surat. In the second half of the 6th century, the Kalacuris settled in the Narmada Valley and occupied northern Mahārāshtra, Gujarāt, and Mālava. They also adopted the Cedi era dating from 248–249. Harassed by the rising power of the Cālukyas and Gurjaras, the Kalacuris moved east to Jabalpur, where they were to come into prominence again in the 9th century.

In the eastern Deccan, the Guntūr and Tenāli districts were ruled by the Ānanda family. In the 4th century Veṅgi came under the control of the Śālaṅkāyanas and, in the next century, passed into the hands of the Viṣṇukuṇḍin family, who ruled there until the early 7th century. The Viṣṇukuṇḍins, like many of the other newly risen dynasties of the peninsula, took great pride in the performance of Vedic sacrifices. They married into the Vākāṭaka family, probably to secure themselves against their neighbours—the eastern Gaṅgas and the Māṭharas ruling in Kaliṅga. The Pitṛbhaktas ruled the intervening territory of Vishākhapatnam. The Māṭharas occupied the Shrikakulam area and appear to have been overthrown by the Vasiṣṭha. An eastern branch of the Gaṅga dynasty established itself in southern Mysore and soon controlled not only the Ganjam district from where they began but Shrikakulam as well. Dakṣiṇa Kosala or southern Kosala (Raipur, Bilāspur, and Sambalpur areas), once part of the Sātavāhana empire, came under the rule of the Śarabhapurīya family. After the mid-6th century, the kingdom passed into the hands of the Pāṇḍuvaṃśis. A branch line of the dynasty appears to have ruled in Mekala (the Maikala Range near Amarakaṇṭaka).

The Cālukyas

The most significant kingdom of the Deccan was that of the Cālukyas, who are associated with Vātāpi (Bījāpur district) in the 6th century AD. The Cālukyas controlled large parts of the Deccan for two centuries. There were many branches of the family, the most important of which were the Eastern Cālukyas, ruling at Piṣṭapura (Pithāpuram in the Godāvari Delta) in the early 7th century; the Cālukyas of Vemulavada (near Karīmnagar, Andhra Pradesh); and the renascent later Cālukyas of Kalyāṇī (between the Bhīma and Godāvari rivers), who rose to power in the 10th century. Cālukya power reached its zenith during the reign of Pulakeśin II (610–642), a contemporary of Harṣa (see above *Successor states*). The early years of his reign were taken up with a civil war, after which Pulakeśin had to reconquer lost territories and re-establish his control over recalcitrant feudatories. Pulakeśin then campaigned successfully in the south against the Kadambas, the Alūpas, and the Gaṅgas. Finally, a matrimonial alliance with the Gaṅgas terminated the campaign. An attack on Konkan resulted in the acquisition of the island of Ghārāpuri (Elephanta Island near Bombay). Leading his armies north, he defeated the Lāṭas, Mālavas, and Gurjara. Pulakeśin's final triumph in the north was the victory over Harṣa of Kannauj. Pulakeśin then turned his attention to the eastern Deccan and conquered southern Kosala, Kaliṅga, Piṣṭapuram, and the Viṣṇukuṇḍin kingdom. He started the collateral branch of the Eastern Cālukyas based at Piṣṭapuram with his younger brother Viṣṇuvardhana as the first king. Pulakeśin then launched another major campaign against the powerful South Indian kingdom of the Pallavas, in which he defeated their king Mahendravarman I, beginning a Cālukya–Pallava conflict that was to continue for many centuries. Pulakeśin II sent an embassy to the court of the Persian king Khusru II. Good relations between the Persians and the Indians of the Deccan were of great advantage to the Zoroastrians of Persia, who, fleeing from the Islāmic persecution in subsequent centuries, sought asylum in India and settled along the west coast of the Deccan. Their descendants today are the Parsi community.

The advantage to the Cālukya king of this conquest was that he was "the lord of the eastern and western waters"; that is, he controlled both coasts of the Deccan. The major river valleys of the northern Deccan—the Narmada, the Tāpti, the Godāvari with its tributaries, and the Krishna were in Cālukya hands, as were the valuable routes in the valleys. This in turn meant the control of the west coast trade with west Asia and the Kalinga and Andhra trade on the east coast with Southeast Asia. The centuries-long conflict between the northern and the southern Deccan, of which the Cālukya–Pallava conflict was but a facet, also had geographical, political, and economic reasons. Any South Indian power wishing to expand would inevitably try to move up the east coast, which was not only the most fertile area of the peninsula but was also rich from the income of trade with Southeast Asia. Therefore, any power wishing to control the northern Deccan had to control the east coast as well, since rivers and routes ran west to east. With the major maritime activity gradually concentrating on southeast Asian trade, in which even the west coast had a large share, the control of both coasts was of considerable economic advantage. It was along the east coast, therefore, that the conflict between the two regions was often expressed. The next 100 years of Cālukya power in the main witnessed the continuation of this conflict, weakening both contenders. Ultimately, in the mid-8th century, a feudatory of the Cālukyas, Dantidurga of the Rāṣṭrakūṭa family, rose to importance and established himself in place of the declining Cālukya dynasty. The Eastern Cālukyas, who had managed to avoid involvement in the conflict, survived longer and came into conflict with the Rāṣṭrakūṭas. Another branch of the Cālukyas established itself at Lāṭa in the mid-7th century and played a prominent role in obstructing the Arab advance, but it too declined soon after.

Southern India. The southern part of the peninsula split into a number of kingdoms each fighting for supremacy. Cēra power was based mainly on a flourishing trade with western Asia. The Cōlas retired into insignificance in the Uraiyūr (Tiruchirāpalli) area. The Pāṇḍyas were involved in fighting the rising power of the Pallavas, and this occasionally led them into alliances with the Deccan kingdoms. In Mysore the Gaṅgas were dominant, but, placed as they were between the Pallavas and the Kadambas, they could hardly expand. Nor did their distant collaterals, the Eastern Gaṅgas, come to their aid in times of distress. The Kadambas came to power in Kuntala after the decline of the Cūtūs in the 4th century. Frequently under attack from the Vākātakas and later the Pallavas, they succumbed finally to the Cālukyas in the 6th century. The Bāṇas occupied the Kolār region adjoining the Pallava kingdom and more often than not were feudatories of the latter.

The rise of the Pallavas

The origin of the Pallava dynasty is obscure. It is not even clear whether the early Pallavas of the 3rd century AD were the ancestors of the later Pallavas of the 6th century, who are sometimes distinguished by the title "imperial." It would seem, however, that their place of origin was Toṇḍaimaṇḍalam, with its centre at Kāñcīpuram (Kāñcī). Prākrit copperplate charters issued by the early kings from Kāñcī often mention places just to the north in Andhra Pradesh, suggesting that the dynasty may have migrated to the Kāñcī area. The Sanskrit and Tamil epigraphic records of the later kings of the dynasty indicate that the later Pallavas became dominant in the

6th century after a successful attack against the Kalabhras, which extended their territory as far south as the Kāverī. The Pallavas reached the height of their power during the reign of Mahendravarman I (*c.* 600–630), a contemporary of Harṣa and Pulakeśin II. Among the sources of the period, Hsüan-tsang's account acts as a connecting link since he travelled through the domains of all three kings. The struggle for Veṅgi between the Pallavas and the Cālukyas became the immediate pretext for a long drawn-out war, which began with the defeat of the Pallavas. Apart from his campaigns, Mahendravarman was a writer and artist of some distinction. His play, the *Maṭṭavilāsaprahasana*, treats in a farcical manner the idiosyncrasies of Buddhist and Śaiva ascetics.

His successor, Narasiṃhavarman I Mahāmalla (*c.* 630–668), avenged the Pallava defeat by capturing Vātāpi. He sent two naval expeditions to Ceylon to assist the king Mānavamma to regain his throne. The expeditions set out from Mahābalipuram, where port facilities had been developed. Pallava naval interests laid the foundation for the extensive use that their successors, the Cōlas, made of the navy. Toward the end of the 8th century, the Gaṅgas and the Pāṇḍyas joined coalitions against the Pallavas. As the Cālukyas declined under pressure from the Rāṣṭrakūṭas, the Pāṇḍyas gradually took on the Pallavas and, by the mid-9th century, advanced as far as Kumbakonam. This defeat was avenged, but, by the end of the 9th century, Pallava power had ceased to matter very much.

Society and culture. Some of the Pallava kings took an interest in the Ālvārs and Nāyaṉārs, the religious teachers who preached a new form of Vaiṣṇavism and Śaivism based on the *bhakti* cult. Among the Śaivas were Appar (who is said to have converted Mahendravarman from Jainism) and Māṇikkavācakar. Among the Vaiṣṇavas were Nammālvār and a woman teacher, Āṇḍāḷ. The movement aimed at preaching a popular Hinduism, in which Tamil was preferred to Sanskrit. Emphasis was placed on the participation of women in the congregations and the concept of the peripatetic teacher. The movement gradually spread northward. The Tamil devotional cult was in a sense competitive with Buddhism and Jainism, both of which suffered a gradual decline. After a long period of quiescence, however, Jainism found a foothold in Rājasthān and Gujarāt, while Buddhism flourished in eastern India in places such as Nālandā, a monastery that attracted vast numbers of students from India and abroad. Buddhism had come to be influenced by various esoteric Tibetan and east Indian cults, particularly the Tantric cults, and a new school called Vajrayāna (Thunderbolt Vehicle) Buddhism developed. The widespread Śakti cult associated with Hindu practice was based on the notion that the male can be activated only by union with the female. Thus the gods were given consorts—Lakṣmī and Śrī for Viṣṇu and Pārvatī, Kālī and Durgā for Śiva—and ritual was directed toward the worship of the mother-goddess. Much of it was derived from the earlier fertility cults and local rites and beliefs that were assimilated into Hinduism. It may also have been due to the incorporation of non-Aryan cultures into Hindu society and the religion that the peoples of these cultures would have brought with them (see also HINDUISM).

At the same time orthodox Brahmanism received encouragement, especially from the royal families. Learned Brahmins were given endowments of land. The new Brahmanism now acquired a locality and an institution in the form of the temple. The earliest remains of a Hindu temple discovered at Sāñcī date to the Gupta period. The structure of these temples was extremely simple and consisted of a shrine room, called a *garbhagṛha* ("womb house"), where the image of the deity was placed and which opened onto a porch. Over the centuries additional structures were added until the temple complexes covered many acres. In the peninsula, the early temples were rock-cut shrines in imitation of Buddhist models. Although the Cālukyas did introduce freestanding temples, most of their patronage extended to rock-cut monuments. The Pallavas also began with rock-cut temples, as at Mahābalipuram, but, when they took to freestanding temples, they produced the most impressive examples of their time.

Temple building

With the growth of temples and monasteries, there also grew up traditions of mural painting and sculpture. Earlier examples of mural painting occur at Bāgh (Dhār district) and Sittanavāsal (Pudukkottai district), and the tradition reached its apogee in the murals at Ajantā (Aurangābād district), the best of which date to Vākāṭaka and Cālukya periods. The style of murals on the walls of Buddhist monasteries travelled from India to Afghanistan and Central Asia and ultimately to China. Equally impressive was Buddhist sculpture at Sārnāth, in Uttar Pradesh. It is possible that the Buddhist images led to the depiction of Hindu deities in iconic form. The symbolism of the Hindu deity, however, took precedence over mere representation, and the deities were portrayed with many arms each carrying a symbolic attribute.

Temples were richly endowed with wealth and land. The large endowments could accommodate the colleges of higher learning (*ghaṭikā* and *maṭha*), primarily for priests. These became responsible for much of the formal education, and inevitably the use of Sanskrit became widespread. There was an appreciable interest in philosophy, with heated debates between Buddhist and Hindu philosophers. Hindu philosophy had by now been classified into six major schools: the Nyāya, Vaiśeṣika, Sāṃkhya, Yoga, Mīmāṃsā, Vedānta. An indication of the growing domination of Brahmanical intellectual life is that the ancient *Purāṇas* were now rewritten substantially in their present form under Brahmanical influence.

Sanskrit literature

The flowering of classical Sanskrit literature also belongs to this period. The plays and poems of Kālidāsa (*Abhijñānaśākuntala*, *Mālavikāgnimitra*, *Vikramorvaśīya*, *Raghuvaṃśa*, *Meghadūta*) are believed to have been written during the time of Candra Gupta II, although Kālidāsa's date is still placed anywhere between the 2nd and 7th centuries AD. In the south, the propagation of Sanskrit resulted in the *Kirātārjunīya*, an epic written by Bhāravi (7th century), and in Daṇḍin's *Daśakumāracarita*, a collection of popular stories (6th century). Tamil literature was equally productive, as is expressed in the composition of two didactic works, the *Tirukkuraḷ* and *Nālaḍiyār*, and in the more lyrical strain of the *Silappadikaram* and the *Maṇimekhalai*, two Tamil epics. Representing a less common genre of literature in the Gupta period was the *Kāma-sūtra* of Vātsyāyana, a manual on the art of love. This was a collation and revision of earlier texts and displays a remarkable sophistication and urbanity.

Science and mathematics

The monasteries and temples were centres of formal learning, and the guilds were centres of technical knowledge. The mixture of the theoretical and practical, however, sometimes occurred, as in the case of medicine, particularly veterinary science. Advances in metallurgy related not only to casting techniques but were also involved in sculpture, as in the Sultānganj Buddha and a famous iron pillar now at Meharaulī (Delhi). Gold and silver coins of the Gupta period show a quality of minting technology that was not to be surpassed for many centuries. Mathematics was particularly advanced, probably more so than anywhere in the world at the time. Indian numerals were later borrowed by the Arabs and introduced to Europe as arabic numerals. The use of the cipher and the decimal system is confirmed by inscriptions. With advances in mathematics there was a comparable advance in astronomy. Āryabhaṭa, writing in AD 499, calculated π to 3.1416, the solar year to 365.3586 . . . days and stated that the earth was spherical and rotated on its axis. That European astronomy was also known is suggested by the 6th-century astronomer Varāhamihira, who mentions the Romaka Siddhānta (School of Rome) among the five major schools of astronomy.

Legal texts and commentaries were abundant—the better known being those of Yājñavalkya, Nārada, Bṛhaspati, and Kātyāyana. The judicial process had become more formalized with a hierarchy of procedures and judges. Also there was a great increase in the amount of legal commentary on social problems and property rights. The post-Gupta period saw considerable social change not only with migrations from outside India but also from the Aryanizing of non-Aryan tribes within India. The expanding village economy opened up new areas geographically, and the increasing importance of guilds in the towns indicated fresh perspectives on social life. New notions of social status either opposed or were adjusted to the old.

750–C. 1200

Northern India. *The tripartite struggle.* The century saw the start of the tripartite struggle for Kannauj between the Pratihāras, the Rāṣṭrakūṭas, and the Pālas dynasties. The Pratihāras, indirectly associated by some historians with the Jodhpur Pratihāras, rose to strength in the Avanti–Jalaor region in the second quarter of the 8th century. They appear to have used western India as a base from which to extend their power through central India into the Ganges Valley. The capture of Kannauj was not in itself of great political importance, but it symbolized the control of the central Ganges Valley, which gave access to the entire Ganges Plain. The Rāṣṭrakūṭa dynasty, a feudatory of the Cālukyas, rose to power during the reign of Dantidurga, *c.* 753, who not only overthrew the Cālukyas but established the new kingdom. The Rāṣṭrakūṭas were the inheritors of the Sātavāhana and Vākāṭaka kingdoms, and their interest in Kannauj was probably to try to capture the trade routes from the Ganges Valley. This was the first occasion on which a power based in the Deccan made a serious bid for a pivotal position in northern India. According to Tāranātha, a 16th-century Buddhist historian of Tibet, the Pālas came from Puṇḍravardhana (Bogra district), and their first ruler, Gopāla (*c.* 750–770), included Vaṅga in his kingdom and gradually extended his control to the whole of Bengal.

Vatsarāja, a Pratihāra ruler who came to the throne *c.* 778, controlled eastern Rājasthān and Mālava. His ambition to take Kannauj brought him into conflict with the Pāla king, Dharmapāla (*c.* 770–810), who had by this time advanced up the Ganges Valley. The Rāṣṭrakūṭa king Dhruva (*c.* 780–793) attacked each in turn and claimed to have defeated them. This initiated the so-called tripartite struggle, at the beginning of which, the Pratihāras were in an inferior position, as the Pālas were able to consolidate their position in eastern India. Dharmapāla soon retook Kannauj and put his nominee on the throne. The Rāṣṭrakūṭas were preoccupied with problems in the south. Vatsarāja's successor, Nāgabhaṭa II (*c.* 793–833), reorganized Pratihāra power, attacked Kannauj, and for a short while reversed the situation. But soon after he was defeated by the Rāṣṭrakūṭa king Govinda III (793–814), who in turn had to face a confederacy of southern powers that kept him involved in Deccan politics, leaving northern India to the Pratihāras and Pālas. Bhoja (*c.* 836–885) revived the power of the Pratihāras by bringing Kālañjara (Bānda district), and possibly Kannauj as well, under Pratihāra control. Bhoja's plans to extend the kingdom, however, were thwarted by the Pālas and the Rāṣṭrakūṭas. More serious conflict with the latter ensued during the reign of Kṛṣṇa II (*c.* 878–914). Initially Bhoja met with success, but later some of the territory he gained had to be returned to the Rāṣṭrakūṭas.

An Arab visitor to western India, the merchant Sulaymān, referred to the kingdom of Juzr (which is generally identified as Gurjara) and its strong and able ruler, who may have been Bhoja. Of the successors of Bhoja, the only one of significance was Mahīpāla (*c.* 908–942), whose relationship with the earlier king remains controversial. Rājaśekhara, a renowned poet at his court, implies that Mahīpāla restored the kingdom to its original power, but this may be an exaggeration.

The Pratihāra feudatories

By the end of the 10th century, the Pratihāra feudatories—the Cāhamānas, Candellas, Guhilas, Kalacuris, Paramāras, and Caulukyas—were asserting their independence, although the last of the Pratihāras survived until 1027. Meanwhile Devapāla (*c.* 810–850) was reasserting Pāla authority in the east and, he claimed, in the northern Deccan. The end of the 9th century, however, saw the decline of the Pāla kingdom with feudatories in Assam and Orissa taking independent titles. Pāla power revived during the reign of Mahīpāla (*c.* 988–1038), although their stronghold now was Bihār rather than Bengal. Further attempts to recover the old Pāla territories were made by Rāmapāla, but, by 1120, even he had failed. After the collapse of the last Pāla king in 1162, the Varman dynasty ruled in Bengal. There was a brief revival of power in Bengal under the Sena dynasty (*c.* 1070–1289). Finally Mithilā (northern Bihār) came under the control of the Karṇāṭa dynasty, probably founded by an officer from Karṇāṭaka.

In the Rāṣṭrakūṭa kingdom, Amoghavarṣa (*c.* 814–878) faced a revolt of officers and feudatories but managed to survive and reassert Rāṣṭrakūṭa power despite intermittent rebellions. Campaigns in the south against Veṅgi and the Gaṅgas kept him preoccupied and prevented him from participating in northern politics. The Rāṣṭrakūṭa capital was moved to Mānyakheṭa (Malkhed, in Andhra Pradesh), doubtless to facilitate southern involvements, which clearly took on more important dimensions at this time. Sporadic campaigns against the Pratihāras, the Eastern Cālukyas, and the Cōlas, the new power of the south, continued (see below *The Cōlas*). Indra III (914–927) captured Kannauj, but, with mounting political pressures from the south, his control over the north was inevitably short-lived. The reign of Kṛṣṇa III (*c.* 939–968) saw a successful campaign against the Cōlas, a matrimonial alliance with the Gaṅgas, and the subjugation of Veṅgi. Rāṣṭrakūṭa power declined suddenly, however, after the reign of Indra, and this was fully exploited by the feudatory Taila.

Taila II (973–997) was of the Cālukya family and ruled a small part of Bijāpur. He traced his ancestry to the earlier Cālukyas of Vātāpi. On the weakening of the Rāṣṭrakūṭa power, he defeated the King, declared his independence, and founded what has come to be called the later Cālukya dynasty. The kingdom included southern Mysore, Konkan, and the territory as far north as the Godāvari. By the end of the 10th century, the later Cālukyas clashed with the expanding power of the Cōlas. The Cālukyas' capital was subsequently moved north to Kalyāṇī (in Bidār). Campaigns against the Cōlas took a more serious turn during the reign of Someśvara I (1043–68), with alternating defeat and victory. The later Cālukyas, however, by and large retained control over the western Deccan despite the hostility of the Cōlas and of their own feudatories. But, in the middle of the 12th century, a feudatory, Bijjala (1156–67) of the Kalacuri dynasty usurped the throne at Kalyāṇī. The last of the Cālukya rulers, Someśvara IV (1181–*c.* 1189), regained the throne for a short period, after which he was overthrown by a feudatory of the Yādava dynasty.

Minor kingdoms

On the periphery of the large kingdoms were the smaller states such as Nepal, Kāmarūpa, Kashmir, and Utkala (Orissa). Nepal had freed itself from Tibetan suzerainty in the 8th century but still remained a major trade route to Tibet. Gradually the *rānas*, the feudal chiefs, gained power and threatened the position of the king. Kāmarūpa with its capital at Prāgjyotiṣa (near Gauhāti) was one of the centres of the Tantric cult. In 1253 a major part of Kāmarūpa was conquered by the Ahoms, a Shan (Burmese) people from whom it derives its present name, Assam. Politics in Kashmir were dominated by turbulent feudatories seeking power. By the 11th century Kashmir was torn between rival court factions, and royal oppression of King Harṣa accentuated the suffering of the people. Smaller states along the Himalayan foothills managed to survive without becoming too embroiled in the politics of the plains.

The Rājputs. In Rājasthān and central India there arose a number of small kingdoms ruled by dynasties that came to be called the Rājputs (literally, sons of kings). The term was used by royal families that claimed Kṣatriya status and linked their lineage with either the Sūryavaṃśi or the Candravaṃśi, the royal lineages of the *itihāsa-purāṇa* tradition; or else with the Agnikula (Fire lineage) based on a lesser myth in which the eponymous ancestor arises out of the sacrificial fire. The four major Rājput dynasties—Pratihāra, Paramāra, Cauhān (Cāhamāna), and Caulukya—claimed Agnikula lineage. The claims made in Rājput genealogies to supernatural ancestry suggest that either they were families of obscure origin—perhaps semi-Hinduized local tribes who gradually acquired political and economic status—or else that they were of non-Indian (probably Central Asian) origin.

The Caulukyas of Gujarāt (also known as the Solaṅkis) had three branches: one ruling Mattamayūra (the Mālava–Cedi region), one established on the erstwhile kingdom of the Cāpas at Aṇahilapāṭaka (Patan), and the third at Bhṛgukaccha (Broach) and Lāṭa in the coastal area. By the 11th century they were using Gujarāt as a base and attempting to annex neighbouring portions of Rājāsthan and Avanti. Kumārapāla (*c.* 1143–72) was responsible for consolidating the kingdom. He is also believed to have become a Jaina and to have encouraged Jainism in western India. Hemacandra, an outstanding Jaina scholar noted for his commentaries on political treatises, was a well-known figure at the Caulukya court. Many of the Rājput kingdoms had Jaina statesmen, ministers, and even generals, as well as Jaina traders and merchants. By the 14th century, however, the Caulukya kingdom had declined.

Adjoining the kingdom of the Caulukyas was that of the Paramāras in Mālava, with minor branches in the territories just to the north (Mount Ābū, Bānswāra, Dūngarpur, and Bhīnmāl). The Paramāras had started as feudatories of the Rāṣṭrakūṭas and rose to eminence during the reign of Bhoja. An attack by the Caulukyas weakened the Paramāras in 1143, and, although the dynasty was later re-established, it remained weak. In the 13th century the Paramāras were threatened by both rising Yādava power in the Deccan and the Turkish kingdom at Delhi; the latter conquered the Paramāras in 1305.

The Kalacuris of Tripurī (near Jabalpur) also began as feudatories of the Rāṣṭrakūṭas. The Kalacuris became a power in central India in the 11th century during the reigns of Gāṅgeyadeva and his son Lakṣmīkarṇa, when attempts were made to conquer territories as far afield as Orissa, Bihār, and the Doab. Here they came into conflict with the Turkish governor of the Punjab, who had extended his territory as far as Vārānasi. To the west, there were conflicts with Bhoja Paramāra, and the Kalacuris declined at the end of the 12th century.

The Candellas, whose kingdom comprised mainly Jejākabhukti (Bundelkhand), were feudatories of the Pratihāras. Among the important rulers was Dhaṅga (*c.* 950–1008), who issued a large number of inscriptions and was generous in donations to Jaina and Hindu temples. Dhaṅga's grandson Vidyādhara (1017–29), often described as the most powerful of the Candella kings, extended the kingdom as far as the Chambal and the Narmada rivers. This brought him into direct conflict with the Turkish leader Maḥmūd of Ghazni, though the battles between them were indecisive. The Candellas had also to face the attacks of the Cauhāns, who were in turn being harassed by the Turks. The Turkish kingdom at Delhi encroached into Bundelkhand, but the Candellas survived until the 16th century, as minor chieftains.

The Kachchhapaghātas ruled at Gopādri (Gwalior), with branches in the neighbourhood at Dubkund and Narwar. They were ultimately conquered by the Turks. The Gāhaḍavālas rose to importance in Vārānasi after that city was sacked by the Turks in 1034. They extended their kingdom up the Doab including Kannauj. The king Jayaccandra (12th century) is mentioned in the poem *Pṛthvīrāja-rāso* of Candbardāi, in which his daughter, the princess Sanyoġita, elopes with the Cauhān king Pṛthvīrāja. Jayaccandra was killed in battle against the Turkish leader, Muḥammad Ghūri, and his kingdom was annexed. The Guhilas became prominent after their capture of Chitor in the 8th century, their original centres having been Nāgahrada (Nāgda) and Āghaṭa (Ahar), which became the nuclei of the region called Medapāṭa (Mēwar). Despite hostilities with the Caulukyas and Cāhamānas, the Guhilas maintained their position. A severe attack from the Turks in the early 13th century was parried under the leadership of Jaitrasiṃha (*c.* 1213–52). In the Śripatha region (Bharatpur) at Bayana ruled the Yaduvaṃśa family, claiming, as the name implies, descent from the ancient Yadu tribe. Their activities were focussed on the area between Āgra and Delhi. The Haryana region north of Delhi was ruled by the Tomara Rājputs who founded the city of Dhillikā (Delhi) in 736. They were originally feudatories of the Pratihāras. In the 12th century they were overthrown by the Cauhāns.

The Cauhāns

Inscriptional records associate the Cauhāns with the lake Śākambharī and its environs (Sāmbhar Salt Lake in Jaipur district). Cauhān politics were largely campaigns against the Caulukyas and the Turks. In the 11th century they founded the city of Ajayameru (Ajmer) along the southern part of their kingdom, and in the 12th they captured Dhillikā from the Tomaras and annexed some of their territory along the Yamuna River. The name of Pṛthvīrāja III has come down both in folk and historical literature as the Cauhān king who resisted the Turkish attacks in the first battle at Tarāin in 1191. Pṛthvīrāja, however, was defeated at a second battle in the same place in 1192, which defeat ushered in Turkish rule in northern India.

The coming of the Turks. The establishment of Turkish power in India is initially tied up with politics in the Punjab. The Punjab was ruled by Jayapāla of the Hindu Shāhiya dynasty, which dynasty had in the 9th century wrested the Kābul Valley and Gandhāra from a Turkish Shāhiya. Relations both political and economic were extremely close between the Punjab and Afghanistan. Afghanistan in turn was closely involved with Central Asian politics. Sebüktigin, a Turk, was appointed governor of Ghazni in 977. He attacked the Hindu Shāhiyas and advanced as far as Peshāwar. His son Maḥmūd succeeded to the Ghazni principality in 998. He went to war with the Shāhiya dynasty and almost every year until his death in 1030 led raids against the rich temple centres in northern and western India, using the wealth obtained from the raids to finance successful campaigns in Central Asia and to build a Central Asian empire. He emerged as a patron of culture and was responsible for sending to India the scholar al-Bīrūnī, whose study, *Ta'rīkh al-Hind* is a source of valuable information. A by-product of temple raiding was that it also credited Maḥmūd with religious merit, since he claimed that he was destroying the idols of the infidels. He left his governors in the Punjab with a rather loose control over the region.

In the 12th century the Ghūrid Turks were driven out of Khorāsān and later out of Ghazni by the Khwārezm-Shāhs. Inevitably the Ghūrids sought their fortune in northern India, where the conflict between the Ghaznavids and the local rulers provided an excellent opportunity. Muḥammad Ghūri advanced into the Punjab and captured Lahore in 1185. Victory in the second battle of Tarāin consolidated his success, and he left his general Quṭb-ud-Dīn Aybak in charge of his Indian possessions. Muḥammad was assassinated in 1206 on his way back to Afghanistan. Quṭb-ud-Dīn remained in India and declared himself sultan of Delhi, the first of the Slave, or Mamlūk, dynasty.

The Deccan and the south. In the northern Deccan the decline of the later Cālukyas brought about the rise of their feudatories, among them the Yādava dynasty (also claiming descent from the Yadu tribe) based at Devagiri (Daulatābād), whose kingdom (Seunadeśa) included the Khāndesh, the Nāsik, and the Ahmadnagar districts. The kingdom expanded during the reign of Siṃhana (*c.* 1210–47), who campaigned against the Hoysaḷa in northern Mysore, against the lesser chiefs of the western coast, and against the Kākatīya kingdom in the eastern Deccan. Turning northward, he attacked the Paramāras, the Caulukyas, and Lāṭa. The Yādavas, however, facing the Turks to the north and the powerful Hoysaḷas to the south, declined in the 14th century.

In the eastern Deccan, the Kākatīya dynasty was based in the Nalgonda and Warangal areas (Andhra Pradesh) and survived until the Turkish attack in the 14th century. The Eastern Cālukyas ruled in the Godavāri Delta, and, in the 13th century, their fortunes were tied to those of the Cōlas. The Eastern Gaṅgas, ruling in Kaliṅga, came into conflict with the Turks advancing down the Ganges Valley to the delta in the 13th century.

The Cōlas. The Cōlas were by far the most important dynasty in the subcontinent at this time, although their activities mainly affected the peninsula and Southeast Asia. The nucleus of Cōla power during the reign of Vijayālaya in the late 9th century was Thanjāvūr, from which they spread northward, annexing in the 10th century what remained of Pallava territory. To the south they came up against the Pāṇḍyas. Cōḷa history can be reconstructed in considerable detail because of the vast number of lengthy inscriptions issued not only by the royal family but also by temple authorities, village councils, and trade guilds. Parāntaka I (907–953) laid the foundation of the kingdom. He took the northern boundary up to Nellore (Andhra Pradesh), where his advance was stopped by a defeat at the hands of the Rāṣṭrakūṭa king Kṛṣṇa III. Parāntaka was more successful in the south, where he defeated both the Pāṇḍyas and the Gaṅgas. He also launched an abortive attack on Ceylon. For 30 years after his death, there was a series of overlapping reigns that did not strengthen the Cōla position. There then followed two outstanding rulers who rapidly reinstated Cōla power and ensured the kingdom its supremacy. These were Rājarāja I and Rājendra.

Rājarāja I's conquests

Rājarāja (985–1014) began with the south and attacked the Pāṇḍyas and Īllamaṇḍalam (Ceylon). In the case of the latter, the old capital at Anurādhapura was destroyed, and a new capital was established by the Cōlas at Polonnaruva. Northern Ceylon became a province of the Cōla kingdom. A campaign against the Gaṅgas and Cālukyas extended the Cōla boundary north to the Tungabhadra River. On the eastern coast the Cōlas battled with the Cālukyas for the possession of Veṅgi. A marriage alliance gave the Cōlas an authoritative position, but Veṅgi remained a bone of contention. A naval campaign led to the conquest of the Maldive Islands. The conquest of these islands as also of the Malabar Coast and northern Ceylon can be explained as necessary to the Cōla control over trade with Southeast Asia and with Arabia and East Africa. These were the transit areas, ports of call for the Arab traders and ships to Southeast Asia and China, the source of the valuable spice sold at a high profit to Europe.

Rājarāja's son Rājendra was associated with the government from 1012 and ruled until 1044. To the north he annexed the Raichūr Doab and moved into Mānyakheṭa in the heart of Cālukya territory. A revolt against Mahinda V of Ceylon gave Rājendra the excuse to conquer southern Ceylon as well. In 1021–22 the now-famous northern campaign was launched. The Cōla army campaigned along the east coast as far as Bengal and then north to the Ganges River—almost the exact reverse of Samudra Gupta's campaign to Kāñcīpuram in the 4th century AD. But the most spectacular campaign was a naval campaign against the Śrivijaya kingdom in Southeast Asia in 1025. The reason for the assault on Śrivijaya and neighbouring areas appears to have been the interference with Indian shipping and mercantile interests seeking direct trading connections with South China. The Cōla victory reinstated these connections, and thoughout the 11th century Cōla trading missions visited China.

The Hoysaḷas and Pāṇḍyas. The succession after Rājendra is confused until the emergence of Kulottuṅga I (1070–1122), who was of mixed Cōla and Eastern Cālukya descent. But his reign was the last of any significance. The 12th and 13th centuries saw a gradual decline in Cōla power, accelerated by the rise of the Hoysaḷas to the west and the Pāṇḍyas to the south.

The Hoysaḷas also claimed Yādava origin and began as hill chieftains, feudatory to the Cālukyas. The core of the kingdom was Dōrasamudra (near Mysore), and the kingdom was consolidated by Viṣṇuvardhana (12th century). The Hoysaḷas were involved in conflict with the Yādava kingdom, which was seeking to expand southward, particularly during the reign of Ballāla II (1173–1220). Hostilities also developed with the Cōlas to the east. The armies of the Turks ultimately diminished the Hoysaḷa kingdom to the point of nonexistence, until, in the 14th century, it gave way to the Vijayanagara kingdom. In the 13th century the Pāṇḍyas became the dominant power in the south, but their supremacy was brief since they were attacked in the 14th century by Turkish armies. Information on the dynasty is supplemented by the account of Marco Polo who visited the region in 1288 and 1293.

Society and culture. *Indian feudalism.* Apart from the political events of the time, a common development in the subcontinent was the recognizable decentralization of administration and revenue collection. From the Cōla kingdom, there are long inscriptions on temple walls referring to the organization and functioning of village councils. Villages that had been donated to Brahmins had councils called the *sabhā;* in the non-Brahmin villages the council was called the *ur.* Eligibility qualifications generally relating to age and ownership of property were indicated, along with procedural rules. The council was divided into various committees in charge of the different aspects of village life and administrations. Among the responsibilities of the council was the collection of revenue and the supervision of irrigation.

Village councils

In the Deccan, the rise and fall of dynasties was largely the result of the feudatory pattern of political relationships. The same held true of northern India and is seen both in the rise of various Rājput dynasties as in their inability to withstand the Turkish invasions. There is considerable controversy among historians as to whether the feudatory pattern can be accurately described as feudalism. Some argue that, although it was not identical to the classical example of feudalism of western Europe, there are sufficient similarities to allow the use of the term. The counter argument is that the emphasis on the economic contract, essential to western European feudalism was absent in India or was, at least, not as clearly stated. In any event, the patterns of land relations, politics, and culture changed considerably, and the major characteristic of the change is decentralization.

The commonly used term for a feudatory was *sāmanta,* a term that designated either a conquered ruler or, more often, a secular official connected with the administration who had been given a grant of land in lieu of a salary and who had asserted ownership over the land and gradually appropriated rights of ruling the area. There were various categories of *sāmantas.* As long as a ruler was in a feudatory status, he called himself *sāmanta* and acknowledged his overlord in official documents and charters. Independent status was indicated by the elimination of the title of *sāmanta* and the inclusion instead of royal titles such as maharaja, *mahārājādhirāja.* The feudatory had certain obligations to the ruler. Although virtually in sole control administratively and fiscally over the land granted to him, he nevertheless had to pay a small percentage of the revenue to the ruler and maintain a specified body of troops for him. He was permitted the use of certain symbols of authority on formal occasions and was required, if called upon, to give his daughter in marriage to his suzerain. These major administrative and economic changes, although primarily concerning fiscal arrangements and revenue organization, also had their impact on politics and culture. The grantees or intermediaries in a hierarchy of grants were not merely secular officials but were often Brahmin beneficiaries who had been given grants of land in return for religious services rendered to the state. Such grants were, in most cases, free of taxes and dues. The grants were frequently so lucrative that the Brahmins could marry into the families of local chiefs, and this explains the presence of Brahmin ancestors in the genealogies of the period.

The economy. Cultivation was still carried out by the peasants, generally Śūdras, who remained tied to the land. Since the revenue was now to be paid not to the king but to the *sāmanta,* the peasants naturally began to give more attention to his requirements. The *sāmantas* copied the life-style of the royal court and tried to set up miniature courts in imitation of the royal model. The culture of the royal court was thus disseminated, but at the same time, the system encouraged parochial loyalties and local cultural interests. One of the manifestations of this local involvement was a sudden spurt of historical literature such as Bilhaṇa's *Vikramāṅkadevacarita*, the life of the Cālukya king Vikramāditya VI, and Kalhaṇa's *Rājataraṅgiṇī*, a history of Kashmir.

This trend toward decentralization was coupled with an apparent tendency toward a decline in trade in all but the fringe areas of the subcontinent. The west coast was active, but Indian traders did not venture out so much, since the Arabs had established trading settlements in India. The Cōla and Pāla kingdoms were exceptions. Powerful trading guilds had the political and military support of the Cōla monarchy. Even the rich Hindu temples of South India invested their money in trade. Pāla contacts were mainly with Śrivijaya and trade combined with Buddhist interests. The monasteries at Nālandā and Vikramásīla (Bihār) maintained close relations. By now eastern India was the only region with a sizable Buddhist interest. The hinterland was devoid of trade, and there seems to have been a decline in commercial centres. The traditional routes were still used, and some kingdoms were based essentially on the revenue from such routes as those along the Arāvalli Range, Mālava, and the Chambal and Narmada valleys. The paucity of coins for this region may be the result of a decline in the volume of trade. Significantly, the major technological innovation, the introduction of the Persian wheel (*araghaṭṭa*) as an aid to irrigation in northern India, pertains to agrarian life and not to urban technology. It has been suggested that these economic and administrative changes introduced the self-sufficient economy of the Indian village.

Social mobility. Historians once believed that the post-Gupta period brought greater rigidity in the caste structure and that this rigidity was partially responsible for the inability of Indians to face the challenge of the Turks. This view is now being modified. The distinctions, particularly between the Brahmins and the other castes, were in theory sharper, but in practice it now appears that social restrictions were not as rigid as believed. Brahmins often lived off the land and founded dynasties. Most of the groups claiming Kṣatriya status were those who had recently acquired it. The conscious reference to being Kṣatriya, a characteristic among Rājputs, is a noticeable feature in post-Gupta politics. The fact that many of these dynasties were of obscure origin suggests considerable social mobility: a person of any caste, having once acquired political power, could also acquire a genealogy connecting him with the traditional lineages and conferring Kṣatriya status on him. A number of new castes such as the Kāyasthas (scribes) and Khatris (traders) are mentioned in the sources of this period. According to the legal sources, they originated from intercaste marriages, but this is clearly an attempt at rationalizing a situation. Many of these new castes played a major role in society. The hierarchy of castes did not have a uniform distribution throughout the country. Thus the Kṣatriya and Vaiśya groups were little emphasized in South India, where the majority were Śūdras and participated in almost all professions. The pre-eminent position of the Brahmin was endorsed not merely by the fact that many had lands and investments but by the fact that they controlled education. Formal learning was almost restricted to the institutions attached to the temples. Technical knowledge was available in the various artisan guilds. Not all Brahmins, however, were prosperous and powerful. Even among the Brahmins there was a hierarchy; some Brahmin castes, who had perhaps been tribal priests before being assimilated into the Hindu tradition, remained ordinary village priests catering to rites and ceremonies and the day to day religious functions.

Religion. The local nucleus of the new culture led to a large range of religious expression, from the powerful temple religion of Brahmanism to a widespread popular *bhakti* religion and even more widespread fertility cult. The distinctions between the three were not clearly demarcated. Rites and concepts from the one flowed into the other. The traditional worship of Viṣṇu and Śiva had the support of the elite and the urban *bhakti* groups. Temples dedicated to Vaiṣṇava and Śaiva deities were the most numerous. But also included were some of the chief deities connected with the fertility cult, and the mother-goddesses played an important role. The *Purāṇas* had been rewritten to incorporate popular religion. Now the *Upapurāṇas* were written to record rites and worship of more localized deities. Among the incarnations of Viṣṇu the most popular was Kṛṣṇa. To the earlier austere hero of the *Bhagavadgītā* was now added the pastoral and the erotic aspect. The love of Kṛṣṇa and Rādhā was expressed in sensitive and passionate poetry and sculpture.

The erotic theme in Hinduism

The introduction of the erotic theme in Hinduism was closely connected with the fertility cult and Tantrism. The latter, named after its scriptures, the *Tantras*, influenced both Hindu and Buddhist ritual. Tantrism originated in eastern India but was associated with the folk religion throughout the subcontinent and, to that degree, represented the conversion of a folk religion into a sophisticated one. The emphasis on the mother-goddess strengthened the status of the female deities and also linked it with the *śākta-śakti* cult. The erotic aspect was also related to the ritual of coition being necessary to full Tantric rites. The depiction of erotic scenes on temple walls therefore had a magicoreligious context.

Vajrayāna Buddhism current in eastern India, Nepal, and Tibet shows evidence of the impact of Tantrism. The goddess Tārā emerges as the saviour and is in many ways the Buddhist counterpart of *śakti*. Buddhism was on the way out—the Buddha had been incorporated as an *avatāra* of Viṣṇu, and it had lost much of its popular appeal, which had been maintained by the simple habits of the monks. Its traditional source of patronage had declined with declining trade. Jainism, however, managed to maintain some hold in Rājasthān, Gujarāt, and Mysore. The protest aspect of these religions, especially the opposition to Brahmanical orthodoxy, had now been taken over by the Tantrics and the *bhakti* cult. The Tantrics expressed their protest through their rather extreme rites: as also did some of the heretical sects such as the Kalamukhas and Kāpālikas. The *bhakti* cult expressed the more puritanical protest of the urban groups, and it gradually spread to the rural areas. Pre-eminent among the *bhakti* groups during this period were the Liṅgāyats, or Vīraśaivas, founded by Basava, who were to become a powerful force in Mysore, and the Pandharpur cult in Mahārāshtra, which attracted preachers such as Nāmadeva.

Literature and the arts. It was also in the *maṭha* and the *ghaṭikā*, attached to the temples, that the influential philosophical debates were carried out in Sanskrit. Foremost among the philosophers were Śaṅkarācārya (9th century), Rāmānuja (1017–1137) and Madhva (13th century). The discussions centred on religious problems, such as whether knowledge or devotion was the most effective means of salvation, and problems of metaphysics, including that of the nature of reality.

Court literature, irrespective of the region, continued to be composed in Sanskrit, with the many courts competing for the patronage of the poets and the dramatists. There was a revival of interest in earlier literature, with copious commentaries on prosody, grammar, and technical literature. The number of lexicons increased, perhaps necessitated by the growing use of Sanskrit by non-Sanskrit speakers. Literary style tended to be pedantic and imitative, although there were some exceptions, such as Jayadeva's lyrical poem on the love of Rādhā and Kṛṣṇa, the *Gītagovinda*. The *bhakti* teachers preached not in Sanskrit but in the local languages, giving a tremendous fillip to literature in these languages. Adaptations of the *Rāmāyaṇa*, *Mahābhārata*, and *Bhagavadgītā* were used regularly by the *bhakti* teachers. In addition, hymns were composed and congregations addressed in the popular language. There was thus a gradual breaking away from Sanskrit and Prākrit via Apabrahmṡa (the "crooked language") and the eventual emergence and evolution of Kannada, Telugu, Marathi, Gujarati, Bengali, Oriya, and the dialects of Bhojpuri, Maithili, and Māgadhī.

Differentiations of languages

The period was rich in sculpture both in stone and metal, each region registering a variant style. Western India and Rājasthān emphasized ornateness, with the Jaina temples at Mount Ābū attaining a perfection of rococo. Nālandā was the centre of striking but less ornate images in black stone and of Buddhist bronze icons. Central Indian craftsmen used the softer sandstone. In the peninsula the profusely sculptured, rock-cut temples such as the Kailāsa at Ellora, with Cālukya and Rāṣṭrakūṭa patronage, created a style of their own. But the dominant style was that of Cōla sculpture, particularly in bronze as typified in the famous Naṭarāja image. The severe beauty and elegance of these bronze images mainly of Śaiva and Vaiṣṇava deities and saints remains unsurpassed. A new genre of painting was the illustration of Buddhist and Jaina manuscripts with miniature paintings popular in Nepal, eastern India and Gujarāt.

Temple architecture was divided into three main styles distinguished by the ground plan of the temple and by the shape of the *śikhara* (tower) that rose over the *garbhagṛha* and that became the commanding feature of temple architecture. The North Indian temples conformed to the *nāgara* style, as is seen at Osiān (Jodhpur district), Khajurāho, Konārak, Bhubaneswara and Puri. The South Indian, or *drāviḍa*, style with its commanding gateways (*gopuram*) can be seen in the Rājarājeśvara and the Gaṅgaikoṇḍacōlapuram temples. The Deccan style, *vasara,* tended to be an inter-mixture of the northern and the southern, with early examples at Vātāpi, Aihoḷe, and Pattadakal and, later, at Halebīd, Belūr, and Somnāthpur in the vicinity of Mysore. Artistic achievement was handsomely rewarded from temple funds, which made the temples the focus of attack from invaders.

The question that is frequently posed as to why the Turks so easily conquered northern India and the Deccan has in part to do with what might be called the medieval ethos. A contemporary observed that the Indians had become self-centred and unaware of the world around them. This was substantially true. There was little interest in the politics of neighbouring countries or in their technological achievement, as is evident, for example, from the slow impact of the use of the stirrup in the early cavalry. The medieval ethos expressed itself not only in the "feudatory" attitude to politics and the parochial concerns that became dominant and prevented any effective opposition to the Turks but also in the trappings of chivalry and romanticism that became central to elite activity.

It has been generally held that the medieval period of Indian history began with the arrival of the Turks (dated to either AD 1000 or 1206) because the Turks brought with them a new religion, Islām, which changed Indian society at all levels. Yet the fundamental changes that took place around the 8th century, when the medieval ethos was introduced, would seem far more significant as a criterion of change than the coming of Islām.

(R.Th.)

III. The early Muslim period, c. 1200–1526

NORTH INDIA UNDER MUSLIM HEGEMONY, C. 1200–1526

The first Muslim conquests in the subcontinent were made by Arabs in Sind during the 8th century, and there had been Muslim trading communities in India at least since that time; but the significant and permanent military movement of Muslims into North India dates from the late 12th century and was carried out by a Turkish dynasty that arose indirectly from the ruins of the ʿAbbāsid caliphate. The road to conquest was prepared by Sultan Maḥmūd of Ghazna (modern Ghaznī in Afghanistan), who conducted more than 20 raids into North India between 1001 and 1027 and established in the Punjab the easternmost province of his large but short-lived empire. Maḥmūd's raids, though militarily successful, were mainly for plunder rather than for conquest. They did reveal the wealth of India, however, and indicated that North India was vulnerable to military attacks.

Permanent Muslim conquest

The Delhi sultanate. The decline of the Ghaznavids after 1100 was accentuated by the sack of Ghazna by the rival Shansabānīs of Ghūr in 1150–51. The Ghūrids, who inhabited the region between Ghazna and Herāt, rose rapidly in power during the last half of the 12th century, partly because of the changing balance of power that resulted from the westward movement of the non-Muslim Karakitai Turks into the area dominated by the Seljuq Turks, who had been the principal power in Iran and parts of Afghanistan during the previous 50 years. The Seljuq defeat in 1141 led to a struggle for power among the Karakitai, the Khwārezm-Shāhs, and the Ghūrids for control of parts of Central Asia and Iran. The Ghūrid invasions of North India are part of this Central Asian struggle, for it was during the last quarter of the 12th century that Ghūrid troops, led by Sultan Ghiyāṡ-ud-Dīn Muḥammad and his brother Muʿizz-ud-Dīn Muḥammad ibn Sām, commonly called Muḥammad of Ghūr, conducted campaigns of expansion both into Khorāsān in the west and into North India in the east.

The Ghūrid conquest. The early Ghūrid invasions of India were led by Muḥammad of Ghūr and his lieutenant Quṭb-ud-Dīn Aybak. After some initial successes, their attempts to follow the southern route into India through the Gumal Pass met obstacles. In 1178 Ghūrid troops, exhausted after crossing the desert of Mt. Ābū, suffered a severe defeat at the hands of the army of Mularaja II, the Cālukya ruler of Gujarāt. The Ghūrids then turned to the northern route, through the Khyber Pass, and destroyed the remnants of Ghaznavid power in India with the capture of Peshāwar (1179), Siālkot (1185), and Lahore (1186).

Destruction of the Ghaznavids

By 1185 the Ghūrids had conquered the local Muslim rulers of the northwest and were in a favourable military position to move against the North Indian Rājput powers. The conquest of the Rājputs was not easy, however, and the Ghūrids were by no means always victorious during the next few years. Muḥammad of Ghūr was defeated by the Cāhamānas (Chauhān) under Pṛthvīrāja in 1191 at Tarāin, northwest of Delhi, but his forces returned the following year to defeat and kill the Rājput king on the same battlefield. The victory opened the road to Delhi, which was conquered in 1193 but left in the hands of a tributary Hindu king. Muḥammad of Ghūr completed his conquests with the occupation of the military outposts of Hānsi, Kuhram, Sursuti, and Sirhind and then returned to Ghazna with a large hoard of treasure, leaving Quṭb-ud-Dīn Aybak in charge of consolidation and further expansion.

Quṭb-ud-Dīn displaced the Cāhamāna chief and made his headquarters at Delhi in 1193, when he began a campaign of expansion. The Gāhaḍavāla chief Jayaccandra was defeated and slain and Banaras taken in 1194. During the next three years Quṭb-ud-Dīn was occupied mainly with battles against Rājput forces that were trying to reconquer Ghūrid-held lands between Delhi and Gujarāt. In 1198–99, however, he subdued Badaun and Kanauj in the upper Ganges region; and in 1202 he conquered part of the Candella kingdom of Bundelkhand, on the southeastern border of Ghūrid possessions, with the capture of Kālinjar.

One of the most interesting and instructive episodes of the Ghūrid conquest was the rapid rise of an obscure military adventurer, Ikhtiyār-ud-Dīn Muḥammad Bakhtiyār Khaljī. After he was refused service in both Ghazna and Delhi, he took a low position under the commander of the Banaras and Oudh (Awadh) division of Quṭb-ud-Dīn's army. He used his small salary to collect a band of soldiers (mostly Khaljī tribesmen, like himself), and *c.* 1200 he began to raid into the Magadha territory in the eastern Gangetic Plain. Bakhtiyār was a brilliant soldier and soon amassed enough plunder to recruit a large force. He received permission from Quṭb-ud-Dīn to continue his campaigns as long as he could finance them through his own resources. By 1202 Bakhtiyār had conquered Nadia, the capital of the Sena kings of Bengal. Within two years, however, the ambitious general had embarked upon what proved to be a disastrous attempt to conquer Tibet. Defeated by the terrain, the weather, and the harassments of the hill tribes, Bakhtiyār managed to return to Bengal with a few hundred men, and there he died in 1206.

Reasons for Ghūrid success

Had it not been for Bakhtiyār Khaljī, the Ghūrids probably would not have conquered Bihār and parts of Bengal during their first thrust into the Gangetic Plain. It is the element of opportunism plus the means by which he gained his success that make Bakhtiyār significant. He combined military genius with the use of extremely mobile cavalry to defeat his foes. He was able to recruit troops, partly because he had money but also because he was successful in his exploits. The availability of a large number of military adventurers from Central Asia who would follow commanders with reputations for success was one of the important elements in the rapid Ghūrid conquest of the major cities and forces of the North Indian plain. Other factors were important as well: better horses contributed to the success of mobile tactics, and the Ghūrids also made better use of metal for weapons, armour, and stirrups than did most of their adversaries. Perhaps most important was the tradition of centralized organization and planning, which was conducive to large-scale military campaigns and to the effective organization of post-campaign occupation forces. While the Rājputs probably saw the Ghūrids as an equal force competing for paramount power in North India, the Ghūrids had in mind the model of the successor states to the ʿAbbāsid caliphate, the old Iranian Sāsānid Empire, and particularly the vast centralized empire of Maḥmūd of Ghazna.

In 1205 Sultan Muḥammad of Ghūr suffered a severe defeat at Andkhvoy (Andkhui) at the hands of the Khwārezm-Shāh. News of the defeat precipitated a rebellion by some of the Sultan's followers in the Punjab, and, although the rebellion was put down, Muḥammad of Ghūr was assassinated at Lahore in 1206. Thus, the Ghūrid possessions were insecure everywhere.

The defeat at Andkhvoy proved to be the beginning of the end of the Ghūrid Central Asian empire, and it was still far from certain that the Ghūrids would be able to consolidate their position in India. They held the major towns of the Punjab, Sind, and of much of the Gangetic Plain, but there were military threats from many quarters, and almost all the land outside the cities still was subject to some form of control by Hindu landholders and chiefs. Even in the Doab (the land between the Ganges and the Yamuna rivers, near Delhi) the Gāhaḍavālas held out against the Turks. Most significantly, the Rājput chiefs of Rājasthān had not been permanently subdued but had retreated to less accessible positions in the hills and forests.

The Muʿizzī (or Slave) dynasty. It is not certain that the Turks' major objective at the time was the consolidation of their Indian conquests, for it appears that the Ghūrids were not ready to give up their struggle against the Khwārezm-Shāhs and that rivalries among the slave successors to Muḥammad of Ghūr were of paramount importance. When Quṭb-ud-Dīn Aybak, Muḥammad of Ghūr's slave and principal commander in India, assumed authority over the Ghūrid possessions in India, he moved from the neighbourhood of Delhi to Lahore. There he set up guard against another of Muḥammad of Ghūr's slaves, Tāj-ud-Dīn Yildiz of Ghazna, who also claimed his former master's Indian possessions. In 1208 Quṭb-ud-Dīn defeated his rival and captured Ghazna but soon was driven out again. He died in 1210 in a polo accident, having made no effort to extend his Indian conquests, but he had managed to establish the foundation of an Indian Muslim state.

Quṭb-ud-Dīn was the first ruler in what has become known, perhaps unreasonably, as the Slave dynasty, even though three families were represented among its nine members, and only Quṭb-ud-Dīn attained a freed status after he had become ruler. Slavery was, however, an integral and important part of the political system. As practiced in eastern Muslim polities of this period, the institution of slavery provided a nucleus of well-trained and loyal military followers for important political figures; indeed, one of the principal objects of this form of slavery was to train specialists in warfare and government, usually Turks, whose first loyalty would be to their masters. Slave status was honourable and was a principal avenue to wealth and high position for talented individuals whose origins were outside the ruling group. It has been observed that a slave was a better investment than a son, whose claim was not based upon proved efficiency. Yet, slaves with high qualifications could get out of control, and often slaves or former slaves controlled their masters as much as they were controlled by them. The beneficial results for the sultanate of this type of political interaction were that some men of talent had room to rise within the system and thus were less tempted to tear it down and that the responsibilities of government tended to rest in the hands of capable men, whether or not they were the actual rulers.

Importance of slavery

The reign of Iltutmish

Iltutmish (reigned 1211–36), son-in-law and successor to Quṭb-ud-Dīn Aybak, was able to consolidate many of the military gains of his predecessors, although the sultanate continued to be hard pressed militarily throughout the 13th century. During his reign Iltutmish was faced with three problems: defense of his western frontier, control over the Muslim nobles within India, and subjugation of the many Hindu chiefs who still exercised a large measure of independent rule. His relative success in all three areas gives him claim to the title of founder of the independent sultanate of Delhi. His reign opened with a factional dispute in which he and his Delhi-based supporters defeated and killed the rival claimant to the throne, Quṭb-ud-Dīn's son, and put down a revolt by a portion of the Delhi guards. In the west Iltutmish was passive at first and even accepted investiture from his old rival, Yildiz; but when Yildiz was driven from Ghazna into the Punjab by the Khwārezm-Shāh in 1215, Iltutmish was able to defeat and capture him at Tarāin. Iltutmish might have faced a threat himself from the Khwārezm-Shāh had it not been for Genghis Khan's attack upon the latter. Again Iltutmish waited while refugees, including the heir to the Khwārezm-Shāhī throne, poured into the Punjab and while Nāṣir-ud-Dīn Qabācha, another of Muḥammad of Ghūr's former slaves, maintained a perilous hold on Lahore and Multān. Iltutmish's political talents were pushed to the maximum as he tried desperately to avoid a direct confrontation with the armies of Genghis Khan. He refused aid to the Muslim Khwārezm heir against the pagan Mongols and yet would not attempt to capture him. Fortunately the Mongols were content to send raiding parties into the Salt Range, which Iltutmish wisely ignored, and eventually the Khwārezm-Shāh prince fled from India after causing enormous destruction within Qabācha's domains. Thus, Iltutmish's cause was advanced, and in 1228 he was able to drive Qabācha from Multān and Uch and, by establishing his frontier east of the Beās River, to avoid a direct confrontation with the Mongols. He was not able to gain effective control of the western Punjab, however, largely because the area was subject to raids by hill tribes.

Iltutmish fared better in the east. In 1225 he launched a successful campaign against Ghiyās-ud-Dīn ʿIwāz Khaljī, one of Bhaktiyār Khaljī's lieutenants, who had assumed sovereign authority in Lakhnāwatī (Bengal) and was encroaching upon the province of Bihār. ʿIwāz Khaljī was defeated and slain in 1226, and in 1229 Iltutmish invaded Bengal and slew Balka, the last of the Khaljī chiefs to claim independent power.

Iltutmish's campaigns against the Rājputs were ultimately less successful, although he temporarily captured Ranthambhor (1226), Mandor (1227), and Gwalior (1231) and plundered Bhīlsa and Ujjain in Mālwa (1234–35). His generals suffered defeats, however, at the hands of the Cāhamānas of Būndi, the Cālukyas of Gujarāt, and the Candellas of Narwar, and his victories were not sufficient to suppress the revival of several Rājput polities.

By 1236 the sultanate of Delhi was established as clearly the largest and most powerful of a number of competing states in North India. The new state had internal momentum as well, surviving severe factional disputes during the next ten years while four of Iltutmish's children or grandchildren were in turn raised to the throne and deposed. This momentum was maintained largely through the efforts of Iltutmish's personal slaves, who came to be known as the Forty (*chihilgān*). A political faction whose membership was characterized by talent and by loyalty to the family of Iltutmish, the Forty managed to fend off or absorb claimants to the throne from other lines. Meanwhile they divided the kingdom among themselves. None was willing to grant supremacy to another of their group, and each sought to build his personal fortune and position; nevertheless, they all appear to have realized that the future of the political system in which they participated depended upon a policy of cooperation in the face of a continued Mongol threat and the danger of revived Rājput power.

Rise of the Forty

The political situation had changed by 1246, when Ghiyāṣ-ud-Dīn Balban, a junior member of the Forty, had gained enough power to attain a controlling position within the administration of the newest sultan, Nāṣir-ud-Dīn Maḥmūd (reigned 1246–66). Balban, acting first as *nā'ib* ("deputy") to the Sultan and later as sultan (reigned 1266–87), was the most important political figure of his time. The period was characterized by almost continuous struggles to maintain Delhi's position against the revived power of the Hindu chiefs (principally Rājputs) and by vigilance against the strife-ridden but still dangerous Mongols in the west. During the first ten years of Maḥmūd's reign, Balban conducted major campaigns against five Rājput chiefs with only partial success. Ranthambhor could not be taken from the Cāhamānas, and, beginning in 1256, Mewāti raids first threatened the environs of Delhi and later actually penetrated the city. Thus, at least until 1266, the power of the sultanate was stagnant if not in decline. The Sultan's authority was challenged in several frontier regions by Hindu chiefs or discontented Muslim nobles, and even in central regions of the state sultanate rule sometimes was challenged by the nobility.

Balban's accession (1266) brought some improvement. He sought to raise the prestige of the institution of kingship through the use of ceremony, the strict administration of justice, and the formulation of a despotic view of the relationship between king and subject. The success of his policy owed much to the death or incapacity of most of the Forty and to the lack of rival claimants to the throne. Probably the most significant aspect of his reign was this elevation of the position of the sultan, which made possible the reorganization and strengthening of the army and the imposition of a tighter administrative apparatus, particularly in the area around Delhi.

Balban's military strategy

Balban's military strategy was to work outward from the capital. First, he cleared the forests of Mewatis; then he restored order in the Doab and Oudh and suppressed a revolt in the Badaun and Amroha districts with particular viciousness. Having established the security of his home territory, Balban then chose to consolidate his rule over the provincial governors rather than to embark upon expeditions against Hindu territories. He argued that Turkish forces in India were insufficient to guard against the Mongol threat, man the existing administrative posts, and also conquer Rājput territories; but probably he saw also that it was in his own interests to strengthen his hold on the outlying territories already held by Muslims. Thus, he reacted vigorously and effectively against an attempt to establish an independent state in Bengal in the 1280s. Balban's policy of consolidation was a wise one; it strengthened sultanate rule and enhanced the power of the ruler so that his successors could undertake a number of successful expansionist campaigns after 1290.

Balban's concern over a shortage of manpower arose in part because the Mongols had severed Delhi's contact with Turkistan. Because few pureblood Turks could be recruited, Afghans and Indian-born Muslims had to be added to the administration and army. Although Balban was opposed to this admixture, necessity forced him to begin a practice that was to become much more significant in later years.

The Khaljīs. Balban's successors were unable to manage either the administration or the factional conflicts between the old Turkish nobility and the new forces, led by the Khaljīs; and, after a struggle between the two factions, Jalāl-ud-Dīn Fīrūz Khaljī assumed the sultanate in 1290. He immediately rewarded his supporters with offices and money and attempted to conciliate members of the old nobility. A number of them, as well as a large part of the populace of Delhi, however, continued to view him as a non-Turkish usurper. During his short reign (1290–96), Jalāl-ud-Dīn suppressed a revolt by some of Balban's officers, led an unsuccessful expedition against Ranthambhor, and defeated a substantial Mongol force on the banks of the river Sind. In 1296 he was assassinated by his ambitious nephew and successor, ʿAlā'-ud-Dīn Khaljī.

The transition to Khaljī rule was more than a dynastic change, because it represented the triumph of new blood and resulted in significant administrative and economic innovations. The view of medieval Muslim historians that the end of Balban's dynasty represented the end of the Turkish sultanate of Delhi is exaggerated, for the administration was neither so racially pure before 1290 nor so racially mixed thereafter as is sometimes stated. Nevertheless, the Khaljīs were not recognized by the older nobility as coming from pure Turkish stock (although they were Turks), and their rise to power was aided by impatient outsiders, some of them Indian-born Muslims, who might expect to enhance their positions if the hold of the followers of Balban and the Forty were broken. To some extent, then, the Khaljī usurpation was a move toward the recognition of a changing balance of power and thus functioned as a cohesive force: those Muslims of talent who were outside the old ruling group were able to alter the system enough so that their efforts would be rewarded. Rebellion against the sultanate was not necessary.

The reign of ʿAlā'-ud-Dīn

By far the ablest of the Khaljīs, if not of all the sultans of Delhi, was ʿAlā'-ud-Dīn Khaljī (reigned 1296–1316). His career demonstrates many features common to ambitious and talented rulers. During his reign the sultanate briefly assumed the status of an empire. In order to achieve his goals of centralization and expansion, ʿAlā'-ud-Dīn needed money, a loyal and reasonably subservient nobility, and an efficient army under his personal control. He had earlier, in 1292, partly solved the problem of money when he conducted a lucrative raid into Bhīlsa in central India. Using that success to build his position and a fresh army, he led a brilliant and unauthorized raid on the fabulously wealthy Devagiri (modern Daulatābād) in the Deccan early in 1296, with the idea that he could gain enough wealth to finance a coup. The wealth of Devagiri not only financed his usurpation but provided a good foundation for his state-building plans. ʿAlā'-ud-Dīn already had the support of many of the disaffected Turkish nobles, and now he was able to purchase the support of more with both money and promotion. He also was able to capture and subsequently to imprison, blind, or kill the sons of Jalāl-ud-Dīn and their supporters.

As sultan, ʿAlā'-ud-Dīn soon initiated a number of military, revenue, and economic reforms that were designed to raise more money, put a greater distance between the Sultan and his nobles, and to sink the roots of the sultanate more deeply into Indian soil. Many land grants and revenue assignments were resumed, and nobles were paid in cash whenever possible. The rate of taxation was increased officially to 50 percent of the produce, and officials were sent out to force local Hindu landholders to pay the revenue demand in full. For the first time in the history of the sultanate, taxation appeared as revenue demand based upon actual measurement of the land in many areas of North India rather than as a kind of tribute collected from local landholders. ʿAlā'-ud-Dīn also introduced a partly successful system of price and wage controls in the Delhi area so that the inflation caused by the sudden influx of both men and money following the organization of a standing army would devalue his treasury as little as possible. These measures were much more oppressive than any attempted by earlier sultans, and it is not entirely clear why ʿAlāʾ-ud-Dīn was able to enforce them as well as he did. His success must have been due in part to his military and administrative ability, but it also depended upon the creation of a substantial standing army—the first that the sultanate had known—which was directly under his command and which he kept at Delhi for extended periods.

The result of ʿAlāʾ-ud-Dīn's reforms and his energetic rule was that the sultanate expanded rapidly and was subject to a more unified and efficient direction than during any other period. ʿAlāʾ-ud-Dīn began his expansionist activities with the subjugation of Gujarāt in 1299. Next he moved against Rājasthān and then captured Ranthambhor (1301), Chitor (1303), and Māndū (1305) and later added Siwāna (1308) and Jālor (1312). These conquests greatly reduced the power of the Rājput chiefs and made them, finally, subject to Delhi. In addition, the Rājput campaigns opened the road for further raids into South India.

Expansionist activities against Rājput chiefs

These raids were not intended to result in occupation of the land but rather in the formal recognition by Hindu kings of ʿAlāʾ-ud-Dīn's supremacy and in the collection of huge amounts of tribute and booty, which were used to finance his centralizing activities in the north. In 1307 his lieutenant Malik Kāfūr again subdued the Yādava kingdom of Devagiri and in 1309 added the Kākatīya kingdom of Telingana. In 1310–11 Malik Kāfūr plundered the Pāṇḍya kingdom in the far south, and in 1313 Devagiri was again defeated and finally annexed to the sultanate.

ʿAlāʾ-ud-Dīn also managed to fend off a series of Mongol attacks, which posed a much more serious threat than those of Balban's reign. Mongol invasions into the Punjab (1297–98) and into Sīwistān (1299) were repulsed, and, while another invasion almost reached Delhi in the same year and the Mongols actually invested the city in 1303, ʿAlāʾ-ud-Dīn finally was victorious on both occasions. Other invasions were repulsed in 1305 and 1306, after which the Mongol attacks subsided, probably as much because of an intensification of internal rivalries as of the lack of Mongol success in India.

Ambition, a talent for ruling, and the gold of South India carried ʿAlāʾ-ud-Dīn a long way, but it is also significant that he was one of the first rulers to deliberately expand political participation within the sultanate government. Not only did he partly open the gates to power for the non-Turkish Muslim nobility—some of whom were even converted Hindus—but he also at least made gestures toward the inclusion of Hindus within the political world he viewed as legitimate. Both ʿAlāʾ-ud-Dīn and his son married into the families of important Hindu rulers, and several such rulers were received at court and treated with respect. Like the Mughal ruler Akbar, 250 years later, ʿAlāʾ-ud-Dīn appears to have had the vision of an empire in which both Hindus and Muslims would participate within the ruling group, although both would be subject to the strict discipline of the ruler. ʿAlāʾ-ud-Dīn's centralizing activities also led, however, to a good deal of oppression of both Hindus and Muslims.

ʿAlāʾ-ud-Dīn's success was not lasting, nor did the sultanate remain in his family for long. The succession dispute following his death in 1316 resulted in the murder of Malik Kāfūr by the palace guards and the blinding of ʿAlāʾ-ud-Dīn's six-year-old son by the Sultan's third son, Quṭb-ud-Dīn Mubārak Shāh, who assumed the sultanate (1316–20). During Quṭb-ud-Dīn's reign, revolts in Gujarāt and Devagiri were suppressed, and Telingana was raided again. Quṭb-ud-Dīn was murdered by his favourite general, a Hindu convert named Khusraw Khān, who had built substantial support among a group of Hindus who were not part of the traditional nobility. Opposition to Khusraw's rule arose immediately, led by Ghāzī Malik, the warden of the western marches at Deopalpur; and Khusraw was defeated and slain after four months. Ghāzī Malik was probably able to gain enough support to overthrow Khusraw because of his own military reputation and because of Khusraw's position as an outsider. It is unlikely, however, that Khusraw's Hindu origin was of major significance (for many Muslims supported him). Historians of the succeeding Tughluq period, however—perhaps in justification of the Tughluq usurpation—made much of the claim that Ghāzī Malik saved the sultanate from domination by infidels.

Succession dispute

The Tughluqs. Ghāzī Malik, who ascended the throne as Ghiyāṣ-ud-Dīn Tughluq (reigned 1320–25), had first risen to prominence during the reign of Jalāl-ud-Dīn Khaljī and had later distinguished himself by his successful defense of the frontier against the Mongols. His reign was short but successful. He sent an expedition against Telingana in 1321–22, captured it in 1323, and then raided into Jājnagar. In addition, another Mongol raid was repulsed, and Bengal, which had been independent under Muslim kings since the death of Balban, was again brought under sultanate rule. While returning from the Bengal campaign, the Sultan was killed when a wooden shelter collapsed on him at Afghānpur, near Delhi. Although some historians have argued that Muḥammad ibn Tughluq plotted his father's death, the case never has been proved.

The reign (1325–51) of Muḥammad ibn Tughluq marked both the high point and the beginning of the decline of the sultanate. The period from 1296 to 1335 can be seen as one of nearly continuous centralization and expansion. A contemporary historian counted 23 provinces at the beginning of Muḥammad ibn Tughluq's reign, and there were few places in the subcontinent where the Sultan's authority could be seriously challenged. Even before 1335, however, things began to go wrong, and, while the sultanate enjoyed its greatest geographical extension during his reign, Muḥammad ibn Tughluq was unable to maintain the momentum of consolidation. By 1351 South India had been lost and much of the North was in rebellion.

Muḥammad ibn Tughluq was an innovative and ambitious ruler; yet his innovations and his ambitions appear to have worked to his disadvantage. Like the Mughal ruler Aurangzeb, more than three centuries later, Muḥammad ibn Tughluq was confronted by problems resulting from expansion into South India, which put him in an untenable military and political position. And, like Aurangzeb, he tried to hold his territories in the Deccan and thus paid for his ambition with a weakened hold on the North and the ultimate independence of the South. Eschewing the Khaljī policy of maintaining Hindu tributary states in the South, Muḥammad ibn Tughluq, while still a prince, had brought two of the three remaining southern Hindu powers under the direct control of the sultanate, and in 1326–27 he subdued the third (Kampili). Direct Muslim rule in the South, however, did not necessarily signify control from Delhi. In an effort both to settle additional Muslim nobles in the South and to maintain his control over them, the Sultan made Daulatābād (Devagiri) a second capital in 1327 and forcibly moved a significant proportion of the unhappy inhabitants of Delhi there. The extent to which Delhi was depopulated by the move is questionable, however, and perhaps the severe famine of 1335–36 was as significant a cause of the city's temporary decline.

No sooner was the Sultan established at Daulatābād than trouble broke out in the North. Rebellions by Kishlū Khān on the western border and by Nāṣir-ud-Dīn in Bengal were put down in 1327–28. The Sultan was less successful against an invasion by the Mongols, however, and was obliged to pay a large tribute after they had come almost to the gates of Delhi. Perhaps in reaction to this invasion, Muḥammad ibn Tughluq raised an army reported to number 370,000 men and said to have been designated for a campaign into Khorāsān, from whence the Mongols had come. It is more likely that the army's object was Ghazna or Peshāwar, but in any case the troops were never used and were disbanded after being paid for a year, thus diminishing the treasury. Another attempt to extend the boundaries of the sultanate some years later—this time in the Kumaon region of the Himalayan foothills—was actually carried out and resulted in the loss of almost an entire army through the ravages of disease and the guerrilla tactics of the hill people.

Loss of the South

By 1335 it was evident that Muḥammad ibn Tughluq's attempt to hold the South was not likely to succeed. The Muslim governor of Maʿbar, the southernmost province of the sultanate, declared his independence in 1334–35 and founded the sultanate of Madura while Muḥammad ibn Tughluq was busy quelling a rebellion in Lahore. Soon rebellions by Hindu chiefs had resulted in the formation of several new states, the most important of which was Vijayanagar. During the next few years, while the Sultan was kept moving from north to south in an attempt to put down rebellions in practically every province, he lost control of the rest of his South Indian possessions after successful rebellions in Gulbarga (1339), Warangal (1345–46), and Daulatābād, which led to the founding of the Bahmanī kingdom. Muḥammad ibn Tughluq spent the last five years of his life trying to suppress yet another rebellion in Gujarāt and thus could not make an attempt to regain Daulatābād.

Muḥammad ibn Tughluq's successor was his cousin Fīrūz ibn Rajab, thereafter known as Fīrūz Shāh (reigned 1351–88). Although this son of a Rājput princess has been depicted by medieval chroniclers as a pious ruler whose reign saw peace and prosperity, he still campaigned in Bengal (1353–54 and 1359), Orissa (1360), Nagarkot (1361), Sind (1362 and 1366–67), Etāwah (1377), and Katehr (1380). Despite these efforts, Fīrūz was unable to recover Bengal for the sultanate, and Sind was no more than a tribute-paying vassal during his reign. Fīrūz's decision (*c.* 1365) not to accept an invitation from a Bahmanī prince to intervene in Brahmanī politics and reconquer the Deccan was probably a wise one. Fīrūz had witnessed the troubles of his cousin and must have seen how difficult if not impossible it would be for even the most talented and energetic of rulers (which he was not) to hold the South and North simultaneously.

The principal reason for Fīrūz's good reputation among contemporary chroniclers was probably his conciliatory attitude toward the two main influential Muslim groups of the period: the Muslim religious leaders and the nobility. While ʿAlāʾ-ud-Dīn Khaljī kept religion and religious leaders apart from his political plans and Muḥammad ibn Tughluq incurred the enmity of at least some Ṣūfīs because of his refusal to give them what they regarded as proper support, Fīrūz rewarded Ṣūfīs and other religious leaders generously and listened to their counsel. He was indeed a pious ruler: he created charities to aid poor Muslims, built many colleges and mosques, abolished taxes not recognized by Muslim law, made largely unsuccessful attempts to convert his Hindu subjects, and sometimes persecuted them.

His weakness as a ruler was politically more significant than was his piety, however, and his weak policy toward his nobility was an important reason for the decline of central authority during his reign.

Decline of central authority

Balban, ʿAlāʾ-ud-Dīn, and Muḥammad ibn Tughluq all had made attempts to check the power of the nobility and to centralize authority; the latter two had also realized the necessity for allowing a certain amount of mobility both into and within the army and civil administration for groups that had come to represent significant and articulated interests. The Khaljī revolution had brought Muslim outsiders into positions formerly enjoyed almost exclusively by Balban and his followers, and during the first 30 years of Tughluq rule the gradual integration of new blood into the nobility had continued. Such a policy also enhanced the power of the sultans over all of the nobility because it unsettled old nobles and provided grateful new ones. Judging by the revolts during his reign, however, Muḥammad ibn Tughluq's policy toward his nobility was too autocratic to succeed. Partly for that reason and partly because of his own proclivities, Fīrūz adopted policies that gave his nobles much more autonomy. He agreed that fewer new nobles of questionable heritage (*i.e.*, Indian Muslims and Hindu converts) should be allowed to have important positions. The result was that the Sultan lost both an important means of leverage and a means of adjusting to new political circumstances. Fīrūz also made little or no attempt to pay officers in cash (rather than in assignments of land revenue), granted hereditary appointments, and extended the system of revenue farming. All of these measures, which reversed policies adopted by one or more of the strong rulers of the previous 50 years, tended to decrease Fīrūz's control over his nobility and over the revenue system. Finally, contemporary chronicles suggest that Fīrūz's generally light hand on the reins of administration led to increasing inefficiency and corruption, especially after the death of his very competent vizier, Khān Jahān I, in 1370.

Fīrūz was justly famous as a builder, however. In addition to a large number of mosques, schools, hospitals, caravansaries, and even towns, he constructed five canals for irrigation, the most important of which ran for 150 miles (240 kilometres), and a number of reservoirs and wells for the same purpose.

Decline of the sultanate. Succession disputes were the rule rather than the exception in the Muslim kingdoms of India, but the death of an old ruler after a long reign often led to more than normally destructive disputes because there could be two generations of grown men with claims to the throne. Such a situation arose after the death of Fīrūz, in 1388, and it was further complicated by the relatively great power of the nobility and by the absence of any claimant who exhibited a superior degree of talent. The sons and grandsons of Fīrūz, supported by various groups of nobles, began a struggle for the throne that rapidly diminished the authority of the sultanate and provided opportunities for Muslim nobles and Hindu chiefs to enhance their autonomy. By 1390 the Muslim governor of Gujarāt had declared his independence, and between 1391 and 1394 the important Rājput chiefs of Etāwah rebelled and were defeated four times. Clearly, the authority of Delhi was in doubt. By 1394 there were two sultans, both residing in or near Delhi. The result was bitter civil war for three years; meanwhile the disastrous invasion of Timur (the Tamerlane of Western literature) grew nearer.

Timur's invasion of India

Timur was a Barlas Turk who rose from an uncertain position as ruler of a small principality in Transoxania to become one of the greatest conquerors the world has known. Timur invaded India in 1398, when he was 62 years old and in possession of a vast empire in the Middle East and Central Asia, and dealt the final blow to the effective power of the Tughluq dynasty and of the sultanate itself. In a well-executed campaign of four months—during which many of the disunited Muslim and Hindu forces of North India either were bypassed or submitted peacefully while Rājputs and Muslims fighting together were slaughtered at Bhatnagar—Timur reached Delhi and, in mid-December, defeated the army of Sultan Maḥmūd, and sacked the city. It is said that Timur ordered the execution of at least 50,000 captives before the battle for Delhi and that the sack of the city was so devastating that practically everything of value was removed—including those inhabitants who were not killed.

After this catastrophe, Delhi became merely one of the regional principalities of North India, competing with the emerging Rājput and Muslim states. After Timur's invasion, Gujarāt, Mālwa, and Jaunpur soon became powerful independent states, old and new Rājput states rapidly emerged, and Lahore, Dīpālpur, Multān, and parts of Sind were held by Khiẓr Khān Sayyid for Timur (and later for himself). In this unstable political situation, many smaller states also began to emerge.

During the 15th and early 16th centuries, no paramount power enjoyed effective control over most of North India and Bengal, although the Lodī sultans of Delhi gradually asserted authority over much of the Gangetic Plain and the Punjab. The lack of unified rule has led some historians to describe the period as one of political anarchy and confusion, in which the inhabitants suffered because there was no strong guiding hand. Such a conclusion is far from certain, however, even for the central areas of the Gangetic Plain where many battles were fought. In areas where effective regional rule either was restored or developed—as in Rājasthān, Orissa, Bengal,

Rise of regional states

Gujarāt, Mālwa, Jaunpur, and various smaller states in the North, as well as in the large and small states of the Deccan—the quality of life may well have been as good or better for cultivators, townspeople, landholders, and nobles than it had been in earlier centuries. Although contemporary sources are scarce, the information available does not indicate a significant decline in total cultivation or trade (despite some alteration of trade routes), and various regional histories suggest that the vigour of local political organization was maintained if not enhanced.

The Sayyids. The last of the Tughluqs died in 1413, and Delhi and a small area surrounding it fell into the hands of the Turk Khiẓr Khān in 1414. The Sayyid dynasty ruled the territory until 1451, trying to obtain tribute and recognition of suzerainty from the nearby Rājput rulers and fighting almost continuously against neighbouring states to preserve their kingdom intact. The last Sayyid ruler, ʿAlāʾ-ud-Dīn ʿĀlam Shāh (reigned 1445–51), peacefully surrendered Delhi to his nominal vassal, the Afghan Bahlūl Lodī, and retired to Badaun district, which he retained until his death in 1478. Meanwhile, the neighbouring kingdom of Jaunpur developed into a power equal to Delhi during the reign (1402–40) of Ibrāhīm Sharqī. Ibrāhīm's successor, Maḥmūd, conducted expansionist campaigns against Bengal and Orissa and, in 1452, initiated a conflict with the Lodī sultans of Delhi that lasted at least until the defeat and partial annexation of Jaunpur by Bahlūl Lodī in 1479.

The Lodīs. Before he moved to Delhi, Bahlūl Lodī had already carved out a kingdom in the Punjab that was larger than that of the Sayyid sultans. During the next 75 years Bahlūl and his two successors, Sikandar (reigned 1489–1517) and Ibrāhīm (reigned 1517–26), continued to hold Delhi and intermittently to expand their control over the surrounding territory. Bahlūl pacified the Doab and subdued Etāwah, Chandwar, and Rewāri. Sikandar completed the pacification of Jaunpur (1493), campaigned into Bihār, and founded the city of Āgra in 1504 as a base from which to launch his ultimately unsuccessful attempt to control nearby Rājput states. By the time of Sikandar's death, the Afghans could claim a somewhat uneven control over the Punjab and most of the Gangetic Plain down to Bihār. Still, the question of Lodī paramountcy in North India was far from settled, for it can be argued that the strongest military force in India on the eve of the Mughal conquest was that of the Rājput confederacy, under Rānā Sāngā, rather than that of the Lodīs. A significant result of the Lodī state's development was the immigration into India of a considerable number of Afghans, who settled in and helped to expand the sultanate and who were the principal rivals to the new Mughal power through most of the 16th century.

Immigration of Afghans

The last Lodī sultan, Ibrāhīm, was more autocratic than his predecessor, and he was ultimately less able to control his skittish nobility, who tended to see the Lodī sultans as first among equals only. He soon faced an Afghan rebellion in the east under the leadership of his brother Jalāl Khān, and, while Ibrāhīm put down this and some other Afghan revolts in the east, the groundwork for the final disaster was laid in the west. Dawlat Khān Lodī, governor of the Punjab, and ʿĀlam Khān Lodī, Ibrāhīm's uncle, appealed to Bābur, the Mughal ruler of Kābul, to aid them in their attempt to overthrow the Sultan. The adventurous Bābur was at that time probably thinking only of annexing the Punjab, but, as his previous history had demonstrated, he was quick to take advantage of political opportunities. In 1524 he led an expedition to Lahore and defeated Ibrāhīm's army. Bābur then passed over his Afghan allies and appointed his own officials in the Punjab. After his allies had indignantly left him, he went on to defeat and kill Ibrāhīm at Pānīpat, near Delhi, in 1526 (see below, *The Mughal Empire*). The Afghan sultanate underwent a short revival under the Sūrs in 1540–55, only to be replaced by the Mughals again under Humāyūn and then Akbar.

Appraisal of the Delhi sultanate. In many ways the sultanate of Delhi can be seen as a continuation of the Hindu political tradition of the preceding period. Except for a brief time under ʿAlāʾ-ud-Dīn Khaljī and the early Tughluqs, the sultanate appeared as one of a number of powers—though usually the greatest—that competed for the paramount position in North India. Although most of the upper level of Hindu chiefs in the plains areas were removed, the Rājput chiefs in the hills and forests were never entirely subdued, and they returned repeatedly to challenge the sultanate. Even in the plains areas, however, it is likely that only a small proportion of the land was directly administered by Muslims, while the rest was left in the hands of Hindu petty chiefs and landholders, who paid what amounted to tribute rather than a tax based upon measurement of the land, except during ʿAlāʾ-ud-Dīn's reign. Even under ʿAlāʾ-ud-Dīn, the area under centralized revenue control was not very large, and Muḥammad ibn Tughluq's attempts to increase the rate of taxation within the area and to expand it helped to ruin agriculture in the Doab and were partly responsible for the revolts of his nobles. Despite these disclaimers, however, the formation of a Muslim political system designed for centralization and the introduction of an Islāmic ruling group and of Muslim culture were extremely important developments in the history of the subcontinent.

THE MUSLIM STATES OF SOUTH INDIA, C. 1350–1680

Sultanate rule in most of South India existed for only a few years and was firmly established only in the Deccan's northernmost province, whose capital was Daulatābād. The forced withdrawal of the sultanate forces from the Deccan between 1330 and 1347 was partly the result of resistance offered by Hindu chiefs and some Muslim nobles. Members of those two groups then established the two strongest states of the South—the Muslim-ruled Bahmanī kingdom and the Hindu-ruled Vijayanagar empire.

The Bahmanī dynasty. The Bahmanī kingdom, which lasted from 1347 to roughly 1527, arose out of a revolt by a group of Muslim nobles against the Delhi sultan, Muḥammad ibn Tughluq, in 1345. The founder of the Bahmanī dynasty, Ḥasan Gangū, ascended the throne at Daulatābād in 1347 as ʿAlāʾ-ud-Dīn Bahman Shāh and soon moved his capital to Gulbarga, centrally located on the Deccan Plateau, where it remained until about 1425. The natural focus for the Bahmanī state was the Deccan Plateau tableland. It was bounded on the north by the Vindhya Mountains and Mālwa; on the west by the Western Ghāts and the steep drop to the coastal plain beyond; on the south by the Tungabhadra River, beyond which lay the much disputed no-man's-land, called the doab, between the Krishna and Tungabhadra rivers, where so many battles were fought with the rulers of the kingdom of Vijayanagar; and on the east, less definitively, by the lower end of the gradually sloping plateau. Much of the political and military history of the Bahmanī sultanate can be described as an attempt to gain effective control of the Deccan Plateau and then, less successfully, to expand outward from it. The period of consolidation was followed by a much longer period of intermittent warfare against Mālwa and Gujarāt in the north, Vijayanagar in the south, and Orissa in the east.

Revolt by Muslim nobles

Bahmanī consolidation of the Deccan. Bahman Shāh spent most of his reign consolidating a kingdom in the area that had formerly been subject to the Delhi sultanate government at Daulatābād and in strengthening his hold over those Muslim nobles who chose to remain in the Deccan rather than to join Muḥammad ibn Tughluq in North India. He adopted the four territorial divisions established by Muḥammad ibn Tughluq for his own administration and established departments and appointed officials similar to those of the Delhi sultanate. Working outward from his capital, he was able to establish his authority over the western half of the Deccan Plateau and to impose an annual tribute upon the Hindu state of Warangal, which had also emerged from the breakup of the Deccan portion of the Tughluq empire. Often, however, the tribute was not paid, and a number of wars were fought over the question of whether the Bahmanīs could maintain a superior position in relation to their eastern neighbour in the following years.

Bahman Shāh was succeeded by his son Muḥammad Shāh I (reigned 1358–75), who began the struggle with Vijayanagar that was to outlast the Bahmanī sultanate and continue, as a many-sided conflict, into the 17th century. The period 1350–1500 saw at least ten wars, most of which were concerned with control over the Tungabhadra-Krishna doab. The doab had been an area of contention long before the foundation of either the Bahmanī kingdom or Vijayanagar. During Muḥammad Shāh's reign institutional and geographical consolidation proceeded to the point where a solid foundation for the kingdom was established. In his wars against Vijayanagar and Telingana (Warangal), Muḥammad Shāh effectively made use of newly organized artillery to defeat an army much larger than his own. His two wars with Vijayanagar gained him little, but his attack on Telingana in 1363 gained him a large indemnity plus possession of the town of Golconda and its dependencies; and in 1365 his rapid response to a rebellion by the governor of Daulatābād and some Marāthā and other chieftains of Berār and Bāglanā led to a quick victory. The Sultan was spared further internal or external threats to his kingdom, and he spent the last ten years of his reign consolidating his hold over the territories in his possession. His well-laid foundations were soon disturbed, however, when his son and successor, ʿAlāʾ-ud-Dīn Mujāhid (reigned 1375–78), was assassinated by his cousin Dāʾūd while returning from a campaign in Vijayanagar. Dāʾūd was in turn murdered by ʿAlāʾ-ud-Dīn's partisans, who then set Dāʾūd's brother Muḥammad II (reigned 1378–97) on the throne and blinded Dāʾūd's son. These political difficulties enabled Vijayanagar to take away part of Goa and other territory along the western coast; but the rest of Muḥammad's reign was peaceful, and the Sultan spent much of his time building his court as a centre of culture and learning.

Political and cultural tendencies

Several political and cultural tendencies were becoming noticeable at this time and had significant effects on the development of the Bahmanī state and its successors. Although the state had been organized by a group of dissident nobles from the Delhi sultanate, differences in both the culture and the membership of the nobilities developed, largely because of differences in recruiting patterns. Soon after the foundation of the Bahmanī state, large numbers of Arabs, Turks, and particularly Persians began to immigrate to the Deccan, many of them at the invitation of Sultan Muḥammad, and there they had a strong influence on the development of Muslim culture during subsequent generations. The new settlers (*āfāqīs*) also had a political effect, as they soon began competing successfully for important positions within the political hierarchy. The original rebels from the Delhi sultanate and their descendants, who came to be called *dakhnīs* (*i.e.*, Deccanis—from the Deccan), thought of themselves as the old nobility and thus resented the success of the newcomers. The situation was not unlike that of the Delhi sultanate, in which a party of established nobles had tried to protect their privileged position against newcomers who were developing claims to power. Thus, the distribution of high offices among Persian newcomers by Sultan Ghiyāṣ-ud-Dīn (Muḥammad II's oldest son, who ruled for about two months) in 1397 was seen as a threat by the old nobles and Turks and was probably a major reason for his assassination. Later, the addition of Hindu converts and Hindus to the nobility complicated the situation further, as it had in the north, but the division between *dakhnīs* and *āfāqīs* (hereafter called newcomers) was most significant and contributed to the disintegration of the Bahmanī state.

Muḥammad II's peaceful reign was followed by a year of succession disputes caused both by party conflicts and by dynastic rivalries. When Muḥammad's cousins Aḥmad and Fīrūz finally gained control, Fīrūz succeeded as Tāj-ud-Dīn Fīrūz. His reign (1397–1422) was a period of notable cultural activity in the Bahmanī sultanate, as well as one of continued development of the trend toward wider political participation. Noted for his intelligence and learning, Fīrūz nurtured the greatest centre of Muslim culture in India at a time when the Delhi sultanate was rapidly dissolving. Perhaps in an effort to balance the continuing influx of Persians, as well as to strengthen his own position as a ruler who was above all the nobles and who recognized the realities of political power, Fīrūz gave a number of high offices to Hindus (Brāhmaṇs) and married several Hindu women, including the daughter of the King of Vijayanagar. Thus, the parallel with the earlier development of the Delhi sultanate nobility continued. The fact that Hindus were becoming politically more significant at a time when the military rivalry with Vijayanagar was renewed suggests a political rather than a religious motivation for that rivalry.

Fīrūz stopped an invasion in the north by the Gond raja of Kherla in Madhya Pradesh and conducted two moderately successful campaigns against Vijayanagar. The first brought him a tribute payment and temporary possession of part of the Andhra country, while the second ended with his marriage to the Vijayanagar king's daughter, another tribute payment, and the establishment of an apparently amicable relationship between the two rulers. The peace lasted for only ten years, however, and a third war (1417–20) ended in a disastrous defeat for Fīrūz by the united forces of Vijayanagar and Fīrūz's former allies, the Velama faction of the Reddi ruling group in Andhra. Although no territory was lost, the defeat so weakened Fīrūz's position that, when the question was raised of whether Fīrūz's son or his brother Aḥmad should succeed him, most of the army supported Aḥmad; and Fīrūz, who was 70 years old and dying, was forced to abdicate in favour of him.

Expansionist ambitions of Aḥmad I

One of the first acts of the new sultan, Shihāb-ud-Dīn Aḥmad I (reigned 1422–36), was to move the capital from Gulbarga to Bīdar, which was surrounded by more fertile ground and had become more centrally located, now that some territory had been gained to the southeast, in Telingana. Perhaps, also, the move signified Aḥmad's expansionist ambitions, for in 1425 he defeated and killed the Velema ruler of Warangal and finally annexed most of Telingana, bringing his eastern border to the edge of Orissa. During the next decade, however, rebellions forced Aḥmad to allow local chieftains to rule as tributaries throughout much of the area.

External and internal rivalries. Although the Bahmanī state had been threatened from the north earlier, it was during Aḥmad's reign that conflicts first broke out with the northern neighbours, Mālwa and Gujarāt. The breakdown of centralized authority within the Delhi sultanate and the consequent rise of provincial kingdoms meant that new rivalries could develop on a regional basis, and the Bahmanī sultans found themselves contending with two of the successor states of the Delhi sultanate in an arena where their expansionist ambitions had some chance of success. A border dispute with Mālwa led to a Bahmanī victory and a short-lived recognition of the chieftainship of Kherla as a Bahmanī protectorate. Aḥmad then forged an alliance with another northern neighbour, Khāndesh, and, on the pretext of giving aid to a Hindu chieftain who had revolted against Gujarāt, he sent unsuccessful expeditions into Gujarāt in 1429 and 1430. The latter defeat was especially significant; it partly stemmed from rivalries between the Deccani officers and the newcomers from the Middle East, a friction that appears to have become gradually more intense from this point until the breakup of the Bahmanī sultanate.

During the last year of his reign, Aḥmad named his eldest son as his heir and gave him full charge of the administration; he parcelled out the provinces among his other sons, exacting from them promises that they would be loyal to the new ruler. Perhaps the scheme was useful; even though Sultan ʿAlāʾ-ud-Dīn Aḥmad II (reigned 1436–58) had to face a rebellion by one of his brothers, a precedent was set for a rule of primogeniture, which seemed to alleviate the problem of succession disputes for the rest of the century. Unfortunately for later Bahmanī rulers, rivalries among the nobility were to prove just as detrimental to the fortunes of the dynasty as family disputes were in many other dynasties of the period.

Aḥmad II proved to be a weaker ruler than his father had been, and during his reign the conflicts among the nobles intensified. Two short wars with Vijayanagar in 1436 and 1443–44 were confined to Krishna-Tungabhadra doab and signified little except the arrival of a new power, the Hindu Gajapati king of Orissa, who allied himself with the Bahmanī ruler in the second campaign. Perhaps more significant in its ultimate effect was the Bahmanī victory over Khāndesh in 1438. The force in that campaign was composed exclusively of newcomers, who had convinced the Sultan that Deccani treachery had been responsible for the defeat in Gujarāt in 1430. The newcomers thereby gained considerable influence with the Sultan but at the same time intensified the resentment of the Deccanis, who retaliated in 1446 by massacring a large number of them, with the malleable Sultan's tacit permission. Later, when the Sultan was convinced that the newcomers had been unjustly killed, he punished many of the responsible Deccanis and promoted the surviving newcomers. During the last years of his reign, Aḥmad had to face a rebellion in Telingana led by his son-in-law, the most noteworthy aspect of which was the military and diplomatic skill displayed by a newly arrived noble, Maḥmūd Gāwān, who had persuaded the rebels to desist and the Sultan to pardon them.

Three sultans reigned between 1458 and 1481, but the most notable personality of the period was the Persian émigré Maḥmūd Gāwān, who was a leading administrator during the reigns of Humāyūn (reigned 1458–61) and his son Niẓām-ud-Dīn Aḥmad III (reigned 1461–63) and was chief minister under Muḥammad III (reigned 1463–82). During Maḥmūd Gāwān's ascendancy, the Bahmanī state achieved both its greatest size and greatest degree of centralization, and yet, partly because of the attempts at centralization and partly because of the continuing rivalry between the Deccanis and newcomers, the period ended with Maḥmūd Gāwān's assassination and the rapid dissolution of the effective power of the Bahmanī state.

Military successes in the west

Militarily, the Bahmanī forces usually were successful. After Maḥmūd Gāwān's installation as chief minister in 1463, a series of expansionist campaigns resulted in the subjugation in the west of most of the Konkan, including the important port of Goa, and the Bombay Carnatic. The frontier with Mālwa in the north was maintained more or less as it was, while an alliance with Vijayanagar proved effective in defeating Orissa in 1470. A later campaign in the east produced some minor advantages for the Bahmanīs in Telingana.

As chief minister, Maḥmūd Gāwān attempted to enhance the power of the crown through a series of administrative reforms and political manoeuvres. Up to the 1470s the kingdom had been divided into four provinces, centring around the cities of Daulatābād, Berār, Bīdar, and Gulbarga, respectively. The governors of the four provinces had control over almost all aspects of civil and military administration within their territorial jurisdictions. Administration was thus decentralized from the beginning, but the relative power of the provincial governors as compared with the centre potentially became even greater as the state expanded and each of the four provinces grew larger. To decrease the power of the governors, Maḥmūd Gāwān created eight provinces in place of the four, reduced the military control of the governors by making the commanders of all forts but one in each province responsible directly to the Sultan instead of to the governor, and tightened central control over the employment and payment of troops within the provinces. In addition, he introduced a system of measurement and valuation of agricultural land and created a large block of crown land within each province. Maḥmūd Gāwān also tried to balance important appointments between Deccanis and newcomers—a policy that suggests not only his desire to reduce disputes among the nobility but perhaps also his intention to enhance the power of the chief minister, who, although a newcomer, had raised himself above party conflicts.

Unfortunately for Maḥmūd Gāwān and for the Bahmanī dynasty, party strife had developed to such an extent that a group of Deccani nobles who were motivated by hostility toward the chief as a newcomer, as well as by dislike of his efforts toward centralization, falsified evidence to make Maḥmūd Gāwān appear a traitor and convinced Muḥammad III to execute him in 1481. All the newcomers and some of the Deccani nobles disapproved of the execution and sided with Yūsuf ʿĀdil Khān, previously Maḥmūd Gāwān's chief supporter. Most of the newcomers returned to their provinces and refused to come to the capital, and the Sultan was left with only the support of the conspirators. When he died in 1482 (of grief over his error in judgment, the chronicles report), the leader of the conspirators, Malik Nā'ib, was able to make himself regent for Muḥammad's minor son, Shihāb-ud-Dīn Maḥmūd (reigned 1482–1518).

Bahmanī decline. Maḥmūd's reign began with an abortive attempt to assassinate Yūsuf ʿĀdil Khān, which resulted in the Khān's agreement to retire to Bijāpur and leave Malik Nā'ib and the conspirators in charge at Bīdar. Now the lack of institutionalized central power and the detrimental effects of the conflict between Deccanis and newcomers rapidly became more apparent. Malik Nā'ib, never popular even with a number of the Deccanis, was put to death in 1486 by the Abyssinian governor of Bīdar, and the Sultan subsequently began to rely on the newcomers for support. An attempt on Maḥmūd's life in 1487 by a group of Deccanis strengthened the Sultan's reliance on the newcomers and led to the slaughter of a great many Deccanis. But by this time it began to become apparent that the power of the Sultan was less than that of several of his nobles, and, although he continued to be a valuable pawn for the provincial governors to try to control, his power to rule was nearly gone. The provincial governors and their followers could not be controlled, nor did they believe that maintaining the centralized Bahmanī state would any longer be in their best interests. Consequently, the governors were usually unwilling to aid the Sultan when he attempted to put down rebellions by other governors or by powerful nobles.

Rebellions by governors and provincial nobles

One of the first revolts was that of a Turkish noble, Qāsim Barīd, who defeated the army sent against him by the Sultan and then forced Maḥmūd to make him chief minister of the state. Qāsim Barīd's attempt to reimpose central authority was opposed by most of the chief nobles, however, who defeated him once and then refused to recognize his authority. Next, Malik Aḥmad Niẓām-ul-Mulk, the son of Malik Nā'ib, began to carve out a territory for himself by conquering Marāthā forts along the western coast. He defeated the two armies sent against him by the Sultan, whom he forced to recognize his conquests, and in 1490 he assumed a practical independence and established his capital at Ahmadnagar. Yūsuf ʿĀdil Khān of Bijāpur and Fatḥ Allāh ʿImād-ul-Mulk of Berār had demonstrated their sympathy for Malik Aḥmad's activities and soon emulated him. Although the three governors still did not assume the insignia of royalty, it was clear by the end of 1490 that Sultan Maḥmūd and the chief minister, Qāsim Barīd, could not command any of them.

Successors to the Bahmanī. During the 1490s the rivalries intensified among the former provincial governors, other high nobles, and Qāsim Barīd, who was the effective head of the government at the Bahmanī capital. Each began to form temporary alliances and to fight battles with other nobles in order to enhance his own position. Gradually the five successor states to the Bahmanī sultanate took shape, as lesser nobles were defeated and their territories were incorporated by the provincial governors or retained by Bīdar. Bijāpur, Berār, and Ahmadnagar were joined by Golconda in 1512, when Quṭb-ul-Mulk of Golconda founded the Quṭb Shāhī dynasty. Although a Bahmanī sultan still remained as a puppet ruler until at least 1545, effective control of the Bīdar government passed into the hands of Qasīm Barīd's son Amīr Barīd upon his father's death in 1505, thus establishing what proved to be a dynastic claim for the Barīd Shāhīs of Bīdar.

Ironically, the conflict between Deccanis and newcomers, which had done so much to destroy the unity of the sultanate, was of little importance after 1492. The major rivalry of the next decade was between two newcomers,

Qāsim Barīd and Yūsuf ʿĀdil Khān. (Qāsim Barīd, however, was supported by the Deccanis of Bīdar in his struggle with another Deccani, Malik Aḥmad of Ahmadnagar.) The shift resulted from the fact that there were no longer parties of nobles but rather semi-independent states whose rulers were attempting to establish and expand their authority. With territorial integrity the primary goal, alliances with any semi-independent rulers outside the territory who might threaten its sovereignty necessarily fell into the field of foreign relations, and they tended to assume the expedient quality of most such relationships.

Unity against Vijayanagar

One issue that occasionally united the Bahmanī successor states was the desire to profit at the expense of Vijayanagar. Perhaps in an attempt to regain some of his lost authority and with the idea that spoils and possibly territory could be gained from raids on Vijayanagar, which was suffering from disunity and weak central control, Sultan Maḥmūd II proposed in 1501 that a policy of an annual *jihād*, or holy war, against the Hindu kingdom be adopted by the Muslim nobles. A number of relatively successful raids were undertaken during the next few years, but in 1509 the new ruler of Vijayanagar, Kṛṣṇa Deva Rāya, repulsed the Muslims with substantial losses. Vijayanagar then grew stronger, and alliances against it increasingly became a matter of necessity, although there were many occasions when a Muslim king would ally with Vijayanagar against another Muslim. Ultimately, the Hindu kingdom fell victim to the expansionist ambitions of Bijāpur and Golconda, when these kingdoms took advantage of Vijayanagar's defeat by an alliance of Muslim armies in 1565.

In the struggle for control of the Deccan after the breakup of the Bahmanī sultanate, the two southernmost of the successor states, Bijāpur and Golconda, ultimately found themselves in the most advantageous position because they were farthest away from the growing power of the Mughal Empire in North India. During the latter part of the reign of the emperor Akbar (reigned 1556–1605), the Mughals began a southward movement that was to end with the annexation of Bijāpur and Golconda in 1686 and 1687. During the intervening period, the Mughal presence became increasingly important to the remaining Deccan kings, who struggled to maintain or expand their position within the Deccan while fending off the advancing Mughal juggernaut.

Balance of power alliances. During the 16th century the strongest and best organized of the Bahmanī successor states was Ahmadnagar, followed by Bijāpur and then Golconda. All three were much larger and more important than Berār and Bīdar, and all three either began with or soon came to accept the Shīʿah form of Islām (the religion of the Persian newcomers) as the official faith of their rulers. During the 16th century the three major states formed shifting patterns of alliances against each other, which sometimes also included Vijayanagar, while the two smaller Muslim states ranged themselves on one side or the other in order to protect their independence. The goal of military campaigns normally was to humble the adversary without doing irreparable harm, for all three major Muslim states feared the supremacy of any one state, and a tripartite division of territory seemed more likely to insure the continued independence of all. This principle appears to have operated, at least temporarily, even in the case of a united campaign against Vijayanagar in 1565, for the destruction of Vijayanagar's power was followed almost immediately by the formation of a series of alliances between Vijayanagar and one or another of the victorious Muslim kings.

The defeat of Vijayanagar opened the way for the southward expansion of Bijāpur and Golconda, and the terms of a 1571 treaty between Bijāpur and Ahmadnagar suggest that it was considered proper to restore a potentially unbalanced political situation by recognizing the right of Ahmadnagar to annex Berār and Bīdar in return for recognition of Bijāpur's right to annex an equivalent amount of territory from Vijayanagar. Ahmadnagar did not annex Bīdar, but it did acquire Berār in 1574. Bijāpur was unable to take full advantage of the opportunities for expansion to the south during the 1570s, partly because of factional disputes among the nobles. Thus, Ahmadnagar managed to retain a slightly superior position. The tide began to turn in the 1580s, however, with the establishment of a stable regency at Bijāpur, fortified by a series of marriage alliances with other royal lines in the Deccan and by the political deterioration of Ahmadnagar under the rule of the slightly mad Murtaẕā. Murtaẕā's murder in 1588, by a son who was more insane than he, set off a chain of events that resulted in simultaneous invasions by Bijāpur from the south and by Murtaẕā's brother Burhān, who had the support of the Mughal emperor Akbar, from the north. Burhān defeated the army of Ahmadnagar, recalled the foreign nobles (as the newcomers of Bahmanī times were now designated) who had been expelled from the kingdom, and assumed the throne in 1591. Campaigns against Bijāpur and against the Portuguese at Chaul, as well as bitter rivalry between the Deccani and foreign nobles, further weakened Ahmadnagar at a time when Akbar's growing interest indicated grave danger. The death of both Burhān and his son in 1595 was followed by increased factionalism and finally by civil war as rival claimants to the throne were put forward. When one party appealed for aid to the governor of Gujarāt, Akbar had an excuse to launch the campaign he had already been planning. The two wars that followed resulted in the Mughal acquisition of Berār, the capture of the ruler of Ahmadnagar, and the defeat and annexation of Khāndesh. A group of nobles, however, led by the Abyssinian Malik ʿAmbār, raised a member of the royal family to the throne at Daulatābād and continued to fight the Mughals.

Political deterioration of Ahmadnagar

Mughal conquests in the Deccan. Largely because of the efforts of Malik ʿAmbār, a former African slave, Ahmadnagar was able not only to halt the Mughal advance into the Deccan during the next few years but also even to recover some of the territory lost before 1600. An extremely able and ambitious man, Malik ʿAmbār instituted revenue reforms, probably modelled after the recently introduced Mughal reforms, strengthened his contingents of Marāthā light cavalry, and emphasized training in guerrilla warfare for them. These preparations, as well as the rivalries among the nobles stationed in the Mughal Deccan during the reign of Akbar's successor, Jahāngīr, enabled Malik ʿAmbār's forces to win several victories and to recover Ahmadnagar city; but the Mughals decisively defeated a combined army from Ahmadnagar, Bijāpur, and Golconda in 1615, and in 1621 Malik ʿAmbār was forced to cede an additional strip of land to the Mughals. For the next five years Malik ʿAmbār held his own, once against an alliance between Bijāpur and the Mughals, although usually in alliance with Bijāpur, whose aid was given more with an eye to gaining territory from Ahmadnagar as it disintegrated than with the idea of stopping the Mughals. Malik ʿAmbār's death in 1626, however, was followed rapidly by disunity among his supporters and by the defeat and capture of the last Niẓām Shāh at Daulatābād in 1633.

Final annexation of Ahmadnagar

The final annexation of Ahmadnagar led to a direct confrontation between the Mughals and Bijāpur, Golconda, and the Marāthā leader, Shāhjī Bhonsle, who had built up a force while in the service of Ahmadnagar and was now operating independently. Bijāpur, weakened by internal dissensions after the death of Sultan Ibrāhīm II in 1626, was unable to resist the Mughal invasion of 1636 and agreed to a peace treaty by which Bijāpur acknowledged Mughal supremacy, agreed to pay an annual tribute and to allow Mughal arbitration of disputes with Golconda, and recognized the old boundary of Ahmadnagar as the limit of Mughal territory. The peace thus established lasted until the death of Sultan Muḥammad in 1656. Next, the Mughals established peace with Golconda on even harsher terms. Thus, although Bijāpur and Golconda continued as independent states for another 50 years and, in fact, continued to make some progress in the south, where Vijayanagar's authority had disintegrated, they were already subject to some terms of Mughal authority by 1636 and were marked for later conquest. Indeed, it was probably only the rivalry among the Mughal emperor Shāh Jahān's sons, his illness in 1656, and the subsequent war of succession that saved the Deccan kingdoms from extinction in the 1650s.

The only force in the south that did not appear ready to fall before the Mughals was the Marāthās. Marāthā soldiers had been serving under the Deccan sultans for some time, but it was the organization of Marāthā forces by Ahmadnagar's Malik ʿAmbār, together with the unsettled conditions caused by the Mughal wars, that appears to have given Marāthā commanders the opportunity to enhance their positions. Foremost among them was Shāhjī Bhonsle, who continued to control, sporadically, a number of forts in their home territory after the fall of Ahmadnagar. For a time Shāhjī was in the service of Bijāpur, but primarily he served himself, organizing his forces and preparing the way for an explosion of Marāthā power under the direction of his more famous son Śivajī after 1650. Before his death in 1680, Śivajī had developed a political organization and a fighting force that proved able to withstand another 27 years of grim warfare against the Mughals and finally to cause a Mughal retreat from the Deccan.

THE VIJAYANAGAR EMPIRE, 1336–1646

The brief period of Mughal rule in South India following the conquest of Bijāpur and Golconda climaxed a movement toward the expansion of Muslim rule that had begun more than three centuries earlier; but during most of that period the far south was controlled by the last great medieval Hindu kingdom, Vijayanagar.

Many details of the founding of Vijayanagar are not known. It is clear, however, that the kingdom arose out of the political confusion resulting from the Muslim incursions into South India during the first part of the 14th century. At that time many existing dynasties were overturned, and shifts in the balance of power occurred within the region. The powerful local landholders (many of whom were called Nāyaks), probably spurred both by unhappiness at the higher revenue demands imposed by the Delhi sultan and by the concurrent revival of Śaivism (doctrine of a Hindu sect devoted to the god Śiva), were able to organize significant military actions soon after Muḥammad ibn Tughluq's departure from the Deccan in 1329.

Founding of the kingdom of Vijayanagar

Development of the state. The kingdom of Vijayanagar was founded by Harihara and Bukka, two of five brothers who had served in the administrations of both Kākatīya and Kampili before those kingdoms were conquered by the armies of the Delhi sultanate in the 1320s. When Kampili fell in 1327, the two brothers were captured and taken to Delhi, where they converted to Islām. They were returned to the Deccan as governors of Kampili for the sultanate with the hope that they would be able to deal with the many local revolts and invasions by neighbouring Hindu kings. They followed a conciliatory policy toward the landholders of the area, many of whom had not accepted Muslim rule, and began a process of consolidation and expansion. Their first campaign was against the neighbouring Hoysaḷa king, Ballāla III of Dōrasamudra, but it stagnated; after the brothers reconverted to Hinduism and proclaimed their independence from the Delhi sultanate, however, they were able to defeat Ballāla and thereby secure their home base. Harihara I (reigned 1336–57) then established his new capital, Vijayanagar, in an easily defensible position south of the Tungabhadra River. Successful revolts against Delhi by several Hindu rulers on the eastern coast of the Deccan and by the Muslim governor of Maʿbar in the extreme south opened opportunities for expansion, and the subsequent struggles among the Hindu and Muslim powers of the south, based more upon political and military than religious lines, resulted in the emergence of both Vijayanagar and its natural rival, the Muslim Bahmanī sultanate.

Conquests. In 1336 Harihara held uneasy suzerainty over lands extending from Nellore, on the southeast coast, to Bādāmi, south of Bijāpur on the western side of the Deccan. All around him new Hindu kingdoms were rising, the most important of which were the Hoysaḷa kingdom of Ballāla and the Andhra confederacy, led by Kāpaya Nāyaka. But Ballāla's kingdom was disadvantageously situated between the Maʿbar sultanate and Vijayanagar, and two years after Ballāla was killed by the sultan in 1343, his kingdom had been conquered by Bukka, Harihara's brother, and annexed to Vijayanagar. This was the most important victory of Harihara's reign; the new state now could claim sovereignty from sea to sea, and in 1346 a great celebration was held, attended by Harihara and his four brothers. In the same year Bukka was established as joint ruler, with his headquarters at Gatti.

Harihara's brothers made other, less significant conquests of small Hindu kingdoms during the next decade. But the foundation of the Bahmanī sultanate in 1347 created a new and greater danger, and Harihara was forced to lessen his own expansionist activities to meet the threat posed by this powerful and aggressive new state on his northern borders.

Administrative foundation of the state

During Harihara's reign the administrative foundation of the Vijayanagar state was laid. Borrowing from the Kākatīya kings he had served, he created administrative units called *sthola*s, *nāḍu*s, and *sima*s and created officials to collect revenue and to carry on local administration, preferring Brāhmans to men of other castes. The income of the state apparently was increased by the reorganization, although centralization probably did not proceed to the stage where salaried officials collected directly for the government in most areas. Rather, most land remained under the direct control of subordinate chiefs or of a hierarchy of local landholders, who paid some revenue and provided some troops for the king. Harihara also encouraged increased cultivation in some areas by allowing lower revenue payments for lands recently reclaimed from the forests.

Consolidation. Harihara was succeeded by his brother, who as Bukka I (reigned 1357–77) engaged in a number of costly and mainly unsuccessful wars against the Bahmanī sultans during the first decade of his reign. His efforts resulted in the establishment of the Krishna River as the boundary between the two kingdoms. The major accomplishments of Bukka's reign were the conquest of the short-lived sultanate of Maʿbar (Madura), 1370, and the maintenance of his kingdom against the threat of decentralization. During Harihara's reign the government of the outlying provinces of the growing state had been entrusted to his brothers—usually to the brother who had conquered that particular territory. By 1357 some of Bukka's nephews had succeeded their fathers as governors of these provinces, and there was a possibility that the state would become less and less centralized as the various branches of the family became more firmly ensconced in their particular domains. Bukka, therefore, removed his nephews and replaced them with his sons and favourite generals so that centralized authority (and his own line of succession) could be maintained. But the succession of Bukka's son Harihara II (reigned 1377–1404) precipitated a repetition of the same action. A rebellion in the Tamil country at the beginning of his reign probably was aided by the disaffected sons and officers of Bukka's deceased eldest son, Kumāra Kampana, who were not ready to acknowledge Harihara's authority. Harihara was able to put down the rebellion, however, and subsequently to replace his cousins with his own sons as governors of the provinces. Thus, the circle of power was narrowed once again. The question of succession to the throne had not been settled, however. On many occasions, the conflict resumed between the King and his lineal descendant, who tried to centralize the state, and the collateral relatives (cousins and brothers), who tried to establish ruling rights over some portion of the kingdom.

The temporary confusion that followed the assassination of the Bahmanī sultan ʿAlāʾ-ud-Dīn Mujāhid in 1378 gave Harihara the opportunity to recapture Goa and some other ports on the western coast. During the next decade pressure increased for expansion against the Reddi kingdom of Kondavīdu in the northeast. The slight gains made in 1390–91 against an alliance of the Velama chieftain of Rājakonda and the Bahmanīs were more than offset, however, when the Bahmanī sultan besieged Vijayanagar in 1398–99, slaughtered a large number of people, and exacted a promise to pay tribute. The tribute was withheld two years later, however, when Vijayanagar made alliances with the sultans of Mālwa and Gujarāt. Nevertheless, Harihara's reign was relatively successful because he expanded the state, maintained internal order, and managed to fend off the Bahmanī sultans. The control of ports on both coasts provided opportunities for the acquisition of increased wealth through trade.

Wars and rivalries. Harihara II's death in 1404 was followed by a violent succession dispute among his three surviving sons. Only after two of them had been crowned and dethroned was the third, Devarāya I (reigned 1406–22), able to emerge victorious. During his reign the involvement of Vijayanagar and the Bahmanī sultanate as backers of different claimants to the throne of the Reddi kingdom of Kondavīdu led to another direct confrontation between the two powers, another siege of Vijayanagar city, and to the eventual partition of Kondavīdu (1420) between Vijayanagar and the Velamas of Rājakonda, who had changed sides during the protracted struggle. This extensive involvement in Telingana brought Vijayanagar into conflict for the first time with the kingdom of Orissa to the north. Although a war was temporarily averted, there began a rivalry that was to last for 125 years.

Rivalry with Orissa

Perhaps Devarāya's most significant achievement was his reorganization of the army. Realizing the value of cavalry and well-trained archers, he imported many horses from Persia and Arabia and hired Turkish bowmen, as well as troopers who were skilled in mounted warfare. Thus, although it appears that he was seldom able to best the Bahmanīs in the field, he had begun to narrow the strategic and technological gap between north and south and to build an army that would be better suited to warfare on open plains.

The short reigns of Devarāya's two sons, Rāmchandra and Vijaya, were disastrous. In a war against the Bahmanīs many temples were destroyed, and Vijaya was forced to pay a huge indemnity. A combined invasion by the King of Orissa and the Velamas of Andhra resulted in the loss of the territories newly gained in the partition of the Reddi kingdom of Kondavīdu. Vijaya's son and successor, Devarāya II (died 1446), however, reconquered the lost Reddi territories and incorporated them into his kingdom, restored the power of his subsidiary Reddi allies at Rājahmundry (*c.* 1428), and, in 1443, defended them again against the incursions of the Velamas and the King of Orissa. Wars with the Bahmanīs in 1435–36 and 1443–44 over control of Raichūr and Mudgal forts in the Krishna-Tungabhadra doab ended inconclusively. Those campaigns, however, led to further improvements in Vijayanagar's military forces when Devarāya proclaimed that Muslims would be welcome in his service and hired a number of Muslim archers to instruct his Hindu troops. Devarāya also levied tribute from Ceylon and campaigned successfully in the Kerala country of the far south, where his victories over local chieftains suggest a process of consolidation. His reign saw both the greatest territorial extension and the greatest centralization of the first period of the history of Vijayanagar.

Decentralization and loss of territory. During the 40 years after Devarāya's death in 1446, the centralized power of the state declined, and a considerable amount of territory along both coasts was lost to the Bahmanī sultans and to the suddenly powerful Gajapati ruler of Orissa. During the 1450s and 1460s Kapilendra, the great king of Orissa, together with his son Hamvira, conquered the Reddi kingdom of Rājahmundry and the Vijayanagar province of Kondavīdu, captured Warangal and Bīdar from the Bahmanīs, and sent a victorious army down the east coast as far south as the Kāverī River.

Although the army of Orissa soon withdrew from the southernmost districts, the raid had a considerable effect upon Vijayanagar. It not only weakened the empire in the east but also indicated that provincial governors might have to fend for themselves if they expected to retain their territories. The fact that Devarāya's son Mallikārjuna (reigned 1446–65) was succeeded by a cousin rather than by his own son was another indication of lessened central control and of the failure of the King and his immediate family to secure their own future, as had been done by many of his ancestors when they removed their cousins from positions of power. The new ruler, Virūpāksha (reigned 1465–85), had been a provincial governor. His usurpation was not accepted by many of the provincial governors on the east and west coasts or by the direct descendants of Mallikārjuna, who retired to the banks of the Kāverī and ruled much of the southern part of the kingdom in a semi-independent fashion.

Beginning in 1470 the Bahmanīs, under the chief minister Maḥmūd Gāwān, began a campaign that succeeded in taking much of the west coast and the northern Carnatic from Vijayanagar. The loss of Goa and other ports was especially disconcerting because it cut off not only an important source of trade and state income but the principal source of supply of Middle Eastern horses for the military as well. The death in 1470 of Kapilendra of Orissa temporarily relieved military pressure in the east; but it was a provincial governor, Narasiṃha Sāluva of Chandragiri, rather than Virūpāksha, who took advantage of the resultant civil war in Orissa to regain lost territory. Narasiṃha also aided the displaced King of Orissa to regain his throne from his brother and consequently became involved in a war with the Bahmanīs (1478–81), who supported the other claimant.

Reconquest of lost territory

Later dynasties. Beginning as a small chieftain about 1456, Narasiṃha had put together a large dominion by 1485 as a result of conquests in the south, as well as campaigns against Orissa; and, although nominally subordinate to Virūpāksha, he was performing more extensive military and administrative functions than was his superior. It is not surprising, when Virūpāksha was murdered by one of his sons, who was in turn murdered by his brother, that Narasiṃha Sāluva (reigned 1485–90) stepped in to remove the new ruler and to begin his own dynasty. Usurpation was easier than consolidation, however, and Narasiṃha spent his reign in relatively successful campaigns to reduce his vassals throughout the kingdom to submission and in unsuccessful attempts to stop the encroachment of the King of Orissa. Narasiṃha also opened new ports on the west coast so that he could revive the horse trade, and he generally revitalized the army. By 1490 the process of centralization was begun again, and both internal and external political circumstances soon would combine to create better opportunities than ever before.

Reconsolidation. Narasiṃha Sāluva left his kingdom in the hands of his chief minister, Narasa Nāyaka, by appointing him regent for his two young sons. The minister, in effect, was the ruler from 1490 to 1503. Court intrigues led to the murder of the elder prince by one of Narasa Nāyaka's rivals and to the capture and virtual imprisonment of the younger by Narasa Nāyaka in 1492. The usurpation (in all but name) resulted in opposition from provincial governors and chiefs that lasted for the rest of Narasa Nāyaka's life. Early in his regency, however, he had the opportunity to take advantage of the beginning of the disintegration of the Bahmanī sultanate. He invaded the much-disputed Tungabhadra-Krishna doab in 1492–93 at the invitation of the Bahmanī minister, Qāsim Barīd, who was trying to subdue the newly independent Yūsuf ʿAdil Khān of Bijāpur. Narasa Nāyaka took the strategic forts of Raichūr and Mudgal; and, although they were lost again in 1502, the growing disunity of the emerging Muslim polities would provide many similar opportunities in the future.

Narasa Nāyaka also campaigned in the south to restore effective control, which had not existed in many areas since the raid from Orissa in 1463–64. He compelled most of the chiefs and provincial governors to recognize his suzerainty in both Tamil country and the Carnatic and nearly restored the old boundaries of the kingdom (the eastern districts were still held by Orissa). By 1503 Narasa had practically completed the process of reconsolidation with which Narasiṃha Sāluva had charged him. He also had made virtually certain, however, that his own line rather than that of his old master would continue to rule. It was during the reigns of his sons that Vijayanagar rose to new heights of political power and cultural eminence.

Narasa's eldest son and successor, best known as Vīra Narasiṃha (reigned 1503–09), ended the sham of regency. After ordering the by-then grown prince's murder in 1505, he ascended the throne and inaugurated the third dynasty of Vijayanagar. The usurpation again provoked opposition, which the new king spent most of his reign attempting to quell. He was successful except in subduing the rebellious chiefs of Ummattūr and Srirangapatnam in the south and in recovering Goa from the Portuguese, with whom, however, he was able to establish relations to obtain a supply of better horses.

Reign of Kṛṣṇa Deva

Growth of power. Vīra Narasiṃha was succeeded by his brother Kṛṣṇa Deva Rāya (reigned 1509–29), one of the greatest of the Vijayanagar kings. During his reign the kingdom became more powerful than ever before, and internal consolidation reached a new peak. Kṛṣṇa Deva spent the first ten years of his reign solidly establishing his authority over his subordinate chieftains and governors while fending off invasions from the northeast. After decisively defeating an invading coalition of Bahmanī forces (who by this time were virtually separated into five states) and capturing Raichūr fort, Kṛṣṇa Deva took advantage of a quarrel between Bijāpur and the Bahmanī ruler to subdue both Gulbarga and Bīdar and to restore the imprisoned Bahmanī sultan to his throne in 1512. During the same period he conducted a successful campaign to subdue Umattūr in the south, and a new province was established there. From 1513 to 1516 Kṛṣṇa Deva campaigned against the Gajapati ruler of Orissa, conquering all that king's territory up to the Godāvari and raiding as far as the Orissan capital at Cuttack. Orissa then sued for peace, and its king gave his daughter in marriage to Kṛṣṇa Deva, who consequently returned to Orissa all the conquered territory north of the Krishna River.

While Kṛṣṇa Deva was fighting in the east, Ismāʿīl ʿĀdil Shāh of Bijāpur had retaken Raichūr fort. In 1520 Kṛṣṇa Deva decisively defeated Ismāʿīl with some aid from Portuguese gunners and recaptured Raichūr. In 1523 he carried the attack further and invaded Bijāpur, captured several forts, and tried again to create dissension among the Muslims by raising a Bahmanī claimant to the throne at Gulbarga. One result of these successful campaigns and of Kṛṣṇa Deva's subsequent haughty behaviour was to point out vividly to the Muslim rulers the dangers posed by Vijayanagar, so that in years to come they thought more and more of concerted action against that kingdom. Kṛṣṇa Deva's highly successful reign thus led to increased danger to his realm. During most of his reign Kṛṣṇa Deva maintained a mutually advantageous relationship with the increasingly powerful Portuguese, whereby he maintained access to trade goods, especially to horses from the Middle East, while the Portuguese were allowed to trade in his dominions.

Vijayanagar was visited by Magellan's cousin, Duarte Barbosa, between 1504 and 1517, and, even allowing for the exaggeration that was often present in European accounts of India, Barbosa's description suggests a prosperous and well-populated country. The capital city had many palaces, wide yet crowded streets, and a wide variety of trading enterprises. The King reportedly paid an army of 100,000 men, although it is unlikely that most were present at the capital except at the beginning of a campaign, and, upon his death, said Barbosa, 400 or 500 women would burn themselves on his funeral pyre.

About 1524–25 Kṛṣṇa Deva abdicated and had his young son crowned king. His son died shortly thereafter, however, reportedly poisoned by the jealous former chief minister. Kṛṣṇa Deva imprisoned the minister and his family and dealt successfully with a serious rebellion three years later—when one of the minister's sons escaped—as well as with Ismāʿīl ʿĀdil Shāh's attempt to take advantage of Kṛṣṇa Deva's troubles to recoup his position. Kṛṣṇa Deva's death in 1529 ended the period of the kingdom's greatest military and administrative success.

Renewed decentralization. Kṛṣṇa Deva had passed over his infant son and his young nephew and picked his half brother Achyuta Deva Rāya (reigned 1529–42) to succeed him. Following a brief succession dispute, Achyuta Deva Rāya was able to reach the capital from Chandragiri, where Kṛṣṇa Deva had kept him and other princes confined, and to ascend the throne. Although he probably was not as dissolute a ruler as the Portuguese writer Alvar Núñez Cabeza de Vaca described him to be, the severe challenges he faced made a successful reign difficult. Kṛṣṇa Deva's death had precipitated renewed attacks by Bijāpur, Golconda, and Orissa and a revolt by the King's minister, Vīranarasiṃha Sāluva, and the southern chieftains of Ummattūr and Tiruvadi. Achyuta dealt successfully with all the enemies until the late 1530s, when he was imprisoned by Rāma Rāya, the chief minister, with whom he had agreed to share power. Opposition to Achyuta's imprisonment by some of the nobles, combined with a revolt in the south, led to his release and the beginnings of civil war; but the new ruler of Bijāpur, Ibrāhīm ʿĀdil Shāh, after early attempts to create divisiveness in Vijayanagar, arbitrated a settlement between Achyuta and Rāma Rāya. Under the settlement it was agreed that Achyuta was king but that he would not interfere with Rāma Rāya's role within his own estate.

Achyuta's reign ended with about the same external boundaries of the kingdom as in 1529; but the struggle with Rāma Rāya plus the activities of other nobles and chieftains weakened the hold of the centre over some of the provinces. The process of decentralization had set in again, but now the strongman who would pull the kingdom together was already on the scene. Rāma Rāya brought himself to the undisputed pinnacle of power in 1542–43, when he defeated his rival in the succession struggle following Achyuta's death and crowned his own candidate, Achyuta's nephew Sadāśiva (reigned 1542–76). After seven or eight years, Rāma Rāya also assumed royal titles, but from the first Sadāśiva was kept under guard, and Rāma Rāya, together with his brothers Tirumala and Venkatadri, ruled the kingdom.

Rāma Rāya was able to control, although not to subdue entirely, rebellious nobles in the east and the extreme south. He also concluded a treaty with the Portuguese (1547), whose settlements had been expanding and who had caused no small amount of damage to indigenous settlements over the past few years. The treaty was broken in 1558, however, and Rāma Rāya then exacted tribute in compensation for damage to temples caused by the Portuguese.

Relations with the Muslim states. Most crucial during the period of Rāma Rāya's rule, however, were Vijayanagar's relations with the Muslim successor states to the Bahmanī sultanate. At least since Kṛṣṇa Deva Rāya's time, Vijayanagar had usually competed on a more than equal basis and in the same system of state rivalries with the five Muslim states. Thus, an invasion from Bijāpur was repulsed in 1543; in 1548 Rāma Rāya aided Burhān Niẓām Shāh of Ahmadnagar in taking a fort from Bīdar, but in 1557 Rāma Rāya allied himself with Bijāpur against the Niẓām Shāh and Golconda. The result of the last war was a collective treaty, by which any of the four parties, attacked unjustly by another, could call upon the other allies to stop the aggressor. When Ḥusayn Niẓām Shāh broke the treaty by invading Bijāpur in 1560, Vijayanagar and Golconda responded with an attack that not only resulted in Ahmadnagar's loss of the fort of Kalyāṇi to Bijāpur but also in an invasion of Bīdar and the defeat of its ruler by Rāma Rāya. Soon, however, the ruler of Golconda, Ibrāhīm Quṭb Shāh, allied himself with Ahmadnagar against Bijāpur, and Rāma Rāya allied Vijayanagar with Bijāpur to severely defeat the aggressors.

The four-party treaty of the mid-16th century

Decline of Vijayanagar. It is likely that the sultans of Golconda and Ahmadnagar, who had lost much at the hands of Rāma Rāya, were primarily responsible for the formation of an alliance that destroyed Vijayanagar's power forever. By 1564 at least four of the five sultans (Berār is questionable) had declared a holy war and had begun their march on Vijayanagar, which resulted early in 1565 in the disastrous defeat of the Vijayanagar forces in the Battle of Talikota and in the subsequent sack and destruction of much of the city of Vijayanagar. Rāma Rāya was captured and killed, but his brother Tirumala escaped to the south with the King and much of the royal treasure.

Military policies. Although Rāma Rāya's efforts toward centralization were not entirely successful, it was his military policies, probably through no fault of his own, that ultimately led to disaster. There were rebellions when he replaced many members of the old nobility with relatives and close associates, but they appear to have been no more serious than many another rebellion of previous periods under similar circumstances. Indeed, judging on the basis of the number and size of the military campaigns that Rāma Rāya was able to launch outside Vijayanagar in later years, it would seem that his internal control was relatively secure. Rāma Rāya has been criticized for allowing Muslims to hold important positions within his administration, and, although his final defeat at Talikota was at least partly attributable to the defection of two of his Muslim generals, the policy appears to have worked well up to that time. Rāma Rāya's early experiences as an official at the court of Golconda appear to have given him ideas for improving the Vijayanagar administration and army. As early as 1535 he had hired 3,000 Muslim soldiers from Bijāpur, and he later tried to make the Vijayanagar state apparatus more like that of the neighbouring Muslim states. In short, he was building a state that would be as competitive as possible in that time and place. It is likely that at first Vijayanagar's Muslim neighbours took a similar view of state relations and that Vijayanagar was seen as just another competing state. Rāma Rāya's military successes plus the knowledge that Vijayanagar was stronger than any one of the sultans led to the Muslim alliance against it. Despite a Muslim historian's claim that the alliance was formed because of Rāma Rāya's bad treatment of Muslims, there is little evidence to indicate that the principal motives were other than political. Furthermore, the subsequent behaviour of the sultans suggests that once Vijayanagar had been humbled they were willing to return to a system of shifting alliances among all the Deccan powers.

Loss of central control. The Battle of Talikota did not result in the destruction of the kingdom of Vijayanagar, although the capital city never fully recovered from the ravages it suffered. Rāma Rāya's brother Tirumala established a new headquarters at Penugonda and began to rebuild the army, but the defeat at Talikota had been so severe that he could no longer maintain control over many of the provinces. Much of the south and southeast was lost as the Nāyaks of Madura, Tanjore (Thanjāvūr), and Jinjī effectively asserted their independence. Rebellions and banditry arose in many areas. Tirumala successfully defended himself against a challenge by his nephew, who was aided by Bijāpur, and then joined with Ahmadnagar and Golconda in a campaign against Bijāpur. Tirumala accepted the new states of Nāyaks of the south, retained the allegiance of Mysore, Vellore, and Keladi, and set his three sons as governors of the three linguistic regions of his kingdom. In 1570 he had himself crowned and thus officially inaugurated the fourth and last Vijayanagar dynasty (although the puppet king Sadāśiva appears to have survived until 1576).

Rebellions and banditry

When Tirumala retired, his son Śrīranga I (reigned 1572–85) tried to continue the process of rebuilding while struggling to maintain his place among the Muslim sultanates. An invasion by Bijāpur was repulsed with the aid of Golconda, but invasions by Golconda resulted in the loss of a substantial amount of territory in the east and the loss of the wealth of the temple of Narasiṃha at Ahobalam, which was plundered by a Marāthā Brāhmaṇ officer in the service of Golconda. Śrīranga's difficulties partly stemmed from the lack of aid from his brothers, who ruled their separate regions, and partly from the dissensions of his nobles and the semi-independent status of some of them. Many nobles had apparently decided that it was no longer in their best interests to give full support to the larger state and that, in the absence of overwhelming power, the development of smaller, subregional states was both possible and potentially more profitable.

Śrīranga died without issue and was succeeded by his younger brother Venkata I (reigned 1585–1614), whose ability and constant activity, combined with a relative dearth of interference by the Muslim sultanates, prevented the further disintegration of centralized authority over the next 28 years. A series of wars between 1580 and 1589 resulted in the reacquisition of some of the territory that had been lost to Golconda in the east, but Venkata spent most of his time attempting to retain his hold over his rebellious chieftains and nobles. Most of the east and the Tamil south was in rebellion at one time or another, the most serious threat occurring in 1601, when the Nāyaks of Madura, Tanjore, and Jinjī came to the aid of the rebellious Lingama Nāyaka of Vellore. The Nāyaks were defeated, and Vellore later was captured, but Venkata's authority was not restored in the far south. The process of decentralization, although halted for a time, could not be reversed. In the northern areas that had been laid waste by invading armies, Venkata undertook a program of restoration by offering lower revenue payments. It would appear that by the time of his death in 1614 he had accomplished enough so that a revival of imperial power and prosperity was possible, but instead rivalries among the nobility rapidly led to further decentralization and to the diminution of the state.

Breakup of the empire. Venkata's nephew and successor, Śrīranga II, ruled only four months. He was murdered, along with all but one of the members of his family, by one of the two contending parties of nobles. A long civil war resulted and finally degenerated into a series of smaller wars among a number of contending parties. By about 1629 the authority of the surviving member of the dynasty, Rama Deva Rāya (reigned 1618–30), was recognized in a much-truncated kingdom along the eastern coast. Although some chieftains continued to recognize his nominal suzerainty and that of his successor for the next few years, real political power resided at the level of chieftains or provincial governors, who were carving out their own principalities. The fourth Vijayanagar dynasty had become little more than another competing provincial power.

Bijāpur and Golconda took advantage of the decline in Vijayanagar's strength to make further inroads into the south, while the King's own nephew Śrīranga allied himself with Bijāpur. In 1642 an expedition from Golconda drove the King from his capital at Vellore. Hearing that his uncle was dying, Śrīranga deserted Bijāpur and had himself crowned. Although he was able to play off Bijāpur and Golconda against each other for a time, he could not gain control over the provincial Nāyaks, who were by then virtually independent; and, when Bijāpur and Golconda finally struck at the same time, Śrīranga was helpless. A last appeal to his Nāyaks to come to the defense of Hinduism resulted instead in his defeat by their combined forces in 1645. Meanwhile, Bijāpur and Golconda advanced, with the blessings of the Mughal emperor at Delhi, who had suggested that they should partition the Carnatic between themselves. The Nāyaks realized the danger too late, and by 1652 Muslim sultans had completed their conquest of the Carnatic. Śrīranga retired to Mysore, where he kept an exile court until his death in 1672.

Muslim conquest of the Carnatic

Administration of the empire. The Vijayanagar empire achieved a degree of political unity over a number of linguistic regions of South India for roughly two centuries and was, to some extent, consciously represented by its sovereigns as the last bastion of Hinduism against the forces of Islām. As with similar Muslim religio-political claims, however, this one often appeared to be more rhetorical than real. The shifting patterns of alliances among Vijayanagar and the sultanates, the occasions on which a rival party of nobles or a claimant to the throne of Vijayanagar would enlist the aid of a Muslim sultan, and the employment of both Hindus and Muslims in the sultanates and Vijayanagar suggests that rivalries were more political than religious. The various progressive reforms of the Vijayanagar army suggest also that efforts were made to transform at least one aspect of the state in order to make it more competitive with its Muslim rivals.

The administration of the kingdom sporadically achieved a relatively high degree of centralization, although centrifugal tendencies regularly appeared. The central administration had both a revenue and military side, but the actual business of raising taxes and troops was mostly the responsibility of the provincial governors and their subordinates. The central government maintained a relatively small body of troops, but it assigned a value to the lands held by the provincial governors and determined the number of troops that were to be supplied from the revenues of each province. This administrative plan led to the development of the Nāyak system, which worked well enough when the central authority was strong but provided territorial bases for the Nāyaks to build semi-independent holdings in times of imperial weakness. The imperial rulers were aware of the power of the provinces and tried to counter it by appointing members of the royal family as governors of the militarily more important (but not necessarily more lucrative) provinces. On the whole, however, the device was not successful because succession rivalries, as in the Muslim kingdoms to the north, tended to produce filial disloyalty to the throne and even rebellion.

Although exact figures are unavailable, the evidence suggests that the level of taxation was close to half of the produce in many areas. Much of the revenue collected did not go to the state, however, because various layers of local landholders took their share first. Although most revenue came from agrarian taxes, commercial and artisan taxes were levied as well. (P.B.Ca.)

IV. The Mughal Empire, 1526–1761

THE ESTABLISHMENT OF THE MUGHAL EMPIRE

The significance of Mughal rule. The establishment of the Mughal Empire (1526) was an event of great national and international importance. The Mughals were not rigid Muslims, and although the first two rulers of the line —Bābur and Humāyūn (Homāyūn)—generally followed policies similar to those of the Delhi sultans, they did not strictly enforce Muslim law. Akbar, the third ruler of the dynasty, almost completely discarded, both in theory and practice, the principles of the Islāmic state; he declared himself to be the impartial ruler of both Hindus and Muslims and accorded them equal rights and privileges. He disestablished Islām as religion of the state and, contrary to the practice of the sultans, placed all religions in the land at par. This policy amounted to a political and social revolution. It generated forces that put the diverse sections and communities of India on the road toward becoming one people, enabling the country to achieve unprecedented unity and political, social, economic, and cultural progress.

Internationally, too, India not only began to regain its position among the nations of Asia and Europe but it actually became one of the richest and most powerful countries in the world. Persia, Transoxania, and Turkey recognized India's position as a great power, perhaps greater than each one of them individually. European nations, such as Portugal, England, France, and Holland, displayed eagerness to have friendly relations with India and to share its wealth through commerce.

Mughal origins. The foundation of the Mughal Empire was not a single or isolated event. The idea was inspired by Timur, who invaded India in 1398 but had no definite ambition to conquer and rule over it. Nevertheless, Timur nominated one Khiẕr Khān Sayyid as his governor of Multān and probably also as his representative in Hindustān. Khiẕr ruled in Timur's name and, after Timur's death in 1405, in that of his son and successor Shāh Rokh Mīrzā (Shāhrukh). Khiẕr Khān's son, however, severed connections with the Timurid dynasty and set himself up as an independent ruler in 1421. In 1503 a direct descendant of Timur, Ẓahīr-ud-Dīn Muḥammad Bābur, heard the story of Timur's invasion of India and formed the resolution of one day repeating the exploit.

Bābur. Bābur was the fifth descendant of Timur on the side of his father and the 14th descendant of Genghis Khan through his mother. He was a Chagatai Turk, so-called because his ancestral homeland, the country north of the Oxus, was the heritage of Chagatai Khan, the son of Genghis Khan. But he was commonly known as the "Mughal." On the death of his father in 1494, Bābur, at age 11, became king of Farghana (Fergana), which formed the northern part of Transoxania (now in the Uzbek S.S.R.). As a boy king he lost Farghana and passed through a period of adversity, having to fight his own paternal and maternal uncles. During 20 years of adversity and warfare Bābur trained himself by appropriating military tactics and modes of warfare of his adversaries—Turks, Mongols, Persians, and Afghans, and he made a scientific synthesis of these systems. He became a good general through a career of many defeats and through years of homeless wanderings, privations, and hardships.

Foiled in his design of recovering his ancestral dominion in Central Asia, Bābur turned his attention to India. His conquest of the Punjab and relations with the Afghan rebels Dawlat Khān and ʿĀlam Khān have been described above.

Having secured the Punjab, Bābur advanced toward Delhi, receiving encouraging offers of support from many Delhi nobles. He routed two advanced parties of Ibrāhīm Lodī's troops and met the sultan's main army, 40,000 (according to Bābur 100,000) strong, east of the town of Pānīpat in April 1526. Bābur claimed to have 12,000 men all told, but historians have placed the Mughal force at 25,000 or more, because a large number of Indian mercenaries had swelled it after Bābur's occupation of the Punjab.

The first Battle of Pānīpat

After eight days of inaction, during which the opposing forces faced each other at a few miles' distance, Ibrāhīm, provoked by an unsuccessful night attack by Bābur's troops, moved forward on April 21. Seeing that the Mughal front line was defended by a formidable row of wagons and breastworks, Ibrāhīm's troops hesitated and lost the advantage of a shock charge. Bābur, taking advantage of this, ordered his men to attack. Ibrāhīm fought bravely, but his swords and arrows could not answer Bābur's guns, and he died with 15,000 of his men. The Delhi army then broke and fled, and Bābur occupied Delhi and Āgra within a few days. His success was the result of a scientific combination of cavalry and artillery, the rapidity of his movement, and his superior generalship.

Bābur, however, had yet to encounter his most powerful Indian adversary, Rānā Sāngā of Mewār, the head of the Rājput chivalry in the country, before he could feel himself secure. The accounts of Rājput bravery made the Mughals nervous; but Bābur raised their morale by a stirring speech and roused their religious feelings by taking a vow in the presence of his troops to behave like a true Muslim, by renouncing wine and by breaking his wine vessels in a dramatic fashion. A very severe contest took place at Khānwā, near Fatehpur Sīkri, on March 17, 1527. Bābur made use of the same tactics as at Pānīpat two years before, and won a similar victory.

After defeating the Afghāns of eastern Uttar Pradesh and Bihār on the confluence of the Ganges and the Ghāgra on May 6, 1529, Bābur was in possession of the country from the Indus to Bihār and from the Himalayas to Gwalior and Chanderi; he had already obtained possession of Multān, and therefore in the northwest corner of India, only Sindh (Thatta) remained beyond his jurisdiction.

Though a very intelligent, shrewd, and highly cultured prince, who left an imperishable record of his adventurous life and a lifelike description of India in his memoirs, the *Tūzuk-e Bāburī*, Bābur was not a constructive genius. He did not create a new system of administration or improve the existing institutions. He squandered the huge wealth piled up in the treasuries of Delhi, Āgra, and other places and died in 1530, before he could consolidate his newly won territories in India.

Humāyūn. Bābur bequeathed to his son Humāyūn a vast though unconsolidated empire and an empty treasury. He gave him the deathbed advice to behave kindly toward his brothers. A dutiful son, the new ruler assigned Kābul, Ghazna (Ghaznī), and Punjab to his next brother, Kāmrān, and made similar assignments for his other two brothers, ʿAskarī and Hindāl. These ambitious men wanted to rule over Hindustān. His cousins, known as the Mīrzās, were equally ambitious and disloyal. Humāyūn's greatest difficulty, however, came from two independent chiefs—Bahādūr Shāh of Gujarāt and Shēr Khān of Bihār—who coveted the throne of Delhi.

Humāyūn's expulsion from India

Humāyūn began badly by invading the Hindu principality of Kālinjar in Bundelkhand, which he failed to subdue. Next he picked a quarrel with Shēr Khān by unsuccessfully besieging the fortress of Chunār (1532). Thereafter he conquered Mālwa and Gujarāt, but he could not hold them. Leaving the fortress of Chunār unconquered on the way, Humāyūn proceeded to Bengal to assist Sultan Maḥmūd of that province against Shēr Khān. He lost touch with Delhi and Āgra, and because his brother Hindāl began openly to behave like an independent ruler at Āgra he was obliged to leave Gaur, the capital of Bengal. Negotiations with Shēr Khān fell through, and the latter forced Humāyūn to fight a battle at Chausa, ten miles southwest of Baksar and a short distance from the Karamnāsa River (June 26, 1539), in which Humāyūn was defeated. He was compelled to cross the flooded Ganges with the help of a water carrier (Niẓām). He did not feel strong enough to defend Āgra, and he retreated to Bilgrām near Kanauj, where he fought his last battle with Shēr Khān, who had now assumed the title of Shēr Shāh. Humāyūn was again defeated and compelled to retreat to Lahore, fleeing from Lahore to Sind, from Sind to Rājputāna and from Rājputāna back to Sind. Not feeling secure even in Sind, he fled (July 1543) to Iran to seek military assistance from its ruler Shāh Ṭahmāsp. The Shāh agreed to assist him with an army on the condition that Humāyūn become a Shīʿah Muslim and return Qandahār to Iran in the event of his successful acquisition of that fortress. In 1544 Humāyūn captured Qandahār from ʿAskarī and then occupied Kābul. Kāmrān fled to Ghazna, and from there to Sind. Humāyūn again lost Kābul to Kāmrān in 1546, but he was able to recover it the next year. Kāmrān continued to give him trouble, but he was ultimately defeated and blinded by Humāyūn's orders.

Shēr Shāh and his successors. During Humāyūn's exile Shēr Shāh established a vast and powerful empire and strengthened it with a wise system of administration.

Sher Shāh's administration

He carried out a new and equitable revenue settlement, greatly improved the administration of the districts and the *pargana*s (village units), reformed the currency, encouraged trade and commerce, improved communication, and administered impartial justice.

Shēr Shāh died on May 22, 1545, and was succeeded by his son Islām Shāh (ruled 1545–53). Islām Shāh, pre-eminently a soldier, was less successful as a ruler than his father. On Islām's death his young son Fīrūz, a boy of 12, came to the throne; but he was murdered by his own maternal uncle, Mubāriz Khān, who captured the throne and assumed the title of Muḥammad ʿĀdil Shāh Sūr. His right to rule was disputed by two other descendants of Shēr Shāh, and a civil war resulted.

Restoration of Humāyūn. From Kābul Humāyūn watched the situation in India. He had been preparing since the death of Islām Shāh to recover his throne. In December 1554 he crossed the Indus and marched to Lahore, which he captured without opposition (February 1555). Meanwhile, Sūr's rivals, Sikandar and Ibrāhīm, were fighting each other near Āgra and failed to put up an effective resistance to the invader. The advance guard of Humāyūn's army occupied Jullundur, Sirhind, and Hissār without striking a blow. When the Mughals pushed toward Delhi after occupying the Punjab, Sikandar sent a large army to intercept them. A battle at Machhīwara on the Sutlej (May 15) ended in Humāyūn's victory. Sikandar himself was defeated at Sirhind on June 22 and fled to the hills of the Punjab. Humāyūn occupied Sirhind and captured Delhi and Āgra in July 1555. He thus regained the throne of Delhi after an interval of 12 years, but he did not live long after his restoration; he died as the result of an accident in Shermandal in Delhi (January 1556). His death was concealed for about a fortnight to enable the peaceful accession of his son Akbar, who was at the time away in the Punjab.

Humāyūn was not a great emperor, and was unlucky despite his name (which means "fortunate"), but his memory was perpetuated by his son, who proved to be one of the greatest rulers of the Mughal empire.

AKBAR THE GREAT

Extension and consolidation of the empire. Akbar (ruled 1556–1605) was proclaimed emperor at Kalanaur in Gurdāspur amid gloomy circumstances. Delhi and Āgra were threatened by ʿĀdil Shāh's minister Hemū, and Mughal governors were being driven from all parts of northern India. Akbar's hold over a fraction of the Punjab—the only territory in his possession—was disputed by Sikandar Sūr and was precarious. To make matters worse, Delhi and the surrounding areas had been in the throes of a devastating famine for about two years, and there was disloyalty among Akbar's own followers. But guided by his guardian, Bayram Khān, the new emperor decided to fight Hemū, who had defeated the Mughal governors of Āgra and Delhi (October 7, 1556), occupied those cities, and was advancing toward the Punjab to drive Akbar out of India.

Threats to the empire

They met in battle on November 5 on the historic field of Pānīpat. Hemū, at the head of 30,000 men, overthrew the Mughal right and left wings and launched an attack on the enemy centre, hurling 1,500 elephants against it. The Mughals were about to give way when Hemū was struck in the eye by an arrow and fell unconscious on his elephant. His army was seized with panic and fled in all directions. The Mughal victory was decisive. They occupied Delhi and Āgra, and Sikandar Sūr was compelled to surrender in May 1557. Muḥammad ʿĀdil Shāh was killed in 1557 at Monghyr. Ibrāhīm, the third Sūr pretender, had to seek asylum in Orissa. Thus within two years of Akbar's victory there remained no rival to contest his claim to the sovereignty of Hindustān.

Until 1560, the administration of Akbar's truncated empire was in the hands of Bayram Khān. Bayram's regency was momentous in the history of India; at its end the Mughal dominion embraced the whole of the Punjab and Multān, the territory of Delhi, the present Uttar Pradesh as far east as and including Jaunpur, and in the southwest Dholpur, Gwalior, Ajmer, Nāgaur, and Jaitaran (in Jodhpur state).

Bayram Khān's regency

Akbar, however, soon became restless under Bayram Khān's tutelage. Influenced by his former nurse, Māham Ānaga, and his mother, Hamīda Bānū Baygam, he was persuaded to dismiss him (March 1560).

Four prime ministers of mediocre ability then followed in quick succession. Akbar was not yet keen to take the reins of government into his own hands, and it was only by the beginning of 1561 that the young ruler began giving some measure of attention to the affairs of government.

Although not yet his own master, Akbar took a few momentous steps during this period. He conquered Mālwa (1561) and marched rapidly to Sārangpur to punish Adham Khān, the captain in charge of the expedition, for improper conduct. Second, he appointed Shams ud-Dīn Muḥammad Atgah Khān as prime minister (November 1561). Third, he took possession of Chunār, which had always defied Humāyūn, at about the same time.

The most momentous events of 1562 were Akbar's marriage with a Rājput princess, daughter of Raja Bhārmal of Amber, and the conquest of Merta in Rājasthān. The marriage led to a firm alliance between the Mughals and the Rājputs. The princess became the mother of the future Jahāngīr, Akbar's heir and successor, and the alliance secured solid military Rājput support for the Mughal throne, contributing greatly to the empire's expansion and stability.

Mughal–Rājput alliance

In 1562 Akbar experienced a remarkable mental change. "On the completion of my 20th year," he said, "I experienced an internal bitterness and from the lack of spiritual provision for my last journey, my soul was seized with exceeding sorrow." A result of this change was the abolition, after April 10, 1562 (his 20th birthday), of the enslavement of prisoners of war and of the forcible conversion of them and their women and children to Islām. By the end of June 1562, Akbar freed himself completely from the influence of the harem. The harem party, headed by Māham Ānaga, her son Adham Khān, and some other ambitious courtiers, murdered the new prime minister, Atgah Khān (May 16). Adham then tried to force his entry into the emperor's room, probably to explain the cause of Atgah Khān's murder and to beg his forgiveness; but he was killed by Akbar. Akbar informed Māham Ānaga of the death of her son. She was then lying ill, and she died on June 24. Akbar forgave the conspirators and appointed a former prime minister, Munʿim Khān, to that office.

Thus from about the middle of 1562 Akbar took upon himself the great task of shaping his policies, leaving them to be implemented by his agents. He embarked on a policy of conquest, establishing control over Jodhpur, Bhātha (modern Rewa), and the Gakkhar country between the Indus and the Beās in the Punjab. Next he conquered the wild but prosperous region of Gondwana in the modern Madhya Pradesh. During this period he removed discrimination against the Hindus by abolishing pilgrimage taxes in 1563 and the hated *jizyah* (poll tax on non-Muslims) in 1564.

Rebellions against Akbar

In 1565 some of the principal Uzbek nobles combined together to raise the standard of rebellion. During this period Mīrzā Sulaymān of Badakhshin invaded Kābul more than once. Mirzā Ḥakīm, Akbar's half-brother, governor of Kābul, feeling unsafe, proceeded to the Indus to appeal to Akbar for help. There he was persuaded by some disloyal Mughals to try to seize Delhi. He crossed the Indus and proceeded to Lahore. When Akbar prepared to resist him, he fled back to Kābul. Mīrzā Sulaymān, who was still near Kābul, then patched up a peace with Mirzā Ḥakīm and retreated to Badakhshan. Taking advantage of the situation, some of Akbar's other relatives tried to play the same game. But Akbar was not the man to tolerate insubordination, and the rebellions were crushed.

Subjugation of Rājasthān. Rājasthān occupied a prominent place in Akbar's scheme of conquest; without establishing his suzerainty over that region, he would have no title to the sovereignty of northern India. Unlike his father and grandfather, Akbar was well aware of the valour and sincerity of the Rājputs; his aim was to subordinate them and win their loyalty. In 1567 he invaded Chitor, the capital of Mewār, whose ruler had scornfully rejected the idea of recognizing Akbar as his overlord. Attacking Chitor's gigantic fort (October), which was well defended and provisioned and was considered impregnable, he had three extensive mines dug under cover of fire from his batteries. These exploded with a terrific noise, shattering the northern bastion of the fort from its very foundation and killing a large number of defenders. At the same time he continued hitting the fort with constant fire from heavy guns. The commander of the fort was killed, and the garrison temporarily lost heart. But the Rājputs donned yellow robes, determined to fight and die a glorious death; they flung open the gate and faced the Mughals sword in hand (February 24, 1568). Most of them were slain, and Akbar ordered the massacre of about 30,000 men. The fort fell into his hands. Chitor was constituted a district, and Āṣaf Khān was appointed its governor. But the western half of Mewār remained in the possession of Rānā Udai Singh.

The fall of Chitor

Soon after the fall of Chitor, Akbar besieged Ranthambhor, a formidable fortress; it surrendered in March 1569. Kālinjar surrendered without fighting in August 1569. In November 1570 Akbar held a conference of Rājput chiefs at Nāgaur, which was attended by the rulers of Amber, Jodhpur, Bīkaner, and Jaisalmer. All these entered into a friendly alliance with Akbar and recognized him as their suzerain. Almost the whole of Rājasthān thus submitted, except the Rānā of Mewār, who continued to offer resistance from his retreat in the hills. Būndi, Dūngarpur, Bānswāra, and Pratapgarh submitted shortly thereafter.

Foundation of Fatehpur Sīkri. Akbar's two sons, Salīm and Murād, were born near the shrine of Shaykh Salīm Chishtī in Sīkri, and he formed the plan of converting that village into a city and making it his residence (November 1571). The hilly eminence, one mile long and a furlong broad, was levelled into a plain, and royal palaces were erected on it. Nobles and officers built mansions for themselves. A city wall with nine gates was erected on three sides, and the fourth side on the southwest was protected by an extensive lake many miles in area.

Conquest of Gujarāt. Akbar's next objective was the prosperous province of Gujarāt, an emporium of commerce with the countries of west Asia and Europe. He found little opposition and easily captured Ahmadābād (November 1572). From there he proceeded to Cambay and defeated Ibrāhīm Mīrzā, one of his kinsmen, at Sarnāl (December). Next he captured Surat after a brief siege in February 1573, and returned to Fatehpur Sīkri.

As soon as Akbar's back was turned, a rebellion broke out in Gujarāt. Ibrāhīm Mirzā, who had fled to Daulatābād, returned and besieged Ahmadābād. Akbar returned in person; he reached Ahmadābād on September 2, having marched 450 miles in 11 days. He crossed the Sābarmati against the advice of his cautious captains and attacked the enemy the same day. Ibrāhīm was defeated and taken prisoner. Gujarāt submitted finally, and Akbar returned to Fatehpur Sīkri on October 5. This expedition is rightly described as "the quickest campaign on record." The conquest of Gujarāt pushed Akbar's western frontier to the sea and brought him into contact with the Portuguese, who made peace with him.

Conquest of Bihār and Bengal. The conquest of Bengal, Bihār, and Orissa, ruled by Dāʾūd Khan, became essential in view of Akbar's new policy, which aimed at the political unity of India. Taking Patna from Dāʾūd, he subjugated Bihār in 1574, and then returned to Āgra. Munʿim Khān was left with instructions to conquer Bengal, which was occupied after the Battle of Tukra (March 3, 1575). Munʿim Khān made peace with Dāʾūd, who had fled to Cuttak and prepared to renew the contest. Dāʾūd was allowed to retain possession of Orissa, but he disregarded the treaty and tried to recover Bengal. Accordingly a fresh campaign was organized, and Dāʾūd was finally defeated and killed in a battle near Rājmahāl in July 1576. Bengal was then annexed, but a few of the local chiefs continued to give trouble for some years more.

Defeat of Dāʾūd Khan

Attempt to conquer Mewār. Udai Singh's son Pratāp, who became Rānā of western Mewār in 1572, continued to offer uncompromising resistance to the Mughals. Akbar was determined to win the remaining part of Mewār by peace or war. He sent four diplomatic missions to persuade Pratāp to recognize his suzerainty, and at the same time tried to isolate him. The missions failed, and in April 1576 Akbar deputed Mān Singh of Amber to capture the remnant of Mewār. A fierce battle took place on June 18, 1576, at the entrance of Haldi Ghati, a spur of the Arāvalli chain, near the village of Khamnaur on the southern bank of the river Banās. So desperate was the Rānā's charge that the Mughal advance guard and left wing were scattered and the right wing and centre were hard pressed. But Pratāp's army was small in number, and he had no reserve or rear guard to back up his initial success. In his attempt to break the Mughal centre and right wing, he hurled his war elephants against them; but arrows and bullets from the imperial side proved too much, and the Rānā's men lost heart and fled from the field. Mān Singh occupied Gogunda, but failed to secure possession of all Mewār.

The Rānā eventually succeeded in recovering a good part of his ancestral territory before his death in 1597. Akbar sent more than one expedition against Amar Singh, son and successor of Pratāp; but his kingdom remained unconquered during Akbar's lifetime.

Annexation of Afghanistan. In 1581, Akbar moved against his rebellious half-brother, Mohammad Ḥakīm of Kabul. Ḥakīm submitted, and Akbar appointed his half-sister, Bakht-un-Nisā' Baygam, governor of Kābul. Ḥakīm died in July 1585, and Kābul was then incorporated in the empire.

Submission of Ḥakīm

Annexation of Kashmir. The ruler of Kashmir, Yūsuf Shāh, declared his submission but did not present himself at the imperial court. Akbar, who was at Lahore in 1585 to safeguard his northwestern frontier from an expected Uzbek invasion and to crush a rebellion of the Pashtun tribes between India and Afghanistan, sent forces to reduce Kashmir to absolute submission early in 1586. Yūsuf Shāh recognized Akbar as his sovereign. But Akbar disapproved of the treaty, and Yūsuf was arrested. His son Ya'qūb escaped to Srīnagar and prepared to resist, but he was compelled to surrender. Kashmir was now annexed to the empire and became a district (*sarkār*) of the province of Kābul. Yūsuf Shāh was released after some time and placed in the Mughal service.

Conquest of Sind. Akbar had acquired the fortress of Bhakkar as early as 1574. He now coveted the southern part of Sind on the mouth of the Indus, without which his supremacy over northwestern India could not be complete. Moreover, he wanted to use Sind as the base of operations against Qandahār. In 1590 he directed ʿAbd-ur-Raḥmān Khān-e Khānān, governor of Multān, to acquire the principality of Thatta (lower Sind) from its ruler, Mīrzā Jānī Beg. The latter was defeated and compelled to surrender his entire territory, including the fortresses of Thatta and Sehwān (1591); he too entered the imperial service.

Conquest of Orissa. Mān Singh, governor of Bihār, invaded Orissa in 1592. Its ruler, Nīṣār Khān, submitted after a feeble resistance and was confirmed as governor. But two years later he rebelled and seized the crown lands of Puri and Jagannātha. Mān Singh defeated and expelled him, and the province was annexed to the empire and became a part of Bengal.

Conquest of Baluchistan. Mīr Maʿṣūm Khān was deputed in February 1595 to conquer Baluchistan, the only principality (except Assam) in northern India that had not yet acknowledged Akbar's authority. Maʿṣūm attacked the fort of Sibi, northwest of Qandahār, and defeated the *amīr*s, who delivered the whole of Baluchistan, including Makrāna, the region near the coast, into the hands of the Mughals.

Qandahār and the Deccan. In April 1595 the Persian governor of Qandahār, Moẓaffar Ḥoseyn Mīrzā, who was not on good terms with the authorities in Teheran, peacefully delivered his province into the hands of Akbar's men. The acquisition of Qandahār completed Akbar's conquests in northern India and gave the empire a natural frontier in the northwest. The late 1590s were taken up with the Deccan campaigns described in the previous section, which resulted in the defeat of Ahmadnagar, and the annexation of Khāndesh and Berār.

Akbar's administration. Emboldened by the successful promulgation, in September 1579, of the *maḥzar* (miscalled the infallibility decree), by which he assumed the right of interpreting Islāmic doctrine whenever there were conflicting opinions about the meaning of the Qur'ān, and sought to end the influence of the *ʿulamā'* (religious divines) in state affairs, Akbar announced a new theory of kingship. He asserted that the king was God's representative on earth and the impartial ruler of all his subjects, irrespective of their religion. He must be absolutely tolerant to every creed, establish universal peace in his dominions, and work ceaselessly for the welfare of all classes of his people. Akbar thus considered himself to be above the Muslim law or the law of any other religion or community. He believed in the unity of leadership, secular and religious.

In trying to implement his theory of kingship, Akbar prescribed a daily routine for himself. He started work at sunrise, when he appeared before his people at the balcony of salute (*jharokha-e darshan*), and he continued working until midnight, with a few hours' gap for meals, rest, recreation, and prayers. He is said not to have slept for more than three hours a night, feeling that hard work was essential for the welfare of the people.

Akbar was wise enough to delegate much of the work to his ministers and officers, keeping in his hands the initiation of policy and the issuing of instructions and seeing that these were properly followed. He successfully exercised the functions of supervision and control over every department of administration.

Central, provincial, and local government. Akbar's central government consisted of four departments, each presided over by a minister: the prime minister (*Wakīl*); finance minister (dewan, or *wazīr*); paymaster general (*mīr bakhshī*); and chief sadr (*ṣadr uṣ-ṣudūr*), who was the chief justice and religious official combined. They were appointed, promoted, or dismissed by the emperor, and their duties were well defined.

The empire was divided into 15 provinces—Allāhābād, Āgra, Oudh (Awadh), Ajmer, Ahmadābād, Bihār, Bengal, Delhi, Kābul, Lahore, Multān, Malwa, Qhāndesh, Berār, and Ahmadnagar. Kashmir and Kandahār were districts of the province of Kābul. Sind, then known as Thatta, was a district in the province of Multān. Orissa formed a part of Bengal. The provinces were not of uniform area or income. There were in each province a governor, a dewan (revenue and finance officer), a *bakhshī* (military commander), a *ṣadr* (religious administrator) and *qāẓī* (agents who supplied information to the central government).

In all parts of the empire there were many subordinate states, whose rulers enjoyed varying degrees of power and prestige. These states were reckoned as so many districts and were attached to the *ṣūbahs* (provinces) within the boundaries of which they happened to be situated.

The provinces were divided into districts (*sarkārs*). Each district had a *fowjdār* (a military officer whose duties roughly corresponded to those of a collector); a *qāẓī;* a *kotwāl*, who looked after sanitation, police, and administration; a *bitikchī* (head clerk); and a *khazānedār* (treasurer).

Every town of consequence had a *kotwāl*. The village communities conducted their affairs through *pañcāyat*s (councils) and were more or less autonomous units.

Fiscal system. The main sources of Akbar's income, besides the land revenue, were from forests, irrigation canals, and fisheries, tributes from feudatory princes, a salt tax, and customs duties. The main features of the land revenue administration were measuring and classifying land into four categories, ascertaining the actual produce of the soil, and preparing separate schedules of rates for produce and of government levies for the fiscal *dustūr*s into which the empire was divided. The average produce and demands were based on the previous ten years' produce and prices; this was known as the ten-year settlement. The government's share was one-third of the produce. Definite rules were laid down for the guidance of collectors. Akbar reformed the currency to make it one of the best then known in the world.

The army. Mostly foreign in personnel, Akbar's army was originally composed of Mongols, Persians, Turks, Uzbeks, and Afghans, who were granted large assignments of land in lieu of salaries. The cavalry was the most important branch, followed by the artillery; the infantry was of little consequence. In 1573 Akbar first introduced the branding of horses and thereafter the *manṣabdārī* system, which graded the list of the officers, or *manṣabdārs* (holders of ranks), ranging from the rank of ten to that of 5,000, subsequently raised to 12,000. There had already been a kind of gradation system, but with Akbar's innovation promotion or demotion from one rank to another was a normal feature. The *manṣabdārs* were required to maintain a fixed number of horsemen, horses, elephants, camels, and carts appropriate to their individual ranks; to bring their contingents for periodical musters; and to get their horses branded.

The *manṣabdārī* system

There were 36 grades of *manṣabdārs*; besides *manṣabdārs*, there were *aḥadī* and *dākhilī* troops, who belonged to a higher rank and were paid higher salaries. The army also used war elephants. There was no navy, but there were boats commodious enough to carry a few elephants each. The *manṣabdārī* system, though not free from defects, was an improvement over the earlier system of tribal chieftainship and the organization of levying contingents. The *manṣabdārs* and their troops were under strict discipline and control of the central authority and were well paid.

The Mughal imperial service was organized on bureaucratic principles and was military in character and outlook. There was no distinction between military and civil services. With the exception of the *qāẓīs*, the *ṣadrs*, and some other religious officers, all had to be enrolled as *manṣabdārs*. Their salaries were determined and their ranks in the service fixed by their numerical designations. There was no specialization of qualification in appointments, and members could be transferred from one duty to another of an entirely different nature. There were no separate educational or medical services, though teachers, physicians, and artists were employed as imperial servants.

Repeal of discriminatory laws

Judicial reforms. Akbar repealed discriminatory laws against non-Muslims and amended the personal laws of both Muslims and Hindus so as to provide as many common laws as possible. He decreed that a man should not marry more than one wife unless his first wife was barren, forbade marriage between cousins and near relatives, and ordered that boys were not to marry before the age of 16 and girls before that of 14. He raised the age of circumcision to 12. The *kotwāls* in the cities were charged with the duty of enforcing these laws. The organization of judicial courts was allowed to remain as it had been under his predecessors, and decisions of the village *pañcāyats* was recognized. Akbar reformed the mode of conducting investigation and insisted that the judges try to find out the truth by every possible device and that they "should not be satisfied with witnesses or oaths, but pursue them by manifold enquiries by the study of physiognomy and the exercise of foresight . . ."

Religious policy. Akbar was interested in the study of the great problems of life and death. Early in 1575 he established at Fatehpur Sīkri a religious assembly hall ('Ibādat-khānah) where discussions on Islāmic religion, law, and tradition were held. He soon became dissatisfied with what he considered the shallowness of Muslim divines and threw open the meetings to learned men of other religions. He invited the Zoroastrian priest Mahyārjī Rānā from Navsāri in 1578–79, three Christian missions from Goa (1580–82, 1591, 1595–1605), and three Jain missions (1582–84, 1592–93, 1593–95) and acquired a good knowledge of these religions. He had already established contact with Hindu pandits. A comparative study of religions convinced him that there was truth in all of them, but that no one of them possessed absolute truth. He therefore disestablished Islām as the religion of the state, extended equal patronage to all faiths, and permitted legitimate religious propaganda and conversion to all. He rejected the Islāmic doctrine of resurrection and judgment and brushed aside revelation. He adopted many Hindu and Parsi beliefs and customs, such as belief in the doctrine of transmigration of the soul and sun worship. He did not subscribe to the five fundamentals of Islām, and he believed in Muḥammad as a prophet but not as the only prophet or the last and greatest prophet. He prayed, unlike a Muslim, four times—at sunrise, noon, sunset, and midnight. But he did not publicly repudiate his belief in Islām; nor did he persecute it, as some modern scholars have assumed.

Dīn-e Ilāhī. Many years' close and comparative study of religions made Akbar feel the insufficiency of Islām for being the national religion of India with its vast Hindu population and its highly developed religions and cultural traditions. Nor did he find Hinduism, Jainism, Zoroastrianism, or Christianity suitable for that purpose. Moreover, the followers of each of these religions (except those of Hinduism) considered their respective faiths alone to be true and the rest unworthy of acceptance. There was consequently a great deal of discord in the religious life of India. This troubled Akbar, because national progress was being hampered on account of religious conflict and disharmony. So he sounded religious leaders of various communities and unfolded a scheme of an eclectic organization (Dīn-e Ilāhī) that would combine the merits of all religions and eliminate their defects. But it was opposed by Raja Bhagwantdās of Amber, and Akbar gave up the idea of pursuing it to its logical conclusion. Instead he created the Dīn-e Ilāhī on the model of a Sūfī order (muslim mystical brotherhood). This new order had its own initiation ceremony and rules of conduct; otherwise, members were permitted to retain their diverse religious beliefs and practices. It was devised with the object of forging the diverse communities in the country's population into one people.

Religious conflict and disharmony

Akbar had succeeded in bringing about the political, administrative, economic, and to some extent the cultural unification of northern India by introducing Persian as the only official language and by bringing about the fusion of Hindu and Muslim architecture, music, and painting and providing a common religious and secular literature. By introducing several social reforms, he attempted to make social unification a reality. But he believed that for this unification to be permanent it must be based on some kind of mutual religious-cum-cultural understanding and appreciation. In short, he wanted a common religious forum for at least the elite of the various sections of the Indian population. The time was not ripe for the successful implementation of an idealistic program of that type; but Akbar's motive, nevertheless, was exceptionally noble.

Akbar's significance. Akbar's idealism, natural gifts, and force of character as well as his concrete achievements entitle him to a high place among the rulers of mankind. He is considered the greatest ruler of the Mughal dynasty and one of the greatest in the entire history of India.

His last days were full of anxiety due to the death of his younger sons and the rebellion of his eldest son, Salīm, who held court at Allahābād as an independent prince. Akbar became furious, and proceeded toward Allahābād to chastise the prince, but he had to return on account of one mishap or another. He thought of appointing Salīm's son Khusraw as his successor; but Salīm submitted in time, and Akbar forgave him and formally appointed him his heir and successor. Akbar fell ill on October 3, 1605. Physicians failed to diagnose the trouble correctly, and Akbar died at midnight of October 25–26.

THE EMPIRE IN THE 17TH CENTURY

The rebellion of Khusraw

Jahāngīr. Within a few months of his accession, Salīm (ruled 1605–27), who assumed the title of Jahāngīr, had to deal with a rebellion led by his eldest son, Khusraw. Khusraw was defeated at Lahore and was seized just after he had crossed the Chenāb, at the ferry of Shāhpur. He was brought in chains before the emperor at Lahore and partially blinded; his followers were given barbarous punishments. Jahāngīr imposed on the Sikh Gurū Arjun a fine of two lakhs of rupees for having blessed Khusraw. On the Gurū's refusal to pay, he was put to death; this act permanently estranged the Sikhs from the Mughals.

Khusraw's rebellion led to a few more risings, which were suppressed without much difficulty. Shāh 'Abbās I of Persia, taking advantage of the unrest, besieged the fort of Qandahār (1606); but abandoned the siege, when Jahāngīr promptly sent an army against him.

Marriage to Nūr Jahān. One of the most important events of the reign was Jahāngīr's marriage to Mihr-un-Nisā'. She had been appointed lady-in-waiting to Jahāngīr's stepmother; the emperor chanced to see her in a festival in March 1611, fell in love with her, and married her that May. The lady became his favourite wife and was honoured with the title of Nūr Jahān.

Nūr Jahān raised her father, brother, and other relations to high positions in the state. She enjoyed great in-

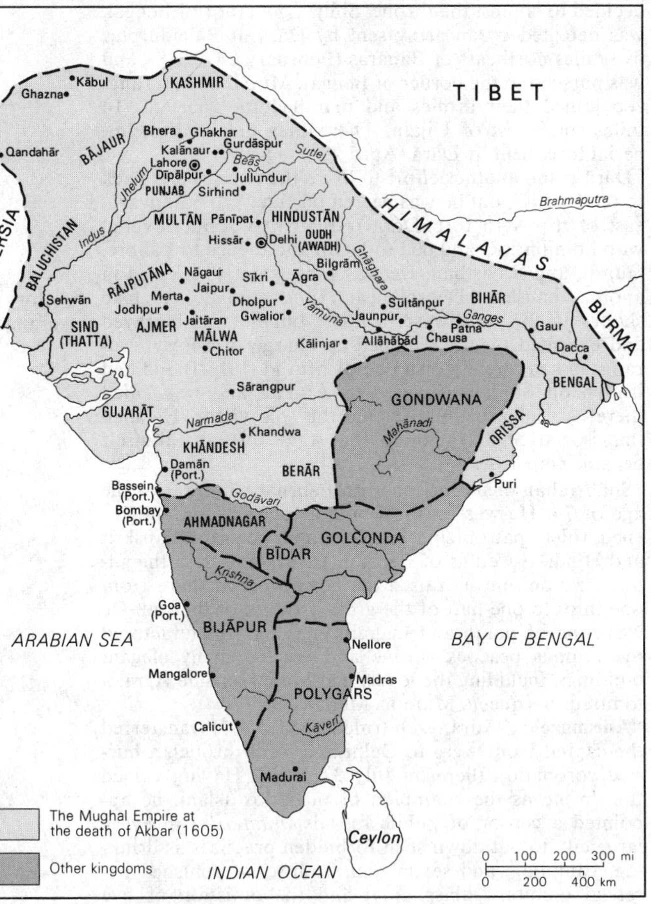

India in 1605.
Adapted from C. Davies, *An Historical Atlas of the Indian Peninsula*, 2nd ed. (1959); Oxford University Press

fluence and authority, formed a clique with her parents, her brother Āṣaf Khān, and Prince Khurram (third son of Jahāngīr), and became a power behind the throne; Khurram, later called Shāh Jahān, married Āṣaf Khān's daughter Arjumand Bānū Baygam, who was later given the title of Mumtāz Maḥal. Nūr Jahān exercised a strong influence on her husband and looked after him with unparalleled care and devotion. Under her influence Jahāngīr restrained himself from excessive drinking. She relieved him of much of the drudgery of administrative routine and anxiety. She enhanced the splendour of the Mughal court and ably seconded the efforts of her husband in patronizing learning and art and disbursing charity. But in politics and administration she encouraged factionalism. From 1611 to 1622 she supported the claims of Khurram to be the heir; but after her daughter by an earlier marriage, Lādlī Baygam, was wed to Prince Shahryār, Nūr Jahān began to back the latter and tried to reduce Khurram's influence. This drove Khurram into a rebellion against his father, and there was a prolonged civil war.

Nūr Jahān's influence

Subjugation of Mewār and Kangra. In pursuance of his father's policy, Jahāngīr dispatched five successive expeditions to subdue Rānā Amar Singh of Mewār, but all these failed. In 1613 Khurram was given the supreme command of the army, and Jahāngīr himself marched to Ajmer to be near the scene of action. The Rānā was then obliged to open negotiations, and Jahāngīr was happy to accept the terms proposed (1615). Amar Singh recognized Jahāngīr as his suzerain and all his territory in Mughal possession was restored, including Chitor, which, however, was not to be fortified. The Rānā was not obliged to attend the imperial *darbār* (administrative council), but his son was to represent him; nor was he required to enter into a matrimonial alliance with the Mughal royal family. Jahāngīr naturally claimed success against the Rānā, whom his great father had failed to subdue. He also took credit for the conquest in 1620 of the hill state of Kangra with the sacred shrine of Jwālāmukhī, which also had defied all previous Muslim invaders, including Akbar. Jahāngīr was right in boasting that except for Assam the whole of northern India was now in his possession.

War in the Deccan and the loss of Qandahār. Jahāngīr considered it his duty to complete the conquest of the Deccan, where, as was mentioned above, he was opposed by Malik ʿAmbar of Ahmadnagar. In 1620–21, Malik ʿAmbar was forced to surrender extensive territories to the Mughals; Byāpur and Golconda also agreed to pay tribute.

In 1622 ʿAbbās of Persia again besieged Qandahār, and Khurram (now Shāh Jahān) was directed to relieve that fortress. But the prince was planning a rebellion against his father and failed to take effective action. The fortress fell after 45 days' siege. Shāh ʿAbbās justified its capture on the plea that it belonged to Persia. Jahāngīr accused the Shāh of treachery and sent forces to recover the fortress, which could not be done successfully owing to Shāh Jahān's rebellion and the illness and death of Jahāngīr himself.

Shāh ʿAbbās' siege of Qandahār

Rebellion of Shāh Jahān. Alienated by the hostility of Nūr Jahān, Shāh Jahān raised the standard of revolt in 1623. After failing to take Fatehpur Sīkri, in April, he retreated to the Deccan, thence to Bengal, and from Bengal back again to the Deccan, being pursued all the time by an imperial force. His plan to seize Bihār, Oudh, Allāhābād, and even Āgra failed; and Mahābat Khān, the imperial general, inflicted defeat after defeat on the fugitive. At last Shāh Jahān submitted to his father unconditionally. Nūr Jahān, who was becoming suspicious of Mahābat Khān's fast-rising power and prestige, demanded that Shāh Jahān surrender Rohtās and Asīr, send Dārā and Aurangzeb, two of his elder sons, to court. Shāh Jahān complied without hesitation. He was forgiven and appointed governor of Bālāghāt. The three-year-old rebellion, which had caused a considerable loss of men and money, came to an end in April 1626.

Mahābat Khān's coup. Immediately on the conclusion of peace with Shāh Jahān, the imperious Queen decided to punish Mahābat Khān for his refusal to take orders from anyone but Jahāngīr and to support Shahryār's claim to the throne. She ordered Mahābat Khān to Bengal and framed charges of disloyalty and disobedience against him. Instead, Mahābat Khān proceeded to Punjab, where the Emperor was encamped. Jahāngīr refused to see him, and the Queen insulted him further by asking him to explain why he had affianced his daughter without previous permission. Mahābat Khān was enraged and decided to secure the person of the Emperor and destroy Nūr Jahān's power. He appeared before the imperial camp at the head of his powerful army, took Jahāngīr back to his own camp, and placed him under surveillance. Nūr Jahān then voluntarily surrendered to Mahābat Khān and was permitted to join Jahāngīr. They remained under the custody of Mahābat Khān for about two months, and they both apparently reconciled themselves outwardly to the general's domination; but Nūr Jahān hatched a plot to secure the release of the Emperor. One day Jahāngīr planned to review his troops and sent word to Mahābat Khān to keep his army at a little distance so as to prevent any possibility of a clash between the two forces. During the review Jahāngīr joined his men, escaping his captor. Thus outwitted, Mahābat Khān submitted to Jahāngīr. But the emperor's health was greatly impaired, and he died on November 7, 1627, near Bhimbar.

Capture of Jahāngīr

Evaluation of Jahāngīr. Although he had rebelled against his father, Jahāngīr cherished the loving memory of Akbar and held him in a great reverence. Mughal painting and music reached high standards of development under his patronage. He usually followed his father's policy of religious toleration and, although he did not have complete faith in the dogmas of any religion, he was certainly a liberal Muslim. He was a fairly successful ruler and a just administrator, and had the good sense to continue the administrative system and policies of his father.

Shāh Jahān. Shāh Jahān (ruled 1628–58) had already had his elder brother Khusraw strangled to death (1622); and under his instructions his father-in-law Āṣaf Khān slew all other royal princes, the possible rivals for the throne. On Shāh Jahān's accession Āṣaf Khān was appointed prime minister and Nūr Jahān was given an adequate pension.

Rebellions against Shāh Jahān

Shāh Jahān's reign was marred by a few rebellions, the first of which was that of Khān Jahān Lodī, governor of the Deccan, who was recalled to court after failing to recover Bālāghāt from Ahmadnagar. He rose in rebellion and fled back to the Deccan, and Shāh Jahān followed, and in December 1629 defeated Khān Jahān and drove him to the north, ultimately overtook him, and killed him in a skirmish at Shihondā in what is now the Bānda district of Uttar Pradesh (January 1631).

The next rebellion was led by the Hindu Orchha chief Jujhār Singh in Bundelkhand. Jujhār was compelled to submit after his kinsman Bhārat Singh defected and joined the Mughals. Jujhār was pardoned on condition of surrendering a part of his territory and proceeding to the Deccan for imperial service. On his return to Orchha he attempted to seize Gondwana; but he was asked to surrender it and pay a fine. Jujhār refused to comply and recalled his troops from the royal service. After a prolonged campaign, he was defeated and murdered (1634). Two of Jujhār's sons were converted to Islām; a third was put to death because he refused to convert. Many Hindu temples in Bundelkhand were wantonly desecrated and demolished. Orchha was made over to Devī Singh, a relative of Jujhār Singh's, who had gone over to the Mughals; the Bundelās refused to acknowledge him as their leader, and trouble continued for some time.

Meanwhile in 1632 Shāh Jahān became involved in a dispute with the Portuguese of Hooghly in Bengal, who were indulging in piracy and who had stolen two slave girls belonging to the Mughals. The Portuguese were obliged to deliver up the slaves and pay a fine, and 400 of them were brought to Āgra, where they were imprisoned when they refused to embrace Islām.

In the Deccan, Shah Jahān's forces captured Daulatābād, the new capital of the Niẓāmshāhī kingdom. This, however, did not bring about the complete extinction of that kingdom; it kept the northern parts of what is now the Poona (Pune) district and the whole Konkan.

Settlement in the Deccan

Bijāpur submitted, acknowledged Mughal suzerainty, and once again agreed to pay an annual tribute. Golconda's sultan also agreed to pay tribute and to assist the Mughals against Bījāpur in case of a war with the latter (May 1636). Relations with the Marāthās (see below *The Marāthās*) also were settled, but not without fighting. For the time being Shāh Jahān was able to settle the affairs of the Deccan to his satisfaction.

Early in 1638 Shāh Jahān succeeded in recovering Qandahār, which had been lost during the last years of Jahāngīr's reign. The Persian governor, ʿAlī Mardān Khān, was on poor terms with the court of Teheran; he intrigued with the Mughal officers and surrendered the fortress to Shāh Jahān. In February 1649 the Shāh recaptured Qandahār after a brief siege. Shāh Jahān made three unsuccessful attempts (1649, 1652, 1653) to recover the fortress. The relations between India and Persia, therefore, became strained.

Central Asian policy. Following in the footsteps of his predecessors, Shāh Jahān hoped to conquer Samarkand, the original homeland of his ancestors. The brother of Emām Qolī, ruler of Samarkand, invaded Kābul and, in 1639, captured Bāmīān, which gave offense to Shāh Jahān. The Emperor directed his son Murād to invade Badakhshan; but Murād failed (1646) and was replaced by another son, Aurangzeb. The latter fought bravely, but the situation was complicated by an alliance between the Uzbeks and ʿAbbās II of Persia, and Shāh Jahān's Central Asian policy ended in failure.

War of succession, 1657–59. Shāh Jahān fell ill in September 1657, and rumours spread that he was dead. He executed a will bequeathing the empire to his eldest son, Dārā. His other sons, Shujāʿ, Aurangzeb, and Murād, who were grown men and governors of provinces, decided to contest the throne. Shujāʿ, governor of Bengal, was defeated by an army sent by Dārā at Bāhādurpur, five miles northeast of Banaras (February 24, 1658), and was pursued to the border of Bengal. Murād and Aurangzeb joined their armies and marched to Dharmat, 14 miles southwest of Ujjain. There they defeated an imperial force sent by Dārā (April 25).

Dārā made another effort to drive the two princes back to the Deccan, but he was beaten on June 8 at Sāmugarh, east of the Āgra fort. Dārā retreated to Āgra, covered with humiliation, and fled to Delhi and thence to Lahore, Gujrāt, and Rājasthān. He was subsequently defeated in another battle at Deorai near Ajmer and fled to take shelter in the northwest frontier; but he was betrayed and executed on the trumped-up charge of heresy. Aurangzeb had already disposed of Murād (July 5) and had beaten off Shujāʿ, who fled to Arakan and was killed there; Aurangzeb thus became the sole victor. He then imprisoned Shāh Jahān in the Āgra fort and himself became emperor.

Victory of Aurangzeb

Shāh Jahān died a prisoner on February 1, 1666, at the age of 74. He was on the whole a tolerant and enlightened ruler, patronizing scholars and poets of Sanskrit and Hindi as well as of Persian. He systematized the administration, but he raised the government's share from one-third to one-half of the gross produce of the soil. He was fond of pomp and magnificence. He manufactured the famous peacock throne and erected many elegant buildings, including the lovely Tāj Mahal outside Āgra, a tomb for his queen, Mumtāz Maḥal.

Aurangzeb. Aurangzeb (ruled 1658–1707) transferred the capital from Āgra to Delhi and went through a hurried coronation there on July 31, 1658. Having gained the throne as the champion of orthodox Islām, he appointed a censor of public morals (*muḥtasib*) in every large city to put down such forbidden practices as drinking, gambling, and sexual immorality; he punished heretical opinions, blasphemy, and the omission of five daily prayers and the fast of Ramaẓān (Ramaḍān) by Muslims. Aurangzeb deliberately reversed the policy of his predecessors toward non-Muslim subjects by enforcing the principles and practices of the Islāmic state. He reimposed the *jizyah* on non-Muslims and saddled them with religious, social, and legal disabilities. To begin with he forbade their building new temples and repairing old ones. Next, he issued orders to demolish all the schools and temples of the Hindus and to put down their teaching and religious practices. He doubled the customs duties on the Hindus and abolished them altogether in the case of Muslims. He granted stipends and gifts to converts from Hinduism and offered them posts in public service, liberation from prison in the case of convicted criminals, and succession of disputed estates. He persecuted the Shīʿah and the Ṣūfīs (nonconformist Muslims) as well.

Aurangzeb's policy toward non-Muslims

This policy of fanaticism led to numerous rebellions. The Jāṭ peasantry of Mathura rebelled in 1669; a Satnāmī rising occurred in 1672; the Sikhs in the Punjab revolted under their Gurū Tegh Bahādur, who was brutally put to death in 1675. But the most prolonged uprising was the Rājput rebellion, caused by Aurangzeb's annexation of the Jodhpur state and his seizure of its ruler's posthumous son Ajit Singh with the intention of converting him to Islām. This rebellion spread to Mewār; and Aurangzeb himself had to proceed to Ajmer to fight the Rājputs, who had been joined by the Emperor's third son, Akbar (January 1681). But by a stratagem Aurangzeb managed to isolate Akbar, who fled to the Deccan and thence to Persia. The war with Mewār came to an end (June 1681) because Aurangzeb had to pursue Akbar to the Deccan, where the prince had joined the Marāthā king Shambhūjī. But Jodhpur remained in a state of rebellion for 27 years more, and Ajit Singh occupied his ancestral dominion immediately after Aurangzeb's death.

Aurangzeb's conquest of Assam proved to be transitory, and his war with the frontier tribes sapped the resources of the empire. But in 1661 Palāmau, or the Rānchi region, was annexed to Bihār, and Mughal suzerainty was re-established in Ladākh.

Aurangzeb spent the last 25 years of his reign in the Deccan, and invaded and annexed Bijāpur (1686) and Golconda (1687). Then he concentrated his might against the recently established Marāthā kingdom, but Marāthā resistance was so stubborn that even after nearly two decades of struggle he failed to completely subdue them (see below). The aged Emperor died on March 3, 1707, and was buried at Khuldābād, four miles west of Daulatābād.

Assessment of Aurangzeb

Aurangzeb possessed natural gifts of a high order. He had assiduously cultivated learning, self-knowledge, self-reverence, and self-control, and he exercised a curb over his tongue and temper. He was extremely industrious, methodical, and disciplined in habits and thoughts, and his private life was virtuous. But his narrow religious bigotry made him ill-suited to rule the mixed population of his empire. He treated all non-Muslims in the country as inferior people. His ambition was to convert India into a purely Muslim country; but in fact he destroyed rather than built. He was suspicious by nature. Besides killing his brothers, he imprisoned his three sons, the eldest of whom died in confinement. Similarly, his daughter Zīb-un-Nisā' ended her life in prison.

A recent attempt has been made to show that Aurangzeb was not as bigoted a Sunnī Muslim as has been represented, and that he granted land to a famous temple of Banaras. A few instances of this kind—which to be sure were due to political reasons—would not make Aurangzeb appear tolerant, when abundant, unimpeachable contemporary evidence proves that he destroyed thousands of Hindu temples and schools and forcibly converted Hindus to Islām. The idea that he pursued these policies only in wartime is a pure invention of his modern apologists and finds no confirmation in contemporary writings.

MUGHAL DECLINE IN THE 18TH CENTURY

Bahādur Shāh I (*Shāh ʿĀlam*). Aurangzeb's eldest son had died in prison. His second son, Muʿaẓẓam Bahādur Shāh, or Shāh ʿĀlam (ruled 1707–12), aged over 63 years, gained the throne after defeating and disposing of his two brothers, Āʿẓam and Kām Bakhsh. He recognized Ajit Singh, in rebellion since birth, as the Maharājā of Jodhpur and made peace with other Rājputs. Then he tried to settle his scores with the Sikhs, who also had rebelled in the Punjab under their leader Bandā Singh Bahādur. After a good deal of initial success, Bandā was defeated and driven into the hills of Jammu. But when Bahādur Shāh died in February 1712, Bandā recovered Sādhaura and Longarh and continued his depredations as before.

Bahādur Shāh was a mild and generous man. Though possessed of dignity of behaviour, he proved to be a weak ruler. He was fond of compromise even in important political and administrative matters. But he followed his father's policy of intolerance, retained the *jizyah*, and did not appoint Hindus to high posts. His short reign was on the whole tolerably successful.

Jahāndār Shāh. There were three wars of succession among Bahādur Shāh's sons; and the eldest son, Jahāndār Shāh (ruled 1712–13), triumphed. He was an incompetent ruler who neglected the business of government. He bestowed his favours on his concubine Lāl Kowr and appointed her low relatives to high posts. The *wazīr* Zūlfiqār Khān sulked at home, thwarted in administrative business by musicians and buffoons. There was confusion all around.

The Sayyid brothers

Jahāndār's claims were disputed by his nephew Farrukh-siyar. He defeated Jahāndār Shāh with the help of the Sayyid brothers (ʿAbdullāh Khān and Ḥusayn ʿAlī Khān) and put him to death on February 11, 1713. Jahāndār was the first ruler of the Mughal dynasty to prove utterly incapable of administering the affairs of the empire and to behave like a foolish upstart.

Farrukh-siyar. Farrukh-siyar (ruled 1713–19) was a young man of 30 at the time of his accession. He was utterly weak, thoughtless, and devoid of physical and moral courage; and his reign was one long attempt at perfidious conspiracy against his *wazīr* ʿAbdullāh Khān and Ḥusayn ʿAlī Khān—the two Sayyid brothers who had been instrumental in raising him to the throne.

The Sayyids reduced Ajit Singh of Jodhpur (May 1714). Another expedition defeated Bandā, the Sikh leader, who was put to a cruel death at Delhi (June 1716). But the Jāṭ leader Churāman could not be suppressed and peace had to be made with him. By this time the quarrel between the Emperor and the Sayyid brothers had come to a head. Ḥusayn ʿAlī Khān brought a Marāthā force to Delhi, deposed the Emperor, and placed Rafīʿ-ud-Darajāt on the throne (February 1719). This boy king was suffering from consumption, and he was removed from the throne. His elder brother Rafīʿ-ud-Dawlah was crowned king on June 16, 1719, with the title of Shāh Jahān II. Rafīʿ-ud-Dawlah too was a sickly youth, and he died on September 17, 1719.

Muḥammad Shāh. On September 28 the Sayyids crowned Rawshan Akhtar (ruled 1719–48), a grandson of Bahādur Shāh, emperor under the title of Muḥammad Shāh. He was a weak and inexperienced prince, and the Sayyids retained all power in their hands. The powerful Niẓām-ul-Mulk I, Mughal viceroy of the Deccan, who was hostile to the Sayyids, captured Khāndesh and defeated and killed two nephews of the Sayyid brothers. Therefore, Ḥusayn ʿAlī Khān and the Emperor proceeded to the Deccan to put down Niẓām-ul-Mulk. On the way Ḥusayn ʿAlī fell victim to a conspiracy (October 1720). Muḥammad Shāh then turned back toward Delhi and defeated and imprisoned the elder Sayyid, ʿAbdullāh Khān (November).

Muḥammad Shāh appointed Niẓām-ul-Mulk *wazīr* of the empire, but the latter found it difficult to function in the midst of youthful, pleasure-loving courtiers and returned to the Deccan (December 1723). Qamar-ud-Dīn Khān was, therefore, appointed *wazīr*. The Niẓām practically became independent in the Deccan (October 1724). Another adventurer, Saʿadat Khān, who was appointed governor of Oudh in September 1722, laid the foundation of the virtually independent Shīaʿh dynasty of that province. Bengal, Bihār, and Orissa, which constituted a viceroyalty during the reign of Bahādur Shāh, became practically independent at this time. The Marāthās diverted their attention to the north at the instigation of the Niẓām, beginning in 1731 annual raids into the Mughal territory in northern India.

Invasion by Nāder Shāh

The central government had become so weak that the country was invaded in 1739 by a Persian adventurer, Nāder Shāh, who had established himself as the ruler of Iran. He captured Qandahār, Ghazna, and Kābul and crossed the Indus at Attock (December 1738). He overpowered the governer of Lahore and defeated Muḥammad Shāh near Karnāl (February 1739). Nāder then marched to Delhi and ordered a general massacre in which 30,000 people were slain. He left Delhi on May 26, laden with a booty amounting to 30 crores of rupees in cash, along with jewels, gold and silver plate, furniture, and other valuable articles, including the famous peacock throne of Shāh Jahān. He deprived the empire of the province of Kābul, which he annexed to Iran.

The invasion paralyzed Muḥammad Shāh and his court and heaped humiliation upon the country. But the Emperor failed to take a lesson from it. Nothing was done to reorganize and reform the administration. Marāthā raids on Mālwa, Gujrāt, Bundelkhand, and the territory north of these provinces continued as before. The Emperor was compelled to appoint the peshwa as governor of Mālwa. The province of Katēhr (Rohilkhand) was seized by an adventurer, ʿAlī Muḥammad Khān Ruhēla, who could not be suppressed by the feeble government of Delhi. The Punjab was invaded by Aḥmad Shāh Abdālī, a lieutenant of Nāder Shāh who became king of Kābul after Nāder's death (June 1747); he sacked Lahore but was defeated by a Delhi army at Mānupur near Machhīwara and compelled to retreat (March 1748). Muḥammad Shāh died in April 1748.

Aḥmad Shāh. Upon Muḥammad Shāh's death, his son Aḥmad Shāh (ruled 1748–54) crowned himself king. He was a young man of 21 who possessed no qualities of leadership. His *wazīr*s, Ṣafdar Jang of Oudh, and Mīr

Bakhshī Saādāt Khān, were also mediocre. Ṣafdar Jang tried to crush the Ruhēla and Bangash Pathans, who had usurped Rohilkhand and Farrukhābād, but suffered a defeat (September 1750). He undertook a second expedition against Rohilkhand and defeated the Ruhēlas with Marāthā assistance (April 1751). He returned to Delhi to find that the Emperor had made peace with Abdālī, who had invaded northwestern India a third time, and ceded to him the Punjab and Multān (March 1752). The *wazīr*, therefore, had the Emperor's favourite adviser murdered, which led to a complete breach between the Emperor and his *wazīr* and resulted in a civil war between them. Ṣafdar Jang was defeated and left for Oudh (November 1753). Power passed into the hands of ʿImād-ul-Mulk, a grandson of Niẓām-ul-Mulk, who entered into an alliance with the Marāthās and with their help became *wazīr*. He deposed the Emperor on June 2, 1754, and placed ʿĀlamgīr II (a son of Jahāndār Shāh) on the throne.

ʿĀlamgīr II. ʿĀlamgīr (ruled 1754–59) was as inept as his predecessor. During his reign the fourth Abdālī invasion took place. The invader was provoked by ʿImād-ul-Mulk's seizure of the Punjab, which had been ceded to Abdālī in 1752. After driving the *wazīr*'s agent from Lahore (November 1756), Abdālī was pressed by Shāh Walī Allāh, the most important Muslim Ṣūfī saint of northern India, to move down to Delhi and help restore effective Muslim rule in the country by crushing the Marāthās, who were dominating all northern India, and the Jāṭs, who had brought the entire country from Bharatpur to Ballabgarh under their rule. Abdālī stayed in India for a few months, married his son Timur to the daughter of ʿĀlamgīr II, and sent an army against Surajmal. He sacked Mathurā and massacred a large number of innocent pilgrims. He then entrusted to the Ruhēla captain Najīb-ud-Dawlah (Najīb Khān) the protection of ʿĀlamgīr II. Najīb proved to be an exacting and rigorous jailer, who meted out rough treatment to ʿĀlamgīr II. There was no love lost between him and the *wazīr*, ʿImād-ul-Mulk, who had once again regained power with Marāthā assistance.

Restoration of Muslim rule

The Marāthā influence was now re-established at the capital, and their leader Raghunath Rāo marched to the Punjab and drove away the Abdālī's son and agent (April 1758). ʿImād-ul-Mulk expelled Najīb to his *jāgīr* (Sahāranpur and Najībābād) and drove the Emperor's eldest son, ʿAlī Gawhar, from Delhi. The prince fled to Sahāranpur, from there to Oudh, and thence to Allāhābād. The Marāthā power had now reached its zenith. Their only potential enemy in northern India was Najīb-ud-Dawlah. Therefore Dattājī Sindhia besieged him at Shakartāl, 18 miles west of Muzaffarnagar, and the siege dragged on through the rainy season of 1759. Najīb appealed to his kinsmen of Rohilkhand—to Shujāʿ-ud-Dawlah of Oudh and Aḥmad Shāh Abdālī of Kābul—to save him from destruction. Shāh Walī Allāh once again besought the Abdālī to come and uproot the Marāthās and the Jāṭs, and promised him heavenly assistance in this sacred mission. So Abdālī undertook his fifth invasion of India. The *wazīr* ʿImād-ul-Mulk, alarmed at the news, had ʿĀlamgīr II assassinated on November 29, 1759. He proclaimed Muḥī-ul-Millat, grandson of Kām Bakhsh, as emperor under the title of Shāh Jahān III. After this he marched toward Shakartāl to join Dattājī Sindhia, who now raised the siege and proceeded toward Lahore to fight the invader.

Abdālī entered Punjab in August 1759 and drove away the Marāthā governor. From Lahore he proceeded toward Delhi, sending a detachment of his army to fight Dattājī Sindhia, who was marching toward Sirhind. He defeated and killed Dattājī at Barārī Ghāt, ten miles north of Delhi, and then occupied Delhi.

Meanwhile, the peshwa had dispatched a strong army under his cousin Sadāshiv Rāo Bhāo to drive away the invader and re-establish Marāthā supremacy in northern India. The Bhāo was joined by Surajmal of Bharatpur; but in view of the Marāthā record in the north, all Rājput and other Hindu chiefs declined to join him. His attempt to win over Shujāʿ-ud-Dawlah of Oudh also failed, and the latter joined the invader, who claimed his cause as one of Islām. Surajmal too deserted the Marāthās because of differences over general policy and the mode of warfare to be followed. The Bhāo expelled the Abdālī agent from Delhi, deposed Shāh Jahān III, and proclaimed the accession of ʿĀlamgīr II's son Shāh ʿĀlam II, who was in the east, planning to invade Bihār. ʿĀlam had already proclaimed himself emperor after his father's death; he made Shujāʿ-ud-Dawlah his *wazīr*.

Accession of Shāh ʿĀlam II

At the end of the rainy season the Marāthās marched from Delhi toward Sirhind in order to occupy the Punjab and cut off the Abdālī's retreat. On October 17 the Bhāo captured the fort of Kunjpurā, six miles northeast of Karnāl, and proceeded to Sārhind. The Abdālī, who had spent the rainy season of 1760 at Sikandarābād, crossed the Yamuna at Bāghpat, 25 miles north of Delhi. On learning of the Marāthā movement toward the Punjab, he deputed a contingent of his troops to pursue the Bhāo. The latter thereupon turned back and encamped at Pānīpat. The Abdālī arrived there three days later. The Marāthās fortified their camp and decided to fight.

The armies lay facing each other for two months, with daily skirmishes occurring between their scouts. The final battle was fought on January 14, 1761, in which the Marāthā army, which had suffered two months' starvation and lack of equipment, was completely routed. The Bhāo died, fighting bravely to his last breath. The peshwa's son Vishwās Rāo, who was the generalissimo of the army, was also slain along with most of the notable officers and chiefs; Mahādājī Sindhia and Malhār Rāo Holkar alone among the notables escaped from the field. The third battle of Pānīpat shattered the dream of a Marāthā empire for all India. It cleared the way for the British, who had already usurped the position of making and unmaking nawabs of Bengal, Bihār, and Orissa, to the sovereignty of northern India. Aḥmad Shāh Abdālī was not anxious to follow up his victory and to occupy and rule India. His troops clamoured and demanded arrears of pay, compelling him to return to Kābul. He recognized Shāh ʿĀlam as emperor and ʿImād-ul-Mulk as *wazīr*. He delivered charge of Delhi to Najīb-ud-Dawlah. The Abdālī's attempt to conclude a peace with the peshwa and Surajmal of Bharatpur failed, and he left Delhi for Kābul in March 1761.

Shāh ʿĀlam being away in Bihār, the throne of Delhi remained vacant from 1760 to 1771. During most of this period Najīb-ud-Dawlah was in charge of the administration of the capital and the dwindling empire. He acted like a virtual dictator and carried on a ceaseless warfare with the Jāṭs and the Sikhs but failed to crush either of them. The nominal empire now consisted of Delhi and a small area around it. (A.L.S.)

V. The Marāthās

EMERGENCE OF THE MARATHA EMPIRE

Mahārāshtra: the land and its people. Mahārāshtra, homeland of the Hindu Marāthās, which the great Marāthā leader and hero Śivajī (1627–80) made the base of an empire, extends from the Arabian Sea on the west to Sātpura Mountains in the north. In the 17th century, Mahārāshtra was surrounded by the independent Muslim kingdoms of Bijāpur and Golconda in the south, by the Mughal Empire in the north, and by a number of European settlements on the west. The Muslim states of the south were in a process of disintegration, and the Mughal Empire, though at its largest during Śivajī's time, declined rapidly after the death of the great Mughal emperor Aurangzeb in 1707. The vacuum created by the fall of the Mughal Empire remained unfilled until the beginning of the 19th century, when the British began to consolidate their position. In this period between the decline of the Mughals and the establishment of British dominance, the Marāthās carved out their empire. A number of earlier ruling dynasties in the region had given it political unity, and the teachings and writings of a number of saints in Marathi, a regional language, gave rise to a cultural and religious unity.

The career of Śivajī. Śivajī's father, Shāhjī Bhonsle, a *jāgīrdār* (holder of the right to collect the land tax from an assigned area), had been prominent in resisting the aggressiveness of the Mughal Empire, which then dominated India. Śivajī's mother, Jijā Bāī, developed in him high moral qualities and a great faith in religion, and all accounts agree in evaluating Śivajī as a born leader of men. In 1647 Śivajī, at the age of 20, assumed the administration of his *jāgīr* and, with the help of a number of neighbouring chieftains scattered over the Sahyādri Ranges, undertook the task of carving out a kingdom for himself in western Mahārāshtra. Fortunately for Śivajī, the neighbouring kingdom of Bijāpur was in decline. Its ruler, Muḥammad Shāh, suffered from a protracted illness and his kingdom was weakened by internal dissensions. Śivajī took advantage of the situation by building up an impregnable chain of strong fortresses, and by 1653 he had set up a kingdom that extended over the entire territory between the Bhīma and Nīra rivers.

Foundation of the Marāthā state

With a strong base in the Sahyādri Ranges, Śivajī turned his attention to the territory west of the Sahyādri. Between 1654 and 1660 he extended his kingdom on the west coast. Many willingly joined him; others, such as the Morays of Javli, were ruthlessly crushed. By 1657 Śivajī was raiding the Mughal territories in the direction of Junnar and Ahmadnagar and the Bijāpur territories in north Konkan. The coastal regions were being occupied at this time by European powers. The English set up a factory at Rājapur in 1648 and the Dutch settled down at Vengurla and the Portuguese at Chaul. It seems that Śivajī was aware of the danger of European power growing on the west coast of India and decided to build up a strong naval power; he established a number of naval fortresses on the western coast over a period of some 30 years.

It was during one of his encounters with Bijāpur forces in 1659 that Śivajī killed Afẓal Khān, one of the leading generals of Bijāpur, who had been deputed to feign friendship with Śivajī and kill him. With alluring promises of confirming Śivajī in the possession of territories he had conquered from Bijāpur, Afẓal Khān invited Śivajī to meet him at Wai, a little south of Poona (Pune). Apprised of Afẓal Khān's intentions, Śivajī reciprocated with an equally feigned fidelity and, in a physical embrace, killed him. He then followed up with a sharp attack on Afẓal Khān's army and the capture of a vast booty. Śivajī's army then poured into south Konkan and the Kolhāpur district and captured the fort of Panhāla. By this time, one Shāyistah Khān had been appointed the Mughal governor of Deccan and, in conjunction with Bijāpur forces, was trying to bring pressure upon the Marāthās. Having driven the Marāthās from the neighbourhood of Poona. Shāyistah Khān was resting comfortably in a house in Poona, in which Śivajī had passed his early youth, when Śivajī made a surprise attack on him. Shāyistah Khān escaped with the loss of a thumb, but one of his sons and a large number of his followers were killed. Such adventures spread Śivajī's fame far and wide and made him feared by his adversaries. His sack of Surat the largest trade mart on the west coast (January 1664), was an act of still greater audacity.

Relations with the Mughals. Having thus failed to check Śivajī, Aurangzeb, the Mughal emperor, turned to other tactics. He appointed Jai Singh, his ablest Hindu general and diplomat and a man of infinite tact and patience, to deal with him. Jai Singh succeeded in convincing the Bijāpurs of Mughal strength and generosity and won them over to his side. This intensified the Mughal thrust against Śivajī. Attacking the important Marāthā fort of Purandhar, Jai Singh forced Śivajī to sue for peace. Jai Singh seems to have decided, as a first step in his Deccan policy, to neutralize the Marāthās and then suppress the kingdom of Bijāpur. This policy suited the immediate interests of Śivajī also, for he was content to allow the Mughal armies to break the back of Bijāpur resistance. In June 1665 a treaty was signed at Purandhar between Śivajī and Jai Singh under which Śivajī was to surrender to the Mughals 23 out of 35 forts conquered by him in Bijāpur and to receive Bijāpur territories worth more than double that amount in lower Konkan and Bālāghāt. Śivajī was also to accept Mughal suzerainty and send his son as his representative to the Mughal court.

Aurangzeb, who distrusted Śivajī, did not accept Jai Singh's proposals with enthusiasm. Jai Singh's subsequent failure to deal effectively with Bijāpur discredited his policies and enabled Aurangzeb's advisors to attribute the failure to lack of support, even to treachery, on Śivajī's part. Under these circumstances, Jai Singh decided to arrange a personal meeting between Śivajī and the Mughal emperor, and, induced by Jai Singh, the Marāthā leader agreed to visit Aurangzeb at Āgra. But the visit misfired, and Jai Singh's entire Deccan policy collapsed. Treated as a hero by his countrymen, Śivajī did not expect to be treated as a mere local potentate, as he was in the eyes of the custodians of procedural propriety at the Mughal court. Finding that others had precedence over him in the audience hall, he flew into a rage, swooned, and was moved, at the Emperor's orders, into an anteroom. His behaviour shocked Aurangzeb, but, fearing that Śivajī's followers might ally themselves with Bijāpur and its supporters, he restrained himself and put Śivajī under simple confinement, from which he made a dramatic escape in a fruit basket.

Śivajī at Aurangzeb's court

Returning from Āgra, Śivajī for some time avoided provoking the Mughals, limiting his energy to consolidation of his power in the immediate vicinity of his homeland. Nor did he repudiate the suzerainty of the Mughal Empire that he had accepted by the Treaty of Purandhar, and he was soon confirmed by the Mughals in his title of raja (king). After more than three years of truce with the Mughal emperor, Śivajī resumed his military adventures in 1670. He soon regained the whole territory of north Konkan, which had been ceded to the Mughals in the Purandhar treaty.

Śivajī's second offensive. On October 3, 1670, Śivajī carried out the second sack of Surat and exacted heavy tribute from the local merchants. On October 17, he invaded Bāglāna and defeated Dā'ūd Khān at Dindori. This was followed by invasions of Khāndesh and Berār. Realizing the gravity of the situation, Aurangzeb sent reinforcements to the Deccan, but, despite the great concentration of the Mughal power in that area, the Marāthās were able to capture the twin towns of Mulher and Salher early in 1672. The Mughal government soon revised its strategy, appointing the capable Bahādur Khān, as sole commander in the Deccan. This led to effective results. Bahādur Khān set up his headquarters at Padgaon, north of the Bhīma River, a place of great strategic importance.

Excluded from Mughal territory by Bahādur Khān, Śivajī now turned toward Bijāpur, where the ruler's death in December 1672 had thrown everything into confusion. Śivajī recaptured Panhālā from Bijāpur early in March 1673 and followed it up by the capture of Sātāra in July. The Mughal preoccupation with the Khyber Afghans in 1674, Aurangzeb's personal move to the northwestern frontier, and the removal of some Mughal forces from the Deccan again emboldened Śivajī to make inroads into Mughal territories. Crowning himself at Raigadh on June 6, 1674, with great pomp and ceremony, Śivajī again moved into Bāglāna and Khāndesh. Fearing that the Mughal effort to contain the Marāthās on the one side and control the Bijāpur kingdom on the other was merely leading to an increase in Śivajī's strength, Bahādur Khān revived Jai Singh's strategy and decided to concentrate on the suppression of Bijāpur and patch up his relations with Śivajī. Śivajī knew that once the Mughals succeeded in destroying Bijāpur it would be his turn next, and he was not confident of being able to withstand a frontal attack by the Mughals on his territories. He devised a new strategy; deciding to build up a second base for Marāthā power, in Karnatak, inaccessible to the Mughals.

Śivajī's coronation

Conquest of Karnatak. Śivajī thought that by allying himself with the kingdom of Golconda he would be able to exercise greater pressure on Bijāpur, and, while the Mughals captured its northern territories, he would be able to conquer for himself the southern and southeastern parts. A joint scheme for the conquest of Bijāpur territories in the south was finally evolved in a personal meeting between Śivajī and the Golconda ruler at Hyderābād. Śivajī also tried to win over to his side some Marāthā leaders allied with Bijāpur. His greatest success in the Karnatak area lay in the conquest of Jinjī, which he made his principal seat of government in the south. Pressed by the Mughal armies, Bijāpur turned to Śivajī for help and confirmed him in the possession of all the territory that he had conquered from it. It was a personal tragedy for Śivajī that, at a time when he appeared to be at the height of his glory, his own son Sambhāji turned against him and joined the Mughals. Sambhāji soon fell out with the Mughals, however, and escaped to Panhālā, where he was kept in confinement. On his way back from Karnatak, Śivajī met Sambhāji at Panhālā and tried his best to win him over, but without much success. Śivajī breathed his last on April 4, 1680, at Raigadh, at the age of 53.

Śivajī's achievements. Śivajī left behind him a well-organized army, a well-settled administration, and a well-endowed treasury. But, during the lifetimes of his immediate successors, the high principles on which he had set up his administration fell into disuse, his armies became instruments of aggression and vandalism, and his treasury was depleted. His kingdom was broken up once in his own lifetime and on several occasions thereafter, but the character of the political system that he established lasted for nearly 150 years.

Śivajī set up his state by welding a scattered group of clans into something resembling a nation, and infused it with an ideal. He was a deeply religious man who respected saintly character, irrespective of caste, community, or religion, but he did not allow religious or moral considerations to interfere with his statecraft and empire building. It was his combination of saintliness and political shrewdness, of gentleness, finesse, and wisdom, of military and administrative abilities, that gave Śivajī a unique position in Indian history.

Śivajī borrowed the pattern of his administration from the Mughals and also tried to bring about a number of reforms. He was against the *jāgīr* system and ruthlessly confiscated the land given to people under earlier regimes. He tried to abolish the numerous middlemen who had come between the cultivators and the government. He believed in making appointments on the basis of merit, which was a remarkable innovation. In the sphere of military administration, Śivajī's main emphasis was on the building of forts. He was a strict disciplinarian, severe punishment being inflicted on any soldier who violated the canons of discipline laid down by him. Unlike the Mughal armies, Śivajī's armies were extremely austere. His camp was generally without pomp, without women, and without baggage. His effort to raise a strong and independent navy of his own was but one example of his grasp of the contemporary situation.

It was the torch of revolt lighted by Śivajī that finally engulfed the entire country and consumed the mighty Mughal Empire, rendering completely ineffective all the efforts Aurangzeb made to save it.

Śivajī was succeeded by his son Sambhāji. It was at this time that one of Aurangzeb's sons, Prince Akbar, deputed to deal with the Rājputs (a group occupying a large area in the northeast), revolted against the Mughal emperor and took shelter with Sambhāji. An alliance between the Rājputs and Marāthās would have been very dangerous to the Mughal Empire, and Aurangzeb was quick to suppress the revolt of the Rājputs and march into the Deccan to take charge of the anti-Marāthā campaigns. Both Bijāpur and Golconda being in an advanced stage of dissolution, the powerful Mughal armies conquered them in quick succession, in September 1686 and October 1687, respectively. The Mughals then concentrated their strength against Sambhāji, who was captured by Aurangzeb's forces and made to walk for miles dressed as a buffoon, with thousands of spectators lining the public roads. But he refused to yield before Aurangzeb, even under torture. His body was hacked to pieces along with those of a number of followers, and their heads, stuffed with straw, were exhibited in the chief towns of the Deccan to the accompaniment of drum and trumpet.

Sambhāji's capture by the Mughals

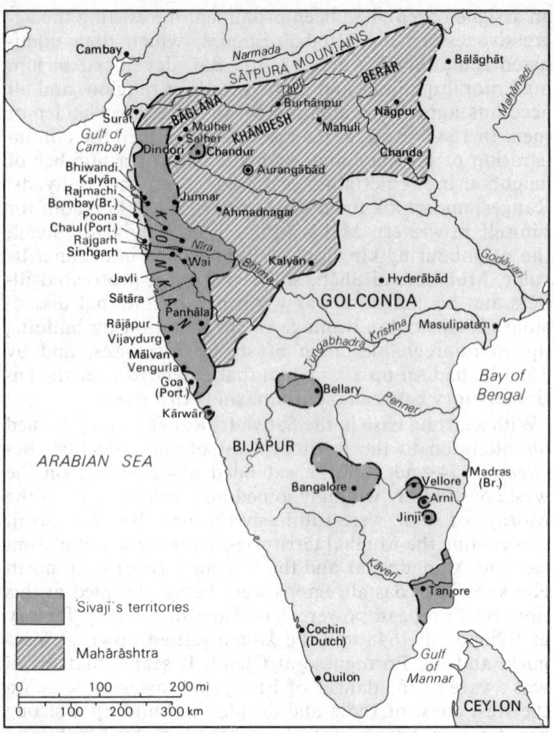

The Marāthā kingdom at the death of Śivajī (1680).
Adapted from C.C. Davies, *An Historical Atlas of the Indian Peninsula* (1959); Oxford University Press

The Marāthā war of independence. For Aurangzeb, however, it proved to be a pyrrhic victory. The atrocities he had committed in the south aroused the Marāthā nation as nothing had done before. Rāja Rām, Sambhāji's younger brother, was quickly proclaimed *chhatrapati* (the Marāthā royal title). The Mughal forces continued to advance. A group of new Marāthā leaders took direction of civil and military affairs in an attempt to save the situation. Guerrilla warfare was employed and rendered the Mughal conquests useless. In the meantime, Rāja Rām was moved for security to the town of Jinjī in the far south, which resisted a Mughal siege for eight years. On Rāja Rām's death in March 1700, his widow, Tārā Bāī, took up the leadership of the entire movement. In the meantime, Shāhū, the eldest son of Sambhāji, and his talented mother, Yesubai, had been captured by Aurangzeb and were moving with his armies from place to place.

The Deccan wars proved to be the undoing of Aurangzeb. Lasting for over 20 years, they were immensely costly, and officers who had marched with the Emperor in their youth to the south became old and worn out with no victory in sight. Aurangzeb's death on February 20, 1707, marked the end of the effort. While the Mughal Empire stood on the verge of collapse, the Marāthās were filled with new hope and vigour.

Bālājī Visvanāth as peshwa. On Aurangzeb's death, Shāhū was able to escape from the Mughal camp and was crowned as *chhatrapati* by the Marāthās. His succession was challenged by Rāja Rām's widow, Tārā Bāī, and he had to spend his energies in internecine quarrels for many years. But he was fortunate in having as his main supporter Bālājī Visvanāth, a Brahmin, who was first appointed as *senakarte* and rose to be the peshwa (prime minister). It was with the help of Bālājī that Shāhū was able to secure the support of Kānhoji Angria, a rebel head of the Marāthā navy. While Angria dealt with the Siddis and later with the Portuguese and the English, the Marāthā armies, taking advantage of the weakness of the Mughal Empire, made inroads into the Mughal-held territories of Mālwa, Gujarāt, Bāglāna, and Khāndesh, but they were repulsed by Sayyid Ḥusayn ʿAlī, the Mughal governor of Deccan, and all the efforts of Shāhū and his talented peshwa to bring order to the chaotic conditions in the Marāthā state met with frustration.

Guided by Shankraji Malhar, a shrewd Maharashtrian

diplomat, Ḥusayn ʿAlī established contacts with Shāhū and signed an agreement with him, under which: (1) Shāhū was recognized as the lawful ruler of territories and forts that had at one time belonged to Śivajī; (2) the Marāthās were confirmed in their legal possession of territories recently conquered by them in Khāndesh, Berār, Gondwana, Karnatak, and other places; and (3) they were allowed to collect certain taxes from all the six Mughal *ṣūbas* (districts) in the south, in return for which they were to serve the Mughal emperor with a contingent of 16,000 troops and pay him an annual tribute. Then, as has been described above, a Marāthā army was quickly collected under Khande Rāo Dābhāde and marched with Ḥusayn ʿAlī to Delhi. With the balance of power in their favour, the Sayyid brothers replaced Farrukh-siyar with their protégé, Muḥammad Shāh (1719).

Intervention in Mughal affairs

Bālājī returned in triumph to Sātāra, where he died shortly thereafter. He was a capable administrator, as is testified by the new methods of revenue collection, based on *sardeshmukhī* and *chauth*, which he set up for the Marāthā state. The *sardeshmukhī* gave its holder (*jāgīrdār*) a right to 10 percent of the taxes collected in his region. The *chauth* was collected from semiconquered territories, where the Marāthās kept the peace but took no responsibility for internal welfare and administration. Marāthā leaders could make inroads into distant territories and, if they succeeded in establishing control as *jāgīrdār*, could treat those territories as their *vaṭans* (domains), to which they could make hereditary claims. Each owed allegiance to Shāhū, who, in turn, owed allegiance to the Mughal emperor. The question of allegiance, however, was academic. The Marāthā Empire was highly decentralized, and each *jāgīrdār* claimed virtual ownership of the territory he controlled.

Bājī Rāo and the expansion of Marāthā power. Bālājī Visvanāth was succeeded as peshwa by his son, Bājī Rāo, who, both as a commander and as a diplomat, far outstripped his father. His immediate concern was with the Niẓām ul-Mulk, the Mughal viceroy in the Deccan, who was in revolt against Muḥammad Shāh. In 1720 the Niẓām had wrested Asīrgarh and Burhānpur from the Mughals and defeated powerful Mughal armies in the battles of Khandwa and Bālāpur. Evading a direct confrontation with the Niẓām, Bājī Rāo decided to turn his attention to Karnatak in the far south and Mālwa and Gujarāt to the north of the Niẓām's territories. Bājī Rāo personally led two successful expeditions in Karnatak in 1725 and 1726, and re-established Marāthā rule there. Taking advantage of the absence of the Marāthā forces, however, the Niẓām had moved his armies in the direction of Junnar and Poona. Bājī Rāo adopted diversionary tactics and, quickly moving from Karnatak, threatened the base of the Niẓām's power in Burhānpur. The Niẓām's forces, quickly retracing their steps, were caught unawares at Pālkhed, 20 miles (32 kilometres) west of Aurangābād, where they found it impossible to extricate themselves. On March 6, 1728, the Niẓām was forced to enter into an agreement with the Marāthās, under which he ratified the Marāthā claims accepted earlier by the Sayyid brothers, agreed to pay up the arrears of *chauth* and *sardeshmukhī*, and recognized Shāhū as the legitimate ruler over the Marāthā dominions.

Expeditions to Karnatak

Following his victory against the Niẓām, Bājī Rāo turned his attention to Mālwa, Bundelkhand, and Gujarāt. His brother, Chimnaji, defeated a Mughal army led personally by the governor of Mālwa at Amjhera near Dhār on November 29, 1728. He then moved into Gujarāt. Bājī Rāo, had, in the meantime, moved on to the support of Chhatrasāl Bundela, then fighting against Muḥammād Khān Bangash, governor of Allahābād, and inflicted severe defeats on Qayām Khān, son of Muḥammad Khān Bangash, and then on Bangash himself.

The rapid successes won by the Marāthās in the heart of the Mughal Empire presented a serious problem to the rulers at Delhi. The Emperor now appointed Muḥammad Khān Bangash as the governor of Mālwa. He defeated a Marāthā force near Ujjain but was soon defeated by another Marāthā army, the Marāthās continuing their advance toward Delhi.

Determined to show the Mughal emperor "flames and the Marāthās at the gates of the capital," Bājī Rāo reached Delhi in March 1737, throwing the capital and its environs into a state of panic and confusion, but, he retreated when a Mughal army moved out of Delhi to meet him. In sheer desperation, the Mughal emperor once again turned toward the Niẓām for help. The Niẓām attempted a pincer movement against the Marāthās, trying to crush them with a large force under his son, Nāṣīr Jang. This was perhaps the largest army put forth against the Marāthās since the days of Aurangzeb. The Niẓām, however, proved no match for the superior military craftsmanship of Bājī Rāo and was defeated by him near Bhopāl. Mālwa was now formally ceded to the Marāthās under the imperial seal. The Niẓām agreed to withdraw completely from the territory between the Jumna (Yamuna) and Narmada, and a substantial sum of cash was to be paid by him to the Marāthās out of the imperial treasury by way of their expenses.

The Niẓām's defeat

After Nāder Shāh's sack of Delhi in 1739 (see above), Shāhū decided that the most realistic way of extending Marāthā power was to adopt a policy of resuscitating the falling Mughal Empire and controlling its administration, rather than attempting to take up the throne. "If we attempt the other course (of aggression)," he told his advisers,

> it would involve us in enmity with all our neighbours, with the consequence that we should be exposed to unnecessary dangers and court a crowd of troubles all round.

Meanwhile the Marāthās had become engaged in a struggle with the Portuguese on the western coast. The policy of raising a strong line of naval defenses on the west coast in order to protect the base of the Marāthā Empire had been laid down as early as Śivajī. In the meantime, the Portuguese were also busy setting up their fortresses in the region. The effort was resumed by the Marāthās as early as 1719 but was taken up in earnest only in the summer of 1737. In April 1739 the Marāthās attacked Portuguese-held Bassein. Bassein surrendered on May 5, 1739, and a peace was finally concluded with the Portuguese. Then, when Marāthā power was at its zenith, Bājī Rāo died on April 28, 1740, at the age of 40.

Bājī Rāo's death closed one important era in Marāthā history. Next only to Śivajī in military genius, he had transformed the Marāthā state into the major power in India. Under his leadership, the Marāthās, once "a cloud no bigger than man's hand," spread all over India. Bājī Rāo is often criticized for his policy of carrying the Marāthā power to Delhi at the cost of its consolidation in Mahārāshtra itself, where it was faced by powerful challenges—from the Niẓām-ul-Mulk in the east and the Portuguese on the west. "Strike, strike at the root, and the branches will fall of themselves," he is supposed to have said. Shāhū, who would have preferred to respect Mughal authority and wished to concentrate on strengthening Marāthā power in the south, was unwilling or unable to control his peshwa. Bājī Rāo's eye was certainly fixed on the revenues of Mālwa and Gujarāt, with the help of which he hoped to bring about a consolidation of the Marāthā kingdom in the south. But, while struggling for the establishment of the Marāthā domination over Mālwa and Gujarāt, Bājī Rāo constantly kept before him the broader political objective of establishing Marāthā hegemony over the Deccan. This is borne out by the texts of several agreements he made with the Niẓām, in each one of which Marāthā claims for *chauth* and *sardeshmukhī* over the Deccan are reiterated, and by several of his transactions with the Mughal emperor, in which he demanded the right of consultation in the appointment of a governor for Deccan.

Assessment of Bājī Rāo

THE MARATHA CONFEDERACY

Bājī Rāo I was succeeded as peshwa by his son Bālājī Rāo, then only 19. His period as peshwa, 1740–61, was marked by the inability of the Marāthā government to control its own chieftains.

The Marāthās, engrossed as they were in distant campaigns, did not seem to realize that Nāder Shāh's invasion of 1739 had opened a window in the northwest of India, through which his successors were keeping a constant watch on the affairs at Delhi. Aḥmad Shāh Abdālī, who succeeded Nāder Shāh in 1747, maintained close relations with the Ruhēlas and the Bangashes, the chief enemies of the Delhi Empire. Ṣafdar Jang, the *wazir* (chief minister), with the approval of the Emperor, sought Marāthā help, while the Pathans turned to Abdālī. The Marāthās under Malhār Rāo Holkar and Jayappa Sindhia, assisted by the Jāṭs, inflicted severe defeats on the Pathans and received from the Emperor half of Rohilkhand as their prize—their first territorial conquest beyond the Jumna. The Pathans, in sheer desperation, turned toward Abdālī for help, thus involving the Marāthās in a clash between the two northern empires.

Conflict with Aḥmad Shāh Abdālī

The Marāthās might still have kept out of it if they had not, in their search for glory, decided to follow Abdālī after he was returning from the sack of Delhi in 1757. Defeating Najīb Khān at Āgra and securing the whole of the Doab, the Marāthā armies marched in the direction of Lahore. In March 1758 they defeated the Governor of Sirhind, and by April 9 they had expelled Abdālī's agents from Lahore. Tukōjī Holkar and Sabaji Sindhia subjugated the whole of Punjab and planted the Marāthā banner on the fort of Attock. They claimed with pride that they had brought the whole of India, from Attock to Cuttack and from Kashmir to Kanyā Kumārī (Cape Comorin) under their control, little realizing how faulty this control was. In 1759, Abdālī, shocked by the Marāthā aggressiveness, returned to India. By October he had taken possession of Lahore and was moving in the direction of Delhi.

Aroused to a supreme effort, the peshwa then dispatched Sadāshiv Rāo with an army against Abdālī. The subsequent campaign and Sadāshiv Rāo's defeat at Pānīpat in January 1761 has been described above. Bālājī Rāo died a few months later.

Challenge and survival. Marāthā power in the north soon revived under Mādhav Rāo I (1761–72). By April 1770, two able commanders, Ramchandra Ganesh and Visaji Krishna had not only captured Āgra and Mathurā but had entered the territory of Aḥmad Khān Bangash and, crushing the joint opposition of Bangash and the Ruhēlas, were able to re-establish the Marāthā position in Rohilkhand. On February 10, 1771, Delhi was taken and Jawan Bakht, the son of Shāh ʿAlām II, was placed on the Mughal throne as a Marāthā client.

But the Marāthās now had a new rival in the British, who had made excellent use of the Marāthā absence from northern India to establish their own power there. At Baksar (Buxar) in October 1764 they defeated the combined armies of the Emperor, the Wazir, and the Ṣūbedār. In 1765, they acquired supreme power from Calcutta to the Doab.

The First Marāthā War

By 1772 the English had fully exploited the weaknesses of the local governments in Bengal and Karnatak by consolidating their power in these regions, and were ready to move against the Marāthās, who were distracted by internal disputes following Mādhav Rāo's death. Capturing Broach in 1772 and Salsette a little later, the British obtained a number of commercial, military, and political advantages on the Bombay coast. They also secured a strong position for themselves in Gujarāt in 1775, but then withdrew under instructions from British East India Company headquarters at Calcutta.

The war was soon resumed, this time by the Calcutta government itself. Using the visit of a French agent at Poona to raise the bogey of a Marāthā alliance with European powers, Warren Hastings, the governor general, made new demands upon the Poona government and, on the latter's failure to implement them, started an offensive against them simultaneously on the diplomatic and military fronts. Madhya Pradesh, Gujarāt, and Konkan were selected for large-scale military operations, but each was tied up with a diplomatic objective. Col. Thomas Goddard, the commander of the British armies marching through Bundelkhand, made an effort to detach Bhonsle, one of the Marāthā leaders, from his allegiance to the Poona government. The effort failed, which put Goddard's expedition into a difficult situation. Another British army ascended the Western Ghāts from the side of Bombay and clashed with the Marāthās at Wadgaon. Here also they were more interested in pushing diplomatic thrusts than in pressing military victories. Their plan of campaign in Konkan and Gujarāt was directed at bringing pressure upon Mahādāji Sindhia.

The anti-British coalition

The British aggression against the Marāthās was met by a spirit of resistance all over the country; and by 1780 Nāna Fadnavis, representing the central government, was able to organize an alliance against the British, consisting of the Marāthā confederacy, the Niẓām, and Hyder (Haidar) Ali. The Niẓām, by constantly writing to Nāna at Poona and Diwakar Pandit at Nāgpur, had played a leading role in setting it up, whereas Nāna Fadnavis was responsible for bringing in Mahādāji Sindhia, Tukōjī Holkar, and other Marāthā leaders. Even those who stood outside the alliance, such as the Nawab Wazīr of Oudh and the Nawab of Bengal, gave it their silent approbation. The Siddis of Janjira, the traditional enemies of the Marāthās, joined the combination by a separate agreement. The Portuguese, the French, and the Dutch were sympathetic. A detailed plan of war was drawn up by the allies: the Bhonsle was to attack the English in the north, Hyder Ali was to bring them under control on the Madras coast, the Poona forces were to oppose them in Gujarāt and Konkan, and the Niẓām was to attack them on the east coast.

The weakness of the alliance—at both the diplomatic and the military levels—soon became clear. The British could bribe Khandoji Bhonsle and induce him to permit a free passage to British armies marching under Gen. Eyre Coote through Orissa in the direction of Madras. The Niẓām not only did not send his armies in the direction of Orissa, as he had agreed to do, but kept himself busy in exploiting the opportunity opened to him by the great military pressure that the Marāthā armies were exerting in Gujarāt. Besides the political weaknesses of the alliance, it suffered from severe military limitations. Its members, with the solitary exception of Hyder Ali, were incapable of taking any military offensive against the English.

It was Hyder Ali, with his Europeanized armies, who was able to inflict some serious reverses on the English in Karnatak. Reaching Madras, Eyre Coote found the British there ill prepared either to repel or resist Hyder Ali's armies. Coote wanted the Bombay government to send some military help to Madras, which it was impossible for them to do, since the military pressure on the Bombay side also was growing. This induced the British to greater diplomatic efforts. On September 10, 1780, a second treaty was signed between the British and Fateh Singh of Gujarāt, under which Fateh Singh agreed to give them military support. Bhonsle then agreed (April 6, 1781) to support the British in their war against Hyder Ali. The growing strength of Hyder Ali's offensive on the Coromandel and the Malabar coasts compelled the British first to reduce their pressure on Mālwa and the Western Ghāts and, later, to withdraw themselves from these regions. It was, however, the difficult military situation on the west coast that forced them to open negotiations with the Marāthās. On May 17, 1782, a treaty was signed between the British and the Marāthās at Salbai. With the solitary exception of Salsette and its adjacent islands, the British were forced to restore every inch of territory they had acquired during the course of a long and nerve-racking war. The weaknesses of the Marāthā state, however, had been exposed, and the British could hope to break up the entire political system in stages.

The Treaty of Salbai

During the period of the first Marāthā War, the imperial forces at Delhi were being looked after by Mīrzā Najaf Khān. On Najaf Khān's death in April 1782, the Emperor decided to invite the Marāthā leader Mahādāji Sindhia to Delhi. Over British opposition, Mahādāji was appointed the *vakīl-e muṭlaq*, the highest executive office in the empire. Mahādāji's task in Delhi was not easy. He had to deal with recalcitrant Mughal chiefs and rebellious Rājput leaders. He sustained a major military defeat at

Lalsot in 1787 at the hands of the Rājputs, who had been joined by Hamdani and his Mughal troops. In this difficult situation, Mahādāji frantically sought help from Poona, but received little. Tukōjī Holkar and ʿAlī Bahādur, who were sent with Marāthā armies to the north, proved obstacles to his plans rather than a help. Nevertheless, while the British were repairing their losses and consolidating their gains in the war with the Marāthās, Mahādāji was able to strengthen his position at Delhi.

Visiting Poona in 1792, he found the atmosphere full of mistrust and suspicion. He succeeded in gaining the confidence and respect of the young Peshwa, but his sudden death on February 12, 1794, at the age of 67, threw all his schemes out of shape. A victory that the Marāthā armies won against the Nizām at the Battle of Kharda in March 1795 could be described only as "the vanishing flicker of the Marāthā glory."

The Battle of Kharda

Decline of Marāthā power. Following the death of Mahādāji Sindhia, the decline of the Marāthā Empire became rapid. Six months after the victory over the Nizām at Kharda, Peshwa Madhāv Rāo died under tragic circumstances, by accident or suicide. The succession devolved upon Bājī Rāo II, a thoroughly incompetent and unscrupulous man but the only legitimate claimant in the peshwa family. Nāna Fadnavis opposed him with all his strength but was finally made to yield under the pressure of Daulat Rāo Sindhia, who was now the most powerful chieftain. The state of uncertainty at Poona and differences among its leaders gave the British governor general, Lord Wellesley, a chance to intervene. He brought increasing pressure on Bājī Rāo to accept an alliance with the British. Nāna was inclined to conciliation, but Bājī Rāo attempted to organize an anti-British confederacy. After Nāna Fadnavis died in 1800, all restraints upon Bājī Rāo were removed. He instituted a reign of terror in Poona; people suspected of the slightest treachery were ruthlessly selected and brutally killed.

In 1795, a war of succession had started in the Holkar state. Daulat Rāo supported Kāsī Rāo. Encouraged by Nāna, Kāsī's three brothers challenged his claims to the throne. Malhār Rāo being killed in a fracas, Jaswant Rāo collected a roving band of adventurers around him and pursued his family's wars against Sindhia and tried to force the Peshwa to side with him.

Bājī Rāo, fleeing from Jaswant Rāo in 1802, went to Wadgaon, then to Sinhagadh, and ultimately into the arms of the British. Boarding a British ship at Suvarnadurg, he reached Bassein on December 16. On December 31, 1802, he signed a treaty with the British at Bassein, which was to prove the death warrant of the Marāthā Empire. Under the Treaty of Bassein, (1) the friends and enemies of one were to be treated as friends and enemies of the other, (2) the British were to protect Bājī Rāo's territory as their own, and (3) a subsidiary force of 6,000 regular infantry, with field artillery, was to be permanently maintained by the British at Poona.

The Second Marāthā War

The British were determined to place Bājī Rāo back in power, under their own tutelage, at Poona. On August 7, 1803, Sir Arthur Wellesley opened war upon Sindhia and Bhonsle by an attack on Ahmadnagar. This was followed by the Battle of Assaye, which proved to be a stiff one, the victory costing a great deal to the British. It was followed by the capture of Burhanpur, Asirgadh, and Gāwīlgarh. Earlier, on September 14, the British, under General Burkin, had already defeated another army of Sindhia and, entering Delhi, had taken the Emperor under their protection. The fighting against Sindhia and Bhonsle soon spread to Gujarāt, where the British captured Baroda, Broach and Champaner, and to Orissa, where they captured Jagannāth and Cuttack. Bhonsle and Sindhia were forced to sign separate treaties with the British—Bhonsle on December 17, 1803, under which he ceded to the British the province of Cuttack with all its forts, and to the Nizām, western Berār up to the Wardha river; and Sindhia on December 30, 1803, by which he ceded to the British the Doab region, parts of Bundelkhand, Broach, and some districts of Gujarāt, the fort of Ahmadnagar, and the Ajantā region up to the Godāvari. He was also asked to renounce his control over the Emperor, relinquish all his claims over the Peshwa, the Nizām, and the Gaekwar, and to recognize the independence of all those feudatories who had made separate engagements with the British.

The British preoccupation with Bhonsle and Sindhia gave Jaswant Rāo Holkar an opportunity to intensify his military raids. Forcing Bhonsle and Sindhia to sign peace treaties, the British turned toward Holkar and warned him of the consequences of his actions. Holkar, it seems, was living in a world of illusions. He did not seem to understand the change that had taken place in Indian politics. With the Peshwa under their control, with the Nizām, Sindhia, Bhonsle, and Gaekwar reduced to the position of subordinate allies, and with complete control over Bengal, Oudh, and Karnatak, the British had become the paramount power in India, whereas all the Indian powers were divided against each other. In 1804, it was sheer foolhardiness for any Indian chieftain to think of resisting them. With the help of his vast, disorganized, and disparate armies, Holkar could elude the British for some time. Plundering Pushkar and Jaipur, he quickly moved on to Mandsaur. He defeated a British force at Banās, sending it into retreat to Āgra. Emboldened by his successes, he captured Mathurā and fell upon Delhi. Encountering stiff resistance there, he moved into the Doab, ruthlessly devastating the British territories. Defeated at Farrukhābād, November 17, 1804, he retreated to Dīg, where he was supported by the Jāṭ Raja of Bharatpur. On December 13, Dīg was captured, but the mud walls of Bharatpur successfully resisted several stormy attacks of the British armies and repulsed them with heavy losses. In the meantime, Sindhia, regaining his confidence, had repudiated the treaties he had signed with the British less than a year earlier and marched against the latter with a large army and 180 pieces of heavy artillery. His army soon joined the 60,000 soldiers under Holkar, and a number of leading Marāthā *sirdār*s collected at Sabalgarh to think out ways and means of driving the British out of the country. Wellesley's rough-and-ready methods had brought about a severe reaction, and the decision makers in London were forced to think of alternative policies.

Appointment of Cornwallis

Realizing that their aggressive policies had created a difficult situation for them in India, the British government quickly changed tactics and slowed down their program of expansion. They now sent Lord Cornwallis once again to India and asked him to restore Indian politics to the point at which he had left them. Cornwallis started with pacifying Sindhia and signing a treaty with him under which the British gave up their recent alliances with the Rājput princes of Udaipur, Jodhpur, Kota, and others in Mālwa and Mewāt and undertook to enter into no engagement with Sindhia's tributaries, nor to interfere with Sindhia's conquests from Holkar between the Tāpti and Chambal. Holkar kept up the fight against the British. Deserted by Sindhia, he proceeded to Ajmer and requested the Raja of Jodhpur to join him. Frustrated there, he moved toward Patiāla, hoping to receive the support of the Sikhs and Afghans. Both Ranjit Singh and the Shah of Afghanistan gave him some encouragement, but, when Holkar found Ranjit Singh secretly entering into a pact with the British, he was left with no alternative but to sign a treaty with them. Completely in control of the situation in India, the British could afford to be liberal and, in return for his surrendering all claims to his territories north and west of Chambal, they guaranteed to him the territories to the south and east of it. All his ambitions of defeating the British having been frustrated, Holkar settled down at Indore, brooding deeply over the national disaster. For some years his sole hobby was to work day and night in a gun factory he had set up at Bhānpura. In October 1808, he went completely mad, and three years later he died, at the age of 30, after a short career of nine years, packed with heroic deeds and terrible disasters. He was succeeded by Malhār Rāo Holkar, a boy of ten years, and his wife Tulsi Bāī carried on the administration.

End of the empire. Lord Wellesley was able to establish the British paramountcy in India, but it was at a terrible cost. He had captured power all over India but had refused to take up responsibility. Bājī Rāo, Daulat Rāo, the Niẓām, and the Nawab Wazīr of Oudh were all like gilded puppets, dancing to the tune of the British but incapable and unwilling to exercise any control over administration. These puppet rulers were provided with British subsidiary forces for their protection, but their own armies, now disbanded and converted into roving Pindari bands, wandered aimlessly through the length and breadth of the country, plundering and destroying whatever came their way. The whole country was thrown into chaos. Within five miles of Poona neither life nor property was safe. The wave of anarchy gradually began to spread to the areas under the direct control of the British and forced them to find a solution.

It was specifically with the object of bringing peace to a country in the worst throes of lawlessness and disorder that Lord Hastings was appointed governor general of India in 1813. On the death of Raghuji Bhonsle in March 1816, he forced his successor, Mudaji Appa Sahib, to sign a subsidiary treaty. In June 1817 Bājī Rāo was asked to sign another treaty with the British by which he surrendered to them whatever phantom of overlordship over Indian chiefs he still possessed. He was forced to give up all his territory outside Mahārāshtra, withdraw all his *vakīls* from foreign courts, and agree not to maintain any correspondence or communication with them. This amounted to a public declaration of the dissolution of the Marāthā confederacy. Bājī Rāo agreed outwardly but, smouldering with anger and frustration within, started inducing other Marāthā chiefs to rise against the British. In September 1817, while Bājī Rāo attacked the Poona residency, Appa Sahib attacked the residency at Nāgpur. Both were foolhardy attempts and ended in failure. Bājī Rāo escaped from Poona and moved toward Nagpur, with a view to joining Appa Sahib, but, learning that he was being carried as a prisoner to Allāhābād, entered the forests of Gondwana and remained in hiding there for two years, supported by the disbanded armies of Poona and Nāgpur along with a number of Pindaris.

The Third Marāthā War

Hastings had, in the meantime, entered into separate treaties with Kota, Būndi, Bharatpur, Udaipur, Jodhpur, Jaipur, and other protégés of Sindhia. Isolated from his supporters and surrounded by the British armies, Sindhia was forced to sign a treaty on November 5, 1817. Thereafter, the British armies moved through the length and breadth of central India, suppressing the Pindaris with a heavy hand. Forcing Amīr Khān, one of the Pindari leaders in collusion with Holkar, to surrender, and conferring upon him the rulership of Tonk, the British attacked Holkar's armies. Malhār Rāo, a boy of 16, and his sister, Bhima Bāī, a widow of 20, rode through the ranks imploring their men not to surrender. But it was an unequal fight, and Holkar was forced to sign the Treaty of Mandsaur on January 6, 1818, under which he ceded to the British territory north of Būndi and south of Sātpura and agreed to maintain a subsidiary force and disband his armies. Bājī Rāo maintained a solitary resistance for some more time, frantically appealing to all and sundry, including the ruler of Burma, for help against the British. Pursued by British troops, he moved from pillar to post between November 1817 and May 1818 and finally surrendered, shamelessly begging for liberal terms. Offered a safe asylum and a liberal pension, he decided, finally, to settle down at Bithur near Kānpur, symbolizing in his misery the end of the Marāthā Empire. (S.P.V.)

VI. India and European expansion, c. 1500–1858

EUROPEAN ACTIVITY IN INDIA, 1498–C. 1760

Earlier links between Europe and India

When the Portuguese navigator Vasco da Gama landed at Calicut in 1498, he was restoring a link between Europe and the East that had existed many centuries previously. The first known connection between the two regions had been Alexander the Great's invasion of the Punjab, 327–325 BC. In the 2nd century BC Greek adventurers from Bactria had founded kingdoms in the Punjab and the bordering Afghan hills; these survived into the late 1st century. This territorial contact in the north was succeeded by a lengthy commercial intercourse in the south, which continued until the decline of the Roman Empire in the 4th century AD. Trade with the East then passed into Arab hands, and it was mainly concerned with the Middle Eastern Islāmic and Greek worlds until the end of the Middle Ages. The only physical contact came from occasional travellers, such as the Italians Marco Polo and Niccolò dei Conti, and the Russian Sergey Nikitin in the 15th century; and these were few because of commotions within the tolerant Arab-Islāmic world created by successive incursions of Turks and Mongols. For Europe in 1498, therefore, India was a land of spices and of marvels handed down from imaginative Greek authors. For Muslims, Europe was the land of Rūm, or the Greek empire of Constantinople (just become Turkish); and for Hindus, it was the abode of the foreigners called Yavanas, a corruption of the Greek word Ionian.

Renewed contact with Europe

The Portuguese. The Portuguese were the first agents of this renewed contact because they were among the few European nations to possess both the navigational know-how and the necessary motivation for the long sea voyage. During the 15th century the land routes for the Indian trade—via the Red Sea and Egypt or across Persia, Iraq, Syria, and Turkey—had become increasingly blocked, mainly by Turkish action. The surviving Egyptian route was subject to increasing exploitation by a line of middlemen, ending with the Venetian monopoly of the European trade. The motive for finding a new route was therefore strong; this task fell to the Portuguese, partly because the stronger Spaniards were absorbed in discovering the New World (a by-product of the same search for an Eastern route). The Portuguese further inherited crusading zeal from wars against the Moors in Portugal and North Africa. Finally, they had learned navigational techniques from the Genoese, who were disgruntled at their exclusion from the Mediterranean carrying trade.

When Vasco da Gama arrived in Calicut, he hoped to find Christians cut off by Muslim action, to deal a blow at Muslim power from their maritime rear, as it were, and to corner the European spice trade. He found his Christians in the Syrian Christians of Cochin and Travancore, he found the spices, and he found Muslim Arab merchants entrenched at Calicut. It was his successors, Francisco de Almeida and Afonso de Albuquerque, who established the Portuguese Empire in the East. Almeida set up a number of fortified posts; but it was Albuquerque (governor 1509–15) who gave the empire its characteristic form. He took Goa in western India in 1510, Malacca in the East Indies in 1511, and Hormuz (Ormuz) in the Persian Gulf in 1515, and he set up posts in the East Indian Spice Islands. The object of these moves was to establish for Portugal a strategic command of the Indian Ocean, so as to control the maritime spice trade and to ruin the Middle Eastern Muslim world by cutting off its trade. Hormuz dominated the Persian Gulf; an attack on Aden was intended to do the same for the Red Sea. While Malacca was the nerve centre for the spice-producing islands of Indonesia and the exchange mart for the trade with the Far East, Goa, not Malacca, was the capital because of Portuguese concern with the Muslims of the Middle East.

The Portuguese reliance on sea power

The Portuguese method was to rely on sea power based on fortified posts and backed by settlements. Portuguese ships, sturdy enough to survive Atlantic gales and mounted with cannon, could easily dispose of Arab and Malay shipping. The bases enabled the Portuguese to dominate the main sea-lanes; but Portugal, with less than 1,000,000 people and involved in Africa and South America as well, was desperately short of manpower. Albuquerque turned his fortresses into settlements to provide a resident population for defense. Intermarriage was encouraged. At the same time, Christianity was encouraged through the church. Goa became an archbishopric. St. Francis Xavier started from Goa on his mission to the south Indian fishermen. The Inquisition was established in 1560. The new mixed population thus became firmly Catholic and provided a stubborn resistance to attacks.

A lack of resources precluded any attempt to establish a land empire. Portugal's control of the Indian Ocean—its period of empire—lasted through the 16th century. During this time it attained great prosperity. Goa acquired the title of Golden, and it became one of the world's wonder cities. Trade with Europe was a royal monopoly, and, in addition, a system of licenses for all inter-Asian trade enriched the royal exchequer. Inter-Asian trade was free to individual Portuguese; and it was the profits of this, combined with trimmings from the royal monopoly, that gave them their affluence.

The three marks of the Portuguese Empire continued to be trade, anti-Islāmism, and religion. The Portuguese early considered that no faith need be kept with an infidel, and to this policy of perfidy they added a tendency to cruelty beyond the normal limits of a very rough age; the result was to deprive them of Indian sympathy. In religion the Portuguese were distinguished by missionary fervour and intolerance. Examples of the former are the Madura mission of Roberto de Nobili (1577–1656), nicknamed the White Brahmin, and the Jesuit missions to the court of the Mughal emperor Akbar (ruled 1556–1605). Of the latter, there was the Inquisition at Goa and the forcible subjection of the Syrian church to Rome at the Synod of Diamper in 1599.

The Portuguese thus had few friends in the East to help them in a crisis, and in 1580 the Portuguese kingdom was annexed to Spain; thenceforth until 1640 Portuguese interests were sacrificed to those of Spain. Because of the Spanish failure to quell a Dutch rising in The Netherlands, and after the defeat of the Spanish Armada in 1588, the route to the East was opened to both English and Dutch. The Dutch arrived first; under their blows in Indonesia and those of the English in India the Portuguese ascendancy crumbled, though they retained Goa until 1961.

This first modern impact on India has left distinct though not extensive traces. The first is the mixed population of Luso-Indians, or Goanese, along the western coast of India and in Ceylon and with them, a lingua franca in the ports and markets. Then came Roman Catholicism, which today has perhaps 5,000,000 followers and an array of churches, convents, and colleges all over India. A by-product has been a tradition of intolerance, which still lingers. More tangible traces include imported articles such as tobacco, potatoes, pineapples, tomatoes, papaya, cashew nuts, and two varieties of chilies, which have become part of the Indian scene.

The Dutch. In the race to the East after the Spanish obstacle had been removed, the Dutch, having larger resources, were the first to arrive. Their first voyage was in 1595, helped by the local knowledge of Jan Huyghen van Linschoten, who had worked for six years in Goa. J. Van Neck's voyage in 1598 was so profitable (400 percent for all eight ships) that the die was cast for a great Eastern adventure. The Dutch objective was neither religion nor empire, but trade; and the trade in mind was the spice trade. They were monopolists rather than imperialists. Empire came later, as a safeguard for monopoly.

Dutch objectives in India

The Dutch, therefore, went directly to the East Indies (Indonesia), the main source of spices, and only secondarily to south India, for pepper and cardamons, and to Ceylon for these and cinnamon. From 1619 their headquarters were fixed at Batavia (now Djakarta) in Java, from which they developed a series of outlying stations in the East Indian islands (*e.g.*, Celebes and the Moluccas) and intermediate ones like Cape Town in South Africa, and Ceylon for supply. This was the work of the governor general J.P. Coen (served 1618–23; 1627–29), and the whole system may be said to have been completed under the governor general J. Maetsuyker (served 1653–78). Monopoly was the keynote of 17th century Dutch activity in the East; empire followed in the 18th.

The Dutch system demanded the control of the Eastern seas, and this meant the elimination of European rivals. Those in possession were the Portuguese. The Dutch succeeded with superior resources and better seamanship, but the Portuguese, though defeated, were not destroyed. Ousted from most strongholds, the Portuguese retained their capital, Goa, in spite of blockades and sieges. The second European obstacle was the English, who followed the Dutch to the East Indies; no match for the Dutch in resources, they were virtually excluded from the East Indies with the Dutch seizure of their factory at Amboina (modern Ambon) in 1623 (see below *The British, 1600–1740*).

It remained for the Dutch to organize their trade, which was operated through the Dutch East India Company, a complicated organization dominated by the maritime state of Zealand. Much larger than the English company, it had the character of a national concern. Dutch sea power, more efficient than that of the Portuguese, secured monopoly conditions in the islands and sea-lanes. It was only in land areas like Travancore that resort had to be made to competition. But there remained the problem of exchange, for the Dutch, like the English, were short of exchange goods. Textiles were needed to buy spices in Indonesia; and silver, to buy textiles (cotton or silk) in India and China. To work the spice monopoly the Dutch developed an elaborate system of Eastern trade from the Persian Gulf to Japan, the ultimate object of which was to secure the goods with which to secure the spices without recourse to scarce European resources. It was this trade that brought the Dutch to India at Surat, the Coromandel coast (Negapatam), Bengal, and up-country at Āgra.

The British, 1600–1740. The English venture to India was entrusted to the East India Company, which received its monopoly rights of trade in 1600. The company included a group of London merchants attracted by Eastern prospects, not comparable to the national character of the Dutch company. Its initial capital of £50,000 was less than one-tenth of the Dutch company's. Its object, like that of the Dutch, was to trade in spices; and it was at first modestly organized on a single-voyage basis. These separate voyages, financed by groups of merchants within the company, were replaced in 1612 by terminable joint stocks, which covered operations over a term of years. Not until 1657 was a permanent joint stock established.

Formation of the English East India Company

The company's objective was the spices of Indonesia, and it went to India only for the secondary purpose of securing cottons for sale to the spice growers. The Indonesian venture met with determined Dutch opposition, culminating in the massacre of Amboina in 1623, when the Dutch seized the English factory there and executed its factors. No redress was ever obtained, though the Dutch occupation was not recognized until 1667.

In India the English found the Portuguese enjoying Mughal recognition at the western Indian port of Surat. Portuguese command of the sea nullified the English embassy to the Mughal court in spite of its countenance by the emperor Jahāngīr. The English victory at Swally in 1612 over the Portuguese, whose control of the pilgrim sea route to Mecca was resented by the Mughals, brought a dramatic change. The embassy of Sir Thomas Roe (1615–18) to the Mughal court secured an accord (in the form of a firman, or grant of privileges), by which the English secured the right to trade and to establish factories in return for becoming the virtual naval auxiliaries of the empire. This success, with England's exclusion from Indonesia by the Dutch in the same period, determined that India, not the Far East, should be the chief theatre of English activity in Asia.

There followed through the 17th century a period of peaceful trading through factories operating under Mughal grants. This held good for Surat and later for Hooghly (1641) in Bengal. In the south, the factory at Masulipatam (1611) was moved to the site of Madras, granted by a Hindu raja (1640); it shortly (1647) came under the control of the sultans of Golconda and thence passed to the Mughals in 1687. The only exception to this arrangement was the island port of Bombay; Bombay was independent, but its trade was small because the Marāthās, soon locked in combat with the Mughals, held the hinterland.

The trade the company developed differed radically

The English company's trade

from that of the Dutch. It was a trade in bulk instead of in highly priced luxury goods; the profits were a factor of volume rather than scarcity; it worked in competitive instead of monopolistic conditions; it depended upon political goodwill instead of intimidation. The English trade became more profitable than that of the Dutch because the smaller area covered and the lack of armed forces necessary to enforce monopoly reduced overhead charges. But it encountered its own difficulties. The Indians would take little other than silver in exchange for their goods, and the export of bullion was an offense to England's reigning mercantilist political economy. Lack of military power meant management of Asian governments instead of their coercion. Lack of home dominance meant compromise and hazard of fortune.

To solve the silver problem the English developed a system of country trade not unlike that of the Dutch, the profits of which helped to pay for the annual investment of goods for England. Madras and Gujarāt supplied cotton goods, and Gujarāt supplied indigo as well; silk, sugar, and saltpetre (for gunpowder) came from Bengal, while there was a spice trade along the Malabar coast from 1615 on a competitive basis with the Dutch and Portuguese. Opium was shipped to the Far East, where it later became the basis of the Anglo-Chinese tea trade. The merchants lived in "factories" or in a collegiate type of settlement where life was confined, colourful, and often short.

Difficulties for the company in England

The company had many difficulties in England. There was mercantilist disapproval and mercantile jealousy of monopoly; there was danger from government at a time of political commotion. King Charles I encouraged the rival Courteen Association (1635), and Oliver Cromwell allowed virtual free trade until 1657. Under the later Stuarts the company prospered, only to have its hopes dashed by a war in India and by the Whig revolution of 1688. The Whigs promoted a new company in 1698, which, however, failed to oust the old one after some years of struggle. In 1702 the government insisted on a merger, which was completed in 1708–09 under the name of The United Company of Merchants trading with the East Indies. This was the body that 40 years later launched on the sea of Indian politics.

A way of harassing the company besides attacks on the export of bullion was to limit the sale of cotton goods in England. In 1700 the sale of Asian silks and printed or dyed cottons was forbidden, but trade continued for re-export to the Continent. After 1700 the company found a new profitable line in the China tea trade, whose imports increased (1706–50) from 54,000 to 2,300,000-odd pounds.

In India, the company suffered a serious setback when it resolved, under Sir Josiah Child's inspiration, to resort to armed trade and attack the Mughals. But the emperor Aurangzeb was too strong, and the venture (1686–90) ended in disaster. Out of this fiasco, however, came the foundation of Calcutta by Job Charnock in 1690—a mud flat that had the advantage of a deep anchorage—and the age of fortified factories surrounded by satellite towns. These were the answers, with Mughal consent, to increasing Indian insecurity. The Madras factory was already fortified, and Ft. William in Calcutta followed in 1696. The company thus had, with independent Bombay, three centres of Indian power.

For the next half century the company confined its relations with the Mughals, who had now spread to the deep south beyond Madras, to disputes over rights and terms of trade at local levels. Fresh privileges were obtained in Delhi, and these they were content to argue about rather than fight for. The factors were learning the art of Indian diplomacy as they had formerly to learn the arts of Indian commercial management.

The French. The French had shown an interest in the East from the early years of the 16th century, but individual efforts had been checked by the Portuguese. The first viable French company was launched by the minister of finance Jean-Baptiste Colbert, with the support of Louis XIV, in 1664. After some false starts, the French company acquired Pondicherry, 85 miles (137 kilometres) south of Madras, from a local ruler in 1674. It obtained Chandernagore (Chandernagar), 16 miles (26 kilometres) north of Calcutta, from the Mughal governor in 1690–92. At first the French initiatives suffered from the mixing of grandiose political and colonial schemes with those of trade. Under the care of François Martin, from 1774, the company turned to trade and began to prosper.

French acquisitions

The progress of the settlements was interrupted, however, by events in Europe. The Dutch captured Pondicherry in 1693; when the French regained it under the Peace of Ryswick (1697), they had gained the best fortifications in India but had lost their trade. By 1706 the French enterprise seemed moribund. The company's privileges were let to a group of Saint-Malo merchants from 1708–20.

After 1720, however, came a dramatic change. The company was reconstituted, and over the next 20 years its trade was expanded, and new stations were opened. Mauritius was finally settled in 1721; Mahe in Malabar and Kārikāl on the eastern coast were acquired in 1725 and 1739. Chandernagar was revived. Though a company in form, the French company remained under the close supervision of the government, which nominated the directors and, from 1733, guaranteed fixed dividends.

In spite of the company's growth and its fostering by government, its sales in Europe in 1740 were only about half those of the English East India Company. Its trade was large enough to be worth seizing but not great enough to rival that of the English.

Other enterprises in India included a Danish East India Company, which operated intermittently from 1616 from Tranquebar in south India, acquiring Serāmpore in Bengal in 1755, and the Ostend Company of Austrian Netherlands merchants from 1723, a serious rival until eliminated by diplomatic means in 1731. Efforts by Swedes and Prussians proved abortive.

The Anglo-French struggle, 1740–63. In 1740 India appeared to be relatively tranquil. In the north the Persian Nāder Shāh's invasion (1739) had proved only to be a large-scale raid. In the Deccan, the viceroy, Niẓām-ul-Mulk, provided a centre of stability. In western India a Marāthā peshwa ruled. But in the south there was competition between Marāthās, Mughals, and local rulers. There was a sense of impending change in the air; the Mughal emperor was sickly, the Niẓām was aged, the Marāthās were active and ambitious.

It was on this scene that events in Europe precipitated an Anglo-French struggle in India. The War of the Austrian Succession began with Frederick II the Great of Prussia's seizure of Silesia in 1740; France supported Prussia, and from 1742 England supported Austria. The stage thus set, the English decided that the French Indian trade was too powerful to be left alone; the neutrality of previous years was therefore abandoned. Both sides depended on sea power for success, but it was the French who moved first—with an improvised fleet from Mauritius, Comte Mahé de La Bourdonnais drove the British in alarm to Bengal and captured Madras after a week's siege in September 1746. Quarrels between La Bourdonnais and the Governor of Pondicherry, Joseph-François Dupleix, marred this unexpected success, but an English attack on Pondicherry was repelled. Then the Treaty of Aix-la-Chapelle (1748), which ended the war, returned Madras to the English in exchange for Cape Breton Island in North America.

It would thus appear that the status quo had been restored. But in fact the situation had radically changed. Madras was now recognized as British by European treaty, and this was accepted by one of the rival Indian chiefs. The French had grown in prestige as skillful soldiers and in power by detachments of the French fleet left behind on La Bourdonnais' departure. Above all, the astute Dupleix had seen the opportunity offered for exploiting the new French reputation in the confused politics of the region. For some years there had been a disputed succession to the governorship of the Carnatic (Karnatak), itself a dependency of the Niẓām of Hyderābād. The Niẓām had installed a new Carnatic nawab in

Dispute over the Carnatic succession

1743, but the dispute smouldered on between the partisans of the two rival families, who looked impartially to Marāthās, Mughals, and the Europeans for help.

In 1748, on the morrow of Aix-la-Chapelle, an occasion for French interference occurred with the death of the aged Niẓām. There was a disputed succession between his second son and a grandson, Muẓaffar Jang. Dupleix, encouraged by his easy repulse of the Carnatic nawab from the walls of Madras, decided to support both Muzaffar and the claimant to the Carnatic nawabship, Chanda Sahib. Dupliex's reward for success would be the means of ruining the English trade in south India and an indefinite influence over the affairs of the whole Deccan. At first fortune favoured him. The Carnatic nawab was killed in the Battle of Ambur (1749), which demonstrated convincingly the superiority of European arms and methods of warfare over those of contemporary India. The threatening invasion of the new niẓām, Nāṣir Jang, ended with the Niẓām's murder in December 1750. French troops conducted Muẓaffar Jang toward Hyderābād; and when Muẓaffar in turn was murdered three months later, the French succeeded in placing the late Niẓam's third son, Ṣalābat Jang, on the Hyderābād throne. Thenceforward, in the person of the skillful Marquis de Bussy-Castelnau, Dupleix had a kingmaker at the centre of Muslim power in the Deccan.

The English response to these dramatic successes was to support for the Carnatic nawabship the son of the late nawab, Muḥammad ʿAlī, who had taken refuge in the rock fortress of Trichinopoly (modern Tiruchchirāppalli). They had already interfered in the affairs of Tanjore (modern Thanjāvūr) and were no strangers to Indian politics. The French supported Chanda Sahib for the nawabship. There thus developed what was really a private war between the two companies.

Bussy-Castelnau was established at Hyderābād, with the revenues of the Northern Sarkārs (six coastal districts) to support his army. In the south the French had only Muḥammad ʿAlī to remove. But from 1751 Dupleix's star began to wane. Robert Clive (*q.v.*), a discontented young British factor who had left the countinghouse for the field, seized the fort of Arcot, political capital of the Carnatic, with 210 men in August 1751. This daring stroke had the hoped-for effect of diverting half of Chanda Sahib's army to its recovery. Clive's successful 50-day defense permitted Muḥammad ʿAlī to procure allies from Tanjore and the Marāthās. The French were worsted, and they were eventually forced to surrender in June 1752. Dupleix never recovered from this blow; he was superseded in August 1754 by the director Charles Robert Godeheu, who made a not unfavourable settlement with the British.

Downfall of Dupleix

The French gained but a brief respite; the Seven Years' War in Europe, in which Britain and France were once more on opposite sides, broke out in 1756. Both sides sent armaments to the East. The first British force was diverted to Bengal, so that the French general Thomas Arthur Lally had an advantage on his arrival in 1758. Lally was brave but headstrong and tactless; after taking Fort St. David, he lost time and credit marching to Tanjore, where he lost Indian sympathy by executing temple Brahmins. Then his attack on Madras (1758–59) miscarried, while Clive's troops from Bengal defeated the French garrison of the Northern Sarkārs. When Sir Eyre Coote arrived with reinforcements, the British defeated Lally decisively at Wandiwash in January 1760. Bussy-Castelnau, who had been recalled from Hyderābād, was captured; and Lally retreated to Pondicherry, where, after an eight-month siege made tense by bitter recrimination, he surrendered in January 1761. The French threat to British power in India had ended.

Reasons for the British victory

This defeat could be partly blamed on Lally, but there were also other more vital causes. An overriding factor was the British command of the sea. Lally could get no allies for lack of money and no money for lack of supply from France. The British could supply Madras from both Britain and Bengal. The French company was under the control of the French government, and the company suffered from the vicissitudes of its politics.

European military superiority. The supremacy in Indian politics, which seemed to come so suddenly to the Europeans in India, also requires explanation. There was the matter of arms. The Mughals imported their cavalry tactics from Turkestan and their artillery from Turkey. But their firearms remained slowfiring and cumbrous, so that they were outclassed both in quick firing and in range by the 18th-century musket and the cannon landed from the fleets. Infantry could fire three times instead of once before the heavy Mughal cavalry could close, and this destroyed at a blow the Indians' traditional dominance. But besides this technical advantage, the Europeans had also the moral one of discipline. Troops with loyalty guaranteed by regular pay were more than a match for the personal retinues or mercenary soldiers of the Indian chiefs, however brave they might be individually. A chronic problem with Indian armies at that time was the lack of means to pay them; campaigns would be diverted for collecting revenue for this purpose (when Europeans later trained Indians in the European manner, their advantage increased; discipline removed the uncertain factor of personal leadership, and regular pay removed the Indian general's bugbear of mutiny). A further advantage was civil discipline; the European forces were directed by men themselves under discipline, who were without hereditary connections or ties (though to modern eyes they often seemed refractory or disloyal, by contemporary Indian standards they were regularity itself). Indian loyalty was to leaders who might be killed, to relatives who might back the wrong side, to governments that might (and often did) fail to pay or be overthrown. On the Indian side, whatever the situation, someone was nearly always looking over his shoulder thinking of the chances of a change of leadership or a successful coup. Thus the European possessed not only an expertise denied to the Indians but also a spirit, a tenacity, and a will to win that was rare in the Indian forces of the time.

Revolution in Bengal. The revolution in Bengal was the product of a number of unrelated causes. The imminence of the Seven Years' War prompted the British to send out Clive with an armament to Madras in 1755. Succession troubles in Bengal combined with British mercantile incompetence to produce a crisis at a moment when the French in south India were still awaiting reinforcements from France.

Causes of the revolution

ʿAlī Vardī Khān—the governor, or nawab, and virtual ruler of Bengal—died in April 1756, leaving his power to his young grandson Sirāj-ud-Dawlah. The latter's position was insecure because of discontent among both his Hindu and Muslim officers and because he himself was both headstrong and vacillating. On an exaggerated report that the British were fortifying Calcutta, he attacked and took the city after a four-day siege, on June 20, 1756. The flight of the British governor and several councillors added ignominy to defeat. The survivors were held for a night in the local lockup, known as the Black Hole; many were dead the next morning.

News of this disaster caused consternation in Madras. An armament preparing to oust Bussy-Castelnau from the Deccan was diverted to Bengal, giving Clive a force of 900 Europeans and 1,500 Indians. He relieved the Calcutta survivors and recovered the city on January 2, 1757. An indecisive engagement led to a treaty with Sirāj on February 9, which restored the company's privileges, gave permission to fortify Calcutta, and declared an alliance.

This was a decisive point in British Indian history. According to plan Clive should have returned to Madras to pursue the campaign against the French; but he did not. He sensed both the hostility and insecurity of Sirāj's position and began to receive overtures to support a military coup. The chance of installing a friendly and dependent nawab seemed too good to be missed. Having taken this decision, Clive chose the right candidate in Mīr Jaʿfar, an elderly general with much influence in the army. In so acting Clive was probably influenced by the example of Bussy-Castelnau at Hyderābād; for seven years Bussy-Castelnau had maintained himself with an Indo-French force, sustaining the niẓām Ṣalābat Jang and maintaining French influence in the largest south Indian state with outstanding success. This system, of a "sponsored" Indian state, controlled but not administered, was the one Clive had in mind for Bengal.

Clive's plans for Bengal

The prospects for success seemed good. The event, however, proved otherwise, and there were reasons for this not realized at the time. The chiefs were so lacking in vigour that they made little resistance to British encroachments. External danger could only come from one direction and source—the Mughal authority—and that was at the moment in dissolution. While Bussy-Castelnau had no French merchants to satisfy, the British merchants in Calcutta were ready and eager to exploit the situation. And, because the British company's government was made up entirely of merchants, it is easy to understand why the sponsored state of 1757 became the virtually annexed state of 1765.

Before breaking with Sirāj, Clive took the French settlement of Chandernagar, which the Nawab left to its fate lest he might need British help to repulse an Afghan attack from the north. The actual conflict with Sirāj, at Plassey (June 23, 1757), was decided by Clive's resolute refusal to be overawed by superior numbers, by dissensions within the Nawab's camp, by Mīr Jaʿfar's failure to support his superior, and by Sirāj's own loss of nerve. Plassey was, in fact, more of a cannonade than a battle. It was followed by the flight and execution of Sirāj, by the occupation of Murshidābād, the capital, and by the installation of Mīr Jaʿfar as the new nawab.

Clive now controlled a sponsored state, and he played the part with great skill. His position was prejudiced at the outset by the Nawab's failure to find the expected hoarded treasure with which to fulfill his financial promises to the British. The Nawab therefore looked for financial support toward his Hindu deputies, with whom saving was a second nature. Clive had therefore to intervene repeatedly. In 1759 he defended Patna from attack by the heir to the Mughal throne, ʿAlī Gawhar (later Shāh ʿĀlam II), who hoped to strengthen his position in the confused world of Delhi politics by acquiring Bihār. Clive also had to deal with the Dutch, who, hearing of Mīr Jaʿfar's restiveness and alarmed by the growth of British power in Bengal, sent an armament of six ships to their station at Chinsura on the Hooghly. Though Britain was at peace with Holland at the time, Clive manoeuvred the Dutch into acts of aggression, captured their fleet, defeated them on land, and exacted compensation. They retained Chinsura but could never again challenge the British position in Bengal.

Clive left Calcutta on February 25, 1760, at the height of his fame and aged only 34, looking forward to an English political career. The Nawab was completely dependent on the British, to whose trade it seemed that the rich resources of Bengal were now open. But the prospect was less brilliant than it looked; and for this, and for the troubles that ensued in the next few years, Clive had a direct responsibility. Two measures undermined the plan of a sponsored state, leading to the company's bankruptcy on the one hand and to the virtual annexation of Bengal on the other. The first of these was an understanding with Mīr Jaʿfar, not mentioned in the actual treaty, that the private internal trade of the East India Company's servants should be exempt from the usual tolls and customs duties (the company's trade with Europe was already exempt from duty under concessions made in 1717). The company's monopoly covered the actual trade with Europe and the articles purchased in India to make up its "investment"; but its servants were free to trade otherwise within Bengal and overseas to Asian countries. It was this private trade that, in the virtual absence of salaries, gave most of them their subsistence and some their fortunes. In Bengal this private trade was subject to internal duties. Mīr Jaʿfar's concession, expressed in the form of *dastak*s, or passes, gave them immense advantages over their Indian competitors. From free trade many passed to intimidation; agents were employed who used the British name to terrorize the countryside and infringe the company's monopoly.

Problems in a sponsored state

The second measure was the taking of presents. This was not forbidden by the company and was, in fact, a recognized custom; but it unlocked the floodgates of corruption. The treasure of Murshidābād was reputed to be worth £40,000,000 sterling. On the strength of this rumour, large amounts were paid to the armed forces and to the company leaders. In addition, Clive obtained a further Mughal title and then claimed a revenue assignment, or *jāgīr*, for its upkeep, which was worth £30,000 a year. In the context of contemporary values these grants equalled nearly one-quarter of the average annual Bengal revenue, or about one-seventeenth of the then annual revenue of Great Britain. With such a vigorous opening of the floodgates, it is not surprising that the other servants of the company asked for more almost as a matter of right and that the company's directors in London, with relatives and connections on the spot, preferred verbal denunciations to any resolute or sustained action. The effects became speedily apparent when in fact the £40,000,000 sterling turned out to be £1,500,000, so that (as Clive later admitted to a parliamentary enquiry), the Nawab had to sell jewels, goods, and furniture to meet his obligations. The results of these measures unfolded themselves in the next decade and continued to be felt for a generation.

THE EXTENSION OF BRITISH POWER, 1760–1856

The period of disorder, 1760–72. The departure of Clive signalled the release of acquisitive urges by the company's Bengal servants. These urges were so strong that the governor, Henry Vansittart (served 1760–64), found himself unable to control them. Under the company's constitution, he had only one vote in a council of up to a dozen and could be overruled by any knot of determined men. During these years a body of English merchants, long separated from British standards and social restraints, suddenly found themselves with real but undefined authority over the whole of a large and rich province. It is not surprising that they thought mainly of getting rich quickly.

The first step was the deposition of the nawab Mīr Jaʿfar on the grounds of old age and incompetence. His supplanter, Mīr Qāsim, was able and anxious to reassert his authority. He paid £200,000 in gratuities, of which Vansittart received £50,000 besides an allowance of £18,000 from the company and private trade on his own account. In addition, he ceded the districts of Burdwān, Midnapore, and Chittagong. Both sides now wanted power; and to this issue was added that of money, of which both sides were short. The Nawab had lost substantial land revenue and the lucrative tolls on the British merchants' private trade; the company was receiving no remittances from Britain, because the directors considered that Bengal should pay for itself. In such a situation a clash was inevitable.

Mīr Qāsim removed his capital to distant Monghyr, where he could not be so easily overseen, asserted his authority in the districts, and raised a disciplined force under an Armenian officer. He then turned to the company and negotiated a settlement with Vansittart, by which the company's merchants were to pay an ad valorem duty of 9 percent, against an Indian merchant's duty of 40 percent. At this the Calcutta Council revolted, reducing the duty to 2.5 percent and on salt only. The breach came in 1763 when Mīr Qāsim, after defeat in four pitched battles, murdered his Indian bankers and British prisoners and fled to Oudh. The next year Mīr Qāsim returned with the emperor Shāh ʿĀlam II and his minister Shujāʿ-ud-Dawlah to be finally defeated at Baksar. This conflict rather than Plassey was the decisive battle that gave Bengal to the British.

These events had been viewed with growing alarm in London. The news of the Mīr Qāsim campaign coincided with the victory of Clive's faction in the company over that of Lawrence Sulivan. Clive used it to appoint himself governor with power to act over the head of the council; he intended an administrative reformation and a political settlement. He arrived in May 1765 to find that the British victory at Baksar had placed Shāh ʿĀlam in his hands but had created a situation of deep confusion

Clive's return to India

in other respects. Mīr Ja'far had been restored and had died; his second son had succeeded at the cost of £139,000 in presents. The British merchants and their agents were the unresisted predators of the Bengal economy, and no one knew the next step to take.

Clive acted with extraordinary vigour. Within four days of arrival he had set up a Select Committee; and, when he left less than two years later, he had effected another revolution. Turning to India's political situation, Clive had to decide where to stop. No one barred his way to Delhi, and he could at that moment have turned the whole Mughal Empire into a company-sponsored state. But he realized that Delhi was easier to have than to hold. He fixed his frontier at the borders of Bihār and Oudh. Shāh 'Ālam was given the districts of Kora and Allāhābād, and he settled in the latter city, with a tribute (or subsidy) of £260,000 from Bengal (nearly 10 percent of its estimated revenue). Shujā' received back Oudh, with a guarantee of defense, in return for paying the troops involved and a cash indemnity. These two were to be buffers between the company and the Marāthās and possible marauders from the north.

Clive's next step was to settle Bengal's own status. The Mughal emperor still had much influence, though little power; his complete discountenance might therefore have done the company more harm than good. Clive's solution was to obtain from Shāh 'Ālam the dewanee, or revenue-collecting power, in Bengal and Bihār (the company was thus the imperial dewan for those two provinces). The Nawab was left in charge of the judiciary and magistracy, but he was helpless because he had no army and could only get money to raise one from the company.

Clive's system of dual government

This was Clive's system of "dual government." The actual administration remained in Indian hands; and for superintendence Clive appointed a deputy dewan, a Persian officer, Muḥammad Riẓā Khān, who was at the same time appointed the Nawab's deputy. The chain was thus complete. The company, acting in the name of the Emperor and using Indian personnel and the traditional apparatus of government, now ruled Bengal. Their agent was Riẓā Khān; the success of the experiment turned on his efficiency and the extent of the governor's support.

Within the company, Clive enforced his authority by accepting some resignations and enforcing others. Presents of more than 4,000 rupees were forbidden, and those between that figure and 1,000 rupees were only to be received with official consent. The regulation of private trade was more difficult, for the company paid virtually no salaries. Clive formed a Society of Trade, which operated the salt monopoly, to provide salaries on a graduated scale; but the company directors disallowed this on the ground of expense, and two years later they replaced it by commissions on the revenue, which cost the company more. Finally, Clive dealt with overgrown military allowances with equal vigour, overcoming a mutiny headed by a brigade commander. He used a legacy from Mīr Ja'far to start the first pension fund for the Indian army.

Clive left Calcutta in February 1767. His work—diplomatic, political, and administrative—was a beginning rather than a complete settlement. But in each direction, instead of looking back to the past, it reached out to the future. This creative period exacted a heavy price. Clive was pursued to England by his enemies, who launched a parliamentary attack, which, though triumphantly repulsed in 1773, led to his suicide the following year. The year 1765 marks the real beginning of the British Empire in India as a territorial dominion.

Enrichment of the company's servants

It is worth noting how the company's servants so enriched themselves at this time that they undermined the economy of Bengal, and those who returned to England became a byword for ostentation. Apart from the great political prizes already mentioned, it must be remembered that all of the company's servants were engaged in private trade on their own account. Their new authority and the company's power enabled them to exploit their trade with little hindrance. They had the means of using intimidation (through their agents) against Indian rivals like the indigo growers, and Indian police, customs, revenue, and judicial officials. Presents and bribes were the price Indians had to pay for freedom from harassment. They were able through their connection with the administration to arrange virtual monopolies for particular articles in particular districts, fixing a low purchase price as well as a high selling price. They could arrange commissions on revenue collection, mercantile transactions, and any form of commercial activity. What was not done through agents could be arranged through intermediaries, who also, of course, had their own compensation. Thus a man could make a fortune, lose it in England, return for another, lose it again, and return for a third. It is significant that from the time of Clive's second governorship lamentations increased that the opportunities for quick fortunes were slipping away.

The Company Bahadur. The regime that Clive established in 1765 was really a private dominion of the East India Company. It was not a British colony, and it fitted into the very flexible structure of the dying Mughal Empire. The structure of the administration was Mughal, not British, and its operators were Indian, personified by the deputy nawab Muḥammad Riẓā Khān. It was a continuation of the traditional state under British control, and it can be aptly described by the company's popular title, the Company Bahadur, the Valiant, or Honourable, Company. This Company Bahadur state continued through Warren Hastings' time and in essence until the early 19th century, although Lord Cornwallis (governor general, 1786–93) substituted largely British for Indian personnel. The revenue was collected by the officers of the deputy nawab; the law administered was the current Mughal (Islāmic) criminal code, with the traditional personal codes of the two communities; the language of administration was Persian. Only the army broke with the past, with its British officers, its discipline, and its Western organization and tactics.

The arrival of Warren Hastings

It was this state that Warren Hastings (*q.v.*) inherited when he became governor of Bengal in 1772. His 13-year rule can be divided into his internal administration, his dealings with his council, and his foreign policy. Hastings inherited a state that in the five years since Clive's departure had stepped back toward the corruption from which Clive had rescued it. But Hastings was armed with authority by the directors, so that the first two years of his government were a period of real reform. He first dealt with the *dastaks*, or free passes, the use of which had crept in again since Clive's departure; they were abolished, and a uniform tariff of 2.5 percent was enforced on all internal trade. Private trade by the company's servants continued, but within enforceable limits. The Bengali began to experience some security and a settled order, if not yet an equitable society. Next, the company "stood forth as *dīwān*," taking over the responsibility for the revenue collection from Riẓā Khān, who was arraigned for corruption; the charges could not be proved, however, even with the approving support of the British authorities. Hastings substituted British for Indian collectors working under a Board of Revenue. In a way this was a retrograde step, for the new collectors were often as corrupt as their predecessors and more powerful; but the change gave legal power to those who already wielded it in fact, and in the future their irregularities could more easily be dealt with than could the surreptitious dealings through the old Indian collectors. Finally, Hastings instituted a network of civil and criminal courts in place of the deputy nawab's. The same law was administered by British judges, who were often incompetent, but a model was provided into which Western ideas and practices could later be fed.

These changes held good through the period of Hastings' rule and may be said to have provided a viable though not yet very competent or equitable state. Criminal and personal law cases were virtually in the hands of Indian assessors to British judges who did not know Persian; revenue administration was distorted by the collectors' desire both for gain and increased returns. Hastings was least successful in his revenue administration, for which he never advanced beyond a condition of trial and error; a five-year settlement made in ignorance proved unsuccessful, and he was finally reduced to annual settlements, which meant hit-and-miss arrangements with the traditional *zamīndārs* (tax collectors).

Hastings was personally incorrupt, but he had to tolerate a good deal in others and to resort to extensive jobbing to placate his supporters both in Bengal and in London. He left a personal legend behind him, but his administration was disorderly as well as strong. A reason for this can be found in his relations with his council. Under the Regulating Act of 1773 Hastings became governor general of Fort William in Bengal, with powers of superintendence over Madras and Bombay. He was also given a Supreme Court, administering English law to the British and those connected with them, and a council of four, appointed in the Regulating Act. The leading council member, Sir Philip Francis, hoped to succeed him; and because Hastings had no power of veto, Francis was able with two supporters to overrule him. For two years Hastings was outvoted, until the death of one member enabled him to use his casting vote. But the struggle continued until Francis returned to London in 1780, to continue his vendetta there. The struggle culminated with charges against Hastings of malversation by an Indian entrepreneur, Nand Kumar, and with the latter's conviction before the Supreme Court of perjury and his execution under English law. The episode exposed the moral weakness of the council majority, which failed to reprieve Nand Kumar, and convinced the Indians of Hastings' overriding power. This struggle, lasting for years, left Hastings triumphant but also embittered; he had not only to deal with the opposition in Calcutta, which never ceased, but also with the constant threat of supersession in the involved politics of London at that time. This strain probably accounts for the acts that formed important items in Hastings' subsequent impeachment—these were the dunning of Raja Chait Singh of Benares (Vārānasi) and his deposition in 1781; and the pressuring of the baygums (princesses) of Oudh for the same reason. Hastings' financial difficulties at the time were great, but such actions were harsh and high-handed.

Hastings' relations with his council

The impeachment of Warren Hastings (1787–95) at the behest of Edmund Burke and the Whigs, which followed his return from India and ended in his acquittal but retirement, was a kind of very rough justice. Hastings had saved for the company its Indian dominions, and he was relatively incorrupt. But the charges served notice that the company's servants were responsible for their actions toward those they governed, and for these actions they were answerable to Parliament. Hastings was so identified with the company's rule that he was the inevitable target for any such assertion of principle.

The company and the state. During the first half of the 18th century the East India Company was a trading corporation with a steady annual dividend of 8–10 percent, offering its servants prospects of a modest fortune through private trade, along with great hazards to health and life. It was directed in London by 24 directors—elected annually by the shareholding body, the Court of Proprietors—who worked through a series of committees.

The Bengal adventure from 1757 turned the two courts—of directors and proprietors—into political bodies, because they now controlled a great Eastern state. Shares became political counters, the purchase of which might secure votes needed to change the company's policy. A second result was the return to Britain of the company's servants with fortunes; their ostentation and lack of restraint earned them the title of nabobs. These events soon produced reactions. The shareholders wanted to share in this new wealth, in the guise of increased dividends; and the directors wanted the company as well as its servants to benefit from this wealth. Two processes were thus set in motion—one a rising pressure for increased dividends and the other an attempt by the company to discipline its servants and to secure some profit for itself. Broadly speaking, it was the success of the first and the failure of the second that provoked state intervention in the company's affairs.

The close personal connection between the "direction" and the company's servants themselves weighed heavily and eventually stultified the directors' efforts. It produced an infirmity of purpose, which led to the return to Bengal by one faction of servants dismissed for irregularities by another—a factionalism epitomized by the struggle between Clive and Sulivan for control of the company. These developments occupied the 1760s, drastically reducing the prestige of the company. On the side of discipline, alarm at the overruling of Vansittart and the wars against Mīr Qāsim and Shāh ʿĀlam led to the dispatch of Clive as governor in 1765. As the effect of Clive's measures diminished after his return to England in 1767, three "supervisors" were dispatched to Bengal in 1769 with plenary powers, but they were lost at sea. Then Warren Hastings was appointed in 1772 with a reform mandate. But it was too late, for bankruptcy was now knocking at the door.

State intervention in company affairs

The company had hoped for large profits from Clive's first control of Bengal. The hopes then shortly dashed were revived by his second governorship. Clive believed that he had secured a revenue surplus of £2,000,000 for the company. On the strength of these expectations, the company's dividend was raised to 12.5 percent in 1767; in the same year the first signs of parliamentary opposition were bought off by the offer of £400,000 a year to the state in return for undisturbed possession of Bengal. As the expectations withered, this became a financial millstone that compelled the company in 1772 to ask for the loan of £1,000,000 to avert bankruptcy. This opened the floodgates of parliamentary criticism, leading to committees of inquiry and revelations of malpractices, to Clive's suicide (1774), and to the beginning of state intervention.

In 1773 the British government gave a loan of £1,400,000 to the company; but its price was the Regulating Act, passed the same year. The act sought to "regulate" the affairs of the company, both in London and India. In London, the qualifications fee for a vote was raised from £500 to £1,000, and the directors' terms were extended from one to four years, with a year's gap before re-election. This ended the jobbing of votes for the control of policy by private interests and gave continuity of policy to the direction. In India, a governor generalship of Fort William in Bengal was established, with supervisory control over the other Indian settlements and Warren Hastings as its first incumbent. Hastings was given four named councillors, but future appointments were to be made by the company. Finally, a Supreme Court with a chief justice and three judges was set up.

The Regulating Act

The Regulating Act was a first step toward taking the political direction of British India out of the hands of the company and of securing a unified overall control. But it had serious defects, which bedeviled administration in Bengal and made India (despite British preoccupation with the American Revolution) a leading subject of political controversy over the next 20 years.

The governor general possessed no veto in his council. With three political councillors from Britain, each ready to take Warren Hastings' place, this led to his virtual supersession by the majority for two years and to a paralysis of the executive. Hastings used the energy in fighting his council that should have gone to reforming Bengal. The superintending power added responsibility with little power to enforce it. The Supreme Court decided to administer English law (the only law it knew) and to apply it not only to all the English in Bengal but also to all Indians connected with them; in practice this meant those Indians in Calcutta, and it led to such grave abuses as the hanging of Nand Kumar for an offense not recognized as being capital in any Indian code.

In 1780 the company's privileges ran out; but this was during the crisis of the American Revolution, so that a decision was delayed until 1784. Charles James Fox's radical measure to transfer the control of British India to seven commissioners was defeated by the King's influence in the House of Lords, but the next year the matter was settled for more than 70 years by the prime minister William Pitt's India Act of 1784. Its essence was the institution of a dual control. The directors were left in

Pitt's Act of 1784

charge of commerce and as political executants; but they were politically superintended by a new Board of Control, the president of which, in the person of Henry Dundas, soon became the virtual minister for India. The directors dealt with the board through a secret committee of three, but their dispatches to India could be altered, vetoed, and dictated by the board. The governor general could be recalled by the crown. In India, the governor's council was reduced to three, including the commander in chief, and by an amending act he acquired the veto, which Warren Hastings had missed so much. Finally, there was to be a parliamentary inquiry before each 20-year renewal of the company's charter.

Pitt's India Act proved to be a landmark because it gave the British government control of policy without patronage. The cumbrous dual system developed into a seesaw arrangement of give and take, becoming ever stronger on the government side as greater ability, influence, and power had their effect. The inquiry provision produced a national inquest on Indian affairs every 20 years, the conclusions of which marked successive stages in the diminution of the company's political power. On the first such inquiry, in 1793, the company repelled an attempt to compel it to support Christian missionary work; this incident led to the foundation of the Church Missionary Society in 1799. In 1813 the company was obliged by Parliament to admit missionaries and was deprived of its monopoly on trade with India. By the Act of 1833 it lost its trade altogether and was thenceforth a governing corporation under increasing state surveillance. In 1853, with the introduction of competitive examinations, the company lost most of its patronage and also had to admit nominated directors. Policies were increasingly dictated to a sulky or apathetic board. The last case of the recall of a governor general by the company was that of Lord Ellenborough in 1844; this was the real swan song of the company, because it was recognized at the time that such a thing could never happen again. The company had become a managing agency on behalf of the British government.

Relations with the Marāthās and Mysore. After Clive's settlement in 1765, the East India Company had no desire for any further acquisitions. Its object was still trade; it regarded the acquisition of Bengal as a political framework for the safe conduct of trade, justified by the danger of near anarchy in its most profitable scene of operations. But such a resolution was easier to make than to keep. Indian states were ever ready to seek European help in achieving their own projects; many of the company's servants looked longingly at territorial revenues that might assist their own enrichment, and the exigencies of Indian politics at times made nonalignment difficult to observe.

The three centres of the company's power

In 1765 the three centres of the company's power were independent of each other, but the post-Mughal Indian pattern was becoming clear. In the north there were the Mughal fragments of Allāhābād, Oudh, and Delhi, with the Sikhs resurgent in the Punjab. In the Deccan the Niẓām of Hyderābād maintained uneasily his Mughal regime. In the west and south were two vigorous and expansive powers—the Marāthās and Mysore.

The Marāthās had made their bid for the Mughal succession in the previous decade, and they were now recovering from a disastrous defeat at Pānīpat (1761). The unified leadership of the peshwa had given way to a confederacy of the peshwa and four military dictatorships developing into monarchies. The Marāthās were restless, energetic, and acquisitive; their greatest enemy was their own divisions. In the south the old Hindu state of Mysore had passed into the hands of a Muslim military adventurer of genius, Hyder (Haidar) Ali Khan, in 1762.

When Warren Hastings took overall control of the company's possessions in 1774, Madras had already stumbled into war with Hyder Ali and had submitted to a virtually dictated peace under the walls of Madras in 1769. The Nawab of Carnatic had become by degrees dependent on the company because he needed its support against the threat of Hyder and the Niẓām. Ingenious and feckless, the Nawab involved Madras in south Indian politics and the company in his affairs by borrowing from its servants.

Hastings had a natural gift for *Realpolitik*, but he was tied to a policy of nonaggression. Much of his diplomatic skill was spent repairing the blunders of others. His major work for British India was preserving the company's dominion against a coalition of country powers, virtually unaided from home at a time when Britain was itself hard pressed both in America and by a European coalition. His first work was to safeguard Bengal from the reviving power of the Marāthās, who had conducted Shāh ʿĀlam to Delhi in 1771. Hastings intervened and handed Allāhābād and Kora to Shujāʿ-ud-Dawlah of Oudh in return for a subsidy and a treaty. The following year he found himself assisting the Nawab of Oudh to crush the Afghan Ruhellas between the Jumna (modern Yamuna) and the Ganges (this stroke was the first item in the indictment at his impeachment, but its effect was to stabilize the north Indian situation for the next ten years).

Hastings' diplomacy

In western India Hastings was the victim of Bombay brashness and of directorial blunders. A succession struggle in Poona (modern Pune) for the peshwaship led Bombay to support Raghunath Rāo in the hope of securing the islands of Salsette and Bassein. When this was countermanded by Calcutta, London intervened to renew the venture. In 1779 a British army was surrounded on its way to Poona, one month before a force sent by Hastings completed a brilliant march across India at Surat. In 1782 the British made peace with the Peshwa, abandoning Raghunath and having only Salsette to show for seven years of war. This first round with the Marāthās was a draw.

While this war was in progress, Hastings was confronted with a far greater menace. In 1780 the ineptitude of Madras provoked a coalition of the Niẓām, Hyder, and the Marāthās, which defeated the company's armies and swept over the Carnatic. Though without hope of succour from Britain, itself hard pressed, Hastings set about sustaining the Madras forces and dividing his foes. In 1781 the military balance was restored, and the next year the Marāthās made peace. Hyder died (1782), French help arrived too late to affect the issue, and in 1784 the Treaty of Mangalore with Hyder's son Tippu (Tipu) restored the status quo. Hastings had thus little to show in the way of empire building. His feat of defense without external aid was nevertheless remarkable. He preserved the British dominion in India, and by so doing he made it possible for others to extend it. The company had become one of the recognized great powers of India.

Pitt's Act of 1784 reiterated the company's own intentions by forbidding aggressive wars and annexations. Lord Cornwallis and his successor Sir John Shore (governor general 1793–98) were eager to comply, but Cornwallis nevertheless found himself involved in the third Mysore war (1789–92) with Tippu Sultan, who possessed his father's ability without his judgment. The cause was a combination of Tippu's intransigence with conflicting obligations undertaken by the Madras government. It took three campaigns before Cornwallis could bring Tippu to bay. Half his dominions were annexed, more as a precaution than as an exercise in imperialism. But Tippu remained formidable and, not unnaturally, more hostile than ever.

The ascent to paramountcy. At this point in time a radical change occurred in British policy. Two causes were principally responsible. There was a growing body of opinion within the company that only British control of India could end the constant wars and provide really satisfactory conditions for trade; full dominion would be economical as well as salutary. The more compelling immediate cause was the transformation of European politics by the French Revolution. A new French threat to India emerged, this time overland, with Napoleon's Egyptian expedition of 1798–99. It was certain that a French army under such a leader would find many friends in India to welcome it, and not least Tippu Sultan.

Moves toward imperialism

The government of Lord Wellesley. The next governor general, Lord Mornington (later title, Wellesley), combined the convictions of the imperialist group with a

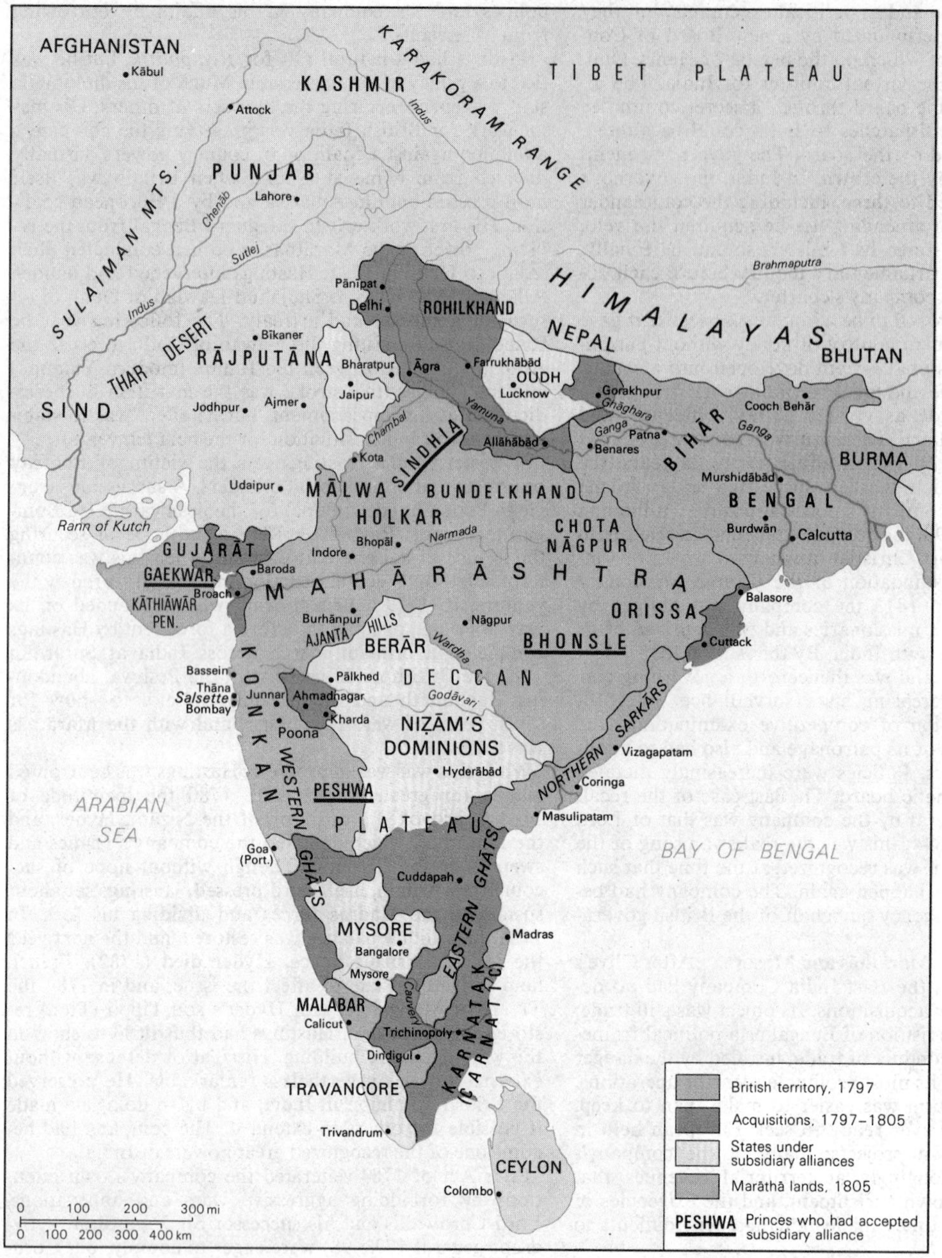

India, 1797–1805.

Adapted from R. Treharne and H. Fullard (eds.), *Muir's Historical Atlas: Ancient, Medieval and Modern*, 9th ed. (1965); George Philip & Son Ltd., London

mandate to deal with the French. Wellesley was thus able to use this fear of the French as a cover for his imperialism until he was near to complete success. His term of office (1798–1805) was therefore a decisive period in the rise of the British dominion.

Wellesley decided first to strike at Mysore, still a formidable military power and avowedly hostile. He had little difficulty getting the Niẓām for an ally and securing the neutrality of the Peshwa. The Niẓām, hard pressed by the Marāthās, was persuaded to disband his contingent of French-trained troops in return for a promise of protection. This was the first of Wellesley's subsidiary treaties (see below). Tippu Sultan had entertained French republican envoys and had planted a tree of liberty at Seringapatam; but when the British stormed Seringapatam in May 1799, he was isolated and at bay, and he found too late that concessions, in the Indian tradition, would not save him. Tippu died fighting in the breach. The British rejoicings over this unexpectedly complete victory emphasized the fear that the Mysore monarchy had inspired. Wellesley tempered his imperialism with diplomacy by restoring the child head of the old Hindu reigning family as the ruler of half of Tippu's dominions; the other half was divided between the Niẓām and the company. This was the real beginning of the Madras presidency as a substantial territorial unit.

Wellesley's use of *Realpolitik*

For the next three years Wellesley was occupied with certain exercises in *Realpolitik* and with developing his device of the subsidiary treaty. The *Realpolitik* was evidenced in four directions. On the death (1801) of the reigning Carnatic nawab Wellesley took over his territories, pensioning the new nawab with one-fifth of the revenue. The same fate befell the small but highly cultivated state of Tanjore, to the south of the Carnatic (1799), and the city–port state of Surat on a disputed succession.

The biggest of these exercises concerned the Mughal successor state of Oudh in northern India, which had been in treaty relationship with the company since 1765. This rich state had fallen into disorder under the listless though cultured rule of Āsaf-ud-Dawlah; on his death in 1797 a succession dispute and an Afghan invasion of the Punjab gave Wellesley a welcome opportunity for interference. He pressed the Nawab to disband his troops and increase his payment to the company for his subsidiary force. When the Nawab offered to abdicate, it was accepted immediately; but, on finding that abdication would mean annexation and not his son's succession, he withdrew it, and Wellesley treated him as contumacious. In 1801 Wellesley annexed half the state, running along the northern and eastern banks of the Ganges, including Rohilkhand. Whatever the verdict on the means employed, this move had important consequences. Oudh was isolated, and a jumping-off place was secured for an attack on the northern Marāthās. The company was no longer looking for buffer states as shields against attack but for territory that would serve as springboards for offensive action.

Development of the subsidiary system

This change of attitude applies to Wellesley's development of the subsidiary system. In the hands of Clive and Warren Hastings it was a defensive instrument to safeguard the company's possessions; in the hands of Wellesley it was an offensive device with which to subject independent states to British control. The essence of the system was that the company undertook to protect a state from external attack in return for the control of its foreign relations. For this purpose it provided a subsidiary force of company troops, who were commonly stationed in a cantonment near the state capital. The state paid for this force by means of a subsidy, which was often commuted into a cession of territory. In order to protect itself from an external enemy, the state in question bound itself irrevocably to the British power, providing at its heart, as it were, the means of its own coercion should it ever wish to resume independence.

Wellesley first applied this system in 1798 to Hyderābād, when the aging Niẓām was in dire fear of the Marathas. In 1800 the subsidy was compounded for the Niẓām's share of the Mysore annexations. The same system was applied to Oudh, when the great annexation of 1801 was said to be on account of the subsidiary force. It was then the turn of the Marāthās—the remaining bastion of Indian independence. Had the Marāthā chiefs remained united, Wellesley could have accomplished little; the death of the young Peshwa released fresh dissensions, however, heightened by that of the minister Nāna Fadnavis in 1800. The chiefs Holkar and Daulat Rāo Sindhia (Sindia) contended for power over the peshwa Bājī Rāo II. On Holkar's success in 1802, Bājī Rāo fled to Bassein and applied for British aid. Such an opportunity at the centre of Marāthā power was not to be missed; in addition there was the justification that Daulat Rāo Sindhia, in the north, had 40,000 French-trained troops under a French commander. The Treaty of Bassein (December 31, 1802) placed, as it were, a time bomb at the heart of the Marāthā confederacy; British troops were stationed at Poona, at the price of a cession of territory, and the Peshwa was reduced to dependency on the British.

This action provoked the Second Marāthā War—at first against Daulat Rāo Sindhia and the Bhonsle and then against Holkar. At first the British won resounding victories. Wellesley's brother Arthur (later the duke of Wellington) defeated the Sindhia–Bhonsle coalition in west central India, while Lord Lake broke up Sindhia's French army, occupied Delhi, and took the aged emperor Shāh ʿĀlam II under protection. Then came a check, however, with the intervention of Holkar using the old Marāthā cavalry tactics, forcing the British to retreat, and besieging Delhi. Though Holkar was later defeated, this was the signal for which exasperated directors and a doubting ministry had been waiting. Wellesley was recalled. His race for hegemony had been lost in the last lap. But Wellesley's work, avowedly imperialistic, made ultimate supremacy inevitable. The Marāthās were too broken to reunite, and there was no one to take their place.

Inevitability of British supremacy

The government of Lord Minto. The next ten years were an interlude, not a new era. During this period both Sindhia and Holkar plundered the chiefs of Rājasthān, thus preparing them mentally for future British overlordship. Meanwhile, bands of freebooters, known as Pindaris, raided the Nāgpur and Hyderābād states in widening circles and thence entered British territory. These were dispossessed villagers and discarded soldiers—the human flotsam and jetsam of the frequent wars. They had the elusiveness of guerrillas; and they received the tacit countenance of the Marāthā princes but not the goodwill of the population, who were their principal victims.

Lord Minto (governor general 1807–13) was occupied with the revived French danger, once more serious with the Treaty of Tilsit (1807) and Napoleon's resulting alliance with Russia. To guard against a French-sponsored Russian attack, British missions were sent to Afghanistan, to Persia, and to Ranjit Singh, the Sikh ruler of the Punjab. The first two proved fruitless, but the Treaty of Amritsar with Ranjit Singh (1809) defined British and Sikh spheres of influence and settled relations for a generation. Minto's other achievement was the capture of the Île de France and of Java from the French-controlled Dutch; the former island became a colony (now the dominion of Mauritius), and the latter was restored under the peace treaty. One result of this episode was the acquisition of the key point of Singapore by Sir Stamford Raffles in 1819.

The government of Lord Hastings. The end of the Napoleonic Wars in 1815 opened a new era in India by strengthening the commercial and economic arguments for completing supremacy and by removing all fear of the French. The Pindari raids, which grew year by year until they affected both the Bengal and Madras presidencies, added further reasons for action. The final act was directed by Lord Hastings (governor general, 1813–23), who came to India as a consolation for his failure to attain the premiership under his friend the Prince Regent. Lord Hastings, however, first had to deal, in 1814–16, with the Gurkhas of Nepal, who inflicted a series of repulses on a Bengal army unprepared for mountain warfare. Each side earned the respect of the other. The resulting Treaty of Kāthmāndu (1816) gave the British the tract of hill country where Simla, the site of the future summer capital of British India, was situated, and it settled relations with British India for the rest of the British period. Nepal remained independent and isolated, supported by the export of soldiers to strengthen the British military presence in India.

The Gurkhas of Nepal and the Pindaris

Lord Hastings then turned to the Pindaris. By a large-scale and well-planned enveloping movement, he hoped to enclose them in an iron net. But this involved entering Marāthā territories and seeking the cooperation of their princes. Sindhia agreed after agonizing indecision, and this really settled the issue. Holkar's state was in disorder and was easily defeated. Both the Raja of Nāgpur and the Peshwa resisted and attacked the British forces stationed under their respective subsidiary treaties. Nāgpur quickly collapsed, but the Peshwa kept up a running fight before surrendering in June 1818. The Pindari bands themselves, chased hither and thither, broke up or surrendered.

The East India Company was thus the undisputed master of India, as far as the Sutlej River in the Punjab. This episode was completed by the acceptance of British suzerainty by the Rājput chiefs of Rājasthān, central India, and Kāthiāwār, as they had formerly accepted the Mughals. Thus the year 1818 marks a watershed, when the British Empire in India became the British Empire of India.

The British Empire of India

The settlement of 1818. The diplomatic settlement of 1818, except for a few annexations before 1857, remained in force until 1947 and is therefore worth some attention. The company, under the influence of its guiding star of economy, was glad to be saved the expense of administering as much of India as possible, especially the less fertile portions. Having controlled the larger states by its subsidiary forces (for which they paid), it was content with tribute from the remainder, with control posts at strategic points. Thus Kāthiāwār was controlled from Baroda; Rājasthān, from Ajmer. There was no thought of integration, as in Mughal days. The states were isolated and excluded from any connection with the British. About half of India remained under Indian rulers, robbed of any power of aggression and deprived of any opportunity of cooperation—in the south were the large units of Mysore, Hyderābād, and Travancore; in the west, the states of Śivajī's family; across the centre to the east,

Nāgpur and a number of poor "jungle" states; in the west and west central areas, numerous Rājput and other Hindu chiefs with the surviving Marāthā states of Sindhia, Holkar, and the Gaekwar; beyond the Jumna, some Sikh princedoms; and in the Ganges Valley, the still prosperous and disorderly state of Oudh. In all there were more than 360 units; politically they were like the surviving fragments of a broken jigsaw puzzle, with all its complexity but without its unity.

The subjection of a whole subcontinent containing a unique civilization has long been a source of historical wonderment. The onetime explanations of innate superiority and of mere fate are no longer seriously entertained. But analysis goes far to dissipate the mystery. In the first place, the feat was not unique; the Turkish Muslims had twice done much the same—for shorter periods, it is true, but also with fewer resources. All these achievements were made possible by the innate divisiveness of Hindu society, rent by class and caste divisions, which rendered it unusually willing to call in unwelcome outsiders to defeat the still more unwelcome neighbour. The foreigners, asked in the first resort to assist in defeating a rival, were in the last resort accepted as masters in preference to dominance by a rival. Thus Marāthās preferred the British to the Mughals or Muslims; and the Niẓām, the British to the Marāthās. Long historical memories can be inhibiting as well as inspiring. Against this setting can be set the company's urge toward unity in the interests of trade. Even when its Indian trade was no longer profitable, India gave profits to others, and its opium bought the China tea, which gave the company its overall profits. Given the fact of expansion, Britain enjoyed the advantage of overseas reinforcement through its sea power and of reserves of power, far greater than that of any Indian prince, through its rapidly expanding industrial economy. A lost battle for the British was an incident in a campaign; for the Indian prince, usually the end of the chapter. Then there were the technical advantages of arms and military discipline and the immense general advantage of a disciplined civilian morale. In the later stages this was boosted by the rising self-confidence of Europeans in general, with its belief that the western European civilization was the only truly progressive one that had ever existed. For the Hindu, on the other hand, his world was at its lowest ebb—in the Kali, or dark age—while the Muslim believed in inscrutable fate. The Hindu's heart was in his religiocultural complex, and political dominion meant little to the ordinary Hindu so long as this remained untouched.

Analysis of the British achievement in India

Organization and policy in British India. The realization of supremacy in 1818 made urgent the problem of the organization of and determination of policy for British India. So far only Bengal had been deliberately organized; the extensive areas annexed after 1799 in the north and the south were still under provisional arrangements. Now the Peshwa's dominions in the west awaited settlement. The administrators of the first 30 years of the 19th century gave British India the form it retained until 1947. Outstanding among them were Sir Thomas Munro in Madras, Mountstuart Elphinstone in western India, and Sir Charles Metcalfe in Delhi; to this trio must be added a fourth—Holt MacKenzie, whose planning determined the lines of settlement from Benares to the Jumna.

The form of British India

Organization. The only area so far definitely settled was that of Bengal, Bihār and Orissa. Lord Cornwallis had been charged by Pitt with the reorganization of Bengal under the new act. Besides being a soldier of distinction, Cornwallis was a man of outstanding integrity, a landlord with rural tastes, and an instinctive Whig. Cornwallis first undertook a cleansing of the existing system. Discipline among the company's servants was enforced at the price of dismissal. Private trade was forbidden to all government officers, and the service was divided into administrative and commercial branches. These measures were coupled with a generous salary system, which removed the temptation to corruption. From this time the company's service began to gain its later reputation for efficiency and integrity. All this could be done because the governor general, with his Council of three and his veto power, was now unassailable to the attacks that had ruined Vansittart and frustrated Warren Hastings.

From this secure base Cornwallis built up the Bengal system. Its first principle was anglicization. In the belief that Indian officials were corrupt (while British corruption had been cured), all posts worth more than £500 a year were reserved for the company's covenanted servants. Next came the frame of government. The 23 districts each had a British collector with magisterial powers and two assistants, who were responsible for revenue collection. The judicial system was organized with district judges for both civil and criminal cases. In civil cases there were four courts of appeal; and in criminal, four circuit courts. Criminal justice was taken over from the nawab's deputy, thus removing the last shred of Mughal authority. The criminal code was the Islāmic, humanely modified. A new police force replaced the former local constables of the *zamīndārs* (tax collectors). This new system, which, with its division of authority, showed its Whig influence, was rounded off by the proclamation of the rule of law, making all governmental acts answerable in the ordinary courts of law. Though hardly noticed at the time by Indians, it was a radical innovation with far-reaching effects. It was a charter of civil as distinct from political liberty.

Cornwallis' permanent settlement of the land revenue is the measure that most deeply affected the life and structure of Indian society, three-quarters of the revenue coming from the land. He found a system of hereditary *zamīndārs*, who had acquired police and magisterial powers as well, and who were much shaken by the frequent changes of revenue policy under the British. The "settlement" was the decision in 1793 to stabilize the revenue demand at a fixed annual figure, with a commission to the *zamīndār* for collection, and to regard him as the owner of his *zamīndāri;* he had the disposal of wastelands within his jurisdiction, but these lands were liable to be sold for arrears of payment. Thus the tax collector became a landlord, with the Achilles heel of sale for arrears, while the tiers of lesser landholders became his tenants. The *zamīndār* reaped the profit of rising prices and of the cultivation of wasteland, while the classes below him lost their occupancy rights. The intended protection of these tenants proved illusory because their rights were customary, unsupported by documents. The legal cases that ensued clogged the courts to the point of breakdown. Initially, the *zamīndār* often lost his holding because the fixed demand was pitched too high. The net result of this measure was the creation of a landlord class, loyal to the British connection but divorced from touch with the cultivators. The government, receiving the revenue from the *zamīndārs*, knew little of the people and could do little for them.

Cornwallis' permanent settlement

At first the Bengal system was thought to provide the key to Indian administration, but doubts multiplied with the years. In Madras, Sir Thomas Munro retained the paternal framework of government but introduced a radically differing method of revenue management known as ryotwar, in which the settlement was made directly with the cultivator, each field being separately measured and annually assessed. The system eliminated the middleman but sometimes placed the cultivators at the mercy of lower officials, who often formed cliques of caste groups. Munro considered that innovation and ignorance were the ruling British vices. His system tended to be static and to allow the subordinate tail to wag the directing British dog.

In western India, Mountstuart Elphinstone had the problem of reconciling to British control the resentful Marāthās of the Peshwa's dominions. With a masterly mixture of tact and firmness he largely succeeded. He retained Indian agency as far as possible, and he allowed the Marāthā nobles, or *jāgīrdārs*, to retain most of their land and many of their privileges. He even continued some donations to Hindu temples. He used the ryotwar method of assessing land revenue, collecting through local officials from the village headmen. In Bombay he encouraged Western learning and science, tempting suspicious Brahmins to open their minds to the West. He

Reconciling the Marāthās

foresaw the ultimate end of British rule through voluntary westernization, and he took the first steps toward introducing the new world without antagonizing the old.

In the north, Sir Charles Metcalfe discovered the largely autonomous village with its joint ownership and cultivation by caste oligarchies. He believed this to be the original pattern of rural organization throughout India, and it became his passion to preserve it as far as possible in current conditions. Like Munro and Elphinstone, he was suspicious of change and wished to leave the villagers alone as far as possible. In this he was powerfully supported by the work of Holt MacKenzie, the Bengal secretary whose memorandum of 1819 set a course of recognition and record of village rights for the whole of the northwestern provinces (as later revised and codified, this marked the end of the Bengal system of permanent revenue settlement).

Administration of British India

The resulting system of administration of British India was still largely Indian in pattern, though it was now British in direction and superintendence. It was paternalistic and hierarchical; and it suffered, like its immediate predecessors, from a chronic tendency to overassess. The emperor was replaced by the mystical entity, the Company Bahadur; and its representative, the governor general, moved about with almost equal pomp. The higher direction was exclusively European, but the officers acted in a Mughal spirit, and the administration at subdistrict and village level went on much as before. But there were also large changes. The British established on a national scale the idea of property in land, and the resulting buying and selling caused large class changes. Their new security benefitted the commercial classes generally, but the deliberate sacrifice of Indian industry to the claims of the new machine industries of Britain ruined such ancient crafts as cotton and silk weaving. The new legal system, with its network of courts, proved efficient on the criminal side but was heavily overloaded on the civil.

The strain and the scandal of this situation created a demand for increased Indian agency and caused the first breaches in the British monopoly of higher office. Indianization began with the confessed inefficiency of the British legal system. The picture is completed by the company's army, separately organized in the three presidencies and officered, like the civil service, exclusively by the British. It was backed by contingents of the British army. The Bengal army preponderated in numbers and fighting spirit. On European standards it was cumbrous and inefficient; some of its defects were exposed in the early days of the Nepal war. But it was more than a match for anything that could be brought against it. Only the Russians, could they have moved so far in force, might have made short work of it.

The determination of policy. The administration of British India thus established was impressive though ponderous. But it was essentially static; it was a repair of the machinery of government without any decision about its direction. Such a situation in a subcontinent could not be viable for long.

The nature of the government in India

In the early 19th century a great debate went on in Britain about the nature of the government in India. The company wanted India to be regarded as a field for British commercial exploitation, with the company holding the administrative whip with one hand and exploiting with the other. This pleased no one but the company itself. As an extension of this, the new regime could be regarded as a law-and-order or police state, holding the ring while British merchants in general traded profitably. But this was assailed from several quarters. There was the Whig demand, first voiced by Edmund Burke in his campaign against Warren Hastings, that the Indian government must be responsible for the welfare of the governed. This was reinforced by Evangelicals in England, both Anglican and Baptist, who added the rider that as the ruler Britain was responsible for India's spiritual and moral welfare as well. The Evangelicals were a rising force, influential in the British "establishment." Their specific for India, as a preparation for conversion, was English education. They were reinforced in this by the rising group of freethinking Utilitarians—followers of Jeremy Bentham and James Mill—who were influential in the company's service, who wished to use India as a laboratory for their theories, and who thought Indian society could be transformed by legislation. Finally, there were radical rationalists who had borrowed the doctrine of human rights from France and wished to introduce them into India; and on the practical side there was a body of British merchants and manufacturers, who saw in India both a market and a profitable theatre of activity and who chafed at the restraints of the East India Company's monopoly.

Some of these influences seeped into the Tory ascendancy, which lasted until 1830. In 1813 the East India Company lost its monopoly of trade with India and was compelled to allow free entry of missionaries. British India was declared to be British territory, and £10,000 was to be set aside annually for the promotion of both Eastern and Western learning. But the real breakthrough came with the governor generalship of Lord William Bentinck (served 1828–35; *q.v.*) and with the Whig government that, from 1830, carried the great Reform Bill.

Reforms of Lord William Bentinck

Bentinck was a radical aristocrat. His administrative reforms were in line with Utilitarian theory but with deference to local conditions and in harmony with his own military sense of command. In Bengal, the collector was made the real head of his district by the addition of civil judgeship to his magistracy; he was also disciplined by the institution of commissioners to superintend him. The judiciary was overhauled with the same eye to a chain of authority.

But it was as a social reformer that Bentinck made an indelible mark on the future of India. He was commissioned by the directors to effect economies in order to show a balanced budget in the approaching charter-renewal discussions. In doing this he incurred much odium; but he was able to take the first steps in Indianizing the higher judicial services. On his arrival Bentinck was confronted with an agitation against *satī*, or the burning of Hindu widows on the funeral pyres of their husbands. In suppressing the practice, he had to face the reproaches of both Hindus and Europeans on the grounds of religious interference. But he was also fortified by the support of the Hindu reformer Rammohan Ray. In thus acting and in prohibiting child sacrifice on Saugor Island and discouraging infanticide—a widespread practice among the Rājputs—Bentinck established the principle that the general good did not permit violations of the universal moral law, even if done in the name of religion. The same principle applied to the suppression of *ṭhagī* (thuggee), or ritual murder and robbery by gangs in central India in the name of the goddess Kālī. On a more positive side Bentinck substituted English for Persian as the language of record for government and the higher courts, and he declared that government support would be given primarily to the cultivation of Western learning and science through the medium of English. In this he was supported by T.B. (later Lord) Macaulay, whose speech in Parliament on July 10, 1833, was the most eloquent expression of the new spirit ever made.

This period saw the British in India committed to promoting the positive welfare of India instead of merely holding a ring for trade and exploitation; to introducing Western knowledge, science, and ideas alongside the Indian, with a view to eventual absorption and adoption, and to the promotion of Indian participation in the government with a view to eventual Indian self-government. It was the changeover from the concept of a Mughal successor state—the Company Bahadur—to that of a westernized self-governing dominion. In the former case, the British were wardens of a stationary society; in the latter, trustees of an evolving one.

Concept of a westernized self-governing dominion

A word should be added about the Indian states. Their place in British India was also a subject of the great debate on the future of India. On the whole, the argument for subordinate isolation held, and no great change occurred in their status until after the Mutiny of 1857 (see below *The mutiny and great revolt of 1857–59*). Out of the discussions, however, came the de facto principle of British paramountcy, which was increasingly assumed though not openly proclaimed. The only important change before 1840 was the takeover of Mysore in 1831 on the ground of misgovernment; it was not annexed, but it was administered on behalf of the raja for the next 50 years.

The completion of dominion and expansion. After the settlement of 1818, the only parts of India beyond British control were a fringe of Himalayan states to the north and a block of territory in the northwest covering the Indus Valley, the Punjab, and Kashmir. To the south Ceylon was already occupied by the British, but to the east lay the valley and hill tracts of Assam and the Buddhist kingdom of Burma straddling the Irrawaddy River.

The Himalayan states were Nepal of the Gurkhas, Bhutan, and Sikkim. Nepal and Bhutan remained independent throughout the British period; but Sikkim came under British protection, providing the hill station of Darjeeling as Bengal's hill capital. The valley and hill tracts of Assam were taken under protection to save them from Burmese attack. From this time the Indian tea plant was cultivated, after the failure of Chinese imported ones, and commenced the great Indian tea industry.

In the early 19th century the Burmese were in an aggressive mood, having defeated the Thais (1768) and subjected Arakan and hill states on either side of the river valleys. Attacks on British territory in 1824 started the First Anglo-Burmese War (1824–26), which, though mismanaged, led to the British annexation of the coastal strips of Arakan and Tenasserim in 1826. The Second Anglo-Burmese War (1852) was caused by disputes between merchants (trading in rice and teak timber) and the Rangoon governor. The governor general, Lord Dalhousie (served 1848–56), intervened, annexing the maritime province of Pegu with the port of Rangoon in a campaign this time well-managed and economical. Commercial imperialism was the motive for this campaign.

Wars with Burma and Afghanistan

To the northwest British India was bounded by the Sikh kingdom of Ranjit Singh, who added Kashmir to his state in 1819 and Peshāwar in 1834. Beyond was confusion, with the Afghan monarchy in dissolution and its lands parcelled between several chiefs and Sind, controlled by a group of *amīrs*, or chiefs. British indifference changed to action in the 1830s, owing to the advance of Russia in Central Asia and to that nation's diplomatic duel with Lord Palmerston about its influence in Turkey. Afghanistan was seen as a point from which Russia could threaten British India or Britain could embarrass Russia. Lord Auckland (served 1836–42) was sent as governor general, charged with forestalling the Russians; and from this stemmed his Afghan adventure and the First Afghan War (1838–42). The method adopted was to restore Shāh Shojāʿ, the exiled Afghan king, then living in the Punjab, by ousting the ruler of Kābul, Dōst Moḥammad. Ranjit Singh cooperated in the enterprise but cleverly avoided any military commitment, leaving the British to bear the whole burden. The route of invasion lay through Sind, because of Sikh occupation of the Punjab.

The *amīrs*' treaty of 1832 with the British was brushed aside, and Sind was forced to pay arrears of tribute to Shāh Shojāʿ. At first things went well, with victories and the occupation of Kābul in 1839. But then it was discovered that Shāh Shojāʿ was too unpopular to rule the country unaided; the British restoring force thus became a foreign occupying army—anathema to the liberty-loving Afghan—and was regularly engaged in putting down sporadic tribal revolts. After two years, a general revolt in the autumn of 1841 overwhelmed the British garrison. Meanwhile, the Russian menace in eastern Europe had receded. Auckland's successor, Lord Ellenborough (served 1842–44), arranged for the evacuation of the country by means of a converging march on Kābul from Qandahār in the south and Jalālābād in the north and a return through the Khyber Pass. Thus honour was satisfied, and the fact of defeat was glossed over. Shāh Shojāʿ was shortly murdered. The episode demonstrated, at a heavy price in terms of money and human suffering, the ease with which Afghanistan could be overrun by a regular army and the difficulty of holding it. The enterprise, though conceived as an insurance against Russian imperialism, developed into a species of imperialism itself. Economics joined with Afghan spirit to put a limit on British expansion in this direction.

Relations with Sind

After the Afghans came Sind. There was little to be said for the *amīrs* themselves—a group of related chiefs who had come to power in the late 18th century and had kept the country in poverty and stagnation. A treaty in 1832 threw the Indus open to commerce except for the passage of armed vessels or military stores; at the same time the integrity of Sind was recognized. Thus Auckland's march through Sind was a clear violation of a treaty signed only seven years before. Sore feelings at the turn of events in Afghanistan produced a final breach. On a charge of unfriendly feelings by the *amīrs* during the Afghan War, Karāchi, occupied in 1839, was retained. Further demands were then made; the moderate resident James Outram was superseded by the militant general Sir Charles James Napier; and resistance was provoked, to be crushed at Miāni in 1843. Sind was then annexed to the Bombay Presidency; after four years of rough-and-ready rule by Napier, it was put on the road to prosperity by Sir Bartle Frere.

There remained the great Sikh state of the Punjab, the single-handed creation of Ranjit Singh. Succeeding to a local chiefship in 1792 at the age of 12, he occupied Lahore in 1799 under a grant from Zamān Shāh, the Afghan king. He could thus pose as a legitimate ruler, not only to his own Sikhs but to the majority of Muslims of the Punjab. From this start he extended his dominions northwestward as far as the Afghan hills and including Kashmir and Jammu and southwestward toward Sind to Multān and near Sheikhpura. The Treaty of Amritsar with the British in 1809 barred his expansion southeastward; besides directing Rānjit's expansionism northwestward, it produced an admiration for the disciplined company's troops, who coolly repelled the wild Sikh Akalis when they attacked the British at Amritsar. From that time dated the formation of the formidable Sikh army with its 40,000 disciplined infantry, 12,000 cavalry, and powerful artillery. It was generally agreed to compare favourably for efficiency with the company's forces.

Relations with the Sikhs

Ranjit Singh employed Hindus and Muslims besides Sikhs, but his regime was in fact a Sikh domination based on tacit Hindu support and Muslim acquiescence. It used most of the revenue to support the army, which made it apparently powerful but retarded development. It was a highly personal system, centred on Ranjit himself. It was thus one that the company would not lightly attack but that had inner weaknesses behind its impressive facade. These weaknesses began to be exposed on the morrow of Rānjit's death in 1839; within six years the state was on the verge of dissolution. Army disbandment or foreign adventure seemed the only way for the Sikhs to deal with this crisis. The former being impossible, at length the Rani (Hindi *rānī*) regent (for the boy prince Dulip Singh), the chief minister, and the commander in chief agreed on a move against the British. The frontier was crossed in December 1845, and a sharp and bloody war ended in a British victory at Sobraon in February 1846. The British feared to annex outright a region full of former soldiers and wished to retain a buffer state against possible attack from the northwest. By the Treaty of Lahore they took Kashmir and its dependencies, with the fertile Jalandhar area, reduced the regular army to 20,000 infantry and 12,000 cavalry, and exacted an indemnity of £500,000. They then sold Kashmir to the Hindu chief Gulab Singh of Jammu, who had changed sides at precisely the right moment. Thus a chronic political problem for the subcontinent was created.

The balance thus created between annexation and autonomy, between Lahore and Jammu and Lahore and the Afghans, did not last. There was no subsidiary force, for fear of antagonizing the Sikhs. Two years later a rising at Multān became a national Sikh revolt, and the Sikh court was helpless. Another brief and still more bloody war, with the Sikhs this time fighting resolutely, ended with their surrender in March 1849 and the British annexation of the state.

Annexation this time proved viable because of the underlying tension between Sikhs and Muslims. The Sikhs preferred a British to a Muslim raj (Hindi *rāj*). The British depressed the sirdars, or Sikh leaders, but left the rest of the community and its religion untouched. The Sikhs sided with the British during the 1857 mutiny; the Muslims, however, could not forget their loss of power to the Sikhs. There was little commercial exploitation of the state, and the Sikhs found employment in the army. Lord Dalhousie (*q.v.*) closely supervised the administration through a like-minded agent, Sir John Lawrence. The pair produced a new model administration, establishing what was known as the Punjab school. It was noted for strong personal leadership, on-the-spot decisions, strong-arm methods, impartiality between the communities, and material development, including irrigation. A canal, a road, or a bridge was the Punjabi officials' delight. The cultivator was preferred to the sirdar (landlord); the countryman, to the townsman. The Punjab system was strong and efficient, creating prosperity; but it never reconciled the communities or welded them into unity. The Punjab feeling thus remained a territorial sentiment, without ever becoming a national spirit. This failure was a basis for later partition.

British annexation of the Sikh state

Lord Dalhousie's reign (served 1848–56) is often regarded as an exercise in imperialism; in fact it was more an exercise in westernism. Dalhousie was a man of great drive and strong conviction. His convictions were westernizing and mainly motivated his actions. In general he considered Western civilization to be far superior to that of the Indian, and the more of it that could be introduced the better. Along these lines he pushed Western education, introducing a grant-in-aid system, which later proliferated Indian private colleges, and planned three universities. Socially, he allowed Christian converts to inherit the property of their Hindu families. Materially, he extended irrigation and the telegraph and introduced the railway.

Politically, British administration was preferable to Indian and it was to be imposed where possible. Externally, this led to annexation as in the Punjab and Burma, rather than to the control of foreign relations or to a British-superintended native regime. Internally, it led to the annexation of Indian states on the ground of misgovernment or the doctrine of lapse. The leading case of misgovernment was the disorderly but prosperous Muslim state of Oudh—the oldest ally of the British. The doctrine of lapse concerned Hindu states where rulers had no direct natural heirs. Hindu law allowed adoption to meet these cases, but Dalhousie declared that such must be approved by the supreme government; otherwise there was "lapse" to the paramount power, which meant the imposition of the usual British administration. The three principal cases were Sātāra in 1848 (the family of the Marāthā hero Śivajī), Jhānsi (1853), and the large Marāthā state of Nāgpur (1854). Finally, Dalhousie abolished the titular sovereignties of the Carnatic and Tanjore, declined to continue the former peshwa's pension to his adopted son, and gave notice of the termination of the Mughal imperial title itself.

The first century of British influence. The onset of British influence in India differed both in manner and in kind from that of other historical invasions. The British came neither as migrating hordes seeking new homes nor as armies seeking plunder or empire. They had no missionary zeal. Yet eventually they did more to transform India than did any previous ruling power. This apparent paradox requires some explanation.

Political effects. At first the British were only one group of foreign traders among several, fortunate to find in the Mughals a firm government ready to foster trade. Their entry into politics was gradual, first as allies of country powers, then as their virtual directors, and only finally as masters. At each step they were assisted by local powers who preferred British influence to that of their neighbours. It was only in the 20 years 1798–1818 that they were consciously imperialistic and only thereafter that they treated India as a conquered rather than an acquired country. The effect of this was to replace the defunct Mughal regime and the abortive Marāthā successor empire with a veiled but very real hegemony.

Indians were used to the idea of political unity and overlordship. They admired the British for being more successful than themselves, while reprobating many of the British habits and doctrines. But the old ruling classes showed little sign of adopting British institutions; after 1818 they withdrew within themselves, nursing their memories rather than feeding their hopes. The Indian regimes of 1857 all assumed a traditional form. The one department in which Western influence was effective was the military. From the time of Mīr Qāsim in Bengal (1760–63), Indian princes began to train troops in the European manner and to form parks of artillery. Some of these bodies, culminating in Ranjit Singh's Sikh army, attained a high degree of efficiency. Their problem was maintenance, for most princes lacked the necessary resources to pay their men and officers regularly and maintain their arms. Indian opinion in general saw the British as the latest holders of the traditional paramount power. There was no novelty in the foreign personnel of the government, for this had been a Mughal practice, too. What was new was the artificial division between British India and Indian-governed India, with virtually no contact between the two. The Mughals practiced partnership for a century; the Turks and Afghans, subordinate cooperation; the British, it seemed, wished to forget the Indian leaders altogether.

Economic effects. Things were quite different, however, in the economic field. Up to 1750 the effect of the East India Company's operations was marginal. Production of cotton and silk goods, of indigo, saltpetre, and, later, opium was stimulated in particular areas like Bengal, Gujarāt, and Mālwa, with some gain to the middlemen but no sign of any general rise in living standards. India then, as now, was mainly agricultural; and its industries, though significant, were marginal to its whole economy. The latter changed, however, with the acquisition of Bengal. The bias in favour of British merchants diverted trade from their Indian counterparts, though some of the profit went back to the British merchants' Indian agents. The extravagant present giving, a large abuse of a traditional system, diverted much money to Britain. Still more, the pressure on the *zamīndārs* for more revenue, and theirs in turn on the cultivators, further diminished the Bengali income. To this must be added the operation of monopolies, public and private. When the Bengal famine of 1770 occurred, reckoned to have swept away one-third of the population, little attempt at relief was made, though this, with Bengal's network of waterways, was practicable. The cruel severity with which the revenue was still collected at this time delayed recovery for many years. Economic recovery was further delayed by Warren Hastings' makeshift revenue arrangements; and much dislocation was caused in the social structure, with its own effect on economic life. Cornwallis' permanent settlement (1793), after an initial period of dislocation, gave relief and security to the *zamīndārs*, who benefitted by the rise in prices and the cultivation of wastelands; the cultivators themselves, now the *zamīndārs*' tenants at will, remained as poor as before. Apart from the *zamīndārs*, the only class to benefit from the British was that of the entrepreneurs of Calcutta, who acted as agents and bankers to the British. Thus both Clive's and Hastings' business managers became wealthy landowners. In Madras little could be done until the incubus of the Carnatic nawab's debts were removed and the country was settled after the Cornwallis–Wellesley annexations (1792–99). There, economic settlement turned on the working of the ryotwar revenue system; regularity of collection was offset by severity of assessment, and the same may be said of both western and northern India.

Effect of the company's operations

After 1800 there was a new factor, in the appearance of machine-made cotton goods from Britain. These steadily undermined the Indian handicraft industries, until all but the highest and coarsest grades of cloth were squeezed out. The district of Dacca in the 1820s was illustrative of this process. From about 1830 the tea industry of Assam began with coffee in the south. Coal mining was begun; but its growth, with that of the jute and cotton-machine industries, had to wait for the second half of the century. The average Indian was far more secure than before, except for famine; but he was not much more prosperous, except in patches. India drifted toward the status of a colonial economy, a supplier of raw materials, a market for manufactured articles, to the profit of the foreigner.

Displacement of classes

Social effects. The social effects of this period were considerable. They took mainly the form of the displacement of classes. As already noted, there was a general disturbance in Bengal caused by the permanent settlement, whereby the lesser landholders were reduced to the condition of tenants at will. But there was also disturbance among the *zamīndārs*. The first upset followed the famine of 1770, when the cultivators were often too few for the revenue demand to be met, and "farming" the revenue for some time took the place of a revenue settlement. The second upset came with the permanent settlement of 1793, when the revenue figure fixed was in many cases too high for the existing cultivation. By 1820 it was calculated that more than one-third of the estates had changed hands through sale for arrears of land tax. The purchasers were in the main the Calcutta entrepreneurs, newly enriched by their contacts with the British. Many were absentees. The social link between landholder and cultivator had been broken, cash nexus replacing traditional rights.

In Calcutta itself, these same rentiers formed a fashionable and intellectual society, from which came the first significant cultural contacts with the West. It was composed of the prosperous section of the three upper Bengali castes, with such others as gained acceptance by their wealth or education. Collectively this literate class was known as the *bhadralok*.

In the north there was less dislocation, though the landholders, many of whom had no title but the sword, tended to be depressed. There was a general recognition of rights and broadly of their protection. The chief sufferers were ruling families, who lost power, and the official aristocracy, who lost office. In the south, chiefs whom Munro dispossessed were largely in the class of robber barons.

In western India, a balance between aristocratic and cultivating rights was perhaps better maintained than elsewhere and relations were harmonious. Of significance there was the rapid development of Bombay from the time it came to possess a large hinterland in 1818. With it came the rise of the enterprising Parsi community.

In general, apart from Bengal, there was some depression of the old aristocracy, a regulation and preservation of lesser landholders' rights, and an encouragement of the commercial classes. Communities did not break up, but their fortunes rose and fell with their ability to adjust to these conditions.

Cultural effects of British influence

Cultural effects. The cultural effects of British influence during the century 1757–1857, though less spectacular, were in the long run farther reaching. At first there was little enough. But as the Europeans grew in political importance, Indians became interested in the causes of the growth, so that the first examples of cultural influence were in the military field. Some Europeans, in their turn, early interested themselves in Indian culture, marked by the foundation of the Asiatic Society of Bengal in 1784, by Sir William Jones, and by the translation of such Sanskrit works as the *Bhagavadgītā* and *Sakuntala* and of Persian works like the *Ā'īn-e Akbarī*.

As the British completed their supremacy, four Indian attitudes could be discerned. There were Indians who rejected all things Western, retiring to their houses and estates to dream of the past. There were those who were clients and employees of the British, as they had been of the Mughals and the Turks before them, without any intention of giving up their traditional culture. But there were also those who, while remaining good Hindus or Muslims, began to study Western ways and thought for careerist purposes. And there was, finally, a small group who sought to study the ideas and spirit of the West, with a view to incorporating in their own society anything that seemed desirable.

The agents of Western influence were government officials, who carried Western ideas, such as utilitarianism, equality before the law, and property into their administration of revenue and the law, and missionaries, who combined hostility to Hinduism and Islām with the presentation of a new ethic—the practice of good works and the promotion of English education as a preliminary for conversion. It was at this point that the Indian careerist and inquirer met the new Western stream of thought. The English language was popular because it opened paths to employment and influence; orthodox Hindus patronized the English schools and promoted the Hindu College (now Presidency College) in Calcutta (1816). This college, along with Alexander Duff's Scottish Churches College, also in Calcutta, became a centre of Western influence and saw the rise of the Young Bengal movement, the westernizing zeal of which denied the Hindu religion itself.

The leadership of Raja Rammohan Ray

But between the complete westernizers and the careerists was a third group, which found a leader of genius in Raja Rammohan Ray. Making a moderate fortune in Calcutta finance, which he invested in *zamīndārīs*, from 1815 Roy advocated reforms in Hindu society and the acceptance of some features of Western thought. He denounced *satī* (the burning of widows) and championed the cause of the Indian widow and wife. He advocated English education as a means of bringing Western knowledge to India. He denounced idolatry and preached monotheism. With his *Precepts of Jesus* he both introduced the Christian ethic into Hindu society and drew the sting of missionary attacks. He finally founded a reforming Hindu body, the Brahmo Samaj (Divine Society), in 1828. Both careerists and Ray's followers cooperated in the spread of English education, but it was the latter who began the movement of borrowing from the West without any feeling of disloyalty to their past.

By the year 1857 the British had established complete political control of the Indian subcontinent, which they ruled directly or through subordinate princes. They had established an authoritarian system of government, making use of Mughal practice and tradition and supported by an efficient civil service and a relatively efficient army. Princely India remained in a stagnant traditionalism; nominal sovereignties were suppressed in the name of progress. In British India land settlements had produced much social dislocation, while purporting to respect traditional rights and to learn from the past; in particular, the Western concept of property in land had led to much social displacement. The westernized legal system was efficient in suppressing crime but dilatory in upholding rights and incomprehensible in its working. Social evils like *satī*, thuggee, and infanticide had been suppressed or discouraged, but Hinduism and Islām were still respected. The revolutionary aspect of the British presence was the decision, taken about the time of Bentinck, to introduce Western knowledge and science through the medium of the English language. Western inventions like the telegraph, scientific irrigation, railways, and steamships followed, throwing India open to the industrial mechanistic and democratic world of the developing West. Along with education went the Christian missionary intrusion, with its moral and ideological challenge. This, in its turn, provoked a creative response from Rammohan Ray's circle, who were laying the foundations of a modernized Hinduism, which was later to find political expression in the Indian National Congress.

THE MUTINY AND GREAT REVOLT OF 1857–59

The mutiny of the Bengal army began on May 10, 1857, at Meerut, when Indian soldiers who had been placed in irons for refusing to accept new cartridges were rescued by their comrades. They shot the British officers and made for Delhi, 40 miles (64 kilometres) distant, where there were no British troops. The Indian garrison at Delhi joined them, and by the next nightfall they had secured the city and Mughal fort, proclaiming the aged titular Mughal emperor as their leader. There at a stroke was an army, a cause, and a national leader—the only Muslim who appealed to both Hindus and Muslims.

Nature and causes of the rebellion. But this movement became much more than a military mutiny. There has been much controversy over its nature and causes. The British military commander Sir James Outram thought it was a Muslim conspiracy, exploiting Hindu grievances. Or it might have been an aristocratic plot, set off too soon by the Meerut outbreak. But the only evidence for either of these was the circulation from village to village of chapatis, or cakes of unleavened bread, a practice known to have taken place at any time of unrest. The lack of planning after the outbreak rules out these two explanations, while the degree of popular support argues more than a purely military outbreak.

Nationalist historians have seen in it the first Indian war of independence. In fact, it was rather the last effort of traditional India. It began on a point of caste pollution; its leaders were traditionalists who looked to reviving the past, while the small new westernized class actively supported the British. And the leaders were not united, because they sought to revive former Hindu and Muslim regimes, which in their heyday had bitterly clashed. But something important was required to provoke so many to seize the opportunity of a military uprising to stage a war of independence.

Military cause of the mutiny

The military cause was both particular and general. In particular, it was the greased cartridges supplied for the new breach-loading Enfield rifles. These had to be bitten off before insertion, and the British manufacturers had supplied a fat of mixed beef and pork—anathema to both Hindus and Muslims. This mistake was retrieved as soon as discovered; but the fact that explanations and reissues could not quell the soldiers' suspicions suggests that the troops were already disturbed by other causes. The Bengal army of nearly 130,000 Indian troops contained about 40,000 Brahmins as well as many Rājputs. The British had accentuated caste consciousness by careful regulations, had allowed discipline to grow lax, and had failed to maintain understanding between British officers and their men. In addition, the General Service Enlistment Act of 1856 required recruits to serve overseas if ordered, a challenge to the castes who composed so much of the Bengal army. To these points may be added the fact that the British garrison in India had been reduced at this time to 23,000 men because of troop withdrawals for the Crimean and Persian wars.

The general factors that turned a military mutiny into a popular revolt can be comprehensively described under the heading of political, economic, social, and cultural westernization. Politically, the princes of India had retired into a sulky seclusion after their final defeat in 1818. But the wars against the Afghans and the Sikhs and then the annexations of Dalhousie alarmed and outraged them. The Muslims had lost the large state of Oudh; the Marāthās had lost Nāgpur, Sātāra, and Jhānsi. Further, the British were becoming increasingly hostile toward traditional survivals and contemptuous of anything Indian. There was, therefore, both resentment and unease among the old governing class, fanned in Delhi by the decision to end the Mughal imperial title on Bahādur Shāh's death.

Economically and socially, there had been much dislocation in the landholding class all over northern and western India as a result of British land-revenue settlements, setting group against group. There was thus a suppressed tension in the countryside, ready to break out whenever governmental pressure might be reduced.

Reactions to Western interventions

Then came the Western innovations of the now overconfident British. Their educational policy was a westernizing one, with English instead of Persian as the official language; the practitioners of the old learning felt themselves slighted. Western inventions like the telegraph and railways aroused the conservative prejudice of a conservative race (though Indians crowded the trains when they had them). More disturbing were the interventions, in the name of humanity, in the realm of Hindu custom —*e.g.*, the prohibition of *satī*, the campaign against infanticide, the law legalizing remarriage of Hindu widows. Finally, there was the activity of missionaries, by this time widespread. Government was ostentatiously neutral, but an increasing number of its officers were friendly, so that Hindu society was inclined to regard them as eroding Hindu society without openly interfering. In sum, this combination of factors produced, besides the normal tensions endemic in India, an uneasy, fearful, suspicious, resentful frame of mind and a wind of unrest ready to fan the flame of any actual physical outbreak.

The revolt and its aftermath. The dramatic capture of Delhi turned mutiny into full-scale revolt. The whole episode falls into three periods—first came the summer of 1857, when the British, without reinforcements from home, fought with their backs to the wall; the second concerned the operations for the relief of Lucknow in the autumn; and the third was the successful campaign of Sir Colin Campbell and Sir Hugh Rose in the first half of 1858. Mopping-up operations followed, lasting until the British capture of Tantia Topi in April 1859.

From Delhi the revolt spread in June to Kānpur and Lucknow. Kānpur surrendered on June 16; but the Lucknow garrison held out in the residency from July 1, in spite of the death of Sir Henry Lawrence on July 4. The campaign then settled down to British attempts to take Delhi and relieve Lucknow. In spite of their apparently desperate situation, the British possessed long-term advantages—they could and did receive reinforcements from Britain; they had, thanks to the resolution of Sir John Lawrence, a firm base in the Punjab, and they had another base in Bengal, where the people were quiet; they had no anxiety in the south and only a little in the west; they had an immense belief in themselves and their civilization, which gave resolution to their initial desperation. The mutineers, on the other hand, lacked good leadership until nearly the end; they had no confidence in themselves and suffered the guilt feelings of rebels without a cause, making them frantic and fearful by turns.

British long-term advantages

In the Punjab were some 10,000 British troops, which made it possible to disarm the Indian regiments; and the recently defeated Sikhs were so hostile to the Muslims that they supported the British against the Mughal restoration in Delhi. A small British army was improvised, which held the ridge before Delhi against greatly superior forces until Sir John Lawrence was able to send a siege train under John Nicholson. With this, and the aid of rebel dissensions, Delhi was stormed and captured by the British on September 20, while the emperor Bahādur Shāh surrendered on promise of his life.

Down-country operations centred on the relief of Lucknow. Setting out from Allāhābād on July 7, the British general, Sir Henry Havelock, fought his way through Kānpur to the Lucknow residency on September 25, where he was besieged in his turn. But the back of the rebellion had been broken and time gained for reinforcements to restore British superiority. The next phase saw the relief of the residency (November 16) and the capture of Lucknow by the new commander in chief, Sir Colin Campbell (March 1, 1858). By a campaign in Oudh and Rohilkhand, Campbell cleared the countryside.

The next phase was the central Indian campaign of Sir Hugh Rose. He first defeated the Gwalior contingent and then, when the rebels Tantia Topi and the Rani of Jhānsi had seized Gwalior, broke up their forces in two more battles. The Rani found a soldier's death, and Tantia became a fugitive. With the British recovery of Gwalior (June 20) the revolt was virtually over.

The restoration of peace was hindered by British cries for vengeance, often leading to indiscriminate reprisals. The treatment of the aged Bahadur Shah was a disgrace to a civilized nation; also, the whole population of Delhi was driven out into the open, and thousands were killed after perfunctory trials or no trials at all. Order was restored by the firmness of Canning, whose title of "Clemency" was given in derision by angry British merchants in Calcutta, and of Sir John Lawrence in the Punjab. Ferocity led to grave excesses on both sides, distinguishing this war in horror from other wars of the 19th century.

Measures of prevention of such crises in the future

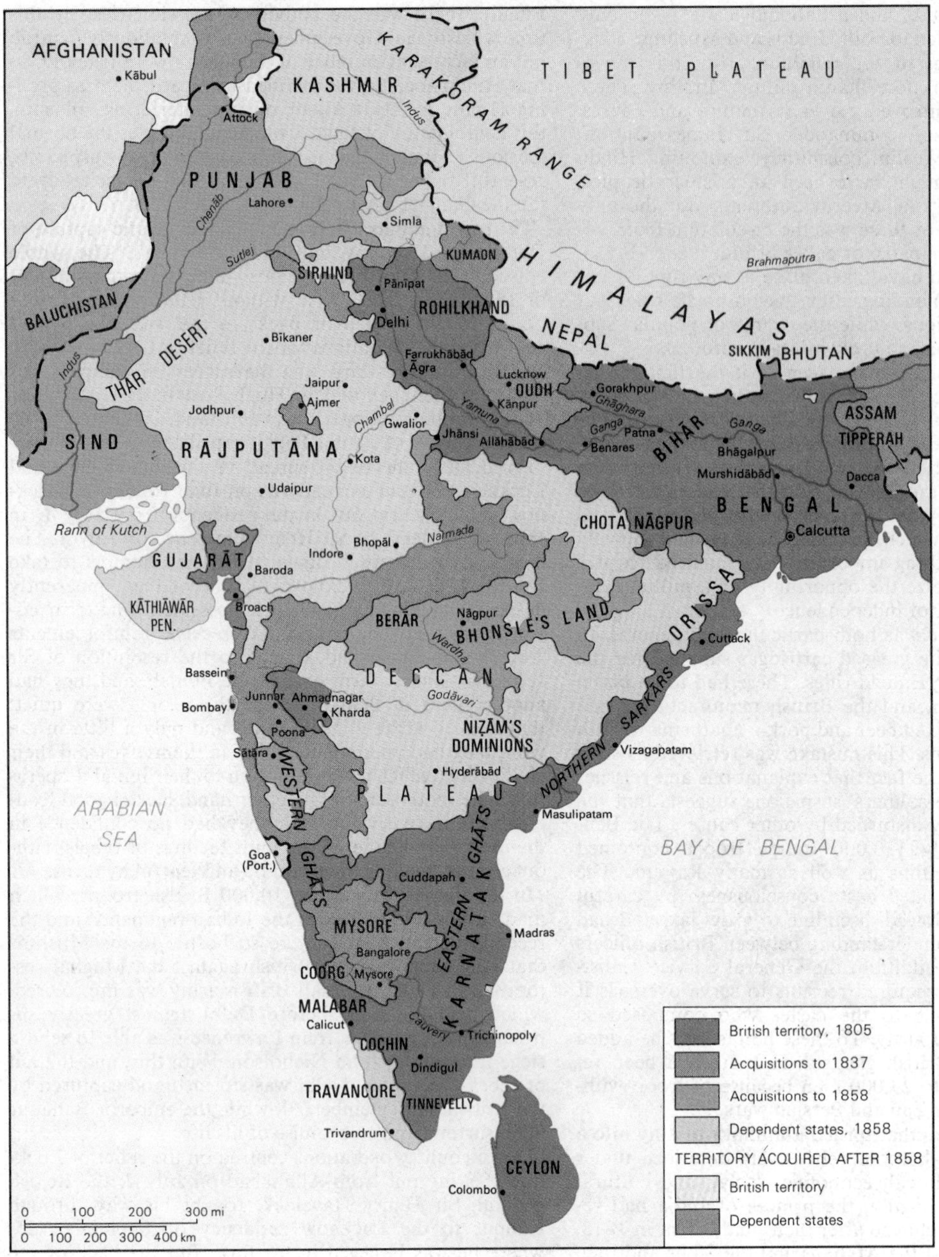

British India to 1858.
Adapted from R. Treharne and H. Fullard (eds.), *Muir's Historical Atlas: Ancient, Medieval and Modern*, 9th ed. (1965); George Philip & Son Ltd., London

naturally began with the army, which was completely reorganized. The ratio of British to Indian troops was fixed at roughly 1:2 instead of 1:5—one British and two Indian battalions were brigaded together so that no sizable station should be without British troops. The effective Indian artillery, except for a few mountain batteries, was abolished, while the Brahmins and Rājputs of Oudh were reduced in favour of other groups. The officers continued to be British, but they were more efficient and more closely linked with their men. The army became an efficient professional body, drawn largely from the northwest and aloof from the national life.

(T.G.P.S.)

VII. British imperial power (1858–1920)

CLIMAX OF THE RAJ

The six decades between the end of the "mutinous" war of 1857–58 and the conclusion of World War I saw both the peak of British imperial power in India and the birth of nationalist agitation against it. The period was haunted by dark memories of the "mutiny" and heartened by dreams of freedom; its first phase was dominated by fear, its later years by hope.

The Government of India Act of 1858. The legacy of the war of 1857–58 was of fundamental and far-reaching importance to British India. On August 2, 1858, less than a month after Charles Canning, first viceroy of India, proclaimed the victory of British arms, Parliament passed the Government of India Act, completing at one legislative stroke the transfer of British power over India from the East India Company to the crown. The company's residual powers and responsibilities over Indian affairs were vested in the secretary of state for India, a minister of Great Britain's cabinet, who would be assisted and advised, especially in financial matters, by a Council of India at Whitehall, consisting initially of 15 Englishmen, seven of whom were elected from among the old company's court of directors and eight of whom were appointed by the crown. Though some of Britain's most powerful political leaders became secretaries of state for India in the latter half of the 19th century, including eminent men like Lord Salisbury (1866–67 and 1874–78) and Lord Kimberley (1882–85 and 1886), actual control over the government of India remained secure in the hands of British viceroys in Calcutta and Simla and their "steel-frame" of approximately 1,500

Indian Civil Service (ICS) officials posted "on the spot" throughout British India. Even after the Liberal philosopher-statesman John Morley (later Lord Morley) took charge of the India Office as secretary of state from 1906 to 1910 and fully asserted the singular constitutional powers bequeathed to that post in 1858, the cumbersome machinery of British India's bureaucracy continued to prove itself virtually intractable.

Social policy. On November 1, 1858, Lord Canning announced Queen Victoria's proclamation to "The Princes, Chiefs and Peoples of India," unveiling a new British policy of perpetual support for "native princes" and nonintervention in matters of religious belief or worship within British India, while reiterating the company's long-standing promise of "impartiality" with respect to "race or creed" in the recruitment of officers for the ICS.

Preservation of maharaja autocracy

The first of these new crown policies put an end to Lord Dalhousie's vigorous prewar policy of political unification through princely state annexation. The Dalhousie doctrine of lapse was abandoned, and princes were left free to adopt any heirs they desired, so long as they all swore undying allegiance to the British crown. In 1876, at Prime Minister Benjamin Disraeli's prompting, Victoria added the title empress of India to her regality. British fears of another "mutiny" and consequent determination to bolster Indian states as "natural breakwaters" against any future tidal wave of revolt thus left more than 560 enclaves of autocratic maharaja rule to survive, interspersed throughout British India, for the entire nine decades of crown rule. The new policy of religious nonintervention was born equally out of fear of recurring mutiny, which many Englishmen believed to have been triggered by orthodox Brahmanic and Mawlawī reaction against the secularizing inroads of utilitarian positivism and the proselytizing of Christian missionaries. Liberal socioreligious reform, which, since the abolition of the custom of *satī* in 1829 had received official British support, came to a halt for more than three decades after the crown took direct control over India. Thirty-five years of official laissez-faire in social reform elapsed between the company's Hindu Widow's Remarriage Act of 1856 and the crown's Age of Consent Act of 1891; yet the latter only timidly raised the age of statutory rape for "consenting" Indian brides from ten years to 12. Not before 1928 would the government of India next find courage to legislate in the sacred realm of marriage, passing at that time its act restraining marriage to a "child bride" under 14. Fearless Indian social reformers such as Mahadev Govind Ranade, Maharshi (Great Seer) Dhondu Keshev Karve, and Behramji Malabari were obliged to lead the struggle for female emancipation through widow remarriage, female education, and agitation against infant marriage, without official support. But many Britishers in India, official as well as nonofficial, privately encouraged these Hindu and Parsi reformers. The Indian National Social Conference, founded by Ranade in 1897, became the leading unofficial Indian agency for coordinating and advancing the vital socioreligious reformation of Hinduism, which after 1920, thanks to the charisma and reforming zeal of Mahatma (Great Soul) Gandhi, merged with the mainstream of political nationalism of the Indian National Congress.

British racial attitudes

Queen Victoria's promise of racial equality of opportunity in the selection of her servants for the government of India was never implemented during this era, and the most tragic legacy of 1857–58 was the unbridgeable gulf of racial hatred left by the "mutiny" between British and "native" communities throughout India. Canning, who won the originally opprobrious title Clemency from his Calcutta countrymen for his humane treatment of Indian prisoners of war, was the aristocratic exception to what became a rule of British racial arrogance and often violent abuse of "natives" in the wake of the war, which may have started as a military mutiny but ended as a bitter racial holocaust. The English writer Rudyard Kipling captured the typical attitude of British officials who went to India in this period, as he put it, to "take up the White man's burden." Britishers lived, by and large, throughout the interlude of their Indian service to the crown as super-Brahmin "Pakka Sahibs," remaining as aloof as possible from "native contamination" and counting the months till they would be eligible to return home to retire in Great Britain on their ICS pensions. British military cantonments (called camps) were constructed beyond the walls of many of the larger "native" cities in this era. They were built initially for the more effective dispersal of military regiments as part of the general reorganization of British India's armies (Bengal, Bombay, and Madras), which in 1857 had only 45,000 British to 240,000 native troops, but which by 1863 had attained their new "safer mix" of 65,000 English to 140,000 Indian soldiers. British camps soon became suburban residential islands for all Europeans, whose social life was centred around the British Club. After 1869, with the completion of the Suez Canal and the simultaneous introduction of steam transport, reducing the sea passage to India from almost three months to as many weeks and less, Englishwomen came East with ever greater alacrity, and the British officials they married found it more tempting to return home with their English families during furloughs than to tour India as their predecessors had done. Fewer and fewer Englishmen dared to consort openly with Indian women, unless they were in remote regions where it might be unsafe to take English ladies. Thus, while the intellectual calibre of British recruits to the ICS in this era was, on the average, probably higher than that of servants recruited under the company's earlier "patronage" system, British contacts with Indian society diminished in every respect, and English sympathy for and understanding of Indian life and culture was, for the most part, replaced by suspicion, indifference, and fear. The competitive ICS examinations were theoretically as open to Indian as they were to British subjects of the crown, but since examinations were given only in London to horse-riding male entrants between the ages of 17 and 22 (in 1878 the maximum age was still further reduced to 19), it is hardly surprising to find that by 1869 only one Indian candidate had managed to clear all these hurdles to win admission to the ICS.

Government organization. From 1858 to 1909 the government of India was an increasingly centralized paternal despotism and the world's largest imperial bureaucracy. The Indian Councils Act of 1861 transformed the viceroy's Executive Council into a miniature cabinet run on the portfolio system, with each of the five ordinary members placed in charge of a distinct department of Calcutta's government—home, revenue, military, finance, and law. The military commander in chief sat with this council as an extraordinary member, and when Lord Kitchener took command in 1902 he soon protested against meeting with a military member who was his junior in battle rank but his equal at least on the viceroy's council. Kitchener demanded, therefore, that the military member of council be replaced with a soldier appointed by army headquarters, directly subordinate to the commander in chief. Lord Curzon, who was then viceroy, most vigorously resisted this attempt by Kitchener to subvert Britain's traditional policy of the subordination of military to civil authority in government, and a titanic struggle ensued at Simla, one that resulted in Curzon's resignation and departure from India in 1905. A sixth ordinary member was assigned to the viceroy's Executive Council after 1874, initially to preside over the Department of Public Works, which after 1904 came to be called Commerce and Industry. Though the government of India was by statutory definition the "Governor-General-in-Council" ("governor general" remained the viceroy's alternate title), the viceroy was empowered to overrule his councillors if ever he deemed that necessary. He personally took charge of the Foreign Department, which was mostly occupied with relations with princely states as well as bordering foreign powers. Few viceroys found it necessary to assert their full despotic authority, since the majority of their councillors usually agreed with every position they took, but in 1879 Viceroy Lytton felt obliged to overrule his entire council in order to accommodate demands for the elimination of

Powers of the viceroy

his government's import duties on British cotton manufactures, despite India's desperate need for revenue in a year of widespread famine and agricultural disorders. From 1854 additional members met with the governor general's Executive Council for legislative purposes, and by the act of 1861 their permissible number was raised to between six and 12, no fewer than half of whom were to be nonofficials. All such legislative councillors were added by appointment of the viceroy, who was empowered to veto any bill passed on to him by this body. But its debates were to be open to a limited public audience, and several of its nonofficial members were Indian nobility and loyal landowners. The legislative council sessions thus served as something of a public-opinion barometer of a very crude sort and the beginnings of an advisory "safety valve" for the government of India, designed to provide the viceroy with early crisis warnings at the minimum possible risk of parliamentary-type opposition. The act of 1892 further expanded this central council's permissible additional membership to 16, ten of whom could be nonofficials, and increased their powers to the extent of allowing them to ask questions of government and formally to criticize the official budget during one day reserved at the very end of each year's legislative session in Calcutta for that purpose. The Supreme Council still remained, therefore, quite remote from any sort of parliament, but its next giant step in that direction, to be taken in the Indian Councils Act of 1909 (popularly called the Morley–Minto reforms), would bring it much closer to parent British prototypes of responsible, though not as yet representative, government.

Influence of the viceroys. The viceroyalty of India was one of the more lucrative plums in the crown's patronage orchard, and with the exception of Sir John Lawrence (viceroy from 1864 to 1869), who had been reared in the company's service, went throughout this era to a curious mixture of lesser British nobility, devoid of Indian experience. Lord Canning (governor general and viceroy from 1856 to 1862) was succeeded by James Bruce, 8th earl of Elgin (1862–63), a lackluster viceroy who died after 20 months in India. Lord John Lawrence, whose work in settling the Punjab had established his reputation for firm and efficient administrative leadership, returned to Calcutta as viceroy in 1864, after having served three years on the secretary of state's council in Whitehall. The Punjab and Oudh Tenancy Acts of 1868 were the major achievements of Lawrence's viceroyalty, for, by assuring tenant peasants of their occupancy rights, they helped to restore stability and revive north India's agricultural productivity. Lawrence's tenure, however, was scarred by severe famine in Orissa as well as Rājputāna. Lord Mayo (viceroy from 1869 to 1872) went to India after serving as chief secretary for Ireland and found similarly violent disaffection from British rule, faced, as he was throughout his viceroyalty, with Wahhābī Muslim uprisings in Bengal and Kuka Sikh raids in the Punjab. Mayo himself was assassinated by the knife of a Muslim prisoner on the Andaman Islands in 1872. Lord Northbrook (viceroy from 1872 to 1876) was sent by Gladstone from the British War Office to succeed Mayo and managed by his policy of inertia to restore calm to India. Disraeli's viceroy, Lord Lytton (1876–80), was a Tory romantic who inaugurated a most costly foreign policy that precipitated the Second Afghan War (1878–80). Lytton's domestic policy was one of laissez-faire for Lancashire cottons and repression of "native" opinion opposed to that policy by the muzzling of India's fourth estate with his unpopular Vernacular Press Act of 1878. The liberal viceroy Lord George Ripon (1880–84) was Gladstone's political counterpart in India and soon came to be as widely revered by India's populace as Lytton was reviled. Ripon repealed his predecessor's legislation against the press and sponsored the first official measures designed to introduce to British India representative institutions at the local district and municipal government levels.

Ripon's attempted reforms

In 1882 Ripon called for the creation of municipal and district government boards, at least two-thirds of whose members would be elected nonofficials. Though his efforts were sabotaged by a jealous bureaucracy and undermined by Indian lack of enthusiasm and experience in self-government, Lord Ripon deserves an honoured place in Indian history as the first viceroy who laboured to plant the seed of independent rule in British Indian soil. Ripon also struck the first official blow against his government's policy of racism in India by urging his law member of council, Sir Courtney Ilbert, to draft a bill that would allow Indian judges in the service to try cases involving Englishmen as well as Indians. This attempt to remove racial bigotry from British India's legal code by the introduction of the Ilbert Bill in 1883, however, almost ended in a white mutiny in Bengal. The British enclave became so outraged and vituperative in its racist clamour against the proposed measure that the bill could only be enacted in a totally emasculated form, with the added stipulation that any "European British" defendant would have the option of standing trial before a jury at least half of which would be of "European complexion." Though Bengal's white supremacists won their battle against Ripon and Ilbert, they inadvertently demonstrated to a generation of young Indian nationalists the tactics of political agitation and protest. If a handful of white lawyers, planters, and publicists could by their shrill and persistent demands force the mighty government of India to reverse itself, there was no reason to believe that millions of Indians could not achieve as much. In 1885, just a year after Lord Ripon left India, the Indian National Congress, prior incarnation of the Republic of India's ruling Congress Party, was born.

Economic policy. Economically, this was an era of increased commercial agricultural production, rapidly expanding trade, early industrial development, and severe famine. The total cost of the war of 1857–58, approximately £40,000,000 and equivalent to a normal year's revenue, was charged to India and paid off from increased revenue resources in four years. The major source of government income throughout this period remained the land revenue, which, as a percentage of the agricultural yield of India's soil, continued to be "an annual gamble in monsoon rains." Usually, however, it provided about half of British India's gross annual revenue, or roughly the money needed to support the army. The second most lucrative source of revenue at this time was the government's continued monopoly over the flourishing illicit opium trade to China; the third was the tax on salt, also jealously guarded by the crown as its official monopoly preserve. An individual income tax was introduced for five years to pay off the war deficit, but urban personal income was not added as a regular source of Indian revenue until 1886. Despite continued British adherence to the doctrine of laissez-faire during this period, a 10 percent customs duty was levied in 1860 to help clear the war debt. It was reduced to 7 percent in 1864 and to 5 percent in 1875. In 1879, the cotton import duty was abolished and not reimposed on British imports of piece goods and yarn until 1894, when the value of silver fell so precipitously on the world market that the government of India was forced to take action, even against Lancashire, by adding enough rupees to its revenue to make ends meet.

Early Indian industrialism

Bombay's textile industry had by then developed more than 80 power mills, and the Indian industrialist Jamsetji N. Tata's (1839–1904) huge Empress Mill was in full operation at Nāgpur, competing directly with Lancashire for the vast Indian market. Britain's millowners again demonstrated their power in Calcutta by forcing the government of India to impose an "equalizing" 5 percent excise tax on all India-manufactured cloth, thereby convincing many Indian millowners and capitalists that their best interests would be served by contributing financial support to the Indian National Congress.

Britain's major contribution to India's economic development throughout the era of crown rule was the railroad net that spread so swiftly across the subcontinent after 1858, when there were barely 200 miles (320 kilometres) of track in all of India. By 1869 more than 5,000 miles of steel track had been completed by British railroad companies, and by 1900 there were 25,000 miles of rail laid. By the start of World War I the total reached 35,000 miles (56,000 kilometres), almost the full growth of India's rail net. Initially, the railroads proved a mixed blessing for most Indians, since by linking India's agricultural, village-based heartland to the British imperial port cities of Bombay, Madras, and Calcutta, they served first of all to accelerate the pace of raw-material extraction from India while speeding up the transition from subsistence food to commercial agricultural production. Middlemen hired by port city Managing Agency Houses rode the trains inland, inducing village headmen to convert large tracts of grain-yielding land to commercial crops. Large sums of silver were offered in payment for raw materials when the British demand was high, as was the case throughout the U.S. Civil War. But when the Civil War ended, restoring raw cotton from the southern United States to Lancashire mills, the Indian market collapsed. Millions of peasants weaned from grain production now found themselves riding the boom-and-bust tiger of a world-market economy. They were unable to convert their commercial agricultural surplus back into food during depression years, and from 1865 through 1900 India experienced the most severe series of protracted famines in its entire history. Though the population of the subcontinent increased dramatically from about 200,000,000 in 1872 (the year of the first census) to over 300,000,000 in 1920, the population actually declined by several millions between 1895 and 1905. The spread of railroads also accelerated the destruction of India's indigenous handicraft industries, for trains filled with cheap competitive manufactured goods shipped from England now rushed to inland towns for distribution to villages, underselling the rougher produce of Indian craftsmen. Entire handicraft villages thus lost their traditional markets of neighbouring agricultural villagers, and craftsmen were forced to abandon their looms and spinning wheels and return to the soil for their livelihood. By the end of the 19th century a larger percentage of India's population (approximately 90 percent) depended directly upon agriculture for support than at the century's start, and the pressure of population upon arable land increased throughout this period. Railroads also provided the military with swift and relatively assured access to all parts of the country in the event of emergency and were eventually used to transport grain for famine relief as well.

Effects of British imports

The rich coalfields of Bihār and Orissa began to be mined in this period to help power the imported British locomotives, and coal production jumped from 500,000 tons in 1868 to over 6,000,000 in 1900 and more than 20,000,000 by 1920. Coal was used for iron smelting in India as early as 1875, but the Tata Iron and Steel Company, which received no government aid, did not start production until 1911, launching India's steel industry in Bihār. Tata grew rapidly after World War I, and by World War II had become the largest single steel complex in the British Commonwealth, its city of location named Jamshedpur, after its founder. The jute textile industry, Bengal's counterpart to Bombay's cotton industry, developed in the wake of the Crimean War (1853–56), which, by cutting off Russia's supply of raw hemp to the jute mills of Scotland, stimulated the export of raw jute from Calcutta to Dundee. In 1863 there were only two jute mills in Bengal, but by 1882 there were 20, employing over 20,000 workers, and by 1908 British India's jute production was greater than Dundee's. The most important plantation industries of this era were tea, indigo, and coffee. British tea plantations were started in North India's Assam Hills in the 1850s and in South India's Nīlgiri Hills some 20 years later. By 1871 there were over 300 tea plantations, covering more than 30,000 cultivated acres (12,000 hectares) and producing over 6,000,000 pounds of tea. By 1900 India's tea crop sufficed to export 137,000,000 pounds to Britain, displacing the tea of China in London. As cheaper Indian tea ousted its Chinese rival from British markets, the Chinese planted opium in land formerly devoted to tea, and during the first decade of the 20th century China's demand for Indian opium dropped so sharply that by the end of World War I, when the League of Nations called upon Britain to stop the opium trade, it had virtually stopped itself. The flourishing indigo industry of Bengal and Bihār was threatened with extinction during the "Blue Mutiny" of 1859–60, but India continued to export indigo to European markets until the end of the 19th century, when synthetic dyes made that natural product obsolete. Coffee plantations flourished in South India from 1860 to 1879, after which disease blighted the crop and sent Indian coffee into a decade of decline. During much of the last decade of the 19th and the first decade of the 20th century, India's economy was ravaged by famine and plague (the bubonic plague entered Bombay in 1896), and it was not until World War I that further strides were made in British India's industrial development and overall economic productivity.

FOREIGN POLICY

The northwest frontier. British India expanded beyond its company borders both to the northwest and the northeast during this initial phase of crown rule. The turbulent tribal frontier to the northwest remained a continuing source of harassment to settled British rule, and Pathan raiders served as a constant lure and justification to champions of the "forward school" of imperialism in Calcutta, Simla, and Whitehall. Russian expansion into Central Asia in the 1860s provided even greater anxiety and incentive to British proconsuls in India, as well as at the Foreign Office in London, to advance the frontier of the Indian empire beyond the Hindu Kush and, indeed, up to Afghanistan's own northern border along the Oxus. Lord Canning, however, was far too preoccupied with trying to restore tranquillity within India to consider embarking upon anything more ambitious than the northwest-frontier punitive-expedition policy (commonly called "butcher and bolt"), which was generally regarded as the simplest, cheapest method of "pacifying" the Pathans. As viceroy, Lawrence continued the same border-pacification policy and resolutely refused to be pushed or lured into the ever-simmering caldron of Afghan politics. In 1863, when the popular old *amīr*, Dōst Moḥammad Khān, died, Lawrence wisely refrained from attempting to name his successor, leaving the Dōst's 16 sons to fight their own fratricidal battles until 1868, when Shīr ʿAlī finally emerged victorious. Lawrence then recognized and subsidized the new *amīr*, and Mayo met to confer with him at Ambala in 1869, reaffirming Anglo-Afghan friendship but resisting all requests for more permanent and practical support by the *amīr* for his still precarious regime.

Action against the Pathans

The Second Afghan War. Russia's glacial advance into Turkistan and Samarkand sufficiently alarmed Disraeli and Salisbury that by 1874, when they came to power in London, they pressed the government of India to pursue a more vigorous interventionist line with Kābul. Northbrook resisted all such cabinet promptings to reverse Lawrence's noninterventionist policy and return to the militant posture of the First Afghan War era, resigning his office rather than accept orders from ministers whose diplomatic judgment he believed to be disastrously distorted by Russophobia. Lytton, however, was more than eager to act as his prime minister desired, and, soon after he reached Calcutta, he rushed to notify Shīr ʿAlī that he was sending a "mission" to Kābul. When the *amīr* refused Lytton permission to enter his hermit kingdom, the viceroy bellicosely declaimed that Afghanistan was but "an earthen pipkin between two metal pots." In 1878, Russia's General Stolyetov was admitted to Kābul, while Lytton's envoy, Sir Neville Chamberlain, was turned back at the border by Afghan troops. The Viceroy decided to crush his neighbouring "pipkin" and launched the Second Afghan War on November 21, 1878, with a British invasion over the high passes. Shīr ʿAlī fled his capital and country, dying in exile early in 1879. The British army occupied Kābul, as it had in the first war, and a treaty signed at Gandamak on May 26, 1879, was concluded with the former *amīr*'s son, Yaʿqūb Khān. Yaʿqūb Khān promised to admit a British resident to his Kābul court and to turn over the direction of Afghan foreign relations to him in return for his British promise of money and arms to support and protect the new *amīr* from his many enemies. A telegraph line was to be strung between Kurram and Kābul, and the former border district of Afghanistan was to be occupied by British troops, as would also be Pishīn, Sibi, and the Khyber and Mishmi passes. In July 1879 Sir Louis Cavagnari, the British resident, reached Kābul and on September 3, 1879, was assassinated there. British troops trudged back over the passes to Kābul, removing Yaʿqūb to India; his throne was left vacant until July 1880, when ʿAbdor Raḥmān Khān, nephew of ShīrʿAlī, became *amīr*. The Second Afghan War, which thus proved to be a Pyrrhic victory, became the leading issue in the British general elections of 1880, after which Disraeli's Tory cabinet was replaced by Gladstone's Liberal government. Lord Ripon tactfully concluded the negotiations with ʿAbdor Raḥmān, by which Britain managed slowly to extricate itself from the military morass into which Lytton had rushed with all the fervour and lack of foresight of a schoolboy. The Khyber and Kurram were left to the Afghans, as was Kābul, and, though British troops remained in Qandahār until 1881, they were withdrawn thereafter and continued to occupy only the border towns of Sibi and Pishīn. ʿAbdor Raḥmān, one of the shrewdest statesmen in Afghan history, remained secure on his throne until his death in 1901. Though Russia defeated the Turkmen and advanced toward Merv in 1881, British India survived that new threat to its security without another Afghan war. Ripon urged instead that an Afghan diplomatic settlement be reached between Britain and Russia. This was accomplished by the Anglo-Russian agreement on Afghanistan's northern border reached on July 22, 1887. Panjdeh was abandoned to Russia and the northwestern corner of Afghanistan fixed at Zulfiqar.

Settlement with Russia

Creation of the North-West Frontier Province. Lord Lansdowne, viceroy from 1888 to 1894, sought to reassert a more forward policy in Afghanistan, following the advice of his military commander in chief, Lord Roberts, who had served as field commander in the Second Afghan War. Sir Mortimer Durand, the government of India's foreign secretary, was sent by Lansdowne on a mission to Kābul in 1893 to open negotiations to delimit the Indo-Afghan border. Demarcation of this "Durand Line" was completed in 1896, adding the tribal territory of the Afrīdīs, Maḥsūds, Wazīrīs, and Swātīs to the domain of British India, as well as the chieftainships of Chitral and Gilgit. The 9th earl of Elgin (1894–99), Lansdowne's successor, devoted most of his viceregal tenure to sending British Indian armies on punitive expeditions along this new frontier. The frontier rising of all Pathan tribes (1897) took no less than 35,000 troops to put down. The fiercely independent tribal peoples of India's northwest-frontier hill country continued to battle in protracted guerrilla campaigns against British arms. Lord Curzon recognized the impracticality of trying to administer the turbulent frontier region as part of the large Punjab province and in 1901 created a new North-West Frontier Province containing some 40,000 square miles (about 100,000 square kilometres) of trans-Sutlej and tribal borderland territory under a British chief commissioner responsible directly to the viceroy. By instituting a policy of regular payments to frontier tribes, the new province reduced border conflicts, though for the next decade British troops continued to fight against Mahṣūds, Wazīrīs, and Zakka Khel Afrīdīs.

The Anglo-Russian Convention of 1907 was the first comprehensive attempt to define central Asian "spheres of influence" effectively enjoyed by the two great European rivals. The Afghan portion of this convention placed Afghanistan outside Russia's sphere but within Britain's, as far as foreign relations were concerned. Though the new *amīr*, Ḥabībollāh Khān (1901–19), refused to sign the convention, this agreement served to ensure Anglo-Afghan peace until after World War I. Following Ḥabībollāh's assassination in February 1919, however, his son and successor as *amīr*, Amānollāh Khān, issued a call to his people to rise up in holy war (*jihād*) against the British. The Third Afghan War, thus started in May 1919, never posed a serious challenge to British India, however, for after British warplanes were used to bomb Kābul and Qandahār the *amīr* appealed for peace at the end of May, and a preliminary treaty ending all hostilities was signed at Rawalpindi on August 8, 1919. The formal treaty ending the Third Afghan War was concluded on November 22, 1921, establishing Anglo-Afghan relations on the basis of "internal and external independence."

The Third Afghan War

The incorporation of Burma. To the northeast, British India's conquest of Burma was completed during this period. The Second Anglo-Burmese War (1852) had left the kingdom of Ava (Upper Burma) independent of British India, under the rule of King Mindon (1853–78). Mindon built his capital at Mandalay and welcomed British steamers, bringing British residents as well as private traders up the Irrawaddy from Rangoon to his peaceful kingdom. In 1871 Mindon convened the Fifth Buddhist Council in Mandalay, the first such council called in some 1,900 years. Mindon was succeeded by a junior son, Thibaw, who in February 1879 celebrated his ascendancy to the throne of Ava by having 80 siblings massacred. King Thibaw refused to renew his father's treaty agreements with Britain, turning instead to seek commercial relations with the French, who were then advancing toward his kingdom from their base in Indo-China. Thibaw sent envoys to Paris, and in January 1885 the French signed a treaty of trade with the kingdom of Ava, dispatching a French consul to Mandalay. This envoy hoped to establish a French bank in Upper Burma to finance the construction of a railway and the general commercial development of the kingdom, but his plans were not permitted to bear fruit. The viceroy, Lord Frederick Dufferin, impatient with Thibaw for delaying a treaty agreement with British India, goaded to action by British traders in Rangoon, and provoked by fears of French intervention in Britain's "sphere," sent an expedition of some 10,000 troops up the Irrawaddy in November 1885. The Third Anglo-Burmese War ended in less than a month with the loss of hardly 20 lives, and on January 1, 1886, Upper Burma, a kingdom larger than Britain and with a population of some 4,000,000, was annexed by proclamation to British India. As in Afghanistan, Britain's military difficulties in Burma began only after its initial conquest, and, though Burmese guerrilla warfare may have been less terrifyingly effective than the Afghan variety, imperial order was only gradually achieved and even by 1890 extended hardly across one-half of the conquered territory. The greater portion of Upper Burma, the Chin Hills and Shan States, was never totally subdued or pacified by the British. From 1886 to 1897 the new province of united Burma was administered by a chief commissioner and after the later date by a lieutenant governor appointed by the government of India.

Burmese overtures to the French

INDIAN NATIONALISM AND THE BRITISH RESPONSE

Origins of the nationalist movement. The Indian National Congress held its first meeting in December 1885 in Bombay city, while British Indian troops were still fighting in Upper Burma. Just as the British Indian empire attained its outermost limits of expansion, the institutional seed of the larger of its two national successors was thus sown. Provincial roots of Indian nationalism, however, may be traced to the beginning of the era of crown rule in Bombay, Bengal, and Madras. Nationalism emerged in 19th-century British India both in emulation of and as a reaction against the consolidation of British rule and the spread of Western civilization. There were, moreover, two turbulent national mainstreams flowing beneath the deceptively placid official surface of British administration: the larger, predominantly Hindu movement, which led eventually to the birth of India, and the smaller Muslim one, which acquired its organizational skeleton with the founding of the Muslim League in 1906 and led to the creation of Pakistan.

Many English-educated young Indians of the postmutiny period emulated their British mentors by seeking employment in the ICS, the legal services, journalism, and education. The universities of Bombay, Bengal, and Madras had been founded in 1857 as the capstone of the East India Company's modest policy of selectively fostering the introduction of English education in India. At the beginning of crown rule, the first graduates of these universities, reared on the works and ideas of Jeremy Bentham, John Stuart Mill, and Thomas Macaulay, sought positions that would help them improve themselves and society at the same time, convinced that with the education they had received and the proper apprenticeship of hard work they would eventually inherit the machinery of British Indian government. Few Indians, however, were admitted to the ICS, and among the first handful who were, one of the brightest, Surendranath Banerjea (1848–1925), was dismissed dishonourably at the earliest pretext and turned from loyal participation within the government to active nationalist agitation against it. Banerjea became a Calcutta college teacher and then editor of *The Bengalee* and founder of the Indian Association in Calcutta. In 1883 he convened the first Indian National Conference in Bengal, anticipating by two years the birth of the Congress on the opposite side of India. After the first partition of Bengal in 1905, Banerjea attained nationwide fame as a leader of the *swadeshi* ("of our own country," or India-made goods) and boycott (of British manufactured goods) movements.

Early figures in the nationalist movement

In Bombay, young leaders of new India were also busily at work in the 1870s, establishing provincial political associations such as the Poona Sarvajanik Sabha (Poona Public Society) founded by Mahadev G. Ranade, who had graduated first in his class from Bombay University's first bachelor of arts class in 1862. Ranade found employment in the educational department in Bombay, taught at Elphinstone College, edited the *Indu Prakash*, helped start the Hindu reformist Prarthana Samaj (Prayer Society) in Bombay, wrote historical and other essays, and became a barrister, eventually being appointed to the bench of Bombay's high court. Ranade was one of the early leaders of India's emulative school of nationalism, as was his brilliant disciple Gopal Krishna Gokhale (1866–1915). Gokhale, revered by Mahatma Gandhi as his political guru (preceptor), taught at Fergusson College and was an editor and social reformer as well as a nationalist political leader. He was elected president of the Congress in 1905. Moderation and reform were the keynotes of Gokhale's life, and by his use of reasoned argument, patient labour, and unflagging faith in the ultimate equity of British liberalism, he achieved more for India, working within the system of British rule, than did any of his contemporaries. Bal Gangadhar Tilak (1856–1920), Gokhale's Poona colleague at Fergusson College, was the leader of Indian nationalism's revolutionary reaction against British rule. Tilak was Poona's most popular Marathi journalist, whose vernacular newspaper, *Kesari* ("Lion"), became the leading literary thorn in the side of the British. The Lokamanya (Revered by the People), as Tilak came to be called after he was jailed for seditious writings in 1897, looked to orthodox Hinduism and Marāthā history as his twin sources of nationalist inspiration. Tilak called upon his compatriots to take keener interest and pride in the religious, cultural, martial, and political glories of pre-British Hindu India, rather than slavishly focussing their attention on foreign learning and emulating the ideas and attitudes of British white Christian oppressors. He helped found and publicize the popular Ganapati and Shivaji (Śivajī) festivals in the 1890s in Poona, former capital of Marāthā Hindu glory. Tilak had no faith in British justice, and his life was devoted primarily to agitation aimed at ousting the British from India by any means and restoring *swarāj* ("self-rule" or independence) to India's people. The militant nature of Tilak's agitation helped stimulate youthful terrorists such as the brothers Chapekar of Poona, who assassinated two British officials on the night of Queen Victoria's Diamond Jubilee (June 22, 1897). The orthodox Hindu character of Tilak's revolutionary revival, moreover, while bringing many non-English-educated Hindus into the nationalist movement, served to alienate India's Muslim minority and to exacerbate communal tensions and conflict.

The viceroyalties of Lytton and Ripon prepared the soil of British India for nationalism, the former by internal measures of repression and the futility of an external policy of aggression, the latter indirectly as a result of the European community's rejection of his liberal humanitarian legislation. One of the key men who helped arrange the first meeting of Congress was a retired British official, Allan Octavian Hume (1829–1912), Ripon's radical confidant. Hume, a mystic reformer and ornithologist, lived in Simla after retiring from the ICS in 1882, studying birds and Theosophy. Hume had joined the Theosophical Society in 1881, as had many young Indians, who found in Theosophy a movement most flattering to Indian civilization. Mme Blavatsky, cofounder of the Theosophical Society, went to India in 1879 to sit at the feet of Swami Dayananda Sarasvati (1824–83), the "Luther of Hinduism," whose "back to the Vedas" reformist Hindu society, the Arya Samaj, was founded in Bombay in 1875. Dayananda called upon Hindus to reject the "corrupting" medieval excrescences of their faith, including idolatry, the caste system, and infant marriage, and to return to the original purity of Vedic life and thought. The Swami insisted that post-Vedic changes in Hindu society had led only to weakness and disunity, destroying India's capacity to resist foreign invasion and subjugation. His reformist society was to take root most firmly in the Punjab at the start of the 20th century, and it became that province's leading nationalist organization. Mme Blavatsky soon left Dayananda and established her own "Samāj," whose Indian headquarters were outside Madras city, at Adyar. Annie Besant (1847–1933), the Theosophical Society's most famous leader, succeeded Mme Blavatsky and became the first and only Englishwoman to serve as president of the Indian National Congress (1917; see also THEOSOPHY).

Influence of Theosophists

The early Congress movement. The first Congress session was convened in Bombay city on December 28, 1885. Womesh C. Bonnerjee, a Calcutta barrister, presided over 73 representatives, as well as ten more unofficial delegates, from every province of British India. Fifty-four of the delegates were Hindu, and only two were Muslim, the remainder being mostly Parsi and Jain. Practically all the Hindu delegates were Brahmins. All of them spoke English. More than half were lawyers, the remainder consisting of journalists, businessmen, landowners, and professors. Such was the first gathering of the new India, an emerging elite of middle class intellectuals devoted to peaceful political action and protest on behalf of their nation in the making. On its last day Congress passed resolutions that embodied the political and economic demands of its members, serving thereafter as public petitions to government for the redress of grievances, while helping to educate the rest of India's population in the meaning of the new national program. These initial resolutions called for the full restitution to Britain's House of Commons of the authority over Indian administrative affairs that the government of India had autocratically usurped; for the abolition of the reactionary council in Whitehall; for the addition of elected nonofficial representatives to the Supreme and provincial legislative councils; and for real equality of opportunity for Indians to enter the ICS by the immediate introduction of simultaneous examinations in India and England. The Congress' economic demands started with a call for the reduction of "Home charges," which included the entire India Office budget and the pensions of officials living in England in retirement. Dadabhai Naoroji (1825–1917), the "grand old man" of Congress who served three times as its president, was the leading exponent of the popular economic "drain" argument, which offered theoretical economic support to nationalist politics by insisting that India's poverty was the product of British exploitation and annual plunder of gold and silver as well as raw material resources. Other resolutions called for the reduction of military expenditure, condemned the Anglo-Burmese War, demanded retrenchment, and urged reimposition of import duties on British

The first demands of Congress

manufactures. Hume attended the first Congress as the only English delegate, while Sir William Wedderburn (1838–1918), Gokhale's closest English adviser and himself later elected twice to serve as president of Congress, and Professor William Wordsworth, principal of Elphinstone College, both appeared as observers. Most Englishmen in India, however, either ignored Congress and its resolutions as the action and demands of a "microscopic minority" of India's diverse millions or considered them the rantings of disloyal extremists. Despite this combination of official disdain and hostility, however, Congress quickly won substantial Indian support and within two years had grown to number more than 600 delegates. In 1888, when Dufferin, on the eve of his departure from India, dismissed it as "microscopic," it mustered 1,248 delegates at its annual meeting.

Curzon's policies. George Nathaniel Curzon, 1st marquess of Kedleston and viceroy from 1899 to 1905, hoped in 1900 that Congress was "tottering to its fall," confessing that one of his great ambitions was to "assist it to a peaceful demise." By the time his viceroyalty ended, however, Lord Curzon had inadvertently infused Congress with unprecedented popularity and militant vitality. Curzon's untiring capacity for administrative labour, combined with his insensitivity to criticism—especially from "natives"—made him at once the most efficient and least popular viceroy in Indian history. Curzon's reign marks the peak of imperial centralization of authority by the government of India and of indifference to public opinion. In foreign policy, Curzon devoted himself to seeking ways of excluding Russian influence from the Persian Gulf and Seistan, Kābul, and Lhasa. In a personal display of imperial pomp, Curzon toured the Persian Gulf in a British warship in 1903, the same year in which he held his extravagant *darbār* (festival and reception of native princes) in Delhi. In 1904 he launched a mission to Tibet, which soon turned into a military massacre and invasion of the Chumbi Valley and Gyantse. It was followed by British Indian armed occupation of that remote region beyond the Himalayan passes. The Anglo-Russian Convention of 1907 stipulated the withdrawal of British troops from Tibet, and this was carried out in 1908. Curzonian imperiousness and impatience in negotiating with Ḥabībollāh, the new *amīr* of Afghanistan, alarmed Prime Minister Balfour's cabinet more than any threat of Russian influence in Kābul did; for, having just extricated Britain from the Boer War (1899–1902), no British statesmen dared contemplate the prospect of a third Afghan War. In 1905 Sir Louis Dane, who was ordered to remain in Kābul despite Curzon's impatience, successfully completed negotiations of a treaty with Afghanistan, which Curzon considered humiliating. That same year, however, the spectre of Russian power over Asia was diminished considerably by Japan's unexpected victory in the Russo-Japanese War (1904–05).

Curzon's principal domestic concern was to improve the efficiency of Indian administration. To this end he created a new province (the North-West Frontier), a new Department at Simla (Commerce and Industry), reformed the Indian police, reorganized the governing bodies of Calcutta University, and partitioned the province of Bengal. Curzon failed to realize in pursuing the latter two administrative "reforms" that human sympathy and understanding are important components of any government's drive toward achieving efficiency. His trenchant speech to the graduates of Calcutta University in support of the Universities Act of 1904 did more to alienate Bengali intellectuals from his government than any official statement made since the "mutiny," and the actual partition of Bengal in 1905 brought that province to the brink of open rebellion. Bengali Hindus viewed the partition, which created a Muslim-majority province of Eastern Bengal and Assam and left a truncated Bihari- and Oriya-speaking Hindu-majority province in West Bengal, as clear evidence of Curzon's policy of divide and rule. Everyone conceded that, with some 85,000,000, Bengal was much too large for a single province, but why, Bengalis asked, was it necessary to divide the territory in such a way as to strip Bengali Hindus of a majority in either new province? Surely, their leaders argued, this was proof of the government's vindictive antipathy toward the outspoken *bhadralok* ("respectable people") intellectuals. Partition, they argued, was really designed to remove them from positions of provincial power. Rallying to the defense of the "mother province," mother-goddess-worshipping Bengali Hindus responded with religious zeal to the mass protest meetings called by Congress leaders before and in the wake of the partition proclamation of October 16, 1905.

The partition of Bengal (1905)

Reaction to the partition of Bengal. Millions of Indians, hitherto unmoved by the austere language of Congress speeches and resolutions, now joined the nationalist movement, swept along by the tide of emotion that rushed over Bengal. "Bande Mātaram" ("Hail to the Mother") became the Congress national anthem, its words taken from a popular Bengali novel by Bankim Chandra Chatterjee, *Ānandamaṭh* ("Abbey of Bliss"), its music written by Bengal's poet Rabindranath Tagore. When Bengalis realized that all of their appeals, the countless petitions they had signed, and the river of rhetoric they had poured from platform and press protesting against partition were of no avail in dissuading government from its ill-conceived plan, they turned to other tactics. First of all, they launched a boycott of British-made goods, dramatizing their determination to live without foreign cloth by igniting huge bonfires of Lancashire goods throughout Bengal. At the same time, they vowed to use only domestic (*swadeshi*) cottons and other goods made in India. Simple India-made saris soon became far more fashionable in Calcutta *bhadralok* society than the finest Lancashire silks. The boycott and *swadeshi* movement spread across India to Poona, Bombay, and Madras and became the major economic plank in Congress' platform. The first partition of Bengal thus served to stimulate indigenous Indian industry, from cloth to matches, from glass products to iron and steel.

Demands for Indian education

Increased demands for national education also swiftly followed partition, and Curzon's outspoken contempt for Indian intellectuals convinced many of them to rely upon themselves rather than depend on government. Pioneers in the development of totally Indian institutions of higher learning in western India were the so-called Indian Jesuits of the Deccan in the 1880s, Vishnu Chiplunkar (1850–82), Gopal Agarkar (1856–95), Tilak, and Gokhale. In Bengal the indigenous education movement spread as swiftly as *swadeshi*. Nor were Bengal and Bombay the only centres of the movement, for in 1910 Pandit Madan Mohan Malaviya founded the private Hindu University in Benares, the revered centre of Hindu culture in the United Provinces. *Swarāj* ("self-rule") was the last major demand to be added to Congress' platform as a result of Bengal's partition. The sacred *mantra* ("holy utterance") of *swarāj* was voiced for the first time at a Congress session in 1906, in the presidential address of Dadabhai Naoroji at Calcutta. The demand for self-rule swiftly swept the country, and Tilak soon claimed it as his "birthright."

Nationalism in the Muslim community. While Congress was calling for *swarāj* in Calcutta, the Muslim League held its first meeting in Dacca, capital of the newly created Muslim-majority province of Eastern Bengal and Assam. Though the Muslim quarter of India's population lagged behind the Hindu majority in uniting to articulate nationalist political demands, Islām had, since the founding of the Delhi sultanate in 1206, provided Indian Muslims with sufficient doctrinal mortar to unite them as a separate religious community. The era of effective Mughal rule (*c.* 1556–1707), moreover, gave India's Muslims a sense of martial and administrative superiority to, as well as separation from, the Hindu majority. In 1857 the last of the Mughal emperors had served as a rallying symbol for many "mutineers," and in the wake of the "mutiny" most Britishers placed the burden of blame for its inception upon the Muslim community. Sir Sayyid Ahmad Khan (1817–98; *q.v.*), India's greatest 19th-century Muslim leader, succeeded, in his "Causes of the Indian Revolt" (1873), in convincing many British officials that Brahmin Hindus, rather than Mughal Muslims, were primarily to blame for the "mutiny." Sir Sayyid had entered the company's service in 1838 and was the leader of Muslim India's emulative mainstream of political reform. He visited Oxford in 1874 and returned to found the Muhammadan Anglo-Oriental College at Aligarh in 1875. It was India's first centre of Islāmic and Western higher education, with instruction given in English and modelled after Oxford. Aligarh became the intellectual cradle of the Muslim League and Pakistan. Sayyid Mahdi Ali, popularly known by his title Mohsin-ul Mulk (1837–1907), was secretary of Aligarh and convened the deputation of some 36 Muslim leaders, headed by the Aga Khan, that called upon Lord Minto (viceroy from 1905 to 1910) to articulate the special national interests of India's Muslim community (1906). Minto promised that any reforms his government would enact (the Indian Councils Act of 1909 was then being fashioned) would surely safeguard the separate interests of the Muslim community. Separate Muslim electorates, formally inaugurated by the act of 1909, were thus vouchsafed by viceregal fiat in 1906. This encouraged the Aga Khan's deputation, so that it issued an expanded call to the first meeting of the Muslim League, which convened in December 1906 at Dacca. The All-India Muslim League was formed as a "Political Association . . . to protect and advance the political rights and interests of Mussalmans of India." Other resolutions moved at its first meeting expressed Muslim "loyalty to the British government," as well as approval of and support for the Bengal partition and condemnation of the boycott movement.

Muslim demands

Reforms of the British Liberals. In Great Britain the Liberal Party's electoral victory of 1906 marked the dawn of a new era of reforms for British India. Hampered though he was by the viceroy, Lord Minto, the new head of the India Office, John Morley, was able to introduce several important innovations into the legislative as well as the administrative machinery of the British India government. First of all he acted to implement Queen Victoria's promise of racial equality of opportunity, which since 1858 had served only to assure Indian nationalists of British hypocrisy. He appointed two Indian members to his council at Whitehall: one a Muslim, Sayyid Husain Bilgrami, who had taken an active role in the founding of the Muslim League; the other a Hindu, Krishna G. Gupta, the senior Indian in the ICS. Morley also persuaded Minto to appoint the first Indian member to the viceroy's Executive Council, Satyendra P. Sinha (1864–1928), in 1909. Sinha (later Lord Sinha) had been admitted to the Bar at Lincoln's Inn in 1886 and was advocate general of Bengal before his appointment as the viceroy's law member, a position he felt obliged to resign in 1910. He was elected president of Congress in 1915 and became parliamentary undersecretary of state for India in 1919 and governor of Bihār and Orissa in 1920. The constitutional precedent established by Morley in adding Indians to the highest councils of Whitehall and Calcutta was never thereafter reversed, and in 1910 Sinha was succeeded by Sayyid Ali Imam, a Muslim barrister who served on the Supreme Legislative Council before moving to the Executive Council. Morley's major reform scheme, the Indian Councils Act of 1909, directly introduced the elective principle to Indian legislative council membership, and, though the initial electorate was a miniscule minority of Indians enfranchised by property ownership and education, in 1910 some 135 elected Indian representatives took their seats as members of legislative councils throughout British India. The act of 1909 increased the maximum additional membership of the Supreme Council from 16 (to which it had been raised by the Councils Act of 1892) to 60. In the provinces of Bombay, Bengal, and Madras, legislative councils had been created in 1861. Their permissible total membership had been raised to 20 by Lansdowne's Act of 1892, and this was increased to 50 in 1909, a majority of whom were to be nonofficials. The act of 1909 also permitted the addition of 50 members to the legislative councils of the United Provinces and Eastern Bengal and Assam and of up to 30 in all other provinces. In abolishing the official majorities of provincial legislatures, Morley followed the advice of Gokhale and such other liberal Congress leaders as Romesh Chunder Dutt (1848–1909), overriding the bitter opposition of the ICS as well as his own viceroy and council. True Liberal that he was, Morley believed that the only justification for British rule over India was to bequeath to the government of India England's greatest political institution, parliamentary government. Minto and his officials in Calcutta and Simla did succeed in watering down the reforms as much as possible by writing stringent regulations for their implementation and insisting upon the retention by the executive of veto power over all legislation. Elected members of the new councils were empowered, nevertheless, to engage in spontaneous supplementary questioning as well as formal debate with the executive concerning the annual budget, debate on which would no longer be limited to the last day of each year's legislative session but would extend over many days. Members were also permitted to introduce legislative proposals of their own. Gokhale took immediate advantage of these vital new parliamentary procedures by introducing his Elementary Education Bill into the Supreme Legislative Council in 1910. That measure called for the inauguration of a system of free and compulsory elementary education throughout British India. Although defeated, it was brought back again and again by Gokhale, who used the platform of the government's highest council of state as a sounding board for nationalist demands. Before the act of 1909, as Gokhale told his fellow congressmen in Madras that year, Indian nationalists had been engaged in agitation "from outside," but "from now we shall be engaged in what might be called responsible association with the administration." This most important forward step in the evolution of Indian self-government was taken as a result of the full cooperation of liberal Englishmen and Indian nationalists of the moderate emulative wing of Congress, which by this time had split apart.

Beginnings of parliamentary practice

Moderate and militant nationalism. The Congress meeting of 1907 never came to order long enough to hear the presidential address of Rash Behari Ghose, the candidate of conservative leaders. The division of Congress reflected broad tactical as well as presidential-candidate differences between the liberal evolutionary and militant revolutionary wings of the national organization. Tilak's New Party militants wanted to extend the boycott movement to the British government, and the cult of the bomb as well as the gun had become popular throughout Bengal and Mahārāshtra. Moderate Congress leaders, who cautioned compatriots against "extreme" speeches that might encourage violence, were themselves attacked as traitors to the motherland. The split left Congress divided for nine years into the influential moderate Conventionists of Gokhale's party and the revolutionary revivalists of Tilak's, who had captured the allegiance of India's youth. Tilak was, however, deported to Mandalay prison for sedition in 1908 and kept there until 1914.

From 1908 to 1910 Bengali terrorism reached its peak of frenzy, as did official repression on the part of Minto's government. At the end of 1910 Lord Hardinge of Penshurst succeeded Minto as viceroy (1910–16) and recommended the reunification of Bengal and the creation of a separate province of Bihār and Orissa. On December 12, 1911, King George V announced the revocation of Curzon's partition of Bengal at his Coronation Darbār in Delhi, which was to be the new capital of British India. By shifting the capital from Calcutta to Delhi, former capital of Mughal glory, the British hoped to placate Bengal's Muslim minority, even as the reunification of their motherland was designed to mollify Bengali Hindus. Eastern Bengal and Assam was dissolved, and Muslims cried bitterly "no bombs, no boons." The following year, in 1912, as he was about to enter Delhi in his regal state procession atop an elephant, Lord Hardinge was wounded by a bomb thrown by a would-be assassin, who escaped.

Reunification of Bengal

The reunification of Bengal had come too late to restore

tranquillity to British India. Edwin Montagu, Morley's protégé at the India Office, who served as parliamentary under secretary of state for India from 1910 to 1914 and as secretary of state from 1917 to 1922, announced in 1912 that the goal of British policy toward India would have to be to meet the just demands of Indians for a greater share in government. Britain was finally awakening to the urgency and intensity of India's political demands on the eve of World War I, when more compelling problems of European diplomacy pre-empted Whitehall's attention.

WORLD WAR I AND ITS AFTERMATH

India's contribution to the war effort. The impact of World War I on India was as pervasive as that of the war of 1857–58 had been. India's contributions to the war were extensive and significant, yet the war's contributions to change within British India were far greater. India's initial response to Lord Hardinge's declaration of his government's entry into World War I in August 1914 was, for the most part, enthusiastically supportive. Maharajas volunteered their men, money, and personal service, while Congress leaders, from Tilak, who had just been released from Mandalay and had wired the King-Emperor vowing his patriotic support, to Gandhi, who toured Indian villages urging peasants to join the British army, were allied in backing the war effort. Only India's Muslims, whose doctrinal allegiance to the Ottoman caliph had to be weighed against their temporal devotion to British rule, seemed hopelessly ambivalent from the war's inception. India's Congress support was primarily offered on the assumption that England would repay such loyal assistance with substantial political concessions—if not immediate independence or at least dominion status following the war, then surely its promise soon after the Allies won victory. No Indian imagined the war could possibly drag on for four years. The government of India's immediate military support was of vital importance in bolstering the western front, and an expeditionary force including two fully manned infantry divisions, the Meerut and Lahore, and one cavalry division left India in late August and early September 1914. They were shipped directly to France and moved up to the battered Belgian line just in time for the First Battle of Ypres. The Indian Corps sustained extraordinarily heavy losses during the winter campaigns of 1914–15 on the western front. The myth of Indian racial inferiority, especially with respect to courage in battle, was thus dissolved in sepoy blood on Flanders fields. In 1917 Indians were at last admitted to the final bastion of British Indian racial discrimination—the ranks of royal commissioned officers. Indian troops were rushed to East Africa and Egypt as well as the western front in the early months of the war, and by the end of 1914 more than 300,000 officers and men of the British Indian Army had been shipped to overseas garrisons and battlefronts. The Indian Army's most ambitious as well as ill-managed campaign was fought in Mesopotamia. In October 1914, before Turkey joined forces with the Central Powers, the government of India launched an army to the mouth of the Shatt al-Arab to further Curzon's policy of control over the Persian Gulf region. Basra was taken easily in December 1914, and by October 1915 the British Indian army had moved as far north as Kut-al-Amara (modern al-Kut), barely 100 miles (160 kilometres) from Baghdad. The prize of Baghdad seemed within reach of British arms, but less than two weeks after Gen. Sir Charles Townshend's doomed army of 12,000 Indians started north in November 1915, they were stopped at Ctesiphon, then forced to fall back to Kut, which was surrounded by Turks in December and fell in April 1916. This disaster became a national scandal for Britain and was appropriately investigated by a royal commission, whose report, published in June 1917, led to the immediate resignation of India's secretary of state, Austin Chamberlain. Edwin Montagu, Chamberlain's successor at Whitehall's India Office, informed the Commons on August 20, 1917, that the policy of the British government toward India was thereafter to be one of

The Mesopotamian campaign

> increasing association of Indians in every branch of the administration, and the gradual development of self-governing institutions, with a view to the progressive realization of responsible government in India as an integral part of the Empire.

Soon after this stirring promise of political reward for India's wartime support, Montagu embarked upon a personal tour of India. During his tour, Montagu conferred with his new viceroy, Lord Chelmsford (viceroy from 1916 to 1921), and their lengthy deliberations bore fruit in the Montagu–Chelmsford Report of 1918, the theoretical basis for the Government of India Act of 1919.

Anti-British activity. Anti-British terrorist activity started soon after the war began, sparked by the return to India of hundreds of embittered Sikhs who had sought to emigrate from their Punjab homes to Canada but who were denied permission to disembark in that country because of their colour. As British subjects the Sikhs had assumed they would gain entry to underpopulated Canada, but after wretched months in cramped and unsanitary conditions, with inadequate food supplies aboard an old freighter, they returned to India as confirmed revolutionaries. The Ghadr (Mutiny) Party had been started by Punjabi Sikhs in 1913, and its leaders journeyed abroad in search of arms and money to support their revolution, the foremost among them, Har Dayal, going to Berlin to solicit aid from the Central Powers. Muslim disaffection also grew and acquired revolutionary dimensions as the Mesopotamian campaign dragged on. Many Indian Muslims appealed to Afghanistan for aid, urging the *amīr* to start a holy war against the British and in defense of the caliphate. After the war, the Khilafat movement, an offspring of growing pan-Islāmic consciousness in India, was started by two fiery orator-journalists, the brothers Shaukat and Muhammad ʿAlī. It lured thousands of Muslim peasants to abandon their village homes and trudge over frozen high passes in a disastrous *hijrah* (flight) from India to Afghanistan. In Bengal terrorist bombings continued to harass officials, despite numerous "preventive detention" arrests made by Indian Criminal Intelligence Division (CID) police under the tough martial-law edicts promulgated at the war's inception. The deaths of Gokhale and Mehta in 1915 removed the most powerful moderate leadership from Congress and cleared the way for Tilak's return to power in that organization after its reunification in 1916. The sessions at Lucknow in December 1916 brought even further unity to India's nationalist forces in the form of a pact outlining a program of minimum immediate national demands and agreed upon by both Congress and the Muslim League. The Lucknow Pact called first of all for the creation of expanded provincial legislative councils, four-fifths of whose members should be elected directly by the people on as broad a franchise as possible. The League's readiness to unite with Congress was attributed to the pact's stipulation that Muslims should receive a far higher proportion of separate electorate seats in all legislative councils than they had enjoyed under the act of 1909. Thanks to such generous concessions of political power by Congress Hindus, Muslim nationalist leaders, including Mohammad Ali Jinnah (1876–1949), later to become the *qāʾid-e aʿẓam* ("great leader") of Pakistan, agreed to set aside doctrinal differences and work with India's Hindu majority toward the attainment of national freedom from British rule. This Congress–League rapprochement was, however, short-lived, and by 1917 communal tensions and disagreements once again dominated India's faction-ridden political scene. Tilak and Annie Besant each campaigned for different home-rule leagues, while Muslims worried more about pan-Islāmic problems than all-India questions of unity. Montagu's August 1917 announcement, followed by his popular tour of India, had also brought the prospect of rapid British concessions of power to many political leaders in India, who now returned to entrenched party positions rather than adhering to idealistic schemes of implausible unity. In July 1918, after returning home, Montagu published his lengthy "Report on Indian Constitutional Reforms,"

The Muslim Khilafat movement

noting that he and Chelmsford agreed that "nationhood within the empire represents something better than anything India has hitherto attained." The report went on to elaborate upon the principles on which the government planned to revise British India's constitution, the most novel of which was that of dyarchy (dual government), whereby power over external, financial, and law-and-order matters would remain in official hands, but other affairs would come under direct control of representatives chosen by an electorate.

Indian contribution to World War I

By Armistice Day, November 11, 1918, more than 1,000,000 Indian troops had been shipped overseas to fight or serve as noncombatants behind the Allied lines on every major front from France to Gallipoli. More than 100,000 Indian battle casualties, over 36,000 of which proved fatal, were sustained during the war. India's material and financial contributions to the war effort were hardly less valuable, with some £80,000,000 worth of military stores and equipment shipped from India's ports to various fronts, nearly 5,000,000 tons of wheat valued at over £40,000,000 sent to Great Britain, some £137,000,000 worth of raw jute and sacks alone exported, and vastly expanded output and export of cotton goods as well as rough-tanned hides, wolfram, manganese, mica, saltpetre, timbers, silk, rubber, and various oils. The government of India paid for all of its troops overseas, adding about £20,000,000 annually to its wartime military expenditure, and before the war ended the viceroy presented a gift of £100,000,000 (actually an imperial tax) to the British government. Tata's Iron and Steel Company received Indian government support once the war started and by 1916 was producing 100,000 tons of steel a year. An industrial commission was appointed in 1916 to survey the subcontinent's industrial resources and potential, and in 1917 a munitions board was created to expedite the production of war materials. Wartime inflation was immediately followed by one of India's worst depressions, which came in the wake of the devastating influenza epidemic in 1918, an epidemic that took a far heavier toll of Indian life and resources than all the casualties sustained throughout the war.

The Amritsar massacre. Politically, as well as economically, the postwar years proved depressing to India's high expectations. After the war British officials, who in the first flush of patriotism had abandoned their ICS posts to rush to the front, returned to oust the Indian subordinates acting in their stead and carried on their prewar jobs as though nothing had changed in British India. Indian soldiers also returned from battlefronts to find that back at home they were no longer treated as invaluable allies but reverted immediately to the status of "natives." Most of the soldiers recruited during the war had come from the Punjab, which, with only 7 percent of India's population, had supplied over 50 percent of the combatant troops shipped abroad. It is thus hardly surprising that the flashpoint of postwar violence that shook India in the spring of 1919 was Punjab province. The actual issue that served to rally millions of Indians, arousing them to a new level of disaffection from British rule, was the government of India's hasty passage of the Rowlatt Acts early in 1919. These "black acts," as they came to be called, were peacetime extensions of the wartime emergency measures passed in 1915 and had been rammed through the Supreme Legislative Council over the unanimous opposition of its Indian members. Indian leaders viewed the autocratic enactment of such legislation, following the victorious conclusion of a war in which India had so loyally supported Britain, as a confession of British treachery and duplicity and the abandonment of the promised policy of reform in favour of a new wave of repression. Mohandas Gandhi (*q.v.*), the Gujarati barrister who had returned from South Africa shortly after the war started and was by then recognized throughout India as one of the most promising leaders of Congress, called upon his countrymen to take sacred vows to disobey the Rowlatt Acts, launching a nationwide movement for the repeal of those repressive measures. Gandhi's appeal received the strongest popular response in the Punjab, where the Arya Samaj leaders Kitchlew and Satyapal addressed mass protest rallies from the provincial capital of Lahore to Amritsar, sacred capital of the Sikhs. Gandhi himself had taken a train to the Punjab early in April 1919 to address one of those rallies, but he was arrested at the border station and taken back to Bombay by orders of the tyrannical lieutenant governor of the Punjab, Sir Michael O'Dwyer. On April 10, in Amritsar, Kitchlew and Satyapal were arrested and deported from the district by Deputy Commissioner Miles Irving, and when their followers tried to march to Irving's bungalow in the camp to demand the release of their leaders they were fired upon by British troops. With several of their number killed and wounded, the enraged mob rioted through Amritsar's old city, burning British banks, murdering several Englishmen, and attacking two Englishwomen. Gen. R.E.H. Dyer was sent with troops from Jullundur to restore order, and, though no further disturbances occurred in Amritsar until April 13, Dyer marched 50 armed soldiers into the Jallianwalla Bāgh (Garden) that afternoon and ordered them to open fire on a protest meeting attended by some 10,000 unarmed men, women, and children without issuing a word of warning. It was a Sunday, and many neighbouring peasants had come to Amritsar to celebrate a Hindu festival, gathering in the Bāgh, which was a place for holding cattle fairs and other festivities. Dyer kept his troops firing for about ten minutes, until they had shot 1,650 rounds of ammunition into the terror-stricken crowd, which had no way of escaping the Bāgh since the soldiers spanned the only exit. About 400 civilians were killed and some 1,200 wounded. They were left without medical attention by Dyer, who hastily removed his troops to the camp. Sir Michael O'Dwyer fully approved of and supported the Jallianwalla Bāgh massacre, and on April 15, 1919, issued a martial-law decree for the entire Punjab province. Lord Chelmsford characterized the general's action as "an error of judgment," but when Montagu finally learned the atrocious details of the slaughter that had occurred in Amritsar he appointed a commission (under Lord Hunter) to hold a full inquiry in India. Dyer defended his action as

British treachery over reform

> the least amount of firing which would produce the necessary moral and widespread effect it was my duty to produce . . . from a military point of view, not only on those who were present, but more specially throughout the Punjab.

Dyer was relieved of his command, but he returned to England as a hero to many British admirers, who presented him with a collected purse of thousands of pounds and a jewelled sword inscribed "Saviour of the Punjab."

Consequences of the massacre

The Jallianwalla Bāgh massacre turned millions of patient and moderate Indians from loyal supporters of the British raj into national revolutionaries who would never again trust to British "fair play" or cooperate with a government capable of defending such action. The following year, Mahatma Gandhi launched his first Indian *satyāgraha* ("hold fast to the truth") campaign, India's response to the massacre in Jallianwalla Bāgh.

The Government of India Act of 1919. Britain's Parliament still hoped to avert the collision course of confrontation with Indian nationalism that had been set by the government of India by rushing through reforms designed to liberalize the autocracy. These were contained in the Government of India Act of December 1919, known familiarly as the Montagu–Chelmsford Reforms. They initiated a healthy devolution of authority from British to Indian hands, and, had they come before April 1919, they would most probably have received a warm welcome from Congress. The viceroy's Executive Council was now to have at least three Indian members, while the Supreme Legislative Council was to be transformed into a bicameral legislature consisting of an imperial Legislative Assembly and a Council of State. The Assembly would have 140 members, 100 of whom would be elected, with no more than 25 of the remaining 40 to be officials. The Council of State would have 60 members, 20 of whom would be appointed officials, the other 40 to be elected by a more carefully restricted electorate than that that would vote for assembly representatives. Enfranchisement continued to be based on property and education, but under the Act of 1919 a total of some

5,000,000 Indians were to become eligible to vote for provincial council representatives in the 1921 elections. Less than 1,000,000 subjects would be permitted to vote for candidates to the Imperial Assembly, and only 17,000 could choose the conservative Council of State members. Dyarchy was to be introduced at the provincial level, at which executive councils would be divided between responsible ministers elected to preside over "transferred" departments (education, public health, public works, and agriculture) and officials appointed by the governor to rule over "reserved" departments of state (land revenue, justice, police, irrigation, and labour). Provincial legislative councils were expanded in membership. At least 70 percent of their members were to be elected and no more than 20 percent reserved for appointed officialdom. The constitution of British India had thus advanced many strides in its gradual metamorphosis from a totally irresponsible autocracy to a fully responsible parliamentary form of government.

Enlargement of the franchise

Gandhi's strategy. But 1920 saw the beginning of the policy of noncooperation by the Congress. Gandhi set August 1 of that year as the day of fasting and prayer that would launch his nationwide *satyāgraha* movement. For Gandhi there was no dichotomy between religion and politics, and his unique political power was in great measure attributable to the spiritual leadership he exerted over India's Hindu masses, who viewed him as a *sādhu* ("saint") and worshipped him as a *mahātma* ("great soul"). He chose *satya* ("truth") and *ahimsa* ("nonviolence" or love) as the polar stars of his political movement because the former was the ancient Vedic concept of the real, embodying the very essence of existence itself, while the latter, according to Hindu (as well as Jain) scripture, was the highest religion (*dharma*). With these two weapons, Gandhi assured his followers, unarmed India could bring the mightiest empire known to history to its knees. His mystic faith magnetized millions, and the sacrificial suffering (*tapasya*) that he took upon himself by the purity of his chaste life and prolonged fasting armed him with great powers. Gandhi's strategy for bringing the giant machine of British rule to a halt was to call upon his countrymen to start a multiple boycott campaign in 1920, boycotting British-made goods, British schools and colleges, British courts of law, British titles and honours, British elections and elective offices, and, should the need arise if all other boycotts failed, British tax collectors as well. The total withdrawal of Indian support would thus stop the machine, and nonviolent noncooperation would achieve the national goal of *swarāj*.

Muslim reaction to Gandhi

The Muslim quarter of India's population could hardly be expected to respond any more enthusiastically to Gandhi's *satyāgraha* call than they had to Tilak's revivalism, but the Mahatma laboured valiantly to achieve Hindu–Muslim unity by embracing the ʿAlī brothers' Khilafat movement as the "premier plank" of his national program. Launched in response to news of the Treaty of Sèvres's dismemberment of the Ottoman Empire in 1920, the Khilafat movement coincided with the inception of *satyāgraha*, thus giving the illusion of unity to India's nationalist agitation. Such unity proved, however, as chimerical as the Khilafat movement's hope of preserving the caliphate itself, and in December 1920 Mohammad Ali Jinnah left the Nāgpur Congress, disgusted by Gandhi's mass following of Hindi-speaking Hindus. The days of the Lucknow pact were over, and by the start of 1921 the forces of Hindu and Muslim agitation destined to lead to the birth of the independent dominions of India and Pakistan in 1947 were clearly set in motion in their separate directions. (S.A.Wo.)

VIII. Prelude to independence

INDIAN NATIONALISM AND THE END OF THE RAJ

The final period of British rule can best be understood by studying the interaction of two trends. First, there was the transformation of British policy: the period opened with Britain in the twilight of an era of Liberal reform; then followed a long, almost uninterrupted government by Conservatives, with Labour finally taking over after World War II to implement a program of radical change. The initial reforming impulse of the pre-World War I Liberal governments was thus followed by caution and an insistence upon "safeguards" in constitutional evolution, with the movement toward a transfer of power making rapid headway only after the election of the Labour government in 1945. The second major trend was the endeavour of the Indian National Congress to mobilize a broadly based nationalist movement that would compel the British to hand over power. This endeavour was constantly hampered by the tendency of different sections of the movement to pull away in different directions. In the end, the Muslim political leadership opted for a separate form of independence—Pakistan. Divisive tendencies, which were only partially arrested by the struggle against the British, reasserted themselves after independence in both the new countries.

Response to dyarchy. The Amritsar massacre of 1919 provided an unpromising prelude to the elections which were to usher in dyarchy (see above *British imperial power [1858–1920]*). Gandhi called upon the Congress to boycott the elections. With the deaths of Mehta, Gokhale, and Tilak there was something approaching a vacuum in the leadership of the Congress at this time, and into this Gandhi moved, never to be completely dislodged. But there were other leaders, and those who had supported the old moderates in their faith in constitutional advance now declared that they would contest the elections and work the dyarchical system in order to fit India for self-government. These leaders may be termed the "old" Congress, for their most venerable spokesman was Surendranath Banerjea, a founder-member of Congress and long known as the Lion of Bengal. Not all, however, were ancients: there was Tej Bahadur Sapru, a brilliant lawyer, S.N. Sastri—almost as celebrated as Gandhi for his work among overseas Indians—and M.A. Jinnah (*q.v.*), called "the apostle of Hindu–Muslim unity." These men now regretfully seceded from Congress, most joining the Indian Liberal Federation. This was the first of many breakaway movements that were to mark the years of Gandhi's leadership. In three major provinces—Bengal, Bombay, and the United Provinces (now Uttar Pradesh)—ministries were formed by distinguished Liberals. Their period of office (1920–21 to 1923–24) was marked by impressive legislative reforms. Elsewhere, politics took on regional patterns. Punjab politics was marked by an urban–rural division. The towns were dominated by Hindus with thoroughgoing Congress views. The countryside was fairly equally divided between Muslims and Hindus, with the Sikhs as a sturdy minority. Rural life was dominated by the great landowners, especially in West Punjab. Rural interests were now brought under one umbrella by the formation of the Unionist Party. This was mainly Muslim, but it enjoyed the loyalty of the Hindu Jat cultivators, while Sikh landlords gave it conditional support. Sikh militants also developed a "direct action" form of politics through the fighting Akalis. The Unionist Party asserted an ascendancy over Punjab politics, basing its appeal on rural development. Politics also assumed a regional form in Madras (now Tamil Nadu). The Congress had never emerged as a strongly organized force in the South and was associated closely with the Brahmin elite, a group comprising less than 3 percent of the population but with a monopoly of power and position. An anti-Brahmin movement grew up in the 20th century, drawing upon a sense of pride in the nonpriestly culture of the non-Aryan Tamils. This movement assumed a political form as the Justice Party, which secured a clear majority in the first Madras dyarchy legislature. The leader was designated chief minister, and a regulated pattern of parliamentary government developed.

Regional politics

Having turned his back upon dyarchy, Gandhi endorsed the strangest cause of his infinitely varied public life: that of the Khilafat, or Muslim unity under the sultan (caliph) of Turkey. The Indian Muslims were anguished by the policy of Prime Minister Lloyd George in backing Greek claims against Turkey. Edwin Montagu's anxiety at his chief's apparent unconcern for the consequences within the Islāmic world caused him to engineer a protest that led Lloyd George to demand his resignation. The Indian

Muslims were stirred up by militant religious organizations that made overtures to the "new" militant Congress. They preached the end of the infidel British rule. Congress simultaneously launched a civil-disobedience campaign designed to compel the British to concede *swarāj*. *Swarāj* had been translated as "home rule," but it now became amplified into independence. The dual campaign was designed to demonstrate the unity of the peoples of India: Hindu-Muslim ek hai ("Hindu and Muslim are one"). But the Khilafat agitation, with its open incitement to religious militancy, stimulated a rising among the coastal Arab–Indian community of South India, the Moplahs, and they fell upon the Hindu population. In the United Provinces, a Congress mob besieged the Chauri Chaura police station and murdered the constables. Once again, Gandhi called off his campaign because the ordinary people could not understand his message. Gandhi was arrested (March 1922), brought to trial, and sentenced to six years' imprisonment. He was actually in jail until February 1924, being released after a serious operation.

Meanwhile, the Congress came under the influence of what may be called the "middle" Congress. A former moderate, Motilal Nehru, had placed himself beside Gandhi. But he found himself increasingly in alliance with C.R. Das of Bengal, when both emerged from imprisonment after the collapse of civil disobedience. Das insisted that the purpose of politics was fundamental change: he inquired,

> How will it profit India if in place of the white bureaucracy that now rules over her, there is substituted an Indian bureaucracy of the middle classes?

He argued that entry into the legislatures could be the means to force the British to accelerate change. He won over Motilal, and at a special session of Congress in September 1923 he secured a declaration that Congress "suspends all propaganda against entering councils." At the elections in September 1923, the Congress (campaigning as the Swarajya Party) made considerable gains, mainly at the expense of the Liberals. In the Central Provinces they commanded a majority, and in Bengal they formed the largest group, C.R. Das being invited to head the ministry. He refused, and the Swarajists were able to bring ministerial government to a stop. In the Punjab, however, the Unionists fought off the attack and moved on, while in Madras the Justice Party also survived as the government.

The Simon Commission

In London the Conservative government and, in particular, the diehard secretary for India, Lord Birkenhead, looked forward to the time when ten years of dyarchy would be completed; that is, to when a constitutional review would be required. In response to Indian wishes the review was advanced by two years, and the Indian Statutory Commission (Simon Commission) was appointed (1927) to look at the working of dyarchy and recommend future policy. As was usual, this was an all-parties Commission, with the Liberal Sir John Simon as chairman and with C.R. Attlee, a Labour member of Parliament, as one of its members. But the commission was entirely drawn from English public life, although even the Montagu–Chelmsford Report had been prepared with the assistance of Indian political leaders. Almost all shades of Indian opinion condemned this racial exclusivism (as it appeared). An almost complete boycott of the commission was mounted throughout its Indian travels. The Liberals and also the Muslim leader Jinnah joined the Congress in their boycott.

The position of the Muslims in politics at this time was ambiguous. The Khilafat campaign had collapsed—the Turkish leader Mustafa, Kemal Atatürk had abolished the office of caliph in 1924. Some Khilafatists nevertheless hung around on the fringe of the Congress. The Muslim League retained a shadowy existence. Its president (1919–30) was Jinnah, but its membership was a few hundred only, and even these were divided. Some Muslims, such as Fazl-i-Husain, the leader of the Punjab Unionist Party, had their own political power base; some were traditionalists, still looking belatedly to the British rulers for patronage. But, across their divisions, most of the Muslims opposed the Simon Commission.

In an effort to reply to British charges that Indians could not agree among themselves, an all-parties committee was set up under Motilal Nehru as chairman, to produce a draft Indian constitution. This emerged as a moderate document. Dominion status—that is, equality with Canada, Australia, New Zealand, and South Africa—was demanded "as the next immediate step." There would be a two-chamber Parliament, but the governor general would remain as the constitutional representative of the British crown. This constitution served to alarm the Muslims and reunite them in their distress. A conference was convened under the Aga Khan, and subsequently Jinnah produced what came to be known as "the 14 points." This was a demand for a weak federation, with autonomy to the provinces and measures to endow the North-West Frontier, Sind, and Baluchistan (the solidly Muslim areas of the northwest) with equal status alongside the other provinces. In the central government, the Muslims wanted at least one-third of the representation, although numerically they formed less than a quarter of the total population.

The Round Table Conferences. In Britain, a Labour government was briefly in office (1929–31). The viceroy, Lord Irwin, was an ultraconservative, but he developed an empathy for the Indian condition that included a personal understanding with Gandhi. Irwin announced that the goal of British policy in India was indeed dominion status. This infuriated the Conservative right wing, led by Lord Salisbury and Winston Churchill. But the Conservative centre (followers of Baldwin), as well as the Liberal and Labour parties, were ready to talk about reform. It was proposed to hold a "Round Table" Conference in London between representatives of the Indian communities and the British political parties. The first session was convened in the autumn of 1930. Meanwhile, the Simon Commission had reported, recommending that dyarchy in the provinces be replaced by full ministerial government. The Commission recoiled from the idea of parliamentary central government and envisaged an enlarged legislature as a forum of debate.

The Congress was suspicious of British tactics and intentions. A new generation of leaders was coming forward. The two new stars riding in the firmament were Jawaharlal Nehru (*q.v.*), regarded as the disciple of Gandhi (though he was an avowed Socialist, whereas Gandhi—if he could be given a label—was an anarchist), and Subhas Chandra Bose, formerly lieutenant of C.R. Das and heir to the militant, physical-force element in Bengali politics. It was a symbol of the new mood that, whereas the older Nehru had been satisfied with dominion status, his son was determined to have a Socialist republic. On January 26, 1930, the Congress, meeting at Lahore, pledged itself to a declaration of independence.

Positions at the first conference

When the first Round Table Conference met (November 1930–January 1931), the Congress was absent. Political India was represented by a group of Liberals—distinguished individuals, but, politically speaking, only middlemen—as well as spokesmen for the minorities, including Jinnah and the Aga Khan for the Muslims. There was another distinct group, for the 600 princes and princelings who still retained their quasi-independent status under British suzerainty (or "paramountcy," as it was termed) had sent their representatives. A few of these rulers (notably the Maharaja of Mysore) had steered their states forward into systems of representative government. But the majority still clung to an arbitrary autocracy, and these included the two largest, Hyderābād and Kashmir. If British India were to move forward to dominion status, where would this leave the princely states? British policy groped toward some means for closer association through the political device of federation. Since Canada adopted federation in 1867, as the solution for provincial differences and difficulties, federation had been invoked as the cure-all remedy for political impasses. Federation had worked in Australia; it had failed in Ireland. Now it was proposed for India. To general surprise, the princes departed from their usual position of immobility to announce that they were prepared to enter a federal form of government.

To the extent that the general principle of an all-India federation was accepted by both sides, the conference was a success, and an atmosphere of goodwill was created. There was a prospect of involving the Congress, even though the party had embarked upon another campaign of civil disobedience. In March 1931 there emerged the Gandhi–Irwin pact, by which Gandhi agreed to call off *satyāgraha* ("nonviolence") in return for the government releasing all political prisoners not guilty of violence and withdrawing pending prosecutions. The objective was for the two sides to meet at a second London conference. This meeting occurred in the autumn of 1931. By then, Britain was just emerging from the trough of the world depression, and the Labour government had given way to a national, Conservative-majority administration. Congress was represented solely by Gandhi, with Sarojini Naidu at his side. He asked for the substance of dominion status; that is, full self-government. The British countered by talk of safeguards and reservations. They were given justification for this strategy, as the representatives of the Muslims and of other minorities, such as the untouchables, stuck rigidly to exactly this demand. The second session closed on a note of anticlimax, and Gandhi returned to India to resume noncooperation.

As a result of this anti-British activity, Gandhi and the other Congress leaders were arrested. But Indian economic conditions had eased somewhat, and the political pressure eased in response. The failure of Gandhian nonviolence to produce short-term results led to pressures within the party. A number of Congress members drifted away to join the Liberals and others in working the legislative system: these were called Responsivists, because they advocated a positive response to dyarchy. In 1934 there was an attempt to swing the Congress in a left, militant direction. A Socialist Party was formed within the Congress, its leaders young intellectuals such as Jayaprakash Narayan and Asok Mehta. Jawaharlal Nehru was identified with the group, while Gandhi was sympathetic and influenced the Socialists away from centralism.

The Communal Award of 1932

While Indian politics was in the doldrums, the government in Britain was laboriously fashioning a constitution to replace dyarchy. The Round Table Conference had struggled on, after the departure of Gandhi, through a third session; but only the persistent Indian Liberals took it seriously. To cut through the deadlock that had settled over the relations between the dominant-caste Hindus, as the British saw the Congress, and the Muslims and untouchables, the prime minister, Ramsay MacDonald, issued a Communal Award in August 1932. This continued the system of separate electorates and separate constituencies for all who might be considered minorities and was viewed by most Indians as a blatant example of the policy of "divide and rule." The main beneficiaries were the Muslims, but the principle also applied to the Sikhs in Punjab, to Indian Christians, Eurasians, the aboriginal tribes, special interests (women, organized labour, business, landlords, universities)—and to the untouchables. Gandhi resented the last award especially, because it directly contradicted his campaign to integrate those he called Harijans (People of God) into the wider community. Gandhi succeeded in bypassing the award by negotiating an agreement with B.R. Ambedkar, the untouchables' leader, dramatizing his stand by yet another fast.

The Government of India Act of 1935. After the Communal Award, the Conservative secretary for India, Sir Samuel Hoare, proceeded with his officials to construct an elaborate structure for the next constitutional advance; this was to become the longest statute ever to be framed by a British Parliament. The Conservative centre gave its support, though this was based on the calculation that the Muslims and the princes would balance the Congress. The right wing, led by Winston Churchill, staged an all-out revolt that nearly secured the backing of the Conservative Party conference, and that helped to delay the passing of the Government of India Act till 1935. Under the act, government in the provinces was handed over to ministries elected on a much wider franchise (the total Indian electorate now numbered 40,000,000). At the centre, a new federation was envisaged, but its introduction was dependent upon the willing accession of one-half of the princes. The act created an elaborate federal structure, including a Supreme Court, and embodied safeguards and reservations designed to take care of any possible contingency. All this ensured Congress' condemnation of the act: Nehru described it as "a Charter of Slavery." What escaped everyone's notice at this time (though it was realized later) was that, if the major political organization in the land should decide to move in and operate the new constitution, there was little the British could do to hold up the inevitable transfer of power. Previous reform measures had included a provision for a further constitutional review; the 1935 act did not, for it was planned as the last installment before full self-government—even though, in the 1930s, the majority of British politicians and officials probably envisaged the final era lasting as long as dyarchy (nearly 20 years).

The elections of 1936

The first elections under the new constitution were held at the end of 1936. Congress hesitated between total boycott (advocated by Nehru) and participation in order to wreck the new constitution. The latter policy prevailed. Congress entered the fight with an integrated organization and a simple, effective appeal to the people. The Muslim League, its would-be rival, was compelled to improvise arrangements in the last few weeks before the poll. There were 1,585 seats open to contest. Congress fought 1,161 and gained 716, winning an absolute majority of seats in five provinces (the United Provinces, the Central Provinces, Bihār, Orissa, and Madras), while just short of a majority in Bombay. Because of inchoate organization, the Muslim League was able to contest only about 150 of the 482 constituencies reserved for Muslims. It won 109 seats, but in no province did the League gain a majority.

The extent of the Congress success surprised all opponents and possibly even its own people. What now? There followed an intraparty debate about accepting office. Nehru and the militants objected, and when overruled insisted that the Viceroy and governors must agree not to use their special powers in face of popular government. No such undertakings were given, but Congress nevertheless proceeded to take office. It was a historic moment. Apart from the brief encounter of the Round Table Conference, the Congress and the British rulers had stood apart. Now they were working together in harness. In addition to the six provinces listed above, Congress was also able to form ministries in Assam and on the North-West Frontier, where the Pathan Red Shirts (Khudai Khitmatgars) adhered to Congress. Only Punjab, still staunchly Unionist, Sind, under local barons, and Bengal, governed by an unstable coalition, eluded the Congress dominance.

World War II. The experience of actually operating the machinery of government consolidated the middle Congress. The organization men, the men of affairs, were in the ascendant—Gandhi was less relevant. But the situation was reversed by an external factor: the outbreak of World War II. The viceroy, Linlithgow, chose to observe the strict formalities of protocol and declared that India was at war with Nazi Germany without first gaining the support of the national leaders toward committing their country to war. The Working Committee of the All-India National Congress (the High Command, as it was often called) ordered all the Congress provincial ministries to resign in protest. There was considerable reluctance to follow orders, but by October all had resigned. The initiative in Indian politics was no longer in Congress' hands.

Jinnah's demand for Muslim sovereignty

Jinnah called on the Muslims to observe a day of thanksgiving when the Congress left office and raised the level of Muslim demands. At their annual gathering, held at Lahore in March 1940, the League passed a resolution demanding that geographically contiguous units be:

> Demarcated into regions which shall be so constituted with such territorial readjustments as may be necessary that the areas in which the Muslims are numerically in a majority, as

in the north-western and eastern zones of India, should be grouped to constitute 'independent states' in which the constituent units shall be autonomous and sovereign.

There could be different interpretations of the intentions of this resolution: were the Muslims seeking separation or a looser federal structure? And how were the Muslim-majority zones to be defined when in both Bengal and Punjab the communities were almost inextricably intermeshed in town and countryside? But the ambiguity was resolved by the press, which labelled this demand as the Pakistan Resolution. Previously, Pakistan (Land of the Pure), as a separate homeland for the Muslims of India, had been dismissed as the dream or illusion of Rahmat Ali, a Muslim exile in Cambridge. But now Pakistan became the talking point in every discussion about India's political future.

Indian constitutional advance was put to one side by the British government while the German armies occupied western Europe, and British Commonwealth forces (including Indian army divisions) chased Mussolini's troops out of North and East Africa. But, when Japan struck down into Southeast Asia at the beginning of 1942, the threat to India galvanized the British war cabinet into reconsidering the political stalemate in India as a matter of urgency. In February 1942, the members of the war cabinet were formed into committees designed to take over responsibility for important areas of policy. The India Committee was presided over by C.R. Attlee, then leader of the Labour Party and also deputy prime minister. His colleagues included Simon, leader of the 1928 commission, several Conservatives, and the Socialist Sir Stafford Cripps. A plan was rapidly submitted by Attlee for a declaration of British policy that would bind the government to setting up an Indian constitutional assembly immediately after the war terminated, to work out the terms of Indian independence. It was to be made clear, however, that any province that did not wish to accept the new constitution might continue, for the time being, under existing arrangements. In return for this commitment it was hoped that the political parties—especially the Congress—would join in the prosecution of the war against Japan. It was decided to send Cripps to India to persuade the politicians to cooperate.

The Cripps mission

Cripps arrived in Delhi on March 23, 1942, and plunged into intensive discussion with all the politicians, especially the Congress. Argument centred mainly on the short-term question of Indian national participation in the war effort. But deadlock was soon reached over the Congress claim—stated by their president Abul Kalam Azad—that Cripps had conceded "a National Government which would function as a Cabinet," from which Cripps backed down. The Cripps mission, as the first of a series of bargaining encounters that were to take place between the British and Indian leaders in the years leading up to independence, showed how misunderstanding would constantly degenerate into deadlock, essentially as both sides were unclear about the consequences of their own and their opponents' plans and proposals. Mutual suspicion could rapidly become mutual hostility. Jinnah and the Muslims had played a waiting game during the Cripps–Congress discussions but had seized upon the proviso that a province might not be compelled, against its own expressed majority opinion, to accept a constitution devised by the rest of India.

The Japanese advance continued, and by May 1942 almost the whole of Burma was within their grasp. But the Japanese attack was halted on the jungle hillsides of the Assam–Burma border. For two years there would be no significant change in the fortunes of war in the Burma theatre. But this was not clear in 1942, either to Indians or to British. Both anticipated an invasion, and Gandhi re-emerged to call upon the British to leave Indians to deal with the Japanese by nonviolent means. The slogan "Quit India" now appeared everywhere. As there was no response, the All-India Congress Committee issued a statement in August 1942 demanding an immediate departure: if this was refused, Congress would begin "a mass struggle on nonviolent lines on the widest possible scale." Two days later Gandhi and the Working Committee were arrested. The leadership of the struggle passed to younger men who intended to fight: "Let us Do or Die" was their slogan. Jayaprakash Narayan, already on the run from the police, led the guerrilla campaign. But, as so often happens when violence is unleashed, the campaign passed largely into the hands of bullies and bandits. Within six weeks the revolt (which was largely confined to the eastern districts of the United Provinces and Bihār) had been suppressed, and for two years there was silence in Indian politics.

The Congress rebellion

THE TRANSFER OF POWER

In October 1943, Field Marshal Lord Wavell, the architect of the early British victories in Africa, became viceroy. He was a distinguished leader but found great difficulty in communicating with any warmth to all but his closest acquaintances. He nevertheless attempted to reopen negotiations with the Congress leaders, who from 1944 were gradually released from internment. The Muslim League had made a considerable impression on the political scene, finding personnel for ministries in several provinces. C.R. Rajagopalachari—who was not interned (the 1942 outbreak hardly affected South India)—came forward in April 1944 with a formula whereby the Muslims would be given the opportunity to decide, by referendum, whether they wanted to form a separate state. After his release, Gandhi met Jinnah (September 1944) to discuss a similar formula, but they were unable to agree. Wavell decided that this might be the moment to take the initiative. After consultations in London, he convened an all-parties conference at Simla in June 1945 to discuss the formation of a government representing the main Indian political groups, but Congress and the League could not agree about the basis on which ministers should be chosen.

Policy of the Attlee government. Soon after Simla there was a general election in Britain in which Labour came to power with a large majority. Attlee became prime minister and reconstituted an India–Burma Committee, with Cripps and the new secretary for India, Lord Pethick-Lawrence, as members. The new government was committed to independence for India but took over the 1942 Cripps position: that no unwilling province should be coerced into accepting an independence that did not safeguard minority rights. What would happen if agreement could not be reached? Lord Wavell had come down firmly on the necessity of Indian unity, but he advised the Cabinet that if Jinnah refused to cooperate with Congress he should be offered a Pakistan that included only the actual Muslim-majority districts. This would mean the division of two great provinces—Bengal and Punjab. Wavell still believed (like most British officials) that Jinnah was bluffing, that he was using Pakistan as a stalking horse in order to gain as many concessions for the Muslims as possible.

The elections of 1946

The Labour Cabinet was not yet ready to test Jinnah's bluff. First, elections to choose a central legislature and legislatures for the provinces were announced. Both the Congress and the League went into the elections with confidence. This time the League had the support of local-level organization, backed by the enthusiasm of active workers, among whom students were numerous. The results simplified Indian politics into a struggle of Congress versus the Muslim League. At the centre, the League won all the seats reserved for Muslims, but Congress won all but five of the nonreserved seats. In the provincial elections—held on a wider franchise, representing 30 percent of the adult population—the League gained 439 of the 494 Muslim seats, while Congress swamped all the other parties and stood to take office in eight provinces. Paradoxically, despite its spectacular success in terms of votes, the League was able to form ministries only in Sind and Bengal, and even then under somewhat unreliable leaders from a party viewpoint. In the Punjab the League was just short of a majority; the Unionists still clung to office.

Against this unpromising background of a confrontation between two monolithic parties, both having an electoral mandate to demand opposing terms, the Labour government decided to send a mission to Delhi to work out constitutional proposals with the Indian leaders. The cabinet mission was led by Lord Pethick-Lawrence, but Cripps was the dominant personality, with A.V. Alexander, minister of defense, as the third member. Because the failure of the 1942 Cripps mission was partly ascribed to estrangement from the then viceroy, the 1946 mission included Wavell as a fourth member for almost all purposes.

The delegates began by listening to all shades of opinion. Attempts to evolve an agreed solution representing the combined views of Congress and the League soon failed, and the mission was compelled to produce its own formula. This was an ingenious plan, devised initially by Cripps, to create three tiers of government, the lowest (provincial) tier being arranged in groups of Hindu- and Muslim-majority provinces. After prolonged discussion and manoeuvring, both the Congress and the Muslim League failed to accept the plan. The League announced that the time had come for Muslim "direct action," and August 16, 1946, was announced as Direct Action Day. It was marked by an impressive display of Muslim solidarity but was overshadowed by riots and atrocities in Calcutta, during which some 4,000 persons were killed in the course of three days.

Muslim Direct Action Day (August 1946)

Immediately after the "Great Calcutta Killing" (as it was soon called), Wavell formed an interim government of Indian politicians. It consisted of eight adherents of Congress and four independents. In October, five Congress nominees resigned to make way for League members, though Jinnah declined to serve alongside Nehru. This did little for interfaith relations, and a wave of killings swept across East Bengal.

Although events were clearly reaching the breaking point, Nehru and Gandhi still resisted any concession affecting the unity of India. But Vallabhbhai Patel and other prominent Congress figures began to realize that the deadlock must be broken somehow or else India would drift into civil war.

Wavell also understood the need for urgency and informed the Labour government that he must have a time limit for the termination of British rule. Attlee had come to feel that Wavell had lost his way, and decided to replace him with Adm. Lord Louis Mountbatten, the former supreme commander of Southeast Asia Command. On February 20, 1947, Attlee told Parliament that it was the "definite intention" of the government to transfer power "into responsible Indian hands by a date not later than June 1948." Because there was no assurance that agreement could be reached on the form of government for the new India, power might have to be transferred to some of the provincial governments. At the end of his statement, Attlee announced that Wavell would be succeeded as viceroy by Mountbatten.

Partition. Very soon after the latter arrived in India in March 1947, he decided that the goal of a united polity (which he was briefed to attain) was no longer feasible. In Punjab, the Unionist ministry had resigned, and the province was ungovernable. No party ministry could contain the rising tide of hatred that was welling up among Muslims, Sikhs, and Hindus. The British governor took over the responsibility for public order, but the riots and killings continued. Mountbatten had to act fast, and he showed a drive and determination that carried others along with him. If Pakistan was to be conceded, then Jinnah had to understand that he must accept the logic of his own doctrine: the non-Muslim districts of Punjab and Bengal would be denied to him. But Jinnah himself saw that there was something more important than territory, for he told Mountbatten: "I do not care how little you give me so long as you give it to me completely."

Behind the scenes, Patel was reconciling his Congress supporters to Pakistan, though he was determined that the Muslims would not receive one scrap more than their due. He was also determined that Indian unity would be preserved by incorporating the 600 princely states into the new union, so that the old patchwork of ambiguities and obsolescences would be replaced by a unified administration. Thus, when Mountbatten set to work to persuade Gandhi and Nehru, he did not have to worry about the rest of the Congress. Gandhi submitted his own plan to win back the Muslims—by voluntarily putting them in control of a united India. Congress would not swallow this experiment in understanding, so Gandhi withdrew himself from the debate. Nehru was persuaded by the argument that communities should not be coerced into joining a political entity against their will. But, while agreeing with Mountbatten, he seems to have still cherished the belief that the Muslim League did not really represent the will of the Muslim masses.

At the end of April, Mountbatten sent a draft plan to London for Cabinet consideration. They made a number of minor modifications but accepted the overall objective: that the peoples of India should themselves choose, through their elected representatives, whether they wanted to partition their land. Mountbatten gave Nehru a preview of the plan and went personally to London to seek Cabinet approval of modifications designed to meet Nehru's objections. On return, he called a meeting of the leaders—Nehru, Patel, Jinnah, and others, with Baldev Singh for the Sikhs. The provinces where actual Congress governments were functioning were assumed to wish to merge in a united India. Sind, Baluchistan, and the North-West Frontier were to make a straight choice: India or a new entity (for Pakistan was still not identified by name). The method of choice varied. The Frontier voters were to take part in a popular plebiscite, and in the two great provinces that might be divided (Punjab and Bengal) there was to be a preliminary meeting of all members of the provincial legislatures to vote on whether to adhere to India or adhere to the new entity as a complete province. Then the legislators were to separate into two groups representing the Muslim- and non-Muslim-majority districts and to decide whether or not their province should be partitioned: a majority in favour of partition in either section would decide the issue. If Bengal decided on partition, then the Sylhet district of Assam, which included a majority of Muslims, was to hold a plebiscite to decide whether or not to join the Muslim-majority part of Bengal. The plan was accepted by the leaders of Congress and the League and was then announced to the world. At the press conference at which the details were discussed, Mountbatten revealed that the date for the transfer of power "could be about the 15th of August" 1947; this allowed less than ten weeks to prepare for possible partition and independence. Events now seemed to take over from people. The ritual of choosing for India or Pakistan was carried out, and there were no surprises. The Bengal and Punjab legislatures met, and a majority (the Muslims) voted that the undivided provinces should leave India. Then they divided into two parts, and the non-Muslim group voted for partition: thus Bengal and Punjab were scheduled for dismemberment. The other Muslim-majority areas opted for the still-unnamed Pakistan. On the Frontier a majority of the total electorate voted for Pakistan.

The Mountbatten plan

There were four great questions to be solved in the ten weeks before partition. The assets of undivided India—financial and material—had to be equitably apportioned between the two new countries; the public services had to be dissolved and reconstituted in two portions; and a frontier had to be demarcated within the mixed Muslim–Hindu–Sikh populations of Punjab and Bengal. The fourth issue was the most elusive. The Mountbatten plan had produced a formula whereby British India could be split into two new polities, but nothing whatever had been decided about the future of the 600 princely states, which, in theory, were in various kinds of feudal relationship with the British crown—and which, in theory, would revert to their pre-British status of sovereignty when paramountcy (the suzerainty of the British king-emperor) lapsed with the end of imperial rule.

The division of the assets was entrusted to a Partition Committee. The bulk of the material assets was in the territory of the future Indian Union, and there it remained. Financial assets were also frozen until, after independence, Gandhi entered into a fast to reconcile India and Pakistan, and then some restitution was made. The allocation of the public services was on a basis of individual choice: Muslim officials who belonged to areas within the future Indian Union could choose to go to Pakistan, and vice versa. The division of the Indian Army was more difficult. Few units were altogether Hindu, Sikh, or Muslim. The officers and men had to choose their option and then await posting to the country of their choice. Meanwhile, a spirit of communal hostility intensified in all the services, most deplorably in the police.

The boundary award

Even more crucial was the delineation of a new frontier that would satisfy the expectations of both the new countries. Two judicial tribunals were appointed, with judges adhering to both the new countries, and with a joint chairman—the English jurist Sir Cyril (later Lord) Radcliffe. The claims on both sides were so extravagant and the judges aligned themselves so obviously in political and not judicial terms that Radcliffe alone had to invent the new frontiers. He did his best, but the communities were so intermeshed and the clashes of interests so irreconcilable that he was compelled to adjudicate under grave disadvantages. He delivered his award to Mountbatten two days before the transfer of power (on August 13). Knowing that the Radcliffe award would offend both sides, the Viceroy delayed its promulgation until after independence. Perhaps with some reason, Pakistan felt that it had received bare justice; but this did not make the new India any more pleased with the award.

The transformation of princely India was not so tidy. Once again Mountbatten exploited the fact that he knew where he wanted to go, whereas almost no one else was so firm of purpose. The British Labour government had formulated no overall policy for the princes. Mountbatten coaxed and cajoled the great majority of them into signing instruments of accession to the new India. The Muslim state of Bawahalpur, which bordered the West Punjab, naturally adhered to Pakistan, as did the Khān of Kalāt in Baluchistan and some other chieftains contiguous to the new West Pakistan. Hyderābād, in the heart of South India, had a population of 16,000,000, predominantly Hindu, under the rule of a Muslim dynasty. The Niẓām (popularly supposed to be the richest man in the world) intended to make himself independent and held out against Indian attempts to bring him in. His plan miscarried, largely because a local populist Muslim leader launched a militant movement (the Razakars) that provided a motive for Indian military forces to intervene and restore order, in September 1948. Hyderābād accepted the same conditions as other former princely states and was later partitioned and disappeared from the map. Kashmir, in the north, presented a similar problem. It had a population of more than 4,000,000, a definite Muslim majority, and a ruler who was a Hindu playboy. He also hoped to become independent and negotiated a "standstill" agreement with both India and Pakistan. Meanwhile, popular movements developed within Kashmir against princely autocracy. The maharaja replied with repression. With the assent of the new Pakistan government, tribal fighters from the hills of the Frontier poured into Kashmir proclaiming *jihād*, a holy war. The maharaja fled to Delhi and acceded to India in return for military assistance. Mountbatten (who continued as governor general of India—without Pakistan—after independence) accepted the accession, subject to this being confirmed by popular referendum. Indian forces arrived by air and threw back the tribesmen. Pakistan replied by infiltrating regular troops, until the new states were locked in an undeclared war. They were saved from escalation of the conflict by the initiative of the United Nations in bringing about a cease-fire in January 1949. The cease-fire line (which left the Vale of Kashmir and the bulk of the state on the Indian side) became the de facto frontier, though neither India nor Pakistan recognized it as such.

The Kashmir problem

India and Pakistan rapidly adapted to nationhood. In India the putative Constituent Assembly became the new parliament, with Jawaharlal Nehru as prime minister. In Pakistan Jinnah chose the more withdrawn office of governor general, leaving his lieutenant, Liaquat Ali Khan, to be prime minister and chief executive. The new India and Pakistan had to face an immediate crisis in the unexpected influx of refugees. Seven to eight million people left their homes in India and fled to Pakistan, and about the same number made the nightmare journey in the other direction. Perhaps 200,000 did not complete the journey and were slain on the way. This was the consequence of the communal conflicts that had preceded independence. At the top level of political negotiation, the transfer of power was conducted with dignity, even nobility; but, at the base level of the man and woman in the street and village in those areas that were partitioned, it was carried out amid suffering, loss, and bitterness.

(H.R.T.)

IX. The new nations

Despite partition, India and Pakistan remain clenched in a mutual relationship, and trends in one country have a powerful effect in the other. India, by reason of its much greater size and by virtue of a much more rapid takeoff into nationhood, has always been dominant.

INDIA

Nehru's premiership. Nehru was already prime minister of India (effectively) at independence, and he retained his arduous office until his death, in May 1964. The burden of leadership—as head of a mighty party, guide to the nation, and international statesman—was intolerably heavy. During the 1950s Nehru demonstrated an extraordinary vitality and endurance, but the unremitting strain inevitably took its toll, and the last years saw a sad decline in his powers, which was inevitably reflected in the quality of national life. By then, however, Nehru had firmly stamped his imprint upon his country. His three major bequests were a democratic, parliamentary system of government, an economy conditioned by Socialism and centralized planning, and a vision of society moving toward secularism and social justice.

India's constitution was completed by November 1949. A federal union of states was held together by a centralized national government, the core of which was the prime minister and the Cabinet, responsible to the Lok Sabha, or central Parliament. The Supreme Court and the president were established as further safeguards of the constitution and the nation, but they function as guardians against misgovernment, not at all as rivals to the parliamentary executive. The constitution provides a charter of rights that have a positive, directive quality. Article 17, for example, declares: "Untouchability is abolished and its practice in any form is forbidden."

The constitution

The elections of 1952. With a new constitution, India prepared (1952) for its first general election to be held on the basis of universal adult franchise. For the lower house of the Lok Sabha, 489 members were to be chosen, while the state assemblies provided places for nearly 3,400 members. The Congress—much more than a political party and usually described as the Freedom Movement—dominated the national and local scene. The leaders had proved their patriotism by demonstration and by incarceration in British jails. They enjoyed the support of the rural masses, and the organization was fortified by funds from businessmen and landlords alike. The minorities looked to the Congress for protection, as previously they had looked to the British raj. In opposition to the Congress there were only minor parties and a host of independents. The great opponent of the Congress—the Muslim League—was disbanded (except in the extreme south, where a Muslim pocket kept a branch going), and most Muslims looked to the Congress for protection. The Socialist Party broke away from the Congress in 1948 and presented an original program. The Communists—who had grown greatly in strength during World War II—were well organized only in certain areas, and the Hindu religious organizations were discredited by the assassination of Gandhi by a Hindu fanatic. Thus, when the nation went to the polls in 1952, the Congress won dramatic victories everywhere. In the Lok Sabha they gained 362 of the 489 seats. The Communists came next (23 seats), followed by the Socialists (12 seats). This commanding position of the Congress was based upon 45 percent of the popular vote. The Communists emerged as the main

Consolidation of Congress

opposition in four states—those areas where they were later to demonstrate grass-roots activism. Elsewhere the opposition was formed from regional or local groups, based mainly on traditional loyalties.

The period between the first elections of 1952 and the second elections of 1957 was one of achievement. The First Five-Year Plan (1950–55) was completed, and development goals were fully achieved, and the second plan (1956–61) was launched with a more ambitious overall target. The second general election in 1957 was an endorsement by the people of the success of Nehru's leadership: there was actually an increase in the government's majority to 366 seats out of a total of 494 in the Lok Sabha, while the Communists made a modest advance to 29 members. The arrival of the right-wing Hindu Jan Sangh Party, with four members, seemed of very little significance.

Reorganization of the states. Although the Congress—and Nehru—were impregnable at Delhi, there were indications that at the state level the pattern of politics might change. In the South of India the speakers of the Dravidian languages (a group quite distinct from the Indo-Aryan languages of northern and central India) began actively campaigning for a redistribution of the existing administrative structure into states based upon the languages: Tamil, Telugu, Kannada, and Malayalam. The first militant movement arose among the Telugu speakers, who were divided between the states of Madras and Hyderābād, and in 1953 Andhra Pradesh came into being as the Telugu state. Following an inquiry by a States Reorganization Commission (1956), the whole political map of India was redrawn, the previous mixture of British-Indian provinces and princely states being reduced to a new pattern of 14 states representing linguistic regions. The transformation was most radical in the south, the northern tier remaining largely unchanged. A question mark remained over two states—Bombay, where two languages, Marathi and Gujarati, coexisted, and Punjab, where Hindi and Punjabi were jointly spoken. Bombay was to witness militant protest by the Marathi speakers until at last the state was partitioned in 1960. In Punjab the Sikhs launched a mass campaign for "Punjabi Suba," a state in which they would be the majority community. Nehru refused to concede this demand, despite extreme political pressure, but the state was eventually partitioned in 1966 in the aftermath of the war with Pakistan—in which the Sikhs had played an important part.

Demands of linguistic minorities

As the states were redefined on the basis of local and regional consciousness, so political parties at this level increasingly adopted postures that were founded in regional issues and that had little relation to overall conceptions of nationalism and Socialism. In Madras an avowedly Tamil separatist party, the Dravida Munnetra Kazagham (DMK), speaking for the lowly castes against the Brahmins, emerged to challenge the Congress. In nearby Kerala the first Communist state government took office under E.M.S. Namboodiripad, a former Gandhian, in 1957.

The elections of 1962. Nehru's last general election in 1962 took place against a background of gathering uneasiness. Foreign policy, based upon nonalignment, appeared to be under strain along the Himalayan frontier with China, and the invasion of Goa in December 1961, though a military success, was a sign of the abandonment of nonviolence. The economic program, though still going forward, had lost its momentum. Most important of all, Nehru was tired and old and relied too much upon his own personal "court." At the national level, nevertheless, the Congress retained a remarkable degree of support. The Lok Sabha then consisted of 516 seats. On a popular vote of 48 percent (the highest so far), the Congress obtained 355 seats. The opposition, previously strongest on the left, split almost equally between left and right. The Jan Sangh increased its membership to 14, while a new secular conservative party, Swatantra (Freedom), gained 22 seats. The Communists remained the largest opposition group, with 29 members.

Foreign policy. Indian foreign policy during the Nehru period may be described as one of nonalignment with either of the two world power blocs. The dispute with Pakistan rumbled on, however, causing a major part of the Indian Army to be permanently deployed in Kashmir and in the Punjab. The northeastern portion of the Kashmir state is a remote Buddhist province, Ladākh, bordering upon Tibet. There the Aksai Chin had been vaguely demarcated on maps, though not upon the actual terrain, as part of the Kashmir domain and therefore appeared as part of the Indian Union. But from 1950 onward the medieval Tibetan state was replaced by the People's Republic of China. Communication between Lhasa and the rest of China had to depend upon a route that ran across the Aksai Chin salient, and the Chinese began to build a modern road. There was another border where conflict might occur, in the hills to the north of Assam. A border had been jointly agreed at a conference in Simla in 1914 between British and Tibetan officials and became known as the McMahon Line, from the name of the British negotiator. Only after World War II was administrative control actually extended to this area, the North East Frontier Agency (NEFA), and only after independence was an Indian official sent to the most advanced point, Tawang, where a great Buddhist monastery dominated the hills.

Friendship with China

In 1954 India and China signed a treaty designed to symbolize the friendship of two newly liberated countries within the "Five Principles of Peaceful Co-Existence" known as Pancha Shila. Relations between the two countries were complicated when in 1959 the Dalai Lama fled with thousands of his supporters into India. China indicated through diplomatic initiatives that a joint review of the frontier ought to proceed in order to demarcate a line representing present agreements rather than past imperial "aggression." India remained deaf to these overtures and insisted upon the legal validity of the McMahon Line. Meanwhile, in 1959 and 1960, China concluded agreements with Pakistan and Burma, respectively, to settle the petty disputes that had prevailed since the British period over certain sectors of their frontiers. India was incensed because the agreement with Pakistan covered sections of the former Kashmir boundary, occupied by Pakistan in 1947 but still claimed as de jure Indian territory.

The Himalaya border conflict of 1962

In the autumn of 1962 orders were issued to consolidate Indian border forces in forward positions. Beyond Tawang, Indian troops moved into what was a disputed area, even according to the 1914 agreements. The Chinese retaliated, both in Ladākh and in NEFA, launching a major offensive that caught the Indians off balance (October 20, 1962). Tawang was occupied, and the Assam plains lay open to attack, while in Ladākh 43 army posts were captured. In this emergency Nehru urgently called for British, Commonwealth, and U.S. assistance. British guns and U.S. bombers were rushed in, but, as unexpectedly as the war began, it ended. On November 7 the Chinese unilaterally announced that they were withdrawing their forces back to the lines of actual control before the conflict, intimating that India must observe a neutralized buffer zone between the frontier forces. China was left in undisputed control of Aksai Chin and the border road. It was a sad finale to the policy of nonalignment.

The war of 1965. After the frontier war with China, morale in India was low. The economic development program was levelling off. Nehru died in May 1964 and was succeeded by a meek but by no means undistinguished Gandhian, Lal Bahadur Shastri. In contrast, Pakistan was conscious of doing very well. For the first time the inferiority complex that had afflicted Pakistan vis-à-vis India was lifted. In this atmosphere Zulfikar Ali Bhutto, then foreign minister of Pakistan, conceived the dangerous plan of forcing India to reconsider the closed subject of Kashmir. Early in 1965 there were border skirmishes between police and military forces in the Rann of Kutch, where there was no clearly demarcated frontier. Pakistan appeared to emerge with a military advantage, and, when the British prime minister, Harold Wilson, suggested that the matter might be referred to international arbitration, both countries agreed. Could not this be repeated in Kashmir?

Bhutto persuaded Pres. Ayub Khan to agree to a plan whereby irregular forces would be infiltrated into Kashmir to promote a guerrilla war, which would expand to the point where the United Nations would intervene. The guerrilla campaign was a failure, however, and India retaliated by an action on the 1949 cease-fire line. Pakistan moved an armoured force to cut off Indian lines of supply in Kashmir, and on September 6, 1965, the Indian Army sought to relieve the pressure by crossing the Punjab frontier in a three-pronged attack on Lahore. The big powers used their persuasion to end the combat. Superior Indian strength would probably have become decisive had not China created incidents on the Himalayan border in Sikkim, which seemed to constitute a threat of war. On September 22 a cease-fire came into effect.

The position was debated at the UN, and Indians were startled to find that many Muslim countries of the Middle East, Asia, and Africa saw them as the aggressors. At last the Soviet Union persuaded Ayub to meet Shastri at Tashkent in January 1966. After enormous effort, Soviet Premier Aleksey Kosygin induced the two sides to sign a peace agreement based on a complete return to the status quo and a vague undertaking to negotiate differences. Shastri, who had been ill, died at Tashkent.

The Tashkent Conference (1966)

Shastri's death caught everyone unprepared. One candidate for the premiership was Morarji Desai, a veteran Gandhian, also a believer in financial orthodoxy and therefore acceptable to important elements in the Congress Party. From among other candidates support polarized around Indira Gandhi, Nehru's only daughter. When the votes of the Congress parliamentary party (the elective body) were counted, Mrs. Gandhi had secured the backing of three-quarters of the members.

Indira Gandhi's premiership. The election of 1967 was preceded by signs that the polity and the economy were in a critical condition. There was a food shortage of unprecedented proportions, with semi-famine conditions in several states, and India appealed to the United States and other grain-growing countries for aid. At the same time inflation and poor industrial performance had led to devaluation of the rupee in June 1966.

In the Lok Sabha, the Congress scraped back with a bare majority: 278 seats out of a total of 520. The largest opposition groups emerged on the right: Swatantra (44 seats) and Jan Sangh (35 seats). The Communists were split into the "Moscow," or right, Communists (22) and the "Peking" Communists (19). The two Socialist parties jointly numbered 36, and Madras state returned a solid block of 25 DMK members. The Congress retained control of half the states; it was decisively defeated in three (also in the Delhi territory).

The period following the 1967 election saw political turmoil at both the state level and in the Lok Sabha and resulted in a major realignment in the Congress Party itself. Mrs. Gandhi's opponents in the party attempted to end her premiership, and Congress was split into opposing and supporting groups. Mrs. Gandhi demonstrated that "her" Congress (designated "ruling") would move toward radical policies such as land reform and the nationalization of banking. Deciding to seek electoral support, she announced that a fifth general election would be held in March 1971.

Mrs. Gandhi's triumph

The result was her personal triumph. The ruling Congress won 350 of the 440 seats contested by the party, giving it a two-thirds majority (out of a total 520 seats) in the new Lok Sabha, enough to carry through desired constitutional amendments. The Old Congress dwindled down to 16 seats. Swatantra crept back to the Lok Sabha with eight members and the Samyukta Socialists with only three. Jan Sangh, with 22 members, was the only right-wing party to maintain some continuity. The DMK returned with 23 members (previously 25). The Communist Party of India (CPI) held firm with 23 seats, and the Moscow-aligned Communists made a distinct impact, winning 25 seats.

On August 9, 1971, a treaty of peace, friendship, and cooperation was signed with the Soviet Union. Much of 1971, however, was dominated by the growing controversy with Pakistan over the status of its eastern province (see below *Pakistan: Civil war*). Both India and Pakistan declared a state of emergency in November, fighting spread to Kashmir, and open warfare existed on both fronts by December 3. The war ended when Pakistani troops in Dacca surrendered to Indian and Bangladesh (East Pakistan) forces on December 16. All Indian troops were withdrawn from Bangladesh by March 12, 1972, and India supplied its neighbour with generous aid. An attempt to relieve the strained relations with Pakistan was undertaken when Mrs. Gandhi and Bhutto met at Simla, India, from June 28 to July 3.

Thereafter, however, Mrs. Gandhi's popularity began to wane. In 1974 the veteran socialist Jaya Prakash Narayan led a campaign against her alleged despotic government that attracted mass support, and in June 1975 her election to the Lok Sabha of 1971 was declared void. Mrs. Gandhi replied by declaring a state of emergency throughout India on June 26. Hundreds of politicians, including Narayan and Morarji Desai, were arrested and jailed; the press was harshly censored, and strikes were declared to be illegal. The sweeping powers Mrs. Gandhi assumed were employed to stop inflation and to improve the administration of public services. Parliament became her servant, and she amended the constitution to strengthen her position.

In January 1977 Mrs. Gandhi suddenly announced that a nationwide election for the Lok Sabha would be held in six weeks. The emergency was relaxed and her political opponents were freed. Many surmised that her intention was to obtain an electoral mandate to invest her son, Sanjay Gandhi, with formal powers, and it was expected that the election results would be manipulated. In actuality, there was no attempt to control the elections. The main opposition groups formed a coalition known as the Janata (People's) Party, with Morarji Desai as the leading contender and Narayan as the voice of the nation's conscience. One of Mrs. Gandhi's closest colleagues, Jagjivan Ram, leader of the Harijans (the former untouchables), formed his own opposition party, the Congress for Democracy.

Once again, Indira Gandhi flung herself unsparingly into the fight, but this time she met defeat, even losing in her own constituency. The Janata candidates won 270 seats, the Congress for Democracy 29, and the Congress 153 (of which 92 came from the four southern states where Mrs. Gandhi's popularity remained undimmed).

Mrs. Gandhi's fall

Immediately after the results were declared, Mrs. Gandhi resigned, and it appeared as though her political career was ended. The remnant of Congress members chose another party president. Morarji Desai became prime minister on March 24, and the new president of India, Neelam Sanjiva Reddy, was elected in July.

The new government established a commission to investigate alleged excesses during the state of emergency. Attempts to prosecute Mrs. Gandhi failed, however, and appeared only to enhance her popularity. When state elections were held in southern India on February 25, 1978, they were contested by a rump Congress Party that acknowledged Mrs. Gandhi as its leader and called itself the Congress (I), "I" standing for Indira. Her candidates did surprisingly well, gaining a majority in the states of Karnataka and Andhra Pradesh. She was once again the most talked-about politician in India, and in November she was reelected to the Lok Sabha. She was ousted the next month, however, and was imprisoned for one week.

The Janata leadership was openly divided over Mrs. Gandhi's continuing challenge. Tension within the party increased steadily, and Desai found himself more and more alienated from his ministers. In July 1979 he was forced to resign, and Chaudhary Charan Singh, who had been one of his chief opponents, succeeded him later in the month. On August 20, however, Charan Singh resigned and asked for new elections. The end of 1979 was a time of political confusion at both the union and state levels. This confusion was swept away in 1980. In the Lok Sabha elections of January, the Congress (I) Party won 351 of the 525 contested seats, and no opposition party won more than 10 percent of the seats. Following this victory, Mrs. Gandhi was again sworn in as prime minister on January 14. Her party continued to win in the midterm state elections held in May, the biennial elections for the Rajya Sabha (upper house of Parliament) in July, and

Mrs. Gandhi's return

state by-elections in November. Legal cases that had been brought against Mrs. Gandhi, Sanjay Gandhi, and associates were withdrawn. Mrs. Gandhi's triumph was marred, however, by the death of Sanjay Gandhi in an airplane crash on June 23.

Mrs. Gandhi again dominated India's national life. In 1981 her party defeated two no-confidence votes in the Lok Sabha, and a resolution introduced in 1978 to expel her from that body was revoked. Major political issues confronting her administration in the early 1980s were the agitation in Punjab for an autonomous Sikh state and the demands in Assam that immigrants from Bangladesh be deported.

PAKISTAN

India received the advantage of Nehru's leadership for almost two decades; Mohammed Ali Jinnah, however, died in September 1948, within 13 months of independence. The leaders of the new Pakistan were mainly lawyers, with a strong commitment to parliamentary government. They had supported Jinnah in his struggle against the Congress not so much because they desired an Islāmic state as because they had come to regard the Congress as synonymous with Hindu domination. They had various degrees of personal commitment to Islām. To some it represented an ethic that might (or might not) be the basis of personal behaviour within a modern, democratic state. To others it represented a tradition, the framework within which their forefathers had ruled India. But there were also groups that subscribed to Islām as a total way of life, and these people were said to wish to establish Pakistan as a theocracy (a term they repudiated). The members of the old Constituent Assembly, elected at the end of 1945, assembled at Karachi, the new capital.

Ambivalent attitudes toward Islām

Jinnah's lieutenant, Liaquat Ali Khan, inherited the task of devising an acceptable formula. Himself a moderate (he had entered politics via a landlord party), he subscribed to the parliamentary, democratic, secular state. But he was conscious that he possessed no local or regional power base. He was a "refugee"; he came from the United Provinces, the Indian heartland, whereas most of his colleagues and potential rivals drew support from their own people in Punjab or Bengal. Liaquat Ali Khan therefore deemed it necessary to gain the support of the religious spokesmen (the *mullah*s or, more properly, the *'ulamā'*). He issued a resolution on the aims and objectives of the constitution, which began, "Sovereignty over the entire universe belongs to Allāh Almighty alone" and went on to emphasize Islāmic values. This led to protests from Hindu members of the old Constituent Assembly; Islāmic states had traditionally distinguished between the Muslims, as full citizens, and *dhimmīs*, nonbelievers who were denied certain rights and saddled with certain additional obligations.

Political decline. Liaquat Ali Khan fell to an assassin's bullet in October 1951. Into his place as prime minister stepped Khwaja Nazimuddin, the leading member of the family of the Nawab of Dacca. He was a Bengali aristocrat and a man of extreme personal piety. Nazimuddin had followed Jinnah as governor general under the interim constitution (virtually the 1935 Government of India Act). He was succeeded as governor general by Ghulam Mohammad, a Punjabi, so that the twin pillars of power represented the two main regional power bases in West Pakistan and East Pakistan.

With Nazimuddin in office, militant Muslims, led by the Ahrars, a puritanical political group, called for the purification of national life. In 1953 they demanded that the Aḥmadīyah sect should be outlawed from the Islāmic community. Nazimuddin temporized, and rioting and arson enveloped Lahore and other Punjabi towns. The secretary of defense, Col. Iskander Mirza, a former political officer, pressed the Cabinet into sanctioning the promulgation of martial law in Lahore, and order was restored. Ghulam Mohammad decided that Nazimuddin must go, although he enjoyed the support of the Constituent Assembly. The dismissal was effected and a new prime minister from Bengal was found in Mohammad Ali Bogra.

Without a constitution, the legislative assemblies, both national and provincial, were replenished ad hoc. But in March 1954 a general election was held in East Bengal (East Pakistan) to choose a new provincial legislature. The contest was between the official Muslim League and a "United Front" of parties from the extreme right (orthodox religious) to extreme left (quasi-Marxist). There was a landslide defeat for the Muslim League. At the head of the victorious opposition stood two politicians who had previously kept one foot in the Muslim League and the other in the camp of the Congress and regional politics; these were the aged Fazl ul-Haq, with his Krishak Sramik (Workers and Peasants) Party, and Hussein Shaheed Suhrawardy, with a new party, the Awami League. The result was a dramatic demonstration of the gulf between West and East Pakistan.

Electoral defeat of the Muslim League (1954)

The Constituent Assembly reflected the new political mood by attempting to curb the powers of the governor general, who retaliated by proclaiming the dissolution of that body. Ghulam Mohammad's action was validated by the Supreme Court, with the rider that a new assembly must be convened. This was produced by a system of indirect election. The ministry of Mohammad Ali Bogra was completely reorganized, with three newcomers introduced as strong men from outside politics: these were Maj. Gen. Iskander Mirza, as minister of the interior, Gen. Mohammad Ayub Khan, commander in chief, as minister of national defense, and Chaudhri Mohammad Ali, a senior civil servant, as minister of finance. Mohammad Ali Bogra had little support in the new assembly, and he was replaced by Chaudhri Mohammad Ali.

Ghulam Mohammad, whose health had broken down, was replaced as governor general in August 1955 by Iskander Mirza. The latter had no regional power base and little in common with any of the politicians. Mirza insisted that his fellow administrator Chaudhri Mohammad Ali remain prime minister, and Chaudhri was able to succeed in one objective over which his three predecessors had failed: he induced the politicians to agree to a constitution (February 1956). In order to create a better balance between the West and East wings, the provinces and parts of West Pakistan were amalgamated into one administrative unit.

The constitution of 1956 embodied the Islāmic provisions of the "aims and objectives" resolution of 1949 and declared Pakistan to be an Islāmic republic. The national parliament was to comprise one house of 300 members, equally representing East and West. Ten seats were reserved for women. In constitutional theory the prime minister and Cabinet were to govern according to the will of the parliament, with the president exercising only reserve powers.

The constitution of 1956

Khan Sahib, a former premier of North-West Frontier Province, was invited by the Muslim League to become the chief minister of the new "one unit" of West Pakistan. Soon after taking office, Khan Sahib was faced with a revolt against his leadership in the Muslim League, but he adroitly turned the tables by forming a new group, the Republican Party, out of dissident Muslim League assemblymen. In the National Assembly also, members adopted the Republican ticket, and Prime Minister Chaudhri Mohammad Ali found himself without a majority. He resigned in September 1956.

Iskander Mirza, then president, was compelled to accept an Awami League government headed by Suhrawardy but dependent on Republican support to retain office. For a time the combination worked, but the flimsy consensus of Pakistan politics soon began to dissolve into factionalism, regionalism, and sectarianism. Khan Sahib found his hold over the West Pakistan legislature slipping, and he asked the President to suspend the constitution. The East Pakistan legislature voted unanimously for autonomy in all matters except foreign affairs, defense, and currency. The country was to hold its first complete general election in 1958, but a dispute over the basis of the constituencies led to Suhrawardy's resignation. His successors proved ineffective and the legislative process came to a halt.

Military government. President Mirza had made no secret of his dissatisfaction with the working of parliamentary democracy in Pakistan. He therefore came to a decision to put an end to politics. On October 7, 1958, a presidential proclamation announced that the political parties were abolished, the constitution abrogated, and the country placed under martial law, with Gen. Mohammad Ayub Khan as chief martial law administrator. Mirza announced that the martial law period would be brief and that a new constitution would be drafted. On October 27 he swore in his new Cabinet.

General Ayub became prime minister, and three lieutenant generals were named to the Cabinet. The eight civilian members included businessmen and lawyers, one being a young newcomer, Zulfikar Ali Bhutto. That same evening the new military ministers called on the President, with contingents of armed soldiers, and informed him that he was to resign. After a short interval, Mirza was exiled to London. A proclamation issued by Ayub announced his assumption of the presidency.

Presidency of Mohammad Ayub Khan

Martial law lasted 44 months. During that time a number of army officers took over vital civil-service posts. A number of politicians were excluded from public life under the Electoral Bodies (Disqualification) Order, or EBDO. A similar purge took place among civil servants.

Ayub had long pondered the problem of creating political institutions that would express Islāmic ideals and foster national development. He came forward with a plan for "basic democracies," directly elected by the people, as local units of development. Elections for the basic democracies took place in January 1960. The Basic Democrats, as they became known, were at once asked to endorse Ayub's presidency and to give him a mandate to frame a constitution. Of the 80,000 Basic Democrats, 75,283 gave him affirmative votes (February 1960). A constitutional commission was asked to advise on a suitable form of government. Ayub accepted some of its proposals and substituted some of his own, aiming, he said, for "a blending of democracy with discipline." In the early days of Ayub's regime there were notable reform measures, such as the Muslim Family Laws Ordinance of 1961, restricting polygamy, but later the President found it necessary to make concessions to Muslims in order to bolster his regime.

One feature of the Ayub regime was the quickening pace of economic growth. During the initial phase of independence, the growth rate was less than 3 percent per annum and scarcely moved ahead of the rate of population growth. During the mid-1950s even this rate declined, but from 1960 to 1965 the rate advanced to more than 6 percent per annum. Development was particularly vigorous in the manufacturing sector.

Disparities between the East and West wings

There was considerable imbalance between East and West; during the 1950s East Pakistan was becoming poorer in per capita terms every year, whereas the West was achieving positive growth. A continuing grievance was the contribution made by East Pakistan to foreign exchange by the export of jute and tea, from which it was felt the West reaped more advantage; the West was also the major beneficiary of foreign aid.

The outstanding example of favoured treatment for the West was the great Indus Basin scheme for hydroelectric development. Pakistan skillfully negotiated for assistance from the World Bank, the United States, and other friends. In addition to economic aid, Pakistan also received immense military aid from the United States.

The war over Kashmir in 1965 (see above *India*) had more far-reaching effects on Pakistan than on India. Ayub received a new mandate from the Basic Democrats in January 1965, when he won decisively against a spirited challenge from Fatima Jinnah, the sister of Mohammed Ali Jinnah. In the early days of his presidency Ayub had moved freely among the rural people, talking to them face to face. After the war he withdrew behind a curtain of dictatorship, becoming a remote figure in a bulletproof limousine. Bhutto, the chief exponent of struggle against India, was relieved of office in 1966. Mujibur Rahman (Sheikh Mujib), who had inherited the leadership of the Awami League, the major force in East Pakistan, was arrested and accused of conspiring with India.

Ayub's autocratic position was suddenly challenged in the autumn of 1968; an unsuccessful attempt on his life was followed by the arrest of Bhutto and other opposition leaders. Ayub attempted to stem the mounting protest by summoning a conference of opposition leaders and by withdrawing the state of emergency under which Pakistan had been governed since 1965. These concessions failed to conciliate the opposition, and in February 1969 Ayub announced that he would not contest the presidential election due in 1970. Protests and strikes flared everywhere, being especially militant in Bengal. At length, on March 25, 1969, Ayub resigned, handing over responsibility for governing to the commander in chief, Gen. Agha Mohammad Yahya Khan. Once again the country was placed under martial law. Yahya assumed the title of president as well as chief martial law administrator. He made it clear that his aim was an early general election, which took place in December 1970.

Decline of Ayub

Civil war. The success of the Awami League in East Pakistan surprised even its friends. Sheikh Mujib emerged with a majority at his command among the membership of the new assembly (167 of the 300 total). But what upset all predictions was the victory in West Pakistan of Bhutto's Pakistan People's Party (PPP), which won particularly heavily in Punjab and gained a clear majority (83) of the representation from the West. Yahya's plan provided that when the new assembly met it must produce a constitution within 100 days. Mujib, however, stood out for complete independence for East Pakistan, except for foreign policy, though the East wanted to make its own aid, trade, and defense agreements. Bhutto rejected these terms and refused to bring his party to Dacca to participate in the assembly. On March 1, 1971, President Yahya announced that the National Assembly would be suspended indefinitely. Sheikh Mujib replied by ordering a boycott and general strike throughout East Pakistan. Bowing to the inevitable, Yahya proceeded to Dacca in mid-March to negotiate a compromise that would concede the substance of Mujib's demands while retaining tenuous ties that might still preserve the name of Pakistan. But compromise proved impossible. President Yahya denounced Mujib and his men as traitors and launched a drive to "reoccupy" the East with West Pakistan troops.

Warfare between government troops and supporters of the Awami League broke out in the East in March. Sheikh Mujib and many of his colleagues were arrested, while others escaped to India, proclaiming East Pakistan an independent state under the name Bangladesh (Bengal Land). As fighting continued, the number of refugees crossing the border into India grew into the millions. In December 1971 India successfully invaded East Pakistan. The establishment of a Bangladesh government with Mujib as prime minister followed in January 1972.

Bhutto's regime. Accepting responsibility for the defeat and breakup of Pakistan, President Yahya resigned on December 20, 1971, and Bhutto became the undisputed leader of former West Pakistan. He secured another election victory for the PPP, opposition being largely confined to the North-West Frontier Province and Baluchistan, where the National Awami Party (NAP) demonstrated support for its autonomy program. Bhutto's declared policy of Islāmic Socialism brought few tangible changes, but his populism was undeniably successful. He became increasingly autocratic, however, suppressing criticism, jailing opponents, and employing militant methods against the restive Pashtuns and Baluchs. A new constitution was adopted on April 10, 1973, and Bhutto became prime minister of Pakistan.

On January 4, 1977, Bhutto announced that elections would be held within two months, unfolding a national charter of peasant reform. Nine opposition parties hastily patched together the Pakistan National Alliance (PNA) and launched a demand for the Islāmic way of life in Pakistan. The campaign was marked by violence, with opposition candidates complaining of brutal discrimination. The results were a sweeping victory for Bhutto's PPP, which obtained 155 of the 200 seats in the legislature.

The results were denounced as fraudulent by the PNA. Mounting protest soon brought chaos to Karachi and other major cities, where Bhutto was compelled to call out the army and proclaim martial law. He tried to buy peace by offering concessions to the PNA leaders (most of whom were under arrest), but they would accept nothing short of a new election. Religious leaders (*maulvis*) declared that Bhutto was an unlawful ruler whom it was no crime to kill.

Zia ul-Haq's regime. To avoid total chaos, the chief of staff of the army, Gen. Mohammad Zia ul-Haq, took over as chief administrator of martial law on July 5, 1977. His early efforts to create an acceptable political alternative had only limited success. He announced that elections would be held in 90 days, but it was clear that Bhutto was the only politician of mass appeal. In September Bhutto was arrested and charged with attempted murder, and he was sentenced to death on March 18. Zia was proclaimed president of Pakistan on September 16.

By this time the PNA was split, with most elements forming an opposition that demanded early elections, withdrawal of the army from Baluchistan, and the introduction of a full Islāmic code of laws. A zealous Muslim, Zia had already imposed Islāmic criminal punishments, such as flogging and maiming, which were formally enacted as law in February 1979. Bhutto was hanged on April 4, 1979, following a Supreme Court review of his case. In October elections were postponed indefinitely, political parties and strikes were banned, and the press was submitted to strict censorship.

The invasion of Afghanistan by the Soviet Union in December 1979 became central to Pakistan's internal and foreign affairs. Claiming that a Soviet attack on his country was possible, Zia embarked upon a military buildup supported by the United States and by other Islāmic countries and feared by India. The influx of millions of refugees from Afghanistan led Zia also to acquire foreign economic aid. On March 24, 1981, Zia announced a provisional constitutional order that allowed the government to be kept under martial law indefinitely and that gave the president power to amend the constitution. A 350-member Federal Advisory Council—whose members were nominated and had no decision-making powers—was established in December and held its first meeting on January 11, 1982. There were periodic outbursts of religious and political violence throughout the year. Against that background, Zia praised the armed forces and sought a role for them in the making of national and international policy.

BANGLADESH

The 1970s. The new nation was faced with great internal problems. Economic assistance was provided by the United Nations, the Soviet Union, and others, but progress was impeded by administrative incompetence. At first Sheikh Mujib functioned as a constitutional leader, answerable to a parliament, but in the face of insoluble difficulties his authority as president after 1974 became almost absolute. Discontent mounted, especially in the army. Stories of waste and corruption increasingly involved Mujib and his wife and relatives. On August 15, 1975, all of them were assassinated. There followed a power struggle in which military officers pushed the politicians aside.

Regime of Zia ur-Rahman

A second coup in November 1975 led to the emergence of Maj. Gen. Zia ur-Rahman as the "strong man" of Bangladesh. Zia reversed the policies of Mujib; relations with India became distant, and leaders associated with the former Pakistani administration were brought back. In May 1977 Zia staged a national referendum that produced a vote 99 percent in his favour, but discontent continued among radical army officers and politicians. On October 2 an unsuccessful attempt was made to seize the Dacca airport, where government leaders were negotiating the release of a hijacked Japanese airliner. The coup was quickly suppressed.

Zia held a presidential election on June 3, 1978. To provide support, he encouraged the formation of a new political organization, the Bangladesh Jatiyabadi Dal (BJD; Bangladesh Nationalist Party), including right-wing elements such as the old Muslim League. The opposition created a similar coalition, Ganotantrik Okkyo Jote (Democratic United Front), bringing together survivors of Sheikh Mujib's Awami League, and attempted to mobilize Mujib's former mass following. Zia won, however, and his party swept the parliamentary elections held on February 18, 1979. In April Zia lifted martial law, which he had declared in 1975. He then began a program of agricultural and rural development to be financed by foreign aid. Drought and famine in 1978–79 and severe flooding in 1980 led to strikes and agitation, and Buddhists in the Chittagong Hill Tracts violently resisted the resettlement of Muslims in that region.

Zia promoted improved relations with China and the United States and with other Muslim countries. Dealings with the Soviet Union were strained, while Bangladesh and India continued to disagree over a maritime boundary and the use of the waters of the Ganges.

The 1980s. Zia was assassinated by army officers in Chittagong on May 30, 1981. He was succeeded by his vice president, Abdus Sattar, who was elected to the presidency on November 15. Sattar refused to give the armed forces a formal role in the government. He was ousted from power on March 24, 1982, by Lieut. Gen. Hossain Mohammad Ershad, who proclaimed martial law, appointed himself chief martial law administrator, and gave himself the powers to make laws and appoint civilian judges. Ershad attempted to improve the country's grave economic problems by denationalizing almost all industry, promoting foreign investment, controlling imports, and enacting other measures.

Regime of Hossain Mohammad Ershad

(H.R.T./Ed.)

BIBLIOGRAPHY

The emergence of civilization in North India: The following are general surveys of the prehistory of the subcontinent of India: BRIDGET and RAYMOND ALLCHIN, *The Birth of Indian Civilization* (1968), with extensive bibliography and list of radiocarbon dates; DOUGLAS H. GORDON, *The Prehistoric Background of Indian Culture*, 2nd ed. (1960); D.D. KOSAMBI, *The Culture and Civilisation of Ancient India in Historical Outline* (1965), a somewhat idiosyncratic, synthetic account that sets out to integrate divergent types of evidence; BENDAPUDI SUBBARAO, *The Personality of India*, 2nd ed. (1958); SIR MORTIMER WHEELER, *Early India and Pakistan, to Ashoka*, rev. ed. (1968), a short and lucid survey by a former director general of archaeology in India. General accounts of the Indus Civilization are SIR MORTIMER WHEELER, *The Indus Civilization*, 3rd ed. (1968), an up-to-date and comprehensive account; STUART PIGGOTT, *Prehistoric India to 1000 B.C.* (1950), still indispensable in spite of much recent work; WALTER A. FAIRSERVIS, "The Origin, Character, and Decline of an Early Civilization" (1967), a short pamphlet that includes much profound and original thought, and *The Roots of Ancient India* (1971); and JEAN-MARIE CASAL, *La civilisation de l'Indus et ses énigmes* (1969).

The development of Indian civilization from c. 1500 BC to c. AD 1200–1300: On historiography, a much-neglected area of Indian history, the standard work is CYRIL H. PHILIPS (ed.), *Historians of India, Pakistan and Ceylon* (1961). FREDERICK E. PARGITER, *Ancient Indian Historical Tradition* (1922, reprinted 1962); V.S. PATHAK, *Ancient Historians of India* (1966); and ROMILA THAPAR, "Interpretations of Ancient Indian History," in *History and Theory*, 7:318–335 (1968), all deal with the various aspects of the historiography of ancient India. Among survey histories of the period may be mentioned ARTHUR L. BASHAM, *The Wonder That Was India*, 3rd ed. (1967); D.D. KOSAMBI (*op. cit.*); and ROMILA THAPAR, *A History of India*, vol. 1 (1966). For political history, H.C. RAYCHAUDHURI, *The Political History of Ancient India*, 6th ed. rev. (1953), remains a standard work. More recent writing is included in the series *The History and Culture of the Indian People*, 11 vol. (1951–77). On economic history, U.N. GHOSHAL, *The Agrarian System in Ancient India* (1930), raises the relevant issues; as does ALINDRANATH BOSE, *Social and Rural Economy of Northern India, c. 600 B.C.–200 A.D.*, 2nd ed. rev., 2 vol. (1961–67). An introduction to political ideas and institutions is R.S. SHARMA, *Aspects of Political Ideas and Institutions in Ancient India*, 2nd rev. ed. (1968). (*1500–c. 600 BC*): N.R. BANERJEE, *The Iron Age in India* (1965), discusses iron technology in India. S.C. MALIK, *Indian Civilization: The Formative Period* (1968), raises the question of relating archaeological evidence to formulations on early Indian society. V. GORDON CHILDE, *The Aryans* (1926, reprinted 1970), remains a standard work on the origin and dispersal of the Aryans. Early views on this period are in VINCENT A. SMITH, *The Early History of India*, 4th ed. rev. (1924, reprinted 1957), but this is now considered somewhat out of date. Kingship is discussed in N.N. LAW, *Aspects of Ancient Indian Polity* (1921). A more detailed discussion on political theories is found in U.N. GHOSHAL, *History of Hindu Political Theories*, 2nd ed. (1927). (*c. 600–150 BC*): Standard works on the Buddhist evidence are T.W. RHYS DAVIDS, *Buddhist India* (1903); B.C. LAW, *Some Kṣatriya Tribes of Ancient India* (1924) and *Geography of Early Buddhism* (1932); more recent studies include DEV RAJ CHANANA, *Slavery in Ancient India, as Depicted in Pali and Sanskrit Texts* (1960); and NARENDRA WAGLE, *Society at the Time of the Buddha* (1966). The interrelation between society and political ideas is discussed by CHARLES DREKMEIER in *Kingship and Community in Early India* (1962). On the Mauryan period, general works include K.A. NILAKANTA SASTRI (ed.), *The Age of Nandas and Mauryas* (1952); VINCENT A. SMITH, *Aśoka, the Buddhist Emperor of India*, 3rd ed. rev. (1920); and ROMILA THAPAR, *Aśoka and the Decline of the Mauryas* (1961). (*c. 150 BC–AD 300*): A.K. NARAIN, *The Indo-Greeks* (1957); J.E. VAN LOHUIZEN DE LEEUW, *The Scythian Period . . .* (1949); and ROMAN GIRSHMAN, *Bégram: Recherches archéologiques et historiques sur les Kouchans* (1946), concern the political history of this period in northern India. The most recent monograph on the date of Kaniṣka is ARTHUR L. BASHAM (ed.), *Papers on the Date of Kaniska* (1968). GULAM YAZDANI (ed.), *The Early History of the Deccan*, 2 vol. (1960); P.T.S. AIYANGAR, *History of the Tamils, from the Earliest Times to 600 A.D.* (1929); N. SUBRAHMANIAN, *Sangam Polity* (1967); and K.A. NILAKANTA SASTRI (ed.), *A History of South India from Prehistoric Times to the Fall of Vijayanagar*, 3rd ed. (1966), deal with the southern parts of the subcontinent. (*AD 300–750*): Political histories include R.C. MAJUMDAR and A.S. ALTEKAR (eds.), *The Vākāṭaka-Gupta Age, Circa 200–500 A.D.* (1967); R.N. DANDEKAR, *A History of the Guptas* (1941); R.K. MOOKERJI, *The Gupta Empire*, 4th ed. (1969); EDWARD A. PIRES, *The Maukharis* (1934); B.P. SINHA, *The Decline of the Kingdom of Magadha (c. 455–1000 A.D.)* (1954); R.S. TRIPATHI, *History of Kanauj to the Moslem Conquest* (1937); D. DEVAHUTI, *Harsha* (1970); and D.C. SIRCAR, *The Successors of the Sātavāhanas in Lower Deccan* (1939). On administration and revenue, see D.N. JHA, *Revenue System in Post-Maurya and Gupta Times* (1967); V.R.R. DIKSHITAR, *The Gupta Polity* (1952); and U.N. GHOSHAL, *Contributions to the History of the Hindu Revenue System* (1929). Social and economic history is the main theme of R.N. SALETORE, *Life in the Gupta Age* (1943); S.K. MAITY, *Economic Life of Northern India in the Gupta Period, c. A.D. 300–550*, rev. 2nd ed. (1970); D.R. DAS, *Economic History of the Deccan, from the First to the Sixth Century A.D.* (1969). (*AD 750–1200*): There are a number of studies of political history relating to this period, some on regions and others on individual dynasties. Among them are A.S. ALTEKAR, *The Rāshṭrakūṭas and Their Times* (1934); A.C. BANERJEE, *Rajput Studies* (1944); H.C. RAY, *The Dynastic History of Northern India (Early Mediaeval Period)* (1931); R.C. MAJUMDAR, *The History of Bengal*, 2 vol. (1943–48); S.K. MITRA, *The Early Rulers of Khajuráho* (1958); N.S. BOSE, *History of the Chandellas of Jejakabhukti* (1956); DASHARATHA SHARMA, *Early Chauhán Dynasties* (1959); PRATIPAL BHATIA, *The Paramaras, c. 800–1305 A.D.* (1970); K.A. NILAKANTA SASTRI, *The Cōlas*, 2nd ed. rev. (1955); and J. DUNCAN DERRETT, *The Hoysalas, a Mediaeval Indian Royal Family* (1957). Related to political institutions is T.V. MAHALINGAM, *South Indian Polity*, 2nd rev. ed. (1967). Two major sources have been translated and make interesting reading: M.A. STEIN (trans.), *Kalhana's Chronicle of the Kings of Kashmir* (1892); and EDWARD C. SACHAU, *Alberuni's India*, 2 vol. (1888; reprinted in 1 vol., 1964). Trade and commerce in the context of Arab trade is discussed by GEORGE F. HOURANI in *Arab Seafaring in the Indian Ocean in Ancient and Early Medieval Times* (1951); the economic background in LALLANJI GOPAL, *The Economic Life of Northern India, c. A.D. 700–1200* (1965); and the exposition of feudalism in India in R.S. SHARMA, *Indian Feudalism, c. 300–1200* (1965).

The early Islāmic period and the Mughal Empire: The most detailed treatment is R.C. MAJUMDAR (ed.), *The History and Culture of the Indian People*, vol. 5–6 (1957–60). Although the articles in this work offer scholarly treatments, they usually tend to present an Indian (as opposed to a Pakistani), and sometimes a Hindu nationalist point of view, and thus tend to emphasize the accomplishments of Hindu culture and of Hindu states, while they sometimes minimize those of the Muslims. For a very short treatment of the period that is slanted in the opposite direction, see I.H. QURESHI, *The Muslim Community of the Indo-Pakistan Sub-Continent, 610–1947* (1962). *The Cambridge History of India*, vol. 3 (1928); and *The Oxford History of India*, 3rd ed. (1958), offer accounts that were written during the period of British rule and that reflect to some extent the British imperial point of view, although they are generally factually accurate. For a relatively short and good factual account written in India since independence, see R.C. MAJUMDAR, H.C. RAYCHAUDHURI, and K.K. DATTA, *An Advanced History of India*, 3rd ed. (1967). Another history of the Muslims in India is S.M. IKRAM, *History of Muslim Civilisation in India and Pakistan* (1961). Good scholarly treatments of many aspects of the period that have to do with Muslims can be found in the *Encyclopaedia of Islam*, new ed. (1960–). A short but stimulating treatment from a Marxist point of view is contained in D.D. KOSAMBI, *An Introduction to the Study of Indian History* (1956). For a sample of the Persian chronicles that are the basic source for most of the history of the period, the reader may consult the translations in the appropriate volumes of HENRY M. ELLIOT and JOHN DOWSON, *The History of India, as Told by Its Own Historians*, 8 vol. (1867–77, reprinted 1966). (*The Delhi Sultanate*): Monographs of varying quality exist for each subperiod. The best is A.B.M. HABIBULLAH, *The Foundation of Muslim Rule in India*, 2nd rev. ed. (1961), which covers the pre-Khaljī period. K.S. LAL, *History of the Khaljis, A.D. 1290–1320*, rev. ed. (1967), provides an adequate political history and an interesting account of Alluddin Khaljī's economic reforms. AGHA MAHDI HUSAIN, *The Tughluq Dynasty* (1963); and K.S. LAL, *Twilight of the Sultanate* (1963), are less interesting although they provide detailed political narratives. PETER HARDY, *Historians of Medieval India* (1960), is a good historiographical treatment; WILLIAM H. MORELAND, *The Agrarian System of Moslem India* (1929), is still the best single account of the economic history. Political and administrative institutions are covered by R.P. TRIPATHI, *Some Aspects of Muslim Administration* (1936); S.P. NIGAM, *Nobility Under the Sultans of Delhi, A.D. 1206–1398* (1967); I.H. QURESHI, *The Administration of the Sultanate of Delhi* (1942); and K.A. NIZAMI, *Some Aspects of Religion and Politics During the Thirteenth Century in India* (1961). Nizami is also useful for social and religious history, and in many ways is one of the most interesting books on the Sultanate. Finally, a most interesting and almost unique attempt to provide a social history of the common people is K.M. ASHRAF, *Life and Conditions of the People of Hindustan*, 2nd ed. (1970). (*The Bahmanīs and successor states*): Practically the only monographic work done on the Bahmanīs has been by H.K. SHERWANI. His writings provide a basic political history, and give a different view of the Bahmanī–Vijayanagar wars than the view presented in *History and Culture of the Indian People*. Otherwise, consult Sastri's *History of South India* or *The Cambridge History of India*. (*Vijayanagar*): Sastri's account again is useful, as are three monographs by T.V. MAHALINGAM: *Administration and Social Life Under Vijayanagar* (1940); *Economic Life in the Vijayanagar Empire* (1951); and *South Indian Polity*, 2nd rev. ed. (1967), although the last work provides a generalized account of a much longer period, and is difficult to disentangle. A very interesting edition of the accounts of two European travellers who visited Vijayanagar is contained in ROBERT SEWELL, *A Forgotten Empire—Vijayanagar* (1900, reprinted 1924). (*The Mughal period*): In addition to the relevant sections of the Cambridge and Oxford histories mentioned above, the following works deal with various aspects of Mughal history: STEPHEN M. EDWARDES and H.L.D. GARRETT, *Mughal Rule in India* (1930, reprinted 1962); IRFAN HABIB, *The Agrarian System of Mughal India, 1556–1707* (1963); IBN HASAN, *The Central Structure of the Mughal Empire and Its Practical Working up to the Year 1657* (1936, reprinted 1970); ISHWARI PRASAD, *The Life and Times of Humāyūn* (1955); J. SARKAR, *History of Aurangzib*, 5 vol. (1912–24; 2nd ed. rev., 1925); *The Fall of the Mughal Empire*, 4 vol. (1932–50); and *Mughal Administration*, 4th ed. rev. (1952).

The Marāthās: The first major work on Marāthā history was JAMES C. DUFF, *History of the Mahrattas*, 3 vol. (1826). J.N. SARKAR made substantial contributions both to the translation and editing of a large number of Persian documents in English and producing first-rate original writings on the subject. Among them are: *Delhi During the Anarchy, 1749–1788, as Told in Contemporary Records* (1921); *Historical Records Relating to Northern India, 1700–1817* (1925); *Delhi Affairs, 1761–1788*, in *Persian Records of Maratha History*, ed. by P.M. JOSHI (1953); *Sindhia as Regent of Delhi, 1789–1791*, in *Persian Records of Maratha History* (1954); *House of Shivaji: Studies and Documents on Maratha History*, 3rd ed. (1955); and *Daulat Rao Sindhia and North Indian Affairs, 1810–1818* (1951). P.M. JOSHI, a Marāthā historian, besides editing some of the works translated by J.N. Sarkar, also published translations in English of several Marāthā documents, including *Expansion of Maratha Power, 1707–1761: Selections from the Peshwa Daftar* (1956), and *Revival of Maratha Power, 1761–1772: Selections from the Peshwa Daftar* (1962). JAMES H. GENSE and D.R. BANAJI (eds.), *The Gaikwads of Baroda: English Documents*, 10 vol. (1937–45), give a great deal of information on the history of the Gaikwad dynasty. RUSTOM D. CHOKSEY (ed.), *The Last Phase: Selections from the Deccan Commissioner's Files—Peshwa Daftar, 1815–1818* (1948), throws valuable light on the last few years of the Marāthā rule in India. The first scientific study of the forces—social, economic, and cultural, as well as political—that led to the building up of Marāthā power was M.G. RANADE, *Rise of the Maratha Power, and Other Essays* (1900, reprinted 1961); which was followed by a critical analysis by G.S. SARDESAI in his *Main Currents of Maratha History* (1926). Other studies include V.G. DIGHE, *Peshwa Bajirao I and Maratha Expansion* (1944); P.C. GUPTA, *Bajirao II and the East India Company, 1796–1818*, rev. ed. (1964); V.V. JOSHI, *Clash of Three Empires* (1941); G.S. SARDESAI, *New History of the Marathas*, 3 vol. (1946–48); J.N. SARKAR, *Shivaji and His Times*, 6th ed. (1961); S.N. SEN, *Administrative System of the Marathas*, rev. ed. (1925), and *Military System of the Marathas* (1958); H.N. SINHA, *Rise of the Peshwas*, vol. 1 (1931); and S.P. VARMA, *A Study in Maratha Diplomacy: Anglo-Maratha Relations, 1772–1783* (1956).

India and European expansion, c. 1500–1858: (*Europeans in India, 1498–1760*): WILLIAM W. HUNTER, *A History of British India*, 2 vol. (1899–1900); CHARLES R. BOXER, *The Portuguese Seaborne Empire, 1415–1825* (1969), an authoritative modern study, and *The Dutch Seaborne Empire, 1600–1800* (1965); H.H. DODWELL, *Dupleix and Clive* (1920, reprinted 1967), a detailed and acute study of the Anglo-French struggle in South India and the British acquisition of Bengal. (*The growth of British India, 1757–1818*): ABDUL MAJEED KHAN, *The Transition in Bengal, 1756–1775* (1969), a detailed study of the transfer of administration from Indian to British hands in Bengal; KEITH FEILING, *Warren Hastings* (1954), a thorough and shrewd study of this enigmatic man; LUCY S. SUTHERLAND, *The East India Company in Eighteenth-Century Politics* (1952), a masterly survey of Indian politics at the British base in the Namier style; SIR C.P. ILBERT, *The Government of India*, 3rd ed. (1915), a constitutional lawyer's classic exposition of the development of the forms of the Government of India; ARTHUR ASPINALL, *Cornwallis in Bengal* (1931), a lucid description of the Cornwallis administrative revolution in Bengal; PAUL E. ROBERTS, *India Under Wellesley* (1929), not wholly satisfactory but the best available study of this empire builder; EDWARD J. THOMPSON, *The Making of the Indian Princes* (1943), a lively account of the eclipse of the independent Indian powers by an imaginative writer turned historian. (*Organization and policy, 1818–57*): T.H. BEAGLEHOLE, *Thomas Munro and the Development of Administrative Policy in Madras, 1792–1818* (1966), a succinct study of the formulation of British policy in southern India by a young scholar; KENNETH A. BALLHATCHET, *Social Policy and Social Change in Western India, 1817–1830* (1957), an authoritative study of Mountstuart Elphinstone's work of reconciling the Marāthās; PERCIVAL SPEAR, *The Twilight of the Mughals* (1951), dealing with Charles Metcalfe's policy in the Delhi Territory and British relations with the Mughals; ERIC STOKES, *The English Utilitarians and India* (1959), an important work on the influence of British ideas in India that enlarges historical perspective; SOPHIA D. COLLET, *The Life and Letters of Raja Rammohun Roy*, 3rd ed. by D.K. BISWAS and P.C. GANGULI (1962), the standard biography of the Indian reformer updated by two scholarly disciples; KHUSHWANT SINGH, *A History of the Sikhs*, 2 vol. (1964–66), the best modern work on the Sikhs as a whole, by a Sikh; WILLIAM LEE-WARNER, *The Life of the Marquis of Dalhousie*, 2 vol. (1904), still the standard work on this key figure. (*The Indian Mutiny*): S.N. SEN, *Eighteen-Fifty-Seven* (1957), the best modern work on the Indian Mutiny by the most distinguished of recent Indian historians; MICHAEL MACLAGAN, *"Clemency" Canning* (1962), which uses Canning's papers to describe his part in the Mutiny crisis.

British India, 1858–1920: The most comprehensive surveys of this period are in *The Cambridge History of India*, vol. 6; *The Oxford History of India;* SPEAR (1958); and *The History and Culture of the Indian People*, vol. 9, *British Paramountcy and Indian Renaissance*, 2 pt. (1963–65), and vol. 11, *Struggle for Freedom* (1969). The first two works relate the history of this period primarily from the British point of view, the last tells the same story from the vantage point of Indian nationalism. For primary sources of this period, see CYRIL H. PHILIPS (ed.), *The Evolution of India and Pakistan, 1858 to 1947* (1962). For the decade immediately after the War of 1857–58, see THOMAS R. METCALF, *The Aftermath of Revolt: India, 1857–1870* (1964). A useful survey of most of this period is SARVEPALLI GOPAL, *British Policy in India, 1858–1905* (1965); and the best economic study is D.R. GADGIL, *The Industrial Evolution of India in Recent Times*, 4th ed. (1942). An excellent monograph on the Indigo revolt is BLAIR KLING, *The Blue Mutiny* (1966). For social history and Imperial "racial" problems, the best work is still E.M. FORSTER, *A Passage to India* (1924). More recent monographic studies are FRANCIS ROBINSON, *Separation Among Indian Muslims* (1975), a history of Muslim politics in the United Provinces from 1860 to 1923; CHRISTINE BOLT, *Victorian Attitudes to Race* (1971); and FRANCIS G. HUTCHINS, *The Illusion of Permanence* (1967). For the genesis of the Indian National Congress and its first meeting, see BRITON MARTIN, *New India, 1885* (1969). The official history of the Congress is B. PATTABHI SITARAMAYYA, *The History of the Indian National Congress*, 2 vol. (1946–47). A good early account of Indian nationalism by one of its leaders is SURENDRANATH BANERJEA, *A Nation in Making* (1925, reprinted 1963). For a study of early Congress factionalism, see STANLEY WOLPERT, *Tilak and Gokhale: Revolution and Reform in the Making of Modern India* (1962). A new study of Lord Curzon's viceroyalty is DAVID DILKS, *Curzon in India*, 2 vol. (1969–70). For Morley and Minto, see JOHN MORLEY, *Recollections*, 2 vol. (1917); MARY MINTO, *India, Minto and Morley, 1905–1910* (1934); and STANLEY WOLPERT, *Morley and India, 1906–1910* (1967). For early Muslim nationalism, see KHALID B. SAYEED, *Pakistan: The Formative Phase, 1857–1948*, 2nd ed. (1968); HAFEEZ MALIK, *Moslem Nationalism in India and Pakistan* (1963); and WILFRED C. SMITH, *Modern Islām in India*, rev. ed. (1946). An excellent new anthology on the "grandfather" of Pakistan is *Iqbal, Poet-Philosopher of Pakistan*, ed. by HAFEEZ MALIK (1971). The best biography of Pakistan's "Quaid-i-Azam" is still HECTOR BOLITHO, *Jinnah: Creator of Pakistan* (1954). For Gandhi, the best introduction remains his autobiography, *The Story of My Experiments with Truth*, 2 vol. (1927–29). A provocative psycho-historical study is ERIK ERIKSON, *Gandhi's Truth: On the Origins of Militant Nonviolence* (1969). For Motilal and Jawaharlal Nehru, see B.R. NANDA, *The Nehrus, Motilal and Jawaharlal* (1962). Nehru also wrote a brilliant autobiography, *Toward Freedom: The Autobiography of Jawaharlal Nehru* (1941). LORD HARDINGE wrote a brief memoir of his viceroyalty, *My Indian Years, 1910–1916* (1948). Montagu has left a vivid account of his visit to India as secretary of state: EDWIN S. MONTAGU, *An Indian Diary* (1930). The Government of India published a short official account on *India's Contribution to the Great War* (1923). The Montagu–Chelmsford *Report on Indian Constitutional Reforms* (1918) is also worth reading. For the postwar massacre at Jallianwala Bāgh in Amritsar, see STANLEY WOLPERT, *An Error of Judgment* (1970).

Emerging nationalism, partition, and independence: PERCIVAL SPEAR, *India, Pakistan, and the West*, 4th ed. (1967); HUGH TINKER, *India and Pakistan: A Political Analysis*, rev. ed. (1967). (*Pre-Independence, 1920–47*): LEWIS S.S. O'MALLEY (ed.), *Modern India and the West* (1941, reprinted 1968); VAPAL P. MENON, *The Transfer of Power in India* (1957), a detailed study of events leading to partition, drawing extensively upon confidential papers; CHAUDHRI MUHAMMAD ALI, *The Emergence of Pakistan* (1967, reissued 1973), a senior Muslim administrator's account; HUGH TINKER, *Experiment with Freedom: India and Pakistan, 1947* (1967); HENRY V. HODSON, *The Great Divide: Britain, India, Pakistan* (1969), the definitive account of events from 1930 onward, especially with reference to Mountbatten's viceroyalty. (*Post-Independence in India*): WYNDRAETH H. MORRIS-JONES, *Parliament in India* (1957, reprinted 1975), a scholarly analysis of the political power structure in Nehru's heyday; SELIG S. HARRISON, *India: The Most Dangerous Decades* (1960), a prophetic work outlining the pattern of politics beyond the Nehru system; GENE D. OVERSTREET and MARSHALL WINDMILLER, *Communism in India* (1959), an account of the rise of Communism to the threshold of power; DONALD EUGENE SMITH, *India As a Secular State* (1963), an extremely valuable study of the interaction of religious and political pressures; MYRON WEINER (ed.), *State Politics in India* (1968), a survey of regionalism in eight states in the 1960s; RAJNI KOTHARI, *Politics in India* (1970), a sophisticated political science textbook; DILIP HIRO, *Inside India Today*, 2nd ed. (1978), a journalist's investigation into Mrs. Gandhi's emergency; DOM F. MORAES, *Indira Gandhi* (U.K. title, *Mrs. Gandhi*, both 1980), a sympathetic political biography; MAYANTARA SAHGAL, *Indira Gandhi: Her Road to Power* (1982), a less complimentary biography and an analysis of contemporary Indian politics; VED MEHTA, *A Family Affair: India Under Three Prime Ministers* (1982), an account of Indian politics from 1975 to the early 1980s. (*Post-Independence in Pakistan*): KHALID BIN SAYEED, *Pakistan: The Formative Phase, 1857–1948*, 2nd ed. (1968), and *The Political System of Pakistan* (1967), an excellent textbook that compresses much detail into a short space; LEONARD BINDER, *Religion and Politics in Pakistan* (1961); IAN M. STEPENS, *Pakistan*, 3rd ed. (1967), combining shrewdness and romantic feeling; MOHAMMAD AYUB KHAN, *Friends Not Masters* (1967), the political testament of the man who ruled Pakistan for 11 years; GOLAM W. CHOUDHURY, *The Last Days of United Pakistan* (1974), in which a participant narrates the sequence of events leading to the breakup of Pakistan and emergence of Bangladesh.

(F.R.Al./R.Th./P.B.Ca./A.L.S./
S.P.V./T.G.P.S./S.A.Wo./H.R.T.)

Indo-European Languages

Indo-European is the name of a family of languages that by 1000 BC were spoken over most of Europe and in much of Southwest and South Asia; from the second half of the 15th century the Indo-European tongues have spread to most other inhabited parts of the world. In German the family is called *Indogermanisch*, which has led to the occasional use of "Indogermanic" in English. The term Indo-Hittite is used by scholars who believe that Hittite and the other Anatolian languages (see below) are not just one branch of Indo-European but rather a branch coordinate with all the rest put together; thus, Indo-Hittite is used for a family consisting of Indo-European proper plus Anatolian. As long as this view is neither definitively proved nor disproved, it is convenient to keep the traditional use of the term Indo-European.

Indo-Hittite hypothesis

Languages of the family. The well-attested languages of the Indo-European family fall fairly neatly into the ten main branches listed below; these are arranged according to the age of their oldest sizable texts.

Anatolian. Now extinct, Anatolian was spoken during the 1st and 2nd millennia BC in what is presently Asian Turkey and northern Syria. By far the best known of its members is Hittite, the official language of the Hittite Empire, which flourished in the 2nd millennium. Very few Hittite texts were known before 1906, and their interpretation as Indo-European was not generally accepted until after 1915; the integration of Hittite data into Indo-European comparative grammar has, therefore, been one of the principal developments of Indo-European studies in this century. The oldest Hittite texts date from the 17th century BC, the latest from the 13th. For more information, see ANATOLIAN LANGUAGES.

Indo-Iranian. Indo-Iranian comprises two main subbranches, Indo-Aryan (Indic) and Iranian. Indo-Aryan languages have been spoken in what is now northern and central India and Pakistan since before 1000 BC. Aside from a very poorly known dialect spoken in or near northern Iraq during the 2nd millennium BC, the oldest record of an Indo-Aryan language is the Vedic Sanskrit of the Ṛgveda, the oldest of the sacred scriptures of India, dating roughly from the centuries around 1000 BC. Examples of modern Indo-Aryan languages are Hindi, Bengalī, Sinhalese (spoken in Ceylon), and Romany, the language of the Gypsies.

Iranian languages were spoken in the 1st millennium BC in present-day Iran and Afghanistan, and also in the steppes to the north, from modern Hungary to Chinese Turkistan. The only well-known ancient varieties are Avestan, the sacred language of the Zoroastrians (Parsees), and Old Persian, the official language of Darius I (ruled 522–486 BC) and Xerxes I (486–465 BC) and their successors. Some modern Iranian languages are Persian, Pashto (Afghan), Kurdish, and Ossetic. For more information on the Indo-Iranian languages, including the Kafiri group, which occupies a special position, see INDO-IRANIAN LANGUAGES.

Greek. Greek, despite its numerous dialects, has been a single language throughout its history. It has been spoken in Greece since at least 1600 BC, and, in all probability, since the end of the 3rd millennium. The earliest texts are the Minoan Linear B tablets, some of which may date from as far back as 1400 BC (the date is disputed), and some of which certainly date from around 1200 BC. This material, very sparse and difficult to interpret, was not identified as Greek until 1952. The Homeric epics—the *Iliad* and the *Odyssey*—composed for the most part in the 8th century BC, are the oldest texts of any bulk. For more information, see GREEK LANGUAGE.

Minoan Linear B texts

Italic. The principal language of the Italic group is Latin, originally the speech of the city of Rome, and the ancestor of the modern Romance languages: Italian, Romanian, Spanish, Portuguese, French, etc. The earliest Latin inscriptions date apparently from the 6th century BC, with literature beginning in the 3rd century. Scholars are not in agreement as to how many other ancient languages of Italy and Sicily belong in the same branch as Latin. For more information on Latin, the languages derived from it, and the other languages that belong or may belong to the Italic branch of Indo-European, see ITALIC LANGUAGES; ROMANCE LANGUAGES.

Germanic. In the middle of the 1st millennium BC, Germanic tribes lived in southern Scandinavia and northern Germany. Their expansions and migrations from the 2nd century BC onward are largely recorded in history. The oldest Germanic language of which much is known is the Gothic of the 4th century AD. Other languages include English, German, Dutch, Danish, Swedish, Norwegian, and Icelandic. For more information on the Germanic languages, see GERMANIC LANGUAGES; ENGLISH LANGUAGE.

Armenian. Armenian, like Greek, is a single language. The Armenians are recorded as being in what is now eastern Turkey and the Armenian Soviet Socialist Republic as early as the 6th century BC, but the oldest Armenian texts date from the 5th century AD. For more information, see ARMENIAN LANGUAGE.

Tocharian. Tocharian, now extinct, was spoken in present-day Chinese Turkistan in the 1st millennium AD. Two distinct languages are known, labelled A (Turfanian) and B (Kuchean); many scholars consider Tocharian A and B to be two dialects of the same language. One group of travel permits for caravans can be dated to the early 7th century, and it appears that other texts date from the same or from neighbouring centuries. These languages became known to scholars only in the first decade of the 20th century; they have been less important for Indo-European studies than has Hittite, partly because their testimony about the Indo-European parent language is obscured by 2,000 more years of change, and partly because Tocharian testimony fits fairly well with that of the previously known non-Anatolian languages. For more information, see TOCHARIAN LANGUAGE.

Tocharian A and B

Celtic. Celtic was spoken in the last centuries before the Christian Era over a wide area of Europe, from Spain and Britain to the Balkans, with a group (the Galatians) even in Asia Minor. Very little of the Celtic of that time and the ensuing centuries has survived, and this branch is known almost entirely from the Insular Celtic languages—Irish, Welsh, and others—spoken in and near the British Isles, as recorded from the 8th century AD onward. For more information, see CELTIC LANGUAGES.

Balto-Slavic. The grouping of Baltic and Slavic into a single branch is somewhat controversial, but the exclusively shared features outweigh the old divergences. At the beginning of the Christian Era, Baltic and Slavic tribes occupied a large area of eastern Europe, east of the Germanic tribes and north of the Iranians, including much of present-day Poland and the western Soviet Union. The Slavic part of this area was probably fairly small, perhaps centred in what is now southern Poland. But in the 5th century AD the Slavs began expanding in all directions, until now the Slavic languages are spoken over the greater part of eastern Europe and northern Asia. The Baltic-speaking area, however, has contracted, so that Baltic languages are presently confined to the two Soviet Socialist Republics of Lithuania and Latvia.

The earliest Slavic texts, written in a dialect called Old Church Slavonic, date from the 9th century AD; the oldest substantial material in Baltic comes from the end of the 14th century, and the oldest connected texts from the 16th century. For more information, see BALTIC LANGUAGES; SLAVIC LANGUAGES.

Albanian. Albanian, the language of the present-day republic of Albania, is known from the 15th century AD. It presumably continues one of the very poorly attested ancient Indo-European languages of the Balkan peninsula, but which one is not clear. For more information, see ALBANIAN LANGUAGE.

In addition to the tongues just listed, there are several poorly documented extinct languages of which enough is known to be sure that they were Indo-European and that they did not belong in any of the branches enumerated above (*e.g.*, Phrygian, Macedonian). Of a few, too little is known to be sure whether they were Indo-European or not (*e.g.*, Ligurian). For all these, see ANCIENT EPIGRAPHIC REMAINS.

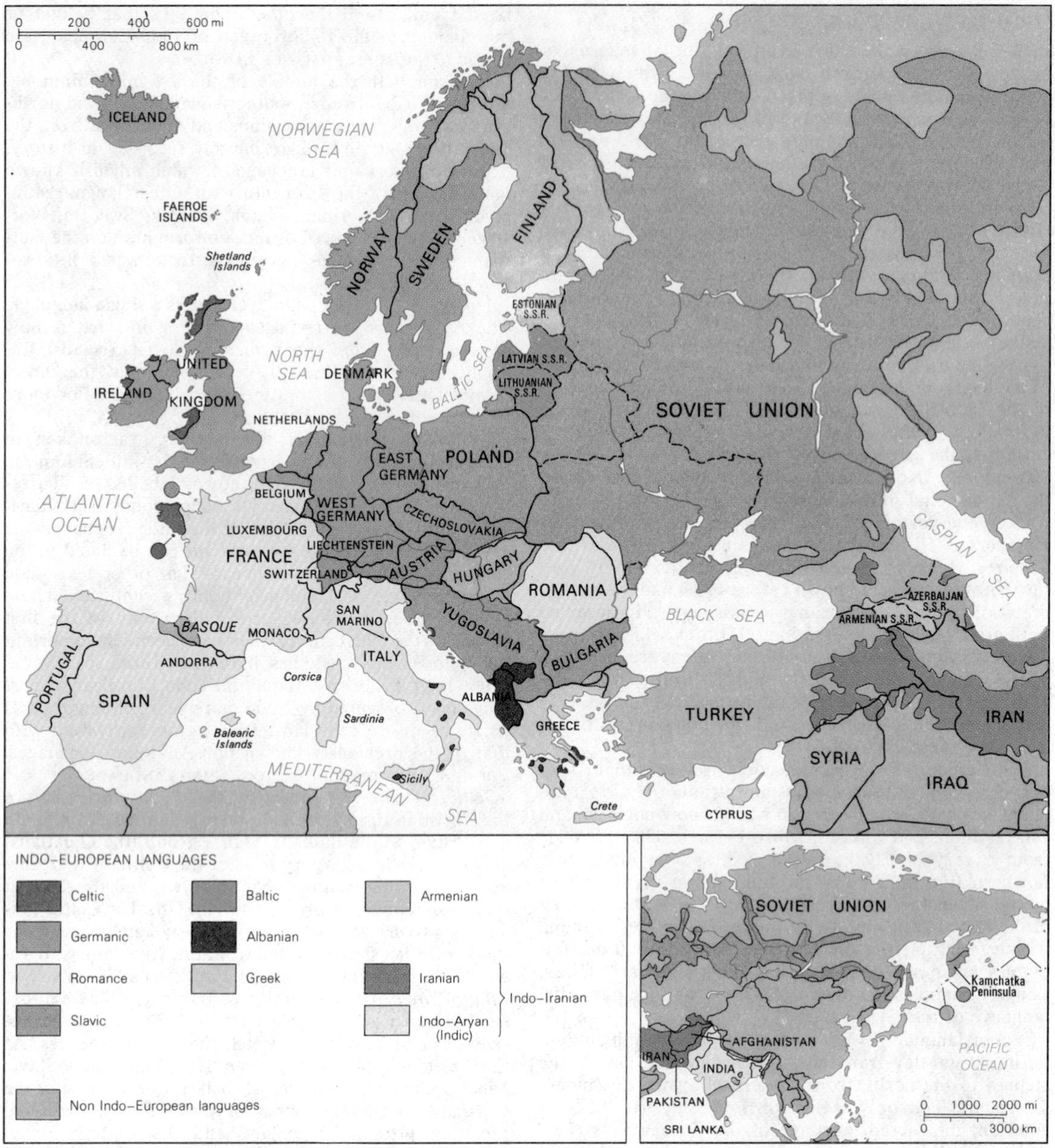

Approximate locations of Indo-European languages in Eurasia in the 20th century.
Adapted from A. Meillet and M. Cohen, *Les Langues du monde* (1952); Editions du Centre National de la Recherche Scientifique, Paris

Reasons for grouping the languages together

Establishment of the family. *Shared characteristics.* The chief reason for grouping the Indo-European languages together is that they share a number of items of basic vocabulary, including grammatical affixes, whose shapes in the different languages can be related to one another by statable phonetic rules. Especially important are the shared patterns of alternation of sounds. Thus the agreement of Sanskrit *ás-ti*, Latin *es-t*, and Gothic *is-t*, all meaning "is," is greatly strengthened by the identical reduction of the root to *s-* in the plural in all three languages: Sanskrit *s-ánti*, Latin *s-unt*, Gothic *s-ind* "they are." Agreements in pure structure, totally divorced from phonetic substance, are, at best, of dubious value in proving membership in the Indo-European family.

Table 1 gives examples of typical vocabulary items widely shared within the Indo-European family that have been decisive in establishing the family. A blank indicates that the language in question does not use the item in the given meaning or that its word for that meaning is unknown.

Similarities in grammatical endings are shown in Table 2 by samples of noun declension and verb inflection in some of the more archaic languages that have kept the inflectional endings of Indo-European relatively unchanged. Note that Old Lithuanian *-į* and *-ų* were nasalized vowels, continuing from the earlier forms **-in* and **-un*. (The asterisk marks a form that is not actually found in any document or living dialect, but is reconstructed as having once existed in the prehistory of the language.)

The statable phonetic rules referred to earlier are not always obvious without careful observation. Note that the English dental consonants *t*, *d*, and *th* do not correspond in a straightforward manner to the Greek dental sounds *t*, *d*, and *th;* that is, English *t* does not occur where Greek *t* appears, nor English *d* where Greek has *d*. But the relationships between the sounds are not random either—English *t* does not correspond to Greek *t* in one word, to *d* in a second, and to *th* in a third, according to no discernible pattern. Rather, where Greek has initial *t*, English has *th*, as in "that" and "three"; where Greek has *d*, English has *t*, as in "tree," "two," and "ten"; and where Greek has *th*, English has *d*, as in "daughter." Note also that phonetic similarity as such is not needed to establish relationship. Thus, many of the Armenian words in Table 1 look quite different from the related words in other Indo-European languages. But here too regular rules of correspondence can be found; *e.g.*, Greek initial *p* corresponds to Armenian *h* or zero (a lack of consonant) in the words meaning "fire," "father," "foot," "five."

Table 1: Widely Shared Indo-European Terms*

	Hittite	Sanskrit	Greek	Latin	English	Armenian	Tocharian B	Old Irish	Lithuanian	Albanian
I	uk	ahám	egō	ego	I	es			àš	
me	ammuk	mā́m	eme	mē	me	is		-m	manè	mua
thou		tuvám	su	tū	thou	du	twe	tú	tù	ti
thee	tuk	tvā́m	se	tē	thee	k'ez	ci	-t	tavè	ty
who?	kuis	kás	tis	quis	who?	ov	kᵤse	cía	kàs	kush
what?	kuit	kím	ti	quid	what?	z-i	kᵤse	cid	kàs	çë
that		tát	to		that	da	te		taĩ	
water	watar	udakám	hudōr		water		war	uisce	vanduõ	ujë
fire	paḫḫur		pūr		fire	hur	puwar			
father		pitár-	pater-	pater	father	hayr	pācer	athair		
mother		mātár-	māter-	māter	mother	mayr	mācer	máthair	mótina	
brother		bhrā́tar-		frāter	brother	elbayr	procer	bráthair	brólis	
sister		svásār		soror	sister	k'oyr	ṣer	siur	seser-	
daughter		duhitár-	thugater-		daughter	dustr	tkācer		dukter-	
son		sūnús	huios		son		soy		sūnùs	
sheep	Luw. ḫawi-	ávis	o(w)is	ovis	ewe			oí	avìs	
cow		gā́v-	bous	bōs	cow	kov	keᵤ	bó	Latv. gùovs	
horse	Hier. Luw. aśuwa-	áśvas	hippos	equus	OE eoh		yakwe	ech	ašvà 'mare'	
pig		sūkarás	hūs	sūs	sow		suwo			thi
dog	Hier. Luw. śuwana-	śvā́n-	kuōn	canis	hound	šun	kwen-	con-	šun-	
wheel		cakrám	kuklos		wheel		kokale 'wagon'			
heart	kart-		kardiā	cord-	heart	sirt		cride	širdìs	
knee	kenu	jā́nu	gonu	genū	knee	cunr	keni	glún		gju
tree,wood	taru	dā́ru	doru		tree			daur 'oak'	OCS drěvo	dru
foot	pat(a)-	pā́d-	pod-	ped-	foot	otn	paiyye			
long	talukis	dīrghás	dolikhos						ìlgas	
new	newas	návas	ne(w)os	novus	new	nor	ñuwe	nue	naũjas	
goes	pa-itsi	éti	eisi	it			yan		eĩna	
is	estsi	ásti	esti	est	is	ē	ste	is	ẽsti	është
eats	etstsi	átti	edei	ēst	eats	utē			ĕda	
carries		bhárati	pherei	fert	bears	berē	parän	berid		bie 'brings'
knows		véda	(w)oide		wot	gitē		ro-fitir	OCS věstŭ	
1		ékas	oi(w)os 'alone'	ūnus	one			oín	víenas	një
2	twi-	duvā́	duo	duo	two	erku	wi	dó	dù	dy
3	tri-	tráyas	treis	trēs	three	erek'	trey	trí	trỹs	tre
4		catvā́ras	tettares	quattuor	four	č'ork'	śtwer	cethair	keturì	katër
5		páñca	pente	quīnque	five	hing	piś	cóic	penkì	pesë
6		ṣáṭ	hex	sex	six	vec'	ṣkas	sé	šešì	gjashtë
7	siptam-	saptá	hepta	septem	seven	ewt'n	ṣukt	secht	septynì	shtatë
8		aṣṭā́	oktō	octō	eight	ut'	okt	ocht	aštuonì	tetë
9		náva	enne(w)a	novem	nine	inn	ñu	noí	devynì	nëndë
10		dáśa	deka	decem	ten	tasn	śak	deich	dẽšimt	dhjetë
100		śatám	hekaton	centum	hundred		kante	cét	šim̃tas	
not	natta	ná		ne-	not			ní-	ne-	

*Words lacking in the language named at the top of the column but found in a closely related language are included, with these abbreviations: Luw. = Luwian; Hier. Luw. = Hieroglyphic Luwian; OE = Old English; Latv. = Latvian; OCS = Old Church Slavonic.

Linguistic studies of the family. The ancient Greeks and Romans readily perceived that their languages were related to each other, and, as other European languages became objects of scholarly attention in the late Middle Ages and the Renaissance, many of these were seen to be more similar to Latin and Greek than, for example, to Hebrew or Hungarian. But an accurate idea of the true bounds of the Indo-European family became possible only when, in the 16th century, Europeans began to learn Sanskrit. The massive similarities between Sanskrit and Latin and Greek were noted early, but the first person to make the correct inference and state it conspicuously was the English Orientalist and jurist Sir William Jones, who in 1786 said in his presidential address to the Asiatic Society that Sanskrit bore to both Greek and Latin

> a stronger affinity, both in the roots of verbs, and in the forms of grammar, than could possibly have been produced by accident; so strong, indeed, that no philologer could examine them all three without believing them to have sprung from some common source, which, perhaps, no longer exists. There is a similar reason, though not quite so forcible, for supposing that both the *Gothick* [*i.e.,* Germanic] and the *Celtick*, though blended with a very different idiom, had the same origin with the *Sanscrit*; and the old *Persian* might be added to the same family . . .

Table 2: Examples of Noun and Verb Inflection

	Hittite paant- (gone)	Sanskrit yant- (going)	Greek iont- (going)	Latin eunt- (going)	Old Lithuanian seser- (sister)
Singular nominative	paant-s	yán	iōn	iēn-s	sesuõ
Singular accusative	paant-an	yánt-am	iont-a	eunt-em	sẽser-į
Singular genitive	paant-as	yat-ás	iont-os	eunt-is	seser-ès
Singular dative	paant-i	yat-é		eunt-ī	sẽser-i
Singular locative	paant-i	yat-í	iont-i	eunt-e	seser-yjè
Plural nominative	paant-es	yánt-as	iont-es	eunt-ēs	sẽser-es
Plural accusative	paant-us	yat-ás	iont-as	eunt-es	sẽser-is
Plural genitive	paant-an	yat-ā́m	iont-ōn	eunt-(i)um	seser-ũ
I go	pai-mi	é-mi	ei-mi	e-ō	ei-mì
You (sg.) go	pai-si	é-ṣi	ei	ī-s	ei-sì
He, she goes	pai-tsi	é-ti	ei-si	i-t	eĩ-ti
We go	pai-wani	i-más	i-men	ī-mus	ei-mè
You (pl.) go	pai-tteni	i-thá	i-te	ī-tis	ei-tè
They go	pa-antsi	y-ánti	i-āsi	e-unt	

The work of Bopp, Rask, and Grimm

The detailed evidence on which Jones based his conclusion was not presented until the 19th century. In 1816 Franz Bopp, the German philologist, presented his *Über das Conjugationssystem der Sanskritsprache in Vergleichung mit jenem der griechischen, lateinischen, persischen und germanischen Sprache* ("On the system of conjugation of the Sanskrit language, in comparison with those of Greek, Latin, Persian, and Germanic"), in which the relation of these five languages was demonstrated on the basis of a detailed comparison of verb morphology (structure). Two years later there appeared the "Undersøgelse om det gamle Nordiske eller Islandske Sprogs Oprindelse" ("Investigation on the Origin of the Old Norse or Icelandic Language"), by the Danish philologist Rasmus Rask, originally written in 1814. This work demonstrated methodically the relation of Germanic to Latin, Greek, Slavic, and Baltic. In 1822 the second edition of the first volume of Jacob Grimm's *Deutsche Grammatik* ("Germanic Grammar") was published (Jacob Grimm was one of the Brothers Grimm of fairy tale fame); in this grammar were discussed the peculiar Indo-European vowel alternations called *Ablaut* by Grimm (*e.g.*, English "sing, sang, sung"; or Greek *peíth-ō* "I persuade," *pé-poith-a* "I am persuaded," *é-pith-on* "I persuaded"). In addition, Grimm tried to find the principle behind the correspondences of Germanic stop and spirant consonants (the first made with complete stoppage of the breath from the lungs, and the second made with constriction of the breath stream from the lungs, but not complete stoppage) to the consonants of other Indo-European languages. The sound changes implied by these correspondences have become known as "Grimm's Law." Examples of it include the stop consonant *p* in Latin *pater* corresponding to the spirant consonant *f* in "father," and the correspondences between English and Greek *t*, *d*, and *th* discussed above.

Bopp demonstrated in 1838 that the Celtic languages were Indo-European, as had been asserted by Jones. In 1850 the German philologist August Schleicher did the same for Albanian, and in 1877 another German philologist, Heinrich Hübschmann, showed that Armenian was an independent branch of Indo-European, rather than a member of the Iranian subbranch. Since then, the Indo-European family has been enlarged by the discovery of Tocharian and of Hittite and other Anatolian languages, and by the recognition, with the aid of Hittite, that Lycian, known and partly deciphered already in the 19th century, belongs to the Anatolian branch of Indo-European.

The Indo-European character of Tocharian was announced by the German scholars Emil Sieg and Wilhelm Siegling in 1908. The Norwegian orientalist Jørgen Alexander Knudtzon recognized Hittite as Indo-European on the basis of two letters found in Egypt (translated in *Die zwei Arzawa-briefe*, 1902; "The Two Arzawa Letters"), but his views were not generally accepted until 1915, when Bedřich Hrozný published, in the *Mitteilungen der deutschen Orient-Gesellschaft*, the first report of his own decipherment of the much more copious material that had meanwhile been found in the ruins of the Hittite capital itself.

First full comparative Indo-European grammar

The first full comparative grammar of the major Indo-European languages was Bopp's *Vergleichende Grammatik des Sanskrit, Zend, Griechischen, Lateinischen, Litthauischen, Altslawischen, Gotischen und Deutschen* ("Comparative Grammar of Sanskrit, Zend, Greek, Latin, Lithuanian, Old Slavic, Gothic, and German"; first edition 1833–52). But this and August Schleicher's shorter *Compendium der vergleichenden Grammatik der indogermanischen Sprachen* ("Compendium of the Comparative Grammar of the Indo-European Languages"; first ed. 1861–62) were rendered obsolete by the major breakthrough of the 1870s, when scholars realized that sound correspondences are not merely rules of thumb that do not have to be strictly observed, and that apparent exceptions to sound laws can often be accounted for by stating them more accurately or by reconstructing additional different sounds in the parent language. The difference between Gothic *d* in *fadar* "father" and *þ* in *broþar* "brother," for example, both corresponding to *t* in Sanskrit, Greek, and Latin, proved to be correlated with the original position of the accent, a discovery known as Verner's Law (named for the Danish linguist Karl Verner). Thus, *d* appears when the preceding syllable was originally unaccented (*fadar* : Greek *patér-*, Sanskrit *pitár-*), and *þ* occurs when the preceding syllable was originally accented (*broþar* : Greek *phrā́ter* "member of a clan," Sanskrit *bhrā́tar-*).

The knowledge and opinions that had accumulated by the end of the 19th century are largely incorporated in the German linguist Karl Brugmann's *Grundriss der vergleichenden Grammatik der indogermanischen Sprachen* ("Outline of Comparative Indo-European Grammar"; second ed. 1897–1916), which remains the latest full-scale treatment of the family. A new *Indogermanische Grammatik* ("Indo-European Grammar"), under the editorship of the Polish scholar Jerzy Kuryłowicz, takes into account the progress that has been made since 1900; it was in the course of publication in the early 1970s.

Proto-Indo-European

The parent language. By comparing the recorded Indo-European languages, especially the most ancient ones, much of the parent language from which they are descended can be reconstructed. This reconstructed parent language is sometimes called simply "Indo-European," but in this article the term Proto-Indo-European is preferred.

Phonology. In Proto-Indo-European there were at least 11 stop consonants. In the following grid these sounds are arranged according to the place in the mouth where the stoppage was made and the activity of the vocal cords during and immediately after the stoppage:

	labial	dental	palatal	labiovelar
Voiceless	p	t	ḱ	kʷ
Voiced		d	ǵ	gʷ
Voiced aspirated (?)	bh	dh	ǵh	gʷh

Labial denotes a sound made with the lips; dental, with the tip of the tongue against the back of the teeth. The palatals were probably made by contact between the upper surface of the tongue and the hard palate (the roof of the mouth), like Hungarian *ty* and *gy* in *atya* and *Magyar*. The labiovelars were probably made by contact between the upper surface of the tongue and the soft palate (the area behind the hard palate), with a concomitant rounding of the lips. Voiceless designates sounds made without vibration of the vocal cords; voiced sounds are pronounced with vibration of the vocal cords. The exact pronunciation of the "voiced aspirates" is uncertain.

There may also have been a voiced labial stop, *b*, but correspondences pointing to this are few, and rarely extend beyond immediately neighbouring languages. Correspondences that some scholars take as evidence for a set of plain velar consonants (made with the back of the tongue touching the soft palate), *k*, *g*, *gh*, are partly, perhaps entirely, the result of special developments of labiovelars and palatals in specific positions. The evidence for a set of voiceless aspirated stops *ph*, *th*, *ḱh*, *kh*, *kʷh* is extremely weak. (Aspirated consonants are sounds accompanied by a puff of breath.)

There was one sibilant consonant, *s*, with a voiced alternant, *z*, that occurred automatically next to voiced stops. The existence of a second apical spirant, *þ* (presumed pronunciation like that of *th* in English "thin"), is extremely uncertain.

Laryngeal theory

Most scholars now agree that the parent language had one or more additional stop or spirant consonants, for which the label laryngeal is used. These consonants, however, have mostly disappeared or have become identical with other sounds in the recorded Indo-European languages, so that their former existence had to be deduced mainly from their effects on neighbouring sounds. Hence, the laryngeal sounds were not suspected until 1878, and even then they were rejected by most scholars until after 1927, when Kuryłowicz showed that Hittite often has *ḫ* (pronunciation uncertain, but perhaps a velar spirant like the *ch* in German *ach*) in places where a "laryngeal" had been posited on the evidence of the other Indo-European languages. There is still considerable disagreement about how many "laryngeals" there were, what they sounded like, what traces they left, and how best to symbolize them. Probably there were three or four, which can be written H_1, H_2, H_3 (and H_4), and probably some or all of them were palatal or (labio-)velar spirants. The principal traces they left outside Anatolian are in the quality and length of neighbouring vowels, H_2 (and H_4) changing a neighbouring *e* to *a*, and H_3 changing it to *o*, while all laryngeals lengthened a preceding vowel. In Anatolian, H_2 and H_3 remained as *ḫ*, at least in some positions; H_4 is tentatively set up to account for words with *a* that lack *ḫ* in Hittite.

When laryngeals between consonants disappeared, a vowel sometimes remained, as in Greek *stasis*, Sanskrit *sthitis*, Old English *stede* "a standing (place)" from Proto-Indo-European *stH_2tis. Scholars who do not posit "laryngeals" reconstruct a separate Proto-Indo-European vowel ə (called *schwa indogermanicum*) to account for these correspondences.

Finally, there were the nasal sounds *n* and *m*, the liquids *l* and *r*, and the semivowels *y* and *w*. When *y* and *w* occurred between consonants, they were replaced by the vowels *i* and *u*. The nasals and liquids functioning as nuclei of syllables in this position (like the final sounds of English "bottom," "button," "bottle," "butter") are traditionally written *ṇ*, *ṃ*, *ḷ*, *ṛ*. Some scholars dispense with these diacritical marks and with the distinction between syllabic *i* and *u* and nonsyllabic *y* and *w*, but this obscures certain distinctions, such as that between *-wṇ-* in *ḱwṇsu "among dogs," Sanskrit *śvasu*, and *-un-* in *tund- "shove," Sanskrit *tundate*.

Ablaut and vowel grades

The vowel system of Proto-Indo-European was dominated by a pattern of alternation called ablaut. The alternant (called a grade) that occurs in a given syllable of a given form is only partly predictable from the shape of the rest of the word. The basic vowel of the system was *e* ("normal grade"), and the changes it could undergo were loss (zero-grade), change to *o* (*o*-grade), lengthening to *ē* (lengthened grade), and lengthening plus change to *ō* (lengthened *o*-grade). The stem *ped-* "foot," for example, appears as such in Latin *ped-is* (normal grade) "of a foot," as *-bd-* in Avestan *fra-bd-a-* (zero-grade) "forefoot," as *pod-* in Greek *pod-es* (*o*-grade) "feet," as *pēd- in Latin *pēs* (lengthened grade) "foot" in the nominative singular, and as *pōd- in English "foot" (lengthened *o*-grade).

Ablauting forms whose basic vowel is *a*, *o*, *ē*, *ā*, or *ō* in the recorded languages (*e.g.*, Greek *ag-* "lead," *op-*"see," *stā-* "stand") are now believed to have had *e* preceded or followed by laryngeal in the parent language; *e.g.*, *H_2eǵ- "lead," *H_3ek^w- "see," *steH_2- "stand." It is uncertain whether there were additional *o* and *a* vowels besides those arising by ablaut and from *e* next to a laryngeal.

The vowels *i* and *u* did not participate in ablaut alternations, but rather functioned primarily as the syllabic realizations of the consonants *y* and *w*, as in *leyk^w- "leave," zero-grade *lik^w-, like *derḱ- "see," zero-grade *dṛḱ-. Long *ī* and *ū* in the recorded languages derive, at least in part, from sequences of *i* or *u* plus laryngeal; *e.g.*, Latin *vīvus* "alive" from *g^{w}iH_3wós.

Thus the parent language had at least the following vowels:

	front	back
high	*i*	*u*
mid	*e*, *ē*	*o*, *ō*

(In forming front vowels, the highest point of the tongue is in the front of the mouth; for back vowels, that point is in the back. High vowels are those in which the tongue is highest—closest to the roof of the mouth; mid vowels are made with the tongue between the extremes of high and low.) Of these vowels, *i* and *u* really functioned as consonants, and *ē*, *o*, *ō* were all conditioned alternants of *e*. But as noted above there may also have been *ī*, *ū*, *a*, and a second *o*.

The accent just before the breakup of the parent language was apparently mainly a pitch accent, rather than one of stress. Each full word had one accented syllable, presumably pronounced on a higher musical pitch than the other syllables.

The Indo-European verb

Morphology and syntax. The Proto-Indo-European verb had three aspects: imperfective, perfective, and stative. Aspect refers to the nature of an action as described by the speaker; *e.g.*, an event occurring once, an event recurring repeatedly, a continuing process, or a state. The difference between English simple and "progressive" verb forms is largely one of aspect; *e.g.*, "John wrote a letter yesterday" (implying that he finished it) versus "John was writing a letter yesterday" (describing an ongoing process, with no implication as to whether it was finished or not). The Anatolian languages lack a dimension of aspect, and it is not yet clear what the earlier system underlying both Anatolian and the rest of Indo-European was.

The imperfective aspect, traditionally called present, was used for repeated actions and for ongoing processes or states; *e.g.*, *sti-steH_2- "stand up more than once, be in the process of standing up," *weǵh-e- "be in the process of conveying," *es- "be." The perfective aspect, traditionally called aorist, expressed a single, completed occurrence of an action or process; *e.g.*, *cteH_2- "stand up, come to a stop," *wēǵh-s- "convey." The stative aspect, traditionally called perfect, described states of the subject; *e.g.*, *woyd- "know," *ste-stoH_2- "be in a standing position."

Verb roots were by themselves either perfective (like *steH_2- "stand") or imperfective (like *weǵh- "convey," *es- "be"). This basic aspect, however, could be reversed by aspect markers; *e.g.*, reduplication for imperfective, as in *sti-steH_2- (reduplication is the repetition of a word or part of a word), and *-s-* for perfective, as in *wēǵh-s-. The stative aspect was always marked by the *o*-grade of the root in the indicative singular (as in *woyd- "know"), and usually also by reduplication (as in *ste-stoH_2-); it had personal endings different from those of the other two aspects.

From one aspect of a given verb the shape and even the existence of the other two aspects could not be predicted; for example, *es- "be" had only the imperfective aspect. Ways of forming imperfectives were especially numerous and often involved, in addition to their imperfective aspectual meaning, some other notion, such as performing the action habitually or repeatedly (iterative), or causing someone else to perform it (causative). One root could thus have several imperfective stems; so to the root *er- "move" there were at least a causative form, *ṛ-new- "set in motion," and an iterative form, *ṛ-sḱe- "go repeatedly."

The Proto-Indo-European verb was also inflected for mood, by which the speaker could indicate whether he was making statements or inquiries about matters of fact; making predictions, surmises, or wishes about the future or about unreal but imagined situations; or giving commands. Compare English "If John is home now (he is eating lunch)" with the verb "is" in the indicative mood, discussing a matter of fact, with "If John were home now (he would be eating lunch)" with the verb "were" in the subjunctive mood, describing an unreal situation. There were two Proto-Indo-European suffixes expressing mood:

Mood in Indo-European

-e- alternating with *-o-* for the subjunctive, corresponding roughly in meaning to the English auxiliaries "shall" and "will," and -yeH_1- alternating with -iH_1- for the optative, corresponding roughly to English "should" and "would." Verbs without one of these two suffixes were marked for mood and tense by their personal endings.

These personal endings basically expressed the person and number of the verb's subject, as in Latin *amō* "I love," *amās* "you (singular) love," *amat* "he or she loves," *amāmus* "we love," and so on. In the imperfective and perfective aspects there were two sets of endings, distinguishing two voices: active, in which typically the subject was not affected by the action, and mediopassive, in which typically the subject was affected, directly or indirectly. Thus Sanskrit active *yajati* and mediopassive *yajate* both mean "he sacrifices," but the former is said of a priest who performs a sacrifice for the benefit of another, while the latter is said of a layman who hires a priest to perform a sacrifice for him. In the stative aspect there was no distinction of voice. (Voice indicates the relationship of the action expressed by the verb to the subject of the statement.)

To mark mood and tense, verbs in the imperfective aspect that did not have a mood suffix had three sets of personal endings in both active and mediopassive voices: imperative, primary, and secondary. Verbs with imperative endings belonged to the imperative mood (used for commands); *e.g.*, *s-dhí "be," *és-tu "let him be." Verbs with primary endings were marked as non-past in tense and indicative in mood; *e.g.*, *és-ti "he is." (Indicative mood signifies objective statements and questions.) Verbs with secondary endings were unmarked for tense and mood, but were most typically used as past indicatives (_e.g._, _*g_^{w}_hén-t_ "he slew") and to fill out gaps in the imperative paradigm (_e.g._, _*s-té_ "be" in the plural, _*g_^{w}_hṇ-té_ "ye slew; slay" in the plural). To mark such forms unambiguously as past indicatives, an augment, usually consisting of the vowel _e_, could be prefixed; _e.g._, _*é-g_^{w}_hen-t_ "he slew," _*ēst_ (= _*é-es-t_) "he was."

Verbs in the perfective aspect without a mood suffix did not occur with primary endings, and so lacked a non-past indicative tense. Verbs in the stative aspect apparently lacked a distinction between primary and secondary endings, so that a form like _*wóyd-e_ "he knows" meant also "he knew."

Noun cases, number, gender

The inflectional categories of the noun were case, number, and gender. Eight cases can be reconstructed: nominative, for the subject of a verb; accusative, for the direct object; genitive, for the relations expressed by English "of"; dative, corresponding to the English preposition "to," as in "give a prize to the winner"; locative, corresponding to "at," "in"; ablative, "from"; instrumental, "with"; and vocative, used for the person being addressed. For examples of some of these see Table 2. Besides singular and plural number, there was a dual number for referring to two items. Each noun belonged to one of three genders: masculine, to which belonged most nouns designating male creatures; feminine, to which belonged most names of female creatures; and neuter, to which belonged only a few words for individual adult living creatures. The gender of nouns not designating living creatures was only partly predictable from their meaning.

Adjectives were nouns that varied in gender according to the gender of another noun with which they were in agreement, or, if used by themselves, according to the sex of the entity to which they referred; thus, Latin _bonus sermō_ "good speech" (masculine), _bona aetās_ "good age" (feminine), _bonum cor_ "good heart" (neuter), or _bonus_ "a good man," _bona_ "a good woman," _bonum_ "a good thing." The neuter of an adjective was identical with the masculine except for having different endings in nominative and accusative cases. Feminine gender was either completely identical with the masculine or derived from it by means of a suffix, the two commonest being _*-eH_$_{2}$_-_ and _*-iH_$_{2}$_-_ (_*-yeH_$_{2}$_-_).

Demonstrative, interrogative, relative, and indefinite pronouns were inflected like adjectives, with some special endings. Personal pronouns were inflected very differently. They lacked the category of gender, and marked number and case (in part) not by endings but by different stems, as is still seen in English singular nominative "I"; oblique "my," "me"; plural nominative "we"; plural oblique "our," "us." (The oblique is any case other than nominative or vocative.)

Syntactic features

Some notable features of Proto-Indo-European syntax are: the non-ergative case system, that is, the subject of an intransitive verb is in the same case as the subject (rather than the object) of a transitive verb; concord (agreement) in case, number, and gender between adjective and noun; and use of singular verbs with neuter plural subjects, as in Greek _panta rhei_ "all things flow," with the same verb as _ho potamos rhei_ "the river (masculine) flows," contrasting with _hoi potamoi rheousi_ "the rivers flow" (indicating that neuter plurals were originally collectives and grammatically singular).

Lexicon and culture. Much less is known about the parent language's vocabulary than about its phonology and grammar. Sounds and grammatical categories do not easily disappear or undergo radical change in so many daughter languages that their former existence can no longer be detected. It is relatively easy, however, for an individual word to disappear or shift meaning in so many daughter languages that its existence or meaning in the parent language cannot be confidently inferred. Hence, from the linguistic evidence alone, scholars can never say that Proto-Indo-European lacked a word for any particular concept; they can only state the probability that certain items did exist, and from these items make inferences about the culture and location in time and space of the speakers of Proto-Indo-European.

Thus is it supposed that the Proto-Indo-European community knew and talked about dogs (_*ḱwón-_), horses (_*éḱwo-_), sheep (_*H_$_{3}$_éwi-_), and almost certainly cows (_*g_^{w}_ów-_) and pigs (_*suH-_). (The Anatolian words for these last two are still unknown, however.) Probably all these animals were domesticated. At least one cereal grain was known (_*yewo-_), and at least one metal (_*H_$_{2}$_eyos_ or _*H_$_{4}$_eyos_). There were vehicles (_*woǵho-_) with wheels (_*k_^{w}_ek_^{w}_lo-_), pulled by teams joined by yokes (_*yugo-_). Honey was known, and probably formed the basis of an alcoholic drink (_*melit-_, _*medhu_) related to the English "mead." Numerals up through 100 (_*ḱṃtóm_) were in frequent use. All this suggests a people with a well-developed Neolithic (characterized by simple agriculture and polished stone tools) or even Chalcolithic (copper- or bronze-using) technology.

Location and date. Linguists have not found a reliable and precise way to determine from linguistic evidence alone the date at which any set of related languages must have begun diverging. The best that can be done is to estimate the degree of difference between the languages in question, taking into account all that is known about them, and then compare this estimate with the estimated degrees of difference within families of languages —such as the Romance family—whose actual time of divergence is approximately known. Using this sort of "dead reckoning," it can be said that the earliest attested Indo-European languages—Anatolian, Indo-Iranian, and Greek—are different enough that the parent language must have been split into several distinct languages well before 2000 BC, but similar enough that the first split into separate languages is not likely to have been much earlier than 3000 BC, and may have been somewhat later.

Division of Indo-European into languages between 3000 and 2000 BC

For further progress the linguistic findings must be correlated with those of archaeologists and paleontologists to see if there was a population group within Eurasia that was relatively small and homogeneous before 3000 BC and that underwent considerable expansion and fragmentation beginning about 3000 BC—give or take a few centuries—such that some of its fragments can be ancestral to components of the cultures of the speakers of the various recorded Indo-European languages. The culture of this population group in the centuries around 3000 BC must also correspond to what can be inferred for Proto-Indo-European from the linguistic data.

At present the archaeological evidence seems to find such a group in the Kurgan culture of the south Russian steppe, east of the Dnepr (Dnieper) River, north of the Caucasus, and west of the Urals. According to the Lithuanian-American archaeologist Marija Gimbutas, in _Indo-European and Indo-Europeans_ (1970), this culture began spreading west _c._ 4000–3500 BC (Kurgan II), and began to occupy a really wide area stretching from eastern central Europe to northern Iran _c._ 3500–3000 BC (Kurgan III). Allowing a few centuries for the speech of widely separated bands to diverge to the point of becoming distinct languages, this agrees tolerably well with the date suggested by the linguistic evidence for breakup of the parent language. So far the Kurgan culture has been traced back to the 5th millennium BC; its earlier antecedents are still unknown.

Remote relationship of Indo-European to the Uralic languages is very likely. Geographically, the earliest reconstructible locations of the two families are contiguous; lexically, there are strong resemblances in a number of basic words or word parts, including personal, demonstrative, interrogative, and relative pronouns, personal endings of verbs, the accusative case ending _-m_, and such words as those for "water" and "name"; typologically, the families are fairly similar (_e.g._, both have many suffixes, but few or no prefixes or infixes—elements inserted within words). The resemblances, however, are too few to permit the reconstruction of a common "Indo-Uralic" parent language; the two families must have separated several thousand years before the breakup of Indo-European.

Possible relationship to Uralic

If Indo-European is related to other language families —_e.g._, to Hamito-Semitic (Afro-Asiatic) or Caucasian— it must have diverged from them much earlier than from

Uralic, because the number of cogent resemblances is much smaller. There is no evidence that Indo-European originated by fusion of components from two or more distinct language families.

Characteristic developments of Indo-European languages. As Proto-Indo-European was splitting into the dialects that became the first generation of daughter languages, different innovations spread over different territories.

Indo-Iranian, Balto-Slavic, Armenian, and Albanian agree in changing the palatal stops *ḱ, *ǵ, and *ǵh into spirants (*s, ś, th*) or affricates; *e.g.*, Sanskrit *aśri-* "sharp edge," Old Church Slavonic *ostrŭ* "sharp," Armenian *asełn* "needle," Albanian *athëtë* "bitter" beside Greek *ákros* "tip," Latin *acidus* "biting," all from a basic element *H_2*eḱ-* "sharp, pointed." (Spirants, also called fricatives, are sounds produced with audible friction as a result of the airstream passing through a narrow, but unstopped, passage in the mouth; *e.g.*, English *s, f, v*. Affricates are sounds that begin as stops, with complete stoppage of the airstream, but are released as spirants, or fricatives; *e.g.*, the *ch* in "church," the *j* in "jam.") The languages that change the palatal stops to spirants or affricates are not separated from one another by any recorded languages that preserve the palatals as stops; so it is therefore inferred that the change to affricates (whence later spirants) occurred just once, and spread over a cohesive dialect area of Proto-Indo-European.

Of the languages that share this change, however, Balto-Slavic shares with Germanic (including English) an *m* in certain case endings where other Indo-European languages, including Indo-Iranian, Armenian, and Albanian, have *bh* or a sound regularly developed from *bh*. Examples of the *m* ending include English "the-m" and Old Church Slavonic *tě-mŭ* "to those ones"; the *bh* and related sounds (*ph, v, b*) are illustrated in the following: Sanskrit *té-bhyas* "to those ones," Armenian *noro-vk'* "with new ones," Albanian *male-ve* "to mountains," Greek *ókhes-phin* "with chariots," Latin *omni-bus* "for all." Because Balto-Slavic and Germanic are neighbours, it is inferred that *m* replaced *bh* in these case endings just once in the parent language, and that the area over which this innovation spread only partly overlapped the area that adopted affricated pronunciation of the palatals.

This pattern is general for changes dating from the time the parent language was breaking up into distinct languages. Each of the resulting languages shares some innovations with some of its neighbours, but only rarely do different innovations shared by two or more branches of Indo-European cover exactly the same territory.

Developments of the separated Indo-European languages

Once the dialects had become differentiated enough to be distinct languages—probably by 2000 BC, at least in most cases—each largely went its own way, and agreements in developments since then are due either to borrowing across language boundaries (as in the notable convergences between Modern Greek, Albanian, Romanian, and the southernmost Slavic languages) or to parallel but independent workings out of the same base material.

Changes in phonology. In phonology, the most striking changes have been loss or reduction in many languages of final or unaccented syllables, and loss in several languages of certain consonants between vowels, often followed by contraction of the resulting vowel sequence. Thus words in modern Indo-European languages are often much shorter than their Proto-Indo-European ancestors; *e.g.*, English "four," Armenian *č'ork'*, colloquial Persian *car* "four" from *k^w*etwóres;* French *vit* (pronounced *vi*) "lives" from *g^w*í*H_3*weti;* Russian *dvesti* "two hundred" from **duwoy ḱm̥toy*.

Changes in morphology. Because much of the marking of Proto-Indo-European inflectional categories was done in final syllables, loss and reduction of these syllables have often had serious grammatical consequences. In the noun, loss of endings has generally led to loss or great reduction of the case and gender systems, while ways have generally been found to salvage the distinction between singular and plural. In Modern Persian, for example, where all final syllables have been lost, the old case and gender distinctions have disappeared also, but plural number is still regularly marked, either with *-an* (originally the genitive plural ending of some nouns) or with *-ha* (of obscure origin).

In the verb, where more endings originally had two syllables, loss of final syllables has had less serious consequences for morphology. Even here, however, some languages, including English, have totally or almost totally given up the marking of subject by personal endings. Compare English "I, we, you, they love" and "he, she loves" with the Spanish conjugation for "love"—*amo, amas, ama, amamos, amáis, aman*—or the Russian version—*ljubljú, ljúbish, ljúbit, ljúbim, ljúbite, ljúbjat*.

Changes in noun inflection have generally involved simplification. Almost everywhere the dual number has been lost; in many languages the noun genders have been reduced from three to two (as in French, Swedish, Lithuanian, and Hindi), or lost entirely (as in English, Armenian, and Bengali). Only Slavic has complicated the gender system, by imposing on the inherited distinctions contrasts of animate versus inanimate or of personal versus nonpersonal.

Reduction in cases

Everywhere except in the oldest Indo-Iranian languages the original eight Indo-European cases have suffered reduction. Proto-Germanic had only six cases, the functions of ablative (place from which) and locative (place in which) being taken over by constructions of preposition plus the dative case. In Modern English these are reduced to two cases in nouns, a general case that does duty for the vocative, nominative, dative, and accusative ("Henry, did Bill give John the letter?"), and a possessive case continuing the old genitive ("Bill's letter"). In languages such as French and Welsh, nouns are no longer inflected for case at all. In some languages, to be sure, nouns have begun fusing with words placed directly after the nouns to create new case systems, coexisting with relics of the old. Thus, Old Lithuanian had in addition to seven inherited cases an illative (place into), made by adding *-n(a)* to the accusative (*peklosna* "into hell"), an allative (place to, toward), made by adding *-p(i)* to the genitive (*Jesausp* "to Jesus"), and an adessive (place at which), made by adding *-p(i)* to the locative (*Joniep* "in John").

Changes in the verb have been more complex. Besides loss or merger of old categories, many new forms have been created and many old forms have acquired new values. In Ancient Greek the focus of the stative aspect (perfect) has largely shifted from the present state ("he is dead") to the previous event that led to this state ("he has died"). As a result, the perfect came to mean the same as the perfective past (aorist), and has therefore disappeared from Modern Greek. New forms created in Ancient Greek include future and future perfect tenses, based on the desiderative present forms (such as "he wants to walk") of the parent language.

In Germanic the principal new creation was the weak past tense (ending in a *t* or *d*), such as English "loved," "thought," German *liebte, dachte*, made by combining the verb stem with a past tense of the Germanic verb for "do." (The strong past tense formed by vowel alternations, like "sing," "sang," "run," "ran," comes from the Proto-Indo-European stative aspect.)

In some languages participles (verbal adjectives) have come to function as finite verbs. Thus in Hindi *mard strī-ko dekhtā* "the man sees the woman," *dekhtā* "sees" is etymologically a participle "seeing," agreeing in number and gender with the subject *mard* "man." In the past tense, *mard-ne strī dekhī* "the man saw the woman," the verb *dekhī* is etymologically a past passive participle "seen," agreeing in gender and number with the object *strī* "woman," and the subject is marked with an instrumental ending.

Vocabulary changes. Changes in vocabulary have been even greater than those in sounds and grammar. Words in modern Indo-European languages have several sources. They may be recognizable loanwords, such as English "skunk," "chain," and "inch" (from Algonkian, French, and Latin, respectively); they may have been formed within the history or prehistory of the language itself, such as English "radar" and "rightness"; they may be of obscure origin, such as English "drink," which is common Germanic but has no cognates outside Germanic, or "boy," which is peculiar to English and Frisian; or they may be inherited words that have changed meaning, such as English "merry" from Proto-Indo-European *mṛǵhu- "short." Only a small fraction of the vocabulary can be traced back to words that can confidently be asserted to have existed in the parent language with approximately their present meaning. The same is true, albeit in a lesser degree, even for the oldest recorded Indo-European languages. None has more than a few hundred words and roots that are clearly inherited from the parent language without essential change of meaning. Table 1 gives examples of words widely retained with little change. Typically they include pronouns; nouns, verbs, and adjectives of relatively simple and ubiquitous meaning; numerals; and simple adverbs and prepositions.

Non-Indo-European influence on the family. Indo-European languages, like all languages, have always been subject to influence from neighbouring languages, both related and unrelated.

Influence of non-Indo-European languages on the sounds and grammar of Proto-Indo-European is not demonstrable, partly because there is no direct evidence about the languages that were in contact with Indo-European before 3000 BC. It can be surmised, however, that some words are loans; *e.g.*, **pelek̑us* "ax," a word for an object likely to be imported or learned of from neighbours with superior technology, and which is not analyzable into a known Indo-European root plus a known Indo-European suffix.

Adoption of loanwords

When Indo-European languages have been carried within historic times into areas occupied by speakers of other languages, they have generally taken over a number of loanwords, as with English and Spanish in the Americas or Dutch in South Africa. Aside from the special case of the pidgin and creole languages, however, there has been very little effect on sounds and grammar. These have been significantly affected within historic times only when an Indo-European language has been spoken in prolonged close contact with non-Indo-European speakers, as with Ossetic (an Iranian language) in the Caucasus, or when its speakers have been very strongly influenced culturally by speakers of a non-Indo-European language, as with Persian, in which Arabic plays much the same role as Latin does in English.

In prehistoric times most branches of Indo-European were carried into territories presumably or certainly occupied by speakers of non-Indo-European languages, and it is reasonable to suppose that these languages had some effect on the speech of the newcomers. For the lexicon, this is indeed demonstrable in Hittite and Greek, at least. It is much less clear, however, that these non-Indo-European languages affected significantly the sounds and grammar of the Indo-European languages that replaced them. Perhaps the best case is India, where certain grammatical features shared by Indo-European and Dravidian languages appear to have spread from Dravidian to Indo-European rather than vice versa. For most other branches of Indo-European languages any attempt to claim prehistoric influence of non-Indo-European languages on sounds and grammar is rendered almost impossible because of ignorance of the non-Indo-European languages with which they might have been in contact.

BIBLIOGRAPHY. The introductory, classic, and most comprehensive works on Indo-European languages are in German and French. Several publications, however, are written in English.

KARL BRUGMANN, *Grundriss der vergleichenden Grammatik der indogermanischen Sprachen*, 2nd ed., 3 vol. (1897–1916), the latest completed full treatment of the whole family; ANTOINE MEILLET, *Introduction à l'étude comparative des langues indo-européennes*, 8th ed. (1937, reprinted 1964), the best introduction to the subject; JERZY KURYLOWICZ (ed.), *Indogermanische Grammatik* (1968–), vol. 2, *Akzent, Ablaut*, by JERZY KURYLOWICZ (1968), and vol. 3, pt. 1, *Geschichte der indogermanischen Verbalflexion*, by CALVERT WATKINS (1969), when completed, this work will present an account of the entire family—less detailed than Brugmann's, but much more up-to-date; JULIUS POKORNY, *Indogermanisches etymologisches Wörterbuch*, 2 vol. (1951–69), the most recent etymological dictionary of the whole family; CARL DARLING BUCK, *A Dictionary of Selected Synonyms in the Principal Indo-European Languages* (1949), a mine of information about Indo-European words for several hundred basic concepts; HOLGER PEDERSEN, *Sprogvidenskaben i dei nittende aarhundrede* (1924; Eng. trans., *Linguistic Science in the Nineteenth Century*, 1931; reissued as *The Discovery of Language*, 1962), a very good account of 19th-century work in the field; GEORGE CARDONA, HENRY M. HOENIGSWALD, and ALFRED SENN (eds.), *Indo-European and Indo-Europeans* (1970), a collection of recent papers on aspects of Indo-European language, culture, and mythology, especially valuable for the attempt to combine linguistic and archaeological evidence about Indo-European prehistory; FREDRIK OTTO LINDEMAN, *Einführung in die Laryngaltheorie* (1970), an excellent brief account of the main advance in Indo-European phonology since 1900.

(W.C.)

Indo-Iranian Languages

The Indo-Aryan and Iranian languages together constitute the Indo-Iranian language group, the easternmost major branch of the Indo-European family of languages. Indo-Aryan (Indic) languages are spoken by approximately 400,000,000 persons in India, Pakistan, Sri Lanka (formerly Ceylon), Nepal, Bangladesh (former East Pakistan), and other areas of the Himalayan region. The Gypsy, or Romany, dialects of the U.S.S.R., the Middle East, Europe, and North America are also of Indo-Aryan origin. Speakers of Iranian number about 50,000,000 and live in areas extending from Pakistan (former West Pakistan) to Iran, Afghanistan, and the southern U.S.S.R. Among the Indo-European languages, only Mycenaean Greek and Hittite possess older records than those of Indo-Iranian.

The Indo-Iranian tongues have been used as both administrative and literary languages. Old Persian was the administrative language of the early Achaemenian dynasty dating from the 6th century BC; and an eastern Middle Indo-Aryan dialect was the language of the chancellery of King Aśoka in India in the mid-3rd century BC. As literary languages, the Indo-Iranian languages have been used in the texts of some of the world's great religions: Indo-Aryan for Buddhism, Hinduism, and Jainism, and Iranian for Zoroastrian and Manichaean texts. The oldest Zoroastrian texts are in dialects included under the name Avestan. Commerce, conquest, and religion spread the influence of these languages. Indo-Aryan languages, for example, penetrated deep into Southeast Asia; names in Indonesia and other areas and Sanskrit texts in Cambodia reflect this influence.

Linguistic features shared by Indo-Aryan and Iranian

Relationship of the Indo-Aryan and Iranian branches. The close relation between the Iranian and Indo-Aryan groups has never been doubted. They share characteristic features that set them apart as a subgroup of Indo-European. The long and short varieties of the Indo-European vowels *e*, *o*, and *a*, for example, appear as long and short *a:* Sanskrit *manas-* "mind, spirit," Avestan *manah-*, but Greek *ménos* "ardor, force." (In the following examples, ¯ indicates a long vowel; ˘ indicates a short vowel. The spellings used in this article for Indo-Aryan and Iranian forms are traditional transliterations for the most part. In some cases, more accurate phonetic symbols are used. These can be found in the International Phonetic Alphabet.) In instances in which some Indo-European languages have an *a* sound, Indo-Iranian has *i* as a reflex of Indo-European sounds called laryngeals; *e.g.*, Greek *patḗr* "father," Sanskrit *pitṛ-*, Avestan and Old Persian *pitar-*. After stems ending in long or short *a*, *i*, or *u*, an *n* occurs sometimes before the genitive (possessive) plural ending *ām* (Avestan *-ąm*); *e.g.*, Sanskrit *martyānām* "of mortals, men" (from *martya-*); Avestan *mašyānąm* (from *mašya-*), Old Persian *martiyānām*.

In addition to several other similarities in their grammatical systems, Indo-Aryan and Iranian have vocabulary items in common—*e.g.*, such sacrificial terms as Sanskrit *yajña-*, Avestan *yasna-* "sacrifice"; Sanskrit *hotṛ-*, Avestan *zaotar-* "a certain priest"; and names of divinities and mythological persons, such as Sanskrit *mitra-*, Avestan *miθra-* "Mithra." Indeed, both the Iranians and the Indo-Aryans used the same word to refer to themselves as a people: Sanskrit *ārya-*, Avestan *airya-*, Old Persian *ariya-* "Aryan."

Indo-Aryan and Iranian also differ in many points. Among them, Indo-Aryan has an *i* sound representing an Indo-European laryngeal sound not only in initial syllables but generally also in interior syllables; *e.g.*, Sanskrit *duhitṛ-* "daughter" (*cf.* Greek *thugátēr*). In Iranian, however, the sound is lost in this position; *e.g.*, Avestan *dugədar-*, *duɣdar-*. Similarly, the word for "deep" is Sanskrit *gabhīra-* (with *ī* for *i*), but Avestan *ǰafra-*. Iranian also lost the accompanying aspiration (a puff of breath, written as *h*) that is retained in certain Indo-Aryan consonants; *e.g.*, Sanskrit *dhā* "set, make," *bhṛ*, "bear," *gharma-* "warm," but Avestan and Old Persian *dā*, *bar*, and Avestan *garəma-*. Further, Iranian changed stops such as *p* before consonants and *r* and *v* to spirants such as *f:* Sanskrit *pra* "forth," Avestan *frā;* Old Persian *fra;* Sanskrit *putra-* "son," Avestan *puθra-*, Old Persian *puṣṣa-* (*ṣṣ* represents a sound that is also transliterated as ç). In addition, *h* replaced *s* in Iranian except before non-nasal stops (produced by releasing the breath through the mouth) and after *i*, *u*, *r*, *k; e.g.*, Avestan *hapta-* "seven," Sanskrit *sapta-;* Avestan *haurva-* "every, all, whole," Sanskrit *sarva-*. Iranian also has both *xš* and *š* sounds, resulting from different Indo-European *k* sounds followed by *s*-like sounds, but Indo-Aryan has only *kṣ; e.g.*, Avestan *xšayeiti* "has power, is capable," *šaēiti* "dwells," but Sanskrit *kṣayati*, *kṣeti*. Iranian was also relatively conservative in retaining diphthongs that were changed to simple vowels in Indo-Aryan.

Iranian differs from Indo-Aryan in grammatical features as well. The dative singular of *-a*-stems ends in *-āi* in Iranian; *e.g.*, Avestan *mašyāi*, Old Persian *cartanaiy* "to do" (an original dative singular form functioning as infinitive of the verb). In Sanskrit the ending is extended with *a*—*martyāy-a*. Avestan also retains the archaic pronoun forms *yūš*, *yūžəm* "you" (nominative plural); in Indo-Aryan the *-s-* was replaced by *y* (*yūyam*) on the model of the 1st person plural—*vayam* "we" (Avestan *vaēm*, Old Persian *vayam*). Finally, Iranian has a 3rd person pronoun *di* (accusative *dim*) that has no counterpart in Indo-Aryan but has one in Baltic.

Original homeland of Indo-Iranian

The original location of the Indo-Iranian group was probably to the north of modern Afghanistan, in the present-day southern U.S.S.R.—the area called Soviet Turkistan—where Iranian languages are still spoken. From there, some Iranians migrated to the south and west, the Indo-Aryans to the south and east. From geographical references in the earliest Indo-Aryan literary document, the Ṛgveda, it is clear that the earliest settlement of Indo-Aryans was in the northwest of the Indian subcontinent. Migration did not take place at once; there was doubtless a series of migrations. The date of entry of the Indo-Aryans into the subcontinent cannot be pinpointed, though the beginning of the 2nd millennium BC is plausible and generally accepted.

There is heated controversy concerning the precise linguistic position of the language of the Indo-Iranian family first attested in Middle Eastern cuneiform texts of *c.* 1450–1350 BC. Some borrowed words and proper names appearing in these Hittite–Hurrian documents have been interpreted as belonging either to Indo-Iranian, to an Indic subgroup of Indo-Iranian that had not yet fully split, or to Indo-Aryan proper. Complete scholarly agreement on this issue has not been reached.

The identification of the Harappan peoples, whose writing has not yet been satisfactorily deciphered, also awaits further research; with it may come a possible answer as to whether Indo-Aryans encountered these people or whether their civilization had passed by the time the Indo-Aryans arrived on the subcontinent. Whatever the answers to these problems may be, the reasons for the split of the Indo-Aryans and Iranians are not known.

In the following presentation regarding Indo-Aryan documents as evidence for linguistic history, it should be borne in mind that almost all dates are approximations.

The article is divided into the following sections:

The Indo-Aryan languages

LANGUAGES OF THE GROUP

Indo-Aryan languages are assigned to three major periods: Old, Middle, and New Indo-Aryan. These periods are linguistic, not strictly chronological. Old Indo-Aryan includes different dialects and linguistic states referred to in common as Sanskrit. The most archaic Old Indo-Aryan is that of sacred texts called Vedas. Classical Sanskrit is the name given to the literary language that represents a polished form of various dialects. The late Vedic dialect described by the grammarian Pāṇini (*c.* 6th century BC) is also commonly called Classical Sanskrit. Middle Indo-Aryan includes both the dialects of inscriptions from the 3rd century BC to the 4th century AD and literary languages. Apabhraṃśa dialects represent the latest stage of Middle Indo-Aryan development. Though all Middle Indo-Aryan languages are included under the name Prākrit, it is customary to speak of the Prākrits as excluding Apabhraṃśa.

New Indo-Aryan is represented by such modern vernaculars as Hindi and Bengali, which began to emerge from about the 10th century AD. These too have earlier and later stages, culminating in the present-day languages.

Modern Indo-Aryan tongues and number of speakers

New Indo-Aryan languages account for about 322,000,000 speakers in India, or approximately 73 percent of the population at the time of the 1961 census. Considering the approximately 50,000,000 Bengali speakers in Bangladesh, approximately 30,000,000 speakers accounted for by Punjabi and Sindhi in Pakistan, and 8,000,000 Sinhalese (Sinhala) speakers in Sri Lanka (formerly Ceylon), the total number of New Indo-Aryan speakers is well over 400,000,000. According to the Indian census of 1961, there are 547 mother tongues of the Indo-Aryan group within the bounds of postpartition (1947) India. Some of these are dialects used by few speakers; others are official state languages having 20,000,000 or 30,000,000 speakers. The major groups of New Indo-Aryan languages are given in Table 1 with census data when available. Structurally and historically, Hindi and Urdu are one, though they are now official languages of different countries written in different alphabets. The term *hindī* (also *hindvī*) is known from as early as the 13th century. The term *zabān-e-urdū* "language of the imperial camp" came into use in about the 17th century. In the south, Urdu was used by Muslim conquerors of the 14th century.

Official state languages

Many of the languages in Table 1 are official state languages, the media of education up to the university level and of official transactions. Hindi, written in the Devanāgarī script, is the co-official language (with English) of

Table 1: Modern (New) Indo-Aryan Languages

key: B—Bangladesh, former East Pakistan (1961); I—India (1961); N—Nepal (1954); P—Pakistan (former West Pakistan, 1961)

language group, language	where principally spoken*	reported number of speakers (000)†	comments
Eastern group			
Assamese	*Assam*, India	6,803 (I)	official language of Assam, India; also‡
Bengali	*Bangladesh; West Bengal, Tripura,* and Assam, India	50,040 (B); 33,889 (I); 46 (P); 45 (N)	official language of Bangladesh and of West Bengal, Tripura, and Manipur, India; also‡
Oriya	*Orissa*, India	15,719 (I); 13 (B)	official language of Orissa, India; also‡
Northwest group			
Punjabi	*Punjab*, Northwest Frontier Province and Karāchi, Pakistan; *Punjab*, Haryana, Delhi, and Ganganagar district of Rājasthān, India; *Jammu* portion of both Indian- and Pakistani-held portions of Jammu and Kashmir	26,200 (P)§; 10,951 (I); statistics not available for Pakistani-held portion of Jammu and Kashmir	official language of Punjab, Pakistan, and, with Urdu, of Jammu section of Jammu and Kashmir
Lahnda	Punjab and Northwest Frontier Province, Pakistan	statistics not available (P)¶; 20 (I)	
Sindhi	*Sind* province and *Las Bela* and other eastern districts of Baluchistan province, Pakistan; Kutch district of Gujarāt, India	4,964 (P); 1,373 (I), mainly immigrants from area now in Pakistan	official language of Sind, Pakistan; also‡
Pahari (a group of languages)			
Eastern Pahari			
Nepali (major east Pahari language)	*Nepal, Sikkim,* Bhutan	4,014 (N); 947 (I); 74 (Sikkim, 1961); statistics not available for Bhutan	official language of Nepal
Central Pahari			
Kumauni	Himalayan Uttar Pradesh, India	1,030 (I)	
Garhwali	Himalayan Uttar Pradesh, India	810 (I)	
Western Pahari (62 languages and dialects according to the Indian census of 1961)	*Himachal Pradesh*, adjoining district of Uttar Pradesh, India; Himalayan districts of Indian- and Pakistani-held Jammu and Kashmir	660 (I); statistics not available for Pakistani-held portion	Pahari is an official language of Himacha Pradesh, along with Hindi
Unclassified and unspecified	(same as Western Pahari, above)	1,026 (I)	
Dardic			
Dard (East Dardic)			
Kashmiri (major language of East Dardic)	*Vale of Kashmir* and adjoining districts to south and west in Indian- and Pakistani-held portions of Jammu and Kashmir	1,965 (I), of which 1,956 are speakers of Kashmiri; 42 (P); statistics not available for Pakistani-held portion of Jammu and Kashmir or for Afghanistan	Kashmiri, along with Urdu, is an official language of the Kashmiri-speaking area of Jammu and Kashmir; also‡
Other Dardic languages:			
Khowari (Central Dardic), Kafiri (West Dardic), and other minor languages	*Gilgit Agency* of Pakistani-held portion of Jammu and Kashmir; adjoining districts of Northwest Frontier Province, Pakistan; and adjoining portion of northeast Afghanistan	173 (P, partial enumeration); statistics not available for Pakistani-held portion of Jammu and Kashmir or for Afghanistan	position of Dardic is disputed: some account for its peculiarities by proposing that it left the Indo-Iranian branch after Indo-Aryan but before all the features particular to Iranian had evolved; others suggest that East and Central Dardic are definitely Indo-Aryan, but that they did not go through the middle Indo-Aryan stage represented in documents; Kafiri occupies a special position
West and Southwest groups			
Gujarati	*Gujarāt*, Bombay district of Mahārāshtra, India	20,304 (I); 241 (P)	official language of Gujarāt, India; also‡
Marathi	*Mahārāshtra* and eight adjoining districts in three older states of India	33,287§ (I)	official language of Mahārāshtra, India; also‡
Konkani	*Goa*, coastal Mahārāshtra south of Bombay, and coastal Mysore, India	1,352¶ (I)	
Sinhalese	*Sri Lanka* (Ceylon)	7,518 (approximate 1963 total based on data of Sri Lanka for Sinhalese by ethnic groups)	official language of Sri Lanka (Ceylon)
Maldivian	*Maldive Islands*	approximately 100	official language of Maldive Islands

*Italic type indicates language is spoken by a majority or plurality of the population in the area; roman type indicates language is spoken by a minority of the population in the area. †Not shown when there are fewer than 10,000 reported speakers in a given country. "Reported" number of speakers is often far different from actual number of speakers. Indian (I) data include census returns for Indian-held portion of Jammu and Kashmir; Pakistani (P) data do not include data for Pakistani-held portion of Jammu and Kashmir. Pakistani data are incomplete for the tribal areas of the Northwest Frontier Province, west Dardic.

the Republic of India and is used as a lingua franca throughout North India. It has varieties according to the mother tongue of the area; *e.g.*, Bombay Hindi and Calcutta Hindi. Each of the major state languages has several other dialects in addition to the standard dialect adopted for official purposes. Including the various dialects down to the village level, it can be said that a chain of communication stretches across North India such that each dialect forms a link with each adjacent dialect. On the level of official languages this is not so: a Gujarati speaker will not readily understand colloquial Bengali.

HISTORICAL SURVEY OF THE INDO-ARYAN LANGUAGES

The points noted above regarding Indo-Aryan migration make it difficult to determine the domain of Proto-Indo-Aryan, the ancestral language of all the known Indo-Aryan tongues, if indeed there was any such single region. All that can be said with certainty is that the Indo-Aryans on the subcontinent first occupied the area comprising most of present-day Punjab (both West and East), Haryana, and the Upper Doab (Ganges–Yamuna interfluve) of Uttar Pradesh. The structure of Proto-Indo-Aryan must have been close to that of early Vedic, with dialectal variations.

Old Indo-Aryan. *Old Indo-Aryan documents.* The most archaic Sanskrit is that of the Vedas, of which there are four major text groups called Saṃhitās: the Ṛgveda, Atharvaveda, Sāmaveda, and Yajurveda. The Yajurveda is in turn divided into two main branches, the White (Śukla) Yajurveda and the Black (Kṛṣṇa) Yajurveda. The Ṛgveda, Atharvaveda, and Sāmaveda are purely metrical texts mainly used by priests in their ritual. The texts of the Black Yajurveda contain both verses used in ritual sacrifice (called *mantras*) and prose sections that are explanatory in nature, giving mythological explanations of sacrifices and objects used in them, together with etymologies (derivations of words). These sections are known as *Brāhmaṇa* portions. Each Veda also has a particular *Brāhmaṇa* connected with it. The early Vedic texts are pre-Buddhistic; a plausible date accepted for the composition of the Ṛgveda is between 1200 and 1000 BC,

Table 1: Modern (New) Indo-Aryan Languages (continued)

language group, language	where principally spoken*	reported number of speakers (000)†	comments
Midland group			
Hindi	*Uttar Pradesh, Madhya Pradesh, Bihār, Haryana, Delhi,* Rājasthān, Punjab, Himachal Pradesh, and in scattered proximate districts of West Bengal and Mahārāshtra, India	123,025§ (I); 141 (B); 80 (N)	co-official language (with English) of the Republic of India and a lingua franca throughout North India; language of official business in area described; Khari Boli, based on a dialect of western Uttar Pradesh to the northeast of Delhi, is considered to be a standard form of Hindi; official language of Uttar Pradesh, Madhya Pradesh, Bihār, Haryana, Rājasthān, and Himachal Pradesh states and of Delhi union territory, India; also‡
Eastern Hindi (incomplete)			
Awadhi (Avadhi)	north central and central Uttar Pradesh, India	528 ‖ (I)	
Bagheli	north central Madhya Pradesh and south central Uttar Pradesh, India	557‖ (I)	
Chattisgarhi	east central Madhya Pradesh, India	2,962§ (I)	
Western Hindi (incomplete)			
Braj Bhasa	western Uttar Pradesh and adjacent districts of Haryana, Rājasthān, and Madhya Pradesh, India	76‖ (I)	
Bundeli (Bundelkhandi)	north central Madhya Pradesh and southwestern Uttar Pradesh, India	22‖ (I)	
Other Hindi languages and dialects (Eastern and Western, including Hindustani)	scattered over much of Uttar Pradesh, Madhya Pradesh, and Haryana and in eastern Rājasthān, India	6,388‖ (I)	
Urdu	*Karāchi* district and Pakistan in general; all but northeastern and southern peninsular India	23,324¶ (I); 2,991 (P), claimed as an additional language by 2,872 others (P); 311 (B); 33 (N)	official language of Pakistan (before 1971 co-official language of Pakistan; recognized in the constitution of India; a form of Urdu known as Dakhini Urdu (Southern Urdu) is still used in the area around Hyderabad; an official language in both the Indian- and Pakistani-held portions of Jammu and Kashmir; also‡
Bihari (a group of languages)			
Maithili	North Bihār, India; adjacent lowland Nepal	4,985 (I)¶; 919 (N)	
Magahi (Magadhi)	central Bihār, India	2,816 (I)‖	
Bhojpuri	western Bihār and eastern Uttar Pradesh, India	7,965 (I)¶; 16 (N)	
Others	Bihār, India	1,041 (I)¶	
Rajasthani (a group of languages)			
Mewati	northeast Rājasthān, India	48‖ (I)	
Ahirwati	northeast Rājasthān	21‖ (I)	
Harauti	southeast Rājasthān	561‖ (I)	
Malvi	western Madhya Pradesh and southeast Rājasthān	1,142‖ (I)	
Nimadi	southwest Madhya Pradesh	528‖ (I) India	
Marwari	western, central, and northern Rājasthān	6,242¶ (I)	
Rajasthani—other and unclassified	over most of Rājasthān, with locally important groups in scattered districts of Mahārāshtra, Andhra Pradesh, and Mysore, India; and both Indian- and Pakistani-held portions of Jammu and Kashmir	6,391¶ (I); 153 (P); statistics not available for Pakistani-held portion of Jammu and Kashmir	Rajasthani, an official language of Rājasthān along with Hindi
Bhili (a group of dialects)	southern Rājasthān, western Madhya Pradesh, eastern Gujarāt, and northwest Mahārāshtra, India	2,440 (I)	
Khandeshi	northwest Mahārāshtra	428 (I)	
Others (inadequately classified or unspecified)			
Tharu	sub-Himalayan Nepal	360 (N); 11 (I)	
Miscellaneous dialects	sub-Himalayan Nepal	891–953 (N), depending on inclusiveness of listing	

languages, and Punjabi. As of 1972, Afghanistan has had no population census, but speakers of various Dardic languages there may number as many as 100,000, while another 10,000–20,000 may speak Indo-Aryan languages. ‡One of the 15 official languages listed in Schedule VIII of the Indian Constitution. §Presumed significant overstatement by census. Punjabi in Pakistan includes Lahnda. Marathi in India includes many speakers of Konkani and possibly also of Khandeshi. "Hindi" (undifferentiated) includes many speakers of all the languages of the Midland group footnoted ‖ or ¶. ‖Presumed gross understatement by census. ¶Presumed significant understatement by census.

though the exact chronology of these early texts is difficult to establish. The prose passages of *Brāhmaṇas* and of the early *sūtra* (aphoristic texts) period may be called late Vedic. Also of the late Vedic period is the grammarian Pāṇini, author of a treatise called *Aṣṭādhyāyī*, who makes a distinction between the language of sacred texts (*chandas*) and the usual language of communication (*bhāṣā*).

Epic Sanskrit is so called because it is represented principally in the two epics, *Mahābhārata* and *Rāmāyaṇa.* In the latter the term *saṃskṛta* "formed, polished" is encountered, probably for the first time with reference to the language. The date of composition for the core of early Epic Sanskrit is considered to be in the first centuries BC.

Classical Sanskrit

Classical Sanskrit is the language of the major poetic works (*kāvya*), drama (*nāṭaka*), tales such as the *Hitopadeśa* and *Pañca-tantra,* and technical treatises on grammar, philosophy, and ritual. It was used not only by the poet Kālidāsa and his predecessors Bhāsa, a dramatist, and Aśvaghoṣa, a Buddhist author, in the first centuries AD but was also continued long after Sanskrit was a commonly used mother tongue; indeed, Sanskrit is a language of learned treatises and commentaries to this day. It is also used as a lingua franca among *paṇḍits* (Brahmin scholars) from different areas of India, and the 1961 census lists 2,544 persons claiming it as their mother tongue.

Linguistic developments. Linguistic developments can be traced from the early Vedic of the Ṛgveda through the later Saṃhitās on to the late Vedic of *Brāhmaṇa* prose and *sūtras*, culminating in the language described by Pāṇini, which is tantamount to Classical Sanskrit. For example, the nominative plural form ending in *-āsas* (*devāsas* "gods") was already less frequent than *-ās* in the Ṛgveda and continued to lose ground later; in *Brāhmaṇa, -ās* (*e.g., devās*) is the normal form. There are numerous other changes evident. For example, the instrumental singular form of *-a*-stems ends both in *-ā* and *-ena* (a pronoun ending) in the Ṛgveda, with the latter

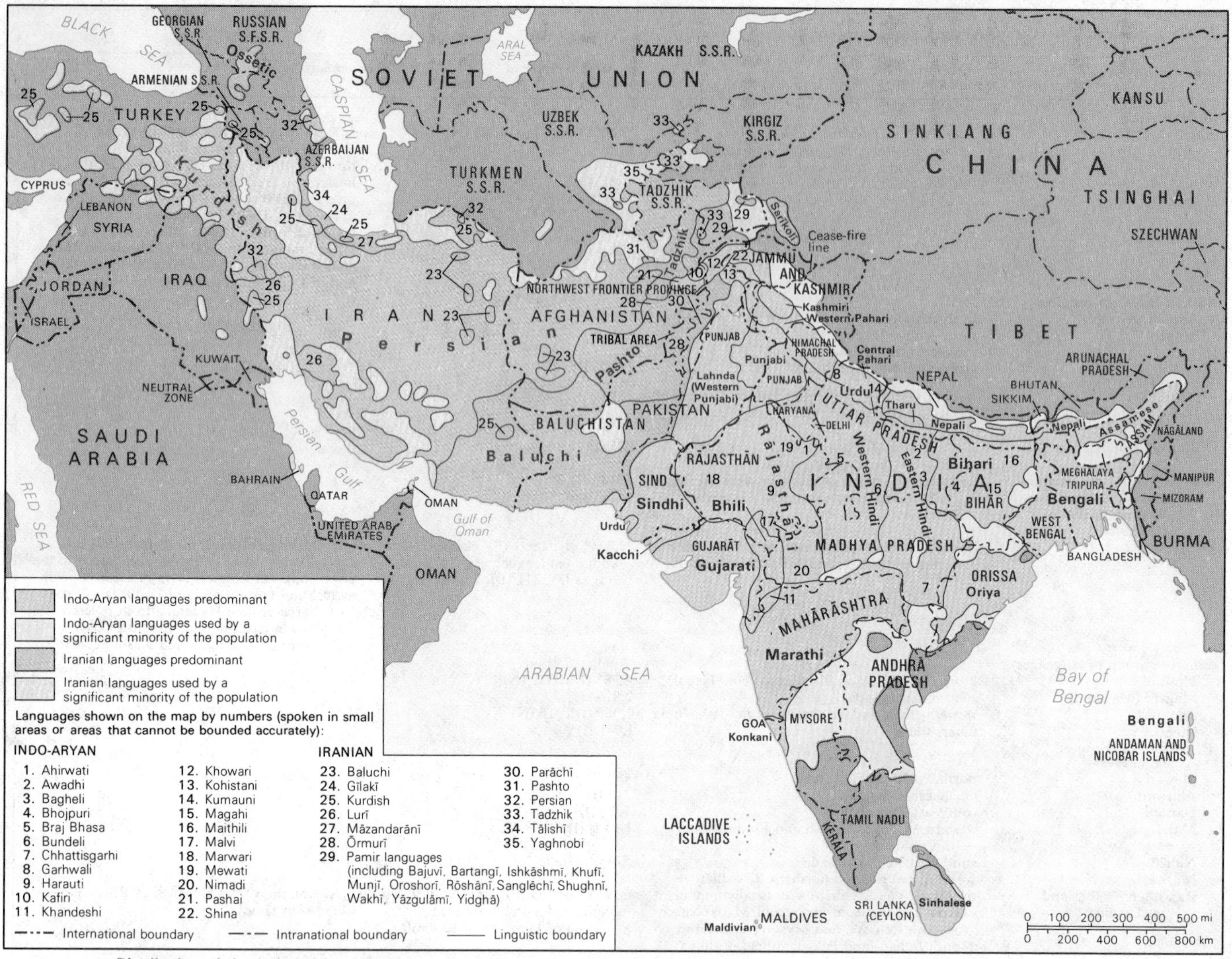

Distribution of the Indo-Iranian languages.
Researched and compiled by Joseph E. Schwartzberg

form predominating; thus, *vīryā* "heroic might" appears once, and *vīryeṇa* occurs ten times (from *vīrya-* "heroic might, act"). In later Vedic *-ena* is the usual ending. All the early Vedic forms are expressly classed as belonging to the sacred language (*chandas*) by Pāṇini.

The verb also shows chronological differences. For example, the 1st person plural ending *-masi* (*e.g.*, *bharāmasi* "we bear") predominates over *-mas* in Ṛgvedic but not in the Atharvaveda; *-mas* becomes the normal ending later. Early Vedic distinguishes between the aorist, imperfect, and perfect tenses. The aorist is commonly used to refer to an action that has recently taken place; the imperfect is a narrative tense referring to actions accomplished in the distant past. The perfect form of the verb originally denoted, as in Greek, a state reached; *e.g.*, *bi-bhāy-a* "is afraid" (root *bhī*). From earliest Vedic, however, this was not always the use of the perfect. Although the grammarian Pāṇini distinguished between the three tenses noted (he said the perfect is used to denote an action beyond one's ken), the perfect and imperfect both came to be used as narrative tenses.

There are also future forms of Vedic, formed with suffixes (*-iṣya* and *-sya*) and used from earliest times. A future form, composed of an agent noun of the type *kartṛ-* "doer" and followed, except in the 3rd person, by forms of the verb *as* "be" (*e.g.*, *kartāsmi* [*kartā asmi*] "I will do"), was recognized as in common use by Pāṇini but is rare in early Vedic.

The injunctive of early Vedic

Early Vedic had a category that went out of use by the late Vedic period of *Brāhmaṇas*—the injunctive, which was formally a form with secondary endings lacking the augment, a prefixed vowel. The injunctive could be used to denote a general truth. A general truth can also be signified by the subjunctive, which is characterized by the vowel *a* affixed to the present, aorist, or perfect stem. Later Vedic retained the injunctive only in negative commands of the type *mā vadhīs* "do not slay." The subjunctive also diminished slowly until it was no longer used; for Pāṇini the subjunctive belonged to sacred literature. The functions of the subjunctive were taken over by the form called optative (and the future form).

Noun forms incorporated into the verb system are numerous in early Vedic. Ṛgvedic has forms with affixes *ya* and *tva* functioning as future passive participles (gerundives); *e.g.*, *vāc-ya-* "to be said," *kar-tva-* "to be performed, done." The Atharvaveda has, additionally, forms with *-(i)tavya* (*hiṃs-itavya-* "to be injured") and *-anīya* (*upa-jīv-anīya-* "to be subsisted upon"). By late Vedic, the type with *tva* had been eliminated; Pāṇini recognized as normal the types *kārya-*, *kartavya-*, *karaṇīya-* "to be done." In Indo-Aryan, from earliest Vedic down to New Indo-Aryan, forms called absolutives (or gerunds) are used to denote the previous of two or more actions performed (usually) by one agent: "having done . . . he did"; for example, *pibā niṣadya* "sit down (*niṣadya* "having sat down") and drink." Ṛgvedic uses *tvī*, *tvā*, *tvāya*, (*t*)*ya* to form absolutives, but these were later reduced to two: *tvā* with a simple verb or one compounded with the negative particle, and *ya* with a verb compounded with a preverb (a preposition-like form).

Early Vedic also uses various case forms of action nouns in the capacity of infinitives; *e.g.*, dative singular *-tave* (*dā-tave* "to give"), genitive singular *-tos* (*dā-tos*), both from a noun in *-tu*, which also supplies the accusa-

Table 2: Sanskrit (Devanāgarī Alphabet and Numerals)

vowels and diphthongs: initial	medial	name	equivalents: EB preferred	alter-natives	approximate* pronunciation
अ		akāra	a		f*u*n
आ	ा	ākāra	ā		f*a*ther
इ	ि	ikāra	i		f*i*ll
ई	ी	īkāra	ī		mach*i*ne
उ	ु	ukāra	u		p*u*ll
ऊ	ू	ūkāra	ū		r*u*de
ऋ	ृ	ṛkāra	ṛ	ṛi, *ri*	litte*r*
ॠ	ॄ	ṝkāra	ṝ	ṛī, *ri*	†
ऌ	ॢ	ḷkāra	ḷ	lṛi, *li*	ab*le*
ए	े	ekāra	e	ē	f*a*de
ऐ	ै	aikāra	ai	āi	s*i*te
ओ	ो	okāra	o	ō	b*o*ne
औ	ौ	aukāra	au	āu	n*ow*

consonants and special signs	name	equivalents: EB preferred	alter-natives	approximate* pronunciation
Gutturals‡				
क	kakāra	k		*k*in
ख	khakāra	kh		blo*ckh*ead
ग	gakāra	g		*g*o
घ	ghakāra	gh		lo*g h*ut
ङ	ṅakāra	ṅ	ñ	si*ng*
Palatals				
च	cakāra	c	ch, *k*	*ch*in
छ	chakāra	ch	chh, *kh*	pi*tch h*ook
ज	jakāra	j	*g*	*j*ob
झ	jhakāra	jh	*gh*	he*dgeh*og
ञ	ñakāra	ñ	n	ca*ny*on
Retroflexed∮				
ट	ṭakāra	ṭ	*t*	po*t*
ठ	ṭhakāra	ṭh	*th*	an*th*ill
ड	ḍakāra	ḍ	*d*	di*d*
ळ	ḷakāra	ḷ	*l*	‖
ढ	ḍhakāra	ḍh	*dh*	a*dh*ere
ण	ṇakāra	ṇ	*n*	ow*n*
Dentals¶				
त	takāra	t		li*tt*le
थ	thakāra	th		boa*t h*ouse
द	dakāra	d		*th*en
ध	dhakāra	dh		an*d h*e
न	nakāra	n		*n*o
Labials♀				
प	pakāra	p		li*p*
फ	phakāra	ph		u*ph*ill
ब	bakāra	b		*b*a*b*y
भ	bhakāra	bh		a*bh*or
म	makāra	m		*m*ai*m*
Semi-vowels				
य	yakāra	y		*y*ard
र	repha	r		*r*a*r*e
ल	lakāra	l		*l*i*l*y
व	vakāra	v		*w*e
Spirants♁				
श	śakāra	ś	ç, *s*	*sh*y (palatalized)
ष	ṣakāra	ṣ	sh	*sh*y (retroflexed)
स	sakāra	s		*s*and
ह	hakāra	h		*h*at
Diacritics				
ः	visarga	ḥ		□
ं	anusvāra	ṃ	n̲	◇
ँ	anunāsika	ṃ	ṁ	◇

numerals

Devanāgarī	Arabic	Devanāgarī	Arabic	Devanāgarī	Arabic
०	0	११	11	२२	22
१	1	१२	12	२३	23
२	2	१३	13	२४	24
३	3	१४	14	२५	25
४	4	१५	15	२६	26
५	5	१६	16	२७	27
६	6	१७	17	२८	28
७	7	१८	18	२९	29
८	8	१९	19	३०	30
९	9	२०	20	१००	100
१०	10	२१	21	१०००	1,000

*These pronunciations apply to Sanskrit. The same symbols sometimes have different values in the modern languages. †Same as *ṛkāra,* but lengthened. ‡Pronounced at back of throat. ∮Pronounced with the tongue curled back against the roof of the mouth. ‖A retroflexed *l*, close to the second *l* in "little." ¶Pronounced with closed teeth. ♀Pronounced with the lips. ♁Breathed. □A diacritical mark indicating aspiration. ◇Diacritical marks indicating nasalization.

tive ending *-tum* (*dā-tum*). There are other types in early Vedic, but the nouns in *-tu* are important; in late Vedic the accusative *-tum* and the genitive *-tos* (construed with *īś* or *śak* "be able, can") became the norm. According to Pāṇini, forms in *-tum* and dative singular forms of action nouns are equivalent variants: *bhok-tuṃ gacchati/ bhojanāya gacchati* "He is going out to eat."

Chronological and dialectical modifications

Dialects. That some forms fell into disuse in the course of Indo-Aryan is natural; the above represent both chronological and dialectal modifications. Such change was recognized by Indian grammarians; *e.g.,* Patañjali, of the mid-2nd century BC, noted that perfect forms of the type *ca-kr-a* "you did, have done" (2nd person plural) were not in use at his time; instead, a nominal (adjective) form *kṛ-ta-vant-as* was used, consisting of the past passive participle *kṛ-ta-* and an adjectival suffix *-vant.* Indian grammarians also recognized the existence of different dialects. Pāṇini noted forms used by northerners (*udīcya*) and easterners (*prācya*), as well as various dialectal uses described by grammarians who preceded him. Earlier documents also afford evidence for dialect variation; *e.g.,* the early Vedic of the Ṛgveda is a dialect in which the Indo-European *l* sound was for the most part replaced by *r*—*prā* "fill," *pūr-ṇa-* "full." This change accords with Iranian; *e.g.,* Avestan *pərəna* "full." These forms contrast with Latin *plenus* and Gothic *fulls,* with *l.* Other dialects kept *l* and *r* distinct. There are also doublets that have both *r* and *l* in words with Indo-European *r: rohita-/lohita-* "red." The variant with *l* can be assumed to belong to an eastern dialect. This variance accords with Middle Indo-Aryan evidence and the fact that such *l* forms become more numerous in the tenth book (*maṇḍala*) of the Ṛgveda, which is demonstrably more recent than the most ancient parts of the

Ṛgveda and dates from a time when the Indo-Aryans had progressed farther east than their original location on the subcontinent. The development of retroflex *ḷ*- and *ḷh*- sounds (produced by curling the tip of the tongue upward toward the hard palate) from the retroflex sounds of *ḍ* (*nīḷa*- "nest" from *nīḍa*-) and *ḍh* when occurring between vowels is another feature characteristic of some dialects, including the major dialect of the Ṛgveda.

Classical Sanskrit. Classical Sanskrit represents a development of one or more such early Old Indo-Aryan dialects. At this state, the archaisms noted above have been eliminated. Moreover, the accentual system of Classical Sanskrit is not the same as that of Vedic, which had a system of pitches; vowels had low, high, or circumflex (first rising, then falling) pitch, and the particular vowel of a word that received high pitch could not be predicted. In Classical Sanskrit, on the other hand, the accent was probably predictable. If the next to the last vowel was long, it received the accent; if not, the vowel preceding it was accented. The Vedic system survived at least to the time of Pāṇini, who described it fully and did not restrict it to sacred language.

Accentual system of Classical Sanskrit

For all this simplification, Classical Sanskrit is considerably more complex than Middle Indo-Aryan. In addition to the vowels *a*, *i*, and *u* (in both long and short varieties), it has *ṛ* and *ḷ* used as vowels. Consonant clusters occur freely, except in word final position, and the system of sound modification conditioned by the context, called *sandhi*, is fully operative. Moreover, in its grammatical system Classical Sanskrit maintains the dual number, seven cases in addition to the vocative form (which marks the one addressed), and a complex set of alternations. For example, to the nominative singular form *agni-s* "fire," correspond the genitive singular *agne-s* "of fire" the nominative plural *agnay-as* "fires," and the instrumental plural *agni-bhis* "with fires," with differing vowels in the second syllable. There are also separate sets of nominal (noun) and pronominal (pronoun) endings. Some nouns and adjectives inflect as pronouns; *e.g.*, *ekasmai*, dative singular masculine-neuter of *eka*- "one."

The verb system of Classical Sanskrit also maintains complex alternations. In the present tense of the type *bhav-a-ti* "becomes, is," the stem (*bhav-a*-) remains unchanged throughout the paradigm except for lengthening of the *-a-* to *-ā-* before *v* and *m*. But other verbs have vowel alternation; *e.g.*, *as-mi* "I am," *s-mas* "we are"; *e-mi* "I go," *i-mas* "we go"; *juhomi* "I pour," *juhumas* "we pour." A distinction is observed between active and mediopassive endings: *jan-ay-a-ti* "engenders" with the active ending *-ti*, but *jā-ya-te* "is born" with the mediopassive ending *-te*. (Mediopassive verb forms are used for the passive, reflexive, and other meanings.)

Classical Sanskrit also has a rich system of nominal and verbal derivatives. Compound words are of the following kinds: copulative (*dvandva*) compounds such as *mātā-pitarau* "mother and father" (also elliptic *pitarau* "parents"); the type like *tat-puruṣa*- "his man," in which the first member is equivalent to a case other than nominative; the type like *bahu-vrīhi* "much-rice," in which the object denoted is other than that of any of the members of the compound (*bahur vrīhir yasya* "He who has much rice"); and adverbial compounds (*avyayībhāva*) of the type *upāgni* (*upa-agni*) "near the fire." In addition, there are derivatives with affixes *-tara-* and *-tama*, such as *priya-tara*- "very dear" and *priya-tama*- "most dear" from the adjective *priya*-. Pronouns have derivatives equivalent to case forms; *e.g.*, *tatra* "there," *yatra* "where," and *kutra* "where?" are equivalent to locative forms such as *tasmin*, *yasmin*, and *kasmin*. These can also be used without a noun.

Among the derivative verbal systems are the causative and the desiderative ("desire to"); the former has an affix *-ay-* (*gam-ay-a-ti* "makes to go," *kār-ay-a-ti* "has do") or, after roots in *-a*, *-pay-* (*sthā-pay-a-ti* "sets in place"). The desiderative is formed with *-sa-* and reduplication (repetition of a part of the root)—*dī-dṛk-ṣa-te* "desires to see" (root *dṛś*). The desiderative also has an agent noun in *-u*—*dī-dṛk-ṣ-u* "who wishes to see."

Middle Indo-Aryan. The Sanskrit word *prākṛta*, whence the term Prākrit, is a derivative from *prakṛti*- "original, nature." Grammarians of the Prākrits generally consider the original from which they derive to be the Sanskrit language as described by grammarians going back to Pāṇini. Most modern scholars consider *prākṛta* to refer to the "natural" languages, the vernaculars, as opposed to Sanskrit, the polished language of literature and the educated (*śiṣṭa*). There is also linguistic evidence to support this view. Several forms in the Prākrits are found in Vedic but not in Classical Sanskrit. As Classical Sanskrit is not directly derivable from any single Vedic dialect, so the Prākrits cannot be said to derive directly from Classical Sanskrit.

The Prākrits

The most archaic literary Prākrit is Pāli, the language of the Buddhist canon (*c.* 5th century BC) and of the later stories and commentaries of Theravāda Buddhism. Pāli represents essentially a western Middle Indo-Aryan dialect, though there are sufficient easternisms in the canon to have led some scholars to the view that the canon as it exists today is a recast of an original in an eastern dialect. To the Buddhist literature also belongs the *Gāndhārī Dhammapada*, the only literary text written in a dialect of the northwest. The Niya documents, official documents written in Prākrit dating from the 3rd century AD, also belong to the northwest. The earliest inscriptional Middle Indo-Aryan is that of the Aśokan inscriptions (3rd century BC). These are more or less full translations from original edicts issued in the language of the east (from the capital Pāṭaliputra in Magadha, modern Patna in Bihār) into the languages of the areas of Aśoka's kingdom. There are other Prākrit inscriptions up to the 4th century AD, and Sanskrit was not used inscriptionally until the first centuries AD. Literary Prākrits other than Pāli were also used in independent works and in dramas along with Sanskrit.

According to Prākrit grammarians, Mahārāṣṭrī ("From the Mahārāshtra Country") is the Prākrit par excellence. It is the language of *kāvya*s (epic poems) such as the *Rāvaṇavaha* (also called *Setubandha*) from no later than the 6th century AD. Mahārāṣṭrī is also the language of lyrics in Rājaśekhara's *Karpūra-mañjarī* (*c.* 900), the only extant drama written completely in Prākrit, and of verses recited by women in the classical drama of Kālidāsa and his successors, though not earlier. The literary dialect used for conversation among higher personages other than the king and his captains in the drama is Śaurasenī, while Māgadhī is used by lower personages.

The language of the early Jaina canon, the final version of which was made in the 5th or 6th century AD, is called Ardhamāgadhī ("Half Māgadhī"); Jaina also used another literary dialect, called Jaina Māhārāṣṭrī in noncanonical works. The oldest poetic work in this is Vimala Sūri's *Paumacariya* (*c.* 3rd century). Of other Prākrit dialects mentioned by grammarians, Paiśācī (or Bhūta-Bhāṣā, both meaning "Language of Demons") is noteworthy; it is said to be the language of the original *Bṛhat-kathā* of Guṇāḍhya, source of the Sanskrit book of stories *Kathā-saritsāgara*.

Buddhist works were also written using a language that has been called Buddhist Hybrid Sanskrit. Among these works is the *Mahāvastu*, the core of which is thought to date from the 2nd century BC. This language is a Middle Indo-Aryan dialect of indeterminate origin, which steadily became more Sanskritized in prose sections of later works.

Buddhist Hybrid Sanskrit

The most advanced stage of Middle Indo-Aryan, Apabhraṃśa, was also used as a literary language. That there was literary creation in Apabhraṃśa by the 6th century is clear from an inscription of King Dharasena II of Valabhī, in which the King praises his father as being adept in Sanskrit, Prākrit, and Apabhraṃśa composition. Moreover, in the fourth act of Kālidāsa's drama *Vikramorvaśīya* there are Apabhraṃśa verses. Because Kālidāsa probably lived in the 3rd or 4th century, literary composition in Apabhraṃśa is earlier still, if these verses are legitimate. There is a great deal of later literature in Apabhraṃśa, for the most part Jaina works; *e.g.*, *Paumacariu* of Svayambhū (8th–9th century), *Harivaṃśa*-

purāṇa of Puṣpadanta (10th century), *Sanatkumāra-cariu* of Haribhadra (12th century).

Linguistic developments. Middle Indo-Aryan is characterized generally by the reduction of the complexities seen in Old Indo-Aryan. The vowel system was reduced by the merger of *ṛ* (and *ḷ*) sounds with vowels and the change of the diphthongs *ai* and *au* to the vowel sounds *e* and *o; e.g.*, Pāli *accha-* "bear" (Sanskrit *ṛkṣa-*), *iṇa-* "debt" (Sanskrit *ṛṇa-*), *uju-* "straight" (Sanskrit *ṛju-*), *pucchati* "asks" (Sanskrit *pṛcchati*), *mettī-* "friendship" (Sanskrit *maitrī-*), *orasa-* "breast-born, legitimate" (Sanskrit *aurasa-*). Moreover, *-aya-* and *-ava-* commonly contracted to *-e-* and *-o-; e.g.*, Pāli *jeti* "conquers" (Sanskrit *jayati*), *odhi-* "limit" (Sanskrit *avadhi-*). Final consonants were deleted, with the exception of *-m*, which developed to an *-ṃ* sound before which a vowel was shortened (Pāli *bhāriyaṃ* "wife"; Sanskrit *bhāryām*). Together with the trend toward replacing variable consonant stems by unchanging stems in *-a-*, this change had serious consequences for the grammar. Consonant stems steadily disappeared and were transformed to stems ending in a vowel; *e.g.*, to Sanskrit *śarad-* "autumn," *sarit-* "stream," and *sarpis-* "butter" correspond the Pāli forms *sarada-*, *saritā*, and *sappi-*. Consonant clusters were also modified in Middle Indo-Aryan; *e.g.*, Pāli *khetta-* "field" (corresponding to Sanskrit *kṣetra-*), Pāli *dakkhiṇa-* "right, south" (Sanskrit *dakṣiṇa*), *aggi-* "fire" (Sanskrit *agni-*), *puṇṇa-* "full" (Sanskrit *pūrṇa*), and *taṇhā-* "thirst" (Sanskrit *tṛṣṇā-*). The shortening of vowels before modified consonant clusters led to the use of short *ĕ* and *ŏ* sounds, which were unknown in Old Indo-Aryan; *e.g.*, Pāli *sĕmha-* "phlegm" (Sanskrit *śleṣman*), *ŏṭṭha-* "lip" (Sanskrit *oṣṭha-*).

The above phenomena are not restricted to Pāli; they are pan-Middle Indo-Aryan. Differences between Pāli and Aśokan and other Prākrits include the retention of voiceless stops (*i.e., p, t, k*) between vowels in Pāli and Aśokan dialects; other Middle Indo-Aryan dialects modify them. The extreme development appears in literary Māhārāṣṭrī, in which unaspirated stops (pronounced without an accompanying audible release, or puff of breath) other than retroflexes (*ṭ, ḍ*) and labials (*p, b*) were deleted, aspirated stops (pronounced with an audible puff of breath) were replaced by *h*, retroflexes (pronounced by curling the tongue upward toward the hard palate) became voiced, and labials were replaced by *v; e.g., loa-* "world" (Sanskrit *loka-*), *loaṇa-* "eye" (Sanskrit *locana-*), *sāhā-* "branch" (Sanskrit *śākhā-*), *paḍhai* "recites, reads" (Sanskrit *paṭhati*), and *savaha-* "curse" (Sanskrit *śapatha-*).

Characteristics of literary Māhārāṣṭrī

Essentially on the same level are the dialects of Jaina texts, but in these a *y* glide prescribed by grammarians occurs when a consonant is elided: *vayaṇa-* "face" (Sanskrit *vadana-*); *sayala-* "whole" (Sanskrit *sakala-*). In Śaurasenī, on the other hand, voiceless stops (*e.g., p, t, k*) between vowels are voiced (*e.g.*, become *b, d, g*, respectively); *e.g., ido* "hence" (Sanskrit *itaḥ*); *tadhā* "thus" (Sanskrit *tathā*). Though Pāli and Aśokan are at an earlier level of development with respect to these changes, they share with the rest of the Middle Indo-Aryan dialects the replacement of voiced aspirated sounds between vowels by *h: lahu-* "light, unimportant" from *laghu-*; *dahati* "gives" (Sanskrit *dadhāti*). Similarly, they share the change of *dy-* to *j: joti-* "light, brilliance" (Pāli *jotati* "shines," Sanskrit *dyotate*). Pāli and Aśokan, however, retain a *y* sound, changed to *j* in most other Prākrits; *e.g.*, the pronoun *ya-* (feminine *yā-*), as in Sanskrit, opposed to *ja-*.

The deletion of stop consonants noted above resulted in vowel sequences within words that were unknown to Old Indo-Aryan. Similarly, the extent of *sandhi* modification was restricted in Middle Indo-Aryan. The Middle Indo-Aryan vowels *ī* and *ū* do not change to *y* and *v* before dissimilar vowels in compounds; *e.g.*, Māhārāṣṭrī *rattī-andhaa-* "dark of night" (Sanskrit *rātry-andhaka-*). In addition, the first of two contiguous vowels in different words is subject to deletion; *e.g.*, Pāli *manas'icchasi* (from *manasā icchasi*) "you wish in your mind."

In its grammatical system, Middle Indo-Aryan also reduced complexities. The dual number no longer exists as a separate category; for Sanskrit *dvābhyām* "by two," Middle Indo-Aryan has *dohi(ṃ)*, with the ending *-hi(ṃ)* equivalent to the instrumental plural *-bhis* of Old Indo-Aryan. Among other changes is the replacement of the dative case by the genitive except in particular usages; *e.g.*, the use of forms corresponding to the Old Indo-Aryan dative to denote a purpose.

In Middle Indo-Aryan, nominal and pronominal forms are no longer strictly segregated; *e.g.*, Aśokan *vijitamhi* "in the kingdom" (also *vijite*) has a pronominal ending equivalent to Sanskrit *-smin*.

Middle Indo-Aryan verb system

In the verb system, the contrast between active (*-ti*) and mediopassive (*-te*) endings was obliterated. Further, the Old Indo-Aryan distinction between aorist, imperfect, and perfect forms was eliminated. With few exceptions, the sigmatic aorist (an aorist form with *s*) provides the only productive preterite of early Middle Indo-Aryan: Aśokan *ni-kkhamisu* "they set out" (Sanskrit *nir-a-kramiṣur*). In later Prākrits verbally inflected preterites were generally eliminated; in their place was used the past participle. For example, in Śaurasenī *devi uva-visa, mahā-rāo vi ā-ado* "Sit down, my queen, the king also has arrived," the past participle *ā-ado* (Sanskrit *ā-gataḥ*) agrees with *mahā-rāo* "king" (Sanskrit *mahā-rājaḥ*) in number and gender. If the verb is transitive, the participle agrees with the direct object, and the agent is denoted by an instrumental form: in Jaina Māhārāṣṭrī, *teṇa vi savvaṃ siṭṭhaṃ* "He has told everything," *teṇa* "by him" denotes the agent, and *siṭṭhaṃ* "told" (Sanskrit *śiṣṭam*) agrees with the neuter singular form *savvaṃ* (Sanskrit *sarvam*). When no object is denoted, the verb is in the neuter singular. Old Indo-Aryan used both the participial construction and the finite verb; thus to Prākrit *so vi teṇa samaṃ gao* "He also went with him" could correspond Sanskrit *so'pi tena saha gataḥ* or *so'pi tena sahāgamat* (*saha agamat*). The Middle Indo-Aryan development eliminated the latter.

Alternations of the Sanskrit type *as-mi, s-mas* were eliminated in Middle Indo-Aryan; the predominant type of present tense was formed from an unchanging vowel stem (Pāli *e-ti, e-nti* "go[es]").

Nominal forms of the verb system are of the same types as Old Indo-Aryan; *e.g.*, the Pāli future passive participle *kātabba-* (Sanskrit *kartavya-*) "to be done," Śaurasenī *karaṇia;* Ardhamāgadhī, Jaina Māhārāṣṭrī, and Māhārāṣṭrī *karaṇijja-* "to be done." The infinitive is commonly formed on the present tense stem, not on the root, as in Old Indo-Aryan. Thus Pāli *pappotum* is formed on the present *pappoti;* Sanskrit *prāptum* is formed on the root *prāp*, present tense *prāpnoti*.

Dialects. Middle Indo-Aryan shows evidence of dialectal differentiation. The earliest documents that allow one to determine roughly the dialect distribution are Aśoka's inscriptions. These represent three major dialect areas: east, as in the inscriptions of Jaugaḍa, Dhauli, and Kālsī; west, in Girnār; and northwest, in Mānsehrā and Shāhbāzgaṛhī. Characteristic of the east dialect area is final *-e*, corresponding to *-o* in the west and *-as* in Sanskrit; in the east dialect area *l* also regularly corresponds to *r* of the west and of Sanskrit. Moreover, in the east dialect area there is a tendency to insert a vowel within consonant clusters, while in the west and northwest one of the consonants is assimilated to the other without an intervening vowel. For example, to Sanskrit *rājñas* "of the king" corresponds Girnār *rañño*, Shāhbāzgaṛhī *raño*, Jaugaḍa *lājine*. Northwest stands apart in retaining three spirant sounds, *ś, ṣ, s*, which merge to *s* elsewhere. Aśoka's eastern dialect, from the Magadha country, shows an *s* sound for Old Indo-Aryan *ś, ṣ, s*, rather than the *ś* sound typical of literary Māgadhī. Grammatical features also show dialectal variation; *e.g.*, the Aśokan dative singular form is *-āya* in the western dialects (Girnār *atthāya* "for the purpose of") but *-āye* in the east (Kālsī, Dhauli *aṭṭhāye*).

Apabhraṃśa. As noted above, the most advanced development of Middle Indo-Aryan is seen in Apabhraṃśa. Sound changes that are typical of Apabhraṃśa include the replacement of the vowel sound *a* by *u* in final syllables; *e.g.*, *karahu* "you do, make," corresponding to *karaha* (*karadha*) in other Prākrits. From stems in *-aya-* develop forms in *-au* and nasalized *-aũ* (nasalization is here indicated by a tilde): *bhaḍārau* "honored one, king" (Prākrit *bhaṭṭārayo*), *haũ* "I" (Aśokan *hakaṃ*). Nasalization also appears in environments in which earlier *m* occurred between vowels; *e.g.*, *gāũ* "village" (from *gāma*, Sanskrit *grāma*). Numerous other sound changes are evident, among them the development of *-s*(*s*)- between vowels into *h: tahŏ* "of him" (from Prākrit *tassa*, Sanskrit *tasya*); *hohinti* "will be" (compare Pāli *-hossati*). Apabhraṃśa contractions, such as *-aya-* changing to *-a* and *-iya* to *-ī*, foreshadow New Indo-Aryan, in which the development was extended; *e.g.*, Apabhraṃśa *pāṇiu* "water" (Old Indo-Aryan *pāniyam*), Gujarati *pāṇī*, Hindi *pānī*.

In other points Apabhraṃśa also presaged New Indo-Aryan. The interest of Apabhraṃśa lies in the fact that contracted forms presage the New Indo-Aryan opposition of masculine, neuter, and feminine nouns; thus, Apabhraṃśa *-au*, *-aũ*, *-ī*, Gujarati *-o*, *-ũ*, *-ī* (*gayo*, *gayũ*, *gaī* "went"), Hindi *-ā*, *-ī* (*gayā*, *gaī*). The case system of Apabhraṃśa is also at a more advanced level of disintegration than that of earlier Middle Indo-Aryan, with the instrumental and locative plurals being identical in form (*-ahĩ* or *-ehĩ* for *-a*-stems) and instrumental singular forms also being used as locatives.

In the Apabhraṃśa verb system, present tense stems in *-a* predominate. Apabhraṃśa verb endings differ from those of other Prākrits. Most interesting is the 3rd person plural type *kara-hĩ* "they do," which coexists with *karanti*. The form *kara-hĩ*, corresponding to the 3rd person singular *kara-i* "he does," is formed on the model of the pair *kara-ũ* (1st person singular, "I do") and *kara-hũ* (1st person plural, "we do"). Here again Apabhraṃśa comes close to New Indo-Aryan. Moreover, Apabhraṃśa has some causative formations that do not occur elsewhere in Middle Indo-Aryan but are known from New Indo-Aryan—*bham-āḍa-i* "causes to turn," Gujarati *bhamāṛe che* "causes to turn round," and *pais-āra-i* "causes to enter," Gujarati *pɛsāre che* "causes to enter, to penetrate."

Apabhraṃśa syntactic patterns

Also noteworthy are two syntactic usages that closely parallel New Indo-Aryan. The present participle is used as a conditional; *e.g.*, *jai haũ mi teṇa sahũ tau karantu to kiṃ asamāhie sahũ marantu* "Even if I had performed (*karantu*) ascetic acts with him, would I have died without mental concentration?" in which the participles *karantu* and *marantu* have conditional value. In Sanskrit the conditionals *a-kar-iṣya-m* and *a-mar-iṣya-m* are used; but in Gujarati one would say *jo hũ . . . karat . . . to marat*, and Hindi would have the forms *kartā . . . martā*. The Apabhraṃśa gerundive in *-iv(v)a* or *-ev(v)a* can be used as an infinitive; *e.g.*, *pi-evae laggā* "began to drink." This is the Gujarati construction *pi-vā lāgyo* "began to drink," in which *pi-vā* is an inflected form of *pi-vũ*, a verbal noun (infinitive) corresponding etymologically to the Apabhraṃśa gerundive.

Influences on Middle Indo-Aryan. In the mid-2nd century BC, the grammarian Patañjali explained that to speak faultlessly the language now called Sanskrit (as described by Pāṇini) one should imitate the correct speakers (called *śiṣṭa* "learned, educated") of Āryāvarta ("Country of the Aryans"). Earlier, the grammarian Kātyāyana (*c.* 3rd–4th century BC) noted that Pāṇini gave lists of verb roots in order that certain Middle Indo-Aryan forms not be classed as correctly derived from a Sanskrit verb root. Moreover, Patañjali noted that one should study grammar in order not to use incorrect words such as *helayaḥ* instead of *herayaḥ* (a phrase used in calling to people) or *gāvī* instead of *gauḥ* "cow"; *gāvī* is a Middle Indo-Aryan word. The observations of these grammarians would lend support to the view that by the 6th or 5th century BC Sanskrit as a medium of learned conversation coexisted with Middle Indo-Aryan. Further, the Pāli canon records that the Buddha enjoined his followers to use the vernaculars in communicating his teachings, and the Jaina canon gives Ardhamāgadhī as the language used for communicating the teachings of Mahāvīra. Similarly, Aśoka used Middle Indo-Aryan, not Sanskrit, in the inscriptions he ordered written throughout his kingdom; Sanskrit does not appear on inscriptions until the early centuries AD (*e.g.*, Rudravarman's inscription at Junagarh, *c.* AD 150). The coexistence of Old Indo-Aryan and Middle Indo-Aryan is to be accepted even for the time when the earliest Old Indo-Aryan texts were put to writing.

Middle Indo-Aryan shows similar evidence of the influence of linguistically more advanced vernaculars on literary compositions. The Prākrits of elegant literary compositions must have been artificial, different in many respects from the vernaculars current at the time, though reflecting languages that were current at some former time. The Old Indo-Aryan and Middle Indo-Aryan stages, then, present a picture of concurrent vernaculars with dialects and literary languages influenced by the vernaculars; it is impossible to compartmentalize the different stages as beginning and ending at any definite date.

Sources of borrowing into Indo-Aryan

The literary languages borrowed from earlier languages. There are Prākritisms (*i.e.*, forms of earlier Prākrits) in Apabhraṃśa; *e.g.*, the genitive singular ending *-ssa* instead of *-hŏ* and 2nd person plural verb forms in *-ha* instead of *-hu*. All the literary Prākrits used Sanskrit as a source for borrowing words. Words that came into the Prākrits from Sanskrit with no change in form are called *saṃskṛta-sama* "identical with Sanskrit" (or *tat-sama* "identical with that") and are contrasted with words termed *saṃskṛta-bhava* (*tad-bhava*) "whose origin is in Sanskrit"—that is, words that the grammarians can derive from Sanskrit by using certain rules. Another class of words, called *deśya* (or *deśī*) "belonging to the area, country," includes items that the grammarians cannot derive easily from Sanskrit and that are supposed to have been in use in particular areas from early times.

Many or most of the *deśya* words are indeed derivable from Sanskrit, but some are of Dravidian origin; *e.g.*, *akka* "sister" (Telugu *akka*), *attā* "father's sister" (Telugu *atta*), *appa* "father" (Telugu *appa*), *ūra* "village" (Telugu *ūru*), *pulli* "tiger" (Telugu *puli*). Borrowing from Dravidian occurred also at earlier times; the Dravidians originally occupied territory much farther north than they did in Middle Indo-Aryan times. The Ṛgveda has such words as *kuṇḍa* "pitcher, pot," which is doubtless of Dravidian origin (Tamil *kuṭam* "pot"). Such borrowings become more numerous in later Sanskrit. It is not always certain that borrowing proceeded from Dravidian to Indo-Aryan, however, because Dravidian languages freely borrowed from Indo-Aryan. Thus, some scholars claim that Sanskrit *kaṭu* "sharp, pungent" is from Dravidian, but others claim that it is a Middle Indo-Aryan form deriving from an earlier **kṛt-u* "cutting" (root *kṛt*). (An asterisk [*] preceding a form indicates that it is not attested but has been reconstructed as a hypothetical form.) Whatever the judgment on any individual word, it is clear that Indo-Aryan did borrow from Dravidian, and this phenomenon is important in considering a group of sounds that sets Indo-Aryan apart from the rest of Indo-European—the retroflexes. Without doubt the influence of Dravidian is to be considered as contributing to the extension of these sounds beyond their limited occurrence in inherited Indo-European items such as *nīḍa* "nest" (from **ni-sd-o*), *iṣ-ṭa* "desired" (from **is-to*), and *stīr-ṇa* "spread out" (from **stṝ-no*). The Munda languages (or, more generally, the Austro-Asiatic languages) are also a source of some borrowing into Indo-Aryan; *e.g.*, Sanskrit *jambāla* "mud" (Santali *jọbọ*).

In the 8th century AD, the philosopher Kumārila mentioned not only Dravidian but also Persian and Greek as sources of foreign words. Such borrowing goes back to early times. In the 6th century BC Darius counted Gandhāra as a province of his kingdom, and Alexander the Great penetrated into northern India in the 4th century BC. From Iranian come words such as that meaning "inscription, writing, script"; in the northwest inscriptions of Aśoka the word is *dipi* (Old Persian *dipi*) and Sanskrit has *lipi*, the form in other Aśokan versions and in Pāli. Also from Persian is Sanskrit *kṣatrapa* "satrap"—Old Persian *xšassa-pāvan-*. Of Greek origin are such mathematical and astronomical terms as Sanskrit *kendra* "centre" (Greek *kéntron*), *jāmitra* "diameter" (*diámetron*), and *horā* "hour" (*hṓra*). *Yavana* "foreigner," originally the Greek word for Ionian, is known from as early as the time of Pāṇini. Later, Arabic words such as *taślī* "trigon" came into Sanskrit.

Division of India into linguistic states

The modern Indo-Aryan stage. The division of the Indian subcontinent into linguistic states and even into countries (Pakistan, Bangladesh, and India) is a recent phenomenon. Even after independence and partition, Bombay state existed until it was split into Gujarāt and Mahārāshtra states in 1960. Punjab was split into Punjab and Haryana states in 1966 as a result of Punjabi agitation for a separate linguistic state. Before independence, under British rule (entrenched from the 18th century), there were princely states within dialect areas; under Mughal rule (16th–18th centuries), Persian was the language of the court and of courts of justice and continued in the latter function for a time under the British. Though Hindi–Urdu may have been a lingua franca, however, the great dialectal diversity of earlier times continued.

Some of the modern Indo-Aryan languages have literary traditions reaching back centuries, with enough textual continuity to distinguish Old, Middle, and Modern Bengali, Gujarati, and so on. Bengali can trace its literature back to Old Bengali *caryā-padas*, late Buddhist verses thought to date from the 10th century; Gujarati literature dates from the 12th century (Śālibhadra's *Bharateśvara-bāhubali-rāsa*) and to a period when the area of western Rājasthān and Gujarāt are believed to have had a literary language in common, called Old Western Rajasthani. Jñāneśvara's commentary on the *Bhagavadgītā* in Old Marathi dates from the 13th century and early Maithili from the 14th century (Jyotīśvara's *Varṇa-ratnākara*), while Assamese literary work dates from the 14th and 15th centuries (Mādhava Kandalī's translation of the *Rāmāyaṇa*, Śaṅkaradeva's Vaiṣṇaviṭe works). Also of the 14th century are the Kashmiri poems of Lallā (*Lallā-vākyāni*), and Nepali works have also been assigned to this epoch. The work of Jagannāth Dās in Old Oriya dates from the 15th century.

Amīr Khosrow used the term *hindvī* in the 13th century, and he composed couplets that contained Hindi. In early times, however, other dialects were predominant in the midlands (Madhyadeśa) as literary media, especially Braj Bhasa (*e.g.*, Sūrdās' *Sūrsāgar*, 16th century) and Awadhi (*Rāmcaritmānas* of Tulsīdās, 16th century). In the south, in Golconda (Andhra, near Hyderābād), Urdu poetry was seriously cultivated in the 17th century, and Urdu poets later came north to Delhi and Lucknow. Punjabi was used in Sikh works as early as the 16th century, and Sindhi was used in Ṣūfī (Islāmic) poetry of the 17th–19th centuries. In addition, there is evidence in late Middle Indo-Aryan works for the use of early New Indo-Aryan; *e.g.*, provincial words and verses are cited.

The creation of linguistic states has reinforced the use of certain standard dialects for communication within a state in official transactions, teaching, and on the radio. In addition, attempts are being made to evolve standardized technical vocabularies in these languages. Dialectal diversity has not ceased, however, resulting in much bilingualism; for example, a native speaker of Braj Bhasa uses Hindi for communicating in large cities such as Delhi.

Attempt to establish one national language

Moreover, the attempt to establish a single national language other than English continues. This search has its origin in national and Hindu movements of the 19th century down to the time of Mahatma Gandhi, who promoted the use of a simplified Hindi–Urdu, called Hindustani. The constitution of India in 1947 stressed the use of Hindi, providing for it to be the official national language after a period of 15 years during which English would continue in use. When the time came, however, Hindi could not be declared the sole national language; English remains a co-official language. Though Hindi can claim to be the lingua franca of a large population in North India, other languages such as Bengali have long and great literary traditions—including the work of Nobel Prize winner Rabindranath Tagore—and equal status as intellectual languages, so that resistance to the imposition of Hindi exists. This resistance is even stronger in Dravidian-speaking southern India. The use of English as an official language entails problems, however, because with the use of state languages for education, the level of English competence is lowering. Another danger faced is the agitation for more separate linguistic states, threatening India with linguistic fragmentation hearkening back to earlier days.

CHARACTERISTICS OF THE MODERN INDO-ARYAN LANGUAGES

The trends noted in Middle Indo-Aryan continue in New Indo-Aryan. The Middle Indo-Aryan vowel sequences *ai* and *au* were changed to single vowels during the development of New Indo-Aryan, final vowels were shortened and deleted, and *ḍ* and *ḍh* sounds between vowels were replaced by the sounds *ṛ* and *ṛh*. The noun cases were further reduced, and the introduction of nominal (noun) forms into the verb system became more pronounced.

Literary languages tend to become somewhat removed from the usual standard colloquial. Literary, or High, Hindi, for example, tends to replace some of the Perso-Arabic vocabulary with Sanskritic items, whereas literary Urdu makes great use of Perso-Arabic words. The gap is formalized in Bengali, in which a distinction is made between the highly Sanskritic language Sadhu-Bhaṣa and the colloquial standard called Calit-Bhasa.

Phonology. [Note: The forms of the words given below reflect actual pronunciation, rather than being transliterated versions of the standard orthographies. For New Indo-Aryan the symbols *ə*, pronounced as the *a* in English "sofa," and *a* are used for the sounds earlier transcribed as *a* and *ā*, respectively; *e.g.*, Gujarati *karū̃* "I do" and *māro* "beat" are now written *kərū̃* and *maro*. This practice permits certain contrasts to be made among sounds that are significant in the description of dialectal features. In Kashmiri words, *a* is short, opposed to *ā*.]

Vowel changes in New Indo-Aryan

Vowels in sequence contracted in early New Indo-Aryan; *e.g.*, Old Indo-Aryan *aśīti* became Middle Indo-Aryan *asīi*, Hindi and Punjabi *əssī*, and Bengali *aśi* "80." Further, *ai* and *au* sounds changed to *e* and *o*, and *aū* to *ū*, while *iu* developed into *ī*. The diphthongs *ai* and *au* were retained well into the New Indo-Aryan period and are still pronounced in some areas; *e.g.*, Braj Bhasa *kərəū̃* "I do," *kərəi* "he does." Middle Indo-Aryan -*ḍ*- and -*ḍh* developed into the flaps *ṛ* and *ṛh*; *e.g.*, Prākrit *sāḍiā* "woman's garment," Kashmiri, Lahnda, Hindi, Gujarati, Bhojpuri, Bengali, Oriya *saṛī* "sari"; and Prākrit *paḍh*- "recite, read," Sindhi *pəṛh-əṇu*, Lahnda *pəṛh-əṇ*, Hindi, Punjabi *pəṛh-na*, Gujarati *pəṛh-vū̃*, Marathi *pəṛh-ṇə* "study."

Stress is not generally contrastive in New Indo-Aryan as it is, for example, in English (*e.g.*, noun "éxport," verb "expórt"), though different areas have different rules for placing major emphasis on a given syllable. For example, in Hindi, in which vowel length is pertinent, *gilá* "swallowed" has major stress on the last syllable, *gī́la* "wet," on the first. In Gujarati, on the other hand, vowel length is not pertinent; the stress position depends on which vowels occur in contiguous syllables and on the structure of the syllables, whether open or closed; *e.g.*, *júno* "old," but *dukán* "store." In Bengali each syllable of a word receives about equal stress.

The sounds that most clearly distinguish Indo-Aryan from the rest of Indo-European are the voiced aspirate stops (*gh* and the like, pronounced with an accompanying audible puff of breath) and the retroflexes (*ṭ* and so on, pronounced by curling the tongue upward toward the hard palate). In the outlying New Indo-Aryan areas, however, the sound system is reduced. Sinhalese has no aspirated stops, Assamese has no retroflexes, and Kashmiri has no voiced aspirates. The geographic position of these languages doubtless contributed to these losses: Sinhalese coexists with Tamil, Assamese is surrounded by Tibeto-Burman languages, and Kashmiri is on the border of the Iranian area.

New Indo-Aryan shows evidence of early dialect distribution; this is discernible by considering sound changes proper to each group. The eastern group (Assamese, Ben-

Early New Indo-Aryan dialect distribution

gali, Oriya) has three important changes. Long and short *i* and *u* merged; *e.g.*, Assamese *nila*, Oriya *niḷɔ* (ɔ is similar to the *o* of "coffee" in some English dialects), Bengali *nil* "blue-black" but Sanskrit *nīla;* Assamese *dhuli*, Bengali *dhulo*, Oriya *dhuḷi* "dust" but Hindi *dhūl* and Sanskrit *dhūli*. The vowel sound *a* of Middle Indo-Aryan was replaced by ɔ in Bengali and Oriya and ɒ (similar to the *o* of "hot" in southern British English) in Assamese in initial position and open syllables; *e.g.*, Bengali *mɔron*, Oriya *mɔrɔn*, Assamese *mɒrɒn* "death"; Sindhi *mərəno* "mortal, death," Sinhalese *mərəṇə*, Gujarati, Marathi *mərəṇ* (compare Sanskrit *maraṇa-*). Moreover, in this group a vowel is affected by the quality of the vowel in a following syllable. For example, in Bengali *ami kori* "I do," the verb root has *o* followed by *i* in the next syllable, but *tumi kɔro* "you do" has an ɔ sound; similarly, *ami kini* "I buy" but *tumi keno*. As a result of vowel assimilation also, Assamese has an ɔ sound instead of ɒ representing Middle Indo-Aryan *a:* Assamese *xɔhur*, Bengali *šɔšur* "husband's father" (compare Hindi *səsur*, Prākrit *sasura-*, Sanskrit *śvaśura-*).

Assamese and Bengali are set off from Oriya. In the former two, Middle Indo-Aryan *ḍ* and *ḍh* merge medially to *ḍ* (then *ṛ*) with a subsequent development to *r* in Assamese; *e.g.*, Oriya *daṛhi*, Bengali *daṛi*, Assamese *dari* "beard"; Hindi, Gujarati *daṛhī*, Prākrit *dāḍhiā*. Assamese is also distinguished from Bengali by several developments, among them the merger of Assamese retroflex sounds with dental sounds; *e.g.*, Assamese *ut* "camel" but Bengali *uṭ*, Oriya *oṭɔ*, Sindhi *uṭhu*, Lahnda, Pahari *uṭṭh*, and so on. Assamese also has *s* for earlier *c* and *ch* sounds and a *z* sound for *j* and *jh; e.g.*, Assamese *kas* "glass," Bengali *kac;* Assamese *azi* "today," Oriya *aji*, Bengali, Hindi *aj*. In addition, Assamese replaced an *s* sound initially by *x* and between vowels by *h—xɔhur*.

Particular sound changes also characterize languages of the northwest. In this group, an older voiceless stop (*e.g.*, *t*) became voiced (*e.g.*, became *d*) after a nasal sound; in other areas, the voiceless stop is retained: Kashmiri *dand*, Punjabi *dənd*, Sindhi *ḍəndu* "tooth" (the *ḍ* in Sindhi is an imploded stop; see below) but Assamese, Bengali, Hindi, Gujarati, Marathi *dāt*, Sinhalese *dətə* (Sanskrit *danta-*). Moreover, in the northwest group a voiced stop (*e.g.*, *d*) preceded by a nasal was assimilated to the latter, resulting in two nasals, which were subsequently reduced to one in some areas; in the rest of New Indo-Aryan, the vowel preceding the nasal was nasalized. Thus, Kashmiri *don* "churning stick," Sindhi *ḍənu* "tribute," Punjabi *dənn* "fine," Lahnda *ḍənn* "force," Kumauni *dan* "roof" contrast with Assamese *dãr* "pole," Bengali *dãṛ* "oar," Hindi *dãḍ* "oppression, fine," and others; all forms derive from Old Indo-Aryan *daṇḍa-* "stick, staff, club, royal power, fine, punishment."

In the sequence of a short vowel followed by two consonants, Pahari differs from the rest of the northwest group and agrees with the rest of New Indo-Aryan. In the northwest this sequence either remained unchanged or the cluster was simplified without lengthening of the vowel; other languages generally simplified the cluster and lengthened the vowel: Punjabi *bhətt*, Sindhi *bhətu*, Lahnda *bhət*, Kashmiri *bati* "cooked rice, food" but Nepali, Kumauni, Hindi, Assamese, Bengali, Gujarati, Marathi *bhat*.

Sound changes in Dardic

Dardic occupies a special position. The sibilant sounds did not all merge here. For example, Kashmiri, a Dardic tongue, has *šurah* "16" with *š* rather than *s*, as in most other Indo-Aryan languages, and *sat* "7" with *s*. Further, voiced aspirated stops merged with unaspirated stops in Dardic; *e.g.*, Kashmiri *gur* "horse" but Hindi *ghoṛa;* Kashmiri *dɔd* "milk" but Hindi *dūdh*.

One major feature distinguishing Sindhi from the rest of the northwest group is the development of a series of imploded stops (also called suction stops and recursive stops), for *b*, *d*, *j*, and *g*. Implosive stops also occur in the Sindhi vicinity; for example, Kacchi has imploded *b*. Another feature that distinguishes Sindhi from other northwest languages, including Kacchi, is the retention of the Middle Indo-Aryan final short vowels; *e.g.*, Sindhi *əkhi* "eye" but Hindi *ãkh* (Middle Indo-Aryan *akkhi-*).

Punjabi is distinguished from other members of the northwest group by its tonal system, having low (\`), mid (¯), and high (´) tones. Initial voiced aspirated stops of earlier Indo-Aryan appear in Punjabi as voiceless stops with low tone on the following vowel; *e.g.*, Punjabi *kòṛa* but Hindi *ghoṛa;* Punjabi *tãĩ* "2½" but Hindi *ḍhāī*. Non-initially, a voiced aspirate became unaspirated and the preceding vowel received high tone; thus, Punjabi *dúd* "milk" but Hindi *dūdh*, and Punjabi *láb* "profit" but Hindi *labh*.

Gujarati, Marathi, and Konkani in the west and southwest differ from the languages of the midlands in that, as in the east, there is no contrast between long and short *i* and *u* vowels. The *i* of Gujarati and Marathi *vis* "20" is pronounced like the *ee* of English "teeth," the *i* of Gujarati *iccha* and Marathi *iččha* "wish" like the *i* of "pitch," but such a difference is not contrastive, as it is in Hindi (*gīla* "wet": *gila* "swallowed"). Gujarati has certain features that, in turn, set it apart from the other languages of this group. In addition to *e* and *o* sounds, it has the open vowels ɛ, ɔ; *e.g.*, *cɔthũ* "fourth" (Middle Indo-Aryan *cauttha*), *bɛs-vũ* "to sit" (Middle Indo-Aryan *baisai* "sits"). Moreover, Gujarati has murmured vowels, generally developed from vowels followed by *h;* *e.g.*, *kɛh che* "says" (*h* represents murmuring of the vowel), Old Gujarati *kahai chai*. Marathi and Konkani have two series of affricate sounds; *e.g.*, *č* (pronounced as the *ch* in English "chat"; the equivalent of *c* in some other languages) and *c* (pronounced as the *ts* of "rats").

There was clearly mutual influence of Indo-Aryan languages at an early time, together with movement of groups of speakers (compare the position of Pahari). Thus, while Punjabi *sacc* "true" is the expected form comparable to Middle Indo-Aryan *sacca-* (Old Indo-Aryan *satya-*), Hindi *səc* "true" does not represent the expected outcome. The item *səc* must come from the Punjabi area.

Gender in New Indo-Aryan

Grammar. Like Middle Indo-Aryan, New Indo-Aryan distinguishes only two numbers—singular and plural. Unlike Middle Indo-Aryan, the New Indo-Aryan languages differ in the degree to which gender distinctions are made. Three genders are retained in the west and southwest (Gujarati, Marathi, Konkani), and this is true also of Sinhalese. Unlike Gujarati, Marathi, and Konkani, in which every noun, whether it denotes an animate being or not, has a particular gender that is unpredictable, Sinhalese restricts masculine and feminine gender to animates and neuter to inanimates. The eastern group (Assamese, Bengali, Oriya) has no grammatical gender distinctions, and two genders are distinguished elsewhere.

Over a large area of New Indo-Aryan the noun has only two cases—direct and oblique. A lack of distinction between direct and oblique cases in the plural is typical of several languages, including forms in Hindi, Gujarati, Marathi, and Bhojpuri. Direct forms are used independently, oblique forms before postpositions (words or word elements following a noun that function similarly to English prepositions) and other affixes; the combination of stem and postposition serves the function of inflected case forms of earlier Indo-Aryan. Thus, to denote an object (direct or indirect) Hindi uses the postposition *ko*, which occurs in direct object constructions normally only with nouns denoting animate beings; *e.g.*, *ləṛke-ko dekh-ta hɛ* "He sees the boy," *ləṛke-ko miṭhaī do* "Give a sweet to the boy." Other postpositions are *mẽ* "in," *pər* "on," *se* "from, with, by means of." A large group of postpositions are linked to the noun with the affix *ka* (oblique form *ke*, feminine *kī*), which also is used to form adjectives (possessives); *e.g.*, *ləṛke-ke sath gəya* "He went with the boy," *ləṛke-ke pas hɛ* "The boy has it" (literally, "It is by the boy"). Many such postpositions represent old nominal (noun) forms. Other New Indo-Aryan languages have systems similar to that of Hindi, though the forms of the postpositions differ.

Though the nominal (noun) system of Punjabi is very close to that of Hindi, it has separate ablative (indicating separation and source) and locative (indicating place) forms in the singular and plural, respectively, for nouns such as *koṭha* "house"; *e.g.*, *koṭhiõ* "from the house," *koṭhī* "in the houses." Some languages have a fuller case system than that noted above; *e.g.*, Bengali has a genitive singular ending, a genitive plural ending, and a locative case. Similarly, Kashmiri has nominative, dative, ablative, and agentive cases. Not all such case forms are inherited from Middle Indo-Aryan. In addition to case endings, these languages also use postpositions; *e.g.*, Kashmiri *garājas-andar* "in the garage," with *-andar* after the dative *-as* ending.

Adjectives behave generally in the same way as nouns but have a syntactic restriction. In Hindi the possessive is in the oblique (non-nominative) form, as is the noun after which it occurs; but in the plural, only the noun has the oblique form. Further, the formation of comparatives and superlatives with derivative affixes has been eliminated. To a Sanskrit sentence such as *ime amū-bhyaḥ āḍhya-tarāḥ* "These (people) are richer than those," in which the comparative *āḍhya-tara* occurs construed with the ablative form, corresponds a Hindi sentence *ye un-se əmīr hɛ̃*, in which no comparative affix is used—literally, "These are rich from (*i.e.*, in comparison with) those." Comparable constructions with a postposition meaning "from" occur elsewhere in New Indo-Aryan.

Comparatives and superlatives

The pronominal system of New Indo-Aryan formally resembles the Middle Indo-Aryan stage more than its noun system. For example, Gujarati *hũ* "I," *mɛ̃* "I" (agentive), *əme* "we" (also agentive) are directly comparable to Apabhraṃśa *haũ, maĩ, amhaĩ*. The number distinctions of the Middle Indo-Aryan pronoun have been replaced, however, by distinctions of familiarity and politeness. For example, Hindi and Bengali have a three-way distinction—Hindi *ap*, Bengali *apni* "you" are polite or honorific forms; Hindi *tum*, Bengali *tumi* are informal forms; and Hindi *tū̃*, Bengali *tui* are used only for inferiors and small children. (Hindi and Bengali differ, however, in the plural forms of these.) In Gujarati, on the other hand, *tū̃* is a very familiar pronoun, whereas *təme* is used generally, covering the approximate domains of Hindi *ap* and *tum; ap*, if used, strikes the hearer as fawning. Marathi has a similar system. Southwestern languages also make a distinction in the 1st person plural between inclusive and exclusive, the exclusive excluding the person spoken to. In the form of the relative pronoun and the 3rd person pronoun, languages differ in the degree to which gender distinctions are made, thus contrasting with Old and Middle Indo-Aryan, in which these forms had three genders. For example, Marathi has masculine, feminine, and neuter for the relative pronoun, while Bengali has animate and inanimate.

New Indo-Aryan languages differ in the degree to which finite verb forms have been replaced by nominal (noun) forms. In Bengali a contrast is made between continuous or actual present (English "be . . . -ing") and non-continuous or habitual present; *e.g.*, *ami kaj kor-i* "I work" (literally, "I do work"), with the ending *-i*, contrasts with *ami kaj kor-ch-i* "I am working," in which *ch* intervenes between the root and the ending. Hindi has a similar contrast but uses nominal forms; *e.g.*, *mɛ̃ kam kar-ta hũ* "I work," *mɛ̃ kam kər rəh-a hũ* "I am working." Both contain the finite form *hũ* of the auxiliary; but *kər-ta* and *rəh-a* are nominal forms, the latter the past of *rəh-* "stay." Gujarati has both types, the present tense using finite verb forms, the imperfect employing nominal forms; *e.g.*, *hũ kam kərũ chũ* "I work, am working" and *hũ kam kər-to hə-to* "I was working, used to work." Even in areas in which finite forms are not used in the present, they occur in the imperative forms and what may be called the subjunctive; *e.g.*, Hindi *tum kam kər-o* "work," *mɛ̃ əndər aũ* "May I come in?"

Person–number system

The person–number system of the New Indo-Aryan verb accords with the use of pronouns. For example, the forms *ja-o, kər-o* in Gujarati *təme kyã jao cho* "Where are you going?" and *šũ kəro cho* "What are you doing?" are historically plurals but are used with reference to one person addressed by the pronoun *təme*. Similarly, in Hindi, in which a person distinction is not made in the plural, *ap kəhã ja rəhe hɛ̃, ap kya kər rəhe hɛ̃*, equivalent in meaning to the Gujarati sentences, have the plural form *rəhe hɛ̃*. Bengali has completely given up any number distinction in verb forms: *ami/amra kori* "I/we do." In the 3rd person a distinction is made between ordinary and honorific: *še* (ordinary)/*tini kɔren*, plural *tara/tāra kɔren*. Other languages (*e.g.*, Hindi) also have honorific forms, for which the plural is used.

In the formation of the future there are again regional differences. Some retain the future in *-s-* (Gujarati *hũ kər-iš*, 3rd person *e kər-š-e*) or *-h-* (*e.g.*, eastern dialects of Braj Bhasa, *cəlihəõ* "I will go"). Characteristic of the Eastern languages and of Bihari (including Bhojpuri, Magahi, Maithili) is the suffix *-b-*; *e.g.*, Bengali *jabe* "will go." All of these are finite forms. On the other hand, in Hindi and adjoining areas, the future is inflected for gender.

A similar contrast between the use of verbal and nominally inflected forms also appears in the past tense forms. The predominant pattern in New Indo-Aryan is that of Middle Indo-Aryan: forms are used that are etymologically participles.

The New Indo-Aryan languages retain the passive and causative forms. The causative is conservative in retaining both the affixes that appear in Middle Indo-Aryan and vowel alternation. The passive is also formed by affixation in some areas. But many languages also have a compound formation involving the verb *ja* "go" and an auxiliary (*hɛ*); *e.g.*, Hindi *yahã hindī bol-ī ja-t-ī hɛ* "Hindi is spoken here."

There are other auxiliaries, which, like *hɛ*, can occur with any verb in the language; *e.g.*, the verb "can," Hindi *sək-*, Gujarati *šək*. A characteristic feature of New Indo-Aryan, however, is the use of certain verbs, variously called vector verbs or compound verbs, in restricted contexts and with particular semantics. For example, one can say *mər gə-ya* "He died," *bhūl gə-ya* "He forgot," *bol uṭh-a* "He blurted out" in Hindi, using the verbs *ja* "go" (masculine singular past *gə-ya*), *uṭh* "stand up." This phenomenon is pan-Indo-Aryan and still requires investigation.

New Indo-Aryan word order

The examples cited above also illustrate the normal word order in New Indo-Aryan languages: subject (including agential forms), object (with attributive adjectives preceding), verb (together with auxiliaries). Adverbials can precede the full sentence or occur after the subject, with slight differences in emphasis; *e.g.*, Hindi *mɛ̃ kəl aũga*, or *kəl mɛ̃ aũga* "I will come tomorrow (*kəl*)." Relative clauses normally precede correlatives: Hindi *jo admī kəl tumhare ghər-mẽ tha vo kɔn hɛ* "Who (*kɔn*) is the man (*admī*) who (*jo*) was in your house yesterday?" A notable exception to the normal final position for verbs occurs in Kashmiri, in which the verb usually occurs in second position after the subject; thus, to Hindi *vo kha rəha hɛ* "he is eating" corresponds Kashmiri *su chu khĭavān* with the auxiliary *chu* after the subject.

Vocabulary. The two most important sources of non-Indo-Aryan vocabulary in New Indo-Aryan are Persian (including Arabic items introduced through Persian), the court language of the Mughals, and English. The Perso-Arabic vocabulary permeates every aspect of New Indo-Aryan vocabulary, especially in the midlands (Uttar Pradesh through the Punjab). There are, of course, Hindi-Urdu words proper to Islām: Hindi *kuran* "Qur'ān," *ʿīd* (name of a holy day), *nəmaz* (certain prayers), *məsjid* "mosque," as well as the word for "religion," *məẓhəb*. In addition, there are numerous Perso-Arabic military and administrative terms (*kila* "fort," *səvar* "horseman," *ədalət* "court of justice"); architectural and geographic terms (*imarət* "building," *məkan* "house," *məhəl* "palace," *duniya* "world," *ilaka* "province"); words having to do with learning and writing (*kələm* "pen," *kitab* "book," *ədəb* "literature, good manners") and with apparel (*jeb* "pocket," *moja* "socks," *rumal* "handkerchief") and anatomy (*khūn* "blood," *gərdən* "neck," *dil* "heart," *bazu* "arm," *sər* "head"). Indeed some of the most common vocabulary is of this origin: *tārīkh* "date," *vəkt* "time," *sal* "year," *həfta* "week," *umər* "age," *admī* "man," *ɔrət* "woman," and others. Even the grammatical apparatus of postpositions and conjunctions reflects Perso-Arabic influence; *e.g.*, *-ke bad* "after," *əgər* "if," *məgər* "but," *ya* "or."

The colloquial language used by any Hindu or Muslim communicating in Hindi–Urdu will contain a large number of such words. There have been efforts to polarize the two, and at times champions of Indo-Aryan have tried to replace Perso-Arabic vocabulary with Sanskritic words. The style that tends toward eliminating all but the most common Perso-Arabic words may be called High Hindi, written in the Devanāgarī script, as opposed to High Urdu, which retains Perso-Arabic of long standing, uses Persian and Arabic for learned vocabulary and is written in the Perso-Arabic script.

Influence of English on vocabulary

The influence of English as a source of borrowing still continues, and it is rare to hear a conversation on any technical subject among speakers of any Indian language in which English words are not liberally used. Among loanwords from English are names of conveyances such as Hindi *rel-gaṛi* "railroad-train" and *ṭɛksī* "taxi"; profession names such as *injinīr* "engineer," *jəj* "judge," *ḍaktər* "Western doctor," *pulis* "police"; and terms of educational administration such as *kaləj* "college" and *yunivərsiṭī* "university." English words are susceptible to replacement in India by Sanskritic ones as are those of Perso-Arabic origin.

Of much lesser magnitude are New Indo-Aryan borrowings from other languages, among them Portuguese and Turkic. From the latter, the word *urdū* came to be used as the name of a language. From Portuguese come such Hindi words as *ənənnas* "pineapple," *paū̃* "(Western style) bread," *kəmīz* "(Western) shirt," *kəmra* "room," and *girja* "(Christian) church."

Writing systems. Ancient India had two main scripts in which Indo-Aryan languages were written. Kharoṣṭi, used in the northwest, is of Aramaic origin and is written from right to left; Brāhmī, of North Semitic origin, is written from left to right and appears earliest on Aśokan inscriptions in areas other than the northwest. Most scripts of New Indo-Aryan are developments of the Brāhmī. The Devanāgarī (or simply Nāgarī), used for writing Sanskrit documents in North India, is the script of Hindi and Marathi as well as Nepali. Gujarati uses a more cursive derivative. Devanāgarī is also used, mainly among Hindus, for Kashmiri, which has, in addition, a traditional script called Sarada, which is not now in common use. The Perso-Arabic script is used instead. Also usually written in Perso-Arabic writing are Urdu and Sindhi (for which the Devanāgarī is also used in schools in India), whereas Punjabi employs it in Pakistan as well as a particular script of its own, known as Gurmukhi ("From the Teacher's Mouth") in the sacred writings of the Sikhs. In the east, the scripts used for Bengali and Assamese are closely related; and that of Oriya, related to the other two, is highly cursive like that of neighbouring Dravidian languages. Such is also the case with Sinhala.

The traditional alphabets are both over-explicit and not clear enough with regard to accurate representation of the spoken word. As systems in which a consonant symbol with no other accessory symbol accompanying it stands for the syllable consisting of the consonant followed by short *a*, they require previous knowledge of items for correct interpretation; Hindi *kərta* is written *ka-ra-tā* in the Devanāgarī, and one must know that the word has only two syllables. Though Bengali has only the spirant sound *š*, the alphabet has symbols for *ś*, *ṣ*, and *s*, as in Old Indo-Aryan; but verb forms such as *kori* and *kəren* are written *ka-ri* and *ka-re-na*, both with the same initial symbol. And, though syllabic *ṛ* was lost as early as Middle Indo-Aryan, the scripts have a separate symbol for this. Script reform has been suggested; it has even been proposed that all Indo-Aryan languages adopt a Latin (roman) alphabet with diacritics, but chances for this are poor. (Ge.Ca.)

The Iranian languages

LANGUAGES OF THE GROUP

The various Iranian languages fall distinctly into three categories—Ancient, Middle, and Modern Iranian.

Avestan and Old Persian

Ancient (Old) Iranian. Of the ancient Iranian languages, only two are known from texts or inscriptions, Avestan and Old Persian, the oldest parts of which date from the 6th century BC. Avestan was probably spoken in northeastern Iran, and Old Persian is known to have been used in southwestern Iran. Other ancient Iranian languages must have existed, and indirect evidence is available concerning some of these. Thus, from the 5th-century-BC historian Herodotus, the Median word for "female dog" (*spaka*) is known, and a number of Median loanwords have been recognized in the Old Persian inscriptions. In addition, a number of Median personal names are attested in various sources. It is likely that all those languages that are known only from the Middle Iranian period were in fact spoken in a less developed form in the ancient period. The same observation may apply to some of those modern Iranian languages that are not attested in the earlier periods.

The degree of mutual intelligibility that existed among the ancient Iranian languages is not known with certainty. The differences in the nature of the surviving sources have to be borne in mind. On the one hand, there is the religious poetry of Zoroaster in the Avestan language and on the other, the official inscriptions of the Achaemenid rulers in Old Persian. Differences in the method of transmission present a further difficulty in the way of direct comparison. Nevertheless, it can safely be stated that the degree of mutual intelligibility must have been much greater between the ancient languages than between the Middle Iranian languages and that those languages geographically closer to each other probably were mutually understood better than those spoken in areas farther apart.

Avestan can hardly be said to be known beyond the ancient period, although only the earliest texts, the Gāthās, are as old as the 6th century BC, and the later texts represent the language of several subsequent centuries. Old Persian, on the other hand, itself spanning the 6th to the 4th century BC, was continued more or less directly by the various forms of Middle Persian. Even here, however, although both Old and Middle Persian represent the language of the royal court, there are considerable differences between them for which no satisfactory explanation has yet been given.

Middle Iranian. Middle Persian is known in three forms, not entirely homogeneous—inscriptional Middle Persian, Pahlavi (often more precisely called Book Pahlavi), and Manichaean Middle Persian. Middle Persian belongs to the period 300 BC to AD 950, and was, like Old Persian, the language of southwestern Iran. In the northeast and northwest the language spoken was Parthian, which is known from inscriptions and from Manichaean texts. There are no significant linguistic differences in the Parthian of these two sources. Most Parthian belongs to the first three centuries AD.

Eastern group of Middle Iranian languages

Middle Persian and Parthian were doubtlessly similar enough to be mutually intelligible, but they differ so greatly from the eastern group of Middle Iranian languages that these must have appeared to be almost foreign languages. The languages of the eastern group, moreover, cannot have been themselves mutually intelligible. The main known languages of this group are Khwārezmian (Chorasmian), Sogdian, and Saka. Less well-known are Old Ossetic (Scytho-Sarmatian) and Bactrian, but from what is known it would seem likely that these languages were equally distinctive. There was probably more than one dialect of each of the languages of the eastern group, although there is certainty only in the case of Saka, for which at least two dialects are clearly attested. The main Saka dialect is known as Khotanese, but a small amount of material survives in a closely related dialect called Tumshuq, formerly known as Maralbashi.

A few words are known in all of these eastern Iranian languages from as early as the 2nd to the 4th century AD, but substantial evidence begins for Sogdian in the 4th century, for Saka probably no earlier than the 7th century (though that for Tumshuq may be a few centuries older), and for Khwārezmian not until the 12th century and later. The principal evidence for Bactrian belongs to the 2nd century. To the same period belong the Scytho-Sarmatian names of the earliest inscriptions.

All the eastern Iranian languages of the Middle Iranian period were spoken in Central Asia, with the exception of the language of the Scytho-Sarmatian inscriptions from southern Russia, north of the Black Sea. More precisely, Bactrian was spoken in northern Afghanistan and in the adjacent parts of what is now Soviet Central Asia. Khwārezmian was the language of Khwārezm (Khiva), now an *oblast* in western Uzbekistan but formerly of greater extent. Sogdian was probably spoken over most of Soviet Central Asia, especially in eastern Uzbekistan, Tadzhikistan, and western Kirgiziya. There were also colonies of Sogdians in various cities along the trade routes to China; in fact, most Sogdian material comes from outside Sogdiana. The Saka dialects, Khotanese and Tumshuq, were spoken in Chinese Turkistan, modern Sinkiang; Tumshuq is the name of a small village in the extreme west of Sinkiang. Khotanese was spoken in Khotan near the modern city of Khotan (Chinese Ho-t'ien) on the southern route across the Takla Makan desert and within about 100 miles (160 kilometres) to the north and to the east of Khotan, where manuscripts have been found, mainly at the sites of former shrines and monasteries.

Modern Iranian. The discontinuity already observed between Old and Middle Iranian is even more striking between Middle and Modern Iranian. There are no modern counterparts at all to Khwārezmian, Bactrian, and Saka, and there is no direct continuity in the case of any of the other Middle Iranian languages. Even Modern Persian does not represent a straightforward continuation of Middle Persian but is rather a koine (a dialect or language of a small area that becomes a common or standard language of a larger area), based mainly on Middle Persian and Parthian but including elements from other languages and dialects. Although Sogdian is known in several forms, possibly representing different dialects, none of these can be considered the direct ancestor of modern Yaghnobi, spoken at present in the valley of the Yaghnob (Yagnob) River, a tributary of the Zarafshān (Zeravshan). Yaghnobi, nevertheless, certainly belongs linguistically to the Sogdian family. Similarly, the languages of the Scytho-Sarmatian inscriptions may represent dialects of a language family of which Modern Ossetic is a continuation, but it does not simply represent the same language at an earlier date.

Modern Iranian state languages

Only four of the many modern Iranian languages are the official languages of the state in which they are spoken. The chief of these is Persian (known in Persian itself as Fārsī), the national language of Iran, which is spoken by about 15,000,000 people as a native language. It is recognized, moreover, as a second language in Afghanistan, where it is spoken in only a slightly different form. The national language of Afghanistan is the East Iranian language known as Pashto, of which there are about 10,000,000 speakers, many living in Pakistan (former West Pakistan). Tadzhik is spoken by at least 1,000,000 people widely spread throughout Tadzhikistan and the rest of Soviet Central Asia and is readily intelligible to speakers of Persian, to which it is very closely related, although it is in some respects more archaic. In addition to being the national language of Tadzhikistan, Tadzhik is important as the lingua franca of the Pamirs, a region where a remarkable variety of Iranian languages and dialects is spoken. Fewer than 500,000 people speak Ossetic. Most of the Ossetes (Osetes) live in two administrative divisions of the U.S.S.R., the North Osetic A.S.S.R. and the South Ossetian autonomous *oblast* of the Georgian S.S.R. Although spoken in the heart of the Caucasus Mountains, Ossetic is an East Iranian language not mutually intelligible with any other Iranian language.

Two other Iranian languages, Kurdish and Baluchi, are spoken over a vast area, although they have not been officially accepted as the national language of an established state. Kurdish is spoken by at least 5,000,000 people living in Iran, Iraq, Turkey, Syria, and Soviet Transcaucasia. More than 1,000,000 people speak Baluchi as their chief language; they are spread widely over parts of eastern Iran, Pakistan, Afghanistan, and southern Soviet Central Asia. In Iran, Baluchi speakers live mainly in the region of Baluchistan, a region in the southeast that now forms part of a province with Seistan. In Pakistan, Baluchi speakers live mainly in the southwestern province of Baluchistan; in Soviet Central Asia, they are found mainly around Merv in southern Turkmenistan; and in Afghanistan, they are widely scattered, mainly over the southwestern portion of the country. There is a sizable Baluchi colony in Oman, and many Baluchi merchants have settled in the sheikhdoms of southern Arabia and along the east coast of Africa as far south as Kenya. Linguistically, Baluchi and Kurdish are both West Iranian languages. Baluchi is thus much more closely related to Kurdish than it is to its close neighbour Pashto. According to the most likely theory, the present eastern location of Baluchi speakers is the result of migrations from the region of the Caspian Sea during the Middle Ages.

Dialects. The six modern Iranian languages discussed above are the only ones that have an established literary tradition. They are not, however, homogeneous, each having its own dialect divisions. No definitive dialect classification has yet been made, nor indeed has any attempt at systematic classification of the whole range of Iranian languages won wide acceptance. The usual practice, followed here, is simply to list the main languages in groups of varying size, arranged on a roughly geographical basis.

Ossetic dialects

There are two main dialects of Ossetic: the eastern, known as Iron, and the western, known as Digor (Digoron). Of these, Digor is the more archaic, Iron words being often a syllable shorter than their Digor counterparts; *e.g.*, Digor *madä*, Iron *mad* "mother." Iron is spoken by the majority of Ossetic speakers and is the basis of the literary language. Chosen in the 19th century for the translation of the Bible, it is still the official language today. Little is known of the other Ossetic dialects. A small amount of the Ossetic dialect of Tual in the south, which differs little from Iron, was published in Georgian script at the beginning of the 19th century.

Yaghnobi is still spoken by a small number of people southeast of Samarkand. It has two main dialects, eastern and western, which differ only slightly. The characteristic difference is between a western *t* sound and an eastern *s* sound from an older *θ* sound (as *th* in English "thin"); *e.g.*, western *mēt*, eastern *mēs* "day," beside Sogdian *mēθ* (Christian Sogdian *myθ*).

Dialects of the Shughnī group are spoken in the Pamirs. Closely related to this group is Yāzgulāmī. A period of a Yāzgulāmī–Shughnī common language (protolanguage) has been postulated by some scholars, after which it separated first into Yāzgulāmī and Common Shughnī; and then Common Shughnī gradually divided into Sarīkolī, Oroshorī-Bartangī, Rōshānī-Khufī, and Bajuvī-Shughnī. Sarīkolī, the easternmost of these dialects, is spoken in Chinese Sinkiang.

Speakers of Wakhī number 10,000 or so in the region of the upper Panj. Vākhān (Wākhān), the Persian name for the region in which Wakhī is spoken, is based on the local name Wux̌, a Wakhī development of *Waxšu, the old name of the Oxus (modern Amu Darya). (An asterisk denotes a hypothetical, unattested, reconstructed form or word.) The Wakhī language is remarkably distinct from its neighbours and has many archaic features.

Around the bend of the Amu Darya and in the valley of the Vardūj River to the southwest, a few people speak dialects of the Sanglēchī-Ishkāshmī group. This group is clearly distinguished from its neighbours but is closely related to the other languages of the Pamirs.

Scarcely more than 2,000 people speak dialects of the Yidghā-Munjī group. Monjān is a very remote valley located in northern Afghanistan, and it is separated by a mountain pass from the Sanglēchī-speaking region. Yidghā is spoken in the valley of the Lutkuh in Chitrāl, which is now in Pakistan. Yidghā-Munjī is most closely related to Pashto.

Pashto dialectal groups

The existence of two dialectal groups within Pashto has long been known. Thus, the word Pashto represents a southwestern dialect form (*paštō*), in contrast to a northeastern form (*paxtō*). According to one hypothesis, Pashto literature was created among the northeastern tribes. Two minor dialects, Wazīrī and Waṉētsī, have some features of special interest.

Although spoken in a few villages in Afghanistan, two languages have features closely associating them with Western Iranian. These are Parāchī, spoken in the Hindu Kush north of Kābul, and Ōrmuṛī, found in two dialects, one in the Lowgar Valley south of Kābul and the other in Kāniguram in Wazīristan.

Farther south is the wholly West Iranian language, Baluchi, mentioned above. Despite the vast area over which Baluchi is spoken, its numerous dialects are all mutually intelligible. The most recent study of the Baluchi dialects divides them into six groups: Eastern Hill dialects; Rākhshānī dialects including that of Merv; Sarawānī; Kechī; Loṭunī; and the coastal dialects. Of these, Rākhshānī is the most widely spoken and is used for broadcasting both in Pakistan and in Afghanistan, but the coastal dialects have the greatest prestige and the most extensive literature.

In the southeastern corner of Iran, Baluchi gradually gives way to the Bashkardī dialects.

In central Iran the influence of Modern Persian is everywhere strongly felt, and it is often difficult to distinguish between dialects of Modern Persian, Persian with dialectal traits, and closely related languages. In Yazd and Kerman the Parsis speak the old Gabrī dialect, whereas the Muslims speak Persian. Among other central dialects are Nāṭanzī, Sōī, Khunsārī, Gazī (near Isfahan), Sīvandī (northeast of Shīrāz), Vafsī, and Ashtiyānī, to name but a few.

Semnānī, spoken east of Tehrān, forms a transitional stage between the central dialects and the Caspian dialects. The latter are divided into two groups, Gīlakī and Māzandarānī (Tabarī). Also closely related is Tālishī, spoken on the west coast of the Caspian Sea on both sides of the border with the U.S.S.R. To this northwestern group belong the so-called southern Tātī dialects spoken south and southwest of Qazvīn, as well as the scarcely known dialects of Harzan and Galinqaya spoken northwest of Tabriz. The name Tātī is usually applied to the dialects spoken in Russian Dagestan and northeast Azerbaijan. They differ little from Modern Persian.

Of the dialects of Fars Province, only Larī, southeast of Shīrāz, is notably distinctive. Kumzarī in Oman and the Lur dialects of the southwest also differ little from Persian.

Kurdish dialects

There are many dialects of Kurdish, the widely spoken West Iranian language that is thought to occupy a dialectal position intermediate between Baluchi and Persian. Three main dialect groups can be distinguished—northern, central, and southern. A systematic study has been made of the dialects of Iraq, which include ʿAqrah (Akre), ʿAmādīyah, Dahūk, Shaykhān, and Zākhū in the northern group, and Irbīl (Arbīl), Bingird, Pishdar (Pizhdar), Sulaymānīyah (Suleimaniye), and Wārmāwah in the central group. The Central Mukrī dialect is spoken in the extreme west of Iran, south of Lake Urmia.

Gorānī is spoken in several dialects, mainly in the Zagros Mountains, and it is strongly influenced by the surrounding Kurdish dialects. The Gorānī dialect of Hawrāman, Hawrāmī, is notable for its many archaic features. Closely related to Gorānī is Zaza (Dimli), spoken west of Iran.

HISTORICAL SURVEY OF THE IRANIAN LANGUAGES

The Iranian protolanguage and its development. By the time Iranian begins to be attested in the 6th century BC, the language is already found differentiated into several distinct languages. Scholars have reconstructed the sound system and some of the grammatical features of Common Old Iranian, the protolanguage that preceded these dialects.

The phonological system that underlay Common Old Iranian was by and large maintained everywhere throughout the Iranian-speaking world. It consisted of the following distinctive consonant sounds:

k	g	x	[ɣ]	ŋ
č	ǰ			
p	b	f	[β]	m
t	d	θ	[ð]	n
š	ž			
y	r	l	w	h

Unfamiliar symbols are taken from the International Phonetic Alphabet, or are conventional transcriptions (*e.g.*, *š* for the *sh* sound in "ship," *ž* for the *z* sound in "azure," *č* for *ch* in "church," and *ǰ* for *j* in "jam"). The voiced fricatives (*i.e.*, the first three consonants represented in the fourth column—ɣ, β, and ð), which are produced with vibrating vocal cords and local friction, may be regarded as variants of the voiced stops (*e.g.*, *g*, *b*, *d*); but they are characteristic of Iranian languages generally and especially of the eastern Iranian languages. In addition to these sounds Old Persian had another sibilant sound, often transcribed as *ç* or *ss*, which developed from the cluster θr (pronounced as the *thr* in "three"). In Middle Persian it fell together with the *s* sound. The most noticeable alteration of the old sound system is the introduction in some languages of additional series of consonants under the influence of neighbouring languages. Thus, Ossetic has a series of ejective sounds (uttered with a simultaneous glottal stop) on the pattern of the unrelated Caucasian languages; and a number of Iranian languages have a retroflex series (produced with the tongue tip curled up toward the roof of the mouth) as a result of contact with Indo-Aryan languages.

Changes from Indo-European sounds to Iranian sounds

Some of the differences between Iranian languages arose as a result of different developments of the earlier sounds. Thus, the Indo-European sounds *ḱ*, *ǵ*, and *ǵh* resulted in Indo-Iranian *ś*, *ź*, and *źh*, which in turn became *s*, *z*, and *z*, respectively, in Avestan but *θ*, *d*, and *d* in Old Persian. Hence, Indo-European **ḱm̥tó-* "hundred" became Indo-Iranian **śatá-*, attested by Old Indo-Aryan *śatá-*, and then Avestan *sata-*, but Old Persian *θata-*. Nevertheless, *θ* and *d* as well as *s* and *z* belong to the basic pattern, the difference being merely distributional.

The main source of differentiation is in the variation of consonant cluster development and that of groups of consonants and semivowels. Here again it is mainly a question of distributional differences. Thus, the Indo-European group **ḱu̯* became Indo-Iranian **śu̯*, retained in Old Indo-Aryan in the spelling *śv* of the standard transcription. Indo-Iranian **śu̯* developed variously in Iranian: *s* in Old Persian, *sp* in Avestan and Median, *ś* (written *śś*) in Khotanese, and *š* in Wakhī. These developments can be seen in the following forms of the Indo-European word **eḱu̯o-* "horse": Old Indo-Aryan *áśva-*, Avestan and Median *aspa-*, Old Persian *asa-*, Khotanese *aśśa-*, and Wakhī *yaš*. Yet another development can be seen in Ossetic, in which the word for "mare," Avestan *aspā-*, appears as Digor *äfsä* and Iron *yäfs*.

The vowel system of Common Old Iranian consisted of short and long varieties of *a*, *i*, and *u*, and a neutral vowel *ə* (similar to the *a* in "sofa"). This analysis assumes that the Indo-Iranian vocalic *r* (r̥) had already developed to *ər* in Proto-Iranian, just as its long counterpart became *ar*. An early and general monophthongization of the diphthongs *ai* and *au* to *ē* and *ō*, respectively, must also be considered characteristic, although it should not be ascribed to Common Old Iranian as is sometimes done. This basic system was almost everywhere maintained, sometimes with the addition of one or two distinctive vowel sounds (phonemes).

For further details concerning the relationship of Iranian to Indo-European and Indo-Aryan, see the introduction of this article.

The Old Iranian stage. Old Persian was the language of the Achaemenid court. It is first attested in the inscriptions of Darius I (ruled 522–486 BC), of which the longest, earliest, and most important is that of Bīsitūn. At Bīsitūn are also inscribed versions of the same text in Elamite and Babylonian, and fragments of an Aramaic version on papyrus documents from Elephantine (modern Jazīrat Aswān) also exist. Old Persian words and names are also to be found in large numbers as loanwords in contemporary Elamite sources and in 5th-century-BC Aramaic documents.

As early as the time of Darius the Great's successor, Xerxes I (ruled 486–465 BC), the inscriptions show linguistic tendencies characteristic of the development from Old to Middle Persian. After Xerxes the production of original Old Persian inscriptions declined, probably as a result of the wider adoption of Aramaic and Elamite as the usual means of writing. With Artaxerxes III (ruled 359/358–338 BC), Old Persian inscriptions came to an end. The break is marked by Alexander's destruction of Persepolis in 330 BC.

Alternate terms for Avestan

By far the largest part of attested Old Iranian is written in the language now usually called Avestan, after the Avesta, the name given to the collection of works forming the scripture of the Zoroastrians. The name itself is Middle Persian. In former times, this language was called Zend, another Middle Persian word, which refers to the Middle Persian (Pahlavi) commentary on the Avesta. Because the homeland of the Avestan language was long thought to be in Bactria, it was often in the past called Bactrian. Bactrian is now used to designate a different Iranian language belonging to the Middle Iranian period.

Since the beginning of the 20th century it has been generally accepted that the homeland of the Avesta was Khwārezm, which in ancient times included both Merv and Herāt. Merv is now in Turkmenistan, Herāt in northwest Afghanistan.

The oldest part of the Avesta is known as the Gāthās, the poems composed by Zoroaster (Zaraθuštra), the founder of the Zoroastrian religion. His date is uncertain but is traditionally ascribed to the 7th to 6th century BC. The so-called *Khurda Avesta* ("Little Avesta") is a miscellany of texts of later date, the oldest parts of which may have been composed about 400 BC. The language of the *Khurda Avesta* is different in many details from that of the more archaic language of the Gāthās, and it may even represent a different dialect. Many uncertainties surround the detailed interpretation of the Avesta as a result of the method of transmission. The Avesta was not recorded until after the language had ceased to be used, except by Zoroastrian priests. The present manuscripts date from the 13th century and later, although they reflect the recording of the priestly tradition in the special Avestan script during the 6th century AD.

The Middle Iranian stage. Middle Persian was the official language of the Sāsānians (AD 224–651) and was used for their inscriptions. The most important of these is the 3rd-century inscription of Shāpūr I, which has parallel versions in Parthian and Greek. Middle Persian was also the language of the Manichaean and Zoroastrian books during the 3rd to the 10th century AD. The extant literature of the Zoroastrian books is much more extensive than that of the Manichaean texts, but the latter have the advantage of having been recorded in a clear and unambiguous script. Moreover, the Middle Persian of the Zoroastrian books, or Pahlavi, as it is usually called, does not simply represent the spoken language of the writers of the 9th-century Zoroastrian texts. It is probable that they spoke early Modern Persian and that their speech often impinged upon their writing but that they strove to write the Middle Persian of several centuries earlier as it was attested in the inscriptions of the early Sāsānian Empire when Middle Persian was the koine. By contrast, in the case of Manichaean Middle Persian, some texts survive unchanged from the 3rd century AD, the time of the Persian teacher Mani himself (AD 216–274).

Records of Parthian

Very little Parthian survives from the pre-Sāsānian period. A large number of Parthian ostraca (inscribed pottery fragments) from the 1st century BC were discovered at Nisa near modern Ashkhabad, but they are inscribed in ideographic Aramaic (*i.e.*, Aramaic writing that uses Aramaic words as symbols to represent Parthian words). Dating before the 3rd century are a document from Hawrāman, some coin legends, and a dated grave stele. The most copious and important material is the work of the Sāsānian kings of the 3rd century, who added a Parthian version to their inscriptions—Ḥājjīābād, Naqsh-e Rustam (Ka'be yi Zardusht), and Paikūla. A few decades later Parthian disappeared as a result of the rise of the Sāsānians and the predominance of their native tongue, Middle Persian. Manichaean Parthian of the 3rd century was preserved as a church language in Central Asia.

The oldest surviving Sogdian documents are the so-called Ancient Letters found in a watchtower on the Chinese Great Wall, west of Tun-huang, and dated at the beginning of the 4th century AD. Most of the religious literature written in Sogdian dates from the 9th and 10th centuries. The Manichaean, Buddhist, and Christian Sogdian texts come mainly from small communities of Sogdians in the Turfan oasis and in Tun-huang. From Sogdiana itself there is only a small collection of documents from Mt. Mugh in the Zarafshān region, mainly the business correspondence of a minor Sogdian king, Dewashtich, from the time of the Arab conquest around 700.

The relationship of the various forms of Sogdian to one another has not yet been sufficiently investigated, so that it is not clear whether different dialects are represented by the extant material or whether the differences can be accounted for by reference to other relevant factors, such as differences of script, period, subject, style, or social milieu. The importance of social milieu can be seen by comparing the elegant Manichaean literature directed to the court with the more vulgar language of the Christian literature directed to the lower classes.

Of the Saka dialect known as Tumshuq very little has survived, and despite its evidently close relationship to the much better known Khotanese dialect, full interpretation has proved difficult. Knowledge of Khotanese is more firmly based on a substantial corpus of material, including extensive bilingual texts. Although the chronological range of the extant Khotanese material is limited to only a few centuries, probably the 7th to the 10th, a rapid development of the language is apparent. At the phonological level, most noticeable is the loss of syllables between the older and later stages of the language. Thus, *hvatana-* "Khotanese" at the oldest stage is successively weakened to *hvatäna-*, *hvaṃna-*, *hvana-*, *hvaṃ*. At the morphological level, most striking is the tendency to simplify the case endings and even to replace them by analytical expressions, constructions of two or more words. Thus, Late Khotanese has *rakṣaysā hīya rāde* "kings of the *rākṣasas*," whereas Old Khotanese would have *rakṣaysänu rrunde*. The Old Khotanese *-änu* ending is unmistakably genitive plural, but the Late Khotanese *-ā* is merely a general oblique plural ending and has been reinforced by *hīya* "own," used to mean "of."

Buddhist influence on Khotanese

Khotan was a great centre of Buddhism during the 1st millennium AD, and all the surviving literature in Khotanese is either Buddhist or coloured by Buddhism. Even in business documents and official letters the Buddhist background is usually not difficult to discern. It can scarcely be coincidental that the Buddhist literature of Khotan, flourishing so vigorously during the 10th century, ended abruptly with the Muslim conquest at the beginning of the 11th.

Little survives of Bactrian and Scytho-Sarmatian. Knowledge of Bactrian is based almost entirely on a single inscription of 25 lines from Āteshkadeh-ye Sorkh Kowtal in northern Afghanistan. Even less is known of Scytho-Sarmatian.

Little is also known of Old Khwārezmian; that is, Khwārezmian written in the indigenous Khwārezmian script. Apart from a few coin legends and inscriptions on silver vessels, the material that survives consists of inscriptions of the 2nd century AD from Topraq-qal'ah (Toprakkala) and of the 7th from Toqqal'ah, archaeological sites in Uzbek S.S.R. Much more is known of Late Khwārezmian, written in the Arabic script. This material is found mainly in two Arabic works, the 13th-century *fiqh* work of Mukhtār az-Zāhidī, called the *Qunyat al-munyah*, and the Arabic dictionary *Muqaddimat al-Adab* of az-Zamakhshari (1075–1143/44), of which a manuscript glossed in Khwārezmian was found.

Modern Iranian. Of the modern Iranian languages, by far the most widely spoken is Persian, which, as already indicated, developed from Middle Persian and Parthian, with elements from other Iranian languages such as Sogdian, as early as the 9th century AD. Since then, it has changed little except for acquiring an increasing proportion of loanwords, mainly from Arabic. Persian has been a literary language since the 9th century, and there is an increasing awareness of the continuity of its literary tradition with the earlier periods. As the national language of Iran in succession to Middle Persian, it has for centuries strongly influenced the other Iranian languages, especially on Iranian territory. In fact, it seems likely that with the increase of modern methods of communication, Persian will eventually supplant entirely most of the other languages and dialects. Against this trend stand only Kurdish and Baluchi, the speakers of which tend to regard their languages as an expression of their particular identities. Nevertheless, even Kurdish and Baluchi have been and are strongly influenced by Persian.

Modern Iranian languages in Afghanistan and the Soviet Union

Outside Iran, the situation is rather different. In Afghanistan the first national language is Pashto, even though Persian is the official second language. Pashto became the official language by royal decree in 1936, and literary activity has been encouraged by the Pashto Ṭolana (Pashto Society) of Kābul. On Soviet territory both Ossetic and Tadzhik have received official encouragement; nevertheless, both languages will in time give way to the Russian language as the language of administration. Other languages also compete with Ossetic and Tadzhik. Ossetic became a literary language only in the second half of the 19th century, but the neighbouring Georgian has a still flourishing ancient literary tradition dating back to the 5th century AD and has many more speakers. Tadzhik, on the other hand, has a lifeline through its close connection with Persian, but it too has been retreating before Uzbek, an unrelated language of the Turkic group.

CHARACTERISTICS OF THE IRANIAN LANGUAGES

All Iranian languages show in their basic elements the characteristic features of an Indo-European language. Apart from the extensive borrowing of Arabic words in Modern Persian, the Iranian languages have scarcely been affected by unrelated languages, with the notable exception of Ossetic, which has been strongly influenced by the neighbouring Caucasian languages. Some dialects of Tadzhik have been very receptive to Uzbek elements. In the case of languages in contact with Indian civilization, the most noticeable non-Iranian feature often taken over is the Indo-Aryan series of retroflex sounds. These are foreign to Indo-Aryan itself, being a result of the influence of the Dravidian languages.

The elaborate phonological and morphological structure of the Indo-European parent language has been progressively simplified in the development of the Iranian languages. The basic phonological structure of Common Old Iranian has on the whole been maintained, but the morphological system has continued to be simplified. There has been a constant move in almost all Iranian languages toward an analytic structure; *i.e.*, the use of prepositions and word order rather than case endings to indicate grammatical relationships.

Phonology. The most characteristic features of the Iranian phonological system are those that distinguish it from the Indo-Aryan system. These are the development of various fricative sounds (indicated in phonetic symbols as x, f, θ, and later ɣ, β, ð), and of the voiced sibilant sounds *z* and *ž*. (See also the introduction to this article.) Even in Iranian, however, these sounds did not persist universally. In western Middle Iranian the *θ* sound was lost, and it is rare in the modern languages. In Pashto the inherited *f* sound has been discarded. Baluchi, except in the extreme east, is entirely without fricatives. Voiced bilabial and dental fricative sounds (β and ð) were recorded in some early manuscripts of Modern Persian, but they became *b* and *d* by the 13th century

Development of Iranian fricative sounds

Two negative features have also resulted in differentiation between Indo-Aryan and Iranian. One is the result of the coalescence in Proto-Iranian of aspirated and unaspirated voiced stops. Thus, Indo-European **b* and **bh* were maintained in contrast in Indo-Aryan as *b* and *bh*, but they fell together in Iranian as *b*. This resulted in an alteration of the phonological structure because the number of consonant contrasts (oppositions) was reduced. The other negative feature is the absence of the retroflex consonants from Iranian except as a later importation in contiguous regions.

Other divergences in development, such as the change of an *s* sound to *h* in Iranian, brought about a difference in distribution rather than in structure because *h* developed also in Indo-Aryan but from Indo-Iranian **źh* and **gh* before front vowels (*e.g.*, *e* and *i*). The features discussed here are illustrated in Table 3.

In Old Iranian the stress lay on the next to the last syllable if it was heavy (*i.e.*, contained a long vowel or was closed by a consonant)—otherwise on the preceding syllable. With the loss of final unstressed vowels in the development of many Iranian languages, the stress often came to be on the final syllable. End stress is characteristic of Modern Persian.

Grammar. In Old Persian the Indo-European inflectional system appears considerably simplified. In particular, the genitive and the dative coalesced into one case and the instrumental and ablative into another. Moreover, in the plural the nominative and accusative cases are not distinguished. This reduced system is still found in the Middle Iranian period in Old Khotanese and to a certain extent in Sogdian. Eastern Iranian is in this respect more conservative than western. By the Middle Iranian period, western Iranian had abandoned nominal (noun, adjective, pronoun) inflection altogether, as is the

Simplification of the case system

Table 3: Phonetic Developments in Indo-Iranian Languages

key: NP—New Persian; Bal.—Baluchi; Yaghn.—Yaghnobi

Sanskrit	Avestan	Old Persian	modern Iranian	English translation
kratu-	xratu-	xratu-	NP xirad	"insight"
viś-	vis-	viθ-	Bal. gis	"house"
jānā́ti ("he knows")	zān(ā)	dān(ā)-	NP dān-	"know"
bandh-	band-	ba(n)d-	NP band-	"bind"
bhūta-	būta-		NP būd	"been"
sacā ("with, at the same time as. . .")	hačā	hačā	NP az	"from"
han-	ǰan-	ǰan-	Bal. ǰan-	"strike"
abhra-	aβra-		NP abr	"cloud"
mṛga- ("deer")	mərəɣa-		NP murɣ	"bird"
nir-ay-		nij-ay-*	Yaghn. nīž-	"go out"
pramāṇa- ("measure, authority")		framānā-	NP farmān	"command"
sthūṇā-	stunā-	stūnā-	NP sitūn	"pillar"

*In Old Persian *nij-ay-* "go out," *j* is written for *ž*, which was not represented in the script.

Table 4: The Persian Alphabet

consonants					equivalents		approximate pronunciation
alone	initial	medial	final	name	EB preferred	alternatives	
ا	ا	ـا	ـا	alef	*		*
ب	بـ	ـبـ	ـب	be	b		*b*a*b*y
پ	پـ	ـپـ	ـپ	pe	p		*p*e*pp*er
ت	تـ	ـتـ	ـت	te	t		*t*ie
ث	ثـ	ـثـ	ـث	s̄e	s̄	s, th	*s*and
ج	جـ	ـجـ	ـج	jīm	j	dj	*j*ob
چ	چـ	ـچـ	ـچ	che	ch	č	*ch*in
ح	حـ	ـحـ	ـح	ḥe hoti	ḥ	ḥ	*h*at
خ	خـ	ـخـ	ـخ	khe	kh	kh	Ger. Bu*ch*
د	د	ـد	ـد	dāl	d		*d*i*d*
ذ	ذ	ـذ	ـذ	ẕāl	ẕ	z, dh	*z*one
ر	ر	ـر	ـر	re	r		*r*ip
ز	ز	ـز	ـز	ze	z		*z*one
ژ	ژ	ـژ	ـژ	zhe	zh	zh	a*z*ure
س	سـ	ـسـ	ـس	sīn	s		*s*and
ش	شـ	ـشـ	ـش	shīn	sh	sh	*sh*y
ص	صـ	ـصـ	ـص	ṣād	ṣ	ṣ	*s*and
ض	ضـ	ـضـ	ـض	ẕād	ẕ	ẓ	*z*one
ط	ط	ـط	ـط	ṭā	ṭ	ţ	*t*ime
ظ	ظ	ـظ	ـظ	ẓā	ẓ	z̧	*z*one
ع	عـ	ـعـ	ـع	ʿeyn	ʿ		†
غ	غـ	ـغـ	ـغ	gheyn	gh	gh, q	‡
ف	فـ	ـفـ	ـف	fe	f	fe	*f*i*f*ty
ق	قـ	ـقـ	ـق	qāf	q	ķ	‡
ك	كـ	ـكـ	ـك	kāf	k		*k*in
گ	گـ	ـگـ	ـگ	gāf	g		*g*o
ل	لـ	ـلـ	ـل	lām	l		*l*i*l*y
م	مـ	ـمـ	ـم	mīm	m		*m*ai*m*
ن	نـ	ـنـ	ـن	nūn	n		*n*o
و	و	ـو	ـو	vāv	v	w	*v*an§
ه	هـ	ـهـ	ـه	he havaz	h		‖
ی	یـ	ـیـ	ـی	ye	y		*y*et¶

vowels, diphthongs, and special diacritical marks		equivalents		approximate pronunciation
letter or sign	name	EB preferred	alternatives	
آ	alef maddeh	ā	á	*a*rm
ىٰ	alef maqṣūreh	ā	á	*a*rm
ا	alef	*		*
و	vāv	ū		f*oo*d§
ی	ye	ī		bl*ee*d¶
ـَ	fatḥeh (or zebar)	a		m*a*p
ـِ	kasreh (or zīr)	e		b*e*t
ـُ	ẕammeh (or pīsh)	o		b*o*ne or *o*range
ی - (ـِی)	kasreh ye	ī		bl*ee*d
و - (ـُو)	ẕammeh vāv	ū		f*oo*d
یْ - (ـَی)	kasreh ye sâken	ey	ay, ai	f*a*de
وْ - (ـَو)	ẕammeh vāv sāken	ow	aw, au	b*o*ne
ـْ	sokūn (or jazm)	omit		♀
ـة	tā marbūṭah	eh, ah, or at		♂
ـّ	tashdīd	double consonant		me*dd*ling, etc.
ء	hamzeh	initial, omit; medial and final, ʾ		□
ـِ ی، —	eẕāfeh	-e, -ye	-i, -yi	◇

*Initially *a* or *e*, pronounced *m*a*p* or *b*e*t*; medially and finally, *ā*, pronounced *a*rm. †A glottal stop, as in New York or Cockney "bottle." ‡A guttural *gh*; also medially and finally often softened as in French *r*ien. §As a consonant, *v*an; as a vowel, f*oo*d. ‖Generally silent in final position; otherwise *h*at. ¶As a consonant, *y*et; as a vowel, bl*ee*d. ♀Used to show that a consonant is not vocalized. ♂Arabic feminine ending usually not pronounced in Persian except as silent *h*. □A pause between two vowels, as in English "di-et," "qui-et." ◇A particle linking a qualifying noun or adjective with a noun; usually not written. Transliterate "-e" (with hyphen) after final consonants (except silent *h*), "-ye" (with hyphen) after silent *h* and vowels.

case with Middle and Modern Persian and with Parthian. In some languages, both western and eastern, two or, rarely, three cases survive. Ossetic is quite exceptional in maintaining an elaborate case system; it is partly a result of secondary, purely Ossetic developments.

The elaborate conjugational system of the Indo-European verb followed a similar path to disintegration. In particular, the whole past tense system was given up by the Middle Iranian period. Only a few relics remain of the Indo-European system, such as the partial survival of the augment (a prefixed vowel or lengthening of the initial vowel) in the Sogdian imperfect tense. But a new past tense system developed, based on the old past participle, which is often combined with auxiliary verbs. Many languages distinguish between transitive and intransitive verbs in the past tense system; and in some languages, such as Khotanese and Pashto, even gender and number are distinguished.

The present tense system was far better preserved. The dual number was in retreat in Old Iranian and is not attested later. The middle voice, a form that indicates that a person or thing both performs and is affected by the action represented, was generally abandoned by the Middle Iranian period, although middle voice inflection is well represented in Khotanese. With these qualifications, the endings of the present indicative (active) have been generally well preserved. A variety of imperative, subjunctive, and optative forms, partly based on inherited forms and partly the result of innovation, is found especially in the eastern languages, including Ossetic.

Rigidity of word order is, on the whole, most characteristic of those languages, such as Persian, that have gone furthest in the reduction of the inherited morphological system.

Vocabulary. The Islāmic conquest of Iran during the 7th century entailed not only a change of religion but also a change of language. The sacred language of Islām was Arabic, and the proportion of Arabic words used in Persian rapidly increased until it reached something like the 40 to 50 percent of the present day. Before the introduction of the Arabic element, most loanwords were mainly from other Iranian languages. Most familiar is the extensive borrowing from Median found in Old Persian. In later periods, Modern Persian borrowed words extensively from Turkish and from European languages. Persian is itself the donor language in the case of the other Iranian languages, all of which have drawn upon its vocabulary.

Buddhism was similarly responsible for the large proportion of Indo-Aryan words, both Sanskrit and Prākrit, found in Sogdian and especially in Khotanese. A considerable Indian element occurs in the vocabulary of those modern Iranian languages that have been or are in contact with modern Indo-Aryan languages in the northwest, such as Lahnda and Sindhi. There the Dardic languages have also been influential. Baluchi has also borrowed from Brahui, a Dravidian language spoken in Baluchistan in Pakistan.

Loanwords from languages of India

Ossetic occupies an exceptional position. Most of its Persian and Arabic borrowings have come to it through Turkish, but more striking are the large number of words borrowed from the Caucasian languages, especially Georgian. In modern times, Ossetic continues to be influenced by Russian.

Writing systems. Iranian languages have been written in many different scripts during their long history, although various forms of Aramaic script have been predominant. Modern Persian is written in Arabic script, which is of Aramaic origin. For writing the Persian sounds *p*, *č*, *ž*, and *g*, four letters have been added by means of diacritical marks. By the addition of further letters, this Perso-Arabic script has been adapted to write not only the other main modern Iranian languages, Pashto, Kurdish, and Baluchi, but also those minor ones that are occasionally recorded. An advantage of the use of this consonantal script is that by not defining vowel qualities it is possible to include local dialect variations to a considerable extent.

Two modern Iranian languages spoken on Soviet territory are currently written in a modified version of the Russian alphabet: Tadzhik and Ossetic. Soviet scholars have, however, tended to use modified Latin alphabets to record the minor languages that have no literary tradition, such as some of the Pamir languages. Ossetic has also been written in the Georgian script.

Old Persian was written with a cuneiform syllabary, the origin of which is still hotly disputed. Middle Persian, Parthian, Sogdian, and Old Khwārezmian were recorded in various forms of Aramaic script. Two forms of this script as they developed for writing Sogdian were adopted by the Uighurs. In its cursive form this script spread even further, to the Mongols and Manchus. Three other scripts are important for the remaining Middle Iranian languages: Greek script for Bactrian, Arabic script for Late Khwārezmian, and varieties of Central Asian Brāhmī script, which are of Indian origin, for Khotanese and Tumshuq.

The Aramaic script was not systematically adapted to the writing of Middle Iranian; and despite the introduction of a variety of diacritical marks to differentiate letters, considerable ambiguity remained. Moreover, several letters tended to coalesce in form. In this respect, the Pahlavi script, used for writing the Middle Persian of the Zoroastrian books, developed furthest. In it, the original 22 letters of the Aramaic alphabet have been reduced to 14, which are further confused by the use of numerous ligatures (linked letters). It was the realization that this script was inadequate to record precisely the traditional pronunciation of the sacred text of the Avesta that led the Zoroastrian priests to devise the elaborate Avestan script, which, with its 48 distinct letters formed by differentiation out of the 14 used for Pahlavi, was well suited to the task.

(R.E.E.)

BIBLIOGRAPHY

Indo-Aryan languages (general works): JULES BLOCH, *L'Indo-aryen du veda aux temps modernes* (1934; rev. Eng. trans., *Indo-Aryan from the Vedas to Modern Times,* 1965), a masterly survey of Indo-Aryan throughout its history; R.L. TURNER, *A Comparative Dictionary of the Indo-Aryan Languages* (1966), an indispensable source in which Sanskrit word headings are given Middle Indo-Aryan forms and New Indo-Aryan cognates; M.B. EMENEAU, "The Dialects of Old Indo-Aryan," in HENRIK BIRNBAUM and JAAN PUHVEL (eds.), *Ancient Indo-European Dialects,* pp. 123–138 (1966), a good summary, with discussion of proposed theories and references.

Old Indo-Aryan: THOMAS BURROW, *The Sanskrit Language,* new and rev. ed. (1973), a summary of the prehistory and history of Sanskrit, with references to Middle Indo-Aryan, which contains somewhat personal views but is valuable for its discussion of non-Aryan influences on Sanskrit; LOUIS RENOU, *Histoire de la langue sanskrite* (1956), an insightful summary of the grammar, vocabulary, and style of different stages of Sanskrit, with text selections and translations; MANFRED MAYRHOFER, *Kurzgefasstes etymologisches Wörterbuch des Altindischen (A Concise Etymological Sanskrit Dictionary),* 4 vol. (1953–80), contains sober etymologies, full references, and a discussion of loanwords and words supposed to have been borrowed from Dravidian.

Middle Indo-Aryan: RICHARD PISCHEL, *Grammatik der Prākrit-Sprachen* (1900; Eng. trans., *Comparative Grammar of the Prākrit Languages,* 2nd ed., 1965), an encyclopedic grammar of all the Prākrits except Buddhist Hybrid Sanskrit and Pāli, which includes a good discussion of the different Prākrits in the introduction (now in need of updating); S.M. KATRE, *Prakrit Languages and Their Contribution to Indian Culture,* 2nd ed. (1964), a general survey of the Prākrits, including Pāli; LUDWIG ALSDORF, *Apabhraṃśa-Studien,* pp. 5–17, 20–37 (1937, reprinted 1966), important studies discussing noun and verb inflection.

Modern Indo-Aryan: JOHN BEAMES, *A Comparative Grammar of the Modern Aryan Languages: To Wit, Hindi, Panjabi, Sindhi, Gujarati, Marathi, Oṛiya, and Bangali,* 3 vol. (1872–79, reprinted 1966); and A.F.R. HOERNLE, *A Comparative Grammar of the Gaudian Languages with Special Reference to the Eastern Hindi* (1880, reprinted 1975), general comparative grammars of the New Indo-Aryan languages—though in need of modernization, still indispensable; SIR GEORGE A. GRIERSON, *On the Modern Indo-Aryan Vernaculars* (1931), a reprint of two long articles, tracing the phonologic developments that led to New Indo-Aryan; S.K. CHATTERJEE, *Indo-Aryan and Hindi,* 2nd rev. ed. (1960), a series of lectures briefly tracing the history of Indo-Aryan, with special emphasis on Hindi, its relation to other Indo-Aryan languages, and the language problem in India.

Iranian languages (general works): An important comprehensive treatment of the Iranian languages in general is WILHELM GEIGER and ERNST KUHN (eds.), *Grundriss der iranischen Philologie*, 2 vol. (1895–1904, reprinted 1974). This invaluable work is now in many respects antiquated, and it contains no account of several Middle Iranian languages that have been made known only in this century. A more recent account in less detail is provided by the *Handbuch der Orientalistik*, vol. 1, sect. 4, *Iranistik*, pt. 1, *Linguistik* (1958). There is an introduction to the subject in Russian: Иосиф Михайлович Оранский, *Введение в иранскую филологию* (1960). Some useful bibliography with brief guidelines is given by D.N. MACKENZIE, "Iranian Languages," in THOMAS A. SEBEOK (ed.), *Current Trends in Linguistics*, vol. 5, *Linguistics in South Asia*, pp. 450–477 (1969).

Old Iranian: All known Old Persian texts except for recent discoveries are given in transcription and translation in ROLAND KENT, *Old Persian*, 2nd ed. rev. (1953). Information on Old Persian linguistic problems is contained in WILHELM BRANDENSTEIN and MANFRED MAYRHOFER, *Handbuch des Altpersischen* (1964). On the Avestan language the article by GEORG MORGENSTIERNE, "Orthography and Sound-System of the Avesta," in *Norsk Tidsskrift for Sprogvidenskap*, 12:30–82 (1942), is of great importance. A useful bibliographical guide to more recent work on Avestan is provided by J. DUCHESNE-GUILLEMIN, "L'Étude de l'iranien ancien au vingtième siècle," *Kratylos*, 7:1–44 (1962).

Middle Iranian: The verbal system is described for Parthian by A. GHILAIN, *Essai sur la langue parthe, son système verbal d'après les textes manichéens* (1939, reprinted 1966); and for Middle Persian by W. HENNING, "Das Verbum des Mittelpersischen der Turfanfragmente," *Zeitschrift für Indologie und Iranistik*, 9:158–253 (1933). A Pahlavi dictionary for students is D.N. MACKENZIE, *A Concise Pahlavi Dictionary* (1971). The grammar of Sogdian has received detailed treatment in ILYA GERSHEVITCH, *A Grammar of Manichean Sogdian* (1954); and of Khotanese in R.E. EMMERICK, *Saka Grammatical Studies* (1968). A brief sketch of Khwārezmian is given in W.B. HENNING, "The Khwarezmian Language," *Zeki Velīdi Togan'a Armağan*, pp. 421–436 (1955).

Modern Iranian: Many works are available for the study of Modern Persian. An important recent work is GILBERT LAZARD, *Grammaire du persan contemporain* (1957). For the early stages of Modern Persian, Lazard's *Langue des plus anciens monuments de la prose persane* (1963) is invaluable. The same author has provided a comprehensive guide to the most important linguistic features of Tazhik in "Caractères distinctifs de la langue tadjik," *Bulletin de la Société linguistique de Paris*, 52:117–186 (1956). A treatment of Baluchi dialects is J.H. ELFENBEIN, *The Baluchi Language* (1966). Of the many works describing Kurdish dialects, a comprehensive modern work is D.N. MACKENZIE, *Kurdish Dialect Studies*, 2 vol. (1961–62). For the history of the Pashto language, GEORG MORGENSTIERNE, *An Etymological Vocabulary of Pashto* (1927), remains standard. Morgenstierne's *Indo-Iranian Frontier Languages*, 4 vol. in 6, 2nd ed. rev. and with new material (1973), is the work most often quoted for most of the minor languages. Ossetic has been described by a native speaker: V.I. ABAEV, *A Grammatical Sketch of Ossetic* (1964; orig. pub. in Russian, 1959).

(Ge.Ca./R.E.E.)

Indonesia

Indonesia, an archipelago in the Indian and Pacific oceans, lies across the Equator for one-eighth of the Earth's circumference off the coast of the Southeast Asian mainland. Its islands can be grouped into the Greater Sunda Islands of Sumatra (Sumatera), Java (Jawa), the southern extent of Borneo known as Kalimantan, and Celebes (Sulawesi); the Lesser Sunda Islands (Nusa Tenggara) of Bali and a chain of islands that runs eastward through Timor; the Moluccas (Maluku) between Celebes and New Guinea; and the western extent of New Guinea known as Irian Jaya (formerly Irian Barat). The country is the largest in Southeast Asia, about 741,000 square miles (1,919,400 square kilometres) in area, with a maximum dimension from east to west of about 3,200 miles (5,100 kilometres) and a dimension from north to south of 1,200 miles. It is composed of 13,667 islands, more than 7,600 of which are unnamed and almost 12,700 of which are uninhabited. Almost 70 percent of the area is included in the three largest islands of Kalimantan, of which about three-quarters, or 208,300 square miles, is part of Indonesia; Sumatra, with 182,900 square miles; and Irian Jaya, with 163,000 square miles. Nearly 85 percent of the total land area is accounted for with the addition of Celebes (73,000 square miles) and Java and Madura (51,000 square miles).

Composition of the Indonesian archipelago

Formerly known as the Netherlands, or Dutch, East Indies, the islands were first named Indonesia in modern times by a German geographer in 1884, although this name is thought to derive from Indos Nesos, "Indian Islands" in the ancient trading language of the region. The capital, Jakarta (Djakarta), is located near the northwestern coast of Java.

Indonesia declared its independence from The Netherlands in 1945, but its struggle for independence continued until 1949, and it was not until the official recognition by the United Nations of Irian Barat as a part of Indonesia in 1969 that the nation took on its present form. From 1949 to 1965 the country followed an erratic path in its development but managed to establish its identity and integrity. After 1965 a more rational development plan helped bring about the stabilization of the currency, the strengthening of the general basis of the economy, and an improvement of the low standard of living. In its development the country relies heavily upon its agricultural capacity and the export of such plantation crops as coconuts, rubber, and tea; its petroleum products, of which it is the major producer in Asia; its rich deposits of tin and other minerals; and timber. High oil prices during the late 1970s produced a balance-of-payments surplus and a balanced budget, but both achievements were adversely affected in the early 1980s both by lower oil prices and by reduced output.

The most populous nation in Southeast Asia, with a population of 147,490,300 reported in the 1980 census, and advantageously located between mainland Asia and Australia, Indonesia has a critical role to play in the development of its part of the world. In keeping with its size and importance, it is active in such regional and international groupings as the Association of Southeast Asian Nations (ASEAN), the Economic and Social Commission for Asia and the Pacific (ESCAP), and the United Nations. (For associated features see CHINA SEA; DJAKARTA; see also INDONESIA, HISTORY OF.)

This article is divided into the following sections:

I. The landscape

THE ENVIRONMENT

General nature of the islands' topography

The major Indonesian islands are characterized by rugged volcanic mountains, covered by dense tropical forests, which slope down to coastal plains often covered by thick alluvial swamps and bordered by shallow seas and coral reefs. Cultivated land is mainly devoted to rice, which in many areas is grown on mountain terraces, or to plantation crops. In the highly populated areas palm-shaded villages are scattered among green rice terraces, which are overlooked by the forest-clad cone of an active volcano.

Relief. The physical structure of the country is unique and complicated because it encompasses the junction of three major sections of the Earth's crust and involves a complex series of shelves, volcanic mountain chains, and deep-sea trenches. Kalimantan and the arc of islands including Sumatra, Java, Bali, and the Lesser Sunda chain sit on the Sunda Shelf, a southward extension of the continental mass of Asia. The shelf is bounded on the south and west by deep-sea trenches such as the Java Trench that form the true continental boundary. Irian Jaya and adjacent islands, possibly including Halmahera, sit on the Sahul Shelf, which is a northeastward extension of the Australian continental mass, in turn bounded to the northeast by a series of deep-sea trenches including the Bismarck Trench.

The third major unit of the Earth's crust in Indonesia is an extension of the belt of mountains of Japan and the Philippines that runs south between Kalimantan and Irian Jaya. It includes a series of mountain volcanoes and deep-sea trenches on and around Celebes and the Moluccas.

The interrelation of these units is not yet clearly understood. The present land–sea relations are somewhat misleading because the seas that lie on the Sunda Shelf and on the Sahul Shelf are shallow and of recent origin; they rest on the continental mass rather than on a true ocean floor. The Sunda Shelf itself has relatively low relief and is not volcanic. The mountain system that is welded along the outer margin of the shelf and comprises the outer edge of the continental mass of Asia, however, is an area of strong relief and is perhaps the most active volcanic zone in the world.

The outer or southern side of the chain of islands from Sumatra through Java and the Lesser Sundas forms the active leading edge of the Southeast Asian landmass. It is characterized by active volcanoes, bounded on the south and west by a series of deep-sea trenches and grading off on the north or inner edge to swamps, lowlands, and the shallow sea. This shallow sheltered sea was formed at the close of the Pleistocene period (10,000 to 2,500,000 years ago) and there is evidence of former land bridges that facilitated the migration of plants and animals from the Asian continent.

Borneo, the third largest island in the world and the main island on the Sunda Shelf, is hilly and mountainous. Its relief, however, seldom exceeds 3,940 feet (1,200 metres), and most of the island lies below 656 feet. Structural trends are not as well defined as on adjacent islands, although a broad mountain system runs roughly from northeast to southwest. It includes the island's highest peak of Mt. Kinabalu, which rises to 13,455 feet north of Kalimantan in Sabah, Malaysia. Indonesian Borneo, or Kalimantan, comprises about 73 percent of the island and is mainly mountainous and forested, with coastal alluvial swamps.

The Kepulauan Riau (Riau Islands) lie between Kalimantan and Sumatra. They have a granite core and can be considered as a physical extension of the Malay Peninsula. Like Malaysia, they are rich in tin, which is recovered both on land and offshore, mainly off the islands of Bangka, Belitung (Billiton), and Singkep.

Sumatra is flanked on its outer western edge by a string of nonvolcanic islands, including Simeulue, Nias, and the Mentawai group, none of which is densely inhabited. Sumatra runs from northwest to southeast for a length of 1,069 miles and a maximum width, including offshore islands, of about 324 miles and is bisected by the Equator. The island divides into four main physical regions: (1) the narrow coastal plain along the west; (2) the Pegunungan Barisan (Barisan Mountains), which extend the length of the island close to its western edge and include 10 active volcanoes; (3) an inner nonvolcanic zone of low hills grading down toward the stable platform of the Asian mainland; and (4) the broad alluvial lowland, as much as 150 miles wide and no more than 100 feet above sea level, that comprises the eastern half of the island.

Sub-regions of Sumatra

Much of eastern Sumatra is a forest-covered swamp that is difficult to penetrate seriously inhibits the development of the inland area. The mountain watershed is close to the west coast, and much of the soil cover in the hills and lowlands is built up by debris from the volcanoes. There are a number of beautiful lakes in Sumatra, the most famous of which is Danau Toba (Toba Lake), which lies in the north at an elevation of 2,953 feet above sea level and covers some 685 square miles.

Java is some 620 miles long and has a maximum width of about 125 miles. Its physical divisions are not as distinct as those of Sumatra because the offshore land zone is part of the island. Java can be broken down into five longitudinal zones. A series of limestone platforms extends along the south coast; in some areas they form an eroded karst region (a limestone region marked by sinks interspersed with abrupt ridges, irregular rocks, caverns, and underground streams) that makes communication and habitation difficult. A southern mountain belt is partially composed of sediments derived from eroded volcanoes; it includes a number of alluvial basins that are heavily cultivated, as around Bandung and Garut. The belt of volcanoes of the third physical region contains 50 active cones and 17 volcanoes with a recent history of eruption. A northern alluvial belt spreads across the Sunda Shelf toward the sea and is extended by delta formations, particularly during volcanic activity. There are deep inland extensions of the alluvial region, which in central Java cut through to the south coast. Finally, there is a second limestone platform area along the north coast of Madura and adjacent section of eastern Java.

The many islands east of Java are much smaller, less densely populated, and less developed than Java. The landscape patterns in Bali and Lombok are similar to those of eastern Java. The Lesser Sunda chain continues through Sumbawa and Flores islands, narrowing progressively until it appears on a map as a spine of volcanic islands that loops north through Pulau Banda (Banda Island), known as a source of nutmeg during the days of the spice trade (14th–18th centuries). The same volcanic system may be considered to reappear in northern Celebes. Sumba and Timor form an outer fringe of nonvolcanic islands, like those off the edge of the Sunda Shelf in Sumatra.

Celebes

Celebes shows some evidence of being squeezed between the conflicting forces of the more stable surrounding masses of the Sunda and Sahul shelves. Its complex shape somewhat resembles a capital K, with an additional long peninsula running northeast from its north–south backbone. There are, therefore, three large gulfs, Tomini, or Gorontalo, on the north, Tolo on the east, and Bone on the south. The coastline is long in relation to the size of the island. Celebes consists of ranges of mountains that are cut by deep rift valleys, many of which contain lakes. The island is fringed by coral reefs and is bordered by deep-sea trenches. Its northeast arm of Minahasa is volcanic and structurally different from the rest of the island, which is composed of a complex of igneous and metamorphic rocks.

The islands of the Sahul Shelf appear to have a structure similar to those of the Sunda Shelf. They include New Guinea and the northern Moluccas. The shelf is bordered on the north by deep trenches and mountains—which in the southeastern part of the island of New Guinea are volcanic along the outer rim—and lowland swamps along the inner rim that faces the Australian mainland across a shallow sea.

Volcanoes. There are some 220 active volcanoes and many hundreds that are considered extinct. They run in a crescent-shaped line along the outer margin of the country through Sumatra and Java as far as Flores and then loop up through the Banda Sea to a junction with the volcanoes of northern Celebes.

Volcanoes play a major role in soil development and enrichment, and there is a strong relationship between agricultural development, density of population, and location of volcanoes. Of the 70 volcanoes that have a recent history of eruption, the greatest concentration (17) is on Java. The greatest population densities occur in such areas as the region south and east of Merapi volcano in central Java, where the soil is enriched by volcanic ash and debris. The same pattern occurs on Bali and in northern Sumatra, where the rich soils are directly related to flows from volcanic eruptions.

Active volcanoes

Volcanic eruptions are by no means uncommon. Merapi, which rises to 9,485 feet near Yogyakarta (Jogjakarta), erupts frequently—often with extensive destruction of roads, fields, and villages but always to the great benefit of the soil. Kelud (5,679 feet), near Kediri in eastern Java, can be particularly devastating because its large crater lake is thrown out during eruption, causing great mud flows (*lahars*) that rush down into the plains and sweep all before them.

Perhaps the best known volcano is Krakatoa (Krakatau), which erupted from the seabed of the Selat Sunda (Sunda Strait) between Sumatra and Java in 1883. All life on the surrounding island group was destroyed. The violence caused tidal waves throughout Southeast Asia, killing tens of thousands of people, and ash clouds that circled the Earth affected the Sun's penetration and produced spectacular sunsets for more than one year. In 1963 Mt. Agung in Bali erupted after being dormant for more than 140 years, causing more than 1,500 deaths and heavy property destruction.

Drainage and soils. There are no long or large rivers except in Kalimantan, where the Kapuas (715 miles long), Barito (560 miles), and Mahakam (480 miles) flow from the interior mountains to the sea. They all have shifting sandbars across their mouths, which restrict their use for transportation.

The seas must also be viewed as a dominant physical feature, having an important effect on climate, transportation, and the development of culture. They serve both as channels of communication and as barriers protecting distinctive features. The shallow seas between many of the islands are a significant future resource not only of offshore oil and tin but also of fisheries and food.

Indonesia illustrates the relation between climate and source rock in the formation of soils. The rocks on Java are primarily andesitic volcanics (dark gray rocks consisting essentially of the minerals oligoclase or feldspar), while rhyolites (the acidic lava form of granite) are dominant on Sumatra, granites on the Kepulauan Riau, granites and sediments in Kalimantan, and sediments in Irian Jaya. The resulting soils in humid regions are mainly lateritic (containing iron oxides and aluminum hydroxide) and of varying fertility depending on the source rock; they include heavy black or gray-black margalite soils and limestone soils. Black soils occur in regions with a distinct dry season, and highly localized soils include the fertile ando soils, which developed on the andesitic volcanic sediments of the northeastern coast of Sumatra.

Soil erosion and leaching

In general, the perpetual high temperatures and heavy precipitation throughout much of Indonesia has led to rapid erosion and deep chemical weathering and leaching, which usually results in impoverished soil. In areas covered with tropical rain forests, such as Kalimantan, the soils are protected by the forest cycle; as plants die, rapid decomposition releases nutrients that are reabsorbed by new vegetation growth. Although such soils support a luxurious growth, they cannot support a large agricultural population because clearing of the forest breaks the cycle and can lead to accelerated soil deterioration.

Minerals that are leached from the soil are replaced by alluvial deposition from rivers, as in some parts of Kalimantan, or by deposition in impounded water or rice terraces. Most valuable in Indonesia is the volcanic ash, which is transported by wind to be deposited as a layer of homogeneous, fresh inorganic material over wide areas; it is also carried as suspended material in streams and irrigation channels. The best soils are derived from or enriched by basic andesitic volcanic material, the ejecta from rhyolitic volcanoes being less rich. The basic volcanoes occur in western Sumatra and especially in Java.

Climate. The climate is controlled by Indonesia's island structure and position astride the Equator, which assure high, even temperatures, and by its location between the two landmasses of Asia and Australia, which strongly influences the monsoonal rainfall patterns. Temperatures are uniformly high and are a function of elevation rather than latitude. They are highest along the coast, where mean annual temperatures range from 74° F to 88° F (23° C to 31° C) and are moderated considerably above 2,000 feet. The only area high enough to receive snow is the Pegunungan Maoke (Snow Mountains) of Irian Jaya. The difference of temperature between night and day in Jakarta is at least five times as great as the difference between high and low temperatures of January and July; the highest temperature ever recorded in Jakarta was 96° F (36° C), and the lowest was 65° F (18° C).

Rainfall patterns

Rainfall is more varied in extremes and distribution. Most of Indonesia receives heavy precipitation throughout the year, the greatest amounts occurring from December to March. From central Java eastward toward Australia, however, the dry season, from June to October, is progressively more pronounced; in Timor and Sumba there is little rain during these months. All of Kalimantan, all of Sumatra except for portions of its northern tip, and much of Java, eastern and southern Celebes, Irian Jaya, and the Moluccas have an average annual rainfall of 80 inches (2,000 millimetres) or more. Eastern Java and northern Celebes receive between 60 and 80 inches, while the Lesser Sunda Islands, closest to Australia, have only 40 to 60 inches.

The absolute daily maximum of rainfall can be extremely high, with a number of stations recording between 20 and 28 inches. Local variations, caused in large part by geographic features, are great. Jakarta, for example, near sea level, has a mean annual rainfall of 75 inches, while Bogor, which is 30 miles south towards the mountains, at an elevation of 873 feet, records 170 inches of rainfall.

Seasonal variations are due to monsoonal Asian air drifts and the convergence of tropical air masses from both north and south of the Equator along an intertropical front of low pressure. The monsoon pattern in any given part of the archipelago depends on location either north or south of the Equator, proximity to Australia or mainland Asia, and the position of the intertropical front. During December, January, and February, the west monsoon, reflecting Asian influence, brings heavy rain to southern Sumatra, Java, and the Lesser Sunda Islands. In June, July, and August, these areas are affected by the east monsoon, which brings dry air from Australia. Only the Lesser Sunda Islands and eastern Java have a well-developed dry season, which increases in length toward Australia. By the time the east monsoon has crossed the Equator—becoming the southwest monsoon of the Northern Hemisphere—its winds have become humid and a source of rain. Sumatra and Kalimantan, which are located close to the Equator and far from Australia, have no dry season, although precipitation tends to be slightly lower

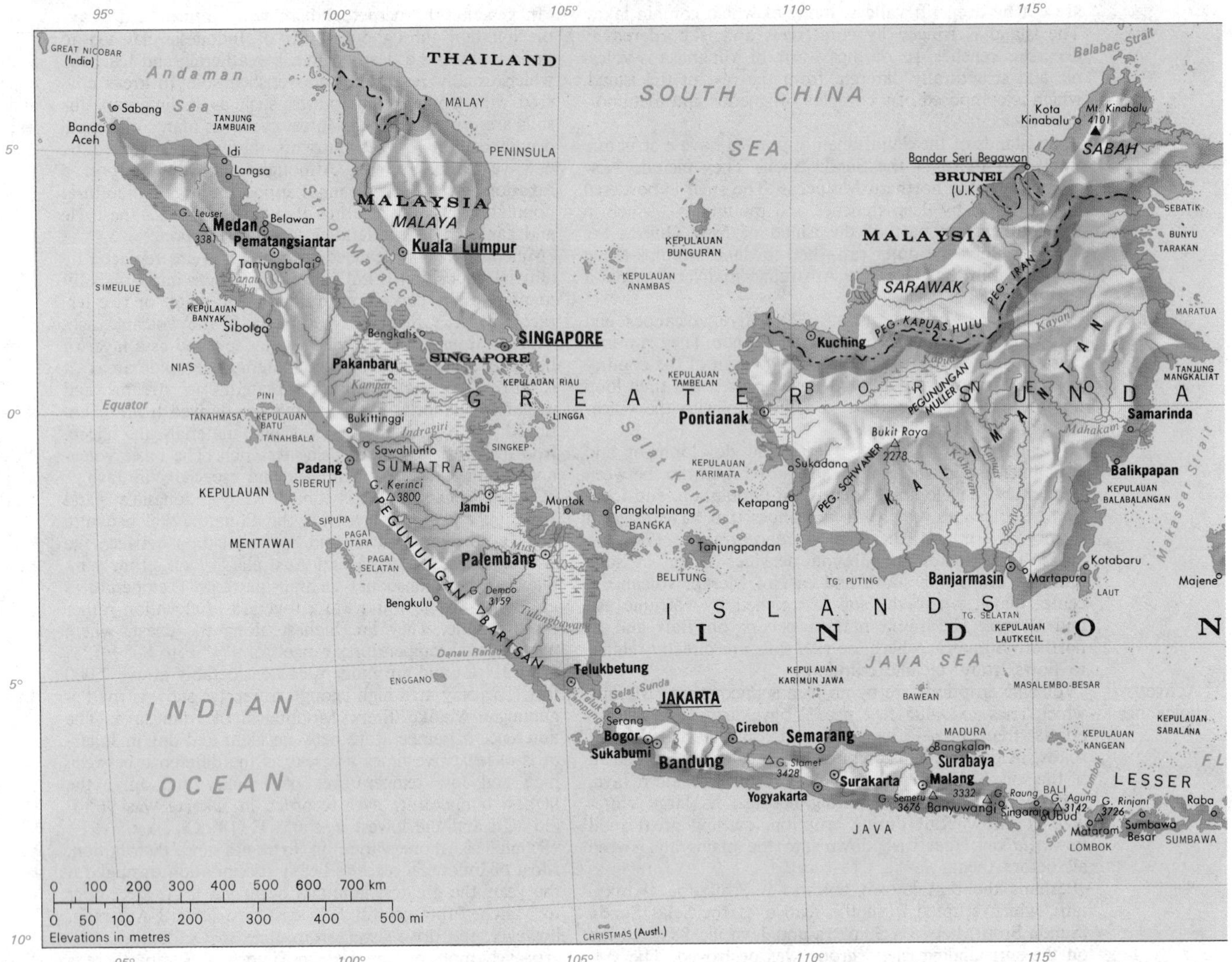

95°
100°
105°
110°
115°
5°
0°
5°
10°
GREAT NICOBAR (India)
Andaman Sea
THAILAND
MALAY PENINSULA
SOUTH CHINA SEA
Balabac Strait
Sabang
Banda Aceh
TANJUNG JAMBUAIR
Idi
Langsa
G. Leuser 3381
Medan
Belawan
Pematangsiantar
Tanjungbalai
Danau Toba
SIMEULUE
KEPULAUAN BANYAK
Sibolga
NIAS
Str. of Malacca
MALAYSIA
MALAYA
Kuala Lumpur
Bengkalis
SINGAPORE
Pakanbaru
Kampar
KEPULAUAN RIAU
PINI
Equator
TANAHMASA
KEPULAUAN BATU
TANAHBALA
Bukittinggi
Indragiri
Sawahlunto
SUMATRA
Padang
SIBERUT
G. Kerinci 3800
Jambi
KEPULAUAN MENTAWAI
SIPURA
PAGAI UTARA
PAGAI SELATAN
PEGUNUNGAN BARISAN
Musi
Palembang
G. Dempo 3159
Bengkulu
Tulangbawang
Danau Ranau
ENGGANO
Telukbetung
Selat Sunda
Teluk Lampung
KEPULAUAN BUNGURAN
KEPULAUAN ANAMBAS
KEPULAUAN TAMBELAN
LINGGA
SINGKEP
GREATER SUNDA ISLANDS
Muntok
Pangkalpinang
BANGKA
Selat Karimata
Tanjungpandan
BELITUNG
Pontianak
KEPULAUAN KARIMATA
Sukadana
Ketapang
Kota Kinabalu
Mt. Kinabalu 4101
SABAH
Bandar Seri Begawan
BRUNEI (U.K.)
SEBATIK
BUNYU
TARAKAN
MALAYSIA
SARAWAK
PEG. IRAN
PEG. KAPUAS HULU
Kuching
Kapuas
Kayan
MARATUA
TANJUNG MANGKALIAT
BORNEO
PEGUNUNGAN MULLER
KALIMANTAN
Samarinda
Mahakam
Bukit Raya 2278
PEG. SCHWANER
Kahayan
Barito
Balikpapan
KEPULAUAN BALABALANGAN
Makassar Strait
Banjarmasin
Martapura
Kotabaru
LAUT
Majene
TG. PUTING
TG. SELATAN
KEPULAUAN LAUTKECIL
INDONESIA
JAVA SEA
KEPULAUAN KARIMUN JAWA
MASALEMBO-BESAR
BAWEAN
JAKARTA
Serang
Bogor
Sukabumi
Bandung
Cirebon
Semarang
G. Slamet 3428
Surakarta
Yogyakarta
MADURA
Bangkalan
Surabaya
Malang
3332
G. Semeru 3676
Banyuwangi
JAVA
KEPULAUAN KANGEAN
KEPULAUAN SABALANA
BALI
G. Raung
Singaraja
G. Agung 3142
Ubud
Lombok
Selat Lombok
G. Rinjani 3726
Mataram
LOMBOK
Sumbawa Besar
SUMBAWA
Raba
LESSER
INDIAN OCEAN
0 100 200 300 400 500 600 700 km
0 50 100 200 300 400 500 mi
Elevations in metres
CHRISTMAS (Austl.)

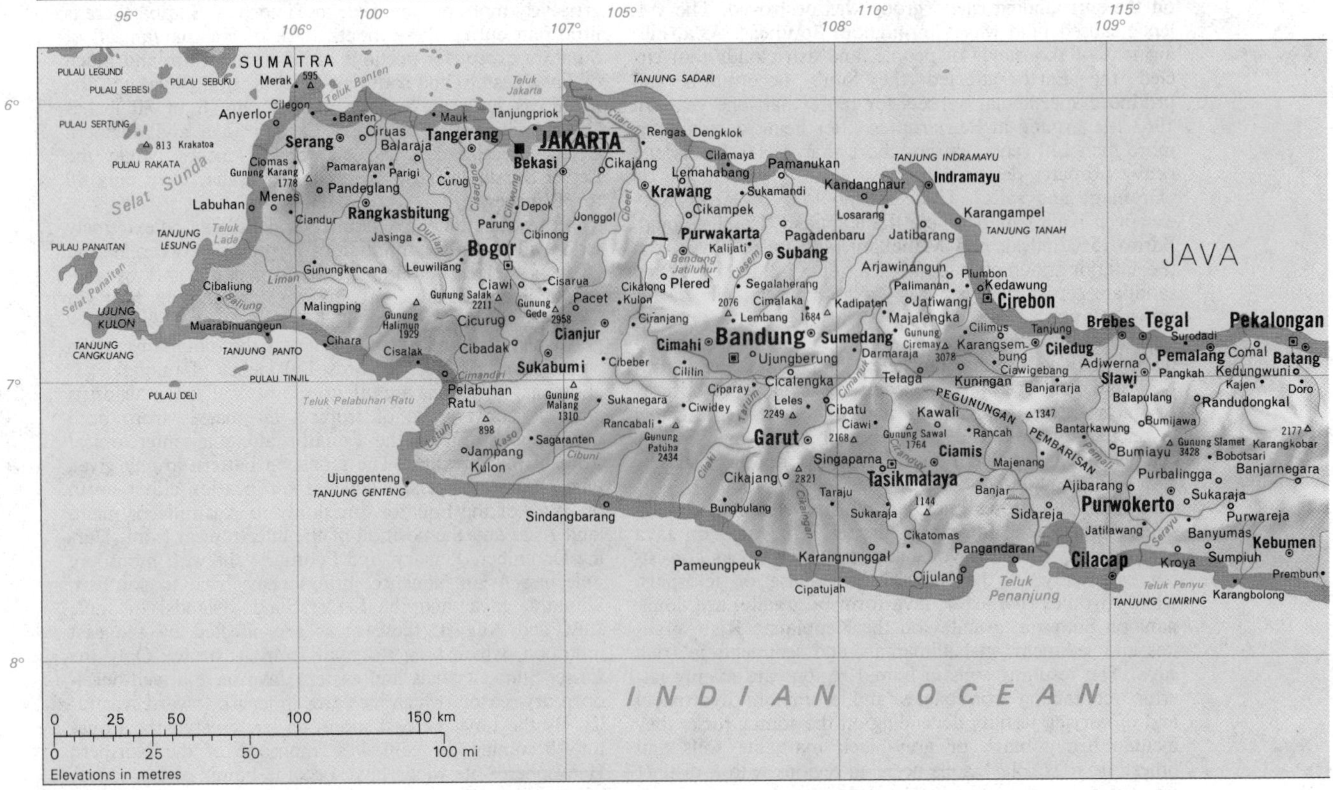

106°
107°
108°
109°
6°
7°
8°
SUMATRA
PULAU LEGUNDI
PULAU SEBESI
PULAU SEBUKU
Merak 595
Teluk Banten
Teluk Jakarta
TANJUNG SADARI
PULAU SERTUNG
Cilegon
Anyerlor
Banten
Serang
Ciruas
Balaraja
Mauk
Tangerang
Tanjungpriok
JAKARTA
Bekasi
Rengas Dengklok
Citarum
Cilamaya
Pamanukan
TANJUNG INDRAMAYU
Indramayu
813 Krakatoa
PULAU RAKATA
Ciomas
Gunung Karang 1778
Pamarayan
Parigi
Curug
Cikajang
Lemahabang
Pandeglang
Selat Sunda
Labuhan
Menes
Ciandur
Rangkasbitung
Depok
Krawang
Sukamandi
Kandanghaur
Karangampel
TANJUNG TANAH
TANJUNG LESUNG
Teluk Lada
Parung
Cibinong
Jonggol
Cikampek
Losarang
Jasinga
Bogor
Purwakarta
Pagadenbaru
Jatibarang
JAVA
PULAU PANAITAN
Selat Panaitan
Gunungkencana
Leuwiliang
Kalijati
Subang
Bendung Jatiluhur
Arjawinangun
Plumbon
Cibaliung
Liman
Ciawi
Cisarua
Cikalong
Plered
Segalaherang
Palimanan
Kedawung
Cirebon
Gunung Salak 2211
Gunung Gede 2958
Pacet
Kulon
2076
Cimalaka
Jatiwangi
Lembang
1684
Kadipaten
Majalengka
UJUNG KULON
Malingping
Gunung Halimun 1929
Cicurug
Cianjur
Ciranjang
Bandung
Sumedang
Gunung Ciremay 3078
Cilimus
Tanjung
Brebes
Tegal
Pekalongan
Surodadi
TANJUNG CANGKUANG
Muarabinuangeun
Cihara
Cibadak
Cimahi
Ujungberung
Darmaraja
Karangsembung
Ciledug
Pemalang
Comal
Batang
TANJUNG PANTO
Cisalak
Sukabumi
Cibeber
Cililin
Cicalengka
Telaga
Ciawigebang
Adiwerna
Pangkah
Kedungwuni
PULAU TINJIL
Cimandiri
Kuningan
Slawi
Kajen
Doro
PULAU DELI
Teluk Pelabuhan Ratu
Pelabuhan Ratu
Gunung Malang 1310
Sukanegara
Ciparay
Leles 2249
Cibatu
Banjarsari
Banjarjarja
Balapulang
Randudongkal
Ciwidey
Cimanuk
PEGUNUNGAN PEMBARISAN
1347
898
Rancabali
Gunung Patuha 2434
Garut
2168
Ciawi
Gunung Sawal 1764
Kawali
Rancah
Bantarkawung
Bumijawa
2177
Sagaranten
Jampang Kulon
Cibuni
Ciamis
Majenang
Bumiayu
Gunung Slamet 3428
Karangkobar
Bobotsari
Ujunggenteng
TANJUNG GENTENG
Singaparna
2821
Tasikmalaya
Banjar
Ajibarang
Purbalingga
Banjarnegara
Cikajang
Taraju
Sukaraja
Purwokerto
Purwareja
Sindangbarang
Bungbulang
Sukaraja
1144
Sidareja
Jatilawang
Banyumas
Kebumen
Cikatomas
Pangandaran
Cilacap
Kroya
Sumpiuh
Pameungpeuk
Karangnunggal
Cijulang
Teluk Penanjung
Teluk Penyu
TANJUNG CIMIRING
Karangbolong
Prembun
Cipatujah
INDIAN OCEAN
0 25 50 100 150 km
0 25 50 100 mi
Elevations in metres

INDONESIA

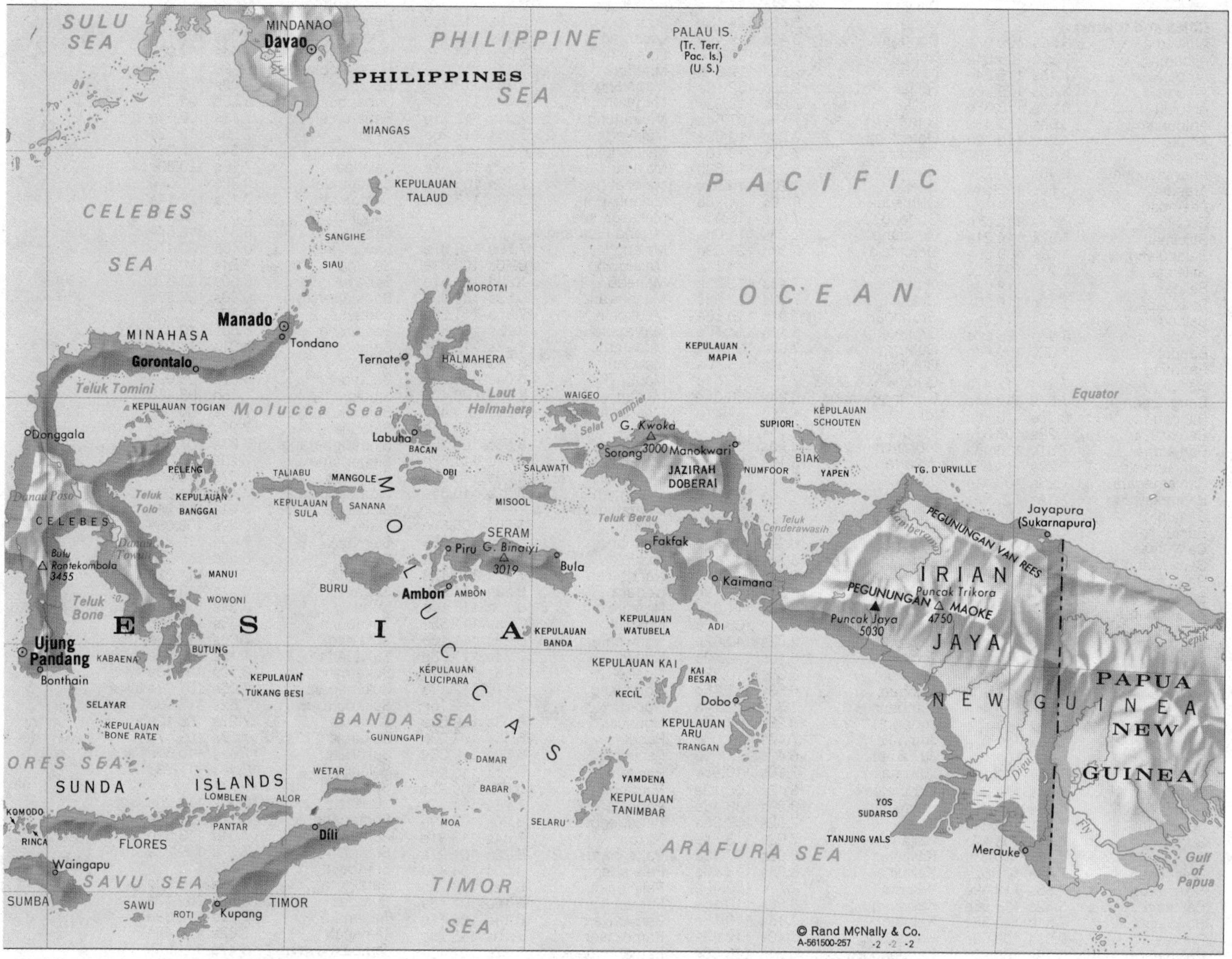
SULU SEA
MINDANAO
Davao
PHILIPPINE SEA
PHILIPPINES
PALAU IS. (Tr. Terr. Pac. Is.) (U.S.)
MIANGAS
KEPULAUAN TALAUD
CELEBES SEA
PACIFIC OCEAN
SANGIHE
SIAU
MOROTAI
Manado
MINAHASA
Tondano
Ternate
HALMAHERA
Gorontalo
KEPULAUAN MAPIA
Teluk Tomini
KEPULAUAN TOGIAN
Molucca Sea
Laut Halmahera
WAIGEO
Equator
Selat Dampier
G. Kwoka 3000
SUPIORI
KEPULAUAN SCHOUTEN
Donggala
Labuha
BACAN
OBI
SALAWATI
Sorong
Manokwari
BIAK
PELENG
TALIABU
MANGOLE
JAZIRAH DOBERAI
NUMFOOR
YAPEN
TG. D'URVILLE
Danau Poso
Teluk Tolo
KEPULAUAN BANGGAI
KEPULAUAN SULA
SANANA
MISOOL
Teluk Berau
Teluk Cenderawasih
Jayapura (Sukarnapura)
PEGUNUNGAN VAN REES
CELEBES
Danau Towuti
SERAM
Piru
G. Binaiyi 3019
Bula
Fakfak
Bulu Rantekombola 3455
MANUI
WOWONI
BURU
Ambon
AMBON
Kaimana
IRIAN
PEGUNUNGAN MAOKE
Puncak Trikora 4750
Puncak Jaya 5030
Teluk Bone
KEPULAUAN BANDA
KEPULAUAN WATUBELA
ADI
JAYA
MOLUCCAS
CELEBES
Ujung Pandang
KABAENA
BUTUNG
Bonthain
KEPULAUAN LUCIPARA
KEPULAUAN KAI
KAI BESAR
KECIL
Dobo
PAPUA NEW GUINEA
NEW GUINEA
SELAYAR
KEPULAUAN TUKANG BESI
KEPULAUAN BONE RATE
BANDA SEA
GUNUNGAPI
KEPULAUAN ARU
TRANGAN
FLORES SEA
DAMAR
SUNDA ISLANDS
WETAR
LOMBLEN
ALOR
BABAR
YAMDENA
KEPULAUAN TANIMBAR
YOS SUDARSO
KOMODO
PANTAR
MOA
SELARU
Dili
TANJUNG VALS
RINCA
FLORES
ARAFURA SEA
Merauke
Gulf of Papua
Waingapu
SAVU SEA
TIMOR SEA
SUMBA
SAWU
ROTI
Kupang
TIMOR
Digul
Fly
Sepik
Mamberamo
© Rand McNally & Co.
A-561500-257

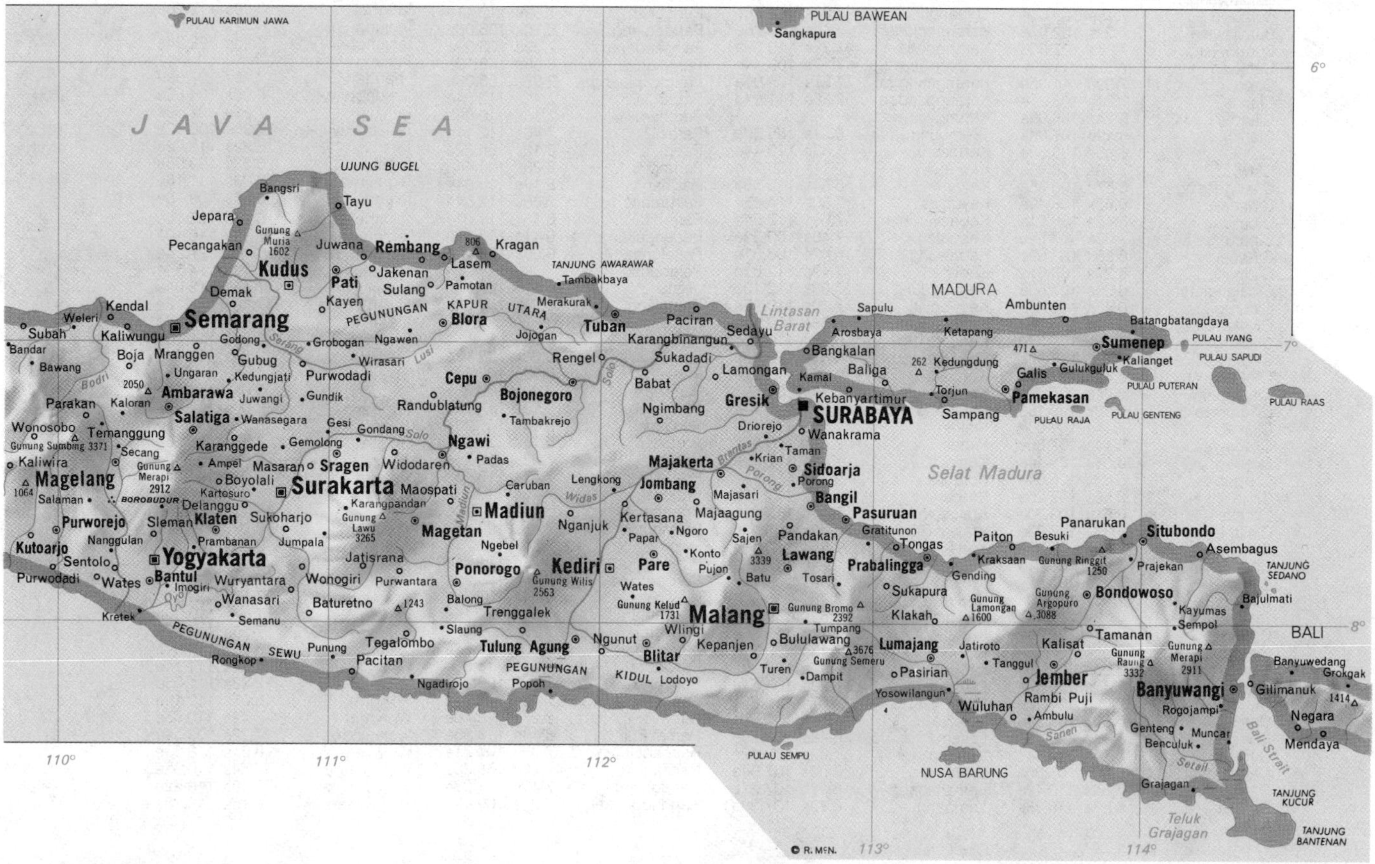
PULAU KARIMUN JAWA
PULAU BAWEAN
Sangkapura
JAVA SEA
UJUNG BUGEL
Bangsri
Tayu
Jepara
Gunung Muria 1602
Pecangakan
Juwana
Rembang
Kragan
Kudus
Pati
Jakenan
Lasem
TANJUNG AWARAWAR
Tambakbaya
Demak
Kayen
Sulang
Pamotan
MADURA
Sapulu
Ambunten
Kendal
Semarang
PEGUNUNGAN KAPUR UTARA
Blora
Merakurak
Tuban
Paciran
Lintasan Barat
Arosbaya
Ketapang
Batangbatangdaya
Subah
Weleri
Kaliwungu
Godong
Grobogan
Ngawen
Jojogan
Karangbinangun
Sedayu
Bangkalan
Sumenep
PULAU IYANG
Bandar
Boja
Mranggen
Gubug
Wirasari
Rengel
Sukadadi
Lamongan
Baliga
Kedungdung
Kalianget
PULAU SAPUDI
Bawang
Ungaran
Kedungjati
Purwodadi
Cepu
Babat
Kamal
Galis
Gulukguluk
PULAU PUTERAN
Ambarawa
Juwangi
Gundik
Randublatung
Bojonegoro
Gresik
Kebanyartimur
Torjun
Pamekasan
PULAU RAAS
Parakan
Kaloran
Salatiga
Wanasegara
Gesi
Tambakrejo
Ngimbang
Driorejo
SURABAYA
Sampang
PULAU RAJA
PULAU GENTENG
Wonosobo
Temanggung
Gondang
Ngawi
Wanakrama
Gunung Sumbing 3371
Secang
Karanggede
Gemolong
Taman
Kaliwira
Gunung Merapi 2912
Ampel
Masaran
Sragen
Widodaren
Padas
Majakerta
Krian
Sidoarjo
Selat Madura
Magelang
Boyolali
Surakarta
Lengkong
Jombang
Porong
Salaman
BOROBUDUR
Kartosuro
Delanggu
Karangpandan
Maospati
Caruban
Majasari
Bangil
Purworejo
Sleman
Klaten
Sukoharjo
Gunung Lawu 3265
Madiun
Nganjuk
Kertasana
Majaagung
Pasuruan
Panarukan
Situbondo
Kutoarjo
Nanggulan
Prambanan
Jumpala
Magetan
Papar
Ngoro
Sajen
Pandakan
Gratitunon
Tongas
Paiton
Besuki
Asembagus
Sentolo
Yogyakarta
Jatisrana
Ngebel
Konto
Lawang
Kraksaan
Gunung Ringgit 1250
Prajekan
TANJUNG SEDANO
Purwodadi
Wates
Bantul
Imogiri
Wuryantara
Wonogiri
Purwantara
Ponorogo
Kediri
Pare
Pujon
Batu
Tosari
Prabalinggo
Gending
Wanasari
Gunung Wilis 2563
Wates
Sukapura
Bondowoso
Bajulmati
Baturetno
Balong
Gunung Kelud 1731
Malang
Gunung Bromo 2392
Gunung Lamongan 1600
Gunung Argopuro 3088
Kayumas
Sempol
Kretek
Semanu
Trenggalek
Wlingi
Klakah
Tamanan
BALI
PEGUNUNGAN SEWU
Slaung
Ngunut
Tumpang
Punung
Tegalombo
Tulung Agung
Blitar
Kepanjen
Bululawang
Gunung Semeru 3676
Lumajang
Jatiroto
Kalisat
Gunung Raung 3332
Gunung Merapi 2911
Banyuwedang
Grokgak
Rongkop
Pacitan
PEGUNUNGAN KIDUL
Lodoyo
Turen
Dampit
Pasirian
Tanggul
Jember
Banyuwangi
Gilimanuk
Ngadirojo
Popoh
Yosowilangun
Wuluhan
Rambi Puji
Ambulu
Rogojampi
Negara
Genteng
Muncar
Mendaya
Benculuk
Bali Strait
PULAU SEMPU
NUSA BARUNG
Grajagan
TANJUNG KUCUR
Teluk Grajagan
TANJUNG BANTENAN
© R. McN.

MAP INDEX

Cities and towns

Adiwerna	6.56s	109.07e
Ajibarang	7.25s	109.04e
Ambarawa	7.15s	110.24e
Ambon	3.43s	128.12e
Ambulu	8.21s	113.36e
Ambunten	6.54s	113.43e
Ampel	7.26s	110.32e
Anyerlor	6.04s	105.56e
Arjawinangun	6.40s	108.25e
Arosbaya	6.56s	112.51e
Asembagus	7.45s	114.12e
Babat	7.07s	112.09e
Bajulmati	7.57s	114.21e
Balapulang	7.03s	109.05e
Balaraja	6.21s	106.26e
Baliga	7.08s	113.03e
Balikpapan	1.17s	116.50e
Balong	7.57s	111.26e
Banda Aceh	5.34n	95.20e
Bandar	7.02s	109.47e
Bandung	6.54s	107.36e
Bangil	7.36s	112.47e
Bangkalan	7.02s	112.44e
Bangsri	6.30s	110.45e
Banjar	7.22s	108.32e
Banjararja	7.01s	108.48e
Banjarmasin	3.20s	114.35e
Banjarnegara	7.23s	109.41e
Bantarkawung	7.14s	108.55e
Banten	6.03s	106.09e
Bantul	7.54s	110.20e
Banyumas	7.31s	109.17e
Banyuwangi	8.12s	114.21e
Banyuwedang	8.08s	114.36e
Batang	6.55s	109.45e
Batangbatang-daya	6.56s	113.59e
Batu	7.53s	112.31e
Baturetno	7.59s	110.56e
Bawang	7.06s	109.55e
Bekasi	6.14s	106.59e
Belawan	3.47n	98.41e
Benculuk	8.26s	114.12e
Bengkalis	1.28n	102.07e
Bengkulu	3.48s	102.16e
Besuki	7.45s	113.41e
Blitar	8.06s	112.09e
Blora	6.57s	111.25e
Bobotsari	7.18s	109.22e
Bogor	6.35s	106.47e
Boja	7.06s	110.06e
Bojonegoro	7.09s	111.52e
Bondowoso	7.55s	113.49e
Bonthain	5.32s	119.56e
Boyolali	7.31s	110.35e
Brebes	6.53s	109.03e
Bukittinggi	0.19s	100.22e
Bula	3.06s	130.30e
Bululawang	8.05s	112.37e
Bumiayu	7.15s	109.00e
Bumijawa	7.09s	109.07e
Bungbulang	7.27s	107.35e
Caruban	7.32s	111.39e
Cepu	7.09s	111.35e
Ciamis	7.20s	108.21e
Ciandur	6.24s	105.59e
Cianjur	6.49s	107.08e
Ciawi	6.40s	106.50e
Ciawi	7.10s	108.09e
Ciawigebang	6.57s	108.35e
Cibadak	6.53s	106.49e
Cibaliung	6.46s	105.51e
Cibatu	7.06s	107.59e
Cibeber	6.55s	107.09e
Cibinong	6.27s	106.51e
Cicalengka	6.59s	107.50e
Cicurug	6.47s	106.47e
Cihara	6.52s	106.06e
Cijulang	7.42s	108.27e
Cikajang	7.23s	107.49e
Cikalong Kulon	6.42s	107.12e
Cikampek	6.24s	107.27e
Cikatomas	7.36s	108.15e
Cilacap	7.44s	109.00e
Cilamaya	6.14s	107.36e
Ciledug	6.54s	108.44e
Cilegon	6.03s	106.04e
Cililin	6.56s	107.26e
Cilimus	6.51s	108.30e
Cimahi	6.53s	107.32e
Cimalaka	6.48s	107.56e
Ciomas	6.12s	106.01e
Ciparay	7.02s	107.42e
Cipatujah	7.45s	108.00e
Ciranjang	6.49s	107.14e
Cirebon	6.44s	108.34e
Ciruas	6.07s	106.15e
Cisalak	6.55s	106.27e
Cisarua	6.40s	106.56e
Ciwidey	7.06s	107.26e
Comal	6.53s	109.31e
Curug	6.15s	106.33e
Dampit	8.13s	112.44e
Darmaraja	6.55s	108.05e
Delanggu	7.36s	110.42e
Demak	6.53e	110.38e
Depok	6.24s	106.50e
Dili	8.33s	125.34e
Dobo	5.46s	134.13e
Donggala	0.40s	119.44e
Doro	7.02s	109.41e
Driorejo	7.20s	112.37e
Fakfak	2.55s	132.18e
Galis	7.08s	113.33e
Garut	7.13s	107.54e
Gemolong	7.24s	110.50e
Gending	7.47s	113.18e
Genteng	8.22s	114.09e
Gesi	7.20s	110.59e
Gilimanuk	8.10s	114.26e
Godong	7.01s	110.45e
Gondang	7.23s	111.06e
Gorontalo	0.33n	123.03e
Grajagan	8.36s	114.11e
Gratitunon	7.43s	113.00e
Gresik	7.09s	112.38e
Grobogan	7.01s	110.56e
Grokgak	8.11s	114.46e
Gubug	7.02s	110.40e
Gulukguluk	7.04s	113.40e
Gundik	7.12s	110.54e
Gunungkencana	6.34s	106.04e
Idi	4.55n	97.47e
Imogiri	7.55s	110.23e
Indramayu	6.20s	108.19e
Jakarta	6.10s	106.48e
Jakenan	6.45s	111.08e
Jambi	1.36s	103.37e
Jampang Kulon	7.16s	106.37e
Jasinga	6.29s	106.28e
Jatibarang	6.28s	108.17e
Jatilawang	7.31s	109.06e
Jatiroto	8.07s	113.19e
Jatisrana	7.48s	111.07e
Jatiwangi	6.43s	108.16e
Jayapura	2.32s	140.42e
Jember	8.10s	113.42e
Jepara	6.35s	110.39e
Jojogan	6.58s	111.46e
Jombang	7.33s	112.14e
Jonggol	6.28s	107.03e
Jumpala	7.42s	111.00e
Juwana	6.42s	111.09e
Juwangi	7.10s	110.45e
Kadipaten	6.46s	108.10e
Kaimana	3.39s	133.45e
Kajen	7.02s	109.35e
Kalianget	7.03s	113.54e
Kalijati	6.32s	107.40e
Kalisat	8.08s	113.48e
Kaliwira	7.27s	109.49e
Kaliwungu	6.56s	110.15e
Kaloran	7.15s	110.15e
Kamal	7.10s	112.42e
Kandanghaur	6.21s	108.06e
Karangampel	6.27s	108.27e
Karang-binangun	7.00s	112.28e
Karangbolong	7.45s	109.28e
Karanggede	7.22s	110.39e
Karangkobar	7.17s	109.44e
Karangnunggal	7.37s	108.06e
Karangpandan	7.36s	111.04e
Karang-sembung	6.51s	108.39e
Kartosuro	7.33s	110.44e
Kawali	7.11s	108.22e
Kayen	6.54s	110.58e
Kayumas	7.50s	114.08e
Kebanyartimur	7.09s	112.54e
Kebumen	7.40s	109.39e
Kedawung	6.42s	108.31e
Kediri	7.49s	112.01e
Kedungdung	7.06s	113.13e
Kedungjati	7.10s	110.37e
Kedungwuni	6.58s	109.39e
Kendal	6.55s	110.12e
Kepanjen	8.07s	112.33e
Kertasano	7.35s	112.06e
Ketapang	1.52s	109.59e
Ketapang	6.54s	113.17e
Klakah	7.59s	113.15e
Klaten	7.42s	110.35e
Konto	7.46s	112.19e
Kotabaru	3.14s	116.13e
Kragan	6.42s	111.37e
Kraksaan	7.45s	113.21e
Krawang	6.19s	107.17e
Kretek	7.58s	110.19e
Krian	7.24s	112.33e
Kroya	7.38s	109.14e
Kudus	6.48s	110.50e
Kuningan	6.59s	108.29e
Kupang	10.10s	123.35e
Kutoarjo	7.43s	109.53e
Labuha	0.37s	127.29e
Labuhan	6.23s	105.51e
Lamongan	7.07s	112.25e
Langsa	4.28n	97.58e
Lasem	6.42s	111.26e
Lawang	7.49s	112.42e
Leles	7.06s	107.54e
Lemahabang	6.17s	107.27e
Lembang	6.49s	107.38e
Lengkong	7.31s	112.03e
Leuwiliang	6.34s	106.37e
Lodoyo	8.10s	112.13e
Losarang	6.24s	108.10e
Lumajang	8.08s	113.13e
Madiun	7.37s	111.31e
Magelang	7.28s	110.13e
Magetan	7.39s	111.20e
Majaagung	7.34s	112.21e
Majakerta	7.28s	112.26e
Majalengka	6.50s	108.13e
Majasari	7.30s	112.31e
Majenang	7.18s	108.45e
Majene	3.33s	118.57e
Makasar, see Ujung Pandang		
Malang	7.59s	112.37e
Malingping	6.46s	106.01e
Manado	1.29n	124.51e
Manokwari	0.52s	134.05e
Maospati	7.35s	111.26e
Martapura	3.25s	114.51e
Masaran	7.27s	110.56e
Mataram	8.35s	116.07e
Mauk	6.04s	106.30e
Medan	3.35n	98.40e
Mendaya	8.23s	114.42e
Menes	6.23s	105.56e
Merak	5.56s	106.00e
Merakurak	6.52s	111.59e
Merauke	8.28s	140.20e
Mranggen	7.01s	110.31e
Muarabinuan-geun	6.50s	105.53e
Muncar	8.25s	114.18e
Muntok	2.04s	105.11e
Nanggulan	7.46s	110.12e
Negara	8.22s	114.37e
Ngadirojo	8.13s	111.19e
Nganjuk	7.36s	111.55e
Ngawen	6.59s	111.18e
Ngawi	7.24s	111.26e
Ngebel	7.46s	111.37e
Ngimbang	7.17s	112.13e
Ngoro	7.41s	112.16e
Ngunut	8.08s	112.00e
Pacet	6.45s	107.03e
Paciran	6.52s	112.20e
Pacitan	8.11s	111.05e
Padang	0.57s	100.21e
Padas	7.25s	111.32e
Pagadenbaru	6.26s	107.49e
Paiton	7.44s	113.31e
Pakanbaru	0.32n	101.27e
Palembang	3.00s	104.45e
Palimanan	6.42s	108.26e
Pamanukan	6.16s	107.48e
Pamarayan	6.15s	106.17e
Pamekasan	7.10s	113.28e
Pameungpeuk	7.37s	107.42e
Pamotan	6.46s	111.29e
Panarukan	7.42s	113.56e
Pandakan	7.39s	112.41e
Pandeglang	6.18s	106.06e
Pangandaran	7.39s	108.39e
Pangkah	6.58s	109.10e
Pangkalpinang	2.08s	106.08e
Papar	7.42s	112.04e
Parakan	7.16s	110.06e
Pare	7.46s	112.11e
Parigi	6.12s	106.22e
Parung	6.25s	106.44e
Pasirian	8.13s	113.04e
Pasuruan	7.38s	112.54e
Pati	6.45s	111.01e
Pecangakan	6.41s	110.42e
Pekalongan	6.53s	109.40e
Pelabuhan Ratu	6.59s	106.33e
Pemalang	6.54s	109.22e
Pematang-siantar	2.58n	99.03e
Piru	3.03s	128.12e
Plered	6.37s	107.22e
Plumbon	6.40s	108.28e
Ponorogo	7.52s	111.27e
Pontianak	0.02s	109.20e
Popoh	8.15s	111.48e
Porong	7.32s	112.20e
Prabalingga	7.45s	113.13e
Prajekan	7.46s	113.58e
Prambanan	7.45s	110.30e
Prembun	7.43s	109.48e
Pujon	7.50s	112.27e
Punung	8.08s	111.01e
Purbalingga	7.24s	109.22e
Purwakarta	6.34s	107.26e
Purwantara	7.50s	111.16e
Purwareja	7.29s	109.25e
Purwodadi	7.05s	110.54e
Purwodadi	7.50s	110.00e
Purwokerto	7.25s	109.14e
Purworejo	7.43s	110.01e
Raba	8.27s	118.46e
Rambi Puji	8.13s	113.36e
Rancabali	7.08s	107.21e
Rancan	7.12s	108.30e
Randublatung	7.12s	111.23e
Randudongkal	7.06s	109.19e
Rangkasbitung	6.21s	106.15e
Rembang	6.42s	111.20e
Rengas Dengklok	6.09s	107.17e
Rengel	7.04s	112.00e
Rogojampi	8.19s	114.18e
Rongkop	8.08s	110.45e
Sabang	5.53n	95.20e
Sagaranten	7.13s	106.54e
Sajen	7.39s	112.32e
Salaman	7.34s	110.08e
Salatiga	7.19s	110.30e
Samarinda	0.30s	117.09e
Sampang	7.12s	113.14e
Sangkapura	5.52s	112.40e
Sapulu	6.54s	112.57e
Sawahlunto	0.40s	100.47e
Secang	7.24s	110.13e
Sedayu	6.59s	112.32e
Segalaherang	6.40s	107.39e
Semanu	8.00s	110.38e
Semarang	6.58s	110.25e
Sempol	8.01s	114.07e
Sentolo	7.50s	110.13e
Serang	6.07s	106.09e
Sibolga	1.45n	98.46e
Sidareja	7.29s	108.46e
Sidoarja	7.27s	112.43e
Sindangbarang	7.27s	107.08e
Singaparna	7.20s	108.06e
Singaraja	8.07s	115.06e
Situbondo	7.42s	114.00e
Slaung	8.01s	111.24e
Slawi	6.59s	109.08e
Sleman	7.42s	110.20e
Sorong	0.53s	131.15e
Sragen	7.26s	111.02e
Subah	6.57s	109.52e
Subang	6.34s	107.45e
Sukabumi	6.55s	106.56e
Sukadadi	7.06s	112.18e
Sukadana	1.15s	109.57e
Sukamandi	6.20s	107.40e
Sukanegara	7.05s	107.08e
Sukapura	7.52s	113.03e
Sukaraja	7.27s	108.12e
Sukaraja	7.27s	109.17e
Sukoharjo	7.41s	110.50e
Sulang	6.48s	111.23e
Sumbawa Besar	8.30s	117.26e
Sumedang	6.52s	107.55e
Sumenep	7.01s	113.52e
Sumpiuh	7.37s	109.22e
Surabaya	7.15s	112.45e
Surakarta	7.35s	110.50e
Surodadi	6.53s	109.17e
Taman	7.22s	112.39e
Tamanan	8.02s	113.48e
Tambakbaya	6.47s	111.50e
Tambakrejo	7.17s	111.36e
Tangerang	6.11s	106.37e
Tanggul	8.08s	113.26e
Tanjung	6.52s	108.52e
Tanjungbalai	3.28n	98.24e
Tanjung-pandan	2.45s	107.39e
Tanjungpriok	6.06s	106.53e
Taraju	7.27s	107.59e
Tasikmalaya	7.20s	108.12e
Tayu	6.32s	111.02e
Tegal	6.52s	109.08e
Tegalombo	8.03s	111.16e
Telaga	6.58s	108.18e
Telukbetung	5.27s	105.16e
Temanggung	7.18s	110.10e
Ternate	0.48n	127.24e
Tondano	1.19n	124.54e
Tongas	7.44s	113.04e
Torjun	7.10s	113.12e
Tosari	7.53s	112.53e
Trenggalek	8.03s	111.43e
Tuban	6.54s	112.03e
Tulung Agung	8.04s	111.54e
Tumpang	8.00s	112.46e
Turen	8.10s	112.41e
Ubud	8.30s	115.16e
Ujungberung	6.55s	107.42e
Ujunggenteng	7.22s	106.24e
Ujung Pandang	5.07s	119.24e
Ungaran	7.07s	110.24e
Waingapu	9.39s	120.16e
Wanakrama	7.18s	112.44e
Wanasari	7.58s	110.35e
Wanasegara	7.17s	110.39e
Wates	7.51s	110.10e
Wates	7.55s	112.07e
Weleri	6.58s	110.04e
Widodaren	7.25s	111.14e
Wirasari	7.03s	111.05e
Wlingi	8.05s	112.18e
Wonogiri	7.49s	110.55e
Wonosobo	7.22s	109.54e
Wuluhan	8.21s	113.33e
Wuryantara	7.54s	110.52e
Yogyakarta	7.48s	110.22e
Yosowilangun	8.15s	113.18e

MAP INDEX (continued)

Physical features and points of interest

Adi, *island*	4.18s	133.26e
Alor, *island*	8.15s	124.45e
Agung, Gunung, *mountain*	8.21s	115.30e
Ambon, *island*	3.40s	128.10e
Anambas, Kepulauan, *islands*	3.00n	106.00e
Andaman Sea	7.00n	97.00e
Arafura Sea	9.00s	135.00e
Argopuro, Gunung, *mountain*	7.57s	113.33e
Aru, Kepulauan, *islands*	6.00s	134.30e
Awarawar, Tanjung, *cape*	6.45s	111.56e
Babar, *island*	7.55s	129.45e
Bacan, *island*	0.35s	127.30e
Balabalangan, Kepulauan, *islands*	2.20s	117.25e
Bali, *island*	8.25s	115.15e
Bali Strait	8.18s	114.25e
Baliung, *river*	6.50s	105.52e
Banda, Kepulauan, *islands*	4.34s	129.55e
Banda Sea	5.00s	128.00e
Banggai, Kepulauan, *islands*	1.30s	123.15e
Bangka, *island*	2.15s	106.00e
Bantenan, Tanjung, *cape*	8.46s	114.32e
Banten, Teluk, *bay*	5.58s	106.13e
Banyuk, Kepulauan, *islands*	2.10n	97.15e
Barat, Lintasan, *channel*	6.52s	112.45e
Barisan, Pegunungan, *mountains*	3.00s	102.15e
Barito, *river*	3.32s	114.29e
Barung, Nusa, *island*	8.28s	113.21e
Batu, Kepulauan, *islands*	0.18s	98.28e
Bawean, *island*	5.46s	112.40e
Belitung, *island*	2.50s	107.55e
Berau, Teluk, *bay*	2.30s	132.30e
Biak, *island*	1.00s	136.00e
Binaiya, Gunung, *mountain*	3.09s	129.28e
Bodri, *river*	6.52s	110.10e
Bone, Teluk, *gulf*	4.00s	120.40e
Bone Rate, Kepulauan, *islands*	7.00s	121.00e
Borneo (Kalimantan), *island*	1.00s	114.00e
Borobudur, *historical site*	7.36s	110.12e
Brantas, *river*	7.28s	112.25e
Bromo, Gunung, *mountain*	7.57s	112.57e
Bugel, Ujung, *cape*	6.24s	111.02e
Bunguran, Kepulauan, *islands*	4.40n	108.00e
Bunyu, *island*	3.33n	117.50e
Buru, *island*	3.24s	126.40e
Butung, *island*	5.00s	122.55e
Cangkuang, Tanjung, *cape*	6.50s	105.15e
Celebes (Sulawesi), *island*	2.00s	121.00e
Celebes Sea	3.00n	122.00e
Cenderawasih, Teluk, *bay*	2.30s	135.20e
Cibeet, *river*	6.16s	107.15e
Cibuni, *river*	7.26s	106.47e
Cikaingan, *river*	7.44s	107.54e
Cikaso, *river*	7.25s	106.40e
Cilaki, *river*	7.30s	107.25e
Ciletuh, *river*	7.11s	106.27e
Ciliwung, *river*	6.08s	106.49e
Cimandiri, *river*	7.02s	106.32e
Cimanuk, *river*	6.14s	108.13e
Cimiring, Tanjung, *cape*	7.46s	109.03e
Ciremay, Gunung, *mountain*	6.54s	108.24e
Cisadane, *river*	6.00s	106.38e
Citanduy, *river*	7.41s	108.47e
Citarum, *river*	5.59s	107.03e
Damar, *island*	7.09s	128.40e
Dampier, Selat, *strait*	0.40s	130.40e
Deli, Pulau, *island*	7.00s	105.34e
Dempo, Gunung, *mountain*	4.02s	103.09e
Digul, *river*	7.07s	138.42e
Doberai, Jazirah, *peninsula*	1.30s	132.30e
Durian, *river*	6.01s	106.24e
D'Urville, Tanjung, *cape*	1.28s	137.24e
Enggano, *island*	5.24s	102.16e
Flores, *island*	8.30s	121.00e
Flores Sea	8.00s	120.00e
Gede, Gunung, *mountain*	6.47s	106.59e
Genteng, Pulau, *island*	7.13s	113.54e
Genteng, Tanjung, *cape*	7.21s	106.24e
Gorontalo, Teluk, see Tomini, Teluk		
Grajagan, Teluk, *bay*	8.45s	114.15e
Greater Sunda Islands	0.00	110.00e
Gunungapi, *island*	6.38s	126.40e
Haliman, Gunung, *mountain*	6.42s	106.26e
Halmahera, *island*	1.00n	128.00e
Halmahera, Laut, *sea*	1.00s	129.00e
Indian Ocean	7.00s	98.00e
Indragiri, *river*	0.22s	103.26e
Indramayu, Tanjung, *cape*	6.14s	108.18e
Iran, Pegunungan, *mountains*	2.05n	114.55e
Irian Jaya (West New Guinea), *physical region*	5.00s	138.00e
Iyang, Pulau, *island*	7.00s	114.11e
Jakarta, Teluk, *bay*	6.05s	106.48e
Jambuair, Tanjung, *cape*	5.15n	97.30e
Jatiluhur, Bendung, *dam*	6.35s	107.20e
Java (Jawa), *island*	7.30s	110.00e
Java Sea	5.00s	110.00e
Jawa, see Java		
Jaya, Puncak, *peak*	4.05s	137.11e
Kabaena, *island*	5.15s	121.55e
Kahayan, *river*	3.20s	114.04e
Kai, Kepulauan, *islands*	5.35s	132.45e
Kai Besar, *island*	5.35s	133.00e
Kalimantan, see Borneo		
Kampar, *river*	0.16n	101.41e
Kangean, Kepulauan, *islands*	6.55s	115.30e
Kapuas, *river*	0.25s	109.40e
Kapuas, *river*	3.01s	114.20e
Kapuas Hulu, Pegunungan, *mountains*	1.25n	113.15e
Kapur Utara, Pegunungan, *mountains*	6.52s	111.30e
Karang, Gunung, *mountain*	6.16s	106.03e
Karimata, Kepulauan, *islands*	1.25s	109.05e
Karimata, Selat, *strait*	2.05s	108.40e
Karimun Jawa, Kepulauan, *islands*	5.50s	110.20e
Kayan, *river*	2.55n	117.35e
Kecil, *island*	5.45s	132.40e
Kelud, Gunung, *mountain*	7.56s	112.18e
Kerinci, Gunung, *mountain*	1.42s	101.16e
Kidul, Pegunungan, *mountains*	8.13s	112.00e
Komodo, *island*	8.36s	119.30e
Krakatoa (Krakatau), *volcano*	6.07s	105.24e
Kucur, Tanjung *cape*	8.40s	114.35e
Kwoka, Gunung, *mountain*	0.31s	132.27e
Lada, Teluk, *bay*	6.28s	105.48e
Lamongan, Gunung, *mountain*	7.58s	113.20e
Lampung, Teluk, *bay*	5.40s	105.20e
Laut, *island*	3.40s	116.10e
Lautkecil, Kepulauan, *islands*	4.50s	115.45e
Lawu, Gunung, *mountain*	7.38s	111.11e
Legundi, Pulau, *island*	5.50s	105.18e
Lesser Sunda Islands (Nusa Tenggara)	9.00s	120.00e
Lesung, Tanjung, *cape*	6.28s	105.40e
Leuser, Gunung, *mountain*	3.44n	97.10e
Liman, *river*	6.29s	105.48e
Lingga, *island*	0.10s	104.35e
Lomblen, *island*	8.25s	123.30e
Lombok, *island*	8.45s	116.30e
Lombok, Selat, *strait*	8.30s	115.50e
Lucipara, Kepulauan, *islands*	5.30s	127.33e
Lusi, *river*	7.05s	110.55e
Madiun, *river*	7.23s	111.27e
Madura, *island*	7.00s	113.20e
Madura, Selat, *strait*	7.25s	113.25e
Mahakam, *river*	0.35s	117.17e
Makassar Strait	2.00s	117.30e
Malacca, Strait of	2.30n	101.20e
Malang, Gunung, *mountain*	7.02s	107.01e
Maluku, see Moluccas		
Mamberamo, *river*	1.26s	137.53e
Mangkaliat, Tanjung *cape*	1.02n	118.59e
Mangole, *island*	1.53s	125.50e
Manui, *island*	3.35s	123.08e
Maoke, Pegunungan (Snow Mountains)	4.00s	138.00e
Mapia, Kepulauan, *islands*	0.50n	134.20e
Maratua, *island*	2.15n	118.36e
Masalembo-Besar, *island*	5.34s	114.26e
Mentawai, Kepulauan, *islands*	2.00s	99.30e
Merapi, Gunung, *mountain*	7.33s	110.26e
Merapi, Gunung, *mountain*	8.03s	114.14e
Miangas, *island*	5.35n	126.35e
Minahasa, *peninsula*	1.00n	124.35e
Misool, *island*	1.52s	130.10e
Moa, *island*	8.10s	127.56e
Molucca Sea	0.30s	125.00e
Moluccas (Maluku), *islands*	1.00s	128.00e
Morotai, *island*	2.20n	128.25e
Muller, Pegunungan, *mountains*	0.40n	113.50e
Muria, Gunung, *mountain*	6.36s	110.53e
Musi, *river*	2.20s	104.56e
New Guinea	4.00s	138.00e
Nias, *island*	1.05n	97.30e
Numfoor, *island*	1.03s	134.48e
Nusa Tenggara, see Lesser Sunda Islands		
Obi, *island*	1.23s	127.45e
Oyo, *river*	7.57s	110.22e
Pacific Ocean	3.00n	140.00e
Pagai Selatan, *island*	3.00s	100.20e
Pagai Utara, *island*	2.42s	100.07e
Panaitan, Pulau, *island*	6.35s	105.14e
Panaitan, Selat, *strait*	6.40s	105.15e
Pantar, *island*	8.25s	124.07e
Panto, Tanjung, *cape*	6.51s	105.55e
Patuha, Gunung, *mountain*	7.10s	107.23e
Pelabuhan Ratu, Teluk *bay*	7.05s	106.25e
Peleng, *island*	1.20s	123.10e
Pemali, *river*	6.47s	109.01e
Pembarisan, Pegunungan, *mountains*	7.13s	108.45e
Penanjung, Teluk, *bay*	7.48s	108.40e
Penyu, Teluk, *bay*	7.45s	109.12e
Philippine Sea	6.00n	130.00e
Pini, *island*	0.07n	98.42e
Porong, *river*	7.32s	112.51e
Poso, Danau, *lake*	1.52s	120.35e
Puteran, Pulau, *island*	7.05s	114.00e
Puting, Tanjung, *cape*	3.31s	111.46e
Raas, Pulau, *island*	7.10s	114.33e
Raja, Pulau, *island*	7.14s	113.47e
Rakata, Pulau, *island*	6.10s	105.26e
Ranau, Danau, *lake*	4.50s	103.55e
Rantekombola, Bula, *mountain*	3.21s	120.01e
Raung, Gunung, *mountain*	8.09s	114.02e
Raya, Bukit, *mountain*	0.40s	112.41e
Riau, Kepulauan, *islands*	1.00n	104.30e
Rinca, *island*	8.41s	119.42e
Ringgit, Gunung, *mountain*	7.43s	113.50e
Rinjani, Gunung, *mountain*	8.24s	116.28e
Roti, *island*	10.45s	123.10e
Sabalana, Kepulauan, *islands*	6.45s	118.50e
Sadari, Tanjung, *cape*	5.58s	107.18e
Salak, Gunung, *mountain*	6.42s	106.44e
Salawati, *island*	1.07s	130.54e
Sanana, *island*	2.12s	125.55e
Sanen, *river*	8.23s	113.37e
Sangihe, *island*	3.35n	125.32e
Sapudi, Pulau, *island*	7.06s	114.20e
Savu Sea	9.40s	122.00e
Sawal, Gunung, *mountain*	7.12s	108.16e
Sawu, *island*	10.30s	121.54e
Schouten, Kepulauan, *islands*	0.55s	135.55e
Schwaner, Pegunungan, *mountains*	0.40s	112.40e
Sebatik, *island*	4.08n	117.47e
Sebesi, Pulau, *island*	5.57s	105.30e
Sebuku, Pulau, *island*	5.54s	105.32e

MAP INDEX (continued)

Sedano, Tanjung, *cape*	7.50s	114.25e
Selaru, *island*	8.09s	131.00e
Selatan, Tanjung, *cape*	4.10s	114.38e
Selayar, *island*	6.05s	120.30e
Semeru, Gunung, *mountain*	8.06s	112.55e
Sempu, Pulau, *island*	8.26s	112.42e
Seram, *island*	3.00s	129.00e
Serang, *river*	6.43s	110.35e
Serayu, *river*	7.41s	109.06e
Sertung, Pulau, *island*	6.06s	105.24e
Setail, *river*	8.30s	114.21e
Sewu, Pegunungan, *mountains*	8.05s	110.35e
Siasem, *river*	6.14s	107.42e
Siau, *island*	2.42n	125.24e
Siberut, *island*	1.20s	98.55e
Simeulue, *island*	2.30n	96.00e
Singkep, *island*	0.30s	104.25e
Sipura, *island*	2.12s	99.40e
Slamet, Gunung, *mountain*	7.14s	109.14e
Snow Mountains, see Maoke, Pegunungan		
Solo, *river*	6.47s	112.33e
South China Sea	7.00n	110.00e
Sula, Kepulauan, *islands*	1.52s	125.22e
Sulawesi, see Celebes		
Sulu Sea	7.00n	120.00e
Sumatra (Sumatera), *island*	0.05s	102.00e
Sumba, *island*	10.00s	120.00e
Sumbawa, *island*	8.40s	118.00e
Sumbing, Gunung, *mountain*	7.23s	110.04e
Sunda, Selat, *strait*	6.00s	105.45e
Supiori, *island*	0.45s	135.30e
Talaud, Kepulauan, *islands*	4.20n	126.50e
Taliabu, *island*	1.48s	124.48e
Tambelan, Kepulauan, *islands*	1.00n	107.30e
Tanah, Tanjung, *cape*	6.28s	108.32e
Tanahbala, *island*	0.25s	98.25e
Tanahmasa, *island*	0.12s	98.25e
Tanimbar, Kepulauan, *islands*	7.30s	131.30e
Tarakan, *island*	3.21n	117.36e
Tenggara, Nusa, see Lesser Sunda, Islands		
Timor, *island*	8.50s	125.00e
Timor Sea	10.00s	129.00e
Tinjil, Palau, *island*	6.57s	105.48e
Toba, Danau, *lake*	2.35n	98.50e
Togian, Kepulauan, *islands*	0.20s	122.00e
Tolo, Teluk *gulf*	2.00s	122.30e
Tomini, Teluk (Gorontalo, Teluk), *gulf*	0.20s	121.00e
Towuti, Danau, *lake*	2.45s	121.31e
Trangan, *island*	6.35s	134.20e
Trikora, Puncak, *peak*	4.15s	138.45e
Tukang Besi, Kepulauan, *islands*	5.40s	123.50e
Tulangbawang, *river*	4.24s	105.50e
Ujung Kulon, *peninsula*	6.45s	105.20e
Vals, Tanjung, *cape*	8.25s	137.38e
Van Rees, Pegunungan, *mountains*	2.30s	138.00e
Waigeo, *island*	0.14s	130.45e
Watubela, Kepulauan, *islands*	4.35s	131.40e
West New Guinea, see Irian Jaya		
Wetar, *island*	7.48s	126.18e
Widas, *river*	7.30s	112.08e
Wilis, Gunung, *mountain*	7.48s	111.45e
Wowoni, *island*	4.08s	123.06e
Yamdena, *island*	7.36s	131.25e
Yapen, *island*	1.45s	136.15e
Yos Sudarso, *island*	7.50s	138.30e

during July and August. Strong cyclones and typhoons, which normally occur in higher latitudes, are absent in Indonesia, but afternoon thunderstorms are common.

Vegetation and animal life. About 75 percent of Indonesia is still covered with the natural growth of tropical rain forest, of which less than 20 percent is primeval forest. Irian Jaya and eastern Kalimantan are about 80 percent forest covered, while on the densely populated islands of Java and Madura more than 20 percent of the land is covered with forest.

Tropical rain forests

The vegetation is similar to that of the Philippines, Malaysia, and eastern New Guinea. There are about 30,000 species of flowering plants, including 5,000 species of orchids, as well as *Rafflesia*, a giant water lily that is the world's largest flower. There are more than 3,000 tree species, including durian, camphor, illipe nut, valuable timber varieties such as teak and ironwood, and rattans. More than 4,000 species are exploited for economic purposes, either directly or indirectly. Major timber operations are located in Kalimantan where the trees are not differentiated but are referred to as "broad-leafed species"; they include, for example, meranti which has a soft, lightweight, pinkish to darkish red wood. Teak, which is also broad-leaved, comes mainly from Java.

The most important vegetation type is the mixed lowland and hill tropical rain forest, which occurs below 5,000 feet. It is characterized by a large number of species, including high-canopied and buttressed trees and woody, thick-stemmed lianas (climbing plants). Epiphytes (plants that derive nourishment from the air and usually live on another plant) such as orchids and ferns, saprophytes (plants that live on dead or decaying matter), and parasites are well developed. Above 5,000 feet this forest gives way to mountain evergreen rain forest dominated by oak, laurel, tea, and magnolia species. Another typical feature of Indonesian vegetation is the mangrove forest, characterized by the formation of stilt- or prop-rooted trees, which grow only in salty or brackish water along muddy shores. Mangrove swamps are extensively developed along the shallow seas on eastern Sumatra and southern Kalimantan.

Only 10 percent of the total land surface is devoted to agriculture. Intensive cultivation is restricted to Java, Bali, Lombok, and certain areas of Sumatra and Celebes. More than 40 percent of cultivated land on Java is in rice, mainly along the northern coastal plain and in the great plains of central Java. In the drier section of eastern Java crops such as corn (maize), cassava, and sweet potatoes are grown, and there are sugar, rubber, tea, and coffee plantations.

Development in Sumatra is less intensive and occurs mainly in the estate section on the east coast of northern Sumatra. Around Medan there are extensive plantations producing tobacco, rubber, palm oil, kapok, tea, and coffee, none of which is native to the region. Rice and general crops are grown in the Padang area in the west and around the oil fields near Palembang in the southeast. There are extensive coconut plantations in many parts of the country.

Indonesia belongs to the two faunal regions of Asia in the west and Australia in the east. The boundary runs between Bali and Lombok, and Kalimantan and Celebes. To the west of this line, called Wallace's line, the Asian animal community includes the rhinoceros, orangutan, tapir, tiger, and elephant. Animals related to Australian fauna are confined to the east and include both birds, such as cockatoos, bowerbirds, and birds of paradise, and marsupials such as bandicoots (small insectivorous, herbivorous, marsupial mammals) and cuscuses (brightly-coloured, woolly-haired arboreal marsupials).

Endemic animal species

Many of the islands contain endemic species. Peacocks are found only in Java and the related kuau only in Sumatra. The mountain goat lives only on the rugged slopes of the Pegunungan Barisan. About 30 specimens of single-horned rhinoceros are restricted to the western tip of Java in the nature preserve of Menanjung Ujung-kulon; this nearly extinct species is one of the highly protected forms of wildlife. A unique species of proboscis monkeys lives only in Kalimantan, and the babirussa (a large hoglike quadruped) and anoa (a small wild ox with nearly straight horns) can be found only in Celebes. A giant lizard—the prehistoric Komodo dragon, which attains a length of 12 feet—occurs on the two islands of Rinca (Rintjah) and Komodo, between Sumbawa and Flores.

There are many unusual species of insects in Indonesia, including giant species of walkingsticks, which can attain eight inches in length, walking leaves, huge atlas beetles, elegant luna moths, and beautiful bird-wing swallowtails.

TRADITIONAL REGIONS

The island structure of Indonesia provides natural boundaries that strongly influence the traditional regions. The coastal strip is inhabited by a somewhat homogeneous amalgam of traders who have spread throughout the islands. The "coastal Malays" have a mixture of Malay, Javanese, and Makasarese (a people of southern Celebes) origins and are characterized by strong Islāmic beliefs. The traders and coastal Malays have tended to insulate the peoples in the interior, who have been allowed to preserve their local customs and traditions. On the smaller islands administrative and traditional regions generally overlap, while on the larger islands the administrative structure was normally established to harmonize with traditional and cultural divisions.

Java. The three provinces of Java—the most populous and culturally sophisticated part of the country—serve to illustrate the coincidence of traditional and administrative regions. Central Java is the centre of Javanese culture, history, and language and is the site of the main Javanese historical monuments. Central Java is an area with a large rural population. East Java is also inhabited by Javanese, with Madurese people in the east; it is similar to central Java, but it includes the industrial city of Surabaya (Surabaja) and places heavier emphasis on plantation agriculture. West Java is the land of the Sundanese, who are related to but quite distinct from the Javanese in language and tradition. In addition, Java contains the strongly contrasting metropolitan district (*daerah khusus ibukota*) of Jakarta, the capital city, which does not coincide with cultural or traditional patterns, and the special autonomous district (*daerah istimewa*) of Yogyakarta, which is still ruled by a sultan and is a stronghold of Javanese culture and tradition.

Sumatra. The provinces on Sumatra (seven provinces plus the special autonomous district of Aceh [Atjeh]) also have a degree of traditional integrity. Located in the north, Aceh is a region of strict Muslims who were long noted for their resistance to European influence. North Sumatra, with its major city of Medan, includes a rich plantation area along the coast and, at a higher elevation, the region inhabited by the Bataks, who were largely isolated until the 19th century. Jambi (Djambi), an oil-rich province in the east, is inhabited by Malay people and is the area in which the Indonesian language developed. West Sumatra is the region of the Minangkabau people, who are devout Muslims and are noted for their matrilineal society in which property is passed on through the female line. Lampung and Bengkulu provinces, in the southern part of Sumatra, are the sites of major oil fields. Riau province includes part of the coastal swamp area of Sumatra, as well as the Riau Islands to the east, which have their own traditions and culture.

The outer islands. On Kalimantan the division is between the coast and the inland region. Chinese and Malays dominate the coastal regions, while a variety of Dayak tribes live in the interior, where they carry out primitive shifting cultivation. A similar pattern applies in Irian Jaya and on many of the other islands where maritime-trading communities have been developed along the coast and agrarian, noncommercial societies, with strongly developed and highly localized customs, inhabit the interior.

Religions on the islands east of Java

East of Java each island or group of islands has maintained its own distinct character, in many cases strongly influenced by religion. Bali is Hindu and is quite different in character and customs from any other part of Indonesia. Lombok is partly Hindu, but the influence of Islām is stronger. Sumbawa is Muslim, Flores is largely Roman Catholic, and Timor contains strong Protestant groups. These variations also prevail in Celebes and the Moluccas, where the Makasarese and Buginese of southern Celebes are Muslims noted as seafarers and shipbuilders, while the Menadonese in northern Celebes (Minahasa) and the Ambonese are Christian.

The barriers of the mountains and the sea have protected the character and traditions of many groups. Away from the major cities and areas of dense population, there are significant variations from one valley to the next and almost from one village to the next. In many cases the tribal groups—the Toraja (Toradja) of Celebes, the Dayak of Kalimantan, and the Gayo, Lampung, and Batak peoples of Sumatra—were relatively untouched by outside influences until the arrival of Christian missionaries during the 19th century, and even today they display a wide range of cultures.

THE LANDSCAPE UNDER HUMAN SETTLEMENT

Rural settlement. Indonesia is primarily a rural country, with almost 80 percent of the population living in agricultural areas. About half the population inhabits the inland wet-rice areas of Java, Madura, and Bali, which have a highly sophisticated rural structure. Other areas of high rural population are found in parts of Sumatra and Celebes. Most of the rest of the country is sparsely settled by tribal groups who engage in shifting cultivation.

The Javanese village

The Javanese rural village is the most common settlement. Green rice fields cover the flat land and rise up the hillsides in terraces as far as the water supply will allow. Within the rice fields are scattered clusters of palm and fruit trees, which indicate the location of the villages. In the heavily populated areas of central and eastern Java, there are thousands of such villages that are contiguous only along the major roads. Most villages have fewer than 100 houses.

The people of each village form a group that is homogeneous both in economic condition and in social interest and outlook. In many cases, and particularly in irrigated areas, there is much mutual exchange of labour. Overpopulation in the densely populated areas has led to the decrease in size of the average farm, which is less than one acre, and to an increase in the numbers of the landless rural group, who work mainly as farm labourers or sharecroppers.

Each village has its source of water, which usually is channelled through the village, a mosque and elementary school, and a network of swept-earth paths. There is little commercial activity; purchases are made from peddlers or from the market towns, which often are also local government centres. Houses are well separated and are normally of frame and bamboo with roofs of red tile or coconut fibres; the village head may live in a masonry house. Goats, chickens, banana and papaya trees, and a host of small children are characteristic of village life.

Rural structure varies considerably from region to region. Bali villages are clusters of walled family complexes with Hindu house temples, public buildings, and larger temples. The Batak villages around Lake Toba in northern Sumatra, Minangkabau villages in western Sumatra, Toradja villages in southern Celebes, and Dayak longhouses in Kalimantan each have their characteristic structure and building style. The social pattern also varies considerably. On Java the pattern is very simple, with few organized groupings above the level of the household, while on neighbouring Bali there are strong groups related to working, dancing, and other functions, many of which are associated with Hindu festivals.

The rural mode of life is controlled by the productivity of the land. It ranges from the semi-nomadic shifting cultivation of tribal groups, through cassava and sago gardening, smallholder plantations, and irrigated rice farming, to large mechanized plantations. In some cases these activities are combined with some form of cottage industry. Most Indonesians are small-scale, independent peasant farmers who operate at or near the subsistence level and sell some produce but do not accumulate capital. In general, the villages are small, independent, and largely self-sufficient.

Urban settlement. Indonesia has not undergone rapid urbanization, despite the rapid growth of its several large cities. Except in Jakarta, which has experienced an influx of population from the country, urban growth is more a reflection of the large total population than of any great movement to the cities. The urban sector accounts for about 23 percent of the total population.

Few of the cities, except for the major ports of Jakarta, Surabaya, and Medan, have the heterogeneity of a true urban centre. They are rather the local governmental, cultural, and social centres for highly populated and distinct regions. The growth of the cities has not been accompanied by a parallel growth of industry, and the outlook of much of the urban population is still rural. Large parts of the population, even in Jakarta, live in replicas of rural villages, or *kampong*s, characterized by rural customs, housing, sanitation, and roads, which are adequate and pleasant in the country, but inappropriate in a crowded city.

Four of the five largest cities, Jakarta (6,503,400), Surabaya (2,027,900), Bandung (1,462,600), and Semarang (1,024,900), are on Java. Medan (1,379,000) is located on Sumatra. These five cities may be considered as metropolitan areas rather than large provincial towns since they contain the major government, financial, and business offices. Other large cities, such as Padang, Yogyakarta, and Palembang, are centres of provincial and regional government and of local trade and have limited international ties or contact with foreign businessmen.

The character of the cities

The cities have individual characters. Jakarta, as the capital and centre of finance, has fine government buildings, impressive avenues and fountains, and an increasing number of multi-story hotels and office buildings. Surabaya is a major port and industrial city. Bandung, a former resort area and military centre, has much light industry and a number of universities. Semarang is the administrative capital and commercial centre of central Java. Yogyakarta, which was the seat of the revolutionary government between 1945 and 1949, is the seat of the ruling family of the sultan of Yogyakarta and remains the centre of Javanese culture. In addition to the wealth of historic monuments in the region, it also is the site of the large Universitas Gajah Mada and schools of art and of traditional dance and music. In Sumatra, Medan is the port for the rich plantation area of the north, and Palembang is the port for the oil fields and refineries of the south.

In a sense the nation's urban structure is decentralized, with the population identifying with their regions. Many people who have been born or raised in Jakarta refer to themselves as Batak, Javanese, or Minahassan and may use their local language rather than Indonesian in their homes.

The evolution of Indonesian cities has not been adequately studied, but they are generally composed of an elite group of government officials, military officers, and business leaders who in the larger cities tends to be Western oriented; a middle-income group of civil servants, teachers, and other professionals who are seriously underpaid and must struggle to maintain their position; and a large group of labourers, servants, and semi-literate and unskilled itinerants who strongly identify with their villages and frequently move back and forth between village and city in harmony with the harvests.

No city has a central sewage-disposal system or adequate basic services for the provision of water, electricity, and telephone. Even these limited services are restricted to those city sectors where the relatively wealthy reside. In Jakarta significant steps have been taken to improve these services and to provide recreational and social welfare facilities and public transportation.

A transient foreign element of diplomats and company representatives plays a minor role in city structure. The permanent foreign element—mainly of Chinese, Indian, and Arab business families—is more fully integrated, but each group maintains its own contacts and patterns of life. The Indonesians have not yet developed their own urban culture, although Jakarta, with its strong international contacts, would certainly be the closest approach. Since association with this international culture implies a degree of wealth, it is largely confined to the families of officials, professionals, and prominent businessmen. The lower income groups have retained their basic ethnic cultures, strengthened by trips to home villages during times of harvest or during the Muslim Ramaḍān, a month-long period of fasting and atonement.

Urban administration

Although social structure is decentralized, the administrative structure is highly centralized, with Jakarta the headquarters of the central government. Most taxes, including land and real estate taxes, are collected by the central government, on which city and regional governments must depend for their revenue.

Major reforms are needed to allow cities to play a more important role in future development. Leadership in this vein has been taken in Jakarta, where the city government has taken active steps to develop an infrastructure of services and facilities. These improvements are financed through such mechanisms as a government lottery and the legalization and imposition of a tax on gambling, which together contribute about 25 percent of the city budget.

II. People and population

The Indonesian motto—"*Binneka Tunggal Ika*" ("Unity in Diversity")—is illustrated by the fact that, within the population of more than 147,000,000, there are more than 300 different ethnic groups and 250 distinct languages and that most of the major world religions are found there, in addition to a wide range of indigenous ones. Within this diversity there are certain groupings and concentrations; thus, most of the people are Malaysian, speak languages that have an Austronesian (Malayo-Polynesian) base, and profess Islām.

POPULATION GROUPS

The Malaysians are related to the Mongoloid peoples of Asia. Racial characteristics are not pronounced, partly because of centuries of mixing with Arabs, Indians, and Europeans. The people throughout most of Indonesia are light brown in skin colour and of slight stature and have straight or slightly wavy black hair. In the eastern islands the people take on the kinky hair, darker skin, and coarser features that are characteristic of the Papuans of the island of New Guinea.

Languages. Most of the languages spoken in Indonesia have an Austronesian base. The major exceptions are those of Irian Jaya, where Papuan languages are used, and some of the Moluccas, where the North Halmaheran language family is found. The Austronesian language family is broken into 16 major groups within which languages are closely related though distinctly different. On Java there are three major languages—Javanese, Sundanese, and Madurese—while on Sumatra there are 15, many of which are divided into a number of distinct dialects. Within the Toraja group, a relatively small population in the interior of Celebes, there are eight languages. In eastern Indonesia each island has its own language, which is often not understood on the neighbouring islands.

The national language

The national language, Bahasa Indonesia, evolved from a Malay dialect spoken in the Jambi area of eastern Sumatra; it has much in common with other Malay dialects that have long served as regional lingua francas. Since it is a relatively simple and widely used language that was not associated with one of the dominant ethnic groups, Bahasa Indonesia has been accepted without serious question and has served as a strong force of national unification. It is now learned by all children in the schools, where the local language is the medium of instruction during the first two years and Bahasa Indonesia is used for the remaining years. In 1972 a uniform revised spelling was agreed to between Indonesia and Malaysia so that communications could be improved and literature more freely exchanged between the two countries.

Major ethnic groups. The diverse ethnic populations may be grouped into three broad groups—an inland wet-rice society, coastal peoples, and tribal groups. The first group, the strongly Hinduized wet-rice growers of inland Java and Bali, make up more than one-half of the national population. With an ancient, highly sophisticated culture of strong social and agricultural traditions, it includes the Javanese, Sundanese, Madurese, and Balinese peoples. The second group of Islāmic coastal peoples is ethnically heterogeneous, including the Malays from Sumatra and, from southern Celebes, the Makasars, who are found in all coastal towns but are a stronger influence outside Java. The third group of tribal peoples has developed in areas where rainfall will not support wet-rice cultivation, and shifting cultivation is practiced. These various ethnic groups tend to be small and isolated and have developed a wide range of cultures.

Besides this cultural categorization there are a number of other major ethnic groups. They include the Bataks and Minangkabaus in Sumatra, the Minahasans in northern Celebes, and the Ambonese.

The Chinese community

The largest nonindigenous group is the Chinese, most of whom have lived in Indonesia for generations. They are mainly descendants of Chinese immigrants who came originally from the provinces of Fukien and Kwangtung, in southeastern China. Of the total Chinese population of about 4,000,000, some 80 percent live in the towns and cities of Java and Sumatra, where they are engaged in trade. The Chinese also form more than 25 percent of the population in western Kalimantan, where many are farmers and fishermen, and in the Kepulauan Riau, where many are engaged in mining.

Most of the former 60,000 Dutch and 200,000 Eurasian residents left Indonesia after independence. Indians, Arabs, and other Europeans are relatively unimportant in numbers, although their influence in business and other elements of Western culture are apparent in the major cities.

Religions. About 90 percent of the population profess Islām, which in most cases is strongly influenced by Hinduism, Buddhism, and older pagan and animistic beliefs. The 3,000,000 Hindus live mainly on Bali, and there are about 12,900,000 Christians scattered throughout the country, more than two-thirds of whom are Protestant and the remainder mainly Roman Catholic. Most Chinese practice Buddhism and Confucianism. In remote areas some tribal religions are practiced.

Successive layers of religious beliefs reach back to the rituals and magic of the original settlers. Remains of *Homo erectus* (originally called Pithecanthropus, or Java man) were found in central Java. There are remnants of an aboriginal people in southern Sumatra. The present population is descended from a series of waves of migrants from Asia, especially southwestern China. There is little recorded history before the 7th century although there is evidence of earlier cultures (Śrivijaya) in Sumatra.

The earliest recorded Indonesian history shows extensive religious influences from India; the early Indonesian states that centred on Java or Sumatra evolved through many forms of Hinduism and Theravāda and Mahāyāna Buddhism. During the 9th century AD both Hinduism and Buddhism were practiced as court religions; Śiva and Buddha were looked upon as manifestations of the same spiritual being. The blending of the two religions continued until the 14th century, when Islām was introduced along the coasts by Muslim traders from India. Throughout all the religious changes on the court level, the common people adopted part of each new religion as an additional layer over their basic traditional and animistic beliefs. Although Islām has become the dominant religion, it includes elements of all past beliefs.

The major religions were all introduced on the coast and, except in such open areas as Java and southern Sumatra, penetrated slowly inland. Regions such as central Kalimantan and Irian Jaya, the mountains of northern Sumatra, and the interiors of other mountainous islands remained virtually untouched. Ritualistic headhunting in Kalimantan and Celebes and cannibalism in northern Sumatra were practiced until the arrival of Christian missionaries in the late 19th century.

Indonesian variants of Islām

Islām is most strictly practiced in Aceh, western Sumatra, western Java, southeastern Kalimantan, and some of the Lesser Sunda Islands. Away from these strongholds, the people consider themselves to be Muslims, but most do not follow the full ritual of fasting and prayers. On Java only about one-third of the Muslims follow orthodox practices; they are referred to as the *santri*. Members of the more Hinduized Muslims, including a majority of white-collar workers, are termed *priayi*. A third tradition, called *abangan*, is strongly influenced by traditional and ancestral spirits and is closely associated with the peasants. These three traditions do not conflict but grow out of one another. Ritual ceremonies, *selamatan*s, are held on all special occasions, the head of a bull is buried at the dedication of a new building, and the many rituals connected with birth, death, and marriage are carefully observed by people at all levels.

DEMOGRAPHY

The population numbered more than 147,000,000 in the census of 1980, an increase of 28,000,000 over that of 1971. Indonesia is the fifth most populous country in the world after China, India, the Soviet Union, and the United States. The average population density is 200 persons per square mile (77 persons per square kilometre).

International migration is not important to the growth and structure of the population. There is probably a good deal of unrecorded illegal movement between parts of Indonesia and adjacent areas of Malaysia and the Philippines.

Internal migration, under which families from overpopulated areas of Java are resettled in less populated parts of the country, such as Sumatra and Kalimantan, is carried out with government support. Before settlements are made, soil and climate surveys are conducted, roads are cleared, and temporary housing is built. These programs were shifting some 100,000 people annually by the late 1970s. They play an important role in the opening of new areas, although they are not sufficient to provide significant relief to overpopulated areas.

Distribution of the population

Population distribution throughout Indonesia is very uneven, so that the country as a whole suffers not so much from overpopulation as from extremely uneven distribution of population. The 1980 census figures reflected the underlying situation: whereas the average density for Indonesia was 200 persons per square mile, for Java and Madura it was nearly 1,800 per square mile. The population on Java is by no means evenly distributed, since much of the land is mountainous and forested, and in some regions it exceeds 3,000 persons per square mile. Java and Madura, with less than 7 percent of the land area, contain three-fifths of the population. At the other extreme, in Kalimantan 5 percent of the national population lives on 28 percent of the land, and in Irian Jaya less than 1 percent occupies some 22 percent of the land.

Indonesia, Area and Population

	area		population	
	sq mi	sq km	1971 census	1980 census
Metropolitan district *(daerah khusus ibukota)*				
Jakarta Raya	228	590	4,579,300	6,503,400
Provinces *(propinsi)*				
Bali	2,147	5,561	2,120,300	2,469,900
Bengkulu	8,173	21,168	519,300	768,100
Irian Jaya	162,928	421,981	923,400	1,173,900
Jambi	17,345	44,924	1,006,100	1,446,000
Jawa Barat	17,876	46,300	21,623,500	27,453,500
Jawa Tengah	13,207	34,206	21,877,100	25,372,900
Jawa Timur	18,503	47,922	25,517,000	29,188,900
Kalimantan Barat	56,664	146,760	2,019,900	2,486,100
Kalimantan Selatan	14,541	37,660	1,699,100	2,064,600
Kalimantan Tengah	58,919	152,600	701,900	954,300
Kalimantan Timur	78,162	202,440	733,800	1,218,000
Lampung	12,860	33,307	2,777,000	4,624,800
Maluku	28,766	74,505	1,089,600	1,411,000
Nusa Tenggara Barat	7,790	20,177	2,203,500	2,724,700
Nusa Tenggara Timur	18,485	47,876	2,295,300	2,737,200
Riau	36,511	94,562	1,641,500	2,168,500
Sulawesi Selatan	28,101	72,781	5,180,600	6,062,200
Sulawesi Tengah	26,921	69,726	913,700	1,289,600
Sulawesi Tenggara	10,690	27,686	714,100	942,300
Sulawesi Utara	7,345	19,023	1,718,500	2,115,400
Sumatera Barat	19,219	49,778	2,793,200	3,406,800
Sumatera Selatan	40,034	103,688	3,440,600	4,629,800
Sumatera Utara	27,331	70,787	6,621,800	8,360,900
Timor Timur	5,743	14,874	—	555,400
Special autonomous districts *(daerah istimewa)*				
Aceh	21,387	55,392	2,008,600	2,611,300
Yogyakarta	1,224	3,169	2,489,400	2,750,800
Total Indonesia	741,101*	1,919,443	119,208,200*	147,490,300

*Details do not add to total given because of rounding.
Source: Official government figures.

Population projections made on the basis of the 1971 census, taking into account continuing decline in mortality with a consequent increase in life expectancy and a declining birth rate (due in part to extensive family-planning programs embarked upon in the 1970s), indicated a growth in the annual rate of population increase. It was estimated that the population would reach 160,000,000 in 1986, 176,000,000 in 1991, and 210,000,000 in 2001. This would represent nearly a doubling of the 1971 population by the end of the 20th century, with no significant change in distribution.

(J.F.McD.)

III. The national economy

Since World War II, Indonesia has played a modest role in the world economy, and its importance has been considerably less than its size, resources, and geographical position would seem to warrant. Years of economic mismanagement and the subordination of development to political ideals during the first 16 years of independence led to financial chaos and to a serious deterioration in the capital stock. With a major change of economic direction after the 1965 military coup, when Suharto began to assume power, some measure of stability was regained, and the conditions for an orderly policy of rehabilitation and economic development were established.

Major economic problems

Although the potential for development is considerable and Indonesia can be expected ultimately to become the major economic force in Southeast Asia, serious problems remain. In the late 1970s, per capita income was significantly lower than in most neighbouring states. The rate of increase in population is perhaps lower than for Southeast Asia as a whole, but it has been accelerating. Population pressure in Java is intense, while the costs of developing the underpopulated outer islands (all islands except Java and Sumatra) impose a substantial burden on the limited development funds available. Urban drift and, in particular, urban unemployment have become major problems.

Although there has been a dramatic increase in the industrial sector, primarily in crude oil production, the economy has remained predominantly agricultural. Independent peasant farmers account for the larger part of production, notably of rice and other food crops, but there is an important estate sector that produces mainly for export. Indonesia is a major supplier of rubber and a less significant producer of a wide range of other commodities, such as coffee, tea, tobacco, copra, spices (cloves and nutmeg), and oil palm products. In contrast to neighbouring Malaysia, however, the estates have failed to modernize, and there has been considerable deterioration. This is also true of export crops in the smallholder sector. There has, however, been an improvement in food crop cultivation, and the government has improved the production, marketing, and distribution of sugar.

Indonesia is a major exporter of petroleum, natural gas, and tin. Widespread exploration for deposits of oil and other minerals has resulted in a number of large-scale projects that have contributed substantially to general development funds. The projects have, however, tended to reinforce the general position of Indonesia as a supplier of raw materials to world markets.

The corollary of the primary economy is that the country has remained a major importer of manufactured goods and of the technical skills and knowledge required for development. In spite of the substantial domestic market, there has been little industrial development, and the industrial base is surprisingly inadequate. A number of new projects were implemented in the early 1970s, and overall investment has risen quickly. It remains small, however, in relation to needs and is biassed toward mineral and forestry production. There is little evidence of much growth in indigenous entrepreneurial activity in manufacturing. Domestic resources are limited, and there is a heavy dependence on inflows of foreign aid and private capital to finance large-scale development.

Natural resources

Indonesia has a large, mostly unprospected variety of mineral deposits, including those of petroleum, tin, manganese, copper, nickel, bauxite, and coal. Lack of communications, political factors, and an absence of systematic planning have together seriously impeded exploration. Since 1965, however, considerable progress has been made in the exploration and development of these mineral deposits, and more than 30 foreign firms are engaged in extensive oil exploration throughout the country and offshore. Tin deposits are found on Bangka, Singkep, and Belitung islands and off the southwestern shore of the Kalimantan. Nickel occurs on Celebes, Halmahera, and other islands of the Moluccas and in Irian Jaya. Manganese deposits are located in central Java and on Sumatra, Kalimantan, Celebes, and Timor. There are copper deposits in the Jayawijaya Mountains of Irian Jaya. Bintan, Bangka, Singkep, and Kalimantan have bauxite, and coal occurs on Sumatra and Kalimantan. There are also deposits of iron, sulfur, gold, and silver.

The consistent monsoon climate and almost even distribution of rainfall make it possible for the same types of crops to be grown throughout the country. About 11 percent of the total land area is estimated to be used by smallholders. Some 34,000 square miles is rice land, and a further 53,000 square miles is used for other crops. About 1 percent of the total area is held by estates.

The natural vegetation of largely tropical rain forest accounts for about 73 percent of the total land area. Forest reserves, including all forest land in Java, accounts for 76,400 square miles, about one-third of which is potentially exploitable. A major boom in forest exploration and exploitation has been in progress since the mid-1960s. There are several small areas of deciduous forest and plantations (notably of teak), but most of the trees are tropical hardwoods.

Hydroelectric potential

Hydroelectric generation on Java is limited by the nature of the river system, although a major project at Jatiluhur (Djatiluhur), with a capacity of 125,000 kilowatts, has been implemented, and there are possibilities for hydroelectic development of the Brantas and Solo rivers. Outside Java there is considerable potential, notably in Sumatra, but the low demand is limiting. Large-scale coal and petroleum deposits provide ready raw material for thermal generation, which is likely to be the basis for most of Java's power generation.

SOURCES OF NATIONAL INCOME

Agriculture, forestry, and fishing. Agriculture accounts for about two-thirds of the work force and contributes one-third of the national income and one-fourth of recorded exports. In Java rice and other food crops such as corn, cassava, sweet potatoes, peanuts (groundnuts), and soybeans dominate the small farms, although such cash crops as tobacco have also been widespread. In the outer islands cash-crop production is relatively more important; rubber and coffee are grown in Sumatra and Kalimantan, and copra is grown in the east. The major estate crops are rubber, oil palms, coffee, tea, sugar, and tobacco. Sumatra accounts for more than half the total area under estate production.

Waldo E. Austin—Black Star

Terraced rice fields on the island of Java.

Before World War II Indonesia was self-sufficient in basic foodstuffs, although some low-quality rice was imported to release some high-quality rice for export. Since 1945 production has failed to keep pace with demand, and grain (mainly rice) has been imported. Yields remained low, and the deteriorating infrastructure has encouraged a shift from rice toward other less demanding basic subsistence crops, such as cassava.

Rice has remained the cornerstone of peasant agriculture, however, and increased production of it has been the most important single aim of every five-year plan. By the late 1970s yields had been increased through various Bimingan Massal (Bimas: "mass guidance") schemes designed to promote the use of high-yielding varieties and fertilizer by increasing the availability of credit. Yields of other food crops have remained low and are expected to improve only with the extension of credit and other government incentives.

The agricultural estates

Before the 1940s Indonesia had one of the largest and most scientifically based estate sectors in the world. After World War II neglect, political factors, and nationalization (since 1957) brought about a general decline in production. The majority of non-Dutch estates had been returned to their original owners, British or American, by the end of the 1960s. The former Dutch estates, retained by the government, accounted for about one-half of the estate output. The estates are grouped on a regional basis, although some products such as sugar and tobacco are treated separately.

Substantial rehabilitation and replanting took place in the early 1970s in both the private and public sectors. Rubber has remained the major commodity, although replanting has been a long-term process. Oil palms have been increasing in importance, and the ailing sugar industry was rehabilitated in the early 1970s to increase production for domestic consumption.

The timber industry grew rapidly from the mid-1960s to the late 1970s. During that period the export of logs and timber rose nearly five times; this rapid exploitation has caused considerable damage, however, and large areas of the country are in need of reafforestation. A sudden slump in the export market in the early 1980s was caused by export restrictions, declining demand, and the increased use of logs for domestic industrial processing to encourage local development of wood-based industries. Foreign investment accounts for nearly one-half the total capital invested in forestry.

Fisheries have been developed on a small scale. With the aid of Japan, there has been an increase in both production and exports. A large part of the inland catch is from irrigation canals; marine fish accounted for about three-fourths of the total catch in the late 1970s.

Mining. Mining has provided a small, rapidly growing contribution to the gross domestic product (GDP). It employs only a limited work force, but through exports and taxation it contributes substantially to foreign-exchange earnings and development. In the past petroleum and tin were the most important, although coal, bauxite, gold, and other minerals have been mined. In the late 1960s and early 1970s exploration led to a number of projects for large-scale production of copper, nickel, manganese, and other commodities.

Petroleum extraction

Petroleum is produced in Sumatra and Kalimantan and on small-scale offshore sites in the Java Sea. Output by the early 1980s was equivalent to about 10 percent of Middle East production and contributed more than three-fifths of Indonesia's gross exports. Refinery production since 1968 has been in the hands of Pertamina, the state oil company. Foreign oil companies operate under a production-sharing formula, by which the ownership of the oil resources remains with the government of Indonesia and the foreign companies act as contractors, supplying the necessary capital.

The islands of Bangka, Belitung, and Singkep were mined for tin long before World War II. Since 1949 tin production has declined, and by the early 1980s it was at about the same level as the early 1950s. Production is largely in the hands of state companies. Nickel is produced on Celebes by a joint Indonesian–Japanese concern, and is also produced in Irian Jaya and in the Moluccas. Bauxite is produced on the Kepulauan Riau. Coal production in Sumatra declined during the 1960s, and the outlook is bleak in view of the competition from other fuels and the deterioration of facilities. The government, however, has taken steps to increase production.

Manufacturing. There was little increase in manufacturing's contribution to the GDP during the 1960s and 1970s. In the early 1980s less than 10 percent of the labour force was engaged in manufacturing, a significant proportion of which was employed in cottage and home industries. Most large-scale industry is state owned. Much small-scale industry is privately owned by the Chinese community. Inefficient state management, government controls, the shortage of finance, and high interest rates have all contributed to small profits, a deterioration in facilities, and substantial subcapacity working. The government has promoted both domestic and foreign investment in industry.

The largest industries are those that process agricultural and mineral products. The estate groups and companies normally control their own facilities, and Pertamina controls petroleum refining. The Pusri (Pasri) fertilizer factory is located close to the Palembang oil and gas field. There are other state-owned chemical fertilizer factories. There is a petrochemical plant at Plaju on southern Sumatra. Other industries receiving government priority include cement manufacture in eastern Java, central Sumatra, and Celebes and steel manufacturing at Cilegon on western Java.

The textile industry

The major industry based on imported raw materials is the textile industry, which is not competitive enough to prevent substantial textile imports. The spinning mills are largely either state owned or in the hands of foreign concerns, while the weaving and finishing factories, which are centred in Bandung, are largely small-scale and privately owned by local entrepreneurs. Batik production—an Indonesian method of hand printing textiles—is concentrated in central Java. Although production of batik remains a major cottage industry, there are also a number of larger scale operations.

Small-scale workshops manufacturing consumer goods and general products (furniture, household equipment, textiles, and printed matter) are largely privately owned. Development has been limited, and there has been little evidence of the entrepreneurial buoyancy found elsewhere in Southeast Asia because of high interest rates, financial difficulties, low working capacity, and government intervention. The main centre of private industry is western Java; considerable development is also taking place in Jakarta.

Energy. Indonesia is self-sufficient in the basic fuels, such as petroleum, coal, and wood. Domestic petroleum consumption exceeds the total ouput of refineries, which use only about 30 percent of the crude oil production. Installed electric-generating capacity at the end of 1980 in the public sector amounted to nearly 3,000,000 kilowatts produced by diesel, steam, hydroelectric, and gas turbine units. A state company has managed and operated these facilities since nationalization in 1969. In addition to the public facilities, about 1,000,000 kilowatts are generated by private units installed largely because of uncertain public supply. This generating capacity is extremely low for a country of Indonesia's size, and substantial expansion is necessary if Indonesia is to meet its growing energy needs.

Financial services. Major public (government-owned) banks include Bank Indonesia, the central bank; Bank Ekspor Impor Indonesia, the export-import bank; Bank Rakyat Indonesia, which specializes in rural credit; Bank Negara Indonesia, which specializes in industrial credit; Bank Bumi Daya, for the estates and forestry; Bank Pembangunan Indonesia, the development bank; Bank Dagang Negara, the state foreign-exchange bank; and Bank Tabungan Negara, the state savings bank. Each bank is diversified and operates independently. Foreign banks were allowed to return to Indonesia in 1966, but after 1969 no new licenses were issued. They tend to specialize in trade and foreign-exchange transactions.

The tight-money policy

Interest rates have remained high. Even such subsidized rates as those available to farmers under the Bimas schemes are 1 percent per month or more. A tight-money policy has been a major instrument in stabilizing the economy and restricting inflation. Confidence has returned, and bank deposits have risen fast, though bank advances remain below potential levels, and the mobilization of domestic savings for development is a serious constraint on growth. Increased bank lending has been directed largely to commercial, agricultural, and other short-term projects.

Nonbanking financial institutions are restricted. Limitations on trading in stocks and shares were lifted in 1970, and a new stock exchange was opened in order to help familiarize the Indonesian public with such investment and attract foreign capital. The stock exchange, however, plays only a minimal role in the mobilization of savings. Insurance, trading, and similar facilities are largely obtained abroad.

Foreign trade. In general, Indonesia exports raw materials, both agricultural and mineral, in return for manufactured goods. There is an import need also for some raw materials, such as cotton, rice, and other food crops. There was no substantial growth in the monetary value of trade between 1950 and 1970, but after 1973, because of the high price of oil, both the value of trade and the balance of payments increased dramatically. Since 1967 both imports and exports have risen, and, because of the development policies in operation, this pattern continued during the 1970s.

Indonesia's most important trading partner is Japan, which at the beginning of the 1980s accounted for nearly 45 percent of exports and imports. The United States accounted for 15 percent of imports and 25 percent of exports. A significant volume of exports continues to be marketed through Singapore, which, with Malaysia, accounted for about 12 percent of the total in the early 1980s. Other important trading partners include the Philippines, Saudi Arabia, Australia, West Germany, The Netherlands, and China. The share of the Soviet Union and eastern Europe has been small.

The composition of exports

Although oil accounts for 50 percent or more of gross exports, its net contribution to foreign-exchange earnings has been substantially lower; imports of goods and services for the oil industry, the transfer of profits, and other factors amount to almost 75 percent of export earnings. Timber products accounted for 30 percent of non-oil exports in the early 1980s. Rubber accounted for approximately 20 percent of nonoil exports and was facing declining prices and competition from synthetics. Other agricultural exports include coffee, copra, tea, pepper, tobacco, and oil palm products. In the long term nonoil minerals will probably be of increasing significance. Imports largely consist of manufactures, capital equipment and consumer goods, and foodstuffs.

MANAGEMENT OF THE ECONOMY

The private sector. Since 1966 the private sector has assumed a more influential role. The five-year plans have emphasized the government's role in developing the economic and social infrastructure of the country, leaving major investments in exploration and exploitation of national resources or in new manufacturing industry to the private sector. Exceptions to this have included the role of Pertamina and the fertilizer, cement, chemical, paper, and textile-spinning industries in which the government, together with foreign aid, has remained a major force. In the public sector, the emphasis increasingly has been on independent, self-financing state enterprises.

The private sector forms three broad categories: foreign; the domestic commercial, industrial, and financial sector; and agricultural activity. Agriculture is dominated by independent peasant small-holders, who account for a large majority of food production and a major proportion of export crops. Official policies in respect of credit and extension services have been vital in forming the framework within which the smallholder makes his decisions, but ultimately it has been private initiative that has determined the growth in production.

There has been a complex and reasonably well-developed commercial sector based on the marketing and export of agricultural produce and on the supplying of consumer goods and services to the domestic market. It has been dominated by the Chinese community, although indigenous participation and unofficial army activity at the lower levels have grown. Consumption and trade credit have been generated largely within the trading system, but there is also a range of private banking and moneylending facilities. Apart from these, the private financial sector has been weak and has played only a modest role in mobilizing domestic resources.

Private industry

The private industrial sector also has been relatively weak. A multitude of controls, inflation, high interest rates, and high unofficial as well as official taxation have all tended to discourage fixed investment and the development of an indigenous entrepreneurial class. The Chinese community in particular has tended to channel its enterprise into short-term trading activities. Since 1966 a much greater reliance has been placed on the market mechanism, and major taxation and other reforms have been introduced. High interest rates and lack of managerial expertise have continued to place domestic industry at a disadvantage.

The public sector. The government has played a crucial role in development. Its primary task in the mid-1960s was to restore stability and to establish the context within which normal economic life would begin. The major inflationary factor of a vast budget deficit produced a strict, balanced budget and tight-money policies, which were coupled with substantial imports to help balance supply and demand. This approach proved successful, but inflation, temporarily brought under control by the early 1970s, continued to trouble Indonesia in the early 1980s.

With overall stability restored, the emphasis shifted toward development. The 1969–74 development plan gave primary attention to the production of crude oil and to the rehabilitation of the economic infrastructure, notably in agriculture, power supply, and communications. In industry the major emphasis was on projects such as fertilizer production that support agriculture and on those such as textiles. In agriculture the major target was self-sufficiency in food grains, and an important subsidiary aim was the rehabilitation of export crops.

A family-planning program was also begun. In general, however, social objectives have received relatively low priority. The 1974–79 and 1979–84 development plans continued to place the highest priorities on agriculture (including irrigation), communications, and tourism. An exception has been the attention given to village and rural development, which, although economic in application, is largely social in inspiration. Defense, though given low priority, has been a substantial drain on the country's resources.

The problem of the bureaucracy

A major restraint on development has been a swollen and ill-paid bureaucracy. The government's ability to organize and implement development projects has also been limited by lack of experience and the unreliability and inadequacy of statistical and other information. A large inflow of foreign technical assistance has been necessary to help devise economic programs and projects, often as a condition of capital aid. Low pay and poor working conditions have fostered corruption that has distorted development and imposed a substantial burden. The nationalization of the administrative structure has been a major long-term task.

Taxation. A rapid increase in taxation receipts has been achieved since 1967 because of the continued rise in prices and the increased ability to mobilize domestic resources. But the tax base has been limited for a country of Indonesia's size, and the demands on government revenue both for development and for purposes such as wages and salaries have been such that local funds have remained a serious problem, exacerbated by corruption and the widespread practice of bypassing the state budget. Since official budget allocations to regional authorities, military formations, and governmental organizations are sometimes felt to be too small, these agencies impose illegal taxes and levies to supplement the state budget. Some progress has been made, however, in keeping such taxes and levies under control.

By the early 1980s receipts were still largely dependent on taxes on foreign trade and on commodity activities, particularly of oil, tobacco, and sugar. Customs, excise, and corporate and other taxes on oil companies accounted for about 70 percent of all revenue in 1981–82.

Trade unions and employers' associations. Organized labour has been weak and still suffers from the repressions of early years in which the main trade union, the All-Indonesia Federation of Labour Organizations (Sentral Organisasi Buruh Selurah Indonesia, or SOBSI), was tied to the Communist Party. Large, politically motivated associations of farmers were loosely knit and did little to promote the welfare of their members. Some Indonesian businessmen have banded together to agitate against the advantages allegedly given to nonnationals, but their organizations are of negligible importance. Since 1965 the government has sought to incorporate functional groups such as those of farmers and fishermen into a quasi-governmental political party, and many organizations and associations (including minority religious groups, such as the Buddhists and women's organizations) have joined.

Economic policies. Indonesian economic policies reflect a desire for financial stability and orderly economic development along orthodox Western lines. The military government has entrusted economic management to a group of professional economists and other experts who have been attempting a pragmatic approach to economic problems with assistance from the World Bank and foreign governments.

Planners have accepted Indonesia's geographical position and historic economic structure as suggestive of a relatively open and free economy. A previous system of intervention and controls has been put into reverse, and foreign investment and aid, subject to development conditions, have been welcomed. The foreign-exchange system in Indonesia has been greatly simplified, repatriation of profits is straightforward, and incentives have been provided for foreign investment. Emphasis was initially placed on exports of traditional products such as copra, rubber, and coffee, although it has become recognized that petroleum, timber, and minerals will become relatively more important.

Indonesia's position as an exporter of raw materials and an importer of manufactured goods is accepted for the foreseeable future. Import substitution and support for the agricultural sector have been the two major aims of industrial policy. Import substitution, however, has been geared to simple commodities such as food, textiles, fertilizers, and cement, and no attempt at a massive, broadly based industrialization policy has been attempted.

Development of a mixed economy

Internally, a mixed economy has been under establishment. The exploitation of natural resources has been left largely to private initiative subject to overall government supervision and contracts. The government has continued, however, to develop large-scale industrial projects, in particular when private enterprise has not been forthcoming. Medium and small-scale manufacturing have been left largely to the private sector—especially in the field of consumer goods. Emphasis in the development plan has been placed on the rehabilitation of the economic infrastructure, irrigation, and communications. The general aims of credit and fiscal policies have been to provide the conditions for the release of private incentive within the context of financial orthodoxy. Subsidized credit and interest rates, however, have been used in accordance with general government priorities. Protection is given on a moderate basis to local industry.

Problems and prospects. This consistent approach to development has carried its own risks. Its emphasis has been on soundness, and it has been heavily dependent on foreign aid and foreign technical assistance. One problem with such an orthodox emphasis on the role of private enterprise has been that it has led to an increasingly inequitable distribution of income. It has not been possible to implement the policies with sufficient force because powerful military interests and a vast inefficient bureaucracy distort the economic structure.

In the short to medium term these problems appear likely to be contained. The chaos and suffering under an earlier regime have been sufficiently close—and the benefits from rehabilitation and quick development sufficiently great—for the vast majority of the people to be relatively content with stability.

In the longer term, however, expectations may exceed the objectives of the government. In the 1970s the increasing income from mineral and timber exploitation went to a small minority, including foreign interests, while the pressure of population growth produced serious unemployment. The resulting rise in popular resentment toward foreign investment and the maldistribution of wealth may become significant factors. In addition, it is possible that general development will slow down once rehabilitation is completed, declining prices for agricultural products will offset increasing productivity in the rural sector, and industry will become more dominated by Chinese and Western interests.

It is difficult to determine if other general policies initiated in the 1970s will effectively address these problems. The growing signs of unrest indicate that reforms need to be pursued with urgency. The need for family planning, for the creation of new jobs, for the nationalization of the civil service, for the end of corruption, for the creation of an entrepreneurial class, and for the correction of the imbalances between Java and the outer islands are all part of accepted dogma. It seems reasonable to argue that the development of Indonesia's natural resources may provide sufficient strength to enable long-term development to succeed, but only if the necessary changes are followed through forcibly.

(E.I.U.)

TRANSPORTATION

Because Indonesia is an island country, sea transport plays a key role in the movement of raw materials and agricultural products from their source to markets. On the islands road transport is dominant. The only islands with even a rudimentary transportation network are Java and Sumatra. On Java, where existing rail and road organization is good and is capable of being expanded to meet growing needs, emphasis has been placed on road transport because of the short distances involved. Road traffic can be increased rapidly as roads are improved and trucks imported, while railroad traffic continues to be hampered by the poor condition of rolling stock. There is, however, an important role for railways both for freight and passengers because the high population density of Java places a limitation on new road construction.

The physical nature of the country favours the development of strong sea links for freight and strong air links for passengers. Most parts of Indonesia have not been adequately served by the transport network, a factor that has critically hampered economic development.

The transportation problem is best illustrated by Jakarta, where miles of paved roads are choked by the high density of traffic. Conditions are compounded by the unregulated stopping, turning, weaving, and manoeuvring of official and private buses, passenger cars, trucks, and the *becak*, a three-wheeled bicycle taxi and its motorized counterpart, the *helicak*. Off the main thoroughfares, the way is crowded by peddlers, who display their wares in wheeled stalls on sidewalks, along fences, and on the roadway, and by masses of pedestrians carrying bulky loads balanced at either end of shoulder sticks. Buses and local trains tend to be greatly overcrowded with people clinging to doors.

The Indonesian State Railway

Railways. The Indonesian State Railway (Perusahaan Jawatan Kereta Api, or PJKA) operates nearly 4,900 miles of track, 3,600 miles of which are on Java and Madura and 1,300 miles on Sumatra. The track on Java is interconnected, but on Sumatra there are four separate systems among which rolling stock cannot be directly transferred.

Geographic features and commodity composition have reduced the competitive position of the railroad. There has been little demand for long-distance bulk movement, normally the mainstay of railroad operation but in Indonesia handled by shipping. In the late 1970s, of the total revenues of the state railways, more than 50 percent was derived from passenger traffic.

The government has undertaken improvements in rail service. These include rehabilitation of existing facilities and the purchase of a limited amount of new equipment to allow the railroads to meet their slowly expanding role. A special feature of the PJKA is a special passenger train that provides daily first-class sleeper service on Java between Jakarta and Surabaya via Yogyakarta.

Roads. The road network consists of some 80,000 miles of roads, of which about 35,800 miles are paved. Most of the paved roads are on Java, where the network of highways is adequate to meet traffic needs in most areas. Much of the remaining paved mileage is on Sumatra. Kalimantan and Celebes have some good roads, but on Irian Jaya and the Moluccas there are few road interconnections between major settled areas.

Most of the paved roads were designed for pre-World War II traffic and are unable to bear the current traffic. An active maintenance and rehabilitation program undertaken in the early 1970s was financed in part by foreign aid.

Of the estimated 3,300,000 road vehicles in the country by 1980, more than one-half were motorcycles, 577,000 were passenger cars, and 453,000 were trucks and buses. Their numbers have increased rapidly each year as new vehicles have been imported and old and obsolete ones have continued to be used. Away from the major cities the variety of vehicles is remarkable, and automobiles that in some countries would be restored as collectors items have been converted into small buses.

Port facilities. Most of the major population centres are close to the sea, where they can be served and linked by coastal and inter-island shipping services. The adjacent seas are relatively calm because Indonesia is outside the belt of typhoons and high winds, and even where docking facilities are not available, it is usually possible for ships to anchor and discharge and load from lighters and other craft.

There are some 300 ports, more than 20 of which have facilities and water depths that allow ships of more than 500 tons to load and unload at quayside. The major dry cargo ports are Tanjungpriok (Tandjungpriok; the outport of Jakarta), Tanjungperak (Tandjungperak; the outport of Surabaya), and Belawan (the outport of Medan). Palembang in southern Sumatra is the major petroleum port. Other major ports include Semarang and Cirebon (Tjirebon), on Java; Telukbayur (the outport of Padang), on Sumatra; Manado, on Celebes; Ambon, on Moluccas; Jayapura (Djajapura), on Irian Jaya; and Banjarmasin, on Kalimantan.

About 60 percent of inter-island shipping in 1969 was maintained within Indonesia, and the rest was with Malaysia and Singapore. One-third of the inter-island trade is carried by powered coastal vessels (small wooden vessels using sails as well as power), one-third by the regular inter-island fleet (consisting of steel ships smaller than those of oceangoing size), one-fifth by domestic and foreign oceangoing vessels, and the rest by barges and sailing vessels. The main commodities carried are petroleum products, rice, copra, cement, flour, fertilizer, coconut oil, salt, rubber, asphalt, logs, and lumber.

There is great room for improvement in inter-island services through the use of modern loading and unloading techniques and some modification of the container concept to meet local needs and conditions. The government has established a body to coordinate shipping and establish schedules.

International air services

Air transport. International air services are confined to Jakarta in Java and Denpasar in Bali. Major cities in Sumatra have limited service to Malaysia, Yogyakarta has limited service to Japan, and Jayapura in Irian Jaya has limited service to Papua New Guinea. Scheduled services within the country are provided by several companies, the most important of which are Garuda, the national airline, and Merpati Nusantara, which is partially subsidized by the government. There are also several nonscheduled airlines.

There were about 40 civil airports and several military or joint military–civil airports by the early 1980s. Of the civil airports, only those of Jakarta, Surabaya, and Yogyakarta on Java, Denpasar on Bali, Medan on Sumatra, Ujung Pandang (Makasar) on Sulawesi, and Biak on Irian Jaya could accommodate large jets.

Improved air service will require not only runway extension but also the installation of telecommunication and navigational aids and lights. Aircraft utilization is low because few airports are equipped and lighted for nighttime operations. The capacity in the country as a whole is adequate to meet existing needs.

IV. Administration and social conditions

THE STRUCTURE OF GOVERNMENT

The Republic of Indonesia (Negara Republik Indonesia) was proclaimed in 1945. Its jurisdiction included the present area from Sabang in Sumatra to Merauke in Irian Jaya, or the entire area of the former Netherlands Indies. The Netherlands retained possession of a large part of this region, however, and a provisional capital was established in Yogyakarta, which was the stronghold of the revolution.

Constitutional development

With the close of the struggle for independence at a Round Table Conference in The Netherlands in 1949, the United States of Indonesia was established. The federal system did not last long, and in 1950 the federated governments unanimously decided to return to a republican form of government. After some difficulties the Republic of Indonesia returned to the constitution of 1945 by presidential decree.

The national government. Executive power lies in the president, who is assisted by a vice president. Both are elected every five years by the Majelis Permusyawaratan Rakyat (MPR; People's Consultative Assembly), and consequently are responsible to, although not subordinate to, that body. The ministers and heads of departments are appointed and dismissed by the president, who is also responsible for the supreme command of the army, navy, and air force. He has the authority to issue regulations, to implement acts, and to make agreements with foreign countries.

The president is assisted by the Dewan Pertimbangan Agung (DPA; Supreme Advisory Council). A maximum of 27 members are appointed by the president for a term of five years. They are prominent figures from all fields with wide experience at the regional as well as the national level. The Badan Pemeriksa Keuangan (BPK; Supreme Audit Board), appointed by the president and having five members, controls state finance and makes regular reports to the Dewan Perwakilan Rakyat (DPR; House of People's Representatives).

Besides holding executive power, the president is the leader of the legislative branch, the DPR, and in case of emergency he may issue governmental regulations with the consent of the DPR as a substitute for legislative acts. If such governmental regulation does not get the consent of the DPR, it is considered revoked.

The People's Consultative Assembly

The People's Consultative Assembly is the highest authority in the state, with the primary responsibilities of electing the president and vice president and determining the constitution and the broad lines of governmental policy. It consists of 924 members, including representatives from the DPR, regional delegates, and representatives of political parties and functional groups such as farmers, businessmen, the armed forces, and students, appointed by the president on the basis of nominations from those respective groups. The term of office of the MPR is five years, and the assembly sits at least once every five years.

The DPR consists of 464 members, 364 of whom are elected on a proportional system and 100 of whom are appointed by the respective groups as representatives of political parties and functional groups. The body sits once a year, and its members serve a term of five years.

The Dewan Perwakilan Rakyat Daerah (DPRD; Regional Council of Representatives) forms the regional government, the regulations and composition of which are determined along lines similar to those of the DPR.

The president is advised and assisted by a cabinet of ministers from the various government departments. Ministries include those for broad areas such as economic, financial, and industrial affairs; political affairs and defense; social welfare; supervision of development and the environment; research and technology; and administrative reform. Each minister is assisted by a secretary general, one or more director generals, an inspector general (if appropriate), and a staff of special assistants.

Regional and local government. The country is divided into 24 provinces, the two special autonomous districts of Aceh and Yogyakarta, each of which is headed by a governor, and the metropolitan district of Jakarta Raya. There are three provinces on Java, seven on Sumatra, four on Kalimantan, four on Celebes, four on Bali and Nusa Tenggara, or east Indonesia, and one each for the Moluccas and Irian Jaya.

The 246 second-order divisions, or *kabupaten*s, are headed by a *bupati*, and the 3,349 third-order divisions, or *kecamatan*s, are headed by a *camat*. In addition, there are 54 cities that have obtained autonomous status and have been recognized as municipalities, or *kotamadya*s, which are headed by a mayor, or *walikota*.

These regional units are all headed by officials of the central government. The village, or *kampong*, is headed by a *ketua*, and a group of villages, or *desa*, is headed by a *lurah;* these officials are elected locally and provide the link between the people and the central government on the *kecamatan* level. Regional and local government is highly dependent on the central government, which controls most appointments and collects more than 95 percent of all revenue.

The political process. The election law states that all citizens who have reached the minimum age of 17 or who have married may vote in general elections. All those who have reached the age of 21 may stand for elections. Voting is direct and by secret ballot.

The history of national elections

The first election after independence was held in 1955. Almost 170 political parties and factions contested, and four major parties obtained the majority of the votes. The election was carried out with little disturbance, but the resulting government was gradually set aside during the closing years of the regime of Sukarno—Indonesia's first national figure and first president, from 1949 to 1967—as the concept of a "Guided Democracy" took hold. At one point there were almost 100 ministries, each competing to build a more impressive edifice. The structure collapsed with an attempted coup d'etat of 1965, which led to the downfall of Sukarno.

After a period of stabilization and restructuring in which the armed forces played a major role, the second election of the DPR was held in 1971. Contesting this election were nine political parties and Sekber Golkar (Sekretariat Besar Golongan Karya), the joint secretariat of 61 nonaffiliated functional groups. These groups include nonparty associations of peasants, fishermen, civil servants, cooperatives, religious groups, students, the armed forces, and veterans that are allowed to contest the elections on the same level as political parties. After the 1965 disturbances the Golkar took on a stronger role, and the various groups combined into Sekber Golkar to present a united front for the 1971 elections, strongly supported by both the government and the military. It is, however, impossible to understand the political working on all levels in Indonesia without being aware of the concept of *mushawarah*, or "consensus," arrived at on the basis of extensive consultations aimed at reaching unanimous agreement. Decisions are seldom arbitrary or made by one person, but are the result of extensive discussions. This is the traditional approach to all problems.

Since the 1971 election, in which the Sekber Golkar won the largest number of votes, there has been extensive consultation on the best form of political structure to further strengthen national rather than group interests. The fragmentation of political parties has tended to emphasize group interests, and in response to government pressure to simplify the party system, during 1973 many of these parties combined to form two officially recognized parties, the United Development Party (Partai Persatuan Pembangunan; PPP), and the Indonesian Democratic Party (Partai Demokrasi Indonesia; PDI).

Justice. The judicial system consists of a Supreme Court (Mahkamah Agung) in Jakarta, which is the final court of appeal; high courts located in principal cities on Java, Sumatra, Celebes, Kalimantan, Bali, Moluccas, and Irian Jaya, which deal with appeals from district courts; and more than 250 districts courts.

The four judicial spheres

There are four judicial spheres (for general, religious, military, and administrative matters), each with its own courts. The religious, military, and administrative courts deal with special cases or particular groups of people, while the general deals with normal cases, both civil and criminal.

There is one codified criminal law for all of Indonesia; the Dutch codified civil code is applied to foreigners. For Indonesians the civil law is *adat*, or traditional, law, which varies from one district or ethnic group to another. The difficult process of codifying the extremely complex and diverse *adat* law was undertaken in the 1970s.

The armed forces. The armed forces of the Republic of Indonesia (Angkatan Bersenjata Republik Indonesia; ABRI) is not a colonial inheritance but was founded as a national armed force soon after independence. It consists of the army, navy, air force, and, since 1964, the state police. The army has a strength of about 195,000 men, about one-third of whom are engaged in civil and administrative duties; the navy has 52,000 men, including 12,000 marines, and has a small number of cruisers, submarines, destroyers, and frigates, as well as many smaller craft. The air force has a strength of 26,000 men and about 50 combat aircraft. Military service is not compulsory, except for university students.

The armed forces have as their primary tasks the defense and security of the country and, in normal times, the preservation of internal security. They are also looked upon as a social and political force and are expected to play an active role in development, particularly in rural areas. Personnel are given special training for the implementation of development activities, and they may serve to stimulate such activity on the village level. Politically, the armed forces have been active both in the maintenance of political stability and in the election process—for example, by participating in preelection preparations such as teaching people party symbols and the method of voting.

Administrative services. *Education.* At independence educational opportunities for Indonesians were limited even on the lower levels and were practically nonexistent on the university level. Since the 1940s the government has placed great emphasis on mass education, and some 80 percent of the children now enter primary schools. Dropout rates have been high, however, and were estimated in 1968 at 67 percent in primary, 25 percent in junior secondary, and 40 percent in senior secondary schools. According to the 1980 census, almost 72 percent of the population over the age of 10 was able to read and write.

Responsibility for education is centred in the Ministry of Education and Culture; the Ministries of Religious Affairs and Agriculture also have extensive educational programs, and most other ministries have training and upgrading programs in specific areas. In the early 1980s approximately 10 percent of primary, 35 percent of junior secondary, and nearly 50 percent of senior secondary students were enrolled in private schools.

The educational system

The educational system involves six years of primary education, followed by three years of junior and three years of senior secondary schools. Each level is divided into general, vocational, technical, and agricultural curricula. About 45 percent of the senior secondary students are in vocational, technical, and teacher-training schools. In general, teachers' salaries are low, and many are forced to take second jobs. Materials and supplies, particularly books, are insufficient, and the quality of education is poor. In addition, curricula have not been closely related to the country's manpower needs.

Where possible, parent–teacher associations supplement the school budget and contribute to better teacher salaries, materials, and supplies. In the early 1970s the total educational structure was redesigned and strengthened through both traditional and innovative techniques. The magnitude of such a project is indicated by the fact that by 1980 on the primary level alone there were some 22,487,000 pupils in 105,000 schools with 665,000 teachers scattered over the 1,000 inhabited islands.

By the early 1980s, higher education included more than 40 public universities—including one in each province—institutes and teacher-training colleges, about 120 other institutes and academies controlled by various government ministries, and more than 350 private institutions of higher learning. Because of the great problem of maintaining adequate staff and standards in such a widespread system, the Ministry of Education and Culture has established five consortia, consisting of representatives from the main universities, to deal with agriculture, science and technology, medicine, social sciences, and education. Postgraduate programs, begun in 1972, are concentrated at these centres, which also provide staff upgrading facilities for other universities. The institutes that were strengthened include the Universitas Pertanian Bogor (Bogor Agricultural University), the Institut Teknologi Bandung (Bandung Institute of Technology), the Universitas Indonesia in Jakarta, Gayjah Mada University in Yogyakarta, and Universitas Airlangga in Surabaya.

Health and welfare services. By 1980 there were an estimated 10,500 doctors, or one doctor for every 14,000 persons. Rural and remote areas were less well served, with an average ratio of less than one physician per 100,000.

The Five-Year Plan for health

A master plan for the rehabilitation of health services was begun in 1969 and has continued in operation under subsequent five-year plans. Its general objective, apart from the rehabilitation of essential facilities, was the provision of integrated health services through the promotion of adequately staffed curative and preventive services, particularly on the district level. The most complete district centres combine existing clinics with maternal and child-health centres and provide services for family planning, school health, nutrition, communicable-disease control, health statistics, environmental health, health education, dental health, and public-health nursing. These centres also supervise less comprehensive centres and subcentres in the villages.

One of the most serious problems is the shortage of medical and paramedical personnel, mainly nurses and midwives. Indigenous midwives (*dukun*s), often with limited training, assist at about 90 percent of the births in Indonesia; extensive training programs have been set up to bring the *dukun*s toward the standards of qualified midwives. Medical training is offered at 11 state schools and a number of private schools. Most of Indonesia's doctors, dentists, and pharmacists are trained at Universitas Indonesia, Airlangga University, Gajah Mada University, and Pajajaran State University in Bandung.

Family planning. The concept of family planning runs counter to traditional views, and there was much early resistance to such a program. A massive program was set up in 1968, at the beginning of the first five-year development plan, to provide information on family planning to women of childbearing age and to establish clinics that would be run by the Ministry of Health. By the early 1980s there were more than 5,000 such clinics, of which 90 percent were in Java and Bali. Thousands of personnel are also trained by the Indonesian Planned Parenthood Association.

The goal for the coordinated programs during 1971–75 was the reduction of the birth rate in Java and Bali by about 9 births per 1,000 population and that for all of Indonesia by 6 per 1,000 by 1976. This ambitious aim was severely limited in its initial stages because of the scarcity of administrative personnel able to successfully implement the new programs.

Housing. In rural areas the floors of dwellings consist of pounded earth or cement, or else of raised wood floors, while wooden framing supports walls of woven bamboo matting, and the roofs are of dried palm fibre or tiles. In urban areas floors are of cement or tile, the framing of the dwellings is of teak or meranti wood, the walls are of brick and plaster, and the roofs of tile or shingle. Although only about 20 percent of the population lives in urban areas, the major housing problems are in the cities, where new arrivals crowd into squalid slums. In their desire to escape the restraints of the traditional rural life and seek the opportunities of the cities, most immigrants find living conditions that are less attractive than those of the country.

Jakarta is the most modern city in Indonesia and the one with the greatest problems. It lacks a dependable supply of electricity, gas, and water, an adequate telephone system, a waste-disposal system, and adequate school and health facilities. Given the present rate of population increase, about 35,000 new households are added to the city each year, but only about 2,500 new permanent housing units are officially approved. Temporary housing, which does not require approval, fills the gap, and it is estimated that perhaps no more than one-fifth of the housing units in Jakarta are permanent.

Although active steps are being taken to improve the services, there is no substantial program to build low-cost housing. Subsidized housing is largely provided by employers, including government ministries, for a limited number of key employees.

SOCIAL CONDITIONS

Indonesia is in the midst of a period of intense social change, in which new ideas and values are being spread throughout the country. The massive rural population, which has the strongest traditional ties, is being reached by such means as agricultural extension workers and rural broadcasting. Farmers are being introduced to the value of improved seeds, fertilizers, and insecticides. The urban population has more contact with modernization and development through improvements in social services and facilities. Conditions in Indonesia are still poor, however, and the problems great.

The economy remains unbalanced, with too great an emphasis on small-scale agriculture; there is limited industry and serious unemployment. These problems have been compounded because of the rapid increase in the birth rate in the years after 1949. The number of youths aged 17 who entered the work force annually before 1966 numbered less than 1,500,000; in 1971 they numbered more than 3,000,000. The majority are semi-literate and unskilled labourers who join the already overcrowded lower economic levels.

Wages and the cost of living

The per capita gross national product, which was U.S. $380 in the early 1980s, is unevenly distributed. In Jakarta an average family, living on the simplest level, requires a much higher income. Few individuals earn an adequate income; many people have two or three jobs, and all members of the family may work and contribute. The central government has nearly 2,000,000 employees, a large percentage of whom receive less than $200 per year, including all allowances such as those of rice and oil. Most devote as little time as possible to their official jobs and as much as possible to supplementary employment.

The situation was improving by the early 1980s through increasing salaries and stabilizing costs. The government provides an annual salary increase for its employees of 33 to 50 percent, and other employers have granted similar increases. Wages of unskilled workers have not made parallel increases; consequently, there remains a large group in the cities that is inadequately housed, fed, and clothed.

The enormous rise in the cost of living in the cities has slowed since 1968, and, although there have been price increases, they have not been as serious. In rural areas the situation is also beginning to improve, and the income of farmers and villagers is increasing. This is evident in the improved appearance of the villages, schools, hospitals, and recreational facilities and by the increase in the number of such items as transistor radios and bicycles.

Health conditions in Indonesia are closely related to problems of diet. The major communicable diseases are well under control, although there are still cases of cholera, malaria, and tuberculosis. In the late 1970s there were some 137,000 persons with leprosy and 25,000 cases of tuberculosis. Although the diet of most of the people is limited to rice, vegetables, and a small amount of fish, it is adequate in most nutritional needs, and the bulk of the people are healthy and strong. In poorer regions and among the urban poor, there are serious nutritional deficiencies, in many cases due to a lack of understanding of needs rather than to a lack of availability of good food.

V. Cultural life and institutions

The diverse cultural heritage

Indonesia exhibits a rich diversity of cultural forms that range from those of the old Malay, which are preserved mainly in the remote interiors of Sumatra and Borneo, through the traditional Javanese and Balinese forms, which are heavily influenced by the Hindu stories of the Mahābhārata and the Rāmāyaṇa, to the modern culture that has evolved from this complex heritage. Claire Holt, in *Art in Indonesia* (1967), has divided cultural life into three overlapping spheres: "the Heritage," which includes the statues and monuments of the past; "Living Tradition," which covers the traditional theatre using shadow plays (*wayang kulit*), puppets (*wayang golek*), or human actors (*wayang orang* or *wayang wong*), and the use of new media to express traditional concepts as in the painting and sculpture of Bali; and "Modern Art," which deals with new forms of painting, sculpture, drama, and dance. For much of the population, particularly in the rural areas, "Living Tradition" is a valid term; for the cultural heritage centred around traditional, highly stylized, and semi-ritualistic forms, such as the shadow play, strongly influences all aspects of their lives.

MONUMENTS

From the 8th through the 10th centuries AD, extensive temple complexes (*tjandis*; *candis*) were built in central Java, most of which are now buried or in ruins. The government has been actively engaged in restoration since the 1950s.

The remains of the first of the great central Javanese monuments, the Śaivite temple of the Dataran-Tinggi Dijeng (Dieng Plateau), date to the early 8th century. The Śailendra dynasty, which ruled Java and Sumatra (8th–9th century), built the great Mahāyāna Buddhist monuments, including that of Borobuḍur, which was constructed around AD 800. Late in the 9th century the kings of Mataram built the Hindu monuments around Prambanan. Chandi Lara Yonggrang (Tjandi Lara Jonggrang), commonly called Prambanan, is the largest and best preserved of a series of Hindu temple complexes in the region. It consists of six main temples; the three large ones along the west are dedicated to Śiva, Viṣṇu, and Brahmā and contain fine statues. Of the three smaller temples along the east, the middle one contains a statue of Nandi, the bull of Śiva. The main temples are heavily ornamented with stone carvings of the gods and other heavenly beings, and there is a series of relief panels depicting the Rāmāyaṇa story.

The temples of Borobuḍur

Borobuḍur is often considered the most significant monument in the Southern Hemisphere and one of the finest Buddhist monuments in the world. It stands on a hill and rises to a height of 115 feet from its base, which measures 403 feet square. The monument consists of a lower structure of six square terraces and an upper structure of three circular terraces, combining the ancient symbols of the circle for the heavens and the square for the Earth. In the centre of each side of the square terraces is a staircase leading to the next level. The inner wall on each level has niches containing statues of Buddha, whose life is depicted in the bas-reliefs that cover both inner walls and balustrades. The circular terraces are not decorated and contain 72 bell-shaped *stūpas*, each containing a statue of Buddha. In the centre of the upper terrace is the main *stūpa*, which stands 23 feet high and is now closed. It was opened in 1842, but no statues or relics were found.

Between the 10th and 16th centuries, the centre of power shifted to eastern Java. Literature in ancient Javanese (*kawi*) flourished during this period, and a number of impressive temple complexes were constructed, none of which, however, approached the grandeur of Borobuḍur or Prambanan. The most imposing complex is Chandi (Tjandi) Panataran near Blitar, which was constructed at the peak of the Majapahit period in the 14th century. With the ascendancy of Islām in the 16th century, the temples fell into ruins, and the main continuity of Hindu influence shifted to Bali.

THE STATE OF THE ARTS

The "Living Tradition" is best represented by the various ways in which the Indian legends of the Rāmāyaṇa and Mahābhārata permeate society. It is in evidence in many Asian countries, but nowhere stronger than in the highly populated rural areas of Java and Bali. The same situations and poses in the carvings on Prambanan are seen in the *wayang* ("play") performances in contemporary villages and cities. The word *wayang* (*wajang*) refers to the flat leather puppet used in shadow plays; in its broader sense it has come to mean the performance itself, whether it involves leather or wooden puppets or human actors.

The *wayang*

In puppet performances the narration and dialogue are recited by a storyteller (*dalang*), who manipulates the puppets and is the artist of the performance. When leather puppets are used, the audience can sit either in front of or behind a screen, thus viewing either the puppets or their shadows. When people perform these dramas, they often wear masks (*wayang topeng*). The performances are accompanied by a gamelan orchestra, which consists almost entirely of percussion instruments such as gongs, the xylophone-like *gender* and *gambang*, a two-stringed instrument called a *rebab*, and a flute.

Performing and decorative arts. Bali will always be of special interest culturally because its Hindu traditions have been preserved, undisturbed by the spread of Islām. Sculpture, wood carving, and painting continue to evolve in an environment that encourages the development of the most colourful and exotic forms. Although continually changing, these forms remain true to the basic traditions and religious beliefs of the people.

There are probably as many distinct dance styles in Indonesia as there are languages and dialects. The most advanced are found on Java, where one of the best-known troupes is the *kraton* (Sultan's Palace) of Yogyakarta, and on Bali, where many villages have their own dance troupes. The dances have common roots and characteristics, including many kneeling and crouching postures; little running, leaping, or spinning; much use of the hands, fingers, and eyes; and, with the exception of some Balinese dances, a slow tempo. Elaborate and traditional costumes are customary, with emphasis on the headdress, which may include flowers, horns, feathers, or incense sticks. Both men and women participate, the men's dances being more varied and vigorous. Although the stylized dances, such as the Balinese *legong* or the Javanese *serimpi*, are the best known, traditional dance styles are found throughout the country. They include the candle and umbrella dances of central Sumatra, the hobbyhorse dances of Java, the trance dances of many regions, and the more primitive tribal dances of the interior of Kalimantan and the eastern islands.

Decorative arts include carvings in stone, wood, bone, and ivory, woven and dyed fabrics, and metalwork. Although some of these owe much to other parts of Southeast Asia, the various sections of Indonesia have produced individual styles. The commemorative and symbolic motifs of both the Dong Son of Indochina and the late Chou of China have strongly influenced Indonesian art. Textile design is regarded as the most varied and attractive artistic achievement.

The art of batik

Batik making, practiced almost exclusively on Java, involves a complex wax-resistance process in which all parts of a cloth that are not to be dyed are coated on both sides with wax before the cloth is dipped into the dye. Using a penlike wax holder called a *canting*, it is possible to create very intricate and elaborate designs. It is a very time-consuming process, and those batiks that are made entirely by hand take several weeks to complete. Much modern batik is made using copper stamps (*caps*) to apply the wax, thereby greatly speeding up the process and lowering the cost.

On woven fabric, which is made everywhere from Sumatra through the eastern islands, the most characteristic element is the key-shaped figure combined with other geometrical figures. The rhombus (an equilateral parallelogram usually having oblique angles) frequently occurs together with straight lines, equilateral triangles, squares, or circles, which permits an enormous number of variations, including stylized representations of human beings and animals. Each island or region has its characteristic patterns, which serve to identify the area in which the cloth is made.

The art of weaving is highly developed. It includes the famous *ikat* ("to bind or tie") method, in which the thread is dyed selectively before weaving by binding fibres around groups of threads so that they will not take up colour when the thread is dipped in the dyebath. This process may be applied to the warp, which is most common and is found in Sumatra, Borneo, and Sumba. Weft *ikat* is found mainly in south Sumatra, and the complex process of double *ikat* is still carried on in Tenganan in Bali, where such cloth has great ceremonial significance.

Museums. Indonesian museums have the nucleus of good ethnographic collections, but they have been neglected. The national museum in Jakarta has an extensive collection of Indonesian carvings, textiles, and artifacts; in addition, it contains models of traditional houses and villages from various parts of the country. The Jakarta Museum, which has been restored, displays historic material of the city.

There are a number of other museums throughout the country, the most notable of which are the Radya Pustaka in Sukakarta (Solo, or Sala) in central Java, the Museum Bali in Denpasar, and the Ratna Warta in Ubud in Bali. All suffer from limited support and can neither display their materials well nor build up their collections. The Presidential Palace in Bogor, which has a fine collection of Indonesian art, is located adjacent to the Botanical Gardens.

PRESS AND BROADCASTING

There are more than 100 daily newspapers, nearly one-quarter of which are published in Jakarta. They represent a variety of factions, including trade unions, student groups, political groups, religious groups, and the armed forces, but most consider themselves to be independent. Most are published in Indonesian, but there are a few newspapers in English, in Sundanese, and Mandarin Chinese. Only a few of the major journals, such as *Merdeka*, *Indonesia Raya*, and *Kompas*, exceed 120,000 copies a day, and the great majority daily print in the range of 15,000 to 30,000 copies or less. There are also several weeklies, some of which are illustrated.

Antara, the Indonesian National News Agency, has branches throughout Indonesia and in major news centres in the world. It is connected with some 25 foreign agencies, and the principal international press services have offices or representatives in Indonesia.

Radio and television are mainly controlled by the government, although there are a large number of independent radio stations that broadcast locally with relatively low-power transmitters. Radio Republik Indonesia (RRI) has transmitters throughout the country; and in addition to national daily broadcasts in Bahasa Indonesia, which include educational programs, there are daily broadcasts overseas in Arabic, Bahasa Malaysia, Chinese, English, French, German, Hindi, Japanese, Thai, and Urdu. The main RRI studio centre in Jakarta was rebuilt early in the 1970s, and there are studio centres and facilities in Yogyakarta, Medan, Ujungpandang, and other cities. Local and regional centres mainly originate their own programs, but all studio centres are equipped to relay broadcasts from Jakarta.

In addition to RRI, there are more than 130 radio stations that have been set up by provincial administrators and more than 500 amateur and commercial radio stations, mostly with low-powered transmitters. In Jakarta and other major cities, commercial radio services are well established.

Yayasan Televisi Republik Indonesia (TVRI) is the only source of television; it transmits (mainly in Bahasa Indonesia) between five and six hours daily on four channels. There are television studios in Jakarta, Yogyakarta, Den pasar, Ujungpandang, Medan, and other cities. Transmitters have been installed on a number of microwave relay stations so that reception is available over much of the flat area of western and central Java, as well as Sumatra, Celebes, and Kalimantan. In 1976 and 1977 Indonesia launched two communications satellites that can handle radio, telephone, and television signals, effectively linking all communications systems in the nation.

VI. Prospects for the future

Indonesia is faced with the interrelated problems of population growth and economic development. Although it became the principal oil producer in the Far East and had rice surpluses during the 1970s, it did not achieve its planned objectives of food self-sufficiency and faster industrial development, especially in manufactured goods. Its third Five Year Plan (1979–84) again concentrated on these areas, especially greater diversity in agricultural output. This is being implemented in part through a government-sponsored program to settle and cultivate virgin territory. The projected annual economic growth rate of 6.5 percent continued to be achieved in the early 1980s, despite a general world recession. The threat of more serious unemployment in cities and rural areas is one of the most serious problems for the future as the population grows, and the distribution of income is in danger of becoming more inequitable. Although it is faced with many problems, the government is following a policy designed to move the country toward the position that its location, resources, and people would warrant.

BIBLIOGRAPHY

General works: RUTH T. MCVEY (ed.), *Indonesia* (1963), is a scholarly reference work with chapters including "Physical and Human Resource Patterns" by KARL J. PELZER and "Indonesian Cultures and Communities" by HILDRED GEERTZ. N.A. DOUWES DEKKER, *Tanah Air Kita: A Book on the Country and People of Indonesia* (1951), is a popular pictorial review of the islands that contains an accurate cultural description. Informative travel guides include: DARBY GREENFIELD, *Indonesia: A Traveler's Guide*, 2 vol. (1975–76), the first volume on Java and Sumatra and the second on Bali and the eastern islands; STAR BLACK *et al.*, *Bali*, 5th ed. (1977); and BILL DALTON, *Indonesia Handbook*, 2nd ed. (1980). The *Ensiklopedi Indonesia* (1980–) is to be complete in 6 vol. For general reference volumes, see the Europa publication *The Far East and Australasia* (annual); NUGROHO, *Indonesia Facts and Figures* (1967); BUREAU OF STATISTICS, *The Statistical Pocketbook of Indonesia* (annual); NENA VREELAND *et al.*, *Area Handbook for Indonesia*, 3rd ed. (1975); DEPARTMENT OF INFORMATION *Indonesia Handbook 1976* (1977); LOUIS FISCHER, *The Story of Indonesia* (1959); B.H. and J.T.D. HIGGINS, *Indonesia: The Crisis of the Millstones* (1963); G.M. KAHIN, *Nationalism and Revolution in Indonesia* (1952); DATUS C. SMITH, JR., *The Land and People of Indonesia*, rev. ed. (1968); B.H.M. VLEKKE, *Nusantara: A History of Indonesia*, rev. ed. (1959); and M.C. RICKLEFS, *A History of Modern Indonesia* (1981).

Landscape: R.W. VAN BEMMELEN, *The Geology of Indonesia* (1949), is an exhaustive survey of the country's geology and natural resources, with detailed information on individual islands. See also WARREN HAMILTON, *Tectonics of the Indonesian Region* (1979); and E.C.J. MOHR and F.A. VON BAREN, *Tropical Soils: A Critical Study of Soil Genesis As Related to Climate, Rock and Vegetation* (1954), with most examples drawn from Indonesia.

Population: N. ISKANDAR, *Some Monographic Studies on the Population of Indonesia* (1970), contains a review of the 1961 census and projections; see also NITISASTRO WIDJOJO, *Population Trends in Indonesia* (1970). UNIVERSITAS INDONESIA, *The Population of Indonesia* (1974), is the World Population Year monography commissioned by the UN Committee for International Coordination of National Research in Demography.

Culture: Cultural material is presented in F.A. WAGNER, *Indonesia: The Art of an Island Group* (1959); CLAIRE HOLT, *Art in Indonesia* (1967); and MIGUEL COVARRUBIAS, *Island of Bali* (1937). Extensive reference may also be made to publications of ECAFE and other United Nations bodies, which often contain detailed reports and analyses on specific subjects, and to the information bulletins of the Ministry of Information.

(J.F.McD./Ed.)

Indonesia, History of

This article covers the history of the peoples of Java, Sumatra, and the neighbouring islands, the area formerly known as the East Indies, and now the nucleus of the Republic of Indonesia. The article is divided into the following sections:

I. Indonesia to the end of the 16th century

THE ARCHIPELAGO AND ITS EARLY HISTORICAL RECORDS

The Indonesian archipelago stretches for more than 3,000 miles east–west and is the largest island complex in the world. The sea has inevitably influenced Indonesian history. Monsoon winds, blowing north and south of the Equator, have facilitated communication within the archipelago and with the rest of maritime Asia; the warm rainfall has nourished rich vegetation. In early times the timber and spices of Java and the eastern islands were known afar, as were also the resins from the exceptionally wet equatorial jungle in the western islands of Sumatra and Borneo. Not long after the beginning of the Christian Era goods were already being shipped overseas, and navigable rivers brought the Indonesian hinterland into touch with distant markets.

Easy navigation did not result in the formation of territorially large kingdoms. The many estuaries of Sumatra and Borneo, facing the inland seas, possessed an abundance of nutritious seafood that made possible a settled mode of life, and the contacts between the people of one estuary and their neighbours were more important to them than those they could make with overseas lands. Indonesian maritime history is the story of the efforts of local groups, endowed with more or less comparable resources, to protect their separate identities. The same local interests prevailed on the island of Java, where the lava-coated soil, watered by gently flowing rivers, encouraged wet-rice production and a patchwork of settled areas in the river valleys separated by mountains and jungle. Long before records begin, many of these coastal and riverine groups were probably evolving an elementary form of hierarchy, accompanied by the craftsmen's tokens of rank. No single group was large enough to overrun and occupy neighbouring territories; its energies were absorbed rather by an ever more intensive exploitation of its own natural resources. Those living on or close to the sea knew that geographical isolation was out of the question but regarded their maritime environment as a means of enhancing their well-being through imports or new skills rather than as an avenue to the world. Looking outward, far from inculcating a sense of belonging to greater communities, was subordinated to local needs.

Political fragmentation

Not surprisingly, Indonesian place-names have often remained unchanged since the beginning of documented history. In these places, not necessarily far apart, each leader saw himself at the centre of the world that mattered to him, which was not, until much later, the archipelago or even a single island but his own strip of coast or river valley. Some centres achieved local hegemony, of course, but never to the extent of being able to extinguish permanently the pretensions of rival centres in the neighbourhood. The early history of Indonesia, therefore, is compounded of many regional histories that only gradually impinge on each other.

Indonesia's languages

The historical fragmentation of the archipelago, sustained by its rich climate and accentuated rather than offset by easy access to the outside world, is reflected in its languages. Scholars have debated the location of the areas outside Indonesia from which the speakers of the Austronesian (Malayo-Polynesian) languages originally came: the Asian mainland and the Pacific islands have been proposed.

What is significant for the historian, however, is that the speakers of these languages almost certainly drifted into the region in small groups over long periods of time and did not suddenly assume a common identity when they reached the coasts and rivers of the archipelago. On the contrary, they remained scattered groups, sometimes coexisting with descendants of earlier Pleistocene populations, who, in their turn, had also learned to make economic use of their environment over an immense span of cultural time. The perhaps 200 languages within the Western, or Indonesian, branch of the Austronesian family are an index of the manner in which the peoples of the Indonesian archipelago submitted to the realities of their landscape.

The historian must remind himself—when he examines the stone or metal inscriptions comprising, along with surviving copies of early religious texts, his important sources of documentary information—that his evidence is always concerned with specific places. He must not suppose that he can supply satisfactory narrative accounts of extensive areas or solve the problems of interregional relationships created by ambiguous inscriptions. His task is the study of cultural history in widely scattered groups of society rather than narrative accounts of still very indistinct kingdoms; it is the investigation of beliefs shared by the ruling classes and the peasantry and of the points of contact between them. The ideas of men of rank were articulated in architecture and literature, reflecting varying degrees of exposure to influences outside the archipelago, but all groups of the population subscribed to basic assumptions concerning mankind's dependence on the goodwill of the gods. Industrial archaeology, undertaken in western Borneo, will probably one day provide knowledge of the technological skills and outside contacts of those peoples who did not leave behind them more conventional records of their past.

INDONESIAN "HINDUISM"

Influence of foreign contacts

It may one day be shown by students of prehistory that Indonesians were sailing to other parts of Asia long before the Christian Era. Records of foreign trade, however, begin only in the early centuries AD. A study of the Roman historian Pliny's *Natural History* suggests that, in the 1st century AD, Indonesian outriggers were trading with the east coast of Africa. Indonesian settlements may have existed at that time in Madagascar, an island with distinct Indonesian cultural traits. The geographer Ptolemy, in the following century, incorporated information from Indian merchants in his *Guide to Geography* concerning Iabadiou, presumably Java, and Malaiou, which, with its variants, may refer to Malayu in southeastern Sumatra.

Regular voyages between Indonesia and China did not begin before the 5th century AD. Chinese literature in the 5th and 6th centuries refers to western Indonesian tree produce, including camphor from northern Sumatra, and also to two Sumatran resins that seem to have been added to the seaborne trade in western Asian resins and were known in China as "Persian resins from the southern ocean." Indonesian shippers were probably exploiting the economic difficulties south China was suffering because it had been cut off from the ancient central Asian trade route. Certain little estuary kingdoms were beginning to prosper as international entrepôts. Their location is unknown, though Palembang's commercial prominence in the 7th century suggests that the Malays of southeastern Sumatra had been active in the "Persian" trade with southern China.

Hindu religious conceptions. The cultural effects of these commercial exchanges, usually described as "Hinduization," have been discussed for many years. It is now held that Hinduism was brought to Indonesia, not by traders as was formerly thought, but by Brahmins who taught the Śaivite message of personal immortality. Sanskrit inscriptions, attributed to the 5th and 6th centuries, have been found in eastern Borneo, a considerable distance from the international trade route, and also in western Java. They have been attributed to the 5th and 6th centuries. They reveal that Indian literati, or their Indonesian disciples, were honoured in some royal courts. The rulers were prominent *rakas*, heads of groups of villages in areas where irrigation and other needs had brought into being intervillage relationships and supravillage authority. The inscriptions, and also Chinese sources, indicate that some rulers were involved in warfare and must have been seeking to extend their influence. The Śaivite Brahmins supervised the worship of Śiva's phallic symbol, the linga, in order to tap the god's favours on behalf of their royal patrons. These Brahmins were representatives of an increasingly influential devotional movement (bhakti) in contemporary Indian Hinduism; they probably also taught their patrons how to achieve a personal relationship with the god through "austerity, strength, and self-restraint," in the words of one inscription from Borneo. The rulers, therefore, were encouraged to attribute their worldly successes to Śiva's grace; the grace was obtained through devotional exercises lovingly offered to Śiva and probably regarded as the guarantee of a superior status in the life after death. These Śaivite cults, marks of a privileged spiritual life, would have been a source of prestige and royal authority.

Indonesian religious conceptions. But the question must be asked to what extent such religious ideas were comprehensible to those who first heard them. Indonesians, who had been accustomed to constructing terraced mountain-like temples, symbolizing holy mountains, for the burial and worship of the dead, would not have been perplexed by the Brahmins' doctrine that Śiva also dwelt on a holy mountain. Natural stones, already placed on mountain terraces for the ritual of megalithic worship, would have been easily identified with Śiva's natural stone linga, the most prestigious of all lingas. Indonesians, already concerned with the passage rites and welfare of the dead, would have paid particular attention to Hindu devotional techniques for achieving immortality in Śiva's abode. The meditative ascetic of Hinduism may have been preceded in Indonesia by the trance-inducing shaman (priest-healer). Again, the notion that water was a purifying agent because it had been purified by Śiva's creative energy on his mountaintop would have been intelligible to mountain-worshipping Indonesians, especially if they already endowed the water flowing from their own gods' mountain peaks with divinely fertilizing qualities.

Mountain temples

Indonesian religious conceptions must certainly have supplied the perspectives of those who first listened to the Brahmins. Confidence in the Brahmins, honoured especially as teachers (gurus), would have depended on their demonstrating means of achieving religious goals already recognized as important in the indigenous system of beliefs. The Brahmins' role was probably prepared during earlier visits by Buddhist missionaries, who also shared the Indian concern for religious salvation.

Adoption of Indian religious form

But Indonesian circumstances and motivation underlay the adoption of Indian forms. The use of Hindu terminology in the inscriptions represents no more than Indonesian attempts to find suitable metaphorical expressions from the sacred Sanskrit literature for describing their own realities. Sanskrit literature, imported from India on manuscripts or by feats of memory, would have been especially culled when courtly literati were seeking to describe those rulers who had achieved an intensive personal relationship with Śiva. One must not be deceived by the accumulating acquaintance with Indian civilization reflected in Indonesian inscriptions and Javanese literature. The Indonesians, like others in early Southeast Asia, had no difficulty in identifying themselves with the universal values of "Hindu" civilization represented by the sacred literature. Indian literary and legal works were to provide useful guidelines for Indonesian creative writing, but they did not bring about the thoroughgoing "Hinduization" of the archipelago any more than Indian Brahmins were responsible for the formation of the early kingdoms of the archipelago.

In the final analysis, therefore, India should be regarded as an arsenal of religious skills, the use of which was subordinated to the ends of the Indonesians. Expanding communication meant that increasing numbers of Indonesians became interested in Indian thought. The first reasonably well-documented period of maritime Malay history provides further evidence of the Indonesian adaptation of Indian religious conceptions.

THE MALAY KINGDOM OF SRIVIJAYA-PALEMBANG

The kingdom of Śrivijaya is first mentioned in the writings of the Chinese Buddhist pilgrim I-ching, who visited it in 671 after a voyage of less than 20 days from Canton. He was on the first stage of his journey to the great teaching centre of Nālandā in northeastern India. The ruler of Śrivijaya, who assisted I-ching on his journey, lived at Palembang in southeastern Sumatra. For four centuries thereafter, Palembang was the major entrepôt in Southeast Asia for merchants from the Indian Ocean who wished to trade with China by sea.

Buddhism in Palembang. Śrivijaya-Palembang's importance is established by Arab and Chinese historical sources spanning a long period of time. Its own records, in the form of Old Malay inscriptions, are limited almost entirely to the second half of the 7th century (682–686). The inscriptions reveal that the ruler was served by a hierarchy of officials and that he possessed wealth, though the source of his wealth is not disclosed. The period when the inscriptions were written was an agitated one. Battles are mentioned, and the ruler had to reckon with disaffection and intrigues at his capital. Indeed, the main theme of the inscriptions is a curse on those who broke a loyalty oath administered by drinking holy water. The penalty for disloyalty was death, but those who obeyed the ruler were promised eternal bliss.

I-ching recommended Palembang, with more than 1,000 monks, as an excellent centre for studying Buddhist texts before proceeding to India. The 7th-century inscriptions, however, are concerned with less scholarly features of Buddhism. They deal with Tantric aids to magical power (see below), in the form of *yantra* symbols, which were distributed by the ruler to faithful servants. Some of his adversaries disposed of them, too. Especially interesting as evidence of the influence of the Mahāyāna form of Buddhism within the context of royal power is the Talang Tuwo inscription of 684, which records the king's prayer that a park he has endowed may give merit to all living beings. The language and style of this inscription, incorporating Indian Tantric conceptions, make it clear that the ruler was presenting himself as a *bodhisattva*—one who was to become a Buddha himself—teaching the several stages toward supreme enlightenment. Here is the first instance in the archipelago's history of a ruler's assumption of the role of religious leader.

Tantric teachings

The inscriptions show that the teachings of the Tantrayāna (Tantric) school of Mahāyāna Buddhism, teaching magical procedures for achieving supernatural ends, had reached Palembang before the end of the 7th century. The Tantrayāna came into prominence in India only in the 7th century, and the synchronism of its appearance in Palembang reflects not only the regularity of shipping contacts between Sumatra and India but, more importantly, the Malays' quick perception of the contribution of the Tantrayāna as a source of personal spiritual power. The word for "curse" in the inscriptions is more frequently a Malay than a Sanskrit one, and it is reasonable to suppose that the Malays grafted Tantric techniques on to indigenous magical procedures. The vitality of Malay religion is probably also reflected in the prestige of its sacred hill, Bukit Seguntang, which was visited by those in search of spiritual power. Bukit Seguntang would not suddenly have become such a centre as a result of traffic in Tantric conceptions during the 7th century. In other words, the disturbances reflected in the inscriptions are less likely to have been the growing pains of a rising kingdom than the efforts of an already important kingdom to achieve, or perhaps recover, hegemony in the region.

The maritime influence. Special circumstances affecting Śrivijaya-Palembang toward the end of the 7th century are consistent with this conclusion. In the centuries before the Chinese undertook long voyages overseas, they relied on foreign shipping for their imports, and foreign merchants, trading with China, required a safe base in Indonesia before sailing on to China. This seaborne trade, regarded in China as "tributary" trade with the "emperors' barbarian vassals," had developed during the 5th and 6th centuries but languished in the second half of the 6th century as a result of the civil war in China that preceded the rise of the Sui and T'ang dynasties. The decline in the China trade was probably accompanied by economic regression in the western Indonesian harbour kingdom near the Strait of Malacca, which had provided the entrepôt. Chinese records for the first half of the 7th century mention several small harbour kingdoms in the region, especially in northeastern Sumatra, that were pretending to be Chinese vassals. The rulers of Palembang, hoping for a revival of trade under the new T'ang dynasty, must have been anxious to monopolize the China trade and eliminate their rivals. They succeeded in doing so. Before I-ching left Southeast Asia in 695, Śrivijaya was in control of the Strait of Malacca; the ruler's determination to control all harbours in the region that might compete in the China trade explains his militancy, as shown in the Old Malay inscriptions.

Importance of the China trade

The subsequent power of the maharajas of Śrivijaya depended on their alliance with those who possessed warships. The fact that Arab accounts make no mention of piracy in the islands at the southern end of the Strait of Malacca suggests that the seafaring inhabitants of these islands identified their interests with those of the maharajas, refraining from molesting merchant ships and cooperating in controlling Śrivijaya's potential competitors in northern Sumatra. The maharajas offered their loyal subjects wealth, posts of honour, and—according to the inscriptions—supernatural rewards. But the coalition of maritime Malays in this geographically fragmented region survived only as long as the Palembang entrepôt was prosperous and its ruler offered enough largesse to hold the elements together. His bounty, however, depended on the survival of the Chinese tributary trading system, which needed a great entrepôt in western Indonesia. Early Malay history is, to an important extent, the history of a Sino-Malay alliance. The maharajas benefitted from the China trade, while the emperors could permit themselves the conceit that the maharajas were reliable imperial agents.

The extent of the Palembang kingdom

The territorial extent of the Palembang kingdom is unknown. The offshore islands at the southern entrance of the Strait of Malacca were essential to its power, but its influence in Sumatra would have been secured by control of the river estuaries, and territorial possessions without specific commercial advantages would probably have been avoided.

Malay unity under the leadership of the maharajas was inevitably undermined when Chinese ships began in the 12th century to sail directly to centres of production in the archipelago and a single entrepôt was no longer needed. But Śrivijaya-Palembang had already, toward the end of the 11th century, ceased to be the chief estuary kingdom in Sumatra. Hegemony had passed, for unknown reasons, to the neighbouring estuary town of Jambi, which was probably controlled by the great Minangkabau country of Malayu in the interior. With the decline of the tributary trade with China a number of harbours in the region became centres of international trade. Malayu-Jambi never had the opportunity to build up naval resources as Śrivijaya-Palembang had done, and in the 13th century a Javanese prince took advantage of the power vacuum.

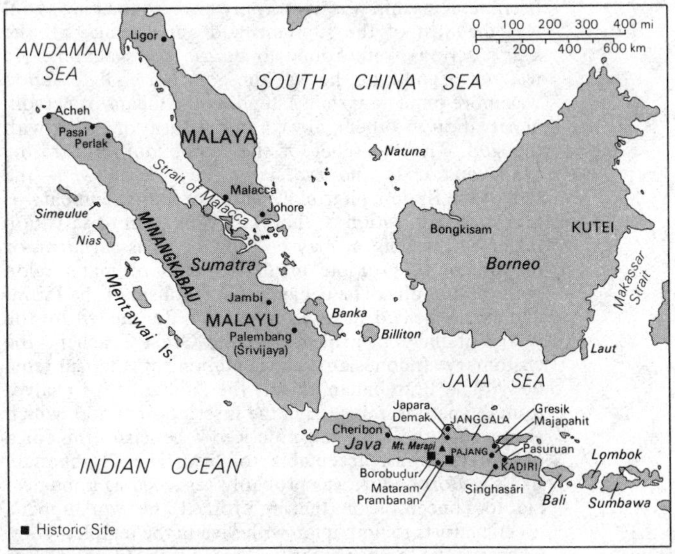

Sites associated with early Indonesian history.

CENTRAL JAVA IN THE 8TH AND 9TH CENTURIES

Eastern Javanese inscriptions throw little light on happenings before the 10th century, but the evidence from south central Java, and especially from the Kedu Plain in the 8th and 9th centuries, is more abundant. This period in central Java is associated with the Śailendra princes. An old Malay inscription from north-central Java, attributed to the 7th century, establishes that the Śailendras were of Indonesian origin and not, as was once suspected, from mainland Southeast Asia. In the middle of the 9th century the ruler of Śrivijaya-Palembang was a Śailendra who boasted of his Javanese ancestors; the name Śailendra also appears on the undated face of an inscription on the isthmus of the Malay Peninsula; the other face of the inscription—dated 775—is in honour of the ruler of Śrivijaya.

In spite of ambiguous references to Śailendra connections overseas, there is no solid evidence that the territories of the central Javanese rulers at this time extended far beyond central Java, including its north coast. Yet the agricultural wealth of this small kingdom sustained vast religious undertakings; the monuments of the Kedu Plain are the most famous in Indonesia. The Borobuḍur, in honour of Mahāyāna Buddhism, comprises 2,000,000 cubic feet of stone and 27,000 square feet of stone bas-relief. It was built about 800—not much more than half a century before Śiva's great temple, the Prambanan, less than 50 miles (80 kilometres) away. The two monuments, which have much in common, help to explain the religious impulses in earlier Javanese history.

Divine attributes of the kings

The Borobuḍur is a terraced temple surmounted by stupas, or stone towers; the terraces resemble Indonesian burial foundations, indicating that the Borobudur was regarded as the symbol of the final resting place of its founder, a Śailendra, who was united after his death with the Buddha. The Prambanan is also associated with a dead king. An inscription of 856, very likely on its foundation stone, mentions a royal funeral ceremony and shows that the dead king had joined Śiva, just as his predecessor, the founder of the Borobuḍur, had joined the Buddha. Divine attributes, however, had been ascribed to the kings during their lifetimes. A Mahāyāna inscription of this period shows that a ruler was said to have the purifying powers of a *bodhisattva*, the status assumed by the ruler of Śrivijaya in the 7th century; a 9th-century Śaivite inscription from the Kedu Plain describes a ruler as being "a portion of Śiva."

The divine qualities of these kings, whether of Mahāyāna or of Śaivite persuasion, had important implications in Javanese history and probably in the history of all parts of the archipelago that professed the forms of Indian religion. The ruler was now and henceforth seen as one who had achieved union with the supreme god in his lifetime. Kingship was divine only because the king's soul was the host of the supreme god and because all the king's actions were bound to be the god's actions. He was not a god-king; he was the god. No godlike action was more important than extending the means of personal salvation to others, always in the form of union with the god. The bas-relief of the Borobuḍur, illustrating Mahāyāna texts and especially the *Gaṇḍavyūha*—the tale of the tireless pilgrim in search of enlightenment—is a gigantic exposition of the Mahāyāna path to salvation taken by the king; it may be thought of as a *yantra*, or instrument to promote meditation and ultimate union with the Buddha. The pedagogic symbolism of the Prambanan is revealed in its iconography, dominated by the image of the four-armed Śiva, the Great Teacher—the customary Indonesian representation of the supreme deity. The Prambanan affirms the Śaivite path to salvation; the path is indicated in the inscription of 856, which shows that the king had practiced asceticism, the form of worship most acceptable to Śiva. The Prambanan, like the Borobuḍur, was probably regarded as a magical aid to concentration that reinforced the worshipper's ascetic efforts to find union with Śiva in the temple.

The significance of royal tombs

These royal tombs taught, and also provided, the means of salvation. The royal role on earth was similar. The kings, not the religious elite, bore the responsibility of ensuring that all could worship the gods, whether under Indian or Indonesian names. Every god in the land was either a manifestation of Śiva or a subordinate member of Śiva's pantheon, and worship therefore implied homage to the king, who was part of the god. The growing together, as a result of Tantric influences, of Śaivism and the Mahāyāna meant that, over the centuries, the divine character of the king became continually elaborated. His responsibility was the compassionate one of maintaining his kingdom as a holy land. The *bodhisattva*-king was moved by pity, as were all *bodhisattvas*, while the Śiva-like king, as an inscription of the 9th century indicates, was also honoured for his compassion. Compassion was expressed by providing an environment wherein religion could flourish. Governing well, keeping the peace, protecting the numerous holy sites, encouraging religious learning, and above all performing purification rituals to render the land acceptable to the gods were different aspects of a single mission; the teaching of the religious significance of life on earth. The lonely status of the ruler did not separate him from the religious aspirations of his subjects; the Prambanan provides a recognition of the community of interest between ruler and ruled. The 856 inscription states that a tank of purifying water, filled by a diverted river, was made available as a pilgrimage centre for spiritual blessings similar to those at Bukit Seguntang in Palembang. Hermitages had been built at the Prambanan, and the inscription states that they were "to be beautiful in order to be imitated."

The divine mission of the kings, as shown in the evidence from the Kedu Plain, does not mean that the Javanese kings had great empires. The king was expected to show his divine qualities before he acquired a following. Only then would his ventures attract those who could confidently believe that they were earning religious merit in supporting him. Perhaps such supporters constructed the small buildings around the main Prambanan complex. The inscription of 856 states that they built "cheerfully."

The great monuments of the 9th century suggest something of the cultural framework within which events took place in Java. The religious preoccupation evident in the symbolism of the Borobuḍur and the Prambanan was shared by the higher groups in society. It was a world view that saw all social phenomena in religious terms, emphasizing the purification and liberation of the soul from mortal ties as the ultimate purpose of life. The gods were to be served by society, but each person had his own responsibility for earning final release in death from the burden of life. The multiplicity of individual religious goals, like the multiplicity of regional centres, strengthened tendencies toward political fragmentation.

EASTERN JAVA AND THE ARCHIPELAGO FROM 1019 TO 1292

The kingdoms of the river valleys

After the beginning of the 10th century, inscriptions and monuments in central Java cease. For more than 500 years little is known of developments in central Java, and nothing of what happened in western Java or in the eastern hook of the island. The evidence for these years comes almost exclusively from the Brantas River Valley and the adjacent valleys of eastern Java. This abrupt shift in the historian's focus of attention has never been satisfactorily explained.

Government and politics. Eastern Java did not form a natural political unit. Those who lived in the more distant hinterland had differences with those who could strengthen their resources through foreign trade. No single town emerged that was so exceptionally endowed in local resources as to become a permanent capital; instead, the residencies of defeated kings were abandoned, and the sites of some of them are unknown. The problems of government in these conditions are illustrated by the events of the 11th century. In 1016 the overlord's city was destroyed in what an inscription of 1041 described as "the destruction of the world," and the kingdom fell apart. The most recent explanation of the episode is that a Javanese vassal had rebelled. The kingdom was restored by the dead king's son-in-law Airlangga, a half-Balinese prince. From 1017 to 1019 he lived with hermits, probably practicing asceticism. In 1019 he was hailed as ruler of the small principality of Pasuruan near the Brantas Delta, but he could not take the military offensive until 1028 and his final success was not before 1035. His victories gradually established his claims to divine power. Airlangga dispatched his last enemy by provoking an uprising against him in the manner taught by Kauṭilya, the master of Indian statecraft who recommended the use of subversion against an enemy. In his famous "Calcutta" inscription Airlangga expressed the hope that all in the land would now be able to lead religious lives.

He then undid the results of his achievement. Foreseeing that two of his sons might quarrel, he divided his kingdom so that one son should rule over the southern part, known as Panjalu, Kaḍiri, or Daha, and the other over the northern part, Janggala. The consequences of this decision are mourned in a 14th-century poem, the *Nāgarakertāgama*. Airlangga's sons refused to honour their father's intentions. Fighting broke out, and the Kaḍiri rulers were unable to establish their uneasy domination over the kingdom until the early 12th century.

Dependence of king as protector

The ideal of a greater Javanese unity, protected by a divine king, was probably cherished most by the villages, since they benefitted from peace and safe internal communications. Javanese inscriptions sometimes acknowledge the king's gratitude for villagers' assistance in times of need. The villages were often prosperous centres of local government, ruled by councils of elders who claimed descent from the founding families. But local lords could make difficulties for the villages by tampering with the flow of the river or exacting heavy tolls from traders. In comparison with these vexations, the royal right to the villagers' services and part of their produce was probably not resented. No document was more respected than the inscription that recorded a village's privileges.

The king's chief secular responsibility was to safeguard his subjects' lands, including the estates of the temples and monasteries that were so conspicuous a feature of the Javanese landscape. When the king wanted to build a temple on wet-rice land he was expected to buy the land, not confiscate it. At court he was assisted by a small group of high officials, among whom his heir seems to have been the most important. Officials were rewarded with appanages from royal lands, for the king, like his noble vassals, was also a regional lord. The council of officials passed on royal decisions to subordinates, but there was no centralized system of government with representatives permanently stationed in different parts of the country. Instead, the officials made a circuit of the country and visited village elders. Royal rule was probably not harsh; the protests that have been preserved were probably prompted by unusually weak government. A reasonable relationship between ruler and villagers may be seen in a Balinese inscription of 1025 that records a king's sale of his hunting land to a village after the villagers had complained of their lack of land. Village elders sat with the officers of royal law in order to guarantee fair trials and verdicts reflecting the consensus of local opinion. Customary law was incorporated in the royal statutes. Aggrieved individuals could appeal to the king for redress; groups of villages sought his assistance for large-scale irrigation works. The villages paid taxes to the ruler, who thus enjoyed an economic advantage over other regional lords. Everything depended on the ruler's energy and a general agreement that his government served the interests of all.

The Kaḍiri princes of the 12th century ruled over a land that was never free from rebellion. In 1222 Kertajaya was defeated by an adventurer, Angrok, and a new capital was located at Kutaraja, later renamed Singhasāri, near to the harbours of east Java. The changed economic circumstances in the archipelago as a whole must now be taken into account, since they have an important bearing on the internal history of Java in the 13th and 14th centuries.

Eastern Java's prosperity

The empire of Kertanagara. During the 12th century, Chinese shipping was becoming capable of distant voyages; one consequence was that the entrepôt services in western Indonesia, formerly provided by Śrivijaya-Palembang, were no longer indispensable to the China trade. Instead, Chinese merchants sailed directly to the numerous producing centres in the archipelago. The eastern Javanese ports became more prosperous than ever before. A smaller entrepôt trade also developed on the coasts of Sumatra and Borneo and in the offshore islands at the southern entrance to the Strait of Malacca. In consequence, the Minangkabau princes in the hinterland of central Sumatra, heirs to the pretensions of the great overlords of Śrivijaya-Palembang, were deprived of the opportunity of developing their port of Jambi as a rich and powerful trading centre. A power vacuum existed in the seas of western Indonesia, and the Javanese kings aspired to fill it.

Java had probably long been regarded as the centre of a brilliant civilization. Old Javanese became the language of the inscriptions of the island of Bali in the 11th century, and in many parts of the archipelago the contacts of trade must have spread Java's reputation as an island of scholars. A recent study of the grafting of Tantric ritual on to a megalithic shrine at Bongkisam in western Borneo, some time after the 9th century, provides a glimpse of cultural diffusion at work on the maritime fringes of Indonesia. Javanese cultural influence in other islands almost certainly preceded political domination.

Disunity in the Malay world and the cultural fame of Java are not sufficient to explain why the Javanese king Kertanagara (reigned 1268–92) chose to impose his authority on Malayu in southern Sumatra in 1275. It has been suggested that the king's concern was to protect Indonesia from the threat of the Mongol ruler Kublai Khan by organizing a religious alliance. But Kertanagara probably imposed his political authority as well, though his demands would have been limited to expressions of homage and tribute.

The king's activities overseas were almost certainly intended to enhance his prestige in Java itself, where he was never free from enemies. His political priorities are reflected in a Sanskrit inscription of 1289, attached to an image of the king in the guise of the Akṣobhya Buddha, claiming that he had restored unity to Java; his overseas exploits are not mentioned.

The king as Śiva

The precise doctrinal contents of Kertanagara's royal cult are unknown. In his lifetime and after his death his supporters revered him as a Śiva-Buddha. They believed that he had tapped within himself demonic forces that enabled him to destroy the demons who sought to divide Java. The 14th-century poet Prapanca, author of the *Nāgarakertāgama* and a worshipper of Kertanagara, admires the king's scholarly zeal and especially his assiduous performance of religious exercises for the good of mankind. The cult may have incorporated hitherto unfamiliar Tantric elements, although the role of the royal ascetic had long been a familiar feature of Javanese kingship. The king who had been buried in the 9th-century mausoleum of the Prambanan was identified with Śiva, the teacher of asceticism. Early in the 13th century King Angrok, according to a later chronicle, regarded himself as the Bhaṭāra Guru and therefore as Śiva, the patron of ascetics. Śaivite and Mahāyāna priests were under royal supervision from at least as early as the 10th century, and the Tantric concept of a Śiva-Buddha, taught by Kertanagara, would not have been regarded as extraordinary. Javanese religious speculation had come to interpret Śaivism and the Mahāyāna as identical programs for personal salvation, with complementary gods. Union with divinity, to be achieved here and now, was the goal of all ascetics, including the king, who was regarded as the paragon of ascetic skill. Kertanagara's religious status, as well as his political problems and policies, are by no means eccentric features in early Javanese history; particular circumstances, stemming from Chinese participation in maritime trade in the archipelago, enabled him to exercise his divine power beyond Java itself. In the 14th century the homage of overseas rulers to the Javanese king was taken for granted.

THE MAJAPAHIT ERA

In 1289 Kertanagara maltreated Kublai Khan's envoy, who had been sent to demand the Javanese king's submission. The Mongol emperor organized a punitive expedition, but Kertanagara was killed by a Kaḍiri rebel, Jayakatwang, before the invaders landed. Jayakatwang in his turn was quickly overthrown by Kertanagara's son-in-law, later known as Kertarajasa, who used the Mongols to his own advantage and then forced them to withdraw in confusion. The capital city was now established at Majapahit. For some years the new ruler and his son, who regarded themselves as successors of Kertanagara, had to suppress rebellions in Java; not until 1319 was Majapahit's authority firmly established in Java with the assistance of the famous soldier Gajah Mada. Gajah Mada was the chief officer of state during the reign of Kertanagara's daughter (*c.* 1329–50), and in these years Javanese influence was restored in Bali, Sumatra, and Borneo. Kertanagara's great-grandson, Hayam Wuruk, became king in 1350 under the name of Rajasanagara.

Hayam Wuruk's reign

Hayam Wuruk's reign (1350–89) is remembered in the archipelago as the most glorious period in Javanese history. Prapanca's poem, the *Nāgarakertāgama*, written in 1365 and surviving in a manuscript found in Lombok at the end of the 19th century, provides a rare glimpse of the kingdom from a contemporary point of view. The poem was originally called the *Deśa warṇana*, or "the description of the country." It endeavours to show how royal divinity permeates the world, cleansing it of impurities and enabling all to fulfill their obligations to the gods and therefore to the holy land—the now undivided kingdom of Java. The poem resembles an act of worship rather than a chronicle. The poet does not conceal his intention of venerating the king, and, in the tradition of Javanese poetry, he may have begun it under the stimulus of pious meditation intended to bring him into contact with divine influences embodied in the king.

Prapanca does not, however, ascribe an unrealistic degree of authority to Hayam Wuruk. Not until the 17th century did Javanese rulers attempt to make regional chiefs into obedient officials. Hayam Wuruk merely required the heads of princely families to live in the capital city, thereby concentrating his power at the centre. Subordinate officials travelled around the kingdom, asserting the royal authority in such matters as taxes and the control of religious foundations. An index of the king's prestige was his decision to undertake a land survey to ensure that his subjects' privileges were being maintained. In the absence of an elaborate system of administration, the authority of the government was strengthened by the ubiquity of its representatives, and no one set a more strenuous example than the king himself. According to Prapanca, "the prince was not for long in the royal residence," and much of the poem is an account of royal progresses. In this way Hayam Wuruk was able to assert his influence in restless areas, enforce homage from territorial lords, reassure village elders by his visits, verify land rights, collect tribute, worship at Mahāyāna, Śaivite, and at ancient Javanese holy sites, and visit holy men in the countryside for his own spiritual enlightenment. His indefatigable travelling, at least in the earlier years of his reign, meant that many of his subjects had the opportunity of coming into the presence of one whom they regarded as the receptacle of divinity.

The New Year ceremony

One of the most interesting sections of the *Nāgarakertāgama* concerns the annual New Year ceremony, when the purifying powers of the king were reinforced by the administration of holy water. The ceremony, attended by scholarly Indian visitors, enables the poet to assert that the only famous countries were Java and India because both contained many religious experts. At no time in the year was the king's religious role more emphatically recognized than at New Year's, when the notables of the kingdom, the envoys of vassals, and village leaders came to Majapahit to pay homage and be reminded of their duties. The ceremony ended with speeches to the visitors on the need to keep the peace and maintain the rice fields. The king explained that only when the capital was supported by the countryside was it safe from attack by "foreign islands."

Since the poem venerates the king, it is not surprising that more than 80 places in the archipelago are described as vassal territories and that the mainland kingdoms, with the exception of Vietnam, are said to be protected by the king. Prapanca, believing that the king's glory extends in all directions, delineates in detail the actual limits of relevant space from a 14th-century Javanese point of view. No less than 25 places in Sumatra are mentioned, and the Spice Islands, whose product was a source of royal wealth, are well represented. On the other hand, northern Celebes and the Philippines are not mentioned.

During Hayam Wuruk's lifetime Javanese overseas prestige was undoubtedly considerable, though the king demanded no more than homage and tribute from his more important vassals, such as the ruler of Malayu in Sumatra. In 1377, when a new Malayu ruler dared to seek investiture from the founder of the Ming dynasty in China, Hayam Wuruk's envoys in Nanking convinced the emperor that Malayu was not an independent country. Javanese influence in the archipelago, however, depended on the ruler's authority in Java itself. When Hayam Wuruk died in 1389, the Palembang ruler in southeastern Sumatra saw his opportunity for repudiating his vassal status. He had noted the Ming dynasty's restoration of the long-abandoned tributary trading system and its prohibition of Chinese voyages to Southeast Asia and supposed that foreign traders would again need the sort of entrepôt facilities in western Indonesia that Śrivijaya-Palembang had provided centuries earlier. He may even have announced himself as a *bodhisattva* and heir of the maharajas of Śrivijaya. The Javanese expelled him from Palembang, whence he fled to Singapore and then to Malacca on the Malay Peninsula.

ISLAMIC INFLUENCE IN INDONESIA

Muslim kingdoms of northern Sumatra. Foreign Muslims had traded in Indonesia and China for many centuries; a Muslim tombstone in eastern Java bears a date corresponding to 1082. But substantial evidence of Islām in Indonesia begins only in northern Sumatra at the end of the 13th century. Two small Muslim trading kingdoms existed by that time at Samudra-Pasai and Perlak. A royal tomb at Samudra, of 1297, is inscribed entirely in Arabic. By the 15th century the beachheads of Islām in Indonesia had multiplied with the emergence of several harbour kingdoms, ruled by local Muslim princes, on the north coast of Java and elsewhere along the main trading route as far east as Ternate and Tidore in the Moluccas.

The establishment of the first Muslim centres in Indonesia was probably a result of commercial circumstances. By the 13th century, in the absence of a strong and stable entrepôt in western Indonesia, foreign traders were drawn to harbours on the northern Sumatran shores of the Bay of Bengal, a good distance from the dangerous pirate lairs at the southern end of the Strait of Malacca. Northern Sumatra had a hinterland rich in gold and forest produce, and pepper was being cultivated at the beginning of the 15th century. It was accessible to all archipelago merchants who wanted to meet ships from the Indian Ocean. By the end of the 14th century, Samudra-Pasai had become a wealthy commercial centre, giving way in the early 15th century to the better protected harbour of Malacca on the coast of Malaya. Javanese middlemen, converging on Malacca, ensured its importance for foreigners and Indonesians alike.

Relocation of centres of trade

Pasai's economic and political fame depended almost entirely on foreigners. Muslim traders and teachers were probably associated with its administration from the beginning and were bound to introduce the religious institutions that made foreign Muslims feel at home. The first Muslim beachheads in Indonesia, and especially Pasai, were to a considerable extent genuine Muslim creations that commanded the loyalty of the local population and encouraged scholarly activities. There were similar new harbour kingdoms on the northern coast of Java. Tomé Pires, author of the *Suma Oriental*, writing not long after 1511, stresses the obscure ethnic origins of the founders of Cheribon, Demak, Japara, and Gresik. These Javanese kingdoms existed to serve the commerce with the extensive Muslim world and especially with Malacca, an importer of Javanese rice. The rulers of Malacca, though of prestigious Palembang origin, had accepted Islām precisely in order to attract Muslim and Javanese traders to their port.

New men could now be expected to contribute impulses to Indonesian life. The northern Sumatran and Javanese coasts seem hitherto to have been on the fringe of the Śaivite-Mahāyāna cultures of southern Sumatra and eastern Java. For the first time in Indonesian history, the possibility existed that the inhabitants of formerly peripheral regions would begin to influence the course of events, inspired by Islām's assertion of the equality of all believers and supported by very profitable communications with the Muslim world throughout Asia.

But Indonesian history is the history of many distinct and often greatly separated regions. The history of early Indonesian Islām is no exception. What happened in the 15th and 16th centuries cannot be explained simply in terms of the influence of new ideas. The political ambitions of many regional princes intervened, and a variety of often rapidly changing and sometimes disturbed situations developed. The historian looks in vain for a uniform pattern of early Muslim life in the archipelago.

Acheh as a Muslim state

Acheh, which succeeded Pasai in the 16th century as the leading harbour kingdom in northern Sumatra, became a self-consciously Muslim state; it had contacts with Muslim India and its own school of Muslim mysticism; its sultans sought an alliance with the Ottoman Turks against the Portuguese, who had conquered Malacca in 1511. The Malay princes of Malacca, on the other hand, were not so unambiguously zealous on behalf of Islām. They installed Muslim vassals on the east coast of Sumatra in the 15th century, but when Malacca was captured by the Portuguese the princes transferred their capital southward to Johore and gradually became involved in a conflict not only with the Portuguese but also with the Achinese for control of the Strait of Malacca. Acheh, for its part, was unable to impose its faith on the Batak highlanders in the interior. The single and notable gain for Islām in Sumatra was in the

Minangkabau country, where Śaivite-Mahāyāna Tantric cults had flourished in the 14th century. Islām's penetration of Minangkabau by way of the Achinese west coast of Sumatra was far advanced by the beginning of the 17th century. Minangkabau, a land of enterprising and mobile traders, was later to exercise a significant influence in the affairs of the archipelago.

Muslims in Java. The Sumatran beachheads of Islām had commercial ties with other parts of the region, but they were not closely involved in events outside their immediate neighbourhoods. In Java, on the other hand, where the distance between the Muslim coastal fringe and the interior was negligible, a tense situation developed. The Muslims did not overthrow the kingdom of Majapahit (see above). Majapahit, weakened by feuds within its royal family and increasingly denied the benefits of overseas commerce, merely withered away and disappeared in the early 16th century. The passing of its hegemony left a power vacuum in Java that set in train a conflict between Islām and the aristocratic traditions of the interior.

In later centuries, the Javanese inland elite chose to bridge over the events of the 15th and 16th centuries and see a continuity between Majapahit and Mataram, the great kingdom of 17th-century Java. This vision of the past, however, conceals a very troubled period in Javanese history. The militant mood of coastal Islām may be seen in the enforced imposition of the new faith on western Java and also on Palembang in southern Sumatra. Quite similarly, the impact of Islām may be gauged by the fury of the 17th-century Mataram kings against the princes and Muslim notables of the northern coast.

The conflict seems to have begun with the determination of the Demak rulers in the first half of the 16th century to rule over a great Javanese kingdom. The coastal princes, especially as their harbours grew richer and their dynasties older and more confident, came to see themselves not only as Muslim leaders but as Javanese princes. Their pretensions are reflected in Tomé Pires' statement that they cultivated the "knightly" habits of the ancient aristocracy. But when Demak sought to expand inland, bringing with it Islām, its armies were halted by Pajang in the middle of the 16th century. Some years later, Mataram, another principality in central Java, came to the fore. The climax of the conflict was in the first half of the 17th century, when Agung, ruler of Mataram, took the offensive and destroyed the coastal states and with them the basis of Javanese overseas trade.

Links with Javanese tradition

It is unlikely that this bitter struggle was fought mainly for religious reasons. Islām came to Indonesia from India, perhaps especially from southern India, and the mood of the mystic Ṣūfī sects of Islām was probably not foreign to the Javanese ascetics. Ṣūfī "saint" (*wali*) and Javanese guru would have understood and respected each other's yearning for personal union with God. The Javanese tradition, in which small groups of disciples were initiated by a teacher into higher wisdom, was paralleled by the Ṣūfī teaching methods. For Muslim theologian and Javanese scholar alike the concern was always less with the nature of God than with skills for communicating with Him. Arabic texts tended eventually to be recited as meditative aids, just as the Tantric *mantras* once had been.

The first Javanese disciples of Islām were probably not the thoughtful representatives of earlier religious systems in Java but humble men of the coast who had been left outside the traditional teachings of the court and the anchorites. These men doubtless saw in Islām a simple message of hope, offering them not only a congenial personal faith but also opportunities of secular advancement in a trading society where rank was not as important as fervour. Early Muslim literature has a theme of the wandering adventurer who comes from obscure origins, makes good, and seeks the consolations of Islām. For Muslim disciples such as these the times offered boundless means for achieving success, either in trade or in the service of ambitious princes. These princes, also the product of Islām, needed guardians of their conscience, courtly advisers, and, above all, military commanders. For the new elite the progress of coastal Islām brought both spiritual and material gain. All of this must have been greatly disturbing to those in the interior who had been nurtured in older traditions and saw no reason for abandoning their Śaivite-Mahāyāna values. For the aristocrats of the interior, the memories of Majapahit's stable and hierarchic system of government under a godlike king represented standards of civilized behaviour that must be asserted at all cost against the forces of confusion released by the coastal population. Contacts between wandering dervishes and the peasants, at a time of acute distress caused by warfare, and the pretensions of Muslim court officials, some of whom claimed a privileged religious status without precedent in Javanese history, must have seemed to threaten the foundations of society. The ruler of the interior kingdom of Pajang is depicted in the Javanese chronicles as an ascetic and as the son and grandson of ascetics. He was, in this respect, a true Javanese king. When, several generations later, the ruler of Mataram destroyed the coastal states he was seeking to destroy the forces that disunited Java. This was in the tradition of earlier Javanese kings. His conquests were as much a part of his mission as Kertanagara's had been in the 13th century.

Thereafter Islām was permitted to survive only on Javanese royal terms. Its innovating effects were postponed until the end of the 19th century. It was now one of several religious activities and therefore tolerable in Javanese eyes. Muslim officials in the court of Mataram became well-rewarded and obedient servants of the ruler. In time, scholars returned to the study of the earlier genre of Javanese literature, including texts that taught the nature of government according to the values of the "Hindu-Javanese" world. In the countryside, Islām remained influential in time of social distress, preaching to aggrieved peasants of the coming of the Messiah. As a literary influence Islām survived in the form of mystical texts and poems, romantic tales, and also in borrowings by later inland-court historians of material from the "Universal Histories" (*Sĕrat Kaṇḍa*) of the coastal culture. The borrowings are testimony of the impact of what had happened in the 15th and 16th centuries, which later historians could reinterpret but not ignore.

The history of 16th-century Java is still not fully understood, but Portuguese intervention seems to have been unimportant. The Portuguese survived chiefly as private traders, and, by the end of the century, the level of Muslim Indonesian trade with the Middle East, and thence with Europe, was greater than it had ever been. In the neighbourhood of the Strait of Malacca, Acheh and Johore were struggling for overlordship, and the scene in Java was being prepared for the final phase in the struggle between coastal Islām and the inland aristocracy. The outcome might have been the emergence of greater Indonesian unities under cover of Javanese claims to leadership. The situation was altered by the appearance of the Dutch at the end of the century. (O.W.W.)

II. Indonesia since 1600

THE GROWTH OF THE DUTCH EMPIRE

The Dutch East India Company. The fall of Malacca to the Portuguese in 1511 is often taken as a turning point in Indonesian history. Over the next century Portuguese efforts were to be directed to securing control of the trade of the Spice Islands. At the end of the 16th century, Dutch and British interests in the region gave rise to a series of voyages: those of James Lancaster in 1591, Cornelis de Houtman in 1595 and again in 1598, Jacob van Neck in 1599, Lancaster again in 1601, and others. In 1602 the Dutch East India Company (Vereenigde Oostindische Compagnie; VOC) received its charter, two years after the formation of the English East India Company, and began to attempt to exclude European competitors from the Indies and to control the trade carried on by indigenous Asian traders. The Company's commercial monopoly later formed the basis of the Dutch territorial empire. For these reasons many historians have tended to see 1511 or 1600 as the beginning of a period of European domination lasting until the 20th century. Since the 1930s, however, some historians have criticized the view of Indonesian history that judges Europeans to have been the major factor in shaping the history of the Indies from the 17th century onward. By contrast, they have stressed an essential continuity of Indonesian history and have argued that the voc at first made little change in traditional political or commercial patterns. Traditional Asian commerce, according to one view, was a noncapitalistic peddling trade, financed by patrician classes in Asian countries and conducted by innumerable small traders who collected spices and pepper in the Indies for disposal in the port cities of Asia. In this view the voc was seen, in effect, as merely another merchant prince, gradually inserting itself into the existing trade patterns of the Spice Islands and accommodating itself to them. As Batavia became the headquarters from which it established factories in the Spice Islands and elsewhere, the company gradually became a territorial power but was, at first, only one power among others and not yet ruler of the Indies. Only during the 19th century did new economic forces, the product of industrial capitalism, burst upon the Indies and submerge them under a new wave of European imperialism.

The theory is an overstatement. If the coming of the Europeans did not represent a sharp break in the continuity of Indonesian history, it did, at least, initiate changes which, in the long run, were to be of enormous importance. The voc itself represented a new type of power in the Indies: it formed a single organization, traded across a vast area, possessed superior military force, and, in time, employed a bureaucracy of servants to look after its concerns in the Indies. In sum, it could impose its will upon other rulers and force them to accept its trading conditions. Under the governor generalship of Jan Pieterszoon Coen (*q.v.*) and his successors, particularly Anthony van Diemen (1636–45) and Joan Maetsuyker (1653–78), the company laid the foundations of the Dutch commercial empire and became the paramount power of the archipelago.

The process, however, was gradual. During the early 17th century the company went far toward establishing its monopoly. It captured Malacca from the Portuguese (1641), confined the British, after a period of fierce rivalry, to a factory at Bencoolen in southwestern Sumatra, and established a network of factories in the eastern islands. Though it may have wished to limit its activities to trade, the company was soon drawn into local politics in Java and elsewhere, and, in becoming the arbiter in dynastic disputes or in conflicts between rival rulers, it inevitably emerged as the main political entity in the islands. In the 1620s, Sultan Agung, ruler of the central Javanese kingdom of Mataram, and representative of the old and highly sophisticated Hindu-Javanese civilization, sought to extend his power over Bantam in West Java. This brought him into conflict with the Dutch, and he laid siege to the Dutch fortress at Batavia. Though Agung's forces were eventually compelled to withdraw, the result of the confrontation was inconclusive and left both the Dutch and Javanese warily respectful of each other's strength. But over the following century, internal dissensions in Mataram led to increasing Dutch involvement, and in the early 18th century a series of wars of succession among pretenders to the throne of Mataram hastened the process. In return for its services in 1674 to Amangkurat I, Sultan Agung's successor, and to his successor, Amangkurat II, shortly afterward, the voc received the cession of the Preanger regions of West Java. This was the first of a series of major territorial advances. In 1704 Dutch forces assisted in replacing Amangkurat III with his uncle, Pakubuwono I, in return for which further territory was ceded. In this way almost all of Java gradually passed under Dutch control, and by 1755 only a remnant of the kingdom of Mataram remained. This was divided into two principalities, Jogjakarta and Surakarta, which survived until the end of Dutch rule. In Sumatra, attempting to control the pepper trade, over the course of the 17th century, the voc established footholds in western Sumatra and Palembang, but the main Dutch expansion there did not take place until the 19th century.

Sultan Agung

Administration. In acquiring these territorial responsibilities, the company did not at first establish a close administrative system of its own in the areas which passed under its control. In effect, the voc replaced the sovereign of the royal court and, in so doing, inherited the existing structure of authority. An indigenous aristocracy administered the collection of tribute on behalf of the company, and only gradually was this system converted into a formalized bureaucracy. For the time being, the traditional aristocracy of local rulers was adequate for the purpose of governing an agrarian society. The voc, like the royal court before it, drew revenue in the form of produce from the peasantry within its domain.

Adapted from Zainu'ddin, *A Short History of Indonesia* (1968); Praeger Publishers

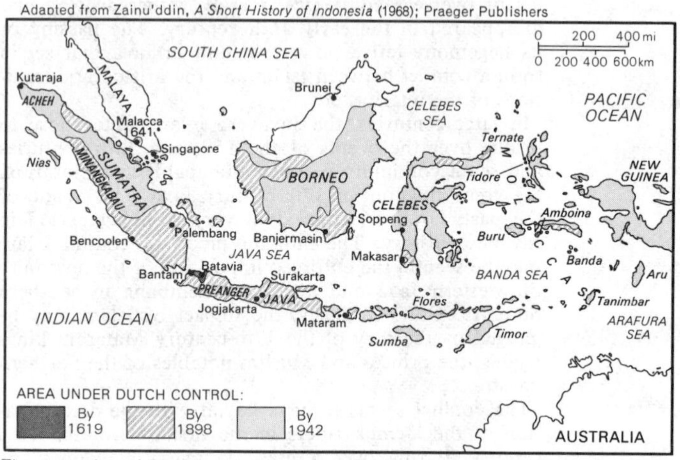

The expansion of Dutch control in Indonesia.

Commercial policy. To implement its commercial monopoly, the voc established company factories (trading posts) for the collection of produce, pressured individual rulers to do business solely with the company, controlled the sources of supply of particular products (clove production, for example, was limited to Amboina, nutmeg and mace to the Banda islands) and, in the 18th century, pushed through a system of so-called forced deliveries and contingencies. Contingencies constituted a form of tax payable in kind in areas under the direct control of the company; forced deliveries were produce that native cultivators were compelled to grow and sell to the company at a set price. There was little difference between the devices. In theory, forced deliveries were thought of as a form of trade in which goods were exchanged, but they were, in fact, as Furnivall has it, "tribute disguised as trade," while contingencies were "tribute undisguised." In effect, the whole system of company trade was designed to extract tribute from the Indies. Produce was drawn from the Indies for disposal on a European market, but without stimulating any fundamental technological change in the area's economy. The profits belonged to the company, not to the producers. The indigenous traders of the region were pushed aside by the voc as it gained control of more and more of the export trade of the archipelago. The growth of Batavia resulted, for example, in the decline of the north coast ports of Java, through which much of the spice trade had been channelled since before the 15th century. In this way the traditional pattern of trade was checked and distorted.

Decline of the voc

During the 18th century, the voc ran into financial difficulties from a variety of causes: the breach of the company's monopoly by smuggling; the growing administrative costs as the company came to shoulder greater responsibilities of government; the corruption of the company's servants; and the increasing pressure of British competition, culminating in 1784 in the Treaty of Paris, which allowed the British to trade in East Indian waters. In 1799, five years after the French invasion of the Netherlands during the Revolutionary Wars, the new Dutch government of the Batavian Republic wound up the affairs of the company (see LOW COUNTRIES, HISTORY OF).

The French and British in Java, 1806–15. The fall of the Netherlands to France and the dissolution of the company led in due course to significant changes in the administration of the Indies. In 1806 Napoleon established the kingdom of Holland, under his brother Louis. The new kingdom was concerned with the defense of the Indies against possible British attack, and one of Napoleon's marshals, Herman Willem Daendels, was appointed as governor general. Daendels strengthened Javanese defenses, raised new forces, built new roads within Java, and improved the internal administration of the island. He anticipated the principles of the later Culture System (see below) by imposing a tax that would be paid in kind and represent a proportion of total production. He expanded the compulsory cultivation of coffee. As part of his attempt at administrative centralization, he tried to formalize the position of the Javanese regents. He paid them salaries and attempted to make them clearly subordinate to Dutch prefects, thus emphasizing their character as civil servants of a central government rather than as semi-independent local rulers. His administrative reforms, however, were not completely implemented.

Raffles' governorship

In 1811 Java fell to a British East India Company force under Lord Minto, governor general of India, who, after the surrender, appointed Thomas Stamford Raffles as lieutenant governor. Raffles approached his task in the conviction that British administrative principles, modelled in part on those developed in Bengal, could liberate the Javanese from the tyranny of Dutch methods; he believed that liberal economic principles, by ending compulsory cultivation, could simultaneously expand Javanese agricultural production, improve revenue, and make the island a market for British goods. Along with his doctrinaire liberalism, he brought to his task a respect for Javanese society. Before his appointment, he had been a student of Malay literature and culture, and during his period in Batavia he encouraged the study of the society he found about him. Raffles rediscovered the Borobuḍur, the ruins of a great Buddhist temple in central Java, and published his *History of Java* in 1817, a year after his return to England.

Raffles carried further the administrative centralization begun by Daendels and planned to group the regencies of Java into 16 residencies. In bringing regents more firmly under central control, he believed himself to be relieving the villagers from what he saw as feudal oppression. By declaring all lands the property of the government and by requiring cultivators to pay a land rent for its use, he proposed to end the compulsory production system. This, he believed, would free the peasants from servility to their "feudal" rulers and from the burden of forced deliveries to the Dutch and allow them to expand their production under the stimulus of ordinary economic motives.

Failure of reforms

Unfortunately, Raffles oversimplified the complexities of traditional land tenure. He misread the position of the regents, whom he at first wrongly believed to be a class of feudal landholders rather than an official aristocracy. (The regents, in fact, had no proprietary rights in the land of their subjects.) He also failed to take account of the necessity for a survey of landholdings if the land-rent system were to be adequately administered. Initially, he had proposed to make village headmen responsible for land rent, but realizing that headmen were not landlords either, he tried to shift responsibility to the individual cultivators. Though the details changed, the intention did not. He was concerned to replace what he saw as a tribute system, paid in the form of forced deliveries, by the payment of a fixed and regular rent that would leave the landholders more free to enjoy the fruits of their enterprise than they had been in the past. But despite a series of adjustments in his original plan, Raffles failed to devise an effective means of applying his theories before the return of Java to Dutch hands as part of the general settlement following the defeat of Napoleon. After Raffles' departure, the land-rent system continued, but with the village, and not the cultivator, as the unit of assessment.

Dutch rule in the 19th century. Before the 19th century, Indonesian societies had experienced considerable pressure from Europeans, but they had not been submerged by Western influences. The political order of Mataram had been eroded, and the first steps had been taken toward administrative centralization in Java. In the outer islands, local rulers had been forced to submit in some measure to the will of Batavia. The trading patterns of the archipelago had been changed and constricted. Nevertheless, these were superficial developments when seen against the continuing coherence and stability of Indonesian societies. They were superficial, also, compared with the Western impact still to come.

When the Dutch returned to Indonesia after the Napoleonic Wars, their main concern was to make the colony at least self-supporting. During the interregnum, both exports and revenue had declined sharply, despite Raffles' hopes for his land-rent system. The costs of government in Java were rising as a result of the growing complexity of administration. In restoring their authority, the Dutch retained the main outlines of the system of residencies, regencies, and lower administrative divisions, though they did not, at first, follow exactly the attempts of Daendels and Raffles to turn the regents into salaried officials, specifically responsible to the residents. Rather, they saw the regent as the "younger brother" of the resident. This difference in theory was perhaps of slight practical effect, since the tendency in lower levels of territorial administration continued in the direction of an increasingly centralized control. Several factors contributed to the trend: one was the need to deal with a series of disturbances, particularly in Java and western Sumatra, but also on a lesser scale in the Celebes, Borneo, and the Moluccas: a second was the new economic policy, adopted in 1830, which placed new economic responsibilities on local officials.

Increasing central control

The Java War of 1825–30 sprang from a number of causes. In part, it was the product of the disappointed ambitions of its leader, Prince Dipo Negoro, who had been passed over for the succession to the throne of Jogjakarta. In part, it sprang from resentment among the aristocratic landholders of Jogjakarta, whose contracts for the lease of their lands to Europeans had been cancelled by the governor general. The immediate trigger of revolt was the government's action in building a road over land bordering on a sacred tomb. There were also, no doubt, hidden factors of the kind often to be found in cases of agrarian protest in Java—factors such as the messianic expectation of the coming of a Just Ruler who would restore the harmony of the kingdom. From these varied causes there sprang a revolt which, through the skillful use of guerrilla tactics, continued to challenge Dutch authority for five years, until the Dutch treacherously seized Dipo Negoro during truce negotiations and exiled him to Celebes.

About the same time, the Dutch in western Sumatra were drawn into the so-called Padri War (named after Pedir, a town in Acheh through which Muslim pilgrims usually returned home). Basically, this was a religious struggle between revivalist Islāmic leaders in Minangkabau and the *adat* (customary law) leaders of the community. Under Imam Bondjol, the Padri forces resisted Dutch pressure from the early 1820s until 1837. The effect of this involvement was inevitably to strengthen the Dutch administrative commitment in western Sumatra. Together with the Java War, it also accentuated the financial difficulties of the government and strengthened Holland's desire to find a means of making the Indies pay.

The formation in 1825 of the Netherlands Trading Company (Nederlandsche Handelmaatschappij; NHM), a company embracing all merchants engaged in the Indies trade and supported by the Netherlands government with the king as its chief shareholder, did not produce the hoped for commercial expansion. In 1830, however, a newly appointed governor general, Johannes Van Den Bosch, devised a new method by which the government could tap the resources of the Indies. This was the so-called Culture System, or Cultivation System (Cultuurstelsel).

The Culture System

The Culture System provided that a village set aside a fifth of its cultivable land for the production of export crops. These crops were to be delivered to the government in lieu of tax. Land rent was to continue at the same time as a complementary part of the system and as a measure of the amount to be produced by each village. Thus, if a village, through the growing of export crops on a fifth of its land, returned an amount in excess of the land rent for which it had been assessed, it would be free of land rent and would be reimbursed to the extent of the excess; on the other hand, if a village produced less than the assessed amount of land rent, it would have to make up the difference.

From the government's point of view the Culture System was an overwhelming success. Exports soared, rising from 13,000,000 guilders in 1830 to 74,000,000 ten years later. The products were disposed of through The Netherlands Trading Company, and between 1840 and 1880 their sale brought to the Dutch treasury an annual average of 18,000,000 guilders, approximately a third of the Dutch budget. The effects of the system for the Javanese were, however, of more dubious value. Though its founder believed that, by stimulating agricultural production, the Culture System would ultimately benefit the people of Java as well as the home government, it came to be considered, in later years, both by Dutch critics and by outside observers, as a particularly harsh and burdensome policy. Van den Bosch's expectations were not entirely false. The policy did extend village production in certain areas, and the population of Java increased from 6,000,000 to 9,500,000 during the full operation of the system. The range of exports from Java was extended. Indigo and sugar were the first items to be made the subject of compulsory cultivation; coffee, tea, tobacco, and pepper were subsequently added. Nevertheless, the system placed a heavy burden on the cultivators, who derived no profits from their activities. The Indies government stood effectively between the producer and his market, and the annual surplus, the so-called *batig slot*, was remitted home to add to Dutch, not Javanese, prosperity. Of more long-term importance was the fact that while the system brought the Indies into contact with a wider overseas market, it did nothing to stimulate technological change in the Javanese economy.

There were other consequences. The Culture System required efficient administration. The regent became the kingpin of the system, responsible to the resident for the delivery of crops from his regency. In some cases, regents, secure in the knowledge they were backed by Dutch power, imposed additional burdens upon their subjects—a development that received trenchant criticism in the novel *Max Havelaar*, written under the pseudonym Multatuli by Eduard Douwes Dekker, a former official of the Indies government. But the long-term effect of the new functions imposed on regents was to reduce their independence and to hasten the process, started by Daendels, by which a loosely structured administrative aristocracy was gradually converted into a salaried civil service. Regents were no longer able to draw their revenues from their subjects, and the lines of authority were clearly drawn. Regents, aided by a junior Dutch official (the *controleur*), became clearly responsible to the Dutch residents above. By 1860 the administrative divisions of Java had been firmly established, and the service that staffed them had acquired the character it was essentially to preserve for the remainder of the colonial period.

In the 1860s the Culture System came under attack not only from humanitarian quarters but also from private business interests in The Netherlands. The latter appealed to liberal economic principles in support of their right to share in the riches of the Indies; and their pressure was effective. Though the Culture System was not abolished and continued for a number of years to make its contribution to the Dutch treasury, the decision was taken to encourage also the entry of private capital. The Liberal Policy, as it was called, was effectively inaugurated in 1870 by the adoption of an agrarian law that provided that European investors could acquire land under long-term leasehold, either from Indonesian landholders, or in the case of unoccupied land, from the government. Certain safeguards were provided for the Indonesian landholder: the provision that Europeans lease, rather than purchase, land was intended to prevent the alienation of Indonesian land, and the government was charged with the responsibility also of preventing Europeans from leasing land needed for the subsistence of village populations. At the same time, provision was made for the recruitment of Indonesian labour, again subject to certain safeguards to protect the workers. Within this framework Dutch capital began to flow to the Indies on a scale that was to transform the character of the Indonesian economy and society. The next 60 years saw a tenfold increase in the value of exports (from 107,000,000 guilders to 1,160,000,000). There was a change, also, in kinds of products exported. Such exports as coffee, sugar, tea, and tobacco continued to expand; but such industrial raw materials as rubber, copra, tin, and oil soon came to dominate the export economy. These remarkable developments were, in large measure, the product of a totally different system of production. Under the company, during the interregnum, and, later, under the Dutch crown working through the Culture System, export crops were grown by Indonesian cultivators on their own land. Under the Liberal Policy, however, the new crops were the subject of estate production. Much economic expansion took place in Sumatra rather than Java and Sumatra's east-coast residency became the seat of a vast new plantation economy. The estates were company owned, and the economic developments of the late 19th century were indeed the product of corporative, rather than individual, enterprise.

The Liberal Policy

Rapid economic development was accompanied by territorial expansion. Though the Dutch had established their control effectively over Java by the mid-18th century and though they had gradually expanded their original holdings in Sumatra over the course of the 19th, their control over the rest of the archipelago was patchy and incomplete. It was exercised, in the main, through agreements with local rulers rather than through direct control over territory. The closing years of the 19th century and the early years of the 20th saw rapid moves to round out the Dutch empire and extend it effectively over the whole of the Indies. In northern Sumatra, warfare with the people of Acheh (Atjeh) lasted with varying degrees of intensity from 1873 to 1908 and brought the northern tip of Sumatra under Dutch control. In Celebes and the Moluccas, where the Dutch had for long exercised a general authority, a new instrument—the Short Declaration (in contrast to the earlier Long Contract)—bound local rulers to accept the control of Batavia. Dutch authority was extended in this way over Bone and Luwu in the Celebes, over central Borneo, over Bali and the Lesser Sunda Islands, and over Ternate, Ceram, and Buru in the Moluccas. Footholds were established also over parts of West New Guinea. Acting from their main base in Java, the Dutch by 1910 had effectively completed the process of converting the Indies into a unified colonial dependency. This was largely the result of the post-1870 expansion. Communications had been developed, also—roads and railways in Java and Sumatra and expanded shipping services to link Java to the outer islands—to serve the needs of the new plantation economy.

Impact of the "new imperialism"

The "new imperialism" of the late 19th century may be seen as part of a worldwide movement whereby the industrial countries of western Europe partitioned among themselves the hitherto undeveloped areas of the globe. In Africa and in the South Pacific, in Burma, Indochina, and Malaya, as well as in Indonesia, a new "forward movement" was taking place that stood in dramatic contrast to the earlier patterns of commercial empire. If the European presence created a watershed in Indonesian history, it is to be discerned about 1870 rather than in 1600.

The social impact of these developments upon Indonesian society was tremendous. The economic and political expansion brought a new Dutch population to the Indies: civil servants to staff the growing services of government, managers to run the new estates, and clerks to staff the import–export houses and other businesses. These came to form a European enclave within the major cities and accentuated the lines of social division in what was increasingly a caste society divided along racial lines. The

Dutch, however, were never a purely expatriate community whose members were anxious to retire as soon as possible to Holland. Many of them regarded the Indies as their home. They made provision there for the education of their children. They proposed to retire there. Their sense of belonging was very different, for example, from that of the British in India, and it was to give an added bitterness to the later struggle to retain the colony after World War II. From the Indonesian point of view, the growing cities became the home of a new urban way of life and stimulated social change. A new elite emerged under the influence of the expanding Western impact. So did a new class of unskilled and semiskilled workers who found employment as domestic servants or as labourers in the light industries that began to develop. Rural society, though more sheltered, was also altered by the currents of change. Although the agrarian law and the later labour legislation had provisions to protect existing customary rights over land and to guarantee fairness of contracts for labourers, the mere fact of contract employment on the estates affected the village society from which workers were drawn and played its part in hastening growth of a rootless and disoriented population, divorced increasingly from the shelter of traditional village society but not absorbed into the new urban culture.

The Ethical Policy. Liberals confidently assumed that, just as freedom of enterprise would maximize welfare at home, so the application of European capital to the task of developing colonial resources would gradually improve the lot of colonial peoples. By the end of the 19th century, the 30 years of the Liberal Policy in Indonesia did not appear to have achieved that miracle. The growth of the estates and the swelling volume of exports from the Indies was, in fact, marked by falling per capita income. By the end of the century, growing criticism of the Dutch record in the Indies was given particularly influential expression by C.T. van Deventer, a Liberal Democratic member of the States General, who argued that Holland had been draining wealth from the Indies and had incurred thereby a "Debt of Honour" that should be repaid. His suggestion was that The Netherlands should turn from its strictly laissez-faire policy in the Indies and pursue instead a positive welfare program supported by funds from the metropolitan treasury. In 1901 a change of government in Holland provided the opportunity for a new departure in policy along the lines suggested by van Deventer. According to the Ethical Policy, as it was called, financial assistance from The Netherlands was to be devoted to the extension of health and education services and to the provision of agricultural extension services designed to stimulate the growth of the village economy.

Van Deventer's reforms

Though self-interested in some ways (the extension of education to Indonesians was, for example, in some measure a response to the growing need for clerks to staff the lower levels of government and business administration), the Ethical Policy was essentially idealistic. In the hopes of its most fervent supporters, it was seen as a noble experiment designed to transform Indonesian society, to enable a new elite to share in the riches of Western civilization, and to bring the colony into the modern world. Its ultimate goals were, of course, not clearly defined. Van Deventer looked to the emergence of a Westernized elite who would be "indebted to the Netherlands for its prosperity and higher Culture" and who would gratefully recognize the fact. Others hoped for the growth, by "cultural synthesis," of a new East Indian society based on blending of elements of Indonesian and Western cultures and able to enjoy a large measure of autonomy within the framework of the Dutch empire.

Despite these rather grandiose visions, the achievements of the Ethical Policy were much more modest. It neither checked declining living standards nor promoted an agrarian revolution. It did, however, provide agricultural assistance and advice, but this was directed to the improvement of techniques of irrigation and cultivation within the existing wet-rice technology of Java. Its effect, therefore, was to confirm the gulf between the European economy of the estates, mines, oil wells, and large-scale commerce and the traditional, largely subsistence, Indonesian economy of wet-rice or shifting cultivation. In education, a little was done to provide a greater degree of opportunity at primary, secondary, and even tertiary levels, but at the end of the 1930s only a handful of high school graduates was produced locally, and the literacy rate was calculated at just over 6 percent.

The goals of the Ethical Policy were set too high, and the devices adopted to implement them were too modest. Given the inertia of traditional societies, it was not to be expected that a new order would be created as easily as the proponents of the Policy had hoped. Nevertheless, during the years of its operation, the Indies did see the release of tremendous forces of social change. These resulted, however, not from the conscious plans of the Ethici but from the undirected force of Western economic development. Java's population, which had risen from about 6,000,000 to almost 30,000,000 over the course of the 19th century, increased to over 40,000,000 by 1920. The population increase, together with urbanization, the penetration of a money economy to the village level, and the labour demands of Western enterprise combined to disrupt traditional patterns. Where the Ethical Policy was most effective, despite the limitations of its educational achievement, was in producing a small educated elite who could give expression to the frustration of the masses in a society torn loose from its traditional moorings. Western currents of thought had their impact also within Islāmic circles, where modernist ideas sought to reconcile the demands of Islām and the needs of the 20th century. It is against this background that a self-conscious nationalist movement began to develop.

The rise of nationalism. Indonesian nationalism in the 20th century must be distinguished from earlier movements of protest: the Padri War, the Java War, and the many smaller examples of sporadic agrarian unrest had been "prenationalistic" movements, the products of local grievances. By contrast, the nationalism of the early 20th century was the product of the new imperialism and was part of wider currents of unrest affecting many parts of Africa and Asia. In Indonesia in the 20th century, nationalism was concerned not merely with resistance to Dutch rule but with new perceptions of nationhood, embracing the ethnic diversity of the archipelago and looking to the restructuring of traditional patterns of authority in order to enable the creation of Indonesia as a modern state. It derived in part from specific discontents, the economic discriminations of colonial rule, the psychological hurt arising from the slights of social discrimination, and from a new awareness of the all-pervading nature of Dutch authority. Important, too, was the emergence of the new elite, educated but lacking adequate employment opportunities to match that education, Westernized but retaining still its ties with traditional society.

Formation of the nationalist movement

The formation in 1908 of Budi-Utomo (High Endeavour) is often taken as the beginning of organized nationalism. Founded by Wahidin Sudirohusodo, a retired Javanese doctor, Budi-Utomo was an elitist society the aims of which, though cultural rather than political, included a concern to secure an accommodation between traditional culture and the modern world. Numerically more important was Sarekat Islām (Islāmic Association) founded in 1912. Under its charismatic chairman, Omar Said Tjokroaminoto, the organization expanded rapidly, claiming a membership of 2,500,000 by 1919. Later research suggests that the real figure was likely to have been no more than 400,000, but even with this greatly reduced estimate Sarekat Islām was clearly much larger than any other movement of the time. In 1912 the Indische Partij (Indies Party)—primarily a Eurasian party—was founded by E.F.E. Douwes Dekker; banned a year later, it was succeeded by another Eurasian party, Insulinde. In 1914 the Dutchman Hendricus Sneevliet founded the Indies Social Democratic Association (ISDV), which became in 1920 the Indonesian Communist Party (PKI).

By the end of World War I there was, thus, a variety of organizations in existence, broadly nationalist in aim, though differing in their tactics and immediate goals and in the sharpness of their perceptions of independent nationhood. In the absence of firm party discipline, it was common for individuals to belong simultaneously to more than one organization and, in particular, the presence of ISDV members in Sarekat Islām enabled them to work as a "bloc within" the larger movement. The idea that the time was not yet ripe for Communist parties to assume independent leadership of colonial nationalism later led the Comintern to formulate the strategy of cooperation with anti-imperialist "bourgeois" parties.

At the end of World War I the Dutch, in an effort to give substance to its promise to associate the Indonesian community more closely with government, created the Volksraad (People's Council). Composed of a mixture of appointed and elected representatives of the three racial divisions defined by the government—Dutch, Indonesian, and "foreign Asiatic"—the Volksraad provided opportunities for debate and criticism but no real control over the government of the Indies. Some nationalist leaders were prepared to accept seats in the assembly, but others refused, insisting that concessions could be obtained only through uncompromising struggle.

In 1921 the tension within Sarekat Islām between its more conservative leaders and the Communists came to a head in a discipline resolution that insisted that members of Sarekat Islām belong to no other party; this, in effect, expelled the Communist "bloc within," and there followed a fierce rivalry between the two for control of the grass-roots membership of the organization. The PKI, once it had committed itself to independent action, began to move toward a policy of unilateral opposition to the colonial regime. Without the support of the Comintern, and even without complete unanimity within its own ranks, it launched a revolt in Java at the end of 1926 and in western Sumatra at the beginning of 1927. These movements, which had elements of traditional protest as well as of genuine Communist insurrection, were easily crushed by the Indies government, and Communist activity was effectively ended for the remainder of the colonial period.

The Bandung "study club"

The defeat of the Communist revolt and the earlier decline of Sarekat Islām left the way open for a new nationalist organization, and in 1926 a "general study club" was founded in Bandung, with a newly graduated engineer, Sukarno, as its secretary. The club began to reshape the idea of nationalism in a manner calculated to appeal to Indonesia's new urban elite. After the failure of the ideologically based movements of Islām and Communism, nationalist thinking was directed to the idea simply of a struggle for independence, without any precommitment to a particular political or social order afterward. Such a goal, it was believed, could appeal to all, including Muslims and Communists, who could, at least, support a common struggle for independence, even if they differed fundamentally about what was to follow. Nationalism, in this sense, became the idea that the young Sukarno used as a basis of his attempt to unify the several streams of anticolonial feeling. The ideas of the Bandung Study Club were reinforced by currents of thought emanating from Indonesian students in Holland. Their organization, reorganized in 1922 under the name of the Indonesian Union (Perhimpunan Indonesia), became a centre of radical nationalist thought and, in the mid-1920s, students returning from Holland joined forces with like-minded groups at home.

The new nationalism required a new organization for its expression, and in July 1927 the Indonesian Nationalist Association, later the Indonesian Nationalist Party (Partai Nasional Indonesia; PNI), was formed under the chairmanship of Sukarno. The PNI was based on the idea of noncooperation with the Indies government and was thus distinguished from those groups, such as Sarekat Islām, that were prepared to accept Volksraad membership. Sukarno, however, while seeking to create a basis of mass support for the PNI, also attempted with some success to work together with more moderate leaders and succeeded in forming a broadly based, if rather precarious, association of nationalist organizations, the PPPKI.

At the end of 1929 Sukarno was arrested with some of his colleagues and was tried, convicted, and sentenced to four years' imprisonment. He was released at the end of 1931, but by then the united movement he had helped to create had begun to disintegrate. The PNI, fearful that Sukarno's conviction had made it an illegal party, had dissolved itself and reformed as Partindo. A number of other groups came to join in a new organization, the Club Pendidikan Nasional Indonesia (Indonesian National Education Club), known as the New PNI. While Partindo saw itself as a mass party on the lines of the old PNI, the New PNI, under the leadership of Mohammad Hatta and Sutan Sjahrir, aimed at training cadres who could maintain a continuing leadership of the movement and who could thus prevent it from being so easily immobilized by the arrest of its leaders.

Arrest of Sukarno

In 1933 Sukarno was arrested for the second time and exiled to Flores and later to Bencoolen (Bengkulu) in South Sumatra. Repressive action followed against other party leaders including Hatta and Sjahrir, who were also exiled. In the later 1930s nationalist leaders were forced to cooperate with the Dutch, and such moderate parties as Parindra accepted Volksraad membership. In 1937 a more radical party, Gerindo, was formed, but it considered support of Holland against the threat of Nazism more important than the question of independence.

War in Europe and the Pacific changed the situation. The fall of the Indies to the Japanese onslaught early in 1942 broke the continuity of Dutch rule and provided a completely new environment for nationalist activity.

Japanese occupation. Japanese military authorities in Java, having interned Dutch administrative personnel, found it necessary to use Indonesians in many administrative positions, thus giving them opportunities that had been denied them under the Dutch. In order to secure popular acceptance of their rule, the Japanese sought also to enlist the support of both nationalist and Islāmic leaders. Under this policy Sukarno and Hatta both accepted positions in the military administration.

Though initially welcomed as liberators, the Japanese gradually established themselves as harsh overlords. Their policies fluctuated according to the exigencies of the war, but, in general, their primary object was to make the Indies serve Japanese war needs. Nationalist leaders, however, felt able to trade support for political concessions. A first attempt to mobilize Indonesian support for the Japanese—the Triple A Movement, based on the crypt slogans "Japan the Leader of Asia, Japan the Protector of Asia, Japan the Light of Asia"—was crudely conceived, and Sukarno was able to convince the administration that Indonesian support could only be mobilized through an organization that would represent genuine Indonesian aspirations. In March 1943 such an organization, Putera (Pusat Tenaga Rakjat; Centre of the People's Power) was inaugurated under his chairmanship. While the new organization enabled Sukarno to establish himself more clearly as the leader of the nation and while it enabled him to develop more effective lines of communication to the people, it also placed upon him the responsibility of trying to sustain Indonesian support for Japan through, among other things, the *romusha* (forced-labour) program. Later in the year Indonesian opinion was given a further forum in a Central Advisory Council and a series of local councils. At a different level, Indonesian youths were able to acquire a sense of corporate identity through membership in the several youth organizations established by the Japanese. Of great importance, also, was the creation in October 1943 of a volunteer defense force composed of and officered by Indonesians trained by the Japanese. The Sukarela Tentara Pembela Tanah Air (Peta) was to become the core of the republic's army during the revolution.

The Triple A Movement

In March 1944 the Japanese, feeling that Putera had served Indonesian rather than Japanese interests, replaced it with a "People's loyalty organization" (Djawa Hokokai), which was kept under much closer control.

In September 1944 the Japanese premier announced the Japanese intention to prepare the Indies for self-government. In the following March an "Investigating Body for the Preparation of Indonesian Independence" (BPKI) was formed, drafted a constitution, and dealt with other matters pertaining to future independence. In August 1945, on the eve of the Japanese surrender, Sukarno and Hatta were summoned to Saigon, where Marshal Terauchi promised an immediate transfer of independence.

Proclamation of independence

On their return to Djakarta (Jakarta; formerly Batavia), Sukarno and Hatta were under pressure to declare independence unilaterally. This pressure reached its climax in the kidnapping of the two men, for a day, by some of Djakarta's youth leaders. After the news of the Japanese surrender had been confirmed, Sukarno proclaimed independence on the morning of August 17, 1945.

The revolution. The proclamation touched off a series of risings across Java that convinced the British troops entrusted with receiving the surrender of Japanese forces that the self-proclaimed republic was to be taken seriously. At the level of central government, the constitution adopted by republican leaders was presidential in form, but a widely representative Central National Committee (KNIP) became, in effect, an ad hoc parliament. Sukarno, as president, agreed to follow parliamentary conventions by making his Cabinets dependent upon their ability to command KNIP confidence.

The spontaneous character of the Indonesian Revolution was demonstrated by a number of incidents, notably in the struggle for Bandung in late 1945 and early 1946 and in the Battle of Surabaya in November 1945 in which Indonesian fighters resisted superior British forces for three weeks. Though the Dutch had expected to reassert their control over their colony without question, and though they were able to play upon Outer Island fears of the Java-based republic, they eventually were compelled to negotiate with republican representatives led by Prime Minister Sjahrir. The Linggadjati Agreement (1946–47), by which the Dutch agreed to transfer sovereignty in due course to a federal Indonesia, appeared to offer a solution to the conflict. (The Dutch claimed that a federation was necessary because of the diversity of the Indies and the difference between heavily populated Java and the more sparsely populated Outer Islands.) Differing interpretations, however, made the agreement a dead letter from the beginning. On July 20, 1947, the Dutch, in an attempt to settle matters by force, initiated what they termed a police action against the republic. Its effect was to evoke UN intervention in the form of a Good Offices Committee, and it ended in the precarious Renville Agreement of January 1948. On December 18, 1948, a second police action was launched.

Meanwhile, the government of the republic faced some domestic opposition. In 1946 a left-wing plot was organized by followers of Tan Malaka, who opposed the policy of negotiation with the Dutch. This so-called July 3 Affair was easily crushed. In September 1948 a more serious challenge in the form of a Communist revolt (the Madiun Affair) was also defeated.

The second police action aroused American concern. It also closed Indonesian ranks firmly behind the republic. In these circumstances, The Netherlands, at a round-table conference at The Hague, finally agreed in August 1949 to transfer sovereignty to an independent United States of Indonesia beginning in December 1949.

INDONESIA SINCE INDEPENDENCE

The years of constitutional democracy. The initial federal constitution of 1949 was replaced in 1950 by a unitary but still provisional constitution. It was parliamentary in character and assigned an essentially figurehead role to the president. It provided for a unicameral legislature to which the Cabinet would be responsible. From the revolutionary period, Indonesia had inherited a multiparty system. The main parties after independence were the major Muslim party, Masyumi (Masjumi); the Muslim theologians' party, Nahdatul Ulama (NU), which seceded from Masyumi in 1952; the Nationalist Party (PNI); the Communist Party (PKI); the "national communist" party, Murba; the lesser Muslim parties, Perti and Partai Sarekat Islam Indonesia (PSII); and the Socialist Party (PSI). Until the first elections were held in 1955, Parliament was filled by appointment under a gentlemen's agreement between parties as to their probable electoral strengths. The elections of 1955, a remarkable and technically successful experiment in the exercise of political choice by a largely nonliterate population, confirmed the position of Masyumi, NU, PNI, and PKI as the country's four leading political parties.

Party alignments

With the exception of the PKI, the parties did not represent clearly opposing interests or programs, though some broad bases of support could be seen. The PNI was particularly strong in the ranks of the civil service, while Masyumi tended to find its support in market towns and among the trading classes; NU was stronger in rural areas. The PSI, an influential party until it was virtually eliminated in the elections, had strong support in the higher ranks of the army and bureaucracy. Also important was the regional distribution of party strengths. The PNI, NU, and PKI were essentially Java-based parties, while Masyumi drew most of its strength from outside Java, particularly in western Sumatra and South Celebes (Sulawes: Selatan). Its support within Java was to be found mainly in West Java (Jawa Barat), the home of the Sundanese and not of the ethnic Javanese. This unevenness in party strengths meant that political rivalry in the early years of independence tended to have a regional flavour, a fact that was of importance when regional resistance to the centre reached the point of open revolt in 1958. In simplified terms, it is possible to see, in the regional distribution of party strengths, a broad opposition between the hierarchical, rice-based society of Java and the more strongly Muslim areas where commerce rather than agriculture has been the basis of historical development. Any interpretation of political conflicts in Indonesia must take account also of the extent to which the parties and their suborganizations reflected major cultural streams (*aliran*) in Indonesian society rather than interests, classes, or even regions. In addition to Masyumi's suspicion of the Javanese parties, the division within Java bewtween *santri* (devout Muslims) and *abangan* (reflecting an earlier, pre-Muslim syncretism) is important in understanding the rivalry of the NU and Masyumi, on the one hand, and the PNI and the PKI, on the other.

Rapid government turnover

In the early 1950s there was a rapid succession of governments—Hatta (December 1949–August 1950), Natsir (September 1950–March 1951), Sukiman (April 1951–February 1952), Wilopo (April 1952–June 1953), Ali Sastroamidjojo (July 1953–July 1955), Harahap (August 1955–March 1956), and Ali Sastroamidjojo's second government (March 1956–March 1957). Though the early governments did attempt to come to grips with major problems—the maintenance of internal security, economic development, civil service retrenchment, army reorganization, etc.—their instability created a growing disillusionment with the fruits of independence and a sense of contrast between the heroism of the revolution and the self-seeking party rivalry that followed it. In particular, conflict between the export-producing Outer Islands and the heavily populated island of Java was becoming more marked. In December 1956 these factors of discontent led to movements of regional dissidence, supported by local military commanders, in West Sumatra (Sumatera Barat), Minahasa (in North Celebes), and elsewhere.

Introduction of Guided Democracy. Against this background, Sukarno (*q.v.*), resentful of his circumscribed position as figurehead president, began to move toward a greater interference with constitutional processes. In February 1957 he announced his own "Concept" for Indonesia. Criticizing Western liberal democracy as unsuited to Indonesian circumstances, he called for a political system of "democracy with guidance" based on indigenous procedures. The Indonesian way of deciding important questions, he argued, was by way of prolonged deliberation (*musyawarah*) designed to achieve a consensus (*mufakat*). This was the procedure at the village level, and it should be the model for the nation. He proposed a government based on the four main parties plus a national council representing not merely political parties but functional groups—workers, peasants, intelligentsia, national entrepreneurs, religious organizations, armed services, youth organizations, women's organizations, etc.—

in which, under presidential guidance, a national consensus could express itself.

In March the resignation of the second Ali government was followed by a proclamation of a "state of war and siege." A new nonpartisan government was formed under Djuanda. At the end of 1957 a further crisis arose after the defeat of a United Nations motion calling for a renewal of negotiations on the question of West Irian (West New Guinea, or Irian Barat, now Irian Jaya). In a series of direct actions across the country, Dutch property was seized, and the government felt itself obliged to accept responsibility for the running of these enterprises. Early in the following year, the dissident leaders of West Sumatra called for the formation of a new central government under Hatta. When their demand was ignored they formed a Revolutionary Government of the Republic of Indonesia (PRRI) in Padang, as an alternative government of the republic. This direct challenge to Djakarta had the support of some senior Masyumi leaders, including the former premiers Natsir and Harahap, and it was backed also by the military commander of North Celebes (Sulawesi Utara).

Seizure of Dutch property

Faced by this open rebellion, the central government acted swiftly. Military action against West Sumatra quickly reasserted Djakarta's authority. The suppression of the revolt in North Celebes followed soon after. In this changed situation, with the regions defeated, the parties discredited, and the army's prestige enhanced by its success against the rebels, Sukarno, in partnership with the army leadership, took up once more the idea of Guided Democracy. By early 1959 he and the army chief of staff, Gen. A.H. Nasution, had become committed to the idea that a return to the revolutionary constitution of 1945 (a presidential-type constitution) offered the best means of implementing the principles of deliberation, consensus, and functional representation. In April 1959 Sukarno urged this course in a speech to the Constituent Assembly, elected in 1955 to draft a permanent constitution. When the assembly failed to agree by the necessary two-thirds majority to adopt the constitution of 1945, Sukarno, despite the dubious legality of such an action, introduced it by presidential decree on July 5, 1959.

Sukarno's alliance with the army

Guided Democracy. Under the 1945 constitution, Sukarno possessed executive responsibility as well as ceremonial functions as head of state. He quickly created a new government with Djuanda, now first minister, at its head. Pending elections under a new electoral law, he appointed members in accordance with the functional representation principle to the bodies for which the constitution provided: the People's Consultative Assembly (Majelis Permusyawaratan Rakyat) and the Supreme Advisory Council (Dewan Pertimbangan Agung). In 1960, when parliament rejected the government's budget, he replaced it with a provisional nominated parliament.

Domestic policies. Sukarno's central purpose was the preservation of national unity and the restoration of a sense of national identity. His integrative skills gave him some success in the pursuit of these goals, though at a price. Under Sukarno's leadership, the political style of Guided Democracy became increasingly flamboyant. Its ideology was enshrined in a cluster of slogans and in the abbreviations and acronyms to which they were reduced: the ideas of continuing revolution, of Manipol (Political Manifesto), Ampera (the Message of the People's Suffering), Nasakom (the unity of nationalism, religion, and communism), and others. Its concern for display was manifested in grandiose buildings, in national monuments, and in such occasions as the Fourth Asian Games (1962), to which Indonesia was host.

Sukarno's influence on political style

Sukarno's concern with symbols of greatness was not accompanied by any attempt to come to grips with the nation's economic problems. The damage done to the economy by the seizure of Dutch enterprises in 1957 and the wasteful extravagances of his later search for grandeur was justified in his eyes as integral to the task of making Indonesians proud of themselves and of their independence. Nevertheless, he was careless of the economic consequences of his policies. He appeared to show no recognition of the inflation that reached new rates of acceleration in the early 1960s. By 1965 exports were falling, and foreign indebtedness stood at $2,400,000,000.

Sukarno's power during the years of Guided Democracy depended in great measure on the preservation of a balance between the army and the PKI. Sukarno consistently protected the PKI from moves made against it by the army, and the period saw a growth in the Communists' prestige. He opposed military attempts to prohibit its congresses and to suppress its newspapers. He banned such bodies as the Democratic League (1960) and the body for the promotion of Sukarnoism (1964), which had been organized to counter PKI power. He advanced PKI leaders to positions within the national leadership. To many observers he appeared to be preparing the way for the Communists to come to power. To others he appeared merely to be redressing a balance that was in constant danger of being tilted against the PKI.

Protection of the Communists

Foreign policy. In the early 1950s Indonesia's main concern was to secure international support for its claim to West Irian, which had been retained by the Dutch in 1949; apart from that, it aimed at a neutralist foreign policy. At the Afro-Asian Conference in 1955 (the Bandung Conference) the country staked a claim to third world leadership. By the early 1960s, however, Indonesia was moving to a new international position. In ideological terms, Sukarno had sketched the world, as he saw it, in terms of a conflict between Nefos and Oldefos (New Emerging and Old Established Forces). In this analysis was embodied his continuing hostility to the West.

The West Irian campaign achieved success in 1962, when an agreement was reached with The Netherlands for the transfer of the territory to Indonesia after a period of temporary UN administration, though with provision for the inhabitants of the territory to make an "Act of Free Choice" before the end of 1969. (This was eventually effected by representative councils, which confirmed West Irian's continuance as part of Indonesia.) The resolution of this issue was followed, however, by the development of Indonesia's opposition to the formation of Malaysia and its commitment, after an erratic series of changes of mood, to a policy of "confrontation" of the new Malaysian federation in September 1963. The confrontation policy was followed two years later by Indonesia's sudden withdrawal from the UN in January 1965 in reaction to the seating of Malaysia on the Security Council.

Policy of "confrontation" with Malaysia

The coup and after. On the night of September 30, 1965, a group of army conspirators, with their headquarters at Halim Air Base, kidnapped and murdered six army generals. A seventh, Nasution, escaped. The following morning the 30th September Movement announced that it had seized power to forestall a coup against the President by a council of generals. In the meantime General Suharto, commander of the army's strategic reserve, began to gather the reins of power into his own hands. By evening he had seized the initiative from the conspirators.

The PKI maintained that the coup attempt was an internal affair of the army. The army leadership insisted that it was part of a PKI plot to seize power, and the following months saw a slaughter of Communists across Java and in Bali, with estimates of those killed ranging from 80,000 to more than 1,000,000. With the destruction of the PKI, one of the elements of balance that had supported the Sukarno regime was eliminated, and the President himself, though he had much strong support, came under increasing pressure. On March 11, 1966, against a background of student action, the army forced him to delegate extensive powers to Suharto, now chief of staff of the army. With these powers, Suharto banned the PKI and arrested 15 of Sukarno's ministers but did not yet act against Sukarno himself. In March 1967 the MPRS, now purged of its left-wing members and with Nasution as its chairman, appointed Suharto acting president. In March 1968 he was appointed to the presidency in his own right. Sukarno was kept under house arrest until his death on June 21, 1970.

Massacre of the Communists

The New Order. Suharto was concerned to reverse many of Sukarno's policies. The confrontation with Malaysia was quickly ended, and Indonesia rejoined the United Nations. But the major policies initiated by Suhar-

Suharto's regime

to's New Order had to do with economic rehabilitation and were adopted under the guidance of a group of American-educated economists from the University of Indonesia. Successful negotiations secured a rescheduling of Indonesia's foreign debts and attracted aid through an intergovernmental group of donor countries. The complex regulations governing economic activity were simplified. In 1967 a new foreign investment law provided a framework for new private capital investment. To all appearances the results of the new economic policies were spectacular. The inflation rate was quickly reduced and the rupiah stabilized. Oil production expanded, thanks partly to exploration by a number of new foreign companies operating through the gigantic state oil corporation, Pertamina. Manufacturing industry also expanded rapidly.

These policies had their critics. To some it seemed that the republic was becoming economically dependent on Western capital and, in particular, on large transnational corporations, that direct foreign investment had created an Indonesian comprador class that battened on foreign companies, and that new wealth had exaggerated existing inequalities rather than removing them.

Though his power depended from the beginning upon the support of the army, Suharto, in the early years of his rule, appeared concerned to preserve the image of caretaker government pending a return to democratic procedures and civilian rule. The appointment of Adam Malik as foreign minister and the Sultan of Yogyakarta (Jogjakarta) as minister for economic, financial, and industrial affairs provided a civilian component in government, and preparations were made for the introduction of a new electoral law. With the passage of time, however, the regime appeared to become more military in character and to display a more authoritarian style. Kopkamtib, the security organization established to restore order in the wake of the coup of 1965, remained as an arm of government. The President was concerned to control and discipline the political parties. He supervised closely the formation of a new Muslim Party, Parmusi, and exercised strict control over it thereafter. He interfered in the internal affairs of the PNI. The elections, held ultimately in 1971, though heralded as a genuine return to democratic procedures, were accompanied in fact by charges of flagrant coercion of voters. Of greater long-term significance was the intervention of the government-sponsored organization Sebker Golongan Karya, or Golkar (Joint Secretariat of Functional Groups). In theory, Golkar was a nonparty organization representing, like Sukarno's functional groups idea of 1957, the groupings of which the nation was really composed. In practice, Golkar was a government party, and its sweeping electoral success (it secured 236 out of 360 seats in 1971) owed much to pressure brought to bear on voters by government agencies. On the heels of the Golkar victory came more drastic action against the political parties in the form of a forced rationalization, so that only two parties were left. In 1973 the four Muslim parties (Parmusi, NU, PSII, and Perti) were amalgamated to form the United Development Party, and the five non-Muslim parties (PNI, Parkindo, Katolik, IPKI, and Murba) were amalgamated to form the Indonesian Democratic Party.

Political controls

These measures of political control did not eliminate all opposition to the regime. There remained elements of Islāmic opposition, reinforced by Outer Islands feelings that the regime was dominated by Java. There were intellectual critics of the regime and, from time to time, movements of student unrest. In 1973 anti-Chinese riots occurred in Bandung. More spectacular were the disturbances of January 1974, when students chose the visit of the Japanese prime minister, Tanaka Kakuei, to demonstrate against both Suharto and the role of foreign capital in the Indonesian economy. Their protest drew wider mass support and developed into open rioting in Djakarta. Army rivalries were also present, especially between Sumitro, head of Kopkamtib, and Ali Moertopo, head of the special operations branch (OPSUS). Though Sumitro was dismissed after the riots, factional differences within the army remained important.

Currents of opposition were strengthened in 1975 when Pertamina, the state oil enterprise, proved unable to meet repayments on short-term borrowings and had to be rescued by the government. The default led to the dismissal of its director general, Lieut. Gen. Ibnu Sutowo, whose extravagant life-style and apparent independence from government control had for long made him a symbol of the irresponsibility and corruption of state enterprises. The government's method of incorporating East Timor (the former Portuguese Timor) into Indonesia in 1975–76 also brought domestic as well as foreign criticism.

Elections in 1977, held again amid charges of improper governmental pressure on the electorate, resulted once more in a sweeping Golkar victory, with 63 percent of the vote. The Muslim vote, however, held firm. The United Development Party surprised observers by obtaining more than 29 percent.

The elections drew attention to the presence of elements of opposition to the Suharto regime. In January 1978, on the eve of Suharto's reelection to the presidency for a third five-year term, the government resorted again to repressive methods, closing down sections of the press and arresting student leaders and intellectuals. These actions reflected its feeling of vulnerability and its recognition that the consensus that had sustained it in the late 1960s and early '70s had evaporated. Lines of cleavage are not easy to define, but insofar as they contain elements of rivalry between centre and regions, opposition between Muslims and non-Muslims, and, in Java, the division between *santri* and *abangan*, as well as between rich and poor, they reflect divisions of long standing within Indonesian society. Nevertheless, Suharto's reelection in March 1978, and Adam Malik's election as vice president, suggested that, for the time being, the regime was stable. (J.D.L.)

BIBLIOGRAPHY

General works: D.G.E. HALL, *A History of South-East Asia,* 3rd rev. ed. (1968), and D.J. STEINBERG (ed.), *In Search of Southeast Asia* (1971), give general treatments of Indonesian history in the context of the broader history of Southeast Asia. B.H.M. VLEKKE, *Nusantara,* 2nd rev. ed. (1959), is a readable general history. W.F. WERTHEIM, *Indonesian Society in Transition,* 2nd rev. ed. (1959), and R.T. MCVEY (ed.), *Indonesia* (1963), provide an introduction to Indonesian society. J.D. LEGGE, *Indonesia,* 3rd ed. (1980), examines some historiographical problems.

Indonesia to c. 1600: F.D.K. BOSCH, *Selected Studies in Indonesian Archaeology* (1961), contains selected translations of some of Bosch's distinguished contributions to the study of Indonesian culture. J.G. DE CASPARIS, "Historical Writing on Indonesia (Early Period)," in D.G.E. HALL (ed.), *Historians of South-East Asia,* pp. 121–163 (1961), is a helpful survey of the development of Indonesian historiography, with ample bibliographic guidance. G. COEDES, *Les États hindouisés d'Indochine et Indonésie,* rev. ed. (1964; Eng. trans., *The Indianized States of Southeast Asia,* 1968), has sections dealing with Indonesia that introduce the basic evidence and discuss its implications in a judicious manner. H. KERN, *Verspreide Geschriften,* 16 vol. (1913–29), are collected studies of Indonesian epigraphy and early history by the pioneer scholar in this field. N.J. KROM, *Hindoe-Javaansche Geschiedenis,* 2nd ed. (1931), is the first and very detailed critical account of the evidence for early Indonesian history. Though parts of the work are now dated, it remains the basic work on the subject. T.G. PIGEAUD (ed.), *Java in the 14th Century,* 3rd ed. rev., 5 vol. (1960–63), the edited and translated text of the *Nāgarakertāgama,* accompanied by an extensive commentary, is indispensable reading for the study of Java, especially in the 13th and 14th centuries. SUDJATMOKO *et al.* (eds.), *An Introduction to Indonesian Historiography* (1965), is a very important survey and discussion of the skills and contributions of a variety of scholarly disciplines in the field of Indonesian history.

Indonesia from the 17th through 20th century: For a discussion of trade patterns of the early period of European contact see J.C. VAN LEUR's essays, *Indonesian Trade and Society* (1955), and M.A.P. MEILINK-ROELOFSZ, *Asian Trade and European Influence in the Indonesian Archipelago Between 1500 and About 1630* (1962). M.C. RICKLEFS, *Jogjakarta Under Sultan Mangkubumi, 1749–1792* (1974), examines 18th-century Javanese politics against the background of the Dutch presence. CLIVE DAY, *The Policy and Administration of the Dutch in Java* (1904; reprinted as *The Dutch in Java,* 1966), remains an interesting treatment of the Culture System and Liberal Policy.

The best survey in English of Dutch economic policies in the 19th and 20th centuries is still J.S. FURNIVALL, *Netherlands India* (1939). See also G.C. ALLEN and AUDREY G. DONNITHORNE, *Western Enterprise in Indonesia and Malaya* (1957); and the collection of Dutch economic writings published as *Indonesian Economics: The Concept of Dualism in Theory and Policy* (1961). R. VAN NIEL, *The Emergence of the Modern Indonesian Elite* (1960), studies the theory and operation of the Ethical Policy. GEORGE MCT. KAHIN, *Nationalism and Revolution in Indonesia* (1952) remains the standard study of the rise of nationalism and the struggle for independence. For a more recent survey of the revolution see A.J.S. REID, *The Indonesian National Revolution, 1945–50* (1974). RUTH T. MCVEY, *The Rise of Indonesian Communism* (1965), is an authoritative history of the PKI to the revolts of 1926–27. BERNHARD DAHM, *Sukarno and the Struggle for Indonesian Independence* (1969), explores the development of Sukarno's thinking up to 1945. The Japanese occupation is examined in HARRY J. BENDA, *The Crescent and the Rising Sun: Indonesian Islam Under the Japanese Occupation, 1942–1945* (1958); and B.R. O'G. ANDERSON, *Some Aspects of Indonesian Politics Under the Japanese Occupation: 1944–1945* (1961). ANDERSON's *Java in a Time of Revolution* (1972) gives a close study of the opening year of revolution. The standard account of the early years of independence is HERBERT FEITH, *The Decline of Constitutional Democracy in Indonesia* (1962). DANIEL S. LEV, *The Transition to Guided Democracy* (1966), carries the story from 1957 to 1959, and REX MORTIMER, *Indonesian Communism Under Sukarno: Ideology and Politics, 1959–1965* (1974), from 1959 to 1965. See also J.D. LEGGE, *Sukarno: A Political Biography* (1972). The essays in CLAIRE HOLT *et al.* (eds.), *Culture and Politics in Indonesia* (1972), provide illuminating treatment of aspects of modern Indonesian history and culture. For the New Order see KARL D. JACKSON and LUCIAN W. PYE (eds.), *Political Power and Communications in Indonesia* (1978).
(O.W.W./J.D.L.)

Indus River

The Indus is a great trans-Himalayan river and one of the longest rivers in the world, having a length of 1,800 miles (2,900 kilometres). It has a total drainage area of about 450,000 square miles, of which 175,000 square miles lie in the Himalayan mountains and foothills and the rest in the semi-arid plains of Pakistan. The river's annual flow is about 274,055,000,000 cubic yards—twice that of the Nile and three times that of the Tigris and Euphrates combined. The river's name comes from the Sanskrit word *sindhu*. It is mentioned in the Ṛgveda, the earliest (*c.* 1500 BC) chronicles and hymns of the Aryan peoples of ancient India, and is the source of the country's name.

Course and tributaries. *The Upper Indus.* The river rises in southwestern Tibet at an altitude of 16,000 feet. For about 200 miles it flows in a northwesterly direction, crossing the southeastern boundary of Jammu and Kashmir at an elevation of about 15,000 feet (4,600 metres). Eleven miles beyond Leh, in Ladākh, it is joined on its left by its first tributary, the Zāskār. Continuing for 150 miles in the same direction the Indus is joined by its notable tributary the Shyok on the right bank. After its confluence with the Shyok, and up to the Kohistān Mountains, it is fed by mighty glaciers on the slopes of the Karakoram Range, the Nānga Parbat Massif, and the Kohistān Ranges. The Shyok, Shigar, Hunza, Gilgit, and other streams carry the glacial waters into the Indus. Since the present-day precipitation of snow in this region is not sufficient to feed these great rivers of ice, it seems clear that the giant ice streams of the Karakoram are survivors of the last Ice Age of the Himalayas.

Glacial meltwater influx in the Upper Indus

The Shigar joins the Indus on the right bank near Skārdu in Baltistān. The Gilgit, farther down, is another right-bank tributary, joining it at Bunji. Some miles farther downstream, the Astor River joins as a left-bank tributary, bringing waters from the glaciers east of Nānga Parbat. The Indus then flows west, crosses the Kashmir border, and turns south and southwest to enter Pakistan. There it skirts around the Nānga Parbat Massif (26,660 feet; 8,126 metres) in gorges as deep as 15,000 to 17,000 feet and 12 to 16 miles wide. Trails cling grimly to precipitous slopes overlooking the river from elevations of 4,000 to 5,000 feet.

After emerging from this region of high altitude, the Indus flows as a rapid mountain stream between the Swāt and Hazāra areas in Pakistan, passing the site of the Tarbela Dam, which was scheduled for completion in 1975. The Kābul River joins the Indus just above Attock, where the Indus flows at an elevation of 2,000 feet and is crossed by the first bridge carrying rail and road. Finally, it cuts across the Salt Range near Kālābāgh to enter the Punjab Plain.

The Lower Indus. The Indus receives its most notable tributaries from the Punjab Plains to the east. These five rivers—the Jhelum, the Chenāb, the Rāvi, the Beās, and the Sutlej—give the name Punjab ("land of five rivers") to the land shared between Pakistan and India.

After receiving the waters of the Punjab rivers, the Indus becomes much larger and, during the flood season (July–September), is several miles wide. It flows here at an elevation of 259 feet. Its slow speed at this stage results in its accumulated silt being deposited on its bed, which is thus raised above the level of the sandy plain; indeed, most of the plain in Sind has been built up by alluvium laid down by the Indus. Embankments have been built to prevent flooding, but occasionally these give way, and large areas are destroyed by inundation. Such floods occurred in 1947 and 1958. During heavy flooding the river sometimes changes its course.

The Indus Delta

Near Tatta the Indus begins its deltaic stage and breaks into distributaries that join the sea at various points south-southeast of Karāchi. The delta covers an area of 3,000 square miles or more, and extends along the coast for about 130 miles. The uneven surface of the delta area is marked by a network of existing and abandoned channels. The coastal strip, from about five to 20 miles inland, is flooded by high tides.

Hydrology. The principal rivers of the Indus River system are snow fed. Their flow varies greatly at different times of the year: the discharge is at a minimum during the winter months, there is a rise of water in spring and early summer, floods occur in the rainy season (July–September), and occasionally there are devastating flash floods. The Indus and its tributaries receive all their waters in the upper hilly parts of their catchments. Therefore, their flow is at a maximum where they emerge out of the foothills, and little surface flow is added in the plains, where much loss of water occurs because of evaporation and seepage. On the other hand, some water is added by seepage in the period after the monsoon months. In the main stream of the Indus, the water level is at its lowest from mid-December to mid-February. After this the river starts rising, slowly at first and then more rapidly at the end of March. The high-water level usually occurs between mid-July and mid-August. The river then falls rapidly until the beginning of October, when the water level subsides more gradually. Annually, the Indus carries about one-half of the total supply of water (144,283,000,000 cubic yards) in the Indus River system. The Jhelum and Chenāb each carries about one-fourth as much as the Indus; and the Rāvi, Beās, and the Sutlej combined comprise about one-fifth of the total supply of the system (271,316,000,000 cubic yards).

Shifting course of the Indus

There is considerable physiographic and historical evidence to prove that since the dawn of civilization—at least since the days of Mohenjo-daro culture, 4,000 years ago—the Indus, from the southern Punjab to the sea, has been shifting its course. It is confined between limestone ridges at Rohri-Sukkur, but thereafter it has wandered, shifting generally to the west, particularly in its deltaic sector, so that about 200 years ago it began to flow into the Rann of Kutch. In upper Sind the Indus has shifted westward a distance of about ten to 20 miles in the last seven centuries. The river is now held back to some extent by higher ground from Sehwān to Tatta at the head of the delta, but the possibility of future shifting cannot be ruled out. There is also evidence of the shifting of the Chenāb, Rāvi, Beās, and Sutlej rivers during the historical period.

Climate. From its source to its mouth, the annual rainfall in the Indus region varies between five and 20 inches (125 to 500 millimetres). Except for the mountainous section of Pakistan, the Indus Valley lies in the driest part of the subcontinent. Northwestern winds sweep the Indus

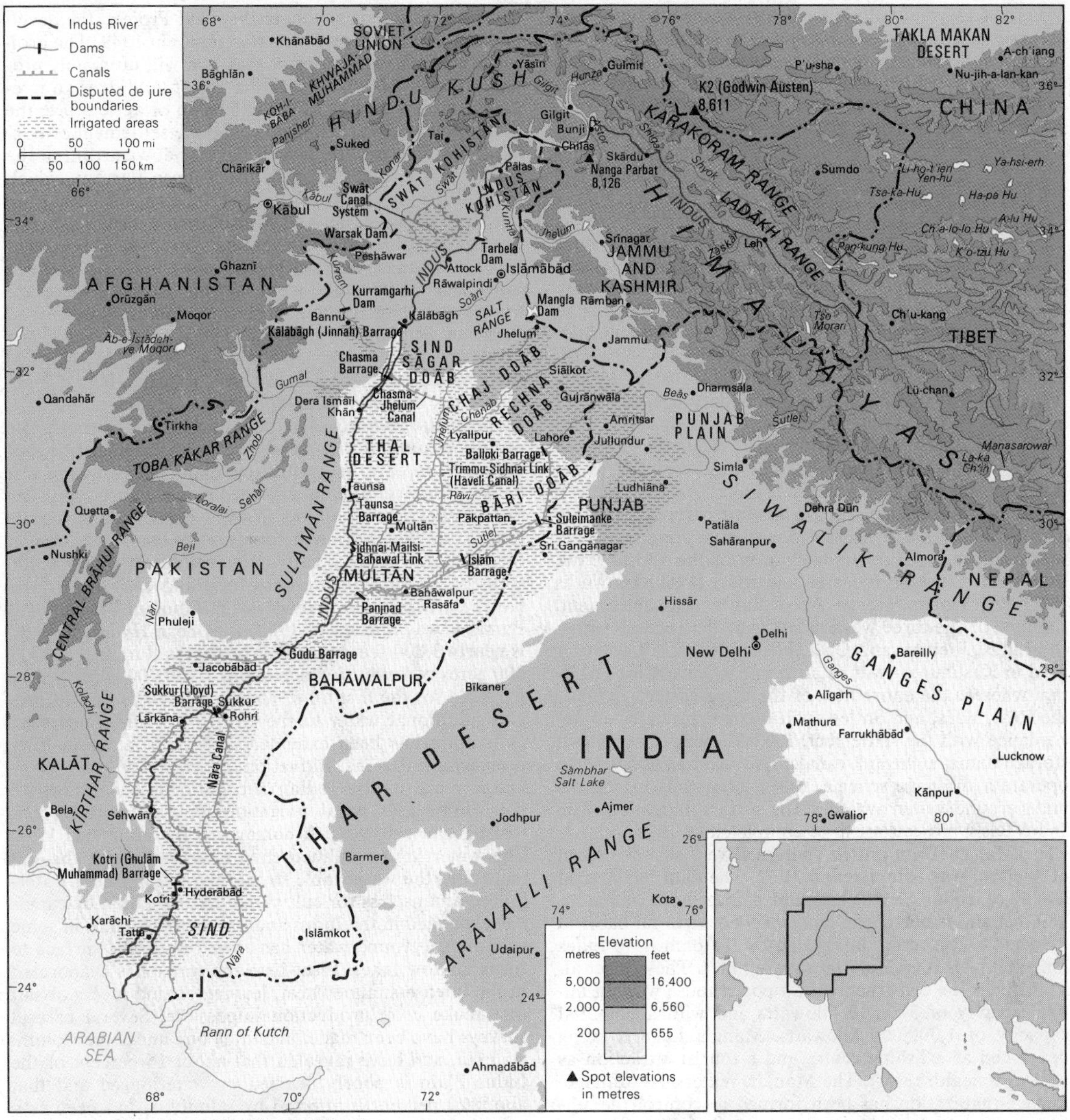

The Indus River Basin and its drainage network.
Irrigation data adapted from N. Ginsberg (ed.), *The Pattern of Asia* (© 1958); Prentice-Hall, Inc.

Valley in winter (December to February) and bring four to eight inches of rainfall—vital for the successful growing of wheat and barley. The mountain region of the valley receives precipitation largely in the form of snow. A large amount of the Indus' water is provided by melting snows and glaciers of the Karakoram, Kohistān, and Himalayan mountains. The monsoon rains (July to September) provide the rest of the flow. The climate of the Indus Valley ranges from that of the dry semidesert areas of Sind and lower Punjab to the severe high mountain climate of Kohistān, Hunza, Gilgit, Ladākh, and western Tibet. January temperatures here are below freezing point in the north, while July temperatures reach a maximum of about 100° F (38° C) in Sind and Punjab. Jacobābād, one of the hottest spots on Earth, is situated west of the Indus River in upper Sind and often records summer maximums of 120° F (49° C).

Vegetation and animal life. There is a close relationship between climate and vegetation in the Indus Valley. In the Lower Indus region of Sind, desert conditions prevail ten to 25 miles away from the river, and the area is dominated by poor grass and sand. Irrigation by floods or canals permits some cultivation. In upper Sind and Punjab, overgrazing and felling timber for fuel has led to destruction of both trees and vegetation. Further, prolonged human interference with natural drainage and deforestation on the Siwāliks has led to marked deterioration in groundwater conditions and so in vegetation. It appears that in prehistoric and earlier historic times the middle Indus region was more wooded than it is at present: accounts of Alexander the Great's Indian campaigns (*c.* 325 BC) and records of Mughal hunts in the 16th century and after suggest considerable forest growth. Even today, in the Indus Plains not far away from the river, there are thorn forests of open acacia and bush and undergrowth of poppies, vetch, thistles, and chickweed. Near the river are stretches of tall pampa-like grass, and streams and canals are often lined with tamarisk trees and some dense scrub, but there is nowhere a natural forest. In recent years afforestation of some parts of the Thal area in the Punjab east of the Indus has been commenced. Cultivated areas close to the river have many trees, and the strip below the mountains has something of the appearance of parkland. Coniferous trees abound in the Pakistan and Kashmir areas of the mountainous parts of the Indus Valley.

The Indus is moderately rich in fish. The best known variety is called *palla* and is the most important edible fish found in the river. Tatta, Kotri, and Sukkur, all in Sind, are the most important fishing centres. Between the Swāt and Hazāra areas the river is noted for trout fishing. In recent years, since the establishment of Pakistan, fish culture has been practiced in the reservoirs of dams and barrages. Close to the mouth of the Indus—

for about 150 miles along the coast—there are numerous creeks and a shallow sea beyond. The area is rich in marine fish, the most important catches including pomfrets and prawns, which are obtained from November to March. The annual catch is said to be about 50,000 tons. A modern fish harbour has been built near the port of Karāchi, providing cold storage and marketing. In recent years an export trade in prawns has developed and sea fish are marketed in different parts of Pakistan.

Economic utilization. Irrigation from Indus waters has provided the basis for successful agriculture since time immemorial. Modern irrigation engineering work commenced around 1850, and large canal systems were constructed by the British administration. In many cases old canals and inundation channels of Muslim and Sikh times were revived and modernized; thus the greatest canal irrigation system in the world was created. At partition in 1947, the international boundary between India and West Pakistan cut the irrigation system of the Bāri Doāb and the Sutlej Valley Project, originally designed as one scheme, into two parts. The headwork fell to India while the canals ran through Pakistan. This led to a disruption in the water supply in some parts of Pakistan. The dispute that thus arose and continued for some years was resolved through the mediation of the World Bank by a treaty between Pakistan and India (1960) known as the Indus Waters Treaty. According to this agreement, the flow of the three western rivers of the Indus Basin—the Indus, Jhelum, and Chenāb (except a small quantity used in Kashmir)—will be utilized exclusively for Pakistan, whereas the entire flow of the three eastern rivers—the Rāvi, Beās, and Sutlej—will be used by India. In accordance with the settlement, Pakistan was to build two storage dams, eight link canals, and five barrages and to operate a drainage scheme, using tube wells that make underground water available for surface irrigation. The Indus Basin projects are to be completed by 1975.

The Indus Waters Treaty

The Mangla Dam on the Jhelum River, near the town of Jhelum, was completed in 1967. The dam has a crest length of about 11,000 feet and a maximum height of 380 feet and is one of the largest rolled earth-fill dams in the world. The reservoir created by the dam is 40 miles long and has an area of 100 square miles. The project also includes the construction of a powerhouse with an initial capacity of 300,000 kilowatts and with a potential capacity of 1,000,000 kilowatts. Mangla Lake is being developed as a fishing centre and a tourist attraction as well as a health resort. The Mangla Watershed Management Organization has been formed to control the silting of the lake by using various techniques of soil conservation and afforestation.

A second gigantic project was taking shape in the early 1970s: Tarbela Dam on the Indus, 80 miles northwest of Rāwalpindi. Work began in 1967; when finished, the dam will be 9,000 feet long and 485 feet high, and its reservoir will be 50 miles long. The project will enable 350,000 acres (140,000 hectares) of land to be developed and will provide 2,100,000 kilowatts of electricity. The dam, of the rock-filled type, is scheduled for completion in 1975.

Eight new link canals and five barrages have been completed by the Pakistan Water and Power Development Authority. The biggest of these link canals is the Chashma-Jhelum link joining the Indus River with Jhelum, with a discharge capacity of 21,700 cubic feet per second. Water from this canal will be used to feed the Haveli Canal and Trimmu-Sidhnai-Mailsi-Bahawal link canal systems, which provide irrigation to the Multān and Bahāwalpur divisions in the lower Punjab.

On the Indus itself, there are five important headworks, or barrages, after the river reaches the plain. In the hilly region, the principal canals west of the Indus are the Swāt Canals, which flow from the Swāt River, a tributary of the Kābul River. These help in the irrigation of the two chief crops of the area, sugarcane and wheat. The Warsak multipurpose project on the Kābul River, about 20 miles northwest of Peshāwar, provides irrigation for food crops and fruit orchards in the Peshāwar Valley and is designed to produce 240,000 kilowatts of electricity. In the plain region, the Kālābāgh or Jinnah Barrage controls the system of canals in the Thal Project, the development authority for which was set up in 1949. The project irrigates a former desert area and will ultimately provide water to about 1,500,000 acres of land. It is an integrated project aiming at the extension of agriculture, the development of rural industry, and the settlement of population in villages and towns. Farther downstream in the Dera Ghāzi Khān district is the Taunsa Barrage, which aims at the irrigation of about 170,000 acres of land in the Dera Ghāzi Khān and Muzaffargarh districts. It was opened in 1959 and will eventually produce about 100,000 kilowatts of electricity. The power will help to operate about 1,000 tube wells. Within the Sind there are three major barrages on the Indus—Gudu, Sukkur, and Kotri, or Ghulām Muḥammad. The Gudu Barrage is just inside the Sind border and is 4,445 feet (1,355 metres) long. When fully completed it will irrigate about 2,800,000 acres of cultivated land in the region of Sukkur, Jacobābād, and parts of Lārkāna and Kalāt districts. The project has greatly increased the cultivation of rice, but cotton is rapidly becoming the major crop on the left bank of the river and has replaced rice as a cash crop. The Sukkur Barrage was built in 1932 and is about a mile long. Four canals originate on the right bank and three on the left. They serve a cultivable area of about 5,000,000 acres of land producing both food and cash crops. The Kotri Barrage, also known as the Ghulām Muḥammad Barrage, was opened in 1955. It is near Hyderābād and is nearly 3,000 feet long. This project will irrigate 2,800,000 acres of land, of which about 1,700,000 acres will be irrigated for the first time. The right-bank canal will provide additional water to the city of Karāchi. Sugarcane cultivation has been extended, and crop increases have been achieved in the cultivation of rice and wheat.

Water-logging and salinity

Experience in the Indian subcontinent and elsewhere has shown that canal irrigation, unless carefully controlled, can cause much damage to the cultivated land. The water in the unlined canals seeps through the soil and raises the water table so that the soil becomes waterlogged and useless for cultivation. As irrigation by canals has expanded in the Indus and its tributary lands, in some areas underground water has appeared on the surface to form shallow lakes. Elsewhere the water has evaporated in the intense summer heat, leaving behind layers of salt that make crop production impossible. Several careful surveys have been made, including one under the Colombo Plan, and have revealed that about 15 percent of the Indus Plain is poorly drained or waterlogged and that about 22 percent is affected by salinity. It has been estimated that nearly 100,000 acres of canal irrigated cultivated lands go out of production every year. To check this, adequate drainage and the construction of a network of tube wells is necessary. The water drawn out of the tube wells lowers the water table and flushes the surface salts down into the earth. An effective drainage system is therefore essential, and schemes are being undertaken in large areas of Pakistan, from the Indus to the Sutlej.

Until about 1880 the Indus and the other Punjab rivers carried some navigation, but the advent of the railways and expansion of irrigation works has eliminated all but small craft that ply the Lower Indus in Sind. There are fishing boats on the Lower Indus, and the upper reaches of rivers and canals above the first railway crossing are now used for floating timber down from the foothills of Kashmir.

BIBLIOGRAPHY. Geographical descriptions and many specific details concerning the Indus are contained in the following: O.H.K. SPATE, *India and Pakistan*, 3rd ed. rev. (1967); KAZI S. AHMAD, *A Geography of Pakistan*, 2nd ed. (1969); and L.D. STAMP, *Asia*, 12th ed. (1967). H.T. LAMBRICK, *Sind: A General Introduction*, vol. 1, *History of Sind* (1964), furnishes details concerning shifts and changes in the course of the Indus and its distributaries and minor channels during the past several centuries. The Pakistan Water and Power Development Authority, with headquarters in Lahore, publishes the monthly journal *Indus* that features special articles and reports dealing with irrigation, harnessing of power, and energy and hydraulic problems.

(N.A.)

Industrial and Organizational Relations

"Industrial relations" or "organizational relations" as a subject of study is concerned with the behaviour of men in organizations in which they work for a living. Its theoreticians attempt to explain patterns of cooperation, conflict, and conflict resolution among workers and among managers and between the two groups; they seek to discover factors determining the outputs of the organization, from physical product to human satisfactions or dissatisfactions; and finally they increasingly concern themselves with the relations between industry and community and with comparative international studies of behaviour in organizations.

The following is a table of contents for this article:

I. The evolution of industrial relations

CONCEPTIONS OF THE WORKER

19th- and early-20th-century views. In classical economics, workers were treated like commodities, subjected to the natural laws of supply and demand. Although classical economists readily acknowledged that men are not motivated by money alone, they abstracted out of reality only the economic factors, which led them to consider workers as undifferentiated and passive instruments in the production process.

In the 1890s an American industrial engineer, Frederick W. Taylor, evolved an engineering approach to what was later called "scientific management." Taylor's approach was similar to that of the classical economists in regarding workers as passive instruments of production, but he did recognize differentiation among workers, at least insofar as degrees of skill were concerned. He developed methods for time-and-motion studies to determine the elements of particular jobs and the way in which these elements should be put together for the greatest efficiency. His approach focussed upon the individual worker; there was no place in his model for group membership or for the effects of groups upon individual behaviour.

A step further in the recognition of differentiation among workers came with the emergence of industrial psychologists, who were concerned with the measurement of the skills and aptitudes of individuals. At least in the early stages of these developments, workers were viewed as isolated individuals, and no attention was given to group phenomena.

Labour economists entered the field before the turn of the century, concerning themselves particularly with the growth of unionization. Recognizing that the earlier approach of classical economics was deficient in treating jobs entirely in terms of supply and demand, labour economists saw workers as banding together as a means of influencing the supply of labour and the terms under which it could be purchased. Although the early labour economists recognized social aspects beyond economics in union organization and collective bargaining, they were concerned almost exclusively with organization at the plant or company level.

The advent of industrial relations. Although scattered courses pertaining to what we now call industrial relations were offered in departments of economics, engineering, and psychology, it was not until the 1940s and 1950s that a distinctive academic field emerged. The primary influence was the research program carried out at the Hawthorne Western Electric plant in Cicero, Illinois, under the direction of Elton Mayo for the Harvard Graduate School of Business Administration. The research program was launched in 1927 with studies of the effects of illumination upon productivity. When investigators were able to find no systematic relations between the quality of lighting and productivity, they moved on to a relay-assembly study, in which five female employees were subjected to varying patterns of rest periods and refreshments, with constant productivity measurements being maintained. In the early periods of this experimental program, the investigators thought that they were witnessing increases of productivity in response to rest periods and refreshments, though it never seemed clear which pattern of changes led to optimum productivity. When rest periods and refreshments were eliminated in the twelfth experimental period and productivity remained at its previous high level, Mayo and his associates recognized that something other than the designed experimental manipulations was influencing these results. They concluded that this "something" must be the social relations among the workers, in combination with the unusual separation of this work group from the normal constraints of factory supervision. The girls appeared to take great pride in membership in a group singled out for the experiment. This unplanned outcome has come to be known as the "Hawthorne effect."

Western Electric–Hawthorne experiments

Although the interpretations that Mayo and his associates made of the test room results have recently come under critical fire, the concern here is not with the validity of the conclusions but rather with the effects of the Hawthorne studies upon the subsequent development of the field. Publication of some of Mayo's writings and of the major research report in *Management and the Worker*, by F.J. Roethlisberger and William J. Dickson in 1939 attracted large numbers of sociologists, social psychologists, and social anthropologists into a field that had previously been limited to economists, engineers, and industrial psychologists.

Four general conclusions were drawn from the Hawthorne studies:

1. *The aptitudes of individuals* (as measured by industrial psychologists) are imperfect predictors of job performance. Although such measures may give some indication of the physical and mental potentialities of the individual, the amount he actually produces is strongly influenced by social factors.

2. *Informal organization* affects productivity. Although previous students of industry had looked upon workers either as isolated individuals or as an undifferentiated mass organized in terms of the formal chart of hierarchi-

cal positions and responsibilities established by management, the Hawthorne researchers discovered a group life among the workers. Though they were not the first to observe that individuals formed groups in industry as well as elsewhere, their report provided by far the most systematic description and analysis of work-group organization yet to appear. The Hawthorne studies also showed that the relations that supervisors developed with workers tended to influence the manner in which the workers carried out—or failed to carry out—management directives.

3. *Work-group norms* affect productivity. The Hawthorne researchers were not the first to recognize that work groups tend to arrive at norms of what is "a fair day's work," restricting their productivity below that point even when they would be physically able to exceed the norm and would be financially rewarded for it. However, the Hawthorne study provided the best systematic description and interpretation of this phenomenon.

4. *The plant is a social system.* The Hawthorne researchers came to view the plant as a social system, made up of interdependent parts. Although there was some vagueness as to the identification of these parts and as to whether the parts should be considered to be in "equilibrium," the emphasis on interrelatedness tended to have a strong influence on subsequent research.

Behavioral scientists had made their entry into the field by attacking the then prevailing oversimplified notions of the individualistic economic man and the formalistic engineering notions of organizational structure, technology, and efficiency. As often happens in arguments between members of competing schools of thought, the force of the behavioral science attack carried some of its proponents so far as to view the work organization as simply a system of social relations. During the 1950s and 1960s the field underwent a major process of redefinition, which consequently affected conceptions of the worker.

Behavioral scientists now recognize the importance of economic factors, but they see material rewards having an impact upon behaviour in combination with social and psychological factors, and they study the pattern in this combination. While not discarding their interest in interpersonal relations, students of organizational behaviour have become increasingly concerned with the ways in which technology and the formal structure of the organization serve to channel those relations.

CONCEPTIONS OF THE MANAGER

Changing conceptions of the behaviour of managers. Classical economists made no distinction between the manager and the entrepreneur, the man who brings together land, labour, and capital and puts them to work for himself. Although experienced businessmen certainly recognized a distinction, it did not take hold in the literature until 1933 and the appearance of the classic study by Adolph Berle and Gardiner Means, *The Modern Corporation and Private Property*. When the authors demonstrated that in most U.S. corporations the owners (that is, the stockholders) played no direct role in the management of the concern and that the managers generally had insignificant holdings of stock, it became apparent that theories of entrepreneurial behaviour had little to contribute to the understanding of the behaviour of managers.

Max Weber's notion of bureaucracy

Sometime earlier, Max Weber (1864–1920), the German economist and sociologist, had approached the study of managerial behaviour through his concept of bureaucracy. To Weber, bureaucracy did not have the negative connotations often heard in casual conversations; he used the term simply to point to a phenomenon of growing importance even in his time: the large organization with fixed positions linked together in a hierarchical pyramid, with specialization and division of labour and with established rules and regulations governing behaviour. To Weber, the manager was the individual who, according to the office he held, interpreted and applied the rules of the organization. Later organizational sociologists, though recognizing the importance of Weber's contribution in focussing attention on the impersonality and rationality of modern industrial and governmental organizations, pointed out that Weber's model failed to take into account some of the most important features of the modern business organization. They argued that it gave an unduly rigid picture of organizations, that it failed to devote attention to processes of change, and that it built so exclusively on the hierarchy of authority as to neglect horizontal and diagonal relations. In any case, Weber's formulations were of interest primarily to social scientists. Practicing managers and students of business in business schools, at least until recently, were likely to have little familiarity with the Weberian approach to managerial behaviour.

The early model of the manager taught in American business schools followed lines of functional specialization. In these terms, he was the one who had mastered such subjects as accounting, marketing, production, finance, and so on. Later, it was recognized by theoreticians and practicing managers alike that management was a good deal more than the sum of these specialized functions, and this realization in turn led to the conception of the manager as generalist, who would understand the various specialized functions and who would be able to effectively and efficiently coordinate these functions and the people engaged in them. The emphasis turned to decision making.

In the academic as well as the business world today, the most widely espoused conceptions of managerial leadership are called "participation management," a term popularized by the American psychologist Rensis Likert, in whose terms the skilled manager is one who talks and acts "in terms of groups," who consults with groups of subordinates and even seeks to involve them in the process of decision making. The approach involves a focus on interpersonal relations, on the quality of communication, and also upon the problem of helping people to penetrate social facades so that they are better able to deal with the real thoughts and feelings of their associates. Participation management thus has no recognized place for management technology and formal organization. The emphasis is entirely upon interpersonal relations.

In the 1940s a competing approach to management arose out of the field of anthropology, when investigators saw that since interpersonal contacts were observable, quantifiable, and tended to follow regular patterns, the study of their patterning could provide a foundation for analyzing any set of social relations. While such investigators concentrated on the observation and measurement of interaction, they gave major emphasis to technology and the formal organizational structure by which such interactions are channelled. They conceived the role of the manager as that of an organizer and monitor of the flow of interactions in his organization.

Changing conceptions of management's responsibilities. Since the early days of the Industrial Revolution, management spokesmen have been concerned with defining and redefining the responsibilities of the company to the community.

The Industrial Revolution brought about great accumulations of wealth and also focussed public attention on the apparent negative effects of rapid industrialization on working people. To what extent workers in the new factories were worse off than they had been in the much smaller scale cottage industries may be a matter of continuing debate, but there is no question that large concentrations of workers—men, women, and children—crowded together in oppressive physical conditions and working long hours for low pay made the problem much more publicly visible. In the earlier period workers had dealt with owners and agents of whom they had some personal knowledge. The establishment of large factories destroyed the direct relationship, and it became less credible for the owner to claim that he took a personal interest in his workers.

In the last two centuries management people have taken,

in general, two broadly different positions regarding management's social responsibilities.

The view of laissez-faire

The laissez-faire attitude. The first stance represents a sort of combination of laissez-faire economic theory and the Protestant ethic. In this view the owner or manager has no responsibility for the welfare of the workers outside the immediate plant situation; man's station in life is a reflection of his intrinsic merit in the eyes of God; the wages and other labour costs incurred by the firm are the result of competitive market conditions. In this view, then, the owner's or manager's responsibility to his employees began and ended with operating the firm in such an efficient manner that it was able to meet competition in the market place, and if all businessmen similarly followed a policy of intelligent self-interest, the broad social interests of society would be better served than by any other policy.

The expression of this point of view has undergone changes in style over the years. Today one hardly expects most businessmen any longer to state the position with religious overtones, and even the most laissez-faire inclined spokesman is likely to concede that there are some social problems that are not resolved by private initiative in pursuit of enlightened self-interest. However, managers with this view of the world tend to take a defensive position regarding the responsibilities of their firm beyond the gates of the plant. They recognize that popular opinion and government policies and programs may require them to take on activities not dictated by immediate material interest, but the tendency is to do what has to be done to keep out of trouble with the outside world and nothing more.

Paternalism. The other stance begins with the assumption that management has a social responsibility to the communities in which its plants are located. If one states the situation in this general way, hardly a management spokesman today would deny this social responsibility, and yet, when one gets beyond rhetoric, one finds a wide variety of views as to what actions—if any—management should take. In assessing the present scene one might do well to examine the historical evolution of conceptions of management's social responsibilities.

The Scotsman Robert Owen (1771–1858) was the first industrialist to back up words about management's broad social responsibilities with a program of action. Although Owen was interested in broad questions of social reform, he did undertake to carry out his philosophy in the area under his immediate control. Having arisen out of the work force in a textile mill himself, he was concerned with the social and economic conditions of the workers and believed that the economic success of the enterprise did not have to depend upon exploitation of workers. In New Lanark he built workers' housing, schools, and a store that were far superior to contemporary standards for workers' communities. He was also an influential figure in the early development of the cooperative movement in England.

Owen's ideas and the successful operation of his plant and community during his lifetime impressed many social reformers and some businessmen as well. His influence can be traced directly to the establishment of the industrial city of Lowell, Massachusetts. Francis Cabot Lowell (1774–1817) had made a trip to England and Scotland to study textile mills and related community problems before launching his own enterprises in Massachusetts. He had found New Lanark far more in harmony with American ideals regarding the dignity of man than the average English industrial plant at the time. Lowell faced a social problem of an immediate practical nature. He had to recruit a labour force, largely female, not available in the towns where he was building his plants. To meet this need the firm built, in what came to be called the city of Lowell, a number of boarding houses especially for young women. Each house was under the control of a woman who was supposed to watch over the moral life of her charges, and the girls were not allowed out of the house after 10 PM except with special permission. Lowell also made liberal provisions for the building of schools and churches. He and his associates stimulated the Middlesex Mechanics Association, which sponsored cultural and educational programs.

Somewhat later, George M. Pullman (1831–97) undertook to build around his Pullman Palace Car Company a complete community (the town of Pullman, now a part of Chicago) that would house all the employees and provide for all the essential facilities. In the early period of the Pullman Company, the quality and condition of worker housing was probably a good deal superior to the average for other industrial workers.

When Henry Ford startled the industrial world with his announcement of the $5-a-day wage in 1914, he followed it with steps designed to help workers make good use of their increasing affluence. The company already had a small legal department set up to help workers with the complicated problem of home buying, and now Ford established what he called a sociology department. It was staffed with social workers who made home visits to workers' families to provide advice and help on family problems. Members of the department were also free to talk with workers within the plant during working hours in efforts to straighten out family problems.

Although many other companies in the industrialized countries pursued programs based on an assumption of managerial responsibility for the conditions of life outside the plant gates, these cases provide illustrations of the types of projects undertaken.

How does one assess the success of such efforts along these lines? In the United States the Lowell project was the longest lived and the most admired by foreign visitors. Charles Dickens compared Lowell very favourably with the typical English industrial city. Nevertheless, the distinctive character of Lowell had been lost before the end of the 19th century. Native New Englanders were replaced in the work force by the new immigrants and their children, and the women of these immigrant families had no rural homes to return to after several years of labour in Lowell, as had the New England girls. The boarding houses thus lost their primary rationale, and by 1900 all of them had been sold by the companies. Even in the early years of the Lowell textile industry, conditions could not have been quite so idyllic as described by some of the visitors, for there were 9 recorded strikes or lockouts in the mills in the period 1834–79. The strikes greatly increased in frequency after this period, when management was faced by changes in the social composition of the work force, with successive waves of immigration.

The Ford experiment in social welfare also was short-lived. Management in the plants argued that the sociology department was interfering with production and that the workers did not like having social workers prying into their personal affairs.

Company towns

It would seem to be more than coincidental that some of the most bitter strikes in the United States—from Pullman in 1894, through the Southern mill towns in the 1930s, to Kohler, Wisconsin, in the 1960s—have taken place in company towns. Whatever economic grievances workers have had in these situations, it is clear that economic exploitation is not a complete explanation of the bitterness of the disputes. However benevolent or oppressive the manager is in the company town situation, he has far more extensive control over the lives of the workers than is found in other towns and cities. In the company town the owner or his agents not only run the plant; they also run the government, provide the local services, run the hospital, and operate the company store. Whatever grievance a resident of the town may have is, in his eyes, the fault of the company. When clashes in labour relations do arise in these situations, they are thus likely to look more like a struggle for independence than a standard union-management dispute.

The rise of unions in the mass-production industries of the United States in the 1930s helped to convince executives that a paternalistic approach to labour and community relations was no longer feasible. Extensions of management's social responsibilities were now achieved through collective bargaining. Still, these broader benefits, such as pensions and health insurance, were limited to the workers and their immediate families. There was a tendency to assume that any responsibilities for the welfare of the community as a whole should be assumed by government.

Conceptions of public relations and community service. Although management's withdrawal from paternalistic community responsibility was accelerated by the growth of unionization, company officials began increasingly to see the need for the company to play a role in the communities where its plants were located. This need grew in part out of the recognition of changes in top management's relations to the industrial communities. In an earlier era factories had been locally owned, and the owners played a prominent role not only in the management of the plants but also in the affairs of the community. Now as local plants became part of large corporate organizations with headquarters in cities far away from most of the plant locations, and the management of the local plants came to consist of corps of college-trained men who moved up the ladder of promotion by moving from plant to plant and city to city, company executives came to recognize the threat of company estrangement from the local communities. Management found itself in an awkward position when local union leaders who had lived all their lives in the community were leading other local residents in a strike against absentee top management and its local temporary representatives.

A common reaction to this estrangement was the development of public relations and community service programs. Public relations men sought to tell the communities how good management was being to them and to inform management about problems in company-community relations. Top management began to redefine the role of plant manager to include the function of representing the company to the community, and this meant participating in community service activities along with locally based business and professional men. Thus, it became common to find the plant manager and other members of the management group playing prominent roles in the community fund drives and other service activities. There were two important characteristics of such community service activities: they had no direct influence upon life inside the factory, and they involved simply a commitment to maintaining the community rather than any initiative toward changing it.

Conceptions of broad social responsibility. In the 1960s management people began to recognize that the community service orientation was not adequate for coping with the problems of cities that were erupting in violence. By this period the leaders of the powerful unions that were negotiating with the leading companies had come themselves to be part of the new industrial elite. No longer were the unions seen as leading a broad movement for social change and a possible radical reordering of society. They came increasingly to be viewed as organizations devoted to the defense and improvement of the status of workers who held a relatively privileged position in society compared to the "underclass" of workers who were employed in low wage situations, who worked only sporadically, or who were unemployed. In this period it became evident that the acute and chronic problems affecting society as a whole and industry in particular were not going to be solved simply by having a "good" management relating to its union and indulging in "good" relations with the communities.

In the past, management's recruitment, selection, and training policies had been based on an unquestioned assumption: that it was the responsibility of management to try to skim the "cream" off the labour market. As technological progress steadily reduced the proportion of unskilled jobs in industry and business, there arose the increasingly severe problem of workers who were not only unemployed but were, in fact, classified as "unemployable." When unskilled jobs had been more readily available, the man with little to offer in educational background or craft training could nevertheless find a place at the bottom in the plant and learn enough on the job to move up into at least semiskilled positions. When this bottom rung of the employment ladder had been knocked out in so many plants, men and women with below-average education and training found sharply reduced opportunities to get a start in industry. So long as each firm sought to skim the cream off the labour market and so long as government employment services sought to refer only the best qualified applicants to employers, hundreds of thousands of people were being systematically excluded from the benefits of an otherwise affluent society.

Recognition of this problem has led to a redefinition of managerial and governmental social responsibilities. Government agencies are beginning to develop programs to give special attention to placing the "hard core unemployed." A number of companies have relaxed their standards of qualifications for employment, at least for a segment of the prospective work force, and have even actively recruited in urban slum areas and developed special training programs so that workers who would otherwise be excluded could be eased into factory jobs.

Helping the disadvantaged

Some companies even went considerably further in the assumption of social responsibilities, as they made changes in plant location or purchasing policy in recognition of new social needs. For example, one major corporation built a new plant in one of the most depressed slum areas of a great metropolitan centre with the explicit purpose of providing employment and training for people who otherwise would never have had an opportunity to work for such a corporation. With this new wave of social concern by leaders of business, many younger executives have become dissatisfied with the old-fashioned service approach exemplified by the community fund and other charitable activities and have begun searching as individuals for ways in which they can help members of disadvantaged groups to develop the knowledge and skills required to launch and develop small businesses. Professors and students in some of the leading business schools have become similarly involved in offering consultation and assistance to the small businessman, especially in the slums of cities. Even if only a small minority have been moving in this direction, this nevertheless marks a distinct change from the earlier implicit assumptions that the only purpose of the business school was to educate men for business leadership—which meant in those days prominent positions in large corporations.

This new business orientation, however, should not be thought of in terms of a broad realignment of ideas and activities. The most far-reaching financial and personnel commitments have been made by those few companies that have such massive resources and such strong competitive positions that great sums of money can be committed to enterprises that are speculative at best from an economic standpoint and can only be justified in terms of meeting management's public responsibilities—and improving the corporate image. Most companies did not go very far or very fast in these new directions. Even when impressive numbers of "hard core unemployed" were hired and retained in the work force for some months, as business activity slackened, these newly hired special problem cases were likely to be the first ones to be laid off.

The responsibilities that some business leaders were claiming for industry clearly cannot be borne by industry alone. A job development program for disadvantaged groups cannot be successful during an economic recession. Even in a prosperous time, companies are not going to commit massive resources and personnel to the task of recruiting and training and counselling and otherwise assisting those who otherwise would not fit in, unless the government provides financial incentives. The future will no doubt see much experimentation between industry and government regarding the distribution of responsibilities, costs, and payments involved in providing economic opportunities for disadvantaged peoples.

However limited the private industry commitment to

broad social and community concerns was in the 1960s, there is no possibility of turning back to the isolation of the old laissez-faire philosophies. If management people felt impelled in the 1960s to take more initiative in tackling the problems of the great cities, lest the cities themselves explode in ethnic and class warfare, in the 1970s industry was facing the challenge of environmental pollution. Public campaigns for the control and reduction of pollution are bound to involve a further redefinition of management's responsibilities to society. Here again one can assume that some industrial leaders will take the initiative in investing large economic and human resources in the reduction of the pollution for which their firms are responsible, and yet the magnitude of the problem will clearly call for a combination of governmental and private company action. One can expect the government to be increasingly active in setting standards, exacting penalties on polluters, and offering financial incentives to those who reduce pollution. Whatever combination of efforts evolves, this newly recognized problem is bound to increase the concern of management people for the social, economic, and environmental problems in which they and their companies are inevitably involved.

Efforts to reduce environmental pollution

The discussion of management's responsibilities has thus far been limited to experience in the United States and Great Britain. In the developing countries, a different situation is found.

The special problems of developing countries

Especially in mining and petroleum operations, the companies (nearly always foreign owned) have found it necessary to build roads and housing for managers and workers, to provide schooling for children of employees and medical care for employees and their families, and so forth. In the face of rising nationalistic sentiments, many such companies have been seeking to disengage themselves from responsibilities not directly connected with their industrial operations. Community facilities cannot be simply abandoned, however, and the companies face difficult negotiations to establish the terms under which the government will take over the responsibilities to be relinquished by the companies.

II. Cross-cultural comparisons

Do the principles of organizational behaviour apply universally, or must they be adapted to different social structures and cultures? Starting with the Hawthorne studies, much of the work in this field has been in the United States. Some of the most important studies have been done in England, but the two countries are culturally sufficiently close to provide little opportunity to test the universality of propositions across cultures. In recent years, however, first-rate field studies in industrial and business organizations have been carried out in Latin America, France, Japan, India, and a number of other countries, so that one is at last in a position to examine the interrelations of behaviour in organizations and the culture and social structure within which the organization lives.

The chief problem is one of moving beyond the anecdotal to the general level. Anyone with experience in a country other than his own can tell how "they do things differently over there," but a series of colourful tales is no substitute for systematic and comparative analysis. For that purpose one needs to look at phenomena in different cultures along the same dimensions. One may look at two dimensions that are provided by the environment of the organization and two dimensions that are provided by the internal life of the organization. The "outside" dimensions are: (1) the social structure of the country and (2) the sentiments and value orientations characteristic of the culture. The "inside" dimensions are: (3) the structuring of interpersonal relations and (4) the distribution of rewards and penalties.

Dimensions for comparative analysis

In terms of this framework, if one examines the interrelations of the organization and the culture and social structure, one is studying the relations of variables in dimensions 1 and 2 to the variables in 3 and 4. When one speaks of "variables," precise measurements are implied. What follows, however, gives only some preliminary interpretations from various studies without presenting the evidence. The discussion begins with comparisons between four countries or culture areas in terms of these four dimensions.

TYPICAL NATIONAL OR REGIONAL SYSTEMS

The United States. The United States is characterized by a social structure that is relatively open and fluid. Social-class differences are recognized, but they are not as marked in terms of differences in clothing and style of life as they are in many other countries. (Afro-Americans are of course the major exception to this generalization, since skin colour and other physical characteristics still have important status implications, and black militants have been developing a characteristic style of dress that sets them apart from whites.)

In sentiments and value orientations the United States is characterized by a general belief in the equality of man (although, of course, some segments of the population have been unwilling to include Afro-Americans in this view of the world). Ideally, the individual is expected to be rewarded in his work and elsewhere according to his achievements and not according to his birth or other ascribed characteristics. A high positive value is placed on work. Although white-collar work has more prestige than blue-collar work, there is less social distinction between these categories than is found in most other countries. Compared to other countries, there is in the United States in general a high level of faith in people. That is, there is a presumption that other people are men of goodwill and can be trusted.

In interpersonal relations within organizations, there is more fluidity in the sense of rapid changes in organizational structure and in the relations among people than is found in many other countries. Authority relations are characterized by the tendency to question orders and yet to work within the system of authority; that is, the right thing to do is to confront your superior with disagreements and to raise suggestions and complaints for face-to-face discussion. Although the United States has well-developed structures and procedures for third-party intervention in union-management relations, there is a high value placed on the parties being able to thrash out their differences among themselves.

Along with this belief in the values of face-to-face discussion and resolution of conflicts goes a strong belief in the values of decentralization and dispersion of power. It is felt that the people directly facing the problems are the ones who should have the responsibility for solving those problems, with "dictation" from above to be avoided as much as possible.

There has been so much geographical mobility in the United States that family ties, beyond parents and children, are often exceedingly weak. Furthermore, it is generally believed that a man should get ahead on his individual merits, and nepotism generally is frowned upon.

Although unionization has had an important influence on the development of trends toward a more collective orientation, systems of distribution of rewards and penalties are still based upon assumptions of achievement motivation, and efforts are generally made to provide individual rewards and penalties that are related to the "merits" of the individual. For example, the individual's pay is determined by the job he holds and, if incentive rates exist, by the amount of his production, without regard for length of service and family responsibilities, which in some other countries may be influential factors. (Of course, length of service may be important in determining access of the individual to a particular job, but he is rewarded or penalized in the performance of that job, without any direct consideration of his length of service.)

Latin America. Compared to the United States, the countries of Latin America have social structures that are closed and rigid—that is, class lines are sharply drawn, and there are difficult barriers to mobility (although mobility in recent years has become somewhat easier). Family ties are strong in the sense that people tend to think and act in terms of family, when they are in other spheres of activity. Family solidarity is built around a dominating father figure and a protective mother figure. When the father dies, the solidarity of the family may break down in competition for the power and resources that he formerly controlled.

Governments tend to be strongly centralized in the capital city, with key local officials being appointed by the central government. On the other hand, the formal centralization of power in the government may not go along with the corresponding power of implementation of government decisions in local areas. Local people who occupy important economic and social positions are often able with impunity to disregard some governmental decisions.

In sentiments and values one finds a higher degree of acceptance of authoritarian leadership and a tendency to value a man for what he *is* rather than for what he *does*. The *is* tends to be defined in terms of certain ascriptive characteristics such as social class position and family membership. There tends to be a sharp distinction between blue-collar and white-collar work. Work in general is not conceived as an end in itself, but as simply a means to an end, so that when a man has accumulated the resources he needs in order to live in the pattern customary to his social status, it is perfectly appropriate for him to reduce his work efforts or turn the work over to somebody else. Latin America is characterized by a low level of faith in people in general and by a tendency to believe that only members of one's family or close friends are to be trusted. There is a high value on individualism, but it is individualism detached from achievement orientation. Here there is an apparent paradox—the general acceptance of authoritarian control as legitimate vies with a desire to avoid the impact of that control. This leads people to value escape from control rather than direct confrontation with those in control.

In interpersonal relations there is a rigidity of social categories with problems of communication between them. The common pattern emphasizes authoritarian control. There tends to be great difficulty in resolving problems between organizational units on the same level, with a consequent dependence upon the arbitration of a superior authority in the case of disagreements. In the field of union-management relations there is seen this same pattern: the avoidance of direct interpersonal confrontation and working out of joint problems in favour of appealing issues to third parties (government officials) for decision.

The distribution of rewards and penalties tends to be on an ascriptive basis. The distribution is in terms of broad social categories, but modified by personal influences. Thus it is common for individual subordinates to be rewarded not so much by merit or performance as by presumed loyalty to the superior who controls the rewards.

Japan. In Japan's social structure, class distinctions are strongly marked, and there is relatively little mobility across class lines within the career of the individual. That is, the young man who begins full-time work in the blue-collar ranks has little opportunity to move into white-collar or managerial positions. On the other hand, the educational system is an important channel of intergenerational mobility. The son of a blue-collar worker who passes his entrance examinations to college and satisfactorily completes a college career is admitted without question into the ranks of management. College entrance is much more competitive than in the United States, for the proportion of high school graduates admitted to college is far lower in Japan. On the other hand, the high school student is not competing with fellow students for the favourable recommendations of his teachers, since admission is determined by scores on a uniform national examination.

In Japan social activities and loyalties centre on the family to such an extent that other institutions tend to be conceived in terms of family relations and obligations.

In the field of government, even in periods of dictatorial government, Japan has been noteworthy for the extent of collective responsibility and group action at the level of the village or neighbourhood.

In sentiments and value orientations one sees considerable respect for hierarchical positions and considerable deference accorded to people of superior status and age. Although there is emphasis upon individual achievement in the educational system, when a man is once in his job he is expected to value his loyalties to the group more highly than his individualistic impulses.

There is a high dignity assigned to work, and in fact it appears that people are expected to work harder than they are anywhere else in the world. The business firm is looked upon as if it were a family, which means that the employees have permanent obligations to the firm, but likewise the executives have permanent obligations to employees. Although there have not yet been adequate surveys taken, Japan probably would score high in faith in people. There seems to be a general assumption that a man will live up to his responsibilities. What is known as the "shame principle" has an impact, and it would appear that the most potent force in bringing a deviant back into line is the expression of disapproval by his associates, which is expected to make him feel ashamed of himself.

In interpersonal relations there appears to be considerable deference to authority, and yet a common system of decision making in organizations (the "ringi system") involves a group of subordinates signing their names to a proposal that they then refer to the next level of authority—and on up the line. When a proposal comes up with the backing of the group involved, it is very difficult for a superior to veto it.

Regarding the resolution of conflicts or disagreements between equals, one finds that Japanese culture discourages the face-to-face thrashing out of differences that is favoured in the United States. On the other hand, the culture also inclines each individual to be especially sensitive to the thoughts and feelings of those with whom he has to work, so that the individual is unlikely to advocate strongly a course of action that would appear to threaten the interests of others. Furthermore, since men move up in the hierarchy primarily through increasing age and seniority, department heads are not in competition with each other in the same sense that they are in some other industrial countries. This movement up by age and seniority means that the people currently working together will already know each other very well from past association and will act in line with the thought that they will be working closely together in the future. This tends to build a sense of collective responsibility and to discourage individualism. (The Japanese have a variety of devices—such as early retirement, assigning men to positions in subsidiaries and suppliers, and promoting men into positions of prestige but little concrete responsibility—to meet the problem of those who, with advancing years, do not show the capacities the company needs in higher positions.)

The family principle applies even to union-management relations. Most Japanese unions are limited in membership to those working in a particular firm, and there is little tendency in union-management relations for unions to seek to organize workers from many firms into one unit. Even when unions strike the efforts seem to be directed not so much at economic damage to the firm as at the public embarrassment of the management. The words and actions of the union leaders are directed at gaining public attention and wide publicity, in the hopes that management will be shamed into being once again a good father to the members of the organizational family.

In Japanese firms the distribution of rewards and penalties is on a highly collective basis. Although incentive rates are gaining some ground in Japan, the prevailing pattern has been to reward people in terms of their membership in the organization, with pay based on a combination of the rate for a particular position, the years of service to the firm, and the employee's family responsibilities. In management also, rewards tend to be of a collective nature, with people moving up according to length of service and seniority. There is a tendency to avoid the assignment of individual responsibilities for decisions. When a decision turns out obviously to be wrong, it is the management group that suffers shame rather than a particular individual. Of course, within the group, there must be some recognition that certain individuals played a more prominent role in making a decision than others, and thus the outcome of a given decision must have some effect upon the way that members of a management group regard each other, but there have as yet been no studies of this aspect of the problem. In any case the management group presents a united front to the outside world.

France. In social structure France appears to have moderately firm social-class divisions with mobility across class lines generally being limited to those who come up through the educational system. On the other hand, France is exceedingly high in intergenerational mobility.

France is characterized by an exceedingly high centralization of political power and administrative organization, with all important decisions being made in Paris. The French bureaucracy appears to operate with greater efficiency than the typical Latin American bureaucracy, for decisions centrally arrived at tend to be more effectively implemented in the provinces. Much of French life is organized around the family.

In sentiments and value orientations France seems to be somewhere between the extremes in achievement-ascription orientation, with the social characteristics of the individual counting strongly for his position in society, but with individual achievement also highly valued. France is characterized by the high value placed on individualism, which in this case is associated with resistance to authority, and by a strong commitment to the social segment in which the individual finds himself, in opposition to outside powers. Although there are no measures of this dimension, one would expect France to come out on the low side in interpersonal trust. In values regarding work one would expect France to fall somewhere between the extremely high values given in Japan and the United States and the extremely low values found in Latin America.

The best existing study of French industry (Michel Crozier's *Bureaucratic Phenomenon*) shows interpersonal relations being channelled within fixed social categories, so that there is extremely little social interaction among them and differences of interest are next to impossible to negotiate. People in each segment of the organization seem to band together to resist higher authority, which makes adaptation difficult in their relations with higher authority or in the horizontal dimension. As individuals have developed their defenses against higher authority, they have tended to cope with the rules and regulations from the top by following the formal rules but often evading the spirit of the regulations.

The distribution of rewards and penalties tends to follow social categories, with little attention to individual performance.

LESSONS TO DERIVE FROM THE TYPICAL SYSTEMS

The relations among dimensions. The profiles presented above are of course highly oversimplified, and in each country or region organizations can be found that do not fit the models presented. Furthermore, each country or region is in the process of change so that the profile of today may not fit the situation of tomorrow. Within these limitations, if one assumes that the profiles are reasonably accurate, a further question remains: what are the relations among the four dimensions?

For example, what is the relationship between the degree of interpersonal trust found within a culture and the characteristic pattern of interpersonal relations found in the organization? It would seem that where interpersonal trust is low the organization will be centralized, with little delegation of authority and responsibility—for delegation does not take place unless superiors have a fair degree of trust in subordinates. Individuals and groups will have difficulty in working out agreements through negotiation, for negotiation again requires a degree of trust, or else the individuals will feel that they cannot count on the concessions that might be offered by the other side in the negotiating process. Centralization is accompanied by authoritarian leadership. This leads subordinates to compete for the favour of the boss, and such competition tends to promote distrust among the competitors. Thus it can apparently be said that a low level of trust tends to foster the development of a certain pattern of interpersonal relations, and that such a pattern tends to reinforce a low level of interpersonal trust.

American and Japanese models of development

Implications for development. In recent years U.S. conceptions of the business enterprise and of business practices have provided the chief model that proponents of aid to the developing countries have sought to export. The U.S. model is based upon certain assumptions regarding human nature, without taking cultural difference into account. When one compares the U.S. with Latin America one might indeed assume that, if certain U.S. value orientations and patterns of interpersonal relations could be exported, the Latin American countries would accelerate their economic development.

When one looks at Japan, this simplistic notion breaks down. Since it began to industrialize, Japan has advanced as rapidly as has the United States and currently appears to be moving ahead even faster. The Japanese experience demonstrates that the U.S. type of individualism with its stress on personal responsibility and rewards and penalties geared to performance is not the only route to development. Japan has had extraordinary material success with a collective orientation and a pattern of distribution of rewards and penalties based on group membership. Nevertheless, although the contrasts are indeed striking, one should not overlook the common elements. Both the United States and Japan place a very high value on the dignity of work—including work with the hands. Furthermore, although the Japanese discourage individualism in the organization, they place a very high value on achievement orientation in the school system.

These observations suggest certain lessons for those seeking to accelerate industrial and economic development in the underdeveloped world. The cultural differences between the United States and Japan make it clear that there is no "one best way" to industrial development. Furthermore, the elements of culture do not operate independently but must be understood in relation to one another. For example, if one were able to build up in country X the high degree of collective orientation found in Japan but failed to produce also the high level of achievement motivation and commitment to hard work characteristic of Japan, one could hardly expect an accelerated rate of development.

Cross-cultural studies do *not* suggest that when one tries to accelerate development for country X one must leave its culture alone. Cultures are constantly changing, but they do not transform themselves overnight. The introduction of modern industry is bound to have effects upon the culture. The industrial developer cannot expect just to do his own project and expect to hold everything else constant. He must understand the cultural context into which his project fits and plan both for the adaptation of the project to the existing culture and for the production of new types of behaviour essential to the project and not previously provided by the culture.

III. Work careers

In general, managers and workers have quite different work careers, so that it is necessary to consider them separately.

THE STRUCTURE OF WORK CAREERS

Managerial careers. Increasingly in all industrialized countries managers are recruited from among those who have graduated from a university or college. Although there is a good deal of variation from industry to industry within the same country, it is increasingly rare for a man to start as a factory worker and to rise beyond first-line supervision and into higher ranks of management. Higher management does recognize, however, that the man fresh out of a university lacks enough detailed knowledge of the problems and possibilities of his company immediately to be worth the salary it is necessary to pay him. There are two common responses to this phenomenon. One is to recognize that the investment will not immediately bear fruit and to make a further investment in the new employee by providing him with an elaborate training program. In addition to formal instruction, the training period may involve rotating the individual through a broad range of jobs, giving him exposure to a variety of experiences, and yet not depending on him to any great extent for performance. The justification for this approach is that the initial investment in the man will make him more valuable to the company in later years. There are two disadvantages: the man may leave the company before the investment in his company education has been recovered, and many claim that the best way to learn on a job is to assume responsibility for results.

Education and training

The other approach is to place a man immediately on a job in which he has responsibility for results. This provides the challenge lacking in the first approach, but it has possible disadvantages. The entry job may be very narrow and limiting and thus may not provide very valuable experience for later development of the executive.

Some managements are coming to take an approach to the training of executives that is different from either of the extremes just discussed. They claim that in a highly industrialized society jobs on the managerial level change so rapidly that a man's practical knowledge can easily become obsolescent when he is ten years out of the university, even if he had learned originally all of the right things in his engineering or business education. The remedy for this obsolescence appears to be to encourage managerial employees to take refresher courses in programs of continuing education from time to time.

To what extent does moving up in the management organization involve moving around the country geographically? A large company is likely to have plants all over the country, and it is taken for granted that any major promotion often involves selling one's house and moving into another community. Even when the executive is working for a small company, he may find that he makes contacts leading to better opportunities in other companies, and so he transfers not only geographically but also from company to company. Although there are yet no international comparative studies on this point, one may assume that the United States is on the high end of the range in the freedom with which executives move from company to company, whereas in Japan the movement from one to another company would be exceedingly rare.

Workplace mobility

Can an executive refuse an offered promotion if it means movement to another city? The answer to that question for the United States is necessarily ambiguous. Rarely is an executive told that he will have to move or else lose his job. In other words, he is not ordered to move. At the same time he may well understand that, if he refuses the offered promotion, he may get the reputation of not being sufficiently ambitious and aggressive or sufficiently loyal to the company. He may then find that, if he later looks for a promotion and is even willing to go to another city, he has gotten into the box of the "not promotable" and is blocked from further career advancement.

Workers' careers. The structure of the blue collar worker's career is quite different. His working career can be divided into four parts: initial period, trial period, stable period, and retired period. In the initial period the worker is still going to school and tries out a number of part-time jobs. Knowledge of what jobs an individual has had in the initial period provides very little predictive evidence regarding the long-run career development of individuals in the United States. In Latin America the future manager is exceedingly unlikely to have had any experience as a part-time manual worker in his youth, whereas in the United States a young man who is aiming for college and, later, management positions may well take on part-time jobs in manual labour before he is through his education, without any feeling that this is inappropriate from a status point of view. In fact the college man who has earned money as a youth as a construction labourer or as a service station attendant may later talk about this experience as if he were proud of it, and indeed he may find that other people give him some credit for the breadth of his experience.

It is when the worker reaches the trial period that the dividing line between future managers and career blue-collar workers is encountered. The college-educated manager abandons manual jobs (except perhaps incidentally during vacations), whereas the manual worker has his first real job (outside of vacation periods) even though he may not yet be committed to that job or that employer. He compares notes with friends and keeps looking around for something better. He may change within a few months of employment. Even in the so-called stable period, there may be a fair amount of movement. A study by the American sociologists Seymour Martin Lipset and Reinhard Bendix in the city of Oakland, California, surveyed 935 male heads of families with an average of 25.3 years experience in the labour force and showed that they averaged nearly five (4.8) distinctly different jobs each. In the retired period, even though the individual severs connections with a regular employer, he may still take on part-time jobs.

Along with stages in the worker's career go shifting attitudes toward his job. When the worker remains with the same company, his attitudes toward the job and the company tend to follow a curvilinear pattern: high at first, then dropping through the middle period, and rising in the later parts of his career. Individuals tend to begin work with such unrealistically high expectations as to the nature of the jobs and the opportunities before them that disillusionment then sets in, but after some years they adjust themselves, lower their expectations, and express more satisfaction with the work situation.

Worker's attitudes toward his job

Geographical mobility seems to vary with the field of work activity and the level of skill. There is a good deal of geographical movement in the construction industry generally, and especially in such lines as the forming of structural steel, the laying of pipelines, and the construction of dams. In terms of skill levels those at the top in certain crafts find that they can readily move around the country and pick up jobs, whereas those in the middle skill levels do not have the abilities to offer that would enable them to be so mobile. Those at the bottom, perhaps because of the combination of enforced layoffs and their own feelings of lack of reward in the job, tend also to be rather mobile.

A number of studies have shown the reluctance of factory workers to leave their community when the plant shuts down. It is now clear that simply the availability of jobs at high levels of pay elsewhere is not enough to move people. Ties with friends and family make workers reluctant to leave, but there can also be good economic reasons. If the worker owns his home in a community where a plant has shut down, he is likely to find the real-estate market so depressed in that community that if he had to sell his house he would get only a fraction of what it would cost to buy a house in a community to which he is moving. Therefore he is likely to conclude that it is best to stay where he is in the hope that the job market will pick up.

SOCIAL MOBILITY BETWEEN THE CLASSES OF WORKERS

Are opportunities for social mobility in the United States much greater than in other parts of the world, as many U.S. citizens have generally been inclined to believe? For lack of truly comparative data, this is a difficult question to answer. On the matter of social mobility within the career of one individual there are very few cross-cultural data. On intergenerational mobility (from father to son), the complexities of comparing whole occupational structures from country to country generally are too great. There are some studies of movement between blue-collar and white-collar work, however. Although the first studies suggested there was little difference among industrialized nations in these rates of movements, further research has tended to confirm the U.S. ranking at the top in upward mobility (high blue- to white-collar, low white- to blue-collar movement). In this regard the U.S. appears substantially above Sweden, England, Japan, West Germany, The Netherlands, and Italy. On the other hand, one study has shown France at approximately the same level with the United States in these mobility rates.

In recent years there has been a popular belief that young persons of humble origins no longer have as many opportunities to reach the top of large business enterprises; the idea is that there are fewer self-made men among the business elite. Scholarly studies comparing recent decades with such periods as the 1920s, however, indicate that social mobility in this respect has remained virtually unchanged. It is true that a college education is far more necessary today, but then more people are going to universities. The rate of social mobility to the top is about the same.

Since rates of mobility depend not only upon the social structures of the countries in question but also upon the rate of industrial expansion (or contraction) and upon changes in the structure of jobs, it is uncertain whether the rate of mobility of country X is characteristic of that country over a number of generations or is a product of economic trends in one period of time. Population trends may also be important. The high upward mobility rate of France may be partly explained by a relatively low rate of population growth over a long period and a high rate of industrial expansion in recent years.

IV. Worker behaviour and formal organization

Some years ago this section would have begun with a discussion of "formal" versus "informal" organization, but more recent research seems to suggest that this dichotomy is a misleading way of looking at the field. Roughly speaking, the dichotomy was this: formal organization comprised the specifications of management; informal organization, on the other hand, included such things as the behaviour of workers as they banded together to determine how much production was a "fair day's work," how they should behave toward the supervisor, and so on. Informal organization also covered the ways in which the foreman actually worked out an adjustment with his workers, quite apart from the specification of his duties by management. The problem with this dichotomy arose in trying to distinguish between the formal and the informal at the level of behaviour. At the extremes there was no problem: one could readily distinguish the behaviour of the foreman giving a worker orders on what to do next and the behaviour of the foreman in conversing with the worker about some athletic event. The difficulties arose as one moved in from those two extremes to the very common situation in which the informal and formal seemed to be mixed together in action. In fact, the better the foreman and the worker were getting along together, the more difficulty one had in distinguishing between formal and informal behaviour.

The way out of this dilemma proved to be to distinguish between behaviour on one hand and formal organization on the other. With this approach formal organizational structure is limited to such elements as can be determined without behavioural observation. For example, the organization chart that is available for inspection in most companies provides official management's conception of the organizational hierarchy. Job descriptions tell (in management's view) what workers are supposed to do and how they are supposed to do it. There are rules and procedures established by management concerning the distribution of authority and responsibility. Where these matters are not written down or drawn on charts (though they are in most large modern organizations), the problem is somewhat more difficult, but one can still approach the study of formal organizational structure through interviewing management people to determine their conceptions of the nature of the hierarchy, of the distribution of authority and responsibility, of the nature of particular jobs, and so on. In other words, with this approach one deals with the formal management theory of the way in which the organization is designed and is supposed to operate.

Using this approach involves no assumption as to what extent observed behaviour will correspond to the formal organizational structure, but there must be the assumption that the formal organizational structure will indeed *tend* to influence the behaviour to be observed. However, we are not here talking about informal versus formal organization but rather about the relationship between the formal organizational structure and observed behaviour.

FACTORS AFFECTING WORKER ATTITUDES AND BEHAVIOUR

What factors affect individual and group behaviour in organizations? It is necessary to consider first certain factors built into the jobs; later the effects of managerial leadership can be considered.

Financial considerations. Wages and fringe benefits are important criteria whereby workers judge whether a job is a good one or a poor one. There is a general expectation that the wages paid should be in line with the prevailing social evaluation of the jobs, so that it becomes impossible to separate the rate paid from the prestige that the job holds. One must distinguish between money as a motivating force for organizational membership or for superior performance. Where the individual is paid a fixed rate for the job he holds, the money itself can serve only as an incentive to maintain a minimum performance level that will keep him in the organization. Greater performance must be elicited through other means. It is only when the money paid bears a relationship to the amount produced that money has a possible motivational effect upon productivity.

Incentive or piece-work systems

Incentive systems have important effects upon the behaviour of workers and supervisors and also upon the problems of plant administration. The effectiveness of the individual incentive system depends upon setting the rates-per-unit-produced high enough to motivate workers to put out extra effort and still not so high as to be unduly costly to management. Rates are set by time and motion study. Once the desired sequence of methods has been determined, it should be a simple technical problem to measure the number of units that the worker produces in a given time period—except that the accuracy of measurements depends upon selecting workers having "average skill" and working at a "normal pace." Workers, of course, recognize that if they are able to maintain a slow pace during observation and yet simulate diligent effort, they are likely to get a price-per-piece that will allow them to make high earnings without excessive effort. Some workers develop great skill in this type of make-believe. Experienced time-study men recognize that workers are trying to fool them, and so they tend to make allowances for the amount that they are being fooled. This transforms what is intended to be a scientific procedure into one that is a mixture of measurement and speculation.

The difficulties of rate setting would be great enough if management had only to set a rate once and then continue the rate for years, but in most modern organizations this is far from the case, for frequent changes in products, technology, and work methods upset the original conditions. When any major change takes place, there is a clear understanding on the part of both labour and management that a new rate is called for, thus setting in motion once again the complicated procedures. Perhaps even more difficult from a social standpoint are those instances in which the changes being introduced are small. Most union contracts hold that piece rates are to be changed only with the introduction of a "major" change in job content, but the parties frequently disagree on whether or not a given change can be classified as major. Then, too, over a period of months management may introduce a series of small changes, every one of which could be considered as minor, but all of which together might add up to "major."

At what point does management claim the right to introduce a new rate? Suppose, for instance, that an improvement in question is something developed by a worker, as often happens. If management allows the improvement to be introduced without a change in rates, then that worker and all others who work on the same job may be able to earn far more than others on similar jobs, thus disturbing the wage structure. On the other hand, if management intervenes and sets a new rate, the workers will feel that they are being deprived of the fruits of their ingenuity and skill. In any event, the complexities of the rate-setting process are such as to elicit pressure tactics on the part of workers against management. Although the overall effect of the piece-rate system in the average case will probably be greater production than could be achieved without it, it also tends to promote a substantial increase in conflict or at least to give the parties a set of difficult problems to resolve.

Motivational and social problems of incentives vary according to whether they are based on the individual, the group, or some larger unit. As a rule, the larger the social unit covered by an incentive system, the simpler the problems of administering the system, but the more remote from the incentive formula is the motivation of the workers. When an incentive formula is based upon the performance of the entire plant, individuals can be motivated only if the formula is linked with a system of continually involving workers and supervisors and management people in discussing ways and means of improving general performance. The individual piece-rate system, on the other hand, has interesting effects upon supervisors. Where a piece rate is in effect, the supervisor does not need to check so often to make sure that people are working. If the particular rates have been accepted by workers as more or less reasonable, they are likely to work at much the same pace whether the foreman is present or not.

Technological considerations. This is not to suggest that the only way to keep workers at work is to give them a financial incentive or check closely on their performance. There are workers so committed to their job that they work diligently regardless of a supervisor's presence. But, in any event, the worker is importantly affected by the technology, the flow of work into which he fits, and the nature of his particular job. This is most clearly evident in automotive assembly-line technology, in which the individual's work is paced by the movement of the conveyor belt that brings to him the machine or part of the machine on which he is to perform his particular operations. The individual himself maintains a relatively fixed position. As he works faster he can move a few feet up the line, and as he works slower he can move a few feet down the line, but he cannot move very far in either direction without interfering with the work of others.

Assembly-line technology

Research has shown that the automotive assembly line is one of the most oppressive industrial environments yet constructed by man. There is also evidence of the particular aspects of the environment that elicit the worker's negative reactions: the pressure to keep up with the line (workers constantly seek to bid on the few jobs available in the assembly plants that will get them off the line); the monotony of constantly repeating a simple task (even on the assembly line there is evidence that satisfaction with the job correlates with the number of operations performed); and the restrictions on social interaction (some research has shown that workers who express a need for social interaction, as most do, are more negative toward the job than those who express no such need).

Although the assembly line provides useful illustrations of the impact of technology upon job satisfaction, one must not think that such technology is representative of modern industry. Actually the machine-paced conveyor belt of the automotive assembly line provides only a small fraction of industrial jobs, and, with advancing technology, that fraction is declining. As several researchers have shown, the satisfactions that workers find in their jobs vary enormously from industry to industry. At the low end of the scale are the automotive plants and textile mills, in which a worker faces constant work pressure, cannot control the pace of his work, lacks a choice of work techniques, and cannot move about very freely. Toward the high end of the scale, there are such industries as chemicals and printing, in which there are higher levels of worker skills, more freedom of physical movement and choice of work methods, and generally greater worker satisfactions. It is interesting to note that the skills involved in these more "satisfying" industries are of two quite distinct types. In chemicals very little hand manipulation is involved, and the skills are of an intellectual sort, the operator having to interpret meters and charts and then, on the basis of this diagnosis of the condition of the process, make the appropriate adjustments. By contrast, the skilled jobs in printing place a premium on hand manipulation. Apparently jobs that require either type of skill can offer important intrinsic satisfaction to workers, and the skill level naturally also provides satisfactions that go with the higher prestige job.

Correlations between skills and mental and physical health

Social researchers have also found a correlation between the level of skill required and the mental health of workers—the higher the skill level the better the mental health. And this correlation extends into management—with higher management people enjoying better mental health than lower level supervisors. The same general conclusion seems to hold for physical health. When a well-known executive suddenly succumbs to a heart attack, one is inclined to attribute the event to the tensions peculiar to the executive life, and yet studies have demonstrated that the incidence of heart attacks is greater at lower management and worker levels than it is among executives. These studies do not *prove* that experiences on the job account for differential health. Studies in various countries have shown a consistent relation between social class and health, both mental and physical—the lower the social class, the poorer the health. Thus, until one can sort out the conditions of family and community life from the plant environment, one will not be able to determine the health effect of a particular job situation, but one can only assume that workers expressing very negative attitudes toward their work are subject to more adverse effects in regard to health.

Organizational considerations. The worker's satisfaction with his job situation is not determined entirely by the characteristics of the particular job he holds. It makes a great deal of difference in his view of himself and his future whether his job is in a line of promotion so that he can look forward to moving up to jobs at successively higher levels. If the individual is on a "dead-end job," however secure it may be, one can expect him to be less satisfied than if he were on a job paying the same money but also offering opportunities of promotion. Industries differ markedly in this regard; some provide an individual with opportunities for a series of promotions up the line, whereas others are so divided up organizationally that individuals are boxed into departments within which only a few promotions are available. The contrast should not be drawn only in terms of the possibility or impossibility of a worker moving up from his job; one must also think in terms of "probabilities" provided by the proportions of jobs in each category. For example, in automotive assembly plants there are jobs off the line, and workers do get promoted to be foremen, but these higher level jobs are so few relative to the number of jobs on the line that the average worker must seek to adjust himself to a working life of trying to keep up with the line.

The *structure* of jobs within a department or other work unit affects worker behaviour too. As Leonard Sayles, the American student of business administration, has shown, where jobs are homogeneous as to work performed, level of skill, rate of pay, and working conditions, there is greater likelihood that the workers will band together to exercise pressure on management in advancing their interests than will be the case with a department in which the jobs are heterogeneous. In the homogeneous situation management finds it difficult to improve the situation of one worker without similarly affecting all of the others, and management similarly has difficulty in making an adverse decision that does not affect all workers in the department in a similar way. The similarity of conditions that workers face thus tends to promote work-group solidarity and effective negotiation with management. In the heterogeneous situation individuals may have opportunities to profit at the expense of fellow workers, so that the worker is tempted to try for individual gains at the expense of group members.

The issue of the relation between satisfaction and motivation

It has been widely assumed that satisfying and dissatisfying elements in jobs fall at opposite ends of the same continuum: that the absence of negatively valued characteristics in a job will lead to job satisfaction and that, similarly, the absence of positively valued characteristics will lead to dissatisfaction. The American industrial psychologist Frederick Herzberg has challenged this apparent truism with a "dual factor" theory of job satisfaction and motivation. His "satisfiers" are related to the nature of the work itself and to the rewards growing directly out of work performance. These are factors such as sense of achievement, recognition, interest in the work itself, and advancement. The "dissatisfiers" are associated with the individual's relation to the environment in which he does his work. Company policies and ineffective administration rank highest in this dimension, followed closely by incompetent technical supervision. Also involved are such items as working conditions, salary, and interpersonal relations with supervisors. Herzberg uses his analysis of satisfaction-dissatisfaction in order to get at motivation. He argues that the *presence* of "satisfiers" tends to motivate people toward greater effort and improved performance, whereas the *absence* of "dissatisfiers" has no effect upon motivation. Subsequent research by others has yielded both confirming and conflicting evidence on the existence of two distinct factors, so that the issue remains open. Nonetheless, Herzberg's separation of satisfaction from motivation promises to clarify future research.

CHARACTERISTICS OF MANAGERIAL LEADERSHIP

Vertical relationships. The man-boss relationship has received more research attention than any other aspect of organizational behaviour. Many students of supervisory leadership have been concerned with ways in which the exercise of authority could be made compatible with democratic ideology. Would the "employee-centred" supervisor, who showed concern for the welfare of his workers, be more highly regarded by the workers than the "production-centred" supervisor, who focussed all his attention on getting out the product? Would the "employee-centred" supervisor also get more production out of his department than the "production-centred" supervisor? In other words, were consistent relations to be found among supervisory style, worker satisfaction, and productivity? Early students of this relationship were hoping to find that virtue paid off—that a good democratic leader not only was better liked by his subordinates but also got more production out of them. The first studies did indeed seem to support this proposition, but in later years many conflicting findings have been reported—so much so that the conclusion must be that no systematic relations between worker productivity and worker satisfaction can be shown.

"Employee-centred" and "production-centred" supervisors

Why has so much research on leadership style by so many able people led to so few firm conclusions? The first answer relates to the particular methodology used in studies of supervisory leadership: the questionnaire survey. With this method, research men drew conclusions not only about worker attitudes but also about the supervisory behaviour that the workers thought that they were experiencing. In other words, the behavioural categorizations of supervisors (as general or close supervisors, for example) were not based upon the direct observation of supervisors but rather upon the inferences of subordinates. The early studies also suffered from a neglect of technology and organizational structure. It was as if workers and supervisors were living and acting exclusively in a world of interpersonal relations. Only gradually, as researchers sought to find explanations for unexpected results, did they take note of the differences in supervisory roles growing out of differences in technology and the nature of the job. For example, in one study it was found that, in *production* departments, foremen who were seen by workers as high in "initiation structure" (telling workers what to do, checking up on performance, etc.) were judged by their superiors to be more effective foremen than those who were lower on "initiation structure" and higher on "consideration," perceived as concern for and responsiveness to workers' needs and desires. On the other hand, in *maintenance* departments, those foremen higher on "consideration" and lower on "initiation structure" were more highly rated by their superiors. Findings such as these suggest that, even if such studies had provided good behavioral descriptions of supervisory leadership styles (which they did not), one could still not hope to show a consistent relation between leadership style and productivity except under certain specified conditions.

Technological considerations

The work of industrial sociologist Joan Woodward in England has related leadership to technological conditions. Woodward and her associates carried out an impressive study of 203 manufacturing firms in south Sussex, eventually concentrating their attention upon the relations between technology and formal organizational structure. In order to compare so many units, Woodward worked out a typology of technologies according to types of production. The unit or small-batch type involves separate production of individual units or production of small numbers of the same unit. Large-batch or mass production involves relatively standardized production of large numbers of the same unit. Continuous process involves industries such as petroleum and chemicals in which the fluids and gases flow through the process in continuous form.

When Woodward lumped all of the plants together, she was able to find no clear structural patterns emerging, but, when she sorted them out into technological types, she discovered that each type had its characteristic ratio of workers to first-line supervisors and also of those reporting directly to the chief executive. Thus in unit or small-batch production plants, the first-line supervisor had an average of 23 persons working for him, whereas the average rose to 50 in large-batch or mass-production plants and dropped to 13 for the first-line supervisor in continuous-process plants. The ratios of those reporting to chief executives ranged from a median of four in unit production to ten in continuous process, with large-batch and mass production falling in between with seven. Woodward also marshalled evidence indicating that these ratios were related to the efficiency of the plants. On the basis of ratings of outside observers regarding the efficiency of the units, she found that those rated "above average" tended to have ratios of workers to first-line supervisors and of executives to chief executives that were close to the average for their category, whereas the firms judged "less successful" tended to be above or below the average figures. Her figures therefore suggest that each type of technology has its own optimum ratios of personnel at the various levels.

Woodward's findings have devastating implications both for the theorists of scientific management and for its principal critics. Scientific management theorists sought to establish, as a universal principle of management, an optimum "span of control" ratio of personnel reporting to a given superior. Woodward demonstrated that the search for such a universal principle was fruitless: there could only be an optimum ratio under certain specified technological conditions; under a different set of conditions a different ratio would apply.

Critics of scientific management had been arguing that the span-of-control ratios advocated in the literature necessarily meant that large organizations must have a long hierarchy of authority. They claimed further that a long line of authority produced the evils of poor communication, excessive control of subordinates, and poor morale of workers and supervisors. They proposed a counter ideal of the organization with a broad and flat organizational structure. Increase the number of people reporting to a superior, they argued, and you reduce the control he can exercise over any of them; and by thus increasing the freedom of subordinates, one can expect to increase their job satisfaction and also their productivity. The claims of these critics, however, are not without problems: although there may indeed be a tendency in large organizations to build a hierarchy of authority excessively long and narrow, just how flat the organization structure should be cannot be determined on the basis of any universal principle but must be determined according to the type of technology involved.

The Woodward study also has important implications for work on supervisory leadership. When one considers the differences in the behavioral requirements for the supervisor directing the work of 13 men and the supervisor directing the work of 50 (with those ratios being determined in part by the technology), one must recognize that universal generalizations regarding the man-boss relationship must be either highly superficial or misleading. This does not mean that generalizations are impossible, but it does mean that propositions regarding supervisory leadership style must be placed in a context of the particular type of technology and organizational structure in which the supervisor functions.

Lateral relations among supervisors

Types of lateral managerial relationships. The literature on supervisory leadership also faces another difficulty. Most of the studies are written as if the organization consisted exclusively of vertical relationships. This is a gross oversimplification. Even at the level of the first-line supervisor, research data suggest that the more effective foremen are not distinguished from the less effective in the amount of time that they spend with their subordinates but rather in the amount of time that they spend with their direct superior and with staff and service people. It is only the beginning of the analysis to point out that the supervisor or manager has many other relationships outside of the direct line of authority. To advance one's understanding one needs to be able to classify these into types. Below, with some modification, is the typology suggested by Leonard Sayles; the manager of a production department in a large complex organization is involved in eight types of lateral relationships: (1) work flow, (2) buy-sell, (3) service, (4) scheduling, (5) auditing and standard setting, (6) stabilization, (7) advisory relations, (8) innovation.

Work flow. Here the manager is engaged in efforts to work out adjustments with managers whose departments both precede him and follow him in the flow of work.

Buy-sell. In this relationship (called trading by Sayles), the manager is engaged in negotiating with the departments that supply him with parts for his operation and perhaps also with the purchasing department in an effort to get materials at prices and quality that will permit him to improve performance of his department. On the selling side, he seeks to persuade the company salesmen or managers of other departments using his production to accept the kinds and quantities of products that his department can most effectively produce. He is also engaged in an exchange of favours with other people in management, seeking to get them to do things for him, responding to their requests, or offering help with the expectation of reciprocity in the future.

Service. In this relationship, the manager seeks to develop such a relation with maintenance crews as to provide for repair and general servicing of his machines according to the most convenient schedule for his production and in line with the quality of performance he needs.

Scheduling. Production planning involves a manager in relations with people in another department who are occupied with determining what his department shall produce and in what sequence the production shall be run. Although the scheduling department must concern itself with the coordination of production throughout the plant, the manager may find that if he develops effective relations with schedulers he can persuade them to make adjustments in the schedule for his production problems.

Auditing and standard setting. This involves the manager of a production department in relations with people who are concerned with checking and recording his costs and with establishing the cost-production standards of performance against which he will be measured. Since a manager's performance is judged by his superiors in terms of his meeting or failing to meet these standards, it is of great importance whether these standards are set in a way that the department manager and his associates can consider "reasonable."

Stabilization. This involves the relations of the department to other units in the plant in cases in which a decision that the manager might make within his department would have repercussions throughout the plant. For example, there may be a policy as to the frequency and amount of pay increases that can be authorized, with the provision that the manager cannot deviate from this policy without approval of the personnel department. Or the manager might conclude that he could reduce his costs if he contracted out for one item used in his production, but he finds that such a decision would involve the plant in problems with the union as well as threaten other relations within management. He must therefore secure approval from some organizational unit dealing with such stabilization problems before making this change.

Advisory relations

Advisory relations. The manager may find a number of people more than willing to offer him advice that he feels he does not need, whereas he has trouble getting the advice that he feels would be really helpful. It is then his problem to work out ways of blocking off the unneeded advice without offending the advisers and developing relations with those who can really help him so that he can call upon them when help is needed.

Innovation. The manager has always to recognize that there are development engineers and applied-research people who are constantly searching for ways of introducing changes in the technology, work flow, or products produced in his department. Any such changes designed to bring about improvement in the future are bound to present some problems for the man who is trying to meet the day-to-day standards of performance. If he simply opposes all efforts to introduce changes into his department, he will get a reputation as an old-fashioned stubborn fellow who is not in line with management's future plans. On the other hand, if he just lets the innovators move things around at will, he may find himself in a position in which his current performance is suffering severely. The department manager therefore must try to fit himself into the innovative process in such a way as to strike a balance between the needs of change and progress and the needs of maintaining current performance.

Status in lateral relations

The complexity of horizontal and diagonal relationships. Although each of the relationships described above influences the vertical relations between the manager and his subordinates and superiors, none of them involves the direct exercise of authority or the submission to authority. To complicate matters further, the relative status levels of the two people in the relationship are crucial. From the standpoint of the manager in question, one may regard a relationship as either diagonally up or diagonally down. For example, a statement from the plant personnel man (ranked below the plant manager) may be taken as advice that the plant manager is free to disregard, whereas the same statement from the vice president for personnel is bound to appear in quite a different light. The plant manager recognizes that technically he has not received an order from the vice president, and yet he knows that if he disregards the statement he is running a serious risk. If there are no observable adverse consequences from his failure to take the vice president's advice, the plant manager may have no problem, but if he gets into some kind of trouble that his superiors think he could have avoided by taking the advice, then he may be severely criticized.

The complex of vertical, horizontal, and diagonal relations

The manager or supervisor is constantly engaged in a complex network of horizontal and diagonal relations. It is of course important how the manager or supervisor gets along with his immediate subordinates, but his relations with his subordinates are strongly influenced by his handling of the other sets of relationships. If the manager cannot organize smoothly the work flow relations between his department and others, his own production will suffer delays, and his subordinates, especially if they work on piece rate, will complain that they are losing money. If he cannot get maintenance service for his machines when needed, he will drop behind in his production and will feel under pressure to try to get his subordinates to put out extra effort. If those setting standards for his department call for a level of production that his subordinates do not think reasonable, he will nevertheless have to try to get it out of them. Furthermore, there are cases in which a good relationship between workers and a foreman has deteriorated in reaction to changes in the foreman's horizontal and diagonal relations with others. Under these circumstances, it is hardly surprising that a focus of research upon man-boss relations in isolation has yielded so few concrete results. If one takes seriously the notion that the organization is a social system made up of interdependent parts, and if one considers the horizontal, diagonal, and vertical relations to be the parts of the organization, then it naturally follows that generalizations regarding one part will be faulty unless they are stated in terms of the conditions of the other parts.

In sum, management involves far more than directing subordinates and being responsive to one's organizational superior. The manager is involved in a complex network of relationships and finds himself frequently in a situation that social psychologists describe as role conflict: people in different positions in the organization have conflicting expectations regarding the way that he should behave. In the long run, he will be judged even by his superiors by the way he appears to get the job done, and getting the job done requires negotiating with people in horizontal and diagonal relationships and developing some reciprocity with subordinates as well as trying to get them to carry out the wishes of his superior. The successful man is not one who unnecessarily antagonizes the people with whom he has to continue to work; neither is he a person who seeks to keep everybody happy, for he realizes that such an outcome is impossible when there are conflicting demands and interests at work. To a considerable extent the successful manager is one who works out his own definition of his job and his relations with those with whom he works. He seeks to recognize and negotiate differences rather than to ignore or suppress them. This kind of performance requires considerable independence of spirit. The man who, consciously or unconsciously, tries to get ahead simply by conforming to the wishes of his boss is not likely to progress or even to survive for very long in the complex and competitive environment of most modern large organizations.

V. Innovation and change in organizations

THE COMPONENTS OF CHANGE

A great deal of literature in industrial relations has revolved around the phenomenon called "resistance to change." The implicit assumption is that it is just human nature for men to resist change and that therefore the agents of change should devise methods of overcoming this resistance. It is then usually pointed out that when the people to be affected by the change have an opportunity to participate in shaping the nature of the change and bringing it about, their resistance is reduced or eliminated. This point of view is faulty in two important respects. It assumes a universal tendency to resist the introduction of change, and it assumes that the nature of the change or the existing state of the social system make no difference: that all that counts is the process whereby the change is introduced.

In modern industry it is misleading to assume any universal tendency toward resistance to change. In fact many plants are constantly undergoing changes, and many such changes are carried out without anything that could be labelled as "resistance to change." Where one does observe disturbances accompanying the introduction of a particular change, calling what happens "resistance to change" simply serves to attach a label that conceals much more than it reveals. For example, in the introduction of the "Amicon tube" (a case study offered by the American researchers in business administration Harriet Ronken and Paul Lawrence), the only phenomenon that might be called resistance to change was manifested by the development engineers, who paradoxically are usually associated with change. The case involved an electronics plant in which changes were constantly being introduced and in which, in the usual flow of activities and interactions, the first steps were always taken by the development engineers. Industrial engineers became involved only later when it came time to work out the methods of production and to establish the piece rates for workers. In the instance of the Amicon tube, however, the original designer happened to be one of the industrial engineers, and the plant manager allowed him to take over and direct the kinds of activities ordinarily initiated by the development engineers. The development engineers objected to this denial of their usual precedence. The whole tangled history of the project must be interpreted against the background of this reversal of the customary flow of work from development into production.

Case studies of change

Another instructive case study (this one by the American student of technology Charles Walker) involves the introduction of a new steel-tube mill, more automatic in operation than an old mill. Eleven workers from the old mill did not originally resist being assigned to the new mill and, in fact, in a few months became accustomed to working with each other in the new pattern and came to consider themselves as a crew. Then, however, management announced a reduction of the crew from 11 to 9 men, and the workers did indeed vigorously resist this disruption of the relations that they had developed. Furthermore, the workers actively pressured management to set new piece rates on production in the new automatic mill, for naturally they sought early installation of rates that would enable them to earn at least as much as they had been taking home at the old mill. As a means of applying pressure on management, the workers held down production, while management resisted setting new incentive rates until there was a longer period of experience to study the problem.

What is involved in the changes in these case studies is not resistance. Rather it is *reaction* to the introduction of change. And to predict reactions one needs systematic information of three types: (1) the nature of the change to be introduced; (2) the state of the social system at the time of introduction; (3) the process whereby the change is to be introduced. The important thing, therefore, is to ask in what ways the nature of the change will affect the customary pattern of human interaction and the organization of activities in the social system. "Change" should not be viewed as a universal abstraction or concept. One should get down to specific cases and specific components and think in terms of the changes in behaviour to be required of people. Then one can make sensible predictions about the reactions of those people and about the ways in which the process of introducing the change should be organized so as to minimize resistance and maximize the support for the new approach.

Reactions to change can also be expected to differ according to past organizational experience with changes. If the organization is one in which changes have been infrequent and therefore any change is a major event, there will probably be more disturbance than would be the case in an organization in which changes are constantly being introduced. In fact, most modern companies have achieved a systematization or institutionalization of the change process. Management sets up a research and development department whose explicit purpose is to bring about the introduction of new technologies, new chemical processes, and new products.

THE RESEARCH AND DEVELOPMENT PROCESS

The stages in research and development

Large modern companies institutionalize the introduction of changes in products and methods of production by setting up units to organize the research and development process. The process may begin with a basic research unit seeking to solve some scientific problems concerning materials or chemical processes that are more or less related to the company's interests. The knowledge gained out of this basic research is then utilized by an applied research unit, which aims to determine the scientific and technical feasibility of utilizing the findings in new product or process development. At this point the development engineers take over, seeking to work out the technical problems by setting up a pilot operation or otherwise testing out various approaches. When the development engineers believe that they have the technical problems of production or processing solved, the industrial engineers step in to work out the methods of production, to determine the nature of the jobs required, to set the incentive rates (if any), and in general to move the new product or process into production. It is only at this point that the impact of the innovation strikes workers and management in production.

It should not be assumed, of course, that all innovations reaching the factory floor follow the complete route, beginning with basic research. Much innovative activity begins with applied research units, where the work involves application of scientific principles that are already known. Still more of the activity may originate with the development engineers, without any foundation in research. Neither is the flow necessarily all in one direction. In some cases a problem that does not yield to solution in applied research may become a project in basic research, or the development engineers may call upon applied research for help on a problem that they have been unable to solve. Whatever the history of a particular project, it must be seen against the background of the company's customary flow of work among units and departments from research into production. As noted in the "Amicon tube" case, when the innovation follows a path incompatible with the established one, difficulties are bound to arise.

Coordination of the various stages

One of the basic problems in the organization of research and development is that effective performance requires human influences to move in both directions: downstream with the progress of the work from research to marketing, upstream from marketing to research. Although the work done nearer research naturally sets limits upon what downstream department members such as salesmen can do, unless key people at upstream positions are aware of the problems and viewpoints farther downstream, much of their work will end in frustration and conflict. For example, if, after the research and development and pilot testing have been done on a proposed new product, management decides that the product cannot be made for a price permitting the high-volume sales that would make it profitable, then thousands of man-hours of work and large amounts of material will have been wasted. Clearly such frustrations cannot be completely avoided, for no management has information at the beginning of research and development that would render possible a marketing decision at the very outset. Nevertheless, rather than thinking of completely separate steps following one another downstream, one should think of policies and procedures that will bring the ideas and worries of downstream people to the attention of upstream people so that each group can work on its own problems with some conception of the problems that other groups will be facing at another time.

Some concerns try to meet the need for coordination through the establishment of liaison positions, consisting of individuals whose job it is to work between two departments, relating one to the other. The difficulty in this solution is that it not only adds additional people to the payroll but may even serve to prevent department managers themselves from getting together to thrash out common problems.

Some interdepartmental problems have to be resolved through an appeal to a higher authority, but if this is the prevailing pattern of problem solving, the research and development process is not functioning effectively. Appeal to higher authority not only involves valuable time lost in decision making but also serves to put decision making in the hands of people who are so far removed from the problem that they lack knowledge adequate to its solution. Furthermore, frequent resort to arbitration by superiors tends to build up a competitive win-lose orientation among subordinates so that they come increasingly to regard people in other departments as opponents rather than as collaborators.

If constant resort to arbitration is to be avoided, department managers must develop some skill in negotiating with other managers, so that a mutually satisfactory arrangement can be worked out without any single negotiator having the final decision over others. The coordination process may also be facilitated if, from time to time, when higher management people recognize problems of communication and cooperation in the research and development process, they call meetings of the key people concerned. If these meetings are conducted in such a way as to diagnose the problems of coordination and collaboration rather than to lay the blame on one individual or another, the meetings may open the way to further discussions in much smaller groups of those people immediately involved in each particular problem.

Finally, some companies are experimenting with an approach that involves the flexible use of personnel along the line of the flow of work. That is, instead of each department maintaining strictly its own personnel on a given project, one man may be detached from his own work group to follow the project several steps downstream. Similarly, a man from a department further downstream may be detached to work on a project two or three steps before it reaches his own department. In this way, as people move back and forth, they serve to broaden their own experience and knowledge and also to facilitate communication among work groups.

VI. Scientists and engineers in the industrial organization

In the early days, research in industrial relations focussed on workers. Gradually attention spread to foremen and then to higher levels of management. Recently, considerable attention has been devoted to the study of scientists and engineers in the industrial organization.

THE SCIENTISTS

The first industrial research departments, of the late 19th and early 20th centuries, were set up in established companies that were really unsure of what they were instituting. Research units were patterned after already existing departments, thus ignoring the important differences between the work involved in research and the work involved in production, assembly, and so on. The major differences can be summed up in these ways:

Differences between scientific research and other plant work

1. *Production of ideas as opposed to the production of objects.* The scientific laboratory's most important product is *ideas*, not objects, and thus the leadership methods used in the production of physical objects are not likely to apply to the production of ideas.

2. *Distribution of education.* In the production organization the average levels of education increase as one goes up the line from workers to first-line supervisors and on into management. In the scientific research unit, however, there are often scientists with doctoral degrees working in the laboratory under the general direction of higher management people who have not gone beyond the first university degree.

3. *Locus of knowledge.* Although workers in the average production shop will have more intimate, detailed knowledge of their tasks than do people at higher levels, the people at successively higher levels will have more systematic or broader technical knowledge regarding the

overall production operations. In the scientific laboratory, on the other hand, the scientists as workers not only know more than their supervisors do about their immediate jobs but also tend to know more about the broader technical and scientific aspects of their projects.

4. *Degree of predictability of outcomes.* Although management people in production departments often complain that they are not getting the output that they expect, usually one finds upon further questioning that the gap between reality and expectation is only a matter of a few percentage points. In the scientific laboratory, on the other hand, outcomes are far less predictable. The scientist may be able to estimate with reasonable accuracy how long it will take him to perform a series of experiments, but if he knew how the work was going to turn out, he would not really be performing experiments. Much of scientific work consists of moving systematically down several pathways that turn out to be blind alleys before the scientist discovers that one pathway that proves productive. Of course, there are great differences within science in this regard. If the scientist is working on the testing or further elaboration of well-established principles, his work is more predictable. If he addresses himself to problems beyond the frontiers of knowledge, his projects become more unpredictable.

5. *Reference groups.* The production foreman and his superiors in line management tend to identify with the organization. That is, they judge their successes and failures in terms of the ways in which they are viewed by people *within* the organization. Scientists have a problem of dual loyalties. They see their success in terms of recognition not only within the company but also within their profession. They belong to professional associations, read the journals of the profession, attend professional meetings, and see their success to some extent determined by what they are able to publish about their work in scientific journals and by the reputation that they gather among scientists outside the company.

6. *Replaceability of personnel.* In most departments, if labour turnover is high, management may have to recognize a serious problem, but it does not have to worry that the resignation of a worker or even of a single first-line supervisor will jeopardize the performance of the plant. In the laboratory, however, the resignation of a single scientist may make the difference between success and failure in an important project. Superiors must therefore be much more seriously concerned with individual adjustment problems among scientists.

Leadership in scientific laboratories

These comparisons suggest that a different pattern of supervisory leadership is called for in the scientific laboratory. Although "close" supervision may be compatible with high production in some factory technologies, it is clear that this approach to the scientific laboratory will stifle creativity and drive scientists out of the company.

The director of a scientific laboratory finds little opportunity to tell subordinates what to do, yet he may play a vital role in helping them to achieve success in their work and in meeting the general goals of the company. It is now well recognized that the laboratory director must make allowance for the problem of dual loyalties, providing opportunities for a scientist to attend professional meetings, to report to his scientific colleagues on his work, and to publish. If he does not allow for such opportunities, the chances are that he will not be able to keep many good scientists.

Beyond providing these outside opportunities, what can the laboratory director do? He can play a very important role as representative of his laboratory to higher authorities. The effectiveness of the performance of his work group and the satisfactions of the members will depend to a large extent upon the projects that they get assigned to their department. The effective manager is in close consultation with the scientists in his department, and, as they develop ideas for projects on which they want to work, he undertakes to sell those projects to higher management. Thus his success in helping his subordinates to get the kind of work that they want to do contributes both to their morale and their productivity.

Although the laboratory manager's powers over his subordinates are far more limited than those of the manager in a production shop, there are important functions that he can perform for his subordinates so as to make them accept and even welcome his leadership. He can see to it that the scientists in his department have access to the goods and services and information that they need in order to do their job well. He can get recognition for the superior performance of his subordinates, bringing it to the attention of his own superiors and seeking rewards for the scientists in terms of increased salary and other symbols of higher status. He can help the scientists to interpret the significance of their work to higher management. The specialized scientist who knows the most about the project he is working on is often not able to communicate its significance effectively to nonspecialists, and the manager can play an important role in translating technical and scientific ideas into terms that make economic sense to laymen.

The composition of scientific work teams

The manager may also be influential in the composition of work teams. Where the outputs of the laboratory are produced by teams rather than by individuals (which is often the case), the results will depend not simply upon the talents and personalities of the team members but also upon the way in which they are able to work together. This means more than compatibility of personality or even the matching of scientific knowledge (*e.g.*, matching chemists with physicists); it means also a melding of "cognitive styles"—joining some scientists who are especially gifted in recognizing and diagnosing the essential elements of a problem with other scientists who perhaps lack this diagnostic skill but are very effective in working out the problem once its diagnosis has been agreed upon. If the team leader does not possess both these skills himself, clearly he must see to it that both skills are represented on the team.

The manager may sometimes have to function as mediator or arbitrator of differences that arise among his subordinates. Although he may try to encourage them to solve their problems among themselves, this may not always be possible, so it is important that he have skill in resolving the conflicts brought to him.

Finally, the effective laboratory manager functions to stimulate the development of ideas among scientists in his department. This seems paradoxical because one is naturally inclined to wonder how a manager who does not have the depth of knowledge of his subordinates in the various specialized activities under his general direction can serve to stimulate the development of their ideas. He does this by stimulating the communication among them in formal and informal discussions of work in progress and planned. As a discussion leader he may not have the competence to propose the solution to any scientific problem, and yet sometimes an intelligent man who is not immersed in a particular specialty can ask provocative questions that would not occur to the specialist.

THE ENGINEERS

Engineers play crucial roles in introducing change, yet their satisfaction in their work does not measure up to the importance of their functions. Although countless surveys have shown a correlation between the status of a position and the satisfaction of the men holding that position, the relationship breaks down for engineers. In surveys, engineers rank only slightly above blue-collar workers in their level of expressed job satisfaction. How is this low level of satisfaction to be accounted for? Some theorists have claimed to find the answer in role conflict—the conflict between the commitment of the engineers to the profession and their commitment to the company. If this diagnosis is correct, then for engineers as well as scientists, solutions should be found in the policy sometimes described as "parallel paths to progress." According to this organizational strategy, the engineer or scientist can achieve success and increasing economic rewards in the company in either of two pathways. One pathway is the usual one of advancement into supervision and management, in which the specialist gets farther and farther re-

Job satisfaction among engineers

moved from his specialty and more and more concerned with the direction of the activities of other men. The other pathway would reward individuals for their superior performance by giving them more prestigious titles and more money but keeping them directly involved in their professional specialties.

Allowing engineers a choice of careers, however, would have meaning only if they do indeed experience a "role conflict." Such an assumption may be doubtful. Because engineering is by nature an applied field, engineers do not face the lure and promised prestige of success in "pure engineering" as do many scientists in "pure science." Most engineers interpret success in terms of moving up in the company and set a relatively low value on recognition by their professional colleagues outside of the company. Moving up means not only more pay but also better opportunities to determine the projects that the engineer and his subordinates will work on. The selection of projects in turn affects the perceived success or failure of the engineering group and its manager. Power cannot be disentangled from the reputation for superior performance.

Relatively few engineers desire to retain the role of specialist at the workbench. This being the case, "staff" positions that are supposed to be rewards for superior technical performance come to be consolation prizes for engineers who are judged by their superiors not to be good enough for promotion into management but still useful enough to be retained within the company.

One must look elsewhere for the causes of dissatisfaction among engineers. Of particular importance are the types of engineering jobs to which men are assigned. In some large companies, numbers of engineers work in the same department on problems of such a routine nature as to be indistinguishable from draftsmen's work. In this setting, the engineer may feel that, like the blue-collar worker, he is just a cog in a machine. Where engineers have organized for collective bargaining purposes, it has been largely from such work situations that membership has been drawn. Even when engineers are not placed in such routine situations, they may be part of such large systems that each engineer cannot so readily feel that he is making a significant contribution.

There is also an important distinction between project organizations on the one hand and service or functional groups on the other. Those working to develop a particular project are likely to be much more satisfied with their work than those in a service department. The engineers in a service organization cannot identify with the product that others are producing; they find that they get little if any favourable recognition for their service; and they are often criticized for their alleged failures.

Compared with most other types of employees, engineers have to contend with an unstable social environment. Their employment may depend on the success of their company in securing contracts. A failure to get a particular contract may result in downgrading or layoffs of engineers. But even where employment and pay are secure, the engineer has difficulty in achieving a kind of social stability: he is assigned to one project group until its work is completed, and then he is likely to find himself on a different project with new associates. In fact, a project may not even be completed but be shut off in midstream by a higher management that rules that even technical success will not lead to an economically feasible product. The engineer thus is constantly faced with a shifting social scene over which he may have little control. Those who do make the most successful adjustment to this problem are the leaders who not only help develop projects but also have the wherewithal to sell higher management on the feasibility of the projects. Thus, building and retaining a stable work group may depend in large measure upon the ability of engineers to become "internal entrepreneurs," developing new project ideas and selling them up the line. This of course leads to increased pay, recognition, and higher positions for the successful engineer, so that success is inevitably tied up with the selection of one's own projects to work upon.

VII. Conflict and conflict resolution: union-management relations

Of the variety of conflicts found in industrial organizations, those involving union-management relations have received the most attention. These relations have to be seen in terms of an evolutionary process beginning with the organization of conflict and carrying on into the development of procedures that, though they may not eliminate conflict, at least provide for orderly procedures for the resolution of particular issues.

THE DEVELOPMENT OF A UNION

Organizing a union

Where the establishment of a union depends upon the vote of workers, in order to have any hopes for success organizers must begin on the basis of widespread dissatisfaction among workers. It is the task of the organizer to bring together workers so that they can make their discontents known to each other and establish bonds that form the basis of the union. In this stage the organizer plays a role described by Leonard Sayles as "the lawyer for the defense." Whatever the issue, the organizer seeks to place the blame on management and to show that only the establishment of a union can lead to the solution of the problem.

Winning recognition for the union and establishing contractual relations

In this stage, within the incipient local union, leadership tends to go toward the aggressive and eloquent. When the union has been recognized by management and collective relations come into being, the scene shifts markedly. Now the union leaders face complexities that were of no concern to them before. When the issue was simply recognition or nonrecognition of the union, union leaders had a single standard against which to judge their activities. When recognition is once achieved, especially if management negotiators have the will and skill to deescalate the hostilities, the union leader then has to discriminate among issues, weighing them in terms of both their importance to the membership and the possibilities of winning cases with management. If he fails to make gains on issues of special importance to the membership or precipitates conflict on issues in which the gains achieved do not turn out to balance the sacrifices of the members, the leader may lose his position.

Along with the shift from open conflict to contractual relations tends to go an increasing centralization and bureaucratization of the local union, especially when large units are involved. In the stage of organizing the union, success depends upon encouraging potential leaders in departments and work groups to define their own issues and mount an attack on management. When contractual relations have developed, the local union leader comes to recognize that an issue raised in one work group or department may have implications for other units of the plant, so that he cannot afford to let the departmental union stewards commit the union on an issue arising within a single work group until that issue has been assessed at the top levels of the local union. This tendency toward centralization is accelerated by parallel shifts in management's policies and procedures. When management recognizes that a decision made by a foreman in one department may commit the company to similar action throughout the plant, managers are inclined to require their foremen to check with higher authority before acceding to any union grievance or proposal. As the union leaders find that the foremen cannot make decisions, they tend to raise issues quickly to the higher levels where plant-wide considerations can be negotiated.

CAUSES OF UNION-MANAGEMENT CONFLICT OR COOPERATION

A great deal of attention has been paid to the causes of union-management conflict or cooperation. Some persons have contended that trust and goodwill are the "causes" of the good relations, but trust and goodwill cannot simply be willed into existence. There have to be prior conditions and experiences that prompt union and management officials to trust each other and entertain sentiments of goodwill.

Similarly, when management people have been asked

for the secret of getting along with a union, many have been inclined to answer, "You have to be firm, but fair." This is no more help than the mutual trust explanation. How is the meaning of firmness or fairness determined? What the manager calls firmness may be looked upon by the union man as blind stubbornness. What the manager calls fairness may be looked upon by the union man as offensive to elemental human rights.

Research suggests that there should be a structural approach to answering this question. In comparing cases in which union and management people seem to be getting along well together with cases in which conflict is apparent, one can expect to find consistent differences in the organization of interaction and activities of union and management officials. It may be useful to examine these differences at the plant level. Until the union enters the scene, management people are predominantly in the position of initiating interaction for workers and also initiating worker activities. Afterward, local union officers and their agents are doing the initiating—seeking out management people to present grievances or getting management to change a policy or procedure or reverse a decision that has been made. To this structural change management may respond in one of three ways. In the first pattern of response, management people seek to satisfy union leaders by yielding to their demands, on the theory that if management is as generous as it can afford to be, the union leaders will be satisfied and abandon their pressures against management. This strategy rewards union leaders in two ways: they get satisfaction both because their superiors in social status and economic resources (that is, management) have responded to their demands and because they have strengthened their position with rank-and-file workers by presenting them with rewards. In other words, management is providing psychological reinforcement for the very behaviour that it is seeking to discourage. This first type of strategy is necessarily short-lived. Management officials eventually discover that their attempts to win over the union leaders through generous concessions are serving only to push the company into a precarious economic condition, so that finally management officials must refuse to give any more. Reversal of past practices can be expected to lead to conflict between union and management.

A second type of strategy is associated with a quite different management theory. The executives see the problem in terms of power and feel that every effort must be made to define and then to defend those prerogatives that necessarily belong to management. This relationship is characterized by a formalization of relations with the union, as management seeks to examine each union initiative strictly in terms of the collective bargaining agreement. According to this approach, contacts with union officers, between the annual bargaining sessions, are confined almost exclusively to grievance meetings. In these meetings, of course, union leaders take the initiative in bringing up problems on which they demand action from management. Management people seek to respond in those cases in which the grievance seems clearly justified in terms of the contract but otherwise to hold firm. Management refuses to be pressured by actions taken outside of the grievance procedure. For example, in the case of a departmental wildcat strike, management people characteristically refuse to enter into any discussion of the underlying problems until the workers in question have gone back to work.

This policy, if consistently applied, may tend to discourage conflict during the life of a collective bargaining agreement. In fact, wildcat strikes tend to occur only if management procedures and policies are unclear and inconsistent. If workers early experience a wildcat strike with the result that they lose pay, fail to get their problems discussed until they go back to work, and perceive that management still treats their problems in terms of a formal interpretation of the contract, they and their union leaders are inclined to lose faith in the utility of wildcat strikes and other such pressures. They stop resorting to them.

Although a strategy that management uses to defend its prerogatives may tend to discourage "disorderly" conflict, it can nevertheless provoke the hostility of union leaders. If they are blocked from taking any initiative with management except in the grievance procedure, they will naturally devote much time and effort to the discovery and development of issues that they can push within the grievance procedure. Moreover, having only these limited means of expressing their sentiments during the long periods between bargaining sessions, they will be inclined to push a tough policy in confronting management at these very sessions in which they bargain for new contracts.

Although the "soft" and "hard" management strategies described above sound quite different, they are similar in important respects and thus yield similar management attitudes. In both cases, management leaves the initiative in the union-management relationship entirely in the hands of the union leaders. With this approach, union leaders are constantly coming to management to demand changes (which may be costly to management). The management people feel on the defensive, complain that the union is not considering the welfare of the total organization, and come to see the union leaders as enemies who—sooner or later—must be resisted. Management people do not see that they are getting any rewards from their dealings with union leaders. At best, they see themselves as paying a price for the maintenance of peace.

Strategies of reciprocity

In cases in which union and management people claim to be getting along well together, one sees that management has abandoned its defensive position. Management people, from the foremen to higher levels, tend to take more initiative in bringing management's problems to the union. For example, the foreman may feel that, according to the contract, he has a right to discipline a particular worker, but he may nevertheless decide that he will first talk with the departmental union steward to see if the steward can help to straighten out the problem. Similarly, at higher levels management may bring to the attention of union officers its problems of productivity, absenteeism, changing of work assignments, and so on. A reciprocity develops between union and management. The management people continue to respond to initiatives from the union officers but they also take initiative with the union people in seeking their help on management problems. An implicit exchange develops, with each party getting something out of the relationship with the other party. When this happens, one sees problems being peaceably resolved to the mutual satisfaction of the parties, and one sees the attitudes of mutual trust and goodwill developing.

This reciprocity may not develop at all levels of the organization, and at points where it is lacking, there will be, predictably, tensions and negative attitudes. For example, there may be a situation of reciprocity at the top level, where union officers and management people develop sympathy for each other's problems and take action on these problems down the line, but the union may then be insufficiently responsive to the problems being experienced and expressed by the rank-and-file members. In this situation the union leaders may be highly critical of the rank and file for not understanding the "true facts" of the functioning of the plant, and the workers will be increasingly hostile to the union leaders for "selling out" to management. Unless the local union leaders can continue to be responsive to the rank-and-file workers, there may be a split in the local union, followed by a contest for local union office and an overthrow of the established leadership.

Approaches to collective bargaining

Analyzing the collective bargaining process between union and management representatives, American behavioural scientists Richard Walton and Robert McKersie have diagnosed two types of bargaining approaches, "distributive" and "integrative." In following the distributive approach, the union is, in effect, saying to management: "Of what you have, let us see how much we can take away from you." And management is naturally inclined to hold back and resist the demands. This approach yields antagonistic sentiments and is likely to lead to open conflict. Following the integrative approach, the parties seek to define and resolve problems whose resolution can be directly beneficial to both parties. Where this approach is followed, management people as well as union leaders are proposing problems that need to be resolved, and the discussion proceeds in an atmosphere of general goodwill. Although one might expect to find some pure cases of distributive bargaining, one is exceedingly unlikely to find any cases in which the entire negotiation process follows an integrative pattern. In some cases the parties may be able to spend much time on issues of mutual concern, but the question of the size of the wage package always poses a distributive problem. Even in the absence of pure cases, one can make some predictions regarding the relative frequency of distributive versus integrative problems in the bargaining process. Cases marked by predominance of distributive problems will be characterized by hostile sentiments between the parties and are likely to be accompanied by such conflicts as planned slowdowns, refusals to accept overtime work when management is behind in its production schedule, and even strikes. As the types of problems move toward the integrative end of the continuum, one can expect to observe more favourable interpersonal sentiments and a lower incidence of conflict behaviour.

This approach to the collective bargaining process is not unlike the day-to-day union-management relations in the plant, even though the setting and structure of interactions are quite different. In both cases, harmonious relations are distinguished by a pattern of reciprocity in which the management as well as the union brings in problems for discussion and action and in which there is an effort to arrive jointly at solutions of mutual advantage.

BIBLIOGRAPHY. M. CROZIER, *Le phénomèna bureaucratique* (1964; Eng. trans. 1964), a classic study of organizational behaviour in France; F. HERZBERG, B. MAUSNER, and B. SNYDERMAN, *The Motivation to Work*, 2nd ed. (1959), systematic statement of the influential and controversial two-factor theory of job satisfaction and motivation; R.R. RITTI, *Engineers and the Industrial Corporation* (1970), an examination of the roles and problems of engineers in a large industrial organization with a high level of technological and scientific development; F.J. ROETHLISBERGER and W.J. DICKSON, *Management and the Worker* (1939), the pioneering study that opened the field to behavioral scientists, still worth reading; L.R. SAYLES, *Managerial Behavior* (1964), an approach to analysis of managerial behaviour emphasizing lateral and diagonal relations; C.R. WALKER, *Toward the Automatic Factory* (1957), a case study of the introduction of an automatic tube mill in the steel industry; R.E. WALTON and R.B. MCKERSIE (eds.), *A Behavioral Theory of Labor Negotiations* (1965), an interpretation of collective bargaining in terms of integrative versus distributive issues; W.F. WHYTE, *Organizational Behavior: Theory and Application* (1969), a textbook that generally follows the approach of this article; J. WOODWARD, *Industrial Organization: Theory and Practice* (1965), the study that provoked a reorientation of research to take into account the behavioral impact of different types of technology; M.Y. YOSHINO, *Japan's Managerial System: Tradition and Innovation* (1968), the best assessment of Japanese management in terms of historical development and current organization and activities.

(W.F.Wh.)

Industrial Design

Everything made by man has been designed somehow, somewhere, by someone; behind every product lies a chain of decisions leading up to its actual physical presence. This obvious point underlines the immense scope of the word design. It may also prepare the reader to accept much broader definitions of the subject than were previously current, for one of the most marked characteristics of the 20th century has been the breaking down of barriers between one discipline and another and the merging of what were once looked upon as separate processes or professions. Just as fine artists seem voluntarily to have departed from their conventional media and thus to have erased their own dividing lines until no one can say for certain whether a work of art is a painting, a sculpture, or even a piece of industrial craftsmanship, so designers have been poaching on each other's formerly established preserves, with the result that familiar elassifications, such as architecture, engineering, or industrial design, are no longer as watertight or meaningful as they once were. Indeed, the designer today may be anything from a typographer to an electronics engineer, and often "the designer" is now, rather than an individual, a team comprising many different specialists.

Role of the designer

Expansion of the designer's role has been worldwide. It has been recognized in the United States by the president of the Organization for Social and Technical Innovation at Cambridge, Massachusetts, Donald A. Schon:

> The modern corporation does not commit itself to a single product line or even to a single technology; its commitment is to a major human function and to the changing technologies and organisational relations required to carry it out. . . . The obsolescence of products—not the obsolescence of particular products but of products as the unit of design—creates the requirement for a new kind of design and designer, namely the design and designer of systems—*e.g.*, of housing, feeding, clothing, etc.—to which business systems are coming to respond. . . . Design becomes indistinguishable from systems developments.

The designer's expanded role is also recognized in Japan, as in a statement by a past chairman of the Japanese Industrial Designers Association, Katsuhei Toyoguchi: "Industrial designers in Japan must not become isolated from wider horizons lest they be left behind through their own specialisations." The Japanese critic Marsaru Katzumie made a similar point in an essay called "Industrial Design and Living Planning" (1964) when he argued that just as architecture has expanded to embrace city planning and graphic design had expanded to embrace corporate images and the visual language of communication, so industrial design must extend beyond the individual product to the "modern living environment." And Dzhermen Mikhaylovich Gvishiani, the vice chairman of the State Committee for Science and Technology of the Council of Ministers of the U.S.S.R., speaking at the Sixth Congress of the International Council of Societies of Industrial Design (1969), declared: "Design is a planning activity which is organically bound up with social, economic, scientific and technological progress."

THE ESSENCE OF GOOD DESIGN

Definitions of good design must therefore depend upon their contexts. They will vary widely from article to article and industry to industry. For instance, the design content in one product may be 90 percent a matter of electrical or mechanical efficiency and only 10 percent a matter of appearance; in another the proportions may be the other way around, with all the emphasis on form or colour. In the former category there may well be objective yardsticks by which to measure the quality of the design. In the latter, assessments will almost certainly be subjective.

Attempts to define good design

There have been in the last 50 years or so valiant attempts to reach a universal definition of good design, many of them with ethical overtones, such as that of William Richard Lethaby, English author and architect: "Good design is the welldoing of what needs doing." Most of these, however, have been so large and self-evident as to be almost platitudinous. But even those that have attempted more precision—such as the aphorism of Frank Pick, onetime head of London's public transport system and president of the British Design and Industries Association: "Good design is intelligence made visible" or the favourite bon mot of Georges Combet, the former president both of the French gas industry and the French Institut d'Esthétique Industrielle: "Good design is economy of means"—need qualification and explanation. In the context of the kind of pop art and youthful fantasy epitomized in the late 1960s by London's Carnaby Street, "intelligence made visible" becomes altogether too sobersided, while in the context of, say, Art Nouveau or a new Baroque, "economy of means" could appear irrelevant. Equally, the classical dictum of the famous modern architect Ludwig Mies van der Rohe—that in architecture and design "less is more"—would apply generally only during phases of simple taste. In a richly ornamental phase, such as the Rococo in Europe or the princely Regency in England, "the more the better" might sound equally convincing as a guide to good design—which is not to say that there are no real values. It is simply to warn that the spirit of the age must be considered.

In this modern age, therefore, when, as Marshall McLuhan, 20th-century Canadian critic, has pointed out, action and reaction occur almost at the same time, it need not be surprising that older, soberer, slower measurements may no longer seem adequate. Appreciation must now be geared to different time scales. Men are changing from a belief in permanent universal values to a recognition that a design may be valid at a particular time for a particular purpose to a particular group of people in a particular set of circumstances, but that outside those shifting limits it may not be valid at all. Thus, there may be coeval but quite dissimilar solutions that can still be equally acceptable to differing groups—a miniskirt (or a maxiskirt) for the teen-ager, something less (or more) revealing for the matron; painted pop furniture for the young marrieds, teak or rosewood for the ageing. A product must be good of its kind for the situation and purpose for which it has been designed.

If cheap paper furniture were to come to stay, man would have to learn to live with its early decomposition and replacement. He might also have to learn to live with an entirely new palette, for bright fairground colours have long marched with ephemeral trivia. It might be wise, in fact, to recognize several planes of creativity and not to try to mold them into one homogeneous whole or to subject them to one universal law. Invention and imagination in outward appearances may well contribute increasingly to the design of consumer goods and indeed to the environment as a whole, even at the apparent expense of logic or of those rational fitness-for-purpose, truth-to-materials principles that were so widely accepted between World Wars I and II as being safe sheet anchors. The kaleidoscopic irreverence of a teen-age boutique and the deliberate gaudiness of a popular restaurant, while appearing to contradict much received opinion of the late 19th century and first half of the 20th concerning the use of ornament ("it would be greatly for our aesthetic good if we could refrain entirely from the use of ornament"—Louis Sullivan [U.S. architect]) may yet in their own impudent way make a positive contribution to the environment. But they will do this only when and because they are convinced, conscientious accomplishments.

Questions of morality and quality in design

And so a return is made almost to moral judgments. The need is still for discipline, for efficiency, and for common sense in the midst of nonsense. The need is to latch on to quality, whether of thought or material or structure; for, as Sir Gordon Russell, a former director of the British Council of Industrial Design, said in the first issue of *Design* magazine (January 1949), "Good design is an essential part of a standard of quality." The dilemma imposed on professional or propagandist design organizations or on educational institutions by the liberation, even license, of a permissive, precocious, commercially abundant popular culture can be resolved only by once more seeking the truth, though this time the truth is likely to be more subjective and elusive. Many would, then, agree that evidence of conviction—conviction made visible—is what schools of art and design centres should look for today, not such mutable values as usefulness or pleasure. Only then, it is suggested, will the contributors be sifted from the charlatans.

Neither should there be forgotten the other half of Confucius' definition of a real artist craftsman—or, say, of a real industrial designer today—namely "his ability to create something new with his traditions that are old," for this ability or inability has been not only at the root of a lot of problems facing the old craft-based industries but is central to design in the newer technological ones, where products must be up to date if they are not to be out of date. These twin pressures—tradition and innovation—have indeed been the main influences on design ever since the Industrial Revolution.

IMPACT OF THE INDUSTRIAL REVOLUTION

Apart from the unconscious sympathy that has united the tastes of different kinds of artists and craftsmen in all great periods of design, two factors characterized the pre-Industrial Revolution era. The first was the close (often personal) relationship between a maker and his customer. The second was the sure eye of the customer himself. In many cases, too, the maker was also the retailer, knowing his customers as well as they knew him. Thus was built up a rare degree of confidence between craftsman and client or between builder and client, and from it stemmed things of such excellence and beauty that people have ever since looked back on those times and those products with nostalgia. Many of these products survived to point the contrast between the handmade and the mass-produced, providing on the one hand a whip with which to beat the machine-made product but on the other a curb with which to inhibit industrial experiment. The very qualities of those handmade designs so impressed succeeding generations of manufacturers that they felt challenged to copy by machine. Not unnaturally the machine-made copy seldom measured up to the original. At the same time, the old personal relationship between maker and consumer began to disappear, specialization and subdivision of activities taking the place of total craftsmanship and regional and, later, national distribution taking the place of personal, parochial dealings.

The crafts-man–customer rift created by the Industrial Revolution

Thus, the Industrial Revolution separated the maker from his customer and, in many cases, even separated the maker from the final product to which he had contributed, so that he saw or knew only a part of the whole. And between maker and customer came a host of middlemen, who, not knowing how things were made, could not know how they should be made and could not set or maintain any standards other than statistical ones; as Lewis Mumford, modern American social critic, has said, they counted figures until only figures counted. And so society gradually slipped from that ideal state of affairs, in which no one would make and no one would sell anything to which he himself would not give house room, into those cynical attitudes whereby a manufacturer would squander his days churning out items of which he was often privately ashamed, while a retailer would spend his time selling merchandise for which he felt no personal responsibility—and all this, then as now, in the name of giving the public what it wanted.

It was this collapse of standards, coinciding in the middle of the 19th century with the emergence of a new rich middle class, which was long on energy but short on education, that spurred such English thinkers of the time as John Ruskin and William Morris into protesting against all manufacturers and into believing the only way to achieve acceptable standards of design was to return to the honest qualities of medieval craftsmanship and, thus, inevitably to medieval appearances. Their contemporaries, however, were more than willing to follow any lead backward into the past, and so what had started as a protest against second-rate machine-made reproductions in fact gave a further fillip to the demand for antiques and commercial variations on the antique. And thus was lost a great opportunity to rethink the product in the light of the new processes by which it could be made. The mid-19th-century manufacturer was unable to perceive that his machine had introduced an entirely new factor into the problems of designing. He accepted without question the easy notion that art was something that could be bought in the marketplace and applied to industry, and thus, as Sir Herbert Read later observed, "by one of those monstrous misapplications of words which can confuse thought for centuries, the epithet 'applied' was taken from ornament and given to art." The advent of what is today known as industrial design was thus long delayed by the ascendancy of this 19th-century conception of applied art.

There was one area of design in the 19th century, however, that was relatively free from historical, romantic, artistic associations. The first people to point to this other stream of mid-19th-century design were the many critics of the exhibits in the famous Crystal Palace of

1851 in London. From this Great Exhibition stemmed many of the heavy, turgid patterns and designs that filled the Victorian catalogues and also many obese shapes in furniture that have lingered on into the 20th century. At the same time, the Great Exhibition opened the door to a flood of amateurish handicrafts full of fantasy and dexterity but with few of the qualities of traditional craftsmanship. These and their machine-made imitations rapidly became the junk that cluttered the Victorian home, particularly the humbler home: as Adolf Loos observed at the end of the 19th century, "the lower the standard of a people, the more lavish are its ornaments"; in other words, the poorer the family, the more conspicuous waste becomes a conventional necessity.

Criticism of Victorian design

It was this element of pretentiousness in Victorian design that Sir Matthew Digby Wyatt, one of the English architects and critics of the mid-19th century, most deplored. He blamed manufacturers for "borrowing ornaments expressive of lofty associations and applying them to mean objects." The members of the official Great Exhibition jury must have felt the same, for in their report they regretted that there had not been

> more specimens of ordinary furniture for general use; work whose merits consist in correct proportion, simple but well-considered design, beauty of material, and perfect workmanship.

One can in those words already begin to hear the voice of the modern designer and, even more clearly perhaps, in another contemporary comment on the same exhibition, which stated:

> Some sections and especially that of machinery, feeling their pre-eminence to be secure and undoubted, were content to be plain and unpretending. The only beauty attempted was that which the stringent application of mechanical science to the material world could supply; and in the truthfulness, perseverance, and severity with which that idea was carried out there was developed a style of art at once national and grand.

If one added to that a passage from a lecture given at the Royal Society of Arts in the early 1860s by the Victorian architect William Burges, one might be led to assume that the Modern Movement of the 20th century had its roots deep in the 19th; for Burges, in seeking the causes for the low standard of design of British manufactures in his time, found the principal one to be "a want of distinctive architecture." "Until the question of architectural style gets settled," he said,

> it is utterly hopeless to think about any great improvement in modern art. It is most sincerely to be hoped that in course of time we may get something of our own of which we need not be ashamed.

Then with remarkable foresight he added, "This may perhaps take place in the 20th century; it certainly as far as I can see will not occur in the 19th."

He was probably right about architecture both for its influence on design in general and for the conflict of styles that lasted well into the 20th century, but, unlike the critics of the Great Exhibition, he had overlooked the prime contribution of many of his own contemporaries, namely the Victorian engineers. These great and typical 19th-century figures had been quietly pursuing their own revolutionary way, designing and building great structures for the railway age that owed almost nothing to past styles and almost everything to the new materials and methods that enabled them to solve hitherto unposed problems. Of all 19th-century edifices it is the great engineering works, the railway tunnels, the suspension bridges, and the cast-iron vaults of the train sheds that have really stood the test of time, for "art" was a long way from the thoughts of their designers. It was only when the architects intervened or when engineers succumbed to some fashionable architectural influence that these fine things faltered and slipped into some fancy dress or other. Equally, it was 19th-century technology, not 19th-century art, that produced the fine engines for factories and the splendid locomotives for the railroads. If one had to isolate the single most constructive influence in 19th-century design, one might not be wide of the mark in choosing the concept of transport or mobility; for it was this that really captured the imagination of the 19th century—and what captures the imagination of any age is certain to produce the most typical and interesting design, whether it is a medieval cathedral or a supersonic jet.

Revolutionary Victorian engineers

Prince Albert, consort of Queen Victoria, must have felt something of this when he said at the Mansion House banquet to launch the Crystal Palace:

Prince Albert's views

> I conceive it to be the duty of every educated person closely to watch and study the time in which he lives. Nobody will doubt for a moment that we are living at a period of most wonderful transition. The distances which separated the different nations and parts of the globe are gradually vanishing before the achievements of modern invention and we can traverse them with incredible speed.

By drawing attention to the new possibilities opened up by new methods of transport, Prince Albert touched on the one development that more than any other was going to colour the century to come; for looking back over the last 100 years, there can be little doubt that the most forthright and typical designs have been by-products of the idea of transport, of travel, of speed, or, more generally, of mobility. And if one extends mobility to cover the related ideas of lightness, flexibility, portability, and even of transience and economy, one begins to arrive at the sort of yardsticks by which 20th-century design can best be measured. But neither the Prince Consort nor any of his contemporaries could see that far ahead, even though Prince Albert had vision enough, when showing Joseph Paxton's plans for the Crystal Palace to Queen Victoria, to say: "Look well on these, my dear, for you may be looking at the architecture of the future." The Crystal Palace was indeed a forerunner of much of the modern architecture of the 20th century; it was the first large building made of metal and glass, prefabricated in standard units to a repeating module and erected in an incredibly short time. Together with the equally original work of the 19th-century engineers, it can claim its place in the family tree of the Modern Movement.

But so can William Morris and the other reformers of his generation, though care should be taken to distinguish between these two Victorian influences—on the one hand, the often anonymous work of the engineers and, on the other, the fully credited work of the artist craftsmen. It took many years for these two streams to come together, for they were hardly on speaking terms at the beginning. Had Ruskin and Morris not been so blinded by distaste for the ordinary commercial products of the Industrial Revolution, they might have understood and welcomed the simple honesty of the engineers and joined forces with them. They might even have accepted the challenge of Sir Henry Cole, English public servant and educator, to the Society of Arts in 1847:

The conflict between commercial and artistic design

> Of high art in this country there is abundance, of mechanical industry and invention an unparalleled profusion. The thing still remaining to be done is to effect the combination of the two, to wed high art with mechanical skill.

Instead they took solace in the belief that only medieval standards of craftsmanship could provide the moral fibre and sincerity that commercialism lacked. Thus, though theirs were the first voices raised in protest, their contribution never came to grips with the real problems of incipient technology but was diverted into the backwaters of the Arts and Crafts Movement which attempted to revive handicrafts in England in the 1880s and '90s.

20TH-CENTURY MOVEMENTS

It is necessary before discussing design in the 20th century to have spent some time on 19th-century Britain, for so much that is essential to modern conceptions of quality and technique stemmed either directly from or in reaction to what had happened in the Victorian Age, whether by way of protest or of practice. Had it not been for the emotional protests of William Morris and his followers or, in the next generation, the more intellectual protests and practice of men like Arthur Heygate Mackmurdo, Charles Francis Annesley Voysey, and Charles Rennie Mackintosh, it is possible that the Art Nouveau movement would not have developed as it did at the turn of the century; while, if it had not been for the anonymous practice of the Victorian engineers, it is possible that the fundamental contribution of the German Bauhaus would have been delayed. Both these movements—Art Nouveau and Bauhaus—have been decisive in directing design in the 20th century and both have a continuing influence. Art Nouveau in its day seemed to bridge the two centuries spiritually as well as chronologically. Some have called it the final fling of 19th-century love of ornament. It could equally be called the first general international revolt, for, although there had since 1850 been more than enough naturalistic floral and vegetal decoration, there had been nothing quite like the twining Art Nouveau tendrils with their highly stylized flowers and foliage. If the 1850s tried to imitate, the 1900s tried to symbolize nature. Also, as if to emphasize organic growth, there was in most cases a markedly linear quality and even a verticality about these designs, whether in book illustration, wrought iron, glass, china, or brass. Although it had its roots in nature, it was emphatically not an imitative, revivalist style, for it broke with many petrified traditions and led architects and designers to think twice about hackneyed historical motifs. It was probably this combination of innovation and exuberance that in the 1960s recommended the style again to many young designers, particularly in graphic and two-dimensional fields. It would be wrong, however, to look upon Art Nouveau simply as a decorative style. Its break with tradition was more fundamental than that, for its architect exponents—Mackintosh and Voysey in Britain, Henry van de Velde and Victor Horta in Belgium, Louis Sullivan and even the young Frank Lloyd Wright in the United States—were all influenced by the organic force of the movement that thus prepared the way for the more radical philosophies of the next generation of reformers.

Art Nouveau

By the end of the first decade of the 20th century, the time was clearly ripe to pull together all these varied influences, each of which had contributed to the liberation of the architect and designer from preconceived notions. There was so much in the air, so many experimental minds exploring new but similar lines of thought, that someone was needed to set the compass and, as so often in history, the times produced the man. His name was Walter Gropius. As a young architect he had worked in the office of Peter Behrens, another great German innovator who, apart from designing many minor electrical appliances, had in 1909 built in Berlin the first really modern factory building, a great hall for making turbines. Behrens introduced the young Gropius to the idea of systematical study of the problems posed by any new building rather than reliance on accepted styles. Gropius became obsessed, as he later wrote, by the conviction that modern constructional technique could not be denied expression in architecture and that that expression might demand the use of unprecedented form—an obsession that he soon put into practice in his first famous buildings in Germany, the Fagus Works at Alfeld-an-der-Leine in 1911 and the office building in the Werkbund Exposition at Cologne in 1914.

Walter Gropius

With the Fagus Works modern architecture as known today had arrived—and so had the philosophy and thinking upon which the Modern Movement in design is based. The important point to note is that the outward forms of the New Architecture should not be the personal whims of individual architects searching for self-expression or novelty for novelty's sake (that would have been as fruitless as the Victorian conception of art for art's sake) but should be, as Gropius wrote, "the inevitable logical product of the intellectual, social, and technical conditions of our age." With the arrival of this new architecture, an entirely different approach to designing could be pursued emphasizing the most logical, practical, and economical solutions. This analytical, structural approach distinguishes the design of the 20th century from previous periods, and from it stems not only the liberation of the modern designer from preconceived notions of styles or forms but also his proper subjugation to practical considerations of use, materials, and manufacture.

The Bauhaus. It was in 1919 that Walter Gropius went to Weimar, Germany, as head of the Arts and Crafts School and also of the Weimar Academy of Fine Arts, his first action being to amalgamate the two institutions into one school of design, known ever since as the Bauhaus. That amalgamation underlined his belief that the divorce between the fine and the not-so-fine arts had been the cause of 19th-century degeneration in design. It was, he said, the rise of the academies, of "salon art," that had spelled the gradual decay of the spontaneous traditional art that had permeated the life of the whole people. In this, of course, he was a follower of Ruskin and Morris; however, unlike them, he insisted that his students should live wholeheartedly in their own age—the machine age.

It was thus from the Bauhaus—first at Weimar, later at Dessau, Germany—that the idea of "industrial design" arrived to change the whole pattern of designing for industry. No longer were manufacturers to buy designs or art produced in studios in the hope of being able to apply them in their works; now the designer himself was to become a complete technician able to design for the machine. The Bauhaus workshops became laboratories working out practical new designs for everyday articles that could be put into mass production, with the students themselves being put through intensive training in handwork in order to learn to handle tools and materials—not so that they should become craftsmen, as such, but so that they should grasp the whole sequence of manufacture. This practical instruction was a stepping stone to understanding of standardization and simplification, the function of handwork being the preparation of prototypes for mass production. Architects and designers worked side by side, because Gropius was convinced not only that architecture would become more and more a matter of industrial prefabrication and standardization (as it has) but also that only by giving architects and designers a common training could the products of industry take their place in the new architecture. "This idea of the fundamental unity underlying all branches of design was," he said, "my guiding inspiration in founding the original Bauhaus." His answer to those who feared a dull uniformity from standardization:

The emergence of Industrial design

> In all great epochs of history the existence of standards—that is the conscious adoption of type-forms—has been the criterion of a polite and well-ordered society; for it is commonplace that repetition of the same things for the same purpose exercises a settling and civilizing influence on men's minds.

Unhappily, the politics of nationalism were soon to disrupt Germany and to drive such sanity underground or abroad, but Germany's loss was the world's gain, for emigrants from the Bauhaus—Ludwig Mies van der Rohe, Marcel Breuer, László Moholy-Nagy, Paul Klee, Wassily Kandinsky, Herbert Bayer, and others, including Gropius himself—carried the message to other lands, where it was to mingle with and enhance indigenous strivings.

Scandinavian developments. In Scandinavia the ground was particularly well prepared, for Sweden had long had an active arts and crafts society (the Svenska Slöjdföreningen, founded in 1845) whose members had taken good note of the founding in 1907 of the Deutscher Werkbund, a voluntary association of German manufacturers, designers, and laymen that had been among the first to welcome the preaching and practice of the Bauhaus. By 1915 the Svenska Slöjdföreningen was actively promoting the idea of beauty and function in everyday things. The conditions in Sweden were especially favourable to this kind of propaganda, for the country, at peace in the middle of war, was emerging from a rural into an industrial economy without losing the countryman's sense of quality and fitness for purpose. At the same time, Sweden remained fundamentally democratic and broadly classless, two characteristics that have strongly coloured modern Swedish design as first unveiled to the world in the great manifesto exhibition of 1930 in Stockholm, organized by pioneers like Erik Gunnar Asplund, Gregor Paulsson, and Sven Markelius. It was from this exhibition and from the teachings of the Svenska Slöjdföreningen and the Konstfackskolan (the Royal College of Art of Stockholm) that stemmed the essential common sense and charm of so much modern

Swedish architecture and design and also the worldwide export, 20 years later, of so many Scandinavian artifacts. Indeed, the Danes and the Finns and, to a lesser degree, the Norwegians were not slow to follow suit—the Danes, with names such as Kaare Klint, Arne Jacobsen, Finn Juhl, Hans Wegner, Børge Mogensen, being pre-eminent in furniture and the Finns, with artists such as Kaj Franck, Tapio Wirkkala, Timo Sarpaneva, and of course the great architect and universal designer Alvar Aalto, excelling in glass.

The Netherlands. Just as Sweden and Denmark took advantage of their neutrality in World War I to develop new standards, so the neutral Netherlands provided a platform for a splendidly revolutionary group of architects, painters, designers, and philosophers who in 1917 launched a publication and a movement called de Stijl in opposition to the then solid, pompous, and bourgeois standards of Dutch architecture and design. The group advocated complete purification of all the plastic arts. The leader of the group, Theo van Doesburg, wrote that only the completely abstract can express the human essence with precision; sensitivity and emotion in the arts were inferior, unworthy attributes. "Art," he said, "should not move the heart." He and his collaborators—painters like Piet Mondrian and Bart van der Leck and architects and designers like Gerrit Thomas Rietveld, Jacobus Johannes Pieter Oud, and Cor van Eesteren—aimed to establish a simple, universal, utopian aesthetic capable in any medium of expressing the essential characteristics of the modern age, among which lucidity and tidiness should take a high place. Mondrian's square, spare, bare abstracts became in a sense the handwriting for the whole group. A chair by Rietveld or a house by Oud would express the same abstraction, for de Stijl was nothing if not consistent. Because it was so consistent and disciplined, its influence spread in the 1920s and '30s far beyond The Netherlands, but whereas the Bauhaus offered freedom of expression, within the limitations of industrial production, de Stijl offered dogmatic straitjackets of verticals, horizontals, and primary colours. It was, as its name implies, a deliberate style and as such was bound to be both short-lived (it folded with its magazine in the mid-1930s) and the subject of later re-examination and imitation (as in the late 1960s).

De Stijl

France. The link between France and The Netherlands in this context could be said to be the painter: just as the Dutch abstractionists epitomized de Stijl, so the Cubists were the first artists between the wars in France to influence design in the wider context; and whereas functionalism was the mainstream of German and Scandinavian design in the 1920s and '30s, expressionism was the main force in France—and later still in Italy. At the 1925 International Exhibition of Decorative Arts in Paris, there was a spate of expressionism, over-ornamented and trivially neo-Cubist but well received commercially. Apart, however, from the jazz-age angularity of many of the exhibits (a feature that found an echo in the late 1960s), the 1925 Paris exhibition was famous for the pavilion of protest, L'Esprit Nouveau, that was staged there by Le Corbusier and his friends. This in its way was as dramatic an expression of modern design as was, four years later, the famous pavilion of Mies van der Rohe at the International Exposition (Barcelona). But major French contributions to modern industrial design had, like the major Italian ones, to wait until after World War II, when names such as Henri Viénot and Roger Tallon in France and Gio Ponti, Enrico Peressutti, Marco Zanuso, Battista Pininfarina, Marcello Nizzoli, and a host of others in Italy claimed the world's attention.

United States. It was, however, in the United States that the actual profession of industrial design was really founded in a search for new products during the Great Depression of the 1930s. If such pioneers as Walter Dorwin Teague, Norman Bel Geddes, Raymond Loewy, and Henry Dreyfuss were in the early days self-confessed streamliners and commercial stylists, they and their successors later steered a more rational, functional course, influenced perhaps by the modern movements in Europe. At all events, it was in the United States that the profession was first recognized and exploited by industry, and it is still to the United States that the world looks for major examples of systems design, company design policies, and corporate identities by men such as Eliot Noyes and Charles Eames. It is notable, too, that in the United States the industrial designer has been regularly called upon in those sophisticated areas of technology and human activity that are the most typical of this century—namely aviation in its widest sense. At least two of the first generation pioneers—Walter Dorwin Teague and Henry Dreyfuss—had worked for leading U.S. aircraft constructors, and Walter Dorwin Teague's office was called in by the United States Air Force to work with the architects Skidmore, Owings and Merrill on the interior design and furnishing of the United States Air Force Academy at Colorado Springs. Even the National Aeronautics and Space Administration has not overlooked the industrial designer's contribution, for very early in the space program President Kennedy called upon Raymond Loewy to help design the human-comfort factors in orbiting space stations.

Importance of aviation in U.S. design

CONTEMPORARY TRENDS

Thus, the designer has progressed in the last hundred years from individual artist craftsmanship to the most advanced realms of modern technology, taking in on the way all manner of essential household goods from irons to refrigerators; every breed of vehicle from tractors to automobiles; every sort of office appliance from typewriter to computer; and, increasingly, many types of capital goods used by industry indoors and out-of-doors from machine tools to cranes and earth movers.

In short, the industrial designer is now an indispensable member of the industrial team. This applies not only in the United States and the older technologically developed countries of Europe or in the more recently industrialized countries like the U.S.S.R. and Japan, in both of which industrial design is a highly regarded pursuit (in the U.S.S.R. more perhaps for the contribution it can make to factory equipment and amenities; in Japan for the great impetus it has given to the export trade, particularly in portable television sets, cameras, and binoculars), but also in the emergent countries.

Industrial design has been recognized as of international educational importance by UNESCO through its support for the International Council of Societies of Industrial Design (ICSID), a worldwide grouping of professional design societies and government-sponsored design councils and centres founded in London in 1957. By 1972 it comprised nearly 60 societies from nearly 40 countries, with new ones applying to join each year. One of the best and most authoritative definitions of industrial design or, rather, of the industrial designer was written into the ICSID Constitution that was adopted at the first general assembly of the organization in Stockholm in 1959. It is worth quoting, perhaps, not because it stood much chance of survival unamended for very long, since such definitions are seldom definitive—indeed, a special commission was soon set up to try to redefine the activity, an attempt that was finally frustrated at the 1971 General Assembly at Barcelona, where it was agreed to drop definitions from the Constitution altogether—but because it well described the scope of designers working for industry at the middle of the century and, by implication, the kind of personal qualifications and professional training needed at that time to make a successful career. It read:

Definition of an industrial designer

> An Industrial Designer is one who is qualified by training, technical knowledge, experience and visual sensibility to determine the materials, construction, mechanisms, shape, colour, surface finishes and decoration of objects which are reproduced in quantity by industrial processes. The Industrial Designer may, at different times, be concerned with all or only some of these aspects of an industrially produced object.

In order to be able to include graphic and other two-dimensional designers, the ICSID definition continued:

> The Industrial Designer may also be concerned with the problems of packaging, advertising, exhibiting and marketing, when the resolution of such problems requires visual appreciation in addition to technical knowledge and experience.

The last paragraph of the definition widened the scope still further, for it stated:

> The Designer for craft based industries or trades where hand processes are used for production is deemed to be an Industrial Designer when the work produced to his drawings or models is of a commercial nature, is made in batches or otherwise in quantity and is not the personal work of the artist craftsman.

That, then, was the widely accepted definition of the role of the industrial designer throughout the 1960s, and, though it came under fire for lack of ethical or political content, it continued to be influential. It was and remained a reasonable summary of the industrial designer's contribution and a fitting tribute to the pioneering endeavors of the early practitioners. The question of the future of industrial design is particularly relevant in the latter third of the 20th century since the state of the art is at a crossroads, both philosophically and materially.

The philosophical problem was in the late 1960s and early 1970s at the root of the worldwide art students' revolt, and it remains part of the universal restlessness at the unparalleled disequilibrium between the haves and the have-nots. The have-nots, object-hungry as they are, quite properly look upon industrial design as an ambition to be urgently fulfilled as a mark of progress and development, while the haves, object-saturated as they are, tend to regard it as an overvalued status symbol that simply underlines the iniquities of affluence amidst poverty. The younger the haves, the less interested they are in products as indicators of a standard of living but, in contrast, the more interested they are in those larger design issues that affect the quality of life. The have-nots, on the other hand, are largely unready for the sort of technological sophistication required to produce the products that they regard as their due. So there arises the ironical situation whereby neither the product-starved nor the product-satiated can effectively grasp the real rewards that should stem from the proper development of the industrial design profession. The product-starved seem destined to pass patiently through the various intermediate stages of technology, concentrating first on those labour-intensive processes that can absorb the greatest number of unemployed hands and thus seek from their designers (or rather, for the time being, from the designers of the more developed countries) relatively simple products that can be made almost by hand, while the product-satiated will presumably increasingly turn away from the design of things to the design of systems to cope with major problems of the environment.

This conflict may, in the long term, prove more apparent than real, since the developed world, sickened as it may be with the visible contrasts between private affluence and public squalor, will solve its major social, economic, and environmental problems and eventually renew the quest for product innovation, though by then on a more public-spirited, less personally ambitious scale; and—again hopefully—the underdeveloped world, learning by others' mistakes, will surely catch up. But whatever the outcome of these theoretical challenges, it is certain that the profession of industrial design will emerge in a very different guise from that which is generally recognized today—a fact well understood by designers themselves, particularly in the United States. Indeed, as was indicated at the beginning of this article, the industrial designer, having earned in the mid-20th century honourable recognition as a professional in his own right, will, by the end of the century, have to accept just as honourable anonymity as a member of the total industrial–social creative team.

That this is already the trend is apparent from the quiet revolution taking place in those colleges or institutions in the West where industrial design is taught. In most countries the subject has historically been accepted as proper to a school of art—design, even industrial design, having originally been thought of in terms of applied art. Most art schools thus opened design departments alongside their fine art studios, but those design departments were almost universally craft based. The subjects taught had little enough connection with real industrial life, and those that did were usually limited to skills related to craft-based industries, such as pottery, glass, cutlery, silverware, textiles, furniture, and typography. It was not really until the 20th century had got into its stride that such products as light fittings, kitchen appliances, office machinery, and other useful or mechanically functional articles, were also studied; by then voices were already being raised to question whether an art school was in fact the right sort of establishment in which to train designers for that sort of product.

It was predictable that as new materials were developed, such as plastics, alloys, foams and laminates, the design schools and their students would begin to desert the old traditional materials and processes. One result of this intense interest in the new technologies was the gradual downgrading, if not denigration, of the old handicraft activities—some schools, indeed, changing their venerable "Arts and Crafts" titles to "Art and Design" or even to "Design" alone. But simultaneously two other developments became manifest, the one in a sense contradicting the other and both at variance with the up until then seemingly logical evolution of crafts schools into design schools.

Handicrafts revitalized

The first development was by way of reaction to the subordination of handwork to industry and was itself reinforced by growing public demand for one-of-a-kind individual possessions in markets flooded with mass-produced products. Many design schools, influenced perhaps by the founding by a knowledgeable American benefactor, Mrs. Vanderbilt Webb, of the World Crafts Council and by the setting up (1971) in Britain of an official Crafts Advisory Committee, began rethinking and upgrading the role of the handicrafts departments with a view to producing graduates capable of supporting themselves as practicing craftsmen, rather than having to return whence they came as teachers of more teachers. At the same time, modest workshops began to multiply, employing perhaps only half a dozen craftsmen but contributing nonetheless in a small way to solving the problem of human redundancy inherent in the advance of technology. And, as so often before, these handworkers began to inject into the marketplace new ideas and designs destined in due course to influence the mass-producers. The toy industries in many countries, for instance, were greatly enriched by the imaginative inventions of individual small-scale producers who were primarily artist craftsmen but whose ideas, having been exposed to interested publics through design centres and other specialist outlets, were taken up and put into larger production by manufacturers already established in the trade. By the early 1970s, therefore, there was a noticeable swingback toward handwork in many schools that had a few years earlier deliberately veered away from it and toward industrial design.

The "anti-design" movement

At the same time, the industrial design departments came under attack from a very different quarter and for a fundamentally different reason. As a side effect of product saturation or even of the product revulsion manifested in politically restless, youthful sectors of the Western world, the whole concept of hardware came, through the proliferation of consumer durables, under attack. Just as "anti-art" became a fashionable, familiar feature of the fine-art schools in the late 1960s, so "anti-design" began to appear in the shape of genuine philosophical questioning of the benefits of technology and thus, indirectly, of design if all that combination could produce was more hardware to mulct the pocket, confuse the mind, and clutter the environment. Perhaps the clearest exposure of this dilemma was made in a paper delivered in November 1970 to the Royal Society of Arts in London by Michael Tree, head of the Information Division of Britain's Council of Industrial Design. Called "Software and Hardware —Changing Attitudes to Design," his paper contrasted the extreme efficiency of many objects as examples of technological prowess with their extreme inefficiency in terms of society or the environment. Discussing television, for instance, he said: "here is a highly sophisticated technology, capable of bringing images in colour across great distances, which performs a daily miracle in millions of homes. Yet where is the country," he asked, that could claim that the standards of its broadcast programmes are anywhere near the level of the technology involved? Once again the hardware is well ahead of the software: the cleverness ahead of the wisdom.

Or later in the same paper:

> We praise and admire a well-designed product and then discover that the manufacturer's packaging or his servicing arrangements fall sadly below its high standards. We welcome the introduction of mechanical safety factors into the manufacture of modern cars and then lament the pollution coming from their exhausts.

In other words, by the early 1970s, those most closely concerned with the subject of industrial design were in a sense questioning its whole social or even ethical foundation, for as the Director (Sir Paul Reilly) of that same Council of Industrial Design said at the opening in April 1970 of the International Design Centre in West Berlin:

> From my experience of running London's Design Centre, I am well aware of a diminishing interest among our younger visitors in displays of individual artefacts, but of an increasing interest in exhibitions that demonstrate inter-relationships between different skills and disciplines—a diminishing interest, that is, in the Design Centre's shop window role, but an increasing interest in it as a sort of social laboratory.

This same thought was expressed in the 1969–70 yearbook of the Swiss Environmental Debate and Action Foundation by Professor Erik Herløw, prominent Danish architect and designer, who wrote:

> Execution of design demands a horizontal, ethical attitude supplemented by a vertical, deep-seated knowledge governed by humanistic ethics . . . the designer himself has succeeded in converting industrial design into a medium for mass production, mass expenditure, mass consumption as well as wholesale murder in innumerable environments . . . If this allegation holds good, it means that "design" can be either a means to self-destruction or a means to survival in a more rational world than we know today.

The opening of new fields for design

And yet, alongside these two streams of thought—the craft-orientated desire for more individual, handmade possessions and the satiated rejection of mass-produced objects (both, of course, being minority attitudes)—another equally important development was taking place in the field of design training and education. In spite of the social disillusionment felt by many young designers leading to their rejection of the growing deification of design for machine production that had been prevalent since the 1850s, serious teachers of the subject began breathing new life into it precisely because they were prepared to abandon old definitions and thus extend the work of the designer into fields formerly closed to him. This change of direction was well described to Scandinavian audiences early in 1972 by a visiting English lecturer, Professor Misha Black, head of the School of Engineering Design at the Royal College of Art in London. He made the point that people no longer look upon typewriters or washing machines as works of art, although they clearly have formal and symbolic qualities, which, as an adjunct to their mechanical efficiency, can give minor aesthetic pleasure. He then emphasized that because mass-produced objects are best judged as technically efficient mechanisms, though sometimes having the additional merits of visual and tactile agreeableness, industrial design must be seen as an aspect of the totality of engineering design; and success in its practice will require deep understanding of the restrictions and potentialities of mechanical and production engineering. "Industrial design," he said,

> must, therefore, in the future be considered as a specialised aspect of mechanical engineering and rooted in its technology as firmly as architecture should spring from the technologies of civil engineering and building construction.

In other words, industrial design for the next generation of students will be a pursuit based less on art, craft, intuition, or fashion than on firm familiarity with contemporary technology and sociology. Or, to quote Professor Black again:

> If we isolate industrial design as a discipline, its future in the 1980s must be based on engineering knowledge and experience; the designer must be a special kind of engineer and should not be educated to conceive of himself as primarily an artist bringing qualities of aesthetic judgment and human understanding to bear, from the outside, on problems of engineering invention and design. We do not want to educate engineers with a smattering of human and aesthetic understanding nor artists with a dilettante knowledge of engineering, but a new kind of engineer able to make aesthetic judgments with the same authority as that with which he makes mechanical and production decisions.

Changes in the education of designers

If that educational target were to be accepted generally, there would be a progressive diminution of the role of the art schools, accompanied by a parallel increase in the importance of technical colleges in the training of designers; moreover, the words industrial design undoubtedly would gradually fall into desuetude as the activity itself became merged with other disciplines. This development was anticipated or at least recognized in Britain when early in 1972 the 27-year-old Council of Industrial Design not only changed its name from the particular to the general, being known from that April onward simply as Design Council, but also, on instructions from the British government, took on responsibility for promoting engineering design as well as industrial design, the two being rightly regarded as inseparable elements of the same creative activity. It should be noted, perhaps, that the same decisions had already been taken in Canada and Australia, where the comparable bodies had been called Design Councils from their inception. The Russian and French equivalents were not so happily placed, not having so succinct or useful a word as "design" but having instead to fall back, respectively, on the rather clumsy phrases Technical Aesthetics and Esthétique Industrielle.

There was, of course, a satisfactory element of wish fulfillment in this long-delayed marriage of industrial and engineering design, for had it happened 100 years earlier, many mistakes and misunderstandings would have been avoided; indeed, the separate profession of industrial design might never have been called into existence, any more than would that of typography have arisen had printers not, in their search for productivity, abdicated their responsibilities for design. In the craft of typography, too, however, the same marriages are taking place as more and more printers are beginning to offer complete services.

These arguments for the totality of design are, however, by no means universally accepted. Old traditions—even those that have not yet reached their century—die hard and entrenched interests will resist change, while misinterpretations will persist long after their source has been rectified. It will take many years before engineers in general will accept responsibility for ergonomics and aesthetics or even before they will welcome the industrial designer into their engineering teams. Despite the cogent argument of those who have followed these developments that the modern industrial designer, as distinct from the commercial stylist, preferring subtraction to addition, will seek economy of means and simplification rather than elaboration and complication, the conservative engineer will tend to regard the industrial designer as some kind of artist brought in at the end of the development to dress up or prettify a piece of functional equipment. The designer may insist, instead, that the truth is the opposite—that the modern industrial designer, as opposed to the first generation of commercial stylists, is probably the true heir to those great Victorian engineers whose exhibits at the 1851 Crystal Palace were so properly praised for being "plain and unpretending," while it is in this generation that the engineer has become the stylist, frequently falling for fashion and favouring voguish (though usually outmoded) shapes, ornament, and lettering. It is a strange reversal of roles since at one time it was certainly the industrial designer who was (and often is still) criticized in engineering circles for being the cosmetician.

THE PATH AHEAD

While recognizing this new totality of design, it might perhaps be profitable to speculate on the role of design in the industrial, commercial world of the near future, for there are already indications of the direction it will take. It has been said that the history of design in manufacture over the last 250 years could be compressed almost into three words—integration, disintegration, and reintegration—for that broadly has been the sequence of development from the days of handcraft, when the designer and maker were one, through the mechanization of the first industrial revolution, when the designer became divorced from manufacture, to the present age of swiftly changing technology, which compels close consultation between all concerned with product initiation, including, of course, the designer—whether the problem concerns engineering design or industrial design.

Integrating design and management

It may be too early to claim that industrial management, in general, accepts the central role of the designer, though increasing lip service is being paid to his importance. It is also too early to claim that the designer yet understands the problems or language of management. But it is not too early to argue that a much fuller integration of design with management is in the offing. This will have come about through several irresistible pressures.

First, modern managers, particularly in large organizations, are broadly market orientated as opposed to production orientated and, as such, are already more conscious of design than was the previous generation. Market orientation enforces concern for the product, for consumer preferences, for customer convenience, for public appearances, visible manifestations, corporate identities, and so forth, all of which are aspects of the design problems and policies of competitive business.

Secondly, the inevitability of technological development and the rising tempo of change appear to demand increasing flexibility in management thinking. This points to large-scale industry becoming directed increasingly toward function and process as opposed to product orientation or even market orientation. There will thus be a basic shift from managerial styles appropriate to stable markets and stable product lines to those appropriate to recognition that the central theme of the modern industrial organization is continuous innovation, whether of product or process. It will follow that design itself will have to expand as a corporate function and must, therefore, become more closely integrated with management.

Thirdly, since change is practically a condition of survival in the modern world, design in this wider sense must become increasingly important, since it is by definition a creative activity and, therefore, inseparably linked to change. It must thus become a matter of paramount concern to management, the more so since management itself is increasingly becoming the management of change.

Fourthly, design will inevitably cease to be an individual pursuit in favour of a group activity as technology becomes more complex and, thus, is bound to impinge on management at many more points than in the days of individual, personal, and signable artifacts.

Probable effects of social pressures

Fifthly, industry, whether public or private, is likely to become increasingly subject to social pressures and to public participation in decision making and, therefore, must become increasingly aware of its social responsibilities. Ecology, amenity, and environment are all going to be given more weight in industrial and commercial planning, and these are all extensions of design. It is not by accident that the word environment has recently gained such widespread currency, for it exactly expresses the coming expansion of design and the extension of the designer. As management's social conscience expands, so will the role of the designer. Indeed, this is already happening, for no major decision on the location or development of an industrial complex, an airport, or even an airplane can take place today without close consultation with many kinds of designers, from urbanists at one end of the scale to typographers at the other.

From the industrial designer's point of view, all these developments are to be welcomed, for he has for too long been pigeon-holed in management's mind as a specialist to be called in fairly late in the decision-making chain—in order to prepare a given product for a given market. The industrial designer has been called in, if at all, toward the end of the sequence of product development. He has seldom been involved in the basic work of innovation and invention. As a consequence, the organization of design in industry has been compartmentalized, stage one being product initiation, stage two product engineering, with industrial design coming in only at stage three. Sometimes the industrial designer may be on a company's staff, but often he will be an outside consultant and thus even further removed from the seats of power and decision. This inability to influence major functions and decisions early enough has tended to relegate the industrial designer to subordinate positions that are related more to merchandising and packaging than to fundamental research and development.

All this, however, is undoubtedly going to change rapidly and radically. With the obsolescence of the product as the main unit of design in corporate thinking and its replacement by processes or systems, the role of the designer is going to come much nearer the centre of the circle, always remembering that "the designer" will no longer be an individual but a team. This interdisciplinary team, comprising many different specialists, will move from its present precarious peripheral perch right to the heart of the matter, for systems design must be a central corporate function, not a belated activity concerned with individual product development. With the rise of systems and the decline of products in the hierarchy of managerial priorities, the designer will come into his own, since, more than most of his industrial colleagues, he will through his very creativity be able to contribute to the management of change. When that happens, not only will the designer be again properly integrated with industry but also he will be properly integrated with management. Indeed, he will be indisputably a member of the management team. And that, in the circumstances of a technological society, will be the nearest feasible equivalent to the complete unity of design and manufacture that was enjoyed before the Industrial Revolution.

Of course, none of this is so speculative as it may sound, for the future is already here, so to speak. The concepts of the process being the product and the design of systems superseding the design of products are already facts. They are already commonplace in America, where, for example, a school-construction program will not be tackled through the design of a building system in the conventional sense but, in the first place, by working out in detail all the uses it will be put to and all the solutions involved in a scheme for the building of many similar schools, each requiring a high degree of flexibility in use. The first-stage result will thus be a series of interlocking performance criteria, giving rise, in turn, to the development of interlocking flexible systems based on standard components. In other words, the designers, having done their creative thinking, will leave the translation of their specifications to the contractor's own technical experts. Essential to this kind of planning is the design of networks or systems allowing standard components to be assembled in a wide variety of relationships. And, as a by-product of such standardization of parts, it becomes possible to combine economical mass production with the kind of individual selection usually associated with custom manufacture, an advantage of considerable value in face of the apparent tug-of-war between the economist and the psychologist in present-day society, the economist finding all manner of good arguments for simplification and standardization, while the psychologist points to the fundamental human need for change and choice and variety.

These new approaches to design and these new methodologies will demand in designers higher levels of mathematical ability, and there is no doubt that this trend will continue, with the computer increasingly relieving the designer of his mathematical donkeywork. The most fundamental challenge to conventional ideas on design has been the growing advocacy of systematic methods of problem solving, borrowed from computer techniques, for the designer today is faced with a fantastic array of choices—of materials, processes, textures, shapes, colours—with which to solve his increasingly various and complex problems. Only the most modern methods will do this, and only through these modern sophisticated techniques will designing for industry reach its real maturity.

BIBLIOGRAPHY. HERWIN SCHAEFER, *The Roots of Modern Design: Functional Tradition in the 19th Century* (1970), an account of interest to both the professional and layman—the strength of the author's thesis lies in his understanding of the motives of 19th-century industrialists and of the 19th-century vernacular tradition; NIKOLAUS PEVSNER, *Pioneers of Modern Design, from William Morris to Walter Gropius*, rev. ed. (1964), a well-researched and scholarly work on those who laid the foundations for modern design education; REYNER BANHAM, *Theory and Design in the First Machine Age*, 2nd ed. (1967), provides background information on both the theories and facts of designing useful in understanding the complexity of trends that form much of 20th-century design; HENRY DREYFUSS, *Designing for People* (1955), a sound work by one of the world's greatest industrial designers; ARTHUR DREXLER and GRETA DANIEL, *Introduction to Twentieth Century Design* (1959), a pictorial guide, with some explanatory text, to some of the classic examples of domestic and small product designs permanently retained at the Museum of Modern Art, New York; LASZLO MOHOLY-NAGY, *Vision in Motion* (1956), a personal statement by the founder of the Institute of Design, Chicago, that directly relates art components in design to industrially-produced objects; PAUL J. GRILLO, *What Is Design?* (1960), a provocative attempt to get both the design student and the layman to think experimentally about some fundamental design concepts; FREDERICK C. ASHFORD, *The Aesthetics of Engineering Design* (1969), a practical study of how the industrial engineer integrates production requirements, ergonomic needs, and aesthetic values so that small- to medium-sized machines become coherent designs; W.H. MAYALL, *Machines and Perception in Industrial Design* (1968), a useful introduction to appreciating the problems and opportunities of industrial design and ergonomics in process machinery; JAMES PILDITCH and DOUGLAS SCOTT, *The Business of Product Design* (1965), a guide to product planning with emphasis on marketing; MICHAEL MIDDLETON, *Group Practice in Design* (1967), a description of how different specialists creating complex projects can, by the employment of systematic team techniques, arrive at successful solutions in various fields; JAMES PILDITCH, *Communication by Design* (1970), a work that encourages businessmen to initiate design programs; JOHN CHRISTOPHER JONES, *Design Methods* (1970), a plea for systematic methods to be applied to designing, with an outline of new methods and their advantages and limitations; K.F.H. MURRELL, *Ergonomics: Man in His Working Environment* (U.S. title, *Human Performance in Industry;* 1965), one of the best general guides to the most commonly encountered problems concerning human factors and the methods of solving them; MICHAEL FARR, *Design Management* (1966), a book for the would-be user of design as an integral component of industry and commerce; FIONA MACCARTHY, *All Things Bright and Beautiful: Design in Britain 1830 to Today* (1972), a well-researched account of the battles for improvement.

Industrialization and Modernization

In the present age, mankind is passing through one of its great transformations. The first transformation was the emergence of the human group itself, in the form of the primitive community. The second transformation was the appearance of civilizations. The third, which is that of the present time, is the crystallization of modern industrial society and its spread over the planet.

The three transformations are usually considered to follow one another in an evolutionary way, although the sequence is not inevitable: some primitive societies and nonmodern societies have survived to the present day without becoming modern. It is not known why several primitive communities mutated into civilizations and why Western culture was the first, if not the only, culture to generate the modern industrial society. There are some plausible hypotheses, but these are as yet unproved.

The superiority or desirability of modernity or industrialism, of progress, or even of civilization remains an open question. There are no generally accepted criteria for evaluating the three societal forms and their numerous varieties. The choices among them exist only in theory, while the actual course of events has been determined largely by the modern industrial complex as it has crystallized in the West. Its tremendous material power and dynamism, along with the magnetic attraction it has exerted upon widely different cultures, have given it an irresistible thrust, transforming all societies and inaugurating the era of universal history.

The article is divided into the following sections:

THE NATURE OF MODERNIZATION

Modernization, westernization, and industrialization

The process of modernization was at first regarded as one of westernization or Europeanization, because it began in Europe and spread outward. But modernization can no longer be regarded as the mere transplanting of European institutions to other parts of the world nor as a transition toward one fixed societal type. The struggles for national independence, the rise of new nations, the continual transformation of capitalist society, the rise of various forms of planned economies, and the fusion of Western with non-Western components in modernizing societies have made it clear that modernization involves a variety of models, all of which are in flux. It is also clear that there are many paths toward modernity. One may hazard a guess that the increasing unification of the Earth will eventually bring about more cultural and social homogeneity. At any rate, the outcome will be a new world civilization, heir to Western and non-Western cultures alike. The process of modernization is a kind of permanent revolution, without any final goal; one can already distinguish "old modern," "transitional," and "new modern" phases, while the contemporary scene even offers glimpses of a "postmodern" one.

Modernization affects all of society, including the economic, political, and social systems. In the economic sphere, modernization takes the form of industrialization. The first modern society was the outcome of the Industrial Revolution in England during the late 18th and early 19th centuries. In the political sphere, while democratic constitutional regimes were formerly thought to be characteristic of modern society, it is now apparent that many types of political system are compatible with modernization so long as they allow reasonably stable economic and social development. In the social sphere, also, various forms of organization are compatible with a modern society so long as they permit the necessary changes in personality, norms, social relations, and institutions. These three spheres, the economic, political, and social, have to be kept distinctly in mind, because they change at different rates and in different sequences under different historical conditions.

Common traits of modern societies

Secularization. One difficulty in defining modernization is that it has many aspects and diverse forms, all of them changing. Another source of confusion is the need to distinguish between the historical process leading to the crystallization of the modern industrial complex, which may be called primordial modernization, and the many other transitions through which modernization spreads over the planet. Modern societies may be thought of as a general category including many different types, all of which have certain common traits distinguishing them from the societies of the past (traditional societies). These traits include the continuous and accelerated expansion of knowledge and its deliberate application to technology in the production of goods and services, with the use of ever new and higher forms of energy, toward the goal of maximizing efficiency. Underlying all this is a tendency that sociologists have termed secularization, in the sense of activities rationally organized around impersonal and utilitarian values and patterns rather than around ceremonial and traditional ones. Secularization is found to some extent in every historical civilization, but it is carried much further in modern societies and has a somewhat different orientation. As used in the following discussion, the term implies certain principles of behaviour and organization that are necessary to the rise and maintenance of any modern society. These principles have to do with (1) the nature of social action, (2) society's orientation toward change, and (3) the degree of differentiation and specialization of institutions.

The nature of social action. One may distinguish theoretically between two opposed types of social action: action that is prescribed and action that is chosen. These are what sociologists call ideal types, meaning that they are conceptual constructs not to be found anywhere in their pure form. Both types of action, like all human behaviour, are socially and culturally conditioned. During his early years the individual acquires certain attitudes, motivations, and knowledge that are required, or tolerated by the society he lives in, and these tend to become an integral part of his personality. They are reinforced from outside by various punishments or rewards—psychological, social, and physical. In the case of prescribed action, the individual is expected to behave in a specific way, while in the case of behaviour that is chosen he selects his own course of action and is obliged only to observe certain general rules in making his choice. For example, in most nonmodern societies the individual must follow the occupation of his father or marry according to traditional prescriptions, while in modern society he is expected, within limits, to choose his own spouse or occupation. Prescribed action may usually be seen as the individual expression of a collective act, while action by choice requires a fully individualized self. Rational action is a particular kind of action by choice, in which the guiding criterion is to choose the optimum means of reaching a given end. Action by choice is very rare in primitive communities and severely restricted in premodern societies.

Orientation toward change. Change is universal, although in some societies it may be extremely slow and interrupted by periods of stagnation or limited to particular areas. Societies differ in their orientation toward it. Primitive communities and premodern civilizations do not accept change in most of their institutions, while in modern societies change is expected or required. The former institutionalize tradition; the latter institutionalize change. As in the case of social action, however, modern societies do not legitimize all change but only change occurring in given areas and according to certain rules.

Differentiation of institutions. Societies vary in the number and nature of the institutions devoted to carrying on such essential functions as the provision of goods and services, reproduction and education, regulation of behaviour, defense against disease and military attack, and the satisfaction of religious, aesthetic, recreational, and other needs. At one extreme, in the primitive community, most of these functions are shared by all of the members. Premodern civilizations show a considerable differentiation of institutions, but these involve only a tiny minority of the population, such as priests and warriors and the urban trades; all institutions in the premodern society are dominated by the same values and norms. In modern society, the differentiation of institutions and social division of labour proceed almost without limit; the institutions become more and more autonomous, all human activities are fragmented by increasing specialization, and even the unity of the individual person seems threatened by a multiplicity of roles. This differentiation is gradually extended to the entire population. Its limit is defined by the need for all the various institutions and role to work together with some degree of compatibility.

The three principles of secularization described above are not, of course, independent of one another. Change and differentiation are facilitated by choosing; both involve innovation, purposeful deviation from established patterns, that can take place only through choice—that is, nonprescriptive action. The central meaning of secularization is that choice, as a deliberate act, requires persons endowed with sufficiently individualized minds to be aware of alternatives. The development of such individualized minds is a complex psychological and historical process that underlies the transition from primitivism to civilization, both Western and non-Western. The former generated a particular kind of civilization, the modern industrial one, not only through an exceptional growth of individuation but also by a specific orientation —by a different way of relating the individual to his own self, to his society, to the natural world, and to the fundamental problems of human existence. An orientation toward knowledge, technology, and economy is basic to modern civilization.

Secularization and stability. Secularization, of course, does not exist by itself. It is part of a total social context and is affected by social transformations. It tends to increase in degree and spread in range once it reaches a level sufficient to generate self-sustaining growth in knowledge, technology, and economy. Increasing secularization leads away from a single system of values toward pluralism in values, and, as has often been observed, such pluralism tends to erode the very foundation of an integrated social system: its common core of shared values and norms. Many contemporary problems have arisen from contradictions among values.

NONMODERN AND PREMODERN SOCIETIES

Primitive and civilized societies. The differences between primitive and civilized societies are fairly clear. Primitive societies usually consist of a few hundred or a few thousand individuals living in a small area, while civilizations may reach hundreds of millions covering a whole continent and including societies varying in size from city-states to empires. Civilization becomes possible when a well-established agriculture and technology give rise to an economic surplus enabling the development of cities and of a written culture. Primitive communities are not static; in fact, they brought the predecessors of civilized man to a human level, and some of them generated the innovations making possible the rise of civilizations. But, once civilization begins, the rate and nature of change are altered. The time scale narrows from tens of millennia to centuries; social and cultural changes acquire a new meaning as civilizations rise and fall and historical cycles, stages, and directionality appear.

Characteristics of civilizations

As noted above, civilizations are accompanied by secularization and individuation. Their psychological basis has already been laid in primitive man by the development of certain ego functions, self-objectification, and some potentiality for self-awareness. But in civilization the subjective experience of the self in relation to the outer world, including other human beings, acquires a new dimension. The change has been variously described as the "dawn of consciousness," the transition from a shame to a guilt culture, a decline in the strength of the collective consciousness, or the individualization of man out of "tribal consciousness." Deliberate action or choice now becomes possible on a much wider scale. In a primitive society, differentiation is essentially biological; the economic, familial, political, military, religious, aesthetic, recreational, and other functions are performed at the primitive level as part of a single web of norms, attitudes, and behaviour patterns. The division of labour barely transcends the categories of age and sex; the social hierarchy, if any, is minimal; the kin group, from the nuclear family to the larger group of common descent, includes the whole community; while religion, magic, and myth permeate all of life and give it meaning.

In civilization the division of labour brings forth a host of specializations, including the separation of agriculture from trade and the crafts, of town from country, the emergence of new forms of property, and the development of upper and lower classes. Institutions such as the family and kinship, religion, law, politics, warfare, and education become distinct from one another, take on different organizational patterns, and develop interrelationships. The development of religion and the appearance of writing are particularly important. Civilized religions, particularly the great historical religions, are universalistic in their application to mankind; they also have a developed conception of the self. Written language acts as a powerful tool to increase social differentiation and complexity—so much so that the terms literate and nonliterate are commonly used as synonyms for civilized and primitive. To these common characteristics of nonmodern civilized societies other general features must be added. Agriculture remains the basis of the economy, occupying as much as 90 or 95 percent of the working population. Economic activity enjoys a lower status than other human activities. Technology is not yet founded on science; it changes very slowly, is local and peculiar to each civilization, and applies to only a few areas of life. Population grows very slowly, and numbers are kept down by high mortality. Social stratification in these premodern civilizations is rigid, with great differences in wealth, income, and social position; and there is very little movement upward or downward from one class to another. Usually there is a tiny elite or upper stratum and a large majority of commoners, the two strata being subdivided into several horizontal and vertical substrata, including a variety of groups and associations. Merchants' and artisans' guilds and cultural, religious, and recreational associations can be found in all civilized premodern societies. Certain categories, generally economic ones such as merchants and artisans, remain low in power and prestige even after they have acquired wealth, while others, such as the religious or cultural elites, enjoy high prestige even if they lack wealth or power. There are also likely to be castes, made up of persons who are excluded or segregated or enslaved. Some civilized societies are more rigid than others: social mobility may be higher in some, particularly in times of political or social troubles; but this mobility is almost always limited to the cities and does not include the great peasant masses. Great variations are also found among nonmodern civilizations in family and kinship structures, particularly within the various strata; the extended family and the large household prevail in the upper strata, while at lower levels the kinship units are smaller. There is variation also in their political systems, which include cities, states, feudal systems, bureaucratic empires, and others.

Diversity of nonmodern civilizations

Oversimplifying a rather complex matter, one may measure the diversity of these nonmodern civilizations along five gradients: (1) They vary in the degree of centralization, ranging from extremely decentralized feudal systems to highly centralized bureaucratic societies. In between there are patrimonial states and city states. (2) They also vary in the degree of differentiation, both political and social. (3) The political structure is usually traditional; that is, founded on inheritance or religious beliefs, although in some cases the leaders are chosen by collective bodies. (4) Participation in political decisions tends to be limited either to the ruler and a small circle of aides or to an upper class. In some nonmodern societies participation is more extensive, including a category of "citizens," as in ancient Greece, but even in these cases the vast majority of the population—peasants, outcasts, and other lower groups—are not included. (5) The amount of bureaucratization varies from none at all to a considerably organized and autonomous bureaucracy.

The social organization of all civilized nonmodern society may be characterized as a mixture of secularized and nonsecularized structures. In every case, the nonsecularized structures predominate. Social relationships depend more on what a person is—in terms of sex, age, social and ethnic origins, and family—than on his capability, efficiency, and relevance; in technical terms, ascription is more important than achievement in determining social relationships. Relations and roles are seen in terms of specific persons (particularism) rather than as formally defined categories (universalism). Finally, roles and relationships tend to be diffuse, rather than specific, and oriented toward emotional or aesthetic expression, rather than toward the accomplishment of a task.

Primitive communities seem to show a higher potential for survival than do civilizations. There is no way of estimating the average life-span of primitive communities, but it should probably be measured in terms of millennia. Civilizations are more adaptable to changes in their environment and to other external challenges than are primitive communities, but they appear to be much more vulnerable to internal stresses. Many theories of history agree that, while secularization increases creativity, it also produces higher stresses and lessens the ability of society to cope with them.

Primordial modernization. *The origin of modernity.* A distinction has been made above between the first historical process that led to modern civilization and the many subsequent transitions to modernity in the rest of the world. The initial transition in the West may be seen as a series of separate trends that merged to produce what is thought of as modernity. Significant contributions were made by other civilizations—the Arabic, the Hindu, the Chinese—but the Western cultural tradition was unique in creating a capacity for self-sustained growth. Only in the West did knowledge take the form of a logically conceived experimental science; only in the West was there a scientific technology and a production-oriented economy. Various theories of history have attributed these peculiarities to certain central values in the Western tradition, especially to its pattern of individuality. Others have attributed them to certain characteristics of Western social organization as it evolved out of the ancient city-state. The question remains open. At the present day it seems impossible to say whether other societies and traditions might eventually have produced a modern industrial civilization of themselves. The West was certainly not unique in the level of scientific, mathematical, and technological development reached in the period before modernization set in. In fact, some crucial inventions, such as the steam engine, had been available since the Hellenistic era. Chinese science and technology maintained between the 3rd and the 13th centuries a level unapproached in the West; among the Chinese technological innovations were three—printing, gunpowder, and the magnet—that Francis Bacon regarded as having "changed the whole face and state of things of the World." But the Hellenistic and Chinese civilizations did not move onward to modernization. It is reasonable to assume that this occurred in the West because of certain basic value orientations working within particular forms of social organization. Social scientists have developed some highly suggestive hypotheses as to the critical features in the political and economic structures of the West.

Modern traits in the classic Western societies. Nowhere did the economy acquire such distinctiveness and prominence as in the commercial capitalism of medieval Europe, which was the immediate predecessor of modern industrial capitalism. Most anthropologists, economic historians, and sociologists stress the fact that only in the West did the economy cease to be oriented mainly toward consumption, prestige, or power and come to place its main emphasis on production as its goal. This involved a shift toward production for further production; that is, capital investment. Before this came about, certain preconditions had to be created, including the institutions of the market and of private property. Markets had existed since primitive times but not in the modern form of an impersonal economic mechanism of demand and supply. Exchange took place, as the Austrian-born British historian Karl Polanyi and others have shown, in the service of other than purely economic purposes, often in the form of reciprocal gift giving. The emphasis on reciprocity can be seen, for example, in the doctrine of the "just price" that survived until the beginning of the modern era; this nonmarket form of exchange exists today only within the family and among other primary groups. As long ago as 5th-century Athens and late republican Rome, the market as an economic mechanism was beginning to emerge, and the two different modes of exchange coexisted throughout classical antiquity. This did not happen in the great capitals of the Asian empires. As Marx and Engels pointed out, the Asian Military societies were based on the primitive community with its low division of labour, common property, and lack of individuation. The ancient cities of the West saw for the first time a dissolution of the bonds of the primitive community with its emphasis on common property; there

The market as an economic mechanism

was a development of private property, which made possible a commercial, quasi-capitalistic economy and an urban commercial class resembling those that were to appear in premodern Europe.

The legacy of Western antiquity was more than intellectual, scientific, and economic. It had a political dimension as well. As the German sociologist Max Weber observed, the classical city-state of the West was the first political entity to establish a real citizenry, as an association of equals. "In China, the magical closure of clans, in India the closure of castes eliminated the possibility of civic confederations. In China the clans as bearers of the ancestor cult were indestructible. In India the castes were carriers of a particular style of life upon the observance of which salvation and reincarnation depended." Only the Western city, both in Rome until the late empire and in the Middle Ages, developed its own army, "a fundamental component in the origin of the corporate, autonomous urban communities." In the East, the armies had depended on the centralized authority of bureaucratic military empires and had been far removed from the control of the commoners.

This brief inventory cannot omit the contribution of Roman rational and universalistic law, the influence of Rome's relatively advanced political organization, and Rome's role in transmitting the Judeo-Christian tradition.

The premodern West and the birth of modern civilization. The European cities of the Middle Ages provided what the classical cities had not, the preconditions for uninterrupted social development. The significant characteristics of the European cities were, in Max Weber's enumeration: (1) the "guild character of the Middle Ages, which helped to create a specific town economy" and "made the surrounding country subservient to the town interests"; in the ancient city the guilds functioned differently; (2) the fact that "the typical citizen of the medieval guild city is a merchant or craftsman" whereas in antiquity "the full citizen is the land holder"; this difference was also reflected in the exercise of the rights of citizenship, which were more equalitarian—at the legal level—in the city of the Middle Ages; (3) the social cleavages of the medieval city, which contained the germ of modern class conflict between workers and employers, whereas in the ancient city the main cleavage had been between the landed and the landless; (4) the basing of wealth on trade and industry, rather than on land and warfare as in the ancient city; (5) the fact that, in the ancient city, trade and industry had been subordinated to military interests; and finally (6) the low status of the nonmilitary arts in antiquity. "Over against the citizen stands the 'low-bred': anyone is low-bred who follows the peaceful quest of profit in the sense of today."

The medieval city

In the medieval urban setting, then, the new class of bourgeoisie created the modern order. The process of secularization described above was carried further than ever before, and it created, in conjunction with the other great religious and political changes, a stable basis for permanent growth. As in all the great cultural revolutions of mankind, the changes were inextricably interwoven. There was, to begin with, a change in the attitude toward manual labour, which no longer had a stigma attached to it. This was not unrelated to the rise of a practical science founded both on conceptual thinking and on the manipulation of matter. The growth of a money economy was reciprocally connected with quantification, an essential element in the new science; with the perception of time; and with the deliberate, rational use of time both in one's personal life and in the business organization. Money, as the German sociologist and philosopher Georg Simmel pointed out, was symbolic of the dynamic character of the emerging new world. Money was a dissolvent of old social bonds. The rise of the money economy, with its commercialization of life and its transformation of all the products of work into merchandise, went hand in hand with the separation of the workers from the means of production, the creation of "free labour," and the emergence of the new dynamic class of capital-goods owners, a change that, according to the Marxian view, played the key role in the rise of industrial society in its early capitalist form.

It is not the purpose of this article to enumerate all the scientific, technological, and social changes or the intellectual and religious transformations that took place in the four centuries preceding the Industrial Revolution. Certain developments, however, were of particular importance not only in the emergence of modern society but also in its later universalization. On the psychological level a new type of personality appeared that incorporated the new behaviour patterns associated with secularization, directing its energies toward productive economic activity. These new behaviour patterns were roughly those described by Max Weber in his discussion of the "Protestant ethic" as a factor in the rise of capitalism. On the structural level, a new political unit and a different political system had to be created; the city-state and the feudal–patrimonial organization of political life were replaced by the centralized bureaucratic state.

All of this and much more went into the creation of the first industrial society. The various trends and innovations must be conceived of as long-term historical processes, taking place to some extent along parallel lines but not continuously or at the same time. They appear in differing forms and intensities, sometimes developing and sometimes declining to re-emerge later in another historical context. While they tend to occur together, to form clusters, so to speak, there are several concrete historical cases in which one of the components was lacking or they were not sufficiently developed to produce the modern industrial complex.

MODERN SOCIETIES

Any description of modern society as a historical category must be kept at a rather high level of generality. This is because the very nature of modernity involves continuous and rapid change and also because the present time is characterized by sharp ideological and military struggles focussed around different types of modern society.

Science and technology. Scientific knowledge is the central dynamic component of modern society, its "prime mover." Science in this context should not be confused with other intellectual activities or forms of knowledge not based on empirical procedures—*i.e.*, philosophy or theology. It represents the principles of secularization applied virtually without limit. The principle of continuous institutionalized change is built into the very methodology of science, all of its propositions being provisional and subject to change according to standardized procedures. Science is also autonomous within society, in that its values and norms cannot be infringed upon without destroying its creativity. Its autonomy, however, does not prevent it from having ethical and social implications, and these are among the main sources of tension in modern civilization.

Modern secularizing tendencies

Technology, like science, represents the secularizing principles. Technology has a centralizing tendency, since it leads to specialization, interdependence, central coordination, and economies of scale, all of which involve increasing concentration of decision making in every sphere of life and over larger and larger geographical areas.

In both science and technology, change takes the form of self-sustained growth, a process almost entirely quasi-automatic and impersonal. In the most advanced societies the coordination of individual action (*i.e.*, purposive, rational action) has led to the collectivization and automatization of choice and change. This is an unexpected and rather contradictory outcome of the extreme individualism that originally generated modern civilization.

The economic system. Secularization is the hallmark of any modern economy, which must operate without much concern for religion, ethics, aesthetics, or considerations of prestige. Its main orientation has to be toward maximum efficiency. In every type of social, political, or economic order, the modern economy must obey these principles. Its essential characteristic is a capacity for self-sustaining growth.

Characteristics of a modern economy

A modern economy will display all or most of the following characteristics. (1) It will have mechanisms for the permanent creation or absorption of innovations in technology and organization. These mechanisms will insure the continuous emergence of new dynamic sectors to replace those that are declining or no longer expanding. (2) It will use increasingly higher forms of energy and more efficient technologies in every branch of economic activity. (3) The production of goods and, later, of services will usually predominate over agriculture, although the latter will be carried on in an increasingly efficient way. (4) Capital-intensive activities will increasingly predominate over labour-intensive activities—*i.e.*, the amount of capital per worker will tend to increase. (5) The size of the productive unit will tend to increase, as will also the economic unit, and there will be increasing technological specialization. (6) Saving and capital investment are increasingly carried on through corporate organizations. (7) Corporate management of production becomes predominant, whether under state ownership, private ownership, or some mixture of public and private ownership; and at the same time there is a divorce between the ownership and the actual management of production, which is increasingly carried on by professional managers. (8) There is more and more national economic planning, although it takes different forms in different economic systems. (9) Political units become more and more technologically and economically dependent upon one another, nationally and internationally. (10) Increasing output per capita becomes the prevailing tendency, along with perhaps a more equitable distribution of it, the latter resulting from deliberate state intervention rather than from the spontaneous forces of the market. There is a tendency in advanced economies, just as in science and technology, for individual entrepreneurship to be replaced by collective management and the "organization man." The orientation of the economy gradually shifts from the production of heavy industrial goods to the satisfaction of consumer demand.

The political system. The main characteristics of modern political systems have been summarized by the U.S. political scientist Lucian Pye as involving three tendencies:

> first, with respect to the population as a whole, a change from widespread subject status to an increasing number of contributing citizens, with an accompanying spread of mass participation, a greater sensitivity to the principles of equality and a wider acceptance of universalistic laws. Second, with respect to governmental and general systematic performance, political development involves an increase in the capacity of the political system to manage public affairs, control controversy, and cope with popular demands. Finally with respect to the organization of the polity, political development implies greater structural differentiation, greater functional specificity, and greater integration of all participating institutions and organizations.

Modern political systems present certain controversial problems. The meaning of political participation in a totalitarian state is quite different from its meaning in a pluralistic democracy. But the position of a person under totalitarian rule is even more different from his "subject" status in a nonmodern political system. In the latter, the ruled are outside the political system; they lack political awareness, and their traditional ideas leave no room for the questioning of authority. In the totalitarian system, on the other hand, the citizenry are highly politicized, are required to give at least lip service to an ideology (presumably as the result of deliberate assent), and take part in highly organized elections. There are also other forms of political participation at various levels.

Another difficult question confronted by any modern political system in some degree is the extent of its capacity for promoting and absorbing change. The need for this is imposed by the dynamic nature of the social and economic systems. Since change usually means conflict, the capacity of a modern system for resolving conflict must be high. In advanced societies, however, there is always some area in which change may involve too much conflict, perhaps even to the extent of causing disintegration or disruption of the social order. There must always be a central core of shared values, and when these are threatened the society may be endangered. An important mechanism of political and social integration is the principle of nationality, an essential component of any modern political system. It is this that maintains the unity and identity of modern society, replacing the primitive bonds of the tribe and the old loyalties to religion and tradition. Historically, in the advanced countries, the acquisition of a national identity began with the bourgeoisie and proceeded to the middle and the lower classes, coinciding with the extension of civil, political, and social rights. In modernizing societies, the main driving force has been nationalism—one of the functional substitutes for the bourgeois Protestant ethic.

Social organization. *The modern personality.* Modern society is secularized at all levels—at the cultural (values, norms, roles, institutions, and groups) and at the psychological (motivations, attitudes, personality, social relations, and behaviour). Such a society requires its own type of personality structure, one capable of self-guidance and decision making, with at least some capacity to confront change. The older, traditional type of personality found it difficult to confront change or unexpected situations without experiencing disorientation and anxiety. This is a challenge to modern man as well, arising from the stresses inherent in the structure of modern society, with its high rate of change and the conflicting demands it makes upon the individual. In fact, the more advanced countries seem already to be generating a new type of personality that differs from the type found in the earlier stages of modernity. Most interpersonal relations are transformed. Secularization is extended well beyond the spheres of knowledge, technology, and the economy. In other words, primary ties based on intimate personal contacts are replaced in many areas by secondary relationships of impersonal character in which individuals are interchangeable, in a way typical of rational bureaucratic organization.

The decline of primary ties

Primary bonds do not disappear, but their scope is reduced. While industrial society emphasizes impersonal roles for the sake of efficiency, there is a point at which the requirements of the individual establish an area, varying with the cultural and social setting, within which the family, kinship networks, friendships, and other primary relations are maintained. The family may be restricted to the nuclear family, and the kinship network may be likewise reduced, but they are never suppressed altogether. Many other primary ties are maintained or recreated or transformed and fused with modern traits; in this way they often turn out to be compatible with the requirements of modern institutions. These adaptations may be seen in the persistence of paternalistic relationships in Japanese industrial enterprises and in the frequent intrusion of expressive behaviour in nonprimary relationships in advanced Latin societies. Such adaptations do not, of course, eliminate the tensions mentioned above in any modern society.

Population and education. An important aspect of social modernization is change in the size, growth, composition, and ecological distribution of the population. In the premodern society, fertility and mortality are high. They both decline during modernization, but the decrease in mortality precedes by many decades that in fertility, so that there is an intermediate phase of high population growth—the so-called population explosion. Even after the decline in fertility, however, the rate of population increase continues to be higher than in premodern societies. The changes in vital rates also greatly modify the age structure of the population.

At the same time, changes in the productivity of agriculture and in the demand for industrial labour result in large-scale migration from rural to urban areas, reversing the rural predominance characteristic of all previous eras. In modernized countries, the great majority of the population live in urban areas—and those who remain rural follow an urbanized way of life. Local roots tend to disappear. People no longer live in a specific city, town, or village; they occupy places in an occupational or organizational network covering the whole nation (and, increasingly, large international areas) and move along the network according to choice or opportunity. This ecological mobility expresses the dynamic nature of modern society and derives from the need to maximize efficiency. New occupations continually replace old ones, and their number increases with greater specialization and the opening of new areas of activity.

Changes in education

Education undergoes corresponding changes. Modern life requires not only universal literacy but also increasing levels of education. While in early modern society a few years of primary school were sufficient for most jobs, in advanced nations secondary school is a universal requirement, and a college education is necessary for many occupations. But the most striking change is in the timing and forms of education. First, education ceases to be only one stage in the life cycle and becomes a permanent need because of the permanent revolution in occupations. Second, education has to reformulate its goals in order to meet the need for plasticity and change. Third, it requires new institutional and pedagogic mechanisms to meet new cultural needs.

Social stratification. The dynamism of modern society has a strong impact on its stratification. This tends to change in the following ways: (1) Most of the population move into the middle strata, with minorities at the top and bottom. (2) There is less discontinuity between strata in terms of income, style of life, education, interpersonal relations, manners, social distance, and prestige, so that clear-cut classes give way to a continuum of strata. (3) Mobility upward and downward becomes greater than in premodern society. (4) Values, attitudes, ideologies, motivations, and expectations take on an equalitarian colour; equality of opportunity and achievement are emphasized. All of this is in response to the underlying changes in production, distribution, education, and politics described above.

But this pattern of stratification is only the visible, socially accepted one and does not in every respect conform to reality. For the degree of equalitarianism actually existing in modern societies is less than that emphasized by the established values and ideologies. There are inequalities arising from family, ethnic, and regional influences, from differences in education, childhood development, and other factors, that run counter to the stress on achievement demanded by the principle of efficiency. It is even possible that the distribution of power is more concentrated in modern society than in premodern society. There may also be greater rigidity in the status differentials at the top and at the bottom.

There are a number of reasons for this discrepancy between the socially accepted image of stratification and the reality of it. The image, of course, tends to give legitimacy to the social order and is therefore valuable to it. Part of the reason for its acceptance is obviously that most persons' perceptions of society are influenced by the prevailing values and ideologies. But these perceptions are reinforced in certain ways by experience. First, there is the external uniformity of life styles, in such things as dress, behaviour, and the interests and activities emphasized by mass recreation and the mass media. Second, there is much equalitarianism in interpersonal relations and manners. Third, the complex organization of society allows the exercise of authority to be shared by people at many different levels. Fourth, most important of all, people feel that they are moving upward in life at a faster rate than is actually the case. This results from three factors: occupational upgrading, through the continuous replacing of lower tasks by machinery (or by immigrants and newcomers from outside); education upgrading, as people stay in school for longer periods of their lives; and consumption upgrading, resulting not only from a general rise in living standards but also from the constant creation of new types of goods and services, which are usually introduced at the top of the social hierarchy and circulate downward. The three kinds of upgrading involve a continual circulation of status symbols from the top of society to the bottom, which is experienced subjectively not as a downward distribution of objects from above but as an upward motion on the social ladder.

The illusion of mobility

Thus, many persons experience personal mobility while actually remaining at the same relative position in society, since it is the whole system that is being moved upward.

The maintenance of this illusion, which may be called that of self-sustained mobility, requires a continuing stream of technological and economic innovations. Even if these are forthcoming, the prestige of the status symbols is likely to become less and less enduring, so that their downward circulation will have to be increasingly accelerated. Succeeding generations, moreover, may cease to be satisfied by the illusion. This is one of the implications of the criticism of the "consumer society" in the 1960s and 1970s.

It is not possible to discern any essential difference in stratification among advanced modern societies. While in Communist countries the ownership of property is more equalitarian than in capitalist countries, there is more concentration of control over the means of production. Income may perhaps be more evenly distributed in Communist countries, but power is monopolized by a small elite. This fact of political power is perhaps the significant difference between the two systems insofar as social mobility is determined by political decisions at the top.

Many aspects of modern social organization have not been covered in the foregoing discussion. Among these are organized religion, the multiplicity of voluntary formal associations and informal groups, recreational institutions, the mass media, art and literature, and the various elites. An analysis of these and other sectors of the complex modern world would reveal the same pattern of accelerated secularization that was underlined above.

PATTERNS OF TRANSITION TOWARD MODERNITY

Modernization follows diverse patterns, and in no two countries does it take the same course. There are, however, certain common factors in the transitions of all countries. One generalization is that modernization or development is never balanced; it is always uneven, because the many social and cultural components do not undergo their transformations simultaneously nor at the same speed, and the various processes do not follow the same sequence. Some countries begin before others, and some regions within countries are ahead of others. The same asynchronism holds at the institutional and psychosocial levels, as well as among social groups, strata, classes, and other sectors of the population. There is an imbalance even within individuals, who display a mixture of modern and archaic attitudes, values, and motivations. The three components of modernization—the economic, the social, and the political—begin in different epochs, proceed at different rates, and follow different sequences. Each component, moreover, consists of a multiplicity of asynchronic sub-processes. The way in which the various processes and sub-processes occur, their acceleration or deceleration, or changes in their sequence, may determine the success or failure of the whole transition.

Main determinants of modernization. The factors that relate to modernization may be classified in the following ways. To begin with, there are the characteristics possessed by each society at the start of its transition.

Countries classified by their characteristics at the start

The starting point. Societies starting their transition to modernity vary in their levels and forms of secularization. Four main groups of countries may be distinguished: (1) Western or European countries; (2) westernized countries—that is, non-European but having European origins or coming under prolonged European influence or both; (3) civilized countries; and (4) primitive countries. Within these four groups, countries may be classified according to the times when they arrived at modernization. The firstcomer, of course, was Great Britain, both politically and economically. France was a firstcomer politically but not economically. Second comers among the Western countries include the central and northern European countries such as The Netherlands, Switzerland, the Scandinavian countries, the German states, and the Austro-Hungarian empire. Second comers among the westernized countries correspond to the offshoots of France and Great Britain overseas: the former colonies that became the United States, Canada, Australia, and New Zealand. Third comers among the Western countries include the southern and eastern European countries and (in part) the Soviet Union. Third comers among the westernized countries are the Latin American countries. A fourth category is Japan, the first civilized non-Western comer. A fifth category is comprised of other civilized non-Western comers, mostly Asian countries; many of these are higher civilizations such as India or China, along with African countries such as Egypt, Morocco, Algeria, and Ethiopia (the latter one of the few surviving archaic civilizations). A final category consists of the surviving primitive societies, most of them in Africa; their transition to modernity began for the most part in the second half of the 20th century.

It should be noted that many of the westernized areas include within them archaic civilizations and primitive societies. This is particularly important in Mexico, Peru, and part of the Caribbean area, where large populations had already reached a civilized level when they were submitted to colonial domination. These pre-Western civilizations had a strong influence in colonial times and have been powerful factors in shaping the nations that emerged after independence. The primitive societies, on the other hand, were largely destroyed by contact with the West, as in the United States, Canada, Argentina, and Uruguay, where the indigenous Indians were practically wiped out. To these local primitive communities must be added, however, the population imported from primitive areas—*i.e.*, the Africans brought to the United States, Brazil, and other American countries, who have exercised a recognizable influence on the shape of the transition there. Finally, in all of the Western countries the great majority of the people, especially the peasantry, lived at the start in premodern and sometimes even in precivilized social and cultural forms. Pockets of these populations and sometimes even whole categories of them remained at a relatively unmodernized level for a long time, and such people may even now be found within the most advanced countries. This is particularly notable among the Western third comers.

Societies at the starting point of modernization vary not only in their levels and forms of secularization, as described in the preceding paragraphs, but also in the extent to which they possess a centralized, bureaucratic state, in their ethnical and cultural homogeneity, and whether they are self-governing or dominated from outside. These three interrelated variables have a strong influence on the nature of the transition. The most favourable configuration is the presence at the starting point of a self-governing centralized bureaucratic territorial state, nationally homogeneous. This was the case with the Western firstcomers and with some of the second and third comers; it was also true of Japan (except for the degree of bureaucratization), China, and a few others. In most of the remaining countries one or more of the traits was lacking. This deficiency varied from very low to very high: it was at a minimum among the Western countries and their westernized offshoots; was higher and more frequent among the non-Western civilizations; and reached a maximum among the decolonized states of Africa, where nation building begins with de-tribalization.

The international system. With the rise of modern civilization, the era of world history began. The first modern industrial society had immediate effects on the rest of the world, and these effects increased during the 19th century, being multiplied by technological innovation and economic growth. The rise of an international system was inherent in the nature of modern industrial civilization. It has led to an international stratification of countries according to their relative political, economic, and military power. Increasingly one can distinguish a centre of the system and a periphery. The centre exercises leadership over the periphery, this being in most cases a kind of formal or informal colonization.

An essential feature of the international system is its continuous change. Change is brought about by developments within the modern industrial civilization itself or by international events such as wars, revolutions, economic crises, and social movements.

Centralization of the international system

World interdependence and centralization have tended to increase since the beginning of modern civilization, but the forms they have taken have changed. In the 19th century the revolution in transportation, together with the high industrial productivity of the centre (chiefly Great Britain, but followed by the Western second comers), led to the integration of the world market through international trade. This involved the transference of much primary production (agriculture, mining, and raw materials) to undeveloped areas of the planet. It was accompanied by the commercial conquest of the peripheral areas by the centre. Most of the peripheral areas, particularly the Latin American countries and most of the non-Western countries, began their economic modernization and their integration into the world system through the development of some form of export economy. The production of primary goods for export, accompanied by extensive private investment from the countries of the centre, became an essential factor in shaping the whole social structure. Politically and militarily, the domination of the centre tended to assume the form of direct colonization in most non-Western civilizations and Africa; only a few large societies, such as Japan or China, escaped colonization. The countries of the centre during this phase included Great Britain and a few other Western second and third comers.

With the two world wars, the international system entered a second phase. The countries of the centre came to include the United States, the Soviet Union, western Europe, and, later, China. There was, of course, a marked cleavage between the Communist countries and the others. The era of direct colonization ended, and practically all areas of the world became organized as nation-states. The countries of the periphery began to industrialize. Internationalization of the economy began to take the form of customs unions and free-trade areas, and there was a growth of international corporations. By the late 1960s and the early 1970s a third phase of the international system had begun: the East–West division between capitalist and Communist countries seemed to be giving way to polycentrism in which one could discern Western, Soviet, Chinese, and "nonaligned" groupings.

Scientific and technological advance has tended to increase the dependence of the peripheral countries upon those of the centre. The new discoveries require increased amounts of capital investment; the countries of the centre have a monopoly on them; and the new technology is adapted to the requirements of advanced societies rather than to those of developing countries. The same considerations apply to organizational innovations in government, business, education, and other sectors.

Changing internal structures

The impact of the international system on the modernizing of individual countries has changed in the course of time as political and social conditions have changed. Only a few examples can be given here. The two world wars and the economic Depression of the 1930s profoundly affected the foreign trade of the central countries. Their trade declined relative to their total economies, a larger proportion of it came to consist of industrial goods, and it tended increasingly to be oriented toward the industrial countries. At the same time, industrialization went ahead in the more advanced peripheral countries. The old international division of labour between industrial countries and raw-material-producing countries was increasingly replaced by new forms of relations. The foreign investment of the central countries shifted from such things as raw materials and railroads to industrial goods, and capital flowed increasingly toward other central countries. The old ideology of free trade and free enterprise was weakened by the increasing intervention of the state, by the consolidation of large corporations, and by the growth of nationalized industries in many countries. The extension of civil, social, and political rights within the countries of the centre, and the growth of mass communication, accelerated the pressure for similar rights among the masses in the peripheral countries and among the elites who occupied positions of leadership.

Changes in modernization patterns. Some reference has already been made to the effects of asynchronism, differences in starting points, and the changing state of the international system upon the modernization of individual countries. Others will be examined in the following discussion.

The type of leadership existing in a country at the time modernization begins may have a critical effect on the process. The bourgeoisie led the movement toward a modern society in Great Britain, France, the central and northern European states, and their overseas offshoots. In Germany, however, the situation was somewhat different, with a weak bourgeoisie and a strong state; there the process was dominated by the state. In Germany and also in countries formerly belonging to the Austro-Hungarian empire, there were additional complications in the lack of one or more of the following factors: (1) the territorial state, (2) nationality, or (3) independence. The Soviet-born U.S. historian Alexander Gerschenkron, in comparing the 19th-century development of European countries, has suggested a typology of "agents" of development: factory in the first comer; bank and factory in the second comers; and state, bank, and factory in the third comers (such as Italy or tsarist Russia). In the Latin American countries, the delay in formation of a national bourgeoisie and its weakness when it did come into existence were still more critical, since the Hispanic heritage and the lack of autonomy, of territoriality, and of nationality were decisively reinforced by the state of the international system at the time. The result there was development of export economies focussed on primary goods, dependence on the countries of the centre, delay or failure in industrialization, and an inability to incorporate large proportions of the population into a viable political and social system.

Patterns in the new countries

The effect of differences in rates and sequences of the component processes of modernization may be seen in a comparison of Latin American and the new countries of Asia and Africa with the Western industrialized countries. In most of these nations the demographic transition has been radically different from the Western example, because the decrease in mortality occurred sooner, and the decrease in fertility was delayed; in consequence, the population explosion has been much greater, and it has occurred earlier in the course of economic development. The same acceleration has occurred in urbanization, resulting in urbanization without industrialization. In the new countries there have been stronger contrasts between levels of modernization within countries, and much larger population segments have remained outside the modernizing sectors; these internal disequilibria have tended to increase over time, creating difficult problems for the governments. There has been a growth of public and private bureaucracies at a pace faster than in the West when it was in the corresponding historical stage; to some extent this serves only to provide employment for some of the excess urban population. In most urban areas the proportion of middle class persons is likewise higher than it was in the West at the same stage. There is a simultaneous occurrence of processes that occurred successively and some distance apart in the West. The new countries tend to be strongly centralized politically and socially while underdeveloped politically and economically. These are a few examples of the considerable differences in the modernization patterns of relatively early and relatively late comers to modernization.

MODERN CIVILIZATION: PROBLEMS AND PROSPECTS

Transitional and structural problems. The problems of modern society are of several kinds. Some arise from the resistance of groups of the population to certain aspects of the transition, often based on the defense of particular characteristics of the old society. This is not merely a matter of interests or of power; for values, attitudes, habits, and intellectual convictions play an equal part. In recent times some of the darker aspects of modernity have given strength to the resistance.

Other problems of the transition are structural, internal, and international. As noted earlier, the process of secularization brings into being many different ethical, aesthetic, and ideological tendencies, making it difficult to find common values in which everyone may share. A modernizing society must find ways of socializing the individual while leaving him the capacity to choose and to change. It must also develop ways of controlling the inevitable conflicts among persons and within persons. Some features of modern society tend to impede its response to these demands; advanced technology and complex organizations have a way of atomizing the individual and leaving him without the ability or the strength to make his own choices. The nightmare visions of George Orwell, Aldous Huxley, and other writers who have depicted societies of the future in which people are subjected to total control through scientific, technological, and organizational devices are not mere fantasies but concrete possibilities.

The future of conflict

Modernization and conflict. All theories of modernization agree that the transition is bound to be full of conflict, often revolutionary and violent. They disagree on the importance of conflict and the form it will take. Marxists see class conflict as the prime mover in historical change, defining classes in terms of their relation to the means of production. Most theories also agree that conflict will decrease or even disappear when the most advanced stage of modernity is finally reached; what conflict remains will be institutionalized and contained within civilized patterns. There is no way of predicting whether or not this will be the case. It may be that the contradictions inherent in modern civilization, added to those inherited from past history, will even produce a higher level of conflict.

The problem of world survival. The most serious questions raised by modernization are on the planetary level. The gap between the advanced and the developing countries has tended to increase rather than diminish. At the same time, the old premodern rivalries of national states continue unabated, while technological progress threatens to destroy man's environment. Since modern civilization is intrinsically planetary, it can endure only through planning on a global scale, based on universalistic values and carried out on behalf of all mankind. If man is to survive, he must invent the social order required by the scientific and technological civilization he has created.

BIBLIOGRAPHY. Two general and nontechnical books on the subject are MYRON WEINER (ed.), *Modernization: The Dynamics of Growth* (1966); and C.E. BLACK, *The Dynamics of Modernization* (1966), the latter focussed on political modernization. Anthologies of a somewhat more technical nature are WILBERT MOORE and BERT F. HOSELITZ (eds.), *Industrialization and Society* (1963); and OTTO FEINSTEIN (ed.), *Two Worlds of Change* (1964). The neo-evolutionary and historical point of view is presented in TALCOTT PARSONS' short books, *Societies: Evolutionary and Comparative Perspectives* (1966) and *The System of Modern Societies* (1971). Economic evolution in a global social context is analyzed by KARL POLANYI, *The Great Transformation* (1944). Various theoretical orientations may be found in S.N. EISENSTADT (ed.), *Readings in Social Evolution and Development* (1970). Two classic works in economic and social history are MAX WEBER, *Wirtschaftsgeschichte* (1923; Eng. trans., *General Economic History*, 1927 and 1958), and *Die protestantische Ethik und der "Geist" des Kapitalismus* (1904; Eng. trans., *The Protestant Ethic and the Spirit of Capitalism*, 1958). Two Marxist classics are KARL MARX and FRIEDRICH ENGELS, *The Communist Manifesto* (1848; Eng. trans., new ed., 1952) and *Die Deutsche Ideologie* (1932; Eng. trans., *The German Ideology*, 1969). On secularization, see GINO GERMANI, "Secularization, Modernization and Economic Development," in S.N. EISENSTADT (ed.), *The Protestant Ethic and modernization* (1967). For an example of the application of a general theory to a specific area, see GINO GERMANI, "Stages of Modernization in Latin America," in *Studies in Comparative International Development* (1969–70). Other treatments by the same author include *Politica y Sociedad en una época de Transición* (1971) and *Sociología de la Modernización* (1971).

(G.Ge.)

Industrial Medicine

Industrial medicine, a relatively new branch of medical science, has among its major concerns the protection of the worker from any hazards that may arise from his occupation or his occupational environment and the handling of any health emergencies that may occur during the hours of his employment. While early writers recognized the ravages of occupational diseases, which were rife among the metal miners of antiquity and the Middle Ages, Bernardino Ramazzini (1633–1714), a professor of medicine at the University of Modena and later at Padua, in northern Italy, was the first to publish a systematic account of trade diseases. He conceived it to be the duty of medical science to cultivate this specialty in order that workers could earn their living without bodily injury. The Industrial Revolution of the 19th century had profound effects on community life and on the health of people in the new factories and mines. There followed legislation to protect women and young persons by prohibiting employment below a certain age and by limiting their hours of work. The rising toll of deaths and serious injuries from accidents and diseases caused by the new machinery and exposure to toxic materials widened the scope of legislation. As knowledge of the effects of work on health increased, enlightened managements set up their own industrial medical services to improve and maintain health, safety, and efficiency. In the Soviet Union, after the October Revolution of 1917, special emphasis was given to preventive medicine and to providing for the health and safety of people at work.

Developments after World War II. World War II, with its enormous demands on manpower for industry and the armed services, encouraged developments that continued during a sustained period of high employment. By the 1970s industrial medicine, which previously had been primarily concerned with the prevention of industrial accidents and diseases among manual workers, was transformed into the wider and more challenging discipline of occupational health, which aims to protect and improve the health of all classes and kinds of workers. With shortages of skilled manpower in many countries, the care of the worker has become an economic necessity, not simply a moral or legal obligation. Developing countries give high priority to occupational-health services. Their national prosperity depends on a rapid process of industrialization in which the health and efficiency of the worker and a good environment are especially important.

Recent shift in emphasis

Relationship with other health services. In most countries in the Western world, services are provided voluntarily by the employer and are separate from other community-health services. In eastern European countries, there is usually one service consisting of two main branches: therapeutic and prophylactic medicine. The former is provided by hospitals, polyclinics, and the medical departments of large plants; and the latter, in the sanitary and epidemiological stations (Sanepids) in towns, rural areas, and, occasionally, in large plants. Physicians in hospitals and other treatment centres are responsible for the medical care of workers and the diagnosis and treatment of occupational diseases. The staff of the Sanepids have, among their other duties, responsibility for the assessment and control of the working environment. (The word Sanepid is derived from the first syllables of the English words sanitary and epidemiological. It is used in World Health Organization reports by Russians translating into English in the Soviet Union.)

Scope of article. This article deals with the aims and functions of occupational-health services and the types of occupational exposures that are hazardous, with examples of the more common occupational diseases, their treatment, outlook, and prevention.

AIMS AND FUNCTIONS OF OCCUPATIONAL-HEALTH SERVICES

The aims of an occupational-health service as defined by the International Labour Organisation are to protect people against any health hazard that may arise out of their work; to contribute toward their physical and mental adjustment by adapting work to suit them and by assigning them to jobs for which they are suited; and to contribute to the establishment and maintenance of physical and mental well-being. These aims are achieved by a medical team made up of occupational physicians and nurses or medical auxiliaries. A recent development, particularly in larger organizations with hazards from exposure to environmental contaminants, has been to appoint an occupational hygienist or health engineer to help with the measurement, assessment, and control of such hazards.

Selection and fitness for work. To help people find suitable work demands a knowledge of job requirements and an assessment of applicants' abilities by vocational selection including medical examinations. Such examinations are particularly important in the case of prospective employees for jobs that carry a risk of occupational disease or accident, or for jobs such as driving public vehicles and food handling, which may entail risks to others.

Continued medical surveillance. Vulnerable groups, including those exposed to recognized occupational hazards, handicapped persons, the young, the aged, and workers with prolonged or repeated absences from work, need to be kept under continued medical surveillance.

Identification of unrecognized hazards. An occupational-health service has a major responsibility for detecting health hazards of all degrees. The methods used are the clinical observation and enquiry about the work of persons who are being given treatment and advice and the observation of groups. Observing a whole group of workers may reveal a high death or sickness rate from a certain disease that is related to work. In this way nasal cancer has been identified as an occupational risk among nickel workers, lung cancer in asbestos workers and miners of hematite (an iron ore), and coronary heart disease as a high mortality risk among workers exposed to carbon disulfide, which is used in the manufacture of viscose rayon. Experts in occupational medicine can make an important contribution to the prevention of health risks in the planning and design of new plant and machinery. Similarly, their advice may be sought on the arrangement of hours of work and shift systems.

Methods of finding hazards

Treatment and counselling. Speedy treatment of injuries or acute poisonings at the place of work can prevent complications and aid rehabilitation. Such an arrangement has economic advantages in that it saves loss of time from travelling and waiting in crowded outpatient clinics and dispensaries. Workers with minor injuries who are referred to outside agencies are often kept off work unnecessarily by physicians and nurses who are not familiar with their patients' working conditions. A treatment service can become the focal point of an occupational-health service by providing evidence of physical and psychosocial hazards. It also offers opportunities for counselling and health education.

In developing countries with inadequate provisions for community health, occupational-health services may have to accept responsibility for general medical care of workers and their families.

SPECIFIC OCCUPATIONAL EXPOSURES

Inorganic and organic chemical compounds. The range of toxic chemicals to which man may be exposed is rapidly increasing. Naturally occurring materials such as lead, mercury, and silica have been sources of occupational disease since antiquity. To these have been added other materials taken from earth, such as asbestos, radioactive ores, and petroleum products, and a growing range of synthetic or artificially produced compounds. Among the more important toxic substances are metals and their compounds, such as lead, mercury, beryllium, cadmium, chromium, manganese, and nickel; compounds of arsenic, phosphorus and silicon; the noxious gases; and aromatic, aliphatic, and halogenated hydrocarbons (examples of the aromatic hydrocarbons are benzene and naphthalene; of the aliphatic, gasoline and fuel oils; of halogenated, trichloroethylene and carbon tetrachloride).

Respiratory tract irritants

The physical state of a material is a major factor in determining its toxic properties. As the respiratory tract is the most important mode of entry of industrial poisons into the body, substances that occur as gases, vapours, and particulate matter are usually more dangerous and difficult to control than compounds that normally occur as liquids.

Liquids can have a direct action on skin and mucous membranes. Some are absorbed through the skin and act as systemic poisons. Liquids that have a local action on the skin may be classified as primary irritants or as sensitizers that produce allergic reactions. Common primary irritants include inorganic acids and alkalis; salts of antimony, chromium, mercury, cadmium, and arsenic; and such industrial solvents as turpentine, trichloroethylene, and alcohol. Petroleum and coal-tar derivatives like pitch, bitumen, and mineral oils are keratogenic (that is, they tend to promote development of the horny layer of the skin) and can cause skin cancers.

There are many chemical substances that can cause sensitization dermatitis. First exposures may be harmless, but with repeated exposure sensitization may develop, and subsequent exposure, even to minute quantities, may cause severe dermatitis. Examples of sensitizers are photographic developers, dyes, oils, resins, and plasticizers (chemicals added to rubber to make it flexible, workable, or stretchable).

Liquids that are readily absorbed through the skin and act as systemic poisons include the nitro and amino derivatives of benzene, phenol, and tetraethyl lead (the latter of which is added to gasoline as an antiknock agent). Poisonous liquids may be swallowed accidentally, but this seldom occurs in industry and is usually the result of bringing food into workrooms.

Airborne contaminants

Airborne contaminants such as gases, vapours, aerosols, and dusts, if inhaled, may produce local effects on the respiratory tract or may act as systemic poisons. Irritants inflame mucous surfaces. Those of a high solubility such as ammonia and sulfur dioxide are absorbed by the moist surfaces of the upper respiratory passages; thus the lungs usually escape damage. Gases of moderate solubility such as chlorine and ozone can damage both the upper respiratory passages and the lungs. Because irritants of low solubility (*e.g.*, nitrogen dioxide and phosgene) have no effect on the upper respiratory tract, there is no warning that the worker has inhaled a poisonous gas. After a delay of several hours, acute pulmonary edema (collection of fluid in the lungs) with asphyxiation occurs, often resulting in death, because the cause of the injury has not been recognized.

Asphyxiants, which exert their effects by interfering with the oxygen supply to the tissues, are of two principal types, simple asphyxiants and chemical asphyxiants. The simple asphyxiants are physiologically inert gases that act by diluting the atmospheric oxygen below the partial pressure required to maintain an oxygen saturation of the blood sufficient for normal tissue respiration. Common examples of simple asphyxiants are carbon dioxide and methane. Chemical asphyxiants act by a chemical action that either prevents the blood from transporting oxygen from the lungs to the tissues or interferes with oxygenation in the tissues. Among the chemical asphyxiants are carbon monoxide; cyanogen and hydrogen cyanide, which inhibit tissue oxidation by combining with cellular catalysts; aniline, which changes hemoglobin to methemoglobin; and hydrogen sulfide, which causes respiratory paralysis. (For the effects of methane, carbon monoxide, and hydrogen sulfide, see below *Diseases due to gas inhalation*.)

A few compounds act primarily as anesthetics or narcotics without serious systemic effects. Examples are acetylene, ethylene, ethyl alcohol, and trichloroethylene, which is widely used as an industrial solvent. Its anesthetic property is by far its most important toxic effect and may cause accidents. Cases of addiction to trichloroethylene occur because continued exposure to low concentrations creates a pleasant feeling of mild intoxication. There are indications that trichloroethylene may also cause ventricular fibrillation, a rapid twitching of the muscle fibres of the lower chambers of the heart, preventing their coordinated contraction.

A large number of substances in the form of gases, vapours, or particulate matter, when inhaled and absorbed into the bloodstream, exert systemic toxic effects on one or more of the organ systems. There is a diverse group that causes anemia and other blood disease. They include inorganic compounds of lead and derivatives of benzene, arsine, and radioactive substances. There is a large group that affects the central nervous system and the peripheral nerves or causes behavioral disorders; important examples are lead, mercury, arsenic, and manganese; trichloroethylene, carbon disulfide, methyl bromide, and chloride; and organophosphorous pesticides. Among the several liver poisons are the halogenated hydrocarbons such as carbon tetrachloride, chloroform, tetrachloroethane, chlorinated naphthalenes, and methyl chloride; and compounds of selenium, antimony, and phosphorus. Substances that attack the kidneys include compounds of mercury and cadmium; and halogenated hydrocarbons. The kidneys and the bladder are also the site of occupational cancers after exposure to chemicals used in the dyestuff and rubber industry; these include naphthylamines, benzidine, and 4-aminodiphenyl. Virtually any system or organ in the body may be damaged by specific industrial exposures. Lead, the chlorinated hydrocarbons, and organophosphorous compounds have general toxic effects. The latter, which are used as pesticides, inhibit an enzyme and cause acetylcholine to accumulate. This disturbs vision, upsets the digestive and respiratory tracts, slows the heart, and paralyzes the limbs.

Substances that affect blood

There are several dusts that have a local action on the respiratory tract and cause disabling and incurable chronic industrial pulmonary diseases. These diseases are more prevalent than any other group of occupational diseases, mainly because they have an extremely gradual onset and are not readily detected, and also because dust particles of respirable size are difficult to control. The most important of these arise from the inhalation of silica, coal dust, and asbestos (see below *Diseases due to dust inhalation*). They occur among miners and workers using these materials in manufacturing processes and building operations. They cause formation of scar tissue that eventually destroys large areas of lung tissue and leads to severe breathlessness. Superimposed pulmonary tuberculosis intensifies these dust diseases and makes the outlook grave. Metals that act upon the respiratory system include beryllium (see below *Metal poisoning*), cadmium, aluminum, and such hard metals as tungsten carbide and cobalt. Vegetable dusts from cotton, flax, and soft hemp give rise to a respiratory disease, byssinosis, characterized by symptoms of chest tightness at the beginning of the working week and eventually leading to chronic bronchitis and emphysema (inflammation of the air passages and abnormal distention of the lungs with air). Other vegetable dusts like bagasse and hay that become contaminated with mold spores produce an allergic alveolitis (inflammation of the air sacs of the lungs) that can be disabling. More recently, hazards of pulmonary disease have been described among workers who make enzyme washing powders and those exposed to organic diisocyanate compounds, used in making paints and lacquers, synthetic rubbers, and adhesives. Occupational cancer of the lung occurs among workers exposed to asbestos, to bichromates, to polycyclic hydrocarbons in gas-retort houses, and to arsenic compounds; it also occurs among workers engaged in the mining of radioactive ores and hematite. Cancer of the sinuses is a hazard among nickel refiners and woodworkers who make furniture from hardwoods.

Mechanical factors causing occupational disorders. Vibrating and rotating tools may cause a condition called dead hand, vibration, or pneumatic-hammer disease. In industries in which repetitive movements of the hands and forearms are common, such as boot and shoe manufacture, assembly-line operations, and net making, the tendon sheaths and the junctions between muscles and tendons may become inflamed, a condition called tenosynovitis. This painful and disabling condition may affect new employees or regular workers who have been assigned to a new process calling for unusual and repetitive movements.

Cramps or craft palsies also occur in occupations that involve complex and rapid repetitive movements. The condition is found in writers, telegraphists, pianists, and in workers in many other trades. Coordinated movement becomes difficult or impossible. There are no organic changes in the nervous system and muscles. The condition is due to a combination of physical and psychological factors. Neurotic symptoms are common among those affected.

Workers who use hard tools such as picks, hammers, and shovels or who habitually kneel at their work are subject to "beat" conditions. Beat hand is a subcutaneous cellulitis (inflammation of tissues under the skin) caused by infection of tissue subjected to constant bruising. It is of frequent occurrence among miners and stokers. Beat knee, which occurs among carpet layers and miners in low seams is the result of repeated pressure and minor injury. It has two forms, a subcutaneous cellulitis, and bursitis (inflammation of the bursa, a small sac containing fluid and situated at points of friction such as the knee or elbow).

Noise. Industrial noise can damage the ears and cause annoyance. There is no clear evidence that it can cause mental or physical illness apart from injury to the hearing mechanism (see below *Mechanical factors*). There is also no evidence from available data that ultrasonic waves (of too great frequency for human hearing) are significantly hazardous.

High and low temperatures. High temperatures occur in a variety of occupations, such as mining, metal refining and casting, brickmaking, construction work in the tropics, and work in engine rooms aboard ships. Common effects are heat cramps from loss of sodium chloride in the sweat; if saline drinks are taken, the cramps can be prevented. In heatstroke, sweating suddenly ceases and the body temperatures may rise as high as 108° F (42° C). If this state is unrelieved, coma and death may ensue. Heat exhaustion occurs during excessively hot weather in workers not acclimatized to heat. Sweating is profuse and body temperatures are normal. It is caused by dilation of the peripheral blood vessels. Recovery is rapid after rest.

Effects of exposure to cold

Exposure to low temperatures occurs among workers in artificially cooled or naturally cold environments. Such persons include building workers, commercial fishermen, food-storage attendants, and Dry Ice makers. The effects are chilblains, frostbite, and immersion foot or trench foot. These conditions may be prevented by protective clothing.

Radiation. Radiation can be classified as ionizing or non-ionizing. Ionizing radiation breaks down the molecules in tissues into electrified particles, or ions. Non-ionizing sources of radiation include ultraviolet light, laser, and infrared. Ultraviolet light produced, for example, in electric arc welding, can cause conjunctivitis—inflammation of the mucous membrane lining the eyelids and covering a portion of the exposed part of the eyeball—and burning of the skin. Laser beams, intense and nonspreading beams of visible light, with applications in industry that include microwelding and micromachining, can cause damage to the eye and produce ionizing radiations. Infrared radiation, as from hot metal and glass, may cause cataract (opacity of the lens of the eye) or systemic effects.

Ionizing radiations include X-rays, gamma rays, and corpuscular radiation (radiation of subatomic particles) emitted from naturally or artificially radioactive sources. Industrial hazards may arise from the use of X-rays, and radioactive isotopes (unstable forms of substances that emit radiation in the process of breaking down into other substances), use of radioactive paint (*e.g.*, to make watch hands luminescent), and mining of radioactive ores. The most serious chronic effects are skin cancers among radiologists (specialists in the medical use of radiation) and radiographers (persons engaged in production of X-ray films); bone tumours among users of radioactive paint; and lung cancer in miners of radioactive ores. Ionizing radiations can also cause leukemia (malignant proliferation of white blood cells), aplastic anemia (underproduction of red blood cells and hemoglobin); nausea, vomiting, diarrhea, and abdominal pain; and brain damage.

High and low pressures. Exposures to high or low atmospheric pressures can cause decompression sickness. It occurs, for example, when workers in compressed air, as in constructing tunnels under rivers, are too rapidly returned to ordinary air pressures, or when airmen ascend too rapidly to high altitudes. The symptoms include pains in the joints and bones; difficulty in breathing, or even asphyxia; and staggers, dizziness, and vomiting. All these symptoms are caused by the release of nitrogen from solution in the blood and tissues and the formation of nitrogen bubbles. (See COMPRESSION AND DECOMPRESSION INJURIES.)

Infectious agents. The most important sources of occupational diseases due to infections are the zoonoses (diseases of vertebrate animals transmissible to man). Examples are anthrax (see below *Infectious agents*), brucellosis, and psittacosis. Brucellosis, or undulant fever, has a worldwide distribution. The disease, which usually results from direct contact with infected cattle, goats, milk, or milk products, is characterized by recurrent attacks of fever and ill health. Psittacosis, infection with an organism variously called *Miyagawanella*, *Bedsonia*, and *Chlamydia*, is acquired through contact with infected wild birds, domestic fowls, parrots, and other cage birds. Fever and sometimes severe lung disease result. Occupational infections may also be acquired from contaminated water, soil, or air.

Leptospirosis, or Weil's disease, is a risk among miners, sewer workers, slaughterers, and fish gutters. The organism *Leptospira icterohaemorrhagiae* is shed in the urine of infected rats and survives in pools or stagnant water or on moist surfaces and so infects man. The disease is characterized by mild fever and jaundice.

Tetanus

Tetanus organisms harboured in the intestinal tracts of many animals are passed in the feces and lie dormant in the soil for long periods. Construction and agricultural workers run the risk of acquiring the disease should tetanus spores contaminate a penetrating wound.

Pulmonary tuberculosis may be contracted by doctors, bacteriologists and nurses in the course of their work; such cases are instances of occupational disease.

SOME REPRESENTATIVE OCCUPATIONAL DISEASES

Diseases due to dust inhalation. Asbestosis is a lung disease caused by inhalation of asbestos dust. Asbestos is the name applied to a variety of naturally occurring silicates that are fibrous, flexible, and resistant to heat and acids. They have many industrial and domestic uses; *e.g.*, as fire-resisting clothing, insulation around steam pipes, brake linings, and coating for bulkheads of ships. When mixed with cement, asbestos is used to make sheets, pipes, and blocks for building work. There are three main types: chrysotile, a magnesium silicate, blue asbestos, or crocidolite, which is mainly a silicate of iron, and amosite, a magnesium–iron silicate. It is only recently that their dangerous properties in the form of dust have been fully recognized. The disease asbestosis is characterized by difficulty in breathing, cyanosis (bluish skin), clubbing of fingers and toes, impairment of respiratory function (release of carbon dioxide from the blood and its taking up of oxygen), and characteristic chest X-rays. Additional hazards of cancer of the bronchus, pleura, or peritoneum may also result. (The pleura and peritoneum are the membranes lining the chest and the abdomen, respectively.) Diagnosis of these malignant forms of asbestos disease is made by chest X-rays and pleural or peritoneal biopsy (examination of specimens of pleura and peritoneum).

Prevention of asbestosis

Prevention of asbestos disease depends on dust control by enclosure and exhaust ventilation of machinery, transport of the material in impervious bags, scrupulous cleanliness of floors, personal protective devices, and the use of nontoxic synthetic materials as substitutes in situations in which dust control is difficult.

Periodic examination of workers at risk enables those with early evidence of disease to be removed from further exposure. This measure, combined with high standards of environmental hygiene, can reduce the risk.

Other forms of industrial lung disease due to dust inhalation are reviewed in the article RESPIRATORY SYSTEM DISEASES.

Diseases due to gas inhalation. Methane (CH_4), a colourless, ordourless gas formed by decaying vegetable matter, may be a hazard in coal mines. It acts as a simple asphyxiant. Miners may be overcome if concentrations are high enough to cause oxygen deprivation; fortunately, in such circumstances the miners fall to the ground, where concentrations are lower because methane is lighter than air, and thus they may recover. Methane, also known as firedamp, produces an explosive mixture with air at relatively low concentrations. Such accidents are now rare, because dangerous concentrations of methane may be detected by flame safety lamps.

Carbon monoxide (CO), the most widely encountered poisonous gas, may be present wherever coal, paper, oil, gasoline, or any other organic material is burned. The gas is colourless and odourless. It reduces the oxygen-carrying capacity of the blood by combining with hemoglobin to form carboxyhemoglobin, and thus it brings about asphyxiation. The carboxyhemoglobin produces a characteristic bright-pink skin. Diagnosis can be confirmed by examination of the blood. Treatment includes removal of the victim to the open air, artificial respiration, and administration of oxygen. Prevention of carbon monoxide poisoning depends on good plant design and adequate ventilation, proper maintenance of the plant, tests for air contamination, and the provision of breathing apparatus for use in case of exposure.

Prevention of CO poisoning

Hydrogen sulfide (H_2S) poisoning occurs in mines in which sulfide ores are found, in the production and refining of petroleum, and in the manufacture of viscose rayon, chemicals, dyes, and glues. The gas is colourless and has an odour resembling that of bad eggs. At low concentrations it produces irritant effects, particularly on the eyes. At relatively high concentrations, it causes headaches, giddiness, depression, and lung irritation. With concentrations above 700 parts per million, acute poisoning occurs, with sudden loss of consciousness and respiratory paralysis. Death follows if the victim is not removed to a clean atmosphere and given artificial respiration, preferably with the administration of oxygen.

Metal poisoning. Examples of metal poisoning are the diseases resulting from exposure to beryllium and lead.

Beryllium has many valuable uses as a hard, corrosion-resistant alloy with copper, aluminum, or nickel. It was at one time used along with phosphorus for coating the tubes of fluorescent lamps, but this practice was abandoned because of beryllium's high toxicity. Exposures may occur during the extraction of the metal from the ore, the manufacture and cutting of alloys, and the making of refractory materials.

Exposure to beryllium can cause acute inflammation of the lungs, the skin, and the conjunctiva. There is a chronic form of beryllium disease that has an extremely gradual onset. It is characterized by severe difficulty in breathing, loss of appetite, and a general feeling of ill health. Diagnosis is made on the basis of a history of exposure, the past course of the illness, X-ray findings, and the presence of beryllium in the urine and the tissues. The outlook is poor in the chronic form of the disease. The use of corticosteroids (hormones produced by the outer substance of the adrenal glands) has improved the outlook and may arrest early cases.

Prevention depends on rigorous dust control and routine medical surveillance.

Lead poisoning, one of the classic occupational diseases, is caused by exposure to a variety of lead compounds that have been exploited by man since ancient times. These compounds may be organic or inorganic.

Exposure to inorganic lead compounds occurs in a number of situations, including metal smelting, making lead-based paints and varnishes and burning them off, and the manufacture of wet-cell storage batteries. The inorganic compounds are absorbed as dust or fumes, mainly through the respiratory tract.

Poisoning by organic lead compounds is a relatively recent hazard introduced by the use of tetraethyl lead as an antiknock additive to motor fuels. It is a highly volatile fluid that may be absorbed by inhalation, ingestion, or through the skin.

The early symptoms of inorganic lead poisoning include fatigue, disturbance of sleep, intestinal colic, and constipation. More prolonged and severe exposure may cause brain and kidney damage and wristdrop or other palsies from muscle damage. Diagnosis can be made on the basis of a history of exposure and of signs and symptoms that include a dark line just below the margin of the gums that is caused by lead deposits.

Avoidance of lead poisoning

Lead poisoning among industrial workers that is severe enough to cause symptoms can be avoided by medical surveillance and by such measures as environmental control of dust and fumes and routine environmental monitoring to ensure that atmospheric concentrations of lead are within acceptable limits. Treatment of lead poisoning is by use of a chelating agent, a substance that forms with lead a stable and harmless compound that can be excreted by way of the kidneys.

Poisoning by organic lead compounds such as tetraethyl lead presents a different clinical picture, which is characterized by mental confusion and agitation. In severe cases there is acute mental disturbance with delirium, convulsions, and coma usually leading to death. Intoxication may occur as a result of accidental spillage or of cleaning storage tanks that have held ethyl gasoline without adequate protection. The most effective treatment is repeated doses of barbiturates for sedation.

Mechanical factors. Among the more important occupational diseases in which mechanical factors play a part are diseases caused by the use of vibrating tools and the injuries to the ears from industrial noise.

Pneumatic hammers such as road drills and rotating tools used for grinding metals or saws for cutting wood can cause vibration disorders that include Raynaud's phenomenon (also called dead hand or pneumatic hammer disease), a disorder affecting the blood vessels. There is intermittent pallor or cyanosis of the hands (a bluish or purplish discoloration of the skin) precipitated by exposure to cold; abnormalities of the bones and joints in the fingers, wrists, and elbows; loss of calcium in the wristbones (which causes no symptoms); and injury to the shoulder joint and soft tissues of the hands.

Diagnosis is made on the basis of the history of exposure to vibration and associated symptoms. Workers can protect themselves by avoiding chilling of hands, wearing protective padded gloves, and avoiding excessive periods of exposure to vibrations.

The effects of noise on hearing are broadly divisible into three categories: temporary and permanent hearing loss and acoustic trauma. The latter is a damage to the ears that results from exposure to a brief intense burst of sound, as from gunfire. The victim may sustain ruptured eardrums and damage to the middle and inner ear. Temporary hearing loss is a short-term effect that is virtually always present during or after exposure to noise. Permanent occupational deafness is caused by continued exposure to high noise levels, which eventually impair the function of the hearing apparatus in the cochlea of the inner ear. The two important characteristics of noise are its frequency, which is measured in cycles per second (or hertz) and determines the pitch or note of the sound, and its intensity or loudness, which is measured in decibels. Most industrial noise is continuous and consists of a broad band of frequencies. If loudness, or sound pressure level, reaches 80 decibels or more for eight hours a day, there is a risk that permanent deafness will occur. The first effect is to reduce hearing acuity at sound frequencies around 4,000 cycles per second or hertz (Hz). If such noise exposures continue over a long period, hearing acuity is reduced over a wider range of frequencies. Since ordinary speech is mainly within a range of 300 to 3,000 Hz, hearing loss in this range must be avoided by reducing the level of noise and the duration of exposure, by providing ear protection, and by audiometric (hearing) examinations to detect persons susceptible to noise.

Types of ear damage from noise

Infectious agents. Among the infections encountered in occupational surroundings is anthrax, caused by *Bacil-*

lus anthracis. It may occur in those who come into contact with animals suffering from the disease, their carcasses, or wool, horsehair, bones, hides, or horn. The bacillus forms resistant spores that survive for many years. The disease occurs in three forms—external or cutaneous, pulmonary, and gastrointestinal. Cutaneous anthrax, or malignant pustule, is by far the most common form of the disease. Infection usually takes place through a skin abrasion on an exposed area. After a few days a small itchy papule (pimple-like elevation) appears and develops into a small blister surrounded by an inflamed, swollen area and covered by a black scab. Diagnosis is made on the characteristic appearance of the lesion and a history of exposure. It can be confirmed by bacteriological investigation. If large doses of penicillin are given early, the outcome is usually favourable and fatalities are rare. Prevention is possible by cleansing of materials from areas with a high anthrax incidence, by scrupulous personal hygiene, and by educating workers at risk in the early recognition of the disease so that treatment can be immediate.

BIBLIOGRAPHY. ETHEL BROWNING, *Toxicity of Industrial Metals*, 2nd ed. (1969), a well-documented, succinct account of the toxicity of metals used in industrial processes; *Toxicity and Metabolism of Industrial Solvents* (1965), comprehensive and also well-documented; WILLIAM BURNS, *Noise and Man* (1968), a well-written scientific appraisal of the effects of noise on humans, including methods of measuring hearing and noise; DONALD HUNTER, *Diseases of Occupations*, 4th ed. (1969), a comprehensive and fascinating account of the occupational diseases (the standard work); INTERNATIONAL LABOUR OFFICE, *Encyclopaedia of Occupational Health and Safety*, 2 vol. (1971–72), comprising more than 900 articles prepared by experts in their fields; FRANK A. PATTY (ed.), *Industrial Hygiene and Toxicology*, 3rd ed., 3 vol. in 4 (1978–81), an excellent reference book on toxicology and environmental control; BERNARDINO RAMAZZINI, *De morbis artificum diatriba* (1713; *Diseases of Workers*, 1713 text rev. with Eng. trans. and notes by W.C. WRIGHT, 1940), one of the most important classics on diseases of workers—fascinating to read; R.S.F. SCHILLING (ed.), *Modern Trends in Occupational Health* (1960), including 21 chapters on the more important occupational hazards and their measurement, with sections on vocational psychology, morale, and machine design; and *Occupational Health Practice* (1973), a comprehensive account of the practice of occupational health.

(R.S.F.S.)

Infectious Diseases

The term infectious disease refers to a process caused by a microorganism that impairs the health of an individual person. The term infection is defined as the invasion of the body by microorganisms and the reaction of tissues to their presence or to the toxins that these organisms produce, irrespective of whether or not the health of the person is affected. When an infection occurs in which there is no alteration of health, the term subclinical infection is used. Thus, a person may be infected but not have an infectious disease. This principle is illustrated by the use of vaccines for the prevention of infectious diseases. For example, a virus such as measles may be partially inactivated (attenuated) and used as an immunizing agent. The immunization is designed to produce a measles infection in the recipient but generally causes no discernible alteration in the state of health. It produces immunity to measles without producing a clinical illness (an infectious disease).

Among the agents of infections disease, microorganisms are the microscopic or submicroscopic "germs" such as viruses, bacteria, and protozoa that enter the body. Higher up the scale are the just visible parasites such as the acari, or itch mites, of scabies, and the helminths, or worms, which may be several feet long. The only characteristic all of these share is that, for part or all of their life, they depend for survival on being able to parasitize or live on a human host. A virus to survive and multiply must get inside a living cell, but many bacteria can live and multiply for a time on nonliving matter, and helminths for part of their life lead an independent existence. Size is often linked with more vital characterstics, but one function that certainly does not correlate with size is the ability to cause serious disease. Many of the most disastrous infections are caused by the smallest of the parasites that attack the body. The virus of poliomyelitis, for example, is only about 25 millimicrons (0.001 inch) in diameter.

The most important barriers to invasion of the human host by microorganisms are the skin and mucous membranes. The mucous membranes are the tissues that line the nose, mouth, and upper respiratory tract. When these tissues are broken or affected by another disease process, invasion by microorganisms may occur. These microorganisms may produce a local infectious disease (*e.g.*, boils) or may invade the bloodstream and be carried throughout the body, producing generalized bloodstream infection (septicemia) or localized infection at a distant site (*e.g.*, meningitis, an infection of the covering of the brain). Infective agents can be swallowed in food and drink to attack the wall of the intestinal tract and cause local or general disease. The conjunctiva, which covers the front of the eyes, may be penetrated by invisible viruses, and these may cause a local inflammation of the eye or pass into the bloodstream and cause a severe general disease such as measles or smallpox. Microorganisms can enter the body through the delicate membranes of the genital tract, setting up the acute inflammatory reaction of gonorrhea in the genital and pelvic organs or spreading out to attack almost any organ of the body with the more chronic but more destructive lesions of syphilis. Even before birth, viruses and other infective agents can pass through the placenta and attack developing cells, so that at birth the infant may already be diseased or deformed.

The hostile environment

From conception to death, then, humans are a target for attack by multitudes of other living organisms, all of them competing for a place in the common environment. The air people breathe, the soil they tread on, the waters and the vegetation around them, the buildings they inhabit and work in, all can be populated with forms of life that are dangerous. Domestic animals may harbour organisms that are a threat, and wildlife teems with agents of infection that can afflict humans with serious disease. Humans are not without defenses against these threats. The body is equipped with sensitive mechanisms that react quickly and specifically against disease organisms when they attack, and survival throughout the ages has depended largely on these reactions. The human environment, in the microbiological sense, is mainly a hostile one. To some extent humans have learned to control it, but they cannot subdue it, and sometimes a minor change in the environment may lead to unforeseen alterations in the balance between humans and their biological competitors.

This article is divided into the following sections:

I. General aspects
- Types of infectious agents
  - Categories of microorganisms
  - Modes of survival
- The human host
  - Commensal organisms
  - Immunity
- The effects of human activities and surroundings
  - Human activity
  - Animals and insects
  - Inanimate environment
- Routes and modes of infection
  - Respiratory route
  - Gastrointestinal route
  - Mucous membranes
  - Skin
  - Transplacental infection
- Prevention
  - Immunization programs
  - Isolation techniques
  - Destruction of infectious agent or carrier

II. Individual systemic diseases
- Respiratory tract
  - Viral diseases
  - Bacterial diseases
  - Fungus diseases
  - Other infections
- Gastrointestinal tract
  - Bacterial diseases
  - Viral diseases
  - Diseases caused by helminths

Skin and mucous membranes
Bacterial diseases
Viral diseases
Diseases caused by protozoa
Diseases caused by rickettsiae
Diseases caused by skin parasites

I. General aspects

TYPES OF INFECTIOUS AGENTS

Categories of microorganisms. Microorganisms, the agents of infection, can be divided into different groups on the basis of their size, biochemical characteristics, and the manner in which they interact with the human host. The groups of microorganisms that cause infectious diseases are categorized as follows: bacteria, viruses, chlamydia, rickettsia, Mycoplasma and Ureaplasma, fungi, and parasites.

Generally, bacteria are large enough to be seen under the light microscope, whereas viruses are not. Streptococci, bacteria that cause scarlet fever, are about 0.75 micrometre (0.00003 inch) in diameter. The spirochetes, which cause syphilis, leptospirosis, and rat-bite fever, are five to 15 micrometres long. Bacteria can survive within the body but outside of individual cells. Some bacteria, classified as aerobes, require oxygen for growth, whereas others, such as those normally found in the small bowel of healthy persons, only grow in the absence of oxygen and therefore are called anaerobes. Most bacteria are surrounded by a capsule that appears to play an important role in the ability of an individual organism to produce disease. A number of bacterial species can elaborate toxins that, in turn, may damage tissues. Bacteria contain both deoxyribonucleic acid (DNA) and ribonucleic acid (RNA) and can be treated with antibiotics.

Differences between bacteria, viruses, and mycoplasms

Viruses typically are intracellular parasites and cannot be grown in the laboratory unless the growing medium contains living cells. Viruses are placed into various groups on the basis of size, shape, and whether they contain DNA or RNA; all contain either DNA or RNA, but not both. Viruses are visible by electron microscopy; they vary in size from approximately 25 millimicrons (poliovirus) to 250 millimicrons (smallpox virus). (One millimicron is 0.001 micrometre.) They cannot be treated with antibiotics.

Chlamydia are obligatory intracellular parasites (*i.e.*, obliged to live in cells) that are 250 to 500 millimicrons in diameter. When they interact with the host cells, cytoplasmic microsomes are produced. Chlamydia contain DNA and RNA and can be treated by antibiotics. Human diseases caused by Chlamydia include conjunctivitis (inflammation of the covering of the eye) in the newborn infant, pneumonia, and genital infection.

Rickettsia are small organisms that range in size from 250 millimicrons to more than one micrometre. They are devoid of a cell wall but are surrounded by a cell membrane. They are obligatory intracellular parasites with the exception of *Coxiella burnetii*, the cause of Q fever. This rickettsial agent can survive in milk, sewage, and aerosols. Most rickettsia are transmitted to humans by an arthropod carrier, or vector, but *Coxiella burnetii* can be transmitted to humans by the tick or can be acquired by inhalation, causing pneumonia. Rickettsial diseases may respond to therapy with appropriate antibiotics.

Mycoplasma and Ureaplasma are the smallest organisms capable of growing in a cell-free medium. They range in size from 150 to 850 millimicrons. These organisms may cause pneumonia, genital infection, or infection of the brain, spinal cord, liver, and other organs. Disease due to Mycoplasma and Ureaplasma may be treated with antibiotics.

Fungi may exist as yeast or molds and may alternate between these forms, depending on the environmental conditions. Yeasts are simple cells, three to five micrometres in diameter. Mold consists of filamentous branching structures called hyphae, two to 10 micrometres in diameter, that are formed of several cells lying end to end. Fungal diseases in humans are called mycoses and include such disorders as histoplasmosis, coccidioidomycosis, and blastomycosis. These diseases can be mild, characterized by an upper respiratory infection, or severe, characterized by involvement of the bloodstream and every organ system. Antibiotics may be effective in their treatment.

Parasites may be subclassified into protozoa (unicellular organisms devoid of a cell wall). One of the most common protozoan parasite diseases of humans is malaria. The various species of malaria parasites are about four micrometres in diameter. Another type of parasite, the tapeworm, can grow to several feet in length. Treatments aim either to kill the parasite or to disturb it so that it dislodges itself from attachment to the human host.

Modes of survival. Infective agents have various ways of achieving survival. Some depend on rapid multiplication and quick spread from one host to another. When the virus of measles enters the body it multiplies quietly for a week or two, then pours into the bloodstream and spreads into every organ of the body. For several days before a rash appears, the surface cells of the respiratory tract are bursting with measles virus, and vast quantities are shed every time an infected person coughs or sneezes. A day or two after the rash appears, antibody rises in the bloodstream; this quickly kills the virus and stops further shedding. The patient rapidly becomes noninfectious but already may have infected others. In this way an epidemic rapidly builds up, and there is an enormous increase in the amount of measles virus in circulation. This picture is true of many other infectious agents—for example, influenza virus. How such viruses exist between epidemics is less clear, for outside the human body their life is precarious. The infection certainly smoulders on, perhaps in human or in animal carriers, and perhaps in some latent form as yet unknown.

In more chronic infections the picture is different. In tuberculosis there is no overwhelming multiplication and rapid shedding of the tubercle bacillus. Instead it remains in the infected person's body for a long time, slowly forming areas of chronic inflammation, which, from time to time, break down and allow bacilli to escape to the outside. There is no need for hurry or for explosive outbreaks.

Some organisms grow spores, a resting or dormant form, resistant to heat, cold, drying, and chemical action. A sporing organism does not need to cause outbreaks in humans, for it has the key to its survival locked up in its own spore, which can survive for months or years under the most adverse conditions, and sporing organisms are not, in fact, highly infectious. The germ of tetanus, *Clostridium tetani*, is present everywhere in the environment—in garden soil, in dust, on window ledges and floors—and yet tetanus is an uncommon disease, especially in developed countries. The same is true of the anthrax germ, *Bacillus anthracis*. It is usually present in abundance in factories where rawhides and animal wool and hair are handled, but it rarely causes anthrax in people working there. In both cases, the germ gains nothing from infecting humans, for it cannot escape from the body whether the person lives or dies from the disease. *Clostridium botulinum*, the germ of botulism, produces one of the most lethal toxins that can afflict humans, and yet the disease is one of the rarest: the germ depends for its survival on its resistant spore. In contrast to these relatively independent organisms, there are others that cannot exist at all outside the human body. The germs of syphilis and gonorrhea, for example, depend for survival on their extreme infectivity and their complete adaptation to a parasitic existence.

Spore-growing organisms

Some organisms have a complicated life cycle and depend on more than one host. The malaria parasite must pass part of its life inside a mosquito, whereas the liver fluke, an occasional human parasite, spends part of its life in the body of a sheep, part in a water snail, and part in the open air as a cyst attached to grasses. Many other life histories, equally or more complicated, could be cited.

THE HUMAN HOST

Commensal organisms. All of the outer surfaces of the body are covered with microorganisms that normally do no harm and may in fact be useful. Such organisms are called commensal. Those on the skin may help to break down dying skin cells or to use up debris secreted by the many minute glands and pores that open on the skin. Many of the organisms in the intestinal tract break complex waste products into simple substances, and others help in the manufacture or synthesis of chemical compounds such as some of the vitamins that are essential to human life. It should be understood in this connection that the gastrointestinal canal is one of the "outer" surfaces of the body. From its upper part, the stomach and duodenum, food is absorbed into the body, and into its lower part, the large intestine, waste products are excreted from the inside of the body. Embryologically, too, the intestinal canal is an external structure formed by the intucking, or invagination, of the ectoderm, or outer surface, of the body. The mouth, the nose, and the sinuses, or spaces inside the bones of the face, are in this context also external structures, in direct contact with the outside environment. They are heavily populated with microorganisms. Some of these are true commensals; they live on humans, deriving their sustenance from the surface cells of the body without doing any harm. Others are disease germs, or indistinguishable from them; they live, like the true commensals, in the nose and throat of a human being and, in spite of their disease potential, may never cause disease. They are capable, however, when the environment is altered, of causing severe illness in their host, or, without harming their host, they may infect a second person with a serious disease. In this case, the first host is the carrier of the microorganism, the second a victim of the microorganismal disease.

Change from commensals to disease-causing organisms

It is not known why, for example, the hemolytic streptococcus can live for months or years in the throat without trouble—in the carrier state—and then suddenly cause an acute attack of tonsillitis, or how an apparently harmless pneumococcus gives rise to pneumonia, or how an indolent throat parasite such as *Haemophilus influenzae* suddenly invades the body and sets up one of the most severe forms of meningitis (inflammation of the coverings of the brain and spinal cord). It may be that such external influences as a change in temperature or humidity are enough to upset the balance between host and parasite or that a new invader such as a virus enters and, by competing for some element in the environment, forces the original parasite to react more violently with its host. The term "lowered resistance," often proffered to help describe conditions at the onset of parasitic disease, is nonspecific and implies any change in the immune system or inflammatory system of the host.

The microorganismal environment can of course be changed radically and obviously. If antibiotics are given to a person, the commensal organisms in his body can be killed, and other organisms, less innocuous, may take their place. In the mouth and throat, penicillin may eradicate pneumococci, streptococci, and other microorganisms that are sensitive to the drug, and microorganisms such as *Candida albicans*, insensitive to penicillin, may then proliferate in the absence of normal competitors and cause thrush, an inflammatory condition of the mouth and throat. In the intestinal canal an antibiotic may easily kill most of the microorganisms normally there and allow dangerous organisms, such as *Pseudomonas aeruginosa*, to multiply and perhaps invade the bloodstream and the tissues of the body. If an infectious agent—for example, a salmonella or food-poisoning germ—reaches the intestinal canal, the giving of an antibiotic may have an effect very different from what could be expected on theory; instead of attacking and destroying the salmonella, it kills the normal inhabitants of the bowel and allows the salmonella to flourish and persist. The relationship of the body to its normal commensal organisms is delicate.

When a pathogenic (disease-causing) microorganism invades the body for the first time, clinically the response of the body may vary from nothing at all through various degrees of nonspecific reactions to a response recognized as a specific infectious disease. Immunologically there is always a response, the purpose of which is defense. This defense may be completely successful, and in this case there is no obvious bodily reaction; partially successful, when the affected person suffers but recovers from an infectious disease; unsuccessful, when in spite of specific immune reactions, the patient is overwhelmed by the intensity of the infectious process and dies.

The two responses, the clinical and the immunological, can be illustrated by the natural history of the disease poliomyelitis. When the virus of this disease enters the body for the first time, it multiplies in the throat and in the intestinal tract. In some people, it gets no further: virus is shed to the outside from the throat and from the bowel for a few weeks, and then all the shedding ceases and the infection is over. The host, however, has responded and has developed circulating antibodies to a type of poliovirus. These antibodies are specific globulin-protein elements in the blood that subsequently prevent disease when poliovirus of the same type is again encountered by that person. In other people, the same process occurs, but, in addition, some virus gets into the bloodstream, where it circulates for a short time before being eliminated from it. In a few, the virus passes from the bloodstream into the central nervous system. There it may enter and destroy some of the nerve cells that control movement in the body and so cause paralysis in some of these patients. This last is by far the least common result of infection with poliomyelitis virus. Most infected persons have no symptoms at all; they are not aware they have been infected. Those whose bloodstream is infected often have a mild illness, consisting of no more than malaise—slight headache and possibly a sore throat. This is known as the "minor illness" of poliomyelitis, and it is unlikely to be recognized as poliomyelitis except among family contacts of a paralyzed patient. When the central nervous system is invaded by the virus, the infected person suffers from severe headache and other symptoms suggesting meningitis. This is known as the "major illness"; such persons are acutely ill, but most of them recover their normal health after about a week. Only a few of those with the major illness suffer from paralysis; the central nervous system has a large reserve of cells, as have most human organs, and only if a great number of cells in any area are destroyed by virus is the nervous system unable to send out its motor energy to the muscles served by that area, resulting in paralysis. Of all the people infected with poliomyelitis virus, not more than one in 100, possibly as few as one in 1,000, suffers from paralysis, although paralysis is the dominant feature of the fully developed clinical picture of poliomyelitis, and although to most people poliomyelitis means paralysis. This wide range of clinical response is true of most infections, though the proportions may vary. Influenza virus, for example, may cause symptoms ranging from a mild cold to a feverish illness, severe laryngitis (inflammation of the larynx, the voice box) or bronchitis, or an overwhelming and fatal pneumonia, and the proportions of persons suffering from these differing effects may vary from one epidemic to another. In measles, on the other hand, the typical symptoms are in fact the commonest: most patients have a rash and some respiratory symptoms, though infections without physical manifestations do occur.

"Minor" and "major" illnesses of poliomyelitis

Immunity. *Natural immunity.* With regard to the operation of the defense mechanisms of the body, the immunological response, there is perhaps more uniformity of pattern. Every species of animal possesses some natural resistance to disease. Humans have a high degree of natural resistance to foot-and-mouth disease, whereas cattle and sheep, with which they may be in daily contact, suffer in the thousands from it. A rat is highly resistant to diphtheria, whereas a child readily contracts the disease. What such resistance depends on is not understood. It must to some degree be genetically derived; it is possible, for example, to produce by selective breeding two strains of rabbits, one highly susceptible to tuberculosis, the other highly resistant. In humans there may be racial differences, but it is always difficult to disentangle such factors as climatic, nutritional, economic, and hygienic from those factors that might be purely racial. In some tropical and subtropical countries, poliomyelitis is a rare clinical disease, though a common infection, but visitors to such countries often contract serious clinical forms of the disease. The absence of serious disease in the residents is not due, however, to natural resistance but, rather, to the fact that from infancy onward they are repeatedly exposed, as a result of poor hygiene, to small doses of poliomyelitis virus and thereby acquire resistance, whereas the visitor from a country with stricter standards of hygiene is protected from such immunizing exposures in childhood and has no acquired resistance to the virus when encountering it as an adult.

Natural resistance does not depend on such exposures. The skin obviously has great inherent powers of resistance to infection, for most cuts and abrasions heal quickly, though often they must be smothered with potentially pathogenic microorganisms. If an equal number of typhoid germs is spread on a person's skin and also on a glass plate, those on the skin die much more quickly than those on the plate, suggesting that the skin has some bactericidal property against typhoid germs. Equally clearly, the skin varies in its resistance to microorganisms at different ages: ringworm is a common fungus infection of children's skin but is rarer in adults, and acne is a common infection of the skin of adolescents but is uncommon in childhood or in older adults. The phenomenon of natural immunity could be illustrated equally well by examples from the respiratory, intestinal, or genital tracts, where large surface areas are exposed to potentially infective agents and yet infection does not occur.

Variations in skin's resistance

If the organism causes local infection or gains entry to the bloodstream, a complicated series of events ensues. Special cells normally manufactured in the bone marrow and circulating in the blood (white blood cells or polymorphonuclear leukocytes) move to the site of infection. Some of these cells reach the site by chance (random migration), since every body site is constantly supplied by the blood in which these cells circulate. Additional polymorphonuclear leukocytes are attracted and directed to the sites of infection (directed migration) by various substances normally found as components of human blood. A number of these components collectively are referred to as the complement system. Several of the complement components (*e.g.*, C3 and C5) specifically act to direct the white blood cell to the site of invasion. Directed migration is called chemotaxis.

When the polymorphonuclear leukocyte reaches the invading organism, the cell attempts to ingest, or eat, the invader. Ingestion of bacteria may require the help of still other components of the blood, called opsonins. An opsonin generally is a protein substance such as one of the circulating globulins or complement components. These materials act to coat the bacterial cell wall and prepare it for ingestion. (The term opsonin is derived from a Greek word meaning to cater or prepare a meal.)

The prepared bacteria, then, is eaten, and once it is inside the white blood cell a complex series of biochemical events occurs. As a result of these biochemical reactions the bacteria may be killed, but its products are passed into the bloodstream, where they come in contact with other circulating cells called lymphocytes. Two general types of lymphocytes are of great importance in protecting the human host: T cells and B cells. When a T lymphoctye encounters the bacterial products, it is sensitized to recognize the material as foreign to the individual. Once sensitized, the T lymphocyte possesses an immunologic memory. Thus, when the T lymphocyte encounters the same bacteria again, it immediately recognizes the organism and sets up an appropriate defense more rapidly than it did on the first encounter. The ability of a T lymphocyte to perform its function normally is dependent on the thymus gland found in most individuals. In a person born without a thymus the body's ability to defend itself against various types of infections is impaired because the T lymphocyte does not function normally. T lymphocytes are responsible for what generally is referred to as "cellular immunity."

After the T lymphocyte has encountered and responded to the foreign bacteria, it interacts with B lymphocytes. B lymphocytes are responsible for producing the circulating proteins of normal human blood called gamma globulins. There are various types of B lymphocytes, each of which can produce only one form of gamma globulin. The gamma globulin classes that have been identified are IgG, IgA, IgM, IgD, and IgE.

When the B lymphocyte has interacted with the T lymphocyte, the first globulin produced is IgM. Subsequently, during recovery from infection, IgG is produced that specifically can kill the invading microorganism. In addition, if the same microorganism invades the host again, the B cell immediately responds with a dramatic production of IgG specific for that organism, rapidly killing it and thereby preventing disease. This defense is defined as immunity to a given disease. The presence in the bloodstream of IgC specific for a certain bacteria, or the ability to rapidly produce the IgC, provides immunity to that specific infection. The presence of circulating gamma globulins is called humoral immunity; it is termed specific, which means that the antibody produced in response to one infectious agent protects against that agent only.

Most infective agents exist in several types or strains. There are three types of poliomyelitis, for example, known as types I, II, and III. Antibody produced against type I protects against type I but not against types II and III. That is why vaccines against poliomyelitis must contain all three types of viruses. There are nearly 100 types of common-cold virus. A common-cold vaccine to be effective would have to contain all of these types, and there are many technical reasons why this cannot be done; or the person to be protected would require a large number of injections, each containing a few common-cold viruses.

Antibodies are produced in the body in response to the stimulus either of infection with an organism or the administration of a suspension of an organism, dead or alive, by mouth or by injection. When alive, the organisms have been weakened, or attenuated, by some laboratory means so that, whereas they still stimulate antibodies, they do not produce their characteristic disease. However stimulated, the antibodies are produced by the body itself and therefore tend to remain in the body indefinitely. Moreover, the antibody-producing cells of the body remain sensitized to the infectious agent and respond to it again, if it attacks the body, by pouring out more antibody. This is why one attack of a disease often renders a person immune to a second attack and is the theoretical basis of active immunization by vaccines. Antibody can be passed from one person to another, conferring protection on that second person; but, in this case, the antibody has not been produced in the body of the second person, nor have the antibody-producing cells been stimulated. The antibody is a foreign substance and is eventually eliminated from the body, so that protection is short-lived. The most common example of this form of passive immunity is the transference of antibodies from the mother through the placenta to the unborn child. This is why a disease such as measles is uncommon in babies less than one year old; after that age, the infant has lost all of its maternal antibody and becomes susceptible to the disease, unless protected by active immunization. Sometimes antibody is extracted in the form of gamma globulin from blood taken from immune persons and is injected into susceptible persons to give them protection against a disease—for example, measles or rubella. Such protection can only be temporary.

Passive immunity

The duration of active immunity. In many cases active immunity is lifelong, as in measles or rubella. In other instances it can be very short-lived, not more than a few months. Most measurements of antibody are of antibody in the blood, or serum antibody, but in some diseases antibody produced elsewhere may be more important. In respiratory viral infections, antibody produced by some of the surface cells of the respiratory tract appears to be a more important part of the defense mechanism than serum antibody, and serum antibody may not be able to reach the respiratory surfaces from the bloodstream. Many respiratory virus infections, including influenza, are primarily surface infections, attacking and multiplying in respiratory surface cells. Vaccines given by injection may stimulate serum antibody only, and this may be one reason why influenza vaccine is not a highly successful vaccine. Vaccines inhaled as mists or sprays may induce the production of local surface antibody and so be more effective than vaccines by injection.

The persistence of acquired immunity is related not only to circulating antibody (gamma globulin) but also to sensitized T lymphocytes (cellular immunity). Although both cellular immunity and humoral (B-cell) immunity are important, their relative importance in protecting a person against disease varies with particular microorganisms. For example, antibody is of great importance in protection against common bacterial infections such as pneumococcal pneumonia or streptococcal disease. In contrast, cellular immunity is of greater importance in protection against viruses such as measles or against the bacteria that cause tuberculosis.

Acquired immune deficiency syndrome (AIDS)

In acquired immune deficiency syndrome (AIDS) the cell-mediated (T-cell) immune regulation and surveillance system of the human body is affected. First recognized in 1979 in the United States, AIDS appears to be a defect that is irreversible once it has been acquired. Persons with AIDS have various degrees of immunologic abnormalities, resulting in illnesses manifested by persistent enlargement of the lymph nodes and chronic or recurrent infections, particularly infections with organisms that generally do not cause disease in the normal host. These persons also are prone to the development of malignancies.

The incidence of the disease increased markedly after its identification, and a rigorous research effort was undertaken to delineate the cause of the disorder.

AIDS initially was described in previously healthy homosexual males who had had extensive sexual encounters with a variety of partners. It has come to be known, however, that this disorder also occurs with increased frequency in persons who abuse drugs intravenously, are hemophiliacs, or have received blood transfusions, as well as in a disproportionate number of people who live in or have immigrated from Haiti or who are of Haitian descent. A heterosexual female whose male partner has AIDS also may be afflicted, as may infants born to mothers who are drug abusers or who are of Haitian descent.

The mechanism by which the disease is transmitted from one individual to another is not known. It appears, however, that the transfer of blood or blood products may be an important vehicle for transmission.

The etiology of AIDS also is not known, but it is presumed to be caused by an infectious agent. Viruses that have been found with great frequency in individuals with AIDS and that have been postulated as playing a causitive role in the syndrome include cytomegalovirus, Epstein-Barr virus (the cause of infectious mononucleosis), hepatitis B virus, or a "new" virus that has the potential for causing malignant change. It also seems likely that both genetic and environmental factors are important since there are variations in the expression of the syndrome.

The incubation period for AIDS appears to vary from six months to two years. During this time there is a gradual deterioration of the immune system, resulting in impaired T-cell regulation and surveillance mechanisms. Those who are afflicted develop recurrent or chronic infections with organisms that are otherwise well tolerated in normal individuals. In patients with AIDS, however, these organisms produce life-threatening disease and frequently cause death.

Many persons with AIDS are at increased risk for malignancies, particularly Kaposi's sarcoma, a cutaneous disorder, with dark blue or purple-brown plaques or nodules on the extremities, which progresses at a more rapid rate than normally seen in individuals who do not have the syndrome. Other malignancies noted with increased frequency in persons with AIDS include lymphomas and squamous-cell carcinomas.

Some persons with AIDS have chronic and recurrent fever, night sweats, weight loss, malabsorption of food from the gastrointestinal tract, and generalized enlargement of the lymph nodes. These symptoms may persist for variable periods of time before malignancies become apparent or before overwhelming infection with an otherwise innocuous organism has been documented.

The diagnosis of AIDS should be considered in persons whose symptoms include recurrent or unusual infections (*pneumocystis carinii*, cytomegalovirus, or cryptococcal disease), weight loss, persistent fever, and lymphadenopathy, particularly if they belong to one of the groups known to be at risk.

Antibiotics, used to treat specific infections, are the only treatment that ameliorates the symptoms of AIDS. The death rate is as high as 50 percent and usually results from infection that either no longer responds to antibiotics or for which no therapy is available.

THE EFFECTS OF HUMAN ACTIVITIES AND SURROUNDINGS

All living matter, humans and their microbes, animals, and plants, must adapt to the environment. Neither the environment nor the adaptations to it are ever static. In Switzerland, for example, swineherds in summer go about their work barefoot, but in winter they wear boots. Swineherd's disease is caused by a germ called *Leptospira pomona*, which enters the body most easily through moist damaged skin. It is not surprising, then, that the disease is much more common in summer than in winter. More subtle is the effect of the salinity or acidity of water. In Aberdeen, Scotland, Weil's disease, a form of jaundice that is caused by *Leptospira icterohaemorrhagiae*, used to be very common in fishworkers; in Grimsby, Lincolnshire, the disease was uncommon, although conditions appeared similar. In Aberdeen, however, tap water was used to sluice the benches and work tables; in Grimsby seawater was used. Leptospira flourish in freshwater but not in salt water.

Effects of differences in environment

In a study conducted in the coal mines of Ita and Akaike, in Japan, 80 percent of the rats monitored passed *Leptospira icterohaemorrhagiae* in their urine; there were 300 cases of Weil's disease in 18 months among mine workers in Ita, but only seven or eight in the same period in Akaike. It was found that the soil was alkaline in the Ita mines but acid in the Akaike mines; leptospira die rapidly in acid conditions and so had little chance to infect the workers in the acid Akaike mines. The environment in the alkaline Ita mines was much more dangerous to the miners, though superficially there was no apparent difference. Whether major or minor, crude or subtle, differences in environment can make vast differences in the outcome of the struggle between man and microbe.

Human activity. *Living conditions*. Human social habits and circumstances greatly influence the spread of infectious agents. Poorer families tend to live in more crowded conditions. Within their homes there is less living space, and their dwellings generally are more densely packed together than are the homes of the rich. Proximity facilitates the passage of disease germs from one person to another, and from one family to another; this is true whether the germs pass through the air from one respiratory tract to another, or whether they are bowel germs and depend for their passage on close personal hand-to-mouth contact or on lapses of sanitation or hygiene.

Family differences

The makeup of the family unit is also an important factor. In families with preschool children, infection spreads more readily, for these young children are both more susceptible to infections and, because of their faulty hygienic habits, more likely to share their microbes with other members of the family and with friends of the same age in the same neighbourhood. Because of this close and confined contact, infectious agents are spread more rapidly.

The virus of poliomyelitis spreads easily in conditions of close contact, but it is a virus that usually causes no active disease. When it does, it attacks older persons much more severely than younger. Children in poorer homes are likely, then, to be infected at an early age, and, if illness results, it is likely to be mild. In wealthier homes young children are less exposed to infection, and, when they first encounter the virus at an older age, they tend to suffer attacks that are more severe than those experienced by children in poorer homes. This difference is seen even more clearly in the outcome of the infection in less developed and in developed countries. In the former, because of poor hygiene and less standardized conditions, poliovirus spreads rapidly in early childhood, leading more often to immunity than to illness; in the developed countries, with high standards of hygiene, young children are less exposed and fewer develop immunity in early life, with the result that paralytic illness, a rarity in the less developed country, is frequently seen in the more developed countries in older children and adults. As a less developed becomes a developing country, the pattern of infection and disease changes toward that of a developed country. Only by artificial immunization can the pattern then be altered and the disease perhaps abolished in both types of community.

Effects of population density and social habits

Population density. In spite of what has just been said, density of population does not of itself determine the ease with which infection spreads through a population. In New York City, for example, with its many high-rise dwellings, the density of the population per square mile is much greater than in some of the world's older cities, but the hepatitis virus, for example, spreads much faster in the latter. A family in a New York City apartment may never see the inhabitants of most of the other apartments in the block, whereas, in an ancient Oriental city, for example, with dwellings built close together, neighbours are in daily contact. In New York state the incidence of infectious hepatitis (infection of the liver) has been shown to vary inversely with the density of the population. In the city itself, with a population density of more than 24,000 to the acre, the annual incidence of the disease between 1954 and 1962, for example, was 10.4 per 100,000: in urban areas of the state, with a population density of 515, the incidence was 19.2, and in rural areas, with a density of 66, it was 42.5. The incidence of the disease reflects, of course, not so much the density of the populations as their social habits and chances of contact.

Social habits. Vampire bats, when they bite cattle in the plains of Brazil, often transmit the virus of rabies to the animals and so cause their death from paralytic rabies. They do not bite Brazilian cattle ranchers, doubtless because in the wide plains there are few ranchers, whereas cattle are plentiful and more attractive to the bat. In Trinidad bat-transmitted rabies does occur in humans, but on that island the herdsman may sleep by his beasts in a shack, and bats in such circumstances may be less fastidious in their choice of blood. The mechanism of infection is the same in Trinidad and Brazil, but the difference in social habits affects the incidence of the disease.

In Malta, in the early 20th century, goats were milked at the customers' doors, and a disease caused by a *Brucella* germ in the milk was so common that it was known as Malta fever. When pasteurization of milk became compulsory, the picturesque method of milk delivery ceased, and Malta fever disappeared on the island except among some of the rural inhabitants, who still, perhaps, drank their milk raw and were in any case in daily contact with their infected animals. The case provides an example, on one small island, of how a change in social habit can affect environment and the incidence of a severe disease.

Less picturesque but no less important alterations in environment occur when children in a modern community first go to school. The child from a poorer, crowded home has had more experience of infection and may, therefore, have more immunity than the child from a wealthier home, so that the latter, encountering many infections for the first time, may develop more illnesses. Coughs, colds, sore throats, and swollen neck glands may occur one after the other. In a nursery school, with children at a tenderer and less hygienic age, outbreaks of dysentery and other bowel infections may occur, and even among older children, if they take their midday meal at school, food-borne infection due to some breakdown in hygiene may sweep through whole classes. These are dangers against which the children are protected to some extent in their homes but against which they have no defense when they move from their home environment to school.

Changing food habits among the general population also affect the environment for man and microbe. Meals taken outside the home in many cases offer more opportunity for food-poisoning germs to get into the food; as long as the standard of hygiene in the food preparation area is sound, there is no danger, but a flaw can produce a disastrous outbreak. Poultry are often heavily infected with food-poisoning *Salmonella* germs. When chickens were customarily bought fresh from a farm or a shop and cooked in the oven at home, food poisoning from eating chicken was almost unknown. Food habits have changed in many countries, however, and poultry is more often sold deep-frozen. The germs survive in the cold, and if the bird is not fully thawed before it is cooked there is a good chance that heat penetration will be poor and salmonellas will survive in the centre.

Effects of changes in habits

Temperature and humidity. Overcrowding is not necessarily a sign of poverty. At a cocktail party the human density per square yard may be much greater than in the poorest home, and humidity and temperature both rise to a level that can be uncomfortable for the human participants but ideal for the microbes that are also present. Virus-containing droplets pass easily from one guest to another, and the party may well be followed by an outbreak of the common cold. In contrast, members of scientific expeditions have spent whole winters in the Arctic and Antarctic without any respiratory illness in spite of the low temperature, only to catch severe colds on the arrival of the supply ship in the early summer. Cold temperature has not much to do with colds, for these are caused by viruses. Colds are commoner in winter because people then tend more to crowd together and so spread their various viruses. In the polar expeditions, however, the members rapidly develop immunity to the viruses they bring with them and, throughout the long winter, encounter no new ones: their colds in the summer are caused by viruses imported by the crew of the supply ship. When the members of the expedition return to temperate zones, they come down again with colds caught from friends and relatives.

Movement. Movement into a new environment often is followed by outbreaks of infectious disease. The crews of supply ships have occasionally been afflicted with colds on arrival at an Arctic base as a result of catching a virus from those whom they came to relieve; it is not always the overwintering scientists who suffer. In mass movements of population infection is always a hazard. On pilgrimages and in wars, improvised feeding and sanitation lead to outbreaks of such intestinal infections as dysentery, cholera, and typhoid, and in war more have sometimes died from these diseases than have been killed by bombs and bullets. In World War I young men from the Highlands and islands of Scotland caught measles when they joined regiments in the cities; in their isolated homesteads they had never encountered the virus and so had no immunity to it. As often happens when a so-called childhood disease strikes adults for the first time, they suffered severe attacks of measles.

Effects of changes in environment

People entering isolated communities may carry measles with them, and the disease may then spread with astonishing rapidity and often with enhanced virulence. In the Faeroe Islands, in 1846, a traveller from Copenhagen carried measles virus with him, and 6,000 of the 8,000 inhabitants caught the disease. Most of those who escaped illness were over 65 years old and had developed immunity during an outbreak of measles on the islands 65 years earlier. In Fiji, in 1875, a disastrous epidemic of measles killed a quarter of the population. These are examples of the effect of a change of environment in favour of a virus: nearly every human being in such "virgin" populations is susceptible to infection, so that the virus can multiply and spread unhindered. In a modern city population the virus affects mainly young susceptible children; when it has run through these, the epidemic must die down through lack of susceptible persons, and the virus does not spread again until a new generation of children is on hand. With the use of measles vaccine, the supply of susceptible children is decreased, and then the virus cannot spread and multiply and must die out.

Many people enjoy leaving their homes in towns and cities to camp for a holiday in the country. Such an innocent change in environment can lead to infection if it brings them in contact with sources of infection that are absent in the town. Picnicking in a wood, one may be bitten by a tick carrying the virus of one of several forms of encephalitis; when swimming in a canal or a river, one risks infection by the organisms of Weil's disease. A hiker may come on some watercress growing wild in the damp corner of a field and may swallow with the cress almost invisible specks of life that will grow into liver flukes in the body and cause illness that is common in sheep but that can also spread to humans when the circumstances are in its favour.

Occupation and commerce. In occupational and commercial undertakings, people often manipulate their environment and, in so doing, expose themselves to infection. A farmer in his fields is exposed to damp conditions in which microorganisms of disease may flourish. In clearing out a ditch, he may be infected with leptospira passed into the water in rats' urine. In his cowsheds he is exposed to infection with brucellosis if his herd is infected or with salmonellosis or Q fever (see below *Cattle, pigs, goats, and sheep*). Abattoir workers run similar risks, and so do veterinarians. A docker or a worker in a tannery may get anthrax from imported hides; an upholsterer may get it from wool and hair; and a worker mending sacks that have contained bone meal may contract the disease from germs still clinging to the sack. Workers in food factories and shops are often infected from the raw meat that they handle; they are sometimes regarded as carriers and causes of outbreaks of *Salmonella* food poisoning, but as often as not they are victims rather than the cause of the outbreak. In poultry plants workers may contract salmonellosis, more rarely psittacosis, from the birds that they handle and sometimes an infection of the eyes from a virus disease of the birds. Forestry workers breaking into a reserve may upset the balance of nature of the area and expose themselves to attack from the undergrowth or the trees by insect vectors of disease that in their undisturbed environment would never come in contact with humans. Whenever humans manipulate the environment—by herding animals together, by importing goods from abroad, by draining a lake, or by laying a pipe through sodden land, and in many other seemingly innocent ways—they run the chance of interfering with microbial life and attracting into their own environment agents of disease that they might not otherwise ever encounter.

Animals and insects. In social habits, work, recreation, and travel, humans can upset or interrupt the cycle of life in which they live. Sometimes they do this knowingly, more often unintentionally; sometimes the alteration is in their favour, more often, perhaps, it is against their own interest. Animals have little control over their environment. They may acquire diseases or carry the agents of disease both in their wild state and when domesticated. In both situations they can act as reservoirs of infection; transfer of infection to humans depends on the extent to which environments overlap.

Environment and salmonellosis

Cattle, pigs, goats, and sheep. Much of the infection in domestic animals comes from domestication itself. Infection with salmonellas, for example, is much more common in cattle and pigs than in sheep, and part of the reason is that cows and pigs are confined together for part of their lives in shelters where infection, once introduced, can build up rapidly, whereas sheep spend nearly all of their lives in open pastures; when they are confined, especially in trucks over long journeys, sheep are just as susceptible to salmonellosis as cattle and pigs are. Q fever spreads very rapidly in cattle, both in pastures and under cover; yet, even so, it usually spreads more slowly in beef herds, which always range in the open, than among dairy herds, which spend part of every day under cover.

Salmonellosis is a serious economic infection among cattle and pigs. It can cause severe disease and death in calves and piglets and sometimes in the grown animals. Many animals that recover remain carriers and excrete the germ in their feces for the rest of their lives. Salmonellas can live for many months in stalls and sties or in animal feces in the open, and farmers, cowmen, and swineherds may be infected directly during their work. The main route of infection from animals to humans is, however, via the abattoir, the food factory, the butcher's shop, the kitchen, and the table. At any stage in that journey, salmonellas can be conveyed from contaminated to sound meat; the greatest danger occurs when they are conveyed from raw to cooked food, for, on the latter, at a favourable temperature, they can multiply and cause disease.

Brucellosis is a common infection of cattle, sheep, goats, and pigs. The organisms that cause it, various species of *Brucella,* tend to settle in the mammary glands and the genital tract and are discharged in enormous numbers in the milk, in vaginal discharges, and in the urine and feces. The disease causes loss in milk production and also abortion or decreased fertility in the animals. Brucellae can exist for long periods outside the animal body, and the whole environment, including the air of a cowshed, may be heavily laden with the live germs. Humans may be infected by drinking raw milk from an infected animal or by direct contact with the animals. It is an occupational risk of veterinarians, who may be infected during obstetrical operations. Farmers may breathe in brucellae in contaminated cowsheds, or the germ may enter their bodies through the conjunctivas of their eyes or through their skin when splashed with milk or discharges. Goatherds and shepherds spend most of their lives alongside their animals and are easily infected by close contact. Abattoir workers can be infected directly from the carcasses, and laboratory workers from cultures of germs on the laboratory bench. Animals contract the disease from their heavily contaminated environment, from licking infected placentas or fetuses, or from breathing in particles of dust contaminated with brucellae from dried urine or feces.

Pigs are more often infected with leptospira than are cattle, sheep, or goats. *Leptospira pomona* is the commonest type in pigs, though pigs, when they are in contact with dogs, may be infected from the dogs with *L. canicola;* from rats they can get *L. icterohaemorrhagiae.* These germs may cause acute disease in the pig or lead to infection of the fetus and abortion in the sow, but often the animals suffer no illness, the leptospira living in the tubules of the pig kidney without affecting renal function. They are passed in large numbers in the urine and can survive for months in the damp environment of sty or field. Swineherds' disease due to *L. pomona* can be caught in such an environment; canicola fever or Weil's disease can also be contracted by piggery workers when one of the other two leptospira is being shed in the pigs' urine. Leptospira may also infect dogs. Humans can be infected from close contact with dog urine that has been contaminated by leptospires; even dogs that have been immunized specifically against leptospirosis may be carriers or spreaders of the organism.

Spread of Q fever

Q fever has already been mentioned; the Q stands for query, for its cause was at first unknown. It spreads rapidly in cows, sheep, and goats, and whole herds, flocks, and districts are often contaminated with the *Coxiella* organisms that cause the disease. The germs are passed in vast quantities in milk, urine, and feces, in vaginal discharges, and on placentas, and they survive for long periods dried in dust; yet they spread to humans unwillingly, though humans are susceptible to the infection. Q fever in humans tends to occur in localized outbursts; in the middle of a heavily infected area, it may break out suddenly on one farm only, affect everyone on it, even chance visitors, and die out again within a few days. The infection has been conveyed in straw used for packing sculpture or machinery, and those who unpacked came down with the disease. It often appears to be a "place" infection: in World War II, in Italy and Greece, the disease broke out in single billets where men slept on straw, but not in adjoining billets where conditions appeared to be identical. Yet the passage of infected sheep through narrow Italian streets has seemed enough to spread the disease to inhabitants of the houses. In some areas blood tests show that the infection has spread widely from animals to humans without causing symptoms; in others, with an equal amount of infection in the animals, there has been no evidence of spread to humans. It may be that the coxiellae can for some unknown reason become more virulent and so more capable of infecting humans; or some subtle changes in the environment may allow them to pass more freely from animal to human.

Rats and other wild mammals. Wild animals, like humans, have commensal microorganisms living in their tissues and can also be devastated by outbreaks of infectious disease. Transfer to humans can be direct, as by a bite, or indirect through a complex of environmental circumstances.

The rat is a common carrier of leptospires. There are many different types of leptospira, and different rats may carry different types. *Rattus conatus* is the rat most often found in the cane fields in Australia. It often is a carrier of *L. australis* and sheds it in its urine on the sharp lower blades of the canes. These blades scratch the legs of workers in the field and they catch cane-field leptospirosis. Sometimes the common rat, *Rattus norvegicus*, invades the cane fields and drives out the native rat and, shedding *L. icterohaemorrhagiae* in place of *L. australis*, infects the workers with Weil's disease in place of the milder cane-field leptospirosis.

The bite of a rat can convey any microorganism that contaminates its mouth, including leptospira, but rat-bite fever is the name applied to two diseases spread by rat bites. In one the germ is *Spirillum minus;* in the other, *Streptobacillus moniliformis.* The rats themselves are usually healthy carriers, even when the organisms are in their bloodstream, but some infected rats suffer from an inflammation of the eyes, conjunctivitis, which may be the source of infection when a rat bites a human.

Rats and mice are often infected with salmonellas. These microorganisms can cause severe disease in the animals; more often they suffer little but excrete the salmonellas in their feces. In this way they can contaminate any foodstuffs to which they have access, including fodder for farm animals, and they may also contaminate the environment of cowsheds and pig sties with their droppings and so infect cattle and pigs directly. Often, however, the rats themselves are the victims of infection on contaminated farms, and, when these are cleaned up, the infection dies out in the rats. Infected rats, if they gain entrance to abattoirs, food factories, bakeries, and shops, can contaminate human food, but, except in very bad conditions, they are not major causes of human salmonellosis.

Rats as carriers of plague

The greatest scourge of mankind conveyed by rats has, of course, been plague, and the history of plague is the history of humans and rats. The microorganism of plague, *Yersinia pestis*, is carried by various rat fleas, especially one called *Xenopsylla cheopis*. The organisms multiply in the proventriculus (front stomach) of the flea, and when the flea bites the rat, the organisms flood through the wound into the rat's bloodstream. The fleas rapidly infect vast colonies of rats. As the animals die off, the fleas are forced to seek another host, and the nearest one is usually human. The ultimate reservoir of *Yersinia pestis* is, however, not the rat. The infection smoulders all over the world in many wild rodents, including voles, bandicoots, ground squirrels, and chipmunks. From the wilderness the infection can be carried by field rats or mice nearer to the haunts of the house rat, and then humans, by commerce and industry, can attract the rats to ports and ships and so to distant parts of the globe. But there is more to the spread of plague than mere contiguity of flea, rat, and human. Temperature and humidity affect the survival of the fleas: when it is hot and dry they do not flourish, so that plague breaks out in the cooler, more humid months of the year and dies down in hot, dry summers.

Foxes carry the germs of brucellosis, leptospirosis, and tularemia, but the main threat to humans from the fox is the dread disease rabies. It seems likely that the fox, the wolf, and other wild canines are not the main reservoir of rabies virus but, rather, that it is maintained in such small carnivores as mongooses and polecats and only occasionally breaks through to foxes and then to dogs and humans. Bats, too, harbour the virus and sometimes convey it to humans.

Birds. Investigation of birds in and around farms has shown that many of them become infected with coxiellae. Of those caught on farms, more than 15 percent have been found infected, whereas more than 4 percent of those caught near farms but fewer than 2 percent of those caught farther away from farms have been found infected, findings that suggest that the birds carry the infection away from the farms rather than bring it in. Poultry on farms may also be infected. In some diseases there is evidence that migrant birds carry infection. Murray Valley encephalitis virus may be borne from northern to southern Australia in migrant birds. Japanese B encephalitis virus sometimes escapes from the paddy-field heronries of Japan, where it is endemic, to the centre of neighbouring towns, where it infects pigs in abattoirs and, thereafter, humans; birds, or parasites on them, may effect its passage. In another form of encephalitis, West Nile fever, there is strong evidence that the hooded crow is the reservoir of infection.

Birds as carriers of psittacosis

The main infection spread by birds to humans is psittacosis. This disease affects at least 70 members of the parrot family, and infection sometimes spreads very readily to humans. In one outbreak, 26 people who passed through a room containing two apparently healthy parrots caught the disease, and in another incident 12 actors on the stage caught the illness from the 13th member of the cast, a parrot. The infection is not restricted to the psittacine, or parrot, family. Pigeons are often heavily infected, as many as 20 percent of wild pigeons and 60 percent of loft or racing pigeons. There is no doubt that the breeding and racing of pigeons have often led to psittacosis in humans; even the guards of railway trains conveying crates of these pigeons have occasionally caught the disease. To what extent pigeons in city squares are a danger to the bystanders who feed them is not known: the strain of *Bedsonia*, the organism of the disease, found in pigeons seems to be less virulent for humans than the parrot strain, and perhaps the risk is small, though the dust from feathers and dried feces could set up a dangerous concentration in the environment of the square, if the pigeons were infected. Many other birds suffer from or carry the infection.

Insects. The relationship between microorganism, insect carrier, and human can be complex. When Q fever was first investigated in Australia, it seemed to be a local disease in abattoir workers infected directly from carcasses. Further investigation showed that it was a disease of bandicoots and opossums, spread among them by a tick, *Haemaphysalis humerosa*. A scrub tick, *Ixodes holocyclas*, carried the infection from these wild animals to cattle, and the cattle tick *Boophilus annulatus* became infected and excreted the virus in its feces, whence, dried in dust, it later spread to humans. By another cycle, the disease also spread from kangaroos and wallabies by a tick, *Amblyomma triguttatum*, to sheep and then to humans. In other countries other ticks have been involved, and it seems likely that ticks play an important part in maintaining the animal reservoir of Q fever coxiellae in some parts of the world, but the mechanism of transfer to humans is not always clear. In Switzerland, for example, Q fever is common, but ticks are rare. Moreover, the disease in humans occurs equally commonly in winter and summer in some countries, though in winter there are few if any ticks on the host animals. Lice, bedbugs, and fleas may all be infected with and excrete coxiellae, but there is no evidence that they spread Q fever to humans.

Conditions affecting insects as disease carriers

For an insect to be an efficient carrier, or vector, of a disease organism, it must be present in the correct place at the correct time and in the correct proportion with regard to the host animals. The season must be right, the temperature and the humidity suitable. The amount of winter rainfall and summer drought affects the vector population, as do the presence of shade or sun, the height of trees, and the thickness of undergrowth and the density of decaying vegetation, as well as the nature of living organisms in the compound—all of these factors may determine whether or not the insect vector can spread an infectious agent in a given environment. The height and duration of virus concentration in the blood of the host animal may be of critical importance. If virus is plentiful and persists for a long time in the host's blood, then whole clouds of insect vectors may become infected and able to spread infection with their next bite; if there is little virus in the host's blood and it disappears quickly, few if any of the biting insects may become infected and the disease does not spread. Some biting insects are highly fastidious and will bite only one or two hosts; others are promiscuous. When humans intrude into a host-vector reserve, the outcome depends on one, several, or all of these factors. Humans may come to no harm, or they may contract a severe disease such as one of the many forms of insect-borne encephalitis.

Malaria is spread by mosquitoes, and an essential part of the life cycle of the malaria parasite takes place in their bodies. Mosquitoes also carry the viruses of several forms of encephalitis and of yellow fever. But not any mosquito will do. Each disease has its own mosquito, and the same mosquito may be an efficient vector of a disease in one locality yet may fail to transmit it in another. Moreover, the same disease may be transmitted by different vectors in different areas. Insects are important agents in the spread of some diseases, but their role is never a simple one. A great deal depends on the relationships of the organisms in the area and on the life history of the infectious agent.

Inanimate environment. Dust cannot cause infectious disease unless it contains the living agents of the infection. Yet the term inanimate is a convenient one to use when infectious disease arises from contact with an environment in which there is no obvious direct living contact between source and victim of an infection. Thus, a pencil is an inanimate object, but if it is first sucked by a child suffering from scarlet fever and then by a second child, the organism causing the disease can be conveyed to the second child. Many such objects, a handkerchief or towel, for example, may convey infection under favourable conditions, and when they do so they are known as fomites.

Dust is perhaps one of the commonest inanimate elements capable of conveying disease. Organisms present in the dust may get on food and be swallowed, settle on the skin and infect it, or be breathed into the respiratory passages. Some germs can live for long periods dried in dust; the germs of anthrax and tetanus, Q fever, brucellosis, and psittacosis have all already been mentioned. Under certain conditions all may be dangerous, but under different conditions there may be no danger. The germ of tetanus, *Clostridium tetani*, is one of the commonest germs in dust, but the incidence of tetanus varies greatly in different parts of the world. In many countries it is rare, in others common, and the difference may be related to slight differences in human behaviour or custom. The wearing of shoes, for example, in temperate climates protects the wearer against many wounds, whereas the barefoot child in the tropics sustains many puncture wounds of the feet that, though minor, may carry tetanus spores into the tissues of the foot where conditions may be ideal for germination and the production of toxin. Obstetrical practices in some parts of the world can lead to infection of the newborn child. Other influences more subtle, such as changes of temperature or humidity, may affect the spread of other diseases by dust. A long, wet winter followed by a dry summer may encourage the growth of molds in hay, and the dust, when the hay is disturbed, may lead to infection of farmers' lungs.

Water-borne diseases

Water is not a favourable medium for the growth and multiplication of microorganisms, and yet many can survive in it for long enough to carry infection to humans. Cholera and typhoid are both waterborne diseases. The virus of hepatitis, too, can survive in water, and waterborne outbreaks of this disease have occurred in various places. But the mere presence of a microorganism in water does not necessarily lead to spread of the disease. People have swum in water polluted with *Salmonella typhi* without getting typhoid, whereas others eating shellfish from the same water have developed the disease. The same may be true of hepatitis; the eating of clams from infected water has often caused disease, whereas swimming has not been proved a hazard. Shellfish concentrate germs in their tissues, and this is probably why they can transmit diseases.

Water is carried to humans in pipes for drinking, but it is also carried away in pipes as sewage. When there are defects in the systems, water may pass from one to the other, and the microorganisms in sewage may then find their way into drinking water. Septic tanks, manure heaps, and garbage heaps may be situated inappropriately with respect to wells and other sources of drinking water, and, in this way, microorganisms of disease may contaminate the water. Even after such contamination, the water can be drunk with safety if it passes first through the reservoir and purification plant of a waterworks, but, if it is drunk directly from the well, disease probably will follow.

ROUTES AND MODES OF INFECTION

Microorganisms can infect the human host via the intact or broken skin, the conjunctiva, the respiratory tract, the gastrointestinal tract, or the mucous membranes of the genitourinary tract; by direct inoculation into the bloodstream; or through the placenta from mother to fetus.

Primacy of the respiratory tract as a portal of entry

Respiratory route. The respiratory tract is the main portal of entry for microorganisms into the body. The passage of air into and out of the body goes on every second of the day and night, and the tract is unceasingly exposed to the outer environment and to any agents of infection that it may contain. The gastrointestinal tract has much greater protection, for humans to a large extent have control, through hygienic measures, over what goes into it. Humans can to some extent control the danger of infection through the genital tract, skin for most of the time is partly covered by clothing, transplacental infection is usually prevented by antibodies already present in the pregnant woman, and the eyelid protects the delicate membranes of the eye in sleep.

Types of disease. Not all of the microorganisms that enter by the respiratory tract cause a respiratory illness. The varicella virus (the cause of chicken pox), for example, enters the bloodstream through the lining cells of the respiratory tract and then spreads to other organs where it multiplies; after an interval, at the height of its multiplication, the virus bursts into the cells of the skin where it causes its most characteristic clinical manifestations. The virus does, indeed, reinvade some of the cells of the upper respiratory tract at the same time that it reaches the skin and may then cause respiratory symptoms, but, at its initial entry, it does not attack the cells of the respiratory tract or cause a local disease there. The viruses of the common cold, by contrast, do not pass farther into the body than the lining cells of the respiratory tract; they multiply there, and the symptoms that they cause are entirely respiratory.

The meningococcus, the germ of one form of meningitis, enters the body by the upper air passages, where indeed it often settles down, causing no trouble at all to its host, though it may escape in the breath to infect other people. The symptoms of the disease are due to the spread of the germ beyond the respiratory tract into the bloodstream and into the central nervous system, where it multiplies exceedingly and causes inflammation of the meninges, the membranes that surround the brain. Diphtheria bacilli and the streptococci of scarlet fever both enter in the breath and attack the upper part of the respiratory tract, causing in each case a form of tonsillitis. Diphtheria bacilli may, indeed, on occasion attack the larynx, the trachea (windpipe), and even the bronchi, but in both diseases the dangerous symptoms are usually caused not by the local inflammatory exudate in the upper part of the respiratory tract but, rather, by the circulation of toxin from that site through the bloodstream to other parts of the body. In diphtheria the heart and the nervous system are mainly attacked; and in scarlet fever the heart, the joints, and the kidneys are affected.

Types of respiratory infections

Psittacosis is more nearly a typical respiratory infection. The germs are inhaled in fine dust or aerial suspensions, and, though the infection causes a generalized illness, respiratory symptoms are usually present, arising from an inflammatory reaction of the cells of the lower respiratory tract that are attacked by the psittacosis germ. Rubella is a respiratory infection in that entry is certainly by the respiratory tract, and at the height of the illness the virus multiplies in the cells of the upper respiratory tract and passes out in the breath to infect other people; but the virus also spreads through the body and is present in the skin rash. The illness is usually mild, and respiratory symptoms are trivial. On the other hand, though measles virus passes through the bloodstream like rubella virus and reaches the skin and most organs of the body, it does produce an acute inflammatory reaction in the cells of the respiratory tract, and respiratory symptoms are always present and often severe. *Bordetella pertussis*, the germ of whooping cough, is a purely respiratory pathogen. It is inhaled in the breath and concentrates its attack on the cells of the respiratory tract and lungs, where it causes extensive damage. Anthrax bacilli, though they most often attack the body via the skin, are sometimes inhaled in fine dust and cause disastrous and usually fatal reactions in the bronchi and lungs, an example of how the route of entry may dramatically affect the nature of an infection.

Although the pneumococcus can cause disease in other parts of the body, especially one form of meningitis, it is typically a pathogen of the respiratory tract only, and is the common cause of lobar pneumonia, the disease in which the cells lining many of the air sacs of the lungs are so swollen by inflammation that air can neither pass in nor out of them; oxygen cannot get through the blocked air sacs into the bloodstream nor can carbon dioxide escape, and the affected person is forced to increase his rate of breathing in an effort to get those gases through the parts of his lungs not affected by the pneumococcus. Such a condition can be caused by other respiratory agents of disease, including those often called the respiratory viruses. Of these the best known is the influenza virus, but there are many others.

The respiratory tract. The respiratory tract is not a homogeneous expanse of living tissue. The type of cell that lines the nose is different from that lining the trachea and bronchi and again very different from the flat cells that surround the air sacs; the cells are different because they have different functions to perform.

Variations of environmental conditions within the respiratory tract

There are changes, too, in temperature from the rather cold conditions in the nostrils to the warmth of the lungs, where the inhaled air has reached the temperature of the inside of the body before it releases its oxygen to the bloodstream. There are differences in humidity; the dry air breathed into the nose takes up moisture as it descends to the lungs. The acidity of the environment alters slightly from one part to another of the tract, the viscosity of the fluid bathing the lining cells varies, and there is a difference in the oxygen concentration at different levels; in the nose it is atmospheric, but in the air sacs the oxygen concentration falls rapidly as it diffuses into the bloodstream. These differences and changes are vital to the ventilation of the body, but they also greatly affect the forms of microorganismal life that may colonize different parts of the respiratory tract.

Rhinoviruses, for example, are at home in the cells lining the human nose; the temperature, the degree of acidity or alkalinity (pH), and the oxygen concentration meet their requirements so well that they are able to flourish and, in doing so, to affect their host with the common cold. In the throat, conditions do not suit them quite so well, and in the lower respiratory tract, where the most obvious differences are a rise in temperature and a fall in oxygen concentration, they are seldom present and do no damage. Another virus, the respiratory syncytial virus, behaves differently. The warm, moist environment and the falling oxygen concentration of the lung recesses suit it admirably, and there it causes inflammation that blocks the smallest air ducts and leads to acute bronchiolitis, a severe and sometimes fatal respiratory disease of infants. The virus does not thrive in the upper air passages, where it causes only mild catarrhal illnesses (*i.e.*, inflammation of mucous membranes), difficult to distinguish from the common cold; it is rarely found in the nose. These upper respiratory illnesses, moreover, occur in older children and adults rather than in infants, so that changes other than obvious physical ones can affect the conflict between microorganism and host. The respiratory syncytial virus, so typically a pathogen of the lower respiratory tract of young infants, can also cause a flare-up of infection in elderly persons with chronic bronchitis, who might have been expected to have antibodies from previous exposure to the virus. Moreover, in these elderly persons, the inflammatory reaction caused by the virus takes place in the lower, not the upper, respiratory tract. Respiratory syncytial virus is not a common cause of infection in the elderly bronchitic, but it illustrates the complexity of the environmental and other factors that determine the outcome when a microorganism gains entry to the human body.

Respiratory syncytial virus

For almost any of the respiratory pathogens an equally complex pattern can be described. Influenza virus, for example, though capable at times of causing worldwide epidemics of severe and often fatal disease, may at other times cause illnesses no more severe than the common cold, and infants may escape whereas adults succumb to the infection.

Haemophilus influenzae is a microorganism named for its occurrence in the sputum of patients suffering from influenza—an occurrence so common that this microorganism was at one time thought to be the cause of the disease. It is now known to be a common inhabitant of the nose and throat that may invade the bloodstream, producing meningitis, pneumonia, and disease of various other organs. In children it is the commonest cause of acute epiglottitis, a condition in which tissue at the back of the tongue becomes rapidly swollen and obstructs the child's airway; it can kill the child if the obstruction is not relieved. It is also a common cause of a flare-up in elderly bronchitics, but, for most of the time and in most people, it leads a harmless commensal existence in the respiratory tract.

Factors influencing spread by respiratory route. It is not known what causes a commensal organism to become virulent nor what external circumstances affect the onset of respiratory virus infections. Low temperature is not the dominating factor in the development of the common cold: vigorous experiments have demonstrated this again and again. People do commonly feel drafts and experience chilling before they develop a cold but probably because they have already caught the cold and are, as a result, abnormally sensitive to drafts. The essential factor for development of the cold seems to be the penetration into the nose of wet droplets containing virus. These are usually large and heavy and fall to the floor of the room quickly; few, therefore, are inhaled. The fine droplets, which float through the air, dry rapidly at room temperature, and, though they are inhaled, do not convey the infection, for the virus does not survive drying. Moreover, in ordinary talking the droplets that escape from the mouth consist mainly of saliva, which contains little virus, and at ordinary distances few of these droplets would reach the listener, though in crowded rooms enough virus may pass to spread the common cold. The real danger comes from coughs and sneezes, when droplets from the deeper respiratory tract are shed; these may contain greater quantities of virus. It seems, however, that another factor is also involved, namely, that some people for some unknown reason are prolific shedders of virus, whereas others with equally bad colds are not; and some viruses, when shed, are good spreaders, whereas others, though shed in equal amounts, are not.

Spread of colds by droplets

Most of the circumstances that bear upon the spread of the common cold viruses operate in the spread of other respiratory viruses as well, though the whole story is rarely known. Adenoviruses, for example, are not a source of great trouble in the general adult population, but in military establishments they are, recruits often becoming ill in large numbers with sharp adenovirus respiratory infections. It is difficult to see why similar outbreaks do not occur in other communities with changing populations.

One thing that must be emphasized regarding the respiratory tract as a route of infection is that climate is relatively unimportant. Those who live in temperate climates tend to regard respiratory virus infections as their especial burden, but evidence from virus surveys in many parts of the world shows that respiratory viral diseases are just as common and take the same form in tropical as in temperate climates.

Gastrointestinal route. Infection by way of the gastrointestinal tract presents fewer problems. The route and mode of infection are usually direct.

Most of the microorganisms that cause gastrointestinal

disease in humans depend for their survival on a parasitic existence in the intestinal tract of humans or other animals. *Salmonella typhi*, the germ of typhoid, is parasitic exclusively on humans. When it first enters the body, it causes a severe disease, for it passes through the intestinal wall and is carried in the bloodstream to many organs. In most persons the germ disappears from the body at the time of recovery, but in a few it settles down in some organ, usually the gallbladder, and may remain there indefinitely without causing any symptoms. From the gallbladder, typhoid germs are constantly excreted down the bile duct into the intestine and then out of the body in the feces. These persons, who themselves have recovered from the disease, have become carriers, and they are the only reservoirs of *Salmonella typhi* in nature. If, by good hygiene and sanitation, the organisms in the feces of carriers can be prevented from getting into food and drink, further cases of typhoid cannot occur, and in countries with high standards of hygiene and sanitation typhoid has become a rare disease.

Typhoid and other salmonellas contrasted

Most other salmonellas are parasites of many hosts. *Salmonella typhimurium*, for example, is a common parasite of humans but also of farm animals, as well as of a wide variety of other hosts such as tortoises, elephants, foxes, pythons, rats, and seals. It is not dependent for its survival on finding a lodging in the human body but, instead, ranges freely and promiscuously through a varied environment and is never without a host. The threat to humans is different from that of *Salmonella typhi*. Human carriers and human feces play only a minor role in the spread of *Salmonella typhimurium;* instead, the threat comes along a chain of infection in animals, from farms through markets to abattoirs and then on to food factories, shops, and kitchens. A sound sewage-disposal system and a safe water supply do not protect humans against this form of salmonella infection. Instead, the control of infection on farms, in markets, in abattoirs, and in poultry plants and a high standard of food hygiene in factories, kitchens, and shops are required. In a sophisticated society typhoid dies out because the typhoid germ cannot circulate, but in the same society sophistication leads to a complicated system of food handling and distribution, and other forms of salmonella infection may increase rather than decrease in consequence.

Adaptation to one specific host is both advantageous and disadvantageous to a microorganism. The main advantage is that it need be present only in rather small numbers in order to infect. This has one important epidemic implication. Microorganisms do not flourish in water in large numbers, although small numbers can survive, sometimes for several weeks. *Salmonella typhi* in water supplies has caused outbreaks of typhoid rather commonly in the past. On the other hand, waterborne outbreaks of other forms of salmonella infection have been rare and have occurred only when there has been gross pollution of drinking water. These other salmonellas, for all their promiscuity, must build up a formidable population before they are able to infect humans, and this they cannot do in water. Moreover, even if they get into food, they must be able to multiply in it, and this requires time and a suitable temperature; they will not multiply inside a refrigerator.

A second possible advantage for the highly adapted microorganism is that, when it meets its single host, it establishes for itself a satisfactory relationship with that host. *Salmonella typhi* does not provoke in humans, as do many other salmonellas, a violent diarrheal disease that might be regarded as a rejection of a parasite by a host. Instead, it slips quietly into the bloodstream and can ensconce itself in the safe shelter of some host tissue cells before the host is aware of the infection. *Salmonella typhimurium*, on the other hand, does not normally invade the bloodstream or the cells of its host; on its entry to the human body it irritates the lining cells of the gastrointestinal tract, and the diarrhea that results leads to its expulsion from the host's body. This is not a complete or absolute picture of the behaviour of the two salmonellas. *Salmonella typhimurium* does sometimes invade the bloodstream, and humans can become carriers of the germ; and, on the other hand, *Salmonella typhi* does sometimes cause diarrhea soon after it infects its host. But the distinction is in general valid; so much so that the term salmonellosis does not cover infection with *Salmonella typhi*. Clinically and epidemiologically it is a separate disease. Salmonellosis covers infection by any one of many other species of salmonellas, and there are about 1,200 different members of the group. Many of them can infect humans; mostly they cause a diarrheal rather than a generalized type of disease.

The great disadvantage of adaptation to one host has already been stated: that the microorganism is entirely dependent on the one host species, and, if its passage from one member of the species to another can be interrupted, it has no other host to turn to and must die out, trapped by the very success of its specific adaptation. This has happened to *Salmonella typhi* in many developed countries.

Other organisms causing intestinal symptoms

Germs other than salmonellas cause intestinal symptoms and are conveyed by food or drink. Staphylococci are very common and ubiquitous: some of them, given the right conditions, can produce a toxin, or poison, that is extremely irritating to the human gastrointestinal tract. (Such toxins are called enterotoxins.) If these organisms get into food and are kept at room temperature, they begin to multiply freely and to produce the enterotoxin. Even if the food is cooked thereafter and all of the staphylococci are killed by the heat, the enterotoxin remains active, for it is heat-stable; when the food is eaten the toxin quickly causes vomiting by irritating the consumer's stomach. Another germ, *Clostridium welchii*, acts in a somewhat similar way. The toxin is again heat-stable, but both the live germs and the toxin must be swallowed to produce symptoms; together they irritate the lower bowel, not the stomach, so that the symptom is diarrhea rather than vomiting, and the onset is later than in staphylococcal food poisoning.

Not all the germs that enter by the gastrointestinal tract cause gastrointestinal symptoms. The virus of poliomyelitis enters by the mouth and multiplies in the pharynx and in the intestine; it causes no intestinal symptoms and often causes no symptoms at all. Before the paralytic symptoms of the disease can develop, the virus must pass from the infected person's intestinal tract into the bloodstream and from there into the central nervous system. Brucellosis can be conveyed by drinking milk, but the symptoms of the illness are of a generalized disease, and there are no intestinal symptoms. Like *Salmonella typhi*, the germ of brucellosis looks for an intracellular lodgment in the host's body. The virus of one form of hepatitis enters by the mouth. It does cause, in the early stages of the illness, vague gastrointestinal symptoms, but its dominant effect is on the liver; it causes inflammation of the liver cells, and this leads to jaundice. The bovine tubercle bacillus, before the days of pasteurization of milk, was one of the most relentless of gastrointestinal invaders. It could indeed cause ulceration of the wall of the intestinal tract and long-drawn-out symptoms of intestinal disease, but much more often it used the gastrointestinal tract solely as a portal of entry and made its way to the bones and joints, there to cause destructive changes. *Clostridium botulinum* is normally a germ of the soil. If it gets into food, however, and is given an atmosphere with low oxygen pressure, it can produce an extremely powerful toxin that, if swallowed in food, passes quickly to the nervous system and produces paralysis of the muscles of swallowing and breathing that is often fatal. *Clostridium botulinum* differs from staphylococci in that the microorganism itself is very resistant to heat, whereas its toxin is quickly destroyed by it. If food containing the toxin is boiled before it is eaten or canned, there is no danger, but if it is eaten without being properly heated, paralysis follows. A mere taste of the food is enough to kill.

Gastrointestinal infections not spread in food or drink

In all of the above examples of gastrointestinal infection, it is assumed that the microorganism is conveyed in food or drink. Sometimes the infection seems even more direct, straight from the environment to the gastrointestinal tract. Around the bed of an infant suffering from gastroenteritis, there is usually a heavy concentration of the infecting germ. Clothing, blankets, dust on floors and ledges, towels, diapers, sinks, taps, soap, dusting powder, and any toilet article may all be contaminated with the microorganism. More important, the hands of nurses, physicians, parents, or other attendants readily pick up organisms such as *Yersinia enterocolitica* or *Campylobacter fetus* from these sites, and hand-to-mouth transfer to other infants can then occur. *Shigella sonnei* usually causes a fairly mild diarrheal disease, but it is highly infectious and spreads by direct hand-to-hand contact in families, nursery schools, and wards. *Shigella sonnei* can live for weeks in dark, damp surroundings. Sonnei dysentery can be conveyed also in food, and other dysentery germs, *Shigella flexneri* and *Shigella shigae*, are often waterborne in areas of poor sanitation, where they cause explosive and severe outbreaks of disease. The germ of cholera spreads in the same waterborne way.

The germs of gastrointestinal infections live in the human environment. They do not leap into the mouth but must be carried there in food or drink or on the hands. Of all of the infections they are perhaps the easiest to control, in theory at least, for the mechanism of control is simple, namely, the provision of safe water and food. In scale, the task can be gigantic.

Mucous membranes. Mucous membranes, the coverings of partly exposed parts of the body over which lies a protective fluid film of mucus, are found in the nose and mouth, the eye, and the genital passages. (Much of the linings of the respiratory and gastrointestinal tracts are mucous membranes, but these routes of infection have already been touched upon.)

The conjunctiva. The conjunctiva is a delicate membrane lining the eyelid and covering the front of the eye. It is protected to some extent by the instinctive action of the eyelids against injury by dust and other particulate matter, but it is more exposed to invisible attack by microorganisms than any part of the body except the skin. It is surprisingly seldom attacked by obvious infections. Conjunctivitis (inflammation of the conjunctiva) is not an extremely uncommon condition, but severe forms are. The eye of a baby passing through the birth canal is probably exposed to many dangerous germs, yet ophthalmia neonatorum, or conjunctivitis of the newborn, is rare, and it was rare even before the days when antibiotics could destroy such dangerous germs as that of gonorrhea in the genital passages. Doubtless the fact that the baby's eyes are closed during childbirth protects the delicate conjunctiva, but it is also probable that the membrane has some natural property, or immunity, to protect it against pathogens. When the defenses are defeated, which rarely occurs, germs can cause severe inflammation of an infant's conjunctiva; this may involve many of the other structures of the eye and lead to blindness.

Herpes infection of the eye

Most people suffer from "cold sores," or herpes of the mouth and lips, from time to time during adult life. These sores are caused by type I of the herpes simplex virus (*Herpesvirus hominis*) and are usually trivial, though irritating and unsightly. Herpesvirus infection of the eye instead of the lips is a much more serious condition, for it can lead to ulceration and to partial loss of sight from the scar that is left when the ulcer heals. The diphtheria bacillus does occasionally affect the eye during an attack of the disease; it produces a milky film, most often on the inside of the eyelid, but rarely causes severe damage. Trachoma, a serious inflammatory disease of the eye caused by a virus, is still a common infection in some tropical countries, perhaps now the only common severe disease of the eye caused by direct attack by a microorganism.

Microorganisms can pass through the conjunctiva and reach the bloodstream. Laboratory workers have found that guinea pigs can be infected with salmonellas much more readily and with much smaller doses of the organisms through the conjunctiva than through the mouth, and measles virus can certainly enter through the conjunctiva. Rubella is another virus that may enter the body through the eye, and sometimes swimmers in contaminated canal water seem to have caught Weil's disease by the passage of leptospira through their conjunctivas.

The nose and mouth. Most of the infections that enter by the nose and mouth have already been considered here as respiratory and gastrointestinal infections. Some microorganisms produce local diseases only. Thrush, for example, is a disease of the mouth and throat caused by yeastlike germs, but these are probably normal inhabitants of the area and cause disease only when the balance of microbial life in the mouth is disturbed, most often by the use of antibiotics for some other disease. Some of the enteroviruses can cause local inflammation of the throat, and streptococci typically attack the tonsils and cause tonsillitis. Diphtheria bacilli grow readily on the tonsils, but, as has been already stated, the danger in this disease comes from the toxin that is formed there and passes into the bloodstream. Syphilis normally enters the body by the genital tract, but sometimes the mouth is the portal of entry, and the primary sore may then be on the lips or tonsils. Tubercle bacilli taken into the mouth in milk can be taken up by the lymphoid tissue of the tonsils. From the tonsils they pass to the lymph nodes of the neck. There they are halted, but they set up a chronic inflammatory reaction, sometimes leading to breakdown of the node and discharge of pus on the surface of the neck. This used to be a common condition when milk containing tubercle bacilli was drunk raw, but it is now rare. Infectious mononucleosis, or glandular fever, is another disease in which the virus appears to enter by the mucous membrane of the mouth and finds its way to the neck nodes and other glands of the body.

Local diseases of nose and throat

Apart from the respiratory viruses that often cause the common cold, microorganisms do not readily attack the nose, though, when a person already has a cold because of a virus, other organisms such as streptococci and staphylococci take advantage of the altered state of the nasal mucous membranes to set up secondary inflammation; this may spread into the sinuses, or air spaces, that open into the nose.

Genital tract. The germs of syphilis and gonorrhea, *Treponema pallidum* and *Neisseria gonorrhoeae*, or the gonococcus, are parasites solely of humans and depend for their survival on passing from one to the other and on multiplying in each new host. The normal pathway is across the genital mucous membrane in sexual intercourse. In the acute stage of each disease, the microorganism is present on the genitals in great numbers and is highly infective for the sexual partner. There are no elaborate environmental requirements other than those provided in the genital tracts, and infection is by simple mechanical transfer.

Miscellaneous genital infections

Other agents of disease can be conveyed in the same way. It is not known which microorganism causes nonspecific urethritis (inflammation of the urethra of unknown cause), and there may be more than one, but the infection is certainly spread during sexual intercourse. *Herpesvirus hominis* type II can cause an infection on the male or female genitalia and be spread from one partner to the other, and a protozoan, *Trichomonas vaginalis*, the cause of acute vaginitis (inflammation of the vagina) in women and mild urethritis in men, also passes across the genital mucous membranes. A rather mysterious microorganism, *Listeria monocytogenes*, an uncommon cause of abortion in women, may be a normal part of the intestinal microbiologic flora (organisms always present in the gastrointestinal tract). It may spread from the gastrointestinal tract and colonize the genital tract; subsequently, it may infect the fetus in successive pregnancies. It has on rare occasions been isolated from the genital tract of the husband of an infected woman, but whether sexual intercourse is the common mode of infection is not known. The organism is a common parasite of many animals.

These are all examples of infections caused by direct contact of the genital mucous membranes. It is possible that during sexual intercourse microorganisms may pass from the bloodstream of one partner to the bloodstream of the other through microscopic tears in the mucous membranes. There is some evidence, for example, that the virus of serum hepatitis (hepatitis B virus) may very occasionally pass in this way from one person to another, and, in a few instances, a leptospiral infection may also have been passed sexually. If this does occur, it seems to be exceptional, but microorganisms have always found new pathways of infection, and the exceptional, if it provides easy passage, may in time become the accepted route. The virus of serum hepatitis has certainly exploited the new routes that injections, blood transfusions, and similar techniques have opened up for it.

Skin. More exposed than any other organ of the body to direct assault by microorganisms, the skin is, at the same time, the organ most resistant to their attack. It is in fact more vulnerable to attack from within than from outside the body; many microorganisms, having entered the body by some easier route than through the skin, multiply and increase their striking power inside the body and then, at the height of the disease, swarm through the bloodstream to attack the skin through the blood vessels on its undersurface, usually with great success. Smallpox and chicken pox behave in this way, and so successfully that they lead to breakdown of great areas of skin. Measles and rubella virus also invade the skin and cause their typical rash but do little damage to its cellular structure, and so do the germs of typhoid, plague, meningococcal meningitis, and many others. When staphylococci get into the bloodstream, they often invade the skin from below and cause large pustules on it; and yet the outside of healthy skin is often covered with staphylococci that live as commensals on it and seem unable to penetrate its covering of horny cells.

Invasion of skin from within

Close and repeated contact, possibly causing minor damage to the outer layer of cells, seems to be necessary to infect the skin. Impetigo, a skin disease caused by staphylococci or streptococci, is readily passed from one child to another, usually in the rough and tumble of daily life and play during which some surface skin cells may be rubbed off. *Bacillus anthracis*, as has been noted, is a spore-forming germ of low infectivity for humans. Although dockers and other workers in ports frequently handle heavily contaminated hides and hair, skin infection is rare and usually occurs on parts of the skin that have been grazed by the contaminated materials. Vaccinia (cowpox) is an infectious disease caused by the insertion of vaccinia virus into the skin during vaccination against smallpox. The virus can spread to other areas of the skin, carried there on the fingers of the patient. In all of these instances, minor invisible damage is probably a necessary factor before the skin gives way to infection.

Some microorganisms may enter by the unbroken skin. The streptococcus is one, and there seems little doubt that the germs of brucellosis and of Q fever can also enter through the skin. (It is not possible in any of these cases to exclude minor skin wounds as the portal of entry.) Some fungi are able to colonize the skin and cause disease. Ringworm is a well-known example, and there is no evidence that a break in the skin is necessary for such organisms to cause disease.

Invasion of broken skin

When the skin surface is seriously damaged, as in grazes and burns, the situation is quite different. Germs on the skin, normally innocuous, invade the denuded area, and germs floating in the air settle on the exposed surface. Indeed, invasion by such germs is one of the major hazards of burns, and great precautions are taken in the treatment of burns to create as far as possible an aseptic atmosphere. Diseases that normally must enter the body by some other route take advantage of broken skin areas. Diphtheria of the skin, although rare in temperate zones, in which people wear clothes and boots against the weather, is not so uncommon in warmer climates. Desert sores of the legs and other parts of the body are often infected with diphtheria bacillus, and its toxin can be absorbed into the body from the skin to cause paralysis elsewhere in the body.

The mite of scabies, *Sarcoptes scabiei* (*Acarus scabiei*), burrows into the skin and takes up its habitation in its deeper layers, and body and head lice live on the skin and get their nourishment directly from it. These mites and lice are true parasites of the skin. Fleas, ticks, mosquitoes, and other biting arthropods are not; they are after the blood beneath the skin, and they pierce through it to get to a blood vessel. Any disease they introduce is therefore a blood-borne, not a skin, infection. The action of their biting parts is, in fact, like that of a syringe, and a contaminated syringe can introduce almost any microorganism into the body. The great hazard of syringe and transfusion therapy is that the virus of serum hepatitis can so readily be introduced thereby. *Clostridium tetani* infects humans only when it is carried into the body in a wound, usually but not invariably a penetrating wound that carries the germ into an area of low oxygen tension where it can multiply and produce its toxin. The virus of rabies gets into the body by the bite of a rabid animal, again not a true infection through the skin. A mere lick by a rabid animal is probably not dangerous unless there is some break in the skin, but such a break might be invisible to the naked eye.

Transplacental infection. The circulation across the placenta carries all of the nutritional and other factors required for the development and growth of the unborn child. Normally it carries, as well, many of the antibodies present in the mother's circulation, and babies are born protected in this way against many infectious diseases. This transfer mechanism may in fact be made use of during pregnancy to protect newborn babies against neonatal infection; if the mother is given a course of tetanustoxoid injections during pregnancy, she will produce antibodies in her blood, and these will reach the baby's bloodstream before birth. If a mother should during her pregnancy become infected with a disease, the germ of that disease, instead of the antibody against it, can reach the infant in her womb. The result may be disastrous. The disease that causes the greatest concern is rubella, or German measles. This disease is usually an extremely mild one in children and adults. If the virus gets through the placenta in the first three months of pregnancy, however, it can attack the cells of the fetus at a stage when vital organs are being formed. The virus penetrates these rapidly dividing cells and disrupts the pattern completely. The eye, the heart, and the inner ear are all developing in these early months, and an infant infected at this stage through the placenta with rubella virus may be born at term, deaf, blind, and with a hole in the heart. Rubella infection of the mother during the last six months of pregnancy may cause less serious disease in the fetus.

Rubella damage to fetus

Two other infections that can lead to disastrous maldevelopment in the fetus are cytomegalovirus disease and toxoplasmosis, both normally common and innocuous infections but highly damaging to immature fetal cells. Some common viruses, such as the virus of chicken pox, vaccinia, and smallpox, can cross the placenta, but they differ from these other infections in that they tend to reproduce the normal type of the disease in the unborn child, though often with fatal severity. A child infected in the uterus with chicken pox, vaccinia, or smallpox may be born dead, covered with a rash typical of the disease. Vaccinia is the disease intentionally given in vaccination against smallpox, and no woman should ever be vaccinated during pregnancy unless she has been or is likely to be in close contact with a smallpox patient.

Other infections of the fetus may be acquired by passage of the infecting agent across the placenta. These include syphilis, malaria, tuberculosis (rarely), leptospirosis, brucellosis, and cryptococcosis. There are still many unexplained mental and physical defects of the newborn. Some may still be due to unsuspected transplacental infection.

PREVENTION

Procedures calculated to prevent infection or lessen its incidence include immunization programs, isolation, disinfection, and disinfestation.

Immunization programs. Immunization procedures can best be considered under two headings: those that must be routine because the risk is universal and those that are required only when there is a special or unusual risk. The two are not completely distinct, for a vaccine may be regarded as routine in one environment and unnecessary in another. For example, yellow-fever vaccine is essential in tropical areas in which the disease is prevalent but pointless in temperate zones where it does not exist.

Routine procedures. All over the world there are certain infectious diseases that menace the health or life of young children, and against these, immunization, if available, must be routine. Diphtheria, whooping cough, and poliomyelitis are obvious examples; they can all attack young children, and all can be severe.

Protective antibody may pass from the mother across the placenta to the fetus. Against some diseases antibody protection acquired in this manner may persist for only a few months. The first vaccine given to a baby is usually a combined one, containing the toxoids (modified toxins) of diphtheria and tetanus bacilli and a suspension of killed whooping-cough (pertussis) germs. Tetanus toxoid is given not because the disease is common but because it is one of the most severe infections at any age. Because the toxoid causes almost no reaction and immunity lasts for many years, it is well to start immunization against the disease as early as possible. The triple diphtheria–tetanus–pertussis vaccine (DTP) must be given in three doses. The first dose sensitizes the cells of the body's immunity mechanism, but little, if any, antibody is produced. The second dose, six to eight weeks later, causes a sharp outpouring of antibody into the bloodstream. A third dose raises the antibody level still higher. The initial three doses of this combined vaccine are recommended at two months, four months, and six months of age. A further dose of combined vaccine is given as a booster at 18 months. At four to six years of age, the DTP vaccine may be given again. Some physicians prefer to omit the pertussis booster at this age and give only the bivalent tetanus toxoid-diphtheria vaccine (Td). An adult-type vaccine containing diphtheria and tetanus toxoids (Td) is recommended at 12 years and again at 18 years of age. The adult form of diphtheria and tetanus toxoid vaccines contains approximately one-tenth the amount of diphtheria toxoid found in the pediatric preparation used for immunizing the younger child but the same amount of tetanus toxoid as found in the pediatric preparation. A repeat dose of Td vaccine is recommended once every 10 years thereafter to maintain protection against diphtheria and tetanus throughout life.

Vaccine for diphtheria, tetanus, whooping cough

Two types of poliomyelitis vaccine are available, live or killed. The live vaccine is given by mouth on a lump of sugar; the killed, by injection under the skin. The vaccine must contain the viruses, live or dead, of the three poliovirus types, I, II, and III. With both vaccines three doses are required. This is unusual with a live vaccine; repeat dosages are given to ensure universal immunity. Most experts now prefer live polio vaccines. A sugar lump is more acceptable than an injection, and it is much easier to use this method in a large-scale vaccination program. Moreover, it produces intestinal immunity as well as body immunity: this means that wild poliovirus cannot establish itself in the intestines of a person immunized with live vaccine. ("Wild" virus means natural virus as it circulates in the community, unmodified by any attenuating laboratory procedures.) It is not as certain that this holds with persons immunized with killed polio vaccine; wild poliovirus might establish itself in the intestines of such a person, and, though he could not, being immune, himself develop poliomyelitis, he might pass the virus on to some nonimmunized contact.

Against measles antibody protection acquired by the fetus from the mother may persist in the infant for 12 months or longer and may interfere with the action of measles vaccine. For this reason measles immunization generally is not recommended until age 15 months. Measles vaccine, a live, attenuated viral vaccine, is given by injection under the skin, and only one dose is required.

Rubella vaccination

Measles vaccine is given to protect the child against a troublesome and sometimes severe illness. With rubella, or German measles, the problem is different. Rubella is a mild, almost trifling illness in children, scarcely worth vaccinating against. The virus can, however, cross the placenta and severely damage the cells of the fetus at the stage when vital organs are being formed. The object of rubella vaccination, then, is to protect the unborn child, not the person receiving the vaccination. It might seem logical to vaccinate all women early in pregnancy or all women of childbearing age. The danger of such a policy is that the vaccine virus, though attenuated, is live and can probably cross the placenta. Whether it can damage fetal cells, as wild rubella virus does, is not known, but the risk is too great to run. The problem can be tackled in two ways. Rubella vaccine can be given widely to young children in the hope of stamping out the virus from the environment and so protecting pregnant women against the danger of infection. The second method is to give the vaccine to girls around the age of 11 to 12 years in the hope of building up a population of women in the childbearing age immune to rubella. Perhaps the best scheme would be a combination of both: to vaccinate all children at an early age in an attempt to eradicate the virus and to revaccinate girls just before puberty for double assurance.

A live attenuated mumps vaccine is available and recommended for administration at 15 months of age. In current practice a single dose of a vaccine containing measles, rubella, and mumps viruses is given at 15 months of age to protect against all three of these diseases.

There can be no doubt about the efficacy of smallpox vaccine. It does protect the vaccinated person against smallpox. Unfortunately, it can have unpleasant complications. It usually gives the vaccinated person a sore arm and often a mild fever. It can cause a spreading ulceration of the skin that can, in the worst cases, be fatal, and it is sometimes followed by encephalitis (inflammation of the brain), which, if not fatal, can cause blindness and paralysis. In 1980 the World Health Organization declared the world to be free of smallpox; smallpox vaccine is no longer recommended. The eradication of smallpox represents a modern medical triumph.

BCG vaccine

A live vaccine is available against tuberculosis. Known usually as BCG (bacille Calmette-Guérin), it consists of attenuated tubercle bacilli. It is given into the skin by scratch or skin puncture. In some countries it is given in the period immediately after birth; in others, around the age of 12 years. The vaccine is not recommended for routine use in the United States. Much depends on local circumstances and the danger of infection. Many children have infections with tuberculosis that cause no symptoms but render them immune, and a simple skin test can be done that shows whether a person is susceptible or immune to tuberculosis, either through unnoticed natural infection or by BCG vaccination.

Influenza vaccines induce immunity to the strains of influenza virus contained in the vaccine that is administered. Unfortunately, the strains of influenza virus that produce disease change continuously. Immunity could be maintained only by repetitive, yearly immunizations with a vaccine that would require yearly changes in its immunizing components. Generally, influenza immunization is reserved for the elderly or for individuals with chronic lung or heart disease.

No vaccines exist for prevention of the common cold. The problem with the common cold is that there are more than 100 viruses that produce symptoms of this disease, and it is neither practical to make a vaccine containing more than 100 viruses nor acceptable to receive hundreds of immunizations.

At least three viruses cause a disease that clinically is called infectious hepatitis. These viruses cause hepatitis A, hepatitis B, and non-A, non-B hepatitis. Non-A, non-B hepatitis may be more than one disease, but the virus or viruses causing non-A, non-B hepatitis have not been isolated. A vaccine has been produced that can protect humans against hepatitis B virus; it is recommended for persons at high risk for hepatitis B infection (dentists, surgeons, those who work with blood in hospitals or laboratories, and kidney dialysis technicians).

Special-risk vaccines. In countries with advanced standards of hygiene and sanitation there is no need for vaccines against typhoid or cholera. In less developed countries both are required. TAB vaccine contains dead bodies of typhoid and paratyphoid A and B germs. It can be given by injection into or under the skin. Two injections, separated by six weeks, give good protection for about three years but will not protect against extremely large doses of the germs. Cholera vaccination also requires two doses of vaccine, but protection lasts for only six months, so that anyone living in a cholera area must be revaccinated every six months. Both cholera and typhoid are diseases of bad hygiene, and a high standard of hygiene and sanitation gives better protection than vaccines.

Vaccination against yellow fever, plague

Yellow fever, by contrast, is a mosquito-borne disease, and humans have much less control over the environmental reservoirs of infection. Yellow-fever vaccine is fortunately one of the most successful live vaccines, and protection lasts for 10 years. Plague vaccine is composed of killed strains of the plague bacillus, *Yersinia pestis;* two injections are required as an initial course and a reinforcing dose should be administered every six months to residents in a plague area. Plague is another disease in which environmental control, in this case the control of rats, is more effective than vaccines in eradicating the disease. Against both louse-borne and flea-borne typhus, a vaccine containing the germs of both diseases, known as rickettsiae, gives some protection; two or preferably three injections are given in the primary course. Thereafter one injection each year is required, but, if typhus becomes epidemic in any area, reinforcing doses may be advised.

The foregoing are all diseases of the environment, and every entrant requires protection. With rabies the situation is different. Humans contract the disease only after a bite from a rabid animal.

Veterinary and quarantine officers, dog handlers in kennels and pounds for strays, laboratory workers handling the virus, and naturalists in areas in which the disease is present in small animals can all be protected in advance of possible bites. They require at least three primary injections and reinforcing doses at intervals of one to three years, according to their antibody response: if a person thus vaccinated is bitten by a rabid animal, he is given a short course of reinforcing injections, for, with a disease as fatal as rabies, it is not safe to rely solely on past vaccinations. When an unvaccinated person is bitten by a rabid animal, he must be given a dose of hyperimmune human antirabies globulin and must also receive immunization with human diploid-cell rabies vaccine. The hyperimmune globulin provides a measure of immediate protection, and the vaccine stimulates the recipient's immune system to produce antirabies antibodies. The incubation period of rabies is usually between one and three months, so that there is time to immunize the person after the bite and before the virus can multiply and overwhelm the body.

The use of a vaccine is an attempt to imitate the antibody response that follows natural infection. In some diseases it is highly successful; in others, less so. It is at most a second best attempt to defeat the disease. The most effective method, though often the most difficult, is to eliminate the infective agent from the environment.

Isolation techniques. *In the hospital.* The successful isolation of an infectious person in a hospital depends partly on separation of the person from others but much more on the way the patient is handled by doctors, nurses, and other attendants. They must know exactly how the infectious agent leaves the body of the patient and how they can prevent it reaching others.

Microorganisms leave the body of an infectious person by various routes—from the respiratory tract in many diseases, in the feces and urine in others, or in any pus or discharge from any part of the body. The skin often becomes contaminated: in an intestinal infection—typhoid, for example—the skin on the buttocks and the lower half of the trunk is usually contaminated with *Salmonella typhi.* The germ of a disease is often present in the patient's bloodstream, so that samples must be taken with great care. Doctors and nurses prevent spread of disease also on the basis of knowledge of how long the patient is infectious. In measles, for example, virus is expelled in vast quantities from the nose and mouth for several days before the rash appears, but this ceases a day or two after the rash; in typhoid fever, by contrast, *Salmonella typhi* is passed in the urine and feces from the early days of the illness for an indefinite period.

The patient's room and everything in it can be rapidly contaminated with germs. It is the responsibility of doctors and nurses to make sure none of these germs gets out of the room into the corridor and from there into another patient's room.

Techniques in the hospital

The technique depends on awareness. An attendant's hands must be washed thoroughly after touching anything contaminated with the isolated patient's germs. As far as possible an attendant's technique must be one of "no touch." Dressings, for example, are removed by forceps and placed at once into disposable bags. Patients' clothing and bed linen are placed in bags sealed at the bedside. Virtually everything used in nursing the patient is disposable—forceps, towels, gauze, needles, and syringes—and all are placed at once after use in disposable paper bags. All the materials that have to be taken out of the room ideally go out through a hatchway to the outside, not to the corridor.

The greatest care is taken in disposing of the patient's excreta—sputum, urine, and feces.

Gowns and masks are traditional in the infectious sickroom. Their value is doubtful. The key to isolation technique is awareness, not paraphernalia: the informed, conscientious nurse can control infection even in simple surroundings.

In the home. In the home the surroundings are simple, but so are some of the problems. There is only one patient and only one disease, so that the great hospital danger of conveying one infection to a patient already suffering from another does not arise. On the other hand, the patient has been in intimate, uncontrolled contact with all of the other members of the household, and in that time he may have been highly infectious, and others may already be infected. The development of the disease in these contacts may, in some infections, be avoided by suitable treatment.

In both the hospital and home disinfection of the room after the patient has been released is of some importance. This varies with the disease. In many diseases the germs die quickly away from the patient so that there is no danger at all. In others it can linger alive on bedclothes, furniture, and dust.

Destruction of infectious agent or carrier. Microorganisms can never be eliminated. They are infinitely more numerous than humans and infinitely more tenacious of life, even in the most hazardous environments. Moreover, they have functions that are vital to the existence of other living beings, including humans. But some, to humans, seem only harmful, and humans have devised means to prevent the entry of such organisms into immediate environment or to destroy them if they do get in.

Destruction of germs

Food, drink, and air. Infectious agents can reach humans in the food they eat and the air they breathe. Over the former humans can exercise considerable control, over the latter very little, and only in special circumstances. Many of the germs in food are killed by the heat of ordinary cooking. Some, such as the germ of botulism, *Clostridium botulinum,* can be killed only by much higher temperatures, and these are attained in high-pressure heat treatment applied in canning factories; most of the safety of food supplies comes from simple hygienic measures—cleanliness and the denial to food-poisoning germs of the conditions they like, mainly gentle warmth and the chance to multiply. Both are denied them inside a refrigerator.

More specific precautions are applied to milk and water. Pasteurization is the process whereby milk is heated to a temperature lethal to disease germs and kept at that temperature until they all die. There are several different methods, all of them a function of temperature and time. In one method the temperature is between 145° and 150° F (63° and 66° C) and the time is 30 minutes; in another the temperature is 161° F (72° C) and the time is 15 seconds. Either method destroys all of the disease germs, but others—the thermophilic or heat-stable germs—survive: these are harmless to humans but cause souring of the pasteurized milk after a few days. All can be destroyed if the milk is subjected to still higher temperatures. This is sterilization; the milk keeps indefinitely, but the flavour is altered.

The purification of water involves three processes—holding, filtration, and chemical treatment. The water is held in reservoirs for several weeks, and in this time most disease germs die, for water is not a good medium for growth. The water is next passed through filters that remove most of the germs still present, and finally, before the water goes into the supply pipes, a chemical is added, usually chlorine, to kill off any disease germs that have escaped. Drinking water so treated is not sterile, for some germs survive all of these treatments; but, fortunately for humans, disease germs do not. Sodium flouride also may be added in appropriate concentration to water that does not already contain natural flouride. Water that has been appropriately flouridated has been shown to be effective in preventing tooth decay when it is ingested regularly by children during the period of time that the deciduous and permanent teeth are forming.

It is not usually practicable to remove disease germs from the air, but skillful ventilation can greatly reduce the danger by diluting their concentration. In special hospital wards—for example, units for the treatment of burns and operating theatres—an attempt can be made by the use of air filters to remove all of the microorganisms, and such attempts are at least partly successful. In very special cases, in which even a mild infection might prove disastrous, the patient in bed can be enclosed in a plastic tent; direct passage of germs from attendant to patient can be blocked in this way, and the air entering the tent can be controlled and filtered so that no germs, other than the patient's own, are present inside the tent. A person suffering from severe burns or recovering from a transplant operation might be treated in this way. In general, however, humans must breathe the air they find around them.

The vector. To stop the spread of disease by insect-borne parasites, humans adopt two main methods: (1) to prevent contact between themselves and insects, and (2) to attempt to destroy insects. Most often both methods are used together. To prevent contact people may site their habitations too far away from breeding grounds for insects to reach them; they may clear areas of shrub and forest in between, so that insects have no shelter to help them across. People should also still practice simple methods around the home: the wearing of protective clothing and boots toward nightfall, screens across windows or around beds, and the use of an insect-repellent lotion on any exposed skin.

Methods of killing insects

Methods used to destroy the insect carrier range from simple domestic procedures to major engineering schemes. A flytrap is a useful method of reducing the number of flies or other carriers in a single household, but it has no effect on the total insect population. Long-lasting lethal sprays on walls of houses and other buildings kill insects that invade buildings, but, to have any permanent effect on the insect population, they must be used on a wide scale on the breeding grounds as well. This may mean the spraying of lakes, swamps, and scrubland by helicopter, and there is a risk of destroying other forms of life besides the insect aimed at. Some of these may be the natural enemies or predators of the carrier, and their destruction could lead to an increase rather than a decrease in its number. A further risk is that just as bacteria may become resistant to antibiotics, so may insects become resistant to insecticides. This has indeed occurred already in some areas, a fact that illustrates the tenacity of life among microorganisms. Insecticides have proved powerful weapons in controlling carriers of disease, but their use illustrates the difficulties and dangers in any attempt to upset the fine balance of nature.

A knowledge of the life and habits of the insect is the basis of biological methods of control. The tsetse fly of trypanosomiasis, or sleeping sickness, feeds largely on the blood of big game animals, and, if humans can drive these off from an area, the tsetse flies must also disappear. *Xenopsylla cheopis*, the plague flea, depends on rats for its meals of blood, and extermination of rats brings an end of the flea and plague in the area. Some species of fish feed on malaria larvae on the surface of lake waters, and stocking the waters with these fish has been successful in cutting down the number of adult mosquitoes that fly off to attack humans. Insects are often highly fastidious in the type of vegetation that they choose as cover or refuge. Some can survive certain climatic conditions only under plants that grow close to the ground; others depend on water plants for protection and oxygen. Clearing away such plants can have a more profound effect on insect population and is more biologically rational than the use of nondiscriminating insecticides. These biological measures may be very simple, but they are derived from detailed study of all of the life of the area. At a more basic level, humans have attempted to interrupt the reproductive cycle of insects by raising large populations of males in laboratories and so affecting their reproductive organs by radiation, chemicals, or crossbreeding that, when released, they are incapable of fertilizing the female.

Effects of major engineering projects

Major engineering undertakings can have massive and sometimes unexpected effects on vector life and human disease. Draining a lake or a swamp, altering the course of a river, clearing a forest area, building a town in a rural area—all of these may be done with no thought of altering the balance of life in the area, but the effect may be profound, and it may be beneficial or harmful: beneficial if it deprives disease carriers of their habitat and harmful if it brings humans nearer to it. Minor works may also bring changes: the filling in of cracks in walls and floors, the draining of pools around a village, and the use of concrete instead of mud for floors or the use of stone instead of wood for walls of huts and other buildings—all of these cut down the chance of insects' breeding near human habitation. Major or minor, such works can alter the biological environment and, carried out with forethought, can greatly benefit human life and health.

Disinfection. In spite of all of the precautions, microorganisms do arrive in the immediate human environment, and people must then employ methods to destroy them. The main weapon is heat. Many microorganisms are easily killed by heat: salmonellas, for example, are killed in 15 minutes at 140° F (60° C). Others, especially spore-bearers, resist boiling for hours. The most effective method of sterilization is the application of steam under pressure. This is carried out in apparatus called autoclaves, from which all of the air can be drawn off by vacuum pump before the steam is introduced under pressure. With a complete vacuum and steam at 15 pounds per square inch (one kilogram per square centimetre), a temperature of 250° F (121° C) is reached inside the autoclave, and this maintained for 20 minutes sterilizes all of its contents. With dry heat the temperature must be much higher, 320° F (160° C) for 45 minutes or 356° F (180° C) for 7½ minutes, and the hot air must be able to circulate freely in the chamber to ensure that all of the articles reach this temperature. Many articles perish or deteriorate if heated in either of these ways—leather, rubber, or some plastics, for example. These may be treated with formaldehyde in special cabinets, an old but fairly efficient method, or exposed to gamma radiation—increasingly used for surgical instruments and materials, especially for disposable plastic syringes, catheters, and dressing utensils. It can also be used for sterilizing meat carcasses and canned foods. Ethylene oxide may also be used for sterilizing without heat, but its use requires special apparatus and skilled technique, for it is a toxic gas.

Often the only available way of dealing with germs is to use chemicals known as disinfectants. The selection is wide. Many can be shown to be effective in laboratory tests with the germs concerned, but they often lose their effect in the presence of blood, pus, feces, and other organic matter. Another disadvantage is that some, whereas very effective against the germ, are also harmful to human tissues. Few, if any, achieve sterility, but only disinfection. Disinfection means the destruction of all of the active disease germs, whereas sterility means the absence of all of the germs. A few spores in a bedpan matter not at all. The same spores on a surgical dressing might bring disaster, for, in the environment of a surgical wound, spores can germinate and cause serious and sometimes fatal infections. Sterility, then, is essential for vital procedures; disinfection is often enough for domestic purposes.

II. Individual systemic diseases

The infective agent, the host, the environment, the routes and modes of infection, and the means of prevention have been touched upon in some detail. It remains to consider what happens when microbes turn human defenses and, for a time at least, achieve dominion over them; in other words, to look at the clinical picture of infectious diseases. It is convenient to do this according to the portal of entry and the type of infectious agent.

RESPIRATORY TRACT

Viral diseases. The viral infections that enter the body through the respiratory tract include those, such as the cold and influenza viruses, that affect the respiratory tract primarily and others, such as infectious mononucleosis, smallpox, and chicken pox, that are systemic in their effects.

Respiratory tract infections. Of the many viruses that can cause disease in the respiratory tract, at least 200 have been identified by virologists. Around 100 of these are rhinoviruses, the organisms that cause the common cold. This is by far the commonest infectious disease to afflict mankind.

Rhinoviruses

When rhinoviruses enter the nose in a wet droplet, they settle on cells lining the airway and immediately penetrate them. This they must do in order to survive, for a virus cannot multiply except inside a cell; in fact, it uses materials in the host cell to form new virus particles. These new virus particles then escape from the first cell and enter neighbouring ones and start the process of multiplication, or replication, all over again. The host cell reacts to the invasion by producing a substance called interferon, which interferes with viral replication inside the cell. Antibody cannot enter cells, but it can attack and destroy viruses as they cross from one host cell to another. Interferon acts against all of the 100 or so rhinoviruses, but antibody can attack one strain of virus only. Whether or not a person gets a cold when a rhinovirus enters the nose depends on how quickly nasal cells form interferon to stop the virus replicating and on whether the person already has the specific antibody in his system with which to destroy migrating virus particles. Both mechanisms eventually work together to bring the infection to an end. It is a question of timing, and rhinoviruses are fast workers.

If the virus gets a good start, its activities irritate the lining cells in the nose, and they respond by pouring out streams of clear fluid. This acts by diluting the virus and getting it out of the nose. The sensory organs in the nose are stung by the inflammatory reaction, and this sets up sneezing, a second method of expelling the virus. If the virus gets deeper into the upper respiratory tract, coughing is added to the patient's symptoms, another mechanism for getting rid of the virus. As the host's defenses increase, the symptoms abate, the clear fluid often changing to thick fluid that is full of the debris of dead cells that have perished in the struggle. The common cold is the expression of an open fight between a rhinovirus and a host's defenses. It takes place in a restricted field, the nasal epithelium (covering layer), but it has, in miniature, all of the characteristics of the wider encounters between human and virus that mark some of the more serious infectious diseases. Influenza is one of these.

Influenza viruses A, B, C

There are three families of influenza viruses: A, B, and C. The A viruses cause the great influenza epidemics, the B viruses cause smaller localized outbreaks, and the C viruses are not important causes of human disease. The A viruses are not a stable family group; in fact, their most constant characteristic is change. The virus was first isolated and identified in 1933 and was simply influenza virus A or, sometimes, AO. It kept changing very slightly for many years but was still recognizable as AO until 1946, by which time its character had changed so much that its designation was changed to A1. This A1 virus held the field for 11 years, continuously changing a little but still obviously an A1 virus. In 1957 another major change took place, and the A2 virus came on the scene; it first appeared in China and so was called the A2 Asian influenza virus. The A2 Asian strain continued to appear, changing slightly year by year, until 1968, when a different strain was isolated in Hong Kong. This, although it differed considerably from the 1957 strain, still had most of the A2 characters. It was called, therefore, not A3 but, rather, A2 Hong Kong 1968.

These changes, or mutations, occur in the antigenic structure of the virus. An antigen is that part of a microorganism that gives it its own specific character and that enables a microbiologist to identify it from a crowd of otherwise similar microorganisms. The antigens of a germ, also closely connected with its infectivity, stimulate specific antibodies in the body of the infected host. These antibodies protect the host for some time against reinfection, and, if a large number of people in a community develop antibodies, the microorganism concerned finds it difficult to spread rapidly. When, however, a microorganism undergoes a major change in its antigenic composition, the antibodies provoked by the older antigens give no protection against the new, and the population is wide open to attack by what is, in the antigenic sense, a completely new microorganism. This has two important results. The new virus can sweep unhindered through the unprotected hosts, and vaccines that gave protection against the old infection are useless against the new one. This happened in 1957 and in 1968, when the new Asian and Hong Kong influenza-virus strains swept across the globe, causing epidemics, or rather pandemics, of the disease.

The symptoms of influenza are always primarily respiratory in character. Some affected persons have little more than a severe common cold, whereas others suffer an overwhelming general infection. It depends on where the virus strikes and how much resistance it meets. The reactions of the respiratory lining cells are the same as in the common cold. They pour out fluid, but, whereas fluid poured into the nose is an inconvenience to the patient, fluid poured into the air cells of the lungs can be disastrous. In the fatal cases there is no inflammatory reaction such as in pneumonia, for the patient, lungs full of fluid, dies before there is time for such a reaction to take place. Influenza is a rapidly disabling illness, but the worst symptoms are usually over in a week, unless complications set in. These are usually caused not by the influenza virus itself but by such microorganisms as pneumococci, staphylococci, and *Haemophilus influenzae.* Often these organisms have lived a harmless commensal life in the patient's respiratory tract and break into the respiratory lining cells only when they find them already damaged by influenza virus. The result may be acute bronchitis or pneumonia, always a serious hazard in the influenza patient and sometimes a fatal one. Most of these secondary invaders are affected by antibiotics, and many persons, though desperately ill, can be saved by their use. The greatest danger from the influenza virus, however, is when it attacks the aged or the debilitated, especially those already suffering from chronic chest or heart diseases. In such patients the cells of the respiratory tract are already damaged by disease and are unable to withstand the further damage caused by the viral attack.

Other respiratory illnesses

The common cold is easy to diagnose and so, in an epidemic, is influenza. But many other acute respiratory illnesses are difficult to distinguish clinically. The symptoms are caused by irritation of the cells of the respiratory tract, and these respond in the same way to different irritants. Most affected persons have a feeling of chilliness, their temperatures are elevated for a few days, and they may have to take to bed. An exact diagnosis can be made if specimens of sputum, nasal discharge, throat washings, and blood are taken, but this entails a vast amount of tedious and expensive laboratory work, and in many cases the sick person recovers long before the results are known. An exact viral diagnosis may help with treatment, however, by enabling the physician to choose from among available drugs those capable of attacking specific viruses.

Infectious mononucleosis. Infectious mononucleosis, often called glandular fever because of the swelling of the nodes in the neck, the armpits, and the groin that occurs in some persons with the disease, incapacitates individuals for varying periods of time. Some affected persons are physically fit for normal activities within two or at most three weeks, whereas others remain ill for as long as two months.

The commonest symptom is sore throat, and there is usually a thick, white coating, or membrane, on each tonsil. This membrane is like that seen early in diphtheria, but it always remains white in infectious mononucleosis, whereas, in diphtheria, after the first day, it turns foul and greenish black. Swelling of the lymph nodes in the neck, the armpits, and the groin occurs only in some persons. There are changes in the white cells of the blood and in the patient's serum, detected by a special test.

Epstein-Barr virus

Epstein-Barr virus is the cause of infectious mononucleosis. The virus was first isolated not from persons with infectious mononucleosis but, rather, from tumour cells in children suffering from a form of cancer called Burkitt's lymphoma. Later research showed that most children throughout the world develop antibodies to this virus early in life, evidence that they have been infected with it, though without suffering any illness and certainly without any signs of tumour growth or of infectious mononucleosis. Infectious mononucleosis is a disease mainly of adolescent and adult life and seems to occur only in persons who have escaped Epstein-Barr virus infection in childhood. Infectious mononucleosis and Burkitt's lymphoma are both diseases of the lymphoid tissues of the body. Some of the unusual blood cells in infectious mononucleosis have properties much like those of cells of Burkitt's lymphoma, and further study of infectious mononucleosis cells may give a clue to the cause of cancerous growth in lymphoid cells.

Smallpox and chicken pox. Smallpox and chicken pox are both diseases in which the virus enters by the respiratory route, multiplies in the internal organs, and, at the height of the infection, causes a rash on the skin. The rashes are at first glance similar. In each the first thing seen is a flat spot, or macule; this changes into a clear blister, or vesicle; the contents become turbid, and the blister is then called a pustule. The pustule dries up, forming a scab, and the scab separates, leaving a scar, or pock. Although the diseases are similar, there are two great differences. In chicken pox the rash is heaviest on the trunk and on the upper part of the limbs; it has a centre-seeking, or centripetal, distribution. In smallpox the rash is heaviest on the face and on the lower parts of the limbs: its distribution is centre-fleeing, or centrifugal. The other fundamental difference is in the rate of progression from macule to pock. In chicken pox the progression is so rapid that the early stages are often not noticed; within a few hours the macules have changed to vesicles, and by the end of 24 hours the first scabs have appeared. In smallpox a macule takes three days to change to a vesicle, and it is eight days before the first scab is formed. No one can say why the two rashes behave so differently, but it is fortunate that they do, for it is usually possible to diagnose the two diseases by examination of the rash. The viruses can be distinguished in the laboratory.

Difficulties of diagnosis do occur, mainly with the mildest or the most severe types of smallpox. The mildest attacks occur in persons who have been vaccinated in the past and are almost, but not completely, immune to the disease. The rash in such patients may consist of a mere sprinkling of spots, even as few as one. At the other extreme, the virus multiplies with such vehemence in the internal organs that, when it pours into the bloodstream, it overwhelms the patient's power of resistance and kills him before the true rash has time to appear. He is, indeed, covered with a rash, but it consists of purple blotches of blood or a red blaze over the whole skin. Time and again in smallpox outbreaks, cases have been missed, either because they were very mild or very severe, for the rashes in such cases resemble not at all the orderly progressive pustular rash of typical smallpox. Less commonly, cases of chicken pox have been mistaken for smallpox, either because the pustular rash was so intense that it looked like smallpox or because there was bleeding into the skin.

Smallpox, which historically was one of the great epidemic diseases of mankind, has now been conquered. From 1967 to 1976 the World Health Organization carried out an eradication program—using mass vaccination, surveillance, and containment—in Africa, South Asia, South America, and Indonesia, the last areas of endemic smallpox. After the end of the program, except for an epidemic in Somalia in 1977, there were reports of only isolated and scattered cases of the disease, and after 1979 there were no reports of smallpox.

Vaccination against smallpox consists of injecting live vaccinia virus into the skin. It multiplies in the skin and forms a local sore on the arm. Its presence causes the body to form antibodies, and these antibodies protect the patient not only against vaccinia but also against smallpox. In the early days of vaccination, material was taken from the vesicle of a smallpox patient and scratched very carefully into the skin of other persons; this was known as variolation, from *variola*, the Latin name for smallpox. Variolation usually did give protection, but sometimes it produced unmodified and even fatal smallpox in the vaccinated person. It was later found that material taken from the vesicles of cowpox, if inserted into human skin, stimulated antibodies against smallpox but never caused that disease in the person vaccinated. This became for a time the accepted method of obtaining a virus for immunization, but the virus now is grown in laboratories in hen eggs and is no longer derived from cowpox. Vaccinia virus, cowpox virus, and smallpox virus are all indistinguishable by most laboratory tests, but they grow slightly differently and at different temperatures in hen eggs.

Bacterial diseases. *Diphtheria.* The human body can resist small doses of diphtheria bacilli, *Corynebacterium diphtheriae*, forming antitoxin against it; though the bacillus may settle down in the nose or in the throat of a person with antitoxin in his blood, its toxin cannot invade his body, and the diphtheria bacillus causes the person no harm at all. He becomes a carrier of the germ, suffers nothing himself but is a great danger to other people, for the disease spreads through a population mainly by means of healthy carriers.

Course of diphtheria

Corynebacterium diphtheriae enters the body of a susceptible person via the respiratory tract, but the symptoms it causes are not usually respiratory. It settles on the tonsils and there creates an inflammatory reaction that leads to the formation of a thick skin, or membrane, which may cover the tonsils and spread on the hard palate and up behind the nose. The diphtheria bacillus remains at this site, but while multiplying there, it produces its powerful toxin, which spreads through the body in the bloodstream and causes great damage to the heart and nervous system. The amount of toxin invading the body depends on the extent of the membrane. If it is confined to the tonsils only small amounts are produced, and the sick person is unlikely to suffer from serious toxic complications. If the membrane spreads beyond the tonsils, either behind the nose or across the hard palate, there are likely to be some of the most dangerous complications.

The membrane separates from the throat by the end of a week or 10 days, but toxic complications come on later in severe cases. The heart suffers first, often in the second or third week. The patient falls into toxic heart failure and may die at this stage. If the person is brought through this dangerous period, the heart recovers completely, and the patient appears well. But this appearance is deceptive, and it is one of the most treacherous aspects of this disease that paralysis due to the action of diphtheria toxin on the nervous system often strikes a person when he seems to have recovered from the early illness. Paralysis of the palate and of some eye muscles develops in about the third week: this is usually transient and not severe. As late as the fifth to eighth week, however, paralysis of swallowing and of breathing comes on in severe cases, and these may kill the patient after weeks of apparent well-being. Later still, paralysis of the limbs may occur, but this is not life-threatening. The only heartening aspect of these paralyses is that they are due to a temporary failure of the nerve supply to muscles. If the patient can be kept alive through the critical phase, he will recover completely. This is very different from the outlook in poliomyelitis, for in that disease a person with severe paralysis, if he survives, is usually left with residual paralysis.

Antibiotics can destroy the diphtheria bacillus in the throat and are given to every patient, but the essential treatment of the patient is to get antitoxin quickly into his body to neutralize the circulating toxin. The antitoxin may save the life of the person, if given early enough, but the body eventually eliminates it as a foreign substance, and it does not give any permanent protection against the disease. For this, the patient must produce his own antitoxin, and his body will do this in response to active immunization with diphtheria toxin. Active immunization carried out on a wide scale eradicates this killing disease.

Pneumococcal, staphylococcal, and streptococcal infections. Coccus means a small round dot or berry. Pneumo is from the Greek word for lungs, staphylo for a bunch of grapes, and strepto for a chain. Thus, the pneumococcus is a dot-shaped germ that attacks the lungs, staphylococci under the microscope look like bunches of grapes, and streptococci form chains. The three microorganisms belong to different biological groups, but in their relations with humans they have many things in common. Often they live as harmless commensals in the upper respiratory tract, but each can quicken into virulent activity and cause such serious conditions as pneumonia, septicemia (invasion of the bloodstream), or meningitis.

Causes of pneumonia, septicemia, meningitis

The pneumococcus is the commonest cause of lobar pneumonia, the disease in which one or more lobes, or segments, of the lung become solid and airless as a result of inflammation. Staphylococci affect the lung either in the course of staphylococcal septicemia, when the germs leak out of the circulating blood and cause scattered abscesses in the lungs, or as a complication of a viral infection of the lungs, commonly influenza, when staphylococci may invade the damaged lung cells and cause a life-threatening form of pneumonia; a similar condition may occur in young infants. Streptococcal pneumonia is less common than the other two and occurs usually as a complication of influenza or other lung disease.

Pneumococci often leak out from inflamed lungs into the bloodstream and cause septicemia, with continued fever but no other special symptoms. Staphylococci produce a hectic type of septicemia with high, swinging fever; the germs reach almost any organ of the body, the brain, the bones, and the lungs especially, and destructive abscesses form in these areas. Streptococci, too, cause septicemia with hectic fever, but the organisms tend to cause inflammation of surface lining cells rather than abscesses, pleurisy (inflammation of the chest lining) rather than lung abscess, peritonitis (inflammation of the membrane lining the abdomen) rather than liver abscess. In the course of either type of septicemia, organisms may leak into the nervous system and cause streptococcal or staphylococcal meningitis (inflammation of the brain coverings), but these are rare conditions. Pneumococci, on the other hand, often spread directly into the central nervous system, and pneumococcal meningitis is one of the common forms of meningitis.

Staphylococci and streptococci are common causes of skin diseases. Boils or impetigo (in which the skin is covered with blisters, pustules, and yellow crusts) may be caused by either. The staphylococcus can also cause a vicious inflammation of the skin that strips the outer skin layers off the body and leaves the underlayers exposed as in severe burns, a condition known as epidermal necrolysis. Streptococci can be the cause of the red inflammation of the skin known as erysipelas. Some staphylococci produce an intestinal toxin and cause food poisoning, whereas streptococci settling on the throat produce a reddening toxin that speeds through the bloodstream and produces all of the symptoms of scarlet fever. How the same germs can act with such divergent intensities is not known. The three organisms can all be attacked with antibiotics. The diseases they cause have not been conquered by antibiotics, but, when antibiotics are used with intelligence, much of the damage done by the organisms can be controlled, and many lives can be saved.

Meningococcal infections. Meningococci are fairly common inhabitants of the human throat, in most cases causing no illness at all. As the number of healthy carriers increases in any population, there is a tendency for the meningococcus to become more invasive. When an opportunity is presented, it launches into the bloodstream, invades the central nervous system, and causes meningococcal meningitis (formerly called cerebrospinal meningitis or spotted fever). When meningococci invade the bloodstream, some meningococci leak into the skin and cause blood-stained spots, or purpura. If the condition is diagnosed early enough, antibiotics can clear the bloodstream of the germ and prevent any from getting far enough to cause meningitis. Sometimes the septicemia takes a mild chronic relapsing form with no tendency toward meningitis; this is cured once it is diagnosed. The meningococcus can cause one of the most fulminating of all the forms of septicemia; the body is rapidly covered with a purple rash, purpura fulminans, and the blood pressure collapses; the heart and blood vessels are affected by shock, and the patient is dead in a matter of hours. Few indeed are saved, despite all the drugs and accoutrements of modern medicine.

Meningococcal meningitis

Meningococcal meningitis, at one time a dread and still a very unpleasant disease, when diagnosed early usually responds to treatment with penicillin.

Tuberculosis. Tuberculosis is one of the great scourges of mankind, and yet, paradoxically, most people infected with the germ do not suffer from the disease. Instead, the germ, *Mycobacterium tuberculosis*, becomes trapped in the tissues of the body, surrounded by defensive cells and finally sealed up in a hard, calcified nodule. This nodule, or calcified tubercle, can be seen on an X-ray film of the lungs as a tiny dense shadow at the edge of the lung field, and often one can see as well a hard shadow in one of the lymph nodes in the centre of the field. These two shadows represent the primary complex of tuberculosis and show that the tubercle bacillus on reaching the lung did travel a short distance through it before the defenses of the body clamped down on it and brought its excursion to an end. This is a common occurrence in childhood, and the child often suffers no obvious illness while it is going on but, as a result of this mild infection, becomes resistant to tuberculosis for the rest of his life. A skin test at any later time will show that he has been infected and is immune. The tubercle bacillus being locked up quickly in the tissues, the child is not usually infectious to others. In some cases, however, the tubercle bacillus is not caught in a primary complex but spreads rapidly in the lungs and out into the bloodstream and so reaches almost any organ of the body, especially the meninges that cover the brain, where it causes tuberculous meningitis. This rapid disease is called miliary tuberculosis because when viewed on an X-ray the many tubercles look like tiny millet seeds. It may result because the child inhales a very large dose of tubercle bacilli or because for some reason, of which malnutrition is one, the resistance of the child's body is low.

In the adult the disease takes a different form, whether due to reactivation of the primary infection or some new heavy infection is not clear. Instead of becoming locked up, the bacillus spreads slowly and widely in the lungs, and, instead of causing a hard, calcified nodule, forms large cheesy, or caseous, masses that break down the respiratory tissues and form cavities in the lung. The disease process eats its way into the bronchi, or air passages, and the tubercle bacillus can then be coughed or breathed out, making the patient infectious to other people. A blood vessel is sometimes eroded by the advancing disease, and then the patient, to his great alarm, coughs up bright red blood. This spreading type of disease is sometimes known as consumption, a name dropping out of use as the disease comes under control but one that vividly describes the destructive progress of the disease. Before curative drugs were available this process was usually, but not invariably, fatal. With rest, good food, and nursing care, patients built up resistance against the tubercle bacillus and eventually sealed it off, though with much scarring of the lungs. In those whose resistance was overcome, the lungs became a mass of caseous material, and the bacilli often spread to the kidneys, the meninges, and other organs before the patient died.

Spread of tuberculosis in adults

Most of the above relates to tuberculosis caused by the human strain of *Mycobacterium tuberculosis*. The bovine strain infects cattle and is excreted in milk. If the milk is

The bovine strain of *M. tuberculosis*

drunk raw, this bovine bacillus readily infects humans. The bovine bacillus may be caught in the tonsils and spread from there to the lymph nodes of the neck, where it causes caseation of the node tissue: the node swells and bulges under the skin of the neck, finally breaking down and bursting through the skin as a chronic discharging ulcer. From the gastrointestinal tract the bovine tubercle bacillus may spread into the bloodstream and reach any part of the body. It shows, however, a great preference for bones and joints, where it causes destruction of tissue leading to gross deformity. Tuberculosis of the spine, or Pott's disease, kept children in hospitals, strapped for years to spinal frames, the purpose of which was to prevent deformity while the body slowly overcame the infective process. Many cases of hunchback were caused by the bovine tubercle bacillus. Pasteurization of milk kills tubercle bacilli and, this, along with the raising of tuberculosis-free herds, has led in many countries to the disappearance of bovine tuberculosis in humans.

Tuberculosis is not, however, a conquered disease. In fact, the prevalence of tuberculosis has increased. The disease is more severe in malnourished persons but may afflict anyone irrespective of the state of nutrition, hygiene, or socioeconomic status. In many parts of the world, especially the less developed countries, it is still one of the major killing diseases. The BCG (bacille Calmette–Guérin) vaccine is an important weapon in areas of the world where this disease is particularly prevalent. As regards treatment of the disease, one of the great advances in 20th-century medicine has been the discovery of antituberculous drugs. Streptomycin was the first, followed by isonicotinic acid and para-aminosalicylic acid. One of the difficulties of treatment is that some tubercle bacilli become resistant to drugs, though there is less danger of this when two or three are given together. In spite of such combinations, some tubercle bacilli still become resistant to them, and then newer, but sometimes more toxic, drugs must be used. The drug treatment of tuberculosis has in the developed countries removed the need for sanatoriums in which patients were nursed and rested for years while the defensive properties of their bodies dealt with the disease. Drugs have cut down the length of treatment to months instead of years, and patients can usually be treated in their homes, after a short course of treatment in a hospital (see RESPIRATORY SYSTEM DISEASES).

Leprosy. Leprosy, or Hansen's disease, is one of the dread diseases, a dread that stretches back into antiquity; the leper has always been regarded as "unclean." Yet it is not a highly infectious disease; prolonged, intimate family contact is needed for its spread from one person to another. Most adults in leprosy areas appear to be immune, but children are very susceptible. The disease has almost disappeared from most temperate countries, but it is still a common disease in Asia, Africa, and Central and South America. At least 2,000,000 people are known to have the disease, and the actual number of infected persons may be as high as 15,000,000. In sheer numbers it presents a serious problem, not lessened by the fact that it is a disabling, deforming disease, slowly progressing throughout the life of the leper but not usually cutting short that life. The management of the leprosy problem involves social, vocational, medical, rehabilitative, orthopedic, and reconstructive surgical services on a large scale.

Location and numbers of leprosy cases

The disease is caused by the leprosy (Hansen's) bacillus, *Mycobacterium leprae*, and has two principal types: tuberculoid and lepromatous. How it gets into the body is not clearly known. The bacillus is discharged in enormous quantities from the nose of patients with one form of leprosy but also from broken-down skin sores; it may therefore be inhaled by contacts of the patient or be spread from skin to skin. The first reaction to its presence takes place in the deep layers of the skin, and the reaction may be one of two kinds. In one form there is a sharp reaction to its presence: body cells crowd into the area in an attempt to seal off the invader, and in these areas very few bacilli can be found. The intense cellular reaction involves all of the thickness of the skin and the tissues under it, the sweat glands, the hair follicles, and the nerve fibrils that end in the skin. This shows on the patient's skin as a firm, dry spot in which there is no sense of heat, cold, or touch. The cellular reaction continues to spread into the main trunk of the nerve, tending to strangle it so that impulses cannot get up or down. This causes loss of power in the muscles of the area, loss of sense of pain, and loss of circulation in the part affected. This is most commonly seen in the forearm or lower leg, and it leads to claw hand and gross deformity of the foot, but paralysis of muscles of the face, eye, and neck may also occur. Because the person cannot feel pain, minor injuries pass unnoticed, and large eroding ulcers can form, causing loss of fingers and toes; sometimes the condition of the limb may be so bad that amputation is the only remedy. This form of leprosy is known as tuberculoid leprosy because of the hard nodules, or tubercles, in the skin. It is ironical that it occurs in patients whose tissues resist the disease, for the intense cellular response is a reaction of resistance, successful insofar as it prevents local multiplication of the leprosy bacillus and spread through the body but unsuccessful in that it grips and destroys the vital tissues in the invaded areas.

Lepromatous leprosy

The second form of the disease is lepromatous, or cutaneous, leprosy. In this there is very little cellular response, and the bacillus can multiply freely. It can always be found in enormous numbers in the deep layers of the affected skin, and it spreads widely in the skin's lymphatic channels. It spreads up the nerves but does not grip them as in the tuberculoid form. It very often spreads to the skin of the face, where it causes thickening and corrugation of the skin and a typical leonine appearance. Soft nodules appear on the ears, nose, and cheeks and sometimes break down into discharging sores. The nose is often teeming with bacilli, and this sometimes leads to destruction of the septum of the nose and the palate.

The progress of leprosy is slow. It may be years before a child infected by a parent shows the first sign of the disease, often a vague, scarcely noticed spot on the skin. Years may pass before any change is noticed, and the child has often grown to an adult before he is recognized as a leper. Patients suffer occasionally from bouts of fever, but the course of the disease is mainly one of increasing disability and disfiguration. Lepers do not often die of their leprosy: they can live a normal span of years and, with proper medical and rehabilitative care, can live in some measure of comfort.

Drugs for leprosy

Drugs do help to arrest the disease and make the patient noninfectious, but none that acts quickly is yet available. Dapsone is one of the more effective, but in the early 1980s a worldwide increase in resistance to dapsone led health officials to predict renewed increase in occurrence of the disease.

One of the difficulties is that so far no one has been able to grow the leprosy bacillus in laboratory plates, and only since 1960 has it been possible to grow it in a laboratory animal. The footpad of a mouse can be infected, and the disease in the mouse resembles the disease in humans, so that the progress of the disease can be studied and the effect of new drugs tried first on the infected mouse.

Apart from the use of drugs, the management of the disease is a vast human problem. The leper must be helped in his disfigurement and his paralyses. The greatest problem is the prevention of infection. A baby born to a leprous mother has little chance of escape unless it is separated from her. A father is almost bound to infect some members of his family unless taken away from them. The fear of separation makes the family conceal the disease and so increases the danger of spread. The ideal must be not a colony for lepers only but, rather, village or other community groups in which whole families can live in good conditions and the leper can be given the treatment he needs and encouraged and enabled to work within his limitations.

Fungus diseases. Fungi are mainly saprophytes; that is, they live on dead and rotting animal and vegetable matter. They are found mostly in soil, on objects contaminated with it, on plants growing from it, or on animals living on it.

There are many airborne fungus diseases: actinomycosis, blastomycosis, aspergillosis, coccidioidomycosis, torulosis,

The important fungus diseases

and histoplasmosis are some of the more important. They have much in common. Most of them have at first been regarded as severe or fatal diseases because these were the only forms that doctors recognized, but many of them have later been shown to be common and mainly trivial infections.

Coccidioidomycosis and histoplasmosis are two rather similar diseases and may be taken as examples. Both can cause severe generalized and fatal infections, but in both a common manifestation is a mild form of pneumonia or pneumonitis. The patient has a chill and cough and is feverish, symptoms indistinguishable from those caused by many other acute respiratory infections. X-ray of the chest may show a localized shadow or a more diffuse mottling of the lungs, but again there is nothing diagnostic in these appearances. Sometimes the X-ray appearances are more like active tuberculosis, and, as the disease dies down, hard, calcified scars can be seen on the film, very much like old, healed tuberculosis. In a very few cases there are widespread areas of destruction in the lungs, and the fungi spread through the body to the liver, spleen, heart, and brain, often causing death. But, most commonly, infection with *Coccidioides immitis* or *Histoplasma capsulatum* causes no symptoms or discomfort at all, and a positive reaction to a skin test with the fungal extracts coccidioidin or histoplasmin is the only way of telling that the fungus has entered the body.

The fungus of both diseases is present in the soil but can be raised in dust into the air and so into the lungs. Coccidioidomycosis is commonest in dry spells, and dust storms have caused outbreaks of infection in humans. During World War II, when such outbreaks occurred among airmen, planting grass in the airfields and oiling dusty roads kept the fungus on the ground and stopped the spread of the disease. *Histoplasma capsulatum* likes moist, shady conditions and is found in woods, caves, cellars, silos, and old chicken houses. The latter seem especially important, for chickens are often infected and pass enormous numbers of the parasites in their droppings, and the use of chicken manure in gardens may sometimes lead to histoplasmosis in gardeners. Dogs, rats, mice, bats, pigeons, skunks, and probably many other animals become infected and may help to spread the disease. But the essential cause is inhalation of the fungi, and humans can breathe the fungus only when it is wafted into the air.

The diseases can be identified by means of skin tests and examination of sputum; sometimes it may be necessary to puncture the bone marrow or take a specimen from a lymph node and look for the fungi there. The fungi are resistant to most antibiotics, but the antibiotic amphotericin is effective; it is a highly toxic substance and is used only in persons with the life-threatening forms of the disease. Most persons with mild attacks recover without special treatment and often without even knowing that they have been infected.

Other infections. *Q fever*. Q fever can be contracted either by inhaling the microorganism *Coxiella burnetii* in fine dust or by drinking it in milk. The source is always some animal, and the disease was first identified in 1937 among abattoir workers in Australia. Its spread to humans must depend on some elusive modulation of the environment, for often when the organisms abound in the atmosphere, they do not spread to humans, whereas at other times when they appear no more abundant, everyone within reach comes down with Q fever.

Symptoms and course of Q fever

The symptoms of the disease are those of a generalized infection: fever, chills, sweating, tiredness, malaise, pain behind the eyes, and often severe headache. There are often no respiratory symptoms, apart from slight cough, and yet an X-ray film usually shows obvious signs of pneumonia or other inflammatory changes. The acute illness lasts about 10 days, but the affected person may feel weak and tired for several weeks longer. Complications are unusual, but very rarely the organisms spread through the blood to the valves inside the heart and cause a very severe and sometimes fatal form of endocarditis (inflammation of the heart lining).

Coxiellae can be grown from blood, sputum, urine, and cerebrospinal fluid, but it is another odd feature of Q fever that, whereas infection of humans is such a chancy, unpredictable affair in everyday surroundings, the handling of the organisms in the laboratory is a dangerous occupation. Most laboratory workers find it safer to examine blood for antibodies only and make no attempt to grow the coxiellae; a rise in blood level of antibodies during the illness is a sufficient aid to diagnosis.

Coxiellae are sensitive to the tetracycline group of antibiotics, and these are effective in treatment. Prevention is difficult: first, because the factors that cause infection in humans are not exactly known, and second, because the infection, though very common in farm animals, does not greatly affect their commercial productivity.

Psittacosis. Psittacosis is similar to Q fever in the symptoms it causes, but indications of chest abnormalities are more obvious, and the person affected often has a troublesome cough. As in Q fever, an X-ray film often shows more extensive signs of lung damage than the symptoms suggest. The illness may be over in a week or 10 days, but sometimes it drags on for weeks or months. In a few cases the central nervous system is attacked, and the patient may be disoriented or stuporose. The disease is seldom fatal, but in a few patients the disease process spreads throughout the lungs, and the patient dies from respiratory insufficiency.

The disease can be diagnosed in the laboratory by growing the germs, bedsoniae, in mice or on hen eggs, but, like coxiellae, they are dangerous to handle, and antibody tests are sufficient for diagnosis. The illness responds to treatment with the tetracycline antibiotics, but severely ill patients require skilled nursing care and oxygen therapy. Prevention depends on (1) informing bird handlers of the danger of psittacosis and (2) the raising of pet birds in hygienic commercial breeding houses where they can be tested for the absence of diseases before sale. With poultry the problem is more difficult, for antibiotic treatment does not clear the birds of infection, and it is difficult to protect workers who handle the carcasses and organs of birds.

GASTROINTESTINAL TRACT

Bacterial diseases. *Typhoid and paratyphoid*. The typhoid bacillus, *Salmonella typhi*, is excreted by a typhoid carrier, and, if it finds its way into food or water, it infects whomever eats or drinks it. There are no animal hosts in the story of typhoid; infection can spread only from one person to another.

Course of untreated typhoid

Typhoid is a generalized, and not merely an intestinal, infection. *Salmonella typhi* after being swallowed enters the bloodstream and reaches almost any organ of the body. In so doing it causes all of the symptoms of a bloodstream infection, or septicemia. The illness begins with headache and generalized discomfort (malaise), the temperature creeps upward day by day, and, by the end of a week, the patient must go to bed. At this stage rose spots may appear on the skin of the chest and abdomen, and the spleen becomes large enough for the physician to feel, signs that the typhoid bacillus has travelled around the body and entered the cells of the skin and the spleen. The bacilli may next attack the wall of the bowel from the bloodstream, producing ulcers at the lower end of the small intestine; one of these may later eat its way through the wall of the bowel—and cause peritonitis—or a blood vessel in the base of the ulcer may burst and cause serious bleeding into the intestinal canal. The illness drags on for several weeks, and the patient lapses into a stuporose state. Slowly, after two or three weeks, the fever leaves, the mind begins to clear, and strength begins to return to the wasted body, but a month or two may pass before the patient feels well again. The patient recovers from the disease but not always from the infection, for *Salmonella typhi* may have settled down inside the cells of an internal organ, usually the gallbladder, and, though it will never trouble the patient again, it will be excreted by way of the bile duct and feces for years and possibly for life, serving as a source of infection to others.

Such was the story of typhoid before the antibiotic chloramphenicol was discovered. Many patients died from the disease, and those who recovered had a long and exhausting illness. Chloramphenicol given by mouth cuts the illness short within a week, one of the most dramatic successes of the antibiotic era. Another drug, trimethoprim sulfamethoxazole, also provides effective treatment. Chloramphenicol, for all of its success in the acute stage of the disease, is useless against carriers. Sometimes a carrier cannot be cured except by removal of the gallbladder.

Salmonella paratyphi, the paratyphoid organism, can cause an illness similar to typhoid, though usually milder. Often, however, the symptoms are those of a short attack of gastroenteritis (inflammation of the stomach and intestine) with much diarrhea but with no symptoms of septicemia. The bacilli can be grown easily from blood, feces, and urine, and antibodies can be detected in the blood serum in both diseases. If a person has been inoculated with typhoid-paratyphoid vaccine (TAB), he may have antibodies in his blood because of this, but, if the person is suffering from typhoid or paratyphoid, the level of antibody will rise during the illness and help the physician to reach a diagnosis. TAB vaccine gives some, but not complete, protection against typhoid and paratyphoid. It does not protect against a massive dose of the disease organisms, such as a person might swallow if he ate food on which the bacilli had had time to multiply.

Bacillary dysentery. The germs of bacillary dysentery are shigellae, of which the commonest are *Shigella shigae*, *Shigella flexneri*, and *Shigella sonnei*. Shigellae have only one host, humans, so that infection passes only from one person to another, and it takes the fecal-oral route. With *Shigella sonnei*, hand-to-hand contact is enough to convey infection from the feces of one person to the mouth of another, but the other two shigellae are usually conveyed in water or food.

The infection is mainly an intestinal one. The shigellae attack the wall of the bowel, causing an inflammatory reaction or even ulceration. The main symptom is diarrhea, and blood is often passed in the stool. The loss of fluid can be so severe that the fluid and salt balance of the body is deranged, and dehydration and gross biochemical upset follow, leading to collapse and prostration in those severely stricken. At the other extreme, the symptoms may be mild or even trivial, as is usual with *Shigella sonnei* dysentery.

Identification of the disease is not difficult; shigellae are present in vast numbers in the feces and grow easily in the laboratory. In patients severely ill, fluid and salt lost in the feces must be replaced quickly by intravenous infusion. Antibiotic therapy generally is provided orally. The sensitivity of shigellae to antibiotics varies from one location to another. Trimethoprim sulfamethoxazole generally is an effective form of antibiotic therapy. Ampicillin treatment may be effective, but up to 30 percent of shigellae in some areas will not respond to treatment with this antibiotic. Treatment with antibiotics shortens the course of disease only slightly but helps to speed the disappearance of organisms from the stools, thereby preventing spread of the disease to others.

Distinction between typhoid and salmonellosis

Salmonellosis and food poisoning. Salmonellosis is human infection with salmonellas other than the typhoid-paratyphoid group. The distinction is useful, for these other salmonellas—and there are about 1,200 different types—usually cause an abrupt diarrheal disease, and not a general systemic disease such as typhoid. The course and method of spread of salmonellas to humans have already been described. Many of the salmonellas are promiscuous as regards hosts, and this complicates the story of their spread to humans. Moreover, not being highly adapted to one host, they must multiply before they can infect, and this means that they must usually get into food and multiply there. In other words, salmonellosis is one form, perhaps the most common form, of what is usually called food poisoning.

A few salmonellas tend to invade the bloodstream and be carried through the body. *Salmonella choleraesuis* is one that does so; very often it causes no diarrhea on entering the body but later causes a septicemic type of illness, and, later still, it may settle down and produce abscesses inside the bones of the limbs or spine. *Salmonella typhimurium*, probably the commonest of all of human salmonellas, also sometimes invades the bloodstream but usually after or during a diarrheal illness, and so may such common salmonellas as *Salmonella enteritidis*, *Salmonella dublin*, and many others.

Almost any microorganism, if it multiplies enough in food, can cause food poisoning, but there are two, besides salmonellas, that cause trouble again and again: staphylococci and *Clostridium welchii*. Staphylococci have already been mentioned as causes of lung and skin infection; some members of the family, given warmth and moisture, produce an enterotoxin (intestinal poison) that causes food poisoning. *Clostridium welchii* also produces a food-poisoning toxin; it is an inhabitant of the bowel of humans and other animals and is a common contaminant of the environment. The property of both these toxins that makes them especially dangerous is that, once formed in food, they are not destroyed by heat, even by boiling. Staphylococci die with such treatment, but their toxin is unchanged.

The symptoms of food poisoning are diarrhea, vomiting, and abdominal pain. The symptoms vary according to the cause. Staphylococcal toxin is a gastric irritant, and, soon after the food is swallowed, the person begins to vomit. This gets rid of much of the toxin, so that little passes into the gut, and diarrhea and abdominal pain are not prominent symptoms in staphylococcal food poisoning. Poisoning by *Clostridium welchii* is caused partly by the preformed toxin, but this seems not to cause symptoms unless there are clostridia multiplying in the intestinal tract as well. The onset is therefore more delayed than in staphylococcal food poisoning, eight to 12 hours compared with two to six. Abdominal pain is characteristic, and there is always diarrhea but rarely vomiting. Symptoms of salmonella infection usually are caused by growth of the germs in the intestinal tract. The onset may be delayed for 12 to 24 hours, and the main symptom is diarrhea. Thus there is a quick onset and vomiting in staphylococcal food poisoning, a slower onset, pain, and diarrhea in clostridial food poisoning, and a longer interval and diarrhea only in salmonella food poisoning. These characteristics are not absolute, but the clinical picture may give a hint of the bacteriological cause.

Treatment and prevention of food poisoning

Food poisoning is an unpleasant and sometimes alarming illness. When severe, it may cause temporary collapse, and, in persons already debilitated by some other illness, it may even cause death. Usually it is inconvenient rather than dangerous. A severe outbreak may lead to dehydration in some persons, and fluid lost in vomit or by diarrhea may have to be replaced by intravenous infusion of the appropriate fluid and salts. Most persons recover rapidly and without such treatment. Antibiotics are not effective.

The prevention of food poisoning lies in good food hygiene and good animal husbandry. Food poisoning cannot always be traced to its exact source, but somewhere along the line of production and distribution there is usually some error or fault that could have been avoided.

Botulism. In 1793 in Wildbad, Germany, 13 people shared one sausage; all became ill and six died. The Latin word for sausage is *botulus*, and the word botulism was first used to describe the illness in these German patients. The sausage was doubtless of the smoked, uncooked variety; there would be very little oxygen inside the sausage skin; and it was probably kept some time before being eaten—all conditions that favour the growth of *Clostridium botulinum*. This is a spore-bearing microorganism present in the soil, which grows only in conditions of low oxygen tension, such as may be found in canned, smoked, or cured food, but not at all in fresh food. When multiplying, it produces a desperately powerful toxin; a mere taste of food containing botulinum toxin is enough to cause death. The toxin is, however, easily destroyed by heat; two minutes at 70° C (158° F) destroys it. The multiplying bacilli are also heat-labile; 10 minutes at 80° C (176° F) kills them. The spores are highly heat-resistant and withstand boiling for hours. To kill them, moist heat at 120° C (248° F) is required. This temperature can be achieved with certainty only in commercial canning plants.

In home canning this safe temperature may be reached if a pressure cooker is used, but merely boiling the cans is not a reliable method.

When *Clostridium botulinum* toxin is swallowed in food, it does not irritate the gastrointestinal tract but is rapidly absorbed and carried in the bloodstream to nerve endings in muscles. Normally, in response to a nerve impulse, the chemical acetylcholine is produced at these sites and causes the muscle to contract. *Clostridium botulinum* toxin attacks the last fine nerve fibrils and stops the impulse from passing along them. No acetylcholine is released and the muscle cannot contract. It is paralyzed. The first sign of the diseases in many is paralysis of the muscles of the eyelid, a sign that may appear within hours of eating the food. Next the paralysis affects the muscles of speech. Swallowing becomes difficult, and finally the breathing muscles stop. The person remains conscious through most of the illness, until suffocation from loss of breathing clouds the brain. Death may occur within a day of onset; persons less severely poisoned may linger for a week. Few who reach the stage of severe paralysis survive. Others who may have taken less of the toxic food develop only the milder forms of paralysis. Mortality in outbreaks varies from 2 to almost 100 percent; in every outbreak some patients die, and in the worst there are no survivors.

Treatment is difficult. *Clostridium botulinum* antitoxin is given in large doses intravenously, but it is doubtful, when the toxin has reached the nerve fibrils, if antitoxin can do anything to dislodge it. A chemical, guanidine hydrochloride, counteracts the action of *Clostridium botulinum* toxin on nerve endings and has been used successfully in treatment, but it is itself a toxic substance to be given only with great care. Paralyzed muscle can recover if the patient can be kept alive, and perhaps the best hope of survival in otherwise desperate cases lies in tube feeding, tracheostomy (making an opening in the windpipe), and artificial ventilation. *Clostridium botulinum* is an inhabitant of the soil, not a parasite of humans. It attacks humans only when they disturb its natural environment.

Brucellosis. Brucellosis, also called undulant, Malta, and Mediterranean fever, is caused by infection with *Brucella melitensis*, *Brucella abortus*, *Brucella suis*, or *Brucella canis*. Of these organisms *B. melitensis* is an infection of sheep and goats; *B. abortus*, of cows; *B. suis*, of pigs; and *B. canis*, of dogs.

In the animals the infection may often not be apparent, for brucellae and the animals that they infect have become fairly well adapted to one another. A drop in milk production or a general lack of condition may be the only signs in the animal, but abortion is also common in cows infected with *Brucella abortus*. The infection is therefore of considerable economic importance, although it causes no dramatic loss of stock, as does, for example, anthrax. Humans, on the other hand, are not a natural host for brucellae, and, when infected, they often react sharply. Acute brucellosis is an illness characterized by sudden chills and rigours, by swinging fevers and drenching sweats, by pains all over the body, and by great weakness and fatigue. This illness lasts for about a fortnight, and the disease may then be over, but the symptoms often return in waves of fever, and these waves are the reasons for the name undulant fever. There are recurring bouts of illness for six months or a year, but then, in most persons, the infection dies out. In a few it persists, often for years. Chronic brucellosis, though not the most common sequel of infection with brucellae, is perhaps the most difficult to deal with, for the patient's symptoms are vague and tiresome and may easily be dismissed as psychological rather than infective in origin.

Course of brucellosis

The infection may cause complications in many parts of the body, in the joints and spine especially, but also in the heart, the eyes, the kidneys, and the lungs. Brucellosis is treated with antibiotics, particularly tetracyclines and streptomycin. Results in the acute form are fairly satisfactory. The chronic form is much more difficult. The solution of the brucellosis problem lies in eradication of the disease in animals.

Viral diseases. *Poliomyelitis.* Poliomyelitis is a disease that causes inflammation and destruction of the anterior horn cells (motor cells) of the spinal cord. But the virus enters by the mouth and multiplies in the throat and the intestinal tract. It is, in the main, a harmless parasite of humans, for in only one in 100, or perhaps in one in 1,000, cases does the virus reach the central nervous system. When it does, it attacks nerve cells and prevents them from sending out impulses to muscles. The result is paralysis of muscles: the extent of the paralysis depends on where the virus strikes and the number of cells that it destroys.

In some persons the virus invades the bloodstream and gets no further. These people often have a vague flu-like illness called, when recognized, the minor illness of poliomyelitis. When the virus enters the central nervous system, patients get signs and symptoms of meningitis, the major illness. They have headache, stiff neck, and vomiting. Many recover at this stage, but an unfortunate few develop paralysis. The impulses that constantly move down the motor nerve from the spinal cord to muscles are cut off in poliomyelitis when the nerve cells are destroyed. As a result the muscles go limp and cannot contract. This is known as flaccid paralysis and is the type found in poliomyelitis. Most commonly, some of the limb muscles are paralyzed. The abdominal muscles or the muscles of the back may be paralyzed, and this paralysis may affect posture. The neck muscles may go, so that the patient cannot raise his head. Paralysis of the face muscles may cause twisting of the mouth or drooping of the eyelids. Paralysis of the throat or of the muscles of breathing can threaten life.

Forms of poliomyelitis

Nerve cells are not always completely destroyed by poliovirus. They can recover with time. By the end of a month power often returns to apparently paralyzed muscle, and by the end of six months recovery can be complete. If the nerve cells are completely destroyed, however, paralysis is permanent.

The virus of poliomyelitis depends for its survival on a parasitic environment in the human intestinal canal. Polio vaccine can make the intestinal canal resistant to the entry of wild poliovirus, so that poliomyelitis is theoretically eradicable.

Hepatitis. Jaundice is the main sympton of hepatitis, or inflammation of the hepar, or liver. Serum hepatitis has been shown to be caused by a virus, called hepatitis B virus. Infectious hepatitis is probably also caused by a virus, called hepatitis A virus. Another common cause of hepatitis has not been isolated and, for lack of a better name, is called non-A, non-B hepatitis.

Infectious hepatitis spreads easily from person to person by the fecal–oral route. It is a disease of close personal contact but can also spread in food and water. Serum hepatitis is more commonly injected into the body, straight into the bloodstream via a vein or, less directly, via the subcutaneous tissues. The virus floats in the blood serum of an infected person and can get out on the point of a syringe needle or other instrument. If the syringe is then used unsterilized on another person, enough virus is injected to infect that person. Blood given in transfusions, for example, may be contaminated with the virus, and serum hepatitis is a hazard of all of the manipulations in which the blood of one person passes into the body of another.

The two diseases are similar. Infectious hepatitis, which is more often mild, frequently attacks children, in whom the inflammation of the liver may be so mild that jaundice is absent. Older people suffer more severely. Serum hepatitis is more commonly a fairly serious illness. In both diseases, the affected person suffers from weakness and sluggishness, with loss of appetite, headache, some fever, and some generalized aches and pains. Jaundice, the main feature, may range from a tinge of yellow in the conjunctivas to a deep orange dyeing of the whole skin. Itchiness of the skin is troublesome when jaundice is severe. After a week or two, recovery begins, although it may be several weeks before the patient is back to normal. Of persons jaundiced with infectious hepatitis, probably not more than one or two per 1,000 die, but, in elderly persons with serum hepatitis, mortality may rise to 20 percent.

Comparison of serum and infectious hepatitis

It is not always easy to decide whether a person has infectious hepatitis or hepatitis B. A history of contact with another patient or of an injection or transfusion may help to decide. A blood test is of some value, for patients with serum hepatitis often have a substance in their blood called Australia, or hepatitis B, antigen, whereas patients with infectious hepatitis do not.

Infectious hepatitis can be controlled by strict personal hygiene and by the provision of safe food and water supplies. The incidence of serum hepatitis can be lessened by scrupulous attention to aseptic technique and by screening of blood donors for hepatitis B antigen.

Diseases caused by helminths. *Trichinosis.* The worm that causes trichinosis, *Trichinella spiralis*, is tiny, not more than four millimetres (0.16 inch) long when fully adult. It infects an enormous number of hosts, from mice and rats to polar bears. In one stage of its existence it settles down as a larva in the muscle of the host animal. There it becomes surrounded by tough fibrous tissues that form a cyst around it, and it may live inside this cyst for months or years. Unless the muscle of the host animal is eaten by another animal, the trichinella dies in the cyst, and the cyst calcifies. If the host animal is eaten, the hard coat of the cyst is dissolved in the stomach, and the larva pierces and settles down in the wall of the intestine of its new host. It grows quickly and mates, and the female then produces eggs from which minute larvae emerge. These pass into the lymph channels of the intestine; from there they enter the main lymph duct of the body, the thoracic duct; this empties into one of the large veins, and the tiny larvae then reach the heart, pass through the lungs, pass into the heart again, and go into general circulation whence they may reach any part of the body. In muscle they encyst, and the cycle begins again.

Development of trichina worm in host animal

Human beings most commonly become infected by eating undercooked pork. A few days after exposure the infected person becomes feverish and has vague abdominal symptoms. These are followed, a few days later, by pains in the joints, headache, and swelling of the face, a characteristic symptom. Great pain develops in the muscles of the limbs, in the chest, and in the eyeballs, and often breathing is painful, for the diaphragm is usually heavily infected. The illness continues for a week or two before it gradually subsides, but in some patients the condition worsens. The outlook depends on the intensity of the infection. In some epidemics, mortality may be as high as 10 to 16 percent in known cases, but many people have attacks so mild that they are not recognized.

Examination of the blood is an aid to diagnosis. Pieces of muscle may be taken for microscopic examination, and cysts may then be seen in the muscle fibres. There is no known specific treatment.

Fascioliasis. *Fasciola hepatica*, the liver fluke, is a leaf-shaped worm about four centimetres (1.6 inch) long that grows in the liver of various animals, especially cattle and sheep. The eggs pass down the bile duct and are excreted in the feces. If the eggs get into pools of water, they hatch after a few weeks, and the larvae, at this stage called miracidia, must find their way into a small water snail, *Lymnaea truncatula*. There, in the course of about two months, they multiply asexually and emerge as free-swimming larvae with tails. These finally attach themselves as cysts to grasses or leaves of plants growing in the water. The cysts resist drying when the waters recede, and, if they are later swallowed on the grass or plants, they hatch out in the host's intestine, migrate across the abdominal cavity, pierce the liver, and settle down in the bile ducts, where they cause obstruction to the flow of bile and inflammation in surrounding liver tissue.

Development of liver fluke

Fascioliasis is a serious economic disease of cattle and sheep. Humans can be infected by eating wild watercress. The cysts hatch in the person's intestine and make mostly for the liver, but some go astray. These migrating larvae may cause unexpected complications; they have been found, for example, in the tissues of the larynx. The symptoms of fascioliasis in humans are fever, sweats, loss of weight, abdominal pain, and anemia, and sometimes a fleeting nettle rash; in the blood there is an increase in white blood cells of the type called eosinophils, a common finding in worm infections. The best way of preventing fascioliasis in humans would be to forbid the sale of watercress, unless it is grown in commercial watercress beds that are protected from pollution by animal feces.

Trichinosis and fascioliasis are but two of many helminth, or worm, infections in which the life cycle of the parasite depends on a chain of environmental circumstances. Break one of the links and the cycle ends.

SKIN AND MUCOUS MEMBRANES

Bacterial diseases. *Anthrax.* Anthrax, named from the Greek word for coal, is so called because a sore with a coal-black centre develops on the skin of the infected person. The disease organism, *Bacillus anthracis*, may escape from the sore and spread up a lymph channel to the nearest lymph node, where it is usually halted. Only seldom does it invade the bloodstream; when it does, it can cause rapidly fatal septicemia, with internal bleeding and sometimes anthrax meningitis. In more than 90 percent of patients the bacilli stay in the skin sore. There is always much swelling around it, and there are bouts of shivering and chilliness, but otherwise there is little general upset.

This is true only of cutaneous (skin) anthrax, which comes from infected animal products, usually hides, wool, and hair or bones. When the anthrax bacillus is breathed in and attacks the lungs, a suffocating bronchitis results from which few survive. This illness is sometimes called woolsorters' disease. Intestinal anthrax, a very rare and often fatal form of the disease that comes from eating the flesh of animals dead of anthrax, inflames the stomach and intestines with ulcers much like the sores on the skin.

Bacillus anthracis is a spore-bearing germ capable of remaining alive for years in pastures. In damp, warm pastures the bacilli multiply rapidly, but when the pastures dry out in the heat of the year the bacilli form spores. As the grasses die down on the parched land, the animals must graze closer to the soil, and then they readily become infected. The disease is often fatal to cattle, sheep, goats, and other herbivores, and they sometimes die in thousands. Their hides, wool, and bones are shipped heavily contaminated with *Bacillus anthracis*. The bacillus is fortunately not highly infectious for humans, but it does not depend on multiplication in humans for its survival.

Skin anthrax usually responds quickly to penicillin. The outlook is nearly always good, provided the patients are treated early. Anthrax in humans can be prevented by vaccination of exposed workers and by sterilization of all of the contaminated materials.

Treatment and prevention of anthrax

Tetanus. Tetanus is like anthrax in many ways. The disease organism, *Clostridium tetani*, is a sporing germ that can live for years in soil and has no need to attack humans in order to survive. Indeed, it gains nothing from such attack, being locked up forever in the tissues of the infected human host. It can be found almost anywhere, in soil, dust, or on window ledges, but, unless it is given very favourable conditions, it is not highly infectious for humans or, indeed, for any animal. It is a self-sufficient microorganism, well able to maintain its place in nature without disturbing other living things that share its environment.

Clostridium tetani multiplies freely only in areas of low oxygen concentration. A deep, dirty wound in the body offers it such conditions. As the germs multiply, they produce their toxin, and this rapidly spreads by way of the bloodstream or directly up a nerve to the central nervous system, where it attacks motor nerve cells and excites them to overactivity. Excessive impulses rush down the nerves, and the muscles at the far end are thrown into convulsive spasm. The convulsions, when severe, can be the most dread and horrible of all afflictions. The commonest spasms occur in the muscle of the jaw, and the first sign of illness is often stiffness of the jaws, or trismus. (Lockjaw is the vivid popular name for the disease.) The muscles of the mouth are often affected, pulling the lips out and up over the teeth into a grimace, the mixture of smile and snarl that heralds the onset of the generalized convulsive stage in the brutal clinical picture of tetanus.

Any muscles can be attacked. Spasm of the muscles of the throat can make swallowing impossible, whereas the muscles of the larynx or of the chest wall can be thrown into such violent spasm that breathing is impossible and the sufferer's life is threatened. This is a common cause of death if untreated, but there are other toxic effects on the heart, blood pressure, and vital cerebral centres that may kill the patient later in the disease.

Prevention of tetanus

Tetanus is a preventable disease. Tetanus vaccine is one of the most successful, least toxic, and most enduring of available vaccines. It should be given to every child and repeated at long intervals throughout life, especially after wounds have been received. Tetanus antitoxin (ATS) is a different product altogether. It contains antibodies against tetanus, and these can be injected as ATS into the body of a wounded person. This gives some protection immediately and can be useful if the individual has not been appropriately immunized. Antitoxin is derived from the blood of humans immunized against tetanus.

Treatment of the disease consists in keeping the patient alive until the disease burns itself out. Tetanus antitoxin is usually given in the hope that it will neutralize toxin in the bloodstream; once the toxin is in the nerve cells, it is beyond the reach of antitoxin. Penicillin is also given in the hope that it will destroy any tetanus bacilli in the wound. Sedatives used in high doses control milder spasms, and, if severe spasms seem imminent, curare is administered. This drug paralyzes all of the external muscles of the body so that they cannot go into spasm. The muscles used in breathing are paralyzed, too, so that respiration must be maintained by artificial means. About three weeks of this treatment must be continued before the spasms tend to disappear. Even the most severely ill patients can be saved when this treatment is skillfully and persistently carried out.

Tularemia. Tularemia, named from Tulare County, California, where the germ *Francisella tularensis* was first isolated in ground squirrels, has been found in a large variety of animals.

In animals, *Francisella tularensis* usually causes an illness characterized by a caseous, or cheesy, degeneration of various glands and the spleen, liver, and lungs. The disease can be spread to humans by the bite of an infected animal, by contact with blood or fine dust from the animal's body during skinning and similar operations, or by the bite of a tick, mosquito, or deer fly. The disease also is acquired by the ingestion of animal products that have been infected by *Francisella tularensis* and have not been cooked appropriately. The disease takes several forms in humans. The commonest is the ulceroglandular type, in which there is a painful sore at the site of the wound and a swelling of the lymph node that drains the area; the sore is often on the finger and the swelling, or bubo, in the armpit. The bubo often breaks down and discharges pus, but sometimes it remains hard and tender for weeks. Along with these local signs the infected person has a sharp, feverish reaction that may last two or three weeks, with headache, vomiting, body pains, and general weakness.

Types of tularemia in humans

Other forms of tularemia include the typhoidal, marked by an exhausting or feverish illness, and the pneumonic, caused by breathing in dust.

Treatment with an antibiotic—streptomycin, tetracycline, or chloramphenicol—is usually successful, but penicillin is of no value. Mortality is sometimes as high as 5 to 7 percent in the typhoidal or pneumonic forms, but in other types the outlook is good.

Viral diseases. *Rabies.* "Rabies" means "madness," especially madness in the rabid dog, and humans have always associated rabies with dogs. The dog is still regarded as the main source of rabies, and, as far as rabies in humans goes, this is true; but rabies virus depends for its survival in nature on the constant and widespread infection of smaller animals, and the disease in foxes, jackals, wolves, and dogs is a mere occasional overspill from this deeper pool of infection in mongooses, polecats, and related animals and among martens, ferrets, skunks, weasels, and bats.

Rabies virus has an odd association with bats, especially vampire bats. These latter feed on the blood of cattle in the wide plains of South America, and the death of cattle from paralytic rabies is a serious economic problem in those areas. The bats themselves become rabid and bite other bats, but the spread of rabies among bats probably takes place mainly through the air in the caves where they roost in millions. In the South American plains bats do not attack humans, probably because there are vast numbers of cattle but very few people. But when bats flew across the Gulf of Paria to Trinidad and settled on the island, they found humans living and sleeping alongside their beasts, so naturally they bit people too and gave them rabies. Bats are gregarious animals; vampire, insect-eating, and fruit-eating bats flock together in caves, and rabies has spread to these other bats, which, driven rabid by the virus, may change their feeding habits; there have been a few cases of rabies in humans due to a bite from a normally insect-eating or fruit-eating bat.

Rabies virus travels quickly in a bitten animal from the bite to the central nervous system. It multiplies in the nerve cells and after a time spreads down some nerves and reaches the salivary glands. When a dog gets rabies, its temper changes quickly. It is often more affectionate for a day or two and given to licking its human contacts, a dangerous practice, for the virus is already in its saliva. Soon it grows restless and wanders off, ready to bite anyone that gets in its way. After a few days it returns home, unable to bite any more because the muscles of its throat are paralyzed; it seeks only a quiet place to hide and dies there from rapid spread of paralysis. Any human being that it has bitten during its short illness will get rabies, unless given energetic preventive treatment.

Rabies symptoms in humans

In humans the illness begins with vague symptoms of malaise, headache, and fever, but in a day or two the stage of excitement comes on. The person becomes anxious, sleepless, and fearful. The muscles of the throat become paralyzed so that he cannot swallow or drink, and this leads to a dread of water, or hydrophobia. The mental state varies from maniacal excitement to dull apathy, but soon the person falls into coma and is usually dead in less than a week.

Once the earliest symptoms have appeared there is probably no cure for the disease, although possible use of curare and artificial ventilation as described for tetanus may be able to save some persons.

The incubation period, or time that elapses between the bite and the first symptom, is usually between one and three months. This gives a chance to interrupt the otherwise inevitable process of infection. The bite should at once be washed, and the bitten patient should as soon as possible be given a dose of antirabies serum. This is usually derived from the blood of an immunized horse (equine antirabies serum), but, if it can be obtained, human antirabies serum is better. The serum provides the patient's body with antibodies, albeit not produced in his own body. Rabies vaccine must also be given. Human diploid-cell rabies vaccine (HDCV) is given immediately and three, seven, 14, and 28 days later. This vaccine is more effective than previous vaccines. The dangerous side effects seen in association with the older rabies vaccines have not been a problem with the use of HDCV.

Herpesvirus. The herpesvirus group comprises DNA viruses that cause several diseases. Those causing infections in humans are varicella zoster (the virus that causes chicken pox and shingles), Epstein-Barr virus (infectious mononucleosis), cytomegalovirus (most often associated with infections of the newborn infant and of persons whose immunological mechanisms have been compromised or impaired), and herpes simplex (cold sores and herpetic venereal diseases). The herpes simplex virus (HSV) has assumed increasing importance because of its ability to cause venereal disease.

There are two serotypes of herpes simplex: HSV-1 and HSV-2. A primary (first-time) infection may be an isolated event. It may be symptomatic (ulcerative lesions with or without systemic illness) or asymptomatic (no obvious illness or lesions).

HSV-1 is the common cause of cold sores. The primary infection usually occurs in childhood and is asymptomatic in 50 to 80 percent of the cases. Ten to 20 percent of the persons affected have recurrences precipitated by emotion or by other illnesses. HSV-1 also can cause infections of the eye, central nervous system, and skin. Serious infection may lead to death in a person whose immunological system has been compromised.

HSV-2 is associated most often with herpetic lesions of the genital area (venereal disease); HSV-1, however, can be recovered from 15 percent of genital lesions. The frequency of asymptomatic venereal infection is not known. Recurrences are the rule, especially with HSV-2.

The lesions are small, red, painful spots that become fluid-filled vesicles, which then rupture, leaving eroded areas that eventually become scabbed. These primary lesions occur two to eight days after exposure and may be present for up to three weeks. Viral shedding and pain usually end in two weeks. When infections recur the duration of the pain, lesions, and viral shedding is approximately 10 days. The involved area includes the vagina, cervix, and occasionally the urethra in the female and the head of the penis in the male. The disease usually is transmitted from one person to another by sexual contact.

Diagnosis is important because infants born through the birth canal, rather than by caesarean section, to mothers with active HSV-2 are at increased risk for generalized infection, including infection of the central nervous system. It can cause death in 60 percent of infants and severe mental retardation in 20 percent of the surviving infants.

Diagnosis is made by finding typical, painful lesions. Examination of the fluid from the vesicles shows viral particles within the nucleus of tissue cells and the presence of multinucleated giant cells. These cells can be seen on a routine Pap smear or with other special staining techniques applied to fluid removed from the vesicle. Diagnosis also can be made by examination of the blood for a change in the serum antibody titers as evidence of active infection. The elevation of antibody titers is not as striking in recurrent infections as it is in the primary infection.

There is no cure once infection has been established, and therapy is directed at relieving symptoms. There is, however, evidence that an antiviral agent, acyclovir, may be effective in diminishing the duration of the symptoms and the period of time during which virus may be recovered from the lesions in patients with primary herpetic infection. Acyclovir interferes with the replication of the virus, but it is effective only before the latency stage is established. (Latency is the ability of the virus to live in tissues, usually nerve tissue, following the primary infection without causing symptoms and with protection against destruction.) Subsequent reactivation of the virus can occur in response to a multitude of stimuli. Therefore, early detection, as well as protected intercourse to prevent spread during viral shedding, are imperative.

Diseases caused by protozoa. *Malaria.* Malaria (from Italian, "bad air") is one of the most serious environmental diseases. Although it has nothing to do with bad air, it does rise from still bodies of water and spread across the surface of the land. Heat and cold and the moisture of the air affect its movement, and even twilight, darkness, and dawn mark the rise and fall of this infection. But the cause of the disease is a unicellular parasite called plasmodium, and it is conveyed to humans by the *Anopheles* mosquito.

The mosquito begins its life as an egg deposited on water. The larva hatches out in two or three days and spends the next few weeks near the surface of the water. It feeds on microorganisms in the water and breathes in oxygen from the atmosphere through a spiracle, or breathing orifice, at one end of its body. After molting four times it changes into a pupa, and from the pupa emerges after a few days the adult mosquito. The young mosquito floats for an hour or so on the pupa case until its wings dry and harden, and then it flies into the air, where the adult female is soon mated by a male. The pairs then separate, the male to seek plant juices as its food, the female to feed on human blood. She is armed with mouthparts specially adapted for cutting into human skin, which she pierces in her search for a blood vessel; at the same time, she squirts some saliva into the wound. When she has had her fill of blood, she flies off to rest, but, if plasmodia, the malaria parasites, were present in her victim, some will have entered her stomach as she sucked the blood. The sexual forms of the parasite, gametocytes, mate in the mosquito's stomach, and the fertilized female gamete (sex cell) encysts in the stomach wall. After one to three weeks the cyst bursts open, and a large number of young sexual parasites, the sporozoites, emerge. These find their way to the salivary glands of the mosquito, and the next time she bites she will inject some of these parasites into her victim. The parasites multiply in the victim's liver for a week or so and then spill into the bloodstream, in the form called merozoites, and enter many of the red blood cells. There they multiply, or sporulate, asexually; after two or three days they burst out of the red cells that they have destroyed and enter some more, repeating the cycle over and over again, destroying red blood cells each time. Eventually some sexual forms emerge, the gametocytes; they do not multiply or mate in the human body, but if the victim is bitten again, they get sucked into the mosquito's stomach, and the life cycle of the malaria parasite begins again.

Development of malaria parasites

Four varieties of *Plasmodium* infect humans: *P. vivax*, *P. ovale*, *P. malariae*, and *P. falciparum*. They all cause malaria, the common feature of which is recurring bouts of fever that shake the sufferer with alternating shivering and sweating. According to the rate in which the asexual parasites multiply and burst out of the patient's red blood cells, these attacks may occur every day (quotidian malaria), every third day (tertian malaria), or every fourth day (quartan malaria); but often different cycles of sporulation are going on in the person's red cells at the same time, and the periodicity of the shivering attacks is blurred. *Plasmodium falciparum* tends to sporulate in 36 rather than 48 hours, and the attacks come on more quickly than every third day; the disease is then called subtertian malaria or, more often, because of its severity, malignant tertian. Malaria can mimic almost any other disease. The infected person becomes anemic from loss of red blood cells and may be jaundiced, have gastroenteritis, show signs of bronchitis, have a hectic, continued fever, or even collapse and be cold, with no fever at all. Any illness in a person who may have been exposed to infection must be regarded as malaria until proved otherwise. In most persons the attacks come to an end even without treatment, though they recur later. But when *Plasmodium falciparum* is the parasite, the fever is often mild for a day or two, with headache, aches and pains, and a little vomiting or diarrhea, and then changes with treacherous suddenness to an overwhelming illness, with signs of liver, kidney, or respiratory failure or with coma from invasion and blocking of the small blood vessels of the brain, a characteristic of cerebral malaria. Persons with these symptoms may die unless they can have the most urgent and skillful medical attention, and it is one of the tragedies of malaria that the early illness of malignant malaria, which is easily treatable, is so often not identified until the unmistakable but desperate stage of cerebral malaria sets in.

Treatment is in theory simple. Excellent antimalarial drugs are available. Chloroquine given by mouth for three days cures early falciparum malaria and brings attacks of the other forms to an end, though they recur later unless the person is treated after the attack with drugs to prevent a relapse. For the treatment of malignant or cerebral malaria, the antimalarial drug must be given intravenously without delay, and measures are taken to restore the red blood cell level, to correct the severe upset of the body fluids and salts, and to get rid of the urea that accumulates in the blood when the kidneys fail.

Prevention of malaria

The prevention of malaria can be tackled in two main ways: by trying to break contact between humans and mosquitoes and by administering drugs to persons exposed to bites to prevent the onset of the disease. The mosquito can be attacked in the larval and adult stage. Antimalarial drugs, if taken regularly, prevent the onset of the disease. They are taken before entry to a malarious area, regularly while in the area, and for some time after leaving it.

The malaria parasite, like most microorganisms, holds stubbornly to life. Malaria parasites resistant to drugs have appeared in several malarious areas, and combinations of old and new drugs have been tried to combat this; more than 100,000 possible drugs have been tested in the United States alone in the search for an effective one. The struggle against malaria is not over.

Diseases caused by rickettsiae. The rickettsiae are a family of microorganisms named for the American pathologist Howard Taylor Ricketts, who died of typhus in 1910 while investigating the spread of the disease. They cause a group of diseases in humans characterized by fever and a rash, and all depend for survival on passing at some stage through the body of a louse, a mite, a tick, or a flea. The great epidemic form of the disease, epidemic louse-borne typhus, is caused by *Rickettsia prowazekii* and differs from most of the others, except trench fever, in that humans are the only host. Humans get the other diseases only when they break into some cycle in nature where they are not needed for the survival of the rickettsia. In murine typhus, for example, *Rickettsia mooseri* is a parasite of rats conveyed from rat to rat by the rat flea, *Xenopsylla cheopis;* it will bite humans if they intrude into its environment. Scrub typhus is caused by *Rickettsia tsutsugamushi*, but it normally parasitizes only rats and mice and other rodents, being carried from one to the other by a small mite, *Leptotrombidium* (previously known as *Trombicula*). This mite is fastidious in matters of temperature, humidity, and food and finds everything suitable in restricted areas, or "mite islands," in South Asia and the western Pacific. It rarely bites humans in their normal environment, but if humans invade its territory en masse it will certainly attack, and outbreaks of scrub typhus follow, large enough to upset the invaders and their projects. The spotted fevers are caused by rickettsiae that spend their normal life cycles in a variety of small animals, spreading from one to the other inside ticks; these bite human intruders and cause African, North Asian, and Queensland tick typhus, as well as Rocky Mountain spotted fever. One other spotted fever, rickettsialpox, is caused by *Rickettsia akari;* this lives in the body of the ordinary house mouse, *Mus musculus*, and spreads from one to another inside the mouse mite *Allodermanyssus sanguineus*. The *Rickettsia* is probably a parasite of wild field mice, and it is perhaps only when cities push out into the countryside that the house mice catch the infection. But the *Rickettsia* of epidemic typhus lives only in the human body and in the louse and needs no other environment than that which humans, when their hygiene falters, provide.

Transfer of typhus by louse

Typhus. Epidemic typhus has also been known as jail fever, war fever, or camp fever, names that suggest overcrowding, underwashing, and lowered standards of living. The body louse, *Pediculus humanus*, has a powerful sucking mouth, lined with fine teeth for gripping the host's skin while it cuts it with a pair of fine stylets. As it sucks the blood of a typhus victim, rickettsiae pass into its pharynx and down into its gut, where they invade the cells lining the intestinal wall. They multiply inside, and the cells burst after a few days, releasing hordes of rickettsiae into the intestinal canal. These either reinfect other cells or are passed out in the feces. Lice leave a body when it gets too hot from fever or too cold from death and crawl to another human host. The clothing of a heavily infested typhus patient is contaminated with louse feces, and careless removal of it may raise a cloud of infected dust in the air and, in this way, spread typhus to others, especially physicians and nurses.

About 10 days after the infected bite the person falls ill. Intense headache and fever are always present, and after a few days a rash comes out on the back and chest and spreads to the abdomen and limbs, but not to the face. The sick person is flushed, and the eyes are bleary. Circulation becomes sluggish, and there may be spots of gangrene on the fingers, genitals, nose, and ears. Signs of pneumonia or of kidney failure are common. Soon the person becomes stuporose and then may lapse into coma and die. Much depends on age: the young tend to recover, the aged to die.

This is the sequence of events if there is no treatment. Tetracyclines and chloramphenicol both have a dramatic curative effect, and, if treated early enough, few persons should die. The disease can be diagnosed clinically during epidemics and by laboratory tests.

The prevention of epidemic typhus calls for the elimination of human body lice. Antityphus vaccine is also effective; two doses are given at a fortnight's interval, and a third is given after three months. Thereafter, doses at several months' intervals are given to exposed personnel. The vaccine gives great protection against attack and almost complete protection against death.

Rocky Mountain spotted fever. Rocky Mountain spotted fever is the Western Hemisphere form of tick-borne typhus. The disease organism, *Rickettsia rickettsi*, is a parasite of many wild animals in North, Central, and South America—rabbits, chipmunks, porcupines, weasels, rats, mice, and possibly also dogs. Many different ticks carry the rickettsiae from one animal to another, and, once infected, the female tick can pass them through the ovaries to her offspring, so that ticks can act both as carriers and as reservoirs of infection. The wood tick (*Dermacentor andersoni*), the dog tick (*Dermacentor variabilis*), the lone star tick (*Amblyomma americanum*), and several others carry the infection to humans in different parts of the Americas; in spite of its name, Rocky Mountain spotted fever is most common on the East Coast of the United States and has been found in every state. It is a disease of the wilds, and humans can be infected only if they enter its reserves. It is a disease of the summer and early fall months, when ticks are active.

Course of Rocky Mountain spotted fever

The illness begins with headache, fever, and chills, soon followed by pains in the bones and joints and great weakness or prostration. A rash comes out in the first week of illness. It is more profuse than the rash of epidemic typhus and affects the face as well as the body. It looks not unlike measles. In some persons the colour deepens after a day or two, and in the worst cases it turns purple with blood. By the end of a week in severe cases, the patient shows signs of brain irritation and may be agitated, sleepless, or delirious. Breathing becomes laboured and circulation poor, and areas of gangrene may develop on the hands and feet. In the worst cases, the patient falls into coma and dies, but in most the fever gradually abates and the patient slowly recovers.

Chloramphenicol and tetracycline are both effective in treatment, provided treatment is early. In the latest stages the sick person may be beyond medical aid, but few should reach that stage before treatment is begun. To avoid infection humans must avoid ticks. If people go into an infected area, for recreation or in their occupation, they need clothing impregnated with insect repellent. If people are exposed constantly in their work, they should be vaccinated against the infection.

Diseases caused by skin parasites. *Scabies.* The parasite that causes scabies, *Sarcoptes scabiei*, is a mite just visible to the unaided eye. In spite of its small size, it has quite formidable mouthparts and eight very powerful legs. With her hind legs the female of the species hitches herself into the perpendicular, and, with her mouthparts thus closely applied to the skin, she cuts her way down into the horny layer. Altering her direction, she then tunnels horizontally and gouges out for herself a burrow up to several inches long and usually not very straight. She prefers the skin between the fingers and the toes, on the wrist and the elbows, in the armpits, below the breast, and on the male genitals. She does most of her moving at night. The burrows can easily be recognized: sometimes the mite can just be seen at the far end of one, and it is easy to pick her up on a needle and examine her under the microscope. She lays up to 30 eggs, four or five a day, and these hatch into larvae in four to five days, undergoing two molts before they become female adults; the male has only one molt. From egg to laying adult female takes about three weeks.

The mite passes from person to person by close contact, and scabies is characteristically a disease of wartime, for living standards then drop, washing may be difficult, and people are crowded together. The burrowing of the mite causes irritation, but in addition a rash breaks out on parts of the body where there are no burrows, on the buttocks, over the shoulder blades, and on the abdomen. The cause of this rash is not obvious; it is probably a reaction to the presence of the parasite on the body. It is intensely irritating and interferes with sleep.

Prevention of scabies

The means of prevention are obvious, consisting of clean underclothes and frequent change of clothing and washing, conditions hard to come by in wars and mass migrations. Effective treatment consists of painting the affected person from neck to feet with a lotion that kills the mite; benzyl benzoate is often used. It is desirable to treat a whole family or a group of people living together, for often the early burrowing stages of the disease cause no irritation, and a person can be infested long before he knows it.

BIBLIOGRAPHY. PAUL D. HOEPRICH (ed.), *Infectious Diseases* (1972); and RALPH D. FEIGIN and J.D. CHERRY (eds.), *Textbook of Pediatric Infectious Diseases*, 2 vol. (1981), are advanced postgraduate textbooks containing material to which the general reader might refer. ANDRÉ SIEGFRIED, *Routes of Contagion* (1965; U.K. title, *Germs and Ideas: Routes of Epidemics and Ideologies*, 1965; originally published in French, 1960); and HENRY E. SIGERIST, *Civilization and Disease* (1943, reissued 1970), nontechnical works that deal with the effect of disease on human life and history. FRANK M. BURNET, *The Background of Infectious Diseases in Man* (1946), outlines the problems presented by infectious diseases in the middle of the 20th century; the fact that many of the problems have since been solved adds to the interest of the book. CLIFFORD HORTON-SMITH (ed.), *Biological Aspects of the Transmission of Disease* (1957), deals with the mechanics and interrelationships of infection in plants, animals, and humans; the level of writing varies from the very technical to the semipopular. WILLIAM H. MCNEILL, *Plagues and Peoples* (1976), a book for the general reader, describes the dramatic impact of infectious diseases on the rise and fall of civilizations; J.F.D. SHREWSBURY, *A History of Bubonic Plague in the British Isles* (1970), gives a scholarly but highly readable description of the plague. PAUL CASSAR, *Medical History of Malta* (1964), deals with the problems of epidemic disease, in war and peace, throughout the history of the island. KENNETH MELLANBY, *Pesticides and Pollution* (1967), reviews the problems presented by pollution in the modern world, many of which derive from attempts to control the spread of disease in humans and nature. JAMES M. ALSTON, *A New Look at Infectious Disease* (1967), shows briefly how, as one problem in the field of infectious disease is solved, another takes its place. J.A. BOYCOTT, *Natural History of Infectious Disease* (1971), discusses infectious disease as just one aspect of parasitism—a study, in simple terms, of host–parasite relationships. ANDREW B. CHRISTIE, *Infectious Diseases, with Chapters on Venereal Diseases*, 5th ed. (1968), gives a simple account of the clinical and social aspects of infectious diseases, and *Infectious Diseases: Epidemiology and Clinical Practice*, 3rd ed. (1980), is an advanced textbook, but with much about the nature of infection that the nontechnical reader can find useful; A.B. and MARY C. CHRISTIE, *Food Hygiene and Food Hazards . . .*, 2nd ed. (1977), discusses in a light, nontechnical manner the problems of food-borne infections. FRANK L. HORSFALL and I. TAMM (eds.), *Viral and Rickettsial Infections of Man*, 4th ed. (1965) is an advanced postgraduate textbook that, especially on epidemiology, contains material to which the general reader might refer.

(A.B.C./R.D.F.)

Inflammation

Like many of the basic concepts in pathology, inflammation resists any all-inclusive definition. A reasonable approximation would be the local reaction of living tissues—especially the small blood vessels, their contents and their associated structures—to injury.

At first sight, the number and diversity of diseases of animals and man classed as inflammatory would seem to exceed the limits of even so broad a definition. It may be shown, however, that tissue reactions ranging from burns to pneumonia, leprosy, tuberculosis, and rheumatoid arthritis, all examples of inflammation, do in fact fit within the definition, although, paradoxically, it is recent evidence that has emphasized this point.

In an analysis of inflammation, the most important step is to separate the stages of the inflammatory process. All inflammation begins as simple acute, "short-lived," inflammation, which proceeds in one of four directions: resolution, organization (building up of new tissue), suppuration (formation of pus), or chronic—"long-lasting"—inflammation. Any noxious process that damages living tissue—infection with bacteria, excessive heat, cold, mechanical injury such as crushing, acids, alkalis, irradiation—or infection with viruses can cause inflammation. The organ or tissue involved makes only minor differences to the inflammatory process.

The four cardinal signs

In ancient times inflammation was recognized as an entity by virtue of simple observation. Thus Celsus (a Roman physician of the 1st century AD) listed the four cardinal signs of inflammation as *calor*, *rubor*, *turgor*, and *dolor* (heat, redness, swelling, and pain). As a description it still cannot be bettered, although a fifth, loss of function, is sometimes added.

The realization that the four cardinal signs were in fact the outward evidence of changes in small blood vessels (the microcirculation) was dependent on the development of the microscope. Early in the 19th century experimentalists began to study the effects of noxious stimuli on translucent living tissues that were suitable for microscopic examination, such as the frog's tongue. The definitive description of the vascular changes of acute inflammation is generally attributed to a German pathologist, Julius Cohnheim.

Cohnheim was convinced that inflammation is purely and simply an automatic response of small blood vessels to injury and that it plays little part in defense against infection. A Russian biologist, Élie Metchnikoff, challenged this view in one of the bitter scientific controversies of the latter part of the 19th century. Metchnikoff's studies on simple forms of life such as the amoebas led him to recognize that the white cells (leukocytes) of the blood like amoebas ingest particulate matter (phagocytosis) and that this process of phagocytosis is vital for preserving mankind from the ravages of bacteria. Metchnikoff drew attention to the key role played by leukocytes in inflammation, although Cohnheim himself had observed the participation of these cells in the response. Nevertheless it was Metchnikoff's work that laid the basis for the modern science of immunology.

THE STAGES OF INFLAMMATION

Simple acute inflammation. The first event after injury is a constriction, or narrowing, of the arterioles; *i.e.*, the microscopic portion of the arterial tree that carries oxygenated blood from the heart to all parts of the body. Arterioles have a coat of muscle that enables them to vary their calibre in response to nervous and chemical stimuli. As a result of constriction there is usually a sharp reduction in the volume of blood flowing through the affected part. The change in calibre is, however, transient and, except in cases of extremely severe damage, lasts no more than a matter of minutes.

As the arteriolar constriction wears off it is replaced by a dilation of the arterioles, with apparent paralysis of the muscle coat. Alterations in blood flow are variable, but usually an increased volume of blood is delivered to the part. It is this augmentation of circulation that explains the enhanced redness and warmth of acutely inflamed tissues. Because of the increased volume of blood delivered in the dilated arteries the entire microcirculation of capillaries (simple, thin-walled vessels linking arteries and veins) and venules (microscopic veins) becomes flushed with blood. In these latter parts of the system, however, the circulation lacks the pulsatile thrust of the arterial tree and tends to slow down so that the blood stagnates and may even coagulate.

Partly as a result of this sluggish flow, the white corpuscles of the blood leave their normal position in the centre of the stream and move to the outer boundary of the stream so that they impinge upon the inner wall of the blood vessel, especially the venule. Motion-picture photographic studies of the inflamed ears of rabbits have shown this phenomenon particularly well, the white corpuscles (leukocytes) being seen to bounce on the cells lining the vessel, to become caught up on projections of these cells, and finally to adhere to them. This adhesion of the leukocytes to the inner lining (endothelium) of venules is known as margination and is a major feature of the

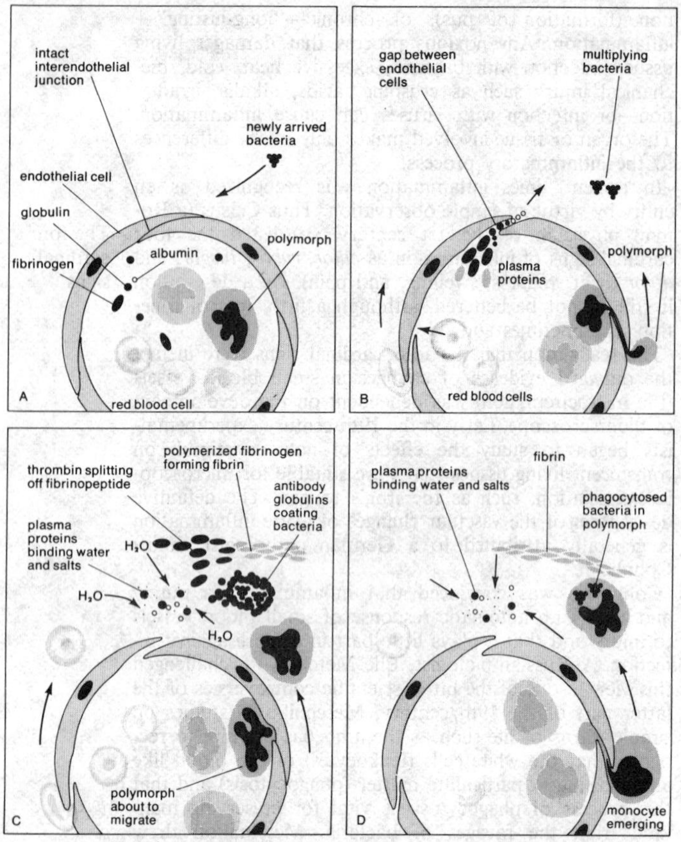

Stages in the formation of an acute inflammatory exudate in response to invasion of the tissues by bacteria.
(A) Normal venule, with polymorphonuclear leukocyte, red blood cell, and three plasma proteins in its channel.
(B) Plasma proteins, red blood cells, and polymorphonuclear leukocyte passing through gap between endothelial cells; the proteins leave at rates inversely proportional to exudate.
(C) Activity in the tissues. (D) The invading bacteria are ingested and destroyed; monocytes emerge, become macrophages, and remove debris.
P. Cull, St. Bartholomew's Hospital Medical College, London

acute inflammatory process. Though in very mild injury the change goes no further than this, margination of leukocytes is usually followed by their emigration. In acute inflammation, the type of leukocyte involved is predominantly the neutrophil polymorphonuclear leukocyte, so named because of its intermediate or neutral staining characteristics with certain dyes, and because of the irregular or polymorphic nature of its nucleus. Emigration involves the passage of these cells from the interior of the vessel to the exterior, so that the leukocytes come to lie in the tissues in the extravascular space. The passage of blood constituents through vessel walls into the tissues is the hallmark of inflammation and the tissue collection so formed is termed the exudate. Leukocytes move through the vessel wall by virtue of their inherent powers of locomotion expressed as amoeboid movement —*i.e.*, the pushing out of footlike processes (pseudopodia) after the fashion of the amoeba.

It is usually at least one to four hours after injury before sizable emigration of leukocytes is obvious. Long before the migration of white cells forms a cellular exudate, however, a fluid exudate has collected. The walls of the small vessels concerned are normally freely permeable to water and salts but allow only small quantities of the proteins in the blood plasma to pass from the circulation. In inflammation the walls of venules and capillaries lose their relative impermeability to protein, which, as a result, escapes from the blood into the tissues; there, because of its ability to take up and hold water (oncotic pressure), it leads to an accumulation of fluid (edema). In normal circumstances when the vessel wall is not leaky, the oncotic pressure of the circulating proteins helps to retain fluid within the blood stream, thus counterbalancing the hydrostatic pressure of the blood itself, which would otherwise tend to push fluid out of the circulation. This balance of forces is stated formally as Starling's law. The accumulation of fluid in inflamed tissues due to leakiness of vessels to plasma protein (increased vascular permeability) is the cause of the swelling that is one of the cardinal signs of inflammation and also a major cause of the pain because of the pressure exerted by the fluid on nerve endings. For this reason inflammation is more painful in regions in which there is little space for the exuded fluid to diffuse. It is also the explanation of the throbbing character of some inflammatory pain, since with each heart beat there is an increase of pressure transmitted to the nerve endings.

Escape of plasma proteins into tissues

The loss of fluid from stagnant reaches of the microcirculation is one explanation of the thickening, sluggishness, and coagulation of the blood in these damaged regions. Much experimentation and argument has gone into the problem of how the protein escapes from inflamed vessels. A major clue seemed to be provided by the observation that the freedom with which individual proteins leave such venules varies inversely with the molecular size of the protein (molecular sieving). This led to the suggestion that vessel walls contain pores of fixed size that restrict passage of proteins in proportion to the size of the molecule. The problem was solved by observations made with the electron microscope that in inflamed venules gaps appear between the junctions of the endothelial cells making up the vessel wall. These gaps were, however, much larger than the theoretical size of the pores needed to explain molecular sieving. It is believed, therefore, that the gaps within the endothelium allow all proteins to pass freely but that the membrane surrounding the outer perimeter of the endothelial cells (basement membrane) acts as some kind of sieve, perhaps by virtue of its meshlike molecular structure. Although venules appear to be the major source of plasma-protein escape in acute inflammation, the capillaries, too, play a part. In spite of the predominance of the venule it is nevertheless still common for the phenomenon to be termed increased capillary permeability purely for historical reasons. Particular mention must be made of the plasma protein fibrinogen, which is the largest of the plasma proteins and has an elongated molecular structure. After passing through the permeable vascular wall, the fibrinogen usually undergoes breakdown by an ubiquitous enzyme (thrombin) in the tissues, the major role of which normally is to control bleeding by accelerating the clotting of blood. In inflammation, the exuded fibrinogen suffers the splitting off of part of its molecule, and the residual fragments then join together to form fibrin by a process similar to that used industrially to produce artificial fibres such as nylon. Fibrin forms strands that produce a characteristic network on and within inflamed areas. Its most classical deposition is seen on the surface of inflamed hearts (pericarditis) or lungs (pleurisy), or in the trachea in diphtheria.

Mechanism of escape of proteins from vessels

Another type of plasma protein that leaks from the vessels during acute inflammation is gamma globulin. The special importance of this group of proteins is that they include the so-called antibodies. Antibodies are produced by the body in response to the presence of foreign material (antigen) and react specifically with the antigen. The leakage of antibodies into tissues infected by bacteria helps to clump the bacteria or dissolve them or accelerate their uptake and digestion by phagocytes.

Route of escape of white cells

The electron microscope also revealed the route by which white cells leave inflamed vessels. The leukocytes do so by inserting footlike projections (pseudopodia) into the tight junction between two endothelial cells. The rest of the leukocyte follows the pseudopod and the whole cell eventually reaches the extravascular space. The interendothelial junction appears to seal up behind the white cell during its progress through the vessel wall. The mechanism whereby the leukocyte penetrates the basement membrane of the vessel is unknown, but it has been suggested that the cell may secrete an enzyme that softens the membrane sufficiently to allow passage.

The sequence of events in simple acute inflammation can then be summarized as follows: transient arteriolar vasoconstriction, sustained dilation of the microcirculation with stagnation of blood in capillaries and increased flow in arterioles, leakage of protein into the tissues because of increased vascular permeability, adhesion of leukocytes to vessel walls, and migration of leukocytes into the tissues. This process would take about three hours but could take longer if some preliminary step were necessary; *e.g.*, local multiplication of bacteria.

Release of chemical substances in injured tissue. Research to determine how the body achieves such a standard response to many diverse types of injury has mainly taken the form of a quest for chemical substances (mediators) naturally present in the body, whose release or activation by injury causes the characteristic changes of inflammation.

Role of histamine

The first step in this process has been the discovery of a natural chemical that can cause all or some of the inflammatory changes. Foremost among these is histamine, a simple molecule derived from the amino acid histidine and found to cause vascular changes akin to inflammation. Histamine-like substances were seen to be released from inflamed areas, and for a time it seemed that much of inflammation could be explained by the release of histamine from certain cells of the body, notably mast cells or platelets. The introduction of the antihistaminics, which counteract the effects of histamine, permitted the theory to be tested. If histamine were the cause of the vascular changes in inflammation, the antihistaminics should prevent their development. In fact they failed to do so in both man and experimental animals. It was not until much later that detailed analysis of experimental inflammation in animals showed, with the aid of antihistaminics, that histamine did in fact play a role, albeit a minor one, in causing the vascular changes that occur in the first 30 minutes or so after injury.

In experiments on the release of histamine-like substances and in other experiments, it was always assumed that other compounds with similar properties were released from injured tissues. Serotonin (5-hydroxytryptamine) is a substance, widely distributed in the body, some of whose properties are akin to those of histamine. With the aid of drugs that antagonize only serotonin (specific antagonists) it can be demonstrated that, while the compound may have some role to play in inflammation in rodents, it does not have one in humans.

Peptides as mediators

Peptides are chains of amino acids that form subunits of proteins. It has been known since the 19th century that inflamed tissues contain peptides, resulting from breakdown of protein. In the 1930s workers extracted certain compounds from such tissues and found that when injected into skin they could cause many of the changes of acute inflammation. It was concluded that the active principle is a peptide (leukotaxine). Twenty years later, it was shown that the extraction procedures used produced a mixture of peptides and that the common characteristics of those which increased vascular permeability was that they were composed of eight to ten amino acids. In addition certain specific peptides were found to be formed in blood serum in the presence of various enzymes or in contact with foreign surfaces. The most noticeable of these peptides is bradykinin (Greek, "slow movement") so called because of its ability to cause a slow contraction of intestinal muscle. Bradykinin is composed of nine amino acids and has been synthesized. It produces vascular changes similar to those of acute inflammation when injected in minute quantities. Nevertheless it has proved difficult to obtain convincing evidence for the actual participation of bradykinin or similar peptides in the inflammatory process. There is in general little correlation between the suppression of bradykinin activity and of inflammation. Increased amounts of the peptide or of the natural enzyme that activates it (kininogenase) have been demonstrated in inflamed tissues, but in these experiments it is difficult to exclude activation by the experimental procedures themselves. Another problem is posed by the rapidity with which such peptides are destroyed in body fluids once they are formed. Kininogenase is found in blood plasma and in tissue cells especially within cytoplasmic structures called lysosomes.

Other possible mediators

Many other candidates for the role of inflammatory mediator exist, especially as regards increased vascular permeability. It has been suggested that local destruction of the adrenal hormone epinephrine by the enzyme monoamine oxidase is a factor in vascular dilation and altered permeability, since epinephrine reverses these changes. More recently, activation of the highly complex complement system of blood plasma has been proposed as a mechanism. (The complement system is discussed in the article IMMUNITY). The complement system is known to be involved when antigen and antibody unite, but there is a possibility that other forms of tissue damage may also bring it into action with consequent liberation of enzymes that could cause inflammatory changes. It has been suggested that injury activates enzymes that cause sustained and greatly augmented local liberation of histamine and that the histamine is in some way inaccessible to antihistamine drugs. Recently a complex group of fatty acids known as the prostaglandins has been advanced as possible mediator of vascular changes in some forms of inflammation. In addition at various times a variety of uncharacterized substances and extracts of tissues or tissue cells have been put forward as mediators of increased vascular permeability after injury, as well as a number of enzymes, especially those that attack proteins, obtained from similar sources.

It is obvious from this profusion of candidates that no certainty exists. What does appear plain is that the major vascular event of acute inflammation, namely increased vascular permeability, is a multiphase phenomenon. The early phase appears to be due to release of histamine, augmented in rodents by serotonin. The mechanism of the subsequent more prolonged phase or phases remains in doubt. Besides all the substances discussed above, there is, of course, also the possibility of direct structural damage to the vessel wall, especially by extremely destructive injury such as burns.

Role of nervous impulses

Since the earliest investigations of inflammation, the role of the nerves that serve particular areas has been studied. It has been shown that the red flare (due to vasodilatation) appearing on lightly damaged skin as part of the so-called triple response can be abolished by cutting the nerves to the affected area or by blocking the nerves with local anesthetic. The other features of the inflammatory reaction were unimpaired. In general, inflammation appears to develop virtually normally in totally denervated areas under experimental conditions. It has, however, been possible to show that in man nervous impulses can in special circumstances play a major part. Thus irritants can be injected into suitable subjects under hypnosis without production of any inflammatory vascular response. It is even possible, by suggestion to such patients in their hypnotic state, to cause one arm to develop inflammatory changes and the other not to, although both arms have been similarly treated.

An interesting feature of the studies just described is the inability of hypnotic suggestion to affect the emigration of leukocytes although it does suppress vascular dilation and protein leakage. This, of course, suggests that the two phenomena have different mechanisms. Originally it was held that the mediators that cause vascular changes are also responsible for white-cell exudation.

On re-examination it was found that the leukocyte accumulations caused by these substances are much too small to be of significance in inflammation and that they are probably a by-product of the vessel's leakiness to protein. This observation stimulated a search for mediators with a stronger action on leukocytes. Bacteria in particular cause especially massive leukocytic exudation in inflammation, and recent studies have revealed that many diverse types of micro-organisms contain chemical substances that can be shown to attract leukocytes even in tissue-culture vessels outside the body. This specific attraction is known as chemotaxis. Bacteria appear to contain two types of chemotactic substance, one acting directly on the leukocytes and of relatively low molecular weight, probably a peptide, and one acting by virtue of its ability to activate a chemotactic substance in blood plasma. This latter bacterial substance is of high molecular weight and is probably a protein. The material that is activated in plasma is probably of more than one type and in some cases appears to be part of the complement system, mentioned earlier. Apart from micro-organisms, certain tissue extracts appear to possess the property of activating serum to produce factors chemotactic to leukocytes. There has been some dispute as to whether any of these factors are truly chemotactic; that is, whether they really set up a specific attraction to the leukocyte or whether they merely accelerate random movement in the cells. At the moment it seems likely that both views have some truth in that mobility is random in the absence of a graded concentration of the attractive substance and directional when such a gradient exists.

At present it is not possible to identify any pure chemical substance in the body with the specific property of causing white cells to emigrate in inflammation. Nevertheless the weak action of vascular mediators on leukocytes, the existence of different powerful factors active on leukocytes, and the separation in time of vascular changes and leukocyte migration in inflammation all indicate the separate identity of the two sets of phenomena.

Leukocytosis, fever, and ESR

The systemic associations of acute inflammation. Acute inflammation is commonly accompanied by a rise in the number of leukocytes circulating in the blood (leukocytosis), by fever, and by an increase in the rate at which the red corpuscles of the blood settle under gravity (raised ESR, or erythrocyte sedimentation rate). All three are widely used as diagnostic tests in medical practice. The mechanism of leukocytosis has defied many attempts at elucidation. No hormone or mediator has been identified, although adrenal and pituitary hormones and stress are known to produce modest changes. Many investigators doubt whether a true leukocytosis mediator exists and suspect that feedback of information to the bone marrow to liberate more leukocytes is accomplished by other means. The mechanism of fever is thought to be the release of a chemical substance from damaged leukocytes and tissue cells (endogenous pyrogen), which acts on the centre in the brain that regulates body temperature. Bacteria contain fever-producing substances (endotoxin, bacterial pyrogen), but these are thought to act mainly by liberating fever-producing substances produced by the body itself. The rise in ESR is due to the presence in the blood plasma of an unduly high proportion of proteins of high molecular weight such as fibrinogen and gamma globulin. This in turn causes the red cells to clump together, and the clumping in turn increases their sedimentation rate. In severe tissue injury other changes occur in the peripheral circulation (shock) and in the body's metabolism but these are beyond the scope of the present article.

Varieties of simple acute inflammation. The essence of uncomplicated acute inflammation is that the injury should not be sufficiently severe to cause abscess formation or scarring (see below), nor sufficiently difficult to eradicate as to lead to chronicity (see below). Mild burns, mechanical injury, frostbite, chemical irritation, bacterial or viral infection, or hypersensitivity (allergy) all come within this compass. Of these only hypersensitivity needs special mention. Acute allergic inflammation can vary from a trivial local increase in vascular permeability leading to urticaria (hives) to a full-blown reaction with much cell exudation. In the first type local release of histamine and other mediators from mast cells and platelets probably constitutes the major mechanism. In the more extensive type the major factor may be local deposition in the vessel wall of soluble antigen-antibody complexes that bind and activate complement, in particular a trimolecular component of complement with a powerful chemotactic effect on polymorphonuclear leukocytes. This mechanism is thought to be important in bringing about the inflammatory changes in acute glomerulonephritis (inflammation of the kidney), especially when it follows streptococcal infection. It is believed that antigen from the bacteria combine with the patient's antibody to form complexes that lodge in the kidney and set up inflammation as described above.

Resolution. The expected fate of simple acute inflammation is resolution, a term which implies disappearance of the exudate and the return of the affected part to normal function and structure. An important preliminary change in resolution is the gradual replacement of the polymorphonuclear leukocytes of the exudate by mononuclear leukocytes. These latter cells are mainly monocytes; *i.e.*, large phagocytic cells with a plain round, oval, or slightly indented nucleus. Usually their emigration from the blood commences at the same time or shortly after that of the polymorphs. When the injurious stimulus ceases or is overcome by the body's defenses, emigration comes to a stop. The polymorphs have a short life span and are highly motile so that they rapidly die, disintegrate, or leave the site of inflammation. The monocytes, however, are less mobile and more long-lived and thus dominate the scene after the first 24 hours or so. Because of their great phagocytic and digestive powers they are ideally suited to clear the area of debris and restore a normal picture. The most dramatic example of resolution is provided by lobar pneumonia in which, once the tide of recovery sets in, a lobe of the lung that was rendered entirely solid by exuded fibrin and leukocytes is rapidly restored to normal. However, with the widespread use of antibiotics this phenomenon is now much less spectacular in its presentation.

Suppuration. When an acute inflammatory reaction progresses to the local formation of pus, an abscess is said to be formed and the process is known as suppuration. Pus is a viscous liquid formed of the digested bodies of dead leukocytes and tissue cells. It contains all the chemical substances of which these cells are formed, namely, proteins, peptides, amino acids, nucleic acids, lipids, carbohydrates, and all their respective breakdown products. Pus is usually creamy yellow or green in colour but may be tinged with blood or mixed with clear mucus. Because of its physicochemical properties and because it may be shut off from the body's defenses, pus may be slow to disappear even when the cause has been eliminated. It is therefore an axiom of surgeons that pus must be drained before healing can occur. In an abscess, the central core of pus is surrounded by inflamed tissue, the microscopic appearance of which will depend on its duration and causation. Pus is formed wherever the injurious stimulus is such that it induces large numbers of polymorphonuclear leukocytes to emigrate into the affected area and leads also, because of its toxicity, to massive killing of these leukocytes and of tissue cells. The commonest cause of suppuration is infection of the tissues with certain bacteria, notably the so-called pyogenic cocci. Of these *Staphylococcus aureus* is now the most important; it gives rise not only to trivial skin pustules as in acne vulgaris but also to fatal pneumonia. There are many other pus-producing organisms. The killing of the leukocytes and tissue cells is accomplished by toxins within the bacteria or produced by them. The liquefaction of the dead cells is brought about by enzymes either of bacterial origin or derived from the dead cells themselves. In the latter instance the enzymes are sited within small particles in the cytoplasm (lysosomes).

Cause of suppuration

Organization. When injury damages a part sufficiently to cause not only inflammation but also destruction of tissue, it is necessary for the defect to be repaired. This is accomplished by the dual processes of regeneration and organization, which together constitute healing. Regeneration involves the repeated division of surviving tissue cells until the breach is made good. Tissues vary widely in their regenerative capacity and some, notably brain, totally lack this ability. In other instances there is a large defect of connective tissue or a mass of blood clot or exudate to be replaced by some form of permanent structure. Organization deals with these problems and is the process whereby new blood vessels and connective-tissue-forming cells (fibroblasts) grow into such an area to form first vascularized connective tissue and then scar tissue.

The process has been well studied with the aid of a transparent observation chamber inserted in a rabbit's ear, and later observations with the electron microscope added little new information. An essential preliminary step is invasion of the site by monocytes (see above). These cells enlarge and become avidly phagocytic (macrophages), thus clearing the area of much particulate debris. From the blood vessels at the margin of the area buds or extensions form and grow inward until they join up with similar buds growing in from other directions. These solid buds then acquire a hollow interior (lumen) and are then known as capillary loops. Some of these newly grown vessels collect a coat of smooth muscle cells by ingrowth from pre-existing vessels and thus become new arterioles. Others become surrounded by fibrous tissue by a similar process and develop into veins. The newly formed vessels are immature and their walls are leaky so that they are surrounded by a zone of exuded blood plasma, red corpuscles, and leukocytes. Once the vessels are formed an extensive remodelling process occurs, with progressive reduction in the number of vessels.

Accompanying the ingrowth of vascular buds there is a migration of fibroblasts formed from the division of similar cells that survived the inflammatory reaction. Once present in the damaged area these cells secrete a protein known as collagen, a fibrillar molecule joined together (polymerized) to form chainlike links of great strength, thus reconstituting the connective tissue lost by injury. New lymphatic channels form by a process similar to that seen in blood vessels. More slowly new nerves grow into the organizing area by budding off from intact nerves at the periphery. It may be many months before normal innervation is restored. The process of organization is accompanied and healing accelerated by contraction of the margins of the wound if such a wound be present. The mechanism of this drawing of the edges of the wound closer together is unknown.

No mediators of the organization process have been discovered, but substances do exist that affect cellular regeneration (chalones). Many factors affect the success of organization, notably blood supply and the presence of bacteria or other irritant material. Vitamin C also is essential for the synthesis of collagen, and certain drugs, especially the corticosteroids such as cortisone, delay organization. Even trivial inflammation—*e.g.*, infected lesions of acne vulgaris—may lead to organization and scarring, but the most dramatic scarring is seen after the extensive destruction of connective tissue that occurs after burns or trauma.

Chronic inflammation. Chronic inflammation denotes a reaction that is long lasting, but because such persistence has characteristic microscopic features, it is these as much as the patient's history that are used by pathologists as a criterion. Chronic inflammation is a category into which fall some of the greatest scourges of mankind such as tuberculosis, leprosy, yaws, syphilis, and rheumatoid arthritis. Other conditions such as chronic nephritis or cirrhosis of the liver or chronic cholecystitis should also properly be included.

The essence of chronic inflammation is that the cause of tissue injury, whether it be the bacillus of tuberculosis or leprosy or a "foreign body" (*i.e.*, irritant solid material of extraneous origin), or a fungus or of unknown nature, be such that it neither quickly kills the patient nor is itself rapidly destroyed or removed by the body's defenses. In the case of living micro-organisms—*e.g.*, those of tuberculosis or leprosy—a symbiotic relationship is thus established between invader and host.

The main pathological feature of chronic inflammation, the more severe varieties of which for historical reasons are termed granulomatous, is infiltration of the affected area by certain types of cells. These are macrophages, epithelioid cells, lymphocytes, plasma cells, giant cells, and fibroblasts, the nature of the exudate varying with the cause of inflammation. Thus in tuberculosis epithelioid cells are prominent, and in syphilis, plasma cells. Lymphocytes and fibroblasts belong to separate cell lines, but most of the granulomatous exudate is now recognized to be derived from the macrophage, which thus becomes the architectural unit of chronic inflammation. Recent work has made it plain that for the most part the macrophage cell is derived not from local tissue but from a precursor in the bone marrow that exists in the circulation as a monocyte and enters the inflamed area in the same fashion as do granulocytes in acute inflammation. Thus, as indicated earlier in this article, current research has demonstrated the validity of the long-established general definition of inflammation as a reaction essentially of small blood vessels and circulating blood cells. Lymphocytes enter existing granulomas and may transform to plasma cells. Macrophages coalesce to form multinucleate giant cells especially in reactions to foreign bodies and in tuberculosis.

Mechanisms and main cause of chronicity

With the origin of macrophages established it remained to determine the mechanisms whereby chronic inflammation persisted for such long periods. Recent research has shown that this is accomplished in three ways, by sustained emigration of monocytes from the circulation into the affected tissues, by proliferation of macrophages in the inflamed zone by mitotic division, and by the ability of such macrophages to live for a long time without dividing, dying, or being replaced. These mechanisms have been worked out in experimental models of chronic inflammation in animals, and the importance of each mechanism varies with the cause of injury. It seems likely that the same three mechanisms would exist in human diseases, again varying in importance according to the cause.

The main reason for inflammation's becoming chronic is failure of macrophages to digest and thereby eliminate the irritant (*e.g.*, bacilli) that they have ingested. In some cases bacilli thrive and multiply within macrophages, as in leprosy and tuberculosis. The cause of the failure is unknown; it may lie in the chemical composition of certain micro-organisms or in deficiencies in the digestive apparatus of some or all of the phagocytes, or in some immunological defect or allergic mechanism as yet obscure. It is possible that, even in foreign body reactions, the body may become hypersensitive to some of its own inflammatory products and that the reaction is prolonged and aggravated as a result.

THE THERAPY OF INFLAMMATION

Wherever possible, treatment is aimed at eliminating the cause of inflammation. Thus bacterial inflammation is dealt with by the administration of antibiotics such as penicillin or tetracycline. Such therapy is usually effective but has become increasingly hampered by the appearance of antibiotic-resistant strains of micro-organisms. Chronic infections such as tuberculosis are also treated by antibiotics such as streptomycin, sometimes in combination with other antituberculous drugs such as isoniazid. Foreign-body reactions are dealt with by surgical removal of the irritant object.

When the cause of inflammation is unknown or not amenable to such specific therapy it is the practice to use anti-inflammatory drugs—*i.e.*, substances that lessen the signs and symptoms of inflammation without necessarily affecting the cause. Such drugs may be given by mouth or by injection, or applied locally. They include the corticosteroids such as cortisone, the salicylates such as aspirin, and more recent introductions such as indomethacin or phenylbutazone. All these compounds are widely used in the rheumatic disorders where the cause of inflammation is unknown but where it is necessary to control inflammatory pain and swelling. Simpler symptomatic treatment of inflammation hallowed by long usage includes the use of hot or cold compresses or hot poultices, or application of embrocations, or counterirritants. Although it is desirable to lessen pain and tissue destruction, no therapy should disregard the defensive role of the inflammatory response and, for this and other reasons, the use of powerful agents such as cortisone is undertaken with great caution, lest the treatment prove more harmful than the disease.

BIBLIOGRAPHY. H.W. FLOREY (ed.), *General Pathology*, 4th ed., ch. 1–6 and 17 (1970), a comprehensive modern text with a good account of acute inflammation, including its historical aspects; B.W. ZWEIFACH, L. GRANT, and R.T. MCCLUSKEY (eds.), *The Inflammatory Process* (1965), an account of all aspects of inflammation, each topic discussed by an appropriate expert, with detailed bibliography; W.G. SPECTOR and D.A. WILLOUGHBY, "The Inflammatory Response," *Bact. Rev.*, 27: 117–154 (June 1963), a review of inflammatory mechanisms, with an extensive bibliography; W.G. SPECTOR (ed.), "The Acute Inflammatory Response," *Ann. N.Y. Acad. Sci.*, 116: 747–1084 (1964), proceedings of a symposium devoted to current aspects of inflammation research, "The Granulomatous Inflammatory Exudate," in *Int. Rev. Exp. Path.*, 8:1–55 (1969), an up-to-date review of current knowledge concerning chronic inflammation, including a full bibliography.

(W.G.S.)

Inflation and Deflation

The terms inflation and deflation have been used in a number of different senses. In the 1960s, "inflation" was taken loosely to mean an inordinate rise in the general level of prices. It was not uncommon, however, to speak of wage inflation or profit inflation in referring to rises in wages or profits. During and after World War II, there was much talk of suppressed inflation; *i.e.*, a situation in which price rises were to a large extent prevented by administrative controls made necessary by a demand for goods and services that was excessive in relation to the available supply (demand inflation), perhaps resulting from an excessive or growing supply of money (currency inflation, or monetary inflation). In some periods, notably between World Wars I and II, it has been common to speak of income inflation, or simply of inflation in the sense of an increase in the flow of money income not necessarily associated with rises in prices. Because of the unpleasant associations of the word inflation, the variant reflation has sometimes been used to describe a contrived or proposed increase in money income not associated with unacceptable rises in prices.

The term deflation should logically denote the opposite of inflation in all these usages, and broadly speaking it does, though in its shorter history (the word dates only from 1919, whereas inflation has been used in an economic context at least from the mid-19th century) it has more often meant reductions of money supply or of income than reductions of the price level. After the great deflations of 1920–25 and 1929–33, it acquired unpleasant overtones, and the euphemism disinflation enjoyed a brief currency.

Generally, therefore, it is possible to say that inflation refers to an increase (especially one that is considered excessive) of money supply, money income, or the price level—phenomena that often but by no means always go together. Deflation refers to the decrease of any or all of these. The aspect of inflation that has attracted most attention is an increase of the general level of prices, whereas the emotive power of the word deflation springs from its association with reductions in employment and buying power.

Insofar as inflation and deflation have to do with changes in price levels, it is useful to have standards for measuring such changes. Index numbers are normally used for this purpose, and whether one diagnoses inflation or deflation and how much may depend to a considerable extent on the particular index one uses. Most indexes are prepared by measuring changes in the price of a selected list, or "market basket," of goods and services (see PRICES, STATISTICS OF). The selection of the goods and services to be included in the price index is important because the prices of different goods move in different degree and even in different directions. Ideally, the quantity and quality of these goods should reflect the spending habits of the community or of a stated section of the community, but unfortunately spending habits may change over a period of time. This gives the question of how much inflation or deflation has occurred over a period an element of ambiguity that cannot be completely removed.

CHANGES IN PRICES AND INCOME LEVELS

Types of inflation. The general level of prices everywhere has shown an upward trend over the last four centuries, though this has not been true for shorter periods. Thus, the general trend of prices in the 19th century was downward, though with many fluctuations, as was that between 1919 and 1939. There was a strong upward trend of prices in western Europe in the 16th century, associated with the inflow of gold and silver from the New World. Shorter but much sharper price rises have occurred in time of war, notably the Napoleonic Wars and World Wars I and II. After World War I, however, the price level fell substantially. In the years after 1939 many countries experienced an inflation that was unparalleled in extent and duration; the price rise from 1953 to the 1970s, in particular, was the biggest inflation (not connected with a major war and its immediate aftermath) in history.

"Creeping inflation" and rapid inflation

Most of the industrialized countries in that time experienced what is usually described as "creeping inflation"—a rise in the general price level averaging between 1 and 6 percent a year. The rate of rise was higher in the 1960s than it had been in the 1950s in all the main countries of this group: in the United States, the average rose from about 1 percent a year in the 1950s to 2 percent a year in the 1960s; in Great Britain, from 2 percent to 4 percent; in Japan, from 2 percent to 5 percent; in West Germany, from a little more than 1 percent to 3 or 4 percent. Until the 1970s the price rises had proved to be tolerable. Although they caused some unease in all the countries affected, this had not been great except where they seemed to lead to balance of payments difficulties—as in Great Britain. It is noteworthy that, in this period, investors indicated their expectation of further inflation by bidding up the prices of equities so far that their yields became regularly lower than those of fixed-interest securities.

A more drastic phenomenon is the chronic, rapid inflation known to Latin America, the extent of which can be seen from the fact that by 1970 the currencies of Brazil, Chile, and Argentina had depreciated to one- or two-thousandths of their 1914 value in terms of the United States dollar. In the 1950s and 1960s the annual rates of increase of cost of living in these countries varied between 10 and 70 percent a year. Rates such as these, once people have become accustomed to them, have a considerable effect on economic behaviour. Longterm lending at fixed rates of interest almost ceases, and people hold little money. Rapid inflation encourages residential building, because a house or a flat is a good hedge against rising prices; on the other hand, it seems to discourage public-utility development, partly because of the difficulty of borrowing the necessary long-term capital and partly because public resistance to rate increases tends to make utilities unprofitable. All of this means considerable distortions in the economies in question, but they seem capable of sustaining high rates of inflation for long periods.

Hyperinflation

The most extreme form of inflation—hyperinflation—in which the rate of price increase accelerates rapidly and the currency very largely ceases to be used, is fortunately rare. It has never occurred in any country that has not been disrupted by war or foreign occupation. A boundary seems to be passed when the price level begins to double in six months or less. At about this point, public behaviour with respect to money undergoes a radical change; foreign currency or goods begin to be used instead of the national currency for some purposes; and wage and salary payments begin to be made at shorter intervals, with frequent revisions. Money circulates much more rapidly, and the purchasing power of the stock of money falls. The increase in the quantity of money, however, is very much greater than the rise in its velocity of circulation. The quantity increases partly because tax collections lag behind expenditure, and governments run large budget deficits that are financed by (in effect) creating money. The quantity of money also increases because, with wages rising very fast (perhaps because they come to be geared to the foreign-exchange rate or to expectations of what that rate will be in a few days or hours), there appears to be a shortage of money for the needs of business. Through such mechanisms as these, the German price level rose thirteen hundred thousand million times in the inflation of 1923 and the Hungarian several million million million times in the inflation of 1945–46. Less spectacular hyperinflations occurred in revolutionary France in 1795–96 and in Russia and Austria after World War I. China and Greece suffered episodes of this kind during or after World War II.

Hyperinflation is largely a matter of loss of confidence in the value of money, and it is usually stopped by the issue of a new monetary unit that the public is somehow persuaded to accept as reliable. In Germany in 1923, the new currency—the Rentenmark—commended itself because it was ostensibly convertible into bonds on which interest fixed in terms of gold was promised. The promise, however, was seldom tested; people accepted the new currency as reliable because they needed it and apparently wanted to believe in its reliability.

Deflation. Deflation includes fewer varieties of economic experience than inflation does. There is no deflationary phenomenon corresponding to hyperinflation or even to chronic, severe inflation of the Latin-American kind. There have been long periods in which prices have shown a gently falling trend; the prices of a fairly extensive collection of commodities fell by about 25 percent between 1820–25 and 1846–50 and by 40 percent between 1874 and 1896. The latter period was not a period of depression in the sense of low business activity or high unemployment, though industrial production may have grown at a rate rather slower than that of the preceding generation. Various explanations of this substantial fall of prices have been advanced: failure of the supply of gold to keep up with the growth of economic activity, the opening up of the agricultural and mineral resources of the Western Hemisphere by railway and steamship, the relative peacefulness of the times, and a slowing of industrial growth. All of these may have had some influence.

Periods of falling prices

The 1920s were also a period of falling prices, combined in the United States and some other countries with a high level of prosperity. As in the late 19th century, improving supplies of primary products, particularly agricultural commodities (the prices of which are much more fluid than those of manufactures), may have been a main factor. The period witnessed some of the most notable and controversial examples of currency deflation. One was the deliberate reduction of Great Britain's money supply in 1925 to permit the country's return to the gold standard at the prewar parity. The result was high unemployment, resulting mainly from the inability of exporting industries to capture, at the old rate of exchange, sufficient markets and also from the tight internal monetary policy that was necessary to guard gold reserves in these circumstances. A more drastic deflationary policy was pursued in Germany after 1928. This was successful in correcting the balance of payments but led through bankruptcies to a collapse of credit, which in turn infected the banking system; the ultimate social and political effects were disastrous.

Deflation of money incomes is usually less a result of deliberate policy than it is a disease that most countries either catch from abroad through reduction in the demand for their exports or contract through some failure of internal expenditure, most commonly expenditure on capital investment. Such reductions in expenditure, from whatever quarter, have some effect in reducing prices; many prices, however, especially those of services and manufactured goods, tend to be inflexible, particularly in a downward direction, so that a reduction in demand leads to a decline in production rather than in price. In the Great Depression of the 1930s, by far the most serious yet experienced, output in the United States fell by about 30 percent between 1929 and 1933, while the general price level fell by only 22 or 23 percent. In examining the fluctuations of money income in Great Britain between 1870 and 1914, it is seen that about three-quarters of their amplitude is attributable to changes in the volume of production and only about a quarter to variation in the price level. That is why deflation, whether deliberately induced or suffered involuntarily, has such unpleasant associations; in the short term (a qualification that must be stressed), it tends to mean a fall in income and employment rather than in the level of prices.

Effects of inflation and deflation. The short-term effect of deflation, in the sense of reduction in expenditure, is thus in large part to reduce production and employment; similarly, the short-term effect of increases of expenditure is normally to increase employment and production, as well as (generally after varying intervals) prices and wage rates. Both deflation and inflation, however, can come, immediately, from impulses other than changes in expenditure. Deflation, in the sense of an influence tending to reduce prices, can come, for instance, from a reduction in the world price levels of the commodities that a country imports, as happened in Great Britain in the late 19th century. The effect of this, by itself, on real income is clearly favourable, since the prices of imported goods for domestic use are lowered. There are also likely to be favourable effects on production, since consumers' purchasing power is increased, profits are raised, and the stage is set generally for the encouragement of domestic investment. Unfortunately, because these conditions often go with reduced purchasing power in the countries that supply the cheaper imports, they become poorer customers.

Effects on production and employment

If an inflationary influence takes the form of a rise in wage rates (perhaps from vigorous trade-union activity), one effect may be to put pressure on profits and thus to discourage industrial investment (as in Great Britain and a number of other countries in 1970–71). This is not inevitably the case: since wage increases are eventually spent, their effect on total demand may offset their effect on profits unless they put the country at a substantial competitive disadvantage in foreign markets. The effects of inflationary and deflationary influences on the level of economic activity thus depend, sometimes in complex ways, on the precise circumstances. The same is true, to some extent, of policy measures that operate primarily upon the supply of money. An increase in the supply of money generally tends to raise expenditure and activity (if the latter is not already at a physical maximum); but a good deal depends on who holds the money, and, in some circumstances, the influence of easy monetary conditions seems to be weak. The effect of monetary stringency in reducing activity is rather more certain, but it is far from being a precise instrument of policy (see MONEY).

The effects of inflation and deflation on the distribution of income within a country similarly depend on the nature of the forces at work. All that can be said for certain is that price inflation reduces the share in the national income of those sections of the community whose money incomes are permanently fixed (*e.g.*, bondholders) or adjust to rising prices slowly and with difficulty. Deflation has the opposite effects. As between wage earners and profit receivers, the balance in an inflation can swing either way. Sometimes aggressive union bargaining is able to keep wages a jump ahead of prices and profits. Sometimes, as in war booms or investment booms, new purchasing power flows first into the hands of public authorities or private corporations, and prices tend to be pushed up ahead of wages. The fact that inflation favours debtors and penalizes creditors tends, if inflation is expected to continue, to be reflected in high interest rates. The rates rarely prove high enough to offset the effects of the inflation. Indeed, when expectations of inflation become universal, they lead to the self-reinforcing phenomena that have been examined above (see *Types of inflation*).

The influences of inflation and deflation on a country's balance of payments, though rather less complex, are not entirely free from ambiguity. Because the balance of payments on current account is identical with the difference between the aggregate value of the goods and services a country produces and that of those it absorbs, it follows

Effects on the balance of payments

that increased internal demand for its products must worsen a country's current balance unless production increases—which is less likely as plant and manpower become more fully utilized. In the absence of rigid controls, increasing internal demand must eventually either draw in additional imports or absorb resources previously used for producing exports. On the other hand, inflation of the level of wages and other costs is less certain in its effects. Raising the price of a country's goods in relation to those of other countries will even improve its balance of payments if the physical volume of its exports is not much reduced and that of its imports not much increased. Only if these volumes are responsive to changes in relative price will a deterioration in the balance follow. Experience suggests that they generally are sufficiently responsive for this to happen but that the response takes some time to come about.

Certain inflationary policies may, in the longer run, accelerate the growth of an economy. When new money flows first into the hands of firms or government agencies that use it to purchase plant and equipment, and the increase of wages lags somewhat behind that of prices, the effect is to divert resources to capital investment; if the capital developments are well chosen, the rate of increase of the economy's productive capacity and income will be raised. Rapid price inflations, however, may encourage kinds of capital investment that are not conducive to the growth of real income—the building of luxurious housing, for example. There is no direct relationship between the rate of price inflation and the rate of economic growth. In Latin America, for example, every conceivable combination of growth or stagnation on the one hand and rapid price inflation or relative price stability on the other was to be seen in the years after World War II.

CAUSES AND MECHANISMS

From a more theoretical view, at least four basic schemata commonly used in considerations of inflation and deflation can be distinguished.

The quantity theory. The first of these and the oldest is the view that the level of prices is determined by the quantity of money. The ratio of the stock of money that people want to hold to the value of the transactions they perform each year (or the inverse of this ratio, called the velocity of circulation) is supposed, in the simplest version of this view, to be fixed by such factors as the frequency of wage payments, the structure of the economy, and saving and shopping habits. So long as these remain constant, the price level will be directly proportional to the supply of money and inversely proportional to the physical volume of production. This is the celebrated quantity theory, going back at least as far as David Hume in the 18th century. But the theory assumes that productive capacity is fully employed, or nearly so. Since, in fact, the extent to which productive capacity is used varies a great deal—indeed, sometimes more than the level of prices—the quantity theory fell into disfavour between World Wars I and II, when the level of activity provided more reasons for anxiety than did the long-run movement of prices.

Money and prices

In a refined version, the quantity theory was revived by Milton Friedman and other University of Chicago economists in the 1950s and 1960s. Their basic contentions were that short-period changes of the money supply are, in fact, followed (after a varying interval) by changes in money income and that the velocity of circulation, though it fluctuates to some extent with the money supply, tends to be fairly stable, especially over long periods. From this, they concluded that the money supply, while not a reliable instrument for controlling short-term movements in the economy, can be effective in controlling longer term movements of the price level and that the prescription for stable prices is to increase the money supply regularly at a rate equal to that at which the economy is estimated to be expanding.

Against this, it has been argued that in highly developed economies the supply of money varies largely with the demand for it and that the authorities have little power to vary the supply through purely monetary controls. The correlations observed by this so-called Chicago school between money supply and money income are attributed by their critics to variations in the demand for money to spend, which elicit partial responses from supply and are followed after an interval by corresponding changes in money income. The relative stability of the velocity of circulation is attributed by them to the facility with which the supply of money accommodates itself to demand; they argue that insofar as supply may be restricted in the face of rising demand, velocity will increase, or (what really amounts to the same thing) new sources of credit, such as trade credit, will be exploited.

The Keynesian theory. The second basic approach is represented by J.M. Keynes's theory of income determination. The key to it is the assumption that consumers tend to spend a fixed proportion of any increases they receive in their incomes. For any level of national income, therefore, there is a gap of a predictable size between income and consumption expenditure, and to establish and maintain that level of national income it is only necessary to fix expenditure on all nonconsumption goods and services at such a level as to fill the gap. Apart from government outlays, the main constituent of this nonconsumption expenditure is private investment. Keynes supposed investment to be fairly sensitive to the rate of interest. The latter, in turn, he supposed to be negatively related, up to a point, to the stocks of "idle" money in existence—in effect, positively related to the velocity of circulation of money. He held, moreover, that there is a floor below which long-term interest rates will not fall, however low the velocity of circulation. These relationships between interest and idle money (or the velocity of circulation) have been pretty well supported empirically (see INCOME AND EMPLOYMENT THEORY).

Determinants of national income

The chief importance of the Keynesian approach and various elaborations of it is that they provide a framework in which governments can endeavour to manage the level of activity in the economy by varying their own expenditures and receipts or by influencing the level of private investment. This has been a principal basis of policy in many industrialized countries in recent decades. Difficulties in practice have sprung from uncertainty about, or changes in, the underlying quantitative relationships and the existence of uncertain time lags in their operation, which make it hard to deal effectively with unforeseen contingencies. The uncertainty and weakness of the relation between interest rates and private investment are another source of difficulty. Many economists believe, however, that the approach has led to better control over short-term changes in employment and real income.

In the form in which it has just been stated, however, the Keynesian approach does not offer much insight into movements of the price level. The simplest variant of it that will do so is based on the view that inflation arises entirely from attempts to buy more goods and services than can, physically, be supplied—*i.e.*, more than can be produced at the "full employment" level of activity. If, for example, government expenditure is higher than the difference between production and consumption at the level corresponding to full employment, there is an "inflationary gap." The working of the market process closes this gap by a bidding up of prices to the point at which the difference between income and consumption, in money terms, is big enough to accommodate the government expenditure. (In an economy open to foreign trade, the gap may be closed wholly or in part by the creation of an import surplus). The theory fails to account for the experience in the decades after World War II of continuous inflation in conditions that do not suggest the existence of an inflationary gap.

The "cost–push" theory. A third approach in the analysis of inflation assumes that prices of goods are basically determined by their costs, whereas supplies of money are responsive to demand. In these circumstances, increasing costs may create an inflationary pressure that becomes continuous through the operation of the "price–wage spiral." The supposition is that wage earners and profit receivers (neglecting for the moment other groups in the

Wages and inflation

economy) aspire to incomes that add up to more than the total value of their production at full employment. One or both groups must, therefore, be dissatisfied at any given time. The wage earners, if dissatisfied, demand wage increases. These are conceded (at least in part) by employers in the course of the bargaining process, initially at the expense of profits. Later, employers increase prices to reflect their higher costs, and, while this restores profits, it also reduces wage earners' real incomes, sowing the seeds of a further round of wage demands. If the supply of money were fixed, this process would lead to increasing monetary stringency; it would become increasingly difficult to finance increases in wages and purchases of goods the prices of which had just been raised or, indeed, to finance production and distribution generally—though, as noted earlier, there are some circumstances in which the velocity of circulation can rise drastically and make a limited money stock go a long way. In practice, money supply responds to demand, partly because monetary authorities do not wish to see the dislocation of capital markets that would follow if monetary stringency produced very large rises in rates of interest.

In the 1960s, there was much discussion of a relation named after the British economist A.W. Phillips (though in a rudimentary form it can be traced to earlier writers), whereby the rate of increase of wages was shown to vary negatively with the level of unemployment. This can be interpreted as signifying that the price–wage spiral proceeds more rapidly at high levels of economic activity than at low ones. The empirical evidence for the "Phillips curve" was not entirely satisfactory; in Great Britain, in particular, the relationship seemed disconcertingly inconsistent in 1967 and some later years. The hopes that had been excited in some quarters that a higher but still politically tolerable level of unemployment would reduce or end inflation were shaken by the rapid wage inflation that occurred during a time of recession in 1970–71.

The structural theory. The fourth basic approach to the inflationary process is not entirely independent of some of those just discussed; its distinguishing feature is its emphasis on structural maladjustment in the economy. One version of it depends upon the simple proposition that resistance to reductions of money wages is so strong that they hardly ever take place. If this is so, then all adjustments of wages to take account of relative changes in the supply of, and demand for, labour in different industries or occupations have to be accomplished through the absolute raising of all wages except those of the group of workers whose market position is weakest. The rate of wage inflation as a whole is then seen as proportional to the rate of structural change in the economy.

Inflation in developing countries

Another version, held to be appropriate to some developing countries, focusses on the gap between imports and exports. Imports tend to increase faster in those countries (because of the rising demand for manufactured goods) than the ability of the traditional exporting industries to pay for them. Difficulty is experienced in substituting home manufactures for imports, partly because home markets are often too small to support the required industries and partly because the development of manufacturing itself requires extensive imports of machinery and structural materials. Consequently, there is a continuous downward pressure on the international value of the country's currency; this is felt in a continuous upward pressure on the country's internal prices. Alternatively, inflation in such countries may result from social and political pressures to provide employment for the overflow into the towns of a rapidly growing rural population; since there is a shortage of savings, this leads to excessive creation of new credit in one way or another and thus to a straightforward "demand–pull" inflation. The chronic inflationary tendencies in some Latin-American countries have been attributed to mechanisms of these kinds.

Since 1939 the threat of inflation has loomed much larger than that of deflation in the world as a whole, and the efforts of economists have been directed to analyzing the former rather than the latter. The most generally accepted explanation of income deflation remains the Keynesian one (in various elaborations); in this view, income deflation will also lead to price deflation as economic activity slows down. Falling prices may also come about as the result of rising productivity: if output per man-hour rises faster than money wage rates, prices will tend to fall. For a long time after World War II, the Soviet Union was able, by central planning, to keep wages and incomes from rising faster than productivity; and some writers hold that increases in productivity were an important factor in the downward trend of world prices in the 19th century.

BIBLIOGRAPHY. The classic account of the German inflation after World War I, with much material on other inflations up to that time, is CONSTANTINO BRESCIANI-TURRONI, *Le Vicende del marco tedesco* (1931; Eng. trans., *The Economics of Inflation*, 1937). A general account of inflation in Europe after World War I is presented in the LEAGUE OF NATIONS, *The Course and Control of Inflation* (1946). Inflationary experience throughout the world between 1939 and 1951 is analyzed in A.J. BROWN, *The Great Inflation: 1939–1951* (1955). West European and North American experience is dealt with in WILLIAM FELLNER *et al.*, *The Problem of Rising Prices* (1961) and ORGANIZATION FOR ECONOMIC CO-OPERATION AND DEVELOPMENT, *Inflation: The Present Problem* (1970). The relationship between inflation and growth is discussed by GEOFFREY MAYNARD in *Economic Development and the Price Level* (1962); and by DUDLEY SEERS in "A Theory of Inflation and Growth in Under-Developed Economies Based on the Experience of Latin America," *Oxford Economic Papers*, New Series, 14:173–195 (1962). The most comprehensive survey of the literature of the theory of inflation is MARTIN BRONFENBRENNER and FRANKLYN D. HOLZMAN, "A Survey of Inflation Theory," in *Surveys of Economic Theory*, vol. 1 (1965), which contains an excellent bibliography. Inflation theory as a whole is discussed in A.J. HAGGER, *The Theory of Inflation* (1964); a more general account, with reference to experience mainly in the United States, Great Britain, and the Soviet Union, is THOMAS WILSON, *Inflation* (1961). Two important theoretical works are: BENT HANSEN, *A Study in the Theory of Inflation* (1951); and HAROLD K. CHARLESWORTH, *The Economics of Repressed Inflation* (1956). A useful account of world price movements from 1820 to 1933 is WALTER T. LAYTON and GEOFFREY CROWTHER, *An Introduction to the Study of Prices*, 3rd ed. (1938).

(A.J.B.)

Information Processing

This article cuts across many disciplines, technologies, and activities concerned with processing information for organization, storage, communication, and use. For information on library classification systems, such as the Dewey Decimal and Universal Decimal systems, see LIBRARY SCIENCE. For information on the computer, its methods of operation, and the social implications of its use in information processing, see COMPUTERS.

Information processing includes most human activity in which language plays a part. Graphics are an adjunct to language; and books, photographs, diagrams, formulas, and maps are among the many graphical forms used to display language. Information is also stored, displayed, and transmitted in many ways other than by graphical processes and by voice and gesture. A phonograph record, a magnetic tape, a punched card, and a gene are only a few of the many other physical forms for information storage.

Physical forms for information storage

Information can always be restated completely and accurately in natural language. Patent diagrams, musical scores, mathematical and chemical formulas, and photographs, for example, can be scanned by optical electronic devices to produce magnetic-tape records as a sequence of magnetized and nonmagnetized spots. These sequences can then be fully described by lengthy sentences.

The information revolution and knowledge explosion. The information revolution comprises the tremendous technological advances made during the past few centuries in human capabilities to encode, record, reproduce, and disseminate information. New technologies for preserving and transmitting aural and visual information have greatly increased information-processing capacity. The electronic computer, together with its peripheral equipment, provides electromechanical capability for modifying and reprocessing stored information to produce vast new stores of information.

The information revolution produced a knowledge explosion. Advances in the development and use of computerized information-processing networks, some of them on a worldwide basis, suggest not only further "explosion" of knowledge but revolutionary steps in generation and reorganization, storage, and distribution. Tutorial instruction in several subjects, bibliographical literature searches, scientific and engineering calculations, translation of technical material from one natural language to another, and playing games, such as chess and checkers, against a computer programmed as an expert opponent are examples of the many capabilities—in various stages of development—of existing information-processing networks. Anything that can be done anywhere in the world with any computing system could now be done at any standard teletypewriter or other operator's console—provided that the communications connections have been made and the computer files and programs modified to permit general access from remote points.

Information network capabilities

Information: the new basic resource. All of these technological advances together have made information a new basic resource that supplements the familiar natural resources of matter and energy. Accumulated world knowledge takes on an entirely new meaning and significance as techniques for mining, storing, sharing, and using information in new ways are learned. Knowledge in the form of newly stored information is not degraded or destroyed with use.

Stores of information represent a new kind of transactable commodity, ranking in future human importance alongside material and energy resources. Control of information stores and processing facilities may well become more important than material and energy resources as a source of social and economic power. This situation may lead to a wider dispersal of human power, as suggested above, and to a reduction in importance of the few specialists who hold power merely because of special knowledge. Easy access to knowledge could become a great equalizer among traditionally unequal intellectual competitors, just as firepower has sometimes served to equalize otherwise unequal physical competitors. (M.M.F.)

INFORMATION MEDIA

Considered below are both the primary forms of information, those in which the records are first disseminated; and the secondary forms, which result from their further analysis, description, and synthesis.

Conventional primary media. Primary media can be classified according to the physical forms in which the information appears (that is, as printed, auditory, or visual media) and, again, according to their format (as textbooks, monographs, periodicals or journals, or as report literature or reprints).

The scholarly journal. The most important form in which new information is disseminated is the learned, scholarly, or scientific periodical or journal. The journal was developed in the beginning of modern science about the middle of the 17th century, when the need arose for rapid dissemination of brief reports on the experiments and observations that were beginning to engage the attention of a part of the scholarly community. The early scientific journals were as much news media as the contemporary newspapers in which they found their models; they more closely resembled modern abstract and review journals than modern primary journals. The antecedents of the journal paper, or article, are not clear; it seems likely that it developed out of the paper prepared for oral delivery before a scholarly society and subsequently published in the society's proceedings, or perhaps it came out of the prize essay that the early societies developed to stimulate and recognize achievements in observation and experiment or to present summaries of the state of knowledge in a particular field. The scientific paper early took on a well-prescribed format that has been more or less traditionally honoured through the ages. The classical scientific paper is said to proceed with the stately dignity of a minuet from the statement of a problem, to a discussion of its background and history, to a review of the literature on the subject (documented with references or citations to the original papers), to a statement of the methodology followed in the experiment or observation, to a report of the results found and the conclusions to be drawn from these results, along with an indication of necessity for future research on the subject—the whole followed by a summary in the form of a coda, which recapitulates all the preceding elements.

Beginnings of the scholarly journal

Format of the scientific paper

The scholarly journal developed both as a vehicle for disseminating information in the form of articles and papers and as a repository of official records that formed a basis for generalizations in science. It developed as an open record in which each scholar submitted his findings and observations to his fellow scientists for their review and criticism. The scholarly journal as it is known today, however, contains not only reports of original research or original observations but also administrative and personal news relating to the special subject or society with which it is associated, abstracts of papers appearing in other media, book reviews, and reports of meetings. Various names are attached to these periodicals, all of which point either to the periodic way in which they are issued or to their historical origins—"bulletin," "journal," "proceedings," "transactions," and the equivalents and cognates in all languages.

Beginning with two journals that started publication in 1665, the number of scientific periodicals has grown to huge proportions, although estimates vary considerably, from 25,000 to over 100,000 titles. The amount of redundancy in this mass is not easy to estimate; it is equally difficult to determine how much of the volume represents important, significant, or even new contributions to knowledge. Analysis revealed that of some 13,000 journals received by one major research library, only about 4,000 could be considered both substantive for, and within the scope of, that collection.

The problem of the proliferation of the literature has traditionally been met by scholars narrowing their fields of interest, that is, by increasing the degree of specialization. Specialization of subject interest, and therefore of communications vehicles or journals, follows two general patterns: fragmentation, in which a subject establishes its own organs apart from the subject with which it has been associated in the past (*e.g.*, when biochemistry or physiological chemistry separated from physiology), and synthesis, in which specialists from different disciplines—for example physics and biology—find common ground in their mutual interest in a problem such as the flow of fluids through restricted channels. The biologist is interested in this subject because of its application to the circulation of blood, the engineer, because it relates to interests such as the industrial transport of fluids. A new subject and a new vehicle with which to exchange information among the workers in that field was thus created and entitled biorheology.

Fragmentation and synthesis

Alternatives to the scientific journal have been proposed. One of the most far-reaching and persistent proposals is to use the separate paper as a primary unit for dissemination and to develop techniques for distributing papers either on demand or to subscribers on the basis of an established reader-interest profile. To some extent these proposals reflect the present widespread use of reprints and preprints of scientific papers. Preprints are sometimes prepared in advance of presentation of a paper before a scientific society, or in advance of publication, for distribution either on demand or to a selected group of the author's colleagues or peers. Most scientific papers are published without payment to the author; in many cases, the author is assessed some of the costs of printing. He usually accepts this as an obligation to his discipline because no research can be considered completed until it has been entered into the record. The author is usually given a number of copies or reprints of the article, which he may distribute to those who request them, having learned of the article's existence through

Alternatives to the scientific journal

secondary information media (see below) or by means of end references in other articles; or the author may use reprints to inform a group of coworkers.

Report literature. Another method of distribution is the so-called unpublished report of sponsored research; the contractor, or grantee, is usually required to submit periodic reports to the grantor (governmental, academic, or industrial) on the progress of his work. These reports are "unpublished" in the sense that they are not printed initially in any periodical—the "open" literature—but are duplicated for distribution either on request or to a mailing list. They are frequently issued in series, each containing a single report or review and, in some instances, restricted to a readership with an established "need to know"—for example, classified reports designated "secret" or "confidential." Separate mechanisms for indexing and distributing these reports have been developed.

Importance of unpublished reports

Unpublished reports are of considerably more significance in industrial research and development than in basic research; and in certain fields, such as biology and medicine, they have been very little used. It has been said that 90 percent of the reports on developmental research contain little information of interest to anyone not intimately concerned with the project. The significant part of the report literature is in most cases rewritten for publication in the open literature.

Information-exchange groups, newsletters, and other media. Information-exchange groups and newsletters developed as a response to both publication delays and new interdisciplinary groupings. Information-exchange groups, in a way, hark back to the early days of modern science, when scientific workers often exchanged observations and reports by letter, sometimes through a corresponding secretary who may have been self-appointed or who served one of the scholarly societies. Modern information-exchange groups have been set up so that a member of the group can send a report of his work to a designated central agency, which then duplicates it and dispatches it to other members. These reports have the status of private communications and can be so cited in the literature. Newsletters are also issued in a large number of fields to subscribers or to a selected mailing list.

Nonconventional primary media. There is a prevalent feeling that new mechanisms are needed to make information more readily accessible and that better techniques are needed to channel it to the ultimate consumer. Radio is still an effective medium for this purpose, and primary information can be disseminated and also stored and retrieved by means of audio discs and tapes. Audio tapes and discs are being used in some cases as auxiliary publication forms to books and journals, particularly when it is difficult if not impossible to transmit the information in any other way; an example is the interpretation of heart sounds. Some audio-tape and disc publication media also represent secondary publication in the forms of abstracts and reviews of the literature in a particular field; they can also represent primary publication—for example, when original panel discussions, conferences, or lectures are recorded for subsequent duplication and distribution.

Information on film

Motion-picture films also represent a medium for dissemination of original information that lends itself primarily to visual presentation, but in most cases films are used principally as teaching mediums. Film has been used extensively also to store images of text in miniaturized form, as on reels as microfilm, or in some kind of sheet form, as microcards or microfiche, for ease in duplication, storage, and dissemination. Except in very few cases, film has not been used widely as a medium of primary distribution. One example is the Library of American Civilization, a retrospective collection on ultramicrofiche of the full original text of about 20,000 titles, published by Library Resources, Inc., a division of Encyclopædia Britannica, Inc.

Many national government agencies and international bodies such as the General Assembly of the United Nations have placed reports and proceedings on microfiche. Efforts have been made toward establishing standard size and reduction ratios, and reading devices for enlarging the image and for printing it on paper have been developed.

Information on magnetic tapes

Magnetic tapes with information in digital form—that is, magnetic dots that are recorded on a coated plastic ribbon and are read and processed by computers—have not yet been used extensively as a primary publication medium. The development of computer-assisted composing equipment, in which the full text of a document is initially stored on magnetic tape, suggests a potential for primary distribution in this medium. It has been predicted that, with the development of new modes of recording and storing information in electronic and miniaturized forms, the printing press may one day cease to dominate the dissemination of information as it does today. The publishing business may gradually be transferred into an information-processing business. It does not seem likely, however, that the printed page will be supplanted in the near future as the paramount method of information storage and dissemination. It is versatile, and it offers economic advantages that few other media approach.

Secondary media—conventional and nonconventional. As the size of a literature grows, the greater becomes the necessity for developing techniques for searching it. The earliest scientific journals, the *Journal des Sçavans* (1665) and the *Philosophical Transactions* of the Royal Society of London (1665), were in a sense abstract and review media that referred to primary publications in other forms. One of the earliest examples of a periodical devoted exclusively to extracting parts of other publications was the *Aufrichtige und unpartheyische Gedancken* ("Sincere and Unbiased Thought"), two volumes of which appeared between 1714 and 1717. During the course of the years a vast system of systems, national and international, has grown up to cope with the problem of indexing and abstracting the literature and of providing data compilations, reviews, and synthesis. The "system" in most countries grew piecemeal, as agencies and services were established to process some segment of the literature as the need arose. The result is a conglomeration of information-processing activities that range widely in subject matter and represent varying degrees of coverage up to the hundreds of thousands of items covered by major indexing and abstracting services such as the *Index Medicus*, the *Bibliography of Agriculture*, *Biological Abstracts*, the *Referativnyi zhurnaly*, and the *Bulletin Signalétique*.

Descriptive and informative abstracts

Abstracts. Traditionally, abstracts have been in two forms: the descriptive abstract, which provides an indication of the information contained in the original communication beyond that provided by the title of the article, and the informative abstract, which usually tries to present all the significant data in the original article. The descriptive, or indicative, abstract ideally should provide the investigator with enough clues to inform him whether the original article will have sufficient information or data pertinent to his inquiry to justify his consulting it. There is a vast proliferation of abstracting services. Broad ones cover whole disciplines, such as chemistry and biology; narrow ones cover such subjects as microelectronics, nuclear resonance, and rare earths. Most specialty journals, the primary purpose of which is to issue original contributions, also supply their readers with reviews or abstracts of recent periodical literature in the specialty. These may range from a few selected abstracts covering some significant recent papers to comprehensive abstracting services that assume an identity quite apart from the original journal; an example of the latter is the *International Abstract of Surgery*, which is published in conjunction with the journal *Surgery, Gynecology and Obstetrics*. Most of the major countries have their own complexes of abstracting services, and they cover the whole range of contemporary knowledge. Such abstracting services are also utilized internationally. Despite the huge overlap of abstracting efforts, the overlap is never absolute. In the United States, *Chemical Abstracts* provides a major abstracting service; published by the American Chemical Society since 1907, it covers more than 200,000 articles a year. *Biological Abstracts*, published since 1926, abstracts more than 100,000 articles a year. British abstracting services include *Nutrition Abstracts and Reviews*, published in Aberdeen since 1931, and *Physics Abstracts* (*Science Abstracts*, Section A), published in London since 1898.

At least two countries have attempted to coordinate and centralize many of their abstracting efforts into a single agency. The Centre de Documentation du Centre National de la Recherche in Paris publishes the *Bulletin Signalétique* in 22 numbered sections and several unnumbered sections covering such subjects as aeronautics, medical entomology, and telecommunications. The Soviet Union has two centralized agencies. The Institute of Scientific Information of the Academy of Sciences, established in 1950, publishes a series of 40 or more *Referativnyi zhurnaly*, some of very large size; the biological section rivals *Biological Abstracts*, with over 150,000 abstracts. In medicine, the Soviet Ministry of Health also publishes a series of *Meditsinskii referativnyi zhurnaly*, similar to the *Excerpta Medica* series published in Amsterdam, which abstracts, in English and in 30 or more sections, a part of the world's literature in medicine.

Abstracts appear in a large variety of forms—card, slip, or fiche form, periodical form, and in hard-cover books—and usually require some auxiliary form of arrangement or indexing to make them readily accessible. They are usually issued or published in a classed arrangement by major-subject groupings, which sometimes makes it necessary to search through a large group of abstracts to find the few that are sought. Card or slip-form services can of course be arranged manually in subject grouping according to a scheme supplied with the system or of the user's own choosing. Abstracts may also be processed by machine if they are reproduced on some kind of machine-readable form, as edge-notched or punched cards. With periodical and book-form abstract services, an index is usually supplied.

Abstracting by machine

Techniques of abstracting by machine tried experimentally have been based on mechanized analysis of the frequency of terms in a text. Those parts of the texts in which the terms are embodied are then selected to provide an "auto-abstract." The magnetic tapes generated in the processing of texts can also be made available for searching on computers at other information-processing centres.

Reviews. A review is an integrated and organized discussion of the literature pertaining to a well-defined subject; it may define the scientific objectives of the field under examination, examine prevailing concepts or hypotheses, and comment critically on the state of existing knowledge. It usually covers a limited period of time, frequently the period since the last comprehensive review appeared. Like abstracts, reviews may be either descriptive or critical. They are valued particularly when they provide thoughtful evaluations of the contributions made in the field and attempt to place them in some kind of relationship to each other. In many fields this operation is done systematically by publishing reviews either in the primary journals in the subject or in periodicals specifically dedicated to this purpose.

Reference books, handbooks, and manuals. Under the rubrics "reference books," "manuals," and "handbooks" could be named a great many different kinds of data collections and evaluative and interpretive surveys of available information. These range from the short monograph or series of data tables covering small aspects of a single subject to encyclopaedic surveys that attempt to bring together available information from a broad universe of knowledge into a comprehensive work (see ENCYCLOPAEDIA). There are voluminous works of this kind in many special fields, some of them published over many years and with revisions of sections or completely new editions from time to time. Sometimes these comprehensive surveys are issued in loose-leaf form, which may be kept current by supplements and replacements for superseded sections. Loose-leaf services are also available with some data-compiling services as well as with comprehensive treatises. On the whole, compilations of data tend to differ from other publications in form because they lend themselves to tabular arrangements and cumulative publication; examples are the tables of constants provided in various fields and the tables for the identification of compounds in chemistry. (D.A.K.)

STORAGE AND RETRIEVAL

Indexes and indexing. A familiar form of index is a list of words or phrases at the end of a book, each word or phrase being associated with the page numbers on which it appears in the text. More generally, an index consists first of an ordered set of words and phrases, called headings, the ordering principle usually being alphabetic. Subheadings may be listed in alphabetic order under main headings, and cross references from one heading to another may be present. Next, each heading or subheading is associated with a designator of the location within a body of literature (which may include many books and periodicals) of information related in some way (for example, by subject) to that heading. This association is essential, for "index" means "to point out" or serve as a guide to location.

Information provided by an index

The heading and location designation are in general accompanied by additional information of two kinds: (1) that which qualifies, or specifies, the particular sense in which the heading is used at the designated location, or which gives the context in which it is used—as in a concordance; (2) that which briefly describes the book or article containing the requested information—often, title and author.

Thus, an index serves to guide its user to the information he seeks and at the same time usually provides some basis for screening or selection before the page or document containing the information is itself sought. Principally an index directs the inquirer to a specific piece of information, but it may also make known to him related items of information brought together by the proximity of their headings. In general, however, items related by subject may appear at points widely scattered in an alphabetic listing. A good index should in that case carry cross references from each one to each of the others and so minimize the disadvantages of such scattering. With the object of bringing together more effectively related material, some indexes are ordered according to a classificatory scheme rather than alphabetically. A classified index is in general more difficult to use than is an alphabetic index. In principle, a well-designed index can incorporate the advantages of both types of arrangement.

Attempts to identify principles and to formulate a theory of indexing have not resulted in any widely accepted and substantive body of knowledge. Subject indexing remains an ill-defined process. Variations exist in opinion and in practice, and experimental tests have shown that great inconsistency often arises even when two indexers apply the same system to the same document.

Early indexes

Published indexes. Book indexing began at least as early as the 16th century. By the end of the 18th, its value had become widely recognized and the practice well established. Many authors and professional bibliographers took pride in compiling a good index, and a body of rules for indexing had by then taken form. In 1878 the Index Society was formed in London, with Henry Wheatley as secretary. The first publication of the society, in that same year, was Wheatley's *What Is an Index?* This 132-page book traces the early history of indexing, contains many references to particular book indexes and opinions of scholars about indexing, outlines rules governing the practice of indexing (rules of compilation, arrangement, and printing), and presents an annotated preliminary list of English indexes. The style of writing is anecdotal and rambling to the point of distraction, but Wheatley's book contains much valuable information.

Wheatley credits the law profession, particularly Sir Henry Thring, for early recognition of the absolute need for indexes and for drawing up and publishing some "masterly instructions" for an "Index to the Statute Law" (*Law Magazine*, vol. 8, p. 491 [August 1877]). In his section on rules of compilation, Wheatley quotes from Thring's instructions:

The basis of an index to a book of the ordinary kind is a series of titles or catch-words arranged in alphabetical order and indicative of the main topics treated of in the book.

The object of an index is to indicate the place in a book or collection of books in which particular information is to be found. Such an index is perfect in proportion as it is concise in expression, whilst exhaustive in its indication of every important topic of the subject to which it is an index. . . .

A complete knowledge of the whole *law* is required before [the indexer] begins to make the index, for until he can look down on the entire field of law before him, he cannot possibly judge of the proper arrangement of the headings, or of the relative importance of the various provisions.

The greatest value of Wheatley's book probably lies in the compendium of early indexes that it presents. Among those mentioned as notable in some respect are:

Concordance of the Bible, compiled by Hugo de St. Caro [*sic*], 1247; possibly qualifies as the earliest index in the presently accepted sense of the word: "five hundred monks are said to have been employed upon it."

First English concordance of the New Testament, printed by Thomas Gybson, 1536 (the earliest index in English mentioned by Wheatley).

English concordance of entire Bible, compiled by John Marbeck, 1550.

A Complete Concordance to the Holy Scriptures of the Old and New Testaments by Alexander Cruden, 1737. "Most of the Concordances published since are founded upon Cruden."

An index to Boccaccio in *Le Ricchezze della Lingua volgare*. Compiled by Francis Alunno, 1545.

Juan de Pineda's *Monarchia Ecclesiastica o historia Universal del Mundo*, Salamanca, 1588; contains a "full and admirably-constructed" index, among the earliest.

Prynne's *Histrio-mastix*, 1633, an early index more readable than the book itself.

Pope's *Homer* contains a "curious poetical index to the Iliad . . . referring to all the places in which similes are used."

A Collection of the moral and instructive Sentiments, Maxims, Cautions and Reflexions contained in the Histories of Pamela, Clarissa and Sir Charles Grandison, digested under proper heads, compiled by Samuel Richardson, 1755.

A General Index to the Spectators, Tatlers and Guardians, compiled by Sir Richard Steele, 1757.

A General Index to the twenty-three volumes of the Parliamentary or Constitutional History of England, compiled by W. Sandby, 1761.

The Statutes at Large, from Magna Charta to 1761, index compiled by Danby Pickering, 1769.

Bibliotheca Botanica, Bibliotheca Anatomica, Bibliotheca Chirurgica, and *Bibliotheca Medicinae Practicae*, all compiled in the 1770s by the great physiologist Albrecht von Haller, exemplifying the importance that he attached to indexing.

A General Index to the Philosophical Transactions (Royal Society), for the first 70 volumes, compiled by P.H. Maty, 1787.

Repertorium Commentationum a Societatibus Literariis editarum, 1800–20, a 16-volume (quarto) index "classified according to the chief divisions of knowledge," compiled by Reuss.

The Complete Concordance to Shakspere, compiled by Mrs. Cowden Clarke, 1845; superseded earlier concordances.

Shakespeare-Lexicon, compiled by Alexander Schmidt, 1874.

The American Journal of Science and Arts, general index to 49 volumes, compiled by B. Silliman and B. Silliman, Jr., 1847; one of the very few American indexes mentioned by Wheatley.

The Encyclopædia Britannica, or Dictionary of Arts, Sciences and General Literature, 8th ed., index by James Duncan, 1860.

Wheatley lists many other concordances and indexes of "Particular Books, Atlases, Publications of Societies, Periodicals, Statutes, Journals of the Houses of Lords and Commons, and Parliamentary Papers." His book contains in all likelihood the first "catalog" or compendium of indexes ever published.

It seems unlikely that any one index will ever be widely agreed upon as being the earliest, for this distinction depends very much on definition and specifications. In "Early Indexing Techniques: A Study of Several Book Indexes of the Fourteenth, Fifteenth, and Early Sixteenth Centuries" (*The Library Quarterly*, vol. xxxv, no. 3, pp. 141–148 [July 1965; University of Chicago Press]), Francis J. Witty concluded that manuscripts exhibiting alphabetic indexing appeared no earlier than the 14th century and cited a similar conclusion reached by Lloyd W. Daly. The same article does make reference, however, to medieval works that "might be considered as indexes" and cites as examples the 8th-century *Sacra parallela* of St. John of Damascus (an alphabetic subject index to the Bible and the Fathers) and the *Milleloquia* of Augustine and Ambrose compiled by Bartholomew of Urbino, which consisted of quotations arranged alphabetically by subject. Witty goes on to comment in detail upon the indexes contained in two 14th-century manuscripts (Egidio Colonna's *Commentarius in primum sententiarum* and Pedanius Dioscorides' *De materia medica*, ed. by Max Wellman), an incunabulum (*Liber cronicarum* of Schedel, printed by Anton Koberger, 1493), and two books printed in the 16th century (Erasmus' edition of St. Augustine [printed by Froben, 1529] and Budé's *De asse et partibus* [the edition of 1541, printed by Vascosanus, Stephanus, and Roigny]). Three conclusions were reached by Witty as a result of this brief study:

Analysis of early indexing methods

First, the arrangement of entries was roughly alphabetical. The key words in the index were arranged alphabetically by their initial letters, but the strictness of the order hardly carried beyond the first syllable and certainly not to the end of the word. The key word dictating this arrangement might or might not be the first word of the entry.

Second, the most frequently employed analytical device was a catchword taken from the text. The majority of the early indexes are lists of sentences—often taken verbatim from the text—and arranged in order by the catchword. One indexer varied the practice of drawing entries from the main text by taking his entries from the marginal summaries accompanying the text. The general approach and appearance of these indexes remind one of the "key-word-in-context" idea, although evidence has not revealed that early indexers theorized about their practices.

Third, the index to the works of St. Augustine edited by Erasmus departed from the total reliance on catchwords to use subject headings. This practice was not a sixteenth-century innovation, because subject headings were used in two early medieval indexes to *authors* (not books). But the evidence at hand shows that before 1550 the use of subject headings for subject indexes to books was uncommon.

The transition from individual book indexes and periodical indexes to indexes that attempted to cover entire branches of disciplines or subjects, regardless of where published, took place in the 19th century.

Modern indexes

The modern history of indexing begins in 1848 when William F. Poole, while still an undergraduate at Yale University, implemented the notion of a single published index to numerous issues of numerous periodicals. The *Readers' Guide to Periodical Literature*, begun in 1900, carried forward this development and was especially significant in the emphasis that it placed on subject access and upon really useful cross references. It marked the beginning of an important series of published indexes such as the *Art Index*, *The Education Index*, *The Book Review Digest*, and *Social Sciences and Humanities Index*. Today, nearly 2,000 periodical indexes are published in more than 40 countries. Government agencies, such as national libraries, compile similar volumes. Mechanized data-processing techniques have been successfully applied to index making (see below *Mechanized storage and retrieval systems*).

The problems and process of indexing. As an approach to understanding the nature and problems of indexing, it is useful to consider the general process as divided into three operations:

1. The text is analyzed in order to select the concepts (or proper names) that seem to the indexer to be of potential interest to the users of the index.

2. The concepts, subjects, or words so identified may then require "translation" into some form of standard or controlled terminology, possibly utilizing a subject-

heading list or an authority list. Thesaurus-like arrangements of words have become widely recognized as important aids to this translation process.

3. Finally, the aggregate of index terms from the entire collection of material indexed must be compiled and arranged according to some set of filing rules.

Indexing exists only for the sake of retrieval, and it is, of course, reasonable to view the performance of indexing systems in that framework. There are two basic categories of failures that could be attributable to a deficient index, namely, the failure to discover information that is relevant to the purposes of the inquirer and the finding of information, pointed out by the index, that is not relevant to those purposes. Either type of failure can occur for a number of reasons, foremost among which is the richness and variety of language for expressing concepts and the concomitant impossibility of one indexer's bringing to bear on the first stage (the "concept selection") of the indexing process all conceivable points of view that a user might have at some future time.

Failures in indexing

The question of index phrase length remains prominent in attempts to develop a theoretical framework for indexing. If one wished, for example, to index information dealing with "hard soldering of aluminum alloys," index entries could appear in the following forms and, accordingly, at different points of an alphabetic ordering scheme:

hard soldering of aluminum alloys
soldering, hard, of aluminum alloys
aluminum alloys, hard soldering of
alloys, aluminum, hard soldering of

Other permutations are possible and probably just as reasonable. Each of the above entries is to a greater or lesser degree useful, depending on the point of view of the inquirer. Each brings the entry into proximity with a different set of possibly related entries. An important question, then, is whether the index should attempt to incorporate all reasonably likely points of view and place each entry in all corresponding positions or whether some preferred permutation of the terms can somehow be agreed upon. There seems to be neither evidence nor general agreement that a useful rule for establishing preferred order for the terms of the index entry can be developed, though efforts to do so nonetheless persist.

Coordinate indexing. The very important notion of coordinate indexing represents an approach to the problems of permutation and combination by avoiding them altogether at the indexing stage and permitting a "post-coordination" (*i.e.*, a specification of co-occurrence) of any combination of terms in the search process. This notion gained prominence with the introduction of Uniterm indexing around 1950. The basic hypothesis of Uniterm coordinate indexing is that, for practical purposes of finding specific information, one can dispense with the recording of relationships among words and index a document with a set of individual, relatively brief terms. In the search process, a document, in order to be retrieved, must contain some specified co-occurrence of index terms—whether or not such terms bear the intended relationship to one another.

Uniterm indexing

Thus, a document indexed "hard," "soldering," "aluminum," and "alloys" will be retrieved in response to a request for all documents described by any one, any two, any three, or all four of those terms. To illustrate the type of failure attributable to lack of relationships, that document would be retrieved in a search based on "hard" and "alloys," though it may be quite irrelevant if the inquirer's intent is to find information on "hard alloys." The fact that irrelevant retrieval can in principle occur through the accidental coordination of unrelated terms should not obscure the pragmatic question of whether this happens to an excessive extent. Any system of indexing and retrieval can be presumed to lead to some amount of irrelevant information, and the inquirer himself must finally judge the usefulness of what is retrieved and screen out material which does not serve his purpose.

The implications for the index itself of an approach that permits post-coordination of term combinations should be a very great reduction in the total number of terms, owing to the elimination of many pre-established combinations and through the elimination of much of the need for cross references. The extent of reduction realizable can be inferred from the results of converting a list of 49,000 Library of Congress subject headings and cross references to just 3,620 unit terms.

Reduction in index terms

Automatic indexing. Relatively simple and inexpensive forms of automatic indexing have reached the point of practical application as published "permuted-title" indexes. Words are selected from titles only and used as index headings. The resulting printed index is arranged so as to display the heading word in the context of the title from which it was selected; thus, a permuted-title index is a title concordance. Two of the major publications of this type are *Chemical Titles* and *Biological Abstracts Subjects in Context* (BASIC). The effectiveness of permuted-title indexing, as well as that of other forms of automatic indexing, is yet to be established. Opinion on the matter varies widely.

The cost of indexing, whether by man or machine, is a matter of some importance. If full text is to be automatically indexed, the cost of encoding it for machine use, for example, on punched cards, is very high. It is common practice in manual indexing to assign from 3 to 30 index terms per document, and the cost of this is much less than the cost of encoding full text, word by word.

If a very large number of index terms is to be assigned, it might reasonably be expected that machinelike diligence would be of considerable advantage. Yet one might not wish to forgo the merits of human judgment. The following prescription for a three-state process combines the advantages of human and machine skills, with due regard for controlling cost. (1) The first stage involves human selection of some relatively small portion (though large compared to the number of index terms normally assigned) of the entire text for indexing. This portion might reasonably include title, abstract (if any), section headings, and selected paragraphs. This initial step of "text reduction" is intended as an economic measure, and, though an element of human judgment is involved, it should not require a high level of skill or subject knowledge. The selected material is then encoded by means of a manual keypunching or keystroke operation. (2) The second stage should be a fully automatic selection and matching process, preferably using a thesaurus or word-and-phrase list as described earlier. (3) The final stage is proposed as a human review of the machine-assigned terms, with any augmentation, deletion, or editing that may be judged desirable, utilizing a high degree of skill and knowledge.

Combining man and machine

The economics of automatic indexing will no doubt be affected eventually by technological development in automatic print reading. When print-reading machines can accommodate to a large variety of type fonts and formats, and when their speed, cost, and reliability result in a sufficiently low cost per word of text read, then the initial manual selection and transcription process can be bypassed.

Citation indexing. Most scientific and scholarly articles cite references to other articles. In this way a link or association, often a subject relationship, is established between an article and each of those it cites. Such links represent the author's judgment that certain other articles would probably be of some interest to those who have interest in his own. In principle, then, reference citations can be utilized for the finding of documents related to one another. It is in fact common practice for scientists to engage in literature search by beginning with a single paper or article and then seeking other articles it cites as references. These, in turn, will cite others, and it is not difficult thus to find one's way into a considerable segment of the literature on any subject.

The act of following a chain of citations itself could be carried out more easily with the aid of a printed author or title or author and title heading list serving as an index, with each heading being associated with the author, title, and location of all references that it cites. A simple rearrangement of the format (which could incidentally be carried out by machine procedures) would permit using a cited article as a heading and associating with it the identification and location of all subsequently published citing articles. This latter form of publication is known as a citation index, or a citator. One publication of this general type, *Shepard's Citations*, well-known to lawyers, has been widely used since 1873. This periodic publication permits finding subsequent law cases, opinions, and articles for which a given case or statute, entered as a heading, is cited as applicable. Eugene Garfield suggested citation indexes for scientific literature and founded the Institute for Scientific Information, which, since 1961, has published a quarterly series, cumulated annually, called *Science Citation Index*. In producing this index, the processes of sorting, arrangement, and composition are carried out by machine.

Files. *File organization.* Whether a publication is classified or indexed, the result of the process is a record that links subject terms (index words, class numbers, etc.) with item descriptions (book author and title, report number, etc.). A particular term may be used for many published items; a given item may be indexed by several terms.

There are two basic modes of recording. In one, each individual record (catalog card, punched card, microrecording, magnetic recording, etc.) relates to a single item and carries all the index terms used for that item. Needle- or machine-sorted punched cards are of this type. In the other, each individual record relates to a single term and carries all the item descriptions for which that term has been used. Peephole cards are of this type.

Arranging the records

A collection of records of either kind is referred to here as a file. The records may be arranged among themselves in various ways, and the arrangement will affect the way in which the file can be searched. If the records are in random sequence, the whole file must be scanned to locate those items relating to a particular term. This operation is known as sequential, or serial, scanning. If the arrangement is based on an ordered sequence of terms, and there is ready random access to any part of the file (as in a card catalog), then fractional scanning can be done in a series of stages.

Numberless variations of these arrangements are possible with different file media. The organization of the file is a physical problem that determines the efficiency of the search procedure. (D.R.Sw.)

Mechanized storage and retrieval systems. Various mechanized storage and retrieval systems have been developed, perhaps the most interesting being the MEDLARS (Medical Literature Analysis and Retrieval System) of the National Library of Medicine in Bethesda, Maryland.

Purposes of MEDLARS

MEDLARS was designed as a dual-purpose system: (1) to produce a published index, *Index Medicus*, widely distributed for manual searching; (2) to provide the capability of searching the same file by machine methods and also of reformatting parts of the file to produce special bibliographies, either on demand or continuously. The contents of some 2,500 periodicals are described by staff indexers who are familiar with the subject matter they handle. They select their descriptors, or subject headings, from a controlled list developed with the assistance of specialists from many fields.

The indexing is performed at two levels, one with a limited number of tags, or descriptors, for each article for the printed index and the other in depth, with many more descriptors for selected articles. Depth indexing is available only for machine searching and for printing special bibliographies. The citations to the journals along with their descriptors are punched on paper tape and then transferred to magnetic tape, which can be processed and reformatted in many ways to produce the various printed indexes and also to perform searches on specific subjects to produce bibliographies for individual users. (For a description of the computer's use in storage and retrieval systems, see COMPUTERS.) (D.A.K.)

Information centres. There is no general agreement on the precise definition of an information centre. It has been defined very broadly as any library or collection of documents that serves more than a few people. This definition is unsatisfactory, for it treats libraries and information centres synonymously, whereas significant distinctions can be made. It is useful to distinguish information centres from libraries on the basis of subject matter, form, services, and equipment. Information centres generally cover a narrow field of science and technology, and they cover it in depth. More than libraries, centres are concerned with handling technical reports and journal articles dealing primarily with current information. Centres also provide a greater range of user services than do most libraries.

Types of information centres

Four types of information centres can be distinguished, based upon the primary activity or service the centre is to provide. Document depots, generally government-sponsored, serve as archives for the acquisition, storage, retrieval, and dissemination of a variety of documents. The depot prepares specialized bibliographies, publishes announcements, indexes, abstracts, documents, and provides copies. Abstracting and indexing services, discussed above, usually provide information in published form. Special libraries are mission or discipline oriented. Information analysis centres issue analyses of their holdings rather than disseminating source documents; they may provide special bibliographies on request. (H.Bo.)

INFORMATION-PROCESSING SYSTEMS: THEORY AND PRACTICE

Basic principles. Schools, banks, libraries, telephone and telegraph systems, research institutes, postal systems, and newspaper offices are familiar information-processing systems. They are all being improved rapidly through use of electronic data-processing technology.

A user's message is input (written, spoken, sent) at a receptor (keyboard, microphone, etc.) of an input terminal, is received, and then is stored in a buffer. The message is then encoded, transmitted, and carried over a channel to a control unit (input) buffer, then decoded and processed by the control unit. Processing by the control processor results in decisions and orders that specified data and instructions stored previously in memory be transferred to the control unit and to the central processor, for logical and arithmetical analyses. These transfers and analyses lead to changes in the contents of various memory elements and then to encoding for transmission in accordance with orders by the control unit. This order leads to transmission over appropriate channels for storage in buffers at one or more specified output terminals. The output terminals receive, decode, and store the messages in their buffers. Effectors then output messages to current users of output terminals.

Small systems may all be in one cabinet in one room and be able to serve only one user at a time. Some larger systems may serve many users, with several of them at a distance from the central processor. Of the special purpose large systems, SAGE (semi-automatic ground environment), developed by the United States Air Force to provide protection against surprise enemy attack, is a well-known example. The SAGE network, consisting of a dozen direction centres scattered throughout the continental United States and Canada, each with a large electronic computer, was designed to be fed data from many elaborate radars and from many other information sources. The data were stored and processed continuously, enabling Air Force personnel to keep the entire air space over and around the continental United States and Canada under constant surveillance. General-purpose large systems are now common. They involve the use of a computer by several parties on a shared-time basis. Sometimes a university may lease a computer, allowing various departments to make use of its memory and computation facilities for given periods of time. Private firms such as banks may also share time on a computer.

Computers in linguistics

Non-numerical information systems. Computers are used as tools for research in linguistics and as components of primitive systems that seek (1) to translate from one natural language to another; (2) to answer questions when adequate linguistic and logical analysis of question-

and-information store is a prerequisite for success; or (3) to yield useful retrieval of relevant items from a large collection indexed either automatically or with human aid. Among the linguistic research areas are: concordances (discussed in earlier sections of this article), statistical determination of authorship, analyses of transformational grammar, and statistical content analyses. This general field has been called computational linguistics (see also LINGUISTICS). (M.M.F.)

BIBLIOGRAPHY

Information media: C.P. BOURNE, "The World's Technical Journal Literature," *Am. Documen.*, 13:159–168 (1962), an analysis of the universe of scientific-technical periodicals, by language, subject, and country of origin; COMMITTEE ON SCIENTIFIC AND TECHNICAL COMMUNICATION, *Scientific and Technical Communication, a Pressing National Problem and Recommendations for Its Solution: A Report* (1969), a comprehensive review of the state of information processing in the sciences and the government's current and potential role; D.A. KRONICK, *A History of Scientific and Technical Periodicals* (1962), documents the origins and growth of the scientific-technical journal up to 1790; R.H. ORR *et al.*, "Communication Problems in Biomedical Research," *Fedn. Proc. Fedn. Am. Socs. Exp. Biol.*, 23:1117–76, 1297–1331 (1964), a thorough study of the needs, mechanisms, and problems of information in a broad special field that has relevance to all scientific communication; R.H. PHELPS and J.P. HERLING, "Alternatives to the Scientific Periodical," *U.N.E.S.C.O. Bull. for Libraries*, vol. 14, no. 2 (1960), a review of the history and nature of these proposals with a discussion of some of the reasons why they have not prospered; *The MEDLARS Story at the National Library of Medicine* (1963), a description of one of the first large mechanized information-processing systems.

Indexes and indexing: ROBERT A. FAIRTHORNE, "Content Analysis, Specification, and Control," *A. Rev. Inf. Sci. Tech.*, 4:73–109 (1969), a discussion of the terminological, conceptual, and philosophic aspects of indexing and classification, with an extensive bibliography; BRIAN C. VICKERY, "The Process of Subject Indexing," and "Controlled Indexing Terminology," in *Techniques of Information Retrieval*, ch. 8–9 (1970), a thorough introduction to indexing and indexing terminology—see also ch. 12, "Files and Search Strategy," on selected aspects of file organization and search logic as related primarily to indexing and to documentation; F. WILFRID LANCASTER, *Information Retrieval Systems: Characteristics, Testing, and Evaluation* (1968), a clear and concise introduction to indexing, index languages, searching, and evaluation of information-retrieval systems, especially of value in explicating the major concepts of the field with minimal demands on the reader's technical vocabulary or prior acquaintance with the subject matter; SUSAN ARTANDI, "Document Description and Representation," *A. Rev. Inf. Sci. Tech.*, 5:143–167 (1970), a review of publications in 1969 on various aspects of indexing, including the indexing and subject analysis process, factors affecting indexing, inter-indexer consistency, index languages, automatic indexing, and the cost of indexing, including a bibliography of 96 entries, most of which concern some aspect of indexing; BRIAN C. VICKERY, "Document Description and Representation," *ibid.*, 6:113–140 (1971), a review of publications of 1970 on indexing and index languages, with particular attention given to studies that bear on basic issues of evaluating word extraction, combining of word forms and synonyms, use of phrases, generic grouping of terms, and term coordination, and including a bibliography of 50 articles or reports on indexing, classification, and retrieval; STELLA KEENAN, "Abstracting and Indexing Services in Science and Technology," *ibid.*, 4:273–303 (1969), a survey of the literature of 1968 on indexing and abstracting services produced by scientific societies, government, and institutions in the United States; PHYLLIS V. PARKINS and H.E. KENNEDY, "Secondary Information Services," *ibid.*, 6:247–275 (1971), based on 133 publications of 1970 covering essentially the same general topic dealt with by Keenan (above); DONALD W. KING and EDWARD C. BRYANT, "Evaluation of Indexing Processes and Indexing Language," in *The Evaluation of Information Services and Products*, ch. 5 (1971), a chapter dealing with issues of experimental design in retrieval tests and in indexing consistency tests, written for the reader acquainted with elementary mathematics; HENRY WHEATLEY, *What Is an Index? A Few Notes on Indexes and Indexers*, 2nd ed. (1879), an annotated compendium of early indexes, primarily of interest to the student of indexing history; FRANCIS J. WITTY, "Early Indexing Techniques: A Study of Several Book Indexes of the Fourteenth, Fifteenth, and Early Sixteenth Centuries," *Lib. Q.*, 35:141–148 (1967), of interest to the student of the earliest history of indexing.

Information centres: ALLEN KENT, *Specialized Information Centers* (1965), a textbook that describes and analyzes the various functions that must be performed in information centres, with case histories used to illustrate the similarities and differences in operational procedures at different centres and to derive general principles; G.S. SIMPSON, JR., and CAROLYN FLANAGAN, "Information Centers and Services," *A. Rev. Inf. Sci. Tech.*, 1:305–330, 335 (1966), a summary of the literature relating to specialized information centres and services in the United States covering document depots, special libraries, abstracting and indexing services, and information-analysis centres; L.F. CARTER *et al.*, *National Document-Handling Systems for Science and Technology* (1967), a description and appraisal of the current system for controlling and disseminating scientific and technical information in the United States; HAROLD WOOSTER, "An Information Analysis Center Effectiveness Chrestomathy," *J. Am. Soc. Inf. Sci.*, 21:149–159 (1970), a discussion of various criteria for evaluating the effectiveness of information analysis centres.

Journals: *Computing Reviews* (monthly), published by the Association for Computing Machinery, New York, includes reviews and abstracts of articles on computers and information processing and samples the world's literature in this field. The international journal, *Information Storage and Retrieval* (bimonthly), is devoted to the publication and dissemination of articles dealing with the theory and methodology of information storage and retrieval. The *AFIPS Conference Proceedings* (semi-annual) is published by the American Federation of Information Processing Societies, New York. The papers given each year at the Spring and Fall Joint Computer Conferences provide current coverage of every aspect of computers and information processing. See also the *Journal of the American Society for Information Science* (bimonthly) and the annual conference proceedings of this society.

(M.M.F./D.A.K./H.Bo./D.R.Sw.)

Information Theory

One of the most prominent features of 20th-century technology has been the development and exploitation of new communications media. Concurrent with the growth of devices for transmitting and processing information, a unifying theory known as information theory was developed and became the subject of intensive research. It is an example of a theory that was initiated primarily by one man, the U.S. electrical engineer Claude E. Shannon, whose initial ideas appeared in an article, "The Mathematical Theory of Communication," in the *Bell System Technical Journal* (1948). In its broadest sense, information is to be interpreted to include the messages occurring in any of the standard communications media, such as telegraphy, radio or television, the signals involved in electronic computing machines, servomechanism systems, and other data-processing devices. The theory is even applied to the signals appearing in the nerve networks of animals and man. The signals or messages do not have to be meaningful in any ordinary sense.

The chief concern of information theory is to discover mathematical laws governing systems designed to communicate or manipulate information. It sets up quantitative measures of information and of the capacity of various systems to transmit, store, and otherwise process information.

Some of the problems treated relate to finding the best methods of using various available communication systems, the best methods for separating the wanted information, or signal, from the extraneous information, or noise. Another problem is the setting of upper bounds on what it is possible to achieve with a given information-carrying medium (often called an information channel). While the central results are chiefly of interest to communication engineers, some of the concepts have been adopted and found useful in such fields as psychology and linguistics. The boundaries of information theory are quite vague. The theory overlaps heavily with communication theory but is more oriented toward the fundamental limitations on the processing and communication of information and less oriented toward the detailed operation of the devices employed (see OPTIMIZATION, MATHEMATICAL THEORY OF).

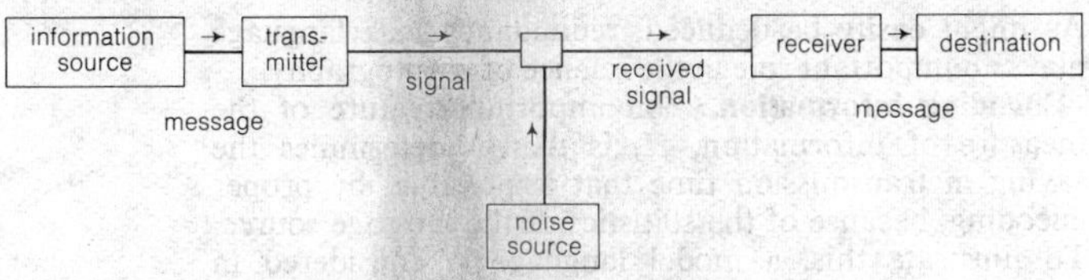

Figure 1: Elements of a general communication system.

Central problems of information theory. The type of communication system that has been most extensively investigated is shown in Figure 1. It consists of the following: (A) An information source that produces the raw information, or "message," to be transmitted. (B) A transmitter that transforms or encodes this information into a form suitable for the channel. This transformed message is called the signal. (C) The channel on which the encoded information, or signal, is transmitted to the receiving point. During transmission the signal may be changed or distorted. The static in radio reception and the snow in television reception are familiar examples of such changes. These disturbing effects are known generally as noise and are indicated schematically in Figure 1 by the noise source. (D) The receiver, which decodes or translates the received signal back into the original message or an approximation of it. (E) The destination or intended recipient of the information.

Elements of a general communication system

It will be seen that this system is sufficiently general to include a wide variety of communication problems if the various elements are suitably interpreted. In radio, for example, the information source may be a person speaking into a microphone. The message is then the sound that he produces, and the transmitter is the microphone and the associated electronic equipment that changes this sound into an electromagnetic wave, the signal. The channel is the space between the transmitting and receiving antennas, and any static or noise disturbing the signal corresponds to the noise source in the schematic diagram. The radio receiver converts the received signal into an audible output from a loudspeaker. The destination is a person listening to the message.

Information as a physical quantity

A basic idea in information theory is that information can be treated very much like a physical quantity, such as mass or energy. A homely analogy may be drawn between the system in Figure 1 and a transportation system; for example, an information source is like a lumber mill producing lumber at a certain point. The channel in Figure 1 might correspond to a conveyor system for transporting the lumber to a second point. In such a situation there are two important quantities: the rate R (in cubic feet per second) at which lumber is produced at the mill and the capacity C (in cubic feet per second) of the conveyor. These two quantities determine whether or not the conveyor system will be adequate for the lumber mill. If the rate of production R is greater than the conveyor capacity C, it will certainly be impossible to transport the full output of the mill; there will not be sufficient space available. If R is less than or equal to C, it may or may not be possible, depending on whether the lumber can be packed efficiently in the conveyor. Suppose, however, that there is a sawmill at the source. This corresponds in the analogy to the encoder or transmitter. Then the lumber can be cut up into small pieces in such a way as to fill out the available capacity of the conveyor with 100 percent efficiency. Naturally, in this case a carpenter would be provided at the receiving point to fasten the pieces back together in their original form before passing them on to the consumer.

If this analogy is sound, it should be possible to set up a measure R, in suitable units, giving the rate at which information is produced by a given information source, and a second measure C that determines the capacity of a channel for transmitting information. Furthermore, the analogy would suggest that by a suitable coding or modulation system, the information can be transmitted over the channel if and only if the rate of production R is not greater than the capacity C. A key result of information theory is that it is indeed possible to set up measures R and C having this property.

Measurement of information. Before considering the question of how information is to be measured, it is necessary to clarify the precise meaning of "information" from the point of view of the communication engineer. Often the messages to be transmitted have meaning: they describe or relate to real or conceivable events. This is not always the case, however. In transmitting music, the meaning, if there is any, is much more subtle than in the case of a verbal message. In some situations the engineer is faced with transmitting a totally meaningless sequence of numbers or letters. In any case, meaning is quite irrelevant to the problem of transmitting the information. It is as difficult to transmit a series of nonsense syllables as it is to transmit straight English text. The significant aspect of information from the transmission standpoint is the fact that one particular message is chosen from a set of possible messages. What must be transmitted is a specification of the particular message that was chosen by the information source. The original message can be reconstructed at the receiving point only if such an unambiguous specification is transmitted. Thus, in information theory, information is thought of as a choice of one message from a set of possible messages. Furthermore, these choices occur with certain probabilities; some messages are more frequent than others.

Choice probabilities

The simplest type of choice is a choice from two equally likely possibilities; that is, each has a probability 1/2. That is the situation, for example, when a tossed coin is equally likely to come up heads or tails. It is convenient to use the amount of information produced by such a choice as the basic unit, and this basic unit is called a bit. The choice involved with one bit of information can be indicated schematically as shown in Figure 2

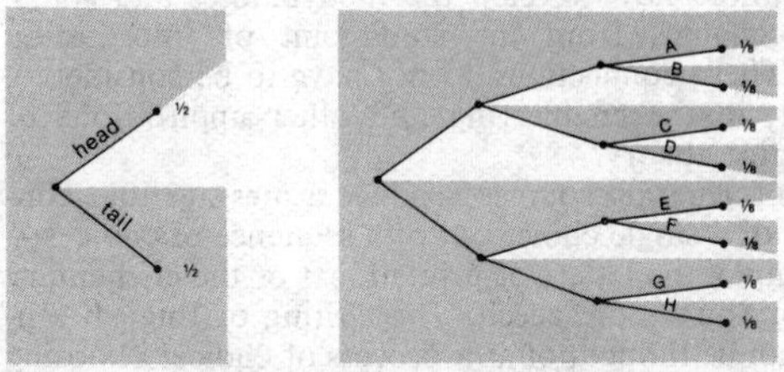

Figure 2: Possible forms of choices.
(Left) A binary choice, as in the flip of a coin, in which head and tail each have probability 1/2. (Right) Three successive binary choices, leading to eight possible outcomes, A through H, each with probability 1/8 (see text).

(Left). Either the upper or the lower line may be chosen with probability 1/2 for each possibility.

If there are N possibilities, all equally likely, the amount of information is given by $\log_2 N$. The reason for this can be seen from Figure 2 (Right), in which there are eight possibilities, each with probability 1/8. The choice can be imagined to occur in three stages, each involving one bit. The first bit corresponds to a choice of either the first four or the second four of the eight possibilities; the second bit corresponds to the first or second pair of the four chosen; and the final bit determines the first or second member of the pair. The number of bits required is $\log_2 N$, in this case $\log_2 8 = 3$.

If the probabilities are not equal, the messages in the set will have different amounts of information associated with them. If the probabilities of the messages are given by $p_1, p_2, \cdots, p_N$, then the amount of information associated with the first message is $\log_2 (1/p_1)$, that of the second is $\log_2 (1/p_2)$, and so forth. The expected value of these amounts of information (see Box formula 1) is called the entropy, H, or the average information of the message set.

The entropy takes on its smallest value, zero, when one message is certain to occur (*i.e.*, has a probability of 1) and all other messages never occur (*i.e.*, have 0 probability). Intuitively, there is no information in a message that is a priori certain. Conversely, the entropy takes on its maximum value, $\log_2 N$, when the N messages in the set are equally likely. Individual messages in the set can have arbitrarily large amounts of information, but these

$$H = p_1 \log_2 (1/p_1) + p_2 \log_2 (1/p_2) + \cdots + p_n \log_2 (1/p_N) \quad (1)$$

messages with large information occur so rarely that the expected value remains bounded by $\log_2 N$.

The parlor game "Twenty Questions" illustrates some of these ideas. In this game, one person thinks of an object, and the other players attempt to determine what it is by asking not more than 20 questions that can be answered "yes" or "no." According to information theory, each question can, by its answer, yield anywhere from no information to $\log_2 2$ or one bit of information on the average, depending upon whether the probabilities of "yes" and "no" answers are very unequal or approximately equal. To obtain the greatest amount of information, the players should ask questions that subdivide the set of possible objects as nearly as possible into two equally likely groups. For example, if they have established by previous questions that the object is a town in the United States, a good question would be "Is it east of the Mississippi?" This divides the possible towns into two roughly equal sets. The next question then might be "Is it north of the Mason and Dixon's line?" If it were possible to choose questions that always had the effect of subdividing into two equal groups, it would be possible to isolate, in 20 questions, one object from 2^{20} (approximately 1,000,000) possibilities. This corresponds to 20 bits.

The formula for entropy in information theory is identical in form to that representing entropy in statistical mechanics. There are a number of other connections between statistical mechanics and information theory, and some authors now develop thermodynamics and statistical mechanics from the standpoint of information theory. These connections do not have to be considered, however, in the engineering and other applications of information theory.

Message sequence

Most information sources produce a message that consists not of a single choice but of a sequence of choices—for example, the letters of printed text or the elementary words or sounds of speech. The writing of English sentences can be thought of as a process of choice: choosing a first word from possible first words with various probabilities; then a second, with probabilities depending on the first; etc. This kind of statistical process is called a stochastic process; and information sources are thought of, in information theory, as stochastic processes. A more general formula for H can be given that determines the rate at which information is produced by a stochastic process or an information source.

Printed English is a type of information source that has been studied considerably. By playing a kind of "Twenty Questions" game, suitably modified, with subjects trying to guess the next letter in an English sentence, it can be shown that the information rate of ordinary written English is not more than about one bit per letter. This phenomenon is a result of the very unequal frequencies of occurrence of different letters (for example, E is very common in English while Z, Q and X are very infrequent), of pairs of letters (TH is very common and QZ very rare), and of the existence of frequently recurring words, phrases, and so on. This body of statistical data relating to a language is called the statistical structure of the language. If all 26 letters and the space in English had equal frequencies of occurrence (*i.e.*, each had probability 1/27) and the occurrence of each letter of text was independent of previous letters, the information rate would be $\log_2 27$, or about 4.76 bits per letter. Because only one bit actually is produced, English is said to be about 80 percent redundant.

The redundancy of English is exhibited by the fact that a great many letters can be deleted from a sentence without making it impossible for a reader to fill the gaps and determine the original meaning. For example, in the following sentence the vowels have been deleted:

MST PPL HV LTTL
DFFCLTY N RDNG THS SNTNC.

As might easily be deduced, redundancy in a language plays an important role in the science of cryptography.

Encoding information. An important feature of the measure of information, H, is that it determines the saving in transmission time that is possible, by proper encoding, because of the statistics of the message source. To illustrate this, a model language is considered in which there are only four letters—A, B, C, and D—with the probabilities 1/2, 1/4, 1/8 and 1/8, respectively. In a long text in this language, A will occur one-half the time, B one-quarter of the time, and C and D each one-eighth of the time. If this language is to be encoded into binary digits, 0 or 1, as for example in a pulse system with two types of pulse, then the most direct code is the following: $A = 00$; $B = 01$; $C = 10$; $D = 11$. This code requires two binary digits per letter of message. By proper use of the statistics, a better code can be constructed as follows: $A = 0$; $B = 10$; $C = 110$; $D = 111$. It is readily verified that the original message can be recovered from its encoded form. Furthermore, the number of binary digits used is smaller on the average. It will be, in fact, $(1)\frac{1}{2} + (2)\frac{1}{4} + (3)\frac{1}{8} + (3)\frac{1}{8} = 1\frac{3}{4}$ where the first term is due to the letter A, which occurs half the time and is one binary digit long and similarly for the others. It may be found by a simple calculation that $1\frac{3}{4}$ is just the value of H, calculated for the probabilities 1/2, 1/4, 1/8, and 1/8. The basic idea here, that of encoding common letters into short messages and uncommon letters into longer messages, is used in Morse Code.

The result verified for the special case above holds generally. If H is the entropy, in bits per letter, of an information source, then every binary encoding that represents the source uses at least H binary digits per source letter on the average. Conversely, binary encodings can be found using as close to H binary digits per source letter as desired. The difference in the general case is that the encoding becomes more complicated as the average number of binary digits per source letter approaches H. Rather than encoding single source letters into sequences of binary digits, it is required to map sequences of source letters into sequences of binary digits.

This important result in information theory gives a direct meaning to the entropy H for a source or a language. It says, in fact, that H can be interpreted as the equivalent number of binary digits required when the language or source is encoded into 0 and 1 in the most efficient way. For instance, if the estimate of one bit per letter, mentioned above as the rate for printed English, is correct, then it is possible to encode printed English into binary digits using, on the average, one for each letter of text; and, furthermore, no encoding method would average less than this.

Transmission of information. The problem of defining information transmission when a message is transmitted over a channel is now considered. If there is no noise and the message is faithfully reproduced at the destination, the problem is simple. The information transmitted (measured in bits) is then the same as the information of the source message, and the average information transmitted is the same as the entropy of the source.

Problem of the noisy channel

For a noisy channel, the situation is more complex. One simple example is called a binary erasure channel. If a source is binary, producing 0's and 1's with equal probability, and nine-tenths of the time the message gets through to the destination correctly, and the other one-tenth of the time, the noise is so bad that a special symbol called "erasure" is delivered to the destination—then it is concluded that nine-tenths of the time, a bit of information is transmitted, and one-tenth of the time no information is transmitted. This leads to an average information transmission of 9/10 bit per message.

Another simple example is known as a binary symmetric channel. When a 0 is transmitted, 0 is received with probability 9/10, and 1 is received with probability 1/10. Similarly, a transmitted 1 is received as a 1 with probability 9/10 and as a 0 with probability 1/10. Assuming the source to produce 0 and 1 with equal likelihood, the entropy, or average uncertainty, of a source message is 1 bit. After a 0, say, has been received at the destination, the a posteriori probability that a 0 came out of the source is 9/10, and that of a 1 is 1/10. Thus, the uncertainty of the source, conditioned on a received 0, is $9/10 \log_2 10/9 + 1/10 \log_2 10$, or about 0.47 bit. The same uncertainty arises if a 1 is received, so that the reception of a symbol reduces the uncertainty of the source message from 1 bit to 0.47 bit. It is reasonable to conclude that 0.53 bit of information has been transmitted over the channel.

The difference between these two examples is quite striking. In both cases 90 percent of the transmitted digits are correctly received; but the binary symmetric channel, in which it is not known what received digits are in doubt, conveys considerably less information than the binary erasure channel, in which dubious digits are overwritten with the erasure symbol. A similar example occurs in a "true-false" examination in which a student who gets 90 questions correct and leaves 10 unanswered appears to know much more than a student who gets 90 correct and 10 wrong.

In general, the average transmitted information through a channel can be found in the same way as in the above examples. For each possible output symbol, there is an uncertainty of the source, based on the a posteriori probabilities for that particular output.

The conditioned entropy of the channel input, given the channel output, is the average of the above uncertainties, weighted by the output symbol probabilities. The average transmitted information is the difference between the entropy of the input and the conditioned entropy of the input, given the output. In the special case when the input is uniquely specified by the output, the conditioned entropy is zero, and the transmitted information is the same as the original uncertainty of the input.

Channel capacity

The most important attribute of a communication channel is its capacity. Capacity is defined as the maximum (over the input probabilities) average transmitted information for a channel. The capacities of the binary erasure channel and binary symmetric channels previously discussed are 0.9 and 0.53 bits per symbol, respectively.

Channel capacity and source entropy are linked together by the noisy-channel coding theorem, which is the fundamental result of information theory. This result states that if the source entropy (in bits per unit time) is less than the channel capacity (in bits per unit time), then encoders and decoders can be constructed such that the source output is re-created at the destination with as small an error probability as desired. Conversely, if the source entropy is greater than the capacity, then the error probability can not be made arbitrarily small.

As an example of this result, the binary erasure channel is considered, and it is assumed that a return channel is available so that whenever an erasure occurs at the receiver, notification of it is sent back to the transmitter, and the offending digit is repeated.

Because the transmitted digit is received correctly nine-tenths of the time and correct digits are never repeated, there are 9 source digits for each 10 transmitted digits on the average. Thus the source entropy and capacity are equal and no errors occur.

The above example is misleading with respect to the ease with which channel noise can be combatted. If the return channel is unavailable, or if the noise is not in known positions (*i.e.*, erasures), the coding and decoding required by the theorem are quite complex and become increasingly complex as the error probability is reduced toward zero.

Coding for error correction. Most techniques for coding to reduce errors are based, at least indirectly, on the concept of parity checks. The parity of a set of binary digits is defined as 1 if the set contains an odd number of 1's and defined as 0 otherwise. Thus the parity of 111 is 1, that of 110 is 0, that of 0001 is 1, etc. A change of any single digit in the set changes the parity of the set. Thus, if a set of digits is transmitted, followed by transmission of the parity of the set (called a parity check digit), a single error in the transmission can be detected by the disagreement between the parity of the received set and the received parity check digit. Naturally, this disagreement does not indicate which received digit is in error, and no correction is possible.

Use of parity checks

The following example shows how parity checks can be used to correct errors. Four source digits (s_1, s_2, s_3, s_4) are transmitted, followed by three parity check digits, p_1, p_2, p_3. The digit p_1 is chosen as the parity of the first three source digits; p_2 as the parity of the first, second, and fourth; and p_3 as the parity of the first, third, and fourth (see formula 2). Then, for example, the source digits 1001 would be encoded into 1001100. If the first source digit s_1 is received in error at the receiver but all other digits are received correctly, then each received parity check will disagree with the parity of the corresponding set of received source digits. Likewise, if the second source digit is received in error, only the first two parity checks will disagree with the corresponding received parities, because s_2 is not in the set used for the third parity check. Similarly, each source digit and parity check digit has its own unique pattern of disagreements, allowing any single error in the seven digits to be corrected. Multiple errors unfortunately cannot be corrected in this example.

The above code is an example of a block code, a code in which the source digits are segmented into sequences of a fixed length (4, for the example), and there is a rule for transforming each source sequence into a sequence of channel digits of fixed length (7, for the example). The block length of the code is the length of the channel sequence, and the code rate (assuming a binary source) is the ratio of source sequence length to channel sequence length. Thus, the example yields 4/7.

The coding theorem asserts that there are block codes with code rates arbitrarily close to channel capacity and probabilities of error arbitrarily close to zero. It can be shown, however, that the required block length increases both as the code rate approaches capacity and as the desired error probability approaches zero.

Codes with long block length and minimum error

A great deal of mathematical research has been devoted to finding constructive procedures to generate codes with large block lengths and low probabilities of error. A variety of relatively practical and effective coding techniques is known. Most of the techniques use parity checks, with the mathematical structure determining which source digits will be checked by each parity check. Surprisingly enough, however, no constructive techniques are known that allow the probability of decoding error to be made arbitrarily small at code rates close to channel capacity. This situation is particularly surprising in view of the fact that the coding theorem is proved by picking codes at random and showing that as the block length increases for a fixed code rate, the probability of decoding error goes to zero. This paradoxical situation is summed up by the oft-repeated quip that "all codes are good except the ones that anybody can think of."

From a practical standpoint, block coding and decoding techniques have not been widely used in the data-communication field. It is quite common, however, to encode data by means of a parity check code and to use the parity checks at the receiver to detect errors. Blocks with errors are then retransmitted.

Most practical applications of coding to correct errors have used convolutional codes instead of block codes. For example, suppose that each source digit entering the encoder is transmitted and then followed by a parity check digit so that the transmitted stream has the form $s_1\, p_1\, s_2\, p_2\, s_3\, p_3 \cdots$. Suppose that each parity check digit is the parity of the two preceding source digits (see 3). Thus, if the first four source digits are 1011, the first eight transmitted digits will be *1*1*0*1*1*1*1*0 (the source digits are italicized).

If noise alters one of the source digits in transmission over the channel, then the parities will not check for the two succeeding parity check digits. On the other hand, if noise alters a parity check digit, only that one parity will fail to check. Thus, any single error (if preceded and followed by at least three correct digits) can be corrected.

To attain very low probabilities of decoding error with convolutional codes, the parity check constraints must extend over more digits. Rather than making p_n the parity of s_n and s_{n-1}, p_n would be the parity of a large set of

$$(2)\quad \begin{cases} p_1 = \text{parity}\ (s_1, s_2, s_3) \\ p_2 = \text{parity}\ (s_1, s_2, s_4) \\ p_3 = \text{parity}\ (s_1, s_3, s_4) \end{cases}$$

$$(3)\quad p_n = \text{parity}\ (s_n, s_{n-1})$$

$$(4)\quad C = W \log_2\left(1 + \frac{P}{NW}\right)$$

previous source digits in a fixed set of positions relative to p_n.

Convolutional codes have been very effective in telemetering data back from space probes. Coding is particularly useful there because the traditional techniques for improving communication, such as increasing power and increasing antenna size, are inordinately expensive.

Band limited channels. The communication channels considered above were all discrete, involving sequences of symbols entering and leaving the channel. In most physical communication channels, however, the input and output are usually continuously varying signals on a wire, cable, or antenna terminal. The devices that convert the discrete sequences into continuous signals and vice versa are known as modems (digital data modulators and demodulators). The modulator converts the discrete sequence into a signal suitable for the channel and the demodulator makes decisions on the received combination of signal and noise and produces a discrete sequence as its output. Modems are sometimes regarded as part of the channel and sometimes as part of the transmitter and receiver. The usual criterion is to regard the channel as the fixed part of the system and the transmitter and receiver as the part to be designed or optimized.

Because of physical limitations of the transmission medium and because of the need to avoid interference with other channels, the transmitted signal on a channel is frequently restricted to lie within a given band of frequencies W hertz wide. For example, radio stations are restricted in this way, each station broadcasting within an area having one of a nonoverlapping set of frequency bands. A result known as the sampling theorem states that a signal of this type is indicated by specifying its values at a sequence of $2W$ appropriately placed sampling points per second. Thus, it may be said that the set of signals limited to a band W hertz wide has $2W$ degrees of freedom per second.

If there were no noise whatever on such a channel it would be possible to distinguish an infinite number of different amplitude levels for each sample. Consequently, in principle, an infinite number of binary digits per second could be transmitted, and the capacity C would be infinite. In practice, there is always some noise; but even so, if no limitations are placed on the transmitter power, P, the capacity will be infinite, because at each sample point an unlimited number of different amplitude levels may be distinguished. When noise is present and the transmitter power is limited, the capacity C becomes finite. This capacity depends on the statistical structure of the noise and the nature of the power limitation.

Gaussian noise

The simplest, and in some ways the most fundamental, type of noise is white Gaussian noise, such as that produced in an electrical resistor by thermal effects. It has the characteristic of being evenly spread out in frequency and is specified by N, its average power per hertz of frequency. Similarly, the simplest limitation on transmitter power is the assumption that the average transmitter signal power is no greater than P.

If the input signal of a channel has a power limitation P and a bandwidth limitation W, and if the output signal is the sum of the input signal and white Gaussian noise of power per hertz N, then the capacity of the channel (measured in bits per second) can be shown to be a simple increasing function of W and of P/N (see 4). The interpretation of C here is the same as before. By proper design of transmitter and receiver, it is possible to transmit up to C binary digits per second with as small a probability of error as desired, while it is not possible to transmit more than C binary digits per second with an arbitrarily small probability of error.

Many physical channels are subject to noise phenomena quite different from that above, and the above expression for capacity does not apply to them. The above formula is inapplicable to high-frequency radio links and tropospheric scatter links, but applicable to satellite communication and communication from space probes.

Figure 3 illustrates the relationship between capacity and bandwidth and between capacity and P/N. Figure 3

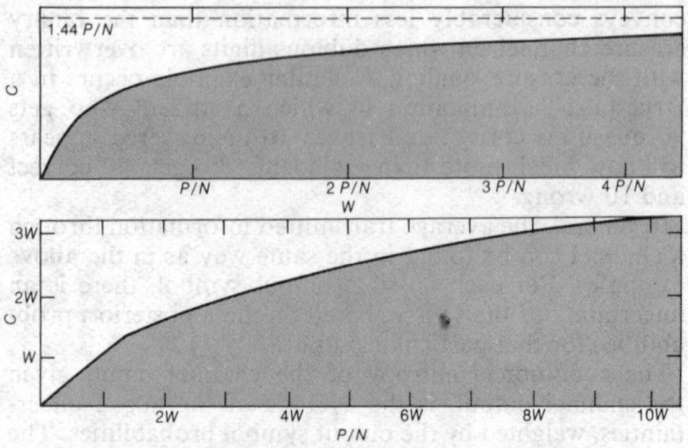

Figure 3: Relationships between bandwidth and capacity or between P/N and capacity (top) when W is much greater than P/N and (bottom) when W is much smaller than P/N.

(top) shows that if W is much greater than P/N (called the power limited regions), then capacity is insensitive to changes in W. From the formula for capacity, given above, it is possible to show that, for very large values of W, the capacity approaches a limiting value of 1.44 P/N. If W is much smaller than P/N (called the bandwidth limited region), then capacity is relatively insensitive to changes in P/N (see Figure 3 [bottom]).

The relation between C, W, P, and N (see 4) can be regarded as an exchange relation between the bandwidth W and the signal-to-noise ratio P/N. Keeping the channel capacity fixed, the bandwidth can be decreased provided the signal-to-noise ratio is sufficiently increased. Conversely, an increase in bandwidth allows a lower signal-to-noise ratio in the channel.

One method of exchanging bandwidth for signal-to-noise ratio is shown in Figure 4. The upper curve represents a signal function with a bandwidth such that it can be specified by giving the samples shown. Each sample has four amplitude levels. The lower curve is obtained by combining pairs of samples from the first curve as shown. If the pair of samples from the upper curve have amplitudes x and y, a single amplitude z for the lower curve is computed by adding $4x$ to y. The four possible values of x combined with the four possible values of y produce

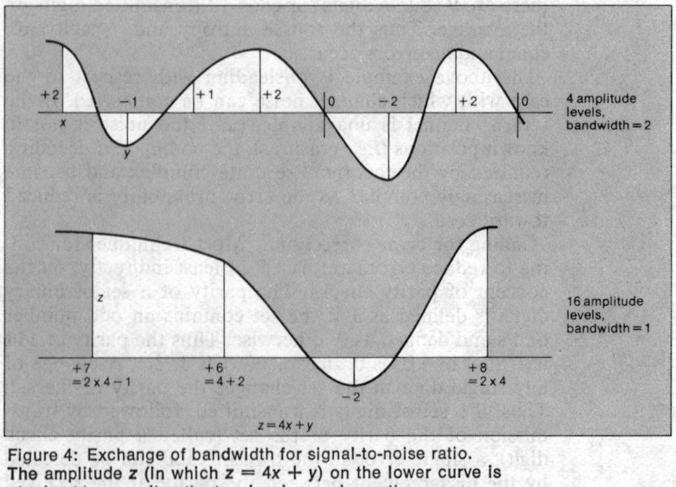

Figure 4: Exchange of bandwidth for signal-to-noise ratio. The amplitude z (in which $z = 4x + y$) on the lower curve is obtained by sampling the two levels x and y on the upper curve whose abscissas lie within the corresponding braces.

16 possible values of z, which must be distinguished. The samples, however, now occur only half as frequently; consequently, the band is reduced by half, at the cost of increasing the signal-to-noise ratio. Operating this in reverse doubles the band but reduces the required signal-to-noise ratio.

For channels in the bandwidth-constrained region, techniques similar to the pulse amplitude modulation of Figure 4 are quite effective in achieving transmission rates relatively close to capacity. Ordinary telephone line channels provide an example of the bandwidth-constrained region, although the capacity formula above is only a crude approximation for such channels. For channels in the power-constrained region, such as deep space channels, such simple techniques as pulse amplitude modulation require about 10 times as much power as predicted by the capacity formula. The use of error-correcting codes can yield significant power savings.

Sources with distortion measures. Many sources, such as voice, television, and the measurement of physical characteristics, are not appropriately regarded as being discrete. Serious problems arise in attempts to define the uncertainty or entropy of such sources. For example, if the source output is the speed of an automobile, which is a priori equally likely to be anywhere between 0 and 100 mph, it takes one bit of information to find out whether the speed lies in the interval 0 to 50 mph or 50 to 100 mph. Similarly, it takes two bits to find out in which 25 mph interval the speed lies and n bits to resolve the speed to an interval of 100 times 2^{-n} mph. Letting n get increasingly larger, the conclusion is that there is an infinite amount of uncertainty in the speed of the automobile. A natural way out of the dilemma lies in the fact that the uncertainty of the speed depends upon the desired resolution.

As a general approach to problems of this sort a distortion measure $D(u,v)$ is defined. For each possible source output u and each possible signal v used at the destination to represent a source output, $D(u, v)$ assigns a non-negative number representing the unacceptability of having source output u represented by signal v. For the automobile example above, u would be the automobile speed, v the approximation to u at the destination; and the distortion might reasonably be chosen as the square of the approximation error (see 5). If the source output is a continuously varying signal $u(t)$, and $v(t)$ is an approximation to $u(t)$ at the destination, then the distortion measure is a function of time and might be chosen as before (see 6).

The distortion measure can be chosen to reflect the importance or meaning of the source output to the destination. For example, in speech transmission the ear is relatively insensitive to phase distortion of the speech signal, and thus an appropriate distortion measure would weight amplitude distortion more heavily than phase distortion. With speech, the relative importance of intelligibility versus speaker recognition and voice quality can be weighed. The choice of an appropriate distortion measure for a source such as speech is very difficult and thus limits the applicability of information theory.

For any given source and distortion measure, it is possible to encode the source output into a binary sequence and, after storage or transmission of the sequence, to decode the sequence into an approximation of the source output. For example, if the source output is limited to a band W hertz wide, the encoding could be the reverse of the procedure in Figure 4. The signal could be sampled $2W$ times per second, and the samples could be quantized to a given number of levels, each level having its own binary code word. The approximation to the source would be constructed by mapping the binary sequences back into sample levels and the sample levels back into a time-varying signal. The approximation would differ from the source output because of the error introduced in quantizing.

The rate R of a source relative to a distortion level D is defined as the smallest number of binary digits per unit time required to encode the source output, subject to the restriction that the average distortion between the source

(5) $$D(u, v) = (u - v)^2$$

(6) $$D[u(t), v(t)] = [u(t) - v(t)]^2$$

output and the final approximation be at most D. With the above definition, the rate of the source becomes a function, $R(D)$, of the allowable average distortion. The larger the allowable distortion D is, the smaller the required number of binary digits is.

Unfortunately, finding the best way to encode a source into a binary sequence for a given allowable distortion is usually at least as difficult as finding good error-correction techniques for noisy channels. Because of this, the above definition is not very helpful in calculating the function $R(D)$. Instead $R(D)$ is found by the following procedure. A hypothetical channel is considered between the source and the destination. Such a channel is defined by the conditional probabilities of outputs given inputs, and corresponding to each such channel there is an average transmitted information per unit time and an average distortion per unit time. It can be shown that $R(D)$ is the smallest average transmitted information per unit time over all such channels for which the average distortion per unit time is at most D.

The fundamental theorem for sources and distortion measures

The fundamental theorem concerning sources and distortion measures can be stated loosely as follows: For a given source and distortion measure, $R(D)$ is the rate in bits per second of the source relative to a distortion level D. The source output is to be transmitted over a channel of capacity C bits per second, and D_c is the distortion level for which $R(D_c) = C$. Then, independent of the transmitter and receiver, the average distortion between source output and destination must be at least D_c. Conversely, transmitters and receivers can be constructed so that the average distortion is as close to D_c as desired. Finally, the transmitter can first encode the source output into at most C binary digits per second and then encode the binary digits for transmission over the channel in such a way that the resulting average distortion is as close to D_c as desired.

Because the minimum average distortion with which a source can be transmitted depends only on the capacity of the channel and not on any other channel characteristics, this theorem gives considerable force to the notion that the capacity is indeed a fundamental parameter of a channel. The theorem also points out that the current trend toward using binary data as a common interface between sources and channels (thus separating the problem of source processing from channel error correction) does not necessarily lead to any degradation in performance.

The theorem does not show how to construct transmitters and receivers that achieve a distortion close to the theoretical minimum. Its major use has been as a standard against which to compare existing systems, thus indicating where major improvements are possible.

Detection, estimation, and prediction. Another type of problem that has been studied extensively in the field of information theory is that of determining the best devices for extracting a message from a noise-corrupted signal. If the message represents a selection from a discrete set of choices, then the process of extracting the message from a noisy signal is known as detection. If the message represents the specification of one or more parameters over a continuous range of values, then the extraction of the message from a noisy signal is called estimation. More generally, in estimation, the message might be a continuously varying function of time, or even a function of time and space. Prediction is an important special case of estimation in which the message of interest is the value of a random signal at some future time (see AUTOMATA THEORY). This future value is to be estimated from the portion of the random signal (perhaps noise-corrupted) that has occurred up to the present time.

A few of the many areas in which detection problems arise are as follows: receivers in digital communication systems, radar receivers, sonar receivers, seismic detectors, oil field exploration, and radio astronomy. In many of these areas there are related estimation problems. If, for example, one uses radar to determine whether there is an object in a particular region of the sky, one has a binary detection problem. If one also wants to know the location, size, and velocity of the object, it becomes an estimation problem, and a different type of radar system is needed.

Conceptually, detection problems are most naturally treated in what is called a Bayesian formulation (see STATISTICS). Here one assumes that there are n possible messages, numbered 0, 1, $\cdots$, $n-1$, and that these messages occur with known probabilities, p_0, p_1, $\cdots$, p_{n-1}. Conditional on each message, there is a known probability distribution on the received noise-corrupted signal. Finally, there is a cost C_{ij} associated with detecting message j if message i is actually present. Within this formulation, the optimum detector can then reasonably be defined as the detector that minimizes the expected cost of incorrect decisions. Such an optimum detector can be implemented by just computing a set of $n-1$ numbers, called likelihood ratios, and then making a decision based on the relative sizes of the likelihood ratios. The ith likelihood ratio is defined as the ratio of the probability of the received noisy message conditional on message i to the probability of the received noisy message conditional on message 0. These likelihood ratios do not depend on the probabilities with which the messages occur nor on the cost function C_{ij}. For this reason, the likelihood ratios are also fundamental in other formulations of the detection problem where one is unwilling or unable to make assumptions about the probabilities of the messages or about the cost function.

Assumptions underlying prediction or filtering

There is one important situation in which the likelihood ratios are quite easy to calculate. Assume there are n known signals, $S_0(t)$, $S_1(t)$, $\cdots$, $S_{n-1}(t)$, corresponding to the n messages. Assume further that the received noisy signal when message i occurs is $S_i(t) + n(t)$, in which $n(t)$ is Gaussian noise. Then each likelihood ratio can be found by passing the received noisy signal through an appropriately chosen linear filter and sampling the output at a given time. More complex detection problems can be handled by extensions of this basic technique.

A few of the many areas in which estimation and prediction problems arise are as follows: control, analogue communication receivers, radar receivers, sonar receivers, seismic array processors, and radio astronomy. As with detection, the simplest conceptual formulation for estimation is the Bayesian formulation, in which one assumes complete probabilistic descriptions of both messages and received signals. If a cost function, such as the squared value of the error, is specified between message and message estimate, then an optimum estimator can be defined as the estimator that minimizes the expected cost.

A classic case of the above formulation is that in which the message and the noise are jointly Gaussian processes and the received signal is message plus noise. The optimum estimator, with an arbitrary delay or prediction interval, was found independently in the United States and the Soviet Union by the mathematicians Norbert Wiener and A.N. Kolmogorov and turned out to be an appropriately chosen linear filter. A later approach by the U.S. mathematicians Rudolf E. Kalman and Richard S. Bucy turns out to have significant advantages in the many applications in which the processes are nonstationary. Curiously enough, the same solution arises if the message and noise processes are not assumed to be Gaussian, but the estimator is restricted to be linear.

Aside from various extensions of the above case, most estimation problems cannot be solved exactly, and one must be content with approximate solutions and with choosing an estimator structure on intuitive grounds and then optimizing some parameters of the structure.

Cryptographic, linguistic, and other applications. Some applications have been made in cryptography and linguistics. It is possible to formulate a theory of cryptography, or secrecy systems, in terms of the concepts occurring in information theory. When this is done, it appears that the information rate R of a language is intimately related to the possibility of solving cryptograms in that language. The smaller this rate, the easier such a solution becomes and the less material is necessary to render such a solution unique. Indeed, within limits, the theory becomes quantitative and predictive, giving means of calculating how much material must be intercepted in a given language and with a given cipher in order to ensure the existence of a unique solution.

Studies have been made of the distribution of lengths and frequency of occurrence of the different words in a language such as English. It has been found, for example, that the relative frequency of the nth most frequent word may be expressed quite closely by a formula of the type $P(n+m)^{-b}$, with suitable constants for P, m, and b. Experimental data of this type can be explained as consequences of the assumption that a language gradually evolves under continued use into an efficient communication code (see LINGUISTICS).

Psychologists have discovered interesting relationships between the amount of information in a stimulus and reaction time to the stimulus. For example, an experiment can be set up in which there are four lights and four associated push buttons. The lights go on in a random order and the subject is required to press the corresponding button as quickly as possible after a light goes on. It is found that the average time required for this reaction increases linearly with an increase in the amount of information conveyed by the lights. This experimental result holds true under a wide variety of changes in the experiment: the number of lights, the probabilities of different lights, and even varying correlations between successive lights.

The results suggest that under certain conditions the human being, in manipulating information, may adopt codes and methods akin to those used in information theory.

BIBLIOGRAPHY. C.E. SHANNON and WARREN WEAVER, *The Mathematical Theory of Communication* (1949), the classic in which information theory was first developed; R.G. GALLAGER, *Information Theory and Reliable Communication* (1968), a comprehensive modern text; J.R. PIERCE, *Symbols, Signals, and Noise: The Nature and Process of Communication* (1961); and G. RAISBECK, *Information Theory: An Introduction for Scientists and Engineers* (1964), two non-mathematical introductions; M.S. PINSKER, *Information and Information Stability of Random Variables and Processes* (1964; orig. pub. in Russian, 1960), a very general and abstract work on the development of coding theorems; JACOB WOLFOWITZ, *Coding Theorems of Information Theory*, 2nd ed. (1964), a classic on the mathematical development of coding theorems; T. BERGER, *Rate Distortion Theory: A Mathematical Basis for Data Compression* (1971), a comprehensive modern treatment of source coding with a distortion measure; E.R. BERLEKAMP, *Algebraic Coding Theory* (1968), a comprehensive modern treatment of block codes; W.W. PETERSON, *Error-Correcting Codes* (1961), an earlier less abstract work on the development of coding techniques; Special Issue on Error Correcting Codes, *IEEE Trans. on Communication Technology* (October 1971), a series of articles dealing with applications of coding techniques; NORBERT WIENER, *Extrapolation, Interpolation, and Smoothing of Stationary Time Series, with Engineering Applications* (1949), a classic on the development of filtering and prediction; A.N. KOLMOGOROV, "Interpolation and Extrapolation of Stationary Random Sequences," *Izv. Akad. Nauk SSSR*, Ser. Mat., vol. 5, no. 3 (1941), a classic on the independent development of filtering and prediction; H.L. VAN TREES, *Detection, Estimation, and Modulation Theory*, 3 pt. (1968–71), a comprehensive treatment of communication applications of filtering and prediction theory; A.M. YAGLOM, *An Introduction to the Theory of Stationary Random Functions*, rev. ed. (Eng. trans. 1962), a comprehensive treatment of filtering and prediction theory; C.E. SHANNON, "Communication Theory of Secrecy Systems," *Bell Syst. Tech. J.*, 28:656–715 (1949), a classic in cryptography; W.R. GARNER, *Uncertainty and Structure As Psychological Concepts* (1962), with some applications to psychology.

(R.G.G.)

Infrared Sources, Astronomical

The infrared region of the electromagnetic spectrum, in very general terms, consists of those wavelengths lying between visible light and radio wavelengths. It includes wavelengths between about 7,000 angstroms (one angstrom, or Å, equals 10^{-8} centimetre) and perhaps a few millimetres, a range of several thousand, which explains why there is ambiguity concerning wavelengths when reference is made to infrared radiation.

Astronomical sources in the region between the visible part of the spectrum and about one micron (one micron is 10^{-4} centimetre, or 10,000 angstroms) have been investigated using techniques that are extensions of those applied to astronomy at visible wavelengths. That is, sources have been observed at these wavelengths using photographic plates and extended-spectral-range photomultiplier tubes. The results obtained have also been an extension of results obtained at visible wavelengths. It is primarily at wavelengths beyond one micron that infrared observations have yielded fundamentally new information about astronomical objects. In addition, it is at wavelengths beyond 10,000 angstroms that the techniques for detecting radiation also begin to change dramatically. The generally accepted definition of infrared radiation extending to radio wavelengths must also be examined in the light of current developments. Radio-astronomical techniques are presently used for detecting radiation at wavelengths of two millimetres, and, therefore, detection of astronomical objects in the millimetre region of the spectrum should now be considered within the realm of radio astronomy.

In light of the above, this article is restricted to observations of infrared radiation from astronomical objects in the region between one micron and one millimetre. In almost all cases, infrared astronomical sources have been found to be associated with objects that have been observed at visible wavelengths and in many cases with objects known to be radio sources; *i.e.*, solar system objects, stars, nebulae, and galaxies.

First discovery of infrared radiation

History. Infrared astronomy originated in the early years of the 19th century with the work of the British astronomer Sir William Herschel, who placed thermometer-like devices at various places along the spectrum of the Sun, obtained by breaking up white light into its components in a spectroscope. His devices indicated that there was energy arriving from the Sun at wavelengths longer than could be detected by the human eye and that this energy was, like light, part of the electromagnetic spectrum.

The detection of infrared radiation from astronomical objects began seriously with the work of the American astronomers W.W. Coblentz, Edison Pettit, and Seth B. Nicholson in the 1920s. These investigators employed thermocouples and discovered that relatively redder stars radiated relatively more infrared radiation. The spectral range of the radiation, however, was not well defined.

Consequently, the results consisted more of measurements of the total radiation from stars than of distribution of energy with wavelength. Investigations by astronomers of the effect of the interstellar medium on wavelengths of radiation motivated further work in the infrared; and in 1948 the extension of observations on the extinction of stars to wavelengths of two microns (one micron is 0.001 millimetre) was reported. Thus, infrared techniques became a tool applied to investigations of astronomical problems.

Modern infrared astronomy began in the early 1960s. The technological developments necessary before this could occur were the use of cryogenic (extremely cold) detector systems. Examples are lead sulfide photoconductors cooled with liquid nitrogen and the gallium-doped germanium bolometer (see below *Principles of detection*) cooled with liquid helium. The development of special interference filters was also necessary. The gallium-doped germanium bolometer developed by F.J. Low ultimately led to detection of radiation out to wavelengths of 20 microns from ground-based telescopes and detection of radiation at 100 microns from balloons and aircraft and was even used for detection of radiation at one-millimetre wavelength. This device formed the basis of infrared astronomy at wavelengths beyond three microns throughout the 1960s and led to vast numbers of new discoveries. Present detectors at these long wavelengths also include copper-doped germanium photoconductors.

In 1965 an unbiassed complete survey of the sky in the Northern Hemisphere was initiated at a wavelength of 2.2 microns by G. Neugebauer and R.B. Leighton. This work resulted in a catalog of thousands of sources of infrared radiation. Most of the sources detected in the survey have been identified and associated with known cool stars, but several objects of peculiar interest were found.

Principles of detection. The progress of knowledge gained about astronomical objects at infrared wavelengths has been determined almost completely by the evolution of detectors and other techniques used in this work. There are two types of detectors presently used in almost all infrared astronomical applications. These are bolometers (primarily the gallium-doped germanium bolometer) and photoconductors made of lead sulfide as well as germanium, doped typically with copper, mercury, or cadmium. The detection of infrared photons (a photon is the quantum of energy associated with electromagnetic waves) in a bolometer is accomplished by measuring the change in resistance of the device when it is exposed to radiation. The absorption of infrared energy leads to an increase in temperature of the piece of semiconductor that is the detector, and this results in decreased resistance of the material, a change that can be easily recorded.

In a photoconductor, the absorption of a photon by the semiconductor material leads to the production of a free negative electron or a "hole"; *i.e.*, a space that acts as a positive charge. The free electrons or holes are then collected by application of a potential difference across the semiconductor.

Problems of reception

The atoms and molecules of the Earth's atmosphere severely limit observations of astronomical sources at infrared wavelengths because each type of molecule absorbs specific wavelengths of radiation, thereby preventing these from reaching Earth-based instruments. Transmission through the atmosphere is very small at many wavelengths between one micron and one millimetre. Atmospheric water vapour is the source of the most serious problem, leading to almost total opaqueness between 40 and 200 microns. Other absorption bands of water vapour and carbon dioxide create regions unusable for observations between one micron and 40 microns as well. The regions that can be used for astronomical infrared measurements from mountaintop observatories lie between the absorption bands of the absorbing atmospheric gases and are commonly referred to as atmospheric windows.

Practically all ground-based observations are obtained through the use of ordinary reflecting telescopes, which focus infrared wavelengths in the same way as visible light. Some gains in sensitivity could be made through the use of cooled telescopes in orbit outside of the terrestrial atmosphere; however, considering the enormous cost of the cryogenic systems that would be required and comparing it with the large amount of work that can be done with ground-based instruments and with those carried high in the atmosphere by balloons, rockets, and airplanes, there is considerable doubt as to whether infrared space telescopes should be constructed. The maintenance of cryogenic systems on space telescopes would be a formidable task.

The detection of small amounts of infrared radiation from specific astronomical objects is difficult because they must be detected against a large background of radiation from the terrestrial atmosphere, the observing telescope, and auxiliary instrumentation, all of which are between 200° and 300° K (on the absolute-temperature scale 0° C is 273° K) and, at these temperatures, radiate energy in the infrared region of the spectrum. A certain amount of such radiation always falls on a detector and degrades its performance.

Special optical devices and techniques are necessary in infrared applications. Exotic materials must be used as windows and lenses, and, in general, they are not as efficient as might be desired. Thus, reflecting components are used to as great an extent as possible. Spectral regions for observation are generally isolated with special interference filters made of infrared-transmitting materials.

Types of infrared sources. *Sources in the solar system.* Some of the brightest infrared astronomical sources are objects within the solar system: the Sun, Moon, planets, and planetary satellites. The Moon, satellites of other planets, and asteroids have generally been found to emit radiation with a spectrum like that of a blackbody. (A blackbody is an object that would absorb all of the radiation falling on it. The energy distribution of radiation emitted by a blackbody is uniquely determined by temperature.) Some interesting properties of the surfaces of some of these solar-system objects seem to be indicated by the spectrum of reflected sunlight at the shorter infrared wavelengths. Observations of the planets have generally yielded information about the abundance of various atmospheric constituents. Further analyses are continuing in efforts to envisage realistic model atmospheres for the planets that are in agreement with observations in the infrared. The thermal emission from comets has also been observed. The radiation from at least one shows characteristics similar to those of the radiation from some type M stars, as described below.

Blackbody concept

Galactic sources. In the observations of objects outside the solar system, many unexpected results have been obtained.

The radiation emitted by many stars has been observed at wavelengths extending far into the infrared region; in many of these cases, the distribution of energy among those wavelengths has been found to correspond closely to that of a blackbody radiator at the effective temperature of the star. It is fortunate, in the light of all the peculiar results that have been obtained in infrared astronomy, that several stars with normal spectra are observed. It would be difficult to have a solid basis for calibration of photometric systems if all objects were abnormal. Frequently, in observations of the cooler stars with normal energy distribution, molecular-absorption bands (wavelengths at which part of the radiation emitted by the stars is absorbed by molecules in their atmospheres) have been studied at infrared wavelengths, leading to information about the composition of stellar atmospheres.

A large number of cool stars of various atmospheric chemical composition (classified as M, S, and C stars; the letters identify specific spectral types) have been found to exhibit infrared radiation in excess of that expected from a blackbody at the effective temperature of the star. The shape of the spectrum of the excess radiation emitted by M stars (those with oxygen-rich atmospheres) is probably the result of thermal emission by solid grains of silicate-type materials that have condensed in the outer atmospheres of these stars. The particles have probably been blown out from the star by radiation pressure and now exist in the space around the star. The grains absorb short-wavelength radiation from the star and re-radiate this energy in the infrared. Stars with carbon-rich atmospheres show similar excess radiation, with the difference that the spectrum of the radiation from the circumstellar grains of these stars differs in shape from that from the grains around M stars. The chemical composition of the grains surrounding these carbon stars thus differs from that of the grains surrounding the M stars.

Some hot stars (massive stars in early stages of stellar evolution, of spectral types O, B, and A) exhibit large excess amounts of infrared energy out to wavelengths of 20 microns. Examples are the O stars in the Orion Nebula. The excess radiation from these stars is probably due to circumstellar grains, a remnant of the interstellar medium from which the stars were formed. In some cases, however—particularly in the results obtained from observations of Be stars (B stars with spectra that exhibit emission lines)—excess infrared radiation must be attributed to free-free emission (produced by moving charged particles that approach one another but do not collide) from the hot ionized gas surrounding the star.

Various stars at intermediate temperature range (classified as F, G, and K) also have been found to exhibit peculiar excess radiation at infrared wavelengths. The T Tauri stars, such as T Tauri itself and R Monocerotis (these are stars thought to be in an early phase of stellar evolution), have been found to emit a large amount of infrared radiation. Some but not all F and G supergiants, such as HD 101584 and 89 Herculis, a star of normal chemical composition, have been found to exhibit large excesses. The RV Tauri stars (classified as spectral type G to K) have also been found to have large amounts of excess radiation in the ten-micron-wavelength region. It is thought that these excesses are also due to thermal re-radiation by circumstellar grains, although the origin of the grains is not completely understood.

Several peculiar infrared sources have been observed. One example is the source NML Cygnus, originally detected in a search for astronomical sources of radiation of two-micron wavelength. This object is stellar and is very faint at visual wavelengths with even large telescopes but is one of the brightest infrared sources outside of the solar system at wavelengths near 10 microns. The object shows spectral characteristics of a late-type star (cool and red). Apparently it is surrounded by such a large amount of dust that the visual wavelengths of light are greatly attenuated. Another extreme example is a stellar object buried in the obscuring matter of the Orion Nebula, from which no visible radiation has ever been observed.

Peculiar infrared sources

Nova Serpentis 1970 has been observed in considerable detail. The amount of energy in the infrared increased from a small fraction of the total luminosity of this nova to more than 90 percent over the period between 35 and 60 days after the outburst. Again, the explanation of the measurements must rest on the formation and heating of small solid particles.

The central region of the Galaxy has also been found to be a source of a large amount of infrared energy at wavelengths as long as 100 microns. It appears that most of the radiation from this region comes from dust particles heated by hot stars in regions of ionized hydrogen that are obscured from view by the strong absorption and scattering of visible light that occur between the Sun and the centre of the Galaxy. Some infrared radiation arises from the Sagittarius A radio source near the galactic centre.

Nebular sources. Nebulae of various kinds within the Galaxy have also been found to be sources of radiation at infrared wavelengths.

Galactic diffuse nebulae are regions in which early-type stars are found. It has been known for some time through interpretation of visual wavelength observations that dust as well as ionized gas exists in these regions. Examples of some galactic diffuse nebulae are the Orion Nebula (M42), the Omega Nebula (M17), and the Lagoon Nebula (M8). At infrared wavelengths these objects have been found to radiate large amounts of energy out to wavelengths as long as 100 microns. It is thought that the radiation is caused by the solid dust particles in the nebulae being heated by short-wavelength radiation from the young hot stars in the region. The grains re-radiate this energy in the infrared. The spectral distribution of the radiation from the Trapezium region of the Orion Nebula has been investigated and found to be the same as that from the circumstellar grains surrounding M stars. These data suggest that grains composed of silicate-like materials also exist in interstellar space, at least in the Orion region.

Planetary nebulae (the ionized gas surrounding some dying stars) have also been found to radiate unexpected amounts of infrared radiation. The brightest planetary nebula at infrared wavelengths is *NGC* 7027, although a large number of others have also been detected at wavelengths as long as 10 to 20 microns. In the case of this class of objects, a question arises as to the origin of the solid particles that apparently are necessary to explain the infrared results. The spectral shape of the ten-micron continuum from *NGC* 7027 does not appear to be similar to that observed in M stars or the Orion Trapezium region.

Radiation from planetary nebulae

Emission lines (radiation at discrete wavelengths caused by discrete atomic or molecular transitions) have been observed from some planetary nebulae. The lines that have been detected are those at 10.5 microns and 12.8 microns, due to ions of sulfur and neon, respectively; *i.e.*, the source itself contains these elements. The existence of these lines is one of the few results of infrared astronomy that was predicted and later confirmed by observations.

The Crab Nebula is the remnant of a supernova explosion and is therefore completely different from any of the thermal sources discussed above. It has been observed out to five microns with results that confirm the generally expected nonthermal spectrum of the source.

Attempts have been made to observe the interstellar medium in absorption spectra against known sources of infrared radiation. In particular, searches have been made for absorption features caused by interstellar grains that might be associated with absorption bands of identifiable solid materials. Since it has long been suggested that a significant constituent of the interstellar grains was water ice, a search for the three-micron band of this material has been made; but no evidence for it in solid form as a constituent of the grains has ever been found. Absorption due to the 11-micron band of silicate-like materials has been found in radiation from the galactic centre and in the spectrum of the invisible point source located in the Orion Nebula. The results indicate that, although silicates do exist as constituents of the interstellar grains, most particles are not composed of this material. (Ultraviolet-wavelength results indicate that another significant constituent is graphite.)

Extragalactic sources. External galaxies have also been found to be sources of infrared radiation. In the case of at least one of these objects (M82), the source of radiation is extended over a relatively wide region (at least 20″ of arc) and is probably caused by thermal re-radiation by dust particles. In the cases of the infrared radiation from the nuclei of Seyfert galaxies (for example, *NGC* 1068 and *NGC* 4151) and quasi-stellar objects (for example, 3C 273), the radiation mechanism producing the infrared has not yet been conclusively determined, and knowledge of the physical conditions in these objects must await further observational evidence. Of particular interest is the detailed spectral shape of the radiation in the infrared and the absence or presence of significant variations of infrared with time.

Non-thermal infrared radiation

A class of objects radiating nonthermal infrared radiation has been discovered. One example is the object that until recently was thought to be a variable star, BL Lacertae. These objects are radio sources that also show no spectral lines at visual wavelengths; and thus it is difficult to deduce a distance for them. (The spectrum of an astronomical body helps to establish its distance from Earth.) They are thought to be extragalactic, and their nature will be the subject of considerable further investigation.

Microwave background radiation. Attempts have been made to extend observations of the microwave background radiation (frequently associated with the remnant of the radiation field of the early history of the expanding universe) into the wavelength region shortward of one millimetre. These observations must be made from space above most of the terrestrial atmosphere and are extremely difficult. Further work must be done in the area before conclusive results can be obtained.

BIBLIOGRAPHY. One of the best books on infrared techniques, although somewhat technical, is P.W. KRUSE, L.D. MCGLAUCHLIN, and R.B. MCQUISTAN, *Elements of Infrared Technology* (1962). Articles on infrared astronomy of a semitechnical nature are B.C. MURRAY and J.A. WESTPHAL, "Infrared Astronomy," *Scient. Am.*, 213:20–29 (1965); and G. NEUGEBAUER and R.B. LEIGHTON, "The Infrared Sky," *ibid.*, 219:50–65 (1968). Current developments, also of a semitechnical nature, are frequently reported on in *Sky and Telescope* (monthly). On a more technical level, several review articles summarize various aspects of infrared astronomy. H.L. JOHNSON has reviewed infrared photometry of stars particularly from the point of view of bolometric corrections and effective temperatures in *A. Rev. Astr. Astrophys.*, 4:193–205 (1966). H.L. JOHNSON in *Stars and Stellar Systems*, vol. 7, *Nebulae and Interstellar Matter*, p. 167 (1968), gives examples of the application of infrared observations of stars to the problem of the interstellar grains. The infrared spectra of stars have been reviewed by H. SPINRAD and R.F. WING, *A. Rev. Astr. Astrophys.*, 7:249–302 (1969). A review of the many interesting and frequently unexpected new results of infrared astronomy has been written by G. NEUGEBAUER, E. BECKLIN, and A.R. HYLAND, *ibid.*, 9:67–102 (1971).

(W.St.)

Ingres, Jean-Auguste-Dominique

For the second third of the 19th century, Jean-Auguste-Dominique Ingres was the leader of the Classical, as opposed to the Romantic, school of painting in France. The champion of line and of firm contour, of subtly graded, clear colour, and of carefully balanced composition, he viewed with contempt the dramatic chiaroscuro (treatment of light), the turbulent movement, and the tense emotional context of his chief enemy, the Romantic painter Delacroix. Time has dimmed the acrimony of the quarrels of his epoch and made clearer the quality of his genuine, if still curiously troubling, genius. His position as one of the great masters in the Western tradition is now secure, and his considerable influence upon later artists, men as different as Edgar Degas, Pierre-Auguste Renoir, and Pablo Picasso, is acknowledged.

Giraudon

Ingres, self-portrait, oil on canvas, *c.* 1800. In the Musée Conde, Chantilly, France.

Early life and works. Ingres's rise from his modest, provincial beginnings to his eminence as a life senator and holder of innumerable honours was slow and fitful, yet from the beginning he was sure of himself, his talents, and his chosen path. He was born August 29, 1780, in Montauban, an ancient city in southwestern France, a little north of Toulouse. His father, a decorative sculptor of considerable talent, a modest portrait painter, a musician, and a member of the local learned academy, was his earliest instructor in the arts. Ingres's actual schooling began when he was six. He was then sent to the Brothers of Christian Doctrine (the Marists). Unfortunately, the disruptions of the French Revolution closed that school four years later. Ingres's formal education was over. The abrupt ending left a lasting mark. He spent his lifetime in never-ending study, in an attempt to secure the learning he desired.

In 1791 he was sent by his father, a Toulousain by birth, to artist friends in that city. The youthful Ingres was entered in the Academy of Toulouse to study drawing, figure painting, and landscape. In his first year, "Ingres fils," as he signed some early portrait drawings made during his Toulouse stay, won third prize. Two years later he was awarded a first prize in figure drawing. For nearly three years, from the age of 13 to 16, he supported himself, occupying the post of second violin in the orchestra of the Capital (the opera). Ingres's violin remained with him until his death, and he continued to play it for pleasure.

In the late summer of 1797 he set out for Paris, where he was received by the leading Neoclassical painter Jacques-Louis David as a student in his famous and lively atelier. Two years later Ingres was accepted in the department of painting at the École des Beaux-Arts. In February 1800 he won the school's first prize for a torso and, in October, the second prize in the Prix de Rome. He and his artist contemporaries were exempted that year from military service. A year later he won the first Prix de Rome with his painting "The Envoys from Agamemnon." The French treasury, however, strained by Bonaparte's wars, was then unable to pay the prize. Instead they provided him with a studio in the former convent of the Capuchins and a modest allowance. In 1804 he signed the "Bonaparte as First Consul," commissioned for the city of Liège (now in Belgium), and painted a portrait of his father (Montauban) and his own self-portrait (Chantilly, France). The following year he completed the three portraits of the Rivière family—father, mother, and daughter—and a year later the curiously hieratic and powerful "Napoleon I on the Imperial Throne."

The first Prix de Rome

Mature life and works. He had become engaged to Anne-Marie-Julie Forestier, the daughter of a judge, who was also a student in David's atelier. When the money for his Rome sojourn finally came through, in the late summer of 1806, he immediately left Paris, arriving in Rome in October. The day after Christmas he was given a studio in the small pavilion of San Gaetano at the edge of the Villa Medici property on the Pincian Hill, a studio with wonderful views over Rome and the villa's extensive gardens. His paintings shown in the Salon of 1806, an exhibition that opened after his departure, were severely criticized as "bizarre" and "revolutionary," criticism that he received with bitterness; but, undeterred by the criticism, he passed four productive years at the villa, fulfilling his obligations by sending the required number of paintings to Paris, among them the famous "Valpinçon Bather."

At the end of his term as a *pensionnaire*, instead of returning to France, he moved to a studio nearby in the Via Gregoriana. His engagement to Julie had been broken in 1807, when he courteously but firmly refused her father's command that he return to Paris immediately. Through his friend the engraver Jacques-Edouard Gatteaux, Ingres became acquainted with the French officials ruling occupied Rome. Several of them, such as Charles-François Marcotte, not only gave him commissions but became lifelong friends. In the convent Sta. Trinità dei Monti he painted for the French authorities two large historical canvases, "Romulus Victorious over Acron" and "Virgil Reading the Aeneid" (version revised later). The Roman years were the ones in which he supplemented his meagre income by making the majority of the pencil portrait drawings that are so much sought after and admired today, although they were scorned by their author as potboilers. An almost uncanny control of delicate yet firm and sure line, an unending, if discreet, inventiveness in posing his sitters in a manner to reveal personality through shrewdly observed characteristic gestures, combined with a capacity to record not only an exact likeness but also the precise social rank and even the nationality of the sitters, make this category of Ingres's drawings unique.

Pencil portrait drawings

In 1813 he had married Madeleine Chapelle, a milliner of Chéret, whom he had never met before her arrival in Italy. She came to Rome at Ingres's request and upon the suggestion of her cousin, Madame de Lauréal, who was a friend of the artist. The marriage, although childless after the death of their firstborn, was one of mutual felicity.

With Napoleon's downfall in 1815, Ingres was left without official orders for paintings, until the new ambassador, some months later, commissioned the "Christ Giving the Keys to St. Peter" (Montauban). During 1816 and 1817 Ingres drew the portraits of many English visitors to Rome. His entries in the Salon of 1819, "The Grand Odalisque" (Louvre, Paris) ,"Philip V Decorating Marshall Berwick" (Duke of Alba, Madrid), and "Roger Delivering Anglica" (Louvre) were as severely attacked as his earlier work had been. Grieved and unhappy, the artist accepted the invitation of his former studio mate and musical companion, the sculptor Lorenzo Bartolini, and moved to Florence, where he remained from 1820 to 1824. Orders from friends for painted as well as drawn portraits and the commission for a large altarpiece, the "Vow of Louis XIII," for the cathedral of Montauban, as well as his work on a number of smaller historical paintings, kept him busy. In the autumn of 1824, he left Florence, taking the large "Vow of Louis XIII," rolled, with him to Paris. He was so uncertain of his welcome that he left his devoted wife behind in Florence. To his surprise the painting was a tremendous success. Charles X personally decorated him with the Cross of the Legion of Honor at the Salon's close. In June of the following year he was elected a member of the Académie des Beaux-Arts, and, at the year's end, he opened a studio for students. Soon he had over 100 pupils, among them his future biographer Eugène-Emanuel Amaury-Duval. Stern, exacting, touchy, and apparently humourless, Ingres yet had qualities that held his followers to him in bonds of friendship and admiration broken only by death.

Election to the Académie des Beaux-Arts

In 1827, as a member of the Académie des Beaux-Arts, he and his wife were given an apartment at the Institut de France. The same year he finished and saw put in place, in the Louvre, the ambitious and complicated "Apotheosis of Homer." In 1829 he was named professor at the École des Beaux-Arts, and in 1833 he served as vice president and in 1834 as president; but, when, toward the close of that year, his Salon offering, "The Martyrdom of St. Symphorien," was coolly received, the unhappy artist asked for and received an appointment as Director of the French Academy in Rome. He arrived in Rome in January 1835, jubilantly received by the students and staff. During his directorship (1835–41) he restored and enlarged the Villa, increased the library, and established a course in archaeology. He also took part in many concerts, more than once accompanying on his violin the young piano-playing Charles Gounod, then one of the *pensionnaires*. His portrait drawing of the youthful composer is in the Art Institute of Chicago. Before his return to Paris in 1841, he completed for Marcotte the "Odalisque with Slave," for the Duc d' Orléans the "Antiochus and Stratonice" (1840; Musée Conde, Chantilly, France), and for Tsar Nicholas I "The Virgin with the Host" (1841; State Pushkin Museum of Fine Arts, Moscow).

Late life and works. His return to Paris was a triumph. It included a large banquet in his honour, an invitation to visit Louis-Philippe at Versailles and Neuilly, and a pass for life to the Comédie-Française, which he proudly used for years. His portrait of the Duc d' Orléans was completed in 1842, two months before the death of the Duke, following a carriage accident. The next year Ingres began work for the Duc de Luynes at Dampierre on a great decorative scheme of two allegorical panels, "The Golden Age" and "The Iron Age." The paintings were still unfinished when, in July 1849, Madame Ingres died from a blood ailment. The despairing artist could not bring himself to return alone to Dampierre to complete the commission, so in 1850 the Duc de Luynes released him from the agreement. (A reduced replica of "The Golden Age," signed and dated 1862, is in the Fogg Art Museum, Cambridge, Massachusetts). A year later, he resigned from the École des Beaux-Arts.

Death of Ingres's wife

In the spring of 1852, on the advice of friends, he married the 43-year-old Delphine Ramel, a relative of his old friend Marcotte. Like his first marriage, the second was also happy. (Three portrait drawings depicting Delphine [1855], her father [1852], and her mother [1852] are in Fogg Art Museum.) In 1853 he received the commission for an "Apotheosis of Napoleon I" for the ceiling of the Emperor's salon in the Hôtel de Ville. The Emperor, the Empress, and their entourage came to Ingres's studio a year later to view the completed work (destroyed in May 1871, with Delacroix's "Peace," in the fire of the Commune). During the late 1840s and 1850s, Ingres painted, although always under protest, an impressive number of superb portraits of men and women, as well as his "Self-Portrait" (1858) for the Uffizi (variant of 1859 in the

Fogg Art Museum). In 1862 he was appointed senator (some years previously he had been raised to the grade of Grand Officer of the Legion of Honor), and in 1865 he was made a member of the Belgian Royal Academy of Fine Arts.

Although he never knew Greek and had only rudimentary Latin, he was, through translations, as intimately familiar with the works of his heroes of antiquity, the poets Homer and Virgil, as he was with the paintings of his idol, Raphael. His steady, earnest, private study and his warm friendships with such learned men as the archaeologists Quatremère de Quincy and Désiré Raoul-Rochette more than filled the lacunae of his early education. Present-day scholars have only recently begun to uncover the allusions, allegories, and symbols of such paintings as the "Napoleon I on the Imperial Throne," the "Stratonice," and the "Virgil Reading the Aeneid." He was still studying the old masters at the age of 87. His last drawing, a tracing after a photograph of a composition by the Florentine painter Giotto di Bondone, was made a week before his death on January 14, 1867.

Allusions, allegories, and symbols

Ingres bequeathed to Montauban, his native city, the contents of his studio. In addition to about 4,000 drawings (the studies, sketches, and working drawings of a lifetime), the bequest included such paintings as the coldly classical "Jesus Among the Doctors," finished in 1862 but still in his studio when he died, and the "Dream of Ossian" (signed and dated 1813), which he bought back in 1835 with the idea of reworking the painting; also included were the early oil studies of the nude and two of his three known small landscapes in circular form, made in Rome in 1807, as well as the reference library he had assembled for his own use, the paintings he had collected, his *cahiers*, or notebooks, the little wooden models for his classical structures, and his famous violin. All of this is now housed in the Musée Ingres.

MAJOR WORKS

"The Envoys from Agamemnon" (1801; École des Beaux-Arts, Paris); "Bonaparte as First Consul" (1804; Musée des Beaux-Arts, Liège, Belgium); "Monsieur Philibert Rivière" (1805); Louvre, Paris); "Mme Philibert Rivière" (1805; Louvre); "Mlle Rivière" (1805; Louvre); "Napoleon I on the Imperial Throne" (1806; Musée de l'Armée, Paris); "François-Marcus Granet" (*c.* 1806; Musée Granet, Aix-en-Provence); "Valpinçon Bather" (1808; Louvre); "Oedipus and the Sphinx" (1808; Louvre); "Monsieur Marcotte" (1810; National Gallery of Art, Washington, D.C.); "Romulus Victorious over Acron" (1812; École des Beaux-Arts, Paris); "Virgil Reading the Aeneid" (*c.* 1812; Musée des Augustins, Toulouse, France); "Roger Delivering Angélique" (1819; Louvre), "Paolo and Francesca" (1819; Musée des Beaux-Arts, Angers, France); "The Sistine Chapel" (1820; Louvre); "Count Gouriev" (1821; Hermitage, Leningrad); "Monsieur Leblanc" (1823; Metropolitan Museum of Art, New York); "Mme Leblanc" (1823; Metropolitan Museum of Art, New York); "Vow of Louis XIII" (1824; Cathedral, Montauban, France); "The Apotheosis of Homer" (1827; Louvre); "Monsieur Louis-François Bertin" (1832; Louvre); "The Martyrdom of St. Symphorien" (1834; Cathedral, Autun, France); "Odalisque with Slave" (1839; Fogg Art Museum, Cambridge, Massachusetts); "Duc d'Orléans" (1842; Count of Paris, Louveciennes, France); "Mme d' Haussonville" (1845; Frick Collection, New York); "Mme Reiset" (1846; Fogg Art Museum); "Mme Moitessier Seated" (1856; National Gallery, London); "La Source" (1856; Louvre); "Self-Portrait, Aged 79" (1859; Fogg Art Museum); "The Turkish Bath" (1862; Louvre).

DRAWINGS: "The Family of Lucien Bonaparte" (1815; Fogg Art Museum; Cambridge); "Study of Horseman for St. Symphorien" (1827; Nelson Gallery and Atkins Museum of Fine Arts, Kansas City); "Mme Désiré Raoul-Rochette" (1830; Cleveland Museum of Art); "Charles Gounod" (1841; Art Institute of Chicago); "Portrait of Monsieur Étienne-Jean Delécluze" (1856; Fogg Art Museum).

BIBLIOGRAPHY. LILI FROHLICH-BUM, *Ingres: Sein Leben und sein Stil* (1924; Eng. trans., *Ingres: His Life and Art*, 1926), one of the earliest biographies to appear in English, adequate if uninspired; WALTER PACH, *Ingres* (1939), an artist's appreciative interpretation; GEORGE WILDENSTEIN, *Ingres* (1954), now the standard work of reference in English for the paintings; ROBERT ROSENBLUM, *Jean-Auguste-Dominique Ingres* (1967), a stylistic analysis of the most important paintings —lively, original, and perceptive, with 190 reproductions, 48 in colour; AGNES MONGAN and HANS NAEF, *Ingres Centennial Exhibition, 1867–1967: Drawings, Watercolors, and Oil Sketches from American Collections, Fogg Art Museum, Harvard University, February 12–April 9, 1967* (1967), fully illustrated with a page of critical text opposite each of the 116 full-page illustrations and an appendix on the artist's drawing technique.

(Ag.M.)

Inheritance

In its broadest sense, inheritance, or heritage, means the transfer of something from earlier to later ages or generations. Thus, one may speak of an individual's inherited traits of body or character and of the cultural heritage of one civilization from another. In a more specific sense, inheritance signifies the devolution of property upon the death of its owner. In modern society this devolution is regulated in minute detail by law. In laws of the continental European pattern the pertinent branch is generally called the law of succession. In Anglo-American laws it was customary to distinguish between descent of real estate and distribution of personal estate. The rules applicable to the two kinds of property have been fused, but no common term is yet universally accepted. In England, books dealing with the subject are varyingly entitled "On Wills," "On Probate," "On Succession," or "On Executors and Administrators." In the United States, the phrase probate law is frequently, although inaccurately, applied to the field as a whole. Following the title of an important statute of the state of New York, the phrase law of decedents' estates has been gaining ground, and occasionally one finds the phrase law of succession. The title of the present article has been chosen in accord with the usage of anthropologists and other social scientists.

The article is divided into the following sections:

I. Inheritance and property rights
- Individual ownership of property
- Critiques of inheritance

II. Prime issues in the law of inheritance
- Freedom of testation
- Divided or undivided inheritance

III. Intestate succession
- History of intestate succession
- Intestacy in present law

IV. Wills
- Formalities of wills
- Invalid wills

V. The machinery of transfer
- Transfer in civil law
- Transfer in Anglo-American law

I. Inheritance and property rights

INDIVIDUAL OWNERSHIP OF PROPERTY

Inheritance of property cannot occur unless goods are regarded as belonging to individuals rather than to groups and unless the goods are of such permanence that they continue to exist and to be useful beyond the death of the owner. Among primitive food-gatherers and hunters it has not been uncommon for such personal belongings as weapons or bowls to be destroyed after the death of the owner in order to protect the survivors from being molested by his spirit. Among the Papua of New Guinea and the Damara (Bergdama) of South Africa the hut of the dead man was abandoned or burned down so as to ban the magic of the disease of which the owner had died. Among the Herero of southwest Africa the dead man's goats were slaughtered and eaten; this custom seems to have been connected with the fear that they were affected by his magic but also with the belief that the spirits of the slaughtered goats would follow the dead owner into the realm of spirits, where he would need them. Belief in providing for the needs of the dead seems to have been the root of the widespread custom of burying with the body or burning victuals, utensils, treasure, slaves, or wives. Tombs have yielded rich evidence of such practices in the cultures of the Stone and Bronze ages as well as in the high civilizations of ancient Egypt or pre-Columbian Mexico. Another way of disposing of a dead man's effects was to distribute them among remote relatives and friends, as in American Indian tribes such as the Delaware and the Iroquois;

Property in primitive and modern societies

distribution of this sort, in the absence of rules of inheritance, could easily lead to quarrel and violence, as was often the case among the Comanche Indians.

The view of some Marxist writers that common ownership of all goods, or at least of land, was once universal among mankind can be neither proved nor disproved. Group ownership has been widespread but by no means universal among primitive and archaic agriculturalists. It has, indeed, persisted into modern times in India and parts of Africa and Asia, and it played a considerable role in the development of the Teutonic and Slavic peoples of Europe. In parts of Yugoslavia, ownership of the land by zadrugas—*i.e.*, large groups of progeny of a common ancestor—continued into the 20th century. In western Europe the common ownership of pastures and woods, which grew out of the former system of common ownership of the land of a village, can still be found, especially in the Alpine regions of Switzerland and Austria. While in earlier times colonization of new land tended to be carried on by groups—for instance, the German settlement of the regions east of the Elbe in the 10th to 13th centuries—the Europeans who settled in North America, Australia, South Africa, and other parts of the world in the 18th and 19th centuries regarded individual ownership of land as most favourable to efficient use. In the 20th century, Socialist ideas, combined with large-scale mechanization, have resulted in new forms of land ownership in common: the *kolkhozy* of the Soviet Union, the communes of Communist China, and the *kibbutzim* of Israel. Wherever land is held in common, the death of a member of the group results not in inheritance but in a rearrangement of duties and of rights of participation in the produce of the land or rights of temporary usage of the land itself.

CRITIQUES OF INHERITANCE

The institution of inheritance has been criticized because it renders possible the acquisition of wealth without work and because it is regarded as a principal source of inequality of income. Such attacks have come not only from radicals to whom complete equality of income appeals as a social ideal but also from more moderate thinkers to whom great differences in the distribution of wealth appear to be incompatible with modern views of the dignity of man. In response to their criticisms, inheritance has been defended on economic as well as on moral grounds.

Inheritance defended

Inheritance has been said to be necessary within the framework of an economy of individual property to guarantee the continuity of enterprise without which long-range economic activity could not flourish. The argument has lost much of its force as large-scale enterprise has come to be carried on in corporate form and thus to be directed not by owners but by specialists in management who succeed each other in the manner of officeholders. There is, however, still force in the argument that without the incentive of handing on the fruits of one's work, competition, and consequently the functioning of the total economy, would be hampered.

It is possible to conceive of a social system in which property rights would end with the owner's death. If the assets left behind were not reassigned to some other individual, the eventual result would be complete ownership of all wealth by the community, and the system of individual property would end. A new individual owner could be determined in one of four ways: ownership by the first taker, a practice that would produce strife and disorder; reassignment by a governmental agency, which would constitute an exercise of power regarded as dangerous in a free society; reallottment in accordance with settled rules generally fixed for all; or reallottment in accordance with the wishes of the decedent. The last two are the ways in which the modern systems of inheritance work: the estate is reallotted according to the rules of intestacy law or according to the will of the decedent.

The only debatable issues within a system of private ownership are: who are to be the takers in intestate succession; and whether or not and within what limits freedom of testation shall be permitted. In all societies, inheritance has developed as an incident of kinship. Even in a society in which ownership of property is regarded as belonging to individuals rather than kinship groups, the feeling of belonging to one's group is still so strong, especially between parents and children, that a man's sense of freedom would not be complete unless he knew that he could pass on his possessions to his children. The question arises, however, whether inheritance shall extend beyond the circle of those persons with whom the decendent was connected by ties of affection or about whose well-being he was, or should have been, concerned. In the urbanized, mobile population of highly industrialized nations, the family as a felt unit has tended to shrink to the small circle of husband, wife, and children. Ties of relationship tend to be weak even among first cousins.

Inheritance law as an instrument of social policy

In an age of expanding demands on government, there has been an inclination to let the estate of a person dying intestate pass to the public treasury rather than go to enrich distant relatives or professional tracers of missing heirs, or be split up in small fractions, or wasted in litigation. In England, the circle of intestate takers has been limited by the Administration of Estates Act of 1925 to the grandparents, uncles, and aunts of the deceased. Even more limiting than those of England are the intestacy laws of the Soviet Union and other Communist countries. Under the law of the U.S.S.R., intestate succession does not extend beyond descendants, the surviving spouse, grandparents, brothers, sisters, and incapacitated persons who were dependent upon the decedent for at least one year prior to his death.

Another way of limiting the rights of remote relatives for the benefit of the public treasury consists in increasing the rates of inheritance taxes in proportion to the remoteness of the relationship between the takers and the decedent. In the United States, although the federal tax on succession depends solely on the size of the estate, the additional inheritance taxes levied by the states are widely patterned upon the closeness of relationship. This method is also employed in numerous other countries but not, since 1949, in England.

Inheritance taxation is also used to reduce inequalities in the distribution of wealth. This may be done by compulsory partitions, as under the laws of the French and the German pattern, or by means of progressive inheritance taxation, as in the United Kingdom or the United States, or by a combination of both. The law of inheritance and inheritance taxation is thus an instrument of social policy.

An impressive illustration of the way in which the law of inheritance serves social policy is the inheritance legislation of the Soviet Union. In the early stage of the Bolshevik Revolution, inheritance was limited to the descent of a modest amount of property to close relatives or to the surviving spouse, provided they were in need. The limit upon the size of the property, 10,000 gold rubles, roughly equal to $5,500 in those years, was lifted in 1926; and the requirement of need was also abolished for inheritance by the surviving spouse, descendants, parents, grandparents, brothers, and sisters. Under the civil code of 1922, power of testation was limited to increasing or reducing the share of particular intestate successors. After 1961 property could be left to any person. Private property cannot exist in the means of production, and therefore inheritance is limited to goods of use or consumption and to savings accounts. Within the limits stated, inheritance and freedom of testation are regarded as constituting useful incentives to productivity without constituting a danger to the Socialist system. Inheritance of private property is thus listed in the constitution of 1936 as one of the rights of citizens.

II. Prime issues in the law of inheritance

In a society in which inheritance exists, two issues are of prime importance for the distribution of wealth and for the social and political structure of the society: the issue of the extent to which owners of property shall have the power by their own decision to determine the course of inheritance, and the issue of whether or not estates shall be allowed or even required to pass undivided to one single heir.

FREEDOM OF TESTATION

The question of the property owner's power

The power of an owner of property to determine who is to have it upon his death is thought to stimulate economic activity: it is also considered desirable that a property owner be allowed to modify the rigid rules of the intestacy laws so as to adapt them to the particular situation of his family by preferring, for instance, a crippled child over one of proven capacity. The freedom to disinherit a child may be used to induce filial obedience, but freedom of testation also implies the freedom of making provision for charity. The possibility of abuse for ends of spite, arbitrariness, or whimsy is the price society has to pay for such power. Freedom of testation developed slowly, and nowhere does it exist without limitations. The questions of what the limits shall be, especially to what extent an owner of property shall be free to disinherit close members of his family and to what extent he shall have the power to tie up property beyond the grave, have been answered in widely diverse ways.

History of the will. In a primitive or archaic society in which property is owned by the kinship or neighbourhood group rather than by individuals, freedom of testation cannot exist. Transition from group to individual ownership has rarely if ever occurred in one single step. As to land, even when its use was regarded as rightfully belonging to an individual, its free alienation by sale or gift, and even more so by will, was for long periods hedged in by superior rights of the kinship group, the village, or the feudal lord. Transition to free alienation has often been achieved by means of subterfuge, such as the adoption of the "purchaser" or "devisee" as a son, or, once free alienation had become possible inter vivos (between living persons) but not yet upon death, by fictitious sale or gift to a middleman who would promise to let the grantor keep the property as long as he should live and upon his death to deal with it as directed by the grantor. Such use of adoption occurred in ancient Babylonia, China, Japan, India, and other societies of an archaic patriarchic order. In ancient Greece effects similar to those of a will were achieved by gift, to take effect upon the death of the donor or, where the only child of the family was a daughter, by giving her in marriage together with the estate. Transfer by use of a middleman became possible among the Germanic peoples following the decline of the Roman Empire.

In ancient Rome the institution of the will appeared at an early stage of cultural development, but there, too, it seems to have been preceded by a stage in which its effects could be achieved only by indirection. The so-called will made in assembly (*testamentum comitiis calatis*) seems to have been the approval by the assembly of the adoption of a son by the childless chief of an aristocratic house so that the house and the worship of its deities would be perpetuated.

By the 5th century BC the head of a Roman family seems to have been able during his lifetime to achieve the purposes of a testamentary transaction by fictitious sale to a middleman, *familiae emptor* (purchaser of the family property). In the period of the early principate (1st century AD), the testament was fully recognized in its proper sense. In the mature form in which it is dealt with in the Corpus Juris (6th century AD), it became in the late Middle Ages the model for continental Europe.

Among the Anglo-Saxons and other Germanic peoples, land was subject to ties of the kinship group and, later, of feudalism, so that there was no place for disposition by will. Chattels were more freely alienable. In establishing freedom of testation a prominent role was played by the church, which desired thereby to obtain funds for its activities, which included the bulk of medieval education, charity, and cultivation of the arts. In England the church succeeded shortly after the Norman Conquest in establishing the jurisdiction of its courts for matters concerning succession upon death to personal property. Through the church the will of the Roman pattern became firmly institutionalized, but a testator still had to leave a "reasonable part of the estate" (ordinarily at least one-third) to his wife and children.

Once the alienation of real property had again become possible by gift or sale, there grew up all over Europe that same practice of indirectly achieving the effects of a will by fictitious grant to a middleman (German *Salmann*, "sale man"; English feoffee to uses) that, in analogous circumstances, had grown up at other times and places. On the Continent, the will as such became again available when Roman law was rediscovered and "received," which occurred from the 11th century onward, first in Italy and then north of the Alps. In France and Germany the will of the Roman pattern was fully recognized in the late 15th century. Just about that time, however, the enfeoffment to uses, which had been popular in England, was abolished by Henry VIII's Statute of Uses in 1535. The King wished to restore to the crown its prospects of escheat and of certain feudal duties, which could be evaded by the alienation to uses. Public indignation was so strong, however, that five years later the King found it advisable, by the enactment of the Statute of Wills, to open the way for true testamentary disposition of land. Restrictions limiting devises of those lands of which ownership was connected with the duty of rendering military service were abolished at the time of the Restoration by the Military Tenures Act of 1662. In Scotland, testamentary disposition of land remained precarious until the enactment of the Titles to Land Consolidation Act in 1868.

Limits of freedom of testation. *General.* Freedom of testation has never been absolutely unlimited. Nowhere is a testamentary provision valid if its enforcement would be shocking to public morals. When a testamentary gift is conditioned upon an act of the beneficiary that in good morals should not be so conditioned, as, for instance, a gift conditioned upon the beneficiary's changing his religion, the gift is either invalid or valid unconditionally. Generally, property given by testament cannot be tied up by the testator for an indefinite future. Under the rule against perpetuities, as developed in England and commonly applied in the United States, a testator may leave property to a person for life and upon the first taker's death to some other person; but the last "remainder" must "vest" not later than, roughly speaking, one generation after the testator's death or, in England, since the Perpetuities and Accumulation Act of 1964, a fixed period of years up to 80. In the civil-law countries of the German system, the freedom to provide for substitutions is limited in similar ways, but in those of the French system it is limited much more strictly.

Provisions against disinheritance. A testator's freedom to disinherit his surviving spouse, children, or other heirs has been more extensive in ancient Roman and modern Anglo-American law than in the modern civil-law countries, but it has always had limits. In republican Rome a testator had the power to disinherit his spouse and children, but if he wished to do this he had to say so expressly in the will. In the period of the principate (27 BC–AD 284), it became necessary to state the reasons because a will disinheriting a close member of the family without reasonable and honest cause was in danger of being declared invalid. In the late Roman Empire the descendants —and if there were no descendants, the ascendants (*e.g.*, parents)—were given the right to a share in the estate (*pars legitima*), of which none of them could be deprived except upon serious cause stated in the will. When, after the fall of the Roman Empire, testamentary disposition came to be recognized again in the later Middle Ages, custom generally required that some minimum share, frequently one-third, be left to the surviving spouse, or the descendants, or both. Upon the revival of Roman law on the European continent and in Scotland, these customs were in various ways combined with the rules of the Corpus Juris.

Protection of the rights of heirs

In the modern civil law, two systems are used to provide protection against disinheritance. Under the French system, a testator who is survived by descendants, parents, or (in some countries) brothers, sisters, or even other close relatives, cannot dispose at all of the "reserved portion" of his estate, the size of which depends upon the number and the degree of nearness of relationship of the surviving "forced heirs." Under the civil code of France, for instance, donations inter vivos or by last will cannot exceed one-half of the property of the disposer, if he leaves at his decease a legitimate child; one-third, if he leaves two children; and one-fourth, if he leaves three or a greater number. The indisposable share is one-half of the property if the disposer, having no children, leaves ascendants of both his father's and his mother's lines. Under the German pattern, the surviving spouse, a descendant or, if there are no descendants, a parent can claim to be paid in money one-half the value of the share that would have been his in the case of intestate succession.

In England those customs that required a minimum share in the personal property to be left to the surviving spouse and descendants disappeared in the 17th and 18th centuries. The interest of dower, which guaranteed a life estate to the widow in the real estate of the predeceased husband, lost its protective effect in 1833. At the turn of the 20th century, freedom of disinheritance was complete in England as well as in the dominions but not in Scotland. There, in the movable estate, the legitim (bairn's part) is still reserved to the children, the *ius relicti* to the widower, and the *ius relictae* to the widow. Until 1964 (in immovables) the widower was entitled to curtesy, a liferent in his wife's heritage (*i.e.*, immovable) property, and the widow had the right of terce—*i.e.*, a liferent out of one-third of her husband's inheritable estate. In England, freedom of testation, while unlimited by law, was kept within narrow limits by the custom among wealthy families of preventing the splitting up or alienation of the family wealth by means of a so-called strict settlement. In each generation, the head of the family would settle the estate upon his eldest son in such a way that it would descend to him undivided but subject to a generous life estate for the widow and to provisions for the daughters, younger sons, and other needy relatives. In the different social climate of New Zealand, a new device for protecting needy family members against disinheritance was invented with the enactment, in 1900, of a statute that empowers the court to order adequate provision for the maintenance of a spouse or a needy child out of the estate of any testator who has not made such provision. Family provision acts of this kind have since been enacted in Australia, Canada, and England.

Under the English Inheritance (Family Provision) Act of 1938, as amended by the Intestates' Estates Act of 1952 and the Family Provision Act of 1966, the court may order that, in case of need, provision be made out of the income and, under certain circumstances, even out of the capital, for the benefit of the surviving spouse, an unmarried daughter, a minor son, or any child, male or female, who is incapable of maintaining himself or herself because of physical or mental incapacity. This principle was extended to include the deceased's divorced former wife or former husband, in certain circumstances, by the Matrimonial Causes (Property and Maintenance) Act of 1958 (superseded by the Matrimonial Causes Act of 1965).

In the United States the surviving spouse is protected against complete disinheritance in every state. As to real estate, dower or curtesy has in one form or another been preserved in the majority of the states. Under this system, each spouse has an "estate" in the realty of the other, a portion of which continues beyond the death of one spouse until the death of the surviving spouse and of which the latter cannot be deprived, without his consent, by will or by sale, gift, mortgage, or any other kind of transaction. Under the system of the indefeasible share, the surviving spouse cannot be completely disinherited, but he is poorly or not at all protected against the other spouse's giving away or using up his property before he dies. In most states the two systems are combined, but New York and a few states in the eastern part of the country have followed the example of England and abolished traditional dower and curtesy, the reason being that their existence renders it necessary in every purchase of land to investigate whether the title might not be encumbered with dower and curtesy rights that are not readily discoverable from the abstract or the title deeds.

Community-property systems

In those U.S. jurisdictions that have adopted the so-called community-property system, an indefeasible share in the family wealth is secured to the surviving spouse by his or her being entitled to one-half of the community property, which generally consists of the property acquired during the marriage by the gainful activities of either spouse. Varying systems of community property also exist in numerous European and Latin American countries. In the countries of the French system, community-property law applies unless it has been expressly contracted out by the parties to the marriage. Under the Scandinavian and German systems the assets of husband and wife remain separate, but upon the termination of the marriage the acquests are distributed among them. Protection of the surviving spouse can, furthermore, be achieved through homestead laws and those laws that guarantee to the widow or the widower an award of income payable out of the estate for a few months immediately following the death of the other spouse. Both types of laws are common in the United States.

The only jurisdictions in the United States that protect descendants against disinheritance by giving them indefeasible shares are Louisiana and Puerto Rico, whose legal systems are not derived from the common law. In the other states the descendants are protected either not at all or only indirectly and incompletely by (1) "pretermitted-heir" statutes, which, like early Roman law, require the testator to state the disinheritance of a descendant expressly in the will; or (2) "afterborn-heir" statutes, under which a child born after the making of the will receives his intestate shares unless a contrary intention is stated in the will; or (3) "charity begins at home statutes," under which no more than a certain fraction (*e.g.*, one-half) of the estate may be given to charity by a testator who is survived by certain close relatives; or (4) "hellfire statutes," which declare ineffective a testamentary provision for charitable purpose made by the testator upon his deathbed, in his last illness, or within a fixed period immediately preceding his death.

In the Soviet Union a compulsory share of two-thirds of his intestate share is guaranteed to each minor child of the decedent and to any of the following who are unable to work: the decedent's children, spouse, parents, and those who were dependent on him.

DIVIDED OR UNDIVIDED INHERITANCE

Like the problem of whether and to what extent freedom of testation shall be permitted, the question of whether a person's estate shall pass undivided to one person or whether it should be divided among several takers has significant political implications. The issue has been especially important in the history of Anglo-American law, where it is usually referred to as the problem of primogeniture. The term is too narrow, however, because the sole heir need not necessarily be the first-born son (*primogenitus*). Under the system of ultimogeniture, which existed in parts of England as the custom of Borough English, and also under the German National Socialist law of 1933, the person favoured was the youngest son; under systems of seniorate or juniorate it is the oldest or youngest member of the family; under that of majorate or minorate, it is the oldest or the youngest person standing in equal degree of consanguinity to the decedent. There have also been cases where certain lands have been reserved to the second-born son and his line (*secundogeniture*) or the third-born and his line (*tertiogeniture*), etc.

Primogeniture

In England, undivided inheritance was applied to real but not to personal property. The distinction between the two kinds of property was important in the struggle for power between church and state. In medieval England the organization of society in general and of the army and the public offices in particular was based upon the distribution of the ownership of the land, over all of which the king was lord paramount. The church, on the other hand, concerned itself with divine worship, the care of the sick and poor, and the cultivation of learning and the arts. After the Norman Conquest a compromise was worked out between the king and the church under which the royal courts exercised jurisdiction over real property, while succession to personal property was to be the concern of the ecclesiastical courts. Until 1926 descent to real property thus was subject to rules different from those applying to the distribution of personal property. For the former, the common-law courts developed a system that tended to maintain the existing military and social order through unpartitioned descent of land to one heir rather than division among several coheirs and, for a long time, by reluctance in admitting freedom of testation.

As to personal property, however, the ecclesiastical courts favoured a freedom of testation that allowed a decedent to leave part of his property to the church for the promotion of its manifold activities. In case of intestacy, the church favoured distribution among family members of equal nearness to the decedent. It applied rules similar to those laid down in the 6th century by the Roman emperor Justinian (see below), which, in 1670, were fixed in the Statute of Distribution. The problem about which the two sets of courts differed—namely, whether an inheritance should be split up among several coheirs or pass undivided to a single heir—has, of course, not been limited to England. Unpartitioned inheritance has occurred in the most diverse civilizations—among the Hottentots of southwest Africa, the Maori of New Zealand, the inhabitants of the Tonga Island, in parts of China and Siberia, and in western Europe.

Why and how primogeniture became the common-law system of inheritance of freehold real estate is not clear. Primogeniture obviously served the needs of feudalism, in which the ownership of a parcel of land tended to be connected with a public office or with military duties that could not be well divided among several people. Partition was also likely to result in confusion regarding the services the peasants were bound to render to the landlord. At the peasant level, primogeniture prevented holdings from being split up until they were too small to allow a family to make a living. Attempts to avoid physical partition by selling the land and dividing the proceeds were impracticable in a society in which it was considered important to preserve family ownership of the farm and in which money was not readily available.

In spite of these circumstances, undivided descent of land to one heir never was the exclusive system among the European peasantry. It became, however, the almost universal system among the nobility, who were anxious to preserve intact the family wealth. In order to achieve this purpose it became necessary, after alienability of land and freedom of testation had developed, not only to establish unpartitioned descent as the rule of intestate succession but also to "entail" the land—*i.e.*, to prevent the owner from selling, giving away, or encumbering the land as well as from disposing of it by will. In England varying legal devices were used from the 13th century on. After the 17th century the so-called strict family settlement became the principal device, while on the Continent the *fideicommissum* of late Roman law was adapted to serve the purpose. The political power secured in this way to the nobility and gentry enabled it, as the necessary counterpart of primogeniture, to secure for the younger sons the lucrative positions in the church, the army, and, on the Continent, the expanding bureaucracy. In the 18th century this system was attacked both by the supporters of democratic ideals and by the economists of the classical school. To the latter, entails were objectionable because they not only stood in the way of mortgaging the land for purposes of improvement but also because inalienability prevented its coming into the hands of the most efficient cultivator. The system was first destroyed in the British colonies in New England, and in the course of the American Revolution it was swept away in the other states. In Europe, it collapsed during the French Revolution, and in the Napoleonic Code care

Entailing the land

was taken to prevent its re-establishment. Not only were all descendants or other relatives of equal degree to take part equally in intestate succession but also, by giving each child the right to a minimum share, a testator was prevented from giving all to one child.

In England the main object of the economists' attack upon settlements was removed when, through a series of successive statutes, especially the Settled Land Act of 1882, settled lands were gradually restored to the market; life tenants were thereby given the power under certain circumstances to mortgage or sell the land. Stocks and bonds, which had become a form of wealth more important than land, could, and still can be, tied up by means of a trust; but through the impact of heavy death duties this power has now been restricted. Primogeniture as the rule of intestacy was abolished by the Administration of Estates Act in 1925.

On the Continent, equal division among descendants and other relatives in equal degree became the general rule in the codes of the 19th century, but in certain countries, especially Austria and Germany, the possibility of entail lingered on as a privilege of the nobility until the revolutionary events of 1918. A new argument came to be used, however, in favour of unpartitioned inheritance of land in the 19th century. First in France and then in central Europe and Scandinavia, the argument was put forward that agricultural holdings were being reduced to less than the size necessary to provide a living for a family and that the old peasantry was thus in danger of being driven from the land. This led to the enactment of special laws on farm inheritance in sections of Austria, Germany, and Scandinavia. These laws, while providing unpartitioned inheritance in the case of intestacy, most often left unimpaired the power to provide for multiple succession by will and the power of alienation by sale. A more radical farm-inheritance law was enacted in Germany in 1933 by the National Socialists. It provided not only for undivided inheritance but also forbade partition by will and even the sale of the farm or its encumbrance by mortgage. The peasantry was to be secured as a social class living on the soil, removed from the vicissitudes and temptations of a market economy, although the law allowed the state to remove an unproductive holder. The law was repealed after World War II, but statutes attempting in milder ways to counteract the partitioning of farmsteads have been enacted. Even in France, the civil code was amended by a chain of laws beginning in 1922 so as to postpone, at least temporarily, the physical partition of a farmstead and certain other small holdings.

III. Intestate succession

Succession and kinship

Insofar as the course of succession is not determined by will, it is regulated by the laws of intestate succession. The legal systems of the world present a bewildering variety of intestacy laws, but they all have one feature in common: the intestate takers of the estate of a decedent are universally persons standing to him in a relation of kinship. Consequently, the composition of the group of successors in a society in which kinship is organized matrilineally is different from that of a society of patrilineal or, in modern society, bilineal kinship organization. Whether or not a surviving spouse belongs to the kin group of the decedent depends again on the way in which kinship is organized in the society in question. In modern laws, the surviving spouse is universally given some place in the table of successors, even though he or she may not be regarded as a kin, or a relative, of the decedent.

HISTORY OF INTESTATE SUCCESSION

In preliterate society the order of succession seems to be basically determined by the kinship structure. But in both archaic and developed societies the laws of intestacy have often been distorted by traditionalism, so that features once well adapted to the structure of the family were preserved into periods in which that structure had assumed new shape. The formalism that is characteristic of archaic legal systems (and often occurs in developed ones) tends to generalize rules that have originated in connection with special situations into applications beyond their initial scope. Intestacy laws have thus frequently looked obsolete, confused, or arbitrary. Even the Roman law of the Twelve Tables (*c.* 450 BC) seems not to have fully accorded with the social needs of its day.

Roman law. The basic unit of society in ancient Rome was the "house," the extended family lorded over by its head, the paterfamilias, to whom his wife, his slaves, and possibly several generations of his descendants were subject and in whom title to all property was vested, so that a son or any other member of the house, even as an adult, did not own anything until he had been released from membership by emancipation. The paterfamilias was responsible for all liabilities incurred by any member. The Roman house of those early times resembled the system that prevailed in Japan until very recently. But whereas in Japan the leader of the house had just one successor, under the system of the Twelve Tables the Roman paterfamilias was succeeded by as many new ones as there were *sui heredes; i.e.*, persons who by the death of the chief were freed from his power and thus became persons *sui iuris*. If a house chief died without being survived by *sui heredes*, the law of the Twelve Tables provided that the estate (*familia*) could be acquired by the nearest agnatic relative; *i.e.*, the person related to the decedent by male descent who would be closest to him. If there was no such person, the estate could be had by the Gentiles, who seem to have been the clanlike group—composed of all descendants of a real or mythical ancestor—that apparently ceased to play a significant role in Roman society even at the time of the Twelve Tables. This arrangement for succession seems to have been so unsatisfactory that it became customary —and even a moral, religious, and political duty—to eliminate its coming into play by the execution of a testament. The very name "intestate succession" (*successio ab intestato*) indicates that dying without having made a will constituted an exceptional situation.

The system of Justinian

As Rome grew into an empire, the system of the Twelve Tables became less and less satisfactory. The house of olden times receded in significance; relationship through females came to play as much a role in the consciousness of the people as that through males; and wives mostly ceased to be subject to the power of their husbands or their husbands' house chiefs. Adaptation of the law to the new structure of the family was made, first by the heads of the judicial system, the praetors, and then by imperial legislation. But the changes were unsystematic and halfhearted. In its final stage, the intestacy law became such a patchwork that in 543 and 548 AD the emperor Justinian found it necessary to make an entirely new beginning. By Novels (*i.e.*, supplements to the Corpus Juris Civilis), a new order of intestacy was established. Relatives of a decedent were divided into four classes: (1) the descendants of the decedent; (2) the ascendants of the decedent, his brothers and sisters of the full blood, and the children of brothers and sisters of the full blood; (3) the decedent's brothers and sisters of the half blood and the children of such brothers and sisters; and (4) the other collaterals of the decedent related to him in the nearest grade of consanguinity. No person in a more remote class was to succeed as long as the decedent was survived by a member of a prior class. The surviving spouse stood outside the four classes of relatives. He or she was to succeed only if there was no relative at all. As long as any relative, no matter how remote, could be found, the family wealth was not to be diverted from the bloodline. But a widow's needs were ordinarily taken care of by the dowry, which, given to the husband, usually by her family, at the time of the marriage, was to be hers after the husband's death. For the exceptional case of a "poor widow"; *i.e.*, a widow without dowry, a share in the estate was provided. Distribution among members of the same class was not in all respects clearly regulated by Justinian's text, and so several points remained controversial.

Common law. Justinian's scheme was influential in the practice of the English ecclesiastical courts in their dealings with personal property. But in England the surviving spouse was treated much more generously. A surviving husband had no need to succeed to his wife's personal property upon her death. With the sole exception of choses in action not reduced to possession (*i.e.*, liabilities due to the wife not yet paid), he already owned all of her personal property by virtue of the marriage. But English custom gave the widow one-third of her predeceased husband's estate if he was survived by descendants and one-half if he was survived by other relatives.

English ecclesiastical court practice

English ecclesiastical court practice also clarified some of the points that had been left open in Justinian's codification, abandoning the distinction between the siblings of the full blood and those of the half blood (although under the Canons of Descent to real property applied by the secular courts, the latter remained excluded). The English ecclesiastical practice was codified in the Statute of Distribution in 1670. It became the model for state legislation in the United States, although the state laws show considerable variation in many respects.

Other systems. While the Anglo-American system has largely adopted the Roman order of succession, many of the civil-law countries appear to have followed the Germanic system of parentelic order.

Germanic systems

The first parentela, or order, consists of the descendants of the decedent; the second, of his parents and their descendants collateral to the decedent; the third, of his grandparents and their descendants collateral to the decedent, etc. As long as there is any person standing in a nearer order, no person standing in a more remote one can succeed. In each parentela, persons of a lower grade exclude those of a higher grade. Variations exist in several respects. A person who stood in the first two orders but who predeceased the intestate is generally represented by his descendants; as to the more remote orders, the legal systems differ, as they do also with respect to the question of whether, insofar as representation takes place, the distribution is by roots or by heads. (When distribution is by roots—per stirpes—the estate is divided into as many parts as there are living and dead, but represented, persons standing in the same grade; when distribution is by heads—per capita—the estate is divided into as many parts as there are living persons entitled to sharing.) Considerable differences also exist in the treatment of the surviving spouse of the decedent.

INTESTACY IN PRESENT LAW

In recent times intestacy has been the subject of much legislation. Since the purpose of intestacy is to fill the void left where a decedent has not effectively disposed by will, lawmakers tend to create rules corresponding to those, which, in their opinion, a reasonable testator would have made. But they may also be inclined to lay down rules that they think testators ought to follow in the interests of social policy.

Modern tendencies. Among the most conspicuous trends of modern legislation is the vanishing concern about keeping property within the bloodline through which it came to the decedent. This traditional idea, which was particularly strong with respect to land, had in the field of intestacy resulted in the so-called rule of ancestral estate. In Anglo-American law, the doctrine of ancestral estate was part of the Canons of Descent of real estate. It meant that if an intestate died without descendants, property that had come to him from ancestors should revert to the line whence it had come. In England the principle was abolished in 1925; in the United States it disappeared gradually, although in 1969 it still played a role in Arkansas, Delaware, Hawaii, Kentucky, North Carolina, and Tennessee. In civil-law countries, where it was once known as *jus recadentiae*, the principle has disappeared, except in the Spanish province of Aragon. But France has preserved the related ideas of the *fente* and the *droit de retour*. Under the former, the estate is divided equally between the paternal and the maternal lines (and under the *refente* between the various lines of grandparents). Under the *droit de retour*, assets that were received as a gift by an intestate who dies without descendants return to the donor. The once widespread

Decline of the principle of ancestral estate

idea that, among collaterals, relatives of the full blood occupy better positions than those of the half blood survives in France, in several Latin American countries, and, in several different forms, in some jurisdictions of the United States.

Changing attitudes about sex and marriage, but also about the equality and dignity of human beings, are widely finding expression in laws assimilating the legal situation of persons born out of wedlock to that of legitimate children. The equation of an illegitimate child with a foundling long ago disappeared from common-law systems, but it still persists in the laws of France and of countries following the French pattern, where a child born out of wedlock lacks legal relationship not only to his father but also to his mother until the relationship is formally recognized by the parent in question; once such recognition has been made, however, the child occupies a position resembling that of a legitimate child, including rights of intestate succession. Judicial determination of paternity, which in France is not possible in all situations, can give the illegitimate child rights of support, but it does not suffice to create rights of inheritance. In contrast, rights of inheritance between the illegitimate child and his mother have long been recognized in other jurisdictions, including those of the common law and of the civil law other than the French type. Impetus to the recognition of inheritance rights between an illegitimate child and his father was given by Norway's Castberg Law of 1915. Similar legislation now exists in the other Scandinavian countries, in the Federal Republic of Germany, in several countries of Latin America, in the countries of eastern Europe, in England under the Family Law Reform Act of 1969, in Scotland under the Law Reform Act of 1968, and in some states of the United States. The statutes vary greatly with respect to such details as the mode in and the time at which paternity must be ascertained, the extent of the child's share in the estate, the question of the extent, if any, to which illegitimate relationship creates rights of intestate succession from or through an illegitimate, and the illegitimate's rights to intestate succession to kindred of his father or mother.

Rights of spouses. There is also a widespread trend toward favouring a surviving spouse along with or even above the decedent's blood relatives. Benefits for a surviving spouse can, of course, be achieved by devices other than rights of inheritance. A method of great antiquity is the giving of a dowry, meant to sustain a woman after the death of her husband. In societies in which dowries are customary, the "poor widow" who lacks a dowry can then be helped by an exceptional right to a share in the estate, as was provided in Justinian's reform of the Roman law; this provision still exists in the state of Louisiana for the widow or the widower. A widow may be given a claim for support out of the estate, as in Austria (and in France between 1891 and 1925). Such support may even be provided for a wider circle of persons dependent upon the decedent, as in the family provision laws of England, New Zealand, and other Commonwealth countries.

Broadening of benefits for spouses

Benefits for a surviving spouse can also be provided through some system of community property, as found in numerous civil-law countries and in some states of the United States. The community fund may consist of the acquests made during marriage through the exertions of either spouse, or, additionally, of the movable assets owned by either spouse at the initiation of the marriage, or even of all property owned by the spouses. Upon one spouse's death, the fund is split into halves. One half constitutes the survivor's share in the community and thus belongs to him, whereas the estate of the predeceasing spouse consists of the other half of the community, along with such assets as the predeceasing spouse may have owned as his separate fund. The law may or may not then grant the surviving spouse an intestate share of the estate. Still another way of providing benefits for a surviving spouse is to give him or her a life estate in certain assets of the predeceasing spouse, as is done in the common-law institutions of dower and curtesy. French law, under certain circumstances, gives the surviving spouse a share in the estate or in a fraction of it.

Of great practical importance are the rights to pensions, social security benefits, and damage claims arising from the death of a married person, which are now universally available to a surviving spouse. Improvements in the right of a surviving spouse to share in the married couple's capital have been brought about in France, England, and in numerous U.S. jurisdictions by giving him a preferred position in the scheme of intestate succession; or, as in Scandinavia, by giving the surviving spouse a share in the acquests made during marriage by the exertions of both spouses; or, as in the Federal Republic of Germany, by a combination of both devices. This revalorization of the surviving spouse is the consequence of several factors, including the weakening of family ties, the decreasing importance of inherited wealth, and the diminishing readiness of children to let aged parents live in their household. In addition, the feeling has grown that a wife who stays at home to run the household and bring up the children, instead of going out and earning a living of her own, enables her husband to act as the breadwinner and is therefore entitled to a share in his accumulated earnings.

Examples of existing laws. Intestacy laws vary widely in detail. The principal features of the intestacy rules of England, New York State, the American Uniform Probate Code, France, and the Russian Soviet Federated Socialist Republic are presented below.

England. The complex provisions of the Administration of Estates Act of 1925, as amended by the Intestates' Estates Act of 1952 and the Family Provision Act of 1966, are based on the following scheme:

Recent English legislation

1. The relatives of the decedent are grouped in seven classes. No member of a class takes in intestacy as long as any member of a preceding class has survived the decedent. The classes are: (a) descendants per stirpes; (b) parents; (c) brothers and sisters of the full blood, a deceased brother or sister being represented by his descendants per stirpes; (d) brothers and sisters of the half blood, such a deceased brother or sister being represented by his descendants per stirpes; (e) grandparents; (f) parents' brothers and sisters of the full blood; and (g) parents' brothers and sisters of the half blood.

2. A surviving spouse takes, if the decedent is survived by descendants: the "personal chattels," *i.e.*, the assets of the household, £8,750, and a life estate in one-half of the remaining part of the estate. If the decedent is not survived by descendants but is survived by parents, or brothers and sisters of the full blood, or descendants of such brothers and sisters, the surviving spouse takes the personal chattels, £30,000, and one-half of the remaining part of the estate. If the decedent is not survived by any of the above, the surviving spouse takes all.

If the intestate share of the surviving spouse, an unmarried daughter, an infant son, or a son or daughter incapable of maintaining himself or herself because of mental or physical disability, is insufficient to provide reasonable maintenance, the court may order that payment for the reasonable maintenance of such persons be made out of the estate.

New York State. Under the New York Estates, Powers and Trusts Law of 1966, as amended in 1969, relatives, grouped under the parentelic system, take by intestacy up to, but not beyond, the parentela of the grandparents. In the first and second parentelas, distribution is per stirpes; in the third it is per capita among persons standing in the same grade. If the decedent is survived by one child or the issue of one child, the surviving spouse takes $2,000 in money or intangible personal property and one-half of the residue; if more than one child or their issue survive, the spouse takes $2,000 in money or intangible personal property and one-third of the residue; if only parents or one parent survive, the spouse takes $25,000 and one-half of the residue; if there is no issue and no parent, the spouse takes all.

Recent U.S. approaches to intestacy

In addition, the surviving spouse or, if there is none, surviving minor children, are entitled to an allowance of $1,000 worth of household chattels, certain books of the family library, $5,000 worth of farm equipment, and $1,000 in money or other personal property insofar as this amount is not needed to pay the reasonable family expenses.

Uniform Probate Code (U.S.). The latest state of U.S. thinking is expressed in the *Uniform Probate Code*, approved in 1969 by the National Conference of Commissioners on Uniform State Laws and the American Bar Association. Its adoption is recommended to all states, but by October 1971 it had been adopted only by Idaho. Its provisions on intestacy are as follows:

The intestate share of the surviving spouse is:

(1) if there is no surviving issue or parent of the decedent, the entire intestate estate;

(2) if there is no surviving issue but the decedent is survived by a parent or parents, the first [$50,000], plus one-half of the balance of the intestate estate;

(3) if there are surviving issue all of whom are issue of the surviving spouse also, the first [$50,000], plus one-half of the balance of the intestate estate;

(4) if there are surviving issue one or more of whom are not issue of the surviving spouse, one-half of the intestate estate.

It also has alternative provisions for states with community-property laws:

(1) as to separate property

(i) if there is no surviving issue or parent of the decedent, the entire intestate estate;

(ii) if there is no surviving issue but the decedent is survived by a parent or parents, the first [$50,000], plus one-half of the balance of the intestate estate;

(iii) if there are surviving issue all of whom are issue of the surviving spouse also, the first [$50,000], plus one-half of the balance of the intestate estate;

(iv) if there are surviving issue one or more of whom are not issue of the surviving spouse, one-half of the intestate estate.

(2) as to community property

(i) The one-half of community property which belongs to the decedent passes to the [surviving spouse].

The part of the intestate estate not passing to the surviving spouse . . . , or the entire intestate estate if there is no surviving spouse, passes as follows:

(1) to the issue of the decedent; if they are all of the same degree of kinship to the decedent they take equally, but if of unequal degree, then those of more remote degree take by representation;

(2) if there is no surviving issue, to his parent or parents equally;

(3) if there is no surviving issue or parent, to the brothers and sisters and the issue of each deceased brother or sister by representation; if there is no surviving brother or sister, the issue of brothers and sisters take equally if they are all of the same degree of kinship to the decedent, but if of unequal degree then those of more remote degree take by representation;

(4) if there is no surviving issue, parent, or issue of a parent but the decedent is survived by one or more grandparents or issue of grandparent, half of the estate passes to the paternal grandparents if both survive, or to the surviving paternal grandparent, or to the issue of the paternal grandparents if both are deceased, the issue taking equally if they are all of the same degree of kinship to the decedent, but if of unequal degree those of more remote degree take by representation; and the other half passes to the maternal relatives in the same manner; but if there be no surviving grandparent or issue of grandparent on either the paternal or the maternal side, the entire estate passes to the relatives on the other side in the same manner as the half. . . .

If there is no taker under the provisions of this Article, the intestate estate passes to the [state]. . . .

If representation is called for by this Code, the estate is divided into as many shares as there are surviving heirs in the nearest degree of kinship and deceased persons in the same degree who left issue who survive the decedent, each surviving heir in the nearest degree receiving one share and the share of each deceased person in the same degree being divided among his issue in the same manner.

Intestate succession in France

France. The French Civil Code was enacted in 1804, and its provisions of intestate succession have been changed many times. With respect to the surviving spouse, one must take into account the one-half share in the marital acquests that belongs to the surviving spouse unless some other arrangement was agreed upon at the time of the marriage.

The relatives are grouped in four classes, and no member of a more remote class succeeds as long as there is one of a prior class. The four classes are: (1) descendants per stirpes; (2) parents, brothers, sisters, and children of brothers and sisters; (3) ascendants other than parents; and (4) collaterals other than group 2, up to and including the 6th grade of consanguinity (*i.e.*, first cousins and grandchildren of great-grandparents).

The surviving spouse's rights in the estate, in addition to his one-half share in the marital community fund, are as follows: (1) if there is legitimate issue of a prior marriage of the decedent, the spouse receives a life estate in a portion of the estate corresponding to the share of the child receiving the smallest, but never more than one-fourth of the estate; (2) if there is issue of the marriage of the decedent and the surviving spouse, that spouse receives a life estate in one-fourth of the estate; (3) if there are recognized illegitimate children, or legitimate issue of such children or if there are parents of the decedent or brothers or sisters, nephews, nieces, grandnephews, or grandnieces, the spouse receives a life estate in one-half of the estate; (4) if there are only other relatives, the spouse receives a life estate in the entire estate; (5) if there are no relatives entitled to succeed in the paternal or in the maternal line, the spouse receives one-half of the estate absolutely; and (6) if there are no relatives within the sixth grade of consanguinity, the spouse receives all.

In Soviet law

The R.S.F.S.R. The civil code of the Russian Soviet Federated Socialist Republic (1964), provides the following order of intestate succession: (1) children, spouse, and parents of the decedent, in equal shares, a deceased child being represented by his child or children, and a deceased grandchild by his child or children; (2) brothers and sisters of the decedent and his paternal and maternal grandfathers and grandmothers, in equal shares.

Intestate takers also include those persons who, unable to work, were dependent upon the decedent for not less than one year prior to his death. If there are other intestate takers, such persons take equally with takers of the class that takes the estate.

Ordinary household furnishings and articles pass to those intestate takers who have lived with the decedent for not less than one year prior to his death, without regard to their class or statutory shares.

IV. Wills

A will, or "testament," is the legal transaction by which an owner of property disposes of his assets for the event of his death. The terms are also applied to the written instrument in which the testator's dispositions are expressed. While in modern usage the terms will and testament are interchangeable, in traditional Anglo-American law "will" referred to the disposition of real property and "testament" to that of personal property.

FORMALITIES OF WILLS

A will must be declared in the form of an instrument in writing. A nuncupative (orally declared) will is exceptionally admitted in some jurisdictions in emergency situations, such as those of the soldier on active war duty, the sailor on board ship, or a person finding himself in immediate danger of death.

Kinds of wills

In their rules establishing the requirements of the execution of a regular testamentary instrument, the legal systems of the modern world usually follow one or more of three forms: (1) the witnessed will as developed in England, especially through the Statute of Frauds of 1677; (2) the unwitnessed holographic will as developed in French customary law; (3) the notarial will as developed in the late Roman Empire. Under the system of the witnessed will, which prevails throughout the United States and in all common-law parts of the British Commonwealth, the instrument, which may be typed or printed or written by anyone, must be subscribed by the testator, and his signature must be attested to by two (in the New England states, three) witnesses, who must also sign their names to the instrument. Under the system of the holographic will, which is available not only in most civil-law countries but also in numerous states of the South and West in the United States, the entire instrument, generally including the date and the indication of the place of execution, must be exclusively in the testator's own handwriting and must also be signed by him; witnesses are not required. The notarial will, which is also available in most civil-law countries, is executed so that the testator either dictates his provisions to the notary or hands him an instrument declaring that it contains his will. In civil-law countries, a notary is not a layman but a respected member of the legal profession who is experienced in matters of drafting wills, estate planning, and conveyancing.

The proper drafting of a will can be difficult. In the United States it is complicated not only by the diversity of the law from state to state but also by the fact that, unless different provisions have been expressly stated in the will, rules that are in many respects obsolete apply to such questions as how to apportion the burden of death taxes among the beneficiaries; in which order creditors ought to be paid; what assets are to be used for the payment of debts; which legacies are to be abated in case of insufficiency of the estate to pay them all in full; and what to do when a beneficiary has predeceased the testator. Unless the testator has given special powers to his executor, it may be necessary for the latter to observe cumbersome and expensive formalities in his administration. In the United States it is therefore unwise to draft a will without expert legal advice; and it is advisable for a testator to have his will periodically checked by a lawyer in order to keep up not only with the changing circumstances of the testator's family circle and of his property but also to keep abreast to the frequent changes in the tax laws in order to avoid unnecessary taxes.

INVALID WILLS

Breaking and revoking wills

A testamentary disposition is not valid if at the time of its execution the testator was mentally incompetent or if he acted under "undue influence"; *i.e.*, coercion, or under fraud. It is difficult, however, to break a will upon such grounds. The courts, especially those of the Anglo-American system, demand strict proof that the testator, when he made the provision, was mentally unable to know what he owned or who were his relatives or was unable to form a reasonable plan for the disposition of his property. The mere fact that the testator laboured under some insane delusion will not affect the validity of his will unless it is proved that this governed the disposition made by him. Coaxing and persuasion are generally not held to constitute undue influence in the absence of actual threats. A testator must not be pushed, but he may be led. Undue influence may be held to exist, however, where a testamentary disposition was brought about by a person upon whom the testator was dependent or whom he was likely to obey blindly.

The statutory formalities prescribed for the execution of a will must be observed meticulously. An unwitnessed holographic will may fail because the instrument contains a printed letterhead or some other words, figures, or signs in print, a rubber stamp, or another person's handwriting. A witnessed will may fail because a witness signed outside the testator's line of sight, or because the witnesses were not told that the instrument was the testator's will, or because a blank space was left between the end of the text and the signature of the testator. The witnesses should be absolutely disinterested; *i.e.*, persons who derive no direct or indirect benefit from any of the provisions of the instrument. A witness may be held to be benefitted indirectly if his spouse is appointed in the will as executor and thus given the opportunity to earn the fees of that office. Ordinarily, attestation of a will by such a disqualified witness will not result in the invalidity of the entire instrument but only of the provision from which the witness would have benefitted.

A will is ambulatory; *i.e.*, it is of no effect until the testator's death, and it can be revoked or changed by him at any time. Revocation is effected either by the testator's physically destroying the instrument or by his executing a new testamentary instrument, the provisions of which are incompatible with those of the earlier one or in which it is simply declared that the will is revoked. In many states of the U.S. a will is also revoked automatically if the testator marries after its execution. In England it is revoked by marriage unless it is stated to be made in contemplation of marriage. Attempts by contractual promise to limit one's freedom of changing or revoking his will are without any effect in those legal systems that follow the pattern of the French civil code. But under the system of the German civil code, a disposition is irrevocable if it is expressed in a hereditary pact (*Erbvertrag*) made with a beneficiary or even with a third person. In Anglo-American law the will remains revocable even if the testator has promised that he will not revoke it; but if he does, his estate will be treated as if the testator had lived up to his promise. In practical effect, a testator may thus bind himself to make and not to revoke a will favouring a person who has promised to take care of him in old age. A husband and wife may promise each other that upon the death of one of them his property shall be enjoyed by the survivor and that upon the latter's death it will go to the children or to certain relatives or charities.

V. The machinery of transfer

Rules of intestate succession and of wills do not by themselves bring about the actual transfer of the decedent's assets to the new owners. A society with an economic system based on credit cannot operate on the once accepted principle that a man's debts die with him. Modern law must provide techniques for making sure that the debts left by a dead man are properly paid. For the purpose of orderly transfer of assets and the proper payment of the debts of a decedent, two different techniques have been developed—one in the civil law and one in the common law.

TRANSFER IN CIVIL LAW

The civil-law technique goes back to ancient Rome. When the head of a house, the paterfamilias, died, his position of headship devolved upon his heir or heirs. The heir, or heres, not only acquired all the ancestor's property but also his duties. The heres became liable for the debts, which meant that he had to dig into his own pocket if the assets of the estate did not suffice. This harsh rule was mitigated by the possibility given to the heir to abstain from, or to decline, the accession to the heirship. Then the option of accepting or declining devolved upon the person or persons next in line under the will or the rules of intestacy. If all declined, the succession ultimately came to the state, which was never liable beyond the value of the assets of the estate. Refusal to accept heirship to a father could appear as a violation of the duty of filial piety. Also, at the time the choice was to be made it might not always be apparent whether or not the estate was solvent. So another protective device was invented by Justinian: if, within a certain period of time, the heir fully and correctly inventoried the assets of the estate, his liability would be limited to the assets of the estate or to their value.

Development of the universal successor in civil law

The Roman system is still basically that of the civil-law countries. There are, of course, many variations in detail, especially in the treatment of the situation of succession by a plurality of coheirs and in the treatment of the period of uncertainty as to who will ultimately accept the succession. There must be a person or a plurality of persons who, like the Roman heres, succeeds to the universality of the decedent's estate; *i.e.*, to the assets as well as to the debts. He or they, as the case may be, is or are determined by the decedent's testament, or by the law of intestacy, or by a combination of both. By his testament the decedent may charge the universal successor or successors with the duty to carry out legacies—*i.e.*, to hand over certain assets of the estate to third persons, or to pay to them certain amounts of money. Any person called to be universal successor is free to accept or to decline the position. If he chooses to accept, he may limit his liability to the assets of the estate either, as under the French system, by declaring his acceptance to be under the benefit of the inventory and by then making the inventory fully and correctly or, as under the German system, by handing over the estate to a judicially appointed administrator.

TRANSFER IN ANGLO-AMERICAN LAW

The Anglo-American system developed along quite different lines. Until the 19th century, liability for the debts of a decedent was limited to the assets of his personal estate. Real property was not liable unless it had been specifically mortgaged, in which case the mortgagee had his remedy of foreclosure. Thus, the title to the real property descended, like title to all assets under the civil law, directly to the heir, who acquired it immediately upon the death of the ancestor. But in order to guarantee the liability of the personal property for the debts of the decedent, as well as its proper distribution among the plurality of distributees, the ecclesiastical courts, which had the jurisdiction to deal with succession to personal property, worked out an original technique. Title was treated as passing from the decedent to the bishop or, later, to his substitute (surrogate) and ultimately to a middleman, on whom it was incumbent to pay the debts of the decedent and other claims that might exist against the estate and then to distribute the surplus remaining among the persons entitled thereto under the will or under the rules of intestacy. The provisions of a testament, however, would not be considered until the instrument had been admitted to probate, which means that it had been found to be properly executed and valid by the ecclesiastical court.

Development of probate in Anglo-American law

Probate. The modern laws of the Anglo-American countries have been developed upon this historical pattern with its peculiar features of probate and administration. In England the jurisdiction of the ecclesiastical courts was continuously narrowed by the royal courts. In the court reform of the 1870s, the new Probate, Divorce and Admiralty Division was established in the High Court. It took over from the ecclesiastical courts the narrow jurisdiction that had been left to them, namely, that of scrutinizing instruments purporting to be testaments; but simultaneously its jurisdiction was extended to wills; *i.e.*, instruments purporting to dispose of real property. Administrators are appointed by the Probate Division, but executors derive their powers directly from the will, so that they can act as soon as it is admitted to probate. If the personal representative wishes to obtain authoritative instructions on a problem occurring in the course of the administration, he can turn to the Chancery Division of the High Court, which also regularly decides controversies that may arise. But as a general rule the personal representative is free to act on his own and under his own responsibility, much as does a civil-law heir.

But in the U.S. branch of the common law a somewhat different machinery came into being. Ecclesiastical courts on the English pattern had not existed in the American colonies. The tasks of probate and of appointing administrators had thus to be performed by other agencies. In some places the job was for some time performed by the governor or some other officer of the executive. But the institution that was peculiarly developed in America was the Probate Court, which in most states is called by that name but in New York is known as Surrogate's Court and in Pennsylvania as Orphan's Court.

The tasks of a U.S. Probate Court are much more extensive than those of its English counterpart. United States Probate Courts usually are concerned with the administration of estates not only of decedents but also of minors and mentally incompetent persons. All of the persons entrusted with these tasks are treated as "officers of the court," who must all be appointed by the court, must give bond, and will be closely supervised by the court. In contrast to the practice in England, an American executor, or administrator, is not permitted to take any step without previous approval of the Probate Court, which normally requires that all interested parties be formally notified. Strictly speaking, no piece of furniture may be sold, no claim be settled, without the consent of the court.

Transactions inter vivos

If, as it is frequently done, the strict rules are not meticulously followed, troublesome complications may arise. In any case, time is needed and expenses have to be incurred. Devices have therefore been developed enabling the parties to dispense with administration or to avoid both probate and administration by resorting to transactions inter vivos that permit a person to give away his property while he is alive but under conditions allowing him to retain for himself not only the income and enjoyment during his lifetime but also the power of management, disposition, and revocation. Through such devices as revocable inter vivos trusts, joint tenancies, or "tentative trusts" of bank accounts (so-called totten trusts), one can achieve the practical effects of a will without probate and without administration. One can also escape those safeguards that have been established for the protection of creditors and forced heirs and for the prevention of tax avoidance. While both the English and the civil-law systems maintain the principle that it is not possible to give and to keep, the ingenuity of U.S. lawyers and the indulgence of U.S. judges have made it possible for an owner to "eat his cake and have it." A wave of reform legislation has resulted in simplifications in a great many American states.

Administration. The Uniform Probate Code published by the National Conference of Commissioners on Uniform State Laws (1969) provides a choice between several systems of administration: simple and inexpensive ones for simple cases and administration supervised by the court and containing elaborate safeguards for estates that are insolvent, under dispute, or that present other difficulties. The scheme of the new code thus assimilates the American law of winding up decedents' estates to those of England and of the civil-law countries, where the simple estate is treated as the normal, where no executor is needed unless he is expressly provided for in the testament, and where judicial administration is limited to cases of exceptional risk or complexity.

Under both the English and the American systems, the winding up of an estate follows essentially the same pattern. Anything looking like a will is filed with the Probate Court. The person named executor by the will, or some other interested person, petitions for the admission of the instrument to probate. The procedure varies in detail but, following English tradition, generally provides the possibility of simple, quick proceedings. These may consist of "probate in the common form," or of the more formal procedures of "probate in the solemn form" for the authoritative decision of disputed issues (frequently called "will contest").

The executor

As executor a testator may choose any person or any corporation engaging in the business of administering trusts and estates. But the law seeks to have the position of administrator filled by that person likely to be the one primarily interested in the estate. The statutes thus contain lists of the persons who have a right to be appointed. The first place is usually given to the surviving spouse, followed by relatives in the order in which they are intestate takers. Each of these persons may either accept the office for himself or nominate a person or corporation of his choice. If there is no surviving spouse or relative, the right to administer devolves to the creditors of the decedent and, in the last line, to a public officer, called public administrator, or public trustee.

Under the laws that prevailed in the United States into the 1950s, real property and personal property were not handled in the same way. Unless a testator disposed otherwise, the payment of claims—*i.e.*, debts, estate taxes, and expenses of administration—was from the personal estate. The real estate was not to be touched until the personal estate had been exhausted. Accordingly, title to only the personal estate passed to the executor or administrator. Title to the real estate descended directly from the decedent to the heir or heirs, or to the devisee or devisees named in the will. If the personal estate was insufficient to pay all the claims the executor or administrator would be authorized by the Probate Court to sell or mortgage as much of the real estate as was necessary. In many, although not all, U.S. jurisdictions this different treatment of real estate and personal estate has been abolished, making both liable for claims on an equal footing and equally subject to administration.

Under the English system an executor derives his position directly from the will; under the U.S. system an executor, like an administrator, must be appointed by the Probate Court, and no appointment will be made if the person is found to be disqualified or until he has taken the oath of office and posted bond. An executor may be exempted from the latter requirement by a provision of the will.

An executor or administrator has to collect the assets of the estate, ascertain and pay the taxes and debts, and distribute the surplus to the legatees, or intestate takers. In the civil-law system proper performance of these functions has its sanction in the personal liability of the heir for the debts of the decedent; if he takes steps to free himself of this liability, he has then to manage the estate like a common-law administrator or to hand over to an administrator appointed by the court.

The office of executor or administrator may involve complex responsibilities. Unless one can be certain that there are no unknown debts, that the estate is solvent, that there will be no dispute about the distribution of the estate, that there are none but the simplest tax problems, and that there are no minors or mentally incompetent persons among the possible takers, one should not act as executor or administrator without the assistance of a lawyer.

BIBLIOGRAPHY

The historical background of modern laws of inheritance: M. KASER, *Römisches Privatrecht*, 3rd ed. (1965; Eng. trans., *Roman Private Law*, 2nd ed., 1968); W.W. BUCKLAND, *Text-Book of Roman Law From Augustus to Justinian*, 3rd ed. (1963); R. HUEBNER, *Grundzüge des deutschen Privatrechts*, 2nd ed. (Eng. trans., *History of Germanic Private Law*, 1918, reprinted 1969); F. POLLOCK and F.W. MAITLAND, *History of English Law Before the Time of Edward I*, 3rd ed., vol. 2 (1968); W. HOLDSWORTH, *History of English Law*, 3rd ed., 9 vol. (1923–32).

Discussions and critiques of inheritance: JOHN STUART MILL, *Principles of Political Economy*, vol. 1 (1848); L. BRENTANO, *Erbrechtspolitik* (1899); J. WEDGWOOD, *The Economics of Inheritance* (1929, reprinted 1971); J.C. STAMP, *Some Aspects of the Inequality of Incomes in Modern Communities* (1929); FRIEDRICH ENGELS, *Der Ursprung der Familie, des Privateigenthums und des Staats* (1884; Eng. trans. from the 4th ed. of 1934, *The Origin of the Family, Private Property and the State*, 1942); and K. RENNER, *Die Rechtsinstitute des Privatrechts und ihre soziale Funktion* (1929; Eng. trans., *The Institutions of Private Law and Their Social Functions*, 1949). M.B. SUSSMAN, J.N. CATES, and D.T. SMITH, *The Family and Inheritance* (1970), is a case study culminating in conclusions about testamentary patterns, practices, and effects of inheritance in American society.

Inheritance in socialist societies: J.N. HAZARD, *Communists and Their Law* (1969) and *Law and Social Change in the U.S.S.R.* (1953).

The current law of inheritance: Monographic treatises on contemporary inheritance laws are collected in M. FERID and K. FIRSCHING, *Internationales Nachlassrecht;* the loose-leaf volumes published so far cover the Federal Republic of Germany, the German Democratic Republic, Austria, Switzerland, Belgium, France, The Netherlands, Italy, Vatican City, Spain, Great Britain, the United States, Bulgaria, Yugoslavia, Poland, Czechoslovakia, the Union of Soviet Socialist Republics, Hungary, Israel, and the Republic of China (Taiwan). Concise digests of the succession laws of all jurisdictions of the United States, Canada, the United Kingdom, and a large number of other countries are published annually in MARTINDALE-HUBBELL, *Law Directory*. For the United States, see: W.H. PAGE, *Law of Wills*, rev. ed. by W.J. BOWE and D.H. PARKER, 8 vol. (1960–65), with annual supplements; M. RHEINSTEIN and M.A. GLENDON, *Law of Decedents' Estates* (1971), an introduction to the field for students and other interested readers; T.E. ATKINSON, *Handbook of the Law of Wills and Other Principles of Succession*, 2nd ed. (1953). For England, see: H. THEOBALD, *Law of Wills*, 13th ed. by G. DWORKIN and S. CRETNEY (1971); D.H. PARRY, *Law of Succession*, 5th ed. (1966); W.J. WILLIAMS, *The Law Relating to Wills*, 3rd ed. (1967; suppl. 1971); E.V. WILLIAMS and H.C. MORTIMER on *Executors, Administrators and Probate*, new ed. by J.H.G. SUNNUCHS and R.L. BAYNE-POWELL (1970). For Scotland: D.M. WALKER, *Principles of Scottish Private Law*, 2 vol. (1970); T.B. SMITH, *Scotland: The Development of its Laws and Constitution* (1962); C. DE B. MURRAY, *The Law of Wills in Scotland* (1945).

(M.Y.R.)

Inner Asia, History of

In its historical application the term Inner Asia designates an area that is considerably larger than the heartland of the Asian continent. Were it not for the awkwardness of the term, it would be better to speak of Central Eurasia, comprising all those parts of the huge Eurasian landmass that have not developed a distinctive, sedentary civilization of their own. Europe, the Near Eastern civilizations (both Semitic and Iranian), India, and East Asia surround Inner Asia, limited in the north by the Arctic, its only natural boundary. But because the hearts of men stake out frontiers more clearly than do mountains, streams, or deserts, the real boundaries of Inner Asia are determined at any given time in history by the relationship between the "civilized" and the "barbarian"—the two opposed but complementary. The equation so often propounded—of the civilized with the sedentary and the barbarian with the nomad—is misleading, however, and does not correspond to historical reality. The most significant distinction between the two groups in Eurasia lies probably in the successful attempt of the civilized to alter and command his physical environment, whereas the barbarian simply uses it, often in a masterly fashion, to his own advantage. In its essence, the history of Inner Asia is that of the barbarian, and its dominant feature is the sometimes latent, sometimes open conflict in which he clashes with the civilized. Following the tides of history, the area of Inner Asia is subject to fluctuations. In the rhythm of expansion and contraction, it is possible to detect the two basic patterns of conquest: that of the barbarian—accomplished with arms and ephemeral in his results—and that of the civilized—slow, rather unspectacular, achieved through absorption and assimilation.

Area of Inner Asia

The principal difficulty for the historian of Inner Asia lies in the paucity and relative lateness of indigenous written sources. The first aboriginal sources—written in a Turkic language—date from the 8th century AD, and source material of similar value does not become available again until the 13th century. Most of the written sources dealing with Inner Asia originate in the surrounding sedentary civilizations and are almost always strongly prejudiced against the barbarian; the most important among them are in Chinese, Greek, Latin, Arabic, and Persian.

Without a sufficient number of indigenous written sources, the language of a given Inner Asian people is difficult to determine. It is, however, reasonable to suppose that many of them spoke a Uralic or an Altaic language, and it can be taken for certain that Paleo-Asiatic languages were in wider use in early times than they are now. While it seems likely that the principal languages of many great nomadic empires were Turkic or Mongol, the attribution of such languages to peoples about whose speech insufficient linguistic evidence exists—as in the case of the Hsiung-nu or the Avars—is unwarranted and misleading; it is wiser to confess ignorance.

Two of the natural vegetation zones of Inner Asia have played a prominent part in history: the forest belt, 500 to 1,000 miles (800 to 1,600 kilometres) wide, and, south of it, the steppe, a vast grassland extending from Hungary to Mongolia, facilitating communications and providing grass, the only raw material absolutely essential to the creation of the great nomad empires. The northern frozen marshes and the southern deserts played a minor role in Inner Asian history.

Role of the forest belt and the steppe

PREHISTORY AND ANTIQUITY

The beginnings of man's history in Inner Asia date back to the late Pleistocene Epoch, some 25,000 to 35,000

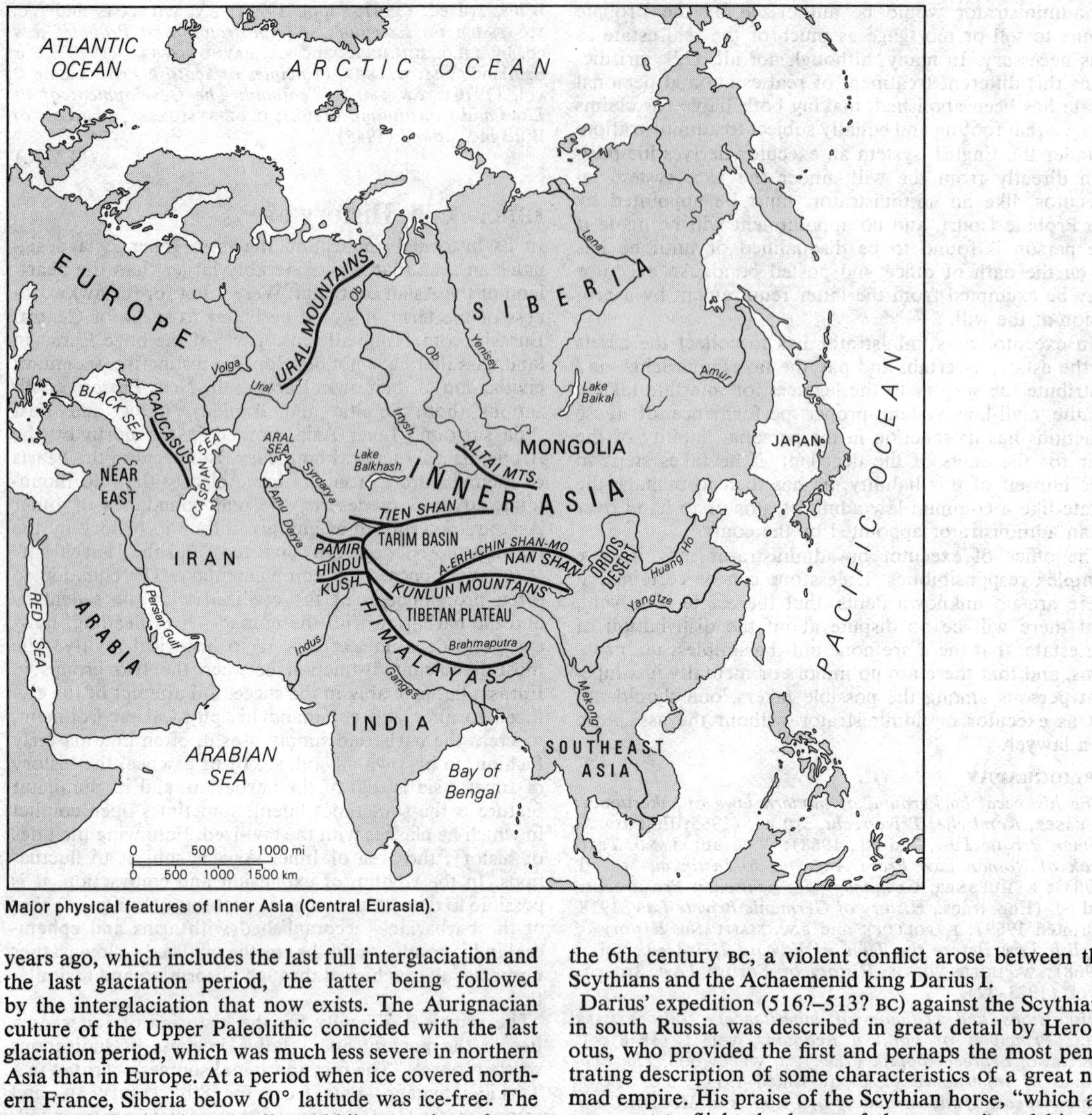

Major physical features of Inner Asia (Central Eurasia).

years ago, which includes the last full interglaciation and the last glaciation period, the latter being followed by the interglaciation that now exists. The Aurignacian culture of the Upper Paleolithic coincided with the last glaciation period, which was much less severe in northern Asia than in Europe. At a period when ice covered northern France, Siberia below 60° latitude was ice-free. The Paleolithic Malta site, 28 miles (45 kilometres) northwest of Irkutsk, is clearly Aurignacian, and it is safe to assume that in this period Siberia and the sub-Arctic areas of Europe belonged to the same civilization. The differentiation between Inner Asia and the surrounding civilization did not begin until Neolithic times, marked by tremendous technical progress and a wide diversification of cultures. This article does not deal with their development or indicate their contacts with eastern, southern, and western cultures; most of the archaeological results, however important, are controversial and are subject to different interpretations in the light of new finds.

Early western peoples. The first human groups to emerge at the dawn of history that are identifiable by name rather than by their artifacts are the Cimmerians and the Scythians, both located in the western half of Inner Asia and reported on by the Greeks.

The Cimmerians. The Cimmerians, whose name appears in the *Odyssey* of Homer, occupied the South Russian Steppe from about 1200 BC. Their civilization, which belongs to the Late Bronze Age, is barely distinguishable from that of other peoples with whom they mingled.

The Scythians. From the second half of the 8th century BC, the Cimmerians were replaced by the Scythians, who used iron implements. The Scythians created the first known typical Inner Asian empire. The chief thrust of their expansion was directed against the south rather than the west, where no major power existed and which thus offered little chance for important booty. In the late 8th century BC, Cimmerian and Scythian troops fought against the Assyrian king Sargon II, and, at the end of the 6th century BC, a violent conflict arose between the Scythians and the Achaemenid king Darius I.

Darius' expedition (516?–513? BC) against the Scythians in south Russia was described in great detail by Herodotus, who provided the first and perhaps the most penetrating description of some characteristics of a great nomad empire. His praise of the Scythian horse, "which always put to flight the horse of the enemy," and his description of Scythian reluctance to engage in direct, open combat and of their preference to harass the enemy are, among others, *loci classici*, applicable to virtually all nomad empires. Herodotus showed the essential conservatism of Inner Asian civilization. The Scythian argument against towns, allegedly put to Darius and reported by Herodotus, "We Scythians have neither towns nor cultivated lands, which might induce us, through fear of their being taken or ravaged, to be in any hurry to fight with you," has its counterpart in Mongol thinking of the 13th century AD. When, in AD 1226, because of Genghis Khan's illness the Mongols hesitated to attack the Tanguts of China, the campaign was postponed on the ground that

Herodotus' description of the Scythians

> The Tangut people have cities surrounded with earthworks and fixed camps. They will not pick up and carry away their walled-in cities, their fixed camps, they will not move away. Let us leave them now and when the khan's health is reestablished we will move again against them.

Equally characteristic is Herodotus' complaint about the Scythians' "insolence":

> For besides the regular tribute, they exacted from several nations additional imposts, which they fixed at pleasure; further they scoured the country and plundered everyone of whatever they could.

In more than one respect the Scythians appear as the historical prototype of the mounted warrior of the steppe; yet in their case, as in many others, it would be mistaken to see in them aimlessly roaming tribes without fixed abodes. The Scythians, like most nomad empires, had permanent settlements of various sizes, representing various degrees of civilization. The vast fortified settlement of Kamenka on the Dniepr, settled since the end of the 5th century BC, became the centre of the Scythian kingdom ruled by Ateas, who lost his life in a battle against Philip II of Macedon in 339 BC.

The Scythians had a highly developed metallurgy, and in their social structure the agriculturalists (*aroteres*), who grew corn for sale, constituted a class of their own. The quality of Scythian art, characterized by a highly sophisticated style called "animal art," remained unsurpassed in Inner Asia. Because its use has been widespread in time and in space, "Scythian art" finds should not necessarily be attributed, as they often are, to the Scythian people. Although the Scythians had no script, it has been established, nevertheless, that they spoke an Iranian language.

There is little trace of aggressiveness in later Scythian history. From the 4th century BC the Scythians were slowly absorbed by the Sarmatians, another Iranian people who were to dominate the South Russian Steppe until the 4th century AD.

Early eastern peoples. From its earliest history China had to contend with barbarian pressures on its borders. In fact, it could be said that the concept of being Chinese was created in opposition to the concept of the barbarian. The group of barbarians called the Hu thus played a considerable role in early Chinese history, leading to the introduction of cavalry and the adoption of foreign clothing, more suitable than its traditional Chinese counterpart for new types of warfare. Around 200 BC a new and powerful barbarian people emerged on China's western borders, the Hsiung-nu. Little is known of T'ou-man, founder of this empire, beyond the fact that he was killed by his son Mao-tun, under whose long reign (*c.* 209–174 BC) the Hsiung-nu became a major power and a serious menace to China. In many respects the Hsiung-nu are the eastern counterparts of the Scythians. The Chinese historian Ssu-ma Ch'ien (145?–*c.* 85 BC) described Hsiung-nu nomadic tactics and strategy in terms almost identical with those applied by Herodotus to the Scythians: the Hsiung-nu "move about in search of water and pasture and have no walled cities or fixed dwellings, nor do they engage in any kind of agriculture."

Emergence of the Hsiung-nu

The centre of the Hsiung-nu Empire was Mongolia, but it is impossible to even approximate the western limits of the land under their direct control. Bactria was not under Hsiung-nu rule; the last Greco-Bactrian kingdom was overrun between 141 and 128 BC by the Iranian Yüeh-chih, chased by the Hsiung-nu from their former country in western Kansu, China. (The Yüeh-chih should be identified with the Tokharians of the Greek sources.) While one part of the Yüeh-chih confederation, the Asi tribe, moved farther westward into the Caucasus, Kujūla Kadphises united the other Yüeh-chih tribes in the 1st century AD and established the Kushan Empire, which expanded into India.) For more than two centuries, the Hsiung-nu Empire, more or less constantly warring with China, remained the major force in Inner Asia. It controlled the slowly growing transcontinental trade linking China with Bactria and Rome. Burial places in Mongolia dating from the early 1st century AD contained a great variety of objects of different origins and some remarkable examples of the indigenous "animal style." In AD 48 the Hsiung-nu Empire, long plagued by internecine struggles, dissolved. Some of the tribes, known as the southern Hsiung-nu, recognized Chinese suzerainty and settled in the Ordos region. The other faction, the northern Hsiung-nu, maintained themselves in Mongolia until about the mid-2nd century, when they finally succumbed to the repeated attacks of the Hsien-pei.

In the middle of the 1st century BC, an unsuccessful political faction of the Hsiung-nu, led by Chih-chih, brother and rival of the ruler, moved westward. With the death of Chih-chih in 36 BC, this Hsiung-nu group disappeared from sight; but, according to one theory that has been put forth, the Huns who appeared on the South Russian Steppe (*c.* AD 370) were descendants of these fugitive tribes.

THE MIDDLE AGES

The last decades of the 4th century AD saw the formation of a new, powerful empire in Mongolia, the political heartland of Inner Asia. The Juan-juan had stepped into the place vacated by the Hsiung-nu. Chinese descriptions barely distinguish them from their predecessors. Their history is an incessant series of campaigns against their neighbours, especially the Chinese.

The Turks. In 552 the Juan-juan Empire was destroyed by a revolution of considerable consequences for world history. The tribe of the Turk (T'u-chüeh in Chinese transcription), living within the Juan-juan Empire and apparently specializing in metallurgy, revolted and seized power. It established an empire that for about two centuries remained a dominant force in Asia. The Turks are the first people in history known to have spoken a Turkic language and the first Inner Asian people to have left a written record. Inscribed funerary

Adapted from A. Herrmann, *An Historical Atlas of China*

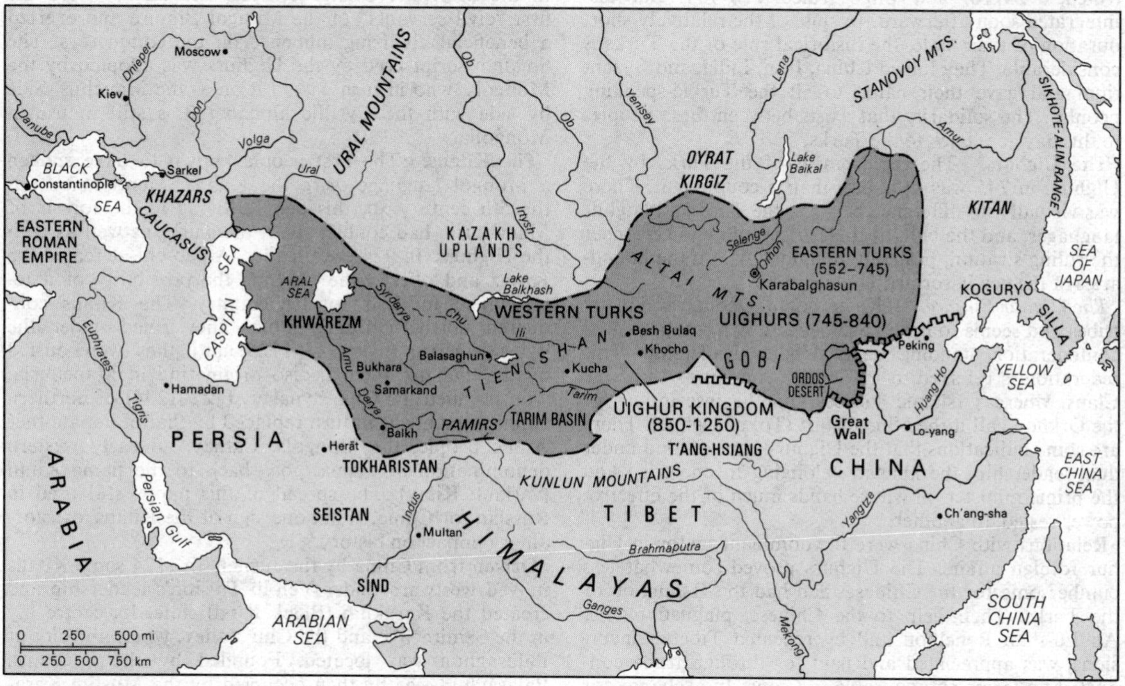

Inner Asia in the Middle Ages.

stelae still standing in Mongolia, mostly near the Orhon Gel (Orhon River), are invaluable from both a linguistic and a historical point of view. These inscriptions give a Turk view of the creation and provide insights into the internal stresses of a pastoral nomad state that, at the height of its power, stretched from the borders of China to those of Byzantium.

Division of the empire. The founder of the Turk Empire, Bumin—who bore the title of khagan—died shortly after his victory. Soon afterward the empire split into two halves. The eastern part, ruled by Bumin's son Mu-han (ruled 553–572), centred on Mongolia; the seat of the western part, ruled by Bumin's brother Ishtemi (ruled 553–573?), lay in Ektagh, an unidentified place, possibly in the Ili or Chu valley. In alliance with the Sāsānids, the Turks attacked and destroyed the Hephtalite Empire (560), thereby gaining control over an important portion of the Silk Road leading from China to Byzantium. Persian reluctance to allow free passage to the Sogdian merchants, who on behalf of the Turks handled the transcontinental trade, led the Turks to seek direct contacts with Byzantium. In 567 a Turk embassy led by the Sogdian Maniakh arrived in Constantinople and was received by the emperor Justin II, who was interested in possible allies situated east of his enemies, the Sāsānids. A series of embassies and counterembassies followed, but they failed to bring about an effective military alliance against the Sāsānids. Under Ishtemi's successor, Tardu (ruled 573–603), the western Turk Empire continued to thrive and, in its westward expansion, reached the borders of Byzantium. In a letter to the emperor Maurice in 598, Tardu refers to himself as "the chief of the seven races and lord of the seven climates of the world." Indeed, by that time the eastern Turk Empire was facing grave difficulties caused partly by internal strife and partly by the vigorous Inner Asian policies of the Chinese Sui dynasty. While the weakening of eastern Turk power gave preponderance to the western Turks, it would seem that basic solidarity between the two parts of the Turk Empire was maintained. They both fell victim to Chinese attacks. In 630 the T'ang emperor T'ai Tsung occupied Mongolia, and in 659, under Kao Tsung, Chinese forces penetrating as far west as Bukhara and Samarkand subdued the western Turks.

Turk revolt against the Chinese

Reunification. In 683 the Turks revolted. The Turk Empire was reborn and reunified under the khagan Elterish (ruled 683–692). Temporary setbacks notwithstanding, the Turk Empire was now centred on Mongolia, and it prospered under the rules of Kapaghan (ruled 692–716) and Bilge (ruled 716–734) but disintegrated soon afterward. In spite of the relatively short duration of their state, the historical role of the Turks is considerable. They linked China, Iran, India, and Byzantium and gave their name to all the Turkic-speaking peoples. The solidarity that exists between these peoples to this day goes back to the Turks.

The Uighurs. The replacement of the Turks by the Uighurs in 745 was little else than a coup d'etat. There was virtually no difference between the Turk and Uighur languages, and the bulk of the Turks, although no longer the ruling stratum, probably remained within the boundaries of the newly formed Uighur state.

The Uighur Empire. This new empire comprised many tribes and seems to have been headed by a smaller tribal confederation standing under Uighur leadership. This federation is referred to in Chinese sources as the Nine Clans, whereas Islāmic sources and the inscriptions of the Orkhon call it the Nine Oghuz (Tokuz Oghuz). There are some indications that the Uighur Empire stood under dual leadership, the khagan belonging to one tribe and the prime minister, in whose hands much of the effective power rested, to another.

Relations with China were the dominant factor in Uighur foreign affairs. The Uighurs proved somewhat less cumbersome for the Chinese than had the Hsiung-nu or the Turks. Their help to the Chinese, plagued by the An Lu-shan Rebellion and by repeated Tibetan incursions, was appreciated and paid for through trade conducted on terms unfavourable to China. In exchange for Uighur horses, often of dubious quality, the Chinese were expected to provide the Uighurs with much-coveted riches. The third Uighur khagan—Mou-yü by his Chinese name (ruled 759–780)—visited Lo-yang in China, where he was converted to an Iranian religion, Manichaeism. Its adoption brought to the Uighur land many Sogdians, whose growing influence on state affairs was resented by the Turkic Uighurs and led to Mou-yü's assassination.

The Uighur Empire was governed from a city, Karabalghasun, the foundations of which were probably laid under the Turks and can still be seen. A Muslim traveller, Tamīm ibn Baḥr, who visited the city around 821, speaks in admiring terms of this fortified town lying in a cultivated country—a far cry from the traditional picture of the pastoral nomad existence.

End of Uighur rule in Mongolia

The Kirgiz invasion. In 840 another Turkic people, the Kirgiz, put an abrupt end to Uighur rule in Mongolia. Coming from the upper reaches of the Yenisey, the Kirgiz represented a lower degree of civilization than the rather sophisticated Uighurs. Their political ambitions did not lead them into campaigns against China, and thus virtually no records exist concerning their activities. Content to stay in the backwaters of history, the Kirgiz are among the very few peoples to have survived the Mongol tide; today theirs is one of the constituent republics of the Soviet Union.

The Uighur kingdom. The Kirgiz invasion, while putting an end to Uighur power, did not annihilate the people. Fleeing Uighur groups settled on the Chinese border in Kansu Province and in Eastern Turkistan in the Turfan region, which had been an Uighur protectorate since the end of the 8th century. Falling back now on the Turfan oases and setting up their capital city in Khocho (Kao-ch'ang, today Karakhoja), the fugitive Uighurs created a remarkably stable and prosperous kingdom that lasted four centuries (*c.* 850–1250). Because of the dry climate of the region, many buildings, wall paintings, and manuscripts written in a great variety of languages have been preserved. They reveal a complex, refined civilization in which Buddhism, Manichaeism, and Christianity lived side by side, practiced by Turks as well as by Tokharians, Sogdians, and other Iranian peoples in the region.

When the time of the Mongol conquests came, the Uighurs lived up to their best cultural traditions. Realizing that resistance would be vain and would only lead to the destruction of his country, Barchuk, the ruler of the Uighurs of Khocho, of his own free will submitted to the Mongols. Uighur officials and scribes were the first "civil servants" of the Mongol Empire and exerted a beneficial civilizing influence on the conquerors. The Sogdian script used by the Uighurs was adopted by the Mongols, who in turn passed it on to the Manchus. Side by side with the Cyrillic alphabet it is still in use in Mongolia.

The Kitans. The first people known to have spoken a Mongol language were the Kitans. Mentioned from the 5th century AD, this people, living in the forests of Manchuria, had contacts with the Turks as well as with the Uighurs. In 924 their leader, A-pao-chi, defeated the Kirgiz and offered the Uighurs the possibility of a resettlement in their former country. The Kitans conquered northern China, which they ruled under the dynastic name Liao (947–1125) until they were ousted by the Tunguz Juchen, also originating in Manchuria, who founded the Chin dynasty (1122–1234) of northern China, which was in turn replaced by that of yet another Altaic people, the Mongols. Cathay, an early western denomination of China, goes back to the name Kitan (variant: Kitay). The spread of this name, still used in Russian for China, is but one sign of the Kitans' extraordinary impact on history.

The Kitans' impact on history

Driven from China by the Juchen, in 1124 some Kitans moved westward under Yeh-lü Ta-shih's leadership and created the Karakitai (Black Kitai) state. Its centre lay in the Semirechye and the Chu Valley, where the city of Balasaghun was located. Founded by the Sogdians, Balasaghun was by then occupied by the Muslim Karakhanids—a Turkic people descended from the Karluks and closely related to the Turks and Uighurs—who, in the middle of the 8th century, had moved west to the Semirechye. In Balasaghun, in 1070, the *Kutadghu Bilig* was written, a lengthy didactic poem, the first product of Turkic literature to show Islāmic influence.

The Seljuqs were another Turkic people on whose land the Karakitai set their eyes. An Oghuz tribe, the Seljuqs moved to the Syrdarya Valley during the 10th century, took the name of their leader, and converted to Islām. They soon became a major factor in the history of the Muslim world. In 1137 Yeh-lü Ta-shih received the submission of the Karakhanid ruler Mahmud, and in 1141, in a battle fought near Samarkand, he decisively defeated the Seljuq sultan Sanjar. The Karakitais thus established themselves in Transoxiana, whence they exerted considerable political influence on Khwārezm. Their rule was shattered in 1211 through the joint action of Küchlüg, a Naiman prince fleeing from the Mongols, and Muḥammad, ruler of Khwārezm.

The Mongol epoch. The creation of the Mongol empire by Genghis Khan was a great feat of political and military skill that left a lasting imprint on the destinies of both Asia and Europe. The geographical basis of Genghis' power, the northwestern parts of which later became known as Mongolia, had been the centre of such Turkic empires as those of the Turks and Uighurs. There are no indications of the time and the manner in which the Mongols took over this region.

Creation of the Mongol Empire. It is probable that Turks were incorporated in the nascent Mongol Empire. In a series of tribal wars that led to the defeat of the Merkits and the Naimans, his most dangerous rivals, Genghis gained sufficient strength to assume, in 1206, the title of khan. Acting in the tradition of previous nomad empires of the region, Genghis' aggressive policies were directed primarily against China, then ruled in the north by the Juchen Chin dynasty. His western campaigns were set in motion quite accidentally by a senseless attack on Mongol forces by the fugitive Naiman prince Küchlüg, and they maintained their momentum through the pursuit of Muḥammad II of Khwārezm, who, in 1218, ordered the execution of Mongol envoys seeking to establish trade relations. As a result, many of the flourishing cities of Khwārezm, Khorasan, and Afghanistan were destroyed, and by 1223 Mongol armies had crossed the Caucasus. Although an important Russo-Kipchak force was defeated May 31, 1223, at the Battle of the Kalka, the Mongols did not make a definite thrust into eastern Europe until the winter of 1236–37. The fall of Kiev in December 1240—with incalculable consequences for Russian history—was followed by a Mongol invasion of Hungary in 1241–42. Though victorious against the forces of King Béla IV, the Mongols evacuated Hungary and withdrew to southern and central Russia. Ruled by Batu (died 1256), the Mongols of eastern Europe (the so-called Golden Horde) became a major factor in that region and exerted a decisive influence on the development of the Russian states.

Mongol thrust into eastern Europe

Simultaneously with these western campaigns, Genghis' successor Ögödei (reigned 1229–41) intensified Mongol pressure in China. Korea was occupied in 1231, and in 1234 the Chin dynasty succumbed to Mongol attacks. The establishment of the Mongol Yüan dynasty in China (1279–1368) was accomplished by the great khan Kublai (ruled 1259–94), a grandson of Genghis.

Mongol rule. The great khan Möngke (ruled 1251–59), who had sent his brother Kublai to conquer China, entrusted another of his brothers, Hülegü, with the task of consolidating the Mongol hold on Iran. In 1258 Hülegü occupied Baghdad and put an end to the ʿAbbāsid caliphate. He laid the foundations of a Mongol state in Iran, known as that of the Il-Khans, which, under Abagha (ruled 1265–82), Arghun (ruled 1284–91), Ghāzān (ruled 1295–1304), and Öljeitü (ruled 1304–15), became both powerful and highly civilized. Although practically independent, the Il-Khans of Persia remained loyal to Möngke and Kublai, but with the passing of Kublai—the last of the great khans still rooted in Mongol soil—the Persian drift toward full independence grew stronger. With Ghāzān's decision to make Islām the state religion—a gesture intended to gain the confidence of the majority of his subjects—a big step toward integration in the purely Iranian (as opposed to Mongol) tradition was taken. A lengthy conflict that opposed the Il-Khans to the Mamlūks of Egypt was not resolved until 1323, when a peace was concluded between the sultan al-Malik an-Nāṣir and Abū Saʿīd (ruled 1316–35), the last of the Il-Khans. After Abū Saʿīd's death the Il-Khanid state, no longer held together by Mongol efficiency, disintegrated.

In Iran and China, the Mongol states that linked their destinies to those of "major" civilizations were gradually losing their identity. But in the steppes of Inner Asia, the descendants of Chagatai and Ögödei, sons of Genghis, maintained an old-fashioned, steppe-oriented policy, increasingly opposed to the "progressive" wing represented in China and Iran by the descendants of Genghis' youngest son, Tolui. After Möngke's death, the steppe candidate Arigböge lost his bid for supreme power to Kublai; further attempts to re-establish the centre of Mongol power in the steppe also failed. The most active and successful protagonist of this policy was Kaidu, a grandson of Ögödei, who made several attempts to carve out an empire for himself from lands ruled by other Mongol princes; he extended his control over Transoxiana, the Ili region, and Chinese Turkistan, and in 1269 he even assumed the title of great khan. The Chagataid khans, to some extent victims of this policy, for lack of better alternatives lent some support to Kaidu; but, after Kaidu's death in 1301, the Chagataid khan Duwa hastened to make his peace with his Mongol kin in both Iran and China. In a letter written to Philip the Fair of France in 1305, the Il-Khan Öljeitü referred to this peace as a portent for universal peace—an overly optimistic statement in view of the many conflicts in the Mongol world, let alone elsewhere.

The Golden Horde

Development within the Golden Horde was on different lines. Its Islāmization, begun under Batu's successor Berke (ruled 1257–67), led to tensions with the Il-Khans but created strong links with the Mamlūks of Egypt, themselves of Kipchak origin. The prosperity of the Golden Horde under ʿAbd Allāh Khan Özbeg (Uzbek; ruled 1313–41) stands in sharp contrast to the disintegrating Il-Khanid state, yet it had its own problems, both internal and external. From within, the growing and unavoidable antagonism between a ruling class that was Muslim-Mongol, but de facto largely Turkic speaking, and the local Christian-Russian elements was aggravated by dissensions within the ruling class. In foreign policy the peace concluded in 1323 between the Il-Khans and the Mamlūks weakened the Golden Horde's influence in Egypt, and the establishment of Ottoman power in the Dardanelles (1354) put a virtual end to the commercial relations between the Volga and the Nile valleys. Perhaps the gravest political mistake of the rulers of the Golden Horde was their failure to recognize that the West—with which, through the Russians, they had excellent links—offered a more fertile ground for further development than the sunbaked deserts of Turkistan. The khans of the Golden Horde, instead of ruling over Russian and Lithuanian princes, were increasingly relying on their help in internal struggles that were rending the state asunder. While their eyes were turned southward, they allowed the rise of dangerous enemies—Russians and Lithuanians—in their rear. The policies of the khan Tokhtamysh (ruled 1377–95) differed from those of his opponents; he enlarged his power base by uniting the Golden Horde with the so-called White Horde, situated farther eastward in West Siberia and on the lower reaches of the Syrdarya. He thus introduced some fresh "steppe power" into the relatively stale, unimaginative military machinery of the Golden Horde. Furthermore, instead of seeking the help of petty east European princes, he hitched his wagon to the rising star of Timur, with whose support Tokhtamysh reasserted Mongol supremacy in Russia.

The aftermath of Mongol rule. Probably Turkic-speaking, and yet claiming to restore the empire of Genghis,

Timur emerged from the general anarchy that characterized Central Asia in the second half of the 14th century. Not certain of his own legitimacy, Timur enthroned puppet emperors, on whose behalf he pretended to act. His whole life was spent in campaigns, among which those against his former protégé Tokhtamysh (defeated in 1395), the Delhi sultanate (1398–99), and Anatolia (1400–02) stand out. Timur's victory over the Ottoman sultan Bayezid I in a battle near Ankara (July 20, 1402) gave much-needed respite to Byzantium and eastern Europe, seriously menaced by the Ottomans. Timur's death in 1405 ended an era of almost two centuries characterized by Inner Asian attempts to create huge if not universal empires. Yet, by the end of the 14th century, the dismemberment of the Mongol Empire was almost complete. After the fall of the Il-Khanids (1335) and the Yüan (1368), only the Golden Horde survived of Genghis' heritage. Itself torn by internal dissensions, the Golden Horde disintegrated in the 1430s, its place taken by the successor khanates of Kazan, Astrakhan, and the Crimea.

Dismemberment of the Mongol Empire

The khanate of Kazan, a multinational and multilingual state, had a relatively short span of life. Its rulers—among whom Mahmutek (ruled 1445–66) was particularly successful—did their best to maintain Kazan's independence in the face of Crimean and Muscovite pressures. When, in 1521, the Crimean Giray dynasty obtained that one of its members, Sahib Giray, be enthroned in Kazan, Ivan IV the Terrible, of Russia, thought the time had come to put an end to Tatar (Mongol) rule in central Russia. In 1552 he occupied Kazan, and, only four years later, he established his rule over Astrakhan, securing thereby for himself the waterway to the Caspian Sea. Under the rule of the Girays, the khanate of Crimea survived until 1783, when it was absorbed by Russia. Moscow continued to pay an annual tribute to the Tatars until 1681.

The 15th century was relatively peaceful on the borderland between Iran and Inner Asia. Timur's son Shāh Rokh Mīrza (ruled 1407–47) in Herat and Shāh Rokh's son Ulugh Beg in Samarkand established centres of civilization that continued to flourish until at least the end of Husain Baykara's (ruled 1469–1506) beneficent rule in Herat. The Timurids, turned sedentary, now constituted a protective layer defending Iran from the barbarians still beyond the pale: the Uzbeks united by Muḥammad Shaybānī. Muḥammad was killed in battle in 1510, but his descendants maintained their grip on Transoxiana until the end of the century. The reserves of nomadic power represented by the Uzbeks, however cumbersome, no longer constituted a serious menace to the existence of strong, sedentary states such as those of the Ṣafavids of Persia or the Ottomans, both capable of repulsing attacks coming from the steppe. Ottomans and Ṣafavids, bitterly opposed to one another, clashed in the Battle of Chāldirān (August 23, 1514); the use of firearms gave the former a decisive victory. Thus appeared in the wings of the Inner Asian scene the faceless protagonist of centuries to come: the gun.

THE MODERN PERIOD; THE AGE OF DECADENCE

From the beginnings of recorded history, pastoral nomadism, practiced on a grandiose scale, was the economic basis of the great Inner Asian empires. Once the domestication of the horse was sufficiently advanced to allow for its use in warfare, the superiority of the mounted archer over the foot soldier or the war chariot was never effectively challenged.

The waning of nomadic military power. When headed by capable leaders, well-trained and disciplined mounted troops were almost invincible. The sedentary civilizations could not, by their very nature, put aside for breeding purposes pastures sufficiently large to sustain a cavalry force that could equal that of the pastoral nomads; hence the latter's military superiority remained a constant for about 2,000 years of Eurasian history.

At its highest degree of development, Inner Asian nomad society constituted a very sophisticated and highly specialized social and economic structure, advanced but also highly vulnerable because of its specialization and the lack of diversification of its economy. Geared almost entirely to the production of war material—*i.e.*, the horse—when not engaged in warfare it was unable to provide the people with anything but the barest necessities of life. To ensure their very existence, Inner Asian empires had to wage war and obtain through raids or tributes the commodities they could not produce. When, owing to circumstances such as severe weather decimating the horse herds or inept leadership, raids against other peoples became impossible, the typical Inner Asian nomad state had to disintegrate to allow its population to fend for itself and secure the necessities for a subsistence. Hunting and pastoral nomadism both need vast expanses to support a thinly scattered population that does not naturally lend itself to strong, centralized political control. The skill of an Inner Asian leader consisted precisely in the gathering of such dispersed populations and in providing for them on a level higher than they had been accustomed to. There was but one way to achieve this: successful raids on other, preferably richer, peoples. The military machinery was dependent on numbers, which then precluded self-sufficiency. In case of prolonged military reverses, the nomadic aggregation of warriors had to disband because it was only in dispersion that, without recourse to war, they were economically autonomous.

Social and economic structure of nomad society

In the course of the 15th century, the steppe territory suitable for great horse herds began to shrink. In the east the Yung-lo emperor of the Ming led five major campaigns against the Mongols (1410–24), all successful but none decisive. Yet when, under the leadership of Esen Khan (1439–55), the Mongol Oirats pushed as far as Peking, they found the city defended by cannons, and they withdrew. In the Middle East, as noted above, the Ottoman and Ṣafavid states barred the road to the no longer invincible nomad cavalry, and, along the western borders of Inner Asia, the Russians were soon to start on their decisive and irresistible march across Inner Asia to the borders of China, India, and Iran.

The triumph of agriculturally based cultures. Their most spectacular advance into Inner Asia carried the Russians eastward through the forest belt, where the hunting and fishing populations offered little resistance and where the much-coveted fur of Siberia could be found in abundance. Acting on behalf of the merchant family Stroganov, in 1578 or 1581 the cossack Yermak moved across the Urals and defeated the Shaybānīd prince Kuchum, who alone represented organized political power in Siberia.

The Russian advance from west to east across Siberia, motivated by commercial rather than political considerations, remains unparalleled in history for its rapidity. The native Finno-Ugric—Samoyed or Tunguz hunters accustomed to paying their fur tribute—were little concerned with the nationality of the tax collectors and found dealing with the Russians no more unpleasant than with Turks or Mongols. Russian penetration was marked by the building of small forts, such as Tobolsk (1587) near the former capital of Kuchum, Tara (1594) on the Irtysh, and Narym (1596) on the upper Ob. The Yenisey was reached in 1619, and the town of Yakutsk on the Lena was founded in 1632. Around 1639 the first small group of Russians reached the Pacific in the neighbourhood of present-day Okhotsk. About ten years later, Anadyrsk was founded on the shores of the Bering Sea, and, by the end of the century Kamchatka was annexed. When advanced Russian parties reached the Amur around the middle of the 17th century, they entered the Chinese sphere of interest; although some clashes occurred, restraint on both sides led to the signing of the treaties of Nerchinsk (1689) and Kiakhta (1727), which remained in force until 1858. To this day the border delineated at Kiakhta has not been altered substantially. It is important to note that Russian occupation of Siberia did not entail the extinction of the native population. Although outnumbered by the colonists as early as the beginning of the 18th century, it continued to grow and, at an estimate, quadrupled since the beginning of the Russian conquest. Many of these peoples have kept their language and their distinctive national identity and, within the framework of the Soviet system, are autonomous.

The thorniest question to be dealt with in the early Russo-Chinese negotiations concerned the Mongols—wedged between the two great powers—who, in the course of the 16th and 17th centuries, reasserted their control over most of the steppe belt. In the 15th century the western Mongols, or Oirats, had become quite powerful under Esen Khan; but, under the strong leadership of Dayan Khan (ruled 1488–1507) and his son Altan Khan (1507–82), the eastern Mongols—and more precisely the Khalkha tribe—gained ascendancy. In 1552 Altan took possession of what was left of Karakorum, the old Mongol capital. Altan's reign saw the conversion of a great many Mongols to the tenets of the Yellow Hat sect of Tibetan Buddhism, a religion that, until the 1920s, played a major role in Mongol life. Ligdan Khan's (ruled 1604–34) attempts to unite the various Mongol tribes failed not only because of internal dissensions but also on account of the rising power of the Manchus, to whom he was forced to surrender. The active Central Asian policy of China's Manchu Ch'ing dynasty brought a lasting transformation in the political structure of the region.

Mongol resurgence

More distant from China, the Oirats could pursue a more independent course. In 1616 one of their tribes, the Torguts, moved westward and settled on the lower reaches of the Volga, where they became known by the name of Kalmyk. The land on which they settled was nominally under Russian control, and the Kalmyks, jealously guarding their independence, were ready to serve the Tsar in his undertakings against the Kazakh and other Turkic tribes. Losing ground to the steady advance of Russian settlers, some Kalmyks tried to return to their former territory, by then under Chinese rule. After a gruelling journey begun in 1770 or 1771, about half of those who set out reached China and were settled in the Ili Valley.

During the century and a half that had elapsed since the Torgut emigration to the Volga, their Oirat brethren had had an eventful history. One of their tribes, the Dzungars, under the leadership of Galdan (ruled 1676–97), created a powerful state that remained a serious menace to China until 1757, when the Ch'ien-lung emperor defeated their last ruler, Amursana, and thus put an end to the last independent Mongol state prior to the creation, in 1921, of Outer Mongolia (the Khalkha princes had submitted to the Manchus in 1691).

The treaties of Nerchinsk and Kiakhta established the northern border of the Chinese zone of influence, which included Mongolia. In the wars against the Dzungars, the Chinese established their rule over Eastern Turkistan and Dzungaria. China's western boundary remained undefined, but it ran farther west than it does today and included Lake Balkhash and parts of the Kazakh Steppe.

Wedged between the Russian and Chinese empires, unable to break through the stagnant but solid Ottoman and Ṣafavid barriers, the Turkic nomads of the steppe lying east of the Volga and the Caspian Sea and south of Russian-occupied Siberia found themselves caught in a trap from which there was no escape. If there is cause for surprise, it lies in the lateness rather than in the fact of the ultimate Russian conquest.

Muḥammad Shaybānī's death did not end Uzbek supremacy in the territories to the south and the east of Lake Aral. Three small, independent Uzbek khanates—from west to east: Khiva, Bukhara, and Kokand—shared the land and vied with one another and with outside foes. To the west of them, between Lake Aral and the Caspian Sea, were the nomad Turkmens, notorious robbers who roamed the inhospitable land. In many respects similar to the Turkmens but better organized, the Kazakhs, since the 17th century divided into three "hordes," nomadized between the Volga and the Irtysh. During the 16th and 17th centuries, they fought Oirats and Dzungars but succeeded in holding their own, and in 1771 Ablay, ruler of the "central horde," located west of the Balkash, was confirmed as ruler both by China and Russia. Yet Russian expansion, motivated by the urge to get closer to the Indian Ocean, forced the Kazakhs to yield. Although some Kazakh leaders, such as the sultan Kinesary, put up spirited resistance (1837–47), the line of the Syrdarya was reached by the Russians toward the middle of the 19th century.

The Uzbek khanates

The Uzbek khanates, militarily less significant and farther from Moscow, survived until the 20th century. Khiva, under the rule of Abulghazi Bahadur Khan (ruled 1643–63), a learned and beneficial ruler, knew a prosperity that was not to return. It became a Russian protectorate in 1873, although the local Kongrat dynasty was not removed until 1920. After the time of the Shaybānīds, Bukhara was ruled successively by two dynasties, the Astarkhanids (1599–1747) and the Mangits (1747–1868). The latter had to recognize Russian suzerainty in 1868 but remained in charge of some local affairs until 1920. Of the three khanates, only Kokand was annexed by Russia (1876).

Despite shortcomings of the Russian administration, the Russians had some proconsuls—such as the governors general Speransky (served 1819–22) and Muraviev-Amursky (served 1847–61) in Siberia and Kaufmann (served 1867–82) in Turkistan—who realized that, once conquered, the interests of the natives coincided with those of the Russians. Lord Curzon, the great British opponent of Russian penetration into Central Asia, noted that

> The Russian fraternizes in the true sense of the word. He is guiltless of that air of conscious superiority and gloomy hauteur, which does more to inflame animosity than cruelty may have done to kindle it. . . .

It was Curzon's judgment that "Russian dominion is not merely accepted by, but is acceptable to the bulk of her Asiatic subjects."

The passing of the three Uzbek khanates, the last remnants of a once considerable political and military power, should not lead to an underestimation of the real achievements of Inner Asia. Although their destruction was the direct result of foreign military intervention, the time was ripe for their demise. Insignificant and narrow-minded, they were not worthy of the finest Inner Asian tradition. The 14th-century Chinese scholar Wang Li, in his remarks about the Mongol Empire, characterized it well:

> All the territory within the Four Seas had become the domain of a single family, civilization had spread throughout, and all barriers were removed. . . . Fraternity among the races had reached a new zenith.

BIBLIOGRAPHY. RENE GROUSSET, *L'Empire des steppes: Attila, Gengis-Khan, Tamerlan* (1939; Eng. trans., *The Empire of the Steppes: A History of Central Asia*, 1970), is the best general history but does not reflect our present knowledge. DENIS SINOR, *Inner Asia: History—Civilization—Languages*, 2nd ed. (1971), is a syllabus for use in college teaching. *Geschichte Mittelasiens*, vol. 5 of the *Handbuch der Orientalistik*, ed. by B. SPULER (1966), is a collective work, very rich in data but uneven in quality; GAVIN HAMBLY *et al.*, *Central Asia* (1969), is easier to read. Some of the great issues of Inner Asia history are admirably treated by OWEN LATTIMORE in *Inner Asian Frontiers of China* (1940) and *Studies in Frontier History: Collected Papers (1929–1955)* (1962). A detailed, heavily annotated bibliographical guide is DENIS SINOR, *Introduction à l'étude de l'Eurasie centrale* (1963).

(D.Si.)

Inner Mongolia

Inner Mongolia (Nei-meng-ku in Wade-Giles romanization; Nei-meng-gu in Pin-yin romanization), one of the five autonomous regions (*tzu-chih-ch'ü*) of the People's Republic of China, is an 800-mile- (1,300-kilometre-) long territory in northern and northeastern China, with an area of 163,900 square miles (424,500 square kilometres). It is bordered to the north by the Mongolian People's Republic; to the east by the Chinese provinces of Kirin and Liaoning; to the south by the Chinese provinces of Hopeh, Shansi, and Shensi and the Ningsia Hui Autonomous Region; and to the west by the Chinese province of Kansu. Since 1954 its capital has been Hu-ho-hao-t'e (Huhehot).

Inner (southern) and Outer (northern Mongolia—now

Modern administrative section of Hu-ho-hao-t'e, the capital of Inner Mongolia.
Marc Riboud—Magnum

the Mongolian People's Republic) have been separate entities since the 17th century. Inner Mongolia's traditional nomadism has been replaced to some extent in the 20th century by agriculture and pastoral farming and by the beginnings of industrialization, largely under Chinese influence.

The Inner Mongolian Autonomous Region was founded by the Chinese Communist regime in 1947, more than two years prior to the establishment of its national government at Peking in 1949. It originally consisted of sections taken from western Heilungkiang Province and from former Chahar Province; some of this core territory is in eastern Inner Mongolia as constituted in the early 1970s. In a series of annexations (1949, 1952, 1954, 1955, and 1956), Inner Mongolia was greatly expanded to the northeast and east, west, and south; from 1956 to 1969, it extended in a great 1,600-mile (2,600-kilometre) arc from east of the Greater Khingan Range in central Manchuria, then dipping southwest and west to the Ala Shan Desert in north central China proper, now in Kansu Province. During this period, more than half of China's frontier with the Mongolian People's Republic was the Inner Mongolian border; at the far northeast, a small section of China's international boundary with the U.S.S.R. along the Amur River was in Inner Mongolia. In 1969, after the Great Proletarian Cultural Revolution, the Peking government reversed its previous policy by sharply cutting down the area of the autonomous region, transferring territory to the surrounding Han (Chinese) provinces in all directions. Only the international frontier with the Mongolian People's Republic remained unchanged. The areas transferred constituted about two-thirds of the former area of the region and contained about 6,000,000 of its former population of about 13,000,000. Inner Mongolia traditionally has been an area of mixture and contact between the agrarian Chinese and the pastoral and nomadic Mongolians. The continuous territorial changes that have affected it have therefore signified the contradiction of diverse cultures and conflicting loyalties. Inner Mongolia has thus served as a testing ground for Chinese efforts to integrate ethnic Chinese and Mongols into a single unified political entity.

Region of Sino-Mongolian intermixture

(For associated physical features, see GOBI; HUANG HO; for historical aspects, see CHINA, HISTORY OF; MONGOLS.)

The landscape. Inner Mongolia, which lies roughly between latitudes 38° and 46° N and longitudes 105° and 120° E, is essentially an inland plateau with a flat surface lying at an elevation of about 3,000 feet and fringed by mountains and valleys. Its southern boundary is formed by a series of high ridges with an average height of between 4,500 and 6,000 feet. To the northwest, the land falls away toward the centre of the Gobi Desert (*q.v.*). An arid zone with low summer rainfall, strong evaporation, almost perpetual sunshine, and constant northwesterly winds, this region provides a natural grassland for pastoral animals. The Huang Ho (Yellow River) provides the major irrigation waterway in the southwestern part of the region. In the centre and the north, rainfall and snow are absorbed by the desert.

Climate. The seasons are marked by sharp fluctuations in the climate. Spring arrives in May and lasts for two months. Summer temperatures are relatively uniform. The July average is about 77° F (25° C) at Hu-ho-hao-t'e in the centre of the region; the yearly variation, however, is about 67° F (37° C). The two hottest months are July and August, when almost 60 percent of the annual rainfall occurs. Winter, which arrives after mid-September and lasts until March, is bitterly cold, with strong, icy winds blowing out of Siberia.

Rainfall is meagre. In the Gobi Desert areas the yearly rainfall is below four inches; the plateau area receives only about 12 inches. The development of farming is handicapped by a frost-free period that lasts only from between 110 to 160 days; the consequent short growing season demands that the harvest occur within a 100-day period after planting. Raising two crops a year is impossible, and droughts occur almost annually.

Soils, vegetation, and animal life. Soils are of two types, either a chestnut-brown soil, in which cereals can be raised by dry farming (technique of farming in non-irrigated, dry soil) once every two or three years after sufficient moisture has accumulated in the soil, or a rich, black soil in the southern extremity of the Mongolian plateau. The prairie on both sides of the great bend of the Huang Ho is known as a "granary of the frontier."

Of the total 163,900 square miles (424,500 square kilometres) of territory in the 1970s, much consists of grassland, which provides pasture for sheep, goats, cattle, and the famous Mongolian horses and camels. Sheep and goats (roughly in equal proportions) are by far the most important, the most ubiquitous, and the most numerous of the animals reared on the grasslands. Mongolian horses are hardy and strong and are reputed to be able to travel from 18 to 25 miles a day for days.

The people. The 1953 census put the population at 6,100,000. By the end of 1957, it had reached an estimated 9,200,000, the increase being due in part to the continuous enlargement of the territory from 1954 to 1956 and also to the increasing migration from China proper to the frontier that had been taking place since 1956. In 1967 official data put the total population at over 13,000,000, representing an increase of 41 percent over the 1957 figure. After the 1969 administrative changes, the population was estimated at about 7,000,000.

Mongols and Chinese compose the bulk of the population. Within the 1957 borders, according to estimates in that year, almost 80 percent were Chinese, 12 percent were Mongols, and the remaining 8 percent consisted of minor groups such as Orochons, Solund, Tungus, Koreans, Dahurs, and Manchus. The changes of 1969 have probably increased the proportion of Mongols and reduced that of the Chinese, Orchons, and other non-Mongol peoples, though it is not known with any certainty by how much.

The population is unevenly distributed, with most of it concentrated in the agricultural southern belt, south of the Ta-ch'ing Shan (Yin-shan Shan-mo) escarpment of the Mongolian plateau, near the Huang Ho. All of Inner Mongolia's other densely inhabited areas were transferred to surrounding provinces. Overall population density in the early 1970s was about 43 persons per square mile, but exceeded 500 around Pao-t'ou and 250 for most of the area along the Huang Ho.

Linguistic groups. Since the Chinese still outnumber the Mongols, the most widely used language is Chinese. The Mongolian dialects belong to the eastern branch of Mongolian languages; they are phonetically, morphologically, and syntactically almost the same as the Khalkha–Mongolian group of Outer Mongolia to the north.

A writing system of the Mongolian language, using the Cyrillic alphabet, was introduced in 1955. The system is identical to the one used for Outer Mongolia. By the second half of 1956, the new Mongolian was taught in the first grade of all schools, and, by 1960, all publications were printed in that alphabet except the classics.

Religious groups. In addition to ancestor worship, most of the Chinese people in the region follow a religion formed of elements of Confucianism, Buddhism, and Taoism. The Mongols are mostly followers of Tibetan Lamaism, with almost every Mongolian family having at least one son in the monastery. Lamaism penetrates into every aspect of Mongol life.

Lamaism and shamanism

Despite the prevalence of Lamaism (a form of Buddhism marked by ritual and a dominant, hierarchical monasticism), some aspects of shamanism (a religion characterized by belief in spirits responsive only to shamans, who are priests using magic) exist. The stronghold of shamanism among the Mongols was in the Hu-lun-pei-erh league (formerly part of Inner Mongolia, now in Heilungkiang Province). About 60,000 Chinese, centred on Hu-ho-hao-t'e, were adherents of Islām. At one time, the Roman Catholic Church exercised some influence, especially in Lin-ho county.

The pattern of settlement. The region remains primarily agricultural and pastoral, with few industrial centres. Within the 1958 boundaries, the ratio of urban to rural population was 21 to 79. The three major urban population centres are: (1) Pao-t'ou—a very large steel-and-iron complex and the terminal of two major railways connecting Peking and Kansu Province. Its population increased from 100,000 in the early 1950s to 490,000 in 1958 and by the 1970s was approaching 800,000. (2) Hu-ho-hao-t'e—capital of the autonomous region and a new cultural and political centre (its 1958 population of 320,000 increased to 700,000 by 1970). (3) Chi-ning, a new commercial centre and the terminal of the Chi-ning–Erh-lien railway, which had a population of 100,000 in 1958.

Administration. The administration differs in name and composition from those in other parts of China. The region is divided into leagues, or *meng*, which are similar to subprovincial units in China proper. The local administrative units are banners (*ch'i*) in the Mongolian areas and counties (*hsien*) in the predominantly Chinese area. In the Mongol areas the banners are subdivided into administrative villages (*gatsaa*) or *aimak* (units of two or three villages); in the nomadic region, the banners are subdivided into *sumun*, which, in turn, are divided into *bag* (groups of nomad farmers), *khoto* (towns), and *ail* (settlements of a few families of nomads).

In accordance with the policy of fostering unity between the nationalities, an effort has been made to set up "democratic coalition governments" in localities where both Mongols and Chinese are represented in substantial numbers.

Conditions of pastoral life

Social conditions. *Health.* Most of the Mongols live in tents, called yurts, that are inadequately ventilated. This, added to a critical shortage of drinking water and the Mongols' reluctance to wash their clothes and bodies, contributes to the spread of epidemic diseases. Syphilis and bubonic plague caused a continuous decline in the Mongolian population in the course of the past century. In 1947 over 60 percent of the pastoral population suffered from syphilis. Though the infant-mortality rate in 1949 was as high as 31 percent, public health has since been greatly improved, and the spread of venereal diseases and plague has been brought under effective control. Energetic promotion of new midwifery methods significantly reduced the rate of infant mortality, and the population decline has come to a halt.

Revolutionary changes in agriculture in the vast pastoral land have impinged on every aspect of Mongolian life. The rapid advance of irrigation and the increasing cultivation of forage crops is steadily reducing nomadism, so that the herdsman is deserting his yurt for a house. Even if he is still nomadic, the old yurt is giving place to a new, plastic type, which has greater resistance to insects and moisture, is lighter and more durable, and has better insulation and ventilation. The diet of the herdsman, which used to consist of mutton, milk, tea, and simple food, is now more varied.

Education. Education has been introduced, mainly through mobile schools and a "half-study, half-work" scheme in which study time is varied according to the requirements of agriculture. According to official government statistics, between 1946 and 1957 the number of elementary schools in the region went up from about 1,600 to more than 9,000, with enrollment increasing from about 140,000 to 860,000; the number of secondary schools rose from about 20 to almost 90 with enrollment up from 4,000 to 60,000. A number of vocational schools and colleges are also in operation.

Welfare. Since the Mongolian family was traditionally small, it was easy for the head of the family to look after the welfare of each of its members, young and old. There were few cases in which a family needed outside help. In the past, the banner government usually levied a tax of about 30 percent of the people's grain in the agricultural area and a tax on cattle from well-to-do pastoral people. A part of the collection served as a relief fund to the poor in time of famine and during the severe winter season. The Communist government, in general, has extended loans to the herdsmen and farmers to help tide them over difficulties, rather than issuing direct relief to the victims.

The economy. *Livestock.* Inner Mongolia has been traditionally renowned for its livestock. In 1952, it produced more than 8 percent of China's cattle, 27 percent of its camels, and 15 percent of the sheep and goats. Despite its prominence, the condition of the livestock indus-

Development of the livestock industry

try was far from satisfactory. Various obstacles (principally depredations by wild animals, diseases, and inadequate weather forecasts) stood in the way of efforts to increase the number of livestock. Some years ago 58,000 head of cattle were slaughtered by wolves. More recently, however, many measures, including large-scale wolf-hunting campaigns and the immunization of cattle, have been taken to improve conditions. Weather stations have also been established to forewarn herders. The introduction of crossbreeding with the Soviet Tsgaisky pedigree sheep by artificial insemination has also brought improvements. According to official data, the total number of livestock rose from about 8,000,000 head in 1947 to 40,000,000 in 1965; the territorial transfers of 1969 reduced these numbers substantially with the transfer of dairying areas in the north to Heilungkiang.

Crops. The harsh climate severely restricts intensive agriculture. In some areas, particularly around the great bend of the Huang Ho, oats, spring wheat, kaoliang, millet, and other grains are cultivated. In irrigated areas, sugar beets and oilseeds are grown.

Minerals. Despite the relative backwardness of its industry, the territory possesses great mineral wealth. Rich iron-ore deposits have been discovered in Pai-yün-o-po near Pao-t'ou. Most coal mining is in Shih-kuai-kou and Kuyang in the vicinity of Pao-t'ou.

Industrial development. From 1953 to 1965 industrial development was centred around Pao-t'ou. During this period the largest project was enlarging Pao-t'ou into one of the major iron-and-steel centres of China. The Pao-t'ou iron-and-steel mills, constructed with Soviet aid and completed in 1961, have the capacity to produce 1,500,000 tons of steel ingots and 1,100,000 tons of finished steel per year. Several dozen modern plants, including those for refractory material (*i.e.*, heat-resistant, nonmetallic, ceramic material), cement, machine building and repairing, textiles, sugar refining, and chemical fertilizer, and two electrical power plants were built in the area, establishing it as one of the most significant industrial bases north of the Huang Ho.

The dairy and chemical industries both have development potential. Since 1950, more than 20 milk-products plants have been built in the grasslands.

The inland drainage of the Mongolian plateau contained a number of salt lakes; owing to evaporation, most have dried up, leaving behind deposits of salt and natural alkali (soda). Initial estimates put the deposits at 200,000,000 tons. These resources are important for the chemical industry in general and the chemical-fertilizer industry in particular.

Transportation and communications. Most of the rail system is in the south, linking the region to the remainder of the national territory. The Feng-t'ai and Pao-t'ou railway starts from Peking and traverses the southern corner.

The rail network

With the advent of industrial development, two new main lines and several forest railways were constructed. The Chi-ning and Ulan Bator International Railway (completed in 1955) connects China with Outer Mongolia and with the Soviet Union. It runs from Chi-ning, an important city in the south of the region, situated along the Peking–Pao-t'ou line, to Erh-lien on the northern border, extending more than 180 miles. This route shortens the rail distance between Peking and Moscow, which otherwise runs via Man-chou-li, by 700 miles. The most important new line, however, is that from Pao-t'ou to Lan-chou in Kansu Province, which runs for more than 600 miles. This completes the rail link between northern and northwestern China. In 1965, before administrative changes, the total rail mileage was about 1,700 miles. Perhaps a third of this was in northern areas transferred to Heilungkiang in 1969.

In addition to the rail network, thousands of miles of highway link most areas. Inland-waterway navigation is somewhat limited. Only the upper course of the Huang Ho, from Lan-chou, in Kansu, to Ho-k'ou-chen, in Inner Mongolia, is navigable. Local airline services include routes from Hu-ho-hao-t'e to A-pa-ha-na-erh-ch'i and Tung-sheng. Telephone and telegraph services are available in most of the banners and counties.

Cultural life. Cultural life bears the deep imprint of Tibetan Lamaist influence. In liturgical music, monastery and temple architecture, scriptural learning and commentary, and religious arts, the Mongols accepted the forms of Tibet. Though the specific content and emphasis of Mongol folk legends vary somewhat with the location and with tribal or clan history concerning their origins, most clans have legends of their founders as either a mythical animal or a hero; others preserve legends about historical figures once prominent in the life of their clan. The subjects and themes of Mongol folktales and other forms of vernacular literature tend to be standard among all the tribes. A very large number concern lamas and religious life. Legends and songs as well as riddles and jokes occupy the leisure time of the night camp and its fireside circle, which form a major aspect of Mongolian life.

Mongolian music is not an independent art but serves solely as accompaniment to songs, dances, and rites. Singing has several functions for the Mongols. It is a form of entertainment, communication, historical recollection, group fellowship, and exuberant expression, and it demonstrates the close affiliation of individual Mongols with their culture and traditions. Mongol singing is generally a gregarious activity, mostly taking place around campfires, after the evening meal.

The Mongols observe seasonal celebrations: the New Year, the celebration of the White Month (signifying rebirth) in spring, the Midsummer Festival on the 12th day of the sixth month, the Autumn Festival (Festival of Fire) on the first day of the eighth month of the Chinese lunar calendar, and the Great Sacrificial Feast to the Fire God on the 23rd day in the lunar 12th month.

Besides the temple festivals, there is the Obo (shrine) Festival, which is held in the fifth month of every year. Toward the end of the ceremonies the festival takes a joyful course without restraint. The best wrestlers chosen from the tribes are matched together; archers gather to shoot at targets; and a race is arranged in which the young men of the tribes, riding their best horses, compete. This is the time for a dashing display of the talent and vigour of the Mongol nomads, and it is the most exciting moment of the year in the annual cycle of the pasturelands.

BIBLIOGRAPHY. UNIVERSITY OF WASHINGTON, FAR EASTERN AND RUSSIAN INSTITUTE, *A Regional Handbook on the Inner Mongolia Autonomous Region* (1956); and *Inner Mongolia Today*, issued by the Peking Nationalities Publishing House (1957), are two basic references that provide general information on Inner Mongolia up to the mid-1950s; SCHUYLER CAMMANN, *The Land of the Camel: Tents and Temples of Inner Mongolia* (1951); OWEN LATTIMORE, *Mongol Journeys* (1941), and *Nomads and Commissars: Mongolia Revisited* (1962); and ROBERT JAMES MILLER, *Monasteries and Culture Change in Inner Mongolia* (1959), deal with the culture, history, religion, and folklore of the Mongols. T.R. TREGEAR, *An Economic Geography of China* (1970), deals with the physical conditions, natural resources, population distribution, and economic development. *The Yearbook on Chinese Communism*, compiled annually by the INSTITUTE FOR THE STUDY OF CHINESE COMMUNISM IN TAIPEI; and *Ten Great Years* (1960), compiled by the STATE STATISTICAL BUREAU IN PEKING provide statistical data. PAUL HYER and WILLIAM HEATON'S article "The Cultural Revolution in Inner Mongolia," *China Quarterly*, 36:114–128 (1968), provides insight into the conditions of the 1960s.

(C.-y.C.)

Innocent III, Pope

Under Innocent III, one of the most gifted and influential popes, the medieval papacy reached the height of its prestige and power.

PREPONTIFICAL LIFE

Lothair of Segni, the future Pope Innocent III, was born in 1160 or 1161 in Gavignano, a castle belonging to his father, Trasimund of Segni, in the Roman Campagna. Through his mother, Claricia Scotti, he was related to many noble Roman families. As a young man, Lothair studied theology in Paris and canon law in Bologna under the great canonist Huguccio of Pisa, whose relatively moderate doctrines on the relationship between the spiritual and temporal authorities provided a long-lasting influence on the future pope. In 1190 Pope Clement III, possibly a relative of Lothair, raised the young subdeacon to the status of cardinal deacon of St. Sergius and St. Bacchus. Lothair played no prominent part in the government of the church during the pontificate of Celestine III and had time to write several theological works; two of them, "On the Miserable Condition of Man" and "On the Mysteries of the Mass," are significant expressions of the ascetic-liturgical inspiration by which this pope, who was so active politically, was animated.

By courtesy of the Vatican Museums

Innocent III, detail of a fresco, 13th century. In the Lower Church of Sacro Speco, Subiaco, Italy.

PONTIFICATE

On the very day of Celestine III's death, Jan. 8, 1198, Lothair was unanimously elected pope after only two ballots; he was ordained priest on February 21 and on the next day was consecrated as bishop of Rome. He reigned as pope until 1216.

The fourth Lateran Council

During Innocent's reign in 1215, there occurred the fourth Lateran Council, which constituted the culmination not only of his pontificate but also of the whole medieval papacy with regard to brilliant attendance and representation of the whole church and, above all, as regards the importance of its decrees. The council promulgated, for instance, the dogma of transubstantiation (the belief that the substance of the bread and wine of the Lord's Supper is changed into the body and blood of Christ), bound every Catholic to confession at least once a year and communion at Easter time, forbade clerical participation in ordeals such as trial by combat and other "judgments of God," and enacted important reforms of clergy and laity without which the medieval church would hardly have withstood internal and external dangers for another 300 years.

Spiritual and temporal powers. Innocent III's very exalted conception of the role of the papacy in the Christian world and his success in making his conception a reality would have been unthinkable without the preparations of the age of Gregory VII, which resulted in an increase of the role of the church and the prestige of the papacy. Innocent's sermons on the day and on the anniversaries of his coronation, as well as the vast corpus of his official letters, blended the legal and philosophical-theological thought of the scholastic age that was characterized by the influence of Aristotelian philosophy with new expressions of mystical fervour and created a language and ideology of unprecedented splendour and majesty for the glorification of the papal office. At the same time, the political constellations within Christendom during his pontificate allowed the Pope to exercise his spiritual authority not only in the inner precincts of the church but also in all vital political questions of the day. Yet he explicitly disclaimed the right and the intention to intervene in temporal affairs as such, with the exception of the Papal States and of those kingdoms that had voluntarily recognized the feudal suzerainty of the papacy. As far as Germany was concerned, Innocent felt that he had very special rights, since the king of Germany was also the emperor of the Holy Roman Empire and, as such, was meant to be the protector of the Roman and universal church. Because the special position of the German king-emperor ipso facto affected the pope's spiritual realm, Innocent believed he had the right to approve or reject dubious elections to the German throne and acted accordingly in the contest over the succession to Henry VI. Otherwise, he was careful to limit his intervention in temporal matters (again, outside the Papal States and the vassal kingdoms) to cases in which political actions had either infringed upon spiritual rights or raised serious moral questions. Nevertheless, the combined authority claimed by the Pope on these various grounds was very great indeed; and he himself often spoke of the pope's sovereign power, though he considered this always as rooted in a *spiritual* power, the power given to Peter by Christ of binding and loosing souls. Papal plenitude of power was for him essentially spiritual sovereignty, however much it could branch out into the temporal sphere for spiritual reasons. It is this claim, not a claim to temporal world rulership, that stands behind some of Innocent's most striking assertions of papal supremacy. They are properly understood, in the whole context of his reign, only as assertions of the ultimate competency of the supreme spiritual authority in any matter whatsoever by which the spiritual concerns of the church (that is to say, faith and morals) are affected.

Problems faced by Innocent. At the beginning of his reign, Innocent III was confronted with three problems: the insecurity of papal sovereignty in the Papal States; the election of two German kings; and the French-English or, to be more exact, the Capetian-Angevin war. At the time of his accession, Rome was practically independent of papal government, but Innocent soon succeeded in reasserting papal rights there. Within a few years, though not without a struggle, he had pacified the rival aristocratic factions and won over most of the people. Moreover, he had been very successful in his policy of recuperation of the Papal States with regard not only to the re-establishment of effective papal government but also with regard to the acquisition of the duchy of Spoleto and the march of Ancona, which together stretched from Rome to the Adriatic Sea and which he claimed on the strength of the heretofore never fulfilled promises of Pepin and Charlemagne. For Innocent, as for the popes of the 12th century, the existence of strong Papal States in the centre of Italy was a vital prerequisite for the independence of the papacy from secular power, and doubly so after the experiences of the last decade, when the union of the Holy Roman Empire with the Sicilian kingdom under Henry VI had nearly paralyzed the papacy's freedom of action.

Sovereignty over the Papal States

The problem of Italy also governed Innocent's policy in the German crisis, when the princes of the Holy Roman Empire, ignoring the claims of Henry VI's son Frederick II, had split over the election of a new German king. One party elected the brother of the deceased emperor, Philip of Hohenstaufen, duke of Swabia; the other elected the duke of Brunswick (son of the great Guelph Henry the Lion and nephew of the English kings Richard the Lion Heart and John), who was to be known as Otto IV. Innocent, fearing the Hohenstaufen tradition, favoured Otto, and the initial actions of Philip and his followers were not calculated to allay his fears; Frederick he hoped to restrict to his Sicilian inheritance and thus to avoid a reunion of the empire with Sicily. Philip, however, was so successful against Otto that Innocent after a few years found it necessary to resume negotiations with him, which might have led to his recognition and to the resig-

The German crisis

nation of Otto or even to the Pope's rejection of the latter, since he already had misgivings about him. Yet Philip unexpectedly disappeared from the scene: he was murdered in 1208 by Otto of Wittelsbach, who had a private grievance against him. Otto IV was then crowned emperor by Innocent III.

In a surprisingly short time, Otto managed to alienate the Pope by his blatant pursuit of plans and actions hostile to papal sovereignty in the Papal States and aiming at the reunion of the empire and Sicily. Innocent excommunicated him after he had embarked, in a flagrant breach of his promises, on the conquest of the Sicilian kingdom and turned to the only other possible candidate for the German and imperial crowns, the young Frederick of Sicily. The Pope had in fact no other choice; he also could hope that he would be able to prevail upon Frederick to keep Germany and Sicily permanently separate. A promise to that effect was no doubt a condition of his support in the German election of 1212 and in 1216. Frederick II, as king of Germany, solemnly promised to transfer full rule over Sicily to his infant son Henry. Meanwhile, Frederick, with the help of King Philip II Augustus of France, had triumped over Otto IV and over Otto's uncle and ally, King John of England, at the Battle of Bouvines (1214). Innocent, who previously had tried to end the war between France and England and had temporarily succeeded in doing so, had at this crucial moment been unable to prevent the fusion of the German throne contest with the French-English (Capetian-Angevin) dynastic conflict.

French-English conflicts

His relationship to both western kings was also complex in other respects. Philip Augustus, who had at all times opposed Otto IV, the relative of his Angevin enemies, had only after a resistance of 12 years obeyed the Pope's demand for reinstatement of his rightful queen, whom he had repudiated. John of England had been excommunicated by Innocent because of his refusal to recognize as archbishop of Canterbury Cardinal Stephen Langton, who had been elected by the monks of the cathedral in accordance with the Pope's wishes. Not until the last moment had John submitted to the Pope and, in order to forestall French invasion of England, declared England a fief of the Holy See (1213). While Innocent did in fact protect John from this latest French design, he could neither deprive his own protégé, Frederick II, of Philip Augustus' military help nor could he expect John to abandon his ally and nephew, Otto. However, when John was forced to sign Magna Carta and then complained to the Pope as to his feudal overlord, Innocent annulled the charter as having been extorted without his consent. Innocent did not and could not see in Magna Carta what later ages were to see in it, an assertion of law against tyranny; he considered it, not altogether without justification, as an attempt at feudal insurrection against royal authority, which he could not ignore.

Fourth and Albigensian Crusades

Of the two Crusades that took place during the pontificate of Innocent III, one—the Fourth Crusade of 1202–04—was diverted to Constantinople, chiefly to suit Venetian interests and against the will of the Pope. Innocent nevertheless accepted the *fait accompli* because he mistakenly believed that the establishment of the Latin Empire and patriarchate of Constantinople would bring about a lasting reunion between the Eastern and Western churches. The other crusade was launched, with Innocent's approval, against the Albigensian heretics, who denied the sacraments and the authority of the ecclesiastical hierarchy. The Pope's decision opened an unhappy chapter in the history of the church by placing under supreme ecclesiastical leadership the repression of heresy by force. It is true that the Albigensian Crusade achieved what two generations of missionaries had been unable to do: it led to the extirpation of heresy in southern France. But the price was much bloodshed, devastation, and injustice, which the Pope, who never demanded the death sentence against heretics, did his best to reduce to smaller proportions, though without much success.

Accomplishments within the church. Innocent recognized that the successes of the Albigensian heretics had been due in part to the fact that not a few of them tried to live in evangelic and apostolic poverty. Innocent, who in his personal life was frugal, encouraged this spirit wherever he found it among the Catholic clergy and laity. In granting lay and clerical communities—such as those of the northern Italian Humiliati (an order devoted to a life of mortification and care of the poor), the Catholic Poor of Durandus of Huesca, the Dominicans, and, above all, the first community of St. Francis of Assisi—permission to preach and teach, Innocent went far beyond what the popes of the 12th century had thought possible and inaugurated the Mendicant orders.

Achievements in canon law and church government

In awareness of the importance of Innocent's legislation in all fields of the church's life, the canonists began to collect and publish his decretals during his pontificate; one of these collections, the so-called *Compilatio Tertia* by Petrus Collivaccinus, received the Pope's official approval. A great number of Innocent III's decretals were later to enter the second part of the *Corpus Juris Canonici* (Body of Canon Law), and Gregory IX's *Liber Decretalium*, or *Liber Extra*. The far-reaching centralization of church government is reflected by Innocent's legislation in general and also by his unlimited claim to fill all vacancies of ecclesiastical offices. The great majority of these provisions, however, were used by Innocent III to support the numerous poor clerics who had been ordained by the bishops but who were either not adequately or not at all supported by them, the rather unhappy stratum of *clerici vagantes* (wandering clerics) well known from the history of literature. Innocent was not successful in his attempt to induce the prelates assembled at the fourth Lateran Council to secure once and for all the support of the Roman Curia by the reservation of a part of their revenues; the plan, if successful, might have prevented the fiscal policies of his successors that were to do so much harm to the papacy's reputation.

In the midst of vast preparations for a new Crusade that he hoped would liberate the Holy Land, Innocent III died suddenly, in Perugia, on July 16, 1216, from one of his frequent attacks of fever, almost certainly malaria. It is hardly possible to refrain from surmising that, had he lived longer, the Fifth Crusade would have had a less unfortunate end or that the all-out struggle between Frederick II and the papacy might have been prevented. No other pope of the 13th century possessed the exceptional blend of strength and profound humaneness that the contemporary sources show Innocent III to have had.

BIBLIOGRAPHY. Innocent's correspondence may be found in J.P. MIGNE, *Patrologia Latina*, vol. 214–217, and his theological works in vol. 217 (1890–91). For Innocent's role in the German throne contest, see *Regestum Innocentii III Papae super Negotio Romani Imperii*, ed. by F. KEMPF in *Miscellanea Historiae Pontificiae*, vol. 12 (1947). Kempf also is the author of one of the three most important recent works on Innocent: *Papsttum und Kaisertum bei Innocenz III* in *Miscell. Hist. Pont.*, vol. 19 (1954); the other two studies are M. MACCARRONE, *Chiesa e Stato nella dottrina di Papa Innocenzo III*, in *Lateranum*, vol. 6 (1940); and HELENE TILLMAN, *Papst Innocenz III* (1954). For Innocent's relations with eastern Christendom, see *Acta Innocentii PP. III . . .*, ed. by P.T. HALUSCYNSKY, in *Pont. Comm. ad Redig. Cod Iur. Can. Orient., Fontes*, ser. 3, vol. 2 (1944); and S. RUNCIMAN, *A History of the Crusades*, vol. 3 (1954), for the Fourth Crusade. For Innocent's relations with England, see C.R. CHENEY and W.H. SEMPLE (eds.), *Selected Letters of Pope Innocent III Concerning England* (1953); and F.M. POWICKE, *Stephen Langton* (1928). For the fourth Lateran Council, see J.D. MANSI, *Sacrorum Conciliorum Nova et Amplissima Collectio*, vol. 22 (1903); and K.J. VON HEFELE and H. LECLERCQ, *Histoire des conciles d'après les documents originaux*, vol. 5 (1913). General works include: A. LUCHAIRE, *Innocent III*, 6 vol. (1906–08); L.E. BINNS, *Innocent III* (1931); J. CLAYTON, *Pope Innocent III and His Times* (1941); and E.F. JACOB in the *Cambridge Medieval History*, vol. 6 (1929).

(G.B.L.)

Innocent IV, Pope

Innocent IV (Sinibaldo Fieschi) was pope from 1243 to 1254, at the climax of the long struggle between the papacy and the Holy Roman Empire. He formulated extreme claims concerning the universal superiority of the pope and deposed his primary opponent, the emperor Frederick II. This led, on the one hand, to the decline of the imperial institution for the rest of the century and, on the other, to the rapid estrangement of the papacy from the political reality, a process that culminated with Pope Boniface VIII. Innocent's understanding of his universal responsibility drove him, more than any other man of his time, to open the church to the problem of evangelizing the East, especially the Mongols and the Muslims, and to seek the unification of the Christian churches.

Early life and early career

He was born Sinibaldo Fieschi in Genoa at the end of the 12th century. His father, Hugo, called Fliscus, was the count of Lavagna and member of a rising family in both the economic and ecclesiastical realms. Sinibaldo, the sixth of ten children, studied at Parma under the direction of one of three uncles who were bishops and then at Bologna in the school of the most illustrious canonists of the age, where he himself became a master of Canon Law. He was a canon of the cathedral of Genoa and later of Parma. He was consecrated bishop of Albenga, Italy, in 1225; in 1227 he was made vice chancellor of the Roman Church and cardinal priest of St. Lawrence in Lucina by Pope Gregory IX. He continued the work and, in great part, the spirit of Gregory IX, first as rector to the March of Ancona (1235–40), where he took up the side of the Guelphs at Camerino and at Ravenna, and later during his own reign as pope.

His study and experience in the field of law (testimony of his expertise exists in his celebrated commentary on canon law, *Apparatus in quinque libros Decretalium*) prepared him to enter as one of the key figures into the conflict between the church and the empire. The emperor Frederick II sought to restructure the imperial authority, with a strong state in Italy as the basis; he was convinced that he had the right to exercise autocratically his imperial power, the *imperialis potestas.* He thus came into head-on collision with the church's claim to universal power, the *universalis potestas,* theoretically elaborated by the canonists of that time, including Sinibaldo Fieschi. According to their theory, the pope possessed universal dominion, which in the abstract juridical order extended to all kingdoms, although in the practical order he had to leave the temporal rule to the emperor and to the kings. On the basis of these two antithetical conceptions, the interests of different parties came into conflict time after time. The last phase of his conflict, which began under Gregory IX, reached its zenith under Innocent IV.

Election as pope

Frederick II was encouraged by the election of Cardinal Fieschi on June 25, 1243, after the see of Rome had been vacant for 18 months following the brief reign of Celestine IV. He immediately entered into negotiations with the new Pope, who took the name Innocent IV, to have the excommunication imposed on him by Gregory IX lifted. The Pope, however, did not trust Frederick, despite an agreement reached on March 31, 1244. He felt unsafe in Rome and secretly fled the city, interrupting the negotiations with the Emperor. Genoese galleys prepared by his relatives were waiting for him at the port of Civitavecchia, to take him to Genoa and then to Lyons (Lyon). Although Lyons was nominally subject to the empire, Innocent IV was under the protection of Louis IX of France.

Late in 1244 the Pope called a general council to meet in Lyons the following summer. Gregory IX had earlier announced such a council, but Frederick II had impeded it by holding as prisoners more than 100 bishops who had fallen into the hands of the Pisans in the naval battle of Meloria. Three themes were to be treated in the council: the question of the Emperor, the liberation of the Holy Sepulchre, and the defense of Christianity against the advance of the Mongols. Thaddeus of Suessa tried in vain to defend the Emperor before the council. Frederick II was solemnly condemned, his subjects were freed from their bond of loyalty to him, and he was deposed on the basis of the triple charge of perjury, sacrilege, and suspicion of heresy. The Pope himself admonished the German princes to elect a new emperor. They named Henry Raspe, landgrave of Thuringia, and, at his death in 1247, William of Holland. The condemnation of Frederick II did not obtain the desired political effects in Germany, but it did show the effectiveness of the network of ties that the papal family had succeeded in tightening in northern Italy, which contributed to the Emperor's defeat at Parma (1247).

Frederick II died on December 13, 1250. The Pope left Lyons and triumphantly returned to Rome in 1253. Meanwhile, he had to continue the struggle against Frederick II's son Conrad IV and also to find a king to whom he could entrust the Kingdom of Sicily as a fief. The Pope offered Sicily first to Richard of Cornwall, then to Charles of Anjou, both of whom refused, and later to Henry III of England, who accepted for his son Edmund. After the death of Conrad IV in May 1254, the papal army was defeated by Manfred, Frederick II's illegitimate son, who had become regent for Conradin, the infant son of Conrad IV. The Pope died soon after at Naples, on December 7, 1254.

Assessment of Innocent IV's pontificate

The struggle against Frederick II brings to light a striking characteristic of Innocent's pontificate and of the period as a whole. A close relationship existed between the political activity and the personal and family fortunes of the Pope and the cardinals. Only relatives and those who received benefices could be counted upon to maintain their political loyalty beyond ideological motivations. That explains the constant presence of Innocent's family in his ecclesiastical, political, and military affairs and his frequent recourse to the distribution of ecclesiastical benefices in their behalf. He took steps to return the expenses incurred by his nephews in their combat with Frederick II, distributed the bishoprics of England and the East to cousins, and supported the creation of a strong family estate at the foot of the Ligurian Apennines, provoking opposition from bishops and lay lords in that area. In this policy of giving church offices to his relatives, Innocent went far beyond what his predecessors had done, and established a pattern of nepotism that came to be recognized as a normal papal prerogative as time went on. In addition, it was his habit to systematically intervene in the affairs of local churches, disposing of ecclesiastical posts in order to settle disputes, to help university students, to reward devout persons, or to help needy clergy. This long distance intervention often made situations worse, because the Pope ended up promising people more benefices than were available. Innocent's successor, Alexander IV, condemned the practice.

Innocent IV's attention to all parts of Christendom and his interventions carried him beyond his conflict with the Emperor to a vivid awareness of other problems that agitated Europe even to its borders. Echoing the appeals of the Christians in Palestine, he induced Louis IX to undertake a crusade, which ended dramatically with the King's imprisonment (1250); he sent a mission (1245–47) to the Grand Khan of the Mongols, led by Giovanni Carpini, in the hope of arresting the advance of the Mongols on eastern Europe; he established contacts with the Eastern Church to prepare for ecumenical union with Russia and the Ukraine. None of these missions attained its desired success, yet he deserves credit for ferreting out the problems in the church and establishing the bases for resolving future conflicts.

The judgment of historians about Innocent IV has been conditioned by their opinion about his struggle against Frederick II. Those who see in Frederick the forerunner of the modern lay state (Jacob Burckhardt and Hermann Kantorowicz) condemn the universalistic claims of the Pope. In general, it is still difficult for German historiographers to form a dispassionate judgment. On the part of ecclesiastics, the tendency is to emphasize Innocent IV's missionary projects and his indisputable qualities as a canonist—his acuteness, openness, and solicitude for human dignity.

BIBLIOGRAPHY. There is no complete, up-to-date biography. The most recent compilation (in Italian) utilizing a variety of sources is that by F. PODESTA, *Innocenzo IV* (1928). Among the general histories that have best elaborated the period and the work of Innocent IV is A. FLICHE and V. MAR-

TIN (eds.), *Histoire de l'église depuis les origines jusqu'à nos jours*, vol. 10 (1950). On Innocent's political relations with the Emperor, see J.M. POWELL, "Frederick II and the Church: A Revisionist View," *Catholic Historical Review*, 48:487–497 (1963), which presents various opinions on the antagonism between the Emperor and the Pope. An important English-language source dealing with the period of Innocent IV is J.A. WATT, *The Theory of Papal Monarchy in the Thirteenth Century: The Contribution of the Canonists* (1966).

(F.Gu.)

Insecta

Insects constitute the class Insecta (or Hexapoda), the largest class of the largest animal phylum, Arthropoda (*q.v.*). Like all arthropods, the insects have segmented bodies, jointed legs, and, when present, external skeletons (exoskeletons). Insects are distinguished from other arthropods by their body, which is divided into three major regions: (1) the head, which bears the mouthparts, eyes, and a pair of antennae; (2) the thorax, which usually has three pairs of legs (hence "Hexapoda," the name that was formerly given to this class) and usually one or two pairs of wings; and (3) the many-segmented abdomen, which contains the digestive, excretory, and reproductive organs.

In a popular sense, "insect" usually means the familiar pests or disease carriers, from bedbugs, houseflies, and clothes moths to Japanese beetles and aphids; the annoyers, such as mosquitoes, fleas, horseflies, and hornets; and the conspicuous butterflies and moths. Many insects, however, are beneficial from man's viewpoint; they pollinate plants, produce useful substances, control pest insects, act as scavengers, and serve as food for other animals (see below *Importance*). Furthermore, insects are valuable objects of study in elucidating many aspects of biology. Much of our knowledge of genetics has been gained from fruit fly experiments, and of population biology from flour beetle studies. Insects are often used in investigations of hormonal action, nerve and sense organ function, and many other physiological processes as well.

This article is divided into the following sections:

I. General features
  Appearance and habits
  Distribution and abundance
II. Importance
  Role in nature
  Commercial significance
  Agricultural significance
  Medical significance
  Control of insect damage
III. Natural history
  Life cycle
  Sensory perception and reception
  Behaviour
  Ecology
IV. Form and function
  External features
  Internal features
V. Evolution and paleontology
  Origin of insects
  Insect fossil record
  Insect phylogeny
  Evolution
VI. Classification
  Distinguishing taxonomic features
  Annotated classification
  Critical appraisal

I. General features

In numbers of species and individuals and in adaptability and wide distribution, insects are perhaps the most eminently successful of all animals. They dominate the present-day land fauna; almost 1,000,000 species have been described, representing about five-sixths of known animal life—the actual number of living species could range from 2,000,000 to 5,000,000, entomologists estimate. The orders that contain the greatest numbers of species are Coleoptera (beetles), Lepidoptera (butterflies and moths), Hymenoptera (ants, bees, wasps), and Diptera (true flies).

APPEARANCE AND HABITS

The majority of insects are small, usually less than six millimetres long. The range in size, however, is wide. Some are almost microscopic, as certain of the feather-winged beetles and parasitic wasps; while some tropical forms attain considerable size, up to 16 centimetres in the hercules beetles, African goliath beetles, certain Australian stick insects, and some Asian and South American moths.

Diversity

In many species the difference in body structure between the sexes is pronounced, and knowledge of one sex may give few clues to the appearance of the other sex. In some, as the twisted-wing insects (Strepsiptera), the female is a mere inactive bag of eggs, and the winged male is one of the most active insects known. Modes of reproduction are diverse, and reproductive capacity is generally high. Some insects, as the mayflies, feed only in the immature or larval stage and go without food as adults. Among the social insects the queen ants and queen termites live for many years (15 to 50); some adult mayflies live less than two hours.

Some insects advertise their presence to the other sex by flashing lights, and many imitate other insects in colour and form and thus avoid or minimize attack by predators that feed by day and find their prey visually, as do birds, lizards, and other insects.

Behaviour is diverse, from the almost inert parasitic forms whose larvae lie in the nutrient blood streams of their hosts and feed by absorption, to dragonflies that pursue victims in the air, tiger beetles that outrun prey on land, and dytiscid beetles that outswim prey in water.

In some cases the adult insects make elaborate preparations for the young; in others the mother defends or feeds her young; and in still others there are complex insect societies, some of which (tropical termites and ants) may reach populations of millions of inhabitants.

DISTRIBUTION AND ABUNDANCE

No scientist familiar with insects has attempted to estimate individual numbers beyond areas of a few acres or a few square miles in extent. Figures soon become so large as to be incomprehensible. The large populations and great variety of insects are related to their small size, high rates of reproduction, and abundance of suitable food supplies. Insects abound in the tropics, both in numbers of different kinds and in numbers of individuals.

If the insects (including the young and adults of all forms from microscopic young springtails [Collembola] to all large adults) are counted on a square yard of rich moist surface soil, 500 are found easily and 2,000 are not unusual in soil samples in the north temperate zone. This amounts to roughly 4,000,000 insects on one moist acre. In such an area only an occasional butterfly, bumblebee, or large beetle—supergiants among insects—probably would be noticed. Only a few thousand species, those that attack man's crops, herds, and products, and those that carry disease, interfere with man seriously enough to require control measures. When they do appear as enemies of man, however, they can build up populations with speed.

Adaptability

Insects are adapted to every land and freshwater habitat where food is available, from deserts to jungles, from glacial fields and cold mountain streams to stagnant, lowland ponds and hot springs. Many live in brackish water up to 1⁄10 the density of sea water, a few live in seawater, and some fly larvae can live in pools of crude petroleum where they eat other insects that fall in.

II. Importance

ROLE IN NATURE

Insects play many important roles in the economy of nature. They aid bacteria, fungi, and other organisms in the decomposition of organic matter and in soil formation. The decay of carrion, for example, brought about mainly by bacteria, is accelerated by the maggots of flesh flies and blowflies. The activities of these larvae, which distribute and consume bacteria, are followed by those of moths and beetles, which break down hair and feathers.

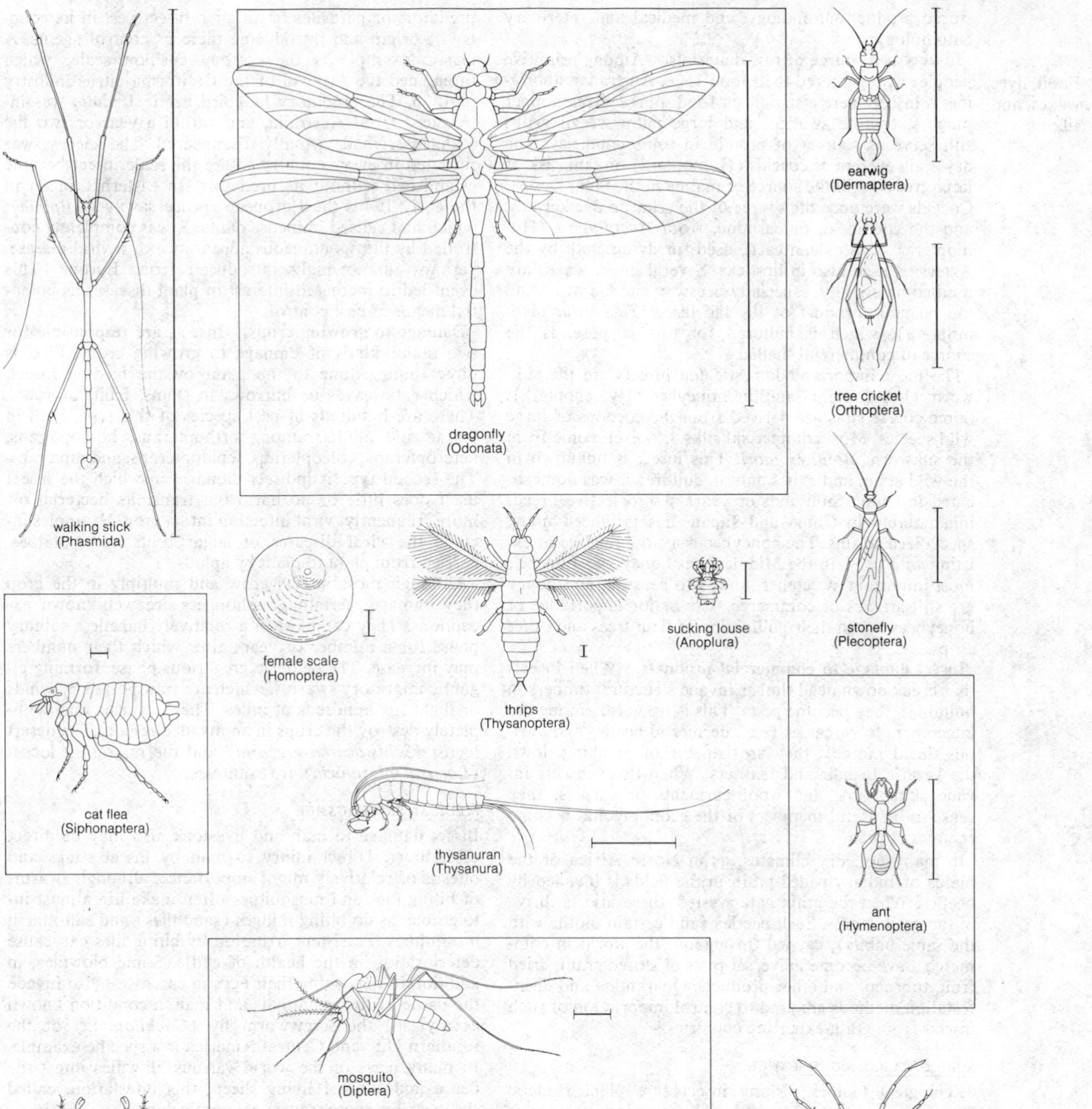

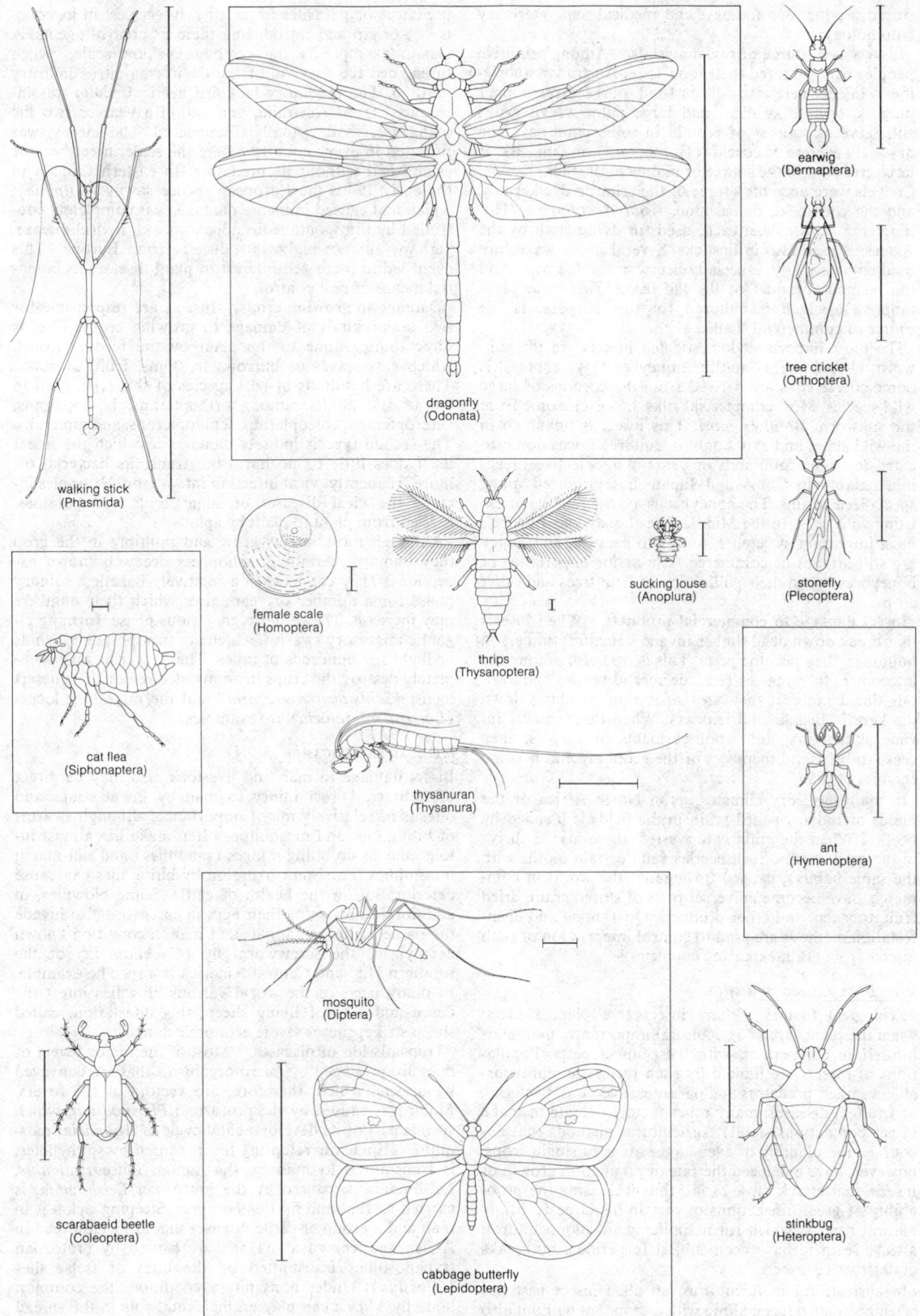

Figure 1: Diversity among adult insects. (Line scales indicate approximate size of each insect.)

Insects and flowers have evolved together. Many plants depend on insects for pollination. Some insects are predators of others (see POLLINATION; SOIL ORGANISM).

COMMERCIAL SIGNIFICANCE

Certain insects provide sources of commercially important products, for example, honey, silk, wax, dyes, pigments; therefore, insects can be of direct benefit to man. Because they feed on many types of organic matter, however, insects cause considerable agricultural damage. Insect pests devour crops of food or timber, either in the field or in storage, and convey infective micro-organisms to crops, farm animals, and human beings. The technology for combatting such pests of man constitutes the applied sciences of agricultural and forest entomology, stored product entomology, and medical and veterinary entomology.

Food, dyes, waxes, and silk

Insects as a source of raw materials. Among primitive peoples who gathered their food (*e.g.*, Australian aborigines), insects were a significant food source. Grasshopper plagues, termite swarms, and large palm weevil grubs still serve as sources of protein in some countries. The dry scaly excreta of coccids (Homoptera) on tamarisk or larch trees is still the source of manna in the Sinai Desert. Coccids were once the source of the crimson dye kermes; and the cochineal, or carmine, from *Dactylopius* (Homoptera) on Mexican cacti, used for dying cloth by the Aztecs, is used also in lipsticks. Several insect waxes are used commercially, especially beeswax and lac wax. And the resinous product of the lac insect *Tachardia* (Homoptera), which is cultured for this purpose, is the source of commercial shellac.

The most important domesticated insects are the silkworm (Lepidoptera) and the honeybee (Hymenoptera). Some coarse silks are derived from the cocoons of large wild species. Most commercial silks, however, come from the silkworm *Bombyx mori.* This insect is unknown in the wild state, and exists only in culture: it was domesticated in China thousands of years ago. Selective breeding, notably in China and Japan, has produced many specialized strains. The honeybee is a close relative of existing wild bees. In the Middle Ages honey was Europe's most important sweetener, and both beeswax and honey are still articles of commerce. The major importance of honeybees lies in their pollination of fruit trees and other crops.

Insect damage to commercial products. When insects that break down dead timber invade structural timbers in buildings, they become pests. This is true also among the latecomers to carcasses (*e.g.*, dermestid beetles and various tineid moths); they are capable of breaking down the keratin in hair and feathers. When these insects invade skins, furs, and wool garments or carpets, they cease to be useful members of the economy and become enemies of man.

In many hot, dry climates, as in North Africa or the plains of India, ripened grain in the fields is invaded by beetles. When the grain is harvested, these insects thrive in the grain stores. Such beetles (and certain moths with the same habits), carried throughout the world in commerce, have become universal pests of stored grain, dried fruit, tobacco, and other products. Quarantine and disinfestation methods are used to control importation of such insects from grain-exporting countries.

AGRICULTURAL SIGNIFICANCE

Ecological factors. Many insects are plant feeders; when the plants are of agricultural importance, man finds himself in competition with these insect pests. Populations of insects are limited by such factors as unfavourable weather, predators and parasites, and viral, bacterial, and fungal diseases; many other factors operate to make insect populations stable. Agricultural methods that encourage the planting of ever larger areas to single crops, however, have enhanced the rate of population growth of insects that attack those crops, thus increasing the probability of great infestations of certain insect pests. Many natural forests, which form similar giant monocultures, always seem to have been subject to periodic outbreaks of destructive insects.

Monocultures

In agricultural monocultures, an alien insect pest has often been introduced along with a crop, but without also bringing along its full range of enemies. This has occurred in the United States with the oyster scale (*Lecanium*) of apple, the cottony cushion scale (*Icerya*) of citrus, the European corn borer (*Pyrausta*), and many more. The Colorado potato beetle (*Leptinotarsa*), which caused appalling destruction a century ago, was a local insect, a native of semidesert country; that beetle, which fed on the buffalo burr plant, adapted itself to a newly introduced and abundant diet, potatoes, and thus escaped from all previous controlling factors. Similar situations often have been controlled by determining the major predators or parasites of an alien insect pest in its country of origin and introducing them as control agents. A classic example is the cottony cushion scale, which threatened the survival of the California citrus industry in 1886. The predatory ladybird beetle *Vedalia* was introduced from Australia, and within a year or two the scale insect had virtually disappeared. The success was repeated in every country where the scale insect became established without its predators. In eastern Canada in the early 1940s the European spruce sawfly (*Gilpinia*), which had caused immense damage, was completely controlled by the spontaneous appearance of a viral disease, perhaps unknowingly introduced from Europe. This event led to increased interest in plant diseases as potential means of pest control.

Damage to growing crops. Insects are responsible for two major kinds of damage to growing crops. First is direct injury done to the plant by the feeding insect, which eats leaves or burrows in stems, fruit, or roots. There are hundreds of pest species of this type, both in larvae and adults, among orthopterans, homopterans, heteropterans, coleopterans, lepidopterans, and dipterans. The second type is indirect damage, in which the insect itself does little or no harm but transmits bacterial or, more frequently, viral infection into a crop. Examples include the viral diseases of sugar beets and potatoes, carried from plant to plant by aphids.

Although most insects grow and multiply in the crop they damage, certain grasshoppers are well-known exceptions. They can exist in a relatively harmless solitary phase for a number of years after which their numbers may increase. They enter a gregarious phase, forming gigantic migratory swarms, which are transported by winds or flight for hundreds of miles. These swarms may completely destroy the crops in an invaded region. The desert locust (*Schistocerca gregaria*) and the migratory locust (*Locusta migratoria*) are examples.

MEDICAL SIGNIFICANCE

Stings and bites

Insect damage to man and livestock also may be direct or indirect. Direct injury to man by insect stings and bites is of relatively minor importance, although swarms of biting flies and mosquitoes often make life almost intolerable, as do biting midges (sand flies) and salt-marsh mosquitoes. Persistent irritation by biting flies can cause deterioration in the health of cattle. Some blowflies, in addition to depositing their eggs in carcasses, also invade the tissue of living animals and man, a condition known as myiasis; the screwworm fly (*Cochliomyia*) of the southern U.S. and Central America is a specific example. In many parts of the world various blowflies infest the fleece and skin of living sheep; this infestation, called sheep-strike, causes severe economic damage.

Transmission of diseases. Most of the major fevers of man are produced by micro-organisms that are conveyed by insects, which, therefore, are vectors of the fevers. Malaria is caused by the protozoan *Plasmodium*, which spends part of its developmental cycle in *Anopheles* mosquitoes. Epidemic relapsing fever, caused by spirochetes, is transmitted to man by the human louse *Pediculus.* Leishmaniasis, caused by the protozoan *Leishmania*, is carried by the sand fly *Phlebotomus.* Sleeping sickness in man and a group of cattle diseases that are widespread in Africa and known as nagana are caused by protozoan trypanosomes transmitted by the bites of tsetse flies (*Glossina*). Under nonsanitary conditions the common housefly *Musca* can play an incidental role in the spread of human intestinal infections (*e.g.*, typhoid, bacillary and amebic dysentery) by contamination of human food. The tularemia bacillus can be spread by deer fly bites, the bubonic plague bacillus by fleas, and the epidemic typhus rickettsia by the louse *Pediculus.* Various mosquitoes spread viral diseases (*e.g.*, equine encephalitis; dengue and yellow fever in man and other animals).

The relationships among the various organisms are complex. Malaria, for example, has a different epidemiology in almost every country in which it occurs, with different *Anopheles* species responsible for its spread.

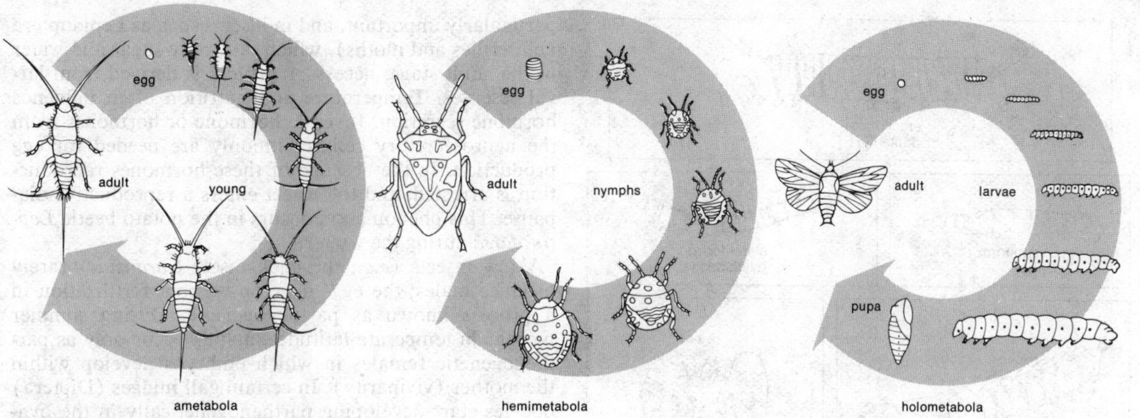

Figure 2: Types of insect development.

These same complexities affect the spread of sleeping sickness. The relationships between man and some diseases are indirect; plague, a disease of rodents transmitted by flea bites, is dangerous to man only when heavy mortality among domestic rats forces their infected fleas to attack man, thereby causing an outbreak of bubonic plague. Typhus, tularemia, and yellow fever also are maintained in animal reservoirs and spread occasionally to man.

CONTROL OF INSECT DAMAGE

The objective of the entomologist is to develop an applied ecology, that is, to introduce modifications into the environment in such ways that diseases will not be spread by insects, and crops will not be damaged. This objective has been achieved in some cases: in many cities flies no longer play a major role in spreading intestinal infections; improved land drainage and improved housing of man and animals has eliminated malaria in many parts of the world.

Massive outbreaks of the Colorado potato beetle in the 1860s led to the first large-scale use of insecticides in agriculture. These highly poisonous chemicals (*e.g.*, Paris green, lead arsenate, concentrated nicotine) were used in large quantities. The continued search for effective synthetic compounds led in the early 1940s to the production of DDT, a remarkable compound that is highly toxic to most insects, nontoxic to man in small quantities (although cumulative effects may be severe), and long lasting in effect. Widely used in agriculture for many years, DDT was not the perfect insecticide. It often killed parasites more effectively than the insects themselves, creating ecological imbalances that permitted new pests to develop large populations. Furthermore, resistant strains of pests appeared. Similar difficulties were encountered with many successors to DDT, such as Dieldrin and Endrin.

Biological control methods

Biological methods of control have become increasingly important as the use of undesirable insecticides decreases. Biological methods include introducing pest strains that carry lethal genes; or flooding an area with sterile males (as was successfully done for the control of the screwworm fly); or perhaps preparing a new kind of insecticide based on modifications of insects' growth hormones. The sugar industry in Hawaii and the California citrus industry rely on biological control methods. Although these methods are not consistently effective, they are considered to be less harmful to the environment than are some chemicals (see PEST CONTROL).

III. Natural history

LIFE CYCLE

Egg. Most insects begin their independent lives as fertilized eggs. The chorion, or eggshell, is commonly pierced by respiratory openings that lead to an air-filled meshwork inside the shell. For some insects (*e.g.*, cockroaches) a batch of eggs is cemented together to form an egg packet or ootheca. Insects may pass unfavourable seasons in the egg stage. Eggs of the lucerne flea *Sminthurus* (Collembola) and of some grasshoppers (Orthoptera) pass summer droughts in a dry shrivelled state and resume development when moistened. Most eggs, however, retain their water although they may pass the winter in a state of arrested development, or diapause, usually at some early stage in embryonic development. Dried eggs of *Aedes* mosquitoes enter a state of dormancy after development is complete; they quickly hatch when placed in water.

The hatching of young larvae is achieved in several ways. Some, such as caterpillars, bite their way out of the egg. Many, such as the flea, have hatching spines with which they cut a slit in the shell; others force off a preformed egg cap. In order to exert this force, the young larva swallows air; after hatching, it continues to distend itself in this way until the cuticle hardens.

Growth and metamorphosis. Once formed, the insect cuticle cannot grow. Growth can occur only by a series of molts (ecdyses) during which new and larger cuticles form and old cuticles are shed. Molting makes possible large changes in body form.

Types of metamorphosis. In the most primitive wingless insects (apterygotes) such as the silverfish *Lepisma*, there is almost no change in form throughout growth to the adult. These are known as ametabolous insects. Among insects such as grasshoppers (Orthoptera), true bugs (Heteroptera), and homopterans (*e.g.*, aphids, scale insects), the general form is constant until the final molt, when the larva undergoes substantial changes in body form to become a winged adult with fully developed genitalia. These insects, termed hemimetabolous, are said to undergo incomplete metamorphosis. The higher orders of insects—*i.e.*, Lepidoptera (butterflies and moths), Coleoptera (beetles), Hymenoptera (ants, wasps, and bees), and Diptera (true flies)—are termed holometabolous because larvae are totally unlike adults. These larvae undergo a series of molts with little change in form before they enter into complete metamorphosis, which includes molting first into pupae and then into fully winged adults.

Types of larvae. Larvae, which vary considerably in shape, are classified in five forms: eruciform (caterpillar-like), scarabaeiform (grublike), campodeiform (elongated, flattened, and active), elateriform (wireworm-like), and vermiform (maggot-like). The three types of pupae are obtect, with appendages more or less glued to the body; exarate, with the appendages free and not glued to the body; and coarctate, essentially exarate but remaining covered by the cast skins (exuviae) of the next to the last larval instar (name given to the form of an insect between molts).

Molting hormone and juvenile hormone

Role of hormones. Both molting and metamorphosis are controlled by hormones. Molting is initiated by a hormone from neurosecretory cells in the brain. The hormone acts upon a prothoracic gland, an endocrine gland in the prothorax; this gland, in turn, secretes the molting hormone, a steroid known as ecdysone, which, by its action on the epidermis, stimulates growth and cuticle formation. Metamorphosis likewise is controlled by a hormone. Throughout the young larval stages a small gland behind the brain, called the corpus allatum, secretes the

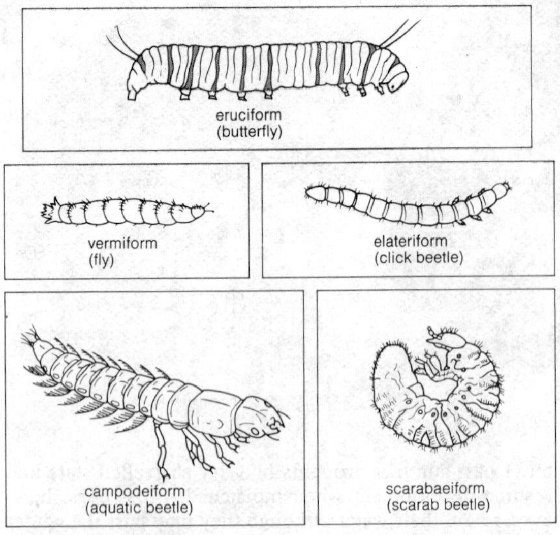

Figure 3: Insect larvae.

juvenile hormone (also known as neotenin). So long as this hormone is present in the blood the molting epidermal cells lay down a larval cuticle. In the last larval stage, juvenile hormone is no longer produced, and the insect undergoes metamorphosis into an adult. Among holometabolous insects the pupa develops in the presence of a very small amount of juvenile hormone.

Although a state of arrested development may occur during any stage, diapause occurs most commonly in pupae. In temperate latitudes many insects overwinter in the pupal stage (*e.g.*, cocoons). The immediate cause of diapause, failure to secrete the growth and molting hormones, usually is induced by a decrease in daylength as summer wanes.

In addition to the changes in form during development, many insects exhibit polymorphism as adults. For example, the worker and reproductive castes in ants and bees may be different; termites have a soldier caste as well as reproductives and persistent larvae; adult aphids (Homoptera) may be winged or wingless; and some butterflies show striking seasonal dimorphism. The general interpretation of all such differences is that, although the capacity to develop different forms is present in the genes of every member of a given species, particular lines of development are evoked by environmental stimuli. Hormones, including perhaps the juvenile hormone, may be agents for the control of such changes. For a discussion of the biochemistry of insect hormones, see HORMONE.

Pheromones

Reproduction. The life of the adult insect is geared primarily to reproduction. Since reproduction is sexual in almost all insects, mating must be followed by impregnation of the female and fertilization of eggs. Usually the male seeks out the female. In butterflies in which vision is important, the colour of the female in flight can attract a male of the same species. In mayflies (Ephemeroptera) and certain midges (Diptera) the males dance in swarms to provide a visual attraction for females. In certain beetles (*e.g.*, fireflies and glowworms) parts of the fat body in the female have become modified to form a luminous organ that attracts the male. Male crickets and grasshoppers attract females by their chirping songs, and the male mosquito is lured by the sound emitted by the female in flight. The most important element in mating, however, is odour. Most female insects secrete odorous substances called pheromones that serve as specific attractants and excitants for males. The male likewise may produce scents that excite the female. Certain scales (androconia) on the wings of many male butterflies function in this way. Assembling scents, active in small quantities, are well known in female gypsy moths and silkworms as male attractants. The queen substance in the honeybee serves the same purpose.

Mating and egg production require appropriate temperatures and adequate nutrition. The need for protein is particularly important, and in insects such as Lepidoptera (butterflies and moths), which take only sugar and water in the adult stage, necessary protein is derived from larval reserves. Temperature and nutrition often influence hormone secretion. Juvenile hormone or hormones from the neurosecretory cells commonly are needed for egg production. In the absence of these hormones reproduction is arrested, and the insect enters a reproductive diapause. This phenomenon occurs in the potato beetle *Leptinotarsa* during the winter.

A few insects (*e.g.*, the stick insect *Carausius*) rarely produce males; the eggs develop without fertilization in a process known as parthenogenesis. During summer months in temperate latitudes, aphids occur only as parthenogenetic females in which embryos develop within the mother (viviparity). In certain gall midges (Diptera) oocytes start developing parthenogenetically in the ovaries of the larvae; the young larvae escape by destroying the body of their mother in a process called paedogenesis.

SENSORY PERCEPTION AND RECEPTION

Touch. Insects have an elaborate system of sense organs. Tactile hairs, concentrated on the antennae, palps, legs, and tarsi, cover the entire body surface. The hairs serve to inform the insect about its surroundings and its body position (a phenomenon known as proprioception). For example, contact between the hairs on the feet and the ground inhibits movement and may lead to a state of sleep in some insects. Modified mechanical sense organs in the cuticle called campaniform organs detect bending strains in the integument. Such organs exist in the wings and enable the insect to control its movements. Campaniform organs, well developed in small clublike halteres (the modified hindwings of dipterans), serve as strain gauges and enable the fly to control its equilibrium.

Sound. Exceedingly sensitive organs called sensilla are concentrated in organs of hearing; *e.g.*, bushy antennae of the male mosquito or tympanal organs in the front legs of crickets or in abdominal pits of grasshoppers and many moths. In moths these sensitive organs can perceive the high-pitched sounds emitted by bats as they hunt by echolocation. Insects complement organs of sound reception with sound-producing organs, which usually are (as in crickets) wing membranes that vibrate in response to movement of a stiff rod across a row of stout teeth. Sometimes (as in cicadas) a tymbal membrane in the wall of the thorax is set in vibration by a rapidly contracting muscle attached to it.

Chemicals. Chemical perceptions by the thin-walled sensilla may be comparable to man's organs of taste or his sense of smell. Many insect chemoreceptors are specialized according to specific behaviour patterns. For example, although approximately equivalent to man in its perception of flower odours and sugar sweetness, the honeybee is exceedingly sensitive to the queen substance, which is scentless to man. And the male silkworm moth is excited by infinitesimal traces of the female sex pheromone, even in the presence of odours that are intensely strong to man.

Sight. Although the insect eye provides very poor form perception, insects by using a process of scanning (*i.e.*, moving the eye rapidly across a field of view) probably can form adequate visual impressions of their surroundings. Insects have good colour vision; colour perception commonly extends (as in ants and bees) into the ultraviolet, although it often fails to extend into the deep red. Many flowers have patterns of ultraviolet reflection invisible to the human eye, but visible to the insect eye.

BEHAVIOUR

Instincts. The insect orients itself by making orientation responses to the stimuli it receives. Formerly, insect behaviour was described as a series of forced movements in response to stimuli. That hypothesis has been supplanted by one that holds that the insect has a central nervous system with built-in patterns of behaviour or instincts that can be called forth by environmental stimuli; these instincts are modified by the insect's internal state, which has been affected by preceding stimuli. Searching for food or an egglaying site, catching prey, and mating are a few examples of complex behaviour. Experimental studies of details of behaviour have provided significant information about the properties of the sense organs. Patterns of behaviour range from comparatively simple reflex responses (*e.g.*, the avoidance of adverse stimuli, the grasping of a rough surface on contact with the claws) to the elaborate behavioural sequences involved in hunting, capturing, and eating prey. The highest developments of behaviour, found in social insects such as the ants, bees, and termites are based on the instinct principle.

Environmental stimuli

An interesting example of a behavioural pattern is that found in the leaf-cutter bee *Megachile*. The female bee first locates a site for her nest in rotten wood and shapes the nest into a long tunnel; then she seeks out preferred shrub leaves from which to build a cell and cuts first a disc for a cell cap, then a series of oval pieces for the walls. After preparing the nest, she stores a mixture of pollen and honey, lays an egg, and finally closes the cell with more cut leaves. The leaf-cutter bee repeats this sequence until the nest is filled. Each act can be performed only in this set sequence. The insect does not stop to repair any damage to the nest but proceeds undeterred to the next step in her behavioural pattern.

The honeybee society is more flexible than that of the leaf-cutter bee. Behavioural sequences of individuals are predictable, but the choice of acts or duties within the hive can be influenced by the needs of the colony. A capacity for learning does exist, and must exist, in any insect that has to find its nest; but learning capacity plays a relatively small part in the overall pattern of honeybee behaviour.

Insect societies. Both in complexity of behaviour and learning capacity, solitary bees and wasps are the equals of social wasps or honeybees. Social insects, however, have developed a division of labour in which the members must do the work required at the proper time. If the society is to succeed, its needs must be communicated to the individual, and the individual must act. These needs may be met by a temporary change in behaviour during which appropriate instinctive acts are performed or by changes in development that lead to the appearance of appropriate castes. Commonly, both behavioural and developmental changes are initiated by pheromones, which act as chemical messengers that convey information from one member of a colony to another.

The queen substance

Insect societies are gigantic families, the offspring of a single female. In the honeybee the single queen in the hive secretes the pheromone known as the queen substance (oxodecenoic acid); it is taken up by the workers and passed throughout the colony by food sharing. So long as the queen substance circulates, all members are informed that the queen is present. If the workers are deprived of queen substance, they proceed at once to build queen cells and feed the young larvae with a special salivary secretion known as royal jelly to produce more queens.

Pheromones liberated by termite soldiers or reproductive adults control the development of soldiers and reproductive forms. Alarm substances and other pheromones control much of the behaviour in ants. A remarkable form of communication is the dance language in the honeybee, in which the direction and approximate distance of a foraging site can be conveyed by one worker to another (see HYMENOPTERA; ISOPTERA; BEHAVIOUR, ANIMAL).

ECOLOGY

Terrestrial insects. Insects feed on every sort of organic matter, and their methods of feeding and digestion have become modified accordingly. The major climatic hazards faced by terrestrial insects are temperature extremes and desiccation. Different species function best at various optimal temperatures. If conditions are too hot, an insect seeks out a cool, moist, and shady spot. If exposed to the sun an insect positions itself so as to present the smallest amount of body surface to the heat. If conditions are too cool, insects remain in the sun to warm themselves. Many butterflies must spread their wings to collect heat before they can fly. A moth raises its temperature by vibrating its wings or "shivering" before taking flight. The heat generated in this way is conserved by hairs or scales that maintain an insulating layer of air around the body. The optimum muscle temperature for flight is from 38° to 40° C.

In extremely cold weather the danger for insects is freezing, and insects that survive winters in cold latitudes are called cold hardy. A few insects (*e.g.*, some caterpillars and aquatic midge larvae) tolerate ice formation in body fluids, although it is probable that the cell contents do not freeze. In most insects, however, cold hardiness means resistance to freezing. This resistance results partly from accumulation of large quantities of glycerol as an antifreeze and partly from physical changes in the blood that permit supercooling, without freezing, to temperatures far below the freezing point. Resistance to desiccation includes development of hard waterproofing waxes and exaggeration of water-conserving mechanisms.

Aquatic insects. Major adaptational changes—apart from remarkable modifications of the legs for swimming—concern respiration of aquatic insects. Some occur in insects that rise to the water surface to take atmospheric air into their tracheal systems. Mosquito larvae use only the last pair of abdominal spiracles, which open at the tip of a respiratory siphon. Water beetles (*e.g.*, *Dytiscus*) have converted the space between the protective sheaths on the hindwings (elytra) and the abdomen into an air storage chamber. Air-breathing insects can prolong the period of submergence by trapping air among their surface hairs. This air film acts as a physical gill and makes possible oxygen uptake from water.

Respiratory adaptations

Other adaptations to an aquatic environment have occurred in larvae that obtain all their oxygen from the water. In midge larvae, abundant tracheae (breathing tubes) supply the entire thin cuticle. Caddisfly larvae (Trichoptera) and mayfly larvae (Ephemeroptera) have tracheal gills. In large dragonfly larvae, the gills are inside the rectum, and the water is pumped in and out through the anus.

Protection from enemies. Insects may derive some protection from a horny or leathery integument; but they also have various chemical defenses. Some caterpillars carry among their body-surface hairs special irritating hairs, which break up into barbed fragments containing a poisonous substance that causes intense itching and serves as a protection against most birds.

Dermal glands of many insects discharge repellent or poisonous secretions over the cuticle; other insects are protected by poisons that are present continuously in the blood and tissues. Such poisons often are derived from the plants on which the insects feed. In many hymenopterans (ants, bees, wasps) accessory glands of the female, which usually pour out a secretion over the egg, have become modified to produce toxic proteins. These poisons, injected into the nervous system of the prey of solitary wasps, paralyze it; in this state the prey serves as food for the wasp larva. Similar stings are used by hymenopterans, including ants, wasps, and bees, for self-defense.

Concealment

Concealment is an important protective device for insects. Vast numbers hide beneath stones or the bark of trees. Others rely on protective coloration. Although insect colours depend partly on pigmentation in the outer body covering (cuticle), the most important pigments occur in epidermal cells below the cuticle. Butterfly and moth pigments are deposited inside flattened hairs, or scales, which cover the wings. Some of the most brilliant insect colours are not the result of pigmentation; they are physical interference colours produced by fine laminae in the surface of the scales. Protective coloration may take the form of camouflage (cryptic coloration) in which the insect is confused with its background. The coloration of many insects copies a specific background with extraordinary detail. Stick insects (*Carausius*) can accommodate their colour to that of a changing background by moving pigment granules in their epidermal cells. Some caterpillars have patterns that develop in response to a background; however, these are irreversible. Insects such as caterpillars, which rely on cryptic coloration, combine it with a rigid deathlike position.

Alternatively, insects that are well provided with chemical defenses generally show conspicuous warning, or aposematic, coloration. Experiments have proved that predators such as birds quickly learn to associate such coloration "labels" with nauseous or dangerous prey. Finally, insects without nauseous qualities may gain protection by mimicry, that is, by developing the conspicuous coloration found in distasteful species (see also COLORATION, BIOLOGICAL; MIMICRY).

Population regulation. The factors that limit the numbers of insect species are complex. Experimental studies of a population of grain beetles in a jar containing wheat show that the complexities increase if a second species is added. With insects in natural habitats, competing not only with members of their own species but with numerous other species as well, the obstacles to survival become increasingly great. Competition among species is reduced to some extent by adaptation of species to niches, or habitats, for which other insects do not compete.

Competition

Formerly, controversy arose over whether numbers were always density dependent (*i.e.*, limited by the density of the species itself) or whether catastrophic actions, notably the vagaries of weather, were often of prime importance. It has since become recognized that the ultimate factor in the control of numbers is competition within the species for food and other needs; but in many circumstances, before competition for food becomes significant, numbers are reduced by external factors. Competition within a species often is reduced by wholesale migration to new localities. Migration may occur by active flight, as in aphids and locusts, largely directed by the wind. Another important factor in the regulation of populations is balanced polymorphism of species, in which the prevalence of individuals with given characteristics changes according to the action of natural selection as the state of the environment changes (see also MIGRATION, ANIMAL; POLYMORPHISM, BIOLOGICAL; POPULATION, BIOLOGICAL).

IV. Form and function

EXTERNAL FEATURES

Cuticle. The insect is covered by the cuticle, a layer of inert material laid down by a single sheet of epidermal cells. It consists mainly of chitin, a carbohydrate also known as polyacetylglucosamine, and sclerotin, a hard substance composed of protein tanned by quinones. The cuticle, which has a superficial layer of waterproofing wax to prevent loss of water by evaporation, also serves as the skeleton to which the muscles are attached. In insects (*e.g.*, caterpillars), in which the cuticle is soft and flexible, the skeleton is of the hydrostatic type; that is, body fluid pressure, maintained by muscle tension beneath the body wall, provides the firmness necessary for the function of muscles involved in movement. In insects with hard bodies, the cuticle is made up of hardened areas called sclerites; the flexible joints between sclerites provide a permanently rigid external skeleton. At the back of the head and in the thorax, hardened ingrowths of the cuticle, known as apodemes, furnish a kind of internal skeleton for muscular attachment.

Head. In present-day insects the primitive segments are grouped into three regions known as head, thorax, and abdomen. The first six segments have fused to form the head; the appendages of these segments have become modified into antennae that bear numerous sense organs and mouthparts that convey food to the mouth. Eyes also are prominent on the head. In most insects the mouthparts, adapted for chewing, consist of several parts; behind the upper lip or labrum is a pair of hard, toothed mandibles. These are followed by a pair of structures called first maxillae, each consisting of a bladelike lacinia, a hoodlike galea, and a segmented palp bearing

Mouth-parts

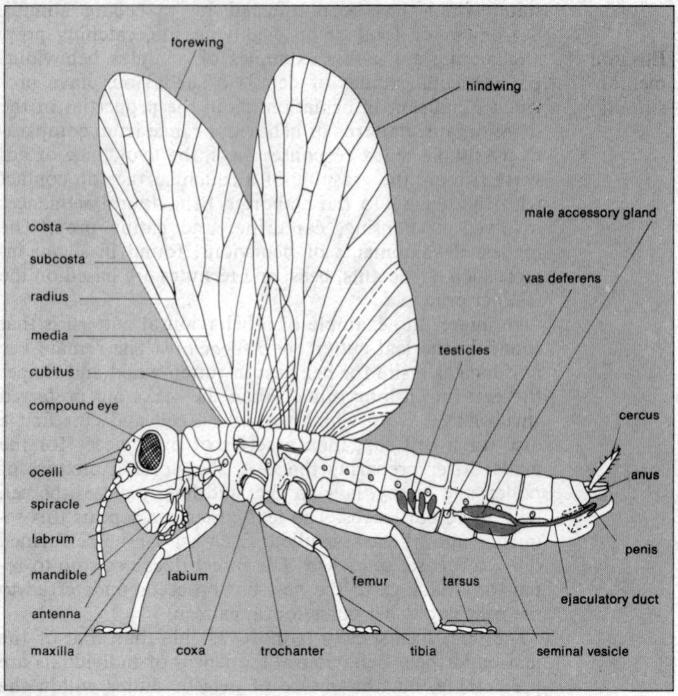

Figure 4: Body plan of a generalized insect, showing external features and male reproductive structures.
From H. Weber, *Grundriss der Insektenkunde* (1966); Gustav Fischer Verlag

sense organ. The paired second maxillae are partly fused in the midline to form the lower lip, or labium. Sometimes a median tonguelike structure, called the hypopharynx, arises from the floor of the mouth.

Insect mouthparts have been modified strikingly and reflect particular methods of feeding. The dipterans (true flies) provide instructive examples. In the primitive bloodsucking flies (*e.g.*, the horsefly *Tabanus*) the mandibles and maxillae form serrated blades that cut through the skin and blood vessels of the host animal. The epipharynx and hypopharynx are elongated and grooved so that, when apposed, they form a tube for sucking blood. The tonguelike labium is used for imbibing exposed fluids. Dipteran mouthparts have evolved in two directions. In the mosquitoes (Culicidae) the mandibles, maxillae, epipharynx, and hypopharynx have become exceedingly slender stylets that form a fine bundle and are used for piercing skin and entering blood vessels. The labium, elongated and deeply grooved, serves only as a sheath for the stylet bundle. In the housefly *Musca*, however, mandibles and maxillae have been lost; the tonguelike labium alone remains and serves for feeding on exposed surfaces. Certain flies related to *Musca* have reacquired a capacity to suck blood; however, since they have lost both mandibles and maxillae, a new bloodsucking mechanism has developed. Labial teeth have evolved for cutting through the skin, and the labium itself is plunged into the tissues. The stable fly *Stomoxys* has an arrangement of this kind. In the tsetse fly *Glossina*, the labium has become a fine, needlelike structure normally protected by a sheath formed from the palps of the lost maxillae.

Other mouthpart modifications of the mouthpart components provide the cutting and sucking mouthparts of fleas (Siphonaptera), plant-sucking insects (Homoptera), bloodsucking bugs (Heteroptera), honeybees (Hymenoptera), and nectar-feeding butterflies (Lepidoptera).

Thorax. The insect thorax consists of three segments (called the prothorax, mesothorax, and metathorax), which may be fused but are usually recognizable. Each segment has four groups of hard plates (sclerites); the groups are the notum (upper), the pleura (sides), and the sternum (underside). Thoracic sclerites are located on a given segment by using an appropriate prefix (pro-, meso-, meta-); for example, the notum (upper sclerite) of the prothorax is the pronotum.

Each segment bears a pair of legs, and, in the mature insect, the mesothorax and metathorax typically carry a pair of wings. Each leg always consists of five parts: a coxa articulated to the thorax, a small trochanter, a femur, a tibia, and a tarsus with one to five segments. The tarsal segments often carry claws with adhesive pads between them (arolia or pulvilli); these enable the insect to hold onto smooth surfaces. The legs may be modified for leaping, burrowing, grasping prey, or swimming in various ways.

From H. Weber, *Grundriss der Insektenkunde* (1966); Gustav Fischer Verlag

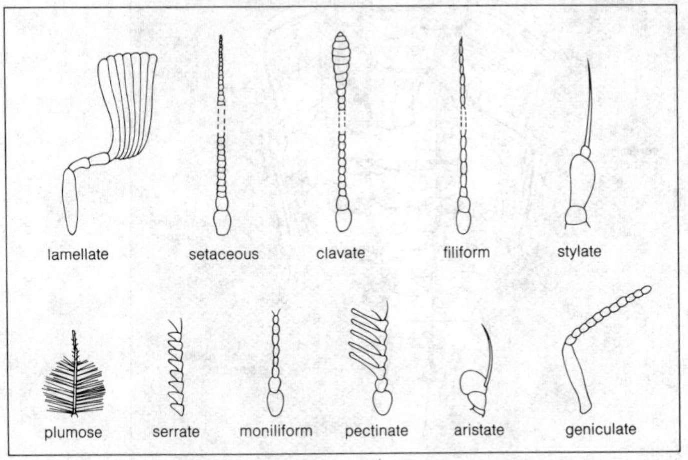

Figure 5: Insect antennae.

The wings at rest may be extended permanently on each side, as in some dragonflies (Odonata), or held erect above the body, as in mayflies (Ephemeroptera); in most insects, however, they are folded against the abdomen. The wing consists of cuticular sacs that bud out from the wall of the thorax; the sacs become flattened during development, and the two membranes, pressed together, are stiffened by thickenings of the cuticle that form cylindrical veins carrying tracheae, nerves, and circulating blood to all parts of the wing. Wings utilized for flight commonly are made of thin membranous cuticle. In some insects, notably beetles (Coleoptera), the wings of the middle segment of the thorax have become thick and horny and serve as protective sheaths (elytra) of the membranous hindwings.

Locomotion and flight

The locomotion of insects is effected by muscles acting on the external skeleton. In leaping insects (*e.g.*, grasshoppers, fleas) the force of muscle contraction is used to compress a pad of an elastic protein, resilin; when the catch mechanism is released, the stored energy in the protein molecule is used to project the insect into the air. Insect flight is achieved by flapping the wings; during these movements the wing blade, twisted as it passes from elevation to depression, produces the same effect as the rotating propeller of an aircraft. Muscles capable of changing this inclination control the direction of flight. The chief flight muscles control flight in one of two ways: in dragonflies, directly on a lever at the base of each wing; but, in most insects, indirectly by deforming the shape of the thorax. The longitudinal muscles of the thorax depress the wings that are articulated with it; the vertical muscles elevate them.

In butterflies, the number of wing beats per second may be as low as 8 to 12, while the rate in mosquitoes may exceed 600. These rates can exceed the frequency of contraction and relaxation of muscles responding to nerves because the muscles, after they have begun contracting and relaxing, respond to the alternating elastic tension in the thoracic wall, where the frequency is determined by the natural periodic oscillation of the thorax. The flight of insects, despite their small size, conforms to the aerodynamic laws that regulate the flight of aircraft.

Abdomen. The abdomen consists of a maximum of 11 segments, although this number commonly is reduced by fusion. Appendages are usually absent except in caterpillars, which use up to five pairs of abdominal prolegs in walking, and in adult insects where the appendages at the hind end have become transformed into external genitalia. In the male these genitalia are paired claspers used to hold the female; in the female, three pairs of valvulae are used to manipulate eggs during oviposition. In some insects, notably crickets and cockroaches, two feelers, or cerci, at the hind end of the abdomen bear sense organs.

INTERNAL FEATURES

Nutritive requirements

Digestive system. The nutritive requirements of insects are much the same as those of mammals—water, inorganic ions, and essential amino acids (*i.e.*, those that cannot be synthesized by the animal). The requirements for preformed fat and carbohydrate vary with the species. Although vitamins of the B group are needed by insects, neither vitamins A nor D are required, and many insects can synthesize ascorbic acid (vitamin C). On the other hand, insects cannot synthesize adequate quantities of cholesterol; thus, in effect, cholesterol can be defined as a vitamin for insects.

Insects that feed solely on some restricted diet (*e.g.*, sterile blood, plant juices, refined flour) have special cells termed mycetocytes that harbour symbiotic micro-organisms; these organisms, transmitted through the egg to the next generation, benefit their host by furnishing it with an internal source of vitamins and perhaps other essential nutrients. If the symbiotic micro-organisms are removed experimentally, an insect fails to grow if not provided with a diet rich in vitamins.

The digestive system consists of a foregut formed from the mouth region (stomodaeum), a hindgut formed similarly from the anal region (proctodaeum), and a midgut (mesenteron). The foregut and hindgut are lined by cuticle continuous with that on the body surface. The mouth is followed by the muscular pharynx, which functions in sucking and swallowing, and the esophagus, which may be enlarged to form a crop. The crop discharges into the midgut, sometimes, as in cockroaches, by way of a muscular gizzard or proventriculus. The termination of the midgut is marked by the attachment of the malpighian tubules, the chief organs of excretion. The hindgut commonly consists of a narrow ileum followed by a larger and often thick-walled rectum, which discharges at the anus.

Digestive enzymes, secreted not only by the salivary glands but also by the cells of the midgut and its diverticula, vary with the diet of the insect. The most important enzyme secreted by the salivary glands is amylase; the midgut secretes several enzymes including protease, lipase, amylase, and invertase. The products of digestion are absorbed chiefly in the midgut.

The hindgut receives food residues from the midgut as well as waste products from the malpighian tubules. The end products of nitrogen metabolism are uric acid, small amounts of amino acids, and urea; in aquatic insects, ammonium salts may be a major form for nitrogen excretion. In the rectum, the epithelial cells lining the gut wall

From H. Weber, *Grundriss der Insektenkunde* (1966); Gustav Fischer Verlag

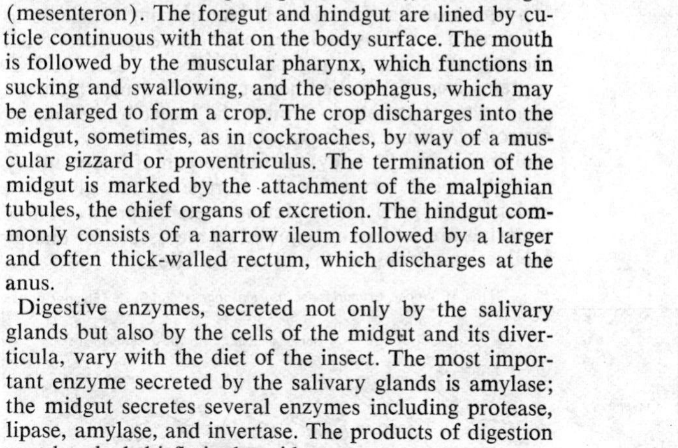

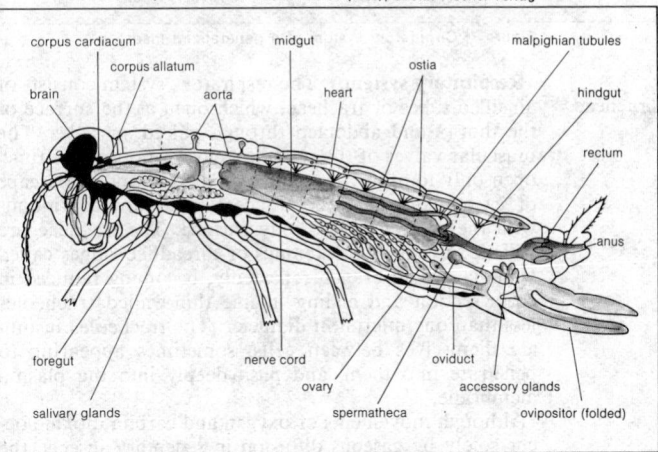

Figure 6: Internal features of a generalized female insect.

often are enlarged, particularly in restricted areas where they form rectal glands. The epithelial cells of these glands are supplied richly with tracheae and function in the reabsorption of water and ions. The rectal contents of insects that inhabit dry environments commonly are reduced to dry fecal pellets prior to discharge. In many insects, particularly those which feed on relatively dry foods (*e.g.*, beetles infesting stored grain), the upper segments of the malpighian tubules are bound by a sheath to the rectal surface and form a cryptonephridial system that serves to increase the capacity of the rectum for reabsorbing water and salts. The products of digestion, discharged into the hemocoele, or general body cavity, are transported by the circulatory fluid, or hemolymph, to the organs.

Circulatory system. The circulatory system is an open one, with most of the body fluid, or hemolymph, occupying cavities of the body and its appendages. The one closed organ, called the dorsal vessel, extends from the hind end through the thorax to the head; it is a continuous tube with two regions, the heart or pumping organ, which is restricted to the abdomen, and the aorta, or conducting vessel, which extends forward through the thorax to the head. Hemolymph, pumped forward from the hind end and the sides of the body along the dorsal vessel, passes through a series of valved chambers, each containing a pair of lateral openings called ostia, to the aorta and is discharged in the front of the head. Accessory pumps carry the hemolymph through the wings and along the antennae and legs before it flows backward again to the abdomen.

The circulating hemolymph, or blood, is not important in respiration but functions in transporting nutrients to all parts of the body and metabolic waste products from the organs to the malpighian tubules for excretion. It contains free cells called hemocytes, most of which are phagocytes that help to protect the insect by devouring micro-organisms. An important tissue bathed by the hemolymph is the fat body, the main organ of intermediary metabolism. It serves for the storage of fat, glycogen, and protein, particularly during metamorphosis. These materials are set free as required by the tissues for energy production or for growth and reproduction.

From H. Weber, *Grundriss der Insectenkunde* (1966); Gustav Fischer Verlag

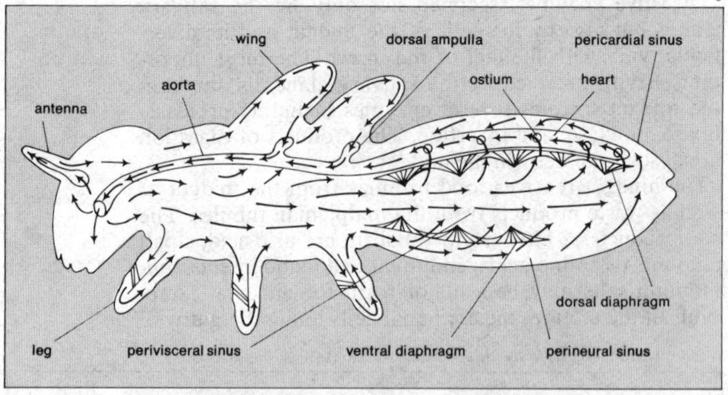

Figure 7: Circulatory system of a generalized insect.

Tracheae

Respiratory system. The respiratory system consists of air-filled tubes or tracheae, which open at the surface of the thorax and abdomen through paired spiracles. The muscular valves of the spiracles, closed most of the time, open only to allow the uptake of oxygen and the escape of carbon dioxide. The tracheal tubes are continuous with the cuticle of the body surface. The tracheae are stiffened by spiral thickenings or threadlike ridges called taenidia, which branch repeatedly, becoming reduced in cross section and ending in fine thin-walled tracheoles less than one micron in diameter. The tracheoles insinuate themselves between cells, sometimes appearing to penetrate into them, and push deeply into the plasma membrane.

Although movements of oxygen and carbon dioxide occur solely by gaseous diffusion in sedentary insects, the system is ventilated mechanically in active species. Pumping movements of the abdomen provide the force necessary to drive out streams of air at some spiracles and suck them in at others. The taenidia keep the tracheae distended, thus allowing free passage of air. In addition, the most active insects have large thin-walled dilatations of the tracheae called air sacs, which serve to increase the volume of air displaced during respiratory movements. Both lack of oxygen and accumulation of carbon dioxide provide stimuli to nerve centres that induce increased respiration during muscular activity.

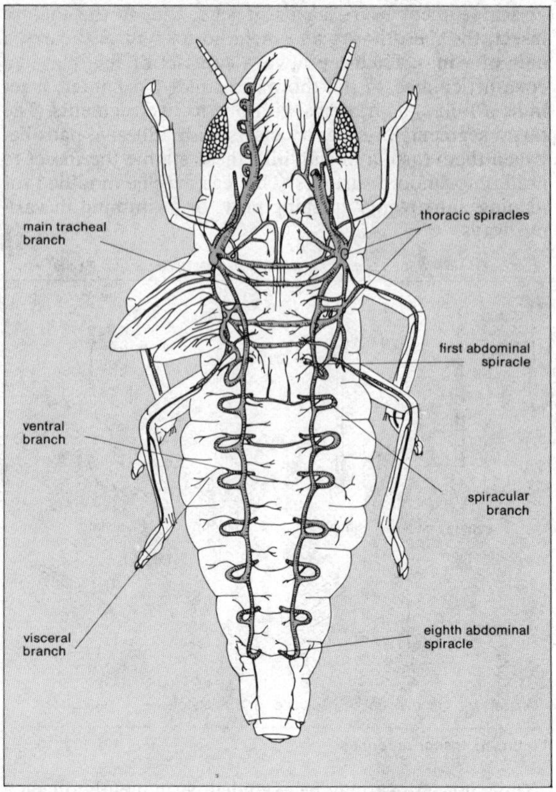

Figure 8: Respiratory system of a generalized insect.
From G. Grandi, *Istituzioni di Entomologia Generale* (1966); Calderini

Reproductive system. The reproductive system consists of the sex glands, or gonads (male testes and female ovaries), the ducts through which the sexual products are carried to the exterior, and the accessory glands. The two testes are made up of a variable number of follicles in which the spermatocytes mature and form packets of elongated spermatozoa. Spermatozoa, liberated in bundles with heads held in a cap of gelatinous material, accumulate in the vesicula seminalis, a dilated section of the male sexual duct (vas deferens).

Each of the two ovaries consists of a number of ovarioles. The ovarioles converge upon the two oviducts, and the oviducts unite to form a common oviduct down which the ripe eggs are discharged. Each ovariole consists of a germarium and a series of ovarial follicles. The germarium is a mass of undifferentiated cells that form oocytes, nurse cells, and follicular cells. The nurse cells provide nourishment for the oocytes during the early stages of their growth; follicular cells, which invest the enlarging oocyte as a continuous epithelium, provide the materials for yolk formation and, in the final stages, lay down the eggshell or chorion. The ovarial follicles increase progressively in size as the oocytes grow to form ripe eggs.

During copulation, bundles of spermatozoa are sometimes introduced directly into the female vagina by means of the male copulatory organ, or aedeagus. Secretions from the accessory glands of the female activate the sperm, the sperm bundles disperse, and the free spermatozoa make their way up to the receptaculum seminis, or spermatheca, where they are stored, ready to fertilize the eggs. In most insects, the male accessory glands secrete materials that form a tough capsule, or spermatophore;

Spermatheca

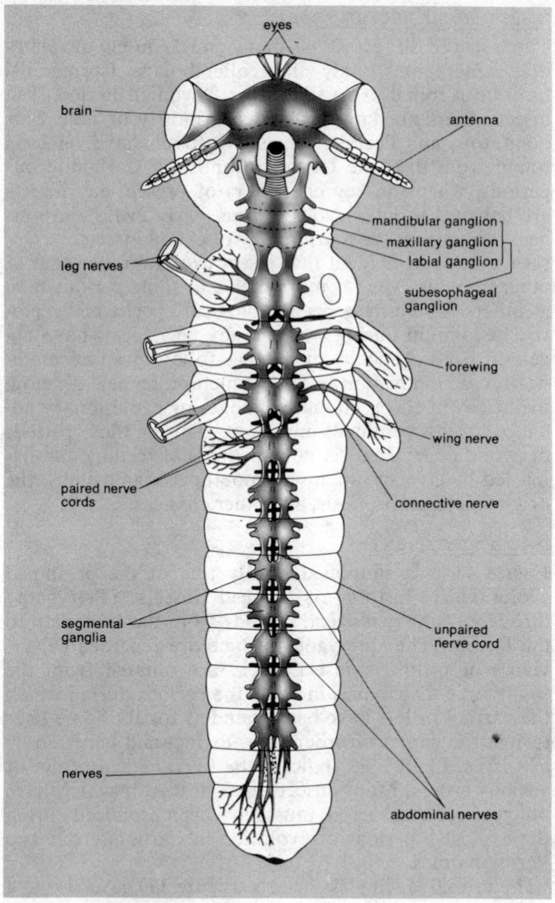

Figure 9: Nervous system of a generalized insect.
From G. Grandi, *Introduzione allo Studio della Entomologia* (1951); Edizioni Agricole

spermatozoa are encased in this spermatophore, which is inserted into the entrance of the vagina. The spermatophore walls commonly contain a gelatinous substance that swells upon exposure to secretions of the female and forces out the spermatozoa. The vagina serves both for receiving sperm and for laying eggs.

The terminal segments of the abdomen of females sometimes are modified to form an ovipositor used for depositing eggs. In butterflies and moths (Lepidoptera) a second copulatory canal independent of the vagina has been evolved, so that the sperm enter by one route, and the eggs are deposited by another.

The eggshell, or chorion, commonly provided with an air-filled meshwork, provides for respiration of the developing embryo. The chorion is also pierced by micropyles, fine canals that permit entry of one or more spermatozoa for fertilization. As the egg passes down the oviduct before egg laying, the micropyles come to lie opposite the duct of the spermatheca; at this stage fertilization occurs. Eggs must be waterproof to prevent desiccation; each egg has a layer of waterproofing wax, sometimes over the entire shell surface, more often lining the inside.

Nervous system. The central nervous system consists of a series of ganglia that supply nerves to successive segments of the body. The three main ganglia in the head (protocerebrum, deutocerebrum, and tritocerebrum) commonly are fused to form the brain, or supraesophageal ganglion. The rest of the ganglionic chain lies below the alimentary canal against the ventral body surface. The brain is joined by paired connectives to the subesophageal ganglion, which is linked in turn by paired connectives to the three thoracic and eight abdominal ganglia (numbered according to segment). In most insects the number of separate ganglia has been reduced by fusion. The last abdominal ganglion always serves several segments. In homopterans and heteropterans all the abdominal ganglia usually fuse with mesothoracic and metathoracic ganglia; and in the larvae of higher flies (Cyclorrhapha), the ganglia of the brain, thorax, and abdomen form one mass.

Each ganglion is made up of nerve-cell bodies that lie on the periphery and a mass of nerve fibres, the neuropile, that occupies the centre. There are two types of nerve cells, motor neurons and association neurons. Motor neurons have main processes, or axons, that extend from the ganglia to contractile muscles, and minor processes, or dendrites, that connect with the neuropile. Association neurons, usually smaller than motor neurons, are linked with other parts of the nervous system by way of the neuropile.

Cell bodies of the sense organs, called sensory neurons, lie at the periphery of the body just below the cuticle. Sensory neurons occur as single cells or small clusters of cells; the distal process, or dendrite, of each cell extends Sensilla
to a cuticular sense organ (sensillum). The sensilla are usually small hairs modified for perception of specific stimuli (*e.g.*, touch, smell, taste, heat, cold); each sensillum consists of one sense cell and one nerve fibre. Although these small sense organs occur all over the body, they are particularly abundant in antennae, palps, and cerci. The sense cell of each sensillum gives off a proximal process, or sensory axon, which runs inward to the central nervous system, where it enters the neuropile and makes contact with the endings of association neurons. Bundles of both sensory axons and motor axons, which are enclosed in protective membranous sheaths, constitute the nerves.

Tactile hairs may be sensitive enough to perceive air vibrations and thus serve as organs for sound reception. Tympanal organs (eardrums) are present in certain butterflies and grasshoppers. Mechanical sensilla (chordotonal organs), which are sunk below the surface of the cuticle, serve for perception of internal strains and body movements.

Eyes. The eyes are of two kinds, simple eyes, or ocelli, and compound eyes. In the adults of higher insects

From V.B. Wigglesworth, *The Life of Insects*, Copyright ©1964 by V.B. Wigglesworth; World Publishing Co.

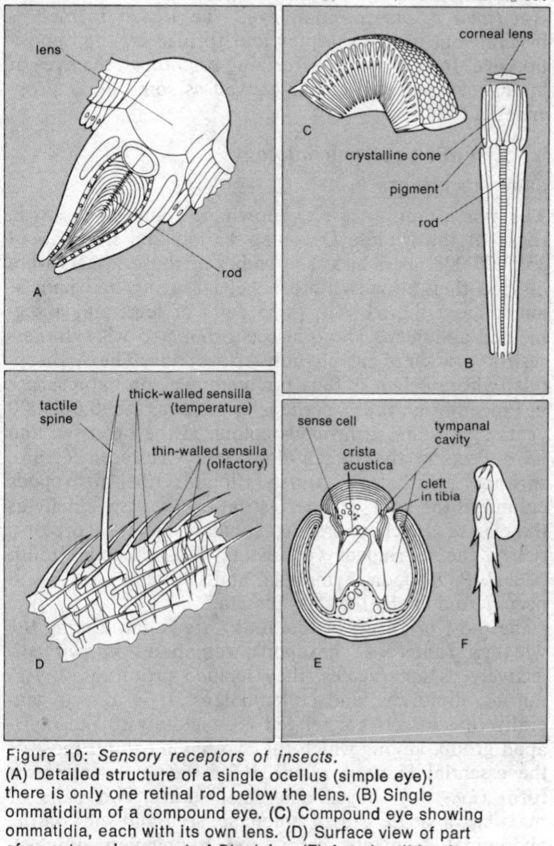

Figure 10: *Sensory receptors of insects.*
(A) Detailed structure of a single ocellus (simple eye); there is only one retinal rod below the lens. (B) Single ommatidium of a compound eye. (C) Compound eye showing ommatidia, each with its own lens. (D) Surface view of part of an antennal segment of *Rhodnius.* (E) Anterior tibia of *Decticus* at the level of tympanal organ. (F) Foreleg of *Tettigonia* showing slitlike openings of tympanal sacs.

both types are present. The visual sense cells are derived from the epidermis, as are those of other sense organs, and are connected to the optic ganglia (a part of the brain) by sensory axons. Each visual sense cell has a zone at its surface, which, on exposure to light, gives rise to chemical products that stimulate the sense cell, called the retinula cell, and initiate the nerve impulse in the sensory axon. The light-receptive zone, or rhabdom, of the retinula cell commonly has a rodlike form; because it lies perpendicular to the surface, light passes lengthwise along it. In the simple eyes (ocelli) a lens-shaped area of cuticle lies over the group of retinula cells that form the retina. Since the optical structure is primitive, the visual image received is crude; ocelli can perceive only light, darkness, and movement.

The compound eye

The compound eye, made up of a number of facets, resembles a honeycomb; each facet overlies a group of six or seven retinal cells that surround the rhabdom. Each of the retinal units below a single facet is termed an ommatidium. The number of facets varies. For example, there are only a few dozen facets in the eye of the primitive apterygote *Collembola,* while the eye of the housefly *Musca* has some 4,000, and the highly developed eye of the dragonfly may contain up to 28,000.

During light reception, rays from a small area of the field of view fall on a single facet and are concentrated upon the rhabdom of the retinula cells below. Since each point of light differs in brightness, all the ommatidia that form the retina receive a crude mosaic of the field of view. Unlike the image in a camera or in human eyes, the mosaic image in the compound eye is not inverted but erect. The fineness of the mosaic and, therefore, the degree of resolution improves with increasing numbers of facets. It is estimated that the eye of the honeybee has visual acuity equal to 1 percent that in man.

Each ommatidium commonly is shielded by a curtain of pigmented cells that prevent the spread of light to neighbouring ommatidia. This is termed an apposition eye. In the eyes of insects that fly at night or in twilight, however, the pigment can be withdrawn so that light received from neighbouring facets overlaps to some extent. This is termed a superposition eye. The image formed is brighter but not as sharp as that formed by the apposition eye. In addition to perceiving brightness, the eyes of insects can perceive colour as well as some other properties of light.

V. Evolution and paleontology

ORIGIN OF INSECTS

The most primitive insects known are found as fossils in rocks of the Middle Devonian Period and lived about 350,000,000 years ago. The bodies of those insects were divided then, as now, into a head bearing one pair of antennae, a thorax with three pairs of legs, and a segmented abdomen. Those insects originated with the terrestrial branch of the phylum Arthropoda. The Arthropoda, whose origin is thus far unknown, probably arose in Precambrian times, perhaps as much as 1,000,000,000 years ago. Some arthropods colonized the open sea and have become the present-day class Crustacea (crabs, shrimps) and the now-extinct Trilobita. Other arthropods colonized the land. This terrestrial line persists chiefly as the classes Onychophora, Arachnida (spiders, scorpions, ticks), the myriapods (consisting of Diplopoda [millipedes], Pauropoda, Symphyla, and Chilopoda, or centipedes), and finally the class Insecta.

Apterygotes

The most primitive insects today are found among the wingless (apterous) hexapods; sometimes known collectively as apterygotes, they include proturans, thysanurans, diplurans, and collembolans. It is agreed generally that insects are related most closely to the myriapod group, among which the Symphyla exhibit most of the essential features required for the ancestral insect form (*i.e.,* a Y-shaped epicranial suture, two pairs of maxillae, a single pair of antennae, styli and sacs on the abdominal segments, cerci, and malpighian tubules). There is, therefore, general agreement that the insects probably arose from an early symphylan-like form.

INSECT FOSSIL RECORD

The insect fossil record has many gaps. Among the primitive apterygotes, only the collembolans (springtails) have been found as fossils in the Devonian Period. Ten insect orders are known as fossils, mostly of Late Carboniferous and Permian times. No fossils have yet been found from the Late Devonian or Early Carboniferous periods, when the key characters of present-day insects are believed to have evolved; thus, early evolution must be inferred from the morphology of extant insects.

It has become evident that insect evolution, like that of other animals, was far more active at some periods than at others. There have been geological epochs of "explosive" evolution during which many new forms have appeared. Those epochs may have followed some modification or innovation in body function, or new developments favoured by climatic changes or evolutionary advances of other animals and plants. During those periods of evolutionary change, new methods of feeding and living led to diversity of insect mouthparts and limbs, the origin of metamorphosis, and other changes.

INSECT PHYLOGENY

Figure 11 is a simplified family tree of the presumed evolutionary history of winged insects (Pterygota) throughout the geological periods from the Devonian to the Recent. The apterygotes, which are regarded as survivors of primitive insect stock, are omitted from the family tree. Dark lines indicate the periods during which the various orders have been found as fossils. Some lines stop at the names of orders now extinct and known only as fossils. Light lines indicate the hypothetical origin of various orders. Many insect types, traces of which have not yet been discovered, must have been produced during the explosive periods of evolution in Carboniferous and Permian times.

The primitive wingless insects (Figure 11) gave rise to a

From J. Smart, "Explosive Evolution and the Phylogeny of Insects," *Proceedings of the Linnean Society of London* (1963)

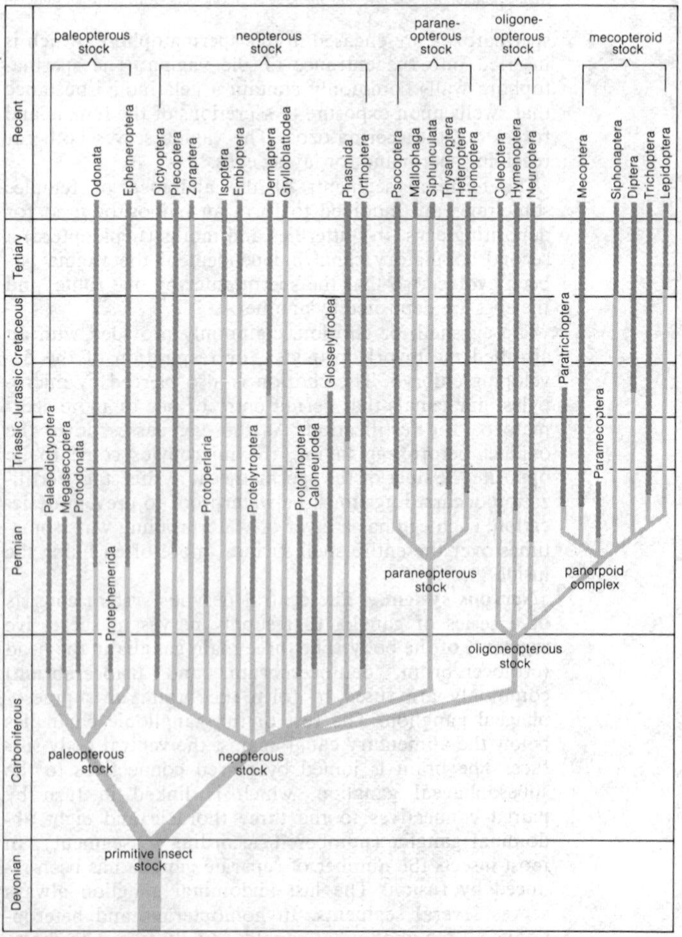

Figure 11: Phylogenetic relationships of insects.

paleopterous stock. Descendants of this stock included ancient fossil types that flourished in Permian times, such as the giant dragonflies or Protodonata (some of which had a wing span of more than half a metre) and dragonflies and damselflies (Odonata) and mayflies (Ephemeroptera), both of which have persisted with little change to the present. The primitive insect stock also gave rise to a neopterous stock, believed to include the progenitors of the remaining insect orders. The Orthoptera (grasshoppers) and the Plecoptera (stoneflies) have been found as fossils even in late Carboniferous times. The Isoptera (termites), Embioptera (webspinners), and Dermaptera (earwigs), though doubtless of ancient origin, have not been found yet as fossils dated earlier than the Mesozoic Era.

The evolutionary radiation (Figure 11), believed to have given rise to the orders listed above in the Middle Carboniferous Period, is thought to have produced also a paraneopterous stock, which formed the base for a new evolutionary radiation during the Permian Period. Present-day derivatives of this stock evolved into the Psocoptera (psocids), Mallophaga (chewing lice), Anoplura or Siphunculata (sucking lice), Thysanoptera (thrips), Heteroptera (true bugs), and Homoptera (*e.g.*, aphids).

Several phylogenetic lines (Figure 11) are exopterygote (*i.e.*, insects with simple metamorphosis) some of which, such as Mallophaga and Anoplura, are secondarily wingless. The remaining orders are endopterygote (insects with complete metamorphosis). They are shown in Figure 11 as derivatives of an oligoneopterous stock, which gave rise to Neuroptera (lacewings), Hymenoptera (ants, wasps, and bees), and Coleoptera (beetles) in the Early Permian Period; the early ancestry of these orders is obscure, however, and the earliest fossils closely resemble present-day forms. One line from the evolutionary radiation (Figure 11) at the beginning of the Permian gave rise to a mecopteroid stock, and there is good evidence that a sub-radiation of these mecopteroid orders (sometimes called the panorpoid complex) provided the origin for the present Mecoptera (scorpionflies), Diptera (true flies), Siphonaptera (fleas), Trichoptera (caddisflies), and Lepidoptera (butterflies and moths; see FOSSIL RECORD; GEOLOGICAL TIME SCALE).

EVOLUTION

Wings and flight. Insect wings develop as paired outgrowths from the thorax, stiffened by ribs, or veins, in which run tracheae. These tracheae follow a consistent pattern throughout the Pterygota, and their specific modifications (known as venation) are important in classification and in estimations of the degree of relationship between groups. The basic consistency of venation suggests that wings have been evolved only once among the insects, that is, all the Pterygota (as shown in Figure 11) arose from a single stem. By the time (toward the end of the Carboniferous) fossil insects are found, wings are developed fully. In the Paleoptera (Figure 11) the wings are held aloft above the back, as in mayflies, or held extended permanently on each side of the body, as in dragonflies. Throughout the Neoptera there is a wing-flexing mechanism (secondarily lost in butterflies) that enables the wings to be folded back to rest on the surface of the abdomen.

First appearance of winged insects

Winged insects must have made their appearance very early in the Carboniferous, more than 300,000,000 years ago; but there is no fossil evidence to show the way they evolved. One hypothesis is that wings arose as fixed planes extending sideways from the thorax and that these planes were used, perhaps in some large leaping insect, for gliding. Later muscles developed, first to control inclination and then to move the wings in flapping flight. Another hypothesis is that wings may have originated from large thoracic tracheal gills, similar to the movable tracheal gills along the abdomen of some mayfly larvae. Such outgrowths could have been useful to insects exposed by the drying up of a temporary aquatic habitat and might have carried them in rain-bearing winds to a new watery home. It is likely that the most primitive symphylan-like insects were terrestrial; throughout insect evolution, however, independent adaptations to aquatic habitats have occurred. Usually the pattern is one in which the adults leave the water and disperse. Many pterygote insects have become secondarily wingless, sometimes as single species or groups of species within large orders, sometimes as entire orders (the parasitic lice, Mallophaga and Anoplura, and the fleas, Siphonaptera).

Metamorphosis. It generally is agreed that insect metamorphosis evolved as adult insects gradually adopted different modes of life from those of larvae. The characters of larva and adult became genetically independent; in response to natural selection, therefore, each was able to evolve independently of the other. Mouthparts, limbs, and other morphological features were modified in different directions and in higher groups. Where these differences were extreme, an intermediate pupal stage evolved to bridge the morphological gap between larva and adult. It seems quite probable that the development of metamorphosis occurred more than once during the evolution of insects.

Feeding methods. Insects did not evolve in a constant environment. Throughout geological time there were prodigious changes in climate; in addition, evolution was continuous among all other animals and plants. Geologically the selection pressures among insects were changing continuously. At the end of the Mesozoic Era the first flowering plants appeared. Insect evolution has paralleled that of the flowering plants; they have evolved together. As Lepidoptera (butterflies and moths), Hymenoptera (ants, bees, and wasps), Diptera (true flies), and Coleoptera (beetles) began to feed upon flowers, nectar, or pollen, flowering plants came to rely more and more upon insects—rather than upon the wind—for transferring their pollen. Flowers evolved nectaries, scents, and conspicuous colours as attractants for those insects that could effect cross-pollination. Insects likewise evolved appropriate mouthpart modifications for extracting nectar from flowers.

Parallel evolution with flowering plants

During the Mesozoic warm-blooded animals (mammals and birds) first appeared; by the dawn of the Tertiary Period, they had become predominant among the earth's large animals. The warm fermenting excrement and the decaying dead bodies of mammals furnished excellent nutrient media for many insect larvae, notably among the Diptera and Coleoptera. The adults in both groups found their nourishment in flowers. Some heteropterans (true bugs) and dipterans pierce the skin of birds and mammals and feed on their blood. The Anoplura (sucking lice) and the Siphonaptera (fleas) have become so specialized for this type of parasitic existence that their relationships to other insects are not yet known with certainty.

Continuing evolution. Evolution is occurring among present-day insects. They exhibit a balanced genetic polymorphism; in other words, in response to small environmental changes, one genetic form, more successful than another, will become more plentiful. Sometimes there is no visible difference between these forms, the advantage presumably lying in some physiological change. It is advantageous for a species to have a gene pool from which favourable characters can be selected so that the species can respond to environmental changes. Changes within a species may occur progressively over a large geographical area. Such a progressive genetic change is termed a cline; in some cases insects at the extremes of the cline are so unlike that they are taken as separate species and may be infertile when crossed.

One well-known example of evolution in action among insects is industrial melanism (accumulation of the black pigment melanin); many butterflies inhabiting industrial areas have become almost black during the past century; black forms are more tolerant of pollution and less conspicuous to predators. Another example of this cline type of evolution is the development of insect strains resistant to an insecticide that has been applied heavily in an area for several years. In many parts of the world houseflies have become highly resistant to DDT.

VI. Classification

DISTINGUISHING TAXONOMIC FEATURES

The class Insecta is divided into orders on the basis of the structure of the head, including eyes, mouthparts, and antennae; the thorax, including legs and wings; and the abdomen, including segmentation, spiracles, and appendages (cerci, styli, furcula). The genitalia and their accessory structures, usually located in the ninth abdominal segment, are important in classification. Other taxonomic criteria include bristles (their form and arrangement are known as chaetotaxy), sensory receptors (spines, hairs, sensilla, tympanal organs), pattern of wing venation, and position of mouthparts. In addition, type of metamorphosis and form of larva and pupa are used to distinguish insects.

ANNOTATED CLASSIFICATION

CLASS INSECTA

Body divided into head, thorax, and abdomen; head with 1 pair of antennae, mouthparts consisting of a pair of mandibles and 2 pairs of maxillae, the 2nd pair fused medially; thorax with 3 pairs of legs and usually 1 or 2 pairs of wings; segmented abdomen lacks walking appendages; genital opening near anus; metamorphosis usually occurs; about 1,000,000 species named; worldwide distribution.

Subclass Apterygota

Primitively wingless; metamorphosis slight or absent (ametabola); adult with 1 or more pairs of pregenital appendages; adult mandibles articulate with head capsule at a single point.

Order Protura. Minute in size; mouthparts entognathous (withdrawn in head capsule) and piercing; no antennae or compound eyes; abdomen with 11 segments, well-developed telson (last abdominal segment); tracheal system present or absent; malpighian tubules reduced to papillae; metamorphosis slight (see APTERYGOTE).

Order Thysanura (bristletails). Mouthparts ectognathous (exposed) adapted for biting; antennae many-segmented, only basal segment with muscles; compound eyes present or absent; tarsi of legs with 2 to 4 segments; 11-segmented abdomen ends in segmented median filament plus a variable number of lateral, styliform, pregenital appendages and a pair of many-segmented cerci; tracheal system and malpighian tubules present; metamorphosis slight or absent (see APTERYGOTE).

Order Diplura (or Entotrophi). Mouthparts entognathous; antennae with many segments, all with muscles; compound eyes and ocelli absent; tarsi of legs with one segment; abdomen without terminal median filament and with lateral styliform appendages on most pregenital segments, ends in paired cerci; tracheal system present; malpighian tubules absent or vestigial (see APTERYGOTE).

Order Collembola (springtails). Mouthparts entognathous, adapted for biting; antennae with 4 segments, the first 3 with muscles; compound eyes absent; abdomen 6-segmented, usually with a ventral tube on segment I, a retinaculum on segment III, and a forked springing organ (furcula) on segment IV; tracheal system usually absent; no malpighian tubules; metamorphosis absent (see APTERYGOTE).

Subclass Pterygota

Winged or secondarily wingless; metamorphosis; adults without pregenital abdominal appendages; adult mandibles (unless greatly modified) articulating with head capsule at 2 points.

Division Exopterygota (hemimetabola)

Metamorphosis simple, sometimes slight; pupal instar rarely present; wings develop externally; immature stages commonly resemble adults in structure and habits.

Order Ephemeroptera (mayflies). Soft-bodies with short setaceous (bristle-like) antennae and vestigial mouthparts; wings held vertically at rest, hind pair much reduced; intercalary veins and many crossveins present; abdomen with long cerci, and with or without a medial caudal filament; larvae (nymphs) aquatic, campodeiform (elongated and flattened) with tracheal gills of varied form; true adult preceded by a subimago (winged instar) (see EPHEMEROPTERA).

Order Odonata (dragonflies). Predaceous insects with biting mouthparts; 2 pairs of elongate membranous wings, each with a complex network of small crossveins and a conspicuous stigma; compound eyes very large and prominent; antennae short and filiform (threadlike); abdomen elongated and slender with male accessory armature on 2nd and 3rd ventral segments; larvae (nymphs) aquatic, with labium modified to form a prehensile organ for catching prey; breathing by rectal or caudal gills (see ODONATA).

Order Plecoptera (stoneflies). Soft-bodied insects, some large with long, bristle-like antennae; mouthparts of biting type, but weak; wings membranous, folded back over the abdomen in repose; tarsi of legs with 3 segments; abdomen usually bears a pair of long, jointed cerci; young (nymphs) aquatic, campodeiform, usually with long antennae, cerci, and tracheal gills of varied type.

Order Dictyoptera (cockroaches, mantids). 2 pairs of wings; thickened forewings called tegmina; hindwings folded longitudinally fanwise; hindlegs similar to middle ones, adapted for running; tarsi of legs 5-segmented; mandibulate mouthparts, adapted for chewing (see ORTHOPTERAN).

Order Grylloblattodea (grylloblattids). Wingless; eyes small or absent; female ovipositor well developed; all legs similar, adapted for running; tarsi of legs 5-segmented; mandibulate mouthparts, adapted for chewing (see ORTHOPTERAN).

Order Phasmida (stick and leaf insects). Often wingless; when winged, tegmina often shorter than wings; all legs similar, adapted for walking; mandibulate mouthparts; no tympanum; female ovipositor short, often concealed (see ORTHOPTERAN).

Order Orthoptera (grasshoppers, crickets). 2 pairs of wings (forewings called tegmina); femur of hindleg enlarged for jumping; tarsi of legs usually with 3 or 4 segments; special auditory and stridulatory (sound-producing) organs often present; mandibulate mouthparts, adapted for chewing (see ORTHOPTERAN).

Order Dermaptera (earwigs). Elongated insects with chewing mouthparts; forewings reduced to very short leathery tegmina devoid of veins; hindwings semicircular with radially disposed veins, folded fanwise and then transversely; many species wingless; cerci unjointed and modified to form heavily sclerotized forceps.

Order Embioptera (webspinners). Gregarious insects inhabiting silken funnels; chewing mouthparts; both pairs of wings similar, with the radial vein (R) greatly thickened, other veins often reduced; short 2-segmented cerci; female wingless, larva-like.

Order Isoptera (termites or white ants). Social insects polymorphic in form (*i.e.*, live in large communities consisting of reproductive forms, wingless sterile soldiers, and young stages, or workers); biting mouthparts; wings alike, elongated, membranous, capable of being shed by basal fractures; anterior wing veins strongly sclerotized; fine network between other veins; cerci short; genitalia rudimentary in both sexes; show affinities with cockroaches (see ISOPTERA).

Order Psocoptera (booklice or psocids). Small or minute insects with long filiform antennae, delicate membranous wings (though many are wingless), head with Y-shaped epicranial suture, enlarged post-clypeus (sclerite on the face); maxilla with a rodlike lacinia (inner lobe) partly sunk into head capsule; labial palps much reduced; cerci absent.

Order Zoraptera. Minute winged or wingless insects with 9-segmented moniliform (beadlike) antennae; Y-shaped epicranial suture; normal maxillae and labial palps; wings with simplified venation, capable of being shed at basal fracture lines; cerci short, with single segment.

Order Mallophaga (chewing lice). Wingless ectoparasites, chiefly on birds; eyes reduced, no ocelli, antennae with 3 to 5 segments; mouthparts modified for biting; prothorax distinct and free; mesothorax and metathorax often partly fused; thoracic spiracles ventral; cerci absent (see PHTHIRAPTERA).

Order Anoplura or Siphunculata (sucking lice). Wingless ectoparasites of mammals; eyes reduced or absent; antennae with 3 to 5 segments; mouthparts, highly modified for piercing and sucking, retracted into head when not in use; thoracic segments fused; thoracic spiracles dorsal; cerci absent (see PHTHIRAPTERA).

Order Thysanoptera (thrips). Minute slender-bodied; short antennae, piercing mouthparts; wings, when present, very narrow with much reduced venation and long marginal setae; cerci absent, metamorphosis includes 1 or 2 inactive pupal instars (see THYSANOPTERA).

Order Homoptera (cicadas, hoppers, whiteflies, aphids, scale insects). Plant feeders; mouthparts adapted for sucking; beak arises from back of head; wings, when present, usually number four; front wings with uniform structure, either membranous or slightly thickened; wings at rest usually held rooflike over body; male scale insects with only 1 pair of wings;

ocelli present or absent; compound eyes usually well developed (see HOMOPTERA).

Order Heteroptera or Hemiptera (true bugs). Mouthparts adapted for piercing-sucking, with slender segmented beak arising from front of head; basal portion of front wing (called a hemelytron) thickened and leathery, with tip membranous; hindwings entirely membranous; wings at rest held flat over abdomen with membranous tips of front wings overlapping; ocelli present or absent; compound eyes usually well developed (see HETEROPTERA).

Division Endopterygota (holometabola)

Metamorphosis complex, accompanied by a pupal instar; immature stages differ from adult in structure and habits; wings develop internally during larval stages.

Order Megaloptera (alderflies, dobsonflies). Head prognathous (mouthparts located anteriorly on a horizontal head); biting mouthparts; filiform antennae; 2 pairs of large similar wings, at rest held rooflike or nearly flat over abdomen; larvae elongated, with biting mandibles (see NEUROPTERAN).

Order Raphidiodea (snakeflies). Head prognathous, elongated; biting mouthparts; filiform antennae; prothorax elongated, cylindrical; 2 pairs of similar elongated wings, at rest held rooflike over abdomen; larvae elongated, flattened, with biting mandibles (see NEUROPTERAN).

Order Neuroptera (lacewings). Head hypognathous (mouthparts located ventrally on a vertical head); antennae varied; 2 pairs of similar wings, at rest held rooflike over abdomen; larvae elongated or broad, with piercing, sucking jaws (see NEUROPTERAN).

Order Mecoptera (scorpionflies). Slender carnivorous insects with elongated filiform antennae, head usually a downward directed rostrum, with biting mouthparts; legs long, slender; wings similar, membranous, carried longitudinally and horizontally in repose; abdomen elongated with short cerci; male genitalia prominent (recalling a scorpion's stinger); larva eruciform (caterpillar-like) with biting mouthparts, sometimes with abdominal feet as well as 3 pairs of thoracic legs; pupae exarate (appendages free).

Order Trichoptera (caddisflies). Small to moderate mothlike insects with bristle-like antennae; mandibles vestigial or absent; wings membranous, hairy, at rest held rooflike over the back; larvae aquatic, more or less eruciform, usually living in cases held by means of hooked caudal appendages; pupae exarate with strong mandibles (see TRICHOPTERA).

Order Lepidoptera (butterflies, moths). 2 pairs of membranous wings, few crossveins; wings, body, and appendages covered with broad scales; mandibles normally vestigial or absent; maxillae forming coiled sucking proboscis; larvae eruciform, with spiracles on most segments, often with 5 pairs of prolegs on the abdomen in addition to the 3 pairs of thoracic true legs; pupae usually obtect (appendages glued to body) (see LEPIDOPTERA).

Order Coleoptera (beetles). Minute to large in size; modified forewings are horny or leathery (elytra), usually meet to form a straight middorsal suture; hindwings membranous, folded below elytra, often vestigial or absent; mouthparts adapted for chewing; prothorax large and mobile, mesothorax much reduced; larvae varied (campodeiform and eruciform), pupae exarate, without articulated mandibles (see COLEOPTERA).

Order Hymenoptera (ants, bees, wasps, sawflies). 2 pairs of membranous wings, venation often much reduced; hindwings smaller and connected to forewings by a row of hooklets; mouthparts primarily of biting type but often adapted for sucking fluids; abdomen usually constricted at the base (except sawflies) with first segment fused to metathorax; ovipositor always present and modified for sawing, piercing or stinging; larvae usually legless with distinct head, in sawflies eruciform with locomotory appendages; pupae exarate, usually in a cocoon (see HYMENOPTERA).

Order Diptera (true flies). 1 pair of membranous wings; hindwings modified to form halteres; sucking mouthparts, usually forming a proboscis, sometimes adapted for piercing; mandibles rarely present; labium usually expanded distally to give a pair of fleshy lobes; prothorax and metathorax small and fused, large mesothorax; larvae eruciform and legless, often with head reduced and retracted; tracheal system varied; pupae either free and exarate or enclosed in the hardened larval cuticle (puparium) (see DIPTERA).

Order Siphonaptera (fleas). Small, wingless, laterally compressed; adults ectoparasitic on warm-blooded animals; compound eyes absent; usually a pair of ocelli; short antennae in grooves on head; mouthparts modified for piercing and sucking; both maxillary and labial palpi present; thoracic segments free; coxae of legs very large; larvae slender, eruciform and legless; pupae exarate, enclosed in cocoon (see SIPHONAPTERA).

CRITICAL APPRAISAL

The classification into orders presented above is acceptable to most entomologists. Although the apterygotes are classified here as four unrelated orders of the subclass Apterygota, three of these groups (proturans, collembolans, diplurans) are considered by some entomologists as three separate classes equivalent to the class Insecta. In such a classification the subclass Apterygota includes only the thysanurans and their relatives. For this alternative classification, see APTERYGOTE.

The order Orthoptera infrequently includes, in addition to the grasshoppers and crickets, three other closely related groups (classified above as distinct orders): dictyopterans (cockroaches and mantids), grylloblattids, and phasmids (stick and leaf insects). The term orthopteran often is used as a common name for these four groups. For an expanded classification of orthopterans as four distinct orders, see ORTHOPTERAN.

The Mallophaga (chewing lice) and Anoplura (sucking lice), classified here as orders, sometimes are grouped as suborders of an order Phthiraptera, a group of obligate permanent ectoparasites of birds and mammals. For this alternative classification, see PHTHIRAPTERA.

The homopterans and heteropterans, here classified as separate orders, sometimes are considered as suborders of an order Hemiptera. Both groups have piercing-sucking mouthparts; for this reason they are believed to be related closely to each other. Some entomologists, however, consider distinguishing features other than the mouthparts sufficiently important to accord full ordinal status to each group. For further discussions of the taxonomic problems involved in classifying Homoptera and Heteroptera, see HOMOPTERA; HETEROPTERA.

The term neuropteran frequently is used to describe three closely related groups, classified here as three distinct orders: Neuroptera (lacewings), Raphidiodea (snakeflies), and Megaloptera (dobsonflies and alderflies). Although the tendency has been to classify these groups as distinct orders, they sometimes are placed in the order Neuroptera. For a more detailed classification of the neuropterans as three orders, see NEUROPTERAN.

Among the lepidopterans, members of the family Micropterigidae are more primitive than existing trichopterans (caddisflies). Although some entomologists treat them as a distinct order (Zeugloptera), see LEPIDOPTERA for a scheme that places them in the order Lepidoptera.

The aberrant parasitic *Stylops* and its allies have been treated as the order Strepsiptera. The tendency now, however, is to include them in the order Coleoptera (see COLEOPTERA).

BIBLIOGRAPHY

General and classification: A.D. IMMS, *A General Text-Book of Entomology*, 9th ed. entirely rev. by O.W. RICHARDS and R.G. DAVIES (1957); V.B. WIGGLESWORTH, *The Life of Insects* (1964); C.T. BRUES, A.L. MELANDER, and F.M. CARPENTER, *Classification of Insects*, 2nd rev. ed. (1954).

Insect form: R.E. SNODGRASS, *Principles of Insect Morphology* (1935); J.S. KENNEDY (ed.), *Insect Polymorphism* (1963).

Insect physiology and biochemistry: M. ROCKSTEIN (ed.), *The Physiology of Insecta*, 3 vol. (1964–65); V.B. WIGGLESWORTH, *The Physiology of Insect Metamorphosis* (1954), *The Principles of Insect Physiology*, 6th ed. rev. (1965), *Insect Hormones* (1970); V.G. DETHIER, *The Physiology of Insect Senses* (1963); D. GILMOUR, *The Biochemistry of Insects* (1961); V.J.A. NOVAK, *Insect Hormones: The Physiology, Morphology, and Phylogeny of the Insect Endocrines* (1966).

Insect behaviour and communications: C.G. JOHNSON, *Migration and Dispersal of Insects by Flight* (1969); C.T. BRUES, *Insect Dietary: An Account of the Food Habits of Insects* (1946); J.W.S. PRINGLE, *Insect Flight* (1957); P.T. HASKELL, *Insect Sounds* (1961).

Economic and ecological importance: C.L. METCALF and W.P. FLINT, *Destructive and Useful Insects: Their Habits and Control*, 4th ed. (1962); J.R. BUSVINE, *Insects and Hygiene:*

The Biology and Control of Insect Pests of Medical and Domestic Importance, 2nd ed. (1966); R.M. GORDON and M.M.J. LAVOIPIERRE, *Entomology for Students of Medicine* (1961); T.R.E. SOUTHWOOD, *Ecological Methods: With Particular Reference to the Study of Insect Populations* (1966).

(V.B.W.)

Insectivora

The mammal order Insectivora includes the shrews, moles, hedgehogs, and several lesser known groups. Of about 400 species in the order, nearly 300 are shrews of the family Soricidae. All insectivores are small, as mammals go, the largest being about the size of a small rabbit. Shrews are probably the smallest of all mammals; some species of *Sorex* and *Crocidura* weigh as little as 2.5 grams. The general body plan (Figure 1) varies greatly within the order. Many shrews are superficially mouselike but may be distinguished from mice and other rodents by the absence of chisel-like incisor teeth. Typical moles (Talpidae) and golden moles (Chrysochloridae) are cylindrical, burrowing animals with short, thick limbs and reduced tails and eyes. Hedgehogs (Erinaceidae) and some hedgehog-like tenrecs (Tenrecidae) are stocky animals whose upper surfaces are covered with short spines. Elephant shrews (Macroscelididae) are rather delicate animals, with long hindlegs like those of kangaroo rats or jerboas. Within the larger families the body plan is quite variable. Most insectivores live at or near ground level, except for the squirrel-like tree shrews and several aquatic moles, shrews, and tenrecs.

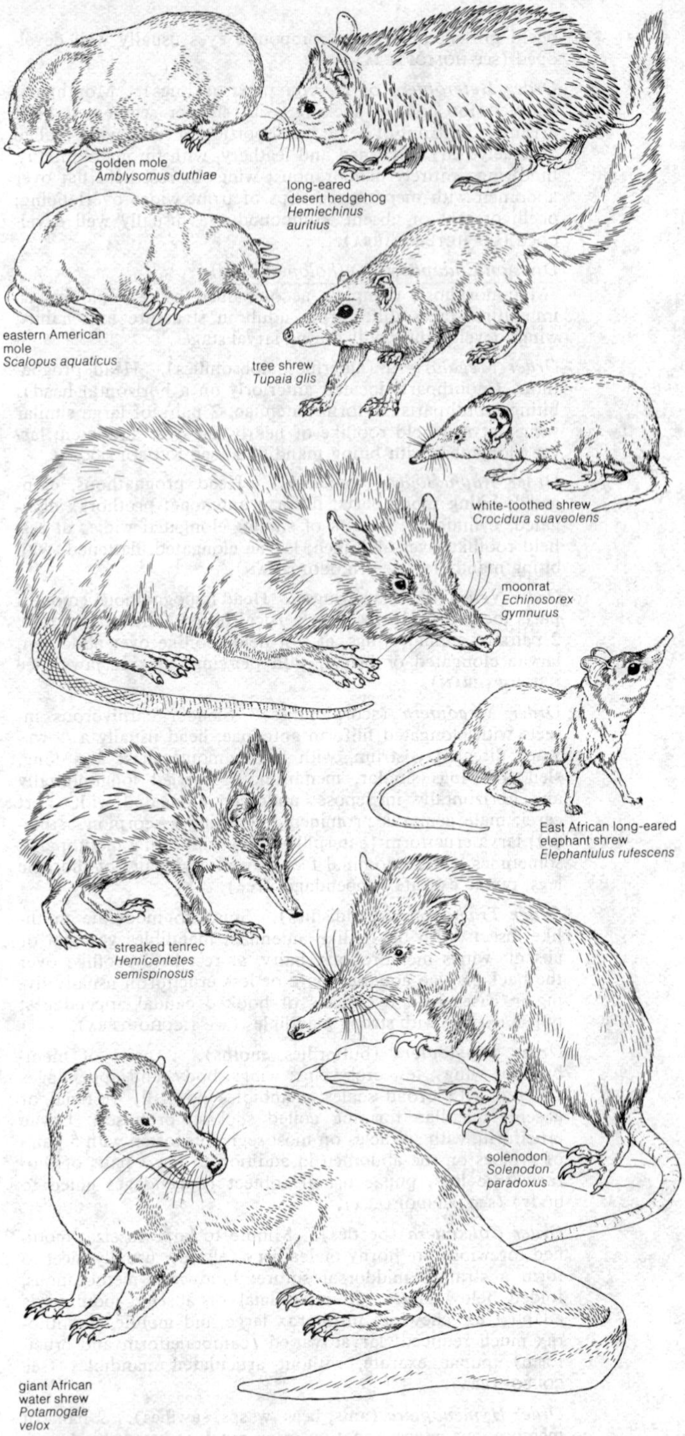

Figure 1: Representative insectivores.

Drawing by R. Keane based on photos courtesy of (golden mole) Herbert Lang through J. Meester, (eastern American mole) *U.S. Fish and Wildlife Service*, (white-toothed shrew) Liselotte Dorfmuller, (streaked tenrec) Howard E. Uible, (solenodon) New York Zoological Society; from (long-eared desert hedgehog, tree shrew, East African long-eared elephant shrew) E.P. Walker, *Mammals of the World*, (giant African water shrew) Grzimeks Tierleben, *Enzyklopadie des Tierreiches*; Kindler Verlag Zurich

Importance to man. Small and secretive, most insectivores are rarely seen by man and are of almost no economic importance. The velvety fur has poor durability, but mole skins have occasionally been used for trimming various garments and for complete coats.

The burrows of moles in lawns may cause the collapse of the turf, and those in fields and gardens provide small rodents with access to plant roots. Indirectly, the more abundant insectivores are ecologically important as consumers of invertebrates and occasionally of small vertebrates and as prey for larger animals. None is an important disease carrier, although elephant shrews harbor malaria, and some soricid shrews may carry plague.

Role of shrews in mythology

A few insectivores are the subjects of aboriginal myths. Some Eskimos believe that the red-toothed shrews (*Sorex*) will attack a man and kill him by burrowing through his body to the heart. The hero shrew (*Scutisorex congicus*), whose backbone of fused and arched vertebrae protects it from crushing, is venerated by central African natives, who believe that consumption of its heart will confer the animal's strength upon the eater.

Distribution. Insectivores are widely distributed but are not found in Antarctica, the Australian region, and South America (except for extreme northern regions). Various marsupials found in Australia are ecologically equivalent to certain insectivores, including a marsupial mole. Why insectivores are absent from South America has not yet been satisfactorily explained.

NATURAL HISTORY

Life cycle. *Reproduction.* Temperate zone insectivores, such as shrews, moles, and hedgehogs, have cyclic reproductive periods. Males develop enlarged testes in late winter or early spring that begin to produce sperm. At the same season females develop enlarged ovarian follicles in preparation for ovulation (release of eggs). Because female hedgehogs may undergo several periods of heat during which copulation does not result in pregnancy, it seems likely that ovulation occurs at a specific time, regardless of other reproductive activities. In shrews and moles, by contrast, every mating results in pregnancy; it has thus been supposed that ovulation in these animals is induced by copulation. An inverse relationship seems to exist between gametogenesis (the production of eggs or sperm) and the development of certain cells in the ovaries and testes. Female moles also exhibit a vaginal cycle, in which the vagina opens to the exterior only during the season of heat, pregnancy, and lactation. The majority of tropical insectivores appear to breed throughout the year; presumably, sperm production is continuous, and ovulation can occur at any appropriate time. Some evidence indicates that, in tropical areas with wet and dry seasons, the majority of births take place with the approach of the rainy season and the accompanying increase in the abundance of invertebrates. In West Malaysia, for example, 41 percent of the recorded pregnancies of one species of white-toothed, or musk, shrew (*Suncus*) occur from October through December, and the peak of the monsoons occurs in January; 19 percent of the pregnancies occur from April through June, before the height of the dry season in July. South African golden moles breed during rainy seasons. Some tenrecs become dormant during the Madagascan dry season, so it is likely that their reproductive period is also related to approaching rains.

Courtship and mating have seldom been observed among insectivores. Males and females of most species remain together for a brief period during which mating takes place. Among tenrecs the male may bite the female's neck; copulation then takes place, with the male mounting the female from behind in all known cases. Shrews may remain locked together for up to five minutes after the male dismounts, while the female drags the male after her. The ejaculate of the male short-tailed shrew (*Blarina brevicauda*) includes a waxy plug that blocks the vaginal orifice, preventing the loss of semen.

Gestation periods

The length of the gestation period varies from two or three weeks in shrews to 50 to 60 days in elephant shrews and tree shrews. In part, the length depends upon the condition of the young at birth; shrews and moles, for example, with a gestation of three or four weeks, have naked, blind, and helpless young. Hedgehogs, with a slightly longer period, have young that, although essentially helpless, do have partially developed spines. Tenrecs may have a 50-day gestation; the young have spines and rather quickly develop neuromuscular integration sufficient to enable them at about four days of age to walk and to exhibit at five days the stereotyped tenrec "bucking" defensive behaviour pattern (see below). Newly born elephant shrews have fur, open eyes and ears, and the ability to follow the parent. That a long gestation does not necessarily produce more developed young in insectivores, however, is shown by tree shrews, which bear helpless young after a relatively long gestation period. After giving birth, females of some species, such as tree shrews and some red-toothed shrews, may immediately mate again.

The number of young produced depends in part on species, latitude, and condition of young at birth. Elephant shrews, tree shrews, otter shrews (Potamogalidae), solenodons (Solenodontidae), and golden moles have one to three young. In the hedgehog family the spiny species have one to seven young; the nonspiny tropical Asian gymnures commonly have two. Moles average two to five young, depending on the species. Shrews have more young in temperate areas than in the tropics. Average numbers recorded range from two to three in Africa; two on the island of Guam; three, four, and five in various parts of India; and seven to eight in Great Britain. Various tenrecs may hold the record for number of young among placental mammals, *Centetes* having as many as 25; the presence of more than 30 embryos has been recorded.

Maturation and longevity. Embryonic development has been studied in only a few insectivores. In most shrews, moles, hedgehogs, and tenrecs, the eyes and ears open in about a week, and the babies are weaned in three or four weeks. Tropical white-toothed shrews reach sexual maturity in about five weeks, as do elephant shrews; tenrecs attain this condition in two months, a time that may also apply to other tropical insectivores. Temperate zone shrews, moles, and hedgehogs attain reproductive maturity in the second year of life. The characteristic chain-forming behaviour of young white-toothed shrews (in which the young form a chain behind the mother, each animal gripping with its teeth the rump fur of the one ahead) may begin after the ears open but before the eyelids part, suggesting that this behaviour is organized by sound stimuli.

The average life-span of most wild insectivores, like that of most small mammals, is probably quite short. It has been estimated at six weeks for shrews. Some individuals of populations of temperate zone shrews and moles, however, must live at least one year in order to participate in reproduction. These species seemingly are programmed for a year of healthy life, but few live beyond this; they succumb from wornout teeth. Captive shrews have survived two and one half years, elephant shrews three years, and hedgehogs ten years.

Response to adverse conditions. As a normal part of their annual cycle, various insectivores have developed strategies for surviving intervals during which food is in short supply. In temperate regions this occurs in winter; in tropical areas dry seasons often are times of privation.

Dormancy in hedgehogs

Hedgehogs cope with the problem of food shortage by seeking a shelter, rolling themselves into a ball, and becoming dormant. Although the temperature of the extremities drops to that of the surrounding air, that of the heart remains at the level of an active animal; in this way energy is used slowly. In the dormant hedgehog, white blood cells concentrate in unusual numbers around the stomach and intestine, the sugar level in the blood drops by one half, and the level of magnesium in the blood rises to twice the normal value. In a normally dormant hedgehog, the Islets of Langerhans, which are tissues in the pancreas that secrete the hormone insulin, are active. Certain tenrecs are the only other insectivores definitely known to become dormant, a state they may enter during the dry season or in cool weather. The body temperature drops to that of the environment, and the respiratory rate may slacken to five or six breaths per minute. One kind of golden mole, *Chrysospalax*, has been reported to become dormant.

Another common stratagem used by many animals to survive lean times, the storage of food, is known for only a few insectivores. Some kinds of shrews store such invertebrates as snails. The European mole (*Talpa europaea*) may paralyze earthworms before burying them in groups in its mound. Energy may be stored as fat by some hedgehogs, tenrecs (*Microgale*), and star-nosed moles (*Condylura*). The last two genera use the tail as a storage organ.

A curious and unexplained aspect of the annual cycle of some temperate zone shrews involves the volume of the brain and the height of the braincase; both decrease to a minimum in midwinter, then increase again.

Behaviour. *Feeding behaviour*. All insectivores feed wholly or partly on animal matter and spend a substantial amount of time foraging. Shrews consume large quantities of invertebrates and occasionally small vertebrates. Moles eat soil invertebrates, including worms. Larger species eat larger prey; hedgehogs, for example, may consume frogs, mice, birds, lizards, and snakes and in captivity will eat bread and milk. The diet of golden moles is not well-known, although some species are known to prefer legless lizards (*Anguis*); others consume earthworms and insect pupae and larvae. Tree shrews are omnivorous, eating many insects as well as fruit; in captivity they thrive on commercial monkey food. Elephant shrews avidly eat locusts and, in captivity, thrive on bird meat. The aquatic tenrec *Limnogale* eats the tubers of the pondweed *Aponogeton*, and also takes fish. The water shrews consume aquatic animals, sometimes even small fish, and the otter shrew eats crabs, fish, and amphibians.

Many insectivores probe through leaf litter or soft soil. Solenodons proceed in this way until the long snout contacts prey; then the forepaws sweep forward and inward, gathering the object into the mouth. So stereotyped is this behaviour that even in captivity the animal captures inert food items in this way. Young solenodons follow the foraging parent and may learn the scent of acceptable food by smelling the mouth of the female. Young tenrecs may also learn to discriminate food by following their mother. Tenrecs, which often forage in groups, become excited at the scent of earthworms and begin to root enthusiastically. The sound of rooting and chewing stimulates other tenrecs in their searching activity. Shrews search through leaf litter or underground passageways of other mammals, locating prey by smell and contact. Moles do much of their hunting in their burrows, which may act as natural traps into which invertebrates fall. Golden moles emerge after rains and forage in the surface soil. Some shrews hold food items in their paws while eating and may carry food to preferred sites to eat it. Tenrecs may use the forefeet to hold down worms while they are torn in pieces.

A number of insectivores are reported to drink water, although elephant shrews probably do not do so. Tree shrews use water for drinking and bathing. Many insectivores may obtain sufficient water from their food or from dew.

Orientation and activity periods. Except for tree shrews and elephant shrews, both of which are primarily diurnal (*i.e.*, active by day), insectivores rely relatively little on vision for orientation. In most species, olfactory, tactile, and auditory cues are most important. Shrews, some tenrecs, and possibly the solenodons use a crude form of echolocation, a process by which objects are located by sound waves reflected back to the animal. Tenrecs produce clicks with the tongue at frequencies from five to seven kilohertz. Spiny tenrecs produce high frequency noises by vibrating together rows of overlapping spines on the middle of the back; the sounds produced in this way probably are used in social communication rather than orientation. Shrews and solenodons produce, probably with the larynx, clicks of ten to 31 kilohertz (in solenodons) and 25 to 60 kilohertz (in shrews). Many insectivores, when exploring strange surroundings, maintain contact with a solid surface such as a wall or a log, which is probably tested with the facial sensory hairs (vibrissae). After a territory has become familiar, many insectivores are able to traverse it by memory and may become severely disoriented if the landscape changes.

Sound production

Most insectivores are active at night, although shrews may be active throughout the 24-hour period. Most elephant shrews and tree shrews are diurnal, but at least one genus in each family is nocturnal. True moles and apparently also the little-studied golden moles are active by day or night.

Locomotion. In walking, most insectivores proceed by moving the right forefoot and left hindfoot, then left forefoot and right hindfoot forward together (crossed extension limb synchrony). Solenodons run with a quadrupedal richochetal (springing) gait, in which both forefeet and then both hindfeet strike the ground together. Other large insectivores also probably run in this way. Elephant shrews may hop bipedally, but their locomotion has not yet been studied. Tree shrews are skillful climbers but spend much of their time on the ground; some tenrecs are also partly arboreal. A few insectivores, such as otter shrews, several species of shrews and moles, and one tenrec, are partially aquatic and swim with alternate strokes of the hindfeet. The American water shrew (*Sorex palustris*) has been observed to scamper over the surface of still water, apparently being supported by the surface tension and the fringe of stiff hairs on its feet. The water tenrec (*Limnogale*) has webbed feet, as do the aquatic moles *Desmana* and *Galemys*. Some aquatic insectivores may use a laterally compressed tail in swimming, such as is found in the water shrew *Nectogale elegans*, the water moles *Desmana moschata* and *Galemys pyrenaicus*, and the otter shrew *Potamogale velox*.

Movements in water

Grooming. All insectivores spend some time in self-grooming. The universality of this behaviour suggests that it is necessary for keeping the hair in proper condition for its role in thermoregulation. Solenodons use only the hindfeet in grooming, perhaps because the forefeet are enlarged for digging, and the elongated snout hinders the use of the mouth in grooming. Shrews use the hindfeet and also the tongue. (Why the forefeet are not used by shrews is not clear.) Hedgehogs likewise do not use the front feet for cleaning. The tenrec *Echinops* uses both hindfeet and front feet. Tree shrews of the genus *Tupaia* use all four feet, but the forepaws and mouth are the dominant cleaning organs. These animals also comb the fur with the lower incisors.

Burrowing and nesting. Probably the most complex insectivore shelters are built by moles. A mole may have an underground nest chamber surrounded by concentric rings of tunnels interconnected by radiating ones. Shallow surface tunnels extend from this deeper complex and are evidenced by raised ridges, which mark their course. The mole may also throw up a large mound of earth on the surface that marks the location of its deep tunnel system. Burrows are dug by using the spadelike forefeet in a manner resembling the breaststroke of swimmers. The golden moles may use the same method, but little is known concerning their excavations. Some shrews dig tunnels, but many species use the runs of other animals. Shrews build surface nests, lined with shredded plant material, in which they rest or bear their young. Solenodons construct nest chambers during the breeding season, as do hedgehogs and tenrecs. The last two also build nests for keeping warm when the temperature drops. Elephant shrews often seek shelter among rocks and probably seldom excavate their own burrows; they may, however, occupy those abandoned by rodents. Tree shrews build nests of leaves and other vegetation, often among roots or fallen timber or in a tree cavity above the ground. When frightened, many insectivores immediately flee to a nearby burrow entrance.

Defensive behaviour. Spiny insectivores, such as hedgehogs and tenrecs, defend themselves by rolling into a ball with the spineless undersurface curled inward. Hedgehogs have a specialized muscle that is capable of pulling the spiny dorsal skin about the animal so that only a small unprotected area remains. Spiny tenrecs, when disturbed, exhibit a stereotyped defense behaviour in which the spines on the head and neck are erected, and the animal "bucks" by throwing its forequarters upward. The action would drive spines into an attacker. Solenodons and tenrecs gape and hiss at intruders, a pattern also seen in the unrelated American opossum, a marsupial. Shrews, when confronted with strangers, open the mouth and emit bursts of high-pitched cries.

Shrews and solenodons have been shown to produce saliva with poisonous properties; it probably functions in quieting large prey animals. Shrew bites may be painful to humans.

Social behaviour. The majority of insectivores are rather antisocial, except at breeding time and in the context of the female–young relationship. Adult shrews and moles tolerate other adults of their species briefly during the period of mating, following which the female and young form a group until the young are full grown; the young rarely appear alone during this interval. Young white-toothed shrews (*Crocidura*) exhibit chain formation, in which each animal grasps the rump fur of another, one grasping the mother, after whom they then trail. Baby shrews are rather indiscriminate and may attempt chain formation with such inappropriate subjects as white mice.

Solenodons have a prolonged period of juvenile dependency during which the young follow the female, perhaps learning to locate favoured foraging areas and to discriminate in food selection. Adult solenodons approach each other with open mouths, perhaps emitting high-frequency clicks. Contact involves one animal closing its mouth over the snout of the other, then pressing the snout against its own flanks and back. Several solenodons may occupy a burrow. Various tenrecs forage in large groups which probably consist of one or more females and young. Elephant and tree shrews live solitarily or in groups of two or three, consisting of a female and her young. Hedgehogs may also form temporary groups of female and young.

Juvenile behaviour

Hedgehogs and spiny tenrecs perform an unexplained "self-anointing" behaviour, which is triggered by the presence of such substances as urine or certain chemicals. The animal licks the material until a frothy spittle is produced; in some species this is then spread over the body by the tongue in typical hedgehogs (*Erinaceus*) or by the mouth and forefeet in tenrecs.

Ecology. *Predation upon insectivores.* Shrews are preyed upon by a variety of birds, mammals, and snakes, but seemingly the strong odour produced by the flank gland of shrews makes them unpalatable to some predators. Skulls of shrews are commonly found in owl pellets (regurgitated indigestible remains of prey). Little is known about the predators of elephant and tree shrews. True moles and golden moles may be safe from many predators because of their subterranean habits; spiny hedgehogs and tenrecs may, for the same reason, be relatively safe. In Madagascar some tenrecs are preyed upon by man. Solenodons seemingly suffered little predation on Cuba and Hispaniola until man introduced dogs, cats, and mongooses there. These carnivores have drastically reduced solenodon populations, probably because the solenodons had evolved no defenses against such predation.

Territoriality. Each adult shrew occupies its own territory of about 0.1 to 0.4 hectare (0.25 to one acre). About 40 percent of its behaviour involves avoiding other shrews. When shrews from adjacent territories encounter one another, they engage in mutual avoidance if possible. Avoidance is made easier by an oily odoriferous substance exuded by the flank glands, which helps to warn off other shrews of the same species. A similar kind of territoriality probably is practiced by moles. Population structure of most other insectivores has not yet been studied. Tree shrews apparently defend nest territories, and males may mark these areas by smearing onto branches the yellow exudate from throat and chest glands.

Habitats. Insectivores utilize diverse habitats. Shrews occupy the ground surface in forests and grasslands but are less common in deserts, although *Notiosorex* and *Diplomesodon* occupy New and Old World deserts, respectively. Moles are largely confined to North Temperate Zone forests and meadows, especially in areas of deciduous forests and adjacent prairies. Hedgehogs live in forests, grasslands, and deserts of the Old World. Spineless hedgehogs (Echinosoricinae) live in tropical rain forests of Asia. Golden moles occupy many habitats in southern Africa. Otter shrews live in riparian situations (*i.e.*, on the banks of natural water courses), in the Congo Basin and environs. Elephant shrews prefer African savanna areas, but some are forest dwellers. The tenrecs live in most habitats on Madagascar; some are partly arboreal. Tree shrews are largely terrestrial in tropical Asian forests, but most can climb well and are partly arboreal. Solenodons are strictly terrestrial foragers in the forests of Cuba and Hispaniola.

FORM AND FUNCTION

The order Insectivora is the most difficult of living mammalian orders to define because the groups included retain traits of primitive placental mammals and are not very specialized. Although each family has specializations, they are not such as to suggest that each group should be raised to ordinal level. Furthermore, many of the families are as old as many mammalian orders, and the evidences of common relationship are often obscured.

Skull. The skull of insectivores is typically low in that the braincase does not rise abruptly from the level of the rostrum (the bony support for the snout), which tends to be long and tapered. Seen from above, the skull is triangular in outline. The cerebral cortex of the brain is not well developed, and the olfactory bulbs are large, in conjunction with the well-developed sense of smell. In addition, the elongated rostrum supports muscles that activate a still longer, highly mobile snout with well-developed tactile capabilities that are useful in probing for food. The middle ear cavity is partly or wholly enclosed by the tympanic bone. In such forms as shrews and hedgehogs, the tympanic bone (surrounding the middle ear) is ringlike and attached to the base of the skull (basicranium) only at one point, probably the primitive situation. Other forms, such as moles and golden moles, have an expanded tympanic bone fused to the basicranium to form an auditory bulla (an enclosed chamber). The bulla of tree shrews and elephant shrews includes an entotympanic bone, a trait also seen in primates. Many insectivores have small external ear pinnae (the projecting "shells" of the ear); this is nearly or quite lacking in burrowing forms such as moles but may be rather prominent in such forms as desert hedgehogs. In shrews and tenrecs, at least, sensitivity to high-frequency sounds is well developed.

Presence of tympanic bone

Orbital fossae (eye sockets) and eyes are variably developed in insectivores, most species having relatively small eyes. In moles and golden moles, in which the eyelids are fused shut, probably only differences in light intensity can be detected. Large eyes and well-developed vision are present only in tree and elephant shrews. In

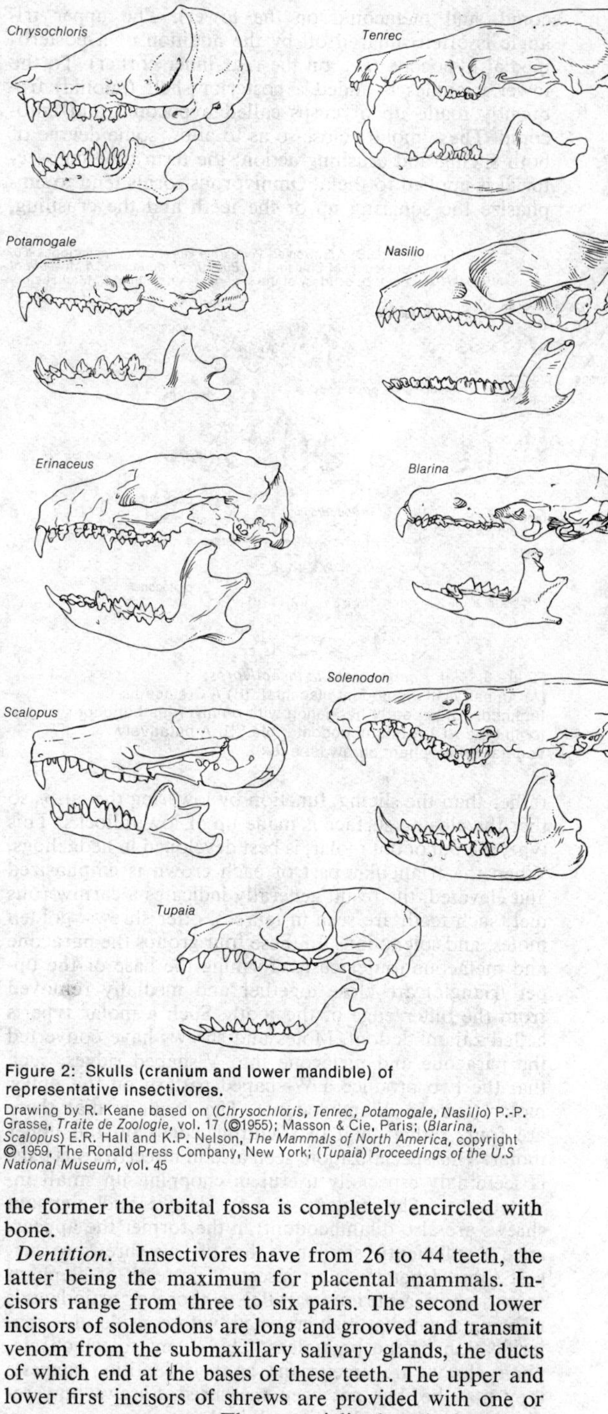

Figure 2: Skulls (cranium and lower mandible) of representative insectivores.

Drawing by R. Keane based on (*Chrysochloris, Tenrec, Potamogale, Nasilio*) P.-P. Grasse, *Traite de Zoologie*, vol. 17 (©1955); Masson & Cie, Paris; (*Blarina, Scalopus*) E.R. Hall and K.P. Nelson, *The Mammals of North America*, copyright © 1959, The Ronald Press Company, New York; (*Tupaia*) *Proceedings of the U.S National Museum*, vol. 45

the former the orbital fossa is completely encircled with bone.

Dentition. Insectivores have from 26 to 44 teeth, the latter being the maximum for placental mammals. Incisors range from three to six pairs. The second lower incisors of solenodons are long and grooved and transmit venom from the submaxillary salivary glands, the ducts of which end at the bases of these teeth. The upper and lower first incisors of shrews are provided with one or more accessory cusps. These specialized teeth close so as to provide the animal with a delicate tool for picking up small invertebrates. The incisors of tenrecs may also be provided with accessory cusps, but tenrecs lack the other dental specializations of shrews. The lower incisors of tree shrews form a comblike structure and are used for grooming the fur. The canine teeth, though present in insectivores, are usually small, rarely extending much above the level of the other teeth; they are not strong and elongated as those in carnivores (an exception is the Palearctic mole *Talpa*). The canine teeth of hedgehogs and moles have double roots, an unusual condition among mammals. Premolars range from the simple one-cusped structures seen in shrews and some moles to multicusped molariform teeth. The molariform premolar is usually the fourth or, more rarely, the third.

Insectivoran molars are of a primitive placental type. The crown supports several usually conical cusps arranged in a triangular pattern (called protocone, paracone, and metacone on the upper teeth; protoconid, paraconid, and metaconid on the lower). The upper triangle is often squared off by the addition of a posteromedial hypocone (*i.e.*, on the rear inner corner). To the lower triangles is added a posterior shelf (talonid) frequently made up of cusps called hypoconid and entoconid. These molars close so as to allow some degree of both slicing and crushing action; the term tuberculosectorial is applied to them. Omnivorous forms tend to emphasize the squaring up of the teeth and the crushing,

From (A,B,C,D) A.S. Romer, *Vertebrate Paleontology*, copyright 1966, University of Chicago; (E) *Bulletin of the American Museum of Natural History* (1942), courtesy of the American Museum of Natural History

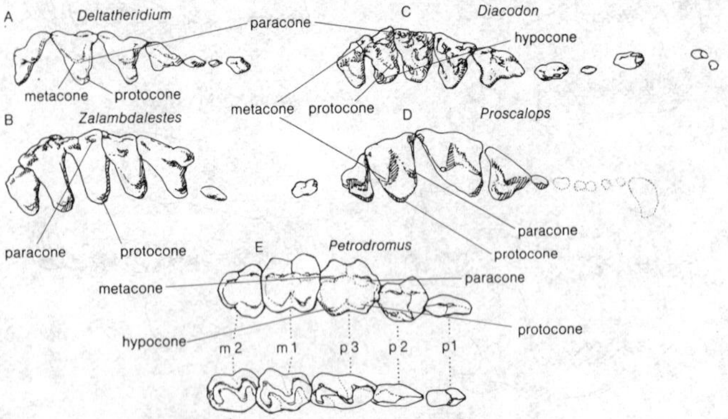

Figure 3: *Major molar types in insectivores.*
(A) An early zalambdodont placental. (B) A Cretaceous leptictid. (C) An early hedgehog with omnivorous bunodont tooth type. (D) A dilambdodont mole. (E) A putatively vegetarian elephant shrew (see text).

rather than the slicing, function by lowering the cusps so that the closing surface is made up of low hillocks. This type, the bunodont molar, is best developed in hedgehogs. When the triangular part of each crown is emphasized and elevated, the result generally indicates a carnivorous diet; such teeth are seen in tenrecs, otter shrews, golden moles, and solenodons. In these four groups the paracone and metacone (outer cusps, forming the base of the upper triangle) are close together and medially removed from the outer edge of the tooth. Such a molar type is called zalambdodont. Moles and shrews have converted the paracone and metacone into V-shaped ridges, such that the two produce a W-shaped pattern on the upper molar (termed dilambdodont). The result is that there are four, rather than two, cutting edges on the upper molar. This specialization, seen also in insectivorous bats, is seemingly especially useful in chopping up small invertebrates. The molars of tree shrews and elephant shrews are also dilambdodont; in the former the appearance is sufficiently similar to that of true shrews to suggest some dependence on insects. The teeth of elephant shrews show a curious parallel to those of artiodactyls in being somewhat high crowned, with considerable molarification of the premolars. The extent to which elephant shrews are vegetarians, as their dentition suggests they may be, has not been measured. Shrews may replace their milk teeth while still in the uterus.

Limbs. The appendicular skeleton of insectivores retains many traits seen in primitive placental mammals. All except the otter shrews retain a clavicle connecting scapula (dorsal part of pectoral girdle) to sternum (breastbone). Since absence or reduction of the clavicle usually characterizes mammals that are specialized for rapid leaping locomotion, such as artiodactyls (antelopes, pigs, and cattle) and perissodactyls (horses, rhinoceroses, and tapirs), its absence in otter shrews, which are reported to be clumsy on land, is perplexing. The humerus (upper bone of the forelimb) of insectivores retains an entepicondylar foramen (an opening in the articular surface), absent in many more specialized mammals. The radius and ulna (bones of the forearm) are separate and well developed. The manus (forefoot) is rarely specialized, usually possessing five digits and a relatively full complement of wristbones (carpals). In some forms (shrews and hedgehogs) one wristbone, the centrale, is missing or fused with an adjacent bone, as it is in most primates. Moles have broad forefeet, in which supernumerary bones are closely knit to form a rigid plane, as in the blade of a shovel. Golden moles have the hand digits reduced to four, two of which are greatly enlarged and bear huge, picklike claws. The pelvic girdle shows no peculiarities. In a few families (shrews, moles, golden moles, and otter shrews) the pubic bones do not form a symphysis (union); in others a short or long symphysis is present. The femur (thighbone) is marked by a laterally placed third trochanter (a ridge) for muscular attachment, presumably a primitive trait but one seen in a variety of other mammals. The tibia and fibula (lower bones of the hindlimb) are usually fused distally (near the ankle), but in solenodons this fusion takes place only with old age and in some tenrecs and all tree shrews not at all. Fusion reduces the lateral mobility of the foot but promotes more efficient forward and backward motion. In hedgehogs and elephant shrews the toes may be reduced to four. All insectivores except elephant shrews have plantigrade foot posture; *i.e.*, the entire sole is placed down in walking. In some species, however, the heel is frequently lifted from the ground.

Fusion of tibia and fibula

Tail. The tail structure varies according to the behaviour of the animal. Burrowing insectivores have little or no tail, in common with most other burrowing animals. Climbing and running species have well-developed tails, haired or nearly naked. The slow-moving hedgehogs generally have short tails. In aquatic forms, such as aquatic shrews, moles, and potamogales, lateral compression of the tail seemingly suits it for steering functions.

Fur texture and coloration. Specializations of the hair are seen in hedgehogs and some tenrecs, which possess spiny hair. Burrowing species have reversible fur, which can lie down either anteriorly or posteriorly as the animal moves forward or backward in the tunnel. The fur of golden moles has a distinctive metallic sheen or iridescence. Few insectivores are strikingly coloured; most are brown, gray, or black with little countershading. Exceptions occur in diurnal species, which may be more brightly coloured and have some indication of patterns.

Digestive and reproductive specializations. Tree shrews and elephant shrews possess a cecum (a blind pouch) at the junction of small and large intestines. An intestinal cecum is not present in carnivorous insectivores, since it serves for storage and continued digestion of plant food. Elephant shrews, whose teeth suggest a diet consisting largely of plants, have a large cecum; tree shrews, which probably eat relatively less plant food, have a small cecum.

A true scrotum containing the testes is present only in tree shrews; in some other forms, such as moles and tenrecs, the testes lie close to the surface in the perineal region (the area ventral to the anus) but do not leave the abdominal cavity. A penis bone (baculum) is found in tenrecs and moles. Elephant shrews have a trifurcate penis, a trait that led some early students to ally them with the marsupials, some of which have a bifurcate structure. The form of the uterus is Y-shaped, or bicornuate, as in many other mammals.

Metabolism. Although insectivoran physiology has been studied in connection with special abilities, such as dormancy in hedgehogs, it is not well-known for the order. Of great interest are the smaller shrews, which, because of their minute size and relatively large ratio of body surface to volume, have an exceptionally high rate of metabolism, necessitated by the high rate of energy loss in the form of heat. As a result shrew life consists largely of a frenetic search for food. A captive female *Sorex* ate 3.3 times her own weight every 24 hours.

EVOLUTION AND CLASSIFICATION

Evolution. In late Cretaceous and early Cenozoic times (beginning about 100,000,000 years ago) a number of primitive placental mammals existed that did not display the specialized characteristics of modern orders; they possessed tritubercular (three-cusped) cheek teeth, with the paracone and metacone well separated and located laterally on the occlusal (closing) surface. These animals, the Leptictidae, some of which persisted until

Oligocene times (about 38,000,000 years ago), were close structurally to Eocene hedgehogs and may well be ancestral not only to many modern insectivores, especially hedgehogs, shrews, and moles, but also to a variety of other modern mammals, such as ungulates and primates. These insectivores, in which the paracone and metacone are well separated and are near the lateral edge of the molar, are thought by some paleontologists to have descended from Late Cretaceous leptictids and to form a separate lineage from the zalambdodonts. The fossil record is fairly clear in showing common ancestry of shrews and moles, and probable derivation from late Eocene or early Oligocene hedgehog-like ancestors (perhaps 40,000,000 years ago). Some paleontologists believe that the presence of zalambdodont molars in tenrecs, otter shrews, and golden moles is indicative of independent descent from the zalambdodont deltatheridiids, a family of doubtful ordinal affinities, of Late Cretaceous time. It has recently been suggested that solenodons also descended from a hedgehog-like ancestor, which reached the Greater Antilles in early Tertiary time. Tree shrews are known from Paleocene time (about 65,000,000 years ago) and probably come closest among living mammals to representing the appearance of the early Cenozoic primitive placentals. Fossil elephant shrews from the African Miocene (about 26,000,000 years ago) offer few clues to the origin of the Macroscelididae, which were in all likelihood derived from the unspecialized Early Cenozoic placental group. Tenrecoids and golden moles have an exclusively African and Malagasy fossil history, also stemming from the Miocene.

Classification. *Distinguishing taxonomic features.* Insectivores are characterized by the lack of distinctive features seen in other mammalian orders rather than by the possession of unifying morphological traits. All possess a low braincase, a rather long conical rostrum (snout) and unspecialized legs, feet, and locomotion. They can be distinguished from similarly built rodents by the lack of the gnawing incisors (followed by a diastema, or space) that characterize the rodents and from similarly built marsupials by the lack of an abdominal pouch.

Annotated classification. Taxonomists disagree on the relative degrees of relationship among insectivoran families (except that shrews, moles, and hedgehogs are conceded to form a cohesive phyletic unit); the classification omits subordinal and superfamilial groupings.

ORDER INSECTIVORA
Primitive placental mammals characterized by a low braincase, conical snout, and lacking locomotor or dental specializations of other mammalian orders; 77 genera, 406 species.

Family Erinaceidae (hedgehogs and gymnures)
Eocene to Recent; Eurasia and Africa. Spiny pelage (covering) present (subfamily Erinaceinae, hedgehogs) or lacking (Echinosoricinae, gymnures); zygomatic arch (below eye orbit) present in skull; molars quadrate, bunodont (see above *Dentition*); auditory bulla a tympanic ring, not fused to cranium. Terrestrial, omnivorous, often hibernating or estivating. Hedgehogs are Eurasian and African; gymnures native to the Asian tropics, often shrewlike. Ten genera, 14 species.

Family Talpidae (moles)
Eocene to Recent; Holarctic. Manus very broad and specialized for digging; molars with W-shaped crests; zygomatic arch present; auditory bulla fused to cranium; eyes minute; ears without pinnae; humerus bone extremely broad and short. Burrowing (fossorial), sometimes aquatic. Fur of some commercial value. Fifteen genera, about 22 species.

Family Soricidae (shrews)
Eocene to Recent; Africa, Eurasia, North America, northern edge of South America. First upper and lower incisors procumbent, multicusped; zygomatic arch lacking; bulla a tympanic ring, unfused to skull; molars with W-shaped crests; small size. Terrestrial, aquatic, or subfossorial foragers in ground litter or water for small invertebrates. Twenty-four genera, approximately 291 species.

Family Solenodontidae (solenodon, almiqui)
Pleistocene to Recent; Cuba and Haiti. Molars zalambdodont; zygomatic arch incomplete; incisors canine-like, lower ones grooved; long scaled tail; long mobile snout. Terrestrial, perhaps nearing extinction. Two genera, 2 species.

Family Tenrecidae (tenrecs)
Miocene to Recent; Madagascar. Molars zalambdodont; zygomatic arch incomplete; bulla composed of a tympanic ring and basicranial elements; form variable from nearly tailless, spiny, rabbit-sized *Tenrec* to long-tailed, soft-furred, shrewlike *Microgale*. *Oryzorictes* is molelike, while *Limnogale* is muskrat-like and a vegetarian. Nine genera, 20 species.

Family Potamogalidae (otter shrews)
Recent; West Africa. Webbed feet, otter-like form; zalambdodont molars. Riparian, aquatic, feeding on aquatic vertebrates and invertebrates. Two genera, 3 species, often included as a subfamily of Tenrecidae.

Family Chrysochloridae (golden moles)
Miocene to Recent; Africa. Two digits on front feet with enormously enlarged claws; proximal segments of arm recessed into sides of thorax; heart and lungs elongated; zalambdodont molars; complete zygomatic arch composed of maxillary rather than jugal bone. Eyes covered with skin; tail rudimentary; pelage with metallic sheen. Fossorial. Five genera, 11 species.

Family Macroscelididae (elephant shrews)
Miocene to Recent, Africa. Cecum well-developed; feet greatly elongated; molars quadrate and high-crowned; eyes large; auditory bullae complete, including entotympanic bone; zygomatic arch complete; resembling long-snouted kangaroo rats or jerboas. Diurnal, terrestrial, saltatory, animalivorous and phytophagous. Five genera, about 28 species.

Family Tupaiidae (tree shrews)
Paleocene to Recent, tropical southeast Asian mainland, Sumatra, Borneo, Philippines. Small cecum; orbital fossa ringed with bone; zygomatic arch complete; molars quadrate with W-shaped crests; eyes large; audital bulla includes entotympanic bone; generally like a long-nosed squirrel in appearance and behaviour. Terrestrial and arboreal; diurnal or nocturnal. Five genera, 15 species.

In addition to the above, 14 families of primitive extinct mammals are sometimes assigned to the Insectivora. These families, with their geologic time spans, are listed below.

Family Dimylidae. Oligocene–Paleocene.
Family Picrodontidae. Paleocene.
Family Zalambdalestidae. Cretaceous.
Family Leptictidae. Cretaceous–Oligocene.
Family Adapisoricidae. Paleocene–Miocene.
Family Pantolestidae. Paleocene–Oligocene.
Family Apternodontidae. Eocene–Oligocene.
Family Apatemyidae. Paleocene–Oligocene.
Family Mixodectidae. Paleocene.
Family Anagalidae. Eocene–Oligocene.
Family Paroxyclaenidae. Eocene–Oligocene.
Family Ptolemaiidae. Oligocene.
Family Pentacodontidae. Paleocene–Eocene.
Family Plesiosoricidae. Eocene–Pliocene.

Critical appraisal. It is possible, though current opinion does not support it, that insectivores with zalambdodont teeth (tenrecs, solenodons, golden moles) form a monophyletic unit descended from either pre-tritubercular Mesozoic (Jurassic, about 190,000,000 years ago) pantotheres or the zalambdodont deltatheridiids of late Cretaceous and Paleocene times. More likely, zalambdodont teeth were derived from the tritubercular type seen in leptictids. Zalambdodont and dilambdodont teeth represent different ways of increasing the length of shearing edge of a tritubercular tooth. Tupaiids and macroscelidids share a number of traits that have led some authorities to separate them as a group called Menotyphla, while grouping the other insectivores as the Lipotyphla. Some authorities have considered the colugos (Cynocephalidae) to belong in the Insectivora, but most now place them in a separate order, Dermoptera. Tupaiids share some traits with primitive primates and have been included in that order by some prominent authorities (see, for instance, PRIMATES). Elephant shrews have many of these same traits, however, and would have to be included in the Primates as well. Some mammalogists treat the elephant shrews as a distinct order, Macroscelidea (see MAMMALIA). A growing body of evidence suggests that soricids, talpids, erinaceids, solenodons, tenrecs, otter shrews, and possibly chrysochlorids form a naturally related group to which the ordinal or subordinal term Lipotyphla should apply. This group, as well as elephant shrews, tree shrews, primates, bats, and others, apparently have been separate from one another since earliest Tertiary times, and consistency may in the end dictate assignment of a separate ordinal name to each.

BIBLIOGRAPHY. A. CABRERA, *Genera mammalium*, vol. 1, *Insectivora*, vol. 2, *Galeopithecia* (1919–25), a Spanish classic—a still unsurpassed illustrated review of living insectivora; PETER CROWCROFT, *The Life of the Shrew* (1957), a review of the biology of the common Eurasian *Sorex araneus;* J.F. EISENBERG and E. GOULD, "The Behaviour of *Solenodon paradoxus* in Captivity with Comments on the Behavior of Other Insectivora," *Zoologica*, 51:49–58 (1966); "The Tenrecs: A Study in Mammalian Behavior and Evolution," *Smithson. Contr. Zool.*, no. 27 (1970), a technical but easily read review of the biology of this family; F.G. EVANS, "The Osteology and Relationships of the Elephant Shrews (Macroscelididae)," *Bull. Am. Mus. Nat. Hist.*, 80:85–125 (1942), a technical comparison of elephant shrews, tree shrews, erinaceids, and lemuroids; GILLIAN GODFREY and PETER CROWCROFT, *The Life of the Mole* (*Talpa europaea Linnaeus*) (1960), a readable, semi-popular account of the common European mole; E. GOULD, N.C. NEGUS, and A. NOVICK, "Evidence for Echolocation in Shrews," *J. Exp. Zool.*, 156:19–38 (1964); K. HERTER, "Das Verhalten der Insektivoren," *Handb. Zool.*, vol. 8, sect. 9, pp. 1–50 (1957), a German language review of the behaviour of all insectivores; M.W. LYON, "Treeshrews: An Account of the Mammalian Family Tupaiidae," *Proc. U.S. Natn. Mus.*, vol. 45 (1913); S.B. MCDOWELL, "The Greater Antillean Insectivores," *Bull. Am. Mus. Nat. Hist.*, 115:117–214 (1958), a technical review of the relationships of solenodons to other insectivores.

(J.Fi.)

Instinct

The word instinct, from the Latin *instinctus* (incited or instigated), often refers to compelling and little understood factors that incite or drive human behaviour. So-called human instincts have sometimes been regarded as substantially emotional (see EMOTION; MOTIVATION). Efforts to give a more precise and clearer meaning to the word have resulted in the formulation of a number of major defining characteristics, which are enumerated below.

Defining attributes

Characteristics of instinctive behaviour. *Heritability.* Instinctive behaviour is largely heritable; *i.e.*, it follows a recognizable and predictable pattern in all normal members of at least one sex of a species. Many of the activities of a species of animal are sufficiently constant and predictable to serve as specific characteristics in the same way, and often to the same degree, as do bodily structures. This is true of the display movements of birds (*e.g.*, peacocks), the web-spinning movements of spiders, the burrowing habits of marine worms, the prey-catching techniques of weasels or wolves, the food-hoarding movements of squirrels, and the browsing methods of antelope.

The genetic or inherited nature of instinctive behaviour is particularly evident in aggressive and submissive sexual behaviour and in fighting of various kinds. Other instinctive activities of this kind serve nutrition, including methods of obtaining and eating food; care of the body surface, including cleaning, grooming, and scratching movements; escape from predators, including methods of concealment, freezing or "playing dead," and taking flight; social behaviour, including ways of responding to others both sexually and regardless of sex; and sleep, including the rhythms of rest and wakefulness and bodily positions assumed in sleep.

Many of these relatively fixed, species-characteristic types of behaviour appear to be primarily inherited; at first sight, at least, they may seem little influenced by the particular experiences of the individual animal. But much instinctive behaviour as, for example, playing or exploring, is, nevertheless, modifiable, and the detailed form of the action taken may vary according to the circumstances of the moment and the individual experience previously encountered.

Complexity of pattern. Instinctive activity is not usually a limited response to a simple stimulus but rather is a sequence of behaviour that runs a predictable course; for example, nest-building behaviour that shows a patterned sequence of acts among many birds and some fishes. Many of these actions are far from being either simple or brief. Extraordinary elaboration may be found, and, although some instinctive behaviours may be complete in seconds, others may take minutes, hours, or days.

Adaptive function. Since instinctive behaviour is assumed to be genetically based and therefore shaped by the pressures of natural selection, it follows that most of the consequences of instinctive activity contribute to the preservation of an individual or to the continuity of the species; that is, instinctive activity tends to be adaptive, contributing to the animal's ability to reach maturity and to breed.

Stability under external change. Ideally, instinctive behaviour seems not to depend on learning or practice (see LEARNING, ANIMAL) but to emerge in full complexity without rehearsal when appropriate stimuli or circumstances are encountered. Often, such stimuli do not guide or mold the instinctive behaviour but seem simply to trigger or release it. This characteristic gives instinct the appearance of driving the animal endogenously (from within); the quality of instinctive activity thus appears to depend only secondarily on exogenous (external) stimulation.

Experiments in which an animal is reared in a very limited environment (perhaps in isolation, as when a songbird is kept alone in a soundproofed chamber from the moment of hatching) may indicate the extent to which behaviour is spontaneous (or endogenous) or is governed (or triggered) by external circumstances. Rather than seeking to distinguish sharply between instinct and learning, however, it may be more useful to assess the degree to which a given item of behaviour is environmentally stable or unstable (labile). Indeed, aspects of behaviour of a single species may differ greatly in this respect; thus, the nesting activity, calls of alarm, and courting behaviour of birds may be extraordinarily constant under varying conditions. On the other hand, food seeking and feeding may be extremely labile (or susceptible to learning), so that geographically disparate groups of individuals belonging to the same species may have very different feeding habits.

Instinct and learning

Varieties of instinctive behaviour. No animal is ever completely isolated from some kind of environment; even in the egg or in the womb it is exposed to environmental variations just as it is after hatching or birth. There is, nevertheless, a sharp distinction between the egg or uterus phase and the free-living, active, sensing animal exposed to environmental stimuli of great diversity. In the case of the egg of an insect enclosed in a largely impervious shell or of a parasitic worm similarly isolated by an impermeable cyst wall, isolation from the environment may be so great that the animal undergoes little more than changes of temperature and oxygen supply. Thus, when such an animal emerges from its egg or cyst, the details of its structure and behaviour would seem maximally attributable to the genetic proteins in its cells; that is, its behaviour appears to be as much inherited as is its bodily structure. This sort of behaviour is environmentally so stable that it is naturally and quite reasonably given the label instinctive.

Reflex activity. A variety of what may be called simple instinctive behaviour has long been known as reflex action. When this term was introduced, it meant the simple and almost invariable response of a simple organ system (*e.g.*, a single muscle) to a simple stimulus, such as a touch or a flash of light. In its most elementary versions, this activity has been seen as the function of an idealized mechanism that has been called the reflex arc. The primary components of the reflex arc have been identified as the sensory-nerve cell (or receptor) that receives the stimulation, in turn connecting (hence the term arc) to another nerve cell that activates the muscle cell (or effector).

Although such a reflex arc might be the simplest imaginable mechanism for inflexibly automatic behaviour, it is a theoretical minimum rather than an actually observed functional arrangement of cells in the body of the animal;

nevertheless, a mechanism but little more complicated than this helps to account for the locomotion of such animals as millipedes. In some insects, for example, the stepping movement of one limb or muscle provides stimuli that set off another limb or muscle on a similar course of movement, providing a kind of feedback system or chain of reflex arc activities. In most cases of this sort, however, the basic physiological mechanism is more complicated than the simple arc theory would suggest. Additional nerve cells capable of communicating with other parts of the body (beyond the receptor and effector) are invariably present in reflex circuits. Such connections are what make possible the conditioning of reflex responses.

Among higher animals, and perhaps many others (such as insects), what once were thought to be chain reflexes are not systems simply linked or chained together; they are systems under the precise control of coordinated complexes of nerve cells in particular parts of the nervous system, such as the spinal cord and brain. Even without evidence of a chain of feedback (or reafferent) stimuli, performance may be smoothly integrated. This is well illustrated by the complex movements of swallowing in mammals; in the dog, for example, 11 separate muscles or muscular systems are found to discharge one after the other, precisely timed to a matter of milliseconds, and all under the control of the central nervous system (CNS: brain and spinal cord). Such complexes of precisely controlled movement, known as fixed action patterns, are thought to form the hard core of the inborn movement forms of instincts. When such fixed action patterns seem to constitute an end point or goal-directed climax of some sort, they are known as consummatory acts.

Consummatory behaviour

Fixed action patterns. Some male spiders perform elaborate courtship actions that affect selectively females that are ready to respond sexually. The male, in testing for a receptive female, first stands out of reach and goes through elaborate precise gestures with limbs, pedipalps, and other body parts that are distinctively shaped or patterned in a manner characteristic of the species. Perhaps even more remarkable fixed action patterns are found in the displays of male fiddler crabs of the genus *Uca*, about 40 species of which are distributed over the Earth's tropical ocean beaches. One of the two claws enormously enlarged, seemingly having been evolved

Adapted from A. Eibl-Eibesfeldt, *Grundriss der vergleichenden Verhaltensforschung: Ethologie*

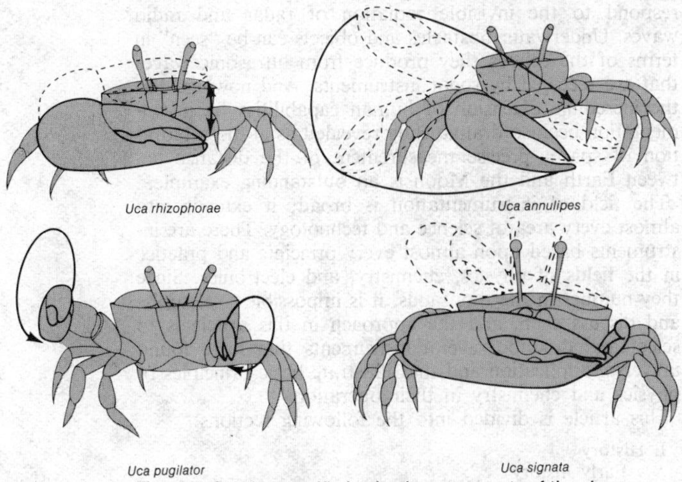

Figure 1: Species-specific instinctive movements of the claws in courtship behaviour movements of fiddler crabs *(Uca)*.

primarily for sexual and aggressive displays, and its ritualistic gestures are quite characteristic of the species. The timing and form of movement are so invariable from one individual to another that an expert can distinguish by this alone the species of crab, whether it comes from the shores of Panama, Tahiti, or Bali.

There must be some very precise, built-in mechanism, presumably some integration of hormonal and nervous-system controls, which ensures that each individual in a species exhibits the distinctive fixed action pattern at the right speed, amplitude, and intensity (*see* BEHAVIOUR, ANIMAL for further discussion of fixed action patterns). Beyond those noted for fiddler crabs and spiders, innumerable examples of such instinctive patterns are found among the elaborate display movements of many other animals, such as insects, fishes, and birds. Among the latter three groups, these movements also are part of the species communications mechanism, serving to permit members of a species to distinguish the signals of their fellows and prospective mates from all other visual stimuli. Thus, there is a system of instinctive perceptual abilities at least as complex as the inborn tendencies to exhibit patterns of motor behaviour. Likewise, the perceptual instincts are of primary importance for the survival of the species.

Modifiable action patterns. Some types of instinctive behaviour, while showing a rigid core of fixed action pattern, are still modifiable by conditioning and other learning processes. A good example is provided by the nest-building behaviour of many birds: after the breeding female has chosen a nest site, she finds and deposits sticks or twigs or pieces of grass there. A jackdaw (*Corvus monedula*) or rook (*C. frugilegus*) standing on a potential nest locality with twigs held in its beak performs a downward and sideward sweeping movement that brings the material into contact with the ledge or the branches on which the nest is to be built. The moment the twig or branch carried by the bird meets resistance, the sideways movements become more vigorous and merge into a series of quick trembling thrusts (so-called Tremble Shoving). When the twig is in a position that offers even more resistance, the efforts become more intense until the twig wedges fast. After this consummatory achievement the bird apparently loses interest in his activities for the moment.

Tremble Shoving

An inexperienced jackdaw at first will try any objects small enough to be handled, even pieces of ice and the metal ends of small electric bulbs. None of these ever becomes lodged firmly enough by the Tremble Shoving to result in a stimulus that is sufficiently consummatory to ensure successful nest building. Such failure quickly extinguishes the bird's tendency to fetch inadequate objects; equally rapid positive conditioning is effected, and the jackdaw learns to be a twig connoisseur, coming to use only those that are just right in shape and flexibility. Indeed, it has been observed that the nests of entire groups of such birds are predominantly constructed of twigs and other pieces that are taken from only one kind of tree, even though there are other building materials that are readily available.

In contrast to jackdaws, many small songbirds do apparently have an inborn tendency to select the kinds of materials that are appropriate for different phases of nest construction. This innate predilection for suitable building materials has been shown dramatically among canaries reared in man-made nests of felt. Even though female canaries thus reared have never encountered anything long and flexible before, when nest-building time comes, they can select materials appropriately. As soon as pieces of grass, bits of string, cotton, or any long flexible objects are placed in the cage, these female canaries display interest and, within seconds, carry the objects to the nest place and commence weaving movements. Once the proper state of construction has been reached, and not before, the birds display an innate tendency to line their nests with feathers, plucking out their own when no others are to be found.

A caged female canary long deprived of nesting material may take hold of one of its own feathers in its beak and, without detaching it, go through the motions of lining the nest with it again and again without, of course, actually lining the nest. Another striking example of complex nest building is found in the extraordinarily complicated movements and responses by which weaver birds build their elaborate hanging nests with such architectural features as roof, egg chamber, antechamber, and entrance tunnel. Research has identified an elaborate system of relations among external stimuli, internal hormonal conditions, neural function, and reproductive development in the behaviour of female canaries during the course of their breeding cycle. Evidence of an elaborate combination of innate physiological activity and individual experience also comes from studies concerning the development of songs and call notes among birds.

A young bird isolated from other members of its kind, or even more rigorously from all patterned auditory stimulation in a soundproofed chamber, produces an extremely limited, basic sound pattern. If the young bird is allowed to develop and sing along with other members of the species, however, the instinctive tendencies seem to be more fully realized through fine adjustments added by imitative learning.

By courtesy of N.E. Collias and E.C. Collias

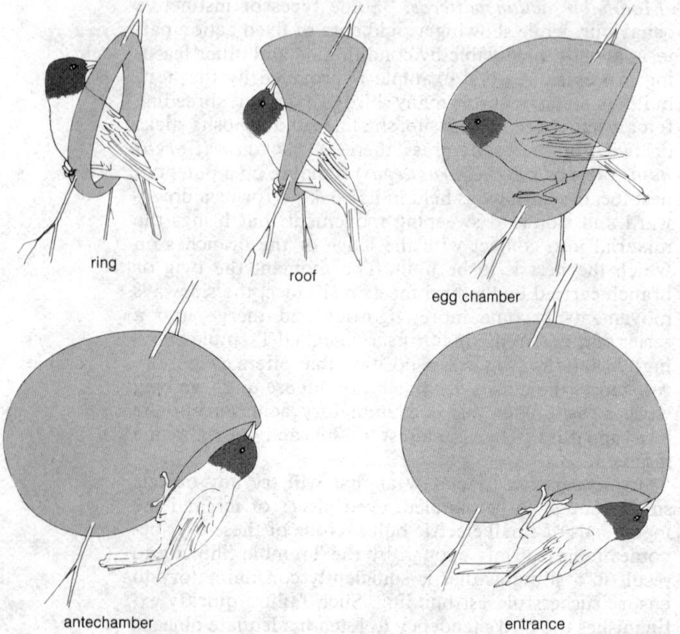

Figure 2: Five stages in the construction of a nest by the male village weaver (*Ploceus cucullatus*)

With more complexity in brain structure and function as is found in many mammals, behaviour is relatively flexible, and fixed action patterns tend to be overlaid by learned patterns and to that extent obscured; nevertheless, an inexperienced brown rat deprived of nest material tends to use its own tail instead, carrying it about in behaviour that is reminiscent of that shown by a feather-deprived canary. After gathering materials, brown rats typically heap them up in a more or less circular wall and then begin to tap down and smooth the inner surface of the nest cavity. When a very inexperienced rat is offered paper strips or other soft material for the first time, it goes into a random frenzy in which the sequence (gathering, heaping, and smoothing) is confused. Yet, each of the three phases is performed to perfection, not differing even on analysis by slow-motion films from those of an experienced rat. After having placed two or three paper strips together flat on the ground, however, the novice rat will perform heaping-up movements in the empty air above them, then apparently pat down a nest wall that is not yet in existence. Only later, after it has had more experience as a builder, does the rat seem to learn to inhibit the instinctive heaping and patting movements until the appropriate stages of construction have been reached.

Nesting rats

The catalog of instinctive behaviour among animals is much richer than the few examples offered here. Despite the clear differences observable in the detailed manifestations of instincts in comparing frog, goldfish, pigeon, cat, rabbit, and human being, for example, all of these behaviours may be seen to hinge on genetically transmitted physiological structures and functions. Indeed, many animal instincts may profitably be compared with some of the built-in forms of behavioral tendency among plants (see STEREOTYPED RESPONSE).

BIBLIOGRAPHY. A nontechnical account of some of the early observations, establishing the newer approach to instinct, is found in KONRAD LORENZ, *Er redete mit dem Vieh, den Vögeln und den Fischen,* 6–8th ed. (1952; Eng. trans., *King Solomon's Ring: New Light on Animal Ways,* 1952; reduced photographic reprint, 1961). Wide-ranging surveys of instinctive behaviour include IRANAUS EIBL-EIBESFELDT, *Grundriss der vergleichenden Verhaltensforschung: Ethologie* (1967); ROBERT A. HINDE, *Animal Behaviour: A Synthesis of Ethology and Comparative Psychology,* 2nd ed. (1970); PETER R. MARLER and WILLIAM J. HAMILTON, *Mechanisms of Animal Behaviour* (1966); WILLIAM H. THORPE, *Learning and Instinct in Animals,* 2nd ed. (1963); NIKOLAAS TINBERGEN, *The Study of Instinct* (1951). Papers and books devoted to special aspects of instinctive behaviour are T.H. BULLOCK, "The Origins of Patterned Nervous Discharge," *Behaviour,* 17:48–59 (1961); and in *Nervous and Hormonal Mechanisms of Integration* (1966); ROBERT A. HINDE (ed.), *Bird Vocalizations: Their Relation to Current Problems in Biology and Psychology* (1969), and *Non-Verbal Communication* (1972); KONRAD LORENZ, "The Innate Bases of Learning," in KARL H. PRIBRAM (ed.), *On the Biology of Learning* (1969); CLAIRE H. SCHILLER (ed.), *Instinctive Behavior: The Development of a Modern Concept* (1957); WILLIAM H. THORPE, *Bird Song: The Biology of Vocal Communication and Expression in Birds* (1961), and "Animal Vocalization and Communication," in FREDERIC L. DARLEY (ed.), *Brain Mechanisms Underlying Speech and Language* (1967).

(W.H.T.)

Instrumentation

The modern level of technology would not have been attained without the development and use of precise measuring instrumentation. Every advance in mankind's technological capabilities from the earliest times was necessarily preceded by the development of instrumentation that enabled people to see, measure, and gain access to the unknown they were probing. In fact, a large part of the advances of human culture and civilization is owed to the incredibly sensitive and powerful instruments of the human body, the senses of sight, sound, touch, smell, and taste.

The principles involved in the use of human senses are employed in the instruments and mechanisms used throughout mankind's technological environment. In the search for the instrumental tools to control and understand the world, people have first turned to those that are derived from these same principles, in the process effectively enlarging their own senses. Instruments enabling aircraft and ships to see through fog and at great distances respond to the invisible radiation of radar and radio waves. Underwater obstacles and objects can be "seen" in terms of the echoes they produce from ultrasonic waves that are received by sonar instruments. And nowhere has the incredible extension of human capabilities by instrumentation been so dramatically revealed as in the exploration of space; precise measurement of the distance between Earth and the Moon is an outstanding example.

The field of instrumentation is broad; it extends into almost every area of science and technology. There are instruments based upon almost every principle and practice in the fields of physics, chemistry, and electronics. Since they number in the thousands, it is impossible to describe and discuss each, and the approach in this article is to select and describe several instruments that have found universal application and that illustrate basic principles of physics and chemistry in their operation.

This article is divided into the following sections:

I. History

EARLY HISTORY

Though modern science and industry are inconceivable without precision instruments, only since the Industrial Revolution and the rise of experimental science have such devices been indispensable. Yet there has always been a need for measuring the dimensions of buildings, the area of fields, the capacity of vessels, the weight of coins, and the passage of time; and from antiquity simple methods and devices have existed. The greatest need for precise measurement in early days occurred in astronomy and navigation, and it was in these fields that the most significant and accurate instruments were invented.

The armillary sphere

The oldest known astronomical device was the armillary sphere, used to represent the great circles of the heavens. A later modification, originating with the ancient Greeks, was the astrolabe, which could be used to determine the time, the length of the day or night, or the rising and setting of a star. The invention of the compass represented a striking advance in instrumentation. This device, which for the first time gave a directional indication without using astronomical indicators, may have originated in western Europe, or it may have been imported there from China. The earliest models consisted of a small bar of magnetized iron floating in a bowl of water on a reed or section of wood.

The invention of the telescope in the early 1600s gave mankind an instrument that extended the most important of the senses, that of sight. Though its invention in about 1608 is generally credited to the Dutch optician Hans Lippershey, Galileo was first to make effective use of it. Using a simple telescope with two lenses that magnified three times, Galileo observed lunar craters, four of the satellites of Jupiter, the phases of Venus, and the star-like nature of the Milky Way. Use of the telescope led to a tremendous growth in astronomical knowledge and measurement ability.

Although most of the early instruments merely provided a necessary measurement, there were instances in which instruments were directly coupled to control functions. Perhaps the earliest known example is the water clock developed by Ctesibius of Alexandria in the 3rd century BC. The water clock consisted of a vessel into which water flowed through an orifice, raising a float connected to a series of linkages that actuated any of a variety of time-indicating mechanisms. The water had to be controlled to flow into the vessel at a constant rate. The device that both monitored and controlled this flow was the float, mounted in a regulating vessel ahead of the metering orifice. This float, projecting into the opening of a conical valve connected to the water supply, throttled the inflow of water as the level rose; as the level lowered, the valve opened, letting water flow in to raise the level again. The arrangement achieved a constant level in the regulating vessel and hence a constant flow through the metering orifice.

Possibly the first instrumentation system to be invented in modern Europe was the thermostatic furnace of Cornelis Drebbel (1572–1634), a Dutch mechanic and chemist. Into a mercury thermometer, half inside and half outside the furnace, was placed a float. This float was connected through rods, levers, and pivots to a damper cover. An increase in heat caused the mercury and float to rise, and that motion was transmitted to the damper cover, which adjusted the draft appropriately.

Similar temperature regulators followed this first attempt. William Henry's sentinel register, first described in 1771, used, instead of mercury, a column of water that rose and fell as the air in the closed vessel surrounding it heated and cooled. Another temperature regulator, patented in 1783, used as its temperature sensor two rods made of metals of maximum difference in their coefficients of thermal expansion (*i.e.*, one metal expanded very much and the other very little in response to heat), one concentrically surrounding the other. The differential expansion and contraction resulting from varying levels of heat was conveyed to the damper cover by a series of levers, which multiplied the original motion by a factor of 100.

Watt's centrifugal governor

The best known early attempt at an instrumentation system was the centrifugal governor invented by James Watt in 1788. Its purpose was to maintain the speed of rotation of a steam engine at a constant predetermined value. It accomplished this by sensing the actual speed and adjusting the steam inlet valve of the engine accordingly. The speed of rotation was measured by a pair of centrifugal pendulums connected with the engine's flywheel by ropes and pulleys and rotating at engine speed. Under the influence of centrifugal force, the pendulums swung farther outward as the speed of the engine increased. A linkage transmitted this motion to a sleeve, which slid up or down along the axis of rotation to control the valve admitting steam to the engine. Decreasing speed caused the flyweights to swing back and thus caused the sleeve to slide in a manner that opened the steam valve and accelerated the engine.

THE 19TH AND 20TH CENTURIES

The development of instrumentation in the 19th and 20th centuries derived impetus from four major historical movements. The first was the Industrial Revolution of the 18th and 19th centuries, with its accompanying scientific advances. The second was the 20th-century growth of modern industry. The third impetus was provided by the introduction of computers in the early 1950s, and the fourth came with the advent of the Space Age.

The Industrial Revolution. The advances during this period were numerous, but they can be illustrated by a discussion of instrumentation in three critical areas: dimensional measurement, electrical measurement, and analytical determination.

The manufacture of both the industrial equipment and the scientific instruments of this period necessitated the adoption of new standards of precision. Devices were urgently needed to measure the dimensions of machine tools and their products. The most commonly used instrument for this purpose, first developed in 1638 for astronomical measurements, was the screw micrometer, in which the turning of a screw is translated into a carefully determined linear movement. As its use became widespread, refinements brought standard models capable of measuring to 0.0025 millimetre (0.0001 inch), and special models measured to 0.000025 millimetre (0.000001 inch). The precision work made possible through use of these instruments paved the way for mass-production methods. No longer was it necessary to build each machine separately; instead, individual parts could be manufactured in large numbers, and the final machine assembled by drawing the necessary components from a stock of interchangeable parts.

The screw micrometer

During the 19th century the principles of electrical phenomena were discovered and applied in the development of the electrical industries. It became necessary to devise instruments to detect and measure electrical phenomena, and these instruments laid the groundwork for the variety of modern instrumentation that depends upon electronic circuitry.

The instrumentation primarily in use during this time measured current, voltage, or resistance. The earliest measurement of current and voltage followed the Danish physicist Hans Christian Ørsted's discovery in 1820 that a current-carrying wire would cause deflection in a nearby pivoted magnet. A number of instruments called galvanometers were then developed that indicated the amount of current or voltage by using the electromagnetic force in a coil of wire carrying a current to move a pointer across a scale. The controlling force against which the pointer operated was either gravity, a spring, or a magnetic field.

Galvanometers

Precision measurement was finally established in 1837 with the invention of the tangent galvanometer, the first such device in which the angle of deflection was directly proportional to the current, which then allowed practical, precision current measurement. The growing demands of the electrical industries led to the invention in 1879 of a portable device to measure current and voltage, the spring ammeter. In this device the attraction of an iron core within a tubular coil compressed a flat strip spiral, resulting in a twist at one end, to which an indicating pointer was attached.

The most important method of resistance measurement was the Wheatstone bridge, first introduced in 1843. This method, which consisted of comparing an unknown resistor with a standard resistance, was used routinely throughout the century for resistance measurement and is still a common basic circuit used in thousands of instruments.

The third important area of instrumentation advance from the time of the Industrial Revolution to the end of the 19th century was in the field of analysis. Analytical instrumentation was primarily used in astronomy, medicine, and chemistry. Improvements in the microscope, which had been invented in the early 17th century, led by 1820 to some spectacular advances in biology and medicine.

The microscope gained use in the detection of adulterated food as well as in crystallography (the scientific study of crystals) and metallurgy. Sugar solutions, such as syrup, were analyzed commercially by the polarimeter, an instrument developed in 1840, which passed polarized light through the solution. The spectroscope, developed in the mid-19th century, uses a prism to separate light into its spectrum of different wavelengths. Study of this spectrum through an optical instrument attached to the spectroscope reveals the chemical elements present in the substance emitting the light. The new instrument's great sensitivity permitted the detection of trace elements previously overlooked. The spectroscope achieved its greatest importance in astronomy, in which it made possible identification of the elements present in the stars.

Modern technology. The rapidly evolving technology of the 20th century furnished an impetus for the development of modern instrumentation, as well as the knowledge required to bring it into being. Though the greatest needs for instrumentation have been in the production and process industries, applications developed in virtually every field. The growth of technology has created a number of new instrumental needs. First, technological growth creates a need for the measurement of more variables: an industry that once needed to monitor only temperature and pressure, as it acquires greater complexity of operation, finds it necessary to monitor flow rate, humidity, acidity, and chemical composition. Second, technological growth creates situations in which old instrumentation is too slow or too insensitive. Finally, situations arise in which measuring instruments must operate or actuate control devices or serve to record various measurements automatically.

Many new instruments and techniques were developed to meet these needs. A U.S. industry survey in the 1960s revealed more than 10,000 different instruments in use, produced by 5,500 different companies.

Electronic circuitry. Instrumentation in the 20th century has been characterized by the increasing use of electronic circuitry. The following is a generalized, simplified description of the operation of electronic instrumentation. First, a transducer (a device for changing energy from one form to another) transforms the variable to be measured into an electrical signal. This signal is then processed and converted into a measure of the variable being studied. This measure may be displayed in a number of ways; it also may be recorded or used to regulate devices that control the measured variable.

Examples of transducers are the thermocouple and the photocell: heat, in the thermocouple, and light intensity, in the photocell, are converted to an electrical voltage. By no means do all transducers operate by a simple and direct conversion of the variable into an electrical signal; many utilize various indirect methods. An example of indirect conversion is the thermistor, which measures flow rate by measuring the amount of electric power needed to maintain its temperature against the cooling effects of a flow of liquid. The faster the liquid flows, the more quickly the thermistor cools, hence the more power is needed to maintain a steady temperature.

Effect of the transistor and integrated circuit

The invention of the vacuum tube greatly increased the capability of electronic instrumentation. An even greater step forward resulted from development of solid-state devices, such as transistors and integrated circuits, which for the most part have completely replaced the electron tube in instrumentation. A single integrated circuit element of very small size can contain several thousand circuit elements. Electronics has made possible the electron microscope, an instrument so powerful that it can be used to examine molecules.

Some of the most profound advances in instrumentation during the growth of technology have been in analyzing the composition of various substances. This widespread and important use of instrumentation gained most momentum in the years following World War II; until that time analysis was carried out for the most part by the older, more traditional noninstrumental methods. Spectacular gains in accuracy, versatility, and speed over the older methods were brought about in the 1940s by the introduction and refinement of such instruments as spectrophotometers, mass spectrometers, and gas chromatographs (see below).

Computers. The commercial introduction of computers in the early 1950s had a revolutionary effect upon instrumentation. Computers easily process, display, or store the output of measuring instruments, and they perform an endless variety of sophisticated functions with measurement data. Such functions include detailed analysis, checking for unusual patterns, virtually instantaneous correlation of the data with information from other measuring instruments, and use of the data for instantaneous initiation of control systems.

The development of the computer revolutionized instrumentation in many ways. The speed of its operation made possible its use in combination with many types of instruments both in the laboratory and in monitoring processes and production lines. The computer's ability to perform complex analyses of the measurement data made possible measurements that formerly had been impossible. The exploration of outer space brought a great demand for miniaturization and computerization of instruments for remote control.

II. Monitoring industrial processes

Instruments that monitor variables in industrial processes originated with very simple devices that provide a measure of temperature, pressure, fluid level, and density. As instrumentation and processes developed it became necessary to measure increasingly complex chemical and physical properties, until today there is an almost endless variety of instruments capable of monitoring process variables and leading to automatic operation. These automation systems increasingly tend to involve the digital computer as an integral component. In almost all instances the monitoring instrumentation is based upon some principle and technique thoroughly developed and previously used in a laboratory.

Monitoring instrumentation is widely used in the production and process industries. Process industries are those that transform raw materials into various chemical products. The primary variables monitored in the process industries are chemical, physical, and environmental properties. The basic chemical property monitored is composition. The physical properties monitored are turbidity, viscosity, density, and flow rate. The environmental properties monitored are temperature, pressure, and humidity.

Instrumentation in production industries

Production industries manufacture a physical product, such as machined parts, plastic items, and electronic components. These industries make wide use of modern instrumentation, although not to the same extent as the chemical process industries. Production applications tend to be more limited, with fewer variables monitored and fewer instruments used. There are two major reasons for this difference. First, the number of variables in production industries is less than in the process industries. Second, because of the sheer number and variety of objects produced, instrumentation is inherently more difficult to apply than in the process industries, which handle large volumes of materials such as liquids and gases having many properties in common.

Nevertheless, the production industries employ instrumentation to monitor such variables as physical dimensions, weight, optical properties, electrical properties, and radiation characteristics. Many of the instrumentation systems in the production industries are highly individual, used perhaps for only one specific item.

MONITORING CHEMICAL PROPERTIES

Chemical and petroleum processing plants play a large role in industry throughout the world. Since their processes involve the continuous flow of large volumes of materials through different steps, they are most amenable to monitoring and control by instrumentation. Indeed, such methods have been used since the beginning of the 20th century. For many years, however, only single-function instruments that measured temperature, pressure, or flow, and actuated simple control mechanisms, were used. By 1945 it had become clear that further progress depended upon development of sensors that would continuously analyze the composition of a given stream of chemicals.

Although automatic analytical instruments used in industry embody principles of laboratory instruments, the industrial devices look quite different. A production instrument must operate continuously over long periods, often in a harsh environment; hence, the instrument must be much more rugged than the laboratory model. Of the many laboratory principles employed in the process analytical instruments, the three in widest use today are refractometry, absorption spectroscopy, and gas chromatography.

Refractometers. Refraction is a term applied to the bending of a light beam as it passes from one material to another; for example, from air to water. Essentially, it is a measure of the difference in the velocity of light in the two materials. This measurement is usually obtained by making use of Snell's law, which gives the refractive index as the sine of the incident angle (the angle at which the light strikes the material) divided by the sine of the refracted angle (the angle at which the light leaves the material).

The refractive index, like molecular weight, density, and boiling point, is a characteristic physical property of matter and has long been used analytically in the laboratory. Since each chemical material has its own specific refractive index, the variation found in mixtures containing different proportions of two compounds becomes indicative of the composition. As a measure of chemical composition the refractive index can generally be applied with assurance only to mixtures of two components (called binary mixtures); measurement becomes ambiguous when more components are present. As an exception, there are instances in which a pseudobinary mixture occurs; the components separate into two distinct groups with each group behaving as one component.

Binary and pseudobinary mixtures

Measurement of the refractive index is simple and can be done to a high degree of sensitivity. It is possible to determine a change of one unit in the sixth decimal place of the refractive index with great accuracy. This was one of the first laboratory methods used by the developers of process monitors. The first such monitor appeared in 1952. To provide high sensitivity and especially to compensate for temperature changes (to which the refractive index is very sensitive), these first instruments operated on the differential cell principle, in which the difference in index between the sample in one part of the cell and a reference material in the other is measured. Early applications involved controlling fractionation of a complex hydrocarbon mixture by choosing the sampling point so that it behaved as a pseudobinary mixture. By 1965 most of these instruments had been replaced by the more powerful chromatographic analyzer, which completely analyzes the process mixture, permitting the use of computers and control techniques that earlier were impossible.

The critical angle refractometer

The critical angle refractometer appeared in 1962. The refractive index is measured by finding the angle at which a light beam striking the point of contact between a glass surface and the solution (or sample) is totally reflected. It is known as the critical angle, since rays at lesser angles permeate the liquid; at greater angles, they are totally reflected. The mechanism for measuring the critical angle is quite simple. A circular beam of light is transmitted to a prism face in contact with a solution, which divides it into a totally reflected light portion and a dark portion, depending on the critical angle value of the solution. As the solution composition changes, so does the dark portion. The position of the dividing line between light and dark in the returned beam is maintained by an automatic motor system in the control electronics and so becomes a measure of critical angle.

Although the critical angle refractometer is less sensitive than the differential instrument (by a factor of 100), the former requires only a surface reflection: no transmission of light through the solution is necessary. Thus dark solutions and suspensions, as well as clear solutions, can be measured directly in the process line. There is no need to use a separate sampling system for the instrument.

The characteristics of the critical angle refractometer make it uniquely suited for the food industry. Sugar solutions are ideal candidates for measurement by refractometers because they are essentially a mixture of two pure substances, sugar and water. In the manufacture of many carbonated beverages a refractometer is used to control preparation of the sugar-water base to within 0.05 percent of the desired concentration.

Infrared analyzers. That part of the electromagnetic spectrum lying between the visible and microwave regions is broadly considered the infrared. The region of greatest practical importance for infrared instrumentation occurs between two and 15 micrometres (one micrometre = 0.001 millimetre) in wavelength, where the strong absorption occurs at specific characteristic wavelengths for most organic and inorganic substances. These spectra are unique to each substance, because the frequency of the absorption bands is determined by the position and configurational relationships of the vibrating atoms in a molecule. Since the amount of energy absorbed by a material at any of its characteristic frequencies is a measure of its concentration in a mixture, a very sensitive and powerful technique is provided for the analysis of mixtures. Infrared instrumentation and these methods are widely used in analytical laboratories.

A laboratory infrared spectrometer has an optical system capable of passing a selected wavelength of light through a substance. Designers of process infrared analyzers, however, did not use such an optical system. The basic principle in the operation of all present-day analyzers is the nondispersive-filter-photometer principle, which allows these instruments to make use of not merely one specific wavelength but rather the total energy absorbed by the sample from a beam containing all wavelengths. To isolate a desired component the analyzer, by the use of filters, is rendered more sensitive to changes in concentration of this component and less sensitive to all other

Nondispersive-filter-photometer principle

interfering infrared absorbers in the mixture. Figure 1 shows the infrared analyzer measuring the concentration of a single component in a process stream. Carbon dioxide, for example, would be measured by sealing a quantity of that gas in the detector. A beam chopper directs infrared radiation alternately through the comparison cell, which contains pure air, and the sample cell, which may or may not contain carbon dioxide. The carbon dioxide in the detector absorbs part of the radiation in a characteristic way. Absorption causes the gas to expand, and the membrane moves accordingly, generating an electrical signal. When carbon dioxide enters the sample cell, it absorbs part of the radiation before the beam from that cell reaches the detector, and uneven pulses result. These can be translated into the percentage of carbon dioxide in the sample stream. Gases with absorption spectra overlapping carbon dioxide can be put in the filter cells, nullifying the interference. With complicated mixtures, it is not always possible to render the analyzer insensitive to certain components. This inability coupled with the great effort sometimes required to reduce interference is the major limitation of the instrument.

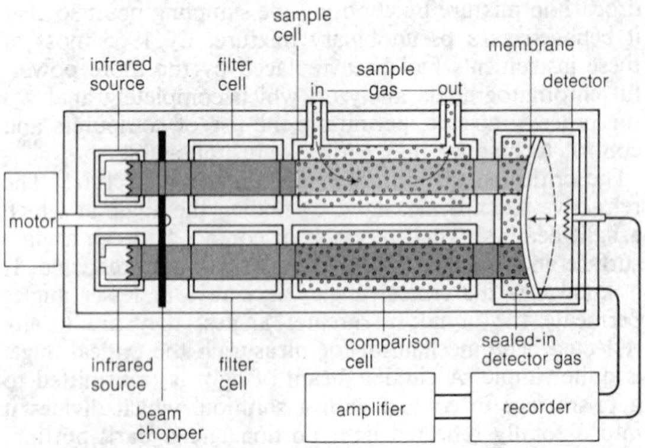

Figure 1: Infrared analyzer (see text).

Like the refractometer, the infrared analyzer is capable only of measuring concentration of a single component in a sample stream. Unlike the refractometer, however, it can isolate that single component from a mixture of many others. Since 1945 the number of applications of the infrared analyzer throughout the world has reached more than 10,000. In the early part of this period, it was employed for a large number of problems, some simple and some very complex. Solutions to the complex problems were not entirely acceptable, either because of insufficient discrimination against interfering compounds by the filtering technique or because the solutions required a multicomponent analysis. When process chromatographs (see below) became available in the mid-1950s, they were applied to the complex problems, leaving for the infrared analyzer the problems it solves best; *i.e.*, those involving an essentially simple mixture in which the desired material possesses strong, isolated absorption bands in the infrared range. A large number of industrially important mixtures in process streams and environmental problems meet this requirement.

Chromatographic analyzer. The process chromatograph, which appeared about 1955, was the first analytical instrument capable of a complete compositional analysis. Yet, it is simple in principle and execution and very broad in scope and analytical power. The development of the chromatographic analyzer and its use in processes has proceeded at an unusual rate. Uses of the analyzer range from the simple monitoring of one component in a mixture to providing a computerized output analysis for 50–100 components in a process stream.

The process chromatograph

Fundamentally, a process chromatograph resembles its laboratory counterpart more closely than do most plant instruments. The differences result from requirements imposed by the plant environment and by automatic operation. The process instrument usually is divided into two distinct units—an analyzer unit located quite near the process stream and a programmer unit that can be placed where needed. The analyzer must obtain its own sample, analyze it, and process the detector information into some useful data. Depending on the intended use, these data are then delivered to either a recorder, a controller, or a computer. The instrument must continue to repeat the same cycle, sometimes as often as once each minute, for many months, without interruption but with a high degree of reliability and fast response.

Gas chromatography is a procedure by which a volatile mixture is separated into its components by being injected into a moving, inert gas phase passing over a stationary absorbent bed in a tubing. The bed may be solid absorbent particles, or those particles coated with an involatile liquid, or the inner wall surfaces of a narrow capillary tube (0.25 millimetre [0.01 inch] in diameter) coated with the liquid. Separation of the sample components occurs by the difference in their absorptivity on the surfaces of the absorbent bed. The separated components pass from the tubing into a detector, where their relative concentration is measured.

While chromatographic analyzers are present in all phases of chemical plant operations, their earliest successful application occurred in the petroleum industry on light hydrocarbon streams. This industry has operations in which high-volume products are amenable to automatic control and are well suited to the chromatograph's analytical ability. The use of these instruments has expanded to many other areas such as air pollution monitoring and control of combustion processes; they are also used for the analytical experiments in space exploration.

Measurement of pH. The pH is a measure of the degree of acidity or alkalinity of a solution. Almost every industrially important product has a characteristic pH value. It must be measured and controlled if it affects the efficiency of the process or product uniformity. This property may also be measured for corrosion inhibition or to control the pH value of discharge from an industrial plant into rivers and sewers.

Glass electrode for pH measurement

The basic sensor used for measurement of pH, a glass electrode or conductor, contains a thin glass membrane that makes it sensitive to the concentration of hydrogen ions (electrically charged particles, H^+) in a solution. Since the early part of the 20th century the glass electrode has been accepted as the standard for pH measurements. The glass electrode can be built to withstand the high-temperature and high-pressure conditions of many plant environments. An acid dissolved in water produces many positively charged hydrogen ions (H^+) in the solution, whereas a base produces many negatively charged hydroxyl ions (OH^-). When the number of hydrogen ions equals the number of hydroxyl ions, the solution is neutral, like pure water, and is defined as having a pH of seven. If there is an excess of hydrogen ions the solution is acidic (range is O–$<$ 7 pH); if there is an excess of hydroxyl ions the solution is basic (range is $>$ 7–14 pH). In order to measure pH, the glass electrode, which is connected to a reference electrode, is immersed in the sample solution, and an electric voltage proportional to the hydrogen ion concentration results. This voltage can be displayed directly on a meter whose scale is calibrated to read a pH value.

MONITORING PHYSICAL PROPERTIES

Turbidity. Turbidity arises from the presence of particulate matter in a liquid, and is a commonly monitored property of chemical materials. The analytical devices for the determination of turbidity make use of visible light—the portion of the spectrum that lies between 400 and 700 millimicrons (one millimicron equals one millimetre $\times 10^{-6}$). The principles of analysis for the visible region are much the same as those for the infrared and ultraviolet regions except for the wavelength of light used.

The turbidimeter

In a typical turbidimeter light from a tungsten source is passed through a filter that selects light of a desired wavelength band for the analysis. The selected light is then passed through the process material, which absorbs it in proportion to its turbidity. The light that is not absorbed but transmitted is detected by a phototube in the detector compartment and electrically amplified. The amplified signal drives both a direct-reading meter on the instrument panel and a recorder. The measurement of both colour and turbidity may be accomplished by the same instrument: the colour is measured by absorption at a specific wavelength, and turbidity is measured by the absorption of light at all wavelengths.

Density. Density, an important physical property of a substance, is generally measured for one of two reasons: either because it is a significant property of the manufactured product, or to help determine composition of a product when the densities of the two components differ significantly.

Several principles are employed in density measuring instruments. Gas densities are generally determined either by measuring the buoyant effect of the gas or by comparing the rotation of a turbine wheel in a standard gas against the rotation in the gas to be measured. The densities of liquids can be measured by an automatic hydrometer (see below), by determination of the mass of a given volume of the liquid, or by measurement of the extent to which the liquid absorbs gamma radiation. And since the pressure of a column of liquid is a function of the density of the liquid, density may also be determined by measuring the pressure exerted by a given height of liquid.

The hydrometer

Of all these methods, one of the most widely used in both gas and liquid density determination is the hydrometer. The operation of a hydrometer is based on Archimedes' law, which states that a body in a fluid is buoyed up by a force equal to the weight of the volume of fluid it displaces. By measuring the buoyant force acting upon an object of known volume immersed in a gas or liquid, one can determine the weight of that volume of the gas or liquid and thus its density.

The gas density balance is an example of the application of this principle. This device consists of a light dumbbell, the two balls of which are hollow, suspended in an atmosphere of the gas being measured. One ball is punctured, and therefore admits the gas; it is thus free of buoyancy effects. The other ball is sealed, and will tend to rise and fall to different degrees as it is buoyed by gases of differing densities. The force necessary to keep the dumbbell suspension from tilting yields a measurement of the force of buoyancy; thus, the density of the gas may be determined.

An example of the application of the hydrometer technique to liquid density measurement employs a different method, although the general principles involved are the same. In this method a probe is inserted into the liquid to be measured. Its tip contains a ball-plummet, which is suspended at an exact position under the pole of an electromagnet. The measurement of the electromagnetic force necessary to suspend the ball in the liquid reflects the force of buoyancy, and thus the density of the liquid. Hydrometers of this type have been used in the formulation of liquid synthetic latex to terminate the reaction at a suitable value of density. Another typical use is in the pumping station of an oil pipeline in order to measure the density of the oil. This instrument is particularly useful in observing the passage of the interface dividing two batches of oil in transit in the pipeline.

Viscosity. The viscosity of a fluid is the degree to which it resists flow under applied force. This property commonly requires measurement during the operation of chemical processes. Viscosity measurements can be used to follow polymerization reactions (in which small organic molecules join together to form larger ones) in order to determine the completeness and degree of polymerization of the product, and in any other process in which viscosity is a characteristic property of the fluid under study.

Viscosity is measured continuously by utilizing any one of the following physical measurements: the amount of damping of mechanical oscillations by the fluid; the drag of the fluid on a rotating cylinder; the drag of a float against a constant flow of liquid; and rate of flow in a confined area.

Of these methods, the measurement of the damping of mechanical oscillations by the fluid is most widely used. A small blade of steel, inserted into the process stream, is made to oscillate by an impulse signal. The oscillation is affected by the viscosity of the liquid in the same way as the ringing of a bell in a liquid: the more viscous the liquid, the faster the ring dies away. The pulse is sent to the probe many times per second from an electronic oscillator through a coaxial cable. The rate of decay of the oscillation is measured, and from this the damping effect of the fluid can be determined. This damping effect is a function of both the viscosity and the density of the fluid, so that a knowledge of the density allows a measurement of the viscosity.

Damping of mechanical oscillations

This method of measurement has many applications in the petroleum and chemical fields. These include automatic blending of lubrication oil and quality control of soaps, detergents, and margarines. Applications in other industries include quality control in the production of starches, glues, adhesives, and paper and textile coatings.

Flow rate. In the chemical industry flow rate measurement is essential in controlling all phases of processing and in determining the material balance for processing units. Once manufactured, the transmission of materials through pipelines between distant places calls for an accurate measurement of flow rate. A multiplicity of techniques is used in this measurement. Flow rate may be determined by measuring the change in pressure caused by either a constriction in a pipe or the insertion of a disc with an orifice into the flow stream. Measuring the impact pressure upon a probe inserted into the process stream will yield the flow rate, as will measuring the change in pressure resulting from a change in the direction of the stream. It is also possible to derive the flow rate by measuring the change in the velocity of sound as it passes through the material.

The turbine flowmeter and the orifice meter

One of the most widely used methods is the turbine flowmeter. A turbine rotor is allowed to rotate freely in the moving fluid, and its rotation causes a sudden distortion in the field of a small, powerful magnet located in a sensor unit outside the pipe. This distortion generates an alternating-current voltage that is transmitted to a small computer. The computer analyzes this information and calculates and displays the flow rate.

Another common flow-rate measuring device is the orifice meter. A plate with a circular orifice at the centre is inserted into the process stream, causing the fluid as it passes through the orifice to increase in velocity and correspondingly decrease in pressure. A differential-pressure measuring device measures the fluid pressure just before and just beyond the orifice. Knowledge of this differential pressure allows calculation of flow rate. This type of flowmeter is the most widely used because it is simple and it has been long established in plant processes.

These devices measure the volume-flow rate. This knowledge is useful in monitoring, for instance, the blending of two fluids the densities of which are known, such as gasoline and tetraethyllead. In other cases, such as that in which a large quantity of raw material is being transmitted by pipeline and sold by weight, determination of the mass-flow rate is vital. This may be found by adding to a volume flowmeter a device that measures the density of the material and then calculating mass flow from these two measurements.

There are also flowmeters that directly measure the mass-flow rate. One of these utilizes two turbines in the flow stream, the first of which, driven at a constant speed, acts as an impeller and imparts a certain velocity to the fluid, depending on the fluid's mass. The second turbine, located downstream, is adjusted to slow the flow to its original rate; in doing so it receives a torque, or turning force, proportional to the force of the flow (angular momentum). The turbine deflects a spring at an angle proportional to the torque exerted upon it by the fluid. The result is a very accurate and direct measure of the mass flow.

MONITORING ENVIRONMENTAL PROPERTIES

Temperature and pressure. The accurate measurement of temperature is important in many chemical processes to avoid harm to materials and equipment resulting from temperatures outside a specified range. Its determination is also necessary in situations in which it is a needed variable in the computation of properties such as pressure, viscosity, or density. Methods of sensing temperature depend upon the measurement of the changes caused by temperature. Many devices, such as the familiar glass-stem thermometer, measure the change in volume of a substance, such as mercury, caused by a change in temperature. Thermistors are devices that measure temperature by the change it causes in their electrical resistance. Temperature may be inferred by measuring the intensity of the total radiation emitted, as radiation pyrometers do, or by observing changes in colour or shape of certain materials. These devices exist in such multiplicity to meet differing requirements of size, accuracy, range, and ability to withstand the testing environment.

The thermocouple

One of the most versatile and widely used of these devices is the thermocouple. It operates on the principle that heat imparted to the junction of two different metals or alloys causes a voltage that varies with the amount of heat applied. The device consists of two wires of different metal, fused together at one end to form a measuring junction. The free ends are connected to a measuring instrument, which converts the voltage at the thermocouple junction into a measurement of the temperature, the two quantities being directly proportional.

Pressure, like temperature, is a variable that must be measured accurately in industry, particularly in the chemical industry. Determination of pressure is vital, for instance, in the control of hydrogenation (addition of hydrogen) and distillation in petroleum processing. Again, like temperature, pressure is a variable needed in the calculation of other properties. Pressure-measuring devices vary with the range over which they are meant to be used. In the vacuum range, gas pressure is detected by measuring the current generated due to ionization of the gas or by measuring the thermal conductivity of the rarified gas. Pressures in this region are also calculated by compressing a known volume of the gas until it reaches a fixed pressure. When the new volume is measured, the original pressure can be computed by use of Boyle's Law, which states that the product of the original volume and original pressure is equal to the product of the new volume and new pressure.

In the atmospheric pressure range and above, elastic pressure elements are widely used; they measure the expansion caused by pressure. While some devices measure the expansion of a diaphragm or a bellows, the most commonly used industrial sensor is the so-called Bourdon tube, consisting of a tube in the form of a 250° arc. The process pressure is connected to the fixed socket end of the tube, while the tip end is sealed and connected via a series of links and gears to a pointer. Because of the difference between its inside and outside radii, the Bourdon tube tends to straighten when pressure is applied. The resulting motion of the sealed tip is a function of this pressure, and thus the position of the pointer yields a measure of the process pressure.

A device that has many applications in this pressure range is the strain gauge, which is based upon the fact that metallic conductors subjected to strain exhibit a corresponding change in electrical resistance. There are many types of strain gauge, but all are constructed so that the process pressure causes a strain, and thus a change in electrical resistance, which is measured for a visual display.

Moisture. Because of the industrial and scientific importance of measuring water, and because of water's almost universal presence, analysis for water content is a widespread necessity. The presence of water in a process stream may be either a necessary or an unwanted factor. A definite concentration may be required for the production of desired properties while, on the other hand, water can cause corrosion and other undesirable side effects in many processes. Moreover, measurements of water as a by-product of a reaction indicate the extent of reaction.

Water possesses relatively unusual properties. Many instruments with widespread applications, such as those based on infrared absorption, mass spectrometry, refractive index, and vapour chromatography, can be used for the monitoring of water. Certain methods, however, have been developed for use exclusively in the detection and measurement of water.

Electrolytic measurement of water

The electrolytic approach (involving electrolysis, or the production of chemical changes by an electric current) involves an electrolytic cell, containing a water-absorbing substance such as phosphorus pentoxide, through which a gas sample is passed at a constant velocity. Conditions are adjusted to ensure fairly complete absorption; the electrolytic decomposition of the water in the sample and the current resulting from electrolysis give a measure of the amount of water electrolyzed. With this quantity and that of the volume of gas flowing through the cell, the concentration of water in the sample can be calculated.

Applications of water-measuring devices of this type include the monitoring of air, ethylene, acetylene, and carbon dioxide in refining and allied petrochemical processing and the monitoring of natural-gas pipelines for moisture content in order to prevent the formation of explosive hydrates. Instruments for different uses may be portable or designed for fixed installation and severe environmental exposure.

Water detection by piezoelectric effect

Water vapour in gases is analyzed by observing the change in frequency of specially coated oscillating quartz crystals (the piezoelectric effect). Water vapour is first adsorbed and then desorbed, causing a change in mass of the coating, which affects the frequency of vibration. The method is very sensitive and can detect the presence of as little as 0.1 part per 1,000,000 of water.

Measurement of moisture in materials moving on a track or web can best be done using the selective absorption of an infrared analyzer. The moisture analyzer is mounted in a rugged transversing system over the web to scan the moving material on it. By measuring an average of the absorption of near-infrared energy by the moving sample, the analyzer provides a continuous, non-contacting measurement of moisture. This system can be used in a wide range of applications. It is capable of measuring webs of material travelling at high speed; conveyed particulate and granular material can be measured at moderate to high speeds. Since the sensing head is mounted several inches from the surface being measured, nothing is introduced that interferes with the process. Typical applications include the measurement of water in paper, cellophane, film, instant coffee, tea, soap, detergents, chemicals, rubbers, sand, clay, tobacco, and fibres.

Water content in sheet materials such as paper can be monitored by measuring capacitance, *i.e.*, the ability of the material to store an electrical charge when it is inserted between the plates of a capacitor. The method is sensitive to small quantities because water introduces high capacitance into the sheeting material's low capacitance: thus, the presence of water in a sample causes its capacitance to increase sharply. Devices that operate on the principle of electrical conductivity measurement have similar applications, particularly in the manufacture of food and such products as tobacco and cottonseed meal.

MONITORING PRODUCTION LINES

Mechanical properties. The need for measurement and control of the dimensions of objects in production industries is obvious. Extremely small differences in product size can be critical for machined items, and occasionally accuracies in the range of 0.000025 millimetre (0.000001 inch) must be maintained for such products as optical devices. Measurements in this range are difficult or impossible to achieve through the use of traditional devices, such as the micrometer, and, therefore, highly accurate new instrumentation has been developed.

The capacitive sensor, used in a wide range of automatic inspection machines, can discriminate down to 0.00013 millimetre (0.000005 inch). This instrument uses the two plates of an electrical capacitor to gauge the size of the measured part. The capacitor forms part of an oscillating circuit, and changes in the spacing of the plates cause a change in the output frequency of the oscillator. The changes in dimensions can be derived by measuring this change in frequency.

Another extremely accurate method is the differential-transformer sensor. It depends upon the fact that the electromagnetic coupling between two coils (the electrical effects of two coils on each other due to their proximity) is influenced by the presence of a magnetic core common to both coils. If this core is moved while an alternating current is passed in one coil, extremely sensitive coupling can be obtained with the second coil, coupling so sensitive that changes in core movement of 0.00005 millimetre (0.000002 inch) may be detected.

The electro-optical gauging system

The dimensions of rapidly moving items on a production line can be measured with an electro-optical gauging system. The system is essentially a sampling-type tracking instrument that gauges the dimensions of an object by sensing the optical discontinuity between the object and its background. By continually monitoring objects, the instrument senses the relative positions of each side of an object during a scan cycle. It then produces voltage signals that directly indicate the size of the object. A deviation from a preset value is indicated on a displacement meter. This instrument has found applications in measuring the formation of wire, the insulation of cable, and the extrusion of plastic and metal rods. The system measures objects as small as 0.05 millimetre (0.002 inch) or as large as 15 metres (50 feet) with an accuracy of 0.2 percent.

In production situations in which thickness of the product is important (such as in the production of sheets of material), nucleonic gauging is often used. In this method nuclear radiation is beamed through the product to be measured, and an automatic device measures the amount of radiation transmitted. For materials of constant density, this transmission gives an indication of the thickness. The thickness of a coating on a base material may also be measured by this method through the use of two gauges: the first examines the uncoated material and acts as a standard, while the second measures the coated material. The difference between the two gives a measure of the thickness of the coating. These techniques are applied especially to the manufacture of metal sheet products and the coating of roll sheet products with plastics and other metals.

Figure 2 shows a computer-controlled rolling mill. The computer compares the actual input thickness with the desired and actual output thickness of the strip, compares them to stored data, and generates correction signals to reset the mill rolls in the event of out-of-tolerance conditions.

Weight measurement is a problem that often occurs in industry. Although the principle of the lever as a means of weighing is attributed to Archimedes (3rd century BC), it was not until the 15th century that something new was added to these fundamentals by Leonardo da Vinci. The basic principle of the lever platform scale, the multiple lever scale, and an indicating scale are all attributed to the genius of Leonardo. Since the 17th century no fundamental changes in the principle of lever scales or spring balances have occurred. It was not until the 19th century, with the advent of the hydraulic-load cell, and, more recently, the discovery and development of the strain gauge, that there have been many significant changes in weighing principles and devices.

From *Control Engineering* (November 1969)

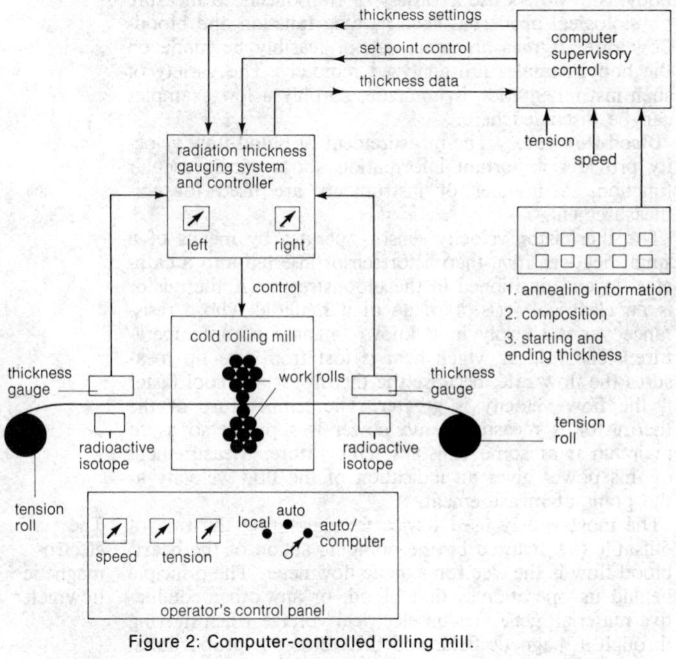

Figure 2: Computer-controlled rolling mill.

Electronic instrumentation is used rather than traditional scales or balances in situations in which speed is an important factor (weighing in roughly ⅒ second can be accomplished). Electronic instrumentation also offers the benefits of a measurement output that can be easily displayed, stored, or utilized in some form of automatic inspection or control. There are three principal methods in use. These are the load cell, in which the weight of the object causes a strain in a supporting member, which is then measured; the pressductor, in which the stress in the supporting member is measured magnetically; and the force balance, in which the weight of the object is supported by an electromagnetically generated equal and opposite force.

The load cell and pressductor

The load cell is a highly developed device working on the strain principle. A column is compressed under the applied weight and the resulting strain is sensed by a wire resistance strain gauge. This gauge is a fine wire, which, when subjected to strain, undergoes a change in resistance. A measurement of this change yields a measure of the weight causing the strain.

The pressductor is a block of magnetic laminations cemented together with four holes drilled through them. A wire carrying alternating current is threaded through two of these holes, and a pickup wire connected to a voltage meter is threaded through the other two. No voltage is detected by this pickup wire in the absence of stress, but stress caused by weight on the supporting column causes a voltage to be developed that is proportional to that weight.

Both the load cell and the pressductor are used in measuring large weights—from one kilogram to many tons. If the very rapid weighing of lighter objects is desired, the force balance is generally used. The object to be weighed is so placed as to deflect a moving coil by its weight. This coil is a conductor carrying a current in a steady magnetic field, and its deflection from rest position is detected and corrected by a balancing current. The current needed is proportional to the deflecting weight, which can thus be determined.

In many manufacturing operations and in process control systems, weight measurement is the most direct and accurate method of control. In the handling of liquids and solids, weight control is relatively independent of process characteristics, physical location, time, atmospheric conditions, and temperature. Units of weight are easily converted to monetary values, thus facilitating economic control. In handling difficult materials, such as chlorine, liquefied petroleum gases, and similar substances, weighing provides a safe and convenient method of control without contact with the product.

Optical properties. Optical properties of products, such as their colour or the degree to which they reflect or transmit light, are important variables that must be controlled in industrial production. Quality control of products such as textiles or optical devices depends upon these measurements. The measurement of colour can also be used in the automatic mechanical sorting of items.

Visible colour depends upon the three primary colours: red, yellow, and blue. The basic method for the determination of the colour of an object makes use of three photocells. One third of the light reflected from the object is diverted to each cell, each equipped with a filter to receive only red, blue, or yellow light, or some equivalent, specific wavelengths related to total colour. Each cell transmits a voltage proportional to the light received, and the ratio of these three voltages is automatically measured. Since each colour category has its own characteristic proportion of these three colours, total colour can be ascertained from this voltage ratio.

Reflected or transmitted light

Measurement of reflected or transmitted light is made if the lightness, darkness, or degree of transparency of a product is important. The basic method consists of shining light onto or through the measured object. The reflected or transmitted light is collected by one or more photocells set to receive all wavelengths of light. The ratio of the energy received by the photocells to the known energy of the light source is a measure of the reflectiveness or transmissivity of the object. Knowledge of this property is useful, for example, in the glass and optical industries, in which the transparency of the object is important, and in production situations such as that of the paper industry, in which defects show up as dark or light spots.

Radiation characteristics. Instruments that measure radiation characteristics are used in the production industries for two major purposes: for the determination of temperature, which is done by instruments that measure infrared emission; and for the detection of product defects, such as faulty wiring, poor internal adhesive bonding, and stress defects, which are found through use of instruments that measure infrared emission, X-ray transmissivity, or sound waves. In most instances these instruments are employed as continuous monitors during high-speed production. Without such instrumentation this detection is impossible or involves destruction of the product.

The radiation pyrometer

An important and versatile device used in production industries to determine and monitor temperatures up to 3,900° C (7,000° F) is the radiation pyrometer. The infrared radiation emitted by the process is focussed upon a detector, which emits a voltage proportional to the intensity of the radiation. This voltage can be converted to a measure of the temperature of the measured object, because temperature is a function of the total radiation emitted. This instrument is used in the detection and control of furnace temperature as well as in a wide range of other industrial situations, especially in the metal processing industry.

The radiation pyrometer, and similar infrared detectors, are also used in production testing for defects, which are indicated by undesirable production of internal heat. An example occurs in the electronics production industries, in which the radiation pyrometer is used in the evaluation of electrical performance through the detection of electrical overstress. This overstress causes excessive power dissipation and thermal interaction, which results in heating of the elements involved. The infrared detector senses this heating as an increase in infrared radiation and thus can be used to pinpoint the defective elements.

A simple thermocouple can be used to continuously measure the temperature of moving strip products such as steel. In galvanizing, the control of this temperature is important just before the sheet moves into a bath to be coated with zinc. The sensor employs a thermocouple embedded in a magnetic block that grips the surface of the moving sheet metal in a free-sliding manner.

In some industries X rays are used to detect product defects. Standard X-ray techniques detect internal configurations, and in situations in which examination of a thin internal section of a multilayered sample is needed, axial transverse laminography can be used. In this method the sample and film are synchronously rotated during X-ray examination, with the result that one plane remains in sharp focus. This plane can be varied to allow inspection of any section of the sample.

Production testing also may use sound waves rather than electromagnetic radiation. Ultrasonic energy (sound waves at frequencies above the limits of human hearing) is beamed into the material, and the reflection, or echo, is detected. Defects are indicated by the appearance of certain characteristic echo patterns; the method is used, for instance, in the detection of poor adhesive bonding or residual stress.

Computerized systems. Computers are used at every stage in the production industries. Though the major area of applicability is in production testing and inspection, they are increasingly used to control virtually all phases of production.

An example of computer use in production testing is found in an automatic test system for electronic and electrical equipment and components. The computer automatically carries out 16 different tests on the unit, including frequency, voltage, and resistance tests. The computer controls the sequence of these tests and evaluates and records the results.

Computerized inspection allows manipulation of situations that might otherwise occur too quickly for control. A computer, for instance, is used to inspect sheet metal travelling at 21 metres (70 feet) per second. The presence of holes or cracked edges is detected by electronic sensors, and the thickness is measured with an X-ray gauge. This information is fed into the computer and stored. The computer automatically measures the total length of sheet metal that passes and commands the system to stop and cut the sheet at a preset length. It then prints out a summary of all the measured characteristics of the sheet; this summary is attached to the coil of sheet metal and serves as a quality-control document throughout the manufacturing process. The computer also provides for the operator a visual display of each of the parameters being measured, with a running total of all the measured characteristics. If a defect such as excessive thickness is detected, the operator orders the computer to rewind the sheet to the spot at which the fault began, cut out the flawed portion, rejoin the ends, and recommence operation.

Production control by computer

In the sheet metal industry, as in many others, computers are used to control many phases of production, not just production testing. Computers in sheet-metal processing track the product through the process, operate the production machinery, control the width and thickness of the metal, regulate furnace temperatures, test the product, and, finally, route it for storage or other processing.

III. Nonmanufacturing applications

BIOMEDICAL INSTRUMENTATION

Throughout history physicians and physiologists have sought information about the workings of the body through the use of their own sense organs. To delve into processes too subtle or too rapid for the human senses, these scientists today utilize some form of transducer to extend their senses and to convert the physiological phenomenon into an electrical signal for measurement.

Examples of biomedical instrumentation are many and varied. Some instruments, such as the electrocardiograph and the electroencephalograph (see below), detect electrical signals generated by the body itself. Others, such as the X-ray machine, operate by beaming radiation into the body. Still others use a variety of transducers to measure physiological properties such as lung function and blood-flow rate. If measurements cannot feasibly be made on the body, samples are analyzed remotely. The variety of such instrumentation is immense, so only a few examples can be discussed here.

Blood-flow rate. The measurement of blood-flow velocity provides important information about cardiovascular function. A number of instruments are used for this measurement.

The thermistor velocity sensor operates by means of a small heat-sensitive thermistor sensor inserted into a catheter tip and positioned in the bloodstream. (A thermistor is an electrical resistor made of a material whose resistance varies sharply in a known manner with temperature.) The rate at which heat is lost from this tip measures the flow rate, because the thermistor will cool faster if the flow velocity is greater. The temperature of the thermistor is measured, and power is supplied so as to maintain it at some constant temperature. Measurement of this power gives an indication of the flow velocity at the point of measurement.

The electromagnetic flowmeter

The most widely used device for measuring the rate of pulsatile (*i.e.*, caused by the pumping action of the heart) blood flow is the electromagnetic flowmeter. The principle behind its operation is that blood, or any other conductive material, generates an electrical voltage when moving through a magnetic field, and this voltage is proportional to the flow rate. There are two major methods of electromagnetic flow determination. In one the artery or vein is surgically exposed, and an electromagnet is fastened around it. The voltage generated by the passage of the blood through the centre of the electromagnet is measured and the flow rate ascertained. In another method a catheter probe is inserted into the bloodstream. The probe tip contains an axially wound coil electromagnet along with two electrodes to measure the voltage produced as the blood flows around the probe. The first method is used primarily in research (on dead tissue) or in surgical situations, whereas the second is utilized in diagnosis.

Heart and brain condition. Two of the most important phenomena monitored by biomedical instruments are heart and brain condition. While a number of instruments and operating principles exist in this area, the two important measuring instruments operate by detecting electric potentials generated within the body.

Experimentation has shown that the surface of the exposed brain generates potential differences of between 300 and 600 microvolts, though the attenuating layer of fluid, bone, skin, and hair reduces this to a maximum of 200 microvolts. These potentials fluctuate rhythmically, and, though not fully understood, may appear in certain patterns that are signs of abnormality. The electroencephalograph measures these patterns through the use of electrodes placed in pairs on the surface of the skull. Each pair of electrodes sends a signal to one recording channel of the electroencephalograph; this signal consists of the voltage difference between the pair. The rhythmic fluctuation of this potential difference is shown as peaks and troughs on a line graph by the recording channel. Any number of electrode pairs and recording channels may be used, but eight-channel instruments are the most common. Electroencephalograms are commonly used in diagnosis, and expert interpretation can find brain disturbances and pin down their exact site long before they are reflected in the patient's behaviour or clinical status. They are also part of the standard equipment of operating theatres. A lessening of the blood supply to the brain, for instance, will show up as a change in the electroencephalogram of an anesthetized patient long before any other outward signs are easily noticeable.

The electrocardiograph

The electrocardiograph operates in a somewhat similar way to measure the electrical impulses emanating from the heart. These impulses originate at the heart's pacemaker (the body part that regulates the heart's rhythmic activity) and move as a wave through the heart, initiating its muscular action. Many qualities of this wave, such as the pattern of initiation and passage through the heart and the general direction of its travel, can be important indicators of heart damage and disease. The electrocardiograph measures this electrical activity through the use of single electrodes placed at various points around the chest. These measure the emitted voltage at each point, and this signal is displayed either on an oscilloscope screen or a line graph. Analysis of the fluctuations in voltage is thus possible, and comparison of the readings from the different locations on the chest yields the general direction, or electrical axis, of the wave.

Along with its many uses as a diagnostic instrument and as a monitor during surgery, the electrocardiograph has a special utility in intensive treatment of coronary patients. The patient is continuously monitored by the electrocardiograph, which feeds its output into a small computer that has been programmed to recognize any dangerous patterns of electrical activity, and to sound an alarm if these should appear. Heart function is also measured by a variety of flow rate and pressure measuring devices, some of which are put into catheter probes and inserted through the blood vessels into the heart itself.

Lung function. Since the 1940s a number of physiological tests have been developed for qualitative and quantitative evaluation of pulmonary functions. Perhaps the most widely used testing instrument is the spirometer, which measures lung capacity by measurement of the height to which the exhaled breath raises a bell turned upside down in water. The impedance pneumograph measures the volume of air inhaled by measuring the degree to which an electric current is impeded in its passage through the chest; the volume of air inhaled can be calculated from the difference in resistance.

The spirometer

Another method for pulmonary function study makes use of radioactive gases. The subject inhales an atmosphere in which all the gases are normal except the nitrogen, some of which is replaced by a radioisotope of the rare gas xenon. Radiation detectors on the chest reveal in which parts of the lung this atmosphere either is failing to penetrate or is present in abnormal volumes. A pattern of the lung areas can be obtained with radioactive sensitive film or on the fluorescent screen of a special scanning instrument.

Laboratory analysis. As knowledge in medical science increases, the need grows for instrumentation in laboratory analysis. In wide use is a device capable of providing 40 to 60 analyses an hour; it consists of a long fine tube through which are drawn samples of such substances as blood serum or urine, separated by quantities of neutral solution (distilled water in most cases). The samples and stretches of water between them are separated by air bubbles. A proportioning pump, by way of a manifold, introduces the air bubbles into the sample streams and advances precise quantities of all solutions and diluents into the system. For specific analyses, reactions are initiated in the samples with reagents that cause a noticeable colour change. These are monitored in a colorimeter, which measures the degree of absorption of this colour by the sample; this measurement is displayed as a peak on a moving graph paper. The degree of absorption is related to the composition of the sample, and the concentration of many constituents, such as albumen and uric acid, can be determined. This type of instrument is especially versatile if a small computer is used to control and record its functions. From each patient a blood sample is sent to a multi-channel analyzer, which provides information to a small computer. The computer not only sets up calibration curves and checks periodically for errors but also provides a tabulation of each patient's results, indicating those surpassing safe levels. About 1,100 tests can be run each hour with such computerized instrumentation.

Few instrumental methods are available to analyze the high molecular weight compounds in the human body, such as proteins in blood plasma and muscle. The white cells (leukocytes) in blood continuously synthesize about 2,000 proteins, which originate by a complex series of biochemical processes using genes (deoxyribonucleic acid; DNA) as a template. These proteins can now be separated and studied by a two-dimensional electrophoresis technique (see Figure 3). In this technique the proteins ex-

By courtesy of the Institute of Clinical Biochemistry, University of Oslo

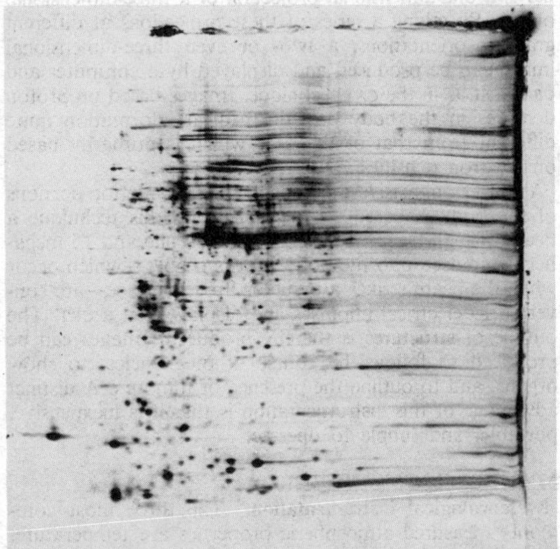

Figure 3: Two-dimensional electrophoresis separation of proteins from human leukocytes. Each spot corresponds to a separated protein.

tracted from blood are first separated according to their isoelectric point by focussing them through a tube filled with a gel. The gel is then extruded and becomes the sample, which is separated in the second dimension by using a voltage applied across a rectangular gel slab. This causes the proteins to migrate down the gel slab and separate according to their molecular weight.

Computer use. The use of computers in the biomedical field is continually growing, most obviously in processing the output of biomedical measuring devices. Computers can record and store the electrical analogue of a physiological event, and play it back later, at a different speed if desired. The computer can also be programmed to recognize certain patterns in the data and to signal this recognition.

Computer-assisted measuring instruments

An example of a computer–measuring-instrument combination using the special abilities of the computer is a system to scan and analyze cell images. The computer is used in conjunction with a vidicon scanner and a high-resolution microscope. A stained blood smear is illuminated with monochromatic light and scanned with a vidicon. The information from some 4,000 points is stored in the computer, which is programmed to analyze it into the five categories of white blood cells.

Computerized axial tomography (CAT) combines the technologies of X-ray, scintillation counting, computer processing, and cathode-ray tube (CRT) display. The result is a picture of a transverse section of a body part that looks like an anatomic section. It is a reconstructed image of the area, formed by the computer's ability to calculate small differences in attenuation of a narrow beam of X rays sweeping through the tissues. These differences cannot be seen by ordinary X-ray techniques. The images formed can show a transverse section of the brain, for example, in which eight slices—each 1.3 centimetres (0.5 inch) thick—will clearly define the condition of the structure. This noninvasive technique can show lesions of the brain, such as tumours, hematomas, cysts, and metastatic diseases. Diagnosis of tumours is about 99 percent accurate. Abnormalities of the liver, pancreas, bladder, and related structures can also be evaluated with CAT.

Another noninvasive instrument, which produces images similar to CAT, is based on nuclear magnetic resonance (NMR). NMR has been used by analytical chemists since the 1950s as a tool to determine molecular structures because it produces a spectrum that uniquely defines protons in a molecule. In the human body proton densities vary from tissue to tissue, and images can be formed that can detect cancerous tissue and outline structures within the body. The NMR image is formed by superimposing a linear magnetic field gradient on the uniform magnetic field gradient applied to the object being studied. The NMR signal is a one-dimensional projection of a three-dimensional object. By taking a series of these projections at different gradient orientations, a two- or even three-dimensional image can be produced and displayed by a computer and CRT, just as in the CAT technique. Images based on proton densities in the body provide medical information quite different from that of the CAT, which is primarily based on electron densities.

A third noninvasive method of imaging interior portions of the body is based on ultrasonics. In this technique a beam of high-frequency energy between one and 15 megahertz is pulsed into the body and its echoes—which occur when the beam strikes a tissue or fluid interface—are converted to electrical impulses and displayed on a CRT. The outline of structures is thereby produced. Images can be produced to follow the course of pregnancies, to show organs, and to outline the presence of tumours. A distinct advantage of this instrumentation is that it is inexpensive, portable, and simple to operate.

ATMOSPHERIC MEASUREMENT

Meteorological instrumentation. The three most commonly measured atmospheric properties are temperature, humidity, and atmospheric pressure. Routine measurement of these properties involves use of such instruments as mercury or alcohol thermometers, wet and dry bulb hygrometers, and mercury barometers. Modern instrumentation must often be used, however, in such situations as remote weather sensing or automatic monitoring of indoor atmospheric variables. An example would be the instruments most often used to monitor these three variables in a radiosonde, or weather balloon. A thermistor measures temperature by the change it causes in its electrical resistance. A hair hygrometer measures humidity by the change it causes in the length of a fibre. Atmospheric pressure is measured by a type of aneroid barometer, which detects the distension that the pressure causes on a metal diaphragm.

Modern instrumentation is also used in meteorology to measure a variety of other atmospheric properties. Automatic systems monitor wind speed and direction, ozone concentration, and total rain falling through the air, in addition to a number of other special variables. Wind direction is most often monitored by the electronic sensing of the orientation of a wind vane; wind speed is monitored by measurement of the pressure it causes, by determination of the rate at which it cools a thermistor, or by sensing the speed of a rotating device used to measure wind speed (cup anemometer). Spectrophotometric techniques (*i.e.*, involving measurement of bands in the light spectrum) are used to monitor ozone concentration, and radar reflection is studied to determine the total rain in the air over large areas, leading to the detection of showers, cold and warm fronts, and cyclones.

Monitoring air purity. Safety engineering often requires monitoring the composition of the atmosphere to determine the concentration of oxygen, carbon dioxide, carbon monoxide, and other gases.

Detecting oxygen deficiency

Oxygen deficiency, for instance, can be encountered in tunnels, ships' holds, storage tanks, and inert-gas-purged rooms. One method of quick detection of subnormal oxygen levels makes use of a fuel-cell detector. This cell consumes oxygen from the atmosphere surrounding the detector and generates a proportional electrical current.

The accumulation of explosive or toxic flammable gases in the air can be measured with an instrument that continuously detects these substances, sounds an alarm, and automatically actuates ventilating devices. The explosion meter functions by drawing a sample of the air to be monitored over a wire heated sufficiently to burn the gases on its surface. The heat of this combustion changes the resistance of the wire, this change being sensed to indicate electrically the amount of explosive gases.

A portable instrument analyzes for traces of many gases in air, such as missile fuel components, ammonia, chlorine, phosgene, hydrogen chloride, and nitrogen dioxide. The instrument incorporates a device called an alpha-particle emitter that ionizes the incoming sample and creates an ion current. A chemical reagent converts the gas to be detected into small aerosol particles, which in turn reduce the ion current in proportion to the number of particles present. This simple device can detect concentrations in the range of parts per 1,000,000 or lower.

Carbon monoxide is the most insidious of toxic gases. It gives no warning of its presence and occurs more frequently than all other dangerous gases. Carbon monoxide can produce serious physical effects at 100 parts per 1,000,000 concentration. The atmosphere in many industrial operations is monitored for this gas with an instrument that functions by the selective absorption principle. The monitored air is drawn through a detector cell containing a catalyst in which a series of thermocouples has been embedded. Absorption of the carbon monoxide liberates heat, which is indicated by the thermocouples.

POLLUTION CONTROL

People are becoming acutely aware of the degree to which they are contaminating the environment. Hundreds, if not thousands, of by-products considered to be pollutants are found in the air, water, and soil and in plants and animals. Awareness of the nature and extent of pollution is largely based on modern analysis instrumentation, which has made detection and study of pollutants possible. Pesticide and mercury pollution, industrial and automobile emission, and many other contaminants require the increasing speed and sensitivity of modern instruments, whether in detection by laboratory analysis or by automatic pollutant monitoring.

Detection. The detection of environmental pollutants involves a multitude of techniques, partly because of the large number of pollutants. In the air alone there are more than 40 separate categories of substances considered to be actually or potentially harmful, with many of these categories containing more than one substance. Examples of techniques employed in the detection of some of the major pollutants, such as mercury and pesticides, illustrate the types of problems encountered.

Detection of mercury. Mercury in many forms is known to occur in trace amounts throughout the environment. Deposits of mercury in inland waters constitute an especially great hazard through the production of the more toxic methylmercury by microorganisms in the bottom mud. Methylmercury and other such organic mercury compounds attack the human central nervous system and remain in the body for long periods of time. Widespread incidents of methylmercury poisoning have been reported only since the mid-20th century. In Japan more than 168 illnesses and 52 deaths were reported in two separate incidents in the 1950s from consumption of mercury-contaminated fish. Since then several hundred persons in a number of countries have died or suffered serious illness from eating seed grain that had been treated with mercury compounds.

Highly sensitive and accurate instruments are needed to measure the concentration of mercury, since the presence of only a few parts per 1,000,000,000 can be significant, and a concentration of only 200 parts per 1,000,000,000 in blood causes noticeable symptoms. Instrumentation is needed not only in the simple detection of mercury but also in tracing its natural cycles through food webs and chains so that it can be determined, for instance, what concentration of mercury in lake water will produce a dangerous mercury concentration in the person who eats fish from that lake. A sensitive instrument used in this measurement is the ultraviolet spectrophotometer. This instrument passes ultraviolet radiation through a sample in which all the mercury has been converted to the elemental vapour form, and the amount of radiation transmitted is then measured. The frequency of radiation chosen, 2,537 angstroms (one angstrom is 10^{-10} metre), is one for which mercury vapour has an intense absorption. The amount of 2,537-angstrom radiation transmitted gives an indication of the concentration of mercury in the sample. Concentrations of mercury below the parts-per-1,000,000,000 range can be measured with this instrument.

The ultraviolet spectrophotometer

Detection of pesticides. Pesticide contamination is another problem that is measured by modern instrumentation. Like mercury, pesticides are found virtually everywhere in the environment. Since they were developed specifically to kill living organisms, it is hardly surprising that many of them are harmful. Some of the basic problems in detection are similar to the problems in mercury detection: the pollutants must be identified in very small concentrations, and their presence in various materials must be sensed so as to gain information about their distribution and cycle patterns. An additional factor with pesticides, however, is their variety; approximately 300 organic chemicals are marketed in more than 10,000 different formulations. Moreover, these pesticides in the environment often change into other substances through chemical reaction. Some of these secondary pollutants, like the polychlorinated biphenyls resulting from DDT (dichlorodiphenyltrichloroethane) reactions, can be dangerous. Thus, detection is often a matter of analyzing not only for a specific pesticide but also for a variety of them plus their by-products.

Given these instrumental requirements for high accuracy and multicomponent analytical ability, the gas/liquid chromatograph has come to be widely used. This instrument operates by passing the sample through a separation column (see above *Chromatographic analyzer*). As the sample passes through the column, individual molecules are absorbed and then released at different times from the column surface. If a column of the proper type is employed, the components of the sample emerge from the column completely separated from each other with the most strongly absorbed emerging last. This emerging stream then passes through a detector, which detects each component by means of its thermal conductivity or reaction to ionization. The relative response is detected and usually presented on a recorder. This instrument can be used in the simultaneous measurement of many components in a sample and can detect concentrations in the parts-per-1,000,000,000,000 range.

The gas/liquid chromatograph

Monitoring. The study and control of pollution often necessitates the use of detection instrumentation for continuous monitoring of pollutant levels in rapidly changing systems. Air-pollutant levels, for instance, may undergo significant change in a matter of hours, and harmful changes at one point of a water pipeline can occur in less than one second. Since the older methods of laboratory analysis take many hours or days, modern instrumentation is desirable not only for its speed but also for its ability to be integrated into a system of automatic control. While continuous monitoring can be useful in virtually any pollution situation, its applications today are primarily in the areas of air and water pollution.

Air-pollution monitoring. Atmospheric monitoring systematically collects and evaluates aerometric (involving the density and weight of gases, such as air) and related data to provide information on pollutant concentrations in ambient air, emissions from polluting sources, and meteorological conditions. Information derived from monitoring is applied in various pollution-control activities: assessing pollution effects on human beings and their environment; studying pollutant interactions and patterns; establishing ambient air-quality standards; developing control strategies and regulations; evaluating the effectiveness of these control strategies when adopted; activating emergency procedures to prevent air-pollution episodes or to reduce their severity; and guiding efforts to minimize the effect of air-pollution by applying mathematical modelling and planning systems.

One of the special problems encountered in air-pollution monitoring is the necessity of virtually simultaneous monitoring over a large area. Indeed, many environmental scientists feel that a global monitoring system is needed. To accomplish this with fixed sampling stations would require vast amounts of money, labour, and equipment. The instrumental alternative involves remote sensing. One method is monitoring by aircraft equipped with a correlation spectrometer, which compares the spectrum of incoming light with a reference spectrum of the pollutant being monitored. Only the light that matches the reference spectrum is detected, the amount of this light being a measure of pollutant concentration. Such systems are used to monitor nitrogen and sulfur oxides. More ambitious systems involving satellites carrying the monitoring instrument are also being used.

Water-pollution monitoring. The aims and uses of water-pollution monitoring are much the same as those of air-pollution monitoring. For compositional analysis many of the same instruments used to monitor air pollutants are used. Other qualities of water besides composition must be monitored. Thus, water-pollution control uses instruments monitoring such qualities as turbidity, colour, pH, and presence of microorganisms. A special requirement in this area is often extreme speed of operation. This need occurs especially in water-treatment plants and in the control of industrial waste water, problems in which large volumes of rapidly moving water in transit lines must be monitored. In these situations the monitoring must be done on-line (*i.e.*, as the water moves through the pipe) because of the large time lag involved in sample removal and remote analysis. An example of on-line analysis is the ultraviolet photometric method of monitoring trace amounts of oil in water. A continuous sampling system divides the water sample into two parts, one of which is filtered to remove undissolved oil. The filtered and unfiltered streams are then run through separate cells of an ultraviolet analyzer in which ultraviolet radiation is beamed through each stream. Since the difference in their absorption characteristics is solely the result of the presence of oil, oil content can be continuously monitored.

Control of industrial waste water

LABORATORY INSTRUMENTATION

From earliest times instruments have been employed in the scientific laboratory. Early instruments were usually quite simple devices, such as thermometers, rulers, optical devices, and meters. As instrumentation became more complex and capable of greater scope, laboratories were developed for specific purposes; products produced elsewhere, either by research groups or in manufacturing, were measured and analyzed with great accuracy. Such analytical instrumentation laboratories, now firmly established as necessary to world technology, take many forms and can best be categorized by function.

Quality control of processes. Manufacturing processes generally involve a number of laboratories associated with the various steps in production. These laboratories are located at the plant facilities in close proximity to the origin of their samples. In large industrial complexes there may also be a centrally located test laboratory.

The tests and analyses, which are made with very simple instruments, are intended to control process variables and the quality of the product. Typical examples of such tests include measurement of liquid density using a hydrometer, determination of the particle size of a granular product using sieves, and measurement of viscosity by timed flow of a liquid through a narrow-bore tubing.

Since many of the quality control tests are done on products that are common among many industries, the problem of standardization of these tests arose long ago. In many countries standards have been established and are regularly brought up to date. In the United States, for example, the American Society for Testing and Materials (ASTM) publishes a multivolume set of specifications of the instrumentation and methods for 4,300 standard tests applied to almost every material used in industry. These tests cover not only chemical but also physical properties of materials, such as paper, ferrous castings, petroleum products, fuels, paints, plastics, electrical components, radioisotopes, and pure chemicals. An example of an ASTM physical test is the ultrasonic inspection of metal tubing for longitudinal discontinuities. Quality control laboratories use these documented testing procedures for much of their work.

Analytical laboratories in industry. Large industrial companies manufacturing chemical, petroleum, or consumable products must have a capable analytical laboratory to supply accurate information on all phases of company activities, from early research on new products to final process control. While some of the older chemical-type analyses are still used, the greater part of the analytical work today is accomplished by instrumental methods. These instruments include spectrometers of various types—infrared, atomic absorption, X-ray, mass, electron, spark emission, Mössbauer, and nuclear magnetic resonance. Other instruments based on the principles of gas chromatography, micromeritics, physical chemistry, magnetic susceptibility, and electron microscopy are also widely used.

Identifying an unknown compound

For qualitative identification of compounds, a combination of results from several complementary instruments is advantageous in rapidly obtaining an answer. Laboratories usually obtain spectra for a given unknown compound on three different instruments: a mass spectrometer, an infrared spectrometer, and a nuclear magnetic resonance spectrometer. Since each instrument functions best for pure compounds, the sample is subjected to a separation and purification step (usually by chromatographic means) before a spectrum is obtained. Each spectrum reveals important clues to the identity of the unknown compound. These instruments are operated by trained personnel, and the combined spectra are interpreted by a specialist, though some functions are now being performed by computer systems.

Gas chromatography. As a method of separating the individual components of a complex mixture, gas chromatography is unequalled. Although the principle of gas–liquid partition chromatography was clearly stated in 1941, the field really opened in 1952 when the simple instrumentation needed to separate and analyze a mixture of fatty acids was described. Since then intensive work with this technique has been carried out in laboratories all over the world, and many instruments, with varying degrees of complexity, have been developed. The present importance of gas chromatography reflects not only the comparative ease of using the technique but also its speed in analyzing very complex mixtures containing a wide range of compounds and concentrations. When the full capability of the method is applied to complex mixtures with more than 100 components, digital electronics can be used to help obtain the analysis. A digital computer built into these devices can accept the chromatogram from a mixture and type out a complete analysis of each component. A complex mixture can be analyzed in minutes, an accomplishment that prior to the discovery of this technique bordered on the impossible, regardless of time. Analyses can be made with gas chromatographs for almost any compound possessing some volatility at 500° C (932° F). Even a large number of metals have been analyzed by first converting them to volatile compound form and obtaining a chromatogram of the compounds. For analysis of nonvolatile compounds a form of chromatography in which the carrier gas is replaced by a carrier liquid is used. Liquid chromatography is extremely useful in the medical field; a complete analysis of an APC (aspirin, phenacetin, and caffeine) tablet can be made in less than five minutes. Chromatography can measure trace concentrations of compounds present in the parts-per-1,000,000 range; for this reason it is useful for measuring pollutants in the environment.

Liquid chromatography

Mass spectrometry. The different masses (isotopes) of an element were first separated in 1910 and the first mass spectrograph was built in 1919. Mass spectroscopy has a long history, but only since 1950 has its powerful ability to determine molecular structure and to identify molecules been developed. This development is due to the increasing capabilities of the instrumentation available. Mass spectrometers are an important analytical tool in most major laboratories.

A mass spectrum is produced when a gas, liquid, or solid is vaporized and injected into an ionizing source (usually an electron beam) under high vacuum. This breaks the molecules into characteristic ion fragments, which are then separated and recorded as the mass spectrum. The first mass spectrometers used a magnetic field to separate the positively charged fragment ions, and present instrumentation is often based on magnetic separation.

By courtesy of Hewlett-Packard Company

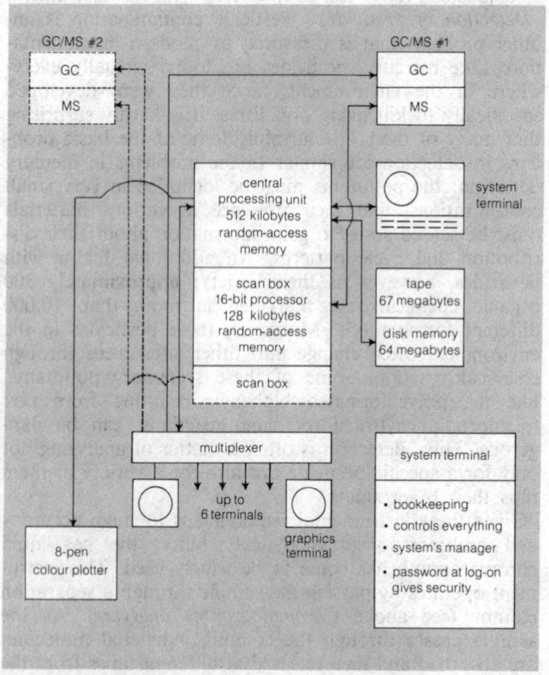

Figure 4: Computerized gas chromatograph / mass spectrometer (GC / MS) system.

GC/MS computer system

A mass spectrum contains a great amount of information about a molecule. From the molecular weight it indicates and from the masses of fragment ions it reveals, the structure of the original molecule can usually be deduced. The instrument can be universally applied to compound identification. Since gas chromatography has separating power and mass spectrometry has identification power, the two instruments are commonly combined into the gas chromatograph/mass spectrometer (GC/MS) system. This provides a uniquely capable instrument for the analysis of complex mixtures.

A GC/MS instrument is such a powerful analytical tool that it is an indispensible instrument in both research and analytical laboratories. So much useful information is produced and so many data analysis techniques are employed that a computer is a necessary part of the GC/MS system. During the 1970s great advances were made in the development of the system (see Figure 4). After injection of a sample of a complex mixture containing 200 compounds into the gas chromatograph, for example, an operator sits in front of a CRT display module to analyze the data produced by the computer. As the more than 2,000 mass spectra associated with the compounds are produced, the computer compares each mass spectrum with more than 80,000 mass spectra of reference compounds and identifies it within seconds. Totally new compounds are also identified by the reconstruction of their molecular structures from their mass spectral patterns. Several operators can work on data or samples simultaneously on the computerized GC/MS, which has revolutionized analysis in fields such as biomedicine, forensics, and environmental pollution.

Infrared spectroscopy. As early as 1905 it was recognized that the selective absorption of infrared radiation arises from the mutual vibrations of the atoms in a molecule (*i.e.*, resulting from the molecules jumping from one energy level to another). The first practical infrared instrumentation was built in 1940 and demonstrated its utility with a number of startling applications. Similar instruments were manufactured, and a revolutionary period of growth for chemical analysis by infrared spectroscopy began. An infrared spectroscopy section is an important part of present-day analytical laboratories.

The atoms forming a molecule can vibrate only in certain fundamental modes characteristic of that molecular configuration. When the frequency of incident radiant energy occurs at the same vibrational frequency as the vibrating atoms, the molecule absorbs that radiation. An absorption spectrum in the infrared region of two to 15 micrometres in wavelength provides a characteristic fingerprint pattern of a compound. This spectrum can be used for qualitative identification and quantitative analysis of a substance. The qualitative aspects have predominated; the characteristic absorption bands of more than 130,000 compounds have been determined and cataloged as reference spectra. These are stored on magnetic tape. By use of a computer system, the spectrum of an unknown compound can be compared with 40,000 reference spectra on the magnetic tape in 40 seconds.

Nuclear magnetic resonance. The spectroscopy of nuclear magnetic resonance (NMR) began in 1946. The energy of radio frequency waves is too small to vibrate, rotate, or interact with atoms or molecules. It is sufficient, however, to affect the magnetic moment (tendency to produce motion) and spin of the nucleus of atoms, so that a resonance absorption of radio frequency radiation by the nucleus occurs when atoms are placed in a magnetic field and irradiated with the proper frequency radio waves. A spectrum is produced by observing resonances for a compound as the magnetic field or radio frequency is scanned.

In analytical chemistry, NMR spectroscopy detects the shape and structure of molecules. Molecules containing hydrogen atoms have the strongest effect, and most instruments are designed to produce NMR spectra of hydrogen atoms. Both qualitative and quantitative information is provided, since each different type of bond of the hydrogen atom gives its own unique resonance. NMR became of vital importance in scientific laboratories as the first commercial spectrometer, appearing in 1953, was followed by a number of other instruments. Some of these are quite complex for research, while others are quite simple for routine analytical work.

Micromeritics. In the next larger size range to the molecule are the clusters of molecules called colloids and then the group of particles with dimensions reaching from microscopic resolution to visibility by the eye, particles of 0.1 to 1,000 micrometres in size. These particles are related to natural phenomena of common experience. In the atmosphere they influence the colour of the sky and sunset. Because of their basic role in industrial processes and their importance in air pollution, particles influence much of modern existence. They are used, for example, as catalysts in processes that are completely altered by a slight change in their properties. The tastes of coffee, chocolate, and peanut butter, for example, are influenced strongly by the fineness of the ground particles in them.

Micromeritics is the technology of fine particles. Instruments to measure the physical characteristics of particles are of prime importance; the physical properties that determine the characteristics of finely divided matter are the primary ones of particle size, surface area, and the sizes of the pores that extend downward from the surfaces.

Surface areas of particles

Enormous surface area can be involved in a small mass of powdered material. A one-centimetre (0.4-inch) cube of finely divided powder may have a surface area as large as 10,000,000 square centimetres (1,550,000 square inches). This surface area is measured by an automatic analyzer that determines the quantity of gas necessary to cover the area with a single layer of molecules of nitrogen gas. The pore structure of a surface area can be measured by simply determining the amount of mercury that can be forced into these pores at various increasing pressures. The particle size of a powder can be determined in an automatic instrument by observing how fast the particles settle through a viscous fluid.

SPACE INSTRUMENTATION

During the 1970s many successful uses of instrumentation in space were developed. These were centred on miniaturization of existing instruments and their adaptation for special uses and remote control, rather than the creation of entirely new instruments. The accomplishments of the 1970s were embodied in the Viking missions to Mars, the Pioneer Venus mission, and the Voyager missions that flew by Mars, Jupiter, and Saturn and its satellites on their way to Uranus and Neptune and the limits of the solar system. In all these space experiments, computers played a key role in control of the instruments and transmission of their data back to Earth.

The Viking missions. Two identical Viking spacecraft, launched 30 days apart in 1975, successfully landed on Mars after almost a year in space flight (see Figure 5). Each carried an impressive array of instrumentation primarily concerned with the detection of life, although other conditions were studied. Each spacecraft had an orbiter section that delivered a lander module to a selected point for descent to the surface and then acted as a relay station to control the lander's functions and transmit data back to Earth. Radio transmission over the 321,860,000-kilometre (200,000,000-mile) distance required 40 minutes round-trip. The orbiter carried television cameras, an infrared thermal mapper, and an infrared spectrometer for water-vapour mapping. By the end of the orbiter mission in August 1980, almost 55,000 pictures of the planet had been taken.

The landers operated for several years and, although no evidence of biological life was detected, a huge amount of information on soil chemistry and meteorological conditions was obtained. Three types of instrumentation systems were mounted on the lander: an X-ray fluorescence spectrometer to analyze surface materials, a module to perform biological experiments, and a molecular analysis module to identify atmospheric constituents and organic molecules in the Martian soil. The lander had a long mechanical arm to scoop up soil from the surface and deliver a sample to the instruments. Surface dust was introduced to the X-ray fluorescence spectrometer. The

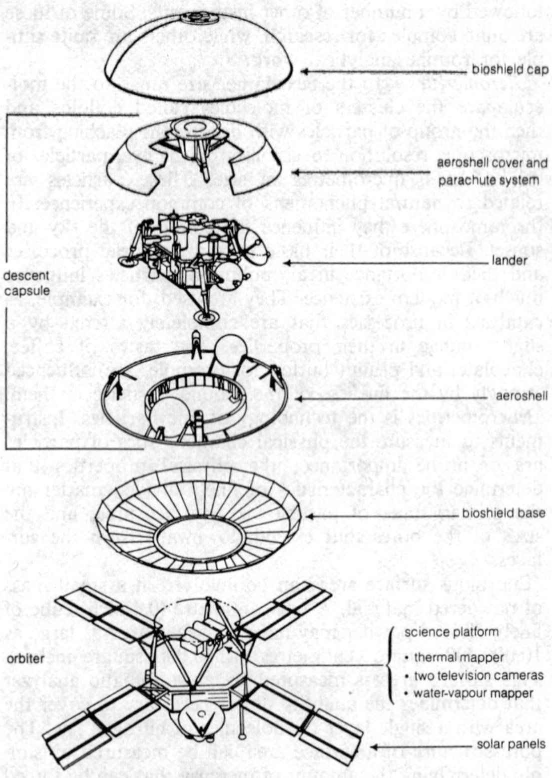

Figure 5: Sections of the Viking spacecraft sent to Mars.
By courtesy of Martin Marietta Corporation

X-ray spectra produced were matched by computer to known spectra for elements of atomic number greater than 11.

The biological module performed three experiments on portions of a common soil sample collected from the Martian surface. The pyrolytic release experiment measured the assimilation of a mixture of radioactive carbon dioxide and carbon monoxide from the atmosphere by living matter after incubation under the Martian atmosphere. The degree of assimilation could be determined by analyzing the gases and pyrolysis products of organic matter that might be present with a gas chromatographic procedure. The labelled release experiment detected assimilation of organic material and its conversion to carbon dioxide by living matter. Martian soil was moistened with a nutrient mixture of simple, radioactively labelled organic compounds, and the headspace gas over the mixture was monitored for an increase of radioactivity with time. The gas exchange experiment was similar; a gas chromatographic analysis was conducted on the headspace gas.

Detection of carbon compounds

The module containing the gas chromatograph/mass spectrometer (GC/MS) unit was designed not only to analyze for atmospheric gases but primarily to detect organic carbon compounds—a necessary condition for the presence of life. The organic compounds were investigated by pyrolyzing a sample of soil to decompose it into compounds easily identifiable by the GC/MS technique. A total of 14 organic analyses were performed on four soil samples and 57 atmospheric samples. The GC/MS analyses showed the soil contained no organic molecules, despite detection sensitivities in the parts-per-1,000,000,000 range. Having successfully completed their mission, the GC/MS instruments were turned off during March–April 1977.

The Pioneer mission. In 1978 the Pioneer Venus spacecraft was launched, requiring six months to reach the planet. The spacecraft, consisting of an orbiter and four probes that landed on the surface, carried numerous instruments. The orbiter used a Bennett-type mass spectrometer to directly measure the ions present in the Venusian ionosphere. Electrons and their temperature were measured electronically. A quadrupole mass spectrometer operating for 243 Earth days measured the neutral gas composition of the upper atmosphere between 150 and 300 kilometres (about 90 and 180 miles). An ultraviolet spectrometer produced valuable information about the sulfur oxide content of the atmosphere and its photochemical changes. A radiometer mapped thermal emission data, providing large-scale meteorological information.

Of the four probes, the sounder probe entered the Venusian atmosphere in December 1979 and descended slowly to the surface (part of the way by parachute), producing data for nearly one hour below an altitude of 62 kilometres (38 miles). A magnetic mass spectrometer measured the composition of gases relative to carbon monoxide, the dominant gas, producing 51 mass spectra before impact. A gas chromatograph provided an alternate method to measure atmospheric gas composition. A solar flux radiometer measured solar radiation as a function of altitude to increase knowledge of the extraordinary surface temperature of Venus.

The Voyager missions. Launched in 1977, each of the two Voyager spacecraft carried sophisticated infrared and ultraviolet spectrometers to explore the outer reaches of the solar system. The infrared spectrometer used was a Fourier transform infrared (FTIR) interferometer type, which extracts the infrared spectrum from an interferogram rather than producing it from an optical scan. It operates from thermal emission of the sample. In this application, the solar bodies being studied are the samples whose emissions are gathered by a telescope.

RESEARCH IN INSTRUMENTATION

In the evolution of instruments for use in research, spectroscopy is increasing in importance; the instruments tend to be of greater complexity and capability, with more automatic operations and more assistance from computers. Among the newer methods of spectroscopy, the emphasis is on the electron and the ion. Photochemical dissociation spectroscopy, a type of chemical spectroscopy, is the product of pulsed high-power lasers, molecular beams, and time-of-flight mass spectrometry. The ion microanalyzer, which combines the functions of a mass spectrometer and an ion emission microscope, provides a visual display of the complete composition of a minute section of a solid surface.

Plasma Chromatography

Ion-mobility spectrometry (IMS) originated in 1970 as plasma chromatography. The simple technique is based on ions reacting with trace molecules at atmospheric pressure. The capabilities of IMS are many: it has uncomplicated instrumentation giving femtogram (10^{-15} gram) sensitivities; it is capable of operating as a five-mode gas chromatographic detector; it can be used to make basic studies on ion-molecule reactions; and it has an ability to selectively monitor ultra-trace components in air. Major advances have been made in development and use of IMS instrumentation in defensive military applications, as a detector of chemical warfare agents, principally the deadly nerve gases.

BIBLIOGRAPHY. F.W. KARASEK, "Notes on Analytical Instrumentation," set of 94 articles, appearing in *Research/Development* (monthly) between 1969 and 1978, that describe a wide range of instrumentation in use in science and industry; BÉLA G. LIPTÁK, *Instrument Engineers' Handbook: Process Measurement*, rev. ed. (1982), a text describing the details of instrument design and application for each of the major classes of automatic process instruments from flowmeters to analytical devices; DOUGLAS A. SKOOG and DONALD M. WEST, *Principles of Instrumental Analysis*, 2nd ed. (1980), a clearly written textbook describing instruments and their uses; ROBERT M. SILVERSTEIN and G. CLAYTON BASSLER, *Spectrometric Identification of Organic Compounds*, 4th ed. (1981), covering the fundamental aspects of spectral interpretation when combining the three spectroscopies of mass, nuclear magnetic resonance, and infrared to identify a compound; M.H. CARR, *The Surface of Mars* (1981), a beautifully illustrated description of the Viking mission to Mars and its results. Refer also to *Scientific American* (monthly), which offers articles on various aspects of instrumentation; *Science* (weekly), a magazine written in technical style; AMERICAN SOCIETY FOR TESTING AND MATERIALS, *Annual Book of ASTM Standards*, a work containing complete details of the instrumentation and tests that are accepted standards of industry in the United States.

(F.W.K.)

Insurance

Insurance is a device to handle risk. Its primary function is to substitute certainty for uncertainty as regards the economic cost of disastrous events. Insurance may be defined more formally as a system under which the insurer, for a consideration, promises to reimburse the insured or to render services to the insured in the event that certain accidental occurrences result in losses during a given time period.

The article is divided into the following sections:

THE NATURE AND ELEMENTS OF INSURANCE

Insurance relies heavily upon the "law of large numbers." In large homogeneous populations it is possible to estimate the normal frequency of common events such as deaths and accidents. Losses can be predicted with reasonable accuracy, and this accuracy increases as the size of the group expands. From a theoretical standpoint, it is possible to eliminate all pure risk if an infinitely large group is selected.

Insurable risk

From the standpoint of the insurer, an insurable risk must meet the following requirements:

1. The objects insured must be numerous enough and homogeneous enough to allow a reasonably close calculation of the probable frequency and severity of losses.

2. The insured objects must not be subject to simultaneous destruction. For example, if all the buildings insured by one insurer are in an area subject to flood, and a flood occurs, the loss to the insurance underwriter may be catastrophic.

3. The possible loss must be accidental in nature, and beyond the control of the insured. If the insured could cause the loss, the element of randomness and predictability would be destroyed.

4. There must be some way to determine whether a loss has occurred, and how great a one. This is why insurance contracts specify very definitely what events must take place, what constitutes loss, and how it is to be measured.

From the viewpoint of the insured person, an insurable risk is one for which the probability of loss is not so high as to require excessive premiums. What is "excessive" will depend on individual circumstances, including the person's attitude toward risk. At the same time, the potential loss must be severe enough to cause financial hardship if a person does not insure against it. Insurable risks include losses to property resulting from fire, explosion, windstorm, etc.; losses of life or health; and the legal liability arising out of use of automobiles, occupancy of buildings, employment, or manufacture.

Uninsurable risks include losses resulting from price changes and competitive conditions in the market. Political risks such as war, punitive taxation, or currency debasement are usually not insurable by private parties but may be insurable by governmental institutions. Very often contracts can be drawn in such a way that an "uninsurable risk" can be turned into an "insurable" one through restrictions on losses, redefinitions of perils, or other methods.

FIRE INSURANCE

Standard fire insurance provisions

The standard fire insurance policy is made up of two parts—the insuring agreement and the conditions and stipulations. The policy coverage is limited to the actual cash value, defined in practice as the replacement cost of the property less an allowance for depreciation. (The subtraction of depreciation from loss settlements may be waived by special provision under an endorsement known as replacement cost insurance.) Settlement must be made within a reasonable time following the loss but without any allowance for increased cost of repair by reason of building codes or other laws. The basic policy does not provide any coverage for indirect loss from fire such as might result from the interruption of a business. This peril can be covered under a separate contract, described below. The insuring agreement covers not only loss from fire and lightning but also losses to property that had to be removed from endangered premises.

Recovery under the basic standard policy is limited to the interest of the insured person. If two individuals own a certain property but only one is insured, and the other is not named in the contract as an insured interest, the limit of recovery is that portion of the property owned by the insured person. The policy refers to all *direct* losses by fire. This implies that if other causes are instrumental in causing the loss, there will be no recovery except for losses due directly from the fire. Thus, if an explosion knocks a building down and it becomes a pile of rubble that later burns, the fire loss is limited to the loss of rubble. Only losses that are *proximately* caused by fire are paid.

Direct losses. Fire insurance policies contain various specific provisions and stipulations. Among the more important provisions are the following:

1. Certain property is declared uninsurable or excluded from the basic coverage. This includes accounts, bills, currency, deeds, evidence of debt, money, or securities. Such property may be covered under a separate form.

2. The basic fire policy customarily excludes loss from certain perils such as war, invasion, insurrection, revolution, usurped power, neglect by the insured, and theft. Thus if the insured sees his property threatened by a fire in a neighbouring building and fails to use preventive measures, he may be denied recovery.

3. Insurance coverage is suspended at any time the insured is increasing the hazard or when the property is vacant or unoccupied beyond a period of 60 days, or during other periods as stated in the policy.

4. The policy may be cancelled by either party for any reason. If the insurer cancels it, however, he must give the insured prior notice.

5. A mortgagee's interest can be protected under the basic fire insurance policy, generally without extra charge.

6. If the insured has other policies of insurance on the same property, each policy contributes to the loss in the proportion that its limits bear to the total limits of all insurance on the property. This prevents the insured from collecting more than his actual cash loss by taking out a number of policies in separate companies.

7. The insured is required to give immediate written notice of the loss and to prove the amount of the loss within a specified period. The policy contains arbitration provisions in the event of disagreement over the amount.

8. The insurer is allowed to rebuild or replace the damaged property with other property of like kind and quality, rather than make a cash settlement. Abandonment of destroyed property to the insurer is not permitted.

9. Legal action to recover loss is not permitted unless all of the requirements on arbitration have been complied with and unless it is commenced within a limited period after the loss.

10. If a party other than the insured burns down a property and is held legally liable for it, the insurer reserves the right to bring a legal action against this third party in the name of the insured. This prevents the insured from collecting twice—once from his insurance company and once from a liable third party.

A widely used clause is the coinsurance clause, used on insurance covering commercial property. Its purpose is to prevent underinsurance. It requires the insured to carry enough coverage to equal a specified percentage, usually 80 to 90 percent, of the true replacement value of the property. If the insured fails to carry this minimum amount, he recovers only that portion of any fire loss equal to the ratio of the amount of insurance actually carried to the amount required under the coinsurance clause.

Fire insurance rates are influenced by four basic risk factors: the fire protection class of the city of location; the type of construction; the class of occupancy of the building; and the degree to which the building is exposed to losses originating outside it. For example, if a city has very little fire protection its insurance rates will be higher than those in a city that is superior in its water supply, fire department, protection and alarm systems, building codes, police protection, and so forth. A building made of fireproof material obviously requires a lower fire rate than one of frame construction. A manufacturer of explosive chemicals would receive a higher fire rate than the owner of a hardware store. If the building is located near another in which explosives are stored, it will carry a higher rate than a building not so exposed.

The standard fire policy insures against only the basic perils of fire, lightning, and removal from the premises. If the insured wishes additional perils to be covered, he must see either that the form lists additional perils or that it is on an "all risk" basis. One of the most common extensions of perils is known as the extended coverage endorsement, which provides coverage against windstorm, hail, explosion, riot, riot attending strike, civil commotion, aircraft, vehicles, and smoke. Each peril is specifically defined and delimited. For example, smoke from a fireplace may not be defined as "smoke."

Indirect losses. An entirely different branch of the fire insurance business has been developed to insure losses that are indirectly the result of one of the specified perils. A prominent example of this type of insurance is business interruption insurance. The insurer undertakes to reimburse the insured for lost profits or for fixed charges incurred as a result of damage. For example, a retail store might have a fire and be completely shut down for one month and partially shut down for another month. If the fire had not occurred sales would have been much higher, and therefore substantial revenues have been lost. In addition, fixed costs such as salaries, taxes, maintenance, and so forth must continue to be paid. A business interruption policy would respond to these losses.

Other forms of indirect insurance include the following: (1) contingent business interruption insurance, designed to cover the consequential losses if the plant of a supplier or a major customer is burned and results in either reduced orders or reduced deliveries that force a shutdown of the insured firm; (2) extra expense insurance, which pays the additional cost occasioned by having extra expenses to pay such as rent on substitute facilities after a fire; (3) rent and rental value insurance, covering losses in rents that the owner of an apartment house may incur if his building is destroyed.

MARINE INSURANCE

Marine insurance is really transportation insurance. After coverage on ocean voyages had been developed, it was a natural step to offer insurance on inland trips. This branch of insurance became known as inland marine. In many policy forms the distinction between inland and ocean marine has disappeared; it is common to cover goods from the time they leave the warehouse of the shipper, even if this warehouse is situated many miles from the nearest seaport, until they reach the warehouse of the buyer, whose warehouse likewise may be located far inland.

Insurance of goods in transit

Ocean marine insurance. Ocean marine contracts are written to cover four major types of property interest: (1) the vessel or hull; (2) the cargo; (3) the freight revenue to be received by the ship owner; and (4) legal liability for negligence of the shipper or the carrier. Hull insurance covers losses to the vessel itself from specified perils. Usually there is a provision that the marine hull should be covered only within specified geographic limits. Cargo insurance is usually written on an *open contract* basis under which shipments, both incoming and outgoing, are automatically covered for the interests of the shipper, who reports periodically the values exposed and pays a premium based upon these values. By means of a negotiable *open cargo certificate*, which is attached to the bill of lading, insurance coverage automatically is transferred to whoever has legal title to the goods in the course of their movement from seller to buyer.

Freight revenue may be insured in several different ways. If there is an obligation by the shipper to pay the carrier his freight bill regardless of whether or not the goods are delivered, the value of the freight is declared a part of the value of the cargo and is insured as part of this value. If the freight revenue is contingent upon safe delivery of the goods, the carrier insures the freight as a part of the regular hull coverage.

Major clauses or provisions that are fairly standardized are (1) the perils clause; (2) the "running down" clause, or R.D.C.; (3) "free of particular average," or F.P.A., clause; (4) the general average clause; (5) the sue and labour clause; (6) the abandonment clause; (7) coinsurance; and (8) express and implied warranties. Each of these will be discussed in turn.

Perils clause. The main insuring clause of modern ocean marine policies is preserved in almost unchanged form from the original 1779 Lloyd's of London form. The clause is as follows:

> Touching the adventures and perils which we the assurers are contented to bear and do take upon us in this voyage: they are of the seas, men-of-war, fire, enemies, pirates, rovers, thieves, jettisons, letters of mart and countermart, surprisals, takings at sea, arrests, restraints, and detainments of all kings, princes, and people, of what nation, condition, or quality soever, barratry of the master and mariners, and of all other perils, losses, and misfortunes, that have or shall come to the hurt, detriment, or damage of the said goods and merchandises, and ship, etc., or any part thereof.

Although the clause reads as if it were an all-risk agreement, courts have interpreted it to cover only the perils mentioned. Essentially, the clause insures the voyage from perils *of* the sea. Perils *on* the sea such as fire are not covered unless specifically mentioned. Furthermore, although the perils clause indicates coverage from "enemies, pirates, rovers, thieves," the policy does not cover losses from war. (War risk insurance is offered in some nations through governmental agencies.)

R.D.C. clause. The R.D.C., or "running down" clause, provides coverage for legal liability of either the shipper or the common carrier for claims arising out of collisions. (Collision loss to the vessel itself is part of the hull coverage.) The R.D.C. clause covers negligence of the carrier or shipper that results in damage to the property of others. A companion clause, the protection and indemnity clause (P and I), covers the carrier or shipper for negligence that causes bodily injury to others.

F.P.A. clause. The F.P.A., or "free of particular average," clause excludes from coverage partial losses to the cargo or to the hull except those resulting from stranding, sinking, burning, or collision. Under its provisions, losses below a given percentage of value, say 10 percent, are excluded. In this way the insurer does not pay for relatively small losses to cargo. The percentage deductible varies according to the type of cargo and its susceptibility to loss.

General average clause. The general average clause in ocean marine insurance obligates insurance policies on various interests to share the cost of losses incurred voluntarily to save the voyage from complete destruction. Such sacrifices must be made voluntarily, must be necessary, and must be successful. For example, if a shipper's cargo is voluntarily jettisoned in a storm in order to save the vessel from total loss, the general average clause requires the insurer of the hull and all other cargo interests to make a contribution to the loss of the shipper whose goods were sacrificed. Other types of losses may also be covered. It has been held, for example, that losses suffered from efforts to put out a fire on shipboard, which result in damage to specific goods, can be included in a general average claim. Similarly, losses from salvage efforts to free a stranded vessel may qualify under a general average claim to which all interests must contribute.

Sue and labour clause. The sue and labour clause requires the ship owner to make every attempt to reduce or save the exposed interests from loss. Under the terms of the clause, the insurer pays for any necessary costs incurred in carrying out the requirements of the sue and labour clause. Thus, if a ship is stranded, under the sue and labour clause the hull owner would be required to hire salvors to attempt to save the ship. Such expenses are paid even if the salvage attempts fail.

Abandonment clause. If salvaging or rehabilitating a ship or cargo following a marine loss costs more than the goods are worth, the loss is said to be constructively total. Under such conditions, the ocean marine policy permits the insured to abandon the damaged ship or cargo to the insurer and make a claim for the entire value. In this case, the salvage belongs to the insurer, who may dispose of it as he sees fit. Abandonment is not permitted in other forms of property insurance.

Coinsurance. Although there is no coinsurance clause as such in the ocean marine policy, losses are settled as though a 100 percent coinsurance clause existed. Thus, if an insured takes out coverage equal to 50 percent of the true replacement cost of the goods he may recover only 50 percent of any partial loss.

Warranties. In the field of ocean marine insurance there are two general types of warranties that must be considered: express and implied. Express warranties are promises written into the contract. There are also three implied warranties, which do not appear in written form but bind the parties nevertheless.

Examples of expressed warranties are the F.C. & S. warranty and the strike, riot, and civil commotion warranty. The F.C. & S., or "free of capture and seizure," warranty excludes war as a cause of loss. The strike, riot, and civil commotion warranty states that the insurer will pay no losses resulting from strikes, walkouts, riots, or other labour disturbances. The three implied warranties relate to the following conditions: seaworthiness, deviation, and legality. Under the first, the shipper and the common carrier warrant that the ship will be seaworthy when it leaves port in the sense that the hull will be sound, the captain and crew will be qualified, and supplies and other necessary equipment for the voyage will be on hand. Any losses stemming from lack of seaworthiness will be excluded from coverage. Under the deviation warranty, the ship may not deviate from its intended course except to save lives. Clauses may be attached to the ocean marine policy to eliminate the implied warranties of seaworthiness or deviation. The implied warranty of legality, however, may not be waived. Under this warranty, if the voyage itself is illegal under the laws of the country under whose flag the ship sails, the insurance is void.

Inland marine insurance. Although there are no standard forms in inland marine insurance, most of the contracts follow a typical pattern. They are usually written on a named-peril basis covering such perils of transportation as collision, derailment, rising water, tornado, fire, lightning, and windstorm. The policies generally exclude losses resulting from pilferage, strike, riot, civil commotion, war, delay of shipments, loss of markets, illegal trade, or leakage and breakage.

Rates are generally negotiated on an individual basis and vary according to the volume of shipments during the year. The final premium is often determined by audit when the volume of the year's shipments are known. The inland transit form also contains a clause covering loss caused by the negligence of third parties. Usually the insurer maintains its right of subrogation against the railroad or other common carrier for all loss for which the carrier is legally liable.

The scope of inland marine is greatly extended by means of "floater" policies. These are used to insure certain types of movable property whether or not the property is actually in transit. Business floater policies are purchased by jewelers, launderers, dry cleaners, tailors, upholsterers, and other persons who hold the property of others while performing services. Personal property floaters are used to cover, on a comprehensive basis, any item of personal property owned by a private individual. They may also cover the property of visitors, or the property of servants while on the premises of the insured. They exclude certain types of property for which other contracts have been designed, such as automobiles, aircraft, motorcycles, animals, or business and professional equipment.

PROPERTY AND LIABILITY INSURANCE

Property and liability insurance, also known as casualty insurance, covers loss associated with hazards to persons and property, including legal hazards as well as those arising from accident and sickness. It does not include life insurance. Major classes are liability (including automobile), theft, aviation, workmen's compensation, credit and title, and a variety of miscellaneous types covering machinery and equipment, plate glass windows, and so forth.

Liability insurance. Liability insurance arises mainly from the operation of the law of negligence. Individuals who, in the eyes of the law, fail to act reasonably or to exercise due care may find themselves subject to large liability claims. Court judgments have been issued for sums so large as to require a lifetime to pay.

There are at least four major types of liability insurance contracts: (1) liability arising out of the use of automobiles, (2) liability arising out of conduct of a business, (3) liability arising from professional negligence (applicable to doctors, lawyers, etc.), and (4) personal liability, including the liability of a private individual operating a home, carrying on sporting activities, and so on.

Some common elements of liability contracts

Practically all liability contracts falling in these four categories have some common elements. One is the insuring clause, in which the insurer agrees to pay on behalf of the insured all sums that the insured shall become legally obligated to pay as damages because of bodily injury, sickness or disease, or wrongful death or injury to another person's property. The liability policy covers only claims that an insured becomes legally obligated to pay; voluntary payments are not covered. It is often necessary to resort to legal or court action to determine the amount of these damages, although in a vast majority of cases the damages are settled out of court by negotiation between the parties.

All liability insurance contracts contain clauses that obligate the insurer to conduct a court defense, pay any settlement including premiums on bonds, interest on judgments pending appeal, medical and surgical expenses that are necessary at the time of the accident, and other costs. Liability insurance has sometimes been termed defense insurance because of this provision. The insurer agrees to defend a suit regardless of whether it is false or fraudulent so long as it is a suit stemming from a peril insured against. The insured is required to cooperate with the insurer in all court actions by appearing in court, if necessary, to give testimony.

Practically all liability insurance policies contain limitations on the maximum amount of a judgment payable under the contract. The cost of defense and supplementary payments are paid in addition to any judgments.

Liability insurance contracts have in common the fact that the definition of "the insured" is broad. Automobile liability policy, for example, includes not only the owner and driver but anyone else operating the car with permission. In business liability insurance, all partners, officers, directors, or proprietors are covered by the policy regardless of their direct responsibility for any act of negligence. Other parties may be included for an extra premium.

Another element common to all liability insurance policies is certain exclusions. Policies covering business activities almost invariably exclude liability arising out of the personal activities of the insured. Each kind of liability contract tends to exclude the liability for which another contract has been devised: a personal liability policy will exclude automobile liability since a special contract has been created for this particular type of liability. Another common exclusion is damage to property under the care, custody, or control of the insured, on the theory that a person cannot be liable to himself for his own negligence; thus if an insured negligently damages his own property, he may not look to his liability policy for recovery but is expected to have some type of physical damage insurance.

Another common element in liability policies is subrogation: the insurer retains the right to bring an action against a liable third party for any loss this third party has caused.

Automobile insurance. Automobile insurance in the United States and Great Britain is commonly written as a comprehensive contract that includes not only liability but also medical payments, theft, and physical damage. Usually the policy defines the insured broadly enough to include anyone who is driving the car with permission of the insured or his spouse. Practices in other countries vary. Compulsory insurance laws obtain in most European countries, and it is not unusual for the language of the contracts to be specified by law.

Business liability insurance. Business liability contracts commonly written include the following: liability of a building owner, landlord, or tenant; liability of an employer for acts of negligence involving employees; liability of contractors or manufacturers; liability to members of the public resulting from faulty products or services; liability as a result of contractual agreements under which liability of others is assumed; and comprehensive liability. The latter contract is designed to be broad enough to encompass almost any type of business liability including automobiles.

Most business liability contracts are written on what has been known as the occurrence basis, under which the business is covered for loss even if the act that produced the claim was not accidental. The only requirement is that the result of the act be accidental or unintended. Thus if a contractor is making an excavation that produces large amounts of dust and this dust causes loss to neighbouring property, his liability policy would respond to claims for loss if it were written on the occurrence basis even though the act that produced the dust was a deliberate act.

Professional liability. Known as malpractice insurance, professional liability contracts are distinguished from general business liability policies because of the specialized nature of the liability. Professional persons requiring liability contracts include physicians and surgeons, lawyers, accountants, engineers, architects, and insurance agents. Important differences between professional and other liability contracts are the following:

1. No distinction is made between bodily injury or property damage liability and there is no limit per accident but rather a limit of liability per claim. This recognizes the fact that one negligent act on the part of a professional person may involve more than one party, each of whom could bring a legal action against the professional person. Thus a doctor might administer the wrong medicine to a number of patients each of whom could bring a legal action.

2. Claims against a professional person may have an adverse effect upon his reputation. The policy therefore permits the insured to carry any action against him to court if he feels it necessary, since an out-of-court settlement might conceivably imply guilt in the eyes of his public or clientele.

In general liability insurance, the policy will defend the insured and pay any judgments rendered against him if it can be shown that negligence existed regardless of any promises made by the insured at the time to the customer.

3. In professional liability insurance there is an exclusion for any agreement guaranteeing the result of any treatment. Suits stemming from clients' dissatisfaction with the service performed are thus not covered.

Personal liability insurance. The most common form of personal liability insurance is issued as a comprehensive personal liability insurance policy. It is an all-risk agreement and contains relatively few exclusions. The policy covers any act of negligence of the insured or residents of his home that results in legal liability. It may also include medical payments insurance covering accidental injury to guests and other nonresidents without regard to the question of negligence.

Theft insurance. Theft generally covers all acts of stealing. There are three major types of insurance contracts for burglary, robbery, and other theft. Burglary is defined somewhat narrowly to mean the unlawful taking of property within a premises that has been closed and in which there are visible marks evidencing forcible entry. This narrow definition is necessary to restrict burglary coverage to a particular class of criminal act. Robbery is defined as that type of unlawful taking of property in which another person is threatened either by force or violence. In the robbery peril, therefore, the element of personal contact is necessary. Theft policies further categorize robbery according to whether it takes place inside or outside designated premises; different premium rates and loss limits apply depending on where the robbery occurs. The insured peril is generally restricted to acts of persons not in a position of trust—"outsiders." Employees, officers, directors, and other "insiders" must be covered under fidelity bonds.

Underwriting is difficult, and rates tend to be high because those businesses most subject to theft are most likely to apply for coverage—liquor stores, pawnshops, jewelry stores, and so forth. Another reason for high rates is that owners tend to underinsure on the assumption that a burglar or robber can steal only so much at any one time.

Major types of theft coverages

Perhaps the most common of all burglary coverages is on safes. Often the loss to the safe itself from the use of explosives and other devices causes as much damage as the loss of the money, jewelry, or securities it contains. Accordingly, the policy covers both types of claims. Another common burglary policy applies to mercantile open stock. In this policy there is usually a limit applicable on any article of jewelry or any article contained in a showcase where susceptability to loss is high. In order to prevent underinsurance the mercantile open stock policy is usually written with a co-insurance requirement or with some minimum amount of coverage.

Another common theft policy for business firms is a comprehensive crime contract covering employee dishonesty as well as losses on money and securities both inside and outside the premises, loss from counterfeit money or money orders, and loss from forgery. This policy is designed to cover in one package most of the crime perils to which an average business is subject.

A broad form of crime protection for individuals is the personal theft policy. This is offered both as a separate contract and as part of a "homeowner's policy." It covers all losses of personal property from theft and mysterious disappearance, including money and securities.

Aviation insurance. Aviation insurance normally covers physical damage to the aircraft and legal liability arising out of its ownership and operation. Specific policies are also available to cover the legal liability of airport owners arising out of the operation of hangars or from the sale of various aviation products. These latter policies are similar to other types of liability contracts.

Perhaps the major underwriting problem is the "catastrophic" exposure to loss. The largest passenger aircraft may incur losses of up to $100,000,000, counting both liability and physical damage exposures. The number of aircraft of any particular type is not large enough for the accurate prediction of losses, and each type of aircraft has its special characteristics and equipment. Thus a great deal of independent individual underwriting is necessary. Rate making is complex and specialized. It is further complicated by rapid technological change and by the constant appearance of new hazards.

Hull insurance for aircraft is generally written on an all-risk basis. Rates are usually expressed as a percentage of the aircraft's replacement value, such as two percent. Policies generally exclude losses from damage that is incurred while the aircraft is being used for unlawful purposes, or outside of the geographical limits specified in the policy, or by someone other than an authorized pilot or for purposes other than those that are authorized in the policy, or in violation of an airworthiness condition or of civil air regulations. Also excluded are losses resulting from war, strike, riot, civil commotion, wear and tear, depreciation, and loss of revenue from failure to use the aircraft.

Policies are written to cover liability of the owner or operator for bodily injury to passengers or to persons other than passengers, and for property damage. Medical costs, including loss of income, are usually paid to passengers suffering permanent total disability without the requirement of proving negligence. This type of coverage has been called admitted liability insurance.

Industrial injury insurance

Workmen's compensation insurance. Workmen's compensation insurance, sometimes called industrial injury insurance, compensates workmen for losses suffered as a result of work-related injuries. Payments are made regardless of negligence. The schedule of benefits making up the compensation is determined by statute.

The scope of employment injury laws, originally limited to persons in forms of employment recognized as hazardous, has, as the result of associating the right to compensation with the existence of a contract of service, been gradually extended to clerical employment, which is safer than being at home or on the street. Nevertheless, the large exception of agricultural employees remains in some underdeveloped countries (*e.g.*, former British colonies), Canada, most of the United States, and the U.S.S.R. (collective farmers). Other classes of exception are employees in very small undertakings and domestic servants. The exclusion of employees with middle class salaries persists in parts of the former British Empire. In a few countries, working employers are enabled to insure themselves as well as their employees.

The notion of employment injury was at first confined to injuries of accidental origin, but during the 20th century it was extended to include occupational diseases in increasing number. To entitle the worker to benefit, the accident must occur during his employment, and many laws also require that the accident should have been caused by the employment in some way; but the trend seems to be toward accepting the former condition as sufficient. Following the German law of 1925, some 30 countries have included accidents occurring on the way to and from work. Injuries due to the employee's willful misconduct are generally excluded. Occupational diseases are covered to some extent by virtually all national laws.

Classes of benefits. Four classes of benefits are provided by compulsory insurance, and, except for certain diseases, a right to them is acquired without any qualifying period of previous employment. First is a medical benefit, which includes all necessary treatment and the supply of artificial limbs. If its duration is limited, the maximum is likely to be one year. Second is a temporary incapacity benefit, which lasts as long as the medical benefit except that a waiting period of a few days is frequently prescribed. Its rate varies in different countries from 50 percent of the employee's wage (*e.g.*, in former British colonies and protectorates, and a few Latin American countries) to 100 percent (in the U.S.S.R., Yugoslavia, Argentina, Brazil, Colombia, and Mexico), with a maximum, and often a minimum, limit (66⅔ percent and 75 percent are the commonest rates). Third is a permanent incapacity benefit, which, unless the degree is very small, when a lump sum is paid, takes the form of a pension. If the incapacity is total, the pension is usually equal to the temporary incapacity benefit. If the incapacity is partial, the pension is proportionately smaller. In some 60 countries an additional pension is granted if the victim needs constant attendance. In cases of death the pensions are distributed to the widow (or invalid widower) and minor children, and, if the maximum total has not then been attained, other dependents may receive small pensions. The maximum is the same as for total incapacity.

In a growing number of industrialized countries (Austria, France, Germany, Ireland, Israel, The Netherlands, and Switzerland) the fourth type of benefit is provided—systematic arrangements for retraining seriously injured persons, and employers may even be required to provide employment to such persons.

Financing and administering employment injury insurance. Almost all systems of employment injury insurance are financed by employers' contributions exclusively, and in almost all of these systems the contribution is proportional to the risk represented by the class of activity in which the employer is engaged. Usually the insurance institution adapts the contribution to the accident experience of the undertaking individually or to any special preventive measures it may have taken. On the other hand, mainly for simplicity, but partly perhaps in order to subsidize basic but dangerous industries, a uniform contribution rate for all classes of activity has been established in Austria, several people's democracies, and many underdeveloped countries.

Social insurance against employment injury, as against other risks, is in most countries administered by institutions under the joint management of employers and employees, and often of government representatives as well; in eastern Europe, however, the administration is entrusted to the trade unions. Disputes are settled by arbitral organs without resort to the courts.

In the United States, an employer may comply with the provisions of most workmen's compensation laws in three ways. He may purchase a private workmen's compensation and employer liability policy from a commercial insurer; he may purchase coverage through a state fund set up for this purpose; or he may set aside reserves sufficient to cover the risks involved. Most workmen's compensation benefits are financed by the first two methods.

State laws in the U.S. are not uniform with respect to the size or length of time for which income payments are made. For example, only 26 states give lifetime income benefits for occupational injuries. In others there is a statutory limitation of between 400 and 500 weeks of payments. Again, most states provide liquidating damages for an injury that is permanent but does not totally incapacitate the worker, such as the loss of an arm or leg. The size of these liquidating damages varies greatly. Most state laws also provide survivors' benefits in the event of the worker's death, and complete medical benefits including rehabilitation expenses.

Coverage of credit risks

Credit insurance. The use of credit in modern societies is so various and widespread that many types of insurance have grown up to cover some of the risks involved. Examples of these risks are: the risk of bad debts from insolvency, death, and disability; the risk of loss of savings from bank failure; the risk attaching to home-loan debts when installments are not paid for various reasons, resulting in foreclosure with subsequent loss to the creditor; and the risk of loss from export credit because of war, currency restrictions, cancellation of import licenses, or other political causes.

Merchandise credit insurance. Credit insurance for domestic buyers and sellers is available in the United States, Canada, Mexico, and most European countries. It is sold only to manufacturers, wholesalers, and certain service agencies, not to retailers. The insurance is designed to enable the seller to recover a certain percentage of losses from insolvency of the debtor, but the contracts list a number of conditions under which the creditor may initiate a claim regardless of the question of insolvency. The policy is designed primarily to meet the needs of those sellers whose business is concentrated among a few buyers, insolvency of any one of which would seriously jeopardize the financial stability of the seller.

Export credit insurance. A special form of credit insurance is available to exporters against losses from both commercial and political risks. In the United States, for example, export credit insurance is written through a consortium of insurance companies organized by the Foreign Credit Insurance Association (FCIA). The Export-Import Bank of Washington assumes the liability for political risks and in many cases part of the commercial risk as well. Coverage is limited to 75–95 percent of the account. Usually, prior approval from the FCIA is required before export credit insurance will be granted. In some cases, the exporter is required to purchase coverage on all of his credit sales in a given country as a device to reduce adverse selection.

Export credit insurance is used more widely in some countries than in others. In Great Britain, approximately a quarter of all export sales are covered, compared with about 6 percent in the United States. Export sales are not eligible for insurance if they are made for cash or financed directly or indirectly through government-guaranteed loans.

Title insurance. Title insurance is a contract guaranteeing the purchaser of real estate against loss from undiscovered defects in the title to property that he has purchased. Such loss may stem from unmarketability of the property because of defective title or from costs incurred to cure defects of the title.

The need for title insurance arises from the fact that real estate transactions are complex and technical. Any legal error, no matter how detailed or minute, may cause a defect in the title that prevents its marketability. Examples of such defects are forgeries, invalid or undiscovered wills, defective probate proceedings, or transfers of property by persons lacking full legal capacity to contract.

Public records contain a description of each piece of real property, and presumably they mention any factor that may cloud the title such as a legal encumbrance, lien, easement, or other matters. When the property is transferred, a search of these records is made, and any defects are recorded on the title. The title insurance policy excludes losses stemming from such recorded defects, since it covers losses only from undiscovered defects. In contrast to most insurance policies, which cover losses occurring during the policy term, title insurance covers only losses that have already occurred but are not known.

Without title insurance the potential buyer of real estate is protected only by a so-called abstract. The abstract is really a legal history of the title. An attorney may examine an abstract and render an opinion as to the validity of the title, but there is no guarantee that the attorney's opinion is correct. Title insurance, which offers such a guarantee, is normally issued by title companies that maintain elaborate records to keep current information on all the property under their surveyance. The premium for title insurance is intended mainly to cover the expenses of maintaining the records. When the property is transferred again, a new policy must be issued and a new premium paid.

Miscellaneous insurance. Special casualty forms are issued covering the hazards of sudden explosions from equipment such as steam boilers, compressors, electric motors, fly wheels, air tanks, furnaces, and engines. Boiler and machinery insurance has several distinctive features. A substantial portion of the premium collected is used for inspection services rather than loss protection. Second, the boiler policy provides that its coverage will be in excess over any other applicable insurance. In this sense, it may be looked upon as an "umbrella policy" to fill in gaps in the insured's program. Third, the policy lists the number of losses that will be paid in the order named, such as: the loss of the boiler or machinery itself due to accident; expediting expenses; property damage liability; bodily injury liability; defense settlement and supplementary payments; automatic coverage of newly installed machinery; business interruption insurance; outage (interruption of service) insurance; power interruption insurance; consequential loss due to spoilage of goods; and furnace explosion. The policy will satisfy each of these claims in the order in which they appear, up to the limit of the coverage.

Boiler, machinery, and plate glass insurance

The extensive use of plate glass in modern architecture has produced a special comprehensive insurance that covers not only plate glass but glass signs, motion picture screens, halftone screens and lenses, glass bricks, glass doors, and so forth. It may be written to cover loss from any source except fire or nuclear reaction.

SURETYSHIP

Surety contracts are designed to protect businesses against the possible dishonesty of their employees. Surety and fidelity bonds fill the gap left by theft insurance, which always excludes losses from persons in a position of trust. A bond involves three contracting parties instead of two. The three parties are: the principal, who is the person bonded; the obligee, the person who is protected; and the surety, the person or corporation agreeing to reimburse the obligee for any losses stemming from failures or dishonesty of the principal. The bond covers events within the control of the person bonded, whereas insurance in the strict sense covers loss from random events generally outside the direct control of the insured. In bonding, the surety always has the right to try to collect its losses from the person bonded, whereas in insurance the insurer may not attempt to recover losses from the insured. Of course, under property and liability policies the insurer may attempt to recover from liable third parties under the right of subrogation, but subrogation rights are often not possible to enforce in practice. Bonds are not usually cancellable by the insurer, whereas most insurance contracts, except life, are cancellable by the insurer upon due notice.

Fidelity bonds and surety bonds

Fidelity bonds are written to cover the obligee, usually an employer, against loss from dishonest acts of employees; surety bonds cover not only dishonesty but also an employee's incapacity to perform the work he has agreed to do, such as constructing a building under contract. Surety bonds are normally written on principals who are acting in an independent or semi-independent capacity, such as building contractors or public officials, whereas fidelity bonds are written on employees acting under the guidance and supervision of their employer. Finally, surety bonds are often issued with the requirement of collateral, whereas fidelity bonds are not. The surety bond is an instrument through which the superior credit of the surety is substituted for the uncertain credit of the principal; hence if the surety is asked to bond a principal of somewhat doubtful credit, the requirement of cash collateral is frequently imposed.

Major types of fidelity bonds. Fidelity bonds differ according to whether specific persons are named as principals or whether all employees or persons are covered as a group. The latter are most frequently used by large employers because they offer automatic coverage on given classes of workers, including new employees, and greater ease of administration, including simpler claims procedures. Fidelity bonds are usually written on a continuous basis—that is, they are effective until cancelled and have no expiration date. The penalty of the bond (the maximum amount payable for any one loss) is unchanged from year to year and is not cumulative. The bonds specify a discovery period (usually two years) limiting the time for discovering losses after a bond is discontinued. When a new bond is put into effect, it can be written to cover losses that have occurred but are undiscovered before the effective issue date of the bond. A salvage clause also is included, stating the way in which any salvage recovered by the surety from the principal is to be divided between the surety and the obligee. This clause is significant, because the obligee may have losses in excess of the penalty of the bond. Some salvage clauses require that any salvage be paid to the obligee until he is fully restored for all of his losses, and others provide that any salvage is to be divided between the surety and the obligee on a pro-rata basis, in the proportion that each party has suffered loss.

Major types of surety bonds. There are various classes of surety bonds. Contract construction bonds are written to guarantee the performance of contractors on building projects. Bonds are particularly important in this field because of the general practice of awarding commercial building contracts to the lowest bidder, who may promise more than he can actually perform. The surety who is experienced in this field is in a position to make sounder judgment about the liability of the various bidders than anyone else and backs up its judgment with a financial guarantee.

Court bonds include several different types of surety bonds. Fiduciary bonds are required for court-appointed officials entrusted with managing the property of others; executors of estates and receivers in bankruptcy are frequently required to post fiduciary bonds. Litigation bonds are court bonds required of plaintiffs and defendants in court actions; examples are bail bonds guaranteeing that a defendant will appear in court, and appeal bonds guaranteeing that a defendant can respond to the extra costs incurred in appealing an adverse decision.

Other types of surety bonds include official bonds, lost instrument bonds, and license and permit bonds. Public official bonds guarantee that public officials will faithfully and honestly discharge their obligations to the state or to other public agencies. Lost instrument bonds guarantee that if a lost stock certificate, money order, warehouse receipt, or other financial instrument falls into unauthorized hands and causes a loss to the issuer of a substitute instrument, this loss will be reimbursed. License and permit bonds are issued on persons such as owners of small businesses to guarantee reimbursement for violations of the licenses or permits under which they operate.

LIFE AND HEALTH INSURANCE

Life insurance. Life insurance may be defined as a plan under which large groups of individuals can equalize the burden of loss from death by distributing funds to the beneficiaries of those who die. From the individual standpoint life insurance is a means by which an estate may be created immediately for one's heirs and dependents. It has achieved its greatest acceptance in Canada, the United States, Sweden, Australia, the United Kingdom, New Zealand, The Netherlands, and Japan, in which countries as of 1968 the value of life insurance policies in force exceeded the national income.

Life insurance in its various forms

In the United States, as of 1970, there were over 355,000,000 policy holders. The assets of 1,790 U.S. life insurance companies totaled nearly $208,000,000,000, making life insurance one of the largest savings institutions in the United States. Much the same is true of other wealthy countries, in which life insurance has become a major channel of saving and investment, with important consequences for the national economy.

Life insurance is relatively little used in poor countries, although its acceptance has been increasing.

Types of contracts. The major types of life insurance contracts are term, whole life, and endowment, but innumerable combinations of these basic types are sold. Term insurance contracts, issued for specified periods of years, are the simplest. Protection under these contracts expires at the end of the stated period, with no cash value remaining. Whole life contracts, on the other hand, run for the whole of the insured's life and gradually accumulate a cash value. The cash value, which is less than the face value of the policy, is paid to the policy holder when the contract matures or is surrendered. Endowment contracts run for a stated period of years and pay their full face value at the end of the period.

Life insurance may also be classified, according to type of customer, as ordinary, group, industrial, and credit. The ordinary insurance market includes customers of whole life, term, and endowment contracts and is made up primarily of individual purchasers of annual premium insurance. The group insurance market consists mainly of employers who arrange group contracts to cover their employees. The "industrial" insurance market consists of individual contracts sold in small amounts with premiums collected weekly or monthly at the policy holder's home. Credit life insurance is sold to individuals, usually as part of an installment purchase contract; under these contracts, if the insured dies before the installment payments are completed, the seller is protected for the balance of his unpaid debt.

Insurance may be issued with a premium that remains the same throughout the premium-paying period, or it may be issued with a premium that increases periodically according to the age of the insured. Practically all ordinary life insurance policies are issued on a level premium basis, which makes it necessary to charge more than the true cost of the insurance in the earlier years of the contract in order to make up "deficits" in the later years; the so-called overcharges in the earlier years are not really overcharges but are a necessary part of the total insurance plan since mortality rates increase with age. The insured is not paying more for his protection than he should because he has a claim on the cash values that accumulate in the early years; if he wishes, he may borrow on this value or may recapture it completely by lapsing the policy. He does not, however, have a claim on all of the earnings that accrue to the insurance company from investing the funds of its policy holders.

By combining term, whole life, and endowment insurance, an insurer can provide many different kinds of policies. Two examples of such "package" contracts are the family income policy and the mortgage protection policy. In each of these, a base policy, usually whole life insurance, is combined with term insurance calculated so that the amount of protection declines as the policy runs its course. In the case of the mortgage protection contract, for example, the amount of the decreasing term insurance is designed roughly to approximate the amount of the mortgage on a property. As the mortgage is paid off, the amount of insurance declines correspondingly. At the end of the mortgage period the decreasing term insurance expires, leaving the base policy still in force. Similarly in a family income policy, the decreasing term insurance is arranged to provide a given income to the beneficiary over a period of years roughly corresponding to the period during which the children are young and dependent.

Some whole life policies permit the insured to limit the period during which he pays premiums. Common examples of these are 20-year life, 30-year life, and life paid up at age 65. On these contracts the insured pays a higher premium to compensate for the limited premium-paying period. At the end of the stated period the policy is said to be "paid up," but it remains effective until death or surrender.

Term insurance is most appropriate when the need for protection runs only for a limited period; whole life insurance is most appropriate when the protection need is permanent. Endowment insurance is primarily designed to ensure that a savings plan will be completed—for example, to build a retirement fund or to provide an educational fund for children.

Settlement options. The death proceeds or cash values of insurance may be settled in various ways. The insured may take his cash value and lapse the policy. A beneficiary may take a lump sum settlement of the face amount upon the death of the insured. He may, instead, elect to receive the proceeds over a given number of years or in some fixed amount such as $100 a month for as long as the proceeds last. He may leave the money with the insurer temporarily and draw interest on it. Or the proceeds may be used to purchase a life annuity, which in effect is another insurance policy guaranteeing regular payments for the life of the insured.

Other provisions. Life insurance policies contain various clauses that protect the rights of beneficiaries and the insured. Perhaps the best known is the incontestable clause, which provides that if a policy has been in force for two years the insurer may not afterward refuse to pay the proceeds or to cancel the contract for any reason except nonpayment of premiums. Thus, if the insured has made a material misrepresentation when he originally obtained the policy, and this misrepresentation is not discovered until after the incontestable period, beneficiaries may still receive the values of the policies so long as the premiums are maintained. Another protective clause is the suicide clause, which states that after a given period, usually two years, the insurer may not deny liability for subsequent suicide of the insured. If suicide occurs within the period, the insurer tenders to the beneficiary only the premiums that have been paid. If the insured has misstated his age when he took out the policy, the misstatement-of-age clause provides that the amount payable is the amount of insurance that would have been purchased for the premium had the correct age been stated. Many life insurance policies return dividends to the insured. These are known as participating policies. The dividends, which may amount to 20 percent of the premiums, may be accumulated in cash left with the insurer at interest, used to buy additional life insurance, used to reduce premium payments, or used to pay up the contract sooner than would otherwise have been possible.

Special riders. The insured may, at a nominal charge, attach to his contract a waiver-of-premium rider under which premium payments will be waived if he becomes totally and permanently disabled before the age of 60. Under the disability income rider, should he become totally and permanently disabled, a monthly income will be paid. Under the double indemnity rider, if death occurs through accident the insurance payable is double the face amount.

The expanding field of health insurance

Private health insurance. In many countries health insurance has become a governmental institution. In some, doctors are employed, directly or indirectly, by a government agency on a full-time or part-time salaried basis, and health facilities are owned or operated by the government. This is the practice in Australia, Brazil, Canada, Chile, Greece, Ireland, Mexico, New Zealand, Sweden, Turkey, and the Communist countries of Europe. In other countries the government pays for medical care provided by private physicians; these countries include Austria, Denmark, West Germany, The Netherlands, Norway, and Spain. In some countries private health insurance programs exist along with, or as part of, the government program. Various combinations of programs are possible, and it is difficult to summarize all the arrangements. The United States provides government-run medical services in veterans' hospitals and mental hospitals; it also has a governmental health insurance program under the Social Security Act amendments of 1965; but most health insurance in the United States still consists of private programs. Much private health insurance in the U.S. is operated on a group basis, generally through groups of employees whose payments may be subsidized by their employer. The following is a description of the principles of private health insurance. (Government medical services are discussed in another article, WELFARE AND SECURITY PROGRAMS.)

Types of policies. There are five major types of health insurance policies: hospitalization, surgical, regular medical, major medical, and disability income. Health insurance contracts are not highly standardized. The statements about policy provisions below should be considered as typical, not universal or comprehensive.

Hospitalization insurance indemnifies for room and board in the hospital, laboratory fees, use of special facilities, nursing care, and certain medicines and supplies. The contracts contain specific limitations on coverage, such as a maximum number of days in the hospital and maximum allowances for room and board. Surgical expense insurance covers the surgeon's charge for given operations or medical procedures, usually up to a maximum for each type of operation. Regular medical insurance contracts indemnify the insured for expenses such as physicians' home or office visits, medicines, and other medical expenses. Major medical contracts are distinguished from other health insurance policies by offering coverage without many specific limitations; usually there is only a maximum per person, a deductible amount, and a percentage deductible called coinsurance under which the insured usually pays 20 percent of each medical bill above the deductible amount. Disability income coverage provides periodical payments when the insured is unable to work as a result of accident or illness. There is normally a waiting period before the payments begin. Definitions of disability vary considerably. A strict definition of disability requires that the insured be unable to perform each and every duty of his regular occupation for a given period, say two years, and thereafter be unable to perform the duties of any occupation for which he is reasonably fitted by training or experience. More liberal definitions of disability state that the insured be unable to perform the duties of his usual occupation.

An important condition of health insurance is that of renewability. Some contracts are cancellable at any time upon short notice. Others are not cancellable during the year's term of coverage, but the insurer may refuse to renew coverage for a subsequent year or to renew only at higher rates or under restrictive conditions. Thus the insured may become ill with a chronic disease and discover that upon renewal the policy excludes all future coverage from this disease. Only policies that are both noncancellable and guaranteed renewable assure continuous coverage, but these are much more expensive.

Problems. Private health insurance contracts are in general quite restricted in coverage, to the point that many consider them to be inadequate for modern conditions. They also lend themselves to abuses such as overutilization of coverage, multiple policies, and insuring for more than 100 percent of the expected loss. Health insurance, by its very existence, helps to escalate rising medical care costs; for example, insured medical losses tend to run higher than noninsured losses because physicians often charge according to "ability to pay," and insurance increases this ability. Through insurance it is also easier to pass on rising hospital costs to the patient. Finally, since there is a tendency for those most likely to have losses to take out health insurance, an element of adverse selection exists. Careful underwriting to screen out those who are trying to take advantage of the insurance mechanism to pay for known bills is considered essential, but this undoubtedly denies coverage to many who need protection.

GROUP INSURANCE

Insurance written for specific groups

Groups have always been important in the insurance field, from the burial societies of the Romans and the insurance funds of the medieval guilds to the fraternal and religious insurance plans of modern times. In recent decades private insurance companies have written large amounts of group insurance, particularly in life insurance, health insurance, and annuities. More than two-thirds of the industrial labour force in the United States in 1968 was covered by group life and health insurance plans established by employers. Much of the impetus for these employee benefit plans came from the labour unions, which pressed for such "fringe benefits" in bargaining with employers.

Group insurance is widely used throughout the world, both in the form of private plans and as social insurance plans. Social security plans with group coverage exist in 132 nations. Private group plans are generally offered wherever private life and health insurance companies operate. Group life insurance is the most commonly offered plan; group health plans are government operated in many nations. In many countries, group pension plans are common as a supplement to social insurance pension schemes.

Group insurance has been especially popular in Japan where many employees serve a company for life. All Japanese life insurance companies offer group life insurance. Health insurance is provided by the government. Funded group pensions became popular after a 1962 tax law made contributions tax deductible for Japanese employers. In addition, virtually all Japanese employers provide lump-sum retirement allowances to their workers.

Group life insurance. Under group life insurance an employer signs a master contract with the insurance company outlining the provisions of the plan. Each employee receives a certificate that gives evidence of his participation in the plan. The amount of insurance depends upon the employee's salary or job classification; usually the employer pays a portion of the premium and the employee pays the rest, but sometimes the employer pays the entire cost of the plan.

A major advantage of group life insurance to an employee is that usually he may obtain coverage regardless of his health. If he leaves the group he may, without a medical examination, convert his insurance to an individual policy. The premiums on group life insurance are considerably less than on comparable individual policies, mainly because the selling and administrative costs are minimal.

Group health insurance. Major types of health insurance written on a group basis include insurance against the losses occasioned by hospitalization, surgical expense, and disability. Hospitalization insurance is designed to cover daily room and board and other expenses. Surgical expense insurance usually provides specified allowances for the physicians' charges for various operation. Regular medical expense coverage is aimed generally at covering part of the costs of medicines and doctor calls. Major medical insurance offers the insured a large monetary coverage, designed to meet catastrophic costs of illness or accident with few restrictions as to the type of medical expense for which reimbursement is allowed. The insured must bear a percentage of any loss, usually 20 percent. Temporary disability income offers the insured a weekly indemnity for a period of up to six months if the insured is temporarily disabled and unable to work. Long-term disability extends the income for periods longer than six months. Accidental death and dismemberment insurance offers an insured or his beneficiary a lump sum; it is used widely as a form of travel accident insurance.

Special protection in group insurance

Under the typical group health insurance contract, the insured person enjoys several elements of protection not obtainable in individual contracts. Cancellation of his coverage is not permitted unless coverage for the entire group is cancelled. He enjoys protection against rate increases unless the rate for all members of his class is increased. He may typically convert his group protection to some kind of individual policy or transfer to another group plan. The insurer tends to be liberal on claims settlement because the typical premium under a group plan is large enough so that the insurer is unwilling to jeopardize the good will of the clientele through miserly claims treatment.

Most group insurance plans require that certain conditions be met. Sometimes there must be a minimum number of persons covered, such as 10 or 25. The group must also have some reason for existence other than to obtain insurance. The most usual types of groups are employees of a common employer, members of a labour organization, debtors of a common creditor, or members of a professional or trade association.

Mention must also be made of nonprofit prepayment plans (such as the Blue Cross plans in the United States), which resemble the above plans in most respects but are not operated by insurance companies. These plans often indemnify the hospital or the physician, on the basis of services performed, rather than the patient. Health insurance plans may also be established independently by large employers, labour unions, communities, or cooperatives. In 1962 there were over 300 such organizations in the United States. In other countries this kind of health insurance has been taken over by government programs. In Sweden, before the enactment of the compulsory insurance program in 1955, 70 percent of the population was covered by private plans. In Great Britain, before the National Health Service was instituted in 1948, about half the population was privately covered. In the Netherlands about half the population was so covered before the government program began, and there were still many private funds run by various groups.

Group annuities. An annuity in the literal sense is a series of annual payments. More broadly it may be defined as a series of equal payments over equal intervals of time. A life annuity, a subclass of annuities in general, is one in which the payments are guaranteed for the lifetime of one or more individuals. A group annuity differs from an individual annuity in that the annuity payments are based upon the assumed length of lives of members of a given group. The size of the payments depends upon several factors: the assumed interest rate, the life expectancy of the individual or individuals making up the group, the length of the period during which any minimum number of payments is guaranteed, the length of time elapsing before the payments begin, and the number of lives on which the payments are continued. For example, if payments are to be guaranteed for 20 years, they will be substantially smaller than if they are guaranteed only for the remainder of a person's life.

The typical group life annuity is written by an employer, who may pay all or part of the cost. Under the usual arrangement, every employee receives each year a credit with the life insurance company for an annuity purchased on his behalf to begin at age 65. The final pension received is made up of the sum of the individual annuities purchased throughout the worker's life. The worker does not as a rule have irrevocable claim to his annuity rights until he has worked with the employer for a given number of years or has reached a given age.

The basic advantage of an annuity is that it provides an income for life that is larger than the amount that the holder would receive if he put his money out at simple interest. It is the reverse of life insurance, in that the insurer pays premiums to the insured; it resembles insurance in that the payment is based on life expectancy.

Variable annuities

The problem of inflation has led to experimentation with variable annuities in order to protect annuitants against decreases in purchasing power. The major distinguishing characteristic of a variable annuity is that the payments vary according to underlying trends in the stock market. Funds paid in for the variable annuity are invested in common stock rather than in bonds, mortgages, or other fixed interest investments as is true of regular annuities. In simplified terms, if the stock market rises 10 percent in one year the annuitant may expect his payments to go up by approximately 10 percent in the following year. Conversely, if the stock market drops 10 percent, the annuitant will suffer a 10 percent reduction in his income. To the extent that the stock market reflects changes in the cost of living, the annuitant's income is automatically adjusted for these changes each year; and if the stock market also reflects increases in productivity in the economy, then the annuitant may expect to receive a share in such increases in the productivity as the economy may gain during his retirement.

Some variable annuity plans are tied directly to a cost-of-living index. In order to finance the increased benefits, the employer invests a portion of the funds in equities such as common stock and real estate. An assumption is made that there will be a sufficient gain from this source to enable the employer to pay the increased cost of living, but the employee is not expected to suffer reductions in his annuity payments.

The problem of adjusting retirement benefits to changes in the economy has been of concern in many countries. In Finland and Israel, the governments have pegged the price of government bonds to the cost-of-living index. Retired individuals purchasing government bonds may then receive automatic increases in interest payments if the cost of living rises. Their interest will not fall below a specified amount. Social security legislation in most parts of the world is geared in various ways to changes in the cost of living. In some cases benefits are directly tied to a price index. In other cases, the legislature from time to time must be asked to make adjustments in social security benefits.

UNDERWRITING AND RATE MAKING

The two basic functions in insurance are underwriting and rating, which are closely related to each other. Underwriting deals with the selection of risks, and rating deals with the pricing system applicable to the risks accepted.

The selection of risks

Underwriting principles. Underwriting has to do with the selection of subjects for insurance in such a manner that general company objectives are met. The main objective of underwriting is to see that the risk accepted by the insurer will correspond to that assumed in the rating structure. There is often a tendency toward adverse selection, which the underwriter must try to prevent. Adverse selection occurs when those most likely to suffer loss are covered in greater proportion than others. The insurer must decide upon certain standards, terms, and conditions for applicants, project estimated losses and expenses through the anticipated period of coverage, and calculate reasonably accurate rates to cover these losses and expenses. Since many factors affect losses and expenses, the underwriting task is complex and uncertain. Bad underwriting has resulted in the failure of many insurers.

In some types of insurance major underwriting decisions are made in the field, and in other types they are made at the home office. In the field of life insurance the agent's judgment is not accepted as final until the home-office underwriter can make a decision, for the life insurance contract is usually noncancellable, once written. In the field of property and liability insurance, on the other hand, the contract is cancellable if the home-office underwriter later finds the risk to be unacceptable. It is not uncommon for a property and liability insurer to accept large risks only to cancel them at a later time after the full facts are analyzed. The insurance underwriter must tread a thin line between undue strictness and undue laxity in his acceptance of risk. His position is not unlike that of the credit manager in a business corporation, in which unreasonably strict credit standards discourage sales but overly weak credit standards invite losses.

An important initial task of the underwriter is to try to prevent adverse selection by analyzing the hazards that surround the risk. Three basic types of hazards have been identified as moral, psychological, and physical. A moral hazard exists when the mental attitude of the applicant is such that he may either want an outright loss to occur or may have a tendency to be less than careful with his property. A psychological hazard exists when an individual unconsciously behaves in such a way as to engender losses. Physical hazards are conditions surrounding property or persons that increase the danger of loss.

An underwriter may suspect the existence of a moral hazard on applications submitted by persons with known records of dishonesty, or when excessive coverage is sought, or when the replacement value of the property exceeds its value as a profit-making enterprise. Underwriters are aware that fire losses are more likely to occur during business depressions. The underwriter has various ways of detecting moral hazard. He may check an applicant's credit. Courthouse and police records may reveal a criminal history or a history of bankruptcy. Other insurance companies can be queried for information when it is suspected that an individual is trying to obtain an excessive amount of coverage or has been turned down by other insurers.

The psychological type of hazard is more interesting. Some persons are said to be "accident prone" because they have far more than their share of accidents, suggesting that unconsciously they want them. It is well known that persons applying for annuities tend to have longer than average lives, and consequently a special mortality table is used for annuitants. Certain types of insanity have to be watched for—notably the impulse to set fires.

Physical hazards include such things as wood-frame construction in buildings, particularly in areas where such properties are densely concentrated. Earthquake insurance rates tend to be high where earth faults exist (as in San Francisco, which is built almost directly over such a fault).

Each kind of insurance has its characteristic hazards. In fire insurance the physical hazards are analyzed according to four major factors: type of construction, the protection rating of the city in which the property is located, exposure to other structures that may spread a conflagration, and type of occupancy.

In underwriting automobile insurance the factors to be considered include the following: the age, sex, and marital status of the driver and members of the driver's household; length of driving experience; occupation; stability of employment and residence; physical impairments; accident and conviction record; extent of use of alcohol and drugs; customary use of the vehicle; age, condition, and maintenance of the vehicle; records of insurance cancellation or refusal. In some cases tests of emotional maturity are administered. Some underwriters even consider such factors as the school records of student drivers, and whether or not driving courses have been taken.

The hazards considered in the underwriting of general liability insurance depend upon the type of business and the record of the businessman applying for coverage. In the field of contracting, for example, the underwriter is interested in the type of equipment owned or rented by the applicant, his losses in the past, his attitude toward safe practice, his cooperation with building inspectors, the stability of his supervisory employees, his financial position and credit standing, and the degree to which he has been a successful contractor in the past.

How insurance rates are established

Rate making. Closely associated with underwriting is the rate-making function. If, for example, the underwriter decides that the most important factor in discriminating between different risk characteristics is age, the rates will be differentiated according to age.

The rate is the price per unit of exposure. In fire insurance, for example, the rate may be expressed as $1 per $100 of exposed property; if an insured has $1,000 of exposed property, his premium will thus be $10. The rate reflects three major elements: the loss cost per unit of exposure, the administrative expenses or "loading," and the profit. In property insurance, approximately one-third of the premium covers expenses and profit, and two-thirds covers the expected cost of loss payments. These percentages vary somewhat according to the particular type of insurance.

Rates are calculated in the following way. A policy, for instance, may be written covering a class of automobiles with an expected loss frequency of 10 percent and an average collision loss of $400. The expenses of the insurer are to average 35 percent of the premium, and there must be a profit of 5 percent. The pure loss cost per unit will be 10 percent of $400, or $40. The gross premium will be calculated by the formula $L/[1 - (E + P)]$, in which L equals the loss cost per unit, E equals the expense ratio, and P equals the profit ratio. In this case the gross premium will be $\$40/[1 - (.35 + .05)]$, or $66.67.

Credibility. A rate is said to be credible when it is based on a number of exposure units large enough to satisfy statistical estimates of accuracy. Thus 10,000 automobiles may be a large enough number to produce a rate that is 99 percent credible, whereas a rate based on 500 may be only 30 percent credible. If an underwriter discovers that his unit costs are averaging 25 percent higher than expected, say $50 instead of $40, and the insured group consists of only 500 autos, he will adjust his rate upward by only 30 percent of the amount that would be required if his higher loss costs were based on an experience of 10,000 autos. The new rate, based on 30 percent credibility, will be calculated according to the formula $L_1 + (L_2 - L_1)\,C/[1 - (E + P)]$, in which L_1 equals loss cost based on existing loss assumptions; L_2 equals loss cost based on new information; C equals credibility of new information; E equals expense ratio; and P equals profit ratio. The new ratio in the above case will be $\$40 + (\$50 - \$40)\ .30/[1 - (.35 + .05)]$, or $71.66. The new gross rate of $71.66 is 7.5 percent above the old rate of $66.67, rather than 25 percent. This increase is 30 percent of the rate increase (25 percent) that would have been made had the new experience been fully credible $(.30 \times .25 = .075)$.

Credibility factors in insurance rate making are developed from statistical theory and the "law of large numbers." Although a full exposition is beyond the scope of this article, it is intuitively easy to see that as the number of exposures increases, the variation of actual losses from probable or expected losses becomes progressively smaller. This assumes that losses occur in a random manner and with frequencies that closely follow some underlying mathematical distribution. Loss predictions become more and more accurate as the number of exposures increases, and credibility factors rise correspondingly.

Four basic standards are used in rate making: (1) the structure of rates should allocate the burden of expenses and costs in a way that reflects as accurately as possible the differences in risk—in other words, rates should be fair; (2) a rate should produce a premium adequate to meet total losses but should not bring unreasonably large profits; (3) the rate should be revised often enough to reflect current costs; and (4) the rate structure should tend to encourage loss prevention among those who are insured.

Some examples will illustrate the nature and application of the criteria outlined above. In life insurance, the rate is generally more than adequate to meet all reasonably anticipated losses and expenses; in other words, the insured is charged an excessive premium, part of which is then returned to him as a dividend according to actual losses and expenses. The requirement that the rate reflect fairly the risk involved is much more difficult to achieve. In workmen's compensation insurance, the rate is expressed as a percentage of the employer's payroll for each occupational class. This may seem fair enough, but an employer with relatively high-paid workers will tend to have fewer employees for a given amount of payroll than one whose workers are paid a lower wage. If the two employers fall into the same occupational class and have the same total payroll, they will be charged the same premium even though one may have a larger number of workers than the other, and hence greater exposure to loss. Fairness may be an elusive goal.

Insurance rates are revised only slowly, and since they are based upon past experience, they tend to remain out of date. In life insurance, for example, the mortality tables used are changed only every several years, and rate adjustments are reflected in dividends. In automobile insurance, rates are revised annually or even oftener, but they still tend to be out of date.

Systems. Two basic rate-making systems are in use: the manual or class-rating method, and the individual or merit-rating method. Sometimes a combination of the two methods is used.

A manual rate is one that applies uniformly to each exposure unit falling in some predetermined class or group, such as people of the same age, workers of one employer, drivers meeting certain characteristics, or all residences in a given area. Presumably the member of each class are so homogeneous as to be indistinguishable so far as risk characteristics are concerned.

Merit rating is used to give recognition to individual characteristics. In commercial buildings, for example, fire insurance rates depend on such individual characteristics as the type of occupancy, the number of and type of safety features, and the quality of housecleaning. A percentage charge or credit may be applied to the base rate for each of these features, in an attempt to reflect the true quality of the risk. Another example is found in employer group health insurance plans where the premium or the rate may be adjusted annually depending on the loss experience or on the amount of claims service provided.

In order to obtain broader and statistically sounder rates, insurers often pool loss and claims experience by setting up rating bureaus to calculate rates based on industry-wide experience. They may have an agreement that all member companies must use the rates thus developed. The rationale for such agreements is that they help insurers meet the criteria of adequacy and fairness. Rating bureaus are used extensively in fire, marine, workmen's compensation, automobile, and crime insurance.

LEGAL ASPECTS OF INSURANCE

Government regulation. The insurance business is subject to extensive government regulation in all countries. In European countries insurance regulation is a mixture of central and local controls. In West Germany, for example, the federal law applies generally to some 9,000 insurers operating in West Germany, most of them small local companies, but only about 10 percent of these insurers are supervised directly by the Federal Insurance Department; the others are all supervised by local agencies.

The various forms of government regulation

In the United Kingdom, regulation generally allows the management fairly complete liberty of action and is concerned only with final business results. In this the U.K. differs from most other European countries, in which the purpose of insurance supervision is to regulate more closely the conditions in which insurers operate.

In the countries of the European Economic Community (under articles 59–60 of the Treaty of Rome) an attempt is being made to obtain greater uniformity among national insurance statutes. This is intended to facilitate the operations of insurers across national borders. Rate regulation, however, remains within the jurisdiction of individual countries, being quite strict in France and Italy and relatively uncontrolled in Germany.

An important legal force influencing insurance regulation in such countries as France, Belgium, Egypt, Greece, Italy, Lebanon, Spain, Turkey, and the former French African colonies is the Code Napoléon. The influence of the Code may be seen, for example, in the matter of third-party liability, in which the burden of proof may be upon the defendant rather than upon the plaintiff.

In some countries not all classes of insurance are regulated. In The Netherlands only life insurance is regulated, and in Belgium only life, industrial injury, and third-party motor vehicle liability insurance. In some countries the scope of supervision may embrace many aspects of the insurance business, but in the United Kingdom and The Netherlands only financial matters are subject to regulation.

In several European countries insurers may not write both life insurance and general insurance (property and liability insurance). Minimum capital requirements vary, depending upon the type of business written, usually being highest for life insurance.

In most European countries policies are submitted to supervisory authorities for approval or for information. In some countries standard clauses or forms of contracts must be used; for example, in Sweden insurers must use a standard compulsory motor vehicle third-party liability policy, and in Switzerland a standard contract for war risks and life insurance is required.

Insurance is often compulsory. In general, laws often require individuals to carry third-party liability insurance and industrial injury insurance. Fire insurance is required on immovable property in Germany. A number of countries require aviation insurance (for accident and sickness) on airline passengers and crewmen.

Although individuals generally have the freedom to select whichever insurer they wish, there are restrictions on freedom in buying insurance from foreign or alien insurers. In some countries, buyers must use domestic insurers for compulsory coverages but are free to take out insurance in foreign or alien insurers when coverage is not available from domestic insurers. In other countries, certain types of insurance may not be placed in foreign countries. About half of the countries of the world prohibit "nonadmitted" insurance, defined as insurance written in contravention of local laws and regulations.

In the United States, where there is relatively close control over rate making by the states, insurance rates must meet three basic requirements: the rates must be adequate to meet losses, must not be excessive, and must not be unfairly discriminatory among different classes of risk. Other aspects of insurance that are subject to regulation by state governments in the United States include: minimum standards of financial solvency; minimum amounts of initial capital; restrictions on the types of assets in which insurance companies may invest; procedures for orderly liquidation of insolvent insurers; minimum levels of security deposits with government insurance commissioners; maximum expense allowances for the acquisition of new business; standard selling practices including agency licensing, policy forms, and provisions; taxation; and service and process procedures governing ways in which suits may be brought to recover losses.

Insurance as a contract

Contract law. In general, an insurance contract must meet four conditions in order to be legally valid: it must be for a legal purpose, the parties must have a legal capacity to contract, there must be evidence of a meeting of minds between the insurer and the insured, and there must be a payment or consideration.

To meet the requirement of legal purpose, the insurance contract must be supported by an insurable interest (see further discussion below); it may not be issued in such a way as to encourage illegal ventures (as with marine insurance placed on a ship used to carry contraband).

The requirement of capacity to contract usually means that the individual obtaining insurance must be of a minimum age and must be legally competent; the contract will not hold if the insured is found to be insane or intoxicated, or if the insured is a corporation operating outside the scope of its authority as defined in its charter, bylaws, or articles of incorporation.

The requirement of meeting of minds is met when a valid offer is made by one party and accepted by another. The offer is generally made on a written application for insurance. In the field of property and liability insurance, the agent generally has the right to accept the insured's offer for coverage and bind the contract immediately. In the field of life insurance, the agent generally does not have this power, and the contract is not valid until the home office of the insurer has examined the application and has returned it to the insured through the agent.

The payment or consideration is generally made up of two parts—the premiums and the promise to adhere to all conditions stated in the contract. These may include, for example, a warranty that the insured will take certain loss-prevention measures in the care and preservation of his property.

Warranties. In applying for insurance the applicant makes certain representations or warranties. If he makes a false representation, the insurer may, at his option, void the contract. Concealment of vital information may be considered misrepresentation. In general, the misrepresentation or concealment must concern a material fact—defined as a fact that would, if it were known, cause the insurer to change the terms of the contract or be unwilling to issue it in the first place. If the agent of the insurer asks the applicant a question the answer to which is a matter of opinion, and the answer turns out to be wrong, the insurer must demonstrate bad faith or fraudulent intent in order to void the contract. If, for example, the agent asks the applicant whether he has ever been seriously ill and the applicant answers no because he mistakenly believes his illness to have been minor, the court may find the statement to be an honest opinion and not a misrepresented fact.

A basic principle of property liability insurance contracts is the principle of subrogation, under which the insurer may be entitled to recovery from liable third parties. In fire insurance, for example, if a neighbour carelessly sets fire to the insured's house and the insurance company indemnifies the insured for his loss, the company may then bring a legal action in the name of the insured to recover the loss from the negligent neighbour. The principle of subrogation is complemented by another basic principle of insurance contract law, the principle of indemnity. Under the principle of indemnity a person may recover no more than his actual cash loss; he may not, for example, recover in full from two separate policies if the total amount exceeds the true value of the property insured.

Insurable interest. Closely associated with the above legal principles is that of insurable interest. This requires that the insured be exposed to a personal loss if the peril insured against should occur. Otherwise it would be possible for a person to take out a fire insurance policy on the property of others, and collect if the property burned. Any financial interest in property, or reasonable expectation of having a financial interest, is sufficient to establish insurable interest. A secured creditor such as a mortgagee has an insurable interest in the property on which he has lent money. In the field of personal insurance an individual is held to have an unlimited interest in his own life. A corporation may take life insurance on the life of a key man. A wife may insure the life of her husband and a father may insure the life of a minor child because there is a sufficient pecuniary relationship between them to establish an insurable interest.

In life insurance, the insurable interest must exist at the time of the contract. Continued insurable interest, however, need not be demonstrated. A divorced woman may continue life insurance on the life of her former husband and legitimately collect the proceeds upon his death even though she is no longer his wife. In the field of property insurance, on the other hand, the insurable interest must be demonstrated at the time of the loss. If an individual insures a home but later sells this home, he may not collect if it burns after the sale, because he has no loss at the time of the fire.

The concept of negligence

Liability law. In most countries, an individual may be held legally liable to another for his acts or omissions and be required to pay damages. Liability insurance may be purchased to cover these contingencies. In some countries (such as the U.S.S.R.) automobile liability insurance is not permitted, on the ground that this would allow the insured to escape the consequences of his negligence; some of the costs, however, are paid by social insurance (in the case of injuries) and by individual accident insurance.

Legal liability exists when an individual commits a legal injury that wrongly invades another person's rights. Such injuries include slander, assault, and negligent acts. A negligent act involves failure to behave in a manner expected when the results of this failure cause a financial loss to others. An act may be classed as negligent even if it is unintentional. Negligence may be imputed from one person to another. For example, a master is liable not only for his own act but also for the negligent acts of servants or others legally representing him. It is not uncommon for a municipality to require that businessmen using city property assume what would otherwise have been the city's negligence for the use of its property. Statutes may impute liability on individuals when no liability would exist otherwise; thus a father may be legally liable for the acts of a minor child who is driving the family automobile.

In common law countries such as the United States and the United Kingdom, three defenses may be used in a negligence action. These are assumed risk, contributory negligence, and the fellow servant doctrine. Under the assumed risk rule, the defendant may argue that the plaintiff has assumed the risk of loss in entering into a given venture and understands the risks. Employers formerly used the assumed risk doctrine in suits by injured employees, arguing that the employee understood and assumed the risks of employment when he accepted the job.

The contributory negligence defense is frequently used to defeat negligence actions. If it can be shown that one party was partly to blame, then he may not collect from any negligence of the other party. Some courts have applied a substitute doctrine known as comparative negligence. Under this, each party is held responsible for a portion of the loss corresponding to the degree of blame attached to him; if a person is 20 percent to blame for an accident he may be required to pay 20 percent of the other person's injuries.

The fellow servant defense has been used at times by employers; an employer would argue in some cases that the injury to an employee was caused not by the employer's negligence but by the negligence of another employee.

Workmen's compensation statutes in some countries have nullified such common law defenses in industrial injury cases.

In many countries the courts have tended to apply increasingly strict standards in adjudicating negligence. This has been termed the trend toward absolute liability, under which the plaintiff may recover for almost any accidental injury, even if it can be shown that the defendant has used "due care" and thus is not negligent in the traditional sense. In the United States, manufacturers of polio vaccine that was found to have caused polio were required to pay large damage claims although it was demonstrated that they had taken all normal precautions and safeguards in the manufacture of the vaccine.

HISTORICAL DEVELOPMENT OF INSURANCE

Ancient origins of insurance

Insurance in some form has been used as long as man has lived in historical society. So-called bottomry contracts were known to merchants of Babylon as early as 4000–3000 BC. Bottomry was also practiced by the Hindus in 600 BC, and was well understood in ancient Greece as early as the 4th century BC. Under a bottomry contract loans were granted to merchants with the provision that if the shipment was lost at sea the loan did not have to be repaid. The interest on the loan covered the insurance risk. Ancient Roman law recognized the bottomry contract in which an article of agreement was drawn up and funds were deposited with a money changer. Marine insurance became highly developed in the 15th century. In Rome there were also burial societies that paid funeral costs of their members out of monthly dues.

The insurance contract also developed very early. It was known in ancient Greece and among other maritime nations in commercial contact with Greece.

England. Fire insurance arose much later, obtaining impetus from the Great Fire of London in 1666. A number of insurance companies were started during the so-called bubble era in England after 1711. Many of them were fraudulent, get-rich-quick schemes, concerned mainly to sell their securities to the public. Nevertheless, two important and successful English insurance companies were formed during this period—the London Assurance Corporation and the Royal Exchange Assurance Corporation. Their operation marked the beginning of modern property and liability insurance.

No discussion of the early development of insurance in Europe would be complete without reference to Lloyd's of London, the international insurance market. It began as a 17th-century coffeehouse patronized by merchants, bankers, and insurance underwriters, gradually becoming recognized as the most likely place to find underwriters for marine insurance. Edward Lloyd would supply his customers with shipping information gathered from the docks and other sources; this eventually grew into the publication *Lloyd's List*, still in existence. Lloyd's was reorganized in 1769 as a formal group of underwriters accepting marine risks. The word underwriter is said to have derived from the practice of having each risk taker write his name under the total amount of risk in the proportion that he was willing to accept at a specified premium. With the growth of British sea power Lloyd's became the dominant insurer of marine risks, to which were later added fire and other property risks. Lloyd's is a major reinsurer as well as primary insurer. It does not itself transact insurance business: this is done by the member underwriters, who accept insurance on their own account and bear the full risk, in competition with each other.

United States. The first U.S. company was organized by Benjamin Franklin in 1752 as the "Philadelphia Contributionship." The first life insurance company in the United States was the Presbyterian Ministers' Fund, organized in 1759. By 1820 there were 17 stock life insurance companies in the state of New York alone. Many of the early property insurance companies failed from speculative investments, poor management, and inadequate distribution systems. Others failed after the Chicago fire of 1871 and the San Francisco fire and earthquake of 1906. There was little effective regulation, and rate making was difficult in the absence of cooperative development of sound statistics. Many problems also beset the life insurance business. In the era following the U.S. Civil War, bad practices developed: dividends were declared that had not been earned; reserves were inadequate; advertising claims were exaggerated; and office buildings were erected, that sometimes cost more than the total assets of the companies. Thirty-three life insurance companies failed between 1870 and 1872, and another 48 between 1873 and 1877.

Modern times

After 1910 life insurance enjoyed a steady growth in the United States. The annual growth rate of insurance in force over the period 1909–69 was approximately 14 percent—amounting to a 100-fold increase for the 60-year period. Over the period 1940–68, property and liability insurance premiums grew more than nine times.

Soviet Union. Following the revolution in 1917, insurance in the U.S.S.R. was nationalized; it is now administered by the organization known as Gosstrakh. Gosstrakh writes two basic forms of coverage, personal and property. Property insurance is the more important and is further divided into two general types: voluntary and required. Property insurance is required on all government-owned property and on certain property of collective farms. Voluntary property insurance is available for non-state-owned livestock, crops, household goods, automotive equipment, and freight.

Personal insurance coverages such as term and whole life insurance, accident insurance, and certain annuity contracts are available on a voluntary basis in the U.S.S.R. In 1959 over 10,000,000 people were reported to be insured by an individual endowment policy with accidental death and disability income protection. Insurance against tort liability is not sold in the U.S.S.R., on the ground that to allow such coverage would permit negligent persons to escape the financial consequences of their behaviour. Reinsurance also does not exist, although Ingosstrakh, which handles all foreign coverages, accepts reinsurance from other world insurance organizations. State-owned enterprises in the U.S.S.R. do not carry insurance as such but use self-insurance in the sense that losses are absorbed in the state budget.

Japan. Insurance in Japan is mainly private enterprise, although government insurance agencies write crop, livestock, forest fire, fishery, export credit, accident and health, and installment sales credit insurance as well as social security. Private companies are regulated under various statutes. Major classes of property insurance written include automobile and workmen's compensation (which are compulsory), fire, and marine. Rates are controlled by voluntary rating bureaus under government supervision. Japanese law requires rates to be "reasonable and nondiscriminatory." Policy forms generally resemble those of Western nations. Personal insurance lines are also well developed in Japan. Ordinary life, group life, and group pensions are all written. Health insurance, however, is incorporated into Japanese social security. Japan ranked second in the world in 1968 in total life insurance in force, and eighth in life insurance per capita.

Worldwide operations. Because of the great expansion in world trade and in the extent to which business firms make investments outside the boundaries of their home countries, the market for insurance on a worldwide scale has been expanding rapidly in recent years. This development has required a worldwide network of offices to provide brokerage services, underwriting assistance, claims service, etc. The world insurance business is concentrated in Europe and North America, which in 1972 had 77 percent of the 13,655 companies. These must service a large part of the insurance needs of the rest of the world. The legal and regulatory hurdles that must be overcome in order to do so are formidable.

It has been suggested that one solution to the shortage of insurance capacity would be to reorganize the worldwide insurance business on a different basis. Some insurers necessarily are more conservative than others and have what others would consider to be unused capacity. At present, the primary insurer underwrites the initial risk and then attempts through reinsurance to redistribute his risk to other insurers in "layers." The capacity of the reinsurance industry to absorb these "layers" has become increasingly strained. An alternative would be to permit each participating organization to absorb a small percentage of the exposure on a direct basis. Thus, in the case of a large loss, each insurer or participating insurer around the world would absorb a fractional percentage of the total. In this way the existing insurance capacity would be more adequately distributed than at present.

Mergers. In recent years there have been numerous mergers and consolidations of insurance companies. In the United States during the period 1955–65 most mergers were between property-liability companies and life insurance companies. After 1965, a new type of merger began to appear: holding companies known as congenerics, with subsidiaries consisting not only of insurance companies but also of companies performing other services such as banking, data processing, loss-prevention engineering, mutual fund management, real estate appraisal, and credit and collection. The advantages claimed for them were various. A life insurance company may find that its total tax burden is less if it is part of a holding company rather than itself owning a number of subsidiary companies. Moreover, a holding company is able to expand by issuing preferred stock, a course not permitted to a life insurance company in many countries. This allows greater "leverage" in financial operations—that is, it can control larger resources with a smaller investment than would otherwise be necessary. There are also merchandising advantages in wide diversification. The sales force can sell not only insurance but mutual funds, loss-prevention engineering, real estate appraisal services, and other financial services.

BIBLIOGRAPHY. Basic surveys of the whole insurance field are given in M.R. GREENE, *Risk and Insurance*, 2nd ed. (1968); J.H. MAGEE and D.L. BICKELHAUPT, *General Insurance*, 7th ed. (1964); and R.I. MEHR and E. CAMMACK, *Principles of Insurance*, 4th ed. (1966). Group insurance is perhaps most completely represented in R.D. EILERS and R.M. CROWE (eds.), *Group Insurance Handbook* (1965); but more specialized treatments are available in D.W. GREGG, *Group Life Insurance*, 3rd ed. (1962); and O.D. DICKERSON, *Health Insurance*, rev. ed. (1963). Recent developments in group coverages in the field of property insurance are covered by I.M. FIELD, *Employee Group Property and Liability Insurance* (1967). Valuable recent treatments of international developments in insurance are by R. WELLS, *Sourcebook on International Corporate Insurance and Employee Benefit Management* (1968); and C.S. HART, *Sourcebook on International Insurance and Employee Benefit Management* (1967). Regulation of insurance is covered in S.L. KIMBALL and H.S. DENENBERG, *Insurance, Government and Social Policy* (1969), which stresses American regulation; and in a study by the ORGANIZATION FOR ECONOMIC COOPERATION AND DEVELOPMENT, *Supervision of Private Insurance in Europe*, 2 vol. (1963), which compares regulation of insurance in major European countries. An authoritative survey of legal aspects of private insurance is found in H.S. DENENBERG, "The Legal Definition of Insurance," *Journal of Insurance*, 31:319–343 (1963).

(M.R.G.)

Integrated Circuitry

An integrated circuit is a combination of interconnected circuit elements, such as transistors, resistors, and diodes, that are inseparably associated with a continuous base material (substrate) by various processing operations that simultaneously form a large number of such elements. Generally, the circuit elements are microscopic in size; hence the term microcircuit is often applied. Conventional circuitry is built by the assembly of separately encapsulated circuit elements and thus differs from integrated circuits.

Integrated-circuit technology provides significant advantages over conventional techniques in many types of electronic systems. The complex digital systems of computers, for example, require vast numbers of circuit elements and would be impractical with any other component technology presently known. The benefits of integrated circuits include smaller size, lower power consumption, often increased speed of operation, improved reliability, and vastly reduced cost. In addition, system design and realization are simplified when using integrated circuits, since most of the required interconnections have already been made within the integrated circuits themselves.

As a result of these advantages, integrated circuits have been the fastest growing segment of electronic component technology since their introduction in 1961. They are responsible in large measure for the broadening of electronics applications to perform better and more efficiently many functions that had previously been accomplished by completely different techniques.

Three basic types of integrated circuits exist: Three basic types

1. Monolithic integrated circuits are formed of elements that are prepared within and upon a semiconductor substrate, at least one of the elements being within the substrate (a semiconductor is a material the electrical conductivity of which lies between that of a good conductor, such as a metal, and an insulator). In almost all cases the semiconductor substrate consists of a thin slice that has been cut from a large single crystal of silicon. The techniques grew out of transistor technology and are often called semiconductor integrated circuits or silicon integrated circuits.

2. Multichip integrated circuits are a micro-assembly of two or more pieces, or chips, of semiconductor material on a substrate. The individual chips may contain single elements or they may be monolithic integrated circuits. The substrate contributes the necessary interconnection and isolation between the chips but does not contain other circuit elements.

3. Film integrated circuits are those the elements of which are formed of films upon an isolating substrate. These are usually restricted to passive electronic components, such as arrays of resistors (devices for impeding the flow of electric current) and capacitors (devices for storing electric charge). This class is divided into thick film and thin film, depending principally upon the technique employed for deposition of the films.

Often these basic types are used in combination. Several monolithic integrated circuits, for example, might be combined with thin-film elements upon the same substrate. Such combinations are called hybrid integrated circuits. In general, a more complete description of the structure of any type of integrated circuit can be given by prefixing additional modifiers to the name.

This article is divided into the following sections:

History
Structure and properties of integrated circuits
  Monolithic integrated circuits
  Thin-film integrated circuits
  Thick-film integrated circuits
  Hybrid integrated circuits
Circuit functions
  Digital circuits
  Analogue circuits
  Microwave applications
Circuit fabrication
  Monolithic integrated circuits
  Film circuits
Future Developments

HISTORY

Since integrated electronics is a melding of many technologies, its beginnings are not clearly defined. The requirement for miniature electronic systems during World War II led to the development of many of the underlying ideas and techniques. During the war, arrays of resistors and interconnections were first fabricated by screen printing patterns of resistive inks and silver paste upon ceramic substrates. This is possibly the first example of the *in situ* (on location) preparation of arrays of electronic elements. It also represents a first use of printing to fabricate electronic parts. Throughout integrated electronics, considerable technology has been adapted from the longer established printing and engraving arts.

Another key event was the invention of the transistor in 1947. For the first time there existed a practical solid-state device capable of amplification. Also in the late 1940s, considerable progress was made on miniature batch-oriented interconnection techniques, including the successful use of etched circuits. In these circuits, inter-

Development of etched-circuit techniques

connection patterns are prepared by etching a metallic foil, which is bonded to an insulating substrate; miniature components are attached by inserting their leads through holes in the substrate and dipping in a bath of molten solder. This has developed into the modern printed circuit board that is utilized extensively for interconnecting integrated circuits. It is also used for electronic components occurring at the next level of system complexity.

The first monolithic integrated circuit was demonstrated in 1958; it was an electronic circuit consisting of a diffused transistor, two resistors, and a resistor–capacitor network. In 1959 an interconnection structure was invented; it utilized thin-film conductors over the oxide insulator that protected the junctions in a planar transistor (see below). About the same time the two principal methods of isolation, junction (see below) and dielectric —that is, separating the components by an insulating material—were patented.

Also during the late 1950s, integrated electronics techniques based upon vacuum deposition of thin films were being developed. The technology was an extension of vacuum evaporation techniques that have for a long time been used to coat mirrors and lenses with metallic and dielectric films.

Thus, by the latter part of the 1950s, the basic approaches to integrated electronics had evolved. Since then, development has been rapid, and the importance of the field has increased so greatly that the majority of circuit elements being produced in the early 1970s were contained in integrated circuits.

STRUCTURE AND PROPERTIES OF INTEGRATED CIRCUITS

Monolithic integrated circuits. Monolithic integrated circuits are formed layer by layer through a complex sequence of materials-processing steps. The resulting structure is a solid three-dimensional network of conductors, insulators, and regions of semiconductor containing proper electrically active impurities. A given processing sequence is capable of producing a variety of circuit functions depending only upon the topological patterns of the various layers, which, in turn, are controlled by a set of masks. These masks are designed to create several different structural features that in combination result in the desired electrical function.

Typically, the mask pattern for a particular layer of a circuit function is repeated in an array in such a way as to cover the entire surface of a semiconductor wafer with a multiplicity of identical patterns. A wafer of silicon two inches (five centimetres) in diameter might contain 100 to 1,000 complete circuits.

Several specific structural features are required to make a complete integrated function. These include the basic circuit elements, such as transistors, diodes, resistors, and capacitors, as well as isolation and interconnection. The following are some of the more important examples:

P–n junctions. Almost all semiconductor devices depend upon positive–negative (*p–n*) junctions for their operation. Regions of semiconductors are *n*-type or *p*-type, depending upon whether the dominant electrical charge carrier is negative (electrons) or positive (holes). This in turn depends upon the dominant impurity contained within the semiconductor. A *p–n* junction is the boundary between two regions of opposite conductivity type. It has the property of conducting when one polarity voltage is applied and serving essentially as an insulator with the opposite polarity.

Transistors. The availability of active devices—that is, devices capable of amplifying electrical signals—is the principal reason for the importance of semiconductor monolithic integrated circuits. Two active devices are important—the junction, or bipolar, transistor and a metal-oxide-semiconductor (MOS), or insulated-gate field-effect transistor. In the former, two *p–n* junctions close to one another in a single semiconductor crystal defining regions of alternating conductivity type, either *n–p–n* or *p–n–p*, can interact so that current supplied to the centre layer will control the flow of significantly larger current between the other two regions. Typical cross sections of such transistor structures are illustrated below in Figure 1A.

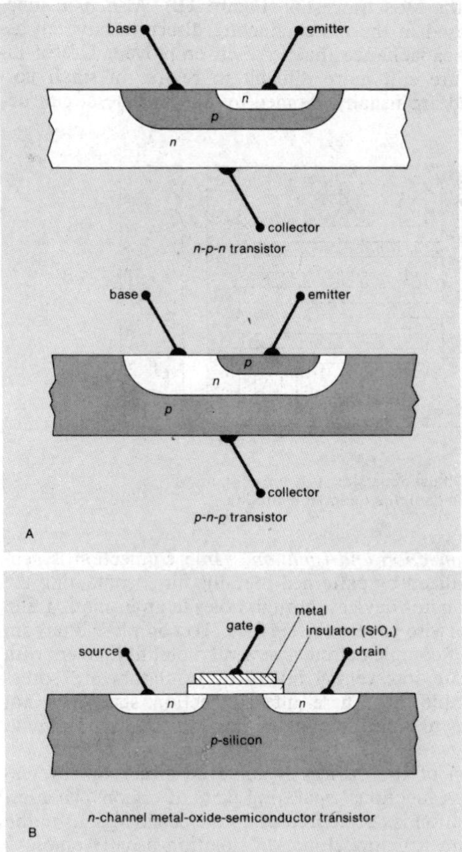

Figure 1: (A) Cross sections through representative diffused transistor structures as employed in integrated circuitry. (B) Cross section through metal-oxide-semiconductor transistor (see text).

The MOS transistor

In the MOS transistor (Figure 1B), two *p–n* junctions are displaced from one another along a surface. The region between them is covered with an insulator and a conducting electrode (metal). Voltage applied to this gate electrode attracts charge carriers to the surface of the semiconductor and may induce and modulate a conducting channel between the source and drain electrodes. Again, two complementary polarity devices are possible, called *p*-channel or *n*-channel, the distinction being dependent upon the conductivity type of the source and drain regions.

Passive elements. Since semiconductors are relatively poor conductors of electricity compared with metals, they are often used for resistors. A region of semiconductor of uniform conductivity type, either *n* or *p*, with appropriate electrical connections, is employed. In its simplest form the resistor is a ribbon of one conductivity type in a sea of the opposite type as shown in Figure 2. The applied voltage during circuit operation must be of such a polarity that the junction forming a boundary of the resistor remains reverse-biased; that is, biased so that no current flows across the boundary. This is termed junction isolation.

More complex resistor structures are also used. In a structure with cross section similar to the transistor of Figure 1A, for example, contacts made to the intermediate layer on each side of the emitter region yield a resistor structure with greater resistance than would result were the emitter region not present, since the conducting cross section is decreased. Such structures are used for large-value resistors in small areas. In certain special cases, thin-film resistors (see below) are deposited onto the monolithic structure.

Only relatively small-valued capacitors can be incorporated in monolithic integrated circuits because of the small volume available in which to store energy. Typical capacitors utilize a metal electrode separated from a semiconductor electrode by a dielectric similar to the gate in the MOS transistor (Figure 1B). Also, *p–n* junctions biased in the nonconducting direction have an associated capacitance that is often employed. Useful inductors are still more difficult to realize in small volumes and are usually avoided by appropriate circuit design.

Capacitors

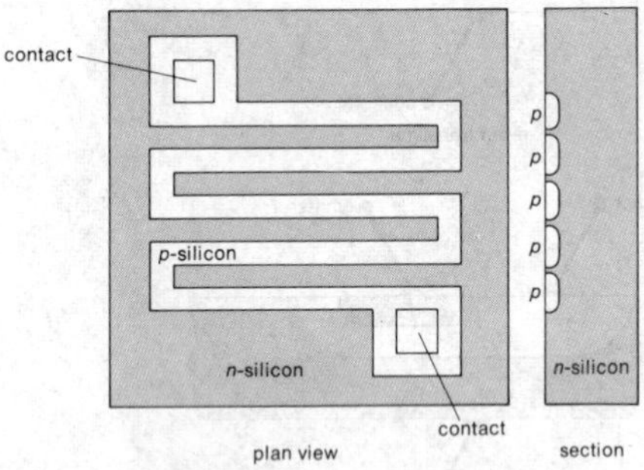

Figure 2: Diffused resistor structure of the type utilized in monolithic integrated circuits.

Interconnection and isolation. Interconnection is generally realized by patterned metallic films contacting the semiconductor devices through holes in an insulating film that otherwise covers the surface. To complete interconnection of complex circuits, several metal film layers with appropriate intervening layers of insulators are sometimes employed. These interconnection structures are analogous to etched circuits prepared *in situ* on a minute scale.

Isolation of the devices is achieved either by reverse-biased *p–n* junctions separating pairs of regions when interconnection is not desired or by dielectric regions in the monolithic structure. Junction isolation usually employs a pair of *p–n* junctions arranged in such a way that no matter which polarity voltage is applied between the regions to be isolated, one or the other junction is reverse-biased.

In the important case of the MOS transistor, the devices are "self-isolating" in that the *p–n* junction forming the source and drain regions is always reverse-biased in operation, so that no special structure need be incorporated. This results in considerable simplification and a correspondingly higher packing density (more components per unit area) for semiconductor components on the semiconductor surface—both considerations having important economic consequences.

Thin-film integrated circuits. Thin-film integrated circuits are formed of elements deposited on an insulating substrate, such as glass or ceramic, by any of a variety of techniques. The simplest and most common circuits are arrays of resistors and capacitors with their associated interconnections. A major limitation in film integrated circuits has been the lack of a generally useful active device, such as a transistor. For this reason, monolithic and hybrid integrated circuits have predominated. Monolithic integrated circuits make extensive use of thin-film structures and share considerable technology with thin-film integrated circuits.

Thin-film resistors

Most thin-film integrated circuits are arrays of passive elements and their associated interconnections. Resistors are made from a variety of materials, including nickel–chromium alloys, tantalum, tantalum nitride, metal silicides, and mixtures of metals and insulators, such as chromium metal and silicon monoxide, called cermets. Conductor patterns are generally aluminum or gold combined with an underlayer of a more active metal to increase adhesion to the substrate. Capacitors and conductor crossovers require the deposition of a layer of dielectric and a second layer of conductor. A thin-film hybrid integrated circuit that has been developed for generating the audio frequencies used in telephone dialing utilizes tantalum nitride films for resistors and tantalum pentoxide for the capacitor dielectric with gold conductors.

A variety of special film structures has been considered, including the utilization of superconducting thin films at cryogenic (very low) temperatures for integrated electronic functions. Unique active elements are possible utilizing the phenomenon of superconductivity; that is, the complete loss of electrical resistance at very low temperatures.

The most successful attempt at developing a thin-film active device has been through growth of a single crystal film of silicon on a synthetic sapphire or spinel substrate. This silicon film can be processed to make high-quality MOS transistors. It is really closer to monolithic technology, however, rather than to the classical thin-film structure.

Thick-film integrated circuits. For thick-film integrated circuits, special inks are printed in patterns through masks in an adaptation of silk-screen printing. When fired, these inks form resistors, conductors, and insulating layers typically several microns (one micron = 0.001 millimetre) thick. Usual minimum line widths are above 100 microns compared with less than 10 microns in the thin-film case. Thick-film technology has proven extremely versatile, and a number of inks, allowing wide ranges of resistance and temperature characteristics, are available.

With film integrated circuits, precise resistor values can be achieved by adjusting the individual elements. With thick films this is usually accomplished by removing a portion of the film with a small grinder or an abrasive jet while monitoring the resistance value. With thin films a laser beam can be utilized to vaporize part of the film, or, in the cases of tantalum and tantalum nitride, electrochemical action is employed.

Hybrid integrated circuits. Film technology is employed principally in hybrid integrated circuits, since it is necessary to add semiconductor chips for good active devices. Figure 3 shows a relatively complex thick-film hybrid containing a variety of chips, including several monolithic integrated circuits and chip ceramic capacitors. Such hybrids can include precision passive elements and can allow the use of combinations of semiconductor elements on the various chips that would be difficult to integrate in a single monolithic structure. They preserve many of the advantages of small size and light weight. Often other miniature components such as ceramic capacitors in chip form are added, extending the range of available elements still further.

By courtesy of Fairchild Camera and Instrument Corp.

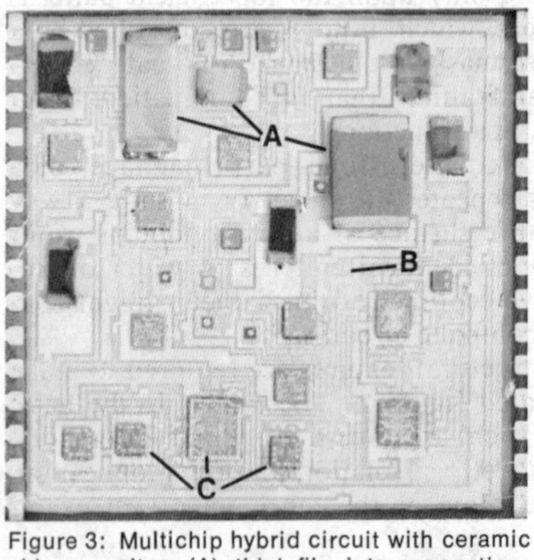

Figure 3: Multichip hybrid circuit with ceramic chip capacitors (A), thick film interconnections (B), semiconductor devices (C).

A problem with hybrid circuits or multichip integrated circuits is the attachment and connection of the semiconductor chips to the films. Three basic approaches are employed (Figure 4). With standard transistor assembly techniques, the back of the chip is soldered to a metallized pad on the substrate, and fine interconnection wires are welded to the chip electrode and proper points on the films.

This "chip and wire" approach is cumbersome if many

chips are required. By making raised contacts coated with solder on the chip and a matching conductor pattern on the substrate, an inverted assembly is possible with the simultaneous attachment of all connections. A third technique makes use of "beam leads," relatively thick metal fingers that protrude beyond the edge of the chip. The free ends of these beams are welded to an appropriate film pattern.

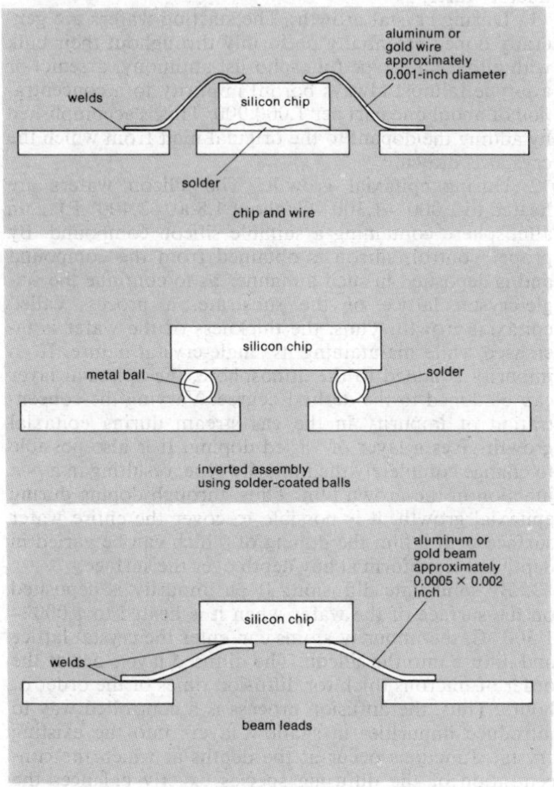

Figure 4: Three methods employed for attaching silicon chips in hybrid integrated circuits.

CIRCUIT FUNCTIONS

Thousands of different electronic functions have been achieved in integrated circuitry. The circuit packages vary in complexity from dual device structures to data storage circuits utilizing several thousand elements. Most of the functions are for signal processing, such as amplification or switching in computers, because these low-power uses benefit most from integration. They include circuits that operate from direct current through microwave frequencies.

Signal processing

Digital circuits. The majority of integrated functions are for digital logic, such as that used in computers and related data processing (see also COMPUTERS). In these kinds of applications, it is necessary only that there be two levels of signal representing a "1" and a "0" be distinguishable.

Several families of integrated logic circuits exist and are used extensively by interconnecting the appropriate circuit functions to realize a logic system. The members of a particular family are designed to drive and be driven by other members of the family. They utilize the same power supply voltages and signal levels. The family members may range in complexity from simple gating functions and other small-scale integrated circuits through more complex single functions called medium-scale integrated circuits (MSI) to complete complex large-scale integrated (LSI) system functions, such as memory arrays that contain the equivalent logical complexity of several hundred gates.

An important group of logic functions utilize the MOS transistor. Often a complete logic system is realized in a small number of MOS–LSI circuits. A photomicrograph of the complete central processing logic for a small computer, for example, is shown in Figure 5. This integrated circuit contains approximately 3,000 transistors. Since small MOS transistors have relatively limited capability

By courtesy of Intel Corp.

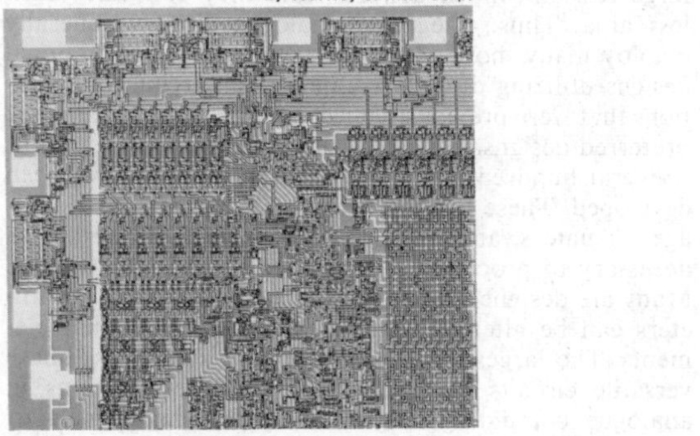

Figure 5: Section of MOS–LSI circuit
Complete circuit consists of 3,000 MOS transistors and their interconnections.

to drive loads, it becomes quite important to minimize the number of devices that must drive external connections.

The large MOS devices that are required to drive external connections consume a disproportionate amount of area. If complex functions are integrated, only a small percentage of the devices need drive any load other than the small capacitances of interconnections and the other devices on the same chip. This has led to extensive use of custom MOS–LSI; that is, LSI circuits designed to perform a specific application for a particular user. Such a custom function utilizing bipolar circuitry would usually be realized by the assembly of appropriate members of a circuit family on a printed circuit board. With MOS, however, it is realized by the generation of a special set of masks that are processed through a standard MOS processing sequence.

MOS circuits are made with either n-channel or p-channel transistors or with both polarities together in complementary MOS. There are a number of variations of the devices on the same chip. This has led to extensive use of different compromises of cost and performance. An important advantage sought in MOS–LSI is low cost because of the high density of circuit functions that can be realized on the silicon. This is partially a result of the self-isolating nature of the MOS transistor and partially because it offers special circuit possibilities. Particularly important are various dynamic circuit schemes that utilize multiple clock phases to transfer information from one circuit stage to the next. They utilize the temporary storage of charge on the gate capacitance of MOS devices to retain the signal between clock phases. Such circuitry requires very little power and can employ minimum size transistors.

Analogue circuits. In analogue circuits such as amplifiers, the magnitude of the signals is important. Monolithic analogue circuits were slow to become important in comparison with digital circuits because the restraints imposed by integration are more limiting. Conventional analogue circuits employ a large variety of circuit elements, including complementary polarity transistors, high-value resistors, precision components, and high-voltage devices, all of these being quite difficult to integrate.

Analogue circuit elements

On the other hand, several new possibilities become available upon integration. While absolute values of various electrical parameters of active and passive elements are quite variable and have large temperature dependences, similar elements in the same monolithic structure generally match well. Pairs of diffused resistors the absolute values of which vary ± 20 percent of nominal, for example, can be expected to match within a few percent. Because of the high thermal conductivity of the silicon and close spacing, the matching is preserved over a wide temperature range. Thus, monolithic integrated analogue circuits can utilize precise resistor ratios but cannot depend upon precise absolute values.

Another significant change in integrated-circuit design compared with design with discrete elements is that active devices, such as transistors, are much less expensive than large resistors or capacitors, since they consume much less area. Thus, integrated analogue circuits generally employ many more active devices than do conventional designs utilizing discrete components. Circuit configurations that were previously uneconomical have become the preferred designs.

Several hundred standard analogue circuits have been developed. These include many types of amplifiers, voltage regulators, and special functions such as the blocks necessary to process the signals in a television receiver. Many are designed so that their specific electrical parameters can be altered by the use of a few external elements. The largest class is operational amplifiers. These versatile circuits are used for arithmetic functions in analogue computing systems, in processing signals of various kinds, and in a wide variety of other applications. By simple external passive feedback networks they can be adapted to a variety of tasks. Integration has resulted in a 100-fold cost reduction that has allowed their use much more extensively than was previously feasible.

When precision components are required, hybrid techniques with film resistor arrays can be employed. Analogue to digital and digital to analogue converters, utilizing a precision resistor array with all of the switching network on a monolithic chip, are examples. Similarly, multichip hybrids can incorporate power transistor chips required in such applications as automobile voltage regulators or the output stage of a radio receiver.

Microwave applications. Hybrid integrated circuit techniques have had a large impact on microwave electronics. Conventional circuit techniques as practiced at lower frequencies are not satisfactory at microwave frequencies because lengths of interconnections are comparable to the wavelength of these high frequencies, resulting in a variety of problems of signal propagation. Formerly, it was necessary to utilize coaxial cable or wave guide for microwave transmission, making the resulting systems bulky and expensive. By employing the miniature sizes possible with integrated circuits, the connections are short compared with the operating wavelength, and open interconnections are possible. A variety of low-power signal sources, detectors, and amplifiers have been developed that eliminate wave-guide interconnections with considerable savings in cost, size, and weight.

CIRCUIT FABRICATION

Monolithic integrated circuits. The starting material is almost always single-crystal silicon. Although many materials are classed as semiconductors, only a few have properties that make them valuable for electronic signal processing. Only germanium, silicon, and gallium arsenide (GaAs) have found commercial applications. Silicon has assumed the dominant position and is the unique candidate for monolithic integrated electronics. This is because of a combination of desirable properties that favour good electrical performance and high chemical stability and also the availability of its dioxide (SiO_2) that is utilized extensively in the complex structures. Many of the procedures are similar to those employed in making transistors and other semiconductor devices (see also SEMICONDUCTOR DEVICES).

The silicon wafer

The starting point for manufacture of monolithic integrated circuits is the silicon wafer. This is a disk perhaps two inches (five centimetres) in diameter and 0.01 inch (0.025 centimetres) in thickness that has been cut from a large single crystal of silicon. These wafers are lapped and polished to remove any crystal damage near the surface from cutting, resulting in a fine mirrorlike surface.

Very important to the underlying economics of integrated electronic fabrication is the fact that many structures are processed at a time. A transistor, for example, might consume only a thousandth of a square millimetre of surface area on the wafer. Thus, if the entire surface (one side) were covered with such transistors, a two-inch wafer could contain over 2,000,000. The processing sequence is designed to make one complete integrated circuit correctly. This single structure occupies only a small portion of the wafer surface. By the batch-processing nature of the technology, this complete structure is repeated over the entire wafer surface so that large numbers are made at the same time.

Doping. There are four important ways of doping; *i.e.*, introducing needed impurities into the semiconductor wafer.

1. During crystal growth: The starting wafers are generally doped essentially uniformly throughout their bulk with either an *n*-type (phosphorus, antimony, arsenic) or a *p*-type (almost always boron) impurity to a concentration of about one part per 1,000,000. This is accomplished by adding the dopant to the original melt from which the crystal is drawn.

2. During epitaxial growth: The silicon wafers are heated to 1,000°–1,300° C (about 1,800°–2,400° F) in an atmosphere containing a suitable silicon compound. By proper control, silicon is obtained from the compound and is deposited in such a manner as to continue the single-crystal lattice of the substrate, a process called epitaxial growth. Thus, the thickness of the wafer is increased while maintaining its single-crystal nature. If an impurity is added to the atmosphere, the epitaxial layer can be doped to the desired degree. Varying the concentration of impurity in the gas stream during epitaxial growth gives a layer of varied doping. It is also possible to change completely the impurity type, resulting in a *p–n* junction in the grown film. Thus, through doping during epitaxial growth, it is possible to cover the entire wafer surface with a film the doping of which can be varied in depth but is uniform at any depth over the surface.

3. By solid-state diffusion: If an impurity is deposited on the surface of the wafer when it is heated to 1,000°–1,300° C, the impurity atoms can enter the crystal lattice and diffuse into the silicon. The diffused layers are of the order of microns thick for diffusion times of the order of hours. Thus, the diffusion process is a controlled way to introduce impurities in shallow layers into the existing crystal. Junctions occur at the depths at which the concentration of the diffusing species exactly balances the doping previously in the crystal, if they are of opposite doping types.

Oxide film mask

A mask can be added so that the impurity enters the surface only in certain regions. This allows a pattern of regions to be diffused into the surface. An effective mask for most important impurities is silicon dioxide, SiO_2. By heating the silicon wafer in an oxidizing atmosphere (oxygen or water vapour), a dense, strongly adherent layer of SiO_2 is formed. Layers up to about a micron in thickness can be grown in an hour at temperatures similar to those employed for diffusion. To carry out a patterned diffusion, the wafer is first oxidized, the desired pattern is etched through the oxide, and the diffusion is performed. The impurity enters the silicon only in the regions in which the oxide was removed. The oxide masking of diffusion is the key to achieving complex structures. It is employed repeatedly to build an integrated structure.

A junction made by diffusion through a hole in an oxide film has a dish shape, with the termination of the junction under the original oxide mask a distance roughly equal to the depth of the junction. The termination of a junction is a region of high electrical field and, therefore, very sensitive to surface cleanliness in its electrical properties. The best termination for a junction that has yet been found is a thermally grown SiO_2 film. If the diffusion mask is allowed to remain over the junction area, it is terminated properly and protected from the environment. This is the basic idea of the planar transistor and a necessary feature for integrated electronic structures.

Diffusions can be performed before epitaxial growth so that an oxide-masked pattern can be buried under an otherwise uniformly doped layer. This is an important combination of steps in achieving some useful isolation structures and for incorporating high conductivity (highly doped) layers buried under devices.

4. By ion implantation: The desired impurity is ionized,

accelerated through 50–500 kilovolts, and allowed to impinge on a silicon wafer. The kinetic energy of the ions causes them to penetrate the crystal to useful depths.

Ion implantation is the only low-temperature process that has been developed and so can be very useful. Every time a wafer is heated, some diffusion takes place wherever a concentration gradient exists in the structure (*e.g.*, at every *p–n* junction). With ion implantation, sharp gradients can be retained. Also, it is possible to control the total impurity concentration electrically, since every ion carries with it a known charge. This results in much more precise doping control than can be achieved by other means, particularly at very low doping levels.

The possibility exists that extremely fine scale patterns can be made on a wafer surface by writing with a focussed beam of ions. Application of ion implantation in integrated structures in the early 1970s, however, remained limited to scanning the wafer surface with a broad beam utilizing a masking film to restrict the areas of penetration.

Photomasking. A major area of the technology relates to forming patterns on the surface. Not only is this important for oxide masking but it is also required to establish interconnection patterns and other thin-film structures. Basically, a highly refined photoengraving process is employed.

A master drawing of the finished structure is created showing how the several layers are superimposed. Typically, this might be done at 500 times final size, so the artwork for an integrated structure that was destined to occupy a tenth inch (2.5 millimetres) square of silicon would be 50 inches (1.25 metre) on a side. A typical interconnection line might be a quarter of an inch wide on the artwork, corresponding to a half mil (0.0005 inch [0.01 millimetre]) in the final structure.

Separate, high-precision drawings of the pattern for each layer are then prepared and reduced to final size photographically. This final image is stepped and exposed many times to cover an area on a photographic plate as large as the silicon wafer. A copy of such a master mask plate is used to photoengrave the film on the wafer.

The wafer surface is first coated with a photosensitive material the solubility of which in appropriate solvents can be altered by exposure to light. It is exposed through the photographic mask, which is usually in contact with the photosensitive film during this exposure. The image is then developed by treatment with solvent, and the developed image is used as an etch mask. Buffered hydrofluoric acid, for example, removes the SiO_2 without reacting with either the remaining photosensitive film or with the underlying silicon crystal.

Selective etching

Presently, lines of five to ten microns are routine for complex structures. Micron lines (0.00004 inch) can be employed for very simple integrated structures. Since this approaches the wavelength of light, it is close to the limit that can be achieved optically.

Film deposition. To complete the integrated structures, it is necessary to deposit and pattern various films of metals, insulators, or semiconductors. Again several techniques are used.

Vacuum evaporation is a common method for most metallic elements and simple alloys. The material to be deposited is heated in an evacuated chamber that also contains the substrate. The material vaporizes and recondenses on the substrate.

Sputtering utilizes an electrical discharge in a low-pressure gas to produce positive ions that bombard a cathode (negative electrode) made of the material to be deposited. This bombardment dislodges atoms from the cathode; they diffuse through the low-pressure gas to the substrate. Usually, the ions are of an inert gas such as argon, but in some cases oxygen or another reactive gas is used, resulting in the deposited film being a compound such as an oxide of the cathode material. Sputtered films are dense and strongly adherent. Mixtures including complex glasses can be sputtered with little change in composition.

Chemical vapour deposition employs chemical reactions at the substrate-gas interface to yield the desired film as a reaction product. Since no vacuum system is required and high-quality films can be produced, this technique is becoming increasingly important.

Another technique for film formation is by oxidation of a previously deposited film to form an insulator. This is accomplished either thermally or electrochemically.

A representative process sequence. As an example of a way in which the process steps might be combined to make a complete monolithic integrated structure, Figure 6 shows successive cross sections through a portion of a silicon wafer that is destined to become a diffused resistor connected to the base of an *n–p–n* transistor. This is a typical sequence utilized for producing integrated circuits. Many possible variations exist, each with its own set of advantages and disadvantages.

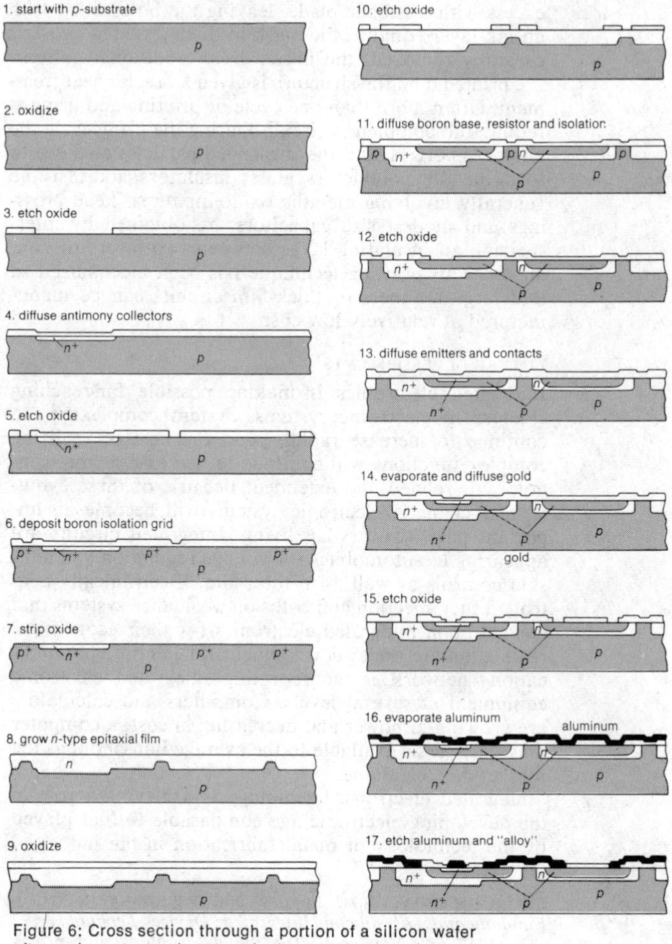

Figure 6: Cross section through a portion of a silicon wafer after various processing steps in the construction of a monolithic integrated circuit. This particular cross section shows construction of an *n–p–n* transistor in an isolated region and a diffused resistor connected in series with the base connection of the transistor. The plus signs following either *n* or *p* indicate a greater than normal concentration of *n*- or *p*- charges (see text).

In this example, step 4 is to introduce a high conductivity region under the transistor to reduce undesirable resistance. The other buried diffusion is done so that isolation can be accomplished by completing the *p*-type barriers between *n*-pockets during the boron base diffusion, step 11. All diffusions are carried out in oxygen, which regrows the oxide layer. Gold diffusion, step 14, increases the switching speed of logic circuits. Gold diffuses into the silicon at a temperature that has little effect on the other impurities.

Upon completion of the processing sequence, each circuit is given an electrical test by means of a multipoint probe contacting the lead-bond pads. Bad circuits are marked for later discard. The wafer is cut into the individual circuits by scratching with a diamond and breaking, by sawing, or by laser cutting. If the circuits are to be individually packaged, they are bonded to the package leads and encapsulated in molded plastic or a hermetic enclosure and subjected to extensive electrical testing to assure that they perform the correct function and exhibit the required parametric values.

Film circuits. Thin-film integrated circuits utilize deposition techniques and photoengraving processes similar to those of the monolithic circuits. Substrate material is generally glass or glazed ceramic, as a smooth surface is necessary to obtain reproducible film properties.

Inks used for thick films

For thick films, inks consisting of a suspension containing an organic binder and the appropriate powdered metal, glass, or other material are printed through a mask or screen. The desired pattern is produced as holes and slots in the mask, which is placed in intimate contact with the substrate. The ink is forced into the holes and levelled with the top mask surface by scraping away any excess with a rubber blade, leaving the holes filled with an ink layer equal to the mask in thickness. The mask is carefully removed, the ink is dried, additional patterns are printed, and the structure is given a precise heat treatment. Often more than one cycle of printing and firing is required to complete a circuit. During the firing cycle the binder vaporizes, and the suspended particles coalesce to form metallic conductors, glassy insulators, and resistors generally involving metallic oxide mixtures. Lead crossings and modest size capacitors are obtained by interspersing an insulating layer between two layers of conductor. This printing technique has been mechanized so that large numbers of thick-film circuits can be manufactured at relatively low cost.

FUTURE DEVELOPMENTS

Integrated electronics is making possible far-reaching changes in electronic systems. System complexity can continue to increase rapidly, and the cost of realizing complex functions will continue to decrease as the technology is refined and extended. Because of these evolutionary changes, electronic systems will become an important part of everyday living. Integrated circuits are appearing in automobiles for voltage regulation and antiskid controls as well as in the radio. Electronically controlled fuel injection and collision-avoidance systems that depend upon integrated electronics for their economical realization are under development. The entire communications network is incorporating integrated electronic equipment at several levels. Computers and calculators are growing in power and decreasing in cost; a computer may become as available to the average household as the present-day telephone.

Integrated electronic technology is achieving a role in the developing electronic age comparable to that played by the technology of metal fabrication in the industrial revolution.

BIBLIOGRAPHY. R.M. BURGER and R.P. DONAVAN (eds.), *Fundamentals of Silicon Integrated Device Technology*, 2 vol. (1967–68), have collected the descriptions and procedures for the manufacture of silicon monolithic circuits and is more complete than R.M. WARNER, JR. and J.N. FORDEMWALT (eds.), *Integrated Circuits, Design Principles and Fabrication* (1965). A.S. GROVE, *Physics and Technology of Semiconductor Devices* (1967), is the best treatment of the underlying science including considerable data and many graphs useful for design. The special issue on integrated electronics of the *Proceedings of the IEEE*, vol. 52, no. 12 (1964), contains reviews of several segments of the field as well as views regarding the long-range significance of integrated electronics. D.K. LYNN, C.S. MEYERS, and D.J. HAMILTON (eds.), *Analysis and Design of Integrated Circuits* (1968), emphasizes the circuit design aspects of integrated circuits. R.H. CRAWFORD, *MOSFET in Circuit Design* (1967), assumes little previous knowledge of MOS devices and goes through elementary circuit designs. M.L. TOPFER, *Thick-Film Microelectronics, Fabrication, Design and Applications* (1971), is the best available collection of information about this important part of hybrid circuit technology.

(G.E.Mo.)

Integumentary Systems

Each organism is separated from its environment by a covering, or integument, that delimits its body. This covering serves several major functions: protection from foreign matter, exclusion from the environment, and communication with the environment. Among single-celled organisms, such as bacteria and protozoans, the integument corresponds to the cell membrane and any secreted coating that the organism produces. In plants and most invertebrate animals, a layer (or layers) of surface (epithelial) cells—often with additional secreted coatings—constitutes the integument. But only among the vertebrates has a boundary covering—with a variety of derived elements such as scales, feathers, and hair—assumed the complexity of an organ system, the integumentary system. For particular aspects of the human integument, see SKIN, HUMAN.

The integument enables an organism to live in a specific environment. The almost impermeable covering of many plants of arid regions helps conserve water, whereas the thin and porous integument of certain tropical forest plants promotes exchange of gases, including water vapour. Among the animals, many lower forms are provided with smooth skins that are bathed in slime, which serves as protection (often with antibiotic qualities) and lubrication.

The wide variety of integuments among vertebrates further exemplifies the adaptive character of the body covering: from the almost impenetrable shield of an armadillo and the dense furry coat of an Arctic bear to the slimy, scaled covering of a cod and the exceptionally smooth skin of a porpoise. Amphibians and fishes often have mucous glands that lubricate their skins and prevent waterlogging and deterioration. Reptiles have thick, leathery skins that help reduce water loss and serve as an armour against enemies. Birds use their feathers—skin derivatives—to fly and to insulate their bodies. The hairy or furry coats of many terrestrial mammals insulate them, shed water, and provide a dense guard against injury.

This article is divided into the following sections:

TERMS AND DEFINITIONS

The integument is composed of cells that range from a single cell thickness, in most plants and in many invertebrates, to multiple cell thickness, in some invertebrates and in all vertebrates. In every case the cells that give rise to the integuments belong to that class of tissue called epithelium. By convention, individual names have been given to the epithelia of different organisms. The epithelium of plants and also of most animals is called epidermis.

Occasionally, the term hypodermis is used for layers beneath the dermis that arise in the same manner as the epidermis; however, hypodermis is also used to identify layers other than epidermal that serve the same function as the epidermis. Some invertebrates and plants are often said to have hypodermes. The dermis underlies the epidermis and supplies it with nourishment. In addition to the cellular layers, the integument often includes a noncellular coating, or cuticle, which is secreted by the epidermis. Such coatings are found in plants and in most invertebrates. The vertebrate skin has generated many kinds of glands and a variety of horny structures but lacks coatings.

A brief survey of the kinds of integuments featured in lower organisms provides an introduction to the vertebrate integumentary system, which is treated in greater detail.

PLANT INTEGUMENTS

The covering layer of plants has the same function as the integuments of animals: the protection of underlying tissue from drying out and from mechanical injury. It is, however, a fragile covering by comparison with animal skins. (The toughened and hardened stems and branches of perennial plants and trees have lost their epidermis proper; the tissues that remain, those of the cortex and other underlying layers, upon exposure become fibrous or corky.)

Lower plants. In lower plants, such as liverworts and mosses, a poorly defined integument exists. Since these plants are small and normally grow in humid locations, the demand of terrestrial life on them is minimal. The flattened, leaflike liverworts have thin-walled superficial cells that may not be distinguishable from deeper lying cells. The upper surface has pores for gaseous exchange between the interior spaces and the environment. Threadlike cells called rhizoids project from the lower surface to the ground. They may act both as anchors and as water-collecting structures. Mosses are somewhat more complex. In many cases all the outer layers of the stem consist of brown, thick-walled, fibre-like cells; they are not distinguishable as living epidermal cells. In some instances, however, a true epidermal layer occurs along the stem. Rhizoids and, often, simple scales extend from the underground portion of the plant.

The "skin" of vascular plants

Higher plants. Among the higher plants—*i.e.*, the vascular plants, including the gymnosperms and flowering plants—the cells of the epidermis are clearly distinguishable. They are alive, more or less regularly shaped, contain a nucleus to one side, and possess a thin layer of cell fluid, or cytoplasm. The central portion of the cells often shows a well-developed vacuole, distinct from the cytoplasm and containing a watery solution. The epidermis of the aerial stems and of the leaves is usually one cell thick; several-layered epidermes are uncommon. Ordinary epidermal cells are devoid of green pigment bodies (chloroplasts) and have the outer walls thickened and waterproofed with a cuticle, which consists of a fatlike substance, cutin, secreted by the epidermis.

The epidermis may be very thin, as on lettuce leaves; quite thick and tough, as on pine needles; waxy coated, as on apples; or powdery dusted, as on grapes. At intervals it is interrupted by small pores (stomates) leading from the exterior to the system of intercellular spaces in the underlying tissues and serving for gaseous interchange between these tissues and outer air. Each stomate is flanked by a pair of modified epidermal cells called

From Adriance S. Foster and Ernest M. Gifford, Jr., *Comparative Morphology of Vascular Plants*, W.H. Freeman and Company, copyright © 1959

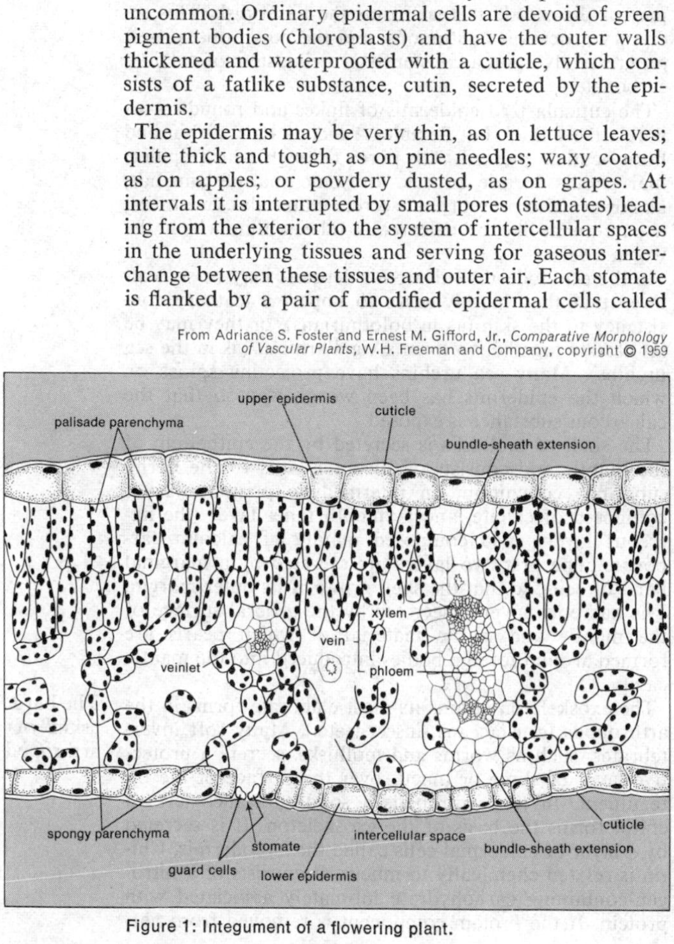

Figure 1: Integument of a flowering plant.

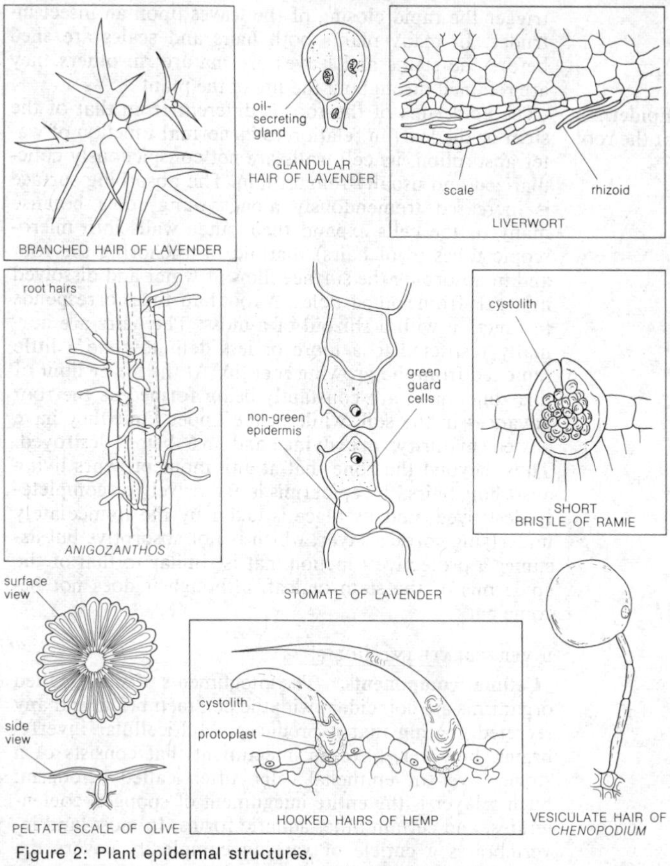

Figure 2: Plant epidermal structures.

From (top left, top centre, middle centre) B. Lloyd, *Handbook of Botanical Diagrams* (1949), University of London Press Ltd.; (top right) G.M. Smith, *Cryptogamic Botany*, copyright © 1955, by courtesy of McGraw-Hill Book Co.; (middle left) *Boston Society of Natural History Proceedings 31* (1904), and (all others) K. Esau, *Plant Anatomy* © 1965, by permission of John Wiley & Sons, Inc.

guard cells, which possess chlorophyll; they open and close the stomate in accordance with the changes in water content of the plant. The stomates of leaves are generally much more numerous in the lower epidermis than in the upper and in some species may be absent in the upper epidermis. The stomates are often situated at the bottom of pits in the leaf surface. Thus, loss of water is checked by the creation of a still atmosphere in the pit around the stomate. Such an arrangement of the stomates is found especially in those plants adapted to growth in regions where the supply of available water is deficient.

In some angiosperms the epidermis is doubled or tripled by divisions in the original layer, resulting in a multiple epidermis, which functions as a water-storage tissue. In many vascular plants epidermal organs known as hydathodes are developed, especially on foliage leaves, and serve for excretion of water in liquid form. The cuticularized epidermis of stems sloughs off in time and exposes underlying cortical cells, which become cork, impregnated with suberin, a fatty waterproofing material. Layers of such cork constitute the bark on older branches.

Trichomes

The epidermis of many species of vascular plants bears appendages called trichomes, which may take the form of hairs or scales of varied shape and function. The simplest hairs consist of single elongated cells projecting above the surface of the epidermis; others consist of simple or branched cell chains. The more complex scales are flat plates of cells commonly inserted on mounds or stalks; they may lie parallel to the leaf surface or project outward from it. In other instances the hairs may be glandular and excrete volatile oils, or be stinging, as in the common stinging nettle, in which the tops of the hairs are brittle and, when touched, penetrate the skin, break, and inject a poisonous liquid into the wound that is thus formed.

The highly touch-sensitive bristles on the leaves of the Venus's flytrap are modified epidermal extensions that trigger the rapid closing of the leaves upon an insect intruder. In many plants both hairs and scales are shed before the stems and leaves are mature; in others they are retained throughout the life of the plant.

Epidermis of the root

The epidermis of the root is different from that of the stem or the leaf. In relation to its normal function of water absorption, its cell walls are not conspicuously cuticularized and usually remain thin. The absorbing surface is increased tremendously along young roots because many of the cells expand their outer walls into microscopic tubes (root hairs) that aid in anchoring the root and in absorbing the surface films of water and dissolved minerals from soil particles. A root hair thus corresponds in function with a rhizoid of a moss. The hairs are normally restricted to a more or less definite zone a little removed from the growing root tip. At the lower limit of this zone, hairs are constantly being formed as the root advances in the soil, while at the upper limit they have passed maturity, are dying, and are being destroyed. Thus, beyond the zone that at any moment bears living absorbing hairs, the epidermis is extensively or completely destroyed, and its place is taken by the immediately underlying cortical layer, which is not absorptive but assumes a protective function that is similar to that of the epidermis of the stem or leaf, although it does not become bark.

INVERTEBRATE INTEGUMENTS

Cellular components. The integuments of single-celled organisms are coincident with the cell membrane and any secreted coating that it produces. Multicellular invertebrates, however, have an integument that consists of a single layer of epithelial cells, often called ectoderm. Such a layer is the entire integument of sponges, coelenterates, and certain other aquatic forms. In most land invertebrates a cuticle of varying complexity covers the ectoderm, thus constituting an epidermis.

Ectodermal and epidermal derivatives may be present in the form of sensory cells, stinging cells, and other specialized cells depending on the species. Gland cells, which may be distinguished in certain invertebrates, are often located in lower tissue but open through the integument. Knobs, ridges, and other excrescences are integumentary features of certain groups of invertebrates. Such sculptural effects may serve as protective devices or as strengthening members of an external skeleton (exoskeleton). Hairlike cilia, bristles, and other fine projections may extend from surface cells. These organelles may serve in locomotion, insulation, respiration (to trap air in aquatic invertebrates), and in feeding (by creating water currents).

From C.K. Weichert, *Anatomy of the Chordates*, 3rd ed., © 1965; used with permission of McGraw-Hill Book Co.

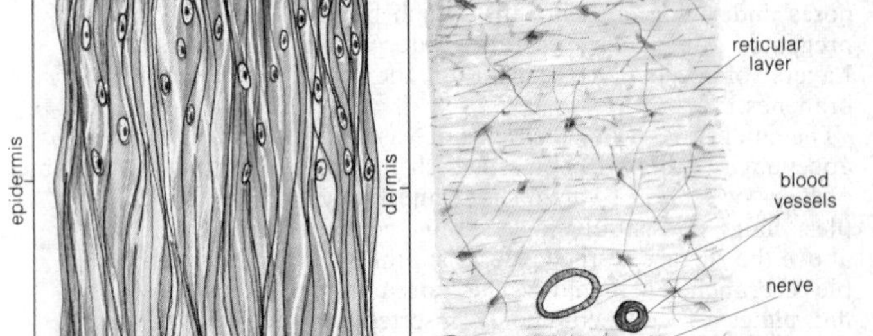

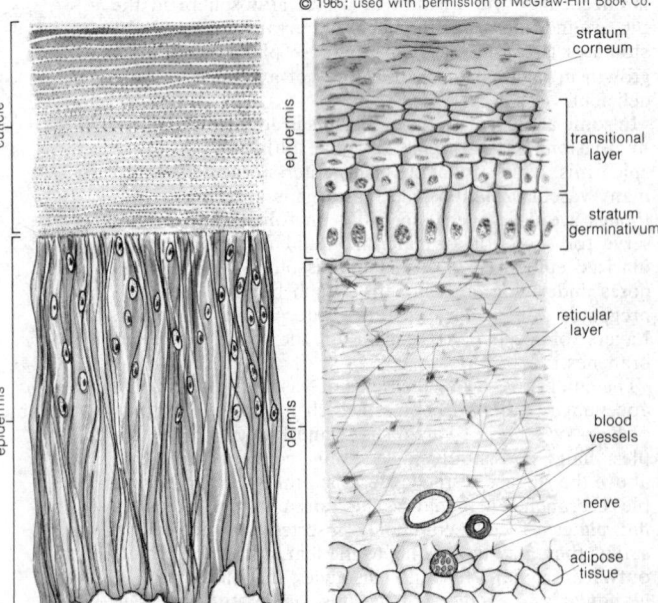

Figure 3: Comparison of (left) invertebrate and (right) vertebrate integuments.

Noncellular elements. The noncellular coatings of the integument of invertebrates are exceedingly varied in composition and extent. These variations cut across taxonomic categories. In the Protozoa, for example, there are all grades between soft forms (*e.g., Amoeba*) and forms with a cuticle that may be proteinaceous (in *Monocystis*) or composed of cellulose (in the plantlike flagellates). Other protozoa have definite shells, composed of protein with various foreign bodies incorporated in it: siliceous plates, calcium carbonate (in most Foraminifera), or cellulose (in the resting stages of slime molds). The Radiolaria have an internal lattice of silica that is laid down inside the cell, a kind of internal skeleton (endoskeleton).

Support and rigidity in invertebrates

The firmness of some invertebrate animals is maintained by a mechanism similar to that in many plants; the individual cells that form the body wall are more or less distended by water to give some degree of rigidity, as in annelid worms (*e.g.*, earthworms, marine worms, and leeches) and in certain mollusks. The annelidan skin is usually a single cell layer with a covering cuticle composed of thin layers of protein fibrils (very small fibres) resembling the collagen fibrils of vertebrates. In many invertebrates, rigid skeletal materials are deposited either on the outer surface of the body or, alternatively, within the cells.

In some animals these rigid structures do not afford attachment for the muscles but merely provide a protective armour. In the arthropods, including crustaceans, insects, and spiders, a many-layered and hardened integument forms the skeletal support as the exoskeleton.

Some sponges deposit needlelike spicules of calcium carbonate in the jelly (mesoglea) beneath the outer epithelium. Similarly, among coelenterates, there are Hydrozoa that have a horny covering protecting the polyps and others with an external calcareous skeleton. Anthozoa show the same diversity. In the common reef-building corals the calcareous skeleton is secreted by that part of the ectoderm that forms the basal disk. This secretory process is continuous, and the polyp raises itself progressively upon a constantly growing stem of calcium carbonate.

The cuticularized epidermis of flukes and roundworms is relatively thick but flexible. Annelids have a thin and horny cuticle pierced with pores through which epidermal glands secrete mucus. In some marine annelids, glands are also present that secrete materials constituting a parchment-like or calcareous tube within which the worm dwells.

In the echinoderms calcareous deposits may be so scattered that they merely serve to impart a leathery consistency to the skin (as in holothurians), or they may be set closely together to form a rigid armour (as in the sea urchins). Many sea urchins have projecting spines on which the epidermis has been worn away so that the calcareous substance is exposed.

The shell of mollusks is secreted by the epithelium of the mantle and consists of an outer layer of the horny substance conchiolin, an intermediate prismatic layer composed of calcite, and a smooth inner layer (the nacreous layer), also composed mainly of calcium carbonate. The first two layers are secreted by a marginal band of cells, so that the shell grows at its outer margin. The nacreous layer is secreted by the general surface of the mantle and is the material of which pearls are formed around foreign bodies introduced into the mantle cavity.

The hard "skin" of arthropods

The exoskeleton attains its most elaborate forms in the arthropods (crustaceans, insects, etc.). Many soft invertebrates, such as worms and mollusks, secrete a protective layer of slime or mucus over the surface of the integument. In the arthropods a solid substance termed chitin forms the basis of the exoskeleton. It is secreted by a layer of epidermal cells called the hypodermis. Chitin is related chemically to mucus. It consists of a nitrogen-containing carbohydrate intimately associated with protein. If the protein component is removed from natural chitin, there remains a material, often called pure chitin, the physical properties of which are very similar to those of the cellulose of plants.

From H. Weber, *Lehrbuch der Entomologie* (1933, reprinted 1968); Gustav Fischer Verlag

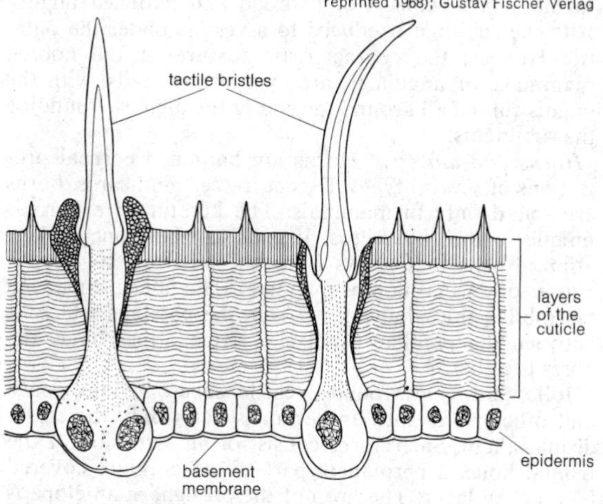

Figure 4: The integument of an insect.

Natural chitin forms a cuticle that is tough but flexible in the integument of caterpillars, which have a hydraulic type of skeleton, also in the joints of the limbs or between one segment of the body and the next. But in most arthropods the segments of the body or of the limbs are in the form of rigid plates that form a true exoskeleton linked to adjacent segments by flexible membranes. The hard material responsible for this change in the chitin is termed sclerotin, and the hardening process is called sclerotization.

The chemical nature of sclerotization is not fully understood, but it is certainly closely related to the hardening of proteins by tanning. Substances capable of causing tanning (notably certain quinones) are almost certainly produced in the cuticle of arthropods during the hardening process. The resulting product (sclerotin) is a kind of natural plastic. In its horny consistency it closely resembles keratin; both are cross-linked, or polymerized, proteins, but the chemical nature of the linkage is different in the two substances. It is probable that other skeletal proteins in invertebrates, such as the spongin of sponges and the conchiolin of mollusks, are also tanned proteins allied to sclerotin.

In many crustaceans (crabs, lobsters, etc.), much of the cuticle is rendered hard by the incorporation of calcareous substances such as aragonite or calcite. But sclerotin is actually harder than calcite, and those parts of crustaceans that need to be of maximum hardness, such as the mandibles and the tips of the claws, are in fact composed of sclerotin. The hardest parts of insects are often the darkest; the hardening and darkening processes are closely associated chemically.

Besides functioning as a skeleton, the cuticle of terrestrial arthropods must act as a waterproof covering in order to prevent these small animals from drying up. This waterproofing is effected by the secretion of a layer of wax on the surface of the cuticle. Such a wax layer, if exposed in an unprotected state would be excessively fragile. It is commonly protected by a thin layer of a cement-like substance that is poured over its surface by small dermal glands. Other glands may discharge quantities of wax, lac, and various other products upon the surface of the insect.

Modifications of the cuticle

The cuticle of arthropods, pierced by ducts of dermal glands that pour out secretions over the surface, is a living structure; it can produce sensory hairs, pigment-bearing scales, claws, wings, and other structures. In some insects it shows brilliant metallic colours that result from the presence of multiple thin plates or ridges in the cuticle. In order that the arthropod may grow, the old cuticle is shed from time to time after a new and larger cuticle has been laid down beneath it. This process is termed molting, or ecdysis. During the time when the new cuticle is hardening, the arthropod is in a very vulnerable condition.

THE VERTEBRATE INTEGUMENTARY SYSTEM

The integument of vertebrates is a vital organ system. It provides protection for the tissue beneath it and a sensory grid to inform the organism of environmental changes. Germproof—and to a great degree waterproof—under normal conditions, it is richly endowed with sensory receptors that respond to external changes. The skin is continuous with the mucous membrane lining the eyelids, mouth, nostrils, rectum, and the openings of the urogenital organs.

Skin layers. In all vertebrates the skin consists of two major layers. The richly cellular, relatively thin outer layer constitutes the epidermis. The thicker and tougher inner portion is the dermis, cutis, or corium. Considerable variation exists in the skins of different classes of vertebrates and is closely associated with the environment of the various groups. The epidermis is the product of the deepest layer of cells, closest to the underlying dermis. This generative layer is called the stratum germinativum. Older cells move toward the epidermal surface with the assistance of the newly forming cells that are produced by the stratum germinativum, being flattened as they move upward through a zone called the transitional layer.

The surface cells of terrestrial vertebrates, mere remnants of once living cells, are scaly and compressed; they constitute the horny layer, or stratum corneum. The cell fragments of the stratum corneum are composed largely of keratin, a tough insoluble protein; this substance provides waterproofing, resistance to mechanical injury, and a barrier to disease organisms. In most land vertebrates the stratum corneum (also called the corneal layer) is shed or molted, either periodically and in large fragments or sheets, as in reptiles, or continuously in small patches or scales, as in mammals.

From C.K. Weichert, *Anatomy of the Chordates*, 3rd ed. © 1965; used with permission of McGraw-Hill Book Co.

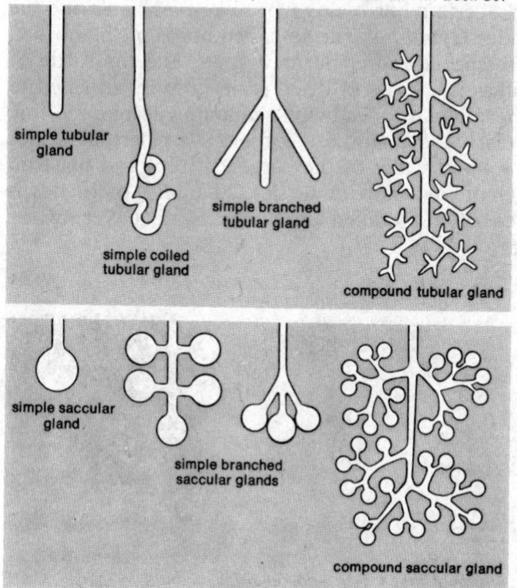

Figure 5: Types of vertebrate integumentary glands.

The dermis, or "true" skin, best developed in mammals, consists largely of fibrous connective tissue (collagen fibres), blood and lymph vessels, smooth muscle cells, and nerve endings. It gives rise to so-called membrane bones—the bony scales of fishes, the bony plates in certain reptiles and mammals, and the membrane bones of the vertebrate skull. Through its blood network the dermis supplies nourishment to the overlying epidermis.

Skin derivatives and appendages. During the course of evolution the skin in vertebrates has undergone remarkable modification, associated with the life habits of the various species. Among the notable changes were the development of pigment structures, skin glands, and other appendages.

The variety of vertebrate skin glands

Skin glands and pigment. Glands serve a secretory function. Those in the skin do not differ essentially from glands found elsewhere in the body, except that they are epidermal derivatives, formed solely from the cells of the stratum germinativum. Skin glands are exocrine glands—*i.e.,* they secrete their products externally through a duct to the epidermal surface. They may (1) be single celled or multicellular; (2) consist of a single blind tube or a clustering of tubes or bulbs; and (3) secrete their product continuously, periodically, or only once.

Mucous glands secrete a protein called mucin, which with water forms the slimy substance known as mucus; mucus serves to lubricate the body, thus lessening friction and aiding locomotion in swimming animals. Serous glands produce a watery secretion; sweat glands of mammals are of this type. Sebaceous glands secrete oil, ceruminous glands secrete wax, mammary glands secrete milk, poison glands secrete a variety of toxins, and scent glands secrete a variety of odoriferous substances. Furthermore, certain epidermal glands may be modified into light-producing structures called photophores, as in the skin of many deep-sea fishes.

Pigment in the skin may be in the form of tiny particles in the lowest cells of the epidermis or in special branched cells (chromatophores) located between the dermis and the epidermis. Chromatophores are common in the lower vertebrates (lampreys, fishes, amphibians, and reptiles) but are not generally present in birds and mammals. In certain animals, depending on the physiological state, the environment, and other factors, the distribution of pigment particles can be changed and the skin lightened or darkened accordingly (Figure 6).

Epidermal scales. Epidermal scales are horny and tough extensions of the stratum corneum. Well developed in reptiles, they are also common on exposed skin in birds and mammals. Such scales are periodically molted or shed gradually along with the rest of the stratum corneum. Epidermal scales are absent in fishes, but dermal, or bony, scales are abundant. Clawlike epidermal scales are present in certain amphibians, including a few toads, certain burrowing wormlike caecilians, and the salamander *Hynobius.* The so-called horns of the horned lizard are specialized epidermal scales, and the rattle of rattlesnakes is a series of dried scales loosely attached to each other, the last one always remaining despite molting of the rest of the stratum corneum. Epidermal scales cover the bony scales of the carapace (top) and plastron (bottom) of the shells of turtles. The beak of turtles is composed of a modified epidermal scale covering the jawbone.

From C.K. Weichert, *Anatomy of the Chordates,* 3rd ed., © 1965; used with permission of McGraw-Hill Book Co.

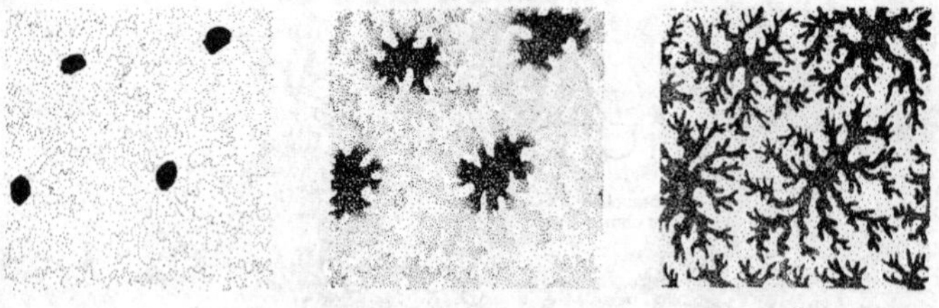

A B C

Figure 6: *Pigment dispersion and resulting change in skin colour.*
(A) Pigment concentrated in centre of cell. (B) Intermediate condition. (C) Pigment dispersed throughout cytoplasm of chromatophores.

Bills in birds are similarly constructed. In birds, epidermal scales are confined to the lower legs, feet, and base of the bill. The spur of some birds is a bony projection covered with a scale-like sheath. The skin of the webs in aquatic birds is also scaly. Except for a few cases, mammals have epidermal scales generally restricted to the tails and paws. The quills of the porcupine and the overlapping horny plates of the pangolin are modified epidermal scales. Mammalian scales are usually associated with hairs.

Claws, nails, and hooves. In many animals, hardened corneal growths occur at the end of the digits. They grow parallel to the skin surface. True claws—found in reptiles, birds, and mammals—consist of a dorsal scalelike plate (unguis) covering a ventral plate (subunguis), the whole capping the bony tip of a digit. Nails—found only in mammals—consist of a broad and flattened unguis, with the subunguis reduced to a vestige under the outer tip. Hooves, the characteristic feature of the hoofed mammals, or ungulates, are exaggerated nails, with the unguis curved all around the end of the digit, surrounding the subunguis.

Horns and antlers. Horns are hardened corneal projections of several types. Except for certain lizards, horns are found only in mammals. The keratin fibre horn is unique to the rhinoceros. It consists of a cone of keratinized cells that grows from an epidermis covering a cluster of dermal bumps (papillae). The fibres, somewhat resembling thick hair, grow from the papillae, and cells between the papillae produce a cement that binds the fibres together.

Hollow horns are found in cattle, sheep, buffalo, goats, and other ruminants. In certain species only the males display them. Such horns consist of an extension of the frontal bone, a permanent part of the cranium covered by a horny layer. The horn of the pronghorn antelope is unique in that the horny covering is shed periodically and a new one is formed from the epidermis that persists over the bony extension.

Antlers

Antlers, which are characteristic features of the deer family, are not integumentary derivatives at all. Fully developed antlers are solid bone, without any epidermal covering. The young antlers, however, are covered with skin having a velvet-like appearance. When the antler is fully developed, the drier skin cracks and is rubbed off by the animal. Antlers in giraffes are small and remain permanently covered.

Feathers and hair. Birds and mammals display remarkable elaborations of the epidermis in the form of feathers and hair, respectively. These distinctive features are dealt with below (see *Birds; Mammals*).

Dermal derivatives. Dermal scales are found almost exclusively in fishes and some reptiles. They are bony plates that fit closely together or overlap and form the dermal skeleton. Highly developed dermal scales are found in turtles, in which the bony plates form a rigid dermal skeleton that is attached to the true skeleton. In other reptiles, dermal scales are small and localized on parts of the body, as in crocodilians, certain lizards, and a few snakes.

Birds lack dermal scales, and only a single living mammal—the armadillo—displays them. Associated with the evolutionary tendency toward elaboration of epidermal extensions in birds and mammals, there has been a corresponding reduction in dermal derivatives. Membrane bones of the skull, the mandible (lower jaw), and clavicles (collarbones) are the remaining vestiges of dermal plates in these groups.

SKIN VARIATIONS AMONG VERTEBRATES

The vertebrates belong to the phylum Chordata and are closely related to a small, fishlike, almost transparent, invertebrate called amphioxus. Amphioxus represents chordate integument at its simplest: an epidermis consisting of one layer of columnar or cuboidal epithelial cells and scattered mucous cells, covered by a thin cuticle, and a thin dermis of soft connective tissue. Beginning with the simplest vertebrates, the cyclostomes (lampreys and hagfishes), the integument becomes complex and pigmented; in successive evolutionary stages a wide array of derivatives appears among the various classes of vertebrates.

Cyclostomes. In the lamprey the surface of the skin is smooth, with no scales. The epidermis consists of several cell layers that actively secrete a thin cuticle. Gland cells producing slime are mixed with the epidermal cells, as in most aquatic vertebrates. The dermis is a thin layer of connective tissue fibres interwoven with blood vessels, nerves, muscle fibres, and chromatophores.

Fishes. Fishes have a more or less smooth, flexible skin dotted with various kinds of glands, both single celled and multicellular. Mucus-secreting glands are especially abundant, particularly in the cartilaginous fishes (*e.g.*, sharks and rays). Poison glands, which occur in the skin of many cartilaginous fishes and some bony fishes, are frequently associated with spines on the fins, tail, and gill covers. Photophores, found especially in deep-sea forms, are thought to be modified mucous glands. They may be used as camouflage or to permit recognition, either for repulsion to delimit territory or for attraction in courtship.

Fish scales

Also formed within the skin of many fishes are skeletal elements called scales. On the basis of composition and structure they may be divided into cosmoid, placoid, ganoid, cycloid, and ctenoid scales. Cosmoid scales, characteristic of extinct lungfishes and not found in any living fish, are similar to ganoid scales. Placoid scales (or denticles), spiny, toothlike projections consisting primarily of enamel and dentine, are found in the skin of many cartilaginous fishes. Ganoid scales, sometimes considered a modification of the placoid type, are chiefly bony but are covered with an enamel-like substance called ganoin. These rather thick scales, found in some primitive bony fishes, are well developed in the gars.

Cycloid scales appear to be the inner layer of ganoid or cosmoid scales. Found in carps and similar fishes, they are thin, large, round, or oval and arranged in an overlapping pattern; growth rings are evident on the free edges. Ctenoid scales are similar to the cycloid, except that they have spines or comblike teeth along their free edges; these scales are found in the higher bony fishes; for example in the perches and sunfishes. Some fishes (*e.g.*, catfishes and some eels) have no scales.

Among the cartilaginous fishes, sharks have a very tough skin. Over it are scattered denticles or placoid

From (quills of the porcupine) W. Montagna, "The Skin," Copyright ©1965 by Scientific American, Inc., All rights reserved; (foot of a bird) A.L. Thomson, *A New Dictionary of Birds* (1964), Nelson, London; (hoof of an ingulate) after Ellenberger in Leisering's Atlas, based on Sisson, *The Anatomy of the Domesticated Animals*, W.B. Saunders Company, from C.K. Weichert, *Anatomy of the Chordates*, Copyright 1965, used with permission of McGraw-Hill Book Company; (others) C.K. Weichert, *Anatomy of the Chordates*, Copyright 1965, used with permission of McGraw-Hill Book Company

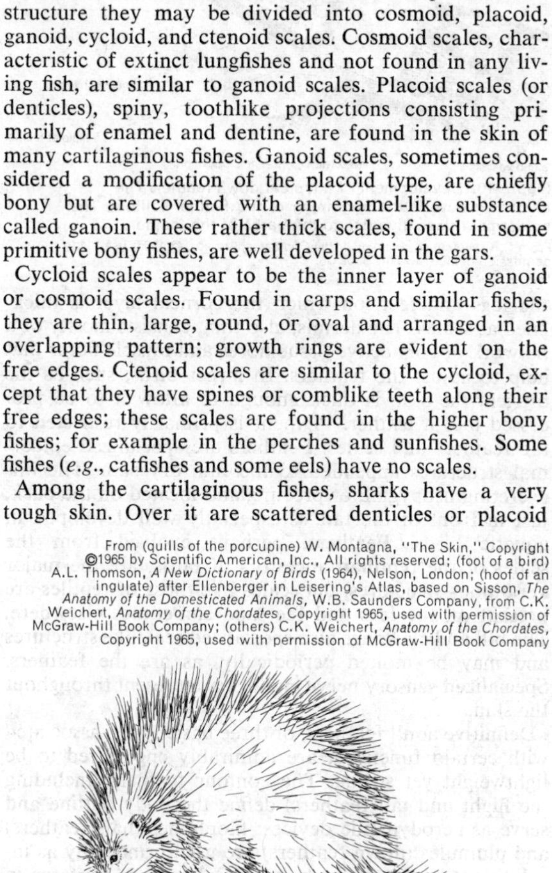

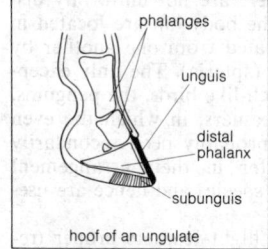

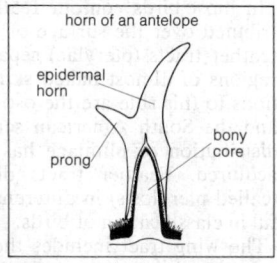

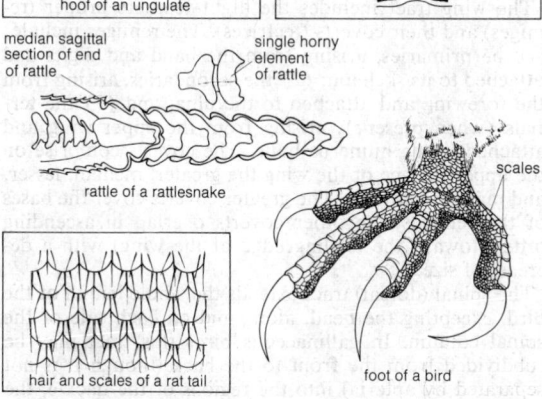

Figure 7: Vertebrate epidermal appendages.

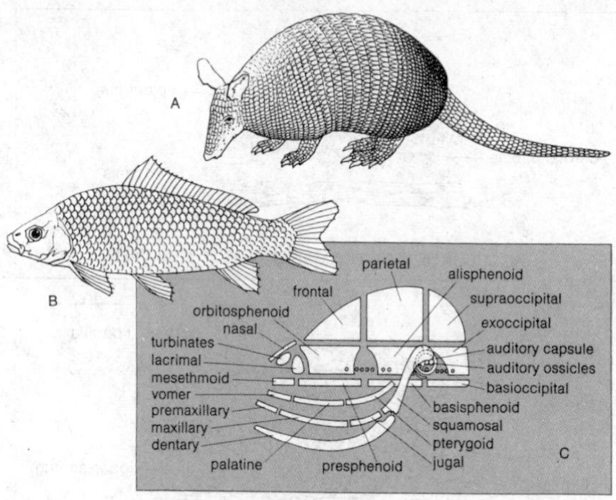

Figure 8: *Vertebrate dermal appendages.*
(A) Armadillo showing scales. (B) Carp with large scales. (C) Membrane bones of mammalian skull.

From (A) W. Montagna, *The Skin*, © 1965 by Scientific American, Inc., all rights reserved; (B) from a painting by Tom Dolan; (C) after Flower, from Kingsley, *Comparative Anatomy of Vertebrates*, The Blakiston Division, McGraw-Hill Book Company, by permission

scales, each with a pulp cavity, around the edge of which is a layer of odontoblasts. These cells secrete the dentine, or calcareous material, of the scale. Outside the dentine is the enamel, secreted by the overlying ectoderm. When the denticles pierce through the ectoderm, no more enamel can be added.

The dominant fishes of the modern era, teleosts, are characterized by bony scales covered with skin. The epithelium of a trout's epidermis provides the animal with an inert covering of keratin. The scales lie in the dermis as thin, overlapping plates with the exposed part bearing the pigment cells. The scale is deposited in a series of annual rings, since its growth is not constant but occurs rapidly in spring and summer and hardly at all in winter.

Amphibians. Modern amphibians have naked skins that lack horny scales, hair, or other protective devices. The amphibian epidermis is composed of several layers of cells and is the first to show a layer of dead epidermal cells in contact with the environment. This horny layer, or stratum corneum, is best developed in amphibians that spend most of their time on land. The dermis is two layered: the stratum spongiosum is an outer and looser layer; and the stratum compactum is an inner, more compact one. The skin of many amphibians is a vital organ of respiration, and the dermis is richly supplied with blood vessels, lymph spaces, nerves, and glands. Chromatophores are located between the epidermis and the dermis.

The first horny skin of amphibians

One small amphibian group, the caecilians, has small fishlike scales embedded in the skin (similar scales occurred in some ancient extinct amphibians). Because of their thinness and position, these amphibian scales provide no protection against drying, one of the principal hazards of life for all animals. This susceptibility to drying out forced (and still forces) amphibians to remain in water or in very humid places, thus limiting their exploitation of the terrestrial environment. The skin must be kept moist in order to serve adequately as a respiratory organ.

Its outer layers are horny—a characteristic typical of land vertebrates. In the adult frog the epidermis is renewed at intervals by a process of molting, which is under control of the pituitary and thyroid glands. The wartiness of the skin of toads results from local thickenings. Both mucous and poison glands derived from the epidermis are present in the skin of amphibians.

Reptiles. The skin of reptiles is dry and contains few or no glands. The epidermis has a well-developed stratum corneum that protects against drying and gives rise to horny scales. The dermis consists of superficial and deep layers, the latter of which are formed mostly of connective tissue. Chromatophores are abundant in the superficial layer in many snakes and lizards. In certain species

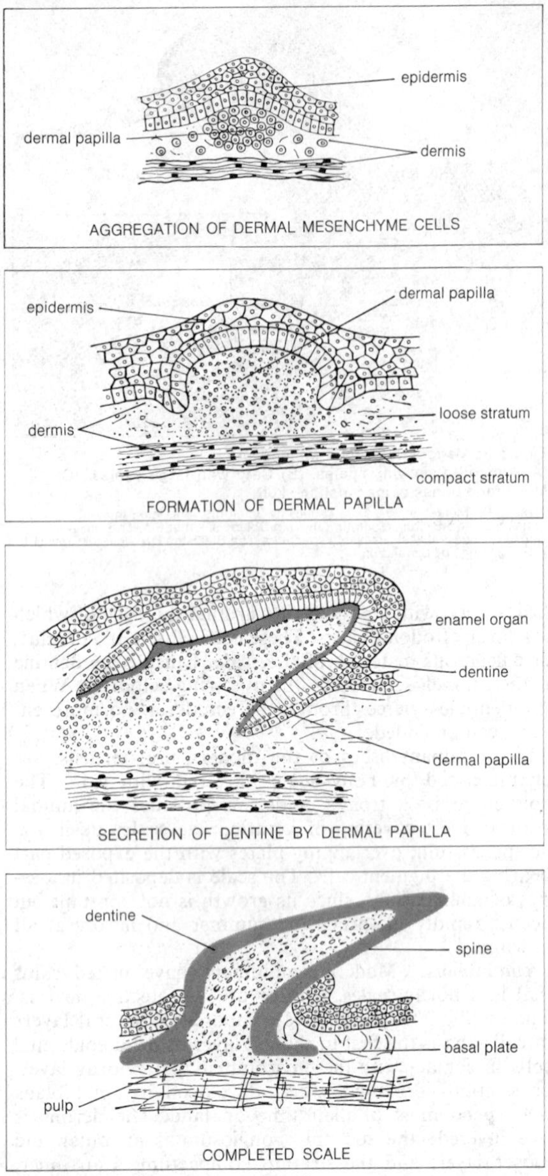

Figure 9: Fish scale development.

From L. Hyman, *Comparative Vertebrate Anatomy*, (©. 1922, 1942) by the University of Chicago; all rights reserved

the skin may be beset with warts or tubercles. In turtles the jawbones are covered over with a modified epidermal scale, forming a beak that is much like the bill of birds.

In most reptiles, the protective layer of horny scales is periodically renewed from beneath, the old layer being sloughed away. The shape and size of the scales vary in the different families and with the mode of life. Maximum flexibility of the skin is achieved by reduction of the scales to small, non-overlapping granules; among desert dwellers there is a tendency for some scales, particularly those on the head and tail, to be enlarged to form spines; burrowing and secretive forms have a slippery body surface because of the presence of smooth, highly polished, overlapping scales. The skin is often reinforced by bony plates, which lie beneath the superficial scales (though corresponding with them in size and shape); these plates may form a continuous protective armour. Other defensive, or sometimes offensive, devices associated with the skin and scales are the occasional development of horns or fringing folds that break up the animal's outline and colouring. The colour pattern may be fixed and concealing by camouflage, or there may be a highly developed mechanism to provide for rapid colour change.

Feathers

Birds. The avian epidermis is thin, delicate, and clothed in feathers, except on exposed regions, such as

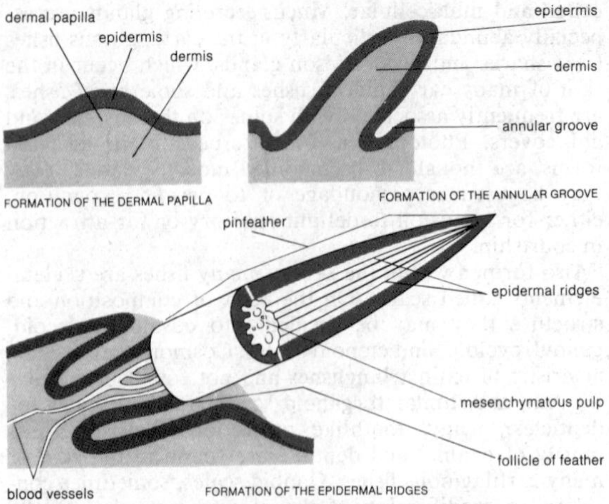

Figure 10: Development of a typical down feather. The annular groove is the beginning of the feather follicle. The epidermal ridges give rise to the barbs of the feather.

From C.K. Weichert, *Anatomy of the Chordates*, 3rd ed., © 1965; used with permission of McGraw-Hill Book Co.

the legs and feet, on which the corneal layer is thickened as scales. The dermis, also thin, consists mostly of a network of connective tissue fibres and muscle fibres that help to adjust the feathers. In larger birds, such as the ostrich, the skin is thick enough to allow it to be processed into a leather. Pigment is primarily restricted to the feathers and scales. Feathers are specialized epidermal structures appended to the thin dry skin. The oil-excreting uropygial, or preen, gland located on the back, just in front of the tail, is especially well developed in aquatic birds. Feathers, perhaps evolved from the scales of the reptilian ancestors of birds, are the major keratinous structures, but scales like those of reptiles are present on the legs and feet and sometimes elsewhere. The bill and claws are also specialized scalelike structures and may be molted periodically, as are the feathers. Specialized sensory nerve endings are present throughout the skin.

Definitive adult feathers, of three basic types, associated with certain functions, are admirably engineered to be lightweight yet strong. The contour feathers (including the flight and tail feathers) define the body outline and serve as aerodynamic devices; filoplumes (hair feathers) and plumules (down feathers) are used principally as insulation, to conserve body heat. Colours and patterns in feathers serve as protective coloration or for sexual display.

In most birds contour feathers are not uniformly distributed over the surface of the body but are located in feather tracts (pterylae) separated from one another by regions of almost naked skin (apteria). The only exceptions to this rule are the ostrich-like birds, the penguins, and the South American screamers, in which the even distribution of plumage has probably been secondarily acquired. Feather tracts differ in their arrangement (called pterylosis) in different species and hence are useful in classification of birds.

The wing tract includes the flight feathers proper (remiges) and their coverts (tectrices). The remiges include: (1) the primaries, arising from the hand and digits and attached to its skeleton; (2) the secondaries, arising from the forewing and attached to the ulna; and (3) the tertials (when present), arising from the upper wing and attached to the humerus bone. The coverts comprise on the upper surface of the wing the greater, median, lesser, and marginal coverts. The greater coverts cover the bases of the remiges; the other coverts overlap in ascending order (toward the leading edge of the wing) with a decrease of size.

The spinal (dorsal) tract extends the whole length of the bird, excepting the head, along and on each side of the spinal column. In gallinaceous birds this tract may be subdivided from the front to the back (though it is not separated by apteria) into the regions of the hackle, the cape, the back, and the saddle; each region is distinguished by the form and pattern of its constituent feathers.

On the ventral surface of the bird are the breast tracts, which are paired, extending from the neck backward in diverging pterylae. Between the breast tracts is a ventral tract, running along either side of the midline along the region of the umbilicus and meeting in front of the anus. The tail tract includes the tail feathers (rectrices) and their coverts. In addition there are the head tract, the humeral tract (scapulars), the femoral tract, and the crural tract.

The three types of definitive adult feathers—contour, filoplume, and plumule—are known collectively as teleoptiles, in contrast to the nestling down feathers, which are called neossoptiles.

Contour feathers

A contour feather of an adult bird tends to be almost bilaterally symmetrical. It consists of a tapering axial rod, the shaft or rachis, to which are attached a large number of tapering parallel rods, the barbs. These in turn carry many minute elongated barbules both on their distal (away from the body) and proximal (toward the body) faces. The distal barbules bear tiny hooklets (hamuli) by means of which they not only overlap but also interlock with grooves on the proximal barbules of the next higher barb, thereby forming the coherent web, or vane, of the feather.

Barbules in the basal portions of feathers are long, delicate threads and do not bind successive barbs together; consequently, this part of the feather is fluffy. The contour feathers collectively define the form, or contour, of the body. The flight feathers (remiges) and tail feathers (rectrices, or steering feathers) are the most striking of the contour feathers. This is because of their size and special use in flight.

The filoplumes, which arise at the bases of contour feathers, are inconspicuous hairlike feathers bearing a small tuft of barbs at their apexes. Filoplumes appear to be present in all birds, but only in certain species do they project beyond the contour feathers (*e.g.*, on the thighs of cormorants).

Plumules, usually completely concealed by contour feathers, are generally scant, but in many birds, such as gulls and ducks, they form a thick, insulating undercovering comparable to the underfur of seals. Their barbs do not form coherent vanes but are long, loose, soft, and fluffy. Their structure is much simplified, and a rachis may be entirely lacking. In herons and some hawks the tips of the plumules disintegrate into a fine scaly powder that becomes distributed over the plumage, providing protection against wetting and giving it a peculiar sheen; accordingly, these specialized down feathers are called powder down.

Mammalian hair

Mammals. The presence of hair attached to the skin is an important distinguishing characteristic of all mammals. In addition to hair, however, there is a variety of horny skin appendages, including scales, nails, claws, hooves, antlers, horns, and glands. Bony dermal plates are found only in the armadillo. The epidermis, composed of several layers of cells, is closely applied to the dermis and is elaborated by a stratum germinativum of columnar cells. The stratum corneum is exceptionally thick and tough in areas exposed to friction. The dead corneal surface is continuously being sloughed off and replaced by cells rising from the layer.

In the thickened areas of skin, the basal layer consists of three subdivisions. Immediately above the stratum germinativum is the prickle-cell layer (stratum spinosum), the cells of which are knit together by cellular projections in close contact. Next above is the granular cell layer (stratum granulosum), in which the epidermal cells die and become laden with particles called keratohyalin granules. The remainder of the transitional layers consists of the clear layer (stratum lucidum), a more or less transparent zone composed mostly of a chemical called eleidin, thought to be an intermediate product in the transformation of keratohyalin granules to keratin.

The dermis forms an elastic layer that constitutes the greater portion of the skin in mammals. It is composed largely of connective tissue fibres, which, when treated with tanning agents, constitute the leather of commerce. Two layers form the dermis: the outer, or papillary, layer lies directly beneath the stratum germinativum of the epidermis; and the inner, reticular layer, which constitutes the remainder of the dermis. The papillary layer is so called for the numerous microscopic structures, or papillae, that rise into the epidermis, especially in areas of wear or friction on the skin; they are arranged in definite patterns beneath epidermal ridges. In man these external ridges constitute the fingerprints and footprints. The reticular layer is made up of coarser collagen fibres than those in the papillary layer; it is in this layer that the various skin glands, vessels, muscle cells, and nerve endings are housed.

Important from the standpoint of survival is the coloration and pattern of coats, which serve both as a camouflage for protection against enemies and as an allurement to mates.

The most important function of hair in most mammals is that of insulation against cold. A second function is that of a sensory organ—large stiff hairs (vibrissae), variously called whiskers, sensory hairs, tactile hairs, feelers, and sinus hairs, are found in all mammals except man and are very helpful to many night-prowling animals. Vibrissae have highly specialized follicles—the root being embedded in a mass of true erectile tissue—and a rich sensory nerve supply. These specialized hairs are few in number, their distribution being chiefly confined to the lips, cheeks, nostrils, and around the eyes, only occasionally occurring elsewhere.

Man's eyelashes consist of sensory hairs that cause the reflex shutting of the eyelid when a speck of dust hits them.

Hair follicles

Mammalian hairs are developed in relatively deep pits in the skin, the hair follicles, which extend downward into the thickness of the dermis or even into deeper tissue. The hair follicle, which is essentially a recess of the skin, is composed of two tissue elements—one, of epithelial origin, closely invests the hair root; the second is connective tissue.

The epithelial layer consists of an outer layer of polyhedral cells forming the outer root sheath and an inner, horny stratum, the inner root sheath, composed of three layers, known, respectively, as Henle's layer (the outermost) of horny, fibrous, oblong cells; Huxley's layer, consisting of polyhedral, nucleated cells containing pigment granules; and the cuticle of the root sheath, composed of a layer of downwardly imbricate scales (overlapping like roof tiles) that fit over the upwardly imbricate scales of the hair proper.

The connective tissue element consists internally of a vascular layer separated from the root sheath by a basement membrane—the hyaline layer of the follicle—and externally has a more open texture corresponding to the deeper part of the cutis containing the larger branches of the arteries and veins.

A small muscle, the arrector pili, is attached to each hair follicle, with the exception of vellous follicles. If this muscle is contracted, the hair becomes more erect, and the follicle is dragged upward; this causes a prominence on the general surface of the skin, producing the temporarily roughened condition that is popularly called gooseflesh.

The hair shaft is composed chiefly of a pigmented, horny, fibrous material, which consists of long, tapering fibrillar cells that have coalesced. Externally, this fibrous substance is covered by a delicate layer of imbricated scales forming the cuticle. In many hairs the centre of the shaft is occupied by an axial substance, the medulla, formed of angular cells containing granules of eleidin (a substance allied to keratin) and quite frequently, in addition, minute air bubbles that give the cells a dark appearance.

The medullary cells tend to be grouped along the central axis of the hair as a core; continuous or interrupted in single, double, or multiple columns. The variations in the medulla may be summarized as: (1) the continuous type, which may be homogeneous or nodose (having a knotty appearance); (2) discontinuous types, which in simple forms may be ovate, elongated, or flattened; and (3) a fragmental type.

Cuticular scales

The dominant form of cuticular scales is an imbricate scale, like a tile or irregular shape, having its edges rounded, minutely notched, or flattened. There are many varieties of the imbricate scale, each typical of its species; thus, in man, chimpanzee, gorilla, and orangutan, the hairs have imbricate scales that are, however, quite distinctive in size, shape, and structure of the edge—slightly oval in chimpanzee, slightly ovate and shallowly notched in man and gorilla, with more deeply notched edges in orangutan.

The second type of cuticular scale is the coronal, in which each cuticular cell completely encircles the hair shaft and may have a smooth or saw-toothed edge. Although the imbricate scale is typical of the higher Primates, the coronal scale in its simpler form is present in the lemurs and tarsiers, becoming in the insectivores more specialized, with saw-toothed edges.

In some Indian bats the cuticular scales are developed as leaflet-like processes arranged in whorls at regular intervals along the hair shaft. In many deer, the cortical substance is nearly indistinguishable, almost the entire hair appearing to be composed of thin-walled polygonal cells. In the peccary the cortical envelope sends inward radial prolongations, the interspaces being occupied by medullary substance; and this, on a large scale, is the structure of the porcupine's quills. One of the most remarkable mammalian hairs is that of the Australian duckbill, or platypus, in which the lower portion of the shaft is slender and wool-like, while the free end terminates as a flattened, spear-shaped, pigmented hair with broad imbricated scales.

In the three-toed sloth, a microscopic alga grows between the cuticular scales of the hairs and appears to be symbiotic, for its presence, giving a curious greenish-gray hue to the coat of the sloth, helps to disguise the animal among the trees.

EMBRYOLOGY AND EVOLUTION OF THE VERTEBRATE SKIN

The skin of vertebrates begins to form very early in the embryo, from a superficial tissue (ectoderm), which spreads over the developing organism almost from its earliest days. Another embryonic tissue, the middle germ layer, or mesoderm, proliferates cells rapidly from segmental building blocks, called somites; these cells then migrate in order to lie directly under the outer ectodermal covering of the embryo. These two embryonic layers —ectoderm and mesoderm—ultimately give rise to the adult skin: the ectoderm produces the epidermis and its derivatives, and the mesoderm produces the dermis and its derivatives.

Differentiation of embryonic tissues proceeds rapidly during the early course of development, and much of what will become adult skin structures—including the glands and appendages—is laid down even before the animal is born, often in a latent or arrested stage, to resume development later, according to the particular species timetable.

Adaptive changes of the epidermis

As a surface constantly exposed to the environment, the epidermis has undergone more adaptive changes during evolution than any other portion of the skin. Ancestral vertebrates, aquatic and fishlike—perhaps resembling amphioxus—faced a limited environmental hazard. They and their fish descendants were buffeted by water, which kept the living surfaces moist, and were covered by a scaly, mucous epithelium that prevented waterlogging and deterioration and assisted swimming. The movement to land was gradual and fraught with risk. Amphibians were among the first vertebrates to explore the terrestrial environment. Many evolved a semi-aquatic lifestyle: they exploited the land for most of their activities but returned to the water for the vulnerable activity of reproduction. Some remained entirely aquatic, and others adapted to a strictly terrestrial life. Their epidermes reflected such habits: aquatic amphibians produced a thin, slimy, dull skin densely covered with mucous glands; terrestrial forms developed a thicker, horny, heavily pigmented skin dotted with poison glands. The reptiles as a class became even more independent of the water. Their skins accordingly assumed a tough, horny, dry form and sometimes received bony contributions from the dermis. Birds evolved a loose, dry skin covered with feathers for insulation and for airfoils and water foils. Finally, mammals adopted a dry, elastic skin, more or less covered with hair. The range of mammalian skin from smooth (glabrous), as in the cetaceans (whales, dolphins, and porpoises), to densely hairy, as in the Arctic bears, is associated with further extension of mammals into a wide range of habitats, many extreme and demanding in terms of the epithelial cloak.

THE BIODYNAMICS OF VERTEBRATE SKIN

The vertebrate skin—despite its variety—serves the two common functions of protection from, and communication with, the environment. In all land vertebrates the uppermost layers of the skin are dead, but the dermis is richly endowed with living tissue that can respond rapidly to change. A variety of nerve endings constantly reports current conditions, and the body makes continuous adjustments in response.

It has been said that the skin is the largest and most versatile organ of the animal body. It shields against injury, against foreign matter and disease organisms, and against potentially harmful rays of the sun. But it also regulates the internal body temperature through its insulative value and its influence on the blood flow. It further embodies the sense of touch and adorns the body; its contours, colour, patterns, and composition aid in species recognition and in sexual attraction. In addition, this extenuated organ has developed to a remarkable degree the ability to regenerate itself and to close any gaps against a hostile exterior.

"Breaks" in the skin's defenses

The effectiveness of the skin as a barrier, however, is not complete. Noxious substances that can gain entry evoke an immune response, and the dermis reddens with the rush of blood to the site. Heat causes expansion of the dermal blood vessels—and in man and horse stimulates the sweat glands to heightened activity—thus increasing the loss of body heat. Conversely, cold causes contraction of the vessels and initiates shivering, thus conserving heat in the first instance and generating it in the second. As a consequence of exposure to the environment and of its peculiar topography of crevices, pores, and wrinkles, the skin is host to an astonishing number of micro-organisms, especially bacteria and fungi. The skin, however, is an unstable environment for this population, which lives on the inert dead epidermal surface that is periodically shed or sloughed off. A normal microcosm thus exists on most epidermal surfaces, the significance and dynamics of which are becoming increasingly clear as investigations proceed. Over the course of evolution an alliance has been made between the skin biota and the epidermal "host" that tends to stabilize the surface; anything that disrupts the skin biota encourages an imbalance and a potential flare-up of certain micro-organisms over others. The human skin, in a real sense "alive" with tiny organisms that generally exist in an ecological balance, has been especially studied in this regard.

BIBLIOGRAPHY

Animals: WILLIAM MONTAGNA, *The Structure and Function of Skin*, 2nd ed. (1962), and "Cutaneous Comparative Biology," *Archs. Derm.*, 104:577–591 (1971), an advanced but readable article on the biological properties and adaptive structure and function of mammalian skin; STEPHEN ROTHMAN, *Physiology and Biochemistry of the Skin* (1954); A.G. LYNE and B.F. SHORT (eds.), *Biology of the Skin and Hair Growth* (1965).

Plants: B.E. JUNIPER, "The Surfaces of Plants," *Endeavour*, 18:20–25 (1959); R.H. SCHIEFERSTEIN and W.E. LOOMIS, "Development of the Cuticular Layer in Angiosperm Leaves," *Am. J. Bot.*, 46:625–635 (1959); D.S. BELFORD and R.D. PRESTON, "The Structure and Growth of Root Hairs," *J. Exp. Bot.*, 12:157–168 (1961).

(Ed.)

Intelligence, Distribution of

Intelligence is a hypothetical construct used to describe individual differences in an assumed latent variable that is, by any direct means, unobservable and unmeasurable. In its popular usage, the concept refers to variations in the ability to learn, to get along in society, and to behave according to contemporary social expectations. Behavioral scientists, psychometrists, and educators will frequently describe individuals with reference to the intelligence quotient (IQ) that is derived from standard tests of intelligence.

The IQ score is an operational, manifest, observable, and measurable *representation* of intelligence. This means that the distribution of intelligence is theoretical and never can be known precisely; however, the worldwide distribution of intelligence quotients empirically can be estimated simply by giving tests to a sample that includes a very large number of people and then constructing graphs (frequency distributions) from the IQ scores. To the extent that the tests are valid measures of intelligence, and provided that the sample selected for testing is representative of the population from which it was drawn, such empirical distributions of IQs will be similar to the population distribution of intelligence.

Normal-curve theory

As with many other characteristics in which individuals differ, intelligence is thought to be distributed in the world population according to a Gaussian (normal) distribution: a grossly bell-shaped curve that extends symmetrically around a central, high-frequency or average value (the arithmetic mean). The spread (or dispersion) of intelligence above and below the average may be expressed as a measure of variability; *e.g.*, the standard deviation (see STATISTICS). Use of the standard deviation results from the necessity to take account of variability (or variances) as well as means (or averages) when comparing different groups of people with respect to intelligence.

On the theoretical assumption of a normal distribution for intelligence, tests designed for its measurement have been constructed in such a way that IQ scores will approximate the normal distribution. Thus, with the mean IQ arbitrarily set at 100 and the standard deviation at 15, about 50 percent of the world's population should have IQ scores between 90 and 110. About 68 percent of all people are expected to have scores between 85 and 115 (one standard deviation above and below the mean). Another 14 percent should score between 70 and 84, with an equal number scoring between 116 and 130. Only 2 percent are expected to obtain scores below 70, with another 2 percent earning higher scores than 130. In practice, however, the distributions derived from large samples of individuals do not conform to these expectations.

The theoretical distribution rests partially on the assumption that the level of general intelligence attained by any individual is genetically determined (has a hereditary basis). There is a growing body of evidence that this is not wholly the case; *e.g.*, one's experiences after birth (indeed, into adult life) appear to play a large part in determining his eventual intellectual status, especially when intelligence is represented by a single global score such as IQ.

Variables that appear to exhibit some influence on intellectual development and on the expression of intelligence include ethnicity, social class, chronological age, race, relative cultural advantage-disadvantage, nutrition, education, general health, and specific child-rearing practices. One obvious factor that contributes to the finding of asymmetrical (lopsided) empirical distributions (those that depart for the normal curve) is represented by the many accidents and diseases that result in brain damage to lower the efficiency of intellectual function. Since none of these disorders is known to produce higher levels of intellectual functioning, only the high end of the distribution is diminished thereby.

MENTAL RETARDATION

Mental retardation is a general term used to refer to hundreds of conditions that share common symptoms of subnormal intellectual functioning and impaired adaptive behaviour, and that seem to originate during the developmental period of the individual. This triple diagnostic criterion has been proposed to acknowledge the imperfect correspondence between one's measured intelligence and his development of social skills, the occurrence of brain damage in adults, and the temporary behavioral deficits that accompany psychiatric disorders. It is estimated that between 1 and 3 percent of the world's population is mentally retarded.

Psychometric specification of level of retardation may be accomplished by calculating how far an individual scores (in standard deviation units) below the population's average IQ score. The Table gives the levels and classifications associated with different IQ ranges, assuming a test with a standard deviation of 15 IQ points. (Thus, −1 means one standard deviation below the average of 100, and so on.) Other systems in current use employ different numerical values, such as 0–20, 20–50, and so on.

Levels and Classifications of Mental Retardation Associated with Ranges of IQ Scores

IQ range	level of retardation	classification
85–100	no retardation	—
70–84	−1	borderline
55–69	−2	mild
40–54	−3	moderate
25–39	−4	severe
Below 25	−5	profound

Older terms for retardation

Although the older terms moron, imbecile, and idiot from the English language were rarely used in Canada and the U.S. during the 1970s, their occasional employment persisted in Great Britain. These classifications were roughly equivalent to the mild, moderate, severe, and profound levels of retardation, respectively. In the Soviet Union, the most common term is "oligophrenia," which groups all intellectually subnormal persons together but focusses primarily on the severe and profound levels. In continental Europe, the term "debile" is used commonly to refer to mildly retarded individuals, with "imbecile" and "idiot" still in use. The World Health Organization has recommended (and uses) a classification system that specifies mild, moderate, severe, and profound degrees of retardation. No standard terminology has yet emerged in Asia.

Levels of retardation. Estimates of the existing prevalence of different levels of mental retardation differ significantly from theoretical expectations based upon the assumption that intelligence is normally distributed. Assuming, for example, a U.S. total population of approximately 200,000,000 persons, normal-curve theory would lead one to expect between 5,000,000 and 6,000,000 persons to score in the mentally retarded range; but, empirically based estimates for that country run as high as 15,000,000, if one includes borderline retardation. In a general way, the observed prevalence agrees with predictions by declining sharply as the associated IQ scores become lower. (There are very many more mild and moderate retardates than there are severe and profound retardates.)

It is also found, however, that the lower the IQ, the greater is the excess of cases in the population over what would be expected from the normal-curve estimates. Thus, in a population of 200,000,000 one would expect to find only 57 persons with IQ scores from 0 to 20; yet, the actual prevalence was estimated to be 100,000, based upon sampling surveys. (Similarly, the normal curve would predict 177,747 cases with IQ scores from 20 to 50, and 5,970,577 cases with IQ scores from 50 to 70, but the actual prevalence was estimated to be 400,000 and 6,030,577 cases, respectively. Including all persons in the U.S. whose IQ scores fell below 70, in a population of 200,000,000 one would expect to find 6,148,382 cases, but the actual prevalence was estimated to be 6,530,577, or 382,195 more cases than were predicted assuming a normal distribution of intelligence.)

In spite of a great accumulation of evidence that it embraces a number of independent abilities, intelligence often is considered in terms of such measures as IQ (as a global, unitary dimension). Some modern intelligence tests reflect attempts to measure abilities, and when this is done it can be seen that each individual may vary considerably in the level of competence he shows for different abilities. One consistency, however, is that individuals whose overall IQ is greater than 100 tend to exhibit higher levels of verbal than of nonverbal (performance) ability; on the other hand, persons whose overall IQ is less than 100 are likely to earn better performance scores than verbal scores.

Causes of retardation. Mental retardation can be classified according to its probable origin (etiology). Most cases of mild retardation appear to be associated with inadequate opportunities to learn, or with subtle sociobiologic effects of poverty, isolation, or cultural deprivation experienced in the first few years of life; among such people there is no obvious neural or physiological pathology. By contrast, individuals who exhibit severe and profound retardation, and many who are moderately retarded, are observed to suffer pathological conditions of the nervous system. Such disorders may be produced by specific genes as in galactosemia, gargoylism, phenylketonuria, or Tay-Sachs disease; by partially gene-dependent mechanisms, as in cretinism, hydrocephaly, hypertelorism, or microcephaly; by chromosomal aberrations, as in Down's syndrome (mongolism) or in Klinefelter's syndrome; by isoimmunization, as in erythroblastosis fetalis; by infections, radiation, or from toxic substances prior to birth; by perinatal factors such as prematurity, head injury, and deprivation or oversupply of oxygen; or by pathological agents during infancy or early childhood, as in meningitis, encephalitis, high fevers, hypercalcemia, hyperbilirubinemia, and lead poisoning. In so-called advanced countries no more than 10–20 percent of the total number of cases of mental retardation can be associated with such known genetic, metabolic, toxic, traumatic, or other biologically definable disturbances. It seems likely that at least 50 percent of the total incidence of retardation in such societies is associated with subtler social and cultural factors (including economic poverty) that do not permit the expression of much intellectual potential that might be genetically possible. By contrast, in places where malnutrition in infancy has been especially widespread (*e.g.*, Biafra, India), such biological disorders as severe protein deficiency (kwashiorkor) seem to be responsible for a substantially high proportion of the retarded population.

Medical factors

With respect to identifiable medical syndromes that produce retardation, there are a number of known and effective treatments. In these cases, as in most medical disorders, early diagnosis is important to successful treatment. The hereditary condition called phenylketonuria (PKU), associated with the inability of the body adequately to metabolize a substance from protein foods called phenylalanine, usually can be diagnosed with a simple test of the newborn's urine or blood. In many European and North American localities tests for its diagnosis have become mandatory. Once the condition is diagnosed, mental retardation from PKU often can be prevented by strict adherence to a diet that is low in phenylalanine. The degree of subsequent intellectual impairment is related to the age of the child at diagnosis and the care with which the prescribed diet is followed.

Syndromes of mental retardation associated with hypothyroidism may be treated by the oral administration of thyroid preparations to replace the missing hormone. Hydrocephaly, characterized by a buildup of cerebral fluid without proper drainage, is best treated early in life by surgical provision for drainage. When drainage is successful, the skull does not continue to enlarge abnormally, the fluid pressure inside the brain cavities (ventricles) is relieved, and further brain damage is forestalled.

Although some hereditary forms of retardation are not directly treatable (*e.g.*, mongolism), their prevalence can be reduced by appropriate genetic counselling. Infants who suffer from mongolism are most likely to exhibit trisomy 21, a disorder in which a surplus (third) chromosome is found with what normally is the 21st pair of chromosomes (see HUMAN BEHAVIOUR, INNATE FACTORS IN). Mongolism in infants becomes more likely as the age of the mother increases. It has been estimated that the incidence of mongolism could be reduced by at least 40 percent if every mother who gave birth after age 30 had her baby five years earlier. In specific cases, a cytogenetic study of the unborn embryo can be done by examining cells recovered hypodermically through the mother's abdomen from the amniotic fluid; if the embryo's karyotype (chromosome picture) is abnormal, abortion may be advised during earlier stages of pregnancy. Prospective parents also can undergo cytogenetic studies, and the chances that they will produce children with particular genetic anomalies often can be specified.

Cultural deprivation

There is increasing evidence that a progressive decline in intellectual functioning throughout childhood is associated with cultural deprivation. In isolated mountain communities, for example, five-year-old children were found to have a mean IQ in the low-average range, while 15-year-olds had a mean IQ in the mentally retarded range. Many children in urban ghettos are one year behind the average in academic achievement by third grade and typically fall three years behind by eighth or ninth grade. Even when gross medical defects seem to be absent, culturally and economically disadvantaged segments of society exhibit a disproportionately large number of mildly retarded persons, producing no greater proportion of severe and profound retardates than do more advantaged groups. Mild retardation is found to be associated with economic deprivation, membership in minority ethnic groups, low educational levels, poor employment opportunities, frequent absence of adult males from the home, many and frequent pregnancies, social discrimination, pregnancies at early ages, poor nutrition, poor general health, inadequate or delayed prenatal care, substandard housing, working mothers, and crowded living conditions. Children tend to become mildly retarded when they have inadequate language models to follow; when they are chronically overstimulated or when they experience an insufficient variety of sensory stimulation; when there is a relatively unstructured and unpredictable environment; and when the child has little opportunity to abstract logical rules by observing order in the behaviour of adults.

With such a conglomerate of correlates, the degree to which any factor acts to lower intellectual levels remains uncertain. In a practical sense, however, the underlying condition is poverty, which seems closely tied to social discrimination. Thus, a concerted attack on these two related problems (economic and social deprivation) may be expected to reduce the proportion of mild mental retardation in any society.

Social factors. Limited efforts to give children a head start by emphasizing early education fall far short of a total attack upon poverty and social discrimination. Such programs, however, do give evidence that carefully planned preschool education (beginning with children as young as three years, concentrated on teaching simple logical skills, language, motivation for achievement, and combined with parent education) can offset at least some of the progressive retardation associated with cultural deprivation. Some of these head-start programs have been shown to have beneficial effects on younger brothers or sisters (siblings) in the so-called target child's own family and, to a lesser extent, on untreated families in the same community.

That mild mental retardation is diagnosed in a number of countries most frequently during the school-age years (between ages 6 and 18) emphasizes the academic referents of the concept of intelligence. Yet, many who have been diagnosed as retarded in school or in special institutions do become relatively independent members of the community at large. Such individuals may, however, need specialized training and follow-up services for vocational habilitation and for helping them develop social skills. Instead of comfortably disappearing into the population, many mildly retarded graduates of special classes and former residents of institutions are found on follow-up to be in the lowest socioeconomic segments, living in substandard housing, earning a marginal livelihood or existing on welfare, having frequent encounters with the law, and being dependent on special help offered by various community agencies (see also MENTAL HEALTH AND HYGIENE).

Adjustment of retardates to community life

Although there is no evidence that psychosis (major psychiatric disorder) is more frequent in the retarded population, such persons have more need of the services of mental-health professionals because of their difficulty in adjusting to the discrepancy between their own resources and the requirements of community living. It is likely that many more mildly retarded and even moderately retarded persons would make successful social adjustments if they were given training specifically designed to prepare them for community life, and if extensive social-casework services are made available to them on a continuing basis. When such services have been combined with vocational habilitation, retarded persons have shown repeatedly that they can hold down many jobs in industrial and service occupations. Working alongside nonretarded workers, they have at least as good a record as their more intelligent associates with respect to quality of work, frequency and severity of on-the-job accidents, absenteeism, and job stability.

Mentally retarded people are not necessarily deficient in long-term memory, and many show no obvious deficiency in ability to learn motor skills. It is most reasonable to expect that they can learn the skills necessary to perform many industrial and service jobs, and that they can remember the routines associated with job performance. Governments in the U.S., Soviet Union, Great Britain, the Scandinavian countries, The Netherlands, and Belgium, for example, have successfully employed thousands of retarded workers in jobs that did not have to be altered to take account of their retardation.

GIFTED PERSONS; GENIUSES; PRODIGIES

In a statistical sense, people who exhibit very high IQs are just as deviant from the "normal" as are the mentally retarded. No internationally accepted classification system seems to be in use for identifying those who have supernormal intelligence; clearly, they do not experience social problems that approach the magnitude of those presented by the intellectually subnormal.

Measurement of intelligence. In psychometric terms, average intelligence usually is associated with IQ scores between 90 and 110. Scores between 110 and 120 roughly constitute the bright-average range. Individuals who score between 120 and 130 are commonly classified as intellectually superior, and those who score above 130 are likely to be identified as intellectually very superior.

A plethora of terms is used rather indiscriminately to refer to persons who show especially high levels of intellectual functioning, including such words as gifted, genius, and prodigy. In English-speaking countries the term gifted generally is applied on the basis of a psychometric criterion alone: a minimum IQ of about 130 is typically required for one to be classified as gifted. The term genius commonly is used to refer to those who manifest very superior general intelligence (often defined as 140 or greater) and who have demonstrated their superiority through an unusually high level of achievement in an intellectually demanding pursuit. The word prodigy is used generally to refer to individuals who have achieved special distinction in a specific enterprise, usually at an early age (*e.g.*, the so-called child prodigy), but without the requirement of superior psychometric (test) intelligence. According to these criteria, a person who shows an IQ greater than 130 could be classified as gifted but would not be classified as a genius unless he had already reached a high level of achievement in an enterprise that required the application of his intellectual powers. To be classified as a prodigy, one would not need to exhibit a very high IQ (although many such individuals do) but would have learned some specific skill rapidly and to a high level, such as would be involved in music, painting, or theatrical arts.

Just as there are theoretically unexpected numbers of mentally retarded people, the prevalence of very high IQ levels is greater than one would anticipate on the assumption that intelligence is normally distributed. In the most superior group, those with IQ scores more than five standard deviations above the mean (175, given a standard deviation of 15 points), the normal-curve expectation is 56 persons in a population of 200,000,000, while the estimated actual prevalence of such high IQ scores is about 200 persons. In the IQ range 161–175, the normal-curve expectation is 5,384 persons in 200,000,000, but the estimated actual prevalence is 36,840. In the IQ range 146–160, the expectation is 264,020, but the estimated prevalence is 514,840. In the IQ range 131–145, the expectation is 4,280,000, but the estimated prevalence is 8,560,000.

Obviously, with frequencies in excess of normal-curve expectations at both the high and low ends of the IQ continuum, there are fewer cases than expected in the middle range. For example, 68,260,000 persons in a population of 200,000,000 are expected to obtain IQ scores between 101 and 115, but the empirical prevalence in this IQ range is 66,424,240, with comparable figures applying to the IQ range 86–100. The overestimation provided by the normal curve continues into the second standard deviation, both above and below the mean. In the IQ ranges 116–130 (and 71–85) prevalence is underestimated, with projections for a population of 200,000,000 being 27,182,000 and 24,463,800 for expected and empirical frequencies, respectively.

The foregoing figures must be interpreted with some caution. They are statistical projections based upon samples that may not have been truly representative of the U.S. population from which they were drawn. Thus, while it is fairly clear that the distribution of IQ scores in that country does not follow the normal curve precisely, perhaps the normal curve would more accurately describe the distribution of intelligence throughout the world, if it were known. (Unfortunately, empirical data on the distribution of intelligence are not available from many lands.) In addition, it is hazardous to assume a constant value of the standard deviation of any group of test scores across chronological ages, social classes, racial groups, and geographic regions. No intelligence test has a standard deviation of exactly 15 points at all ages and at all score levels. Finally, data on the distribution of intelligence are derived entirely from scores on tests that may be quite imperfect representations of hypothesized intelligence (the latent, theoretical variable). Thus, even though IQ seems not to be normally distributed, intelligence theoretically is.

Heredity and environment

Sir Francis Galton observed in *Hereditary Genius* (1869) that significant social achievement tends to run in particular British families. Galton used this evidence to argue for the inheritance of intelligence. What is less clear is whether the eminence achieved by individuals in certain families is more accurately attributed to superior genetic endowment or to the environmental advantages of growing up in surroundings that include intelligent and achievement-oriented adults, good educational opportunities, and even family influence in obtaining opportunities to achieve. The most prevalent modern view is that at least bright-average intelligence is necessary (but not sufficient) for achieving eminence in socially significant affairs. Gifted individuals, geniuses, and prodigies have come from the homes of highly successful parents and also from slums and from marginal farms.

Social and academic aspects. Persons who would be classified as gifted on the basis of IQ scores have come from both ends of the socioeconomic scale, but few from either group achieve genius or prodigy status. While achievement may be a highly desirable social goal, the mechanisms for turning intelligence (or achievement potential) into actual achievement are not well understood. Nevertheless, the potential for achievement that is found in young individuals in all segments of society is actual-ized to a far more nearly universal extent in the culturally and economically advantaged classes than among the disadvantaged members of any society. This suggests that advantages unfortunately concentrated in the middle and upper social classes of many contemporary cultures (*e.g.*, stimulating home environments, good educational opportunities, good nutrition and health care, and cultural enrichment) exert positive, selective influence on the development of individual potential.

Intelligence as academic aptitude

Intelligence test scores show a substantial degree of correlation (coefficients usually between +.60 and +.70) with those on standard tests of school achievement. Indeed, intelligence tests show greatest validity in predicting elementary and secondary school achievement. As a group, gifted children tend to earn high grades in school with relatively little effort. In spite of their relationship to immediate academic performance, intelligence test scores are only moderately efficient predictors of relatively long-range measures of social success.

Prediction of academic success is even less efficient for criteria of excellence in graduate and professional schools. Nevertheless, long-term (longitudinal) studies have shown that gifted children tend to earn above-average incomes as adults, enjoy better than average health (medical and psychiatric) in their mature years, and are likely to attain higher levels of academic and occupational achievement than do persons whose IQs fall in the average range. Gifted individuals are comparatively more able to achieve their aims vocationally; the options available to them are relatively more numerous. Nevertheless, all gifted children do not eventually become particularly successful contributors to society; differences from one person to another in personality, in motivational factors, and in vocational and educational opportunities can reduce individual potentials considerably.

Gifted individuals do present some unique problems, especially in education. One survey indicated that, among a sample of urban junior-high-school children, those with IQs above 140 had only a 50 percent chance of passing to the next grade. It was suggested that, for this sample of individuals, the attention of teachers was directed toward children of average intelligence, producing chronic boredom among the gifted youngsters. Such problems usually may be reduced by constituting special classes for gifted children (with teaching geared to a relatively high level of difficulty and abstraction); or by individualizing instruction within the classroom and by providing enriched assignments and experiences for the gifted.

GROUP DIFFERENCES IN INTELLIGENCE

The distribution of measured intelligence is not uniform across the various segments of society. There are significant differences across age groups, socioeconomic classes, ethnic groups, occupational categories, and between the sexes. To understand these differences, or to study them properly, it is helpful to distinguish intellectual *level* from intellectual *pattern*. Intellectual level is represented by a unitary, global score derived from an intelligence test. Intellectual pattern refers to variations within the same individual among different dimensions of general ability. It is a specification of intellectual level to say that a person scored at an IQ of 114; but it is a description of intellectual pattern to say that his verbal talent is superior to his nonverbal ability or that he achieves a higher score on numerical tasks than on those involving spatial relationships.

Age and class differences

Age affects both intellectual level and intellectual pattern. Individual differences appear in motor abilities during infancy, before children have acquired any verbal skill. When language develops, larger individual differences appear. Intellectual level grows at different rates from one individual to the next; this rate of growth is what presumably is measured and represented in the IQ. There is evidence that such growth continues to adulthood, and even into middle and old age for those who remain intellectually active; however, the rate of development declines after about age 25 across the population as a whole. In old age, skills that derive from earlier learning (*e.g.*, vocabulary knowledge) tend to decay slowly, while those that require new learning (as in solving unfamiliar logical problems) grow more difficult to acquire and to retain.

The effects of socioeconomic class upon intelligence are difficult to isolate. Class itself is a complex variable that defies clear definition, especially in societies that are characterized by considerable social mobility. Nevertheless, some group generalizations can be offered. At a gross level of distinction, it frequently has been observed that lower class children tend to earn lower scores on intelligence tests than do middle class children. The average difference tends to remain even after allowances are made for the cultural content of the tests, these being likely to favour middle class and upper class children. When fathers' occupations are arranged hierarchically, from those with the highest social status to the lowest, a regular decline is observed in the children's average IQ scores. In such samples the mean IQ of children whose fathers were in professional occupations was about 115, while the mean IQ of children whose fathers were in unskilled labouring occupations was about 94. Mean IQ values for the intervening occupational categories were: semiprofessional and managerial, 112; clerical, skilled trades, and retail business, 109; semiskilled, minor clerical, and minor business, 104; farm owners, 98; slightly skilled, 97. While this relationship has been confirmed in several studies of intellectual level, it did not hold for all components in the intellectual pattern; *e.g.*, in mechanical ability, lower class boys achieved higher scores than did middle class and upper class boys in some studies.

Class differences are particularly pronounced with respect to verbal ability. Working class young men in England tend to exhibit higher nonverbal than verbal ability, while the pattern is reversed for young men from the so-called privileged classes.

It is even more difficult to determine whether there are racial or ethnic differences in intelligence. In almost every multiracial nation in the world, race is almost hopelessly confounded with social class. In testing programs it is very nearly impossible to distinguish the effects of race from those of socioeconomic level, social discrimination, examiner's race, language differences, geographic influences, and other variables that might modify the subject's score. Further, the determination of racial groupings is exceedingly complex; efforts to locate genetically "pure" racial groups seem futile.

Racial differences

In studies of racial differences in intelligence in countries where white culture is dominant, it has been a very consistent finding that groups classified as Negro or black are likely to achieve lower scores on standard intelligence tests than do groups of whites or Caucasians. Yet, despite typically significant differences between the mean scores of the two so-called racial groups, the ranges (*i.e.*, the spread between the lowest score and the highest score in each group) are usually found to be about the same, revealing extensive overlap in the score distributions of the two groups. Indeed, even in studies in which average scores strongly seemed to favour whites, considerable numbers of black subjects achieved higher scores than those of the average white.

Such studies have been sharply criticized since in most of them all subjects were tested by white examiners. In studies made to assess the effect of the examiner's race on the subject's scores, black children tended to earn higher scores when they were tested by black examiners than when they were tested by whites. Examiner effects should be controlled in seeking to discover possible racial differences in intelligence test scores; otherwise the results are likely to be misleading.

Black children in Northern cities of the U.S. tend to exhibit higher IQs than do black children in Southern cities; the scores achieved by Northern black children who have migrated from the South tend to increase with the length of time they have lived in the North. Controlling for such influences serves to diminish apparent racial differences considerably. Yet, when tests designed to be relatively free of cultural and language biases are used, smaller racial-group differences appear. Such differences still may reflect environmental effects upon the development of the skills necessary to achieve high scores on intelligence tests, since representation of blacks in the lower social strata throughout U.S. society in the 1970s was disproportionately large.

Thus, while it has been argued that IQ data constitute support for theories of genetic racial inferiority, it seems more likely that the differences reflect persistent social and economic discrimination. Under legal or de facto segregation in many countries, educational facilities for blacks rarely have been equal to those provided for whites (*e.g.*, South Africa, Angola). There is considerable evidence that the growth of intelligence, as reflected in the IQ, is influenced significantly by the quality of available educational resources regardless of race. For example, lower class whites also show lower average IQ scores than do middle class whites in European and North American countries.

Social class and race compared

In studies in which children have been matched on socioeconomic level (usually by family income, education, occupation, and housing), social class has shown a stronger influence on intelligence test scores than has race. For example, intelligence tests were given in Tennessee to black middle class and lower class children and white middle class and lower class children; they were of both sexes in grades four, six, and eight. Significant effects were found for social class, race, age, and sex, the largest part of the differences in test score being associated with social class and the smallest being related to sex. In each comparison, high scores were likely to be earned by middle class, white, male, older children. White middle class children showed a mean IQ of 118 in the fourth grade, 117 in sixth grade, and 118 in the eighth grade. Scores over the three grade levels for black middle class children were 97, 112, and 108. For white lower class children, the scores were 98, 97, and 104, while the scores for black lower class children were 88, 94, and 94. Overlap in the distributions by race was very large, especially within social classes.

Another test given to all four groups measured attitudes toward task achievement. Mean values on that test followed the same general pattern as did the IQ scores, with white middle class children showing the greatest task-related motivation, and black lower class children the least. When IQ scores were adjusted statistically for these motivational differences, racial differences in IQ shrank within social classes, but the social-class difference remained quite large. Such evidence suggests that nonintellective variables associated with social class account for much of the apparent racial differences in IQ that emerge from the usual, poorly controlled studies.

There is growing support for the notion that social-class factors influence intellectual level, and that ethnic factors influence intellectual pattern. Intelligence tests that yield separate scores on four dimensions of ability were administered to middle class and lower class first graders of Jewish, Chinese, Negro, and Puerto Rican origin in New York City. Across all four areas of ability (verbal, reasoning, numerical, and spatial tests), in each ethnic group the middle class children were prone to achieve higher scores than did the lower class children. The social-class difference was greatest within the Negro sample and smallest in the Chinese sample. Jewish children tended to perform best on the verbal test, Chinese children had lower average scores on the verbal test than on any of the other three tests, and Negro children tended to earn better verbal than numerical scores. The rank order of the four groups varied, depending upon the kind of ability being measured, and, as usual, there was considerable overlap among the ethnic groups. From such evidence, it seems likely that the deleterious effects of the lower class environment may be rather generalized across areas of ability. By contrast, specific ethnic differences in cultural emphases and child-rearing practices may produce distinctive patterns of ability, exerting less effect on general intellectual level than do social-class differences.

Sex differences

Sex differences in intelligence are almost as difficult to isolate as are those attributed to race. Tradition has held that the variability of intelligence is greater among men and boys than among women and girls, with relatively more males in both the gifted and severely retarded categories, and with comparatively more females in the average range. Support for this position derived primarily from early studies in which inadequate sampling techniques were used. No completely reliable data were available in the 1970s to demonstrate sex differences in average intelligence levels or in variability. However, some differences have been found in ability patterns; males generally tend to be superior to females in gross motor skills, spatial orientation, mechanical aptitude, and numerical reasoning; females excel on the average in perception of detail, verbal facility, and memory. These sex-group distinctions which exist in patterns of ability may reflect differences in social expectations and in child-rearing practices.

The difficulties encountered in differentiating intellectual differences associated with race, ethnicity, and geography are matched by problems of at least equal difficulty in interpreting such differences. The observed differences often are small and inconsistent; overlap in the distributions of compared groups on any one of these variables is large. Tests used to measure intelligence are imperfect and tend to be biased toward the dominant culture; in Europe, the Americas, and many countries of Asia and Africa with colonial histories, the tests tend to stress white, middle class values. The very concept of intelligence as IQ (as a global, unitary, academically oriented dimension of behaviour) requires further examination before definitive studies can be made with respect to group differences. A shift of emphasis from the study of variations between groups in intellectual level to the study of group differences in intellectual pattern (and the social, genetic, and psychometric correlates of such differences) almost certainly will produce advances in more enlightening directions.

BIBLIOGRAPHY. A. ANASTASI, *Differential Psychology*, 3rd ed. (1958), a comprehensive work on individual differences, containing group comparisons on intelligence by age, sex, race, social class, occupation, and geographic origin, as well as discussions of the nature and organization of intelligence; S. WISEMAN, *Intelligence and Ability* (1967), a compilation of classical papers on individual differences; H.C. HAYWOOD *et al.*, *Social-Cultural Aspects of Mental Retardation* (1970); and J. ZUBIN and G.A. JERVIS (eds.), *Psychopathology of Mental Development* (1967), treatments of the development of intelligence in a social context; G.A. JERVIS (ed.), *Expanding Concepts in Mental Retardation* (1968), a broad sampling of contemporary research on the various biological and social influences on the development of intelligence, with emphasis on developmental anomalies; H.F. DINGMAN and G. TARJAN, "Mental Retardation and the Normal Distribution Curve," *Amer. J. Ment. Defic.*, 64:991–994 (1960), a model for prevalence estimation; H.C. HAYWOOD (ed.), *Psychometric Intelligence* (1970), includes a chapter by L.S. WRIGHTSMAN who presents a scientifically defensible and reasoned view of race differences in intelligence; A.R. JENSEN, "How Much Can We Boost IQ and Scholastic Achievement?," *Harv. Educ. Rev.*, 39:1–123, 449–483 (1969), a discussion of the interaction of scientific and social considerations with respect to race differences and the respective contributions of genetic and experiential factors in the development of intelligence.

(H.C.H.)

Intelligence, Theories of

While the idea of a unitary coordinating "mental" faculty has origins in the writings of ancient Greek philosophers and of medieval Scholastics, systematic theories and extensive empirical investigation of intelligence developed mainly after 1850. The principal formulators of the modern concept were Herbert Spencer (1820–1903) and Sir Francis Galton (1822–1911).

Definitions and conceptions of intelligence. Definitions vary, but common elements clearly may be discerned. Intelligence is defined as a cognitive disposition (knowing) distinct from the affective (emotional) or motivational. It is thought of as exceedingly general and, in contrast to more specific abilities, as influencing a broad range of human performance. Defined primarily as capacity or potentiality, rather than fully developed attainment, it is almost universally accepted as having a biological basis. Cognition manifestly is a function of the central nervous system and individual differences are related to biological-genetic endowment.

Such definitions must be treated with caution; they purport to describe a kind of entity that is at best an abstraction from behaviour, and to say that a human being possesses such-and-such a degree of intelligence may mislead. Intelligence is a disposition or tendency—not a tangible (or even intangible) possession; but the word provides a convenient portmanteau description of the highest level of coordinated thinking by an individual.

Definitions and conceptualizations of intelligence are primarily biological, psychological, and operational. The biologist who focusses on the evolution of species emphasizes the development of intelligence as a powerful tool of adaptation and survival. But concern here will be with human beings as an existing species.

Many psychological definitions throw light on important aspects of human intelligence—*e.g.*, "the ability to carry on abstract thinking" (L.M. Terman), "the capacity to acquire capacity" (H. Woodrow)—but none has been universally accepted. Psychologists have been obliged to attempt tying down the concept to observable behavioral performance. It is possible to define intelligence as "innate general cognitive ability" (C.L. Burt), but investigators have failed to assess this ability in any individual uncontaminated by the effects of upbringing, experience, and education. One line of escape from this dilemma is to propound two definitions of intelligence, referring (a) to the basic given characteristics of the individual's central nervous system and (b) to developed intelligence as molded by experience, learning, and environmental factors. These two aspects have been called "Intelligence A" and "Intelligence B" (D.O. Hebb), and "fluid and crystallized intelligence" (R.B. Cattell).

An alternative is to adopt an operational definition of intelligence in terms of performance on a particular test or battery of tests. This approach is the almost universal practice of experimental psychologists and has achieved impressive results (*e.g.*, in predicting occupational success and other forms of achievement), but there is no single agreed yardstick of measured intelligence. Considerable progress, however, has been made in determining the validity of the available instruments, and an agreed operational definition is by no means impossible in principle.

Structural theories. About 1900 development of psychological tests (*e.g.*, by J. McKeen Cattell in the U.S., by A. Binet in France, and by C. Spearman and Burt in England) led to empirical study of the organization or structure of human abilities. Theory since then has been influenced by statistical techniques (correlation and factor analysis) that help reveal the extent to which varieties of intellectual performance are covariant (or overlap) and that serve to assess their relative importance.

General intelligence versus primary abilities

From about 1910 to 1950 there was wide controversy: some (*e.g.*, Spearman) maintained that a massive statistical factor (interpreted as general intelligence) adequately accounted for the observed data, and that more specialized abilities were relatively unimportant; others (*e.g.*, L.L. Thurstone) found the concept of intelligence superfluous and split it into six or seven virtually independent "primary abilities," such as spatial, inductive, numerical, and verbal. By the 1970s there was general agreement that both positions are simplistic and untenable. The conflict seems to have arisen from the use of alternative methods of mathematical analysis; from differences among the groups of people studied, particularly in range of ability and education; and from the theoretical preconceptions of the investigators. It has become generally accepted that a sample of people who represent a broad range of ability, tested with instruments that cover a wide range of cognitive skills, will yield evidence for both general intelligence and more specific abilities. The apparent relative importance of general and specific factors in any study reflects the sampling of people and of tests.

J. P. Guilford's theory

From about 1950 to 1970, major influence came from work of J.P. Guilford, who theorized that "intelligence" is multidimensional to an unprecedented degree, embracing 120 highly specific abilities. Evidence for these abilities did not derive primarily from an inductive program of original experiments; they were formulated on logical (in many ways, a priori) grounds. A group of these abilities concerned with divergent or creative thinking has become the subject of extensive, fruitful research.

The 120 abilities were theoretically distinguished through a cross-classification of cognitive activities into logically discernible processes—*e.g.*, remembering, divergent thinking; into the kinds of information processed —*e.g.*, letters, words, numbers; and into the products of such processing—*e.g.*, classes, systems, relations. Similar analyses were suggested independently by L.G. Humphreys and N. Guttman (facet analysis) but were not as thoroughly developed.

Guilford's work revitalized research into creativity, generating disputes in the 1970s on the status of creativity as a general, pervasive trait and on its relation to measured intelligence. Studies relating measures of creativity and intelligence produced diverse results, some showing great overlap, others suggesting that the two qualities are virtually independent. Contributions to such divergences probably stem from the nature of creativity; it seems to straddle both cognitive and temperamental differences. It also is widely accepted that measures of creativity and intelligence overlap very considerably at low and average levels but diverge so markedly as to be almost independent among uniquely gifted individuals.

Heredity and environment. It has been demonstrated repeatedly that intelligence as assessed by the most highly regarded tests reflects substantial genetic influence. A common finding in European and North American research is that about 70–80 percent of human variation in measured intelligence is ascribable to genetic differences, only 20–30 percent to environmental factors.

Bold conclusions from these data require major qualification. The evidence applies to groups of people and does not specify any given individual. It represents a sample drawn from each society or culture at a given time, and environmental conditions (*e.g.*, availability of food) may change rapidly within a society to alter the ratio. For example, severe protein deficiency among infants tends to abort genetic potentials for intelligent behaviour. Thus, these results should not be held to apply to populations that have been less carefully studied; *e.g.*, peoples of Asia, Africa, and South America among whom malnutrition is widespread. Besides, computation of such a ratio rests on such arguable technical assumptions as that endorsing the application of an additive variance model to the assessment of these effects (J. McV. Hunt, 1961).

Such estimates mainly derive from comparisons of monozygotic (identical) and dizygotic (fraternal) pairs of twins in terms of similarity of performance and from rare cases of monozygotic twins reared apart. Possibly more convincing additional evidence comes from observed similarities in measured intelligence among people of established degrees of consanguinity. L. Erlenmeyer-Kimling and L.F. Jarvik (1963) reviewed 52 such studies and found marked support for a substantial genetic effect in measured intelligence. While little was known about the genetic details, it seemed likely that many genes act to generate individual differences in the normal range of intelligence, mental retardation and specific disorders being more directly related to a few major genes.

Intelligence level has been shown not only to be heritable but also to correlate positively with socioeconomic class. It therefore has been feared in Western industrial societies (where birth rate has been highest in "lower" social classes) that national intelligence might be declining. Hardly any such evidence has been found; indeed, the three or four major relevant studies available by 1970 revealed small average gains in population performance over 30 or 40 years in these countries. It is probable that the gains reflect social and environmental improvement rather than genetic change.

Beneficial effects of superior environment and opportunity on measured intelligence seem to be shown in studies of U.S. blacks. Average IQ scores were higher among blacks in New York and Illinois than among whites in the economically poorer Southern states of Mississippi and Georgia. Although some of this effect was attributed to selective migration, average score among the northern blacks also was consistently related to length of residence in Northern states.

Attempts to design "culture-fair" tests

Efforts to compare national and racial groups chronically have faced the problem of designing appropriate tests. Although some cognitive tests are undoubtedly more "culture-fair" than others, cultural and environmental differences are so complex (P.E. Vernon, 1969) that test constructors with claims to know "culture-fair" characteristics should be treated with skepticism. Even within one culture it is extraordinarily difficult to devise measures that are acceptably "fair" to all social groups and that at the same time are effective indicators of intelligence. Since verbal skills tend to be particularly susceptible to early deprivation and environmental handicap, nonverbal tests seem to provide a most limited solution.

Development and decline of intelligence. Predictive estimates of intelligence in later life can be made with a fair degree of success at about the age of four or five, but little earlier. B.S. Bloom (1964) estimated that about 50 percent of variation in intelligence at age 17 is predictable at age four. Research into native language acquisition in infancy was active in the 1970s, revolutionized by progress in psycholinguistics, and was expected eventually to influence developmental theories of intelligence.

Measures of general intelligence proved serviceable for predicting a variety of performance over the life-span, as shown by Terman's massive studies, but the measures are too crude for detailed accounts of development. Nevertheless, developmental curves for separate test components differ markedly; for instance, verbal scores on the Wechsler Adult Intelligence Scale typically remain fairly constant throughout adult life, particularly among high scorers (whose verbal skills may increase up to late middle age), while average Wechsler performance scores decline with increasing steepness between ages 20 and 60.

As long as enough time is allowed, problem-solving ability tends to deteriorate relatively little before old age, but speed in dealing with unfamiliar problems drops sharply. This difference appears to be closely associated with a diminishing scope of attention and decline in short-term memory span. Persons who show higher intelligence in early life tend to hold up best, curves of high and low scorers fanning out more widely with increasing age.

These statistical trends from intelligence testing have been enriched by the clinical methods of Jean Piaget, in which cognitive development among children is intensively studied. In some respects this *méthode clinique* is relatively subjective and is limited to comparatively small samples of subjects.

The theories of Piaget. Piaget's work produced an overall picture of human cognitive development up to adolescence, as contrasted with earlier piecemeal analyses of individual differences. His theory is a unique effort to synthesize biology and epistemology. Problems in epistemology (*e.g.*, how people can think of a perfect circle when they have never seen one) were a classic concern of philosophers, who generally knew little about early cognitive development. Piaget's approach was to tackle such problems by detailed observation of individual children.

He concluded that intelligent behaviour depends on an initially precarious, increasingly stable equilibrium between contrasting intellectual functions that he called assimilation and accommodation; every human being passes through specifiable phases of cognitive development in a fixed order that corresponds moderately well to chronological age; such development is hierarchical in that each phase incorporates rather than supplants those preceding; the cognitive structures available often can be described in terms of mathematical groups and lattices.

While much of this work is highly technical and by no means easy to follow, Piaget's conception of qualitative changes in cognitive performance won wide acceptance. Numerous cross-cultural studies later lent support to the general applicability of Piaget's findings.

The influence of computers. The already considerable influence of high-speed computers in the study of intelligence seems likely to increase. Beyond the enormous computational facilities they provide, such computers are of value in generating mathematical models of intelligence and in simulating complex cognitive performance. Even in its infancy, the study of machine intelligence has produced striking results.

Computers already can play checkers (draughts) better than their programmer. They can give correct answers to items from intelligence tests that are difficult enough to be useful in the selection of university students. More general computer programs serve to solve a very wide range of logical problems; for instance, these machines discover proofs of geometrical theorems.

Computer developments by the 1970s had not produced any single widely accepted theory of intelligence, but current ideas about brain mechanisms are expressed with growing frequency in cybernetic terms, offering close analogies to computer operation. Systematic trial-and-error loops in computer programs are clearly similar to human processes in solving problems and in testing hypotheses. Individual differences in intelligence are coming to be expressed in such computer terms as basic speed of operations, quick access to memory storage, number and complexity of programs or schemata on file, and adequacy of programming language.

BIBLIOGRAPHY. The pioneer work of Binet is well summarized in J.W. REEVES, *Thinking About Thinking* (1965). Early statistical views are described in C.E. SPEARMAN, *The Abilities of Man* (1927). A useful summary of early U.S. research into intelligence and of the development of major theories is by R.D. TUDDENHAM in L. POSTMAN (ed.), *Psychology in the Making* (1961). An excellent survey of the logic and principles of factor analysis is provided in C.L. BURT, *The Factors of the Mind* (1940). A comprehensive account of a multifactorial theory of intelligence is in J.P. GUILFORD, *The Nature of Human Intelligence* (1967). An eclectic overview of the literature, including that on creativity and on machine intelligence is provided by H.J. BUTCHER, *Human Intelligence* (1968), and in BUTCHER and D.E. LOMAX, *Readings in Human Intelligence* (1971). Other useful collections of readings are S. WISEMAN (ed.), *Intelligence and Ability* (1967); and L.E. TYLER (ed.), *Intelligence: Some Recurring Issues* (1969). Accounts emphasizing the importance of heredity are by A.R. JENSEN, "How Much Can We Boost IQ and Scholastic Achievement?," *Harvard Educational Review*, 39:1–123, 449–83 (1969); and of cultural and environmental influences by J.MCV. HUNT, *Intelligence and Experience* (1961); and P.E. VERNON, *Intelligence and Cultural Environment* (1969). A definitive summary of Piaget's earlier work is in J.H. FLAVELL, *The Developmental Psychology of Jean Piaget* (1963).

(H.J.B.)

Intelligence and Counterintelligence

Intelligence means, basically, evaluated information. As used in this article it denotes a wide variety of governmental activities related to national security and foreign policy. A statesman's day often begins and ends with the reading of intelligence reports. While accurate information may not guarantee an optimum decision, incorrect or inadequate information has demonstrably caused disaster. Thus it is not enough that accurate information exists somewhere in government files: such information must be properly interpreted and be in the right hands at the right time.

The most important category of intelligence activity is information gathering (by various means, including espionage), along with the analysis and communication of such information. Another aspect is counterintelligence, a police and security function that is concerned primarily with defensive, protective activities. Finally, some national intelligence services are used for covert political action that involves intervening in a variety of clandestine ways in the internal affairs of other nations.

NATURE OF INTELLIGENCE

The various categories of intelligence are potentially endless. A defense department needs military intelligence, an atomic energy commission needs scientific information, a foreign office needs political information, and a premier or president needs an amalgam of these and many more. Consequently, intelligence activity has become a vast international "industry." Total U.S. governmental expenditures on intelligence in 1970 may be roughly estimated at around $5,000,000,000. Employed in this work were possibly as many as 150,000 persons in the United States and many thousands more overseas. The intelligence activities of the Soviet Union were of comparable dimensions.

Types of intelligence that are sought. Political intelligence is at once the most sought after and least reliable of the various types. Obviously, no one can predict what the outcome of political forces in a foreign country will be, and the analyst is reduced to making estimates of alternatives based on what he knows about political trends and patterns. His most concrete data will include such things as voting records, the details of party organization and leadership, and sophisticated analyses of political documents. A prime source of political intelligence has long been the reports of diplomats; the diplomats normally gather data from open sources in the country where they are stationed, and send back reports to their governments. Their work is supplemented by that of the professional intelligence apparatus. Much military intelligence is gathered by military attachés, who have formal diplomatic status but are known to be chiefly concerned with intelligence. Ironically, military information is often more difficult to obtain in peacetime than during war. In wartime much is learned from captured equipment, captured enemy forces, and information gained from patrols. The kinds of information considered to be of greatest value pertain to military organization and equipment, procedures and formations, and the number of units and total personnel.

Sources of information

Economic factors are crucial to a nation's military strength, its political development, and the conduct of its foreign policy. Unemployment in Japan, a food shortage in India, rice production in Southeast Asia, a balance of payments crisis in the United States or Great Britain—each has obvious relevance to the conduct of foreign policy. Intelligence organizations, therefore, give major importance to the collection of data on trade, finance, natural resources, and industrial capacity, and to complex analyses such as the estimation of gross national product.

Technological advance has produced an ongoing race between military capabilities and defensive measures, and between new methods of collecting intelligence and new techniques of protecting secret information. Consequently, intelligence systems must be on guard against scientific or technological breakthroughs that may give one country a decisive advantage over another. They must be kept abreast of foreign advances in nuclear energy, in the electronic, chemical, and biological sciences, and along all other frontiers of scientific knowledge.

If an intelligence system is to make estimates of a foreign nation's future behaviour, it obviously needs detailed information about the personal characteristics of national decision makers. The scope of biographical research has broadened with the growth of international organizations, since negotiators need to be "briefed" with information about their foreign counterparts.

Intelligence agencies constantly work at compiling data on foreign populations, topographies, climates, and an increasingly wide range of ecological factors. The questions asked of the intelligence analyst may range from "What is the nature of the water supply in Addis Ababa?" to "What are the prospects for economic growth next year in Outer Mongolia?"

Three categories of intelligence

Types of intelligence in terms of scope. Intelligence is often classified in three categories: strategic (sometimes called national), tactical (or combat), and counterintelligence. Of these, the broadest in scope, strategic intelligence, covers information about the capabilities and intentions of foreign nations. Tactical intelligence, sometimes called operational or combat intelligence, is information required by field commanders. The distinction between strategic and tactical, in certain respects, may be vanishing, because in an age of rockets, missiles, and jet aircraft what is of importance to the field commander may be of equal importance to the highest command. A major field commander may require today much the same kind of information as a president and his national security council, and vice versa.

Counterintelligence is information and activity related to protecting one's own information and the secrecy of one's own intelligence operations. It is largely a police function, although counterintelligence operations often result in the discovery of positive intelligence. The adversary's efforts to penetrate one's own security may give clues as to what information the adversary needs, as well as information about his techniques, equipment, and operational procedures.

Sources of intelligence. While the public sees the intelligence operative as a "cloak and dagger" secret agent, in fact the largest amount of intelligence work is an undramatic search for information from public sources. These include the monitoring of foreign radio broadcasts; the analysis of the contents of foreign publications of all kinds; and the sifting of reports from diplomats, businessmen, accredited military attachés, and other observers. Most intelligence work is performed by university-trained research analysts in quiet offices.

Covert sources of intelligence are more dramatic, falling into three major classifications: aerial and space reconnaissance, electronic "eavesdropping," and the secret agent working at the classic spy trade. Broadly speaking, the value of each as a source of crucial information is probably in descending order as listed. This is because a photographic report constitutes hard intelligence, whereas the report of a secret agent may be speculative, difficult to prove, and therefore "soft." Public and secret sources will be discussed in greater detail below.

A BRIEF HISTORY OF INTELLIGENCE ACTIVITIES

Intelligence in premodern periods. The earliest counterparts of the modern intelligence agency were perhaps the ancient soothsayers who claimed to be able to communicate with the gods and therefore often were said to have the power of predicting the future. As in modern times, their reports were often ignored by the decision makers. The Bible contains references to an intelligence function, such as the Lord's advice to Moses (Num. 13) that he send agents to "spy out the land of Canaan." Twelve agents were sent who returned after 40 days to report that the people in the land flowing with milk and honey were more powerful than the Israelites—for which intelligence they were punished by the Lord.

Another ancient commentator on intelligence and counterintelligence was Sun Tzu, whose book *Ping Fa* (*The Art of War*), written about 400 BC, is said to be widely read by contemporary Chinese Communist strategists. Sun Tzu refers in his book to five kinds of secret agents, corresponding to modern concepts of "agents in place," "double agents," "deception agents," "expendable agents," and "penetration agents." Sun Tzu stressed the importance of good intelligence organization, and he also wrote of counterintelligence and psychological warfare.

In the Middle Ages

In the Middle Ages intelligence began to be used systematically in western Europe, although it was crudely organized. On the one hand it was usually impossible to conceal the massing of troops or ships, making strategic surprise difficult to achieve in military operations; on the other hand, communication was slow, and thus a fine balance often existed between the information available about the enemy and the ability to communicate it in time. The Mongol leader Subotai, in directing an invasion of Europe in the 13th century, made good use of the highly organized intelligence system of the Mongols to achieve spectacular military successes. One historian has observed: "Whereas Europe knew nothing about the Mongols, the latter were fully acquainted with European conditions, down to every detail, not excepting the family connections of the rulers." (Michael Prawdin, *The Mongol Empire*; G. Allen, London, 1940 p. 254.)

Intelligence in the West was deficient in many respects. According to Allen Dulles in *The Craft of Intelligence*, European rulers in the Middle Ages "were not very well informed about the Byzantine Empire and the Eastern Slavs; they knew even less of the Moslem world, and they were almost completely ignorant of anything that went on in Central and East Asia." Italian merchants had contacts with the East but there was no systematic way of communicating their knowledge to policy makers. The lack of intelligence resulted in strategic defeats for the West on numerous occasions.

In the 15th century the Italian city-states began to establish permanent embassies in foreign capitals. The Venetians used such outposts as intelligence sources and even developed codes and ciphers by which information could be secretly communicated. By the 16th century other European governments had followed suit.

From the Renaissance to the Franco-Prussian War

The growth of nationalism and intelligence systems. The rise of nationalism, punctuated by the Peace of Westphalia in 1648, saw the growth of standing armies and professional diplomats. These brought a need on the part of statesmen for evaluated foreign information and so organizations and procedures for its procurement began to be developed. Queen Elizabeth I maintained a notable intelligence organization. Her principal state secretary, Sir Francis Walsingham, developed and maintained—partly, it is said, out of his own personal fortune —a network of several score intelligence agents in foreign lands. He recruited able graduates of Oxford and Cambridge, developed the black arts of espionage and foreign political intrigue, and even had tools and techniques for making and breaking codes. Walsingham's was clearly a forerunner of contemporary intelligence systems. Later the cardinal de Richelieu and Oliver Cromwell, whose intelligence chief, John Thurloe, is often cited as an early master spy, developed notable intelligence systems.

Not until the late 18th century, however, did sharp organizational distinctions arise between internal security (a policy or counterintelligence function) and external foreign intelligence. The populace began to give its allegiance to the state rather than to dynasties or religious leaders. As a result, national leaders concerned themselves increasingly with foreign "public opinions," producing both a new diplomacy and new intelligence needs.

Major innovations in organization and doctrine during this period have been credited to Frederick the Great. Under Frederick, and later under Bismarck's aide Wilhelm Stieber, the Prussians organized the intelligence function as an integral part of the general staff. This called for a single military intelligence agency to serve as the nation's eyes to the outside world. Under Stieber perhaps the first large-scale espionage system emerged. According to Allen Dulles, "Stieber went after the farmers and the storekeepers, the waiters and the chambermaids. He used these methods in preparing for the Prussian attacks against both Austria in 1866 and France in 1870."

Modern power politics and intelligence systems. European power politics, the pursuit of imperialist foreign policies, and advances in military technology required an increasing amount of strategic intelligence. Intelligence bureaus spread throughout Europe, producing a corresponding growth in counterintelligence activity.

During World War I

Nevertheless, most European nations entered World War I with inadequate intelligence services. That war is now often cited as one that none of the combatant nations intended, suggesting in itself a tragic intelligence failure. The French intelligence service had been torn by internal intrigue, after having already been weakened by the Dreyfus affair, and other services had been shaken by scandal. Miscalculation of German military strength in 1914 was a prime example of intelligence failure.

German intelligence, which in 1870, under Stieber, was reputed to be the best on the continent, had also deteriorated. The German General Staff of 1914 evidently placed little faith in the information supplied to it. For the Germans, policy seemed to dominate intelligence.

The Russians had great initial success against the Austrians because of the treason of an Austrian general staff officer, but subsequently Russian intelligence performed no better than that of other nations in World War I. The British were successful in breaking German naval codes, and in their Middle Eastern intelligence operations. The Germans carried on successful activities in Persia and scored limited espionage successes in the United States. The United States had no central intelligence. At the beginning of the war army intelligence was a small section within the general staff, comprising two officers and two clerks; by the war's end, this service had grown to 1,200 officers and civilians. Patently, most were amateurs. Navy intelligence was equally deficient.

Most of the evidence strongly suggests that the leaders of the major powers were supplied with inadequate information all during the war. It has even been asserted that not a single strategic action in the war was decisively influenced by any of the military intelligence services.

World War II

The intelligence lessons of World War I, along with advances in technology, especially electronics and aircraft, resulted in a proliferation of intelligence agencies in the 1920s and 1930s. The growth of such agencies was further stimulated by the advent of regimes with expansionist foreign policies in the U.S.S.R., Italy, Germany, and Japan. These produced, in reaction, counterintelligence organizations in the democracies.

World War II led to the creation and expansion of intelligence services everywhere. The United States, which had virtually no peacetime intelligence services, created in the Office of Strategic Services (OSS) its first full-fledged organization for intelligence and secret operations. The war imposed intelligence requirements never before faced by the major warring powers. This was primarily the result of accelerating technology: air warfare in particular required vast new offensive and defensive intelligence operations, and the growth of radio broadcasting produced a new art of psychological warfare that demanded intelligence services for the analysis of its effects. Even with all the new developments, intelligence forecasting remained a precarious trade. The Pearl Harbor attack in December 1941, the German attack on the U.S.S.R. in 1941, the Battle of the Bulge in 1944, the unexpected German resilience under Allied bombing attacks—in these and other instances the decision makers failed to profit from their elaborate intelligence networks.

World War II was followed by the "Cold War," in which the intelligence organizations of opposing blocs became combatants. In every major nation huge new bureaucracies were created. Usually these consisted of interlocking and often competitive secret agencies, vying with each other for new assignments and sometimes withholding information from each other.

The world soon became familiar with the Central Intelligence Agency (CIA) of the United States. Somewhat less well known were Great Britain's MI-5 and MI-6; the KGB and the GRU of the Soviet Union, the SDECE of France, China's Social Affairs Department, and the Shin Bet of Israel. The main function of these and numerous other espionage networks was to engage in a wide assortment of clandestine activities, ranging from espionage to covert political action and psychological warfare in foreign lands.

At the same time, the exploits of spies and counterspies became a subject for mass-media fiction. Books, movies, and television moved the spy to centre stage, sometimes in a comic but often in a dead-serious role. All of this tended to glamorize what is most often a painstakingly tedious, or even at times a disgustingly immoral and distasteful, occupation. Of writers of spy fiction it has accurately been said, "Never have so many been misled by so few."

NATIONAL INTELLIGENCE ORGANIZATIONS

In a world in revolutionary ferment, the authentic intelligence officer occupies the centre of great debates over national security policy. At issue in most of the debates are questions of *power*, *probability*, and *time*. A prime task of the modern professional intelligence officer, military or civilian, is to try to answer questions for the policy maker about power and about behaviour probabilities, within a time scale. For a chief of state trying to decide some question relating to nuclear armaments, an ideal intelligence system would provide precise knowledge of a potential enemy's *power*, the *probability* of that enemy's behaviour or reaction in given contingencies, and a *time* schedule for the most likely sequence of events.

Policy questions

These are basic, even classic problems for all intelligence services. Information as to how these services address their problems is highly uneven. More is generally known about the American system than any other, a good deal about that of the Soviet Union, and comparatively less about other systems. Intelligence systems fall into three general types: the American, which has been followed by nations such as Germany, Japan, and South Korea since they came under American influence after World War II; the Soviet, which is imitated in large measure by most Communist-governed nations; and the British, on which are patterned most of the Western European systems.

The United States. In September 1967 the Central Intelligence Agency (CIA) observed its 20th anniversary. The CIA grew out of the nation's wartime experience with the Office of Strategic Services (OSS) and a postwar decision to create a central security organization comprising a Department of Defense and a National Security Council, under which the CIA was to function. One of the lessons of World War II had been that there was a need for a central organization to coordinate for the president all information on foreign affairs and to perform certain functions best done centrally. There were heated debates at war's end as to how much centralization was needed. Some wanted a central intelligence setup that would eliminate Army, Navy, State Department, and other separate units. Others wanted to turn over all but technical military intelligence functions to the State Department. The outcome was a compromise in which the Central Intelligence Agency was created under the National Security Act of 1947, but other departments and agencies continue to maintain their own intelligence sections. Since then the idea of a single entity has given way to the concept of an "intelligence community" comprising the CIA, the Defense Intelligence Agency (DIA), separate Army, Navy, and Air Force intelligence staffs, State Department intelligence, the National Security Agency (NSA), an Atomic Energy Commission (AEC) intelligence unit, and the Federal Bureau of Investigation (FBI). The latter is primarily a domestic internal security agency engaged in counterintelligence activity, with few assignments overseas. The National Security Act of 1947 which remained in the 1970s the basic charter for the organization, assigned to the CIA five specific functions: (1) advising the National Security Council (NSC) on intelligence matters related to national security; (2) recommending to the NSC measures for efficient coordination of the intelligence activities of departments and agencies of government; (3) correlating and evaluating intelligence and seeing that it is properly communicated within the government; (4) carrying out for existing intelligence agencies any additional services the NSC determines can best be performed centrally; and (5) carrying out such other functions and duties related to national security intelligence as the NSC may direct.

Out of this assignment of basic functions grew a large new agency with an annual budget sometimes approaching $1,000,000,000 and with assignments around the globe. The CIA is believed to employ about 15,000 full-time employees in the United States, mainly in Washington, D.C., and several thousands more in overseas posts. Its annual budget in the late 1960s was believed to be in the vicinity of $750,000,000, but that did not include the numerous functions performed by military and paramilitary units functioning under the CIA's direction and control. Specific operational guidelines for the CIA are contained in some two-score secret directives—called National Security Council Intelligence Directives—defining its functions and establishing jurisdictions in areas in which other intelligence agencies might have a functional claim.

The Central Intelligence Agency

Since 1947, the CIA has come to perform three major assignments: (1) foreign intelligence gathering, evaluation, and communication; (2) counterintelligence operations overseas; and (3) secret political intervention and psychological warfare operations in foreign areas. The first two functions are clearly stipulated in the congressional statute creating the CIA; the third was assumed as a Cold War necessity and on the basis of a very free interpretation of the original charter.

The CIA is managed by a director and a deputy director, both appointed by the president and subject to Senate confirmation. The director of Central Intelligence in fact wears two hats. He is head of the Central Intelligence Agency, as well as the president's principal intelligence adviser, and thus theoretically the number one man in the intelligence community—theoretically, because each of the other major units, such as the Federal Bureau of Investigation, the National Security Agency, or the Defense Intelligence Agency, operates somewhat autonomously. The head of the CIA is, in fact, "first among equals."

The major divisions of the CIA are those for intelligence, plans, science and technology, and administration. The intelligence division, the largest, is responsible for the production of finished intelligence in its various forms—from instant news flashes to encyclopaedic surveys. Most of the thousands of workers in the intelligence division are research analysts. By contrast, the plans division, sometimes called the "Department of Dirty Tricks," has handled various clandestine operations such as high-altitude reconnaissance flights over the U.S.S.R., the attempted invasion of Cuba in 1961, and paramilitary missions in Laos and the Congo (Kinshasa; now Zaire). The science and technology division concerns itself both with new techniques of intelligence gathering and with the technological developments of other nations that may have impact upon American security. The administration division is concerned with recruitment and training, library services, including information storage and retrieval, and various other housekeeping activities.

One of the most important sections of the CIA is the Office of National Estimates, presided over by a Board of National Estimates. This board, made up of veteran intelligence specialists, is concerned with the production of National Intelligence Estimates (NIE's) that represent the best information available from all sources on a given subject. For example, if the president should ask for an estimate of the nuclear capacity of mainland China in 1975, an NIE might be produced giving the best answer available. Before going to the president the estimate would have to be approved by the U.S. Intelligence Board, at which time any member of the intelligence community would have a chance to add comments and appraisals of its own.

The U.S. Intelligence Board may be described as the "Supreme Court" of the intelligence community. Its chairman is the director of the CIA and includes representatives from the State Department, the Defense Intelligence Agency, the National Security Agency, the Federal Bureau of Investigation, and the Atomic Energy Commission.

The FBI's jurisdiction in the intelligence community pertains mainly to efforts of foreign intelligence agents to penetrate government security systems in the United States. Such counterintelligence often produces significant information about a foreign nation's intentions, its level of information on a given topic, or its operational procedures. During World War II the FBI had a major, positive intelligence role in Latin America. Afterward, its operations were restricted to the United States and, with an occasional exception, have remained so ever since.

The National Security Agency

The National Security Agency is the largest, most expensive, and perhaps least known of all American intelligence organizations. Its basic functions are cryptological—the making and breaking of codes and ciphers and the security problems connected with them. One way to view this huge agency is to see it as an omnipresent electronic eavesdropper on all the world's major secret government-related communications. From its headquarters near Washington, D.C., the NSA conducts an immense variety of electronic espionage activities. Estimates of its size and budget generally set its number of employees at around 20,000 and its annual expenditures in excess of $1,000,000,000. But its activities also involve thousands of armed-service personnel, supervised by the NSA. Devices for electronic espionage of various sorts are placed in planes, on ships, or at ground installations overseas. This kind of intelligence work was brought to world attention when the USS "Pueblo" was seized by the North Koreans in 1968 and its crew detained for a year. The subsequent Navy and congressional inquiries revealed that the ship was on assignment for the National Security Agency, with a mission to collect data on North Korean and Soviet naval operations in the Sea of Japan.

The vast secret communications and surveillance apparatus of the NSA today contrasts sharply with the situation of the late 1920s when the American cryptographic agency, known as the "Black Chamber," was abolished with the explanation by a secretary of state that the United States must not read "other persons' mail."

The Defense Intelligence Agency is the newest major member of the U.S. intelligence community. It was established in 1961 as a culmination of the increasing centralization in the Department of Defense, which began with the "unification" measures of 1947. The DIA was set up by the secretary of defense to improve the intelligence product available to him and to the Joint Chiefs of Staff. Another purpose was to eliminate costly duplication and a tendency of the separate armed services to use their own intelligence data as ammunition in the annual competition for budget allocations. This tendency had resulted in the Army exaggerating the number of Soviet divisions, the Navy overstressing the dangers of Soviet submarines, and the Air Force overestimating the production of Soviet aircraft and missiles. The separate Army, Navy, and Air Force intelligence branches ceased to have a major role in producing national or high-level policy intelligence. Their functions were confined to tactical and technical intelligence and counterintelligence.

The director of the DIA is the principal intelligence adviser to the secretary of defense and to the chairman of the Joint Chiefs of Staff. He represents all the armed services on the U.S. Intelligence Board.

In many ways the DIA plays a role for military intelligence similar to that of the CIA in the wider intelligence community. In addition to coordinating and supervising military intelligence functions, the DIA has been assigned other functions thought best performed centrally. These have included photographic intelligence, consolidation of dissemination facilities, and the management of automated data-handling projects and services.

By 1970, the DIA had been unsuccessful in persuading Congress to appropriate $25,000,000 for a new building. In the same year its direct budget was around $70,000,000 with total personnel of about 7,000.

The Department of State, through its Bureau of Intelligence and Research, collects, analyzes, and disseminates large amounts of political, economic, and cultural information about those nations in which the United States has accredited representation.

The bureau, referred to as INR in the intelligence community, operates under a director whose rank since 1963 has been that of assistant secretary of state. The bureau has the double function of meeting the requirements of the intelligence community as set by the National Security Council and those of the State Department's own intelligence needs. Area specialists constitute the bulk of the INR staff, which is small by comparison with those of other intelligence agencies.

The Atomic Energy Commission has long been a producer and a consumer of information in the important field of nuclear energy. Its intelligence division contributes technical guidance to the CIA and armed services intelligence units, which gather raw data on foreign nuclear developments. The AEC is an intelligence producer in the sense that it analyzes data gathered by other agencies and processes and disseminates intelligence on foreign atomic weapons capabilities and other developments in the nuclear field.

The AEC is accordingly listed as a "member" of the U.S. intelligence community and is represented on the U.S. Intelligence Board.

Military intelligence services

The creation of the Defense Intelligence Agency sharply reduced the role of the separate armed forces in the high-level intelligence system. Yet each of the armed services maintains a major intelligence division for tactical and technical intelligence and for counterintelligence activities.

Army intelligence is organized under the assistant chief of staff for intelligence, traditionally referred to as G-2. It directs the work of Army attachés in foreign embassies as well as highly technical activities such as mapping, communications, and electronics. Each of the seven technical services of the Army—chemical, engineers, ordnance, quartermaster, signal, transportation, and medical—has a particular intelligence function.

One of the best-known branches of Army intelligence is the counterintelligence division, commonly referred to as CIC. Its members are trained in investigative and security techniques and are concerned with the detection and prevention of attempts at treason, espionage, sabotage, and the more common problems of service-related black markets, gambling, and prostitution. It is the Army's counterpart of the civilian FBI, and carries out many similar functions in foreign areas.

The Navy has a natural intelligence mission. Its submarine forces engage in reconnaissance and surveillance of large sea areas—in itself a basic intelligence activity. In addition, submarines can land amphibious patrols and underwater teams and furnish facilities for periscope surveillance and photography of seacoasts. Carrier striking forces can conduct aerial photography as well as visual and electronic reconnaissance. The Marine Corps can serve as an additional intelligence arm in its operations under general Navy direction. Navy intelligence activities are directed by the assistant chief of naval operations (Intelligence) who heads the Naval Intelligence Command (NIC). There is also the assistant chief of naval operations for communications under whose command is a Navy Security Group with cryptologic functions.

The NIC has three basic divisions: (1) Naval district intelligence officers operating in designated geographic areas; (2) intelligence units with the forces at sea serving directly under unit commanders and indirectly under the NIC; and (3) naval attachés who serve under the multiple direction of the NIC, the State Department, and the Defense Intelligence Agency.

The Air Force, like the Navy, has been accorded by technology a front-line intelligence position. The assistant chief of staff, intelligence, is charged with the responsibility for planning, directing, and supervising Air Force policies and organizations covering a worldwide range of intelligence activities. A special responsibility is to be a sentinel against technological, strategic, or tactical surprise. Explicit functions assigned to the Air Force intelligence system are: (1) coordination of collection, evaluation, and dissemination of all air intelligence; (2) maintenance of up-to-date target dossiers for worldwide deterrence purposes; (3) liaison between foreign military groups and the Air Force; (4) supervision of the Air Security Service, the principal organization for Air Force counterintelligence; and (5) representation of the Air Force on numerous interagency boards and committees within the intelligence community.

The Soviet Union. The Committee of State Security (KGB [Komitet Gosudarstvennoy Bezopasnosti]) resembles the America CIA and FBI and Secret Intelligence Service rolled into one. This combination of foreign intelligence, counterintelligence, and internal security roles is unusual, although the Soviet system has set the pattern for intelligence services in other Communist countries.

From Cheka to KGB

The lineage of the KGB begins with the Cheka, the secret police established by the Bolsheviks in 1917. In 1922 the Cheka was reorganized into the GPU (State Political Administration) and in 1934 was renamed the NKVD (People's Commissariat for Internal Affairs). During World War II several further reorganizations occurred, out of which grew the MGB (Ministry of State Security).

The current organization, the KGB, was created in 1954. It is commonly believed to dominate the entire Soviet intelligence system, and some analysts picture the KGB chief as a man of immense potential power in the political sphere. Nonetheless, other separate intelligence agencies do exist in the U.S.S.R., including that of the Foreign Ministry, but most particularly the Central Intelligence Office (GRU [Glavnoye Razvedyvatelnoye Upravleniye])—the chief intelligence directorate of the Army general staff. The GRU deals primarily with military intelligence, and although at times there have been indications of competition and conflict with the KGB, the latter is thought to have predominance.

The KGB is organized into a number of major Directorates. The First Chief Directorate carries out primarily counterintelligence missions. This pervasive section of the KGB performs an internal security function similar in some ways to that of the American FBI but not limited to domestic jurisdictions.

The Second Chief Directorate is responsible for foreign intelligence and is believed to have a wide variety of subsections dealing with particular areas (such as an American section) and specific functions (such as psychological warfare in foreign areas).

The Third Chief Directorate is believed to encompass Smersh, popularized in the 1960s by the British novelist Ian Fleming. The real Smersh—derived from the Russian Smert Shpionam meaning "Death to Spies"—has as its principal assignment maintaining security within the armed forces and watching for potential traitors within the military and intelligence services.

A number of other chief directorates exist, each with specialized intelligence functions and particular geographical jurisdictions. Many Soviet officials serving abroad have been thought to have some direct connection with the KGB or the GRU, some of them as actual agents using various forms of "cover"; and it has been alleged that some Soviet ambassadors have held rank within the KGB. Soviet diplomats assigned to the United Nations occasionally have been discovered to be intelligence agents, but the same is assumed to hold true for the diplomats of most other major nations.

Estimates of the size and annual cost of Soviet intelligence are highly speculative. Since the KGB encompasses internal security, border guards, and foreign-intelligence personnel, the total cost probably runs into billions of dollars, with perhaps 100,000 or more employees, not counting paramilitary detachments. But there is no reliable information on these matters.

Great Britain. British intelligence was organized along modern lines as early as the days of Queen Elizabeth I, and their experience has influenced the structure of most other systems. Unlike those of the United States and the Soviet Union, British intelligence agencies have preserved through most of their history a high degree of secrecy concerning their organization and operations.

The two principal British intelligence agencies are the Secret Intelligence Service (sometimes referred to under its wartime designation as MI-6) and the Security Service (commonly called MI-5). The obsolete labels, still used, derive from the fact that the Secret Intelligence Service was once "section six" of military intelligence and the Security Service, "section five."

Today MI-6 is a civilian organization with functions resembling those of the American CIA. The British intelligence community, however, is even more of a confederation of separate agencies than is that of the United States. The Secret Intelligence Service (MI-6) is charged with gathering information overseas and with other strategic services ranging from foreign espionage to covert political intervention. The director of the SIS is commonly referred to as "C" and remains an anonymous figure in British governmental life. A high wall of secrecy likewise surrounds his organization; the government barely acknowledges its existence, although an annual lump-sum appropriation request must be presented publicly to Parliament. This sum, about $30,000,000 in recent years, fails to cover all the expenditures on the secret services, but it does indicate that the British services are much smaller, perhaps by a factor of 20, than those of either the U.S. or the Soviet Union.

Security Service

Also included in the annual budget submitted to Parliament is the Security Service (MI-5). This is roughly equivalent to the American FBI, or the internal security section (counterintelligence) of the Soviet KGB. It differs from the FBI in performing certain counterintelligence functions overseas. Its main charge is to protect British secrets at home from foreign spies and to prevent domestic sabotage, subversion, and the theft of state secrets. The Security Service is headed by a director general, whose code name in years gone by was "K"—a designation derived from the name of Sir Vernon Kell, its head from 1909 to 1940. The Security Service makes no direct arrests, working secretly behind the more publicized "Special Branch" of Scotland Yard. The director of the Security Service reports to the prime minister through the home secretary.

The supervision of the Secret Service is the duty of the Joint Intelligence Committee, a Cabinet subcommittee under the chairmanship of the permanent undersecretary of the foreign office. Another layer of control is exerted by the Cabinet secretary in the case of the Secret Service and by the permanent head of the Civil Service in the case of the Security Service.

Another principal member of the British intelligence community is the Defence Intelligence Staff, resembling the American Defense Intelligence Agency. This integrates intelligence specialists of the Royal Army, Navy, and Air Force within the Ministry of Defence. Still another service is Communications Intelligence, an organization for electronic surveillance and cryptology resembling the National Security Agency of the United States, but much smaller in size and scope. Its operations are concentrated in what is called the Government Communications Centre.

The Joint Intelligence Committee combines all of the British intelligence agencies and performs functions of overall policy control and of approval of "national estimates" similar to those carried out by the U.S. Intelligence Board.

The British system may also be more responsibly run than the United States or the Soviet Union.

France. The French, like the British, have been more successful than other major nations in maintaining secrecy for their intelligence system. This is attributable, in part, to tighter censorship control.

One of the two principal agencies for foreign intelligence in France is the SDECE (Service de Documentation Extérieure et de Contre-Espionnage). It was created in the same year as the CIA, 1947, and is roughly equivalent to the CIA. SDECE combines foreign intelligence and counterintelligence, including political operations and psychological warfare overseas. It is headed by a *directeur-général*. SDECE is believed to have worked closely in the

1950s with the CIA and with other North Atlantic Treaty Organization (NATO) intelligence agencies that were dominated by the United States. French agents were important in alerting American officials to the presence of Soviet missiles in Cuba in 1962. After 1962, however, the CIA and the SDECE ceased their close collaboration when France developed a more independent foreign policy.

Another major French intelligence agency is the Second Division of the National Defense Staff, combining, to some degree, formerly separate Army, Navy, and Air Force specialists. The traditions and doctrines of the old French Army's Deuxième Bureau (Military Intelligence) no doubt influence the general staff's Second Division. Its functions are to gather foreign military intelligence. A third important member of the French intelligence system is the DST (Direction de la Sécurité du Territoire) charged with internal security. It is the French equivalent of the American FBI and operates under the administrative control of the Ministry of the Interior.

The SDECE was shaken in 1968 by the publication of the memoirs of Philippe Thyraud de Vosjoli, who had been an important officer in the French intelligence system for 20 years. De Vosjoli asserted that SDECE had been deeply penetrated by the Soviet KGB in the 1950s, an allegation that the government denied. He also indicated that there had been periods of intense rivalry between the French and American intelligence systems. There have been other indications that SDECE experienced a number of major intelligence failures, structural reorganizations, and changes of leadership in the period between 1950 and 1970. The French services have been no more successful than those of other countries in remaining clear of political intrigue, both internal and international.

China. Mainland China's intelligence system resembles closely that of the Soviet Union, although not much is known about it. Less distinct lines exist in China between the professional intelligence function and Communist Party administrative functions. This may reflect the fact that the Chinese revolution still is in a much earlier stage than that of the Soviets. The best information suggests that the intelligence organization consists of four major units: those of the Party, the State Council (the governmental bureaucracy), the military establishment (Defense Ministry), and the Ministry of Foreign Affairs.

Dominance of the party

Under the title Social Affairs Department, the intelligence unit of the Central Committee of the Communist Party attempted for some years to exert dominant control over the entire intelligence system, much in the fashion of the Soviet KGB. This department, with perhaps 25,000 employees, is thought to have been abolished during the Cultural Revolution of the late 1960s. It is probable that only its name was changed. As in the U.S.S.R., the Army—through the Defense Ministry's large intelligence staff—is potentially a strong competitor of the civilian intelligence agencies. The Army chief of staff in China also runs the Military Secret Police and heads the "Political Department" of the Defense Ministry. Clearly there are two main functions within the military: first, to assure the reliability and loyalty of the Chinese military establishment—in effect, an internal security function—and second, to secure positive intelligence about foreign military systems. The State Council operates a Ministry of Public Security that concerns itself mainly with internal security. Finally, there is the Foreign Intelligence Department in the Ministry of Foreign Affairs, responsible for intelligence gathering and other overseas activities including covert political action. It is roughly the equivalent of the American CIA. Its agents operate, like those of most other nations, through embassies, legations, the New China News Agency (used as "cover"), the overseas Chinese, and other obvious channels.

Observers outside of mainland China have speculated about the quality of Chinese foreign intelligence, and some have suggested that Peking's leaders are poorly informed about the outside world as a consequence of a party-dominated intelligence system reporting what its leaders want to hear. If this is true, it is an exaggeration of a fault common to all intelligence systems, aggravated by the isolated and doctrinaire character of the Chinese leadership.

Israel. The state of Israel, since its creation in 1948, has met its obvious need for intelligence and counterintelligence with intelligence services that have gained a first-class reputation. One mark of their professionalism is that less is known about them than about other systems. They consist of five major organizations.

The Central Institute for Intelligence and Security has a director who is chairman of a committee presiding over the entire Israeli intelligence system. The Central Institute, much like the CIA, operates primarily in foreign areas, gathering information through all the techniques used by modern intelligence systems. It carries out covert political operations which require clandestine activity. The numerous Israeli secret agents living in Arab lands, for example, are under the supervision of the Central Institute. Its director is responsible to the prime minister. A second agency, perhaps Israel's best-known security unit, is the Shin Bet, after the Hebrew initials for General Security Services. Its main function is counterintelligence. Shin Bet is also an investigative agency concerned with potential sabotage, Arab terrorist activities, and security matters having a strong political flavour. A third major Israeli agency is the Intelligence Corps of the Defense Forces. Its chief is the military intelligence adviser to the defense minister. The Research Department of the Foreign Ministry is a fourth agency. Resembling the Bureau of Intelligence and Research in the U.S. State Department, this relatively small unit focusses on political information, including policy-oriented studies and the evaluation of information supplied through diplomatic channels. The fifth member of the system—the Special Investigations Department of the Israel Police Force—is concerned with investigations inside Israel's boundaries.

Shin Bet

Israel's successes to date in her wars with Arab countries may be attributed in large measure to the efficiency of her intelligence system. But it has not been without its scandals. The most dramatic was the "Lavon affair," which led ultimately to the resignation of Prime Minister David Ben-Gurion. This is said to have been an attempt in 1954 to blow up American and British information offices in Egypt in order to arouse Western public opinion against the Egyptians. But for the most part the secret services of Israel have operated without exposure and with apparent success. Israeli law prohibits domestic publication of information about the intelligence agencies.

Israeli intelligence has the advantage of a cosmopolitan population, providing persons whose language and experience enable them to pose as citizens of Chicago, Munich, London, Rome, or even Cairo. Recruitment is thought to be from three main sources: the Haganah, the one-time illegal Jewish army in Palestine, with its allied intelligence agency; ex-members of the Irgun and Stern groups, that also operated in the prestate era; and the newer immigrants.

HOW INTELLIGENCE IS GATHERED

Good intelligence management must begin with the determination of what needs to be known. Unless precise requirements are set, data will be collected unsystematically and the decision maker left, in the end, without the required information. Once data are collected they must be evaluated and transformed into a usable form (and sometimes stored for future use). Evaluation is essential because of the wide variety of sources, many of them of doubtful reliability. A standardized system is used. Source reliability may be rated A, B, C, etc., down a scale. Information accuracy may likewise be rated 1, 2, 3, etc., with 1 representing confirmed information and 3 denoting a "possibly true" accuracy. Thus the classification of a bit of information as C-3 would mean it came from a fairly reliable source and was possibly true.

With organizational sophistication, refined procedures,

and the most advanced technology, intelligence still falls into two categories—the "knowable" and the "unknowable." It is possible to obtain "hard" intelligence on the number of Soviet intercontinental ballistic missiles. But it is not possible to predict, with precision, the political intentions of Soviet leaders.

Most valuable information comes from overt sources, that is to say, from sources accessible without resort to illegal methods. Open sources probably contribute more than 80 percent of the input to most intelligence systems. This will vary according to the subject country, since clearly there are far fewer state secrets in some countries than in others. Foreign mass media, including press, radio, and TV, are a standard source, and they require a massive effort in recording, translating, and storing information.

Covert sources and clandestine collection methods provide the basis for much of the drama and romance accorded intelligence work in fiction. The classic espionage agent is now obsolescent. His place is being taken by inanimate operators such as orbiting reconnaissance satellites, long-range cameras, and a variety of sensing, detecting, and acoustical instruments. Now it is possible to see and hear at a distance in the night and to photograph from an altitude of hundreds of miles. A kind of race has developed between the use of technology to uncover secrets and its use to make secrets more secure. Techniques of reconnaissance have advanced dramatically since the 1940s when the Soviets accused the United States, accurately, of drifting balloons carrying special cameras across Soviet territory to photograph Russian military and industrial installations. The Peking Military Museum is said to have on display American "drone" aircraft, downed over China, that had been used for photoreconnaissance missions. Everyone has heard of the American U-2 aircraft, capable of flying at very high altitudes while taking photographs of ground installations that experts can read with great accuracy. Orbiting satellites, continuing advances in photographic capabilities and sensing devices, and the growth of computer technology radically changed intelligence and counterintelligence capabilities in the 1960s. The USS "Pueblo," captured by the North Korean government in January 1968, might accurately be described as an electronic scavenger sent out to collect information about North Korean radio communications procedures, Soviet naval equipment and procedures, and other kinds of intelligence such as Soviet submarine signatures—telltale and unique signals permitting their later identification. Computers can be used to analyze complex data on industrial production, missile launchings, and economic growth rates. High-altitude photographs taken from aircraft or satellites yield information on crops, floods, drought areas, or even plant diseases, which in turn can be used to assess the economic prospects of a country.

Use of aircraft and satellites

So vast is the intake of information that intelligence systems have been threatened by inundation. In the years since World War II great efforts have gone into the development of efficient means for cataloging, storing, and retrieving on demand the gigantic volume of data being amassed. Intelligence agencies have led in developing new indexing and codifying techniques and machinery for the electronic analysis, storage, and location of specific information.

CURRENT CONSIDERATIONS

Since World War II, intelligence has come to constitute one of the world's largest industries, employing hundreds of thousands on a professional basis. Annual expenditures for governmental and nongovernmental intelligence run into many thousands of millions of dollars. Under contemporary political and technological conditions, intelligence systems are likely to grow in size and scope. They have already taken on assignments that go beyond their informational and security functions, such as secret political and paramilitary operations. These activities will probably continue, since they are preferable to overt warfare between nuclear powers.

In most countries, intelligence services have probably outgrown their optimal size. Secret bureaucracies tend to grow beyond the point of efficiency, especially when they can argue that the fate of the nation depends upon their budgetary health. There is also the problem of control. In some respects this is similar to the problem of civil-military relations, aggravated by the secrecy factor. To put the matter simply: knowledge is power, and secret knowledge is secret power. Historically secret services have often been vehicles of conspiracy and political intrigue. Control is difficult to apply, both in democracies and authoritarian systems, since a secret service can logically demand secrecy for its operations. In an age of accelerating technology, it seems quite likely that the power of intelligence systems will grow vis-à-vis political authority. Presidents and prime ministers, in order for them not to become prisoners of their intelligence systems, will of necessity have to find ways of enforcing effective policy controls.

BIBLIOGRAPHY

General works: WILLIAM J. BARNDS, "Intelligence and Foreign Policy: Dilemmas of a Democracy," *Foreign Affairs*, 47:281–295 (1969); PAUL W. BLACKSTOCK, *The Strategy of Subversion* (1964), primarily a historical survey of secret operations by intelligence agencies engaged in intervention in foreign lands; JOHN M. CARROLL, *Secrets of Electronic Espionage* (1966) and *The Third Listener: Personal Electronic Espionage* (1969), surveys of electronic developments that have assisted intelligence and counterintelligence professionals; DAVID J. DALLIN, *Soviet Espionage* (1955); ALLEN W. DULLES, *The Craft of Intelligence* (1963), an unsystematic and somewhat anecdotal survey of intelligence work by the man who most influenced the organization and development of the U.S. Central Intelligence Agency in the important years of the 1950s; DAVID KAHN, *The Code Breakers: The Story of Secret Writing* (1967), a unique comprehensive history of codes, ciphers, and cryptanalysis from ancient to modern times; KLAUS KNORR, *Foreign Intelligence and the Social Sciences* (1964), a scholarly analysis of the potentialities and limitations of social science research techniques and findings for intelligence work; RICHARD W. ROWAN, *The Story of Secret Service* (1937), a historical survey of intelligence activities, stressing espionage and counterespionage prior to World War II; HAROLD L. WILENSKY, *Organizational Intelligence* (1967), a sociological survey of the use of intelligence in complex organizations; DAVID WISE AND THOMAS B. ROSS, *The Espionage Estabishment* (1967), a popularized description of the intelligence systems of the U.S., Great Britain, Russia, and China.

United States: SHERMAN KENT, *Strategic Intelligence for American World Policy* (1949), a professional intelligence analyst's description and explanation of the intelligence process and the role of intelligence in national policy making; YOUNG HUM KIM (ed.), *The Central Intelligence Agency: Problems of Secrecy in a Democracy* (1968), a collection of essays dealing with the policy, organization, and control problems of secret services in a democratic society; LYMAN B. KIRKPATRICK, JR., *The Real CIA* (1968), an organizational history by a man employed by the CIA for 20 years; HARRY H. RANSOM, *The Intelligence Establishment*, rev. ed. (1970), a careful analysis of the issue of secrecy; DAVID WISE and THOMAS B. ROSS, *The Invisible Government* (1964), a journalistic disclosure of the organization and activities of the CIA and related agencies; ROBERTA WOHLSTETTER, *Pearl Harbor: Warning and Decision* (1962), the best study available on the intelligence failure at the time of Pearl Harbor in 1941; JACK ZLOTNICK, *National Intelligence* (1964), a guarded but authoritative description of the U.S. intelligence system and some of its procedures.

Great Britain: R.V. JONES, "Scientific Intelligence," *Journal of the Royal United Service Institution*, 92:352–369 (1947), a unique essay describing the applications of science to intelligence operations in World War II: DONALD MCLACHLAN, *Room 39: A Study in Naval Intelligence* (1968), an authoritative account of some of the work of the British Navy in intelligence operations in World War II; BRUCE PAGE, DAVID LEITCH, and PHILLIP KNIGHTLEY, *The Philby Conspiracy* (1968), a detailed account of the case of H.A.R. Philby, who infiltrated the British intelligence service for the Soviet Union, and of the history and organization of the secret services in Great Britain; KENNETH STRONG, *Intelligence at the Top: The Recollections of an Intelligence Officer* (1968), an autobiographical account of 40 years in British military intelligence.

(H.H.R.)

Interior Design

Although man's desire to create a pleasant environment is as old as civilization itself, interior design, the conscious planning and design of man-made spaces, is a relatively new field.

In recent years the term interior decorator has been so loosely applied as to be nearly meaningless, with the result that other, more descriptive terms have come into use. The term interior design indicates a broader area of activity and at the same time suggests its status as a serious profession. In some European countries, where the profession is well established, it is known as interior architecture. Recently, those who are concerned with the many elements that shape man-made environments refer to the total field as environmental design.

The following article deals with principles of good design that are applicable to all design activities, but special emphasis is on interior design, particularly as a creative and problem-solving activity. Specific components relating to interior design are discussed in some detail. This is followed by a discussion of design procedure for interiors and a discussion of specific types of interiors. The final section of the article treats the historical development of interior design.

Principles of interior design

It is important to emphasize that interior design is a specialized branch of architecture or environmental design; it is equally important to keep in mind that no specialized branch in any field would be very meaningful if practiced out of context. The best buildings and the best interiors are those in which there is no obvious disparity between the many elements that make up the totality. Among these elements are the structural aspects of a building, the site planning, the landscaping, the furniture, and the architectural graphics (signs), as well as the interior details. Indeed, there are many examples of distinguished buildings and interiors that were created and coordinated by one guiding hand.

Importance of total design

Because of the technological complexity of contemporary planning and building, it is no longer possible for a single architect or designer to be an expert in all the many aspects that make up a modern building. It is essential, however, that the many specialists who make up a team be able to communicate with each other and have sufficient basic knowledge to carry out their common goals. While the architect usually concerns himself with the overall design of buildings, the interior designer is concerned with the more intimately scaled aspects of design, the specific aesthetic, functional, and psychological questions involved, and the individual character of spaces.

Although interior design is still a developing profession without a clear definition of its limits, the field can be thought of in terms of two basic categories: residential and nonresidential. The latter is often called contract design because of the manner in which the designer receives his compensation (*i.e.*, a contractual fee arrangement), in contrast to the commission or percentage arrangement prevalent among residential interior decorators. Although the volume of business activity in the field of residential interiors continues to grow, there seems to be less need and less challenge for the professional designer, with the result that more and more of the qualified professionals are involved in nonresidential work.

The field of interior design already has a number of specialized areas. One of the newer areas is "space planning"—*i.e.*, the analysis of space needs, allocation of space, and the interrelation of functions within business firms. In addition to these preliminary considerations, such design firms are usually specialists in office design.

Specialized design firms

Many design firms have specialized in such fields as the design of hotels, stores, or shopping centres. Others work primarily on large college or school projects, and still others may be specialists in the design of hospitals and nursing homes. Design firms active in nonresidential work range from small groups of associates to organizations with 50 to 100 employees. Most of the larger firms include architects, industrial designers, and graphic designers. In contrast, residential interior designers are likely to work as individuals, possibly with two or three assistants. The size of these firms is a clear indication of the relative complexity of large nonresidential design commissions. In addition to being less complex, residential design is a different type of activity. The residential interior is usually a highly personal statement for both the owner and the designer, and it is doubtful that a client who wished to engage the services of an interior designer for his home would be happy with an organized systems approach.

In recent years most large architectural firms have established their own interior-design departments, and smaller firms have at least one specialist in the field. There are no precise boundaries to the profession of interior design nor, in fact, to any of the design professions. Furniture design, for example, is carried out by industrial designers and furniture designers as well as by architects and interior designers. As a rule, furniture designed for mass production is designed by industrial designers or furniture designers; the interior designer or architect usually designs those special pieces that are not readily available on the market or that must meet specific needs for a particular job. Those needs may be functional or aesthetic, and often a special chair or desk designed for a specific job will turn out to be so successful that the manufacturer will put such pieces into his regular line. The same basic situation holds generally true in the design of fabrics, lighting devices, floor covering, and all home-furnishing products. All design activities are basically similar, even though the training and education in the different design fields varies in emphasis. A talented and well-trained designer can easily move from one specialized area to another with little difficulty.

In the discussion of the general aspects of design, it is important to note that there is an important distinction between art and design. A designer is basically concerned with the solution of problems (be they functional, aesthetic, or psychological) that are presented to him. The artist is more concerned with emotive or expressive ideas and with the solution of problems he himself poses. A truly great or beautiful interior can indeed be called a work of art, but some would prefer to call such an interior a "great design."

Distinction between art and design

AESTHETIC COMPONENTS OF DESIGN

General considerations. A general definition of beauty and aesthetic excellence would be difficult, but fortunately there are a number of generally accepted principles that can be used to achieve an understanding of the aesthetic considerations in design. One must note, however, that such understanding requires exposure and learning; an appreciation of any form of art needs such a background.

A thorough appreciation of design must go beyond the first impression. The first impression of the interior of a Gothic cathedral might be that it is somewhat dark or gloomy, but, by the time the visitor senses its majestic proportions, notices its beautiful stained glass windows and the effect of light, and begins to understand the superb structural system that permitted builders of cathedrals to achieve their lofty goals, he can truly begin to appreciate the overall aesthetic qualities (Figure 1).

One of the key considerations in any design must be the question of whether a design "works" or functions for its purpose. If a theatre has poor sight lines, poor acoustics, and insufficient means of entry and egress, it obviously does not work for its purpose, no matter how beautifully it might be decorated. Such a design could be considered good only if it were thought of abstractly as a kind of walk-in sculpture. In some cases the building is meant to be sculpture rather than architecture. The Statue of Liberty, for instance, is primarily intended as a monument, despite the fact that it contains rather tortured interior spaces.

Importance of function

To use function as the only aesthetic criterion would be limiting, but it certainly is a valid consideration to be

Figure 1: Majestic overall aesthetic quality of a Gothic interior: nave and choir, cathedral of Notre Dame, Paris, 1163–*c.* 1200.
Shostal

kept in mind. Designers are often tempted to overdesign or "style" an object or interior rather than design it. Some of the most beautiful objects of the 20th century are beautiful because they were the result of purely functional considerations. It is conceivable that future art historians will consider a modern jet plane the crowning artistic achievement of the middle of this century, rather than any building, interior, or conscious art form.

The aesthetic response to an interior and its furnishings must take into consideration the social and economic conditions as well as the materials and technology of the time. The elegant or ornate interiors that are usually associated with the 18th and 19th centuries were appropriate to the social and economic conditions of the nobility or the wealthy bourgeoise who were the original occupants. The chairs were designed for formal living, and the elaborately carved furnishings were designed to be cared for by many servants (Figure 2, left). Such an interior is alien to the 20th-century way of life and would be totally inappropriate for a contemporary middle class family. It would also be inappropriate to use modern materials and processes to imitate earlier materials and processes (Figure 2, right). Many manufacturers try desperately to make plastic look like wood, stone, or just about anything plastic. All aesthetic criteria have something to do with honesty. Some aestheticians have compared beauty to truth, and there can be little doubt that honestly expressed functions and honestly expressed materials and manufacturing processes are far more beautiful than fakery and imitation.

Relation of interior to basic structure

All interiors, by definition, occur inside buildings and therefore have a very real relation to these buildings. The best interiors today, as well as in the past, are those that relate well in character and appropriateness to the particular building. The furnishings designed and scaled for spacious country homes or palaces would obviously be out of place in a small urban apartment or suburban home. A strong and unusual piece of architecture such as New York City's Trans World Airlines terminal (at John F. Kennedy International Airport) could not be properly furnished with standard commercial furniture and products. The building, as well as the interiors, was conceived as a total design by the Finnish-born architect Eero Saarinen. Whether the observer agrees with the architect's concept or not, he clearly senses the strong interrelationship between the exterior and the interior—and therefore the aesthetic unity and success. Another successful interior and building is the Ford Foundation headquarters in New York City, the work of architects Kevin Roche and John Dinkeloo, with interiors by Warren Platner. The design is notable for its handsome spaces opening out toward an enclosed garden space (Figure 3). This obviously would not have been possible or appropriate if the view from the offices had been unattractive.

The interiors within indifferent or unattractive buildings must strive to make up for the lack of design qualities in the structures. Thus, it is sometimes necessary to ignore the ugliness of the building and create an inward-looking beauty if no architectural character exists.

By courtesy of (right) Knoll International, Inc.; photograph, (left) Louis Reens

Figure 2: *Social and economic considerations in interior design.*
(Left) Elaborate mid-19th-century dining room in the Gothic Revival style, Lyndhurst, Tarrytown, New York, designed by Alexander J. Davis. (Right) Simple pedestal table and chairs appropriate to the dining room of the mid-20th century family, designed by Eero Saarinen, 1956–59. Synthetic materials and mass production methods are used to achieve furniture suited to its function.

Figure 3: Aesthetic unity in the interrelation of exterior and interior space: Ford Foundation headquarters, New York City, designed by Kevin Roche and John Dinkeloo, 1967.
J. Zimmerman—FPG

The most difficult aesthetic consideration is the problem of appropriateness. The appropriate atmosphere or character of an interior must take all the foregoing points into consideration. The architectural character of the TWA terminal would make it inappropriate for use as an office building. The appropriateness of individual, more intimate, and small-scaled interiors is more subtle. The interior design of a discotheque would hardly be appropriate for a research library, and a college classroom would hardly provide the desired atmosphere for a kindergarten. Many of these responses and relationships are complex and have psychological as well as aesthetic factors.

Elements of design. Of all the component elements that together form a completed interior, the single most important element is space. Spaces can be exhilarating or depressing, cheerful or serene, all depending upon the use the designer has made of the various elements that form the whole. Space is, in modern times, a costly commodity. The beautiful space of the Gothic cathedral achieved its success through generous proportions and lofty heights (see Figure 1). Due to the vast increase in construction costs in contemporary structures, spaces tend to be smaller and less generous; more skill on the part of the designer is required to give such limited spaces a particular atmosphere or character. On the other hand, sheer volume of space is not sufficient. There is hardly a larger space than the interior of one of the structures at the John F. Kennedy Space Center in Florida, yet obviously the aesthetic impact of that immense interior is negligible. A space need not be large and monumental to be aesthetically successful. The handling of mass and form even within a small structure can become exciting and beautiful. Frank Lloyd Wright was masterful in creating beautiful spatial sequences, even within residential-scale buildings (Figure 4). The previously mentioned Ford Foundation building is a relatively small structure among the huge buildings of New York City, yet the experience of that space is real and pleasurable.

Characteristics of space

Space can be thought of as the raw material which must be molded and shaped with the designers' tools of colour, texture, light, and scale. The interrelationship of design elements can be clarified by visualizing the result if the interior of St. Peter's in Rome were painted in garish colors or painted all black or sprayed with a foamy texture covering all surfaces or flooded with enormously intense floodlight that eliminated all play of dark and light. Obviously, any of these modifications would totally destroy the beauty and success of that space.

Colour is the quality of light reflected from an object to the human eye. When light falls upon an object, some of it is absorbed, and that which is not absorbed is reflected, and the apparent colour of an object depends upon the wavelength of the light that it reflects. The scientific attributes of colour and light in interior design are, however, less important than the skillful combination of colour values, hues, tones, shades, and above all textures. Although there can be no strict rules about colours and textures, it is well to remember the famous statement of the modern architect Mies van der Rohe that "less is more." His Crown Hall at Illinois Institute of Technology in Chicago, built in 1956, is elegant, understated, subtle, and is notable for its careful handling of textures and materials. To accept "less is more" as the sole guideline to design, however, would be a serious fallacy. Space, which is the essence of a meaningful interior, would be dull indeed if it were never varied—if there were no intimate spaces with low ceilings, in contrast to large spaces of greater height, and if spaces did not interrelate to provide the user with a sequential experience of moving from one to another. Monotony would also result if all interiors in a given building were of the same colour, material, and textural quality. Man needs variety and change.

The use of colour

The manipulation of space is a matter of both aesthetic and functional consideration. A small entrance vestibule in a building is needed to keep out wind and cold or heat and rain, yet it is equally important in providing a visual transition from outdoors to the interior of the building. The sheltered sleeping alcoves in early cave dwellings served not only to express man's desire for smaller and more intimate spaces for personal use but gave protection from draft or cold.

Much in our man-made structures is built of natural materials, and it must be remembered that these materials have natural colours and textures that usually are superior to anything man can create artificially. Competent designers are very much aware of the innate qualities and textures of all materials, especially natural ones (see Figure 4). For instance, a sensitive designer would

Value of natural properties

Hedrich-Blessing photo

Figure 4: Carefully modulated spatial sequences in residential scale exemplified by the living room designed by Frank Lloyd Wright for his home and studio, Taliesin East, at Spring Green, Wisconsin; photograph, 1939.

choose a simple oil finish on wood to bring out the beauty and quality of the grain rather than use the once-fashionable high-gloss finish that tended to obscure and change the texture. Textures are important not only for their appearance but also for their sense of touch, and for their effect on light absorption or reflection. Abrasive surfaces or very rough plaster would obviously be unpleasant to the touch and possibly dangerous in an interior, depending upon the use the interior is intended for. Textures can evoke feelings of elegance (such as silks) or informality (such as rough, tweedy materials).

Light, both natural and artificial, is one of the most important design elements, but unless surfaces are appropriate in colour and texture, the control and effect of light will be lost. The beautiful quality of space in a Gothic cathedral is very much related to the handling of light (see Figure 1). The source of daylight, high overhead or filtered through stained glass, creates exciting patterns of light and shade and a variety of intensities and pools of light. This same principle can be used in all interior spaces, and contemporary interiors often have skylights or high windows to provide variety and changing patterns of light. Artificial lighting is equally important, and, again, the same considerations of highlights, good overall illumination, and variety are important.

Concepts of design. The scale and proportion of any interior must always relate to the architecture within which the interior exists, but the other important factor in considering the scale of man's environment is the human body. Throughout the ages, designers and architects have attempted to establish ideal proportions. The most famous of all axioms about proportion was the golden section, established by the ancient Greeks. According to this axiom, a line should be divided into two unequal parts, of which the first is to the second as the second is to the whole. Leonardo da Vinci developed a figure for the ideal man based on man's navel as the centre of a circle enclosing man with outstretched arms. The French architect Le Corbusier developed a theory of proportion called Modulor, also based on a study of human proportions. Yet, at best, these rules are merely guidelines. They can never substitute for the eye and judgment of the designer, and it is reasonable to predict that attempts to make the all-powerful computer a substitute for the designer's sensitivity are also bound to be far from perfect.

The search for ideal proportions

It was stated earlier that the need for a changing scale and spatial relationship in the environment seems a natural one, almost a physiological as well as a psychological one. Perhaps the need for "personal" environment and scale can best be understood by considering some extreme examples. To a person flying at 30,000 feet in an airplane, the scale of anything seen on the ground appears so small that he loses touch with the reality of objects. People who fear heights are rarely bothered by the view out of an airplane because the distance to the objects on the ground has transcended normal perceptions of scale. In a similar manner, a person's reaction to the scale of a small house is quite different from his reaction to a large high-rise building. Details of pattern, texture, and material are accepted and expected in the small structure since they are in a meaningful scale with respect to man. By the same token, the sculptural ornaments on the tops of early skyscrapers seem absurd today.

Almost all principles of design for interiors can be comprehended with clear analytic understanding and common sense, without regard to dogmatic rules. If a beautiful 18th-century breakfront (which might be over eight feet tall) is placed in an apartment with a ceiling height just an inch higher than the piece of furniture, it would obviously look out of scale. If a space is planned so that all the heavy and massive pieces of furniture are pushed toward one end of the room, with nothing on the other side, the room would obviously look out of balance. Yet balance and symmetry applied as inviolate design principles would result in very formal, very traditional, and somewhat dull interiors. Careful symmetry was a generally accepted rule during the Renaissance, and in any classic building one can be sure to find a carefully balanced and symmetrical facade, just as most formal and classic interiors have rigidly balanced plans. It is now recognized that balance can also be based on asymmetry. Both architecture and interior design in the 20th century have consciously broken with the many rules handed down from past eras. It is more important for a building or space to be expressive of its purpose. At one time, it was traditional for a theatre, opera house, or concert hall to embody certain forms and shapes without any real consideration of sight lines, seating distance from the stage, or acoustics. On the other hand, the Berlin Philharmonic Concert Hall (1964) works beautifully as a concert hall and expresses its purpose and function clearly in an exciting and dynamic way (Figure 5).

Departures from the rules in the 20th century.

Balance and symmetry, colour, pattern, and repetition used to be a matter of adherence to a tradition. Until fairly recently, many interiors were painted in dark colours, often ignoring the fact that light reflection was adversely affected and that no real contrast or sparkling accent was achieved. In many contemporary rooms, however, most surfaces are kept in neutral or light colours, possibly with one wall accented in a strong colour or texture. An interior with uniform overhead lighting might be an efficient work space but would lack the character that can be achieved by providing some accent lights in small areas.

The designer's concern for honesty of materials and textures has brought about changing attitudes toward some of the conventional practices of interior decoration, such as the use of strongly patterned wallpapers and flowered prints. Any interior that has too many different patterns, too many textures, and too many repetitive features of any kind will appear overpowering, overly busy, overdesigned, and confusing. A designer often attempts to have a dominant theme or idea, be it colour, form, texture, or some rhythmic pattern. It must be noted also that design is influenced by changing attitudes and fashions. The movements in art and architecture of the 1950s and 1960s have influenced interior design in the direction of an emphasis on pure form, the absence of superfluous decoration, and expressiveness of materials. Recently, however, a kind of countermovement in the field of painting and sculpture has been influential. For instance, the use of large-scale graphic elements (supergraphics) in interiors has become popular and accepted, in spite of the fact that its very idea often consciously denies or destroys the visual clarity of existing architectural design features. Some of the leading designers in the United States and in several European countries have also become very interested in large patterns, rhythmic geometries, and decorative surfaces, and this may point toward a new trend (Figure 6).

Sequential relationships

Most interiors consist of a series of interrelated spaces. It is important that the various spaces be designed in a sequential relationship to each other, not only in terms of planning but also in terms of the visual effect. A successful interior should be cohesive within each area and cohesive as a totality. It must above all relate to the building and to the architectural concept. A good example is the previously mentioned TWA terminal by Eero Saarinen. In spite of the extremely complex sculptural forms used, there is a sequence and clearly balanced rhythm that not only unifies the total composition but clearly relates it to the total architecture.

The best examples of design are those in which no visible difference exists between the interior and the exterior, between the building and its site, and between the many parts or spaces to each other and the total building. An example is the house of the American architect Philip Johnson in New Canaan, Connecticut. Johnson's home and its setting appear effortlessly united, with individual parts subordinated to the success of the whole (Figure 7).

Design relationships. The real and conscious relationship between art, architecture, and design is of long standing. Though mural painting was largely neglected in the mid-20th century, in the past great murals have been the planned focal points of interiors and have in a way determined the architecture (Figure 8). Similarly, sculpture or sculptural forms, as fixed and permanent

Figure 5: Dynamic, asymmetrical architecture creating an unconventional yet functional interior design space: Berlin Philharmonic Concert Hall, designed by Hans Scharoun, 1964.
By courtesy of the Staatsbibliothek Preussischer Kulturbesitz Bildarchiv, Berlin

aspects of buildings, can be the most important design features if planned that way by the architect together with the interior designer and artist. Perhaps the best design is one in which there is no visible difference between architecture and interior and in which even the artwork is incorporated as an integral part of the total (see Figure 14, left).

Jeremiah O. Bragstad

Figure 6: Supergraphic interior emphasizing decorative rather than architectural design: Hear-Hear Record Shop, San Francisco, designed by Daniel Solomon, graphics designed by Barbara Stauffacher, 1969.

The design relationship of interiors to architecture can be clarified by citing an extreme example: the stage set. A set for a theatrical production is a form of interior design but, unlike all other aspects of interior design, it attempts to create its own world and atmosphere concerned only with the play and not at all related to the world or even reality. The creation of a world of make-believe is precisely the function of a stage, but in real life it is impossible to divorce a particular interior from everything else around it. Sometimes a designer may attempt to create a "theatrical" interior, but the point being made strongly and unequivocally here is that every interior must relate to the architecture and to the nearby environment.

Art objects and interior design

Design relationships of individual works of art (paintings, prints, or sculptures) to interiors are most significant in terms of scale and placement, rather than in terms of subject matter, colour, or style. A very old painting, if it is good, will look well within a contemporary interior; a very modern piece of sculpture can be beautiful within an interior furnished with some beautiful traditional pieces. Any work of art, if successful within itself, is "correct" with any interior if properly placed or selected to work with the total space. Certainly there is no need to match colours of paintings to interiors or to select subject matter in works of art that reflect a particular theme, such as food for dining rooms or hunting scenes for the den.

Interiors as they relate to landscape or cityscape are sometimes misunderstood by architects. A crass but typical example is the ubiquitous picture window in suburban housing tracts. Often the only view from the window is the picture window of the neighbouring house. When the view is a beautiful one, it should be possible to plan the interior with the furniture plan and orientation such that seating arrangements can take advantage of the view and yet work for other functions, such as relation to a fireplace or a conversation group, as well.

Graphics in interior design

In many areas of interior design the field of graphics is taking on increasing importance. In every public or institutional building, signs, directories, and room identifications play an important visual part. Good architectural graphics have only been stressed in recent years, as a result of the increasing size and complexity of structures. Buildings such as airports depend upon clear and handsome graphics to make the spaces work and to make them aesthetically cohesive. A related aspect of graphics is the printed matter that is part of certain interior functions. Interior designers must be concerned with the design of menus, wine lists, napkins, and matchbooks in a well-designed restaurant. Designers dealing with stores or

Figure 7: *Interrelation of interior and exterior space.*
Harmony of landscape, architecture, and interior design: Glass House, New Canaan, Connecticut, designed by Philip Johnson, 1949. (Left) Exterior. (Right) Interior.
Russ Kinne—Photo Researchers.

shops are concerned with the graphics of shopping bags, signs, and posters. Often the interior designer is the actual graphic designer, or he works together with the graphic designer, just as the architect works with the interior designer or landscape architect.

Modes of composition. It must be emphasized that there are many different moods, or modes of composition, that are possible in interior design. The recognition of this fact makes it difficult to apply valid critical criteria to these modes, since many of them are intensely personal. What may appear to be picturesque to one person might be ugly or cluttered to another. Each person brings to interior design his own cultural mores and his own prejudices, and in many ways he is psychologically conditioned and influenced to accept certain things and to reject others. In discussing various modes of composition, one must therefore take into consideration the occupants and their backgrounds, the locale and site, and then try to apply the most basic design principles as general guidelines.

SCALA, New York

Figure 8: A simply designed interior space made vivid and compelling by frescoes on the ceiling and walls: Sistine Chapel, Rome, by Michelangelo, 1508–12, 1533–41.

Formal and informal compositions

Formal and informal compositions are relatively easily defined and classified; in fact, this distinction is useful throughout the history of furniture and interiors. Formal styles are usually associated with life at court or furnishings for the palatial homes of nobles or a moneyed elite. The informal periods usually are associated with rural living or the simpler pieces of furniture made by the local craftsmen in rural areas, where they plied their trade with limited tools, using local woods. Formal furniture, as a rule, leads to formal interior compositions. Balance and symmetry certainly tend to lead to formal compositions. Formality is not associated with any particular period. In fact, a very famous contemporary chair, the Barcelona chair by Mies van der Rohe, is an extremely formal and elegant piece. It would seem wrong to use that chair in a casual catercorner room arrangement.

Setting strongly influences the character of a space. By its very definition, a rustic setting would be rural and informal and would seem wrong and incongruous in a formal townhouse or city apartment. Since most business and public interiors are located in urban centres, any attempt to make such interiors look rustic or homey would be an aesthetic paradox. By the same token, it would appear equally incongruous to design a restaurant located in an old mill or barn in New England in a formal and urban character with elegant furnishings, whether they were contemporary or antiques of a formal nature.

Functional compositions

Certain modes of composition are determined by the function of the spaces as much as by the location and by the architecture. For example, a cozy or homey interior is normally associated with residential interiors or similarly intimate interiors, such as restaurants that may wish to appear "cozy." Some interiors, such as discotheques, require excitement and other interiors, such as funeral parlors, require serenity or dignity. One expects certain modes of composition for certain functions, but one's expectations are subject to many external influences, such as personal background, location, psychological associations, and changing fashions. For instance, the typical bank interior until about 1950 was expected to be solid, dignified, awe-inspiring, formal, and above all confidence inspiring. Contemporary design for business and industry has become accepted by all, and the early 1950s saw the logical extension of these firmly established design principles into the area of bank design. One of the first radical departures of traditional design for banking spaces was the Manufacturers Trust Company Manhattan office designed by Skidmore, Owings and Merrill in the early 1950s. It was the first widely published "glass" bank, and it set a trend that has become the new mode of composition for banks.

Fashion or design trends influence one's reactions to many kinds of designs. The term clutter is usually associated with Victorian design of the 19th century. Under the usual definition of the term clutter, one thinks of home interiors with collections of accessories and with an overabundance of knickknacks—the typical Victorian home (Figure 9). In the mid-1960s a new approach to office design, reflecting the "cluttered" approach, was developed. This office appears disorganized at first glance. Actually, the system (called office landscape; see below *Kinds of Interiors: Public Interiors: Space Planning*) is very efficient and for that reason is deemed acceptable, even if the visual impact tends to be chaotic. Traditionally, office and business interiors were pristine, orderly, and very organized, and the idea of a cluttered appearance would have been anathema to designers.

Frank Lerner

Figure 9: A cluttered Victorian interior in the exotic Moorish style, designed by landscape painter Frederick Edwin Church for his home, Olana, at Hudson, New York, 1870–72.

Exotic compositions

The most difficult mode of composition for objective analysis is one that some people call exotic. The chances are that all exotic interiors are highly personal statements and cannot be rationally understood in theoretical design terms (Figure 9). To begin with, what may appear exotic to the average American could be very ordinary or even homey to another culture. Japanese or oriental design in general serves as an example. A Japanese style interior is extremely subtle, serene, and understated, yet to the uninitiated such an interior will appear exotic. Undoubtedly that same phenomenon holds true in reverse. Oriental people have often been impressed with Western-style design and have adopted it presumably because to them it appeared exotic. The increased mobility of the middle classes of many nations today has made foreign travel possible for more and more people, thereby tending to soften some of the very strong regional differences in design. The modes of composition are still discernible nationally or certainly by major geographic and ethnic divisions, but they tend to be less distinct. Many subtle differences exist within the same country, some of which are based on varying socio-economic backgrounds, much in the manner of the traditional difference between formal styles (at court and in homes of nobility) and informal modes of composition for the country people and middle classes. The labels that one applies to these modes of composition are often only descriptive. They must not be confused with objective evaluation of design values. An interior that is by the creator's definition exotic or picturesque may or may not be a well-done exotic design.

Symbolism and style. There are many historic examples of symbolism in design, but often the symbolism is not a conscious statement so much as a more subtle reflection of style. Religious buildings, especially churches, have until recently been consistently traditional expressions of style or symbolism. The church and church architecture flourished during the Middle Ages, and the style of church architecture that became the dominant symbol was the Gothic style. Until the recent past, churches were still designed, as a matter of course, in Gothic style. It is interesting to note that a "Gothic" church designed and built in 1820 can be clearly identified as such, and a "Gothic" church from the year 1920 has the imprint of that year as obviously as the date on its cornerstone. There has been a similar symbolic or stylistic tradition in the design of public or governmental buildings. Both interiors and exteriors of city halls, court buildings, and major government structures were usually in the "classical" style, symbolizing authority, power, and stability, based on our long historic association of these concepts with Greco-Roman antiquity and Renaissance thought.

Symbolism in religious buildings

Another form of symbolism in interior design has been the creation of interiors around specific themes or concepts. Among the earliest examples is the Egyptian tomb. The interior design and decoration depicted the life of the king or special events from his life, and the total interior was intended as a kind of magic to assure the occupant's journey into life after death and guarantee his happiness there. Another example of a symbolic interior created for a specific purpose is the Roman hunting lodge, Piazza Amerina, in Sicily, which has splendid murals and floors depicting animals and hunting. A more recent example of a similarly symbolic interior on the same subject is Theodore Roosevelt's home at Oyster Bay on Long Island, built in 1880. It is full of hunting trophies and mementos symbolizing his personal interests and his personality (Figure 10).

The styles that developed in interiors and in interior furnishings were always symbolic of the social structure of the society that created them. It is easy, for instance, to look at the graceful, feminine lines of a Louis XV chair, delicately curved and luxuriously upholstered, and to see it as a symbolic expression of the superficialities of court life. One can also look at some of the crudely fashioned early American furniture and see in one's mind the life of the settler who fashioned it. Life was harsh, time was precious, and articles of furniture were confined to essentials. The need for economical use of space was symbolized by dual-purpose, functional pieces such as dough boxes that served as tables and tables that turned into chairs and had storage compartments for the family Bible as well.

Symbolism in business offices

As functional and efficiency-oriented as business and office design is today, it is full of unwritten rules relating to symbolism. The design of an office reflects the status of the occupant. Top executives are located in the largest corner offices with the best views of the city and invariably are on the top floors of the corporate headquarters. The size of desks is a symbolic indication of the executive's importance in the hierarchy of the firm. The very top officers may, however, do away with desks altogether and have offices resembling living rooms—to symbolize

Figure 10: An interior shaped by objects symbolizing Theodore Roosevelt's personal interests and personality, North Room, Sagamore Hill, Oyster Bay, Long Island, 1880.
By courtesy of United Airlines, Inc.

the fact that they are beyond routine paperwork and above the need for standard office furnishings. The fashions (or styles) of design vary and develop even within a brief period of ten or 20 years. Thus, another symbol—carpeting—has become somewhat outdated. Until recently, top executives expected wall-to-wall carpeting in their offices. Today such offices may have wood or other natural floors, perhaps with beautiful area rugs. The very idea of a private office is, of course, the most important symbol in a status-conscious business community (Figure 11). Designers have found, however, that the need for communication between executive and staff, including visual contact, often makes private offices less than efficient.

Symbolism in residential interior design occurs on many levels but again tends to be influenced by changing styles.

By courtesy of Dallek Inc., Design Group

Figure 11: Executive office resembling a residential interior: Faberge Corporation Headquarters, New York City, designed by Dallek Inc., Design Group, 1968.

When television first became available, the home screen became a symbol of prosperity and at the same time became the focal point of residential interiors. By the 1970s a television set had become a standard possession and was no longer a compositional emphasis; in fact, it was often concealed or casually incorporated into the total design.

A homeowner is likely to be very conscious of the image his house or apartment conveys. Traditional furniture, for instance, is still associated with elegance in the minds of many laymen, a situation that can lead to the acquisition of poor reproductions or meaningless imitations of nonexistent styles. To most people a real fire in a fireplace is a delightful physical and visual experience that often has nostalgic associations. Since they are no longer needed to heat houses, fireplaces in the 20th century increasingly have become a luxury and thereby a symbol of substance to many people. These circumstances have often resulted in imitation fireplaces of the worst possible design, with simulated fires.

Contemporary symbolism

From the designer's point of view, design symbolism in public spaces is valid at times but can and should be used in contemporary terms rather than as stylistic imitation of past eras. An example of the success of such design can be seen in the new Boston City Hall, built in 1968, which symbolizes government, authority, and dignity in totally original and contemporary terms. There is little valid reason to consciously introduce symbolism into residential interiors, unless it is the kind of cultural symbolism exemplified in Japanese interiors, such as that of the Zen tea house (*cha-shitsu*), where certain design features reflect a way of life and have ceremonial meanings.

PHYSICAL COMPONENTS OF DESIGN

Architectural components. The foregoing section on aesthetic components stressed the fact that, in design, the whole or total effect is more important than the specific device or element used. The same is true of architectural components, and this should be kept in mind in the following discussion.

Ceilings. Although ceilings are in most interiors the largest unbroken surface, they are often ignored by amateur designers and even by professional designers. The result, especially in public and office interiors, is frequently a mass of unrelated lighting devices, air conditioning outlets, and the like. Ceilings were emphasized in the Baroque and 18th-century traditions: beautiful interiors of these periods had highly ornate, decorated ceilings, with painted surfaces or with intricate plaster details and traceries (Figure 12, left).

Value of the plain white ceiling

Few modern designers take advantage of the design possibilities offered by ceilings. One such possibility is the creation of textural effects with wood. Of course, one must respect the effect of a simple plaster ceiling in an otherwise well-designed interior; often the white plaster ceiling is needed to reflect light and to provide a calm cohesiveness to the space (Figure 12, right). Since most modern ceilings are low, a heavy texture or a strong colour could create a depressing feeling; hence, the popularity of a plain white ceiling. It is important for a plain ceiling to be just that: a surface without blemishes, without bumps, and without small unrelated areas of different height.

In contemporary public buildings there is frequently a "hung" ceiling below interior concrete structural slabs. The space between the slab and the "hung" ceiling is needed for mechanical equipment as well as to allow for the recessing of the lighting system.

An earlier section of this article discussed the variation of heights in relation to scale and space. It is important to keep such varying ceiling heights related to the plan of the room if such a device is to succeed. A lowered ceiling in a dining area, for instance, can be pleasant and intimate, but a lowered ceiling covering only part of the area can be most distracting.

Floors. Basically, there are two kinds of floors for interiors: those that are an integral part of the structure and those that are applied after the structure is completed. Interior designers working together with archi-

Figure 12: *Ceiling design.*
(Left) Highly ornate Rococo ceiling, Pilgrimage Church *Wies*, Upper Bavaria (Germany), designed by Dominkus Zimmerman, 1745. (Top) Simple, white plaster ceiling, Christ Lutheran Church, Minneapolis, Minnesota, designed by Eliel and Eero Saarinen, 1950.
(Left) Toni Schneiders, (right) Balthazar Korab

tects have the opportunity to specify flooring such as slate, terrazzo, stone, brick, concrete, or wood, but in most interiors the flooring is designed at a later stage and is often changed in the course of a building's life. Sometimes it is possible to introduce a heavy floor, such as terrazzo or stone, in a finished building or during remodelling, but these materials, beautiful as they are, tend to be too costly as surface applications.

Resilient flooring materials

Man-made, or synthetic, floor coverings are usually classified as resilient floors. The oldest of this type is linoleum. The resilient flooring materials marketed in the 1970s include asphalt, vinyl asbestos, linoleum, cork, and vinyl. Cork, which is not a synthetic, is handsome but not very durable. Basically, resilient floor tiles are excellent materials that are economical and easily maintained. They can be given almost any appearance, which is a temptation that manufacturers are unable to resist. When the tiles are plain, in good colours or textures, they are very attractive and appropriate, but when they are made to imitate stone, brick, mosaic, or other materials, the results are disastrous. Pure vinyls are the most expensive of the resilient floorings and have been the most tortured in terms of "design." The vinyls are the softest and most resilient of the tiles and are very easy to maintain. Asphalt tile is the least expensive and most widely used resilient flooring; it is quite brittle and hard underfoot. Vinyl asbestos is somewhat softer underfoot and, being grease resistant, is easier to maintain than asphalt but higher in cost. Linoleum, which ranges in cost between the asphalt and pure vinyl floorings, is strong and suitable for heavy-duty uses.

Ceramic tiles and quarry (unglazed) tiles are made not only for such areas as bathrooms but, particularly in the case of quarry tiles, are suitable for almost any space. Installation usually requires a cement bed over the existing subfloor, making this material difficult to use in existing buildings. Like other natural materials, quarry-tile floors possess a natural beauty and have the additional advantage of easy maintenance.

Wood floors still account for a very large percentage of all floors, especially in residences. In addition to the strip oak floors, the standard for many apartment houses or homes, many beautiful prefabricated parquet patterns are available in a variety of woods and in many shapes and sizes. These wood tiles can be installed, just like the resilient floor tiles, over existing floors. Wood floors have great warmth and beauty but have the disadvantage of needing more care than do some of the synthetic tiles or quarry tiles.

Walls. Every wall is a material in itself and ideally no material, if properly used, need be covered up. Some elegant buildings since 1960 use concrete in its natural texture—*i.e.*, showing the formwork left by wooden forms as a conscious expression of the material. During the 19th century, fakery in design was very popular, and part of the concern with the true expression of materials today is a revolt against the earlier tradition. In the 20th century, for instance, brick walls are considered very beautiful and desirable, yet many old townhouses have layers of plaster and paint or wallpaper on top of attractive brickwork.

It is not unusual for a decorative detail or device to survive long after the valid reason for it has disappeared. Wall panelling has been popular for hundreds of years, and, indeed, a natural wood texture adds warmth and elegance. The only way the craftsmen of earlier periods were able to apply wood panelling was in frames (stiles and rails) or wainscotting, since wood panelling was made of solid wood and had to be broken up into narrow dimensions in order to prevent warping and shrinking. Out of that need developed beautiful details of moldings, carved details, and carefully proportioned panelling. A similar art developed somewhat later in plaster. Obviously, 20th-century building costs and methods rarely permit real quality in elaborate panelling or highly ornate plasterwork (Figure 13), nor would this sort of imitative design be appropriate in a modern building. But wood panelling and plywoods in many beautiful veneers are readily available and provide a vast range of beautiful, if expensive, wall surfacing for important spaces. Prescored, pre-finished inexpensive plywoods, on the other hand, are often used as finishing materials for basement rooms in American homes.

Walls of wood veneer

The use of fake moldings, with printed moldings or panelling or with any of the countless imitation wall-surfacing materials from brick wallpaper to artistically poor wall murals, is the kind of decoration that a good designer avoids. Even so, not every interior should be a

Figure 13: Ornate plasterwork to decorate wall and ceiling: dining room from Kirtlington Park, Oxfordshire, designed by Thomas Roberts, completed 1748. In the Metropolitan Museum of Art, New York City.
By courtesy of the Metropolitan Museum of Art, New York, Fletcher Fund, 1931

plain space with nothing but the natural walls. Highly decorative wallpapers have long been available in bold and exciting patterns. Often in 20th-century design a strong paper is employed on one wall only, instead of having the whole space surrounded by a dominant pattern. Many wallpapers, such as grasscloth and shiki silk papers from the Far East, have natural textures. For public spaces and for any space requiring easy maintenance and special cleanliness, a number of wallpapers have been developed that are completely washable and sanitary. Most of these are vinyl-coated fabrics, and some of them are extremely strong and durable and are particularly suited for such spaces as hospital or hotel corridors. Because these vinyl-coated wall fabrics are usually specified by designers and architects, the level of design is far superior to those made for the home.

There are many wall-surfacing materials using fabrics laminated to paper. These coverings provide warmth and texture, as well as acoustic properties. Fabrics in general have been used widely as wall-coverings in the past and continue to be popular.

A designer's imagination and the client's budget are the only limitation on the materials that may be used for wall surfacing. Some, such as ceramic or mosaic tiles, are extremely practical; some, such as cork, have excellent acoustical characteristics. For functional or for aesthetic reasons the designer may elect to use such materials as leather, metals, plastic laminates, or glass. No wall in itself should be designed or selected without relation to the total scheme.

Windows and doors. Windows and doors in contemporary design are not placed as decorative elements or as parts of symmetrical compositions but are primarily considered as functional elements and are expressed as such. If windows are carefully designed and placed for light, for ventilation, for air, and for view, decorative treatment is often unnecessary and a simple device such as a shade or shutter will suffice to control light and privacy. Most buildings, however, need window treatments, since no particular care in the placement of fenestration was taken by the builders.

The most frequently used devices are curtains and draperies. Although semantically there is no clear distinction between the two, drapery implies more elaborate treatments with lining, overdrapes, valances, and tassels. A curtain, on the other hand, is lighter, more direct, less theatrical, and more functional. Frequently, a light material is chosen to provide privacy or light control with minimum emphasis. Curtains, however, offer only partial control over light, glare, and privacy; complete control or privacy often requires shades, blinds, or shutters. Window shades without overly ornate borders and tassels are a perfectly good device for those controls, and Venetian blinds are also a most acceptable treatment.

Curtain characteristics

Since the 1960s designers have tried to simplify window treatments, and, if curtains, shades, or blinds were not deemed appropriate for functional or aesthetic reasons, devices such as chains or beads on windows or very simple sliding panels were found to be more effective than more elaborate treatments.

The essential considerations for windows must be based on the functional needs and on the overall aesthetic intent. If a space is well designed in architectural terms and presents a cohesive image, it rarely makes sense to feature a window or door. Poorly detailed windows in office buildings or apartment houses are often overcome or played down by using a simple curtain material covering a complete window wall. The wall-to-wall and floor-to-ceiling treatment of a window wall is frequently the only way to screen out unattractive details.

Planning for doors

Doors must be carefully planned, relating the swing and location to the functional needs, and their heights, colour, material, or textures to the adjoining wall surfaces or design elements in the space. Most doors used in the 20th century are "flush" doors—that is, they have unbroken surfaces made of wood or metal; even where glass is used the attempt is usually made to have maximum glass area unbroken by frames and moldings. Sometimes the entrance doors to important spaces are designed or decorated as compositional focal points, but usually the emphasis is on excellence in detailing and hardware rather than on decorative surface designs.

Other components. The detailing referred to in connection with the handling of doors is one of the most important factors in interior design. Every architectural component must be detailed well. Poor details make for poor design. The meaning of detailing in a design sense is more than the graphic explanation of certain components on a drawing. It means the way materials are put together, the way one part is fastened to another, the way parts and materials are expressed and articulated. Stairs or ramps are architectural components of great importance, whether in stores, in public buildings, or in homes. Since these structural features represent large vertical forms in space, they often become the dominant design feature in an interior space (Figure 14). Stairs in hotel lobbies, for example, are usually in very prominent locations. The actual stair design, however, is surprisingly restrictive and set. The height of riser and its relation to the tread is fixed, and variations for normal vertical circulation are extremely limited. Matters of detail involve such considerations as whether the stair is open or enclosed, whether it is a bold sculptural form or an airy dynamic shape (resulting from the use of open treads without risers), whether the stair honestly expresses its material (be it wood, steel, or marble), or is wrapped in carpeting. The many detailing possibilities present a real challenge to designers and, unlike mass-produced windows, light switches, or plumbing fixtures, give designers a chance to design in a completely personal or creative way.

Components such as heating units, electric outlets, and telephone connections offer no design choice other than limited selection among mass-produced products and the best placement within the space. The pattern created by placement of fixtures is as important with walls or any

Figure 14: A ramp functioning as the focal element of an interior: the former V.C. Morris Shop, San Francisco, designed by Frank Lloyd Wright, 1948.
Maynard L. Parker

Placement of utility fixtures

other surfaces as it is for ceilings. A given wall may have doors, windows, electric outlets, switches, air-conditioning registers, and heating units (radiators or convectors). It is the designer's job to deal with all of these components by design, by organization, by placement or elimination, and by detailing. Often, the more bulky components, such as radiators, are "eliminated" by building the unit into the wall or, in existing, poorly detailed buildings, by creating a "built-in" appearance through some design feature. Radiators or convectors are often housed in neatly detailed enclosures that may run the whole length of a window wall and may at the same time provide an additional surface under the windowsill. Depending on the location, a continuous enclosure may contain some shelving or storage elements making use of the extra space not needed for the actual heating unit (or air-conditioning unit).

In large, nonresidential interiors, the mechanical components are often massive. For instance, the telephone installation needed in an office for several hundred people requires a very large space and a complex installation of conduits and other elements that affect the interior design. The air-conditioning or heating unit for a simple store may be fairly bulky, and again the designer deals with the allocation of space as well as with the mechanical function of the equipment. All of the mechanical equipment for buildings is specified or engineered by specialists, but it is essential that an interior designer have the basic knowledge and understanding to be able to coordinate the various specialties. The many pipes, stacks, and vents that go into a plumbing system, although not exposed and shown as a rule, are of real concern to the designer. Whether architectural components are expressed and detailed, whether they are concealed or built-in, they are incorporated in the design.

Furniture and accessories. To the layman, furniture is the most important aspect of interior design. It is a significant component of design to the professional as well, since it is the most personal and intimate product relating man to a building. It is also personal because it can be moved from one home to the next and handed on from generation to generation, and often furniture takes on important sentimental value. Accessories are even more personal, but they are less significant to the overall effect of the interior, since they are by nature smaller than furniture. Almost anything that people own or collect could be called an "accessory," including functional objects, such as ashtrays, and decorative objects, such as porcelain, glass, or ceramics.

Personal nature of furniture

Although some quite sophisticated furniture existed in ancient Egypt, the use of furniture was rare during the Middle Ages and only became significant during the Renaissance. During most subsequent periods there have usually been close interrelations between architectural and furniture styles and modes of interior design. (That aspect of furniture will be discussed below under *Historical and stylistic developments of interior design.*) The 20th-century pioneers of design and architecture—such as Mies van der Rohe, Le Corbusier, and Marcel Breuer—were not able to find any suitable contemporary furniture available in the 1920s and 1930s when they built structures without historical references. They designed much of their own furniture, and some of these modern "classics" are still very much in demand. Well-designed modern furniture developed in Scandinavian countries in the 20th century out of the long tradition of craftsmanship and design prevalent in those countries. The real beginning of modern furniture in the United States came only after World War II, and much of it was first developed for nonresidential uses. Charles Eames, George Nelson, and Florence Knoll are among the distinguished American designers who have pioneered furniture design and manufacturing processes. Their furniture primarily was introduced to the public through use in public or work spaces. A large segment of furniture manufacturers has still not been touched by design of any kind, and furniture under such invented names as "Mediterranean" or "Italian Provincial" (both nonexistent historic styles) is still being foisted upon the public.

Whatever material or manufacturing process may be used, the important criteria that must be applied in furniture are function, comfort, and durability, together with aesthetic considerations. Architects and interior designers often prefer to build in furniture wherever possible, and, indeed, some of the best historic and contemporary interiors contain little movable furniture. An interior without any furniture or accessories would probably appear stark and uninviting, and it is clear that the personal touches possible through selection of appropriate furniture and accessories are very important.

Use of built-in furniture

One can use a vast array of decorative objects or plants as accessories. In a way, every accessory used in a home, office, or public space is in some way a part of the total composition, and must therefore be selected with care. No rules exist on what is "proper" other than the basic principles of design that were discussed earlier.

Lighting. Light is one of the key elements of interior design. Most 20th-century interior spaces are used as much with artificial light as with daylight, and lighting has become a very significant tool for the interior designer. There are three major aspects to lighting: function, aesthetics, and health. The latter factor is often ignored, but insufficient illumination can cause eyestrain and physical discomfort. Illuminating engineers have established recommended standards of illumination for various tasks and have also provided rules and standards relating to brightness of the source of lighting and controls for shielding the eye from direct glare. Light can be diffused and can, in general, be controlled very accurately.

Types of lighting

Two basic types of lighting are used in modern interiors: incandescent and fluorescent. The former is somewhat redder than daylight but contains all colours of the spectrum. Since fluorescent light has an uneven spectrum, colours tend to appear distorted. A mixture of the two is often the best way to achieve colour accuracy. Some of today's fluorescent lamps are close to daylight accuracy, and manufacturers continue to improve the quality of available lamps. Both types of light can be used in "direct" or "indirect" lighting in interiors or in a combination of these methods known as semidirect or semi-indirect (Figure 15).

Designers and architects strive to build in lighting as much as possible. Recessed lighting, lighting coves, and architectural lighting in general can be controlled much more efficiently than portable lamps.

Figure 15: Fluorescent, incandescent, and neon light used to create a particular atmosphere or mood: Ocean Tank, New England Aquarium, Boston, architects and designers, Cambridge Seven Associates, Inc., 1967. The dim light of the aquarium is immediately evocative of the dark, mysterious underwater world.
By courtesy of the Cambridge Seven Associates, Inc.; photograph, Norman McGrath

A good lighting scheme must provide some variety in highlights, shadows, and accent lights to avoid monotony. An even, overall lighting system, such as a luminous ceiling, can be highly efficient, but it lacks character and interest. Most interiors require a certain flexibility for different functions within the space at different times of day and night. In certain interiors, such as stores and shops, lighting becomes a display and sales tool, and in festive spaces, such as ballrooms or theatres, the quality of light can provide sparkle and mood more effectively than any other component of design. One can think of the potential of lighting in terms of the theatre. Some productions are staged without formal sets, yet the changing mood and setting can be suggested by controlled illumination.

Design in portable lamps

Most intimate interiors depend to some extent on portable or fixed (ceiling and wall-mounted) lamps. The design of lamps, especially table lamps for homes, has somehow brought forth a vast array of bad designs, together with a smaller number of good ones. Many lampshades are similarly banal in design, but a shade as such is an excellent diffusor of light and shield against glare. Some lamps and shades are designed for specific tasks, others for accent lighting.

Fabrics. There are three basic aspects that determine appearance and suitability of fabrics for interior use: fibre content, weave, and pattern. Fibres are either natural or man-made. The important natural fibres are cotton, wool, linen, and silk. Although silk has long been considered the most elegant and desirable of all natural fibres, it does not stand up well under direct sunlight and heat and, in general, requires more care than most other fibres. Wool, like silk, is an animal fibre; depending upon its weave, it can be made into extremely strong and beautiful fabrics and is therefore very much in demand for contemporary interiors. Both cotton and linen are made from vegetable fibres and are both durable and pliable. Unless cotton and linen are interwoven with other fibres, however, they are not generally as strong as wools or man-made fibres and tend to be restricted to light-duty interior purposes.

Families of man-made fibres

Man-made (synthetic) fibres in the 20th century abound under a variety of trade names, and new synthetics are continuously being developed. Some of the major families of synthetic fibres are glass fibres, acetate, acrylic and modacrylic, nylon, olefin, polyester, rayon, and saran. The chemical composition and processes used in the manufacture of man-made fibres make possible a variety of specific qualities. Some offer strength and elasticity; some offer resistance to fire, stain, mildew, sun, or abrasion; and some offer resistance to moisture and organic agents, others to crushing and wrinkling.

Many fabrics are woven in a combination of two or more fibres in an attempt to improve the appearance or utility or both. Another factor in selecting or specifying fabrics is the touch of the fabric, or the "hand." Certain fabrics made from man-made fibres seem unpleasant to the touch compared to silk or wool fabrics.

Weaving is an ancient art, and fundamentally there is little difference between the very early handlooms and the power looms found in major textile plants today. The three most common weaves in use are plain weaves, which include basket weaves; floating weaves, which include twill and satin weaves; and pile weaves, which include both cut and uncut weaves. Weaving techniques of lesser importance to interior design include knitting, twisting, forming, and felting.

The pattern of textiles, especially in contemporary terms, is frequently the natural pattern created by the weave of the fabric, although patterns are also created by printing. In traditional textile terms, reference to pattern usually meant a historic style. The history of textiles ranges from early Egyptian and Oriental patterns to the present. Each era has developed fashionable and popular patterns. Contemporary textile designs, for instance, are usually abstract or geometric, but floral and large flowing patterns were also popular in the 20th century.

Colour in fabrics

Colour is one of the most important aspects of fabrics in interior design, inasmuch as the colours of fabrics are frequently the most important areas of colour in interiors. Dye colours can be added to unspun fibres, spun yarns, or woven textiles. Colour fastness is a major concern to interior designers, for faded fabrics can be quite detrimental to an interior.

Natural elements. No man-made object can equal the beauty found in nature, and it is not surprising that the introduction of natural elements into interiors has always been considered desirable. In spite of their beauty, one cannot arbitrarily introduce a plant, a tree, or rocks, or water into an interior. The foremost considerations must be the location of the space, its climate, and its relationship to the outdoors.

Climatic considerations determine the kind of plant, flower, or tree that can prosper in an interior. The most beautiful plant will not survive long under adverse conditions, and a dying tree or plant certainly offers no decorative advantage.

The location and orientation of interior to exterior spaces is another important consideration in the introduction of natural elements. In warmer climates, it is possible to have a gradual transition between interior and exterior, and plants providing this natural transition will look well and will prosper. In colder climates a real barrier of glass or a solid wall separates the indoors from outdoors, and at best the transition can be made visually.

There are a number of simple devices that make it possible to keep delicate plants and flowers alive under controlled conditions. Greenhouses in all sizes, ranging from window size to room size can be the most delightful areas of an interior, but obviously special conditions and maintenance must be provided. The scale of plants or small trees must be considered. One large indoor tree can be a beautiful accent in even a small space. Too many trees or plants in a small space would be overpowering, unless indeed the space is designed primarily as a greenhouse space or plant room.

Natural elements other than plants and flowers that can be used in interiors are water, rocks, stones, or pebbles, and planting areas in natural soil. For large spaces, usually public buildings, pools or contained areas of water can be extremely beautiful and exciting. Some interior features have been created with running water and small recirculated waterfalls. Sometimes a small area of pebbles with a few plants or carefully chosen rocks can add a touch of real beauty to an interior. Even collections of rocks, minerals, seashells, and other natural elements provide the touch of nature that can make an interior come alive.

PROCEDURE

Professional interior-design assignments may range from the design of a small apartment to extremely large and complex jobs such as the planning and design of all of the floors in an office building or the design of all the spaces in a hotel or resort. The procedures vary somewhat from one job to the next and depend upon the size of the design organization, but the following basic outline covers the usual procedures followed by professional designers.

Interview with the client

Preliminary phases. The first step is the interview with the client. This is often a series of conversations and must eventually lead to a mutual agreement. Clients usually have a good idea of their needs and preferences, yet an experienced designer frequently sees some needs not envisioned by the client, and often he must re-educate the client's attitude about preferences. Obviously, the interview must also convince the client that the designer is the right one for his needs. Most established professionals do not commence any design work nor engage in prolonged meetings and conversations without a retainer for their services. Depending upon the scope and complexity of the job, agreements between clients and interior designers range from simple letters written by the designers to lengthy legal documents, covering precisely the services to be rendered, as well as the procedures and responsibilities. The designer makes a survey, including an analysis of the client's present program, and he often prepares a new program. Frequently, for instance, a designer upon surveying existing facilities finds that the redesign of these facilities would be more suitable to the client's needs and more economical than the leasing of a new space or the adding of additional space. More often the situation is reversed: the client does not realize that investing in a major renovation of his space does not permit room for future change or expansion, and upon the design firm's advice new premises are obtained or built. Sometimes there is a question of whether a particular interior of some value or meaning should be restored or reconstructed, and again the experience of the interior designer is needed for those decisions.

When the job involves redesigning existing spaces, at a very early stage the interior designer will require very accurate plans of existing conditions. In many older buildings, there are no up-to-date plans, and the design firm must take exact field measurements in order to obtain plans and elevations for the existing spaces. These plans must also reveal whether walls are bearing (supporting) or whether they can be demolished. The electrical and mechanical system must be carefully evaluated, sometimes by engineers.

The need for up-to-date plans

For large jobs pre-architectural planning and programming can consume many months or even years. Major corporations contemplating major building projects need precise programs, analyses of existing facilities and equipment, and a number of alternate schemes and proposals. Based upon the functions performed by the various departments of a corporation and the interrelation of these departments to each other, designers actually prepare a schematic building shape (such as a high-rise building or a series of smaller structures), including a basic system for offices or other functions.

The final program outline is eventually presented to the client for approval prior to any actual design work. The budget obviously is a paramount consideration. Together with the program analysis, designers must frequently prepare an approximate budget or attempt to make their proposals based upon a budget set by the client.

Among the additional factors that must be considered are availability of materials and furnishings, maintenance of the interior, and the character or appropriateness of the planned scheme. Business interiors often represent large investments for the clients, and a delay of several weeks in the completion of a job, due to the non-availability of products or furnishings, could represent a sizable loss. In public interiors, such as hotels, stores, or educational institutions, the maintenance factors must be carefully analyzed. On a smaller scale, residential interiors must be considered with similar care. Maintenance factors for the floors of kitchens or children's rooms are important.

Maintenance factors

Design and presentation. After the completion of a program and the acceptance of the program by the clients, the actual design work can begin. Designers usually work on many alternative schemes. A single space such as a restaurant or a carefully designed store takes many days of preliminary design studies. As the size of the job increases, the interrelation of individual spaces increases the complexity of these studies, and it is quite likely that the designer will need a rough study model in order to visualize the spaces three dimensionally. Drawing and drafting at that stage is the designer's way of visualizing his own ideas and at the same time putting them in such a form that they can be communicated to his associates for discussion and eventually communicated to his clients. All the aesthetic components come into play at that stage of design, including colours, lighting, and textures, although at the early design stages no precise selection of materials or objects is made. Obviously, this creative phase of interior design is based on thorough research and critical analysis and is not simply the result of a sudden flash of inspiration.

The preliminary presentation

Once the designer or the team of designers feels that a scheme has been arrived at within the stated objectives, a preliminary presentation will be prepared. Although a competent designer will try a number of possible schemes for every job, he will, as a rule, decide which of the many ideas he explored in rough form is the most successful and that will be prepared for a preliminary presentation. For important commissions, such a presentation might consist of a number of sheets or presentation boards showing plans, elevations, sketches, and renderings, and, in many cases, models as well. Most clients are not trained to visualize space from plans and elevations, and perspective sketches and renderings are necessary to fully explain a scheme. At the preliminary presentation the specific colours, furnishings, and details are not resolved yet, since the aim at that stage is to obtain the basic approval from the client.

Final drawings and specifications. If a preliminary presentation has been completely accepted, the designers can proceed to the final design stages. If changes have to be made, another meeting (or meetings) with changed presentations may be necessary.

The next stages of the design may consist of a series of drawings done by professional draftsmen or by the interior designer himself, if he works as an individual. Depending on the type of job, final drawings may consist of just a few sheets or a very large number of drawings. Plans, elevations, details, sections, and specifications are the language of architectural and design offices, and they are prepared with carefully drawn dimensions and notes for the many contractors who carry out the actual construction. Certain drawings may be done by subcontractors or related trades; for instance, the air-conditioning system is usually designed by air-conditioning engineers, and the duct work must be designed in connection with the lighting system in order to assure that lighting fixtures do not conflict with ducts. Similarly, mechanical equipment—such as heating or plumbing pipes, telephone cables, and electrical lines—must be coordinated to avoid conflicts and problems. Before outside firms or subcontractors become involved, the designer or design firm usually prepares the design drawings with sufficient information to enable various contractors to submit bids. Almost all major jobs are sent out for bid to several contractors, in order to provide the client or the designer as his agent with a series of competitive estimates.

Preparation of final drawings

On complex and costly design commissions a final and elaborate presentation may be prepared after the acceptance of the preliminary presentation. This might include very carefully drawn perspective renderings in colour. Many presentations include scale models and may consist of nothing but carefully crafted models.

Together with the preparation of final drawings, interior designers begin the process of final selection and specification of all furnishings. The process of selecting and ordering fabrics, furniture, lighting, and all other furnishings requires a thorough knowledge of available products. In large cities there are often hundreds of sources, but, in spite of the vast product choice available, it is not always possible to find just the right fabric or just the right piece of furniture. In such cases interior designers may have to design special furniture, floor coverings, lighting fixtures, or fabrics. Most interior designers are familiar with quality products and maintain within their offices samples and catalogs of furnishings that they consider of merit. The products that have been selected by the designer are usually submitted to the client either as part of the original design presentation or in a separate approval step. Methods of placing purchase orders vary. Many design firms and individual designers prefer to limit their activity to selection and specification and arrange to have the client's purchasing office place the orders. In other cases the designer places the purchase orders but then submits the invoices to the client for direct payment. In either case ordering and specifying is an exacting task. Delivery and availability is an important concern that the interior designer is responsible for. If a hotel is scheduled for opening at a specified date, it may be necessary to place orders for furniture and furnishings as early as two years before completion date in order to assure delivery on time.

Selection and specification of furnishings

Construction. The actual building of the interior, be it a renovation or a new construction, needs considerable supervision by the designer, although constant on-site supervision is not always required. For an office or residence, a few visits may be sufficient. The thoroughness of working drawings and details influences the degree of supervision that is needed: the more complete the drawings and specifications for a particular job, the less time must be spent on the site during the building stage.

Building supervision

In spite of the fact that the workers are usually highly skilled craftsmen, there are questions that can only be answered on the site, and there are always unforeseen problems that require changes or on-the-spot decisions. Many interior designers have considerable understanding of construction and building technology, can communicate with tradesmen intelligently, and are able to offer valuable advice and suggestions. The situation can also be reversed. Many construction workers are very skilled and knowledgeable and are able to offer suggestions that designers are happy to accept. The supervision must proceed through all stages of a job. Knowledgeable designers spare no effort to see that every phase of the job is done in the best possible way.

As with other furnishings, interior designers select, commission, or purchase artwork, plants, and accessories. In residential interior design, clients usually own many of these things or will certainly be involved in the selection and purchasing, but in interior design for commercial or public spaces this responsibility is in the hands of the designer.

From the foregoing discussion, it will be clear that the design of large interior jobs involves many detailed considerations from the inception to the completion. For this reason most large design firms dealing with hotels, governmental or institutional clients, or large business firms have developed work sheets and checklists for all aspects of the work. Each phase of a job is usually under the supervision of a job captain or chief designer, and each checklist or form is controlled and checked repeatedly in order to assure that everything has been considered and that the job is moving smoothly to completion.

Work-sheets and checklists

KINDS OF INTERIORS

Although the foregoing sections have mentioned different kinds of interiors, in reference to both aesthetic and physical components of design, there has been no specific discussion of different design considerations for varying interiors. The aesthetic criteria suggested in earlier sections are subject to considerable variation, depending on the kind of interior involved.

Residential interiors. Residential interiors are obviously much freer and much more personal for both the interior designer and the occupants than other types of interiors. In fact, homes that have been designed unconsciously by creative occupants without any standard decorative rules are often the most beautiful ones. Certain planning and functional considerations are constant in any residence, and, although these too may be ignored by the occupant who wishes to be strongly individualistic, they can provide at least basic guidelines.

The planning of modern houses or apartments must take into consideration the location of certain needs in relation to others. The dining space should be near the food-preparation area, and the food-preparation area should be accessible to the entrance used to bring in food supplies and remove waste. Access to children's sleeping areas should not be through the adults' living spaces. Access to bathrooms should be close to the bedroom areas and should not be through living or dining spaces.

Relation of one space to another

The furniture arrangement for a living space must take into account the occupant's life-style and preferences. If a space is planned for young people, no seating might be provided other than the floor, but, for the more conservative or older occupants, comfortable seating for conversation and other activities is essential. Open-plan houses (living, dining, eating facilities without separate rooms) work splendidly and beautifully for some people but might not be the ideal answer for a family with many children and a desire for privacy at the same time. The special storage needs that must be considered for many homes vary from bookshelves to storage areas for bicycles, from facilities for recorded music to storage of sporting equipment. Such facilities can often be added by interior designers, if not provided by the architect.

There are several types of residence, and each one may require a different approach, partially based on economic considerations. The private house owned by the occupant warrants not only built-in designs and other permanent design features (lighting, flooring, etc.) but, in general, lends itself naturally to anything within the imagination of the designer and the budget of the owner. Cooperative apartments are prevalent in larger cities, and those that are bought outright by the owners can be designed and changed as long as the structure of the building is not tampered with. A different approach is usually called for in rented apartments or houses. Major changes and special furniture and other built-in features would be considered a poor investment by the client and would, as a rule, be frowned upon by the landlords.

In the past, professional help for residences has been basically reserved for wealthy clients. The residences involved were often status symbols, and the furnishings were to a large extent traditional furnishings and antiques. The best of such ornately designed homes are authentic, museum-like interiors, which indeed only the very affluent can afford. (Most status-conscious interiors, however, consist of reproductions and imitations and have little to do with good design.)

Residences as status symbols

Today, instead of being limited to the service of the wealthy, the designer has a widening and important opportunity in a totally different aspect of residential interiors: mass housing and low-income housing. Although only in recent years have some designers involved themselves in this area, with an increasing concern on the part of both government and private enterprise for the effect of environment, the field should offer a growing opportunity for challenging creative work. Such designers, as well as helping to create more liveable spaces for those with limited housing budgets, can also be of great help in assisting occupants to choose simple, sturdy, attractive, and functional furnishings. A major problem for many people, on a variety of income levels, is the high cost of furnishings; mistakes in judgment are too costly to be discarded and thus must be endured. The help of professionals can minimize this problem and also protect low-income families from being induced to buy installment-plan furnishings of poor quality and design.

Public interiors. *Space planning.* Although many designers are engaged in residential interior design, there has been a marked shift away from that field since 1950, and more designers than ever work in the design of public, institutional, and commercial spaces. Space planning for business firms, governmental agencies, and institutions is a significant aspect of office design and is concerned primarily with planning, allocation of spaces, and interrelations between offices, departments, and individuals. The aesthetic or design phase varies with the degree of importance attached to offices by the clients. In a large firm, the clerical, accounting, or filing areas tend to be well designed in terms of lighting, efficiency, space, and function but have few frills or design features. The executive offices, reception areas, and conference rooms, on the other hand, are frequently elaborately and luxuriously designed, since they serve as images for the corporations as well as status symbols for their occupants. Decisions relating to size of offices and their furnishings are basically arrived at through functional considerations. An executive frequently must seat groups of people in his office. A department manager or clerk will rarely need more than one or two extra chairs.

Pre-architectural planning has taken on such importance that many design firms provide this service. Through careful study and analysis, standards of typical offices, relationships of offices and departments to each other, the need for flexibility and storage, and many other aspects of work within a given business can be arrived at, and such a study then becomes the program for the actual design of a new building or premises. When truly large firms or governmental agencies are involved, space studies preceding the actual design may take several months or even years.

Office landscape

A rather recent innovation in office design is known as office landscape (from the German word *Bürolandschaft*). Above, in *Modes of composition*, it was noted that the appearance of a "landscaped" space might seem chaotic. Actually, however, the system was developed in the 1960s by a German team of planning and management consultants who made intelligent use of computer technology to arrive at predictable relationships between persons and departments in a given organizational structure. Office landscape also takes into consideration the high cost of building and the continuous need for change in large corporations. The solution offered by these planners was not to build the traditional permanent walls and private offices but to arrange a large open space in a purely functional plan. Divisions between people and departments are created by free-standing screens, and plants are often used to divide and enhance space. Office landscape has been used in several major installations in the United States, following considerable popularity in Europe, but there are skeptics who question the basic claims of office-landscape supporters that less space is required and that the resulting democratization creates a better spirit and working relationship among staff members.

It is interesting to note that even in conventional office planning there is controversy about whether or not the occupant of an office should be involved in its design. Designers tend to insist on making all decisions, and management usually supports that point of view, yet psychologists, among others, counsel that a greater involvement of the individual with his own personal environment would be desirable.

Governmental interiors. A notable characteristic of interior design for public buildings—such as court rooms, assembly halls (on all levels of government including the United Nations), city halls, and cultural buildings—is that the consumer is excluded from participation in decision making. Another is that in all cases the interiors try to present a very definite image or symbol. Governmental buildings, especially in the past, were designed to present a solemn, awe-inspiring, majestic, and even slightly ominous look, both in their architectural composition and their interior treatment of spaces. For centuries, marble, stone, lofty ceilings, and imposing architectural elements have been traditional.

The image of government buildings

Institutional interiors. Schools, hospitals, and universities are examples of institutions now extensively using the services of interior designers and architects. Many universities have staff designers dealing with the institution's many design needs, from office spaces to dormitories. Certain institutional needs, such as operating rooms in hospitals, are strictly functional, yet the patients' rooms and many other hospital facilities are very much within the scope of interior design. Until recently, however, such involvement was not prevalent, and it has been common to refer to a sterile, dull-looking space as "looking like a hospital." A greater recognition of the influence of the environment upon human behaviour has brought about increased emphasis on interior design for all kinds of institutional interiors. Indeed, even though up to now little work has been done by designers in penal institutions, it is a safe prediction that in a short time there will be considerable concern for the environmental qualities of these institutions, as well.

Commercial interiors. Contemporary designers are much involved with commercial spaces—such as stores, hotels, motels, and restaurants. Many designers and design firms specialize in highly specific spaces such as restaurants, and others may become specialists in the design of showrooms for the garment industry. Frequently, the design of a restaurant, shop, or hotel must be keyed to a theme. It might be a nautical theme for a yacht club or a theme based on the artifacts of the particular region in which a hotel is located. Obviously, all commercial spaces must be designed in a highly functional way. A store with a beautifully designed interior will fail if it does not work for circulation of customers, for display, for storage, and above all for sales. Some of these functional needs create difficult design problems. A hotel or motel room, for instance, must be designed for use by individuals, couples, and family groups. Maintenance is also an important factor in the design of commercial spaces.

Use of a theme

Religious interiors. Religious architecture is heavily influenced by symbolic concepts as well as by the ritual and traditions of a particular faith. Designers of religious interiors must, therefore, base their approach on a set of rules preceding all other design considerations. The simple and modest Quaker prayerhouses, for instance, express the tenets of that faith as clearly as some of the richly appointed Roman Catholic and Eastern Orthodox churches.

Industrial interiors. Industrial interiors do not usually involve interior designers. There are, of course, many industrial spaces, such as workshops, laboratories, and factories, that have been planned by architects and designers, and there are a few that have stressed some aesthetic considerations. By and large, however, industrial interiors are created as strictly functional spaces. For this very reason, some of these spaces are quite beautiful. This may sound paradoxical, but, like the modern bridge or airplane, they can be extremely handsome without the conscious attempt to create beauty.

Special interiors. Although an attempt was made to classify the kinds of interiors that are the prevalent concern of interior design, there are many kinds of special interiors that at times fall within the larger field of environmental design and that do not fit into a particular category or even a professional subspecialty. Transportation design may be part engineering, part industrial design, part architecture, and part interior design. Interiors of ships are certainly interior design, but the interiors of automobiles, aircraft, and trains are often a combination of many specialties. The advent of large commercial aircraft has taken the aircraft interior out of the area of the strictly functional, and, indeed, the introduction of these large planes has seen an intense competition among the airlines to create spaces that go beyond the concept of mere seating. Also included in transportation design are the terminal buildings associated with air, road, and water transportation systems.

A less spectacular example is the field of exhibition design, another area of design having interfaces with other fields, including, in this case, graphics and advertising. Related to this field are museum design and exhibition and the preservation and restoration of historic buildings.

It is clear that any man-made interior or exterior space is influenced by design or its absence. More important than a listing of the various kinds of special interiors is the underlying fact that designers are becoming involved in all aspects of the environment. (A.A.F.)

Historical developments

The art of interior design encompasses all of the fixed and movable ornamental objects that form an integral part of the inside of any human habitation. It is essential to remember that much of what today is classified as art and exhibited in galleries and museums was originally used to furnish interiors. Paintings were usually ordered by size and frequently by subject from a painter who often practiced other forms of art, including furniture design and decoration. Sculptors in stone or bronze were often goldsmiths who did a variety of ornamental metalwork. The more important artists had studios with assistants and apprentices and often signed cooperative work. Many architects also designed interiors, including the accessories—furniture, pottery, porcelain, silver, rugs, and tapestries. Paintings often took the form of cabinet pictures, framed to be hung on a wall in a particular position, such as over a door. Murals were painted on a diversity of subjects; during the period of the Baroque style in the 17th century, murals sometimes were painted to look like an extension of the interior itself, making it appear more spacious. Mirrors were employed for the same purpose of adding space to an interior.

The deliberate use of antiques as decoration was unusual in most periods. Generally, in older houses elements of the previous decorative scheme were relegated to less important rooms when new decoration was undertaken to bring an old interior into line with current fashion. In this way many antiques have been preserved. The art market has existed from the earliest times for the purpose of providing both new and antique works for the decoration of interiors, but in early times the market in old work was usually limited to paintings by admired masters and goldsmith's work.

Only within the recent historic past have any interiors but those belonging to the rich and powerful been considered worthy of consideration. Still more recent is the collection of the interior furnishings of the past by museums and galleries, where they are studied in scholarly isolation. The segregation of such objects in galleries, however, has led to an increasing misunderstanding of their original purpose; and the division of the arts by museum curators into the fine arts and the decorative (or industrial) arts has helped to obscure the original functions of interior furnishings.

Museum collections of furnishings

To some extent the present attitude has resulted from the rise of the specialist collector since the 1840s. Porcelain and silver, for instance, no longer fulfill their original purpose as part of the household furnishings but are collected into cabinets, since they are so precious. Similarly, the small porcelain figures of Meissen, which were originally part of a table decoration and an integral part of a service, are now too highly valued to be so used.

ORIGINS OF INTERIOR DESIGN

The notion of interior design historically has arisen as part of a settled agricultural way of life. The tents of nomadic peoples were hardly suitable for the more permanent forms of decoration. Among Central Asian nomads, however, carpets and rugs have been employed to decorate and provide comfort in tents and portable dwellings, usually taking the form of coverings for floor and bed, and these have been the principal form of art of the peoples concerned. The oldest nomadic carpet, found in Central Mongolia, dates to the 5th century BC, but geometrically patterned stone reliefs from Assyria in the 7th century BC are thought to be based on earlier carpet patterns.

Hunting peoples living in caves decorated the walls with paintings as early as 20,000 years ago, but these were almost certainly votive paintings rather than decoration, and no trace of movable furniture has survived.

Primitive peoples. Although the practices of present-day primitive peoples sometimes shed light on the historical origins of those practices, there is too little art and decoration in such communities today to illuminate the beginnings of interior decoration. No clear-cut progressions of styles, like those that occurred in Europe, can be identified except among peoples who could hardly be regarded as primitive, such as the former civilizations of South America or the Benin culture of Africa. Nevertheless, even the poorest and most primitive peoples devote some time to the production of works that give them pleasure, and these works often are employed to decorate interiors. Primitive painting often consists of a series of abstract patterns, such as that on the pottery of the Pueblo Indians. Furniture, such as wooden stools, usually has some ornamental carving. Basketwork, wooden vessels, and pottery are decorated with abstract geometrical patterns, and an insistence on symmetry is the rule. Since most of these patterns—especially those to be found in basketry and textiles—bear no resemblance to natural forms, they probably arose from the nature of the techniques employed in making the objects in question.

Ornament based on natural objects more or less realistically depicted probably had a magical connotation; animals, for instance, are intended to promote success in hunting. Even the most abstract and geometric of motifs have a symbolic meaning, which can be interpreted by those who know the key, and this meaning is almost always magical. There are few objects or motifs that do not have some meaning, and the making of objects that have no other purpose than the pleasure taken by their creator in executing them is very rare.

Connotations of ornament

Origins in Western antiquity. Excavations in ancient Mesopotamia and Egypt suggest that the earliest equivalent of furniture consisted of platforms of bricks, which served as chairs, tables, and beds, no doubt spread with textiles or animal skins. There is also good reason to think that walls were painted and, in the case of more important buildings, decorated with mural paintings. Movable furniture first occurred only in the most important residences, such as palaces, and in public buildings. Furniture is of considerable antiquity, though it is known, for the most part, only from wall paintings, sculpture, and vase paintings. Some furniture survives from ancient Egyptian tombs from about 3000 BC in the form of beds, chairs, tables, and storage chests. It is in such furniture that decoration is first seen—in the leg of the bull and the lion employed as a furniture support, especially for beds. It is from this point in the ancient past that the development of interior design can be traced historically.

INTERIOR DESIGN IN THE WEST

Ancient world. *Egypt.* In contrast with the monumental tombs and temples of stone, many of which remained intact to the 20th century, Egyptian houses were built of perishable materials, and, therefore, few remains have survived. Sun-dried or kiln-burnt mud bricks were used for the walls; floors consisted of beaten earth, and a thin coat of smooth mud plaster was often used as an internal wall finish.

In its simplest form the applied decoration was a plain white or coloured wash, but, in larger houses, patterns in varying degrees of elaboration were painted on the plaster. Rush matting was hung across most internal door openings and used as screening inside the small, high windows. It is probable that decorative wall hangings and floor coverings were made of rushes or palmetto woven into a pattern, since painted representations of such hangings have survived from 5th-dynasty tombs at Saqqārah. In the workmen's village of Kahun, built in the 12th dynasty (*c.* 1900 BC), some of the more well-to-do houses contained rooms decorated with brown-painted skirting, one foot (0.3 metre) high, then a four-foot (1.2-metre) dado (the lower portion of wall that is decorated differently from that above it) striped vertically in red, black, and white. Above this the walls were buff coloured with brightly painted decorative panels in the more important rooms, and ceilings were also often of painted wood. It may be assumed that the lavish tomb decoration of all periods was basically derived from the domestic interiors of their time.

Use of natural forms for decorative motifs

Many Egyptian decorative motifs are stylized from natural forms associated with the life-giving Nile. The lotus bud and flower, the papyrus, and the palm appear constantly with borders of checkered patterns or coiled, ropelike spirals, giving an air of space and elegance. The palace of the pharaoh Akhenaton and other large houses at Tell el-Amarna (*c.* 1365 BC) reflect a tendency toward naturalism in their ornamentations. Akhenaton, his queen Nefertiti, and their daughters are frequently represented, usually grouped affectionately together. Other painted panels show animals and birds with twining borders of vegetation. Molded, coloured, glazed ware was introduced to give a brilliant inlay of grapes, poppies, cornflowers, and daisies, all in natural colours. The use of square ceramic tiles as a wall surfacing was uncommon but not unknown. Primary colours were the most common, a brilliant yellow being among the most frequently used, but terra-cotta, gray, black, and white were all added to give contrast. Even floors were delicately painted to represent gardens or pools. One of these at Tell el-Amarna shows a rectangular tank with swimming fish and waterfowl, bordered with lotus and papyrus marshland, with an outer band showing more birds and young cattle in the meadows beyond. Furniture ranged from the simplest benches and ceramic pots to beautifully designed chairs, small tables, and beds in the homes of the rich, where many vases, urns, ceramic, wood, and metal utensils evince a fastidious, luxurious way of life.

Mesopotamia. Very little furniture survives from ancient Mesopotamia, principally because climatic conditions are not conducive to the preservation of wood. What is known has been learned principally from reliefs and cylinder seals. Furniture mounts of bronze and ivory have been excavated, however, and fragments of furniture were uncovered in the royal tombs at the city of Ur, in ancient Sumer. In quality of craftsmanship and decoration, Mesopotamian furniture was comparable to that of Egypt.

The mud-brick houses of the Sumerian and Old Babylonian periods in the Tigris–Euphrates valley resembled their modern counterparts in their rectangular outline and the groupings of rooms about a central court, which was either roofed or open. In the majority of houses, decoration probably was confined to a wide black or dark-coloured skirting painted in diluted pitch with a band of some lighter colour above. Door frames were sometimes painted red, probably as a protection against evil influences, and where doors were used they may have been of palm wood. The poorer houses were simply whitewashed inside and out.

Assyrian relief panels and friezes of ceramic tiles

In the most elaborate Assyrian palaces the main decorative features were panels of alabaster and limestone carved in relief, the principal subjects being hunting, ceremonial, and war, as in the palace of the warrior king Sargon II at Khorsabad (705 BC). Panels and friezes of ceramic tiles in vivid colours decorated the walls inside

EB Inc. with permission of the Staatliche Museen zu Berlin-GDR

Figure 16: Brilliantly coloured glazed brick decoration, facade of the throne room, palace of Nebuchadrezzar II, Babylon, *c.* 600 BC.

and out, and it is evident that this brilliance of colour was a feature of much Assyrian and Babylonian decoration (Figure 16). Carved stone slabs were used as flooring, with typical Mesopotamian rosette and palmette (stylized palm leaf) borders. Occasionally, Egyptian lotus motifs also appear.

Vigorous and warlike figures characterize both Assyrian and Babylonian work, and the standard of execution was extremely high. Naturalistic detail was often engraved on the surface of the figures and animals, which themselves were in relief. After the Persian conquest (539–331 BC) this vigour declined. The palaces built by the Persian kings Darius and Xerxes I at Persepolis show a lighter use of animal figures. Glazed and enamelled tiles were used on the walls, while timber roof beams and ceilings were painted in vivid colours. (E.C.De./Ge.S.)

Crete. The most important buildings of the pre-Hellenic Minoan and Mycenaean periods were the citadel complexes, housing the entire court of the ruler. The palace of King Minos at Knossos in Crete (*c.* 1700–1400 BC) gives evidence of a small but sophisticated society with a taste for luxury and entertainment and a corresponding skill in applied decoration. Frescoes (paintings executed with water soluble pigments on wet plaster) and some panels of painted relief decorated the walls of living rooms and ceremonial rooms, which were grouped asymmetrically round a series of courtyards (Figure 17). Many aspects of Cretan life were depicted, the recurring theme being the acrobatic bullfighting on

Cretan use of painted decoration

Bernard G. Silberstein—Rapho Guillumette

Figure 17: Frescoed throne room, palace of King Minos at Knossos, Crete, *c.* 1700–1400 BC.

which a religious cult was probably centred. Even the backgrounds of friezes and panels, which depicted many-coloured painted birds, animals, and flowers, were given an effect of movement, being divided into light and dark areas. Plain dadoes and borders provided an effective foil and gave articulation to the interiors.

As seafarers, the Cretans could import a rich variety of materials for building and decorative purposes; a wealth of ideas can be seen in the fine pottery, carved ivories, and beaten gold, silver, and bronze with which their palaces were ornamented.

The pottery and metalwork of the Minoans was technically in advance of other Mediterranean peoples of the time, and they were especially expert in firing such large pottery objects as storage jars and baths. Some furniture, especially storage chests, was made of terra-cotta. A chalice made of obsidian, a volcanic glass about as hard as jade, could only have been shaped by grinding with an abrasive such as emery procured from Cape Emeri on the island of Náxos; the form was apparently based on metalwork. Excavations have proved the existence of an advanced sanitary system, with baths either of marble or terra-cotta.

Greece. A period of so-called dark ages in Greece followed the destruction of Knossos in *c.* 1400 BC, but Cretan civilization had already influenced the mainland before then. Small terra-cotta models of furniture and fragments of tables and chairs dating from as early as 1350 BC have been found. Homer's epic *Odyssey*, dating from the 9th–8th century BC, speaks of a chair inlaid with ivory and silver, and sheet copper was used to sheath beams and architraves. The description of a bed reveals it to have been a rectangular wooden frame with coloured leather thonging, like the usual Egyptian bed, and inlaid with silver and ivory. At this time also, wooden vessels were decorated with sheet-gold ornament with repoussé work (ornament in relief made by hammering the reverse side).

Little or no Greek furniture survives from the classical period (5th century BC), but there is ample evidence that it was well constructed and elaborately decorated. The large number of surviving painted vases are a valuable source of information about many aspects of Greek life, and furniture of all kinds—chairs, tables, day couches used for dining, and a large number of accessories—can be identified. These paintings, in fact, were among the major influences on the French Empire style of the early years of the 19th century. Egyptian influence can be traced in some of the early pieces of furniture, an example being a type of chair having a single leg with a lion's head at the top and a single paw at the bottom. This also was to be a favourite theme of the Empire style.

In the Hellenistic period (323–31 BC), domestic comfort and decoration were considered once more. Mosaic floors were an important decorative device, originally made of pebbles as at Olynthus but later developing into the black-and-white or coloured mosaics that were widely used throughout the Roman Empire (see MOSAIC). A central, finely designed panel with realistic motifs and a wide, more coarsely executed border of scroll or key patterns acted as a focus for the arrangement of furniture, which was still limited in quantity.

Hellenistic mosaic floors

Rome. Much more is known about Roman interior decoration, and Roman furniture was based on earlier Greek models. From the beginning of the Christian era the predominant Western style was that derived from ancient Greece by way of Rome. Classical styles were based on mathematically expressed laws of proportion that were applied not only to buildings as a whole but also to much of the interior decoration.

Roman interior decoration is known both from literary sources, such as Pliny's *Natural History* and the *Histories* of Suetonius, and from excavations, such as those that uncovered the remains of the Golden House of Nero soon after 1500 and those at Pompeii and Herculaneum in Italy in the 18th century.

Today, there are many misconceptions about the decoration of the period, most of which date from the 18th century and the classical revival that began soon after 1750. Many excavated bronze objects, including statues, and any bronze that remained above ground, such as the roofing of the Capitol, were melted during medieval times for new work, since bronze was a scarce and expensive metal. This led to the assumption that marble was the predominating material, which is not necessarily true, especially in the case of statuary. Time and exposure to the weather has removed the colour from much of the marble that has survived, but in classical times it was commonly painted and sometimes gilded. Wall paintings at Pompeii and Herculaneum are ample testimony to this. Wall decoration began there about 150 BC, and, by about 80 BC, plastered walls were being made to look like masonry. Such decoration was combined with the true architectural features—*e.g.*, doors and pilasters (flattened columns attached to the wall). The panels are painted variously in yellow, black, magenta, and red, with some imitation marbling indicating an earlier custom of applying marble veneers. Rich colour was also supplied by superbly executed mosaic floors, elegant couches with coloured cushions, and bronze tripods and lamps, such as in the cubiculum of a villa at Boscoreale near Pompeii preserved in the Metropolitan Museum in New York City (Figure 18).

Roman wall painting depicted columns, niches, and open windows with elaborate imaginary views and figures beyond. Painted ruins, such as those in the Villa of Livia, Rome, were the precursors of the 18th- and 19th-century Romantic taste in western Europe.

It has been said that Augustus, who was emperor from 27 BC to AD 14, found Rome of brick and left it of marble, and certainly the interior decoration of imperial Rome expressed the emergence of the city as a world power toward which flowed much of the wealth of the empire. Exotic marbles began to be imported, and brick walls were faced with polished slabs of white and coloured stone. In the more luxurious interiors or for special purposes, obsidian, a natural volcanic glass dark green or purplish-brown in colour, and copper-green malachite were occasionally to be found in the capital. A limited amount of window glass—mostly small, thick, and discoloured panes—was used, for sheet glass was difficult to manufacture. Large translucent crystals of selenite (a kind of gypsum) were sometimes employed to admit light.

Roman marbles and other decorative stone

Some of the large houses contained a picture gallery, known as the *pinacoteca*, for the display of easel pictures. These have now virtually disappeared, but mural paintings are fairly common. Pictorial decoration for floors

Figure 18: Frescoed room, from a villa at Boscoreale, near Pompeii, 1st century AD. In the Metropolitan Museum of Art, New York City.
By courtesy of the Metropolitan Museum of Art, New York, Rogers Fund, 1903

and walls was supplied by mosaics, the picture built up of small fragments (tesserae) of coloured stones, mostly marble, or of small pieces of coloured glass backed by gold foil to increase its reflective power. The subjects are very diverse. Floor-mosaics in dining-rooms were sometimes decorated with simulated fragments of food, as though they had dropped from the table.

Roman furniture was made of stone, wood, or bronze. Villas were largely open to the air, and stone benches and tables were common. Wooden furniture has not survived, but bronze hardware for such furniture is well-known. Buffets with tiers of shelves were used to display silver. Tables were often made of exotic woods and veneers, with ivory, bronze, or silver trim. Tortoiseshell veneers were popular. The dining couches, which replaced chairs, were richly decorated, often with gilded silver or bronze. Chairs followed earlier Greek forms, and while no fixed upholstery was provided, cushions were plentiful.

Roman textiles

The art of tapestry came to Rome from Egypt, where the craft was an ancient one. Few Roman textiles have survived, and those have mostly been found in Egypt and were probably made there. Rugs woven on a linen foundation were imported from Egypt, and fabrics, including rugs, were imported from the Near East. The richest carpets came from Pergamos, in Asia Minor, and were the most highly valued. They were probably woven with gold and silver thread. Nothing survives of these rich textiles because they were all burned long ago to extract the metal. Roman walls were hung with tapestries, and pillars were decorated with textiles. Silk was imported from China until the time of Justinian, in the 6th century, when silkworms were clandestinely brought from East Asia and the industry was established in Europe.

The Romans were highly skilled glassworkers. Domestic glass was made in large quantities, both utilitarian and decorative, and factories were established for the purpose. Mirrors, however, were normally made of polished bronze or silver; if glass mirrors existed at all, they must have been very small.

The amount of bronze employed in household equipment of all kinds was vast. Small pieces of furniture, such as stools, were made wholly of bronze, and a few specimens have survived. Saucepans were made in factories, some bearing what appears to be the trademark of a swan. Lighting fixtures were also made in quantity, of prefabricated parts, and they played a large part in the decoration of the interior. By the 1st century AD enormous quantities of silver went into the making of such objects as large and heavy platters displayed on the buffets. Bowls and similar pieces of hollow ware were commonly decorated with repoussé ornament, less often with engraving, which is usually to be found on the backs of bronze hand mirrors. Antique silver commanded a high price.

Statuary in bronze, from Etruscan sources or looted from Greece and the Greek colonies, decorated the more important interiors. The theatre of Scaurus, for instance, housed 3,000 bronze statues. Some Roman statues have been excavated at Pompeii and elsewhere, but most were remelted. Only one Roman bronze statue has remained above ground in Italy since it was made—the equestrian Marcus Aurelius in Rome.

Pottery was not among the luxuries of ancient Rome. Vessels such as storage jars (amphorae), lamps, bricks, pipes, and architectural ornament were made in factories. Pottery for the table was usually of the so-called Samian ware, although it was made in many other places than Samos; this had a red polished surface and, often, molded relief decoration reminiscent of contemporary silver. Tableware, too, was made in factories and often marked with the name of the potter. Pottery vases of fine quality were made in imitation of those of Greece. They include most of the familiar Greek types, especially the krater (with a large round body, large mouth, and small handles), although the form often varies. The decoration is principally of the red-figure type (black with decorations in red) but is usually much more elaborate than on the Greek originals.

Classical themes and motifs

Themes of decoration are many, and most come from Greek sources. They became part of the vocabulary of classical ornament that was employed during later classical revivals, such as the Renaissance and the Neoclassical movement of the 18th century. The acanthus leaf is by far the most common, and it was in almost continuous use from the 5th century BC in Greece to the 19th century in the West. The Greek and Byzantine acanthus leaf is inclined to be stiff and formal; the Roman and Renaissance form is much more natural. The vine-leaf and grapes motif is also common, and the palmette occurs especially on painted vases. The ivy, laurel, olive, and honeysuckle (anthemion) are usually to be found as frieze ornament, sometimes in stylized form. Festoons, garlands, and swags of laurel were common decorative elements in relief sculpture. "Cable," or "twisted rope," a kind of plaited ornament, was often used for the same purpose. Rosettes—stylized simple roses with equally spaced petals—were widely used. Originally an Assyrian design, they have continued in use to the present. Egg-like forms alternating with tongue- or dart-shaped ornaments originally were a carved stone architectural ornament; they were taken over in later times as part of interior plasterwork.

The lion was very popular, especially the mask and paws, and was employed over a long period, as late as the 19th century, as a furniture ornament or as a door-knocker or handle. Mythological animal forms included the griffin and the chimera, both of Mesopotamian origin, and the sphinx, from Egypt and Corinthian Greece. The head of the ram, a sacrificial animal, commonly ornamented altars and candelabra. The ox skull and horns occur during Roman times, but not often thereafter. The eagle, representing Jupiter, was the symbolic motif of the Roman legions. The human mask surrounded by foliage was common and is usually derived from the masks employed in the theatre or from the head of Medusa, which was especially used as a shield ornament. Atlantes and caryatids, male and female human figures, respectively, were originally used instead of plain columns on building exteriors but were later employed for a variety of ornamental purposes—for example, as part of the decoration of some Renaissance cabinets of architectural form. Trophies were always popular. Weapons arranged in a pattern were carried in the Roman triumphs and later sculptured on monuments. This classical form of ornament was later extended to other groups of implements: in the 18th century, for instance, rustic trophies were formed by grouping agricultural implements, such as spades, beehives, and rakes, into a decorative pattern, and musical trophies were made of musical instruments for the same purpose.

A common type of decoration surviving especially in Pompeii is the frieze of small putti, or cupids, in a variety of guises and at work at a large number of different tasks. These persisted in popularity until well into the 18th century, when porcelain figures of putti in disguise or in an allegorical pose became common. They were also painted on furniture or as part of wall decoration.

Grotesques

Equally popular, but remaining virtually unknown till the discovery of the Golden House of Nero *c.* 1500, are the ornamental motifs known as grotesques (because they were found below ground in a "grotto," a word that strictly means an excavated chamber containing murals). Roman grotesques were fantastic figures, human and animal, that terminated in leafage (usually the acanthus leaf) or in a fishtail, in conjunction with floral and foliate ornament and arabesques. Revived by Raphael about 1517 for the decoration of the loggia of the Vatican, these motifs became widely popular, in many different forms, from the first decade of the 16th century until late in the 18th.

Middle Ages. From the fall of Rome, when the city was finally sacked by Odoacer in 476, to the 15th century, when the Renaissance was already well advanced, information about the decoration of interiors is scarce. Its history has to be pieced together from surviving objects and illuminated manuscripts.

Byzantium. The capital of the Eastern Roman Empire, Constantinople (formerly called Byzantium, later Stamboul, presently Istanbul) was a convenient meeting place for East and West. It felt the influence of Persian art and transmitted it to early medieval European Christian styles. Most surviving Byzantine interiors are ecclesiastical, although secular wall paintings and especially mosaics continued to be popular. The Iconoclasts of the 8th century, however, not only proscribed the making of images but destroyed most of those already existing. Ivory carving was highly developed, and furniture was inlaid with ivory plaques and decorated with carvings. Goldsmith's work, which had existed in large quantities in ancient Rome, was equally popular in Constantinople. Decoration was usually of the repoussé type, with subjects from classical mythology. Very few gold objects have survived, and most bronze work has also been lost. Decorative textiles of fine quality were common, and a few fragments have survived. It is in some of the rare fragments of patterned silks of the 7th or 8th century that the Persian influence is most often to be found. Silk at one time was imported in vast quantities from China.

Constantinople tended to become increasingly an Oriental city as the Greek influence introduced by Alexander the Great waned in the Near and Middle East and the new civilization of Islām was established. (Ge.S.)

Early medieval Europe. In the constant warfare that was waged in Europe in the early medieval period, material possessions dwindled to a minimum: a man did not own for long anything he could not defend and had little use or opportunity for interior decoration. If he possessed more than one house, his furniture and possessions would go with him from place to place. During this time, the arts came to be monopolized by the church, which grew to dominate all aspects of the medieval world.

By the 9th century the Romanesque style was well established in northern Europe. It made far greater use of the semicircular arch and vaulting than had the Imperial Roman style. Much of the sculpture decorating buildings was influenced by the Middle East. The court of Charlemagne in the 9th century was in communication with that of the caliph Hārūn ar-Rashīd, in Baghdad, and the Arabs had opened up a sea route between the Persian Gulf and China. Oriental textiles, imported through Venice and Genoa, began to be found in the more luxurious European interiors, and in the 13th century the first piece of Chinese porcelain, brought back by Marco Polo, found its way to the West and is still preserved in the treasury of St. Mark's, Venice.

Castle interiors

Late into the medieval period, the larger houses, generally called castles, were designed according to military rather than aesthetic principles. The main room was a spacious hall with timber or stone walls (sometimes plastered), an open-beamed roof, narrow slit windows (as yet unglazed), and a floor of stone slabs, tiles, or beaten earth. In the earlier houses the fire burned in the centre of the floor, and the smoke either drifted through a central hole in the roof or dispersed among the rafters; but wall fireplaces soon replaced this unsatisfactory system. Furniture was probably limited to plain stools, benches, and trestle tables, made of local timber, and some heavy chests in which personal possessions were stored. The feudal lord and his lady sat on more elaborate chairs on the dais (raised platform), and a coloured hanging of plain fabric sometimes decorated the wall behind them. Wall hangings and tapestries became more common in Norman times (1066–1189), when stone carving on doorways, fireplaces, window openings, column capitals, and arcading superimposed on the inside walls was also introduced. Such hangings can still be seen in the Norman castles of Rochester, Kent, and Chepstow in England. The whole community often lived and slept in the one hall, but as time went on, two main rooms—the hall and the chamber—were provided. At first, rooms were divided by woolen hangings, hung from iron rods or from the rafters. The houses of the poor were simple, timber-framed shelters with bare earth floors and undecorated walls. Such conditions, with variations according to local circumstances, were generally prevalent in western Europe until the end of the 12th century.

Late medieval Europe. During the 12th and 13th centuries those who had taken part in the Crusades learned something of luxurious living in the Near East, and as a more secure way of life was becoming possible at home, they began to improve their own living conditions. The castle slowly evolved into the manor house. Household equipment became more elaborate and important, no doubt partly because the women had played a greater part in household management since the absence of the men on the Crusades.

Curtains of finer texture began to replace wooden window shutters or heavy homespun hangings. Tapestries relieved the bareness of the walls and gave additional warmth to rooms, and other textiles and tapestries were draped over chairs and tables, and brightly coloured woven or embroidered cushions were used. The fine wood ceilings of the large rooms were sometimes coffered and often painted in bright colours, particularly in France. The disappearance of much of this colour with the passage of time lends a false austerity to surviving medieval interiors.

Development of specialized rooms

A greater number of rooms, serving special needs and giving increased privacy, came into use, although the house was still not planned as a whole. The kitchen, buttery, and pantry were placed at the lower end of the hall beyond a carved timber or stone screen, which, in larger houses, supported a minstrel's gallery. At the opposite end, there was a chamber, or withdrawing room, perhaps with a solar (upper room) above it, used as a bedroom or as a special apartment for the ladies. A guest room was occasionally provided. In the 13th and 14th centuries, the wardrobe was a room with presses for storing curtains, hangings, bed and table linen, as well as the clothing and materials needed by the members of the household. Here sewing and tailoring were carried on, and the room became a combined workroom and storeroom, furnished with heavy, plain tables and chairs.

In the kitchen, rotating spits and adjustable hooks for suspending cooking pots were fixed into a vast hooded or recessed wall fireplace. Plain but pleasing utensils of wood, copper, and iron were kept on hooks on the walls, and enormously solid tables stood on the stone or tiled floor, which was strewn with sawdust or rushes (Figure 21). In the hall the rushes were mixed with fragrant herbs and helped to absorb some of the dirt, smells, and grease. By the 15th century plaited rush mats were common (Figure 19). The introduction of linen tablecloths resulted in a great improvement of manners and cleanliness at meals.

Ornaments and various luxuries, which had become more common during the time of the Crusades, prolifer-

Figure 19: Gothic courtly dining hall with tapestry covered walls, plaited rush mats, trestle table set with gold and silver tableware, and a side table for displaying household plate; Duc de Berry at table from the illuminated manuscript *Très Riches Heures du duc de Berry* by Pol de Limburg and his brothers, France, before 1416. In the Musee Condé, Chantilly, France.
Giraudon

ated in subsequent centuries as commerce with the Near East increased. Household plate, of gold or silver, was frequently displayed on dressers or cupboards as decoration and to impress visitors (Figure 19), it was not unknown for these possessions to be roped off to prevent pilfering. Indoor arrangements for washing and bathing were considered a luxury. A flat-sided metal bowl was sometimes fixed to the wall of a living room with a swinging ewer or a small cistern with a tap over it and a towel on a hinged rod. Small convex mirrors were hung in the walls as early as the 15th century, such as the one in the background of Jan van Eyck's "The Marriage of Giovanni Arnolfini and Giovanna Cenami" (Figure 20).

The Gothic style

The Gothic style first made its appearance in the Ile de France, toward the end of the 12th century. It derived originally from Middle Eastern sources and was developed by Islāmic builders. It came to be widely employed in western Europe, where, for uncertain reasons, it gained the name Gothic by the 17th century. It is characterized by the extensive use of the pointed arch, by spacious interiors, and by walls pierced with numerous windows, often of stained glass (see Figure 1). The style had no fixed rules governing proportion, and decoration, generally, was the free expression of craftsmen within the limits of current fashion and the purpose of the building.

Use of hangings

Knowledge of Gothic interiors derives from illuminated manuscripts (Figure 19) and panel paintings (Figures 20 and 21) from the few surviving *objets d'art.* Much use was made of textiles for covering walls, especially tapestries (Figure 19); the principal medieval centres of tapestry manufacture were Paris and Arras (see TAPESTRY). European courts at this time were very mobile and moved from place to place: tapestries were remarkably versatile, for they could be taken down and rehung elsewhere. They were employed to partition rooms, and were sometimes suspended under a high roof to act as a ceiling. Rugs and carpets had been brought back from the East by the crusaders and were at first employed as a covering for a divan or, in the case of the finer varieties, as bed and table coverings. The carpet for the floor was introduced comparatively late (Figure 20). Weavers of Saracen origin had settled in Sicily and on the Italian mainland, and they produced all kinds of rich fabrics, such as silk and velvet.

Furniture was not present in such quantities as in later centuries, chairs especially being fairly rare. Tables were long and rectangular, laid on trestles, with benches for seating (Figure 19). At the head of the table, for the principal person of the household, was a straight-backed chair. Chairs, generally, were the subject of a certain etiquette, being reserved for the most important people, and they were often surmounted by canopies. Retainers had to stand (Figure 19); less important members of the household were sometimes supplied with stools. Folding chairs, like the old Roman curule chair, appeared in the 14th century. Although a few chairs had seats and arms stuffed with rushes, it was more common to drape them with textiles and put cushions on the seats. Buffets, often superbly carved, were used as a stand for silver and for serving food.

Medieval bedsteads, with highly carved posts and canopies, were often of great size, and they were customarily occupied by several persons—as well as the favourite dogs, who slept on top (Figure 20). The Great Bed of Ware in the Victoria and Albert Museum, London, is reputed to have held six couples in comfort.

Goldsmiths' work was often decorated with enamel, and bronze was similarly treated. The usual technique was the champlevé type, in which the metal is engraved or carved and the spaces then are filled with powdered coloured glass, subsequently fused by firing. At Limoges and in the Rhineland a wide range of objects were executed: quite large works, such as tombs, as well as smaller pieces, such as *chasses* and reliquaries. Lighting appliances were made of bronze or wrought iron. Those for suspension were usually intended for oil lamps, and standing candlesticks and candelabra were provided with spikes onto which the candle was forced (pricket candlesticks).

Gothic decorative pottery

Very little decorative pottery was made, although the colourful dishes and vases of Moorish Spain are an exception. Tiles were extensively employed for both walls and floors in houses of the better class, and there was a proverb in Spain to the effect that a poor man lived in a house without tiles (see Figure 30). The technique of manufacture was often quite complex and included inlaying with clay of a different colour. The vogue for tiles was imported from Islām by way of Moorish Spain. Chi-

By courtesy of the trustees of the National Gallery London; photograph, J.R. Freeman & Co. Ltd'

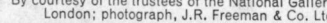

Figure 20: Northern Gothic bedroom with canopied bed, convex mirror, Oriental carpet, and brass chandelier, "The Marriage of Giovanni Arnolfini and Giovanna Cenami(?)," panel by Jan van Eyck, 1434. In the National Gallery, London.

nese porcelain was known in western Europe by the late 14th century but was, of course, extremely rare; indeed, specimens were often mounted in silver in the same way as the semiprecious hard stones such as amethysts, garnets, and peridots.

The Gothic style lingered in England and northern Europe much longer than it did in the south, and many more examples of it escaped destructive wars than on the Continent. The panelled room characteristic of the style and the period has survived more or less intact in England, where panelling with traces of paint can still be found.

Gothic ornament sometimes makes use of motifs similar to those of classical interiors, such as the acanthus leaf and the rosette, but the treatment is very different. The Gothic craftsman liked to abstract certain features of his model and emphasize them in a stylized manner, as in the heraldic eagle, especially as it is used on the reverse of dishes from Moorish Spain and in coats of arms like that of the Holy Roman emperor. It no longer bears any resemblance to the naturally depicted Roman eagle but is stylized, with a geometrically drawn tail. Similarly, the lion has its open mouth, tongue, mane, tail, and claws treated in the same way. Compass work is a marked feature of much Gothic ornament. The cross, for instance, is never a plain cross but is ornamented with geometric motifs; it may represent a re-emergence of some old Celtic motifs, which were often based on compass work. Much Gothic ornament is floral and foliate, freely and naturally treated in some cases but stylized in others. Like interiors, paintings were in bright colours. Some of the ornamental motifs to be found in objects intended for interior furnishing are architectural, like the crocket (projections in foliate form), the panelling of chair backs, and the doors of buffets (Figure 21).

Islāmic countries. The Arab conquest in the 7th century AD and, in the 8th century, Muslim expansion into India and Spain had profound influence on the decorative arts throughout the known world, especially as most of the long-distance trading routes passed through Arab lands. The skills of the conquerors fused with the traditional skills of their subject peoples, and because Islām forbade the portrayal of human or animal form, whether for religious or artistic purposes, and encouraged the incorporation of Qur'ānic texts into design, religion played a considerable and direct part in the development of design. As with nearly every other society, the finest and most lasting buildings were of a religious nature, and, unfortunately, few domestic dwellings have survived.

By courtesy of the Museo del Prado, Madrid

Figure 21: 15th century Flemish interior with Gothic ornamented furniture: "St. Barbara," oil on panel, attributed to Robert Campin, 1438. In the Prado, Madrid.

Figure 22: Manuscript illumination depicting the intricately patterned geometric and floral ceramic tilework characteristically used in 16th-century Persian interiors. "Bahram Gur in the Yellow Pavilion on Sunday," illustration from the *Khamseh* of Nezāmī, Ganjavī, Tabriz School, 1524–25. In the Metropolitan Museum of Art, New York City.

By courtesy of the Metropolitan Museum of Art, New York, gift of Alexander Smith Cochran, 1913

Architectural quality and form were subordinated to intricate and richly coloured surface decoration. Perhaps the finest results were achieved in Persia, where a high level of technical ability already existed in combination with great lyrical sensitivity. There the principal decorative features were the ceramic tiles and tile mosaics that encrusted floors, walls, roofs, and domes both inside and out (Figure 22). The mosques of Isfahan, Meshed, and Tabriz, ranging in date from the 13th to the early 17th centuries, demonstrate a completely satisfactory use of colour in architecture. Lustred tiles with a combination of floral and geometric design date from the 10th and 11th centuries, and naturalistic flowers frequently give a gardenlike effect to the tile decoration. Iris, rose, carnation, tulip, pomegranate, pine, and date are depicted, always with delicately interlacing stems, and contained within plain or patterned borders. Blues of all shades, from turquoise to a deep ultramarine, are characteristic.

Islāmic tiles and mosaics

Patterns for tilework and patterns for the Persian carpets are frequently interchangeable. Carpet designers soon managed to circumvent the Muslim ban on the use of animal forms: lions, deer, leopards, ornamental birds, and, occasionally, even mounted huntsmen were depicted, the figures always judiciously placed to give the maximum decorative effect. Artistic achievement reached its peak under Shah Abbās I (AD 1588–1629), but well before this time Persian carpets, silks, and pottery were known and valued among Europeans, as they still are in the 20th century.

In Egypt and Sicily one of the results of Muslim domination was the introduction of a high degree of ornamentation on wall surfaces, once again principally by means of vividly coloured ceramic tiles. The patterns are more solid than those of Persia, filling up the areas between the containing arabesques and with less open backgrounds. Moorish design in Spain shows even more complex interlacing geometrical framework, which is filled in with formalized leaves, flowers, or calligraphic inscriptions. Ceilings and the upper parts of walls were modelled in flat relief with coloured and gilded arabesques, while the lower wall areas were tiled. The decoration was partly hand chiselled and partly molded. Such decorations may be seen in the Alhambra, built at Granada in the 15th century, a pleasure palace whose arcaded courts and halls are embellished with stuccoed decoration in honeycombed ceilings, stalactite vaults and capitals, tiers of horseshoe-shaped or stalactite-fringed arches, and pierced or latticed windows.

Decoration in the Alhambra

In the mosques of Turkey, walls were veneered with marble, and ceramic tiling was introduced only in small areas. Colours, too, are less exuberant in the large mosques, where a sense of space rather than of overwhelming decoration is pre-eminent. Domestic buildings were largely of wood, looking inward to secluded courtyards and gardens, but with elaborately latticed windows projecting at upper-floor level over the street. As in most other Islāmic countries, the wealthy furnished their houses with velvet and silk hangings, couches, and innumerable cushions (Figure 22).

Islāmic influence in India appears at its finest in the interiors of mosques, tombs, and palaces built during the Mughal period (1556–1707).

Renaissance to the end of the 18th century. The Renaissance was a revival of the old classical styles, and it is not surprising that it first showed itself to a marked degree in Italy. The Gothic style had made comparatively little headway in Italy, where it was regarded as barbarous except in some of the more northerly towns, such as Milan and Venice. The style had more or less coincided with a period of primitive commerce. With the Renaissance the complex commercial organization of ancient Rome began to be revived by the towns of Tuscany, especially Florence. Feudalism disappeared, and the bourgeois merchants and financiers of the town rose to power and influence. Money began to circulate, banks were established, checks and bills were honoured over long distances, factories were opened, and men grew rich enough to buy and commission works of art for interior furnishing from those who owned their own workshops, employed assistants, and were no longer reliant on a system of patronage. With the rise of the town and the invention of gunpowder, the fortified country house became obsolete.

Social influences on design

In and around Florence the new commercial civilization was most highly organized. The old Greek and Roman manuscripts had been preserved, not only by the Christian monasteries but to an even greater extent by the Muslims, and soon after 1350 these began to find their way into northern Italy. Men became increasingly dissatisfied with the spiritual outlook of medieval Christianity, and the old Greek curiosity and philosophical speculation began to revive.

The Renaissance was, in fact, a return to the mainstream of Western art after what could fairly be described as the Gothic interregnum. Nevertheless, a thousand years lay between the fall of the Roman Empire and the Renaissance, and the classical styles of the Renaissance bear the same kind of resemblance to those of Rome as modern Italian bears to Latin. They are similar, but by no means the same thing.

The Renaissance brought back the Roman vocabulary of ornament, although the emphasis was now sometimes in different places (Figure 23). The classical orders (columns with base, shaft, capital, and entablature) were borrowed, and adapted to dress the new architectural style. Architects became highly skilled in the treatment of space, and decoration often played a major part in defining and enriching their vigorous spatial effects. Classical architectural forms were used in plasterwork, inlaid woodwork, and painted decoration as well as for staircases, doors, windows, and fireplaces, which formed increasingly important and elaborate features of interior design. Decorative details inspired by the antique were also used, executed in a wide variety of techniques; garlands, caryatids (statues of women used as supporting pillars), lion masks, grotesques, reclining amorini (cupids), cornucopia (horns overflowing with flowers or fruit), arabesques (entwining scroll and plant motifs), and trophies of arms are among the most familiar. Floors of coloured and patterned marble paving are frequently integrated with the overall decorative scheme. Modelled stucco, sgraffiti arabesques (made by cutting lines through a layer of plaster or stucco to reveal an underlayer), and fine wall painting were used in brilliant combinations in the early part of the 16th century.

Figure 23: Classical ornament used in Italian Renaissance interiors; "Dream of St. Ursula," canvas by Vittore Carpaccio, Italy, *c.* 1495. In the Accademia, Venice.
SCALA, New York

In Venice the transition from Gothic to Renaissance building came less abruptly, as demonstrated in the Doge's Palace, where a Gothic exterior is found in combination with a late 15th-century facade on the east of the courtyard and a series of High Renaissance council chambers, famous for wall paintings by the Venetian painters Paolo Veronese and Tintoretto. Wood panelling with flat pilasters and a molded frieze forms the lower part of the interior wall decoration, with the fine series of historical and allegorical paintings, above, divided into panels between painted and gilded moldings and pilasters. The ceilings of a later date are particularly richly painted, their heavily scrolled carved and gilt cornices and framing introducing a touch of the Baroque style. Windows with twin semicircular headed frames surmounted by a lunette (a semicircular wall area) and fitted into a third, larger round-arched opening are a typically Venetian feature of the waterside palaces. In these, as in all the great Italian houses of the time, the works not only of the finest painters of the period but of the sculptors, goldsmiths and silversmiths, wood-carvers, bronzework-

Venetian interiors

ers and ironworkers were used to embellish the principal rooms. Silks, embroideries, and cut velvets were used as hangings and upholstery, together with elaborately cut and framed looking glasses and carved gilt pendant chandeliers, as in the Palazzo Corner-Spinelli, Venice (1480). Costly carpets were imported, and much fine linen was in use. Trompe l'oeil (realistic) effects of perspective were achieved in the painting of walls and ceilings and also with intarsia (inlaid wood) decorated panelling such as in the study of Federico da Montefeltro, formerly at Gubbio, Italy and now in the Metropolitan Museum, New York City (Figure 24) or in the Palazzo Ducale, Urbino (completed about 1500), where a startling effect is created simulating open cupboards full of books.

By courtesy of the Metropolitan Museum of Art, New York, Rogers Fund, 1939

Figure 24: Intarsia panels from the small study of Federico da Montefeltro, duke of Urbino, at Gubbio, attributed to Francesco de Giorgio of Siena, *c.* 1480. In the Metropolitan Museum of Art, New York City.

During the Renaissance, Venice became a glass-making centre and introduced many new techniques. Blue glass with fine enamel painting dates from the end of the 15th century. Excellent engraving was done with a diamond point as soon as glass of sufficiently good colour was produced, by using manganese to neutralize the colour introduced by impurities in the raw materials. Such glass, which was called *cristallo* from its fancied resemblance to the hardstone known as rock crystal, is the origin of modern crystal glass. The Venetians also imitated coloured hardstones in glass. Glass made white and opaque with tin oxide was sometimes used for enamel painting in the style of porcelain, and clear glass with opaque white threads embedded in it in lace-work patterns was called *vitro di trina*. The Venetians also made mirror glass of excellent quality; in the 17th century they supplied the mirrors for the Galerie des Glaces of the palace of Versailles. Large sheets, however, were not practicable until the French discovered a method of making plate glass late in the 17th century, when the national factory of Saint-Gobain was founded.

Italian woodworking

During medieval times, Italian wood-carvers had achieved a high level of skill in the decoration of churches; now they turned to secular furniture, for which they employed oak, walnut, cypress, and a new, rare, and expensive wood—ebony. (In 17th century France, the craftsmen skillful enough to be entrusted with this wood —who were also makers of cabinets—came to be called *ébénistes*, a term that remains the French equivalent of the English "cabinetmaker.") Many ancient Roman furniture-decorating techniques were revived. Inlaying with a variety of coloured woods, with ivory, mother-of-pearl, and tortoiseshell, with a mosaic of coloured stones known as *pietra dura*, and with painting and gilding in addition, ornamented the finest furniture. The chest (cassone), often commissioned on the occasion of a wedding, was decorated with elaborate painting and gilding, sometimes with a large pictorial subject and sometimes with elaborately carved work, which was later coloured. Italian furniture in its design often made use of architectural motifs. Cabinets were often exceptionally luxurious, with such elements as caryatids flanking central doors, arcades of semicircular arches, and triangular pediment tops. The interiors were sometimes small models of architectural interiors, with mirrors inset to give an impression of spaciousness. Silver furniture, no longer extant, was used in considerable quantities in late Renaissance times, usually crafted from plates of silver beaten over wooden formers.

Majolica

An innovation in Italy, which rapidly spread throughout the rest of Europe, was tin enamelled pottery, known in Italy as majolica and farther north as faïence or delft. Colourful dishes were often painted in a style known as *istoriato* (history painting) with mythological and biblical subjects. As some of the subjects were taken from engravings of Raphael's work, this pottery became known during the 18th and 19th centuries as Raffaelle ware. The majolica potters, the best of them located in Tuscany, made extensive use of grotesques, which show the style at its best.

The old Roman fashion for small bronze figures was revived during the Renaissance, and the fashion for these in interior decoration continued almost to the end of the 19th century. The earliest were fairly exact copies of excavated classical bronzes and may have been forgeries intended for sale at the time as genuine Roman work. The art developed rapidly. Before the 16th century, bronzework was done by the goldsmiths, and, as in most goldsmiths' work, general effect was subordinated to meticulous detail. After 1500, when bronze became popular for lamps, candlesticks, sconces, inkstands, small freestanding decorative figures, and furniture mounts, treatment of suitable subjects developed along the lines laid down for full-sized sculpture. Many small bronzes were made, some of them in the grotesque style.

At the beginning of the 16th century, the revived classicism of the Renaissance began to be modified, and eventually the style divided into two distinct paths. One remained faithful to tradition. The architect Andrea Palladio took ancient Roman works as a model, basing his designs on the theory of proportion laid down by Vitruvius in the 1st century BC in the *Ten Books on Architecture*. The second path was initiated by Michelangelo and led by way of Mannerism to the Baroque style. In both these latter styles, a deliberate exaggeration of forms displaced the strict logic and precision of the High Renaissance and aimed to convey freedom of movement and to involve the spectator in the drama of the design. Mannerism had only a limited influence on interior furnishing, as in the bronzes by Cellini and by Giambologna. Poses are often strained, the torso twisted, and the musculature emphasized; the favourite Mannerist subjects are violent ones, such as the rape of the Sabines and Hercules slaying Anteus.

Characteristics of the Baroque

Baroque was the style of the Counter-Reformation and was intended by the Jesuits to express the temporal power and riches of the Catholic Church in contrast to the austere doctrines of Protestantism. The theatricality of the baroque style soon attracted the attention of princes, who wanted it to be used in the palaces they built (Figure 25). Coloured marbles were used extensively, frequently in combination with bronze and rich gilding. Coloured glass windows were often used for lighting special features. Walls were sometimes painted to appear to be a continuation of the interior, giving an impression of spaciousness. Certain materials were often simulated by others: *scagliola*, for example, is a mixture of marble chippings, gypsum, and glue that was widely employed to

Figure 25: Baroque cupids supporting painted and gilded ceilings in the theatrically conceived bedroom of the Palazzo Sagredo, Venice, c. 1718. In the Metropolitan Museum of Art, New York City.

By courtesy of the Metropolitan Museum of Art, New York, Rogers Fund, 1906

imitate brecciated marble. What appeared to be richly coloured marbles were often no more than painted wood. Drapery was frequently imitated in carved marble, and wooden columns, the purpose of which was purely decorative, were painted like marble or some other exotic stone. Marble or stucco was made to imitate brocaded hangings, as in the Sala Ducale, Vatican, where an effect of space from limited means is created. Basic techniques were unaltered, but all restraint in their use vanished in bold theatrical effects and sensual luxuriance of modelling. Walls became curved, pediments were broken (*i.e.*, with central part omitted), columns and pilasters twisted until the buildings seem to come alive with movement. Bernini exuberantly combined rockwork, figures, and draperies with columns, panelling, and vaulting.

From Italy these styles spread across Europe, where they were absorbed in varying degrees and tempered by the national or local taste and genius. Many Italian designers and craftsmen travelled and worked abroad in France, England, Austria, and Spain.

France. From the middle of the 15th century, ideas from Italy began to change the face of French buildings; this change came gradually, first in the applied decorative detail superimposed on basically Gothic designs, then extending to a symmetry and regularity of the whole. Indeed, one of the basic differences between the Renaissance in France and in Italy is that in the latter the revolution in style involved, from the very outset, the whole conception of design. The centralization of power and the brilliance of French court life was consolidated under Francis I (1515–47) and had already resulted in patronage of artists and craftsmen from Italy. Since the need for churches had been fulfilled in the great age of Gothic building, the king and his court rivalled one another's magnificence in building new châteaux in the early Renaissance style. Stone and timber were readily available, with masons and carpenters skilled in their use.

Style of Francis I

Among the earliest attempts in the new manner are the additions made by Francis I to the Château de Blois. The spiral staircase, with its own open stonework tower, may have been designed by Leonardo da Vinci, who died nearby at Amboise in 1519. Even at this early stage, the decoration of the staircase ceiling with carved bosses (an ornamental ceiling projection) featuring the monogram and heraldic device of the king shows a typical French contribution to Renaissance decoration. Such shields and monograms formed an important element in many decorative features, being used in wall and ceiling panel design or on the large carved stone chimneypieces. The fine galleries of Francis I and Henry II (1547–59) in the royal Palais de Fontainebleau illustrate the increasing elaboration of applied decoration and colour (Figure 26). The flat ceilings are of wood, coffered, coloured, and gilded in a variety of geometrical forms outlined with fine moldings. Molded panels enclose paintings on the upper section of the walls, and molded or carved wood panelling the lower parts, as in Italy. Floors are of hardwood strips, sometimes repeating the pattern of the coffered ceiling above. Benches supported on consoles (ornamental brackets) are designed as part of the overall scheme of wall panelling. Italian artists had been employed at Fontainebleau and elsewhere, influencing the contemporary French architects toward a more Italian conception. Rosso Fiorentino and Francesco Primaticcio decorated the Galerie de François I, while the hexagonal coffered ceiling in the Galerie de Henri II was designed by the French architect Philibert de l'Orme. The architects Sebastiano Serlio and Giacomo da Vignola, together with the goldsmith Benevenuto Cellini, all worked for a time in France, and much of the decorative work in the châteaux of the Loire valley was executed by Italian craftsmen.

In the early 17th century and during the long reign of Louis XIV (1643–1715), formality and magnificence became paramount in the life of the court. Suites of large rooms elaborately decorated provided an opulent background for "Le Roi Soleil" ("The Sun King") and his courtiers, such suites usually consisted of a vestibule, antechamber, dining room, salon, state bedroom, study, and gallery. Staircases were stately and spacious, offering a fitting approach to the main rooms. Decorative schemes incorporated the fittings, hangings, and furniture with that of the room itself.

Versailles

The Baroque style was admirably fitted to express ideas of luxury and pomp. It inspired the building of some of the finest palaces erected in Europe since the days of Imperial Rome. The palace of Versailles built in the mid-17th century and widely imitated, led to the French court style in interior decoration and furnishings. Versailles was intended to be the outward and visible expression of the glory of France, and of Louis XIV, then Europe's most powerful monarch. His finance minister, Colbert, set up a manufactory that made works of art of all kinds, from furniture to jewellery, for interior decoration. A large export trade took French styles to almost every corner of Europe, made France a centre for luxuries, and gave to Paris an influence that has lasted till the present day. The vast initial cost of Versailles has been more than recouped since its completion. Even Louis XIV's most violent enemies imitated the decoration of his palace at Versailles. In 1667 Charles Le Brun was appointed director of the Gobelins factory, which had been bought by the King, and Le Brun himself prepared designs for various objects, from the painted ceilings of the Galerie des Glaces (Hall of Mirrors) at Versailles to the metal hardware for a door lock. (It should be noted that at the Gobelins, as elsewhere in France, furniture was designed by artists or architects who had no practical experience of manufacture, whereas, in the great age of furniture making in England, most designs were made and executed by the cabinetmaker himself, with an intimate knowledge of his material.)

Though the Baroque trend is well established in the Versailles interiors, generally speaking it was regulated in France by an underlying restraint that seldom permitted decoration or movement to dominate entirely. Besides the Galerie des Glaces at Versailles (Figure 27), the

Figure 26: Elaborately carved and painted gallery characteristic of French Renaissance design: Palais de Fontainebleau, Galerie de François I, *c.* 1533–45.
Giraudon

Galerie d'Apollon at the Louvre is an example of magnificence in decoration. The vastness of these rooms and the lavish use of marble, plasterwork, and painted ceilings (with the addition at Versailles of mirror glass panels) created an effect of overwhelming grandeur.

Giraudon

Figure 27: Formality and magnificence appropriate to the court of Louis XIV: Galerie des Glaces (Hall of Mirrors), Versailles, designed by Jules-Hardouin Mansart, ceiling painted by Charles Le Brun, 1678.

Among the architects and artists working at this time were Jean Berain, André-Charles Boulle, Jean le Paultre, Robert de Cotte, and Jules Hardouin-Mansart. Their work continued in the later period in which Baroque ornament was transformed into the airy, delicate Rococo of the mid-18th century (Figure 28). The beginning of this more fluent treatment can be seen in the work of Robert de Cotte at Versailles and the Hôtel de Toulouse, Paris. An immense variety of materials was used for the inlaid and decorated furniture; in a piece by Boulle, for instance, the designer employed—in addition to the tortoise-shell and brass inlay—ebony, copper, lapis lazuli, green-stained ivory or horn, and mother-of-pearl.

Transition from Baroque to Rococo

Despite its freedom from onerous restrictions, the Baroque style had preserved the classical idea of symmetry. It was not until the early decades of the 18th century that there were marked departures from the notion that an object divided vertically should consist of two halves that are mirror images of each other. The Louis XIV style had a passion for symmetry, and it was not until the Regency of the duc d'Orléans, which began in 1715, that asymmetry became one of the features of contemporary decoration. It is one of the principal aspects of the Rococo style. The principal designer in this style, who was largely responsible for its development, was Juste-Aurèle Meissonnier, who was a goldsmith and *ornemeniste*. Thus it is no accident that many objects in Rococo style, including furniture, look as though they had been designed by a metalworker. It has been said that Rococo began when the scrolls stopped being symmetrical. The influences that brought about this revolutionary ornamental concept are worthy of consideration.

The influence of oriental porcelain

Beginning in the early decades of the 17th century, Chinese porcelain and lacquer were imported into Europe in ever-increasing quantities. Porcelain, especially, attracted many distinguished collectors, including most of the royalty of Europe. This increasing use of Chinese art objects in European decorative art provided a powerful influence with no trace of classical tradition. Soon after 1650 the Dutch began to import porcelain from Japan, at first decorated in blue, but toward the end of the century in polychrome, either painted by, or in the manner of Sakaida Kakiemon. This was widely sought, and even more highly valued than Chinese porcelain. When Augustus the Strong, elector of Saxony and king of Poland, bought a palace early in the 18th century to house his collection,

Figure 28: A delicacy of decorative motif in panelling and furniture characteristic of the Rococo design of the Louis XV style: room from the Hôtel de Varengeville, Paris, design attributed to Nicolas Pineau, *c.* 1735. In the Metropolitan Museum of Art, New York City.

By courtesy of the Metropolitan Museum of Art, New York, acquired with funds given by Mr. and Mrs. Charles B. Wrightsman

for instance, he called it the Japanische Palais, and in France Louis-Henri de Bourbon-Condé, duc de Bourbon, established a factory at Chantilly to imitate Japanese porcelain. The decorations of Kakiemon were markedly asymmetrical, as were the painted lacquer panels that were imported to be made into screens and furniture, and there seems no doubt that this feature also influenced European Rococo art.

Despite the quantities in which it was imported, the demand for Oriental porcelain could not be satisfied, and European potters sought desperately to discover the secret. The first factory to make porcelain in the Oriental manner was at Meissen in Saxony, patronized by Augustus the Strong, but soon many small factories began to spring up in Germany, Austria, and Italy. France had several factories making a modified type of porcelain, the most important being the Sèvres factory, owned by Louis XV and patronized by his mistress, Mme de Pompadour. The first English factory, at Chelsea, was established as late as 1745. Porcelain was probably the most important expression of the Rococo style in the first half of the 18th century, with bronze and goldsmiths' work closely following in second place; indeed, this period might well be called the age of porcelain. Rooms entirely decorated with porcelain still exist. These included not only vases and figures, but also mirror-frames, scrollwork, cornices, and even small console tables. A very fine example still survives at the Palazzo di Capodimonte (Museo e Gallerie Nazionale di Capodimonte) in Naples.

The French style developed, in the 18th century, into a very skillful synthesis of materials in which bronze and porcelain played an important part. Furniture was elaborately mounted in bronze with a marble top and was often decorated with porcelain plaques, as well. Clocks were made from porcelain vases. Jardinieres and vases were filled with porcelain flowers with bronze stalks and leaves. Veneering with rare woods reached its height, and decorative marquetry, often elaborately pictorial, was practiced. Much sought at this time was the marquetry of brass and tortoiseshell, which began with Boulle, although it was a revival of an Imperial Roman fashion. Tapestries covered the walls when these were not decorated with carved wood-panelling known as boiserie. Another form of wall-decoration, also employed in the making of furniture, was vernis Martin (Martin's varnish), an imitation of Oriental lacquer that was extremely popular after 1730. The large *salon de reception* of the 17th century gave place to smaller, more intimate rooms, and more of them, and the furniture and decoration of the period are also on a smaller scale.

The Rococo style is remarkable for its flowers and its curves. Furniture legs were gracefully curved, and tops were cut into serpentine shapes. It is easy to see when the Rococo style ends, because chairlegs at once become straight.

Typical Rococo features are seen in the interiors of the architect and decorator Germain Boffrand for the Hôtel de Soubise, Paris (begun 1732), where architectural form has been subordinated to the demands of the decoration; the cornice has disappeared, and walls curve into the ceiling, appliquéd with ragged C scrolls, garlands of flowers decked with ribbons, sprays of foliage, trellising, and shell motifs. The reduced scale of rooms and the reaction from monumental design result in elimination of the classical orders. Relatively small painted panels, idealizing peasant life, were enclosed in flattened moldings, silvered or gilt; pastel-coloured backgrounds prevented the smaller size of the salons from becoming too evident. The use of Chinese motifs typifies the search for novelty and blends well with the general lightness of style. The Cabinet de la Pendule (Room of the Clock) at Versailles (1738), designed by J. Verberckst, is another excellent example of French Rococo interior design. Gilles-Marie Oppenordt and François de Cuvilliés also were distinguished designers who worked with the best artists and craftsmen of the time.

The Rococo fashion spread across Europe to the courts of minor royalties, where many Frenchmen were employed to provide up-to-date buildings and schemes of decoration. In France the Gobelins factory became restricted mainly to the output of tapestries; equally fine work is seen in Aubusson and Beauvais carpets and tapestry. Improvement in glass manufacture resulted in larger mirror panels and brilliant crystal chandeliers.

Neoclassicism of the Louis XVI style

The Louis XVI, or Neoclassical, style began, in fact, to take root before the death of Louis XV in 1774; Mme de Pompadour and her brother, the Marquis de Marigny, were among the first to be attracted by the new classical style in the 1750s. From 1748 onward the characteristically French regard for formality was stimulated by the archaeological discoveries at the sites of the ancient Roman cities of Herculaneum and Pompeii and by the other surveys of classical remains published at this time.

It is sometimes forgotten that contemporary English styles also had influence in France, mainly through the published works of the architects Robert and James Adam. The asymmetrical, sinuous lines of the Rococo were slowly replaced by a more restrained form of decoration based once again on straight lines, right angles, circles, and ovals, arranged symmetrically. The lightness and fine moldings were retained, but the decorative forms were once more contained by the architectural framework. New motifs, many of them selected from antique Roman wall painting, decorated the panelling, in paint or in flat relief; palmettes, husks, urns, tripod stands, sphinxes, trophies of arms or musical instruments were frequently combined in the decorative schemes (Figure 29). Gilt bronze was used with wood and plasterwork for moldings and ornamental fillets, emphasizing the rectilinear character of the design. The work of J.-A. Gabriel in both the Chambre du Conseil at the École Militaire (begun 1751) and the Galerie Dorée, Ministère de Marine (begun 1762) may be cited as Parisian examples. The keynote of colouring, as well as design, is refined simplicity. Silk tapestry wall hangings with fine flower and ribbon motifs appear in pale blues, greens, rose, and lilac. Similar colourings were used for satin and velvet upholstery. The fine wood carving of the brothers Rousseau, gilt bronze work by Clodion (Claude Michel), and furniture pieces by David Röntgen, C.E. Riesener, and

Figure 29: Symmetrical, restrained motifs based on the antique designs characteristic of the early Neoclassical Louis XVI style: Boudoir of Mme. de Serilly, Hôtel de Soubise, Paris, *c.* 1732. In the Victoria and Albert Museum, London.
By courtesy of the Victoria and Albert Museum, London; photograph, John Webb

Jean Oeben show Louis XVI decoration at its highest. Apartments for Queen Marie-Antoinette at Versailles and her boudoir at Fontainebleau are full of this extravagant delicacy, soon to be obliterated in the French Revolution.

Spain. In Spain, Moorish influence mingled with subsequent Western classical styles to produce a unique flavour in decorative design. The style known as Mudejar (*c.* 12th–17th centuries) was the early outcome of these blended Christian and Arab ideas and consists in essence of tiled floors and skirtings in polychrome (Figure 30), plain white walls, carved stucco friezes, and intricately decorated beamed wooden ceilings. The Duke of Alba's palace, Seville, contains fine interiors decorated in this style.

The Mudéjar style

Yellow tiles decorated with freehand motifs in blue became common in the 16th century. Tiles were often used on the ground floor of summer living rooms. Since fireplaces were seldom used in southern Spain, these rooms were vacated in the winter for the upper rooms.

The discovery of the New World, with the riches Spain subsequently drew from Mexico and Peru, created a period of Spanish ascendancy in the 16th century that encouraged building and coincided with the spread of Renaissance ideas throughout Europe. The influence of decorative craftsmen from Italy, together with the abundance of precious metal, encouraged the development of Plateresque ("silversmith-like") decoration. This type of Renaissance decoration was first seen in church interiors, in the form of tombs, *retablos* (a decorative structure behind an altar), and ironwork screens. The Italian motifs were used in a totally non-Italian manner, encrusting the surfaces as in the late Gothic or Mudéjar style.

This unique Spanish blend of widely separate styles produced the fine interiors of the late 15th-century Panteón de los Duques del Infantado, Guadalajara, by Vazquez, and the Palacio de Peñaranda de Duero (*c.* 1530), probably by Francisco de Colonia, where interlaced ceiling beams and timber panels were supported on honeycomb cornices and finely ornamented friezes. (Unfortunately, much of this work is now damaged or destroyed.)

Smaller houses as well as palaces were built around a patio, usually colonnaded and with modelled or carved friezes, columns, and bracket capitals.

Window grilles, or *rejas*, often form an important part of the decorative scheme, the ironwork being traditionally of a high degree of excellence. Love of closely patterned decoration, enveloping all surfaces that could easily be carved or modelled, is an important characteristic of early Renaissance work in Spain, and of the contemporary Manueline style in Portugal. Similar, if rather coarser, work in this style flourished in the American colonies.

High Renaissance decoration in Spain was influenced deeply by the austere character of Philip II and his vast combined palace and monastery, El Escorial (1559–84), near Madrid (Figure 30). This was built for him by Juan Bautista de Toledo and Juan de Herrera. Much of the granite of which the monastery is built is left unadorned, and frescoed vaulted ceilings are the main decorative features of interior design.

By courtesy of the Newsweek Book Division; photograph, Michael Holford

Figure 30: Austere Spanish interior of the Renaissance period; apartments of Philip II: El Escorial, near Madrid, second half of the 16th century.

A revival of decorative arts took place in the late 17th century under the influence of José Benito Churriguera, his family and followers. The Churrigueresque, which also remained a peculiarly Spanish style, expressed the Baroque feeling of the 17th century in extravagant polychrome. Surfaces were broken into scrolls, rosettes, volutes, and fantasticated moldings; bunches of fruit and flowers hung from broken or inverted cornice moldings; and the whole interior—for example, the Sacristy of the Cartuja, Granada (1727–64)—appears to drip with ornament. Here, even cupboards and doors were inlaid with silver, tortoise shell, and ivory, and the only plain surface is the checkerboard tiled floor. Remarkable among domestic examples of this style is the Palacio del Marqués de Dos Aguas, Valencia (1740–44).

The Churrigueresque style

Under the Bourbons, French and Italian influence increased, as can be seen in the interiors of the Royal Palace at Madrid (1738–64), with its handsomely painted ceilings and brocade wall hangings. Here, also, subsequent changes of taste are echoed in the lighter Rococo treatment of the Gasparini Saloon. Toward the end of the 18th century the Neoclassical movement gained a limited footing, though regional styles continued to incorporate the Baroque and older forms.

Fine examples of Spanish colonial work exist in Mexico, Peru, and other South American countries where the Baroque was allied, as in Europe, with the Jesuits. Churches are painted and gilded with an exuberance equal to or even greater than that found in the mother country. Sometimes the churches are encrusted with tiles, and they always possess elaborate *retablos*.

Northern Europe. After spreading from Italy to France, Renaissance influence began to filter to Belgium and Holland, later reaching the various Germanic states and finally dying out in Scandinavia and Russia.

In the Low Countries and northern Germany during the 16th-century Renaissance, ornament was adapted to form an entirely individual style, which can be seen in the pattern books of the artists Hans Vredeman de Vries and Wendel Dietterlin. Strapwork (interlacing bands) and raised faceted ornament were widely employed, together with muscular, grotesque masked caryatids and distorted architectural features arranged in undisciplined designs (Figure 31). Chimney pieces, with overmantels carried to the ceiling, were embellished with marble columns and elaborate strapwork patterns, while similar ornaments flanked the doorways and enriched the ceilings. The great tapestries for which the Netherlands had long been famous were still in use, and Oriental carpets were spread as table covers and not used on the floors. Many town houses and civic buildings were comfortably appointed, yet without spectacular extravagances, and give an impression of modest prosperity. In Belgium the Musée Plantin-Moretus, Antwerp (1550), is unusually richly decorated, showing the influence of Spanish rule in the use of embossed leather as a wall covering. Large windows, with rectangular leaded lights, are again typical of a northern climate. Ceilings are beamed or plastered, and floors most frequently are of tiles on the ground floor and timber on upper floors.

Use of strapwork

The later styles of Baroque and the 18th-century tastes are copied from French models, particularly in Belgium. The Dutch, after achieving independence in the latter part of the 16th century, developed their decoration on more individual lines. Typical domestic interiors on a small scale are familiar through the paintings of the 17th-century artists Jan Vermeer and Pieter de Hooch (Figure 32). The fine series of town houses by Daniel Marot and his sons in The Hague illustrate the cross–currents of the various styles; built at the turn of the 17th century, they were conceived in the Louis XIV, or Régence, manner, yet could be set down in 18th-century London without incongruity (and Marot did, in fact, work for a time in England). Fine stuccoed ceilings and overdoors, largely uncoloured, and wrought iron balustrading are characteristic.

Marot town houses

In Germany the general trend was similar, but in southern Germany and Austria fresh impetus and individuality were given to Baroque and also Rococo design. French and Italian craftsmen worked throughout the 17th century on the many Catholic churches built in south Germany, Austria, Bohemia, and Moravia. The use of colour, fresco, and stucco that they introduced has its own particular flavour when seen in cool northern light (see Figure 12, right).

Secular building from the early 18th century, in the hands of such architects as Johann Lucas von Hildebrandt and Johann Bernhard Fischer von Erlach, makes use of much sculptural detail. Windows are round or oval, figures strain to support capitals, balustrades are carved in sculptural manner, and modelled niches contain larger than life-sized figures; all these give a feeling of movement reminiscent in its impact of Bernini's work in Rome. Another characteristic was the enormous staircase hall, or *Treppenhaus*, which was one of the most notable interior features of German and Austrian Baroque and Rococo architecture. In the halls, colour was frequently confined to the painted ceilings, giving increased force to the novel and delicious colours of the rooms beyond. A vermilion dado or olive-green panels may be contrasted with white and gold. In the Nymphenburg palace, near Munich (1734–39), by the Frenchman François de Cuvilliés, the Rococo reaches its crowning achievement: mirrors are framed in freely scrolled moldings, which in their turn are interspersed with trellising, garlands, baskets of fruit and flowers, cupids, birds, and fountains in silvered stucco on a pale blue or yellow ground, the whole evoking the essence of pastoral Romanticism (Figure 33).

Mingled influences from France, Holland, and England reached Sweden and Denmark in the mid-17th century and are seen in the Baroque and Louis XIV interiors of the Riddarhus and Royal palace in Stockholm and in the chinoiserie (Chinese-influenced decoration) of the Royal Palace of Drottningholm. Scandinavian interiors, however, largely continued to be of the traditional exposed timber boarding, hung perhaps with painted linen panels and brightened by woven chair and cushion coverings (Figure 34).

Scandinavian interiors

Russia imported foreign designers and styles in the late 17th and 18th centuries for the palaces built under the westernizing influence of Peter I the Great, his daughter Elizabeth, and Catherine II the Great. In the mid-18th century the Italian Bartolomeo Francesco Rastrelli designed the Tsarskoye (Detskoye) Selo (now called Pushkin), Peterhof, and Winter palaces in or near St. Petersburg, and A.B. Kvasov, S.I. Chevakinsky, and Rastrelli designed the Hermitage, also in St. Petersburg. Each worked largely according to his own current national styles. The same is true of the work of the British architect Charles Cameron at Tsarskoye Selo Palace and Pavlovsk Palace.

In many areas of Europe, Renaissance, Baroque, and Rococo had little effect on interior decoration. In the Alpine lands, where wood was cheap and plentiful, tra-

By courtesy of the Musee National Suisse, Zurich

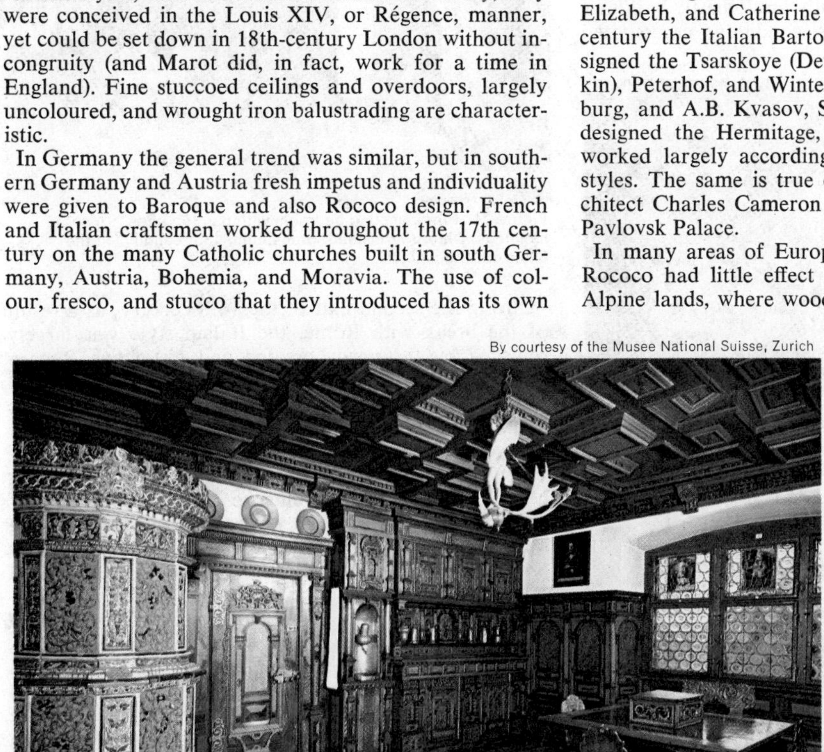

Figure 31: Strapwork and faceted ornament: Swiss Renaissance room from the Rosenburg at Stans, Switzerland, 1602.

Figure 32: Domestic interior typical of the 17th-century Dutch home; "Maternal Duty," canvas by Pieter de Hooch (1629–*c.* 1683). In the Rijksmuseum, Amsterdam.
By courtesy of the Rijksmuseum, Amsterdam

ditional medieval methods continued for a long time. Wooden floors and ceilings and panelled walls, or partly panelled with plain plaster above, were the general rule. The moldings were bold, but carving was usually in low relief and often the woodwork was painted in bright colours.

England. The breakup of the feudal system during the Wars of the Roses and under Henry VII in the late 15th century had far-reaching effects on the social structure of the time and consequently on domestic buildings and their decoration. The new conditions necessitated a larger number of rooms, and a great hall, though still an important apartment, was no longer the focus of indoor life. Wider distribution of wealth gave rise to numerous country houses, and for the next 400 years the English excelled in their building and decoration.

Adoption of Italian ornament

The Italian style reached England in the early 16th century; the earliest example is the tomb of Henry VII in Westminster Abbey, designed by Pietro Torrigiani of Florence at the command of Henry VIII and completed in 1518. For the next 40 years or so, English craftsmen borrowed from the repertoire of Italian ornament, at first inspired by and imitating the Italian artists and craftsmen employed on royal works at Hampton Court Palace, Middlesex, and the Palace of Westminster, London, who used arabesque decoration, medallion heads, and amorini on panelling and plasterwork, often mingling them with the traditional Gothic motifs. The great hall at Hampton Court (1515–30) shows a combination of Renaissance carved and gilded detail with the traditional type of open timber roof, known as the hammerbeam roof, and windows divided into sections by vertical posts (mullions). In spite of Henry VIII's example, however, the Gothic style died hard in England, lingering in the remoter districts well into the 17th century.

Gunther Schmidt—EB Inc

Figure 33: Sinuous, intricate curves characteristic of the Rococo decorative vocabulary: circular mirror room in the Amalienburg pavilion, Nymphenburg Palace, near Munich, designed by François de Cuvilliés, 1734–39.

By courtesy of the Nordiska Museet, Stockholm

Figure 34: Pine panelled bedroom with painted linen hangings, Oktorp farmstead, Stockholm, 18th century. In the Skansen, Stockholm.

During the second half of the 16th century, as a result of the break with Rome, the Italian style was largely replaced by the newly created and distinctive Renaissance style of the Low Countries and Germany, fostered as it was by the close religious, political, and economic relations between England and the Low Countries, the influx of immigrant workmen, and the circulation of Flemish and German pattern books. This new manner became the dominant influence in the decoration of panelling and plasterwork, characteristic features being intrinsic strapwork patterns, pyramid finials (sculptured ornaments used to terminate roof gables), raised faceted ornament, masks and caryatid figures, scrolls, and pilasters. Both the Italian and Flemish styles were adapted and naturalized to some extent by the English craftsmen, producing a new style that is peculiarly English.

At this time, also, the internal porch was introduced into many houses; this device excluded drafts from the room and also in some cases made it possible to reach a second room without passing through the first.

Tudor wall decoration

The frescoing of walls continued; of the few remaining examples, some show scenes from biblical and classical sources and incidents from local folklore. A good Elizabethan example depicting scenes from the story of Tobit was found at the White Swan inn at Stratford-on-Avon. Embossed, painted, and gilt leather was less used in England than on the Continent, but tapestries and such woven fabrics as velvet and damask for the wealthy and "says" (fabrics resembling serge) and "bayes" (baize) for people of more modest means were widely used as wall coverings. The inventories of Henry VIII's palaces show the vast number of tapestries and various hangings possessed by kings and great men. Hangings of painted cloth were widely used as a cheaper substitute for tapestry; these, too, depicted incidents from biblical and classical sources and employed decorative motifs ranging from Gothic to Renaissance subjects. Nearly all of this "counterfeit arras" has perished. The plaited rush matting continued to be used as a floor covering in Elizabethan interiors.

Great chambers and long galleries, usually on the upper floors, are distinctively Elizabethan or Tudor and were used in many cases for work and recreation in bad weather (Figure 35). Barrel-vaulted ceilings occupying the roof space often increased the height of the rooms, as at Chastleton House, Oxfordshire (*c.* 1603). The plaster ceilings were treated elaborately; narrow interlaced bands formed geometrical patterns, with semi-stylized floral, arabesque, or heraldic motifs in the panels between.

Staircase design

The steep medieval winding newel stair (stair with central pillar from which steps radiate) in wood or, more often, stone was abandoned for the more spacious staircase with straight flights of stairs, easier in gradient and planned round an open well. This was most frequently constructed of oak, with carved newel posts (the upright terminating a flight of stairs) and balusters (individual columns in a balustrade) making the most of the opportunity offered for decoration and enrichment.

Toward the middle of the 16th century, a feeling for classic reserve was spreading and the late Renaissance period might have flowered under Charles I had not political upheaval checked the zest for fine building. The architect and stage designer Inigo Jones twice visited Italy and was one of the few north European architects completely to absorb the spirit and decorative repertoire of Italian Renaissance classicism. He introduced the new style in the Banqueting House at Whitehall, the Queen's House at Greenwich; and with his associate and kinsman, John Webb, built Wilton House, Wiltshire.

At Wilton the incomparable Double Cube Room (*c.* 1649) shows the nobility of effect Jones was able to achieve in quite a small compass, for the dimensions of the room—60 by 30 by 30 feet (18 by 9 by 9 metres) —are not large, comparatively speaking (Figure 36). The basic influence is Italian, but the final result—with wide oak-boarded floor, and white- and gold-plastered and panelled walls designed to accommodate the fine portraits by Sir Anthony Van Dyke, the white marble fireplace, and the Corinthian doorcases—is truly English. The coved and painted ceiling, executed by Edward Pierce and Emanuel de Critz, is less distinguished than the decoration below cornice level, but plays a vital part in balancing the proportions of the room. Though Renaissance principles are demonstrated in design such as this, they were not fully developed in the country at large until the 18th century and the advent of the Palladian school of architecture and decoration (influenced by the 16th-century Italian architect Andrea Palladio), under the aegis of the architect Lord Burlington.

After the unsettled period of the Commonwealth, the Restoration introduced new Baroque influences from the Continent. These were fused with the restraining classicism (which was still considered to be a new style) to produce a successful balance of contrast. The designs of the great architect Sir Christopher Wren, though mainly for church and monumental buildings, relied for a great deal of their embellishment on the work of the fine artist-craftsmen such as Grinling Gibbons, sculptor and wood-carver, and Jean Tijou, ironworker, whose work can be seen in close association in St. Paul's Cathedral. In the many country houses, large plain-surfaced oak wall panels provided the perfect foil to the grace and liveliness of Gibbons' carved limewood swags (festoons), garlands, and picture borders, which incorporated flowers, fruit, musical instruments, cherubs, and monograms. In the words of the 18th-century writer Horace Walpole, Gibbons "gave to wood the loose and airy lightness of flowers, and chained together the various productions of the elements, with the free disorder natural to each species." At Petworth house, Sussex, Gibbons' genius may best be seen in the series of perfectly executed picture borders, which date from about 1690. Chimney pieces and doorcases were also decorated in Gibbons' manner, and similar floral motifs can be seen on the plaster ceilings at Ham house, Wiltshire. This house, relatively modest in size, represents without ostentation or extravagance the height of luxurious interior decoration in the late 17th century and incorporates many of the decorative innovations of that time. Among these are the practice of painting wood panelling in imitation of marble or wood graining and of gilding the moldings. Wall hangings include tapestry, gilt and painted leather, and silk damask; there is elaborate parquetry (floors inlaid with woods in contrasting colours).

Decorative genius of Grinling Gibbons

By courtesy of the Birmingham Museum and Art Gallery, England

Figure 35: Panelled walls, tapestries, and intricately molded plaster ceilings characteristic of the most sumptuous Jacobean interiors: The Long Gallery at Aston Hall, Birmingham, England, 1618. In the Birmingham Museum and Art Gallery, England.

Figure 36: Double Cube Room at Wilton, Wiltshire, England, designed by Inigo Jones, *c.* 1649.
A.F. Kersting

Paintings of allegorical subjects by Sir James Thornhill and Antonio Verrio ornament some of the more important buildings of the age, including the Painted Hall at the Royal Hospital in Greenwich, Wren's additions to Hampton Court, and the great chamber at Chatsworth House, Derbyshire. The intricate work of Daniel Marot, a French Huguenot architect who had worked for William III in Holland (see above *Northern Europe*), had a modest influence on the design of many small fittings and shelved cabinets to display china—the collecting of which was a favourite pastime of Queen Mary II. Imported lacquer panels were sometimes used for the panelling of rooms, in accordance with the Chinese taste of the period.

In the last years of the 17th century and in the early 18th century the woodworker found his domain contracting. Through the influence of the grand tour and under the patronage of Lord Burlington, Italian influence predominated, the work of Inigo Jones was studied, and stone and stucco became more widely used, particularly in larger houses. The influence of the architect spread from the outside of the house to the interior decoration and even to the design of the furniture itself. Where wooden panelling was used, it was set in a simple framework. Pine largely replaced oak, and it was painted green, blue, brown, and other colours; walnut and mahogany were occasionally used for panelling. The increased use of stone and marble began with Sir John Vanbrugh, playwright turned architect, who, in his first commission at Castle Howard, Yorkshire (1699), showed an individual and masterly interpretation of Baroque, sculptural and yet with a certain grim epic quality. Applied decoration was kept to a minimum, a practice that he followed later at Blenheim Palace, Oxfordshire, where the severe and spacious entrance hall, with marble-paved floor, ashlar-faced (*i.e.*, faced with thin slabs of hewn stone) walls and columns, wrought-iron gallery railing, and frescoed dome, is the most impressive apartment in the building.

Stone staircases with wrought-iron balustrading came into common use, and by the latter part of the 18th century had almost entirely replaced the earlier, heavier timber stairs such as those at Wolseley Hall, Staffordshire, or Eltham Lodge, Kent, which had carved openwork balustrades or heavy timber balusters. In the smaller houses of the early 18th century, woodwork continued to provide the main decorative features. Wall panelling, moldings, window shutters, and many chimney pieces in simple painted pine echoed the comfortable elegance of the tall sash windows and well-proportioned rooms. Wealthier classes still employed Italian craftsmen, particularly for stuccowork, and the now familiar repertory of garlands, masks, and putti (cupids) was applied not only to the designs of Nicholas Hawksmoor, James Gibbs, and other architects of the quasi-Baroque group but also to the interiors of William Kent and the Palladian architects, whose influence became dominant toward the middle of the century (see Figure 13). In such houses as Holkham Hall, Norfolk, designed in strictly classical manner by Kent in 1734, can be seen the results of extensive travel by both architect and owner. The magnificent entrance hall is again one of the most important rooms, designed on the general lines of a Roman basilica with apse (recess) and side colonnades. At Houghton hall, also in Norfolk, Kent designed fine suites of furniture for Colin Campbell's interiors; these pieces are usually gilt, with acanthus scrolls, consoles, heads, and sphinxes; with feet and legs scrolled or of ball and claw type; and with upholstery in velvet or silk. The plaster ceilings are by Italian craftsmen, with gilded and painted ornament; the walls are dressed with classical plinth, pilasters, and frieze; and pedimented marble chimneypieces contain bas-relief panels above the mantelshelf.

Continuing use of wood in the 18th century

Wall hangings were of tapestry, cut velvet, or watered silk and damask. Elsewhere, hand-coloured, wood-block-printed papers and papers with flocking (pulverized cloth) were coming into use as an economical substitute.

Although the Rococo style never fully established itself in England, many interiors were influenced by the asymmetrical motifs (rocaille) found in the designs of such French decorators as Nicholas Pineau and J.A. Meissonier. The stucco and carved decoration became lighter, more fanciful, and more tortuous in design. Though many Baroque motifs were still used, they were more delicately modelled, and the Rococo style was characterized by elaborate patterns of interlacing C scrolls combined with such naturalistic ornaments as flowers, foliage, shells, and rocks, arranged subtly in asymmetrical yet balanced patterns. The plasterwork and carved panelling were often painted in light colours and the detail picked out in gold.

Popularity of chinoiserie

Closely allied to the introduction of the French rocaille was the revival of the Chinese taste, or chinoiserie, for architects and designers, in search of further novelty, turned again to China for inspiration. Books on travel and topography, notably Jean-Baptiste du Halde's *General History of China*, published in Paris in 1735 and translated into English in 1736, gave added stimulus. Pagodas, mandarin figures, icicles and dripping water, and exotic foliage and birds reached the height of Rococo invention. Chinoiserie was particularly popular for bedrooms, where elaborate chimneypieces and doorcases were set against the background of imported or imitation Chinese wallpapers, and the beds and windows were hung with Eastern textiles. Window hangings, with carved and gilded pelmets (valances), were becoming increasingly important, and at Harwood House, Yorkshire, the furniture designer Thomas Chippendale executed a series of pelmets with mock draperies also carved in wood and coloured to deceive the eye completely.

Gothick taste

The Gothick taste, a further variation of the Rococo, was peculiar to England at this time. The Gothic Revival, engendered by antiquarian scholarship at the turn of the 17th century, later spread to literature and during the 1740s appeared in the more concrete forms of architecture and interior decoration. By the middle of the century the fashion was widely popular, and many houses, large and small, were in part Gothicized, both inside and out. As with chinoiserie, the products of this

18th-century vogue bore little resemblance to the original medieval models. Gothic details, originally worked in stone, were borrowed, adapted, often mingled with rocaille and Chinese motifs, and were executed in wood and plaster. At Strawberry Hill, Twickenham, Middlesex, Horace Walpole, leader of the "true Goths," borrowed the designs of medieval tombs and turned them to designs for fireplaces and bookcases. Though this vogue fell out of general fashion in the 1760s, a few enthusiasts remained who carried the Gothick taste through until it was vigorously revived again in the 19th century.

Contributions of Robert Adam

About 1760 the Rococo style, with all its vagaries of taste, began to give way before the Neoclassical style, largely inspired and introduced by the architect Robert Adam, whose work reflected the newly awakened interest in classical remains. Adam returned from Italy in 1758, and, strongly influenced by both Roman architecture and interior decoration, he evolved a new style based on classical precedent, using as ornament a medley of paterae (plate-shaped motifs), husk chains, the ram's head, the formalized honeysuckle, and other elements. His style of interior decoration was deeply influenced by the gay and delicate patterns of arabesques and grotesque ornament that he had seen in various classical remains in Rome and that had already been copied during the Renaissance by Raphael and others. Adam strongly criticized the Burlington (Palladian) school for using heavy architectural features in their interiors and replaced them with delicate ornament in plaster, wood, marble, and painting, against which, in its turn, criticism was levelled. Much of his work, it may be said, is applied decoration—pretty but without basic architectural quality. With Adam, the despotism of the architect over the craftsman was complete. No detail of decoration or furnishing escaped him; his rapid and precise draftsmanship covered the whole scheme, from the overall treatment of the walls and ceiling to the decorative details of the pelmets and grates. Even carpets were made to order, and often they repeated or echoed the design of the ceiling, bringing the whole room into harmony, as in the green drawing room in the manor house of Osterley Park in Middlesex or in the dining room at Saltram House in Devonshire (Figure 37). Wood was not often left unpainted, and, although the joinery was still admirable, the enrichment was frequently in composition or metal inlay. There were especially designed temple-fronted bookcases, and the plasterwork was often made a frame for the decorative paintings of such artists as Antonio Zucchi or Angelica Kauffmann.

A. F. Kersting

Figure 37: Neoclassical early style dining room at Saltram House, Devonshire, England, designed by Robert Adam, plasterwork and paintings by Antonio Zucchi, 1768.

At this time, cheaper and quicker methods of decoration began to be introduced; a considerable amount of the plaster decoration was cast from molds, and a composite imitation marble called scagliola was sometimes used for floors and columns, while cheaper woods were disguised by marbling and graining.

At the close of the century the Neoclassical style was further refined, the plaster relief decoration being simplified and lightened. The best of this style, strongly influenced by French decoration, can be seen in the work of the architect Henry Holland, who enlarged Carlton House, London, for the Prince Regent and built Southill in Bedfordshire. Holland, like Adam, was inspired by the classical monuments in Italy, where for some time he maintained a draftsman whose drawings of classical detail Holland incorporated in his plasterwork.

United States. The story of the domestic interior and its decoration in the United States is inseparable both from its own architectural development and from the story of English architecture and decoration, from which it was largely derived even long after the American Revolution. Any discussion of United States decorative design, therefore, must refer constantly to the architectural ideas that prompted change on both sides of the Atlantic Ocean.

Contrary to popular legend, the log cabin was not the earliest shelter of the first English settlers. The turfed-over dugout hut of mud-chinked saplings, not unlike the Indian wigwam with the addition of a clay-daubed wooden chimney at one end, was probably the first home of the settlers in both Jamestown and Plymouth.

Early domestic interiors

These primitive dwellings were speedily replaced by frame structures, copying the traditional small house of southeast England. At first a single room was flanked by a massive chimney (where brick quickly replaced wood and clay), but a second room was soon added on the opposite side of the chimney. The attic, later expanded into an overhanging second story, was reached by narrow winding stairs between the central entranceway and the chimney stack.

This development in New England is well represented by such vestiges as the Capen House, Topsfield, Massachusetts (1683) or the Old Iron Works (ironmaster's) House, Saugus, Massachusetts (1636). The interior clearly reflects the structure, with its massive exposed oak corner posts, beams, and joists and its huge open fireplace, which served as the cooking and heating centre of the household. Inside walls were usually of undecorated lath and plaster, covering the studs and their clay or brick filling. Windows were small and originally of casement type, with small leaded panes in a wood frame. Small windows with low ceilings were needed to conserve heat in the severe winters. Floors of wide riven boards of pine, smoothed and sanded, replaced the beaten clay of the first shelters (Figure 38).

The furniture, with few exceptions, was simple and sparse. It was decorated with simple carved and turned ornament and touches of earth colours.

By the end of the 17th century, homespun textiles were supplemented by imported woven materials in the houses of the more affluent; these were used for curtains, table covers, bed hangings, and seat pads. Richly coloured damasks and velvets, enhanced by the unpainted wood and plaster surfaces, were found in Puritan New England and, probably to a greater extent, among the less austere New York Dutch and the comparatively wealthy tobacco planters of Virginia.

In the early dwellings south of New England, brick and stone tended to replace wood as a building material, though many smaller timber constructions must have been used that have now largely disappeared. In the Hudson River region, the traditional cottage of the Flemish and Huguenot settlers, long and low with steep

Figure 38: Simply furnished New England domestic interior: Great Room, Old Iron Works (ironmaster's) House, Saugus, Massachusetts, 1636.
Richard Merrill

pitched roof and extended eaves, became the typical farmhouse. At the same time, the narrow Dutch town house of brick with its stepped gable ends gave New Amsterdam, even after the English occupation, an appearance completely different from that of the English settlements to the north and south.

Dutch features in New York

In the Dutch houses, windows tended to be larger and ceilings higher. The early fireplace, with its tiled border, surmounted with a deep hood, was flush with the wall instead of deeply recessed. Dutch features such as the horizontally divided door, the monumental cupboard, or *kas*, the built-in bed, and tiling and dishes of delftware gave the early New York interior an individuality that withstood English influence until well into the following century.

Similar national characteristics must have distinguished the early Swedish settlement on the Delaware, where, later in the century, the log cabin of pioneer tradition may have appeared for the first time. But the Swedish contribution was only temporary, for the settlement was speedily absorbed by both the Dutch and the English. The early settlements of the English in east New Jersey were mainly founded by migrants from New England who at first designed typical central-chimney houses but before the end of the century largely abandoned them for the Flemish type of house in the neighbouring Hudson River region. The first settlers in Pennsylvania, arriving in Philadelphia at the end of the century, built the type of town dwelling devised for the rebuilding of London after the Great Fire of 1666.

In Virginia and the South, scant evidence remains of the early 17th-century house. Bacon's Castle in Surry County, Virginia, with its projecting two-story porch in front and rear stair tower, built in brick about 1665, is all that remains of a colonial version of the small English Jacobean manor, though there must have been several other examples. From surviving evidence and deduction it is believed that panelled walls, carefully designed beamed ceilings, and ornamental plasterwork in colour were employed in larger Virginia houses. Yet, while the milder climate made loftier ceilings and larger rooms possible, it is unlikely that the ordinary early dwelling differed from its Northern contemporary except in its greater use of brick and in placing chimneys at the ends instead of at the centre of the structure.

Among the wealthy the principal articles of furniture were undoubtedly English imports; the more humble settler probably had to make do with articles of the simplest sort, but since few articles survive from this period, little is known about it. Certainly the scattered or rural character of the Southern settlements and their concentration on tobacco planting failed to encourage the early development of skilled crafts found in villages and towns of the Northern communities. By 1720 the design innovations of Inigo Jones and Sir Christopher Wren, as reflected in the Queen Anne style with its strong mingling of Dutch and Flemish elements, had already crossed the Atlantic. Wren's influence is increasingly evident in the tendency to employ symmetrical design around an accented central feature and, particularly in the interiors, in the greater insistence on classic arrangement in the positions of openings and of panelling. Panelling, usually of pine in the north, was generally painted. Relatively deep and strong tones—red, blue, green, brown, and yellow—were used either singly or in combination, producing an effective background for the walnut furniture of the period.

Influence of Wren and Jones

Additional colour was introduced by more elaborate use of woven and embroidered textiles, in upholstery as well as draperies. Though woven carpets for floor coverings were rare even at midcentury, frequently their effect was achieved by stretched canvas painted with allover repeat patterns.

Colonial furniture

Throughout the colonies, furniture became more plentiful and varied. Chairs without arms took the place of stools, the cabriole (curved leg) largely replaced the turned leg, and small drop-leaf tables replaced the fixed-frame type. Bedroom furniture became differentiated with the development of the high chest (highboy) and the dressing table (lowboy), and later the case-top desk or secretary became the principal ornament of the living room. Tall mirrors with crested tops replaced the small, square, Jacobean style looking glasses of the 17th century, and portraits and prints came into more general use, sharing the wall space with bracketed candle holders or sconces. Artificial light still came mainly from small wick and grease lamps, but tallow and wax candles held in sconces, in adjustable metal and wood floor stands, or in candlesticks of brass or pewter (and occasionally in brass chandeliers) were used by the wealthier.

Though domestic comfort was improving, north of Virginia the large formal house or mansion remained a rarity until about 1750. In the South the wealth of the slaveholding planter made it possible for him to copy the early Georgian type of manor house in England. Great houses of two or three stories with side dependencies (outbuildings) became numerous. Stratford in Westmoreland County and Westover in Charles City County, Virginia, built about 1735 by the Lee and Byrd families, are early examples of the type. The elaborately panelled rooms of these mansions were furnished according to the latest London fashion. Probably only later in the century were these English pieces mingled with those from the cabinetmakers of Philadelphia, New York, and Boston. Between 1750 and the Revolution this Georgian phase reached its highest development. Though generally smaller and lacking the forecourt and dependencies of the southern mansion, the larger houses of the north, such as the Wentworth house in Portsmouth, New Hampshire, mark perhaps the most distinctive achievements of colonial design and decoration by their apt translations into wood of brick and stone Georgian forms.

English Rococo in Philadelphia

In the Middle Atlantic colonies, particularly in Philadelphia (which by 1760 had assumed urban leadership in the colonies), a type of domestic design midway between that of New England and Virginia had developed. There the English Rococo decorative style publicized by Thomas Chippendale received its most competent and original interpretation. This is well seen in Philadelphia interiors such as those of the Powel House (1765) and Mount Pleasant (1762) and in the work of cabinetmakers such as Thomas Affleck and Benjamin Randolph (Figure 39). By this time mahogany, with its fine grain, so receptive to carving and high finish, had largely replaced walnut as the principal cabinet wood. Inspired by this material and the challenge of London design, these Philadelphia craftsmen and their northern contemporaries, particularly John Goddard and Job Townsend of Newport, Rhode Island, brought their art to the highest level of perfection.

During the third quarter of the 18th century, the panelled interior reached its most elaborate form in the

Figure 39: Middle Atlantic adaptation of the English Rococo style using Philadelphia Chippendale furniture: Great Chamber at Mount Pleasant, Philadelphia, 1762.
By courtesy of the Philadelphia Museum of Art

colonies. North of Virginia a fully panelled room was exceptional; wood panelling was reserved for the chimney breast and its flanking recesses or cupboards. In Virginia and the South, full panelling remained the rule. (At colonial Williamsburg, Virginia, surviving houses have been carefully restored and furnished, giving a complete picture of the comfortable panelled rooms dating from the middle decades of the 18th century.) In both North and South, however, the mantel and its overmantel were emphasized as a decorative unit, and the Baroque broken pediment became the usual crowning feature of both overmantel and doorway. Painted woodwork remained popular, but with softer and lighter tones, tending toward white and gray. Plaster wall surfaces were also painted. Block-printed and painted wallpapers were frequently used in the main rooms of these houses, and there are indications that fabric wall hangings were used also.

Plaster ceilings completely concealed the floor beams by the second quarter of the century, and after 1750 these were frequently decorated with ornament in low relief in the French or Rococo manner and hung with many-branched chandeliers of crystal. Floors of hardwood, occasionally parquetry, were more frequently covered with patterned rugs of European or Oriental origin.

Use of textiles

During the 18th century imports of printed cottons or chintz in the Indian taste, and silk brocades and damasks, largely replaced the linen and woolen weaves of earlier days. Upholstered furniture, wing chairs and sofas, and elaborate draperies increased still further the richness of the fashionable interior.

As in Europe, the growth of tea and coffee drinking encouraged production of suitable silverware and the import of English and Oriental porcelains, which required corner and wall storage cupboards. Demand was also created for a variety of small movable tables and stands for tea and coffee services.

During this century the German settlers in Pennsylvania added their traditional styles of design to the dominantly English tradition of the colony, the effects being more evident in folk arts than in formal decoration. It was to this style and its development after the Revolution that the first American decorative glass of Henry William Stiegel and Frederick Amelung must be credited, as well as most of the decoration on early American pottery.

19th and early 20th centuries in Europe. Neoclassicism predominated in France till the rise of Napoleon, when to Roman styles were added Egyptian motifs from his Egyptian campaign of 1798. This was known in France as the Empire style, after the First Empire of France (1804–14), and in England as Regency, for the period (1811–20) when George III was too deranged to rule. Furniture design, for the most part light and graceful during the early part of the Neoclassical period in France, had become more consciously luxurious as the Revolution was approached. During the Empire period it became massive, imposing, dark, and pompous (Figure 40). The usual vocabulary of classical ornament is to be found in both Empire and Regency, with some modifications from earlier times. The cabriole leg of the Rococo style became straight, and curves tended to disappear in all furniture. Symmetry of ornament replaced the asymmetrical curves. In England, in the latter part of the 18th century, porcelain became less and less fashionable, and its place was taken by the cream-coloured earthenware (creamware) of Josiah Wedgwood, and by his jasper and basaltes stonewares, all admirably adapted to the new style. Greek vase-shapes and classical ornament were commonly used in the decoration of Wedgwood wares of all kinds. In England, the work of Thomas Hope, a wealthy amateur architect, gained much attention through the publication of his *Household Furniture & Interior Decoration* (1807). He enlarged and decorated his London home in Duchess Street, Portland Place, and also his country house, Deepdene, in Dorking, Surrey, with somewhat heavy and pedantic design that was at variance with the general trend of the time but influenced later work.

In Germany the solid bulk of the Biedermeier style, with its thick curtains, draperies, antimacassars, and padded upholstery, gave evidence of material prosperity. Many of these features were to become commonplace in Victorian England, but in the meantime, the Regency style was prevalent and contributed many masterpieces of design. Brighton Pavilion (begun 1815) was built by John Nash for the Prince Regent. Much lacquered and bamboo furniture was used, blending with Chinese wallpapers, fanciful treatments of palm trees as columns, and the most extravagant of crystal chandeliers (Figure 41). In general, however, the Regency style strove for elegance without extravagance; innumerable smaller houses were built and decorated with fine wrought-iron balustrades on curving stone staircases, pleasing carved wood or marble mantelpieces of modest sizes, and plain or

The Regency style in England

By courtesy of the Musee National du Chateau de Malmaison; photograph, Studio Laverton

Figure 40: Roman decorative motifs characteristic of the Empire style: bedroom of the Empress Josephine in the Château de Malmaison, near Paris, 1810.

Figure 41: Regency style interior utilizing bamboo and lacquered furniture; decorated with chinoiserie motifs: the Prince Regent's bedroom, royal Brighton Pavilion, Brighton, England, designed by John Nash, begun 1815.
By courtesy of the Royal Pavilion, Brighton, England

panelled walls of light colouring, on which the use of wallpaper was becoming more common.

By the latter part of the 18th century, the Industrial Revolution was slowly developing, particularly in England, and machinery was increasingly producing many objects of interior decoration, modifying their form to suit the new methods and reducing the price to make them available to new markets, a situation envisaged by Wedgwood. The less affluent of the middle classes became the largest section of consumers, and manufacture was increasingly directed toward catering to their tastes. In the early years of the 19th century a new concept was beginning to take shape—the notion of eclecticism, which propounded that any style was as good as another. This led to the idea that styles could legitimately be mixed together. In this way Horace Walpole's nightmare of a garden-seat—Gothic at one end and Chinese at the other—became, in principle, an accomplished fact: one firm, for instance, made a classical urn on a Gothic base.

Eclecticism as a style

In the early decades of the 19th century, in addition to the Empire and Regency styles, there was a Greek style of marked simplicity, and an Italian style described as 'picturesque with Palladian detail' (a contradiction in terms), as well as an "Elizabethan" style, a "Tudor" style, a "Baronial" style (under the influence of Sir Walter Scott), an "Abbotsford" style (also resulting from Scott's influence, based on his house of that name), and a revived Gothic style, far removed from Walpole's modest and amusing essay. The revived Gothic was at first inspired by James Wyatt's pseudo-cathedral built for the author William Beckford at Fonthill Abbey, with interiors of cathedral-like amplitude and about a 300-foot tower.

The Gothic Revival

This Gothic Revival produced a small number of houses in which the pointed arch together with fan vaulting and crocketed (carved with foliated ornament) or deeply undercut moldings were used with some taste and discretion. Toddington Manor, Gloucestershire (1829), by the architect Charles Barry (who, with A.W.N. Pugin, designed the Houses of Parliament), and Hughenden Manor, the house of British prime minister Benjamin Disraeli, exemplify a style used later in the century with greater ostentation and coarseness of detail.

In the principal European countries, interior decoration grew increasingly heavy and elaborate. Ornament came to be considered synonymous with beauty, and pattern covered every possible surface. The products of industrial manufacture were mostly very crude, and their use resulted in loss of refinement; for example, aniline dyes, which are harsh in colour, were first made in 1856 and soon replaced the softer, more harmonious colours. Architects decked out their buildings according to whim in a variety of styles.

In less ambitious schemes of decoration brightly coloured wallpapers with bold patterns were widely used, and the white plaster ceilings were relieved by modelled cornices and often also by some central feature, frequently in a coarsened Rococo design, which made a background for the elaborate light fitting. Rooms became crowded with furniture, and fireplaces were often mounted with elaborate overmantels, fitted with mirror panels and a multitude of shelves and brackets for the display of knickknacks. Both furniture and fittings were draped in dark-coloured plush with heavy fringes. Varnished pitch-pine dadoes, stained-glass windows, and encaustic-tiled floors were also popular.

By the 1830s there was a revival of Rococo, to be seen in the porcelain of the period and the chairs of John Belter of New York, and there was something called the "Louis XIV" style, which that monarch would have found difficulty in recognizing. Throughout this period there was a limited amount of pseudo-Chinese decoration, principally on pottery and porcelain and papier-mâché. After 1853, when Commodore Matthew C. Perry of the U.S. Navy reopened Japan to Western trade and influence, a new kind of Japanese art began to be exported, such as the vases of unprecendented ugliness decorated in Tokyo and called Satsuma, or enormous, grossly over-decorated vases from Seto in Owari (presently Aichi Prefecture), none of which would have found a buyer in the Japanese home-market.

The 19th century was an age of electicism. Decorators introduced the custom of having a different style for each room—"Gothic," "Elizabethan," or "Old English" for the dining-room; "Queen Anne," "Chippendale," or "Louis XVI" for the drawing-room; with pseudo-Elizabethan furniture for the library. Design reached its nadir with the Great Exhibition of 1851, in London, the low-water mark in the history of European taste in interior decoration, from which there was no conceivable direction except upward.

In France, where there was a sounder tradition and Gothic had not been influential for centuries, 19th century taste was not quite so debased as in England. A light and amusing version of Gothic known as the Troubadour style made its appearance in the 1830s, perhaps an international tribute to the contemporary fame of Sir Walter Scott. Rococo was revived as the Pompadour style, and there was a neo-Renaissance period, with furniture designs based on 16th century Italian work. On the whole, the furniture of the second empire (1852–70) was very acceptable in design, although these pieces were based largely on the 18th century; these styles harmonized well with the contemporaneous music of Jacques Offenbach and the brilliance of the court of Napoleon III.

In England there were a few people who recognized the depths to which taste had fallen. The designer and writer William Morris advocated a return to fine craftsmanship in furniture, textiles, and wallpaper, and started his own firm in 1861. Under the influence of the Pre-Raphaelite Brotherhood, artists who advocated a return to medieval principles, his furniture designs were based on actual surviving specimens instead of on Gothic architecture of the most florid periods. Morris's productions were well-made and well-proportioned, often with painted decoration in the old style (Figure 42). He helped

By courtesy of the Victoria and Albert Museum, London; photograph, John Webb

Figure 42: Outstanding craftsmanship and design based upon medieval aesthetic principles: mid-19th century arts and crafts movement English room decorated by William Morris with furniture by Philip Webb. In the Victoria and Albert Museum, London.

to organize the Arts and Crafts Society with the object of improving design. His influence was limited, however, because, like his contemporaries, he looked backward for inspiration and in doing so refused to accept the possibilities of machine production.

Influence of William Morris

The 1870s and 1880s saw a fashion for reproductions of 18th century furniture, especially the designs of Chippendale, Hepplewhite, and Sheraton, in which a few minor crudities, of a kind thought to be inseparable from hand-work, were added to machine-production. Much of the "18th century" furniture that decorates today's interiors is no older than this vogue. A fashion arose in the 1880s for Japanese fans and screens and blue and white porcelain, in conjunction with bamboo and lacquer furniture, a taste to some extent influenced by the paintings of James Whistler.

The influence of Whistler, Morris, and others may be seen in the Art Nouveau style of decoration, which was developed in the 1890s by the Belgian architect and designer Henry van de Velde and the British designer Arthur Heygate Mackmurdo. This was a style in interior decoration which went under various names at the time —Art Nouveau in England, Modern Style in France, the Jugendstil in Germany, and the Stile Liberty in Italy, in reference to the influence of the London firm of Liberty & Co. in promoting the style. Art Nouveau was most reminiscent of Gothic, with overtones of the Japanese art imported during the last quarter of the 19th century. Its ornament is markedly asymmetrical, and principally floral, particular use being made of the lily. It is strongly curvilinear, and there is hardly a straight line to be seen. It often derives its effect from an incongruous juxtaposition of decorative motifs. In furniture, for instance, the asymmetry of Rococo is to be found in its ornament, but in Art Nouveau the whole piece of furniture in some cases is asymmetrical, one side being higher than the other. Although the style created much interest at the Paris Exhibition of 1900, it never became very widely established but was one of several leavening agents in the sphere of design. Nonetheless, its influence extended beyond World War I into the 1920s, when the Art Deco style from Paris became current (see below). Its influence can also be found in such relatively modern designs as the Barcelona chair of Mies van der Rohe of 1929.

Reaction against overcrowded, fussy interiors gathered strength. Plain interior walls in white or very light colours, natural woods, and simple doors and fireplaces were among the changes introduced by the more advanced designers in an attempt to create an original style suited to the changed circumstances of life in the first part of the 20th century.

Late 18th to early 20th centuries in the U.S. *Classic movement after the Revolution, 1785–1835.* Even after the American Revolution, English decorative influence predominated in the United States, in spite of greatly increased contacts with French thought and ideas. Although many leaders like Thomas Jefferson wished to see a complete break with English traditions, the Georgian forms of colonial days persisted in common usage till 1800 or after. By 1785, however, the reaction in Europe against the rather heavy classic style called free Palladianism and its Rococo and Baroque elaborations began to affect design in the United States.

Jefferson, largely under French influence, became the leader of one aspect of the new movement in the South that combined practical planning with a literal classicism based on the direct study of ancient monuments. While Jefferson's interest in strict classic form was felt particularly in architecture, the decorative phase of the movement, both North and South, was dominated by the freer and more personal interpretation of classic motifs based on the work of the Adam brothers in England, before and during the American Revolution. This was the principal influence in the designs of the Boston architect Charles Bulfinch and his followers and was popularized about 1800 in the builders' pattern books of William Pain and Asher Benjamin.

The houses of Boston, Salem, and Portsmouth that were built around 1800–10 by or under the influence of Bulfinch and Samuel McIntire, an architect of Salem, are the best examples of the changes wrought by the fine scale and delicate precision of their Adam-inspired designs, producing what has become known as the early Federal style. In the houses of the time, the circle, the ellipse, and the octagon were introduced as occasional variations in the plan, and the flying or freestanding staircase became a characteristic of the entrance hall (Figure 43).

Federal style

In interior decoration, wood panelling was practically abandoned or was restricted to the area below the chair rail—*i.e.*, the wall molding at the height of the chair back. Decorative emphasis was concentrated on the mantel and overmantel, the doors and window frames, and the cornice, all usually of wood and enriched with delicate repeat ornament (either carved or applied). Rich colour in draperies and upholstery was set off by wall surfaces and decoration in light tones, grayed tints, or white. Block-printed wallpapers with classical motifs were frequently used, as were stencilled decorations in the simpler homes.

In general, geometric forms and the urn, swag, patera,

Figure 43: American neoclassical room in the manner of the Adam brothers, Oval Music Room, Nathaniel Russell House, Charleston, South Carolina, *c.* 1800.
By courtesy of Antiques Magazine; photograph, Helga Studio

and wreath were employed. The taste for lightness and attenuation verging on dryness was reflected in the furniture. The designs of the English furniture manufacturers George Hepplewhite and Thomas Sheraton, influenced by Louis XVI and Directoire forms, found American versions around the turn of the century in the work of Samuel McIntire of Salem, John Seymour of Boston, Duncan Phyfe of New York, Henry Connelly of Philadelphia, and the cabinet shops of Baltimore and Charleston. At first, light woods and finishes and decorative inlays were preferred, but by 1820 French Empire influence substituted dark reddish mahogany, carved and gilded ornament, and heavy, often ill-proportioned forms considered more in keeping with classic taste.

Greek Revival style

After 1820 the early Federal style waned, and Jeffersonian classicism was modified by the introduction of Greek and even Egyptian detail, constituting the so-called Greek Revival. Accompanied by furnishings and draperies in the heavier Sheraton-Empire taste, the classic pattern established in the 1820s became the basic style in building and decorative design. Stimulated by the Greek struggle for national independence, it lasted until about 1850 and constituted for the time a national style without parallel in Europe. In its later decorative aspect, however, the Greek Revival became a fashion rather than a style. As such it marks not only the end of the 18th-century Neoclassicism but the beginning of the Romantic movement.

The Romantic movement and the battle of the styles, 1835–1925. The ordered symbolism of the Roman classic style had been envisaged by Jefferson as a proper expression of the American national ideal; but by 1835 its restraints had grown tedious. Social and economic changes already initiated by the Industrial Revolution encouraged reaction. This found more or less romantic and emotional expression in a series of style revivals ill-adapted to actual conditions.

The Greek Revival was diluted almost immediately by the antiquarian Romanticism of the "Gothic," "Tuscan," and "country cottage" fashions. These offered opportunity to the undercurrent of practical utilitarianism, repressed or thwarted by the classic formula, and also gave a fertile field for the novel or exotic in decorative taste fostered by a wealth-induced appetite for comfort and display (see Figure 2, left and Figure 9). By the middle of the century the last vestiges of order in early Victorian Romanticism had disappeared under a plethora of decorative motifs and objects easily and inexpensively produced by machine (Figure 44). Colour became confusedly drab or brilliant and generally out of character, as a result of the introduction of uncontrolled chemical dyes and the magic of the Jacquard loom, which permitted the weaving of intricate patterns. Increased travel and ease of communications made American styles hardly distinguishable from those of Europe.

Machine-produced decoration

This decorative salad of classic and medieval motifs was supplanted by the revival of the 18th-century forms which temporarily triumphed in the "second Rococo" of the 1850s, when rosewood and walnut took the place of mahogany. This was succeeded by fashions based on the 17th century and the later Renaissance, until the Philadelphia Centennial Exhibition of 1876 brought to America the "craft" medievalism and a new series of more literal style revivals including that of colonial times. These in turn absorbed the exotic Eastern influence of the Aesthetic movement of the later 19th century.

In the first quarter of the 20th century this confusion culminated in antiquarianism for the wealthy and, for most people, period reproductions provided by the wholesale decorator and manufacturer. These 90 years of

By courtesy of the Brooklyn Museum

Figure 44: Victorian parlour with characteristic tufted upholstered chairs, medallion portraits, corner whatnot, and floral carpeting: Robert J. Milligan House, Saratoga, New York, *c.* 1853. In the Brooklyn Museum.

Figure 45: "Design for a Living Room," by Will Bradley, commissioned by *Ladies Home Journal* magazine, 1902. In the early 1900s *Ladies Home Journal* published a series of simplified, contemporary house designs appropriate to the needs and taste of the new century. In the Metropolitan Museum of Art, New York City.
By courtesy of the Metropolitan Museum of Art, New York

enormous technical and financial development are too confused and complex for further analysis here. Almost from the beginning, however, a body of criticism and rational experiment was developing both in Europe and America that was to find effective expression in the early 1920s amid the social and economic upheavals following World War I.

20th century. The principle behind a great deal of 20th century interior decoration was first expounded in Chicago in 1896 in a magazine entitled the *House Beautiful*. This journal opposed both the perpetuation of vulgar display and the excess of ornament that had characterized most of the 19th century. Other American magazines like *Ladies Home Journal* soon followed *House Beautiful*'s lead and published articles on modern decorating (Figure 45). In Europe a group of architects and designers whose thesis was that "form follows function," started the Bauhaus, a school of design founded in 1919 at Weimar, Germany. With such pioneers of modern art and design as Walter Gropius, Paul Klee, Laslo Moholy-Nagy, and others on its staff, it sought to teach the combining of art with craft, and to combat the dehumanizing effect of the machine.

Influence of the Bauhaus

The struggle between the desire to cling to tradition and the necessity of accepting a society based on mechanized industry came into the open between World War I and World War II. The aim of the Bauhaus group was to adapt industrial techniques to meet the needs of a society impoverished spiritually and materially by war. Their work was the culmination of the numerous reform movements of the late 19th and early 20th centuries; cathartic and analytical in its methods, on one hand it shocked the conservative into immoderate fury and on the other converted its radical adherents into equally uncompromising iconoclasts. Many of the "functionalist" ideas they employed were inspired by the subtle simplicities of the Japanese tradition and by the innovations and writings of the Chicago architect Louis H. Sullivan. Functionalism demanded a complete break with the ornamental motifs of the past and a quickened response to form, proportion, line, and texture. It also aimed at a scientific study of human behaviour, correlating psychological responses to physical stimuli of all kinds. The acceptance of its thesis ran parallel to the growth of interest in abstract art, and, although the uncompromising application of so intellectual a program proved immediately impracticable, its bold challenge to convention resulted in notable changes in interior design.

International Style

The style that emerged from the Bauhaus, called the International Style, was felt by many to be lacking in human warmth. Its box-like forms, its hard and glassy surfaces, its use of metal tubing and plywood, its lack of colour and of ornament were received with mixed feelings. The French architect Le Corbusier adhered to similar principles. His famous dictum that the house is a machine brought the retort that most people do not like living in machines. Functionalist thinking, however, led to an increasing use of the materials the machine is capable of producing, such as plastics, synthetic fibres, acrylic paints, and so forth, but these materials were still too often used to simulate other materials.

German Functionalism was slow to establish itself in Europe and hardly affected American design until its leaders found refuge in the United States from Nazi oppression. There the movement was brought to public attention in the mid-1930s by the need for new stimuli in the trough of economic depression, by the educational campaigns of the Museum of Modern Art in New York City, and by the re-establishment of the Bauhaus teachings in the Institute of Design in Chicago.

Art Deco style

In the decade following the Exposition Internationale des Arts Decoratifs et Industriels Modernes, held at Paris in 1925, progressive Western design was influenced principally by the less radical productions of the French luxury crafts, based on a modified Art Nouveau, and by the Swedish success in combining and developing craft traditions in cooperation with industry. These influences, which developed the Art Deco style, were, however, confined to relatively small and semiprofessional coteries, while the market as a whole continued to concentrate on traditional forms, producing and adapting them at various levels of quality and taste (Figure 46). By 1935 the Functionalist movement, led by the disciples of the Bauhaus program, had gained a substantial following among the younger architects and designers. During World War II development virtually ceased in most European countries, and subsequently attention turned

Figure 46: Lavish Art Deco bathroom designed by Armand-Albert Rateau for Jeanne Lanvin, Paris, 1920–22. In the Musée des Arts Décoratifs, Paris.
Photo Fratelli Fabbri Editori, Milan, Italy

again to the Scandinavian countries, particularly Sweden, where strict consideration of function led to simple furnishing schemes which relied on natural wood grains, clear colouring, and texture for their effect. Pattern was subdued and, where used, uncomplicated in outline.

Meanwhile, in the U.S., during and after World War II, the Functionalists, still with the help of the museums and the more progressive schools and periodicals, had gained the interest of a considerable proportion of both the wealthier members of society and the manufacturers who catered to them.

The most obvious changes resulting from the Functionalist movement were mechanization, redistribution of interior space, and elimination of formal barriers between indoors and outdoors. These developments, most prevalent in the United States but disseminated throughout much of the world, were accompanied by radical changes in decoration and the design and use of furniture and fittings. Equipment for heating and lighting, sanitation, and food preparation, all derived from inventions of the 19th century, were brought to a high degree of mechanized efficiency taking full advantage of advanced production methods. Since convenience and economy became principal considerations, utility units were fitted into living space instead of being hidden in otherwise unused areas, as in the traditional room arrangement. By insisting on simplicity of form, colour, and texture, they were made to obtrude as little as possible. In particular, the appearance of the kitchen was studied carefully, especially in smaller houses.

Under the influence of electric power, liquid fuels, flexible controls of temperature, ventilation, and lighting and countless labour-saving devices, the mid-20th century house began to fulfill Le Corbusier's dream of an efficient "machine for living."

Reconsideration and correlation of the space needed in living areas broke down traditional room divisions. The new interior, with its invitation to movement, both actual and implied, was in harmony with the times. Decoration became concerned with function (see Figure 2, right), and, because a living area served more than one purpose, it was frequently irregular in plan and impossible to treat as a unit in the traditional formal matter. Changes of colour, texture, and materials consequently became the chief resources of decorative design, taking the place of ornament (Figure 47). Earlier attempts at the functional mode suffered from too much anxiety over simplicity and unity and thus became monotonous and cold.

The demands of space made it necessary to keep movable pieces of furniture to a minimum and encouraged the use of built-in units. An earlier overemphasis on straight lines and angles was countered by greater use of curved and molded forms in furniture design. As the average house became smaller and more efficient in its use of enclosed space and as the desire for outdoor living grew, there was a tendency to replace at least one of the enclosing walls of both livingroom and bedroom with glass. With a well-arranged plan, this gave each room an everchanging mural and better light, and it also extended the apparent size of the interior. The illusion of bringing the outside indoors gave a feeling of freedom, but it also created practical and psychological problems (see Figure 7).

Despite the reaction that developed against it, the functional modern movement had served an important purpose. Although it produced no recognizable themes of ornament, it did eliminate the *horror vacui* that afflicted the Victorians and Elizabethans alike. It cleared the way for a fresh look at the art of interior decoration as a whole, and for the fresh inspiration that came in the 1950s from Scandinavia and Denmark, which retained the human qualities that much of the work of the Bauhaus was felt to lack. At the same time there was a revival of interest in true Japanese art in interior decoration, which has a certain affinity with Scandinavian. In the 1960s patterns began to return—abstract patterns such as those to be found in Op art. Elegant materials, easily washable, became available for upholstery, and

Photo R. Guillemot—TOP

Figure 47: Dining room and living area designed by Claude Lombardo for his apartment outside of Brussels, 1969. Supple, rounded forms made of cement reinforced with fibreglass are used to create a free-moving, open plan interior.

easy cleaning made it practical for them to be produced in pastel shades and light colours.

That large numbers of people had found it difficult to live with modern austerity became apparent with the immense growth after World War II of the trade in old furnishings of all kinds, with ever-increasing prices. A parallel vogue resulted in an increase in the manufacture of reproductions of all kinds, especially furniture, made partly by machine and partly by hand, leading to the revival of some of the old handcrafts.

INTERIOR DESIGN IN THE EAST

East Asian motifs of decoration bear no relationship to those of the West, although many of them are familiar from *objets d'art* and decoration exported during the last five centuries. No such conflict of styles as those to be observed in the West has existed.

Eastern motifs

The motifs of Eastern art are many and varied, such as the dragon (a ubiquitous and beneficent creature), the so-called phoenix (actually the Chinese long-tailed pheasant), and creatures of all kinds, actual and legendary. Flowers and foliage are part of an elaborate flower-symbolism, and there are many abstract motifs, all of which are part of a complex and rich symbolism, which can usually be interpreted if the key is known. The Chinese language contains many identical words, which have completely different meanings that are identified in speech by intonation; the word *fu*, for example, can mean either a bat or happiness. Therefore, a decoration of bats symbolizes happiness. This is not true in the Japanese language, but the Japanese have taken over many Chinese motifs, such as the bat (*kōmori*). The purpose for which a Chinese object decorated with a dragon was originally intended may often be deduced from the number of claws to the foot—five for the Emperor, four for princes of the blood, and three for officials. The pine, willow, and bamboo in conjunction are termed the "three friends," and represent Buddha, Confucius, and Lao-tzu.

Scrolls of painting or calligraphy are characteristic of interior design in the East. They are changed from time to time to give freshness to the decorative scheme and also to emphasize their quality. Similarly, a vase with a single branch of peach blossom or other flowers may be set out with care. Cabinets and storage chests are of great importance and are often made of camphor wood. An important feature in the houses of north China and Korea is the *k'ang*, or heated brick platform, on which the family sleeps or sits in the cold northern winter.

China. Possessing the oldest Eastern civilization, China has powerfully influenced the others. Forms and motifs of decoration, which began as early as the Shang dynasty (*c.* 1766–*c.* 1122 BC), or even before in the legendary Hsia dynasty, persist throughout Chinese history. Early forms of bronze altar vessels, for example, are found in porcelain in the 18th and 19th centuries, slightly altered in profile but still recognizable.

Materials are very different from those of the West. The Chinese have always been masters of the ceramic art, and their skill spread northward to Korea, north-eastward to Japan, and south to the countries of Southeast Asia. Nearly all the more important techniques—majolica excepted—came from China. The T'ang dynasty (618–907) was renowned for fine earthenwares; the Sung dynasty (960–1280) for superb stonewares; and from the Yüan dynasty (1279–1368) onward the Chinese have led the world in the manufacture of porcelain, the secret of which reached Europe only after the porcelain had been imported for several centuries. Bronze was employed for vessels rather than figure sculpture. Originally purely religious in connotation, bronze vessels were given as gifts of emperors to their favoured subjects by the Chou dynasty (*c.* 1122–*c.* 221 BC), and from that time on were commonly employed for secular purposes. During the T'ang dynasty, handsome mirrors as well as such useful and decorative things as toilet-boxes were commonly made.

Chinese textiles

China was known for its silk in the West in ancient Roman times. Fragments of silk were found in Chinese Turkistan dating to the 1st century BC with motifs of design strongly resembling those of the 20th century. The Chinese have always been noted for superb silk embroideries, highly detailed in a manner requiring a multitude of tiny stitches. Painted silks have been produced in large quantities. Velvet weaving, usually in long strips as chair covers, was an art probably learned from the West, but the art of tapestry (*k'o-ssu*), may go back as far as the Han dynasty (206 BC–AD 220). Carpet-knotting of the highest quality, no doubt learned from Persia, cannot be proved to date before the 17th century, but it may have started at a much earlier date. Rare carpets are knotted with silk and gold, but those with a woollen pile are of fine quality. Pillar-carpets, woven to encircle pillars, are a distinctively Chinese type. Motifs of decoration are those common to other materials.

Jade (nephrite and jadeite) is carved in China into objects with many different purposes. In early times, like bronze, it was mainly used for religious purposes, but it later came to be employed for a variety of secular objects, principally those intended to furnish the scholar's table, such as brush-pots, ink-slabs, water-droppers, table-screens, and paper-weights. In the 18th century especially, bowls and covers, handsomely carved and pierced with a variety of motifs and patterns, were made for interior decoration as incense burners.

Lacquer, the solidified sap of a tree (*Rhus vernicifera*), has been widely employed for a variety of decorative purposes on a foundation of wood or, less often, hempen fabric. Lacquer is employed as a form of paint, or applied in thick layers that can be carved with knives. It is also used to decorate structural timbers in the interior. The finest lacquer came from Japan in the 17th and 18th centuries.

Enamelling on metal is an art that the Chinese learned from Europe, but, in the 18th century especially, some very large bronze vessels in a variety of ornamental forms were covered with enamel utilizing the cloisonné technique. Painted enamels came from Canton in the 18th century, and resemble in style contemporary porcelain enamelling from the same place.

Paintings are usually on silk, and most are in the form of scrolls to be hung on the wall. A long and narrow form is customary. The best of Chinese painting is superb in quality, but criteria of judgment are very different from those applicable to Western art. Style is to a considerable extent affected by calligraphy, and the quality and type of brushstroke plays an essential part. Subjects are usually the poetic delineation of landscape, floral and foliate sprays, and, less often, pavilions. Chinese painting is often pervaded by a subtle and gentle humour hardly seen in Western art. Calligraphy plays an important part in the art of the East; scrolls decorated with an admired calligraphy are hung on walls. Calligraphy often plays a part in the decoration of bronzes and porcelain, and inscriptions on paintings are not uncommon.

The Chinese house

The East Asian house is usually constructed of wood and tiles. The ridge-tile in China, made of glazed stoneware, is often very handsome. Architecture has never been the principal medium for the expression of the Chinese artistic impulse; conservatism, perhaps rooted in ancestor worship, has been paramount and stylistic innovation practically unknown. The basic structure of the Chinese house has remained almost unchanged at least from the Shang dynasty (*c.* 1766–1122 BC). In all types of buildings the roof is the most important feature, and by the T'ang dynasty (AD 618–907) the characteristic upturned eaves and heavy glazed and coloured tile covering had developed. The roof is chiefly supported by timber posts on stone or bronze bases, and the walls of the building serve merely as screens in brick or timber. Floors are often of beaten earth packed tightly into a timber border. Usually, a family house was composed of a series of buildings or pavilions enclosing a garden courtyard and surrounded by a wall. The courtyard played an immensely important part, because of the ever-present ideal that man should live in harmony with nature: a small pool with a lotus plant, a tree, and large rocks symbolized the whole natural landscape, and it was on these features that most care was lavished.

Figure 48: Chinese scholar's study, Peking, late 18th or early 19th century. In the Philadelphia Museum of Art.
By courtesy of the Philadelphia Museum of Art, given by Wright S. Ludington (in memory of his father)

The supporting pillars and brackets of important buildings were carved and painted, many of the designs being similar to those made familiar by Chinese pottery and porcelain. The yellow dragon symbolizes the power of the spirit, the tiger the forces of animal life. Windows were latticed with strips of wood in varying patterns over which translucent white paper was stretched. In addition to the lattice-work patterns, the windows themselves took on great variety of outline, for instance that of a diamond, fan, leaf, or flower. Doorways, too, were fancifully shaped in the form of the moon, lotus petal, pear, or vase, for structural support was not required from the light panel-type walls. Some walls may have been removable altogether, as they were subsequently in the Japanese house; others were of painted wood, hung with tapestries or paintings on silk and other materials.

A description of a Ming (1368–1644) home of the leisured class mentions ceilings with cloisons (compartments) in yellow reed work, papered walls and pillars, black polished flagstones, and silk hangings. Richly coloured rugs, chair covers, and cushions contrasted with dark furniture, which was arranged according to the strict ideas of asymmetrical balance.

Chinese furniture

Little is known of early Chinese furniture, apart from what may be gathered from paintings and similar sources. Low stools and tables were early in use, and chairs, dressing tables, altar tables, and canopied beds were common by the Former (early) Han dynasty (206 BC–AD 8). Designs and materials underwent very little change in the intervening years. Rosewood has always been widely employed, and in the palaces elaborate pieces were encrusted with gold and silver, jade, ivory, and mother-of-pearl. The Chinese interior was more extensively furnished with chairs, tables, couches, beds, and cabinets of cupboards and drawers than was the custom elsewhere in the East (Figure 48). As in Europe, the chair with arms was thought to be a seat of honour. The woods employed are native to the country and were hardly ever exported to the West, though Chinese rosewood is fairly well known in the West because most exported furniture was in this wood. Carved lacquer furniture, like the throne of Ch'ien Lung in the Victoria and Albert Museum, London, was reserved for the emperor and high officials, and the massive incised lacquer screens, known in the West as Coromandel screens, were occasionally exported. Furniture of bamboo, principally intended for garden use, has hardly survived, but barrel-shaped seats of porcelain for the same purpose are not uncommon. Carved decoration on furniture is nearly always extremely simple in design and limited to some form of interlacing fret.

Japan. Interior decoration in Japan was much influenced by Chinese ideas, especially between the 8th and 12th centuries, but it developed along lighter, more austere and elegant lines. As in China, it has altered little since medieval days. The most important differences in modern design are that the matting has been extended to cover the whole of the wooden floor, and sliding doors have replaced single-leaf screens or curtains. Two sides of a Japanese house frequently have no permanent walls, and interior partitions are of paper on a wood frame which admits a soft, diffused light on which shadows fall. These partitions are usually moveable, allowing the interior to be rearranged (Figure 49).

Comparison of Chinese and Japanese design

The Japanese interior is a carefully thought-out arrangement. Wall-decoration hardly exists, and the walls provide a neutral background for the rest. Since the Japanese invariably cover their floors with rice-straw mats and sit on them instead of on chairs, tables are low, and are also used as an arm-rest. Tiers of shelves are common, usually covered with lacquer, and painted decoratively. They occur in a variety of forms, and the asymmetrical quality of Japanese art may be seen in these pieces of furniture, the number and position of the shelves differing on either side, and set at different heights.

In contrast to Western practice, the Japanese do not decorate their rooms with several works of art, but have a special place in the room, a focal point, at which one work of quality is displayed, and this is changed from time to time. Both the Chinese and the Japanese venerate the work of former times, and the Japanese possess the oldest art collection in the world, in the Shōsō-in repository at Nara, which was formed by the Emperor Shōmu in the 9th century AD.

At that time, doors were pivoted in the Chinese manner, and instead of the sliding *shōji*, windows were made of wooden latticing that pushed outward, as may still be seen in shrines and temples. There was a curtained dais for the most important person and separate mats on the wooden floor for others. Then, as now, there was a connecting corridor outside the rooms. The Seiryo-den, or ordinary residence of the sovereign in the Kyōto Imperial Palace, belonged to this period and was recon-

Figure 49: Japanese pleasure house; "Moonlight Revelry at the Dozō Sagami," ink, colour, and gold on paper by Kitagawa Utamaro (18th century). In the Freer Gallery of Art, Washington D.C.
By courtesy of the Smithsonian Institution, Freer Gallery of Art, Washington, D.C.

structed in the 19th century on the model of the original. A present-day family could live quite comfortably in its simple suite of rooms with walls and standing screens decorated with pictures in the Chinese classic manner.

Late in the 15th century the interior began to assume its present form as a result of a slow blending of the older court style with the more austere type of house favoured by the military caste, which was much influenced by Zen Buddhist architecture. Toward the end of the 16th century came the rise of the tea masters. These connoisseurs of the "way of tea," which involves the construction of the tearoom and its garden and correct deportment in them, established hereditary families and schools who remained the aesthetic advisers on most aspects of domestic architecture, interior decoration, and garden planning. They aimed to achieve beauty with frugality, asymmetry, and economy of movement, and much of the simple grace of Japanese interiors is due to them.

Influence of the tea ceremony

In a modern Japanese house, decoration is almost entirely structural, and the residences of all classes are equally neat and free from vulgarity. Their harmony and delicacy derive from an endless variation of detail in a setting that is completely standardized. Ordinary rooms are multiples of the floor-mat unit, six by three feet (1.8 metres by 0.9 metre); the sliding doors five feet eight inches (1.7 metres) high by three feet wide; the supporting pillars four to five inches (ten to 13 centimetres) square, set at six-foot intervals; and the ceiling boards one foot to 1.5 feet (30 to 45 centimetres) wide. All woodwork is unpainted and rarely lacquered, but there is great variety in the *fusuma*, or sliding doors, which divide the rooms and which are covered with paper of many patterns or decorated with paintings or calligraphy. Thus, the whole side of a room may present a landscape either in black and white or in colours, often on a silver or gold background. A change of these *fusuma* will alter completely the appearance of a room, and their removal will convert two or more rooms into one. All rooms can be used as bedrooms, since the bedding is stored in spacious cupboards. The reception rooms provide more scope for decoration than the others, for one end of the room is occupied by a *toko-no-ma*, an alcove with a canopy above it supported by a pillar of fine or uncommon wood, in which is hung the picture or set of pictures that, with the flower arrangement that usually accompanies it, is the only ornament. Both are changed frequently according to the season or mood. Next to the *toko-no-ma*, there is often a built-in writing table. Beside this is usually a *chigai-dana*, an asymmetric arrangement of cupboards and shelves somewhat like a sideboard. Between the top of the *fusuma* and the ceiling is often a *ramma*, an openwork frieze carved with patterns or landscapes in wood or bamboo. A framed tablet with a poem or painting on it sometimes may be placed there. Other walls are of plain plaster in subdued shades, mostly of gray or brown. The ceilings are usually of thin boards, slightly overlapping, upheld by bars about an inch (three centimetres) square, the whole suspended from the roof or floor beams. In large apartments, as in shrines and temples, the coved and coffered "Chinese ceiling," with lacquered woodwork and pictures and patterns in the coffers, is sometimes found. Fancy varieties made of bamboo and reeds and plaited wood are not uncommon. Bamboo has many uses in the Japanese house as pillars and window bars and ceiling material, when split and flattened, it may take the place of boards. Windows are of many shapes—round, square, bell-shaped, jar-shaped, gourd-shaped, diamond-shaped, fan-shaped, and purely asymmetric—and make centres of interest in a blank wall.

Types of ceilings

The furniture in a Japanese house is sparse, perhaps consisting of a cabinet of blackwood or lacquer, a low writing table or a screen, either twofold or sixfold (the latter generally in pairs), decorated with landscapes on a gold or silver background and mounted in brocade. A single-leaf screen sometimes stands in the entrance hall. Among the well-to-do, other valuables such as scroll pictures, braziers, pottery, spare *fusuma*, books, and curios are kept in a detached fireproof storehouse and produced only occasionally to ensure a constant variety in the rooms. It is a principle that rooms that are only occasionally occupied may be more showy and fanciful than ordinary living rooms, and these are most often met with in hotels and restaurants and other places of entertainment. Just as much care is taken with the interiors of the bathroom as with the other rooms, and the doors and windows and walls of these are usually of excellent workmanship.

India. Words of Indian origin such as calico, chintz, and palampore indicate the importance of Indian textiles in the history of western interior design. Yet the Indians themselves have never been very conscious of this role, their own domestic interiors being of the utmost simplicity, with hardly more than a carpet or prayer mat to offset stone floors and plain white walls (Figure 50). The impermanence of the materials used for the majority of dwellings may have been a contributory factor. In more palatial buildings, however, and commonly in both Hindu and Buddhist temples, walls were painted, a practice that, according to literary references, may go back to the Maurya period (321–185 BC). Paintings that survive in cave temples of the Gupta period (AD 320–600) usually depict groups of active mythical or human figures and

Figure 50: Simplicity of domestic Indian interior, Chamba school miniature of a lady suffering the sorrows of love, late 8th century. In the National Museum of India, New Delhi.
Smeets Lithographers, Weert, Holland

are characterized by their sinuous lines. A late example occurs in the unfinished early 17-century murals of the Mattāncheri palace, Cochin, Madras. Inlay of semiprecious stones, carved and bracketed pillars and capitals, and openwork marble panels also adorned the palaces of local rulers. (Ge.S./Ed.)

BIBLIOGRAPHY

General works: ARNOLD FRIEDMANN, JOHN F. PILE, and FORREST WILSON, *Interior Design: An Introduction to Architectural Interiors* (1970), an introduction to the field of interior architecture written for students of design; SHERRILL WHITON, *Elements of Interior Design and Decoration*, 3rd ed. (1963), a scholarly text; RAY and SARAH FAULKNER, *Inside Today's Home*, 3rd ed. (1968), a thorough and well-illustrated book on the interior design of homes; DIANA ROWNTREE, *Interior Design* (1964), a brief and personal view of interior design written primarily for British readers; EDGAR KAUFMAN, *What Is Modern Interior Design?* (1953, reprinted 1969), a very brief but perceptive treatise.

Special types of interiors: MICHAEL SAPHIER, *Office Planning and Design* (1968), a clear overview of the field of business and office interiors; BETTY ALSWANG and AMBUR HIKEN, *The Personal House* (1961), a photographic collection of very personal interiors primarily designed by the artist-occupants, rather than professional interior designers. The photographs and comments contained in the following works make them significant sources for the study and understanding of special interiors: WILLIAM WILSON ATKIN and JOAN ADLER, *Interiors Book of Restaurants* (1960); HENRY END, *Interiors Book of Hotels and Motor Hotels* (1963); JOHN F. PILE, *Interiors Second Book of Offices* (1969); MORRIS KETCHUM, *Shops and Stores*, rev. ed. (1957); GEORGE NELSON (ed.), *Living Spaces* (1952); MARY GILLIATT and MICHAEL BOYS, *English Style in Interior Decoration* (1967).

Special subjects: JOHANNES ITTEN, *Kunst der Farbe* (1961; Eng. trans., *The Art of Color*, 1961); FABER BIRREN, *Color for Interiors, Historical and Modern* (1963); LESLIE LARSON, *Lighting and Its Design* (1964); JOHN F. PILE (ed.), *Drawings of Architectural Interiors* (1967); MARIO G. SALVADORI and ROBERT HELLER, *Structure in Architecture* (1963), a very readable introduction to structural principles understandable to laymen, but written on a very professional level; MARIO DAL FABBRO, *Modern Furniture*, 2nd ed. (1958).

Historical developments: GEORGE SAVAGE, *A Concise History of Interior Decoration* (1966), is the only English-language work that summarizes the history of the subject. Information about the earliest furniture may be found in HOLLIS S. BAKER, *Furniture in the Ancient World* (1966); and the *Natural History* (various editions) of PLINY THE ELDER, which contains much information in the final volumes on the Roman scene. Books about the Middle Ages are not numerous, but the *Guide to the Early Christian and Byzantine Antiquities* of the British Museum (1921), is a useful work. There are many books dealing with various aspects of the Renaissance, such as PETER and LINDA MURRAY, *The Art of the Renaissance* (1963); FRIDA SCHOTTMULLER, *Furniture and Interior Decoration of the Italian Renaissance* (1921); PIERRE DU COLOMBIER, *Le Style Henri IV–Louis XIII* (1941); GERMAIN BAZIN, *Classique, baroque et rococo* (1964; Eng. trans., *Baroque and Rococo*, 1964); and VICTOR TAPIE, *Baroque et classicisme* (1957; Eng. trans., *The Age of Grandeur*, 1960). PIERRE VERLET, *Le Mobilier royal français* (1945; Eng. trans., *French Royal Furniture*, 1963) and *Les Meubles français du XVIIIe siècle* (1956; Eng. trans., *French Furniture and Interior Decoration*, 1967), are important works by a great authority dealing with 18th-century developments. GEORGE SAVAGE, *French Decorative Art, 1638–1793* (1969), discusses most of the objects in general use for interior decoration. FISKE KIMBALL, *The Creation of the Rococo* (1943), is an important examination of the sources of this style; TERISIO PIGNATTI, *Il Rococò* (1967; Eng. trans., *The Age of Rococo*, 1969), is a scholarly picture-book based on an exhibition so titled. ADRIEN FAUCHIER-MAGNAN, *Les Petites Cours d'Allemagne au XVIIIe Siècle* (1947; Eng. trans., *Small German Courts in the Eighteenth Century*, 1958), is valuable for information about the pervasion of French art and culture. The Wallace Collection (London) catalog of *Furniture* by F.J.B. WATSON (1956), and the catalog of *Sculpture* by JAMES G. MANN (1931), are scholarly works essential to the study of their subject; see also F.J.B. WATSON, *Louis XVI Furniture* (1960). On English decoration the works of MARGARET JOURDAIN: *English Decoration and Furniture of the Early Renaissance* (1924), *Regency Furniture, 1795–1820* (1934), and *The Work of William Kent* (1948), are all worth consulting. PERCY MACQUOID and RALPH EDWARDS, *The Dictionary of English Furniture from the Middle Ages to the Georgian Period*, 2nd ed. rev., 3 vol. (1954), is a scholarly and important work. THOMAS A. STRANGE, *English Furniture, Decoration, Woodwork, and Allied Arts* (1900 reprinted 1950), reproduces many pages from 18th-century English design books, including Chippendale's *Director;* and HUGH HONOUR, *Neo-Classicism* (1968), discusses the style in its international implications, as well as dealing with that of the brothers Adam. For the Gothic revival there is no better source than SIR KENNETH CLARK, *The Gothic Revival* (1928, reprinted 1970). JOSEPH DOWNS, *American Furniture* (1952), is a standard work. GEORGE SAVAGE, *The Dictionary of Antiques* (1970), discusses former objects of interior decoration and their style from the Renaissance onwards, and includes a very extensive bibliography. *Art nouveau* has been the subject of a number of books in recent years. Among the best are MARIO AMAYA, *Art nouveau* (1966); MARTIN BATTERSBY, *The World of Art nouveau* (1968); and STEPHEN TSCHUDI MADSEN, *Sources of Art nouveau* (1956). There are no works discussing Oriental interior decoration only, and information must, for the most part, be gleaned from books discussing specific types of objects, such as painting, procelain, furniture, and bronze. By far the best source is *Chinese Art*, 4 vol. (1960–65), an international symposium by several well-known Orientalists that discusses almost everything of importance to the subject. A useful general survey is LEIGH ASHTON (ed.), *Chinese Art*, by several well-known authorities (1935), which summarizes in one volume the salient facts about works in many differing materials. For Japanese art, MARCUS B. HUISH, *Japan and Its Art* (1889), is an excellent general work, but few books that can be recommended for the present purpose have been published in English. On Islāmic art, an excellent work is DAVID TALBOT RICE, *Islamic Art* (1965); a more detailed survey is MAURICE S. DIMAND, *A Handbook of Muhammadan Art*, 3rd ed. rev. (1958). A.U. POPE and PHYLLIS ACKERMAN, *A Survey of Persian Art from Prehistoric Times to the Present*, 14 vol. (1938–67), should be consulted for this aspect. FRANZ BOAS, *Primitive Art*, new ed. (1955), discusses the principles behind the decoration of a wide variety of art of this kind, with special attention to the North Pacific Coast of North America.

(A.A.F./Ge.S.)

International Agreements

International agreements may be defined as instruments by which states and other subjects of international law, such as certain international organizations, regulate matters of concern to them. The agreements assume a variety of form and style, and their terminology is extremely varied. The common denominator is that they are all governed by the law of treaties, which is part of customary international law.

INSTRUMENTS OF AGREEMENT

Treaties

A treaty, the typical instrument of international relations, is defined by the 1969 Vienna Convention on the Law of Treaties as an "agreement concluded between States in written form and governed by international law, whether embodied in a single instrument or in two or more related instruments and whatever its particular designation." It is well understood, however, that the rules set forth in this convention may also apply to agreements between a state and such other subjects of international law as international organizations, the Roman Catholic Holy See, and insurgents, as well as to agreements between two international organizations. The agreements between international organizations, sometimes called interagency agreements, have acquired a significant role since the founding of the United Nations and its specialized agencies, such as the World Health Organization and the Food and Agriculture Organization.

Taking the number of parties to an agreement as the distinguishing characteristic, it is possible to separate bilateral from multilateral treaties. In the case of the former, only two states or a state and an international organization are parties. Multilateral treaties are those to which several states are parties. Another distinction that is frequently made is between contractual and lawmaking treaties. The former is a class of treaties by which the parties agree to exchange pieces of territory or settle a dispute or claims—that is, by which they deal with a particular kind of business. Lawmaking treaties, which have grown tremendously in number and significance since World War II, are instruments in which the parties formulate principles or detailed rules for their future conduct. Such treaties may be bilateral or multilateral. A typical modern treaty of commerce, friendship, and navigation thus contains a large number of articles stipulating how the parties shall behave in the future with respect to trade, tariffs, treatment of foreign nationals and ships, and related matters.

A distinction that is relatively easy to apply to multilateral agreements is their degree of "openness." Some multilateral instruments are open to all states. States that have not participated in the drafting of an agreement thus may become parties by accession once the treaty has entered into force. Some multilateral treaties, on the other hand, may be closed, so that only the original signatories may become parties through ratification. A treaty also may be relatively open. Thus the North Atlantic Treaty (1949) is open to any European state that is invited by the original parties to accede to it if it is found to be ". . . in a position to further the principles of this Treaty and to contribute to the security of the North Atlantic area . . ." (article 10). Some treaties may be deceptively open but are in fact designed to exclude certain states.

Thus the Vienna Convention on the Law of Treaties is open for signature or accession by "all States Members of the United Nations or of any of the specialized agencies or of the International Atomic Energy Agency or parties to the Statute of the International Court of Justice, and . . . any other state invited by the General Assembly of the United Nations. . . ." The states that are thus excluded, unless they are invited by the General Assembly, are the Communist sections of the so-called divided states: above all, North Korea and North Vietnam.

Some multilateral agreements set up an international organization for a specific purpose or a variety of purposes. They may therefore be referred to as constituent agreements. Such agreements may be regional or worldwide in scope. The International Telecommunication Convention of 1965 (which treats telephone and radio as well as telegraphy) is the constituent instrument of the International Telecommunication Union. The United Nations Charter (1945) is both a multilateral treaty and the constituent instrument of the United Nations. An example of a regional agreement that operates as a constituent agreement is the charter of the Organization of American States (Charter of Bogotá), which established the organization in 1948. Constituent instruments are governed both by the law of treaties and by their own specific rules.

The constitution of an international organization may be part of a wider multilateral treaty. The Treaty of Versailles (1919), for example, contained in Part I the Covenant of the League of Nations and in Part XIII the constitution of the International Labour Organisation.

Complexity of international agreements

One of the striking features of most contemporary treaties is their extraordinary complexity. This complexity results from the highly technical nature, especially in the economic and scientific fields, of the matters with which many modern treaties deal and is reflected in their length, number of provisions, detail, and terminology. Some treaties, such as the Paris and Rome treaties of the European Economic Community, are comparable to the most intricate domestic statutes. The Bretton Woods agreements (1944), establishing the International Monetary Fund and the International Bank for Reconstruction and Development, require a high level of legal and economic expertise in their interpretation. To be sure, some bilateral agreements are still relatively simple, but the language of bilateral agreements relating to taxation or treaties of commerce dealing with unfair competition and restrictive business practices calls for the skill of specialists. To reconcile national tariff policy with the rules of the General Agreement on Tariffs and Trade (GATT), for example, requires expertise of the highest order. It is no accident, therefore, that the modern multilateral agreement almost invariably establishes an institution, the function of which is to clarify and interpret the agreement.

The term supranational is of recent origin and is used to describe the type of treaty structure developed originally by six western European states: France, Germany, Italy, The Netherlands, Belgium, and Luxembourg. The first treaty was that of Paris, signed in 1951, establishing the European Coal and Steel Community (ECSC); the second, the Rome treaty, signed in 1957, establishing the European Economic Community (EEC); the third, the Rome treaty of the same date establishing the European Atomic Energy Community (Euratom). The term supranational appears in the ECSC treaty but not in the other treaties, in connection with the decision-making powers of the executive organ of the community known as the High Authority. The members of the executive organs of the ECSC shall, according to the terms of the treaty, "exercise their functions in complete independence, in the general interest of the Community. In the fulfilment of their duties, they shall neither solicit nor accept instructions from any Government or from any organization." This clause, which provides for the complete independence of the members from the governments that appoint them as well as from the governments of which they are and remain nationals, is strengthened by the undertaking of the member states "to respect this *supranational* character and to make no effort to influence the members of the High Authority in the execution of their duties" (article 9; italics added).

Some authorities see in the powers conferred upon the executive organ a transfer of sovereignty from the member states to the High Authority. This view is valid to the extent that certain functions normally exercised by the states are henceforth to be exercised by an independent organ. In this sense supranationality involves a partial transfer and not merely a limitation of sovereignty as is the case with ordinary treaties. The agreements setting up the European community are, therefore, rightly called supranational.

Treaties, however, are not the only instruments by which international agreements are concluded. Depending on the subject matter, the occasion, the desired effect, and the preferences of the chancelleries concerned, other means may be employed. There are single instruments that lack the formality of a treaty called agreed minute, memorandum of agreement, or modus vivendi; there are formal single instruments called convention, agreement, protocol, declaration, charter, covenant, pact, statute, final act, general act, and concordat (the usual designation for accords with the Holy See); finally there are less formal agreements consisting of two or more instruments, such as "exchange of notes" or "exchange of letters." However confusing and inconsistent the practice of nations, the important point is that the binding force does not depend upon the name but upon the substance and intent of the parties.

Other instruments of agreement

Although written instruments are the rule in international intercourse, governments also may make oral agreements. They, too, are governed by the law of treaties, but there may be difficulty in proving that an oral statement has been made in fact and with what intent.

FUNCTIONS OF INTERNATIONAL AGREEMENTS

In the absence of an international legislature, the multilateral treaty is the chosen instrument for adapting international law to changing circumstances brought about by rapid technological developments and the ever-growing interdependence of nations. This growing interdependence of nations is illustrated by the fact that, whereas for the period 1864 to 1914 one authority identified 257 multilateral instruments, the *United Nations Treaty Series* (1946–67) contains 8,887 bilateral and multilateral instruments. The large increase in instruments is, of course, partly attributable to the fact that the number of existing states is more than twice what it was in the period of the League of Nations.

The subject matter covered by international agreements has grown so large as to make classification difficult. States have contracted bilateral and multilateral obligations relating to such diverse matters as commerce, navigation, diplomatic relations, consular relations, mutual assistance in criminal matters (including extradition), judicial assistance in civil matters (including execution of foreign judgments), nationality and statelessness, economic cooperation, air service and air transportation, hydroelectric power, atomic energy, fisheries and conservation of marine resources, cultural exchanges, social insurance, passport and visa requirements, taxation, labour, and copyright and patents and trademarks. This is far from being an exhaustive list as it does not include matters of traditional concern to states such as alliances, boundaries, arbitration, and adjudication nor treaties dealing with the conduct of war and the renunciation of war as an instrument of national policy.

Functions of international agreements

Despite the extreme diversity of international agreements, however, it is possible to classify them according to the functions that they serve in international society. Three such broad functions may be discerned; namely, the development and codification of international law, the establishment of new levels of cooperation and integration between states, and the resolution of actual and potential international conflict.

Development and codification of international law. An important group of multilateral agreements, concluded under the auspices of the United Nations, deals with basic aspects of customary international law. The texts of these agreements have been carefully prepared by the International Law Commission (ILC), submitted to governments for comments, and discussed by the legal committee of the United Nations General Assembly. Codification means "the more precise formulation and systematization of rules of international law in fields where there already has been extensive state practice, precedent and doctrine"; progressive development means "the preparation of draft conventions on subjects which have not yet been regulated by international law or in regard to which the law has not yet been sufficiently developed in the practice of States" (article 15 of the Statute of the ILC, adopted by the General Assembly November 21, 1947).

An outstanding feature of the legislative work of the United Nations has been the participation of nearly all states that have come into existence since the end of World War II. The agreements therefore represent a consensus of very diverse viewpoints and interests. They include important conventions on the law of the sea, on diplomatic and consular relations, and the law of treaties.

Law-making agreements in which the progressive development of international law is the dominant aim are usually in new areas of international concern. Many states have thus subscribed to the 1967 Treaty on Principles Governing the Activities of States in the Exploration and Uses of Outer Space, including the Moon and Other Celestial Bodies (Outer Space Treaty), and the 1968 Agreement on the Rescue of Astronauts, the Return of Astronauts, and the Return of Objects launched into Outer Space.

The establishment of new levels of integration. In common parlance the term integration implies the making of a whole out of parts. This meaning applies also to the use of the term in the context of international relations: when states become so mutually interdependent that they can properly be viewed as constituting a single international community based on peaceful cooperation and accommodation, then integration has been achieved. International agreements, clearly, are instrumental in such a process. Every international agreement is intended to bring the parties to it closer together in the pursuit of some mutual interest. The interdependence that exists is given expression in the agreement, and the agreement in turn serves to further the interdependence. This is particularly true of those agreements that are the constituent instruments of intergovernmental organizations, although nongovernmental organizations have been increasingly relevant in fostering integration in many areas of international interest.

The European Economic Community has inspired most of the theories of integration. The reason for this becomes apparent from the supranational character of the treaties (see above) as well as from the larger aims that they are to serve. The basic idea was to bring France and Germany so close together that war would become impossible. Supranational control over the industries that normally serve military preparation—coal and steel—was considered the means to the end. Beyond this, the signatory states, according to the preamble to the treaty establishing the ECSC,

> Resolved to substitute for historic rivalries a fusion of their essential interests; to establish, by creating an economic community, the foundation of a broad and independent community among peoples long divided by bloody conflicts; and to lay the bases of institutions capable of giving direction to their future common destiny.

Resolution of actual and potential conflict. Since time immemorial international agreements have been the means of settling differences between states or of creating procedures for the settlement of possible future interstate disputes. Bilateral and multilateral agreements such as peace treaties, boundary treaties, claims agreements, and others have dealt with conflicts that have already arisen. Other agreements, again both bilateral and multilateral, have laid down procedures for the peaceful settlement of disputes. Constituent instruments of organizations such as the League of Nations, the United Nations, the Organization of African Unity, and the Organization of American States include provision for the peaceful settlement of disputes. Many lawmaking agreements contain a so-called compromissory clause, whereby the parties agree to submit disputes concerning the application and interpretation of the treaty to arbitration or to the International Court of Justice. In recent years it has become necessary to place the provisions for dispute settlement in a separate "optional protocol." This procedure was applied in connection with the Geneva Conventions on the Law of the Sea, the Vienna Convention on Diplomatic Relations, and the Vienna Convention on Consular Relations. The reason for this was that some states objected strongly to the usual compromissory clause, which provides for the compulsory jurisdiction of the International Court of Justice, and threatened that they would not ratify the conventions if such a clause were included. The optional protocol, predictably, was accepted by only a small number of the parties to the conventions, as few states are prepared to submit to compulsory jurisdiction.

The Vienna Convention on the Law of Treaties contains a compromissory clause for certain types of disputes and a procedure of conciliation for others. The problem with conciliation is that it may, but does not necessarily, settle the dispute as arbitration and adjudication by the court would, but it thus is a little more acceptable to states than compulsory adjudication. The resistance of states to compulsory arbitration or adjudication is indicative of their limited commitment to universal integration through the rule of law. In this respect the European Economic Community is an exception, providing as it does for the compulsory settlement of disputes arising under the three constituent treaties by the Court of Justice, which is open even to individuals.

The scope for international cooperation and integration is, of course, unlimited, but states seem to have gone as far as is compatible with their desire to preserve as much freedom of action as possible in their agreements. An agreement on the standardization of weights and measures does not entail an intolerable limitation on the sovereignty of states. An effective agreement for the control of narcotic and other dangerous drugs, on the other hand, would require a greater degree of limitation than governments have been willing to accept. The result is that after 70 years of international endeavor in this matter, there is still no adequate system of control. The control and eventual reduction of armaments has been on the agenda of international conferences since The Hague Peace Conference of 1899. The Nuclear Test Ban Treaty and the Nuclear Nonproliferation Treaty are seen as encouraging achievements but no more than that. A customs union requires willingness to accept far-reaching limitations upon the sovereignty of states, and some states have been willing to pay the price. Many more may become convinced that larger markets and a larger scale of production are the preconditions of greater economic and social welfare. The customs union within the European Economic Community is an indication that there are no inherent limitations upon the capacity of states to absorb limitations upon their sovereignty. It may be noted that western Europe was the cradle of nationalism and the doctrine of the sovereignty of states. Now it may have become the cradle of supranational integration.

BIBLIOGRAPHY. LORD MCNAIR, *The Law of Treaties* (1961), a standard work on the subject; C.W. JENKS, *Social Justice in the Law of Nations* (1970), a useful, succinct survey of the work of international organizations in the field of social and labour law; R.C. LAWSON (ed.), *International Regional Organizations* (1962), a handbook of the constitutional instruments of contemporary regional organizations; J.L. BRIERLY, *The Law of Nations*, 6th ed. by SIR H. WALDOCK (1963), an outstanding, scholarly survey of international law; A. NUSSBAUM, *A Concise History of the Law of Nations*, rev. ed. (1954), a useful survey of the development of international law from the earliest times.

(L.G.)

International Court of Justice

The International Court of Justice, the principal judicial organ of the United Nations, succeeded the Permanent Court of International Justice after World War II. For generations eminent statesmen, private persons, and various organizations—national and international—have sought to institute some acceptable means for the peaceful settlement of disputes between nations. Methods that have been advocated or resorted to include the use of good offices by other states, commissions of inquiry and conciliation, arbitration, and judicial settlement.

Arbitration as a form of judicial settlement has been used by states over a long period of time—not generally but frequently. Many bilateral and a number of multilateral treaties and conventions providing for arbitration have been concluded from time to time, some relating to then-existing disputes and others relating to disputes or categories of disputes which might arise in the future. Of the multilateral conventions providing for arbitration those that stand out are the Conventions for the Pacific Settlement of International Disputes concluded at the first and second peace conferences held at The Hague in 1899 and 1907. The Convention of 1899 contains provisions on the use of good offices and mediation, international commissions of inquiry, and elaborate provisions designed to regularize arbitral procedure. It also provides for the establishment by the signatories of a panel of jurists called the Permanent Court of Arbitration (although in no sense a court) to which each state, party to the convention, should appoint four members, and from which governments desiring to arbitrate might choose competent arbitrators.

The work of the Permanent Court before World War II

Although many international arbitrations both before and following the Hague conventions constitute landmarks in the process of peaceful settlement of disputes, and the tribunals in such cases made notable contributions to an international jurisprudence, it was recognized that with all its virtues a system in which reliance is placed on ad hoc tribunals, as distinguished from an established court of justice, was not all that might be desired. Elihu Root, the U.S. secretary of state, observed in his instructions to the U.S. delegation to the second Hague conference that the principal objection to arbitration rested not upon the unwillingness of nations to submit their controversies to impartial arbitration, but upon an apprehension that the arbitrators would not be impartial. He instructed the delegates to try to have the Permanent Court of Arbitration developed into a permanent tribunal composed of judges "who are judicial officers and nothing else, who are paid adequate salaries, who have no other occupation, and who will devote their entire time to the trial and decision of international causes by judicial methods and under a sense of judicial responsibility."

The 1899 convention was revised, but as revised it fell far short of the pattern outlined by Root. It did not provide for full-time judges, but rather continued the system of a panel of jurists from which arbitrators might or might not be chosen for particular cases.

The 1907 conference, however, prepared and recommended a draft convention to establish a court of arbitral justice composed of judges to be appointed for fixed periods of service and on a salary basis. But the project was not adopted by the states and the court was never established. Nevertheless, the draft had its influence on subsequent developments.

PERMANENT COURT OF INTERNATIONAL JUSTICE

The next notable step in the process of developing an international judiciary was taken by the League of Nations in 1920, when, pursuant to article 14 of the Covenant of the League, it took steps to establish the Permanent Court of International Justice.

Article 14 provided:

> The Council shall formulate and submit to the Members of the League for adoption plans for the establishment of a Permanent Court of International Justice. The Court shall be competent to hear and determine any dispute of an international character which the Parties thereto submit to it. The Court may also give an advisory opinion upon any dispute or question referred to it by the Council or by the Assembly.

In February 1920, the council appointed a committee of jurists to prepare a plan that it could submit to members of the League for adoption. The committee, following meetings at The Hague in June and July of that year, submitted to the council a draft scheme that, with certain modifications, was adopted by the council, and with still further amendments was approved by the assembly on December 13, 1920. The text was attached to a protocol of December 16, 1920, for signature and ratification by the members of the League. By September 1921, the requisite number of states, a majority, had given their approval, and the draft became the statute of the Permanent Court of International Justice.

The statute prescribed the qualifications for the judges, the method of election and tenure of office, the court's jurisdiction, and its mode of procedure. The first court, consisting of 11 judges and four deputy judges, was elected by the council and the assembly on September 14–16, 1921. Later, in 1930, the assembly elected 15 judges and four deputy judges. Still later, following the coming into force in 1936 of amendments to the statute, the deputy judges were eliminated and the court was composed of 15 judges elected as theretofore by the council and the assembly.

The court held its first meeting at The Hague, its seat, on January 30, 1922. It held regular meetings thereafter until its work was interrupted by World War II. Its last meeting, an administrative one, was in October 1945.

The Hague conventions

During its existence it rendered 31 judgments and gave 27 advisory opinions. The court was open to members of the League and also to states mentioned in the annex to the Covenant. The conditions under which it should be open to still other states were to be laid down by the council. Acceptance of the jurisdiction of the court was not compulsory, and states were free to submit their disputes or not as they might see fit. They were privileged, however, under the optional clause of article 36 of the statute, to declare, either when signing or ratifying the protocol to which the statute was adjoined, or at a later moment, that they recognized as compulsory ipso facto and without special agreement, in relation to any other state accepting the same obligation, the jurisdiction of the court in any or all of certain specified categories of disputes. Such declarations might be made unconditionally or on condition of reciprocity on the part of several or certain states or for a certain time. During the existence of the court some 54 states signed the optional clause of article 36, thereby accepting compulsory jurisdiction in varying forms and for varying periods of time. During this same period 59 states signed the Protocol of 1920, to which the statute was annexed, and all but nine ratified it.

The United States did not become a party to the Statute of the Permanent Court. A senate resolution for adherence that came to a vote on January 29, 1935, failed to obtain the requisite two-thirds vote, and no further action was taken. Yet throughout the period of the court a U.S. jurist was on the bench.

FORMATION OF THE INTERNATIONAL COURT OF JUSTICE

Following World War II and the advent of the United Nations, the League of Nations was dissolved and with it the Permanent Court of International Justice. But that court was not dissolved until the new one—the International Court of Justice—had been established. By this time the nations, including the United States, were thoroughly convinced that a court of justice must have first rank in any organization for the maintenance of peace. Article 92 of the Charter of the United Nations states:

> The International Court of Justice shall be the principal judicial organ of the United Nations. It shall function in accordance with the annexed Statute, which is based upon the Statute of the Permanent Court of International Justice and forms an integral part of the present Charter.

Article 93 provides that all members of the United Nations are ipso facto parties to the statute and that states not members may become parties on conditions to be determined in each case by the UN General Assembly upon recommendation of the Security Council. The court consists of 15 judges, no two of whom may be nationals of the same state, elected by the General Assembly and the Security Council. They do not have life tenure but are elected for periods of nine years and are eligible for reelection.

The seat of the court is at The Hague, but it may hold sessions elsewhere whenever it considers it desirable. Its first session was held at The Hague in April and May 1946.

It is a continuing body. The statute provides that it shall remain permanently in session, except during judicial vacations. It is also an autonomous body. It elects its president and vice president, appoints its registrar, and provides for the appointment of such other officers and clerical staff as may be necessary. The president and the registrar are required to reside at The Hague.

The judges. The judges, who must possess certain specified qualifications, do not represent the states from which they are chosen. They represent the entire international community of states. They are not selected by the governments of their states or even nominated by them; they are nominated rather by the national groups in the Permanent Court of Arbitration referred to above, or, in the case of states not represented on the Permanent Court of Arbitration, by national groups appointed for that purpose by their governments, the purpose being to remove the nominations as far as possible from political considerations.

Comparable safeguards were provided for the election of the judges. The statute stipulates that in such elections the General Assembly and the Security Council shall proceed independently of each other, and that at every election the electors should bear in mind not only that the persons to be elected shall individually possess the qualifications required "but also that in the body as a whole the representation of the main forms of civilization and of the principal legal systems of the world should be assured." Those candidates who obtain an absolute majority of votes in both the General Assembly and the Security Council are to be considered as elected. Further procedure is provided for the situation where, after the first meeting for the purpose of the election, one or more seats remain to be filled.

Impartiality of the judges

The judges receive annual salaries reasonably commensurate with their status. But they must be prepared to accept certain restrictions; *i.e.*, they must refrain from all activities incompatible with their judicial functions. The purpose of the statute is to have at all times a court that is entirely free from bias or any preconceived notion as to the merits of any case coming before it. Each member is required, before taking up his duties, to "make a solemn declaration in open court that he will exercise his powers impartially and conscientiously." In order to facilitate the proper exercise of their judicial functions the members, when engaged in the business of the court, enjoy diplomatic privileges and immunities. Members are bound to hold themselves permanently at the disposal of the court.

While nine judges constitute a quorum, the statute requires that the full court shall sit except when it is expressly provided otherwise. The court may dispense with the sitting of one or more judges "according to circumstances and in rotation," provided the number of available judges is not thereby reduced below 11. In practice, the full court sits in all cases except where a judge is disqualified by reason of some previous connection with the case or is prevented by illness or other serious reasons from attending. No judge may be dismissed unless in the opinion of all the others he has ceased to fulfill the required conditions. Vacancies resulting from death or other causes must be filled by the same method as that laid down for the first election. A member elected to replace a member whose term of office has not expired holds office for the remainder of his predecessor's term.

Obviously, since there are only 15 judges, cases are sometimes presented by states which have no national on the court. While the statute provides that judges of the nationality of each of the parties retain their right to sit in the case before the court, it also provides that, if the court includes upon the bench a judge of the nationality of one of the parties, the other party may choose a person to sit as judge, also that, if the court includes upon the bench no judge of the nationality of either party, each of the parties may choose a person to sit as judge. This privilege frequently is exercised.

Competence. Since the function of the court is to pass judgment upon disputes between states, only states may be parties in cases before the court. It is open to all states parties to the statute and to such other states as comply with conditions laid down by the Security Council, which conditions must not, in any case, place the parties in a position of inequality before the court.

At the time that the statute was being drafted, there was strong sentiment on the part of certain states, particularly the smaller ones, for giving the court compulsory jurisdiction; *i.e.*, making it possible for any state to bring an action against any other state without the latter's consent. The opponents of this view felt that some states were not yet ready to accept compulsory jurisdiction and that to try to force it upon them might cause them to decline to accept the statute at all. They favoured the adoption of the optional provisions in article 36 of the Statute of the Permanent Court. This was agreed upon and that article became, for the most part, article 36 of the new statute. Under it parties to the statute may at any time file with the secretary general of the United Nations a declaration accepting compulsory jurisdiction. Some four dozen states have done so. The declaration may be made unconditionally or on condition of reciprocity on the part of other states, or for a certain time. It was further provided that declarations made under the old statute conferring jurisdiction on the Permanent Court that were still in force should be deemed, as between the parties to the new statute, to be acceptances of the compulsory jurisdiction of the new court.

Reservations about jurisdiction

In 1946, when the U.S. Senate was considering the exact nature of the court's jurisdiction, a resolution was introduced providing that the United States should be free to determine for itself what matters were of an essentially domestic nature and thus outside the jurisdiction of the court. It was argued that such a self-judging reservation was necessary because the court might take a broad view of what was an international question and thus interfere with U.S. policy on immigration, tariffs, and the Panama Canal. Several other countries followed the U.S. example and reserved the right to determine what matters fell within their domestic jurisdiction. But criticism of this position was frequently voiced in the United States and in other countries as being inconsistent with the principle that no one should be a judge in his own cause, and as indicating a lack of confidence in the court. The self-judging reservation was also criticized by members of the court in individual opinions in *Certain Norwegian Loans* (France v. Norway) (1957) and *Interhandel* (Switzerland v. United States) (1959). Several countries that originally adopted the self-judging reservation later reconsidered and withdrew it.

The court's jurisdiction was still further extended by article 37 of the statute, which stipulates that whenever a treaty or convention in force "provides for reference of a matter to . . . the Permanent Court of International Justice, the matter shall, as between the parties to the present Statute, be referred to the International Court of Justice."

States which have not accepted compulsory jurisdiction may not be sued without their consent. A state may give its consent by entering into an agreement with another state or otherwise indicating its willingness to submit the dispute to the court.

In 1954 the United States filed with the court two applications instituting proceedings against the Soviet Union and Hungary, respectively, and in 1955 like action was taken against Czechoslovakia and the Soviet Union, respectively, each complaint relating to certain aircraft incidents; also in 1955 Great Britain filed two applications instituting proceedings against Argentina and Chile, respectively, concerning sovereign rights in the Antarctic. None of the defendant states had accepted compulsory jurisdiction, and on being informed of these actions by the registrar of the court, each in turn specifically declined to submit the dispute to the court.

In 1959 the court held that it lacked jurisdiction over the claim of Israel for damages from Bulgaria for an airliner shot down over Bulgarian territory. In 1931 Bulgaria had accepted the cumpulsory jurisdiction of the Permanent Court of International Justice without time limit. The court held that this acceptance did not carry over to the present because Bulgaria had not joined the United Nations until after the statute of the old court had come to an end. In 1961 the court rejected an argument by Thailand that the effect of this decision rendered ineffectual Thailand's declaration of 1950 purporting to renew a previous acceptance of the court's compulsory jurisdiction. In *Barcelona Traction, Light, and Power Co., Ltd.* (Belgium v. Spain) (1964), the court, in a lengthy analysis of article 37 of the statute, rejected a preliminary objection presented by Spain in reliance on the decision in the Bulgarian case, which the court held should be distinguished and was not controlling in the circumstances of the Barcelona case.

The statute declares it to be the duty of the court to decide disputes in accordance with international law. It applies (1) international conventions establishing rules recognized by the contesting states, (2) international custom, as evidence of a general practice accepted as law, and (3) the general principles of law recognized by civilized nations; and (4) it may look to judicial decisions and the teachings of the most highly qualified publicists of the various nations as subsidiary means for determining rules of law. It may also decide cases *ex aequo et bono* (that is to say, on the basis of a fair solution), if the parties agree. In the absence of such an agreement it must apply rules of law.

Procedure. The official languages of the court are French and English; either may be used by the parties. Written pleadings and oral arguments presented in one language are translated into the other. Beginning with the oral argument in the South West Africa case (1965–66), the court for the first time utilized simultaneous translations in its public hearings. The judgments and opinions are in both French and English.

Cases are brought before the court either by the notification to it of a special agreement concluded by the parties or by the unilateral action of one of them through a written application addressed to the registrar. The proceedings are in two parts, written and oral.

The court may also hear witnesses and appoint commissions of experts to make investigations and reports when necessary. Both these procedures were followed in *Corfu Channel* (United Kingdom v. Albania) (1949). Experts and witnesses presented by the parties were also heard by the court in *Temple of Preah Vihear* (Cambodia v. Thailand) (1962) and in *South West Africa* (Ethiopia and Liberia v. South Africa) (1966). In the South West Africa case, the court decided not to accede to a request by South Africa that the court should itself make an on-site inspection.

The deliberations of the court are in private, but the judgments, which are by a majority vote, are read in open court. In case of a tie, the president may cast a deciding vote; this was done in *South West Africa*, when the judges divided 7–7. Any judge may file a separate opinion if he does not agree in whole or in part with the decision. Few decisions represent the unanimous opinion of the judges. The judgment is final and without appeal.

Enforcement of decisions

The question is frequently asked as to how decisions of the court are enforced. This also troubled the minds of some of the delegates at the United Nations Conference on International Organization, held at San Francisco, California, when the statute was under consideration. To meet their wishes there was incorporated in article 94 of the charter an undertaking on the part of each member of the United Nations "to comply with the decision of the . . . Court . . . in any case to which it is a party," and a further provision that:

> If any party to a case fails to perform the obligations incumbent upon it under a judgment rendered by the Court, the other party may have recourse to the Security Council, which may, if it deems necessary, make recommendations or decide upon measures to be taken to give effect to the judgment.

It should be remarked, however, that by 1967 there had been only one known instance of the failure of a party to a case before the court, or before its predecessor, the Permanent Court of International Justice, to carry out a decision of either court. In the Corfu Channel case,

Albania failed to pay £843,947 awarded to the United Kingdom by the court as compensation for damages suffered.

Advisory opinions. The court is authorized by article 65 of the statute to give advisory opinions on any legal questions at the request of whatever body may be authorized by or in accordance with the Charter of the UN to make such a request.

Article 96 of the charter provides that such opinions may be requested by the General Assembly or the Security Council; also that they may be requested by other organs of the United Nations and specialized agencies, when authorized by the General Assembly. Such requests must be laid before the court by means of a written request containing an exact statement of the questions, accompanied by all documents likely to throw light upon them. From this point on, the procedure before the court is somewhat analogous to that followed in contentious cases. States and organizations presenting written or oral statements are allowed, within a specified time, to comment on those submitted by others. Advisory opinions, like judgments, are delivered in open court.

Membership. Article 13 of the statute provides that the members of the court shall be elected for nine years and may be re-elected, but in order to avoid the necessity of electing an entirely new court at the end of each nine-year period and to ensure that there shall be on the bench at all times a majority of experienced judges, it was further provided that of the judges elected at the first election, the terms of five should expire at the end of three years and the terms of five more should expire at the end of six years; also that the judges whose terms were to expire at the end of the said periods of three and six years should be chosen by lot to be drawn by the secretary general of the United Nations immediately after the first election had been completed.

The first election was held on February 6, 1946, at the London meeting of the General Assembly and the Security Council. Fifteen judges were elected. The procedure provided in article 13 was applied and five judges drew three-year terms and five others drew six-year terms.

BIBLIOGRAPHY. SHABTAI ROSENNE, *The Law and Practice of the International Court*, 2 vol. (1965), the most complete and authoritative treatise on all aspects of the International Court; EDVARD HAMBRO, *The Case Law of the International Court: A Repertoire of the Judgments, Advisory Opinions and Orders of the Permanent Court of International Justice and of the International Court of Justice* (1952, with supplements), a repertoire, prepared by a former Registrar of the Court, arranged to enable the reader to find the views expressed by the Court and by individual judges on all topics of international law with which the Court has dealt; C. WILFRED JENKS, *The Prospects of International Adjudication* (1964), a profound analysis of this subject by an outstanding international lawyer; SIR HERSCH LAUTERPACHT, *The Development of International Law by the International Court*, rev. ed. (1958), a learned and forward reaching study of the work of the Court by a former Judge of the Court.

(P.C.J./G.H.H.)

International Educational Relations

International education has had a variety of meanings; its emphasis and activities have been molded over time by the problems its exponents have considered most pressing. Since its formation in 1945, the United Nations Educational, Scientific and Cultural Organization (UNESCO) has grown in importance as nations from all areas of the globe have brought their particular educational problems to it. This situation has made more and more apparent the need for a working definition accurately encompassing its broad range of activities. One way to see how its focus has evolved and both sharpened and narrowed since 1945 is to compare two of its meanings, one given in 1950, the other in 1968:

> The term "international education" may be applied to the various educational and cultural relations among nations . . .; it refers to international efforts at cooperation and harmony in the exchange of teachers and students, rehabilitation of backward cultural areas, mutual understanding through school instruction, and the like. (From W. Brickman in *Encyclopedia of Educational Research;* New York, 1950.)

> International education . . . is seen as the field concerned with cross-national relations and cooperation and exchanges of educational information and personnel. The three major areas of interest associated with international education are international relations and cooperation in education; cross-national movements of educational materials, students, teachers, consultants, and aid; and education for international and cross-cultural understanding. (From S. Spaulding, J. Singleton, and P. Watson, "The Context of International Development Education," *Review of Educational Research*, June 1968, pp. 201–12.)

In the earlier definition the ambiguous term cultural relations tended to include within the field's purview the exchange of artists and performers. But unless such arts are used to teach something, they are not related to international education. Moreover, the Western orientation of the phrase rehabilitation of backward cultural areas overlooked the enormous benefits that accrue to the donor nation, which often learns as much as it teaches. The more recent definition, on the other hand, limits international education specifically to educational activity and conveys a clearer idea of the content of the field. It points out the areas of interest and major activities and suggests ways of viewing educational relations across national boundaries.

HISTORICAL BACKGROUND

International education has its roots in the 17th century, when John Amos Comenius, a Moravian churchman and teacher, put forward one of the first and most lasting hopes of international education. He envisioned an international Pansophic College dedicated to the advancement of mutual understanding among peoples. In succeeding centuries Montaigne, Rousseau, Kant, and Fichte envisioned international educational cooperation as a step in the direction of world peace. After the Napoleonic Wars a French educator, Marc-Antoine Jullien, stressed in his works the need for an international commission on education to compile, analyze, and disseminate statistics and other educational data for the improvement of all educational systems. He envisioned not only a useful exchange of information but also the growth of mutual trust and understanding among educators. If it were possible to bring educators together, he said, then it might also be possible to bring nations together, and this was his ultimate goal. Later in the century, Herman Molkenboer, a Dutch lawyer and educator, published another imaginative plan for an international education agency and started a periodical, *Journal of Correspondence on the Foundation of a Permanent and International Council on Education*, to publicize it.

In the 20th century the efforts were intensified. In 1908, Edward Peeters founded a publishing firm in Oostende, out of which grew the International Bureau of Education. The threat of World War I and the lack of financial support forced the bureau's activities to a stop less than ten years later, but not before it had issued monographs on education in areas of Europe, Asia, Africa, and South America and had created considerable world interest. A contemporary of Peeters, a Hungarian educator, Frances Kemeny, also gave direction to the development of international education. International education, according to Kemeny, could be advanced in at least six ways: (1) the publication of purely descriptive reports on education in various countries, (2) the organization of international conferences for teachers, (3) the development of international agreements on the organization and structure of education (Kemeny considered this basic to all), (4) the formulation of international statements on the rights of man, (5) the revision of textbooks to eliminate hatred and emphasize mutual trust, and (6) a concentrated effort to eradicate racial prejudice among all peoples.

Kemeny's ideas and others related to them were frequently reflected in questions raised before the League of Nations from 1919 to 1921. Thus the League's Council considered a proposal that a committee of educators and scientists be appointed to study "international cooperation and education." But the word education proved controversial since many nations, jealous of their sovereignty, feared possible infringement on their school systems. In the end the League's Assembly established a Committee on Intellectual Cooperation but decided not to include education in its responsibilities. Despite the handicaps under which it operated, the committee did make a number of lasting contributions. Its work in sponsoring international conferences later became a central function of UNESCO. Its mission to China in 1931 to aid in educational reconstruction helped to establish the principle that international organizations could support the work of the committee and, later, of course, of UNESCO.

Many of the early supporters of the committee viewed its final form with disappointment. They feared that it would limit itself to strictly "intellectual" matters and not extend its interests to preuniversity educational activities. Further, the committee seemed unable to perform the clearinghouse functions that these educators regarded as essential. Consequently, an international group of educators founded the International Bureau of Education as a private organization in 1925. Once again financial support was a problem and governmental interest was hard to enlist. Because of the quality of its studies on comparative education, its professional training of teachers and use of school libraries, and its dynamic leadership, the bureau grew in importance and influence.

Development of UNESCO

The devastating effects of World War II renewed educators' interest in establishing an organization for world-educational cooperation. During the war the Allied Ministers of Education in Exile met in London to discuss the rebuilding of education in Europe after the war was concluded. In April 1944 the Allied Ministers and the U.S. proposed the establishment of a United Nations Organization for Educational and Cultural Reconstruction. The word education again proved a problem, but this time agreements were reached, and at the Conference for the Establishment of the United Nations Education, Scientific, and Cultural Organization, held in London in 1945, the constitution of the new organization was drafted and signed. UNESCO was born.

ACTIVITIES IN INTERNATIONAL EDUCATION

A survey of the programs being undertaken in various nations all over the world indicates that the most common activities are (1) conferences and seminars on education; (2) technical assistance projects for instilling positive attitudes toward modernization or building and adapting institutions abroad, including teacher and student exchanges; and (3) the development of preuniversity world-culture curriculum projects and university-level area-studies centres and programs of international affairs.

Conferences and seminars. International conferences and seminars deal with a wide range of topics—such as problems in the subject areas of mathematics or foreign language or the coordination of educational research in universities—and are held frequently in locations all over the world. They are sponsored by groups and individuals with diverse educational interests: the Association of Universities of the British Commonwealth, for instance, holds regular conferences for the exchange of ideas and for consultation among Commonwealth colleagues; Chinese scientists in 1966 sponsored a science and physics symposium attended by professionals from four continents; President Lyndon Johnson of the U.S. encouraged an International Conference on the World Crisis in Education in Virginia in 1967 to reassess the capabilities of education for meeting the rising expectations of people everywhere for a better life; more recently, the Association for Supervision and Curriculum Development sponsored an international meeting in California with the theme, "In the Minds of Men: Educating the Young People of the World."

Technical assistance and foreign study. Technical-assistance programs are generally the most visible and widely known aspect of international education. They provide scholarships, study grants, and other programs designed to transfer attitudes, technology, and institutions from one country to another. Basically, "technical assistance" has come to be defined rather broadly as the transmission of skills, attitudes, and knowledge that lead to development. Thus, whereas education tends to be identified strictly with formal schooling, technical assistance also includes such educational processes as informal field operations in agriculture or informal projects in intellectual relations. Knowledge, skills, and attitudes can be transmitted in many ways—in a Western-style classroom, a village marketplace, or the office of a government employee. A good case in point is to be found in the work of the Community Development Division of the onetime International Cooperation Administration (U.S.): the division evaluated its programs in terms of the changes that took place in the people inhabiting the areas it aided, because it believed that new schools or roads or an increase in crop yields were important only insofar as they provided tangible evidence of the development of persons.

Technical assistance differs from all other activities in international education in that its objectives are to improve the technical, professional, and managerial skills and knowledge of those assisted. The programs are designed primarily to introduce attitudes, skills, and knowledge that are essential to economic development. The programs are usually geared to specific development activities, such as the establishment of a local training school or the education of business managers, the overhaul of fiscal operations, or the setting up of an industrial productivity centre.

One of the most common types of technical assistance is the project whereby specialists from one country assist their colleagues in another in developing and adopting applicable technology or building institutions. The French in the early 1960s, for example, believing that educating foreign students in France was not the best approach to their former colonies' educational needs, supported programs for establishing universities and other institutions of higher learning in the former colonies themselves. In the early 1970s the Foundation of Higher Education of Central Africa, which unites four institutes of higher and technical education in Bangui, Fort-Lamy, Brazzaville, and Libreville, was under the temporary administration of a French rector. French professors were members of the faculties, but all the institutes had added courses in agriculture, engineering, or teacher training for their African constituencies, and it was planned that these programs and schools would eventually be truly African. Similar programs are found on a school-to-school basis: Cornell University in New York, for instance, pioneered a cooperative program with the University of the Philippines, combining technical assistance and student-faculty exchange with research and training activities in both countries.

Such international education programs are not limited to aid projects between former colonialists and their excolonies. Europe's Organization for Economic Co-operation and Development (OECD) has stimulated joint educational undertakings among its own members, the most ambitious being perhaps the Mediterranean Regional Project, first organized in 1960. Since 1960 Portugal, Italy, Spain, Greece, Yugoslavia, and Turkey have undertaken with OECD assistance a complete assessment of their scientific and technical manpower needs, their educational needs, and the organizational changes needed to meet these needs. Each country developed a national team of five or six planners, economists, and educationists, jointly financed by the home government and the OECD. National plans have been developed and published.

Student-scholar exchange programs

Another type of technical assistance consists of "study abroad" or student-scholar exchange programs. There is probably no nation that does not send at least a few of its students and scholars out of the country on specific educational programs, which can range from brief educational travel tours to four years or more of course work, internship, and research. Although the diversity of such programs makes it difficult to calculate exactly how many students have been involved and how they have been affected, nevertheless a few educators have offered examples and statistics suggesting the variety and popularity of projects:

In recent years the Soviet Union has moved into the ranks of countries with programs of studies for substantial numbers of students from all over the world. A recent UNESCO report indicates the U.S.S.R. now ranks among the five main contributors to the world wide process of international education. The U.S.S.R. ranks fourth in foreign students (21,000) and third in scholarships for foreign nationals (15,000). Approximately 11,000 are from other Communist countries and about 10,000 from Asia, Africa and Latin America. Less than 200 are from western countries. By 1968 the number of foreign students from Communist countries in the U.S.S.R. reached 13,000 and presumably there were similar increases from other areas. (From S. Rosen, "The USSR and International Education; a Brief Overview," *Kappan*, pp. 247–250.)

In Britain about 5% (7,800) of the undergraduates are from other countries, mainly Commonwealth nations. 30% of all post graduate students are from overseas. (From B. Holmes, "International Education in Great Britain," *Kappan*, pp. 267–270.)

In the U.S. there were 110,315 foreign students enrolled in U.S. institutions of higher learning in 1967–68. 22% receive financial aid from U.S. colleges and universities while 38% are self-supporting. The remainder receive financial help from governments or private groups. (From A. Michie, *Higher Education and World Affairs;* New York, 1968.)

During 1967–1968 there were 4,775 U.S. scholars abroad. Nearly half, 49%, were in Europe, the remainder in other continents. 50 were in Vietnam. (*Ibid.*)

The proportion of U.S. college and university students planning to become teachers and the proportion of faculty members specializing in professional education (both coming and going) are extremely small. Only about 1% of American students abroad in 1966–67 were in education. The majority were in the humanities, social sciences and medicine. Only 5% of the foreign students in the U.S. were in education. The majority were in engineering, humanities, the sciences and the social sciences. At the faculty level only 2% of foreign scholars were in education; 8% of American scholars were in education. (From R.F. Butts, "America's Role in International Education: A Perspective," *68th Yearbook of the National Society for the Study of Education;* Chicago, 1969.)

World culture curricula. The third major activity of international education is the attempt to internationalize curricula at all educational levels—a direct consequence of the science and technology that have made people more aware of their relations to societies. Thus at the elementary and secondary level, world-culture courses have been inaugurated; in colleges and universities, centres for area studies and programs involving multidisciplinary international studies have been opened. These trends are especially evident in the United States, where almost every state has at least one project whose goal is the integration of "Third World" courses with the social studies curricula. In the U.S.S.R. the Institute of Economics of the Academy of Sciences has added the Institute of World Economics and International Relations and the Institute of Economics of the World Socialist Systems to enlarge its scope for research.

International education also encompasses numerous other related activities. Academic journals and popular magazines often publish summaries of important papers given at international conferences and the results of cross-national educational studies. Research is carried out on the effects of technical assistance both on the recipients and donors, while surveys are conducted to assess the changing attitudes of students who study other cultures. International education's activities today are far removed from the simple proposals of Comenius and Jullien; all testify to the field's flexibility and promise.

RECENT DEVELOPMENTS IN INTERNATIONAL EDUCATIONAL RELATIONS

Politics and international education. Since World War II the forces of international politics have compelled nations to appreciate the need to work more closely together to solve common economic, political, and social problems; and, as this appreciation has grown, so has the emphasis on international education. Additional motivation has been provided by the desire of many a developed nation to project a favourable picture of itself to people living round the world. Cross-national educational projects effectively combine these factors—the realistic need for cooperation to help meet the revolution of rising expectations and the desire of the developed nation to be viewed as a friendly power. International education programs often represent a combination of various motives. If the motivation of some developed nations is simply to engage in public relations, however, there are others who also prize the opportunity to advance international understanding and world peace and to share human knowledge; and, in any event, aid often does further economic and social development and, in the process, can contribute to international understanding. It should also be noted that religious bodies and business firms similarly establish programs to promote their own image and purposes. Thus missionaries establish schools to stimulate conversions as well as to educate children, and in areas where schools are needed and desired, missionaries are indeed usually welcomed. Businesses often build or contribute to hospitals, libraries, and schools near their plants to attract workers with families. Government aid often operates on the same principles. The aim is clearly enunciated in the United States in the Mutual Educational and Cultural Exchange Act of 1961, from which so much American foreign educational assistance flows: cross-cultural activities serve to "strengthen the ties which unite us with other nations by demonstrating the educational and cultural interests, developments, and achievements of the people of the United States."

Current bilateral technical-assistance and intellectual-relations programs provide ample evidence of the importance of the promotion of national interests in international educational affairs. In short, more and more nations (and national groups) believe that they must implant their beliefs abroad or at least defend them intellectually, whether the challenge takes place in the General Assembly of the United Nations or in the remote villages of Borneo. France, for example, gives the largest share (in 1963, 95 percent) of her public aid to countries in the franc area. This is defended by the French who couch their explanation in terms of the historical and traditional ties they have with former colonies, which, they point out, prefer their aid. The cultural bond that has existed between the donor and recipients is, they believe, strengthened by aid.

Such programs have introduced a new diplomacy that has extended beyond the diplomat and the conference room to include more of the average citizens. Technical assistance now often goes past governments to the citizenry to win their favour by projects directly affecting them. "Visible" signs of the donor—hospitals, schools, and welfare buildings—dot Asia, Africa, and Latin America, reminding people that a foreigner has responded to their needs. Another noteworthy development is the creation of elaborate overseas information services, including libraries, exhibits, film showings, lectures, and concerts promoted by nations of every political persuasion. The growth of these programs has given an added dimension to media, for journalism, radio, television, and the performing arts have all become vehicles of foreign policy—Radio Free Europe being a dramatic example. Political education under this guise has as its object the presentation of a particular position. The line between information and propaganda is often blurred.

Most developing countries of the world nevertheless welcome international-educational activities, for they recognize that they can use the projects for their own ends. Often, too, the donor's aims are not stated or are only implied, while the recipient's desires are emphasized. This is especially true in the area of student- and scholar-aid programs. The U.S.S.R., in its effort to court Asian, African, and Latin American students, set up in 1960 a special university in Moscow to cater to their needs—Patrice Lumumba People's Friendship University, with six specialized faculties (engineering, agriculture, medicine, physico-mathematical and natural sciences, history and philology, economics and law), all for non-Russian students. The university has a preparatory faculty, too, where students learn the Russian language prior to beginning course work. This arrangement allows students with various backgrounds to pursue their particular educational objectives without the frustration of competing with "native speakers" and with the added advantage of being able to compare their experiences with others whose home-country problems are more similar to theirs than the Russians'.

Courting allies through educational means has, in some cases, however, worked against the donors. In the early 1960s China managed to alienate the African students that it had attracted to its universities—chiefly because they were allowed little association with Chinese students and were subjected to rather obvious political indoctrination. The students lived in special dormitories and had their meals in segregated dining rooms: their monthly allowance of 100 yuan also classed them financially above and beyond the Chinese students, who received only 10 yuan a month. The heavy political indoctrination extended to all classrooms and tended to eat away time for appointed subjects.

As a result over 90 percent of the African students left in disgust or anger, and temporarily at least the student-exchange program ended in failure.

U.S. Peace Corps

Probably the best-known technical-assistance project advanced by the United States is the Peace Corps, whose purpose is "the provision of qualified men and women to interested countries to help those countries meet their needs for trained manpower, the promotion of a better understanding of the American people on the part of the peoples served, and the promotion of a better understanding of other peoples on the part of the American people." The main field of Peace Corps activity since its inception in 1961 has been education (elementary, secondary, university, English language, adult, physical, vocational, and agricultural). In 1970 over 11,000 volunteers were currently working in Africa, Latin America, and Asia, and by 1970 some 50,000 had returned from two years' service in more than 50 countries. Although the Peace Corps' impact on host countries is still unclear, there is ample evidence that returning Peace Corps volunteers frequently seek more university study in the area of their service and thus encourage the expansion of area programs in colleges and universities. They themselves become area specialists and, by often turning to teaching, add a new dimension to discussions of international relations both in the classroom and in the community.

In an effort to avoid the charge that foreign assistance is simply self-advancement, many critics have urged that all assistance be administered by nonpartisan international agencies such as UNESCO or similar multinational agencies. Instead of a donor giving directly to a recipient, aid is channelled through an agency that selects, funds, and often staffs feasible programs. One such experiment is the UNESCO Associated Schools Project, which in over 50 countries has tested new educational approaches to international understanding, involving such themes as the study of foreign countries, basic human rights, and women's rights. Overall, UNESCO has developed programs in six major areas: education, the natural sciences, the social sciences, international-cultural activities, mass communication, and technical assistance. The natural-science division emphasizes scientific research in the solution of social and economic problems, the dissemination of scientific information through conferences and monographs, and the publishing of materials designed to improve the teaching of science in schools. The social-science division has similarly concentrated on the publication of research monographs, the application of the social sciences to social problems, and the development of international understanding in the schools. The arts division has produced volumes on the art treasures of many countries and has also been concerned with the role of the museum as an educational agency. As a result of UNESCO's success in applying academic learning to the solution of human problems, demands on the organization have increased; and with the increased membership of technologically less-developed countries, additional attention will undoubtedly be devoted to efforts at economic and social development.

Other international agencies

Other international agencies also sponsor conferences bringing together people from a wide range of nations to discuss common problems and their solutions. The World Bank's Economic Development Institute, for instance, in 1968–69 sponsored courses in economic development attended by 149 persons from 65 developing countries. The World Health Organization has offered fellowships and travel grants to doctors interested in international programs. The Organization of American States has developed its own Regional Educational Development Program, which makes determinedly multinational efforts to improve educational administration, curriculum planning to meet development needs, and educational technology. Each project, to be approved, must meet the priorities established by the Declaration of the Presidents of OAS in 1967. The declaration stated that projects should (1) encourage and supplement national and multinational efforts in the field of education, (2) intensify inter-American cooperation in educational matters, and (3) promote the integration of Latin America through education in order to raise the economic and social level of the region. Therefore, for a national project to be approved it must be (1) multinational in nature, (2) in agreement with the Declaration of the Presidents, and (3) considered as having significant multiplier effects.

Expansion of education. But no matter what type of aid is preferred by donors and recipients—bilateral or multilateral—all are aware of the increasing imbalance in the distribution of the world's riches. Since there is widespread belief that education contributes to the improvement of society and the equalization of wealth, many nations have focussed on the expansion of education as a first and basic step to economic, social, and political development. Such terms as human resources, political socialization, and social capital have become common among social scientists, educators, and politicians as they try to make their schools serve their societies' goals of modernization. Indeed, recent efforts have begun to concentrate on programs of a decidedly practical nature, with measurable outcomes. Instead of simply granting scholarships randomly, for instance, many donors now try to place foreign students in courses useful to the developmental needs and goals of their country. Israel, for example, concentrates on technical-assistance programs concerned with specialized skills. Farmers, agronomists, carpenters, metallurgists, electricians, agricultural mechanics, trade unionists, social workers, midwives, nurses, and public-health officials from all over the developing world are trained in special accelerated courses in Israel by instructors who demonstrate how Israelis themselves have used applicable techniques.

Other donor nations concentrate on aiding the educational development of only a few nations, usually those considered to be of particular interest to them. Australia's financial aid, for example, is mainly sent to Papua and New Guinea and countries of the former British Indian Empire. In 1968–69 almost half of its aid to the latter states was given to provide training for over 8,000 Asians in Australia or to finance correspondence courses for people in that region. One thousand three hundred Australians were also sent to Asia to act as advisers or instructors for government administrators while equipment for schools, universities, and other training institutions was sent to cooperating Asian countries.

Closely related to the belief that education advances development is the faith of many that education can help to spread world peace and world understanding. Efforts to implement this goal are evident in the work of the UN and such specialized bodies as UNESCO's Major Project on Mutual Appreciation of Eastern and Western Cultural Values and in the work of such private foundations as the Carnegie Endowment for International Peace, founded to hasten "the abolition of international war, the foulest blot on our civilization." But as indicated in the *Report on the Fiftieth Anniversary of the Endowment*, progress toward Andrew Carnegie's aim has been limited. The Endowment has therefore revised its purpose. Instead of aiming for "unconditional peace," it is working to realize some demonstrable progress toward peace and toward development of institutions that will allow humanity not only to survive but to prosper in a less than perfect world. These goals are much more modest than those voiced by many. But they represent an honest confrontation with the realities of our age of competitive coexistence.

Not all programs for international understanding, however, are directed to an audience beyond national boundaries. All nations engage, officially and unofficially, in activities to extend among their own nationals an understanding of other nations. In West Germany, for instance, school social studies have been conceived in both national-international and social dimensions. Teachers not only strive to foster the idea of closer European unity and international cooperation but also, in teaching history, attempt to show leaders not as charismatic heroes but as individuals influenced by the society to which they belonged. In the United States there has been increased emphasis on foreign-language training and on curricula broadened to include studies of African and Asian as well as Western cultures on all levels of schooling; the problem, however, is that only from 3 to 5 percent of U.S. teachers have taken courses in non-Western subjects, world cultures, or international issues, even though there is a definite trend toward incorporating the international dimension into graduate professional education and giving more attention to problems in developing nations.

These "internationalizing" enterprises, even when they do quicken peoples' awareness of cultures other than their own, by no means necessarily result in understanding or peaceful disposition toward the cultures studied. There have been enough studies of prejudice and ethnocentrism to show that teaching how other people live does not necessarily lessen prejudice or ethnocentrism. Prejudice and indifference may run too deep in the fabric of most cultures to be changed by a class assignment or a series of international conferences. Suspicion, hostility, and intolerance will persist as long as men neglect to put every attitude to the test of rationality. Very little comes from a proliferation of activities built simply on the assumption that "even strange people can be friendly."

The psychology of prejudice and ethnocentrism

Research exchange. The advancement of human knowledge and competence has become more important in the past 15 years with the increasing number of fellowships and travel grants and with the encouragement of private international organizations, science cooperation offices, seminars, symposiums,, conferences, clearinghouse activities, yearbooks, journals, art reproductions, television, radio, press, and museum programs. Developing countries with scarce resources are particularly interested in such exchanges of educational information. And the variety of international educational research projects is vast. A comprehensive mathematics study in the mid-1960s, for example, assessed the mathematical ability and aptitude of over 133,000 students in more than 5,000 schools of western Europe, Japan, Israel, and the United States; it attempted to relate educational inputs (curriculum, class size, teaching methods, socioeconomic status) to oututs as seen in achievement tests. The International Institute for Educational Planning in Paris has investigated the uses of technology in education—such as the uses of radio, television, audiovisual materials, and programmed instruction for extending literacy, upgrading teacher training, and enhancing community development instruction in developing countries. Some researchers have tried to study childhood experiences as related to national growth.

On the whole, nevertheless, research has been insufficient to change school systems and introduce educational innovations. Few studies have dealt with teacher education in developing countries; few have tried to assess the results of innovations in school systems; few have succeeded in accurately describing the relations between education and development. In short, there is scant documentation of the long-range processes or effects of education.

Research exchange

To facilitate research and to keep countries informed about one another's progress, many organizations sponsor educational conferences and publish research findings. Probably the largest such organization is UNESCO, which frequently sponsors conferences for national ministers of education on a wide range of topics from the quality of university education to the essential rural-development function of primary education in developing countries. It is also involved in pilot projects for improved science and mathematics education, literacy, educational planning, and other contemporary problems (many of these programs have built-in means of disseminating the findings to all interested parties) and plays a major role in standardizing educational research and statistical analysis. In conjunction with the International Bureau of Education, UNESCO publishes surveys of education in countries throughout the world; and through its regional offices in Asia, Latin America, and Africa, it disseminates studies on such matters as child development, adult education, and community development.

The International Bureau of Education, based in Geneva, is the oldest organization in the field concerned with international cooperation in education and the sharing of knowledge; it has been active since 1925 (even during World War II, when it provided educational programs for prisoners of war). Since UNESCO's inception it has jointly sponsored the yearly International Conference on Public Education. Because the IBE has no political base, it has consistently served as a neutral forum for the exchange of educational ideas among states of diverse economic and political interests.

There are also scores of periodicals, journals, and other publications disseminating the results of educational research. Europe's Organization for Economic Co-operation and Development has published guides to its holdings in its Paris library and maintains a clearinghouse service for inquiries from researchers on international educational problems. The Council of Europe also puts out a volume summarizing educational research in various countries of the world. Editors of *The World Yearbook of Education*, published in London and New York, each year select educational topics with a universal interest and invite educators from numerous countries to contribute essays expressing their particular problems and noting their educational progress.

Declines in funds

Interestingly enough, however, although international education activities have increased since 1945, the amount of funding has not increased correspondingly. Certainly more people are able to study abroad now because of economic growth. Certainly radios and television sets can be found even in remote Asian and African villages, and jumbo jets and wider nets of transportation are enabling more people to move about easily and learn about their neighbours first hand. Nevertheless, governments and foundations are allocating less and less money to further such activity. Although a number of factors are undoubtedly responsible, an important one involves the financial crises and accompanying stringent economic measures that have hamstrung many nations. A report published by the U.S. Advisory Commission on International Educational and Cultural Affairs, noting the incongruity of improving international programs and decreasing funds, was entitled, "Is Anyone Listening?" The International Education Year of 1970 was preceded by a year in which expenditures on educational exchange were at the lowest ebb in recent history. This entire dilemma re-emphasizes the necessity for evaluative techniques and serious research into the activities of international education. Until more is known about the impact of cross-national programs, it will be impossible to decide intelligently whether they are fulfilling their purposes.

PROFILES OF STUDENTS AND TEACHERS INVOLVED IN EDUCATIONAL EXCHANGE

As noted earlier, an especially significant development in the second half of the 20th century has been the growth of programs of exchange of persons between nations for educational purposes. From the wandering scholar of classical times to the Fulbright fellow and the Rhodes scholar of the 20th century, men have ignored national boundaries in their search for knowledge. But it is only in recent years that educational exchange has enjoyed the interest and active support of governments, academic institutions, and other elements of society.

One of the basic problems in researching the effects of such exchange programs involves trying to separate the plethora of aims and objectives of the sponsoring bodies. True, the sponsoring agency usually has as one of its goals "educational exchange as a promoter of peace," but it would be impossible to research such a broad and amorphous goal. Moreover, although it should be possible to measure attitudinal changes resulting from the "exchange" experience, most such evaluations have been conducted by the sponsoring groups themselves and thus are often slanted toward developing a favourable image of the donor or host country. Another problem is that there have been few empirical studies of foreign students in countries other than the United States. Thus what is known about the attitudes, expectations, and experiences of persons studying outside their native land is almost completely based on data concerning a stay in America and, consequently, of minimal value for hypothesizing about experiences in other countries.

Nevertheless, considerably more is known about the exchange aspects of international education than about the nature and effectiveness of many other programs. The research, first of all, indicates that the aims of international educational activities may be too ambitious. Researchers have found, for instance, that the generally assumed view that exchange-of-persons activities increase international understanding is oversimplified and overly optimistic. In fact, there is evidence that being in another country even for an extended period of study may have very little effect on the attitudes of the visitor toward the country visited. One worker found in a study made in 1956 that the impressions of a group of Frenchmen who had been in the United States on a training mission were not significantly different from the opinions held by a group who had never been to the country. Visits, in short, can sometimes have no effect at all.

Many studies of foreign students are made with reference to their national background. It has been found, for instance, that Scandinavians studying in the United States were usually not detected as foreigners and thus could adjust to the American scene with remarkable ease. Other studies have concentrated on the foreign students' experiences and attitudes after their return home. One of these, for example, found that students returning to India were able more easily to use their generalist skills than their specialist skills; also, their personal motivations were influenced more by their national, local, and familial milieu than by their foreign educational experience. This type of research eventually should contribute greatly to the efforts of universities designing academic programs for foreign students and devising mechanisms for selecting students for study abroad.

Another aspect of educational exchange that has prompted research is the phenomenon known as "culture shock," or the sense of alienation a visitor feels in a foreign country when he is constantly surrounded by actions, beliefs, and values radically different from his own. The attitudinal U-curve, which describes students' enchantment, disenchantment, and coming to terms with a foreign culture, has been tested on a number of diverse foreign student groups in the United States. To help students through the "disenchantment" period, universities and private organizations have set up orientation programs to prepare the visitor for the new culture. Because the severity of "culture shock" can impede a student, researcher, or expert adviser in his day to day tasks, more behavioural research is needed to identify the sociological and psychological factors involved in this alienation.

Related to the feeling of culture shock are the various forms of racial prejudice that foreign students meet while studying abroad. José Laurel, puppet president of the Philippines during the Japanese occupation of World War II, made it clear that his distaste for Americans stemmed from his student days at Yale, where he experienced discrimination.

This type of experience undoubtedly leaves a lasting impression on the victim. Ways of avoiding or countering such incidents and their effects must be found if educational exchange is to have positive attitudinal results.

The "brain drain"

Lastly, there is the problem known as the "brain drain," the migration of highly skilled people from their homelands (often developing countries) to more advanced countries where their personal fortunes appear to be brighter. Thus in the United States and European nations many foreign students obtaining a specialized or advanced degree frequently stay on to work in the host country after graduation. The figures on this counterflow of brainpower are incomplete, but research based on numbers culled from a variety of embassies and colleges suggests that 90 percent of the Asian students who go to the U.S. to study never return home. Other countries that have experienced difficulty in convincing students to return home after completing their studies include Iran and Lebanon, to which only 50 percent of their nationals return. The problem has reached serious proportions in India, the Philippines, Pakistan, Egypt, Colombia, Argentina, and Greece. To this sombre picture must be added the figures found in a UNESCO report: between 1949 and 1961, 43,000 scientists and engineers emigrated to the United States—many of them from developing countries.

These "brain drain" statistics call into question the effectiveness of educational exchange as a means for promoting development. They point out that the *results* of U.S. aid often run counter to the *aims* of its exchange policies. Moreover, they support the allegation that migration can be damaging to the national interests of the countries of emigration. The money spent educating the emigrants might more usefully be invested elsewhere in the home country, or it might be "tied" into a contract requiring the student to return home after the completion of his education.

Economists, admittedly, are not all agreed that the problem is as serious as educators feel it is. Many contend that immigrants advance their fields in the countries of their adoption and enable the countries to expand economically, contributing to the progress of other areas of the globe. They apply the "supply and demand" theory to emigration: if British scientists migrate to the United States, the market in the U.S. will become saturated, whereas the demands and salaries will go up in the country of emigration, thereby attracting qualified foreign personnel. The actual picture of the "brain drain" probably is a combination of cultural and economic aspects.

If any one theme has developed in international education since the idea's formulation some centuries ago, it is the one that has become especially clear since man landed on the moon: children must be educated more broadly —*i.e.*, more globally. There has indeed been an expanding volume of human interaction around the world because of the growth of communications. There has indeed been an increasing similarity in social behaviour and an increasing commonality due to expanding bureaucratization and technology. Consequently, there has indeed been an increasing similarity among the problems facing all educators.

BIBLIOGRAPHY. A comprehensive survey of the entire field of international education, together with an extensive bibliography, may be found in D.G. SCANLON and J.J. SHIELDS (eds.), *Problems and Prospects in International Education* (1968). Two important works on student and teacher exchange programs are C.E. SPEAKMAN, *International Exchange in Education* (1966); and OTTO KLINEBERG, *International Exchanges in Education, Science, and Culture,* (UNESCO, 1966). A somewhat broader treatment of "cultural relations," including educational relations, is contained in PHILIP H. COOMBS, *The Fourth Dimension of Foreign Policy* (1964).

(D.G.S.)

International Language

An international, or universal, language is a language—natural or artificial—that serves as a means of communication among peoples of differing native languages.

Early solutions to the problem of communicating within linguistically diverse groups included the use of single languages of empire (*e.g.*, Greek, Latin, Arabic, Hindustani, Mandarin) or languages of colonization (Portuguese, Spanish, English, French, Russian). Commercial contacts resulted in pidgin languages, simplified trade languages based on such tongues as Portuguese, Spanish, English, French, and Dutch. Some of these pidgin languages eventually became the mother tongues of groups of multiple ethnic origins, but such languages, called creoles, are not widely used outside of their current restricted areas (New Guinea; East, South, and West Africa; and the Caribbean). And, although multiple bilingualism for some small fraction of the population of the world's more developed areas now seems possible, for the larger numbers of the world's citizens another solution to the universal problem of practical, commercial, and scientific communication has been suggested: a single universal second language.

Suggestions for a universal second language have been many and diverse. Natural languages, in clear political ascendancy, have, at propitious times, been proposed: first French and then English have been prime candidates. Among natural languages, certain lingua francas (such as Melanesian pidgin, Sierra Leonese Creole, or Sranan [Taki-Taki] of Surinam) have functioned, in a limited way, as second languages, and some dead languages have been revived and put to certain restricted uses (Hebrew in Israel, Latin in the Catholic Church). An attempt to lessen the considerable burden of acquiring a natural language as a second language is to be found in a modified natural language; *e.g.*, Basic English. Abstract logical or scientific notations also provide considerably greater precision than is possible in natural languages. Finally, attempts at combining greater simplicity and regularity with greater precision and accuracy have produced constructed languages that are derived from or based on natural languages.

Common features of constructed languages

In constructed languages, both those derived from and those actually based on natural languages, a number of common features can be found. (1) They strive for simplicity (being five to 15 times easier to learn than a natural language). (2) They seek to take advantage of previously established language habits (those acquired by the speakers of common European languages: Latin, French, English, German, Russian), maximizing the use of cultural vocabulary common to such languages (for the most part of Latin and Greek origin), reducing the number of indicators of grammatical categories to a minimum consistent with certain freedom of word order, limiting the number and variety of sounds to a level not inconsistent with that manifest in these European languages, and limiting the representation of these sounds to letters not uncommon to the alphabets of these same languages. (3) They strive to limit the composition of elements in these languages on all structural levels to that degree of redundancy that makes for greatest flexibility and adaptability. (4) They strive to adhere as closely to natural language models as these prior requirements will allow.

Esperanto. Esperanto, the best known of the constructed languages, was invented by a physician, Dr. Ludwik Zamenhof, in Białystok, Poland. The first book on it appeared in 1887, published over the orginator's pseudonym of Doktoro Esperanto. The initial vocabulary contained 921 word roots and an outline of the grammar and the system of sounds (see Tables 1 and 2).

Table 1: Endings Used in Esperanto

<table>
<tr><td>Noun</td><td>*-o*</td><td rowspan="2">plural *-j*</td><td rowspan="3">accusative *-n*</td><td></td></tr>
<tr><td>Adjective</td><td>*-a*</td><td></td></tr>
<tr><td>Adverb</td><td>*-e*</td><td></td><td></td></tr>
<tr><td>Infinitive</td><td>*-i*</td><td></td><td></td><td></td></tr>
<tr><td>Present</td><td>*-a-*</td><td rowspan="4">finite *-s*</td><td rowspan="4">active participle *-nt-*</td><td rowspan="4">passive participle *-t-*</td></tr>
<tr><td>Past</td><td>*-i-*</td></tr>
<tr><td>Future</td><td>*-o-*</td></tr>
<tr><td>Conditional</td><td>*-u-*</td></tr>
<tr><td>Imperative</td><td>*-u*</td><td></td><td></td><td></td></tr>
</table>

Esperanto vocabulary has grown, since 1887, to over 6,000 officially recognized basic roots and to between 40,000 and 50,000 roots from the generally accepted international scientific terminology. Esperanto roots are inherently nominal (*i.e.*, nouns), adjectival, adverbial, or verbal. The characteristic endings that mark these roots reaffirm the inherent root category when added to roots of the same category; *e.g.*, *martel-o* "hammer," *bel-a* "beautiful," *tro-e* "excessively," *lern-i* "learn." When added to roots of a different inherent root category, these endings are derivative in function; that is, they change the function, or part of speech, of the root—*martel-i* "to hammer," *bel-o* "beauty," *tro-a* "excessive," *lern-o* "learning." The resulting forms are somewhat nonspecific but may be made more precise by additional endings—*bel-ec-o* "beauty," *bel-ul-o* "[a] beauty," *bel-aĵ-o* "a beautiful thing," *lern-ad-o* "[continuous] learning." The endings themselves may also be used independently; thus, *ec-o* "property," *ul-o* "person," *aĵ-o* "thing."

Word-formation in Esperanto

Plural adjectives modify plural nouns; *e.g.*, *bel-a-j man-o-j* "beautiful hands," in which *-j* indicates plural, *-a-* indicates adjective, and *-o-* marks the noun. Syntactically, active verbs are linked with their objects (*lern-i lekci-o-n* "learn a lesson").

An original set of stems in which five roots (*i-* "some," *ki-* "what," *ti-* "that," *ĉi-* "all," *neni-* "no") are combined with nine endings (*-a* "kind," *-al* "reason," *-am* "time," *-e* "place," *-el* "manner," *-es* "one's," *-o* "thing," *-om* "quantity," *-u* "person") to form a highly regular system has since been extended by the users of the language to include forms such as *ali-es* "someone else's" and *ali-e* "elsewhere" from *ali-a* "other." Beside complex *inspekt-ist-o* one also finds *inspektor-o* "inspector," and beside *mal-diligenta* the simpler *pigr-a* "lazy" also occurs, introduced by users with special problems of translation or original composition, in closer imitation of natural language forms. Among the sounds, *dz* is rare, and *ĥ* has been largely replaced by *k*.

Table 2: Sounds of Esperanto*

consonants						vowels		
p	t	c	ĉ	k		i		u
b	d	dz	ĝ	g		e		o
f		s	ŝ	ĥ	h		a	
v		z	ĵ					
m	n							
ŭ			j					
	l							
	r							

*Stress falls regularly on the penultimate syllable of the word.

Esperanto has currently upwards of 100,000 users in 83 countries, organized in 50 national associations, 22 international professional groups, and more than 1,200 local clubs and societies. More than 10,000 varied items, both original compositions and translations, have been printed in it to date, including a sizable number of technical dictionaries. Current periodicals number over 100. Such continued vitality for over almost a century is remarkable in the face of Esperanto's repeated failure to achieve official status, either internationally (with the League of Nations or with the United Nations) or within particular countries. Although Esperanto has been particularly favoured in areas in which no single world language is dominant (or in which the presence of a particular world language is overwhelming, such as central Europe and Japan), it has many adherents elsewhere.

Other constructed languages. Other constructed languages have been devised and tested in practice, to greater or lesser degrees, during the same period.

Volapük. Volapük, devised by Johann Martin Schleyer, a German bishop, and brought to wide attention in 1880, achieved some popularity during the following decade. Heavily anglicizing in its largely monosyllabic root inventory, it makes much use of inflected forms in its word-formation. Nouns are inflected for case (nominative, genitive, dative, and accusative) and number (plural),

Volapük inflections

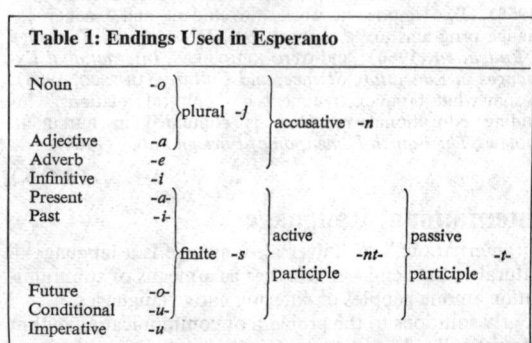

and verbs are conjugated for voice (passive), tense (present, imperfect, preterite, pluperfect, future, and anterior future), aspect (durative), and mood (infinitive, participle, potential, subjunctive, optative, imperative, and jussive). Its root for pronouns, *o-*, is inflected for person (1st, 2nd, 3rd) and for number (plural); in the 3rd person, gender is distinguished (masculine "he," feminine "she," and neuter "it"). Volapük makes heavy use, furthermore, of derivational affixes to characterize whole categories of entities (diseases, animals, elements, continents). Its sound system is generally west European, but it includes the English *ch* and *j* sounds and German *ä, ö,* and *ü.*

Ido. Ido, among a number of other attempts to revise Esperanto, was launched in 1907 by the logician Louis de Beaufront and acquired a certain following in the years before and after World War I. Eclectic in its choice of root inventory (deriving words, like Esperanto, from a variety of European languages), it is only mildly synthetic in its word-formation (also like Esperanto); that is, it uses only a limited number of inflections. Nouns are inflected for number (plural) and, in a very limited way, for case (accusative, only for marking direct objects that precede subjects); adjectives are marked for neither. Ido forms anterior and passive verb forms both with suffixes and with auxiliary verbs; thus there are two ways to express "had been"—*es-ab-is* and *es-is es-inta*—and two forms for "had been done"—*fac-es-is* and *es-is fac-ita.* Its sound system is almost identical with that of Esperanto, but it permits naturalistic irregularities in representation (*qu* = *kw*, *x* = *ks*, *u* = *w*, *i* = *y*) and in accent (*famílio* versus Esperanto *familío*).

Novial. Novial, constructed by the Danish linguist Otto Jespersen, was put forward in 1928 but was very little used except on an experimental basis. Also eclectic in its selection of its root inventory, it incorporates rather more Germanic features than does Esperanto or Ido, although such features in Novial are more easily recognizable than similar features in Volapük. Much more analytic than any of the previous international languages, it makes extensive use of auxiliary elements of Germanic origin (*ha, sal, vud, did, bli, let, mey*) in its conjugation of verbs. The past tense of verbs is either synthetic (using *-ed* or *-d* endings) or analytic (using *did* plus the verb). Its nouns are inflected for number (plural *-s*) and case (genitive *-en, -n*) and, in a limited way, for natural gender (masculine *-o*, feminine *-a*, neuter *-e*). Except for such gender indications, noun bases are, for the most part, endingless. Adjectives terminate in *-i*, which can also be dropped. Novial's apparatus of particles is in fair part Germanic (*irge* "any," *dise* "this," *self* "self"), and its pronouns are inflected for plural number and genitive case (*vu* "you [singular]," *vus* "you [plural]," *vusen* "your [plural]"). Its sound system is similar to that of Esperanto and Ido. Like Ido, it allows irregularities in representation (*qu* = *kw*, *x* = *ks*, *u* = *w*, *i* = *y*) and in accent (stress on the vowel before the last consonant of the stem; *e.g., konstrúkt: konstrúkted*).

Analytic character of Novial

Interlingua (Latino sine Flexione). Interlingua (Latino sine Flexione), initiated in 1903 by a mathematician, Giuseppe Peano, was put to some continued use over a number of years, and its principles were revived in a new Interlingua in the late 1940s and early 1950s. Peano took the vocabulary of Classical Latin as a base and admitted all Latin-derived scientific vocabulary since invented into its basic word-stock. He simplified its grammar to a minimum: noun stems are taken directly from the ablative case, verb stems from the imperative. Nouns are inflected for plural (*-s*). Verb conjugation is analytic (that is, it uses auxiliary words rather than endings); *e.g.,* past, *jam* . . .; future, *i* or *vol, debe, fi,* or *habe ad,* . . .; anterior, *habe . . . o.* Possession may be either synthetic (*e.g., nostro* "our") or analytic (*e.g., de nos* "of us"). Participles, likewise, may be either unitary (active, *ama-nte* "loving"; passive, *ama-to* "loved") or phrasal (active, *qui ama* "who loves"; passive, *qui es amato* "who is loved"). The orthographical system is that of Latin, but it permits certain simplifications (*ph* = *f*, *th* = *t*, *œ* = *e*, *æ* = *e*).

Occidental. Occidental, devised by Edgar de Wahl, was presented in 1922 but had little currency aside from its author's publications. It emphasized the imitation of West European patterns of word derivation, at the expense of generality and simplicity.

Basic English. In Basic English, advanced in 1932 by a British psychologist and educator, Charles Kay Ogden, an attempt was made to find a simplified common core in English usage and to create a form of English embodying that core. Reducing its vocabulary to 850 words, it has 100 terms for operations, 400 for general things, 200 for picturable things, 100 for general qualities, and 50 for opposite qualities. Using these 850 terms in accordance with a few simple rules of grammar (plurals in *-s*, derivatives in *-er, -ing, -ed* from 300 nouns, adverbs in *-ly*, degree with *more* and *most*, questions by inversion and *do*, operators and pronouns conjugated in full), it also permits terms of measurement, numerals, currency, calendar, and all international terms in their English form, thus considerably augmenting the vocabulary at its disposal. The following text shows how little a text in Basic English departs from normal standard English:

The 850 words of Basic English

These changes in the system of thought-connection in the brain, which are now in process, put before us—long before we have any chance of developments in birth-selection—the hope that an increase in brain-power may be possible on a scale which at present we have no idea of. For this to come about we will have to take control of events which at present we have no control over at all.

Basic English met most of the criteria characteristic of other constructed languages, but its reception has not been enthusiastic enough to sustain it.

Future prospects. Although the search for a single universal second language continues, and although one of the languages (Esperanto) has had a certain limited success in practice, it is not thought likely that the search will come to an end in the near future. It is more probable that an extended period of increasing multilingualism—both in languages of wider communication and in those of more restricted local usefulness—will precede any serious attempt to choose and propagate any single second language. The amount of pressure that would be prerequisite to any serious attempt at gaining worldwide communication through a truly international language is not calculable. It is unlikely that the logical necessity of a universal second language will hasten that attempt.

The following are examples of the Lord's Prayer in several constructed international languages.

Esperanto:

Patro nia, kiu estas en la ĉielo, sankta estu via nomo; venu reĝeco via; estu volo via, kiel en la ĉielo, tiel ankaŭ sur la tero. Panon nian ĉiutagan donu al ni hodiaŭ; kaj pardonu al ni ŝuldojn niajn, kiel ni ankaŭ pardonas al niaj ŝuldantoj; kaj ne konduku nin en la tenton, sed liberigu nin de la malbono. Ĉar via estas la reĝeco, la povo kaj la gloro eterne. Amen!

Volapük:

O Fat obas, kel binol in süls, paisaludomöz nem ola! Kömomöd monargän ola! Jenomöz vil olik, äs in sül, i su tal! Bodi obsik vädeliki givolös obes adelo! E pardolös obes debis obsik, äs id obs aipardobs debeles obas. E no obis nindukolös in tentadi, sod aidalivolös obis de bad. Jenosöd!

Ido:

Patro nia, qua esas en la cielo, tua nomo santigesez; tua regno advenez; tua volo facesez quale en la cielo, tale anke sur la tero. Donez a ni cadie l'omnidiala pano, e pardonez a ni nia ofensi, quale anke ni pardonas a nia ofensanti; e ne duktez ni aden la tento, ma liberigez ni del malajo. Nam tua esas la regno, la povo e la glorio eterne. Amen!

Interlingua (Latino sine Flexione):

Patre nostro, qui es in celos, que tuo nomine fi sanctificato. Que tuo regno adventi; que tua voluntate es facta sicut in celo et in terra. Da hodie ad nos nostro pane quotidiano. Et remitte ad nos nostros debitos, sicut et nos remitte ad nostros debitores. Et non induce nos in tentatione, sed libera nos ab malo. Amen.

English (King James Bible version):

Our Father, which art in heaven, Hallowed be thy name. Thy kingdom come. Thy will be done in earth, as it is in heaven. Give us this day our daily bread. And forgive us our debts, as we forgive our debtors. And lead us not into temptation, but deliver us from evil: For thine is the kingdom, and the power, and the glory, for ever. Amen.

BIBLIOGRAPHY

General works: ALBERT L. GUERARD, *A Short History of the International Language Movement* (1922); HENRY JACOB, *A Planned Auxiliary Language*, with a preface by HAROLD E. PALMER (1947); NÓRMAN A. MCQUOWN, a review of Jacob's "A Planned Auxiliary Language," *Language*, 26:175–185 (1950); EDWARD SAPIR, "The Function of an International Auxiliary Language," *Psyche*, 11:4–15 (1931); INSTITUTE OF EDUCATIONAL RESEARCH (Teachers College, Columbia University), *Language Learning: Summary of a Report to the International Auxiliary Language Association* (1933).

Esperanto: LUDWIK LAZAR ZAMENHOF, *An Attempt Towards an International Language* (1889); LEAGUE OF NATIONS, *Esperanto As an International Auxiliary Language* (1922); EDMOND PRIVAT, *Historio de la Lingvo Esperanto* (1927); V. VARANKIN, *Teorio de Esperanto* (1929); LOUIS COUTURAT, *Étude sur la dérivation en Esperanto* (1907).

Volapük: JOHANN MARTIN SCHLEYER, *Mittlere Grammatik der Universalsprache Volapük* (1887).

Ido: LOUIS DE BEAUFRONT, *Complete Manual of . . . Ido*, 3rd ed. (1919).

Novial: OTTO JESPERSEN, *An International Language* (1929).

Interlingua (latino sine flexione): ALEXANDER GODE and HUGH E. BLAIR, *Interlingua: A Grammar of the International Language* (1951); GUISEPPE PEANO, *Key to and Primer of Interlingua* (1931).

Occidental: EDGAR DE WAHL, *Occidental* (1925).

Basic English: CHARLES K. OGDEN, *The System of Basic English* (1934).

In addition to the publications above, there are numerous other grammar books and dictionaries of the individual international languages.

(N.A.McQ.)

International Law

International law is the body of legal rules that apply between sovereign states and such other entities as have been granted international personality (status acknowledged by the international community). The term was coined by Jeremy Bentham and is synonymous with the term law of nations and its equivalents in other languages.

Like precepts of international morality, the rules of international law are of a normative character; *i.e.*, they prescribe standards of social conduct. They distinguish themselves, however, from such moral rules by being, at least potentially, designed for authoritative interpretation by an independent judicial authority and of being capable of enforcement by the application of external sanctions.

International law means public international law, as distinct from *private* international law or the conflict of laws, which deals with the differences between the municipal laws of different countries.

Definitions and distinctions

International law forms a contrast to *municipal* law. While international law applies only between entities that can claim international personality, municipal law is the internal law of states that regulates the conduct of individuals and other legal entities within their jurisdiction.

International law should also be distinguished from *quasi*-international law; that is to say, the law governing relations similar to those covered by international law, but outside the pale of international law because at least one of the parties lacks international personality. Concession agreements between oil companies and sovereign states fall into this category. In case of doubt, they are subject to the municipal law of the state granting the concession.

Transnational law is a purely negative term. It is intended to convey that, in accordance with the intention of contracting parties, a transaction of a consensual character is not or should not be subject to municipal law.

INTERNATIONAL LAW IN PERSPECTIVE

A view of international law in three complementary perspectives will assist in the better understanding of the subject. In the *sociological* perspective, it is possible to offer an explanation of the social functions fulfilled by international law. The *historical* perspective provides insight into the growth potential of international law. The *ethical* perspective furnishes a normative measuring rod by which to test the moral adequacy of any particular system and rule of international law.

International law in sociological perspective. Law is primarily conditioned by its social environment rather than the reverse. In particular, this applies to law in *unorganized* international society as well as in specific international societies organized on the *confederate* model, such as the League of Nations and the United Nations. Under such circumstances, the chief participants—the sovereign states, and especially the strongest among them—tend to view themselves as ultimate ends and are inclined to insist on control of the means indispensable for their survival in any crisis, especially their freedom to arm themselves. They form alliances and counteralliances for aggressive and defensive purposes, create precarious systems of balance of power and, as they see fit, pursue policies of involvement or isolation.

In such situations, the primary function of law is that of a law of *power; i.e.*, the law assists in maintaining the supremacy of force and the hierarchies established on the basis of power and gives to such quasi-orders the respectability and sanctity of law. International law in *unorganized* international society serves these purposes in a variety of ways; *e.g.*, the independence of states is one of the cornerstones of international customary law. This includes freedom of armaments, access to raw materials and markets, and the admission of immigrants. Similarly, whether a state decides to participate in an international congress or conference depends on its own will. Moreover, in the absence of agreement to the contrary, unanimity is required for any decision reached in the assembly of any such international gathering. Finally, any binding third-party settlement of a dispute by reference to law or equity depends on the consent of the parties concerned.

By building international *customary* law on the foundation of state sovereignty, states make certain of reserving to themselves the choice between peace and war. Moreover, international *customary* law puts at the disposal of its subjects the right to apply measures short of war by way of reprisal against alleged breaches of international law.

In international confederations such as the League of Nations and United Nations, the rights of sovereign states to threaten, or resort to, the use of force are limited by consensual undertakings. Yet, voting procedures providing for unanimity or reserving veto rights, and wide escape clauses (such as those contained in Articles 51 and 107 of the UN Charter) tend to reduce such peace-keeping systems to relative ineffectiveness, in particular in relation to the major world powers.

In fields less central to the systems of open power politics or power politics in disguise, international law is permitted also to fulfill the functions of a law of *reciprocity* and a law of *coordination*. Thus, for example, on the basis of innumerable treaties, an international customary law of diplomatic immunity, codified in the 1961 Vienna Convention on Diplomatic Relations, has developed. Similarly, over the centuries, a body of international maritime law, now largely codified in the 1958 Geneva Conventions on the Law of the Sea, has grown up.

Occasionally, the law of reciprocity—that is, a set of legal rules, compliance with which rests normally on the expectation of mutual advantages, rather than the fear of the application of external sanctions—intrudes even into spheres that are closer to actual power politics. This is always possible on a consensual basis, as in peace treaties (see WAR, LAWS OF) and, occasionally, has happened, as in the various conventions concluded at Lausanne in 1923 that terminated a war between Greece and Turkey. The laws of war are illustrations from international customary law. Herein, are the application of legal rules in wars fought for limited purposes, where both sides have exhausted the means of escalation available in systems of power politics, but resist the temptation of total war with no legal restraints.

In an unorganized international society based on entities that tend to put their own interest before the commonweal, the scope of a law of coordination or community law, in which the common interest overrides any incompatible sectional interests, is limited. An impressive illustration of this type of law is the gradual outlawry of the slave trade by bilateral and multilateral consensual undertakings, especially the Treaty of Paris (1815) and the Slavery Conventions of 1926 and 1956.

International law in historical perspective. Since the dawn of history, embryonic and arrested systems of international law have come into existence in many parts of the world. While they are of comparative interest, most have not exercised any influence on the evolution of contemporary international law. Leaving aside the borrowing of some Roman-law terminology and legal techniques, such continuity as exists in the *practice* of international law dates from early medieval international law.

Historical foundations

International law is the product of a threefold process initiated in the Western world: the disintegration of the medieval European community into a European society, the expansion of this European society, and concentration of power in a developing world society in the hands of a rapidly declining number of major world powers.

The historical premises of medieval international law were of stark simplicity: (1) In the absence of an agreed state of truce or peace, war was the basic state of international relations even between independent Christian communities. (2) Unless exceptions were made by means of individual safe conduct or treaty, rulers considered themselves entitled to treat foreigners at their absolute discretion. (3) The high seas were no man's "land," where anyone might do as he pleased.

Treaty law was the predominant feature of medieval international law. Sanctions varied from the exchange of hostages, the pledging of towns, castles, and territories, and the mortgaging of the personal property of kings, or their subjects, to the appointment of guardians, or the addition of the signatures of powerful dignitaries representing the various estates of a prince's realm. Supernatural sanctions, such as solemn oaths or excommunications of a guilty party, were also employed. Ultimately, the observance of treaties and other engagements under medieval international law rested on the same basis as it did in subsequent phases of international law: self-interest, especially in relation to obligations of a reciprocal character, and the value attached by an obligated party to his moral credit and his respect for the principle of good faith.

International law and the expanded world of nation-states

With the expansion of European society, the spiritual basis of inter-Christian international law was weakened but not eliminated. In particular, the universalist spirit that imbued the naturalist doctrine of international law gave to international law the elasticity needed to adapt itself to a constantly widening international environment. Even so, international law primarily served the purposes of assisting in the process of Western expansion.

In the process of the transformation of international law into a world law, international law exchanged its Christian foundation for that of a law among states that were civilized in a highly formal sense. Civilization was understood as compliance with the minimum requirements of the Rule of Law, as this term, or its continental equivalents, was used in pre-1914 days in the Western world, especially regarding the treatment of the persons and property of foreign nationals. It took merely a further step to make sovereignty the decisive test of full international personality. In the pre-1939 era of the coexistence of democratic communities with totalitarian states, such as the Soviet Union, Fascist Italy, Nazi Germany, and militarist Japan, international law had become a law among sovereign states.

While the coexistence of sovereign states in a legal system postulates equality, this equality in international law is of a purely formal character. Thus, while the number of sovereign and equal states sharply increased, that of greater powers shrank to a handful. The veto power of the permanent members of the UN Security Council, the weighting of votes according to the financial interest taken in the International Monetary Fund, and the special position accorded to states of chief industrial importance (as in the International Labour Organisation) are indicative of this trend.

The development of the doctrine of international law followed only slowly in the wake of the practice of international law. In the early days of international law, it sufficed to have lawyers trained in the canon and civil law. They tended to apply to novel situations the concepts of municipal law with which they were familiar. This accounts for the long continued overemphasis in the doctrine of international law on analogies from more mature systems of internal community law to a differently structured society law.

The beginnings of European international law and relations are to be found in the microscopic interstate system of the Italian city-states. Here may be seen the beginnings of the doctrine of international law, especially in the writings of two of the Italian lawyers, Bartolo da Sassoferrato (1314–57) and Baldo degli Ubaldi (1327–1400). When, in the late 15th and 16th centuries, Spain became the leading Western power, Francisco de Vitoria (*c.* 1486?–1546) founded the Spanish school of international law. In the 17th century it came to be rivalled by the Anglo-Dutch school, particularly in the persons of Alberico Gentili (1552–1608) and Hugo Grotius (1583–1645).

The early theorists

While neither Grotius nor any other exponent of international law was the "father" of international law, Grotius' *De Jure Belli ac Pacis* (1625) acquired a fame far greater than that of the works of his predecessors. This was due to a combination of factors that appealed to his contemporaries and subsequent generations: he stressed the self-defeating character of war, accepted sovereign states as the basic unit of international law, and skillfully blended natural law, Roman law, and state practice in a manner that left in vital matters sufficient discretion to governments to do, without legal hindrance, what they thought opportune.

Samuel von Pufendorf (1632–94), the German publicist and jurist, espoused the priority of natural law over positive law. An extreme *naturalist* school followed in his footsteps and attempted to identify international law with natural law. In England, Richard Zouche (1590–1661), laid the foundations of *positivism* in international law, drawing a sharp distinction between the postulates of natural law and international law as actually supplied in state practice. An *eclectic* school, sometimes described as Grotian, tried to find a golden mean between the extremes of naturalism and positivism by relying on both natural and positive law. Christian Wolff (1679–1754) and Emerich de Vattel (1714–67) were two of its early exponents.

Contemporary approaches

The one-sidedness and subjectivity of these techniques led to new departures on inductive, interdisciplinary, and relativist lines. The essence of the *inductive* approach is in the ascertainment of the rules of international law exclusively by means of generally accepted and rationally verifiable evidence. In particular, this involves recognition that the principles, as distinct from the rules, of international law normally are merely abstractions from these rules but do not constitute legitimate law-creating processes. The *interdisciplinary* treatment of international law makes it possible to view international law from the outside, especially in sociological historical, and ethical perspectives. Finally, the exploration of the possible forms of the development of international law in a relativist way, that is making available, side by side, various patterns that always exist for the solution of any social problem, provides a detached but constructive approach to problems of international law in the making.

International law in ethical perspective. In its own speculative framework, the naturalist doctrine of international law provided both sociological and ethical perspectives of the subject. Subsequently, during the reign of positivism, the fulfillment of these tasks was neglected.

A less subjective ethical measuring rod than those applied by naturalist writers is that of civilization itself, which may be viewed as essentially an ethical phenomenon. Links between international law and civilization exist not only historically but also explicitly in one of the three law-creating processes that the International

Court of Justice is charged to apply: the general principles of law recognized by *civilized* nations as distinct from savage and barbarian groups.

Civilization in this sense is more than a mature and rational apparatus of thought and action. It is a continuous process toward, and away from, community relations; that is, relations ultimately based on free cooperation and fellowship, as distinct from fear.

The legal systems of savage and barbarian groups are proof, however, that law can exist without civilization. Similarly, the relations between international law and civilization have varied considerably throughout the history of international law. Ample evidence of this is furnished by state practice regarding the recognition of new governments, states, or nations; the large-scale disregard of the minimum standard regarding the treatment of foreigners; and the ambivalent attitude of states to the legality of weapons of mass destruction. Thus, the relation between international law and civilization is tenuous at the best of times, and it is advisable for any ethical evaluation of contemporary international law to err on the side of caution.

FOUNDATIONS

Basic questions

Certain basic questions call for discussion: the law-creating processes of international law; the law-determining agencies of international law; the relations between international law and municipal law; and the nature of and the relations between rules, principles, and standards of international law.

The law-creating processes of international law. These are the forms in which rules of international law come into existence; *i.e.*, treaties, rules of international customary law, and general principles of law recognized by civilized nations. It is the merit of article 38 of the Statute of the International Court of Justice that this exclusive list of *primary* law-creating processes has received almost universal consent. States that have assented to, or acquiesced in, resolutions adopted unanimously by the UN General Assembly and stated to be declaratory of existing international law may be thought to be prevented in good faith from contesting any longer the existence of a formerly controversial rule of international law. On a consensual basis and, thus, in accordance with one of the primary law-creating processes, this and other *secondary* law-creating processes can, and have, come into existence.

International customary law. This is essentially the international law of unorganized international society, and its rules can be summarized under the heads of seven fundamental principles. The two constitutive elements of international customary law are (1) a general practice of states on a universal, general, or regional basis, and (2) the acceptance by the states concerned of this practice as law.

The origin of international customary law is frequently found in earlier treaty clauses, which, subsequently, were taken for granted, as with the rules regarding the minimum standard applicable to foreign nationals and their property. Occasionally, as in the law of the sea and the law of armed conflict, individual rules of international law have developed out of roughly parallel practices of the leading powers.

Treaties. Treaties and other consensual engagements are legally binding undertakings by which, without any requirements of form under international customary law, the subjects of international law may declare, modify, or develop existing international law as they see fit or agree on transactions; *e.g.*, of a territorial character. They are thus able to transform *jus strictum* into *jus aequum*, *jus dispositivum* into *jus cogens*, and vice versa, and unorganized international society into global or regional international societies on confederate or supranational levels of integration.

The general principles of law recognized by civilized nations. Such principles must fulfill two requirements. To qualify under this heading, a legal principle must be a *general* principle of law, as distinct from a legal rule of a more limited functional scope. It must be recognized and shared by a fair number of civilized nations, and these probably include at least all the world's principal legal systems.

The general principles of law come into play only as a subsidiary law-creating agency; *i.e.*, in the absence of competing rules of international customary law or treaty law. Their existence in the background forestalls any argument that supposed gaps in international law prevent international judicial organs from deciding on the substance of any dispute submitted to their jurisdiction.

The law-determining agencies of international law. These agencies furnish the evidence for the existence of asserted rules of international law. The totality of the subjects of international law constitute the relevant agency for any rules of *universal* customary international law. A convincing majority of subjects of international law provide the requisite evidence for the existence of an alleged rule of *general* customary international law. The ensemble of the parties to a treaty fulfill the same function in relation to any particular consensual engagement. The body of civilized nations, as distinct from savage and barbarian groups, forms the relevant law-determining agency regarding general principles of law recognized by civilized nations.

The decisions of international and national courts and tribunals plus the doctrine of international law (*i.e.*, the teachings of the most highly qualified publicists) constitute what are described in article 38 of the Statute of the International Court of Justice as "subsidiary" means for the determination of the rules of international law.

In practice, consensus scarcely ever exists in any of these law-determining agencies. Thus, it is necessary to determine the relative evidential value of any pronouncements made by the *elements* of law-determining agencies; *i.e.*, the views of individual parties to treaties, relevant diplomatic material, and pertinent decisions of international and national judicial organs. To obtain as objective as possible an evaluation, it is advisable to subject each case to a threefold scrutiny: the degree of generic and individual independence of the element of the law-determining agency concerned, its international outlook, and its professional attainments.

International law and municipal law. International law applies in the relations between the subjects of international law. The relations between subjects and objects, and between objects alone, of international law are governed by municipal law or quasi-international law.

The relation between municipal and international law

While international law is a legal system that actually exists, the term municipal law is an abstraction from the multitude of legal systems that are internal to the individual subjects of international law. Thus, actual conflicts can only arise between international law and *individual* legal systems other than international law, such as United States law or Soviet law. How such conflicts are resolved depends on the level on which they arise. Ultimately, any municipal organ is governed by its own municipal law and must, if needs be, give priority to it. Similarly, international organs such as the International Court of Justice may have to give priority to international law and treat municipal law as inferior in an accepted hierarchy of interlocking legal systems. They may even view international law as being exclusive of all other law and treat municipal law as a mere set of facts, which, as the case may be, complies with or contravenes the international obligations of a subject of international law.

Other basic questions of international law. *Rules, principles, and standards.* The rules of international law are the legal norms that can be verified as the products of one or more of the three generally recognized law-creating processes. For purposes of systematic exposition and legal education, it is also valuable to abstract *principles* from legal rules. Such principles of international law provide the common denominator for a number of related legal rules. They must not be abused by reversing the procedure for the purpose of deriving from them additional legal rules that cannot be verified independently by reference to the primary or secondary law-creating processes of international law. The more fundamental the rules that underlie any particular principle, the more a justification exists for seeing the principle itself as funda-

Underlying norms

mental. It is possible to summarize the whole of international customary law in a number of fundamental principles, and attempts even have been made to reduce all these rules to a single fundamental principle or *Grundnorm* such as Consent, *Pacta sunt servanda*, Recognition and Good Faith.

By way of treaty, subjects of international law are free to create additional principles; *e.g.*, those of freedom of commerce or navigation, or a principle such as that of peaceful coexistence embodied in article 2 of the Charter of the United Nations. Unless parties desire to give unconditional effect to any such optional principle, they have at their disposal counterparts to compulsory rules in the form of optional *standards*, such as those postulated by most favoured nation and preferential treatment.

Jus dispositivum and jus cogens. In a terminology derived from Roman law, a distinction is made in mature legal systems of municipal law between rules that may be altered by contracting parties (*jus dispositivum*) and others that may not (*jus cogens*). As distinct from legal systems with a centralized legal order, around which such *jus cogens* has grown, international customary law, as the law of unorganized international society, does not know of any such peremptory rules. Limitations on the freedom of states imposed by common sense, self-interest, and other pragmatic considerations must not be mistaken for *jus cogens*. Yet, nothing prevents sovereign states from creating peremptory international law by way of treaty; *e.g.*, the seven principles formulated in article 2 of the United Nations Charter.

Jus strictum and jus aequum. Also derived from Roman law, this distinction indicates differences between two other types of rule. Rules of *jus strictum* (*e.g.*, the rules of international customary law on the right of a state to request the recall of a foreign envoy as *persona non grata*) must be interpreted strictly and literally as embodying absolute rights. Others, such as those providing for freedom of communication, must be interpreted as rules of *jus aequum; i.e.*, in a reasonable and equitable manner.

INTERNATIONAL LAW IN UNORGANIZED INTERNATIONAL SOCIETY

The basic rules of international customary law can be summarized in the following fundamental principles: sovereignty, recognition, consent, good faith, freedom of the seas, international responsibility, and self-defense. In this survey are also included post-1945 codifications of the relevant rules of international customary law.

Sovereignty. Initially, a subject of international law is bound only by applicable rules of universal or general international customary law. Additional international obligations may be imposed on any subject of international law only with its consent. Unless the territorial jurisdiction of a state is excluded or limited by rules of international law, its exercise is exclusively the concern of the state in question. Subjects of international law may *claim* potential jurisdiction over persons or things outside their territorial jurisdiction. In the absence of permissive rules to the contrary (*e.g.*, the right of hot pursuit from the territorial sea to the high sea, or the right of reprisal) they may exercise such jurisdiction only inside their territories. It follows from the coexistence of sovereign states under international law that, in principle, they are all equal in status.

Territorial jurisdiction

Recognition. The rules governing recognition cover situations such as the co-option of new subjects of international law, the recognition of territorial claims of another state, the grant and withdrawal of nationality, and the recognition of the maritime flag of a land-locked state.

In principle, recognition is discretionary, but premature recognition of belligerents and insurgents runs counter to the exclusive domestic jurisdiction of the other state concerned and is illegal. The scope and effects of recognition must be ascertained according to the tenor of the act of recognition and its context. It may be unconditional or conditional and may be explicit or implied.

The devices of *protest* and *reservation of rights* may be used to prevent silence from being misinterpreted as an implied recognition of a situation or transaction. Notification is a means of bringing a situation or transaction to the attention of a third power with the intent to invite recognition or some other articulate reaction.

The uses of recognition

In practice, the chief functions of recognition are to acknowledge the existence of an entity as a subject of international law or to acknowledge its head as a representative with whom another state desires to maintain diplomatic relations. The main forms of recognition are recognition of a state or government as exercising de facto or de jure authority in a territory or, as it is simply called, de facto and de jure recognition. De facto recognition implies acceptance of the claim of the recognized government to exercise jurisdiction within its own territory. De jure recognition, however, usually implies acceptance of the claim of the recognized government to exercise extraterritorial jurisdiction over, for example, nationalized companies that own ships entitled to sail under the flag of the recognized state.

Recognition, being a matter of intent, may fall short of full recognition and be limited to recognition of a group as belligerents or as insurgents, if such rebels are in de facto control of part of the territory of another state.

Sovereign states are the principal subjects of international law. Yet, nothing prevents states from recognizing dependent states with limited international personality, such as international protectorates or the former mandates of the League of Nations. None of the trust territories of the United Nations have international personality. They are, however, under the control of the United Nations. Similarly, states are free to recognize, for all or limited purposes, nontypical subjects such as the Holy See, international institutions, and even individual persons as subjects of international law. In each case, whether any entity has been so recognized is merely a question of evidence.

Consent. The rules on consent enable subjects of international law, when entering into agreement, to modify and to supplement as they see fit, but without prejudice to the rights of third parties, any of the rules of international customary law, or the general principles of law recognized by civilized nations.

Sovereign states have full capacity to enter into any kind of consensual engagement. The capacity of others with international personality to undertake consensual commitments under international law is limited according to the scope of their international personality. In the absence of evidence to the contrary, consensual engagements between subjects of international law are governed by international law, but consensual engagements between subjects and objects, or between objects of international law, are outside the pale of international law.

The ambit of agreement

Failing prior obligations to the contrary, as contained for example in an undertaking to negotiate or conclude another agreement, the entry into consensual engagements is purely optional.

International customary law does not prescribe any particular form for consensual engagements, unless the parties desire not to create legal obligations. The effect of consent given in accordance with the requirements of international law is to create legal rights and duties between the contracting parties. In the absence of any contrary intention of the parties, the suspension, revision, and termination of consensual engagements depend on the consent or acquiescence of each of the contracting parties.

Excepting agreements entered into by international organizations, the subject of the law of treaties is now codified in the 1969 Vienna Convention on the Law of Treaties.

Good faith. In the early phases of the evolution of international law, good faith meant, primarily, the absence of bad faith. Gradually, however, good faith was identified with the requirements of reasonableness, common sense, and equity.

Thus, parties to consensual engagements and parties responsible for duly communicated unilateral acts, which they intend to have legal effect, must interpret and execute such engagements in good faith. If a consensual engagement that is subject to international ratification has been ratified, good faith regulates also the relations between the parties prior to final ratification. In the absence of more specialized provisions, acts committed contrary to good faith by any international institution, all of which derive their authority from consensual engagements, are void. Excess of jurisdiction by an international judicial organ or corruption of judges by one of the parties falls in this category. Rules of *jus aequum* must be interpreted as relative rights; *i.e.*, their arbitrary or unreasonable exercise is an abuse of right and a tortious act. In the case of rights derived from rules of *jus strictum*, a harsh exercise of such rights is not illegal but amounts to an unfriendly act; *i.e.*, it is open to retorsion, meaning lawful, but unfriendly acts of retaliation. On the international judicial level, the consensual nexus within which judges and parties operate tends to transform any absolute rights into relative rights, subject to judicial balancing processes in which considerations of good faith, common sense, and reasonableness play a prominent part.

Equitable principles

Freedom of the seas. The inclusion of the rules on the freedom of the high seas (*i.e.*, those parts of the interlinking chain of oceans that lie to seaward of the territorial sea) among those of a fundamental character would be justifiable on the ground alone that they apply geographically to two-thirds of the globe. These rules preclude the appropriation by any individual subject of international law of any portion of the high seas as distinct from the subsoil and bed of the sea. The exercise of permitted jurisdiction varies according to the state of peace, intermediacy between peace and war (*status mixtus*), or war between the states concerned. Subject to a number of exceptions, in time of peace a state may exercise jurisdiction only over ships entitled to fly its own flag. In a state of intermediacy, states are free, under international *customary* law, to interfere with one another's shipping by way of reprisal. In time of war, permissible interference with enemy and neutral shipping is regulated by the rules of sea warfare and prize law. The use of the high seas, the air space above the high seas, and the sea bed must be exercised with reasonable regard for the interests of others. The Conventions of 1954, 1962, and 1969 for the Prevention of Pollution of the Sea by Oil provide a limited implementation of this rule. Piracy *jure gentium* (*i.e.*, illegal acts of violence, detention, or depredation for private ends committed on the high seas), and slave trading are illegal forms of the use of the high seas under international customary law.

The subject is now largely codified in the 1958 Geneva Conventions on the High Seas and on Fishing and Conservation of the Living Resources of the High Seas.

International responsibility. The rules governing the principle of international responsibility are the complement of all other rules of international law. They transform otherwise merely admonitory precepts into legal forms, and, in this sense, may also be described as sanctions of international law.

The rules on international responsibility can be reduced to two propositions: (1) the breach of any international obligation by the organ of a subject of international law constitutes an *illegal act* or *international tort*, and (2) the commission of an international tort involves the duty to make reparation. These are rules of international customary law. Thus, the obligations they create arise independently of the will of any particular subject of international law, and they may be modified by consent and acquiescence. In particular, they can be strengthened by consensual rules that provide for penalties corresponding to those in municipal criminal law (sometimes also described as *international criminal law*) but, actually, constituting merely internationally postulated rules of municipal law, which may be waived by acquiescence and nonprosecution of claims (also described as *extinctive prescription*).

Other rules, such as the powers exercised by states in relation to pirates, blockade runners, and war criminals constitute extraordinary forms of the exercise of national jurisdiction. They are lawful because the home states of these three groups of individuals may not in good faith contest the exercise of such jurisdiction.

Self-defense. In unorganized international society, the distinction between the lawful and unlawful use of force was accepted in state practice in situations of *status mixtus*. In a state of war, any limitations of the right to wage war (*jus ad bellum*) remained a largely ignored postulate of naturalist doctrine on the distinction between just (and legal) and unjust (and illegal) war. The realization of this objective had to await later multilateral treaties, which, by reference to the test of self-defense, incorporated the distinction between legal and illegal wars and other use of force.

The use of force

Under international customary law, measures of self-defense may be taken against illegal acts that are attributable to another subject of international law; against acts of individuals, ships, or aircraft that disentitle any other subject of international law from the grant of protection; and against acts of objects of international law that lack a subject of international law that is entitled to give them diplomatic protection.

The need for self-defense must be compelling and instant. Measures of self-defense comprise any action, including hot pursuit from the territorial sea into the high seas, which is necessary to repel an imminent or present invasion of the rights of a subject of international law.

In cases not covered by the conditions of lawful self defense, the threat or use of force under international *customary* law may amount to a legitimate form of self-help. If a subject of international law has committed an international tort and refuses to make reparation, the other party may resort to acts of retorsion or reprisal.

The legal effects of resort to war under international *customary* law are to bring into operation the laws of war and neutrality (*jus in bello*).

Interaction of the rules governing the fundamental principles of international law. The sphere of freedom of action for subjects of international law—what, in relation to typical international persons may also be termed unlimited state jurisdiction—is governed primarily by the rules on sovereignty. Limitations of this jurisdiction come about as the result of the interplay of the rules underlying some of the other fundamental principles with those on sovereignty.

This interaction of rules has brought about secondary rules and legally determined situations. Five of these are of especial significance: territory, diplomatic law, and immunity; the protection of nationals abroad; freedom of commerce and navigation; extradition and asylum; and succession to international rights and obligations.

Territorial control

Territory. Owing to the preponderance, in a world largely appropriated by sovereign states, of territorial, over personal, jurisdiction, the rules governing title to territory are of major importance. There are significant exceptions, however, such as the high seas; Antarctica, barred from further exclusive appropriation by the 1959 Antarctic Treaty; and outer space and celestial bodies, excluded under the 1967 Outer Space Treaty. The rules relating to territory rest firstly on *sovereignty:* occupation, addition by natural causes of new land to riverbanks (accretion, accession, or alluvion) and assumption, under international *customary* law, of sovereignty over territories the state apparatus of which has been destroyed by conquest (*debellatio*); secondly, on recognition, which stops third parties from contesting the validity of a recognized title; and, thirdly, on consent—namely, the cession of territory.

The legal function of *frontiers* is to settle the exact extent of contiguous territories by unilateral action, express consent, recognition, or acquiescence.

The *air space* above, and the subsoil below, national territory, including the territorial sea, are treated as appurtenances of a state's territory.

Internal waters include ports, harbours, all waters on the landward side of the base line of the territorial sea, and historic bays; *i.e.*, bays which, irrespective of their width, are treated, on grounds of acquiescence or recognition, as subject to the jurisdiction of the coastal state.

The normal *base line* of the territorial sea is the low-water line along a state's seacoast. It is generally recognized that the minimum *breadth* of the territorial sea is three miles. The *outer limit* of the territorial sea, which constitutes also the frontier between national territory and the high sea, is drawn by reference to the base line.

Most of the sea matters are not codified in the 1958 Convention on the Territorial Sea and Contiguous Zone. While it has proved impossible to reach agreement on the breadth of the territorial sea, it is laid down in the above convention that the *contiguous* zone—*i.e.*, a geographically limited zone of the high seas contiguous to the territorial sea, in which coastal states exercise a limited jurisdiction over foreign ships—should not extend beyond 12 miles from the base line of the territorial sea.

Diplomatic law and immunity. States and international institutions can act only through individuals. Thus, relations between states—and international institutions—are based on the principle of *necessary* representation. The chief representative of a state is the head of state who, in principle, has plenary powers to commit his state. After a number of earlier attempts—especially the *règlement* adopted at the *Congress of Vienna (1814–15)* to settle continuous disputes over the precedence of diplomatic envoys—ambassadors, nuncios, and ministers accredited to heads of state, and chargés d'affaires accredited to the foreign ministers of their countries of residence—the classes of diplomatic envoys and their privileges and immunities are now codified in the 1961 Vienna Convention on Diplomatic Relations.

Protection and status of citizens and economic interests abroad

Similarly, the rights and immunities of consuls—resident officials stationed abroad with the consent of the receiving state for purposes of promoting trade and assisting nationals of the sending country—are codified in the 1963 Vienna Convention on Consular Relations.

The protection of nationals abroad. The relevant rules for such protection grew out of individual safe-conducts and innumerable bilateral treaties of commerce and navigation and, between civilized nations, were gradually taken for granted as rules of international customary law or general principles of law recognized by civilized nations.

These rules imply the application of a minimum standard that complies with the rule of law, as understood in liberal and democratic Western countries, regarding the protection of the life, liberty, dignity, and property of foreign nationals. Regarding property, the freedom of states to expropriate or nationalize private property in the public interest with full (or adequate), prompt, and effective compensation, is generally accepted as a rule of international customary law. The rule has behind it the authority of the Permanent Court of International Justice and a considerable number of international tribunals. Doubts that have been raised against the continued validity of the rule (especially in Communist and capital-importing states) are related to the application of the rule in cases of doubtful titles to property rather than to the existence of the rule itself. There is also a widespread mixture of politics, trade, and aid that, on pragmatic grounds, frequently makes inadvisable an insistence by capital-exporting states on strict compliance with the rule.

Freedom of commerce and navigation. Under international customary law, the right of foreign nations to trade in a country and use its means of communications, such as roads, river, and air space is within the exclusive jurisdiction of the territorial sovereign. By way of treaty, such rights of commerce and navigation are granted normally on relative terms; *i.e.*, by reference to optional standards. The classical standards of international treaty law in these fields are those of *most favoured nation* treatment (treatment on the basis of *foreign* parity), *national* treatment (treatment on the basis of *inland* parity) *identical* treatment, *equitable* treatment, *good-neighbourly* treatment, *open-door* treatment (equal treatment of all concerned in a third sovereign state or a territory such as a United Nations trust territory), and *preferential* treatment. In state practice, some of these standards are employed cumulatively or alternatively in one and the same treaty.

Extradition and asylum. In accordance with a long-established practice, states have concluded extradition treaties, enabling them to secure the return of fugitives from their own territorial jurisdiction. In states in which the rule of law in the Western sense applies, considerable care is taken to define precisely the offenses for which extradition may be granted, and extradition normally is limited to nonnationals of the country requested to grant extradition. While a number of states take a different view of political crimes, it is a liberal Western tradition to exclude political offenders from extradition unless they are charged with an attack on life.

Treatment of fugitives

In the absence of consensual undertaking to the contrary, any state may grant *asylum* in its own territory to any individual. This territorial asylum must be distinguished from diplomatic asylum; *i.e.*, asylum that is granted in diplomatic premises situated in another state's territory. In the absence of express treaty rights to this effect, diplomatic asylum may not be granted but, on humanitarian grounds, the territorial sovereign frequently acquiesces in such action.

Succession to international rights and obligations. It is necessary to distinguish three typical situations: (1) *revolution*—this, in principle, is treated as a purely internal affair and, whether successful or not, does not affect the obligations of the subject of international law concerned; (2) *territorial changes*—if two states decide on the cession of a relatively insignificant portion of territory, the matter is settled between the parties by the rules on consent and, in relation to third parties, by those on recognition; if a state agrees to its own truncation, or a composite state is dismembered, the legal consequences of such changes are settled by way of treaty, recognition, or acquiescence; (3) in the case of *belligerent occupation* falling short of *debellatio*, any territorial changes are treated as purely temporary while the war lasts. There are other aspects to be considered. In accordance with a widespread practice, it is presumed that, in the absence of any express settlement in a treaty of cession, the *public property* of the ceding state becomes automatically the property of the cessionary state, and the *public law* of the ceding state is replaced by that of the cessionary state.

There is no general rule of international customary law imposing automatic succession by the cessionary state to the *state debts* of the ceding state. On *equitable* grounds however, a rule to the opposite effect is frequently asserted regarding strictly *localized* debt. Cessionary states are under no obligation to assume any responsibility for tortious acts or omissions of the ceding state.

In principle, treaties are binding only between the contracting parties. Thus, if one of the parties cedes part of its territory, existing treaties are interpreted according to the rule of movable treaty frontiers; *i.e.*, the territorial scope of treaty obligations is presumed to be automatically adjusted to subsequent territorial changes. In cases in which the nonexistence of rules of international law on the automatic succession to international obligations would lead to harsh results, these are likely to be mitigated by the need of the new subject of international law concerned to be recognized and the freedom of existing subjects to make recognition dependent on compliance with justified expectations.

INTERNATIONAL LAW IN ORGANIZED WORLD SOCIETY

Global multipurpose institutions such as the League of Nations and the United Nations are best understood as organizational superstructures of international customary law on a consensual and confederate basis. Their impact on international law is threefold: modification by express consent of the rules underlying the fundamental principles of international law, indirect modification of these rules by acquiescence on the part of member states in the action of organs not actually authorized to exercise law-making functions, and initiation of the further codification and development of international law.

Express modifications. The chief modification introduced by the United Nations Charter is the limitation of the rights of subjects of international law under international customary law to threaten or resort to armed reprisals and war. This extends the duties of the former members of the League of Nations and parties to the Kellogg Pact of 1928. The prohibition now covers the threat or use of force in circumstances falling short of war in the formal sense.

Indirect modifications. The principal means of indirect law making in the United Nations are resolutions of the General Assembly that are adopted unanimously or with the two-thirds majorities required for important questions. If such resolutions purport to be declaratory of international law, it is difficult for member states who voted for them to claim that, on the matters involved, the General Assembly is limited to the mere task of making recommendations. If the organs of the United Nations concerned act consistently on particular resolutions, eventually a time comes when even those states that have voted against them will be deemed to have acquiesced in such resolutions. Nonmember states that are admitted to membership in the United Nations after such resolutions have been adopted may find themselves in a similar situation. They have obtained their recognition on the assumption that they will abide by the generally accepted rules of international law and, increasingly, member states that grant recognition may equate the near-universal law and practice of the United Nations with general international customary law. Moreover, new members must expect that they join this global confederation as they find it.

A number of resolutions passed by the General Assembly fall into this in-between category of law-in-the-making—*e.g.*, those on the Nuremberg Principles that dealt with crimes against peace, war crimes, and crimes against humanity (Res. No. 95[II], 1946); genocide (Res. No. 96[I], 1946); the Universal Declaration of Human Rights (Res. No. 217[III], 1948); the right of peoples and nations to self-determination (Res. No. 637[VII], 1952); permanent sovereignty over natural resources (Res. No. 1803[XVII], 1962); denuclearization (Res. No. 1884 [XVIII], 1963); and nonintervention (Res. No. 2131[XX], 1965).

In some instances, as before the adoption of the Universal Declaration of Human Rights, the almost unanimous protestations by speakers in the General Assembly regarding the purely moral character of the precepts enshrined in the declaration provide adequate evidence of the nonlegal character of the resolution in question. In others, such intention may become evident from the self-contradictions contained in the resolutions themselves. In still others, the intimation of the need for further study and the request for codification of the subject may suggest the political, rather than legal, character of a particular resolution. But if, at any subsequent stage, it can be shown that large and consistent majorities of the principal organs of the United Nations accept rules laid down in such resolutions as legally binding, the transition from law-in-the-making to new law—at least for purposes of the work of the international institution concerned—tends to be made sooner or later.

The codification and development of international law. The International Law Commission, an auxiliary but autonomous organ of the General Assembly of the United Nations, consists of 25 members of recognized competence in international law (Article 2[1] of the Commission's Statute). It has initiated codification and development in a number of fields of international law. In practice, the commission does not distinguish between its efforts on the codification (*i.e.*, the restatement of existing international law) and the development of international law by draft rules involving changes in existing international customary law. Thus, any of the rules proposed by the commission must be examined from this point of view.

In the field of humanitarian law (*i.e.*, the protection of the individual) the International Convention on the Elimination of All Forms of Racial Discrimination of 1965 and the International Covenants on Civil and Political and on Economic, Social, and Cultural Rights, opened for signature in 1966, were channelled from the United Nations Commission on Human Rights to the General Assembly of the United Nations through the Economic and Social Council. On a level of closer constitutional and ideological homogeneity, the Council of Europe adopted the Rome Convention for the Protection of Human Rights and Fundamental Freedoms of 1950, as subsequently amended, and, in the European Commission of Human Rights and the European Court of Human Rights, provided the most effective means yet put into operation for the implementation of the protection of human rights.

On specialized topics, such as the law of the sea, international labour law, and international private law, the Inter-Governmental Maritime Consultative Organization, the International Labour Organisation, and the Hague Conference of Private Law, respectively, fulfill drafting functions of a quasi-legislative character comparable to those of the International Law Commission. In all cases, however, it remains for the sovereign states concerned to decide whether they desire to limit their freedom of action by such further consensual commitments.

Future development

If this will exists, states are not limited to the development of international law on a confederate level. They are free to transform regional, continental, or global areas into federations of a territorial type such as the United States of America or the Commonwealth of Australia. They may also try the pattern of functional federation on the model of one of the European supranational organizations such as the European Economic Community. Under these conditions, the wheel has come full circle, and international law turns again into municipal law, but until such a development becomes universal, international law is likely to remain indispensable in the relations between such sectional groupings.

BIBLIOGRAPHY

Collections of treaties: Consolidated Treaty Series 1648–1919, ed. by C. PARRY (1969–); *League of Nations Treaty Series: Treaties and International Engagements Registered with the Secretariat of the League of Nations*, 205 vol. (1920–46); *United Nations Treaty Series: Treaties and International Agreements Registered or Filed and Recorded with the Secretariat of the United Nations* (1946–); *United Nations, List of Treaty Collections* (1956); M.O. HUDSON and C.B. SOHN (eds.), *International Legislation, 1919–1945*, 9 vol. (1931–50).

Reports of judicial case law: UNITED NATIONS, *Reports of International Arbitral Awards* (1948–); LONDON SCHOOL OF ECONOMICS AND POLITICAL SCIENCE, *International Law Reports* (1950–); A.M. STUYT, *Survey of International Arbitrations, 1794–1938* (1939).

Digests of state practice: A.C. KISS (ed.), *Répertoire de la pratique Française en matière de droit international public*, 6 vol. (1962–69); E. LAUTERPACHT (ed.), *British Practice in International Law* (1963–); J.B. MOORE (ed.), *A Digest of International Law*, 8 vol. (1906); G.H. HOCKWORTH (ed.), *Digest of International Law*, 8 vol. (1940–44); M.M. WHITEMAN (ed.), *Digest of International Law* (1963–). The last three sources deal with the United States.

Dictionaries: K. STRUPP, *Wörterbuch des Völkerrechts*, 2nd ed. by H. SCHLOCHAUER *et al.*, 3 vol. (1960–62); UNION ACADÉMIQUE INTERNATIONALE, *Dictionnaire de la terminologie du droit international* (1960).

General treatises: J.L. BRIERLY, *The Law of Nations*, 6th ed. by H. WALDOCK (1963); C.C. HYDE, *International Law, Chiefly as Interpreted and Applied by the United States*, 3 vol. (1947); M.S. MCDOUGAL *et al.*, *Studies in World Public Order* (1960); D.P. O'CONNELL, *International Law*, 2 vol. (1965); L.F.L. OPPENHEIM, *International Law*, 8th ed. by H. LAUTERPACHT, 2 vol. (1955); G. SCHWARZENBERGER, *A Manual of International Law*, 5th ed. (1967); M. SORENSEN, (ed.), *Manual of Public International Law* (1968); (in French:) P. REUTER, *Droit international public*, 3rd ed. (1968); C. ROUSSEAU, *Droit international public* (1953); (in German:) G. DAHM, *Völkerrecht*, 3 vol. (1958–61); A. VERDROSS, *Völkerrecht* (1964); (in Italian:) D. ANZILOTTI, *Corso di diritto internazionale* (1964); A.P. SERENI, *Diritto internazionale*, 4 vol. (1956-65); (in Spanish:) C. SEPULVEDA, *Derecho internacional público*, 3rd ed. (1968); (translations from Russian:) ACADEMY OF SCIENCES OF THE U.S.S.R., *International Law* (1967); G.I. TUNKIN, *Droit international public* (1965).

Periodicals: American Journal of International Law (1907–); *Archiv des Völkerrechts* (1948–); *British Yearbook of*

International Law (1921–); *Indian Yearbook of International Affairs* (1952–); *Japanese Annual of International Law* (1957–); *Revue générale de droit international public* (1894–); *Soviet Yearbook of International Law* (1958–); *Zeitschrift für ausländisches öffentliches Recht und Völkerrecht* (1929–).
Bibliographies: Reports on Legal Aspects of World Affairs in *Year Book of World Affairs* (1947–); J. ROBINSON, *International Law and Organization* (1967).

(G.Sc.)

International Relations

This article is intended to provide a narrative and an analysis of international relations since World War II, though in order to do this it will be necessary to refer briefly to the relations among the nation-states before that war. For theoretical aspects, see INTERNATIONAL RELATIONS, THEORIES OF. Related articles that have some interest in this context are EUROPEAN DIPLOMACY AND WARS (*c.* 1500–1914) and WORLD WARS.

The article is outlined as follows:

I. International relations before and during World War II

THE EUROCENTRIC WORLD

Modern international relations—the great system of states and empires that by the end of the 19th century comprehended the entire globe—had its origins in Europe. It began as Eurocentric and until after World War II was dominated by European powers. By the end of the 19th century, hardly any region of the world had escaped the influences of European exploration and civilization. Individual nation-states—notably Great Britain, France, The Netherlands, Spain, Portugal, and Russia—acted as the political agents for this outburst of European energy, spirit, organizational and entrepreneurial skill, scientific technique, and military power. The consequence of this global transformation was more than the sum of the activities of these sovereign parts.

In the 18th and 19th centuries, millions of Europeans emigrated voluntarily from their homelands to settle elsewhere, particularly in the New World and in Oceania; they thus filled in and brought European civilization to the large, sparsely settled overseas sectors of the temperate zone and soon manifested strong desire for self-rule or even independence from their colonial governments.

After the Napoleonic Wars of the early 19th century, the European system of international relations displayed two powerful but contradictory tendencies. Within Europe proper, the emerging system of politics was that which had evolved from formal principles of state sovereignty manifested much earlier (1648) in the Peace of Westphalia; the structure of politics was decentralized, based upon many discrete territorial states. The chief actors in this system came to be referred to as the Great Powers (Britain, France, Spain, the Habsburg Empire, Prussia, and Russia); European politics consisted in the competitive and cooperative interaction among these separate sovereign parts, none of which proved capable of commanding and dominating the others. As each of these entities progressed politically, economically, and culturally, so did each differentiate itself from the others. On the principle of national self-determination, each state thus increasingly based (and claimed legitimacy for) itself upon a nationality principle rather than upon cosmopolitan, or multinational, or universalist principles, which had been implicit in previous empires and in the very idea of Christendom itself. Thus the peace of Europe came to rest upon the constant search for equilibrium among its separate parts: the so-called balance of power.

The Great Powers

That the nationality principle was greatly affected by the spread of democratic and liberal ideas had the (curious) consequence that liberal or populist nationalism during the 19th century replaced the principle of dynastic sovereignty as the basis both of the European political order and of European internal tensions and antagonisms. The machinery of the dynastic state increasingly came to be commanded by forces manifesting particularistic national cultures. Thus the chief state casualties of World War I were the German, Habsburg, Ottoman, and Russian empires, all of which were overthrown, broken up, and supplanted by explicitly nationalist political orders. By the 1920s, Europe more than ever was a Europe of nations.

Contradictions of European politics

Outside Europe proper, however, the expansion of European civilization took the form not of particularistic national states but of empires. By 1918 the non-Western world, aside from the Americas, Australia, and New Zealand, was being, or had been, subjugated and annexed by the major European powers. All of Africa, save for Liberia and Ethiopia, was under direct or indirect European rule; the Middle East and South and Southeast Asia were provinces of metropolitan powers; tsarist Russia spread its authority eastward through Siberia and Central Asia to the Pacific, annexing vast provinces of subordinate nationalities; China, afflicted by and disintegrating from these tendencies, became the object of imperial rivalry among outside powers. In all the non-Western world, Japan was the only major territory that proved capable of successfully resisting the political encroachments of Europe, and it did so only by borrowing the organizational and technological skills of Europe and adapting them to its own state necessities. (See further COLONIALISM.)

In the early 19th century, however, the New World of the Americas began to assert its own capacities for self-government and independence even before Europe's "conquest of the world" had been completed. But British America's successful revolt in 1776 and the subsequent rebellions in Central and South America and the Caribbean against Europe were led by transplanted Europeans, chiefly Spaniards and Englishmen. The political ideals that inspired the demand for self-government in the British North American colonies were specifically European in their origins; the American patriots, as Edmund Burke observed, were demanding for themselves the rights of Englishmen. The infectious principles of civil government that spread through the Americas were those of Locke, Montesquieu, and Rousseau, and thus Europe's own emerging political theories of self-determination began to subvert Europe's political dominion of the world even before that dominion had been fully established. The United States of America became the world's "first new nation," in overthrowing European political control and asserting its own national destiny against the pretensions of empire.

THE COLLAPSE OF THE EUROCENTRIC WORLD

In the great wars of modern times, before the attack on Pearl Harbor, the battlegrounds were (with a few exceptions, such as China during the Taiping Rebellion and the U.S. during the Civil War) in Europe; the character of these wars, and the political stakes, were determined by European governments. Although military operations in both world wars reached global scope, both originated in specifically European contests for power and influence. But the ramifications of general European wars in modern times—as truly for the 18th century as for the 20th—were felt in many parts of the

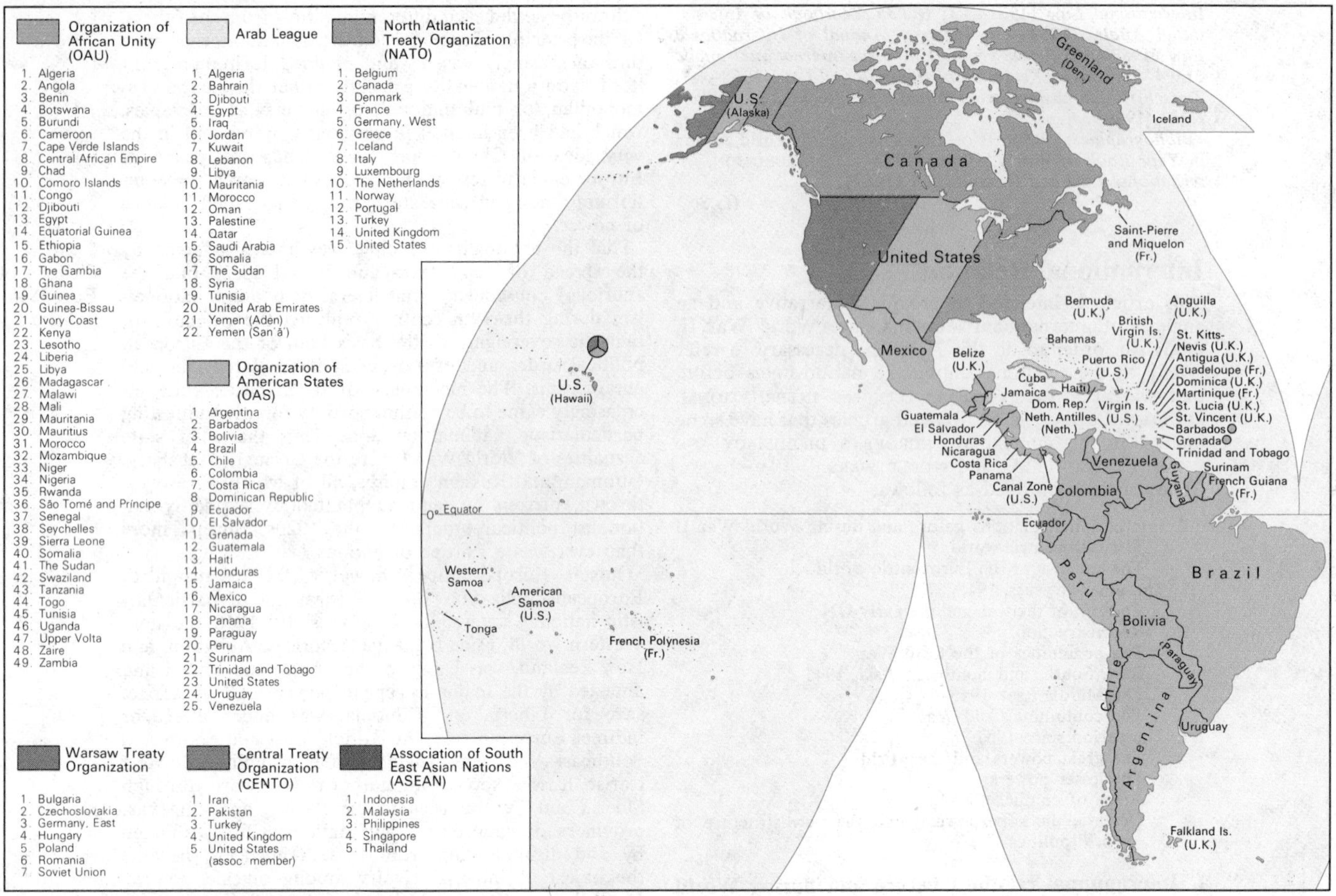

Mutual assistance agreements and regional alliances, 1977.

world far removed from Europe. The struggle for mastery among the European states in Europe was watched and might be participated in but could not be controlled by the rest of the world. Thus the United States before World War II—even after the vast expansion of its industrial power and geographic extent by the late 19th century—remained on the periphery of world politics, playing no significant role in European power politics in the Old World and refusing to ally itself with any European nation for any purpose.

Ideologies in World War II. World War II, like previous worldwide conflicts, originated in Europe; its basic cause lay in the deliberate attempt by Nazi Germany to impose its authority over the entire European continent, reducing the other nations to vassalage. Before 1939 the Western democracies—France and Britain—sought to appease the German dictator Adolf Hitler's territorial demands, hoping thus to moderate his appetites; but neither this policy nor last-minute efforts in 1939 to deter his further aggressions succeeded. In August of that year, Nazi Germany startled the world by concluding a nonaggression pact with the Soviet Union, providing for their joint conquest and partition of Poland. This stroke of diplomacy seemingly opened the way for German domination of all of central Europe. The war that began in September 1939 was to last six years; it was to be the last European war; and its reverberations were wholly to transform world politics. No part of the world was to escape the catastrophic consequences of this contest. The battlefield spread to Asia, where Japan's war for dominion in the Far East and Southeast Asia became linked with Germany's imperial aims in Europe. The Nazi conquests of Denmark, Norway, The Netherlands, France, and Yugoslavia in 1940–41 were preparatory stages in Hitler's plan to subjugate Britain and to destroy the Soviet Union, which on June 22, 1941, German troops attacked. The spread of Japanese military power in China and Southeast Asia, effectively resisted only by American diplomacy, led, on December 7, 1941, to the attack on Pearl Harbor. At that point, what had begun as a regional European conflict became a truly global war, engaging every major power.

Nazi–Soviet pact

While this war, like previous European wars, possessed all the essential characteristics of a *Realpolitik* struggle for power among nations, it also had profound ideological aspects. It aroused fierce passions, both nationalist and universalist. Hitler's purpose, for instance, was not merely to conquer Europe but also to transform it, even to obliterating whole ethnic groups.

The war as fought in Europe pitted the Axis nations —Germany and Italy—against a coalition of the Western democracies and the Soviet Union, but the Spanish historian Salvador de Madariaga later noted a triangular quality in it: the chief belligerents were the liberal, Fascist, and Marxist powers. The struggle was not merely among nations but among differing ideas about the ways in which advanced societies should be governed. Liberal, Fascist, and Marxist ideologies cut across state boundaries.

Liberal–Fascist–Marxist struggle

During the brief Nazi–Soviet alliance of 1939–41, for instance, Communist parties in the West tried to sabotage the war against Germany. Later, when Hitler, betraying his pact with Stalin, launched his attack on the Soviet Union, he sought and found widespread European support outside Germany for an ideological war on Bolshevism. Similarly, when the U.S. and Britain finally joined forces, their war aims—enunciated in the Atlantic Charter issued by Pres. Franklin D. Roosevelt and the British prime minister Winston Churchill in 1941—were basically liberal. Paradoxically, among the major European belligerents, only the Soviet Union minimized universalist ideology; once the war came to Russia, Stalin abandoned all references to Marxism and Communism in his effort to rally the Russian people in a patriotic war. Old symbols of Russian glory were resurrected from

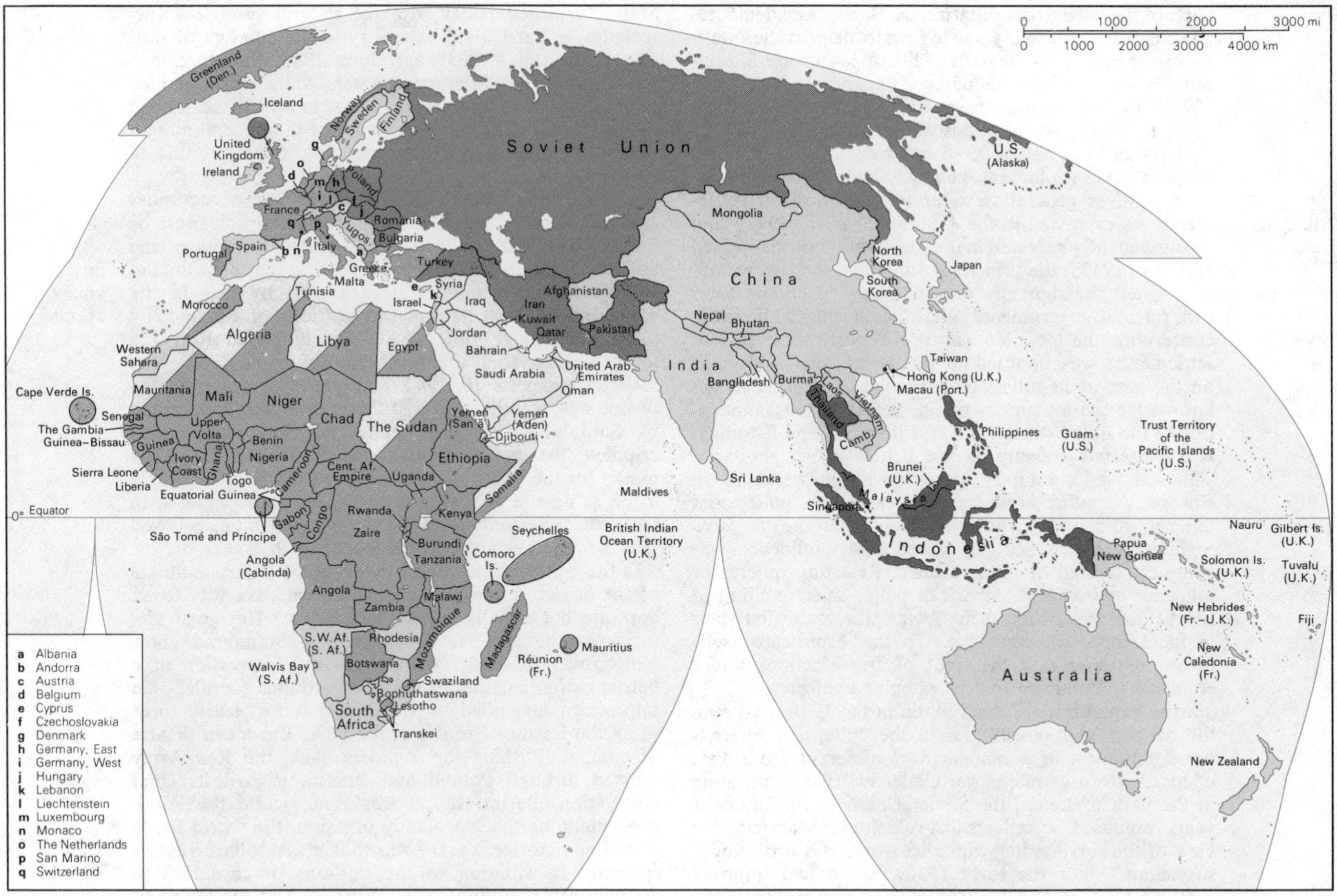

tsarist times, to gain support from a people subject for nearly 25 years to brutal Soviet rule. Not until the war was at an end, in 1946, did the Soviet leadership reanimate its Marxist rhetoric and doctrine.

Roosevelt and Churchill. One formula—unconditional surrender—held together the wartime coalition against Nazi Germany. No equivalent formula was to be found to perpetuate the coalition in the peace that followed. One reason for this was that the war so fundamentally transformed world politics that no statesman, not even Churchill, could comprehend the shape that the future would take. At the three wartime conferences of Allied leaders—at Tehrān (Teheran), Yalta, and Potsdam—the discussions were confined almost exclusively to strategic matters and to the question of treatment of Axis states after their defeat. For his part, Churchill sought, from 1943 onward, to alert his American allies to the possible configurations of European power politics that might result from alternative Anglo-American and Soviet strategies. In secret talks with Stalin during the war, he had explored the spheres of respective British and Soviet influence that might be established in eastern Europe and the Balkans. His advocacy of an Anglo-U.S. assault on southern Europe through the Balkans sprang in part from a belief that such an invasion might somewhat check the westward expansion of Soviet power in Europe.

Roosevelt, for his part, had refused to discuss the postwar settlements, particularly the crucial territorial settlements, until a postwar peace conference could be held. Roosevelt and Cordell Hull, his secretary of state, were profoundly suspicious of Churchill's tentative spheres-of-influence policies as they pertained to Europe, and in trilateral Anglo-U.S.-Soviet meetings at Tehrān and Yalta Roosevelt cast himself in the role of intermediary between Churchill and Stalin. His suspicion of Churchill's motives arose from a fundamental misapprehension both of the aims of British statecraft and of future British influence in the world. Mindful of his predecessor Woodrow Wilson's failure at peacemaking in 1919 (and remembering how the linkage of the

Roosevelt's doubts about Churchill

utopian Covenant of the League of Nations to the particular realities of the Treaty of Versailles had led to the U.S. Senate's rejection of both), Roosevelt sought also to isolate the question of a future international collective security organization from the specific substantive matters of a peace settlement. In his role as wartime leader, furthermore, Roosevelt from the beginning exclusively focussed upon the defeat of the Axis powers—a defeat to be so definitive as to preclude the possibility of any future revival of German or Japanese power. This unwillingness to allow long-range political considerations to deflect attention from military victory was later to be criticized by political strategists, who suggested that it led to far deeper incursions of Soviet power in Europe than were necessary and to the annihilation of constructive power in central Europe. Wishing to avoid the mistakes of his predecessor, Roosevelt fell victim to his own different mistakes, though he did not live to witness their consequences.

One of these consequences, however, was that the conflict was brought to an end more quickly than it might otherwise have been. Roosevelt and his generals George C. Marshall and Dwight D. Eisenhower rejected the idea of a more prolonged "indirect" attrition strategy against Nazi Germany, preferring to strike decisively against the very centre of German military strength on the English Channel coast. His success in mobilizing the vast resources of America, furthermore, was astonishing; by 1945 the United States had assembled the mightiest and most far-flung military force the world had ever known. The sheer abundance of U.S. material and the lavish and swift distribution of it accounted largely for both the rapidity of victory and the relatively low casualties that American forces suffered.

U.S. mobilization

The U.S. view of national self-determination. The refusal of American statesmen to devote wartime attention to the content of a peace settlement did not apply to plans for the occupation of defeated Axis states. At Yalta, and subsequently at Potsdam, U.S. statesmen succeeded in persuading their British and Soviet counterparts of the need to demilitarize, de-Nazify, and democratize a defeated Germany and to install "democratic," anti-Fascist regimes in other parts of liberated Europe. Similar policies were devised for postwar Japan.

While the "shaping of the peace" was, in the American view, to be reserved for postwar conferences, the U.S. as early as 1941 had adopted one particular high moral purpose that, while very abstract, had a profound influence on its general views *about* such postwar settlements. As expressed in the Atlantic Charter (1941) and as subsequently reflected in the Declaration of the United Nations (1942), the principle of national self-determination meant the right of "peoples freely to choose their own form of government." Washington thus, while silent concerning the possible nature of postwar territorial settlements, was opposed to territorial *faits accomplis* on the part of its allies. In particular, it refused to acknowledge the legitimacy of the Soviet (1940) annexation of the Baltic states (Latvia, Lithuania, and Estonia), and it exerted pressure on the British to act similarly. Thus, as Soviet military forces advanced westward in Europe, a conflict arose between basic U.S. policy and the new and real particulars of an emerging *de facto* regime in eastern Europe, where Soviet influence was being established or re-established. Rejecting spheres of influence as immoral, American policy makers clung to liberal doctrines while their Soviet allies extended their political influence westward. To the Americans, self-determination meant the right of free elections under conditions conducive to free popular choice.

Atlantic Charter

Soviet expansion. Joseph Stalin in the 1930s had seen the dangers and possibilities in the collapsing international situation in a manner very different from that of his Western counterparts. Under his rule, continuing in the path of Lenin, the Soviet Union in the interwar years espoused a universalist ideology, Marxism; its view of the surrounding capitalist world was profoundly suspicious. Since the early 1930s, Stalin had imposed a terror on both the Russian people and minority nationalities. His purges of the Communist Party and Red Army had exterminated rivals and destroyed an entire generation of Bolshevik leadership; the survivors were reduced to servile adjutants. Abroad, Stalin conducted a similar purge within the Communist (Third) International, or Comintern, the Kremlin's worldwide apparatus of subversion and revolution. But Stalin miscalculated the significance of the rise of National Socialism and failed to perceive in time Hitler's capacities and goals. Thus under orders from the Soviet Union the German Communist Party collaborated with the Nazis to destroy the Weimar Republic; in Stalin's view, Nazism represented the highest form of monopoly capitalism, and its coming to power represented a necessary phase preceding the final crisis of the bourgeois order. Not until Hitler had gained full control over Germany did Stalin, in 1935, respond to the threat posed by the Third Reich and call upon the western European Communists to cease their attacks on parties of the democratic left and establish Popular Front coalitions against Fascism. Stalin's chief diplomat, Maksim Litvinov, at the League of Nations pressed for collective measures against Hitler. Pacts were concluded with France and Czechoslovakia to supplement the Soviet Union's own capacities.

Stalin and the Nazis

For Stalin, the Munich Agreement of 1938, in which the democracies sacrificed Czechoslovakia to appease Hitler, was a diplomatic catastrophe. Excluded from these proceedings, the Soviet Union was now wholly isolated from the affairs of Europe. Stalin thereupon abandoned his quest for collective security, dismissed Litvinov, and dealt directly with his ideological enemy. By means of the German–Soviet Treaty of Nonaggression (August 23, 1939), the Soviet Union agreed to support economically the Third Reich's war plans, Poland was partitioned, and eastern Europe was divided into spheres of influence. Stalin successfully diverted Hitler's plans westward, and World War II began. Perhaps Stalin overestimated the military capacity of the West to resist Hitler. In any event, throughout Europe the Communist parties once more turned against the democracies, while Stalin furnished Hitler with the natural resources (petroleum, in particular) necessary to the conduct of war.

Between August 1939 and June 1941, therefore, one possible future international system was a world divided among the great totalitarian states, in which the United States might be the sole remainder of the once dominant liberal societies. But Hitler was not to permit this to happen.

Against these potentialities the ensuing catastrophes and trends of World War II and its aftermath must be judged. By 1940, Stalin had pushed the borders of the Soviet Union westward by annexing eastern Poland (1939) and the Baltic states (1940); by war in the winter of 1939–40 he annexed portions of Finland; by blunt diplomacy (June 1940) he compelled Romania to cede Bessarabia and northern Bukovina.

Soviet annexations

Western experts in 1941 had greatly misjudged the Soviet state's ability to resist German attack. Decimated by Stalin's purges, the Red Army was regarded as crippled; the experts thought the Soviet Air Force no match for the Luftwaffe and believed the Russian people to be as hostile to Stalin as to Hitler. Some experts, in fact, when Germany invaded the Soviet Union, believed that Soviet resistance would collapse in weeks.

As the war progressed, however, this Western estimate of the Soviet Union as a crippled giant gave way to an opposite but equally questionable view. The great victories of the Red Army, notably at Stalingrad (now Volgograd) in 1943, created the new impression of a heroic nation capable of the most arduous sacrifice—an impression magnified by the fact that for nearly three years the Eastern Front was the chief European theatre of combat. Pushing the invaders back, the Red Army pressed through Poland and Prussia toward its chief destination, Berlin. In all this time, while the Allies were planning the Normandy invasion, the world heard of Soviet victories. Yet the war took a vast toll of Russian strength. In addition to the millions of casualties in combat, more millions of civilians died at the hands of the invaders or from disease and famine. Great cities were reduced to ruins. The industrial base of the Soviet economy was destroyed. In many areas, notably the Ukraine, open rebellion against Soviet authority took place; nationality groups were forcibly uprooted from their homelands and their survivors resettled in remote regions. So fearful was the Soviet leadership of the effects of Western cultural contamination upon captured Russian troops that returning thousands of them were executed or transported to labour camps. Internal resistance to Soviet authority continued as late as 1947 in the Ukraine. Outwardly to the world, the Soviet Union in 1945 commanded respect as a great power; inwardly it was in chaos.

The new great powers in Europe. In diplomatic matters, however, it was the outward appearance that counted. The rule of the Russian Communists, once confined to the eastern reaches of Europe, by May 1945 extended into the very heart of the Continent. In that part of Europe where the Red Army was dominant, a new empire was to be established.

Since in the West it was American military power that had forced its way upon the Continent, likewise penetrating to its heart, the old European order had now been overwhelmed by two great powers that long had existed on Europe's periphery. In 1945 all the great empires of Europe had been either crushed, like Germany, or pitifully reduced. The historic Eurocentric world had ceased to exist, although few at the time recognized the fact. The political question was what kind of order would supplant it.

II. The postwar years, 1945–57

THE END OF THE WAR AND THE EARLY UN

The German surrender on May 7 (effective midnight May 8), 1945, marked the end of the European part of the war, the Japanese surrender on September 2 the Asian; World War II was over. The last months were not without surprise. On August 6, 1945, the U.S.

dropped an atomic bomb on Hiroshima; three days later another was dropped on Nagasaki, and what some came to call the Atomic Age had begun. The two Japanese cities joined the long list of those wholly devastated by wartime air attack, but the devastation this time was accomplished by only two bombs. Recognition of this awesome power gave the peace forces in Japan a strong argument for immediate surrender.

In San Francisco, 13 days after Roosevelt's death, the United Nations Conference on International Organization opened on April 25. The new organization, replacing the League of Nations, was in large measure the result of unremitting American effort. Roosevelt had regarded it as the cornerstone of postwar collective security under law; a cooperative organization of sovereign nations, it would serve to deter military aggression and to make possible a durable peace.

The U.S. government, shy about the specific features of a postwar settlement, nevertheless was insistent on establishing structures to govern the peace. During the war it had supported international organizations to deal with specific problems of the postwar era. At Hot Springs, West Virginia, in 1943, the U.S. acted as host nation to the Conference on Food and Agriculture that led to the formation of the Food and Agriculture Organization (FAO) two years later; and in 1944, at Bretton Woods, New Hampshire, it sponsored the United Nations Monetary and Financial Conference that led to the formation of two important organizations, the International Bank for Reconstruction and Development (IBRD) and the International Monetary Fund (IMF). In 1943 the United States sponsored the organization of the United Nations Relief and Rehabilitation Administration (UNRRA) to administer the delivery of food and other commodities to the peoples of Europe and Asia.

Truman's fundamental principles

Harry S. Truman, Roosevelt's successor, in a speech in October 1945 laid out 12 fundamental points of U.S. foreign policy, which included avoidance of territorial aggrandizement; disapproval of territorial changes not based on popular consent; nonrecognition of governments imposed by foreign powers; freedom of the seas; equal access to trade and raw materials; freedom of expression and of religion; the establishment of democratic regimes in former enemy countries; and cooperation within the United Nations to preserve the peace. These principles had not been new even to Roosevelt; though their language differed, they were essentially the same as those that Woodrow Wilson had offered in 1918 in the form of his Fourteen Points. The fact that they were once more given such significance was an indication that liberal America would occupy the most conspicuous seat at the forthcoming peace conference.

Roosevelt, however, unlike Wilson, had been realist enough to know that the success of such international designs and principles depended on the power that supported them. In his view, the authority of the new United Nations would lie in the great powers; thus, while a principle of universality of membership lay in the quasi-parliamentary UN General Assembly, in which each member state would have one vote, the real power would lie in the Security Council, in which five great powers—the U.S., the United Kingdom, the Soviet Union, France, and Nationalist China—would share the chief responsibility for peacekeeping and for measures to restore peace. Since each would have the right of veto, measures to keep the peace in effect required unanimity of the five as well as votes of other states sufficient for a majority. And this of course meant that the UN's success or failure depended upon the extent of cooperation or conflict among the great powers and the courtesy powers.

The earliest United Nations organization, one of whose four major purposes was "to save succeeding generations from the scourge of war," had a basic membership qualification, namely, that only those states that had declared war on the Axis powers were eligible. While certain states not previously belligerent, such as Argentina, displayed their peace-loving nature by 11th-hour declarations of war, the organization from its beginning was by no means universalist or comprehensive. As a continuation of a wartime coalition, it originally excluded not only such nations as Italy and Hungary, wartime partners of the Third Reich and Japan, but also such neutral states as Sweden and Switzerland. More important, vast territories of Asia, Africa, and Oceania had no representation other than through European colonial metropoles. Thus while the Soviet Union, augmented by two of its "sovereign" constituent republics (Belorussia and the Ukraine), China, India, Iran, South Africa, Ethiopia, Liberia, Egypt, and a few other Asian states were among its original members, the UN at its inception was predominantly Western, reflecting Western traditions of liberalism and constitutionalism. This was not to be the case later, when the membership came to include more Communist and many new Third World states.

The UN as a Western organization

RECONSTRUCTION

The United States alone among the powers emerged from the war with enormous capacities and resources, its economy vastly enlarged and its homeland unscathed. Postwar reconstruction was thus initially dependent on American decisions and priorities. The devastated Soviet Union proved to be a consumer, not a donor, of resources for reconstruction. This contrast in the conditions of the two powers had far-reaching implications for their respective reputations and influence. In all areas of Europe and the Far East under control of the Red Army, the Soviet Union foraged for material necessary to its own reconstruction; whole industrial complexes, railroad rolling stock, and rail lines were commandeered, dismantled, and removed. While many of these spoils of war were seized as reparations from former enemy states, friendly governments were not spared. In Manchuria, for instance, once it was freed from Japanese occupation, the Chinese were plundered as were the Germans in Europe; steel mills, the potential base for Chinese recovery, were removed, and the economy was wholly deranged.

In contrast, the United States early concentrated its attention upon the reconstruction of areas now under its influence. Seeking no reparations, it tolerated reparations to others. As the "arsenal of democracy" during the war, the United States had furnished nearly $50,000,000,000 worth of military supplies and other necessary commodities to its European and Asian allies, including the Soviet Union. At the war's end the statutory authority for these deliveries ceased, save for material already in movement, and much uncertainty existed as to future U.S. intentions. By 1947, however, it became clear that the damage to Europe was far more profound than any but a few extreme pessimists had foreseen. The destruction visited upon Germany adversely affected the economies of neighbouring nations; Britain, once the world's banker, was now on the brink of bankruptcy, most of its overseas investments having gone to finance its war; the prospect of economic collapse faced all of western Europe.

European political instability

This economic devastation coincided with an unstable political situation in Europe, which in turn was complicated by the growing signs of serious disagreement between the United States and the Soviet Union. In France and Italy, for instance, the two years immediately after the war saw, in the vacuum created by the destruction of the right-wing parties, confrontation between parties of the centre and of the left for control. The Communist parties emerged from the war with organizations far stronger than those of their democratic adversaries. In France, the Communist Party on orders from Moscow briefly collaborated in Charles de Gaulle's first government, but its conditional support was soon to be withdrawn, and in 1947 Communist-led strikes paralyzed the fragile French economy. In Italy, as parliamentary elections approached, the prospect of a Communist victory was very real. In these circumstances, many feared the emergence of a new Europe, dominated in the east by the Red Army (renamed Soviet Army in 1946) and local Communist collaborators and in the west by totalitarians of the left. Were that to occur, much of western Europe would come under Soviet influence if not domination.

It was in this uneasy situation that the economic power of the United States again came into play, culminating in 1948 in the Marshall Plan (formally, the European Recovery Program), in which western European states designed their national economic programs and U.S. material assistance (amounting eventually to $17,000,000,000) filled the gap between their maximum abilities and their minimum needs, to restore their economies to levels of productivity they had enjoyed before the war. By 1952 this goal was reached, and the political crises in Italy and France subsided. European economic recovery became a fact.

THE BEGINNINGS OF THE COLD WAR

Consolidation of Soviet power in eastern Europe. The Yalta Conference—the last meeting of Roosevelt, Churchill, and Stalin, held in February 1945—has been regarded by some as the high point of collaboration among Britain, America, and the Soviet Union. At this conference the three leaders planned their final moves against Germany; delineated their zones of occupation (the U.S. zone being reduced in size to allow for a French zone); and jointly endorsed plans for the establishment of the United Nations. Yet even at Yalta it was clear that Western principles (one of them the right of every people to choose its own form of government) represented in the Atlantic Charter conflicted with the Soviet Union's purposes in eastern Europe.

The focal point was Poland. The Western powers had been committed to the establishment of an independent postwar Polish state. Through the war a government in exile, based in London and composed of émigré political leaders of various parties, had served as rallying point for Polish resistance. It was expected that this regime (like similar Norwegian, French, and Dutch groups in London) would constitute the initial core of postwar government. Britain, after all, had gone to war with Hitler over Poland's right to exist, and the issue for the British was not unaffected by considerations of honour.

The Polish problem

As the Red Army swept westward through Poland, the Soviet authorities established in 1944 a Polish Communist puppet regime (the Polish Committee of National Liberation) in the city of Chełm (later Lublin) and thereafter looked upon this and not the London-based provisional government as the rightful claimant to Polish sovereignty. Angered by the London group's revelations of Soviet murders of Polish officers (the so-called Katyn Massacre of 1940–41) and by the group's stubborn position concerning postwar Polish boundaries (which the Russians wished shifted westward with compensation from Germany for territory lost), Stalin refused to admit its legitimacy. At Yalta, the Western leaders submitted not only to Stalin's territorial plans but also to his demand that the Lublin group constitute the core of the new Polish regime, on condition that it hold "free and unfettered" elections at the earliest possible moment. As a concession to Western sensibilities, to this core were added a few representatives of the London group, including the Peasant Party leader, Stanisław Mikołajczyk. The Soviet Union soon revealed its attitude toward free elections, violating what the West had supposed to be the central issue of principle. Following this Polish example, Soviet authorities elsewhere in eastern Europe where the Red Army was in control thereafter established Soviet-dominated regimes, eliminating political forces that resisted. Thus by 1948 Romania, Bulgaria, Hungary, and Poland were all safely reduced to satellite status: opposition political leaders had been executed, imprisoned, or exiled, and new "people's democracies" had become part of what was, *de facto,* a Soviet empire. In 1948 in Czechoslovakia, a Western-style parliamentary democracy under Edvard Beneš was subverted. With this final coup, an "iron curtain," as Churchill had said in 1946, was truly drawn across the face of Europe, stretching from Stettin (Szczecin) in the north to the Adriatic Sea in the south.

The "iron curtain"

The consolidation of Soviet domination in the east had brought the Soviet state into the heart of Europe. Aside from the U.S. occupation forces stationed in Germany, there was no military force in Europe strong enough to offset the Soviet Army. In 1948 the Swiss Army was probably the most effective western European fighting force. With Germany demilitarized, divided, and ruined, no western European state had the power to defend itself. Nor was there guarantee that the U.S. forces stationed in Germany would remain there long. At Yalta, Roosevelt openly had confessed to Stalin his doubts as to whether the American public would approve any continued U.S. occupation force in Europe. By the later 1940s, in fact, the giant U.S. military machine had been demobilized; from 12,500,000 men, it had shrunk to about 1,500,000, and there remained no U.S. combat-ready forces in Germany. Yet the Soviet Union continued to claim more than 160 combat divisions in its army alone, at least 75 to 80 of which (1,000,000 to 1,500,000 troops) were in eastern Europe and East Germany. Attempts on the part of Britain, France, The Netherlands, and Belgium in 1947 to combine their armed forces only emphasized their feebleness.

The Cold War as Realpolitik and as ideology. If the Cold War is defined as a condition of competition, tension, and conflict short of actual war, engaging the energies and attention of the United States, the Soviet Union, and the forces associated with them, it is analytically uncertain what the Cold War was about. The angry protests in Washington against Soviet violations of the Yalta agreements and the Atlantic Charter were protests of principle, based upon widely accepted views of American (and United Nations) war aims. Despite protests, however, the American government watched passively as the consolidation of Soviet rule in occupied eastern Europe took place. A few American politicians, military officers, and writers in 1947–48 urged a "rollback" of Soviet power, to be obtained by employing threats and ultimatums. But in foreign policy as in other areas of public policy, preferences are tempered by possibilities and costs: the risk of starting a new major war was unacceptable to most Americans, now experiencing the pleasures of peacetime. Nor, as came to be understood later, was there significant risk that the Soviet leaders, outside their vast sphere of virtually unchallenged dominion, would behave recklessly, as Hitler had earlier, in exploiting the weakness of the West. (In marginal and unsuccessful forays during these years, as in Iran, Turkey, and Greece, Stalin displayed prudence when met by determined opposition.)

From one point of view, the Cold War represented an evolving competition for dominance between the two great superpowers and thus was another episode in the long history of *Realpolitik.* But this was only one—if a critical—aspect of it. In Europe in particular, the struggle was perceived by many as a threat to Western civilization from Eastern barbarians; the Soviet Army was thus perceived as the arm of a brutal despotism. But the competition also was ideological. Almost concurrently with the end of hostilities, Stalin abandoned his wartime themes of patriotism and coexistence and reverted to familiar, harsh Marxist–Leninist themes. The new position dictated by Moscow to Communist parties and "fellow travellers" (a translation of the Russian *poputchiki*) in the West again stressed the imminent collapse of capitalism, the impossibility of coexistence, the intrinsic significance of Fascism as a necessary phase of capitalistic development, and the inevitability of war. Soviet economists such as Yevgeny S. Varga, who in wartime had suggested a less catastrophic fate for Western economies, were repudiated, and conciliatory Western Communist figureheads, such as the American party leader Earl Browder, were deposed. In 1947 Stalin's then-favourite aide, Andrey A. Zhdanov, set forth a "two camp" theory to explain the new alignment of forces in world politics, between the peace-loving and progressive camp, led by the Soviet Union, and that of reaction and imperialism, led by the United States.

Zhdanov's "two camp" theory

This ideological offensive was not confined to the realm

of ideas; among other things, it also pertained to the ways in which the economies of advanced—and also emerging—nations should be organized. Where Soviet authority reached, Marxist–Leninist economic doctrines were felt, as state power was asserted over national economies, and private ownership of the means of production and distribution was eliminated. In the West, where Moscow-oriented Communist parties were strong, the effects of this Marxist doctrine could be felt even though Soviet power was not directly present.

These challenges elicited strong responses in the West. Speaking at Fulton, Missouri, in early 1946, Winston Churchill in a strongly anti-Soviet speech called attention to the "iron curtain" dividing Europe and to the threat that Soviet power posed to the West. In March 1947 President Truman in a special emergency address to a joint session of Congress proclaimed what came to be called the Truman Doctrine, asserting the determination of the United States to help "free peoples" resist "attempted subjugation by armed minorities or by outside pressures." The swift decline of British power brought the U.S. into even closer confrontation with the Soviet Union. The Truman Doctrine was no mere abstract proclamation; it was specifically asserted as response to a growing crisis in the eastern Mediterranean, as the Soviet Union, via guerrilla proxies and its army, sought to assert dominion over Greece and Turkey. When Britain, in acute economic distress in early 1947, notified the U.S. government that it could no longer resist these encroachments, the U.S. then assumed the classic British role of balancer. From that point forward, the U.S. Navy was to play the dominant role as protector of Western interests in the Mediterranean.

The Truman Doctrine

The confrontation in Germany. The Zhdanov and Truman doctrines both raised serious questions as to the geographical dimensions of the Cold War, the degree of gravity of the competition between the U.S. and the Soviet Union, and the ultimate objectives of the two rivals. Was the competition between them geographically ubiquitous? Were the differences fundamentally irreconcilable? What forms would this competition take in the future? And, above all, would the outcome be another world war?

The point of closest proximity of Soviet and American power lay exactly where Soviet and American troops had first met in 1945: in Germany. In the Cold War, the central German question to the West was a question not merely of principle but also of power: what form would postwar Germany take, and how would it be oriented between the two "camps"?

The German question had been of central importance to the great powers all along; at Yalta and Potsdam they had agreed on the division of the Reich into zones of military occupation; they had agreed also on programs of de-Nazification, democratization, and demilitarization. Furthermore, Germany as a whole was territorially reduced to a fragment of what it had been. Silesia and much of East Prussia were handed over to Polish administration, and an eastern border was established at the Oder and Neisse rivers; the ancient East Prussian capital, Königsberg, was annexed to the Soviet Union; Austria was detached, once more to be an independent, sovereign state. Berlin, the capital of Prussia, imperial Germany, and the Third Reich, now lay within the Soviet zone of occupation and was divided into occupation sectors as Germany was into zones.

Yalta and Potsdam agreements on Germany

In theory the four occupying powers (including France) were to adjust their policies to reflect consistent programs for Germany as a whole. From the beginning, however, major disagreements developed. These initially centred upon the question of war reparations. While no upper ceiling was set on what Germany should pay for its war crimes, Britain and the U.S. agreed at Yalta to the Soviet proposal of $20,000,000,000 as the basis for subsequent negotiations; this was a concession that they were later to regret. Almost immediately, sharp contrasts appeared in economic and political policies pursued in the four zones. As the Western occupation authorities saw it, the punitive spoliation of Germany—wholly aside from humanitarian considerations—would have grave repercussions on European economic recovery. While determined that Germany should never again recover as an independent great power, they came to see that protracted payment of reparations would require infusions of capital from Western governments if the country were to recover—Western taxpayers (notably Americans) would indirectly pay for Hitler's crimes. The Soviet Union, on the other hand, began the ransacking of its zone for capital equipment, while in addition seeking an indefinite lien on current German production, even in the Western zones.

Thus Western and Soviet occupation policies diverged; with no progress made on agreement as to the future shape of the country as a whole, Germany was reshaped in its component parts. By 1948, the British and American zones, by agreement, were merged as an economic unit, a common currency was introduced, and the nucleus of a future German government was formed—signals of unilateral action to which the Soviet Union quickly retaliated. Berlin lay deep within the Soviet zone, and in June 1948 Soviet authorities blockaded West Berlin, choking off supplies, a measure designed to force the Western powers from the capital or to compel them to abandon plans for West German integration. In the meantime, in the Soviet zone, measures were taken to Sovietize the civilian German authorities. As action and counteraction proceeded, the sentiments of Germans, East and West, turned more and more toward the Western powers. The contest for Berlin, between the threatened starvation of its population by the Soviet Union and the almost miraculous relief of its condition by a Western "airlift," had profound psychological effects. When in mid-1949 the Soviet authorities lifted the blockade, the moral initiative lay with the Western powers. By then, a new state, the Federal Republic of Germany, composed of the three Western zones, had come into being, with an elected national parliament, three major political parties, and a chancellor, Konrad Adenauer, firmly committed to Germany's free association with the West, to a market economy, and to principles of democracy under the rule of law. In response, the Soviet authorities created in their zone the German Democratic Republic, to join the other Soviet satellites as a synthetic nation with little popular support. Two German states were created, but with the difference that the West German state by its constitution was popularly based and committed to the goal of ultimate reunification of the nation.

Berlin blockade

The formation of NATO. The Berlin crisis, coming on the heels of other East–West crises, was the immediate cause of an even more crucial Western initiative: the creation of the North Atlantic Treaty Organization (NATO). In April 1949, only weeks before the Berlin blockade ended, ministers of Belgium, Canada, Denmark, France, Iceland, Italy, Luxembourg, The Netherlands, Norway, Portugal, the United Kingdom, and the United States met in Washington. The North Atlantic Treaty that they signed there (and that came into force in July) bound each to the basic principle of collective defense: an armed attack on one or more of them in Europe or North America would be considered an armed attack on all. By signing this treaty, the U.S. had completed a revolution in foreign policy: it had irrevocably abandoned its traditional policy of no entangling peacetime alliances, and in so doing had accepted a position of power in western Europe. In its quest for security, the United States had abandoned isolationism and, as some critics charged, its commitment to universal collective security under the United Nations Charter.

North Atlantic Treaty

EAST, SOUTH, AND SOUTHEAST ASIA, 1945–57

The colonial territories of Asia. One goal of Japanese wartime expansion had been to seize control of British, Dutch, and French colonial possessions in East and Southeast Asia. The Japanese capture of Singapore, Britain's major Asian naval base, in early 1942 was not merely an important military victory; it symbolized the humiliation and overthrow of European imperial power in Asia. The Japanese conquest of the Philippines, Indochina, Burma, and the Dutch East Indies was depicted as the triumph of Asians over Westerners rather than as the act of simply another imperialist power.

Japan's war against China—which in actuality had begun 10 years before Pearl Harbor—by 1942 was stagnant. In Manchuria, the Japanese occupied and developed a major mainland industrial base; all principal Chinese seaports and major inland cities were under their control. But they signally failed to eliminate their two adversaries, the Communists and the Nationalists. These two rival claimants to Chinese sovereignty were pressed back, respectively, to Yen-an, in Shensi Province, and to Chungking, in Szechwan Province—remote bases of defiance. In China, as in Yugoslavia, the struggle in World War II was essentially triangular, involving an invading foreign power and two indigenous claimants. The armies of Mao Tse-tung and Chiang Kai-shek conserved their forces in battle with the common enemy, each anticipating the time to come when they would be left to deal with each other.

With the collapse of Japan in 1945, two major questions of great international importance appeared: the fate of former Western colonies in Asia and the fate of China. The United States immediately fulfilled an earlier promise of independence by liberating the Philippines in 1946, but this example was not followed by the Europeans. The French, Dutch, and British, seeking to restore their colonial authority, encountered resistance from indigenous nationalist forces that had benefitted politically from the four years of their rulers' absence. As a signal of change in Asia, the new postwar British Labour government under Clement (later Lord) Attlee did not subscribe to Churchill's pledge not to preside over the dissolution of the empire. By 1947 India's independence became a fact; two nations, Muslim Pakistan and Hindu India, inherited sovereignty.

India and Pakistan

With self-determination established for South Asia's most populous and influential nation, it was now only a matter of time before the principle was extended elsewhere. The European imperial powers, with great problems of reconstruction at home, hardly could have been expected to divert significant effort and resources to the reconquest of the colonies. British withdrawal proved to be more graceful than that of the French and Dutch. By 1949 the Dutch admitted the futility of trying to subjugate the East Indies, and the new state of Indonesia emerged. In Indochina, the French mounted with no decisive results a counterinsurgency against nationalist forces, including Communists under the leadership of an old pro-Soviet Comintern agent, Ho Chi Minh. By 1950, however, national self-determination had been effected in most of South and Southeast Asia. Only Europe's oldest and most backward imperial power, Portugal, neutral and unscarred by war, retained hold on its vast, scattered Asian and African possessions, testifying to the influence which, elsewhere, the war had had in accelerating independence from European belligerents.

The new India, under the parilamentary government of the Congress Party and Jawaharlal Nehru, emerged as the moral leader of newly independent Asia. While his government patterned its institutions closely upon Western constitutional forms, Nehru chose to steer an independent course for India in world politics. As the Cold War rivalry between the Soviet Union and the West intensified, Nehru announced for India a policy of "nonalignment"—a position that often was to tilt against the West and toward the new Communist states in the conflicts of the 1950s.

Civil war in China and Communist rule. The victory of Mao Tse-tung and the Communists in China constituted the most far-reaching change in Asian politics, coming on the heels of Soviet expansion in Europe. Rightly or wrongly, many U.S. statesmen and other observers in 1949 saw in this development a vastly enlarged extension of Soviet power and in Mao himself yet another Soviet puppet. As later was to become clear, however, neither Stalin nor his successors were entirely happy about this turn of events. They had dealt with the Nationalist government of Chiang Kai-shek in wartime, and Stalin was not pleased to have a new rival in the Communist movement. Yet at critical junctures in the Chinese civil war, the Soviet Union threw its weight toward the Communists. In the contest between the Nationalist and Communist forces for control of Manchuria beginning in 1945, for example, the Russians provided the Communists with arms, including those surrendered by Japanese forces.

The Chinese Communists and the Soviet Union

During the civil war in China, whatever germs of rivalry existed between Stalin and Mao in no way diluted the animus that Mao showed toward the United States. American support for the Nationalist government during and after the war, while hardly sufficient to establish that government's authority, sufficed to increase the hostility of the Communists. Halfhearted attempts by the Truman administration, in the mission of General Marshall to China in 1946, to reconcile the irreconcilable factions were accompanied by equally feeble U.S. aid to Chiang—a policy that demoralized the Nationalists and enraged the Communists.

By 1947, in fact, though the Truman administration never explicitly stated it, U.S. international resources were almost wholly concentrated on the reconstruction of Europe; as regards Asia, it was only in Japan, where Gen. Douglas MacArthur carried out occupation policies aimed at the establishment of a peaceful, democratic society, that U.S. attention was positively directed toward unambiguous results. Given the pro-Europe bias of U.S. statesmen (earlier evident in Roosevelt's wartime priorities), it hardly could have been expected that America would conduct an even-handed "war of reconstruction" on both the Asian and European mainlands. The defeat of the Nationalist Chinese forces therefore might be considered partly a consequence of American Eurocentric cultural bias as well as of intrinsic weakness of the Nationalist regime. That regime, nonetheless, American statecraft had befriended consistently—against the Germans, Japanese, British, and French—since the time of Woodrow Wilson, a half century of support for the integrity of a united China supposedly destined to be a major mainstay of peace in Asia. Pursuit of that object in the 1930s, by both Hoover and Roosevelt, had in fact led directly to Pearl Harbor in 1941. The collapse of the Republic of China was therefore especially shocking to the U.S.

The Korean War. Hard on its heels came the Korean War in 1950. After the Communist victory in China, U.S. statesmen had expected a breathing spell in East Asia. As Dean Acheson, secretary of state, put it, the United States would "wait for the dust to settle," while consolidation occurred, before considering its future relationship with China. In early 1950 it was generally assumed that the United States would do nothing to assist the remaining Nationalist forces, now reassembled in disarray on Taiwan; that the Communists would soon take over the island and complete their victory; and that then some form of diplomatic relationship between the U.S. and China would be possible. These expectations led Acheson, with the concurrence of the joint chiefs of staff, early in 1950 to depict American interest in the Far East as extending to Japan, Okinawa, and the Philippines but excluding Taiwan and South Korea.

In Korea, divided at the 38th parallel of latitude between Soviet and U.S. military occupation forces, two separate polities had been created in 1948. The possibility of peaceful reunification of the country was remote, since each regime claimed authority for the whole peninsula. While the Republic of Korea, in the south, was more broadly based than the Democratic People's Republic of Korea, in the north, and had stronger popular support, it was U.S. policy to ensure that the country not be reunified by force. In 1948–49, by agreement, both the Soviet Union and the U.S. had withdrawn most of their forces from the peninsula.

Two Koreas

On June 25, 1950, strengthened by Soviet heavy military equipment, North Korean forces invaded the south. Quickly Truman ordered U.S. forces into battle to repel aggression and successfully sought UN sanction for this decision. (The Soviet delegate, absent from the Security Council in protest against the UN's failure to admit the People's Republic of China, was not present to veto the council's decision.)

Meaning of the war. The significance of this war, in the generally deteriorating state of East–West relations at the time, was ominous but unclear, and it remains unclear. Both the role and the motives of the Soviet Union were obscure, as were those of the Chinese Communists. That the North Korean Communist leader, Kim Il-sung, miscalculated the U.S. response to the invasion of the south is fairly certain; less certain is whether or not he did so with encouragement from Moscow or from Peking. In Washington, however, the significance of this new war was not viewed in isolation from events elsewhere. Some saw it as a Soviet-instigated feint to deflect American attention and military resources from Europe, others as a Soviet attempt to enlarge its own East Asian perimeter in the direction of Japan; still others regarded it as a Soviet attempt to pre-empt Korea from Chinese control and as part of a larger design to consolidate its now waning authority in North China.

Truman's view

In Truman's mind, however, this action of aggression (as the Security Council termed it) stirred memories of analogous events in the international politics of the early 1930s. Then, when Japanese and Italian aggressive wars met with no resistance from the League of Nations or from the Western democracies, the stage was set for grosser assaults on the world order. In this view, aggression tolerated was aggression encouraged; the United Nations now was subject to the test that the League had failed, and Truman was determined that this time the principle of collective security should prevail and, in particular, that America should not repeat its earlier mistake of refusing to lend support to emerging structures of world peace and international law. The Korean War in this sense was invested with far more than its immediate significance. The fact that Truman found support for this view from all his principal advisers on foreign affairs testifies to their collective perception of America's dereliction of international duty in the interwar years.

Course of the war. Devastating as it was to the people of Korea, the war nevertheless proved to be limited, both geographically and technologically. The Americans fought it with World War II technology, without recourse to their new "absolute" weapon. The Soviet Union gave unremitting military assistance short of committing Soviet troops. Its preferred strategy, as often proved the case later, was to wage "proxy war," arming and sustaining client armies—guerrilla or conventional—while remaining in the background. But in one respect the Korean War—on the southern side—became a truly collective enterprise. While forces of the U.S. and the Republic of Korea composed the main body of military power, General MacArthur (assigned to UN command) presided over British, Australian, and New Zealand soldiers and even Turkish and Ethiopian units.

After initial setbacks, the United Nations forces in the autumn of 1950 nullified the force of the invasion. By bold landings north of and behind the main battlefront, MacArthur cut off front-line North Korean forces and by the winter of 1950–51 had forced his way far into North Korea. UN forces now pressed northward toward the Chinese Manchurian border.

For two reasons, these battlefield victories both breached the cohesiveness of United Nations support for the war and created new dangers. MacArthur's rapid northward advance challenged the assumptions of some that the UN effort was merely to restore the *status quo ante* and raised the likelihood that victory would result in liberation of the north; indeed, the General Assembly on October 7, 1950, created a United Nations Commission for the Unification and Rehabilitation of Korea. MacArthur now pursued the North Koreans toward the Chinese border on the Yalu River, and in November the Chinese, fearful of invasion, launched an attack, inflicting defeats on the UN forces and driving them southward again. Now there were two adversaries, and it was clear that without some new and major changes the war might continue indefinitely or end in U.S. defeat.

China enters the war

MacArthur's dismissal and the end of the war. Several contradictions now developed for the U.S. in its conduct of the war. In Korea, MacArthur demanded authority (which Truman refused) to carry the war to Chinese territory, blockading its coasts and bombing the "privileged sanctuaries" whence the Chinese forces made their sorties. Such action risked not only enlargement of the war but also the estrangement or defection of America's allies. MacArthur, going over the head of his commander in chief, appealed to a personal American constituency. Faced by insubordination in his command and danger of defection of support in the United Nations, Truman in April 1951 relieved MacArthur of his commands. Soon thereafter, in July, cease-fire negotiations began, with the adversaries now aligned on a battlefront nearly identical with the 38th parallel, where the war had begun. Two years of diplomatic deadlock and sporadic conflict were to pass before the final cessation of hostilities in 1953. When the war ended, the political issues that had given rise to it in the first place still remained. Korea was more divided than ever. The best that could be said was that aggression had been checked.

Two consequences of the war. The Korean War had one consequence of fundamental importance: the gulf between the United States and the Communist government of China, deep even before the war, widened during it, and the manner in which an end was brought to hostilities perpetuated it. In early weeks of the war, the U.S. interposed its 7th Fleet in the Formosa Strait, to serve the double purpose of discouraging an attack upon Taiwan from the mainland and of reducing the risk that the Nationalists themselves might set off a larger war by an attempt to invade the mainland. U.S. force was interposed between the "two Chinas," and thenceforth the Republic of China, in insular exile, became a ward of the United States, bound to it by a mutual security treaty signed in 1954. Many of America's European allies made their separate diplomatic accommodations with Peking, but the United States by its link to Taiwan continued to deny Peking's maximum territorial claims.

The U.S. and the two Chinas

A second and unanticipated consequence of the war was the transformation of the American role in Southeast Asia. The People's Republic of China, as seen in Washington, now loomed over this part of the world as Japan had earlier. Insurgent Communist movements in Indochina, Singapore and Malaysia, Burma, and Thailand seemingly presaged the advance of Communist power over the entire area. These geographically distinct movements were perceived in Washington not as isolated phenomena but as part of a correlated movement and related to all the other places in the world—Europe, the Middle East, and Latin America—where Soviet-sponsored insurgencies were manifested. In Malaysia, British forces successfully checked and ultimately defeated local Communist insurgents, bringing peace to that region. In Indochina, however, the situation was far different. There, indigenous Vietnamese nationalist forces, originally for the most part not Communist, were transformed into Communist cadres intent on imposing on Indochina a political system closely resembling that of China. Before 1950, the U.S. had supported the French only reluctantly and chiefly because the French threatened otherwise to alter their position on western European defense. After the Korean War, however, the U.S. began to see its own interests as adversely affected by the developments in Indochina. After severe reverses, culminating in their defeat at Dien Bien Phu, the French in 1954 sought a quick end to their involvement. The modalities of their withdrawal from Vietnam were negotiated with the Viet Minh, and in Indochina a new divided country came into being: in the north a harsh little Communist state and in the south an artificial and unstable Republic of Vietnam that soon was added to the growing list of America's clients. In Laos and Cambodia, similar insurgencies also stimulated American reaction. In the same year (1954), American diplomacy created the Southeast Asia Treaty Organization (SEATO), again to

Two Indochinas

exemplify American commitment to halt the spread of Communism.

THE MIDDLE EAST, 1945–57

The Middle East, like other non-Western parts of the world before World War II, had been an object of European power rivalries rather than a region of authentic independent nations. Predominantly (apart from Iran) Arabic in culture and primitive in economy, this region possessed special strategic importance. For Russia, it meant access to the Mediterranean; for the British Empire, it was a crucial link to extensive Asian possessions, particularly India; the influence exerted there by other European states, such as France, had obscure historical origins. The Holy Land held special significance to Roman Catholic, Orthodox, and Protestant Christians, as well as to Muslims, while to Jews in the Diaspora Jerusalem was the eternal focus of religious and national hopes.

For more than four centuries the conflicting European aspirations were restrained by the extensive if loosely administered Ottoman Empire. As long as the lethargic authority of Constantinople survived, it subdued parochial indigenous rivalries among its subjects, while serving as buffer to Russian expansion and permitting a complex and wary coexistence among rival faiths in the holy places of Palestine. Indigenous Arabs, once the great civilizing influence of the Mediterranean world, remained in subjection to all these influences.

The stagnant Ottoman regime, however, was not long to survive the many 20th-century pressures on it; nationalism and defeat in war broke control of the Porte in both the Balkans and the Middle East, and in 1918 the empire distintegrated. Its predominantly Arab parts, from the eastern Mediterranean to the Persian Gulf, in 1919 fell under the joint rule of Britain and France, which as victors in war seized title or informal hegemony over Syria, Palestine, Mesopotamia, and the sheikhdoms of the Arabian Peninsula. In World War I, under Gen. Sir Edmund (later Field Marshal Lord) Allenby, the British successfully awakened and exploited nascent Arab national aspirations in the war against the Turks; rival principalities became clients of the Western imperial states. Finally, in the Balfour Declaration of 1917, the British, in response to European Zionist appeals, introduced yet another element into Middle Eastern politics by endorsing the establishment of a "national home for the Jewish people" in Palestine. The post-World War I peace settlements before 1939 thus created an unstable situation in which rekindled national sentiments among indigenous peoples collided with outside rival powers. The borders of Middle Eastern territories, arbitrarily sketched by European diplomats, were as tentative and uncertain as the destinies of the peoples they held.

Balfour Declaration

The U.S. in the Middle East. The Axis defeat (1945) released in this region as elsewhere new combinations of rivals for postwar influence. One newcomer was the United States. From 1942 onward, its regional wartime influence was exercised by the Middle East Supply Centre, based in Egypt; by 1945 U.S. naval power in the Mediterranean was rivalled only by the rapidly declining British forces, and U.S. firms were exploring the oil resources of the Arabian Peninsula. The first (1943) wartime summit conference of Roosevelt, Churchill, and Stalin was held in Tehrān, unintentionally symbolizing the new importance that the Middle East was to have in world politics after the war. Western influence in the region, it became clear, would be chiefly American, even though the French and British did not withdraw immediately.

The Iranian and Turkish cases. The first postwar test between the Soviet Union and the West took place in Iran in 1946. Contrary to wartime agreement, the Soviet authorities failed to withdraw their military forces from the northwestern region, Azerbaijan, and instead installed local pro-Soviet officials and pressed the Iranian government for oil concessions. The Western response to this was immediate; on the agenda of the first regular meeting of the UN Security Council in 1946, the Iranian "case" brought a surprisingly easy diplomatic victory for the West. Soviet forces withdrew, and the Iranian government regained full authority over Azerbaijan and its oil resources. Other Soviet attempts in the immediate region were checked. Soviet pressure on the Turkish government to hand over the eastern province of Kars (which adjoined the Armenian Soviet Socialist Republic) and to establish a Soviet-Turkish condominium over the Dardanelles was met in 1946–47 by firm Western resistance. U.S. military aid to Turkey and Greece strengthened the resistance of both to Soviet threats. A three-year civil war in Greece ended in collapse of Communist forces. By 1949 U.S. power had replaced that of Britain in the eastern Mediterranean, from which the Soviet Union was firmly excluded.

Azerbaijan incident

Palestine: Israel and the Arabs. In Palestine at the same time, as British authority declined, another quite different struggle for power emerged. Since 1920, Palestine, once an Ottoman province, had been governed as a mandate under the League of Nations by the British, who found themselves caught in the cross fire between Arabs and Jews, neither of whom regarded British rule as legitimate but each of whom knew the other to be a rival for the inheritance of legitimacy. The persecution of eastern European Jews had led many of them to emigrate to Palestine long before Hitler's time; the massacre of Jews in Europe by the Nazis after 1933 increased this movement from a trickle to a flood, which greatly complicated the futile attempt by the British to maintain some form of equilibrium between the two communities. The new settlers, many of them Zionists by conviction, brought to Palestine the talents of Europeans. Their technology caused deserts to bloom; their organizational skills and national fervour exceeded those of the indigenous Arabs. Exploiting the ambiguous Balfour Declaration, Zionist leaders made the British commitment to a "national home" the basis for claim to sovereign independence. One logical possible resolution to the rival claims of Arabs and Jews was the partition of Palestine between them. Subject to attack from both sides and incapable of checking the inward flow of Jewish refugees, the British authorities referred the problem to the United Nations. But "legitimate" international partition of Palestine by the United Nations was not acceptable to the Arabs. The remote possibility of a confederal Palestinian state disappeared, and in May 1948 the State of Israel was proclaimed, embracing all the areas gained by contest of arms.

Palestine immigration

The first Arab–Israeli war was no simple civil war confined to Palestine proper. The struggle engaged the diplomacy of the two superpowers and the armies of neighbouring Arab states. The Arab League, a new, loose aggregation based in Cairo and under Egyptian sponsorship, served as rallying point for Arab resistance to Israel. Israeli battlefield victories were thus won not simply over indigenous Palestinian Arab nationalists but over an ill-coordinated coalition of Egyptian, Transjordanian, Syrian, Lebanese, and Iraqi forces.

On this one issue, for quite different reasons, the governments of the Soviet Union and the United States found themselves on the same side. Soviet support for Zionism and then for the new Israeli state arose from a wish to exploit British losses in the region and to exacerbate local conflicts. (At that time, the Soviet Union enjoyed little influence in the Arab world; Communism was anathema to orthodox Muslims and particularly to the conservative, traditionalist regimes in Iraq, Transjordan, Saudi Arabia, and the emirates on the Persian Gulf. Awakening Arab nationalism was centred on literate and economically advanced urban dwellers who had no admiration for the Soviet Union.)

The United States' response to this crisis was divided. American diplomats sought to maintain normal ties with the Arab states, partly because of the newly found oil resources of Arabia and partly because the anti-Soviet bias of Arab regimes seemed to promise future containment of Russian influence in the region. In this view, the Arab–Israeli conflict was at best an unnecessary distraction and at worst a dangerous threat to Western purposes. On the other hand, there was strong public sentiment in the U.S.—confined to neither political party and widespread through all regions—in favour of Zionist aspirations for an independent state, which for the most part was welcomed also by the American Jewish community. This American sentiment was nourished both by the now wholly revealed spectacle of Hitler's genocide policies and by the new image of Jews heroically rebounding from the threat of their destruction as a people.

Recognition of Israel

The Soviet Union and the United States both recognized Israel immediately. President Truman was influenced in his decision to do so by political considerations; with an election campaign before him and with his popularity at a new low, Jewish support was essential. That Republicans failed to make this an issue against him in the ensuing presidential campaign was further sign of the state of American thought on the subject.

With both the superpowers supporting the new state, and with decisive Israeli victories in the field, the United Nations suceeded in imposing an agreed cease-fire; there was peace of sorts as the new state consolidated itself and the Arabs, smarting, regrouped. None of the Arab states would recognize Israel's sovereign legitimacy; all, including the most moderate, went on record as favouring its destruction. Large numbers of Palestinian Arabs, many of whom had been persuaded by Arab governments to abandon their homes, crowded into refugee camps, wards of United Nations agencies, prostrate and hopeless. Neither Israel nor Arab governments accepted responsibility for their plight; the perpetuation of these camps and the refusal of Arab governments to resettle and assimilate their inhabitants provided a continuing irritant.

Nasser and the Suez crisis. More than any other single element, the Arab humiliation by Israel quickened the pulse of Arab nationalism. In Egypt, Syria, and Iraq, new political forces arose against more traditionalist leadership, exploiting military defeat as evidence of political weakness and corruption at home. The new forces, because of European and American support for Israel, took a new, stronger anti-Western position. In Egypt, in 1952, a coup of army officers overthrew the old government; King Farouk fled into exile, and in 1954 Col. Gamal Abdel Nasser emerged as the first "populist" leader of the Arab world. Nasser, who saw himself as the logical leader of pan-Arab forces, destined to bring unity and full independence to the region, was not without rivals in other Arab states. His anti-Western speeches were echoed by revolutionaries challenging the traditionalist regimes in Iraq and the Persian Gulf and the moderate pro-Western King of Jordan. The Soviet Union, for its part, came to see Egypt under Nasser's leadership as the place to begin its Middle East penetration. In the mid-1950s the first shipments of Soviet arms to Nasser took place, via Czechoslovakia.

Soviet arms to Egypt

Nasser began his attack on surviving vestiges of European control by nationalizing, in July 1956, the Suez Canal Company, an act that had far-reaching consequences. U.S. plans to give assistance in the construction of Nasser's favourite project, the Aswān High Dam, were abandoned, while the Eisenhower administration, under John Foster Dulles' leadership, sought to devise a new international canal regime acceptable to the Egyptians, the French and British governments (principal stockholders in the nationalized company), and the canal's principal commercial users. These conciliatory plans collapsed. Without the knowledge of the U.S., the British and French governments began preparations to seize and reoccupy the canal by force. In concert with them, the Israelis, long tormented by Egyptian forays, launched (October 29) an invasion of Egypt, the two European powers suddenly making an appearance in the canal zone to reassert control of the waterway.

Both Eisenhower and Dulles, furious at this surreptitious Anglo-French aggression, condemned the Suez expedition as a violation of the UN Charter. The British and French retreated in humiliation from Suez. Under heavy diplomatic pressure, the Israeli Army withdrew from its advance positions, and a new cease-fire line was drawn to separate Arabs from Jews in the Sinai Desert, this one supervised by UN peacekeeping contingents.

The principal architects of this second Middle East peace—Dulles, UN Secretary General Dag Hammarskjöld, and UN General Assembly Pres. Lester Pearson—were to hail it as another triumph of universal collective security. But UN peacekeeping forces now interposed between Arabs and Jews in Egypt were placed and remained there only on the sufferance of Nasser. (They were to remain for 11 years, until Nasser in 1967 peremptorily dismissed them and a third round of war began.) The humiliation to Britain and France hastened their decline as European powers and increased the prominence of the United States.

The Suez crisis and that in Hungary, which took place in the same year (see below), revealed an emerging double standard in the United Nations. Under the moral tutelage of Nehru's India, in 1956 many new non-Western UN members were quick to condemn actions of Western colonial powers but reluctant to deplore the Soviet Union's actions in Hungary.

THE CONTINUING COLD WAR

The Korean War, itself a major event in world politics, also had important effects on the domestic policies of the superpowers. Before 1950, the United States had reduced its military forces to skeleton peacetime proportions. Though it was the chief founder of NATO, it had virtually no military force in Europe. The original U.S. monopoly on nuclear weapons had ended when the Soviet Union successfully tested an atomic bomb in 1949. Superior to the Soviet Union in naval and air power, America retained some of its historic geopolitical assets as a protected hemispheric power, while far inferior to the Soviet Union in land forces. The Korean War provoked U.S. debate over future strategies and disposition of American military forces. Yet whatever outcome that debate took, the U.S. Congress and public now sanctioned vast increases in defense budgets, as they were to continue to do until the eary 1970s. The draft, scheduled to expire in June 1950, was extended and revitalized.

The U.S. policy of containment. An intellectual catalyst in the debate was an American foreign service officer, George F. Kennan. One of a small band of U.S. diplomats with extensive experience in Moscow and eastern Europe, Kennan in July 1947 published a seminal article, "The Sources of Soviet Conduct," in the American journal *Foreign Affairs,* in which he addressed the major issue confronting U.S. postwar policy: what strategy should be adopted in the face of Soviet expansion and pressures to expand? Faced with an adversary whose view of the world was suspicious and belligerent, said Kennan, the U.S. should steer a course intermediate between craven withdrawal and outright war. His formula—the vigilant containment by counterforce of Soviet power at a constantly shifting series of geographical and political points—called for a high degree of flexibility and alertness. Rejecting the idea of a "rollback" of Soviet power, Kennan nevertheless held forth the notion of the United States as principal and resolute deterrent of further Soviet encroachments. In time, he predicted, spontaneous internal changes might bring to power more moderate Soviet leadership or might even result in revolutionary collapse. In suggesting such possibilities, Kennan was at pains to point out the limitations on the actual power the Soviet government had at its disposal. "The hardships," he wrote, "of their rule and the vicissitudes of international life have taken a heavy toll of the strength and hopes of the great people on whom their power rests."

Kennan's view

Kennan's article clarified the perceptions that many Americans had of the situation their country faced; "containment" became the organizing slogan around which subsequent policies developed. But not surprisingly it elicited strong criticisms as well. John Foster

Dulles denounced it as amoral, in that it accepted Soviet rule of "captive nations," holding out no prospects for their liberation. The political writer Walter Lippmann pointed out that containment easily could dissipate and dilute U.S. influence, by stretching it indiscriminately around the entire Soviet Union, entailing equally indiscriminate engagements with any kind of client state, however corrupt or unimportant, that found itself subject to Soviet threats. Kennan himself later, in the 1960s, was to say that theorists had read into his prescriptions meanings that he never intended.

Lippmann's view

The late Truman administration. One view that figured in the U.S. debate over foreign policy in the early 1950s was that offered by a coalition of American former isolationists and air force enthusiasts. For them, U.S. air supremacy suggested a policy of "hemispherism." They were opposed to the stationing overseas of U.S. ground forces and, in particular, to the maintenance of U.S. forces in Europe, since the cost would weaken the American economy and since nuclear power gave the U.S. the capacity to deter or punish Soviet aggression.

The views of Truman (and later Eisenhower) differed radically from those of the "Fortress America" advocates. Truman's strategy became that of posting U.S. forces alongside those of allies, in both Asia and Europe, to be visible witness to American commitment. Moreover, both Truman and Eisenhower cultivated a range of formal alliances in Europe, Asia, Oceania, Latin America, and the Middle East. In addition to NATO (1949) and the Southeast Asia Treaty Organization (1954), the U.S. signed alliance agreements with Australia and New Zealand (the ANZUS pact; 1951); pressed for closer hemispheric ties under the Inter-American Treaty of Reciprocal Assistance (also called the Pact of Rio; 1947); and in the Middle East sponsored but did not join the Baghdad Pact (1955). After the signing of the Japanese peace treaty in 1951, the U.S. undertook the guarantee of Japanese security; in 1954 a mutual defense treaty bound it to the Republic of China on Taiwan. Its evolving, though informal, commitment to Israel became perhaps a firmer link than explicit ties were with other states. Having once avoided alliances with any nation, the U.S. now had alliances worldwide. The tension among these commitments, and the reconciliation of sets of urgent priorities, posed dilemmas for U.S. policy makers. But the central assumption in each set was that American security required intimate U.S. involvement in the areas of the world out of which threats to security might arise; the successful control and management of local crises would prevent their growth.

New U.S. alliances

The Eisenhower years and McCarthyism. The death of Stalin in 1953, nearly coinciding with a new Republican (the first Eisenhower) administration, marked the end of one chapter in the Cold War. The two transfers of power meant changes in both American and Soviet domestic politics. The new Republican emphasis on fiscal conservatism, however, was not reflected in U.S. expenditures on defense, nor did the Republican administration significantly change foreign policy. More moralistic than his predecessor, Acheson, Dulles as secretary of state employed slogans that alarmed some of America's allies ("massive and instant retaliation," support of "captive peoples," etc.) but carried forward the general lines of policy that a Democratic administration had inaugurated. As a gesture of appeasement to right-wing elements in the Republican Party, however, Dulles launched a purge in the Department of State, directed chiefly at "old China hands" accused of holding "soft" views on Communist China. In the nation as a whole, something of an anti-red hysteria already had been under way in Truman's last two years in office. Sen. Joseph R. McCarthy of Wisconsin became the symbol if not the leader of a coalition of disparate anti-Communists, to many of whom the setbacks to freedom in the world were as much the consequence of American failures as of Soviet successes. According to their view, Roosevelt at Yalta had betrayed eastern Europe into Soviet bondage, American diplomats in Washington and abroad had connived in the triumph of Mao Tse-tung, Communists and fellow travellers in high American office (such as Alger Hiss, Harry Dexter White, and others) were not merely spies but symptoms of the left-leaning of the New Deal. This militant right wing saw in worldwide Communist gains the hand of American statecraft; a chief target, among many, of their attacks was Dean Acheson, whose refusal to condemn Hiss was taken as evidence of his own guilt. McCarthy charged the administration with harbouring as many as 205 Communists in the State Department (a number which he evidently invented), and Truman's refusal (on grounds of executive privilege) to divulge contents of loyalty files was seen only as confirmation of such charges.

The U.S. militant right

The new Republican administration was no better able to fend off these domestic attacks than its predecessor had been. The moderate internationalism of Eisenhower proved to be almost as intolerable to the militant right as that of Roosevelt and Truman. As chairman of a special Senate subcommittee, McCarthy interrogated high administration officials in hearings that divulged no new evidence of Communist influence but that besmirched the reputations of many innocent Americans. That Communists had played a sometimes influential role in New Deal reform and in wartime Washington was a fact well known to many liberals and labour union officers who had fought them and who with equal vigour now fought McCarthy. The two trials of Alger Hiss—a former diplomat accused of Soviet espionage and finally convicted (1950) of perjury—put, as a British commentator then wrote, a "generation on trial," dividing unrepentant Communists and fellow travellers from liberals and former Communists whose illusions, if any, about the Soviet Union had been shattered by events.

Abroad, the anti-red hysteria in the U.S. was exploited by Soviet propaganda, which now vividly depicted America's conversion into a Fascist police state. The conviction (1951) and execution (1953) of Julius and Ethel Rosenberg as spies for the Soviet Union became cause for worldwide anti-American demonstrations; campaigns were waged, in Europe and elsewhere, against America's nuclear power, NATO, the rearmament of Germany, and U.S. repression of "popular" movements and support of "corrupt and repressive" regimes.

The Rosenbergs

De-Stalinization. Stalin's death and the advent of a new Soviet leadership resulted within three years' time in noticeable though hardly basic changes in the character of the Soviet regime. Always suspicious of his colleagues, Stalin in his last years showed increasing paranoia and isolation. The KGB reigned unchecked, its chieftain, L.P. Beria, in constant attendance on Stalin. With Stalin gone, the new Soviet leaders turned on Beria, who was arrested, tried, and executed in a move that displayed an alliance of Communist Party leaders and the army against the secret police. This was a harbinger of great relaxation in Soviet domestic terror; during the late 1950s, many thousands whom Stalin had sent to forced labour camps were quietly released and rehabilitated. In 1956 N.S. Khrushchev, in a speech at the 20th congress of the Communist Party of the Soviet Union, denounced the former dictator for his despotic acts, his shortcomings as statesman and military leader, and his self-glorification in the "cult of personality." Thenceforth Stalin's name was erased from Soviet public memory; the national hymn, a panegyric to him, was suppressed; Stalingrad was renamed Volgograd; Stalin's embalmed body was removed from its honoured spot next to Lenin's, and statues of him were torn down.

Unrest among the satellites. De-Stalinization had electrifying consequences in the Communist world. The removal of some of Stalin's supporters from party and government posts in eastern Europe set in motion a crisis of legitimacy for Soviet rule. As early as June 1953, long before Khrushchev's speech, abortive uprisings had taken place in East Germany. Outside the sphere of direct Soviet rule, de-Stalinization had the further effect of encouraging what the Italian Com-

Communist polycentrism

munist Party leader Palmiro Togliatti now referred to as "polycentrism"; rule of the world Communist movement from Moscow, challenged since 1948 by Tito in Yugoslavia, was now seriously defied. Throughout the Communist world, a complex struggle began between "liberalizers" and "national Communists," on the one hand, and conservatives and "Stalinists" on the other. If there was more than one "road to socialism," as Tito said, the prospect of disintegration of the Communist world was very real. By October 1956 these events culminated in Hungary in a supreme test of both Soviet authority and Communist legitimacy. A popular uprising in Budapest (led by a coalition of workers, intellectuals, and students similar to that in the first uprisings against tsarist authority in St. Petersburg in 1917), coinciding with the Suez crisis, overthrew the Communist regime, and a Western-oriented government under Imre Nagy came to power.

There were limits beyond which even "national Communists" would not go in this crisis. Both Tito and the Chinese now condemned the Hungarian uprising, as did Communist parties of the West. In early November, Soviet tanks moved into Budapest, reimposing Soviet control. Any hopes for liberation that might have existed in the satellite countries were dashed.

NATO and European economic recovery. These eastern European events had little effect on the East–West configuration of power. Throughout the 1950s, as western Europe's economic recovery proceeded, so also did its political and military position improve. The Marshall Plan encouraged moves toward European economic integration. In Rome in 1957 the European Economic Community was established and with it a European Common Market for most of western Europe (but not including Britain, reluctant to break economic ties with the Commonwealth). NATO, originating as a classic alliance of sovereign national entities, developed under U.S. leadership a strong infrastructure of command and control. Under an American commander, the air, naval, and land forces of the U.S., Canada, Britain, and their continental allies were coordinated. Although attempts to establish an integrated European army under a European Defense Community, and thus to make use of West German contingents under control of an all-European command failed, the Federal Republic of Germany joined NATO as a full partner, with its own national military units. The United States in 1951 sent six combat-ready divisions to Germany, to act as a visible deterrent to Soviet forces in eastern Europe. In a military version of Kennan's containment policy, the U.S. Air Force established air bases around the Soviet Union. NATO forces remained greatly inferior in numbers to those of the Soviet Union and its satellites, but in the mid-1950s tactical nuclear weapons were introduced in advanced Western positions, vastly augmenting Western firepower.

Coordination of NATO forces

The deployment of tactical nuclear weapons had the effect of blurring the distinction between unconventional (*i.e.,* nuclear strategic) and conventional (non-nuclear) weaponry. Such a distinction, in the minds of some military analysts, was critical; for one thing, there was the ever-present danger that in Europe as elsewhere a local conflict, arising by deliberation or accident, might expand, transcending the political purposes of either combatant. So long as a clear "firebreak" between non-nuclear and nuclear weapons was maintained, and the latter were firmly controlled by the highest political authority (in this case, the president of the United States), unintended nuclear war, set off in the heat of battle by theatre commanders or their deputies, could be prevented. Yet there was logic in deployment of tactical nuclear weapons. The governments of the West displayed no enthusiasm for matching, in numbers, the ground forces of the Soviet Union, which would have made claims on their societies that probably would have been rejected. Nuclear weaponry in the West thus became a relatively cheap substitute for manpower.

Soviet response. The Soviet Union now found itself reacting to rather than acting upon quickly changing European events. Its diplomatic and propaganda campaign to prevent the establishment of a West German state and West German rearmament had had the effect of hastening what it was designed to prevent. Soviet threats provided incentive for the consolidation of NATO and the European Economic Community, approved in western European parliaments by wide majorities. In all of western Europe, Communist parties, while still strong in France and Italy, showed no promise of commanding electoral majorities except in some municipalities. Their identification with the purposes of the Soviet Union enhanced their reputations as parties with divided allegiance.

Efforts to disrupt Western integration having had opposite effects, the Soviet Union resorted to imitation. In 1949 it promulgated its own German government, the German Democratic Republic, in the Soviet zone; in 1955 it established the Warsaw Treaty Organization, its version of NATO, incorporating under Soviet command all eastern European Communist states except Yugoslavia; in 1949 it established the Council for Mutual Economic Assistance (Comecon), an eastern European variant of the Marshall Plan, to integrate the economies of the satellite states with its own.

Thus by the late 1950s two Europes faced each other, displaying vivid contrasts in life-style, level of economic development, and degree of human freedom. Severe constraints on the movement of persons across national boundaries were enforced by Soviet authority not only on the borders of East and West but on those separating eastern European states. Only in Berlin—where it was still possible to move freely from the Soviet sector to Western sectors—was there an opportunity for eastern Europeans to escape life under totalitarian rule. Here, many disaffected East Germans found an escape route; since many of them were highly valued professionals, their departure in growing numbers was not only a constant cause of mortification to the new East German regime but also an intellectual and economic loss that could not be tolerated indefinitely.

Flight of East Germans

The problem of nuclear energy. By 1946 it was apparent to the whole world that the control of nuclear energy constituted in many ways the most important problem facing the human race. During World War II, both the United States (in concert with Britain and Canada) and the Soviet Union had embarked on programs of nuclear development, scientists in each country being fully aware of the great military implications of atomic energy. But the United States, the first to develop and use an atomic bomb, for the first four years of the postwar period enjoyed a monopoly of what some called the "absolute" weapon.

From the outset, however, there was widespread disagreement, even among specialists, as to what should be done to control the use of atomic energy to prevent planetary destruction. Some, looking to the time when America's monopoly would end, pressed for an international agreement to establish supranational controls to prohibit the use of atomic weapons. Others urged continued nuclear development to guarantee a commanding lead by the United States over its most likely nuclear rival, the Soviet Union. Some pessimists, particularly within the American scientific community, asserted that "the bomb," unless its use was effectively prohibited, would mean the destruction of civilization itself. For some, the new situation called for a leap to world government.

In 1946 the U.S. government, in an initiative which its nuclear monopoly permitted, advanced the first proposals for international control to the United Nations Atomic Energy Commission. The Baruch Plan, so-called after its chief American sponsor, Bernard Baruch, entailed establishment of an international agency with authority over the production of fissionable material and the licensing and supervision of peaceful nuclear facilities. No nation could possess nuclear weapons or the means to build them. The vital feature of this plan was its provision for stringent international inspection of national industrial sites and authority to punish infrac-

The Baruch Plan

tions of the agreements. Whether or not this radical proposal would ultimately have been accepted by the U.S. Senate and the American people will never be known. The Soviet Union immediately rejected the plan's inspection and control features. As in later negotiations over arms control, the Soviet authorities regarded the principle of international inspection as subversive of national sovereignty and the Baruch Plan as an instrument of espionage. They proposed as an alternative an international treaty, with no inspection features, to prohibit the production of nuclear weapons and to require the destruction of existing stocks.

This impasse was never resolved. Instead, technology revealed further possibilities: the refinement of nuclear weapons, resulting in smaller devices and in a truly awesome hydrogen device that was capable of releasing in each blast more energy than all the conventional explosives discharged in World War II.

During the years of its nuclear monopoly, the U.S. government was at a loss as to what to do with this addition to its arsenal. The very existence of the bomb in American hands magnified the country's international prestige. It early became clear, however, that whatever else the atomic bomb was, it was hardly an "absolute" weapon. In the first years, to begin with, there were actually very few such devices at the disposal of the United States, and they were no match for the vast conventional ground forces with which the Soviet Union could easily overrun western Europe. In addition, the very crudeness of this huge weapon made its use in battlefield conditions difficult to imagine. Furthermore, the power of nuclear weapons for destruction was so great that the ruin caused by a nuclear explosion might, in theory at least, transcend any political ends that it was intended to further. Thus the classic view of war, first enunciated by Carl von Clausewitz, as the extension of politics "with an admixture of different means" might be subverted and war become an exercise in purposeless destruction.

In any event, the successful Soviet testing of a nuclear device in 1949 brought an end to American sole possession. By 1950 the central nuclear energy issue in the U.S. was whether to proceed in the development of the fusion-type hydrogen bomb. The decision was affirmative.

The hydrogen bomb

In the deliberations concerning the hydrogen bomb there was less than unanimous agreement among U.S. nuclear scientists. The physicist J. Robert Oppenheimer (called the father of the A-bomb for his wartime supervision of the Los Alamos Scientific Laboratory) led the opposition to the superbomb as chairman of the General Advisory Committee of the U.S. Atomic Energy Commission. Some of his opponents, gaining access to information about Oppenheimer's wartime private life and personal idiosyncrasies, succeeded in 1953 in having him removed from his post as a security risk. The "Oppenheimer case," coming as it did at the height of McCarthy's depredations, gravely split the American scientific and intellectual communities, at the same time raising questions about the U.S. government's internal security program and about the right of principled dissent in the government itself. Under the direction of another physicist, Edward Teller, the program was completed and a hydrogen bomb was successfully tested in late 1952, in the Pacific. A similar Soviet blast, in Siberia, followed in mid-1953.

The Soviet "peace" campaign. Lagging behind the U.S. in the development of nuclear weapons, the Soviet Union in Europe, particularly in Italy, France, and Britain, worked to inspire neutralist and anti-American sentiment. Every Soviet satellite government, each Communist party, and countless front organizations had as an object the depiction of the United States as the home of Fascists, imperialists, and warmongers. In this activity, the Soviet authorities recruited many Western intellectuals to the cause of "peace" and an assault on American imperialism. Fear, frustration, and revulsion at prospects of nuclear war were moods to be exploited in the West. Parallel campaigns were mounted within the Soviet Union to display the "solidarity of the masses" in progressive and peace-loving sentiment. In 1950 the Stockholm Appeal, initiated by Frédéric Joliot-Curie and presented by the Partisans of Peace, claimed the signatures of 273,470,566 persons, including the entire adult population of the Soviet Union. In the West, this document embarrassed many public figures; to refuse to sign it would be to appear opposed to peace, to sign it would be to further Soviet foreign policy.

The balance of terror. By the mid-1950s, what Churchill described as a balance of terror came to characterize the relationship between the two superpowers and their allies. When the Soviet Union on October 4, 1957, launched the first artificial Earth satellite, Sputnik 1, the impregnability of North America to attack from overseas may be said to have come to an end (though the Sputniks themselves were of course unarmed). An unstable and dangerous relationship came into being, characterized as a reciprocal "first strike capability." By pre-emptive surprise attack, one of the superpowers might annihilate the other's vulnerable nuclear strike force. What some also came to call the "arms race" now was fully under way. Ever-larger rocket missiles, with ever-increasing range, were built on both sides of the "iron curtain." In the late 1950s, U.S. intelligence concluded that a "missile gap" favouring the Russians existed between Soviet and American intercontinental forces. Measures were undertaken promptly to narrow the "gap." The Americans now diversified their military forces; after Hiroshima, the U.S. nuclear delivery system had consisted of a bomber force, stationed at bases throughout the world, some in close proximity to the Soviet Union. Thenceforth U.S. power came to rest upon a "triad" composed of manned bombers and intercontinental and submarine-launched ballistic missiles (ICBM's and SLBM's). ICBM's, housed in hardened underground silos, were shielded from all but direct hits; SLBM's had the advantage of both mobility and stealth.

Sputnik 1

While the technological advances consequent on the arms race resulted in the acquisition of enormous capacity for destruction by both sides, some of these advances led to greater stability in the relationship. The protection afforded each side by silo hardening diminished the temptation of a "first strike"; now, according to U.S. analysts, the test of reciprocal stability lay in the possession of a "second strike capacity"—a force surviving a theoretical "first strike" sufficient to devastate the first striker. It was this that lent credence to Churchill's formulation; the balance of terror became in itself a pillar of peace.

Recognition of common mortality began to dawn on the two superpowers. In Stalin's time, Soviet theoreticians continued to propound the doctrine of the inevitability of war as a necessary consequence of contradictions inherent in the capitalist system and as the midwife of revolution. Major war favoured the "progressive forces" in world history. This doctrine was now challenged by a problem deriving from thermonuclear realities: how could Soviet socialism prosper if the industrial base necessary to it were destroyed by enemy attack? Soon after Stalin's death, his successors began to back away from the theme of war as inevitable; even in capitalist systems, it was suggested, forces were at work to hold warmongers in check. Khrushchev reinterpreted official doctrine and began to speak of "peaceful coexistence." Henceforth, nuclear war was bad; wars of national liberation in peripheral areas remained good. This reinterpretation of Marxist–Leninist doctrine by the Soviet leadership produced the first overt conflict between Stalin's heirs and Lenin's Chinese apostle, Mao Tse-tung, who denounced them as revisionists.

Soviet revisionism

France as a nuclear power. The new stalemate between the superpowers had a particular effect on America's relationship with its western European allies. From the outset, the linchpin of the NATO alliance was not merely an American military guarantee but an American nuclear guarantee of European defense: certain U.S. reprisal in event of Soviet attack. This was called deterrence. But America's own continental invulnerability had disappeared. Was it to be supposed that an American president under these changed circumstances would risk American cities to honour a European commitment? This Achilles heel of the Atlantic alliance was first pointed out by a French officer, Gen. Pierre Gallois; the dissemination of doubts thus inspired served now to justify a new development that somewhat shook the NATO alliance: France would develop its own nuclear weaponry; America now had a competitor as nuclear guarantor. Thus the early signs of Sino-Soviet conflict were matched in the late 1950s by signs of Franco-U.S. rivalry, and both owed their origins, at least in part, to the awesome questions to which nuclear power had given rise.

The Austrian treaty and the German problem. In the mid-1950s appeared a few indicators that some East–West issues were susceptible to negotiated settlement. The most important diplomatic development came in 1955, when the Soviet Union agreed to an Austrian peace treaty, entailing Austria's neutralization and the withdrawal of occupation forces. In the United Nations, a deadlock concerning admission of new members was broken, permitting client states of each superpower to enter.

But the central issues of contention remained unresolved, chief among them the German problem. At summit and foreign ministers' conferences, East and West conferees repeated endlessly their incompatible proposals for a German peace settlement and a new order in Europe. In 1955 the Western powers advanced their German formula: creation through free elections of a unified and sovereign Germany, with which a peace treaty would be negotiated; several different plans were offered to prevent the rise of militarism again in the country, and the Western powers would guarantee the Soviet Union support against future German acts of aggression.

German reunification

This proposal was of course rejected. The Soviet authorities were unwilling to subject their East German satellite state to the test of free elections, which it certainly could not survive. Instead, displaying an interest in "European security" rather than in Germany, they proposed the dissolution of military blocs and withdrawal of foreign (*i.e.,* U.S.) troops from Europe proper (Soviet troops, being European, would remain). This proposal was unacceptable to the West: the dissolution of NATO would have the effect of eliminating the West's defense infrastructure; the dissolution of the Warsaw Treaty Organization would not mean loss of the Soviet Union's control of satellite military forces. Even if Soviet and American forces were withdrawn from Europe, the Russians would merely retire behind their borders; the Americans would withdraw across 5,000 miles of ocean.

III. The period since 1957

THE GREAT POWERS AND THE WORLD

The Korean War and the postwar recovery of Japan both drew attention to the growing importance of East Asia in world affairs. Yet the two superpowers' interests continued to confront each other most acutely in Europe and the Atlantic region. The two blocs—NATO and the Warsaw Treaty Organization—owed their *raison d'être* to the special conditions of Europe, and from the perspectives of the Soviet Union and the United States all other geographic areas and their special problems were subordinate. Europe had lost its paramountcy in world politics, but it retained its position as the central zone of rivalry. The North American–European zone (now with Japan added) also remained the world's industrial core and the chief zone of world commerce in manufactured goods. Europe and North America contained (apart from Japan) the world's most prosperous nations. Although Khrushchev had said that the Soviet Union would overtake the United States in industrial and agricultural production in a period of competitive coexistence, the Soviet gross national product continued to lag far behind the American. Only in the machinery of warfare did Soviet technology rival that of the West. Inefficient Soviet agriculture even by 1953 had failed to recover the level of production it enjoyed in 1913, the last peacetime harvest of the tsarist regime. Whatever international reputation the Soviet planned economy had once enjoyed now gave way to a new image as an awkward bureaucracy, deficient in new technology and incapable of meeting the elementary consumer wants of an advanced industrial nation. The per capita income of two of the Soviet Union's eastern European satellites, Czechoslovakia and East Germany, greatly exceeded its own.

Postwar economic growth. The superior performance of Western economies was further demonstrated by the fact (knowable only in retrospect) that they now enjoyed a period of uninterrupted growth. Prewar classical economists had virtually taken the business cycle for granted; economic activity, it was thought, occurred in phases of prosperity and depression. But in the years after World War II, only minor and brief recessions (such as that of the mid-1950s) took place. Most Western governments also avoided both uncontrolled inflation and high unemployment. In fact, in most Western societies the avoidance of high unemployment was a primary objective of national policy.

The consequence of all this was that the postwar period saw very great improvement in the material conditions of human life. No better indicator of this could be found than the decline of infant mortality and increased life expectancy in nearly every country of the world. While, for example, Liberia had not seen its first automobile until 1938, by the late 1960s its capital city, Monrovia, enjoyed traffic jams. In advanced societies, growth—and the expectation of more of it—had the political consequence that struggles over distributive justice were mitigated by a pervasive optimism. The result of this was a period of prosperity the duration and nature of which the world had never before witnessed. Between 1948 and 1973 the world gross domestic product increased by more than three times, at a world rate of more than 5 percent per annum. Even the very poor countries shared in this increase, though at a much lower rate.

Material conditions of life

U.S. economic dominance. This worldwide boom occurred in an international framework that reflected United States economic paramountcy and marketing practices. Leaving aside the Communist countries, whose state trading practices continued to be autarkic and bilateral, the international market economy was truly multilateral. The U.S. and other major trading nations were mindful of, and avoided, practices that in the past had exacerbated the Great Depression of the 1930s. The unilateral attempts of each in the 1930s to "export depression" had led to mutually debilitating tariff wars and self-defeating competitive currency depreciation. The U.S. in 1930 had legislated the Hawley–Smoot Tariff, the highest in American history, at a time when foreign indebtedness and a favourable trade balance should have dictated opposite action.

Economic reasons did not alone account for the profound postwar reversal of U.S. economic policy. American statesmen, with the perspective of years, regarded the prewar lapse of the world economy into autarky as a major cause of World War II. Even though it is conceivable that New Deal protectionist policies on balance may have served the American economy well, such practices had led other states, Japan in particular, to abandon the international market economy in favour of aggressively imposed spheres of regional economic dominance. Thus under U.S. leadership the postwar world structure of trade and finance was deliberately grounded on institutions to facilitate multilateral trade expansion, currency stability, and international capital investment.

Postwar U.S. economic policy reversal

Aside from the Communist states, whose share of international trade was insignificant, some nations enthusiastically accepted this new order, others rejected it. Japan, whose Greater East Asia Co-prosperity Sphere lay in ruins, became one of the world's chief beneficiaries of the new internationalism, its manufactures of high-technology consumer goods penetrating all Western markets. Some Latin-American nations, led in the late 1940s by Argentina, steadfastly resisted this liberal internationalism, preferring instead to rely upon mercantilist policies to conserve foreign exchange and foster internal economic development. Yet by and large the new international economic order, managed chiefly by the United States and its Western partners, dominated the world. The U.S. dollar became the world's monetary standard. New multinational firms, most of them American, emerged, some, such as General Motors, with an annual output exceeding the GNP of most sovereign states. While there were limits to the extent of U.S. political influence, it could not be denied that in economic matters a Pax Americana now ruled the world.

A question to which these developments gave rise was whether America's global political and economic reach was (as Marxists alleged) designed to sustain the capitalist world order or whether the latter was a by-product of the former. One little noticed feature of America's relationship to the world economy was its own constancy. In these postwar years, the ratio of U.S. foreign trade to its gross national product remained almost exactly what it had been in the pre-depression years, little more than 4 percent. This modest figure attested to the fact that the country itself was still a vast, self-contained economic system. Furthermore, America's chief trading partners, and the locales of most U.S. foreign investment, still were its neighbour Canada, Japan, and the nations of western Europe. Such economic interests as the U.S. had in what were now euphemistically called less developed (or underdeveloped, or developing) countries were chiefly concerned with primary products. Returns on U.S. investments in all of Asia (except Japan) in the late 1960s were scarcely larger than the annual operating budget of the University of California. While U.S. private investment in areas such as Latin America was exploitive, U.S. capital in general increasingly came to prefer locales of proved political stability, more so as many regimes in Latin America and elsewhere in the underdeveloped world harassed and expropriated foreign direct investments. If U.S. profit margins in some backward areas were significantly higher than elsewhere, so were the risks.

U.S. foreign investment

The American business community in fact exhibited ambivalence about the new U.S. political role in the world. In the 1940s, for instance, important segments of business were strongly noninterventionist; the isolationist America First Committee in 1941 was chiefly financed by Midwestern industrialists. Important spokesmen for American business, such as the National Association of Manufacturers, remained protectionist in the 1940s long after Roosevelt and Truman began to change tariff policy. Conservative politicians representing important business interests, such as Sen. Robert A. Taft, had fought the Marshall Plan and the stationing of U.S. troops in Europe. To such conservatives at that time, U.S. overseas expenditures were seen as crippling the economy and speeding the drift toward state socialism.

Other business interests, notably banking and the automobile industry, were more disposed to support an activist, international foreign policy, though subtle differences of opinion underlay their world view. Their chief *raison d'être* was profit, and this was not always or necessarily congruent with political purposes and strategies as conceived in Washington. If the Arabian American Oil Company (Aramco) had dictated U.S. policies in the Middle East, Israel probably would have been abandoned. Many U.S. corporations could easily put ideological considerations aside in their eagerness to join in the development of the Soviet economy. For its part, Washington did not always support the interests or aspirations of U.S. firms overseas; often also, as subsequent Central Intelligence Agency (CIA) revelations were to show, it made use of business for political purposes.

Profit versus political purpose

The anomaly in the relationship of the U.S. to the world economy lay in the fact that a relatively self-sufficient America presided over an emerging interdependent international system. The fraction of its trade with the outside world remained insignificant in proportion to its internal transactions; yet such was the sheer size of American industry, in relation to that of the rest of the world, that it had a profound effect internationally. As often in the past, such supremacy provoked not only fear and respect but also envy and dislike. As "Yankee imperialism" in Latin America had been exploited in the 1930s by the Axis powers and their local political supporters, now it was seized upon by Marxists for much the same reasons. As the world's dominant economic power, America inherited the opprobrium that historically had been attached to all imperial powers.

Decolonization. In the years that followed the Suez crisis of 1956, the great European empires were dissolved, leaving behind a throng of new sovereign states and a loose, inchoate aggregation called the Third World (*i.e.*, nations distinct from both the developed West and the Communist bloc). The Third World derived an uncertain identity from the facts of its relative poverty and backwardness; its previous subjection to Western rule; its fate to lie for the most part in inhospitable tropical regions; and its non-Caucasian ethnic composition. Little else made the Third World an aggregation; the new nations born of decolonization had in other respects little in common. Their independence—in most cases won bloodlessly, almost effortlessly, and in great haste—gave rise to a throng of little-anticipated problems. In giving up authority to the new regimes, the main European colonial powers wished to leave as legacy a permanent imprint of their good intentions and the better features of their civic cultures; they were to be disappointed.

Decolonization (leaving aside the Portuguese empire, certain Spanish African protectorates, and many small islands) was chiefly accomplished in the 1960s. In the early phases, the European powers had hoped to retain close association with their former colonies. The British, for instance, hoped that the Commonwealth of Nations, a loose association under the crown, with close economic ties and shared sympathies for constitutional government, would provide a bond of unity with the former mother country. The French had somewhat bolder aspirations for a loose confederal relationship; some of their colonies, such as Algeria, they regarded as organic parts of the metropole. The Belgians and Portuguese were more obdurate. The latter—whose colonial establishments in Asia and Africa long antedated those of the other European nations—actually regarded their possessions as bound in perpetuity to the home country. Unlike the British and French, the Belgians and Portuguese made no plans for even gradual devolution of authority, and when they finally relinquished their hold, they did so abruptly, leaving anarchy behind. The Russians, with a vast, contiguous, and polyglot Asian empire, maintained the fiction of a multinational union of republics. The Stalin constitution of 1936 (and its successor in 1977) specifically provided for the right of secession, but all national forces that Soviet authorities perceived as moving in this direction were crushed.

The Soviet Asian empire

The Soviet Union and national liberation. The Soviet Union nevertheless regarded "national liberation" as a major objective of the Soviet state and the Communist Party of the Soviet Union and its worldwide clients. In the early 1920s Lenin had developed the guide for Comintern activities in European colonial areas: to weaken the capitalists' hold on their empires and thus their hold on the metropoles of Europe. This strategy frequently entailed Communist collaboration with "bourgeois-nationalist" forces in colonial areas; once independence had been achieved, these forces could be eliminated.

In the postwar period, the Soviet Union identified, inspired, or created clients in colonial areas, providing them with funds, material, and training to wage war against imperialist forces or successor regimes. After 1949 China joined with Moscow in these colonial ventures, but as rivalry between the two nations intensified they became rivals in fostering guerrilla-type movements, notably in Southeast Asia but in Africa as well. These adventures for the most part met with little success in predominantly Muslim countries, where religious beliefs were inconsistent with Marxism. But protracted guerrilla wars in many places served Soviet purposes by weakening the European powers at home and, as in the case of France in Indochina, sometimes creating intolerable domestic political turmoil.

These wars of "national liberation," however, presented a certain dilemma to the Soviet Union. Soviet foreign policy always had operated on two levels: that of state to state and that of party to party. Considerations of state were not always reconcilable with the ideology of revolution. Stalin had subordinated the Comintern to state purposes, even, as Trotsky pointed out, betraying revolution when this was expedient. In Soviet activities in the "emerging nations," the dilemma took the form: should Soviet policy concentrate on cultivating good relations with predominantly non-Communist new regimes, or should it persist in subversion in the hope of transforming them into Marxist systems? Further, too belligerent policies could damage state to state relations with colonial powers with which good relations were desired. This last point was exemplified in Soviet postwar dealings with Gaullist France; France being a useful adversary of British, U.S., and German elements in NATO, there were always certain limits to the extent that the Soviet Union might wish to offend it.

Two levels of Soviet foreign policy

There was no way in which the Soviet authorities could resolve this dilemma. In practice, they constantly readjusted ideological with state-to-state components of foreign relations. (For insurgency and wars of national liberation, see further below, *Consequences of the Sino-Soviet rift in other parts of the world.*)

The new states: nonalignment and domestic problems. For the most part, independence was attained by Asian and African states in smooth devolution of power, though sometimes (as in India in 1947) devolution led to violent upheavals and conflicts among contending liberated forces. For the most part, the new nations did not choose Marxism or alignment with the Soviet Union in the Cold War. Following the example of Jawaharlal Nehru in India, many of their leaders explicitly chose "nonalignment" in the East–West struggles. Wishing to legitimate domestic authority by evoking an image as hero in anti-Western struggles, however, more than one of them came down against the West on many international issues. Nehru's minister of defense and ambassador to the UN, V.K. Krishna Menon, exemplified this bias; quick to condemn Western powers' policies when these offended his conscience, he remained quiet in the face of such actions as the Soviet invasion of Hungary.

Nonalignment

With important exceptions, the new political leaders of the Third World found their most pressing problem to be that of staying in power long enough to consolidate statehood. The new regimes faced formidable domestic difficulties. India had been particularly fortunate in that a century of direct British rule had seen the gradual construction of an edifice of Indian self-government and the establishment of a reasonably effective civil service and of an impressive military organization. Indian statesmen were schooled in parliamentary government, and the dominant political party, the Indian National Congress, was a Western-style, constitutional party, tolerating opposition and allowing and enforcing free elections. Finally (despite internecine struggle between Muslims and Hindus, which reached a violent peak after the partition into India and Pakistan), India had a historical identity as a great civilization.

Few of the other new states shared these advantages. In Africa and the Middle East, their borders were artificial contrivances of the European colonial powers, having little relevance to indigenous tribal realities. The chief task, then, of the new rulers of most of these countries was to establish a condition and sense of nationhood where none existed before; and, in particular, to compose the relations among competing ethnolinguistic and religious groups. All too frequently, as in the Middle East, new, synthetic nationalisms territorially based on European administrative districts became sources of rival factions aspiring to create new empires. In sub-Saharan Africa, most of the new leaders, aware of the fragility of their territorial claims, prudently checked any temptation to alter them. Thus, for instance, when the Nigerian authorities fought the secession of Biafra in the late 1960s, all but four African states either supported the Nigerian government or remained silent.

Synthetic nationalism

One difficulty for leaders of many of these new states arose from the fact that they were nationalists without nations. Most were European-educated; they viewed their role as that of nation builders; with few resources at their disposal, they for the most part wished to modernize their countries. But all this meant the risk of estrangement from the peoples they sought to govern. To reinforce their authority, most of them reached outward for technical assistance and material help and frequently became dependent on non-African or non-Asian governments for the military force necessary to subjugate domestic rivals. Themselves among the most Westernized of their people, they found an anti-Western position to be a means of linking themselves with their people, the better to accomplish the goal of modernization. These regimes often were overthrown and replaced, increasingly, in Africa particularly, by military juntas or dictatorships of one sort or other. By the early 1970s there were few Western-style parliamentary governments left in Africa. By that time also, India and Japan were the only significant non-Western states whose governments were based upon constitutional norms, and in India in the mid-'70s constitutionalism was jeopardized.

Aid programs for developing nations. Many non-Western nations derived substantial benefits from the Cold War. Beginning in the early 1950s, the U.S. government came to recognize the political influence that foreign aid might have on the orientation of the new states. Flushed with the economic and political successes of the Marshall Plan in Europe, some U.S. theoreticians now felt that development assistance to new states would inspire them to resist Communism and to "move into the 20th century" as national economies compatible with U.S. interests. There was also, however, a strong element of humanitarianism in the American technical and economic aid program. As President Truman in his *Memoirs: Years of Trial and Hope* (vol. 2, 1956) later said of his Point Four program for aid to underdeveloped countries, "The alternative, as I saw it, was to continue to allow those vast areas to drift toward poverty, despair, fear, and the other miseries of mankind which breed unending wars." But humanitarianism was not a strong enough basis for the large sums the U.S. Congress annually authorized for these programs. Aid became one of the U.S. weapons of influence, and the chief beneficiaries were those states most directly threatened by Communist aggression or subversion. Though much of it was purely military, U.S. aid had a significant effect on the economies of many new states as well as the nations of Latin America. Many economists based their support for aid programs upon the assumption that the appeal of Communism would diminish as non-Communist governments successfully made the transition to truly modern economies.

Functions of U.S. aid

The new nations were quick to realize the benefits to be derived from this aspect of the Cold War. The Soviet Union also introduced aid programs, though they were considerably more selective and smaller than their U.S. counterparts. The competition in aid programs of the two superpowers was most clearly exemplified in 1956, when the U.S. abandoned the Aswān High Dam project in Egypt; the Soviet government swiftly stepped into the breach, and from that time till Nasser's death Egypt was a client of Moscow and U.S.–Egyptian relations were strained.

The Russians were more solicitous than the Americans, however, of the need of some Third World leaders for outward and costly displays of authority. For Sukarno in Indonesia they constructed a sports coliseum; for Kwame Nkrumah in Ghana they built a palace big enough to house all African chiefs of state and their retinues. U.S. aid programs tended to reflect a desire for gradual development, those of the Soviet Union a preference for heavy industry. In India, with Soviet support, steel mills arose; U.S. aid to that country, in contrast, consisted mainly of grain. The monumental character of many such Soviet donations made them more conspicuous than their American counterparts and thus compensated somewhat for their smaller quantity. Both the U.S. and the Soviet Union developed educational and cultural programs, bringing thousands of young non-Westerners to study in their colleges and universities.

The Third World as a zone of conflict in the Cold War. The Third World, while remaining peripheral to the central theatre of Cold War contention, became a subsidiary zone of the conflict. In parts of it—Malaysia, Indonesia, Indochina, and the Congo, for example—it became impossible to separate the indigenous from the external sources of conflict; civil conflict was enmeshed in larger international issues. In Malaysia, a long internal guerrilla war in the 1950s and early '60s (ultimately won by government forces) was an ethnic struggle between Malays and Chinese, but it was much more a war between Communist and anti-Communist forces.

Indonesia

In Indonesia before 1965, manoeuvrings among contending political and military forces involved civil versus military, separatist versus centralist, ethnic group versus ethnic group, and religion versus religion, yet here, too, world politics entered. President Sukarno at first managed to play off various foreign influences against one another; subsequently he joined forces with the Chinese Communists, conceiving a military adventure against Malaysia and cosponsoring an international organization to rival the UN, the New Emerging Forces (Nefo). But in 1965 he was overthrown, and thousands, perhaps hundreds of thousands, of Indonesian Communists and resident Chinese died at the hands of Indonesian mobs.

In the Belgian Congo (now Zaire), the Belgian colonial authorities departed abruptly in 1960, leaving a chaotic situation. A civil war ensued. Western powers supported a multinational United Nations force, which saw its function as that of creating order by lending support to a new central government. But its authority was defied both by separatist Katangese rebels (aided by European mercenaries) and by forces under the leadership of the former prime minister and radical nationalist Patrice Lumumba. The war created at least two martyrs; Dag Hammarskjöld died in an airplane crash in the Congo, and Lumumba was murdered, probably by the Katangese. Ultimately, after great loss of life, the authority of government was asserted.

Indochina

The war in Indochina was the most protracted of all non-Western conflicts save that in the Middle East. Here the struggle involved internal and external forces in many complex ways, though by the early 1950s it was clear that the principal juxtaposition was that in Vietnam between French and French-led local forces and the Communist forces of Ho Chi Minh. Ho's forces, well disciplined and persistent, wore down the morale of the French. At home, French public opinion, weary of any form of war and especially of this one (which had been going on since 1946), by the 1950s became unwilling to tolerate continued French involvement. After one major and symbolic Communist victory at Dien Bien Phu in 1954, a new French government under Pierre Mendès-France went to the conference table in Geneva (where settlement of the Korean War was also on the agenda). The resulting Geneva Accords created two provisional Vietnamese regimes, Communist in the north and non-Communist in the south, separated by an internationally supervised demilitarized zone at the 17th parallel of latitude; within two years, general elections were to be held and the nation was to be reunited. The Geneva Accords were a victors' peace; the signatories were the respective French and Viet Minh military commanders. The non-Communist (South) Vietnamese delegation present at Geneva not only refused to sign but protested the French intrusion in political matters. These military–political accords were nevertheless sanctioned by the great powers of both East and West, except for the United States, which, however, had an observer at the signing ceremonies. A provisional peace of sorts came into being, and, though almost from the beginning the new Communist regime began to infiltrate armed cadres into the south, it lasted until 1960. At this point the Hanoi leadership, its control of the north consolidated, could devote its attention to the south. (The renewed war, with U.S. participation, is discussed below under *Areas of conflict: Southeast Asia.*)

Latin America in the Cold War. In Latin America, on January 1, 1959, a new element entered the Cold War in the Third World when the Cuban dictator Fulgencio Batista, his regime weakened by corruption and by withdrawal of U.S. support, fled the country, leaving it to insurgency forces commanded by Fidel Castro. Little was known of the political nature of Castro's guerrillas, but their leader's defiance of the dictator and his forays against Batista's forces in the mountains of eastern Cuba gained him an international reputation as a kind of Robin Hood. He presented himself as a populist democrat, denouncing tyranny and demanding a new constitutional order with free elections and civil rights. In power, he proved to be otherwise, quickly purging his movement of democratic elements. Streams of refugees flowed out of Cuba, mostly to the United States, where they formed a community always ready to do what it could to undermine the new Cuban regime. The refugees included a large fraction of Cuba's professional classes, whose departure deprived the nation of many needed skills, but among them also were persons from all walks of life, holding many political views.

Fidel Castro

By nationalizing hundreds of millions of dollars worth of U.S. property, Castro antagonized the United States, which in 1960 reduced the quota of sugar imported from Cuba, in January 1961 broke off diplomatic relations, and during 1961 established a total trade embargo.

Castro's rise to power came at a time when "polycentrism" had introduced an element of nominalism into Communist affairs. Latin-American Communist parties, including that of Cuba, had been among the most orthodox in the world, but the Soviet Union, unwilling to offend the U.S. unduly, before Castro's appearance had behaved with prudence in the Caribbean. U.S. intervention in Guatemala in 1954 to crush the left-wing government of Jacobo Arbenz, for example, had been accepted by Moscow. Now, Castro announced himself to be a convinced Marxist–Leninist, and Cuba became a centre for Communist subversion throughout Latin America. By the end of 1961, 13 countries in the Americas had broken relations with Cuba, which had established relations with most governments of the Communist bloc.

By the time that Pres. John F. Kennedy was inaugurated, plans were being made in Washington to launch a movement to remove Castro from office. These ended ignominiously in the late spring of 1961 in the Bay of Pigs disaster; an invading force of about 1,500 Cuban refugees from the U.S. landed on the south coast, and a few days later the survivors surrendered. Washington's refusal to provide air cover or other direct military assistance doomed the ill-conceived invasion to failure; the conviction that it would provoke mass uprisings proved to be wholly unfounded.

This disaster represented the severest shock to American international prestige thus far in the Cold War, and it cemented the already close relationship between the Soviet Union and Cuba. Further, Castro's moral triumph over Yankee imperialism echoed throughout Latin America. The Kennedy administration quickly moved to strengthen ties elsewhere in the hemisphere, launching a new multinational cooperative venture, the Alliance for Progress, and increasing counterinsurgency assistance to Latin-American governments. Through the Organization of American States (OAS), the Kennedy administration took measures against Rafael Trujillo, the dictator of the Dominican Republic, which led to the diplomatic isola-

The Alliance for Progress

tion and overthrow of his regime, to his own assassination (1961), and to the establishment of a (short-lived) liberal regime in 1963.

Despite these efforts, the U.S. could not free itself from its reputation as a supporter of right-wing juntas, a reputation which Communist propaganda nourished and which in fact had some basis in reality. Any liberal administration in Washington faced a fundamental policy dilemma: it could, as in the Dominican Republic, use the mailed fist and impose democracy, thus enhancing its reputation as an imperialist power; it could let right-wing dictators rot by neglect and risk another Castro; it could tolerate and even support right-wing regimes, thus checking Soviet expansionism while reinforcing its own reputation as a sponsor of Fascism. The Kennedy administration chose its Alliance for Progress formula as a benign reformist venture to try to overcome these perplexities; but they remained. The fact that authentic democratic forces were weak throughout Latin America was as intractable as the fact that the giant shadow of the U.S. over the continent made it seem culpable for anything bad that took place.

The Berlin Wall and the Cuban Missile Crisis. In Vienna, in the spring of 1961, Khrushchev and the new American president met for the first time, a meeting that proved to be tense and inconclusive, the two issues of Berlin and Cuba being prominent at the time. Talking of West Berlin's "abnormal" status in Europe, the Soviet Union had been working to "normalize" the situation, while threatening to turn over all authority over Berlin to East Germany, repudiating joint four-power authority over the city as a whole.

The Berlin Wall

During the night of August 12–13, 1961, the East Berlin authorities, with Soviet sanction, threw a barbed-wire barricade (later replaced by a wall) along the Soviet sector line, sealing off the western sector of the city. The intended effect of this action, against which the Western powers merely protested, was to close the one remaining loophole in the chain of fortifications by which Communist authorities insulated the peoples of eastern Europe from the West. Through that loophole countless numbers of East Germans had escaped to the West. With the loophole closed, only the most courageous persisted in attempts to escape. Hundreds were killed by East German police as they sought to penetrate the barrier, and a few succeeded.

In the early autumn of 1962, unconfirmed reports reached Washington of hasty Soviet construction of military bases in Cuba. The Soviet government, when asked, denied that these were offensive missile sites, but subsequent U.S. aerial reconnaissance confirmed that they were. The presence of Soviet nuclear bases only 90 miles from the United States was unacceptable to the U.S. government. Rejecting proposals of either invasion of Cuba or destruction of the bases from the air before they became operational, President Kennedy chose instead to place a naval cordon around the island, to prevent entry of Soviet vessels carrying missiles; at the same time he demanded that the missile bases be removed. In publicly revealing this decision, Kennedy presented to the Soviet Union a *fait accompli* and an ultimatum; Soviet vessels already were approaching Cuba. Kennedy, in announcing the air–naval "quarantine" on October 22, stated that the object was to secure the withdrawal of the bases from the Western Hemisphere. The launching of any nuclear missile from Cuba against any Western Hemisphere nation, he declared, would be regarded as "an attack by the Soviet Union on the United States requiring a full retaliatory response upon the Soviet Union."

For nearly a week a fearful world waited to see how the Soviet Union would respond. One thing was certain: in this nuclear confrontation the United States enjoyed great superiority; it had twice as many intercontinental ballistic missiles as the Soviet Union had; its Polaris missiles carried on nuclear-powered submarines, now operational, and its Strategic Air Command ruled out the possibility of a successful Soviet "pre-emptive strike." Sino-Soviet relations now were so strained that there was little possibility that the Chinese would come to the aid of their former ally. Moreover, the Soviet Union's reputation as a participant in international society was so damaged by the revelation of the bases that few, even among the world's neutralists, would lend support, moral or otherwise.

Khrushchev's capitulation

On October 28 Khrushchev agreed to dismantle the bases and to permit UN inspection to confirm compliance. The danger of a thermonuclear war was over; for a week, however, the leaders of the Communist and non-Communist worlds had gazed into a maelstrom. Mortified by the disclosure of its military inferiority, the Soviet Union was thenceforth to intensify its efforts to attain military parity with or superiority over the U.S.

Some consequences of the missile crisis. Whatever else this experience taught the Russians and Americans, it brought to the attention of both the faulty communications link between Moscow and Washington; the impossibility of direct and immediate communication between the two leaders had enhanced the possibility of unintended war as a consequence of misperception and miscalculation. In 1963 the two superpowers remedied the situation by establishing a "hot line" teletypewriter link.

In Cuba, Fidel Castro apparently took the Soviet capitulation to be a sign of weakness. Thereafter, while not antagonizing the Soviet Union, he turned also toward China for support. Cuban subversive activities in Latin America also increased, to the degree that in mid-1963 a committee of the Organization of American States recommended that stern countermeasures be taken. In general, a consequence of Cuban-subsidized insurrectionist movements was to push many Latin-American regimes further to the right; the overthrow of Juan Bosch's democratic experiment in the Dominican Republic (1963) was evidence of the reaction.

Quemoy–Matsu affair

Sino-Soviet relations. During 1958 the People's Republic of China had intensified its attacks on Nationalist-held offshore island bases, bombarding Quemoy and Matsu and risking war with the United States. The Soviet Union's refusal to be drawn into this dangerous affair was interpreted by the Chinese as indication of betrayal and cowardice. Khrushchev's behaviour in the Cuban Missile Crisis of 1962 confirmed Peking's view.

The sources of Sino-Soviet rivalry were many. Some were ideological; others arose from a steady accumulation of slights and grievances, many of them long concealed from the rest of the world; some arose from ancient border disputes; some were ethnic. Taken together, they created a serious conflict between two great powers.

Moscow had lent the new Chinese revolutionary regime military, economic, and technical aid in the early 1950s. Stalinist ideas of design were to be seen in the heavy and sombre buildings that arose in Peking, in monuments, in colossal placards and rallies; Stalinist also were the outpouring of propagandist literature and the cult of personality that came to surround Mao, and the party–state structure in China closely resembled that of the Soviet Union. Many outside observers concluded in 1949 that the Communist triumph in China represented another Soviet victory. The unity that Peking and Moscow displayed during the Korean War, and the lengths to which the Russians went in their sponsorship of China's application for membership in the UN, strengthened the impression of solidarity; a formal alliance in 1950 cemented what appeared to be a *de facto* comradely relationship.

The relationship withered during the 1950s. The Soviet Union had never been willing to tolerate a coequal in the Communist world, as the rift with Yugoslavia had shown. But Tito was far less of a challenge than Mao. China was not a small Balkan country but a vast civilization of half a billion people. To some extent also Communist Party dogmatists had succeeded in stigmatizing the Yugoslav Communists as "revisionists" who had betrayed revolutionary goals; the stigma became more credible when Yugoslavia in the 1950s accepted U.S. military and economic aid.

China and Stalinism

Moscow was soon to be stung by the same accusations; Peking after Stalin's death persisted in a Stalinist orthodoxy that was unpalatable to the new Soviet leadership. China, for instance, viewed with growing contempt the first signs of Muscovite revisionism on the issue of the inevitability of war (see above, *The postwar years, 1945–57: The continuing Cold War: The balance of terror*). Faced by the post-World War II realities of nuclear power, the new Soviet leadership came gradually to reject that basic tenet of Communist revolutionary theory. Mao, on the other hand, in many of his speeches showed no such fear of nuclear disaster. The doctrinal rift widened after 1956, when Khrushchev denounced Stalin and the "cult of personality." Even when their break with the Soviet Union took on a strong anti-Russian cast, the Chinese leadership continued to revere Stalin alongside Marx and Lenin; pictures of him figured prominently in Chinese celebrations, and his tracts continued to be issued by Chinese printing houses.

To ideological friction were added more mundane sources of conflict. In its occupation of Manchuria, the Soviet Union had stripped North China of much of its postwar industrial base by removing industrial plant and railroad equipment, actions resented by the Chinese. Clumsy in their administration of aid programs, the Russians offended Chinese recipients. The Soviet Union also was reluctant to assist its ally in development of nuclear weapons. In 1960 it abruptly withdrew all technical advisers and cancelled all Soviet development programs in China. Previous Soviet "peaceful" nuclear assistance, however, had made it possible for the Chinese to develop a nuclear bomb, the prototype of which was successfully tested at Lop Nor (Lop Lake, in the Sinkiang Uighur Autonomous Region) in 1964. By then, relations had so disintegrated that the event gave rise to a new concern: China could actually pose a military threat to Soviet security.

A further source of conflict meanwhile arose over the long and in places quite indeterminate border shared by the two states. Tsarist 19th-century expansion into Asia penetrated territories once claimed as part of Ch'ing China, and the new Chinese regime was not pleased at Soviet hegemony over these areas. Accordingly, both countries began attempts to win the allegiance of ethnic groups and nationalities living on the borders. In Moscow the concern was purely Russian nationalist. Russian settlement in Eastern Siberia, remote from and only tenuously connected to the Russian heartland in the West, was scattered and thin. Attempts to encourage "pioneers" to settle these territories (the Virgin and Idle Lands Campaign) were not particularly successful; an inhospitable climate and geographic remoteness discouraged even the boldest settlers. Now, Russian observers viewed the contrast between the sparse population of their Asian realm and the multitudes of Chinese across the border. In 1961 the Soviet Union began public polemic against the Chinese point of view, shattering the pretension of a single Marxist–Leninist world view.

Public Sino-Soviet rift

Consequences of the Sino-Soviet rift in other parts of the world. The worldwide effect of the Sino-Soviet quarrel was to divide national Communist parties into pro-Moscow and pro-Peking movements, competing for constituencies. In western Europe, the parties for the most part maintained their affinity to Moscow; the loyalty of the eastern European Communist regimes (other than those of Yugoslavia and Albania) was little affected. Albania, however, became an enclave of Maoism in the Balkans.

The effects of the party division were most evident in the Third World, where it was manifested in doctrinal clashes over strategy and tactics. Funds and material assistance flowed from Moscow and Peking to their respective clients. Nor was the division limited to a confrontation between purely Soviet and Maoist factions. In Ceylon, for instance, a dominant Trotskyite party managed to insinuate itself between the two camps. China succeeded to some extent in establishing itself as the friend of the impoverished Third World masses. An Asian–African Conference planned to be held in Algiers in 1965 was disrupted when the Chinese argued for the exclusion of the Soviet Union because it was neither African nor Asian. Quarrels between pro-Soviet and pro-Chinese groups in the same year nearly wrecked a World Peace Congress convened in Helsinki.

Certain Third World states drew comfort from the Sino-Soviet quarrel by more closely aligning themselves with the one least threatening to their interests. (India, for example, once a sponsor of Peking, in 1962 found itself waging border war with China on the Himalayan frontier; thereafter, it associated itself more closely with the Soviet Union.)

India and China

It might have been supposed that the non-Communist world would derive advantage from these developments. Communist forces in some countries were weakened by fragmentation. The United States' fears of a renewed general East Asian war with the two giants diminished. North Korea now wavered uncertainly between its two sponsors. In Japan, the division of the Communist Party into two rival wings reduced its prospects of electoral successes.

In other respects, however, the rivalry had the effect of animating the worldwide activities of Communist movements. A historical parallel could be drawn between the Sino-Soviet rift and the rift in Christendom occasioned by the Protestant Reformation in the 16th century. The Reformation had divided Europe into warring camps and provoked generations of passionate and inconclusive warfare; yet it also had served to enliven the spirit of Christians in both camps and to enhance the proselytizing zeal of both. So it was now with the legatees of Marxism.

Since both Peking and Moscow sought to dominate what each regarded as wars of national liberation in the colonial and former colonial areas, their rivalry often found expression in support of contending liberation forces or in competition for a single one. Their competition strengthened indigenous Communist forces. Both Peking and Moscow wished to avoid any accusation of insufficient revolutionary enthusiasm, and thus their rivalry often caused an increase in the scale and scope of conflicts in the Third World. Each established its own training schools for subversion and insurgency in which nationals of many countries could receive instruction. Each exported technical advisers to assist in the conduct of guerrilla wars. From Southeast Asia to Latin America, the effects of this competition were felt.

Counter-insurgency

The major Western powers responded by establishing programs of counterinsurgency, struggling with insurgents for the allegiance and active support of local populations. The revolutionaries employed a mixture of terror and propaganda, exploiting grievances and linking them to theories of human poverty, the sources of which they found in colonialist exploitation, in monopolistic patterns of landholding, and in the interlocking directorates of Western imperialists and their local lackeys. In these contests, the practices and doctrines of Mao Tse-tung usually proved more appropriate to insurgents than those of the Soviet Union. Mao's strategy, until the last phases of the Chinese civil war, had involved the encirclement of power centres; the capture of the village preceded the downfall of the city. His battle plan emanated from the countryside; it was a patient warfare of attrition, designed to wear down the will of the opponent and also to incite him to acts of indiscriminate retaliation that would alienate the population. More traditional Marxist–Leninist revolutionary strategy emphasized the city; the cadre that Lenin and later Stalin identified as the bearer of revolution was the urban proletariat. The Soviet model was European, derived from the examples of revolutionary France in 1789, from the Commune of Paris of 1871, and from St. Petersburg in 1917. Mao's was more recent and more appropriate to the economically backward and relatively nonurbanized Third World. Mao's revolutionary was the peasant, not the steelworker; the visible enemy was the landlord, not the factory owner. The successes of rural insurgency in Cuba and Algeria lent further credence to his views.

Third World insurgency in the 1950s and '60s, however, did not owe its occasional successes solely to Soviet and Chinese support. In many instances the roots were entirely indigenous; furthermore, the evident anti-Western animus in many revolutionary uprisings obtained much of its intellectual armament from the West itself. Some postwar insurgent movements—*e.g.*, that in Algeria—not only were not Communist but derived moral and material support from the West.

The United States did not invariably find itself on the side of counterinsurgency movements. In some zones of conflict, it displayed ambivalence born of conflicting motives and interests. In Algeria, for example, where the French waged a protracted and ultimately unsuccessful war to retain control, Washington early judged the French position as probably hopeless and surreptitiously made advances to the rebel forces. In the 1960s the U.S., mindful of Portugal's critical importance to NATO security, lent military support to the Salazar regime while covertly supporting anti-Portuguese rebels in Africa; hundreds of young Angolan rebels, for instance, were brought to the U.S. for university education.

In any event, the sentiments of important American political leaders, including Kennedy and Nixon, were anticolonial. Kennedy, when a senator in the late 1950s, had delivered a speech favouring Algerian independence, and Nixon as vice president courted the Tunisian leader Habib Bourguiba. American action in these colonial matters often operated on two levels, the Department of State supporting the colonial powers as its European allies, and U.S. covert organizations supporting anticolonial forces in attempts to gain friends for America in the postcolonial period.

THE LESSER POWERS

Peace in postwar Europe. The 1950s and '60s have come to be characterized as the time of the Cold War, but this designation is not entirely appropriate for postwar Europe. Outside the contentions of the superpowers and the confrontations of NATO and the Warsaw Treaty Organization, new configurations of order arose in Europe that resulted in a curious anomaly. While Europe remained the focus of rivalry, it experienced no war; conflict raged in Asia, North Africa, and the Middle East, but Europe was generally peaceful, the insurrections in eastern Europe in 1953 and 1956 being brief and localized. Tranquillity characterized the relations among European states as well as their domestic political conditions.

By comparison with the 1930s, there was a certain orderliness in the politics of the European states, once the necessary postwar reconstruction had been accomplished. Much of this could be attributed to the fact that the "strategic" matters affecting the destiny of Europeans were no longer in their own hands but in those of two essentially non-European powers. The long rivalry between France and Germany had been over the question of which would dominate Europe, an issue that no longer had meaning. In eastern Europe, subjection of the historically combative national states to Soviet domination meant an end to the contentions between Poles and Czechs, Hungarians and Romanians, and so forth, that had been typical in the early part of the 20th century. Divided Germany itself need no longer be feared by its neighbours. Europe's historic issues now were subordinated to much more comprehensive issues that were mediated, ultimately, in Washington and Moscow. The Cold War imposed on Europe two orders where historically there had been many.

There were other reasons for the tranquillity of Europe, however. In a sense, the Hitler period represented for Europeans the peak of chauvinistic nationalism. No one European nation had had a monopoly on this cultural blight; even the peaceable Czechs had once shared in it. But Hitler had pushed nationalism to its furthest limits, to genocide; the memory of Hitler and Nazism now served as an enduring reminder to Europeans of the possibilities that lay in the singleminded fanaticism of national pride. The Nazi concentration camps had contained representatives of all the nations, parties, and religions that Nazism had proposed to subjugate or eliminate; they remained as memorials to postwar Europeans of the solidarity that shared fear can inspire. In no postwar European country did Nazism or any of its several non-German variants survive as a political force.

Chauvinistic nationalism

Integration movements in western Europe. Centrist parties constructed the new Europe. Early postwar leaders such as Robert Schuman of France, Alcide De Gasperi of Italy, and Konrad Adenauer of West Germany, embodying a new European spirit, were architects of new institutions of European cooperation. All of these statesmen were Christian Democrats, Catholic moderates, and their prominence in the movement toward European integration showed the revived influence of Roman Catholic internationalism. Their chief opposition parties at home, the Socialists, also came to accept the ideal of European unity. For differing reasons, Charles de Gaulle (and Gaullism) in France, successive British governments, and western European Communist parties resisted these new tendencies, but they could not halt them. The chief French proponent of a united Europe, Jean Monnet, favoured its construction gradually and functionally, in a kind of technocratic progressivism. In his view, integration should proceed by steps, linking European states together ever more tightly by pragmatic bonds, avoiding the sensitivities of national sovereignty and achieving the ultimate political goal, as it were, by the back door.

Jean Monnet and European unity

Stalin and his successors played an indirect role in these events. The presence of Soviet power in central Europe and the fears aroused over the Berlin issue convinced non-Communist Europeans that they faced a common peril. But in addition the Soviet government and the Communist parties of western Europe attacked the idea of a united Europe and proposals to give it organizational life, seeing in these moves links with Western military integration and U.S. power. Intermittent threats from the Kremlin reminded Europeans of their vulnerability and of the way in which their disunity contributed to it.

Forms of integration. Moves toward integration took many forms. Advocates of unity stressed that continuation of European influence in world politics required broad integration, amalgamating the economic, political, and military resources of all the nations. Progress was greater in economics and politics than in military matters. The proposal to establish a European Defense Community (EDC), with a European army into which new German forces could safely be incorporated, was defeated when the French National Assembly rejected it in 1954. But progress in economic cooperation was steady. The French and German governments in amalgamating their coal and steel resources laid the groundwork for a European Coal and Steel Community, which in turn was the basis for the comprehensive European Economic Community, the EEC. In Rome in 1957, six major European nations joined to establish the international legal basis for a Common Market, the essential purpose of which was the gradual lowering of restrictions on the movement of capital, manpower, and goods among them. Britain, reluctant to join this new organization, joined with six other continental states in the European Free Trade Association (EFTA).

The EEC

In Strasbourg the skeletal form of a European political community was to be seen in the establishment of the Council of Europe in 1949. At that time, it was an object of the French and other continental governments to establish a kind of European parliament with considerable freedom of expression. The British, however, still reluctant to enter Europe, insisted that any European assembly be kept under strict governmental control. By a resulting compromise, a governmental committee of ministers and a Consultative Assembly were set up, composed of national representatives chosen by either the government or the national parliament.

Pro and con on European integration. Centripetal and centrifugal forces contended in these European developments. In each country, there were economic interests that would be affected one way or another by free trade and the free movement of labour and capital. In each country also there were forces fearful of the political consequences of, as there were others eager to press forward toward, a "new Europe." German Socialists initially feared that the Common Market would be dominated by big business. In France, Gaullist opposition to the European community played on patriotic themes. Insofar as de Gaulle was willing to subscribe to any conception of a Europe transcending France, it was a *Europe des patries,* a Europe of sovereign nations; and this Europe, to him, extended as far as the Ural Mountains to include historic Russia.

Britain and Europe

The British ambivalence was exemplified by Churchill's vacillation on the subject. As leader of the Conservative opposition, Churchill in a speech in Zürich on September 19, 1946, called for political action directed toward European union. Back in power as prime minister in 1951, however, he refused (as the Labour government had) to join Britain with any system of political federation, common market, or purely continental scheme for European defense such as the proposed European Defense Community. British reluctance to associate more closely with Europe sprang in part from the persistence of traditional insularity from continental affairs, but practical contemporary interests also counselled the country to remain aloof. For one thing, the government cherished its special relationship to the United States, which in wartime had reached an extraordinary degree of intimacy. Close Anglo-American cooperation in military matters sustained Britain's declining international influence; sentimental attachment to the English-speaking world in turn overlapped with British ties to the Commonwealth of Nations, which were of a practical economic nature as well. Not until much later, in 1973, under another Conservative government, was Britain finally to enter the Common Market.

Attitudes among the continental European states toward Great Britain in Europe varied according to rivalries for prestige and influence. Smaller nations such as The Netherlands welcomed British participation as a counterweight to German power and Italian political instability; West Germany saw the British as moderating French influence; France under de Gaulle viewed Britain's entry as the Trojan horse of an Anglo-American conspiracy, while post-de Gaulle France later welcomed it as a balance to an increasingly strong West Germany.

Gaullism. De Gaulle's return to leadership in France in 1958 had a powerful negative effect on all the processes of European integration. He assumed power during a period of domestic upheaval and instability magnified by emotions generated in the Algerian war, and he reorganized France's political system to strengthen executive authority. The shabby record of the postwar Fourth Republic, with its constantly rising and falling governments, gave way for a time to stable constitutional order under the Fifth Republic, largely reflecting de Gaulle's own quasi-monarchical conceptions. Ending the Algerian war by conceding Algerian independence (1962), which won him the enmity of important elements in the French Army, he brought peace to France for the first time since 1939. He then turned to European affairs.

De Gaulle and European unity

Gaullism affected the new Europe in contradictory ways. Having brought peace to France, a condition essential to western European stability, de Gaulle set himself on a course of resistance to both Atlantic and European integration. Unalterably opposed to U.S. power in NATO affairs, he turned also against the "Eurocrats of Brussels" who, in his view, managed the Common Market in defiance of the popularly responsible European governments. In 1966 he abruptly withdrew France from NATO's collective defense forces and expelled NATO headquarters from France. He did not actually withdraw France from the alliance as he defined it but rather sought to restore the NATO treaty to what he viewed as its essential purpose: an alliance of sovereign, independent states. In his travels across the Continent, he continued to talk of *Europe des patries,* taking this message to Warsaw, Bucharest, and Moscow as well as to the capitals of western Europe. Again, the consequences of his statecraft were contradictory. Reviving French overtures to eastern Europe (a familiar feature of prewar French policy), he quickened hopes among the Soviet satellites by reminding them of the time when Europe had not been divided between East and West. His visits inspired growing sentiment in Romania and Poland for greater freedom from Soviet control. By appearing to Moscow as *enfant terrible* of the NATO alliance, de Gaulle established more intimate ties with the Soviet leadership, thus strengthening his own position at home vis-à-vis the French Communist Party. The Soviet Union valued him for his disruption of Western unity more than it feared him as a threat to the solidarity of its own satellites. In the grave crisis of the Fifth Republic in 1968, when radical student uprisings accompanied by industrial unrest threatened to bring down the government, the French Communist Party remained passive, permitting de Gaulle to reassert his authority.

The new Europe. A new Europe was nevertheless emerging. In all countries of the European Economic Community, great strides were made in productivity. The Common Market became a powerful competitor to North America in world trade; higher living standards and state welfare programs transformed the condition of Europe's population. The new Europe in its several parts became devoted to the pursuit of affluence.

Regional separatism

One aspect of this new condition, however, was that Europe's postwar architects of unity found upper limits to the popularity of their ideal, and a contrary idea, that of regional separation, emerged. Separatist movements arose in France in Brittany and in Britain in Scotland and Wales; in Belgium there were conflicts between Flemish- and French-speakers; in Italy there were regional tensions between north and south. In the 1960s the complexities of domestic politics rather than trans-European matters absorbed more and more of the attention of Europe's leaders. While each NATO member-state in Europe contributed a share of its gross national product to collective defense, and the cohesiveness of the alliance was unimpaired (France excepted), no significant attempts were made by Europeans to assume collectively the burdens of European defense and lessen their dependence on the United States. Furthermore, western Europeans displayed less and less interest in acting as extra-continental, much less global, powers. The rebuff the British and French had received at the hands of their American ally at Suez in 1956 reinforced their inclination to constrict their zones of military interest. British withdrawal from overseas military activity took place gradually and with dignity. French withdrawal, though accompanied by battles, defeats, and recriminations in Indochina and Algeria, was equally definitive. The United States was left as the only Western nation with worldwide interests and with widely scattered military forces. The European nations were still confronted in the East by a strong Soviet Empire, which they lacked capacity to counter. In the view of many American policy makers, Europe had the resources to play a far more significant role in its defense but had no will either to mobilize those resources or to create the machinery by which to coordinate them politically.

A passive Europe

Eastern Europe. In eastern Europe, meanwhile, after 1956, the fact of Soviet dominance was rarely challenged, the one-party regimes regulating their domestic and international affairs so as to give the Soviet Union no occasion to intervene. The idea of liberation, once a lively café topic, had been proved fanciful in 1956. For the most part, police-state vigilance was relaxed, but it was attended by no significant reforms. Gradually, however, different patterns and contrasts emerged among the satellite states. Until 1968, Romania was the only one of these that significantly differentiated itself; situated in a region of secondary strategic importance, it successfully managed to defy Moscow's military authority in the Warsaw Treaty Organization while remaining in the alliance. At the same time, Romania remained loyal to Marxist–Leninist tenets in more orthodox fashion than was now customary in most other Soviet-dominated states. The Romanian policy posed no particular threat to Soviet interests and was accepted.

The Soviet variety of imperialism. The Soviet Union's domination of eastern Europe did not conform to standard conceptions of imperialism. An imperial power is generally presumed to be both stronger and wealthier than those under its subjection, but several eastern European nations were more advanced economically than the Soviet Union. In the Council for Mutual Economic Assistance (Comecon), the economic relationship between, say, East Germany and the Soviet Union resembled that of an advanced industrial state to an underdeveloped country, the former exchanging high technology manufactures in return for natural resources. On several occasions when popular protest against high food prices shook the regime in Poland, the Soviet Union sent substantial food shipments, despite the superiority of Polish to Soviet living standards.

In its dealings with its eastern European allies, however, the Soviet Union faced the dilemmas known to all imperial powers. It obviously could not rule perpetually with an iron fist, yet how far might each state be permitted to pursue a national course? There were, for example, strong incentives in eastern Europe to restore or improve economic ties with the West. How far might these tendencies be allowed to proceed? Economic experimentation designed to lessen the rigidities of socialist planning ran the risk of introducing market economy principles. Finally, the relaxation of iron rule, though it might enhance the popularity of a regime, might also arouse new demands for greater freedom.

Czechoslovakia. In 1968, 12 years after the uprising in Hungary, the Soviet Union experienced a new test of its authority, this time in Czechoslovakia. Since the time of Klement Gottwald, Czechoslovakia had been, next to Bulgaria, the most compliant of the satellites. With the removal, early in that year, of Antonín Novotný, Gottwald's Stalinist successor, 20 years of rigid bureaucratic rule seemingly came to an end. His successor, Alexander Dubček, introduced a series of domestic reforms in the direction of democratization and, especially, freedom of speech, which quickly revealed the basic problems to which political and ideological relaxation gave rise. A wave of spontaneous public demonstrations for greater political freedom took place that Dubček could not control. Nor was the new Czech leader willing to submit to Soviet dictation in dealing with this crisis of authority, though many conferences between the two countries took place. After months of apparent indecision, the Soviet Union (with Poland, East Germany, Hungary, and Bulgaria) on August 20–21 invaded an unresisting Czechoslovakia and reimposed its authority.

The Prague Spring

The Sino-Soviet division had revealed the fundamental socio-economic, historical, and cultural disunity between the Soviet Union and China. From the Chinese point of view (shared by many Third World revolutionaries), the Soviet leadership appeared to be presiding over a revisionist country, in process of becoming bourgeois. The Czechoslovak threat was directed against another aspect, the backward and backward-looking characteristics of the Soviet Union. It expressed the rejection by the eastern European countries, with their distinctive traditions and structures, of the transplanting of the Soviet Union's ponderous bureaucratic system.

The Kremlin apologists saw nationalism as the common characteristic of the Chinese and Czechoslovak as well as Romanian and Yugoslav deviations. This did not alter the fact that the two challenges combined to bring about a sort of return to Stalinism in the Soviet Union. China's ceaseless condemnation of revisionism obliged Soviet leaders to emphasize the Marxist–Leninist purity of their doctrine and the primacy that they were giving to the struggle against imperialism. In fact, Czechoslovak de-Stalinization gathered strength at the very moment when Soviet policy was in process of returning to the habits and forms of the Stalinist era.

The Czechoslovak leaders, although aware of the risks they were taking by relaxing restrictions, were convinced to the very end that they would be able to exercise political leadership through a policy that would be supported by the population as a whole. Unfortunately for Dubček, the Soviet leaders could see only the dangers of counterrevolution involved in the experiment.

To dress the invasion in the garments of Marxism–Leninism, for the benefit of sister parties, a new doctrine of limited sovereignty and of double responsibility had been worked out and expressed in a letter of the "Five" (the Soviet Union and the four allies referred to above) to the Czechoslovak Central Committee on July 15:

Doctrine of limited sovereignty

> Each of our parties is responsible not only to its working class and its people, but also to the international working class, the world Communist movement. . . . Therefore, we must be solid and united in defending the gains of socialism, our security and the international positions of the whole of the socialist community.

This implied the right of intervention in cases where the essential common interests of other Communist countries were threatened by developments in one of them. To mitigate the arbitrary character of this theoretical construction, the Soviet Union attempted to justify the Czechoslovak intervention by an "appeal for aid" that had allegedly been made. But as it was unable to produce any authors of this appeal, the argument rebounded. The military success was transformed into a political fiasco that seriously damaged Soviet prestige and aggravated divisions in the Communist movement. Two Communist countries, Romania and Yugoslavia, protested and rejected the "new doctrine." China characterized the invasion as social–imperialist.

It was the anti-Khrushchevite and anti-progressive nature of the Soviet action that disturbed relationships between Moscow and the Communist parties of the West. Furthermore, an increasing number of Western Communists had realized that what had just been condemned in Czechoslovakia was basically what they themselves were defending. In 1948 all the Communist parties joined in the condemnation of Yugoslavia. In 1956 the crushing of the Hungarian uprising produced some upheavals, but no Western party protested publicly. In August 1968 all except the West German Communists expressed objections.

Whether they liked it or not, they were now forced to admit that the myth of the identification of their interests, and of the working-class interests they hoped to represent, with those of the Soviet Union had had its day. They could not accept the doctrine of limited sovereignty and would be increasingly vulnerable to the tendency to nationalize Communism that first had appeared in Communist countries in direct contact with Soviet hegemony—Yugoslavia, China, Albania, and finally Czechoslovakia.

AREAS OF CONFLICT

Southeast Asia. In 1961, when John F. Kennedy succeeded Eisenhower as president, the United States had extensive commitments overseas. Mutual security alliances linked it with more than 40 countries, and it had an informal yet deep commitment to Israel. The 6th Fleet commanded the Mediterranean, the 7th the western Pacific. U.S. conventional military forces, numerically still inferior to those of the Soviet Union, had technological superiority in all categories. On many occasions since the end of World War II the U.S. had threatened the use of its military strength as an effective means of influence in crises. The American public, to judge by opinion polls, supported these undertakings. In his inaugural address, Kennedy reaffirmed American pledges to its allies. The U.S., he said, would "pay any price, bear any burden, meet any hardship, support any friend, oppose any foe to assure the survival and the success of liberty."

Divided Vietnam

One of the commitments overseas was that in Southeast Asia. The Geneva Accords of 1954 had brought temporary peace to Vietnam while in no way resolving the issues that troubled that nation. North of the 17th parallel of latitude was a Communist regime, south of it a non-Communist regime. The Geneva Accords—to which South Vietnam had never agreed—had specified that the country be unified by means of free, nationwide elections, but neither north nor south displayed interest in this.

For six years after the Geneva agreements, the government of North Vietnam refrained from attacking the south, giving priority to internal consolidation as opposed to external expansion; for one thing, peasant resistance to collectivization of agriculture had to be overcome. In 1960, however, the Hanoi government created the National Liberation Front (NLF), whose object, aided by Soviet and Chinese war material, technical advice, and international propaganda facilities, was to overthrow the southern regime and reunite the country under a Communist government.

Washington, since 1954 guardian of South Vietnam, observed these developments with growing concern. Not only would Communist control in Southeast Asia be another defeat for U.S. foreign policy, but also, it was widely believed, a Communist victory would have the further effect of inspiring aggression elsewhere—the so-called domino effect. But the Americans remembered one lesson from the Korean War: MacArthur's "forward strategy," carrying the war to the very border of China, had resulted in Chinese intervention. It was decided, therefore, that so long as South Vietnam, with economic and military help from the U.S., could successfully fend off Communist attacks, this would be sufficient. This decision gave Hanoi the initiative in the conflict.

Throughout the Kennedy administration, the U.S. was represented in Vietnam only by small groups of counterinsurgency forces, political and military advisers, and officials of the Agency for International Development (AID). By the mid-1960s, it was estimated, there were 40,000 Viet Cong (the guerrilla military arm of the NLF) members in the south, supported by an extensive secret political apparatus. Such was their success that by 1964 roughly 80 percent of the population of the Mekong Delta was under their control. In Saigon there was political chaos. Military coups followed one another as rival factions fought for control. In 1964 Pres. Lyndon B. Johnson increased U.S. support for the faltering government. In August he announced that North Vietnamese torpedo boats had attacked U.S. destroyers patrolling in the Gulf of Tonkin and put before Congress a resolution approving and supporting the President in measures he might take to prevent further aggression. The so-called Gulf of Tonkin Resolution was passed by both houses on August 7. "It should be made . . . clear to [the Communist] regimes, if it is not yet sufficiently clear," said Senator J.W. Fulbright, "that their aggressive and expansionist ambitions, wherever advanced, will meet precisely that degree of American opposition which is necessary to frustrate them." In the following year, the Johnson administration made the decision to greatly enlarge U.S. military forces in Vietnam and by means of carefully timed air raids on North Vietnam to indicate to the North Vietnamese the punishment that was in store for them if the war continued. By July 1965 there were 75,000 U.S. combat troops in Vietnam.

Gulf of Tonkin Resolution

From this time forward, Johnson, while for a time enjoying congressional and public support, found far less enthusiasm abroad for this venture, and much opposition. In Europe, de Gaulle pressed his own formula for peace—"neutralization" of all of Indochina—a formula that barely concealed his own view that a Communist victory was inevitable. International pressures on the U.S. to cease its aerial bombardment were rarely matched by demands that the north cease its invasion. The war was widely viewed as a civil war in which a foreign superpower struggled with brave and poorly equipped patriots whose aim was to build a new nation. Though a few non-Communist nations (such as South Korea and Australia) contributed military forces, the U.S. did not receive the support that it had received from its allies in the earlier Korean war. (For the progress of the war, see VIETNAM, HISTORY OF.)

The war provided a striking contrast between an open, democratic and a closed, totalitarian society. From the onset of the offensive in the south, the North Vietnamese imposed a total censorship concerning their involvement, maintaining the fiction that the conflict was a wholly indigenous uprising against a corrupt, reactionary regime; despite hundreds of thousands of casualties, the North Vietnamese people were not even told officially that they were engaged in battle; masses of North Vietnamese troops were sent south, along the so-called Ho Chi Minh Trail, in a continuous surreptitious infiltration that U.S. and South Vietnamese troops were unable to check. In contrast, the war was brought by television into American living rooms, and for seven years the U.S. public daily and painfully observed the horrors of war.

The reportage of the war in America could not convey its course accurately. In early 1968 North Vietnam launched its long-planned major effort, what came to be called the Tet Offensive (in reference to the lunar new year, with which it coincided), in which regular combat units struck at major cities while simultaneous uprisings of Communist cadres tried to seize power within them. The offensive was a military disaster for the north, and the Viet Cong was never able to recover from the losses it sustained. Yet, as reported to and perceived by a war-weary American public, the offensive was taken to be a defeat for the defending forces: a military defeat for North Vietnam became a psychological defeat for the U.S. Faced with increasing antiwar demonstrations, violence on university campuses, growing opposition in Congress, and unrest in the cities, Johnson in March 1968 announced his decision not to seek reelection to the presidency, to deny requests for additional troops, to reduce U.S. bombing raids on the north (they were stopped a few months later), and to offer to negotiate with North Vietnam. The offer did not bring immediate peace, but it signified the administration's determination to extricate U.S. ground forces from the war.

U.S. domestic social change

What made the war a political disaster for the Johnson administration was the fact that it coincided with great domestic social changes in the United States. As it wore on, it accentuated internal problems that originated in other sources. There was unrest among black citizens and among white youth, both exacerbated by the war. Novel social theories appeared, sanctioning violence as a legitimate form of protest and change while challenging the right of public authorities to respond to it effectively. By the late 1960s, it became difficult to distinguish a widespread peace movement from these violent manifestations of self-expression. A consequence of all this was a polarization in American culture that had no historical parallels. Not until the cease-fire was signed, in January 1973, did this divisive cultural crisis finally begin to subside.

For 25 years, since 1941, the American people by and large had lent sanction to far-reaching U.S. involvement in world politics. They had supported the actions of five administrations in committing the U.S. to resist the spread of expansionist, aggressive forces abroad. American troops had fought three wars—one victorious, another inconclusive, and the third a defeat—to sustain the security of free societies. Now the future role of the U.S. in world politics seemed uncertain. Its material resources were still great, but its willingness to employ them in far-flung international activities now was uncertain.

The Middle East. *The Arab–Israeli war of 1967.* In June 1967, at the height of the Vietnam War, the Middle East once again became the scene of renewed Arab–Israeli conflict. In the years since the Suez Crisis (1956), many changes had taken place in the Arab world. In Iraq, Syria, Egypt, and Algeria, leftist regimes with close connections to the Soviet Union were in power. Elsewhere, as in Saudi Arabia and Jordan, conservative dynasties reigned. Radical Arab governments, though increasingly tied to Moscow, were neither satellites nor Marxist. They were hostile toward the U.S. and Israel, but their appeal was to Arab Muslim populations, and in none of them, much less in Saudi Arabia or Jordan, were regular Communist parties tolerated. Israel was the only Middle East country that had a legal pro-Soviet Communist party. Soviet aid to Arab leftist regimes took the form chiefly of military equipment and training.

None of the Arab states, radical or conservative, except Tunisia, had accepted the view that Israel had a right to exist, but Saudi Arabia and Jordan took a more moderate position than did the regimes in Egypt, Syria, and Iraq. It was the object of Soviet diplomacy to keep the conflict alive (since this was a necessary political condition for Soviet influence in the Middle East) but under control. Either a decisive Arab victory over Israel or a negotiated permanent peace would have meant an end to Arab dependence on the Soviet Union. Now, however, China began to support extremist Arab movements, particularly paramilitary terrorist organizations, some of which were as much of a threat to Arab governments as to Israel. The plight of the Palestinian refugees attracted discordant factions, extremist, moderate, and conservative, with the Palestine Liberation Organization (PLO) serving as umbrella; in its name, terrorists undertook missions of violence, not only in the Middle East but in Europe as well, to advertise their cause.

Soviet diplomacy in the Middle East

Since the Suez crisis, a constant element and source of tranquillity in the region had been the UN peacekeeping forces that acted as buffer between Egypt and Israel. But Nasser, his army now well supplied with Soviet arms and advisers, in late spring of 1967 demanded that these forces be removed, and the UN Secretary General complied. Nasser then closed the Strait of Tirān (the entrance to the Gulf of Aqaba and thus to the Israeli port of Elat) to Israeli shipping and to all other vessels carrying strategic material to Elat. The Israelis, fearing attack (which Nasser had specifically threatened), immediately launched a "preventive" war and in six days of fighting (June 5–10) broke the Egyptian armies, destroyed Nasser's air force, and crossed the Suez Canal. Substantial injury was also inflicted on Syria in the north; the road to Damascus was open. At this point, the UN Security Council once more intervened, and a new cease-fire was ordered. Israeli forces now occupied West Bank regions previously under Jordanian control, the Sinai, and all of Jerusalem. Vast amounts of equipment were taken from the Arab armies. For the third time the combined forces of the Arab world had been beaten in battle by a single small, beleaguered state.

The Six-Day War

Postwar confrontations. During the next six years, as Arab states regathered their strength, international diplomacy again sought without success to resolve the basic issues of the conflict. U.S. influence in the Arab world, already reduced, sank even lower. Nasser, seeking to explain the debacle, claimed that U.S. military forces had engaged in air operations alongside the Israelis and broke diplomatic relations with Washington. The Soviet Union once more began to resupply the shattered Arab states.

The UN resolution that brought the cease-fire had, among other things, directed Israel to withdraw from territories seized in the war; this the Arab states and the Soviet Union took to mean all territories. The Israeli government, while willing to consider withdrawal from some of the territories as part of a general settlement, insisted on retaining all of Jerusalem as well as the Golan Heights in the north and the West Bank of the Jordan.

The U.S. found itself in a difficult position. It was committed to the survival of Israel, and its continuing military aid was a *sine qua non* of Israel's existence. Increasingly, however, in the UN and elsewhere, the U.S. on this issue stood in isolation even from some of its closest European allies. In Europe, West Germany and The Netherlands remained close friends of Israel. Britain's position was intermediate, while the French moved into ever closer relations with the Arab "confrontation states," denying Israel commercial access to the French arms industry. The humiliated Arab states, the radicals in particular, succeeded in linking their cause with Third World ideological movements, and Israel now was depicted by Arab propaganda as an outpost of Western imperialism, a remaining enclave of colonialism. The acts of terrorism committed by PLO groups were represented as those of heroic freedom fighters. This view gained credence not only in the Communist world but also in non-Communist parts of Asia and Africa.

The new role of petroleum. Moreover, there was a new factor in the situation after 1967. Since 1947 there had been tension between U.S. petroleum interests in the Middle East and U.S. policy of support for Israel. By the late 1960s, however, the character of the oil interest began to change and, as it did, so did the shape of international politics.

U.S. oil interests in the Persian Gulf had been confined chiefly to Saudi Arabia; the oil reserves in the Gulf and under the desert had been developed on leasehold from the Saudi government by the Arabian American Oil Company (Aramco). This oil went principally to European markets, the United States relying chiefly on domestic and Venezuelan oil. In the era of ample proved oil reserves and abundant world production immediately after World War II, the oil-exporting nations of the world had been at the mercy of U.S. oil import policies, and to benefit U.S. oil producers the Eisenhower administration had established stringent import quotas. In response to this and at the initiative of the Venezuelan government, a protective association of oil-producing states (including Arab states and Iran), the Organization of Petroleum Exporting Countries (OPEC), was formed in 1960.

Formation of OPEC

During the 1960s the world's greatly increased energy requirements transformed a buyer's into a seller's market. During the same period, furthermore, strict legislation to protect the environment in the U.S. caused an increase in the demand for petroleum of low sulfur content—chiefly to be found in Libya. In 1969 the Libyan monarchy was overthrown by military officers, and the new regime subsequently nationalized the importation, sale, and distribution of, and raised the price of and taxes on, Libyan oil. In earlier days such action would have resulted in swift response from major Western powers; the regime of Mohammad Mosaddeq in Iran, which had done the same thing 19 years earlier, had met with concerted Anglo-U.S. resistance and had finally been overthrown. This time, no Western response came; the oil-importing nations acquiesced, and other Arab states also started to raise their oil prices.

The Arab–Israeli war of 1973. After another Arab–Israeli war in October 1973, members of the Organization of Arab Petroleum Exporting Countries (OAPEC) imposed an oil boycott on the U.S. and other nations charged with supporting Israel; of all the Persian Gulf suppliers, only Iran continued its deliveries. The following January, OPEC tripled the posted price of oil produced by its members.

This crisis starkly revealed the depth of Europe's dependence on Middle Eastern oil for its basic energy requirements and revealed the Americans' rapidly growing dependence on oil imports. The increase in prices intensified inflation in the advanced industrial nations and created severe balance-of-payments difficulties for some nations of Europe; it caused havoc in the economies of many less developed nations, dependent upon petroleum-derived fertilizers. The vast revenues now accruing to Persian Gulf and North African oil states almost overnight transformed them into major factors in the world economy.

The use of the "oil weapon" by Arab states in the fourth Arab–Israeli war had no direct bearing upon the outcome. Initial victories revealed surprising improve-

The Yom Kippur war

ment in Arab fighting abilities, but within two weeks after fighting began Israeli forces had turned back the invasion, though suffering severe losses. Again Israeli forces swept broken Egyptian armies back across the Suez Canal and established themselves on its western bank. Reports reaching Washington of possible direct intervention by Soviet troops and nuclear units led the Nixon administration to order a worldwide precautionary alert (October 25) of U.S. forces. The Soviet Union, which early had called for total Arab participation in the war and praised the oil embargo, demanded immediate peace now that the tide of battle had turned.

Israel in the "Yom Kippur war" survived a fourth contest at arms with its Arab neighbours, but this one took a far heavier toll of its armed forces than any other had. Aware of the likelihood of an Arab surprise attack, Israel this time had not struck first, fearing the effects on public opinion abroad. The ambiguous battlefield outcome now placed the U.S. in a position as diplomatic arbiter and gravely weakened the Soviet Union's prestige in the Middle East. The war also revealed the impotence of the West to take concerted action against the Arab oil states. The U.S. in particular accepted the new oil situation in the Persian Gulf as a *fait accompli*. Many observers saw the OPEC victory as a historical triumph of Third World forces over the West and as an example to other underdeveloped countries in their struggle against "neocolonialism." The possibility that oil again would be used as a weapon in some future war against Israel was further increased as U.S. dependence on Middle Eastern oil grew.

DÉTENTE, THE SUPERPOWERS, AND THE NEW STRUCTURE OF WORLD POLITICS

By the early 1970s, the structure of world politics had greatly changed. U.S. setbacks in Southeast Asia gave rise to mounting public pressure within the United States to reduce the nation's external commitments. The flagging Soviet economy prompted the Soviet leadership to look abroad for capital and technological assistance. The Sino-Soviet conflict reached even higher levels of bitterness, as open border fighting broke out along the Ussuri River in 1969. In the United Nations, the admission of dozens of new members radically transformed the General Assembly and specialized agencies; an Afro-Asian voting bloc now greatly outnumbered the founding members. The last vestiges of colonialism all but disappeared. The western European nations, increasingly preoccupied with domestic problems, showed less and less inclination to play a significant role in world politics.

Transformation of the UN

A worldwide energy crisis, which the Middle Eastern war of 1973 made worse, cast a new shadow over international politics; three decades of uninterrupted world economic growth imposed heavy demands upon known material resources. Fears of impending scarcity, or even exhaustion, of vital raw materials led some economists to predict an end to global economic expansion. Economic disparities between the advanced Western nations (and Japan) and the underdeveloped world increased. In the United Nations, a new bloc of less developed countries—the Group of 77—took the lead in demanding reformation of the international economic order to reduce the disparities. To the tensions of postwar relations between the Communist and non-Communist worlds now was added another factor as the Third World appeared in an adversary role in international meetings. The nations of the world were increasingly interdependent, yet interdependence, in the abstract, seemed irrelevant to the critical question of international war and peace.

Peaceful coexistence. International politics was particularly obscured by a new atmosphere of relaxation between the two great rivals, the United States and the Soviet Union, and their respective allies. This atmosphere, which came to be called détente, encompassed many fields; many Westerners saw in it an end to the Cold War and an occasion for resolving the most acute conflicts.

In the Soviet vocabulary, however, détente was synonymous with the older doctrine of peaceful coexistence, framed by Lenin in the early 1920s and from time to time employed to signify peaceable relations between states with differing social systems. To the Soviet Union, the doctrine had no absolute, intrinsic worth; it was employed to signify a phase in the always conflictual relationship between socialist and capitalist states, a phase in which outright warfare was avoided while the revolutionary struggle was continued by different means. In a public speech on June 21, 1960, Khrushchev had reaffirmed his view that Lenin's theory of the inevitability of war under capitalism no longer applied. On December 5 was published a 20,000-word statement of international Communist policy adopted by representatives of 81 Communist parties assembled in Moscow, in which the term "peaceful coexistence" was used. The statement asserted that, in view of Communist successes and the extent of Communist influence, "a real possibility will have arisen of excluding world war from the life of society even before Socialism achieves complete victory on earth, with capitalism still existing in a part of the world." The key to the victory of socialism, Khrushchev said later, was "peaceful coexistence." Exceptions to this rule were "national liberation wars," in which the Soviet Union would actively assist forces engaged in throwing off the domination of colonial powers. "The slogan of struggle for peace," Khrushchev continued, "does not conflict with the slogan of struggle for communism."

The broad lines of this doctrine were continued by his successor, Leonid I. Brezhnev, in the years after Khrushchev's downfall. In Brezhnev's view, frequently reiterated in the 1960s and '70s, détente had been made possible by forces of socialism now so powerful that the capitalist world could not check their advance. Détente, in this version, applied strictly to state-to-state relations between the Soviet Union and its chief ideological adversaries in the West. In all other respects, in détente the "ideological struggle" and ideological vigilance were to be intensified.

The U.S. view of détente. In the United States, however, détente came to be seen quite differently, both as a process of diplomacy and as a goal. Some saw it as a means by which permanent reconciliation with the Communist powers could be achieved. Others saw social forces at work within the Soviet Union and the United States, both advanced industrial societies, that would bring about a "convergence" of their social systems, presumably resulting in the disappearance of fundamental sources of conflict. Still others placed chief blame upon the United States for having brought about the Cold War in the first place, by overreacting to essentially defensive Soviet postwar policies. Others who observed the Soviet–U.S. arms competition asserted that in the action–reaction cycle it was U.S. initiatives in weapons development that provoked the Soviet Union to respond. Such views reinforced each other and were strengthened by a widespread domestic mood of disillusionment concerning America's use of force in international politics after the war in Indochina. An opinion poll taken in 1972 showed that a majority of Americans were willing to use armed force to defend only one foreign country, Canada, from attack. Under intense public pressure, the U.S. government abandoned universal military service.

The Nixon administration (beginning January 1969), responding to this change in public opinion, was not long in devising new rationales to support its policies abroad. Speaking in Guam shortly after his inauguration, the President revealed what came to be called the "Nixon Doctrine," under which the U.S. would readjust its relationships with its allies, reducing American contributions to their defense and urging them to bear a larger part of the burden of collective defense. In 1970 the President announced that an "era of negotiation" now would supersede an "era of confrontation." Under increasing pressure from Congress to withdraw U.S. troops from Europe, the administration succeeded in persuading

Nixon and the era of negotiation

the Soviet government to join discussions aimed at reciprocal reduction of forces in that area. In 1972 Nixon revealed his own notions about the necessary conditions for a stable world order: a pentagonal structure of peace, based upon the responsible exercise of power by five centres, the U.S., the Soviet Union, the People's Republic of China, Japan, and western Europe.

Resolution of the German problem. In a strictly chronological sense, the stage for Nixon's "era of negotiation" already had been set in Europe during the late 1960s, as the German problem, the focal point of East–West tensions, gradually abated. With U.S. approval, the Federal Republic of Germany had pursued a policy of cautiously normalizing its relationships with its eastern neighbours, Poland and the German Democratic Republic in particular. This policy was approved by the Soviet Union, which long since had reconciled itself to the existence of West Germany as a sovereign state and which was anxious to establish trade relations with West German industrial firms. In negotiations with Poland, Chancellor Willy Brandt agreed to recognize the Oder–Neisse Line as Poland's western boundary, thus accepting as final what the great powers at Yalta in 1945 had agreed to provisionally. Abandoning the so-called Hallstein Doctrine (under which West Germany would sever ties with any state that recognized East Germany), Brandt established diplomatic relations with all eastern European members of the Warsaw Treaty Organization. Negotiations were undertaken with the East German regime leading to formal ties and to means by which West Germans might legally visit relatives in the east.

The Brandt government's acceptance of the German Democratic Republic as a legal state signified abandonment of West German insistence upon all-German free elections leading to national unification. The goal of one united and democratic Germany receded; for the present, two Germanys would coexist, each accorded identical diplomatic status in international organizations.

Two Germanys

The resolution of this issue was closely linked to four-power negotiations over Berlin. When the Soviet Union abandoned its blockade of West Berlin in 1949, it had done so unilaterally, reserving the privilege of future recourse to this weapon of strangulation. Later, by periodic harassment of rail and auto traffic between Berlin and the West, it had displayed willingness to exploit the city's vulnerability to bring pressure on the West in pursuit of Soviet policy. Now, eager to obtain diplomatic recognition for East Germany, the Soviet Union agreed to recognize formally the legitimacy of West Berlin's access to the West. Thus the two questions, of the legal status of the German Democratic Republic and the legal status of West Berlin, were diplomatically linked and both were resolved. Tacitly accepting the Soviet decision to employ East Berlin as capital of East Germany and to maintain the Berlin Wall in violation of four-power rights over the whole city, the Western powers at least were able to assure the necessary conditions for West Berlin to survive in freedom as an island deep within a Soviet sphere. By 1973, when both Germanys were admitted simultaneously to the United Nations, the East German regime was well on the way to complete recognition as a sovereign state in the international community. In 1974 the U.S. established diplomatic relations with it and opened an embassy in the eastern sector of Berlin behind a fortified wall separating it from the U.S. sector.

These agreements in no way affected the internal character of the two German states or their respective alignments in Eastern and Western camps. The agreements, however, placed the stamp of normality upon the situation and hence were criticized by some West Germans as certifying abandonment of hopes for national reunification. The Soviet Union in agreeing to them, however, forfeited one propaganda asset that it long had been able to use in eastern Europe to sustain its rule: having assisted in the normalization of relations between West Germany and the satellites, it could no longer depict West Germany as a bastion of monopoly capitalism and of Fascist revanchists intent upon reimposing a Hitlerian rule over eastern Europe.

The Helsinki conference and MBFR. This central European settlement opened the way for a more comprehensive diplomacy of normalization. For nearly 20 years an object of Soviet diplomacy in Europe had been to obtain general sanction for Soviet dominance in eastern Europe. Since 1954 the Soviet Union had called for the convening of an all-European conference on security and cooperation, which would lead to dissolution of the two blocs, the removal of U.S. forces from the Continent, and general recognition of the inviolability of European national boundaries. The United States would be excluded from such an all-European conference. In 1972, however, the Soviet government conceded the right of the U.S. to participate in such a ceremony and laid aside its insistence on dissolution of the blocs; the Nixon administration, agreeing to the convening of such a conference, obtained Soviet agreement to a separate, parallel conference on reduction of military forces in Europe. In 1973 these two conferences were convened, the 35-nation Conference on Security and Cooperation in Europe at Helsinki and the 11-nation conference dealing with mutual and balanced force reductions (MBFR) at Vienna, with NATO and Warsaw Treaty Organization members in attendance. The signing of the Final Act of the Helsinki conference in 1975 gave the Soviet Union the long-awaited general approval of its territorial hold on eastern Europe; thenceforth all European borders were to be deemed inviolable. In other provisions of the accord, however, the Soviet government conceded the principle that human rights in each European country were a matter of all-European concern. In Vienna, meanwhile, the conference on MBFR stagnated; even as it continued, Soviet forces in Europe were greatly increased, appearing now as a greater threat to western European security than they had been before détente began.

The Helsinki accord

Later years. As these diplomatic developments in Europe appeared to signify the beginning of a new era of peaceable relations, the Soviet Union continued to sponsor offensive actions in the Middle East, Southeast Asia, and Africa. It sanctioned the October war of 1973, an offensive against Israel; in early 1975 North Vietnam, equipped with Soviet weaponry, finally brought down South Vietnam; in Africa, Soviet-supported insurgents took control of Angola and Mozambique, and Soviet-oriented regimes came to control the Horn of Africa, commanding a vital maritime link from the Suez Canal to the Indian Ocean. In the time of détente, the Soviet Union had become a global power, with military capacities rivalling those of the United States in nearly all categories.

Policy makers in Washington sought to effect a diplomatic redress of world power. In the summer of 1971 the U.S. secretary of state, Henry A. Kissinger, visited Peking as a step toward "normalizing" relations between the U.S. and the People's Republic of China. Warmly received by Premier Chou En-lai, Kissinger set in motion a new triangular relationship of rivalry among Moscow, Washington, and Peking. In the same year, Soviet and American negotiators in the Strategic Arms Limitation Talks (SALT) reached agreement on limiting antiballistic missiles. American business, seeing great new opportunities from economic détente, began making arrangements with Soviet authorities to hasten the modernization of the Soviet economy, thus somewhat alleviating the strain imposed on the Soviet citizenry by the armament program. In encouraging such economic initiatives, Kissinger and the Nixon administration hoped to support Soviet moderation while more and more linking the Soviet economy to the normal operations of a peaceable world community.

The U.S. and China

Sino-Soviet rivalry now was the major component of a global balance of power. Peking, once viewing America as its prime enemy, now watched in consternation as U.S. power receded in Asia. The People's Republic of China now began to display concern for a strong system of Western defense in Europe and in its Asian policies sought to discourage attempts by indigenous forces to compel further withdrawal of U.S. bases. Worldwide, however, China, in its struggle with the Soviet Union for pre-eminence in the Communist movement, still found it necessary to support anticolonialist offensives.

The question remained in the mid- and later 1970s as to what new configurations might emerge in world politics in consequence of America's decline as a world power, of Communist polycentrism, and of the seeming rise to prominence of a new Third World. Would the international system, in becoming more diffuse and decentralized, become more anarchic or more stable? Would the diminution of America's international commitments encourage a healthier multipolar world or invite new threats to peace? Or were the perceived changes themselves deceptive, concealing the persistence of the Cold War?

One permanent change was clear to any close observer of international politics: world politics now was wholly global; more than ever before in human history, local events in any part of the world could gain worldwide significance as elements in an interlocking whole that was regulated by no single centre of authority. The Western democratic nations were now a small minority of states in a world otherwise dominated by authoritarian or totalitarian regimes, their influence over world events largely deriving from their continuing economic vitality. Above all of this remained the vivid awareness of the potential destructiveness of nuclear war, inspiring both prudence and fear.

BIBLIOGRAPHY

1945–c. 1957: Major contributions to thought about international relations in the post-World War II period have been made by Raymond Aron, Arnold Wolfers, Hans Morgenthau, Klaus Knorr, and others. On the decline of Europe as the historical centre of world politics, see HAJO HOLBORN, *The Political Collapse of Europe* (1959), and JOHN LUKACS, *The Last European War: September 1939–December 1941* (1976). On the revolutionary transformation of America's role in world politics during and after World War II, see NICHOLAS SPYKMAN, *America's Strategy in World Politics* (1942; reprinted 1970); WILLIAM G. CARLETON, *The Revolution in American Foreign Policy: Its Global Range,* 2nd ed. (1967); REINHOLD NIEBUHR, *The Irony of American History* (1952); and GEORGE F. KENNAN, *American Diplomacy: 1900–1950* (1951). For Marxist versions of this same transformation, see GABRIEL KOLKO, *The Roots of American Foreign Policy: An Analysis of Power and Purpose* (1969), and WILLIAM A. WILLIAMS, *The Tragedy of American Diplomacy* (1959). A comprehensive treatment of world politics in the postwar period is RAYMOND ARON, *Paix et guerre entre les nations,* 6th rev. ed. (1968; Eng. trans., *Peace and War: A Theory of International Relations* (1966). On the origins and nature of the United Nations, see INIS L. CLAUDE, *Swords into Ploughshares: The Problems and Progress of International Organization,* 4th ed. (1971). On the causes and evolution of the Cold War, see HERBERT FEIS, *From Trust to Terror: The Onset of the Cold War, 1945–1950* (1970); JOHN L. GADDIS, *The United States and the Origins of the Cold War, 1941–1947* (1972); JOHN LUKACS, *A New History of the Cold War,* 3rd rev. ed. (1966); and PAUL SEABURY, *The Rise and Decline of the Cold War* (1967). Revisionist versions of Cold War history include D.F. FLEMING, *The Cold War and its Origins, 1917–1960* (1961); GAR ALPEROVITZ, *Atomic Diplomacy: Hiroshima and Potsdam* (1965); and DAVID HOROWITZ, *The Free World Colossus: A Critique of American Foreign Policy in the Cold War,* rev. ed. (1971). The best critique of Cold War revisionist works is ROBERT J. MADDOX, *The New Left and the Origins of the Cold War* (1974). The most comprehensive account of U.S.–Soviet relations is ADAM B. ULAM, *The Rivals: America and Russia since World War II* (1971). On the restoration of western Europe after 1945, see THEODORE H. WHITE, *Fire in the Ashes: Europe in Mid-Century* (1953), and GEORGE LICHTHEIM, *The New Europe: Today, and Tomorrow* (1963). On the collapse of European empires after 1945, see RUPERT EMERSON, *From Empire to Nation: The Rise to Self-Assertion of Asian and African Peoples* (1960), and JOHN STRACHEY, *The End of Empire* (1959). On revolution and anti-Western developments in the Third World, see MORTON A. KAPLAN (ed.), *The Revolution in World Politics* (1962), and FRANTZ FANON, *Les Damnés de la terre* (1961; Eng. trans., *The Wretched of the Earth,* 1965). On international politics in Asia, see HAROLD VINACKE, *The United States and the Far East, 1945–1951* (1952); TANG TSOU, *America's Failure in China, 1941–1950* (1963); DONALD C. HELLMANN (ed.), *Southern Asia: The Politics of Poverty and Peace* (1976); and ROBERT A. SCALAPINO, *Asia and the Road Ahead: Issues for the Major Powers* (1975). On strategy in the postwar period, see URS SCHWARZ, *American Strategy: A New Perspective* (1966); BERNARD BRODIE, *Strategy in the Missile Age* (1959); HENRY A. KISSINGER, *Nuclear Weapons and Foreign Policy* (1957); HERMAN KAHN, *Thinking about the Unthinkable* (1962); RAYMOND ARON, "De la guerre," in *Espoir et peur du siècle* (1957; Eng. trans., *On War,* 1958, reprinted 1968); THOMAS C. SCHELLING, *Arms and Influence* (1966, reprinted 1976); and SIR ROBERT THOMPSON, *Defeating Communist Insurgency: Experiences from Malaya and Vietnam* (1966). The standard Soviet text on strategy is V.D. SOKOLOVSKY, *Soviet Military Strategy* (1975). On moral aspects of modern war, see ROBERT E. OSGOOD and ROBERT W. TUCKER, *Force, Order, and Justice* (1967), and PAUL RAMSEY, *The Just War: Force and Political Responsibility* (1968).

Since c. 1957: RAYMOND ARON, *République impériale: Les États-Unis dans le monde, 1945–1972* (1973; Eng. trans., *The Imperial Republic: The United States and the World 1945–1973* (1974), is probably the best analysis of the contemporary period. The Kennedy presidency is comprehensively presented in ARTHUR SCHLESINGER, *A Thousand Days: John F. Kennedy in the White House* (1965); the Cuban Missile Crisis of 1962 is analyzed in GRAHAM ALLISON, *Essence of Decision: Explaining the Cuban Missile Crisis* (1971). In the vast literature inspired by the Vietnam War, CHESTER COOPER, *Lost Crusade: America in Vietnam* (1970); BERNARD B. FALL, *Street Without Joy: Insurgency in Indochina, 1946–63,* 3rd rev. ed. (1963); and DAVID HALBERSTAM, *The Best and the Brightest* (1972), are recommended. A critique of the treatment of the war by the U.S. communications media can be found in PETER BRAESTRUP, *Big Story,* 2 vol. (1977). In the literature about America's international commitments inspired by that war, the following represent major and contrasting perspectives: J. WILLIAM FULBRIGHT, *The Arrogance of Power* (1967); NOAM CHOMSKY, *American Power and the New Mandarins* (1969); GEORGE LISKA, *Imperial America: The International Politics of Primacy* (1967); and EUGENE ROSTOW, *Peace in the Balance: The Future of American Foreign Policy* (1972). Treatments of world economic problems and their political ramifications include RAYMOND VERNON, *Sovereignty at Bay: The Multinational Spread of U.S. Enterprises* (1971); RICHARD BARNET and RONALD MÜLLER, *Global Reach: The Power of the Multinational Corporations* (1974); ROBERT KEOHANE and JOSEPH NYE (eds.), *Transnational Relations and World Politics* (1972); EDWARD FRIEDLAND, PAUL SEABURY, and AARON WILDAVSKY, *The Great Détente Disaster: Oil and the Decline of American Foreign Policy* (1975); LESTER BROWN, *World Without Borders* (1973); RICHARD N. COOPER, *The Economics of Interdependence: Economic Policy in the Atlantic Community* (1968); and ROBERT W. TUCKER, *The Inequality of Nations* (1977). Later works on the strategic balance of Soviet and American forces include INTERNATIONAL INSTITUTE FOR STRATEGIC STUDIES, *The Military Balance, 1977–78* (1977); JAMES SCHLESINGER *et al., Defending America* (1977); and RAY S. CLINE, *World Power Assessment* (1975).

(P.SE.)

International Relations, Theories of

In both popular and academic usage, the term international relations communicates several meanings. The commonest reference is to the affairs between the governments of independent nations. Regularly used as synonyms under this meaning are international politics, world affairs, foreign relations, external affairs, world politics, international affairs, foreign affairs, and interstate relations. International relations also is used as a family name in the classification of particular studies and academic specializations such as international economics, international politics, international organization, international law, intercultural relations, international education, international communications, and diplomatic history.

Concepts referring to international relations

Recently, some writers have sought to maintain a distinction between international relations and international politics, on the one hand, and world affairs and global politics, on the other. They intend the first to describe the international anarchy of sovereign states competing for power and advantage and the second to characterize an emerging world order in which domestic and foreign affairs tend more and more to blend together and international interdependency increasingly attenuates the sovereignty of states.

Some people think of international relations as strictly political intergovernmental phenomena, while others conceive an inclusion of cross-national relationships between individuals, private groups, and nonpublic organizations, as well as those of government bodies. The former has been called an interstate orientation and the latter an intersocial orientation. Semantic confusion arises readily from differences in fundamental perspective on the subject. Because no general theory of international relations has appeared and gained widespread acceptance around the globe, multiple conceptions and definitions coexist; awareness of this fact remains the best protection of readers of international-relations literature against semantic confusion.

The concept of the "international system" gained currency during the 1960s. One of its several advantages is the basic requirement that the system analyst specify the components and relationships of whatever system is conceived and investigated. Thus the system approach, to be discussed later in more detail, gives some promise of clarifying definitions and terms of reference and, at the same time, permitting many conceptions of the basic nature of international relations.

Since the beginnings of recorded history, interest in conditions in foreign lands and in the relations between peoples has attracted both description and critical analysis. Ancient writing from China, India, the Mediterranean region, and the river-valley civilizations of western Asia contains many references and passages to what, today, would be called the elements of international relations. Certain recurring themes have been observed in these treatments of conditions and relationships of countries from ancient times to the present. Descriptions of international events, especially those of wars and conquest, rendered in chronological narrative form, constitute a major source of knowledge of what happened between nations and states in history. A second theme is reflected in rich and varied analyses of statecraft by writers who have sought to explain how rulers should conduct affairs in dealing with other rulers and with subjects under their control, both at home and abroad. A third preoccupation has been with the collecting and interpreting of rules of legitimate conduct in the transactions between states—developing a corpus of international law. A fourth theme illuminates the constant preoccupation over the ages with the problem of attaining peace and security through the unity and collaboration of all mankind.

This article provides a brief survey of the variety of relations among peoples in history followed by an examination of the flowering of international-relations studies in the 20th century into a distinct and largely autonomous branch of knowledge.

HISTORICAL TYPES OF INTERNATIONAL RELATIONS

Universalist and comparative views of the international scene

No single type of international relations has prevailed across 6,000 years of world history. Nevertheless, writers and commentators have had a perennial tendency to assume that the particular ordering of relations between states and between peoples familiar to them at their own time and place in history has been universal. The Latvian-born American historian Adda Bozeman has performed a great service to the contemporary generation of international-relations scholars by piecing together the fragments of historical evidence that indicate that many different arrangements of relations have existed in the past. This fact had been all but forgotten during some 400 years of "Europeanization" of the globe.

With such long spans of time and so many varied cultural contexts to consider, it is impossible to arrive at an accurate typology that would cover the many historical configurations of international relationships. If the fact that endless variations and differences have existed is kept in mind, a few broad and prevalent types of international structures are worth noting. They serve, at least, as a reminder that the contemporary ordering of international relations has not always existed and, in all likelihood, will give way eventually to different structures.

The imperial system. Conquest states or empires have often established the patterns of relationships in large geographical regions, sometimes for a period of several centuries. Typically, a sustained military campaign would subjugate numerous communities and peoples and place them all momentarily under a centralized military control. The Assyrian and Persian empires had this character and so also did the empire forged by Alexander the Great. The conquests of Muslim armies as they marched from the Arabian peninsula to Spain in the 8th century and the Mughāl conquest in India in the 16th and 17th centuries constitute further examples.

One of a few possible developments would follow the accession to power of an imperial regime. New challengers might arise on the borders to initiate a period of turmoil in the empire, while a military struggle for supreme power and control played itself to a conclusion. Alternatively, the imperial regime might stabilize itself sufficiently to establish bureaucratic management for tax collections and manpower levies in the central territories and to install a hierarchical international system with states on the borders paying homage and tribute to the emperor. A theory of rights and obligations between overlord and subordinates sometimes would help to strengthen the hierarchical pattern, as it did in many periods in ancient China and in medieval Europe. Another outcome was the collapse of imperial unity and the rise of competing and warring states led by lieutenants of the original conquering emperor, as happened in the Alexandrian empire. A multistate system of competing powers thus would emerge from the dissolution of an empire.

The commercial city-state system. Just as empire building by military conquest produced several historically prominent kinds of international-relations structures in the aftermath, so also the expansionism of trading cities created, historically, a different set of international-system types. In earlier times, city-states tended to grow up in geographical locations that were exchange points in long-distance trading. Where specialized manufacturing and commerce developed in ancient, medieval, and early modern times, international political systems also would often emerge.

Two-directional problems of power and security

Political power and security concerns commonly extended in two directions. Occupying relatively small territories, the trading city-states had cause to worry about their hinterlands and about physical and political control over the access routes to and from their centres. An active international politics generally resulted, taking the familiar forms of diplomacy, rule making, alliance building, negotiations, balance of power calculations, and warfare.

Territorial expansion characteristically had to do with competition over ownership and control in the hinterlands adjacent to the cities. One example among many was the diplomatic and military activity that the Venetian trading enterprises of the late Middle Ages devoted to the safeguarding of the immediate land and sea approaches to the city-state. A second involvement of the trading city-states related to colonization. As long-distance trading networks grew, the outposts and marketplaces far removed from the home cities became important. Here, colonies were formed and populated by city-state migrants and became extensions of the home cities. The evolution of international systems with foundations in trading activities tended to become complex.

Complicated structures incorporating cooperative as well as conflictual practices grew up in the relations between city-states and in the territories adjacent to them and in their colonial extensions. Sometimes, the "classical" form of the state system emerged featuring the power politics of diplomatic calculation and military sanctions among states having roughly equal resources, population, and organization. A relatively nonhierarchical structure generally emerged, and diplomatic practice among "sovereign equals" ordinarily was attuned to compromise and accommodation. Nevertheless, the state of peace frequently was broken by the outbreak of war. The systems of international relations of the ancient Greek city-states and the Italian city-states of the Renaissance are cited frequently as examples of the classical model.

Blends of imperial and city-state systems

Although it is helpful to separate different structural types of international relationships according to their genesis in conquest-based empires or in long-distance trading systems, it is important to stress again that these types most often have been mixed together in history. The Roman Empire, for example, when viewed from the angle of the territorial expansion of the republic and early empire, provides an excellent illustration of the conquest state that achieved effective bureaucratic control over a large territory for a period of several centuries. When viewed in the perspective of the far-flung trading network that carried in its wake a system of administrative, legal, and political regulation over many peoples, the Roman Empire appears as a structure of some 30 important trading centres engaged in vigorous commercial activities.

The modern state system. When the consolidation of territorial states began in earnest in western Europe in the 13th and 14th centuries, the multipurpose character of the ancient Roman example was often held up as the ideal. Since 1648, the time of the Peace of Westphalia that brought the Thirty Years' War to an end, the Western state system has had an unbroken succession, according to the commonplace interpretation of diplomatic historians. In theory, the modern state system is an association among sovereign and equal powers governed both by the separate interests of its individual members and by the rules of international law and served by regularized procedures of diplomacy. The basic concept of the modern state system much resembles that of the commerce-based international political structures of the city-state variety. On the other hand, the building of sovereign states since early modern times has incurred much territorial aggrandizement through the use of armed force and, in addition, has spurred a remarkable period of expansionism, primarily through conquest, in all parts of the world beyond western Europe. It was, indeed, the building of overseas empires by the most powerful states of western Europe that spread the state system to a global basis by the end of the 19th century.

One finds in the development of the modern state system a merging of most of the functions and characteristics of other known structures of earlier international relations. The tenacity of this system is shown by the survival of its basic form through several major ideological upheavals, through the transformation of its "actors" from dynastic states to nation-states, through a vast increase in world population, through the massive shifts from agrarian to industrial economies, through the extensive popularization of domestic governments, through scientific and technological revolutions of great scope, and finally, through the expansion of the system, itself, from one corner of the world in the European peninsula to all lands.

The notion of "laws" of international relations

The apparent ultrastability of the state system has led many scholars to conclude that immutable rules, or laws, must govern its operation. From its inception, the state system has been the subject of criticism and discontent. It has been condemned for breeding violence, destruction, and insecurity. It has been blamed for the inequalities among societies and for its failure to provide for fundamental welfare for all peoples. In the nuclear age, it has been characterized as a system that guarantees the ultimate suicide of mankind. The inability of any nation or group of nations to bring any basic change to the structure of international politics of the state system, despite endless and fervent demands for a better system, further suggests that the system must operate according to underlying principles akin to the laws of nature.

The notion of immutable rules is unacceptable from the historical point of view, however, which holds that the contemporary state system, like all social creations, is subject to change and must eventually give way to other arrangements arising from human design and effort. The notion of immutable rules is incompatible also with the social philosophy that man has the intelligence and capability of guiding his destiny and the foresight to make changes to insure survival and to advance welfare.

THE DEVELOPMENT OF STUDIES OF INTERNATIONAL RELATIONS

Three contemporary forces go far to account for the impressive growth of scholarly studies of international relations and foreign policy in the 20th century. An autonomous academic discipline has emerged, related to geography, history, law, sociology, psychology, general political science, philosophy, and other fields, yet belonging to no one of these. The first impelling force was noted above: the growing demand to find better, less dangerous, more effective means of guiding relations among peoples, societies, governments, and economies. A second force is the result of the monumental upwelling of intellectual activity in modern times based on the belief that systematic observation and inquiry will dispel ignorance and serve the betterment of mankind. One sentence by Diderot characterizes this force as well today as when it was written in the 18th century: "Everything must be examined, everything must be shaken up, without exception and without circumspection." The third force is the consequence of the popularization of political affairs, including one of its most important sectors, foreign affairs. Only late in the 19th century did the traditional view that foreign and military matters should remain an exclusive preserve of rulers and special elites yield to the opposite belief that such matters constitute an important concern and responsibility of all the people. This popularization of international relations made logical the idea that education should include instruction in foreign affairs and that knowledge in the field should be advanced in the interests of public control over international political and military matters. The experience of World War I, the war to make the world safe for democracy, strengthened the conviction that not enough was known about international relations and that the universities should reduce ignorance in the field through more research and teaching.

The popularization of foreign and military affairs

Between the two world wars. A strong impulse toward the development of international studies in universities came in the 1920s. New centres, institutes, and schools devoted to teaching and research in international relations were founded. Courses were organized and general textbooks on the subject began to appear. Private organizations were formed, and large grants of philanthropic funds were channelled to the support of scholarly journals, to the advancement of citizenship in world affairs through special training institutes, conferences, and seminars, and to the stimulation of university research.

Initially, three subject areas commanded the most attention. All three had roots in the period of World War I. In the revolutionary upheavals at the end of the war, great portions of the government archives of imperial Russia and imperial Germany were opened and made public in a series of documentary publications. Very exciting scholarly work began to appear that pieced together the hitherto-unknown history of prewar alliances, secret diplomacy, and military planning. These materials were integrated to provide explanations of the origins of World War I. The two decades between the two great wars were the heyday of diplomatic history, and the most famous of the students of international affairs were historians. With great ingenuity and industry, they presented the world with superb examples of the art and science of diplomatic history.

The second subject that captured attention was bound up with the hope and expectation of a new world order in the making through the League of Nations. Some of the schools of international relations that were founded in the 1920s had the explicit purpose of preparing civil servants for what was expected to be the dawning age of international government. Thus the genesis and organization of the League, the history of earlier plans for international federations, and the analysis of the problems and procedures of international organization and international law were investigated with enthusiasm.

The third study of consequence during the early part of the interwar period was an offshoot of the peace movement and was concerned with scholarly investigations of international warfare: its cause, its costs, and its sociological and psychological aspects. Besides the data and the interpretations dredged up in the study of war, the interest in the question "why war?" brought new social scientists—economists, sociologists, and psychologists—into active participation in international studies for the first time. They were pioneers in what was later called the "behavioral approach" to international relations.

Realpolitik in the 1930s

The breakdown of the League, the rise of the aggressive dictatorships, and the coming of World War II in the 1930s caused a reaction against the international government and peace-inspired themes in the study of international relations. Idealism and moralism were criticized, and "realism" became the new thought in the field. The image was built at that time that the first stage of academic development of international studies was the handiwork of starry-eyed idealists and peace visionaries who contributed little more than preaching in behalf of international cooperation and world peace and who ignored the hard facts of international politics. This characterization is untrue, the fact being that the scholarship on world affairs of the '20s and the '30s was extensive and sound in the organization of data and in the development of some fundamental concepts.

In the European tradition since early modern times, the knowledge of international relations had been loosely ordered in two branches of learning. The first is diplomatic history, which has been considered to reflect the variety of political experience, the particularity of events, and the contingencies in the actual practices of diplomacy and war. The second is international law, which has been viewed as registering the "residue of history"—the fundamental principles of conduct, the uniformities in international phenomena, and the permanent aspects of practice. The effect of the new field of international relations was to broaden the traditional organization almost beyond recognition.

New areas of inquiry during the interwar period

The interwar literature ranged into areas that hitherto had not been considered part of international affairs. Some of the topics that today are considered novel and of recent origin were being explored vigorously in those two decades; by the time of World War II, they already had acquired large bibliographies. It is instructive to recall a few of those topics in order to correct the stereotype that moralist teachings were then entirely dominant: the relationship of problems of racial and ethnic minorities to international affairs, the effects of the population explosion on foreign policies, the linkage between raw materials and other of the "life-support systems" of the planet with the structure of action of nations, the effects of imperialism and colonialism on the world, the strategic aspects of international relations including the effects of geographical location and space on military power and the influence on governments of what has come to be called the "military-industrial complex," the economic inequalities of nations, and the role of public opinion, national differences, and cultural orientations in world affairs. If these studies tended to be short on theory and long on description, nevertheless the topics investigated remain relevant.

Certain individual scholarly contributions of the 1930s deserve particular notice because they were forerunners of what was to be developed after World War II. Harold D. Lasswell was making explorations of the relationships between world politics and the psychological realm of symbols, perceptions, and images. Abram Kardiner and his associates were laying the groundwork for a psycho-anthropological approach to the analysis of national behaviour and culture, which later became a popular but short-lived theory of international relations. Frederick L. Schuman was producing foreign policy analyses that synthesized analytic comment with accounts of current international events. Schuman thus set the style that is still followed by government interpreters of foreign policy developments and by the news analysts of world affairs.

Quincy Wright was leading one of the first team research projects in the field and was investigating numerous aspects of international behaviour in a very broad approach to the study of war. Carl J. Friedrich, Frederick L. Schuman, Harold Sprout, Nicholas Spykman, E.H. Carr, Brooks Emeny, and others were developing the main lines of analysis of what became the power-politics explanation of international relations.

Some 30 years later, one begins to appreciate that the general definition of the study of international relations and the widening of its scope far beyond the traditional European conception were the fundamental contributions of the scholars of the interwar period. Many of the innovators of the 1930s found their services enlisted by governments during World War II for work in intelligence, propaganda, and political analysis. In this respect, the war stimulated systematic social-science investigations of many international phenomena. On the other hand, World War II became a great divide for academic international relations.

The war made a drastic change in the agenda of world politics. The postwar intellectual climate shifted in a way to cause a rapid forgetting of many of the earlier interests, emphases, and problems. There was a readiness in the early post-World War II years for an analysis that would cut through the details of studies of myriads of international topics and that would provide a focussed view of the fundamental nature of international politics. An intellectual hunger for theory existed.

The postwar ascendancy of political realism. Hans Morgenthau's *Politics Among Nations,* first published in 1948, met this need for theory. Writing in 1959, Stanley Hoffmann expressed what was, in all likelihood, the opinion of most students of international relations:

Hans Morgenthau and the "realist" theory of power politics

> The theory which has occupied the center of the scene in this country [the United States] during the last ten years is Professor Morgenthau's "realist" theory of power politics.

At the time of this writing, the influence of the Morgenthau text continues to be strong in most countries outside the Communist world. The realist theory still requires the attention of new students of international relations. A reader is best advised to explore the theory at its source. *Politics Among Nations* remains an impressive study; it is clearly conceived and well argued.

At the heart of the realist theory is the concept of interests. Politics is defined as the struggle for power, whether in domestic or international settings. The struggle for power is part of human nature and takes form in society according either to the competition or to the alignment of interests. Collaboration occurs when parties find their interests are coinciding. Rivalry, competition, and conflict result from the clash of interests. Accommodations are possible through the application of political skill.

In an international system composed of sovereign nation-states, the survival of both the states and the system depends on the intelligent pursuit of national interests and on the realistic calculations of national power. As long as the state system persists, the only truly constructive way to participate in international politics is through skilled diplomacy. Religious and ideological crusades threaten the ruin of both the individual states and the system, and disasters follow from attempts to reform nations toward the ideal of universal trust and cooperation.

Thus the realist theory of power politics was brought forward in the late 1940s to stand guard against idealists: those who would think and act in the visionary ways of moralism and legalism in world affairs. No impressive new formulation of political idealism appeared to carry the challenge to the realist position, and the "great debate" of realism versus idealism gradually faded from the scene.

Many scholars of international relations neither opposed nor accepted the power-politics theory. Some simply were engrossed in other aspects of international-relations teaching and research. Large sums of money were made available in the 1950s for the development of foreign-area studies, and general theoretical concerns played little part in the growth of area specialization. Other scholars agreed with Morgenthau's statement that theory and research should have a "concern with human nature as it actually is, and with the historic processes as they actually take place," but they did not believe that the realist conceptualization provided a sufficient explanation of observed international behaviour.

The behavioral decade: mid-1950s to mid-1960s. An important new influence was the arrival in the field of a number of fresh ideas, conceptualizations, models, and paradigms that were loosely identified in ensemble as behavioral theory. The new movement distracted attention from the realist–idealist question. The unanticipated appearance in the mid-1950s of a large number of possible alternative ways to organize international data and to orient inquiries in international relations soon appeared to threaten the very foundations of scholarly communication. Simply to list a number of the conceptual innovations suggests the reason for the anxiety that the discipline might lapse into complete incoherence. In addition to power theory, there appeared a welter of theories, each with its distinctive label: decision making, system, conflict, deterrence, capabilities, field, communication, integration, development, environmental, cognitive, and, finally, game theory. Much of the intellectual effort of the "behavioral decade" went into the task of attempting to understand, compare, interpret, and integrate all these ideas. The scholarly goal of the period became to build an integrated framework of theories—to carry out conceptual mapping.

The behavioral aim to integrate the mass of ideas

To describe the efforts at theoretical integration that were made and the problems that were encountered would require book-length treatment. Suffice it to say that the comparing and integrating of the elements of theory turned out to be difficult. The more the matter was investigated, the more the specialists in theory questioned the necessity of arriving at one comprehensive structure of theory. The international realities that theory is supposed to reference and explain are varied and diverse, so why should one not expect that a number of separate theories would be needed to account for different parts and aspects of international relations? Many purposes are served by international activity, and many different motivations and expectations lie behind the undertakings and enterprises between nations. Given such multidimensionalities of international relations, one requires multiple theories to understand and account for many-sided phenomena.

Increasingly, explanations that trace the forces of international relations to any single source have been seen to be unsatisfactory. The struggle for power among nations, for example, can be accepted as a fact in past and current international politics, but to theorize that all other factors are subordinate to or dependent upon this one is to exclude too much that is important and interesting in international phenomena. Similarly, the formulation that asserts that the character of nations and, hence, the character of their participation in international relations are determined by child-rearing practices is simple, appealing; at the same time, however, it is unacceptable because it theorizes a single cause where multiple causation prevails. The Communist theory that international relations are the historical expression of the class struggle also falls into the single-source classification of theory.

The attitude nurtured in the behavioral decade emphasized the necessity of recognizing social multidimensionality and, therefore, multiple causation and the multiple forms of explanation and theory. Under this perspective, one might well conclude that the concept of the struggle for power among nations and the idea that international relations is really a manifestation of a global struggle between social classes both relate to human conflict and that a theory of conflict should encompass these as well as other conflict interpretations. Indeed, the anticipated integrating effect on theory and research in international relations was a main motive in advancing general conflict theory in the '60s, but it is important to add that conflict theory came to coexist with integration theory and game theory, both of which approach some conflict phenomena from different conceptual angles. Similarly, the rejection of the concept that child-rearing practices are at the root of international behaviour stemmed, not from the judgment that there is nothing in the idea, but instead that there are many additional cultural influences within national societies that bear on the external activities pursued by their governments in international politics. There is even room for cultural theory in the study of international relations, although very few promising contributions have been made in this area of inquiry.

Development of the theory of conflict

By the end of the behavioral decade, the multiple-theory perspective had come into the ascendancy in North America and western Europe. International-relations scholars in the Soviet Union who were following closely the Western literature in the field reported with some satisfaction that Western theory had become eclectic and was in disarray in contrast to their own, which they declared to be based on the unified theory of the science of Marxism. At the same time, they gave indications that some of the Western trends in international-relations thinking were being introduced in socialist countries and that a muted contest between traditional and behavioral approaches was underway.

By the 1970s only the realist theory of power politics survived as a relatively simple, persuasive, and comprehensive explanation of international politics in a conceptual environment that otherwise had become pluralistic and complex to the extent that "theory" could no longer be outlined quickly or conveniently in a classroom or before a large audience. A situation had begun to develop that put the question of "What is the theory of international relations?" into about the same class as the question, "What is the theory of biology?" The obvious response to the latter question is not a descriptive statement but another question: "What branch or aspect of biology do you have in mind?" A similar response must be made today for the theory question in international relations.

Contemporary perspectives in international relations. *Foreign-policy and international-systems perspectives.* One important clarification developed from the effort of the behavioral decade to bring the various theories together in a unified structure. It was the consensus that the academic organization of the discipline has two principal parts. It is convenient to call each part a perspective on the subject. The parts are called the foreign-policy and the international-system-analysis perspectives.

The foreign-policy perspective covers many theory and research interests. Fully generalized, it embraces all the inquiries that look into the domestic sources of external or international phenomena. Thus, a study of any set of traits, structures, or processes arising within a national society or polity that can be demonstrated to determine or influence importantly how that society or polity participates in international relations belongs to the foreign-policy perspective. The decision-making approach to international politics meets the requirement, for example. The analysis of the information that decision makers use, of their perceptions and motives, of the influences on them exerted by public opinion, and of the organizational settings in which they operate is a manifestation of the foreign-policy perspective. Studies that seek to relate the facts of wealth and power of a nation to its international status and role provide other illustrations.

Comparative foreign-policy analysis is a new area of theory and research effort that has appeared since the mid-1960s. Its objectives are, first, to examine the data of domestic sources of external conduct country by country using standard criteria of data selection and analysis, and, then, to compare across countries for generalized findings on foreign-policy performances. When the details of the domestic sources and the external performances have been compared, theoretical statements about the domestic–external linkages and about the groupings of countries according to the types of linkage are expected to develop. The comparative foreign-policy approach, so described, is a strategy for developing theory through inductive research procedures.

The second perspective is that of international system analysis. Whereas foreign-policy analysis concentrates on the actors, international system analysis is preoccupied by the interaction. The term "interaction" suggests challenge and response, give and take, or move and countermove. Diplomatic histories feature the narratives of action and response in international situations and interpret the meanings in the exchanges. The theory of the balance of power is an example of an international-system conception. Explanations and descriptions of bargaining in international negotiations fit the perspective and so also do studies of arms races and other escalating processes. A model of the international trading system would be an example of a structural approach to international system studies, while an examination of how and why a coalition of states disintegrates would represent a process approach to international system analysis.

Toward a definition of the international system

The theorist of international systems may gain a general outlook on the phenomena he studies through a system perspective, but he must bring in a certain amount of empirical details when he identifies the components, relationships, and environments of the system that is the object of his theoretical inquiry. A definition of the international system in its broadest reach is expressed in terms such as those in the following passage, but actual theory building must start with some more focussed and circumscribed statement:

> The outermost boundaries of international relations are suggested if we imagine *all* of the exchanges, transactions, contacts, flows of information, and actions of every kind going on at this moment of time between and among the separately constituted societies of the world. To this picture in the mind we should add the effects created within societies from all such interflowing events in earlier times, both of the immediate and the more remote past. Finally, the stream of these actions and responses should be conceived as moving on to the future of tomorrow and beyond, accompanied by the expectations, plans, and proposals of all observers of the phenomena. (From Charles A. McClelland, *Theory and the International System;* The Macmillan Co., 1966.)

System theory does not turn out to be any single formulation; it is more in the nature of a conceptual anchoring point for a variety of specific formulations. Thus one system theorist may define the components of his system as geographical nation-states related according to rules and political structures, whereas another theorist may define the components of his system as nonterritorial, nonstate transactional units only partly related by the influences wielded by national governments.

The general system perspective. Although the theoretical development of the system idea may lead to very diverse outcomes, another more general concept—that of open, adaptive systems—may provide the most promising approach to a comprehensive understanding of the dynamics of relations among nations. Without imposing any single school of thought or any single interpretation of world affairs, it has a loosely unifying effect on the outlook of students of the field. The general system perspective on international relations may be compared to the map of a little-explored continent. Outlines, broad features, and a continental delineation are not in question, but everything else remains in doubt, is subject to controversy, and awaits exploration. One commentator has remarked that general system theory is not really a theory but instead is "a program or a direction in the contemporary philosophy of science." (From Anatol Rapoport, "Systems Analysis," in *International Encyclopedia of the Social Sciences*, vol. 15, p. 452, 1968.)

General concept of open, adaptive systems

As noted above, the quest for theoretical unification during the behavioral decade resulted in the widespread acceptance of two perspectives—a foreign-policy approach and an international-system approach. The general concept of open, adaptive systems provides a conceptual bridge connecting the two perspectives and creates a loose bond joining many of the diverse theoretical formulations prevailing in the field. An examination of the line of general thinking that builds the bridge and provides the bond is, therefore, well worth attention.

One begins to think about almost any open, adaptive system that involves human beings as a living system. If the system is living, its pervading characteristic is activity. Acting units, however they are recognized and defined, are doing things, participating in events, carrying forward processes, and creating effects. The effects created by activity include progressive influences on the actors. That is to say, the acting unit is immune neither to the effects of its own participation nor to the participatory influences generated by other acting units. It is this situation that establishes the condition of the openness of a system. Streams of influencing activity contain two kinds of processing: the first kind is regular, which is to say, governed by rules and repetitive in form, and the second kind is unexpected, irregular, and variant.

It is the second type that stimulates change and that initiates the special processing called adaptation. A living system is open and is able to adapt, however, only if it in some way has gained access to information on the state of affairs that joins it with its environment and, further, in some way has achieved means to direct and to change its stream of activity. Thus in addition to the fundamental concept terms of openness and adaptation, the general system perspective incorporates the ideas of communication and corrective action or, more generally, of communication and control.

All this is nothing much more than a contemporary expression of the ancient philosophical notion that life is a flowing river, never in being in any fixed, concrete sense, but always in motion and always becoming. To this old view, the modern rendering adds yet one other fundamental feature: the observation that there is a systematic deception afflicting human understanding when the unit of action—the actor or the initiator—is seen as an entity. For social phenomena, the system perspective advises us that we make a grievous error when we identify individual persons, groups, organizations, nations, and so on as separate, uniquely named things. Recognized correctly, all these are nothing other than organized and interlocking activity flows, proceeding across historical time in somewhat regularized fashion. John Doe is to be described, literally, as an organized packet of active processes in exchange with an environment and utilizing communication and control to survive and adapt. The same description fits Japan: an incredibly complex network of related action much more than a place, a people, or a name.

Not only does the general system perspective urge that the "actor" be considered as a configuration of activity but it also prompts a recognition that, most often, the configuration itself has a hierarchical organization. In fact, the use of the term "system" is ordinarily an effort to convey the meaning that smaller organized activity flows serve larger activity flows and that the functional linking of subordinate parts to the operating whole is the process that defines what an actor really is. Thus the conventional explanation is that any recognizable living system is made up of related "components" and that each component, when examined at its own level, is found to be a functioning system in its own right. It also may be called a "subsystem." The specialized literature on the nature and operations of open, adaptive systems at large proceeds from the basis outlined here to explorations of more detailed aspects of structures, functions, processes, and effects of system maintenance and system change and also into particular phenomena of communication and corrective action. Enough of the system conceptualization has been suggested here, however, to show next how these fundamentals have been translated for the purposes of international-relations theory.

In world history, the earth has been populated by hundreds of separate and relatively isolated social systems. Each system, as a somewhat ordered stream of interrelated activities, has had exchanges with its particular environment in its own time and in its own way and has employed communication and control capabilities either to succeed at adaptation or to fail at it and, therefore, perish. What today is called international relations is that sector of exchange of a social system with its particular environment that has to do with interlinked action flows to and from other separate social systems. The knowledge problem of international relations is to understand, describe, and explain such flows to and from social systems from their source to their termination. Social systems thus consist of complexes of "internal" interacting subsystems or components, only some of which connect their processes with the action flows between that social system and another.

Internal processes and interactive processes of nations

The next logical thought then is that there can be only two sources of international conduct. One originates in the activity complexes within each participating social system and the other arises from the effects of the interlinked action flows to and from the participating social systems that together make up the membership of an international system. Hence, two basic perspectives of theory and research on international relations are distinguished by the primary attention given either to the origins of conduct arising from internal processes or to origins of conduct arising from the effects of the processes of exchange between social systems—or, to put it more succinctly, from the effects of interaction.

Obviously, the two perspectives are related because each casts its beam on a sector of a whole phenomenon of action and interaction. If he expects to be understood, the theorist must specify not only the basic perspective he wishes to emphasize but also particular identifications of the "units" of action, the kinds of action flows, and the linkages of processes and effects in this particular conception of the system that concerns him. In a multidimensional social world, the theorist can exercise his choice of a focus of inquiry in many different ways. Multiple theories are the outcome that may be expected from the introduction of the concept of general systems into the study of international relations.

The rise of quantitative research and computers. The emphasis on theory building and theory integrating after World War II was perhaps a reaction against the emphasis on methodology inherent in the historical and institutional studies of the 1930s. In turn, the renewed interest in empirical research after the behavioral decade probably was a reaction against the excessively intensive theorizing. Only part of the renewal of interest in data gathering and data analysis can be accounted for in this way, however. The marked increase in quantitative data studies after the mid-1960s has resulted from the direct influence of the computer.

Computerization came late to the field of international relations; how to use the machines to good advantage was not apparent at first because most observations on the conditions of international relations are recorded in narrative or literary form. The belief was strong that computers could handle only strictly numerical data. Some conservatives argued that the most important aspects of foreign policy and international politics could never be analyzed except by impressions developed in diplomatic work or through inspired insights. Further, the data problems in the study of international relations are particularly trying because so much vital information on diplomatic and military activities is held in secret by governments. The ability to observe only the visible portion of the iceberg and yet to have the responsibility to account for all of it tends to dampen the enthusiasm for research based on the minute analysis of detailed facts. It seems easier and sometimes more satisfying to produce speculative analysis than to build interpretations based strictly on available data. Investigations made in the mid-1960s revealed that the discipline was doing an inadequate job in the management of the data that were accessible. Bibliographical services and other fundamental informational resources were evaluated and found to be disorganized and inefficient.

Uses of computers in international relations

The first big discovery about computers in the study of international relations was that they could be made to serve the function of marvelously efficient librarians. By placing data collections under computer management, researchers could improve their investigations by incorporating vastly larger collections of facts in their work. Facts that had a narrative, nonquantitative form could be included in storage and retrieval systems almost as readily as numerical data. The second revelation was that by systematic coding and counting, many kinds of nonquantitative data could be transformed into quantitative indicator information and then be condensed and evaluated by mathematical and statistical procedures. Vistas on new research possibilities were opened and exploratory studies were made in a number of directions.

The growth of quantitative, computer-assisted research is the most prominent new development in the field. Although quantitative, computer-assisted research is commonly associated with the "behavioral movement," in many respects it harkens back to the "traditional" concerns and problems of diplomatic history. Detailed, painstaking examination of historical records has again become important. The new research is interesting in at least one other respect: it gives promise of bringing the interests of academic theory and research into closer accord with the interests of government analysts and the practitioners of diplomacy.

THE RELATIONSHIPS OF SCHOLARSHIP AND ACTION IN FOREIGN AFFAIRS

The differences between the interests of scholars and practitioners of international affairs have appeared to be more prominent than the similarities. A steady concern of scholars has been to avoid both the fact and the reputation of serving as apologists for official foreign policies. One of the first teachings of the idealism of the discipline's founding period at the time of World War I was to maintain an attitude of future-oriented reform of the international order. Existing systems had lesser importance according to the early objectives of the field. The principle of scientific detachment in social-science research also has contributed to the scholarly effort to evaluate international events and developments from a global standpoint rather than from the perspective of any one country's foreign-policy position. On the other side, practitioners have been inclined more to indifference than to hostility in their attitudes toward academics in international relations. They frequently have professed that for their day-to-day work they have found little of value in the theory and research contributions of the field. One looks in vain, therefore, for many signs of direct influence in either direction. An indirect and subtle exchange has occurred, nevertheless, and it has had importance in the direction of foreign affairs.

Mutual influences of government and academia

New international programs or new foreign-policy directions undertaken by governments often have attracted so much interest in the universities that research programs have been initiated and special subfields of international studies have resulted. Examples of such subfields include: (1) "national development" stimulated by the foreign-assistance programs to aid underdeveloped countries; (2) the "area studies" that emerged from World War II because of the problems that Western governments had in finding knowledgeable personnel who understood the languages, histories, cultures, geography, and politics of Asian, African, and Latin American regions; and (3) "national security," resulting from the heavy influence of military factors on foreign policy and especially from the nuclear-control problem in the post-World War II period.

The indirect influence flowing in the other direction from university studies into governmental thinking may be traced in a number of noteworthy examples during the past two decades: first, the realist formulation of the power-politics theory has filtered into the foreign-policy thinking of the United States government to such an extent that most foreign-policy decisions have been defended by arguments of national interest and power calculation and opposing views have been discounted for reflecting insufficient "hard-nosed" realism. Another interesting example was the preoccupation of Pres. John F. Kennedy's administration with the details of the process of foreign-policy decision making in crisis periods. This orientation can be traced to the popularity of decision-making theory advanced in the academic field in the preceding decade. One other example has been identified in the Soviet Union's revision of foreign-affairs doctrine to accommodate the deterrence theory of nuclear defense. Concepts drawn from the literature of American "defense intellectuals" can be readily seen in Soviet works on military doctrine.

Although the past relations of scholars and practitioners of international relations have been relatively mild and indirect, the future may change this customary relationship. The implications of system theory can be expected to percolate slowly but deeply into the understanding of both officials and the public. As this occurs, there will be greater appreciation of how truly complex and far-reaching the flows of international events are. The problems of survival and adaptation will be seen in a new light and the realization of how interdependent modern nation-states are—how much they are bound to a common fate—should lead to more careful, better researched, and more deliberate formulations of foreign policy. The search for more accurate appraisals of the state of the world in its international aspect, which is the vocation of theory and research in academic international relations, should bring officials and researchers together.

On the other side of the relationship, the surge of growth in quantitative, computer-assisted studies in the universities is creating an increasing appetite for more frequent and more exact reports on the state of the world and in more and more of its aspects. The academic community in whatever country one might name lacks the resources and trained manpower to satisfy this growing appetite for data. The demand could well lead to increased responsiveness of the data-gathering services of national governments and to large reductions both in secrecy and in governmental interference with free public communication among nations. The current practice of withholding large amounts of information about developments in the flows of international events is an atavism left over from the era of aristocratic diplomacy. Today it has become a threat to the survival of mankind.

If the data on the conditions and relationships of the world's social systems (now made more manageable and more available for immediate use through computer systems) are brought into full and untrammeled circulation, the academic field of international relations and the governmental analysis and planning agencies will have much more in common than they have had. The end result, as much to be hoped for as predicted, should be the development of entirely new, more competent, and more realistic approaches to the formulation and execution of foreign policies.

BIBLIOGRAPHY. ADDA B. BOZEMAN, *Politics and Culture in International History* (1960), is the best guide to histories and concepts of past international systems. Other useful references that survey premodern international relations are: COLEMAN PHILLIPSON, *The International Law and Custom of Ancient Greece and Rome*, 2 vol. (1911); RICHARD L. WALKER, *The Multi-State System of Ancient China* (1953); GEOFFREY F. HUDSON, *Europe and China: A Survey of Their Relations From the Earliest Times to 1800* (1931); and FRANK M. RUSSELL, *Theories of International Relations* (1936). SHMUEL N. EISENSTADT, *Political Systems of Empires* (1963), has much information on concepts and organizations of ancient empires. Accounts of the earlier development of the academic study of international relations may be found in EDITH E. WARE, *A Study of International Relations in the United States: A Survey for 1937* (1938); SIR ALFRED ZIMMERN, *The Study of International Relations* (1931); and GRAYSON L. KIRK, *The Study of International Relations in American Colleges and Universities* (1947). Representative of the work of the 1930s that widened the scope of the field are HAROLD D. LASSWELL, *World Politics and Personal Insecurity* (1935; paperback ed., 1965); FREDERICK L. SCHUMAN, *International Politics: An Introduction to the Western State System and the World Community*, 6th ed. (1958); C.K. LEITH, *World Minerals and World Politics* (1931, reprinted 1970); W.S. THOMPSON, *Danger Spots in World Population* (1929); PAUL RADIN, *The Racial Myth* (1934); NICHOLAS SPYKMAN, *America's Strategy in World Politics* (1942, reprinted 1970); CARL J. FRIEDRICH, *Foreign Policy in the Making* (1938); BROOKS EMENY, *The Strategy of Raw Materials* (1935); ABRAM KARDINER, *The Psychological Frontiers of Society* (1945); QUINCY WRIGHT, *A Study of War*, 2nd ed., 2 vol. (1965); and E.H. CARR, *The Twenty Years' Crisis, 1919–1939*, 2nd ed. (1946, reprinted 1964). The idealist attempt to answer the challenge of political realism may be traced in THOMAS I. COOK and MALCOLM MOOS, *Power Through Purpose: The Realism of Idealism As a Basis for Foreign Policy* (1954); and JOHN H. HERZ, *Political Realism and Political Idealism* (1951). Four books on the psychological and cultural aspects of the behavioral study of international relations are an excellent introduction: J. DAVIS SINGER, *Human Behavior and International Politics* (1965); OTTO KLINEBERG, *The Human Dimension in International Relations* (1964); JOSEPH H. DE RIVERA, *The Psychological Dimension of Foreign Policy* (1968); and HERBERT C. KELMAN, *International Behavior* (1965). The most famous book of its time on a psychocultural interpretation of national behaviour was RUTH BENEDICT, *The Chrysanthemum and the Sword* (1946, reprinted 1967). RICHARD C. SNYDER, H.W. BRUCK, and BURTON SAPIN, *Decision-Making As an Approach to the Study of International Politics* (1954), is still basic reading on the decision-making approach, but see also the data in GLENN D. PAIGE, *The Korean Decision* (1968). The most convenient compilation of varied examples of the theory and research of the behavioral decade is JAMES N. ROSENAU, *International Politics and Foreign Policy*, rev. ed. (1969). For conflict theory and international applications of game theory, see KENNETH E. BOULDING, *Conflict and Defense: A General Theory* (1962); THOMAS C. SCHELLING, *The Strategy of Conflict* (1960); and ANATOL RAPOPORT, *Fights, Games and Debates* (1960). An introduction to general system theory in the social sciences is WALTER BUCKLEY, *Sociology and Modern Systems Theory* (1967). MORTON A. KAPLAN, *System and Process in International Politics* (1957); and CHARLES A. MCCLELLAND, *Theory and the International System* (1966), take different approaches to the applications of general systems ideas in the study of international relations. The first published collection of quantitative studies of foreign policy and international relations was J. DAVID SINGER, *Quantitative International Politics* (1968), but more sophisticated analyses have been made since. The selections in the volume do not represent, therefore, the current state of the art. No good survey of how computers relate to research on international relations has appeared, but important material is included in DAVIS B. BOBROW and JUDAH L. SCHWARTZ, *Computers and the Policy-Making Community; Applications to International Relations* (1968).

(C.A.McC.)

Interplanetary Medium

The planets of the solar system, moving in their regular orbits, traverse a vast space containing so little matter that for some purposes it may be considered empty. There is not enough matter in it, for example, to slow the planets' motions noticeably, even over periods of many millions of years. By definition, the interplanetary medium includes whatever matter does exist between the planets and the other bodies of the solar system and includes the gravitational, electric, and magnetic forces that pervade the volume of space dominated by the Sun.

The gravity and radiation effects of the Sun are not confined to the relatively thin, disk-shaped zone in which all the planets have their orbits, but dominate a probably spherical volume of space called the solar cavity (see below *The solar-wind plasma*), which is centred on the Sun and has a diameter probably greater than that of the largest planetary orbit. The term interplanetary medium is used in an extended sense to describe the forces and the thinly scattered matter existing throughout this entire volume.

MATERIAL COMPONENTS AND FIELDS

Interplanetary dust and minor objects. The interplanetary material includes small quantities of dust that probably was produced by collisions between minor planets (asteroids) and that appears to be of much the same material as meteorites. The density of the matter within particles lies in the range of two to eight grams per cubic centimetre, roughly similar to the densities of earthly rocks. Some material, discharged from comets, has a lower density. Most dust particles appear to be orbiting the Sun in planes near the zone of planetary orbits. Other kinds of interplanetary matter include: neutral (*i.e.*, not ionized) hydrogen gas; a plasma gas of electrically charged particles consisting mainly of protons and elec-

Particle Density in Interplanetary Space

particles	number/cm³	remarks
Dust	10^{-12}	radii above 3×10^{-5} cm
Protons	8	varies moderately during the solar cycle
Electrons	8	varies moderately during the solar cycle
Cosmic rays	6×10^{-11}	from galactic sources
Hydrogen	0.01	interstellar value = 0.7/cm³

trons formed by the ionization of hydrogen emitted by the Sun; and cosmic rays, which are mainly positively-charged atomic nuclei moving at high speeds. Most of the cosmic rays arrive in the solar cavity from outside the solar system and the rest are emitted by the Sun. The Table shows the densities of the various kinds of matter in interplanetary space, at approximately Earth's distance from the Sun. For purposes of comparison it may be noted that air at sea level contains approximately 2.5×10^{19} molecules per cubic centimetre. This is on the order of 10^{18} times more than the number of particles of all kinds to be found per cubic centimetre in interplanetary space outside the planetary atmospheres. Yet discoveries made since 1955 have shown that this tenuous interplanetary matter, particularly the charged particles of the plasma, is responsible for many phenomena observed in space and in planetary atmospheres (see below).

The Sun has magnetic fields of force at its surface. These and the presence of many charged particles in interplanetary space necessarily form electrical and magnetic fields there, while the Sun and planets produce strong gravitational fields. Which of these forces will chiefly control the motions of an interplanetary particle depends on the particle's nature. A charged particle with a small mass will have its behaviour strongly affected or even dominated by electromagnetic fields; on the other hand, the motion in space of the larger electrically neutral bodies is dominated by gravitational forces. The motion of small particles (radius less than or equal to 10^{-5} centimetres) near the Sun may be influenced chiefly by still other forces, the pressure of the Sun's radiation tending to force them outward, and a loss of momentum through re-emission of light (the Poynting-Robertson effect, named for a British physicist, John Henry Poynting, and a U.S. physicist, Howard Percy Robertson) tending to move them closer to the Sun.

The flux of particles in space (*i.e.*, the number of them that cross a unit area in a unit time) may be measured by several methods. Equipment on spacecraft, for example, can count certain kinds of particles directly. Observations from the Earth of astronomical phenomena produced by interplanetary particles such as the zodiacal light, and of meteors (see below), and examination of meteorites and meteor craters found on Earth's surface all suggest that the cumulative flux of particles, or objects, with mass greater than any chosen value (measured in grams) is such that its logarithm can be expressed $\log I = -14.0 - \log m$, in which I is the cumulative flux and m is the mass. $I(m)$ is measured in particles per square metre per second per hemisphere of the Earth. The equation is thought to hold for regions along the orbital path of Earth (when Earth itself is elsewhere on the orbit; particles accumulate more densely near a planet) and for values of m between about 10^{-12} gram and 10^{12} grams. The smallest of these "particles" have radii of about 0.000025 centimetre and the largest are minor planets with radii of about 25 metres. Large flux variations observed from spacecraft indicate that dust particles form streams similar to meteoroid streams.

Particle flux close to the Earth

Rocket and satellite observations indicate that the flux close to Earth is considerably higher than the above in the narrower mass range between 10^{-13} gram and 10^{-6} gram (with an uncertainty of about a factor of ten), and, thus, in the vicinity of Earth there appears to be an accumulation of dust due to the Earth's gravitational effects. Many particles are swept up by the Earth and some are seen as incandescent meteors. Those smaller than about 0.0005 centimetres in radius are not burnt up or melted on entering the atmosphere and penetrate to Earth to deposit some 5×10^9 kilograms of material each year.

The solar-wind plasma. The ionized components in space near the Sun come principally from its corona (*i.e.*, its outer atmosphere), a completely ionized gas with a density of about 1,000,000 electrons and 1,000,000 protons per cubic centimetre and a temperature close to 1,000,000° C (see SUN). The flow of this gas, which expands continuously into the surrounding space, constitutes what is known as the solar wind.

The average solar-wind speed increases at first with increasing distance from the Sun until it reaches a point after which it remains substantially constant. Typically, this speed is 200 kilometres per second at a distance of 0.1 astronomical unit (an astronomical unit is the average Sun–Earth distance, 1.5×10^8 kilometres) from the Sun increasing to about 350 kilometres per second at one astronomical unit. Plasma particles also have random velocities within the stream that are specified in terms of a temperature, at Earth's orbit, of about 100,000° C (this corresponds to a mean random proton speed of 50 kilometres per second, and a mean random electron speed of 2,000 kilometres per second. The particle density decreases with increasing distance, r, from the Sun in proportion to one over the distance squared times the velocity, V, or, in symbols, as $1/r^2V$ and is about eight protons per cubic centimetre and eight electrons per cubic centimetre at Earth's orbit. The kinetic temperature also decreases as the distance from the Sun increases.

When the velocity exceeds the local speed of sound (*i.e.*, the average speed of random particle motion) in the plasma, the flow is said to be supersonic, a condition that first occurs at a distance of about 0.03 astronomical unit. This supersonic flow is expected to become subsonic rather abruptly at a distance somewhere between 10 astronomical units and 100 astronomical units from the Sun. The region inside this transition boundary, referred to as the solar cavity, is probably approximately spherical. The corona is slightly less extensive near the Sun's polar regions, however, and there are corresponding variations in the position of the boundary of the solar cavity. The energy essential to maintain the solar wind is continually transferred to it from the Sun. This energy enables the coronal particles to escape; without it they would be bound to the Sun by its gravitational attraction. The Sun loses about 10^9 kilograms of material to the solar wind each second; this amount is too small compared to its total mass to affect its evolution significantly.

The solar-wind plasma consists primarily of protons (H^+) and electrons; also present is approximately 4.5 percent (by number) of helium ions (He^{++}) and less than 0.5 percent of other positive ions. A few of these have been identified (five, six, and seven times ionized oxygen and triply ionized carbon, O^{5+}, O^{6+}, O^{7+}, C^{3+}). All of the ions present in the corona (see SUN) are likely to be present in the solar-wind plasma, but not necessarily in the same proportions.

Changes in solar-wind plasma

Conditions within the solar cavity are not steady. Though the Sun's output of radiation is essentially constant, moderate changes occur continually in the activity of its surface; the solar-wind speed and the density of ions similarly vary continuously in a moderate way. The intensities of the magnetic and electric fields associated with the solar-wind plasma also change. Occasional major variations occur when very large outbursts on the surface of the Sun (frequently associated with sunspots) hurl great masses of plasma into space. These masses move radially outwards with speeds of up to 1,000 kilometres per second and may carry relatively intense magnetic fields with them.

Magnetic fields. The plasma near the Sun consists of electrically charged particles and, even though of extremely low density, constitutes an electrical conducting medium when considered on the interplanetary scale. Its conductivity is responsible for the presence of magnetic fields of force in the solar cavity, and because of it, magnetic fields of force are transported with the plasma ions as if "frozen-in" to the plasma.

Thus, magnetic fields of force present at the surface of the Sun are carried outward with the solar wind; the magnetic lines of force remain attached to the surface of the Sun and, because of its rotation, take up a spiral form in space called Archimedes' spirals. The magnetic-field lines in the plane of the ecliptic (*i.e.*, the Earth's orbital path) are shown in Figure 1; at Earth they make an angle of approximately 55° with the Sun–Earth line. Out of the ecliptic plane the magnetic lines of force are spirals, each of which lies on the surface of a cone with axis coincident with the axis of rotation of the Sun.

The intensity of the magnetic field varies across the surface of the Sun and varies correspondingly in space; the whole pattern of magnetic lines of force in space co-rotates with the Sun. When the intensity of the magnetic field in gauss (a unit of magnetic intensity) at the surface of the Sun is one gauss (a typical value), the corresponding intensity at a point of Earth's orbit is about 5×10^{-5} gauss, a value that may be compared with 0.3 gauss for the intensity of the Earth's magnetic field at the Equator. The magnetic-field pattern in space is rather more irregular than that shown in Figure 1, having many small-scale irregularities superimposed on the regular pattern; these irregularities are also transported outward with the solar wind.

From E. Parker, *Astrophysical Journal* (1958); University of Chicago Press

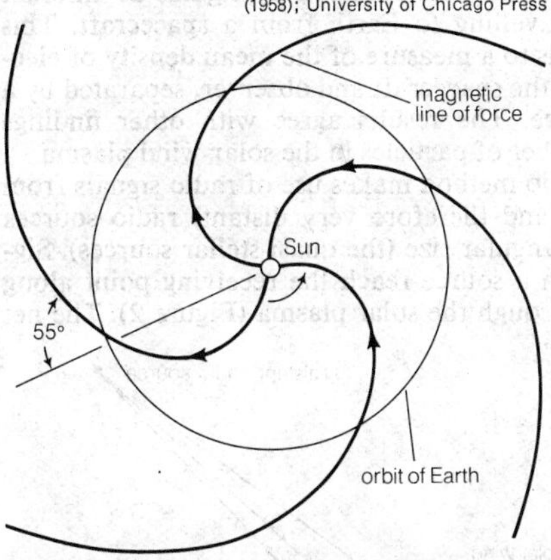

Figure 1: Pattern of the interplanetary magnetic field in the ecliptic plane (simplified).

Electric fields. Associated closely with the magnetic fields in space are electric forces; *i.e.*, forces that act to attract or repel electrically charged particles. The intensity of the electric field is proportional to the velocity, to the intensity of the magnetic field, and to the sine of the angle between the solar-wind direction and the magnetic-field direction (Figure 1). The field has a typical value of .001 volt per metre at the orbit of Earth, with the direction of the force perpendicular to the plane of the ecliptic.

Hydrogen. The presence of about one neutral hydrogen atom per cubic centimetre of interstellar space has been established. Some of this hydrogen enters the solar cavity but is then reduced in quantity by two processes. (1) Photo-ionization changes the neutral hydrogen to ionized hydrogen (protons) by the action of ultraviolet radiation from the Sun; this effect increases closer to the Sun. (2) Charge exchange with the solar wind causes some ingoing hydrogen atoms to exchange electrical charge with outgoing solar-wind protons to produce ingoing protons and outgoing hydrogen atoms. At five astronomical units from the Sun the neutral-hydrogen concentration has been reduced to about 0.03 atom per cubic centimetre, and at the orbit of Earth (one astronomical unit) the concentration is about 0.01 atom per cubic centimetre.

Cosmic rays. Like the solar wind, the cosmic-ray component of the interplanetary medium consists of electrically charged particles, mostly protons (H^+) and helium nuclei (He^{++}), with relatively small quantities of many other elements such as lithium, boron, carbon, oxygen, neon, sulfur, and iron. Cosmic rays are distinguished from the solar-wind particles by their speeds near that of light and kinetic energies measured in millions of electron volts. Solar-wind protons have kinetic energies of about 800 electron volts. An electron volt is the unit of electron energy and represents the energy acquired by an electron in passing through an electric potential difference of one volt.

Cosmic rays are few in number compared with the solar-wind particles (see Table) and have virtually no effect on the structure of the solar wind and the associated magnetic fields. Continuous measurements of cosmic-ray flux in interplanetary space show that the flux has two main parts; one that is fairly steady over months and one that is transient. The cosmic rays of the steady component with kinetic energies greater than about 10^8 electron volts come, initially, from galactic or interstellar space surrounding the solar system; those of lower energy are partly of galactic origin and partly of solar origin. The transient cosmic-ray particles, of solar origin, originate from explosive eruptions on the Sun that generate particles with sufficient energy to escape into interplanetary space. Typically, near Earth, a sharp peak in the cosmic-ray flux occurs between 20 minutes and three hours after such an explosion at the Sun, followed by a slow decrease, lasting from many hours to a few days, to the normal level. The number of transient cosmic-ray events recorded depends upon the kinetic energy of the particles being observed. The largest solar outbursts (see SUN) generate cosmic rays with kinetic energies up to a maximum of approximately 10^9 electron volts, and occur only once or twice per year. At kinetic energies of about 5×10^6 electron volts there is a transient event associated with small solar outbursts every few days.

Cosmic rays from the Sun

The number of galactic particles observed in the steady component of the cosmic-ray flux changes with the general level of activity on the surface of the Sun. This activity has an 11 year periodicity known as the solar cycle (see SUN), and the flux of cosmic-ray particles decreases as the solar activity increases. For example, at the orbit of Earth the flux of cosmic-ray protons with kinetic energies near 10^8 electron volts may change by a factor of about ten during the solar cycle, and that of 10^9 electron-volt protons by a factor of about two. This effect is produced by the fields of magnetic force that are being transported through the solar cavity by the solar wind. Increases in the irregularity of the interplanetary magnetic field, associated with an increase in solar activity, make it more difficult for the galactic cosmic-ray particles to penetrate the solar cavity to near Earth, say, and thus, fewer of them are observed. In other words, electrically charged particles moving in a magnetic field of force are acted upon by forces that modify their trajectories.

The first cosmic-ray particles that arrive near Earth from an eruption on the Sun are known usually to be following the Archimedean spiral of the interplanetary magnetic field (Figure 1). The observation of this fact provided the first confirmation of the spiral structure of the interplanetary magnetic field.

In general, the study of variations in the cosmic-ray flux provides useful information about the magnetic-field conditions that exist in the solar cavity.

PHENOMENA CAUSED BY THE INTERPLANETARY MEDIUM

Most of the components of interplanetary space have been measured from spacecraft but are not visible directly. Some phenomena produced by these components, however, are visible directly from Earth, and, even before the advent of spacecraft, the presence of interplanetary dust and the ejection of plasma from the Sun had been inferred from such evidence. The first two of the following subsections deal with phenomena due to uncharged components (the dust and grains) and the remainder with phenomena resulting from the solar-wind plasma, whether or not these are visible from Earth.

The zodiacal light and gegenschein. At the end of twilight, and before dawn, a faint band of light can be seen above the horizon in clear skies away from city lights. It extends upward above the Sun's position and along the line of the ecliptic plane. The band, called the zodiacal light because it appears within the region of sky occupied by the constellations of the zodiac, fades off with increasing angular distance from the Sun and with distance perpendicular to the ecliptic plane. At its brightest the zodiacal light is about as bright as the Milky Way. This occurs when the ecliptic plane is perpendicular to the horizon; *e.g.*, for observers in northern midlatitudes, during March and April evenings and the mornings of September and October. The band is up to 20 percent polarized; that is, the intensities of the light vibrations in perpendicular planes differ by 20 percent; it can be traced photoelectrically and photographically throughout the night sky. In the direction opposite to the Sun this light forms a hazy area about 8° long and 6° wide known as the gegenschein, or counterglow. The gegenschein, some 15 to 30 times fainter than the zodiacal light at its brightest, is difficult to detect with the unaided eye. In quantitative measurements, these effects must be separated from the bright starlight, the faint stars, the scattered starlight, and the airglow (light emitted in the upper atmosphere).

Origin of the zodiacal light

The zodiacal light is believed to be due to scattering (re-emission or reflection in a new direction) of light from the Sun by interplanetary particles with radii of about 10^{-5} centimetre. Quantitative studies show that the particulate material is confined near the ecliptic, and that the density falls off with distance from the Sun as the inverse of the third power of its square root. The scattering particles are dielectric (nonconducting) rather than metallic; and quantitative theories of the scattering predict the observed form of the light intensity and polarization characteristics. Solar-wind electrons are thought to contribute a negligible amount to the polarization; and some workers in this field consider that at least 10 percent, and perhaps more, of the polarization may come from the highly concentrated region of dust known to be present near Earth.

The theoretical studies noted above also account for the gegenschein because they predict an enhancement of light from the direction opposite the Sun. Other, but less likely, possibilities are that the gegenschein is an extension of the Earth's dust cloud due to solar radiation pressure, or an accumulation of dust at a point 0.01 astronomical unit behind Earth in Earth's orbit where the gravitational forces of Earth and Sun cancel each other.

Noctilucent clouds. Noctilucent (night luminous) clouds are remarkable phenomena. Thought to be due to the penetration of small interplanetary dust particles into the atmosphere of Earth, they are not well understood.

Cloud formation and characteristics

The clouds form in a band a few kilometres thick at an altitude of 82 kilometres, where the air temperature passes through a minimum (the mesopause) before increasing again at higher altitudes. They can be distinguished from normal clouds only when they are seen against a dark sky and when, at a greater height than most of the air, they are illuminated by the Sun while the lower air is not. For this to occur the Sun must be between 6° and 16° below the horizon. Below latitude 50° the total possible viewing time available is about two hours each day. This generally increases at higher latitudes because of the tilt of the Earth's axis. In the Northern Hemisphere, most of the noctilucent clouds occur between June 1 and August 15 with a peak in late July; the observed occurrence is greatest between latitude 50° N and 70° N. Although generally rare, under optimum conditions (late July, 60° N) noctilucent clouds can be seen during 75 percent of the clear nights. Some displays cover an area of 2,000,000 to 3,000,000 square kilometres, 11 such events being recorded during 1963–65. A single cloud may last for several hours.

Rocket-borne instruments have established that the clouds are composed of particles with diameters between 0.1 and 0.3 micron (one micron is one-millionth of a metre). Many are coated with a layer presumed to be ice that increases their diameters two to five times to roughly the wavelengths of visible light.

Comet tails. When moving to within the orbit of Mars, a comet may develop a visible tail that often subdivides into two or three tails (see COMET). The principal tail is of ionized material and because of its continuous interaction with the solar wind always points directly away from the Sun. This phenomenon presents the simplest known demonstration of the existence of the solar wind. Observed accelerations of the material of the comet tail have been related to a source of increase in flow of the solar-wind plasma, such as an earlier active region or outburst on the Sun. The speed of travel of the plasma from the Sun to the comet can then be inferred.

Studies of comet tails led to the postulate of a continuous emission of particles from the Sun. A theory announced in 1958 demonstrated that a steady outward flow of coronal material was possible, and direct observations of such a flow were reported first from a U.S.S.R. space probe in 1960. Verification of the solar-wind plasma flow was obtained in 1962 through measurements made on a spacecraft of the U.S.

Radio dispersion and scintillation. In radio observations use is made of the fact that the presence of electrons in space reduces the speed of propagation of radio signals. The speed of propagation decreases as the frequency of the radio signals increases, an effect called dispersion. It is possible to make precise measurements of the difference in time required by signals at different frequencies travelling to Earth from a spacecraft. This difference leads to a measure of the mean density of electrons between the spacecraft and observer, separated by a known distance. The results agree with other findings about the number of particles in the solar-wind plasma.

Signals from quasi-stellar sources

A second radio method makes use of radio signals from extragalactic (and therefore very distant) radio sources of very small angular size (the quasi-stellar sources). Signals from such a source reach the receiving point along many paths through the solar plasma (Figure 2). The net

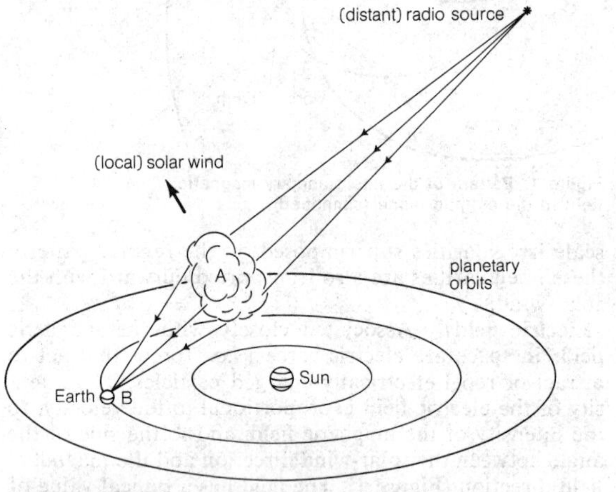

Figure 2: Solar-wind plasma, shown at A, produces scintillation of radio signals from distant source, recorded on Earth, at B.

radio signal fluctuates (scintillates) randomly, just as the light from stars scintillates, or, twinkles as a result of the deflection of some rays passing through the atmosphere of Earth. The principal contribution to the scintillation of the quasi-stellar sources at Earth comes from the plasma in region A of Figure 2 and provides information on the plasma in that region. The arrival of an enhanced plasma cloud at A after a solar outburst is one extreme example.

There is also a pattern of radio signal strength across the Earth's surface at the receiving position, B in Figure 2. As the plasma moves past A, the pattern of signal strength moves correspondingly across the surface at B. Simultaneous observation from three surface stations, B_1, B_2, and B_3, some 100 kilometres apart, provides data from which the solar-wind speed at A can be deduced. By means of these radio techniques and the observations of comet tails, the plasma outside the ecliptic plane, and at distances not explored by spacecraft, can be more or less continuously monitored.

The Earth's magnetosphere. The solar-wind plasma interacts with the magnetic field of force of Earth to form a region called the magnetosphere from within which the plasma is excluded almost completely. The magnetosphere forms because electrically charged particles moving through magnetic fields experience a force that changes their direction. In this way the ions and electrons of the solar-wind plasma are deflected by the magnetic field of Earth; the deflected particles produce electrical currents that, in turn, modify the magnetic field of Earth. The solar wind is deflected, excluded from Earth, and flows around the boundary of the magnetosphere; its speed of flow becomes subsonic during its journey. The front point of the boundary of the magnetosphere is at a distance of about 64,000 kilometres; that is, ten times the Earth's radius from the centre of Earth.

The magnetic-field pattern of Earth is completely changed by the interactions, for, in the absence of solar plasma, it would everywhere have the shape of the inner regions. The outer magnetic lines of force, however, now stretch out behind Earth, and away from the Sun, to form a magnetic tail. The magnetic-field structure, which results from this interaction of the solar wind with Earth, is of major importance in many of the physical phenomena that occur in the near vicinity of Earth.

Auroras. The interplanetary plasma is not entirely excluded from within the magnetosphere. Some of its particles penetrate the magnetospheric boundary, diffuse into the rear portion and then move along the magnetic lines of force and deposit in the polar regions, where they form auroras (see the article AURORAS).

The atmospheres of planets and comets, and the solar wind. Jupiter, which has a magnetic field somewhat like that of Earth, also has a magnetosphere; planets with atmospheres but no significant magnetic fields (*e.g.*, Mars) have solar-wind plasma deposited continuously into their atmospheres, parts of which are also stripped off. The Moon, with no permanent atmosphere and only insignificant local magnetic fields, simply absorbs the impinging particles and forms a region of depleted plasma in space on the side away from the Sun. In each of these cases a taillike region is formed. The comet tail, the magnetospheric tail, the atmospheric tail, and the lunar tail each resemble a giant windsock in space, but only the comet tail is visible to the eye.

THE DIRECT DETECTION OF INTERPLANETARY COMPONENTS

General methods used. Many of the phenomena discussed above provide indirect evidence of the presence of interplanetary matter and plasma. Conclusive evidence of their existence and properties came from direct observations from spacecraft. Until 1970, however, spacecraft had been flown only in the plane of the ecliptic and between heliocentric distances of 0.7 astronomical unit and 1.5 astronomical units, though future spaceflights will undoubtedly extend this range.

Measurements from space probes

Spacecraft used to measure interplanetary conditions may be of satellite type (*i.e.*, in orbits bound to Earth, partly within the magnetosphere), or they may be deep-space probes such as the U.S. spacecraft sent to Mars in 1965 and the U.S.S.R. spacecraft sent to Venus in 1967.

The ionized component of interplanetary matter can now be directly measured fairly readily and by 1970 almost continuous data regarding solar-wind speed, density, and composition was available. Extensive observations of the magnetic-field intensity and the cosmic-ray flux over a wide range of energies are also available. Continuous data about particulate matter, especially particle size and speed, are more difficult to obtain over the wide range of masses of interest.

The general method is to provide suitable detectors on board spacecraft, and to arrange for the data to be radioed to Earth and recorded for subsequent analysis. The principles of some detectors are described below. Many (*e.g.*, the electrostatic solar-wind analyzer) are directional detectors accepting particles from a limited range of directions only; often this directionality can be utilized in conjunction with the spinning motion of a spacecraft to sample many directions in space sequentially.

Principles used in the detection of interplanetary grains and minor objects. The dustlike material in interplanetary space is detected, in general, by registering the impact of the particles with some form of sensor (see SPACE EXPLORATION). A wide range of sensors has been used, the choice depending on the particles to be observed. They are cumulative-flux detectors in that they respond to all particles that produce an impact greater than some threshold value. Measurements at several thresholds are required to determine the distribution of particle masses. The total number of particles and, consequently, of impacts is very small. Contributing also to the difficulties of measurement is the great range of masses found among the "particles" to be studied, from microscopic dust components of 10^{-13} gram to rare objects as masssive as 10^{12} grams.

Space between planets

The low counting rate of impacts in space limits the useful observations that can be made with spacecraft detectors and provides confirmation of the extreme emptiness of interplanetary space. On a spacecraft that travelled past Mars in 1965, only 215 impacts of particles with mass greater than 2×10^{-11} gram were registered in seven months. The counting rate with the same detector for particles with mass greater than 10^{-5} gram would be about one-millionth of the above, so that the flux of particles could not be measured adequately. For particles with mass greater than 10^{-5} gram and diameter greater than 0.01 centimetre a very large sensor is required; and this in effect is provided by the atmosphere of Earth, in which particles with mass greater than 10^{-5} gram become visible as meteors. Flux measures for particles with mass between 10^{-5} gram and 10^{2} grams are obtained by carefully analyzing visual, photographic, and radar observations of the meteor trails. Objects with mass in the range 10^{4} grams to 10^{11} grams pass through the atmosphere and are found as meteorites on the surface of Earth. Estimates of the number that reach the ground are used to infer the interplanetary flux of particles of this size. Large objects (*i.e.*, those with mass greater than 10^{4} grams) are counted by the craters they produce.

Principles used in detection of solar-wind plasma and cosmic rays. Until 1970 two principal types of detector had been used to measure the solar-wind plasma particles from spacecraft: plasma cups (or ion traps) and electrostatic analyzers. The principle of the collection method in each is the selection of specific ions (*e.g.*, H^+, He^{++}) and measurement of the current produced at a collector. The electrostatic analyzer, in contrast to the plasma cup, accepts only particles from a narrow range of directions and a small range of speeds. It is less sensitive than the plasma cup but is more useful for a detailed analysis of the plasma constituents.

All ions entering the analyzer and having the same ratio of kinetic energy to electrical charge are recorded, and by varying the electric potential, the distributions of these two quantities for the incoming ions can be determined. A typical measurement would show a clearly defined major peak in collector current and a secondary peak, attributed respectively to protons (H^+) and helium ions (He^{++}); the mean speed of each of these ion species is usually about 350 kilometres per second; and the width of the peaks would show that the individual ion speeds are grouped closely about the mean speed. The collector currents at each peak are used to determine the ratio of the number of ions of different species; typically, the He^{++}/H^+ ratio is 5 percent. Further minor peaks in collector current would indicate the presence of small quantities of the following ions: doubly ionized helium (the isotope with atomic weight 3), six times ionized oxygen, singly ionized helium-4, triply ionized carbon, and four times ionized oxygen.

Cosmic rays are also charged particles but their considerably higher speed and kinetic energy make different methods of detection necessary. The two principal classes of detectors are ionization-chamber detectors and solid-state detectors; the latter are preferred on spacecraft because of their smaller size. It is possible to arrange that the response will be only to particles arriving from a limited range of directions; *i.e.*, the detector becomes a cosmic-ray telescope. Observations of this type are important in studies of the interplanetary region.

Cosmic rays with a wide range of kinetic energies are

detected by such means; the lowest energy is set by the material enclosing the gas or the material of the solid-state detector. It may be as low as 100,000 electron volts.

BIBLIOGRAPHY. There are no satisfactory general treatments available of the material in this article. Readers wishing more information on particular topics may consult the following review periodicals: *Reviews of Geophysics* (quarterly); *Space Science Reviews* (irreg.); and the *Annual Review of Astronomy and Astrophysics.*

(L.J.G.)

Interstellar Medium

The interstellar medium is the region between the stars. Vast and at first appearance empty, it actually contains enormous, diffuse clouds of matter consisting mainly of hydrogen gas, with a small proportion of heavier atoms and molecules such as those of calcium, sodium, water, ammonia, and formaldehyde. It also contains large quantities of microscopic solid dust particles of uncertain composition. In addition, magnetic fields thread their way throughout interstellar space. The amount of matter in the interstellar medium within the Galaxy is estimated at about 10^{10} times that contained in the Sun (that is, about 5 percent of the Galaxy's total mass). Interstellar matter, both gas and dust, often occurs in cloudlike concentrations, which sometimes condense sufficiently to form stars, and the stars in turn continually lose mass, sometimes through small eruptions, sometimes in catastrophic explosions called supernovae. The mass is thus fed back to the interstellar medium where it mixes with the matter that has not yet formed stars. This circulation of interstellar matter through stars determines to a large extent the amount of the heavier elements in the clouds. The stars, and in particular the supernovae, appear to be the prime generators of more complex atoms by nuclear processes in their interiors.

Interstellar matter is primarily situated in the outer parts of the Galaxy in the so-called spiral arms, described below, which also contain many young stars and diffuse nebulae. Such spiral arms are clearly identified in other spiral galaxies—they extend as curved streaks of brightness winding around an even brighter central region in galaxies such as the Andromeda Nebula. All this material is closely concentrated in a plane, a flat region often called the galactic disk. Owing to the solar system's location with respect to the disk of the Galaxy, of which the Milky Way is the disk seen edge on, its spiral arms lie hidden, one behind the other, in the direction of the bright band of the Milky Way (Figure 1). The constituent of interstellar matter that absorbs starlight is the dust that prevents astronomers from seeing very deep into the Milky Way. The dark bands noticeable on a clear night near the centre of the Milky Way are produced by enormous clouds of this dust. There is a relatively dust-free direction in the Milky Way toward the constellation of Carina, where a line of sight from the observer through a great depth of star-filled space is open along a spiral arm for up to 30,000 light-years' distance.

The interstellar medium can be studied by various techniques. Before 1950 most knowledge was obtained by examining the effects of intervening matter on the light from distant stars, using optical telescopes. Since the development of radio telescopes, astronomers have been able to interpret the radio waves reaching Earth from these tenuously occupied interstellar regions.

Optically, the presence of interstellar matter is manifested in several of the following ways:

1. General absorption of starlight: Light at all wavelengths is absorbed by dust particles, causing an overall dimming of the light over much of the sky, with total absorption in some regions.
2. Selective absorption or reddening of starlight: Because of the smallness of the dust particles, blue light is reflected from them more readily than red light, which has a longer wavelength. If a star is observed through a region of dust the red light is more readily transmitted, whereas the blue light is scattered; hence the star appears redder than it actually is. A similar effect can be seen on Earth at sunset when the Sun appears much redder than it did during the middle of the day because it has to shine through a greater depth of dust when near the horizon.
3. Line absorption of starlight: The atoms and molecules in the interstellar medium are, like those of all gases, capable of absorbing light at certain discrete wavelengths. Electrons, by absorbing light of the correct wavelength, are excited to different levels (or orbits) around the atomic nuclei and the effect of such transitions is observable as a number of dark lines in the spectrum of a star.
4. Polarization of starlight: Starlight in passing through dust clouds becomes polarized—*i.e.,* those light waves parallel to one particular plane are passed more freely than those in other directions—as a result of the interception and redistribution of waves by elongated dust particles (scattering) that have been aligned by a magnetic field in the cloud.
5. Emission and reflection nebulae: The former are produced when young hot stars heat interstellar gas to such an extent that it emits its own light and radio radiation. The latter are dust clouds lit up around cooler stars and shining by reflected starlight much as fog or mist glows around street lamps or automobile headlights.

Types of emission of radio waves

Some constituents of the interstellar medium can be studied through their emitted radio waves—that is, energy waves of wavelength many times longer than that of light. The various types of emission are named or described in the following ways.

1. Continuum radio emission: This can be compared to white light, and is radio energy emitted over a complete wave band region (see ELECTROMAGNETIC RADIATION). Interstellar space is filled with high-energy particles moving nearly at the speed of light called cosmic rays. When these cosmic rays encounter interstellar magnetic fields the particles cannot move in a straight line but are forced to spiral about the lines of magnetic force. In this way, the cosmic rays lose energy that is emitted and that can be observed as radio waves over much of the radio spectrum. Like the starlight mentioned above, this radiation is also polarized.

By courtesy of Bart Bok and A. Rodgers, Mt. Stromlo Observatory, Australia

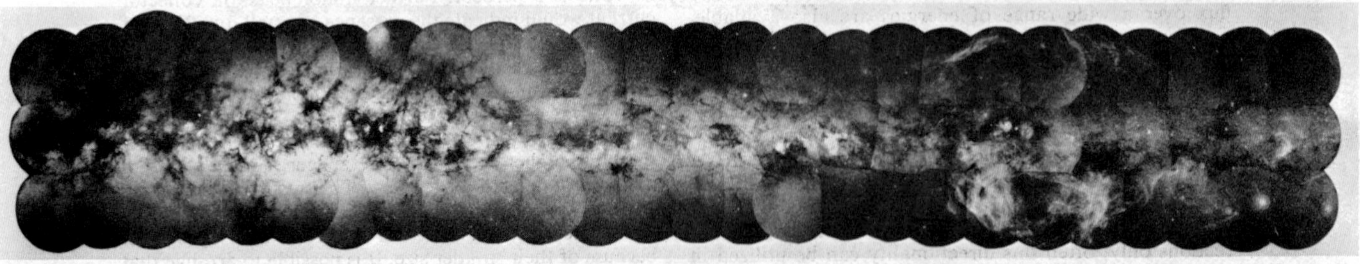

Figure 1: *Southern Milky Way.*
Extensive interstellar dust clouds indicated by dark areas and lanes. Bright area (left side) is the region of the galactic centre in the constellation Sagittarius. The large nearly circular nebulosity (far right) is the Gum Nebula, an irregular nebula, which may be a supernova remnant. An emission nebula, Eta Carinae, is seen as a bright patch (centre right). The Coalsack (centre left) is a dense, obscuring dust cloud. Montage based on *An Atlas of H-Alpha Emission in the Southern Milky Way.*

2. Emission from interstellar hydrogen: Neutral (unionized) hydrogen atoms can absorb or emit tiny amounts of radio energy of a particular wavelength, 21 centimetres. By measuring at this point and comparing with nearby wavelengths, radiating or absorbing hydrogen clouds can be detected.

3. Emission from molecules: The combination of oxygen and hydrogen (OH, the hydroxyl radical referred to as a molecule) can emit or absorb radio waves at many wavelengths, in particular around 18 centimetres. Through measurements at this important wavelength, OH has been found to be common in many parts of the Milky Way. Other molecules such as water, ammonia, and formaldehyde emit radio waves in the wavelength range of one to six centimetres.

The optical and radio emissions have provided most information on the interstellar medium. Balloon, rocket, and satellite astronomy in the ultraviolet, X-ray, gamma-ray, and infrared parts of the spectrum can also provide information, but in the past these methods have contributed relatively little knowledge in this field of astronomy. The use of ultraviolet and X-ray telescopes on satellites should in future lead to an enormous increase in knowledge of the properties of the interstellar medium, in particular the relative abundances of the elements.

It is difficult to observe interstellar matter and magnetic fields, and astronomers therefore do not yet have a complete picture of the precise nature of the dust particles or of the abundances of various elements and molecules in the gas clouds. Only recently have the more complex molecules been discovered, and the first direct measurements of the magnetic-field strengths were made only in 1968. Research into the properties of the interstellar medium is one of the most active areas in astrophysics today and progress is remarkably rapid and stimulating.

EARLY HISTORY OF THE STUDY OF THE INTERSTELLAR MEDIUM

Early photographs

One of the first photographs of illuminated interstellar matter was described by Edward E. Barnard in 1889 in the following way:

> . . . the entire (Pleiades) group of stars is filled with an entangling system of nebulous matter which seems to bind together the different stars with misty wreaths and streams of filmy light clearly all of which is beyond the keenest vision and the most powerful telescopes.

Since 1889 astronomers with larger telescopes have succeeded in studying these interstellar clouds in great detail.

In 1880 the first photograph of the Orion Nebula was described as follows: The Nebula is principally gaseous, a mixture of hydrogen and other gases unknown as yet, in a glowing state. There is food for imagination here and room for questions to satisfy the most speculative minds. To what end is this vast expanse of fiery mist? What mighty and mysterious forces are at play? Are these gigantic outer wreaths moving outward or falling in toward the center? Is this the beginning of worlds or is it the end?

It is known that these emission nebulae are indeed associated with the beginning of worlds, since it is here where the hottest stars heat the surrounding interstellar gas to incandescence that stars have most recently formed.

Not until well into the 20th century were all astronomers satisfied that there was matter of any sort in interstellar space. Earlier discoveries that some regions in the Milky Way appeared to be devoid of stars were accounted for in a different way as is illustrated by William Herschel's comment in the 18th century on finding these dark regions—"Surely this is a hole in the heavens!" This concept, that the dark areas were regions totally devoid of stars like so many tunnels through the Milky Way, persisted well into this century. In about 1909 Barnard, the most famous observer of dark obscured regions, finally accepted the idea that these dark areas were probably due to intervening masses of obscuring matter.

On several occasions well-known astronomers claimed to have proved the existence of interstellar matter before it was scientifically possible to do so. For instance, in 1895 the Dutch astronomer Jacobus Cornelis Kapteyn, famous for his studies of the structure of the galaxy, discovered that the stars in the Milky Way were bluer than those at high galactic latitudes—*i.e.*, well away from the Milky Way. He concluded that the presence of red stars at high latitudes was due to intervening dust clouds that reddened the light from these stars. This implied that the dust occurred in regions well away from the Milky Way. Actually the opposite is true; it is now known that the interstellar dust is concentrated in the direction of the Milky Way, which is practically a plane in space, the plane of the galactic equator, and that what Kapteyn had observed was the predominance of young, hot, and therefore blue stars in the Milky Way and older, cooler, red stars well away from it. In 1908 photographic plates on a given region of sky exposed for successively longer periods of time showed numbers of stars that did not increase in the predicted way. This was interpreted as being due to the presence of absorption that affected the more distant stars more strongly, but it was in fact due to faults in the photographic emulsions. In 1915 better evidence for a lack of interstellar absorption was produced from a study of globular clusters of stars. This was quite correct, but since most of these clusters occurred well away from the Milky Way, the results could not be extrapolated to apply to all regions of interstellar space.

OPTICAL OBSERVATIONS OF INTERSTELLAR MATTER

General absorption. There were basically three ways in which the existence of a large scale distribution of absorbing material was proved. The most dramatic of these was the discovery by Edwin Hubble (1926) at the Mount Wilson Observatory that the apparent distribution of external galaxies was such that when one looked along the Milky Way there appeared to be a "zone of avoidance" in which no galaxies could be seen or photographed. Since it was unreasonable to expect that galaxies should be distributed in a way determined by the orientation of our own galaxy, it was concluded that the effect was caused by the presence of large amounts of obscuring material in the disk of the Galaxy, the Milky Way.

Zone of avoidance

In 1930 Robert J. Trumpler, the Swiss-American astronomer famous for his work on interstellar absorption and clusters of stars, was able to demonstrate directly the presence of large-scale interstellar absorbing material by its effect on the apparent diameters of open-star clusters. He examined the types of stars within a number of open clusters and was able to prepare a Hertzsprung–Russell diagram—*i.e.*, a plot of luminosity against temperature—for each cluster (see STAR). As, for any given cluster, the distance might not be known, the vertical axis of the H–R diagram, which is related to the apparent brightness of the member stars, has to be adjusted according to its distance. As the clusters Trumpler studied were thought to be physically similar to one another, it was expected that the displacement of the stars along the vertical axis would be directly related to their distances. The more distant clusters should appear fainter, and, assuming that they were of similar physical size, they would also appear to have a smaller diameter in photographs. Trumpler found, however, that the apparent diameters of the fainter clusters were systematically larger than predicted. This was the result of interstellar absorption, which dims the light from distant stars and makes them appear farther away than they really are, so that their diameters appear larger than expected. Trumpler was also able to show that the absorbing material responsible for this effect was confined to a thin layer extending along the Milky Way that dimmed the light of the stars by a factor of slightly less than two (0.67) magnitudes per kiloparsec (1,000 parsecs, or about 3,200 light-years) of distance.

A third result, confirming these two, was reported in 1937 by the Mount Wilson astronomer Alfred Joy, who studied the distances of certain variable stars, called Cepheid variables or Cepheids, by several methods. Cepheid variables change brightness in a regular manner, and the regular period depends characteristically on the average

Cepheid variables

intrinsic brightness, or luminosity. The classical method of determining the distance of a Cepheid was to derive its absolute magnitude (a measure of brightness at a standard distance) from its apparent magnitude and its period of variability (see STAR). Joy also measured the velocity of the stars relative to the Sun and from his results, and knowledge of the Galaxy's rotation, was able to make a second distance estimate for the stars. He found that there were systematic differences between the two distance estimates and that these were produced by about 0.6 magnitudes of absorption per kiloparsec (see above), which dimmed the light from the Cepheids and thus produced errors in the determination of their luminosity.

Dust clouds. *Dark clouds of absorbing material.* Besides producing large-scale general absorption in the Milky Way, interstellar dust appears in the form of dark absorbing clouds, often showing distinct boundaries. Such dust clouds are very obvious in telescopic observation, and some are visible even to the naked eye. In the Northern Hemisphere one can observe a "dark rift" running along the Milky Way from the constellation of Cygnus to Sagittarius. E.E. Barnard produced an atlas of these dark nebulae but in 1908 was still unable to accept the idea that they were due to the presence of absorbing material. Closer examination of photographs of such regions revealed that faint stars were often visible within the boundaries of these clouds, suggesting that they were in fact regions of increased absorption due to the presence of matter between the more distant stars and the Sun.

Wolf diagrams

The presence of less obvious dust clouds can be revealed by plotting Wolf diagrams (named after their inventor, Max Wolf), in which the numbers of stars per square degree of sky in successive equal magnitude intervals are plotted against apparent magnitude. Normally, that is, the numbers of stars with successive equal brightness ratios (a ratio or factor of 100 in brightness is equivalent to a magnitude difference of 2.5) are plotted against the apparent brightness measured as a magnitude. A smooth curve should be obtained in an unobscured field. The presence of absorbing clouds is manifested by discrete steps in this curve caused by jumps in the apparent brightness of stars just behind a cloud compared to those just in front. Though the approximate distance to a cloud can in theory be obtained from the value of the magnitude at which the corresponding step occurs, in practice the technique is difficult to apply.

Reflection nebulae. Often, clouds of interstellar dust are illuminated by stars in their immediate neighbourhood. Edwin Hubble noted that when the surface temperature of such a star was less than 18,000° K (about 32,000° F) the spectrum of the nebulosity consisted chiefly of dark lines on a bright background, or continuum, and was exactly similar to the light from the stars. The dust clouds were clearly reflecting the starlight.

From the reflection properties of these nebulae astronomers are able to discover something about the nature of the scattering and absorbing material. The dust, as it is loosely called, was thus shown to consist of highly reflecting particles about 0.00001 inch in diameter and probably comparable to snow in reflective power. The particles, or grains, most probably consist of simple molecular compounds coated by ice, although other suggestions have been made. Perhaps one of the most surprising of these is that the dust particles may be very small diamonds. The problem may be solved when scientists are able to produce particles in the laboratory under conditions similar to those in interstellar space; that is, with the same absorptive and reflective properties as those observed astronomically.

Composition of dust

Completely obscured regions—dark lanes and globules. The most dramatic examples of interstellar dust clouds are the totally dark obscuring lanes seen silhouetted in front of most large-scale bright regions such as the hot-emission nebulae described below. Photographs of the Orion Nebula, the North America Nebula, and many in the catalogue compiled by the 18th-century astronomer, Charles Messier, all show intensely dark structures totally devoid of stars. The Merope Nebula, part of the Pleiades cluster, plainly shows filaments of absorbing material that are apparently related to the magnetic field in the Pleiades region. Many other regions of the sky exhibit long filaments of dense obscuring matter, sometimes seen weakly illuminated by nearby stars, at other times manifested only by the complete absence of stars. For example, in the constellation Taurus there are extensive lanes of obscuring matter. Very small, apparently circular, obscuring clouds known as globules were discovered in 1947. Good examples of both globules and more extended regions of complete absorption lie in front of the Rosette Nebula. Globules may represent a stage in the evolution of a protostar, the condensation of gas and dust from which a star is thought to form.

Globules

Globules are the smallest known dark nebulae. The size of the smallest globules is of the order of a few thousand astronomical units (an astronomical unit is the mean Sun–Earth distance, 93×10^6 miles). Observations of the radio emission from hydroxyl radicals in some globules has led to temperature estimates that indicate that the dust cloud is probably between 5° and 10° K above absolute zero. Fairly complex molecules could form in these dense cold globules, and formaldehyde has already been identified in one such object (see below). The total amount of matter in globules can only be estimated by making uncertain assumptions about the amount of molecular hydrogen and other molecules likely to be present. Best estimates of the masses of the globules range from about half a solar mass for the small globules to 35 solar masses for intermediate size objects. These have a diameter of about 100,000 astronomical units. Large globules, such as the Coalsack, are often seen along the band of the Milky Way, especially in the regions of dark nebulosity such as the constellations Taurus and Ophiuchus. The smaller globules, seen in the direction of emission nebulae, are sharply defined and often appear round, although photographs taken with larger telescopes suggest a "windblown" appearance for the objects. These objects may well be protostars that will become stars when they have attained a mass sufficiently great to allow gravitational contraction to take place.

In photographs, globules not associated with any other object do indeed give the appearance of dark holes, and it is easy to see why Barnard and others felt that they might well be looking through tunnels between the stars to empty space beyond.

Interstellar reddening. In its path through the interstellar dust clouds, starlight is reddened; that is, part of the blue light is scattered and does not reach the observer. Astronomers are able to measure the relative amounts of red and blue light in unobscured stars of given types, and the ratio of these quantities is called the "colour index" of the star. When an intervening dust cloud reddens the starlight the apparent colour index is changed. Comparison between the observed colour index and the predicted value in the absence of obscuration gives a quantity called the "colour excess." By measuring the colour excess of stars over large areas of the sky astronomers are able to map out the boundaries of the obscuring dust clouds.

Colour excess

Polarization of starlight. In general, starlight is said to be randomly polarized or unpolarized. This statement means that the electrical vibrations, which can be thought to represent the radiation, occur in all directions. An analogy can be drawn between the transmission of starlight and the way energy is transmitted along a rope by causing it to vibrate up and down while one end is held. The vibration of the rope can only take place in one direction, say vertically or horizontally, at any given instant. In the case of unpolarized light the oscillations occur in all directions equally. When the light is polarized its oscillation may be likened to that of the rope in that the radiation is oscillating mainly in one plane—*e.g.*, vertically or horizontally. It is possible to construct an optical filter that will accept only light polarized in a certain way. For example, the first of two pairs of polarizing sunglasses, held one in front of the other, will polarize the light passing through it; and the second can be rotated to allow this polarized light to be transmitted, or it can be rotated by 90° so that no light is transmitted.

In the interstellar medium dust clouds polarize the light. The astronomer can observe this light with a polarized filter, rotating it until he obtains the maximum transmission of radiation. In this way he can measure the direction of the plane of polarization and the amount of polarization.

In 1944 it was predicted from theory that, because of processes in the stellar atmosphere, starlight might be polarized at the limb (apparent edge) of the stars. Observations of binary (physically related double) stars would allow this to be detected when one member partially eclipsed the other so that only part of the limb of the latter star was visible. Stellar polarization was first detected in 1948, but it did not depend on the phase of the binary as predicted and was present in nearby single stars. Furthermore, the amount of polarization was correlated with the colour excess of the stars, known to be a measure of the amount of dust in front of the star. Clearly, polarization was being introduced by the intervening dust clouds. In 1949 it was discovered that, in the presence of a magnetic field, suitably shaped dust particles could be aligned so as to produce polarization in a direction parallel to the magnetic field in the clouds. Large-scale observations of stars in the Milky Way showed that through much of the Galaxy the magnetic field appeared to be nearly parallel to the main band of the Milky Way.

It has not been possible to derive the strength of the magnetic field responsible for this alignment of particles since the nature of the particles is not well enough known, but magnetic fields between 10^{-6} and 10^{-5} gauss are probably sufficient to produce this effect.

Spectroscopic absorption lines. Apart from the dust clouds that absorb and polarize starlight, there are large quantities of gas in the interstellar medium. The presence of the gas is indicated by absorption lines at very specific wavelengths in the spectrum of starlight. Such absorption lines are also formed by processes acting in the stars' own outer atmospheres, but the interstellar lines show subtle differences. The German astronomer Johannes Hartmann, while studying such stellar absorption lines of binary stars in 1904, noticed that the line produced by ionized calcium did not show the periodic changes in wavelength of the other lines in the spectrum of Delta Orionis, which were caused by the Doppler effect arising from the binary star's motion. It was assumed, therefore, that the "stationary" calcium lines were not associated with the star but must have been produced somewhere between the star and the observer.

Stationary lines

Hartmann interpreted the spectrum as that of a typical star shining through a cloud of interstellar calcium gas. This conclusion was supported by the American astronomer Vesto M. Slipher in 1909 but was not generally accepted for another 15 years. Stationary lines of sodium were discovered in 1919, and in the early 1920s most astronomers accepted as fact the existence of interstellar gas and dust in the Galaxy. Many kinds of interstellar material have since been discovered by this method, including potassium; titanium; and the compound radicals of carbon, nitrogen, and hydrogen (C, N and H) denoted by CN and CH. Many still unidentified lines are currently being studied. Some of these have been known for 50 years, but no convincing explanation for their existence has yet been produced. The most famous of these is a broad, diffuse line with a wavelength of 4,430 Angstroms (4.43×10^{-4} millimetres). Since the unidentified lines are closely correlated with colour excesses of the stars in whose spectra they are seen, they probably arise in the same dust clouds and are probably due to complex molecules whose spectra have not yet been duplicated in the laboratory.

In 1961, an examination of the absorption lines of many stars at high galactic latitude showed that the absorption is indeed produced in discrete clouds. This confirmed earlier observations by Walter S. Adams in 1949, who had also found that some stars showed several well-separated absorption lines in the spectrum, suggesting that there were well-separated clouds in the interstellar medium with different velocities in the line of sight. New experimental techniques, which were developed in 1968, show that most of the multiple absorption lines observed in 1961 break down further into several distinct components, the study of which provides much more information about the small scale structure of these interstellar gas clouds.

From a detailed analysis of the absorption lines produced in the interstellar medium astronomers can obtain an idea of the relative amounts of sodium, calcium, and other elements and molecules present in interstellar space. This is done by measuring the "equivalent width" of the lines. Equivalent width is defined as the width of a sharp-edged ideal absorption line that would completely absorb starlight and would produce the same amount of darkening in the spectrum as the observed line. These equivalent widths can be theoretically related to the number of atoms present in the absorbing cloud in front of the star.

Interstellar atoms and molecules known to produce optical absorption lines are listed here. Many of the unidentified lines will probably turn out to be those of more complex molecules.

Table 1: Interstellar Atoms and Molecules Detected Optically

in interstellar space		in emission nebulae	
Calcium	(Ca)	Helium	(He)
Sodium	(Na)	Hydrogen	(H)
Potassium	(K)	Oxygen	(O)
Titanium	(Ti)	Silicon	(Si)
Iron	(Fe)	Sulfur	(S)
CH		Nitrogen	(N)
CN		Carbon	(C)
H_2		H_2 (?)	

The nature of the interstellar grains. In the late 1930s it was discovered that the amount of absorption of starlight, or extinction as it is usually called varied inversely as the wavelength (symbol λ). Later work showed that the "extinction curve" can have many different forms in different parts of the Galaxy. Often it shows two distinct wavelength ranges with different dependences of extinction on wavelength. The border between these regions lies in the wavelength region in which the unidentified interstellar absorption lines are found.

The form of the extinction curve

The nature of the extinction curve gives the most direct information on the nature of the interstellar grains in the sense that if the physicist can duplicate such a curve in the laboratory then he will have had to virtually duplicate the conditions in interstellar space as well as the particles. This has been done with only partial success. Some aspects of the extinction curve can be reproduced using grains of graphite, others by ice-covered graphite, and small diamonds have been suggested, but the precise nature of the dust particles, or grains, remains unknown. An early suggestion was that the grains resembled very small meteoroids, or micrometeorites; in later work (1938) metallic particles were considered. The grains are now generally believed to be mostly ices (dielectric, or nonconducting, grains) with graphite and metallic constituents to explain the polarization, but knowledge of the nature of the grains does not supply an answer to the question of how they form. It is likely that they form by collisions of constituent atoms and molecules; much light will be cast on this problem as the science of astrochemistry develops and new and different interstellar molecules are discovered.

The grains, once formed, will act as important cooling agents for the cloud of gas in which they are located. They will also act as "anchors" for molecules and atoms; that is, other free atoms or molecules might collide with them and combine relatively easily with them to form more complex molecules.

Hot interstellar matter. *Bright emission nebulae.* Thirty-three bright diffuse nebulae with absorption lines in their spectra have a nearby star, showing a spectrum similar to that of the nebulae, and they are thus reflection nebulae. In 29 cases in which the star was younger and hotter, with surface temperatures greater than 18,000° K, the nebular spectrum showed characteristic bright lines. Emission lines from nebulae had been known since the work of Sir William Huggins in 1864, but as late as 1922, they were, except for those of hydrogen and helium, still largely unidentified. The similarity between these nebular spectra and the spectra of planetary nebulae, which were known to be shells of gas glowing with energy emitted by their central stars, demonstrated the existence of "emission nebulae," or H II regions as they are often called. H II denotes ionized hydrogen whereas H I indicates neutral hydrogen. A relationship between the angular extent of the nebula and the magnitude of the parent star was also noted. In the 1930s Bengt Strömgren, a Danish-American astronomer, found that the emitting region around many isolated young stars was sharply bounded and that its radius depended on the temperature of the star and the medium's density. For instance, a very hot star could ionize matter out to a distance of 1.5 parsec (pc) in a cloud whose density is 1,000 atoms per cubic centimetre, whereas the cloud would be ionized out to 150 parsecs if its density were one atom per cubic centimetre. For the same clouds a cooler star of the right temperature would only ionize out to 0.3 and 30 parsecs respectively. An emission nebula is formed when the ultraviolet radiation from the parent very hot star ionizes the surrounding gas cloud, which is mainly hydrogen. The ultraviolet energy available in the starlight is used up in producing ionization, and there appears a rather sharp boundary beyond which the hydrogen is neutral (un-ionized). This forms the so-called Strömgren sphere of ionized material. Temperatures inside the Strömgren spheres range from 5,000° to 10,000°. In general, because the gas density around any hot star is not uniform, the emission nebulae are seldom symmetrical. Furthermore, several hot stars in a cluster may produce ionizing radiation so emission nebulae may take varied and picturesque shapes. An example is the Orion Nebula, which can be seen with good binoculars.

Strömgren spheres

Often bright rim structures are found at the edge of emission nebulae. These structures, consisting of dark matter, absorb the light from behind them and are bordered by a bright rim on the side facing the exciting star. They often point to this star and sometimes have the shape of elephant trunks. They are pockets of very high density compared with their surroundings, and they resist the tendency of the H II region to expand into the surrounding dust and gas clouds. Figure 2 shows the Trifid Nebula (also known as NGC 6514), an emission nebula, with dark dust lanes lying in front of it. Elephant trunks and a bright rim structure can clearly be seen.

By courtesy of Bart Bok

Figure 2: *Trifid Nebula (NGC 6514).*
Dark dust lanes cross the bright emission from incandescent interstellar gas. Elephant-trunk structures and a bright rim are evident. Made with 90 in. reflector at Steward Observatory, Tucson Arizona.

Filamentary and irregular nebulae. In many parts of the sky one finds emission nebulae with filamentary or veillike structures but without any associated hot star. Good examples of these are the Veil Nebula in Cygnus and the Crab Nebula in Taurus. These are the remains of gigantic stellar explosions, called supernovae, in which most of the matter from a star has been ejected into the interstellar medium and that are now seen to be many tens of light-years in diameter. The spectra of these nebulae do not show simple emission lines but a more continuous broad band of radiation, which is usually polarized. The emission arises from the interaction of high-energy particles with the magnetic fields in the supernova remnants.

RADIO OBSERVATIONS OF THE INTERSTELLAR MEDIUM

Continuum radiation and its polarization. Observation of the Galaxy at radio wavelengths began in 1932 when the U.S. radio engineer Karl Jansky discovered steady radio noise emanating from the centre of the Milky Way. Grote Reber, a radio amateur in Illinois, built the first of the dish-type radio telescopes now so familiar to modern radio astronomy observatories and from about 1940 proceeded to map this radiation systematically at several wavelengths, all of the order of many metres. He showed that the Milky Way was indeed emitting radio waves and that the source of the most intense radiation was in the constellation Sagittarius, near the centre of the Galaxy.

Several smaller sources were also detected, but it was many years before a theory was proposed that satisfactorily explained this radiation from the Milky Way and other points.

Interaction between cosmic rays and the magnetic field of the Galaxy now seems to be responsible for the radio emission. As stated above, the polarization of light shows that interstellar magnetic fields exist. Some cosmic rays are known to be high-energy electrons, and it is possible to show theoretically that these will be forced to spiral around lines of magnetic force and that in so doing they will produce intense radio waves.

If the magnetic field is strong enough the cosmic-ray electrons may radiate light as well. This process, called synchrotron emission, produces radiation from the supernova remnant, the Crab Nebula in the constellation Taurus; and in 1949 the Soviet astrophysicist I.S. Shklovsky concluded that it is the chief energizing mechanism for many radio sources outside the Galaxy. Synchrotron radiation is linearly polarized at right angles to the direction of the magnetic field, and this polarization can be measured with suitable radio telescopes. Recent maps of the Milky Way show that the radiation is concentrated in the plane of the Galaxy and also that the polarization is indicative of magnetic fields directed along this plane.

Synchrotron radiation

Toward the centre of the Milky Way, the radiation is extremely intense with a very small bright region in the direction of the galactic centre.

Emission from interstellar neutral hydrogen gas. *General properties.* The presence of neutral hydrogen atoms in the interstellar medium had long been suspected as the element was known, from spectroscopic observation at optical wavelengths, to exist there in combination with carbon. No way exists, however, for astronomers optically to observe the neutral, or cold, hydrogen. Hot ionized hydrogen produced optical spectral lines that could be seen in emission nebulae, but away from hot stars the gas was invisible. In 1944 Henk C. van de Hulst showed theoretically that the cold form of the gas would radiate a spectral line with a wavelength of 21.2 centimetres. In 1951 such radiation emitted by large clouds of neutral hydrogen in the Milky Way was detected and van de Hulst's prediction confirmed. The radiation results from a "spin-flip" transition in the ground state of the atom, which means that the spin of the electron orbiting the proton changes from the same rotational direction as the proton spin to the opposite direction. This latter configuration gives a lower total energy for the atom and the energy difference, corresponding to a wavelength of 21.2 centimetres or a frequency of 1420.4056 MHz (megahertz—1,000,000 cycles per second), is radiated away. If the radio astronomer views a strong source through a cloud of hydrogen gas, he will "see" the cloud because it absorbs radiation of the same frequency emanating from the source. This implies that the "spin-flip" transition has occurred in the opposite direction with the atom absorbing the energy and jumping to the higher energy state.

A single atom absorbs or emits at a very precise wavelength, producing a very narrow emission line. In a cloud of atoms such as exists in the Milky Way, however, individual atoms have a wide range of motions with respect to one another so that they absorb or emit over a range of wavelengths, due to the Doppler effect. A cloud of hydrogen many light-years in diameter will produce a broad emission line, usually several tens of kilohertz wide in frequency. The spread in wavelengths or frequency can be directly related to the spread in velocities of the atoms within the cloud, usually several kilometres per second. These velocities in turn are related to the temperature in the cloud, usually about 50° K or more.

The study of emission spectra therefore gives information on the temperatures of the clouds. The way in which the observed intensity varies with position provides information about the structure of the clouds. Lastly, when these clouds have systematic motions away from or toward the Earth, the Doppler effect creates an apparent wavelength change and this Doppler shift can be related to the velocity of the cloud relative to the observer.

Rotation of the Galaxy

The Galaxy rotates in such a way that the Sun moves in a roughly circular orbit at about 250 kilometres per second about the centre, which is located in the constellation Sagittarius. By considering the rotation of the Galaxy, radio astronomers can convert the apparent velocity shift of the spectra of hydrogen clouds to a distance estimate, so that one can plot the location of the clouds in the plane of the Milky Way and thus obtain a map of the Galaxy as seen from outside. Since radio waves are not easily absorbed by interstellar dust, the radio astronomer can "see" right through the Galaxy and obtain a relatively good picture of its structure.

Maps of the Galaxy obtained in this way, combined with other data, show that the hydrogen gas extends to at least 15,000 parsecs (48,900 light-years) from the centre. The Sun is located about 10,000 parsecs (32,600 light-years) out. The thickness of the gaseous disk is about 200 parsecs (652 light-years), and these are found to be spiral arms of gas with widths of about 1,000 parsecs in the plane of the Galaxy. The average density of the neutral hydrogen gas throughout the Galaxy is about one to two atoms per cubic centimetre; from this, it can be calculated that there is an amount of neutral gas equal to between 0.3 and 1×10^{10} times the mass of the Sun in the Milky Way, making up somewhat less than 5 percent of its total mass. By comparison one solar mass unit is 2×10^{33} grams, and the air at Earth's surface contains about 10^{19} molecules per cubic centimetre.

Mapping the Milky Way structure by these methods is difficult. There are regions, especially toward the centre, where no velocity discrimination is obtained. Most of the matter there is expected to be moving along lines parallel to the Sun, and it is therefore difficult to derive an accurate picture of the hydrogen distribution. The interpretation is further confused by the presence of a large region of hydrogen gas, possibly a spiral arm, which has a velocity of 54 kilometres per second toward the Earth. It is probably expanding away from the galactic centre at this velocity; it is thought to be about 4,000 parsecs from the centre. Also, there is some evidence for a small rotating disk of gas at, or around, the centre.

Neutral hydrogen clouds and the intercloud medium. When observed with high radio resolution, the interstellar gas shows much irregularity on a small scale, just as do the dust clouds seen in photographic plates. This is loosely interpreted as being indicative of a similar "cloud" structure in the hydrogen. At present the precise structure of the clouds is uncertain, and their correlation with dust, or even with sodium or calcium clouds, is not always apparent. There are very cold "clouds" with temperatures of the order of 50° K or less, and there is a much hotter and more diffuse, but still neutral, medium between the clouds, the so-called intercloud medium. The densities in the clouds range from about one to several hundred atoms per cubic centimetre. The intercloud medium contains about 0.1 (or less) atoms per cubic centimetre with a temperature of several thousand degrees. This temperature may be maintained by the heating effect of low-energy cosmic rays or X-rays that penetrate most of interstellar space. Since the discovery of pulsars, rapidly varying radio sources with an extremely precise period of change, in 1967, much indirect evidence concerning the temperatures and densities in interstellar space has been obtained from them. Observations of hydrogen emission and absorption spectra give information on the total number of hydrogen atoms in the direction of observation, although the distance of the hydrogen is not always known, nor the actual size of the clouds. At the same time, the signals from pulsars are known to be dispersed (*i.e.*, some wavelengths are delayed more than others), and the dispersion is a direct measure of the total number of electrons in the path to the pulsar, whose distance is also unknown in most cases. Rough quantitative comparisons of the number of hydrogen atoms and the number of electrons reveal some information about ionization conditions in the interstellar medium. Outside the clouds it may be about 1 percent ionized, whereas the clouds themselves have probably less than one-tenth of 1 percent of their atoms ionized, a fact that has important consequences for the stability of the clouds and their ability to form stars.

As described above, a result of galactic rotation is that the hydrogen emission near the Milky Way plane is seen at wavelengths determined by the distance and direction of motion of the clouds with respect to the Sun. In 1963 radio astronomers in The Netherlands found large regions of hydrogen emission well away from the galactic disk with unexpectedly large negative velocities with respect to the Sun. These large negative velocities were surprising because at high galactic latitude one generally observes only nearby (within 1 or 200 parsecs, about 3 to 600 light-years) hydrogen, which has comparatively a very small velocity with respect to the Sun. The Dutch astronomers, however, found clouds with velocities of approach ranging from 50 to 200 kilometres per second. One suggestion is that the approach velocities are simply those of material falling into the Galaxy from outside, but the true explanation for the phenomenon could be one of several other alternatives; *e.g.*, the clouds with the largest velocities could be entirely outside the Milky Way, somewhere in the intergalactic space.

Neutral hydrogen absorption lines. A cloud of hydrogen gas projected in front of a strong distant radio source will absorb the radio waves from the source at the wavelength at which the hydrogen can emit radiation. An absorption spectrum at radio wavelengths is produced in the same way as an optical absorption spectrum. Investigation of such absorption spectra can be used to find the distance of some galactic radio sources, such as a supernova remnant, in the constellation Cassiopeia. The distance of this object could not be derived until its hydrogen absorption spectrum had been observed. As the absorption in this spectrum due to the local spiral arm of the Galaxy and to a more distant one could be identified in its spectrum while the hydrogen in a third arm produced no absorption, the distance of the source could be derived from a knowledge of the structure of the Galaxy. This technique has also been used to determine the distance to some emission nebulae that are obscured by intervening dust but can be detected radio astronomically.

Lastly, absorption lines provide a better estimate of the

total number of hydrogen atoms present in the absorbing clouds than is possible exclusively from observations of emission spectra.

Magnetic fields. So far, the only direct way of measuring the strength of the magnetic field in interstellar space is to measure the so-called Zeeman effect in neutral hydrogen spectra. In 1896 the Dutch physicist Peter Zeeman discovered that spectral lines produced in the laboratory were split into several components when the emitting source was subjected to a magnetic field (see ASTRONOMICAL SPECTROSCOPY, PRINCIPLES OF). When the source is observed in a direction parallel to the magnetic field, the spectrum will be split into two sets of lines shifted with respect to one another. This frequency shift is very small for the tiny magnetic fields of interstellar space and for the 21-centimetre lines; the small corresponding Zeeman effect cannot be measured absolutely because it is swallowed up in the much greater spread caused by the thermal motion of the atoms. Fortunately, the two displaced Zeeman spectra are polarized in opposite senses; one shows left-hand and the other right-hand polarization. This polarization can be measured as a difference across the neutral hydrogen spectrum, and such measurements lead to the derivation of the magnetic-field strength in the cloud producing the radiation. This method, similar to that used for measuring sunspot magnetic fields optically, was first successfully applied to interstellar gas clouds in 1968, after many years of effort on the part of many observers when Gerrit L. Verschuur, the author of the present article, directly measured interstellar magnetic fields in three regions. In one region he found a field with a strength of about 3×10^{-6} gauss (3 microgauss); in the others the fields were 10 and 20 microgauss; for comparison, the strength of the Earth's magnetic field is given below. Due to the difficulty of the measurements however, astronomers may never have a complete map of the magnetic field of the Milky Way, as the Zeeman experiment can only sample those points in interstellar space where suitable hydrogen clouds are situated.

Zeeman effect

Pulsars have indirectly contributed to knowledge of the galactic magnetic field. Their pulsed radiation is polarized, and as it passes through interstellar space the angle of the polarization direction rotates as the result of interactions between the magnetic field and the electrons in the medium. This effect is known as Faraday rotation; from its measurement a value for the average magnetic field between the pulsar and Earth can be derived, taking into account the dispersion data that independently gives the number of electrons in the path. It has been found by this method that the strength of the average interstellar magnetic field is generally lower than that found in the cold hydrogen clouds; *i.e.*, it is of the order of a few times 10^{-6} gauss or less. For comparison, the field strength at the Earth's surface is about one-tenth of a gauss.

Faraday rotation

Interstellar molecules. Many kinds of molecules have been discovered and studied by radio methods. The first of these was the hydroxyl radical (OH), a combination of an oxygen and a hydrogen atom that exhibits many complex transitions between different internal energy states as a result of interactions between the molecular rotation and the spin of the electron associated with the hydrogen atom. Calculations of the radiation expected from the OH molecules first indicated that four discrete emission lines near 18 centimetres (1,800 MHz) would be radiated. These were at approximately 1,612, 1,665, 1,667, and 1,720 megahertz, and their intensities were expected to be in the ratio of about 1:5:9:1.

Table 2: Interstellar Atoms and Molecules Detected with Radio Telescopes

Neutral hydrogen	(H I)
Ionized hydrogen	(H II)
Helium	(He II)
Carbon	(C II)
OH	($O^{16}H$ and $O^{18}H$)
Water	(H_2O)
Ammonia	(NH_3)
Formaldehyde	($H_2C^{12}O$ and $H_2C^{13}O$)
Carbon monoxide	($C^{12}O^{16}$, $C^{13}O^{16}$ and $C^{12}O^{18}$)
Cyanide	(CN)
Hydrogen cyanide	(HCN)
Cyanoacetylene	(HCCCN)
Methyl alcohol	(CH_3OH)
Formic acid (?)	(HCOOH) (?)
Carbon monosulfide	(CS)

Hydroxyl radical. In 1963 OH was detected in several cold interstellar clouds of hydrogen. Other work led to the remarkable discovery that OH in many regions was behaving abnormally, radiating several hundred times more intensely than predicted. The study of these sources is continuing with the regular discovery of new centres of emission. New theories to explain the intensity of this OH emission have so far had only limited success. It is generally agreed that a maser-type amplification must be taking place in some regions of space, and this means that the molecules, instead of populating various energy levels in the expected way, have been stimulated to higher energy states by some as yet unknown resonance mechanism and that as they lose energy they emit the unexpected surplus radiation. Such anomalous OH emission sources, as they are called, have been found mainly near emission nebula and in the direction of infrared stars, but the precise nature of such anomalous sources is not yet clear.

Maser amplification

These OH sources are often extremely small. Their diameters can be measured by a pair of radio telescopes located many hundreds of miles apart operating as an interferometer of very high resolution. These measures indicate that while in many cases the different peaks in a complex OH spectrum are separated in position in the sky by several tens of seconds of arc, individually the peaks may arise in centres having diameters of less than one-hundredth of a second of arc. In the case of the sources in the neighbourhood of IC 1805, a well-known emission nebula, this implies a diameter for the OH emitter of less than that of our solar system.

Other recent discoveries. In late 1968 and early 1969 another set of observations revealed the presence of interstellar ammonia and, later, interstellar water. The detection of interstellar formaldehyde followed. Spectral lines of ammonia and water were detected at about 1.3-centimetre wavelength, and of formaldehyde, near six centimetres. Carbon monoxide was detected in April 1970. Extensive surveys of these molecular lines are now being conducted both in emission and absorption. The presence of a relatively complex organic molecule such as formaldehyde in interstellar space may be significant to the understanding of the origin of life in the Galaxy. The water emission line, too, must be stimulated in some way by maser amplification. The water lines also originate in centres whose size is comparable to or less than the Sun–Earth distance. This emission varies drastically in intensity from day to day, an observation that is consistent with the small size of the sources.

Some clouds of formaldehyde appear to be colder than the space surrounding them, which, intuitively, seems impossible. During a search for new OH sources in 1967, several very dense dust clouds that previously had been discovered optically were examined. It was found that many of these dust clouds appeared to contain much OH that was emitting more or less normally, and astronomers searching for the formaldehyde emission lines also turned their telescopes to these dust clouds. Instead of finding the formaldehyde line in emission as expected, however, they found it in absorption. This seemed unreasonable, as there was no radio source behind the cloud whose radiation could be absorbed. The whole universe, from the point of view of Earth at any rate, is bathed in low intensity radiation thought by some to be the remains of the original "big bang," the supposed violent expansion of the universe at the beginning of time, from which everything might have started. Whether such an origin of the radiation is correct or not, Earth seems to be entirely surrounded by a radio source that has a temperature of 2.8 degrees above absolute zero. The formaldehyde in the dust cloud appeared to be absorbing this

Formaldehyde clouds

radiation, as if the cloud were colder than its surroundings. How a cloud bathed from all sides by 2.8-degree radiation could drop to a temperature of less than 2.8 degrees is a question, the answer to which is not yet forthcoming; but it is probable that the explanation involves an inverse maser-type effect (that is, that the population of the energy levels in the molecules inside a shielding layer of dust has been disturbed in some way).

The discovery, in rapid succession, of the presence of ammonia, water, and formaldehyde in interstellar gas clouds led to an eager search for additional lines and molecules. The detection of formaldehyde that contained the isotope carbon-13 instead of carbon-12 soon followed. The comparison of the amounts of the two kinds of formaldehyde provides a good method for measuring the relative abundances of the two isotopes of carbon. Carbon monoxide and cyanide were found in 1970; these radiate at millimetre wavelengths. No estimates of the wavelengths at which many of the more complex molecules that might exist in interstellar space would radiate are yet available. Lacking such estimates, it is nearly impossible to search large wavelength ranges for new weak spectral lines, and progress in this area is not likely to be rapid.

Lists of new frequencies are constantly being calculated for some of the more complex molecules. In mid-1970 the first molecule containing five atoms was added to the list of molecules known to exist in interstellar space when the presence of cyanoacetylene (HC_3N) was detected in the direction of the galactic centre.

Molecular hydrogen. Neutral hydrogen gas consists of single protons, each with its own orbiting electron. The combination of two such hydrogen atoms in a close bond produces a molecule of hydrogen. Such combinations are already noted in more complex interstellar molecules such as water and formaldehyde, but it has so far been very difficult to make any direct observations of interstellar molecular hydrogen. It is, nonetheless, possible that a considerable fraction, if not the largest fraction, of matter in interstellar clouds is molecular hydrogen.

The first identification of interstellar molecular hydrogen was in mid-1970, following the use of rocket-borne equipment capable of measuring absorption lines of starlight in the ultraviolet part of the spectrum. The first result indicated that at least 50 percent of the gas in a dense absorbing cloud in front of the star Xi Persei is in molecular form.

Radio waves from emission nebulae. Apart from emitting the discrete optical lines mentioned above, emission nebulae radiate a continuous spectrum of light and radio waves due to interactions between free electrons in the ionized gas. This so-called free-free process produces only a small part of the light from the nebulae, but most of the continuous-spectrum radio emission. Inside the Strömgren spheres around the parent stars the hydrogen is fully ionized, which means that the electrons move freely instead of being bound to individual protons. Electrons sometimes are captured by protons and remain in one of the outer energy levels of the hydrogen atom. The electrons can also drop to lower energy levels closer to the proton. Such transitions give rise to the hydrogen spectrum that contains many hundreds of lines at radio and optical wavelengths. These "recombination" lines are readily observed by radio astronomers.

Free-free process

Recombination lines from ionized helium atoms have also been observed, and a line from a third element has been found, tentatively attributed to carbon atoms. Observations of the recombination lines as well as the total radiation from the nebulae gives information about the physical conditions inside the nebulae such as temperature, density, and motions. Densities found in this way range from several times 10^3 to several times 10^6 particles per cubic centimetre and the temperatures from 5,000° to 15,000°.

THE STRUCTURE OF THE INTERSTELLAR MEDIUM

The distribution of matter and stars in spiral arms. Young stars, gas, and associated dust tend to coexist in space within the Galaxy. They all form what is called the Population I component of matter in the Galaxy, and they occur in those regions of space in which star formation has only just occurred or is still taking place. Emission nebulae and the stars that excite this emission range in age from 10^4 to several times 10^6 years. This compares with an age for the Galaxy of about 5×10^9 years.

Examination of nearby external galaxies shows that the relatively young matter in them (very hot stars and the gas and dust) occur in definite armlike structures spiralling about their nuclei. Since Earth is located inside the disk of the Milky Way, astronomers cannot readily unscramble the distribution of stars, gas, and dust as seen from the solar system so as to present a simple picture of the spiral structure in the Milky Way system. But as mentioned above, observations of neutral hydrogen do enable radio astronomers to assemble a plan view of the Galaxy, indicating roughly where the main concentrations of hydrogen are located. Astronomers can also determine the distance to many emission nebulae, dust clouds, and young stars within about 1,000 to 3,000 parsecs of the Earth. By and large, these coincide in position with the regions containing most neutral hydrogen.

The best information concerning the distribution of interstellar dust in galaxies comes from studying other galaxies nearby. In 1961 it was noted that the spiral pattern for galaxies thought to be similar to the Milky Way first becomes apparent near the centre of such galaxies as two principal dust lanes. The luminous spiral arms only appear at larger distances from the nucleus.

In many galaxies the spiral arms break up into a more complex structure with "feathers" of material bridging the gap between adjacent arms. From Earth's location this pattern cannot be seen clearly in the Milky Way nor can it be determined whether Earth is in a region where such interarm bridges occur, although there is some evidence from neutral hydrogen data that it is not located in a simple spiral arm structure.

Spiral pattern

The reason for a spiral pattern in some galaxies is not completely understood. One theory involves the propagation of some sort of spiral density wave that can be maintained in a disk of gas and stars. How such a wave can be generated is not understood, but if its existence is allowed, star formation is expected to occur in the regions of highest density where matter has been pushed by the wave. According to this theory spiral arms are not permanent structures in the Galaxy but, rather, regions in which star formation is currently taking place. Their pattern will move around the centre of the Galaxy causing star formation as it goes.

A simple examination of the present velocity patterns within the Galaxy leads to the conclusion that the spiral-arm pattern should wind itself up, much like a watch spring, as the Galaxy rotates, unless something operates to prevent this happening. Since the Galaxy is thought to have rotated at least 100 times during its existence, an open spiral structure should long ago have ceased to exist. Magnetic fields have been proposed as a force that could hold the arms out against the effect of the rotation of the Galaxy. These magnetic fields would however have to be at least ten times larger than are now measured (see above), and this seems not feasible. Furthermore, optical polarization measurements of about 7,000 stars reveal that the magnetic field, certainly that part of it within several hundred parsecs of the Sun, does not simply lie along the local spiral arm. A helical-shaped model of the magnetic field within 250 parsecs of the Sun that is consistent with the optical and radio polarization measurements has been proposed. It has been realized for some time that, on a smaller scale, the magnetic fields control the shapes of dust clouds. These are often elongated in the direction of the magnetic field in their vicinity, as derived from the polarization properties of the stars near them.

The current picture of the spiral structure of the Galaxy places the Sun near the edge of an arm, although there is a possibility that in the solar neighbourhood there is mainly matter associated with a spur joining two major spiral arms. The local arm, or spur, is about 1,000 parsecs wide and 200 parsecs thick. Beyond an interarm region of another 2,000 parsecs or so in width, in directions away from the galactic centre, lies the so-called Perseus spiral arm, which contains very large numbers of young stars. Such objects as the double cluster h and Chi Persei lie in this arm. Toward the galactic centre there is another arm, called the Sagittarius arm, about 1,000 parsecs away from the Sun's location at the inner side of the local arm. The Sagittarius arm extends from the constellation of Aquila through Sagittarius to Carina. The local spiral arm appears to be directed toward Cygnus at one end and somewhere between Puppis and Orion at the other end.

These patterns are obtained from a study of young, hot stars and nebulae within about 3,000 parsecs of the Sun. The hydrogen data does not present such a clear picture yet. Study of other galaxies, and to a lesser extent of the Milky Way, suggests that the main dust lanes lie on the inside edges of the spiral arms, with more dust the closer one gets to the nucleus of the Galaxy.

The galactic halo. Optical studies reveal a large, nearly spherical distribution of globular star clusters (relatively old objects) around the Milky Way centre that are distributed through a region that is sometimes called the corona or halo of the Galaxy. It is not known whether there is any interstellar matter in this halo. There is evidence, however, that the neutral hydrogen in some spiral arms may extend several thousand parsecs above the Milky Way plane before it ceases to be detectable.

The galactic centre region. The Milky Way system and several other spiral galaxies show at their centres very dense clusters of old stars with a relative lack of interstellar gas, such as neutral hydrogen. It is very difficult, however, to interpret the distribution of hydrogen emission, continuum emission, and radiation from complex molecules in the direction of the galactic centre in terms of a simple picture. There are motions of matter away from the centre that some astronomers interpret as an indication of explosive events at some distant time in the past. There are several very small radio sources at or near the galactic centre, and there is also a considerable amount of OH gas, not all of which is associated with hydrogen clouds in these directions. The hydrogen distribution in the galactic centre seems to be consistent with the presence of a rudimentary bar of matter reminiscent of those seen in barred spiral galaxies.

At least one cloud of gas, possibly located in the nuclear region, contains hydrogen, OH, and formaldehyde and is one of the few in which ammonia has been found. It shows no water spectrum, however. It is an interesting cloud because of the range of complex molecules it contains and because of its location in the Galaxy. In future years it may well produce further surprises for astronomers studying spectral lines.

INTERRELATION BETWEEN STARS AND THE INTERSTELLAR MEDIUM

Formation of stars. It is often stated that hydrogen is the basic building block of the universe. It is believed that stars produce all other elements by synthesis of nuclei through thermonuclear reactions beginning with hydrogen. Since only about 5 percent of the mass of the Galaxy is hydrogen gas, most of it must already have gone into the formation of stars. It is therefore not surprising to find that the regions where young stars are located (*i.e.*, where star formation is taking place) also contain most of the remaining neutral hydrogen.

Element production

It can be shown that within a relatively homogeneous medium containing cold hydrogen, such as a gas cloud in interstellar space, gravitational forces acting between the atoms will cause the cloud to contract. As the result of temperature or density inhomogeneities, smaller clouds may be produced within the original complex, and these may continue contracting individually. As they do so the matter heats up as a result of increased numbers of collisions between the component atoms.

After several times 10^6 years a stage is reached at which the object can be called a star. Young stars are often found in groups called clusters or associations, having formed from many subcondensations of an original large cloud. At some earlier point during the evolution of the contracting cloud the object may be referred to as a protostar. Such protostars may be visible as very small, compact, dark objects, and it is thought that the globules seen in some emission nebulae are examples of protostars.

Protostars

The most massive stars are also the hottest and radiate the most energy. They form in regions of great hydrogen density, and the hydrogen around them that has not yet formed into protostars or stars tends to become ionized by their radiation. This process produces an emission nebula. In a region around a smaller, cooler star a reflection nebula may result.

One problem not yet solved is why the stars are not prevented from forming by the magnetic fields in their parent clouds. It can be shown that in any cloud of neutral gas a very small amount, less than one-tenth of a percent probably, is ionized. This means that there are some free electrons in any neutral hydrogen cloud. The electrons are tied to the magnetic field by mutual interactions. There is also friction between the electrons and the neutral atoms, and the electrons, therefore, form a physical link between the magnetic fields and the hydrogen, neither of which can move without causing the other to follow suit. As the cloud contracts the magnetic fields' lines are forced closer together, which means that the magnetic-field strength increases inside the cloud. It can readily be shown that the magnetic fields should increase to well over 1,000 times the values observed in stars and should prevent contraction of the cloud beyond a certain point. Since stars obviously are formed, it is plain that this does not happen, but no satisfactory theory of why it does not happen has yet been proposed.

T Tauri stars and circumstellar dust. In some parts of the sky, in particular in regions containing much dust, small nebulosities are sometimes found in association with a class of variable star called the T Tauri stars after the name of their prototype. It is thought that these are very young stars, evolving rapidly, still undergoing a process of contraction under the influence of gravitational forces. Several T Tauri stars are known to have around them flattened, disk-shaped clouds of dust, which are possibly the first stages in the formation of planetary systems. (A parallel phenomenon is that of the variable stars called flare stars. These show many similarities to the T Tauri stars without the presence of nebulosity.) In 1946–1947 a T Tauri-type nebulosity was discovered that contained a single star. In 1954 the American astrophysicist, George Herbig, photographed the object again, and two stars were evident. This may constitute evidence of the actual birth of a star.

Planet formation

In 1967 a report that in all clusters and associations containing stars less than 100,000 years old the most luminous stars were most heavily reddened was published. It was suggested that the very young luminous stars are surrounded by obscuring clouds with diameters less than one parsec and masses of the order of 30 solar masses. At a later stage of evolution of the stars these dust clouds somehow become unobservable, possibly as a result of their contraction to disks around the stars. A surprising detail was that there were extensive regions of the Galaxy, with galactic longitude greater than 140°, in which such objects were not found at all and in which, by implication, no stars are currently being born. These findings apply to that part of the sky visible from the Northern Hemisphere.

The formation of a star from interstellar matter. From the discussions above a sequence of events may be suggested, leading from interstellar hydrogen clouds to the birth of a star. Various stages are as follows: (1) a cold neutral-hydrogen cloud containing dust starts to contract; (2) as the density increases, the shielding effect of the dust allows the interior to cool off sufficiently to permit the formation of molecules, such as molecular hydrogen and formaldehyde; (3) the cloud becomes so dense that it is totally absorbing and has the appearance of a globule; (4)

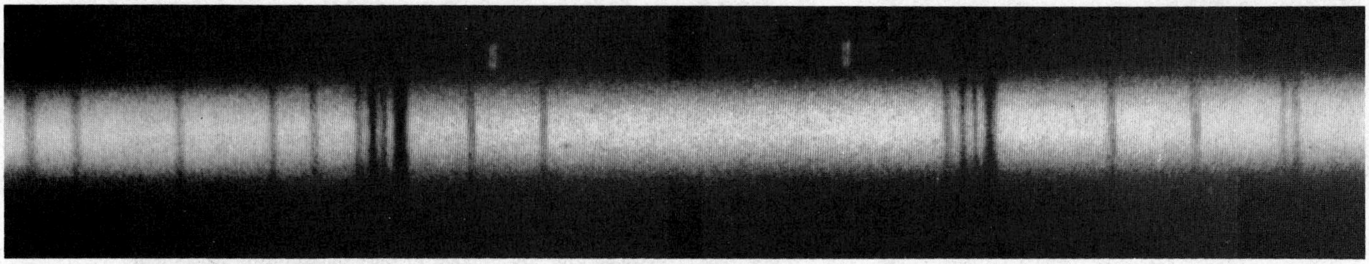

Figure 3: *Optical spectrum showing absorption lines D_1 and D_2 (two bands of darker lines) due to interstellar sodium.*
Bright horizontal band is starlight including many wavelengths. Dark vertical absorption lines are produced by interstellar clouds. The various components are contributed by several clouds between the star and Earth. Spectrum obtained in the direction of the star Epsilon Persei with the Mount Wilson 100-in. telescope.
By courtesy of Hale Observatories

further contraction results in formation of a star that can illuminate the surrounding matter. This may be the T Tauri stage (and possibly the flare star stage); (5) very luminous Wolf–Rayet stars (very hot variable stars, named after two astronomers who pioneered their research) may be produced by parallel development or in a successive state; (6) next, a star embedded in dust, not a variable but still very luminous, appears; (7) the dust disperses or contracts to a disk or planetary system, and the formation of the star is now complete.

Mass exchange. The average star continually loses mass by means of the stellar wind produced by radiation pressure from the star. Such "winds," streams of charged particles, emanate from the Sun. During increased solar activity denser clouds of particles are blown into interplanetary space. There they ultimately blend with the matter already in the surrounding interstellar space. Stars such as novae, supernovae, and the central stars of planetary nebulae also lose differing proportions of their mass catastrophically. There is thus a constant replenishing of interstellar material by injection of matter from stars. This mass loss from stars may roughly balance the present rate at which matter is used up in star formation. Planetary nebulae are estimated to inject about 10^{-13} solar masses of matter per cubic parsec per year, and the estimated injection from the O and B stars in the Galaxy is about the same. Supernovae, being much less numerous, contribute an estimated one-tenth this amount and novae only half as much as the supernovae. M stars must also be important contributors to the replenishment of the interstellar medium, probably as important as the planetary nebulae and O and B stars.

Solar and stellar winds

Apart from the normal processes of contraction in interstellar clouds that result in star formation, interstellar matter may probably also be collected up and remain as part of existing stars or protostars as they move through the interstellar clouds. This process is known as accretion. The amount of interstellar matter gathered up by these objects is still quite uncertain, but the process definitely does occur.

COMPOSITION OF THE INTERSTELLAR MEDIUM

Chemical abundances. At least one more element that contributes considerably to the mass of matter in interstellar clouds must be considered. This is helium, whose spectral lines are seen clearly in the light of stars and emission nebulae. There is, thus, good reason to believe that it occurs throughout the interstellar medium, making up about 10 percent by volume or 30 percent by mass of interstellar matter. In general, the abundances of elements in the interstellar medium are thought to be similar to those in the diffuse emission nebulae. Values found for these nebulae are given in Table 3.

Helium

The relative abundances of the elements in the cold interstellar clouds have been estimated by comparing the strengths of optical absorption lines and neutral hydrogen emission lines of radio wavelengths. Information is obtained only about the relative abundances of calcium, sodium, and hydrogen; and, as is often the case in astronomy, the work is more difficult in practice than in theory. What does emerge from such studies is that the relative abundances of sodium and calcium, with respect to hydrogen, vary greatly from cloud to cloud. This may be dependent on the way in which the dust grains in the clouds absorb these atoms (see Figure 3).

Temperature. The temperature of interstellar matter ranges from a few degrees above absolute zero to about 10,000° K. The very cold regions are often associated with dense dust clouds in which OH emission is detected. The properties of the OH emission make estimates of the temperature possible. Although neutral hydrogen clouds with temperatures as low as 20° K (20° above absolute zero) have been found, their typical internal kinetic temperatures may be around 50° to 100° K. These kinetic temperatures are measures of the amount of thermal motion within the gas clouds. Low-energy cosmic rays, which penetrate most of interstellar space, collide with and ionize hydrogen atoms. This results in the apparent heating of the medium, an effect particularly important for the low density regions between the cold clouds, where kinetic temperatures are probably in the range of 1,000° to 10,000°. In the hot ionized-emission nebulae the kinetic temperatures may be as great as 15,000°. The temperature of matter between the spiral arms is not known as yet, but presumably it is of the order of several thousand degrees, the temperature associated with the intercloud medium.

Density. The average density of interstellar material in spiral arms is about one to two atoms, or about 10^{-24} grams, per cubic centimetre. The density in stars is about one gram per cubic centimetre; the entire range of densities between these values must exist in the interstellar medium. Neutral hydrogen clouds have densities between 2 and 1,000 atoms per cubic centimetre, and the ionized matter in emission nebulae ranges from 10^3 to 10^6 atoms per cubic centimetre. The hot intercloud medium contains about one atom per 10, or 100, cubic centimetres. The number of electrons in the neutral interstellar space may be one-tenth of these values. Clearly then, by comparison with stars or the solid earth, interstellar space is nearly empty and close to absolute zero in temperature, and any effort to detect interstellar matter by actually trying to scoop up some would be impossible at present. In dealing with enormous volumes of this space, however, astronomers are still dealing with vast numbers of

Table 3: The More Abundant Elements in Some Diffuse Emission Nebulae

element	relative number of atoms
Hydrogen (H)	100
Helium (He)	10
Carbon (C)	0.025
Nitrogen (N)	0.013
Oxygen (O)	0.079
Neon (Ne)	0.063
Sodium (Na)	0.00013
Calcium (Ca)	0.00016

atoms or molecules and can, therefore, observe their combined effect.

BIBLIOGRAPHY. B.J. and P.F. BOK, *The Milky Way*, 5th ed. (1981), a description of the contents of our galaxy; O. STRUVE and V. ZEBERGS, *Astronomy of the 20th Century* (1962), a historical approach; G.O. ABELL, *Exploration of the Universe*, 4th ed. (1982), a comprehensive textbook of astronomy for introductory college courses; J. DUFAY, *Nébuleuses galactiques et matière interstellaire* (1954; Eng. trans., *Galactic Nebulae and Interstellar Matter*, 1957), a discussion mainly of early optical data; H. SHAPLEY (ed.), *Source Book in Astronomy, 1900–1950* (1960), a readable description of the basic contributions to astronomical research; B.M. MIDDLEHURST and L.H. ALLER (eds.), *Nebulae and Interstellar Matter* (1968), a series of advanced review papers; J.S. HEY, *The Radio Universe*, 2nd ed. (1976), an introduction to the field of radio astronomy; H. VAN WOERDEN (ed.), *Topics in Interstellar Matter* (1977), a collection of papers presented at an International Astronomical Union symposium. See also B.E. TURNER, "Interstellar Molecules," *Sci. Am.* 228:50–69 (March 1973).

(G.L.Ve.)

Ion-Exchange Reactions

Ions are positively or negatively charged atoms, or groups of atoms, that result from the loss or gain of electrons, respectively, from their neutrally charged parents. In pairs they make up the substance of many crystalline materials, including table salt. When such an ionic substance is dissolved in water, the ions are freed—to a considerable extent—from the restraints that hold them within the rigid array of the crystal, and they move about in the solution with relative freedom. Certain insoluble materials bearing positive or negative charges on their surfaces react with ionic solutions to remove various ions selectively, replacing them with ions of other kinds. Such processes are called ion-exchange reactions. They are used in a variety of ways to remove ions from solution and to separate ions of various kinds from one another. Such separations are widely utilized in the scientific laboratory to effect purifications and to aid in the analysis of unknown mixtures. Ion-exchange materials are also employed commercially to purify water (among other uses) and medically to serve as artificial kidneys and for other purposes (see also ZEOLITES).

Early history. Surprisingly, recognition of ion-exchange processes antedates the great Swedish chemist Svante Arrhenius, who formulated the ionic theory. In 1850, nine years before Arrhenius was born, separate papers appeared in the *Journal of the Royal Agricultural Society of England* by the agriculturist Sir H.S.M. Thompson and the chemist J.T. Way, describing the phenomenon of ion exchange as it occurs in soils. In his paper, entitled "On the Power of Soils to Absorb Manure," Way addressed himself to the question of how soluble fertilizers like potassium chloride were retained by soils even after heavy rains. To answer that question, Way took a box with a hole in the bottom, filled it with soil, and poured onto the soil a solution of potassium chloride, collecting the liquid that flowed out of the bottom. He then washed the soil with rainwater and analyzed the water he had collected, from both the solution and the rainwater. The water turned out to contain all of the chloride that had been originally added but none of the potassium; he found that the potassium had been replaced by chemically equivalent amounts of magnesium and calcium. He called the process "base exchange" because of the basic (nonacidic) character of the exchanged elements. That term persisted until after 1940, by which time the process had become universally known as ion exchange.

In modern parlance, the process would be described in the following way: potassium ions enter the soil and displace calcium and magnesium ions. The chloride ions have no part in the operation and pass through unchanged. In terms of a chemical equation, the process is $2K^+ + Ca^{2+}$ (soil) $\rightleftharpoons Ca^{2+} + 2K^+$(soil), in which the double arrow indicates that the exchange is reversible. In Way's experiment, the process was pushed to completion (that is, the equilibrium was pushed to the right) because the water trickling through the soil continually came in contact with fresh calcium-loaded soil. As Way also ob-

Base exchange

served, the potassium could be regained by washing the soil with a solution of calcium chloride (which pushed the equilibrium in the opposite direction).

Ion-exchange materials. Soil is able to bind positive ions (like K^+ and Ca^{2+}) because it contains clay minerals and organic humic acids. Both of those substances are insoluble materials that carry, as a part of their molecular framework, negatively charged ionic groups. In clays, for instance, such groups are the ends of silicon–oxygen chains—either oxygen atoms that carry an extra electron because they are bonded to only one atom instead of the usual two or aluminum atoms bonded to four oxygens instead of the usual three. The following schematic representation shows both kinds of ionic structure as they occur in an almost infinite variety of silicates and aluminosilicates, both natural and artificial.

$$
\begin{array}{ccc}
 & K^+ & \\
 & | & \\
 & O & O \\
 & | & | \\
-O-Al-O-Si-O^-K^+ \\
 & | & | \\
 & O & O \\
 & | & | \\
\end{array}
$$

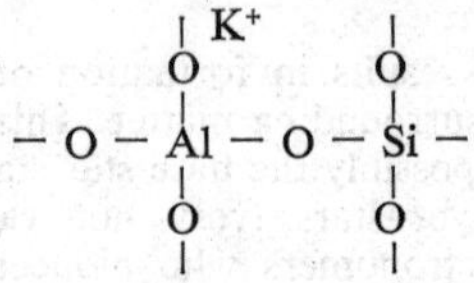

The negative ions are part of the framework; the positive ions, shown here as potassium, are small and can change places with other positive ions if the solid is placed in contact with a solution. The small positive ions must be able to move in and out; they must therefore be located on surfaces or in the interstices of the open lattice structure.

The two requirements for ion exchange—fixed ionic charges on a supporting material and permeability of the material to a solution—are met in a surprisingly large number of materials. The fixed charges may be negative, as in the above example, or they may be positive. The mobile ions must be of opposite charge to the fixed ions. Materials with fixed negative charges exchange positive ions, or cations, and the process is called cation exchange. Those having fixed positive charges correspondingly exchange negative charges, or anions, and are said to undergo anion exchange.

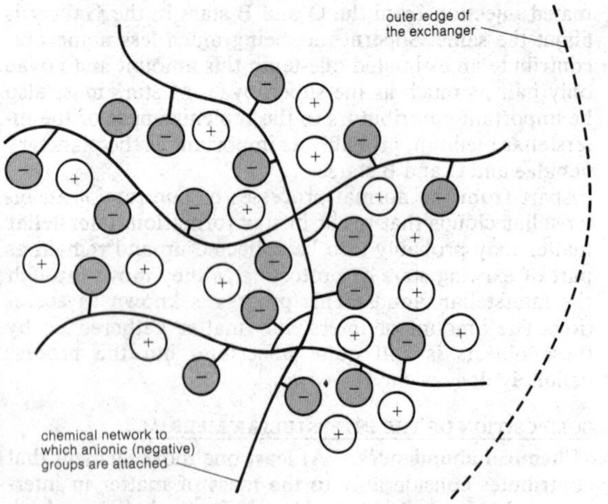

Chemical structure of cation exchanger. The exchangeable ions are marked +. The whole structure is permeated by solvent molecules, usually water (not shown).

A big improvement in ion-exchange technology came about in 1935, when the first ion-exchange resins were discovered by the English chemists Basil Albert Adams and Eric Leighton Holmes. The resins were chemical relatives of the plastic Bakelite and were made by condensing polyhydric phenols or phenolsulfonic acids with formaldehyde.

In 1944 Gaetano F. D'Alelio patented styrene–divinylbenzene polymers, substances with large, network-like molecules, into which ionic groups were introduced by chemical treatment. The structure of these compounds may be represented thus:

Ion-exchange resins

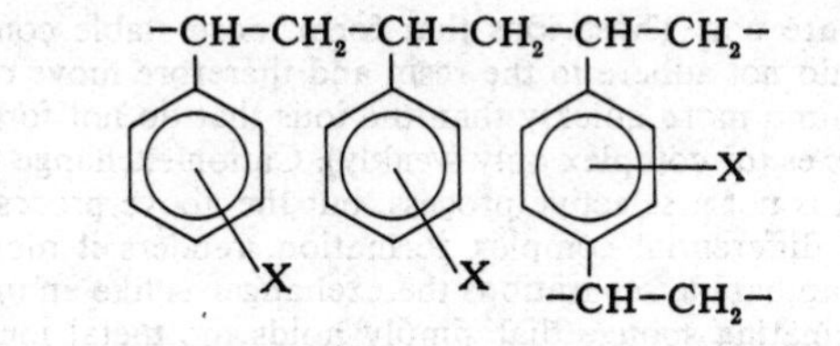

in which X represents the ionic groups, which may occur at various locations on the benzene rings. In the formula as shown, the first two benzene rings come from styrene, whereas the third is from divinylbenzene. Divinylbenzene thus provides cross-linking between the polystyrene chains, joining them into a three-dimensional network that can be tight or loose, depending on the ratio of divinylbenzene to styrene. This ratio can be varied at will; the usual commercial proportion is 8 percent. The ionic groups may be sulfonic acid groups, namely $-SO_3^-H^+$ or quaternary ammonium groups, $-CH_2N^+(CH_3)_3Cl^-$. These two types account for some 90 percent of all ion-exchange resins produced. The hydrogen ions and chloride ions may be replaced by other ions, such as Na^+ (sodium) or OH^- (hydroxide); the hydrogen and hydroxide forms of these resins are very strong acids and bases, respectively.

Styrene and divinylbenzene are liquids and are polymerized as spherical droplets, with the result that the resins have the form of beads that are almost perfect spheres. The beads swell when placed in water, and though they look smooth and impermeable, they are actually very permeable to water and small ions. They may have diameters ranging from a few microns (thousandths of a millimetre) to one to two millimetres. Different sizes are used for different purposes.

Ionic groups other than sulfonic acid and quaternary ammonium salt may be introduced into the resin structure. A useful one is iminodiacetate, $-CH_2N(CH_2COOH)_2$, which forms chelated complexes (structures held together by secondary bonds) with all metals except the alkali metals. The stability of these complexes varies widely from metal to metal. The chelating resins are used in chemical analysis to separate and concentrate trace metals.

Resins carrying the carboxyl group, $-COOH$—useful in medicine and biochemistry—are based not on polystyrene but on polymethacrylic acid:

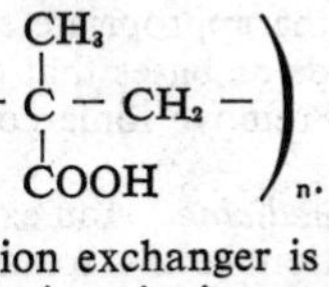

Still another kind of ion exchanger is made from cellulose by introducing various ionic groups into the cellulose molecules. Since the ions are on the surface of the threadlike molecules, instead of being inside molecular frameworks, they are accessible to large ions and molecules. Cellulose-based exchangers are especially useful in biochemistry.

Synthetic inorganic ion exchanges

Synthetic inorganic exchangers have been known since 1903. The first ones were aluminosilicates. About 1955 it was found that phosphates, arsenates, and molybdates of titanium, zirconium, and thorium were good cation exchangers; and many such materials have been prepared, some commercially. They are useful in the nuclear-power industry for they are resistant to radiation and selective to certain radioactive wastes, particularly the long-lived fission product cesium-137. They serve to separate that isotope from other less dangerous fission products.

Another class of inorganic ion exchanger is the molecular sieve. These materials are crystalline aluminosilicates with well-defined structures containing pores of definite sizes that permit only certain ions to enter. When the water is removed from the pores, these substances become selective adsorbents for gas molecules of certain sizes and shapes. They also are powerful catalysts.

The substances termed liquid ion exchangers possibly should be classed as organic solvents, rather than ion exchangers, in spite of their name. The molecules of such substances contain long hydrocarbon chains, which make them insoluble in water, but they also carry ionic groups that attract ions of opposite charge. An example of a liquid ion exchanger is dinonylnaphthalene sulfonic acid, *i.e.*, $(C_9H_{19})_2C_{10}H_5SO_3H$.

Ion-exchange procedures. Only rarely are ion exchangers used in stepwise procedures, in which the resin is mixed into a container of solution and then removed for further treatment. Much more frequently the exchanger is packed into a tube or column through which the solution is made to flow.

Ion-exchange columns

The column arrangement forces the ion-exchange reaction, which is intrinsically reversible, to go to completion in the desired manner. The solution flowing down the column continually meets fresh exchanger, and a reaction that goes half way in the first centimetre of the column may be three-quarters completed in the second centimetre, seven-eighths in the third, and so on. In a short time, the exchangeable ions that entered the column have been adsorbed and become undetectable analytically. When the exchangeable ions do start to emerge from the end of the column, however, the column has become completely saturated with them. It may be restored to its original condition, or regenerated, by passing through it a solution of the ions that it originally contained.

Ion-exchange columns are easy to use, but the theory behind their use is extremely complicated. A column with a solution flowing through it is a nonequilibrium system, and its interpretation must consider not only equilibrium distributions but rates of transfer of material and statistical variations in the paths of liquid flow between the granules that make up the exchanger. There are two chief theories of ion-exchange processes related to the two principal ways in which the columns are employed. In the first procedure, displacement, the column originally contains mobile ions of one kind that are pushed down the column by the steady flow of a solution of ions of a second kind. The theory for this procedure deals with the rate at which the "front" (the boundary between the different classes of ions) advances and its concentration profile (whether the front stays sharp as it moves down the column or whether it becomes progressively more diffuse). In the second process, elution, a thin layer of ions is introduced at the top of a column already saturated with ions of a second kind; it then is washed down the column with the same kind of ions that saturated the column at the start. In elution, the theory must account for the rate of movement of the narrow band of ions and its spread as it proceeds down the column.

When a mixture of two kinds of ions that are held by the exchanger with differing strengths is introduced at the top of a column, the mixture of ions separates as it moves down the column, with the result that the original single band of ions is resolved into two separate bands. This process is called ion-exchange chromatography. Ion-exchange chromatography is an important tool in chemical analysis because it permits separation of materials that are very difficult to separate by other means. It can be applied to organic and inorganic ions and even to substances that are not ionic. It is often used to separate mixtures of many components.

Ion-exchange columns are made in all sizes, from the large tanks used to soften the water supply of great cities to the tiny columns holding less than a cubic centimetre of resin that are used for recovering short-lived radioactive elements in the laboratory. (The element mendelevium was discovered by the isolation of a few atoms on an ion-exchange column.)

Preparation of columns

Care is needed in preparing columns for the laboratory. Dry resin must be stirred with water to let it swell before it is poured into the column. Air bubbles must not be allowed to form in the resin bed for they interfere with the liquid flow. It is desirable to backwash the column—that is, to pass liquid upward to expand the resin bed—in order to release air bubbles and to segregate the resin particles according to size before the column is used. The aim of the preparation procedure is to assure even packing and even flow. For difficult chromatographic separations, resins having uniform, very small particles are used to facilitate mass transfer and give sharper bands. As fine particles offer much resistance to flow, solutions must be forced through under pressure. One procedure is to use long, narrow columns of stainless steel (like those used in a related process called gas chromatography) and to hasten mass transfer by using, instead of resin beads, glass spheres coated with ion-exchange resin.

Ion exchangers, especially inorganic and cellulose-based exchangers, are used in thin-layer chromatography. Chromatographic paper for this purpose is manufactured from finely ground resins and cellulose fibres. One use for this procedure is to filter small traces of metal ions from large volumes of solution.

Ion-exchange membranes

Ion-exchange resins also may be fabricated into thin sheets, although it is not easy to make a sheet of ion exchanger that is strong and flexible and at the same time permeable; development of ion-exchange membranes has been slow for this reason. Ion-exchange membranes are used, however, to separate the electrodes of fuel cells and to remove salts from water by the physical processes termed reverse osmosis and electrodialysis. The former is a kind of filtration process—water is squeezed through the membrane under pressure while the dissolved salts are left behind. The reaction can be carried out, for example, by placing a membrane of cation-exchange resin loaded with sodium ions in contact with a dilute solution of sodium chloride. Because of the characteristics of the ion-exchange process, neither the sodium nor the chloride ions can enter the membrane. Water molecules can penetrate the membrane, however; and because of the pressure exerted on the system, they do so, crossing to the other side. The result is the removal of salt from the water without distillation (the usual desalting process).

Electrodialysis is a process somewhat similar to reverse osmosis. Ions are able to enter an ion-exchange membrane if they are simultaneously removed from it at the other side; the effect is the same as passing an electric current through the membrane. In practice electrodialysis is carried out by placing a cation-exchange membrane on one side of the solution to be desalted and an anion-exchange membrane on the other and then passing an electric current through the system. The result is that positive ions pass through the membrane on one side and negative ions pass through the membrane on the other. Pure water is left eventually in the area between the membranes.

Applications of ion exchange. *In the laboratory.* Ion exchange is used for both analytical and preparative purposes in the laboratory, the analytical uses being the more common. An important use of ion-exchange chromatography is in the routine analysis of amino-acid mixtures. Columns of cation-exchange resin are used, and the solutions are maintained sufficiently acid that the amino acids are at least partly in their cationic forms. The 20 principal amino acids from blood serum or from the hydrolysis of proteins are separated in a few hours, and their concentrations are determined automatically by light-absorption methods. Such analysis is used in clinical diagnosis.

In a less routine and highly important application of ion-exchange chromatography, the products of hydrolysis of nucleic acids are analyzed. In this way, information is gained about the structure of these molecules and how it relates to their biological function as carriers of hereditary information. Cation-exchange resins are used for this purpose as well. Because of their use in analyzing the structures of complex biological materials, ion-exchange chromatographic procedures have been of great importance in the development of modern molecular biology—the explanation of biological processes in terms of the interactions of molecules.

Separation of inorganic ions

Inorganic ions also can be separated by ion-exchange chromatography. The lanthanides, or rare-earth elements, are separated on columns of cation-exchange resin. Solutions of citrates, lactates, or other salts whose anions form negatively charged complexes with the lanthanide ions are used to wash the ions from the column. The metal ions themselves are held by the resin; the complexes are not. Those ions that form more stable complexes do not adhere to the resin and therefore move off the column more quickly than the ions that do not form complexes (or complex only weakly). Cation exchange in general is not a selective process, but the above process, termed differential complex formation, renders it more so. In lanthanide separations the exchanger is like an undiscriminating sponge that simply holds the metal ions, whereas the real separation of the various metals is accomplished by the weakness or strength of the complexes formed.

Anion exchange in hydrochloric acid is an effective way to separate metal ions. Most metals form negatively charged chloride complexes that can be held by anion-exchange resins carrying quaternary ammonium groups (NR_4^+). These complexes differ greatly in their stabilities in solution and in their affinities for the resin. The distribution of metal ions between the solution and the resin depends on the hydrochloric acid concentration and the identity of the metal ion. Impressive separations of metal ions can be achieved by manipulating the hydrochloric acid concentration.

Ion-exchange separations of this kind are widely used; they can be modified by using mixed solvents, like acetone–water, and great selectivity is possible. In the process called "activation analysis," an unknown sample to be analyzed is bombarded with neutrons, and the radioactive elements thus formed are separated by anion-exchange procedures. Such analysis is especially valuable in separating minor metallic constituents from samples containing large amounts of other substances. The technique has been used to analyze lunar rocks.

Chelating resins are used to collect trace metals from seawater. Further, a copper-loaded chelating resin also adsorbs, by coordination, traces of amino acids from seawater. Miscellaneous analytical uses of ion exchange include the dissolving of sparingly soluble salts like calcium sulfate, the determination of total dissolved salts in natural waters (by passing them through hydrogen-loaded, cation-exchange resins and titrating the acid formed), and the identification of minute traces of ions (by absorbing them onto a single resin bead along with a colour-producing reagent).

Preparative uses of ion exchange in the laboratory are not many, but on occasion unusual acids, such as hydroferrocyanic acid, or unusual bases, like cesium hydroxide, are prepared from their salts by passing solutions of the salts through the appropriate resins. Resins also are used to purify acids or bases that contain nonionic contaminants, and to remove ionic contaminants from solvents.

Water softening by ion exchange

In industry and medicine. Ion exchange finds its major industrial application in the treatment of water. Hard water—caused by the presence of calcium and magnesium ions, which form insoluble precipitates with soaps—is softened by exchanging its calcium and magnesium ions with sodium ions. To accomplish this, the hard water is passed through a column of cation exchanger containing sodium ions. After the column has been in use for some time, calcium and magnesium begin to appear in the water leaving the column. Then the column must be regenerated by passing a concentrated solution of common salt slowly through the column; the excess sodium ions displace the ions that produce the hardness so that, after flushing with water, the bed of exchanger is ready to be used again. At first, the exchangers used for this purpose were natural aluminosilicates; but later, synthetic resins came to be used instead.

For special purposes, such as use in the laboratory, water is deionized—that is, freed entirely from dissolved ions of all kinds. This is accomplished by passing the water through two resin beds in separate columns. The first bed contains a cation-exchange resin bearing hydrogen ions and converts the dissolved salts to their free acids. The second contains an anion-exchange resin loaded with hydroxyl ions; it neutralizes the acids, holding back their anions, and leaves nothing in the water but nonionic impurities. The beds are regenerated by strong acid and strong alkali, respectively. An alternative procedure, "mixed-bed" deionization, uses only one column containing the two resins mixed. Since the resins must be separated for regeneration, however, mixed beds are used chiefly in disposable cartridges for small laboratory units.

Resins used for water treatment should last for many years, but their life may be shortened either by accumulation of colloidal matter (prevented by adding activated carbon filters) or by oxidation caused by the dissolved chlorine in the water. Quaternary-base anion-exchange resins carrying hydroxyl ions also deteriorate; they decompose slowly to give tertiary amine polymers and methanol.

In an even older use of ion exchange, salts are removed from sugar juices to raise the yield of crystallized sugar. Deionization also can improve the flavour and storage time of pineapple juice and wine. In these and other beverage applications, ion exchange removes traces of heavy metals, which not only taste bad but also catalyze oxidation.

In hydrometallurgy, the treatment of ores with water solutions, ion exchange helps to recover valuable metals like copper, silver, and gold from waste waters. Uranium can be recovered from low-grade ores by leaching with dilute sulfuric acid—oxidizing if necessary to convert uranium(IV) to uranium(VI)—and then absorbing the negatively charged uranium sulfate complex ions on a quaternary-base anion-exchange resin. This highly selective absorption process thereby separates the uranium from iron and other metals. The uranium is later removed from the resin with dilute nitric acid.

On an industrial scale, cation exchange separates rare-earth elements by means of a displacement technique in which each element displaces elements bound less strongly than it is as it proceeds down the column. The elements emerge (the one with the weakest bond first) one after the other in high purity.

Ion exchangers can function as catalysts. Strong-acid cation-exchange resins loaded with hydrogen ions catalyze certain chemical reactions carried out in the liquid phase, such as hydrolysis (the splitting of molecules with addition of water) and esterification (ester formation). The advantage of the resin over hydrochloric acid as a catalyst in these reactions is that it is present as a separate phase that does not contaminate the product. In addition, the ion-exchange process lends itself to continuous-flow techniques. Gas-phase reactions catalyzed by metal ions, like the cracking of petroleum fractions to produce gasoline, also can be catalyzed by metal-loaded inorganic exchangers, the molecular sieves being particularly suitable for this purpose since their open crystalline structure makes every metal ion accessible.

Ion exchange in medicine

Ion-exchange resins have a limited use in medicine. Carboxylic resins containing hydrogen or ammonium ions, taken by mouth, remove sodium ions from the gastrointestinal tract and control edema; other resins are consumed to lower acidity in the stomach and hence to soothe stomach ulcers. Interest in these treatments has declined, however, because of the resins' undesirable side effects. Resins also are incorporated into artificial kidneys outside the body to remove ammonium and potassium ions from the blood. The most important medical applications of ion exchange, however, have been made in clinical analysis procedures that depend on ion-exchange chromatography.

Equilibria and kinetics. *Ion-exchange equilibria.* The reversibility of ion-exchange reactions greatly affects the behaviour of ion-exchange systems. Typical ion-exchange reactions can be written as follows:

$$A^+ + B^+Res^- \rightleftharpoons B^+ + A^+Res^-$$
$$C^{2+} + 2B^+Res^- \rightleftharpoons 2B^+ + C^{2+}(Res^-)_2,$$

in which Res^- stands for an ion fixed in the resin or other type of exchanger and A^+ and B^+ are univalent cations (monopositive ions) while C^{2+} is a divalent cation.

As is generally true of reversible reactions, equations can be written describing the relative concentrations (amount of material per unit volume) of the various species in equilibrium—that is, when the rate of the forward reaction is equalled by that of the reverse reaction. For the ion-exchange processes indicated above, the following equations demonstrate the relations of the materials present under the conditions of equilibrium:

$$K_1 = \frac{[B^+]\,[A^+Res^-]}{[A^+]\,[B^+Res^-]};\quad K_2 = \frac{[B^+]^2\,[C^{2+}Res_2^-]}{[C^{2+}]\,[B^+Res^-]^2}.$$

In these equations, the constant K_1 is a pure number without units (such as feet per second) because the units on the right side of the equation cancel. The numerical value of K_2, however, as well as its units, depends on the units chosen to express the concentrations on the right side of the equation. Since the constant K_1 or K_2 is the most useful simple description of the equilibrium conditions of an ion-exchange reaction (and knowledge of its value permits calculation of the concentrations of the various substances in equilibrium under specified conditions), determinations of K values are fundamental steps in the study of ion-exchange reactions. For concentrations in the resin, the proportions of mobile ions to the resin framework (in grams or in chemical equivalents of fixed ions) can be used, or one can refer the amounts of mobile ions to the weight of water that the resin contains. More constant values of K_2 can be obtained by reference to the resin rather than to the water, which is fortunate, because the water content of a swollen resin depends on the mobile ions it contains and it is hard to measure. As experimentally determined, however, the values of K_1 and K_2 are not constant but vary with the proportions of exchangeable ions in the resin. This result leads to the unsurprising conclusion that the interior of the resin is not an ideal solution.

The distribution of ions of unequal charge, like B^+ and C^{2+} above, depends on the total concentration of the solution. The more dilute the solution, the greater the tendency for the ions of higher charge to accumulate in the exchanger. One doubly-charged ion entering the exchanger sends two singly-charged ions back into the solution, and the more dilute the solution, the more likely is this replacement to happen. This effect, called "electroselectivity," is used in water softening. Calcium ions are taken up from hard water, which is a dilute solution, whereas they are removed from the resin by regenerating with a solution of sodium chloride that is concentrated.

Many studies have been made of ion-exchange equilibria and the factors that influence the values of K. Different ions are held by exchangers with different strengths. As yet it is impossible to predict a priori the magnitude of K, but one can make certain generalizations, which are different for cation and anion exchange.

Cation exchange

For the alkali and alkaline-earth metal ions, the strength of binding varies inversely as the ionic hydration. Thus, lithium ions, the most strongly hydrated of the alkali metal ions, are the most weakly held by resins, followed in order by sodium, potassium, rubidium, and finally cesium, which forms the strongest bond with the resins. In the alkaline earths the increasing order runs from beryllium to magnesium, calcium, strontium, barium, and to radium, which is the most strongly held.

These sequences are characteristic of resins whose functional group is the sulfonate ion. Resins bearing carboxylate ions, or with fully ionized phosphonate ions, exhibit different sequences. The electrostatic field strength of the fixed ion on the resin determines the order of separation. When the charge on the fixed ion is small and spread over a large area, as in the sulfonate ion, $-SO_3^-$, the field strength is weak and the mobile ions keep their primary hydration shell—that is, the water molecules they hold by direct coordination. The more strongly hydrated ions migrate to where there is more water—that is, out of the resin and into the surrounding solution.

When the ionic charge is concentrated, however, as it is around the terminal oxygens of silicate networks, the mobile cations are attracted so strongly that the primary hydration shell may be squeezed out. The fixed and mobile ions then come into direct contact. The smaller the mobile ion the closer it gets to the fixed ion and the greater the force that holds it. When the ionic charge is extremely concentrated, the alkali-metal sequence is completely reversed: lithium is held most strongly and cesium the least strongly. Intermediate sequences are possible. In this way the selectivity orders in glass electrodes and biological membranes, both of which function by competitive surface adsorption of positive ions, can be explained. This theory is of little help, however, in explaining selectivity orders of heavy-metal ions; in this case, other factors, as yet unknown, seem to be at work.

Anion exchange

The selectivity sequence for halide ions in resins with quaternary-ammonium fixed ions is fluoride, chloride, bromide, and iodide, with fluoride being held the most weakly. This resembles the cation selectivity order, in which the smallest ion also is held most weakly. On the other hand, the differences between the various ions in degree of attachment to the resin is much greater in the series of halide anions than in the series of alkali-metal cations. Iodide is held a hundred times as strongly as fluoride in an 8 percent cross-linked quaternary-ammonium resin; whereas in an 8 percent cross-linked sulfonic resin, cesium is held four times as strongly as lithium.

It is significant that anions are larger than cations (in their crystal-lattice radii) and that they interact with water in a different way. Instead of attracting dipolar water molecules around them, anions tend to break up the hydrogen-bonded structure of liquid water, with the result that the bigger they are, the more difficult it is for them to enter the water. Large ions are thus driven out of the water and into the resin—a phenomenon of great practical value in achieving separations. Perchlorate ions, ClO_4^-, are held ten times as strongly as iodide ions. This effect extends to complex ions such as the chlorides of iron and gold, $FeCl_4^-$ and $AuCl_4^-$, which are held very strongly by quaternary ammonium-type anion-exchange resins. The effect of large size may sometimes be offset by an increased ionic charge, which tends to orient the water molecules and stabilize the dissolved ion. Thus, the higher charged zinc complex $ZnCl_4^{2-}$, with its double negative charge, is more weakly bound by the resin than the iron complex $FeCl_4^-$, with its single negative charge.

Very large ions, of course, cannot enter the resin network. With ions of moderate size, the entry of the ion into the network may become a limiting factor, and it becomes important to distinguish between unfavourable equilibrium, on one hand, and slow exchange, on the other. The equilibrium absorption may be large, but it may take a long time to reach it because the ion has difficulty entering the resin.

Ion-exchange kinetics. Generally, ion exchange is fast. No electron-pair bonds need be broken, and the rate of the process is limited only by the rate at which ions can diffuse in and out of the exchanger structure. The openness of the resin structure, however, depends on the degree of its swelling and on its water content. When both swelling and water content are small, diffusion rates are correspondingly slow. This is true of carboxylic-acid resins and of chelating resins in their acid (hydrogen-ion) form, for these acids are weakly ionized. It is also true of metal-loaded chelating resins. These types of exchangers require ample time for reaction; thus, it is advisable to use a resin with fine particles. High temperature also hastens diffusion. Nonetheless, the general rapidity and efficiency of their actions have brought widespread acceptance and use of ion exchangers.

BIBLIOGRAPHY. F. HELFFERICH, *Ion Exchange* (1962), the standard reference work on the theory of ion exchange; R. KUNIN, *Ion Exchange Resins*, 2nd ed. (1958), a short practical guide to ion-exchange resins and their use; Y. MARCUS and A.S. KERTES, *Ion Exchange and Solvent Extraction of Metal Complexes* (1969), a thorough discussion of extraction and ion-exchange methods; J. KORKISCH, *Modern Methods for the Separation of Rarer Metal Ions* (1969), a practical discussion of ion exchange and solvent extraction; W. RIEMAN and H.F. WALTON, *Ion Exchange in Analytical Chemistry* (1970), a discussion of the theory and types of ion exchangers.

(H.F.W.)

Ionic Crystals

A perfect crystal is a solid in which the atoms, molecules, or charged atoms (ions) are arranged in a regular manner. Crystals with a high degree of perfection are generally not found in nature but must be prepared in the laboratory. Imperfections include impurities and disturbances in the regularity of the lattice, such as, for example, a missing atom.

GENERAL CONSIDERATIONS

Bonding in crystals. All solids consist of atoms bound together by forces that hold the atomic nuclei at fixed distances from one another. Several types of bonds are defined and can be measured, but all are the result of attraction and repulsion between charged particles—*i.e.*, between the positive charges on the nuclei and the negatively charged electrons that surround each nucleus. Electrons are attracted toward their own nucleus as well as toward neighbouring nuclei and, at the same time, they are repulsed by one another. Thus, a certain state of equilibrium must be achieved by any substance in order to exist as a solid but, since solids can be melted or distorted or the configuration of their constituents altered in several ways, it is clear that the state of equilibrium is one that can be affected from without. Crystals are solids that have special properties resulting from the spatial organization of their constituents. Three general classes of bonds in solids are known: covalent, ionic, and metallic (see CHEMICAL BONDING). The free atoms of nearly all elements tend to be unstable enough that they will accept a few electrons to become negatively charged ions (anions) or they tend to lose a few electrons and become positively charged ions (cations). The electrons gained or lost are called valence electrons. Atoms that gain electrons are in some cases capable of forming a bond with similar atoms in which each will share one of its electrons with the other. These shared electrons will thus spend time in the sphere of influence of both nuclei. This is called a covalent bond, and the atoms are considered to form a molecule. In covalent solids (*e.g.*, silicon), covalent bonds exist between each atom and its neighbours. Single atoms (*e.g.*, of carbon) are also capable of forming solids through covalent bonds between them.

Classes of bonds

Ionic bonds. Ionic bonds are formed when two atoms react so that the valence electrons of one are actually transferred to the other, forming two oppositely charged ions. Such bonds, and resulting compounds, are also called electrovalent. In the gaseous and liquid states, ions are free to move about singly although they do tend to associate. When the ionic compound freezes, however, the Coulomb forces of attraction between opposite charges and repulsion between similar charges orient the ions in such a way that every positive ion is surrounded by negative ions and vice versa. In both ionic and covalent solids, all of the electrons are tightly held by their nuclei; in what is called the metallic state, the bonds are such that some valence electrons are left free to move about in the structure, and these give the metal its electrical conductivity. Chemically pure covalent and ionic crystals are, therefore, nonmetallic and, in most cases, behave as thermal and electric insulators.

Ion arrangement. An ionic crystal, therefore, is composed of ions, so arranged that the positive and negative charges alternate and balance one another so that the overall charge of the whole crystal is zero. For example, sodium chloride (table salt) crystals are composed of positive sodium ions and negative chlorine ions, the net charge on each ion being plus or minus one. Other combinations of alkali metals (*e.g.*, lithium, potassium, and rubidium) and halogens (fluorine, chlorine, bromine, or iodine) form similar ionic compounds and are known as alkali halides. More complex ionic crystals contain several types of ions. Barium titanate, for example, is composed of barium (with a charge of $+2$), titanium (with a charge of $+4$), and oxygen (with a charge of -2); the formula for the compound is written $BaTiO_3$.

Uses. Although ionic crystals are important in many industries and in technology (*e.g.*, in photography and as detectors of high-energy radiation), scientists have studied them primarily because both perfect and imperfect simple ionic crystals exhibit a wide range of physical phenomena. Man's understanding of them has deepened his knowledge of atomic structure, chemical bonds, radiation, electricity, magnetism, solubility, etc. These phenomena are difficult to understand in the more complicated (and often more useful) solids, but can be understood in the relatively simple ionic solids. Thus, it is relatively easy, for example, to calculate the approximate energy involved in the formation of a simple ionic crystal from a gas or the energy required to create a vacancy.

It now seems likely that ionic crystals will be increasingly employed in solid-state devices, for example, as photochromic devices (*i.e.*, systems which reversibly change colour when illuminated by certain wavelengths of light). A program is under way to use ionic crystals containing imperfections in information-storage systems, with laser light used to transmit and obtain the information.

Information storage

THE STRUCTURE OF IONIC CRYSTALS

Perfect ionic crystals. The requirements of regularity of the lattice and alternation of charge for the simpler crystals limit the possible arrangements which the ions in an ionic crystal may take up. It is found that the most common arrangement in such cases is the sodium chloride structure, in which the crystal can be thought of as consisting of adjacent cubes, whose corners are alternately occupied by positive and negative ions. A second common structure is the cesium chloride structure in which ions of one sign occupy the corners of cubes and a single ion of opposite sign is at the centre of each cube. Other arrangements, such as those called zinc blende and wurtzite, are possible, but these usually exist in solids in which covalent bonding (due to sharing of electrons; see CHEMICAL BONDING) between ions is important. In more complicated crystals, many structures are found.

X-ray diffraction. The structures of these crystals, as of other solids, may be measured by X-ray-diffraction techniques. In effect, the crystal acts toward X-rays in much the same way as a diffraction grating (consisting of a plate engraved with parallel lines) acts toward light, and the patterns that the diffracted X-rays make upon a screen or photographic plate yield information about the crystal's structure and also about the location of the electrons in the crystal. Each atom consists of a nucleus carrying a specific number of positive charges that identifies the elements, surrounded by an equal number of negative electrons; an ion has either more or less electrons, and, because it is interaction of the electrons with the X-ray beam that causes the X-rays to be diffracted, detailed analysis of X-ray patterns can yield information about how electrons are distributed in the solid. It is found that in the simpler ionic crystals the electrons are quite strongly localized within the ions; therefore, the concept of the ionic crystal as a collection of slightly distorted free ions is rather accurate. This is in contrast to semiconductors, such as silicon, in which the electrons of adjacent atoms form covalent chemical bonds, and to metals, such as copper, in which some electrons behave as though they were not bound at all to individual atoms but were free to move about.

Coulomb energy. Early in the 20th century, a German physicist, Max Born, and others made reasonably accurate calculations of cohesive energy—*i.e.*, the energy involved in the formation of crystals from a gas. Though these calculations have since been considerably refined, many of the early results are not significantly modified by the refinements. As has been indicated, the strongest force holding the ions together is the Coulomb force between opposite charges. Since crystals are stable the ions must stabilize at a certain distance from one another (the Coulomb force does not pull them so close together that there is no space at all left between them), and clearly there must exist repulsive forces of a different nature which become important whenever the ions are close together. Furthermore, the fact that noble gas atoms (such as neon) do not form ions but do crystallize at extremely low temperatures indicates that other, weaker attractive forces must also exist and come into play between atoms or ions under certain conditions. Finally, there exists a second repulsive force that arises from the zero-point energy and represents a quantum-mechanical effect associated with lattice vibrations (see below). It is most important for relatively light ions.

Calculation of the Coulomb energy is straightforward in principle but somewhat difficult in practice. The Coulomb energy between two ions is proportional to the product of their charges (q_1 and q_2) and inversely proportional to the separation (r) which may be represented as q_1q_2/r, and must be summed over all possible ion pairs in the crystal. Furthermore, because the energy falls off only rather slowly with increasing separation, the sum cannot be approximated by neglecting pairs separated by large distances. It was early recognized that a three-dimensional lattice sum could be evaluated rather precisely by the use of mathematical methods which involved sorting the ions into neutral groups. The resulting energy, called the Madelung energy, is inversely proportional to the distance between neighbouring positive and negative ions; and in the equation relating these quantities, the proportionality constant is called the Madelung constant. The Madelung constant that results from the lattice sum characterizes all crystals of a given structure; for the sodium chloride structure, for example, it is 1.747558, whereas for the cesium chloride structure it is 1.762670. The Madelung constant has been computed for many complex structures as well.

Madelung energy

Pauli exclusion principle. If ions in a crystal were regarded as hard spheres, their equilibrium separations could be determined by their radii. This is a relatively accurate picture, as discussed later in this section, but for a better understanding, it is necessary to consider the forces which cause the ions to repel one another. The exact calculation of the most important repulsive force is very difficult; its source is quantum-mechanical, and detailed quantum-mechanical calculations for many-electron systems are quite involved. The major contribution to this repulsive energy arises from the Pauli exclusion principle, which says that no two electrons may have all of their energy states, which are represented by quantum numbers, equal. When two electron "clouds," which envelop their respective nuclei, begin to overlap, there is a tendency for the electrons from one atom to occupy energy states of the other and vice versa, but the tendency is offset by a repulsive force which tends to minimize the overlap of the electron clouds of neighbouring ions. (In simple lattice calculations, this repulsive term is described by a rapidly varying function of ion separation.)

Van der Waals energy. The other attractive energy, already mentioned, called the Van der Waals energy, arises from a quantum-mechanical effect. Although on average, the electronic charges are distributed symmetrically on the atoms, at any given instant the distribution may be slightly nonsymmetrical or asymmetrical—*i.e.*, polarized. A polarized atom has a concentration of negative charges somewhere and, at a distance from it, a concentration of positive charges. This asymmetry generates an electric field, which in turn polarizes neighbouring atoms. These polarized atoms attract each other through an energy that varies inversely as the separation to the sixth power. This energy falls off sufficiently rapidly with distance so that ion pairs with large separations need not be included in the calculation.

The four parts of the total potential energy of the crystal (including the zero-point energy), all have so far been pictured as depending on ionic separation. Like a ball which rolls down a hill, the crystal finds an equilibrium configuration in which its potential energy is a minimum that may be calculated by varying the value for the ion separations until a minimum energy is found. This gives the equilibrium separation and the cohesive energy. It is possible also to calculate other quantities, such as a crystal's elastic stiffness or resistance to compression.

Other calculations

A more ambitious program of calculations would involve repeating the above approach for a given substance in different crystal structures so as to predict the crystal structure on the basis of a minimum energy criterion. Such an approach gives fairly unambiguous results for alkali halides, when, for example, sodium chloride is compared with zinc blende lattices but does not work at all well in distinguishing between halide—*e.g.*, sodium chloride and cesium chloride—structures. The cohesive energies in the latter case are very close, and subtle effects, not all of which are known, determine the equilibrium structure. Most important is the presence of covalent bonds formed between atoms by the sharing of electrons, rather than by a transfer of electrons as in ionic (or electrovalent) bonds, so that covalent molecules in a crystal are neutral. For more complicated ionic crystals, including those that are partially covalent, the question of crystal type formation—*i.e.*, of the manner in which the molecules, atoms, and ions are packed—becomes important. Octahedral coordination of units, in which each unit is surrounded by six neighbours, as in sodium chloride, forms a structure that tends to be associated with ionic bonding; tetrahedral coordination of units, in which each has four nearest neighbours instead, as in zinc blende, is a structure formed by covalent bonding; and, for some cases a rather delicate balance between the two occurs. Silver chloride and silver bromide, for example, have the sodium chloride structure, whereas silver iodide, which is less strongly ionic, has the zinc blende structure.

Pauling's rules

Ionic radii. Years ago a U.S. chemist, Linus Pauling, developed semi-empirical rules to guide the choice in studying crystal structure. The rules are based on the concept of ionic radii—the idea that each ion can be regarded as a hard sphere of a definite radius. Although the charge distribution of electrons in ions is a continuous function of distance, the concept of ionic radii is useful. With a set of radii for different ions, the ions of a crystal can be arranged into different structures: in some cases, the positive and negative ions touch; whereas in others, the smaller positive ions do not touch the negative ones, but the negative ions touch each other. Pauling observed that stable crystal structures tend to be those in which positive and negative ions touch each other and in which the number of nearest neighbours is largest. Simple geometrical calculations of different modes of arranging ions with different diameters suggest that if the positive-to-negative ion-radius ratio is less than 0.414, the structure will be like zinc blende; if it is between 0.414 and 0.732, the structure will be like sodium chloride; and if greater than 0.732, it will be like cesium chloride. But since the rules do not include the tendency for some ions to form covalent bonds, they do not work in all cases. The concept can, with some modification, be extended to treat more complex ionic solids.

Defects in ionic crystals. So far, only perfect ionic crystals have been considered. Real crystals, however, contain defects, and these defects are of particular importance in many properties of ionic crystals. It is informative to consider a pure ionic crystal and assume that it has the simplest defects, which involves the displacement of one or more atoms from their normal positions. There are two common situations. The first, called a Frenkel defect, involves an ion displaced from its normal position into an interstitial position, which is any position not normally occupied. The second, called a Schottky defect, involves an ion displaced from its normal position to the surface. Because each region of the crystal tends to remain electrically neutral, Schottky defects in alkali halides often occur in positive–negative pairs.

Frenkel and Schottky defects

The energy required to create such a defect may be calculated in a manner similar to that outlined in the calculation of cohesive energies. The energy may be supplied in several ways, one of which is thermal. At any temperature, the lattice has heat, or vibrational, energy, and there is a probability that enough of this thermal energy will be given to an ion to create a defect. Defects will occur at any temperature, although the number of defects will increase with increasing temperature. The more energy required to create the defect, the fewer defects there will be. For this reason, the type of defect that takes the least energy to create will predominate when the crystal is in thermal equilibrium. It is found that in most alkali halides, Schottky defects predominate, while in silver halides, Frenkel defects are most common. These defects may also be produced nonthermally, their type and number depending on the mechanism, and the resulting species may not be in thermal equilibrium. The most important nonthermal source of defects is radiation. Effective forms of radiation range from ultraviolet through X-ray to gamma-ray electromagnetic radiation and also include particles such as neutrons (neutrons and protons form the nuclei of atoms), electrons, and alpha particles (helium nuclei, one of the products of radioactive decay). Because incident neutrons or alpha particles have masses comparable to that of the ions, elastic ("billiard-ball") collisions may occur to displace ions into interstitial positions. In other cases, such as ultraviolet and X-ray irradiation, however, the primary process is ionization—that is, the freeing of electrons from their nuclei in the crystal. How this, in turn, leads to defects is a complicated process which is understood to some extent as it occurs in the halides. It appears that a halogen ion possesses considerable potential energy for the formation of a covalent bond with another halogen ion (the result may be called a molecule–ion). This potential energy, however, may be converted to kinetic energy which is then absorbed by one of the halogen ions, carrying that ion out of its position and leaving behind a halogen vacancy. While the details are still unclear, it appears that it is the primary mechanism for the formation of halogen vacancies by ultraviolet and X-ray irradiation.

Colour centres. Among the most important defects in ionic crystals are colour centres, so called because, in many cases, the defect imparts a particular colour to the crystal. There are many kinds of colour centres that have been extensively studied, of which only a few appropriate to the alkali halides will be listed. Their optical properties will be discussed later.

The simplest of these, called the *F* centre, consists of an electron trapped at a halogen vacancy. If the *F* centre traps a second electron, it becomes an F' centre. Two adjacent *F* centres form an *M* centre, while three *F* centres form an *R* centre. The *F* and *M* centres in an alkali halide are shown in Figure 1A.

A second class of colour centres is electron deficient. One of these, the so-called V_k centre (Figure 1B) involves the covalently bonded halogen molecule–ion mentioned above. An *H* centre is similar, except that one of the halogens is in an interstitial position. In the terminology discussed below, these involve self-trapped holes.

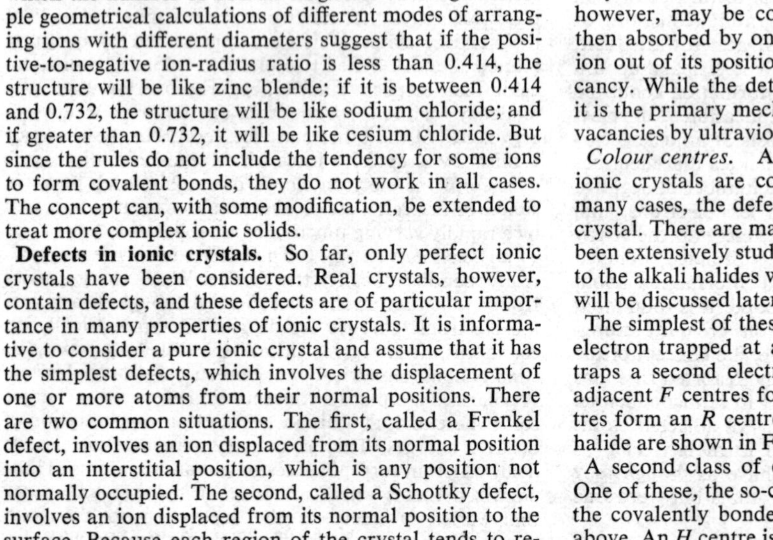

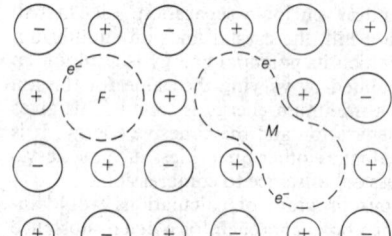

Figure 1: *Colour centre defects.*
(A) The *F* centre, consisting of an electron trapped at a halogen vacancy, and the *M* centre, which is two adjacent *F* centres. (B) The electron-deficient V_k centre produced by formation of a covalent bond by halogen ions.

Colour centres can be produced in a variety of ways. One method, involving ionizing radiation, is an extension of the vacancy formation mechanism discussed above. The electrons that are freed in the ionization process are trapped at the halogen vacancies to form *F* centres. At the same time, self-trapped hole centres can be formed, since halogen molecule–ions are involved in formation of the vacancy.

A second technique for producing *F* centres in alkali halides is called additive coloration. In this method, the crystal is heated in an alkali vapour. Alkali atoms stick to the surface and combine with halogen ions that migrate from the interior to form new atomic layers of crystal but, in the process, leave behind halogen vacancies which can trap electrons to become *F* centres.

A third class of defects involves impurity ions. In this instance, there are many possibilities; positive silver and thallium ions are among the most widely studied. The most common way of adding impurities is addition while the crystals are molten. If the molten crystal is cooled properly, the resulting crystal will contain a random distribution of impurities. In certain cases, the process will not work, because certain impurities will tend to aggregate instead of randomly mixing during crystallization. In such cases, impurities may be added by techniques such as ion implantation, in which the ions are essentially shot into the crystal.

PROPERTIES OF IONIC CRYSTALS

Many properties of ionic solids depend on the nature of their vibrational and electronic states. This topic will be treated briefly here (see SOLID STATE OF MATTER).

Vibration in the lattice

It has been shown how ions can interact, through attractive and repulsive forces so that an equilibrium configuration exists. To a first approximation, the lattice can be treated as though the ions were fastened together by coil springs; if one ion is caused to vibrate, other ions will vibrate as well, because the "springs" will transmit the forces through the lattice. In any system of this type there is a number of ways that the system can vibrate, and each of these ways is called a normal mode. In a perfect solid, the normal modes involve vibrations of all the ions; since ions of a given type are identical and regularly arranged, it is impossible to cause one to vibrate without causing the rest to vibrate as well.

Acoustic and optical bands. In a solid there are many modes, three for each ion, and in a perfect solid the frequencies of these vibration modes are grouped to form bands. In a typical alkali halide there exists a wide band of frequencies ranging from zero to about 10^{12} per second called the acoustic band, and at somewhat higher frequencies there exists what is called an optical band. The acoustic band involves vibrations in which the ions of different charge tend to vibrate together; these vibrations are involved in the transmission of sound waves. The optical band involves vibrations in which the ions of opposite charge tend to vibrate against each other; these vibrations can be excited by light, as will be considered later. The normal modes of vibration are sometimes called phonons to emphasize the quantum properties of the vibrations that behave as waves and units, or quanta of energy (as does light).

Electrical conductivity band. The arrangement of electrons and their energy states in solids must be described by means of quantum theory; in connection with the perfect crystal, this is referred to as energy band theory. Energy states are referred to as energy levels and can be represented by horizontal lines whose levels or elevations are proportional to their energies. The energy levels of a solid form bands in much the same way and for much the same reason as the frequencies of lattice vibrations form bands. An electron in a filled band (a band in which all quantum levels are occupied) cannot conduct electricity, whereas one in a partially filled band can. If one electron is removed from a filled band, the remaining electrons may conduct electricity by "jumping" into the empty state; it is convenient to describe this process as though the empty state were a charged, mobile particle, called a hole. Figure 2A illustrates a theoretically perfect electronic insulator—a filled valence band and an empty conduction band, separated by a region in which no energy levels exist, called an energy gap. Figure 2B shows an electron removed from the valence band (leaving a hole) and placed in the conduction band. Both the electron and hole can now conduct. If impurities are introduced into the crystal, they may have energy levels within the energy gap. This situation is illustrated in Figure 2C. Normally, the lowest impurity level, or its ground state, will be occupied by one or more electrons, and the higher levels, or excited states, will be empty.

Empty states: holes

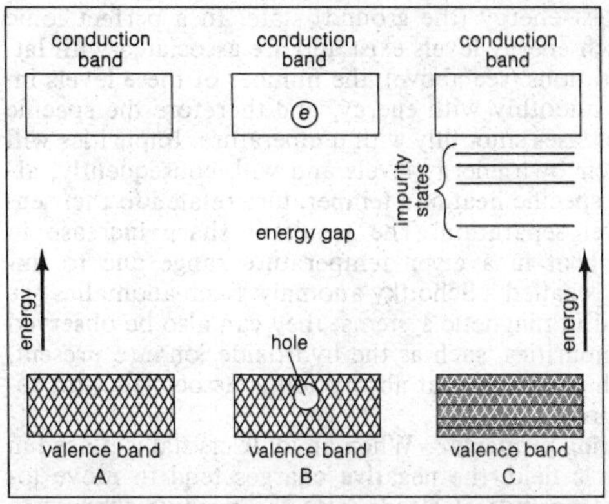

Figure 2: *Energy bands of an insulating crystal.* (A) A perfect insulator: all energy levels of the valence band are filled, and no electrical current can flow. (B) An insulator with one electron removed from the valence band, leaving a hole, and placed in the conduction band; both electron and hole conduct. (C) Impurities in the crystal may have energy levels within the energy gap.

Thermal properties. The conduction of heat, or thermal conductivity, by a crystal is equal to a constant times the spatial rate of change of the temperature, or by the equation $Q = K\,dT/dx$, in which Q is the heat energy transmitted across a unit area in a unit time, dT/dx is the change in temperature per unit distance, and K is the thermal conductivity. Whereas in metals the conduction electrons contribute to the thermal conductivity, in ionic crystals very few of these electrons exist because the valence bands tend to be filled and the conduction bands empty. The other system which can participate in heat conduction is the lattice ions, through their vibrations. Lattice vibrations do not conduct heat as well as do free electrons; ionic crystals are therefore better thermal insulators than are metals. Only a brief explanation of the process may be given here.

It is possible to visualize how, if heat is applied to one end of a crystal, causing the ions to vibrate, the pulse of heat energy can be transmitted through the lattice by means of the vibrations. If this were all there is to it, however, the solid would quickly achieve a uniform temperature, whereas experimentally it is found that in a solid whose ends are kept at different temperatures, the temperature within varies smoothly from one end to the other. The behaviour of the solid lies in the fact that the ions do not interact exactly as if they were connected by springs; so-called anharmonic forces exist which cause the different vibrational waves, or phonons, to interact with one another. This interaction, in turn, enables the phonons to transmit energy to the crystal as a whole, and this leads to the establishment of a smooth temperature variation throughout the solid.

Effect of imperfections. The phonons which carry the heat energy can also interact with imperfections; whereas phonons travel without impedance in a perfect crystal, they can be scattered by imperfections. At very low temperatures the process of thermal conductivity becomes ineffective, and in a small lattice pure crystal thermal conductivity is determined by interaction of the phonons with the surface and thus depends upon the size of the specimen.

Impurities can also lead to changes in the thermal conductivity. Adding small amounts of silver chloride to potassium chloride, for example, leads to a decrease in the thermal conductivity versus temperature. The presence of the silver impurity ions leads to another process for scattering phonons that decreases the conductivity. The dip in the curve is apparently involved with a vibrational wave in which the silver ions vibrate the most; in a sense the silver ion momentarily traps the phonon, which leads to a decrease in the thermal conductivity.

Specific heat. The specific heat, or heat capacity, of a solid is the amount of heat absorbed when the temperature is raised one degree. The ability of a solid to absorb heat depends on how many quantum-mechanical energy levels it has which are approximately an energy kT above the lowest energy (the ground) state. In a perfect ionic solid such energy levels exist and are associated with lattice vibrations (see above); the number of these levels increases smoothly with energy, and therefore the specific heat increases smoothly with temperature. Impurities will have their own energy levels and will, consequently, affect the specific heat at a temperature related to their energy-level separation. The resultant sharp increase in specific heat in a given temperature range due to impurities is called a Schottky anomaly. Such anomalies are observed in magnetic systems; they can also be observed when impurities, such as the hydroxide ion, are present, in which case, the heat absorption is associated with reorientation of the ion.

Polarizing property. When an ionic crystal is placed in an electric field, the negative charges tend to move toward the positive electrode, and the positive charges to move toward the negative electrode. If the charges are not free to move through the crystal, their displacements will be small; such a solid is said to be polarized. The amount of polarization per unit of applied field is related to an electrical property of a solid, called its dielectric constant.

The amount of polarization depends not only on the magnitude of the electric field but also on how rapidly it changes. If the field is constant or changes slowly, both the electrons and the ions as a whole will be displaced, and the solid is characterized by a dielectric constant that remains static. If the field varies rapidly, however, the relatively massive ions cannot move sufficiently rapidly to respond to it, and only the electrons are displaced. Then the solid is characterized by an optical, or high-frequency, dielectric constant.

Impurities such as the hydroxide ion can change the dielectric properties of crystals. In these molecules the positive and negative charges are displaced from one another, and, consequently, the molecules can be made to reorient in an electric field. This reorientation leads to changes in the dielectric constant.

Diffusion properties. So far, only stationary defects have been considered. In certain situations, defects may move through the crystal. This movement can occur in several ways, the most important of which are by interstitial and vacancy mechanisms. In the former, an interstitial ion jumps into an adjacent interstitial site; in the latter, an ion jumps into a vacancy, thereby creating a vacancy in the former position of the ion. Most substitutional impurities diffuse by a vacancy mechanism, and in alkali halides self-diffusion—that is, diffusion of the normal ions—is also by the vacancy mechanism.

Fick's law

The process of diffusion is governed by Fick's law, which states that the number of ions crossing a unit area in a unit time is equal to a constant (indicated by D), called the diffusivity, times the change in concentration per unit distance in the direction of the diffusion.

Diffusion can be measured by several methods, one of which involves radioactive-tracer ions. Radioactive ions are incorporated into the crystal, and their motion is detected by measuring changes in the intensity of radioactivity throughout various regions of the crystal.

Ionic conduction. In an insulator, since there are normally only a few electrons which can conduct electricity, the main electrical conduction process in ionic crystals is not electronic but, instead, involves the motion of ions, and is called ionic conductivity. The phenomenon is closely related to diffusion, since both involve the motion of ions; in fact, the diffusivity and the ionic mobility (symbolized by μ [mobility equals the velocity of the particle per unit of applied electric field]) are related through the Einstein relation, which states that the product of the ionic mobility, Boltzmann's constant, and absolute temperature is equal to the product of the ionic charge and the diffusivity—in equation form, $\mu kT = qD$, in which k is Boltzmann's constant, T is the absolute temperature, q is the charge of the ion, and D is the diffusivity.

Doping

It is found that ionic conductivity is enhanced by the addition (called doping) of doubly charged positive ions to alkali halides—*e.g.*, adding calcium chloride to potassium chloride. The simplest explanation of this is that the doubly charged calcium ions of calcium chloride are more mobile than the singly charged potassium ions, but this is not the explanation. Rather, since the crystal tends to remain electrically neutral, there will tend to be a positive ion vacancy associated with each calcium ion (Figure 3). Conductivity will then occur through the vacancy mechanism.

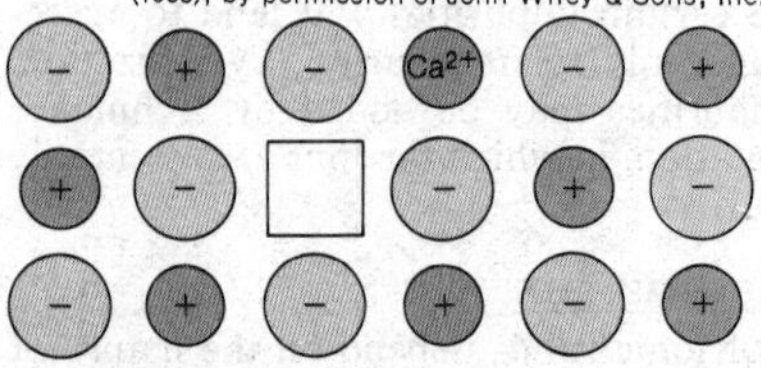

Figure 3: Production of a vacancy to enhance ionic conductivity by adding calcium chloride to potassium chloride. For each calcium ion (Ca^{2+}) there tends to be a positive ion vacancy, indicated as a square, which permits conductivity through the vacancy mechanism.

A practical aspect of both ionic and electronic conductivity of insulators comes from so-called space-charge effects. For example, if it is assumed that conduction is by positive vacancy migration and that the crystal is in an electric field but that the electrodes do not touch the crystal; then, after some time, there will exist a layer of positive charge in the crystal near the negative electrode and a layer of negative charge near the positive electrode. These space charges will set up an electric field inside the crystal in the direction opposite to that of the applied field, which will decrease the ionic currents. Similar problems are associated with electronic conductivity in insulating crystals and can occur even when the electrodes touch the crystal. In some cases, in fact, the building of space charge is an important factor in lowering the conductivity of the crystal.

Optical properties. *Radiation absorption.* "Optical," in this case, refers to an electromagnetic spectrum extending from the infrared through the X-ray region, not specifically to visible light. The interaction of optical electromagnetic radiation with matter, specifically ionic crystals, may be divided into two parts, dispersion and absorption. In the former, radiation is transmitted by the solid, but its characteristics are somewhat changed; in the latter, it is absorbed by the solid. These phenomena are related, as are two others, namely, reflection and luminescence (*q.v.*). Dispersion need not be discussed in any detail here.

A detailed quantum-mechanical treatment of optical properties of solids will show that the existence of absorption depends upon satisfying certain selection rules, the most fundamental of which involves the conservation of energy. The energy of a photon is equal to the product of Planck's constant times the radiation frequency (or $h\nu$, in which h is Planck's constant, and ν is the frequency of the electromagnetic wave). For this photon to be absorbed, when it impinges on a solid, the absorber must have an empty energy level (designated E_2) a distance $h\nu$ higher than an occupied energy level (E_1); then the energy-conserving absorption process involves the energy difference of the two levels: $h\nu = E_2 - E_1$. If no energy levels separated by energy $h\nu$ exist, radiation of this frequency will not be absorbed.

In many ionic crystals, the electronic energy gap (see Figure 2) corresponds to the ultraviolet region of the spectrum. These crystals, if perfect, will not absorb visible light that shines on them and will therefore appear to be transparent. (Imperfections may have levels in the gap and therefore absorb visible light [see below].) As the wave frequency decreases to the infrared, however, the crystals begin to absorb (and reflect) incident radiation, because of the interaction of the radiation with the phonons. The phonon energy of a level is equal to Planck's constant times the phonon frequency, and hence the energy-selection rule is $h\nu = E_2 - E_1 = h(\nu_2 - \nu_1)$, or $\nu = \nu_2 - \nu_1$, in which ν_1 is the initial phonon frequency and ν_2 the final phonon frequency. At low temperatures, there will be few initial phonons, so the initial phonon frequency (ν_1) is approximately zero; thus, $\nu = \nu_2$, which means a photon of frequency ν is absorbed and a phonon of frequency ν_2 is created. Other selection rules indicate that it is the optical phonons that are created, which can also be seen from the fact that the electric field of the radiation interacts with the electric charge displacement associated with the optical mode.

Phonon energy

Infrared absorption thus occurs when the light frequency is comparable to the frequency of the optical modes. Reflectivity is also large in this region, which is maximum for light of frequency ν_t, called the residual ray, or the Reststrahl frequency.

As has been pointed out some impurities tend to trap phonons or to have their own modes of vibrations. These modes can also absorb photons, and in fact, one way of detecting the presence of impurities is to measure their infrared spectrum.

Ionic crystals are strongly absorptive in the ultraviolet region, largely because of the absorption of a photon and the excitation of an electron from the valence band to the conduction band. The onset of this strong absorption depends on the band gap of the crystal. Along with band-to-band transitions, which produce conduction electrons and valence holes, absorption may occur at slightly lower photon energies, leading to the creation of so-called excitons, electron–hole combinations. An exciton can exist because of the Coulomb attraction between electron and positive hole. This represents a bound state between particles, much like a hydrogen atom.

Excitons

In recent years, interest has developed in the interaction of ionic crystals with spectral frequencies from ultraviolet to X-ray. This interest has coincided with the development of sources of radiation in this region generated by electron accelerators called synchrotrons, which are used for high-energy physics research. Scientists are able to study the conduction bands in detail over a wide range of photon frequencies and to compare the results with theory.

If imperfections such as colour centres exist in a crystal, absorption may occur in the visible part of the spectrum. The crystal then may appear coloured; the *F* centre has different characteristic colours in different alkali halides. This absorption arises from transitions from the ground state of the colour centre to an excited state (see Figure 2C for a schematic representation of the energy levels).

Luminescence. In many cases luminescence is present. Luminescence is the inverse of absorption; the crystal system makes a transition from an excited state to the ground state, and a photon is emitted. It is generally found, however, that the frequency of the emitted photon is considerably smaller than that of the absorbed photon. This is called a Stokes shift, and it arises because of the interaction of the electrons with the phonons. When an ion or colour centre is excited, it is no longer in equilibrium with neighbouring ions; the ions are impelled to take on new equilibrium positions and emit phonons. Thus, some of the electronic energy is dissipated as heat energy.

The electron–phonon interaction also causes the absorption and emission bands to be wide. This widening occurs because, as the lattice vibrates, the environment of the ion or colour centre is constantly changing, and therefore the separations of the energy levels change, producing fluctuations in the transition energies.

Conductivity. Although electrons able to conduct do not normally exist in ionic crystals, band-to-band optical transitions produce conduction electrons and valence holes, and these can conduct electricity. Conduction electrons can also be produced by the ionization of impurities or colour centres.

Having produced either these electrons or holes or both, it is possible next to measure their conductivity. Several effects may be found. First, holes in alkali halides tend to become self-trapped at low temperatures and so to have zero conductivity. A similar phenomenon appears to occur in the silver halides, although the evidence is not as strong.

Conductivity of the electrons will be limited by their scattering from phonons and from imperfections, as in any crystal. A peculiar property of conduction electrons in ionic crystals, however, is that they do not behave as though they were of proper mass (see SOLID STATE OF MATTER); but instead, their mass typically appears to be about twice what it is expected to be. This behaviour occurs because the electron interacts with the ions in its vicinity in such a way that it tends to attract the positive ions and repel the negative ions. At any instant, then, there exists around the electron a region of the crystal in which the ions are temporarily polarized, *i.e.*, slightly displaced, and when the electron moves, it must carry this polarization "cloud" along with it. The electron plus its polarization cloud is called a polaron, and the apparent mass of the system is the polaron mass.

The most important optical process involving ionic crystals is the photographic process. When a photographic emulsion containing tiny silver halide crystals is exposed to light, the crystals are decomposed to produce a latent image of tiny specks of metallic silver. Succeeding steps in the process involve further chemical reduction of the silver halide and increase in the size of the silver specks to visibility.

Use of ionic crystals in photography

The steps involved in the primary process of producing grains of metallic silver are not known with certainty. The first step, however, appears to be the creation of a conduction electron and a valence hole by a photon (the energy gap of silver bromide is sufficiently narrow for visible light to achieve this). It is probable that the conduction electron is then trapped at an imperfection, such as at a surface; thereupon an interstitial positive silver ion is trapped at the electron site, forming a neutral silver atom. Repetition of this process at the site leads to a grain of metallic silver. Whether or not the order of the process is correct is uncertain, but it is clear that the clustering of silver ions and electrons to form silver is involved. At the same time, the holes must be trapped, or they will tend to recombine with the electrons. The hole trapping may occur at imperfections or in impurities which are deliberately added for this purpose.

BIBLIOGRAPHY. ALAN HOLDEN, *The Nature of Solids* (1965), an elementary, general work on solids, with considerable information relevant to ionic crystals; CHARLES KITTEL, *Introduction to Solid State Physics*, 4th ed. (1971), a standard introductory solid-state text, containing much material on ionic crystals; F.C. BROWN, *The Physics of Solids* (1967), extensive coverage of ionic crystals, with a good discussion of the theory of the photographic process; LINUS PAULING, *The Nature of the Chemical Bond*, 3rd ed. (1960), a classical work on chemical bonding, including an extensive discussion of bonding and the structure of simple and complex ionic crystals; N.F. MOTT and R.W. GURNEY, *Electronic Processes in Ionic Crystals*, 2nd ed. (1940, reprinted 1964), a classical work on ionic crystals, and though old, still contains much usable material; N.B. HANNAY, *Solid State Chemistry* (1967), much information relevant to ionic crystals, including material on diffusion; J.H. SCHULMAN and W.D. COMPTON, *Color Centers in Solids* (1963), a standard introductory work in the field of colour centers in solids; W. BEALL FOWLER (ed.), *Physics of Color Centers* (1968), a detailed account of recent research in the field of colour centers.

(W.B.F.)

Ionosphere

The ionosphere is an upper region of the Earth's atmosphere in which many of the atmospheric atoms and molecules have become electrically charged by the addition, or more often the removal, of electrons to produce ions, and in which the ions and freed electrons coexist. It is, therefore, said to be ionized. The ionosphere is sometimes defined as the body of ionization itself: the total population of ions and electrons, as distributed throughout the ionospheric region. The lower boundary of the ionosphere lies at heights of about 55 kilometres (34 miles) above the Earth, where the electron concentrations are sufficient by day to affect radio propagation. The concentration of electrons increases irregularly with height, to a maximum at elevations of 200–600 kilometres (125–375 miles). Above that, the concentration decreases once again, but more slowly and over a much greater height span. Relative to the layered regions of the atmosphere, the ionosphere begins at a base near the stratopause (at the top of the stratosphere), rises through the mesosphere (a middle region) to a peak in the thermosphere (a region of increasing temperature), and extends upward to overlap the exosphere (a region of relatively few particles). (See the article ATMOSPHERE, which describes the nature of these regions.) It terminates ultimately at heights of several Earth radii (one Earth radius equals 3,960 miles, or 6,370 kilometres) in a complex of interactions with ionization flowing out from the Sun.

History of ionospheric investigation. Discovery of the ionosphere extended over a century. As early as 1839, a German physicist, Carl Friedrich Gauss, speculated that an electrically conducting region of the atmosphere could account for observed variations of the Earth's magnetic field. This theme was developed by a Scottish physicist, Balfour Stewart, in 1882, in an article for the *Encyclopædia Britannica* (9th edition), which is often taken to mark the start of ionospheric science. The notion of a conducting region was invoked once again in 1902, by an electrical engineer of the United States, Arthur Edwin Kennelly, and an English physicist, Oliver Heaviside, to account for the success of an Italian physicist, Guglielmo Marconi, in transmitting radio signals from England to Newfoundland "round the protuberance of the earth," in 1901.

Early skepticism as to the reality of the conducting region ended in 1925 when unambiguous radio reflections from the Kennelly-Heaviside layer (as it was first known) were reported, and the term ionosphere was introduced.

Gross features. Detailed study of the ionosphere by radar revealed a layered structure. First to be identified was a layer of molecular ionization, called the E layer because of the electric field of the reflected radio wave. It has since given its name in turn to the so-called E region of the atmosphere, which extends over the height range 90–140 kilometres (56–90 miles). A D region underlies this, and, during daylight hours, contains a ledge of electron concentration that merges into the base of the E layer. Overlying the E region is the F layer of ionization, the major layer of the ionosphere, starting at about 140 kilometres (90 miles).

In the height range 100–150 kilometres (62–93 miles), strong electric currents are generated by a process analogous to that of a conventional electric generator, or dynamo (see below). This region, in consequence, is often termed the dynamo region. It is virtually identical to the E region in terms of elevation. Extending upward from it is the magnetosphere, in which the Earth's magnetic field, called the geomagnetic field (see EARTH, MAGNETIC FIELD OF), is dominant in the control of ionization movement. This geomagnetic control is so important for some purposes that the terms F region and even ionosphere are often abandoned completely in favour of magnetosphere for all heights appreciably above the peak of ion concentration in the F layer.

Dynamo region

Contained within the magnetosphere, but contributing relatively little to its ion content, are the highly energetic charged particles of the Van Allen radiation belts (*q.v.*). A protonosphere is often identified at heights above 1,000 kilometres (620 miles) or so; it is the region in which protons (the nuclei of hydrogen atoms) constitute the dominant ionic species. The concentration of these protons, and of the accompanying free electrons, drops radically at the plasmapause, which at low latitudes lies at distances of four to five Earth radii from the Earth's centre but which follows the curvature of the geomagnetic field lines (directions along which a magnetic force acts) to lower elevations at higher latitudes (see Figure 3). Residual ionization is found beyond the plasmapause, arising both from terrestrial and from solar sources in variable but as yet unknown proportions.

At distances of 8 to 14 Earth radii on the Sunward side, and at even greater distances on the flanks and on the night side, the geomagnetic field terminates at the magnetopause. This in turn is surrounded by a magnetosheath of irregular ionization flowing outward from the Sun, the Earth's ionosphere having given way to the Sun's.

The ionospheric regions have been of importance to man since his origin for it is in them that many of the Sun's harmful radiations are absorbed. The ionosphere's existence is in fact a direct consequence of this absorption in the earth's cover of air; man's existence could not continue without it.

Ever since Marconi's pioneering work with wireless transmission, the ionosphere has had an immense commercial importance as well: it has guided radio waves around the curvature of the Earth. The E and F layers are most important in this regard, for it is they that reflect radio signals in the broadcast and short-wave bands that carry much of man's communications to distant points on the Earth. Ionization of the D region acts to attenuate these signals by day but effectively disappears with the setting of the Sun and so permits broadcast reception over much greater ranges at night, when, particularly, radio signals may follow more than one path from transmitter to receiver, and the received signals may interfere constructively or destructively (*i.e.*, the waves are in phase or out of phase with each other); as the ionospheric paths change, the received signals fade in and out, sometimes rhythmically. Ionization in the D region serves as a reflector for long-wave-band signals by day, without introducing serious attenuation of them. This band provides stable communications as a result and so is employed for special purposes; accurate transoceanic navigation by ships and aircraft, for example, is accomplished in part with its aid.

Fading of radio signals

Disturbances of the ionosphere arise from a number of sources and act in various ways to disrupt (or occasionally to improve) radio communications. At times the disturbances produce strong fluctuations of the geomagnetic field, much as Gauss had postulated more than a century ago. Today these fluctuations are of importance in mineral prospecting and submarine detection. The extreme form of ionospheric disturbance, or storm, is accompanied by brilliant displays of auroras (see AURORAS), which have awed man through his history and which cause him even now to debate their nature in detail.

FORMATION AND CHARACTERISTICS

Ionospheric processes. The ionosphere results from processes of ion production, balanced by those of ion loss. The balance is achieved through a complex of intermediate steps, not yet entirely understood. It varies markedly throughout the day, and to a lesser extent through the year and solar cycle.

Of the production processes, the most important by far is photo-ionization initiated by solar radiation. In it, a photon (or quantum of radiation) from the Sun interacts with some parent atom or molecule to strip off an orbital electron (negatively charged) and leave a positively charged ion of the parent species, or occasionally a dissociated atom-ion pair. The photon may be totally annihilated (*i.e.*, absorbed) in the process, or, if its initial energy is sufficiently great and it cannot be absorbed, it may simply be scattered as a photon of less energy. In either event, the stream of ionizing radiation is attenuated as it progresses (see PHOTOELECTRIC EFFECT).

In order to ionize a molecular or atomic particle, a photon must carry an energy at least equal to that which binds the electron to the parent particle. Though this will differ from one species of particle to another, in general the radiation must be of short wavelength, specifically, in the extreme ultraviolet (UV) or X-ray portion of the spectrum. The most important atmospheric species are molecular oxygen that occurs low in the ionosphere, atomic oxygen that occurs at greater heights, and molecular nitrogen that can be found throughout. When initially in their states of lowest energy, these can be ionized only by photons at wavelengths shorter (higher energies) than the ultraviolet wavelengths 1027, 911, and 796 angstroms (1 angstrom = 10^{-8} centimetre) respectively. Longer wavelengths can be effective if the neutral particle is initially in an excited state, the most important example being provided by oxygen in a metastable (*i.e.*, long-lived) form whose ionization limit lies at 1118 angstroms. Again, nitric oxide is an important contributor even though it is a minor constituent: its ionizing limit lies at 1345 angstroms and it is therefore susceptible to ionization by a certain intense solar emission at 1216 angstroms.

Ion production rate

High in the atmosphere, all neutral constituents are of course extremely rarefied. The production rate of ionization—*i.e.*, the number of electrons or ions released per cubic centimetre per second—is correspondingly low, and the attenuation of the incoming radiation virtually negligible. As the solar photons penetrate deeper, they encounter increasing concentrations of ionizable particles; the production rate increases as a result, and the photon flux (number of these photons passing through a unit of area) is more rapidly attenuated. The decrease of this flux eventually overcompensates the increase of atmospheric concentration: the production rate passes through a maximum at some height, dependent on the ionizing radiations and the ionizable particles, and then subsides rapidly to the point of vanishing.

Examples of this general behaviour are presented in Figure 1, in which the total production rate inferred for the case of an overhead sun, designated as q_0, is shown together with the component contributions that are normally made by four bands of solar radiation and by the strong emission at 1216 angstroms. Similar production profiles (curves) may be deduced for the Sun somewhat away from overhead, though the peak contributions then occur at greater heights and with diminished intensities. The production profiles are markedly different when the Sun is at or near the horizon. Within the Earth's shadow, on the night side, there is of course no direct solar radiation: and so production, if there is any, must arise by other means.

Cosmic rays from the depths of space, consisting mostly of fast-moving atomic nuclei, penetrate well into the atmosphere and produce ionization by bombardment, equally by day and by night. An estimate of their contribution to the production rate of ionized particles is included in Figure 1, labelled C.R. Less energetic protons and electrons, either precipitated from the Van Allen belts or newly arrived from the Sun, also produce ionization by bombardment; their contribution is more erratic, and most important at higher altitudes at high latitudes. Bremsstrahlung radiation (*i.e.*, X-rays produced by electrons as they are decelerated) is a further source of photoionization.

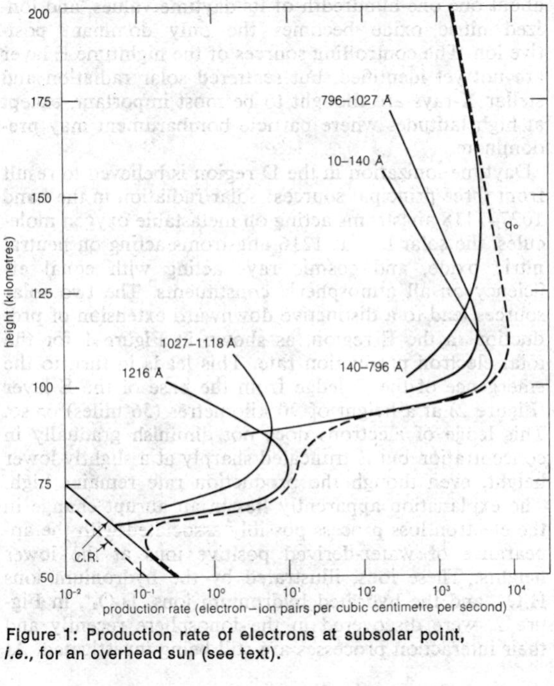

Figure 1: Production rate of electrons at subsolar point, *i.e.*, for an overhead sun (see text).

Hydrogen, and perhaps helium, within and beyond the atmosphere, can scatter appreciable amounts of solar ultraviolet radiation into the Earth's shadow cone. Certain stars, which emit X-ray energy with abnormal intensity, provide a further source of ionization by night, as by day. Molecules disassociate themselves from meteoroids, as the latter pass through the E and D regions; and because many are ionized in the process, they constitute a source of metallic ions that would not otherwise be found at such heights. Finally, certain chemical reactions of the D region are sufficiently energetic in themselves to cause ionization, though their contribution to the production rate may be insignificant.

Recombination of ions and electrons

Against all these sources of ionization must be set the balancing processes of recombination. By diverse means, these processes reunite free electrons with positive ions to produce neutral atoms and molecules once again.

Radiative recombination is a process complementary to simple photo-ionization: a free electron joins a positive ion to produce a neutral particle, and a photon is emitted. In practice the process would occur only in the case of atomic ions, notably ionized atomic oxygen; but before their recombination can be effected in this way, they are converted predominantly by charge-transfer processes (such as the reaction between ionized atomic oxygen and neutral molecular oxygen, to form neutral atomic oxygen and ionized molecular oxygen, written in symbolic form: $O^+ + O_2 \rightarrow O_2^+ + O$, in which O^+ is ionized oxygen, O_2 is neutral molecular oxygen, O_2^+ is ionized molecular oxygen, and O is neutral atomic oxygen; or the reaction between ionized atomic oxygen and neutral molecular nitrogen, forming nitric oxide and atomic nitrogen: $O^+ + N_2 \rightarrow NO^+ + N$, in which O^+ is ionized atomic oxygen, N_2 is neutral molecular nitrogen, NO^+ is ionized nitric oxide, and N is atomic nitrogen).

Molecular ions are inherently more susceptible to dissociative recombination, represented by the combination of positively ionized molecular oxygen with an electron to produce neutral atomic oxygen: $O_2^+ + e \rightarrow O + O$, in which O_2^+ is ionized molecular oxygen, e represents an electron, and O is neutral atomic oxygen; or the combination of positively ionized nitric oxide with an electron to produce neutral atomic nitrogen and oxygen: $NO^+ + e \rightarrow N + O$, in which NO^+ is ionized nitric oxide, e represents an electron, and N and O are neutral atomic nitrogen and oxygen, respectively. Nitrogen ions may recombine similarly, but some other removal process appears to be more rapid in practice, such as the combination of ionized molecular nitrogen and neutral atomic oxygen to form ionized nitric oxide and neutral atomic nitrogen: $N_2^+ + O \rightarrow NO^+ + N$, in which N_2^+ is ionized molecular nitrogen, O is neutral atomic oxygen, NO^+ is ionized nitric oxide, and N is neutral atomic nitrogen.

These relationships indicate the ways in which ionization produced from forms of oxygen and nitrogen are removed, and they include the ultimate recombinative processes for most of the ionosphere.

Ion–ion neutralization provides a further loss mechanism, of some importance in the D region. This process depends upon the presence of negative oxygen ions, the formation of which is probably initiated by the attachment of electrons to neutral oxygen molecules. In principle, these negative ions could neutralize positive ions directly, forming neutral oxygen molecules, expressed by the reaction: $O_2^+ + O_2^- \rightarrow O_2 + O_2$, in which O_2^+ is positively ionized molecular oxygen, O_2^- is negatively ionized oxygen, and O_2 is neutral molecular oxygen, but in practice ionized molecular oxygen reacts primarily with neutral species, either to release the extra electron once again or to transfer it. In the latter event, a sequence of transfer reactions may ensue, leading in the end to terminal species whose only available transfer process is that of ion–ion neutralization.

In the D region negative ions play a subsidiary but distinctive role as repositories of free electrons. By their detachment they provide a source of such electrons, and by their formation they provide a sink; negative ions therefore enter into the balancing of electron production and loss. This balancing has a special significance for many processes, such as those concerned with radio propagation, for which the electrons alone are significant.

Loss rates

General relations, specifying all important interactions and their rates, are difficult to establish and are only partially known. Nevertheless, the loss rate of electrons at most heights within the ionosphere may be expressed in one of two simple forms that help to account for ionospheric properties. The first arises, for example, when the dominant ions are positive molecular ions of either oxygen or nitric oxide. The frequency of occurrence of the recombinative reactions, which then control the loss, must be proportional both to the positive-ion concentration (indicated n_+) and to the electron concentration (n_e), while these two concentrations must be equal in order to maintain charge neutrality. The loss rate of electrons must then be proportional to the product of the positive and negative concentrations, (expressed n_+n_e) or, equivalently, to the square of the electron concentration (n_e^2); it is denoted αn_e^2, in which alpha (α) is a constant. The second simple form occurs when the concentration of positive ions is dominated by atomic ions, notably of oxygen. The frequency of occurrence of the charge-transfer reactions is proportional to the concentration of the neutral species that participate (n_n), and to the positive-ion concentration. The latter can be replaced by the electron concentration, and the frequency of charge-transfer is equal to their product and a proportionality constant gamma (γ), namely, $\gamma n_n n_e$. The subsequent true recombinative stage proceeds at the same rate in an equilibrium state.

Maintenance of a quasi-equilibrium, between a production rate and a loss rate equal to alpha times the electron concentration squared, would require that the electron concentration be equal to the square root of the ratio: production rate divided by the constant alpha (α), expressed by the equation $n_e = \sqrt{q/\alpha}$, in which n_e is the electron concentration and q is the production rate. Profiles of the production rate, such as those of Figure 1, could be converted into profiles of electron density by virtue of this relation. Clearly, they would imply a layering of the electron concentration, which would increase with height to some peak value and then diminish again. On the other hand, when the production rate must be balanced by a loss rate equal to the product of gamma and the neutral particle and electron concentrations, $\gamma n_n n_e$, the resultant electron concentration is equal to the ratio of the production rate to the product of gamma and the neutral particle concentration, namely, $n_e = q/\gamma n_n$, in which n_e is the electron concentration, q is the production rate, and n_n is the neutral particle concentration. Because the concentration of neutral particles depends on elevation, the layering is not immediately obvious in this case. In practice, considerations additional to those of local production and loss become relevant in these circumstances, as will be discussed.

Vertical structure of the ionosphere. Layer structure, first detected in the ionosphere by radio methods, was defined in terms of the electron distribution. Initially, the E and F layers were distinguished, each with its own peak value of electron concentration. On occasion, the F layer appeared to be split into two, termed F1 and F2; but the normal F1 layer is now known to contain no peak intensity of electron concentration and is identified instead as a ledge at the base of the F2 layer. Daytime ionization in the D region includes a D ledge at the base of the E layer, similar in appearance but quite different in origin. The protonosphere constitutes a further distinctive feature above the F2 peak, again, of a different nature. These divisions are illustrated in Figure 2, for low latitudes near noon. The existence of a weak daytime C layer, at heights of 50–60 kilometres (31–37 miles), is suspected but not firmly established as a distinct entity.

Below the F2 peak, the layered structure results entirely from complexities in the local balancing of production and loss processes. Complexities arising in part from height variations of the ionizable constituents, in part from the spectral distribution of the ionizing radiations, and in part from variations in height of the loss mechanisms, lead to a strongly layered distribution of individual positive-ion species, also illustrated in Figure 2. It is advisable to consider even the electron concentration, layers, and ledges in terms of the sources and structure of the positive-ion distributions.

E-layer ionization

Solar ultraviolet radiation in the band 796–1027 angstroms, including in particular a strong line at 1026 angstroms, is a major contributor to the production of the daytime E layer. Photons in this band carry insufficient energy to ionize molecular nitrogen and so avoid loss through that process at higher altitudes. At wavelengths below 912 angstroms photons do ionize atomic oxygen even in the F region and so help to provide a smooth transition from the F layer to the E layer. The longer wavelengths ionize only molecular oxygen, and they encounter this species in appreciable concentrations only after penetrating to the E region. The net contribution of the whole band to the total ion production is indicated in Figure 1 for an overhead Sun.

A second major contribution, also illustrated, is made by solar X-rays in the range 10–140 angstroms. Primarily, this band produces positive molecular nitrogen ions, with an admixture of ionized atomic and molecular oxygen in proportion to the corresponding neutral species; but other reactions act rapidly in the E region to replace the ionized molecular nitrogen and atomic oxygen by ionized nitric oxide and additional ionized molecular oxygen. The latter ions, in fact, dominate the balance achieved in the daytime E layer, as seen in Figure 2.

Recombination in the E layer leads to a loss rate of alpha times the square of the electron concentration (αn_e^2), and an equilibrium electron density equal to the square root of q divided by α ($\sqrt{q/\alpha}$). The elevation angle of the Sun changes throughout the day, and with latitude at a fixed time; the production rate then changes as previously described, and with it the electron concentration. In the absence of any nighttime source of ion production, continued recombination would lead to the virtual extinction of the layer within a few hours after sunset. In fact, however, a new equilibrium appears to become established in which the electron concentration may have about one one-hundredth of its daytime values, and ionized nitric oxide becomes the only dominant positive ion. The controlling sources of the nighttime E layer are not yet identified, but scattered solar radiation and stellar X-rays are thought to be most important, except at high latitudes where particle bombardment may predominate.

D-region ionization

Daytime ionization in the D region is believed to result from three principal sources: solar radiation in the band 1027–1118 angstroms acting on metastable oxygen molecules, the solar line at 1216 angstroms acting on neutral nitric oxide, and cosmic rays acting with equal efficiency on all atmospheric constituents. The two solar sources lead to a distinctive downward extension of production in the E region, as shown in Figure 1 for the total electron production rate. This leads in turn to the emergence of the D ledge from the base of the E layer (Figure 2) at a height of 90 kilometres (56 miles) or so. This ledge of electrons does not diminish gradually in concentration but is truncated sharply at a slightly lower height, even though the production rate remains high. The explanation apparently lies in an abrupt change in the electron loss process possibly associated with the appearance of water-derived positive ions at the lower heights. These ions, illustrated by the hydronium ions H_3O^+, and the hydrated hydronium ions, $H_5O_2^+$, in Figure 2, were discovered in the ionosphere recently and their interaction processes are still being investigated. At

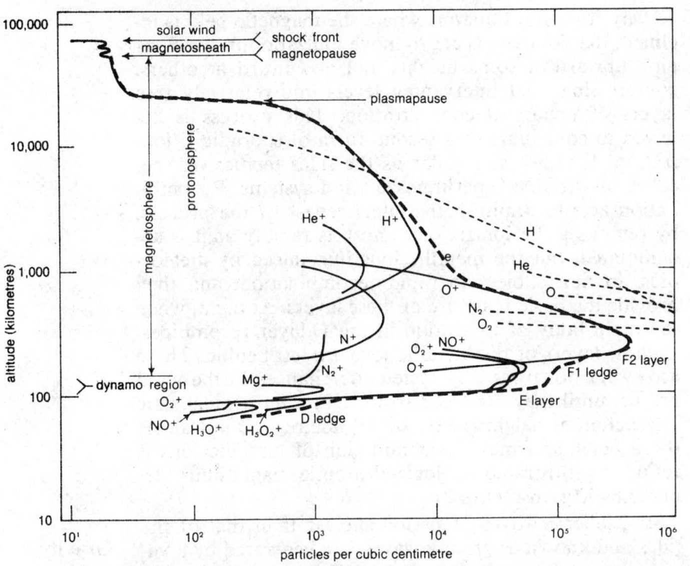

Figure 2: Daytime ionosphere at low latitudes and low solar activity (see text).

night, the direct solar radiations are, of course, cut off, and the D ledge of electrons essentially disappears through rapid recombination and attachment.

The cosmic-ray source remains constant through day and night, but the electron C layer it produces—or the ledge, at least—disappears rapidly at sunset and reappears rapidly at dawn. The absence of any significant electron concentration at night is believed to result from a rapid rate of conversion of electrons to form negative ions, predominantly some terminal species (end products) such as nitrogen trioxide. This conversion could be offset during the day by photodetachment of the negative ions, to produce free electrons once again; or it could be inhibited during the day by an interruption in the chain of negative-ion reactions, most likely by virtue of detachment of electrons from the initial negative ions of molecular oxygen in the course of an interaction with daytime oxygen atoms. The ion chemistry of the region is extremely complicated and not at all well understood.

F-layer ionization

Ionization in the F layer contains a significant contribution from the bands 10–140 angstroms and 796–1027 angstroms that produce the E layer, but its principal source is the intermediate band 140–796 angstroms, acting on both oxygen and molecular nitrogen, with the positive ions of molecular nitrogen being converted rapidly to those of nitric oxide. Demarkation of the F from the E layer results largely from the fact that the transitional band of radiation at 110–170 angstroms, whose maximum production rates would lie at intermediate heights, is very weak in the solar spectrum.

Low in the F region, the equilibrium attained between electron production and loss is of the type already described for the E layer. Taken by itself, this would suggest that the electron concentration should decrease with increasing height above the F1 ledge, just where the F2 layer in fact exhibits a dramatic increase. The increase is explained by a transition to atomic oxygen as the dominant positive ion at greater heights. The electron concentration profile adopts a different form, given by the ratio of the production rate to the product of gamma and the concentration of the neutral species that participate ($q/\gamma n_n$). The neutral particle concentration decreases rapidly upward; it more than offsets the decrease of the production rate to produce an increase of the electron concentration.

At and above the F2 peak, new processes come to control the distribution of ionization. The local balancing of production and loss, which prevails at lower levels, gives way to a balancing that involves movement of ionization. In the first instance, diffusion comes to control: diffusion downward under the pull of gravity, and upward in response to pressure exerted by the ionization itself. A diffusive equilibrium is established when these two effects are in balance, and the balance requires that the concentration of ionization shall decrease with increasing height, just as the neutral species decrease. The form of the electron-concentration profile at lower levels, with its increase of concentration with height, gives way to the diffusive profile with its decrease, and the transition is marked by the maximum of the electron concentration at the F2 peak (see Figure 2).

A requirement for charge neutrality imposes special conditions on the diffusion of ionization, for it demands that the distribution of electrons should match that of the positive ions despite the disparity of the electron and ion masses. A compromise is effected by means of an electric field, self-generated by the ionization, which supports half the weight of the dominant positive ions and in effect adds it to the weight of the electrons. In the region above the F2 peak, hydrogen ions are produced by charge-transfer between ionized atomic oxygen and neutral hydrogen. The electric field, of a strength to support half the weight of the oxygen ions, more than supports the weight of the much lighter hydrogen ions and so carries them upward. They accumulate at high levels, becoming dominant in the protonosphere as shown in Figure 2. The electric field there is weaker, being required to support only half the weight of the hydrogen ions; the upward decrease of ionized atomic oxygen concentration now accelerates, and that of the hydrogen ion concentration begins. Helium ions, of intermediate weight and subject to the same electric fields, echo this behaviour as depicted in Figure 2. It may be that, on some occasions, they become the dominant ions over a shallow height range just below the protonosphere.

Recombination proceeds fairly rapidly at F1 heights, and during the night it erodes much of the ionization there. Ions in the F2 layer are much less subject to local loss processes, but they tend to diffuse downward as the underlying ionization is reduced, and there they too are recombined. This movement proceeds more slowly than might be anticipated, however, apparently because of certain winds in the neutral gas that act on the ions in conjunction with the geomagnetic field to offset the pull of gravity. In any case, the ion content above the F2 peak undergoes only small diurnal changes, though there is a substantial redistribution associated with day–night changes of temperature.

The abrupt decrease of proton and electron concentration at the plasmapause may be understood with the aid of Figure 3. The region beneath the plasmapause, which has already been discussed, is represented in equatorial section by a shaded ring extending outward from the Earth to a distance of a few Earth radii. Through it run geomagnetic field lines, arching up and over the Equator from hemisphere to hemisphere; a few of them are indicated above the equatorial plane, looking much like spider legs. Magnetic field lines that rise at higher latitudes, and so reach farther out over the Equator, are deformed by the effects of ionization flowing outward from the Sun. Some of them, illustrated by lines B and C, are swept away into a geomagnetic tail, extending to great distances on the night side and ultimately merging with interplanetary magnetic fields.

Effects of the geomagnetic tail

Ionization on all these outer field lines is in a continual state of motion from one field line to another: for example, that on line A is swept to line B, to line C, to the "reconnected" line at D, and thence back to line A on a sequence of field lines that follow the path e. Other ionization follows other paths, shown only in part by their equatorial traces, f, f′, g, g′.

During its interval on open field lines such as B and C, the ionization can escape into interplanetary space and evidently does so: the plasmapause appears to mark the transition between an inner domain of ionization that never has this opportunity to escape, and an outer domain that does. When mapped along the geomagnetic field lines, the plasmapause reaches ordinary heights in the F layer at (geomagnetic) latitudes of 50°–60° typically. A sharp trough is seen in the concentration in the F2 layer at these latitudes, particularly at night, and this is believed to be a consequence if not a direct manifestation of the plasmapause. The polar F region lies in the

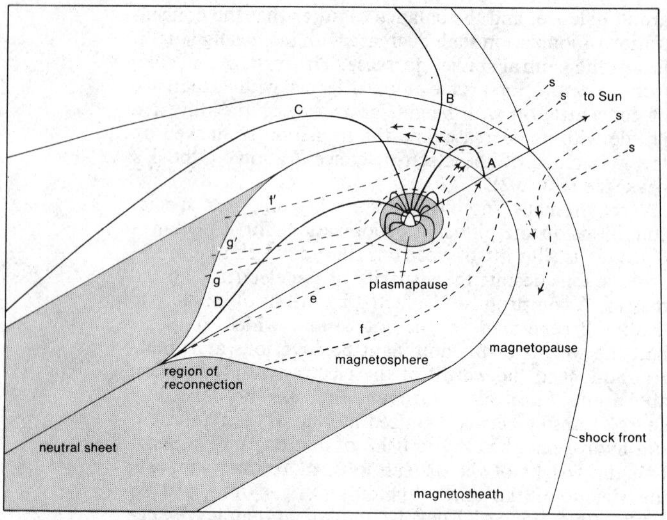

Figure 3: Deformation of geomagnetic field lines (such as A, B,C) and generation of the Earth's geomagnetic tail (extending beyond the region of reconnection) due to the interaction of the solar wind and the Earth's upper atmosphere.

outer domain. Its ionization distribution is often irregular and in some respects anomalous, probably in response to the opportunity of ion escape and, equally, to the intrusion of solar particles in a reverse process.

IONOSPHERIC VARIATIONS AND DISTURBANCES

Of atmospheric origin. The ionosphere is a dynamic region, subject to fluctuations of greater or lesser magnitude, regularly and irregularly. These originate in a variety of causes, not all of them identified. The processes that are at least partially understood can be divided roughly into two groups, those that originate with disturbances on the Sun and those that result from meteorological phenomena in the Earth's atmosphere. The latter are ever present and generally more moderate; they will be described first.

Regular atmospheric oscillations are produced by the daily heating and cooling of the atmosphere at and beneath the lower levels of the ionosphere. These oscillations propagate as waves up into the ionosphere, and the winds that they generate tend to increase in amplitude with height as the gas density decreases. A 24-hour tide dominates in tropical latitudes at altitudes low in the E region, with wind speeds of some tens of metres per second (or miles per hour) there, while a 12-hour tide is more prominent in higher latitudes.

The tidal winds in the dynamo region tend to carry ionization with them. This movement occurs, however, in the presence of the geomagnetic field; electromagnetic dynamo processes intervene, and well-defined streams of ions and electrons—*i.e.*, electric currents—are generated. These currents create electric fields and in consequence modify their own form. The fields in turn modify the motion and general distribution of the ionization. As a result, the layer shapes previously described are deformed in various ways. One important example is associated with an upwelling of ionization in the F layer over the Equator during the day, accompanied by a diffusion of the raised ionization downward along magnetic field lines to higher latitudes: peak daytime electron concentrations are found at latitudes several degrees away from the (geomagnetic) Equator, in consequence, and peak values at the Equator are found only late in the afternoon, at very great heights.

The tide-induced dynamo currents lead to magnetic variations that can be detected at ground level. The currents themselves are greatly enhanced in an Equatorial electrojet, with which is associated an intrinsic instability in the distribution of ionization. Small-scale irregularities are formed, stretched out along the (nearly horizontal to the ground) magnetic field lines. These irregularities act to scatter radio waves and so contribute one form of sporadic E disturbance.

Away from the Equator, where the magnetic field is inclined, the tidal winds act to move ionization in the E region upward at some heights and downward at others, compressing it at intervening levels into relatively thin layers of enhanced concentration. This process is believed to contribute to a second form of sporadic E ionization. It is not as regular as the tides themselves, because of variable superimposed wind systems. Recombination acts to diminish the effectiveness of the process, by removing the ionization almost as rapidly as it is accumulated; but the metallic ions introduced by meteoroids are not subject to rapid recombination, and they provide the basic structure of these layers. At night, when the main body of ionization in the E layer recombines, shallow layers of the metallic ions are left behind. These are swept downward by systematic changes in the wind profile, until they are freed from significant geomagnetic interaction at heights near 100 kilometres (62 miles). At those heights, a major accumulation of metallic ions is found, as illustrated by ionized atomic magnesium (denoted by Mg^+ in Figure 2).

Gravity waves

Atmospheric waves of period shorter than that of the tides and known as gravity waves, are generated by a variety of meteorological processes. They, too, tend to increase in amplitude with height, until dissipation or reflection occurs. They provide a broad spectrum of irregular fluctuations at ionospheric levels, superimposed on the more regular variations of the tides. Isolated waves may be observed occasionally, with wavelengths perhaps 100 kilometres (62 miles) and wave fronts ten times as long, oscillating with periods of about one hour. These are seen as travelling ionospheric disturbances in the F layer, and they may move ionization of that layer upward and downward over tens of kilometres as they themselves progress horizontally over thousands.

The tides, gravity waves, and perhaps other wind systems, act to destabilize the atmosphere at heights below 105 kilometres (65 miles) or so. Turbulence is the result. Turbulent eddies, and to some extent the other motions, serve to mix the atmospheric constituents. Vertical mixing may produce changes in the local concentration of minor constituents in the D and lower E regions, for such constituents often have rapid height variations. As has been seen, the D-region ionization is strongly dependent on these constituents and must be variable with them. At middle and high latitudes, anomalous distributions of this ionization are frequently found during the winter, at times of anomalous meteorological conditions at much lower heights. Dynamical processes, either of the general circulation or of wave-induced mixing, seem likely to provide the causal linkage from the lower levels to the D region. Seasonal variations in the terminal level of turbulent mixing probably occur and may account for some seasonal changes in the composition and so in the ionization of overlying levels.

Irregularities of electron distribution are produced by turbulence, where the latter exists, and they will be borne along by the local wind. Others, produced by the broad spectrum of waves, may propagate through the same region with different speeds. The motion of these irregularities introduces fluctuations in the reflection of radio waves, which may then be used for their study.

Of solar origin. Solar activity follows an 11-year cycle of intensification and decay. The spectral distribution (wavelength intensities) of solar radiation changes with this cycle, and so too do the details of ionospheric layer formation. At maximum solar activity, for example, electron concentrations are generally enhanced, and the F1 ledge rarely appears below the F2 layer. Again, an increased outflow of solar ionization leads to an improved screening out of cosmic rays, and so their contribution to ionospheric production diminishes (as indicated in Figure 1). But the major ionospheric modifications appear as isolated disturbances associated with specific events on the Sun, or as series of such disturbances.

Solar flares

The most dramatic of solar events are the explosive flares that appear suddenly, rise rapidly in intensity, and then decay away in the course of many minutes or a few hours. The stronger flares are accompanied by sudden ionospheric disturbances over the sunlit portion of the Earth. These are characterized by major increases of ionization in the D region down to heights of perhaps 75 kilometres (47 miles), and by smaller fractional increases at greater elevations, occasionally up to the F2 peak. The change is brought about predominantly by solar X-rays in the wavelength band one to ten angstroms, whose intensity may increase by a factor of a hundred or more even though the flare itself may be confined to one-thousandth of the solar disk. Sudden ionospheric disturbances are accompanied on occasion by magnetic crochets; that is, minor fluctuations that result from a change in the dynamo current system, associated in turn with changes of electron concentration in the E region.

Major flares are often followed by polar cap absorption events, named after their effect upon radio waves that traverse high latitudes. A polar cap absorption event is initiated by solar particles—principally protons—ejected from a flare region with energies comparable to those of cosmic rays. Protons that reach the vicinity of the Earth do so only after an initial delay of some minutes or even hours, but they may then continue to arrive in strength for many days on end. They are deflected by the Earth's magnetic field, and some travel in spiral paths along the field lines to ionospheric heights. Except for the most energetic of them, their access is limited to paths along open field lines such as B and C in Figure 3, or more generally along high-latitude field lines that extend well out toward the magnetopause. They are, as a result, strongly channelled into the polar ionospheric regions. Their energies are adequate to penetrate the E region with little loss and then in the D region produce ionization by bombardment of the atmospheric constituents. This can lead to greatly increased electron concentrations by day, and to a lesser extent by night despite the competing effects of attachment. The excess electrons lead to severe absorption or even blackout of radio waves in the broadcast and short-wave bands, and so disrupt communications on vital high-latitude links such as those that traverse the North Atlantic. Long-wave transmissions may be enhanced, because of improved reflection in the D region, but unfortunately their capacity for information transfer is extremely limited and they cannot make up the loss.

A third class of ionospheric disturbance is accompanied by magnetic and auroral storms, initiated by a complex interaction of ionosphere, magnetosphere, and magnetosheath activity whose intricacies are by no means understood. They are not strongly flare associated but instead depend upon magnetically abnormal sunspots and other solar irregularities as yet ill defined. The solar abnormality, whatever its nature, results in an alteration of the general outflow of solar ionization at moderate energies, and in changed magnetic fields carried by that ionization. After a travel time of a day or two, the ionization impinges on the magnetopause and alters the interaction process. The storm may then proceed as a single event with a smooth onset, main phase and decay, extending over some hours or days, or it may be interrupted by a sequence of irregular substorms triggered by instabilities of the whole complex system.

In a typical storm, the magnetopause is pressed in to envelop the Earth more closely. The flow illustrated in Figure 3 is distorted and accelerated, uniformly or in bursts. Solar ionization is caught up in it and carried to the magnetospheric interior. Ionization, both of solar and of terrestrial origin, is energized, with some fraction contributing to the Van Allen belts but a greater portion bombarding the polar ionosphere. The energized protons and electrons move round the Earth differently and so produce a magnetospheric ring current of electrical charge. The enhanced motions are accompanied by strong electric fields, which in turn produce strong electric currents in the polar dynamo region and even at lower latitudes. Where bombardment occurs, new ionization is produced; the electric fields are altered, and the currents are intensified into an auroral electrojet. All of these changes, superimposed, lead to major magnetic fluctuations at ground level: a magnetic storm occurs.

The bombardment, and perhaps collisions induced by the electric fields, lead to an increased energy, or excitation, of atmospheric constituents. The excited particles, and the recombining ionization, emit their excess energy as visible light of many wavelengths: an auroral storm results. If the storm is intense, the pattern of motion depicted in Figure 3 penetrates more deeply toward the Earth, carrying the plasmapause with it and bringing the region of strong magnetic and auroral activity from the normal auroral zone to much lower latitudes.

Auroral storms

The ionospheric storm itself appears primarily in the F region, although particle bombardment at high latitudes does introduce yet another type of sporadic E ionization and some effects in the D region. Motion of the trough in the F layer to lower latitudes accompanies the inward displacement of the plasmapause. Poleward of the trough, the F layer loses almost all resemblance to its normal form, and even Equatorward it is greatly deformed. The polar processes are so complex and overlapping that there is no sorting them out in detail, but great heating is a prominent contributor to the ionospheric changes. Heating occurs at lower latitudes as well and may account for much of the deformation there, but the causes of this heating are obscure. Major travelling ionospheric disturbances are launched from the auroral electrojet and produce transient distortions of the F layer as they propagate to lower latitudes; they may account for the heating there, by deposition of their energy.

And then the storm subsides and normalcy is regained; but if the solar abnormality remains in existence for some months, the storm may repeat itself in similar form at 27-day intervals, each time the Sun rotates to expose the same face to the Earth. Other centres of activity may develop, each with its own outpouring of modified ionization and magnetic fields, to produce a complex interweaving and overlapping of disturbance conditions and storm responses. Such activity continues until the solar cycle reaches its quiescent phase once again, and then disturbances occur infrequently if at all.

PROBING THE IONOSPHERE

Man's interest in the ionosphere developed largely because of radio communications, the improvement of which depended on an increased knowledge of ionospheric behaviour. To acquire that knowledge, man has exploited the radio waves themselves and developed complementary techniques.

Radio waves interact with the ionosphere by setting free electrons into an oscillatory motion; the electrons then reradiate and modify the initial waves. The modification is normally slight at frequencies such as those that make up the very high frequency and ultrahigh frequency bands of standard television channels but becomes severe at lower frequencies. The electron motion is influenced by the geomagnetic field, with the result that waves of a given frequency divide into two modes of propagation, each with its own properties. Collisions of electrons with neutral particles, most frequent in the D region, extract energy from the radio waves and lead to their attenuation. The positive ions play no parallel role, except at very low frequencies, because their relatively great masses inhibit their oscillatory response to the passing radio waves. They may nevertheless be studied to some extent by radio techniques, by virtue of their interactions with electrons. Also, by extension, certain properties of the neutral gas may be inferred.

Some effects of the ionosphere on conventional communication systems have been noted already. These effects and others are employed, with the aid of specialized equipment, for scientific study of the ionosphere. A few examples may be given.

Waves in the very high frequency band, though normally able to pass through the ionosphere, may be reflected or scattered by strong, sporadic E formations and by ionized meteor trails; their arrival at some ground-based receiver, beyond the optical horizon (line-of-sight) of a ground-based transmitter, then gives evidence of the occurrence of such features in the ionosphere. Extremely sensitive receivers, operated in conjunction with large antennas and powerful transmitters, can detect minute amounts of energy scattered from the E and F regions, and from them one can determine a wide variety of information. Signals reflected from the Moon, or transmitted from artificial satellites, may be monitored to detect slight differences in the two modes of propagation, and from them may be determined the total number of electrons along the path of the ray.

Scattering from E and F regions

Radio waves at somewhat lower frequencies, impinging on the ionosphere from below, are reflected back by ionization beneath the F2 peak. By varying the frequency of the transmission and by timing the delay of the reflected signal, observers may determine the electron concentration at corresponding heights; and by repeating the process with equipment in artificial satellites well above the F2 peak, they may extend their measurements into the overlying region.

Sudden ionospheric disturbances, polar cap absorption events, and auroral ionization may all be monitored by the absorption that they introduce, even at frequencies into the very high frequency band when the others are blacked out, and by the improved reflection they occasionally provide in the long-wave band at much lower frequencies. Absorption and other processes may be modified artificially by heating the ionosphere with powerful radio transmissions, and the consequences may then be probed by auxiliary systems in order to gain further information.

Lightning flashes generate strong bursts of radio waves at very low frequencies. Some energy escapes reflection in the D region and passes into the higher ionospheric regions, where it follows magnetic field lines from one hemisphere to another and back again. The higher frequencies in the burst travel faster than the lower and so are received sooner. The radio signal is therefore converted from the sound of a click into a swish of descending tone, called a whistler. Whistlers provide vital information about their propagation path: historically they revealed the existence of the protonosphere and plasmapause, and they continue to afford a routine means of monitoring these features.

Whistlers

Complex instabilities and energy-exchange processes of the magnetosphere generate a variety of other signals in the whistler mode and produce unusual responses to electronically produced radio waves. These signals are studied for their own sake, inasmuch as they reveal interactions that are new to human experience. They provide valuable information about the positive ions of the region as well.

Artificial satellites have enhanced the expansion of radio measurements, as already indicated, by placing radio equipment within the ionosphere. They have also permitted the deployment of photometers that measure spectral intensities, mass spectrometers that measure ion masses, and other instruments more usually associated with laboratory studies, to allow direct measurement of the ionospheric properties. They provide global coverage and temporal continuity and are complemented in this respect by rocket-borne instruments that yield detailed information about the vertical sections of the ionosphere that they traverse.

All of these measurements are supported, in turn, by laboratory studies of many types. The rates of ionization reactions must be known if the relevant sequences are to be identified, and these rates can be established accurately only by laboratory experiments. Further experiments are designed to identify the photon emissions that would result from various reaction processes and to correlate them with nighttime and auroral emissions from ionospheric levels. Radio emissions in the whistler mode are explored in laboratory ionization chambers, and even some scaled modelling of the magnetospheric motions depicted in Figure 3 has been attempted in such chambers. Mathematical investigations are conducted in all aspects, to develop the theories and to permit testing them against observation.

In these diverse ways, human beings, encouraged in part by their desire to communicate, are enhancing their power to understand; natural wonders such as the aurora are coming within the grasp of human knowledge, and more complex ones are being exposed to the enquiring human mind.

BIBLIOGRAPHY. J.A. RATCLIFFE, *Sun, Earth and Radio* (1970), is one of the most suitable introductions to the ionosphere and magnetosphere for nonphysicists or for physicists with a casual interest. The following are introductory texts designed for physicists: C.O. HINES *et al.* (eds.), *Physics of the Earth's Upper Atmosphere* (1965); H. RISHBETH and O.K. GARRIOTT, *Introduction to Ionospheric Physics* (1969); and R.C. WHITTEN and I.G. POPPOFF, *Fundamentals of Aeronomy* (1971). More specialized texts in the subject areas indicated by their titles include: J.W. CHAMBERLAIN, *Physics of the Aurora and Airglow* (1961); K. DAVIES, *Ionospheric Radio Propagation* (1965); R.A. HELLIWELL, *Whistlers and Related Ionospheric Phenomena* (1965); J.W. KING and W.S. NEWMAN (eds.), *Solar-Terrestrial Physics* (1967); S. MATSUSHITA and W.H. CAMPBELL (eds.), *Physics of Geomagnetic Phenomena*, 2 vol. (1967); J.A. RATCLIFFE (ed.), *Physics of the Upper Atmosphere* (1960); R.C. WHITTEN and I.G. POPPOFF, *Physics of the Lower Ionosphere* (1965); and D.J. WILLIAMS and G.D. MEAD (eds.), *Magnetospheric Physics* (1969).

(C.O.H.)

Iowa

Iowa is one of the north central states of the United States, forming a bridge between the forests of the east and the grasslands of the high prairie plains that lie to the west. The state's gently rolling landscape rises slowly as it extends westward from the Mississippi River, which forms its entire eastern border. The state is bounded on the north by Minnesota, on the east by Wisconsin and Illinois, on the south by Missouri, and on the west by Nebraska and South Dakota. Its 56,290 square miles (145,790 square kilometres) had a population in 1980 of 2,913,387. Des Moines has been the capital since 1857, 11 years after Iowa was admitted as the 29th state of the Union.

The popular image of Iowa—one of corn (maize) and hogs, flat prairies, and conservative people—is not altogether incorrect, but it masks both a subtle variety and the fact that Iowa and its people are very much in a middle position—economically and politically as well as geographically. With 94 percent of its land cultivable—third highest among the states—Iowa became, in the 20th century, a major breadbasket of the United States and of the world, ranking with the much larger states of California and Texas in combined agricultural output. In addition, a large part of its industry is directly related to the field of agriculture, and the population is about equally divided between its rural and urban areas. Iowans are strongly Republican in most years, but they exhibit a lively independence when they feel that the times dictate a different tack. Although Iowa has not shared the full benefits that have accrued from economic and demographic expansion, neither has it been crushed by the periodic economic downswings that have afflicted some of the other regions of the nation. (For information on related topics, see the articles UNITED STATES OF AMERICA; UNITED STATES, HISTORY OF THE; NORTH AMERICA; GREAT PLAINS; and MISSISSIPPI RIVER.)

HISTORY

From territory to statehood. The first Europeans to reach Iowa were probably the French explorers Louis Jolliet and Jacques Marquette in 1673. Permanent settlement, however, did not take place until the early 1830s, though Spanish land grants were occupied in the late 1700s, principally to exploit the lead-mining potential around the site of Dubuque. In the interim, both pioneers and Indians moved through the area exploring or hunting. The combined French and Indian history can be seen in geographical names throughout the state: for example, Des Moines, Dubuque, and Le Mars; Ottumwa, Keokuk, and Onawa.

The area that includes the modern state of Iowa was included in the Louisiana Purchase from France in 1803, and during the War of 1812 a U.S. garrison was driven from Ft. Madison on the Mississippi River. Following the purchase of eastern Iowa from the Sauk and Fox Indians in the 1830s, U.S. settlers rapidly moved in to till the land. The Territory of Iowa was established in 1838, with

Rapid settlement

a population of 23,242. In 1846 Iowa was admitted to the Union as part of a compromise that was reached between the slaveholding South and the free North. By 1860 there were nearly 675,000 people in the state, and with the construction of railroads the frontier was pushed further westward. The population of Iowa more than tripled during the 1850s, and the Spirit Lake Massacre in 1857 marked the final instance of Indian hostility in the state. The years immediately prior to the Civil War were Iowa's frontier days, however, with lawlessness, vigilantes, and lynchings accompanying the unsteady beginnings of a settled society.

Iowa was deeply involved on both sides of the issues that led to the Civil War, to which the state contributed more troops in proportion to its population than any other state. No battles were actually fought in Iowa, though a Confederate guerrilla raid from Missouri occurred in 1864.

Economic stabilization. The coming to an end of the Civil War, railroad expansion, and the removal of the Indian threat opened the prairie to settlement by massive waves of immigrants from states to the east and also from northwestern Europe. By 1900 claims to the land had filled the state, and the population showed a slight decline in the decade that followed. The wide use of barbed wire permitted diversified agriculture, and the draining of wetlands began the development of an efficient agricultural production that often threatened the financial stability of the state with too plentiful a harvest. Corn was the basis of Iowa's agriculture from the beginning, nearly all the crop being fed to livestock in order to fatten them for market.

World War I created short-term demands for maximum production and high prices, and since then the state has been plagued with recurring agricultural surpluses, low prices, and high land values. The various economic panics and depressions of the 19th and 20th centuries were only temporary impediments to this pattern of growth. In the past century Iowa politicians have appeared most prominently on the national scene when farm crises have been major issues.

The last significant case of exploitation of natural resources occurred in the coalfields of southern Iowa, beginning in the mid-19th century and reaching its peak in the first two decades of the 20th century. Most of the coal was quickly exhausted, however, and the miners moved on, leaving behind decaying towns and a deteriorating landscape.

After World War I population growth of Iowa slowed considerably. Attempts were made to entice industry into the state to diversify the economy, as animal feeding had diversified agriculture half a century before. Such attempts were not entirely successful, and there is a growing feeling that lack of population growth may be a blessing in disguise—that Iowa can escape many of the problems of environmental pollution and severe economic rises and falls by not encouraging large-scale urban and industrial growth.

THE NATURAL AND HUMAN LANDSCAPE

Geological history. Iowa's terrain and rich soils are the products of the continental ice sheets that covered the state during the Pleistocene Epoch, between 2,500,000 and 10,000 years ago. All four of the major glacial stages are represented by drift deposits or glacial debris in some portion of the state. The first, or Nebraskan, ice sheet covered the entire state but was in turn covered by the younger Kansan drift, except in the northeastern portion near the Mississippi River. These two drifts filled the preglacial stream valleys, and little evidence of them remains.

Glaciation

The Illinoian ice sheet covered a small area of southeastern and extreme eastern Iowa, and in so doing it diverted the Mississippi and created a temporary valley along its western front that can still be seen. Some 20,000 to 25,000 years ago, the Wisconsin ice sheet moved southward in a lobe that ended at about the site of the present city of Des Moines. Accompanying the last two stages of glaciation were extensive deposits of windblown silt, or loess, which in the western portion of Iowa were derived from the glaciation of the Great Plains further west. As the ice sheets retreated, tremendous quantities of drift carried by the melting waters were deposited in the valleys. These various deposits form the basis of the Iowa landscape and make up the parent materials of the present soils.

Relief and soils. The most varied relief anywhere in Iowa is in the northeastern part of the state, which was covered by Nebraskan ice but escaped Kansan glaciation. The region has been studied intensively by geologists because it retains so much of the character of the preglacial land. There tributaries of the Mississippi cut deeply into the underlying bedrock. The Mississippi bluffs stand 300 to 400 feet (90 to 120 metres) above the valley, and the network of tributaries creates a scenic and hilly landscape.

Surface features

Most of the state is underlaid by Kansan drift, which has been eroded for at least a few hundred thousand years by a network of streams that is extremely dense for a glaciated region. Lakes or swamps that were left by the ice have long since been drained by natural erosion, and the result is a rolling landscape of great uniformity throughout most of the state. Near the Missouri River Valley on the western border, the loess was piled 80 to 100 feet over the underlying drift surface, producing a line of bluffs 100 to 200 feet high. The highest point above sea level (1,675 feet) is in the northwest. The broad, flat uplands—which form the popular image of Iowa—are found mainly in the Des Moines lobe, a gently sloping, poorly drained drift plain that covers 12,300 square miles in the central and north central portions of the state. Most of Iowa's lakes are in the northwestern part of this lobe.

Most of the soils of Iowa, formed under prairie vegetation, are thick, dark in colour, and rich in organic matter and minerals. Only in the rough northeast and along the dissected river valleys of the south and southeastern portions of the state are there lighter coloured and less fertile forest soils.

Climate. Iowa's climate reflects the state's position deep in the interior of the continent. Winters are cold, with January temperatures averaging about 15° F (−9° C) in the northwestern section and 25° F (−4° C) in the southeast. Snowfall is relatively light when compared with the amount received in states to the east and north. Summers are warm and more humid, with daytime temperatures throughout the state averaging 75° F (24° C) in July but varying from region to region. Maritime tropical air masses from the Gulf of Mexico bring frequent thunderstorms, with precipitation in June four times that of the winter months. Precipitation ranges from less than 28 inches (700 millimetres) in the northwest to more than 34 inches in the southeast.

Vegetation and animal life. Countless species of wildflowers cover the prairies, and, though most of Iowa's virgin timber was cut long ago, almost 1,500,000 acres (600,000 hectares) are still forested. The only evergreen is the red cedar, which was once found in profusion along the Cedar River. The state's streams are well stocked with dozens of species of fish, and trapping of muskrat and raccoon for furs is still widespread. The ring-necked pheasant—imported early in the 1900s—and quail are the major game birds, replacing the nearly extinct wild turkey. Small animals and a wide variety of other birds are also found.

Patterns of human settlement. Although Iowa is not a featureless plain, the relative homogeneity of physical characteristics has led geographers and other social scientists to use the state as an example of large-scale uniformity. Quarter sections of 160 acres formed the basis of much of the original settlement pattern. Consequently, farmsteads and the smaller towns generally are evenly spaced in the form of a grid, and most of the roads in the state follow a north–south or east–west line. Farmhouses amid the square or rectangular patterns usually have a row of trees serving as a windbreak, as well as providing shade from the bleakly pervasive midcontinental sunlight. The largest city, Des Moines, is sited approximately in the middle of the state, above the widening of the Des Moines River known as Lake Red Rock. The other large cities are on the Missouri and Mississippi rivers at the western and eastern boundaries, or on the Cedar River in the east.

THE PEOPLE OF IOWA

Ethnic and religious groups. Iowa was settled largely by immigration from states lying directly to the east of it and from northwestern Europe. Until 1850 the southern third of Iowa received many settlers from the border states of the South, particularly Kentucky; but the influx from Ohio, Indiana, and Illinois and the New England and Middle Atlantic states was more important in the northern area. Settlers from Europe took on greater significance after 1850. The single most numerous group came from Germany, but Britain and Ireland were well represented. In the later years of the century, many Scandinavians settled throughout the western and central parts of the state. By 1915 there were few foreign-born people in southern Iowa, except Austro-Hungarians and Italians in the coalfields and Dutch near Pella. The larger of Iowa's cities, particularly those on the Mississippi, attracted a variety of groups.

Sources of immigrants

Several ethnic and religious groups—a good example is the Czech population of Cedar Rapids—are still present in Iowa. Among several experiments in communal living, the only survivors of the first years of pioneer hardship are the Amana colonies, a religious group originally from Germany that migrated to Iowa from Buffalo, New York, in 1855. This group changed to a corporate form in 1932 and has been quite successful in maintaining its integrity while modifying its economy to fit the changing times. The strong religious and social traditions of the Amish group living south of Iowa City and near Independence have come into conflict with modern society over state education laws. Mormons fled through Iowa on their way to Utah to escape further persecution in Illinois and New York, and one large group remained behind at Lamoni, in southern Iowa. Quakers were important in the Springdale–West Branch area east of Iowa City in the mid-19th century. This area was an important link in the Underground Railroad, which helped slaves escape from the South before the Civil War. John Brown often visited there, and Pres. Herbert Hoover was born there of Quaker parents. West Branch is the site of the Hoover Presidential Library.

The only notable immigration into Iowa during the 20th century has been that of blacks to the larger urban centres. About 11 and 12 percent of the populations of Des Moines and Waterloo, respectively, were nonwhite in 1980. Despite state and national civil rights laws, blacks generally live in the decaying urban areas, and in the 1960s there were numerous cases of racial confrontation. Most Indians moved westward after federal land purchases in the 19th century, but some, unhappy with life on the plains, returned to purchase a small reservation near Tama.

Most of Iowa's population is Protestant, because major immigration was from northwestern Europe. Roman Catholics are strong in the northeast, in the Dubuque area, and in the larger cities. In its outlook southern Iowa is more Fundamentalist; this had such social ramifications as the prohibition of liquor by the drink until 1963. The political strength of the more conservative rural areas was weakened considerably by reapportionment of the legislature in the 1960s.

Demography. Iowa's population is evenly distributed, a factor that, together with the relative uniformity of the state's physical conditions, has made Iowa an excellent location for the testing of geographic and economic theories. Des Moines has more than 190,000 citizens. Sioux City (82,000) and Council Bluffs (56,000) are the only large population centres in the western part of the state. Cedar Rapids (110,000) and Waterloo (76,000) are in the east, as are the Mississippi River cities of Davenport (103,000) and Bettendorf (27,000), which with Rock Island and Moline, Illinois, comprise the Quad City complex. Most of the remainder of the population lives in scattered, evenly spaced small towns or in dispersed farmsteads.

Population distribution

During the 1970s population of Iowa increased by only 3 percent, a figure that was well below the national rate of 11.4 percent. The fastest growing areas included the suburbs of Des Moines and Cedar Rapids and the counties encompassing the University of Iowa and Iowa State University. The rural population figures continued their century-long decline, however; more than half of the exclusively rural counties experienced losses. The population also declined in many of the state's larger central cities.

The statewide death rate in 1980 was 9.2 per 1,000 people, a figure that has fallen somewhat since 1925. The birth rate rose from 13.6 in 1973 to 16.5 in 1980, after years of steady decline during the 1960s. Unlike birth rates in many other areas of the United States, Iowa's is generally highest in the counties with metropolitan centres and lowest in the rural counties. Since the death rate shows the opposite pattern, it appears that many of the rural counties are experiencing natural rates of decrease as well as emigration.

THE STATE'S ECONOMY

The popular image of Iowa as basically an agricultural state is—unlike many such popular images—entirely correct.

Industry. Iowa is located on the western fringe of the American manufacturing belt, and, although its manufacturing and trade exceed farming in income, much of the former is devoted to food processing or to the manufacture of agricultural machinery. In only a few instances does Iowa contribute significantly to the national economy in areas not related to agriculture. The production of electronic materials in Cedar Rapids, household appliances in Newton, refrigeration equipment in Amana, tires in Des Moines, writing instruments in Fort Madison, and rolled aluminum in Bettendorf are a few exceptions. Exploitation of mineral resources, except for portland cement and gypsum, plays a relatively minor role in the state's economy.

Agriculturally based economy

Agriculture. The agricultural position of Iowa on the national scene is based on the feeding and selling of animals. During the late 1970s Iowa ranked second in the nation in total value of all livestock, first in hogs (having nearly six for each human resident), and second in cattle and calves. Iowa also ranked first in corn for feed, second in soybeans, and third in oats and hay. Higher income from farming helped Iowa's per capita income rise above the national average in the late 1970s, illustrating the importance of farming to Iowa's economy.

Economic management. The state attempts to aid industrial development and improve the general economic situation in Iowa in a number of ways, including the establishment of trade missions and the Industrial Development Commission. Corporate income taxes contribute a very small part to revenues. The government's debt is low, and the overall labour picture is relatively bright. Unemployment rates and work stoppages tend to lag behind national trends.

Transportation. In the 1920s Iowa developed an extensive rural road system designed to serve the relatively low population density. It now has about 112,000 miles (180,200 kilometres) of road, ranking tenth nationally in total mileage and seventh in surfaced-road mileage. There are approximately 5,805 miles of first- and second-class railroad track, in which the state ranks tenth. The amount of railroad track in active use, however, has decreased over the years, and many Iowa towns have lost all railroad service. The state also has more than 240 public airports. Inland waterway traffic is important along the Mississippi River, and a nine-foot-deep channel runs up the Missouri to Sioux City.

ADMINISTRATION AND SOCIAL CONDITIONS

Governmental structure. Iowa's constitution at the time of admission in 1846 proved to be unsuitable, and a second version was drafted and ratified in 1857. This remains the fundamental law of Iowa, though it has been amended numerous times. The constitution provides for a separation of governmental powers into executive, legislative, and judicial components.

The executive. In the executive branch the governor, lieutenant governor, secretary of state, auditor, treasurer, secretary of agriculture, and attorney general are elected for four-year terms. A number of commissions, boards, and departmental executives are appointed by the governor, though most employees of the state departments are under a civil-service system. The Iowa Civil Rights Commission investigates charges, holds hearings, and gives decisions on complaints of discriminatory practices in public accommodations, housing, employment, and education.

The legislature. The bicameral General Assembly meets every year; longer sessions are held in odd-numbered years, when major budget items are decided. The House of Representatives has 100 members elected for two-year terms, while the Senate has 50 members elected for four-year terms. Both bodies are reapportioned every 10 years to ensure compliance with the "one man, one vote" decision of the U.S. Supreme Court.

The judiciary. The state judiciary is headed by the Supreme Court, which has considerable jurisdiction over the lower courts. The nine members of this body elect their own chief justice. Justices are appointed by the governor, are subject to a confirming popular vote one year later, and after an eight-year term may declare their candidacy for another term. There are 13 judicial districts in the state, with the number of judges varying according to population and case load. Most larger cities have municipal courts; the others have police and mayor's courts. Justices of the peace are elected in those townships that lack municipal courts.

Local government. Local authority is vested in each county's board of supervisors, under which serve the elected auditor, sheriff, recorder, treasurer, clerk of district court, and county attorney. The county government collects municipal, school, county, and state taxes; manages welfare; and operates the road system in cooperation with the State Highway Commission. Municipalities, deriving their authority from the General Assembly, have only those powers that have been specifically granted to them. This was an issue of considerable contention when the legislature was controlled by rural forces, but after reapportionment in the 1960s the urban–rural discord was much reduced. Most of the smaller incorporated towns have a mayor–council form of government, whereas most of the larger cities have a council–manager or commission administration.

Republican voting record

Politics. Iowa's political tradition has been more or less Republican. Between 1848 and 1968, only seven Democrats represented Iowa in the U.S. Senate. The Democrats failed to elect a candidate to the governorship until the Depression of the 1930s. Disquiet over farm prices, however, has elicited a substantial Democratic vote on several occasions. Iowans elected Democrats to the U.S. Senate in 1968, 1972, and 1974.

The social environment. Iowa ranks above the median for the United States in family income, but this is largely due to the significant fraction that is derived from agriculture. The cost of living is generally less than that in metropolitan centres of the East and far West but above that of the South and Southwest.

Welfare is managed on the county level, as are many health services, though federal and state funds support these activities. Health facilities are generally adequate in the larger cities, and especially in the University of Iowa medical centre in Iowa City, but rural areas suffer from a lack of doctors and hospitals. Intensive efforts have been taken to rectify this situation. Hospitals are being upgraded, often with federal support. Most methods to lure doctors into rural practice have proved relatively unsuccessful: about two-thirds of the doctors trained in Iowa medical schools establish their practices in other states.

Education. For many years Iowa's rate of literacy has been the nation's highest. Its first public school was opened in 1830, and its system of tax-supported schools dates from 1834. Iowa ranks above more than half of the other states in per-pupil expenditure, with financing from local property taxes and state and federal supplements. The University of Iowa (founded 1847), in Iowa City, is especially noted for the programs in fine arts, and Iowa State University (1858), in Ames, has shown national and international leadership in the basic sciences, agriculture, veterinary medicine, and related fields. There are also a great number of other public and private institutions of higher learning; nearly all of the latter have religious affiliations.

CULTURAL LIFE AND RECREATION

A widely dispersed population with relatively small urban centres makes it difficult for Iowans to support many of the cultural amenities that exist in large urban settings. Travelling shows, including theatre and dance, symphonies, and guest artists visit many places in the state each year. The major cultural centres are the large state and smaller private universities and colleges. The fine arts are notably supported at the University of Iowa, where the regional painter Grant Wood (1892–1942) did much of his work and where the Writer's Workshop enjoys a national esteem. Art museums of significance are found in Iowa City and Des Moines. Such towns as Cherokee and Decorah have museums emphasizing the area's presettlement character or the early European settlers, while Davenport, Des Moines, Cedar Rapids, Sioux City, Dubuque, and Fort Dodge have museums or art galleries.

Sporting life. In a region generally lacking large urban centres, sporting events furnish much of the cultural life. The University of Iowa has long been one of the national leaders in basketball and football attendance. In every college town in the state, football weekends form the centre of the autumn social season. High school basketball and wrestling tournaments evoke great community enthusiasm near the end of the long, cold winters. Outdoor sports of all types are extremely popular, with hunting, fishing, boating, and camping especially prevalent.

Folk culture. Folk traditions are maintained in the Amana colonies (Oktoberfest); in the Dutch community of Pella, with its annual tulip festival; among the Czechs of Cedar Rapids; and in other localities.

Communications. Iowans are served by 19 television stations, 120 radio stations, 41 daily newspapers, and some 340 weekly newspapers.

PROSPECTS

The population of Iowa is nearly stable, with little growth likely in the future unless there are dramatic changes in the pattern of American life. The economy, not likely to boom, is tied closely to the fortunes of the agricultural sector, which battles the twin evils of low prices for its products and high prices for the materials and equipment it needs. Lack of an organized common front in either purchasing or sales hampers the efforts of the rural people in their struggle to acquire the goods and services that more highly urbanized areas take for granted. But progress is not an unmixed blessing in the minds of many Iowans, who cherish the relative freedom from crowding, pollution, and other difficulties that beset more urbanized environments.

BIBLIOGRAPHY. CYRENUS COLE, *Iowa Through the Years* (1940), a highly readable account of the history of Iowa, largely politically oriented; FEDERAL WRITERS' PROGRAM, *Iowa: A Guide to the Hawkeye State* (1949, reprinted 1973), one of the WPA series of state guides, still quite useful and the only comprehensive guide to the background of many localities in the state; PHILIP FRANKLAND and STEPHEN AIROLA, *Atlas of Selected Iowa Services* (1978); *Iowa Official Register* (biennial), voting records, political history, administrative structure of the state, and capsule summaries of history and other related fiMARSHALL MCKUSICK, *Men of Ancient Iowa* (1964), on archaeology and historical Indians, their culture, movements, and artifacts; H.L. NELSON, *A Geography of Iowa* (1967), a nontechnical survey of the agriculture, physical resource base, manufacturing, commerce, and cities of Iowa; ROBERT V. RUHE, *Quaternary Landscapes in Iowa* (1969), a discussion of the effects of the Pleistocene Epoch on the landscape of Iowa, together with consideration of the development of the land surface and soils since the Pleistocene.

(N.E.S.)

Iqbāl, Muḥammad

Muḥammad Iqbāl, an Indian poet and philosopher, is famed for his influential efforts to direct his fellow Muslims toward a renewed activism. His writings influenced the movement that eventually led to the creation of the nation of Pakistan. He attempted to arouse the Muslim people to a new sense of their destiny, one that would enable them to transcend their depressed condition and to evolve new and better manifestations of what he called "that spiritual democracy which is the ultimate aim of Islām." In 1922 he was knighted by the British government in recognition of his eminence as a poet.

Iqbāl was born at Siālkot, India (now in Pakistan), probably in 1877, of a pious family of small merchants and was educated at Government College, Lahore. In Europe from 1905 to 1908, he earned his degree in philosophy from Cambridge University, qualified as a barrister in London, and received a doctorate from the University of Munich. His thesis, *The Development of Metaphysics in Persia*, revealed some aspects of Islāmic mysticism formerly unknown in Europe.

Early poetry

On his return from Europe, he served briefly as professor of philosophy and English literature at Government College. His livelihood was then gained in the practice of law, but his fame came from his poetry, which was written in the classical style for public recitation. Through poetic symposia and in a milieu in which memorizing verse was customary, his poetry became widely known, even among the illiterate. Almost all the cultured Indian and Pakistani Muslims of his and later generations have had the habit of quoting Iqbāl.

Before he visited Europe, his poetry affirmed Indian nationalism, as in *Nayā shawālā* ("The New Altar"), but time away from India caused him to shift his perspective. He came to criticize nationalism for a twofold reason: in Europe, it had led to destructive racism and imperialism; and in India, it was not founded on an adequate degree of common purpose. In a speech delivered at Alīgarh in 1910, under the title "Islam as a Social and Political Ideal," he indicated the new Pan-Islāmic direction of his hopes. The recurrent themes of Iqbāl's poetry are a memory of the vanished glories of Islām, a complaint about its present decadence, and a call to unity and reform. Reform can be achieved by strengthening the individual through three successive stages: obedience to the law of Islām, self-control, and acceptance of the idea that everyone is potentially a vicegerent of God (*nā'ib* or *mu'min*). Furthermore, the life of action is to be preferred to ascetic resignation.

Three significant poems from this period, *Shikwah* ("The Complaint"), *Jawāb-e shikwah* ("The Answer to the Complaint"), and *Khiẓr-e rāh* ("Khiẓr, the Guide"), were published later in 1924 in the Urdu collection *Bāng-e darā* ("The Call of the Bell"). In those works Iqbāl gave intense expression to the anguish of Muslim powerlessness. Khiẓr (Arabic Khiḍr), the Qur'ānic prophet who asks the most difficult questions, is pictured bringing from God the baffling problems of the early 20th century.

> What thing is the State? or why
> Must labour and capital so bloodily disagree?
> Asia's time-honoured cloak grows ragged
> and wears out . . .
> For whom this new ordeal, or by whose hand prepared?
> (Eng. trans. by V.G. Kiernan.)

Notoriety came in 1915 with the publication of his long Persian poem *Asrār-e khūdī* ("Secrets of the Self"). He wrote in Persian because he sought to address his appeal to the entire Muslim world. In this work he presents a theory of the self that is a strong condemnation of the self-negating quietism (*i.e.*, the belief that perfection and spiritual peace are attained by passive absorption in contemplation of God and divine things) of classical Islāmic mysticism; his criticism shocked many and excited controversy. Iqbāl and his admirers steadily maintained that creative self-affirmation is a fundamental Muslim virtue; his critics said he imposed themes from the German philosopher Friedrich Nietzsche on Islām.

The dialectical quality of his thinking was expressed by the next long Persian poem, *Rumūz-e bīkhūdī* (1918; "Mysteries of Selflessness"). Written as a counterpoint to the individualism preached in the *Asrār-e khūdī*, this poem called for self-surrender.

> Lo, like a candle wrestling with the night
> O'er my own self I pour my flooding tears.
> I spent my self, that there might be more light,
> More loveliness, more joy for other men.
> (Eng. trans. by A.J. Arberry.)

The Muslim community, as Iqbāl conceived it, ought effectively to teach and to encourage generous service to the ideals of brotherhood and justice. The mystery of selflessness was the hidden strength of Islām. Ultimately, the only satisfactory mode of active self-realization was the sacrifice of the self in the service of causes greater than the self. The paradigm was the life of the Prophet Muḥammad and the devoted service of the first believers. The second poem completes Iqbāl's conception of the final destiny of the self.

Later, he published three more Persian volumes. *Payām-e Mashriq* (1923; "Message of the East"), written in response to Goethe's *West-östlicher Divan* (1819; "Divan of West and East"), affirmed the universal validity of Islām. In 1927 *Zabūr-e ʿAjam* ("Persian Psalms") appeared, about which A.J. Arberry, its translator into English, wrote: "Iqbāl displayed here an altogether extraordinary talent for the most delicate and delightful of all Persian styles, the *ghazal*," or love poem. *Jāvīd-nāmeh* (1932; "The Song of Eternity") is considered Iqbāl's masterpiece. Its theme, reminiscent of Dante's *Divine Comedy*, is the ascent of the poet, guided by the great 13th-century Persian mystic Jalāl ad-Dīn ar-Rūmī, through all the realms of thought and experience to the final encounter.

Iqbāl's later publications of poetry in Urdu were *Bāl-e Jibrīl* (1935; "Gabriel's Wing"), *Zarb-e kalīm* (1937; "The Blow of Moses"), and the posthumous *Armaghān-e Hijāz* (1938; "Gift of the Hejaz"), which contained verses in both Urdu and Persian. He is considered the greatest poet in Urdu of the 20th century.

Philosophical position and influence

His philosophical position was articulated in *The Reconstruction of Religious Thought in Islam*, a volume based on six lectures delivered at Madras, Hyderābād, and Alīgarh in 1928–29. He argued that a rightly focussed man should unceasingly generate vitality through interaction with the purposes of the living God. The Prophet Muḥammad had returned from his unitary experience of God to let loose on the earth a new type of manhood and a cultural world characterized by the abolition of priesthood and hereditary kingship and by an emphasis on the study of history and nature. The Muslim community in the present age ought, through the exercise of *ijtihād*—the principle of legal advancement—to devise new social and political institutions. He also advocated a theory of *ijmāʿ*—consensus. Iqbāl tended to be progressive in adumbrating general principles of change but conservative in initiating actual change.

During the time that he was delivering these lectures, Iqbāl began working with the Muslim League. At the annual session of the league at Allahābād, in 1930, he gave the presidental address, in which he made a famous statement that the Muslims of northwest India should demand status as a separate state.

In the following years, he participated in two conferences in London and visited France, Spain, and Italy; he also attended a Muslim conference in Jerusalem. In the autumn of 1933, he went to Afghanistan to discuss the foundation of a university in Kābul.

After a long period of ill health, Iqbāl died on April 21, 1938, and was buried in front of the great Bādshāhī Mosque in Lahore. Two years later, the Muslim League voted for the idea of Pakistan. That the poet had influenced the making of that decision, which became a reality in 1947, is undisputed. He has been acclaimed as the father of Pakistan, and every year Iqbāl Day is celebrated by Pakistanis.

BIBLIOGRAPHY. MUHAMMAD IQBAL, *The Reconstruction of Religious Thought in Islam* (1934, reprinted 1962); *Letters of*

Iqbal to Jinnah (1942). English translations of Iqbāl's poetry: A.J. ARBERRY (trans.), *Complaint and Answer* (1955), *Javidnamah* (1966), *The Mysteries of Selflessness* (1953), and *Persian Psalms* (1948, reprinted 1961); V.G. KIERNAN (trans.), *Poems from Iqbal* (1955); R.A. NICHOLSON (trans.), *The Secrets of the Self*, rev. ed. (1940, reprinted 1960). K.G. SAIYIDAIN, *Iqbal's Educational Philosophy*, 6th rev. ed. (1965), a standard analysis of the relevance of Iqbāl's ideas about education written by a distinguished Indian educationist; ANNE-MARIE SCHIMMEL, *Gabriel's Wing* (1963), a thorough analysis of Iqbāl's religious symbolism, including the most comprehensive bibliography in English; WILFRED CANTWELL SMITH, *Modern Islām in India*, rev. ed. (1946), an influential analysis of the apparent contradictions in Iqbāl; S.A. VAHID, *Iqbal: His Art and Thought*, rev. ed. (1959), a standard introduction.

(S.McD.)

Iran

Iran is an Islāmic republic in southwestern Asia. It has an area of 636,296 square miles (1,648,000 square kilometres) and an estimated population of more than 40,000,000 people. It is bounded on the north by the Soviet Union and the Caspian Sea, on the east by Pakistan and Afghanistan, on the south by the Persian Gulf and the Gulf of Oman, and on the west by Turkey and Iraq. Iran also controls about a dozen islands in the Persian Gulf. More than 30 percent of its 4,865-mile (7,829-kilometre) boundary is seacoast. The capital is Tehrān (Teheran).

Known to the West as Persia until 1935, Iran was occupied by a group of closely related Aryan tribes as early as the 9th century BC. The Medes, who first established an empire, were superseded in 550 BC by the Persians. Their name, still retained in the present province of Fārs (Persia), was applied by the West to the entire country. Iran, land of the Aryans, has always been the official name. Today, both names—Persia and Iran—are used.

Although Iran became the world's largest oil-exporting country after World War II, its economy remained predominantly agrarian. A planned economy, inaugurated in 1949, was intended to diversify the sources of national income through industrialization and the exploitation of natural resources other than oil. While the level of progress was uneven, the foundation of an industrial state had been laid by the late 1970s. The overthrow of the monarchy in January 1979, however, halted economic activities and was followed by chaotic political and economic conditions, separatist movements, and an extremely costly war with Iraq.

Revolution of 1979

The constitution of 1979 declares that absolute sovereignty belongs to God; that God's principal representative on Earth is the highest executive, judicial, and legislative authority in the land; and that none of the three branches of government can take any action that is in conflict with Islāmic criteria or in violation of the constitution. (For historical aspects, see IRAN, HISTORY OF; ISFAHAN; TEHRĀN.)

THE LANDSCAPE

The natural landscape. *Relief.* A series of massive mountain ranges surrounds Iran's high interior basin. Most of the country is above 1,500 feet (400 metres), one-sixth of it over 6,500 feet. In sharp contrast are the coastal regions outside the mountain ring. In the north the 400-mile strip along the Caspian Sea, never more than 70 miles wide and frequently narrowing to 10, falls sharply from the 10,000-foot summits to the marshy lake's edge, 90 feet below sea level. Along the southern coast the land drops away from a 2,000-foot plateau, backed by a rugged escarpment three times as high, to meet the Persian Gulf (*q.v.*) and the Gulf of Oman.

The Zagros Mountains

The Zagros range stretches from the border with the Armenian Soviet Socialist Republic in the northwest to the Persian Gulf, and thence eastward into Baluchistan (Balūchestān). As it moves southward, it broadens into a 125-mile-wide band of parallel ridges lying between the plains of Mesopotamia and the great central plateau of Iran. It is drained on the west by streams that cut deep, narrow gorges and water fertile valleys. The land is extremely rugged, difficult of access, and populated largely by pastoral nomads.

Pastoral nomads near the ancient site of Naqsh-e Rostam in the Zagros mountain region.
Inge Morath—Magnum

The Elburz Mountains (*q.v.*), narrower than the Zagros but equally forbidding, run along the south shore of the Caspian to meet the border ranges of Khorāsān (Khurasan) to the east. The highest of the chain's many volcanic peaks is 18,386-foot (5,604-metre), snow-clad Mt. Damavend. On the border of Afghanistan the mountains fall away into barren sand dunes.

The arid interior plateau, which extends into Central Asia, is cut by two smaller mountain ranges. Portions of this desert region, known as *dasht*, are covered by loose stones and sand, gradually merging into fertile soil on the hillsides. Where freshwater can be trapped, oases have existed from time immemorial, marking the ancient caravan routes. The most remarkable feature of the plateau is a salt waste 200 miles long and half as wide, known as the *kavīr*. It remains unexplored, since its treacherous crust is formed by large, sharp-edged salt masses overlying mud. Cut by deep arroyos (channels of intermittent streams), it is virtually impenetrable. According to popular belief, the eastern portion, known as Kavīr-e Lūṭ, is the site of the lost legendary city of Lūṭ (Lot), mentioned in the Qurʾān, which the Bible identifies as Sodom. Folklore holds that the hand of God, which destroyed the city, laid a curse upon the entire area, turning it to salt.

Kavīr-e Lūṭ

Drainage and soils. The few streams emptying into the desiccated central plateau dissipate themselves in saline marshes. The general drainage pattern is down the outward slopes of the mountains, terminating in the sea. There are three large rivers, but only one—the Kārūn—is navigable, for the others (the Atrak and the Safīd system) are too steep and irregular. The Kārūn itself varies in its rate of flow from 7,000 to 75,000 cubic feet (200 to 2,120 cubic metres) per second. All streams are seasonal and variable: spring floods do enormous damage, while in summer many streams disappear. Water is, however, stored naturally underground, finding its outlet in springs and being tapped by wells.

Soil patterns vary widely. The abundant subtropical vegetation of the Caspian's coastal region is supported by rich brown forest soils. Mountain soils are shallow layers over bedrock, with a high proportion of unweathered fragments. Natural erosion moves the finer textured soils into the valleys. These alluvial deposits are mostly chalky, and many are used for pottery.

The semiarid plateaus lying above 3,000 feet are covered by brown or chestnut-coloured soil that supports grassy vegetation. The soil is slightly alkaline and contains 3 to 4 percent of organic material. The saline and alkaline soils in the arid regions are light in colour and infertile. The sand dunes are composed of loose quartz and fragments of other minerals. Except where protected by vegetation, they are in almost constant motion, driven by high winds. In the low-lying parts of valleys and in the *kavīr* there are flooded areas of salt marsh.

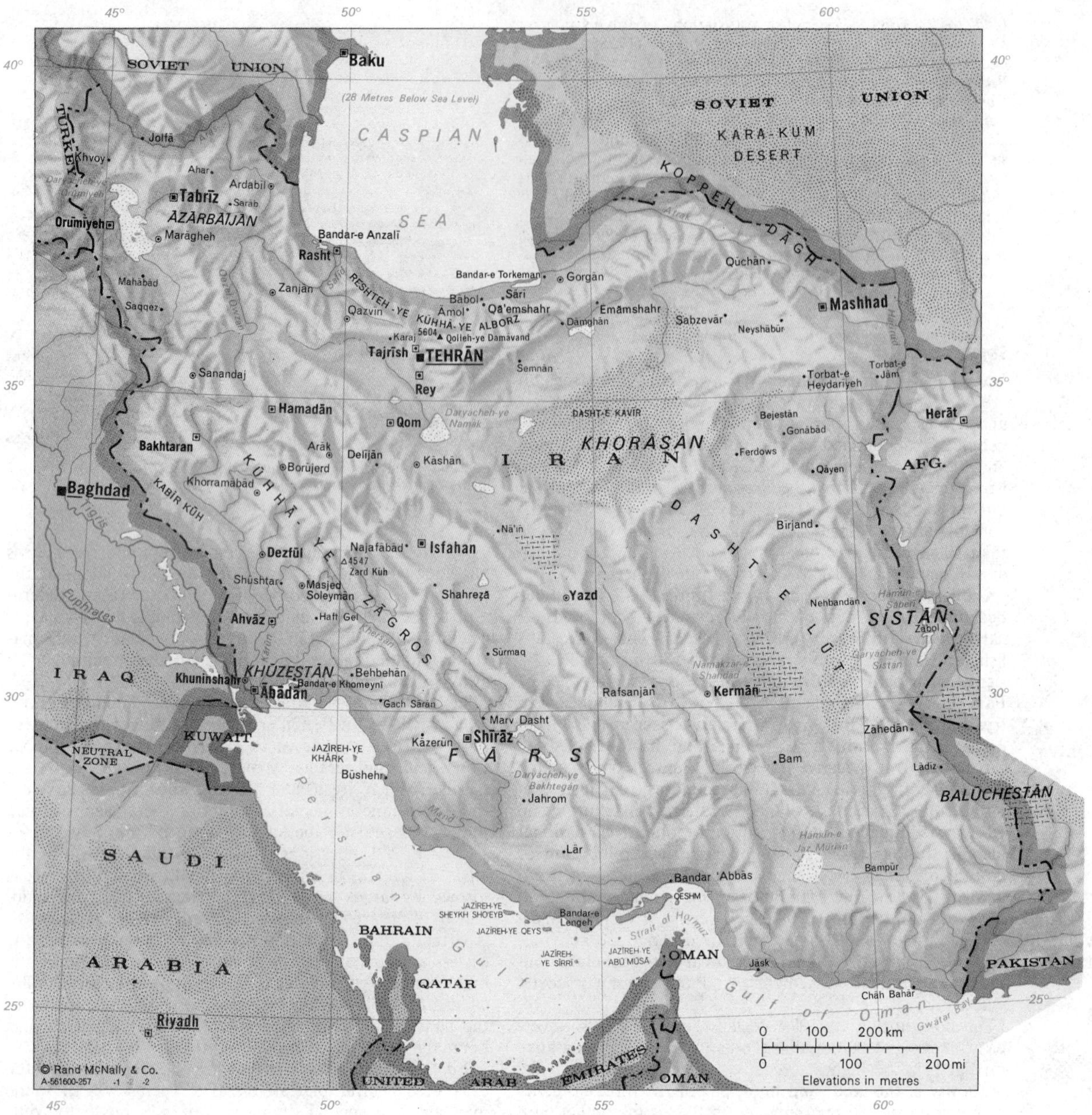

IRAN

MAP INDEX

Cities and towns

Ābādān . . . . .30·20n 48·16e
Ahar . . . . .38·28n 47·04e
Ahvāz . . . . .31·19n 48·42e
Āmol . . . . .36·23n 52·20e
Arāk . . . . .34·05n 49·41e
Ardabīl . . . . .38·15n 48·18e
Bābol . . . . .36·34n 52·42e
Bakhtaran . . . . . . .34·19n 47·04e
Bam . . . . .29·06n 58·21e
Bampūr . . . . .27·12n 60·27e
Bandar 'Abbās . . .27·11n 56·17e
Bandar-e Anzalī . . . . .37·28n 49·27e
Bandar-e Khomeynī . . . . . .30·25n 49·05e
Bandar-e Lengeh . . . . .26·33n 54·53e
Bandar-e Pahlavī, see Bandar-e Anzalī
Bandar-e Shāh, see Bandar-e Torkeman
Bandar-e Shāhpūr, see Bandar-e Khomeynī
Bandar-e Torkeman . . . . . . .36·54n 54·04e
Behbehān . . . . .30·35n 50·14e
Bejestān . . . . .34·31n 58·10e
Bīrjand . . . . .32·53n 59·13e
Borūjerd . . . . .33·54n 48·46e
Būshehr (Bushire) . . . . . . .28·59n 50·50e
Chāh Bahār . . . . . .25·18n 60·37e
Dāmghān . . . . .39·09n 54·22e
Delījān . . . . .33·59n 50·40e
Dezfūl . . . . .32·23n 48·24e
Emāmshahr . . . . . .36·25n 54·58e
Ferdows . . . . .34·00n 58·09e
Gach Sārān . . . . . .30·12n 50·47e
Gonābād . . . . .34·20n 58·42e
Gorgān . . . . .36·50n 54·29e
Haft Gel . . . . .31·27n 49·27e
Hamadān . . . . .34·48n 48·30e
Isfahan . . . . .32·30n 53·00e
Jahrom . . . . .28·31n 53·33e
Jāsk . . . . .25·38n 57·46e
Jolfā . . . . .38·57n 45·38e
Karaj . . . . .35·48n 50·59e
Kāshān . . . . .33·59n 51·29e
Kāzerūn . . . . .29·37n 51·38e
Kermān . . . . .30·17n 57·05e
Kermānshāh, see Bakhtaran
Khorramābād . . . .33·30n 48·20e
Khorramshahr, see Khuninshahr
Khuninshahr . . . . .30·25n 48·11e
Khvoy . . . . .38·33n 44·58e
Lādīz . . . . .28·56n 61·19e
Lār . . . . .27·41n 54·17e
Mahābād . . . . .36·45n 45·43e
Marāgheh . . . . . . .37·23n 46·13e
Marv Dasht . . . . . .29·50n 52·40e
Mashhad . . . . .36·18n 59·36e
Masjed Soleymān . . . . . .31·58n 49·18e
Nā'īn . . . . .32·52n 53·05e
Najafābād . . . . . . .32·37n 51·21e
Nehbandān . . . . . .31·32n 60·02e
Neyshābūr . . . . . .36·12n 58·50e
Orūmīyeh . . . . . . .37·33n 45·04e
Qā'emshahr . . . . .36·28n 52·53e
Qāyen . . . . .33·44n 59·11e
Qazvīn . . . . .36·16n 50·00e
Qom . . . . .34·39n 50·54e
Qūchān . . . . .37·06n 58·30e
Rafsanjān . . . . . . .30·24n 56·01e
Rasht . . . . .37·16n 49·36e
Rey . . . . .35·35n 51·25e
Reẕā'īyeh, see Orūmīyeh
Sabzevār . . . . .36·13n 57·42e
Sanandaj . . . . .35·19n 47·00e
Saqqez . . . . .36·14n 46·16e
Sarāb . . . . .37·56n 47·32e
Sārī . . . . .36·34n 53·04e
Semnān . . . . .35·33n 53·24e
Shāhī, see Qā'emshahr
Shahreẕā . . . . .32·01n 51·52e
Shāhrūd, see Emāmshahr
Shīrāz . . . . .29·36n 52·32e
Shūshtar . . . . .32·03n 48·51e
Sūrmaq . . . . .31·03n 52·48e
Tabrīz . . . . .38·05n 46·18e
Tajrīsh . . . . .35·48n 51·25e
Tehrān . . . . .35·40n 51·26e
Torbat-e Heydarīyeh . . . . .35·16n 59·13e
Torbat-e Jām . . . . .35·14n 60·36e
Yazd . . . . .31·53n 54·25e
Zābol . . . . .31·02n 61·30e
Zāhedān . . . . .29·30n 60·52e
Zanjān . . . . .36·40n 48·29e

Physical features and points of interest

Abū Mūsā, Jazīreh-ye, *island* . . . . .25·52n 55·03e
Alborz, Reshteh-ye Kūhhā-ye, *mountains* . . . . . .36·00n 53·00e
Aras, *river* . . . . . . .39·45n 48·00e
Atrak, *river* . . . . . .37·28n 53·57e
Āzarbāījān (Azerbaijan), *historic region* . . . . .38·00n 47·00e
Bakhtegān, Daryāchen-ye, *lake* . . . . .29·20n 54·05e
Balūchestān, (Baluchistan), *historic region* . . .28·00n 63·00e
Caspian Sea . . . . .38·00n 52·00e
Damāvand, Qolleh-ye, *mountain* . . . . . . .35·56n 52·08e
Demavend, see Damāvand, Qolleh-ye
Elburz, see Alborz, Reshteh-ye Kūhhā-ye
Fārs, *historic region* . . . . .29·00n 53·00e
Gwātar Bay . . . . . .25·04n 61·36e
Harīrūd, *river* . . . . .36·35n 61·05e

MAP INDEX (continued)

Hormuz, Strait of	26·34n 56·15e
Jaz Mūrīan, Hāmūn-e, *salt marsh*	27·20n 58·55e
Kabīr Kūh, *mountains*	32·25n 46·45e
Kārūn, *river*	30·25n 48·12e
Kavīr, Dasht-e, *desert*	34·40n 54·30e
Khārg, see Khārk	
Khārk, Jazīreh-ye, *island*	29·15n 50·20e
Khersan, *river*	31·33n 50·22e
Khorāsān, *historic region*	34·00n 56·00e
Khurasan, see Khorāsān	
Khūzestān, (Khuzistan), *historic region*	30·30n 50·00e
Koppeh Dāgh, *mountains*	37·50n 58·00e
Lūt, Dasht-e, *desert*	33·00n 57·00e
Mand, *river*	28·11n 51·17e
Namak, Daryācheh-ye, *lake*	34·45n 51·36e
Namakzār-e Shahdād, *salt flat*	30·30n 58·30e
Oman, Gulf of	24·30n 58·30e
Orūmīyeh, Daryācheh-ye (Urmia, Lake)	37·40n 45·30e
Persian Gulf	27·00n 51·00e
Qeshm, *island*	26·45n 55·45e
Qeys, Jazīreh-ye, *island*	26·32n 53·56e
Qezel Owzan, *river*	36·45n 49·22e
Reẓā'īyeh, Daryācheh-ye, see Orūmīyeh, Daryācheh-ye	
Ṣāberī, Hāmūn-e, *lake*	31·30n 61·20e
Safīd, *river*	37·25n 49·30e
Seistan, see Sīstān	
Sheykh Sho'eyb, Jazīreh-ye, *island*	26·48n 53·15e
Sīrrī, Jazīreh-ye, *island*	25·55n 54·32e
Sīstān, *historic region*	30·30n 62·00e
Sīstān, Daryācheh-ye, *lake*	31·00n 61·15e
Urmia, Lake, see Orūmīyeh, Daryācheh-ye	
Zāgros, Kūhhā-ye, *mountains*	33·40n 47·00e
Zard Kūh, *mountain*	32·22n 50·04e

Climate. Iran's complex climate ranges from subtropical to subpolar. In winter a high-pressure belt, centred in Siberia, slashes west and south to the interior of the Iranian Plateau, while low pressures develop over the warm waters of the Caspian, the Persian Gulf, and the Mediterranean. In summer one of the lowest pressure centres in the world prevails in the south. Low pressures in Pakistan generate two regular wind patterns: the *shamāl*, which blows from February to October northwesterly through the Tigris–Euphrates Valley, and the "120-day" summer wind, which sometimes reaches velocities of 70 miles per hour in the Sīstān (Seistan) region near the Pakistan frontier. Warm Arabian winds bring heavy moisture from the Persian Gulf. Heat and humidity are unbearable in the Gulf area, while in the Caspian coastal region moist air from the sea mingles with the dry air currents from the Elburz to create a comfortable nightly breeze.

Temperature and rainfall

Temperatures vary from a high of 123° F (51° C) in Khūzestān (Khuzistan) at the head of the Persian Gulf to a low of −35° F (−37° C) in Azerbaijan (Āzārbāījān) in the northwest. Precipitation also varies widely, from less than two inches (50 millimetres) in the southeast to about 78 inches in the Caspian region. The annual average is about 14 inches. Winter is normally the rainy season for the country as a whole. Frequent spring thunderstorms, especially in the mountains, bring destructive hailstones, some as large as four inches (10 centimetres) in diameter. The northern coastal region presents a sharp contrast. The high Elburz Mountains, which seal off the narrow Caspian Plain, wring moisture from the clouds, trap humidity from the air, and create a fertile semitropical region with luxuriant forests, swamps, and rice paddies. Temperatures may soar to 100° F (38° C), the humidity to 98 percent. Frost is extremely rare.

Vegetation and animal life. Topography, altitude, water supply, and soil determine the character of the vegetation. Approximately 12 percent of Iran is forested, most extensively in the Caspian region. Here are found broad-leafed, deciduous trees—oak, beech, linden, elm, walnut, ash, and hornbeam—and a few broad-leafed evergreens. Thorny shrubs and ferns also abound.

The Zagros Mountains are covered by semihumid oak forests, together with elm, maple, *Celtis* (a hackberry), walnut, pear, and pistachio trees. Willow, poplar, and plane trees grow in the ravines, as do many species of creepers. Thin stands of juniper, almond, berberis (a prickly-stemmed shrub with yellow flowers), cotoneaster (an Old-World flowering shrub of the rose family), and wild fruit trees grow on the intermediate dry plateau. Thorny shrubs cover the steppes, while artemisia (a kind of wormwood) grows at medium elevations of the desert plains and the rolling country. There are acacia, dwarf palm, and kunar (Jerusalem thorn) trees and scattered shrubs below 3,000 feet. Desert sand dunes, which hold water, support thickets of brush. Forests follow the courses of surface or subterranean waters. Oases support vines and tamarisk, poplar, date palm, myrtle, oleander, acacia, willow, elm, plum, and mulberry trees. In swamp areas reeds and grass provide good pasture.

The wildlife includes few tigers but many wolves, foxes, leopards, and lynx. Deer and gazelles abound, in addition to wild goats, sheep, and boars. Rodents are ubiquitous, and there are 98 varieties of lizard. Domestic animals include horses, donkeys, cattle, water buffalo, sheep, goats, both species of camel, dogs, and cats.

The landscape under human settlement. *Rural settlement.* Traditionally, the country has been sharply divided along cultural, ethnic, and linguistic lines. In the popular mind the people of each region, frequently associated with a particular city, have specific attributes. The Isfahani is known as a shrewd businessman, witty and industrious; the Yazdi as a hardworking agriculturalist. Azerbaijan produces soldiers and merchants. A Kurd is religiously independent, a fanatical fighter, while the Shīrāzī is a poet by nature and temperament.

Regional characteristics

The topography and the water supply determine the regions fit for human habitation, the character of the people, and their types of dwellings. The deep gorges and defiles, the unnavigable rivers, the empty deserts, and the impenetrable *kavīrs* all result in insularity, tribalism, and a concentration of population around the periphery and in the oases. The felt yurts (circular dwellings) of the Turkmens, the black tents of the Bakhtyārī, and the osier (willow) huts of the Baluchs are typical, as the tribesmen roam from summer to winter pasture. In the vast central and southern plains there are a number of oasis settlements with scattered rudimentary hemispherical or conical huts. In modern times migrations have shortened and the nomads have settled in more permanent villages.

Plain villages follow an ancient rectangular pattern. High mud walls with corner towers form the outer face of the houses, which have flat roofs of mud and straw supported by wooden rafters. In the open centre of the village is a mosque serving also as a school. The cattle that used to be herded there are now usually kept outside.

Mountain villages are situated on the rocky slopes above the valley floor, surrounded by terraced fields, usually irrigated, of grain and lucerne (alfalfa). The houses are square, mud-brick, windowless buildings with flat or domed roofs. The stable is usually under the house.

Caspian villages are completely different. The scattered hamlets have two-storied wooden houses. Separate outbuildings (barns, henhouses, silkworm houses) surround an open courtyard.

Urban settlement. Tehrān, the capital and largest city, is separated from the Caspian by the Elburz Mountains. Isfahan (Eṣfahān), the second largest city, about 250 miles south of Tehrān, is famed for its architecture. There are few cities in central and eastern Iran, where water is scarce, although lines of oases penetrate the desert. Most towns are supplied with water by *qanāt*, an irrigation system by which an underground mountain water source is tapped and the water channelled down through a series of tunnels, sometimes 50 miles in length, to the town level. Towns are, therefore, often located a short distance from the foot of a mountain. The essential feature of a traditional Iranian street is a small canal.

Islāmic city plan

Islāmic influence has determined city layout. There is still strict hierarchical division into separate quarters—the governmental, the residential, and the business sector, or bazaar. The latter, fronting on a central square, is a maze of narrow arcades lined with small individual shops, grouped according to the type of product sold. Today, modern business centres have grown up outside the bazaars. Dwellings are built largely within closed courtyards, with a garden and a pool. Public baths are in all sections of the cities.

Construction of broad avenues and ring roads to accommodate modern traffic has changed the appearance of the large cities. Their basic plan, however, is still that of a labyrinth of narrow, crooked streets and culs-de-sac.

PEOPLE AND POPULATION

Groups historically associated with the contemporary country. *Ethnic and linguistic groups.* Iran is a multilingual and diverse cultural society. About 50 percent of the people speak Persian (Fārsī). The Kurds, whose language has seen scant modification over the centuries, are a fierce nomadic people dwelling in the western mountains of Iran and in Iraq and Turkey. They constitute about 5.5 percent of Iran's population. They have resisted the Iranian government's efforts, both before and after the revolution of 1979, to assimilate them into the mainstream of national life. After the rejection of their demands for autonomy in 1979, they took up arms against the Islāmic republic and, despite harsh military measures, Tehrān failed to establish its full authority over Kordestān (Kurdistan) province. Also inhabiting the western mountains are seminomadic Lurs (5.5 percent), thought to be aboriginal Persians. Closely related, and known as Great Lurs until the 15th century, are the Bakhtyārī tribes, who live in the Zagros Mountains west of Isfahan. Both speak Luri, a Persian dialect, as do the Baluchs (2.3 percent), the agrarian, seminomadic group famed for their superb horsemanship, who inhabit Baluchistan, the eastern part of which is Pakistani territory.

The Kurds

Although the proportion of Turkic ethnic stock is small, approximately 22 percent of the Iranians speak Turkish, a result of the long imposition of Turkish rule on the Persians in the north. The two Turkic ethnic groups are the Qashqā'īs in the Shīrāz area to the east of the Persian Gulf and the Turkmens of Khorāsān in the northeast.

The Armenians, with a different ethnic heritage, have maintained their Indo-European linguistic identity. They are concentrated in Tehrān, Isfahan, and Azerbaijan and are engaged primarily in commercial pursuits. A few isolated remnants of Dravidians are found in the Sīstān region to the east.

Semites—Jews, Assyrians, and Arabs—constitute only a small percentage of the population. The Jews, like the Armenians, have retained their ethnic, linguistic, and religious identity and traditionally have clustered in the largest cities. The Assyrians are concentrated in the northwest, and the Arabs live primarily in the Persian Gulf islands and in Khūzestān. The Arabs' demand for autonomy, their armed attack against government installations, and the suppression of their uprising were among the factors that led to the Iran-Iraq war of the early 1980s.

Semites in Iran

Wars, intermarriage, and commerce have resulted in the intermingling of both blood and vocabulary. Before the revolution of 1979, English and French, and to a lesser degree German and Russian, were widely used by the educated class. Since 1979 Arabic has received priority because of its religious significance.

Religious groups. The vast majority of Iranians are Muslims, mostly of the Shīʿah branch of Islām; Shīʿī Islām is the official state religion. The Kurds and Turkmens are Sunnī Muslims, and among Iran's Arabs the Sunnī and other sects are represented. (For a discussion of Islāmic sects, see ISLĀM; ISLĀMIC THEOLOGY AND PHILOSOPHY.)

Major religious minorities are Christians, Jews, and Zoroastrians. Christians comprise the largest minority group, of whom Orthodox Armenians constitute the bulk. The Assyrians are Nestorians, Protestants, and Roman Catholics, as are a few converts from other ethnic groups. The Zoroastrians are largely concentrated in Yazd in central Iran, Kermān to the south, and Tehrān.

Religious toleration, one of the characteristics of the monarchy, came to an end with the Islāmic revolution in 1979. While Christians, Jews, and Zoroastrians are recognized in the constitution of 1979 as official minorities, the revolutionary atmosphere in Iran was not conducive to equal treatment of non-Muslims. Among these, Iran's Bahā'īs were the greatest victims of persecution. Emigration greatly reduced the Jewish population, which had numbered perhaps as high as 80,000 before 1979.

Demography. The total population of Iran numbered more than 33,700,000 in the 1976 census. According to United Nations estimates, the total population in 1982 was more than 40,000,000; no reliable information on vital statistics or on the number of exiles was available. It was estimated that more than 2,000,000 Iranians lived abroad in the early 1980s, mostly in the United States, Canada, and western Europe.

The people of Iran are extremely youthful. According to the 1976 census, about 45 percent of the population was under 15 years of age, 25 percent between 15 and 29, 25 percent between 30 and 59, and only 5 percent over 60. Males outnumbered females—17,356,347 to 16,352,397.

Population density is not high overall, being only 61.8 persons per square mile (23.9 per square kilometre). The main concentrations are in Azerbaijan, the Caspian region, the watered mountain valleys, and the oases. Many areas are totally uninhabited.

Iran, Area and Population

	area		population	
	sq mi	sq km	1966 census	1976 census
Provinces (*ostāns*)				
Āzārbāījān-e Bākhtarī	15,141	39,216	1,087,000	1,408,000
Āzārbāījān-e Khāvarī	25,908	67,102	2,636,000	3,198,000
Balūchestān va Sīstān	70,108	181,578	503,000	664,000
Bovīr Aḥmadi va Kohkīlūyeh	5,506	14,261	191,000	244,000
Chahār Maḥāll va Bakḥtīārī	5,722	14,820	301,000	394,000
Eṣfahān	36,857	95,459	1,424,000	1,970,000
Fārs	51,467	133,299	1,585,000	2,036,000
Gīlān	5,680	14,711	1,294,000	1,582,000
Hamadān	7,788	20,172	890,000	1,088,000
Hormozgān	26,437	68,472	349,000	462,000
Īlām	7,353	19,045	213,000	246,000
Kermān	74,509	192,978	842,000	1,091,000
Kermānshāhān	9,138	23,668	819,000	1,031,000
Khalīj-e Fārs (Būshehr)	10,677	27,653	259,000	348,000
Khorāsān	120,979	313,335	2,521,000	3,264,000
Khūzestān	24,967	64,664	1,707,000	2,187,000
Kordestān	9,652	24,998	620,000	782,000
Lorestān	12,117	31,384	767,000	934,000
Markazī (Tehrān)	29,799	77,180	4,985,000	6,962,000
Māzandarān	18,288	47,365	1,845,000	2,387,000
Semnān	37,797	97,894	208,000	492,000
Yazd	21,968	56,896	281,000	357,000
Zanjān	8,436	21,848	462,000	581,000
Total Iran	636,295*	1,647,998	25,789,000	33,709,000*

*Figures do not add to total given because of rounding.
Source: Official government figures.

In 1976 Iran's urban population totalled 15,854,680, of whom 9,491,232 lived in 22 cities of more than 100,000, and 17,854,064 were village dwellers and nomads. Tehrān, by far the largest city, had a metropolitan population of more than 4,500,000 in 1976 and an estimated 7,000,000 in 1982. The principal causes of the sudden increase were internal strife and the war with Iraq. Isfahan in 1982 had a population estimated to be 675,000. Rapid population increase and a steady rural exodus to the cities (an average of 250,000 per year through the late 1970s) created intolerable social and economic problems, such as unemployment, congestion, and shortages in housing and educational, hygienic, and transit facilities. These problems, in turn, fueled the flames of the revolution of 1979.

Urban population

THE NATIONAL ECONOMY

In 1963 per capita income at current prices in Iran was U.S. $200 per year. In 1978 the figure was slightly more than $2,500. During 1968–73 the average annual rate of growth for the gross national product was 11.2 percent, but a sudden increase in oil prices in 1973 pushed the growth rate up to 41 percent in 1974–75 before it levelled off at 17 percent or less during the remaining four years of the monarchy.

Prosperity, however, was superficial. The social and political problems created by rapid industrialization, widespread unemployment, and the sluggishness of the agricultural sector led to the political upheavals of 1978 and the overthrow of the monarchy the following year. The Islāmic regime abandoned a planned economy and either cancelled or suspended work on projects initiated in 1973–78 that were aimed at converting Iran into a major industrial power by the year 2000. It committed itself to heavy investment in selected industries (copper, petrochemicals, and steel) and a massive infusion of funds in the agricultural sector. The adoption of any meaningful economic measures seemed unlikely in the early 1980s, however, because of the ongoing war with Iraq and chaotic internal conditions.

Sources of national income. *Agriculture, forestry, and fishing.* The economy is predominantly agrarian, characterized by a low standard of living compared to that of the Western world. Soil continues to be the most exploitable asset. Of the total 407,000,000 acres (165,000,000 hectares) only one-tenth is under cultivation, and more than one-half is considered to be uncultivable, nonagricultural land. While agricultural activities employ about 30 percent of the economically active population, they provide only 13 percent of the gross domestic product. By far the largest acreage is devoted to cereal crops (principally wheat, barley, and paddy rice), followed by cotton and sugar beets and, in much smaller acreages, tobacco. Olives, a wide variety of fruits and nuts, tea, spices, and medicinal herbs are also commercial crops.

The relative neglect of agriculture under the monarchy resulted in a heavy reliance on imported foodstuffs, which by 1979–80 had reached 16 percent of all imports. The principal causes of the problem were lack of transportation and the inadequacy of water resources. For example, figures published in 1976 indicated that 66 percent of all villages lacked commercial roads and that 25 percent of Iran's 60,000 *qanāts*, 13 percent of its deep and medium wells, 15 percent of its artesian wells, and 6–10 percent of its streams, springs, and shallow wells had either dried up or were unusable for lack of care.

Forestry production

Forests cover approximately the same amount of land as agricultural crops—some 45,000,000 acres. The largest and most valuable forests are in the Elburz Mountains, where nearly 40 percent of the 8,500,000 acres is commercially exploitable. The annual yield of timber, about 237,000,000 cubic feet (6,700,000 cubic metres), is used for the domestic building trade and for the manufacture of wood products. Until 1979 some timber was exported.

The forests have been depleted because they have been used indiscriminately for fuel, especially in the form of charcoal; but wood is being replaced as a fuel by oil and natural gas. The former regime, which nationalized the forests in 1963, regulated the sale and export of lumber, introduced forest management, and undertook extensive reforestation. The same policies have been followed by the revolutionary government as conditions permit.

Fishing is important, and fish are caught both for domestic consumption and for export. The industry produces around 5,500 tons per annum from the Caspian in wide variety—sturgeon, bream, whitefish, salmon, mullet, carp, catfish, perch, and roach, the sturgeon yielding its roe for caviar (amounting to about 200 tons per year). More than 200 species of fish are found in the Persian Gulf, 150 of them edible. There the annual catch is about 14,000 tons, with a potential for extensive export of shrimp and prawns.

Of the country's livestock, sheep are by far the most numerous, followed by goats; cattle and buffalo; asses, horses, and mules; and hogs. Camels and poultry are also found in large numbers.

Oil production

Mineral resources. In the early 1980s Iran was among the world's 10 largest producers of oil. Its known reserves were estimated to be 57,000,000,000 barrels, almost one-tenth of the world total, exceeded only by those of Saudi Arabia, Kuwait, and the Soviet Union. Production and exploration were concentrated in the southwest, but oil has also been discovered in Qom and the Kavīr-e Lūṭ, as well as under the offshore waters of the Persian Gulf.

An oil concession to foreign interests (1901), which originally covered 448,000 square miles (1,160,000 square kilometres), was greatly reduced during the 1950s and assigned to a consortium of eight Western companies (U.S., British, Dutch, and French). In 1973 the government nationalized the oil industry, further reduced the consortium's area, and placed its facilities and operations under the control of the government-owned National Iranian Oil Company (NIOC). In 1979 NIOC began selling oil directly to individual companies and countries.

In 1971, before nationalization, oil production was about 4,000,000 barrels a day; between 1974 and 1977 production reached a peak of 6,000,000 barrels a day and was never less than 5,000,000. After the overthrow of the monarchy the Islāmic regime declared a policy of conservation, and the daily production ceiling for 1979–80 was set at 4,000,000 barrels, with 3,000,000 marked for export. Internal political problems and the deterioration of relations with the United States resulted in the loss of traditional markets, and by May 1980 the shipment of 1,700,000 barrels per day to western Europe, Japan, and the United States came to a halt. These problems were further aggravated by the war with Iraq, which created serious shortages in foreign exchange. Production in 1982 averaged 1,500,000–2,000,000 barrels per day, which, according to official statements, was adequate for the needs of the war economy.

Natural gas

Natural gas, found in the south as well as in the Elburz Mountains and in Khorāsān, is also a valuable asset. Reserves, estimated at 480,000,000,000,000 cubic feet (13,700,000,000,000 cubic metres), are the second largest in the world. A 708-mile pipeline runs from the southern oil fields to the Soviet town of Astara on the western shore of the Caspian. Gathering and distributing spur lines run to Tehrān, Kāshān, Isfahan, Shīrāz, Mashhad, Ahvāz, and the industrial city of Alborz, near Kazvin. This state-owned system, known as IGAT I, is one of the largest gas lines in the Middle East. Plans for the construction of IGAT II, a second line to the Soviet Union, and the indirect export of natural gas to western Europe were abandoned with the revolution, and disputes over pricing and the war with Iraq interrupted the flow of gas through IGAT I.

The petrochemical industry, concentrated in the south, was rapidly expanding before the revolution. The largest plant, at Bandar-e Khomeynī (formerly Bandar-e Shāhpūr), produced ammonia, phosphates, sulfur, and other products. The plants of Khārg Island in the Persian Gulf turned out sulfur, liquid gas, and light oil. The war with Iraq, begun in September 1980, led to massive destruction of the petroleum and petrochemical industries.

Iran's other mineral resources are largely undeveloped. Coal is mined in small quantities near Tehrān and in Kermān. Total coal reserves are estimated at 1,000,000,000 tons, but until these are developed, high-grade coal must be imported for industrial use. Chromium deposits north of Bandar ʿAbbās are estimated at 7,000,000 tons, in addition to those in the Elburz Mountains: 80,000 tons were mined in 1980.

Lead, in combination with zinc and other minerals, is widely scattered. A mine at Bafg, near Yazd, produces lead and zinc, and another major complex at Delījān, south of Qom, has a considerable output of concentrated lead and barite (barium sulfate).

Copper deposits

Copper was obtained for centuries from small mines before major deposits were discovered in a belt extending from the Pakistani border to the Soviet border. The Sar Chashmeh deposits in Kermān are estimated at 470,000,000 tons, averaging 1.2 percent copper content, with another 400,000,000 tons a grade lower. Ahar has deposits of higher grade ore, estimated at 10,000,000 tons.

Iron ore, mined at Bafq, at Arāk (southwest of Tehrān), and in southern Kermān, feeds the Isfahan steel plant, which opened in 1971. Rolling mills went into operation two years earlier. An Ahvāz factory produces steel pipe.

Cement production is centred in the provinces of Tehrān, Fārs, and Khūzestān and in the region of Kazvin, west of Tehrān. Fireclay, chalk, lime, gypsum, ochre, and kaolin (china clay) are also produced in commercial quantities. Other mineral resources include magnesite, antimony, manganese, tin, mica, alum, marble, turquoise, and emeralds. Textile mills are centred in Isfahan and the Caspian region.

Hydroelectric and other power resources. The increase of Iran's power supply was considered essential to the country's long-range industrial and agricultural development. Consequently, after the construction of the Amir Kabir Dam on the Karaj River (north of Tehrān) in 1961, similar projects were launched and completed in several provinces, including Azerbaijan, Hamadān, Eṣfahān, Fārs, and Khūzestān. By 1970 the foundation of a national electrification network had been laid, and the expectation was that by the late 1970s inexpensive electrical power would be available for domestic and industrial use and that rural electrification would become an accomplished fact.

Failure of energy policy

Not only were these goals not accomplished, but, in many of the areas where transmission lines were installed and power was available, demand far exceeded capacity. The regular blackouts of the late 1970s in Tehrān and other major urban centres were indications of poor planning and mismanagement. The monarchy's laws for the development of atomic energy were considered by the Islāmic regime to be unnecessary, or at least poorly timed, and the plans were scrapped, the unfinished plants gathering dust in the sun.

Manufacturing. Beginning in 1949, and especially after increased oil revenues became available in 1954, a great deal of emphasis was placed on industrialization. By 1978 Iran's young industries produced a wide variety of products, such as automobiles (mostly assembled), electrical appliances, machine tools, tobacco, food, wood and leather goods, textiles, pharmaceuticals, petroleum, and petrochemical products. Carpet weaving, a traditional Iranian industry, remains very important. Not only does it employ more than 800,000 workers and substantially contribute to incomes in rural areas, but, with 80 percent of carpet production exported, it is Iran's second largest export industry.

Foreign trade. Despite the drive of the monarchy for self-sufficiency, the value of Iran's imports more than doubled between 1974 and 1978, with machinery and transport equipment leading the list, followed by basic manufactures and foodstuffs. Chief sources of supply were West Germany, the United States, and Japan. What created a favourable balance of trade was the huge income derived from the export of petroleum products. Other exports included carpets, cotton, fruits, textiles, minerals, and chemicals.

The constitution of the Islāmic republic greatly emphasizes economic independence. This, however, remained an elusive goal in the early 1980s.

Financial services. In compliance with the Islāmic constitution, all private banks were nationalized in 1979. This was followed by the nationalization of insurance companies and foreign trade. The latter, however, had not been implemented by 1982. The Islāmic Bank of Iran was established in Tehrān, with branches throughout the country; it was later reorganized as the Islāmic Economy Organization. Under Islāmic criteria the interest rate on loans was replaced by a 4 percent commission; banks pay a "profit" of 7–8.5 percent to depositors and become shareholders in large industries to which they lend money. Banks are divided into categories—such as commercial, industrial, and agricultural—but all are subject to the same regulations.

Islāmic Economy Organization

Management of the economy. *The public and private sectors.* Planned economic development, initiated in 1949, was terminated in 1978. The management of the economy under the republic is subject to Islāmic criteria as determined by the Council of Guardians and approved by the legislature. The constitution establishes specific guidelines for the administration of the nation's economic and financial affairs. The ultimate objective is economic independence, full employment, and a comfortable standard of living. The economy is divided into three sectors: public, which includes major industries, banks, insurance companies, utilities, communications, foreign trade, and mass transportation; cooperative, which includes production and distribution of goods and services; and private, which consists of all activities that supplement the first two.

In general terms, all former laws or any sections of them that violated the principles of Islāmic law were declared null and void. After the nationalization of private banks and insurance companies, the government's efforts to put all exports and imports under state control met with stiff resistance, and private firms have continued their activities in this field. As to the rest of the economy, most of the items listed for nationalization were already under state control when the monarchy was overthrown. The various departments of the central government in Tehrān, as well as their provincial and local offices, are either headed by mullahs (religious teachers) conversant with Islāmic law or are advised by religious leaders in the communities concerned.

Islāmic taxes

Taxation. In Islām, the taxes assessed and imposed include an income tax (*khums:* "one-fifth"); a tax for charitable causes (*zakāt*), which has a variable rate and is frequently in kind; and a land tax (*kharāj*), the rate of which has also been based on the principle of *ūshr*, 10 percent of the value of the crops, unless the land is tax-exempt. There is also a poll tax (*jizya*) imposed on members of recognized minority groups, such as Christians, Jews, and Zoroastrians.

The tax laws of the monarchy remained in effect after the revolution but they were enforced more stringently. Tax evasion, widespread before 1979, now may be regarded as a capital crime. The government's tax revenues in 1980–81 almost equalled those of 1977–78, despite war and the disrupted economy.

Trade unions and employer associations. The controlled unions, established under legislation enacted after 1941, constituted one of the major pillars of the revolution. After the collapse of the monarchy in 1979, disputes developed between some members of unions in the oil industry and the representatives of the Islāmic regime. These were settled, sometimes forcibly, and all unions became subject to Islāmic criteria.

Transportation. Iran's large centres of population are widely scattered. There are no navigable rivers except the Kārūn, and rail and air transportation systems are inadequate. Consequently, the nation's roads are of primary importance.

Trans-Iranian highways

Road networks. Main highways connect Tehrān with the provincial capitals, each the hub of a network in the surrounding country. Two trans-Iranian paved highways connect the eastern and western frontiers—Turkey to Afghanistan and Iraq to Pakistan. In 1980 there were 39,218 miles of all-weather roads, of which only 15,414 miles were paved. In 1981, 1,079,000 automobiles and 406,000 trucks and buses were in use.

Railways. The principal line of the state-owned railway system spans the 895 miles between the Caspian Sea and the Persian Gulf, with spur lines to some of the provincial capitals. In 1982 there were 2,855 miles of rail lines.

In 1971 the railway was linked through Turkey with the European system; the link stimulated trade and tourism appreciably, undercutting air fares and materially reducing sea-transportation time. An extension eastward to Singapore was projected under the auspices of the United Nations Economic and Social Commission for Asia and the Pacific (ESCAP). The Iranian portion was completed as far as Mashhad by 1971. There is also a connection with the Soviet rail system via Jolfā in the northwest.

Persian Gulf ports

Port facilities. Before the outbreak of war with Iraq, Iran was served by five major ports on the Persian Gulf. There were also oil terminals at Abadan and Khārg Island, which were destroyed in the fighting in 1981. Khuninshahr (formerly Khorramshahr) and Bandar-e Khomeynī also lay in the war zone, and Iraq threatened to sink any ship attempting to dock there. The largest port, Bandar ʿAbbās, was relatively safe but could not itself accommodate foreign trade. Construction of a major military port, Chāh Bahār in the southeast, was interrupted by the revolution.

Caspian seaports are primarily used for trade with the Soviet Union. Notable among them are Bandar-e Anzalī (formerly Bandar-e Pahlavī) and Bandar-e Torkeman (formerly Bandar-e Shāh).

Air Transport. Major cities and provincial capitals are served by the state-owned Iran Air, and all have airports capable of handling jets. A huge international airport under construction south of Tehrān remained unfinished in the early 1980s. U.S. carriers no longer serve Iran; some major European airlines continue to do so, but with curtailed service, as do major airlines from Asia and Africa. Iran Air cancelled its service to the United States but continued to serve European cities.

ADMINISTRATION AND SOCIAL CONDITIONS

The structure of government. *Constitutional framework.* Iran is an Islāmic republic, with a president, a cabinet, a unicameral legislature (Majles), and a separate judicial branch. The *faqih*, in the early 1980s the *ayatollah* Ruhollah Khomeini, is considered to be the representative of the Twelfth Imam and as such has final authority in all executive, legislative, and judicial matters. After the *faqih*'s death, experts (jurists) elected by the people are to consult and select his successor, to be designated as the new "Leader." In case no single individual is available to fill the position, a Council of Leadership of three to five theologians is to be established, subject to popular approval.

The *faqih*

The president, elected for four years, is largely a figurehead. He appoints the prime minister, who in turn selects his cabinet with the advice and consent of the Majles. None of these can be chosen without the prior approval of the *faqih;* any can be dismissed upon the recommendation of either the Supreme Court or the Majles.

The 270-member Majles is elected by secret ballot for four years; recognized minorities have token representation. A 12-member Council of Guardians with staggered terms determines the constitutionality of all laws passed by the Majles, as well as their conformity to Islāmic principles; six theologians are appointed by the *faqih*, and six other Islāmic jurists are nominated by the High Council of the Judiciary and approved by the Majles. No legislation may be enacted unless the council is in session.

The judiciary consists of a Supreme Court, a Supreme Judicial Council, and lower courts. The Ministry of Justice is the watchdog for all matters concerning the relationship between the legislative and executive branches and the judiciary. The chief justice and the prosecutor general must be Shīʿah jurists (*mujtahids*). Individual rights—such as freedom of press, assembly, and expression—are guaranteed within the framework of Islāmic law.

Regional and local government. The 23 *ostāns* (provinces) are subdivided into *shahrestāns* (counties), *bakhshs* (districts), and *dehestāns* (villages). Governors are nominated by the minister of interior and appointed by the president. At each level there is a council, and the Supreme Council of Provinces is formed from representatives of the provincial councils.

Elections and parties. Under the constitution elections are to be held at least every four years, supervised by the ministry of interior. All important matters are subject to referenda. Candidates for the presidency and the legislature are nominated by political parties. The most important among these is the Islāmic Republican Party, which in the early 1980s had a majority in the Majles and de facto control of the other two branches of the government. The Muslim People's Party, which once claimed more than 3,000,000 members, was inactive after 1981. The Tudeh (Communist) Party, outlawed under the monarchy, was active until May 1983, when it was again outlawed and its leaders were arrested on charges of espionage. The Mujāhedin-i Khalq (Fighters for the People) Party was outlawed, but its armed resistance to the Islāmic regime continued in the early 1980s, as did that of the outlawed Democratic Party of Iranian Kurdistan. Among other parties is the Party of God, whose members are frequently referred to as "club-wielders" because of their violent street fighting.

Islāmic Republican Party

De facto political developments. In the absence of an organized ecclesiastical hierarchy, the religious scholars (*ulema*, or mullahs) have always been respected throughout the world of Islām. In Iran their position is symbolized by the turban, a black one signifying direct descent from the Prophet Muḥammad. At all levels of government the mullahs carry a great deal of influence either through direct participation in the political process or because of their local power. In December 1982 an eight-point program was aimed at checking their abuse of power.

The mullahs

Justice. Under the Islāmic republic all Islāmic judges rely on the Sharīʿa (Islāmic law) as interpreted by the Shīʿah branch of Islām. Any portion of the law codes of the monarchy that in the opinion of the presiding judge is non-Islāmic is either declared null and void or is unenforced. The severity of punishment over the first four years of the revolutionary regime was, in the opinion of some observers, hardly "Islāmic," but rather "cruel and unusual." The practice of Muslim judges in revolutionary Iran in meting out punishment was seen by some as exceedingly harsh.

Armed forces. The first act of the revolutionary government in 1979 was to eliminate the leadership of the monarchy's armed forces. With few exceptions, all high-ranking officers either faced the firing squad or fled the country, and those of lower rank with royalist tendencies were purged. The Revolutionary Guards (Pāsdārān-i Inqilāb), organized in the early days of the republic, received strong support and fast became the country's most effective military force. Security forces involved in the war against Iraq or in fighting against the Kurds and other dissidents were either accompanied by Revolutionary Guards or led by them.

Revolutionary Guards

Administration. Historically, secessionist movements and foreign intrigues have developed whenever the central administration has been weak. In the first four years of the Islāmic republic Tehrān had not succeeded in establishing its control over the entire country. Several tribal insurrections were dealt with but, in addition to sporadic fighting in major cities, the armed resistance of the Kurds to the central government continued.

Local administrative officials are responsible to their counterparts at the provincial level, who in turn report directly to their respective ministries in Tehrān. The constitution requires that at each level the local council be consulted and that its "decisions be respected."

Police services. A national, well-equipped, centrally administered police force was established under the monarchy and continued after the revolution to serve municipalities and to patrol the highways, albeit under the supervision of the Revolutionary Guards. *Komitehs* (revolutionary committees) wield a great deal of authority; they determine the fate of those within their jurisdiction and rely heavily on the Revolutionary Guards for the implementation of their decisions. Police responsibilities also include intelligence, the control of passports and visas, immigration, criminal investigation, the administration of prisons and of the Police University, and the censorship of motion pictures.

Police functions in rural regions are the responsibility of the more than 40,000 gendarmes posted throughout the country. They are principally engaged in the suppression of smuggling, especially of narcotics, which carries the death penalty. The former National Intelligence and Security Organization, Savak, established in 1957, was reorganized and renamed Savama. The head of the new organization reports directly to the president of the republic and the *faqih*. The existence of Savama is not openly acknowledged.

Education. Compulsory education, established in 1943, continued after the revolution, but the system underwent drastic changes. The curricula of elementary and high schools were purged of non-Islāmic materials, and Islāmic subjects and the Arabic language were added as requirements in the first to the 12th grades. Universities and colleges, closed in April 1980, were reopened in December 1982, except for those in Shīrāz, Ahvāz, and Hamadān. Their curricula were revised and all key personnel were replaced.

Health. Health conditions appreciably improved after World War II through the combined efforts of the government, international agencies, and philanthropic endeavour. By 1964 smallpox had been eradicated, plague had disappeared, and malaria had been practically wiped out. Cholera, believed to have been controlled, broke out in 1970 but was speedily checked. Health facilities were far from adequate at the time of the revolution, however, and deteriorated thereafter. In the early 1980s there was a severe shortage, especially in rural areas, of doctors, nurses, and medical supplies.

Advances in public health

Housing. The continuous migration of the rural population to urban centres following World War II had created severe shortages in housing by 1973. The development plan of 1973–78 failed to solve the cities' housing problems, and the population of urban slums, particularly in Tehrān, augmented the ranks of the dissidents who overthrew the monarchy. Housing has continued to be inadequate, even though conditions for the lower classes have shown some improvement.

In the major cities purified water is piped into houses, while small towns and villages rely on wells, *qanāt*s, springs, or rivers. Central heating is not common, except in modern buildings in the major cities. Portable kerosine heaters, iron stoves using wood and coal, and charcoal braziers are the common sources of heat. Fuel was rationed in the early 1980s, primarily because of the war with Iraq.

Social conditions. The constitution of 1979 guarantees basic necessities for all citizens. The former Pahlavi Foundation was renamed the Bonyad-e Mustazʿafin (Foundation for the Downtrodden). A minimum income is promised for all citizens over 60 years of age, and is paid whenever possible. The aim is to close the income gap between the rich and the poor. Unconfirmed reports indicated a high degree of corruption and the emergence of a new class of nouveau riche among the mullahs.

Traditionally, Iran has been a patriarchal society, with a concept of the family that is more comprehensive than that of the Western world. The reforms undertaken by the monarchy did little to change this, and the constitution of 1979 reaffirms that the family is the most important component of society and that its protection is the duty of the state.

Despite the recognition of religious minorities, discrimination persists. The constitutional requirement that all high public officials belong to the Twelver sect of Shīʿah Islām is rigidly enforced.

CULTURAL LIFE AND INSTITUTIONS

Suffering, tears, self-flagellation, and martyrdom are the essential elements of the Shīʿah culture. As members of a minority religion and a protest movement in the early years of Islām, the Shīʿī were frequently persecuted by the Sunnī majority. The martyrdom of Ḥusayn ibnʿAlī in AD 680 at Karbalāʾ, Iraq, at the hands of the Umayyads, the sufferings of Ḥusayn's household, and the massacre of his followers became the rallying point for a national revival after the establishment of the Ṣafavid Empire in 1501. The Shīʿah Persians were then pitted against the Sunnī Ottomans. At the beginning of each lunar Islāmic year the Karbalāʾ tragedy is commemorated by *taʿziya* (passion plays) and self-flagellation with chains, scimitars, and bare hands. The participants either are half-naked or are clothed in bloody shrouds signifying the blood-stained soil of Karbalāʾ and their willingness to join the ranks of the martyrs.

The martyrdom of Ḥusayn

The commemoration of Karbalāʾ has permeated all of Persian culture and finds expression in poetry, music, and the pessimistic Shīʿah view of the world. No religious ceremony is complete without a reference to Karbalāʾ, and no month passes without at least one day of mourning. None of the efforts of the monarchy, such as the annual festivals of art and the encouragement of musicians and native craftsmen, succeeded in changing this basic attitude, which finds laughter and joy undesirable and, in some circles, even sinful.

Traditional crafts. Carpet looms dot the country. Each locality prides itself on a special design and quality of carpet that bears its name, such as Kāshān (Kashan), Kermān, or Isfahan; the carpets are used locally as well as exported.

Carpet weaving and cloth manufacture

The handwoven-cloth industry has survived stiff competition from the country's modern textile mills. By the 1970s there were approximately 45,000 weavers producing velvets, printed cottons, wool brocades, shawls, and cloth shoes. Felt is made in the south and sheepskin is embroidered in the northeast.

A wide range of articles, both utilitarian and decorative, are made of various metals. The most famous centres are Tehrān (gold); Shīrāz, Isfahan, and Zanjān (silver); and Kāshān and Isfahan (copper). Khorāsān is known for its turquoise industry, as is the Persian Gulf region for natural pearls. The craft techniques are as divergent as the products themselves. Articles may be cast, beaten, wrought, pierced, or drawn (stretched out). The most widespread techniques for ornamentation are engraving, embossing, chiselling, damascening (producing wavy lines), encrustation, or gilding.

Numerous decorative articles in wood are produced for both the domestic and export markets in Isfahan, Shīrāz, and Tehrān (inlay) and in Rasht, Orūmīyeh (formerly called Reẓāʾīyeh), and Sanandaj (carved and pierced wood). Machine-made ceramic tiles are produced in Tehrān, but handmade tiles and mosaics, known for their rich designs and beautiful colours, continue to supply a growing market.

Stone and clay are also used for the production of a wide range of household utensils, trays, dishes, and vases. Mashhad is the centre of the stone industry. Potteries are widely scattered throughout the country, Hamadān being the largest centre.

The fine arts. Under the monarchy two architectural trends developed—an artificial imitation of Western styles that had little relevance to the country's climate and an attempt to revive indigenous designs. The National Council for Iranian Architecture, founded in 1967, discouraged blind imitation of the West and promoted Iranian styles modified to serve modern needs. The latter trend was intensified after the revolution.

Architecture

The rigid Islāmic interpretation of the Second Commandment actually discouraged painting and sculpture. This, however, did not prevent Iranian artists from working in other media, such as calligraphy, illumination, and carpets. Western classical painting and sculpture were introduced in the late 19th century and adapted to Iranian themes.

For centuries musical development was inhibited because of Islāmic injunctions. Folk songs and ancient Persian classical music were preserved only through oral transmission from generation to generation. It was not until the 20th century that a music conservatory was founded in Tehrān and that Western techniques were used to record traditional melodies and encourage new compositions. This trend was reversed, however, in 1979, when the former restrictions on music were restored.

Music

Press, broadcasting, and television. The country's daily newspapers and periodicals are published primarily in Tehrān and must be licensed under the press law of 1979. The publication of any anti-Islāmic sentiments is strictly forbidden. Iran operates its own news agency, IRNA. Foreign correspondents are allowed into the country on special occasions.

In 1982 there were more than 10,000,000 radio receivers. Powerful broadcasting stations (medium-wave and shortwave) serve Iran and have special worldwide programs. In addition to Persian and foreign languages, the country's 52 transmitters broadcast in local languages and dialects. There are two television networks, with 18 local stations serving 2,100,000 sets. Because of widespread illiteracy, audiovisual media are much more effective than the press in the dissemination of information.

Radio and television

BIBLIOGRAPHY. *Constitution of the Islamic Republic of Iran* (1980), an English translation, by HAMID ALGAR, of Iran's constitution; SHAHROUGH AKHAVI, *Religion and Politics in Contemporary Iran: Clergy-State Relations in the Pahlavī Period* (1980), a highly informative study of the political power of the Shīʿī establishment; A.J. ARBERRY, *The Legacy of Persia* (1953, reissued 1968), a penetrating study of the origins of Persian civilization; EDWARD G. BROWNE, *The Persian Revolution of 1905–1909* (1910, reprinted 1966); DANIEL CRAIG, "The Impact of Land Reform on an Iranian Village," *Middle East Journal*, 32:141–154 (Spring 1978), a typical example of the problems created by the monarchy's land reform; WILLIAM B. FISHER (ed.), *The Cambridge History of Iran*, vol. 1, *The Land of Iran* (1968), a collection of extremely detailed essays; "Iran," in *The Middle East and North Africa* (annual), a country survey with up-to-date statistical data; ROBERT GRAHAM, *Iran: The Illusion of Power*, rev. ed. (1980), a devastating report on the White Revolution of the early 1960s; CHARLES P. ISSAWI (ed.), *The Economic History of Iran: 1800–1914* (1971), containing documents, statistical data, and commentary on economic conditions prior to World War I; NIKKI R.

KEDDIE, *Roots of Revolution: An Interpretive History of Modern Iran* (1981), a critical study, and "Stratification, Social Control and Capitalism in Iranian Villages: Before and After Land Reform," in RICHARD ANTOUN and ILIYA HARIK (eds.), *Rural Politics and Social Change in the Middle East* (1972), a study based on field research; RUHOLLAH KHOMEINI, *Islamic Government* (1979), the *ayatollah*'s concept of the nature and function of an Islāmic state; ANN K.S. LAMBTON, *The Persian Land Reform, 1962–1966* (1969), a study based on field research; GEORGE LENCZOWSKI (ed.), *Iran Under the Pahlavis* (1978), a collection of essays on conditions in Iran from 1900 to the late 1970s; S.H. NASR, "Ithnā ʿAshariyya," in *The Encyclopaedia of Islam*, new ed., vol. 4 (1978), an article on the beliefs of the Twelvers; ARTHUR U. POPE, *Masterpieces of Persian Art* (1945, reissued 1970), illustrated; BARRY M. RUBIN, *Paved with Good Intentions: The American Experience and Iran* (1980), a critical examination of U.S.–Iran relations and the causes of the revolution; PIERRE SALINGER, *America Held Hostage: The Secret Negotiations* (1981), an authoritive report on the hostage crisis of 1979–81; HANS E. WULFF, *The Traditional Crafts of Persia* (1966), a well-documented study of traditional arts and crafts, with illustrations; SEPEHR ZABIH, *The Communist Movement in Iran* (1966), a lucid analysis of its origin and development. For a discussion of Iran in a regional context, see *Middle East Contemporary Record* (annual).

Iran, History of

Though Iranians have traditionally called their country by its present name, it was known in the West as Persia (or some variant of that name) until 1935, when the usage was changed at the request of the Iranian government. The name Persia originally designated a region situated in southern Iran formerly known as Persis (modern Fārs), but its usage was extended by the ancient Greeks and other Western peoples to apply to the whole Iranian Plateau.

The Iranian people have inhabited that area at least since the early 1st millennium BC. Under the Achaemenid dynasty (6th–4th century BC), they united the Near East. The Iranians had an important influence on the Mediterranean peoples. In medieval times Iran became one of the chief centres of Islāmic civilization and extended its cultural influence into India.

This article covers the history of the Iranian Plateau from the beginning of recorded time until the present, as well as the succession of ancient empires centred there, whose borders extended beyond those of the present country.

The article is divided into the following sections:

- I. The Elamites, Medians, and Achaemenids
  - The Prehistoric period
    - The Paleolithic
    - The Neolithic
    - The 5th to mid-3rd millennia
    - The late 3rd and 2nd millennia
  - The Elamites
    - The Old Elamite period
    - The Middle Elamite period
    - The Neo-Elamite period
  - The protohistoric period and the kingdom of the Medes
    - The coming of the Iranians
    - The kingdom of the Medes
    - The rise of the Persians under Cyrus II
  - Cyrus' successors: the Achaemenid dynasty
    - Cambyses
    - Darius I
    - Xerxes I
    - Artaxerxes I to Darius III
  - Achaemenid society and culture
    - Language
    - Social organization
    - Religion
    - Art
  - The organization and achievement of the empire
- II. The Hellenistic and Parthian periods
  - Alexander and his successors
    - The nobles and the nomads
    - The Seleucids
    - The movement of Iranian peoples
    - Revolt of the high satrapies
  - The rise of the Parthians
    - Invasion of the Parni
    - Formation of the Parthian state
  - The "phil-Hellenistic" period (*c.* 171 BC–AD 10)
    - Mithradates I
    - Phraates II
    - Mithradates II
    - Wars with Rome
    - Settlement with Rome
  - The "anti-Hellenistic" period (AD 2–162)
    - Artabanus III
    - Dissolution of the Parthian state
    - Peace with Rome
  - The end of the Parthian Empire (AD 162–226)
- III. The Sāsānian period
  - Foundation of the empire
    - Rise of Ardashīr I
    - Wars of Shāpūr I
    - Organization of the empire
  - Religious developments
    - Zoroastrianism
    - Christianity
    - Manichaeism
  - Art and literature
  - Foreign policy
    - Conflicts with Rome
    - Intermittent conflicts from Yazdegerd I to Khosrow I
    - Conflicts with the Turks and Byzantium
    - Triumph of the Arabs
- IV. Iran from 640 to the present
  - The advent of Islām (640–821)
    - Abū Muslim's revolution
    - The ʿAbbāsid caliphate (750–821)
  - The "Iranian Intermezzo" (821–1055)
    - The Ṣaffārids
    - The Sāmānids
    - The Iranian renaissance
    - The Ghaznavids
    - The Būyids
  - The Seljuqs and the Mongols
    - The Seljuqs
    - The Ismāʿīlīyah
    - The Khwārezm-Shāhs
    - The Mongol invasion
    - The Il-Khans
  - The Timurids and Turkmen
  - The Ṣafavids (1502–1736)
    - Shāh ʿAbbās I
    - The Afghan interlude
  - Nāder Shāh (1736–47)
  - The Zand dynasty (1750–79)
  - The Qājārs (1779–1925)
    - Āghā Moḥammad Khān
    - European penetration
    - Popular protest and the constitution
    - Rise of Reza Khan
  - The Pahlavi dynasty (1925–79)
    - Reza Shah
    - Mohammad Reza Shah
  - The Islāmic republic
    - Revolution of 1978–79
    - The republic

The early history of Iran may be divided into three phases: (1) the prehistoric period beginning with the earliest evidence of human beings on the Iranian Plateau (*c.* 100,000 BC) and ending roughly at the start of the 1st millennium BC; (2) the protohistoric period covering approximately the first half of the 1st millennium BC; and (3) the period of the Achaemenid dynasty (6th to 4th century BC), when Iran enters the full light of written history. The civilization of Elam, centred off the plateau in lowland Khuzistan, is an exception, for written history begins there as early as it does in neighbouring Mesopotamia (*c.* 3000 BC).

The sources for the prehistoric period are entirely archaeological. Early excavation in Iran was limited to a few sites. In the 1930s archaeological exploration increased rapidly, but work was abruptly halted by the outbreak of World War II. After the war ended, interest in Iranian archaeology revived quickly, and since 1950 numerous excavations have revolutionized the study of prehistoric Iran. Archaeological sources

For the protohistoric period the historian is still forced to rely primarily on archaeological evidence, but much information comes from written sources as well. None of these sources, however, is both local to and contemporary with the events described. Some sources are contemporary but belong to neighbouring civilizations that are only tangentially involved in events in the Iranian Plateau; *e.g.*, the Assyrian and Babylonian cuneiform records from lowland Mesopotamia. Some are local but not contemporary, such as the traditional Iranian legends and tales that supposedly speak of events in the early 1st millennium BC. And some are neither contemporary nor local, but are nevertheless valuable in reconstructing events in the protohistoric period (*e.g.*, the 5th-century-BC Greek historian Herodotus).

For the centuries of the Achaemenid dynasty there is sufficient documentary material that, for the first time, archaeology is not the primary source of data. Economic texts from Mesopotamia, Elam, and Iran; historical inscriptions such as that of Darius the Great at Bīsitūn; contemporary and later classical authors; and later Iranian legends and literature contribute, among other sources, to the understanding of the Achaemenid period.

I. The Elamites, Medians, and Achaemenids

THE PREHISTORIC PERIOD

The Paleolithic. Enigmatic evidence of man's presence on the Iranian Plateau as early as Lower Paleolithic times comes from a surface find in the Kermanshah Valley. The first well-documented evidence of human habitation is in deposits from several recently excavated cave and rock-shelter sites, mainly located in the Zagros Mountains of western Iran, dated to Middle Paleolithic or Mousterian times (*c.* 100,000 BC). There is every reason to assume, however, that future excavations will reveal Lower Paleolithic man in Iran. The Mousterian flint-tool industry found there is generally characterized by an absence of the Levallois technique of chipping flint and thus differs from the well-defined Middle Paleolithic industries known elsewhere in the Near East. The economic and social level associated with this industry is that of fairly small, peripatetic hunting and gathering groups spread out over a thinly settled landscape.

The Mousterian culture

Locally, the Mousterian is followed by an Upper Paleolithic flint industry called the Baradostian. Radiocarbon dates suggest that this is one of the earliest Upper Paleolithic complexes; it may have begun as early as 36,000 BC. Its relationship to neighbouring industries, however, remains unclear. Possibly, after some cultural and typological discontinuity, perhaps caused by the maximum cold of the last phase of the Würm glaciation, the Baradostian was replaced by a local Upper Paleolithic industry called the Zarzian. This tool tradition, probably dating to the period 12,000 to 10,000 BC, marks the end of the Iranian Paleolithic sequence.

The Neolithic. Evidence indicates that the Near East in general was one of the earliest areas in the Old World to experience what the Australian archaeologist V. Gordon Childe called the Neolithic revolution. That revolution witnessed the development of settled village agricultural life based firmly on the domestication of plants and animals. Iran has yielded much evidence on the history of these important developments. In the early Neolithic (sometimes called the Mesolithic), evidence of significant shifts in tool manufacture, settlement patterns, and subsistence methods, including the fumbling beginnings of domestication of both plants and animals, comes from such important western Iranian sites as Āsīāb, Gūrān, Ganj-e Dareh, and Ali Kosh. Similar developments in the Zagros, on the Iraqi side of the modern border, are also traceable at sites such as Karīm Shahīr and Zawi Chemi–Shanidar. This phase of early experimentation with sedentary life and domestication was soon followed by a period of fully developed village farming as defined at important Zagros sites such as Jarmo, Sarāb, upper Ali Kosh, and upper Gūrān. All of these sites date wholly or in part to the 8th and 7th millennia.

By approximately 6000 BC these patterns of village farming were widely spread over much of the Iranian Plateau and in lowland Khuzistan. Tepe Sabz in Khuzistan, Hajji Firuz in Azerbaijan, Godin Tepe VII in northeastern Luristan, Tepe Sialk I on the rim of the central salt desert, and Tepe Yahya VI C–E in the southeast have all yielded evidence of fairly sophisticated patterns of agricultural life (Roman numerals identify the level of excavation). Though distinctly different, all show general cultural connections with the beginnings of settled village life in neighbouring areas such as Afghanistan, Baluchistan, Soviet Central Asia, and Mesopotamia.

The 5th to mid-3rd millennia. Rather less is known of the cultures in this time range in Iran than of contemporary cultures elsewhere in the ancient Near East. Research has tended to concentrate on the Neolithic and protohistoric periods, and the scattered evidence for important cultural and artistic developments in the Chalcolithic and Early Bronze ages resists coherent summary. It is clear that trends that began in the late Neolithic period continued in the millennia that followed and that the rugged, broken landscape of the Iranian Plateau forced man into a variety of relatively isolated cultures. In no instance, with the important exception of Elam (see *The Elamites* below), did Iran participate in the developments that led to fully urban civilization in lowland Mesopotamia to the west or in the Indus Valley to the east. Throughout prehistory the Iranian Plateau remained at the economic and cultural level of village life achieved in the Neolithic. The separate cultural areas on the plateau are as yet barely understood by the modern archaeologist in any terms other than through the painted pottery assemblages found at several sites throughout Iran. Though developing in comparative isolation, each of these areas does yield some evidence for cultural contact with its immediate neighbours and, in some striking cases, with developments in the centres of higher civilization in Mesopotamia. Trade would appear to be the principal mechanism by which such contacts were maintained, and often Elam appears to have acted as an intermediary between Sumer and Babylon on the one hand and the plateau cultures on the other. Trade across the northern part of the plateau, through the sites of Hissar and Sialk, most probably involved the transshipment from Afghanistan to Mesopotamia of semiprecious stones such as lapis lazuli. The appearance of proto-Elamite tablets in Sialk IV may bear witness to such trade. So also may the appearance of similar proto-Elamite tablets at Tepe Yahya south of Kerman and in the great central desert provide evidence of trade connections between Mesopotamia and the east —in this case a trade that may have centred on specific items such as steatite and copper. The province of Fars perhaps also participated in such trade networks, as is suggested by the appearance there, alongside strictly local ceramics, of wares that have clear Mesopotamian affinities. In the west central Zagros, outside influences from both the north and the west can be traced in the ceramic record; such is also the case for local cultures in Azerbaijan, to the northwest. In general, however, these millennia represent a major dark age in Iranian prehistory and warrant considerably more attention than they have recently received.

Trading contacts

The late 3rd and 2nd millennia. The beginning of this period is generally characterized by an even more marked isolation of the plateau than earlier, while the latter half of the period is one of major new disruptions, heretofore unique in Iranian history, that laid the groundwork for developments in the protohistoric period. In northwestern and central western Iran, local cultures, as yet barely defined beyond their ceramic parameters, developed in relative isolation from events elsewhere. All occupation had ceased at Tepe Sialk, but the painted pottery cultures characteristic of earlier Hissar and of the sites on the Gurgan Plain in the northeast continued. Little Mesopotamian influence is evident, though some contacts between Elam and the plateau remain. Perhaps beginning as early as 2400 BC but more probably somewhat later, a radical transformation occurred in the culture of the northeast: earlier painted potteries are entirely replaced by a distinctive gray or gray-black ceramic that is associated with a variety of other artifacts, primarily weapons and ornaments in copper or bronze, also unique. Whether this cultural change represents a strictly local development or testifies to an important intrusion of new peoples into the area is still under debate. In any case, none of these developments can be traced to Mesopotamia or to other areas to the west, regions which had previously been the source of outside influences on the Iranian Plateau. Somewhat later, the local cultures of central and northwestern Iran were apparently influenced by developments in northern Mesopotamia and Assyria along patterns of contact that were well established in earlier periods. Yet this contact, as it is observed at Godin III, Ḥasanlu VI, and Dinka Tepe, did not cause any major dislocation of local cultural patterns. In the second half of the 2nd millennium, however, western Iran—at first perhaps gradually, and then with striking suddenness—comes under the influence of the gray and gray-black ware cultures that had developed earlier in the northeast. Here the impact of these influences are such as definitely to suggest a major cultural dislocation and the introduction of a whole new culture and probably a new people into the Zagros. It is this development that marks the end of the Bronze Age in western Iran and ushers in the early protohistoric period.

THE ELAMITES

Whereas the Iranian Plateau did not experience the rise of urban, literate civilization in the late 4th and early 3rd millennia on the Mesopotamian pattern, lowland Khuzistan did. Here was centred Elamite civilization.

Geographically, Elam included more than Khuzistan; it was a combination of the lowlands and the immediate highland areas to the north and east. Elamite strength was based on an ability to hold these various areas together under a coordinated government that permitted the maximum interchange of the natural resources unique to each region. Traditionally this was done through a federated governmental structure.

Law of succession

Closely related to that form of government was the Elamite system of inheritance and power distribution. The normal pattern of government was that of an overlord ruling over vassal princes. In earliest times the overlord lived in Susa, which functioned as a federal capital. With him ruled his brother closest in age, the viceroy, who usually had his seat of government in the native city of the currently ruling dynasty. This viceroy was heir presumptive to the overlord. Yet a third official, the regent or prince of Susa (the district), shared power with the overlord and the viceroy. He was usually the overlord's son or, if no son was available, his nephew. On the death of the overlord, the viceroy became overlord. The prince of Susa remained in office, and the brother of the old viceroy nearest to him in age became the new viceroy. Only if all brothers were dead was the prince of Susa promoted to viceroy, thus enabling the overlord to name his own son (or nephew) as the new prince of Susa. Such a complicated system of governmental checks, balances, and power inheritance often broke down despite bilateral descent and levirate marriage (*i.e.*, the compulsory marriage of a widow to her deceased husband's brother). What is remarkable is how often the system did work; it was only in the Middle and Neo-Elamite periods that sons more often succeeded fathers to power.

Elamite history can be divided into three main phases: the Old, Middle, and Late, or Neo-Elamite, periods. In all periods Elam was closely involved with Sumer, Babylonia, and Assyria, sometimes through peaceful trade, more often through war. In like manner, Elam was often a participant in events on the Iranian Plateau. Both involvements were related to the combined need of all the lowland civilizations to control the warlike peoples to the east and to exploit the economic resources of the plateau.

The Old Elamite period. The earliest kings in the Old Elamite period may date to approximately 2700 BC. Already conflict with Mesopotamia, in this case apparently with the city of Ur, was characteristic of Elamite history. These early rulers were succeeded by the Awan (Shustar) dynasty. The 11th king of this line entered into treaty relations with the great Naram-Sin of Akkad (*c.* 2254–*c.* 2218 BC). Yet there soon appears a new ruling house, the Simash dynasty (Simash may have been in the mountains of southern Luristan). The outstanding event of this period was the virtual conquest of Elam by Shulgi of the 3rd dynasty of Ur (2094–2047 BC). Eventually the Elamites rose in rebellion and overthrew the 3rd Ur dynasty, an event long remembered in Mesopotamian dirges and omen texts. About the middle of the 19th century BC, power in Elam passed to a new dynasty, that of Eparti. The third king of this line, Shirukdukh, was active in various military coalitions against the rising power of Babylon, but Hammurabi (*q.v.;* more correctly, Hammurapi, *c.* 1792–1750 BC) was not to be denied, and Elam was crushed in 1764 BC. The Old Babylon kingdom, however, fell into rapid decline following the death of Hammurabi, and it was not long before the Elamites were able to gain revenge. Kutir-Nahhunte I attacked Samsuiluna (1749–1712 BC), Hammurabi's son, and dealt so serious a defeat to the Babylonians that the event was remembered more than 1,000 years later in an inscription of the Assyrian king Ashurbanipal. It may be assumed that with this stroke Elam once again gained independence. The end of the Eparti dynasty, which may have come in the late 16th century BC, is buried in silence.

Conquest by Ur

The Middle Elamite period. After two centuries for which sources reveal nothing, the Middle Elamite period opens with the rise to power of the Anzanite dynasty, whose homeland probably lay in the mountains northeast of Khuzistan. Political expansion under Khumbannumena (*c.* 1285–*c.* 1266 BC), the fourth king of this line, proceeded apace, and his successes were commemorated by his assumption of the title "Expander of the Empire." He was succeeded by his son, Untash-Gal (Untash (d) Gal, or Untash-Huban), a contemporary of Shalmaneser I of Assyria (*c.* 1274–*c.* 1245 BC) and the founder of the city of Dur Untashi (modern Choga Zanbil). In the years immediately following Untash-GAL, Elam increasingly found itself in real or potential conflict with the rising power of Assyria. Tukulti-Ninurta I of Assyria (*c.* 1244–*c.* 1208 BC) campaigned in the mountains north of Elam. The Elamites under Kidin-Khutran, second king after Untash-GAL, countered with a successful and devastating raid on Babylonia. In the end, however, Assyrian power seems to have been too great. Tukulti-Ninurta managed to expand, for a brief time, Assyrian control well to the south in Mesopotamia, Kidin-Khutran faded into obscurity, and the Anzanite dynasty came to an end.

Period of military greatness

After a short period of dynastic troubles, the second half of the Middle Elamite period opened with the reign of Shutruk-Nahhunte (*c.* 1160 BC). Two equally powerful and two rather less impressive kings followed this founder of a new dynasty, whose home was probably Susa, and in this period Elam became one of the great military powers of the Near East. Tukulti-Ninurta died in *c.* 1208 BC, and Assyria fell into a period of internal weakness and dynastic conflict. Elam was quick to take advantage of this situation by campaigning extensively in the Diyālā River area and into the very heart of Mesopotamia. Shutruk-Nahhunte captured Babylon and carried off to Susa the stele on which was inscribed the famous law code of Hammurabi. Shilkhak-In-Shushinak, brother and successor of Shutruk-Nahhunte's eldest son Kutir-Nahhunte, still anxious to take advantage of Assyrian weakness, campaigned as far north as the area of modern Kirkūk. In Babylonia, however, the 2nd dynasty of Isin led a native revolt against such control as the Elamites had been able to exercise there, and Elamite power in central Mesopotamia was eventually broken. The Elamite military empire began to shrink rapidly. Nebuchadrezzar I of Babylon (*c.* 1124–*c.* 1103 BC) attacked Elam and was just barely beaten off. A second Babylonian attack succeeded, however, and the whole of Elam was apparently overrun, ending the Middle Elamite period.

It is noteworthy that during the Middle Elamite period the old system of succession to, and distribution of power appears to have broken down. Increasingly, son succeeded father, and less is heard of divided authority within a federated system. This probably reflects an effort to increase the central authority at Susa in order to conduct effective military campaigns abroad and to hold Elamite foreign conquests. The old system of regionalism balanced with federalism must have suffered, and the fraternal, sectional strife that so weakened Elam in the Neo-Elamite period may have had its roots in the centrifugal developments of the 13th and 12th centuries.

The Neo-Elamite period. A long period of darkness separates the Middle and Neo-Elamite periods. In 742 BC, a certain Huban-nugash is mentioned as king in Elam. The land appears to have been divided into separate principalities, with the central power fairly weak. The next 100 years witnessed the constant attempts of the Elamites to interfere in Mesopotamian affairs, usually in alliance with Babylon, against the constant pressure of Neo-Assyrian expansion. At times they were successful with this policy, both militarily and diplomatically. But on the whole they were forced to give way to increasing Assyrian power. Local Elamite dynastic troubles were from time to time compounded by both Assyrian and Babylonian interference. Meanwhile, the Assyrian army whittled away at Elamite power and influence in Luristan. In time these internal and external pressures resulted in the near total collapse of any meaningful central authority in Elam. In a series of campaigns between 692 and 639 BC, in an effort to clean up a political and diplomatic mess that had become a chronic headache for the Assyrians, Ashurbanipal's armies utterly destroyed Susa, pulling down buildings, looting, and sowing the land of Elam with salt.

Defeat by the Assyrians

THE PROTOHISTORIC PERIOD AND THE KINGDOM OF THE MEDES

The beginning of the Iron Age is marked by major dislocations of cultural and historical patterns in western Iran (almost nothing is known of the eastern half of the plateau in the Iron Age). The Iron Age itself is divided into three periods: Iron Age I (*c.* 1300–*c.* 1000 BC), Iron Age II (*c.* 1000–*c.* 800/750 BC), and Iron Age III (*c.* 750–*c.* 550 BC). The latter is the archaeological equivalent of what historically can be called the Median period.

The coming of the Iranians. Though isolated groups of speakers of Indo-European languages had appeared and disappeared in western Iran in the 2nd millennium BC, it was during the Iron Age that the Indo-European Iranians rose to be the dominant force on the plateau. By the mid-9th century BC two major groups of Iranians appear in cuneiform sources: the Medes and the Persians. Of the two, the Medes were the more widespread and, from an Assyrian point of view, the more important group. When Assyrian armies raided as far east as modern Hamadan they found only Medes. In the more western Zagros they encountered Medes mixed with indigenous, non-Iranian peoples. Early in the 1st millennium, Iranian Medes already controlled almost all of the eastern Zagros and were infiltrating, if not actually pushing steadily, into the western Zagros, in some areas right up to the edge of the plateau and to the borders of lowland Mesopotamia. Persians (Parsua, Parsuash, Parsumash) also appear in roughly the same areas, though their exact location remains controversial. At times they seem to have settled in the north near Lake Urmia, at times in the central western Zagros near Kermanshah, later certainly in the southwestern Zagros somewhere near the borders of Elam, and eventually, of course, in the province of Fars (Parsa). It has been argued that these various locations represent a nomadic tribe on the move; more likely they represent more than one group of Persians. What is reasonably clear from the cuneiform sources is that these Medes and Persians (and no doubt other Iranian peoples not identified by name) were moving into western Iran from the east. They probably followed routes along the south face of the Elburz Mountains and, as they entered the Zagros, spread out to the northwest and southeast following the natural topography of the mountains. Where they could, as for example, along the major pass across the mountains from Hamadan to Kermanshah, they infiltrated further west. In doing so they met resistance from the local settled populations, who often appealed to Urartu, Assyria, and Elam for assistance in holding back the newcomers. Such appeals were, of course, most welcome to the great powers, who were willing to take advantage of the situation both to advance their interests vis-á-vis each other and to control the Iranian threat to themselves.

Penetration into the Zagros

It has been suggested that the introduction of gray and gray-black pottery into western Iran from the northeast, which signals the start of the Iron Age, is the archaeological manifestation of this pattern of a gradual movement of Iranians from east to west. The case is by no means proven but is a reasonable reading of the combined evidence. If it is so, then the earliest Iranians in the Zagros can be dated to Iron Age I times, *c.* 1300 BC. Archaeologically, the culture of Iron Age II times can be seen as having evolved out of that of the Iron Age I period, and, though the development is less clear, the same can be said of the relationship between the cultures of Iron Age II and III. The spread of the Iron Age I and II cultures in the Zagros is restricted and would appear to correspond fairly well with the distribution of Iranians known from the written documents. The distribution of the Iron Age III culture on the other hand is, at least by the 7th century, much more widespread and covers almost the whole of the Zagros. Thus, the argument that links these archaeological patterns with the Iranian migration into the area associates the Iron Age I and II cultures with the early penetration of the Iranians into the more eastern Zagros and with their infiltration westward along the major routes crosscutting the main mountain alignments. Those areas where traces of the Iron Age I and II cultures do not appear were the regions still under the control of non-Iranian indigenous groups supported by Urartu, Assyria, and Elam. The widespread Iron Age III culture is then associated with the rise to power of the Median kingdom in the 7th and early 6th centuries BC and the Iranianization of the whole of the Zagros.

The kingdom of the Medes. Traditionally, the creator of the Median kingdom was one Deioces who, according to Herodotus, reigned from 728 to 675 BC and founded the Median capital Ecbatana (modern Hamadan). Attempts have been made to associate Daiaukku, a local Zagros king mentioned in a cuneiform text as one of the captives deported to Assyria by Sargon II in 714 BC, with the Deioces of Herodotus, but such an association is highly unlikely. To judge from the Assyrian sources, no Median kingdom such as Herodotus describes for the reign of Deioces existed in the early 7th century BC; at best, he is reporting a Median legend of the founding of their kingdom.

Foundation of the capital

According to Herodotus, Deioces was succeeded by his son Phraortes (675–653 BC), who subjugated the Persians and lost his life in a premature attack against the Assyrians. Some of this tale may be true. Assyrian texts speak of a Kashtariti as the leader of a conglomerate group of Medes, Scythians, Mannaeans, and miscellaneous other local Zagros peoples that seriously threatened the peace of Assyria's eastern borderlands during the reign of Esarhaddon (680–669 BC). It is possible that Phraortes is this Kashtariti, though the suggestion cannot be proven either historically or linguistically. That a Median king in this period exerted political and military control over the Persians is entirely reasonable, though it cannot be proven.

Beginning as early as the 9th century, and with increasing impact in the late 8th and early 7th centuries, groups of nomadic warriors entered western Iran, probably from across the Caucasus. Dominant among these groups were the Scythians, and their entrance into the affairs of the western plateau during the 7th century may perhaps mark one of the important turning points in Iron Age history. Herodotus speaks in some detail of a period of Scythian domination, the so-called Scythian interregnum in Median dynasty history. His dating of this event remains uncertain, but traditionally it is seen as falling between the reigns of Phraortes and Cyaxares and as covering the years 653 to 625 BC. Whether such an interregnum ever actually occurred, and, if it did, whether it should not be dated later than this, are open questions. What is clear is that, by the mid-7th century BC, there were a great many Scythians in western Iran; that they, along with the Medes and other groups, posed a serious threat to Assyria; and that their appearance threw previous power alignments quite out of balance.

Herodotus reports how, under Cyaxares of Media (625–

585 BC), the Scythians were overthrown when their kings were induced at a supper party to get so drunk that they were then easily slain. It is more likely that about this time either the Scythians withdrew voluntarily from western Iran and went off to plunder elsewhere, or that they were simply absorbed into a rapidly developing confederation under Median hegemony. Cyaxares is a fully historical figure, who appears in the cuneiform sources as Uvakhshatra. Herodotus speaks of how Cyaxares reorganized the Median army into units built around specialized armaments: spearmen, bowmen, and cavalry. The unified and reorganized Medes were now a match for the Assyrians. They attacked one of the important Assyrian border cities, Arrapkha, in 615 BC, surrounded Nineveh in 614 BC but were unable to capture it, and instead successfully stormed the Assyrian religious capital, Ashur. An alliance between Babylon and the Medes was sealed by the betrothal of Cyaxares' granddaughter to Nabopollassar's son, Nebuchadrezzar II (604–562 BC). In 612 BC the attack on Nineveh was renewed and the city fell in late August (the Babylonians arrived rather too late to participate fully in the battle). The Babylonians and the Medes together pursued the fleeing Assyrians westward into Syria. Assyrian appeals to Egypt for help came to nought, and the last Assyrian ruler, Ashur-uballit II, disappeared from history in 609 BC.

Defeat of the Assyrians

The problem now, of course, was how to divide the spoils among the victors. The cuneiform sources are comparatively silent, but it would seem that the Babylonians fell heir to all of the Assyrian holdings within the fertile crescent, while their allies took over all of the highland areas. The Medes gained control over the lands in eastern Anatolia that had once been part of Urartu and eventually became embroiled in war with the Lydians, the dominant political power in western Asia Minor. In 585 BC, probably through the mediation of the Babylonians, peace was established between Media and Lydia, and the Halys River was fixed as the boundary between the two kingdoms. Thus a new balance of power was established in the Near East among Medes, Lydians, Babylonians, and, far to the south, Egyptians. At his death, Cyaxares controlled vast territories: all of Anatolia to the Halys, the whole of western Iran eastward, perhaps as far as the area of modern Tehrān (Teheran), and all of southwestern Iran, including Fars. Whether it is appropriate to call these holdings a kingdom is debatable; one suspects that authority over the various peoples, Iranian and non-Iranian, who occupied these territories was exerted in the form of a confederation such as is implied by the ancient Iranian royal title, king of kings.

Astyages followed his father Cyaxares on the Median throne (585–550 BC). Comparatively little is known of his reign. All was not well with the alliance with Babylon, and there is some evidence to suggest that Babylonia may have feared Median power. The latter, however, was soon in no position to threaten others, for Astyages was himself under attack. Indeed, Astyages and the Medians were soon overthrown by the rise to power in the Iranian world of Cyrus II the Great of Persia.

The rise of the Persians under Cyrus II. The ruling dynasty of the Persians settled in Fars (Parsa) in southwestern Iran (possibly the Parsumash of the later Assyrian records) traced their ancestry back to an eponymous ancestor Hāxamanish or Achaemenes. There is no historical evidence of such a king's existence. Traditionally, three rulers fall between Achaemenes and Cyrus II: Teispes, Cyrus I, and Cambyses I. Teispes, freed of Median domination during the so-called Scythian interregnum, is thought to have expanded his kingdom and to have divided it on his death between his two sons, Cyrus I and Ariaramnes. Cyrus I may have been the king of Persia who appears in the records of Ashurbanipal swearing allegiance to Assyria after the devastation of Elam in the campaigns of 642–639 BC, though there are chronological problems involved with this equation. When Median control over the Persians was supposedly reasserted under Cyaxares, Cambyses I is thought to have been given a reunited Persia to administer as a Median vassal. His son, Cyrus II, married the daughter of Astyages and in 559 BC inherited his father's position within the Median confederation. Cyrus II certainly warranted his later title, Cyrus the Great. He must have been a remarkable personality, and certainly he was a remarkable king. He united under his authority several Persian and Iranian groups who apparently had not been under his father's control. He then initiated diplomatic exchanges with Nabonidus of Babylon (556–539 BC), which justifiably worried Astyages. Eventually, he openly rebelled against the Medes, who were beaten in battle when considerable numbers of Median troops deserted to the Persian standard. Thus, in 550 BC, the Median Empire became the first Persian Empire, and the Achaemenid kings appeared on the international scene with a suddenness that must have frightened many.

Rise of Cyrus the Great

Cyrus immediately set out to expand his conquests. After apparently convincing the Babylonians that they had nothing to fear from Persia, he turned against the Lydians under the rule of the fabulously wealthy Croesus. Lydian appeals to Babylon were to no avail. He then took Cilicia, thus cutting the routes over which any help might have reached the Lydians. Croesus attacked and an indecisive battle was fought in 547 BC on the Halys River. Since it was late in the campaigning season, the Lydians thought the war was over for that year, returned to their capital at Sardis, and dispersed the national levy. Cyrus, however, kept coming. He caught and beseiged the Lydians in the citadel at Sardis and captured Croesus in 546 BC. Of the Greek city-states along the western coast of Asia Minor, heretofore under Lydian control, only Miletus surrendered without a fight. The others were systematically reduced by the Persian armies led by subordinate generals. Cyrus himself was apparently busy elsewhere, possibly in the east, for little is known of his activities between the capture of Sardis and the beginning of the Babylonian campaign in 540 BC.

Nowhere did Cyrus display his political and military genius better than in the conquest of Babylon. The campaign actually began when he lulled the Babylonians into inactivity during his war with Lydia, which, since it was carried to a successful conclusion, deprived the Babylonians of a potential ally when their turn came. Then he took maximum advantage of internal disaffection and discontent within Babylon. Nabonidus was not a popular king. He had paid too little attention to home affairs and had alienated the native Babylonian priesthood. Second Isaiah, speaking for many of the captive Jews in Babylon, was undoubtedly not the only one of Nabonidus' subjects who looked to Cyrus as a potential deliverer. With the stage thus set, the military campaign against Babylon came almost as an anticlimax. The fall of the greatest city in the Near East was swift; Cyrus marched into town in the late summer of 539 BC, seized the hands of the statue of the city god Marduk as a signal of his willingness to rule as a Babylonian not as a foreign conquerer, and was hailed by many as the legitimate successor to the throne. In one stride Cyrus carried Persian power to the borders of Egypt, for with Babylon came all that it had seized from the Assyrians and had gained in the sequel.

The fall of Babylon

Little is known of the remainder of Cyrus' reign. The rapidity with which his son and successor, Cambyses II, initiated a successful campaign against Egypt suggests that preparations for such an attack were well advanced under Cyrus. But the founder of Persian power was forced to turn east late in his reign to protect that frontier against warlike tribes who were themselves in part Iranians and who threatened the plateau in the same manner as had the Medes and the Persians more than a millennium earlier. One of the recurrent themes of Iranian history is the threat of peoples from the east. How much Cyrus conquered in the east is uncertain. What is clear is that he lost his life in 529 BC, fighting somewhere in the region of the Oxus and Jaxartes rivers.

CYRUS' SUCCESSORS: THE ACHAEMENID DYNASTY

Cambyses. On the death of Cyrus the Great the empire passed to his son, Cambyses II (529–522 BC). There may have been some degree of unrest throughout the empire at the time of Cyrus' death, for Cambyses apparently felt it necessary secretly to kill his brother, Bardiya (Smerdis), in order to protect his rear while leading the campaign against Egypt in 525 BC. The pharaoh Ahmose II of the 26th dynasty sought to shore up his defenses by hiring Greek mercenaries, but was betrayed by the Greeks. Cambyses successfully managed the crossing of the hostile Sinai Desert, traditionally Egypt's first and strongest line of defense, and brought the Egyptians under Psamtik III, son and successor of Ahmose, to battle at Pelusium. The Egyptians lost and retired to Memphis; the city fell to the Persians and the Pharaoh was carried off in captivity to Susa. Three subsidiary campaigns were then mounted, all of which are reported as failures: one against Carthage, but the Phoenician sailors, who were the backbone of the Persian navy, declined to sail against their own colony; one against the oasis of Amon (in the Egyptian desert west of the Nile), which, according to Herodotus, was defeated by a massive sandstorm; and one led by Cambyses himself to Nubia. This latter effort was partly successful, but the army suffered badly from a lack of proper provisions on the return march. Egypt was then garrisoned at three major points: Daphnae in the east delta, Memphis, and Elephantine, where Jewish mercenaries formed the main body of troops.

Cambyses' campaign against Egypt

In 522 BC news reached Cambyses of a revolt in Iran led by an impostor claiming to be Bardiya, Cambyses' brother. Several provinces of the empire accepted the new ruler, who bribed his subjects with a remission of taxes for three years. Hastening home to regain control, Cambyses died—possibly by his own hand, more probably from infection following an accidental sword wound. Darius, a leading general in Cambyses' army and one of the princes of the Achaemenid family, raced homeward with the troops in order to crush the rebellion in a manner profitable to himself.

Cambyses has been rather mistreated in the sources, thanks partly to the prejudices of Herodotus' Egyptian informers and partly to the propaganda motives of Darius I. He is reported to have ruled the Egyptians harshly and to have desecrated their religious ceremonies and shrines. His campaigns out of Egypt were all reported as failures. He was accused of suicide in the face of revolt at home. It was even suggested that he was mad. There is, however, little solid contemporary evidence to support these charges.

Darius I. Darius I (*q.v.*), later called the Great, tells the story of the overthrow of Bardiya and of the first year of his own rule in detail in his famous royal inscription cut on a rock face at the base of Bīsitūn mountain, a few miles east of modern Kermanshah. Six leading Achaemenid nobles assisted in slaying the false Bardiya and together proclaimed Darius the rightful heir of Cambyses. Darius was a member of the Achaemenid royal house. His great-grandfather had been Ariaramnes, son of Teispes, who had shared power in Persia with his brother Cyrus I. Ariaramnes' son, Arsames, and his grandson, Hystaspes (Darius' father), had not been kings in Persia, as unified royal power had been placed in the hands of Cambyses I by Cyaxares. Neither is named a king in Darius' own inscriptions. Hystaspes was, however, an important prince of the blood, who, at the time of revolt of the false Bardiya had apparently been the governor of Parthia. Darius himself was in the mold of Cyrus the Great—a powerful personality and a dynamic ruler.

It took over a year (522–521 BC) of hard fighting to put down revolts associated with Bardiya's claim to the throne and Darius' succession to power. Almost every province of the empire was involved, including Persia and, most particularly, Media. A balanced policy of clemency backed by the swift and thorough punishment of any captured rebel leader, combined with a well-coordinated and carefully timed distribution of loyal forces, eventually brought peace to the empire and undisputed power to Darius. He then turned his attention to the organization and consolidation of his inheritance, and it was for this role—that of lawgiver and organizer—that he himself, to judge from his inscriptions, most wished to be remembered.

Such activities, however, did not prevent Darius from following an active expansionist policy. Campaigns to the east confirmed gains probably made by Cyrus the Great and added large sections of the northern Indian subcontinent to the list of Persian-controlled provinces. Expansion in the west began about 516 BC when Darius moved against the Hellespont as a first step toward an attack on the Scythians along the western and northern

Darius' campaign of expansion

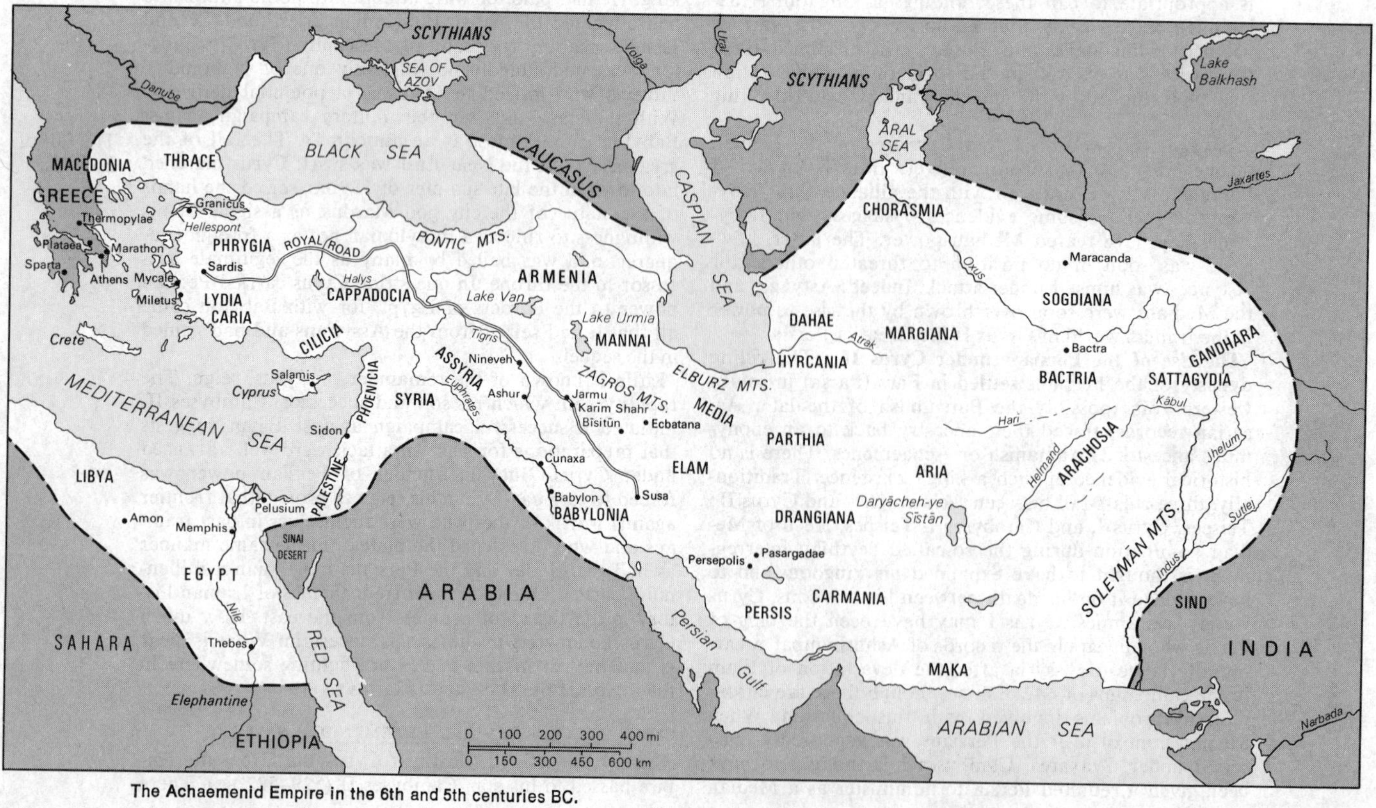

The Achaemenid Empire in the 6th and 5th centuries BC.

shores of the Black Sea. The real strategic purpose behind this move probably was to disrupt and if possible to interrupt Greek trade with the Black Sea area, which supplied much grain to Greece. Crossing into Europe for the first time, Darius campaigned with comparatively little success to the north of the Danube. He retreated in good order, however, with only limited losses, and a bridgehead across the Hellespont was established.

Perhaps in part in response to these developments, perhaps for more purely internal reasons, the Ionian Greek cities on the west coast of Asia Minor revolted against Persian rule in 500 BC. The Persians were apparently taken by surprise, and at first the rebellion prospered. The Ionians received some limited assistance from the Athenians and in 498 BC felt strong enough to take the offensive. With one hand Darius negotiated, with the other he assembled a counterattack. The first Persian military efforts proved only partially successful, however, and the Ionians enjoyed another respite in the years 496–495 BC. A renewed Persian offensive in 494 BC was successful. The Greek fleet was badly beaten off Miletus, and the Persian land army began a systematic reduction of the rebel cities. In *c.* 492 BC Mardonius, a son-in-law of Darius, was made special commissioner to Ionia. He suppressed local tyrants and returned democratic government to many cities. In time the wounds caused by the revolt and its suppression healed, and by 481 BC Xerxes was able to levy troops in this region with little trouble.

By 492 BC Mardonius had also recovered Persian Thrace and Macedonia, first gained in the campaign against the Scythians and lost during the Ionian Revolt. There followed the Persian invasion of Greece that led to Darius' defeat at the Battle of Marathon on August 12, 490 BC. The "Great King" was forced to retreat and to face the fact that the Greek problem, which had probably seemed to the Persians a minor issue on the western extremity of the empire, would require a more concerted and massive effort. Thus began preparations for an invasion of Greece on a grand coordinated scale. These plans were interrupted in 486 BC by two events: a serious revolt in Egypt, and the death of Darius.

Xerxes I. Xerxes (486–465 BC), Darius' eldest son by Queen Atossa, was born after his father had come to the throne; he had been designated official heir perhaps as early as 498 BC, and while crown prince he had ruled as the King's governor in Babylon. The new King quickly suppressed the revolt in Egypt in a single campaign in 485 BC. Xerxes then broke with the policy followed by Cyrus and Darius of ruling foreign lands with a fairly light hand and, in a manner compatible with local traditions, ruthlessly ignored Egyptian forms of rule and imposed his will on the rebellious province in a thoroughly Persian style. Plans for the invasion of Greece begun under Darius were then still further delayed by a major revolt in Babylonia about 482 BC, which also was suppressed with a heavy hand.

Invasion of Greece

Xerxes now turned his attention westward to Greece. He wintered in Sardis in 481–480 BC and thence led a combined land and sea invasion of Greece. Northern Greece fell to the invaders in the summer of 480, the Greek stand at Thermopylae in August of 480 came to nought, and the Persian land forces marched on Athens, taking and burning the Acropolis. But the Persian fleet lost the Battle of Salamis and the impetus of the invasion was blunted. Xerxes, who had by now been away from Asia rather long for a king with such widespread responsibilities, returned home and left Mardonius in charge of further operations. The real end of the invasion came with the Battle of Plataea, the fall of Thebes (a stronghold of pro-Persian forces), and the Persian naval loss at Mycale in 479 BC. Of the three, the Persian loss at Plataea was perhaps the most decisive. Up until Mardonius was killed the issue of the battle was probably still in doubt, but once leaderless, the less organized and less disciplined Persian forces collapsed. Time and again in later years this was to be the pattern in such encounters, for the Persians never solved the military problem posed by the disciplined Greek hoplites (see also GRECO-PERSIAN WARS).

The formation of the Delian League, the rise of Athenian imperialism, troubles on the west coast of Asia Minor, and the end of Persian military ambitions in the Aegean followed rapidly in the decade after Plataea. Xerxes probably lost interest in the proceedings and sank deeper and deeper into the comforts of life in his capital cities of Susa, Ecbatana, and Persepolis. Harem intrigues, which were steadily to sap the strength and vitality of the Achaemenid Empire, led to the assassination of the Great King in 465 BC.

Artaxerxes I to Darius III. The death of Xerxes was a major turning point in Achaemenid history. Occasional flashes of vigour and intelligence by some of Xerxes' successors were too infrequent to prevent eventual collapse but did allow the empire to die gradually. It is a tribute to Cyrus, Cambyses, and Darius that the empire they constructed was as resilient as it proved to be after Xerxes.

The three kings that followed Xerxes on the throne—Artaxerxes I (464–425 BC), Xerxes II (425–424 BC) and Darius II (423–404 BC)—were all comparatively weak individuals and kings, and such successes as the empire enjoyed during their reigns were mainly the result of the efforts of subordinates or of the troubles faced by their adversaries. Artaxerxes I faced several rebellions, the most important of which was that of Egypt in 459 BC, not fully suppressed until 454 BC. An advantageous peace (the Peace of Callias) with Athens was signed in 448 BC, whereby the Persians agreed to stay out of the Aegean and the Athenians agreed to leave Asia Minor to the Achaemenids. Athens broke the peace in 439 BC in an attack on Samos, and in its aftermath the Persians made some military gains in the west. Xerxes II ruled only about 45 days and was killed in a drunken stupor by the son of one of his father's concubines. The assassin was himself killed by Darius II, who rose to the throne through palace intrigue. Several revolts marred his reign, including one in Media, which was rather close to home.

The Peloponnesian War

The major event of these three reigns was the Peloponnesian War between Sparta and Athens that lasted, with occasional pauses, from 460 to 404 BC. Here was a situation ripe for exploitation by the famous "Persian archers," the gold coins of the Achaemenids that depicted an archer on their obverse and that were used with considerable skill by the Persians in bribing first one Greek state and then another. Initially, the Persians encouraged Athens against Sparta, and from this gained the treaty of Callias. Then, after the disastrous Athenian campaign against Sicily in 413 BC, the Persians intervened on Sparta's side. By the treaty of Miletus in 412 BC, Iran recovered complete freedom in western Asia Minor in return for agreeing to pay for seamen to man the Peloponnesian fleet. Persian gold and Spartan soldiers brought about Athens' fall in 404 BC. Despite the fact that the Persians played the two sides against each other to much advantage, they should have done better. One observes a certain lack of control from Susa by the king in these proceedings, and the two principal governors in Asia Minor who were involved, Tissaphernes of Sardis and Pharnabazus of Hellespontine Phrygia, seemed to have permitted a personal power rivalry to stand in the way of a really coordinated Persian intervention in the Greek war.

Artaxerxes II came to the throne in 404 BC and reigned until 359 BC. The main events of his long rule were the war with Sparta that ended with a peace favourable to the Persians; the revolt and loss to the empire of Egypt; the rebellion of Cyrus the Younger, brother of the king; and the uprising known as the revolt of the satraps.

Sparta, triumphant over Athens, built a small empire of its own and was soon involved in a war against the Persians, the principal issue again being the Greek cities of Asia Minor. While Sparta played one Persian governor in Anatolia against the other, the Persians spent gold in Greece to raise rebellion on Sparta's home ground. The Persians rebuilt their fleet and placed a competent Athenian admiral, Conon, in command. The contest continued from 400 to 387, with Sparta forced to act on an ever-shrinking front. A revitalized Athens, supported by

Persia, created a balance of power in Greece and eventually Artaxerxes was able to step in, at Greek request, and dictate the so-called King's Peace of 387–6 BC. Once again the Greeks gave up any claim to Asia Minor and further agreed to maintain the status quo in Greece itself. When Egypt revolted in 405 BC, Persia was unable to do much about it, and from this point forward Egypt remained essentially an independent state.

Cyrus the Younger, though caught in an assassination attempt at the time of Artaxerxes' coronation, was nevertheless, forgiven, thanks to the pleadings of the Queen Mother, and was returned to the command of a province in Asia Minor. But he revolted again in 401 BC and, supported by 10,000 Greek mercenaries, marched eastward to contest the throne. He was defeated and killed at the Battle of Cunaxa in Mesopotamia in the summer of 401. The Greek mercenaries, however, were not broken and, though harried, left the field in good order and began their famous march, recorded in the *Anabasis* of Xenophon, north to the Black Sea and home. Probably no other event in late Achaemenid history revealed more clearly to the Greeks the essential internal weakness of the Achaemenid Empire than the escape of so large a body of men from the very heart of the Great King's domain.

Since 379 BC Greek mercenaries had been gathered together in order to mount a campaign against Egypt. An attack in 373 failed against the native 30th dynasty. On the heels of this failure came the revolt of the satraps.

Revolt of the satraps

Several satraps, or provincial governors, rose against the central power, and one Aroandas, late satrap of Armenia, went so far as to stamp his own gold coinage as a direct challenge to Artaxerxes. The general plan of the rebels appears to have been for a combined attack. The rebel satraps were to coordinate their march eastward through Syria with an Egyptian attack, under the pharaoh Tachos (Zedhor), supported by Greek mercenaries. The Egyptian attack was called off because of a revolt in Egypt by Tachos' brother, and Artaxerxes managed to defeat the satraps who were left alone to face the Great King's wrath. How different would have been the wrath of Darius! Several of the satraps, including Aroandas, were actually forgiven and returned to their governorships. In general the impression is that, in the end, rather than fight the central authority, the satraps were willing to return to their own provinces and plunder there in the name of the Great King. Perhaps they saw that they actually had more authority and more control over real events in their own provincial territories than Artaxerxes had in his empire.

Reign of Artaxerxes III

Plot and counter plot, harem intrigue, and murder brought Artaxerxes III to the throne in 359 BC. He promptly exterminated many of his relatives who might have challenged his rule—all to no avail, for revolts continued to rock the empire. A fresh attempt to win back Egypt was thrown back in 351–350. This setback encouraged revolt in Sidon and eventually in all of Palestine and Phoenicia. Parts of Cilicia joined the rebellion but the revolt was crushed the same year it had begun, 345 BC. But peace was achieved only temporarily; mercenaries from Thebes and the Argives, as well as from the Greek cities of Asia Minor, gathered for a new attempt on Egypt, which, led by Artaxerxes III himself, succeeded in 343 BC. But the local dynasty fled south to Nubia, where it maintained an independent kingdom that kept alive the hopes of a national revival. Persia then misplayed its hand in Greece by refusing aid to Athens against the rising power of Philip II of Macedon. In 339 BC Persian troops were fighting alone in Thrace against the Macedonians, and in the following year, at the Battle of Chaeronea, Philip extended his hegemony over all of Greece—a united Greece that was to prove impervious to Persian gold.

Artaxerxes was poisoned by his physician at the order of the eunuch Bagoas. The latter made Arses king (338–336 BC) in hopes of being the power behind the throne, but Arses did not bend easily to Bagoas' will. He attempted to poison the kingmaker but was himself killed in retaliation. Bagoas then engineered the accession of Darius III, a 45-year-old former satrap of Armenia. So many members of the royal house had been murdered in the court intrigue that Darius probably held the closest blood claim to the throne by virtue of being the grandnephew of Artaxerxes II. Darius was able to put down yet another rebellion in Egypt under Khababash in 337–336 BC, but the beginning of the end came soon afterward, in May 334, with the loss of the Battle of Granicus to Alexander the Great. Persepolis fell to the invader in April 330, and Darius, the last Achaemenid, was murdered in the summer of the same year while fleeing the conqueror. His unfinished tomb at Persepolis bears witness to his lack of preparation.

The invasion of Alexander the Great

Alexander did not win his victories easily, however, and the catalog of troubles that marks the latter part of the Achaemenid Empire—rebellions, murders, weak kings trapped in the harem, missed chances, and foolish policies—cannot be the whole story. The sources, mostly Greek, are often prejudiced against the Persians and tend to view events from but a single point of view. No government could have lasted so long, found its way somehow through so many difficulties, and in the end actually have fought so hard against the conqueror without having much virtue with which to balance its vices.

ACHAEMENID SOCIETY AND CULTURE

Achaemenid society and culture was in reality the collective societies and cultures of the many subject peoples of the empire. From this mosaic it is sometimes difficult to sort out that which is distinctively Persian, or distinctively a development of the Achaemenid period, and therefore perhaps an early Iranian contribution to general Near Eastern society and culture.

Language. The languages of the empire were as varied as its peoples. The Persians, at least originally, spoke Old Persian, a southwest dialect of Iranian (Median was a northwest Iranian dialect), but were illiterate. Their language was first written when Darius commanded that a script suitable for this purpose be invented so that he might inscribe the record of his rise to power at Bīsitūn (the inscriptions in Old Persian are attributed to earlier kings as either late historical forgeries or were probably written during the reign of Darius). That few could read Old Persian might be the reason why Darius at Bīsitūn established the tradition that royal inscription should be trilingual in Old Persian, Babylonian, and Elamite. Old Persian was never a working written language of the empire. Elamite, written on clay tablets, appears to have been the language of many of the administrators in Fars and, it may be assumed, in Elam. Archives of administrative documents in Elamite have been found at Persepolis. Aramaic, however, was the language of much of the empire and was probably the language most used in the imperial bureaucracy. The beginnings of the strong influence of Aramaic on Persian, which is so evident in the Middle Persian of Sāsānian times, can already be seen in the Old Persian royal inscriptions of late Achaemenid times.

Social organization. Little is known of Iranian social organization in the period. In general, it was based on feudal lines that were in part drawn by economic and social function. Traditional Indo-Iranian society consisted of three classes, the warriors or aristocracy, the priests, and the farmers or herdsmen. Crosscutting these divisions was a tribal structure based on patrilineal descent. The title king of kings, used to this day by the shah of Iran, implies that the central authority exercised power through a pyramidal structure that was controlled at levels below the supreme authority by individuals who were themselves, in a certain sense, kings. Traditionally the king was elected from a particular family by the warrior class; he was sacred, and a certain royal charisma attached to his person.

Kingship

Such a method of organizing and controlling society undoubtedly changed under the influences and demands of imperial power and underwent much modification as Iranians increasingly borrowed social and political ideas from the peoples they ruled. Nevertheless, even in later times there is evidence that the original Iranian concepts of kingship and social organization were still honoured and remained the ideals of Persian culture.

Religion. Iranian religion in the pre-Achaemenid and Achaemenid periods is a subject on which there is little scholarly agreement. When the Iranians first entered the semilight of the protohistoric period, they were certainly polytheists whose religious beliefs and practices closely paralleled other Indo-Iranian and Indo-European groups at the same stage in history. Their gods were associated with natural phenomena; with social, military, and economic functions; and with abstract concepts such as justice and truth. Their religious practices included, among others, animal sacrifice, a reverence for fire, and the drinking of the juice of the haoma plant, a natural intoxicant.

Zoroastrianism

Probably around 600 BC there arose in the northeast of the plateau the great Iranian religious prophet and teacher, Zoroaster. The history of the religion that he founded is even more complicated and controversial than the history of pre-Zoroastrian Iranian religion. Yet certain features of his religious reform stand out. He was an ethical prophet of the highest rank, stressing constantly the need for man to act righteously, speak the truth and abhor the lie. In his teaching the lie was almost personified as the Druj, chief in the kingdom of the demons, to which he relegated many of the earlier Indo-Iranian deities. His god was Ahura Mazdā, who, it seems likely, was a creation in name and attributes of Zoroaster. Though in a certain sense technically monotheism, early Zoroastrianism viewed the world in strongly dualistic terms, for Ahura Mazdā and the "Lie" were deeply involved in a struggle for the soul of man. Zoroaster, as might be expected, attempted to reform earlier Iranian religious practices as well as beliefs. He first rejected and then perhaps allowed the practice of the haoma cult in a modified form; he clearly condemned the practice of animal sacrifice; and he elevated to central importance in the ritual a reverence for fire. Fire worship, however, is a misnomer since the Zoroastrians have never worshipped fire but rather have revered it as the symbol *par excellence* of truth.

The crucial question is: were the Achaemenids Zoroastrians or at least followers of the prophet in the terms in which they understood his message? Possibly Cyrus the Great was, probably Darius I was, and almost certainly Xerxes and his successors were. Such a simple answer to the question is possible, however, only if we understand that Zoroastrianism as a religion had already undergone considerable development and modification since Zoroaster's lifetime, influenced by beliefs and practices and by the religions of those people of the Near East with whom the expanding Iranians had intimate contact.

The god of the Achaemenid kings was the great Ahura Mazdā, from whom they understood they had received their empire and with whose aid they accomplished all deeds. Xerxes and his successors mention other deities by name, but Ahura Mazdā remains supreme. Darius I names only Ahura Mazdā in his inscriptions. More significant, however, is Darius' tone, which is entirely compatible with the moral tone of Zoroaster and, in some instances, even compatible with details of Zoroaster's theology. During the reigns of Darius and Xerxes the archaeological record reveals that religious rituals were in force that were also compatible with an evolved and evolving Zoroastrianism. The haoma cult was practiced at Persepolis, but animal sacrifice is not attested. More important, fire clearly played a central role in Achaemenid religion.

There may have been religious overtones in the quarrel between Cambyses and Darius on the one hand and the false Bardiya, a Magian or Median priest, on the other. Certainly there were religious as well as political motivations behind Xerxes' suppression of the Daeva worshippers and the destruction of their temple. It is possible that there was some conflict among the royal Achaemenids, who were followers of one form of Zoroastrianism, the supporters of a different version of Zoroastrianism as practiced by other Iranians, believers in older forms of Iranian religion, and foreign religions, which in the light of the Prophet's teachings were reprehensible. Compromises and syncretism, however, probably could not be prevented. Though the Zoroastrian calendar was adopted as the official calendar of the empire in the reign of Artaxerxes I, by the time of Artaxerxes II, the ancient Iranian god Mithra and the goddess Anahita had been accepted in the royal religion alongside Ahura Mazdā.

Thus, in a sense, the Achaemenid kings were Zoroastrians, but Zoroastrianism itself was probably no longer exactly the religion Zoroaster had attempted to establish. What the religion of the people beyond court circles may have been is almost impossible to say. One suspects that a variety of ancient Iranian cults and beliefs were prevalent. The Magi, the traditional priests of the Medes, may have wielded more influence in the countryside than they did at court, and popular beliefs and practices may have been more deeply influenced by contact with other peoples and other religions. Later classical Zoroastrianism, as known in the Sāsānian period, is an amalgam of such popular cults, of the religion of the Achaemenid court, and of the teachings of the Prophet in their more pure form (see also ZOROASTRIANISM AND PARSIISM).

Art. Achaemenid art, like Achaemenid religion, was a blend of many elements. In describing, with justifiable pride, the construction of his palace at Susa, Darius says,

The palace at Susa

> The cedar timber—a mountain by name Lebanon—from there it was brought . . . the *yakā*-timber was brought from Gandara and from Carmania. The gold was brought from Sardis and from Bactria . . . the precious stone lapis-lazuli and carnelian . . . was brought from Sogdiana. The . . . turquois from Chorasmia . . . The silver and ebony . . . from Egypt . . . the ornamentation from Ionia . . . the ivory . . . from Ethiopia and from Sind and from Arachosia . . . The stone-cutters who wrought the stone, those were Ionians and Sardians. The goldsmiths . . . were Medes and Egyptians. The men who wrought the wood, those were Sardians and Egyptians. The men who wrought the baked brick, those were Babylonians. The men who adorned the wall, those were Medes and Egyptians.

This was an imperial art on a scale the world had not seen before. Materials and artists were drawn from all the lands ruled by the Great King, and thus tastes, styles, and motifs became mixed together in an eclectic art and architecture that in itself mirrored the empire and the Persians' understanding, of how that empire ought to function. Yet the whole was entirely Persian. Just as the Achaemenids were tolerant in matters of local government and custom, as long as Persians controlled the general policy and administration of the empire, so also were they tolerant in art so long as the finished and total effect was Persian. At Pasargadae, the capital of Cyrus the Great and Cambyses in Fars, the Persian homeland, and at Persepolis, the neighbouring city founded by Darius the Great and used by all of his successors, one can trace to a foreign origin almost all of the several details in the construction and embellishment of the architecture and the sculptured reliefs, but the conception, planning, and overall finished product are distinctly Persian and could not have been created by any of the foreign groups who supplied the king of kings with artistic talent. So also with the small arts, at which the Persians excelled: fine metal tableware, jewelry, seal cutting, weaponry and its decoration, and pottery. It has been suggested that the Persians called on the subject peoples for artists because they were themselves crude barbarians with little taste and needed quickly to create an imperial art to match their sudden rise to political power. Yet recent excavations at sites from the protohistoric period show this not to have been the case. Cyrus may have been the leader of Persian tribes not yet so sophisticated nor so civilized as the Babylonians or Egyptians, but when he chose to build Pasargadae, he had a long artistic tradition behind him that was probably already distinctly Iranian and that was in many ways the equal of any. Two examples suffice: the tradition of the columned hall in architecture and fine gold work. The former can now be seen as belonging to an architectural tradition on the Iranian Plateau that extended back through the Median period to at least the beginning of the 1st millennium BC. The rich Achaemenid gold work, which inscriptions suggest may have been a specialty of the Medes, was in the tradition of the delicate metal work found in Iron Age II times at Ḥasanlu and still earlier at Marlik. In its carefully proportioned and well-organized ground plan, rich architectural ornament, and magnificent decorative reliefs, Persepolis, primarily the creation of Darius and Xerxes, is one of the great artistic legacies of the ancient world.

THE ORGANIZATION AND ACHIEVEMENT OF THE EMPIRE

At the centre of the empire sat the king of kings. Around him was gathered a court composed of powerful hereditary landholders, the upper echelons of the army, the harem, religious functionaries, and the bureaucracy that administered the whole. This court lived mainly in Susa but in the hot summer months went to Ecbatana (Hamadan), probably in the spring to Persepolis in Fars, and perhaps sometimes to Babylon. In a smaller version it travelled with the king when he was away in the provinces.

The satraps

The provinces, or satrapies, were ruled by governors (satraps), technically appointed by the central authority but who often became hereditary subkings, particularly in the later years of the empire. They were surrounded and assisted in their functions by a court modelled on that of the central government and were powerful officials. The great king was nevertheless theoretically able to maintain considerable control in local affairs. He was the last court of appeal in judicial matters. He controlled directly the standing military forces stationed in the provinces, though as time went on, the military and civil authority in the provinces tended to become combined under the satrap. The king was also aided in keeping control in the provinces by the so-called king's eyes, or better, the king's ears, officials from the central government who traveled throughout the empire and who reported directly back to the king on what they learned. The number of satrapies and their boundaries varied greatly from time to time; at the beginning of Darius' reign there were 20 provinces. In general, as time went on, the number of satrapies increased, partly because of the need to reassert control over the satraps by decreasing their power base, partly because the feudal structure that underlay Persian society required rewarding more and more people with a role in government, and partly because the original 20 satrapies were undoubtedly simply too large to permit efficient administration.

The army

The army was a particularly important element within the empire. It, too, developed and changed with time. After Cyrus, the Persian tribal levy, based on the responsibility of all male Persians to fight for the king, was replaced by a professional army supplemented by a troop levy from the subject peoples in time of intensive military activity. The elite of the standing army were the 10,000 "immortals" composed of Persians and Medes, 1,000 of whom were the personal guard of the king. The person who controlled this elite, as did Darius on the death of Cambyses, usually controlled all. The troops of the imperial levy fought with the regular army in national units, were armed according to their individual customs, but were usually officered by Persians. Permanent bodies of troops were stationed at strategic points throughout the empire, and, to judge from the garrison at Elephantine in Egypt, these were actually military colonies, firmly settled into the local countryside. Greek mercenaries were used with increasing frequency in later years and many Greeks fought faithfully for Persian silver.

Both the civil and the military administration, as well as public and private trade, were greatly facilitated by the famous royal Achaemenid road system. Communications throughout the empire were better than any previous Near Eastern power had maintained. The famous road from Susa to Sardis in western Asia Minor is the best known of these imperial highways. It was an all-weather road, maintained by the state. Over it ran a governmental postal system based on relay stations with remounts and fresh riders located a day's ride apart. The speed with which a message could travel from the provinces to the king at Susa was remarkable.

On the whole, Persian rule sat lightly on the subject peoples, at least under the early Achaemenids. It was a conscious policy of Cyrus and Darius to permit conquered nations to retain their own religion, customs, their methods of doing business, and even to some extent their forms of government. Cyrus' attitute toward the Babylonians, which led to his being accepted as the rightful successor of Nabonidus, his willingness to permit the Jews to return to Palestine and to their own way of life, and his successors' concern that this promise be honoured; Cambyses' behaviour in Egypt and his acceptance by the Egyptians as founder of a legitimate new Egyptian dynasty; and the policy adopted under Mardonius toward the Ionian cities following their rebellion are all examples of such a policy. Perhaps even too often in the later empire, rebellious peoples, governments, and leaders were forgiven and not suppressed with the thoroughness sometimes characteristic of other regimes. Lapses from this policy, such as Xerxes' violent reaction to rebellion in Babylon, stand out in the record.

Law

Law played an important role in the administration of the empire, and stories of Persian justice abound in the Greek sources. Darius particularly wished to be remembered as the great lawgiver, and law reform was one of the cornerstones in his program for reorganizing the empire. To judge from the Babylonian evidence, two sets of law, possibly administered by two sets of courts, were in force in the provinces. One was the local law undoubtedly based on custom and previous local codifications; the other was the Persian, or imperial law, based ultimately on the authority of the great king. A new word for law appeared in the Near East in Achaemenid times, the Iranian *dāta*, and was borrowed by the Semitic languages used in the empire. In Babylonian and Aramaic, sources give evidence for Persian judges called by the Iranian word, *dāta-bar*. These were probably the judges of the imperial courts. With legal reform came reform and unification of tax structures. The tax structure of the empire was apparently based on the principle that all the conquered lands were the actual property of the king. Thus taxes were rather rents, and the Persians and their land, Fars, by virtue of not being a conquered people, were always tax-free. Each satrapy was required to pay a fixed yearly amount in gold or silver and each vassal state paid a fixed tribute in kind. Again going on the Babylonian evidence, where in previous times agricultural taxes were levied in fixed amounts regardless of the fluctuating quality of the harvest, under Darius all land was surveyed, an estimate of its yield based on an average of the harvests over several years was from time to time established, and taxes were levied in fixed amounts based on a percentage of that average yield. This was not quite an income tax, since it was not based on a percentage of each year's production but was at least a reasonable figure based on a reasonable average production.

Breakdowns often occurred in the Achaemenids' effort to maintain a productive balance between local social structures, customs, laws, and government, and the demand of the empire. The failure of the Persians to find such a balance when dealing with what was, for them, that extremely strange system of social and political organization, the Greek polis, or city-state, probably lay at the heart of their never-ending troubles in Ionia as much as did the power and ambitions of mainland Greeks. Yet even the Ionians, at the best of times, often realized the mutual advantages and benefits of the king's peace and a unified western Asia under a tolerant central administration.

The economy

The economy of the empire was very much founded on that king's peace; it was when the peace broke down with ever-increasing frequency during the last century of Achaemenid rule that the economy of the empire went into a decline that undoubtedly contributed significantly to eventual political and military collapse. Wealth in the Achaemenid world was very much founded on land and on agriculture. Land was the principal reward that the king had available for those who gave service or who were in positions of great political or military power in the empire. Under Darius there was a measure of land called a "bow" that was originally a unit considered sufficient to support one bowman, who then paid his duty for the land in military service. At the other end of the scale were enormous family estates, which often increased in size over the years and which were or became hereditary holdings. They were often administered by absentee landlords. Such major landholdings were, as one would expect, usually in the hands of Iranians, but non-Iranians were also able to amass similar wealth and power, testifying again to the inherent tolerance with which the empire was administered. The Achaemenids themselves took a positive role in the encouragement of agriculture by investing state funds and effort in irrigation and the improvement of horticulture.

They also invested in and endeavoured to encourage trade, a major source of imperial wealth. The effect of the state-maintained road system on the encouragement of trade has already been mentioned. Equal attention was paid to the development of sea-borne trade. State-sponsored voyages of exploration were undertaken in order to search for new markets and new resources. Darius completed a project, begun by the Egyptians, of linking the Nile with the Red Sea by a canal, so that routes across the Arabian Sea and into the Persian Gulf could be used to link the eastern and western ends of his empire. As part of the same program, port development on the Persian Gulf coast was encouraged. An imperial standardization of weights and measures, efforts to encourage the development and use of coinage, and the standardization in the king's name of that coinage were all policies intended to encourage commerce and economic activity within the realm. Banking played a role in the economy. Documents have survived from a family banking business in Babylonia—the house of Murashu and Sons of Nippur—covering the years *c.* 455–403 BC; the firm evidently prospered greatly by lending money and by acting as a middleman in the system of tax collection. Interest rates were high, but borrowers were numerous.

As time went on, there were more and more such borrowers, for the later empire is marked by a general economic decline. The principal cause for this decline was the unsettled political conditions, but other, more indirect causes were unwise government interference in the economy, overtaxation, and the removal of too much hard money from the economy. Gold and silver tended to drain into the treasury of the central government from the provinces, and too little found its way back into the economy. Disastrous inflation was the result. The large sums of money paid to foreign mercenaries and as bribes to foreign governments must have also contributed to an unfavourable balance of payments that in turn stimulated inflation. Such conditions hardly strengthened the empire and must have contributed, in ways that cannot be documented with certainty, to the political unrest that was their own main cause.

The significance of the Achaemenids

Ultimately, the achievement of the Achaemenid Persians was that they ruled with much creative tolerance over an area and a time that, for both the Near East and for Europe, saw the end of the ancient and the beginning of the modern world. In one sense, the ancient Near East died when Cyrus marched into Babylon. Others would argue that its death came when Alexander burned Persepolis. The question remains open. What is clear is that the Achaemenid Empire, the largest anyone had ever yet tried to hold together and one that was not to be surpassed until Rome reached its height, was a profound force in western Asia and in Europe during an important period of ferment and transition in human history. That period witnessed major developments in art, philosophy, literature, historiography, religion, exploration, economics, and science, and those developments provided the direct background for the further changes, along similar lines, that made the Hellenistic period so important in history. Hellenism probably would not have been possible, at least not in the form we know it, if it had had to build directly on the rather more narrow and less ambitious base of the individual civilizations of Bablyon, Egypt, or Greece. In a sense the Achaemenid Persians passed on a concept of empire that, much modified by others, has remained something of a model throughout history of how it is possible for diverse peoples with variant customs, languages, religions, laws, and economic systems to flourish with mutual profit under a central government. In narrower terms, but for the Iranians themselves no less important, the Achaemenid Empire was the beginning of the Iranian nation, one of the pivotal peoples in the modern Near East. (T.C.Y., Jr.)

II. The Hellenistic and Parthian periods

ALEXANDER AND HIS SUCCESSORS

Between 336 and 330 BC Alexander completed the conquest of the whole Achaemenid Empire. (For the story of the conquest see ALEXANDER III THE GREAT.) Alexander's burning of the royal palace at Persepolis in 330 symbolized the passing of the old order and the introduction of Greek civilization into western Asia. Greek and Macedonian soldiers settled in large numbers in Mesopotamia and Iran. Alexander encouraged intermarriage and fostered Greek culture, but he also retained a large part of the Achaemenid administrative structure and introduced Oriental elements and Greek political institutions.

Alexander left no heir. His death in 323 BC signalled the beginning of a period of prolonged internecine warfare among the Macedonian generals for control of his enormous empire. By the end of the 4th century BC Seleucus I Nicator had consolidated his control over that part of Alexander's territory that had corresponded to the Achaemenid Empire (see also SELEUCID KINGDOM).

Seleucus, who, with his son Antiochus I, assumed supreme power, established a government with two capitals: Antioch on the Orontes River in Syria and Seleucia on the Tigris River in Babylonia. The greatest part of Asia—from the Aegean to the Punjab—belonged to this vast kingdom, and to its diverse and varied populace must be added several allied Greek cities, both in Greece and in Asia Minor.

The nobles and the nomads. As he was finishing the conquest of eastern Iran—and at a moment when his attention was being drawn toward the conquest of India—Alexander was confronted by two human factors that were of the greatest importance for the future of his empire. The first of these was the powerful local aristocracy of this part of the Achaemenid Empire, an aristocracy that held enormous properties and dominated the indigenous population; the second was the nomad population that for centuries had wandered along the northern and northeastern frontiers of Iran.

Alexander and the Iranian nobility

Alexander seems to have admired greatly the barons of eastern Iran; he had taken note of their ardour during the two years of hard and constant fighting in his conquest of northeastern Iran. Realizing how such a force could benefit the future of his empire, Alexander convoked an assembly of Bactrian nobles. He ordered 30,000 young men to be chosen for training in the Macedonian military disciplines. He understood the importance of the Iranian light cavalry armed with the bow, and his army would make use of this training in its march toward the plains of India. And finally, he married Roxana of Sogdiana, daughter of a chief of one of the conquered countries, symbolizing the union of the two races.

But Alexander was not unaware that other measures were needed to ensure his control of these vast territories. He founded many new cities, or refounded some already in existence. Many of these were placed along the northern frontiers as protection. Almost half of these new cities were located in the "high (eastern) satrapies." This policy of Alexander's was soon abandoned by the Seleucids, whose efforts at city planning were mostly confined to their western possessions.

In contrast with Alexander, the Seleucids were unable to maintain the good rapport with the eastern Iranian nobility that Alexander had believed essential. And this deficiency, a result of the Seleucids' "pro-Macedonian" policies, was one of the principal causes for the progressive decline of the Seleucid Empire.

The second of the human factors was the nomads who inhabited the immense territories beyond the northern frontiers. They fought constantly with the settled populations, but could nevertheless occasionally ally with them in the face of necessity. When Alexander arrived on the banks of the Jaxartes River, it marked the limit of the "civilized" world; beyond stretched the Eurasian wilderness. The Roman historian Quintus Curtius recounts Alexander's meeting with a delegation of Scythians who gave him a warning. They told him,

> Just cross the Tanais [properly the Jaxartes] and you will see how far Scythia stretches. You will never conquer the Scythians. Our poverty makes us quicker than your army, which bears plunder from so many nations. Just when you think we are far away, then will you see us in your camp. We know how to pursue and how to flee with the same swiftness. [One recalls here the famous "Parthian shot."] We seek out those deserts totally devoid of human culture rather than the cities and the rich countryside.

These words sum up what the nomad world represented to an empire that stretched several thousand miles from east to west. The non-nomad population knew the threat only too well. Alexander was not the first to cross swords with the nomads. Cyrus, founder of the Achaemenid Empire, had paid with his life while fighting them; and Darius, believing he could take them from behind through southern Russia, suffered a crushing defeat in his campaign against the Scythians along the shores of the Black Sea.

If the nomads and the eastern Iranian nobility were the two dominant factors in the decline of the Seleucid kingdom, and if the events they provoked were some of the principal causes for the exhaustion and eventual fall of that state, these same causes played a not inconsiderable role in the collapse of Parthian power. This power was undermined by an aristocracy that retained its military power and refused to bend before the royal will or to give up its meddling in the country's politics.

In the meantime, the kingdom's unruly neighbours to the north and the northeast, at the cost of the lives of several Parthian sovereigns, weakened the kingdom and sometimes added a complementary element to the often numerous intrigues of the pretenders to supreme power during the course of the almost half a millennium of the existence of the Parthian kingdom.

The Seleucids. In the struggle for power after Alexander's death, Seleucus I brought under his control the whole eastern part of Alexander's empire. But even before he had consolidated his control over this territory, the eastern provinces on the Indian frontier had begun to revolt. By about 304 BC Seleucus was forced to abandon these to Candragupta Maurya, the founder of the great Indian Maurya Empire. This was a serious loss to the Seleucids, for they lost not only the Indian territory conquered by Alexander but also frontier districts west of the Indus. As recompense for his losses, Seleucus received 500 elephants, which he took back with him to Syria. From this time on, the west was dominant in the Seleucids' politics to the detriment of their eastern possessions. This near disinterest of the Seleucids in these far-off eastern regions must have alienated the Greeks of these communities who had settled far from their homeland; and the thought of taking back their full independence could not have been far from their minds.

Loss of eastern provinces

Soon afterward, toward 290–280 BC, the two eastern provinces of Margiana and Aria suffered an invasion by nomads. But the invasion was repelled and the nomads pushed back beyond the Jaxartes. Demodamas, general to the first two Seleucid kings, crossed the river and even put up altars to Apollo, ancestor of the dynasty. Alexandria of Margiana and Heraclea of Aria, founded by Alexander, were rebuilt by Antiochus I under the names of Antioch and Achaea, and a wall nearly 100 miles (160 kilometres) long was put up to protect the oasis of Merv against future invasions, the menace of which was never far. Patrocles received a commission to explore the Caspian Sea.

Seleucus I and his successors hoped to Hellenize Asia and held the conviction that the Greeks and Macedonians were a superior race and the bearers of a superior civilization. A network of cities and military colonies was built to assure the stability of a state whose inhabitants would be Asians. The Greek language made deep inroads, especially among the families of those numerous Greeks who married the local women and among those engaged in commerce. But after the 2nd century BC and the slowing of the Greco-Macedonian immigration, the Greek language lost ground and the local element became dominant.

The people of Iran, particularly those in the upper stratum of society, borrowed nothing from Hellenism but its exterior forms. Even the Iranians who lived in such cities as Seleucia or Susa do not seem to have been deeply affected by Greek ideas.

Superficial Hellenization

The movement of Iranian peoples. The victories of Alexander had brought the Greeks to the limits of the known world. But less than a century after Alexander's death there began a great movement back, propelled by stirring of peoples in the Iranian world. In a movement westward, and from the 3rd century BC, the Sarmatians occupied the northern shore of the Black Sea. While driving back their close relatives, the Scythians, they succeeded in "sarmatizing" the Greek cities along its shores. At the end of the 3rd century, there began in Chinese Turkistan a long migration of the Yüeh-chih, an Iranian people who about 130 BC invaded Bactria, putting an end to the Greco-Bactrian kingdom there. (In the 1st century AD they created the Kushan (Kuṣāṇa) Empire, which extended from Afghanistan to the Ganges and from Russian Turkistan to the estuary of the Indus.) Finally, in the mid-3rd century BC, taking a median direction between the other two movements described, the Parni, a nomadic or seminomadic people from the confines of Iran, took over the Seleucid satrapy of Parthia and created the Parthian kingdom. Restoring Achaemenid power for nearly half a millennium, the arrival of the Parthian state coincided with the expansion of Rome and played a role of the greatest significance in the destinies of the world during the three centuries before Christ and the two centuries that followed.

Revolt of the high satrapies. The empire of the Seleucids, like that of the Achaemenids before them, was shaken by revolts of the satraps. The difficult situation in the west and the grave reverses suffered by the royal house accelerated the weakening of the Macedonian kingdom. The loss of its eastern possessions in the third quarter of the 3rd century BC proved fatal to the Seleucid cause. Andragoras, satrap of Parthia, led a revolt about 245 BC; and Diodotus, a Greek who found himself at the head of the satrapy of Bactria, followed his example about 239 BC. About a year later the Parni, led by their chief, Arsaces, invaded Parthia.

Parthia was the first province to detach itself from the Seleucid Empire, just as it had been the first to rise up on the occasion of the accession of Darius the Great. Andragoras, although he did not declare himself king, showed his independence by minting his own coins. At this time Parthia was one of the poorer of the high satrapies. Caught between the mountains and the great central desert, without large agricultural resources, this satrapal independence might seem surprising if it were not for the fact that the main route for the silk trade crossed right through Parthia over a distance more than 100 miles. The tolls the caravans paid must have produced a sizable income.

Parthian independence

The defection of Diodotus is still easier to understand. Bactria, a vast country of a "thousand cities," was located at the junction of the routes to China and India, and it was rich in cultivable land. The Greco-Bactrian kingdom founded by Diodotus expanded rapidly, embracing Sogdiana, Aria, and extending southward and southeastward.

Being at some distance from the west, Diodotus and his successors adopted little by little the customs and life styles of their subjects. The closer these ties were drawn, the stronger became the loyalty of the Bactrians. It is believed that the separation of Diodotus from the Seleucids might, over the long term, have seemed to the Bactrians and Sogdians as the realization of their national destiny, and they might have looked on these satraps as men acting in their interest. For more than a century (230–130 BC) this kingdom held the frontiers and barred the route to the nomads.

THE RISE OF THE PARTHIANS

Invasion of the Parni. Arsaces, who was chief of the Parni, a member tribe of the Dahae confederation, must have begun his struggle against the Seleucids from 247 BC, the year from which the Parthians dated their history. This does not necessarily mean that Arsaces was crowned king in 247. Other Iranian dynasties (*e.g.*, the Sāsānids; see below) dated the beginning of their eras from the time when they began to establish their power rather than from the time of coronation of the first monarch of their line.

Daho-Parno-Parthian tribes "chose chiefs for war and princes for peace" from among the closest circle of the princely family. They were famous for their breeding of horses, for their combat cavalry, and for their fine archers. Alexander encountered them during his Bactrian campaign, and the Greek writers who recorded his reign remarked on their agility and effectiveness as horsemen. They were a people who kept the traditions of patriarchal tribal organization. The Parni, with Arsaces at their head, took the province of Parthia after having beaten Andragoras; soon, neighbouring Hyrcania was annexed and the Caspian reached. Arsaces had himself crowned in the city of Asaak, and the tribe took the name of the Parthians, their close relatives, a name that meant "exiled." Their language was closely related to Scythian and Median. The dynasty these people produced never broke its links with the people, and rare was the Arsacid dynastic sovereign who did not turn to his people in time of danger.

Formation of the Parthian state. The two new kingdoms, that of Arsaces I's Parthians and the Greco-Bactrian kingdom of Diodotus, sprang up almost simultaneously and very near each other; there were, however, notable differences between them. The motivating force behind the rebellion in Bactria was an association—or perhaps even a collaboration—between the local nobility (large landholders who dominated the whole indigenous population) and the local Greek community. Both groups were opposed to the Macedonian domination represented by the Seleucid dynasty.

Relations with the nomads

The makeup of the Parthian kingdom seems to have been different. It was essentially built on the relationship of the inhabitants of Parthia to the neighbouring tribes outside the static frontiers, an ethnic mass, half nomad, half settled, that inhabited the north of Iran. The success of Arsaces and his men was based on their strength, their spirit, and the weakness of their enemies. The Greek element present in Parthia does not seem to have played a role similar to that played by their counterparts in Bactria. In fact the Parthians, at least initially, may have been hostile to the local Greek populations. During their war with the Seleucid king Antiochus III (see below), they massacred all the Greek inhabitants of the city of Syrinx in Hyrcania.

Arsaces. Arsaces seems to have enjoyed great fame among the tribes. His name remained linked with the names of the sovereigns of this dynasty, who succeeded each other for the four and a half centuries of the Parthian state. His image regularly appeared on the obverse of Parthian coins right down to the end of the period.

The rupture of the communications link between the Seleucid capitals and the east caused by Arsaces' success placed Diodotus in a difficult situation. He seems to have wanted to collaborate with Seleucus II in a campaign he was preparing against the Parthians. The death of Diodotus (*c.* 234 BC) and the succession of his son, Diodotus II, reversed matters, for the young successor changed his father's policy and joined with Arsaces. It was not until 232 or 231 BC that Seleucus arrived in the east to put down the rebellion. Arsaces, who had remained closely allied with the nomads to the north, sensing his own weakness in the face of Seleucus' army, fled to the home of the Apasiacae, or "Scythians of the Waters." Seleucus II tried to cross the Jaxartes but, having suffered losses at the hands of the nomads, decided to return to Syria after receiving alarming news from the west. He made peace with Arsaces, who recognized his suzerainty.

From this time on, Arsaces changed his policy: he no longer acted as a nomad but rather as a chief of state, a worthy successor to the Seleucids, whose example he followed. He had himself crowned; besides Asaak and Dara (an impregnable fortress), he founded such cities as Nisa, where he would be buried. These new cities were usually named after the king or the dynasty. Arsaces seems not to have infringed upon the rights of the Greeks and Macedonians living in these cities, perhaps hoping to win their support. From the beginning, while maintaining the autonomy of the cities, he made use of propaganda to ensure their continuing obedience. He installed his capital at Hecatompylos, on the silk route. His death is dated between 217 and 211 BC.

Founding of new cities

Artabanus. His successor, Artabanus I (sometimes known as Arsaces II, reigned *c.* 211–191), continued the work of consolidation. Being already solidly established in Parthia and Hyrcania, Artabanus tried to extend his possessions toward Media. But events in the neighbouring Greco-Bactrian kingdom worked against him: Diodotus II lost his throne, accused, it is thought, of treason to Hellenism through his alliance with the nomads. His throne had passed to Euthydemus when the Syrian army of Antiochus III arrived in Hyrcania.

The wave of revolts by the eastern satraps, which began a movement away from unity in the state, also affected western Iran. The beginning of the reign of the young Antiochus III the Great (223–187 BC) was marked by the dissidence of Molon and his brother Alexander, satraps of Media and Persis. Antiochus III did not undertake his campaign for recovery of the high satrapies—a project his father had planned and never carried out—until 212 BC.

It is admitted that at this time his kingdom in the east did not stretch farther than Media, Persis, Susiana, and Carmania. His operations against Artabanus I were successful; he took Hecatompylos and crossed the mountains separating that province from Parthia, which he occupied. Artabanus, in spite of a lively resistance, fled and took refuge with the friendly Apasiacae, as had his father, Arsaces I. The conflict between the Seleucids and Parthia, however, was ended by a compromise, just as it had been at the time of the invasion of Seleucus II. A much more important struggle against the Bactrian kingdom of Euthydemus awaited Antiochus III. He preferred to make peace with Artabanus, to whom he accorded the title of king in exchange for recognition of his fealty, and obliged the Parthian to send troops to reinforce the Syrian army. The rear of the Seleucid king was safeguarded, but the two provinces held by Artabanus were definitively lost by the Macedonians.

The period following Antiochus' campaign was marked by a strong resistance by the Bactrian cavalry at the frontier and by the siege of Bactra, for two years the capital (208–207 BC). There, too, the Seleucid king made peace with Euthydemus, who, like Artabanus, kept his title of king. Demetrius, son of Euthydemus, married a daughter of Antiochus the Great, thus preserving his political prestige.

Having acquired war elephants and provisions for his army in Bactria, Antiochus crossed the Hindu Kush into the Kabul Valley, where he concluded a pact with the Indian king Sophagasenos, secured still more elephants, and returned by way of southern Iran. The results of this long campaign were meagre. Antiochus recognized the independence of two kingdoms, that of the Parthians and that of Euthydemus, which had been no more than satrapies. The struggle must have weakened these two, but after receiving legalization of their status, the two states proceeded to the reestablishment of their material and military resources.

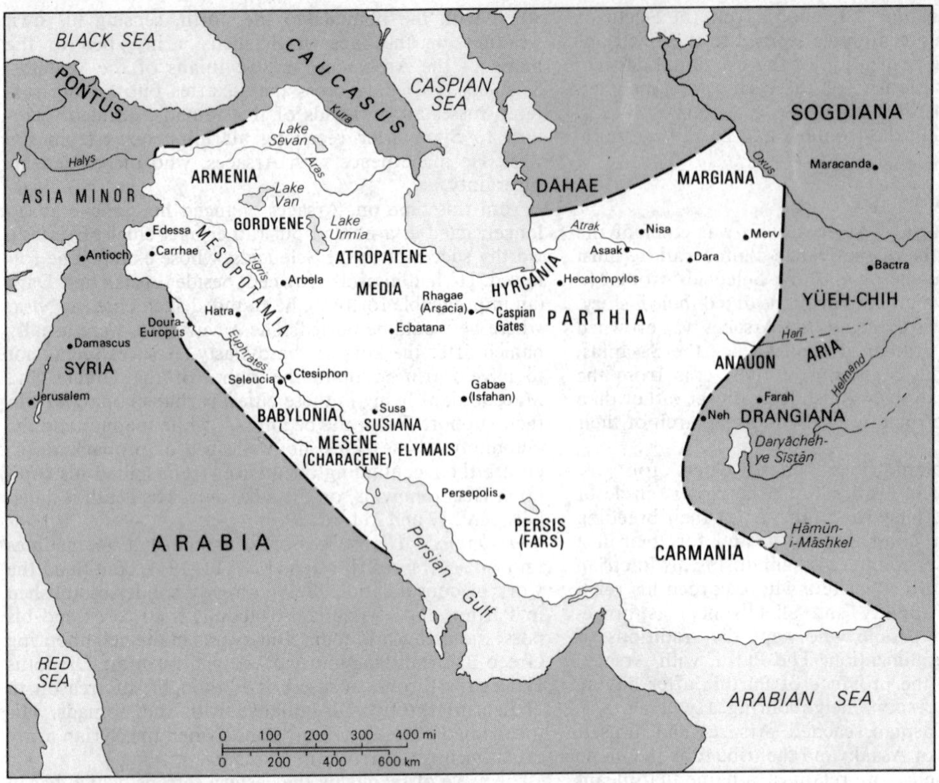

The Parthian Empire in the 1st century BC.
From *Grosser Historischer Weltatlas*, vol. I, *Vorgeschichte und Altertum* (1972); Bayerischer Schulbuch-Verlag, Munich

Phraates I. Precise information is not available concerning the reign of Priapatius (*c.* 191–176 BC), who succeeded Artabanus and whose name appears in documents found in excavations at Nisa. Under his son Phraates I (*c.* 176–171 BC), the young Parthian kingdom seems to have recuperated sufficiently to have taken up once again its expansionist activities. It attacked Media and was successful in the conquest of the Mardi tribe near the Caspian and set up a defense of the "Caspian Gates," an important strategic point of penetration in Phraates' possessions. Overturning tribal tradition, which reserved the succession to the throne to the eldest son, he designated as a successor—even though he had several sons—his brother Mithradates. His choice was no mistake.

Parthian expansion

THE "PHIL-HELLENISTIC" PERIOD (C. 171 BC–AD 10)

The accession of Mithradates I opens a new period in the destinies of the kingdom, which historians call "phil-Hellenistic" and which lasted from the accession of this prince (*c.* 171 BC) until *c.* AD 10. This period was characterized by a strong Hellenistic cultural influence, manifested in the use of the Greek language and in particular in the arts, where, however, national traditions were not completely abandoned.

Mithradates I. From the accession of Mithradates I an expansion of Parthian power in the military, political, and economic domains was manifest. The king began with an attack on the Greco-Bactrian kingdom, which was going through a period of weakness; then he turned against the west and declared himself independent of the Seleucids. To show his complete independence—the first of the Parthian sovereigns to do so—he began issuing coins bearing his likeness, wearing a royal diadem like the Seleucid kings. On the reverse side was a representation of Arsaces, ancestor of the dynasty, seated on an omphalos (hemispheric altar) and holding a bow, in imitation of Seleucid coins that showed Apollo in the same way, as the ancestor of the Seleucids.

The action Antiochus IV Epiphanes undertook against Mithradates ended with the death of Antiochus at Gabae (probably present Isfahan). His death brought a widespread dislocation of the Macedonian kingdom, which crumbled into several smaller states. Toward 160 BC most of the "high satrapies" and the eastern satrapies were apparently lost to the Seleucids. The power that could unite them into one could only be that of the Parthians, who, under Mithradates I, began the assault. In 155 BC Media was occupied, which opened the route to Mesopotamia. In 148–147 BC Mithradates reached Ecbatana, where he moved his capital. Rhagae was "refounded" and given the dynastic name of Arsacia. In 141 BC Mithradates took Seleucia on the Tigris and was recognized king of Babylonia. His forces conquered Susiana and Elymais, either at this time or after 139. In the same year (141), he was obliged to leave Hyrcania for his eastern possessions, which were evidently being menaced by hostile movements of the nomads. There he spent the remainder of his reign.

Demetrius II, probably acquainted with Mithradates' difficulties in the east, undertook an effort to retrieve the situation and recover Mesopotamia, but after a few successes he suffered defeat and was taken prisoner (139 BC). Sent to Hyrcania, he was married there to a daughter of Mithradates, who, by this union, became related to the house of Seleucus. The army of Demetrius included Greco-Bactrian and Elymaian troops—which is understandable—as well as men from Persis, or Persians, who by their cooperation with the Macedonians seem to indicate their opposition to the expansionism of the Parthians, whom they considered foreigners and conquerors. Persia under the Parthians was an empire, but not yet a nation.

Persian resistance to Parthia

Phraates II. Like his father, Mithradates I, Phraates was to remain for some time in the eastern provinces. He was also to endure a last Macedonian attempt to break the Parthian advance. Antiochus VII Sidetes, brother of Demetrius II, who had been taken prisoner, assembled a powerful army, which once more included men of Persis and Elymais. The strength in numbers and the wealth of this army made an impression on contemporaries, who reported that even the simple soldiers wore shoes cobbled with gold. Phraates was beaten in several battles, but time worked on his side. With the arrival of winter, Antiochus quartered his troops in several localities in Media. The local population, exasperated by the undisciplined Syrian soldiery, rose up in revolt. Antiochus was killed and his son taken prisoner (129 BC). Thanks to the loyalty of the Medians, whose sentiments contrasted with those of the Persians, Phraates was victorious. The year 129 BC was a turning point in the history of the eastern Mediterranean: Greco-Macedonian domination received a decisive blow, which it would survive for only 46 years.

The route to great acquisitions in the west seemed to open before Phraates, if the nomads did not stop him. Weakened in his struggle against Antiochus VII, he called upon the Śaka nomads to the north of his frontiers for aid, promising them payment. The reinforcements arrived too late to be of use; he sent them back which provoked them to revolt and pillage the countryside. The Greek prisoners drafted by Phraates into his army participated in the pillage, and Phraates lost his life fighting them. The same fate was reserved for his successor and uncle, Artabanus II (*c.* 128–124/123). The Śakas were pushed back with some difficulty toward Drangiana, to which they gave their name Seistan (Sakastan). Another branch of the vast nomad movement crossed the Oxus and put an end to the Greco-Bactrian kingdom, on the ruins of which the powerful kingdom of the Kushans was to be built.

The second stage of the phil-Hellenistic period extends from the first quarter of the 2nd century until about 30 BC and embraces a period when Parthia reached the apogee of its power and worldwide territorial expansion.

Mithradates II. The reign of this prince constitutes the most glorious chapter of Parthian history. It put an end to the ambitions of Artabanus' son Himerus, left by his father as governor of Mesopotamia, and brought back Hyspaosines, king of Characene, who had extended his possessions too far toward the north, into submission. In the east, the Śakas were on the move—soon an independent state would be formed there that would push toward eastern Iran and India; in the 1st century BC, two dynasties, the Indo-Scythian and the Indo-Parthian, whose members would remain closely linked to the Arsacid dynasty, were to reign in this region. They would disappear after having been absorbed by the kingdom of the Kushans.

The eastern frontiers of Mithradates II incorporated Margiana and Aria. Once order was restored in the east, the King turned toward the west: he placed Tigranes II the Great on the throne of Armenia, and, extending his hegemony over this kingdom and over eastern Asia Minor, he organized pressure on the last Seleucids; among them, a pretender, Demetrius III, was taken prisoner. A meeting with Rome, which had already formed a "Province of Asia" in Asia Minor, became inevitable and took place in 92 BC on the Euphrates between the Roman general Sulla and the Parthian ambassador Orobaze. Mithradates II wisely refused to agree to follow in the Roman path and preferred to retain his neutrality in the struggle between Rome and Mithradates VI of Pontus. Rome in the west and Parthia in the east met as Alexander's successors and, with a common accord, settled the inheritance. The two parties recognized the Euphrates as a common frontier. It seems there was no longer a question either of an alliance or of a signed convention. Upon his return, Orobaze paid with his head for the *lèsemajesté* he had committed by accepting a seat lower than Sulla's at their meeting.

Relations with China

For the first time, Parthian power entered into direct contact with the Chinese empire and received an embassy from the Han emperor Wu Ti (140–87 BC), who dispatched to meet them an escort of 20,000 men. The Chinese were particularly interested in the horses raised in Fergana, which they needed to create a cavalry to fight the nomadic Hsiung-nu, or Huns, on their northern border.

At the zenith of his power, Mithradates II took the title of "king of kings"; in the East, as well as in the West, his empire achieved a position of a power and stability previously unknown. He maintained diplomatic relations with the two greatest world powers, Rome and China. Mithradates I, Phraates II, and Mithradates II were the true creators of the Parthian state, winning for it military and economic victories and raising it to a level comparable to that of the Achaemenid Empire. After the death of Mithradates II, a short period of intrigue and rivalry saw the succession, in turn, of Gotarzes, Orodes I, and Sanatruces. The latter came to power late in life and was replaced in 70 BC by his son, Phraates III (70–58/57 BC), under whom took place sustained contacts with Rome. (For the background of the Roman advance, see ROME, HISTORY OF.)

Wars with Rome. The Roman general Lucullus, in charge of looking after Roman interests in the East (69 BC), hoped to lure Phraates III into an alliance that would help Rome in its struggle against Pontus and Armenia, but the Parthian king, while still maintaining "friendly" relations with Rome, retained his neutrality. An agreement with the Romans renewed the Euphrates line as a frontier. Three years later, in 66 BC, the Roman general Pompey replaced Lucullus and succeeded in concluding a real alliance with Phraates III. This proved, however, to be of short duration, for affairs in Armenia, aggravated by Roman operations on Parthian territory, had brought the two empires to a parting of the ways. To Phraates' protestations Pompey replied with the occupation of Gordyene, a vassal state of the Parthians, and treated with Phraates using the simple title "king." Pompey did not trouble himself over entering into direct relations with the sovereigns of Media and Elymais, vassals of Phraates. The position taken by the Romans toward the king of kings was rather more like that of conquerors than of allies. Pompey's policy became clear: from the Caucasus to the Persian Gulf he hoped to create a wall of states friendly to Rome that would encircle Parthia, in preparation for Roman conquest.

That action fell within the jurisdiction of the Roman triumvir Crassus. As early as 57 BC a conflict with Rome broke out over the case of Mithradates III (58/57–55 BC) who, opposing Orodes II (*c.* 57–37/36 BC), his brother, a parricide like himself of their father Phraates III, fled to Syria and asked the legate Gabinius for aid and asylum. The Roman Senate forbade Gabinius to involve himself in the dispute over the succession to the Parthian throne. Three years later the tension between the two powers was settled in bloody fashion, and the rupture consummated in 53 BC. Without provocation, the army of Crassus—the only one of the triumvirs with Caesar without military glory (Caeser was conqueror of Gaul, and Pompey conqueror of the Near East)—crossed the Euphrates. Orodes II protested and invoked the treaty of friendship in vain. Crassus refused to reply until he arrived at Seleucia on the Tigris. It was a brutal breaking of all the agreements concluded in 69 and 66 BC.

The Battle of Carrhae

The battle near Carrhae (53 BC), led by Surenas with his light and heavy cavalry, cost Rome seven legions and the lives of Crassus and his son. Through Surenas' brilliant victory the routes to Iran and India were closed to Rome, and its ambitions in the Orient were so weakened that the Euphrates became not only a political but also a spiritual frontier; no effort at latinization was possible any longer. A united Greco-Iranian Asia front protected against the Romanization of Iranianized Hellenism and destroyed the myth of Roman invincibility.

The insignia of the Roman legions fell into Parthian hands, and 10,000 Roman prisoners were sent into captivity in Margiana. The victory over Crassus had great repercussions among the peoples of the East. It shook the Roman position in Asia Minor, Syria, and Palestine, while it restored the Parthians' confidence in their power and in their ability to resist Rome, promising them a dominant position among the peoples of the East. According to the Greek writer Plutarch, the severed head of Crassus was brought to Orodes like a hunting trophy while he was attending a presentation of Euripides' play *The Bacchae*.

The Parthian counterthrust in 52–50 BC under the command of Prince Pacorus (Pakores) was not crowned with success. The Arsacid army did not know how to organize long campaigns or how to lay siege to fortified cities. But soon, civil war in Rome reinforced the position of the

Parthians, and Pompey, after being defeated by Caesar, thought of taking refuge among them. It is thought that Orodes, taking advantage of this lull, succeeded in resolving difficulties in the east with the Yüeh-chih, or even perhaps the Kushans. In 48 BC, with Pompey dead, Caesar was absolute master of the Roman world and was preparing to revenge Crassus' defeat when he was assassinated in 44 BC. The duty of following through on Caesar's project fell to Mark Antony. Pacorus, anticipating Antony, crossed into Syria after having concluded an agreement with Quintus Labienus, a Roman commander on the side of Caesar's assassins who had gone over to the Parthians. The successes of the two armies were startling: Labienus took all of Asia Minor, Pacorus all of Syria and Palestine. For nearly two years all the western provinces of the Achaemenids remained in Parthian hands. In Rome it was rumoured that the Parthians were planning to invade Italy itself. But the successes of the Arsacid armies were as ephemeral as they were remarkable. Disagreement between the two generals weakened their effect. In 39 BC Labienus was conquered and slain. Asia Minor was recovered by the Romans, and the following year the same fate struck Pacorus and his conquests.

The defeat of Pacorus and Labienus

Under Orodes II the Parthians had reached the zenith of their power: in the west, the Arsacids had for a short time re-established the empire of the Achaemenids almost in its entirety. Their successes in the east seem to have been equally important. Their capital was moved to Ctesiphon, where the military camp was transformed into a great metropolis, facing Seleucia across the Tigris. At Nisa the city was expanded, the royal palaces made larger, and the royal hypogea were enriched with precious pieces of fine Greco-Iranian art.

In 37 BC Orodes was assassinated by his son Phraates IV, who also did away with his brothers and his eldest son. In 36 BC Mark Antony began to carry out the revenge Caesar had planned. He brought his army to Armenia, through which he planned to enter Media and attack Parthia from the north. But cold weather and Phraates' cavalry combined to force Antony to abandon the fight and return to Syria. In 34 BC he launched another campaign and again suffered heavy losses, and his power struggle with Octavian forced him to abandon his plans for war against the Parthians.

Toward 30 BC Tiridates II, a pretender to the throne of Parthia supported by Rome, obliged Phraates IV to leave Mesopotamia and take refuge with his eastern neighbours, the Scythians, who restored him to power. Driven out, Tiridates took refuge at Rome. He returned again in 28–27 BC, after which Phraates was able to definitively re-establish his power at the same time Octavian was inaugurating the imperial period of Roman history.

Settlement with Rome. The new stage in the phil-Hellenistic period began toward 31 BC, when, after his victory over Antony, Octavian (now Augustus) was sole master in Rome. Before that, however, he had already proposed to Phraates an alliance and a treaty ending the war. The Battle of Carrhae and Antony's defeat raised Parthia to a major power in the eyes of Rome. A renewed "friendship" would permit the return of Roman prisoners and insignia. Augustus put pressure on Phraates through the pretender Tiridates and even tried military intervention. In the end a pact was signed in 20 BC that allowed the return of Roman prisoners and the insignia of the conquered legions. A new stage began in relations between the two states, marked by the conclusion of a real peace that recognized the Euphrates as a frontier between them. Phraates IV was dealt with as the sovereign of a great nation. Rome renounced its ambitions in the east, and Augustus inaugurated a policy of respect. The two states could do nothing but profit from the agreement, for a defeat would have been fatal to either power, and a victory hazardous. The caravan route to India and China was opened. Augustus received ambassadors from the many eastern peoples, including the Indo-Scythians and the Sarmatians. The only country in the east where Rome remained active was Armenia.

Recognition of the Euphrates frontier

All obstacles, however, were not necessarily eliminated. There remained the question of Armenia, which, if controlled by Rome, would be a channel for penetration into Parthia from the north, but if controlled by Parthia would offer an outlet on the Black Sea, over which Rome asserted its authority. The rivalry of the two powers over this country would remain for centuries a stumbling block to peace.

Toward 10 or 9 BC Phraates sent his four sons and grandsons to Rome, a gesture that must be understood as one of confidence in a "friendly" power but also as a guarantee that his throne would pass to his son by Musa, an Italian slave girl given him by Augustus. This son, Phraates V, would assassinate his father with his mother's help and occupy the throne from 2 BC to AD 4 after having married his mother.

The end of this "phil-Hellenistic" period is marked by the clash of the ruling class with foreign influences that had penetrated life in Parthian society. These influences came from Rome and were often introduced by princes of the Arsacid house returning from stays abroad. The short reign of Orodes III (AD 4–6/7) was followed by that of Vonones (7/8–11), son of Phraates IV, who because of his Roman habits was driven out by the Parthian nobility, whose role at this time became dominant in internal politics and dynastic questions. Vonones' fall brought a change in the destinies of the country.

THE "ANTI-HELLENISTIC" PERIOD (AD 2–162)

The new and very important period in Parthian history, often called "anti-Hellenistic," embraces a century and a half, from AD 2 to 162. It is characterized by an expansion of the Parthian national culture and an opposition to all things foreign. The weakness of the reigning dynasty opened wide avenues to the nobility to involve themselves in the official existence of the state. They chose the sovereign whose reign opened the first stage in this new period.

Rise of the nobles

Artabanus III. The king chosen by the barons to replace Vonones was Artabanus III (12–38). They were certainly mistaken in believing they would find in him an easy instrument to manipulate. Artabanus was the son of a viceroy of Hyrcania and was only Arsacid on his mother's side. Under his rule Parthia entered a brilliant but troubled era, one completely dominated by the personality of this violently anti-Roman sovereign, who was eager to drive Rome out of Asia. After an abortive attempt to place his son on the throne of Armenia. Artabanus avoided precipitating matters with Rome and dedicated himself to internal reforms, among which centralization occupied the place of first importance.

The humbling of the great nobles, an enterprise in which he was sustained by the lesser nobles, became necessary. He had to reduce the hereditary privileges the barons had carved out for themselves. It was also necessary to reorganize the states that made up the kingdom. He put princes of his family on the various thrones of these states: Mesene, Persis, Elymais, Atropatene, all these little states were governed by men loyal to the throne. But it proved impossible for him to put down a revolt in the eastern possessions, where the Indo-Parthian king Gondophares declared himself independent (*c.* 19) and took the title "king of kings."

It is thought that the position taken toward the city-states, about which precise information is lacking, was the reason for the seven-year long revolt of Seleucia on the Tigris. The fighting took place there between the Greek and Hellenized elements and the Semites, who demanded their right to participate in the autonomy of the city and who supported pretenders against Artabanus III.

A new attempt to place a son on the throne in Armenia angered Rome, which, with the aid of the nobility, sent for Tiridates III, a pretender the barons had crowned at Ctesiphon, obliging Artabanus III to take refuge with the Dahae, who helped him win back his throne. In 37 a meeting with a representative of Rome on a bridge in the middle of the Euphrates allowed an agreement to be reached that maintained the status quo in Armenia and recognized the Parthian sovereignty with the river as the frontier.

The strong personality of Artabanus III did not seek to impose his kingdom as a world power, but he did not hesitate to make plans to regain the western province, the former Achaemenid possessions.

Dissolution of the Parthian state. The period from 51 to 122 shows a slow dissolution of the Parthian state and its decomposition into several small countries. This was an inevitable result of the weakness of the central power. In the 1st century AD the Parthian Empire, according to the Roman historian Pliny, was composed of 18 kingdoms, 11 in the north and seven in the south, some governed by Arsacid princes and others by local dynasties. In 58 Hyrcania became independent. In the realm of external affairs an effort was made to maintain good relations with Rome, especially because of the new kingdom of the Kushans, which was causing concern on the eastern frontiers. It might be for this reason that in 87 Parthia sent an embassy to neighbouring China to the east of the Kushans. Internally, the nationalistic upsurge became more accentuated.

Pliny's description of Parthia

After the short reign of Vonones II (51), the throne passed to Vologases I (51–77/78), an ardent anti-Roman. One of his brothers, Vonones, was made king of Media. Vologases I wanted his second brother, Tiridates, to be king of Armenia, which put him in the position of a break with Rome, which opposed him militarily. Upon orders from Nero, Corbulo undertook operations broken off by the exchange of ambassadors. An agreement was finally reached: in 66 Tiridates left for Rome with his whole family surrounded by a retinue of princes and 3,000 Parthian nobles. He received from Nero the crown of Armenia, and an end to hostilities was announced by the closing of the doors to the Temple of Janus.

Nationalist sentiment, which under Artabanus III had found expression in the invention of a genealogical table proving the Achaemenid descent of the Arsacid house, manifested itself under Vologases I by the compilation of the Avesta, the holy book of the Iranians, and by the issuance of coins on which, for the first time, Pahlavi characters were added to the Greek legend.

In 78 Pacorus II came to the throne, to be replaced in 79 by the ephemeral Artabanus IV (80/81), who was then replaced permanently by Pacorus II. During his reign the country showed signs of a profound decomposition. The barons refused to obey the crown. In the provinces the army and finances were in the hands of the nobility. Aristocrats occupied the highest positions, and these positions became hereditary. Plots with Rome were hatched, and the nobility felt itself the equal of the dynasty, ready to revolt in defense of their privileges. Externally, the dynasty was unable to count on Rome, which constantly plotted in support of new pretenders. In 109/110 Pacorus II was replaced by Osroes, his brother or brother-in-law.

Invasion of Trajan

In 114 the emperor Trajan invaded Armenia. In vain did the King put his crown at Trajan's feet—he was defeated by the Roman soldiery. With Armenia occupied, the Emperor descended with his army into Mesopotamia. All Babylonia was taken and Ctesiphon, the capital, fell into the hands of the Romans, who carried off a daughter of Osroes and the golden throne of the Parthian kings. Victorious, Trajan went as far as the Persian Gulf. Iranian reaction was not late in coming. Faced with the gravity of the Roman offensive, all the princes of the royal house, formerly divided by internal strife, united against the invader. At Ctesiphon Trajan crowned a new vassal king, but revolt was in the wind and attempts to disunite the Parthian chiefs failed. The Romans suffered losses, and, after a reverse on the walls of Hatra, Trajan abandoned the campaign and died on his way home. Trajan's successor, Hadrian (117–138), abandoned all pretensions to Armenia, Mesopotamia, and Assyria.

Hadrian's desire for peace seems to have been sincere. He sent back Osroes' daughter, promised to return the golden throne, and did not try to profit from the long power struggle between Osroes and Vologases II. He even invited Osroes to come to Rome.

Peace with Rome. This was a time of 40 years of peace with Rome. The status quo it maintained with its western neighbour seems even to have been a necessity for the Parthian kingdom, the expansion of the kingdom of the Kushans on the eastern frontiers having reached the peak of its power under King Kaniṣka (Kanishka). Accurate information about the relations between the Kushans and the Parthians is not available but this long peace sought with Rome suggests that certain precautions were necessary for the kingdom of Iran.

THE END OF THE PARTHIAN EMPIRE (AD 162–226)

The 40 years' peace was succeeded by almost uninterrupted hostilities with Rome, with varied success, Iran remaining more vulnerable because of the exposed position of its capital.

The reign of Vologases II (105/106–?147) and especially that of Vologases III (148–192), the latter not having to dispute the throne with a pretender, could by their length be a sign of a certain stability the country might have experienced. But underneath the apparent calm the intrigues continued, with Rome receiving embassies from the Hyrcanians, the Bactrians, and doubtless from the Kushans.

Apparent stability in the 2nd century

A new clash with Rome came in 161, this time upon the initiative of Vologases III, who considered himself strong enough to attack. He occupied Armenia, crossed the Euphrates, and invaded Syria, which for two centuries had not seen Parthian cavalry. And although the country had been Roman since the time of Pompey, the Syrian population, which included Jews driven from Palestine by the Romans, received the Iranians as liberators. The situation became so serious that Lucius Verus, coemperor with Marcus Aurelius, was dispatched to the east with strong reinforcements taken from the fronts on the Danube and Rhine. The Romans retook Armenia (163) and succeeded in a campaign similar to Trajan's: Dura-Europos was taken and remained Roman until its destruction by the Sāsānids; Seleucia on the Tigris, despite the welcome it reserved for the Romans, was sacked; and in 164 or 165 for the second time Ctesiphon fell into the hands of Romans, who razed the royal palace.

But once more success was not continuous. The Roman army had come from Armenia and had crossed through Azerbaijan, known even today as a country where plague is endemic. Contaminated, the Roman army was sorely tried by disease and obliged to retreat, but not definitively. Lucius Verus, repeating his campaigns in Armenia and northern Mesopotamia, inflicted heavy losses on the Parthians.

The tensions between the two states did not diminish when Vologases IV (191–207) supported a pretender (Niger) against the emperor Septimius Severus. The latter became emperor in 193 and began operations that permitted him to occupy first northern and then southern Mesopotamia and, for the third time in a century, Ctesiphon.

The Parthians in their retreat adopted a scorched-earth policy. As under Trajan, the starving Roman army went back up the Tigris, failed in its attempt to take Hatra, and left the country.

Vologases V, son of the previous king, succeeded him (207–222), and his throne was contested from 213 by another prince, Artabanus V (213–224), who was able to maintain himself thanks to the support of the kingdom of Media. A new invasion of Mesopotamia took place under Caracalla, the *casus belli* being the refusal of Artabanus V to give Caracalla his daughter in marriage. The young Roman emperor dreamed of rebuilding Alexander's empire but succeeded only in the pillage of Media and the destruction at Arbela of the hypogea of the Arsacid kings, whose bones he scattered.

Invasion of Caracalla

The Parthian reply was harsh. Artabanus V avenged himself by invading the Roman provinces and destroyink several cities. Rome sued for peace. Artabanus' conditions were too hard and were refused. Hostilities were taken up again and turned in favour of the Parthians, who obtained such a success that the emperor Macrinus paid 200,000,000 sesterces to make peace.

Since 208 Papak, a lesser prince of Persis, had been

preparing a revolt, which his son Ardashir finally declared openly. A battle took place between him and Artabanus V in 224; the Parthian was killed and the throne of Iran passed into the hands of the Sāsānids, a new national dynasty, originally from Fars, cradle of the Achaemenids.

The Iran of the Parthians, a region strategically crucial for international commerce, maintained open roads, created cities, and encouraged exchanges that were the lifeblood of this great nation stretching from the portals of China and India to the Roman Empire. Tolerant in religion, it was Parthia that contributed to the dissemination of Buddhism to China, where a Parthian prince spread the word of Buddha near the middle of the 2nd century AD. For nearly half a millennium Parthia pursued its great ambition to recover the western provinces of the Achaemenids. An empire of the middle, between Rome on the west and the Kushans on the east, undermined by internal weaknesses, Parthia finally succumbed, leaving its great dreams to its successors, the Sāsānids. (R.Gh.)

III. The Sāsānian period

FOUNDATION OF THE EMPIRE

Rise of Ardashīr I. At the beginning of the 3rd century AD, the Arsacid Empire had been in existence for some 400 years. Its strength had been undermined, however, by repeated Roman invasions, and the empire became once more divided, this time between Vologases V (207–222), who seems to have ruled at Ctesiphon, on the left bank of the middle Tigris in what is now Iraq, and Artabanus V (*c.* AD 213–224), who was in control of Iran and whose authority at Susa, in southwestern Iran, is attested by an inscription of AD 215.

It was against Artabanus V that a challenger arose in Persis (Fars). Ardashīr I, son of Bābak (Pāpak) and a descendant of Sāsān, was the ruler of one of the several small states into which Persia had gradually been divided. His father had taken possession of the city and district of Istakhr (Estakhr), which had replaced the old residence city of Persepolis, a mass of ruins after its destruction by Alexander the Great in 330 BC. Bābak was succeeded by his eldest son, who was soon killed in an accident, and in AD 208 Ardashīr replaced his brother. He first built for himself a stronghold at Gūr, called after its founder Ardashīr-Khwarrah (Ardashīr's Glory), now Fīrūzābād, southeast of Shīrāz in Fars. He subdued the neighbouring rulers and disposed, in the process, of his own remaining brothers. His seizure of such areas as Kerman, Isfahan, Elymais, and Characene (Mesene), to the east, north, and west of Fars, respectively, led to war with Artabanus, his suzerain. The conflict between the two rivals lasted several years, during which time the Parthian forces were defeated in three battles. In the last of these, the battle in the plain of Hormizdagān (AD 226), Artabanus was killed.

Numismatic evidence concerning Ardashīr

There is evidence to support the assumption that Ardashīr's rise to power suffered several setbacks. Thus, Vologases V struck coins at Seleucia, on the Tigris, as late as AD 228/229 (the Seleucid year 539). Another Parthian prince, Artavasdes, a son of Artabanus V, known from coins on which he is portrayed with the distinguishing feature of a forked beard, seems to have exercised practical independence even after AD 228. Numismatic evidence further reflects the stages of Ardashīr's struggle for undisputed leadership. He appears on his coins with four different types of crown: as king of Fars, as claimant to the throne before the battle at Hormizdagān (AD 226), and as emperor with two distinctly different crowns. It has been suggested that this evidence points to two separate coronation ceremonies of Ardashīr as sovereign ruler, the second, perhaps, indicating that he may have lost the throne temporarily.

According to aṭ-Ṭabarī, the Arabic historian (9th–10th centuries), Ardashīr, after having secured his position as a ruler in western Iran, embarked on an extensive military campaign in the east (AD 227) and conquered Seistan (Sakastan), Gorgān (Hyrcania), Merv (Margiana), Balkh (Bactria), and Khwārezm (Chorasmia). The inference that this campaign resulted in the defeat of the powerful

Table 1: Sāsānian Dates Established on Direct Ancient Evidence

event	reign years	Seleucid Era	Christian Era
Accession of Artabanus (Ardawān) V	1		212/213
Inscription of Khwasak at Susa names Artabanus "king of kings"			215
Birth of Mani	5	527	216/217
Artabanus V overthrown and killed by Ardashīr			224
Official first year of Ardashīr		538*	226/227
Last coin of Vologases V, minted at Seleucia		539	228/229
Mani, in 13th year, receives divine revelation		539	228/229
Official first year of Shāpūr I		553	241/242

*Syrian reckoning.

Kushan Empire is supported by the further statement of aṭ-Ṭabarī that the king of the Kushans, probably Vasudeva, was among the eastern sovereigns, such as the rulers of Tūrān (Quzdar, south of modern Quetta) and of Makrān, whose surrender was received by Ardashīr. These military and political successes were further extended by Ardashīr by his taking possession of the palace at Ctesiphon, by his assuming the title "king of kings of the Iranians," and by his refounding and rebuilding of the city of Seleucia, located on the Tigris River, under the new name of Weh-Ardashīr, the Good Deed of Ardashīr.

Sāsānian chronology

The chronology of events in the early Sāsānian period was calculated by the German orientalist T. Nöldeke in 1879, and his system of dating is still generally accepted. The discovery of fresh evidence in manuscript materials dealing with the life of Mani, a religious leader whose activities fall in the early Sāsānian period, led to a reassessment of Nöldeke's calculations by W.B. Henning, by which the principal events are dated about two years earlier. Another alternative has been proposed by S.H. Taqizadeh, who prefers a sequence by which the same events are placed about six months later than the dates established by Nöldeke. Since the dating systems employed by the Sāsānians themselves were based on the regnal years of the individual kings, whose exact coronation dates are often subject to dispute, several details remain uncertain, and their definite solution is not yet possible. A firmer basis of calculation is obtained when the ancient sources quote dates in terms of the Seleucid era, either according to the computation that prevailed in Babylonia, which started from 311 BC, or after the Syrian reckoning, beginning in 312 BC. Tables 2 and 3 give the dates as they can be established on direct numismatic or literary evidence in the differing chronological systems of Nöldeke, Henning, and Taqizadeh.

Wars of Shāpūr I. Shortly before his death, probably because of failing health, Ardashīr abdicated the throne in favour of his chosen heir, his son Shāpūr I. The latter assumed the responsibilities of government but delayed his coronation until after his father's death. Coins thus exist showing Ardashīr together with his son as heir apparent and Shāpūr alone wearing the eagle cap, indicating the exercise of royal rule before his coronation—besides the normal series of Shāpūr crowned as king.

Shāpūr's defeat of the Romans

Shortly after his accession, Shāpūr was faced with an invasion of Persia by the emperor Gordian III (238–244):

> . . . the emperor Gordian levied in all of the Roman empire an army of Goths and Germans and marched against Asūristān [Iraq], the empire of Iran and us. On the border of Asūristān, at Massice [Misikhe on the Euphrates], a great battle took place. The emperor Gordian was killed and we destroyed the Roman army. The Romans proclaimed Philip [the Arab; 244–249] emperor. The emperor Philip came to terms, and as ransom for their lives he gave us 500,000 dinars and became our tributary. For that reason, we renamed Massice Fīrūz-Shāpūr ["victorious (is) Shāpūr"].

Several years later, in AD 256 (or AD 252), another con-

Table 2: Chronological Systems of Nöldeke, Henning, and Taqizadeh

event	Nöldeke	Henning	Taqizadeh
Ardashīr's first year begins		Sept. 27, 223	Sept. 26, 226
Ardashīr's actual accession	Sept. 26, 266	April 28, 244	April 6, 227
Shāpūr's first year begins		Sept. 23, 239	Sept. 22, 241
Shāpūr's actual accession	Sept. 22, 241		
Shāpūr's coronation		April 12, 240	April 9, 243
Shāpūr's death		May 270	April 273
Accession of Hormizd I	Sept. 14, 272		
Hormizd I's death		June 271	April 274
Accession of Bahrām I	Sept. 14, 273		
Death of Mani (about age 60)		March 2, 274	Feb. 26, 277
Death of Bahrām I		Sept. 274	July 277
Accession of Bahrām II	Sept. 13, 276		

frontation between the Persians and Romans occurred:

> We attacked the Roman empire and we destroyed an army of 60,000 men at Barbalissus [in Syria]. Syria and its surrounding areas we burned, devastated and plundered. In this one campaign we captured of the Roman empire 37 cities . . .,

including Antioch, the capital of Syria, itself. A third encounter took place when the emperor Valerian (253–260) came to the rescue of the city of Edessa, in Syria, which was besieged by the Persian army:

> He (Valerian) had with him (troops from) Germania, Rhaetia . . . [follow the names of some 29 Roman provinces], a force of 70,000 men. Beyond Carrhae and Edessa there was a great battle between the emperor Valerian and us. We made the emperor Valerian prisoner with our own hands; and the commanders of that army, the praefectus praetorii, senators and officers, we made them all prisoner, and we transported them to Persia. We burned, devastated and plundered Cilicia and Cappadocia . . . [follow the names of 36 cities].

The source for these quotations is Shāpūr's own account of the events. It was unknown until 1938, when expeditions of the Oriental Institute in Chicago discovered a long inscription on the walls of an Achaemenid building known as the Kaʿbe-ye Zardusht (Kaʿba of Zarathushtra). The text is in three languages, Sāsānian Pahlavi (Middle Persian), Parthian, and Greek. Besides the narrative of the military operations, the inscription provides a description of the Persian Empire of the time and an inventory of Zoroastrian religious foundations established by Shāpūr I to commemorate his victorious wars. These foundations were fire temples dedicated to the "soul" (memory) of the founder himself, of members of the royal family, and of prominent officials who had served under Shāpūr and his predecessor. The list of the officials who are specified by the positions they held throw light on the administrative organization of the empire.

Organization of the empire. In contrast to his father, who claimed to be "king of kings of Iran" (*shāhanshāh ērān*), Shāpūr I assumed the title "king of kings of Iran and non-Iran" (*shāhanshāh ērān ud anērān*). This formula was retained by his successors as the regular designation of the Sāsānian emperors. The hereditary local dynasties, which under the Arsacids had ruled many of the most important provinces, were to a large extent abolished. Instead, such areas as Maishān (Mesene), in western Iran, and Sakastān (Seistān), in eastern Iran, were now ruled by members of the Sāsānian family, who were appointed by the sovereign with the title of *shāh* (king). Among such provincial governors, precedence was often given to the heir to the throne, who was placed in control of large territories, such as the former Kushan Empire (Kūshānshahr) and Armenia, with the title "great king" (*wuzurg shāh*). This arrangement lasted until the early 4th century AD, and such emperors as Shāpūr I and Hormizd II are known to have first held the title *kūshānshāh* as governors of the areas of Bactria, Sogdiana, and Gandhāra. Next in the hierarchy came a few remaining hereditary vassals, such as the kings of Iberia (now Georgia) in the Caucasus, and the chief nobles of the empire, among whom the Warāz, Sūrēn, and Karēn families retained their prominent position from Parthian times. Next in line were the satraps, whose importance had diminished and who were no more than the administrators of larger cities or court officials.

The extent of Shāpūr I's empire

The list of provinces given in the inscription of Kaʿbe-yi Zardusht defines the extent of the empire under Shāpūr I, in clockwise geographical enumeration: (1) Persis (Fars); (2) Parthia; (3) Susiana (Khuzistan); (4) Maishān (Mesene); (5) Asūristān (Iraq); (6) Adiabene; (7) Arab-

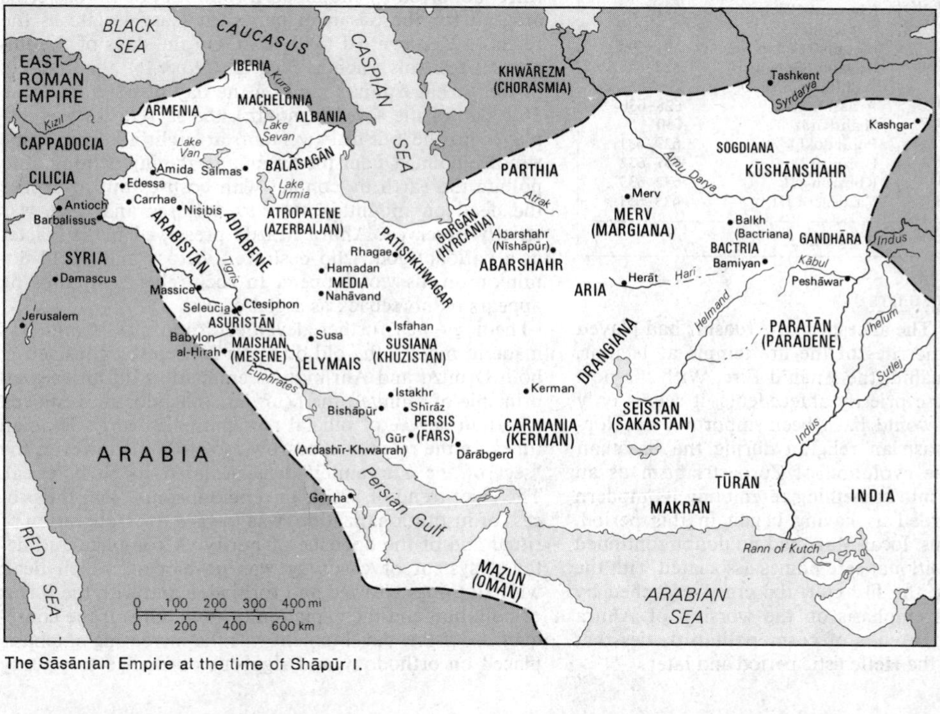

The Sāsānian Empire at the time of Shāpūr I.

istān (northern Mesopotamia); (8) Atropatene (Azerbaijan); (9) Armenia; (10) Iberia (Georgia); (11) Machelonia; (12) Albania (eastern Caucasus); (13) Bālasagān up to the Caucasus Mountains and the Gate of Albania (also known as Gate of the Alans, now the Darreh Āhū Pass in the central Caucasus); (14) Patishkhwagar (all of the Elburz Mountains); (15) Media; (16) Hyrcania (Gorgān); (17) Margiana (Merv); (18) Aria; (19) Abarshahr; (20) Carmania; (21) Sakastān (Seistān); (22) Tūrān; (23) Makrān; (24) Paratān (Paradene); (25) India (probably restricted to the Indus Delta area); (26) Kūshānshahr, until as far as Peshāwar and until Kashgar and (borders of) Sogdiana and Tashkent; and (27), on the further side of the sea, Mazun (Oman). This empire, considerably more extensive than that controlled by the Arsacid dynasty, was governed by members of the royal family and by appointed officials directly responsible to the throne. The greater degree of centralization thus attained by the Sāsānian government partly explains its increased military effectiveness in comparison with the Arsacid administration. Tight organization of the numerous central and provincial officials, whose ranks in the bureaucratic structure on different levels were strictly defined, also contributed toward general administrative efficiency.

Another trend that developed in the Sāsānian period, although it had already made itself felt under the Arsacids, was a strict principle of dynastic legitimacy. For a usurper not of the royal blood to come to the throne was an extremely rare occurrence, though it was in fact accomplished by Bahrām IV Chūbīn. Loyalty was given, however, to the whole royal house, rather as it was in the later Ottoman Empire. The person of the individual ruler was a matter of comparatively lesser importance, and one member of the dynasty could readily be removed and replaced by another. In accordance with this principle of legitimacy, Persian tradition carried the Sāsānian line back to the Achaemenids and, ultimately, to the kings of the legendary period.

Table 3: Sāsānian Kings*

name	reign years	name	reign years
Defeat of Artabanus V (Ardavan)	226	Kavadh (Qobād) I (first reign)	488–496
Ardashīr I	224–241	Jāmāṣb	496–499
Shāpūr I	241–272	Kavadh (second reign)	499–531
Hormizd I	272–273	Khosrow I	531–579
Bahrām I	273–276	Hormizd IV	579–590
Bahrām II	276–293	Khosrow II Parvīz (first reign)	590
Bahrām III	293	Bahrām VI	590–591
Narses	293–302	Khosrow II Parvīz (second reign)	591–628
Hormizd II	302–309	Bestām (rebel in Media)	591–596
Shāpūr II	309–379	Kavadh (Qobād) II Shīrūye (Siroes)	627–628
Ardashīr II	379–383	Ardashīr III	628–630
Shāpūr III	383–388	Shāhrbarāz	630
Bahrām IV	388–399	Pūrāndokht	629–631
Yazdegerd I	399–420	Hormizd V	631–632
Bahrām V Gūr	420–438	Khosrow III	632–633
Yazdegerd II	438–457	Yazdegerd III	633–651
Hormizd III	457–459		
Fīrūz	457–484		
Balāsh	484–488		

*Based mainly on T. Nöldeke's chronology.

RELIGIOUS DEVELOPMENTS

Zoroastrianism. The ancestors of Ardashīr had played a leading role in the rites of the fire temple at Istakhr, known as Ādur-Anāhīd, the Anāhīd Fire. With the new dynasty having these priestly antecedents, it seems only natural that there would have been important developments in the Zoroastrian religion during the Sāsānian period. In fact, the evolution of Zoroastrianism as an organized religion into something resembling its modern form can be regarded as having begun in this period. Under the Parthians, local Magi had no doubt continued to perform the traditional ceremonies associated with the old Iranian deities, the fire cult, the creed preached by Zoroaster, with its emphasis on the worship of Ahura Mazdā, and even the cults of cosmopolitan deities that were introduced in the Hellenistic period and later.

Religion and the state

Under the Sāsānians, stress came to be placed on the fire cult and the worship of Ahura Mazdā. Strong mutual relationships, furthermore, were developed between religion and the state, and an ecclesiastical organization was set up in which every local district of any importance had its own *mobed* ("priest"; originally *magupat*, "chief priest"). At their head stood the *mobedān mobed* ("priest of priests"), who, in addition to his purely religious jurisdiction, appears, especially in later times, to have had a more or less decisive voice in the choice of a successor to the throne and in other matters of state. There is also some evidence that the *mobeds*, by virtue of their proficiency in reading and writing in general and in the interpretation of the sacred scriptures in particular, performed the offices of registrars and scribes in semireligious or nonreligious matters, after the fashion of the Christian clergy in medieval Europe. This situation in turn makes it likely that the priestly library buildings not only contained the sacred texts, charters, and other church records but also served as repositories of local archives, title deeds, and other documents of a legal nature. The building known as Kaʿbe-ye Zardusht and referred to as a *bun-khānag* ("foundation house") may well have served this very purpose.

In the matter of religious practice, the theology of the Sāsānians appears to have developed from that previously current in their home province of Persis (Fars). There, extraneous religious influences were limited. The opposition between the good spirit of light and the demons—between Ormizd (Ahura Mazdā) and Ahriman (Angra Mainyu)—remained the essential dogma. All the other gods and angels were restricted to the role of subordinate servants of Ormizd, whose highest manifestation on earth was not so much the sun or the sun god Mihr (Mithra) but rather the holy fire guarded and attended by his priests. At the same time the names of such deities as Wahrām (Verethraghna), Mihr, and Anāhīd (Anahita) were still associated with the names of fire temples or classes of fires. Divine names were also used to designate the 30 days of each month and of the 12 30-day months of the year, plus five epact days called *gahānīg*, to align the lunar with the solar year.

Ritual practice

All the prescriptions of purity were scrupulously observed. The elaborate ritual still maintained in modern times by the Parsi for the purification and custody of the sacred fire was no doubt observed under the Sāsānians. The officiating priest was girt with a sword and carried in his hand the *barsman* (*barsom*), or bundle of sacred grass. His mouth was covered to prevent the sacred fire from being polluted by his breath. The practice of animal sacrifice, abhorred by the modern followers of Zoroaster, is attested for the Sāsānian period at least as late as the reign of Yazdegerd I (399–420). On the days of the important festivals, such as *Nōgrūz* (*Nowrūz*), the first day of the vernal equinox, and on the day of *Mihragan* (the 16th day of the seventh month), the sacred fire was displayed to the faithful (*wehden*) at nightfall from some vantage point. Under the Sāsānians, the injunction not to pollute the earth by contact with corpses but to expose the dead on mountain tops to vultures and dogs was strictly observed. Ahura Mazdā preserved his character as a national god, who bestowed victory and world dominion on his worshippers. In rock-relief sculptures he appears on horseback as a god of war.

Theology was further developed, and an attempt was made to modify the old dualistic concept by considering both Ormizd and Ahriman as emanations of an original principle of infinite time (Zurvān). This doctrine enjoyed a certain degree of official recognition in early Sāsānian times. In the reign of Khosrow I (531–579), however, the "sect of the Zurvanites" was declared to be heretical. The chief trend of Sāsānian religion, apart from the process of institutionalization, was toward the elaboration of ritual and of the doctrine of purity. A complete and detailed system of casuistry was developed, which dealt with all things allowed and forbidden and with the forms of pollution and the expiation of each. One of the consequences of this development was the increasing emphasis placed on orthodoxy and rigorous obedience to priestly injunctions. Nonorthodox and heretical cults and forbidden manners and customs came to be regarded as a pollution of the land and a serious offense to the true God. It was the duty of the believer to combat and destroy the unbelievers and the heretics. In short, the tolerance of the Achaemenids and the indifference of the Arsacids were gradually replaced by religious intolerance and persecution.

Despite his priestly family origin, Ardashīr himself seems not to have been the person responsible for initiating these new directions in religious affairs. It was once believed that the institutionalization of the Zoroastrian church and the codification of its scriptures and beliefs was the work of a high priest named Tansar, a contemporary of Ardashīr I, of whose activities an account is preserved in the *Letter of Tansar*, contained in the history of Ṭabaristān by the Persian writer Ibn Isfandiyār (12th–13th centuries). New inscriptional evidence, however, rather suggests that, if Tansar was, in fact, a historical personage, his role in religious matters was overshadowed by Kartēr (Karder). The latter, a *herbed* ("teacher priest") and *mobed* ("priest") already prominent under Shāpūr I, appears during the reigns of Bahrām I (273–276) and Bahrām II (276–293) as the dominant figure in the Zoroastrian church. As stated in the Kaʿbe-ye Zardusht inscription of Kartēr, he claims credit for the suppression of non-Zoroastrian religious communities in Iran ("and Jews, Buddhists, Brahmins, 'Nazoreans,' Christians . . . were struck upon"), for the imposition of orthodoxy and discipline on the priesthood ("the heretics [*ahlomog*] . . . who in the Magus estate did not attend to the Mazdean religion and the services to the gods with discrimination, I struck them with punishment and I castigated them"), and for the establishment of royal foundations for the maintenance of priests and of sacred fires.

Role of the priest Kartēr

Christianity. The reference in the Kartēr inscription to two sects of Christians continues the indications from Syriac sources that Christianity had by this time, the second half of the 3rd century, gained a firm footing in the lands of the Tigris and the Euphrates, where it was strongest among the Aramaic-speaking communities. Ultimately, Christian missionary effort came to expand over the whole of Iran and even beyond. As long as the Roman Empire remained pagan, the Christian communities of Iran lived undisturbed by persecution, while the Christians themselves showed outspoken hostility toward such heterodox sects as the Manichaeans and the Gnostic followers of Marcion and Bardesanes, who existed side by side with them. Once the emperor Constantine the Great (306–337) made Christianity the official religion of the Roman world, the Iranian Christians were, on the one hand, drawn to feel a certain sympathy for their foreign coreligionists, while, on the other, political significance came to be attached by the Sāsānian rulers to these religious connections with an often hostile foreign power. After 339 the Christians of Iran were subjected to severe persecutions at the hands of Shāpūr II and his successors. Substantial Christian communities survived, nonetheless, in parts of Iran long after the end of the Sāsānian dynasty.

Manichaeism. During the reign of Shāpūr I a new religious leader and movement made their appearance. Mani (between 216? and 274?) was the offspring of a Parthian family resident in Babylonia ("a thankful disciple I am, risen from Babel's land") but himself a speaker of Aramaic. In the early 20th century, knowledge of his teachings was greatly increased by the discovery of many fragments of Manichaean literature in eastern Turkistan. Subsequently, a large part of the *Kephalaia*, a collection of the religious injunctions of Mani, was recovered in a Coptic version, found in Egypt. These texts can now be collated with the versions of Manichaean doctrines as reported by the Church Fathers, including St. Augustine. From this cumulative documentation, to which other sources can be added, it appears, among other things, that Mani's teachings were formulated under the strong influence of Gnostic ideas and philosophy. Mani proclaimed himself to be the last and greatest Apostle of Jesus as well as the paraclete announced in the Gospel of St. John. With the Gnostic interpretation of the Gospel, Mani tried to combine the doctrines of Zoroaster and Jesus in order to create a new religion of a universal character. There is a tradition that he made his first appearance as a teacher on the coronation day of Shāpūr I (April 12, 240, or April 9, 243), but other evidence suggests that Mani was not necessarily in Iran at the time and may have been on a sea journey to India when he started preaching. He later returned and found many followers, among whom were Fīrūz (Pērōz) and Mihrshāh, governor of Maishān (Mesene), both brothers of Shāpūr I. Even the King himself is said to have been impressed and to have granted the prophet several personal interviews. On the last such occasion, Mani presented the King with his first book, the *Shāpuragān* (*Shabuhragan*), a summary of his teachings ("dedicated to Shāpūr") written in the Middle Persian language, further evidence of a degree of royal favour. During Shāpūr's reign the religion of Mani was thus propagated in and beyond Iran. The heir to the throne, Hormizd I, was also favourably disposed toward him. Shāpūr's younger son, Bahrām I, however, yielded to pressure from the priestly establishment, and Mani was executed. After that, Manichaeism was persecuted and destroyed in Iran. Yet it maintained itself not only in the West, penetrating far into the Roman Empire, but also in the East, in Khorāsān and beyond the boundaries of the Sāsānian Empire. There the seat of its pontiff was at Samarkand, whence it penetrated into Central Asia.

Suppression of Manichaeism

ART AND LITERATURE

Perhaps the most characteristic and certainly among the most impressive relics of Sāsānian art are the great rock sculptures carved on the limestone cliffs that are found in many parts of the country. The best known groups are at Naqsh-e Rostam and Naqsh-e Rajab, both near Persepolis, and at Bishāpūr, an ancient city a few miles north of Kāzerūn in Fārs. At Fīrūzābād, the ancient Gūr, also in Fārs, are two reliefs of Ardashīr I, one depicting the overthrow of Artabanus V, the other an investiture scene. Not far away, in the valley at Sar Mashhad, a representation of Bahrām II shows that king in the process of slaying two lions. At Dārābgerd, about 180 miles southwest of Shīrāz, Shāpūr I is shown triumphing over three Roman emperors, Gordian III, Philip the Arabian, and Valerian. At Naqsh-e Bahrām, north of Kāzerūn, Bahrām III is depicted enthroned. The same ruler appears at Qaṣr-e Abū Nasr, near Shīrāz, and at Gūyom, not far from there. Sāsānian sculptured reliefs are less numerous outside Fārs, but a Sāsānian equestrian that once existed at Rayy (ancient Rhagae), southeast of Tehrān, was replaced in the 19th century by a representation of Fatḥ ʿAlī Shāh, a member of the then-ruling Qajar dynasty. At Shāhpūr (formerly Salmas), on Lake Urmia, Ardashīr I is shown on horseback while receiving the surrender of a Parthian personage. There are also later Sāsānian sculptures at Ṭāq-e Bostān, near Kermanshah, showing Ardashīr II, Shāpūr III, and Khosrow II. In many of these representations the Sāsānian kings can often be identified by their individual crowns.

The most ambitious and celebrated architectural achievement of the dynasty is the vast palace at Ctesiphon, built by Khosrow II (590; 591–628), of which a part is still standing. It is known as the Ṭāq Kisrā and is notable for its great barrel vault in baked brick, a typically Sāsānian architectonic device. Many Sāsānian buildings can also be seen in Fars, where the characteristic construction is of limestone blocks embedded in strong mortar. The most important of these are the palace of Ardashīr I at Fīrūzābād, south of Shīrāz, and a small, well-preserved palace at Sarvestān, southeast of Shīrāz, in which the rooms are roofed with domes and squinches, features often found in Sāsānian architecture. Excavations at Shāhpūr, near Kāzerūn, have revealed some mosaic floors and other features of this important Sāsānian town. Numerous fire temples of the period survive, especially in Fars; these are square buildings roofed by a dome over four arches. Sāsānian remains of considerable

Architecture

extent also exist at Qaṣr-e Shīrīn, on the road from Baghdad to Tehrān, and at Gondēshāpūr, modern Shāhābād, south of Dezfūl.

Metalwork and coinage

Generally speaking, the Sāsānian era was one of a renascence in Iranian art, which, if not quite on the same level as the Achaemenid achievement, was of no small importance. Metalwork reached a high level of artistry and craftmanship; its most characteristic decorative themes are hunting scenes portraying the Sāsānian kings in action. A gold and enamel drinking vessel (now in the Bibliothèque Nationale in Paris) from the time of Khosrow I (531–579)—known as the "Cup of Solomon" and, according to one tradition, a gift of the caliph Hārūn ar-Rashīd to Charlemagne—is perhaps the most sumptuous specimen of Sāsānian metalworking. The art of gem engraving produced many fine intaglio stamp seals and cameos. The coins invariably bear a Pahlavi (Middle Persian) inscription; on the obverse is the head of the king, wearing his characteristic crown, accompanied by his name and title, on the reverse the fire altar with its guardians and the legend "Fire of Ardashīr, Shāpūr, etc." or, in the later period, an abbreviated mint name and the regnal date.

The acquaintance with Greek language and literature maintained by the Arsacid court had begun to decline during the last century of that dynasty. Greek versions nonetheless accompany the Parthian and Middle Persian texts of the inscriptions of Ardashīr I and Shāpūr I, as in the case of the Kaʿbe-yi Zardusht inscription. Later inscriptions, however, are only in Parthian and Middle Persian, as in the case of the inscription of Narses at Paikuli.

Literature

Most of the comparatively few remains of literature in (Book) Pahlavi—a form of Middle Persian somewhat different from that used in the Sāsānian inscriptions—is of late or post-Sāsānian date in its actual form, if not in content. This is partly due to the fact that the transition from an oral to a written literary tradition took place in the later part of the Sāsānian era. This is true of both religious and secular compositions. A passage in a religious text states that "it is proper to consider the living spoken word more weighty than the written." It should be added that most Sāsānian literary remains are primarily of religious and historical rather than of literary interest. Just as foreign learning appears in religious works, likewise foreign prose works of entertainment came to Persia, where they were translated; among them, in the time of Khosrow I, were Hellenistic romance literature and Indian books of tales, such as *Kalīlag and Dimnag*, based on the Indian *Pañca-tantra* or the legends of *Barlaam and Josaphat* (*Balauhar and Budasaf*).

FOREIGN POLICY

In foreign policy the problems under the Sāsānian kings remained, as of old, the defense and, when possible, the expansion of the eastern and western frontiers. The successful military campaigns in the eastern areas by Ardashīr I and Shāpūr I, which resulted in the annexation of the western part of the Kushan Empire, have already been mentioned.

Conflicts with Rome. In the west, the old contest for northern Mesopotamia with the fortified cities of Carrhae, Nisibis, and Edessa continued. The Sāsānians were all the more eager to regain and retain control of Armenia because there the Arsacid dynasty still survived and turned for protection to Rome, with which, in consequence, new wars continually broke out. In the reign of Bahrām II (276–293), the emperor Carus (282–283) invaded Mesopotamia without meeting opposition and reached Ctesiphon. His sudden death, however, caused the Roman army to withdraw. Bahrām II had been prevented from meeting the Roman challenge by the rebellion of his brother, the *kūshānshāh* Hormizd, who tried to establish an independent eastern empire. This attempt ended in failure, however, and Bahrām II appointed his younger son, the future Bahrām III, as viceroy of Sakastan (Seistan). After Bahrām II had died (293), Narses, the youngest son of Shāpūr II, contested the succession of Bahrām III and won the crown. In memory of his victory, Narses erected a tower at Paikuli, in the mountains west of the upper Diyālā River, which was discovered in 1843 by the English Orientalist Sir Henry Rawlinson. Decorated with busts of Narses, the monument has a long inscription in Parthian and Middle Persian that tells the story of the events. In 296, Narses was forced to conclude a peace treaty with the Romans by which Armenia remained under Roman suzerainty and certain areas in northern Mesopotamia were ceded to Rome. By this treaty, which lasted for 40 years, the Sāsānians withdrew completely from the disputed districts. The Roman Empire had meanwhile become Christian, and the Syro-Christian populations of Mesopotamia and Babylonia began to feel sympathy with Roman policies for religious reasons. Christianity also became predominant in Armenia after King Tiridates adopted the Christian faith in 294. The Sāsānian emperors consequently felt the need to consolidate their Zoroastrianism, and efforts were made to perfect and enforce state orthodoxy. All heresy was proscribed by the state, defection from the official faith was made a capital crime, and persecution of the heterodox, the Christians in particular, began. Competition between Iran and Rome–Byzantium thus took on a religious dimension.

Religious factors in foreign policy

A new war was inevitable. It was begun by Shāpūr II in 337, the year of the death of Constantine the Great. Shāpūr besieged the fortress city of Nisibis three times without success. The emperor Constantius (337–361) conducted the war weakly, but Shāpūr was distracted by the appearance of a new enemy, the nomadic Chionites (Huns), on his eastern frontier. After a long campaign against them (353–358), he returned to Mesopotamia and, with the help of Chionite auxiliaries, captured the city of Amida (modern Diyarbakir) on the upper Tigris, an episode vividly narrated by the Roman historian Ammianus Marcellinus (*c.* 330–400). The emperor Julian the Apostate (361–363) reopened hostilities after the death of Constantius (361) but died after having reached the vicinity of Ctesiphon. His successor, Jovian (363–364), was forced to give up the Roman possessions on the Tigris, including Nisibis, and to abandon Armenia and his Arsacid protégé, Arsaces III, to the Persians. The greater part of Armenia then became a Persian province.

Intermittent conflicts from Yazdegerd I to Khosrow I. After about two decades of disturbed reigns (Ardashīr II, Shāpūr III, Bahrām IV), Yazdegerd I came to the throne. His reign is viewed differently by Christian and Zoroastrian sources. The former praise his clemency; the latter refer to him as "Yazdegerd the Sinful." His initial inclination toward tolerance of the Christian and Jewish religions was met by resistance on the part of the nobility. Because of their attitude and because of the growing fanaticism of the Christians, Yazdegerd was forced to turn to repression. After his death (420), the nobles refused to admit any of Yazdegerd's sons to the throne. But one of them, Bahrām V, had the support of al-Mundhir, Arab prince of al-Ḥīrah (east of the lower Euphrates) and a Sāsānian vassal, and also, apparently, of Mihr-Narseh, chief minister of Yazdegerd's last years who was retained in office, and eventually won the throne. As King Bahrām V, surnamed Gūr (Wild Ass), he became the favourite of Persian popular tradition, which exuberantly celebrates his prowess in hunting and in love. Unsuccessful in war with Byzantium (421–422), Bahrām V made a 100-year peace and granted freedom of worship to the Christians. In the east he did succeed in repelling an invasion by a new wave of Hephthalites. In the following decades, however (second half of the 5th century), Hephthalite attacks continued to harass and weaken the Sāsānians. Fīrūz (457–484) fell in battle against them; his treasures and family were captured, and the country was devastated. His brother Balāsh (484–488), unable to cope with continuing incursions, was deposed and blinded. The crown fell to Kavadh (Qobād) I, son of Fīrūz. While the empire continued to suffer distress, he was dethroned and imprisoned (496), but he escaped to the Hephthalites and was restored (499) with their assistance. The Nestorian doctrine (claiming that divine and human persons remained separate in the incarnate Christ) and by now become dominant among the Christians in Iran and was definitely established as the accepted form of Christianity in the Sāsānian Empire.

Reign of Kavadh I

Kavadh I proved himself a vigorous ruler. He restored peace and order in the land. A campaign against the Romans (502) resulted in the destruction of Amida, but another inroad by the Hephthalites in the east compelled him to ratify a peace treaty with the Byzantines. Toward the close of his reign, in 527, he resumed the war and defeated the Byzantine general Belisarius at Callinicum (531) with the support of al-Mundhir II of al-Ḥīrah. Earlier in his reign he had moved away from the Zoroastrian church and favoured Mazdak, the founder of a new socio-religious movement that had found support among the people. The crown prince, Khosrow, however, was an orthodox Zoroastrian; toward the end of his father's reign, in collaboration with the chief *mobed*, he contrived the condemnation of the Mazdakites, who were destroyed in a great massacre (528). On his father's death, after acceding as Khosrow I (531–579), he concluded peace with the Byzantine emperor Justinian (532). He reestablished Zoroastrian orthodoxy, and, although some persecution of Christian communities occurred during periods of tension with Byzantium, the restoration of peace brought about a considerable amount of religious tolerance.

Khosrow I was one of the most illustrious Sāsānian monarchs. From his time dates a new and more equitable adjustment of the imperial tax system. The levying of land revenue in kind was replaced by a fixed assessment in cash, and these assessments continued in force later under the Arab administration. His reputation as an enlightened and just ruler was high during his lifetime and later became legendary. When Justinian, in 529, closed the philosophy school in Athens, the last Neoplatonists turned to Khosrow in hopes of finding in him the true philosopher-king. Though disillusioned by conditions at his court, their gratitude was great when Khosrow obtained for them the right to return. From 540 onward Khosrow had been conducting a long war against Justinian, which, although interrupted by several armistices, lasted until the 50 years' peace of 561. Khosrow also extended his power to the Black Sea and inflicted heavy defeats on the Hephthalites. These military successes are in part the result of several reorganizations of the armed forces and the chain of command that were achieved during Khosrow's long reign.

Conflicts with the Turks and Byzantium. About 560, a new nation, that of the Turks, had emerged in the east. By concluding an alliance with a Turkish leader called Sinjibu (Silzibul), Khosrow was able to inflict a decisive defeat on the Hephthalites, after which event a common frontier between the Turkish and Sāsānian empires was established. Inevitably, this alliance became a source of possible friction, and the Turks sometimes acted as an ally of Byzantium against Iran in a second war (572–579).

Revolts of Bahrām Chūbīn and Bestām

Khosrow bequeathed this war to his son Hormizd IV (579–590), who in spite of repeated negotiations failed to re-establish peace between Byzantium and Iran. Hormizd was unable to display the same authority as his father, and he antagonized the Zoroastrian clergy by failing to take action against the Christians. He finally fell victim to a conspiracy headed by the general Bahrām Chūbīn. Hormizd's son, Khosrow II, was set up against his father and forced to acquiesce in Hormizd's execution. New unrest broke out, in which Bahrām Chūbīn—though not of royal lineage—attempted to secure the throne. Simultaneously another pretender, Prince Bestām, decided to try his luck. Khosrow fled to Byzantium, and the emperor Maurice (582–602) undertook his restoration by military force. Bahrām Chūbīn was routed (591) and fled to and was killed by the Turks, and Khosrow again ascended the throne in Ctesiphon. Bestām held out in Media until 596.

Khosrow II (590; 591–628), surnamed Parvīz (the Victorious), achieved unprecedented splendour and material wealth. The assassination of Maurice (602) impelled him to a war against Byzantium, in the course of which his armies penetrated as far as Chalcedon (opposite Constantinople), ravaged Syria, and captured Antioch (611), Damascus (613), and Jerusalem (614); in 619, Egypt was occupied. The Byzantine Empire was, indeed, at its lowest ebb.

It took the great emperor Heraclius, who was crowned in 610, many years to rebuild the nucleus of a new army. This done, however, he set out in 622 and retaliated vigorously against the Persians. Their armies were defeated everywhere. In 624 Heraclius invaded Atropatene (Azerbaijan) and destroyed the great Zoroastrian fire temple; in 627 he entered the Tigris provinces. Khosrow II attempted no resistance; a revolution followed in which he was defeated and slain by his son Kavadh (Qobād) II (628). When Kavadh died a few months later, anarchy resulted. After a succession of short-time rulers, Yazdegerd III, grandson of Khosrow II, came to the throne in 633.

Triumph of the Arabs. All of these prolonged and exhausting hostilities had drastically reduced the powers of both Byzantium and Iran. The door was open to a newly emerging force that now challenged both states and religions—the Arabs. After several encounters, the fate of the Sāsānian Empire was decided in the battle of al-Qādisīyah (636/637), on one of the Euphrates canals, not far from al-Ḥīrah, during which the Sāsānian commander in chief, Rustam, was killed. Ctesiphon with its treasures was now at the mercy of the victors. Yazdegerd fled to Media, where his generals tried to organize new resistance. The battle fought at Nehāvand (642), south of Hamadan, put an end to their hopes. Yazdegerd sought refuge in one province after another, until at last, in 651, he was assassinated near Merv.

End of the Sāsānian Empire

With the fall of the empire, the fate of its religion was also sealed. The Muslims officially tolerated the Zoroastrian faith, though persecutions were not unknown. Little by little it vanished from Iran, except for a few surviving adherents who remain to the present day in Yazd and a few other places. Other Zoroastrians emigrated to western India, where they are now chiefly concentrated in Bombay. These Parsis (Persians) have preserved only a relatively small portion of their sacred writings. They still number their years by the era of Yazdegerd III, the last king of their faith and the last Sāsānian sovereign of Iran. (A.D.H.B./M.J.Dr.)

IV. Iran from 640 to the present

THE ADVENT OF ISLAM (640–821)

The Arab invasion of Iran made a break with the past that affected not only Iran but all of western Asia and resulted in the assimilation of peoples who shaped and vitalized Muslim culture. The Prophet Muḥammad had made Medina, his adopted city, and Mecca, his birthplace, centres of an Arabian movement that Muslim Arabs developed into a world movement by the conquest of Iranian and Byzantine territories. Neither the Iranian nor Byzantine empires had been unfamiliar to those Arabs who were the former's Lakhmid and the latter's Ghassānid vassals, the two empires' frontier guardians against fellow Arabs who roamed deeper in the Arabian Desert. Also, Meccan and Medinese Arabs had established commercial connection with the Byzantines and Sāsānids. The immunity of Mecca's ancient sanctuary against outlawry and outrage had promoted this city's commercial importance. The Kaʿbah, as the sanctuary was called, was cleansed of idols by Muḥammad, who had himself once been engaged in commerce. He made it the sanctuary of a monotheistic faith whose sacred writings were impregnated with the injunctions and prohibitions needed by a business community for secure and stable trading.

Arab tribalism beyond urban fringes was less easily broken than idols. It was embedded in the desert sparsity that led to warfare and careful counting of a tribe's male offspring. After Mecca and Medina had become Muslim, to secure the routes they depended upon necessitated winning the desert Arabs' allegiance. In the process of doing this, wars over water holes, scanty pastures, men-at-arms, and camels were enlarged into international campaigns of expansion.

Sāsānid weakness

The vulnerability of Sāsānid Iran assisted the expansionist process. In AD 623 the Byzantine emperor Heraclius reversed Persian successes over Roman arms, namely: the capture of Jerusalem in 614 and a victory at Chalcedon in 617. His victim, Khosrow Parvīz, died in 628 and left Iran a prey to a succession of puppet rulers who were frequently deposed by a combination of nobles and Zoroastrian clergy. Thus, when Yazdegerd III, Iran's last Sāsānid and Zoroastrian sovereign, came to the throne in 632, the year of Muḥammad's death, he inherited an empire weakened by Byzantine wars and internal dissension.

The former Arab vassals on the empire's southwest border realized that their moment had arrived, but their raids into Sāsānid territory were quickly taken up by Muḥammad's caliphs, or deputies, at Medina—Abū Bakr and ʿUmar (632–634; 634–644)—to become a Muslim, Pan-Arab attack on Iran.

An Arab victory at al-Qādisīyah in 637 was followed by the sack of the Sāsānid winter-capital at Ctesiphon on the Tigris. The Battle of Nahāvand in 642 completed the Sāsānids' vanquishment. Yazdegerd fled to the empire's northeastern outpost, Merv, whose *marzbān*, or march lord, Mahūyeh, was soured by Yazdegerd's imperious and expensive demands. Mahūyeh turned against his emperor and defeated him with the help of Hephthalites from Bādghis. The Hephthalites, an independent border power, had troubled the Sāsānids since at least 590, when they had sided with Bahrām Chūbīn, Khosrow Parvīz's rebel general. A miller near Merv murdered the fugitive Yazdegerd for his purse.

The Sāsānid end was ignominious, but it was not the end of Iran. Rather, it marked a new beginning. Within two centuries, Iranian civilization was revived with a cultural amalgam, with patterns of art and thought, with attitudes and a sophistication that were indebted to its pre-Islāmic Iranian heritage—a heritage changed but also stirred into fresh life by the Arab-Muslim conquest.

Background of the revolution

Abū Muslim's revolution. Less time was needed before the Arabs' assimilation with Iranians in regions they colonized caused a new Islāmic beginning, Abū Muslim's movement, which began in Khorāsān, in 747. This revolution followed years of conspiracy directed from Medina and across to Khorāsān along the trade route that linked the Far East to Merv and thence with the West. Along the route merchants with contacts in the Mesopotamian Arab garrison cities of Kūfah, Wāsiṭ, and Basra acted as intermediaries. Iranians who by converting to Islām had become clients, or *mawālī*, of Arab patrons played direct and indirect parts in the revolutionary movement. The movement also involved Arabs who had partnered Khorāsānian and Transoxanian Iranians in ventures in the great east–west trade and intercity trade of northeast Iran. The revolution was, nevertheless, primarily an Arabo-Islāmic movement, aimed to supplant a militaristic, tyrannical central government whose fiscal problems made it avid for revenue by one more sympathetic to the needs of the merchants of eastern Islām. Abū Muslim, a revolutionary of unknown origin, was able in Merv to exploit the discontent of the merchant classes as well as that of the Arab and Iranian settlers. The object of attack was the Umayyad government in Damascus.

When Muḥammad died in 632, his newly established community in Medina and Mecca needed a guiding counsellor, an imam, to lead them in prayers and an *amīr al-muʾminīn*, "Commander of the Faithful," to ensure proper application of the Prophet's divinely inspired precepts. As the Prophet, Muḥammad could never be entirely succeeded, but it was accepted that men who had sufficient dignity and who had known him could fulfil the functions, as his caliphs (*khulafāʾ*), or deputies, and imams. After Abū Bakr and ʿUmar, ʿUthmān was chosen for this role.

By ʿUthmān's time, factionalism was growing among Arabs, partly the result of the jealousies and rivalries consequent upon acquiring new territories, and partly the result of the competition between first arrivals in them and those who followed. There was also uncertainty over the most desirable kind of imamate. One faction, the Shīʿah, supported ʿAlī, the Prophet's cousin and husband of his favourite daughter, Fāṭimah, for the caliphate, since he had been an intimate of Muḥammad and seemed more capable than the other candidates of expressing Muḥammad's wisdom and virtue as the people's judge. The desire for such a successor points to disenchantment with ʿUthmān's attempt to strengthen the central government and impose demands on the colonies. His murder in 656 left his Umayyad relatives poised to avenge it, while ʿAlī was raised to the caliphate. A group of his supporters, the Khārijites, desired more freedom than ʿAlī was willing to grant, with a return to the simplest interpretation of the Prophet's revelation in the Qurʾān, along puritanical lines.

The Khārijites

A Khārijite killed ʿAlī in 661. The Shīʿah thenceforth crystallized into the obverse position of the Khārijites, emphasizing ʿAlī's relationship to the Prophet as a means of making him and his descendants by Fāṭimah the sole legitimate heirs to the Prophet, some of whose spiritual power was even believed to have been transmitted to them. This Shīʿism centuries later became the official Islāmic sect of Iran. In the interim, Shīʿism was a rallying point for socially and politically discontented elements within the Muslim community. In addition to the Khārijites, another minority sect was thus formed, hostile from the beginning to the Umayyad government that seized power on ʿAlī's death. The majority of Muslims avoided both the Shīʿite and Khārijite positions but followed instead the *sunnah*, or "tradition," as these orthodox believers conceived the Prophet to have left it and Abū Bakr, ʿUmar, ʿUthmān, and ʿAlī, too, the "rightly guided" first caliphs, had observed and codified it.

Abū Muslim's revolutionary movement was as much as anything representing Medinese mercantile interests in the Hejaz, dissatisfied with Umayyad inability to shelter Middle Eastern trade under a Pax Islamica. To promote the revolution aimed to destroy Umayyad power, the movement exploited Shīʿite aspirations and other forces of disenchantment. The Khārijites were excluded, since their movement opposed the idea of a caliphate of the kind Abū Muslim's adherents were fighting to establish—one that could command sufficient respect to hold together an Islāmic universal state. A discontented element ready to Abū Muslim's hand in Khorāsān, however, was not a religious grouping but Arab settlers and Iranian cultivators who were burdened by taxation.

In Iran, the first Arab conquerors had concluded treaties with local Iranian magnates who had assumed authority when the Sāsānid imperial government disintegrated. These notables—the *marzbāns* and landlords (*dehqāns*)—undertook to continue tax collection on behalf of the new Muslim power. The advent of Arab colonizers, who preferred to cultivate the land rather than campaign farther into Asia, produced a further complication. Once the Arabs had settled in Iranian lands, they were required to pay the *kharāj*, or land tax, collected by Iranian notables and their agents under treaty with the Muslim government. The Iranian collectors proved extortionate and aroused the hostility of both Arab and Persian.

Another source of discontent was the head tax, or *jizyah*, which was applied to non-Muslims of the tolerated religions—Judaism, Christianity, and Zoroastrianism. Thus, on conversion to Islām, Iranians expected exemption from this degrading tax. But the Umayyad government, burdened with imperial expenses, often refused exemption to the Iranian converts.

The tax demands of the Damascus government were as distasteful to those urbanized Arabs and Iranians in commerce as they were to those in agriculture; and hopes of easier conditions under the new rulers than under the Sāsānids were not fully realized. The Umayyads ignored Iranian agricultural conditions, which required constant reinvestment to maintain irrigation works and to halt the encroachment of the desert. This no doubt made the tax burden, from which no returns were visible, all the more odious. Furthermore, the regime failed to maintain the peace so necessary to trade. Damascus feared the breaking away of remote provinces where the Arab colonists were becoming assimilated with the local populations. The government, therefore, deliberately encouraged tribal factionalism in order to prevent a united opposition against it.

Thus the revolution set out to establish an Islāmic oecumene above divisions and sectarianism, the Pax Islamica already referred to, which commerce required and which Iranian merchants without status in the Sāsānid social hierarchy looked to Islām to provide. Ease of communication from the Oxus to the Mediterranean was wanted but without what seemed like a nest of robbers calling themselves a government straddling the route at Damascus. In 750 Umayyad power was destroyed and the revolution gave the caliphate to the ʿAbbāsids (see CALIPHATE, EMPIRE OF THE).

Hejazi commercial interests had in a sense overcome the military party among leading Muslim Arabs. Greater concern for the East was manifested by the new caliphate's choice of Baghdad as its capital, situated on the Tigris a short distance north of Ctesiphon and designed as a new city, to be free of the factions of the old Umayyad garrison cities of Kūfah, Wāsiṭ, and Basra.

The ʿAbbāsid caliphate (750–821). The revolution that established the ʿAbbāsids represented a triumph of the Islāmic-Hejazi elements within the empire; the Iranian revival was yet to come. Nevertheless, ʿAbbāsid concern with fostering eastern Islām made the new caliphs willing to borrow the methods and procedures of statecraft employed by their Iranian predecessors. At Damascus the Umayyads had imitated Sāsānid court etiquette, but at Baghdad Persianizing influences went deeper and aroused some resentment among the Arabs, who were nostalgic for the legendary simplicity of human relations among the desert Arabs of yore. Self-conscious schools of manners grew up in the new metropolis, representing the competitive merits of the Arabs' or Persians' ancient ways. Regard for poetry—the Arabs' vehicle of folk memory—increased, and minds and imaginations were quickened. Philosophical enquiry was developed out of the need for precision about the meaning of Holy Writ and for the establishment of the authenticity of the Prophet's dicta, collected as *ḥadīth*s, or sayings traditionally ascribed to him, and recollected and preserved for posterity by his companions. An amalgam known as Islāmic civilization was thus being forged in Baghdad in the 8th and 9th centuries. The Iranian intellect, however, played a conspicuous part in what was still an Arab milieu. Works of Indian provenance were translated into Arabic from Pahlavi, the written language of Sāsānid Iran, notably by Ibn al-Muqaffaʿ (720–756/757). The wisdom of both the ancient East and West was received and discussed in Baghdad's schools. The metropolis's outposts confronted Byzantium as well as infidel marches in Afghanistan and Central Asia. Cultural influences came from both directions. Curiosity in the pursuit of knowledge had been enjoined by the Prophet "even as far as China." This cosmopolitanism was not new to the descendants of the urban Arabs of Mecca nor to the Iranians, whose land lay across the routes from the Pacific to the Mediterranean. Both peoples knew how to transmute what was not originally their own into forms that were entirely Islāmic. Islām had liberated men of the scribal and mercantile classes who in Iran had been subject to the dictates of a taboo-ridden and excessively ritualized Zoroastrianism and in Arabia had been inhibited by tribal feuds and prejudices.

Islāmic civilization

Despite the development of a distinctive Islāmic culture, the military problems of the empire were left unsolved. The ʿAbbāsids were under pressure from the infidel on several fronts—the Turks in Central Asia, pagans in India and in the Hindu Kush, and Christians in Byzantium. War for the faith, or *jihād*, against these infidels was a Muslim duty. But while the Umayyads had been expansionists and had seen themselves as heads of a military empire, the ʿAbbāsids were more pacific and saw themselves as the supporters of more than an Arab-conquering militia. Yet rebellions within the imperial frontiers had to be contained and the frontiers protected.

Rebellion within the empire took the form of peasant revolts in Azerbaijan and Khorāsān, coalesced by popular religious appeals centred on men who assumed or were accorded mysterious powers. Abū Muslim, executed in 755 by the second ʿAbbāsid caliph al-Manṣūr, who feared his influence, became one such messianic figure. Another was al-Muqannaʿ, "the Veiled Prophet of Khorāsān," who used Abū Muslim's mystique and whose movement lasted from 777 to 780. The Khorram-dīnān, "Glad Religionists," under the Azerbaijanian Bābak (816–838) also necessitated vigorous military suppression. Not until two decades had elapsed was Bābak caught. He was brought to Baghdad for torture and death after so long defying the caliph in Azerbaijan and west Persia. These heresiarchs revived such creeds as that of the anti-Sāsānid religious leader Mazdak (died AD 528 or 529), expressive of social and millennial aspirations that were later canalized into Ṣūfism on the one hand and into Shīʿism on the other.

Revolts within the empire

Seistan, Iran's southeastern border area, had a tradition of chivalry as the ancient homeland of Iranian military champions. Their tales passed to posterity collectively in the deeds of Rostam, son of Zāl, in Ferdowsī's *Shāhnāmeh* ("Book of Kings"), the Persian national epic. On the route to India, Seistan also had trade. Its agrarian masses were counterbalanced by an urban population whose economy could be bolstered by forays into still non-Muslim areas under the southern Hephthalites, the Zunbīls of the Hindu Kush's southwestern flanks, whose command of trade routes with India had to be contested when partnership in this command broke down.

Early exploitation of the province's agriculture by Arab governors had, however, debilitated the rural life, and Khārijites, who found refuge in Seistan from the Umayyads, organized or attracted bands of local peasants and of vagabonds who had strayed south from Khorāsān. The presence of these groups indicates agricultural depression following the first century of rule by nonagricultural Arabs who had failed to grasp the needs of the Iranian cultivator. Khārijite bands isolated the cities and threatened their supplies. Seistan needed an urban champion who could come to terms with the Khārijites and divert them to what could legitimately be termed *jihād* across the border, forming the gangsters into a well-disciplined loyal army. Such a man appeared in Yaʿqūb ebn Leys̄, who founded the first purely Iranian dynasty and threatened the Muslim empire with the first resurgence of Iranian independence.

THE "IRANIAN INTERMEZZO" (821–1055)

Yaʿqūb ebn Leys̄'s movement differed from Ṭāhir ibn al-Ḥusayn's establishment of a dynasty of Iranian governors over Khorāsān in 821. The latter's rise marks the caliph's recognition, after the difficulties encountered in Iran by Hārūn ar-Rashīd (786–809), that the best way for the imam and *amir al-muʾminīn* at Baghdad to ensure military effectiveness in eastern Islām was by appointing a great general to govern Khorāsān. Ṭāhir had won Baghdad from Hārūn's son al-Amīn in favour of his other son al-Maʾmūn in the civil war between the two after their father's death. Ṭāhir was descended from the *mawālī* of the great Arab leader to whom his forbears had become clients in east Khorāsān. He was, therefore, of Iranian origin, but, unlike Yaʿqūb, he did not emerge out of his own folk and because of a regional need. He rose as a servant of the caliphate, as whose lieutenant he was, in due course, appointed to govern a great frontier province. He made Nīshāpūr his capital. Though death followed his assumption of the right of having his name mentioned after the caliph's in the *khuṭbah* (the formal sermon at the Friday congregations of Muslims when those with authority over the community were mentioned after the Prophet), his family was sufficiently influential and respected at Baghdad for the governorship to continue in it until the Ṭāhirids were ousted from Nīshāpūr by Yaʿqūb in 873. Thereafter, they retired to Baghdad.

The Ṭāhirids

Discussion of the rise of "independent" Persian dynasties such as the Ṭāhirid in the 9th century has to be qualified not only by consideration of skillful ʿAbbāsid statecraft but also by recognition of the Muslims' need for legality in a juridical-religious setting. The majority of Muslims considered the caliph as the legitimate head of the Faith and the guarantor of the law. Such a guarantee was pre-eminently the need of merchants in the cities of Seistan, Transoxania, and central Iran.

In the Caspian provinces of Gilan and Ṭabaristān (Mazanderan) the situation was different. The Elburz Mountains had been a barrier against the integration of these areas into the caliphate. Small princely families—the Bāvands, including the Kāʾūsīyeh and the Espahbadīyeh (665–1349) and the Mosāferids also known as Sallārids, or Kangarids (916–*c.* 1090)—had remained independent of Damascus and Baghdad in the mountains of Daylam. When Islām reached these old Iranian enclaves, it was brought by Shīʿite leaders in flight from metropolitan persecution. It was not the Islām of the Sunnī state.

The Ṣaffārids. Yaʿqūb ebn Leyṡ began life as an apprentice *ṣaffār* ("coppersmith"), hence his dynasty's name, Ṣaffārid. Taking to military freebooting, he mustered an army that he disciplined and regularly paid in cash, absorbing many Khārijites into its ranks. This and his extension of Islām into pagan areas of Sind and Afghanistan earned him the *amīr* al-Muʾminīn's gratitude, which Yaʿqūb courted by sending golden idols captured from infidels to be paraded in Baghdad. Yaʿqūb's attitude toward the imam's claiming political subservience was, nevertheless, strikingly similar to that of the caliph-rejecting Khārijites. He turned his attention inward instead of outside the pale of Islām. He seized Baghdad's breadbaskets—Fars and Khuzistan. He drove out the Ṭāhirid emir from Nīshāpūr. His march on Baghdad itself was halted only by the stratagem devised by the caliph's commander-in-chief, whereby Yaʿqūb's army was inundated by burst dikes. Yaʿqūb died soon after, in 879. He had made an empire, minted his own coin, fashioned a new style of army loyal to its leader rather than to any religious or doctrinal concept, and required that verses in his praise be put into his own language—Persian—from Arabic, which he did not understand. He began the Iranian resurgence.

Yaʿqūb's empire

The collapse of the Ṭāhirid viceroyalty left Baghdad faced with a power vacuum in Khorāsān and southern Persia. Yaʿqūb's brother ʿAmr was confirmed as governor of Fars and Khorāsān, albeit reluctantly. The caliph's recognition of the upstart was thrice withdrawn, ʿAmr's authority being disclaimed to the Khorāsānian pilgrims to the Hejaz when they passed through Baghdad. But so long as Khorāsān was victimized by the rebels ʿAbd Allāh al-Khujistānī and, for longer, Rāfiʿ ibn Harthama, ʿAmr was useful to Baghdad. After Rāfiʿ had been finally defeated in 896, ʿAmr's broader ambitions gave the caliph al-Muʿtaḍid (892–902) his chance. ʿAmr conceived designs on Transoxania, but there the Sāmānid ʿAbbāsid vassals held the caliph's license to rule, after having nominally been Ṭāhirid deputies. When ʿAmr demanded and obtained the former Ṭāhirid tutelage over the Sāmānids in 898, Baghdad could leave the Ṣaffārid and Sāmānid to fight each other, and the Sāmānid Esmāʿīl (892–907) won. ʿAmr was sent to Baghdad, where he was put to death in 902. His family survived as Sāmānid vassals in Seistan and were heard of until the 16th century. Yaʿqūb remains a popular hero in Iranian history.

The Sāmānids. There was nothing of the popular hero in the Sāmānids' origin. Their eponym was Sāmān-Khudā, a landlord in the district of Balkh and, according to the dynasty's claims, a descendant of Bahrām Chūbīn, the Sāsānid general. Sāmān became Muslim. His four grandsons were rewarded for services to the caliph al-Maʾmūn (813–833) and received the caliph's investiture for areas that included Samarkand and Herāt. They thus gained wealthy Transoxanian and east Khorāsānian entrepôt cities, where they could profit from trade across Asia, even as far as Scandinavia, and the provision of Turkish slaves, much in demand in Baghdad, while they protected the frontiers and provided security for merchants in Bukhara, Samarkand, Khojand, and Herāt. With one transitory exception, they upheld orthodoxy and at each new accession paid a tribute to Baghdad for the tokens of investiture from the caliph whereby their rule represented lawful authority. Thus, legal transactions in Sāmānid realms would be valid, and Baghdad received tribute in return for the insignia prayed over and signed by the caliph. This tribute took the place of regular revenue, so that it represented a solution of those taxation problems and the consequent resentments that had bedeviled the Umayyad regime. In modern assessments of imperial power, Baghdad may seem to have been politically the weaker for this type of arrangement, but ensuring the reign of Islām in peripheral provinces was important to the caliphs. Islām's portals to the Far East were adequately guarded, the supply of Turkish slaves was maintained, and Turkish pagan tribes were converted to Islām under the Sāmānid aura.

Tribute to the caliph

The Iranian renaissance. This Sāmānid aura lasted from 819 until eclipsed in 999. Its supremacy in northeastern Islām began in 875, when the Sāmānid emir, Naṣr I, received the license to govern all Transoxania. Sāmānid emirs succeeded the Ṭāhirid-Ṣaffārid power in Khorāsān, and under them, the Iranian renaissance at last came to fruition. Shaped out of the vernacular of northeastern Iranian courts and households and making skillful use of additional Arabic vocabulary, the Persian language emerged as a literary medium. Persian notation had been used in the first Muslim *dīwān*s, or chancelleries, in accountancy, because the first civil servants in the old Iranian areas had been Iranians. In 697 the ruthless Umayyad governor Ḥajjāj ibn Yūsuf had ordered the change to Arabic notation, marking the final dethronement of Pahlavi characters. When "New Persian" began to emerge as a written language two centuries later, its alphabet was Arabic. It emerged as poetry, by which it was disciplined into a most expressive and flexible tongue, with the flexibility resulting from perfect control of a highly formal medium. The discipline was that of Arabic prosody, to which scenes of a verdure unknown to the Arab poet in the desert added, in the words of Iranian poets, a new and lustrous imagery. To rival the Arabs' tales of ancient valour, the Iranian legend was versified under Sāmānid impetus in the *Shāh-nāmeh*. Iran's "national epic" was completed by Ferdowsī of Ṭūs in Khorāsān in 1009/10.

Under the Sāmānids, Bukhara rivalled Baghdad as a cultural capital of Islām. Besides the Persian poet Rūdakī (died 940/941), who had crystallized the language and imagery of Persian lyrical poetry as Ferdowsī (died between 1020 and 1026) was to do for that of the epic, patrons such as Naṣr II (914–943) attracted Arabic poets and scholars to Bukhara, and many were bilingual. A written Persian evolved that has survived with remarkably little change.

The Ghaznavids. Rūdakī, in a poem about the Sāmānid emir's court, describes how "row upon row" of Turkish slave guards were part of its adornment. From these guards' ranks two military families arose—the Sīmjūrids and Ghaznavids—who ultimately proved disastrous to the Sāmānids. The Sīmjūrids received an appanage in the Qohestān region of southern Khorāsān. Alptegin founded the Ghaznavid fortunes when he established himself at Ghazna (modern Ghazni, Afghanistan) in 962. He and Abū ol-Ḥasan Sīmjūrī, as Sāmānid generals, competed with each other for the governorship of Khorāsān and control of the Sāmānid empire by placing on the throne emirs they could dominate. Abū ol-Ḥasan died in 961, but a court party instigated by men of the scribal class—civilian ministers as contrasted with Turkish generals—rejected Alptegin's candidate for the Sāmānid throne. Manṣūr I was installed and Alptegin prudently retired to his fief of Ghazna, where he founded what was eventually to become an independent dynasty. The Sīmjūrids enjoyed control of Khorāsān south of the Oxus but were hard-pressed by a third great Iranian dynasty, the Būyids, and were unable to survive the Sāmānid collapse and rise of the Ghaznavids.

The struggles of the Turkish slave generals for mastery of the throne with the help of shifting allegiance from the court's ministerial leaders both demonstrated and accelerated the Sāmānid decline. Sāmānid weakness attracted into Transoxania the Qarluq Turks, who had recently converted to Islām. They occupied Bukhara in 992 to establish in Transoxania the Qarakhanid, or Ilek Khanid, dynasty. Alptegin had been succeeded at Ghazna by Sebüktigin (died 997). Sebüktigin's son Maḥmūd made an agreement with the Qarakhanids whereby the Oxus was recognized as their mutual boundary. Thus the Sāmānids' dominion was divided and Maḥmūd was freed to advance westward into Khorāsān to meet the Būyids.

The Būyids. The Būyids share with the Sāmānids the palm for having brought to fruition the Iranian renaissance. They achieved Iranian political reascendancy by doing what Ya'qūb ibn Leys̄ had failed to do and what the Sāmānids would probably have considered it illegal to do: they captured Baghdad and made the caliph their puppet. As far east as the city of Rayy, west, central, and southern Iran were once more ruled by an Iranian family. At the peak of the Būyid Empire, second to Baghdad the Būyid base became Fars, whence the Achaemenids and the Sāsānians had sprung. Politically, the Būyids effected the Iranization of the metropolitan government. Yet by the very fact that they saw in the caliphate an institution of enough purely political significance to merit its dramatic take-over, they paradoxically left the caliphate's political role emphasized by what at first sight might seem to have been deepest humiliation. Spiritually, the caliphate held no appeal for the Būyids, who were Shī'ite. Politically and juridically, as the stabilizing factor over the Islāmic peoples, the Būyids, in spite of their own religious affiliation, maintained the caliphate.

The homeland of the Būyids (or Buwayhids) was Daylam, in the Gilan uplands in northern Iran. There, at the end of the 9th century, hardy valley dwellers had been stirred into martial activity by a number of factors, among them the rebel Rāfi' ibn Harthama's attempt to penetrate the region, ostensibly with Sāmānid support. 'Amr ebn Leys̄ had pursued the rebel into the region. Other factors had been the formation of Shī'ite principalities in the area and the continued Sāmānid attempts to subjugate them. After the Ṭāhirid collapse, the lack of stability in northern Iran south of the Elburz Mountains attracted many Daylamite mercenaries into the area on military adventures. Among them, Mākān ebn Kākī served the Sāmānids with his compatriots, the sons of Būyeh, and their allies the Zeyārids under Mardāvīz. Mardāvīz introduced the three Būyid brothers to the Iranian Plateau, where he established an empire reaching as far south as Isfahan and Hamadan. He was murdered in 935 but his Zeyārid descendants sought Sāmānid protection. They adhered to the Sunnī orthodoxy and maintained themselves in the region southeast of the Caspian. The Zeyārid Qābūs ebn Vashmgīr (978–1012) built himself a tomb tower, the Gonbad-e Qābūs (1006–07), which remains one of Iran's finest monuments. Also still extant is his descendant 'Onṣor ol-Ma'ālī Keykāvūs' (1049–90), *Qābūs-nāmeh*, a prose "Mirror for Princes," which is a valuable document on the social and political life of the time.

Foundation of Būyid power

Mardāvīz' expansionism south of the Elburz was taken up by his Būyid lieutenants: the eldest brother, 'Alī, consolidated power for himself in Isfahan and Fars and obtained the Caliph's recognition; another brother, Ḥasan, occupied Rayy and Hamadan; the youngest brother, Aḥmad, took Kerman in the southeast and Khuzistan in the southwest. The caliphs al-Muttaqī (940–944) and Mustakfī (944–946) were at the mercy of the Turkish slaves in their palace guard. The generals of the guard competed with each other for the office of *amīr al-umarā'* (commander-in-chief), who virtually ruled Iraq on behalf of the caliphs. When Aḥmad gained Khuzistan, he was close to the scene of the *amīr al-umarā'* contests, which he chose to settle by himself. Aḥmad entered Baghdad in 945 and assumed control of the caliphate's political functions. The caliph became the Būyid's protégé, and conferred on Aḥmad the title of Mu'izz ad-Dawlah. 'Alī became 'Imād ad-Dawlah, and Ḥasan, Rukn ad-Dawlah. All of these titles implied that the Būyids were the upholders of the Muslim 'Abbāsid *dawlah*, or state. In practice, however, the *dawlah* became the "Daylamite State." It should be noted that the titles did not include the word *dīn*, or faith, which was still in the caliph's sphere of action.

Later, Būyid titles increased in grandeur. Even the old Achaemenid title of *shāhanshāh*, King of Kings, reappeared—a title Aḥmad may have thought appropriate for an Iranian whose family reconquered Iran south of the Elburz. As suggested above, Būyid titles emphasized political and territorial sovereignty. This sovereignty reached its greatest extent under Rukn ad-Dawlah's son, 'Aḍud ad-Dawlah, who, after the deaths of his father and uncles, ruled an empire that comprised all of Persia west and south of Khorāsān and included Iraq, with Baghdad at its heart. 'Aḍud ad-Dawlah pursued peace negotiations with Byzantium, perhaps to free himself for his cherished project of an Egyptian campaign against the rival caliphate of the Fāṭimid Shī'ites, established in North Africa in 909, which had been relocated in Egypt in 969 (see FATIMIDS). 'Aḍud ad-Dawlah's concern with the middle kingdom and its westward extension toward the Mediterranean increased his hostility toward the Fāṭimids, despite his own Shī'ī persuasion. In the north, he drove the Zeyārids out of Ṭabarestān, which struck a blow against the Sāmānids' influence in the Caspian area.

Aḍud ad-Dawlah is celebrated for public works, of which the dam he built across the River Kor near Shīrāz, the "Band-e amīr," Emir's Dam, remains. He embellished the tomb of 'Alī at an-Najaf in Iraq, where he himself is buried. He built libraries, schools, and hospitals, and he was the patron of Arabic poet Mutanabbī. Some Arabic verses of his own are still extant. Although 'Aḍud ad-Dawlah was undoubtedly one of Iran's greatest rulers, his fratricidal wars, conducted with terrible intractability on his way to power, initiated Būyid decline. The descendants of the early Būyids reversed the mutual fidelity of the first three brothers. The power this fidelity had achieved and 'Aḍud ad-Dawlah had made into a world force crumbled after his death in 983.

His base had been Shīrāz, which he beautified and established as a cultural centre, but he died at Baghdad, where he chose to keep close to the caliph, whose daughter he married and from whom he took the title "The Crown of the Community" and the privilege of, like the caliph, having drums beaten at his gate on the calls to prayer. He also had his name mentioned after that of the Caliph aṭ-Ṭa'i' in the *khuṭbah*. The Būyids avoided the policy, which would have disrupted the empire, of favouring the Shī'īs. Instead, they offered consolations of an emotional sort to the Shī'īs in the form of public rites on the anniversaries of the Shī'ī martyrs, notably the one commemorating the massacre of 'Alī's son Ḥusayn and his followers under the Umayyads at Karbalā' in Iraq.

Būyid decline

Although the Būyids were careful to avoid sectarian strife, family quarrels weakened them sufficiently for Maḥmūd of Ghazna to gain Rayy in 1029. But Maḥmūd (998–1030) went no further: his dynasty paid great deference to the caliphate's legitimating power, and he made no bid to contest the Būyids' role as its protectors. Maḥmūd's agreement with the Sāmānids' Ilek Khanid successors, that the Oxus should be their and his boundary, held, but south of the river the Ghaznavids had to contend with their own distant relatives, the Oğuz Turks. Contrary to the sage counsel of Iranian ministers, Maḥmūd and his successor Mas'ūd (1031–41) permitted these tribesmen to use Khorāsānian grazing grounds, which they entered from north of the Oxus. United under descendants of an Oğuz leader named Seljuq, between 1038 and 1040 these nomads drove the Ghaznavids out of northeastern Iran. The final encounter was at Dandānqān in 1040.

After their defeat by the Seljuqs, the Ghaznavids, patrons of Islāmic culture and letters, were deflected eastward into India, where Maḥmūd had already conducted successful raids. The raids took the form of *jihād*, or holy war, and the Ghaznavids carried Islām and Perso-

Muslim art to the Indian subcontinent. In Iran, it was the Seljuqs' turn to create a new imperial synthesis with the ʿAbbāsid caliphs. Toghrïl Beg, the Seljuq sultan, entered Baghdad in 1055 and Būyid power was terminated, thus ending what Vladimir Minorsky, the great Iranologist, called the "Iranian intermezzo."

THE SELJUQS AND THE MONGOLS

The Seljuqs. Toghrïl I had proclaimed himself sultan at Nīshāpūr in 1038 and had espoused strict Sunnī orthodoxy by which he gained the caliph's confidence and undermined the Būyid position in Baghdad. The Oğuz Turks had accepted Islām late in the 10th century, and their leaders displayed a convert's zeal in their efforts to restore a Muslim polity along orthodox lines. Their efforts were made all the more urgent by the spread of Fāṭimid propaganda by underground means in the eastern caliphate and by the threat posed by the Christian crusaders from the west.

The Būyids' usurpation of the caliph's secular power had given rise to a new theory of state formulated by al-Māwardī (died 1058). Al-Māwardī's treatise partly prepared the theoretical ground for Toghrïl's attempt to establish an orthodox Muslim state in which conflict between the caliph-imam's spiritual-juridical authority on the one side and the secular power of the sultan on the other could be resolved, or at least regulated, by convention. Al-Māwardī reminded the Muslim world of the necessity of the imamate; but the treatise realistically admitted the existence of, and thus accommodated, the fact of military usurpation of power. The Seljuqs' own political theorist al-Ghazālī (died 1111) carried this admission further by explaining that the position of a powerless caliph, overshadowed by a strong Seljuq master, was one in which the latter's presence guarantees the former's capacity to defend and extend Islām.

The caliph al-Qāʾim (1031–75) replaced the last Būyid's name, al-Malik ar-Raḥīm, in the *khuṭbah* and on the coins with Toghrïl Beg's; and after protracted negotiation ensuring restoration of the caliph's dignity after Shīʿī subjugation, Toghrïl entered Baghdad in December 1055. The caliph enthroned him and married a Seljuq princess. After Toghrïl had campaigned successfully as far as Syria, he was given the title of "King of the East and West." The new situation was justified by the theory that existing practice was legal whereby a new caliph could be instituted by the sultan, who possessed effective power and sovereignty but that thereafter the sultan owed the caliph allegiance because only so long as the caliph-imam's juridical faculties were recognized could government be valid.

Toghrïl Beg died in 1063. His heir, Alp-Arslan, was succeeded by Malik-Shāh in 1072, and the latter's death in 1092 led to succession disputes out of which Berk-yaruq emerged triumphant to reign until 1105. After a brief reign, Malik-Shāh II was succeeded by Muḥammad I (1105–18). The last "Great Seljuq" was Sanjar (1118–57), who had earlier been governor of Khorāsān. Alp-Arslan nearly annihilated the Byzantine Army at Manzikert in 1071, opening Asia Minor to those dependent tribesmen of the Seljuqs of whom Iran and the world were to hear more in the period of Ottoman power. Transoxania was subdued, the Christians in the Caucasus chastised, and the Egyptians expelled from Syria. An empire was for a short time achieved whose extent and stability enabled Alp-Arslan's and Malik-Shāh's great minister, Niẓām al-Mulk (died 1092), to pay an Oxus ferryman with a draft cashable in Damascus.

Battle of Manzikert

The building and maintenance of such a great empire necessitated a military regime and a vast war machine. The price to be paid later was oppression by military commanders and their units, set free after the machine fell out of the grasp of powerful sultans to compete with each other and harry the land. The soldiers had been remunerated by grants of land called *iqṭāʿ*s. The grants later became nuclei out of which petty principalities grew with the decline of the central power. The cultivators were left at the mercy of military overlords in possession of the soil.

The great minister Niẓām al-Mulk was typical of the Iranian bureaucracy which, in an area prone to invasion, was often called upon to attempt to cushion the impact of the brute military force of invaders and contain it within the bounds of administrative, economic, and cultural feasibility. He wrote a "Book of Government" (*Seyāsat-nāmeh*) for his Turkish masters in which he urged the regulation of court procedures in line with Sāmānid models and the restriction of the arrogance and cupidity of the military fief holders. His book is the measure of the Seljuqs' failure to provide enduring stability and equitable government. Had they done so, such a work would have been unnecessary.

The Ismāʿīlīyah. Of one disruptive force the book, in terms betraying near-panic, is dramatically descriptive. The Seljuqs failed to nip in the bud the power of the Ismāʿīlīyah, originally spread by Fāṭimid propagandists, but later split from the mainstream of events in Egypt to become an underground organization within the Seljuq Empire. This movement exercised power by terrorism, so that a nickname, *ḥashīshīyūn* ("hashish smokers"), for its adherents has contributed the word "assassin" to the English language. The movement was a highly intellectual form of extremist Shīʿism, which recognized only seven of the imams in descent from ʿAlī and Fāṭimah, whereas the Shīʿism of the Būyids and of Iran later on recognized 12. The movement was brought to Iran by Ḥasan-e Ṣabbāḥ, who had been trained in Fāṭimid Egypt. In 1090 Ḥasan gained the castle of Alamūt in the Elburz Mountains and the order's principal cells were thereafter situated, so far as possible, in similar impregnable mountain strongholds. From these centres, *fidāʾī*s, or devotees ready to sacrifice their lives, issued forth and permeated society, spreading their mission as peddlers and itinerant tailors and gaining influence among the urban artisan and weaving classes. They were often able to win also the confidence of many highly placed ladies and children, whom they could please with novelties of dress or toys. Niẓām al-Mulk himself was assassinated by one of the *fidāʾī*s, but it is possible that this was done with the connivance of Malik-Shāh's wife, whose son the vizier did not support for the succession.

The "assassins"

The Ismāʿīlīyah were able to puncture Seljuq power but not destroy it. In the end, the Seljuq Empire collapsed where it had begun—in Khorāsān, where Sultan Sanjar ultimately failed to control Turkmen tribes related to him by blood. Sanjar could not rely on military commanders his family had raised to high posts and had rewarded with land and provincial powers. The tribesmen refused to be coerced into paying taxes. In 1153 they captured the old sultan and, although allowing him all the respect of his regal position, kept him captive for three years.

The Khwārezm-Shāhs. Atsiz was the military leader who, after Sultan Sanjar's death in 1157, succeeded in supplanting Seljuq power in northeastern Iran. His ancestor, Anūştegin, had been keeper of Malik-Shāh's kitchen utensils and had been rewarded with the governorship of Khwārezm on the Oxus, where he founded the Khwārezm-Shāh dynasty (1077–1231). Regions elsewhere in Iran, on the passing of Seljuq supremacy, became independent under *atabeg*s, who were originally proxy fathers and tutors sent with young Seljuq princes when these were deputed to govern provinces. At first the *atabeg*s took power in the names of Seljuq puppets. When this fiction lapsed, *atabeg* dynasties such as the Ildeguzids of Azerbaijan (1137–1225) and Salghurids of Fārs (1148–1270) split Iran into independent rival principalities.

Atabeg rule

The Salghurid court in Shīrāz especially fostered the arts, as parvenu, competitive courts are wont to do. The poet Saʿdī (died 1292) was a contemporary in Shīrāz of the Salghurid *atabeg* Abū Bakr ebn Saʿd ebn Zangī (1231–60), to whom he alludes by name in his *Būstān* ("The Orchard"), a book of ethics in verse. Abū Bakr's father, Saʿd, after whom Saʿdī took his pen name, conferred great prosperity on Shīrāz.

Saʿd ebn Zangī came to terms with the Khwārezm-Shāhs. Their power in Transoxania was secured by acceptance of tributary status to the infidel Karakitais of Central Asia. They endeavoured to emulate the Seljuqs by following an expansionist policy in Iran south of the Oxus. Saʿd ebn Zangī, in his relations with the Khwārezm-Shāh, set the pattern his successor Abū Bakr followed later. These *atabegs* saved Fars from outright invasion by northern military powers by paying heavy tribute. This tribute was the price of Shīrāz's remaining the peaceful haven of the arts in which Saʿdī and after him Ḥāfeẓ (died 1390) flourished, to continue the Persian literary tradition begun under the Sāmānids and continued under both the Ghaznavids and the Seljuqs.

The collapse of the Karakitai Empire northeast of the Oxus was partly accelerated by the unsuccessful bid of Khwārezm-Shāh ʿAlāʾ ad-Dīn Muḥammad (1200–20) to win Muslim approval while releasing himself from the Khwārezm-Shāhs' humiliating tributary status to an infidel power. But the *coup de grace* to the Karakitai Empire was delivered by its Gurkhan's own vassal from the east, Küchlüg Khan. Thus, the Khwārezm-Shāh was from 1211 onward faced by another hostile opponent in Central Asia—Küchlüg Khan. The Karakitai settlement had been destroyed; but the situation on the Khwārezm-Shāh's eastern border had worsened.

Meanwhile, Sultan ʿAlāʾ ad-Dīn Muḥammad quarrelled with the caliph; he set up an anti-caliph of his own and further antagonized his Muslim subjects, unremittingly suspicious of a regime once subject to the Karakitai infidels and whose Kipchak mercenary militia and brutal commanders brought cruelty and desolation wherever they marched. Sultan Muḥammad Khwārezm-Shāh was unable to control his army leaders, who had tribal connections with such influential people at court as his own mother. The post-Karakitai wars between him and Küchlüg Khan damaged the safety of the Central Asian trade arteries from China to the West. The great Mongol leader Genghis (Chinghiz) Khan took Peking in 1215 and as Lord of China was concerned with Chinese trade outlets. The situation between Küchlüg and Sultan Muḥammad afforded scope as well as a pretext for the Mongols' westward advance, if only to restore the flow of trade.

The Mongol invasion. Misunderstanding of how essentially fragile Sultan ʿAlāʾ ad-Dīn Muḥammad Khwārezm-Shāh's apparently imposing empire was, its distance away from the Mongols' eastern homelands, the strangeness of new terrain, all doubtless induced fear in Mongols, and this might partly account for the terrible events with which Genghis Khan's name has ever since been associated. The terror his invasion brought must also be ascribed to his quest for vengeance. Genghis Khan's first two missions to Khwārezmia had been massacred; but the place of commercial motives in the Mongol's decision to march to the west is indicated by the fact that the first was a trade mission. The massacre and robbery of this mission at Utrār by one of Sultan Muḥammad's governors before it reached the capital made Genghis single out Utrār for especially savage treatment when the murder of his second, purely diplomatic, mission left him no alternative but war.

Reasons for Mongol vengeance

His guides were Muslim merchants from Transoxania. They had to witness one of the worst catastrophes of history. The years 1220 and 1221 saw the razing of Bukhara, Samarkand, Herāt, Ṭūs, Nīshāpūr, and the slaughter of whole populations. The Khwārezm-Shāh fled, to die on an island off the Caspian coast. His son Jalāl od-Dīn survived until murdered in Kurdistan in 1231. He had eluded Genghis Khan on the Indus, across which his horse swam, enabling him to escape to India. He returned to attempt the restoration of the Khwārezmian Empire over Iran, but he failed to unite the Iranian regions, although Genghis Khan had withdrawn to Mongolia, where he died in August 1227. Iran was left divided, Mongol agents remaining in some districts, local adventurers profiting from the lack of order in others.

The Il-Khans. A second Mongol invasion began when Genghis Khan's grandson Hülagü Khan crossed the Oxus in 1256 and destroyed the Assassin fortress at Alamūt. With the disintegration of the Seljuq Empire, the caliphate had created a state in the area around Baghdad and in southwestern Iran. In 1258 Hülagü besieged Baghdad, where divided counsels prevented the city's salvation. Al-Mustaʿṣim, the last ʿAbbāsid caliph of Baghdad, was executed by being kicked to death. Eastern Islām fell to pagan rulers.

Hülagü hoped to consolidate Mongol rule over western Asia and to extend the Mongol Empire as far as the Mediterranean, an empire that would span the earth from China to the Levant. Hülagü made Iran his base, but the Mamlūks of Egypt (1250–1517) prevented him and his successors from achieving their great imperial goal. Instead, a Mongol dynasty, the Il-Khans, or "deputy khans" to the Great Khan in China, was established in Iran to attempt repair of the damage of the first Mongol invasion. But it failed in repeated attempts to reach the Mediterranean. The injuries Iran had suffered went deep, but it would be unfair to attribute them all to Ghengis Khan's invasion, itself the climax to a long period of social and political disarray under the Khwārezm-Shāhs and dating from the decline of the Seljuqs.

The Il-Khanid dynasty made Azerbaijan its centre, and established Tabriz as its first capital until Solṭānīyeh was built early in the 14th century. At first repair and readjustment of a stricken society was complicated by the collapse of law. The caliphate, as the symbol of Muslim legality, had been eroded by Sultan Moḥammad Khwārezm-Shāh and by its own withdrawal into a temporal state in Iraq and the Tigris-Euphrates estuary region. But it had retained enough vitality for Sultan Muḥammad's action in setting up an anti-caliph to have alienated influential members of his subject people. After 1258 it was gone altogether, while Hülagü Khan showed considerable religious eclecticism and had, in any event, the *yāsā* of Genghis Khan to apply as the law of the Mongol state, in opposition to, or side by side with, the Sharīʿah, the law of Islām.

The Il-Khans' religious toleration released Christians and Jews from their restrictions under the Islāmic regime. Fresh talent thus became available, but competition for new favours marred what good effects this release might have had. It took time for Iranian administrators to resume their normal role after the invasion and to restore some semblance of administrative order and stability. Their process was impeded by the paganism of the new conquerors as well as by jostling for influence among classes of the conquered, not in this instance exclusively Muslim. At the same time, a shattered agrarian economy was burdened by heavy taxes, those sanctioned by the Sharīʿah being added to by those the *yāsā* provided for, so that the pressure of exploitation was increased by Mongol tax innovations as well as by the invaders' cupidity.

The pressure was increased beyond the economy's endurance: the Il-Khanid government ran into fiscal difficulties. An experiment with paper money, modelled on the Chinese money, failed under Gaykhatu (1291–95). Gaykhatu was followed briefly by Baydu (died 1295) who was supplanted by the greatest of the Il-Khans, Maḥmūd Ghāzān (1295–1304). Ghāzān abandoned Buddhism, the faith in which his grandfather Abagha, Hülagü's successor (1265–82), had reared him, and adopted Islām. One of his chief ministers was also his biographer, Rashīd od-Dīn, of Jewish descent. He seems deliberately to have striven to present Ghāzān, whom he styles the "emperor of Islām" (*pādshāh-e islām*), as a ruler who combined the qualities and functions of both the former caliphs and ancient Iranian "great kings."

The reign of Ghāzān

Ghāzān made strenuous efforts to regulate taxes, encourage industry, bring wasteland into cultivation, and curb the abuses and arrogance of the military and official classes. Facilities for home and foreign merchants were furnished. Buildings were constructed and irrigation channels dug. Medicinal and fruit-bearing plants were imported and the cultivation of indigenous ones was encouraged. Observatories were built and improved—a sure indication of concern with agricultural improvement, for seasonal planning required accurate calendars. He fostered Muslim sentiment by showing consideration for those who claimed descent from the Prophet's family, the Sayyids, and it seems probable that he wished to eradicate or overlay Shīʿī-Sunnī sectarian divisiveness, for Ghāzān's Islām appears to have been designed to appeal equally to both persuasions. Any slight bias in favour of the Shīʿah might be attributed to a desire to capture the emotions and imagination of many of the humble people who had reacted against the Seljuqs' orthodoxy and craved a teaching that included millennial overtones. Shīʿism had been liberated by the fall of the ʿAbbāsid Caliphate. Its belief in the reappearance of the Twelfth Imam, who was to inaugurate peace and justice in the world, satisfied this popular craving for religious solace.

Ghāzān's work was carried on but less successfully by his successor Öljeitü (1304–16). Between 1317 and 1335, though he finally relinquished the expensive campaigns against Egypt for the opening to the Mediterranean, Abū Saʿīd was unable to keep the Il-Khanid regime consolidated, and it fell apart on his death. Ghāzān's brilliant reign survives only in the pages of his historian, Rashīd od-Dīn. Wars against Egypt and their own Mongol kinsmen in Asia had in fact hampered the Il-Khans in accomplishing a satisfactory reintegration of an Iranian polity.

As the *atabegs* had done after the Seljuqs, after 1335, Il-Khanid military emirs began to establish themselves as independent regional potentates. At first, two of them, formerly military chiefs in the Il-Khans' service, competed for power in western Iran, ostensibly acting on behalf of rival Il-Khanid puppet princes. Ḥasan the Small of the Chūpānids was eventually defeated by Ḥasan the Tall of the Jalāyirids, who set up the Jalāyirid dynasty over Iraq, Kurdistan, and Azerbaijan; it lasted from 1336 to 1432. In Fars, Il-Khanid agents, the Injuids, after a spell of power during which Abū Isḥāq Injū had been the poet Ḥāfeẓ's patron, were ousted by Abū Saʿīd's governor of Yazd, Mobārez od-Dīn Moẓaffar. Thus in 1353 Shīrāz became the Moẓaffarid dynasty's capital, which it remained until conquest by Timur (Tamerlane) in 1393.

THE TIMURIDS AND TURKMEN

Timur claimed descent from Genghis Khan's family. The disturbed conditions in Mongol Transoxania gave this son of a minor government agent in the town of Kish the chance to build up a kingdom in Central Asia in the name of the Chagatai Khans, whom he eventually supplanted. He entered Iran in 1380 and in 1393 reduced the Jalāyirids after taking their capital Baghdad. In 1402 he captured the Ottoman Sultan Bayezid at Ankara. He conquered Syria and then turned his attention to campaigns far to the east of his tumultuously acquired and ill-cemented empire: he died in 1405 on an expedition to China. He left an awesome name and an ambiguous record of flights of curiosity into the realms of unorthodox religious beliefs, history, and every kind of enquiry concerning lands and peoples. He showed interest in Ṣūfism, a form of Islāmic mysticism that varied from a scholastic study of ascetic techniques for mastering the carnal self to complete abandonment of all forms of authority in the belief that faith alone is necessary for salvation. Ṣūfism had increased in the disturbed post-Seljuq era as both the consolation and refuge of desperate people. In Ṣūfism Timur may have hoped to find popular leaders whom he could use for his own purposes. His encounters with such keepers of the consciences of harried, exploited, and ill-treated Iranians proved that they knew him perhaps better than he knew himself. Whatever his motives may have been, the reverse of stability was his legacy to Iran. His division of his ill-assimilated conquests among his sons served to ensure that an integrated Timurid Empire would never be achieved.

Character of Timur

The nearest a Timurid state came to being an integrated Iranian Empire was under Timur's son Shāh Rokh Shāh (1405–47). Shāh Rokh endeavoured to weld Azerbaijan and western Persia to Khorāsān and eastern Persia to form a united Timurid state for a short and troubled period of time, but he only succeeded in loosely controlling western and southern Iran from his beautiful capital at Herāt. Azerbaijan demanded three major military expeditions from this pacific sovereign and even so could not long be held. Herāt he made the seat of a splendid culture, the atelier of great miniature painters (Behzād notable among them), and the home of a revival of Persian poetry, letters, and philosophy. This revival was not unconnected with an effort to claim for an Iranian centre once more the palm of leadership in the propagation of Sunnī ideology: Herāt sent copies of Sunnī canonical works on request to Egypt. The reaction in Shīʿism's ultimate victory under the Ṣafavid shahs of Persia was, however, already in preparation.

Western Iran was dominated by the Kara Koyunlu, the "Black Sheep" Turkmen. In Azerbaijan they had supplanted their former masters the Jalāyirids. Timur had put these Kara Koyunlu to flight, but in 1406 they regained their capital, Tabriz. On Shāh Rokh's death, Jahān Shāh (1438–68) extended Kara Koyunlu rule out of the northwest deeper into Iran at the Timurids' expense. The Timurids relied on their old allies, the Kara Koyunlus' rival Turkmen of the Ak Koyunlu, "White Sheep" clans, who had long been established at Diyarbakır in Turkey. The White Sheep acted as a curb on the Black Sheep, whose Jahān Shāh was destroyed by the Ak Koyunlu Uzun Ḥasan by the end of 1467.

"Black Sheep" and "White Sheep"

Uzun Ḥasan (1453–78) achieved a short-lived Iranian Empire and even briefly deprived the Timurids of Herāt. He was, however, confronted by a new power in Asia Minor—the Ottoman Turks. His relationship with the Christian Emperor at Trebizond (Trabzon) through his Byzantine wife, Despina, involved Uzun Ḥasan in attempts to shield Trebizond from the ineluctable Ottoman advance. The Ottomans crushingly defeated him in 1473. Under his son Yaʿqūb (1478–90), the Ak Koyunlu state was subjected to fiscal reforms associated with a government-sponsored effort to reapply rigorous purist principles of orthodox Islāmic rules for revenue collection. Yaʿqūb attempted to purge the state of taxes introduced under the Mongols and not sanctioned by the Muslim canon. But the inquiries made by the orthodox religious authorities antagonized the vested interests, damaged the popularity of the Ak Koyunlu regime, and discredited Sunnī fanaticism.

This attempt to revive religious orthodoxy through revenue reform or to effect the latter under the guise of religion no doubt gave impetus to the spread of Ṣafavid Shīʿī propaganda. Another factor must have been related to the same general economic decline that made Sultan Yaʿqūb's fiscal reforms necessary in the first place. Sheykh Ḥeydar led a movement that had begun as a Ṣūfī order under his ancestor Sheykh Ṣafī od-Dīn of Ardabīl (1252–1334). This order may be considered to have originally represented a puritanical, but not legalistically so, reaction against the sullying of Islām, the staining of Muslim lands, by the Mongol infidels. What began as a spiritual, otherworldly reaction against irreligion and the betrayal of spiritual aspirations developed into a manifestation of the Shīʿī quest for dominion over a Muslim polity. By the 15th century, the Ṣafavid movement could draw on both the mystical emotional force and the Shīʿī appeal to the oppressed populace to gain a large number of dedicated adherents. Sheykh Ḥeydar inured his numerous followers to warfare by leading them on expeditions from Ardabīl into the nearby Caucasus. He was killed on one of these campaigns. His son Esmāʿīl was to avenge his death and lead his devoted army to a conquest of Iran whereby Iran gained a great dynasty, a Shīʿī regime, and in most essentials its shape as a modern nation state.

Esmāʿīl

In 1501 Esmāʿīl supplanted the Ak Koyunlu in Azerbaijan. Within a decade, he gained supremacy over most of Iran as a ruler regarded as divinely entitled to sovereignty. The Ṣafavids claimed descent, on grounds that modern research has shown to be dubious, from the Shīʿah imams. Islām in Iran, therefore, could regard itself as at last having a legitimate imam-ruler, who, as a descendant of ʿAlī, required no caliph to legitimate his position. Gone were the days of rule by converted and zealous Sunnī Turks or by Mongols of ambiguous spiritual allegiance. Iran's defilement was removed by the swelling tide of Shīʿism, which bore Esmāʿīl to the throne his family was to occupy until 1722, in one of the greatest epochs of Iranian history.

THE SAFAVIDS (1502–1736)

The new Iranian empire lacked the resources that had been available to the caliphs of Baghdad in former times through their dominion over Central Asia and the West: Asia Minor and Transoxania were gone; also the rise of maritime trade in the west was detrimental to a country whose wealth had depended greatly on its position on important east-west overland trade routes. The rise of the Ottomans impeded Iranian westward advances and contested with the Ṣafavids' control over both the Caucasus and Mesopotamia. Years of warfare with the Ottomans had imposed a heavy drain on the Ṣafavids' resources. The Ottomans threatened Azerbaijan itself. Finally, in 1639 a treaty gave Yerevan in the southern Caucasus to Iran and Baghdad in Mesopotamia to the Ottomans.

Shāh ʿAbbās I. The Ṣafavids were still faced with the problem of making their empire pay. The silk trade, over which the government held a monopoly, was a primary source of revenue. Esmāʿīl's successor, Shāh Ṭahmāsp (1524–76), encouraged carpet weaving on the scale of a state industry. Shāh ʿAbbās I (1587–1629) established trade contacts directly with Europe, but Iran's remoteness from Europe, behind the imposing Ottoman screen, made maintenance and promotion of these contacts difficult and sporadic. Shāh ʿAbbās I also transplanted a colony of industrious and commercially astute Armenians from Jolfā in Azerbaijan to a new Jolfā adjacent to Isfahan, the city he developed and adorned as his capital. The Ṣafavids had earlier moved their capital from the vulnerable Tabriz to Kazvin. Since the Uzbek menace from east of the Caspian had been overcome, ʿAbbās could move his capital south to Isfahan, more centrally placed than Kazvin for control over the whole country, and for communication with the trade outlets of the Persian Gulf. ʿAbbās engaged English help to oust the Portuguese from the island of Hormuz in 1622. He also strove to lodge Ṣafavid power strongly in Khorāsān, where he developed the shrine of ʿAlī ar-Riḍā at Mashhad, the eighth Shīʿah imam, as a pilgrim centre to rival Shīʿī holy places in Mesopotamia, where visiting pilgrims took currency out of Ṣafavid into Ottoman territory.

Army reforms

Under Shāh ʿAbbās I Iran prospered. The old Ṣūfī bands, which had been formed into artificial tribal units for military purposes during the dynasty's formative period, were replaced by a standing army trained and equipped on European lines with the advice of Robert Sherley. Sherley was an English adventurer versed in artillery tactics who, accompanied by a party of cannon founders, reached Kazvin with his brother Anthony in 1598. The bureaucracy, too, was carefully reorganized, but the seeds of the sovereignty's weakness lay in the royal house itself, which lacked an established system of inheritance by primogeniture. A reigning shah's nearest and most acute objects of suspicion were his own sons. Among them, brother plotted against brother over who should succeed on their father's death. Intriguers, ambitious for influence in a subsequent reign, supported one prince against another. Shāh ʿAbbās did not adopt the Ottoman sultans' practice of eliminating royal males by murder (as a child he had been within a hair's breadth of being a victim of such a policy). Instead, he instituted the practice of immuring infant princes in palace gardens away from the promptings of intrigue and the world at large. As a result, his successors tended to be indecisive men, easily dominated by powerful religious dignitaries to whom the Ṣafavids had accorded considerable influence in an attempt to make Shīʿism the state religion.

The Afghan interlude. Shāh Solṭān Ḥoseyn (reigned 1694–1722) was of a religious temperament and especially influenced by the divines, whose conflicting advice, added to his own procrastination, sealed the sudden and unexpected fate of the Ṣafavid empire. One Maḥmūd, a former Ṣafavid vassal in Afghanistan, captured Isfahan and murdered Solṭān Ḥoseyn in his cell in the beautiful mosque-school, or *madrasah*, built in his mother's name.

The Afghan interlude was disastrous for Iran. In 1723 the Ottomans took advantage of the disintegration of the Ṣafavid realm and invaded from the west, ravaging western Persia. Nāder, an Afshārid Turkmen from northern Khorāsān, was eventually able to reunite Iran, a process he began on behalf of the Ṣafavid prince Ṭahmāsp II (1722–32), who had escaped the Afghans. After he had cleared the country of Afghans, Nāder was made governor of a large area of eastern Iran.

NADER SHAH (1736–47)

Nāder later dethroned Ṭahmāsp II in favour of another Ṣafavid puppet. His successful military exploits, however, which included victories over rebels in the Caucasus, made it feasible for this stern warrior himself to be proclaimed Shah in 1736. He attempted to mollify Perso-Ottoman hostility by establishing in Iran a less aggressive form of Shīʿism, which would be less offensive to Ottoman susceptibilities; but this experiment did not take root. Want of money drove him to embark on his celebrated Indian campaign in 1738–39. His capture of Delhi and of the Mughal emperor's treasure gave Nāder booty in such quantities that he was able to exempt Iran from taxes for three years. His Indian expedition temporarily solved the problem of how to make his empire financially viable.

Attack on India

How large this problem loomed in Nāder's mind is demonstrated by his increasingly morbid obsession with treasure and jewels. After suspecting his son of complicity in a plot against him in 1741, Nāder's mind seems to have become unhinged; his brilliance and courage deteriorated into a meanness and capricious cruelty that could no longer be tolerated. In 1747 he was murdered by a group of his own Afshārs, together with some Qājār chiefs—a sad end to one of Iran's greatest leaders.

Nāder had been the first modern Iranian leader to perceive the importance of having his own navy, and in 1734 he had appointed an "Admiral of the Gulf." Ships were purchased from their British captains, and by 1735 the new Iranian navy had attacked Basra. What really mattered, however, were the land forces. Nāder's reign exemplified the fact that to be successful, a Shāh of Iran had to prove himself capable of defending his realm's territorial integrity and of extending its sources of wealth and production by conquest. To these ends, Nāder built up a large army comprised of tribal units under their own chiefs, such as his Afshārid kinsmen, and the Qājārs, and Bakhtyārīs.

But on Nāder's death, his great military machine dispersed, its commanders bent on establishing their own states. Aḥmad Durrānī founded a kingdom in Afghanistan based on Qandahār. Shāh Rokh, Nāder's blind grandson, succeeded in maintaining himself at the head of an Afshārid state in Khorāsān, its capital at Mashhad. The Qājār chief Moḥammad Ḥasan took Mazanderan south of the Caspian Sea. Āzād Khān, an Afghan, held Azerbaijan, whence Moḥammad Ḥasan Khān Qājār ultimately expelled him. The Qājār chief, therefore, disposed of this post-Nāder Afghan remnant in northwestern Iran, but was himself unable to make headway against a new power arising in central and southern Iran, that of the Zands.

THE ZAND DYNASTY (1750–79)

Moḥammad Karīm Khān Zand began his career as an ally of the Bakhtyārī chief ʿAlī Mardān Khān in a bid to oust Shāh Rokh's nominee, Abū ol-Fatḥ Bakhtyārī, from Isfahan. Victory over this representative of the Mashhad regime having been achieved, it was agreed that Shāh Solṭān Ḥoseyn Ṣafavī's grandson, a boy named Abū Ṭarāb, should be proclaimed Shāh Esmāʿīl III; but ʿAlī Mardān Khān broke the compact and was killed. Karīm Khān gained supremacy over central and southern Iran and reigned as regent or deputy (*vakīl*) on behalf of the powerless Ṣafavid prince, never arrogating to himself the title of shah. Karīm Khān made Shīrāz his capital and did not contend with Shāh Rokh (1748–95) for the hegemony of Khorāsān. He concentrated on Fārs and the centre, but managed to contain the Qājārs in Mazanderan, north of the Elburz Mountains. He kept Āghā Moḥammad Khān Qājār a hostage at his court in Shīrāz, after repulsing Moḥammad Ḥasan Qājār's bids for extended dominion. Karīm Khān's geniality and common sense brought peace and popular contentment, and he strove for commercial prosperity in Shīrāz, a centre accessible to the Persian Gulf ports and the Indian trade. After Karīm Khān's death in 1779, Āghā Moḥammad escaped to the Qājār tribal country in the north, gathered a large force, and embarked upon a war of conquest.

Prosperity under Karīm Khān

THE QĀJĀRS (1779–1925)

Āghā Moḥammad Khān. Between 1779 and 1789 the Zands fought among themselves over their legacy. In the end, it fell to the gallant Loṭf ʿAlī, the Zands' last hope. Āghā Moḥammad Khān relentlessly hunted him down until he overcame and killed him at the southeastern city of Kermān in 1794. In 1796 Āghā Moḥammad assumed the imperial diadem, and later in the same year he took Mashhad. Shāh Rokh died of the tortures inflicted on him to make him reveal the complete tally of the Afshārids' treasure. Āghā Moḥammad was cruel and he was avaricious. Karīm Khān's commercial efforts were nullified by his successors' quarrels. With cruel irony, attempts to revive the Persian Gulf trade were followed by a British mission from India in 1800, which ultimately opened the way for a drain of Persian bullion to India. This drain was made inevitable by the damage done to Iran's productive capacity during Āghā Moḥammad's campaigns to conquer the country.

European penetration. Fatḥ ʿAlī Shāh (ruled 1797–1834), in need of revenue, relied on British subsidies but lost the Caucasus to Russia by the treaties of Golestān in 1813 and Turkmanchay in 1828. The last gave Russian commercial and consular agents entrance to Iran, and this began a diplomatic rivalry between Russia and Britain that victimized Iran. This rivalry was eventually resolved when in 1907 an Anglo-Russian convention established, in Iran, Afghanistan, and Tibet, exclusive Anglo-Russian spheres of influence.

Anglo-Russian rivalry

Moḥammad Shāh's (ruled 1834–48) minister Ḥājjī Mīrzā Āghāsī tried to activate the government in a revival of the sources of production and to cement ties with lesser European powers, such as Spain and Belgium, as an alternative to Anglo-Russian dominance, but little was achieved. Nāṣer od-Dīn Shāh (ruled 1848–96) made Iran's last effort to regain Herāt, but 1857 saw the end of such expansionist efforts. Popular and religious antagonism to the Qājār regime increased as Nāṣer od-Dīn Shāh strove to raise funds by selling concessions, ostensibly for the development of his country's resources, to Europeans. The money paid for concessions was squandered by the court and on the Shah's journeys to Europe.

Popular protest and the constitution. The effect of popular protest in bringing about cancellation of a tobacco concession in 1890 demonstrated two factors of crucial significance for the future: first, that unified popular protest could limit despotism's scope; and second, that a mercantile class of sufficient prosperity existed in Iran to make use, with support from religious orators, of popular feeling. The Shah's suppression of the Bābī and Bahāʾī heterodoxies had not, in spite of its ugly severity, ingratiated the regime with the orthodox *ʿulamāʾ*.

The "Tobacco Riots" were the prelude to the constitutional revolution of the reign of Moẓaffar od-Dīn Shāh (ruled 1896–1907). Iran remained on silver after the failure of bimetallism and the world slump in silver values from the 1870s onward. Silver bullion drained out of the country and copper money proliferated, causing bread riots. In 1906 the ailing Shah granted a constitution. In October of that year the first National Consultative Assembly (the Majles) was opened. In 1908, under Moḥammad ʿAlī Shāh (ruled 1907–09), the Majles was suppressed with the aid of the Persian Cossack Brigade. The Majles was revived after a civil war that culminated in Moḥammad ʿAlī's deposition.

Constitution of 1906

Rise of Reza Khan. During World War I, Iran was the scene of rival intrigues by pro-British and pro-German groups among the notables, a class that had succeeded in gaining control of the Majles. The disruption was exacerbated by famine and national bankruptcy.

In 1919 the Majles refused a British offer of financial and military assistance, and British financial and military experts were withdrawn from the country. Salvation came from another quarter, in the person of an Iranian officer, Reza Khan, of the Persian Cossack Brigade. In collaboration with a political writer, Sayyid Zia od-Din Tabataba'i, he staged a coup d'etat in 1921 and took control of all the military forces. Reza Khan's efforts between 1921 and 1925 as, successively, war minister and prime minister under Aḥmad Shāh, resulted in the formation of an army loyal to him, the achievement of order, and finally, in 1925, the deposition of the last Qājār shah and the transference of sovereignty to himself.

THE PAHLAVI DYNASTY (1925–79)

Reza Shah. During the reign of Reza Shah Pahlavi (*q.v.*; Reza Khan's imperial style), educational and juridical reforms were effected that lessened the influence of the religious classes and laid the basis of a modern state. Women were freed from the veil and divorce laws were modified in their favour. The nation's independence from foreign political interference was restored. In 1933 improved terms were gained for Iran on the oil concession granted to a British company in 1901. Iran's first railroad was inaugurated in 1938. Unfortunately, trade necessities, fear of the Soviet grip on the routing of Iranian goods to Europe, and fear of British influence in the south and of Soviet influence in the north made Reza Shah turn to Nazi Germany. His refusal to abandon what he conceived to be obligations toward numerous Germans in Iran in 1941 occasioned an Anglo-Soviet invasion of the country, to ensure the safe passage of American supplies to the Soviet front through Iran. In September 1941 Reza Shah abdicated and left Iran.

Mohammad Reza Shah. In wartime conditions, Reza Shah's son, Mohammad Reza Shah Pahlavi, succeeded to the throne. The Soviet Union and a Communist "popular" regime were removed from Azerbaijan (then the Northwestern Province of Iran) in 1946. In 1951 the Majles passed an act, introduced by Mohammad Mosaddeq, nationalizing Iranian oil; the British Oil Company withdrew. The disturbed political situation during Mosaddeq's premiership turned his nationalization triumph into a Pyrrhic victory. His period in office ended in turmoil in 1953.

The Shah's reforms. By 1961 the Shah was able finally to take the initiative. Dissolving the 20th Majles in May of that year, he cleared the way for the first Land Reform Law, enacted in 1962. The landed minority had to give up its lands to the government for redistribution to cultivators. (Among those stripped of land was the Shiʿah Muslim religious establishment.) Profit sharing in industry was introduced, and the former landlords could receive compensation for their holdings in the form of shares in industries. Cultivators and workers were given more voice in national affairs, and cooperatives in rural areas began to replace the former landowners as sources of capital for irrigation and agrarian maintenance and development. A campaign was organized to reduce illiteracy, and education was further removed from the control of the clergy. The country's power structure was radically changed in a program termed the "White Revolution."

The White Revolution

On January 26, 1963, the White Revolution was overwhelmingly endorsed by the nation. By 1971, when land distribution ended, about 2,500,000 families, comprising a farming population of more than 12,000,000, were estimated to have benefitted from the reforms. During 1960–72 the percentage of owner-occupied farmland in Iran rose from 26 to 78 percent.

Per capita income rose from about \$176 in 1960 to about \$2,500 in 1978. During 1970–77 the gross national product was reported to have increased to an average annual rate of 7.8 percent. Oil revenues financed the extraordinary growth of investment under Iran's successive development plans, rising from \$68,455,000 under the 1949–56 plan to \$9,802,300,000 (50 percent from oil) under the Fourth Plan of 1968–73 and to some \$68,600,-000,000 (more than two-thirds from oil) under the Fifth Plan of 1973–78.

Foreign affairs. Improvement and construction after 1961 were accompanied by an "independent national policy" in foreign relations. The main principles of this foreign policy were support for the United Nations and peaceful coexistence, with a positive approach in cementing friendly and mutually beneficial ties with other nations. Relations with the United States remained close. Iran played a major role in the Central Treaty Organization (Cento) and Regional Co-operation for Development (RCD) with Turkey and Pakistan. It also embarked upon trade and cultural relations with eastern Europe, the Soviet Union, France, Germany, and Scandinavia.

Cento and RCD

Economic developments. Iranian oil development was accelerated after 1954 by a multinational Western consortium led by British Petroleum. The National Iranian Oil Company (NIOC) embarked on all-round expansion. It formed a petrochemical subsidiary and concluded agreements, mainly on the basis of equal shares, with several international companies for exploitation of oil outside the area of the consortium.

National Iranian Oil Company

In July 1973 a new 20-year oil agreement with the consortium of Western firms was concluded. It had the effect of initiating a plain seller-buyer relationship between Iran and the oil companies and of giving Iran control over field operations. These operations, along with all facilities and installations previously worked by the consortium, were vested in NIOC. The consortium agreement was cancelled in 1979, leaving NIOC in control of the Iranian oil industry.

World monetary instability and fluctuations in Western oil consumption dangerously threatened an economy rapidly expanded since 1954 and directed on an unprecedented scale to high-cost development programs. Acutely aware of the danger of dependence on a diminishing asset, the Shah pursued a policy of diversification. Assembly of motor vehicles started in 1957, and in the early 1970s Iran became an exporter of motor vehicles to Egypt and Yugoslavia. Copper reserves were exploited, and in early 1972 Iran's first steel mill began producing structural steel. Iran purchased a major share in the Krupp firm of West Germany in 1974 and continued to press for barter agreements for the marketing of its oil and gas.

Population continued to rise, and the flight from rural areas to towns, particularly to the capital and other northern centres, presented a serious problem. Employment was artificially increased by loans and credits, while businesses were obliged to offer 49 percent of their stock for sale to workers. In 1975 a government-sponsored war on high prices resulted in arrests and fines of traders and manufacturers, injuring the market's confidence.

(P.W.A./Ed.)

THE ISLĀMIC REPUBLIC

Revolution of 1978–79. The sense that in both the agricultural and industrial spheres too much had been attempted too rapidly and that mistakes had been made and expectations disappointed was manifested in demonstrations against the government in 1978; many people were killed, and martial law was imposed in the major cities in September. This ended the relaxation of government controls, begun in 1977, that had encouraged protests and that had led to the emergence of religious activists allied with extremist "Dedicated Fighter" groups, the Mujāhhedin; these groups were opposed to the influx of foreigners, particularly Americans, and to a Westernization they saw as threatening to those traditional values subsumed under the cloak of Shīʿah Islām.

Ruhollah Khomeini, an Islāmic jurist accorded the honorific title of *ayatollah* ("Sign of God"), coordinated an upsurge of opposition—first from Iraq, where he had gone into exile in 1964, and then from France, after 1978—demanding the Shah's abdication. On January 16, 1979, under constitutional procedures, the Shah left Iran; he died in Egypt on July 27, 1980.

The Regency and Supreme Army Councils established for the Shah's absence proved unable to function, and Prime Minister Shahpur Bakhtiar was unable to effect compromise with his former National Front colleagues or with Khomeini. Crowds in excess of 1,000,000 demonstrated in Tehrān, proving the wide appeal of the *ayatollah*, who arrived in Iran amidst wild rejoicing on February 1, 1979. Ten days later Bakhtiar went into hiding, eventually to find exile in Paris.

The republic. On April 1, after a landslide victory in a national referendum, Khomeini declared an Islāmic republic, subsequently invested with a new constitution reflecting his ideals of Islāmic government. Fundamentalist measures followed, with rules for the comportment and veiling of women and the repeal of modern divorce laws. Efforts were made to suppress Western influence, and many of the Western-educated elite fled the country.

In November 1979 supporters of the revolution took control of the U.S. embassy in Tehrān, seized 66 U.S. citizens there and at the foreign ministry, and, with the exception of 14 who were granted early release, held them hostage until January 20, 1981. Also in November 1979, the republic's first prime minister, Mehdi Bazargan, resigned. The republic's first president, Abolhassan Bani-Sadr, opposed the holding of the U.S. embassy. He was forced to flee to France, together with opposition leader Massoud Rajavi of the Mujāhhedin-i Khalq (Fighters for the People) faction. The Mujāhhedin stepped up a campaign of sporadic and highly demoralizing bombing in Tehrān, including the bombing on June 28, 1981, of the headquarters of the ruling Islāmic Republican Party.

In September 1980 the president of Iraq ordered the invasion of the southwestern oil-producing Iranian province of Khuzistan, but a supposedly weakened Iranian army achieved surprising defensive success. By summer 1982, Iraq's initial territorial gains were recaptured by Iranian troops stiffened with Revolutionary Guards and, to a disturbing degree, young village boys attracted by a promise of rewards after life. The Iranians passed to the offensive, threatening Iraqi territory, but they made little headway. Prolongation of the war despite Iraq's desire for peace caused Arab and international anxiety, centred on the possible threat to oil sheikhdoms on the Persian Gulf.

Factionalism and corruption pointed to increased disillusionment by 1983. The numbers of extremely young casualties in the Iran–Iraq war affected public morale, but the government was careful to provide for the poor through mosque-based *Komitehs* (committees). Imports of foodstuffs were still high and, coupled with war expenditures, created a drain on an economy already stricken by a declining world demand for oil and by severe war damage to oil installations. Unrelenting executions on sometimes trivial allegations, rumours of torture, persecution of Bahāʾīs, arbitrary arrests, and bad prison conditions indelibly tarnished the reputation of the republic's leaders.

War with Iraq

(P.W.A.)

BIBLIOGRAPHY

Iran to the end of the Achaemenid Period: RICHARD N. FRYE, *The Heritage of Persia*, 2nd ed. (1976); ROMAN GHIRSHMAN, *Iran from the Earliest Times to the Islamic Conquest* (1954), a useful introduction; GEOFFREY HANDLEY-TAYLOR, *Bibliography of Iran: Coronation Edition*, rev. ed. (1967). (*Prehistory*): R.H. DYSON, JR., "Problems in the Relative Chronology of Iran, 6000–2000 B.C.," in ROBERT W. EHRICH (ed.), *Chronologies in Old World Archaeology* (1965), an authoritative summary of prehistoric Iranian chronology; and "The Archaeological Evidence of the Second Millennium B.C. on the Persian Plateau," *Cambridge Ancient History*, 3rd ed., vol. 2, part 1 (1973); L. VANDEN BERGHE, *Archéologie de l'Iran ancien* (1959), a fairly complete survey by province and by period of Iranian archaeology for all periods to the Sāsānian, with a good bibliography. (*Elam*): PIERRE AMIET, *Elam* (1966), a survey of Elamite art, containing good pictures and a good bibliography; GEORGE G. CAMERON, *History of Early Iran* (1936, reprinted 1976), a good general survey; WALTHER HINZ, "Persia *c.* 2400–1800 B.C.," *Cambridge Ancient History*, rev. ed., fasc. 19 (1963); "Persia *c.* 1800–1550 B.C.," *Cambridge Ancient History*, 3rd ed., vol. 2, part 1 (1973); and RENÉ LABAT, "Elam *c.* 1600–1200 B.C.," *ibid.*, vol. 2, part 2 (1975), authoritative reviews. (*Protohistory*): R. LABAT, "Elam and Western Persia *c.* 1200–1000 B.C.," *ibid.*, a fine survey of Elamite history in the period; T. CUYLER YOUNG, JR., "A Comparative Ceramic Chronology for Western Iran, 1500–500 B.C.," *Iran*, vol. 3 (1965), an attempt to combine archaeological and written sources in a historical reconstruction. (*The Achaemenids*): ANDREW R. BURN, *Persia and the Greeks: The Defense of the West, c. 546–478 B.C.* (1962), a fairly balanced view of the

Achaemenids in their dealings with the Greeks; *Cambridge Ancient History,* vol. 4, *The Persian Empire and the West* (1939), a standard summary of events but in some respects out-of-date; ALBERT T. OLMSTEAD, *History of the Persian Empire* (1948, reissued 1978), a good introduction.

The Parthian Period: The publications of M.E. MASSON and of G.A. PUGACHENKOVA are indispensable for an acquaintance with this period, as are the works of G.A. KOCHELENKO. A detailed Russian bibliography may be found in GREGOIRE FRUMKIN, *Archaeology in Soviet Central Asia* (1970). See also FRANZ ALTHEIM, *Weltgeschichte Asiens im griechischen Zeitalter,* 2 vol. (1947–48), a brilliant study of Hellenism in the Orient, with particular attention to the role of the Iranians; FRANZ ALTHEIM and RUTH STIEHL, *Geschichte Mittelasiens im Altertum* (1970); N. DEBEVOISE, *A Political History of Parthia* (1938, reprinted 1969); JOSEF DOBIAS, "Les Premiers Rapports des Romains avec les Parthes et l'occupation de la Syrie," *Archiv Orientální,* 3:215–256 (1931), well-documented research; ALFRED VON GUTSCHMID, *Geschichte Irans und seiner Nachbarländer von Alexander dem Grossen bis zum Untergang der Arsaciden* (1888); and GEORGE RAWLINSON, *The Sixth Great Oriental Monarchy; or, The Geography, History and Antiquities of Parthia* (1873), both old but still valuable; MIKHAIL ROSTOVTSEV, "The Sarmatae and Parthians," *Cambridge Ancient History,* vol. 11 (1936), of capital importance for Parthian history; WERNER SCHUR, "Parthia," *Pauly-Wissowa Real-Encyclopädie,* vol. 36, col. 1987–2029 (1949); W.W. TARN, "Parthia," *Cambridge Ancient History,* vol. 9 (1932), and *The Greeks in Bactria and India,* 2nd ed. (1951), works based on vast expertise, though certain details are still not universally accepted; JOSEF WOLSKI, "The Decay of the Iranian Empire of the Seleucids and the Chronology of the Parthian Beginnings," *Berytus,* 12:35–52 (1956–57); K.H. ZIEGLER, *Die Beziehungen zwischen Rom und dem Partherreich* (1964), a valuable work with a pro-Roman bias; G.L. RIDER, *Suse sous les Séleucides et les Parthes* (1965), with an important listing of coins.

The Sāsānian Period: (*History*): THEODOR NOLDEKE, *Geschichte der Perser und Araber zur Zeit der Sasaniden aus der arabischen Chronik des Ṭabarī* (1879), German trans. of aṭ-Ṭabarī's (9th–10th century) history, with commentary—still essential; ARTHUR CHRISTENSEN, *L'Iran sous les Sassanides,* 2nd ed. rev. (1944), the only comprehensive history; FRANZ ALTHEIM and RUTH STIEHL, *Feudalismus unter den Sasaniden und ihren Nachbarn* (1954), and *Finanzgeschichte der Spätantike,* pp. 5–114 (1957); N. PIGULEVSKAJA, *Les Villes de l'état iranien aux époques parthe et sassanide* (1963; originally published in Russian, 1956); JEAN GAGE, *La Montée des Sassanides et l'heure de Palmyre* (1964), with translations from several original sources; GEO WIDENGREN, *Der Feudalismus im alten Iran* (1969). (*Chronology*): KURT ERDMANN, "Die Entwicklung der sasanidischen Krone," *Ars Islamica,* 15:87–123 (1951); ROBERT GOBL, *Sasanidische Numismatik* (1968), tables 1–14. (*Inscriptional materials*): ERNST HERZFELD, *Paikuli: Monument and Inscription of the Early History of the Sassanian Empire,* 2 vol. (1924), the first, now somewhat superseded, interpretation of the inscription of Narses; MARTIN SPRENGLING, *Third Century Iran: Sapor and Kartir* (1953), the first interpretation of inscriptions of Shāpūr I and of Kartēr.

Iran since c. AD 600: SIR PERCY M. SYKES, *A History of Persia,* 3rd ed., 2 vol. (1969), a general history; ALESSANDRO BAUSANI, *The Persians* (1971, originally published in Italian, 1962); E. DENISON ROSS, *The Persians* (1931); WILHELM BARTHOLD, *Turkestan Down to the Mongol Invasion,* 4th ed. (1977; originally published in Russian, 1898–1900), the essential survey of northeastern Iranian history from *c.* AD 600 to the 13th century; later research is represented by MUHAMMAD A. SHABAN, *The ʿĀbbasid Revolution* (1970). The *Cambridge History of Iran,* vol. 5 (1968), covers the 12th–14th centuries; MARTIN B. DICKSON, *Sháh Tahmásb and the Úzbeks* (1958), on the history of the first half of the 16th century; LAURENCE LOCKHART, *Nadir Shah* (1938, reprinted 1973), and *The Fall of the Safavī Dynasty and the Afghan Occupation of Persia* (1958), deal with the period 1722–46; PETER W. AVERY, *Modern Iran* (1965), is a general work on the 19th and 20th centuries to 1963. See also JULIAN BHARIER, *Economic Development in Iran: 1900–1970* (1971); and AMIN BANANI, *The Modernization of Iran: 1921–1941* (1961). L.P. ELWELL-SUTTON, *Modern Iran* (1941), covers the period 1924–41, and his *Guide to Iranian Area Study* (1952) has a useful chronological table and bibliography. Dynastic tables and essays on different aspects of Iranian history and culture are in A.J. ARBERRY (ed.), *The Legacy of Persia* (1953, reissued 1968). Sound modern research has produced articles on Iran in *The Cambridge History of Islam,* 2 vol. (1970, reissued 1977). An essential reference work is *The Encyclopaedia of Islam,* 4 vol. and suppl. (1913–38; new ed., 1960–). VLADIMIR F. MINORSKY, *Iranica: Twenty Articles* (1964), *Tadhkirat al-Mulūk* (1943), and *Persia in A.D. 1478–1490* (1957), are the fruits of great insight and the highest quality of research. Other works recommended include ANN K.S. LAMBTON, *Landlord and Peasant in Persia* (1953, reprinted 1969), and *The Persian Land Reform, 1962–1966* (1969); GEORGE LENCZOWSKI (ed.), *Iran Under the Pahlavis* (1978); ROUHOLLAH K. RAMAZANI, *The Foreign Policy of Iran: A Developing Nation in World Affairs, 1500–1941* (1966), and *Iran's Foreign Policy, 1941–1973* (1975); SHAHRAM CHUBIN and SEPEHR ZABIH, *The Foreign Relations of Iran* (1974), a prerevolutionary source; FIRUZ KAZEMZADEH, *Russia and Britain in Persia 1864–1914* (1968); MARVIN ZONIS, *The Political Elite of Iran* (1971); SEPEHR ZABIH, *The Communist Movement in Iran* (1966); ERVAND ABRAHAMIAN, *Iran Between Two Revolutions* (1982); SHAHROUGH AKHAVI, *Religion and Politics in Contemporary Iran: Clergy-State Relations in the Pahlavī Period* (1980); JAMES A. BILL, *The Politics of Iran: Groups, Classes and Modernization* (1972); ROBERT GRAHAM, *Iran: The Illusion of Power* (1978); FRED HALLIDAY, *Iran: Dictatorship and Development* (1979); AMIN SAIKHAL, *The Rise and Fall of the Shah* (1980); MICHAEL M. J. FISCHER, *Iran: From Religious Dispute to Revolution* (1980); NIKKI R. KEDDIE, *Roots of Revolution: An Interpretive History of Modern Iran* (1981); MICHAEL A. LEDEEN and WILLIAM LEWIS, *Debacle: The American Failure in Iran* (1981); HOMA KATOUZIAN, *The Political Economy of Modern Iran* (1980); LOIS BECK and N.R. KEDDIE (eds.), *Women in the Muslim World* (1978); MICHAEL E. BONINE and N.R. KEDDIE (eds.), *Modern Iran: The Dialectics of Continuity and Change* (1981); and FEREIDUN FESHARAKI, *Development of the Iranian Oil Industry* (1976).

(T.C.Y.,Jr./R.Gh./M.J.Dr./P.W.A.)

Iranian Cultures

There have been and are several distinctive yet interrelated cultures in Iran. The country's present-day borders coincide to a considerable extent with naturally distinctive features of the terrain, and the country is thus to a considerable degree a natural cultural area. Its main geographical features are: (1) an interior desert basin, ranging in altitude from 1,000 to 4,000 feet (300 to 1,200 metres) above sea level; (2) the Zagros Mountain system on the west and southwest, enclosing the interior basin; (3) the Elburz Mountains on the north; and (4) a series of less massive and more intermittent mountains on the east. The high interior basin and the adjoining mountain systems are the natural habitat of the Iranian cultures, the only extensions of the cultures beyond it being found on the Caspian shoreline north of the Elburz and along a section of the Tigris–Euphrates plain immediately west of the middle Zagros and north of the Persian Gulf. These two areas are the only truly lowland regions within the borders of Iran, and they are of limited extent. The Iranian mountains rise abruptly from the Caspian Sea, the Persian Gulf, and the Tigris–Euphrates plain, thus clearly setting the Iranian area apart. In the northwest the Zagros and Elburz mountains converge with each other and with the mountains of eastern Turkey and the Caucasus region of the Soviet Union. The rugged terrain of peaks, ridges, and high plateaus has facilitated the maintenance of an Iranian culture distinct from Turkish and Caucasian cultures. An exception to this pattern of nationally distinctive cultures is represented by the Kurds, who inhabit not only portions of northwestern Iran but adjacent portions of Turkey and Iraq as well.

In the northeastern, eastern, and southeastern regions of Iran the less massive mountains result in a somewhat less definite and distinctive Iranian cultural border. Thus, in the northeast, there are Turkmen tribesmen not only in Iran but also in the Soviet Union. In the east there are Afghan (Pashtun) tribesmen living in Iran as well as in adjacent parts of Afghanistan, and in the southeast there are Baluch tribesmen living not only in Iran but also in Pakistan. These, however, are among the most sparsely inhabited regions of Iran.

Influence of other Middle Eastern cultures

While the cultures of Iran are distinctive and, for the most part, associated with an area that is, on the whole, naturally distinguishable, they also have much in common with the non-Iranian cultures of the Middle East. One reason for this is that the people of Iran have long been in contact with other Middle Eastern peoples, influencing them and being influenced by them in many ways. Primarily because of invasions and conquests, for example, most Iranians, like most other Middle Eastern peoples, are Muslims; there are Turkish- and Arabic-speaking Iranians; and there are speakers of Fārsī (the most important and most specifically Iranian language) living in Iraq and Afghanistan.

The other reason is ecological: the entire region from Morocco to the Indus River is basically hot, arid, and desert-like, with precipitation occurring primarily in the mountains. Water supplies sufficient for human habitation are thus available only in some mountain valleys, in rivers and oases whose water flows from mountains, and in some plains of restricted extent where there is some rainfall. These areas are interspersed with each other and with uninhabitable deserts. The Iranian cultures represent the same adaptations to these conditions that have been made by all the other inhabitants of the Middle East and North Africa. Most of the people are village-dwelling farmers practicing a precarious agriculture that is heavily dependent on irrigation and threatened by drought and various predators, human and otherwise. A few people are pastoral nomads—taking advantage of areas too dry for agriculture for the herding of sheep, goats, camels, and cattle. Other people live in towns and cities where processing and long-distance trade are concentrated and where the centres of economic, religious, and political power are located.

PEOPLES AND LANGUAGES

According to the official census of 1966, more than 25,000,000 people lived in Iran in that year. Of this number, about 61 percent lived in rural communities and about 39 percent lived in towns and cities having populations of 5,000 or more. Not specified in this enumeration are the various tribal groups of Iran, but they are presumably included in the rural population. According to some authorities, they number about 3,000,000, of whom apparently about 460,000 are nomadic tent dwellers. Virtually all of the other rural people, tribal and nontribal, live in small villages. These figures are approximate and must not be assumed to be stable. The population of Iran is increasing at the rate of about 3 percent per year, and there is a tendency for pastoralists to become villagers and for villagers to move to cities.

The great majority of the populations of Iran speak Fārsī, the Persian language proper, but approximately 5,000,000 who live in the northwestern province of Azerbaijan speak Azerbaijani (Azeri), a Turkish dialect closely related to the predominant language of Turkey and to the languages of the Qashqai tribesmen of southern Iran and of the Turkmen. Turkish is a member of the Ural-Altaic family of languages and totally unrelated to Fārsī and to Arabic. It was brought into the Middle East by invading tribes after the founding and spread of Islām. Fārsī belongs to the Indo-European family of languages to which English as well as most of the other European languages belong. Fārsī has a number of regional dialects of which that of Fars Province is supposedly the "purest," while Gīlaki and Māzandarānī, spoken along the Caspian shore, are among the most divergent. Fārsī has a long history and a rich literary tradition of which the Iranians are very conscious, and it is the official language of the government. It is, however, written in a slightly modified version of the Arabic alphabet, a fact that has led to a widespread idea that it is similar, or related, to Arabic; it is not, but it does contain a large number of words borrowed from Arabic.

Luri and Bakhtyārī, spoken by adjacent pastoral tribes of the same names in the Zagros, are closely related to Fārsī, though the extent to which they are mutually intelligible with it seems to be a matter of differing opinion. Two other pastoral tribes, the Kurds who live north of the Lurs, and the Baluch, who live in southeastern Iran, each speak their own Indo-European languages, which are not mutually intelligible with Fārsī.

Arabic, while recited on religious occasions by all Muslim Iranians, is regularly spoken only by a few pastoral tribes, mostly of the Khamseh Confederation in the south.

All of these language groups are Muslim, and all except the Baluch, Kurds, and Turkmen belong to the Shīʿah branch of Islām, which is one of the distinctive features of Iran. About 1 percent of the total population is not Muslim. These people are Jews and Zoroastrians, who do not speak distinctive languages of their own, and Christians, mostly Armenians with their own language (Indo-European but not closely related to any of the others). There are also some Assyrian Christians in the northwest who speak Aramaic, an almost-extinct Semitic language related to Hebrew and Arabic.

While these many languages and dialects contribute to the divisions in Iranian life, many Iranians speak at least two of them fluently.

CULTURE PATTERNS

General characteristics: ethos. Iranian cultural patterns will be described in what follows as they were observed in the middle third of the 20th century. It was during this period that many innovations were introduced into Iranian cultures under the leadership of two monarchs, Reza Shah Pahlavi (1925–41) and his son, Mohammad Reza Shah Pahlavi (1941–). These innovations, known collectively as "modernization," have had varied effects on the already existing cultures. These effects are in very transitional stages and their outcome cannot yet clearly be foreseen. At the same time, many of the previously existing cultural patterns continue to characterize most people's lives, and it is these continuing, specifically Iranian, cultural patterns, as observed in a period of great change, that will be emphasized, although not to the exclusion of new developments.

Ethos of insecurity

A pervasive sense of insecurity and a set of resilient adaptations to it—these are perceived by many observers to be facts of Iranian cultures that recur in many different contexts of life. The insecurities of life range from fear of physical harm from the harsh environment or the depredations of other people to apprehensions concerning the unreliability and self-interest of other people. Since, many agree, these insecurities are actual, the sense of insecurity is continually reinforced by reality. On the whole, the adaptations to this pervasive insecurity—such as *taʿrof*, elaborate verbal ceremoniousness and deference, and *taqīyah*, concealment of one's true feelings—do not reduce it; and some adaptations may actually reinforce it. The ramifications of this ethos of insecurity are many, and they have been portrayed and discussed at some length by a number of observers.

Social structures. *Family and kinship patterns.* Membership in a family, consciousness of family ties as potential means of enhancing one's good fortune and position, and concern for family honour are basic elements in the Iranian's identity and in Iranian social structure.

The organizational principle of Iranian kinship is patriliny. This means several things: (1) Formal authority is vested in males. (2) Males are the primary property holders and property inheritors. (3) Membership in the kinship group is determined by descent through males but not through females. The principle on which surnames among English-speaking peoples are acquired is patrilineal, and a simple genealogical chart of parents, grandparents, aunts, uncles, and first cousins, all with the same surname, will yield a small patrilineal group of the type known technically as an extended family. Normally, however, in the West, there are no legal obligations among all the members of the extended family, except between parents and children, and usually no particular sense of membership. Among Iranians, however, there definitely are such obligations and sentiments.

If patrilineal ties are traced back to more distant ancestral generations than grandparents, patrilineal links with a correspondingly larger number of living relatives, descended from more remote ancestors, can be identified. Such larger kinship units are known as patrilineages, patriclans, or patrilineal tribes, depending on the degree of remoteness of the ancestor from whom membership is derived. All of the descendants of a great-great-grandfather, for example, may be considered to be members of a single clan; but this man may have had three sons, and the descendants of each son may constitute a separate lineage. Each of these three lineages is, therefore, a section of the larger clan.

The tribal organizations of the pastoral-nomadic cultures of Iran are founded on various versions and modifications of this basic principle. One of the most important modifications is that nomadic bands have often shifted their allegiance from one tribal section chief to another, and so the membership of many people in many of the sections is, in fact, not based on genealogy. Nevertheless, the principle of very extended genealogical groupings is present in the thinking of the people. Many Iranians associate this thinking with the pastoral nomads and refer to it as "tribal," but it is not by any means absent from village and city life. It has been reported that village populations are frequently divided into *boneh*, which are patrilineally related groups—each living in its own section of the village. Networks of patrilineally related kinsmen, also concentrated in particular quarters, have been reported from some towns and cities. It is not at all clear, however, from the little information that is available, how frequent these kinship structures are or what proportion of the people are involved in them.

Marriage to cousins is a common practice permitted by Islām. Forty-one percent of a sample of working-class married couples in the city of Isfahan were, in a recent study, found to involve cousin marriages. Opinions as to the desirability of such marriages differed very widely among these people, but the practice is traditional and is generally assumed to be a reinforcement of kinship solidarity.

Role and influence of women

While traditionally the civil rights of women have been minimal, women as individuals are often not as completely passive and subordinate as is sometimes assumed. The influence of mothers on their sons is reported to be profound and persistent; very commonly, in marriage arrangements, it is women who are influential in the choice of brides for their sons; relatives on one's mother's side apparently are often as significant as relatives on one's father's side; and women can and do inherit and manage property. In other words, the image of a rigidly and unexceptionally male-dominated system is exaggerated.

Local and territorial organization. The village is the most important local and territorial organization for most Iranians. The village does not, however, conform to the much idealized "folk community" in which complete unity of values gives all inhabitants equality and a secure life-style. On the contrary, village populations are usually divided into quarreling factions and into different social classes.

Urban territorial organization has been suggested, but not described in any detail, in terms of the *maḥallah*, or quarter, which has its own name, reputation, mosque or shrine, public bath, headman, and ceremonial groups such as those that take part in the processions and pageants of important holidays. How extensive such a system of quarters was in the past, how much of it now remains in the older parts of Iranian cities—which have undergone drastic changes in the 20th century—is not clear.

It is the territorial organization of the pastoral nomadic tribes that has received the most attention. Each tribe and each subsection of it must maintain its rights to its winter (lowland) and summer (highland) grazing territories and its passage rights through whatever territory intervenes between the two. This involves constant negotiation with other tribal groups, with villages which lie in or near the transit zone or the winter or summer grazing areas, and with the imperial government and its local officers. It is in the course of such negotiations that tribal groups may shift their allegiance from one leader to another in the hopes of more advantageous arrangements. During much of Iranian history, major tribal leaders have, in effect, been the rulers of the tribal territories and have been quite autonomous from the city-based government of the Shah. In the middle of the 20th century, that autonomy had been greatly reduced, but the tribes still occupy extensive territories at various times of the year.

Stratification. There are a number of social class groups in Iran, and Iranians are very conscious of social class distinctions. They are also particularly aware of the considerable instability of membership in the upper classes. This is true in part because of the extensive redefinitions of status that have accompanied modernization, but the instability of high status positions is traditional, too. It has been observed, for example, that though absentee landlords have been important upper class elements, a landed aristocracy lasting over many generations has never developed because the Iranian inheritance system (which is also the general Muslim system) has divided estates among many heirs and because the monarchy has repeatedly confiscated the holdings of major landlords. The monarchy itself is the pinnacle of the social class system, and there have been Iranian monarchies for 2,500 years. There have been at least ten conventionally recognized dynasties, however, several of them interspersed with troublesome interregnum periods. The founders of the dynasties have often been from obscure and humble origins, and the descendants of deposed dynasties have not enjoyed any special privileges.

Social status rankings

The urban social statuses can be listed thus, in order of precedence: the royal lineage; important merchants, clergy, landlords, and government ministers; high status modern professionals, such as physicians, engineers, and army officers; bazaar merchants and skilled artisans who are self-employed; medium status modern professionals, such as teachers and other civil servants whose jobs require literacy; service specialists—bakers, tailors, masons, automobile repairmen, drivers, peddlers, etc.; factory operatives; and unskilled labourers.

Village social statuses can be highlighted in these terms: farm operators who not only own their own farms but can also employ others to work for them; peasants—mostly tenant farmers—who have rights to shares in village lands; farm labourers who have no rights as members of village communities.

Pastoral-nomadic social statuses have been described as including: tribal chiefs (*īl-khān*s) and their families, who are likely to be resident in cities; the *kalantar*s (leaders of clans) and their families; the *kadhodā*s (the term is also used for village chiefs and leaders of the urban *maḥallah*) and their families, who are the heads of subclans; the ordinary tribesmen; subordinate persons, such as Gypsies and former slaves, who provide services but are not regarded as members of the tribe.

It is the higher status urban residents who dominate the culture; and it is the peasants, landless village labourers, urban bazaar merchants, urban service specialists, and labourers who constitute the majority of the population.

The *dowreh* ("circle") is a group of friends who meet regularly at each others' houses for conviviality and mutual support. Among upper class people and perhaps others, *dowreh*s may be political caucuses. Other groups are the *heyāṭ*, which meets for religious edification, and the *rowẓeh khvānī*, which is an open-house or private prayer and memorial meeting for the major Shīʿah martyrs. Besides their religious import, these meetings also reinforce social solidarity. The *zūrkhāneh* ("house of strength"), an urban men's club which meets to perform highly ritualized, traditional calisthenics, has been said to bring together people of different social classes. So, in principle and in fact, do the congregational prayers in the major mosques on Fridays. Perhaps these observances mitigate the extremes of social-class differences, yet those differences remain very great.

Socialization and education. In Iran, as in other Middle Eastern countries, the birth of boys is said to be greeted with greater rejoicing than the birth of girls. It is also said that girls are often neglected to the point that there is a higher death rate among small girls than among boys. Since reliable and detailed studies on this and related subjects are not available, it is impossible to evaluate such often-stated impressions. It does seem clear, however, that sharply differentiated male and female roles are characteristic of Iranian cultures and that the differentiation starts at birth.

According to some observers, both small boys and girls are primarily in the charge of their mothers or of older brothers or sisters delegated by the mothers, but not very often in the charge of their fathers. From this beginning it has been suggested that girls receive strict and direct training from their mothers, preparing them to become the efficient and dutiful daughters-in-law of other women. From the same mothers, it has been suggested, boys receive very indulgent treatment, either because the mother seeks to make of her son an ally against the father or because the son—even at an extremely early age—is allowed to bully the mother, confident in the support of the father against her. Either way, the resulting "spoiled son" is a personality frequent enough in reality to have been identified by some Iranians themselves, as well as by other observers. Nevertheless, corporal punishment is widely employed, and strict adherence to various rules of formal comportment in interaction with social superiors is generally inculcated, though it would be difficult to prove that positive respect for authority figures is generally internalized.

Marriage practices

Except for the required Muslim circumcision of boys, which generally occurs early in childhood, there are no other "rites of passage" early in life until marriage, which, for most Iranian women takes place between the ages of 13 and 18 and for men on the average roughly seven years later than for women. It is true that for some time the legal minimum marriage age for women has been 15, but permission can be obtained for their marriage as early as 13; and many observers agree that various subterfuges can be and often are used to present prospective brides to the authorities as being older than they actually are. In a study of four villages near Shīrāz in 1963, the median age of women's marriage was found to be between 13 and 15, and in a study of working class families in the city of Isfahan in 1970–71, it was found that 80 percent of the wives had married between the ages of nine and 16, inclusive, most of them within the previous 20 years. The prevailing pressures in the culture —westernized upper class people excepted—are for getting one's daughters married off as soon as possible. Yet the honourable search is to find wives for one's sons, not husbands for one's daughters. The virginity of the bride is an explicitly important criterion of desirability, which in itself reinforces the pressures for the marriage of women at as early an age as is possible. Bridegrooms are expected but not required to be virgins at marriage, extramarital sexuality on the part of men being formally disapproved of by religious and other conventional authorities. The double standard, however, is in operation.

The general characteristics of weddings that emerge from the available source materials include negotiations by the parents and other relatives; signing of the marriage contract, which includes the promise of cash payments (*mahr*) to the bride and her family under various contingencies, including divorce; and the consummation festivities in which the bride is ceremonially conveyed from her parents' to her husband's (or husband's parents') house. Display to close relatives of a bloodstained cloth, as testimonial of the bride's virginity, is a conventional expectation of these proceedings—the actual frequency of which is unknown. Westernized women have been reported to obtain a physician's certificate of virginity before their marriage in order to forestall both the display and the possible claims of subsequently divorce-minded husbands that their brides were not virgins.

Muslim tradition allows a man to have as many as four legal wives at the same time and to divorce a wife unilaterally without cause. The excessive behaviour that these traditions suggest has probably never been typical, and recent Iranian laws explicitly forbid men from having more than two wives at a time. In fact, men with more than two wives have always been extremely rare, and, although accurate figures are not available, it is quite clear that polygamy is a very exceptional practice. Divorce may no longer be effected unilaterally by the husband.

Formal education

Formal education has traditionally conferred prestige in Iran, and until recently it has been available to only a very small proportion of the population. Traditional formal education consisted primarily of learning to read and write in order to learn the holy scriptures of Islām, which are in Arabic. There has been, throughout the 20th century, a steady increase in the number of modern primary and secondary schools as well as universities. The government puts great emphasis on the achievement of literacy. Being able to send one's children to school to as advanced a level as possible is high in the stated priorities of many parents, but the opportunities for the attainment of such goals are relatively limited. Observers are generally agreed that the principles of rote memorization and imitation of authority have been carried over from the traditional schools to the modern ones at all levels. The slow, rhythmical pacing back and forth of university students, not to mention schoolboys, memorizing their course notes out loud is a common sight in the parks and other public places in Iranian cities.

Funeral rites

The deaths of Muslim Iranians are recognized by funeral rites that, insofar as they have been reported in detail, appear to be fairly standard for the country and for Muslims generally. Burial takes place preferably on the same day as death or on the following morning at the latest. Memorial services and ceremonial visits with the bereaved take place on the third, seventh, and 40th days after death. The simplicity or elaborateness of these observances varies greatly, depending upon the status of the deceased and the poverty or affluence of the survivors.

Economic systems. *Settlement patterns and housing.* The basic type of house of the pastoral nomads is a rectangular tent made of dark-coloured goat's hair cloth, supported on poles and secured by ropes. It is very similar to the tent of the Arab Bedouin. Most tents are inhabited by small conjugal families (husband, wife and unmarried children), but the encampments (groups of tents of people who care for their flocks together and move together) generally have a core of men, most of whom are close relatives, such as brothers and cousins. An exception to the goat's hair tent is used by the Turkmen of the northeast. It is the yurt, which has a circular upright frame over which covers of felt are fitted.

Typically, Iranian villages (like Middle Eastern ones generally) consist of clusters of houses built closely together, the fields and orchards lying outside the cluster. Some villages, especially in areas in which raids by pastoral nomads have been a recurrent problem, are fortified, with the houses enclosed either behind a wall or provided with a small citadel for refuge. Village houses characteristically consist of rooms around a courtyard or a structure with a walled yard—in either case an enclosure that presents a solid wall with a heavy, thick wooden gate to the alley by which it is approached. The most common building material is sun-dried or low-fired brick. Roofs are either flat (timbers and packed earth) or domed and vaulted brick. Some village houses have a pillared porch at ground level. Prevailing colours are various shades of tan, set off by the pale blue, in which colour many plastered walls around doorways and in courtyards are painted, and (in season) the shimmering green of poplar and sycamore trees and field crops.

Characteristics of Iranian cities

Of Iran's ten largest cities, only Abadan is entirely new (because of the petroleum industry). All of the others have pre-industrial city characteristics to a greater or lesser degree, in combination with modern characteristics. The modern features consist primarily of: (1) wide, straight avenues, connected by traffic circles, which have been cut through the old traditional cities; (2) industrial areas located on the outskirts; and (3) upper class and lower class residential areas on the outskirts. The far-flung suburbs characteristic of Europe and the United States are unusual.

Traditional city-housing and street patterns are essentially the same as those in villages: walled compounds facing on very narrow streets or alleys. The old courtyards characteristically have a fountain, pool, fruit trees, and flower beds—more or less extensive and well kept, depending upon the means of the inhabitants. The separate rooms around the courtyard may, to mention two extremes, house a single palatial ménage or a separate, poverty-stricken family in each room.

Modern housing in cities consists of a one- or two-story house attached to a walled garden, usually on the south side of the house. The house probably is constructed with more glass, stone, metal, and tile than the traditional house, and, if middle or upper class, is accessible to automobiles; but it retains the same walled-in, intensely private character of the traditional house. Free-standing villas with unwalled grounds and high-rise apartment blocks exist, but they are rare.

Production and technology. The main products of Iran's farmers are wheat and barley. Most of the agriculture is not mechanized, but much of it is irrigated by an ancient system of underground aqueducts called *qanāts*.

Beyond agriculture, Iran's productive technology has for some decades been dominated by the extraction and refining of petroleum in the southwest and, most recently, by the gas-pipeline and steel-production complex that has been worked out in cooperation with the Soviet Union. Iran also assembles and exports motor vehicles designed on European models. Such activities as these demand and provide new types of productive skills. Less modern industries, however, such as textile manufacture, employ a large number of people, and the traditional skills, such as carpet weaving, remain important for large segments of the population. A much larger proportion of the population than in Western countries is available for semiskilled and unskilled labour.

As far as distribution is concerned, small, specialized retail stores are predominant. Many of these are still concentrated by type of commodity in the traditional bazaars that are a very important part of the old sections of most of the cities. There are few department stores or supermarkets, in the Western sense, even in the most modernized areas such as some parts of Teheran.

Property and exchange systems. Much real property in Iran is owned by the crown, and there is a tradition of the monarchy continually reassigning tracts of this property to various persons as reward for their loyalty and support. Such beneficiaries have been prominent among the absentee landlords who, until the early 1960s, were a dominant element in Iran's social class system and economy. Absentee landlordism has been greatly modified but not eliminated by the implementation of land reform in the 1960s. Other extensive properties are owned and administered by the religious organizations (*waqf*) that are generally centred in the larger cities. *Waqf* properties have for many centuries been donated as acts of piety, and the proceeds from them are used for the support of the clergy, maintenance of mosques and shrines and cemeteries, and other sectarian purposes. Whole blocks of villages have been owned by *waqf* organizations and administered in ways that were hardly different from those of secular absentee landlords as far as the tenant farmers were concerned. The land reforms of the 1960s have undoubtedly increased the number of small-scale freeholders in the country. It has been estimated, however, that 40–50 percent of Iran's rural population (one-fourth of the total population of the country) are propertyless labourers unaffected by land reform. They constitute a substantial proportion of the unskilled proletariat that is migrating to the cities.

Some observers report that barter is, or has been, a very important means of exchange, especially among poor Iranians. It is impossible to estimate the relative importance of this. Iran has also had a cash economy for many centuries, and the amount of money in circulation has increased enormously in recent decades, facilitated by petroleum revenues and the introduction of paper money and coins made of nonprecious metals in the 1930s. It is of note that this money is reported to be backed by the great collection of crown jewels, which is kept and exhibited in a special vault in the headquarters building of the Bank Markazi (Central Bank) in Teheran.

Belief and aesthetic systems. Most Iranians are Shīʿah Muslims, and this gives them considerable distinctiveness. There are Shīʿah Muslims living in other Middle Eastern countries, but only in Iran do they constitute an overwhelming majority. Shīʿah Muslims share with Sunnī Muslims (who predominate among the Arabs, Turks, and Pakistanis) belief in Muḥammad as God's prophet and in the Qurʾān, the corpus of Muḥammad's prophecy. This means that Iranians share with other Muslims observance of Ramaẓan, the month of daytime fasting; daily prayers done in a prescribed manner; congregational prayers on Fridays, pilgrimage to Mecca, if possible; and other observances.

Emotional exhibitionism at religious festivals

The emotional outpourings that characterize religious festivals, in particular, the martyrdom days of important Shīʿah saints, are in part conventional, but they are also massive. Men and women weep and moan, smite their foreheads, and, in rhythmical unison, beat their chests. Similar behaviour takes place all the time at the shrines that people visit in fulfillment of vows. Some observers think that these expressions of emotion have social psychological importance, that they are releases of the frustrated and pessimistic feelings that are continually engendered by the ethos of insecurity. There exist hundreds of *emāmzādeh*s (shrines) in Iran, to which long- and short-distance pilgrimages are constantly being made by thousands of people. This cult of saints is anathema to orthodox Sunnī Muslims, although it occurs, in somewhat different form, in North Africa.

Many Iranian people observe customs that are not related to Islām. The most distinctive is the New Year celebration, which begins at the spring equinox, March 21. Symbols of health, well-being, fertility, and renewal accompany this "new day" (Now Rūz) celebration. It ends on the 13th day of the new year (April 2), when special plantings of new wheat are cast out (preferably on moving water) and the misfortunes of the coming year are symbolically banished from the house. Very ancient Zoroastrian themes have been discerned in Now Rūz, a happy time, which, when it coincides with unhappy Muslim periods such as Muḥarram, is felt by many to be dampened thereby.

Of more than incidental interest are the widespread beliefs in, and ritual protections against, the "evil eye," which are not peculiar to Iran but, on the contrary, are generally Middle Eastern. Evil-eye beliefs basically are expressions of fear of the damage that other peoples' envy may, consciously or unconsciously, do to one. Far from being bizarre, these beliefs and practices are wholly compatible with the ethos of insecurity. Consequently, they tend to be immune to the supposedly rational influences of "modernization" except insofar as those influences may be able to relieve the ethos of insecurity; and those influences have not, so far, done this to any appreciable extent.

As in medieval and Renaissance Europe, much of Iran's finest architecture and artistic expression—from ceramic tiles, to miniature paintings, carpets, and poetry—has been inspired by religion, and commissioned by, or dedicated to, religious institutions. On the other hand, all these art forms also have a specifically Iranian character and genius.

EVOLUTION OF THE CULTURE TODAY

The traditionally disintegrating factors in Iranian cultures have included the often autonomous tribes, the provincialism of cities and regions, the sharp division between social classes and the two sexes, and, above all, the ethos of insecurity.

Among the potentially integrating factors have been Islām, the monarchy, and a general consciousness of Iranian identity.

The Pahlavi dynasty has attempted to maximize the integrating factors at the same time that Iran, like many other countries, has been exposed to the influences of western industrialization. Unlike many other countries, Iran has a valuable asset, petroleum, profits from the sale of which have brought large amounts of money into the economy and into the government's treasury. On this basis, the monarchy has developed massive military forces, supplemented by an internal security organization. With these instruments the monarchy has greatly reduced the autonomy of the tribes. Public health and educational institutions have been greatly developed throughout the country. Highways and the telephone and telegraph, radio and television have decreased distance and augmented the accessibility of large proportions of the population to expressions of national identity and unity. The latter are now widely symbolized to an extent and with an intensity probably unique in Iranian history.

Cultural adjustments necessitated by economic development

Two aspects of the ethos of insecurity, fatalism and evasive deference to authority, are characteristic of Iranian cultures, and neither is conducive to individual and institutional innovations. An important question is whether "modernization" can proceed very far or deeply without innovations. This is perhaps the major question which, unanswered, faces the Iranian peoples and their cultures, for if the primary goal of modernization is to increase the gross national product through industrialization and modern business procedures, it is reasonable to ask how the fruits of this goal are to be shared with the landless, propertyless, and unskilled masses of the population, or who will introduce innovations in order to achieve a generalized improvement of the quality of life which, in turn, might ease the ethos of insecurity, and lessen fatalism and evasive deference to authority.

The Iranian government has in fact initiated changes that could be revolutionary if vested interests in the status quo are unsuccessful in subverting them. One is land reform; another consists of the several service corps in which young men and women perform their national service (a new concept) as teachers, public health aides, and the like, in areas in which such services are very much needed; and another is the family planning program the official goal of which is to reduce the country's rate of annual population increase from more than 3 percent to 1 percent by about the year 1990. The purpose of this last goal is to give more people a real chance for improvement in the quality of life as the economy develops. In order to achieve it, the men and women of Iran will very likely have to learn new life-styles, in which women participate more with men in positions of public responsibility.

BIBLIOGRAPHY. W.B. FISHER (ed.), *The Cambridge History of Iran*, vol. 1 (1968), is perhaps the single most comprehensive and informative work on geography and social ecology. HENRI MASSE, *Croyances et coutumes persanes, suivies de contes et chansons populaires*, 2 vol. (1938; Eng. trans., *Persian Beliefs and Customs*, 1955), is a detailed compendium of particular usefulness to those who know Iran. Prominent among histories that are also informative on contemporary Iranian cultures are PETER AVERY, *Modern Iran* (1965); ANN K.S. LAMBTON, *Landlord and Peasant in Persia* (1953); JOSEPH M. UPTON, *The History of Modern Iran: An Interpretation* (1961); and DONALD N. WILBER, *Iran: Past and Present*, 4th ed. (1958). Three novels that are widely considered to be very realistic in regard to various aspects of Iranian life are VINCENT CRONIN, *The Last Migration* (1957); F.M. ESFANDIARY, *Identity Card* (1966); and JAMES MORIER, *Hajji Baba of Ispahan* (1937), a famous classic originally published in 1824. Notable among the books on pastoral nomads are FREDRIK BARTH, *Nomads of South Persia* (1961), perhaps the most comprehensive of any single work on a nomadic group; and MERIAN C. COOPER, *Grass* (1925), a dramatic, eyewitness account of the spring migration of a Bakhtyārī group over the Zagros in 1924, illustrated with stills taken from a moving picture made by Cooper's party. Other useful works on nomads are M.T. ULLENS DE SCHOOTEN, *The Lords of the Mountains: Southern Persia and the Kashkai Tribe* (1956), with colour photographs; WILLIAM IRONS, "The Turkmen Nomads," *Nat. Hist.*, 77:44–51 (1968); and BRIAN J. SPOONER, "Politics, Kinship and Ecology in Southeast Persia," *Ethnology*, 8:139–152 (1969). Three works on the modern family, fertility, mortality, and related matters, are ALI A. PAYDARFAR and MAHMOOD SARRAM, "Differential Fertility and Socioeconomic Status of Shirazi Women: A Pilot Study," *J. Marriage and the Family*, 32:692–699 (1970); PAUL VIEILLE, "Birth and Death in an Islamic Society," *Diogenes*, 57:101–127 (1967); and *Some Demographic Aspects of the Population of Iran* (1968), a collection of articles written mostly by Iranian social scientists. JOHN I. CLARKE, *The Iranian City of Shiraz* (1963); and PAUL W. ENGLISH, *City and Village in Iran: Settlement and Economy in the Kirman Basin* (1966), are two of the best books on modern Iranian cities. Although comprehensive village studies are lacking, these four articles are valuable: ISMAIL AJAMI, "Social Classes, Family Demographic Characteristics and Mobility in Three Iranian Villages," *Sociologia Ruralis*, 9:62–72 (1969); JOHN HANESSIAN, JR., "Yosouf-Abad: An Iranian Village," *Southeast Asia Series*, vol. 12, no. 1–6 (1963); WILLIAM G. MILLER, "Hosseinabad: A Persian Village," *Middle East J.*, 18:483–498 (1964); and XAVIER DE PLANHOL., "Aspects of Mountain Life in Anatolia and Iran," in S.R. EYRE and G.R.J. JONES (eds.), *Geography As Human Ecology: Methodology by Example*, pp. 291–308 (1966). ROGER STEVENS, *The Land of the Great Sophy* (1962), is a superior travel book with wide perspectives on Iranian art and history and some penetrating observations on present-day life. ARTHUR UPHAM POPE, *Persian Architecture* (1965), is concise and magnificently illustrated. For analyses of the problems of cultural stability, ferment, and adaptability for the future, these works are highly informative: MARVIN ZONIS, *The Political Elite of Iran* (1971); NIKKI R. KEDDIE, "The Iranian Power Structure and Social Change, 1800–1969: An Overview," *Int. J. Middle East Stud.*, 2:3–20 (1971); REINHOLD LOFFLER, "The Representative Mediator and the New Peasant," *Am. Anthrop.*, 73:1077–1091 (1971); WILLIAM G. MILLWARD, "Traditional Values and Social Change in Iran," *Iranian Stud.*, 4:2–35 (1971); and PHILIP C. SALZMAN, "National Integration of the Tribes in Modern Iran," *Middle East J.*, 25:325–336 (1971). Two books that systematically consider many aspects of Iranian culture in depth and in the context of change are NORMAN JACOBS, *The Sociology of Development: Iran As an Asian Case Study* (1966); and EHSAN YAR-SHATER (ed.), *Iran Faces the Seventies* (1971).

(J.Gu.)

Iranian Religions

The religions of the Iranian peoples, including the peoples of Iran proper, the Scythians, Sarmatians, and Alani, are characterized by a development of doctrines of salvation, a battle between good and evil, the afterlife, and a concept of a Saviour. Various forms of fire worship and burial rites that reflect certain eschatological views also are important in understanding the religions of the Iranian peoples that eventually exerted an influence on the religions of the Western world.

NATURE AND SIGNIFICANCE

The religious conditions of the ancient Iranian peoples who emerged out of a common Indo-Iranian origin sometime after 1700 BC to form the Iranian nation are largely unknown. The historical importance of the Iranian religions lies in the great role they played in Iranian developments and in the significant influence Iranian types of religion exercised in the West, especially on postexilic Jewish religion; on Hellenistic mystery religions, such as Mithraism; on Gnosticism; and on Islām, in which Iranian ideas are found both in Shīʿah, the most important medieval sect, and in popular eschatology (doctrines dealing with the last times).

In Iran itself the influence of the old religions lived on, not only in Zoroastrianism and in the various politico-religious movements that disturbed Iran during the first centuries of its Islāmic history but also in the cultural heritage of medieval and modern Iran, especially in art and literature.

The problems in the study of Iranian religions lie mainly in the sources and their character. To a great extent the sources are foreign to Iran and extant in many languages. What purely Iranian sources there are date from many periods of the Iranian languages and are full of philological difficulties. Beside the written sources, extremely valuable testimonies are offered by art and archaeology.

The most difficult problem of all is associated with the history of the Avesta, the holy book of the modern Parsis (Zoroastrians of India). Only the fourth part of the original Sāsānian (3rd–7th centuries AD) Avesta was saved after the Arab conquest of Iran in the 7th century. An enormous mass of religious traditions is preserved in Pahlavi (the language of the Sāsānian period) and new Persian literature. Hence the cardinal problem: how much of this textual matter may be traced back to lost Avestan tracts? The evaluation of the Iranian influence in older times depends on the answer to this question.

Characteristics

This influence is explained in terms of the characteristics of Iranian religions, which include: speculative vigour (*i.e.*, macrocosmic-microcosmic speculation); a theological conception of history; dualism; an optimistic monism; and eschatological and apocalyptic speculation (revelations on the character of the last times). The doctrines of

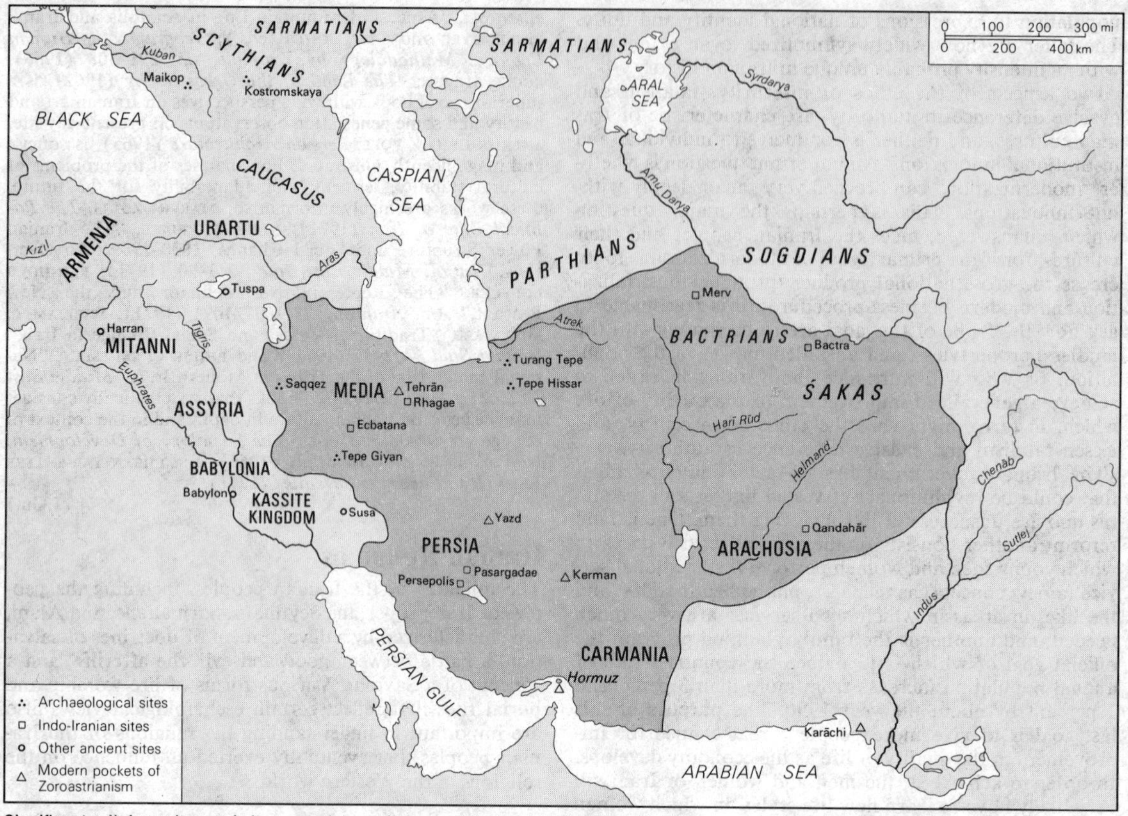

Significant religious sites and sites containing religious artifacts of ancient Indo-Iranian peoples, including those of peoples of adjacent areas and modern Zoroastrians.

the ages of the world and of the bodily resurrection of mankind are typical doctrines that had a great success outside Iran.

All Iranian religions are religions of salvation. Everything is centred on individual and collective salvation. A central place is assumed by a Saviour, who is commissioned by God to bring revelation. Cyclical ideas about the history of the world are combined with the belief that the Saviour has been incarnated in human shape in order to bring a definite revelation. A special emphasis is given here to the concept of "mankind," for Primordial Man, who is the first Saviour, is called Mortal Life. Thus, divinity and humanity interpenetrate each other. The divine Saviour descends to the earth and is born in a human individual as his higher, spiritual element. Such is the background of the famous doctrine of "the saved Saviour." From this idea follows a belief in the ascension of the soul back to its original celestial home.

The idea of the king as a divine person owes a great deal to the expectation of a future Saviour. According to the royal legend, the birth and education of the king are characterized by miracles. When he is born his divine star appears in the sky. The king is thus conceived as a Saviour, and his enthronement introduces a new era, the return of a golden age. The ruler is possessed of the royal glory, the *khvarnah*, which gives him good luck.

The Iranians' attitude to the world is coloured by either pessimism or optimism, according to the emphasis placed on the actual battle between Good and Evil in this present age and on the temporal triumph of Evil or on the definite victory of Good in the final period—yet to come. From the pessimistic attitude the Iranian type of Gnosticism (a religious world view in which matter is viewed as evil and the spirit good) is born. Gnosticism derives from Iran its basic and much of its technical language.

HISTORICAL DEVELOPMENT

Early Indo-Iranian religion. Of the religion of the early Indo-Iranians there is little direct evidence, other than theophorous (god-bearing) personal names of the feudal nobility of the Mitanni kingdom, and the treaty of Suppiluliumas with Mattiwaza, king of Mitanni, dating from about 1380, in which are listed Mitra, Varuna, Indra, and the two Nāsatyas, the twin gods. To these is added a goddess with a Mesopotamian name, Allatum or Ellat. These deities represent the three cosmic and social functions: Mitra-Varuṇa are the rulers, of whom Mitra represents the juridical and Varuṇa the magic-priestly aspect; Indra is the god of the warrior function; Nāsatya and the goddess represent the nourishing function and the collective character of society.

Indo-Iranian deities

The theophorous personal names of Indo-Iranian type include also the names of the western high god Zurvān (time); Vayu, the god of the atmosphere, with affinities to the warrior function; and Arta, the cosmic order, representing such ethical concepts as right and truth.

Scythian religion. Of the north Iranian tribes the Scythians are best known from the religious point of view. Source material consists of Greek and Latin texts and inscriptions, theophorous personal names, monuments of art, tombs, and modern Ossetic (the language of the Ossetes, an Alan people of the Central Caucasus) folklore.

The pantheon, presented in accordance with the Indo-Iranian three-functional system (*i.e.*, the ruling, warrior, and supportive or collective functions), is introduced by Tabiti, the "flaming" goddess. Then follow a god of heaven, called Papeus, "Father," and a god corresponding to Mitra, whose name is either Oetosyrus or Goetosyrus, both representing the ruler function. The warrior function has as its representative a god corresponding to Verethraghna (the Iranian god of victory) in eastern Iran. His Scythian name is unknown. The goddesses Apia, "Water," and Artimpasa (Aphrodite Urania), "she who pays attention to Arti" (a notion signifying luck and fecundity), represent the third, the fertility and collective function. In the inscriptions there is mentioned a "Virgin," who probably is of the same type (or possibly identical with one of them). The enigmatic Thagimasadas (Poseidon), god of the running waters, to be compared with the Ossetic Don Bettyr, probably also belongs to the third function.

Herodotus (5th-century-BC Greek historian) stated that the Scythians had no temples, altars, or statues. The war god, however, had as his sanctuary an enormous heap of bundles of firewood. Atop it was put an iron *akīnakēs* (East Iranian word for a short sword) as the symbol of this god, to which the Scythians sacrificed every year sheep, horses, and captive enemies. They cut off the joined right arm and shoulder of every sacrificed enemy and threw it in the air. Ossetic folklore shows these huge bundles of wood to be destined for a gigantic pyre. From the animal sacrifices a priest offered a small part of the flesh and the bowels to the god, throwing it on the ground before him. No fire was used at sacrifices. Great sacrifices of horses were offered in connection with the funeral ceremonies.

Sacrifice and divination

Among ritual customs divination was prominent. Scythian diviners used rods of salix wood, of which the priest made a bundle. While pronouncing certain conjuration formulas, the priest placed the rods severally one on the other and then again put them together in a bundle. The diviners were called by Herodotus *enareans*, "manwomen" as he translates this term. He stated that the Great Goddess had given them the power of divination. They practiced another divination method, using linden bark. The name *enarean* itself is Iranian: *a-nar(a)-*, corresponding to *anandrieis*, as Hippocrates more accurately translated it. They outwardly changed their sex by dressing and speaking as women.

The cult of the hearth fire, especially that of the king, played a central role. Oaths of an especially solemn character were taken at the royal hearth.

A social-religious custom, confirmed by Ossetic folklore, was the yearly drinking party in every district, when only those who had killed an enemy during the past year were allowed to drink, while the other warriors, covered with shame, were relegated to a separate place. The giant bowl from which the heroes drank among the Ossetes is called *nārt-āmongä*, "indicator of the heroic man."

Death rites and customs

Funeral customs and eschatology are the best known parts of north Iranian religion. Excavations have in every point confirmed the descriptions given by Herodotus. Mourning rites were excessive; *i.e.*, they were expressions of sorrow given in a conventional ceremonial form. Herodotus mentioned these rites only in connection with royal funerals, but Ossetic customs show them to have been regularly practiced. Men beat themselves in their faces, scratched their noses and cheeks, cut their hair, put arrows through their left hands, even cut away pieces of their ears. Women, besides scratching their faces, cut away their tresses or pulled out some of their hair and denuded their bosoms. A scene from a Buddhist painting in Central Asia shows Scythians indulging in such rites of mourning, which have been prevalent in all non-Zoroastrian forms of Iranian religion.

The disposal of the dead followed a certain pattern. There was, however, a difference between the burial of a king and a commoner. The royal tombs were covered with big mounds. A grave was dug that was supported by beams. The tomb itself was constructed with stones. Outside this grave chamber there were graves for the following of the king, people who were slaughtered in connection with the funeral. A corridor, covered by wood, led to the grave. Above the tomb a great tumulus (artificial mound) was heaped up.

The corpse was never burned, but the king was embalmed with wax. With the corpse were buried his arms and personal ornaments. In addition to his servants, horses also were slaughtered and buried.

Eschatological ideas among the Scythians can only be reconstructed from specimens of art, in which there is a scene representing the king before the seated Great Goddess in an act of communion, obviously after death. This scene must be compared with similar scenes described in the Zoroastrian text *Hadōkht Nask*.

North Iranian wall paintings from the graves of Panticapaeum depict banquet scenes. The motif of the funerary banquet has been depicted in a great many areas of the Iranian west.

Myth and art

Not much is known of the myths in general. Primordial Man, called Targitaos, had three sons: Lipoxais, Arpoxais, Kolaxais. Objects of gold fell from heaven: a golden bowl, a hatchet, and a plow and yoke. These objects symbolize the three social functions respectively. It is said that the youngest son, Kolaxais, got hold of these burning objects that had fallen from heaven, because before him the fire was extinguished. Kolaxais, the youngest son, accordingly served as the model for the two other sons.

Another mythical legend tells of the adventures of Heracles. Behind the Greek name may be surmised some Scythian form of Verethraghna, the god of the warrior function.

Religious art is dominated by representations of the ruler. He is, for example, seen on a rhyton (drinking horn) being given a beverage by the deity in a scene of investiture. Both the high god and the king are depicted on horseback, a type of representation later found on Sāsānian (3rd to 7th centuries AD) rock reliefs, where a nomadic influence may be seen. The ruler-god Mithra is also depicted as a horseman on coins from Pontus in post-Achaemenid and Parthian times (late 4th century BC to the 3rd century AD).

Paul Popper

Investiture on horseback of Ardashīr I, founder of the Sāsānian Empire, by the god Ormazd, or Ahura Mazdā. Rock relief at Naqsh-e Rustam, Iran.

In scenes of investiture goddess figures are depicted handing over the rhyton to the king. The Great Goddess is often represented in art, sometimes seated on a throne and holding in her left hand a long sceptre. It is noteworthy in this connection that the royal glory still preserves its common Iranian name, *farr*, in Ossetic folklore, though with a weakened meaning.

A male deity whose type is reminiscent of that of Helios Apollon (a sun deity) may be seen driving his chariot. This type appears also in eastern Iran both in texts (Yasht 10) and in art (among the Śacas).

Sarmatian and Alani religion. Sarmatians and Alanis were closely related to the Scythians and their religion was of the same type. Of the Sarmatians little is known other than that their sepulchres were much simpler than those of the Scythians. More important are the Alanis because of their late descendants, the Ossetes of the Caucasus. Modern Ossetic folklore confirms the descriptions given by classical authors, chiefly Herodotus. These folk traditions fill out the gap of missing myths, for the legends about the Narts (heroic men) preserve many nature myths—for example, those demonstrating that the lightning represents the true nature of Batradz, and the sun that of Sozryko. A kind of trickster is Syrdon, of whom many adventures are told. Undoubtedly the three social groups among the Narts—the Boriats, the Alägats, and the Äxsärtägkats—represent the three social functions.

Eschatology

Important for the understanding of eschatology is the ceremony among the Ossetes called *bähfäldīsyn*. Here a speaker at the funeral gives a speech, called the "Horse-Speech," in which he describes the fate of the dead man and his way on horseback to the world of the Narts. In this description are mentioned the bridge over the river that he has to traverse and the interrogation of the soul at this bridge. If the dead man has been righteous the bridge is easy to pass; but if he has been unrighteous it is impossible to pass, because the bridge breaks down. The "Horse-Speech," for the popular eschatology of Iranian peoples, is highly instructive.

Median and Persian religion. The religions of the Medes and Persians in the pre-Zoroastrian periods were characterized by the presence of a powerful priesthood, the Median Magi. Their support of the Median Gaumāta's (pretender to the Achaemenid throne in 522 BC) seizure of power denied them their influence only for a short time, for already during the reign of Darius I (reigned 522–486), and still more under Xerxes I (reigned 486–465), they regained their position. The religion of the Magi has been styled syncretistic, and without doubt it was a blend of Zoroastrianism and the old religion of western Iranians. The high god of the Medes was Zurvān, god of time and destiny. Among the Persians, on the other hand, the major god was Ahura Mazdā. This fact constantly led to the assumption that the Achaemenid kings were Zoroastrians, but all we know about them speaks against their Zoroastrianism. The deities Mithra and Anāhitā, not accepted by Zoroaster, were worshipped in the west. The position of Mithra especially was very strong, as witnessed by his name being part of theophorous names of priests and nobles. The great festival Mithrakāna was dedicated to him.

Zurvān and Ahura Mazdā, and Mithra and Anāhitā

While Ahura Mazdā and Mithra represented the first (ruling) function, Anāhitā was a goddess representative of the third (social) function. Her worship was characterized by cult images and also by small representations on gems. Equally revolutionary is the fact that temples appeared for the first time in Iranian religion in Achaemenid times.

The Parthian period (2nd century BC to 3rd century AD) shows above all the spread of the cults of Mithra and Anāhitā, in Asia Minor called the "Persian Goddess" and identified with Artemis. Their worship was propagated by the Magi.

Mithra's character as a Saviour god was more accentuated in this period, especially in the so-called "Oracles of Hystaspes," in which prophecies about the birth of the saving god are preserved in the writings of Lactantius (Latin Christian writer, *c.* AD 240–*c.* 320). Other late texts (*e.g.*, *The Chronicle of Zuqnin*, a Syriac Christian historical tract containing much legendary material) speak of the birth of the Saviour in a star falling from heaven. Mithra's worship evidently was concentrated in Armenia and northwestern Iran. There he occupied a strong position in the Zurvanite sect, in which—below Zurvān—he acted as mediator between the two representatives of good and evil, Ormazd (Ahura Mazdā) and Ahriman (Ahra Mainyu). The devotion to Mithra eventually expanded beyond the borders of the Parthian Empire (see also MITHRAISM).

The Sāsānian period is noted for the rise of a Zoroastrian state church and the creation of a written canon, the Avesta. From this holy book, which underwent various redactions, or compressions, Zurvanite myths were purged. They can, however, be reconstructed, partly from Pahlavi texts and partly from Christian polemical writings in the various Syriac acts of martyrs. This period was also characterized by the fusion of the two mighty priesthoods, the Median Magi and the Persian *hērbads.* On the basis of this fusion, the influential *hērbad* Kartēr in the late 3rd century AD laid the foundations of the Sāsānian Church, which had to defend its existence against various denominations within the borders of the empire, such as Jews, Christians, Manichees, and Buddhists (in the east). The fight was difficult against Christians and Manichees, who were severely persecuted. Nevertheless Christianity gained more and more ground and toward the end of the Sāsānian period seemed near a decisive victory, a development stopped by the Arab invasion, which ultimately led to the conversion of nearly the whole Iranian population and the emigration to India of many faithful Zoroastrians, the Parsis (see also ZOROASTRIANISM AND PARSIISM).

MYTHOLOGY

Creation. Creation myths have been preserved primarily in Zurvanite religion. Plutarch stated in *De Iside et Osiride* that Oromazes (the god of good) was born from the purest light but Areimanios (the spirit of evil) from the gloom, and that they strove in war with one another. The good god Oromazes created six gods: of good will, truth, good government, a maker of wisdom, maker of wealth, and maker of pleasures in beautiful things. These gods corresponded with the Zoroastrian *amesha spentas.* Areimanios created rival artificers, also six in number.

Struggle between good and evil

Oromazes withdrew himself from the sun by as much as the sun is withdrawn from the earth and adorned the sky with stars. He then created 24 other gods and put them in an egg. But the gods born from Areimanios, being of the same number, bored through the egg, whence evil things have been mixed with the good.

A time fixed by Destiny will come, however, when Areimanios, bringing plague and famine, must be utterly destroyed by these and forced to vanish. The earth having become flat and level, men shall have one life and one commonwealth, all being blessed and speaking one tongue.

According to the Magi, for 3,000 years in succession Oromazes or Areimanios rules and the other is ruled; for the next 3,000 years they fight and destroy one another's works, but finally Hades (*i.e.*, Areimanios) will fail. Men will become happy, neither needing food nor casting shadow, while Oromazes, the god who brought these things to pass, is quiet and at rest for a time.

The latter part of Plutarch's text goes back to the authority of the Greek historian Theopompus (*c.* 350 BC), whereas the origin of the former part is uncertain but also dates from Achaemenid times. The doctrines contained there are, however, old—and they are Zurvanite. Heaven, according to the Pahlavi religious text *Mēnōk i Khrat* ("Spirit of Wisdom"), is shaped as an egg. In the Zurvanite religious text of *Zātspram* I is described the attack launched by Ahriman (Areimanios) and his following against Ormazd (another name for Ahura Mazdā or Oromazes) in his heavenly light. It can be demonstrated on philological grounds that this text is based on lost Avestan passages, and these passages must have existed in oral tradition before the fall of the Achaemenid empire.

The two gods, the good one and the evil, are considered both as gods and as enemies, on an equal footing. The god of time and destiny, placed above them, is only hinted at, when it is said that there will come a time, fixed by destiny, when Areimanios will be utterly destroyed. The deity of destiny (Zurvān) accordingly decides the outcome of the war between good and evil, an outcome that will make an end of the "mingling" of evil with good (this "mingling," *gumēchishn*, is often alluded to in Pahlavi texts).

Supplementary details were offered by Eudemus of Rhodes (before 300 BC) in an observation preserved by the Greek philosopher Damascius (AD 453–*c.* 533). He stated:

> The Magi . . . call the intelligible and unified Whole, some (of them) Time, others (of them) Space. This results in a distinction either between a good god and an evil daemon, or between light and darkness. And the same people, after thus dividing the indivisible Nature, make a twofold classification of the more important elements, and set Oromazes over the one, and Areimanios over the other.

In Damascius' work the highest deity is time, also called space (in Pahlavi *swāsh*, or *spihr*, and *zamān*). Both Ormazd and Ahriman are represented, the one as the good and light, the other as the evil and dark. But Ahriman is here called not a god but only a daemon.

Cosmology. Cosmology (concerning the order of the universe), among the Magi in the west, is thus entirely dominated by Zurvanite conceptions, implying a double creation, one brought about by the good and the other by the evil principle.

Another aspect of cosmology is the macrocosmic-microcosmic speculation, now extant in the Pahlavi (late

Zoroastrian) book *Bundahishn* XXVIII and other late writings. There is also correspondence between Man as a small World, and the World as a great Man. "Man's body, is a counterpart of the earthly World."

Creation out of God himself

In the Iranian cosmology, God brought forth the whole creation by bearing it in his own body and producing everything from himself. First he created heaven from his head, earth from his feet, water from his tears, plants from his hair, and fire from his mind.

The fact that God has created the universe out of his own body is alluded to in *Bundahishn* I, in which it is said that Ormazd by his act of creation has the position of "father and mother of creation." There the deity is conceived of as bisexual, a Zurvanite doctrine, for Ormazd obviously has taken the place originally occupied by Zurvān, who according to the myths clustering around him is both male and female. The birth of the cosmos as an embryo, proceeding from conception to birth, is a Zurvanite doctrine, for Zurvān is male-female, bearing in his womb the twins Ormazd and Ahriman. This is the myth propagated by the Magi. Originally the myth may have related only that the high god, being bisexual, produced from his womb the whole universe, composed of the elements. These elements, in non-Zoroastrian sources (*e.g.*, Manichaean texts), are called *mardaspanti* or *amahraspandān (amesha spenta)*. The elements (*amahraspandān*) together form the universe, the body of the godhead; even in Zoroastrianism the *amesha spentas* are the various aspects of Ahura Mazdā. Zurvān out of himself produced Ormazd, who is composed of the elements; *i.e.*, the universe.

The gods. The deities in Iranian religions are to be classified according to the three-functional systems. Outside the north Iranian territory their names are: Mithra-Ahura Mazdā, representatives of the sovereign function; Verethraghna (in older times, Indra), representative of the warrior function; Vayu, a deity introducing the series of gods, associated with the same function; Anāhitā, the goddess of fertility, associated with the twin gods, Nāñhaithya, the social function. Already in remotest times the twin gods were probably called Haurvatāt (Health) and Ameretāt (Immortality). The functional series is concluded by the god of fire, here called Ātar, not the Indian Agni (but Agni once was a living deity in Iran, as well as India, as testified by the name Dāshtāgni). Some of these deities were accompanied by minor deities, such as Mithra, who had as his following, on the one hand, Sraosha ("Obedience," originally), Airyaman, and Rashnu ("the Righteous"), who, together with him, decided the fate of the deceased; and, on the other hand, the fertility goddess, Pārendi. The gods were divided in two classes: *ahura* and *daēva*, good ones and evil ones (the opposite of the Indian *asura* and *deva*). All the gods were interpreted spiritually by Zoroaster, but their functions were still preserved in his theological system.

Primordial Man was placed between gods and men. Various such primordial figures met in various parts of Iran: Yim, or Yima (child of the sun), Hōshang, and Gayōmart (first man). Yima was also the first ruler, the model of a sacral king. Gayōmart plays a major role in Zurvanite texts, extant in Pahlavi writings but based on lost Avestan passages.

Man. Man was composed of various spiritual forces, for which "soul conceptions," in referring to man's higher element, is a very inadequate term. Many of them belong to the common Indo-Iranian heritage. Most important of these spiritual forces are *ahu*, *vyāna*, *khratu*, *manah*, *urvan*, *tanu*, *kehrp*, and quite especially *daēnā*. The individual *manah* is part of the cosmic *manah*, in Manichaeism called the "Great Vohu Manah."

The *fravashi* and the *daēnā*

Still more significant is the *fravashi* (properly *fravarti*), meaning "protection," a kind of genius and at the same time the higher spiritual ego of man and his primordial spiritual being. As ancestor-spirits the *fravashis* enjoyed worship in popular religion. The medieval Persian author al-Bīrūnī described the Fravardīgān festival, when food and drink were offered to the spirits of the dead, who during these days used to visit their families and occupy themselves with their affairs, although invisible to them. The *fravashis* are, however, also pre-existent heavenly beings and as such visualized as spear-carrying horsemen. In the great war between good and evil they are the allies of God. They are an Iranian equivalent of the Indian Maruts (followers of Indra, god of the warrior function) and of pre-Zoroastrian origin, chiefly associated with the second social function.

The notion of *daēnā* is also highly complex. In the text *Hadōkht Nask* II, in which the fate of the dead after death is related, the soul (*urvan*) of the righteous spends three nights near the corpse. Toward the end of the third night as dawn begins, a sweet-smelling wind is carried to the soul from the South. In this wind the soul sees its own *daēnā* in the shape of a beautiful 15-year-old virgin. Thanks to the good actions of the righteous soul, she has grown very beautiful. The soul then ascends through the three spheres of heaven, those of the stars, the moon, and the sun, and finally arrives at "the Lights without beginning," the paradise, the place of the Godhead. This way upward is beset with perils, for demons are lying in ambush. Ahura Mazdā orders "spring butter" to be given to the soul, obviously some kind of food or drink of immortality.

The *daēnā* in this case should probably be compared with the paradise virgins of Indian eschatology who meet the ascending soul. The text, *Hadōkht Nask*, was probably written in the priestly Magian circles.

The bridge, *Chinvat peretu* (the "Bridge of the Requiter"), that is to be passed by the dead belongs to the Indo-Iranian heritage. The characteristic that it is sharp as a sword to the unrighteous and therefore impossible to pass appears also in Indian texts, and hence may be regarded as a common Aryan conception.

Eschatology. From individual eschatology the perspective widens to include the fate of the world and humanity. This general eschatology comprises what is called apocalyptic, in which God intervenes in history at the end of time. The world's process of development is conceived as a succession of four periods. A symbol of these ages of the world is the cosmic tree, on which there were four branches, one each of gold, silver, steel, and iron. These four branches were interpreted as corresponding to four periods of the world's history. The world, accordingly, had a brilliant beginning in a descending scale until its end. Zoroastrian tradition interpreted this symbol as a series of four successive reigns, starting with the period when Zoroaster received his revelation. Comparison with the corresponding Indian cyclical scheme, as well as with Zurvanite conceptions, however, demonstrates this fourfold scheme to comprise originally 12,000 years with 3,000 years in every period. It is probable that—as in India—each 3,000-year period was characterized by a certain colour as an alternative of a certain metal. The last period is, among other things, characterized by the fact that mankind is born smaller, with strength also being less than before. This characteristic must be a common Indo-Iranian notion, for it is paralleled by the Indian idea that in every age of the world men are born ever smaller and weaker. Pahlavi apocalyptic literature, in which these conceptions are also found, is based on lost Avestan texts, as can be proved by linguistic and literary analysis. Older attempts to assign Iranian apocalyptic speculations to a post-Christian or even post-Sāsānian age have thus been discredited.

The ages of the world

The last period is characterized by the final struggle between all good and evil powers. A symbol of evil is Azhdahāk (Avesta Azhi Dahāka), the Dragon, fought by the hero Thraētaona (or in other traditions Keresāspa). The Dragon here corresponds to the Indian dragon Ahi, or Vṛtra, killed by Indra. In the final battle a prominent place is taken by Mithra. Azhdahāk was not killed, but only fettered on the Mountain of Demavend. Now he is let loose and brings devastation everywhere, until Keresāspa kills him with his mace. This final battle is called the Great War and survives both in Zoroastrian and Manichaean traditions.

A central role is played by Mithra in the so-called Oracles of Hystaspes, spread in Greek language in the West more than 2,000 years ago. In it the birth of Mithra is alluded to, for it is said that God—to save the righteous among persecuted mankind—will send the "Great King" from heaven, who will annihilate the evil powers with fire and sword. This Great King is no one but the reincarnated Mithra.

Coming of the Saviour

Several Christian texts, based on Iranian traditions, describe the Saviour's miraculous birth. His star appears in the sky, bearing the image of a small boy, and descends in a column of light into a cave, where he is born out of the rock as a small child. The Magi, year after year, wait on the "Mount of Victories," hoping that the Saviour will be born. They present golden crowns as gifts to the newborn Saviour Mithra.

WORSHIP, PRACTICES, AND INSTITUTIONS

Temples and shrines. Indo-European peoples originally lacked temples, idols, and written religious traditions. The same holds true for the Iranian tribes who, however, in the west entered into contact with the Near Eastern culture and were influenced by it. For this reason in Achaemenid times temples existed (for example, in Susa and Persepolis) of modest size, protected by a roof, and housing the holy fire. Reliefs show the Great King officiating before the fire altar. Such altars are extant in Median territory from about 550 BC. The holy fire was also carried on portable altars.

Priesthood and soothsayers. Priests were of the same type as those in Vedic India and usually carried the same names. Thus there were *kavi*, *usig*, and *vifra*, all of whom possessed Indian correspondences. Both *kavi* and *vifra* denote the priest as an inspired person; *kavi* also is the appellation of members of a legendary dynasty. The term *usig* seems to signify a sacrificial priest. The *karapan*, mentioned together with *usig*, is to be connected with the Indian *kalpa* ("rite") and therefore may have been occupied with ritual practice in general. More specialized is the *zaotar*, the correspondence of the Indian *hotṛ*. His task probably was to praise the deity and carry out the libation. Zoroaster was a *zaotar*. At the sacrifice the *staotar* and the *zbātar* also fulfilled the function of praising the godhead. The *mathran* recited special formulas, as in India. The *āthravan* is likewise the same as the Indian *átharvan*, but it is impossible to define his special functions. All these categories are found in eastern Iran.

Western Iran was dominated by the Median Magi, as mentioned before. They were characterized by syncretistic, often deep speculations, coupled with a spirit of fanaticism. They were ancestors of the Sāsānian *mobeds* ("priests"), who had their centre in Shiz and propagated Zurvanite ideas and customs (*e.g.*, next-of-kin marriage). Their later subordinate colleagues, the *herbads* of Fars, were fire priests like the Magi, and also carriers of oral tradition. Like the Magi, they accepted Zoroastrianism and had as their ancestors the *Haēthra paitis* (possibly "fire priests").

Sacrifice. The priest, when sacrificing, recited with "a loud prayer" several sacrificial formulas. The *barsman*-bundle, his special attribute, was much used also among the northern tribes, even as an instrument of divination practice. It corresponds exactly with the Indian *barhis*. The twigs, kept together in a bundle, were spread out on the ground when a sacrifice was offered. The Magi killed the sacrificial animal with a mace, not a knife.

In addition to the *barsman*, the chief elements at a sacrifice were fire, the drinking of *haoma* (the juice of a mild narcotic plant), and libation. Fire was, however, not used to consume the sacrificial victim, which was not burned at all, but to call down the deities from heaven. The fire, Ātar, was the hearth fire. The fire ritual was organized in accordance with the three-functional system, the hearth fire being the starting point, from which the three fires were taken. Later they were associated with the three classes of society. Fire must always be burning and never quenched; it was a perpetual fire. The fire altar was the centre when the Iranian started constructing cult buildings. The *haoma* is the dialectal correspondence of Indian *soma* and was originally an alcoholic drink, conceived of as a drink of immortality, for it was called "averter of death," *haoma dūraosha*. Sacrifices of cattle, celebrated in honour of Mithra, the Slayer of the Bull, and excessive drinking of *haoma* were essential parts of a ritual looked upon by Zoroaster with great horror.

Rites and burial customs. Ritual acts besides sacrifice were above all purification ceremonies and ordeal customs. The elements of purification were fire and water. Of these, fire was the more important. To prove a person's freedom from guilt, it was necessary for him to pass through a real pyre, nourished by fire taken from the sacred fire of a cult place. The deity was invoked to assist at the ordeal. In Zoroastrianism an ordeal with molten metal was used, and eschatological conceptions of how earth is purified through a huge stream of fire hinted at the importance of the ordeal fire.

Ordeals

Burial customs possessed a ritual character but were of different kinds in different parts of Iran. Four types were used: (1) exposure of the corpses so that the fleshy parts were consumed by dogs and birds of prey; (2) burning of the body, after which the ashes were collected in an urn; (3) burial in the ground, attested above all among northern tribes; and (4) embalming and burial in rock tombs, chiefly used in the burial of kings.

CONCLUSION

The evaluation of the influence exercised by Iranian religions depends upon a correct evaluation of the Pahlavi sources. The endeavour to analyze Avestan portions of this literature began only in the second half of the 20th century. When this task has been completed scholars will be in a position to form a more correct opinion of Iranian religion and to state with more certainty its importance as a type of religion independent of Zoroastrianism.

BIBLIOGRAPHY. E. BENVENISTE, *The Persian Religion According to the Chief Greek Texts* (1929), the first effort to analyze the Greek texts; J. BIDEZ and FRANZ CUMONT, *Les Mages hellénisés*, 2 vol. (1938), fundamental for an understanding of the religion of the Magi outside Iran; A. CHRISTENSEN, *Les Types du premier Homme et du premier Roi*, 2 vol. (1918–34), a collection of texts in translation (slightly out of date, but the only existing work of this kind); G. DUMEZIL, *Légendes sur les Nartes* (1930), a collection of Ossetic texts with an analysis of their importance for the Scythian religion, and *Naissance d'archanges* (1945), fundamental for an understanding of the role of the *amesha spentas;* M. ROSTOVTZEFF, *Iranians and Greeks in South Russia* (1922), fundamental for Scythian culture and religion; G. WIDENGREN, *The Great Vohu Manah and the Apostle of God: Studies in Iranian and Manichaean Religion* (1945), an analysis of the concept of messenger and bringer of salvation in Iranian religion; *Iranisch-semitische Kulturbegegnung in partischer Zeit* (1960), the first effort to analyze cultural contacts between Parthian and Semite civilizations; and *Die Religionen Irans* (1965), a comprehensive textbook; O.S. WIKANDER, *Der arische Männerbund* (1938), fundamental for an understanding of the role of the social and cultic organizations in ancient Iran; R.C. ZAEHNER, *Zurvan: A Zoroastrian Dilemma* (1955), an important collection of Zurvanite texts.

(G.Wn.)

Iraq

Iraq (al-Jumhūrīyah al-ʿIrāqīyah) is an independent Arab country of the Middle East, situated at the northwest end of the Persian Gulf. It is bounded on the north by Turkey, on the east by Iran, on the southeast by the Persian Gulf, on the west by Syria and Jordan, and on the south by Kuwait and Saudi Arabia. It covers an area of 168,878 square miles (437,393 square kilometres) and had a population of nearly 12,200,000 in 1978. Baghdad is the national capital. Called Mesopotamia (the Land Between the [Two] Rivers) by the classical world, the country became known as Iraq in the 7th century.

Although basically an agricultural nation, Iraq is internationally important as a major source of the world's oil. Its considerable wealth of oil reserves has enabled the country to embark upon economic development and land-reform programs. It has, however, been subject to political instability since the overthrow of the monarchy in 1958. The army and the Baʿth Party have progressively increased their hold over the political and economic structures of the country and in the 1970s were its strongest guiding forces. Iraq, part of the Arab world, has attempted to affirm its unique national culture, stressing its past and its own identity. For related physical features, see PERSIAN GULF; TIGRIS–EUPHRATES RIVER SYSTEM; see also BAGHDAD; for a discussion of the nation's history, see MESOPOTAMIA AND IRAQ, HISTORY OF. (I.A.A.-L.)

THE LANDSCAPE

Relief and drainage. The fundamental elements in Iraq's physiography are the twin valleys of the Tigris and Euphrates rivers. Joined in the south but diverging in the north, they are separated by a tongue of higher land stretching southward from the Anatolian foothills to just north of Baghdad and known as al-Jazīrah (the Island).

The Tigris and Euphrates

Lower Iraq. The region begins at the ridge between ar-Ramādī and Baghdad and extends about 330 miles southeastward to the Persian Gulf. The Tigris and Euphrates diverge east and west, respectively, below Baghdad, which is therefore in a narrower waist of lowland. Here the Tigris has a particularly tortuous course, and the river is marked by large numbers of meander channels and oxbow lakes. Because of the natural levees (raised embankments on either side of the river) and the difficult entry for tributary streams, there is much marsh. Many subsidiary rivers empty into the Hawr ("lake" or "marsh") as-Suwayqīyah depression, and navigation of the mainstream is difficult because of sharp bends and strong current. Below al-Kūt the course of the Tigris is much straighter and flatter. In its lowest section, especially from al-ʿAmārah southward, much of the waters are dispersed into distributary channels and marshes.

From ar-Ramādī southward the Euphrates flows at first in a well-defined channel. Natural levees occur, as on the Tigris. Between al-Musayyib and as-Samāwah the river discharges into various distributaries; the remnants of a previous swamp include old channels, levees, cutoffs, and lakes. From as-Samāwah there is a well-defined channel as far as an-Nāṣirīyah, or even Sūq ash-Shuyūkh, lying within an open plain that is now largely arid and almost featureless. Below an-Nāṣirīyah distributary channels take off the whole of the Euphrates water, which ultimately drains into Hawr al-Ḥammār, a vast expanse of reedy swamp. From al-Qurnah, the point of junction between the waters of Hawr al-Ḥammār and the Tigris, the river is known as the Shatt al-Arab. Away from the rivers, patches of swamp and marsh are separated by ridges.

Upper Iraq. This region comprises the valleys of the two main rivers, together with the somewhat higher ground that stretches southeastward between them. At its entry into Iraq, the Euphrates has cut a broad, flat valley with steep sides. Rejuvenation of the Euphrates led to many meanders being incised into the flat floor, giving a second set of terraces. Irregularities in rock strata have produced rapids and shoals, and the river tends to hug the western bank, producing a marked escarpment on the west and more open country to the east. The Tigris on leaving Turkey has cut an irregular winding passage among low foothills and ridges. Where the river flows southeastward, it tends to have a wide, shallow bed, with steep-sided low hills on the western (right) bank and open rolling country to the east. Separating these reaches are defiles that run from north to south, the narrowest of which is at Bāghloja, about 14 miles below the confluence with the Nahr al-Khābūr on the Turkish–Iraqi frontier. Here the Tigris is only 120 feet wide, with a series of rapids that are almost cascades. Such conditions continue as far as Mosul, after which relief becomes much less accentuated, ultimately falling away to open steppe through which the Tigris flows in a broader channel. There the Tigris is joined by the Great and Little Zab rivers. One last, isolated defile occurs where the river breaks through the Jabal Ḥamrīn (Ḥamrīn Mountains) above Baʿījī at a gorge that is now used to carry the Iraqi oil pipelines from Kirkūk to the Mediterranean. From Tikrīt southward the Tigris wanders on a flat plain, breaking up into several arms.

Al-Jazīrah region

Between the Euphrates and Tigris and bounded on the north by the Jabal Sinjār lies al-Jazīrah, a region of undulating steppe, small-scale ranges, and closed drainage basins. The warping of the whole area has produced closed drainage basins, the largest of which is the Wādī ath-Tharthār (a long defile running more or less parallel to the Tigris about 20 to 40 miles west of the river), now part of the Tigris flood-control project.

The northeastern region. Fronting the Tigris on the east, between the Turkish frontier and the broad Diyālā Valley paralleling the Iran border, is an upland area roughly rectangular in shape that rises in steps eastward from river level. The first step is the Jabal Ḥamrīn, and behind it lies an undulating territory of river basins, rolling plateaus, and irregular hills that ultimately pass into the main Zagros range in Iran. The lower (western) part, broken by the valleys of the Great and Little Zab, is the ancient region of Assyria. Farther east, as the mountain zone begins, there is an alternation of high ridges aligned northwest to southeast and separated by river basins. This is often spoken of as Iraqi Kurdistan. Here, the mountain ridges have a summit average of about 8,000 feet (2,440 metres). They attain elevations of 10,000 to 11,000 feet in a few places, culminating in Rawāndūz (12,001 feet; 3,658 metres), the highest point in Iraq. Between the ridges are trough valleys usually occupied by rivers that have eroded out basins. All the streams weave a tortuous way south and southwest toward the lowlands and are marked by gorge and defile sections (*darband*) where they skirt or cut through ridges. In a few places, such as as-Sulaymānīyah, al-ʿAmādīyah, and Rawāndūz town, patches of lowland allow cultivation, but much of Kurdistan is given over to nomadism.

The western desert. Lying to the west of the riverine lowlands, this region extends from Kuwait and Saudi Arabia on the south as far as Jordan and Syria. In the region of the Jordan frontier is the Bādiyat ash-Shām (Syrian Desert). The desert area slopes gently upward from the Euphrates lowland and is formed of ancient rocks that are often exposed as irregular pavement. In the extreme south, part of the frontier with Kuwait is formed by Wādī al-Bāṭin, a rift structure three miles wide running inland from az-Zubayr as far as central Arabia. To the northwest lies Ṣaḥrā' al-Ḥijārah, in the main a region of shallow, mud-lined depressions, rocky outcrops, and loose sand. An extensive swamp lies northeast of this area, paralleling the Euphrates.

Farther north lies the Wādīyah region, with steeper slopes. Because of its steepness, normal drainage developed, and there is a network of dry valleys aligned northeastward to the Euphrates that carry floodwater for an hour or two each year. The region takes its name from these valleys, or *wādī*s. Since there is no fringe of continuous sand or salt marsh, as there is farther south, the Wādīyah offers more practicable routes westward and is now used for oil pipelines.

Soils. The soils fall into two contrasted groups—heavy alluvial deposits associated with the main rivers and very light soils in the rest of the country. The alluvial soils contain a significant proportion of humus and clay and dry out to a hard, tenacious mass that can be used for building. The light soils are deficient or entirely lacking in humus and have a low clay content, but they may contain a proportion of wind-deposited minerals, some of which are valuable plant nutrients.

The problem of soil salinity

For both groups of soils, there is an acute problem of salinity induced by conditions of sharply seasonal rainfall followed by a hot, arid season. This produces evaporation of soil moisture and consequent accumulation of alkaline salts at or near the surface in quantities sufficient to inhibit cultivation. On entering Iraq, the Tigris and Euphrates contain about 30 parts per 100,000 of salts; in their lower courses this proportion trebles. It was estimated in 1949 that 60 percent of all irrigated land in Iraq had become salinated, and an overall assessment is that 1 percent of the total cultivated area is abandoned each year because of salinity.

Climate. Because of the simplicity and regularity of relief, Iraq has a straightforward climatic regime. In the lowlands two contrasting seasons occur: a dry and intensely hot summer from May to October and a relatively cool, humid winter from December to March, with short transitional periods. Altitude exerts a considerable effect in the mountain zones, where winters can be severe.

From May onward the predominating climatic element is a persistent and regular northwesterly wind (*shamāl*) over the whole of Iraq. Because these air currents come from land areas, they are dry and few clouds form, so that for several weeks or even months the sun beats down uninterruptedly, producing extremely high temperatures. At Baghdad, July and August daily temperature means are about 95° F (35° C) and 88° F (31° C), respectively; mean daily maxima are about 110° F (43° C). Some drop is apparent close to water surfaces because of high evaporation, but the effect is hardly improved because of greater relative humidity. Strong winds produce blowing dust or sandstorms; July is the worst month, with an average of five storms at Baghdad and eight at ash-Shu'aybah. Usually, no rain falls between May and the end of October.

Conditions are more variable during the winter season, when the *sharqī*—a cool, damp southeasterly wind—brings rain. At other times a cold air mass from the interior of Asia may extend westward, bringing fine but cold conditions. Hot air masses from the south may also affect Iraq; January temperatures of more than 81° F (27° C) are known, but frost may occur anywhere, even at Basra. Such extremes, however, are rare. The northeast has its own climatic conditions; as much as 30 to 40 inches (760 to 1,000 millimetres) of rain occur on the highest mountains, with 15 to 25 inches in the northeastern piedmont (region at the base of mountains).

Two climatic provinces

There are therefore two climatic provinces within Iraq; the hot, arid lowland and the damper northeast, where rainfall is sufficient for cultivation without irrigation, summer temperatures are slightly lower, and a colder, continental winter brings up to three months of snow in some places. The northeast and Kurdistan apart, the main features of Iraqi climate are aridity and overwhelming summer heat, the difficulties of which are intensified by high atmospheric humidity near the rivers.

Vegetation and animal life. Iraq is a meeting place of two major plant groups, both of which show the predominating influence of drought. Toward the north and east, there is a steppe vegetation of perennial bushes and low shrubs, with mugwort (*Artemisia*), goosefoot (Chenopodiaceae), and grass species dominant, together with a "flush" of short-lived creepers and grasses that amounts to about two-thirds of the total vegetation. Toward the south and west, vegetation is often restricted to thorns (chiefly tamarisk and species of *Haloxylon*, commonly called saxual), a few shrubs such as rhanterium, papposum, and other salt-resistant plants. Poplar, willow, licorice, and tamarisk flourish in small clumps near the rivers. Below al-Qurnah, the marshland is an area of reeds, tall grasses, and sedge. The open oak forest on the Zagros Mountains, at altitudes between 2,000 and 6,000 feet, has been mostly reduced to scrub by intensive cutting and unrestricted grazing. Above this region is an Alpine zone of cushion (clumped and compacted) plants and dwarf species broadly similar to those of Alpine Europe.

Animal life has been much reduced. The oryx (a kind of gazelle), ostrich, and wild ass are now practically extinct, and the last known lion was killed around 1910. Bats, rats of various species, jackals, hyenas, and wildcats are the most common mammals, with wild pigs and gazelles in remoter regions. Reptiles are numerous and include lizards, the largest reaching four feet; snakes, mainly "racer"

MAP INDEX

Political subdivisions
al-Anbār.........33·45n 42·40e
al-Baṣrah........30·30n 47·47e
al-Muthannā.......30·30n 45·00e
al-Qādisiyah.....31·35n 45·00e
an-Najah.........31·59n 44·20e
as-Sulaymānīyah.............35·40n 45·30e
at-Ta'mīm.......31·35n 44·35e
Bābil............32·40n 44·35e
Baghdād..........34·00n 43·16e
Dahūk...........37·00n 43·15e
Dhī Qār..........31·00n 46·00e
Diyālā...........34·00n 45·00e
Irbīl.............36·10n 44·00e
Karbalā'.........32·15n 43·07e
Maysān..........32·00n 47·00e
Nīnawā..........36·10n 42·35e
Ṣalāh ad-Dīn.....34·30n 43·49e
Wāsiṭ...........32·45n 45·25e

The names of the political subdivisions do not appear on the map when they are the same as the names of their capital cities.

Cities and towns
Abū al-Khaṣīb...30·27n 47·59e
ad-Dīwānīyah....31·59n 44·56e
'Afak............32·04n 45·15e
Ain Ghazal......36·14n 41·59e
al-'Amādīyah....37·06n 43·29e
al-'Amārah......31·50n 47·09e
al-Bādī...........35·56n 41·32e
al-Baṣra, see Basra
al-Baṭhā'........31·06n 45·53e
al-Fallūjah.......33·20n 43·46e
al-Fāw...........29·58n 48·29e
al-Ḥadīthah.....34·07n 42·23e
al-Ḥaḍr..........35·35n 42·44e
al-Ḥalfāyah.......31·49n 47·26e
al-Ḥayy..........32·10n 46·03e
al-Ḥillah..........32·29n 44·25e
al-Hindīyah......32·33n 44·13e
'Ali al-Gharbī....32·27n 46·41e
al-Kāẓimīyah.....33·22n 44·20e
al-Khāliṣ.........33·49n 00·00e
al-Kifl...........32·14n 44·22e
al-Kūt............32·25n 45·59e
al-Ma 'ānīyah....30·44n 43·00e
al-Maḥmūdīyah..33·03n 44·21e
al-Mawṣil, see Mosul
al-Miqdādīyah...33·59n 44·56e
al-Musayyib......32·47n 44·18e
al-Qā'im.........34·21n 41·07e
al-Qurnah........31·00n 47·26e
Āltūn Kūprī.......35·45n 44·09e
al-'Uzayr.........31·19n 47·25e
Amarah, see al-'Amārah
'Ānah............34·28n 41·56e
an-Najaf..........31·59n 44·20e
an-Nāṣirīyah.....31·02n 46·16e
an-Nu'mānīyah...32·32n 45·25e
'Aqrah..........36·45n 43·54e
ar-Ramādī........33·25n 43·17e
ar-Rumaythah...31·32n 45·12e
ar-Rustamīyah...33·17n 44·31e
ar-Ruṭbah........33·02n 40·17e
ash-Shabakah...30·49n 43·39e
ash-Shāmīyah...31·57n 44·36e
ash-Sharqāṭ......35·27n 43·16e
ash-Shaṭrah.....31·25n 46·10e
ash-Shināfīyah...31·35n 44·39e
ash-Shu'aybah...30·25n 47·38e
as-Sa'dīyah......34·11n 45·07e
as-Salmān........30·30n 44·32e
as-Samāwah......31·18n 45·17e
as-Sulaymānīyah.............35·33n 45·26e
'Ayn Zālah.......36·43n 42·33e
az-Zubayr........30·23n 47·43e
Badrah...........33·06n 45·58e
Baghdad..........33·21n 44·25e
Ba'ījī............34·56n 43·29e
Balad............34·01n 44·09e
Ba'qūbah........33·45n 44·38e
Baṣra............30·30n 47·47e
Dahūk (Dhok)....36·52n 43·00e
Dokan, see Dukān
Dukān (Dokan)...35·56n 44·58e
Ḥalabjah.........35·10n 45·59e
Ḥilla, see al-Ḥillah
Hīt...............33·38n 42·49e
Irbīl..............36·11n 44·01e
Jadīdah..........34·01n 42·28e
Jalībah..........30·35n 46·32e
Jalūlā'...........34·16n 45·10e
Jāsimīyah........33·45n 44·41e
Karbalā'.........32·36n 44·02e
Khān al-Baghdādī........33·51n 42·33e
Khānaqīn.........34·21n 45·22e
Kibāsī............30·34n 47·50e
Kifrī.............34·42n 44·58e
Kirkūk...........35·28n 44·28e
Kūt al-Imārah, see al-Kūt
Kūysanjaq........36·05n 44·38e
Mandalī..........33·45n 45·32e
Mosul (al-Mawṣil)......36·10n 42·35e
Nafṭ Khāneh.....34·02n 45·28e
Nasiriya, see an-Nāṣirīyah
Nukhayb.........32·02n 42·15e
Qal'at Ṣāliḥ......31·31n 47·16e
Qal'at Sukkar....31·51n 46·05e
Qayyārah.........35·48n 43·17e
Ramadi, see ar-Ramādī
Rāniyah..........36·15n 44·53e
Rāwah...........34·28n 41·55e
Rawāndūz.......36·37n 44·31e
Rumaylah.........30·47n 47·37e
Ṣafwān..........30·07n 47·43e
Sāmarrā'.........34·12n 43·52e
Shaykh Sa'd.....32·34n 46·17e
Shithāthah.......32·33n 43·29e
Sinjār............36·19n 41·52e
Sulaymaniyah, see as-Sulaymānīyah
Sūq ash-Shuyūkh........30·53n 46·28e
Tall 'Afar........36·22n 42·27e
Tall Kayf.........36·29n 43·08e
Ṭaqṭaq...........35·53n 44·35e
Ṭāwūq...........35·08n 44·27e
Tikrīt............34·36n 43·42e
Tukayyid.........29·47n 45·36e
Ṭūz Khurmātū...34·53n 44·38e
Zākhū............37·08n 42·41e

Physical features and points of interest
'Abd Allāh, Khawr, *channel*.29·50n 48·20e
Abū Ahl, *well*....34·06n 43·45e
Adab, *historic site*............31·59n 45·45e
al-Athāmīn, *mountains*......30·22n 43·40e
Albū Gharz, Sabkhat, *salt lake*........34·45n 41·15e
al-Furāt, see Euphrates
al-Ḥajarah, *desert*.........30·00n 44·00e
al-Jazīrah, *historic region*...35·10n 42·00e
Arab, Shatt al-, *river*.........31·00n 47·29e
az-Zāb al-Kabīr, see Great Zab
az-Zāb aṣ-Ṣaghīr, see Little Zab
Babylon, *ruins*...32·33n 44·24e
Bāṭin, Wādī al-, *watercourse*.....29·35n 47·00e
Buṭmah, *oil deposit*......36·43n 42·42e
Darband-e Khan Dam............35·18n 45·47e
Dijlah, see Tigris
Diyālā, *river*......33·14n 44·31e
Euphrates (al-Furāt), *river*.........31·00n 47·25e
Gharrāf, Shatt al-, *river*........32·30n 45·48e
Great Zab (az-Zāb al-Kabīr) *river*...........36·00n 43·21e
Ḥabbānīyah, Hawr al-, *lake*...33·17n 43·29e
Ḥammār, Hawr al-, *lake*.........30·50n 47·10e
Hamrīn, Jabal, *mountains*.......34·30n 44·30e
Ḥawrān, Wādī, *watercourse*.......33·58n 42·34e
Ḥijārah, Ṣaḥrā' al-, *desert*...........30·25n 44·30e
Khābūr, Nahr al-, *river*........37·07n 42·21e
Kurdistan, *historic region*...37·00n 44·00e
Little Zab (az-Zāb aṣ-Ṣaghīr) *river*.35·12n 43·25e
Mesopotamia, *physical region*..34·00n 44·00e
Nineveh, *historic site*.....36·25n 43·10e
Persian Gulf.....29·00n 49·00e
Razzāzah, *lake*...33·45n 43·45e
Sham, Bādiyat ash-, *desert*.....32·00n 40·00e
Sinjār, Jabal, *mountain*.......36·23n 41·52e
Sunaysilah, *salt lake*.........35·35n 41·53e
Suwayqīyah, Hawr as-, *lake*...32·40n 46·03e
Takhādīd, *well*...29·59n 44·30e
Tharthār, *lake*....34·00n 43·15e
Tigris (Dijlah), *river*.............31·00n 47·25e
'Ukāsh, Wādī, *river*...........34·15n 40·35e
Umma, *ruins*.....31·40n 45·52e
Ur, *ruins*.........30·57n 46·09e

species and sand snakes; and two types of tortoise, of which one is peculiar to Iraq. Many kinds of fish occur, including the "Tigris salmon," a barbel that can attain seven feet in length. Iraq is also visited by vast numbers of migrant birds.

Traditional regions. Traditionally, the country may be divided into the valleys of the two large rivers, which are relatively densely populated, and the deserts of the west, where nomadism is important. In the northeast (including Kurdistan), where rainfall is sufficient for cultivation to be practiced without irrigation, a pattern of mixed agriculture and herding is found; this region therefore contrasts sharply with the riverine and desert areas.

The landscape under human settlement. Towns play an important part in Iraq. Baghdad, the capital, is by far the largest; other large cities are Basra, Mosul, Kirkūk, al-Ḥillah, Irbīl, Karbalā', and an-Najaf. The rest are spread fairly evenly throughout the riverine areas. Special features of the settlement pattern are the number and even spread of towns of relatively small size (from 10,000 to 25,000 inhabitants) and the extent to which the populations of even large towns are partly agricultural. There is much less of the sharp distinction between town and country that is characteristic of Western countries.

Nomadism is important not only in the western deserts but also between the two rivers, both in al-Jazīrah and the drier and sandier parts as far south as the Shaṭṭ al-Gharrāf. Nomads are also an important element in the towns, which they frequent in large numbers at certain seasons. Religious pilgrimages to Karbalā', an-Najaf, and Sāmarrā' swell the local population. In Kurdistan, seasonal migration mainly from winter (lowland) to summer (upland) pastures is widely practiced. Some Kurdish tribes cross the frontiers into Iran and Turkey. Nomadism (W.B.Fi.)

PEOPLE AND POPULATION

Ethnic and religious characteristics. *Cultural origins.* The population, while increasingly assuming greater homogeneity, still reflects a certain degree of ethnolinguistic and religious diversity. The ancient peoples of Iraq, the Babylonians and the Assyrians, who were Semitic, have long been assimilated and absorbed by successive waves of migration and settlement.

Arabs and their descendants, along with the Arabized

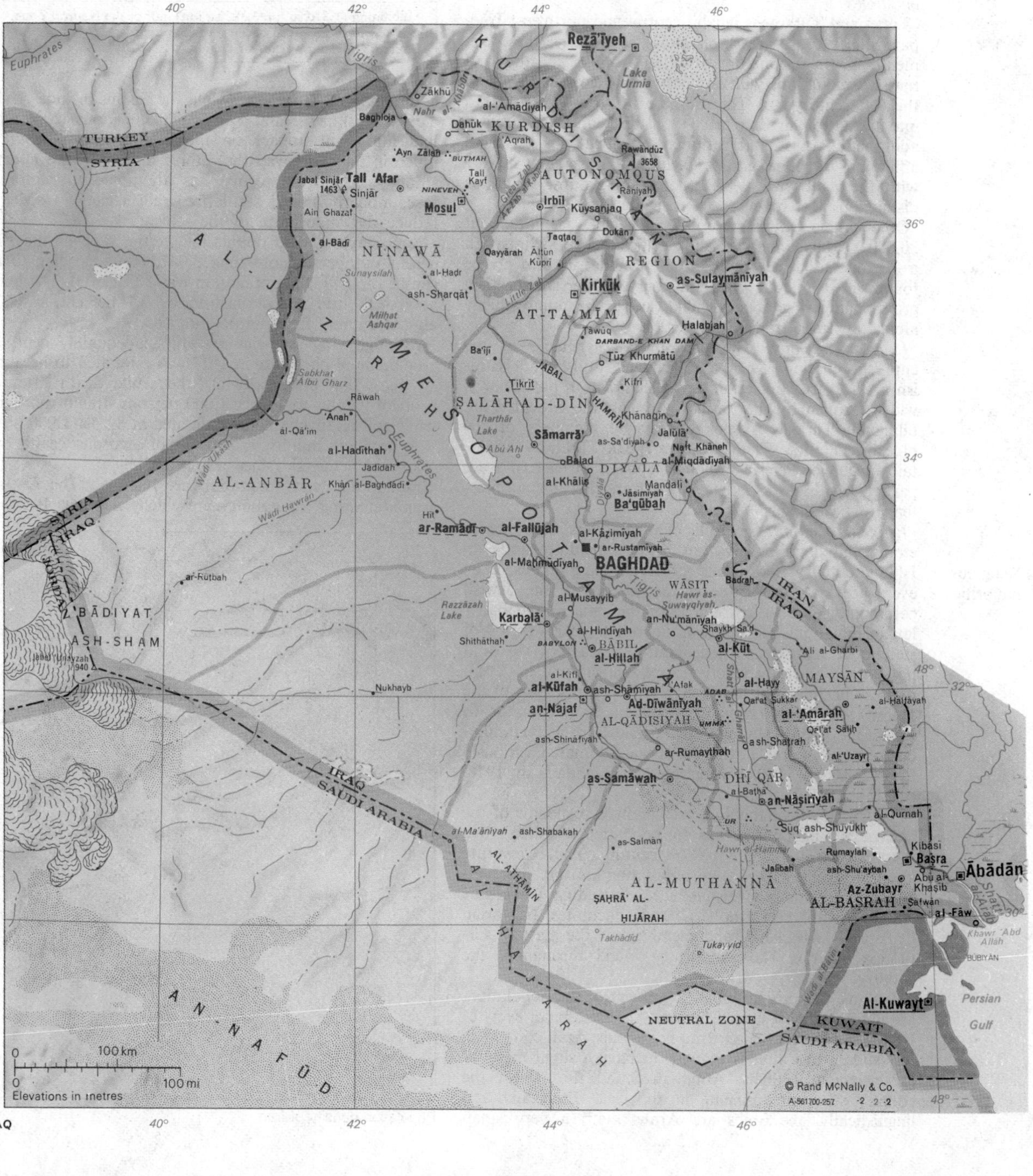

IRAQ

population, are to be found throughout Iraq, and they constitute an overwhelming majority in the central and southern regions. They are estimated to comprise slightly more than three-quarters of the population.

Ethnic minorities

Throughout the centuries, Iraq's contiguity with Iran has brought constant streams of Persian migrants who settled principally in the east. From 50,000 to 60,000 of these, however, were deported to Iran in late 1971 and early 1972. Migrations from Central Asia also brought successive waves of Mongols, Turks, Turkmens, Kurds, and Circassians. Although the Mongols lost their special character as a result of fusion with the dominant population, this was less true of the Kurds, Turks, and Turkmens.

The Kurds, inhabiting the mountainous regions of the north and northeast, retain their separate communal and individual qualities, continue to speak their own language, and are the most visible and articulate of the ethnic minorities. Their demands for autonomy, official recognition of their language, and the right to be educated in Kurdish were met by a constitutional amendment in 1974, although the guerrilla war waged by the Kurds did not end until 1975. (For a further discussion, see MESOPOTAMIA AND IRAQ, HISTORY OF: *Iraq since 1918: The Kurdish question.*)

Turks and Turkmens inhabit central and northwest Iraq, particularly those areas contiguous to Turkey; these elements in the population resulted from a lengthy and massive migration, with the first settlements dating from the 9th century AD. The ultimate incorporation of Iraq into the Ottoman Empire in the 16th century resulted in additional Turkish and Turkmen settlements. The Muslim affiliation of these groups facilitated their intermixture with the Arabs and with other Iraqi groups, so ethnic distinctions lost much of their significance.

Other ethnic groups are quite small. They include about 30,000 Yazīdīs living west and north of Mosul, who speak a Kurdish dialect. About 4,000 Mandaeans are to be found in Baghdad, while the Lurs, a Persian-speaking group numbering about 10,000, are to be found chiefly along the Iraqi–Iranian frontier.

Linguistic groups. The predominant language of the entire population is Arabic, although Turkish and Kurdish are still used in certain areas. Kurdish in particular is widely spoken by the Kurds, although the educated are bilingual. Turkish is spoken only by members of the oldest generation. The Turkmens speak Turkmen, an Altaic language. Persian is widely spoken in eastern Iraq, particularly in areas adjacent to Iran; Persian speakers tend to be bilingual.

Religious affiliations. Religious variation cuts across ethnic and linguistic divisions. Iraq is predominantly an Islāmic country. Jewish and Christian communities, however, are still to be found. Some among the Jewish community date their origin from the time of the Babylonian Exile (586–516 BC). Throughout the early period of statehood, Jews constituted about 2 percent of the total population. With the emergence of Zionism and the eventual establishment of Israel in 1948, the major part of the Jewish community chose or was induced to emigrate to Israel, the United States, Canada, and Europe. The number of Jews in Iraq in the 1960s was estimated variously from 2,000 to 5,000, concentrated in Baghdad. By 1978, only about 450 remained.

Religious minorities

The Christian communities are chiefly descendants of the ancient population that was not converted to Islām when it took root in Iraq in the 7th century. They constitute about 4 percent of the total population and are subdivided among various Christian sects, including Chaldeans affiliated with the Catholic Church, Jacobites, Nestorian Christians (Assyrians), and members of the Eastern Orthodox Church. They are to be found throughout the country.

Muslims, comprising about 95 percent of the population, are divided almost evenly between the two major sects of Islām—Sunnī and Shīʿah. Iraq is the only Arab country in the Middle East that is thought to have a slight majority (52 percent) of Shīʿīs. Although found throughout the country, they predominate in the east. Ethnically and linguistically, the Shīʿīs are Arabs, with a very small community of Turkmens, while the Sunnīs include Arabs, Turks, Turkmens, and Kurds. The religious schism has had important impact on the politics of the country, much in the same way that ethnic divisions have affected stability. The Iraqi regime has attempted to centralize, fuse, modernize, and secularize Iraqi society in order to reduce the importance of the schism.

Iraq, Area and Population

	area		population	
	sq mi	sq km	1965 census	1977 census
Governorates (*muḥāfaẓāt*)				
al-Anbār	32,332	83,740	307,000	466,000
al-Baṣrah	7,363	19,070	669,000	1,009,000
al-Muthannā	18,962	49,111	143,000	216,000
al-Qādisiyah	3,285	8,507	400,000	423,000
an-Najaf	10,615	27,494	—	390,000
at-Ta'mīm	3,729	9,659	474,000	495,000
Bābil	2,035	5,270	488,000	592,000
Baghdād	1,988	5,150	2,045,000	3,190,000
Dhī Qār	5,261	13,626	499,000	623,000
Diyālā	7,452	19,301	397,000	588,000
Karbalā'	22,348	57,880	340,000	270,000
Maysān	5,445	14,103	345,000	373,000
Nīnawā	13,794	35,726	743,000	1,106,000
Salāh ad-Dīn	11,198	29,004	—	364,000
Wāsiṭ	6,683	17,308	334,000	415,000
Kurdish Autonomous Region				
as-Sulaymānīyah	6,083	15,756	400,000	691,000
Dahūk	3,407	3,824	146,000	251,000
Irbīl	5,587	14,471	356,000	541,000
Total Iraq	168,878*†	437,393*	8,047,000†	12,000,000†

*Including (1,310 sq mi, 3,393 sq km) half of the Neutral Zone. †Detail does not add to totals given because of rounding.
Source: Official government figures.

Demography. The population at the time of the 1965 census numbered more than 8,047,000. According to the census of 1977, the population was 12,029,700. The annual growth rate is reckoned to be 3.1 percent, resulting almost entirely from natural increase.

Although vital statistics are still inadequately kept, the crude annual birth rate in 1977 was estimated to be about 47 per 1,000 persons, while the crude death rate was probably closer to 14 per 1,000 persons. Infant mortality, while still relatively high—estimated at 89 per 1,000 births —is declining rapidly as a result of vigorous health programs implemented since the 1960s.

Immigration and emigration are minimal. The few migrants entering the country are chiefly nomadic Bedouins

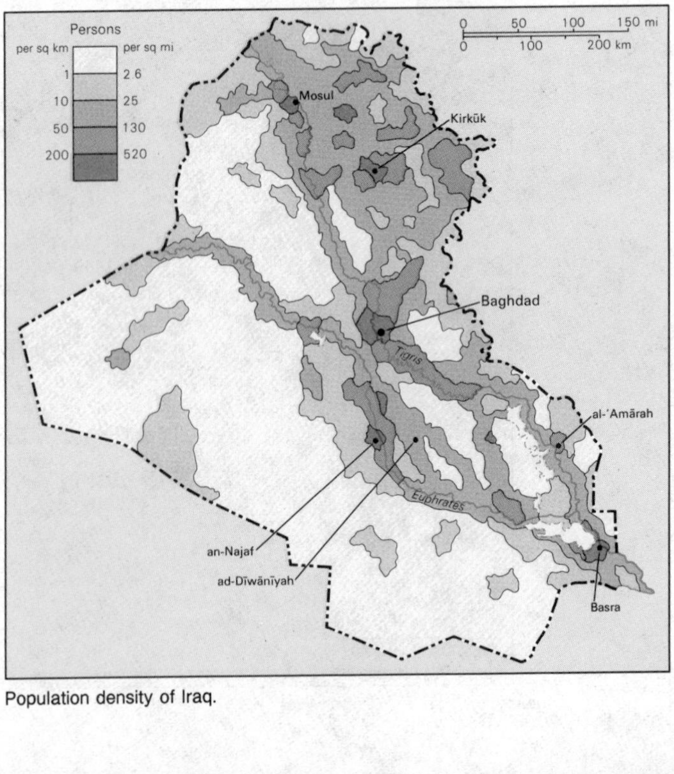

Population density of Iraq.

from Saudi Arabia and the Syrian Desert. The only significant emigration in recent times was that of many Iraqi Jews to Israel.

As is true in other developing countries, there is considerable internal migration. Migrants are chiefly rural people attracted by better employment opportunities in the cities. As a result, Iraqi cities and towns have experienced considerable growth since the late 1950s.

Growth of the urban areas

According to current estimates, nearly 64 percent of the Iraqi population lives in cities and towns, while the rest are considered rural. The ratio has altered in favour of the urban sector as a result of increasing industrial and commercial activities. In 1977, eight cities had populations in excess of 100,000 each—Baghdad, Mosul, Basra, an-Najaf, Kirkūk, al-Ḥillah, Irbīl, and Karbalā'.

By conventional standards, and especially in comparison with other countries of the region, Iraq has a relatively low ratio of people to land. Its developing economy is therefore expected to meet the demands of its increasing population, and, in that sense, future prospects are encouraging.

THE ECONOMY

Iraq had an almost exclusively agricultural economy until expansion in manufacturing, service industries, and nonagricultural activities began in the 1950s. The successive governments have committed themselves to industrial growth, as is made clear by the economic plans of 1965–69, 1969–74, and 1976–80. Increasing income from oil production has enabled the Iraqi government to devote a considerable percentage of the national budget to industrial development and to modernization of its agricultural base. Land-distribution reforms initiated in 1959 and amended by the 1970 Agricultural Act, cooperative rural associations, and the decline of the landed aristocracy contributed to improved agricultural productivity and to a more equitable distribution of income.

The extent and distribution of resources. With the exception of oil, Iraq has modest mineral resources. They include iron ore, chromite, copper, lead, and zinc deposits in the north. Limestone, gypsum, phosphates, and sulfur are abundant. The most important single mineral, however, is oil, which is exploited in the north, northeast, and south. Other oil deposits are known to exist in central Iraq but are uneconomic to exploit. The nation's proven oil reserves in 1979 amounted to more than 4,711,000,000 tons, or nearly 6 percent of the world total.

Oil deposits

The country has suffered from the absence of strict controls over its biological resources. Trees have been greatly exploited as a form of wealth and as sources of fuel, although in 1968 about 7,000 square miles were forested. Afforestation plans produced no visible results in the 1970s. Important wild plants include licorice, which grows along the main rivers, and the valonia oak, which grows in the northeastern mountains and yields a tanning extract. Gum tragacanth is derived from the *Astragalus* (loco) bush, which occurs in the dry steppe regions.

The Tigris and Euphrates rivers constitute Iraq's main sources of hydroelectric power. They are limited, however, by seasonal flow and the largely level valleys through which they flow. The Tigris tributaries that flow from the Zagros Mountains—the Little Zab and Diyālā rivers—have been developed for power generation, as has the Tigris. Thermal power resources are also limited; deforestation has led to the importation of wood, and coal resources are small. Oil for domestic use is supplied by a field near Mandalī and is refined at Khānaqīn.

Sources of national income. *Agriculture, forestry, and irrigation.* Two types of agricultural activity predominate—the one dependent upon rainfall in the north; the other dependent upon irrigation in the south. The best known agricultural product is the date, which is the largest source of foreign-currency revenue after oil. One of the world's largest producers of dates, Iraq grows approximately 578,310 tons annually, largely around the Shatt al-Arab area in the south. Other crops include barley, wheat, linseed, lentils, and beans, as well as rice, sesame, maize (corn), and millet. Cotton production is hampered by soil salinity and declined in the late 1970s.

The diversified landscape has proved hospitable to livestock in greater varieties and quantities than is possible in many other Arab countries. Sheep, goats, camels, cattle, and donkeys are abundant. Trade in animals is traditional, and milk, wool, meat, and other animal products are extensively used. Wool is exported to Europe, and animals are exported to neighbouring Arab countries. In the late 1970s, about 17,500 metric tons of freshwater fish were landed in Iraq.

Forestry is negligible as an industry; building timber must be imported.

The problems of irrigation are complex because flooding usually occurs before many crops have completed their growing season, and excess water must be retained within the river between high banks. Variation in water levels allows for free-flow irrigation in some areas, while in others pumping is necessary. Stagnant water must be led back to the rivers as rapidly as possible, in order to avoid salination.

The largest river-control project is that of the Wādī ath-Tharthār, completed in 1956. A canal 40 miles long leads from the Tigris at Sāmarrā' to the basin of the *wādī*, which thus accumulates floodwater. The project is also being used for the generation of electricity. A smaller project is located on the Euphrates at ar-Ramādī, where water is led into two basins at Hawr al-Ḥabbānīyah and Hawr Abū Dibs. Other dams, the largest of them to be located on the Great Zab at Bekhme and on the Tigris above Mosul, have been objects of lengthy planning and should be under construction in the early 1980s. These and schemes at Mandalī and Jāsimīyah are primarily for irrigation, with flood control and electricity generation as subsidiary features.

The Wādī ath-Tharthār project

The irrigation works at Hindīyah directs the Euphrates water into an older channel running through al-Ḥillah. Also on the Euphrates are the Musayyib project and smaller works at the head of Hawr al-Ḥammār. At al-Kūt, on the Tigris, a barrage that is three times the size of the Hindīyah dam will ultimately improve irrigation to the south and southeast, but there is a restricted volume of water available in summer. The entire low-season flow of the Diyālā River below the Jabal Ḥamrīn is diverted for irrigation. Other irrigation works on a smaller scale are planned or in construction around Hawr al-Ḥammār, the Shatt al-Arab, as-Sulaymānīyah, Irbīl, and Mosul. There are also land-drainage projects to counter salination and windbreaks to prevent the silting up of irrigation and drainage channels.

Mining and quarrying. Small amounts of brown coal are mined at Kifrī between Baghdad and Kirkūk, and scattered deposits of rock salt are exploited under government supervision.

Although oil was first discovered at Naft Khāneh in 1909, the first commercial oil field was developed at Kirkūk between the Zagros Mountains and the Mesopotamian plain in 1927. It has remained the country's main source of oil. The second largest field is located at Zubayr-Rumaylah near Basra. The Mosul field became operative in 1952 and produces lower grade oil, while the small field at Naft Khāneh, near Mandalī, produces oil for domestic consumption. Fields have also been developed at ʿAyn Zālah and Buṭmah, north of Mosul, and elsewhere.

Oil extraction

Oil from the Zubayr field is shipped by tanker through the Persian Gulf. Production from Kirkūk, however, is transported by overland pipeline to Tripoli, Lebanon, and Bāniyās, Syria. The inauguration in 1977 of the oil pipeline between Kirkūk and Dörtyol, Turkey, and the completion in 1976 of a pipeline from Kirkūk to Basra minimized Iraq's previous dependence on Syrian pipeline facilities.

Until 1961, the prospecting, extracting, and exporting of oil were monopolized by the Iraq Petroleum Company (IPC), or its affiliates; mostly British owned, it was finally nationalized on July 1, 1972. In 1967 and 1969 agreements were reached with French and Soviet companies. Further agreements were reached in 1972 with Italy, France, and the Soviet Union for the purchase of nationalized oil. The National Petroleum Authority is the supreme agency concerned with the oil industry. In 1979 Iraq produced 175,000,000 metric tons of oil.

The industrial sector

Manufacturing and energy. Textile factories are becoming increasingly important for the Iraqi market; several were built, especially at Mosul, with assistance from the Soviet Union. Steel mills are in operation at Baghdad and Khawr az-Zubayr, producing more than 1,000,000 tons annually. Power plants, water-supply facilities, breweries, cigar factories, spinning and weaving factories, and brick and cement establishments are located in the Baghdad metropolitan area. A bitumen plant at Qayyārah, south of Mosul, produces more than 75,000 tons of asphalt annually, and two cement plants produce about 1,000,000 tons of cement, which is sufficient for the home market. Sugar plants around Mosul were constructed with the assistance of the Soviet Union, and two additional plants were constructed at Missan, near Karbalā', and at as-Sulaymānīyah. There are also fertilizer factories and a paperboard factory around Basra. Approximately half of the existing manufacturing plants are to be found in Baghdad.

The petroleum and natural-gas industries support domestic and export-based refining and petrochemical industries, with major refineries at Basra and Dawrah, and five smaller facilities elsewhere. Petrochemicals, including fertilizers, urea, sulfuric acid, and ammonia gas, are produced well in excess of domestic agricultural needs at Abulfiluz, south of Basra.

The production of hydroelectric power is centred upon the Tigris River and its tributaries. Power dams are located on the Tigris at Wādī ath-Tharthār, on the Little Zab River at Dukān, and on the Upper Diyālā River at Darband-e Khān.

Financial services and trade. All banks and insurance companies, both domestic and foreign, were nationalized in 1964. The Central Bank of Iraq has the sole right of issuing currency. There are two commercial banks—the Commercial Bank of Iraq and the Rafidain Bank—and specialized banks for agriculture, construction, real estate, and industry. There are three insurance companies.

The chief imports are manufactured goods, machinery, engines, automobiles, and pharmaceuticals. Iraq also imports some foodstuffs such as grains, sugar, and tea. After oil and dates, the chief exports are raw cotton, wool, hides and skins, fertilizers, essential oils and perfumes, and cement. Although Iraq's external trade was previously chiefly with western Europe, an increasing emphasis in the early 1970s on diversification of trading partners resulted in some alteration in the trade patterns. The Soviet Union and other Socialist states, the Far East, and neighbouring Arab countries now account for considerable trade. Iraq is a member of the Arab Common Market and has a special customs pact with Kuwait.

Management of the economy. The role of the state, which is committed to Socialism, increased in the 1970s, and welfare services provided by the regime were expanded. More than 50 percent of the state's revenue is derived from oil royalties. The remainder of the revenue is raised by both direct and indirect taxation.

Trade unions

Iraq has had a vigorous although somewhat checkered trade-union movement since the 1930s. In 1977, about 921,240 workers, mostly in urban manufacturing plants or the oil industry, were union members; trade-union organizations numbered about 137. The strongest unions were those of workers in the oil industry. All the various trade unions are organized in the General Federation of Iraqi Trade Unions, which is a member of both the World Federation of Trade Unions and the International Confederation of Arab Trade Unions.

Employers' associations are relatively weak; they include the Iraq Federation of Industries and the Baghdad Chamber of Commerce. Similarly, peasant unions are somewhat less vigorous than urban-based trade unions. The General Federation of Peasant Societies, established in 1959, comprises about 734 peasant societies. Other organizations include a teachers' union, a lawyers' association, and 273 urban and rural cooperative societies.

Iraq aimed at the transformation of its economy to attain industrialization, socialism, and economic growth through national planning. These plans included an increased gross national product, expansion of the public sector, and attainment of a higher standard of living. The rate of real growth of about 11 percent per annum was achieved between 1970 and 1976.

Transportation. Increasing modernization is reflected in changes of emphasis given to different parts of the transport system. Until the mid-20th century, transport was either by water or by animal. River transport had developed over the centuries to carry goods and persons, particularly from central to southern Iraq. The use of camels, horses, and horse-drawn carts complemented this system. Both of these modes were adequate for a traditional economy, but increasing commercialization and industrialization and the increasing scale of economic interaction between Iraq and its neighbours brought about fundamental changes.

There are about 13,000 miles of roads in Iraq, more than 30 percent of which are paved. Also, the desert land is sufficiently hard to allow cars, trucks, and buses to travel across it. The most developed parts of the road system are in central, northern, and southern Iraq. The opening of the Basra bridge in 1978 provided a direct link between Iraq's road network and the Asian Highway.

Three major railway lines connect the principal cities, and they all converge on Baghdad and Basra. Two narrow-gauge lines connect Baghdad with Basra, and link Baghdad with the northeast provinces east of the Tigris, and a standard-gauge railway connects Baghdad with Mosul and other northern cities and then continues on to Syria, Turkey, and beyond.

Five ports

Iraq's connection with the outside world through the seas is limited to five ports—one at Basra, 85 miles upstream on the Tigris from the Persian Gulf on the Shatt al-Arab; another at Umm Qaṣr, five miles from the Kuwait border; and three marine oil terminals at Fāw, Khor al-Amya, and Mina al-Bakr. All are accessible to oceangoing vessels; the facilities at Mina al-Bakr can accommodate supertankers. The Tigris is navigable by steamer from Basra to Baghdad; smaller power craft can travel upstream as far as Mosul. Only small local rivercraft use the Euphrates. Large rafts, however, carry goods downstream on both rivers.

Baghdad has two airports, one of which is international, and there is an international airport at Basra. The nation's one airline is controlled and owned by the Iraqi government and operates flights to airports in Asia, the Middle East, and Europe. Various Middle East and some major international airlines have landing privileges at Baghdad airport. Internal air traffic is insignificant.

ADMINISTRATION AND SOCIAL CONDITIONS

The structure of the government. While Iraq has had a series of constitutions—the most recent being that of 1970—for all practical purposes Iraq is governed by an ad hoc constitution. It is officially a republic, with legislative power theoretically vested in an elected legislature, executive power in a president and a Council of Ministers, and judicial power in an independent judiciary. Because of the revolutionary nature of Iraqi politics since the overthrow of the monarchy in 1958, however, the political system operates with little reference to constitutional provisions. All legislative and executive powers are in fact exercised by the Council of Command of the Revolution, which since the early 1970s has been composed of 22 members, all of whom were members of the Regional Command of the Baʿth Arab Socialist Party and many of whom were army officers. The chairman of the council is also president of the republic, prime minister, and the commander of the armed forces. The president and the Council of Ministers are accountable to the Council of Command of the Revolution. Actual implementation and execution of broad policies are the function of each relevant minister. While each ministry is headed by a minister, an administrative officer, usually known as director general, is the actual day-to-day administrator. All employees of ministries are appointed civil servants.

The Council of Command of the Revolution

The country is divided for administrative purposes into 18 *muḥāfaẓāt* (governorates), three of which comprise the Kurdish Autonomous Region. Each *muḥāfaẓah* has a governor, or *muḥāfiẓ*, appointed by the minister of the interior, as chief administrative officer. Constitutional provision is made for an elective general council to assist the governor, but this provision had not been implemented by 1980. Each *muḥāfaẓah* is administratively subdivided into districts headed by a *qāʾim-maqām;* in 1979 there were 101 such districts. Each district is then divided into *nāḥīyah*s headed by a *mudīr*, or director. The Kurdish Autonomous Region was formed by government decree in 1974. It contains the predominantly Kurdish provinces of Dahūk, as-Sulaymānīyah, and Irbīl, and is governed by a legislative council that meets in Irbīl city.

Towns and cities have their own municipal councils, each of which is directed by a *raʾīs al-baladīyah*, or mayor. The capital has special status and its own governor.

The political process. Political parties were outlawed with the overthrow of the monarchy in 1958. After the overthrow of Abdul Karim Kassem (Qassim) in 1963 by supporters of the Baʿth (an independent branch of the Syrian-based Baʿth Arab Socialist Party), Iraq became a one-party state. In 1970 the Democratic Kurdistan Party obtained permission to operate, primarily in the north. While the country is actually governed more by the armed forces than by the party, members of the Baʿth have nevertheless penetrated the armed forces. Nominally, all governing institutions espouse the Baʿthist ideology, which includes Socialism and a pan-Arab ideal. Constant turmoil and attempts by successive regimes to consolidate power have been used as justifications for perennial delay in resuming the conduct of normal political and constitutional processes. As a consequence, although Iraqis are assured of their rights to office and to voting, no election was held from 1958 until 1980, when a national legislature was elected.

Dual system of justice

Justice. Theoretically, Iraq has an independent judiciary, which combines French, Islāmic, and revolutionary elements. The system is supervised by a Judicial Council, headed by the minister of justice. There are three types of jurisdiction with corresponding court systems—the civil, religious, and special courts.

Civil courts deal with civil litigation, as well as all criminal cases. The courts of sessions hear serious criminal cases and serve as appellate courts in all criminal cases. Judgments in civil cases are appealed to the courts of appeal. The Court of Cassation is the highest court of the land and has original jurisdiction in crimes committed by public officials.

Each of the religious communities has its own religious court, which is governed by its respective religious law and which deals with all questions of personal status, marriage, and inheritance.

Special courts were formed in pursuance of the National Security Act of 1965. They have original jurisdiction in all cases involving state security. Usually the majority of the judges are military officers.

The armed forces. The Iraqi Army is essentially the creation of the ousted Hashimite monarchy in its attempt to increase the power of the central government. It is a professional army whose officers are trained both in Iraq and in other countries. Modernized and expanded, in 1979 the army had about 190,000 soldiers and officers. Since 1934 Iraqi males have been liable to a compulsory two-year service.

The army's military performance has been affected by the intervention of its officers in politics; since the mid-1930s, there has been a series of coups d'etat. These have generated tensions and have resulted in periodic dismissals of large numbers of officers. While the army is the most important branch of the defense force, there is a well-equipped air force and a small navy consisting of a few submarine chasers and torpedo boats. The Iraqi Army has seen action in the government's attempts to stem the secessionist activities of the Kurds. The air force in 1979 had a strength of about 28,000 men, and had more than 300 combat aircraft. There was also a paramilitary People's Army of 75,000 and a security force of 4,800.

Social milieu. *Educational services.* Before 1921 the educational system was minimal, except for traditional, and particularly religious, instruction. Educational facilities were gradually expanded under the monarchy, and rapid expansion followed the revolution in 1958. It was anticipated that, in the 1980s, Iraq would be able to fully implement its universal compulsory education act.

About 92 percent of school-age boys and about 50 percent of school-age girls were enrolled in primary and secondary schools in the late 1970s. In the academic year of 1978–79, there were more than 2,450,000 pupils in the primary schools, 781,800 at the secondary level, and 91,700 in higher education. Females represented 43 percent, 30 percent, and 30 percent of the totals, respectively. The eradication of illiteracy is a major goal of the national government, and it was estimated that 1,300,000 persons would complete literacy courses in 1980.

Higher education

Higher education is available at six Iraqi universities, located in Baghdad (three), Mosul, Basra, and as-Sulaymānīyah, and a technical institute. An agricultural college at Irbīl and various teachers' and technical colleges provide specialized instruction. The entire educational system is controlled closely by the Ministry of Education and the Ministry of Higher Education and Scientific Research, which also send considerable numbers of students to European and American universities for graduate training.

Health and welfare services. The increasing Socialist commitment of the government has resulted in the expansion of welfare services, including health facilities and housing projects for the poor, particularly in Baghdad. The Law of Social Security of 1956 provides benefits for old age and illness. Other legislation provides for unemployment benefits and minimum wages and has established cooperative societies and industrial trade unions. In 1977 there were about 2,350 health facilities, of which 188 were fully equipped hospitals and 1,650 were dispensaries.

Social changes

Social and economic divisions. The social system—characterized in the past by rigid social and economic differentiation and ethnic, linguistic, and religious schisms—is being altered fundamentally by new, largely Western and Soviet ideologies, institutions, and cultural pursuits. The rapid expansion of the educational system, basic alterations in the system of landholding, and a greater commitment of the state to economic development are affecting Iraqi society and institutions. Poverty, though still prevalent, is declining. The gap is being narrowed between the rich few, who controlled the principal means of wealth and the political superstructure, and the many poor, primarily the peasants and the urban workers. An Iraqi middle class comprising the professional sector has emerged and is exercising a levelling effect on society. It controls the political system through the army and the Baʿth Party and is supported by the peasantry and workers.

CULTURAL LIFE AND INSTITUTIONS

Cultural traditions. Traditional arts and crafts, including the weaving of world-famous rugs and carpets, derived their impetus from a rich, predominantly Arab, cultural legacy; best known are those from Kurdistan. Iraqis, like other Arabs, showed particular concern with poetry and prose literature; in that sense Iraq was but one part of Arab culture as a whole from which it derived and to which it contributed. Until the 20th century, cultural pursuits centred around religious schools and mosques. Folk tradition and dancing were also prevalent, particularly in the village and mountain areas of the country.

Increasing commercial, industrial, and urban activities and rapid changes in education and cultural orientation affected the traditional culture significantly. An increasing concern with Western-inspired models of culture, literature, and the arts began to take hold, and traditional arts experienced a decline.

Government support of traditional culture

The government, anxious to preserve some of the traditional creativity of the culture, assumed an increasingly active role in preserving and strengthening traditional folk arts and crafts. The Ministry of Culture and Information sponsored theatre and art groups whose purpose was to support traditional, as well as modern, cultural art and forms. The National Group for Acting, the Rashīd National Group, the Folklore Group, and the United Artists were established between 1965 and 1967 specifically to encourage the development of a "national" Iraqi culture. Both traditional and modern artistic and literary expressions are juxtaposed in contemporary Iraq, and the population supports each, according to its degree of modernization.

The government and several societies patronize the arts; magazines and radio and television stations periodically present performances or reviews of important cultural events. The Ministry of Culture supervises the country's excellent historical museums, such as the Iraqi Museum and the Mosul Museum, as well as the National Library in Baghdad and the public libraries. An Institute of Fine Arts, established in 1939 in Baghdad and strengthened after 1968, trains Iraqis in music, drama, and the plastic arts. Training in ballet and music is also offered by the School of Ballet and Music, the Institute of Rhythmical Studies, and the Institute of Fine Arts. Iraq has produced several excellent poets, such as Jawahiri and Nazik al-Malaa'ikah, and sculptors and painters, such as Khaled ar-Rahhal, Jawad Salim, Akram Shukri, and Hafidh ad-Durubi.

The mass media have been nationally controlled since 1967 and are closely supervised by the Ministry of Culture. About 22 newspapers are issued in Iraq; of the six dailies, four are written in Arabic, one in Kurdish, and one in English. The central radio station in Baghdad broadcasts daily in Arabic (21 hours), while programs in Kurdish (16 hours), Turkmen (three hours), and Assyrian (two hours) are broadcast from Kirkūk. In a country characterized by a moderate rate of literacy, estimated at 47 percent in 1977, radio and television play a particularly significant role in the dissemination of information and the mobilization of public support. There are approximately 1,700,000 reported radio sets and 425,000 television sets. Four television stations in Baghdad, Mosul, Kirkūk, and Basra and two relay stations in al-ʿAmārah and as-Samāwah serve the needs of the country. The film industry is in its formative stage; Iraq produces about 12 Arabic films annually.

Prospects for the future. With a young population, some agricultural wealth, and mineral resources, Iraq has considerable potential for growth. The government's commitment to economic development has contributed to an improved standard of living and higher per capita income for the population and to the increasing modernization of its social, cultural, and administrative institutions. Political problems, however, continue to affect the development of the country. While Iraq is gradually succeeding in creating a nationally homogeneous society, the establishment of an internally stable political system continues to elude its leaders. Iraq's commitment to a unified and progressive Arab world is, furthermore, jeopardized by intense political conflicts within Iraq itself, as well as by those within the Arab world. Iraq, nonetheless, among the several Arab states, is one of those that have their more promising future prospects.

BIBLIOGRAPHY. The best general summary in English is RICHARD F. NYROP (ed.), *Iraq, a country study* (1979), part of the U.S. Department of the Army's command information "Area Handbook" series. Also useful is *The Middle East and North Africa* Europa publication. A general political history in the 20th century is GEORGE LENCZOWSKI, *The Middle East in World Affairs*, 3rd ed. (1962). Geography and related aspects are presented in G.B. CRESSEY, *Crossroads: Land and Life in Southwest Asia* (1960); *Asia's Lands and Peoples*, 3rd ed. (1963); and S.H. LONGRIGG, *The Middle East*, 2nd ed. (1970). Information on the people, population characteristics, and the social system are found in DORIS G. ADAMS, *Iraq's People and Resources* (1958); FUAD BAALI, *Relation of the People to the Land in Southern Iraq* (1966); GABRIEL BAER, *Population and Society in the Arab East* (1964; orig. pub. in Hebrew, 1960; repr., 1976); FREDRIK BARTH, *Principles of Social Organization in Southern Kurdistan* (1953; repr., 1977); E.S.S. DROWER, *The Mandeans of Iraq and Iran* (1962); ROBERT A. FERNEA, *Shaykh and Effendi: Changing Patterns of Authority Among the El Shabana of Southern Iraq* (1970); and S.M. SALIM, *Marsh Dwellers of the Euphrates Delta* (1962). Information on the national economy and related questions is found in S.N. ALITOVSKY, *Agrarian Changes in the Republic of Iraq, 1958–1965* (1966, orig: pub. in 1966); KATHLEEN M. LANGLEY, *The Industrialization of Iraq* (1961); FAHIM I. QUBAIN, *The Reconstruction of Iraq, 1950–1957* (1958); A.R. AL-RUBAAI, *The Monetary and Banking System in Iraq* (1962); TAHER HAMDI KANAAN, *Input-Output and Social Accounts of Iraq, 1960–1963* (1965); UNITED STATES DEPARTMENT OF AGRICULTURE, *The Agricultural Economy of Iraq* (1965); and DOREEN WARRINER, *Land Reform and Development in the Middle East: A Study of Egypt, Syria, and Iraq*, 2nd ed. (1962; repr., 1976). Political, social, and administrative questions are dealt with in KAMEL ABU JABER, *The Arab Baʿth Socialist Party: History, Ideology and Organization* (1966); ARAB INFORMATION CENTER, *Education in the Arab States* (1966); H. BATATU, *The Old Social Classes and the Revolutionary Movements of Iraq* (1978); E. BE'ERI, *Army Officers in Arab Politics and Society* (1970; orig. pub. in Hebrew, 1966); LORD BIRDWOOD, *Nuri al-Said: A Study in Arab Leadership* (1959); C.J. EDMONDS, *Kurds, Turks and Arabs* (1957); S.N. FISHER (ed.), *The Military in the Middle East: Problems in Society and Government* (1963); W.J. GALLMAN, *Iraq Under General Nuri: My Recollections of Nuri al-Said, 1954–1958* (1964); G.M. HADDAD, *Revolutions and Military Rule in the Middle East* (1965); MAJID KHADDURI, *Independent Iraq, 1932–1958: A Study of Iraqi Politics*, 2nd ed. (1960), *Republican Iraq: A Study in Iraqi Politics Since the Revolution of 1958* (1969), and *Socialist Iraq: A Study in Iraqi Politics Since 1968* (1978); DERK KINNANE, *The Kurds and Kurdistan* (1964); A. KELIDAR, *The Integration of Modern Iraq* (1979); S.H. LONGRIGG, *Iraq, 1900–1950: A Political, Social and Economic History* (1956); and with FRANK STOAKES, *Iraq* (1958); ABID AL-MARAYATI, *A Diplomatic History of Modern Iraq* (1961); F.J. SNELL ("CARACTACUS"), *Revolution in Iraq* (1959); DESMOND STEWART and JOHN HAYLOCK, *New Babylon: A Portrait of Iraq* (1956); and the UNITED STATES DEPARTMENT OF LABOR, *Labor Law and Practice in Iraq* (1962).

(I.A.A.-L.)

Ireland

The republic of Ireland, also known by its Irish name of Éire, is an ancient nation that nevertheless had a background of less than a century of independent political development by 1980. It occupies the greater part of an island of rare natural beauty lying to the west of Great Britain, from which it is separated—at distances ranging from 20 to 120 miles—by the Irish Sea. Located in the temperate zone between latitude 51°30′ and 55°30′ N, and longitude 5°30′ and 10°30′ W—as far north as Labrador or British Columbia in Canada, and as far west as Portugal, or the West African state of Liberia—it is the westernmost outpost of the Atlantic fringe of the Eurasian landmass. Ireland, which, like Britain, once formed part of this landmass, lies on the European continental shelf, surrounded by seas that are generally less than 600 feet (180 metres) in depth. The greatest distance from north to south in the island is 295 miles (475 kilometres), and from east to west it is 171 miles (275 kilometres).

The magnificent scenery of Ireland's Atlantic coastline faces a 2,000-mile expanse of ocean, and its geographical isolation has helped it to develop a rich heritage of culture and tradition linked initially to a separate language. By the 1970s, the perennial concerns of the republic—emigration, cultural and political identity, relations with Northern Ireland (that portion of the island remaining within the United Kingdom)—had been augmented by economic and political problems linked both to a deterioration in the international competitive position of the nation, and to its entry in 1973 into the European Economic Community. The discussions and political developments discernible within the nation as a result of these difficulties evoked a high level of public interest not unaccompanied by a measure of emotion and conflict.

Ireland was an integral part of the United Kingdom from 1800 to 1922 when, by virtue of the Anglo-Irish agreement of December 6, 1921, the Irish Free State was established as an independent member of the British Commonwealth. A new constitution, adopted by the people in a 1937 plebiscite, declared Ireland to be "a sovereign, independent, democratic state," and the last remaining link with the Commonwealth was severed by the Republic of Ireland Act of 1948.

Political origin

Although the constitution of 1937 defines the national territory of the republic as consisting of "the whole island of Ireland, its islands and the territorial seas," in actual fact the present land jurisdiction of the republic covers only 26 counties (or 26,600 square miles [69,000 square kilometres]) out of the 32 counties (or 32,595 square miles [84,400 square kilometres]) into which Ireland is divided. Of the four traditional provinces of Ireland, the republic comprises the whole of Leinster (counties Carlow, Dublin, Kildare, Kilkenny, Laoighis (Leix), Louth, Longford, Meath, Offaly, Westmeath, Wexford, and Wicklow), the whole of Munster (counties Clare, Cork, Kerry, Waterford, Limerick, and Tipperary), the whole of Connacht (counties Galway, Leitrim, Mayo, Roscommon, and Sligo) and three counties (Cavan, Donegal, and Monaghan) of the nine counties of Ulster. The remaining six counties of Ulster constitute Northern Ireland.

Ireland is not a member of the North Atlantic Treaty Organization, and its policies at the United Nations, and in world affairs generally, have been characterized by a high degree of independence of action and outlook. In recent years, trade and economic relations between the republic and Britain, always close, have become still closer. In December 1965 an agreement was signed in London providing for the establishment of a free trade area between the two countries by 1975. In 1967, moreover, the republic joined with Britain, Norway, and Denmark in applying for membership of the European Economic Community.

This article surveys contemporary life in the republic of Ireland; for historical development, see BRITAIN AND IRELAND, HISTORY OF; see also DUBLIN. For a survey of the six counties of Ulster, see NORTHERN IRELAND; UNITED KINGDOM. Additional material on the physical environment of Ireland can be found in the articles IRISH SEA; EUROPE.

THE LAND

Relief features. The territory of the republic consists of a broad and undulating central limestone plain, ringed almost completely by coastal highlands, which vary considerably in geological structure. The flatness of the central lowland—which lies for the most part between 200 and 400 feet above sea level—is relieved in many places by low hills between 600 and 1,000 feet high, while a multiplicity of lakes, large bog areas, and low ridges lend it considerable scenic attractions. The principal mountain ranges are the Wicklow Mountains (Lugnaquilla 3,039 feet [926 metres]), the Macgillicuddy's Reeks in Kerry (Carrantuohill 3,414 feet [1,041 metres]), the Knockmealdown and Comeragh mountains in Waterford, and the Twelve Pins in Connemara. In the west and southwest the wild and beautiful coast is heavily indented where the mountains of Donegal, Mayo, and Kerry thrust out into the Atlantic, separated by deep, wide-mouthed bays, some of which—Bantry Bay and Dingle Bay for example—are, in fact, drowned river valleys. Bantry Bay, which is 20 miles long and between 3 and 5 miles wide, is one of the principal deep-sea anchorages in western Europe. The oil terminal at Whiddy Island in the bay is capable of handling the largest tankers afloat. The east coast, on the other hand, is little indented, but most of the country's trade passes through its ports because of their proximity to British and continental markets.

The western coastline

The coastal mountain fringe illustrates the country's complex geological history. The mountain ridges of the south are parallel east–west foldings of Old Red Sandstone rock, separated by limestone river valleys. Granite predominates in the mountains of Galway, Mayo, and Donegal in the west and northwest, and in Wicklow in the east. Ireland experienced two general glaciations, one covering most of the country and the other extending as far south as a line linking Limerick, Cashel, and Dublin. The characteristic diversity of Irish scenery owes much to the glacial influence, and the large areas of peat bog to be found throughout the country are a notable feature of the landscape. In the past they were the rural population's principal—if not its only—source of domestic fuel. By the 1970s, 90 percent of rural households were connected to the national electricity network, and peat production had been mechanized and industrialized. Over 3,500,000 tons are harvested mechanically each year, for conversion into electricity and for horticultural purposes.

Drainage patterns. The rivers that rise on the seaward side of the coastal mountain fringe are naturally short and rapid. The inland streams, however, flow slowly, often through marshes and lakes, and enter the sea—usually by way of waterfalls and rapids—long distances from their sources. The famed Shannon, for example, rises in the plateau country near Sligo Bay and flows sluggishly for 161 miles, reaching tidewater level at Limerick, and draining a wide area of the central lowland on its way. Other major inland streams—some of them famous for their salmon fisheries—are the Slaney, Liffey, and Boyne in the east; the Nore, Barrow, and Suir in the southeast; the Blackwater, Lee, and Bandon in the south, and the Corrib and the Moy in the west. Because of the porosity of the underlying Carboniferous limestones, an underground drainage system has developed, feeding the interlacing surface network of rivers and lakes. The state has implemented major arterial drainage projects, preventing flooding—and making more land available for cultivation—by improving the flow of water in the rivers and thereby lowering the levels of lakes. There are also state-aided farm drainage schemes designed to bring wasteland and marginal land into production.

Drainage improvement

Soils. Most Irish soils originate from drift, the ice-scoured waste formerly frozen to the base of the advancing glaciers. Some of the older rocks in the country's geological formation—quartzites, certain granites, and shales—weather into infertile and unproductive soils. In many places, however, these have been overlaid by patches of the ice-borne drift, mostly limestone-bearing, which are farmed with considerable success. The bare limestone regions remaining in western areas are a reminder of how much glacial drift cover has meant to the Irish agricultural economy.

Climate. Ireland has an equable climate of the type known to geographers as western maritime. The island lies in an area of mild southwesterly winds, and it comes under the influence of the warm drifting waters of the Gulf Stream. No part of the country is more than 70 miles from the sea, and temperature is almost uniform over the entire island. Average air temperatures lie mainly between limits of 39° and 45° F (4° and 7° C) in January and February, the two coldest months of the year. In July and August, the two warmest months, temperatures usually range between 57° and 61° F (14° and 16° C), although occasionally considerably higher readings are recorded. The sunniest months are May and June, when there is an average sunshine duration of 5.5 and 6.5 hours a day, respectively, over most of the country, and the ancient patchwork of fields and settlements making up the landscape glow under a clear, vital light. Average annual rainfall varies from about 30 inches (760 millimetres) in the east, to more than 60 inches (1,525 millimetres) in the western areas exposed to the darkening clouds that often come scudding in from the Atlantic. The rainfall, combined with the equable climate, is particularly beneficial to the grasslands, which are the mainstay of the country's large livestock population. Snow is infrequent except in the mountains; when it does occur, it is rarely prolonged or severe.

Plant and animal life. Ireland was almost completely covered by the ice cap during the glacial period, and its plant and animal life are consequently mainly—but not quite entirely—the result of the migration of species from other areas. As long as there was a land connection between Ireland and what was to become the rest of the British Isles, most species arrived overland from northern Europe. Irish plant and animal life nevertheless possesses certain unique features due partly to climatic conditions, and partly to the fact that Ireland became separated from Britain by the Irish Sea some time before Britain itself became separated from the European continent. Common English animals such as the weasel and the mole do not exist in Ireland, which also has no snakes; tradition ascribes their absence to banishment at the hands of St. Patrick, the island's patron saint. In addition, there are only two kinds of mice—as against four in Britain—while the only reptile found in Ireland is the newt. Apart from flora imported from northern Europe,

Migration of species

IRELAND

MAP INDEX

Political subdivisions

Carlow	52·50n	7·00w
Cavan	53·55n	7·30w
Clare	52·50n	9·00w
Cork	52·00n	8·30w
Donegal	54·50n	8·00w
Dublin	53·20n	6·15w
Galway	53·20n	9·00w
Kerry	52·10n	9·30w
Kildare	53·15n	6·45w
Kilkenny	52·40n	7·20w
Laoighis	53·00n	7·30w
Leitrim	54·20n	8·20w
Limerick	52·30n	9·00w
Longford	53·40n	7·40w
Louth	53·55n	6·30w
Mayo	53·50n	9·30w
Meath	53·35n	6·40w
Monaghan	54·10n	7·00w
Offaly	53·20n	7·30w
Roscommon	53·40n	8·30w
Sligo	54·10n	8·40w
Tipperary, North Riding	52·45n	8·00w
Tipperary, South Riding	52·25n	7·50w
Waterford	52·10n	7·40w
Westmeath	53·30n	7·30w
Wexford	52·20n	6·40w
Wicklow	53·00n	6·30w

Cities and towns

Abbeyfeale	52·24n	9·18w
Abbeyleix	52·55n	7·20w
Achill	53·56n	9·54w
An Uaimh	53·39n	6·41w
Ardee	53·52n	6·33w
Arklow	52·48n	6·09w
Athboy	53·37n	6·55w
Athenry	53·18n	8·45w
Athlone	53·25n	7·56w
Athy	53·00n	7·00w
Baillieborough	53·55n	6·58w
Balbriggan	53·37n	6·11w
Ballina	52·49n	8·26w
Ballina	54·07n	9·09w
Ballinasloe	53·20n	8·13w
Ballinrobe	53·37n	9·13w
Ballybunion	52·31n	9·40w
Ballyhaunis	53·46n	8·46w
Ballymote	54·06n	8·31w
Ballyshannon	54·30n	8·11w
Baltimore	51·29n	9·22w
Banagher	53·11n	7·59w
Bandon	51·45n	8·45w
Bantry	51·41n	9·27w
Belmullet	54·14n	10·00w
Birr	53·05n	7·54w
Boyle	53·58n	8·18w
Bray	53·12n	6·06w
Buncrana	55·08n	7·27w
Bundoran	54·28n	8·17w
Caher	52·21n	7·56w
Cahersiveen	51·57n	10·13w
Callan	52·33n	7·23w
Carlow	52·50n	6·55w
Carndonagh	55·15n	7·15w
Carrickmacross	53·58n	6·43w
Carrick on Shannon	53·57n	8·05w
Carrick on Suir	52·21n	7·25w
Cashel	52·31n	7·53w
Castlebar	53·52n	9·17w
Castleblayney	54·07n	6·44w
Castleisland	52·14n	9·27w
Castlereagh	53·46n	8·29w
Castletown Berehaven	51·39n	9·55w
Cavan	54·00n	7·21w
Ceanannus Mór	53·44n	6·53w
Clara	53·20n	7·36w
Claremorris	53·44n	9·00w
Clifden	53·29n	10·01w
Clonakilty	51·37n	8·54w
Clondalkin	53·19n	6·24w
Clonmel	52·21n	7·42w
Cobh	51·51n	8·17w
Collooney	54·11n	8·29w
Cootehill	54·04n	7·05w
Cork	51·54n	8·28w

MAP INDEX (continued)

Daingean 53·18n 7·17w
Dingle 52·08n 10·15w
Donegal 54·39n 8·07w
Drogheda 53·43n 6·21w
Droichead Nua 53·11n 6·48w
Dublin 53·20n 6·15w
Dundalk 54·01n 6·25w
Dungarvan 52·05n 7·37w
Dun Laoghaire 53·17n 6·08w
Edenderry 53·21n 7·35w
Ennis 52·50n 8·59w
Ennistymon 52·57n 9·13w
Fermoy 52·08n 8·16w
Foynes 52·37n 9·06w
Galway 53·16n 9·03w
Glengarriff 51·45n 9·33w
Glenties 54·47n 8·17w
Gort 53·04n 8·50w
Gory 52·40n 6·18w
Granard 53·47n 7·30w
Gweedore 55·03n 8·14w
Kanturk 52·10n 8·55w
Kenmare 51·53n 9·35w
Kildare 53·10n 6·55w
Kilkee 52·41n 9·38w
Kilkenny 52·39n 7·15w
Killala 54·13n 9·13w
Killaloe 52·48n 8·27w
Killarney 52·03n 9·30w
Killorglin 52·06n 9·47w
Killybegs 54·38n 8·27w
Kilrush 52·39n 9·30w
Kinsale 51·42n 8·32w
Leitrim 54·00n 8·04w
Letterkenny 54·57n 7·44w
Lifford 54·50n 7·29w
Limerick 52·40n 8·38w
Listowel 52·27n 9·29w
Longford 53·44n 7·47w
Loughrea 53·12n 8·34w
Louth 53·37n 6·53w
Macroom 51·54n 8·57w
Mallow 52·08n 8·39w
Manorhamilton 54·18n 8·10w
Maynooth 53·23n 6·35w
Midleton 51·55n 8·10w
Milltown Malbay 52·52n 9·23w
Mitcheltown 52·16n 8·16w
Moate 53·24n 7·58w
Monaghan 54·15n 6·58w
Mountmellick 53·07n 7·20w
Moville 55·11n 7·03w
Mullingar 53·32n 7·20w
Naas 53·13n 6·39w
Nenagh 52·52n 8·12w
Newcastle West 52·27n 9·03w
Newmarket 52·13n 9·00w
New Ross 52·24n 6·56w
Oldcastle 53·46n 7·10w
Passage West 51·52n 8·20w
Portarlington 53·10n 7·11w
Port Laoise 53·02n 7·17w
Portumna 53·06n 8·13w
Rathdrum 52·56n 6·13w
Rathkeale 52·32n 8·56w
Rath Luirc 52·21n 8·41w
Roscommon 53·38n 8·11w
Roscrea 52·57n 7·47w
Rosslare 52·17n 6·23w
Schull 51·32n 9·33w
Shillelagh 52·45n 6·32w
Skibbereen 51·33n 9·15w
Sligo 54·17n 8·28w
Swinford 53·57n 8·57w
Swords 53·28n 6·13w
Templemore 52·48n 7·50w
Thomastown 52·31n 7·08w
Thurles 52·41n 7·49w
Tipperary 52·29n 8·10w
Tralee 52·16n 9·42w
Tramore 52·10n 7·10w
Trim 53·34n 6·47w
Tuam 53·31n 8·50w
Tubbercurry 54·03n 8·43w
Tullamore 53·16n 7·30w
Tullow 52·48n 6·44w
Waterford 52·15n 7·06w
Westport 53·48n 9·32w
Wexford 52·20n 6·27w
Wicklow 52·59n 6·03w
Youghal 51·51n 7·50w

Physical features and points of interest

Achill Head, *headland* 53·59n 10·13w
Achill Island 54·00n 10·00w
Allen, Lough, *lake* 54·08n 8·08w
Annalee, *river* 54·03n 7·24w
Aran Island 54·58n 8·33w
Aran Islands 53·07n 9·43w
Atlantic Ocean 55·00n 10·00w
Ballinskelligs Bay 51·50n 10·15w
Bantry Bay 51·38n 9·48w
Barrow, *river* 52·30n 6·57w
Bear Island 51·40n 9·48w
Black Rock 54·04n 10·19w
Blacksod Bay 54·08n 10·00w
Blackwater, *river* 51·51n 7·50w
Blackwater, *river* 53·39n 6·43w
Blarney Castle, *state park* 51·56n 8·34w
Bloody Foreland, *headland* 55·09n 8·17w
Bluestack, *mountain* 54·45n 8·05w
Boyne, *river* 53·43n 6·15w
Brandon Bay 52·15n 10·05w
Brandon Mountain 52·14n 10·15w
Broad Haven, *bay* 54·18n 9·55w
Caha Mountains 51·45n 9·45w
Cahore Point 52·34n 6·11w
Carnsore Point 52·10n 6·22w
Carrantuohill, *mountain* 52·00n 9·45w
Carrowmore Lake 54·12n 9·47w
Clare, *river* 53·20n 9·03w
Clare Island 53·48n 10·00w
Clear Island 51·26n 9·30w
Clew Bay 53·50n 9·50w
Clogher Head, *headland* 53·48n 6·12w
Clonakilty Bay 51·35n 8·50w
Comeragh, *mountains* 52·19n 7·35w
Conn, Lough, *lake* 54·04n 9·20w
Connemara, *historical region* 53·25n 9·40w
Cork Harbour 51·45n 8·15w
Corrib, Lough, *lake* 53·05n 9·10w
Derg, Lough, *lake* 53·00n 8·20w
Dingle Bay 52·05n 10·15w
Donegal Bay 54·30n 8·30w
Downpatrick Head, *headland* 54·20n 9·20w
Dundalk Bay 53·57n 6·17w
Dungarvan Harbour 52·10n 7·35w
Dursey Head, *headland* 51·35n 10·14w
Errigal, *mountain* 55·02n 8·07w
Erris Head, *headland* 54·19n 10·00w
Fastnet Rock 51·24n 9·35w
Feale, *river* 52·28n 9·40w
Finn, *river* 54·50n 7·29w
Foyle, Lough, *lake* 55·07n 7·08w
Galty Mountains 52·25n 8·10w
Galway Bay 53·10n 9·15w
Grand Canal 53·15n 7·15w
Great Blasket Island 52·05n 10·32w
Greenore Point 52·15n 6·18w
Gweebarra Bay 54·52n 8·20w
Hags Head, *headland* 52·57n 9·30w
Hook Head, *headland* 52·07n 6·55w
Inishbofin, *island* 53·37n 10·15w
Inishmaan, *island* 53·05n 9·32w
Inishmore, *island* 53·07n 9·45w
Inisheer, *island* 53·02n 9·26w
Inishtrahull, *rock* 55·26n 7·14w
Inishturk, *island* 53·43n 10·08w
Irish Sea 53·45n 5·30w
Keeper Hill 52·45n 8·16w
Kerry Head, *headland* 52·25n 9·57w
Kilkieran Bay 53·15n 9·45w
Killala Bay 54·15n 9·10w
Killarney, Lakes of 52·01n 9·30w
Knockmealdown, *mountains* 52·14n 7·57w
Lambay Island 53·29n 6·01w
Leane, Lough, *lake* 52·05n 9·35w
Lee, *river* 51·55n 9·00w
Leinster, Mount, *mountain* 52·37n 6·44w
Liscannor Bay 52·55n 9·25w
Loop Head, *headland* 52·34n 9·56w
Loughros More Bay 54·47n 8·35w
Lugnaquillia Mountain 52·58n 6·27w
Macgillicuddy's Reeks, *mountains* 52·00n 9·45w
Malin Head, *headland* 55·23n 7·24w
Mask, Lough, *lake* 53·35n 9·20w
Melvin, Lough, *lake* 54·26n 8·10w
Mizen Head, *headland* 51·27n 9·49w
Moy, *river* 54·12n 9·08w
Mweelrea, *mountain* 53·38n 9·50w
Nephin, *mountain* 54·01n 9·22w
Nore, *river* 52·25n 6·58w
Old Head of Kinsale, *headland* 51·36n 8·32w
Poulaphouca Reservoir 53·08n 6·31w
Ree, Lough, *lake* 53·35n 8·00w
Robe, *river* 53·37n 9·16w
Rossan Point 54·42n 8·48w
Royal Canal 53·30n 7·30w
Saint George's Channel 52·00n 6·00w
Saltee Islands 52·07n 6·36w
Shannon, *river* 52·36n 9·41w
Shannon, Mouth of the, *bay* 52·30n 9·53w
Sheep Haven, *bay* 55·10n 7·52w
Skellig Rocks 51·48n 10·31w
Slaney, *river* 52·21n 6·30w
Slea Head, *headland* 52·06n 10·27w
Sligo Bay 54·20n 8·40w
Slyne Head, *headland* 53·24n 10·13w
Suck, *river* 53·16n 8·03w
Suir, *river* 52·15n 7·00w
Swilly, Lough, *inlet* 55·10n 7·38w
Tralee Bay 52·15n 9·59w
Twelve Bens, The, see Twelve Pins, The
Twelve Pins, The, *mountains* 53·32n 9·50w
Valentia Island 51·52n 10·20w
Waterford Harbour 52·10n 6·55w
Wexford Harbour 52·20n 6·55w
Whiddy Island 51·41n 9·30w
Wicklow Head, *headland* 52·58n 6·00w
Wicklow Mountains 53·02n 6·24w
Youghal Bay 51·52n 7·50w

several plants common in Ireland are believed to have reached the country from the Mediterranean, along a subsequently drowned coastal route, and others appear to have migrated from North America, probably by way of Greenland and Iceland.

Regional distinctions. The smallness of the country makes for homogeneity and helps explain the nation's distinctive character; it also militates against the development of significant regional or local divisions. One important regional distinction is provided by the contrast between the part of the country east of the Shannon—with its expanding industrial employment, fertile farmlands, economic growth, and rising standard of living—and the poorer areas of the west—particularly west Donegal, Leitrim, west Mayo, west Galway, Clare, west Cork, and south Kerry—where incomes are among the lowest in the country, and the fertility of the land is in many cases insufficient to provide an acceptable standard of living for the people. These western areas include the districts, known collectively as the Gaeltacht, in which the Irish language and the traditional national culture are best preserved. Heavy emigration continues to constitute a threat to the survival of this cultural heritage, paralleling the experience of the other Celtic nations, Wales and Scotland.

THE PEOPLE

Religious and linguistic background. Although Ireland has been invaded and colonized within historic times by Celts, Norsemen, Normans, English, and Scots, no racial or ethnic distinctions exist in the republic today. Little changed from their proportions at the 1961 census, almost 95 percent of the republic's population at the start of the 1970s were Roman Catholics, with other religious groups (including Church of Ireland Episcopalians 3.7 percent; Presbyterians 0.7 percent; Methodists 0.2 percent; and Jews 0.1 percent) very much in a minority. There is no established church in Ireland; freedom of conscience and the free practice of religion are guaranteed by the constitution.

The Irish language

The constitution provides that Irish, as the national language, is the first official language; it recognizes English as the second official language. All official documents are published in both Irish and English. The Irish language, which is very similar to Scots Gaelic, was widely spoken up to the time of the Great Famine of the 1840s and the subsequent emigrations. From then on, its use declined until 1922, when the teaching of Irish was introduced into all schools. Although, by the 1970s, its use as a vernacular had decreased, it is certainly more widely read, spoken, and understood today than at any previous time in

Ireland, Area and Population

	area		population	
	sq mi	sq km	1966 census	1971 census
Provinces				
Connacht				
Counties				
Galway	2,293	5,939	148,000	149,000
Leitrim	589	1,595	31,000	28,000
Mayo	2,084	5,398	116,000	110,000
Roscommon	951	2,463	56,000	54,000
Sligo	693	1,796	51,000	50,000
Leinster				
Counties				
Carlow	346	896	34,000	34,000
Dublin	356	922	795,000	852,000
Kildare	654	1,694	66,000	72,000
Kilkenny	796	2,062	60,000	61,000
Laoighis	664	1,719	45,000	45,000
Longford	403	1,044	29,000	28,000
Louth	317	821	70,000	75,000
Meath	903	2,338	67,000	72,000
Offaly	771	1,998	52,000	52,000
Westmeath	681	1,763	53,000	54,000
Wexford	908	2,351	83,000	86,000
Wicklow	782	2,025	60,000	66,000
Munster				
Counties				
Clare	1,231	3,188	74,000	75,000
Cork	2,880	7,460	340,000	353,000
Kerry	1,815	4,701	113,000	113,000
Limerick	1,037	2,686	137,000	140,000
Tipperary N.R.†	771	1,996	54,000	54,000
Tipperary S.R.†	872	2,258	69,000	69,000
Waterford	710	1,838	73,000	77,000
Ulster				
Counties				
Cavan	730	1,891	54,000	53,000
Donegal	1,865	4,830	109,000	108,000
Monaghan	498	1,291	46,000	46,000
Total Ireland	26,600‡	69,893	2,884,000‡	2,978,000‡

†The north and south ridings of Tipperary are administered separately. ‡Figures do not add to total because of rounding.
Source: Official government figures.

the present century. English is also taught in all the schools and is universally spoken.

Demographic characteristics. The census taken in 1971 showed a population of 2,978,248, an increase of 94,246 or 3.3 percent in five years. All previous censuses since 1841, with the exceptions of those of 1951 and 1966, had shown a decline in population. In fact, the population of the republic in the early 1970s was little more than half what it was in 1841, although the populations of most other west European countries had at least doubled over the same period. The explanation lies in an exceptionally high rate of emigration, historically to the United States, and later to Britain. Although the population rose by 94,246 in the period 1966–71, births exceeded deaths in the same period by 148,152, indicating an emigration of 53,906 persons. The republic's marriage, birth, and death rates are broadly comparable with those of neighbouring countries, but the rate of emigration continues to be greatly in excess of the next highest rate in Europe. As a result of emigration, the number of Irish-born people living outside their native land is reckoned to total about 50 percent of the population of the republic.

Emigration

There have also been significant internal movements of population. At the end of the 19th century, 25 percent of the republic's population lived in urban districts and 75 percent in rural areas. Three-quarters of a century later, 52 percent lived in towns of 1,500 or more inhabitants, and 48 percent in the country. The political and commercial capital of the country is Dublin (*q.v.*; pop. 680,000), while other major urban centres are Cork (134,000), Waterford (34,000), and Galway (29,000). With farm mechanization and the consolidation of small holdings as contributing factors, agricultural employment still tends to decline, and the movement of population from the country to the town—particularly from the poorer districts on the west coast—continues. The expansion of industrial employment (which rose from 244,000 to 315,000 during the 1960s) has provided much-needed alternative employment at home, but emigration, albeit on a reduced scale, continues as a major national problem. As the stark statistics indicate, the ratio of those in the active age groups (15–64) to those in the dependent age groups (0–14 and 65 and over) is the most adverse in Europe, while the republic's population density per square mile remains at 112—lower than that of any other country in western Europe except Sweden and Norway, both of which have large areas of uninhabitable land. This drain on human resources has significantly marked the character and outlook of the nation.

THE ECONOMY

Overall factors. The republic has a mixed economy. The constitution provides that the state shall favour private initiative in industry and commerce, but when the necessary private initiative is not forthcoming, the state itself undertakes essential services and promotes development projects. Thus state corporations operate the country's air services; its rail and road transport; its television and radio stations; its electricity generation and distribution system; its sugar industry; its peat industry; and other major national undertakings. State companies are also active in the fields of agricultural and industrial credit, food processing, fertilizers, hotels, and life insurance. In some cases, these companies are in direct competition with private enterprise.

State and private enterprise

The gross national product (GNP) in 1971 was £1,858,000,000 ($4,459,000,000), or £625 per head of the population. Government current expenditure in that year was 30 percent of GNP, and 40 percent of the gross capital liabilities of the state, while the average annual rate of growth in real GNP in the late 1960s and early 1970s was almost 5 percent. The average annual trade deficit during this period was £154,000,000, but average net "invisible" receipts, mainly from tourism, were £129,000,000, making an average current deficit on external account of £25,000,000. Paradoxically, the country's external monetary reserves actually increased throughout the period at an average annual rate of £16,700,000, indicating an appreciable capital inflow.

Trading position. The closeness of the economic relations between the republic and the United Kingdom is illustrated by the intensity of their trade exchanges. About 53 percent of the republic's imports come from Great Britain and Northern Ireland, and about 66 percent of its exports are marketed in that area. (The corresponding figures for the member countries of the European Economic Community, taken as a whole, are 15 percent and 11 percent, and for North America, 10 percent and 12 percent, respectively.) Tourism and business relations are facilitated by the absence of a passport barrier between the two countries. Banking and financial relations are also no doubt greatly facilitated by the membership of the republic in the sterling area, and by the fact that Irish and British pounds have remained on a parity footing since 1922.

Resources. The country is not rich in mineral resources. Recent discoveries of silver, lead, and zinc have nevertheless been successfully developed, and annual exports of minerals, metal ores, and concentrates increased from a value of £20,000 in the early 1950s to £10,000,000 twenty years later. The country's dependence on imports for its energy requirements is high, and tending to increase. Of the annual electricity consumption, 17 percent is produced by native waterpower, 36.6 percent from peat, 1.3 percent from native coal, and 45.1 percent from imported oil.

Agriculture. Agriculture is the mainstay of the national economy and, under such circumstances, the country's greatest asset is undoubtedly its climate. This produces abundant vegetable and plant growth and is particularly beneficial to the rich grasslands that enable grazing stock to be kept on pasture almost all the year round, only a limited amount of animal housing being required in winter. Agriculture accounts for about a fifth of the national income and nearly 60 percent of total exports. It employs 29 percent of the working population, although this proportion is tending to decline.

By the early 1970s, there were 260,000 farms of more than five acres in the republic. The size of the average farm is about 40 acres, which, by west European standards, is not small. Most farms are family farms; only 12 percent of those employed in agriculture work as hired labour. Mixed farming is the general pattern, with the production of fat cattle tending to predominate in the midlands and dairy farming in the south. Cereal growing is an important activity in the east and southeast. Sheep raising is widespread on the rugged and sometimes desolate hills and mountain slopes throughout the country and particularly in the western area. About 80 percent of the gross agricultural output consists of livestock and livestock products, cattle being the biggest single item, followed by milk and pigs. Other important products are cereals, sheep and wool, poultry and eggs, and root crops. Enough beets are grown to meet the country's sugar requirements. The bloodstock industry is a thriving sector of the agricultural economy and has won worldwide fame for the Irish horse. Adverse conditions in export markets following World War II handicapped the expansion of Irish agriculture, and the subsequent growth of agricultural output was notably slower than that in the industrial and service sectors. This situation could alter significantly with the republics entrance into the European Economic Community in 1973.

The family farm

When the nation was founded, woodland represented less than 1 percent of the total land area, but since World War II, state replanting has raised the acreage under forests and woodland from 166,000 in the early 1950s to 480,000, or about 3 percent of the total land area, by the early 1970s. The sea-fishing industry, on the other hand, remains relatively underdeveloped. About 1,700 full-time and 3,600 part-time fishermen land catches worth over £2,500,000 each year, the main varieties being herrings, whiting, plaice, cod, haddock, and a wide range of shellfish. Judged by west European standards, home consumption of fish, particularly shellfish, is remarkably low. About 35 percent of the landings of fish, and 90 percent of those of shellfish, are exported. Ireland is surrounded by excellent sea fisheries, and the industry is obviously capable of considerable further expansion. A state board was set up for this purpose in 1963.

Industry. Until World War II, and for some years after it, official policy in relation to manufacturing was nationalistic and protectionist. Young industries, established behind high tariff and quota walls, provided badly needed employment and helped to supply the home market, but they had little or no export potential. From the middle 1950s onward, this policy was progressively reversed. The principal basis of the government's three programs for economic expansion—the first issued in 1958, the second in 1963, and the third in 1969—was an industrial development policy. This was designed, by means of tax concessions, financial grants, and other incentives, firstly to encourage existing industries to increase their competitive strength and seek markets abroad, and secondly to attract new manufacturing enterprises, whether foreign or Irish owned, to the republic. The policy achieved considerable initial success. Over 500 new industrial enterprises, most of them export-oriented, were set up during the 1960s. The average annual rate of growth in the industrial sector throughout the period was 7 percent, while industrial exports rose £41,000,000 to £214,000,000, an estimated increase of 240 percent in real terms. Employment in manufacturing industry rose by 44,000 to 207,000 and emigration fell from 44,000 in 1960 to 15,000 in 1969. In the early 1970s, the republic exported a wide range of manufactured products, including processed foods, beer and spirits, clothing, footwear, machinery, metal ores and concentrates, glassware, pharmaceuticals, floor coverings, and electrical goods and apparatus.

Protectionist and expansionist policies

In the second half of 1969, acute inflationary pressures began to endanger the success of the third program. Inordinate increases in money incomes were judged to be primarily responsible for this situation. Other contributing factors were excessive credit for consumer purposes during 1969 and mounting government expenditure—current and capital—which rose from a total of £166,000,000, or 25 percent of GNP, in 1959–60, to a total of £588,000,000, or 41 percent of GNP, in 1969–70. This rise in government expenditure was largely met by increases in indirect taxes, which accounted, by the early 1970s, for about 66 percent of tax revenue—a remarkably high percentage. The higher prices resulting from increased indirect taxation helped to lend further impetus to demands for even higher increases in personal incomes. In turn, the continued upward trend in personal incomes inevitably led to an expansion of consumer demand, which was quickly reflected in an increase of the balance-of-payments deficit. This rose from £16,000,000 in 1968 to £69,000,000 in 1969, but increased exports in 1970 nearly balanced imports, which had themselves increased by more than 20 percent in value. In this connection, the government has announced its intention of replacing the existing retail turnover and wholesale taxes by a value-added tax—the form of indirect taxation favoured by the EEC. The nation entered the decade with a prices and incomes problem of serious proportions. The gravity of the situation stemmed from an imperative need to check the loss of competitiveness occasioned by cost and price inflation. A competitive economy was all the more desirable in view of a governmental obligation to demobilize protective tariffs in accordance with the Anglo-Irish Free Trade Agreement, to say nothing of the effect of Ireland's entry into the EEC.

Industrial bargaining

By the early 1970s there were 88 registered trade unions in the republic with a membership of about 340,000 craft, semiskilled, and general workers. Almost all Irish trade unions are affiliated to the Irish Congress of Trade Unions (ICTU). There are also nearly 40 employers' unions with a membership of about 13,000, some organized on a craft, and others on a regional, basis. The employers' central negotiating organization is the Federated Union of Employers. Wages and conditions of employment are normally matters for free collective bargaining, although industrial disputes may be referred to the Labour Court, an official body set up in 1946 with the main function of helping disputants to reach agreements. There has been much unrest on the industrial relations front in recent years, especially since the mid-1960s, with annual labour stoppages involving the loss of over 4,000,000 working days in 1970, but only about one-quarter of that in 1971. In 1970 one stoppage paralyzed the cement industry for more than 21 weeks and another brought the commercial banking system of the country to a virtual standstill for 40 weeks.

Monetary authority. The Central Bank of Ireland is the national monetary authority and has responsibilities in regard to safeguarding the integrity of the currency. It does not transact business with the public, but it exerts a considerable influence on the volume of bank credit through the "advice" it gives to the commercial (or, to use the Irish term, the associated) banks. These are the Bank of Ireland (with over 280 branches in the republic), Allied Irish Banks (over 260 branches), the Ulster Bank (some 60 branches), and the Northern Bank (30 or so branches). All four institutions have branches in Northern Ireland as well. The Bank of Ireland and Allied Irish Banks are Irish-owned, while the other two banks are subsidiaries of London clearing banks. Four U.S. banks and one Canadian bank also have offices in Dublin. By the start of the 1970s, deposits in the "associated" banks totalled nearly £500,000,000, those in other licensed banks over £230,000,000 and those in the Post Office Savings Bank over £150,000,000. Installment buying and merchant banking facilities are freely available, and Irish and foreign insurance companies offer all types of coverage throughout the country. There are stock exchanges in Dublin and Cork.

TRANSPORTATION

Roads and vehicles. As a result, no doubt, of its scattered rural population, Ireland has a higher mileage of roads per 1,000 population and per 1,000 vehicles than most European countries. By the early 1970s, the total road mileage exceeded 54,000, nearly a fifth of which was made up of main and trunk roads. Most local roads are well surfaced, and continuous progress is being made toward bringing the arterial roads up to the best modern standards, not just as an aid to tourists exploring the countryside. Ireland entered the 1970s with well over 500,000 licensed road vehicles in the country, over 70 percent of which were private cars—an average of 122 per 1,000 population.

The public system. The public transport system in the republic, including both rail and road services, is operated by a state company, Córas Iompair Éireann (CIE). There are rail services between the principal cities and towns, but, as in other countries, many branch lines have become uneconomical and have been replaced by road services for passengers and goods. The mileage of the reduced rail system, which has been modernized and greatly improved, totalled more than 1,900 by the early 1970s. The city bus services in Dublin and the larger towns as well as a country-wide network of bus services are operated by the CIE. In addition, under contracts with the appropriate government authorities, it provides a free transport scheme for schoolchildren and free travel for old age pensioners. In the early 1970s, the rail system, on average, carried 9,000,000 passengers and 3,000,000 tons of freight annually, while the road system carried 300,000,000 passengers (220,000,000 of them in Dublin) and nearly 4,000,000 tons of freight.

Waterborne traffic. There is no longer any commercial traffic on Irish canals. Of the two major canals in the country, the Royal, which joins the River Shannon with the Irish Sea via Mullingar and Dublin, is closed to navigation, but the Grand Canal, which also runs from the Shannon to the Irish Sea with a branch to the River Barrow, is maintained in a navigable condition.

Some of the smaller ports are of considerable importance to the local business communities concerned, but most of the country's seaborne trade tends to be conducted through the principal east and south coast ports, particularly Dublin, Waterford, and Cork. Dun Laoghaire, Dublin, Rosslare, and Cork are served by cross-channel passenger services to Britain, and Cobh and Galway are ports of call for transatlantic passenger liners, especially in the tourist season. Overseas traffic in owner-driven automobiles has greatly increased since the introduction of ferry services to Britain at Dublin and Dun Laoghaire, and to Britain and the European continent at Rosslare. Tourism is the largest item in the country's net invisible earnings. Its value has increased considerably in recent years, due mainly to the promotional efforts of the Irish Tourist Board (Bord Fáilte Éireann) and to that body's work in encouraging new hotel construction, developing resort areas, extending sporting facilities, and increasing tourist amenities. Income from tourism reached £100,000,000 annually by the early 1970s.

Tourist facilities

The two principal shipping companies are both state-owned. Irish Shipping, Ltd., which has a dry-cargo fleet of 14 vessels with a total deadweight tonnage of almost 200,000, is mainly engaged in the deep-sea tramping and charter trades. It also operates a fast liner service from Irish and British ports to the United States and Canada in association with British shipping companies. The British and Irish (B & I) Steam Packet Company carries passengers, merchandise, and road vehicles between Irish and British ports. The trend toward larger vessels and the shipment of goods in containers has adversely affected the smaller Irish ports, as well as the smaller privately owned shipping companies. About half of the trade between the republic and continental ports is still carried in Irish ships, but the percentage of the country's total foreign trade carried in Irish vessels is considerably less.

Air facilities. There are international airports at Dublin, Shannon, and Cork. Shannon was the world's first duty-free airport; a state-sponsored company offers substantial tax and other advantages to manufacturing and warehousing concerns proposing to establish plants within the duty-free industrial estate at the airport. Aer Lingus–Irish International Airlines, a state-owned company, operates a network of services linking 33 cities in 11 countries in the Old and New Worlds.

ADMINISTRATION AND SOCIAL CONDITIONS

Constitutional framework. The Irish republic is a parliamentary democracy, although, unlike the United Kingdom, it has a written constitution.

The president of Ireland is head of state and first citizen. He is elected by direct vote of the people for a term of seven years and is eligible for re-election for a second term. He normally acts on the advice of the government but acts in consultation with an advisory Council of State in the exercise of certain of his functions. The president signs and promulgates bills passed by the Oireachtas (Parliament) and, when so advised by the *taoiseach* (prime minister), he summons and dissolves Parliament. He may, however, refuse to dissolve Parliament on the advice of a *taoiseach* who has ceased to command a majority in the Dáil (House of Representatives). The president is the guardian of the constitution and may, in certain circumstances, submit a bill passed by Parliament to the people in a referendum, or refer it to the Supreme Court to decide on its constitutionality.

The president's role

There are two houses of the Oireachtas—the Dáil and the Seanad (Senate). Members of the Dáil are elected by adult suffrage in a secret ballot held at least every five years. The republic entered the 1970s with 38 constituencies, each of which, voting by proportional representation, elects three, four, or five members, according to its population. A proposal to abolish proportional representation in favour of straight majority voting was rejected by the people in a referendum held in 1959 and again in a second referendum held in 1966. There are 145 members of the Dáil and 60 members of the Seanad—11 appointed by the *taoiseach*, 6 elected by the Irish universities, and 43 elected to represent various economic, vocational, and cultural interests. The Seanad may delay, for a period of 90 days, bills passed by the Dáil, or it may suggest changes in them, but it cannot indefinitely block their passage into law.

The government, which consists of not less than 7 or more than 15 members, is headed by the *taoiseach*, who presides over its meetings. The *taoiseach*, the *tánaiste* (deputy prime minister), and the minister for finance must be members of the Dáil. The other ministers must be members of either house, but not more than two of them may be senators.

Political parties. Ireland entered the 1970s with a Dáil consisting of 75 seats held by the Fianna Fáil Party, 50 seats held by the Fine Gael Party, and 18 seats held by the Labour Party. Fianna Fáil is a republican party founded by Éamon de Valéra, who opposed the Anglo-Irish Treaty of 1921. The party boycotted the Dáil until 1927 but won the general election of 1932, when de Valera became prime minister, a position he held, with two intermissions, until 1959, when he became president. Fine Gael is the party of the Irish nationalists Arthur Griffith, Michael Collins, and W.T. Cosgrave, who supported the Treaty of 1921 and founded the Irish Free State. Fine Gael held office from 1922 to 1932 and, following World War II, participated in two coalition governments opposed to Fianna Fáil as did the Labour Party. In recent years, the latter group has laid increased stress on its advocacy of socialism.

Coalition government

Local government. By the early 1970s, the local government system comprised 27 counties, 4 county boroughs, 7 boroughs, and 49 urban districts. Each of these areas has a council elected, at regular intervals, by adult suffrage. In addition, there are 28 towns governed by town commissioners. County councils are responsible for physical planning, roads, health and public assistance services, sewerage and water supplies, housing, public libraries, fire services, and courthouses. County boroughs have the same functions except that, in their case, health and public assistance are the responsibility of ad hoc authorities. Noncounty boroughs, urban districts, and towns have more limited duties and, in regard to functions outside their scope, they form part of the administrative counties in which they are situated. Local government authorities in the republic have no functions in relation to police or education.

Important policy decisions—on local taxes, borrowing, the making of bylaws, etc.—are made by the elected councils. Administration, on the other hand, is the responsibility of the county (or city) manager, who usually consults with members of his council before discharging important executive functions. There is a city manager for each county borough council and, for each county council, there is a county manager, who also acts as manager for the lesser local authorities within the country. Local government current expenditures in the early 1970s amounted to over £140,000,000 annually, half of which was met by state grants, £44,000,000 by local taxation, and the remainder by miscellaneous receipts. The local government system generally is supervised by the national Department of Local Government.

Selection of judges

The legal system. Irish law is based partly on common law and partly on statute law. All judges are appointed by the president and normally serve until death or retirement. They may be removed from office only in the case of incapacity or misdemeanour and then only by resolution of both houses of the Oireachtas.

There are 24 district courts, 8 circuit courts, a high court, and a supreme court that acts as the court of final appeal. The high court has a president, six ordinary judges, and two ex officio judges—the chief justice of the supreme court and the president of the circuit court. The supreme court consists of the chief justice, four ordinary judges, and the president of the high court. The circuit court has jurisdiction to try all serious offenses except murder and treason. Such trials take place before a jury. The central criminal court, which has unlimited criminal jurisdiction, consists of a high court judge sitting with a jury. Appeal lies from its decisions to the court of criminal appeal, which consists of a supreme court judge and two high court judges chosen by the chief justice. All members of the judiciary, including district justices, have prescribed legal qualifications: there is no equivalent in the republic of the lay magistracy in England.

There are no local police forces in the republic. The Gárda Síochána (Civic Guard) is a nationwide force of about 6,500 men headed by a commissioner who is responsible to the minister for justice. About 500 members of the force are assigned to detective duties; they usually wear plain clothes and, when necessary, are armed. The rest of the force is uniformed and unarmed. Women police are employed on special duties.

Defense. The defense forces, including the air corps and the naval service, had a strength in the early 1970s of about 8,200 officers and men, with the reserves numbering about 19,000 officers and men. In recent years, Irish military personnel have played an active part in United Nations peace-keeping operations. Irish officers served as UN observers in Lebanon in 1958; in West Irian in 1962; in India and Pakistan in 1965–66; and in the Middle East up to April 1968. Irish troops served with the UN force in the Congo (now Zaire) from 1960 to 1964 and formed part of the UN peace-keeping operation in Cyprus from the latter year on. The Irish chief of staff commanded the UN force in the Congo in 1961–62. There is no conscription in the republic—enlistment in the defense forces, and participation by enlisted men in overseas operations, is voluntary.

Education. Primary education is free, compulsory, and almost entirely denominational. There are about 4,300 primary schools with about 15,000 state approved teachers and an average daily attendance of over 500,000 pupils. There are six state-aided teachers' training colleges. The secondary school system, which is almost entirely denominational and privately owned, comprises nearly 900 schools with about 11,223 teachers and an average daily attendance of approximately 192,000 pupils. State grants are available to most secondary schools to enable them to waive payment of fees. Parallel to the secondary schools are the vocational schools, which are designed to provide primary schools leavers with apprentice training and courses leading to qualifications in architecture, accountancy, engineering, and similar professions. The vocational education system, which includes schools of art, music, domestic science, and hotel training, provides courses at about 800 different centres, employs over 5,200 whole-time and part-time teachers, and has an average enrollment of over 100,000 students. Eight regional technical colleges provide advanced courses for vocational school leavers. University education is given at the University of Dublin (the famous Trinity College), founded in 1591, and at the National University of Ireland, founded in 1909. The latter has three constituent colleges, at Dublin, Cork, and Galway, respectively, and a recognized college, St. Patrick's College, at Maynooth. A higher education authority has been established to deal with the financial and organizational problems of higher education. The number of full time university students amounted to almost 18,000 at the start of the 1970s. An annual expenditure on education of about £50,000,000—over 10 percent of total government expenditure—indicates the importance of education in the national life.

University enrollment

Social services. Health services are administered by the country councils (or local health authorities) under the general supervision of the minister for health. School health examinations, child welfare clinics, and the treatment of tuberculosis and infectious diseases, are available to all without charge. Otherwise, the cost of public health services to the patient depends on his means. Persons who cannot afford to pay are entitled to a comprehensive health service free of charge. A middle income group—insured workers, smaller farmers, and others of restricted means—are entitled to a free maternity and child welfare service and to hospital and specialist services at a low charge. People who are more comfortably off normally arrange and pay for their own medical advice and hospital services; but a voluntary health insurance scheme, established by law in 1957 and now self-supporting financially, met with considerable success and had a membership of over 420,000 by the early 1970s. Due in large measure to the world-famous Irish Hospitals' Sweepstake, the republic maintains an excellent system of hospitals.

The Irish Sweepstake

Social Welfare Insurance is compulsory for all manual workers and for nonmanual workers earning not more than £1,200 per annum. Contributions are shared between employer, employee, and the state. Benefits include widows' and orphans' pensions, unemployment and disability benefits, and old age pensions. Persons of inadequate means receive certain benefits on a noncontributory basis. These include widows' and orphans' pensions, old age pensions, home assistance, unemployment assistance, and pensions for those disabled or blind. Children's allowances are paid to all households for each child under 16, irrespective of means.

Of the 676,000 dwellings in the republic at the start of the 1970s, about 25 percent were over 100 years old and nearly 60 percent over 50 years old—a comparatively high proportion of old houses by international standards. The building of new houses and the reconstruction and improvement of existing dwellings are encouraged by state grants and subsidies, which total about £6,000,000 (or 0.3 percent of the gross national product) per annum. In an average year in the early 1970s, some 12,000 new houses were built, 11,000 reconstructed, and 9,000 improved by the installation of water and sewerage facilities. The demand for housing accommodation has tended to run ahead of the supply, however, due to internal migration, earlier marriages, reduced emigration, and increasing obsolescence of buildings. Over 60 percent of all dwellings in the republic are owner occupied.

CULTURAL LIFE AND INSTITUTIONS

The cultural milieu. Although a few highly successful novels and plays have been written in Irish, the language has yet to produce a modern literature of significant proportions. The language steadily lost ground during the 18th and 19th centuries, but it never ceased to exert a strong, if imperceptible, influence on the English-speaking culture that was progressively taking its place. Many of the traditional modes of thought and expression char-

Vale of Glendalough, a glaciated valley in the mountains of County Wicklow, famous for ecclesiastical ruins, including the 110-foot-high round tower (centre).
By courtesy of Irish Tourist Board; photograph, Bord Failte Photo

acteristic of the Irish language were gradually absorbed into the English spoken in Ireland, and they served to enrich the creative imaginations and the powers of expression of those who wrote and spoke it. The remarkable contributions that Anglo-Irish literature and drama have made to the Western world may be ascribed, at least in part, to this cross-fertilization of two cultures. Be this as it may, it is noteworthy that so small a country should have nurtured so much creative literary genius—men like the great satirist Jonathan Swift, the orator and political theorist Edmund Burke, the novelist George Augustus Moore, the poet William Butler Yeats, and the modern prose masters James Joyce, Liam O'Flaherty, Frank O'Connor, Sean O'Faolain, and Samuel Beckett. In the theatre, too, Irish talent has won world acclaim in the persons of William Congreve, Oliver Goldsmith, Richard Brinsley Sheridan, Oscar Wilde, George Bernard Shaw, and Sean O'Casey.

Literary heritage

The theatre. The theatre continues to enjoy strong popular support. Dublin's famous Abbey Theatre, now rebuilt, stages Abbey classics as well as the work of new dramatists, in Irish as well as English. The Peacock Theatre, incorporated in the new Abbey building, concentrates on experimental theatre and theatre in Irish. There are a half dozen other small experimental theatres in Dublin alone, while Galway has a semiprofessional theatre devoted to plays in Irish, and a vigorous amateur dramatic movement has spread throughout the country. The Wexford Opera Festival, held each year in the autumn, has an international reputation.

Folk traditions. Many cultural institutions are specifically concerned with the popularization and preservation of various aspects of the traditional national culture—the Gaelic Athletic Association with the encouragement of the vigorous national games of hurling and football; the Gaelic League and other organizations with the spread of the Irish language; other bodies with the organization of folk-song and folk-music festivals or fetes (*feiseanna*) at which there are competitions in traditional storytelling and dancing as well as in music and singing. Some of these activities command large followings, particularly among the young.

Folk festivals

Cultural institutions. Other institutions are concerned with more general cultural interests—the Royal Irish Academy (1785) with science and polite learning; the Royal Hibernian Academy (1823) with the fine arts; the Royal Dublin Society (1731) with the advancement of agriculture and the promotion of art and science, and the Royal Irish Academy of Music. The Arts Council, established by the government in 1951, receives an annual grant from the state and in its turn assists the arts and artists by way of grants, scholarships, and awards.

There is a healthy and increasing activity in the fine arts, and many younger artists and designers have gained international acclaim. The work of Irish painters, sculptors, and stained-glass artists is shown each year at three major exhibitions—the Exhibition of the Royal Hibernian Academy, the Oireachtas Exhibition, and the Exhibition of Living Art. The preservationist propaganda of the Georgian Society and An Taisce (the National Trust of Ireland) has not been without impact in countering the effects of the enterprise of property developers on the architectural heritage of Dublin—one of the best preserved 18th-century cities in Europe.

Press and broadcasting. The Irish press is noted for high literary standards, and Dublin has three morning and two evening newspapers. The morning papers are the *Irish Independent* (nonparty and with the largest circulation; in excess of 170,000), the *Irish Press* (independent), and the *Irish Times* (liberal). The *Irish Independent* has an evening paper, the *Evening Herald*, and the *Evening Press* is associated with the *Irish Press.* There are also two Sunday papers—the *Sunday Independent* and the *Sunday Press* with circulations of 300,000 or 400,000. Cork has two daily papers—the morning *Cork Examiner* (independent) and the *Evening Echo.* The *Cork Examiner Weekly* has a substantial readership among Irish emigrants in Britain, while some British periodicals and daily and Sunday papers of varying quality have quite appreciable circulations in the republic. Waterford, Limerick, Galway, and other towns have local newspapers, most of them published weekly or twice weekly.

All radio and television stations in the republic are operated by Radio Telefis Éireann, an autonomous statutory body financed, as to capital, by repayable state grants, and as to current expenditure, by revenue from licenses and the sale of advertising time.

PROBLEMS AND PROSPECTS

The grave disturbances that began in Northern Ireland in 1968 created many difficulties and embarrassments for the republic and resulted in a Cabinet crisis in 1970. Mounting crisis in the north endangered the republic's policies of restraint and moderation as well as the maintenance of good relations between Dublin and London. Adverse economic effects, particularly as regards the tourist trade, were also apparent. In the domestic sphere, progress toward curbing inflation was made at the end of

1970, when the employers and trade unions reached a voluntary national agreement determining general pay levels for the following 18 months. In view of this, the government dropped its Prices and Incomes Bill, which would have enabled it to limit wage increases by order. If the precedent set by this agreement is followed in the future, it could do much to safeguard the competitiveness of the economy and stabilize its rate of growth.

The challenge of the EEC

Negotiations on Ireland's application for admission to the EEC began during 1970, resulting in entry on Jan. 1, 1973. The country expects to enter a new chapter in its history—a prospect promising wide opportunities but also problems of adaptation and adjustment that will tax the national energies and resources to the full.

BIBLIOGRAPHY. BASIL CHUBB (ed.), *A Source Book of Irish Government* (1964), a useful selection of basic official and other texts; T.P. COOGAN, *Ireland Since the Rising* (1966), a narrative account of political and other developments; U.M. ELLIS-FERMOR, *The Irish Dramatic Movement*, 2nd ed. (1954), a study of the origins and development of the movement up to and including the work of J.M. Synge; *Encyclopaedia of Ireland* (1968), articles on a wide variety of different subjects by acknowledged experts in their respective fields; E.E. EVANS, *Irish Folk Ways* (1957), a discussion of traditional patterns of life in the Irish countryside described by an eminent folklorist; ROBIN FLOWER, *The Irish Tradition* (1947), a review of Gaelic Ireland's contribution to western European culture, written by a sympathetic English authority; T.W. FREEMAN, *Ireland: A General and Regional Geography*, 3rd ed. (1965), an outstanding work in its field; KATHLEEN HOAGLAND (ed.), *1000 Years of Irish Poetry* (1947), a comprehensive anthology; JAMES MEENAN, *The Irish Economy Since 1922* (1970), a well-documented, comprehensive survey; *Shell Guide to Ireland* (1967), a mine of historical, archaeological, topographical, and other information with attractive illustrations.

Official publications: Constitution of Ireland, Dublin, Stationery Office; *Irish Statistical Bulletin* (quarterly); *Statistical Abstract of Ireland* (annual); reports of the National Industrial Economic Council; Central Bank of Ireland, *Quarterly Statistical Bulletin* and *Annual Report*.

(F.H.B.)

Irenaeus, Saint

Irenaeus, bishop of Lugdunum (modern Lyon, France) after 177, was one of the leading theologians of the 2nd century AD, the period when the Bible canon was settled, when the first attempts were made to formulate a creed with three articles (*i.e.*, centring on God the Father, the Son, and the Holy Spirit), and when the bishopric became the backbone of the church's organization. In these matters Irenaeus became a teacher for the whole church, both in the East and in the West.

Early career and conflicts

Though his exact birth date is unknown, Irenaeus was born of Greek parents in Asia Minor about 120/140. His own works establish a few biographical points, such as that as a child he heard and saw Polycarp, the last known living connection with the Apostles, in Smyrna, before that aged Christian was martyred in 155. Eusebius of Caesarea also notes that after persecutions in Gaul in 177 Irenaeus succeeded the martyred Pothinus as bishop of Lugdunum.

According to Eusebius, who wrote a history of the church in the 4th century, Irenaeus, prior to his becoming bishop, had served as a missionary to southern Gaul and as a peacemaker among the churches of Asia Minor that had been disturbed by heresy.

The known biographical data—if taken together with his published works—are sufficient to give a picture of an unusual life. Historical sources testify to a close cultural connection between Asia Minor and southern France (the Rhône Valley) during the 2nd century. According to tradition, the Apostle John, as a very old man who had "seen the Lord" (*i.e.*, Jesus), lived at Ephesus in the days when Polycarp was young. Thus, there were three generations between Jesus of Nazareth and Irenaeus of southern France.

The era in which Irenaeus lived was a time of expansion and inner tensions in the church. In many cases Irenaeus acted as mediator between various contending factions. The churches of Asia Minor continued to celebrate

Irenaeus as bishop (centre), detail of a stained-glass window, 13th century. In the cathedral of Saint-Jean, Lyon, France.

J. Baur and A. Lennoz

Easter on the same date (the 14th of Nisan) as the Jews celebrated Passover, whereas the Roman Church maintained that Easter should always be celebrated on a Sunday (the day of the Resurrection of Christ). Mediating between the parties, Irenaeus stated that differences in external factors, such as dates of festivals, need not be so serious as to destroy church unity.

Irenaeus adopted a totally negative and unresponsive attitude, however, toward Marcion, a schismatic leader in Rome, and toward Gnosticism, a fashionable intellectual movement in the rapidly expanding church that espoused dualism. Because Gnosticism was overcome through the efforts of the early Church Fathers, among them Clement of Alexandria and Irenaeus, Gnostic writings were largely obliterated. In reconstructing Gnostic doctrines, therefore, modern scholars relied to a great extent on the writings of Irenaeus, who summarized the Gnostic views before attacking them. After the discovery of the Gnostic library near Najʿ Ḥammādī (in Egypt) in the 1940s, respect for Irenaeus increased: he was proved to have been extremely precise in his report of the doctrines he rejected.

All his known writings are devoted to the conflict with the Gnostics. His principal work consists of five books in a work entitled *Adversus haereses* (*Against Heresies*). Originally written in Greek about 180, *Against Heresies* is now known in its entirety only in a Latin translation, the date of which is disputed (200 or 400?). A shorter work by Irenaeus, *Demonstration of the Apostolic Preaching*, also written in Greek, is extant only in an Armenian translation probably intended for the instruction of young candidates for Baptism.

Influence on the canon, creed, and episcopal authority

Irenaeus asserted in a positive manner the validity of the Jewish Bible (the Old Testament), which the Gnostics denied, claiming that it upheld the laws of the Creator God of wrath. Though Irenaeus did not actually refer to two testaments, one old and one new, he prepared the way for this terminology. He asserted the validity of the two testaments at a time when concern for the unity and the difference between the two parts of the Bible was developing.

Many works claiming scriptural authority, which included a large number by Gnostics, flourished in the 2nd century; by his attacks on the Gnostics, Irenaeus helped to diminish the importance of such works and to establish a canon of Scriptures.

The development of the creed and the office of bishop also can be traced to his conflicts with the Gnostics. On the basis of the New Testament alone, which is concerned with the salvation of man, the creed would not be expected to begin with an article about the creation of the world and man. But, because the Gnostics denied that the God revealed in the New Testament was the Creator, the first article of the creed was for polemical reasons directly connected with Genesis ("In the beginning God created the heavens and the earth"). Irenaeus refers to the creed as a "Rule of Truth" used to combat heresy.

The oldest lists of bishops also were countermeasures against the Gnostics, who said that they possessed a secret oral tradition from Jesus himself. Against such statements Irenaeus maintains that the bishops in different cities are known as far back as the Apostles—and none of them was a Gnostic—and that the bishops provided the only safe guide to the interpretation of Scripture. With these lists of bishops the later doctrine of "the apostolic succession" of the bishops could be linked. Even the unique position of authority of the bishop of Rome is emphasized by Irenaeus, though in an obscure passage.

Though there is no evidence, other than legendary, about his death, the last decade (*c.* 200/203) of the 2nd century is generally assumed to be the period in which Irenaeus died. His feast day is June 28.

BIBLIOGRAPHY. A good biography is F.R.M. HITCHCOCK, *Irenaeus of Lugdunum* (1914). The best edition of *Adversus haereses* is that of W.W. HARVEY (1857; Eng. trans. in the "Ante-Nicene Christian Library," 1868–69). See also the English translation of his *Demonstration* by J.P. SMITH (1952). A very detailed and readable article may be found in the reference work *Catholicisme, hier, aujourd'hui, demain*, pt. 6, "Irénée de Lyon" (1963–67). For Irenaeus' theology, see J. LAWSON, *The Biblical Theology of St. Irenaeus* (1948); G. WINGREN, *Man and the Incarnation: A Study in the Biblical Theology of Irenaeus* (Eng. trans. 1959); A. BENOIT, *Saint Irénée, introduction à l'étude de sa théologie* (1960).

(G.Win.)

Iridales

The flowering plant order Iridales is composed of four families: the Iridaceae with 58 genera and about 1,500 species, the Burmanniaceae with 16 genera and about 130 species, the Corsiaceae with two genera and ten species, and the Geosiridaceae with one genus and species.

The order derives its name from the iris family, Iridaceae, which is of economic importance for its ornamentals. Many species are known for their commercial and medicinal uses. The families Burmanniaceae, Corsiaceae, and Geosiridaceae are primarily of academic interest.

GENERAL FEATURES

Size range and distribution. The order Iridales is mostly composed of herbaceous annuals—short-lived, nonwoody plants or long-lived perennials that inhabit the tropics, subtropics, and temperate zones of the world. A few South African genera (*Aristea*, *Klattia*, and *Witsenia*) of the family Iridaceae are shrubs. The genus *Geosiris* is interesting from a distributional viewpoint because it is restricted to Madagascar.

Utility and economic importance. Horticulturists have for many years cultured and bred members of the Iridaceae, particularly the genera *Iris* and *Gladiolus*. Numerous hybrids and cultivated varieties exist, and newcomers appear almost every year. The hybrids and varieties, with the many different shades of their falls and standards—the outer and inner members of the perianth, corresponding to sepals and petals, respectively—have become so popular that many of the less showy nonhybrid species are ignored by all but professional botanists.

Cultivated iris and gladiolus hybrids

The iris varieties are generally categorized as bearded (referring to a hairy region on the upper surface of the falls), beardless, and bulbous forms. The bearded forms are either tall or dwarf. Examples of the beardless form include the Japanese *Iris kaempferi* and the Siberian *I. sibirica*. The Dutch, Spanish, and English varieties are bulbous; and the so-called German iris is a tall, bearded form.

Iris and *Gladiolus* have become the flowers of specialists, and national societies sponsor periodical exhibitions of the flowers in some Western countries.

Other plants of the family Iridaceae that are popular among gardeners are the genera *Antholyza*, *Belamcanda*, *Crocus*, *Freesia*, *Ixia*, *Moraea*, *Nemastylis*, *Neomarica*, *Romulea*, *Sisyrinchium*, *Tigridia*, and *Tritonia* (*Montbretia*), among others.

The dried rhizomes—horizontal, creeping, rootlike stems—of *Iris florentina*, *I. pallida*, and *I. germanica* have a sweet odour that is associated with volatile and nonvolatile oils. The dried material is orrisroot, which is widely used commercially; for example, it is utilized in the manufacture of perfumes, powders, soaps, and dentifrices. Orris oil is used in flavouring candies, soft drinks, and gelatine desserts; however, because it apparently contains allergy-causing components, its use for these purposes has been discouraged. Orris also possesses mild medicinal properties and is used in the treatment of disorders such as bronchitis and dropsy and those involving the liver. In the form of a powder or in poultices, it is applied to sores.

The stigmas, feathery extensions of the female flower parts, of *Crocus sativus*, the saffron of commerce, yield a yellow dye. Saffron, which is valued for its flavouring

Drawing by M. Moran; (far right) from J. Hutchinson, *Families of Flowering Plants*, © 1959 by The Clarendon Press, Oxford, reprinted by permission

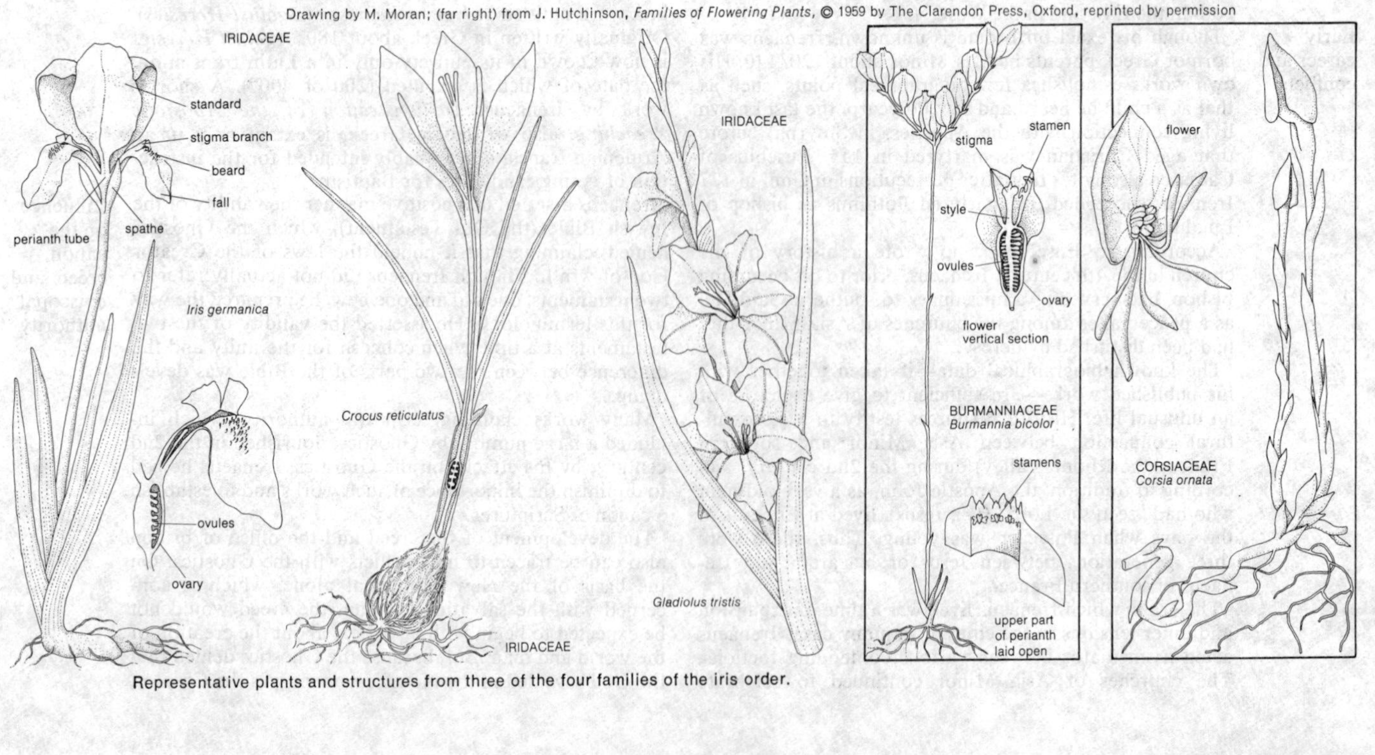

Representative plants and structures from three of the four families of the iris order.

and colouring properties, is used to colour butter, cheese, confections, and medicines. It is used as a remedy for catarrhal affections (inflammation of mucous membranes) of children, for melancholia (mental depression), and to treat enlargement of the liver. It is a nerve sedative and also promotes menstrual discharge. Bulbs of the saffron crocus are toxic to animals, and overdoses of the stigmas are narcotic.

Belamcanda chinensis, the leopard lily, is a remedy for tonsillitis in Chinese medical practice. It is also used to treat chest and liver complaints. The leaves of *Iris germanica* contain ascorbic acid (vitamin C); they are also used to treat frozen feet.

The leaves of *Iris kumaonensis* and *I. ensata* are used as animal feed. Those of the latter, the plants of which are reported to be fibrous, are also used for thatching, matting, and basketwork.

Poisonous substances

Starchy corms—bulblike stem structures—and rhizomes of some members of the iris family are edible. On the other hand, fatal cases of iris poisoning of cattle have been reported from Canada. The rootstocks of the blue flag, *Iris versicolor*, contain a poisonous irritating substance (iridin) that affects the digestive organs and gastrointestinal tract. Poisoning is, however, rare, as the rootstocks are seldom eaten in large quantities. Some allergic individuals suffer skin rashes as a result of handling certain irises.

NATURAL HISTORY

Life cycle. The order Iridales (except for the family Iridaceae) and the order Triuridales are saprophytes, plants that obtain their food from dead organic matter rather than by photosynthesis. In addition, they are mycotrophic, which means that their roots are in close association (mycorrhizal association) with the mycelia (filamentous bodies) of a fungus that generally helps the plant to absorb nutrients and receives some benefit from the plant in return. The plants, in keeping with their saprophytic and mycotrophic modes of nutrition, have reduced scalelike leaves and an undifferentiated embryo contained in a very small seed. These are also features of the orchid order, the most highly evolved group of petaloid monocotyledons—plants with one seed leaf and parallel-veined leaves whose flowers have sepals that are showy and look like petals (see ORCHIDALES).

The family Iridaceae is autotrophic—it produces its own food by photosynthesis—and exploits the growth habits characteristic of the families Liliaceae and Amaryllidaceae, in which the underground food-storage parts are rhizomes, corms, or bulbs. The roots have a velamen, a thick corky epidermis or covering, as in the Liliaceae, the Amaryllidaceae, and the Orchidaceae. Members of the iris family propagate vegetatively, although they also reproduce by seeds. In many species, germination of the seed is slow and irregular; the seeds of some species also require a moist-chilling treatment prior to planting.

The saprophytic and mycotrophic families Burmanniaceae, Corsiaceae, and Geosiridaceae grow in the shade of forests and require a fungal symbiont-partner—at an early stage in development. Only in some species of the Burmanniaceae that grow in open situations are the leaves green and capable of photosynthesis.

Most flowers of the order are brightly coloured and are generally pollinated by insects. Interesting pollination adaptations that impede self-pollination and ensure cross-pollination are present in the Iridaceae. The shape of a flower, for example, bears a close relation to its insect visitor. Pollination in *Freesia refracta* and in some species of *Gladiolus* is by the moth. The flower is adapted to the flight of the moth, which hovers while its tongue probes to the base of the floral tube. Pollen deposited on the moth during the process is transferred to another flower on the next visit. The flowers of *Lapeyrousia* have a long floral tube and are adapted to pollination by a long-tongued fly. The blue-flag beetle makes many punctures in the nectary of *Iris versicolor*, and the nectar that flows out attracts many other insects, especially flies, which may provide pollination services.

Insect pollination

The pollination mechanism in *Iris pseudacorus* (water flag) is unique. The flowers are pollinated by a hover fly or a bumblebee. When the flowers open, the styles, the upper parts of the female pistils, stand about one centimetre (0.4 inch) above the falls (the outer members of the perianth, corresponding to sepals), facilitating pollination by the bee alone. As the flower ages, the petallike styles gradually come to lie close to the falls, thereby leaving a narrow passage insufficient for the bee. The fly pollinates such flowers.

Members of the Iridaceae are susceptible to diseases and pests. *Septoria gladioli*, a fungus, attacks the leaves and the corms, causing hard rot; *i.e.*, the corms wrinkle and harden. The leaves of many *Iris* species are subject to leaf-spot and rust diseases caused by the fungi *Didymellina macrospora* and *Puccinia iridis*. *Fusarium* wilt is another fungus-caused disease resulting in the yellowing of leaf sheaths. Bacterial soft rot caused by *Erwinia caratovora* is a foul-smelling rot of the rhizome; it is spread by the iris borer. Small gradiolus thrips suck the juice from leaf sheaths and flower buds. Most of these diseases and pests are easily controlled by conventional methods.

Ecology. The three mycotrophic families usually grow under the shade of tropical and subtropical rain forests, and most favour acid soils. The family Iridaceae is composed of tropical and temperate plants. Its species prefer sunny habitats and also grow in temperate deserts and alkaline soils. The evolution of the cormous and the bulbous habits has enabled the members of the iris family to grow in some of the most arid regions of the world. Areas in the Mediterranean region in which forests have been destroyed are rapidly colonized by the sunny habitat genera of the family; *e.g.*, *Iris* and *Crocus*. The water flag, *Iris pseudacorus*, forms part of the swamp flora along waterways and is characteristic of sedge-reed zones and boggy poolsides.

Hybridization as an aid in habitat exploitation

Members of the Iridaceae are prone to hybridization, which enables them to become established in different ecological habitats. This appears to have contributed to their wide distribution and evolution.

The minute size of the seeds of the mycotrophic families affords wide dispersal by wind. The need for the specific fungal symbiont on which the plants are physiologically dependent, however, has resulted in a comparatively limited geographical range for the members of these families.

FORM AND FUNCTION

Vegetative and floral characteristics. Plants of the order Iridales are caulescent or acaulescent—stemmed or stemless—herbs with radical (basal) or distichous (in two vertical rows), parallel-veined leaves.

The flowers are mostly bisexual (both sexes in one flower) and radially or bilaterally symmetrical; they have a petaloid perianth—the sepals and petals look alike or are both showy and petallike (that is, generally united at the base). There are three (less commonly, six) stamens (male pollen-producing structures) that are attached to the upper surface of the tepals (the showy petallike sepals and petals when considered together, as in this case, in which the attachment may be with the sepals or petals or with both when the stamens are six in number). The anthers, or pollen-bearing parts of the stamen, are two-celled; and the pollen grains are mostly binucleate. The ovary in most species is inferior—that is, it is enclosed within the basal portions of the sepals and petals; it is three-celled, and the ovule attachment is axile or along the central axis. In some species the ovary is one-celled, in which the ovule attachment is parietal (to the inner ovary walls). The fruit is a capsule.

Physiological and biochemical features. Many species in the order respond to environmental factors; for example, high intensities of light are necessary for well-developed flowers in *Gladiolus*. Temperature has an effect on the flowering of the Wedgwood iris; at extremely high or low temperatures no flower formation occurs. It is possible to make the irises bloom year round by lifting the bulbs prematurely and storing them at a controlled temperature.

The opening and closing of the flowers of the crocuses are dependent on temperature. This is because of the differential growth rate of certain inner cells of the tepals (sepals or petals when both look alike) according to temperature. *Crocus* is sensitive to even as small a change as 0.5° C (0.9° F).

Among the known chemical components of the family Iridaceae, the glycosides (sugar-containing compounds), resinoids (gummy substances insoluble in water), anthocyanins (reddish or purplish pigments), flavonoids (base compounds of certain yellow pigments), volatile and nonvolatile oils, and seed fats rich in linoleic acid are worthy of note. The blue flag *Iris versicolor* contains the resinoid iridin (which should not be confused with the glycoside, also called iridin, found in *I. florentina*). The floral pigments are mostly anthocyanins. Coumarin glycosides (compounds with a vanilla-like odour sometimes used in flavourings) are present in some species; *e.g.*, *I. wattii*.

Chemical similarities among related species

Chemical similarities among related species is of diagnostic value in the genus *Iris*. The species in the *pogoniris* and *evansia* sections of the genus, for example, do not contain leuce-anthocyanins or flavonols (organic compounds containing the ring-structured molecule phenol); in those of the *sibirica* and *californica* groups, however, both the compounds are consistently present. Species of the subsection *spuria* have only leuce-anthocyanins. It is of interest that the two isoflavones, iridin and tectoridin, that are found in species of the *pogoniris* and *evansia* groups, respectively, have not yet been found in any other plant.

EVOLUTION AND PHYLOGENY

In earlier classification systems, the family Iridaceae was considered to be derived from the Amaryllidaceae, a view chiefly based on the common character of the inferior ovary. The importance given to the position of the ovary has been questioned, however, and, even though the Tasmanian genus *Isophysis* has a superior ovary, it has been transferred from the family Liliaceae (order Liliales) to the Iridaceae; the genus therefore is iridaceous in all respects except the superior ovary. Furthermore, it is now widely believed that, although the families Amaryllidaceae and Iridaceae are similar, they have evolved separately from the Liliaceae.

The tiny seeds with an undifferentiated embryo and mycotrophy are features that the family Burmanniaceae shares with the orchids. The two families are closely allied, and the orchids, in older classification systems, are considered to be derived from the Burmanniaceae. Current phyletic appraisals, however, have resulted in the shifting of the Burmanniaceae from the orchid order to the order Iridales, or, in some classification systems, to the order Liliales.

Evidence based upon variations in the development of the stomatal complex (*i.e.*, the stomates, the microscopic pores in the leaves, and the cells near them) among the monocotyledons is valuable in considerations of phylogeny. All the studied plant groups of the order have a stomatal complex with two guard cells (the cells that control the size of the stomate opening) and no subsidiaries (cells that surround the guard cells). This type is regarded to have arisen only once in the evolutionary history of the monocotyledons. Furthermore, the plant groups with this type of stomatal complex usually are closely related. Floral features are thought to have developed along one or, at most, only a few related and parallel lines of increasing specialization, starting with the more primitive order Liliales. According to recent authorities the families of the iris order are derived from the family Liliaceae. Furthermore, the Burmanniaceae and the Corsiaceae are now considered to represent a parallel evolutionary line with the orchids.

Relation to iris order

CLASSIFICATION

Distinguishing taxonomic features. The important distinguishing features useful in delimiting the families of the iris order include the growth habit of the plants, nature of the leaves, symmetry of the flowers, arrangement of the sepals in the bud, number and position of the stamens, and number and structure of the seeds.

Annotated classification. The classification adopted here is a recent one; however, the inclusion of autotrophic and mycotrophic families in the iris order is a situation about which there is no unanimity of opinion among botanists at present.

ORDER IRIDALES

Annual or perennial herbs. Leaves basal or on a definite stem, parallel-veined, linear. Flowers mostly bisexual, radially or bilaterally symmetrical; perianth (sepals and petals) of 6 segments in 2 whorls, mostly basally fused, petaloid (petal-like in structure and appearance). Stamens 3 or 6, arising from the tepals; anthers 2-celled, splitting lengthwise or transversely; pollen mostly with 2 nuclei and 1 germinal furrow or pore. Ovary mostly inferior, 3-chambered, with axile placentation (ovules attach along central axis of ovary) or 1-chambered with ovule attachment to ovary walls; ovules few to many or numerous, mostly anatropous (inverted and straight); fruit a capsule. There are 4 families, about 77 genera, and about 1,640 species distributed in the tropics and subtropics of both hemispheres.

Family Iridaceae (Iris family)

Perennial herbs with rhizomes, corms, or bulbs; with or without a definite stem. Leaves linear to sword-shaped, parallel-veined, basal or in 2 vertical rows. Arrangement of flowers racemose (along a central axis with flowers maturing from the bottom upward) or paniculate (in many-branched clusters). Flowers subtended by 2 prominent bracts (leaflike appendages), showy, radially or bilaterally symmetrical. Stamens 3, opposite the sepals and attached to them, sometimes basally fused into a tube; anthers extrorse. Style 1, often 3-branched. Ovules few to many. Fruit a 3-valved loculicidal capsule (*i.e.*, it opens dorsally into the chamber); seeds with small embryo and copious endosperm. There are 58 genera and about 1,500 species with centres of distribution in South Africa and South America.

Family Burmanniaceae

Slender, often saprophytic herbs. Leaves basal or the upper leaves alternate, minute. Inflorescence racemose or cymose (similar to a raceme but with the flowers maturing from the top downward) in a 2-cleft cincinnus (helicoid cyme). Flowers radially symmetrical. Stamens 3 or 6; anthers opening laterally or toward the central axis of the flower (introrse), anther connective (the tissue between the 2 anther lobes) often appendaged. Style 1, 3-branched. Fruit a loculicidal capsule or pyxis (a capsule that opens circumscissilely—the top comes off as a lid); seeds numerous, minute; endosperm scanty; embryo undifferentiated. There are 16 genera and about 130 species with centres of distribution in the tropics and subtropics of the world.

Family Corsiaceae

Small rhizomatous or tuberous saprophytes. Leaves reduced to scales. Flowers solitary, terminal, bilaterally symmetrical, bisexual or unisexual; the median sepal large and enclosing the remaining 5 perianth members. Stamens 6, exserted (extending beyond perianth members); anthers extrorse. Style 3-parted. Fruit a capsule opening by 3 valves; seeds numerous, minute; endosperm scanty; embryo undifferentiated. There are 2 genera and 10 species distributed in Chile and New Guinea.

Family Geosiridaceae

Small saprophytic herbs with scaly rhizomes. Stems simple or branched; leaves alternate, squamiform (scalelike). Inflorescence loosely cymose. Flowers radially symmetrical, bisexual. Stamens 3, opposite the sepals; anthers extrorse. Fruit 3-angled, inversely conical, and crowned with an annulus; seeds numerous, minute; embryo undifferentiated. One genus and species (*Geosiris aphylla*) with natural distribution restricted to Madagascar.

Critical appraisal. In an older classification system, the family Burmanniaceae and the family Orchidaceae were placed together in a single order, the Microspermae. The genus *Geosiris* was removed from the Iridaceae, where it was placed by its author and included in the Burmanniaceae. The family Iridaceae of that system then formed a suborder, Iridineae, under the order Liliiflorae.

Eventually each of the three tribes of the family Burmanniaceae (Euburmannieae, Thismieae, and Corsieae) was raised to the rank of a family. A new order was proposed for them—the Burmanniales. The family Iridaceae was also elevated to the level of an order representing a distinct group.

Other authorities included the tribes Euburmannieae

and the Thismieae in a newly circumscribed family, Burmanniaceae, and treated the tribe Corsieae as a separate family, Corsiaceae. The genus *Geosiris* was also raised to the rank of a family.

All four families are now placed in the order Liliiflorae of one widely accepted classification system. The Burmanniaceae and the Corsiaceae are included in the suborder Burmanniineae of that system, and the Iridaceae and the Geosiridaceae are placed in the suborder Iridineae. A different, also widely accepted classification system places the Iridaceae in the order Liliales and the three mycotrophic families in the order Orchidales. In the scheme adopted here, the four families compose the order Iridales.

The above taxonomic and phylogenetic controversies result, at least in part, from the nonavailability of allegedly primitive and critical genera and species for morphological study. Studies in the vegetative and floral anatomy, embryology, and cytology (structure and function at the cellular level) of the various groups of the order are necessary for detailed phyletic and taxonomic appraisals.

BIBLIOGRAPHY. L.H. BAILEY (ed.), *Standard Cyclopedia of Horticulture*, 2nd ed., 3 vol. (1958), a standard work with a wealth of information on the cultivation of ornamental, vegetable, and fruit plants of the United States and Canada, including a treatment of the iris-order plants of economic importance; L. DIELS, "Iridaceae," in A. ENGLER and K. PRANTL, *Die natürlichen Pflanzenfamilien* (1930), a descriptive monographic treatment of the iris family; A. ENGLER, "Burmanniaceae," in *Die natürlichen Pflanzenfamilien*, vol. 2, pt. 6 (1889), a descriptive and taxonomic treatment still useful; J.B. HARBORNE, *Comparative Biochemistry of the Flavonoids* (1967), a modern textbook on flavonoids describing their presence in major plant groups and their use in taxonomy; R.E. HOLTTUM, "Growth-Habits of Monocotyledons: Variations on a Theme," *Phytomorphology*, 5:399–413 (1955), an important treatment of the unusual growth forms of the monocots—grasses, lilies, irises, orchids, and others; J. LOWE, "The Phylogeny of Monocotyledons," *New Phytol.*, 60:355–387 (1961), an authoritative treatment of the evolutionary position of the monocotyledons.

(R.M.P.)

Irish Sea

The Irish Sea is an arm of the North Atlantic Ocean that separates Ireland from Great Britain. Since prehistoric times, it has functioned as the maritime core of what has often been characterized as "Atlantic Britain" —a region of coastal lowlands marked by a distinctive cluster of peoples and cultures. In classical times it was known as Oceanus Hibernicus. Postglacial changes in sea level are believed to find a reflection in the myths about a "drowned kingdom" prevalent among the Celtic peoples of the area.

The Irish Sea is bounded by Scotland on the north, England on the east, Wales on the south, and Ireland on the west. The sea is connected with the Atlantic by the North Channel between Northern Ireland and Scotland (minimum width 13 miles) and by St. George's Channel between the southeastern tip of Ireland and southwestern Wales (minimum width 47 miles). As thus defined it is about 130 miles (210 kilometres) long and 150 miles (240 kilometres) wide. Its total area is about 40,000 square miles (100,000 square kilometres).

There are two islands. The Isle of Man (Manx-Gaelic *mannin*, "island"), a distinctive crown possession (*i.e.*, not part of the United Kingdom), lies in the centre of the northern part. Anglesey is close to the coast of North Wales; its Welsh name is Môn (from *mon*, "island"), as in its ancient name Môn mam Cymru, (Mona the Mother of Wales).

Physiography. The greater part of the sea floor lies between zero and 300 feet. Greater depths are restricted to a narrow channel parallel to the east coast of Ireland, where 576 feet has been recorded. There is a series of linear sandbanks near and parallel to the Irish coast and others off the Isle of Man and the English coast. Coarse sand and gravel form the sea floor in the south central Irish Sea. To the north and south there is a decrease in grain size where mud is accumulating. The eastern half of the sea is largely floored by gravels, sand, or muddy sand that has resulted from the reworking of glacial deposits.

Geology and geological history

The Irish Sea is flanked by land almost wholly composed of Paleozoic (225,000,000 to 570,000,000 years old) or older rocks, the exception being the coast of northwest England formed of Triassic rocks (190,000,000 to 225,000,000 years old), which also occur at the northeastern end of the Isle of Man.

The Irish Sea is largely underlain by rocks much younger than those that surround it. Direct evidence comes from a few boreholes and sea-floor samples south and east of the Isle of Man and from a deep borehole at Mochras, off the Welsh coast in northern Cardigan Bay, which, in 1969, proved 1,974 feet of Tertiary and Quaternary rocks (younger than 65,000,000 years old) underlain by 4,281 feet of Lower Jurassic age (up to 190,000,000 years old) and ended in Upper Triassic strata. The borehole site must be separated by a major fault from the older rocks on shore. Other evidence for young rocks comes from geophysical data, chiefly from gravity and magnetic surveys. These have revealed six basins underlain by rocks dating from 65,000,000 to 325,000,000 years old.

The Irish Sea is likely to have originated by rifting during the Tertiary Era (65,000,000 to 26,000,000 years ago), and subsidence of the basins was probably initiated or renewed at this time.

Currents, tides, and salinity. Surface tidal currents reach about five miles per hour in St. George's Channel, near the Irish coast, and are locally strong elsewhere. Currents are weakest (less than one mile per hour) in the west central Irish Sea. The greatest ranges of tide, about 27 feet, occur on the northwest English coast and the smallest, about four feet, on the southeastern Irish coast. Tidal streams enter the Irish Sea from both the north and the south, meeting near latitude 54° N, just south of the Isle of Man. Surface salinity is least, 32 parts per thousand, in the northwestern Irish Sea, presumably due to the inflow of rivers. It rises to about 34.5 in the centre of St. George's Channel. The salinity of the open North Atlantic is 35.5.

Economic activity. On the sea's eastern shores, Liverpool is the largest British port with a net tonnage of shipping of over 60,000,000 entering every year; Manchester is joined to the Irish Sea by the Manchester Ship Canal. On the west, Dublin, with extensive quays on the River Liffey, handles more than half of the cargo trade of the republic of Ireland. Herring are fished in summer months and whiting in winter, and there is some trawling for cod and flatfish, but the Irish Sea catch is only about one-tenth of that of the North Sea. Fleetwood, 37 miles north of Liverpool, is the chief British fishing port, and Dun Laoghaire and Howth, both near Dublin, are important fishing ports for the republic. There are a number of small local fisheries.

Gas and oil resources

The sedimentary basins in the Irish Sea have attracted attention as possible sources of hydrocarbons (petroleum and natural gas), but activity has been small in comparison with the North Sea. Some concessions have been let in the area of the East Irish Sea Basin, and wells have been drilled, but no finds have been reported. It is not possible to assess future hydrocarbon prospects with confidence.

BIBLIOGRAPHY. D.T. DONOVAN and L.H.N. COOPER, "Irish Sea and Celtic Sea," in R.W. FAIRBRIDGE (ed.), *The Encyclopedia of Oceanography*, pp. 408–413 (1966), summarizes the oceanography. A more detailed though earlier account is by K.F. BOWDEN, "Physical Oceanography of the Irish Sea," *Fishery Invest.* (*Lond.*), 18:1–67 (1955). The most recent summary of geology and geophysics is in an article by R.A. EDEN *et al.*, "The Solid Geology of the East Atlantic Continental Margin Adjacent to the British Isles," in *Report No. 70/14*, Institute of Geological Sciences, London, pp. 115–128 (1971). Recent sediments are summarized in another paper in the same volume, by R.H. BELDERSON *et al.*, "Holocene Sediments on the Continental Shelf West of the British Isles," pp. 157–170.

(D.T.D.)

Iron Mining and Processing

Iron is the most useful of the metallic elements and the second most abundant in the Earth's crust, after aluminum. In its elemental form or as steel iron has supplied civilization with most of its tools and machinery, many of its products, and the bulk of its structural elements in large-scale construction. It weighs 491 pounds per cubic foot (7,865 kilograms per cubic metre) at 20° C (68° F) and is a solid at temperatures below 1,535° C (2,795° F). Pure iron has a silvery lustre and takes a high polish. It is highly ductile at ordinary temperatures, becoming brittle only at the temperature of liquid air (−150° C [−238° F]) or at white heat just below its melting point. Except in meteorites, it is rarely found in its elemental form but occurs widely in chemical compounds in the Earth's crust.

Table 1: Iron Ore, Concentrates and Agglomerates*
(000 metric tons)

country	1970	1980†
Soviet Union	195,492	243,370
Brazil	34,758	107,186
Australia	57,110	95,534
United States	91,200	70,407
Canada	47,459	49,812
India	31,368	40,668
France	57,402	29,199
Sweden	31,509	27,184
Liberia	23,256	18,350
Venezuela	21,864	13,681
Chile	11,265	8,960
Spain	7,000	8,865
Mexico	4,045	8,149
Peru	9,713	5,679
Yugoslavia	3,694	4,539
World Total	773,400	883,200‡

*Fifteen largest producing countries and world total. †Preliminary figures. ‡1979 preliminary figure.
Source: West German Statistisches Bundesamt, Aussenstelle Dusseldorf, *Eisen Und Stahl.*

HISTORY

Iron was probably discovered accidentally late in the Bronze Age when, after fires were built on outcroppings of red iron ore (iron oxide), metallic iron was found in the ashes of these fires. With the useful properties of iron thus realized and the red ore, known as paint rock, identified as the source, iron production began. Fires were built against banks of ore exposed to prevailing winds; later, crude rock furnaces were built, and their fires were fanned by bellows to reduce iron oxide to metallic iron. Iron tools and weapons ushered in a new age in both the Near East and the Far East. As recorded in Genesis (4:22), Tubal-cain, the eighth-generation descendant of Adam, was a forger of instruments of bronze and iron. Iron has been found at many sites in Egypt, including two pieces in the Great Pyramid of Giza, built about 2900 BC. Hittite artifacts, from 1900 to 1200 BC, include a cast-iron ring. Several iron-smelting furnaces dating from about 1300 BC have been uncovered in Israel.

Iron ore was discovered independently in China at an unknown date; before the beginning of the Christian era the Chinese had also independently invented the blast furnace and cast iron. In the West the Romans inherited ironworking techniques from the Greeks, carried them to a high degree of perfection, and spread their knowledge to northern Europe. Roman castings have been found in Czechoslovakia, France, and Great Britain. Pliny the Elder (AD 23–79) devotes two chapters of his Natural History to an account of iron production and use.

The Iron Age

Though the Iron Age is usually dated by archaeologists as beginning about 1200 BC, it was not until the European Middle Ages, with the introduction of iron cannon, that iron actually overtook copper and bronze to achieve first place among metals in use. Iron remained unknown in the Americas until the arrival of Columbus.

Before the 18th century charcoal was universally used as fuel for blast furnaces, but about 1708 Abraham Darby of Coalbrookdale, England, submitted coal to the same process used on wood to make charcoal and produced the first coke. Substitution of coke for charcoal took place quickly in coal-rich England but much more slowly in areas where forests abounded, such as North America.

The first American ironworks was built in Virginia in 1621 but was destroyed by an Indian raid a year later. The Massachusetts Bay Colony imported an English iron master and built an ironworks on the Saugus River, 10 miles (16 kilometres) north of Boston, in the 1640s. The operation, fed with bog iron (a hydrated iron oxide), was highly successful. Some direct casting of implements and utensils was done, but the furnace primarily turned out cast-iron bars to be worked by local forges.

In the 19th century the invention of the Bessemer and Siemens-Martin processes, making possible the large-scale production of steel, especially for structural purposes, created an enormously expanded demand for iron (see also STEEL PRODUCTION). This demand was met by more intensive ore extraction in Great Britain, continental Europe, and elsewhere, and the discovery and exploitation of new ore fields, most notably the great Mesabi Range in the north central United States.

Principal 20th-century developments have centred on improved mining machinery and larger capacity blast furnaces; one constructed in Japan in the 1960s is capable of producing 7,000 tons of iron in a 24-hour day.

Production of iron ore and pig iron by the major producing countries are shown in Tables 1 and 2.

IRON ORES: MINING AND PREPARATION FOR PROCESSING

Common ores. The most common compounds from which iron is produced are oxides, carbonates, and sulfides.

Hematite. Red hematite (Fe_2O_3), when pure, contains 70 percent iron. When mined, the content may be as low as 25 percent. It is found mainly in Sweden, Belgium, Western Australia, and the Alabama and Lake Superior regions of the United States. It may readily be distinguished from magnetic and titanium-bearing iron ores by its red streak. Hematite is sometimes mixed with sufficient magnetite to cause it to adhere to a magnet.

Limonite or brown hematite. The hydrated variety of hematite ore is called limonite, or brown hematite ($2Fe_2O_3 \cdot 3H_2O$), and contains about 60 percent iron, when pure. An important ore, it is yellowish to brown in colour. The chief constituent of bog iron ore, it is found in East and West Germany, France, Spain, Western Australia, the Soviet Union, and the United States.

Bog iron ore

Magnetite. Magnetite, a magnetic iron ore, is a natural black oxide of iron (Fe_3O_4); it is often called black sand. Magnetite is found in Sweden, Norway, the Soviet Union, and the United States.

Table 2: Pig Iron and Ferroalloys*
(000 metric tons)

country	1970	1980†
Soviet Union	85,933	107,282
Japan	68,048	87,040
United States	83,294	78,928
China	16,200	35,400
West Germany	33,627	33,873
France	19,221	19,159
Italy	8,354	12,219
Brazil	4,205	11,918
Poland	6,984	11,104
Canada	8,433	10,906
Belgium	10,955	9,845
Czechoslovakia	7,548	9,819
Romania	4,210	9,012
India	6,901	8,767
Australia	6,148	7,811
World Total	428,200	529,000

*Fifteen largest producing countries and world total. †Preliminary figures.
Source: West German Statistisches Bundesamt, Aussenstelle Dusseldorf, *Eisen Und Stahl.*

Table 3: Typical Percentage Composition of Iron Ores

	Swedish magnetite	red hematite (U.K.)	brown hematite U.K.	brown hematite Spanish	German spathic iron ore	clay ironstone American	clay ironstone Yorks
Ferrous oxide (FeO)	28.42	—	—	—	55.64	36.14	39.92
Ferric oxide (Fe_2O_3)	62.06	86.50	90.05	78.80	—	1.45	3.60
Manganous oxide (MnO)	—	0.21	0.08	0.65	2.80	1.38	0.95
Alumina (Al_2O_3)	—	—	—	3.50	—	6.74	7.86
Calcium oxide (CaO)	—	2.77	0.06	—	0.92	2.70	7.44
Magnesium oxide (MgO)	1.44	1.46	0.20	—	1.77	2.17	3.82
Carbon dioxide (CO_2)	—	2.96	—	—	38.35	26.57	22.85
Ferrous sulfide (FeS)	0.07	—	—	—	—	0.10	0.11
Phosphoric anhydride (P_2O_5)	—	—	0.09	0.07	—	0.34	1.86
Silica (SiO_2)	7.60	6.55	1.07	5.55	—	17.37	7.12
Water	—	—	9.22	11.65	—	1.77	2.97
Organic matter	—	—	—	—	—	2.40	1.64

Carbonate. Carbonate ores include siderite and spathic iron ore ($FeCO_3$) and contain 48 percent iron when pure. These ores are mostly clay ironstone and blackband ironstone found in the United Kingdom.

Taconite. This ore consists of an iron-bearing chert derived from ferrous silicate that encloses the Mesabi ores in the United States. In U.S. practice, taconite is any grade of extremely hard, lean iron ore that has its iron either in banded or in well-disseminated form, and which may be hematite or magnetite, or a combination of the two within the same ore body. When leached by hydrothermal methods, it yields a satisfactory ore, the iron remaining as hematite. Leaching is the recovery of usable constituents from heterogeneous material by dissolving in water, dilute acid, or other chemical solution.

Mining techniques. A substantial amount of iron ore is recovered by surface methods, usually known in metal mining as open-pit or opencut. For deeper lying deposits in which the ore and wall rocks are firm, open stopes—a series of descending steps—are cut; in cases of small deposits, the entire ore body may be removed from wall to wall without leaving any pillars. Where the ore body lies buried in rock, deep underground, shaft mining is employed; the vertical shaft may go down several thousand feet. Horizontal tunnels from the shaft follow the ore deposits as they are mined, with locomotives and cars on tracks used to move the ore to the shaft elevators.

Ores with a low sulfur content are more suitable for smelting. Formerly, only ores containing more than 30 percent iron could be smelted profitably, but because of various upgrading processes lower grade ores can now be used. The value of an ore deposit depends on geographic location and accessibility.

Upgrading ores (beneficiation). As the high-grade deposits became more inaccessible or exhausted and as shipping costs increased, it became necessary to separate and discard unusable materials from the iron ores at, or near, the mines. Processes broadly termed beneficiation were developed to upgrade the ore before shipment. Concentration or other preparation of ores is accomplished by

Flotation

leaching and drying, flotation, agglomeration, or magnetic separation. Flotation is an ore-dressing process by which finely pulverized ore is agitated in a mixture of oil and water. Constituent minerals are separated from one another by virtue of their respective abilities to be wetted by water and by their specific gravities. Agglomeration is a concentration process based on making large particles out of smaller particles. Magnetic separation, widely used to separate magnetic material from nonmagnetic, is especially effective in the beneficiation of iron ores.

Sintering. In order to prepare or pre-reduce ore further, sintering and pelletizing were developed. The sintering process is used mainly with fine iron ore that would not be suitable for blast furnace reduction because it would pack too closely to allow counterflow of gases. The fine grains are mixed with coke and ignited, producing semifused lumps that are satisfactory for smelting. Most sintering is done at blast-furnace plants.

Pelletizing. Pelletizing on a commercial scale was begun in the mid-1950s. In this process, iron ore concentrates are ground to powder, mixed with a binder such as bentonite and a small amount of water, and fed into a balling mill that forms the mixture into small biscuit-shaped pieces. These are baked to expel the moisture and to harden sufficiently to withstand shipment and subsequent handling up to the blast furnace. The pelletizing process is now completely automated in many places.

Again, because of the transportation costs, it has been found economical to locate the pelletizing plants at or near the mines. Self-fluxing pellets have been developed by mixing limestone or dolomite with the ore concentrate, an action that minimizes the amount of flux that must be added to the blast-furnace charge and lessens the amount of slag produced. In turn, the tonnage of iron produced by a blast furnace in a given period is increased.

An example of the progress that has been made in the beneficiation of low-grade ores located in inaccessible regions is the Savage River project in Tasmania. The iron-ore deposits there are in a rugged, almost impenetrable region in the northwestern corner of the island. The Savage River deposits, known by 1877, were reconnoitered many times but they defied economical exploitation. The ore is low grade, averaging 38 percent iron; it contains troublesome impurities, particularly titanium, and is locked in bands of rock in a remote, dense forest where average rainfall is more than 100 inches (2,540 millimetres) per year.

Finally, a study developed the feasibility of overcoming the titanium impurity by magnetic separation and by upgrading the low iron content to 67 percent for pelletizing. The remaining transportation problem, with the nearest accessible coast 53 miles away and with mountains and gorges between, was solved by a slurry pipeline. At Savage River a plant was built to crush the ore to powder, magnetically separate the iron-rich particles, and mix them into a slurry with a 40 percent water content that could be pumped to the coast through a nine-inch pipeline. Another plant was built on the coast to dry the ore concentrate and bake it into pellets. Finally, a mile-long jetty and conveyor were constructed to load ships. The operation produced a high of about 2,000,000 tons of pellets during the 1970s.

Pipeline slurry

ORE PROCESSING

Blast-furnace construction and operation. *Structural details.* A blast furnace is constructed from a steel shell lined with refractory brick that resists high temperatures. Spaced around the lower part of the furnace are water-cooled tuyeres (nozzles), usually copper castings, to introduce the air blast. The charge, called the burden, which is dumped into the top of the furnace, consists of alternate layers of charcoal or coke, raw ore, sinter or pellets, and flux. Ironmaking in a blast furnace is a continuous process, furnaces usually being shut down only for major repairs, such as relining with refractory. The modern furnace is some 80 to 100 feet (24 to 30 metres) high, with a hearth diameter of about 30 feet (9 metres).

At the bottom of the furnace is the hearth, built of graphite or refractory brick, which collects the molten iron as it drips down from the reduced ore. Progressing upward are the tuyere zone; the bosh zone (the region where iron and slag begin to melt), extending upward to the plane of maximum diameter; the mantle, or region immediately above, where iron and slag first begin to melt; and, finally, the stack. The stack houses the bells (cone-shaped inserts) that regulate the downward flow of the burden. From this section, the blast-furnace gas, produced by the partial combustion of the coke during the ore reduction, is piped off. Such gas is combustible, though of comparatively low heat value, and is used as a fuel for preheating the air blast.

To prevent spalling (chipping), the refractory brick furnace lining is cooled by a flow of cold water through hollow copper castings inserted at regular intervals.

Stoves

Adjacent to the furnace are stoves to preheat the air blast; these have steel shells, lined with refractory brickwork, and are fired with the blast-furnace gas and coke-oven gas from the coke plant The hot blast is piped into the furnace through the tuyeres.

Coke. A coke-making plant, usually included as part of a blast-furnace plant, produces coke strong enough to withstand the burden in the furnace and of sufficient size and porosity to leave openings for the upward passage of the gases. Because of the scarcity of bituminous coal suitable for making good coke, various methods have been tried for reducing the tonnage of coke required per ton of iron. The most common is to introduce a supplementary fuel through the tuyeres, which may be gas, fuel oil, or finely pulverized coal. In addition, the hot-air blast may be enriched by the addition of oxygen.

Operation. The molten iron is tapped from the blast furnace at regular intervals and the accumulation of slag is drawn off. The iron is either sent in large ladles directly to steel-making furnaces or is pigged (cast into ingots) and stored for later shipment to foundries.

Direct-reduction processes. Because of the high capital investment necessary for blast-furnace construction, many direct-reduction iron-making processes have been tried. By the early 1970s none had been successful in producing economically the tonnage levels of a modern blast furnace, but research continued under the added stimulus of problems of air and water pollution and the shortage of metallurgical coke for furnace operation. Two basic approaches offer promise of delivery to the foundry of hot iron of the proper composition and temperature for direct casting of gray, ductile, and malleable iron: these are the rotary kiln and the travelling grate.

Rotary kiln. A rotary kiln and solid-carbon fuel can prereduce ores that are in lump or pellet form. Rich ore lumps, 0.2–0.8 inch (5–20 millimetres) in size, or iron pellets 0.4–0.6 inch (10–15 millimetres) are fed into the rotary kiln, along with pieces of lump coal and flux about 10 millimetres in size. The temperature of the kiln is maintained at 1,050° to 1,100° C (1,922° to 2,012° F). Since the ore is prereduced, iron particles are produced that are approximately the same size as the charged ore or pellet particles. The product of this method is a molten high-carbon metal.

Problem of ore size

One major disadvantage of this process is that fine ores cannot be used. Other problems include the frequent shutdowns needed for maintenance, the degradation of the charge in the kiln, and the difficulty in maintaining carbon-to-oxygen ratio control.

Travelling grate. In the travelling-grate machine used for prereduction of the iron ore, carefully sized raw materials are not required. Fine ore, coal, and flux are proportioned and ground together. After filtering to remove water, the filter cake is formed into pellets about one inch (25 millimetres) in diameter, which are fed continuously onto the travelling grate machine. After drying, igniting, and carbonizing, the pellets are discharged at about 1,800° F (982° C) into a closed submerged electric-arc furnace and smelted to a controlled grade of high-carbon foundry iron.

In the commercial plant the composite pellets are ignited and carbonized, prereduced, and heated on the travelling grate in less than 20 minutes. Metallurgical control is obtained primarily by varying the proportioning of the raw materials. A major advantage of this process is its ability to use ore of any size and type. Another advantage is that the operation of the travelling-grate machine can be interrupted, whereas a kiln, to be economical, must be kept in constant operation.

Foundries. Throughout history, iron castings have been made by direct casting from smelting furnaces. During the past century or two, the direct casting of iron has given way to indirect methods in order to achieve more precise control.

Foundries remelt the iron either in cupolas or electric furnaces for the manufacture of castings. The most common product of the cupola is gray iron (an iron-carbon alloy containing two to four percent carbon), though the carbon content can be regulated and various metals, such as chromium, nickel, or magnesium, can be added in small quantities to yield mechanical and physical properties needed for specific uses.

The jobbing foundry. In a jobbing foundry that makes small numbers of castings of many different designs, patterns are usually made of wood. These are placed in boxes called flasks, and damp sand is rammed around them to make the molds. The surface must be such that the pattern can be withdrawn without damage to the mold. An opening, or gate, is cut in the mold for entry of the molten iron. Because of the shrinkage of the iron as it solidifies, other openings called risers often are left. These fill with molten iron that feeds down into the casting and prevents voids. When the castings are cooled, they are shaken out of the molds, and the gates and risers are cut off. The molding process, long a handcraft, is becoming more and more mechanized.

Casting molds

The production foundry. Production foundries are those that make hundreds of thousands of castings from the same pattern. Today these are often completely automated, and many of the processes such as molding-sand preparation, cupola charging, and iron pouring can be computer-controlled. Many castings are now made with permanent molds of iron or steel that can be used repeatedly, whereas a sand mold is destroyed when the casting is withdrawn from it.

Modern versions of the lost-wax (cire perdue) process, which consisted of making the patterns of wax, instead of wood or metal, have been developed. The process is reputed to have been discovered by the Sumerians early in the 3rd millennium BC, though some historians place the date earlier in China. Many fine metal works made by this process still survive. The wax patterns do not have to be withdrawn from the molds, since they melt and vaporize on contact with the molten metal. Hence, many complicated shapes can be cast.

The modern term for the lost-wax process is investment casting, and in addition to wax, the patterns are now being made from various volatilizable plastics.

IRON PRODUCTION

Wrought iron. Wrought iron is a form of iron containing less than 0.3 percent and usually less than 0.1 percent carbon, and carrying also 1.0 or 2.0 percent of slag mechanically mixed with it. Wrought iron finds product applications because of its inherent properties of ductility, ease of working, and welding, and superior resistance to service conditions involving corrosion, shock, and fatigue.

Catalan forge. The Catalan forge, which originated about 1300 in Catalonia, Spain, represented a major advance in the manufacture of wrought iron directly from ore. This forge has a siliceous bottom lined with charcoal, with a tuyere inclining downward. The front of the forge is piled with ore and the back with charcoal, the whole being covered with fine mixed ore and charcoal dust, moistened with water.

Puddling. In the 18th century, Henry Cort, in England, invented what is known as the puddling process, still in use. Pig iron is melted in a furnace with iron ore added. The operation is carried out in an oxidizing atmosphere in which silicon, manganese, sulfur, and part of the phosphorus are oxidized and removed in the slag. The temperature is then raised, promoting interaction between the iron oxide and carbon. Carbon monoxide is evolved, causing violent boiling of the charge, which is then worked with a rabble, or rake. As the iron becomes purer, it no longer remains liquid at the working temperature and the entire mass becomes pasty and is separated into portions and hammered and rolled into shapes.

Working with rabble

Table 4: Simple Visual Tests for Identifying Irons

	white cast iron	gray cast iron	malleable iron	wrought iron
Fracture	very fine, silvery white, silky crystalline formation	dark gray	dark gray	bright gray
Unfinished surface	evidence of mold; dull gray	very dull gray	dull gray	light gray, smooth
Newly machined surface	rarely machined	fairly smooth, light gray	smooth surface, light gray	very smooth surface, light gray
Appearance of chips	small broken fragments	partially broken chips but smooth groove	chips do not break short	smooth edges where cut
Size of chips	—	⅛ in.	¼–⅜ in. (0.6–1.0 cm)	continuous
Speed of melting	moderate	moderate	moderate	fast
Colour change while heating	dull red before melting	dull red before melting	red before melting	bright red before melting
Appearance of molten metal	fluid and watery; reddish white	fluid and watery; reddish white	fluid and watery; straw colour	liquid; straw colour

Cast iron. Cast iron is a generic term describing a family of iron alloys containing 1.8 to 4.5 percent carbon. These alloys are usually made into specified shapes for direct use or for further processing by machining or heat treating.

Gray iron. Gray iron covers a wide range of basically iron–carbon alloys containing 2 to 4 percent carbon, in which nearly all the carbon not included in pearlite (an aggregate of ferrite, which is a salt of a ferric hydroxide acting in its capacity of an acid, and cementite, which is iron carbide, Fe_3C) is present as graphitic carbon. Gray iron is produced from pig iron and scrap, or from scrap iron alone. In modern practice, it is customarily melted in a hot-blast cupola, which is supplied with heated air blast as in blast-furnace practice. Various additives to enhance its properties may be introduced into the cupola, after the iron is molten, or into the ladle, before pouring it into molds.

Because of the presence of graphite, the fracture has a gray colour. Gray irons are the most widely used of the cast irons because of their relatively low cost, ease of melting, and excellent casting characteristics.

The engineering properties of gray cast iron took on even greater significance in the 1960s and early 1970s. From simply being a material that was inexpensive, easy to cast, and readily machinable, gray iron has become an important engineering material whose composition, structure, and physical and mechanical properties can be carefully controlled to obtain the best combination of strength and service. While certain mechanical properties, such as tensile strength, improve to a moderate extent by natural aging, heat treatment—followed by quenching and tempering—accomplishes much better results in a few hours. For applications involving wear, such as in machine beds, the wearing surface is now commonly hardened by flame or induction heating.

Technical developments in founding have permitted considerable reduction in machining allowances in finished castings, and they are now produced with a much greater prospect of complete soundness.

White iron. White iron, also named for its fracture colour, contains practically all its carbon in combined forms as cementite (iron carbide, Fe_3C) and pearlite. Low silicon content is usually required, and such stabilizing elements as chromium are added when white iron is to be used in the "as cast" condition. It is frequently alloyed with nickel and chromium for applications involving wear resistance. It is extremely hard, difficult to machine, and not malleable at any temperature.

Ductile, nodular, or spheroidal graphite cast irons. In these variously named cast irons the graphite is transformed from the long, thin flakes typical of gray iron into discrete spheroids. Spheroidal graphite structure can be produced by adding either cerium or magnesium. In both cases, the addition of the nodularizing agent is followed by the addition of ferrosilicon. Spheroidal graphite iron possesses the advantages of superior strength and impact resistance.

Malleable cast iron. Malleable cast iron is a cast iron made by a prolonged anneal of white cast iron in which decarburization (removal of carbon) or graphitization (conversion into graphite), or both, takes place to eliminate some, or all, of the cementite. The graphite is in the form of temper carbon (clusters of finely divided graphite). If decarburization is the predominant reaction, the product, when fractured, shows a light colour, and is called whiteheart malleable; otherwise, the fracture is dark, and the iron is called blackheart malleable.

Alloys. Iron alloys can be grouped by their commercial applications as magnetic alloys, electrical-resistance alloys, heat-resisting alloys, corrosion-resisting alloys, and thermal-expansion alloys.

Magnetic alloys. Magnetic alloys may be classified in accordance with their magnetic properties as soft, or nonretentive of magnetism, and hard, or retentive. The soft alloys range from cast iron, the most retentive, to the iron–nickel alloys, the least retentive. These alloys find widest application in communications and electric-power equipment. Some possess certain properties that make them peculiarly suited for specific applications. The magnetic properties of the alloy containing about 70 percent iron and 30 percent nickel, for example, vary with the temperature. This alloy is used in shunts in electrical and other instruments to compensate for ambient temperature variations. Although the soft alloys generally are used as solid metals, they are sometimes employed in a finely divided condition for inductance cores in telephone and radio-frequency circuits where they minimize eddy-current losses.

Hard alloys

The hard, or retentive, alloys, which remain magnetized after application of a magnetic field, are used in applications in which a constant magnetic field is required but in which it is impractical to establish an electromagnetic field, as in electrical measuring instruments. Hard iron alloys may be made from cast or wrought iron or prepared from powder by sintering.

Electrical-resistance alloys. The electrical-resistance iron alloys are best known for their use as heating elements in radiant heaters, electric ranges, and toasters. Of a number of iron-containing alloys that find wide application in this field, the most popular contain, in addition to the iron, 60 percent nickel and 16 percent chromium; 38 percent nickel and 19 percent chromium; and 22 percent chromium, 5 percent aluminum, and 1 percent cobalt.

High-temperature alloys. In the choice of iron alloys for high-temperature service, the material not only must retain substantially its original identity in the atmosphere and at the temperature of operation, but it must also possess sufficient strength and shock resistance to meet service requirements. The high-temperature alloys are broadly classified as iron-base, cobalt-base, or nickel-base, depending upon the predominant element, but all contain some iron. They are mainly used for turbine blades and components in exhaust superchargers in aircraft engines.

Corrosion-resisting alloys. The term corrosion resisting, as generally used for alloys, means the resistance to corrosion attack by liquids and gases other than air or oxygen. The intensity of such attack is dependent on several factors, such as the alloy concerned, the particular corrosion medium under consideration, its concentration, and the oxidizing or reducing conditions. A large number of the alloys considered corrosion resistant contain iron in amounts varying from 2 percent to over 50 percent. Nickel and chromium are common constituents, together with additions of molybdenum, cobalt, copper, tungsten, and silicon, or combinations of these.

Because of the several factors involved, no single alloy so far has been found that resists adequately all forms of corrosion. An iron alloy with 15 percent silicon, for example, is widely used in vessels for handling many alkalies and acids but is quite unsatisfactory in resisting hydrochloric acid. With the addition of about 4 percent molybdenum, however, the same alloy resists this acid. Many corrosion-resistant alloys are also heat resistant, and the borderline between the two groups is not clearly drawn.

Thermal-expansion alloys. A group of iron-containing alloys has uniquely low thermal-expansion properties. Usually containing a high percentage of nickel, these alloys are used in rods and tapes for geodetic work, compensating pendulums, balance wheels in clocks and watches, and in delicate instruments.

Bimetals

In these so-called bimetals, temperature change causes movement, which is the basis of applications in thermal switches and temperature regulators. In one example, the low-expansion alloy contains approximately 45 percent iron, 52 percent nickel, with additives of titanium and aluminum. It is paired with a high-expansion alloy that contains 49.5 percent iron, 42 percent nickel, 5.5 percent chromium, and again additives of titanium and aluminum.

Thermal-expansion alloys are used in the manufacture of various types of vacuum tubes in which seals must be made between glass and metal. An alloy for this application must have an expansion curve similar to that of glass and must exhibit a high degree of resistance to thermal shock. An alloy possessing these properties is 54 percent iron, 29 percent nickel, and 17 percent cobalt.

Powdered iron. In powder metallurgy—a relatively new process that is growing in importance—iron powder, pulverized to talcum-powder fineness, is used pure or mixed with other metals or nonmetals to form alloys. The process permits alloy proportions that would not be possible using conventional means.

The iron or iron mixture is combined with a binder and pressed in dies or metal molds into desired shapes and sintered. The resulting alloy can be rolled into sheet or drawn into wire. Most importantly, complicated shapes can be formed to very accurate dimensions. Such shapes have good surface characteristics and require little, if any, machining. The physical and mechanical properties of powdered-iron products, in most cases, equal those of castings.

Iron compound applications. In addition to its alloys, iron forms many useful compounds. Some of these are among the naturally occurring compounds, such as ferrous phosphate, which occurs as the ore known as vivianite, and ferrous carbonate, which occurs naturally as spathic iron. The former is one of a number of compounds useful medically. Ferric ammonium citrate is used as an appetite stimulator. Ferrous gluconate, ferrous sulfate, and ferric pyrophosphate are among compounds used to treat anemia. Ferric salts, which act as coagulants, are applied to wounds to promote healing.

Many iron compounds are used industrially; for example, in abrasives, pigments, and magnetic tapes. Ferric carbide and ferrous carbonate have been widely used in the steel industry; ferrous carbonate was for some time a principal constituent of tool steels.

Iron compounds are also widely used in agriculture. For example, ferrous sulfate is applied in spray to acid-loving plants, and various other compounds are used as fungicides.

BIBLIOGRAPHY. The *McGraw-Hill Encyclopedia of Science and Technology*, revised about every four years, contains articles of interest on iron and steel at a fairly high technical level. Abstracts from technical periodicals, foreign as well as domestic, and engineering societies' proceedings and transactions may be found in *Engineering Index* (monthly). These abstracts include identification of sources and authors and therefore afford quick access to articles, papers, and lectures. *The Dictionary of Mining, Minerals and Related Terms*, issued by the UNITED STATES BUREAU OF MINES (1968, revised periodically), provides definitions of terms used in iron mining and processing.

(H.A.W.)

Irrawaddy River

Irrawaddy, the principal river of the Union of Burma and its most important commercial waterway, is about 1,300 miles (2,090 km) long. Its name is believed to have derived from the Hindu *airāvatī* meaning "elephant river." From its sources to its numerous mouths, the river flows wholly within Burmese territory. Its total drainage area is about 158,700 square miles. Its valley forms the historical, cultural, and economic heartland of the Union. The river is formed by the confluence of the Nmai Hka and the Mali Hka (*hka* being the Kachin word for river). Both branches rise in the glaciers of the high and remote mountains in northern Burma in the vicinity of 28° north. The eastern branch, the Nmai, rises in the Languela glacier and has the greater volume of water but is virtually unnavigable because of its strong current. The Mali, the western branch, has a gentler gradient and, although interrupted by rapids, has some navigable sections.

Course of the river. About 30 miles south of the confluence is Myitkyina, the point of the northernmost limit of seasonal navigation by the Irrawaddy steamers. Bhamo, about 150 miles south of the confluence, marks the northern limit for year-round navigation. Between the confluence and Bhamo, the width of the river during the low-water season varies between a quarter of a mile and half a mile. The depth of the main channel averages about 30 feet.

Between Myitkyina and Mandalay, the Irrawaddy flows through three well-marked defiles (narrow passages or gorges). Just south of Sinbo the river enters the upper, or third, defile—a navigational hazard, with a channel only 50 yards wide at its narrowest. Below Bhamo the river makes a sharp westward swing, leaving the Bhamo alluvial basin to cut through the cretaceous limestone rocks of the second defile. The second defile is about 300 feet wide at its narrowest and is flanked by vertical cliffs about 200 to 300 feet high. South of Thabeikkyin the river enters the first defile, which is broader and easier to navigate. Between Katha and Mandalay, the course of the river is remarkably straight, flowing almost due south, except near Kabwet, where a sheet of lava has caused the river to bend sharply westward. Leaving the first defile at Kyaukmyaung, in the Shwebo District, the river follows a broad, open course through the Dry Zone—the ancient cultural heartland—where large areas consist of alluvial flats. From Mandalay, formerly the capital of Upper Burma, the river makes an abrupt westward turn before curving southwest to unite with the Chindwin River in the Pakokku District, after which it continues in a southwesterly direction. It is probable that the upper Irrawaddy originally flowed south from Mandalay, discharging its water through the present Sittang River to the Gulf of Martaban, and that its present westward course is geologically recent. After its confluence with the Chindwin, the Irrawaddy continues to meander through the densely populated Dry Zone to the vicinity of Yenangyaung, after which it flows generally south. In its lower course, between Minbu and Prome, it flows through a narrow valley between forest-covered mountain ranges—the Arakan Yoma ridge to the west and the Pegu Yoma ridge to the east.

The delta of the Irrawaddy may be said to begin about 58 miles above Henzada. The apex of the delta is about 180 miles from its curved base facing the Andaman Sea. The sides of the delta are formed by the southern extremities of the Pegu Yoma on the east and the Arakan Yoma on the west. The westernmost distributary of the delta is the Bassein River. The easternmost stream is the

Rangoon River, on the left bank of which the Burmese capital city of Rangoon is built. As the Rangoon River is only a minor channel, the flow of water is insufficient to prevent Rangoon Harbour from silting up, and dredging is consequently necessary.

Physical characteristics. The volume of the Irrawaddy and its tributaries fluctuates greatly through the year due to the monsoon rains, which occur between June and September. The rapid melting of glaciers during the summer adds still further to the volume. The average discharge of the river near the head of the delta varies between 82,000 and 1,152,000 cubic feet per second; the annual average discharge is 460,000 cubic feet per second. The range between high and low water is also great. Annual variations between low-water level and flood level of 31.7 feet and 37.3 feet have been recorded at Mandalay and Prome respectively. The lowest water level occurs in February, and the highest in August. In general, from December to March the river varies between the lowest level and five feet above it, while from mid-June to mid-October the river is 20 to 30 feet above the lowest level. The river ports therefore find it necessary to have separate high- and low-water landing points.

The river ports

Shipping, transportation, and commerce. The main river ports on the Irrawaddy, from north to south, are Myitkyina, Bhamo, Katha, Mandalay, Myingyan, Chauk, Yenangyaung, Minbu, Magwe, Thayetmyo, Prome, Henzada, and Yandoon. Of these, Mandalay, Chauk, Prome, and Henzada have good landing facilities. The remaining ports have landing facilities for only one or two barges or lighters—the vessels mooring alongside the riverbank in most places. Despite the fact that Mandalay is the chief rail and highway focus in upper Burma, a considerable amount of passenger and goods traffic moves by river. The Chindwin valley has no railroad and relies heavily on river transport. Chauk, downstream from the confluence in the oil-field district, is a petroleum port. Prome, about 140 miles to the south, is linked to Rangoon by road and rail. Henzada, near the apex of the delta, is the rail junction for lines leading to Kyangin and Bassein. A ferry operates between Henzada on the west bank and the railway station at Tharrawaw on the east.

Regular steamer service on the Irrawaddy is maintained by the Inland Water Transport Board (IWTB), which has improved service by introducing diesel engines in place of coal-fired ones. Commercial transportation is maintained for about 800 miles. From Henzada to Bhamo (670 miles), commercial traffic is maintained throughout the year, but from Bhamo to Myitkyina (125 miles), for only seven months. Over 2,000 miles of navigable waterways exist in the Irrawaddy delta. On the Chindwin River transportation is carried on by steam or diesel vessels throughout the year up to Homalin—about 400 miles from its confluence with the Irrawaddy. Seasonal navigation is carried on into Tamanthi, which is 57 (river) miles above Homalin.

As the Irrawaddy delta is one of the world's major rice-growing areas, rice is a major item of commerce on the river. Also transported are other foodstuffs, petroleum, cotton, and local commodities. Teak logs—of which Burma is the world's major exporter—are floated downstream in the form of large rafts. In the delta region, the rice is carried in small country boats to local markets, from where it is shipped to Rangoon for export.

The Irrawaddy is crossed by only a single bridge—the Ava Bridge, which spans the river below Mandalay.

People of the river. The peoples living on the river's banks are culturally diverse. On the upper reaches, the Kachins, who practice shifting agriculture, predominate. In the river valley itself, the Burmans are the dominant group, cultivating wheat, cotton, and oilseeds in the Dry Zone, and rice to the south and in the delta region, where rainfall is more plentiful. Also to the south, and particularly in the delta proper, a considerable minority of Karens and some Indians are to be found among the Burman majority.

Irrigation. While the Irrawaddy has been little used for irrigation in the Dry Zone, its tributary, the Mu River, has been used for this purpose since the 9th century. The current Mu Valley Irrigation Project, financially supported by the UN Development Programme, is the largest in the country, and is ultimately intended to irrigate over 1,000,000 acres. It will permit the dry-season cropping of maize (corn), groundnuts (peanuts), sesame, millet, and other dry crops. If the Irrawaddy and Chindwin waters were also to be utilized, it is estimated that a further 2,800,000 acres might be brought into production.

The soils of the delta are enriched every year by the fertile alluvium carried down by the river. The river waters themselves are used to flood the delta rice paddies. "Irrawaddy" is also the name of an administrative division of the delta, which includes the districts of Bassein, Henzada, Ma-ubin, Myaungmya, and Pyapon.

BIBLIOGRAPHY. BURMA (UNION), ECONOMIC AND SOCIAL BOARD, *Pyidawtha, the New Burma: A Report from the Government to the People of the Union of Burma on our Long-term Programme for Economic and Social Development* (1954), a useful general source on development policy; H.L. CHHIBBER, *The Geology of Burma* (1935), a basic work on geology and the river system; D.W. FRYER, *Emerging Southeast Asia: A Study in Growth and Stagnation*, ch. 8 (1970), a chapter on Burma and an irrigation and transport map; L.D. STAMP, "The Irrawaddy River," *Geogrl. J.*, 95:329–352 (1940), an authoritative and detailed article; KNAPPEN–TIPPETTS–ABBETT–MCCARTHY, *Economic and Engineering Development of Burma* (1953), a comprehensive report assessing Burma's resources, with a chapter on inland waterways.

(S.M.B.)

Irrigation and Drainage

Irrigation is the artificial application of water to land. Drainage is the artificial removal of excess water from land. Though either practice may be, and both often are, used for nonagricultural purposes to improve the environment, this article is limited to their major application, to agriculture. Some land requires irrigation or drainage before it is possible to use it for any agricultural production; other land profits from either practice to increase agricultural production. Some land, of course, does not need either practice.

Irrigation and drainage improvements are not necessarily mutually exclusive. Often both may be required together to assure sustained, high-level production of crops.

This article will review the history of the development of these practices, the planning and construction of present-day systems, and the general scope of these practices in the world.

HISTORY

Irrigation. Prehistoric tablets and carvings indicate that early civilizations developed along rivers that supplied irrigation water to the fields. Although no one really knows when or where irrigation originated, it is reasonably clear that the Egyptians used water from the Nile to irrigate adjacent fields as early as 5000 BC. Records show that King Menes, who lived around 3100 BC, had a large masonry dam built to control the Nile River and provide water for irrigation. A millennium later, the Nile at flood was diverted through a 12-mile- (19-kilometre-) long channel into Lake Moeris, so that after the flood, water in the lake could be released for irrigation.

Babylonian irrigation system

The ancient Babylonians developed a flourishing civilization based on an irrigation agriculture. Discoveries in ancient Babylonian ruins in Iraq reveal that irrigation works were in use before the time of King Hammurabi, about 2200 BC, and Hammurabi is known to have caused a major irrigation canal to be constructed and to have issued regulations governing the maintenance and operation of irrigation ditches.

It is believed to be likely that the practice of irrigation spread to China from Babylonia. The Chinese are known to have had irrigation before 2200 BC. Famous Chinese irrigation works include the Tu-kiang Dam, built about 200 BC, which provided water for about 500,000 acres (200,000 hectares), and the 700-mile- (1,100-kilometre-) long Grand, or Imperial, Canal built AD 589–618.

To the west of Babylonia, the Phoenicians became skilled irrigators before 1500 BC and were probably responsible for the spread of irrigation along the southern shores of the Mediterranean, through their maritime trading.

Irrigation in ancient Peru

In the Western Hemisphere, too, irrigation was practiced at an early date. The Peruvians built elaborate irrigation works in the Pisco Valley before the time of Christ. In Mexico, Hernán Cortés found an ancient agricultural civilization based upon extensive and skillful irrigation. In North America, archaeologists have uncovered a system of reservoirs and canals in what is now the southwest United States that is believed to be 2,000 years old. From ruins it has been estimated that more than 250,000 acres of land in the Salt River Valley of Arizona were irrigated by about 1,000 miles (1,600 kilometres) of canals and ditches.

Ancient systems, structures, and devices. It is possible that irrigation started when prehistoric man planted crops in low areas that trapped floodwaters. From this may have emerged the idea of building a bank around an entire field so that floodwaters could be trapped and permitted to soak into the soil. This practice ultimately led to the development of basin irrigation, which is known to have existed in ancient Egypt and China.

In the basin system, large areas were enclosed by earthen banks; floodwaters were carried into the basin by canals. Main canals carried the water from a river. Distribution canals fed the water from the main canals into the basins. On flat floodplains, the water moved slowly and spread easily over large areas, whereas in mountainous areas elaborate systems of terraces were built to control the water. After the soil was thoroughly soaked, the excess water was drained off and crops that would be able to grow without further water were sown. Because the basin system depended on floodwaters to fill the canals, the fields could be irrigated only during flood times (see Figure 1).

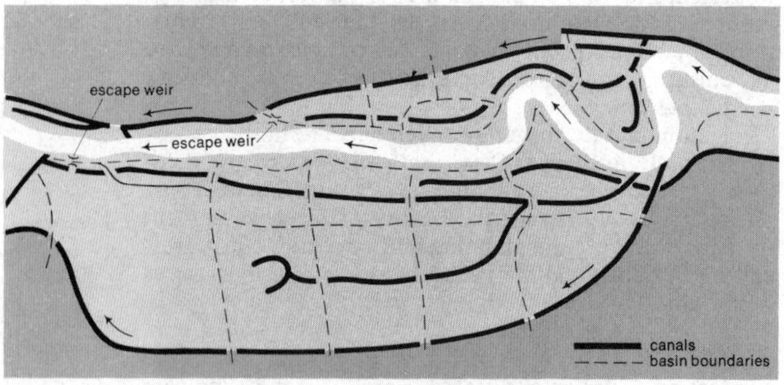

Figure 1: Basin system of irrigation.

Eventually, the realization that water was needed for crops after the beginning of the growing season led to the development of lifting devices and storage reservoirs. Lifting techniques were developed, beginning with the one-man scoop and progressing to counterweighted and animal-powered devices and to the portable Archimedes screw (see WATERWHEEL).

Minneriya tank

Reservoirs were developed in many ancient civilizations; one of the earliest was the tank, or jheel, of India and Ceylon, some of which were extraordinarily large. The Minneriya tank in Ceylon, built in AD 900, had surface dimensions of six miles (ten kilometres) by two miles (three kilometres) and a capacity of 66,000 acre-feet (81,410,000 cubic metres) of water. An acre-foot is the amount of water necessary to cover an acre (43,560 square feet or 4,047 square metres) to a depth of one foot (305 millimetres).

The Persians developed underground sources of water by digging tunnels, or *kanats*, into the hills, often several hundred feet below the surface and as much as 12 miles (19 kilometres) long. It is estimated that over 20,000 *kanats* are still in operation today.

Perennial irrigation developed with the spread of lifting devices and stored water supplies. The new system, more costly than the basin system, was also more flexible and dependable. The canal network did not greatly differ from that of canals for a basin system. A more extensive system of branch canals was needed because the water was distributed throughout the entire area to be irrigated, rather than having the area flooded at a time of high water.

Drainage. The practice of land drainage is also ancient but was evidently viewed as less important than irrigation. At any rate much less is recorded about its early history. The 5th-century-BC Greek historian Herodotus referred to drainage in the Nile Valley, and 200 years later in Rome, Cato the Elder described drainage practices as they were applied in Eastern countries. A later Roman writer, Varro, in his book *On Agriculture*, recorded some of the earliest instructions for constructing drains.

The first drains probably were ditches or canals built to carry floodwaters back to the rivers. Ancient improvements on individual farms consisted of the placing of stones, gravel, logs, and roots and other organic matter in trenches and covering them up. The first known use of tile for drainage was in 1620 in France. Almost 200 years passed before tile was used in England, and it appeared in the United States only in 1835. The basic materials and practices have changed little since then.

A major change in drainage techniques was introduced in the United States after World War II. Equipment that had been used to smooth land for surface irrigation was brought into humid areas to grade land so that it would drain uniformly. The success of the experiment stimulated widespread interest in surface drainage, particularly for soils with slow interval water movement; that is, soils of low permeability.

Multipurpose improvements. For centuries land-reclamation projects were built with the sole objective of irrigation. Similarly, drainage projects were for drainage only. The Boulder Canyon Project in the United States in 1928, whereas it did not actually combine irrigation and drainage goals, represented the first step toward the aim of total water development in a river basin, a goal actively pursued all over the world in the 1950s and 1960s. The objectives of basin projects today in the United States, Soviet Union, People's Republic of China, Africa, and Europe include irrigation, drainage, flood control, public water supply, power generation, navigation, sediment control, salinity control, sanitation, recreation, and fish and wildlife conservation. While it is not possible to achieve all of these objectives in one project, all are usually considered in planning, in which, for example, the low water level desirable for flood-control reservoirs must be balanced against the full level required for water-supply reservoirs.

MODERN IRRIGATION-SYSTEM PLANNING AND CONSTRUCTION

Water supply. The first consideration in planning an irrigation project is developing a water supply. Water supplies may be classified as surface or subsurface. Though both surface and subsurface water come from precipitation such as rain or snow, it is far more difficult to determine the origin of subsurface water.

Studying stream-flow

In planning a surface water supply, extensive studies must be made of the flow in the stream or river that will be used. If the streamflow has been measured regularly over a long period, including times of drought and flood, the studies are greatly simplified. From streamflow data, determinations can be made of the minimum, maximum, average daily, and average monthly flows; the size of dams, spillways, and downstream channel; and the seasonal and carry-over storage needed. If adequate streamflow data are not available, the streamflow may be estimated from rain and snow data, or from flow data from nearby streams that have similar climatic and physiographic conditions.

The quality, as well as the quantity, of surface water is a factor. The two most important considerations are the amount of silt carried and the kind and amount of salts dissolved in the water. If the silt content is high, sediment will be deposited in the reservoir, increasing maintenance costs and decreasing useful life periods. If the salt con-

One of the modern concrete-lined canals of the Israel National Water Carrier that carries water from Lake Tiberias in the north to the Negev, the arid lands of the south.
Riwkin—Pix

centration is high, it may damage crops or accumulate in the soil and eventually render it unproductive.

Subsurface sources of water must be as carefully investigated as surface sources. In general, less is known about subsurface supplies of water than about surface supplies, so, therefore, subsurface supplies are harder to investigate. Engineers planning a project need to know the extent of the basic geological source of water (the aquifer), as well as the amount the water level is lowered by pumping and the rate of recharge of the aquifer. Often the only way for the engineer to obtain these data reliably is to drill test wells and make onsite measurements. Usually, a project is planned so as not to use more subsurface water than is recharged. Otherwise, the water is said to be "mined," meaning that as a natural resource it is being used up.

Two sources of water not often thought of by the layman are dew and sewage. In certain parts of the world, Israel and part of Australia, for example, where atmospheric conditions are right, sufficient dew may be trapped at night to provide water for irrigation. Elsewhere the supply of waste water from some industries and municipalities is sufficient to irrigate relatively small acreages. Recently, due to greater emphasis on purer water in streams, there has been increased interest in this latter practice.

Determining water rights

Before a water supply can be assured, the right to it must be determined. Countries and states have widely varying laws and customs that determine ownership of water. If the development of a water supply is for a single purpose, then the determination of ownership may be relatively simple; but if the development is multipurpose, as most modern developments are, ownership may be difficult to determine, and agreements must be worked out among countries, states, municipalities, and private owners.

The area that can be irrigated by a water supply depends on the weather, the type of crop grown, and the soil. Numerous methods have been developed to evaluate these factors and predict average annual volume of rainfall needed. Some representative annual amounts of rainfall needed for cropland in the western United States are 12 to 30 inches (305 to 760 millimetres) for grain and 24 to 60 inches (600 to 1,525 millimetres) for forage. In the Near East, cotton needs about 36 inches (915 millimetres), whereas rice may require two to three times that amount. In humid regions of the United States, where irrigation supplements rainfall, grain crops may require six to nine inches (150 to 230 millimetres) of water. In addition to satisfying the needs of the crop, allowances must be made for water lost directly to evaporation and during transport to the fields.

Transport systems. The type of transport system used for an irrigation project is often determined by the source of the water supply. If a surface water supply is used, a large canal or pipeline system is usually required to carry the water to the farms because the reservoir is likely to be distant from the point of use. If subsurface water drawn from wells is used, a much smaller transport system is needed, though canals or pipelines may be used. The transport system will depend as far as possible on gravity flow, supplemented if necessary by pumping. From the mains, water flows into branches, or laterals, and finally to distributors that serve groups of farms. Many auxiliary structures are required, including weirs (flow-diversion dams), sluices, and other types of dams. Canals are normally lined with concrete to prevent seepage losses, control weed growth, eliminate erosion hazards, and reduce maintenance. The most common type of concrete canal construction is by slip forming. In this type of construction, the canal is excavated to the exact cross section desired and the concrete placed on the earth sides and bottom.

Water pipelines

Pipelines may be constructed of many types of material. The larger lines are usually concrete whereas laterals may be concrete, cement–asbestos, rigid plastic, aluminum, or steel. Although pipelines are more costly than open conduits, they do not require land after construction, suffer little evaporation loss, and are not troubled by algae growth.

Water application. After water reaches the farm it may be applied by surface, subsurface, or sprinkler-irrigation methods. Surface irrigation is normally used only where the land has been graded so that uniform slopes exist (see Figure 2). Land grading is not necessary for other methods. Each method includes several variations, only the more common of which are considered here.

Surface irrigation systems are usually classed as either flood or furrow systems. In the flood system, water is applied at the edge of a field and allowed to move over the entire surface to the opposite side of the field. Grain and forage crops are quite often irrigated by flood techniques. The furrow system is used for row crops such as corn, cotton, sugar beets, and potatoes. Furrows are plowed between crop rows and the water is run in the furrows. In either type of surface irrigation systems, waste-water ditches at the lower edge of the fields permit excess water to be removed for use elsewhere and to prevent waterlogging.

Subirrigation is a less common method. An impermeable layer must be located below, but near, the root zone of the crop so that water is trapped in the root zone. If this condition exists, water is applied to the soil through tile drains or ditches.

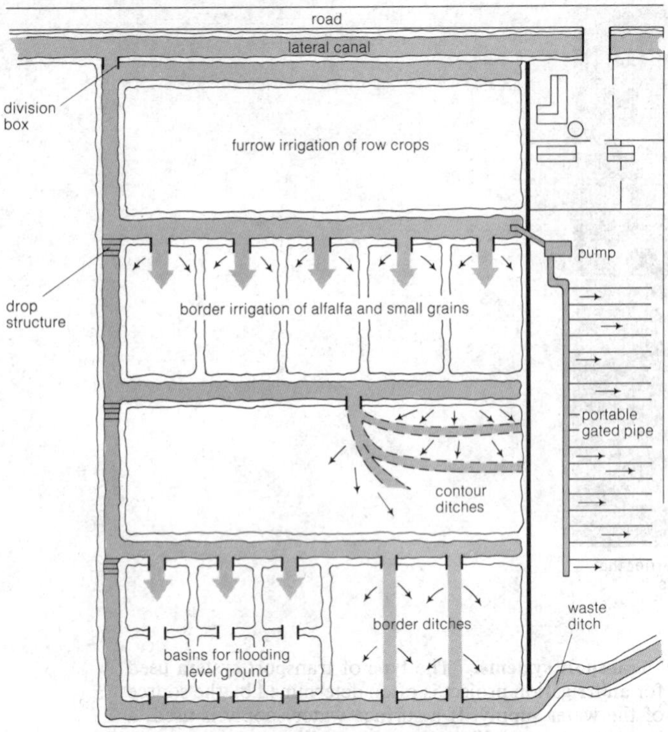

Figure 2: Surface methods of applying irrigation water to field crops.
By courtesy of U.S. Soil Conservation Service

In recent years sprinklers have been used increasingly to irrigate agricultural land. Little or no preparation is needed, application rates can be controlled, and the system may be used for frost protection and the application of chemicals. Sprinklers range from those that apply water in the form of a mist to those that apply an inch or more per hour.

Evaporation and seepage control. Various techniques have been tried to reduce losses of irrigation water. Two major sources of loss, particularly from surface supplies and surface systems, are evaporation and seepage from reservoirs and canals. Many studies have been made of techniques to suppress evaporation. One of the more promising appears to be application of a special alcohol film on the surface, which retards evaporation by about 30 percent and does not reduce the quality of the water. The primary problem in its use is that it is fragile; a strong wind can blow it apart and expose the water to evaporation.

Seepage has largely been controlled by lining main and distribution channels with impervious material, typically concrete. Other materials used are asphalt and plastic film, though plastic tends to deteriorate if it is exposed to sunlight.

In some countries, Egypt for example, sewage is a valuable source of water. In others, such as the United States, irrigation is looked upon as a means of disposing of sewer water as a final step in the waste-treatment process. Unless the water contains unusual chemical salts, such as sodium, it is generally of satisfactory quality for agricultural irrigation. Where the practice is used primarily as a means of disposal, large areas are involved and the choice of crop is critical. Usually only grass or trees can withstand the year-round applications.

Typical systems. The typical surface irrigation system utilizes a publicly developed water supply—*e.g.*, a river-basin reservoir. The public project also constructs the main canals to take water from the reservoir to the agricultural land. In general the canals flow by gravity, but lift stations are often required. Supply and field canals are used to bring the water to the individual field, where it is applied to the land either by furrow or by flooding method.

Sprinkler irrigation

Until recently most sprinkler-irrigation systems depended on privately developed water supplies, but many modern sprinkler systems have been able to draw on public water supplies. In either case, a pump is required to pump water from a large (1,000 gallons, or 3,785 litres, per minute and larger) well or a supply canal. The water goes into the system main and thence to a sprinkler unit. Many automatic or semiautomatic moving sprinkler systems travel over the field applying water. Two common units are the so-called centre pivot and the travelling sprinkler. The centre-pivot unit is anchored at the centre of the field; a long lateral (arm) with sprinklers mounted on it sweeps the field in a circle. The system has the disadvantage of missing the corners of a square field. A travelling sprinkler is mounted on a trailer and propelled across the field in a lane that has been left unplanted. The unit drags a flexible hose connected to the main supply line. When it reaches the end of the lane, it is automatically shut off and can be moved to the next lane. Despite some shortcomings, all sprinkler systems are effective in applying a controlled amount of water at a high level of efficiency with a minimum of labour.

MODERN DRAINAGE-SYSTEM PLANNING AND CONSTRUCTION

Planning a system. The planning and design of drainage systems is not an exact science. Although there have been many advances in soil and crop science, techniques have not been developed for combining the basic principles involved into precise designs. One of the primary reasons for difficulty in applying known theory is the capricious variability of natural soil in contrast to the idealized soils required to develop a theory.

The type of drainage system designed depends on many factors, but the most important is the type of soil, which determines whether water will move through rapidly enough to use subsurface drainage. Soils that have a high percentage of sand- and silt-size particles and a low percentage of clay-size particles usually will transmit water rapidly enough to make subsurface drainage feasible. Soils that are high in clay-size particles usually cannot be drained by subsurface improvements. It is essential to consider soil properties to a depth of five to six feet (1.5 to 1.8 metres) because the layer in the soil that transmits water the slowest controls the design, and subsurface improvements may be installed to these depths.

The topography or slope of the land is also important. In many cases, land in need of drainage is so flat that a contour map showing elevations one foot (300 millimetres) or 0.5 foot (150 millimetres) apart is used to identify trouble spots and possible outlets for drainage water. Often an outlet can be developed only by collective community action. The rainfall patterns, the crops to be grown, and the normal height of the water table are also considered. If heavy rainfall is not probable during critical stages of crop growth, less extensive drainage improvements may suffice. The capacity of the system is governed in part by the growth pattern of the crop, its planting date, critical stages of growth, tolerance of excess water, harvest date, and value.

In some areas the normal water level in the soil is high, in others low; this variable is always investigated before a drainage system is planned.

Types of drainage systems. Drainage systems may be divided into two categories, surface and subsurface. Each has several components with similar functions but different names. At the lower, or disposal, end of either system is an outlet. In order of decreasing size, the components of a surface system are the main collection ditch, field ditch, and field drain; and for a subsurface system, main, submain, and lateral conduits from the submain. The outlet is the point of disposal of water from the system; the main carries water to the outlet; the submain or field ditch collects water from a number of smaller units and carries it to the main; and the lateral or field drain, the smallest unit of the system, removes the water from the soil.

Drainage system outlet

The outlet for a drainage system may be a natural stream or river or a large constructed ditch. A constructed ditch usually is trapezoidal in section with side banks flat enough to be stable. Grass may be grown on the banks, which are kept clear of trees and brush that would interfere with the flow of water.

A surface drainage system removes water from the surface of the soil and to approximately the bottom of the field ditches. A surface system is the only means for drainage improvement on soils that transmit water slowly. Individual surface drains are also used to supplement subsurface systems by removing water from ponded areas.

The field drains of a surface system may be arranged in many patterns. Probably the two most widely used are parallel drains and random drains. Parallel drains are channels running parallel to one another at a uniform spacing of a few to several hundred feet apart, depending on the soil and the slope of the land. Random drains are channels that run to any low areas in the field. The parallel system provides uniform drainage, whereas the random system drains only the low areas connected by channels. In either case, the channels are shallow with flat sides and may be farmed like the rest of the field. Crops are usually planted perpendicular to the channels so that the water flows between the rows to the channels.

Some land grading of the fields where surface drains are installed is usually essential for satisfactory functioning. Land grading is the shaping of the field so that the land slopes toward the drainage channels. The slope may be uniform over the entire field or it may vary from part to part. Before the advent of the digital computer, the calculations necessary for planning land grading were time-consuming, a factor that restricted the alternatives available for final design. Today, computers rapidly explore many possibilities before a final land grading design is selected.

In a subsurface drainage system, often called a tile system, all parts except the outlet are located below the surface of the ground. It provides better drainage than a surface system because it removes water from the soil to the depth of the drain, providing plants a greater mass of soil for root development, permitting the soil to warm up faster in the spring, and maintaining a better balance of bacterial action, the air in the soil, and other factors needed for maximum crop growth.

The smallest component of the subsurface system, the lateral, primarily removes water from the soil. The laterals may be arranged in either a uniform or a random pattern. The choice is governed by the crop grown and its value, the characteristics of the soil, and the precipitation pattern.

Depth of spacing of laterals

The primary decision required for a system with uniform laterals is their depth and spacing. In general, the deeper the laterals can be emplaced, the farther apart they can be spaced for an equivalent degree of drainage. Theoretical studies have shown that laterals can be spaced 24 feet (7.3 metres) apart for each foot of depth. Laterals usually are spaced from 80 to 300 feet (24 to 91 metres) apart and three to five feet (0.9 to 1.5 metres) deep.

Subsurface drainage systems are as important in many irrigated areas as they are in humid areas. A drainage system is needed on irrigated lands to control the water table and ensure that water will be able to move through a soil, thus keeping salts from accumulating in the root zone and making the soil unproductive.

Construction and maintenance. Most subsurface drains are constructed by excavating a trench, installing a tile, and backfilling the trench. Work is in progress in the United States and in Europe to develop machines that will install drain tubes without excavating the trench. Control of the machines to assure proper slope of the drain has been a major problem, but recent development in excavation technology, including the use of laser beams for grade control, have helped to solve it. Traditionally, clay or concrete tile has been the principal material used, but many types of perforated plastic tubes are now employed. An advantage is the reduction in weight of the material handled.

With proper maintenance, drainage systems give relatively long life. Selected herbicides are applied to keep woody growth and water weeds out of the channels. Grates are usually installed over outlets to prevent rodents and burrowing animals from building nests.

Surface drainage systems need almost yearly maintenance to assure the slope and cross section of the channels and the slope of the graded areas because the slopes are so flat that small changes in the ground surface can make marked changes in the ability of a system to function.

Subsurface systems need periodic inspection but usually require little servicing. The outlet of the system and infrequent structural failure of the material are the usual points for service.

LAND RECLAMATION THROUGH IRRIGATION AND DRAINAGE

The need for increased food and fibre production in the 1970s requires the continued development of new agricultural lands. Development of such land is rarely possible without irrigation or drainage systems or both. Easily recognized improvements are the large-scale river-basin projects designed for flood control, irrigation, and power generation. Such projects are in various stages of design or construction in many countries of the world —for example, the Soviet Union, the People's Republic of China, India, Egypt, Iran, Australia, and the United States. In almost all cases, drainage of the irrigated lands is considered a companion requirement. If possible, the drainage improvements are subsurface.

Reclaiming salty soils

A combination of drainage and irrigation is being used to reclaim large areas of land that have been abandoned because of salt accumulation. In this case subsurface drainage systems must be installed, so that high water tables are lowered and pure water flushed through the soil, dissolving the salts and carrying them away in the drainage water. Large areas in the United States, India, and the Near East are potentially available for reclamation by this technique.

The people of The Netherlands have reclaimed land from the sea by the use of drainage. Since the IJsselmeer (formerly Zuiderzee) barrier dam was closed in 1932, converting this large body of water into a freshwater lake, the Dutch have been continually enclosing and reclaiming smaller bodies (polders). After dikes are built around a polder, the area is drained by pumping out the water. Drainage channels and often subsurface drains are installed so that the root zone of crops is drained. After this, cropping is started as the last step in the reclamation process.

The development of land-clearing machinery and surface-drainage techniques has made it possible to clear and drain tropical lands for agricultural production. The first step is the removal of trees, brush, and other tropical growth. Outlet ditches are constructed, followed by drains. In some cases subsurface drains are possible, but more often the soils and rainfall conditions combine to make this improvement impractical. Surface drains are installed on a uniform pattern and the land is smoothed or graded. Drainage systems on newly reclaimed tropical land require special attention while the soils are stabilizing, and some reconstruction is often needed after the soil stabilization is complete.

IRRIGATION AND DRAINAGE THROUGHOUT THE WORLD

Although the Food and Agriculture Organization of the United Nations (FAO) keeps some statistics on irrigated lands, there are no precise, uniform data available on the scope of irrigation in the world. The United States Bureau of Reclamation estimates that in the entire world 385,000,000 acres (155,700,000 hectares) are irrigated. FAO data, supplied by each country, indicate that the largest areas under irrigation are located in the People's Republic of China, India, Pakistan, the Soviet Union, and the United States. A total of 118 countries reported some acreage under irrigation. The smallest area reported was 740 acres (300 hectares) in Barbados, and the largest was estimated as 183,000,000 acres (75,980,000 hectares) in the People's Republic of China. Asia, excluding the Soviet Union, irrigates approximately 73 percent of the total area of the world that is irrigated; most of this is the large surface-irrigated, rice-producing areas of the People's Republic of China, India, Pakistan, and Southeast Asia. The United States and the Soviet Union have about 8 and 5 percent, respectively, of the world's irrigated areas. Europe has about 5 percent, South America and Africa each about 3 percent, and Central America about 2 percent. The remaining 1 percent (or less) is mostly in Australia and New Zealand. Sprinkler irrigation is used throughout the world, but the largest acreage is the approximately 9,000,000 acres (3,640,000 hectares) in the United States.

Popperfoto

Inundation canals running from the Euphrates River, Iraq, that fill when the water level of the river rises.

Statistics on drainage improvements are sparser than statistics on irrigation. It may safely be said that drainage in one form or another is practiced in almost every country of the world. It is now universally accepted that drainage is needed as much on irrigated as on nonirrigated land. Countries such as India that have large-scale river-basin developments planned with irrigation also have companion drainage systems planned, so that the land will not be damaged by salt accumulation.

Some indication of the world picture may be gained from the last drainage census in the United States (1959), which showed that about 92,000,000 acres (37,200,000 hectares) were drained through organized projects, about 10 percent of the land in agriculture. A rule of thumb states that there is at least one acre of privately drained land for each acre in an organized project, indicating about 185,000,000 acres (75,000,000 hectares) of agricultural land drained in the United States at that time.

It is almost certain that the land area of the world improved by irrigation and drainage will continue to increase because these two practices are two of the most basic means of reclaiming and improving agricultural lands.

BIBLIOGRAPHY. L.M. CANTOR, *A World Geography of Irrigation* (1967), a general discussion of the development of irrigation followed by a detailed discussion of its current status by world geographical regions; R.M. HAGAN, H.R. HAISE, and T.W. EDMINSTER (eds.), *Irrigation of Agricultural Lands* (1967), a thorough, technical compilation of information on all aspects of irrigation, including soils, crops, climate, economics, and engineering; J.N. LUTHIN (ed.), *Drainage of Agricultural Lands* (1957), a thorough, technical compilation of information on all aspects of drainage, including soils, crops, economics, and engineering, and *Drainage Engineering* (1966), a recent text; A.R. GOLZE, *Reclamation in the United States* (1952), a general, nontechnical discussion of the evolution of reclamation in the United States as a result of the activities of the Bureau of Reclamation; provides concise factual history of project-by-project development.

(B.A.J.)

Irving Family

Stage family headed by Sir Henry Irving, who was the leading figure of the English-speaking stage during the final quarter of the 19th century. His theatrical company, based on the Lyceum Theatre in London, set a style of production that drew great acclaim from a wide section of the Victorian public; and his success brought him the first knighthood ever bestowed upon an English actor. This success was continued by his two actor sons.

Henry Irving. John Henry Brodribb was born on February 6, 1838, at Keinton Mandeville, Somerset. His father, Samuel Brodribb, was a salesman who collected orders for the tailoring department of the local store. His mother, Mary, was the daughter of a Cornish farming family. In 1842 Samuel found better employment in Bristol; and, rather than risk the child's health in the damp and dirt of the city, the parents decided to send their young son to Mary's sister, Sarah Penberthy, in Cornwall. For the next six years John was brought up by his aunt and her husband, Isaac, the captain of a Cornish tin mine at Halse Town near St. Ives. Growing up in Cornwall endowed John with a strong constitution. Cornish Methodism, to which his mother was a dedicated adherent, gave him his first taste of spell-binding oratory—the language of John Wesley. When Isaac died suddenly in 1848, Sarah could no longer carry responsibility for the child and returned him to his parents, who by this time had moved to London. There John attended Dr. Pinches' private school.

After leaving school he entered a merchant's office as a clerk, but his spare time and thoughts centred on the plays and players of the London theatre. In 1856 a Brodribb uncle gave him a legacy of £100, which he invested in theatrical necessities such as wigs, swords, and costumes. The legacy also allowed him to buy the leading part in an amateur production of *Romeo and Juliet* at the Royal Soho Theatre. As was the custom of the day, he adopted a stage name—Irving—his choice determined by the romances of Washington Irving and the evangelical sermons of the Scottish preacher Edward Irving. A warm reception of his performance gave him the encouragement he needed. He gave up clerking and joined a theatrical stock company in Sunderland in the north of England as a "walking gentleman" (*i.e.*, in non-speaking parts).

By courtesy of the National Portrait Gallery, London

Henry Irving, pencil sketch by Phil May, 1889. In the National Portrait Gallery, London.

The stock companies that travelled from town to town throughout England at this time constituted the only theatrical academy for a young aspiring actor. In three years Irving played more than 400 different parts in 330 plays, including most of the Shakespeare repertoire. This apprenticeship continued for ten years in the provincial towns of England, Scotland, and Ireland. His first success in London came in 1866 in a play called *Hunted Down*.

During a Dublin tour the following year he was introduced to Florence O'Callaghan, the daughter of a surgeon general; in July 1869 they were married. A leading part in a long-running comedy titled *Two Roses* sustained the young couple over the birth of their first son, Henry Brodribb, the following August; but a quarrel following the first night of *The Bells* precipitated a permanent separation a month before the birth of their second son, Laurence Sidney.

The Bells, staged by the American impressario H.L. Bateman at the Lyceum Theatre, was an instant success, and Irving emerged as one of the leading actors of his day. The part of Mathias, an unconvicted murderer haunted by his conscience, suited Irving's gift for the macabre and the melodramatic; and the play was to remain a feature of Irving's repertoire until his death.

For four years Henry Irving was the star of Bateman's company, and in October 1874 he tackled his severest test as an actor when he appeared as Hamlet. Irving's Hamlet has been described as the gentle prince whose failure to do the great things demanded of him arose not from a weakness of will but from an excess of tenderness. This reading departed from the traditional portrayal of the tragic prince, and the humanity and distinction of the performance sharply divided the critics and puzzled the audiences. Nevertheless, Irving won public acknowledgment as the leader of his profession.

Actor-manager of the Lyceum Theatre

When Bateman died in 1875, Irving continued to play under the management of Bateman's widow until 1877. In 1878 Irving became lessee and manager of the Lyceum Theatre and built around him a dedicated if subservient company. He possessed a strong personal vision of the best that could be accomplished: he paid prodigious attention to detail, took no account of expense for settings and costumes, and hired the best designers and musicians in the country. The Victorian public responded to his lead with packed houses, for the romantic historical fare satisfied their concept of what the theatre ought to be. Although he was criticized for his unusual diction, his special mannerisms, and the shakiness of his literary scholarship, Irving took note of the press only as a useful instrument in support of his grand design. Box-office figures spoke louder than the word of the critics, and success brought acclaim from the rich and the famous. The Lyceum became the scene for sumptuous post-performance supper parties at which society was further entertained at Irving's expense.

In 1878 he engaged Ellen Terry as his leading lady and thereby began one of the most famous partnerships in the history of the English stage. Their theatrical qualities complemented each other admirably: he the brooding introvert, she the spontaneous, impulsive creature whose charm won every heart. Together, as Hamlet and Ophelia, Shylock and Portia, they drew enormous audiences.

In 1883 Irving embarked on an American tour with the whole company of actors and technicians, as well as the scenic and lighting effects for which his theatre was famous. His reputation had gone before him, and the company enjoyed a triumphal winter season.

For the next few years Irving and the Lyceum company were at the height of their financial success. Each new production sought to outshine the existing repertory in sumptuousness and elaboration, though each absorbed the profits of the previous season. The plays themselves were of no lasting literary merit, as a young critic named George Bernard Shaw pointed out. He regretted that an actress so talented as Ellen Terry should waste her time on such ponderous trifles. Shaw had written a play, *The Man of Destiny*, that he hoped Irving and Terry might perform. Irving read it, gave Shaw a retainer, and forgot about it. Shaw then accused him of suppressing the play. Irving's retainer, however, had been only a kind gesture to a struggling young author. The two men now became antagonists.

Knighthood

In July 1895, when Irving was honoured by Queen Victoria with a knighthood (the first ever given to an English actor), his status as a national institution made a more inviting target for Shaw. At the same time, through Ellen Terry, Shaw implored Irving to consider the work of the Norwegian playwright Henrik Ibsen. She managed to read Irving two acts of Ibsen's *John Gabriel Borkman*, but Irving's comment was "Threadworms and leeches are an interesting study, but they have no interest to me." Irving's success had been built on the strength of his own theatrical presence expressed through dramatic vehicles of a certain type. With all the signs of popular success around him, he saw no reason to change the formula. His conception of the theatre was that of an "actor's theatre," in which the dramatist was the servant of the performer. Shaw and Ibsen marked the emergence of the "author's theatre," whereby an actor was judged on the fidelity with which he interpreted the vision and message of the playwright.

In 1897 Irving suffered three severe blows. A production by his son Laurence of a play about Peter the Great was a financial disaster. A far more devastating blow was the loss through fire of all the stored scenery for many of the classic productions in the Lyceum repertory. Insurance coverage was inadequate, and the capital loss was crippling. Then, in 1898, Irving had his first serious illness. The company toured without him, and the box-office receipts fell accordingly.

The final years of Irving's life became a struggle to keep the Lyceum company a going concern. New productions of Shakespeare's *Coriolanus*, as well as of the French playwright Victorien Sardou's play on Dante, hastened rather than stemmed the decline. Tours to America were exhausting, without compensating profits. In 1902 the company went into liquidation, and Irving's reign at the Lyceum ended. On October 13, 1905, after a performance of Alfred, Lord Tennyson's *Becket* at the Theatre Royal in Bradford, Irving died, penniless, at the age of 68. He was buried in the Poets' Corner in Westminster Abbey. His personal effects were auctioned to help provide for his widow, whom he had not seen for over 30 years. His obituaries spoke of "The Knight from Nowhere," who left behind him only the memory of his theatrical performances.

Henry Brodribb Irving and Laurence Sidney Irving. Henry Irving's sons, born in 1870 and 1871, had been deserted by their father; and their upbringing was inevitably affected by the parental rift.

Early lives

They relied greatly on each other's company and consequently grew up in London as very close friends. At Marlborough, one of England's more rigorous private schools, Harry's ability to neutralize the potential bully with a stream of improvised storytelling protected both brothers from the worst effects of the system. During the holidays they received tantalizing glimpses of the heady world behind the doors of the Lyceum Theatre. In spite of their mother's denigration of actors and acting, Harry was determined to follow his father's footsteps. Irving would not hear of it, and pressure was brought on the young man to point him in the direction of Oxford and a degree in law. Laurence was sent to Paris and St. Petersburg to study Russian in preparation for a diplomatic career.

Career of H.B. Irving. At Oxford, Harry's career centred more on the Oxford University Dramatic Society than on the law school, and as a result, his father changed his mind and offered both boys places in the Lyceum company. Harry preferred instead to accept an offer from another London company, run by John Hare—a part in the play *A Fool's Paradise*. His debut was not successful, chiefly because he lacked experience, and at the end of the season he returned to the law and was called to the bar. In 1894, however, he joined Ben Greet's company; and there he met a young actress named Dorothea Baird, whom he married in 1896. He appeared as Hamlet in Sunderland and Edinburgh, and the performance evoked praise from critics who noted his clear elocution and the general intelligence of his reading of the part. At the end of the touring season he left the Ben Greet company and joined the company of George Alexander, playing leading parts that further extended his experience. Leaving that company in 1901, he had his first real success in the title role of J.M. Barrie's *Admirable Crichton*. During this time he was working on a biography of Judge George Jeffreys (published 1898), whose notoriously severe sentences were passed on many rebels of the Duke of Monmouth's Rebellion in 1685. Throughout his career he continued his interest in criminology and wrote a number of books on the subject, one of the earliest of which was *French Criminals of the Nineteenth Century* (1901).

Following the death of his father in 1905, Harry formed his own company and attempted to revive some of the now-disbanded Lyceum company's most famous productions, with himself in his father's roles. This bold course met with both praise and unfavourable comparisons. An American tour was only partially successful. Harry's interest in criminology was expressed through his dual performance in an adaptation of Robert Louis Stevenson's *The Strange Case of Dr. Jekyll and Mr. Hyde*. The power of the character change was such that Harry's performances began to influence his personal life, much to the anxiety of his wife and his friends.

Actor-manager of Savoy Theatre

In 1913 he took a lease on the Savoy Theatre, but his choice of plays was not to the public's taste; he sublet the theatre and embarked on a tour of the vaudeville circuit, playing farce with the comedian Tom Reynolds from the old Lyceum company. An engagement in the play *The Silver King* for another management ended shortly after the outbreak of World War I, and Harry returned to the Savoy. A number of other productions ended in 1916 with revivals of *The Bells* and of *Hamlet*, which signalled Harry's farewell to the stage. At the age of 46 he was drafted and given work in the Admiralty. He took up writing criminology again and completed his *Book of Remarkable Criminals* (1918). Following the armistice, Harry's health began to fail. He was able to finish his last book, *Last Studies in Criminology* (published 1921), before he died in London in October 1919. He was buried in Finchley Cemetery.

Career of Laurence Irving. After leaving Marlborough College, Laurence first studied French and Russian in Paris in preparation for a diplomatic career and then moved to St. Petersburg for more intensive Russian studies. With a growing command of Russian, he was able to take part in the exciting artistic life of the city, and he acquired a taste for Russian literature that never left him. He returned to England and began his career as an actor with Frank Benson's Shakespearean company. The parts were less than he had expected, however, and in a moment of desperation he attempted suicide. After recovering from a self-inflicted chest wound, he joined the company of J.L. Toole, an old friend of his father's. Laurence's attitude toward his father was divided between affection and admiration and the residue of years of denigration of his father by his mother; but the tension gradually resolved itself over the years. The boys' attitude toward Ellen Terry also changed. Although they always referred to her as "The Wench," she and Laurence became particularly close in later years.

Collaboration with H.B. Irving

In 1893 Laurence and Harry collaborated on a stage adaptation of Sheridan Le Fanu's *Uncle Silas*. A single matinée gave them experience rather than success. Nor was Laurence's first attempt at original dramatic writing, *Time, Hunger and the Law*, any more successful. Following a number of occasional parts in touring companies, Laurence started work on another play, based on the Russian tsar Peter the Great. He corresponded at length with Count Leo Tolstoy, eventually finished the work, and persuaded his father to include its production in the 1898 Lyceum season. The play did not run and resulted in a financial loss for the Lyceum; but his next play, a translation of Sardou's *Robespierre*, met with greater success. After an American tour with the Lyceum, he returned to England and took part in the first production of Shaw's *Captain Brassbound's Conversion*, mounted by the Stage Society, a newly formed group that sought to promote new plays and playwrights. Although in a letter Shaw detailed Laurence's shortcomings as an actor, their friendship remained intact.

At this time Ellen Terry and Henry Irving parted company after playing together for 20 years. To replace her, Irving engaged a young Welsh actress, Mabel Hackney, whom Laurence married in 1903. The young couple left the Lyceum to perform on music-hall tours in the hope of raising enough money to permit them to establish independent management. The money came in, but subsequent productions of *Peg Woffington* and *Richard Lovelace* failed to draw provincial audiences. Laurence then began work on a dramatization of Fyodor Dostoyevsky's *Crime and Punishment*, combining his love of Russia, his interest in psychological complexities, and his growing ability as a playwright into an enterprise that was well ahead of its time. *The Unwritten Law* was an immediate success when it appeared in London in 1910. Laurence himself played the part of Raskolnikov, and his performance was acclaimed by the critics. The confidence that success gave him increased his stature as a dramatic actor. He played Iago to Sir Herbert Beerbohm Tree's Othello, but his playing was out of key with the rest of the company. For Laurence here marked the transition between the acting style of the old school and the new philosophy of naturalism in acting expounded by Stanislavsky at the Moscow Art Theatre.

A leading part in Ibsen's *The Pretenders* further enhanced his reputation during 1913. The next year he and Mabel set out with their company for a Canadian tour with *The Unwritten Law* and *Typhoon*. At the end of the tour, on May 28, 1914, he and Mabel embarked from Montreal on the "Empress of Ireland." Fogbound in the St. Lawrence River, the liner was struck by a coal ship and sank with a loss of more than 1,000 persons, among whom were Laurence and Mabel Irving.

BIBLIOGRAPHY. For Henry Irving the definitive work is *Henry Irving, the Actor and His World* by LAURENCE IRVING (1951). Earlier biographies were AUSTIN BRERETON, *The Life of Henry Irving*, 2 vol. (1908); and BRAM STOKER, *Personal Reminiscences of Henry Irving* (1906). Highly subjective books by EDWARD GORDON CRAIG include *Henry Irving* (1930, reprinted 1969), *Ellen Terry and Her Secret Self* (1931), and *Index to the Story of My Days* (1957). Ellen Terry's own *Memoirs* were edited by EDITH CRAIG and CHRISTOPHER ST. JOHN (1932); St. John also edited *Ellen Terry and Bernard Shaw: A Correspondence*, 2nd ed. (1949). The Irving–Shaw controversy is well covered in ST. JOHN ERVINE, *Bernard Shaw: His Life, Work and Friends* (1956). Another illuminating book on this group is EDWARD A. CRAIG, *Gordon Craig: The Story of His Life* (1968). For the sons H.B. Irving and Laurence Sidney Irving, the only full works are LAURENCE IRVING, *The Successors* (1967) and *The Precarious Crust* (1971). The BBC has a recording of MAX BEERBOHM describing H.B. Irving at Oxford. Beerbohm's *Around Theatres, 1898–1910*, 2 vol. (1930), are collected reviews of the period. Also useful is *A Bridges-Adams Letter Book* (1971), published by The Society for Theatre Research.

(J.H.B.I.)

Isabella I the Catholic, of Castile

As queen of Castile from 1474 and of Aragon from 1479, Isabella ruled jointly with her husband, Ferdinand II of Aragon (Ferdinand V of Castile). Known as the Catholic Kings, they joined their kingdoms in a personal union and thus paved the way for the formation of the Spanish nation-state. Isabella was an outstanding ruler, responsible for beginning political, social, and religious reforms; it was she who gave permission for Christopher Columbus' voyage of discovery to the New World.

Early life. Isabella was born at Madrigal on April 22, 1451, the daughter of John II of Castile and of his second wife, Isabella of Portugal. Three years later her half brother became king as Henry IV. Despite the fact that she had a younger brother, Alfonso, and that her early years were spent quietly with her mother at Arévalo, Isabella was soon drawn into the web of Castilian politics. She was brought to court when she was 13 in order to be under the King's eye. At first the opposition to Henry IV gathered round Alfonso, but when the latter died in July 1468, the rebellious magnates naturally turned to Isabella. She did not, however, play the role thus designed for her, and the fruit of her political wisdom was to be recognized as his heiress by Henry IV at the agreement known as the Accord of Toros de Guisando (September 19, 1468).

As heiress of Castile, the question of Isabella's future marriage became a matter of increasing diplomatic activity at home and abroad. Portugal, Aragon, and France each put forward a marriage candidate. Henry seems to have wanted his half sister to marry Afonso V, King of Portugal. As between the Portuguese and Aragonese candidates, she herself, no doubt assisted in her decision by her small group of councillors, came down in favour of Ferdinand of Aragon. A third suitor, the French Duc de Guienne, was sidestepped, and without her brother's approval she married Ferdinand in October 1469 in the palace of Juan de Vivero, at Valladolid. The prospect of an Aragonese consort led to the development of an anti-Aragonese party that put forward the claims of a rival heiress, Henry's daughter Joan, known by those who believed that her true father was Beltrán de la Cueva, duque de Alburquerque, as la Beltraneja. The King encouraged this group by going back on the accord of 1468 on the grounds that Isabella had shown disobedience to the crown in marrying Ferdinand without the royal consent. He now rejected Isabella's claim to the throne and preferred that of Joan, for whom he sought the hand of the Duc de Guienne. Though Isabella and Henry were to some extent reconciled, the long-threatened war of succession at once broke out when the King died in 1474.

Marriage to Ferdinand

Archivo Mas, Barcelona

Isabella I, portrait by an unknown artist. In the Real Academia de la Historía, Madrid.

Reign. Isabella was at the time in Segovia, which was secured for her claim. She was supported by an important group of Castilian nobles, including Cardinal Mendoza, the constable of Castile (a Velasco), and the Admiral (an Enríquez), who was related to Ferdinand's mother. The opposing faction, which put forward the counterclaims of Joan, included the Archbishop of Toledo, the master of Calatrava (an influential military order), and the powerful young Marqués de Villena; they were supported by Afonso V of Portugal, who hastened to invade Castile and there betrothed himself to Joan. The first four years of Isabella's reign were thus occupied by a civil war, which ended in defeat for her Castilian opponents and for the Portuguese king (February 24, 1479). With the death of John II of Aragon in the same year, the kingdoms of Castile and Aragon came together in the joint persons of their rulers.

Spain had emerged as a country. But it was to be long before this personal union would lead to effective political unification. Ferdinand, indeed, in his first will (1475) made Isabella his heir in Aragon and openly declared the advantages his subjects would derive from the union with Castile. But each kingdom continued to be governed according to its own institutions. Both sovereigns were certainly united in aiming to end the long process of *Reconquista* by taking over the last Muslim stronghold in Spain—the Kingdom of Granada. In the event, however, the conquest (which began in 1482) proved difficult and drawn out, and strained the finances of Castile to the utmost. Although some of the features of the campaign were medieval (like the order of battle), others were novel. Isabella took a close interest in the conduct of the war and seems to have been responsible for improved methods of supply and for the establishment of a military hospital. In 1491 she and Ferdinand set up a forward headquarters at Santa Fe, close to their ultimate objective, and there they stayed until Granada fell (January 2, 1492).

While she was at Santa Fe another event with which the Queen was to become personally associated was in the making, for Columbus visited her there to enlist support for the voyage that was to result in the discovery of America. Although the story of her offering to pledge her jewels in order to help finance the expedition cannot be accepted, and Columbus secured only limited financial support from her, Isabella and her councillors must receive credit for making the decision to approve the momentous voyage. The terms on which the expedition was to set out to discover a new route to the Indies were drawn up on April 17, 1492. The New World that was discovered as a result of that decision was, with papal confirmation, annexed to the crown of Castile, in accordance with existing practice in regard to such previous Atlantic discoveries as the Canary Islands.

Approval of Columbus' voyage

The Queen and her advisers hardly needed Columbus to remind them of the opportunity now offered for the spreading of Christianity. Yet, the unexpected discoveries quickly brought fresh problems to Isabella, not the least of which was the relationship between the newly discovered "Indians" and the crown of Castile. The Queen and her councillors were more ready to recognize the rights of the Indians than was Columbus; she ordered some of those he had brought back as slaves to be released. The Queen was still concerned with these problems when she died in 1504.

Meanwhile, in 1480 the Inquisition had been set up in Andalusia. There is little doubt that this represented the culmination of a long and popular movement against non-Christians and doubtful converts, which had manifested itself frequently in the late Middle Ages in Castile. The expulsion of those Jews who refused conversion was the logical result of the establishment of the Inquisition. Yet, however meritorious the expulsion may have seemed at the time in order to achieve greater religious and political unity, judged by its economic consequences alone, the loss of this valuable element in Spanish society must have been a serious mistake.

It is difficult to disentangle Isabella's personal responsibility for the achievements of her reign from those of Ferdinand. But, undoubtedly, she played a large part in setting up the court as a centre of influence. With her blue eyes, her fair or chestnut hair, and wearing jewels and magnificent dresses, she must have made a striking figure. At the same time display was matched with religious feeling. Her choice of spiritual advisers brought to the fore such different and remarkable men as Hernando de Talavera and Cardinal Cisneros. A policy of reforming the Spanish churches had begun early in the 15th century. But the movement gathered momentum only under Isabella and Talavera. When in 1492 Talavera became archbishop of Granada, his place at the Queen's side was taken by Cisneros, for whom the monarchs secured the crucial position of archbishop of Toledo in 1495. The monarchs were interested in the reform of the secular clergy and still more in that of the orders of monks, friars, and nuns; Isabella took a particular interest in the reform of the Poor Clares. Although when she died there was still much to be done, the rulers and Cisneros together had gone far toward achieving their goals.

Though intensely pious and orthodox in her beliefs and though granted with Ferdinand the title of the "Catholic Kings" by Pope Alexander VI, Isabella could be both imperious and pertinacious in her dealings with the papacy. This was particularly true when she thought the Pope was making bad appointments to Spanish benefices or in any way encroaching on the customary rights of the crown over the Spanish churches. For the vacant see of Cuenca in 1478, for instance, she rejected the Italian cardinal appointed by the Pope, who four years later accepted her alternative Spanish candidate. Subsequently, she successfully rejected the suggestion that the Pope's nephew should become archbishop of Seville. In seeking to control appointments to Castilian sees, the Queen was not simply inspired by national sentiments. She also sought candidates of high standards; judged by her choices of men such as Talavera and Cisneros, Isabella was, indeed, remarkably effective in achieving her objective.

Isabella was almost as interested in education as she was in religion. After she reached the age of 30, she set herself the task of acquiring proficiency in Latin and succeeded in her aim. At court she encouraged such notable scholars as Pietro Martire d'Anghiera, whom she set up as the head of a new palace school for the sons of the nobility. Naturally, many of the outstanding literary works of her reign, such as Antonio de Nebrija's *Gramática Castellana* (1492; "Castilian Grammar"), were dedicated to her. She was also the patron of Spanish and Flemish artists; part of her extensive collection of pictures survives.

Family sorrows at the end of her reign

The last decade of her reign took place against a background of family sorrows brought about by the successive deaths of her only son and heir, Juan (1497), of her daughter Isabella, queen of Portugal, in childbirth (1498), and of her grandchild Miguel (1500), who might have brought about a personal union between Spain and Portugal. Instead, her daughter Joan, wife of Philip I and mother of the Emperor Charles V, became the heiress of Castile; but this offered little comfort to the Queen because Joan had already, by 1501, shown signs of the mental imbalance that would later earn her the title of "the Mad."

One of the achievements of Isabella's last decade was undoubtedly the success with which the Catholic Kings, acting on her initiative, extended their authority over the military orders of Alcántara, Calatrava, and Santiago, thus giving the crown control over their vast property and patronage. These orders had been for too long exploited by the nobility and were the subject of intense rivalry among those who sought to be elected master of one or other of them. In 1487 Ferdinand became grand master of Calatrava, and by 1499 he had acquired the grand masterships of Alcántara and Santiago. With the capture of Granada, the main work of the orders had been done; and a process that envisaged their ultimate absorption into the lands of the crown was logical and sensible.

Assessment. Good sense and statesmanship were equally reflected in Isabella's will and codicil. Because she left no memoirs, her will is in many ways the most reliable picture of her. In it she sums up her aspirations and her awareness of how much she and Ferdinand had been unable to do. With prudence she comments on the basis of her political program—the unity of the states of the Iberian Peninsula, the maintainance of control over the Strait of Gibraltar, a policy of expansion into Muslim North Africa, of just rule for the Indians of the New World, and of reform in the Church at home. If the overall impression is inevitably piecemeal, it is also clear that she gave to her successors an exceptional document. It assures scholars that, in allotting to Isabella the foremost place among their rulers, Spaniards do not misjudge this remarkable woman. She died in the castle of Medina del Campo on November 26, 1504.

BIBLIOGRAPHY. The standard biography in English remains W.H. PRESCOTT, *History of the Reign of Ferdinand and Isabella, the Catholic* (1838; rev. ed. by J.H.F. KIRK, 1908). Though antiquated it is reasonably reliable. There are good modern summaries of the reign by J.M. BATISTA I ROCA in *The New Cambridge Modern History*, vol. 1 (1957); and J.H. ELLIOT in *Imperial Spain, 1469–1716* (1963).

(J.R.L.H.)

Isaiah

Isaiah (Hebrew *Yesha'yahu*, "God is salvation") was a prophet of ancient Israel, after whom one of the great prophetic books of the Bible is named. (Only some of the first 39 chapters are now considered to be his work; see BIBLICAL LITERATURE.) He was reputed to be in touch with God and gifted with the capacity to speak for God, and his image of himself was in accord with his repute. His message constitutes a significant and lasting contribution to the Jewish and Christian spiritual traditions.

Initial vision and mission

Personal life. The earliest recorded event in his life is his call to prophecy as now found in the sixth chapter of the Book of Isaiah; this occurred about 742 BCE (before the Common Era = BC). The vision (probably in the Jerusalem Temple) that made him a prophet is described in a first-person narrative, for only Isaiah could tell of this intimate personal experience.

According to this account he "saw" God and was overwhelmed by his contact with the divine glory and holiness. He became agonizingly aware of God's need for a messenger to the people of Israel, and, despite his own sense of inadequacy, he offered himself for God's service: "Here am I! Send me." He was thus commissioned to give voice to the divine word. It was no light undertaking; he was to condemn his own people and watch the nation crumble and perish. As he tells it, he was only too aware that, coming with such a message, he would experience bitter opposition, willful disbelief, and ridicule, to withstand which he would have to be inwardly fortified. All this came to him in the form of a vision and ended as a sudden, firm, and lifelong resolve.

Presumably, the man Isaiah was already prepared to find meaning in the vision. It would be good to know about his life before the arrival of that decisive moment. There is, unfortunately, little direct information, mainly inferences to be drawn from the biblical text. At times the prophet's private life shows through the record as an aspect of his public message. Once when he went to confront a king, he took with him, to re-enforce his prophetic word, a son with the symbolic name Shear-yashuv ("a remnant shall return"). Again, to memorialize a message he sired a son on the "prophetess" (his wife) and saddled him with his message as a name: Maher-shalal-hash-baz ("Speed-spoil-hasten-plunder"), referring to the imminent spoliations by the Assyrians. If the sons had not been wanted as walking witnesses to the prophet's forebodings, posterity would not know of this wife or these sons.

Of Isaiah's parental home it is known only that his father's name was Amoz. Since he often spoke with kings, it is sometimes suggested that Isaiah was an aristocrat, possibly even of royal stock. The same reasoning, however, might apply to any number of prophets; from Nathan in David's time onward, prophets had dealings with kings and were, like Isaiah, well informed about public affairs. Moreover, Isaiah's sympathies were emphatically with the victimized poor, not with the courtiers and well-to-do. Also, it is sometimes argued that he was of a priestly family; but his knowledge of cultic matters and the fact that his commissioning seemingly occurred in the Temple in Jerusalem are slender evidence for his priestly descent as against his unreserved condemnation of the priests and their domain; "I am fed up with roasting rams and the grease of fattened beasts," he has God proclaim in a famous passage in the first chapter.

Relation to other prophets

One could argue with equal force that Isaiah is descended from a family of prophets (though his father, the otherwise unknown Amoz, is not to be confused with the prophet Amos). He is thoroughly schooled in the traditional forms and language of prophetic speech. It is an educated speech—strong, vivid, the finest of classical Hebrew. Isaiah is particularly well acquainted with the prophetic tradition known to his slightly older contemporary, Amos. Four eminent Hebrew prophets addressed themselves to the people of Israel and Judah in the latter half of the 8th pre-Christian century: Amos, Hosea, Micah, and Isaiah. Strangely, no evidence suggests that any of these knew in person any of the others. Seemingly, they were apart and alone, yet Isaiah and Amos follow essentially the same lines of thought and differ significantly only in that Amos had addressed the northern kingdom (Israel) while Isaiah would emphatically include Judah and Jerusalem. The basic similarities in style and substance strongly suggest influence, direct or indirect, of the one on the other—and both invoke a recognizable Israelite tradition.

Isaiah's experience bridges the classes and occupations. Whatever his family circumstances, still in his youth he came to know the face of poverty—and the debauchery of the rich. He was at home with the unprotected, the widowed and orphaned; with the dispossessed, homeless, landless; and with the resourceless victims of the moneyed-man's court. He was also acquainted with the rapacious authors of the prevailing misery: promulgators of discriminatory laws, venal judges, greedy landgrabbers, fancy women, thieving and carousing men of means, and irresponsible leaders, both civil and religious. In other words, he was intimately aware of the inequities and evils of human society—which may have been no worse in Israel in the 8th century before Christ than many critics believe they are almost everywhere in the 20th century after Christ.

Theology. It is in his theology that Isaiah leans most heavily on Israelite tradition and shows an acquaintance with the thoughts of Amos. Isaiah shared with him and with the people the long-standing tradition that a special bond united Israel and its God. Since patriarchal times there had been an agreement, a solemn "Covenant" between them: Israel was to be God's people and he their God. He had picked and cared for them. How solicitous he had been for their welfare! Such was the traditional message. Isaiah knew and honoured this ancient tradition; but, more significantly, he also shared the conviction of Amos that this arrangement was wholly conditional, contingent on the people's conduct. Behaviour such as Amos saw about him in Samaria and Isaiah saw about him in Jerusalem could cancel that Covenant—had in fact done so; that is the meaning of the vineyard parable in the fifth chapter of Isaiah. There God is compared to the careful and industrious cultivator of a vineyard—Israel—who, angry at the "wild grapes" of injustice and violence that is his crop, threatens to take away his care and protection.

As Isaiah knew him, Israel's God simply did not fit into the picture of utter injustice and consequent misery rampant in 8th-century Israel. To that people's God, as Isaiah knew him, persons mattered. God was, in fact, more concerned about people than about how his subjects performed for him their oft-rehearsed rituals. A literal interpretation of the 13th verse of chapter 29 and verses 10 to 15 of chapter one would suggest that God finds the motions of worship simply repugnant, and this may well have been Isaiah's meaning. He was overawed by the holiness—the otherness—of his God and must have thought that the customary gifts of meat, grain, and flattery were unseemly, or, at the least, irrelevant. Although, like Amos, Isaiah appears most often to speak in absolutes, it is indeed possible to interpret these two passages less strictly (as some scholars do) and to say that he spoke here in relative terms and that, in his scale of religious values, he merely ranked moral conduct above ritual conformity.

Isaiah's theology included as well the sometimes comforting view that God shapes history, traditionally entering the human scene to rescue his people from national peril. But, according to Isaiah's discomfiting surmise, God could intervene quite as properly to chastise his own aberrant nation, and he could employ a human agent (*e.g.*, a conquering foe) to that end.

Assyria, the rod of God's anger

More readily than Amos, perhaps because a decade had passed, Isaiah could identify the agent: Assyria. Isaiah's call to prophecy roughly coincides with the beginning—after a period of relative inactivity—of the westward expansion of the Assyrian empire under the victorious generalship of Tiglath-pileser III (reigned 745–727 BCE). Current events did not escape the prophet's attention. Isaiah appears to have read the omens, as Amos had done; he could clearly see in Assyria the instrument of God's wrath: "Ah, Assyria, the rod of my anger, the staff of my fury! Against a godless nation I send him . . ." (10:5–6).

Preaching and teaching. If, then, Isaiah was prepared by schooling in tradition and life for the vision that set him on his prophetic course, the preparation involved the mingling in his nature of such elements as those sketched above. In the year that King Uzziah died (742 BCE), according to chapter 6, Isaiah was one of a crowd gathered for an occasion at the Jerusalem Temple when of a sudden it occurred—and he became a prophet: "Go, and say to this people . . . ." The experiences that had gone into the shaping of his young life: his acquaintance with the arrogant rich and the suffering poor; his seeming knowledge of Amos and his heritage of tradition, ethnic and religious; his dismay at the threat of Assyria; above all, perhaps, a new and overwhelming sense of the majestic holiness of God—all merged, coalesced; and he knew that his God was sending him with words for his people and that, reluctant or not, he was compelled to go. From the start or retrospectively, he was aware of a frantic need—impossible to satisfy—to call his people back from the brink of peril. His vision was his moment of insight and resolve when, with complete clarity and instantaneously, he knew what he must do and say.

In its present sophisticated form the record of this experience is hardly contemporary with the event; he did not go home from the Temple and write down chapter 6. The record is the reflection not of a confident and eager youth but of a man buffeted by long experience, embittered and despairing. Three times in other chapters the prophet says of his people that they have "refused" to hear him; it was as though he, a messenger, had been ordered irrationally to "close their minds, plug their ears, veil their eyes," as he says in chapter 6 of his errand to those to whom he was sent. The message that he had to deliver was bad news—unwelcome tidings. And when he spoke of it, as repeatedly he did, he chose such unambiguous language and spoke with so much moral certainty that, as men normally do, his hearers tuned him out; he was foredoomed to speak unheard. A great deal of anguished living intervened between the vision itself and the writing of it. His words "How long, O Lord?" are an expression of utter weariness.

The judgment oracle in chapter 22

If chapter 6 marks the beginning of his career as prophet, the judgment oracle about the conquest of Jerusalem in chapter 22 probably brings his grim story to a close. It is at any rate the latest Isaianic product that can be dated with any degree of certainty. Dates are scarce in Isaiah's book, and the compositions are arranged in no discernible chronological order. The vision in chapter 6 is dated in the year of King Uzziah's death, and the occasion for the utterance in chapter 22 appears to be the unawaited departure of the besieging army of the Assyrian Sennacherib from before the gates of Jerusalem in the year 701. There is nothing to suggest either when Isaiah was born or when he died. The tradition that he died a martyr's death at the hands of Manasseh, king of Judah (*c.* 687–642 BCE), is simply an apocryphal legend, found in the so-called *Martyrdom of Isaiah* and in the Talmud (a postbiblical compendium of Jewish law, lore, and commentary), but with no specific support in Hebrew Scripture.

The last recorded words of Isaiah, in chapter 22, do nothing to relieve the sombre tone of his message, but they do shed further light on his mood and personality. After he had exclaimed in the vision in chapter 6, "How long, O Lord?" he learned to his dismay that even a last remaining tenth of the populace must in turn succumb; just so here the oracle ends with assurance of total disaster: the nation's guilt can be purged by nothing short of death—"Surely this iniquity will not be forgiven you till you die. . . ." Chapters 6 and 22 set the tone of his message and the hue of his mood, and from the first to the last the gloom has not lifted.

This 22nd chapter contains the most personally revealing of all Isaiah's words. Quite unexpectedly the Assyrians have lifted the siege and departed, and the amazed defenders of Jerusalem, flushed and jubilant, give way to celebration; Isaiah cannot share the holiday spirit since for him there has been only a postponement. Nothing has changed, and in his "valley of vision" he sees the day of rout and confusion that God yet has in store for Zion. And so it is that he lays bare his private grief:

> Look away from me, let me weep bitter tears; do not labor to comfort me for the destruction of the daughter of my people.

Response to the historical situation. The historical allusions in the scattered chapters of Isaiah's work agree with the title verse, according to which he was a contemporary of the Judaean kings Uzziah, Jotham, Ahaz, and Hezekiah. His prophetic call is precisely dated by him "in the year that King Uzziah died." At least a part of chapter 7 refers to the event of the year 734 when Ephraim and Syria jointly threatened King Ahaz of Judah. In 732 Tiglath-Pileser conquered Damascus, the fall of which Isaiah had anticipated. In 722 Samaria, the capital of Ephraim, fell to King Sargon of Assyria, which event Isaiah had also foreseen. By the end of the century (701) Sennacherib had laid siege to Jerusalem—and had subsequently withdrawn. Chapters 1:4–8; 10:27–34; 28:14–22; 30:1–7; and 31:1–4 point to those difficult days when Jerusalem was beleaguered and King Hezekiah feverishly sought help from Egypt. Isaiah brought sparse comfort to his kings—even when the siege was lifted, as noted in the passage cited from chapter 22.

The critical alternative: national disaster or return to God

It would be wrong to suppose that Isaiah came to Israel simply to announce the approaching disaster. Painfully sensitive to the rottenness of his society, Isaiah foresaw its consequent collapse. But he also knew and offered an alternative to tragedy: his people's survival depended on their acceptance again of the ancient moral demands. By returning they might be saved. To obtain their return was his program. Or, differently and more properly stated, because he spoke for God and of God, his goal was to redirect his people into the ways acceptable to the God whom by their conduct they had alienated, and so to save them from catastrophe. He screamed dread warnings and pleaded for amendment. He gave way to despair only because his program had no success. His people seemed to him bent on self-destruction; that was the sickening course of their destiny as he saw it unfolding. What Isaiah saw he did not like, and there was no spite in his tidings.

His impossible program comes through in the crisis of 701, during which he stands in violent opposition to the generals ready to go to Egypt for help against the Assyrians laying siege to Zion. Isaiah looked neither to allies nor to armaments for security; these were not the way. If it is God who decides the destiny of nations, security is for God to grant and for men to deserve. Isaiah held the daring view that the best defense is no defense—none other than the reconciling response to the moral demand. No men are secure when some are denied security. "This," he said, "is rest [*i.e.*, this is security]: give rest to the weary."

A case can be made for a theory that Isaiah drew back at the brink, incapable of conceiving a world wholly emptied of his people. What supports this view is a paradox: the observation that, irrationally, he entrusted his rejected message to his disciples and preserved it in a book for the instruction of the survivors of a people doomed, according to his prophecy, to leave no survivors.

There is no consensus as concerns the precise limits of the words of the 8th-century Isaiah or the degree of consistency with which he sustained his tragic monotone. Certainly in his book as it has come down, his nature is elusive—both stern and tender. Magnificently hopeful passages constantly mingle with the prevailing atmosphere of doom. Probably his son's name, Shear-yashuv, means something like "a mere fragment will survive," but possibly it has a hopeful ring: no total disaster—some shall survive. Possibly the name Immanuel ("God is with us"), prophesied for the child who shall be a sign from God that Judah will not be overcome by Israel and Syria, expresses the confidence that God will never forsake his people. And possibly other such assurances are in fact words of Isaiah himself, compelled by his love to palliate the blow.

Isaiah's disciples and the Isaianic tradition

But there is an alternative solution. Although Isaiah was far from popular in his day, he does appear to have attracted some disciples: "Seal the teaching among my disciples." These may have been the circle that kept alive his name and his words—in writing or learned "by heart"—the nucleus of what was to become, through a developing tradition over a long period of time, the biblical Book of Isaiah. And quite possibly successive generations of such Isaiah-men, piously keeping his words alive through radically changing times, added the sustaining messages of hope, well designed to seize the fancy of suffering humanity down the centuries.

Later interpretations of Isaiah's message. Ironically, perhaps, the Book of Isaiah is most widely known and loved just for those comforting words—which may not be his. A passage in the Babylonian Talmud (one of the two Talmud compilations, the other being Palestinian) can say that from beginning to end the book is consolation. The presence of Isaiah scrolls in the archives of the Qumrān (Dead Sea) community is not surprising. By that time (*c.* 1st century BCE–1st century CE) it had become the fashion to assume that prophets spoke not to their times only but of things to come in the far future; and in times of stress men studied prophetic texts intent on learning when redemption was to come. The Greek translation of Isaiah by Jewish scholars (the Septuagint version), accomplished before the Christian Era, reflects a developing tradition of interpretation; it renders the Hebrew term *ʿalma* ("young woman") as *parthenos* ("virgin") in the verse (7:14) about Immanuel, thus drawing Isaiah further into the messianic ring. Now it is a virgin who "shall conceive and bear a son." The promise of a more than ordinary king, a "messiah," was especially enticing. According to the New Testament accounts, when Jesus entered a synagogue in Nazareth and got up to read they handed him a scroll of Isaiah. He read the beginning of chapter 61: "The Spirit of the Lord God is upon me, because the Lord has anointed me . . ." and he said: "Today this scripture has been fulfilled." The Gospels lean more heavily on the Book of Isaiah than on any other prophetic text. Beyond any denominational differences is the utopian dream, the "swords-into-plowshares" passage in Isaiah 2. These and many gleaming words from the expanded Book of Isaiah live on in the present day and today's culture. The word "prophetic" has now become a value-term, closely associated with the primacy of the moral demand and the bearing of justice on the stability of nations, quite in accord with the emphasis of the early Isaiah.

BIBLIOGRAPHY. J. LINDBLOM, *Prophecy in Ancient Israel* (1962), an excellent general introduction to Israelite prophecy; OTTO EISSFELDT, *Einleitung in das Alte Testament*, 3rd ed. (1964; Eng. trans., *The Old Testament: An Introduction*, . . . , pp. 301–346, 1965), on the history of interpretation, with bibliography; ERNST SELLIN, *Einleitung in das Alte Testament*, 10th ed. rev. and rewritten by GEORG FOHRER (1965; Eng. trans., *Introduction to the Old Testament*, 1968), on the structure of the book, with bibliography; R.B.Y. SCOTT, "The Book of Isaiah," in *The Interpreter's Bible*, vol. 5, pp. 151–164 (1956), for literary analysis; S.H. BLANK, *Prophetic Faith in Isaiah* (1958), stressing thought and significance; E.J. KISSANE, *The Book of Isaiah*, 2 vol. (1941–43, vol. 1 revised edition, 1960); BRUCE VAWTER, *The Conscience of Israel* (1961); and F.L. MORIARTY, "Isaiah 1–39," in *The Jerome Biblical Commentary*, vol. 1 (1968), these three quite different in approach.

(S.H.Bl.)

Isfahan

Isfahan (Eṣfahān) is a city of Iran 5,216 feet (1,590 metres) above sea level along the north bank of the Zāyandeh Rūd (rūd, "river"), about 252 miles (405 kilometres) south of Teheran. Formerly capital of the Seljuq and Ṣafavid empires, today it is a provincial centre. The population in 1966 was 424,045.

History and architecture. Little is known of Isfahan before Sāsānian times (after *c.* AD 224 to *c.* 651). Queen Shushan-Dukht, the Jewish consort of Yazdegerd I (AD

339–420), is said to have settled a colony of Jews there in a suburb called Yahūdīyeh (the establishment of this colony has also been attributed to Nebuchadrezzar, but this seems far less probable). The Shahrestān Bridge, which spans the Zāyandeh Rūd a short distance east-southeast of the city, dates from the Sāsānian era; the piers are, however, all that remain of the original structure, the upper part having often been rebuilt. When the Arabs captured Isfahan in 642, they made it the chief city of the great central province of al-Jibāl ("the mountains"), which covered much of former Media.

Under the Būyid (Buwayhid) rulers of Persia (10th century), who rose to power when the temporal authority of the ʿAbbāsid caliphate was on the decline, Isfahan became extremely prosperous. In the middle of the 11th century the Turkish conqueror Toghrïl Beg, the founder of the Seljuq Empire and dynasty, captured Isfahan and made it the capital of his vast domains, and under his grandson Malik-Shāh I (1072–92), the city increased still further in size and splendour. In those days the central point of the city was a square, or rectangle, situated some distance to the north of the later Meydān-e Shāh (square of the Shah). It was bordered on the north by the great Masjed-e-Jāmeʿ, the cathedral mosque, which is still one of the chief architectural glories of the city; at the southern end was the Masjed-e-ʿAlī (Mosque of ʿAlī), of which only the tall minaret remains of the original building. Neẓām ol-Molk (Niẓām al-Mulk), Malik-Shāh's chief minister and the patron of Omar Khayyam, added a dome chamber of great beauty to the Masjed-e-Jāmeʿ. Not to be outdone, his rival Tāj ol-Molk then built close to it a smaller but even more beautiful dome chamber that is said to have attained "the perfection of architecture."

After the fall of the Seljuq dynasty (*c.* 1200), Isfahan was eclipsed by other Persian cities such as Tabriz and Kazvin, but it regained its pre-eminent position during the Ṣafavid period (1501–1736).

The city's golden age began in 1598 when Shāh ʿAbbās the Great (1587–1629) made it his capital in place of Kazvin. He largely replanned and rebuilt it, making it one of the largest and most beautiful cities of the world at that time. As a fitting centre for his capital, he created the immense Meydān-e-Shāh, a courtyard that measures 1,674 by 540 feet (512 by 159 metres). At the southern end of the Meydān is the famous Masjed-e Shāh, or royal mosque, begun in 1611/12 but not finished until after Shāh ʿAbbas' death. This building, decorated with enamelled tiles of great brilliance, has in the 20th century been carefully repaired. On the eastern side stands the Masjed-e Sheykh Loṭfollāh, the mosque used by the Shāh ʿAbbās for his private devotions. On the western side of the Meydān is the ʿAlī Qāpū ("the lofty gate"), a high building in the form of an archway crowned in the forepart by an immense *tālār*, or covered balcony, that served as an audience hall and as a vantage point from which the shah and his courtiers or guests could watch games of polo or gladiatorial combats below. This archway leads into the gardens of the former royal palace, which covers a large area with courts and pavilions, one of which, the Chehel Sotūn ("forty columns"), was famous as a verandah and throne room of Shāh ʿAbbās. At the northern end of the Meydān is a tiled gateway leading to the Qayṣarīyeh, or royal bazaar. The spaces between these buildings are filled by two-storied buildings with arched recesses, all of uniform design.

Nearly 600 yards (549 metres) west of the Meydān-e Shāh and connected with it by a side road is the Chahār Bāgh ("four gardens"), the avenue that Shāh ʿAbbās made to give access to his capital from the south (the shah had to purchase four gardens in order to construct it). The Chahār Bāgh runs southward to the Zāyandeh Rūd, which it crosses by means of a fine bridge built by Allāhverdi Khān, one of Shāh ʿAbbās' generals. The northern part of this avenue, nearly 1 mile (1.6 kilometres) long and 200 feet (61 metres) wide, consisted of two alleyways with a promenade between; down the centre was a watercourse with basins and fountains at intervals. Shade was provided by rows of trees. The two roadways and the promenade remain, but the watercourse and fountains have disappeared.

A French Huguenot jeweler, Jean Chardin, spent ten years in Isfahan between 1664 and 1677 and in his *Voyages* gave a detailed and graphic description of the city as it was at its zenith. It had then, he said, 162 mosques, 48 colleges, 273 baths, and more than 1,802 caravansaries (hostels).

In 1722 the Ghilzai Afghāns, led by Maḥmūd, defeated the Persian army a few miles to the east of Isfahan and took the city after a long siege, in the course of which more than 100,000 of the inhabitants perished from famine and pestilence. Isfahan never fully recovered from this calamity. For many years the greater part of the city was a heap of rubble, and its population dwindled to a fraction of what it had once been.

In the reign of Reza Shah Pahlavi (1925–41) an industrial quarter was built there, and many of the historic buildings were restored.

Laurence Lockhart

Dome of the Lotfollāh Mosque, Isfahan, early 17th century.

Isfahan is on the main north–south highway from Teheran to Shīrāz and the Persian Gulf and is linked by a road east and southeast to Yazd, Kermān, Zāhedān, and so to Pakistan.

The city is famous for its handicrafts, such as silverware, copper work, and brass work, as well as for its pottery. The old art of tile making has been successfully revived in order to enable the ancient monuments to be adequately repaired. Isfahan is also well known for its rugs and its *qalamkārs* (cotton fabrics handprinted with various designs). Modern industry is represented by the textile mills to the south of the river.

Isfahan "ostān" (province). Isfahan is situated in central Iran and bounded southwest by Khūzestan, west by the mountainous general governorship of Chahār Mahal (formerly Bakhtīarī) and that of Lorestān, north by Kāshān (part of Māzandarān *ostān*) and by Semnān-Dāmghān general governorship, east by Khorāsān, southeast by Kermān, and south by Fārs. The country is mountainous to the west and south, but Isfahan city stands on the eastern edge of the Zāgros Mountains in a fertile basin. The climate is relatively temperate.

BIBLIOGRAPHY. ANDRE GODARD, "Isfahan," in *Athār-ē Īrān*, vol. 2 (1937); LAURENCE LOCKHART, "Isfahan," in *Persian Cities*, ch. 3 (1960).

(L.L.)

Islām

Arising in Arabia in the 7th century AD as a result of the preaching and teaching of the Prophet Muḥammad, Islām, with its emphasis on an uncompromising monotheism and a strict adherence to certain religious practices, spread rapidly from the Atlantic to the Pacific and from Africa and Europe to China and Indonesia. Though there have been many Islāmic sects and movements, all followers are bound by a common faith and a sense of belonging to a single community.

This article is divided into the following sections:

GENERAL CHARACTERISTICS AND ETHNIC-GEOGRAPHIC EXTENT

Islām is a major world religion belonging to the Semitic family; it was promulgated by the Prophet Muḥammad in Arabia in the 7th century AD. The Arabic term *islām*, literally meaning "surrender," points to the fundamental religious idea of Islām, namely that the believer, called a Muslim (being the active participle of *islām*), accepts surrender to the will of Allāh (Arabic: God). Allāh is viewed as the unique God—Creator, sustainer, and restorer of the world. The will of God, to which man is to submit, is made known through the Qur'ān (often rendered Koran, the Islāmic scriptures), the Book revealed to his messenger, Muḥammad, who is believed to have been the last of a series of prophets (Adam, Noah, Moses, Jesus, and others) and whose message at the same time consummated and abrogated the "revelations" vouchsafed to the previous prophets. The basic belief of Islām is expressed in the *shahādah*, the Muslim confession of faith: "There is no god but God; Muḥammad is the prophet of God." From this fundamental belief are derived beliefs in (1) angels (particularly Gabriel, the Angel of Revelation), (2) the revealed Books (the Qur'ān and sacred books of Judeo-Christian revelation described in the Qur'ān [*q.v.*]), (3) a series of prophets (particularly eminent among whom are Judeo-Christian figures—although it is believed that God has sent messengers to every nation), and (4) the Last Day (Day of Judgment). Acceptance of this essential creed involves further duties that are to be strictly observed: five daily prayers, a welfare tax called the *zakāt*, fasting, and a pilgrimage to Mecca, all of which—including the profession of faith—are called the Five Pillars.

Basic beliefs deriving from the *shahādah*

From the very beginning of Islām, the Prophet Muḥammad had inculcated a sense of brotherhood and a bond of faith among his followers, both of which helped to develop among them a feeling of close relationship that was accentuated by their experiences of persecution as a nascent community in Mecca. The conspicuous socioeconomic content of Islāmic religious practices (*e.g.*, the *zakāt*) cemented this bond of faith. In AD 622, when the Prophet fled to Medina, his preaching was soon accepted, and the community-state of Islām emerged. From the date of Muḥammad's flight, called the *hijrah*, Muslims begin their calendar—AH (Anno Hegirae) 287, for example, is the same as AD (Anno Domini) 900. During this early period, Islām acquired its characteristic ethos as a religion uniting in itself both the spiritual and temporal aspects of life and seeking to regulate not only the individual's relationship to God (through his conscience) but human relationships in a social setting as well. Thus, there is not only an Islāmic religious institution but also an Islāmic law, state, and other institutions governing society. Only recently have the religious (private) and the secular (public) been distinguished by some Muslim thinkers and separated formally, as in Turkey.

This dual religious and social character of Islām, expressing itself as a religious community commissioned by God to bring its own value system to the world through the *jihād* ("holy war" or "holy struggle"), explains the astonishing success of the early generations of Muslims. Within a century after the Prophet's death in AD 632, they had brought a large part of the globe—from Spain across Central Asia to India—under a new Arab Muslim empire. The period of Islāmic conquests and empire building marks the first phase of the expansion of Islām as a religion. Islām's essential egalitarianism within the community of the faithful and its official discrimination against the followers of other religions won rapid converts. Jews and Christians were assigned a special status as communities possessing scriptures and called the "people of the Book" (*ahl al-kitāb*) and, therefore, were allowed religious autonomy. They were, however, required to pay a per capita tax called *jizyah*, as opposed to pagans, who were required to either accept Islām or die. The same status of the "people of the Book" was later extended to Zoroastrians and Hindus, but many "people of the Book" joined Islām in order to escape the disability of the *jizyah* tax. A much more massive expansion of Islām after the 12th century was inaugurated by the Ṣūfīs (Muslim mystics), who were mainly responsible for the spread of Islām in India, Central Asia, Turkey, and sub-Saharan Africa.

Relationship to other religions

Besides the *jihād* and Ṣūfī missionary activity, another factor in the spread of Islām was the influence of Muslim traders, who not only introduced Islām quite early to the Indian east coast and South India but who proved as well to be the main catalytic agents (besides the Ṣūfīs) in converting people to Islām in Indonesia, Malaya, and China. Islām was introduced to Indonesia in the 14th century, hardly having time to consolidate itself there politically before coming under Dutch colonial domination.

The vast variety of races and cultures embraced by Islām (estimated to total from 600,000,000 to 800,000,000 persons worldwide) has produced important internal differences. All segments of Muslim society, however, are bound by a common faith and a sense of belonging to a single community. With the loss of political power during the period of Western colonialism in the 19th and 20th centuries, the concept of the Islāmic community (*ummah*), instead of weakening, became stronger and helped various Muslim peoples in their struggle to gain political freedom and sovereignty in the mid-20th century.

DOCTRINAL AND SOCIAL VIEWS

Sources. Islāmic doctrine, law, and thinking in general are based upon four sources, or fundamental principles (*uṣūl*): (1) the Qur'ān, (2) the *sunnah* ("traditions"), (3) *ijmā'* ("consensus of the community"), and (4) *ijtihād* ("individual thought").

The Qur'ān (literally, Reading, or Recitation) is regarded as the Word, or Speech, of God that was delivered to Muḥammad by the angel Gabriel. Divided into 114 *sūrahs* (chapters) of unequal length, it is the fundamental source of Islāmic teaching. The *sūrah*s revealed at Mecca during the earliest part of Muḥammad's career are concerned with ethical and spiritual teachings and the Day of Judgment. The *sūrah*s revealed at Medina at a later period in the career of the Prophet are concerned with social legislation and the politico-moral principles for constituting and ordering the community. The *sunnah* ("a clear and well-trodden path") was used by pre-Islāmic Arabs to denote their tribal or common law; in Islām it came to mean the example of the Prophet; *i.e.*, his words and deeds.

Ḥadīth, or collection of the Prophet's sayings

The Ḥadīth (a Report, or collection of sayings attributed to the Prophet) provide the means by which the Prophet's words and deeds are made known. Six of these collections, compiled in the 3rd century AH (9th century AD), came to be regarded as especially authoritative by the largest group in Islām, the Sunnī. Another large group, the Shīʿah, has its own Ḥadīth.

The doctrine of *ijmāʿ* was introduced in the 2nd century AH (8th century AD) in order to standardize legal theory and practice and to overcome individual and regional differences of opinion. Though conceived as a "consensus of scholars," in actual practice *ijmāʿ* was a more fundamental operative factor. From the 3rd century AH, *ijmāʿ* has amounted to a principle of rigidity in thinking; points on which consensus was reached in practice were considered closed and further substantial questioning of them prohibited. Accepted interpretations of the Qurʾān and the actual content of the *sunnah* (*i.e.*, Ḥadīth and theology) all rest finally on the *ijmāʿ*.

Ijtihād, meaning "to endeavour" or "to exert oneself," was required to find the legal or doctrinal solution to a new problem. In the early period of Islām, because *ijtihād* took the form of individual opinion (*raʾy*), there was a wealth of conflicting and chaotic opinions. In the 2nd century AH *ijtihād* was replaced by *qiyās* (reasoning by strict analogy), a formal procedure of deduction based on the texts of the Qurʾān and the Ḥadīth. The transformation of *ijmāʿ* into a conservative mechanism and the acceptance of a definitive body of Ḥadīth virtually closed the "gate of *ijtihād*." Nevertheless, certain outstanding Muslim thinkers (*e.g.*, al-Ghazālī, died AD 1111) continued to claim the right of new *ijtihād* for themselves, and reformers of the 18th and 19th centuries, because of modern influences, have caused this principle to once more receive wider acceptance.

Doctrine. *God*. The doctrine about God in the Qurʾān is rigorously monotheistic: God is one and unique; he has no partner and no equal. Trinitarianism, the Christian belief that God is three persons in one substance, is vigorously repudiated. Muslims believe that there are no intermediaries between God and the creation that he brought into being by his sheer command: "Be." Although his presence is believed to be everywhere, he does not inhere in anything. He is the sole Creator and sustainer of the universe, wherein every creature bears witness to his unity and lordship. But he is also just and merciful: his justice ensures order in his creation, in which nothing is believed to be out of place, and his mercy is unbounded and encompasses everything. His creating and ordering the universe is viewed as the act of prime mercy for which all things sing his glories. The God of the Qurʾān, described as majestic and sovereign, is also a personal God; he is viewed as being nearer to man than man's jugular vein, and, whenever a person in need or distress calls him, he responds. Above all, he is the God of guidance and shows everything, particularly man, the right way, "the straight path."

The God of the Qurʾān

This picture of God—wherein the attributes of power, justice, and mercy interpenetrate—is related to the Judeo-Christian tradition, whence it is derived with certain modifications, and also to the concepts of pagan Arabia, to which it provided an effective answer. The pagan Arabs believed in a blind and inexorable fate over which man had no control. For this powerful but insensible fate the Qurʾān substituted a powerful but provident and merciful God. The Qurʾān carried through its uncompromising monotheism by rejecting all forms of idolatry and eliminating all gods and divinities that the Arabs worshipped in their sanctuaries (*ḥarams*), the most prominent of which was the Kaʿbah sanctuary in Mecca itself.

The universe. In order to prove the unity of God, the Qurʾān lays frequent stress on the design and order in the universe. There are no gaps or dislocations in nature. Order is explained by the fact that every created thing is endowed with a definite and defined nature whereby it falls into a pattern. This nature, though it allows every created thing to function in a whole, sets limits; and this idea of the limitedness of everything is one of the most fixed points in both the cosmology and theology of the Qurʾān. The universe is viewed, therefore, as autonomous, in the sense that everything has its own inherent laws of behaviour, but not as autocratic, because the patterns of behaviour have been endowed by God and are strictly limited. "Everything has been created by us according to a measure." Though every creature is thus limited and "measured out" and hence depends upon God, God alone, who reigns unchallenged in the heavens and the earth, is unlimited, independent, and self-sufficient.

Man. According to the Qurʾān, God created two apparently parallel species of creatures, man and *jinn*, the one from clay and the other from fire. About the *jinn*, however, the Qurʾān says little, although it is implied that the *jinn* are endowed with reason and responsibility but are more prone to evil than man. It is with man that the Qurʾān, which describes itself as a guide for the human race, is centrally concerned. The Judeo-Christian story of the Fall of Adam (the first man) is accepted, but the Qurʾān states that God forgave Adam his act of disobedience, which is not viewed in the Qurʾān (in contradistinction to its understanding in the Christian doctrine) as original sin.

In the story of man's creation, angels, who protested to God against the creation of man, who "would sow mischief on earth," lost in a competition of knowledge against Adam. The Qurʾān, therefore, declares man to be the noblest of all creation, the created being who bore the trust (of responsibility) that the rest of the creation refused to accept. The Qurʾān thus reiterates that all nature has been made subservient to man: nothing in all creation has been made without a purpose, and man himself has not been created "in sport," his purpose being service and obedience to God's will.

Despite this lofty station, however, the Qurʾān describes human nature as frail and faltering. Whereas everything in the universe has a limited nature, and every creature recognizes its limitation and insufficiency, man is viewed as rebellious and full of pride, arrogating to himself the attributes of self-sufficiency. Pride, thus, is viewed as the cardinal sin of man, because by not recognizing in himself his essential creaturely limitations he becomes guilty of ascribing to himself partnership with God (*shirk:* associating a creature with the Creator) and of violating the unity of God. True faith (*īmān*), thus, consists of belief in the immaculate Divine Unity and Islām in one's submission to the Divine Will.

Pride, the cardinal sin

Satan, sin, and repentance. In order to communicate the truth of the Divine Unity, God has sent messengers or prophets to men, whose weakness of nature makes them ever prone to forget or even willfully reject the Divine Unity under the promptings of Satan. According to the Qurʾānic teaching, the being who became Satan (Shayṭān or Iblīs) had previously occupied a high station but fell from divine grace by his act of disobedience in refusing to honour Adam when he, along with other angels, was ordered to do so. Since then, his work has been to beguile man into error and sin. Satan is, therefore, the contemporary of man, and Satan's own act of disobedience is construed by the Qurʾān as the sin of pride. Satan's machinations will cease only on the Last Day.

Judging from the accounts of the Qurʾān, the record of man's accepting the prophets' messages has been rather dismal. The whole universe is replete with signs of God; the human soul itself is viewed as a witness of the unity and grace of God. The messengers of God have, throughout history, been calling man back to God. Yet very few men have accepted the truth; most of them have rejected it and become disbelievers (*kāfir*, plural *kuffār:* literally meaning "ungrateful"—*i.e.*, to God), and when man becomes so obdurate, his heart is sealed by God. Nevertheless, it is always possible for a sinner to repent (*tawbah*) and redeem himself by a genuine conversion to the truth. There is no point of no return, and God is always willing and ready to pardon. Genuine repentance has the effect of removing all sins and restoring a person to the state of sinlessness with which he started his life.

Prophecy. Prophets are men specially elected by God to be his messengers. Prophethood is indivisible, and the Qur'ān requires recognition of all prophets as such without discrimination. Yet they are not all equal, some of them being particularly outstanding in qualities of steadfastness and patience under trial. Abraham, Noah, Moses, and Jesus were such great prophets. As vindication of the truth of their mission, God often vests them with miracles: Abraham was saved from fire, Noah from the deluge, and Moses from the Pharaoh. Not only was Jesus born from the Virgin Mary, but God also saved him from crucifixion at the hands of the Jews. The conviction that God's messengers are ultimately vindicated and saved is an integral part of the Qur'ānic doctrine.

Muḥammad as the last prophet

All prophets are human and never part of divinity: they are simply recipients of revelation from God. God never speaks directly to a human: he either sends an angel messenger to him or makes him hear a voice or inspires him. Muḥammad is accepted as the last prophet in this series and its greatest member, for in him all the messages of earlier prophets were consummated. He had no miracles except the Qur'ān, the like of which no human can produce. (Soon after the Prophet's death, however, a plethora of miracles was attributed to him by Muslims.) The angel Gabriel brought the Qur'ān down to the Prophet's "heart." Gabriel is represented by the Qur'ān as a spirit, but the Prophet could sometimes see and hear him. According to early traditions, the Prophet's revelations occurred in a state of trance when his normal consciousness was in abeyance. This state was accompanied by heavy sweating. The Qur'ān itself makes it clear that the revelations brought with them a sense of extraordinary weight: "If we were to send this Qur'ān down on a mountain, you would see it split asunder out of fear of God."

This phenomenon at the same time was accompanied by an unshakable conviction that the message was from God, and the Qur'ān describes itself as the transcript of a heavenly "Mother Book" written on a "Preserved Tablet." The conviction was of such an intensity that the Qur'ān categorically denies that it is from any earthly source, for in that case it would be liable to "manifold doubts and oscillations."

Eschatology. In Islāmic doctrine, on the Last Day, when the world will come to an end, the dead will be resurrected and a judgment will be pronounced on every person in accordance with his deeds. Although the Qur'ān in the main speaks of a personal judgment, there are several verses that speak of the resurrection of distinct communities that will be judged according to "their own book." In conformity with this, the Qur'ān also speaks in several passages of the "death of communities," each one of which has a definite term of life. The actual evaluation, however, will be for every individual, whatever the terms of reference of his performance. In order to prove that the resurrection will occur, the Qur'ān uses a moral and a physical argument. Because not all requital is meted out in this life, a final judgment is necessary to bring it to completion. Physically, God, who is all-powerful, has the ability to destroy and bring back to life all creatures, who are limited and are, therefore, subject to God's limitless power.

According to strict Qur'ānic doctrine, there is no intercession, although God himself, in his mercy, may forgive certain sinners. Those condemned will burn in hellfire, and those who are saved will enjoy the abiding pleasures of paradise. Hell and heaven are both spiritual and physical. Besides suffering in physical fire, the damned will also experience fire "in their hearts"; similarly, the blessed, besides physical enjoyment, will experience the greatest happiness of divine pleasure. Quite early, however, Islāmic tradition developed the notion of intercession, probably in answer to the Christian doctrine of redemption.

God in the role of commander

Social views. Because the purpose of the existence of man, as of every other creature, is submission to the Divine Will, God's role in relation to man is that of the commander. Whereas the rest of nature obeys God automatically, man alone possesses the choice to obey or disobey. With the deep-seated belief in Satan's existence, man's fundamental role becomes one of moral struggle, which constitutes the essence of human endeavour. Recognition of the unity of God does not simply rest in the intellect but entails consequences in terms of the moral struggle, which consists primarily in freeing oneself of narrowness of mind and smallness of heart. One must go out of oneself and expend one's best possessions for the sake of others.

The doctrine of social service, in terms of alleviating suffering and helping the needy, constitutes an integral part of the Islāmic teaching. Praying to God and other religious acts are deemed to be a pure facade in the absence of active welfare service to the needy. In regard to this matter, the Qur'ānic criticisms of human nature become very sharp: "Man is by nature timid; when evil befalls him, he panics, but when good things come to him he prevents them from reaching others." It is Satan who whispers into man's ears that by spending for others he will become poor. God, on the contrary, promises prosperity in exchange for such expenditure, which constitutes a credit with God and grows much more than the money people invest in usury. Hoarding of wealth without recognizing the rights of the poor is threatened with the direst punishment in the hereafter and is declared to be one of the main causes of the decay of societies in this world. The practice of usury is forbidden.

The concept of a community of the faithful

With this socioeconomic doctrine cementing the bond of faith, the idea of a closely knit community of the faithful who are declared to be "brothers unto each other" emerges. Muslims are described as "the middle community bearing witness on mankind," "the best community produced for mankind," whose function it is "to enjoin good and forbid evil" (Qur'ān). Cooperation and "good advice" within the community are emphasized, and a person who deliberately tries to harm the interests of the community is to be given exemplary punishment. Opponents from within the community are to be fought and reduced with armed force, if issues cannot be settled by persuasion and arbitration.

Because the mission of the community is to "enjoin good and forbid evil" so that "there is no mischief and corruption" on earth, the doctrine of *jihād*, in view of the constitution of the community as the power base, is the logical outcome. For the early community it was a basic religious concept. *Jihād* means an active struggle using armed force whenever necessary. The object of *jihād* is not the conversion of individuals to Islām but rather the gaining of political control over the collective affairs of societies to run them in accordance with the principles of Islām. Individual conversions occur as a by-product of this process when the power structure passes into the hands of the Muslim community. In strict Muslim doctrine, conversions "by force" are forbidden, because after the revelation of the Qur'ān "good and evil have become distinct," so that one may follow whichever one may prefer (Qur'ān), and it is also strictly prohibited to wage wars for the sake of acquiring worldly glory, power, and rule. With the establishment of the Muslim empire, however, the doctrine of the *jihād* was modified by the leaders of the community. Their main concern had become the consolidation of the empire and its administration, and thus they interpreted the teaching in a defensive rather than in an expansive sense. The Khārijite sect, which held that "decision belongs to God alone," insisted on continuous and relentless *jihād*, but its followers were virtually destroyed during the internecine wars in the 8th century.

Besides a measure of economic justice and the creation of a strong community ideal, the Prophet Muḥammad effected a general reform of the Arab society, in particular protecting its weaker segments—the poor, the orphans, women, and slaves. Slavery was not legally abolished, but emancipation of slaves was religiously encouraged as an act of merit. Slaves were given legal rights, including the right of acquiring their freedom against payment, in installments, of a sum agreed upon by the slave and his master out of his earnings. A slave woman who bore a child by her master became automatically free after her master's death. The infanticide of girls that was practiced among certain tribes—out of fear of poverty or a sense of shame—was forbidden.

Distinction and privileges based on tribal rank or race were repudiated in the Qur'ān and in the celebrated "Farewell Pilgrimage Address" of the Prophet shortly before his death. All men are therein declared to be "equal children of Adam," and the only distinction recognized in the sight of God is to be based on piety and good acts. The age-old Arab institution of intertribal revenge (called *tha'r*)—whereby it was not necessarily the killer who was executed but a person equal in rank to the slain person—was abolished. The pre-Islāmic ethical ideal of manliness was modified and replaced by a more humane ideal of moral virtue and piety.

FORMS OF ISLAM: TENSIONS AND SCHISMS

Khārijism. Despite the notion of a unified and consolidated community, as taught by the Prophet, violent differences arose among Muslims within a few years after his death. These differences were in the first instance political, arising out of the question of the leadership of the community. During the reign of the third caliph (deputy or successor of Muḥammad), ʿUthmān, certain circles accused the Caliph of nepotism and misrule, and the resulting discontent led to his assassination. The rebels then recognized the Prophet's cousin and son-in-law, ʿAlī, as ruler but later deserted him and fought against him, accusing him of having committed a grave sin in submitting his claim to the caliphate to arbitration. The word *khurūj*, from which *khārijī* is derived, means in this context "rebellion," and Khārijīs were, therefore, people who believed in active dissent or rebellion against a state of affairs they considered to be gravely impious.

The question of leadership

The basic doctrine of the Khārijīs was that a person or a group who committed a grave error or sin and did not sincerely repent ceased to be Muslim. Mere profession of the faith—"there is no god but God; Muḥammad is the prophet of God"—did not make a person a Muslim unless this faith was accompanied by righteous deeds. In other words, good works were an integral part of faith and not extraneous to it. The second principle that flowed from their aggressive idealism was militancy, or *jihād*, which the Khārijīs considered to be among the cardinal principles, or pillars, of Islām. They interpreted the Qur'ānic command about "enjoining good and forbidding evil" to mean the vindication of truth through the sword. The placing of these two principles together made the Khārijīs highly inflammable fanatics, intolerant of almost any established political authority. They incessantly resorted to rebellion and as a result were virtually wiped out during the first two centuries of Islām.

Because the Khārijīs believed that the basis of rule was righteous character and piety alone, any Muslim, irrespective of race, colour, and sex, could, in their view, become ruler—provided he or she satisfied the conditions of piety. This was in contrast to the claims of the Shīʿah (the party of ʿAlī) that the ruler must belong to the family of the Prophet and to the doctrine of the Sunnīs (followers of the Prophet's way) that the head of state must belong to the Prophet's tribe, *i.e.*, the Quraysh.

A moderate group of the Khārijīs, the Ibāḍīs, has avoided extinction, and its members are to be found today in North Africa and in Oman and other parts of East Africa, including Zanzibar Island. The Ibāḍīs do not believe in aggressive methods and, throughout medieval Islām, remained dormant. Recently, however, because of the interest of Western scholars in this sect, the Ibāḍīs have become active and have begun to publish their classical writings and their own journals.

The permanent influence of Khārijism on Islām

Although Khārijism is now essentially a story of the past, it has left a permanent influence on Islām, because of reaction against it. It forced the religious leadership of the community to formulate a bulwark against intolerance and fanaticism. Positively, it has influenced the reform movements that have sprung up in Islām from time to time and that have treated spiritual and moral placidity and status quo with a quasi-Khārijī zeal and militancy.

The Muʿtazilah. The question of whether works are an integral part of faith or independent of it, as raised by the Khārijīs, led to another important theological question: are human acts the result of a free human choice, or are they predetermined by God? This question brought with it a whole series of questions about the nature of God and of man. Although the initial impetus to theological thought, in the case of the Khārijīs, had come from within Islām, full-scale religious speculation resulted from the contact and confrontation of Muslims with other cultures and systems of thought.

As a consequence of translations of Greek philosophical and scientific works into Arabic during the 8th and 9th centuries and the controversies of Muslims with Dualists (*e.g.*, Gnostics and Manichaeans), Buddhists, and Christians, a more powerful movement of rational theology emerged; its representatives are called the Muʿtazilah (Seceders). On the question of the relationship of faith to works, the Muʿtazilah—who called themselves "champions of God's unity and justice"—taught, like the Khārijīs, that works were an essential part of faith but that a person guilty of a grave sin, unless he repented, was neither a Muslim nor yet a non-Muslim but instead occupied a "middle ground." They further defended the position, as a central part of their doctrine, that man was free to choose and act and was, therefore, responsible for his actions. Divine predestination of human acts, they held, was incompatible both with God's justice and with human responsibility. The Muʿtazilah, therefore, recognized two powers, or actors, in the universe—God in the realm of nature and man in the domain of moral human action. The Muʿtazilah explained away the apparently predeterministic verses of the Qur'ān as being metaphors and exhortations.

Emphasis on reason

They claimed that human reason, independent of revelation, was capable of discovering what is good and what is evil, although revelation corroborated the findings of reason. Man is, therefore, under moral obligation to do the right even if there were no prophets and no divine revelation. Revelation has to be interpreted, therefore, in conformity with the dictates of rational ethics. Yet revelation is neither redundant nor passive. Its function is twofold. First, its aim is to aid man in choosing the right, because in the conflict between good and evil man often falters and makes the wrong choice against his rational judgment. God, therefore, must send prophets, for he must do the best for man; otherwise, the demands of divine grace and mercy cannot be fulfilled. Secondly, revelation is also necessary to communicate the positive obligations of religion—*e.g.*, prayers and fasting—which cannot be known without revelation.

God is viewed by the Muʿtazilah as pure Essence, without eternal attributes, because they hold that the assumption of eternal attributes in conjunction with Essence will result in a belief in multiple coeternals and violate the pure, unadulterated unity of God. God knows, wills, and acts by virtue of his Essence and not through attributes of knowledge, will, and power. Nor does he have an eternal attribute of speech, of which the Qur'ān and other earlier revelations were effects; the Qur'ān was, therefore, created in time and was not eternal.

The promises of reward that God has made in the Qur'ān to righteous people and the threats of punishment he has issued to evildoers must be carried out by him on the Day of Judgment. For promises and threats are viewed as reports about the future, and if not fulfilled exactly those reports will turn into lies, which are inconceivable of God. Also, if God were to withhold punishment for evil and forgive it, this would be as unjust as withholding reward for righteousness. There can be neither undeserved punishment nor undeserved reward; otherwise, good may just as well turn into evil and evil into good. From this position it follows that there can be no intercession on behalf of sinners.

When, in the early part of the 9th century, the ʿAbbāsid caliph al-Ma'mūn raised Muʿtazilism to the status of the state creed, the Muʿtazilite rationalists showed themselves to be illiberal and they persecuted their opponents. Aḥmad ibn Ḥanbal (died 855), an eminent orthodox figure founder of one of the four orthodox schools of Islāmic law, was subjected to flogging and imprisonment for his refusal to subscribe to the doctrine that the Qur'ān, the word of God, was created in time. In the 10th century a reaction began against the Muʿtazilah that culminated in the formulation and subsequent general acceptance of another set of theological propositions, which thus became Sunnī, or "orthodox" theology.

Sunnism. The issues raised by these early schisms and the positions adopted by them enabled the Sunnī orthodoxy to define its own doctrinal positions in turn. Much of the content of Sunnī theology was, therefore, supplied by its reactions to those schisms. The term *sunnah*, which means a "well-trodden path" and in the religious terminology of Islām normally signifies "the example set by the Prophet," in the present context simply means "the conspicuous and well-defined way." In this context, the term *sunnah* usually is accompanied by the appendage "the consolidated majority" (*al-jamāʿah*). The term clearly indicates that the conspicuous and well-defined way is the way of the consolidated majority of the community as against peripheral or "wayward" positions of sectarians, who by definition must be erroneous.

Emphasis on the way of the majority

With the rise of the orthodoxy, then, the foremost and elemental factor that came to be emphasized was the notion of the majority of the community. The concept of the community so vigorously pronounced by the earliest doctrine of the Qur'ān gained both a new emphasis and a fresh context with the rise of Sunnism. Whereas the Qur'ān had marked out the Muslim community from other communities, Sunnism now emphasized the views and customs of the majority of the community in contradistinction to peripheral groups. An abundance of tradition (Ḥadīth) came to be attributed to the Prophet to the effect that Muslims must follow the majority's way, that minority groups are all doomed to hell, and that God's protective hand is always on (the majority of) the community, which can never be in error. Under the impact of the new Ḥadīth, the community, which had been charged by the Qur'ān with a mission and commanded to accept a challenge, now became transformed into a privileged one that was endowed with infallibility.

At the same time, while condemning schisms and branding dissent as heretical, Sunnism developed the opposite trend of accommodation, catholicity, and synthesis. A putative tradition of the Prophet that says "differences of opinion among my community are a blessing" was given wide currency. This principle of toleration ultimately made it possible for diverse sects and schools of thought—notwithstanding a wide range of difference in belief and practice—to recognize and coexist with each other. No group may be excluded from the community unless it itself formally renounces Islām. As for individuals, tests of heresy may be applied to their beliefs, but, unless a person is found to flagrantly violate or deny the unity of God or expressly negate the prophethood of Muḥammad, such tests usually have no serious consequences. Catholicity was orthodoxy's answer to the intolerance and secessionism of the Khārijīs and the severity of the Muʿtazilah. As a consequence, a formula was adopted in which good works were recognized as enhancing the quality of faith but not as entering into the definition and essential nature of faith. This broad formula saved the integrity of the community at the expense of moral strictness and doctrinal uniformity.

On the question of free will, Sunnī orthodoxy attempted a synthesis between man's responsibility and God's omnipotence. The champions of orthodoxy accused the Muʿtazilah of quasi-Magian Dualism (Zoroastrianism) insofar as the Muʿtazilah admitted two independent and original actors in the universe: God and man. To the orthodox it seemed blasphemous to hold that man could act wholly outside the sphere of divine omnipotence, which had been so vividly portrayed by the Qur'ān but which the Muʿtazilah had endeavoured to explain away in order to make room for man's free and independent action. The Sunnī formulation, however, as presented by al-Ashʿarī and al-Māturīdī, Sunnī's two main representatives in the 10th century, shows palpable differences despite basic uniformity. Al-Ashʿarī taught that human acts were created by God and acquired by man and that human responsibility depended on this acquisition. He denied, however, that man could be described as an actor in a real sense. Al-Māturīdī, on the other hand, held that although God is the sole Creator of everything, including human acts, nevertheless, man is an actor in the real sense, for acting and creating were two different types of activity involving different aspects of the same human act.

Formulators of Sunnī doctrine

In conformity with their positions, al-Ashʿarī believed that man did not have the power to act before he actually acted and that God created this power in him at the time of action; and al-Māturīdī taught that before the action man has a certain general power for action but that this power becomes specific to a particular action only when the action is performed, because, after full and specific power comes into existence, action cannot be delayed.

Al-Ashʿarī and his school also held that human reason was incapable of discovering good and evil and that acts became endowed with good or evil qualities through God's declaring them to be such. Because man in his natural state regards his own self-interest as good and that which thwarts his interests as bad, natural human reason is unreliable. Independently of revelation, therefore, murder would not be bad nor the saving of life good. Furthermore, because God's Will makes acts good or bad, one cannot ask for reasons behind the divine law, which must be simply accepted. Al-Māturīdī takes an opposite position, not materially different from that of the Muʿtazilah: human reason is capable of finding out good and evil, and revelation aids human reason against the sway of human passions.

Despite these important initial differences between the two main Sunnī schools of thought, the doctrines of al-Māturīdī became submerged in course of time under the expanding popularity of the Ashʿarite school, which gained wide currency particularly after the 11th century because of the influential activity of the Ṣūfī theologian al-Ghazālī. Because these later theologians placed increasing emphasis on divine omnipotence at the expense of the freedom and efficacy of the human will, a deterministic outlook on life became characteristic of Sunnī Islām—reinvigorated by the Ṣūfī world view, which taught that nothing exists except God, whose being is the only real being. This general deterministic outlook produced, in turn, a severe reformist reaction in the teachings of Ibn Taymīyah, a 14th-century theologian who sought to rehabilitate human freedom and responsibility and whose influence has been strongly felt through the reform movements in the Muslim world since the 18th century.

Shīʿism and its subsects. The Shīʿah are the only important surviving sect in Islām. They owe their origin to the hostility between ʿAlī (the fourth caliph and son-in-law of the Prophet) and the Umayyad dynasty (661–750). After ʿAlī's death, the Shīʿah (Party; *i.e.*, of ʿAlī) demanded the restoration of rule to ʿAlī's family, and from that demand developed the Shīʿite legitimism, or the divine right of the holy family to rule. In the early stages, the Shīʿah used this legitimism to cover the protest against the Arab hegemony under the Umayyads and to agitate for social reform.

Gradually, however, Shīʿism developed a theological content for its political stand. Probably under Gnostic (esoteric, dualistic, and speculative) and old Iranian (dualistic) influences, the figure of the political ruler, the *imām* (exemplary "leader"), was transformed into a metaphysical being, a manifestation of God and the primordial light that sustains the universe and bestows true knowledge on man. Through the *imām* alone the hidden and true meaning of the Qur'ānic revelation can be known, because the *imām* alone is infallible. The Shīʿah thus developed a doctrine of esoteric knowledge that was adopted also, in a modified form, by the Ṣūfīs. The orthodox Shīʿah recognize 12 such *imām*s, the last (Muḥammad) having disappeared in the 9th century. Since that time, the *mujtahids* (*i.e.*, the Shīʿah divines) have been able to interpret law and doctrine under the

Emphasis on the *imām*

putative guidance of the *imām*, who will return toward the end of time to fill the world with truth and justice.

On the basis of their doctrine of imamology, the Shīʿah emphasize their idealism and transcendentalism in conscious contrast with Sunnī pragmatism. Thus, whereas the Sunnīs believe in the *ijmāʿ* ("consensus") of the community as the source of decision making and workable knowledge, the Shīʿah believe that knowledge derived from fallible sources is useless and that sure and true knowledge can come only through a contact with the infallible *imām*. Again, in marked contrast to Sunnism, Shīʿism adopted the Muʿtazilite doctrine of the freedom of the human will and the capacity of human reason to know good and evil, although its position on the question of the relationship of faith to works is the same as that of the Sunnīs.

Parallel to the doctrine of an esoteric knowledge, Shīʿism, because of its early defeats and persecutions, also adopted the principle of *taqīyah*, or dissimulation of faith in a hostile environment. Introduced first as a practical principle, *taqīyah*, which is also attributed to ʿAlī and other *imāms*, became an important part of the Shīʿah religious teaching and practice. In the sphere of law, Shīʿism differs from Sunnī law mainly in allowing a temporary marriage, called *mutʿah*, which can be legally contracted for a fixed period of time on the stipulation of a fixed dower.

Introduction of the passion motive

From a spiritual point of view, perhaps the greatest difference between Shīʿism and Sunnism is the former's introduction into Islām of the passion motive, which is conspicuously absent from Sunnī Islām. The violent death (in 680) of ʿAlī's son, Ḥusayn, at the hands of the Umayyad troops is celebrated with moving orations, passion plays, and processions in which the participants, in a state of emotional frenzy, beat their breasts with heavy chains and sharp instruments, inflicting wounds on their bodies. This passion motive has also influenced the Sunnī masses in Afghanistan and the Indian subcontinent, who participate in passion plays called *taʿziyahs*. Such celebrations are, however, absent from Egypt and North Africa.

Foto Features

Muslims carrying the *taʿzīyah* to their cremation during a procession commemorating the martyrdom of Ḥusayn, in Jaipur, India.

Although the Shīʿah number only about 40,000,000 (Shīʿism has been the official religion in Iran since the 16th century), Shīʿism has exerted a great influence on Sunnī Islām in several ways. The veneration in which all Muslims hold ʿAlī and his family and the respect shown to ʿAlī's descendants (who are called *sayyids* in the East and *sharīfs* in North Africa) are obvious evidence of this influence.

Ismāʿīlīs. Besides the main body of Twelver (Ithnā ʿAsharīyah) Shīʿah, Shīʿism has produced a variety of more or less extremist sects, the most important of them being the Ismāʿīlī. Instead of recognizing Mūsā as the seventh *imām*, as did the main body of the Shīʿah, the Ismāʿīlīs upheld the claims of his elder brother Ismāʿīl (disowned by the Twelvers for drinking wine) and, since his disappearance, await his return; hence their appellation the Seveners (Sabʿīyah). The Ismāʿīlī teaching spread during the 9th century from North Africa to Sind, in India, and the Ismāʿīlī Fāṭimid dynasty succeeded in establishing a prosperous empire in Egypt. Ismāʿīlīs are subdivided into two groups—the Nizārīs, headed by the Aga Khan, and the Mustaʿlīs in Bombay, with their own spiritual head. The Ismāʿīlīs are to be found mainly in East Africa, Pakistan, India, and Yemen.

In their theology, the Ismāʿīlīs have absorbed the most extreme elements and heterodox ideas. The universe is viewed as a cyclic process, and the unfolding of each cycle is marked by the advent of seven "speakers"—messengers of God with Scriptures—each of whom is succeeded by seven "silents"—messengers without revealed scriptures; the last speaker (the Prophet Muḥammad) is followed by seven *imāms* who interpret the Will of God to man and are, in a sense, higher than the Prophet because they draw their knowledge directly from God and not from the Angel of Revelation. During the 10th century, certain Ismāʿīlī intellectuals formed a secret society called the Brethren of Purity, which issued a philosophical encyclopaedia, *The Epistles of the Brethren of Purity*, aiming at the liquidation of positive religions in favour of a universalist spirituality.

The late Aga Khan III (1887–1957), grandfather of the incumbent of the early 1970s, had taken several measures to bring his followers closer to the main body of the Muslims. The Ismāʿīlīs, however, still do not have mosques but *jamāʿat khānahs* ("gathering houses"), and their mode of worship bears little resemblance to that of the Muslims generally.

Other Shīʿah sects. Several other sects arose out of the general Shīʿite movement—*e.g.*, the Nuṣayrīs, the Yazīdīs, and the Druzes—out of which only the Druzes have any considerable following. The Druze sect arose in the 11th century out of a cult of deification of the Fāṭimid caliph al-Ḥākim. Some authorities believe that the growth of the Freemasonry movement was influenced by Druze rituals.

Druzes and Bahāʾīs

During a 19th-century anticlerical movement in Iran, a certain ʿAlī Moḥammad of Shīrāz appeared, declaring himself to be the Bāb ("Gate"; *i.e.*, to God). At that time the climate in Iran was generally favourable to Messianic ideas. He was, however, bitterly opposed by the Shīʿah *ʿulamāʾ* (council of learned men) and was executed in 1850. After his death, his two disciples, Ṣobḥ-e Azal and Bahāʾ Allāh, broke and went in different directions. Bahāʾ Allāh eventually declared his religion—stressing a humanitarian pacificism and universalism—to be an independent religion outside Islām. The Bahāʾī faith won a considerable number of converts in North America during the early 20th century (see also DRUZES and BAHAʾI FAITH).

Ṣūfism. Ṣūfism emerged out of early ascetic reactions on the part of certain religiously sensitive personalities against the general worldliness that had overtaken the Muslim community and the purely "externalist" expressions of Islām in law and theology. These persons stressed the Muslim qualities of moral motivation, contrition against overworldliness, and "the state of the heart" as opposed to the legalist formulations of Islām. Ṣūfism evolved through three distinct phases: asceticism, a purely moral phase; ecstasy, an emotionalist phase in which the subject sought communion with God through states of ecstasy; and the cognitive phase, in which an intuitive knowledge or gnosis (esoteric knowledge) was the ideal. This last phase was a parallel development of Shīʿism, a phenomenon that made Ṣūfism a bulwark against large-scale expansion of Shīʿah Islām. The Ṣūfī adepts (persons skilled in mystical techniques) believe that they have a privileged inner knowledge called *kashf*, or "revelation" (*i.e.*, intuition, which is very distinct from the prophetic revelation, called *waḥy*). The concept of *kashf*, beyond and inaccessible to intellectual penetration, posed a threat to the theologians, who never accepted this form of knowledge as having any objective validity.

In the 11th century the Ṣūfī theologian al-Ghazālī attempted a synthesis between the formal Sunnī theology and Ṣūfism and won for the latter an honourable place within the orthodox structure of ideas. Al-Ghazālī, who was aware of the power of the Ṣūfī experiential method, told the theologians that, unless theology created for itself a base in the "science of the heart," its doctrines could not become religious verities but would remain bare shells that would be devoid of any inner life. At the same time, al-Ghazālī made an effort to keep Ṣūfism within orthodox bounds and rejected its more extravagant claims with regard to the fusion of the human self, or ego, with the divine.

Soon after al-Ghazālī's death, however, Ṣūfism was developed into a pantheistic theosophy at the hands of Ibn al-ʿArabī (died 1240), a Spanish mystic who preached the "unity of all existence" (*i.e.*, of the world and God). The most serious threat of the new Ṣūfī challenge to orthodoxy was that the Ṣūfī ideal of sainthood was advanced as a rival to the prophethood, and the question was posed: is the prophet or the saint spiritually greater? Ibn al-ʿArabī espoused the view that the saint was greater, because he obtained knowledge directly from God, whereas the prophet received his knowledge from the Angel, and because a prophet, insofar as he promulgated the law, was "with men," whereas the saint was "with God." This grave conflict was ultimately resolved by the doctrine of the dialectic of "spiritual states," according to which Ṣūfī experience was conceived as a rhythmic movement between the "inner" and the "outer," "unity" and "multiplicity." This synthetic movement was held to culminate in the prophetic experience. A number of orthodox Ṣūfīs, the most important of whom was the Indian Aḥmad Sirhindī (died 1625), contributed to this synthesis (see also ISLAMIC MYSTICISM).

The ideal of sainthood as rivalling the prophethood

Other forms. *The Aḥmadīyah.* In the latter half of the 19th century in Punjab, India, Mirza Ghulam Ahmad claimed to be an inspired prophet. In his earlier career he had been a defender of Islām against Christian missionaries and had adopted certain doctrines of the Indian Muslim modernist Sayyid Ahmad Khan, namely, that Jesus died a natural death and was not assumed into heaven as the Islāmic orthodoxy believed and that *jihād* "by the sword" had been abrogated and replaced with *jihād* "of the pen." His aim appears to have been to synthesize all religions under Islām, for he declared himself to be not only the manifestation of the Prophet Muḥammad but also the Second Advent of Jesus, as well as Kṛṣṇa for the Hindus, among other claims. He did not announce, however, any new revelation or new law.

In 1914 a schism over succession occurred among the Aḥmadīs. One group that seceded from the main body, which was headed by a son of the founder, disowned the prophetic claims of Ghulam Ahmad and established their centre in Lahore (in modern Pakistan). The main body of the Aḥmadīs evolved a separatist organization and, following the partition of India in 1947, moved their headquarters to Rabwah in what was at that time West Pakistan.

Both of these groups are noted for their missionary work, particularly in the West and in Africa. Within the Muslim countries, however, there is fierce opposition to the main group because of its claim that Ghulam Ahmad was a prophet (the Muslim community believes in the finality of prophethood with Muḥammad) and because of its separatist organization. Outside the Muslim countries, however, the Qadiani group (as the main body is called, Qadian being the birthplace of the founder and first centre of the sect) acts more like a movement than a sect, with a relatively loose connection with its centre in Pakistan.

The Black Muslims. After World War II an Islāmic movement arose among blacks in the U.S.; members called themselves the National of Islam, but they were popularly known as Black Muslims. Although they adopted some Islāmic social practices, the group was in large part a black separatist and social-protest movement. Their leader, Elijah Muhammad, who claimed to be an inspired prophet, interpreted the doctrine of Resurrection in an unorthodox sense as the revival of oppressed ("dead") peoples. The popular leader and spokesman Malcolm X (el-Hajj Malik el-Shabazz) broke with the Black Muslims and adopted more orthodox Islāmic views before his assassination in 1965. After the death of Elijah Muhammad in 1975, the group was renamed World Community of Islam in the West and officially abandoned its separatist aims.

PRACTICES AND INSTITUTIONS

The Five Pillars. During the earliest decades after the death of the Prophet, certain basic features of the religio-social organization of Islām were singled out to serve as anchoring points of the community's life and formulated as the "Pillars of Islām." To these five, the Khārijī sect added a sixth pillar, the *jihād*, which, however, was not accepted by the general community.

The anchoring points of the community's life

The profession of faith. The first pillar is the profession of faith: "There is no god but God; Muḥammad is the prophet of God," upon which depends membership in the community. The profession must be recited at least once in one's lifetime, aloud, correctly, and purposively, with an understanding of its meaning and with an assent from the heart.

Prayer. The second pillar consists of five congregational prayers in a day, although they may be offered individually if one cannot go to the mosque for some reason. The first prayer is performed in the morning before sunrise, the second just after noon, the third in the later afternoon, the fourth immediately after sunset, and the fifth before retiring to bed (only three prayers, however, are mentioned in the Qur'ān: morning, evening, and the middle prayer in the afternoon).

Before a prayer, ablutions are performed by washing the hands, face, and feet. The muezzin (the one who gives the call for prayer) chants aloud from a raised place (such as a tower) in the mosque. When prayer starts, the *imām*, or leader (of the prayer), stands in the front facing Mecca, and the congregation stands behind him in rows, following him in various postures. Each prayer consists of two to four genuflection units (*rakʿah*); each unit consists of a standing posture (during which verses from the Qur'ān are recited, in certain prayers aloud, in others silently), as well as a genuflection and two prostrations. At every change in posture, "God is great" is recited. Tradition has fixed the materials to be recited in each posture.

Brian Brake—Magnum

Muslims at prayer, Kashmir, India.

Special congregational prayers are offered on Friday instead of the prayer just after noon. The Friday service consists of a sermon (*khuṭbah*), part of which consists of preaching in the local language and part of recitation

Nature of sermons

of certain formulas in Arabic. In the sermon, the preacher usually recites a verse of the Qur'ān and builds his address on it, which can be of a moral, social, or political content. Friday sermons have usually considerable impact on public opinion regarding sociopolitical questions.

Although not ordained as an obligatory duty, nocturnal prayers (called *tahajjud*) are encouraged, particularly during the latter half of the night. During the month of Ramaḍān (see below *Fasting*) lengthy prayers are offered congregationally before retiring and are called *tarāwīḥ*.

In strict doctrine, the five daily prayers cannot be waived even for the sick, who may pray in bed and, if necessary, lying down. When on a journey, it is recommended that the two afternoon prayers be combined into one and the sunset and late evening prayers into one prayer as well. In practice, however, much laxity has occurred, particularly in modern times, although Friday prayers are still attended by large numbers.

Lehnert & Landrock

Interior of the ʿAmr Mosque, Cairo, showing the *miḥrāb* (prayer niche) and the *minbar* (pulpit).

The zakāt. The third pillar is the obligatory tax called *zakāt* ("purification," indicating that such a payment makes the rest of one's wealth religiously and legally pure). This is the only permanent tax levied by the Qur'ān and is payable annually on food grains, cattle, and cash after one year's possession. The amount varies for different categories. Thus, on grains and fruits it is 10 percent if land is watered by rain, 5 percent if land is watered artificially. On cash and precious metals it is 2½ percent. *Zakāt* is collectable by the state and is to be used primarily for the poor, but the Qur'ān mentions other purposes: ransoming Muslim war captives, redeeming chronic debts of people, tax collectors' fees, *jihād* (and by extension, according to Qur'ān commentators, education and health), and creating facilities for travellers.

After the breakup of Muslim religio-political power, payment of *zakāt* has become a matter of voluntary charity dependent on individual conscience. Some Muslim countries are seeking to reintroduce it, and in several Middle Eastern countries *zakāt* is officially collected, but on a voluntary basis.

The fast of Ramaḍān

Fasting. Fasting during the month of Ramaḍān (ninth month of the Muslim lunar calendar), laid down in the Qur'ān (2:183–185), is the fourth pillar of the faith. Fasting begins at daybreak and ends at sunset, and during the day eating, drinking, and smoking are forbidden. The Qur'ān (2:185) states that it was in the month of Ramaḍān that the Qur'ān was revealed. Another verse of the Qur'ān (97:1) states that it was revealed "on the night of determination," which Muslims generally observe on the night of 26–27 Ramaḍān. For a person who is sick or on a journey, fasting may be postponed until "another equal number of days." Daily feeding of one poor person is also prescribed "for those who can afford it."

The ḥajj. The fifth pillar is the annual pilgrimage (*ḥajj*) to Mecca prescribed for every Muslim once in a lifetime—"provided one can afford it" and provided a person has enough provisions to leave for his family in his absence. The pilgrimage rite begins every year on the 7th and ends on the 10th of the month of Dhū al-Ḥijjah (last month of the Muslim year). When the pilgrim is about six miles (ten kilometres) from the Holy City, he enters upon the state of *iḥrām:* he wears two seamless garments and neither shaves nor cuts his hair or nails until the ceremony ends. The principal initial activities consist of a visit to the Kaʿbah sanctuary or the Sacred Mosque; the kissing of the Black Stone (Ḥajar al-Aswad); seven circumambulations of the Kaʿbah; and the ascent of and running between Mt. Ṣafā and Mt. Marwah (which are now, however, mere elevations) seven times. At the second stage of the ritual, the pilgrim proceeds from Mecca to Minā, a few miles away; from there he goes to ʿArafāt, where it is essential to hear a sermon and to spend one afternoon. The last rites consist of spending the night at Muzdalifah (between ʿArafāt and Minā) and offering sacrifice on the last day of *iḥrām*, which is the *ʿīd* ("festival") of sacrifice.

By courtesy of the Saudi Arabian Information Service, Royal Embassy of Saudi Arabia

Worshippers encircling the holy Kaʿbah, Mecca, Saudi Arabia.

Many countries have imposed restrictions on the number of outgoing pilgrims because of foreign-exchange difficulties. Because of the improvement of communications, however, the total number of visitors has greatly increased in recent years. In 1965 the number of visitors was estimated to be about 1,500,000, approximately 600,000 of them from outside Arabia. All Muslim countries send official delegations on the occasion, which is being increasingly used for religio-political congresses. At other times in the year, it is considered meritorious to perform the lesser pilgrimage (*ʿumrah*), which is not, however, a substitute for the *ḥajj* pilgrimage.

Sacred places and days. The most sacred place for Muslims is the Kaʿbah sanctuary at Mecca, the object of the annual pilgrimage. It is much more than a mosque; it is believed to be the place where the heavenly bliss and power touches the earth directly. According to Muslim tradition, the Kaʿbah was built by Abraham. The Prophet's mosque in Medina is the next in sanctity. Jerusalem follows in third place in sanctity as the first *qiblah* (*i.e.*, direction in which the Muslims offered prayers at first, before the *qiblah* was changed to the Kaʿbah) and as the place from where Muḥammad, according to tradition, made his ascent (*miʿrāj*) to heaven. For the Shīʿah, Karbalāʾ in Iraq (the place of martyrdom of ʿAlī's son, Ḥusayn) and Meshed in Iran (where Imām ʿAlī ar-Riḍā is buried) constitute places of special veneration where the Shīʿah make pilgrimages.

Shrines of Ṣūfī saints

For the Muslim masses in general, shrines of Ṣūfī saints are particular objects of reverence and even of veneration. In Baghdad, the tomb of the greatest saint of them all, ʿAbd al-Qādir al-Jīlānī, is visited every year by large numbers of pilgrims from every corner of the Muslim world.

The Ṣūfī shrines, which were managed privately in earlier periods, are almost entirely owned by governments in the 20th century and managed by departments of *awqāf* (plural of *waqf*, a religious endowment). The official appointed to care for a shrine is usually called a *mutawallī*. In Turkey, where such endowments constituted a very considerable portion of the national wealth, all were confiscated by the regime of Mustafa Kemal Atatürk (president, 1928–38).

The general religious life of the Muslims is centred around the mosque, and in the days of the Prophet and early caliphs the mosque was, indeed, the centre of all community life. Small mosques are usually supervised by the *imām* (one who administers the prayer service) himself, although sometimes also a muezzin is appointed. In larger mosques, where Friday prayers are offered, a *khaṭīb* (one who gives the *khuṭbah*, or sermon) is appointed for Friday service. Many large mosques also function as religious schools and colleges. Mosque officials are appointed by the government in most countries. In some countries, *e.g.*, Pakistan, most mosques are private and are run by the local community, although some of the larger ones are being increasingly taken over by the government departments of *awqāf*.

The Muslim calendar (based on the lunar year) dates from the emigration (*hijrah*) of the Prophet from Mecca to Medina in AD 622. The two festive days in the year are the *ʿīds*, ʿĪd al-Fiṭr celebrating the end of the month of Ramaḍān and the other, ʿĪd al-Aḍḥā (the feast of sacrifice), marking the end of the pilgrimage. Because of the crowds, *ʿīd* prayers are offered either in very large mosques or on specially consecrated grounds. Other sacred times include the "night of determination" (believed to be the night in which God makes decisions about the destiny of individuals and the world as a whole) and the night of the ascension of the Prophet to heaven. The Shīʿah celebrate the 10th of Muḥarram (the first month of the Muslim year) to mark the day of the martyrdom of Ḥusayn. The Muslim masses also celebrate the death anniversaries of various saints in a ceremony called *ʿurs* (literally, "nuptial ceremony"). The saints, far from dying, are believed to reach the zenith of their spiritual life on this occasion.

The family. A basic social teaching of Islām is the encouragement of marriage, and the Qurʾān regards celibacy definitely as something exceptional—to be resorted to only under economic stringency. Thus, monasticism as a way of life was severely criticized by the Qurʾān. With the appearance of Ṣūfism, however, many Ṣūfīs preferred celibacy, and some even regarded women as an evil distraction from piety, although marriage remained the normal practice also with Ṣūfīs.

Pre-Islāmic practice of polygamy and the Qurʾān

Polygamy, which was practiced in pre-Islāmic Arabia, was permitted by the Qurʾān, which, however, limited the number of simultaneous wives to four, and this permission was made dependent upon the condition that justice be done among co-wives. The Qurʾān even suggests that "You shall never be able to do justice among women, no matter how much you desire." Medieval law and society, however, regarded this "justice" to be primarily a private matter between a husband and his wives, although the law did provide redress in cases of gross neglect of a wife. Right of divorce was also vested basically in the husband, who could unilaterally repudiate his wife, although the woman could also sue her husband for divorce before a court on certain grounds.

The virtue of chastity is regarded as of prime importance by Islām. The Qurʾān advanced its universal recommendation of marriage as a means to ensure a state of chastity (*iḥṣān*), which is held to be induced by a single free wife. The Qurʾān states that those guilty of adultery are to be severely punished with 100 lashes. Tradition has intensified this injunction and has prescribed this punishment for unmarried persons, but married adulterers are to be stoned to death. A false accusation of adultery is punishable by 80 lashes.

The general ethic of the Qurʾān considers the marital bond to rest on "mutual love and mercy," and the spouses are said to be "each other's garments." The detailed laws of inheritance prescribed by the Qurʾān also tend to confirm the idea of a central family—husband, wife, and children, along with the husband's parents. Easy access to polygamy (although the normal practice in Islāmic society has always been that of monogamy) and easy divorce on the part of the husband led, however, to frequent abuses in the family. In recent times, most Muslim countries have enacted legislation to tighten up marital relationships.

Rights of parents in terms of good treatment are stressed in Islām, and the Qurʾān extols filial piety, particularly tenderness to the mother, as a very important virtue. A murderer of his father is automatically disinherited. The tendency of the Islāmic ethic to strengthen the immediate family on the one hand and the community on the other at the expense of the extended family or of the tribe did not succeed, however. Muslim society, until the encroachments that have been made upon it by modernizing influences, has remained basically one composed of tribes or quasi-tribes. Despite urbanization, tribal affiliations offer the greatest resistance to change and development of a modern polity. So strong, indeed, has been the tribal ethos that, in most Muslim societies, daughters are not given their inheritance share prescribed by the sacred law in order to prevent disintegration of the joint family's patrimony.

The Sharīʿah and jurisprudence. The most important and comprehensive concept of Islām at the practical level is that of the Sharīʿah. The term literally means "the path leading to the watering place"—in other words, the source of life. In religion the term means "the highway of righteous life leading to God," or the sum total of divine commands to man. In its comprehensiveness it includes law, moral principles, and the creed to which every Muslim must subscribe. In the 9th century, when the theological formulation of Islām first crystallized and the term Sharīʿah first came into systematic use, it was used restrictively for law, and theology was excluded from it. This practice was the orthodox legacy from the Muʿtazilah, who had opposed the Sharīʿah (law) to theology and tradition to reason. However, the conservative orthodox group, the *ahl al-Ḥadīth*, had never accepted the validity of this dualistic principle, and, for them, all reason worked within the framework of faith or revelation (see also HADITH).

Relationship between theology and law

The Sharīʿah thus became the supreme integrative concept of Islām for later theologians and jurists, such as Ibn Taymīyah and ash-Shāṭibī (died 1388). A conscious relationship between theology and law, which had not existed in the earlier centuries of Islām, came to be established with claims that theology supplied the metaphysical basis for law. Yet, as critics of the Sunnī theology such as Ibn Taymīyah had pointed out, there were certain palpable contradictions between theology and assumptions of law. Theology taught that the producer of human actions was not man but God—although man was morally responsible for his own actions. Law, on the other hand, assumed that man was the producer of his own actions—otherwise, he could not be held responsible for them. Ashʿarite theology taught that divine commands had no purpose and that they deserved absolute obedience because they were divine, and not because they had a purpose. Law, however, was rendered futile if it was not purposeful. Most later theologian-jurists, therefore, developed a new branch of religious knowledge called the "science of the objectives of the Sharīʿah." The most eminent names in that development are al-Ghazālī, Ibn Taymīyah, ash-Shāṭibī, and the Indian Shāh Walī Allāh of Delhi (died 1762).

The Sharīʿah thus came to be conceived less as the letter of the law than it was as a system of values that the law aims at realizing. Pure literalism was condemned. Yet no attempt was ever made by these savants to rethink and remold the law. That law actually ought to change with changing conditions, while the objectives remain eternal, was never seriously contemplated. Shāh Walī Allāh, perhaps the boldest exponent of this trend, defined law as the "quantitative expression" of the Sharīʿah values. Yet, far from attempting to show the possibility of change in the "legal quantities," he declared these quantities to be eternal because they were so revealed. Indeed, despite this revolt against pure literalism, the literalist rigidity had become the basic temper of the legal tradition, and, thus, the Sharīʿah remained confined to the letter of the law.

No effective attempt having been made to separate the moral targets from the legal injunctions of the Qurʾān and the *sunnah*, Muslim law (*fiqh*) retained its original informal character as a blend of morality and law. Because Islāmic law governs all human acts, public or private—"duties toward God" and "duties toward man"—it is essentially a system of "oughts" rather than a specific legal code. For many offenses, instead of strict legal sanctions a private atonement (*kaffārah*) is called for in terms of fasting, freeing slaves, or feeding the poor. Indeed, the evaluation of all human acts is made dependent on the motive or the inner will of the agent, a factor that in many cases conditions the legal judgment. As a consequence, much of this Islāmic law is not enforceable in a court.

The methodology of deduction in Islāmic law is the general methodology applicable to all strictly Islāmic thought and practice, although it is applied to law more specifically. This methodology, which evolved during the first two and a half centuries of Islām, consists of four principles called "the roots of the law." The first two roots are the Qurʾān and the Prophet's *sunnah*. This means that, if a belief, a practice, or a point of law has been clearly enunciated in a text of the Qurʾān or the Prophetic *sunnah*, it must be accepted as absolutely binding. The third principle, or root, is called *qiyās* (analogical reasoning) or *ijtihād* (a personal effort to think out a point on the basis of the relevant teaching of the Qurʾān and the *sunnah*). This means that, if a new case or issue arises that is not textually covered by the Qurʾān and the *sunnah*, the issue may be settled by arguing analogically from such texts or cases that resemble the new issue, allowing for differences.

The four "roots of the law"

The fourth principle is *ijmāʿ*, or consensus. In terms of actual efficacy, consensus is the most important factor of all, for, in effect, even the validity of the Qurʾān and the *sunnah* themselves is dependent on the consensus or general acceptance of the community. But consensus is in particular the agency that validates or rejects the results of individual thought or reasoning (*i.e.*, *qiyās* or *ijtihād*). Consensus is not institutionalized in Islām through any council or committee and works rather silently or informally, but it is on its basis that new laws are made or new ideas accepted. It can be defined as the general will of the community, and its efficacy can be seen from the fact that some schools of law have been accepted and others have disappeared. The general acceptance of Ṣūfism (initially opposed by the orthodox *ʿulamāʾ*), the rejection of rationalist trends in Islām in medieval times, and the acceptance or rejection of modern ideas and values all ultimately rest on the principle of *ijmāʿ*, or consensus.

Four schools of law have survived in Sunnī Islām. The Ḥanafī school (after Abū Ḥanīfah, 8th century) holds sway in India, Pakistan, Afghanistan, Central Asia, Turkey, and Lower Egypt; the Mālikī school (after Mālik ibn Anas, died late 8th century) is operative in North and West Africa and in Upper Egypt; the Shāfiʿī school (after ash-Shāfiʿī, 9th century) is popular in Southeast Asia; and the Ḥanbalī school (after Aḥmad ibn Ḥanbal, 9th century) is officially accepted in Saudi Arabia. The Shīʿah school of law is ascendant in Iran and its Zaydī version in the Yemen (see also ISLAMIC LAW).

The state. Because Islām draws no distinction between the religious and the temporal spheres of life, the Muslim state is by definition religious. The main differences between the Sunnī, Khārijī, and Shīʿāh concepts of rulership have already been pointed out above. It should be noted that, although the office of the Sunnī caliph (*khalīfah*, one who is successor to the Prophet in rulership) is religious, this does not imply any functions comparable to those of the pope. The caliph has no authority either to define dogma or, indeed, even to legislate. He is the chief executive of a religious community, and his primary function is to implement the sacred law and work in the general interests of the community. He himself is not above the law and if necessary can even be deposed, at least in theory.

Sunnī political theory is essentially a product of circumstance—an after-the-fact rationalization of historical developments. Thus, between the Shīʿah legitimism that restricts rule to ʿAlī's family and the Khārijī democratism that allowed rulership to anyone, even to "an Ethiopian slave," Sunnism held the position that "rule belonged to the Quraysh" (the Prophet's tribe)—the condition that actually existed. Again, in view of the extremes represented by the Khārijīs, who demanded rebellion against what they considered to be unjust or impious rule, and Shīʿites, who raised the *imām* to a metaphysical plane of infallibility, Sunnites took the position that a ruler has to satisfy certain qualifications but that rule cannot be upset on small issues. Indeed, under the impact of civil wars started by the Khārijīs, Sunnism drifted to more and more conformism and actual toleration of injustice.

Political conformism of Sunnism

The first step taken in this direction by the Sunnites was the enunciation that "one day of lawlessness is worse than 30 years of tyranny." This was followed by the principle that "Muslims must obey even a tyrannical ruler." Soon, however, the sultan (ruler) was declared to be "shadow of God on earth." No doubt, the principle was also adopted—and insisted upon—that "there can be no obedience to the ruler in disobedience of God"; but there is no denying the fact that the Sunnī doctrine came more and more to be heavily weighted on the side of political conformism. This change is also reflected in the principles of legitimacy. Whereas early Islām had confirmed the pre-Islāmic democratic Arab principle of rule by consultation (*shūrā*) and some form of democratic election of the leader, those practices soon gave way to dynastic rule with the advent of the Umayyads. The *shūrā* was not developed into any institutionalized form and was, indeed, soon discarded. Soon the principle of "might is right" came into being, and later theorists frankly acknowledged that actual possession of effective power is one method of the legitimization of power.

In spite of this development, the ruler could not become absolute because a basic restraint was placed upon him by the Sharīʿah law under which he held his authority and which he dutifully was bound to execute and defend. When, in the latter half of the 16th century, the Mughal emperor Akbar in India wanted to arrogate to himself the right of administrative–legal absolutism, the strong reaction of the orthodox thwarted his attempt. In general, the *ʿulamāʾ* (religious scholars) jealously upheld the sovereign position of the Sharīʿah against the political authority.

The effective shift of power from the caliph to the sultan was, again, reflected in the redefinition of the functions of the caliph. It was conceded that, if the caliph administered through *wazīrs* (viziers or ministers) or subordinate rulers (*amīrs*), it was not necessary for him to embody all the physical, moral, and intellectual virtues theoretically insisted upon earlier. In practice, however, the caliph was no more than a titular head from the middle of the 10th century onward, when real power passed to self-made and adventurous *amīrs* and sultans, who merely used the caliph's name for legitimacy.

Education. Muslim educational activity began in the 8th century, primarily in order to disseminate the teaching of the Qurʾān and the *sunnah* of the Prophet. The first task was to collect and systematize the knowledge that was handed down by the previous generations concerning the meaning of the Qurʾān and the activity and precepts of the Prophet. Thus, in the early period, the character of learning was traditional. That tradition was committed to writing in the 2nd century AH and systematized and developed in the 3rd century AH. This vast activity of "seeking knowledge" (*ṭalab al-ʿilm*) resulted in the creation of specifically Arab sciences of tradition, history, and literature.

When the introduction of the Greek sciences—philosophy, medicine, and mathematics—created a formidable body of lay knowledge, a creative reaction on the traditional religious base resulted in the rationalist theological movement of the Muʿtazilah. Based on that Greek legacy, from the 9th to the 12th century AD a brilliant philosophical movement flowered and presented a challenge to orthodoxy on the issues of the eternity of the world, the doctrine of revelation, and the status of the Sharīʿah (see also ISLAMIC THEOLOGY AND PHILOSOPHY).

The orthodox met the challenges positively by formulating the religious dogma. At the same time, however, for fear of heresies, they began to draw a sharp distinction between religious and secular sciences. The custodians of the Sharīʿah developed an unsympathetic attitude toward the secular disciplines and excluded them from the curriculum of the *madrasah* (college) system. Their exclusion from the Sunnī system of education proved fatal, not only for those disciplines but, in the long run, for religious thought in general because of the lack of intellectual challenge and stimulation. A typical *madrasah* curriculum included logic (which was considered necessary as an "instrumental" science for the formal correctness of thinking procedure), Arabic literature, law, Ḥadīth, Qur'ān commentary, and theology. Despite sporadic criticism from certain quarters, the *madrasah* system remained impervious to change.

Distinction between religious and secular sciences

One important feature of Muslim education was that primary education (which consisted of Qur'ān reading, writing, and rudimentary arithmetic) did not feed candidates to institutions of higher education, and the two remained separate. In higher education, emphasis was on books rather than on subjects and on commentaries rather than on original works. This, coupled with the habit of learning by rote (which was developed from the basically traditional character of knowledge that encouraged learning more than thinking), impoverished intellectual creativity still further.

Despite these grave shortcomings, however, the *madrasah* produced one important advantage. Through the uniformity of its religio-legal content, it gave the *ʿulamāʾ* the opportunity to effect that overall cohesiveness and unity of thought and purpose that, despite great variations in local Muslim cultures, has become a palpable feature of the world Muslim community. This uniformity has withstood even the serious tension created against the seats of formal learning by Ṣūfism through its peculiar discipline and its own centres.

In contrast to the Sunnī attitude toward it, philosophy continued to be seriously cultivated among the Shīʿah, even though it developed a strong religious character. Indeed, philosophy has enjoyed an unbroken tradition in Persia down to the present and has produced some highly original thinkers. Both the Sunnī and the Shīʿah medieval systems of learning, however, have come face to face with the greatest challenge of all—the impact of modern education and thought.

Organization of education developed naturally in the course of time. Evidence exists of small schools already established in the first century of Islām that were devoted to reading, writing, and instruction in the Qur'ān. These schools of "primary" education were called *kuttāb*s. The well-known governor of Iraq at the beginning of the 8th century, the ruthless al-Ḥajjāj, had been a schoolteacher in his early career. When higher learning in the form of tradition grew in the 8th and 9th centuries, it was centred around learned men to whom students travelled from far and near and from whom they obtained a certificate (*ijāzah*) to teach what they had learned. Through the munificence of rulers and princes, large private and public libraries were built, and schools and colleges arose. In the early 9th century, a significant incentive to learning came from the translations made of scientific and philosophical works from the Greek (and partly Sanskrit) at the famous *bayt al-ḥikmah* ("house of wisdom") at Baghdad, which was officially sponsored by the caliph al-Ma'mūn. The Fāṭimid caliph al-Ḥākim set up a *dār al-ḥikmah* ("hall of wisdom") in Cairo in the 10–11th centuries. With the advent of the Seljuq Turks, the famous vizier Niẓām al-Mulk created an important college at Baghdad, devoted to Sunnī learning, in the latter half of the 11th century. The oldest surviving university, al-Azhar at Cairo, was established by the Fāṭimids, but Saladin (Ṣalāḥ ad-Dīn al-Ayyūbī), after ousting the Fāṭimids, consecrated it to Sunnī learning in the 12th century. Throughout subsequent centuries, colleges and quasi-universities (called *madrasah* or *dār al-ʿulūm*) arose throughout the Muslim world from Spain (whence philosophy and science were transmitted to the Latin West) across Central Asia to India. In Turkey, a new style of *madrasah* came into existence; it had four wings, for the teaching of the four schools of Sunnī law. Professorial chairs were endowed in large colleges by princes and governments, and residential students were supported by college endowment funds. Myriads of smaller centres of learning were endowed by private donations.

Ṣūfī orders and folk Islām. From the 12th century, Ṣūfism transformed itself from the doctrine and practice of small circles into a mass religious movement, and Ṣūfī orders or brotherhoods spread from Morocco to Indonesia. The orders were centred around their founders, with their shrines constituting the places of pilgrimage for their followers. "No salvation without following a Ṣūfī *shaykh*" became a universally accepted maxim in late-medieval Islām. The Ṣūfī monastery (called *zāwīyah* or *tekke*) became the centre of public religiosity, nearly overshadowing the mosque. The techniques of inducing autohypnotic states (called *ḥāl;* plural *aḥwāl*) through certain practices of concentration or frenzied dancing and chanting of certain formulas became the expression *par excellence* of popular religiosity, along with the accompanying beliefs in superstitious cults, various kinds of miracles, and saint worship. The *shaykh* (Persian *pīr*) initiated the novice into the practice of *dhikr* ("remembrance"; *i.e.,* of God) and chalked out the path of his spiritual journey, during which the disciple was required to have unquestioning faith in the master.

Transformation of Ṣūfism into a mass movement

Some Ṣūfī orders are local or regional; others are global. The earliest and the most universal order is associated with the name of ʿAbd al-Qādir al-Jīlānī, who died at Baghdad in 1166. Called the Qādirīyah order, it is moderate and stresses a humanitarian approach. The order, which was not actually established by the great Ṣūfī scholar himself but by his son, soon spread through the Middle East, later to India, to Southeast Asia, and finally to West Africa through North Africa. Because of its global dimensions, the relationship of the branches with the central organization is loose. The present head, a descendant of the celebrated saint and also named ʿAbd al-Qādir al-Jīlānī, has been the ambassador of Iraq to Pakistan for nearly two decades; the parent organization at Baghdad is largely maintained through subsidies from the Muslims of the Indian subcontinent.

Ṣūfī orders can be broadly divided into urban and rustic orders, the Qādirīyah order being an urban order. Whereas the urban were more or less close to the orthodoxy, influenced as they were by the *ʿulamāʾ*, the rustic ranged from less orthodox to completely unorthodox. The most orthodox among urban orders is the Naqshbandi order, which even forbids music (*samāʿ*), which is universally legalized by all other orders. The Bektāshīyah order of Turkey was one of the most important rustic orders, influenced by Christian practices and Shīʿah ideas. The so-called irregular (*bi-sharʿ*) orders of India contained a mixture of Muslim and Hindu practices and were riddled with occultisms, superstitions, and unorthodox practices.

The services of the Ṣūfī brotherhoods, however, have been multiple. Not only have they been instrumental in spreading humanitarian ideas (along with latitudinarianism and moral relativism in some cases), but, because of their association with guilds, they have been important vehicles of social-protest movements—and, as in Turkey, of rebellions. Since the 18th century, more orthodox

Ṣūfī brotherhoods have arisen; they are Ṣūfī in form but orthodox in content, such as the Sanūsīs of Libya. Under the impact of modern education and reform, the influence of Ṣūfī orders has visibly declined. In Turkey the regime of Mustafa Kemal Atatürk suppressed all orders and confiscated their vast properties in the 1920s.

Cultural diversity. Underneath the legal and creedal unity, the world of Islām harbours a tremendous diversity of cultures, particularly in the outlying regions. As mentioned earlier, Islām's spread can be divided into two broad periods. In the first period of the Arab conquests, the assimilative activity of the conquering religion was far-reaching. Although Persia resurrected its own language and a measure of its national culture after the first three centuries of Islām, its culture and language had come under heavy Arab influence. Only after Ṣafavid rule installed Shīʿism as a distinctive creed in the 16th century did Persia regain a kind of religious autonomy. The language of religion and thought, however, continued to be Arabic.

In the second period, the spread of Islām was not conducted by the state with *ʿulamāʾ* influence but was largely the work of Ṣūfī missionaries. The Ṣūfīs, because of their latitudinarianism, compromised with local customs and beliefs and left a great deal of the pre-Islāmic legacy in every region intact. Thus, among the Central Asian Turks, shamanistic practices were absorbed, while in Africa the holy man and his *barakah* (an influence supposedly causing material and spiritual well-being) are survivors from the older cults. In India there are large areas geographically distant from the Muslim religio-political centre of power in which customs are still Hindu and even pre-Hindu and in which people worship a motley of saints and deities in common with the Hindus. The custom of *satī*, under which a widow burned herself alive along with her dead husband, persisted in India even among some Muslims until late into the Mughal period. The 18th- and 19th-century reform movements exerted themselves to "purify" Islām of these accretions and superstitions.

Ṣūfī compromises with local customs

Indonesia affords a striking example of this phenomenon. Because Islām reached there late and soon thereafter came under European colonialism, the Indonesian society has retained its pre-Islāmic world view beneath an overlay of Islāmic practices. It keeps its customary law (called *adat*) at the expense of the Sharīʿah; many of its tribes are still matriarchal; and culturally the Hindu epics *Rāmāyaṇa* and *Mahābhārata* hold a high position in national life. Since the 19th century, however, orthodox Islām has gained steadily in strength because of fresh contacts with the Middle East.

Apart from regional diversity, the main internal division within Islāmic society is brought about by urban and village life. Islām originally grew up in the two cities of Mecca and Medina, and as it expanded, its peculiar ethos appears to have developed in urban areas. Culturally, it came under a heavy Persian influence in Iraq, where the Arabs learned the ways and style of life of their conquered people, who were culturally superior to them. The custom of veiling women (which originally arose as a sign of aristocracy but later served the purpose of segregating women from men—the *pardah*), for example, was acquired in Iraq.

Another social trait derived from outside cultures was the disdain for agriculture and manual labour in general. Because the people of the town of Medina were mainly agriculturists, this disdain could not have been initially present. In general, Islām came to appropriate a strong feudal ethic from the peoples it conquered. Also, because the Muslims generally represented the administrative and military aristocracy and because the learned class (the *ʿulamāʾ*) was an essential arm of the state, the higher culture of Islām became urban based.

This city orientation explains and also underlines the deep cleavage between the orthodox Islām of the *ʿulamāʾ* and the folk Islām espoused by the Ṣūfī orders of the countryside. In the modern period, the advent of education and rapid industrialization threatens to make this cleavage still wider, but at the same time this process seems to be changing the old pattern of stratification. As old Ṣūfī orders disintegrate, the village has become the home of orthodox conservative Islām, as the cities absorb the new industrial culture and modern education.

RELIGIOUS SYMBOLISM AND ART

The visual arts. The Arabs before Islām had hardly any art except poetry, which had been developed to full maturity and in which they took great pride. The themes of their poetry were love, chivalry, and personal and tribal pride, although immediately before Islām there was some religious poetry as well.

Like other forms of culture, the Arabs also borrowed their art from Persia and Byzantium. Whatever elements the Arabs borrowed, however, they Islāmized in a manner that fused them into a homogeneous spiritual— aesthetic complex. The most important principle governing art was aniconism; *i.e.*, the religious prohibition of figurization and representation of living creatures. Underlying this prohibition is the assumption that God is the sole author of life and that a person who produces a likeness of a living being seeks to rival God. The tradition ascribed to the Prophet that a person who makes a picture of a living thing will be asked on the Day of Judgment to infuse life into it, whether historically genuine or not, doubtless represents the original attitude of Islām. In the Qurʾān (3:49, 5:113), reflecting an account in a New Testament apocryphal work, it is counted among the miracles of Jesus that he made likenesses of birds from clay "by God's order," and, when he breathed into them, they became real birds, again, "by God's order."

Aniconism as a governing principle of art

Hence, in Islāmic aniconism two considerations are fused together: (1) rejection of such images that might become idols (these may be images of anything) and (2) rejection of figures of living things. Plato and Plotinus, Greek philosophers, had also dismissed representative art as an "imitation of nature"; *i.e.*, as something removed from reality. The Islāmic attitude is more or less the same, with the added element of attributing to the artist a violation of the sanctity of the principle of life. The same explanation holds for the Qurʾānic criticism of a certain kind of poetry, namely, free indulgence in extravagant image mongering: "They [poets] recklessly wander in every valley" (26:235).

This basic principle has, however, undergone modifications. First, pictures were tolerated if they were confined to private apartments and harems of palaces. This was the case with some members of the Umayyad and ʿAbbāsid dynasties, Turks, and Persians—in particular with the Shīʿah, who have produced an abundance of pictorial representations of the holy family and of the Prophet himself. Second, in the field of pictorial representation, animal and human figures are combined with other ornamental designs such as fillets and arabesques —stressing their ornamental nature rather than representative function. Third, for the same reason, in plastic art they appear in low relief. In other regions of the Muslim world—in North Africa, Egypt, and India (except for Mughal palaces)—representational art was strictly forbidden. Even in paintings, the figures have little representational value and are mostly decorative and sometimes symbolic. This explains why plastic art is one of the most limited areas of Islāmic art. The only full-fledged plastic figures are those of animals and a few human figures that the Seljuqs brought from eastern Turkistan.

Much more important than plastic art were paintings, particularly frescoes and later Persian and Perso-Indian miniatures. Frescoes are found in the Umayyad and ʿAbbāsid palaces and in Spain, Iran, and in the harem quarters of the Mughal palaces in India. Miniature paintings, introduced in Persia, assumed much greater importance in the later period in Mughal India and Turkey. Miniature painting was closely associated with the art of book illumination, and this technique of decorating the pages of the books was patronized by princes and other patrons from the upper classes.

Miniature painting

Music. Instrumental music was forbidden by the orthodox in the formative stages of Islām. As for vocal music, its place was largely taken by a sophisticated and artistic form of the recitation of the Qur'ān known as *tajwīd*. Nevertheless, the Muslim princely courts generously patronized and cultivated music. Arab music was influenced by Persian and Greek music. Al-Fārābī, a 10th-century philosopher, is credited with having constructed a musical instrument called the *arghanūn* (organ). In India, Amīr Khosrow, a 14th-century poet and mystic, produced a synthesis of Indian and Persian music and influenced the development of later Indian music.

Among the religious circles, the Ṣūfīs introduced both vocal and instrumental music as part of their spiritual practices. The *samāʿ*, as this music was called, was opposed by the orthodox at the beginning, but the Ṣūfīs persisted in this practice, which slowly won general recognition. The great Ṣūfī poet Jalāl ad-Dīn ar-Rūmī (died 1273)—revered equally by the orthodox and the Ṣūfīs—heard the divine voice in his stringed musical instrument when he said "Its head, its veins (strings) and its skin are all dry and dead; whence comes to me the voice of the Friend?"

Literature. In literature, drama and pure fiction were not allowed—drama because it was a representational art and fiction because it was akin to lying. Story literature was tolerated, and the great story works of Indian origin—*The Thousand and One Nights* and *Kalīlah wa Dimnah*—were translated from the Persian, introducing secular prose into Arabic. Didactic and pious stories were used and even invented by popular preachers. Much of this folklore found its way back into enlarged editions of *The Thousand and One Nights* and, through it, has even influenced later history writing. Because of the ban on fictional literature, there grew a strong tendency in later literary compositions—in both poetry and prose—toward hyperbole (*mubālaghah*), a literary device to satisfy the need of getting away from what is starkly real without committing literal falsehood, thus often resulting in the caricature and the grotesque. Poetry lent itself particularly well to this device, which was freely used in panegyrics, satires, and lyrics. As a form of effective expression, poetry is eminently characteristic of the East. The Arab genius is almost natively poetical with its strong and vivid imagination not easily amenable to the rigorous order that reason imposes upon the mind. This borderline attitude between the real and the unreal was particularly favourable to the development, in all medieval Islāmic literatures of the Middle East, of the lyric and panegyric forms of poetry wherein every line is a self-contained unit. Much more importantly, it afforded a specially suitable vehicle for a type of mystic poetry in which it is sometimes impossible to determine whether the poet is talking of earthly love or spiritual love. For the same reason, poetry proved an effective haven for thinly veiled deviations from and even attacks on the literalist religion of the orthodox.

Poetry as a characteristic of the East

Architecture. Architecture is by far the most important expression of Islāmic art, particularly the architecture of mosques. It illustrates both the diversity of cultures that participated in the Islāmic civilization and the unifying force of Islāmic monotheism that is represented by the spacious expanse of the mosque—a veritable externalization of the sense of all-enveloping divine unity, heightened by the sense of infinity of the arabesque design. The arabesque, though it is ornately decorative, spiritually represents the infinite vastness of God.

Among the earliest monuments are the mosque of ʿAmr built in Egypt in 641–642 and the famous Dome of the Rock of Jerusalem (finished in 691), which, however, is not a mosque but a monument, a concentric-circular structure consisting of a wooden dome set on a high drum and resting on four tiers and 12 columns. The Umayyad ruler al-Walīd (died 715) built the great mosque at Damascus and al-Aqṣā Mosque at Jerusalem with two tiers of arcades in order to heighten the ceiling. The early Syro-Egyptian mosque is a heavily columned structure with a pulpit (*miḥrāb*) oriented toward the Kaʿbah sanctuary at Mecca.

In Spanish and North African architecture these features are combined with Roman–Byzantine characteristics, the masterpieces of Spanish architecture being the famous Alhambra Palace at Granada and the Great Mosque of Córdoba. In the famous Persian mosques, the characteristic Persian elements are the tapered brick pillars, the arches (each supported by several pillars), the huge arcades, and the four sides called *eyvāns*. With the advent of the Seljuqs in the 11th century, faience decoration (glazed earthenware) of an exquisite beauty was introduced, and it gained further prominence under the Timurids (14th–16th centuries). In the number and greatness of mosques, Turkey has the pride of first place in the Muslim world. Turkey began with a Persian influence and then later Syrian in the 13th and 14th centuries, but Turkey developed its own cupola domes and monumental entrances. The Turkish architects accomplished symmetry by means of one large dome, four semidomes, and four small domes among them. In the Indo-Pakistan subcontinent, Muslim architecture first employed Hindu architectural features (*e.g.*, horizontal rather than arcuate, or bowlike, arches and Hindu ornamentation), but later the Persian style predominated.

REFORM AND MODERNISM

The static condition of law and theology, the accompanying stagnation of education, and the general deterioration of Muslim society in the late-medieval period had led, by the 17th–18th centuries, to a consciousness among certain outstanding men that the process of petrification should be halted and that Islāmic society should be reformed by a rethinking of the received content that had been formulated by the medieval schools. For these men, the work of the 14th-century theologian Ibn Taymīyah acted as both an inspiration and a guide in emphasizing the role of *ijtihād* (individual effort at original thinking). It also inspired the Wahhābī reformist movement that erupted in Arabia in the 18th century under the influence of Muḥammad ibn ʿAbd al-Wahhāb. In India, after the efforts of Aḥmad Sirhindī and others to infuse moral life into society in the 17th century, the reformist school of Shāh Walī Allāh of Delhi arose in the 18th century, finally giving rise to a militant puritanical movement in the 19th century.

This puritanical reformism, which became ubiquitous in the 19th century, was characterized by (1) purification of popular Islām from accretions, superstitions, and degenerate beliefs and practices to which Ṣūfism, as a folk religion, had been accommodative; (2) questioning or rejection of the authority of medieval schools and insistence on *ijtihād*, or original thinking, and a reassertion of pure monotheism; (3) focussing attention on the socio-moral aspects of Islām rather than eschatology and metaphysical issues; and (4) adoption of militant methods to impose its ideology. By accepting the authority of the "early generations" (*salaf*), however, all these movements created a barrier against further thought and thus actually militated against *ijtihād*. One result of such reformism was, however, that of discrediting much of the legacy of Ṣūfism and, in some instances, of forming neo-Ṣūfī orders. These new orders had a Ṣūfī form and organization but had an orthodox content and orientation; they were generally activist, and, in varying degrees, maintained a militant position. Instances of such groups are the Sanūsīs of Libya, the Fulani of Nigeria, and the Mahdists of Sudan.

Puritanical reformism of the 19th century

On the foundations of this reformist legacy, modernist reformism arose under the influence of Western ideas during the second half of the 19th century. Jamāl ad-Dīn al-Afghānī (died 1897) summoned the Muslim peoples to unite politically against the West under the banner of pan-Islāmism, to create constitutional governments in their countries, and to reform education. Muḥammad ʿAbduh (died 1905) in Egypt, Sir Sayyid Ahmad Khan (died 1898) and Sayyid Amir Ali (died 1928) in India, and Namık Kemal (died 1888) in Turkey all undertook to reinterpret Islām with the dual purpose of accommodating modern ideas and outlooks within the framework of Islāmic principles and at the same time ensuring to the Muslim that Islām was capable of a modern orientation. These two aspects may be characterized as reformist and apologetic. The apologetic aspect was combined with criticisms of the West and controversies against Western critics of Islām, a factor that ultimately created tension with reformist purposes.

Reforming theology, politics, and social institutions

The main areas of reform were theology, politics, and social institutions. In the field of theology, the role of reason was given prominence, as against medieval doctrine. It was urged that reason and science, far from militating against faith, were the allies of faith. The modernists resurrected the teachings of the Muʿtazilah school and even, to some extent, of the medieval Muslim philosophers Avicenna (Ibn Sīnā) and Averroës (Ibn Rushd). In the realm of politics, the original democratic elements in Islām were given emphasis and interpreted in terms of modern theories of a social contract between the ruler and the ruled, along with a violent criticism of autocratic rule, which had characterized Islām since the medieval period. In the area of social institutions, the elements that received special stress were modern education, attitudes on labour, and the status of women. On this last issue, the modernists contended that Islām purported to ban polygamy since the Qurʾān had made the permission for polygamy dependent upon justice between co-wives, and the Qurʾān itself had stated "You shall never be able to do justice among women, no matter how much you desire."

Plausible as some of the modernist positions may be, they obviously implied that medieval Muslims had departed from the Islāmic ideals. Because of this implication, the conservative *ʿulamāʾ*, representing the vast majority of the masses, opposed modernism and accused its champions of being unfaithful to Islām in favour of Western ideas. This new reactionary orientation began during the second decade of the 20th century, when Muslims began to struggle for freedom from Western rule and were politically anti-Western as well. In this new mood, Muslims withdrew from the earlier liberal modernist stand into a conservative or quasi-conservative position, and the apologetic tendencies already present in the earlier modernism became much more powerful than the reformist orientation. The new mood was given powerful expression by men such as Muḥammad Iqbāl (died 1938), an Indo-Pakistani poet-philosopher, and Muḥammad Rashīd Riḍā (died 1935), an Egyptian theologian. Under the impact of such reaction, strong revivalist movements arose, among them the Muslim Brotherhood in the Middle East and the Jamāʿat-e Islāmī of Indo-Pakistan. These movements, representing the middle and lower middle classes of Muslim society, are not only essentially antimodern and anti-Western, but they are also pitched against their own governments, because the ruling elite in all these countries are educated according to modern concepts and are Western trained. Hence, in the eyes of the new revivalist movements, the nations' rulers are both unfaithful to Islām and unrepresentative of the Muslim masses. To the revivalist, the most unacceptable aspect of modern Western life is its social ethics, characterized, in their eyes, by an increasing permissiveness and a breakdown of the family institution.

In Turkey, the struggle between the old and the new came to an end outwardly in the 1920s with the strong and suppressive measures of Mustafa Kemal Atatürk, who abolished the age-old institution of the caliphate, declared the Turkish republic to be a secular state, ousted the Sharīʿah law, adopted a Western civil code, liquidated the Ṣūfī brotherhoods, abolished the old Islāmic institutions of learning, and replaced the Arabic script with Latin script. Under the pressure of popular opinion, however, some measures were modified after 1950. Nevertheless, the struggle continues, largely underground, and several Ṣūfī orders have become active again. Religious education has also been revived; the effects of the Kemalist social reforms are mostly confined to cities, the countryside still following the old ways.

Elsewhere in the Muslim world, secularism has not been officially adopted, but large-scale social reforms have been introduced. In the field of personal law, most Muslim countries have adopted measures to strengthen the family structure. Polygamy has been banned in Tunisia and has been restricted and discouraged by legal measures in several other countries. Similar restrictions have been put upon the unilateral repudiation of marriage by the husband. Though some Muslim countries have vested the right of granting divorce in courts, others have created quasi-judicial measures to regulate the procedure of divorce.

Attempts at reforms in education

In the area of education, with the exception of Turkey, the new Muslim governments have not abolished the old systems of education but have attempted to reform them by a readjustment of their curricula. Nevertheless, there still exists a dualism in education; the old institutions have not yet fully absorbed the new reforms, and the modern universities do not have adequate arrangements for the teaching of the traditional Islāmic learning. Indeed, this dichotomy in the field of education has created a deep spiritual cleavage between the two sectors of Muslim society and constitutes a grave problem for Islāmic societies—particularly those in Pakistan, Iran, and India, where the traditional system is hardly touched by modern education, and the two systems, therefore, run side by side with each other, resulting in virtually two societies.

In one area, the doctrine of liberal democracy, the earlier posture of liberal modernism has been reversed, at least in practice. The struggles for freedom in all Muslim countries have generated an idea of nationalism that means fighting against the foreign colonial power and ameliorating the economic condition of the masses. The doctrine of the betterment of economic life of the masses is not the idea of the people themselves but of the modern elite ruling them. The ruling elite, in order to push the masses toward economic creativity and betterment and to break their traditional inertia in this field, is often compelled to resort to measures that go against the ideal of liberal democracy. This bid for a quick improvement in the economic field has resulted in a plethora of writings on "Islāmic Socialism." These theories reject both Communism and exploitative capitalism as materialistic (insofar as both systems limit themselves to the economic aspects of life by excluding the moral side of man). At the same time, however, such theories facilitate and defend the assumption of totalitarian powers by the Muslim governments in the name of the masses. The results of this newest development are not yet apparent.

In Central Asia, the Communist regime of the Soviet Union, fearful of the possible consequences of the pan-Islāmism or pan-Turkism that prevailed in that region in the early years of the 20th century, has adopted a deliberate policy of obstructing the growth of an independent Islāmic modernist or nationalist movement and has compromised with the traditionalist conservatives, thus attempting to absorb Islām into Communism in time.

ISLAM'S RELATION TO OTHER RELIGIONS AND SOCIETIES

The rise of Islām and an organized Muslim community raised the problem of relations with other communities and religious groups. The older monotheistic communities, the Jews and the Christians, who possessed a revealed Scripture, were given the status of "the people of the Book" (*ahl al-kitāb*), and their religious and cultural autonomy was recognized. But the pagans were given only two alternatives: either to accept Islām or to die. Before the Prophet's death, most Arab tribes had opted for Islām but had apparently not accepted the idea of a centralized community. Thus, immediately after Muḥammad's death, some tribes, even though they did not renounce Islām as a personal religion, refused to pay the *zakāt* tax to the central political authority that was set up at Medina. (Other tribes had set up their own tribal prophets, and one of them, Musaylimah, already had become a claimant to prophethood during Muḥammad's lifetime.) All of these tribes eventually were reduced to submission.

From this early experience, the orthodox concluded (1) that rebels within a Muslim state must be brought back to submission through *jihād*, a conclusion that appears to be corroborated by the Qurʾān, and (2) that a nonrepentant apostate must be put to death. Whereas the orthodox law still holds both these views, the modernist Muslims accept only the first, rejecting the second on the ground of the Qur'ānic declaration "There is no compulsion in faith." The modernists accuse the orthodox of confusing political policy with matters of personal faith.

Relationships to Jews and Christians

As for Jews and Christians, the Prophet's original intention was probably to regard them as of equal civil status with the Muslims. The "Charter of Medina" promulgated by him soon after his arrival in Medina declares the Jews of that town to be "a community at par with Muslims." His political experiences with the Jews, whom he repeatedly found betraying the pacts for a joint defense of Medina against his Meccan foes, however, led to the gradual adoption of a severe policy of expulsion and execution of Jewish males at Medina. The Jews of Khybar were required also to pay a "poll tax," the *jizyah*. From this precedent, the orthodox concluded that Jews and Christians must pay *jizyah* to the Muslim state.

With the conquest of Iran and India, the principle of "the people of the Book" was extended to Zoroastrians and Hindus, but this recognition was essentially political. The invitation issued by the Qur'ān to the Christians and the Jews to cooperate on the basis of monotheism—"O people of the Book! let us come together on a principle that is common between us—that we shall not worship anyone besides God and shall not associate anyone with him . . ."—was inapplicable to Hinduism and Zoroastrianism.

The status of *dhimmīs* ("protected people"), as the "people of the Book" were called, though still maintained by the orthodox, has been rejected by modernist Muslims, who have been anxious to grant equality of status to all citizens irrespective of religious persuasion in the new Muslim states. They have argued against the orthodox, pointing out that the special status of non-Muslim communities in the classical Muslim state sprang from the fact that *dhimmīs* could not be enlisted in the armed forces and, therefore, had to pay the *jizyah* instead. With the emergence of nation-states, however, there is no necessity for this practice. This argument sounds plausible but probably does not close the issue. The possibility for Muslim nation-states to choose to come together in some kind of a religio-political unity is still open and is being much discussed among Muslims, although, for the present at least, it remains largely pious hope.

A similar shift took place in the doctrine of *jihād*. The classical Islāmic position holds that the world is divisible into three spheres: the zone of Islām (*dār al-Islām*); the zone of peace (*dār aṣ-ṣulḥ*)—*i.e.*, those nations with whom Muslims had peace pacts; and the zone of war (*dār al-ḥarb*)—*i.e.*, the rest of the world. The position on the last zone (of war), however, had already undergone practical modification in the sense that no power was regarded as potentially hostile unless it was actively so. In modern times, *jihād* has appeared as a defense against colonialism rather than as a program of offense.

Islām's attitude toward foreign civilizations has been positive in history. In its early stages, Islām absorbed a whole series of institutions, customs, and laws from neighbouring civilizations, and this process continued throughout the medieval period. In the modern period, it has shown an openness to Western influences at the purely intellectual and technological levels; but, after a temporary 19th-century Westward orientation in the field of social and ethical values, Islām has steadily withdrawn from those modern views. Although political bitterness has been a factor, this factor does not wholly explain Islām's change of attitude toward the West. One may conclude that spiritually and morally the world of Islām is engaged in an anxious soul-searching to find a new stand; and its creativity and possible contribution to a new world order will depend on its ability to discover that new stand. From its historical experience, Islām has acquired both a toughness and a flexibility necessary for creative adjustments, but the nature and dimensions of its present crisis are doubtlessly novel and grave.

BIBLIOGRAPHY

The Qur'ān: The Qur'ān is the basic source of Islāmic doctrine and law. English translations include *The Meaning of the Glorious Koran*, by MARMADUKE PICKTHALL (1930, reprinted 1957); and *The Koran Interpreted*, by A.J. ARBERRY (1964).

General works: Cambridge History of Islam, vol. 2, pt. 8 (1970), an excellent survey; H.A.R. GIBB, *Mohammedanism*, 2nd ed. (1953, reprinted 1963), a penetrating and concise account of the development of Islām; LOUIS GARDET, *Connaître l'Islam* (1958; Eng. trans., *Mohammedanism*, 1961), a systematic presentation of Islām, with religious insight; FAZLUR RAHMAN, *Islam* (1966), a historical and systematic interpretation of Islām by a modern Muslim, and *Islamic Methodology in History* (1965), a critical appraisal of the development of *sunnah, ijmāʿ*, and *ijtihād;* IGNAC GOLDZIHER, *Muhammedanische Studien*, 2 vol. (1888–90; Eng. trans., *Muslim Studies*, 1966), a classic work on the early development of Ḥadīth, reflecting the early history of religious ideas in Islām; R. LEVY, *An Introduction to the Sociology of Islam*, 2 vol. (1931–33), useful account of the development of Islāmic society and institutions.

Theology: D.B. MACDONALD, *Development of Muslim Theology, Jurisprudence and Constitutional Theory* (1903, reprinted 1965), a perceptive presentation of the subject; A.J. WENSINCK, *The Muslim Creed* (1932, reprinted 1965), a basic work on the early development of Sunnī Islām as a reaction to heretical doctrines; W. MONTGOMERY WATT, *Free Will and Predestination in Early Islam* (1948), an excellent treatment of the formative period of Islāmic theology; A.A.A. FYZEE (ed. and trans.), *A Shiʿite Creed* (1942), an annotated translation of a standard Shīʿite creed by Ibn Bābawayh.

Law: J. SCHACHT, *The Origins of Muhammadan Jurisprudence* (1950), a pioneering work on the origins of Islāmic law (for the specialist), and *An Introduction to Islamic Law* (1964), and N.J. COULSON, *A History of Islamic Law* (1964), two satisfactory accounts of the character and development of Islāmic law for the general reader.

Ṣūfism: R.A. NICHOLSON, *The Mystics of Islam* (1914, reprinted 1966); *Studies in Islamic Mysticism* (1921); A.J. ARBERRY, *Sufism* (1950), a brief but good account of the history of Ṣūfī spiritualists; O. DEPONT and X. CAPPOLANI, *Les Confréries religieuses musulmanes* (1897), the most comprehensive account of Ṣūfī brotherhoods.

Education: A.S. TRITTON, *Materials on Muslim Education in the Middle Ages* (1957), an informative, useful compilation; BAYARD DODGE, *Muslim Education in Medieval Times* (1962), a useful sketch.

Political theory and institutions: E.I.J. ROSENTHAL, *Political Thought in Medieval Islam* (1958), a good general survey of the subject.

Islāmic arts: In view of the wealth of descriptive treatments, rather than theory, it is difficult to point to a single source. K.A.C. CRESWELL, *A Bibliography of the Architecture, Arts and Crafts of Islam to 1st Jan. 1960* (1961), contains all the necessary references. See also *Studies in Islamic Art and Architecture* (1965), a volume in honour of K.A.C. Creswell.

Islāmic modernism: The most important interpretive statements by Muslims are: M.S. AMIR ʿALI, *The Spirit of Islām*, rev. ed. (1922, reprinted 1935), concerning the social content of Islām; and SIR MOHAMMAD IQBAL, *The Reconstruction of Religious Thought in Islam* (1934), a theological–philosophical modern interpretation of Islām. Critical presentations by Western scholars are: H.A.R. GIBB, *Modern Trends in Islam* (1947, reprinted 1964); and W.C. SMITH, *Islam in Modern History* (1957). Regional presentations are: W.C. SMITH, *Modern Islām in India* (1946); C.C. ADAMS, *Islam and Modernism in Egypt* (1933, reprinted 1968); C. SNOUCK HURGRONJE, *De Atjèhers*, 2 vol. (1893–94; Eng. trans., *The Achehnese*, 2 vol., 1906), an excellent account of the impact of Westernism on Islām in Indonesia (there is no recent comparable account); and N. BERKES, *The Development of Secularism in Turkey* (1964).

(F.R.)

Islām, History of

Islām, one of the great world religions, began in Arabia and spread to all parts of the world. Because of its emphasis on "community," which includes political, religious, social, and economic aspects, the history of Islām necessarily relates the religious to other aspects of culture. For Islāmic doctrines, practices, and institutions, see also ISLAM; ISLAMIC THEOLOGY AND PHILOSOPHY; and ISLAMIC MYSTICISM.

This article is divided into the following sections:

THE PRINCIPAL PERIODS OF ISLAMIC HISTORY

The classical period. Islām, a religion numbering approximately 600,000,000 adherents in all parts of the world, was brought into being by a call to commitment to the one God preached by the Prophet Muḥammad in the 7th century AD and has been perpetuated through the community of men called to this commitment. Historically, this community (the *ummah*) developed into a world civilization with extraordinary rapidity in the course of less than 100 years. In its formative first four centuries, the civilization displayed remarkable adaptive powers, absorbing many disparate peoples into a single coherent cultural unit stretching from Spain to Central Asia and northern India.

The medieval period. In the 11th century AD, there began a series of disruptive barbarian invasions, first by tribal groups who had been partly Islāmized, then by hostile groups bent on exploiting or even destroying the civilization they encountered. The 500 years that followed, the Middle Ages of Islām, witnessed a series of successful adaptations and internal transformations to accommodate this situation, while at the same time the original unity of culture was replaced by distinct local cultural zones.

The meaning of the AH dating

The 10th and 11th centuries of the Muslim era (denoted AH, Anno Hegirae, "year of the *hijrah*"—the emigration of Muḥammad from Mecca to Medina in AD 622), corresponding with the 16th and 17th centuries AD, witnessed the rise of several great land-based Muslim empires within these zones, which for a time successfully challenged the expansion of the European powers.

The modern period. By the 18th century AD, the failure of the empires to meet the technological challenge of Europe was parallelled by growing Muslim dissatisfaction with the state of religious, social, and political institutions. In the modern period, political collapse, Western imperialism, and internal religious reform were the pressing problems of the Muslim peoples. In the latter half of the 20th century, with political independence won in most areas, the accommodation of the Islāmic community to modernity and the question of how much of the religious tradition is necessary in re-creating the purity of the original religious commitment have continued to exercise the best energies of Muslims. Though in the 20th century Islām as a social unity appears to be in confusion, as a system of faith Islām continues to be vital and expanding.

THE CLASSICAL PERIOD

Historical background. In the century before the rise of Islām, the Arabian Peninsula was the scene of the collapse of the 1,000-year-old civilization of al-Yaman (Yemen), Arabia Felix, the fertile southern tip of the Arabian Peninsula. Abyssinia (Ethiopia), once colonized by South Arabians, had been Christianized by missionaries from Roman Egypt in the 4th century AD and, in the 6th century, was attempting to invade and dominate South Arabia. The Abyssinians hoped to reorganize to their own advantage the lucrative caravan trade that supplied the incense of Arabia and the spices of India to the Mediterranean world. The South Arabians looked for aid to the Persian Sāsānian Empire (which was Zoroastrian—*i.e.,* following the teachings of the 6th-century BC Iranian prophet and religious reformer Zoroaster), one of the two major powers of western Asia. The other great power, the Christian Byzantine Empire, which controlled Syria, Egypt, and North Africa, was an ally of the Abyssinians.

Within the Arabian Peninsula, the economic decline that accompanied the wars of Persia and the Byzantines to the north and the collapse of the Ḥimyarī kingdom—the last of several tribal kingdoms in South Arabia—had been paralleled by a rise in the numbers of population and by exacerbated conflicts among the tribes of Arabia. This period has been remembered as the *jāhilīyah*, the age of barbarism.

Though there were still towns and settlements in the oases, it was the Bedouins—the wild, lawless, and predatory Arab nomads—who were in the ascendant. Although they worshipped star gods, sacred stones, and idols, their highest loyalty was to the tribe or clan, groups claiming descent from a common ancestor. Their greatest achievement was an oral literature, a poetry of extraordinary quality, declaimed in a "high speech" known to all the tribesmen, that celebrated the deeds of the tribes and heroes.

The importance of pre-Islāmic Mecca

In an especially favoured position among the sedentary people were the tribe of Quraysh, who inhabited the well-watered stony valley of Mecca and had come to control what was left of the old caravan trade. Relatively prosperous, they were the chief obstacle to the Abyssinian trade policy and were respected for their managerial ability and their quality of *ḥilm* ("urbanity"). The area of Mecca was a sacrosanct territory that other tribes feared to attack, and its little temple, the Kaʿbah, sacred to a shadowy deity known simply as "the god" (Allāh, probably from al-Ilāh, the god, and cognate with Aramaic Alāhā), had been skillfully raised by the Quraysh to the position of an Arabian pantheon in which all the gods were worshipped (it even included Christian icons, or pictures) and to which the Arab tribes came on pilgrimage to worship and to trade (see also ARABIAN RELIGIONS).

By the time that Muḥammad was born, around AD 570, the influence of both Judaism and Christianity was experienced even in the inner areas of Arabia. A general notion of a supreme and sovereign deity seems to have been held by many Arabs, and some were identifying the God of the Jews and Christians with Allāh, the Lord of the Kaʿbah. Muḥammad was an orphan from a Qurayshī clan (Hāshim) that had a record of opposition to the leading clans of the Quraysh (such as Umayyah and Makhzūm), who had concentrated wealth in their own hands and exploited their tribal brethren.

The prophetic message and arbitration of Muḥammad

Muḥammad's prophetic message was to insist upon the goodness and power of the one God, who is also the Lord of the Kaʿbah. The proper response of man to this goodness is generosity (especially to the poor and the weak) and fair dealing—experiences that Muḥammad, as an orphan member of a lesser clan, had found wanting. Tribal and family ties, he proclaimed, will avail no more than wealth or idols on the Day of Judgment. The revelations, which Muḥammad always perceived as coming into his consciousness from "outside," shared much of the striking, forceful language and imagery of the pre-Islāmic poets.

As a party began to grow up around Muḥammad, the Quraysh leaders of Mecca grew steadily more apprehensive at the social content of his message. At last their harassment forced him and his followers to emigrate in AD 622 to Yathrib, later called "Medina [City] of the Prophet," an oasis 250 miles (400 kilometres) north of Mecca, where he had been invited to come as an arbitrator in the feuds of two large Arab tribes (the Aws and the Khazraj) who, together with three Jewish clans, inhabited the oasis (see also MUHAMMAD).

Birth of the Islāmic community: the ummah. With the founding of the *ummah*, the Muslim community, in the autumn of 622, the Islāmic era begins. The anarchic condition of Arabian society and the absence of any stable institution but that of the tribe had apparently already convinced Muḥammad that, if his religious mission was to succeed, it was necessary to create an ordered community and, eventually, a state.

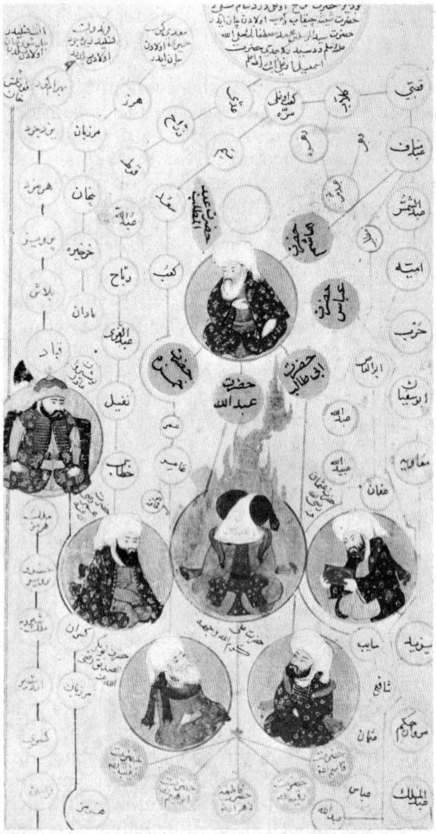

Genealogy of Muhammad from *Zubdat at-tawārīkh*, miniature by an unknown Turkish artist, *c.* 1600. Though dominant Muslim thought is opposed to representation of the human figure or (especially) face, works such as this have sometimes been painted by Muslim artists; note, however, that the Prophet's face is veiled. In the Chester Beatty Library, Dublin (MS. 423).
By courtesy of The Chester Beatty Library, Dublin

Although at first he was only one of the powerful notables of the oasis, the acceptance of his teachings, his own ability, the need for a firmer social structure, and the talents of his followers made him the paramount chief in less than two years. The Jews of Medina met Muḥammad's claim to be a prophet of the God of Abraham with opposition and ridicule, and they intrigued with his enemies both in Mecca and Medina. In time, therefore, the main groups of the Jews were driven out, and one clan, the Qurayẓah, was destroyed by putting the men to death and enslaving the women and children. Lesser groups of Jews continued to live in Medina and are expressly mentioned as forming one *ummah* (community) with the Muslims.

Mecca as a pilgrimage site

At first, the Muslims had turned toward Jerusalem to pray, but through revelations Muḥammad now instructed them to turn toward the Kaʿbah in Mecca and to fulfill there the ancient pilgrimage rites, which, according to tradition, had been instituted by Abraham and Ishmael, the ancestors of the Arabs.

Mecca was still governed by the hostile Quraysh and not accessible to Muḥammad's followers. This situation provided an impetus to subdue Mecca, and also, because of the importance given to the Kaʿbah by Muhammad, the Meccans were assured that their city would not suffer as a cult centre under the new religion. Muḥammad also encouraged his followers to intercept and raid the caravans of the Meccan merchants—the beginnings of the *jihād* ("holy war")—and, by a skillful combination of military pressure and diplomacy, he at last convinced the great majority of Meccans to come over to him as willing co-workers. Medina, however, remained the capital. Just at this period, Persia was weakened because of its wars with the Byzantine Empire, and most of the Arabian communities that had been ruled by pro-Persian factions now entered the collectivity headed by Muḥammad, pledging not to oppose the spread of his religion. By the time of his death in 632, he had gathered together a larger part of Arabia than any Arab before him, the pagan cults were dying out, and the numbers who professed that he was God's messenger were increasing everywhere.

The *ummah*, made up of freemen under God with their households, was a supertribe, to which all the loyalties once given to the tribe were to be transferred. Muslims, those who live in Islām (*i.e.*, commitment to God), were to be brothers, united more closely by religion than by blood, and were firmly prohibited from fighting each other; but they could raid non-Muslims, and this aided the community to expand. Islām has done more to develop confessional pride and communal solidarity than perhaps any other religion. Moreover, the *ummah* accepted social and moral obligations toward those who believed in God and a scripture but did not become Muslims, provided they accepted the social system, paid taxes, and kept the peace. This point was to be of great importance in the future relation of Muslims with other religions.

There were in the community men of faith, who had made a total and sincere conversion, and there were also men, such as the Meccan traders, who found outward conformity profitable and thus contributed willingly of their time and efforts to further the system. Finally, there were people such as the nomads, whose adherence had occurred only under the threat of superior force.

Adaptation and expansion (1st and 2nd centuries AH). *Expansion under the Companions of the Prophet (AD 632–661).* The Prophet's unexpected death (AD 632) at Medina was the first great crisis for the community. What then happened has been hotly disputed by his followers.

The origin of the Sunnīs and the Shīʿites

According to the Sunnīs, the "traditionalists," who make up the majority party of Muslims, the Prophet had left no successor. Immediately, the Medinans began to elect a separate chief. Because he would not have been accepted by the Quraysh, the *ummah* would have fallen apart. Therefore, two of Muḥammad's fathers-in-law, highly respected early converts and trusted lieutenants, prevailed upon the Medinans to elect a single leader, and the choice fell upon Abū Bakr, father of the Prophet's favoured wife, ʿĀʾishah. All of this occurred before the Prophet's burial (under the floor of ʿĀʾishah's hut, alongside the courtyard of the mosque).

According to the Shīʿah, or "Partisans" of ʿAlī, the Prophet had already designated as his successor his cousin and son-in-law ʿAlī ibn Abī Ṭālib, husband of his daughter Fāṭimah and father of his only surviving grandsons, Ḥasan and Ḥusayn. His preference was general knowledge; yet, while ʿAlī and the Prophet's closest kinsmen were preparing the body for burial, Abū Bakr, ʿUmar, and Abū ʿUbaydah from Muḥammad's Companions in the Quraysh tribe, met with the leaders of the Medinans and agreed to elect the aging Abū Bakr as the successor (*khalīfah*, hence "caliph") of the Prophet. ʿAlī and his kinsmen were dismayed but agreed for the sake of unity to accept the *fait accompli* because ʿAlī was still young.

Already, the Bedouins were beginning to repudiate their ties with Medina. Some began to follow other leaders who claimed to have prophetic powers like those of Muḥammad. Abū Bakr (caliph 632–634) responded resolutely with swift military expeditions under experienced Qurayshī leaders. As soon as the tribes had been subdued, he announced a program of expansion to the north. The tribes of the northeast then began to invade the area that is now Iraq, more or less on their own initiative, but, upon meeting with difficulty, they were forced to request the aid and organization of Medina.

Organization of the Arab Muslim empire

Medina's chief efforts went into organizing spectacularly successful raids upon Syria, whose Monophysite Christian population (those who believed that Christ has only one nature) resented the Orthodox Byzantine domination. Before Abū Bakr died, he forestalled a new caliphal election by appointing ʿUmar (634–644) his successor. It was under ʿUmar that the Arab Muslim empire was organized. The Byzantine army evacuated Syria in 636, and Ctesiphon, the Persian winter capital in Iraq, fell in the same year. In 641 Egypt was conquered, with the approval of its Monophysite Christian inhabitants, and in 642 Arab forces overran the Persian plateau. The result of these great victories was to turn the Bedouins to an enthusiastic acceptance of at least the outward aspects of Islām, which had brought them such advantages under Meccan leadership.

ʿUmar's constitution of the Arab empire was logical and simple, expressing both Arab and Islāmic features. The conquered peoples were to live in peace, be protected, keep their own religions and laws, and pay taxes often less onerous than they had paid in the past. The Muslim Arabs were to dwell apart in newly constructed garrison towns on the edge of the desert as a privileged caste supported by the taxes of the conquered. The business of Muslims would be war and religion.

The tribesmen, living in unaccustomed confinement in the garrison towns and observing the growing wealth of the Meccan leadership, increasingly resented what they saw as exploitation of their services. This unrest came to a head under ʿUmar's successor.

When ʿUmar died by the dagger of a Persian slave (not without some suspicion of a plot), he appointed six of the leading Companions of the Prophet to elect a new leader. The electors passed over the claims of ʿAlī to elect the Prophet's other son-in-law, ʿUthmān (caliph 644–656), an early convert from the aristocratic clan of Umayyah, which had once led opposition to Muḥammad. From the first, he affirmed a policy of control of the empire by the Meccans, particularly by the members of his own family, the Umayyads. This antagonized not only the tribesmen but also many of the most devout first Muslims. ʿAlī had been deeply offended by the election and was known to oppose most of ʿUthmān's policies.

When ʿUthmān was murdered by tribesmen from the garrisons of Iraq and Egypt in 656, it seemed natural to the deeply shocked people of Medina to hail ʿAlī as caliph, but ʿĀ'ishah, daughter of Abū Bakr, along with a number of leading Meccans, accused ʿAlī of complicity in the assassination and went to Iraq to raise an army against him. When he, too, went to Iraq to rally his followers against theirs, the result was the Battle of the Camel (so called because it took place around the camel where ʿĀ'ishah sat calling encouragement to her allies), a sanguinary battle between Muslims. The real unity of the *ummah* had been broken, never to be re-established. Henceforth, no caliph would be able to rule without an army, and, because military force had moved to the provinces along with economic power, the capital would move, too. ʿAlī established his capital at the garrison town of Kūfah in Iraq, where he had many partisans.

Disruption of the unity of the *ummah*

He was at once challenged by Muʿāwiyah I, the able governor of Syria, a brother-in-law of the Prophet and cousin of ʿUthmān, whose disciplined army of semisedentarized Syrian Arabs was the best in the empire, and who also had the backing of the most capable Meccan generals, traders, and administrators. Against this coalition ʿAlī could only oppose anarchic and undisciplined tribesmen. When ʿAlī, under pressure, agreed to negotiate with his enemies, the Khārijīs (Seceders) left ʿAlī's party to oppose both him and Muʿāwiyah. Muslim sympathies swung mainly to Muʿāwiyah, because he appeared to offer the best hope of stability and growth. When ʿAlī was assassinated in January 661 by a Khārijī, some of his partisans paid allegiance to his eldest son, Ḥasan, but Ḥasan was easily persuaded to abdicate by Muʿāwiyah, who had already been hailed by the Syrian tribes as caliph in Jerusalem.

Expansion under the Umayyads (661–750). Muʿāwiyah was a superb statesman and succeeded in setting up a stable government, recommencing military expansion, and establishing his dynasty with the help of the tribes of Syria, where the caliphs now resided. Three vital questions, however, remained in abeyance: (1) the relation of the caliphate with the tribes; (2) its relation with the religious leaders; and (3) the relation of Arabs with non-Arabs. The last question was to grow steadily in importance as more and more of the conquered peoples became converts, attracted by the simplicity and success of Islām as well as by the privileged position of the Muslims. This trend, of course, met with the approval of the religious party, but it was often discouraged by the government, and most of the Arabs contemptuously refused to treat the converts with the fraternalism enjoined by Islām.

Integration of Islāmic society

The great problem of the Umayyads was to integrate the society of the empire, and although the basic solutions were found—to allow Arabs to be absorbed into urban societies, to assimilate Muslim Arab landowners with Muslim non-Arab landowners and tax them equally, exempting them from the personal taxes paid by non-Muslims—the solutions were applied too late and too sporadically to save the dynasty.

The caliphate continued to deal with the tribal problem by wars of expansion, with the opportunities for plunder thus offered, while at the same time centralizing its authority. The development of a deadly feud, between the tribes of northern Arabian descent and those of Yamanī (southern) origin, forced the Umayyads to rule by playing the two parties off against each other, a policy that proved unsatisfactory in the long run.

The chance to conciliate the Shīʿah was lost when ʿAlī's surviving son, Ḥusayn, was ambushed and killed in 680 by Umayyad supporters at Karbalā', in Iraq, along with most of the men of his family, while on their way to participate in a revolt at Kūfah. The activist Shīʿīs and the Khārijīs both continued to appeal to the Bedouin element, both led revolts, and both championed the demand of the converts for social justice, thus finding a broader political base in their opposition to the Umayyads.

The religious party included many who were sympathetic to the cause of ʿAlī's family but not yet ready to champion civil war. Most of them distrusted the secular tendencies of the Umayyads, whom they saw as creating a temporal sovereignty at the expense of the prophetic revelation, but were unwilling to endanger the unity of the community. As a distinctive Islāmic civilization grew up under the caliphate and the ethical principles of Islām began to affect the dynasty as well as society at large, the religious teachers were somewhat disposed to give support and consent to Umayyad government. At the same time, non-Arabs were playing an increasingly important role in the religious party by the end of the 1st century AH, and these men brought their own skills to focus on the most universal aspects of Islām. They attempted to systematize the legal and ethical teachings of the Prophet and the early Muslims, as a form of opposition to the caliphate, and many of them protested against the materialism of the day by an ascetic simplicity. Ḥasan al-Baṣrī (died AH 110 [AD 728]), the most renowned teacher and preacher of his day, taught that God gives men the power to disobey him and that the faithful should hold themselves aloof from all religious quarrels and rebellion, being content with voluble protests and passive resistance against tyrannical rulers.

Decline of the Umayyads

By 714, Arab armies had overrun Spain, advanced to Kashgar in Central Asia, and taken Sind and Multān in India. This was the high point of expansion; the euphoria of apparent invincibility was to give way to questioning as Muslim armies began to meet reverses and to be absorbed in their own quarrels, and this placed greater pressure upon the caliphate to find religiously acceptable solutions to social problems. It was an obligation that few caliphs were ready to accept. In 749/50, a general revolt among the converts of eastern Persia (Khorāsān), calling for "an *imām* ["leader"] of the Prophet's family" and joined by most of the Yemeni faction of Arabs with the support of the Shīʿah and most religious scholars, brought down the Umayyad caliphate.

The early ʿAbbāsids. The revolution had been engineered by secret agents, not for the ʿAlids, the descendants of ʿAlī, but for the descendants of the Prophet's uncle ʿAbbās. It was an ʿAbbāsid whom the revolutionaries brought to the caliphate in Iraq. In 763, a new capital, Dār as-Salām, was constructed on the site of a village called Baghdad, not far from the older cities of Babylon, Seleucia, and Ctesiphon.

From the beginning, the ʿAbbāsids realized the importance of conciliating and co-opting the religious teachers who had developed into a distinct group in the late Umayyad period. These scholars were made judges and legal advisers, and heavy emphasis was placed on the religious character and authority of the caliphate, "the shadow of God over his earth." Though the caliphs were Arabs, the Arabs were no longer a privileged elite, and the arts of peace superseded those of war as the preferred pursuit of Muslims. The dynasty maintained a multiracial standing army and made heavy use of the old Sāsānian bureaucratic class, recently converted to Islām.

The results of this change were several: (1) The civilization of Islām was now opened to many cosmopolitan influences and developed swiftly, selecting what it found useful from a variety of cultures. (2) The Quraysh townsman influence had always been important, but Islām was now to develop as a city-building civilization. Wherever Muslims went, they built towns and stimulated commerce and production. (3) Persian traditions predominated in the court and administration, making the caliph always more remote from the Muslims, an Oriental king of kings—surrounded by ceremonial and intrigue—ruling over a centralized and highly taxed empire. (4) The Shīʿah were bitterly disappointed and continued to make agitation and periodic revolts for leaders from the ʿAlids. (5) The remnants of the Umayyad supporters rallied around an Umayyad prince in distant Spain and thus remained aloof from the ʿAbbāsid Empire. (6) Because religion, rather than race, now identified the empire, the position of non-Muslims, declining since the late Umayyad period, deteriorated even more. (7) The identification of orthodoxy with the caliphate might seem to offer greater religious unity; in fact, however, it threatened the development of a true consensus of faith and morals. For one thing, all political dissent would tend to seek justification in a religious sect. For another, the state would tend naturally to champion those doctrines dearest to the caliphate, regardless of the claims of the religious teachers. Finally, the immediacy of the prophetic message was in real danger of being subordinated to the temporal needs of rulers who, despite their show of piety, were at heart no better Muslims than the Umayyad had been.

If the ʿAbbāsids proved the longest lived dynasty in Islām, it is because the conditions of their power changed dramatically. The brilliant and luxurious reign of Ḥārūn ar-Rashīd (786–809) saw the creation of virtually independent vassal states in the frontier provinces, a measure that in the long run could only weaken the unity of the empire. Under Hārūn's son al-Maʾmūn (813–833), a great patron of learning, a clash with the religious teachers occurred when he tried to make the rationalist doctrines of the Muʿtazilah school of theology, which claimed that reason was equal with revelation, definitive for the whole *ummah*. He proposed to withdraw official recognition or support from all who taught that the Word of God (*i.e.*, the Qurʾān) was uncreated. His brother al-Muʿtaṣim (833–842) continued the controversy but felt so insecure that he created a new elite guard of caliphal slaves, Turks from Central Asia, and isolated himself from the people even more in a new capital, Sāmarrāʾ (the capital 836–892).

Religious controversy centring about Muʿtazilah doctrine

The conflict ended with the victory of the traditionalists (Sunnī) and proved that the religious teachers, not the successors of the Prophet, were the final authority on Islāmic faith and practice. Another important conflict was that between the ideals of Persian culture and literature, patronized by the bureaucracy and many great landowners of Persia, and the cultural system based on religious studies and Arabic language, poetry, and genealogy, which was favoured by the religious leaders. The result, paradoxically, was to affirm forever the place of the pagan poets and traditions of the Arabs against which early Islām had reacted and to accommodate a discordant Persian secularism in the culture of the eastern provinces of Islām.

After 861, the Turkish officers of the elite guard made themselves masters of the caliphs, dethroning them at will, plundering their palaces, and appropriating the imperial revenues. Governors and warlords asserted their authority in the provinces, and social and religious revolts appeared again. Because the caliphate had identified itself with orthodoxy and had failed to deliver the perfect social justice it had promised, it was perhaps natural that these revolts came from the activist wing of the Shīʿah.

The 4th century AH (10th–11th centuries AD). In AD 909 (AH 296) a successful revolt among the Kutāmah Berbers of Kabylie brought to power in Tunisia a dynasty of caliphs claiming descent from "the children of Fāṭimah," the Prophet's daughter, and ʿAlī, through Ismāʿīl, a descendant of Ḥusayn. These Ismāʿīlī anticaliphs, the Fāṭimids, conquered most of North Africa and, in 969, were able to conquer Egypt and create a brilliant Islāmic capital at Cairo. In 929 the Umayyad princes of Spain realized an old ambition when, in view of the Fāṭimid threat, the Spanish Sunnī religious leaders agreed to recognize the Umayyads as caliphs in their own right. Their capital, Córdoba, was already the most cultured European city west of Byzantium, and this second Umayyad caliphate endured until 1031.

The rise of the Ismāʿīlī Fāṭimids

Thus, the 4th century AH saw three caliphates: a token of the disunity of the *ummah*. Nonetheless, the theory that government, to be valid, must be derived from the Prophet's successor held good. The establishment of several great capitals was a factor in the great cultural achievements of this period. Islāmic philosophy flourished and aroused the hostility of the religious teachers. In Khorāsān and Transoxania (the area east of the Oxus River—modern Amu Darya—in Central Asia), the Sāmānid princes, nominal Sunnī vassals of Baghdad, patronized a revival of Persian culture and literature until their overthrow in 999. In Mosul and Aleppo, Shīʿī Arab princes, the Ḥamdānids, patronized a revival of Arabic literature (see also ISLAMIC THEOLOGY AND PHILOSOPHY; ISLAMIC MYSTICISM).

The 4th century AH was also a time of heterodoxy. From 945 to 1055, a dynasty of Shīʿite Persian warlords, the Būyids, controlled the ʿAbbāsid caliph and ruled in Iraq and western Persia. They did not belong to the sect of the Fāṭimids and kept the caliph in order to placate their Sunnī subjects, but their misrule and their official support of Shīʿism and Muʿtazilism were generally unpopular.

Intellectually, a few Sunnī scholars—such as al-Ashʿarī at Baghdad (died 936), who broke with Muʿtazilism by claiming that divine justice could not be defined in human terms, and al-Māturīdī at Samarkand (died 944), who emphasized the omnipotence of God while still maintaining the efficacy of the human will—laid the groundwork of a rational defense of traditional Sunnism, but the real fruit of their work was to appear only in the next century.

Among the Ṣūfīs, or mystics, preoccupation with their own insights led to friction with the doctors (teachers) of the religious law. When a prominent Baghdad mystic, al-Hallāj, was accused of blasphemy and heresy and put to death in 922, many embittered Ṣūfīs moved to the Sāmānid realm (a native Persian Muslim dynasty), where they were tolerated. They also converted numbers of Central Asiatic Turkish tribesmen to their own antinomian (anti-legal) version of Islām.

In this period of freethinking and heterodoxy, Muslim sympathies turned again to the ʿAbbāsids as a visible sign of unity and Sunnī orthodoxy. They could no longer pose any real threat to the religious teachers.

THE MIDDLE AGES OF ISLAM

The 5th century AH (11th–12th centuries AD). In the 11th century AD, great movements of tribal peoples occurred, and the resulting social and political dislocation hastened processes already at work.

Sāmānid Transoxania was invaded by the Qarakhāns, leaders of a confederation of Qarlug Turkmens already converted to a form of Islām by Ṣūfī missionaries.

The Ghaznavids. Khorāsān was seized by Maḥmūd, prince of Ghazna (in Afghanistan) and descendant of a Sāmānid Turkish slave officer, who had made himself

Religious policies of the Ghaznavids

independent. The Ghaznavids acted as a bridge between the Sunnī Persian civilization of the Sāmānids and the fervour and fierceness of the tribal Turkmens. Maḥmūd (reigned 998–1030) began raiding and conquering northern India in the greatest expansion of Islāmic territory since Umayyad times. He was the first Muslim prince to be called the *sulṭān* ("authority") by his contemporaries. Hitherto, the word had been used in a general sense for the Islāmic state and its agencies. Sunnism was part of Ghaznavid policy: orthodoxy was to assist political and social stability, and in Khorāsān this included a role for the mystics.

The Seljuqs. In 1040, the hold of the Ghaznavids on eastern Iran was broken by a new confederation of immigrating Turkmens, the Oğuz, led by the family of Seljuq. Well before the decisive battle of Dandānqān (north of Merv, in Khorāsān), this family had begun to identify its rule with law, order, protection of property, and Islāmic orthopraxy (right practice). They thus ran counter to the plundering instincts of their own tribal followers—and unruly Turkmens were always to be a Seljuq problem—but the Seljuq leaders had contracted an alliance with the religious and urban classes of Persian Sunnī Islām. By 1044 they had occupied most of the Iranian plateau; in 1049 and 1054, to divert other Turkmen tribes from Islāmic territory into lands of the traditional enemy, large raids into Armenia and Byzantine Anatolia took place.

The Būyid general, al-Basāsīrī, who held power in Iraq, now recognized the Fāṭimid caliphate to win its support against the growing Seljuq threat. Thus, the Seljuq leader Toghrïl Beg came to occupy Baghdad in 1055 as the saviour of the Sunnī caliphate. In 1058 the ʿAbbāsid caliph al-Qāʾim crowned Toghrïl Beg "King of the East and the West" and invested him with his own sultanate, or temporal authority, enjoining him to protect the *ummah* and fight the holy war. The new sultan was succeeded in 1063 by his nephew Alp Arslan.

The first sultans were illiterate and relied heavily on Khorāsānī administrators, Persians such as Niẓām al-Mulk, who was virtual ruler from 1073 to 1091. Besides attempting to school his masters in the ideals of Oriental despotism, he did much to reorganize the economy of the empire, assigning grants of land to military chiefs in return for service and thus hastening the sedentarization of the tribesmen.

Effects of the Battle of Manzikert

The Seljuqs continued to divert troublesome Turkmens to Anatolia, and in August 1071 the Byzantine field army, under the command of the new emperor Romanus IV Diogenes, met with the army of Alp Arslan at Manzikert, near Lake Van in Anatolia. The result was a catastrophic defeat for Byzantium. The Emperor was captured, his army decimated, and the Turkmens spread into the plateau. Before long, a cadet member of the Seljuq family had been set up by Turkmens as their sultan in Byzantine territory. Anatolia was being conquered piecemeal for Islām. The Byzantine government appealed to the Pope and Europe for aid, and the appeal was met by the First Crusade at the end of the century.

The alliance of the ruling class with the religious leaders under the Seljuqs bore fruit in the creation of *madrasah*s (theological schools), under the initiative of the vizier (confidential administrator) Niẓām al-Mulk; the *madrasahs* were institutions for training *ʿulamāʾ*, men learned in religious matters, as well as a new "orthodox" bureaucracy.

Abū Ḥāmid al-Ghazālī (AH 505 [AD 1111]), a respected Khorāsānī who taught at the Niẓāmīyah Madrasah in Baghdad for a time, distilled in his *Iḥyāʾ ʿulūm ad-dīn* (*The Revival of the Religious Sciences*) the religious spirit of the age: a synthesis of the ideas of the Ashʿarī school of Sunnī theology, the Law, Hellenistic (Greek cultural) thought, and Ṣūfism. His teachings dominated Sunnī *madrasah* education until modern times. Muslims turned to mysticism and to the veneration of the "friends of God"; *i.e.*, holy men, living and dead. Relations between *ʿulamāʾ* and Ṣūfīs became markedly more cordial, and Ṣūfī missionaries carried Islāmic preaching to the urban proletariat and the countryside.

The Almoravids. In the western areas of the Islāmic world, similar developments were taking place. The Lamtūnah people of the Ṣanhājah Berbers, the "veiled men" of Mauretania and Senegal in Africa, stirred by the preaching of ʿAbd Allāh ibn Yāsīn, a Mālikī Sunnī legalist (*i.e.*, one who based his doctrine on the teachings of the 2nd-century-AH teacher Mālik ibn Anas), found a new sense of unity and purpose. By AD 1058 they attacked both the Negro kingdom of Ghana, below the Sahara, and Morocco, where they founded a new capital, Marrakesh (Marrākush). They called themselves al-Murābiṭūn, the "*ribāṭ* people" (*ribāṭ:* a frontier fortress for the holy war). These Almoravids (from Spanish "Almoravides") imposed their militant Sunnism on the Moroccans, who had largely followed Khārijism, Shīʿism, or peculiarly Berber heresies until the conquests by the Lamtūnahs.

Activities of the Almoravids in Morocco and Spain

By 1072, the movement's northern, or Moroccan, wing was in the hands of a great chief, Yūsuf ibn Tāshufīn, who by 1082 had extended his power as far east as Algiers.

In 1086, he invaded Muslim Spain to assist the petty Muslim states that had sprung up in the anarchy of the breakdown of the Umayyad caliphate of Córdoba and that were unable to meet the offensive of the Christian King Alfonso VI of Castile. Yūsuf ibn Tāshufīn inflicted a severe defeat upon the Castilians at az-Zallāqah, but later the quarrels of the Muslim dynasts drew him back to Spain, and this time he dethroned the "party kings" and annexed their territories. Up to this point the Almoravids had simply been barbarian conquerors, fired by religious zeal. In Spain they found an old and refined Muslim civilization, and gradually its charm and luxury seduced them. They imported Andalusian administrators, architects, scholars, and musicians wholesale to Morocco, which had remained rough and relatively primitive. In religion, the Almoravids retained a legalistic narrowness of spirit, but the Almoravid *amīr* ("commander") claimed to rule in the name of the ʿAbbāsid caliph in Baghdad.

Developments in eastern North Africa. In the eastern half of Barbary (in North Africa), too, there was a return to Sunnism, although a heavy price was exacted for it.

Breakdown of Fāṭimid control in Tunisia

When the Fāṭimid caliphs left Tunisia in 973 to fix their residence at Cairo, their viceroys in al-Qayrawān, the *amīrs* of the Ṣanhājah Berber clan of the Banū Zīrī, were at first officially Shīʿites, but the sentiments of their people turned against the Fāṭimids. From 1015 to 1152, a rebellious branch of the Zīrids, the Ḥammādids, seized control of eastern Algeria and ruled independently there from their fortress-city of al-Qalʿah (1015 to 1152), in the name of the ʿAbbāsid caliph. The fourth Zīrid *amīr* of al-Qayrawān, Muʿizz ibn Bādīs, in order to consolidate his hold on his own rich kingdom, formalized the de facto breach with Cairo from 1041 to 1051 and returned his country to the ʿAbbāsid allegiance. The North African Ismāʿīlīs were massacred in popular uprisings, and the Fāṭimids were solemnly cursed in the mosques. The Fāṭimid government replied by giving title to North Africa to two great Bedouin Arab tribes, the Banū Hilāl and Banū Sulaym, thus ridding itself of a troublesome presence in its own territory and punishing an unruly vassal at no cost to itself. The result was a catastrophe for North Africa. Despite attempts by the Zīrids to pacify them, the invaders overwhelmed a combined Zīrid-Ḥammādid army at Ḥaydarān, near Qābis (Gabes, in Tunisia), in 1052. Within five years, al-Muʿizz was obliged to flee with his court to the coastal fortress-city of Mahdīyah. The Bedouins were only very superficially Islāmized and cared nothing for the Fāṭimid creed, but they gladly pillaged the towns and villages of the interior, pastured their flocks on the cultivation, and created havoc and anarchy. Those cities able to survive became city-states under local strongmen, and a near-feudal economy was introduced. By 1065, the Ḥammādid princes of al-Qalʿah were so hemmed in by the Bedouin predators that they began to reside at Bejaïa (Bougie) on the coast, in an area that offered little foothold for nomadism. Sunnism remained the creed of the people, but the blow to their civilization had been severely crippling.

Sicily had been conquered for Islām by the Aghlabīs of al-Qayrawān and ruled for the Fāṭimids by the Kalbī *amīrs*, but Sicily was conquered by the Christian Normans from 1060 to 1091. The tolerant Norman Christian kings of the island and their descendant the emperor Frederick II of Hohenstaufen (1215–50) patronized Muslim culture, but gradually Islām died out in Sicily. Norman attempts from 1087 to 1148 to conquer the seacoast of North Africa were finally successful, but not for long. In 1159 the Almohad caliph ʿAbd al-Mu'min came from Morocco in response to urgent Tunisian pleas to drive the Sicilians out.

The Almohads. The Almohad (al-Muwaḥḥid) Empire, like that of the Almoravids, was a militantly Islāmic state built by Berber tribesmen, though not strictly Sunnī. Its founder was a Berber from the Atlas Mountains (in North Africa), Ibn Tūmart, who had studied the theology of al-Ashʿarī and al-Ghazālī in the East. Upon returning in 1121 to his home in the Sūs district, he won a reputation for sanctity and gained a following among the Maṣmūdah Berbers, who resented the domination of the Almoravid Lamtūnah. His claim to be the *mahdī*, the divinely inspired leader awaited by the Muslim masses who is to bring perfect Islām and social justice before the end of the world, was regarded by Sunnīs as heterodox. After uniting the Maṣmūda as the *muwaḥḥidūn*, or unitarians, he sent them against the Almoravids, whom he accused of idolatrous views as to the real nature of God.

Ibn Tūmart, the *mahdī*

Ibn Tūmart died in AD 1130, and his disciple and successor ʿAbd al-Mu'min took the title of *khalīfah* ("successor") of the *mahdī*. The period 1132 to 1212 was a high point of Muslim culture in the West, for ʿAbd al-Mu'min built an empire comprising all of North Africa and Spain. But the chaotic situation in Tunisia was only temporarily assuaged, and after AD 1184 a civil war there, aided by the Arab Bedouins and by the Ṣanhājah, sapped Almohad strength. Despite Almohad puritanism, this unification of the Muslim West brought a period of elegance and intellectual culture.

Philosophy, almost extinct in the East after al-Ghazālī, found a home under the Almohads; Ibn Rushd (Averroës), Abu Bakr ibn Ṭufayl ("Abubacer"), and Ibn Zuhr ("Avenzoar") were all physicians famous to the late Middle Ages for their achievements under the patronage of the Almohad caliphs. The Jewish philosopher Maimonides (Ibn Maymūn) was also trained in Spain before moving to Cairo as court physician to Saladin.

Under ʿAbd al-Mu'min's great-grandson an-Nāṣir, a combined Spanish Christian Crusade shattered the Almohad army at the Battle of Las Navas de Tolosa (in Spain) in 1212. The Caliph evacuated his troops from Spain and left the Spanish Muslims to settle their affairs as best they could. Only the Naṣrid *amirs* of Granada were able, as vassals of the king of Castile, to preserve some autonomy from AD 1230 to 1492, when their power was finally suppressed by the Christian monarchs Ferdinand and Isabella.

The Almohad dynasty survived in Marrakesh until 1269, but before that, three dynasties—the Ḥafṣids (Banū Ḥafṣ) of Tunis, the Banū ʿAbd al-Wādids of Tlemcen, and the Marīnids (Banū Marīn) of Fez—had divided the territories among themselves. The Mālikī form of Sunnism eventually replaced Almohad heterodoxy.

The Fāṭimid caliphate at Cairo (AD 969–1171). In Egypt, also, there occurred a loss of caliphal authority, a rise of military dictatorship, and, eventually, a return to Sunnism. The first period of the Fāṭimids, from the latter part of the 10th to the middle of the 11th century AD, belongs among the golden ages of Islāmic culture. Nonetheless, the eccentric behaviour of the caliph al-Ḥākim bi-Amr Allāh (996–1021), who persecuted Sunnīs and Christians, helped to bring about the Crusades by destroying the Church of the Holy Sepulchre in Jerusalem, and finally proclaimed his own divinity, helped lessen the religious appeal of the movement (see also DRUZES).

The career of al-Ḥākim

By 1072, six years of famine had paralyzed the economy, civil order had broken down, the Berber soldiery and the Turkish and Sudanese slave troops were creating dreadful disorders, North Africa and Sicily had been lost, the Seljuqs had taken Palestine, and the ʿAbbāsid caliph was being recognized in Arabia. In 1073 the caliph al-Mustanṣir called in the governor of Acre (in Palestine), Badr al-Jamālī, a brilliant Armenian general, to restore order. Badr became a vigorous absolute dictator, checked the Seljuq advance, and restored Fāṭimid power in Egypt and on the Syrian coast. When his son and successor al-Afḍal placed the Caliph's younger son, al-Mustaʿlī, on the throne in AD 1094, he was able to enforce his decision in the territories he ruled, but elsewhere the Ismāʿīlīs, the Shīʿah sect to which the Fāṭimids belonged, rallied to the claim of the elder son, an-Nizār. From mountain strongholds in Syria and Persia, the Nizārīs carried out well-planned murders of political enemies, such as Niẓām al-Mulk (the Persian vizier of the Seljuqs), and became known to history as "the Assassins" (from *hashīshīyīn:* "hashish users," a derogatory name given them by their enemies).

In AD 1099 the crusaders took Jerusalem, which the Fāṭimī had only recently recovered, and by 1118 they were attempting to invade Egypt itself.

The work of the Seljuqs in Syria was continued by the Turk Zangī, Seljuq *atabeg* (or regent) in Mosul and Aleppo (in Syria), who in AD 1144 overran the crusader state of Edessa. His son, Nūr ad-Dīn, was able to unite most of the quarrelling Muslim principalities of Syria and gain control of the important city of Damascus by 1154. A Kurdish officer of his court, Saladin (Ṣalāḥ ad-Dīn al-Ayyūbī), was sent to Egypt with forces to assist the tottering Fāṭimid regime against the crusaders; in 1171 he was able to gain control of the country and restore it to the Sunnī allegiance. After this, the Ismāʿīlīs lingered only in remote areas, such as the mountains of Iran, the Yemen, or the Gujarāt coast of India (see also CRUSADES).

The expansion of Islām in other areas. In the 12th century AD, military regimes, frequently alien, ruled everywhere, usually with the cooperation of the *ʿulamā'*, who considered that even tyranny was more tolerable than anarchy and religious disunity. Increasingly, ruling elite and subjects alike found that the only thing they shared was their religion. One military dynasty replaced another amid general indifference, as long as trade, city life, and religious institutions were safeguarded. Still, the social consensus given by the Law was maintained, the arts flourished, Islām spread into new territories, and the ʿAbbāsid caliph was even able, when the Seljuq sultans grew weak, to emerge as a political power in Iraq. This late flourishing of the ʿAbbāsids occurred chiefly in the reign of the caliph an-Nāṣir (AD 1180–1225). The 12th and early 13th centuries AD were generally an age of elegance and refinement. Islāmic civilization found a permanent base in the heart of India with the establishment of the sultanate of Delhi (AD 1206), and Islām as religion was carried by traders deep into the sub-Sahara and Central Asia and across the sea routes to Sumatra (in Indonesia).

The later Middle Ages (7th–11th centuries AH, 13th–17th centuries AD). *The 7th century AH (13th century AD).* In the 13th century AD, changes took place in the Islāmic world, almost as great as those of the 11th. The collapse of the Almohads between 1212 and 1269 was paralleled by the destruction of Muslim power in the East by the Mongols. In Syria and Egypt in 1250, the end of the Ayyūbid period initiated by Saladin and the rise to power of military slaves (*mamlūks*) occurred.

The effective rule of the Seljuqs in Iran had collapsed in a Turkmen rebellion in Khorāsān in 1157. The son of a former Seljuq officer, who had been given the title of *shāh* ("king") of Khwārezm (the irrigated delta of the Oxus), occupied Khorāsān, defeated the Turkmens, and by 1194 was able to defeat the last Seljuq sultan at Rayy and expand his domain to western Iran. This made his dynasty the enemies of the ʿAbbāsid caliph an-Nāṣir and cost them the support of the *ʿulamā'* and pious Muslims.

The conquests of the Mongols

His son Muḥammad (1200–20) built an empire in Iran and Central Asia with the help of a great army of Turkish slaves. He then unwisely chose to defy the newly risen might of Genghis the Mongol Khan, who had conquered Peking and northern China in 1215. Genghis and his Mongols arrived in 1220, and one by one the cities of Khorāsān and Transoxania were destroyed in blood and flames. After contemptuously laying waste to the Shāh's empire, the Great Khan withdrew. The Khwarezmī army fled to Iraq and Syria, causing great disorders for years as mercenaries and brigands.

In 1243, the Mongols forced the Seljuq sultan of Anatolia to become their vassal. In 1256, Hülegü Khan, grandson of Genghis, was dispatched to the West with a Mongol army, at the same time that his brother Kublai was invading southern China. He first destroyed all the fortresses of the Nizārī Ismāʿīlīs, who had angered him, and in February 1258 he devastated Baghdad, putting the caliph al-Mustaʿṣim to death and sparing only Christians and some of the Shīʿites. The historic heartland of the Islāmic world had become only a province in the Mongol Empire. In 1259 part of Hülegü's army moved on into Syria and were met by the Mamlūk army of Egypt, the best trained professional corps in the Muslim world. At ʿAyn Jālūt, in Galilee, in September 1260, the Mongols were routed, and the Euphrates became the frontier between Mongol and Mamlūk territory.

The rise of the Mamlūks

The Cairo Mamlūks, slave soldiers of Ṣaliḥ Ayyūb, last Ayyūbid sultan of Cairo, had assumed power at his death during the invasion of Egypt by King Louis IX of France in 1250. After their victory over the crusaders, they became a self-perpetuating corporation, choosing a sultan from among their officers, or selecting one of his sons to rule them, and renewing themselves by the purchase and training of foreign slave boys. Sons did not inherit the position of fathers in this military elite. In their beginnings they were a formidable corps, the cultural heirs of the Ayyūbids, and highly conservative.

The real founder of Mamlūk power was Baybars I, who had helped murder the Ayyūbid heir to the throne of Cairo and had distinguished himself at the victory of ʿAyn Jālūt, which had expelled the Mongol army from Syria. He then murdered the Mamlūk sultan Quṭuz and usurped his throne. The Ayyūbid principalities of Syria were annexed, and in 1261 Baybars set up a member of the ʿAbbāsid line as caliph in Cairo to add lustre and legitimacy to his reign. This second ʿAbbāsid caliphate in Cairo was to endure as long as the Mamlūk empire, until 1517, politically powerless but recognized by sultans from many areas. Cairo was by this time the centre of the Islāmic world.

Baybars was both gifted and ruthless. He made an alliance with the Mongols of the Golden Horde in Russia, who had converted to Islām, against the House of Hülegü in Persia and Iraq, and he vigorously attacked the crusader states of the Syrian coast, in order to prevent the threatening alliance of Latin Christendom and the Mongols. The kingdom of Cilician Armenia, allied with both crusaders and Mongols, was systematically ravaged, and in 1268 the Latin principality of Antioch was overrun. The Nizārīs of Syria were forced to become his vassals in 1270, and, one by one, important crusader fortresses were crushed from 1265 to 1275. The Euphrates frontier was strengthened, and Mongol raids turned back. Baybars died in 1277 and, in 1279, was followed by a Mamlūk general, Qalāʾūn, whose descendants reigned intermittently with Mamlūk officers until as late as 1390. In this first period, the Mamlūks were chiefly dominated by the Turkish element, and the empire was the guardian of the old Islāmic order. The close alliance of throne and Sunnī *ʿulamāʾ* was maintained, and the sultans vied with their predecessors in endowing splendid *madrasah*s for *ʿulamāʾ* and convents for Ṣūfīs in Cairo and the chief cities of Syria. The last crusaders were expelled from Syria, and under Mamlūk patronage occurred the "Alexandrian age" of Arab Islāmic culture, in which the legacy of the past was collected, systematized, and imitated.

The other side of the Euphrates formed a much more chaotic, but also more innovative, cultural zone. Here, the Arabic literary tradition was relatively unimportant, and the Persian language was the idiom of literature, even in Anatolia or India.

In Persia, the Il-Khans, descendants of Hülegü after his death in 1265, ruled a separate Mongol kingdom, often at war with the Mongols of Russia or of Turkistan. Hülegü had leaned toward Buddhism but politically favoured the Near Eastern Christians and non-Sunnī Muslims, who had least reason to mourn the passing of Sunnī power. There were many Central Asiatic Muslims in the Mongol army, as well as Buddhists and Christians. As the Il-Khans grew more isolated from Mongolia and thus more dependent upon the agriculture and industry of the natives for the financial support of their army, the attractions of the majority religion grew. Ghāzān Khan (reigned 1295–1304) was able to embrace Islām amid general acceptance by his army, and his successors were all Muslims. Within less than 40 years after Hülegü's terrible invasion, his descendants had become patrons of Muslim culture, endowing mosques and *madrasah*s and building new centres of culture at Tabriz and Solṭānīyeh. The Shīʿites continued to enjoy favour, and campaigns against the Mamlūks went on. This was the first step in an evolution that, by the 16th century AD, would make Persia a Shīʿite state, cut off from much of the rest of the Muslim world.

Mongol acceptance of Islām

Despite the loss of population and productivity in the early Mongol period, Persia flourished culturally under the Il-Khans. The influence of China was felt in all the visual arts, and vigorous new forms were developed. Commerce flourished through trade relations with the Italians, by way of Trebizond on the Black Sea, and with China. In literature, it was a great age, producing some of Persia's greatest poets and historians. Shaken to its roots and exposed to new influences, the Islāmic culture of Persia responded in the most positive fashion.

In Anatolia, vassalage to the Mongols weakened the Seljuq sultanate of Konya, assisted the unruly Turkmens to rebel, and enabled local forces to assert themselves. Anatolia still, however, participated in the flowering of Persian literature. The great mystical poet and teacher Jalāl ad-Dīn ar-Rūmī and his son Sulṭān Walad both wrote in the 13th century; and organized Ṣūfism here, as in Persia, helped to fill part of the vacuum left by the destruction of stable government and social institutions.

The 8th century AH (14th century AD). The Mongols could not create a stable regime in Iran; as they became assimilated to the culture of the settled people, their barbaric spirit also decreased. By the middle of the 14th century, the Il-Khan line was extinct, and a number of successor states had risen in their empire. Important culturally were those of the Moẓaffari *shāh*s of Shīrāz and the Jalāyirid sultans of Baghdad.

Renaissance of medieval Muslim culture

The 8th century of Islām witnessed a renaissance of its medieval culture from Spain and Morocco to India. After the setbacks of the previous century, Islāmic civilization everywhere gathered its forces. Splendid monuments, religious scholarship, cultural refinement that was not yet effete, and the conversion of barbarian tribes and newly conquered territories marked most of the century. Religiously, Islām expanded in the Malay Archipelago, in Africa south of the Sahara, in India through the conquests of the sultans of Delhi and the missionary activities of the Ṣūfī teachers, and in southern Russia, Anatolia, and Nubia. Internally, the function of maintaining unity in the community passed to the Ṣūfī "paths," or orders, which had appeared in the previous century. These did much to give cohesion to Islāmic society, though, because international Ṣūfism developed as a distinctive literature and intellectual system, many of the highest energies of Muslims were drawn off into antirational and highly subjective speculation. Here and there protests were raised; notable were those of the Syrian Ḥanbalī fundamentalist teacher Ibn Taymīyah (died AH 728 [AD 1328]). Ibn Taymīyah, a follower of the 9th-century-AD traditionalist Aḥmad ibn Ḥanbal, challenged the whole evolution of Islām since the time of al-Ghazālī and may be compared with the figure of Martin Luther in Western

Christianity. Unlike Luther, the times were against him, and he was regarded as a crank in his own day. Only four centuries later was the revolutionary impact of his teaching fully felt.

Politically, the tension observed since the 11th century AD was greater than ever; the rulers of Islām were everywhere only a few steps removed from barbarism, a professional class who maintained themselves by exploiting communities with whom they had nothing in common but religion. Beneath the refinement of the century, there was violence on the one hand and quietism on the other.

The 9th century AH (15th century AD). These contradictions brought new collapse, as destructive as that of the 13th century. A Turkish warlord, Timur (Tamerlane) arose in Transoxania around 1369 to rid the country of its Mongol rulers with the approval of the *ʿulamāʾ* and settled people. He gathered masterless men from all over Central Asia into a formidable army and—always advancing pious motives—went on to sack and destroy most of the Islāmic cultural centres of Asia, carrying off their artists and artisans to beautify his capital of Samarqand (now in the Soviet Union). The great Muslim city of Delhi, which had done so much to advance the cause of Islām in India, was destroyed with its people in 1398 on the pretense that they had left India full of infidels. The Sarbedārs of Khorāsān were destroyed because they were Shīʿīs; Mamlūk Syria was plundered (and Damascus burned) in 1401 because it had once sided with Muʿawiyah against ʿAlī. The Ottoman state, founded in what is now Turkey by Osman I *c.* 1300, was ravaged in 1402, and its ruler taken prisoner because he had fought against Muslims and was not pursuing the holy war in Europe with sufficient vigour.

The rise and effects of Timur

Within two years after Timur's death in 1405, his great "empire" had fallen apart. East Persia and Transoxania remained with his descendants, some of whom were notable patrons of the arts. Despite the culture of the "Timurid Renaissance"—in which Persian Islām attempted again to recover its former glory after much devastation—nomad invasions, and the fratricidal wars of the Timurids produced great political instability; and in 1507 the Uzbek (Özbeg) Mongols, descendants of the Golden Horde, overran the stronghold of the Timurids in Iran, the kingdom of Herāt. Nonetheless, Bābur, a Timurid prince, was able in 1526 to invade and conquer the sultanate of Delhi, in disarray after Timur's invasion, and to found the Great Mughal Empire in India.

The later Mamlūks

In the Mamlūk realm, too, the military guardians became more and more predatory. After 1382, the Circassian element, sold by their parents in the Caucasus to the wider opportunities of the Cairo slave barracks, dominated the Mamlūk empire. Under the Circassian an-Nāṣir Faraj, after 1399, the shortsighted and intriguing Mamlūk officers allowed the alliance with the Ottomans against Timur to lapse, so that Timur was able to deal with both states separately. He devastated Syria, abandoned to him by Faraj, but still hesitated to deal with the main Mamlūk army in Egypt. The loss of Syria's prosperity was followed by a low Nile flooding of the tillable land in Egypt, then famine and pestilence. The Mamlūk government turned to the sale of offices, extortion of private fortunes, ruinous taxation, and state monopolies in trade. That the Mamlūk empire survived until 1517 was largely due to the wealth gained from Eastern trade by way of the Red Sea: spices, aromatics, and silk for resale to Europe. Mamlūk extortion, however, led the Europeans to seek direct routes to the East around Africa, and in 1498 the Portuguese closed the Red Sea route to the Mamlūks, whose economic collapse was thus assured. The conservative corps had also refused to adapt to firearms in the 15th century. The Ottomans were easily able to defeat the archaic Mamlūk army and annex Syria and Egypt in 1517.

Only in Anatolia did the general downward trend of the 15th century seem to be replaced by more hopeful events. A local dynasty of *gazis*, fighters for the holy war against the Byzantines, displayed particular cohesion and vigour. These were the Ottomans of the western marches, with their capital at Bursa, who by 1380 had control of an embryo empire on both sides of the Hellespont (between Europe and Asia Minor). In 1389 they had consolidated their position in the Balkans by defeating the Serbian empire at Kossovo. The fourth ruler of the line, Bayezid I, defeated a European crusade at Nicopolis in 1396 but was defeated and captured by Timur in 1402. His Anatolian conquests returned to the old princely families, but a strong Ottoman state re-emerged in 1413 under his son, Mehmed I. This was possible because of the centralized administration set up under Bayezid I and the slave household, the *kapı-kulus*, of the sultans. A new European crusade at Varna in 1444 was defeated by Mehmed's son Murad II. The prestige of the Ottomans as the champions of militant Islām grew, and in 1453 Murad II's son Mehmed II crowned their conquests by capturing—with the help of firearms—the great walled city of Constantinople, the last remnant of the once-mighty Byzantine Empire. Though only the Ottoman lands appeared well governed, the 15th century was an age of cultural refinement. Some of the greatest poets and artists that Iran produced flourished at the court of Herāt, and, despite setbacks, Arabic learning and literature and fine architecture continued in the Mamlūk state.

The rise of the Ottomans

In Morocco, the authority of the Marīnid sultans was eclipsed by the power of their relatives and regents, the Waṭṭāsids in Fez, and the Ṣūfī brotherhoods assumed more and more power in the countryside. In particular, the *sharīfs*, or descendants of the Prophet, commanded the loyalty of the people. The Banu Hilāl Bedouins, who had come into the country under the Almohads also caused great disorders, and the Portuguese seized and held Sabtah (now Ceuta, a Spanish enclave in Morocco) in 1415. By the end of the century, there were Portuguese fortified trading stations all along the Atlantic coast.

The age of empires: 10th century AH (16th century AD). By the end of the 15th century AD, the Byzantine world, deeply divided against itself, had been—with the exception of Orthodox Russia, at that time small—absorbed and pacified by the Ottoman state, which now threatened central Europe. The conquered Christians were treated as junior partners within the empire, under the government of their own patriarchs and bishops. The arrangement was a satisfactory one, at least until the 18th century when Ottoman administration decayed, and it continued until the French Revolution (1789–99), which brought ideas of nationalism to the subject peoples. An important feature of the empire at its height was the *devşirme* system, by which the sons of the Christians could be levied for the ruler's *kapı-kulus* and household troops (*e.g.*, the Janissaries). Educated as Muslims in a complex merit system, some would be trained in the palace school, the best in the empire. From there they could rise to the highest posts, and some became sons-in-law of the sultan. Frequently, they advanced the interests of their Christian relatives.

Participation of Christians: the *devşirme* system

The real imperial age of the Ottomans started with the establishment of the capital at Istanbul. By 1517, they had taken Syria and Egypt and were absorbing the states of the North African coast, which were threatened by Spanish invasions. Here the Turkish corsairs appeared as heroes of Islām, displacing corrupt local rulers, and by 1551 all of North Africa except Morocco was under Ottoman sovereignty.

Ottoman culture was to a considerable degree a syncretism of Persian-Islāmic and Byzantine culture, with old Turkish tradition. This appears very clearly in Ottoman art and architecture. The early Ottomans had had the frontiersman's contempt for religious orthodoxy, and this appears in the religious practices of the common people and even of the court. The influential Bektāshī brotherhood, to which the Janissaries and *kapı-kulus* belonged, combined old Central Asian Ṣūfī antinomianism with Shīʿite heterodoxy and, for its initiates, offered a celibate clergy, ritual confession, communion, and a trinitarian theology. Christian and Muslim peasants quite frequently venerated the same saints and holy places.

Nonetheless, the Ottomans came into conflict with the Shīʿite Ṣafavid dynasty rising in eastern Anatolia and

Persia, and this, more than any other factor, led the Ottoman emperors to emerge as the champions of Sunnī orthodoxy.

The rise of the Ṣafavids in Persia

The rise of the Ṣafavids is a conspicuous example of how the close personal relation of Ṣūfī *shaykh* ("leader") and disciples, together with the missionary spirit found in Ṣūfism, could operate in a time of political instability to build new political structures.

The hereditary heads of the Ṣafavid brotherhood claimed descent from the *imāms* of the "Twelver" sect of Shīʿīs, which teaches that the twelfth *imām* is still alive, ruling the world in occultation (hidden from view), until he reappears in the *mahdī*. Both Mongols and Timurids patronized these *shaykhs*, and in the later 15th century, the order, headquartered at Ardabīl in Azerbaijan, was a considerable local power; its leaders appeared sometimes as allies and sometimes as rivals of the rulers of the Ak Koyunlu (White Sheep) and Kara Koyunlu (Black Sheep) Turkmen confederations. Their followers among the tribes of Anatolia and Azerbaijan were called Kizilbash (redheads) from the distinctive red Ṣafavid headgear. In 1501, the young *shaykh* Esmāʿīl I defeated the Ak Koyunlu and entered Tabriz, the old Mongol capital, proclaiming himself *shāh*. He made Twelverism the state religion and, during the next ten years, went on to impose it by force in all Persia. Many Sunnī *ʿulamāʾ* and *shaykhs* of other Ṣūfī orders were put to death. Khorāsān and Herāt were taken from the Uzbeks.

Within the borders of Ottoman Anatolia, many Turkmens followed the Ṣafavid *shaykhs*, and the Bektāshīs were well-disposed toward the movement. The aggressive and revolutionary Ṣafavid propaganda was combatted by aggressive Sunnīsm, and, before moving against Persia, the Ottoman sultan Selim I massacred all the Shīʿites of Anatolia on whom he could lay hands. Until modern times, the Kizilbash of Anatolia were forced to exist as an underground movement.

In August 1514 Ottoman artillery defeated Ṣafavid cavalry at Chāldirāns in northwest Azerbaijan, and Ottoman authority in Anatolia was re-established. The Ṣafavid empire remained, but the blow to Esmāʿīl's prestige and self-confidence led to a growth in the power of the chiefs of the Kizilbash tribes and of the educated Persian bureaucracy and to frictions among them. Esmāʿīl's son, Shāh Ṭahmāsp I (reigned 1524–76), was able to assert his authority only after serious difficulties. Despite serious internal weakness until 1590 and repeated invasions by Uzbeks in the East and Ottomans in the West, Persia held firm as a Shīʿite empire; this fact radically divided areas that were closely related historically and culturally.

The Mughal Empire: 10th–11th centuries AH (16th–17th centuries AD). The sultanate of Delhi had been captured with small forces using firearms, under the brilliant leadership of Bābur, at Pānīpat in 1526. He thus became the first Mughal emperor of India. His first five successors were remarkable men who built up a great empire at the expense of the Hindu states and other Muslim kingdoms.

Islām in India

Islām in India has been deeply, and permanently, affected by Ṣūfī missionaries from Iran, such as those of the Chishtī brotherhood, whose mysticism, asceticism, and universalism struck a deep chord in the Indian temperament. These Ṣūfī teachers made the greatest possible contrast to the aloofness, elitism, and contempt for all things Hindu of the first destructive waves of Muslim warriors. With time, great numbers of native Indians, often from the lower castes, converted to Islām. Religious syncretism began to seem a possibility. The Mughal emperor who did most to build the state, Akbar the Great (1556–1605), was a religious personality and was accused by his detractors of trying to displace Islām with a new syncretistic religion. In fact, however, he and his circle only emphasized the more universalist aspects of Indian Islām as they found it. This tendency much perturbed orthodox Sunnīs, who realized that Islām in India could be vitiated and Muslim society eroded by accommodation with idolatry. With the passing of time, the power of the orthodox reaction grew and was largely responsible for the coming to power of the sixth Mughal emperor, Aurangzeb, over his brother, Dārā Shikōh, a princely mystic whom he tried and executed on a charge of heresy in 1659.

"The Devotee," miniature by an unknown Mughal artist, showing a prince visiting a dervish, *c.* 1605–10. In the British Museum.
Pramod Chandra

Mughal civilization in India fused indigenous artistic traditions with new inspirations from Iran and Central Asia and achieved great and distinctive elegance in painting, architecture, literature, gardening, and music. India flourished, was united, and saw great imperial splendour under the early Mughals. Under Aurangzeb (1659–1707), however, long and disastrous internal wars sapped the economy and the morale of the army and ruling class. The Hindu Rājput military, who formed a vital part of the army, were in large part alienated by his policies, and many rebelled. Aurangzeb also attempted to conquer the two Shīʿī kingdoms of southern India, Bījāpur and Golconda in the Deccan; but the victories proved disastrous. He was also confronted by the rise of the Marāthā Hindus in the south, against whose guerrilla tactics the Mughal field army was helpless. To his descendants he left a troubled inheritance.

New forms of confrontation with Europe. The 16th-century wars between Francis I of France and the Habsburgs of the Holy Roman Empire offered Süleyman I the Regulator (he was called the Magnificent in Europe), of the Ottoman Empire, an alliance with France in the Mediterranean and opportunities for further expansion in the Balkans. Belgrade, key to central Europe, fell in 1521, and thereafter Süleyman became involved in a struggle with the Habsburgs over Hungary, which each empire had regarded as lying in its own sphere of influence. In 1526, Süleyman invaded Hungary, killed its king at Mohács, and let an anti-Habsburg magnate, John (János) Zápolya, be placed on the throne. In 1529, he drove out a Habsburg army and besieged Vienna for three weeks. In 1532 he reinvaded Austria in answer to Habsburg provocation in Hungary. Zápolya's death in 1540 brought a new war. Süleyman incited the Protestant princes of Germany against pope and emperor and made Ottoman Hungary a stronghold for Calvinists and Unitarians; for a century and a half, support of Protestantism and the alliance with France were basic Ottoman

Expansion of Islām into Europe

policy. France had already been given important trading concessions in the eastern Mediterranean, and after 1580 England and then Holland, both Protestant powers, were given special status and favoured trading positions that greatly aided their mercantile development.

The Ottomans were unable to wholly recapture the Indian Ocean trade from the Portuguese, but they did re-establish Muslim authority in the Red Sea and win a share of the spice trade. The Muslims were not to be finally deprived of the Indian trade routes until the 17th century, when the Dutch and the English appeared in the Indies. In the mid-16th century Russia began to threaten the Ottomans by pressure against Muslim states in the Crimea and Caucasus.

Süleyman's death in 1566 was followed by a series of inferior sultans. The "Long War" with the Habsburgs from 1593 to 1605 exhausted the state and aggravated a complex internal crisis resulting from inflation, disorder in the provinces, corruption in the court, and other problems. The crisis was in part surmounted, but the empire was no longer the optimistic and expanding state it had been. The ruling class, including the *kapıkulus*, were demoralized and fought any remedy that threatened their privileges. A dynasty of reforming grand viziers, the Köprülüs, brought order; but, after 1680, an ill-considered new war against the Habsburgs dissipated the gains made. An Ottoman army was defeated at Vienna in 1683, and all the Ottomans' enemies then leagued against them. In 1699 they were forced to cede Hungary to Austria at the Treaty of Carlowitz. This time the empire was not to recover. Its policy became one of peace, diplomacy, and survival.

Ṣafavid revival in Iran

Developments in Iran. Iran experienced a brilliant revival under Shāh ʿAbbās the Great (1587–1629), who, from his new capital of Isfahan, sought European alliances against the Ottomans. He reorganized the state, relying upon native Iranians and Georgian and Circassian household troops to curb the anarchic Kizilbash. He made military reforms with the aid of English soldiers of fortune, repelled the Uzbek and the Ottomans, and built by commerce by a system of royal factories. Ṣafavid splendour has lingered in the Persian imagination, and Twelverism, the creed they imposed on the country, remains a potent force in Persian nationalism.

Decline began under ʿAbbās' successor and grandson. In 1722 an Afghan revolt broke the royal power and brought desolation to Isfahan. A Turkmen adventurer restored order in the name of a Ṣafavid prince and later usurped the throne as Nāder Shāh Afshār in 1736. After driving out the Afghans, he recovered provinces seized by the Ottomans and Russians during Afghan rule. Nāder was the last great Oriental conqueror. In 1739 he sacked Delhi, further weakening the troubled Mughal Empire; and in 1740 he conquered Transoxania. His successes were quite deceptive; they exhausted an already weakened country. The kingdom fell apart after his assassination in 1747. By 1795, the chief of the Qājār Turkmens made himself *shāh*, with his capital at Tehrān in the north. The Qājārs had the old problem of reconciling tribal interests with those of the state as a whole, but in addition they faced great external pressures.

The Muslim empires of the 16th century had failed to find new means of production and had lost control of vital routes and of the seas while appearing to be splendid and successful. Through the 18th century, imperial authority declined and was replaced by local despots.

Economically and intellectually, the *ummah* had stood still or regressed; politically, socially, and religiously, its unity seemed to be lost.

THE MODERN PERIOD

The 12th and 13th centuries AH (18th–19th centuries AD). Many Muslim spokesmen deplored the situation of the Muslim community in the 18th century AD (12th century AH). Characteristically, the protest was made first of all in religious terms. Outside the area of Ottoman authority, in central Arabia, the House of Saʿūd, a petty amirate, made an alliance in 1744 with Muḥammad ibn ʿAbd al-Wahhāb, a strict fundamentalist Ḥanbalī who had been inspired by the writings of the 14th-century-AD Ḥanbalī Ibn Taymīyah. According to Ibn ʿAbd al-Wahhāb, all veneration of living or dead saints was attacked; the authority of the sultan did not derive from God or from the consensus of the community; the whole Ottoman religious establishment was viewed as an un-Islāmic development or "innovation," and the activities of the Ṣūfīs were regarded as reprehensible. By 1805, the Wahhābīs controlled Mecca and Medina and were raiding the Shīʿite holy places in Iraq.

Renewal and reform

In Iraq and Iran, Muḥammad Bāqir Bihbihānī at the end of the 18th century AD was attacking Ṣūfism and insisting that the *mujtahids*, (religious scholars who interpret the law) must be the real leaders of Shīʿite Islām. He is considered a renewer of Shīʿism.

Ideas of renewal were also coming from the Naqshbandīyah Ṣūfī brotherhood. Shāh Walī Allāh of Delhi (died 1762), a Ṣūfī and theologian, discarded traditionalism, asserted the supremacy of the Sharīʿah (Law), and showed how society and government might be amended by truly Islāmic principles. His student, Sayyid Murtaẓā, taught at the al-Azhar University in Cairo, and his writings show erudition and good sense quite uncommon in his day. The *mujaddidī* (renewer) branch of the brotherhood, encouraged by Shāh Walī Allāh, strengthened Sunnī orthodoxy, attacked Shīʿism, and spread into the Ottoman Empire and its Arab provinces, even into Central Asia and China. Naqshbandism played an important part in 19th-century movements for orthodoxy and unity in Indonesia and Malaya, and Shaykh Shāmil, a Naqshbandī of Dāghistān (modern Dagestan) in the Caucasus, led 30 years of resistance to tsarist Russian forces.

The threat most deeply felt was the aggressive expansion of the European powers. Napoleon I of France invaded Egypt in 1798, and after the French were expelled by the British and Ottomans in 1801, it was possible for an Albanian Ottoman officer, Muḥammad ʿAlī Pasha, to seize control in 1805, be recognized as viceroy of Egypt, begin to modernize its army and agriculture, and transmit his power to his descendants.

Intervention by European powers

Russian ambition to dominate the Black Sea, the Straits (leading from the Black Sea to the Mediterranean Sea), and the Balkans was a major concern of Ottoman diplomacy in the 19th century, and the Turks were forced to meet it by alliances with France and England. The Balkan Christians took easily to the ideas of liberty and nationalism and were encouraged by Christian powers to rebel. Through the century, one territory after another achieved independence.

In North Africa, the French occupied the old Regency of Algiers in 1830. It was not possible to isolate Algiers, and with time, despite the opposition of other European powers, France was led to intervene and establish itself in Tunisia (made a protectorate in 1881) and in Morocco (protectorate in 1912). Tripolitania and Cyrenaica were lost to Italy in 1912.

Russia had annexed the Crimea in 1783. The Kazakhs of northern Central Asia were under Russian "protection" by 1755, and in the 1840s their territories were annexed. The khanates of Bukhara, Khiva, and Khokand were next overcome. Khokand was annexed, and Bukhara and Khiva became protectorates in 1873. The border between Russian Central Asia and Afghanistan, in the British sphere of influence, was drawn in 1888.

India had been gradually infiltrated by the British East India Company, which had come to be treated as one local power among others, to whom provinces might be assigned and of whom services might be requested. By 1803 the Mughal emperor had been put under its "protection." When, in 1857, a Muslim-led rebellion broke out, it briefly united Indians of all classes and religions against the British. After the failure of the rebellion, the last emperor was banished, and control of India was assumed by the British crown.

Pan-Islāmism and Islāmic nationalism

In the latter part of the 19th century, the Muslim scholar Jamāl ad-Dīn al-Afghānī (died 1897) vigorously promoted ideas of Muslim unity: the Muslims were one nation and one civilization, intrinsically superior to the West, if correct leadership could be found.

The 14th century AH (20th century AD). The reactionary Ottoman sultan Abdülhamid II (reigned 1876–1909) capitalized on the feelings of the Sunnīs of the east, who regarded him as the caliph, to shore up his empire (*e.g.*, by building a railway to Hejaz, in Arabia, with their contributions in 1900), thus strengthening Turkish sovereignty in Syria, Arabia, and Yemen.

The Muslim masses thus found themselves caught up in alien international forces that could neither be evaded nor controlled. The division between traditional culture, with all its hallowed associations, and modernity was increasingly obvious. Muslims did not have the technological or military strength or the intellectual vigour as yet to resist effectively. Muslim rulers were forced to barter away the substance of sovereignty for the titles or try to balance the Europeans off against each other, as Persia did with the Russians and British or Turkey did with the several European powers. As groups of Muslims in separate states met the tensions and problems of modernity separately, nationalism developed almost by default. Still, no Muslim people has developed a sense of nationalism that involves loyalty to a community transcending the bounds of Islām. It is also important to remember that, though Muslims have been thrown on the defensive during much of the modern period, Islām has not lost adherents; on the contrary, it is a rapidly expanding faith. In recent times, it has begun to make significant numbers of converts in industrialized societies.

The Arabs, who desired independence from the Turks, found that their countries were partitioned among European powers after World War I. This was followed by even greater disillusionment when Palestine was opened to Zionist (Jewish) colonization, and Israel was established with Western financial and diplomatic support after World War II. This has forced the Arabs, through no desire of their own, to depend more and more on the Soviet Union for assistance against imperialism. This situation was dramatized for them by the attack of the U.K., Israel, and France upon Egypt following the nationalization in 1956 of the Egyptian-chartered Suez Canal Company and by the great sums of American aid given to Israel.

The Turks of Anatolia followed their revolutionary leader Mustafa Kemal Atatürk after World War I in repelling invaders and building a strong nation. The country's elite followed his plans for the rejection of traditional culture, despite the scandal thus caused among Muslims. The extension of the universal franchise after World War II has shown, however, that the traditional ties are deep and uncritical among the masses.

The success of the majority of India's Muslims in 1947 in achieving a separate state, Pakistan, is to some measure offset by a tragic lack of agreement as to how to attain their social and political aspirations and by the deep cultural differences between East and West Pakistan. In 1971, East Pakistan broke away from the West to form the new state of Bangladesh.

The old desire for strong one-man leadership plays a role in modern Muslim politics. The corporate responsibility of the *ummah* for its members is in many contexts translated into Socialism. The old longing for a deliverer who will bring perfect social justice still haunts the popular imagination and to some degree undercuts attempts to ameliorate present realities; what is less than perfect can only be passively and critically endured.

Although Muslims in virtually every area of the world except Russian and Chinese Central Asia have obtained independence from foreign domination in the 20th century—Islam's 14th—industrialization, rapid population growth, and Great Power rivalries create severe problems for Muslim states. Modern technology has given the Muslim countries control of the nomads, revolutionary possibilities in agriculture, and enormous new sources of mineral wealth. The landowning class that controlled early modern governments is being set aside. The new middle classes demand modernity, independence, and a wider material existence. They also remain loyal to Islāmic principles, as they understand them. The new intellectual elite that can free what are viewed as perennial truths from the cultural impediments of the past is only just beginning to emerge.

ISLAM TODAY: DEMOGRAPHIC AND SOCIAL ASPECTS

Reliable census figures are not available for many areas, yet there are perhaps 600,000,000 Muslims in the world today. The majority are Sunnīs. The population of Iran is about 93% Shīʿī, mostly Twelver, and other Twelver communities are found in Lebanon, Syria, India, and Pakistan. The Ismāʿīlīs, or Sevener Shīʿā, are in two principal divisions, the Nizārīs, numerically larger, whose *imām* is the Aga Khan, and the Mustaʿlīs, in several sects. Ismāʿīlīs are found principally as minorities on the west coast of India and Pakistan, in Central Asia, East Africa, and Syria. Some are found in Yemen (Ṣanʿāʾ). The Zaydī Shīʿites, close in practice to the Sunnīs, predominate in the highlands around Ṣanʿāʾ.

Sunnī and Shīʿa population strengths

Of the Khārijīs, only the moderate Ibāḍī sect has survived to modern times: their communities are found in the isle of Jarbah, Tunisia; in the Mzab Oases, Algeria; and in Oman and Zanzibar.

Islām has been expanding in sub-Saharan Africa since the 11th century AD and, as an "African" religion, makes more rapid progress than Christianity in many areas.

It is estimated that about 10% of the total population of both China and India are Muslims. Indonesia, with over 90% of its population Muslim, is the most populous Muslim country. In both Malaysia–Indonesia and China, Islām was accepted as their religion by people who did not give up their pre-Islāmic civilization, a fact that makes for considerable cultural variation. To some extent, the same was true of the Bengali Muslims of eastern India and Bangladesh.

An interesting development of recent years is the growth of Islām among the black population of the United States. Although this at first took the heterodox form called the Black Muslims, there is a marked tendency for these Muslims to turn to more orthodox practice as they come into contact with international Islām.

There are over 30,000,000 Muslims in the Soviet Union; and Muslim majorities exist in Albania, Bangladesh, Chad, The Gambia, Lebanon, Malawi, Malaysia, Niger, Senegal, The Sudan, and Syria. The Arabian Peninsula, Afghanistan, Algeria, Iran, Libya, Mauritania, Morocco, Somalia, Tunisia, and Turkey are nearly 100% Muslim. Indonesia, Iraq, Jordan, Mali, Pakistan, and Egypt are all preponderantly Muslim (90% or over).

BIBLIOGRAPHY. CHARLES J. ADAMS (ed.), *A Reader's Guide to the Great Religions* (1965), contains excellent bibliography on Islām as religion; for Islāmic history, the bibliography of JEAN SAUVAGET and CLAUDE CAHEN, *Introduction à l'histoire de l'Orient musulman* (1961; Eng. trans., *Introduction to the History of the Muslim East*, 1965), though already dated, is almost indispensable. *The Cambridge History of Islam*, 2 vol. (1970), consisting of articles of greatly varying quality, is the best single history available. *The Encyclopaedia of Islām*, 4 vol. and suppl. (1913–38; new ed. in progress, 3 vol. completed, 1960–), has articles arranged according to their Oriental names, thus making it somewhat difficult for Western laymen to use. The new edition contains much more material than the first but has not been completed. On the religious tradition, H.A.R. GIBB, *Mohammedanism*, 2nd ed. (1953; reprinted with revisions, 1961), is the classic exposition by a Western author. J.A. WILLIAMS (ed.), *Islam* (1961), consists of translated original texts arranged so as to let the religious tradition speak from its own perspective. W.M. WATT, *Muhammad: Prophet and Statesman* (1961), is a concise biography of the prophet that reflects modern scholarship and the author's much more detailed earlier studies. H.A.R. GIBB, *Studies on the Civilization of Islam* (1962), contains some excellent articles on the interpretation of Islāmic history, historiography, political thought, religion, and Arabic literature. G.E. VON GRUNEBAUM, *Medieval Islam*, 2nd ed. (1953), gives a general view of Muslim culture in the Middle Ages. S.D. GOITEIN, *Studies in Islamic History and Institutions* (1966), considers medieval institutions and social history. J.A. WILLIAMS (comp.), *Themes of Islamic Civilization* (1971), examines through original texts Islāmic ideas on the community, political philosophy, law, man's freedom, messianism, holy war, and mysticism. E.I.J. ROSENTHAL, *Political Thought in Medieval Islam* (1958), examines the ideas of prominent political theorists. REUBEN LEVY, *The Social*

Structure of Islam (1957), is an attempt to show the effects of Islām on the social structure of the human societies that have accepted it. M.M. SHARIF (ed.), *A History of Muslim Philosophy*, 2 vol. (1963–66), is a grandiose attempt to examine the whole history of Muslim speculative thought down to modern times through articles of varying quality. For Islām in the modern world, two books are particularly recommended: H.A.R. GIBB, *Modern Trends in Islam* (1947); and W.C. SMITH, *Islam in Modern History* (1957).

(J.A.Wi.)

Islāmic Law

Islāmic law as used in this article is the system of duties that are incumbent upon a Muslim by virtue of his religious belief. Total and unqualified submission to the will of Allāh (God) is the fundamental tenet of Islām: Islāmic law is therefore the expression of Allāh's command for Muslim society. Known as the Sharīʿah, a derivative of a root Arabic word meaning track or road, the law constitutes a divinely ordained path of conduct that guides the Muslim toward a practical expression of his religious conviction in this world and the goal of divine favour in the world to come.

NATURE AND SIGNIFICANCE OF ISLAMIC LAW

Sharīʿah and *fiqh*

Muslim jurisprudence, the science of ascertaining what the precise terms of the Sharīʿah are, is known as *fiqh* (literally "understanding"). The historical process of the discovery of Allāh's law (see below) was regarded as completed by the end of the 9th century when the law had achieved a definitive formulation in a number of legal manuals written by different jurists. Throughout the medieval period this basic doctrine was elaborated and systematized in a large number of commentaries, and the voluminous literature thus produced constitutes the traditional textual authority of Sharīʿah law.

In classical form the Sharīʿah differs from Western systems of law in two principal respects. In the first place the scope of the Sharīʿah is much wider, since it regulates man's relationship not only with his neighbours and with the state, which is the limit of most other legal systems, but also with his God and his own conscience. Ritual practices, such as the daily prayers, almsgiving, fasting, and pilgrimage, are an integral part of Sharīʿah law and usually occupy the first chapters in the legal manuals. The Sharīʿah is also concerned as much with ethical standards as with legal rules, indicating not only what man is entitled or bound to do in law, but also what he ought, in conscience, to do or refrain from doing. Accordingly, certain acts are classified as praiseworthy (*mandūb*), which means that their performance brings divine favour and their omission divine disfavour, and others as blameworthy (*makrūh*), which means that omission brings divine favour and commission divine disfavour; but in neither case is there any legal sanction of punishment or reward, nullity or validity. The Sharīʿah is not merely a system of law, but a comprehensive code of behaviour that embraces both private and public activities.

The second major distinction between the Sharīʿah and Western legal systems is the result of the Islāmic concept of law as the expression of the divine will. With the death of the Prophet Muḥammad in 632, communication of the divine will to man ceased so that the terms of the divine revelation were henceforth fixed and immutable. When, therefore, the process of interpretation and expansion of this source material was held to be complete with the crystallization of the doctrine in the medieval legal manuals, Sharīʿah law became a rigid and static system. Unlike secular legal systems that grow out of society and change with the changing circumstances of society, Sharīʿah law was imposed upon society from above. In Islāmic jurisprudence it is not society that moulds and fashions the law, but the law that precedes and controls society.

Such a philosophy of law clearly poses fundamental problems of principle for social advancement in contemporary Islām. How can the traditional Sharīʿah law be adapted to meet the changing circumstances of modern Muslim society? This is now the central issue in Islāmic law. (See *Reform of Sharīʿah law* below).

HISTORICAL DEVELOPMENT OF SHARIʿAH LAW

For the first Muslim community established under the leadership of the Prophet at Medina in 622, the Qurʾānic (Islāmic scriptural) revelations laid down basic standards of conduct. But the Qurʾān is in no sense a comprehensive legal code. No more than 80 verses deal with strictly legal matters; while these verses cover a wide variety of topics and introduce many novel rules, their general effect is simply to modify the existing Arabian customary law in certain important particulars.

During his lifetime Muḥammad, as the supreme judge of the community, resolved legal problems as they arose by interpreting and expanding the general provisions of the Qurʾān, and the same *ad hoc* activity was carried on after his death by the caliphs (temporal and spiritual rulers) of Medina. But the foundation of the Umayyad dynasty in 661, governing from its centre of Damascus a vast military empire, produced a legal development of much broader dimensions. With the appointment of judges, or *qāḍīs*, to the various provinces and districts, an organized judiciary came into being. The *qāḍīs* were responsible for giving effect to a growing corpus of Umayyad administrative and fiscal law; and since they regarded themselves essentially as the spokesmen of the local law, elements and institutions of Roman-Byzantine and Persian-Sāsānian law were absorbed into Islāmic legal practice in the conquered territories. Depending upon the discretion of the individual *qāḍī*, decisions would be based upon the rules of the Qurʾān where these were relevant; but the sharp focus in which the Qurʾānic laws were held in the Medinian period had become lost with the expanding horizons of activity.

Development of a judiciary

Development of different schools of law. A reaction to this situation arose in the early 8th century when pious scholars, grouped together in loose, studious fraternities, began to debate whether or not Umayyad legal practice was properly implementing the religious ethic of Islām. Actively sponsored by the ʿAbbāsid rulers, who came to power in the mid-8th century pledged to build a truly Islāmic state and society, the activities of the jurists (*faqīh*, plural *fuqahāʾ*) in these early schools of law marked the real beginning of Islāmic jurisprudence. Their aim was to Islāmize the law by reviewing the current legal practice in the light of the Qurʾānic principles and then on this basis adopting, modifying, or rejecting the practice as part of their ideal scheme of law.

Of the many early schools of law the two most important were those of the Mālikīs in Medina and the Ḥanafīs in al-Kūfah, named after two outstanding scholars in the respective localities, Mālik ibn Anas and Abū Ḥanīfah. Inevitably the Mālikī and Ḥanafī doctrines, as they were then being recorded in the first compendiums of law, differed considerably from each other, not only because free juristic speculation was bound to produce varying results but also because the thought of the scholars was conditioned by their different social environments. A deep conflict of juristic principle emerged within the schools between those who maintained that outside the terms of the Qurʾān scholars were free to use their reason (*raʾy*) to ascertain the law and those who insisted that the only valid source of law outside the Qurʾān lay in the precedents set by the Prophet himself.

The jurist Shāfiʿī (died 820) aimed to eliminate these schisms and produce greater uniformity in the law by expounding a firm theory of the sources from which the law must be derived. Shāfiʿī's fundamental teaching was that knowledge of the Sharīʿah could be attained only through divine revelation found either in the Qurʾān or in the divinely inspired precedents (*sunnah*) of the Prophet as ascertained through authentic reports (Ḥadīth). Human reason in law should be strictly confined to analogical deduction, or *qiyās*—problems not specifically answered by the divine revelation were to be solved by applying the principles upon which closely parallel cases had been regulated by the Qurʾān or *sunnah*.

The role of divinely inspired precedent

Shāfiʿī's insistence upon the importance of the *sunnah* as a source of law produced a great activity in the collection and classification of Ḥadīths, particularly among his own supporters, who formed the Shāfiʿī school, and the followers of Aḥmad ibn Ḥanbal (died 855) who formed the Ḥanbalī school. Muslim scholarship maintained that the classical compilations of Ḥadīths—especially those of Bukhārī (died 870) and Muslim (died 875)—constituted an authentic record of the Prophet's precedents. The general view of Western orientalists, however, is that a considerable part of the *sunnah* represents the views of later jurists fictitiously ascribed to the Prophet to give the doctrine a greater authority.

Later developments. Shāfiʿī's thesis formed the basis of the classical theory of the roots of jurisprudence (*uṣūl al-fiqh*), which crystallized in the early 10th century. Juristic "effort" to comprehend the terms of the Sharīʿah is known as *ijtihād*, and legal theory first defines the course that *ijtihād* must follow. In seeking the answer to a legal problem the jurist must first consult the Qurʾān and the *sunnah*. Failing any specific solution in this divine revelation he must employ analogy (*qiyās*) or certain subsidiary principles of reasoning—*istiḥsān* (equitable preference) and *istiṣlāḥ* (the public interest). The legal theory then evaluates the results of *ijtihād* on the basis of the criterion of *ijmāʿ*, or consensus. As an attempt to define Allāh's law the *ijtihād* of individual scholars could result only in a tentative conclusion termed *ẓann* ("conjecture"). But where a conclusion became the subject of unanimous agreement by the qualified scholars, it became a certain (*yaqīn*) and infallible expression of Allāh's law. Two major effects flowed from this classical doctrine of *ijmāʿ*. It served first as a permissive principle to admit the validity of variant opinions as equally probable attempts to define the Sharīʿah. Second, it operated as a restrictive principle to ratify the status quo; for once the *ijmāʿ* had cast an umbrella authority not only over those points that were the subject of a consensus but also over existing variant opinions, to propound any further variant was to contradict the infallible *ijmāʿ* and therefore tantamount to heresy.

Ijmāʿ set the final seal of rigidity upon the doctrine, and from the 10th century onward independent juristic speculation ceased. In the Arabic expression, "the door of *ijtihād* was closed." Henceforth jurists were *muqallids*, or imitators, bound by the doctrine of *taqlīd* ("clothing with authority") to follow the doctrine as it was recorded in the authoritative legal manuals.

Sharīʿah law is a candidly pluralistic system, the philosophy of the equal authority of the different schools being expressed in the alleged dictum of the Prophet: "Difference of opinion among my community is a sign of the bounty of Allāh." But outside the four schools of Sunnī, or orthodox, Islām stand the minority sects of the Shīʿah and the Ibāḍīs whose own versions of the Sharīʿah differ considerably from those of the Sunnīs. Shīʿī law in particular grew out of a fundamentally different politico-religious system in which the rulers, or *imāms*, were held to be divinely inspired and therefore the spokesmen of the Lawgiver himself. Geographically, the division between the various schools and sects became fairly well defined as the *qāḍīs*' courts in different areas became wedded to the doctrine of one particular school. Thus Ḥanafī law came to predominate in the Middle East and the Indian subcontinent; Mālikī law in North, West, and Central Africa; Shāfiʿī law in East Africa, the southern parts of the Arabian peninsula, Malaysia, and Indonesia; Ḥanbalī law in Saudi Arabia, Shīʿī law in Iran and the Shīʿī communities of India and East Africa; Ibāḍī law in Zanzibar, ʿUman, and parts of Algeria.

Distribution of various schools of Islāmic law

Although Sharīʿah doctrine was all-embracing, Islāmic legal practice has always recognized jurisdictions other than that of the *qāḍīs*. Because the *qāḍīs*' courts were hidebound by a cumbersome system of procedure and evidence, they did not prove a satisfactory organ for the administration of justice in all respects, particularly as regards criminal, land, and commercial law. Hence, under the broad head of the sovereign's administrative power (*siyāsah*), competence in these spheres was granted to other courts, known collectively as *maẓālim* courts, and the jurisdiction of the *qāḍīs* was generally confined to private family and civil law. As the expression of a religious ideal, Sharīʿah doctrine was always the focal point of legal activity, but it never formed a complete or exclusively authoritative expression of the laws that in practice governed the lives of Muslims.

THE SUBSTANCE OF TRADITIONAL SHARĪʿAH LAW

Sharīʿah duties are broadly divided into those that an individual owes to Allāh (the ritual practices or *ʿibādāt*) and those that he owes to his fellow men (*muʿāmalāt*). It is the latter category of duties alone, constituting law in the Western sense, that is described here.

Penal law. Offenses against the person, from homicide to assault, are punishable by retaliation (*qiṣāṣ*), the offender being subject to precisely the same treatment as his victim. But this type of offense is regarded as a civil injury rather than a crime in the technical sense, since it is not the state but only the victim or his family who have the right to prosecute and to opt for compensation or blood money (*diyah*) in place of retaliation.

Fixed punishment

For six specific crimes the punishment is fixed (*ḥadd*): death for apostasy and for highway robbery; amputation of the hand for theft; death by stoning for extramarital sex relations (*zinā*) where the offender is a married person and 100 lashes for unmarried offenders; 80 lashes for an unproved accusation of unchastity (*qadhf*) and for the drinking of any intoxicant.

Outside the *ḥadd* crimes, both the determination of offenses and the punishment therefore lies with the discretion of the executive or the courts.

Law of transactions. A legal capacity to transact belongs to any person "of prudent judgment" (*rāshid*), a quality that is normally deemed to arrive with physical maturity or puberty. There is an irrebuttable presumption of law (1) that boys below the age of 12 and girls below the age of 9 have not attained puberty, and (2) that puberty has been attained by the age of 15 for both sexes. Persons who are not *rāshid*, on account of minority, mental deficiency, simplicity, or prodigality, are placed under interdiction: their affairs are managed by a guardian and they cannot transact effectively without the guardian's consent.

The basic principles of the law are laid down in the four root transactions of (1) sale (*bayʿ*), transfer of the ownership or corpus of property for a consideration; (2) hire (*ijārah*), transfer of the usufruct (right to use) of property for a consideration; (3) gift (*hibah*), gratuitous transfer of the corpus of property, and (4) loan (*ʿāriyah*), gratuitous transfer of the usufruct of property. These basic principles are then applied to the various specific transactions of, for example, pledge, deposit, guarantee, agency, assignment, land tenancy, partnership, and *waqf* foundations. *Waqf* is a peculiarly Islāmic institution whereby the founder relinquishes his ownership of real property, which belongs henceforth to Allāh, and dedicates the income or usufruct of the property in perpetuity to some pious or charitable purpose, which may include settlements in favour of the founder's own family.

The Islāmic law of transactions as a whole is dominated by the doctrine of *ribā*. Basically, this is the prohibition of usury, but the notion of *ribā* was rigorously extended to cover, and therefore preclude, any form of interest on a capital loan or investment. And since this doctrine was coupled with the general prohibition on gambling transactions, Islāmic law does not, in general, permit any kind of speculative transaction the results of which, in terms of the material benefits accruing to the parties, cannot be precisely forecast.

Family law. A patriarchal outlook is the basis of the traditional Islāmic law of family relationships. Fathers have the right to contract their daughters, whether minor or adult, in compulsory marriage. Only when a woman has been married before is her consent to her marriage necessary; but even then the father, or other marriage guardian, must conclude the contract on her behalf. In Ḥanafī and Shīʿī law, however, only minor girls may be contracted in compulsory marriage, and adult women may conclude their own marriage contracts, except that the guardian may have the marriage annulled if his ward has married beneath her social status.

Husbands have the right of polygamy and may be validly married at the same time to a maximum of four wives. Upon marriage a husband is obliged to pay to his wife her dower, the amount of which may be fixed by agreement or by custom; and during the marriage he is bound to maintain and support her provided she is obedient to him, not only in domestic matters but also in her general social activities and conduct. A wife who rejects her husband's dominion by leaving the family home without just cause forfeits her right to maintenance.

Law of divorce

But it is in the traditional law of divorce that the scales are most heavily weighted against the wife. A divorce may be effected simply by the mutual agreement of the spouses, which is known as *khulʿ* when the wife pays some financial consideration to the husband for her release; and according to all schools except the Ḥanafīs a wife may obtain a judicial decree of divorce on the ground of some matrimonial offense—*e.g.*, cruelty, desertion, failure to maintain—committed by the husband. But the husband alone has the power unilaterally to terminate the marriage by repudiation (*ṭalāq*) of his wife. *Ṭalāq* is an extrajudicial process: a husband may repudiate his wife at will and his motive in doing so is not subject to scrutiny by the court or any other official body. A repudiation repeated three times constitutes a final and irrevocable dissolution of the marriage; but a single pronouncement may be revoked at will by the husband during the period known as the wife's *ʿiddah*, which lasts for three months following the repudiation (or any other type of divorce) or, where the wife is pregnant, until the birth of the child.

The legal position of children within the family group, as regards their guardianship, maintenance, and rights of succession, depends upon their legitimacy, and a child is legitimate only if it is conceived during the lawful wedlock of its parents. In Sunnī law no legal relationship exists between a father and his illegitimate child; but there is a legal tie, for all purposes, between a mother and her illegitimate child. Guardianship of the person (*e.g.*, control of education and marriage) and of the property of minor children belongs to the father or other close male, agnate relative, but the bare right of custody (*ḥaḍānah*) of young children, whose parents are divorced or separated, belongs to the mother or the female, maternal relatives.

Succession law. An individual's power of testamentary disposition is basically limited to one-third of his net estate (*i.e.*, the assets remaining after the payment of funeral expenses and debts) and two-thirds of the estate passes to the legal heirs of the deceased under the compulsory rules of inheritance.

Sunnī inheritance laws

There is a fundamental divergence between the Sunnī and the Shīʿī schemes of inheritance. Sunnī law is essentially a system of inheritance by male agnate relatives or *ʿaṣabah*—*i.e.*, relatives who, if they are more than one degree removed from the deceased, trace their connection with him through male links. Among the *ʿaṣabah*, priority is determined by: (1) class, descendants excluding ascendants, who in turn exclude brothers and their issue, who in turn exclude uncles and their issue; (2) degree, within each class the relative nearer in degree to the deceased excluding the more remote; (3) strength of blood tie, the germane, or full blood, connection excluding the half blood, or consanguine, connection among collateral relatives. This agnatic system is mitigated by allowing the surviving spouse and a limited number of females and nonagnates—the daughter; son's daughter; mother; grandmother; germane, consanguine, and uterine sisters; and uterine brother—to inherit a fixed fractional portion of the estate in suitable circumstances. But the females among these relatives only take half the share of the male relative of the same class, degree, and blood tie, and none of them excludes from inheritance any male agnate, however remote. No other female or non-agnatic relative has any right of inheritance in the presence of a male agnate. Where, for example, the deceased is survived by his wife, his daughter's son, and a distant agnatic cousin, the wife will be restricted to one-fourth of the inheritance, the grandson will be excluded altogether, and the cousin will inherit three-fourths of the estate.

Shīʿī law rejects the criterion of the agnatic tie and regards both the maternal and paternal connections as equally strong grounds of inheritance. In the Shīʿī system the surviving spouse always inherits a fixed portion, as in Sunnī law, but all other relatives, including females and nonagnates, are divided into three classes: (1) parents and lineal descendants; (2) grandparents, brothers and sisters, and their issue; (3) uncles and aunts and their issue. Any relative of class one excludes any relative of class two, who in turn excludes any relative of class three. Within each class the nearer in degree excludes the more remote, and the full blood excludes the half blood. While, therefore, a male relative normally takes double the share of the corresponding female relative, females and nonagnates are much more favourably treated than they are in Sunnī law. In the case mentioned above, for example, the wife would take one-fourth, but the remaining three-fourths would go to the daughter's son, or indeed to a daughter's daughter, and not to the agnatic cousin.

Under Shīʿī law the only restriction upon testamentary power is the one-third rule, but Sunnī law goes further and does not allow any bequest in favour of a legal heir. Under both systems, however, bequests that infringe these rules are not necessarily void and ineffective; the testator has acted beyond his powers, but the bequest may be ratified by his legal heirs.

Further protection is afforded to the rights of the legal heirs by the doctrine of death sickness. Any gifts made by a dying person in contemplation of his death are subject to precisely the same limitations as bequests, and, if they exceed these limits, will be effective only with the consent of the legal heirs.

Procedure and evidence. Traditionally, Sharīʿah law was administered by the court of a single *qāḍī*, who was the judge of the facts as well as the law, although on difficult legal issues he might seek the advice of a professional jurist, or *muftī*. There was no hierarchy of courts and no organized system of appeals. Through his clerk (*kātib*) the *qāḍī* controlled his court procedure, which was normally characterized by a lack of ceremony or sophistication. Legal representation was not unknown, but the parties would usually appear in person and address their pleas orally to the *qāḍī*.

Burden of proof

The first task of the *qāḍī* was to decide which party bore the burden of proof. This was not necessarily the party who brought the suit, but was the party whose contention was contrary to the initial legal presumption attaching to the case. In the case of an alleged criminal offense, for example, the presumption is the innocence of the accused, and in a suit for debt the presumption is that the alleged debtor is free from debt. Hence the burden of proof would rest upon the prosecution in the first case and upon the claiming creditor in the second. This burden of proof might, of course, shift between the parties several times in the course of the same suit, as, for example, where an alleged debtor pleads a counterclaim against the creditor.

The standard of proof required, whether on an initial, intermediate or final issue, was a rigid one and basically the same in both criminal and civil cases. Failing a confession or admission by the defendant, the plaintiff or prosecutor was required to produce two witnesses to testify orally to their direct knowledge of the truth of his contention. Written evidence and circumstantial evidence, even of the most compelling kind, were normally inadmissible. Moreover, the oral testimony (*shahādah*) had usually to be given by two male, adult Muslims of established integrity or character. In certain cases, however, the testimony of women was acceptable (two women being required in place of one man), and in most claims of property the plaintiff could satisfy the burden of proof by one witness and his own solemn oath as to the truth of his claim.

If the plaintiff or prosecutor produced the required degree of proof, judgment would be given in his favour. If he failed to produce any substantial evidence at all, judgment would be given for the defendant. If he produced some evidence, but the evidence did not fulfill the strict requirements of *shahādah*, the defendant would be offered the oath of denial. Properly sworn this oath would secure judgment in his favour; but if he refused it, judgment would be given for the plaintiff, provided, in some cases, that the latter himself would swear an oath.

In sum, the traditional system of procedure was largely self-operating. After his initial decision as to the incidence of the burden of proof, the *qāḍī* merely presided over the predetermined process of the law: witnesses were or were not produced, the oath was or was not administered and sworn, and the verdict followed automatically.

LAW IN CONTEMPORARY ISLAM

The scope of Sharīʿah law and the mode of its administration. During the 19th century the impact of Western civilization upon Muslim society brought about radical changes in the fields of civil and commercial transactions and criminal law. In these matters the Sharīʿah courts were felt to be wholly out of touch with the needs of the time, not only because of their system of procedure and evidence but also because of the substance of the Sharīʿah doctrine, which they were bound to apply.

As a result, the criminal and general civil law of the Sharīʿah was abandoned in most Muslim countries and replaced by new codes based upon European models with a new system of secular tribunals to apply them. Thus, with the notable exception of the Arabian peninsula, where the Sharīʿah is still formally applied in its entirety, the application of Sharīʿah law in Islām has been broadly confined, from the beginning of the 20th century, to family law, including the law of succession at death and the particular institution of *waqf* endowments.

The decline of Sharīʿah

Nor, even within this circumscribed sphere, is Sharīʿah law today applied in the traditional manner. Throughout the Middle East generally Sharīʿah family law is now expressed in the form of modern codes, and it is only in the absence of a specific relevant provision of the code that recourse is had to the traditionally authoritative legal manuals. In India and Pakistan much of the family law is now embodied in statutory legislation, and since the law is there administered as a case-law system, the authority of judicial decisions has superseded that of the legal manuals.

In most countries, too, the court system has been, or is being, reorganized to include, for instance, the provision of appellate jurisdictions. In Egypt and Tunisia the Sharīʿah courts, as a separate entity, have been abolished, and Sharīʿah law is now administered through a unified system of national courts. In India, and, since partition, in Pakistan it has always been the case that Sharīʿah law has been applied by the same courts that apply the general civil and criminal law.

Finally, in many countries, special codes have been enacted to regulate the procedure and evidence of the courts that today apply Sharīʿah law. In the Middle East documentary and circumstantial evidence are now generally admissible; witnesses are put on oath and may be cross-examined, and the traditional rule that evidence is only brought by one side and that the other side, in suitable circumstances, takes the oath of denial has largely broken down. In sum, the court has a much wider discretion in assessing the weight of the evidence than it had under the traditional system of evidence. In India and Pakistan the courts apply the same rules of evidence to cases of Islāmic law as they do to civil cases generally. The system is basically English law, codified in the Indian Evidence Act, 1872.

Reform of Sharīʿah law. Traditional Islāmic family law reflected to a large extent the patriarchal scheme of Arabian tribal society in the early centuries of Islām. Not unnaturally certain institutions and standards of that law were felt to be out of line with the circumstances of Muslim society in the 20th century, particularly in urban areas where tribal ties had disintegrated and movements for the emancipation of women had arisen. At first this situation seemed to create the same apparent impasse between the changing circumstances of modern life and an allegedly immutable law that had caused the adoption of Western codes in civil and criminal matters. Hence, the only solution that seemed possible to Turkey in 1926 was the total abandonment of the Sharīʿah and the adoption of Swiss family law in its place. No other Muslim country, however, has as yet followed this example. Instead, traditional Sharīʿah law has been adapted in a variety of ways to meet present social needs.

From the outset the dominating issue in the Middle East has been the question of the juristic basis of reforms—*i.e.*, granted their social desirability, their justification in terms of Islāmic jurisprudential theory, so that the reforms appear as a new, but legitimate, version of the Sharīʿah.

In the early stages of the reform movement, the doctrine of *taqlīd* was still formally observed and the juristic basis of reform lay in the doctrine of *siyāsah*, or "government," which allows the political authority (who, of course, has no legislative power in the real sense of the term) to make administrative regulations of two principal types.

The first type concerns procedure and evidence and restricts the jurisdiction of the Sharīʿah courts in the sense that they are instructed not to entertain cases that do not fulfill defined evidential requirements. Thus, an Egyptian law was enacted in 1931 that no disputed claim of marriage was to be entertained where the marriage could not be proved by an official certificate of registration, and no such certificate could be issued if the bride was less than 16 or the bridegroom less than 18 years of age at the time of the contract. Accordingly the marriage of a minor contracted by the guardian was still perfectly valid but would not, if disputed, be the subject of judicial relief from the courts. In theory the doctrine of the traditional authorities was not contradicted, but in practice an attempt had been made to abolish the institution of child marriage.

Egyptian reforms

The second type of administrative regulation was a directive to the courts as to which particular rule among existing variants they were to apply. This directive allowed the political authority to choose from the views of the different schools and jurists the opinion that was deemed best suited to present social circumstances. For example, the traditional Ḥanafī law in force in Egypt did not allow a wife to petition for divorce on the ground of any matrimonial offense committed by the husband, a situation that caused great hardship to abandoned or ill-treated wives. Mālikī law, however, recognizes the wife's right to judicial dissolution of her marriage on grounds such as the husband's cruelty, failure to provide maintenance and support, and desertion. Accordingly, an Egyptian law of 1920 codified the Mālikī law as the law henceforth to be applied by the Sharīʿah courts.

By way of comparison, reform in the matters of child marriage and divorce was effected in the Indian subcontinent by statutory enactments that directly superseded the traditional Ḥanafī law. The Child Marriage Restraint Act, 1929, prohibited the marriage of girls below the age of 14 and boys below the age of 16 under pain of penalties; while the Dissolution of Muslim Marriages Act, 1939, modelled on the English Matrimonial Causes Acts, allowed a Ḥanafī wife to obtain judicial divorce on the standard grounds of cruelty, desertion, failure to maintain, etc.

In the Middle East, by the 1950s, the potential for legal reform under the principle of *siyāsah* had been exhausted. Since that time the basic doctrine of *taqlīd* has been challenged to an ever-increasing degree. On many points the law recorded in the medieval manuals, insofar as it represents the interpretations placed by the early jurists upon the Qurʾān and the *sunnah*, has been held no longer to have a paramount and exclusive authority. Contemporary jurisprudence has claimed the right to renounce those interpretations and to interpret for itself, independently and afresh in the light of modern social circumstances, the original texts of divine revelation: in short to reopen the door of *ijtihād* that had been in theory closed since the 10th century.

Syrian and Tunisian reforms

The developing use of *ijtihād* as a means of legal reform may be seen through a comparison of the terms of the Syrian law of Personal Status (1953) with those of the Tunisian Law of Personal Status (1957) in relation to the two subjects of polygamy and divorce by repudiation (*ṭalāq*).

As regards polygamy the Syrian reformers argued that the Qur'ān itself urges husbands not to take additional wives unless they are financially able to make proper provision for their maintenance and support. Classical jurists had construed this verse as a moral exhortation binding only on the husband's conscience. But the Syrian reformers maintained that it should be regarded as a positive legal condition precedent to the exercise of polygamy and enforced as such by the courts. This novel interpretation was then coupled with a normal administrative regulation that required the due registration of marriages after the permission of the court to marry had been obtained. The Syrian Law accordingly enacts: "The *qāḍī* may withhold permission for a man who is already married to marry a second wife, where it is established that he is not in a position to support them both." Far more extreme, however, is the approach of the Tunisian reformers. They argued that, in addition to a husband's financial ability to support a plurality of wives, the Qur'ān also required that co-wives should be treated with complete impartiality. This Qur'ānic injunction should also be construed, not simply as a moral exhortation, but as a legal condition precedent to polygamy, in the sense that no second marriage should be permissible unless and until adequate evidence was forthcoming that the wives would in fact be treated impartially. But under modern social and economic conditions such impartial treatment was a practical impossibility. And since the essential condition for polygamy could not be fulfilled the Tunisian Law briefly declares: "Polygamy is prohibited."

With regard to *ṭalāq* the Syrian law provided that a wife who had been repudiated without just cause might be awarded compensation by the court from her former husband to the maximum extent of one year's maintenance. The reform was once again represented as giving practical effect to certain Qur'ānic verses that had been generally regarded by traditional jurisprudence as moral rather than legally enforceable injunctions—namely, those verses that enjoin husbands to "make a fair provision" for repudiated wives and to "retain wives with kindness or release them with consideration." The effect of the Syrian law, then, is to subject the husband's motive for repudiation to the scrutiny of the court and to penalize him, albeit to a limited extent, for abuse of his power. Once again, however, the Tunisian *ijtihād* concerning repudiation is far more radical. Here the reformers argued that the Qur'ān orders the appointment of arbitrators in the event of discord between husband and wife. Clearly a pronouncement of repudiation by a husband indicated a state of discord between the spouses. Equally clearly the official courts were best suited to undertake the function of arbitration that then becomes necessary according to the Qur'ān. It is on this broad ground that the Tunisian law abolishes the right of a husband to repudiate his wife extrajudicially and enacts that: "Divorce outside a court of law is without legal effect." Although the court must dissolve the marriage if the husband persists in his repudiation, it has an unlimited power to grant the wife compensation for any damage she has sustained from the divorce—although in practice this power has so far been used most sparingly. In regard to polygamy and *ṭalāq* therefore, Tunisia has achieved by reinterpretation of the Qur'ān reforms hardly less radical than those effected in Turkey some 30 years previously by the adoption of the Swiss Civil Code.

Pakistani reforms

In Pakistan a new interpretation of the Qur'ān and *sunnah* was the declared basis of the reforms introduced by the Muslim Family Laws Ordinance of 1961, although the provisions of the Ordinance in relation to polygamy and *ṭalāq* are much less radical than the corresponding Middle Eastern reforms, since a second marriage is simply made dependent upon the consent of an Arbitration Council and the effect of a husband's repudiation is merely suspended for a period of three months to afford opportunity for reconciliation.

Judicial decisions in Pakistan have also unequivocally endorsed the right of independent interpretation of the Qur'ān. For example, in *Khurshīd Bībī* v. *Muḥammad Amīn* (1967) the Supreme Court held that a Muslim wife could as a right obtain a divorce simply by payment of suitable compensation to her husband. This decision was based on the Court's interpretation of a relevant Qur'ānic verse. But under traditional Sharīʿah law this form of divorce, known as *khulʿ*, whereby a wife pays for her release, is a contract between the spouses and as such entirely dependent upon the husband's free consent.

These are but a few examples of the many far-reaching changes that have been effected in the Islāmic family law. But the whole process of legal reform as it has so far developed still involves great problems of principle and practice. A hard core of traditionalist opinion still adamantly rejects the validity of the process of reinterpretation of the basic texts of divine revelation. The traditionalists argue that the texts are merely being manipulated to yield the meaning that suits the preconceived purposes of the reformers, and that therefore, contrary to fundamental Islāmic ideology, it is social desirability and not the will of Allāh that is the ultimate determinant of the law.

As regards the practical effect of legal reform, there exists in many Muslim countries today a deep social gulf between a Westernized and modernist minority and the conservative mass of the population. And reforms that aim at satisfying, and are largely inspired by, the standards of progressive urban society have little significance for the traditionalist communities of rural areas. It is also often the case that the *qāḍīs*, through their background and training, are not wholly sympathetic with the purposes of the modernist legislators—an attitude often reflected in their interpretations of the new codes.

Such problems are, of course, inevitable in the transitional stage of social evolution in which Islām finds itself. But the one supreme achievement of jurisprudence over the past few decades has been the emergence of a functional approach to the question of the role of law in society. Jurisprudence has discarded the introspective and idealistic attitude that the doctrine of *taqlīd* had imposed upon it since early medieval times and now sees its task to be the solution of the problems of contemporary society. It has emerged from a protracted period of stagnation to adopt again the attitude of the earliest Muslim jurists, whose aim was to relate the dictates of the divine will to their own social environment. It is this attitude alone that has ensured the survival of the Sharīʿah in modern times as a practical system of law and that alone provides its inspiration for the future.

BIBLIOGRAPHY. A general survey of the Islāmic legal system, covering its historical development, jurisprudential theory and the most important spheres of the substantive law, is contained in J. SCHACHT, *An Introduction to Islamic Law* (1964); J.N.D. ANDERSON, *Islamic Law in the Modern World* (1959); and N.J. COULSON, *History of Islamic Law* (1964). The reader is referred to the bibliographies of these books, particularly for the numerous articles written by J.N.D. Anderson on the subject of modern developments in the law. J. SCHACHT, *Origins of Muhammadan Jurisprudence* (1950), is the fundamental work of modern research on the early development of legal theory written by the pioneer scholar of this subject. A sound analysis of traditional legal theory is presented in A. RAHIM, *Muhammadan Jurisprudence* (1911); and in F.J. ZIADEH, *The Philosophy of Jurisprudence in Islam* (1961), an Eng. trans. of the Arabic text of an outstanding Muslim jurist, Subhi Mahmassani. M. KHADDURI and H.J. LIEBESNY (eds.), *Law in the Middle East* (1955), includes chapters by Muslim scholars and Western Orientalists on the various spheres of substantive Islāmic law, traditional and modern. A.A.A. FYZEE, *Outlines of Muhammadan Law*, 3rd ed. (1964), is the standard text dealing with Islāmic law as it is applied today in India and Pakistan. *The Encyclopaedia of Islam* (1913–42; 2nd ed., 1960–continuing), contains numerous articles on individual legal topics.

(N.J.C.)

Islāmic Mysticism

Islāmic mysticism refers to that aspect of Islāmic belief and practice in which Muslims seek to find the truth of divine love and knowledge through direct personal experience of God. It consists of a variety of mystical paths that are designed to ascertain the nature of man and God and to facilitate the experience of the presence of divine love and wisdom in the world.

Islāmic mysticism is called *taṣawwuf* (the act of devoting oneself to the mystic life) in Arabic, but it has been called Ṣūfism in Western languages since the early 19th century. An abstract word, Ṣūfism derives from the Arabic term for a mystic, *ṣūfī*, which is in turn derived from *ṣūf*, "wool," plausibly a reference to the woollen garment of early Islāmic ascetics. The Ṣūfīs are also generally known as "the poor," *fuqarā'*, plural of the Arabic *faqīr*, in Persian *darvīsh*, whence the English words fakir and dervish.

Origins and influence

Though the roots of Islāmic mysticism formerly were supposed to have stemmed from various non-Islāmic sources in ancient Europe and even India, it now seems established that the movement grew out of early Islāmic asceticism that developed as a counterweight to the increasing worldliness of the expanding Muslim community; only later were foreign elements that were compatible with mystical theology and practices adopted and made to conform to Islām.

By educating the masses and deepening the spiritual concerns of the Muslims, Ṣūfism has played an important role in the formation of Muslim society. Opposed to the dry casuistry of the lawyer-divines, the mystics nevertheless scrupulously observed the commands of the divine law. The Ṣūfīs have been further responsible for a large-scale missionary activity all over the world, which still continues. Ṣūfīs have elaborated the image of the prophet Muḥammad—the founder of Islām—and have thus largely influenced Muslim piety by their Muḥammad-mysticism. Without the Ṣūfī vocabulary, Persian and other literatures related to it, such as Turkish, Urdu, Sindhi, Pashto, and Panjabi, would lack their special charms. Through the poetry of these literatures mystical ideas spread widely among the Muslims. In some countries Ṣūfī leaders were also active politically.

HISTORY

Islāmic mysticism had several stages of growth, including (1) the appearance of early asceticism, (2) the development of a classical mysticism of divine love, and (3) the rise and proliferation of fraternal orders of mystics. Despite these general stages, however, the history of Islāmic mysticism is largely a history of individual mystic experience.

The first stage of Ṣūfism appeared in pious circles as a reaction against the worldliness of the early Umayyad period (AD 661–749). From their practice of constantly meditating on the Qur'ānic (Islāmic scriptural) words about Doomsday, the ascetics became known as "those who always weep" and those who considered this world "a hut of sorrows." They were distinguished by their scrupulous fulfillment of the injunctions of the Qur'ān and tradition, by many acts of piety, and especially by a predilection for night prayers.

Classical mysticism. The introduction of the element of love, which changed asceticism into mysticism, is ascribed to Rābi'ah al-'Adawīyah (died 801), a woman from Basra who first formulated the Ṣūfī ideal of a love of God that was disinterested, without hope for paradise and without fear of hell. In the decades after Rābi'ah, mystical trends grew everywhere in the Islāmic world, partly through an exchange of ideas with Christian hermits. A number of mystics in the early generations had concentrated their efforts upon *tawakkul*, absolute trust in God, which became a central concept of Ṣūfism. An Iraqi school of mysticism became noted for its strict self-control and psychological insight. The Iraqi school was initiated by al-Muḥāsibī (died 857)—who believed that purging the soul in preparation for companionship with God was the only value of asceticism. Its teachings of classical sobriety and wisdom were perfected by Junayd of Baghdad (died 910), to whom all later chains of the transmission of doctrine and legitimacy go back. In an Egyptian school of Ṣūfism, the Nubian Dhū an-Nūn (died 859) reputedly introduced the technical term *ma'rifah* ("interior knowledge"), as contrasted to learnedness; in his hymnical prayers he joined all nature in the praise of God—an idea based on the Qur'ān and later elaborated in Persian and Turkish poetry. In the Iranian school, Abū Yazīd al-Bisṭāmī (died 874) is usually considered to have been representative of the important doctrine of annihilation of the self, *fanā'* (see below); the strange symbolism of his sayings prefigures part of the terminology of later mystical poets. At the same time the concept of divine love became more central, especially among the Iraqi Ṣūfīs. Its main representatives are Nūrī, who offered his life for his brethren, and Sumnūn "the Lover."

Mystical love

The first of the theosophical speculations based on mystical insights about the nature of man and the essence of the Prophet were produced by such Ṣūfīs as Sahl at-Tustarī (died *c.* 896). Some Hellenistic ideas were later adopted by al-Ḥakīm at-Tirmidhī (died 898). Sahl was the master of al-Ḥusayn ibn Manṣūr al-Ḥallāj, who has become famous for his phrase *anā al-ḥaqq*, "I am the Creative Truth" (often rendered "I am God"), which was later interpreted in a pantheistic sense but is, in fact, only a condensation of his theory of *huwa huwa* ("He he"): God loved himself in his essence, and created Adam "in his image." Ḥallāj was executed in 922 in Baghdad as a result of his teachings; he is, for later mystics and poets, the "martyr of Love" par excellence, the enthusiast killed by the theologians. His few poems are of exquisite beauty; his prose, which contains an outspoken Muḥammad-mysticism—*i.e.*, mysticism centred on the prophet Muḥammad—is as beautiful as it is difficult.

Ṣūfī thought was in these early centuries transmitted in small circles. Some of the *shaykhs*, Ṣūfī mystical leaders or guides of such circles, were also artisans. In the 10th century, it was deemed necessary to write handbooks about the tenets of Ṣūfism in order to soothe the growing suspicions of the orthodox; the compendiums composed in Arabic by Abū Ṭālib Makkī, Sarrāj, and Kalābādhī in the late 10th century, and by Qushayrī and, in Persian, by Hujvīrī in the 11th century reveal how these authors tried to defend Ṣūfism and to prove its orthodox character. It should be noted that the mystics belonged to all schools of Islāmic law and theology of the times.

The last great figure in the line of classical Ṣūfism is Abū Ḥāmid al-Ghazālī (died 1111), who wrote, among numerous other works, the *Iḥyā' 'ulūm ad-dīn* ("The Revival of the Religious Sciences"), a comprehensive work that established moderate mysticism against the growing theosophical trends—which tended to equate God and the world—and thus shaped the thought of millions of Muslims. His younger brother, Aḥmad al-Ghazālī, wrote one of the subtlest treatises (*Sawāniḥ;* "Occurrences" [*i.e.*, stray thoughts]) on mystical love, a subject that then became the main subject of Persian poetry.

Rise of fraternal orders. Slightly later, mystical orders (fraternal groups centring around the teachings of a leader-founder) began to crystallize. The 13th century, though politically overshadowed by the invasion of the Mongols into the Eastern lands of Islām and the end of the 'Abbāsid caliphate, was also the golden age of Ṣūfism: the Spanish-born Ibn al'Arabī created a comprehensive theosophical system (concerning the relation of God and the world) that was to become the cornerstone for a theory of "Unity of Being." According to this theory all existence is one, a manifestation of the underlying divine reality. His Egyptian contemporary Ibn al-Fāriḍ wrote the finest mystical poems in Arabic. Two other important mystics, who died c. AD 1220, were a Persian poet, Farīd od-Dīn ʿAṭṭar, one of the most fertile writers on mystical topics, and a Central Asian master, Najmuddīn Kubrā, who presented elaborate discussions of the psychological experiences through which the mystic adept has to pass.

The mystical poetry of Jalāl ad-Dīn ar-Rūmī

The greatest mystical poet in the Persian language, Jalāl ad-Dīn ar-Rūmī (1207–73), was moved by mystical love to compose his lyrical poetry that he attributed to his mystical beloved, Shams ad-Dīn of Tabriz, as a symbol of their union. Rūmī's didactic poem *Mas̄navī* in about 26,000 couplets—a work that is for the Persian-reading mystics second in importance only to the Qurʾān—is an encyclopaedia of mystical thought in which everyone can find his own religious ideas. Rūmī inspired the organization of the whirling dervishes—who sought ecstasy through an elaborate dancing ritual, accompanied by superb music. His younger contemporary Yunus Emre inaugurated Turkish mystical poetry with his charming verses that were transmitted by the Bektāshīya order of dervishes and are still admired in modern Turkey. In Egypt, among many other mystical trends, an order—known as Shādhilīyah—was founded by ash-Shādhilī (died 1258); its main literary representative, Ibn ʿAṭāʾ Allāh of Alexandria, wrote sober aphorisms (*ḥikam*).

At that time, the basic ideals of Ṣūfism permeated the whole world of Islām; and at its borders as, for example, in India, Ṣūfīs largely contributed to shaping Islāmic society. Later some of the Ṣūfīs in India were brought closer to Hindu mysticism by an overemphasis on the idea of divine unity which became almost monism—a religiophilosophic perspective according to which there is only one basic reality, and the distinction between God and the world (and man) tends to disappear. The syncretistic attempts of the Mughal emperor Akbar (died 1605) to combine different forms of belief and practice, and the religious discussions of the crown prince Dārā Shukōh (executed for heresy, 1659) were objectionable to the orthodox. Typically, the countermovement was again undertaken by a mystical order, the Naqshbandīyah, a Central Asian fraternity founded in the 14th century. Contrary to the monistic trends of the school of *waḥdat al-wujūd* ("existential unity of being"), the later Naqshbandīyah defended the *waḥdat ash-shuhūd* ("unity of vision"), a subjective experience of unity, occurring only in the mind of the believer, and not as an objective experience. Aḥmad Sirhindī (died 1624) was the major protagonist of this movement in India. His claims of sanctity were surprisingly daring: he considered himself the divinely invested master of the universe. His refusal to concede the possibility of union between man and God (characterized as "servant" and "Lord") and his sober lawbound attitude gained him and his followers many disciples, even at the Mughal court and as far away as Turkey. In the 18th century, Shāh Walī Allāh of Delhi was connected with an attempt to reach a compromise between the two inimical schools of mysticism; he was also politically active and translated the Qurʾān into Persian, the official language of Mughal India. Other Indian mystics of the 18th century, such as Mīr Dard, played a decisive role in forming the newly developing Urdu poetry.

Trends in modern Ṣūfism

In the Arabic parts of the Islāmic world, only a few interesting mystical authors are found after 1500. They include ash-Shaʿrānī in Egypt (died 1565) and the prolific writer ʿAbd al-Ghanī an-Nābulusī in Syria (died 1731). Turkey produced some fine mystical poets in the 17th and 18th centuries. The influence of the mystical orders did not recede; rather new orders came into existence, and most literature was still tinged with mystical ideas and expressions. Political and social reformers in the Islāmic countries have often objected to Ṣūfism because they have generally considered it as backward, hampering the free development of society. Thus, the orders and dervish lodges in Turkey were closed by Kemal Atatürk in 1925. Yet, their political influence is still palpable, though under the surface. Such modern Islāmic thinkers as the Indian philosopher Muḥammad Iqbāl have attacked traditional monist mysticism and have gone back to the classical ideals or divine love as expressed by Ḥallāj and his contemporaries. The activities of modern Muslim mystics in the cities are mostly restricted to spiritual education.

SUFI LITERATURE

Though a prophetic saying (Ḥadīth) claims that "he who knows God becomes silent," the Ṣūfīs have produced a literature of impressive extent and could defend their writing activities with another Hadīth: "He who knows God talks much." The first systematic books explaining the tenets of Ṣūfism date from the 10th century; but earlier, Muḥāsibī had already written about spiritual education, Ḥallāj had composed meditations in highly concentrated language, and many Ṣūfīs had used poetry for conveying their experiences of the ineffable mystery or had instructed their disciples in letters of cryptographic density. The accounts of Ṣūfism by Sarrāj and his followers, as well as the *ṭabaqāt* (biographical works) by Sulamī, Abū Nuʿaym al-Iṣfahānī, and others, together with some biographies of individual masters, are the sources for knowledge of early Ṣūfism. Early mystical commentaries on the Qurʾān are only partly extant, often preserved in fragmentary quotations in later sources. With the formation of mystical orders, books about the behaviour of the Ṣūfī in various situations became important, although this topic had already been touched on in such classical works as *Ādāb al-murīdīn* ("The Adepts' Etiquette") by Abū Najīb as-Suhrawardī (died 1168), the founder of the Suhrawardīyah order and uncle of the author of the oft-translated *ʿAwārif al-maʿārif* ("The Well-known Sorts of Knowledge"). The theosophists had to condense their systems in readable form; Ibn al-ʿArabī's *al-Futūḥāt al-Makkīyah* ("The Meccan Revelations") is the textbook of *waḥdat al-wujūd* (God and creation as two aspects of one reality); his smaller work on the peculiar character of the prophets—*Fuṣūṣ al-ḥikam* ("The Bezels—or cutting edges—of Wisdom")—became even more popular.

Later mystics commented extensively upon the classical sources and, sometimes, translated them into their mother tongues. A literary type that has flourished especially in India since the 13th century is the *malfūẓāt*, a collection of sayings of the mystical leader, which are psychologically interesting and allow glimpses into the political and social situation of the Muslim community. Collections of letters of the *shaykh*s are similarly revealing. Ṣūfī literature abounds in hagiography, either biographies of all known saints from the Prophet to the day of the author, or of saints of a specific order, or of those who lived in a certain town or province, so that much information on the development of Ṣūfī thought and practice is available if sources are critically sifted.

Poetical, national, and regional literature

The greatest contribution of Ṣūfism to Islāmic literature, however, is poetry—beginning with charming, short Arabic love poems (sometimes sung for a mystical concert, *samāʿ*) that express the yearning of the soul for union with the beloved. The love-relation prevailing in most Persian poetry is that between a man and a beautiful youth; less often, as in the writings of Ibn al-ʿArabī and Ibn al-Fāriḍ, eternal beauty is symbolized through female beauty; in Indo-Muslim popular mystical songs the soul is the loving wife, God the longed-for husband. Long mystic–didactic poems (*mas̄navīs*) were written to introduce the reader to the problems of unity and love by means of allegories and parables. After Sanāʾī's (died 1131) *Ḥadīqeh ol-ḥaqīqat* ("Orchard of Truth"), came ʿAṭṭar's *Manṭeq oṭ-ṭeyr* ("The Birds' Conversation") and Rūmī's *Mas̄navī-ye maʿnavī* ("Spiritual Couplets"). These three works are the sources that have furnished poets for centuries with mystical ideas and images. Typical of Ṣūfī poetry is the hymn in praise of God, expressed in chains of repetitions.

The mystics also contributed largely to the development of national and regional literatures, for they had to convey their message to the masses in their own languages: in Turkey as well as in the Panjabi-, the Sindhi-, and the Urdu-speaking areas of South Asia, the first true religious poetry was written by Ṣūfīs, who blended classical Islāmic motifs with inherited popular legends and used popular rather than Persian metres. Ṣūfī poetry expressing divine love and mystical union through the metaphors of profane love and union often resembled ordinary worldly love poetry; and nonmystical poetry made use of the Ṣūfī vocabulary, thus producing an ambiguity that is felt to be one of the most attractive and characteristic features of Persian, Turkish, and Urdu literatures. Ṣūfī ideas thus permeated the hearts of all those who hearkened to poetry. An example is al-Ḥusayn ibn Manṣūr al-Ḥallāj, the 10th-century martyr-mystic, who is as popular in modern progressive Urdu poetry as he was with the "God-intoxicated" Ṣūfīs; he has been converted into a symbol of suffering for one's ideals.

SUFI THOUGHT AND PRACTICE

Important aspects. The mystics drew their vocabulary largely from the Qur'ān, which for Muslims contains all divine wisdom and has to be interpreted with ever-increasing insight. In the Qur'ān, mystics found the threat of the Last Judgment, but they also found the statement that God "loves them and they love him," which became the basis for love-mysticism. Strict obedience to the religious law and imitation of the Prophet were basic for the mystics. By rigid introspection and mental struggle the mystic tried to purify his baser self from even the smallest signs of selfishness, thus attaining *ikhlāṣ*, absolute purity of intention and act. *Tawakkul* (trust in God) was sometimes practiced to such an extent that every thought of tomorrow was considered irreligious. "Little sleep, little talk, little food" were fundamental; fasting became one of the most important preparations for the spiritual life.

Central concern of Ṣūfism

The central concern of the Ṣūfīs, as of every Muslim, was *tawḥīd*, the witness that "There is no deity but God." This truth had to be realized in the existence of each individual, and so the expressions differ: early Ṣūfism postulated the approach to God through love and voluntary suffering until a unity of will was reached; Junayd spoke of "recognizing God as He was before creation"; God is seen as the One and only actor; He alone "has the right to say 'I'." Later, *tawḥīd* came to mean the knowledge that there is nothing existent but God, or the ability to see God and creation as two aspects of one reality, reflecting each other and depending upon each other (*waḥdat al-wujūd*).

The mystics realized that beyond the knowledge of outward sciences intuitive knowledge was required in order to receive that illumination to which reason has no access. *Dhawq*, direct "tasting" of experience, was essential for them. But the inspirations and "unveilings" that God grants such mystics by special grace must never contradict the Qur'ān and tradition and are valid only for the person concerned. Even the *malāmātīs*, who attracted public contempt upon themselves by outwardly acting against the law, in private life strictly followed the divine commands. Mystics who expressed in their poetry their disinterest in, and even contempt of, the traditional formal religions never forgot that Islām is the highest manifestation of divine wisdom.

Such manifestation was also connected with the person of the prophet Muḥammad. Though early Ṣūfism had concentrated upon the relation between God and the soul, from AD 900 onward a strong Muḥammad-mysticism developed. Very early the alleged divine address to the Prophet—"If thou hadst not been I had not created the worlds"—was common among Ṣūfīs. Muḥammad was said to be "Prophet when Adam was still between water and clay." Muḥammad is also described as light from light, and from his light all the prophets are created, constituting the different aspects of this light. In its fullness such light radiated from the historical Muḥammad and is partaken of by his posterity and the saints; for Muḥammad has the aspect of sanctity besides that of prophecy. An apocryphal tradition makes even God attest: "I am Aḥmad (= Muḥammad) without 'm' (*i.e.*, Aḥad, 'One')."

The *walī*, or saint

A mystic may also be known as *walī*. By derivation the word *walī* ("saint") means "one in close relation; friend." The *awliyā'* (plural of *walī*) are "friends of God who have no fear nor are they sad." Later the term *walī* came to denote the Muslim mystics who had reached a certain stage of proximity to God, or those who had reached the highest mystical stages. They have their "seal" (*i.e.*, the last and most perfect personality in the historical process; with this person, the evolution has found its end—as in Muḥammad's case), just as the prophets have. Woman saints are found all over the Islāmic world.

The invisible hierarchy of saints consists of the 40 *abdāl* ("substitutes"; for when any of them dies another is elected by God from the rank and file of the saints), seven *awtād* ("stakes," or "props," of faith), three *nuqabā'* ("leader"; "one who introduces people to his master"), headed by the *quṭb* ("axis, pole"), or *ghawth* ("help")—titles claimed by many Ṣūfī leaders. Saint worship is contrary to Islām, which does not admit of any mediating role for human beings between man and God; but the cult of living and even more of dead saints—visiting their tombs to take vows there—responded to the feeling of the masses, and thus a number of pre-Islāmic customs were absorbed into Islām under the cover of mysticism. The advanced mystic was often granted the capacity of working miracles called *karāmāt* (*charismata* or "graces"); not *mu'jizāt* ("that which men are unable to imitate"), like the miracles of the prophets. Among them are "cardiognosia" (knowledge of the heart), providing food from the unseen, presence in two places at the same time, and help for the disciples, be they near or far. In short, a saint is one "whose prayers are heard" and who has *taṣarruf*, the power of materializing in this world possibilities that still rest in the spiritual world. Many great saints, however, considered miracle working as a dangerous trap on the path that might distract the Ṣūfī from his real goal.

The path. The path (*ṭarīqah*) begins with repentance. A mystical guide (*shaykh*, *pīr*) accepts the seeker as disciple (*murīd*), orders him to follow strict ascetic practices, and suggests certain formulas for meditation. It is said that the disciple should be in the hands of the master "like a corpse in the hand of the washer." The master teaches him constant struggle (the real "Holy War") against the lower soul, often represented as a black dog, which should, however, not be killed but merely tamed and used in the way of God. The mystic dwells in a number of spiritual stations (*maqām*), which are described in varying sequence, and, after the initial repentance, comprise abstinence, renunciation, and poverty—according to Muḥammad's saying, "Poverty is my pride"; poverty was sometimes interpreted as having no interest in anything apart from God, the Rich One, but the concrete meaning of poverty prevailed, which is why the mystic is often denoted as "poor," fakir or dervish. Patience and gratitude belong to higher stations of the path, and consent is the loving acceptance of every affliction. On his way to illumination the mystic will undergo such changing spiritual states (*ḥāl*) as *qabḍ* and *basṭ*, constraint and happy spiritual expansion, fear and hope, and longing and intimacy, which are granted by God and last for longer or shorter periods of time, changing in intensity according to the station in which the mystic is abiding at the moment. The way culminates in *ma'rifah*, ("interior knowledge," "gnosis"), or in *maḥabbah* ("love"), the central subject of Ṣūfism since the 9th century, which implies a union of lover and beloved, and was therefore violently rejected by the orthodox, for whom "love of God" meant simply obedience. The final goal is *fanā'* ("annihilation"), primarily an ethical concept of annihilating one's own qualities, according to the prophetic saying "Take over the qualities of God," but slowly developing into a complete extinction of the personality. Some mystics taught that behind this negative unity where the self is completely effaced, the *baqā'*, ("duration, life in God") is found: the ecstatic experience, called intoxication, is followed by the "second sobriety"; *i.e.*, the return of the completely transformed mystic into this world where he acts as a living witness of God or continues the "journey in God." The mystic has reached *ḥaqīqah* ("reality"), after finishing the *ṭarīqah* ("path"), which is built upon the *sharī'ah* ("law"). Later, the disciple is led through *fanā' fī ash-shaykh* ("annihilation in the master") to *fanā' fīar-Rasūl* ("annihilation in the Prophet") before reaching, if at all, *fanā' fī-Allāh* ("annihilation in God").

The practice of *dhikr*

One of the means used on the path is the *dhikr* ("remembrance"), derived from the Qur'ānic injunction "And remember God often" (*sūrah* 62:10). It consists in a repetition of either one or all of the most beautiful names of God, of the name "Allāh," or of a certain religious formula, such as the profession of faith: "There is no God but Allāh and Muḥammad is his prophet." The rosary with 99 or 33 beads was in use as early as the 8th century for counting the thousands of repetitions. Man's whole being should eventually be transformed into remembrance of God.

In the mid-9th century some mystics introduced sessions with music and poetry recitals (*samā'*) in Baghdad in order to reach the ecstatic experience—and since then debates about the permissibility of *samā'*, filling many books, have been written. Narcotics were used in periods of degeneration, coffee by the "sober" mystics (first by the Shādhilīyah after 1300).

Besides the wayfarers (*sālik*) on the path, Ṣūfīs who have no master but are attracted solely by divine grace are also found; they are called Uwaysī, after Uways al-Qaranī, the Yemenite contemporary of the Prophet who never saw him but firmly believed in him. There are also the so-called *majdhūb* ("attracted") who are often persons generally agreed to be more or less mentally deranged.

Symbolism in Ṣūfism. The mystic was in need of symbols. The divine truth was at times revealed to him in visions, auditions, and dreams, in colours and sounds, but to convey these nonrational and ineffable experiences to others the mystic had to rely upon such terminology of worldly experience as that of love and intoxication—often objectionable from the orthodox viewpoint. The symbolism of wine, cup, and cupbearer, first expressed by Abū Yazīd al-Bisṭāmī in the 9th century, became popular everywhere, whether in the verses of the Arab Ibn al-Fāriḍ, or the Persian 'Irāqī, or the Turk Yunus Emre, and their followers. The hope for the union of the soul with the divine had to be expressed through images of human yearning and love. The love for lovely boys in which the divine beauty manifests itself—according to the alleged Ḥadīth "I saw my Lord in the shape of a youth with a cap awry"—was commonplace in Persian poetry. Union was described as the submersion of the drop in the ocean, the state of the iron in the fire, the vision of penetrating light, or the burning of the moth in the candle (first used by Ḥallāj). Worldly phenomena were seen as black tresses veiling the radiant beauty of the divine countenance. The mystery of unity and diversity was symbolized, for example, under the image of mirrors that reflect the different aspects of the divine, or as prisms colouring the pure light. Every aspect of nature was seen in relation to God. The symbol of the soulbird—in which the human soul is likened to a flying bird—known everywhere, was the centre of 'Aṭṭar's *Manṭeq oṭ-ṭeyr* ("The Birds' Conversation"). The predilection of the mystical poets for the symbolism of the nightingale and rose (the red rose = God's perfect beauty; nightingale = soul; first used by Baqli [died 1206]) stems from the soul–bird symbolism. For spiritual education, symbols taken from medicine (healing of the sick soul) and alchemy (changing of base matter into gold) were also used. Many descriptions that were originally applied to God as the goal of love were, in later times, used also for the Prophet, who is said to be like the "dawn between the darkness of the material world and the sun of Reality."

Symbolism of union with the divine

Allusions to the Qur'ān were frequent, especially so to verses that seem to imply divine immanence (God's presence in the world), such as "Whithersoever ye turn, there is the Face of God" (*sūrah* 2:109), or that God is "Closer than your neck-vein" (*sūrah* 50:8). *Sūrah* 7:172—*i.e.*, God's address to the uncreated children of Adam ("Am I not your Lord" [*alastu birabbikum*])—came to denote the pre-eternal love relation between God and man. As for the prophets before Muḥammad, the vision of Moses was considered still imperfect, for the mystic wants the actual vision of God, not His manifestation through a burning bush. Abraham, for whom fire turned into a rose garden, resembles the mystic in his afflictions; Joseph, in his perfect beauty, the mystical beloved after whom the mystic searches. The apocryphal traditions used by the mystics are numerous; such as "Heaven and earth do not contain me, but the heart of my faithful servant contains Me"; and the possibility of a relation between man and God is also explained by the traditional idea: "He (God) created Adam in His image."

THEOSOPHICAL SUFISM

Ṣūfism, in its beginnings a practical method of spiritual education and self-realization, grew slowly into a theosophical system by adopting traditions of Neoplatonism, the Hellenistic world, Gnosticism (an ancient esoteric religiophilosophical movement that viewed matter as evil and spirit as good), and spiritual currents from Iran and various countries in the ancient agricultural lands from the eastern Mediterranean to Iraq. One master who contributed to this development was the Persian Suhrawardī al-Maqtūl ("killed"), executed in 1191 in Aleppo. To him is attributed the philosophy of *ishrāq* ("illumination"), and he claimed to unite the Persian (Zoroastrian) and Egyptian (Hermetic) traditions. His didactic and doctrinal works in Arabic among other things taught a complicated angelology (theory of angels); some of his smaller Persian treatises depict the journey of the soul across the cosmos; the "Orient" (East) is the world of pure lights and archangels, the "Occident" (West) that of darkness and matter; and man lives in the "Western exile."

Contributions of Ibn al-'Arabī

At the time of Suhrawardī's death the greatest representative of theosophic Ṣūfism was in his 20s: Ibn al-'Arabī, born at Murcia, Spain, where speculative tendencies had been visible since Ibn Masarrah's philosophy (died 931). Ibn al-'Arabī was instructed in mysticism by two Spanish woman saints. Performing the traditional pilgrimage to Mecca, he met there an accomplished young Persian lady who represented for him the divine wisdom. This experience resulted in the charming poems of the *Tarjumān al-ashwāq* ("Interpreter of Yearning"), which the author later explained mystically. Ibn al-'Arabī composed at least 150 volumes. His magnum opus is *al-Futūḥāt al-Makkīyah* ("The Meccan Revelations") in 560 chapters, in which he expounds his theory of unity of being.

The substance of theosophic Ṣūfism is as follows. According to the Ḥadīth *qudsī*, or "holy tradition"—"I was a hidden treasure and wanted to be known"—the absolute, or God, yearned in his loneliness for manifestation and created the world by effusing being upon the heavenly archetypes, a "theophany (a physical manifestation of deity) through God's imaginative power." The universe is annihilated and created every moment. Every divine name is reflected in a named one. The world and God are said to be like ice and water, or like two mirrors contemplating themselves in each other, joined by a sympathetic union. The Prophet Muḥammad is the universal man, the perfect man, the total theophany of the divine names, the prototype of creation. Muḥammad is the "word," each particular dimension of which is identified with a prophet, and he is also the model for the spiritual realization of the possibilities of man. The mystic has to pass the stages of the Qur'ānic prophets as they are explained in the *Fuṣūṣ al-ḥikam* ("Bezels of Wisdom") until he becomes united with the *ḥaqīqa Muḥammadīya* (the first individualization of the divine in the "Muḥammadan Reality"). Man can have vision only of the form of the faith he professes, and Ibn al-'Arabī's oft-quoted verse, "I follow the religion of love wherever its camels turn," with its seeming religious tolerance means, as S.H. Nasr puts it: "the form of God is for him no longer the form of this or that faith exclusive of all others but his own eternal form which he encounters." The theories of the perfect man were elaborated by Jīlī (died *c.* 1424) in his compendium *Al-insān al-kāmil* ("The Perfect Man") and became common throughout the Muslim world.

Ibn al-'Arabī's theosophy has been attacked by orthodox Muslims and mystics of the "sober" school as incongruent with Islām because "a thoroughly monistic system cannot take seriously the objective validity of moral standards." Even the adversaries of the "greatest master" could not, however, help using part of his terminology. Innumerable mystics and poets propagated his ideas, though they only partly understood them, and this circumstance led also to a misinterpretation of the data of early Ṣūfism in the light of existential monism. Later Persian poetry is permeated by the pantheistic feeling of *hama ost* ("everything is He").

Ibn al-ʿArabī's contemporary in Egypt, the poet Ibn al-Fāriḍ, is usually mentioned together with him; Ibn al-Fāriḍ, however, is not a systematic thinker but a full-fledged poet who used the imagery of classical Arabic poetry to describe the state of the lover in extremely artistic verses and has given, in his *Tāʾiyat al-kubrā* ("Poem of the Journey"), glimpses of the way of the mystic, using, as many poets before and after him did, for example, the image of the shadow play for the actions of the creatures who are dependent upon the divine playmaster. His unifying experience is personal and is not the expression of a theosophical system.

SUFI ORDERS

Organization. Mystical life was first restricted to the relation between a master and a few disciples; the foundations of a monastic system were laid by the Persian Abū Saʿīd ebn Abī ol-Kheyr (died 1049), but real orders or fraternities came into existence only from the 12th century onward: ʿAbd al-Qādir al-Jīlānī (died 1166) gathered the first and still most important order around himself; then followed the Suhrawardīyah, and the 13th century saw the formation of large numbers of different orders in the East (for example, Kubrawīya in Khvārezm) and West (Shādhilīyah). Thus, Ṣūfism ceased to be the way of the chosen few and influenced the masses. A strict ritual was elaborated: when the adept had found a master for whom he had to feel a preformed affinity, there was an initiation ceremony in which he swore allegiance (*bayʿat*) into the master's hand; similarities to the initiation in Ismāʿīlism, the 9th-century sect, and in the guilds suggest a possible interaction. The disciple (*murīd*) had to undergo a stern training; he was often ordered to perform the lowest work in the community, to serve the brethren, to go out to beg (many of the old monasteries subsisted upon alms). A seclusion period of 40 days under hard conditions was common for the adepts in most orders.

Initiation and investiture

Investiture with the *khirqah*, the frock of the master, originally made from shreds and patches, was the decisive act by which the disciple became part of the *silsilah*, the chain of mystical succession and transmission, which leads back—via Junayd—to the Prophet himself and differs in every order. Some mystical leaders claimed to have received their *khirqah* directly from al-Khiḍr, a mysterious immortal saint.

In the earliest times, allegiance was sworn exclusively to one master who had complete power over the disciple, controlling each of his movements, thoughts, visions, and dreams; but later many Ṣūfīs got the *khirqah* from two or more *shaykhs*. There is consequently a differentiation between the *shaykh at-tarbiyah*, who introduces the disciple into the ritual, forms, and literature of the order, and the *shaykh aṣ-ṣuḥbah*, who steadily watches him and with whom the disciple lives. Only a few members of the fraternity remained in the centre (*dargāh*, *khānqāh*, *tekke*), close to the *shaykh*, but even those were not bound to celibacy. Most of the initiated returned to their daily life and partook in mystic services only during certain periods. The most mature disciple was invested as *khalī-fah* ("successor") to the *shaykh* and was often sent abroad to extend the activities of the order. The *dargāhs* were organized differently in the various orders; some relied completely upon alms, keeping their members in utmost poverty; others were rich, and their *shaykh* was not very different from a feudal lord. Relations with rulers varied—some masters refused contacts with the representatives of political power; others did not mind friendly relations with the grandees.

Discipline and ritual. Each order has peculiarities in its ritual. Most start the instruction with breaking the lower soul; others, such as the later Naqshbandīyah, stress the purification of the heart by constant *dhikr* ("remembrance") and by discourse with the master (*ṣuḥbah*). The forms of *dhikr* vary in the orders. Many of them use the word Allāh, or the profession of faith with its rhythmical wording, sometimes accompanied by movements of the body, or by breath control up to complete holding of the breath. The Mawlawīs, the whirling dervishes, are famous for their dancing ritual, an organized variation of the earlier *samāʿ* practices, which were confined to music and poetry. The Rifāʿis, the so-called Howling Dervishes, have become known for their practice of hurting themselves while in an ecstatic state that they reach in performing their loud *dhikr*. (Such practices that might well degenerate into mere jugglery are not approved by most orders.) Some orders also teach the *dhikr khafī*, silent repetition of the formulas, and meditation, concentrating upon certain fixed points of the body; thus the Naqshbandīs do not allow any emotional practices and prefer contemplation to ecstasy, perhaps as a result of Buddhist influence from Central Asia. Other orders have special prayers given to the disciples, such as the protective *ḥizb al-baḥr* ("The protective armour of the sea"; *i.e.*, for seafaring people—then extended to all travellers) in the Shādhilīyah order. Most of them prescribe for their disciples additional prayers and meditation at the end of each ritual prayer.

Function and role in Islāmic society. The orders formed an excellent means of bringing together the spiritually interested members of the community. They acted as a counterweight against the influence of hairsplitting lawyer-divines and gave the masses an emotional outlet in enthusiastic celebrations (*ʿurs*, "marriage") of the anniversaries of the deaths of founders of mystic orders or similar festivals in which they indulged in music and joy. The orders were adaptable to every social level; thus, some of them were responsible for adapting a number of un-Islāmic folkloristic practices such as veneration of saints. Their way of life often differed so much from Islāmic ideals that one distinguishes in Iran and India between orders *bā sharʿ* (law-bound) and *bī sharʿ* (not following the injunctions of the Qurʾān). Some orders were more fitting for the rural population, such as the Aḥmadīyah (after Aḥmad al-Badawī; died 1286) in Egypt. The Aḥmadīyah, however, even attracted some Mamlūk rulers. The Turkish Bektāshīyah (Haci Bektaş, early 14th century), together with strange syncretistic cults, showed a prevalence of the ideals of the Shīʿites (from Shīʿah—the followers of ʿAlī, first cousin of the prophet Muḥammad, whose descendants claimed to be rightful successors of the Prophet to the religious leadership of Islām). The figure of ʿAlī played a role also in other fraternities, and the relations between Ṣūfism in the 14th and 15th centuries and the Shīʿah still have to be explored, as is also true of the general influence of Shīʿite ideas on Ṣūfism. Other orders, such as the Shādhilīyah, an offshoot of which still plays an important role among Egyptian officials and employees, are typically middle class. This order demands not a life in solitude but strict adherence to one's profession and fulfillment of one's duty. Still other orders were connected with the ruling classes, such as, for a time, the Chishtīyah in Mughal India, and the Mawlawīyah, whose leader had to invest the Ottoman sultan with the sword. The Mawlawīyah is also largely responsible for the development of classical Turkish poetry, music, and fine arts, just as the Chishtīyah contributed much to the formation of classical Indo-Muslim music.

Adaptation to levels of society

The main contribution of the orders, however, is their missionary activity. The members of different orders who settled in India from the early 13th century attracted thousands of Hindus by their example of love of both God and their own brethren and by preaching the equality of men. Missionary activity was often joined with political activity, as in 17th- and 18th-century Central Asia, where the Naqshbandīyah exerted strong political influence. In North Africa the Tijānīyah, founded in 1781, and the Sanūsīyah, active since the early 19th century, both heralded Islām and engaged in politics; the Sanūsīyah fought against Italy, and the former king of Libya was the head of the order. The Tijānīyah extended the borders of Islām toward Senegal and Nigeria, and their representatives founded large kingdoms in West Africa. Their influence, as well as that of the Qādirīyah (see below), is still an important sociopolitical factor in those areas.

Statistical data. It would be impossible to number the members of mystical orders in the Islāmic world. *The Encyclopaedia of Islam* holds that about 3 percent of the total Muslim population belong to mystical orders; the number of those in some way attached to them is surely higher. Even in such countries as Turkey, where the orders have been banned since 1925, many people still cling to the mystical tradition and feel themselves to be links in the spiritual chains of the orders and try to implement their ideals in modern society. The most widely spread group is, no doubt, the Qādirīyah, whose adherents are found from West Africa to India—the tomb of ʿAbd al-Qādir al-Jīlānī in Baghdad still being a place of pilgrimage. The areas where the Sanūsīyah live are restricted to the Maghrib, the Atlas Massif, and the coastal plain from Morocco to Tunisia, whereas the Tijānīyah has some offshoots in Turkey. Such rural orders as the Egyptian Aḥmadīyah and Dasūqīyah (named after Ibrāhīm ad-Dasūqī; died 1277) are bound to their respective countries, as are the Mawlawīs and Bektāshīyah to the realms of the former Ottoman Empire. The Bektāshīyah had gained political importance in the empire because of its relations with the Janissaries, the standing army. Albania, since 1929, has had a strong and officially recognized group of Bektāshīyah who were even granted independent status after World War II. The Shaṭṭārīyah (derived from ʿAbd ash-Shaṭṭār; died 1415) extends from India to Java, whereas the Chishtīyah (derived from Khwājah Muʿīn-ud-Dīn Chishtī; died 1236 in Ajmer) and Suhrawardīyah remain mainly inside the Indo-Pakistan subcontinent. The Kubrāwīyah reached Kashmir through ʿAlī Hamadhānī (died 1385), a versatile author, but the order later lost its influence.

Geographical extent of Ṣūfī orders

The great variety of possible forms may be seen by comparing the Haddāwah, vagabonds in Morocco, who "do not spoil God's day by work" and the Shādhilīyah with a sober attitude toward professional life and careful introspection. Out of the Shādhilīyah developed the austere Darqāwīyah, who, in turn, produced the ʿAlāwīyah, whose master has attracted even a number of Europeans. The splitting up and formation of suborders is a normal process, but most of the subgroups have only local importance. The High Ṣūfī Convent in Egypt counts 60 registered orders.

SIGNIFICANCE

Ṣūfism has helped to shape large parts of Muslim society. The orthodox disagree with such aspects of Ṣūfism as saint worship, visiting of tombs, musical performances, miracle mongering, degeneration into jugglery, and the adaptation of pre-Islāmic and un-Islāmic customs; and the reformers object to the influences of the monistic interpretation of Islām upon moral life and human activities. The importance given to the figure of the master is accused of yielding negative results; the *shaykh* as the almost infallible leader of his disciples and admirers could gain dangerous authority and political influence, for the illiterate villagers in backward areas used to rely completely upon the "saint." Yet, other masters have raised their voices against social inequality and have tried, even at the cost of their lives, to change social and political conditions for the better and to spiritually revive the masses. The missionary activities of the Ṣūfīs have enlarged the fold of the faithful. The importance of Ṣūfism for spiritual education, and inculcation in the faithful of the virtues of trust in God, piety, faith in God's love, and veneration of the Prophet, cannot be overrated. The *dhikr* formulas still preserve their consoling and quieting power even for the illiterate. Mysticism permeates Persian literature and other literatures influenced by it. Such poetry has always been a source of happiness for millions, although some modernists have disdained its "narcotic" influence on Muslim thinking.

Industrialization and modern life have led to a constant decrease in the influence of Ṣūfī orders in many countries. The spiritual heritage is preserved by individuals who sometimes try to show that mystical experience conforms to modern science. Today in the West, Ṣūfism is popularized, but the genuinely and authentically devout are aware that it requires strict discipline, and that its goal can be reached—if at all—as they say, only by throwing oneself into the consuming fire of divine love.

BIBLIOGRAPHY

Introductory works: E.H. PALMER, *Oriental Mysticism: A Treatise on Sufiistic and Unitarian Theosophy of the Persians* (1867), 2nd ed. by A.J. ARBERRY (1938, reprinted 1969), an exposition of later mystical ideas; R.A. NICHOLSON, *The Mystics of Islam* (1914), outdated in some aspects, but still a very readable introduction to classical Ṣūfism and Ṣūfī poetry; A.J. ARBERRY, *Sufism: An Account of the Mystics of Islam* (1950), an historical survey of classical Ṣūfism; G.C. ANAWATI and L. GARDET, *Mystique musulmane* (1961), an excellent study of the major trends and leading personalities in classical Ṣūfism; R.C. ZAEHNER, *Hindu and Muslim Mysticism* (1960), a thought-provoking study of the possible relations between Indian and early Muslim mysticism.

History: M. SMITH, *Rābiʿa the Mystic and Her Fellow-Saints in Islam: Being the Life and Teachings of Rābiʿa al-ʿAdawiyya al-Qaysiyya of Basra, Together with Some Account of the Place of the Women Saints in Islam* (1928), the first study of the herald of mystical love in Islām; J. VAN ESS, *Die Gedankenwelt des Ḥārit al-Muḥāsibī anhand von Uebersetzungen aus seinen Schriften dargestellt und erläutert* (1961), an excellent introduction to the theology and psychology of early mystical thought in Islām; L. MASSIGNON, *La passion d'al-Hosayn ibn Mansour al-Hallāj, martyr mystique de l'Islam*, 2 vol. (1922), an indispensable source book for the history of Ṣūfism in the classical period; A. SCHIMMEL, *Al-Halladsch, Märtyrer der Gottesliebe* (1968), a German translation of parts of Ḥallāj's poetry and prose, and a study of his influence on the literatures of the different Islāmic peoples; S. DE LAUGIER DE BEAURECEUIL, *Khwādja ʿAbdullāh Ansārī (396–481 H./1006–1089): Mystique Hanbalite* (1965), a biography of the author of the beautiful Persian *munājāt* (prayers) and other mystical books; J.A. WENSINCK, *La Pensée d'al-Ghazzālī* (1940), a short and reliable introduction to Ghazālī's thought; J. SUBHAN, *Sufism: Its Saints and Shrines* (1938), a useful survey of the later development of Islāmic mysticism.

Ṣūfī literature: H. RITTER, *Das Meer der Seele* (1955), an exhaustive work on Farīd ud-Dīn ʿAṭṭār's thought as reflected in his mystical poetry; JALAL-UD-DIN RUMI, *The Mathnawi-yi Maʿnawi*, ed. with critical notes, translation, and commentary by R.A. NICHOLSON, 8 vol. (1925–40), the encyclopaedia of mystical thought in the 13th century in masterly translation; H.T. SORLEY, *Shah Abdul Latīf of Bhit* (1940; reprinted 1966), a study of the greatest mystical poet of Sind with translations of some of his poems.

Ṣūfī thought and practice: B. REINERT, *Die Lehre vom Tawakkul in der klassischen Sufik* (1968), the first fundamental study of a single concept central to early Islāmic mysticism, built upon a critical analysis of all available sources; A.J. ARBERRY, *The Doctrine of the Sūfīs* (1935), a useful translation of Kalābādhi's *Kitāb at-taʿarruf*, one of the early treatises on Ṣūfī thought; *The Kashf al-Maḥjūb: The Oldest Persian Treatise on Sufism* by ʿAli b.ʿUthmān *al-Jullābī al-Hujwīrī*, trans. by R.A. NICHOLSON (1911; reprinted 1969), a masterly translation of the voluminous 11th-century account of Ṣūfī thought; G.H. BOUSQUET, *Ih'yâ ʿouloûm ed-dîn; ou Vivification des sciences de la foi* (1955), an analytical index of the most widely read work on moderate mystical thought, prepared with the assistance of numerous scholars; C.E. PADWICK, *Muslim Devotions* (1961), the only account of the popular mystically tinged piety of the Muslims as reflected in their prayer books.

Theosophical Ṣūfism: A.E. AFFIFI, *The Mystical Philosophy of Muhyīd Dīn-Ibnul ʿArabī* (1939), the first attempt, in a Western language, to systematize the pantheistic system of the 13th century theosophist; H. CORBIN, *L'imagination créatrice dans le Soufisme d'Ibn ʿArabi* (1958), a congenial interpretation of Ibn al-ʿArabī's system of thought; R.A. NICHOLSON, *Studies in Islamic Mysticism* (1921), a study of Abū Saʿīd and a discussion of Jīlī's Perfect Man and of Ibn al-Fāriḍ, with a superb translation of most of his odes.

Ṣūfī orders: H. RITTER, "Der Reigen der tanzenden Derwische," *Oriens*, vol. 17 (1964), an account of the ritual dance of the Mawlawīs in Konya for the annual celebration of Rūmī's death anniversary; H.J. KISSLING, "Die Wunder der Derwische," *ZDMG* (*Zeitschrift der deutschen morgen-*

ländischen Gesellschaft), vol. 107 (1957), a fully documented account of the kinds of miracles performed by dervishes; K.A. NIZAMI, *The Life and Times of Shaikh Farid-'ud-din Ganj-i-Shakar* (1955), a good survey of the life of one of the leading Chishtī saints in India; R. BRUNEL, *Le Monachisme errant dans l'Islam: Sīdi Heddi et les Heddāwa* (1955), a penetrating study of a little known fraternity of dervishes in North Africa; J.M. ABUN-NASR, *The Tijaniyya: A Sufi Order in the Modern World* (1965), a study of the development of political activities of this 19th century order in the northern and western parts of Africa; J.S. TRIMINGHAM, *The Ṣūfī Orders in Islam* (1971), the first attempt to give a survey of all orders in Islām, and, as such, quite useful.

(An.Sc.)

Islāmic Myth and Legend

Islām has not developed a proper mythology. Its strict monotheism does not allow for much mythological decoration, and only reluctantly were the Qur'ānic (Islāmic scriptural) revelations embellished and enlarged by commentators and popular preachers. Thus, in the first three centuries, a number of ideas from the ancient Near East, from Hellenistic and especially from Judeo-Christian traditions were absorbed into Islām and given at least partial sanction by the theologians. At the same time, legends were woven around the Prophet Muḥammad (to whom the Qur'ān was revealed) and the members of his family. Though inconsistent with historical reality, these legends formed for the masses the main sources of inspiration about the famous figures of the past and only in recent decades has a new historical approach begun to free the Prophet's personality from a legendary crust and to venture a demythologizing interpretation of the Qur'ān.

Role of storytellers

Since early times Islāmic theologians have sought to disregard the Qur'ānic interpretation of both storytellers and mystics. The *quṣṣāṣ*, or storytellers, made the Qur'ānic revelation more understandable to the masses by filling in the short texts with detailed descriptions that were not found in scripture. Though the mystics tried to maintain the purity of the divine word, they also attempted a spiritualization of both the Qur'ān and the popular legends that developed around it. Their way of giving to the Qur'ānic words a deeper meaning, however, and discovering layer after layer of meaning in them, sometimes led to new quasi-mythological forms. Later Islāmic mystical thinkers built up closed systems that can be called almost mythological (*e.g.*, the angelology—theory of angels—of Suhrawardī al-Maqtūl, executed 1191). An interesting development is visible in poetry, especially in the Persian-speaking areas, where mythological figures and pious legend often were turned into secular images that might awaken in the reader a reminiscence of their religious origin. Such images contribute to the iridescent and ambiguous character of Persian poetry.

SOURCES OF MYTH AND LEGEND

The sources of Islāmic mythology are first of all the Qur'ānic revelations. Since, for the Muslims, the Qur'ān is the uncreated word of God (the text revealed to Muḥammad is an earthly manifestation of the eternal and uncreated original in heaven), it contains every truth, and whatever is said in it has been the object of meditation and explanation through the centuries. Thus, since the 9th century, commentators on the Qur'ān have been by far the most important witnesses for Islāmic "mythology." They wove into their explanations various strands of Persian and ancient oriental lore and relied heavily on Jewish tradition. For example, the Jewish convert, Kaʿb al-Aḥbār brought much of the *Isrā'īliyāt* (things Jewish) into Islāmic tradition. Later on, the mystics' commentaries expressed some gnostic (a dualistic viewpoint in which spirit is viewed as good and matter as evil) and Hellenistic concepts, of which the Hellenistic idea of the Perfect Man—personified in Muḥammad—was to gain greatest prominence. Commentaries written in the border areas of Islāmic countries now and then accepted a few popular traditions from their respective areas; however, the formative period was finished quite early. Traditions about the life and sayings of the Prophet grew larger and larger and are interesting for the study of the adoption of foreign mythological material. A valuable source for Islāmic legends are the *qiṣaṣ al-anbiyā'*, or stories of the prophets, such as those by Thaʿālibī (born 1035) and Kisā'ī (11th century); traditions concerning the prophets of yore in which a large number of pre-Islāmic and non-Islāmic ideas have been incorporated.

Trans-cultural prolifera-tion

From the 11th century onward, the biographies of the mystics often show interesting migrations of legendary motifs from one culture to another. For the Persian-speaking countries the *Tazkerat ol-Owlīyā'* ("Memoirs of the Saints") of Farīd od-Dīn ʿAṭṭār (died *c.* 1220) has become the storehouse of legendary material about the early Ṣūfī mystics. ʿAṭṭār's Persian epics (especially his *Manṭeq ot-ṭeyr*, the "Birds' Conversation") also contain much material that was used by almost every writer after him. *The Maṡnavī* (a sort of poetic encyclopaedia of mystical thought in 26,000 couplets) of Jalāl od-Dīn Rūmī (died 1273) is another important source for legends of saints and prophets. For the Iranian world view, Ferdowsī's (died *c.* 1020) *Shāh-nāmeh* ("Book of Kings") gave a poetical account of the mythology of old Iran, and its heroes became models for many poets and writers. The whole mythological and legendary heritage is condensed in allusions found in lyrical and panegyrical poetry. The Persian poet Ebrāhim ebn ʿAlī Khāqānī's (*c.* 1121–*c.* 1199) works, *qaṣīdahs* ("Odes"), are typical.

Muslim historians interested in world history often began their works with mythological tales; central Asian traditions were added in Iran during the Il-Khanid period (AD 1256–1335). Folk poetry, in the different languages spoken by Muslims, provides a popular representation of traditional material, be it in Arabic, Persian, Turkish, the Indian and Pakistani languages (Urdu, Bengali, Sindhi, Panjabi, Baluchi, etc.), or the African languages; in all of them allusions to myth and legend are found down to the level of riddles and lullabies. Typical of the legendary tradition of the Shīʿahs (Muslims who give special importance to the Prophet's cousin ʿAlī and his descendants) are the *taʿziya*s ("passion-plays") in Iran, commemorating the death of Husayn ibn ʿAlī in Karbalā' (680) and the *marṡīyehs* (threnodies or elegies for the dead), which form an important branch of the Urdu poetry of India and Pakistan (see also ISLAMIC PEOPLES, ARTS OF).

VARIETIES OF MYTH AND LEGEND

Cosmogony and eschatology. The world was created by God's word *kun* ("Be") out of nothing; after the creation of the angelic beings from light, Adam was formed from clay and destined to be God's vicegerent, *khalīfah*. All of the angels obeyed God's order to prostrate themselves before Adam, except Iblīs (Satan), who refused and was cursed; due to Iblīs' instigation Adam ate the forbidden fruit (or grain) and was driven out of paradise. Questions of original sin or of Eve's role do not arise. Satan's disobedience has been explained by the mystics as actually an expression of his obedience to the divine will that does not allow worship of any but the Lord and that conflicted with the order that Satan prostrate himself before Adam.

Before the creation, God addressed the posterity of Adam: "Am I not your Lord," *alastu birabbikum*, and they answered "Yes" (Qur'ān, *sūrah* 7:172). This pre-eternal covenant is the favourite topic of mystical poetry, especially in the Persian-speaking areas for expressing pre-eternal love between God and man, or the unchangeable fate that was accepted that very day, the Yesterday as contrasted to the Tomorrow of resurrection. Angels and jinns (genies) are living powers that become visible in human life; they are accepted as fully real.

Every destiny is written on the "well-preserved tablet," and now "the pen has dried up"—a change in destiny is not possible. Later mystics have relied on an extra-Qur'ānic revelation in which God attests: "I was a hidden treasure" and have seen the reason for creation in God's yearning to be known and loved. For them, creation is the projection of divine names and qualities onto the world of matter.

Satan's refusal to worship Adam, depicting the rebellious angel Iblīs, or Satan, as the human figure on a prayer rug (right). From a 17th-century manuscript of Majāles ol-'Oshshāq. In the Bibliothèque Nationale, Paris (Supplément Persan 1559).

By courtesy of the Bibliotheque Nationale, Paris

Centrality of death and resurrection

The central event of Islām is death and resurrection. The dead will be questioned by two terrible angels (that is why the profession of faith is recited to the dying); only the souls of martyrs go straight to heaven where they remain in the crops of green birds around the divine throne (green is always connected with heavenly bliss). The end of the world will be announced by the coming of the mahdī (literally, "the directed or guided one")—a messianic figure who will appear in the last days and is not found in the Qur'ān but developed out of Shī'ah speculations and sometimes identified with Jesus. The mahdī will slay the Dajjāl, the one-eyed evil spirit, and combat the dangerous enemies, Yājūj and Mājūj, who will come from the north of the earth. The trumpet of Isrāfīl, one of the four archangels, will awaken the dead for the day of resurrection, which is many thousands of years long and the name of which has come to designate a state of complete confusion and turmoil. The eschatological inventory as described in the Qur'ān was elaborated by the commentators: the scales on which the books or deeds are weighed (an old Egyptian idea), the book in which the two recording angels have noted down man's deeds, and the narrow bridge that is said to be sharper than a sword and thinner than a hair and leads over hell (an Iranian idea). The dreadful angels of hell and the horrors of that place are as thoroughly described by theologians as the pleasures of paradise, with its waters and gardens and the houris who are permanent virgins. Pious tradition promises space in heavenly mansions, filled with everything beautiful, to those who repeat certain prayer formulas a certain number of times, or for similar rewarding deeds, whereas the mystic longs not "for houris some thousand years old" but for the vision of God, who will be visible like the full moon. In the concept of the *sidrah* tree as the noblest place in paradise a remnant may be found of the old tree of life. God's throne is on the waters (Qur'ān, *sūrah* 11:9) in the highest world, surrounded by worshipping angels. The created world, the earth, is surrounded by the mountain Qāf and enclosed by two oceans that are separated by a barrier. Mecca is the navel of the earth, created 2,000 years before everything else, and the deluge did not reach to proto-*Ka'bah*. Often the world is conceived as a succession of seven heavens and seven earths, and a popular tradition says that the earth is on water, on a rock, on the back of a bull, on a *kamkam* (meaning unknown), on a fish, on water, on wind, on the veil of darkness—hence the Persian expression *az māh tā māhī*, from the moon to the fish; *i.e.*, throughout the whole world.

Tales and legends concerning religious figures. The majority of popular legends concern the leading personalities of Islām.

Muḥammad. Muḥammad, whose only miracle, according to his own words, was the bringing of the Qur'ān, is credited with innumerable miracles and associated with a variety of miraculous occurrences: his finger split the moon, the cooked poisoned meat warned him not to touch it, the palm trunk sighed, the gazelle spoke for him; he cast no shadow; from his perspiration the rose was created, etc. His ascension to heaven (*mi'rāj*) is still

By courtesy of the Bibliotheque Nationale, Paris

Muhammad's visit to Paradise, depicting Muhammad (right) upon the human-headed steed Burāq and the archangel Gabriel (left). Houris (bottom) exchange nosegays of flowers signifying Friday as the Islāmic holiday. From a 15th-century manuscript of the Mi'rāj-name. In the Bibliothèque Nationale, Paris (supplément Turc 190).

celebrated: he rode the winged horse Burāq in the company of the angel Gabriel through the seven spheres, meeting the other prophets there, until he reached the divine presence, alone, even without the angel of inspiration. Since representations are unlawful in Islām, the Prophet Muḥammad was represented in words: in many a house one finds a beautifully written plaque with a description of his lofty qualities. Muḥammad-mysticism proper was developed in the late 9th century; he is shown as the one who precedes creation, his light is pre-eternal, and he is the reason for and goal of creation. He becomes the perfect man, uniting the divine and the human sphere as dawn is between night and day. His birth was surrounded by miracles, and his birthday (12. Rabī' I) became a popular holiday on which numerous poems were written to praise his achievements. The hope for him who has been sent as "mercy for the worlds" and will intercede for his community on Doomsday is extremely strong, especially among the masses, where these legends have completely overshadowed his historical figure.

Muḥammad-mysticism

Other Qur'ānic figures. In addition to Muḥammad himself, his cousin and son-in-law 'Alī, the Shī'ah hero, has been surrounded by legends concerning his bravery, his miraculous sword, Dhūal-fiqār, and his wisdom. 'Alī's son, Ḥusayn, is the subject of innumerable poems that concern the day of his final fight in Karbalā'.

Almost every figure mentioned in the Qur'ān has become the centre of a circle of legends, be it Yūsuf, the symbol of overwhelming beauty, or Jesus with the life-giving breath, the model of poverty and asceticism. Of special interest is Khiḍr, identified with the unnamed companion of Moses (Qur'ān, *sūrah* 20). He is the patron saint of the wayfarers, connected with the colour green, appearing whenever a pious person is in need, and immortal since he drank from the fountain of life, which is hidden in the darkness. In many respects, he is the Islāmic counterpart of Elijah. Strong influences of the Alexander romances (a widely distributed literary genre dealing with the adventures of Alexander the Great) are visible in his figure.

Mystics and other later figures. The great religious personalities have become legendary, especially the martyr-mystic Ḥallāj (executed in Bagdad, 922). His word *anā al-Ḥaqq*, "I am the Creative Truth," became the motto of many later mystics. His death on the gallows is the model for the suffering of lovers, and allusions to his fate are frequent in Islāmic literature. An earlier mystic, Abū Yazīd al-Bisṭāmī (died 874), was the first to speak about the ascension of the mystic to heaven which is a metaphor for higher unitive, mystical experience. A variation of the Buddha legend has been transferred onto the person of the first Ṣūfī (mystic) who practiced absolute poverty and trust in God, the Central Asian Ibrāhīm ibn Adham (died *c.* 780). The founders of mystical orders were credited by the followers with numerous miracles, such as riding on lions, healing the sick, walking on water, being present at two places at the same time, and cardiognosia (knowledge of what is in another's heart; thought reading). ʿAbd al-Qādir al-Jīlānī (died 1166), the founder of the widespread Qādirīyah order of mystics, and many others have attracted upon themselves a large number of popular stories that formerly had been told about pre-Islāmic saints or about some divinities, and these motifs can easily be transferred from one person to the other. In this sphere the survival of pre-Islāmic customs and legends is most visible. The idea of the hierarchy of saints, culminating in the *quṭb*, the pole or axis, thanks to whose activities the world keeps going, belongs to the mythology of Ṣūfism (Islāmic mysticism).

The mystics as miracle workers

Mythologization of secular tales. A special feature of Islāmic mythology is the transformation of formerly unreligious stories into vehicles of religious experience. The old hero of romantic love in Arabic literature, Majnūn, "the demented one," became a symbol of the soul longing for identification with God, and in the Indus Valley the tales of Sassui or Sohnī, the girls who perish for the sake of their love, and other romantic figures, have been understood as symbols of the soul longing for union with God through suffering and death.

Tales and beliefs about numbers and letters. Many Muslim tales, legends, and traditional sayings are built upon the mystical value of numbers, such as the threefold or sevenfold repetition of a certain rite. This is largely explained by examples from the life of a saintly or pious person, often the Prophet himself, who used to repeat this or that formula so and so many times. The number 40, found in the Qur'ān (as also in the Bible) as the length of a period of repentance, suffering, preparation, and steadfastness, plays the same role in Islām where it is connected, for example, with the 40 days' preparation and meditation, or fasting, of the novice in the mystical brotherhood. To each number, as well as to each day of the week, special qualities are attributed through the authority of both actual and alleged statements of the Prophet. Many pre-Islāmic customs were thus justified. The importance given to the letters of the Arabic alphabet is peculiar to Muslim pious thought. Letters of the alphabet were assigned numerical values: the straight *alif* (numerical value one), the first letter of the alphabet, becomes a symbol of the uniqueness and unity of Allāh; the *b* (numerical value two), the first letter of the Qur'ān, represents to many mystics the creative power by which everything came into existence; the *h* (numerical value five) is the symbol of *huwa*, He, the formula for God's absolute transcendence; the *m* (numerical value 40) is the "shawl of humanity" by which God, the One (al-Aḥad), is separated from *Aḥmad* (*Muḥammad*). *M* is the letter of human nature and hints at the 40 degrees between man and God. The sect of the Ḥurūfīs developed these cabalistic interpretations of letters, but they are quite common in the whole Islāmic world and form almost a substitute for mythology.

Number symbolism

GEOGRAPHIC DISTRIBUTION AND REGIONAL VARIATION

The classical mythology of Islām, as far as it can be properly called so, is spread over the whole area of Islām, since its main source book, the Qur'ān, is the basis of the entire Islāmic culture and is, together with the prophetic traditions, found everywhere. The miracles and legends around a particular Muslim saint are found chiefly in the area of his special influence (especially where his order is most popular). However, legends about the great masters of Ṣūfism are as common in north Africa as they are in India and Pakistan. Even if the names of the saints differ, the legends woven around them are very similar to each other and almost interchangeable. In the area where Persian was read—from Ottoman Turkey to India—the mythological concepts of Ferdowsī's *Shāh-nāmeh* are found side by side with the legends taken from ʿAṭṭār's and Rūmī's works.

The close connection of the Ṣūfī orders with the artisans' lodges and guilds was instrumental in the dissemination of legendary material, especially about the alleged founder, or patron, of the guild (such as Ḥallāj as patron of cottoncarders and Idrīs as patron of the tailors). A proper study of the distribution of most aspects of mythology in the various Muslim areas has not yet been undertaken, since much of the popular material is rarely available in print or is written in less-known languages (a good example is the extremely rich collections of legends and popular pious works in the Pakistani language, Sindhi).

ILLUSTRATION OF MYTH AND LEGEND

Since the art of representation is opposed in Islām, illustrations of mythological and legendary subjects are rarely found. Miniature painting developed only in the Persian and, later on, in the Turkish and Indo-Muslim areas. Books such as Zakarīyāʾ ebn Moḥammad al-Qazvīnī's *Cosmography* contain in some manuscripts a few pictures of angels, like Isrāfīl with the trumpet, and histories of the world or histories of the prophets, written in Iran or Turkey, also contain in rare manuscripts representations of angels or of scenes as told in the Qur'ān, especially the story of Yūsuf and Zalīkhā, which inspired many poems. The *Shāh-nāmeh* has been fairly frequently illustrated. When the Prophet of Islām is shown at all, his face is usually covered and in several cases his companions or his family members are also shown with veiled faces. The only subject from the legends surrounding Muḥammad that has been treated by miniaturists several times is his ascension to heaven. There are a number of splendid Persian miniatures depicting this. In poetical manuscripts that contain allusions to legends of the saints, these topics were also sometimes illustrated (*e.g.*, Jonah and the great fish or scenes from the wanderings of Khiḍr). Several miniatures deal with the execution of the mystic al-Ḥallāj. Mythological themes proper are found almost exclusively in the paintings of Mughal India; especially in the period of Jahāngīr, in which the eschatological peace of lion and lamb lying together is illustrated as well as the myth of the earth resting on the bull, on the fish, etc. But by that time European influence was also already visible in Mughal art.

Persian, Turkish, and Indian Mughal miniature painting

SIGNIFICANCE AND RECENT INTERPRETATIONS

Mythology proper has only a very small place in official Islām and is mostly an expression of popular traditions through which pre-Islāmic influences seeped into Islām. Reformers tried to purge Islām of all non-Qur'ānic ideas and picturesque elaborations of the texts, whereas the mystics tried to spiritualize them as far as possible. Modern Muslim exegesis attempts to interpret many of the mythological strands of the Qur'ān in the light of modern science, as psychological factors, like Muḥammad's ascension to heaven, and especially deprives the eschatological parts of the Qur'ān of their religious significance. Cosmic events are interpreted as predictions of modern scientific research. To some interpreters, jinns and angels are spiritual forces; to others, jinns are microbes or the like. Thus the religious text is confused with a textbook of science. Popular legends surrounding the Prophet and the saints are still found among the masses but are tending to disappear under the influence of historical research, though many of them have formed excellent models for the behaviour and spiritual life of the Muslim believer.

BIBLIOGRAPHY. I. GOLDZIHER, *Die Richtungen der islamischen Koranauslegung* (1920), interpretations of the Qur'ān in classical time; TOR ANDRAE, *Die Person Muhammads in Glauben und Lehre seiner Gemeinde* (1918), on the development of Muḥammad-mysticism; E. FRIEDLANDER, *Die Khidr-Gestalt und der Alexander-Roman* (1913), on the relation between the Alexander romance and the figure of Khiḍr; A. SCHIMMEL, *Al-Halladsch, Märtyrer der Gottesliebe: Leben und Legende* (1968), on the development of the veneration of al-Ḥallāj in Islāmic literatures; M.J.H. HORTEN, *Die religiöse Gedankenwelt der gebildeten Muslime in heutigen Islam* (1916), an account of popular Islām, and *Die religiöse Gedankenwelt des Volkes im heutigen Islam*, 2 pt. (1917–18), an account of the ideas of educated people in Islām; A.J. WENSINCK, "The Ocean in the Literature of the Western Semites," *Verhandelingen der Koninklijke Akademie van Wetenschappen*, vol. 19 (1918), and "The Ideas of the Western Semites Concerning the Navel of the Earth," *ibid.*, vol. 17 (1916); S.H. NASR, *Three Muslim Sages* (1964), an account of the theories of Suhrawardī al-Maqtūl and Ibn 'Arabī; J. HOROWITZ, "The Growth of the Mohammedan Legend," *Muslim World*, 10:49-58 (1920), stresses the haggadic influences; WALTER EICKMANN, *Angelologie und Dämonologie des Koran* (1906), a study of the Qur'ānic concepts of angels and demons; HANS ZBINDEN, *Die Djinn im Islam* (1953), a study of the different types of spirits in Islāmic folklore and tradition; RUDOLF KRISS and HUBERT KRISS-HEINRICH, *Volksglaube im Bereich des Islam*, 2 vol. (1960–62), useful studies in Islāmic folklore, with extensive bibliographies; TAUFIC CANAAN, *Mohammedan Saints and Sanctuaries in Palestine* (1927), on Palestinian folklore; articles in the *Shorter Encyclopaedia of Islam* (1953), the most authoritative collection of information, each article furnished with an extensive bibliography.

(An.Sc.)

Islāmic Peoples, Arts of

The vast populations of the Middle East and elsewhere that adopted the Islāmic faith from the 7th century onward have created such an immense variety of literatures, performing arts, visual arts, and music that it virtually defies any comprehensive definition. In the narrowest sense, the arts of the Islāmic peoples might be said to include only those arising directly from the practice of Islām; more commonly, however, the term is extended to include all of the arts produced by Muslim peoples, whether connected with their religion or not. In this article, the subject includes the arts created in pre-Islāmic times by Arabs and other peoples in Asia Minor and North Africa who eventually adopted the Islāmic faith. On the other hand, arts produced in cultural areas that were only partially Muslim, such as South Asia, Southeast Asia, Central Asia are discussed primarily in articles on arts of those regions (SOUTH ASIAN PEOPLES, ARTS OF; SOUTHEAST ASIAN PEOPLES, ARTS OF; and CENTRAL ASIAN PEOPLES, ARTS OF).

It is difficult to establish a common denominator for all of the artistic expressions of the Islāmic peoples. Such a common denominator would have to be meaningful for miniature painting and historiography, for a musical mode and the form of a poem. The relationship between the art of the Islāmic peoples and its religious basis is anything but direct.

The prohibition on representation

Like most prophetic religions, Islām is not conducive to fine arts. Representation of living beings is prohibited—not in the Qur'ān but in the prophetic tradition. Thus, the centre of the Islāmic artistic tradition lies in calligraphy, a distinguishing feature of this culture, in which the word as the medium of divine revelation plays such an important role. Representational art was found, however, in some early palaces and "at the doors of the bathhouses," according to later Persian poetry. After the 13th century a highly refined art of miniature developed, primarily in the non-Arab countries; it dwells, however, only rarely upon religious subjects. The typical expression of Muslim art is the arabesque, both in its geometric and in its vegetabilic form—one leaf, one flower growing out of the other, without beginning and end and capable of almost innumerable variations—only gradually detected by the eye—which never lose their charm. An aversion to empty spaces distinguishes that art; neither the tile-covered walls of a mosque nor the rich imagery of a poem allows an unembellished area; and the decoration of a carpet can be extended almost endlessly without limit.

The centre of Islāmic religion is the clean place for prayer, enlarged into the mosque, which comprises the community and all its needs. The essential structure is similar throughout the Muslim world. There are, of course, period and regional differences—large, wide court mosques of early times; court mosques, with big halls, of Iran and adjacent countries; central buildings with the wonderfully shaped domes of the Ottoman Empire. The implements, however, are the same: a niche (*miḥrāb*)—pointing to Mecca—made of wood, marble, mosaic, stone, tiles; a small pulpit for the Friday sermon; minarets, locally differently shaped but always rising like the call to prayer that is uttered from their tops; the wooden carved stands for the Qur'ān, which is to be written in the most perfect form; sometimes highly artistic lamps (made in Syria and proverbially mentioned all over the Muslim word); perhaps bronze candlesticks, with inlaid ornaments; and rich variations of the prayer mats. If any decoration was needed, it was the words of God, beautifully written or carved in the walls or around the domes. At first connected with the mosques and later independent of them are schools, mausoleums, rooms for the students, and cells for the religious masters.

The poetry of the Arabs consisted in the beginning of praise and satirical poems thought to be full of magic qualities. The strict rules of the outward form of the poems (monorhyme, complicated metre), even in pre-Islāmic times led to a certain formalism and encouraged imitation.

Goethe's statement that *The Arabian Nights' Entertainment* have no goal in themselves shows his understanding of the character of Arabic belles-lettres, contrasting them with the Islāmic religion, which aims at "collecting and uniting people in order to achieve one high goal." Poets, on the other hand, rove around without any ethical purpose, according to the Qur'ān. For many pious Muslims, poetry was something suspect, opposed to the divine law, especially since it sang mostly of forbidden wine and of free love. The combination of music and poetry, as practiced in court circles and among the mystics, has always aroused the wrath of the lawyer divines who wielded so much authority in Islāmic communities. This opposition may partly explain why Islāmic poetry and fine arts took refuge in a kind of unreal world, using fixed images that could be correctly interpreted only by those who were knowledgeable in the art.

The ambiguity of Persian poetry, which oscillates between the worldly, the divine, and often the political level, is typical of Islāmic writings. Especially in Iran and the countries under its cultural influence, this kind of poetry formed the most important part of literature. Epic poetry of all kinds developed exclusively outside the Arabic-speaking countries; Western readers look in vain for an epical structure in such long poems (as in the case of the prose-romances of the Arabs) and find, instead, a rather aimless representation of facts and fictions. A similar characteristic even conditions innumerable historical works in Arabic, Persian, and Turkish, which, especially in classical times, contain much valuable information, put together without being shaped into a real work of art; only rarely does the historian or philosopher reach a comprehensive view. The first attempt at a philosophy of history, Ibn Khaldūn's *Muqaddimah*, in the 14th century, was rarely studied by his Arab compatriots.

The accumulation of large amounts of material, which is carefully organized up to the present, seems typical of all branches of Islāmic scholarship, from theology to natural sciences. There are many minute observations and descriptions but rarely a full view of the whole process. Later, especially in the Persian, Turkish, and Indo-Muslim areas, a tendency to overstress the decorative elements of prose is evident; and the contents even of official chronicles are hidden behind a network of rhymed prose, which is difficult to disentangle.

The characteristic lack of structure

This tendency is illustrated in all branches of Islāmic art: the lack of "architectural" formation. Instead, there is a kind of carpet-like pattern; the Arabic and Persian poem is, in general, not judged as a closed unity but rather according to the perfection of its individual verses. Its main object is not to convey a deep personal feeling but to perfect to the utmost the traditional rules and inherited metaphors, to which a new image may sometimes be added; thus the personality of the poet becomes visible only through the minimal changes of expression and rhythm and the application of certain preferred metaphors, just as the personality of the miniature painter can be detected by a careful observation of details, of his way of colouring a rock or deepening the shade of a turban. The same holds true for the arabesques, which were developed according to a strict ritual to a mathematical pattern and were refined until they reached a perfection of geometrical complicated figures, as in the dome of the Karatay Medrese in Konya (1251); it corresponds both to the most intricate lacelike Kūfic inscriptions around this dome and to the poetical style of Jalāl ad-Dīn ar-Rūmī, who wrote in that very place and during those years. His immortal mystical poems comprise thousands of variations on the central theme of love. Although such a perfect congruency of poetry and fine arts is not frequently found, the precept about Persian art that "its wings are too heavy with beauty" can also be applied to Persian poetry. Thus, the tile work of a Persian mosque, which combines different levels of arabesque work with different styles of writing, is reminiscent of the way Persian poetry combines at least two levels of reality. And a perfect harmony is reached in some of the miniature manuscripts of Iran, Muslim India, or Ottoman Turkey, which, in their lucid colours and fine details of execution, recall both the perfection of the calligraphy that surrounds them on delicate paper and the subtlety of the stories or poems that they accompany or illustrate.

Those accustomed to the Western ideals of plasticity or form in the fine arts and literature or to the polyphonic interweaving of melodic lines in music have some difficulties in appreciating this art. The palaces seem to be without a fixed architectural plan; rooms and gardens are simply laid out according to daily needs. The historian offers an astounding amount of detailed reports and facts but with no unifying concept. The Muslim writer prefers this carpet-like form; he adds colour to colour, motif to motif, so that the reader only understands the meaning and end of the whole web from a certain distance. Music, differentiated as it may be in the countries between Morocco and India, follows the same model: variations of highest subtlety on a comparatively simple given subject or theme.

Man, a puppet; God, the only actor

Drama and opera never developed in the Islāmic countries; and the art of the novel is a very recent development. There was no reason for drama: God is the only actor who can do whatever he pleases, whose will is inscrutable. Man is, at best, a puppet on a string, behind whose movement those with insight detect the hand of the play master; neither is the problem of personal guilt and absolution posed as it is in the West, nor is a catharsis, or purging of emotion needed through drama. The atomist theory, widely accepted in Islām since the 10th century, leaves no room for a "dramatic" movement; it teaches that God creates everything anew in every moment, and what is called a "law of nature" is nothing but God's custom, which he can interrupt whenever he pleases. The theological and philosophical view that the smallest units, added together in the end, will form a certain unity is reflected in the different arts—painting, music, and literature. But such a world-view does not allow of a drama in the Western sense.

It is true that certain other forms are found in the more folkloristic arts of Islām. Every region has produced poetry, in regional languages, that is more lively and more realistic than the classical court poetry; but such poetry tends to become restricted to certain fixed forms that can be easily imitated. The only attempts at drama in Islām come from these more popular spheres in Iran, where the tragic events of the murder of Ḥusayn (680) at Karbalā' were dramatized in strange forms, using the vocabulary and machinery of traditional Persian poetry and theology. Thus, strangely hybrid forms emerge in the Islāmic arts, highly interesting for the historian of religion and the student of literature but not typical of the classical Islāmic ideals. Popular illustrations of tales and legends and those of some of the Shīʿah heroes are similarly interesting but atypical. In modern times, of course, there have been imitations of all forms of Western literary and visual arts: paintings in the Impressionist or Cubist style, the use of free verse instead of the stern classical forms; and novels, dramas, and music combining Western and Eastern modes. Belief in the Qur'ānic dictum "Whatever is on earth will perish save His face" discouraged artistic endeavour on a large scale; but the Prophetic tradition "Verily God is beautiful and loves beauty" has inspired numberless artists and artisans, writers and poets, musicians, and mystics to develop their arts and crafts as a reflection of that divine beauty. A theory of aesthetics comprising the various artistic expressions of the Muslim peoples has yet to be written. Although there have been a number of studies in literary criticism, the formal indebtedness of some of the best modern poets and painters to the Islāmic heritage has never been studied in full.

In conclusion, it is notable that the arts of the Islāmic peoples have had relatively little impact on other cultures, certainly far less than their artistic merit would appear to warrant. While warmly admiring some manifestations of these arts, Europeans generally have regarded them with neither understanding nor appreciation and at times with outright hostility.

Islāmic art in the West

Europe has known art objects of Islāmic origin since the early Middle Ages, when they were brought home by the crusaders or manufactured by the Arabs in Sicily and Spain. Much admired and even imitated, they formed part of the material culture in those times, so much so that even the coronation robes of the German emperor were decorated with an Arabic inscription. At the same time, Islāmic motives wandered into the belles-lettres of Europe, and Islāmic scientific books formed a basis for the development of Western science. Islāmic culture as such, however, was rather an object of hatred than of admiration; a more objective appreciation of both the works of art and of literature did not start until the mid-17th century, when travellers told of the magnificent buildings in Iran and Mughal India, and the first works from Persian literature were translated, largely influencing German classical literature. Indian miniatures inspired Rembrandt, just as European paintings were imitated by Islāmic artists. Persian carpets were among the most coveted gifts for princes and princesses.

A bias against the cultures of the East persisted, however, until after the 18th-century Age of Enlightenment; the indefatigable work of the British scholars at Fort William at Calcutta brought new literary treasures to Europe, where they were studied carefully by specialists in the emerging field of Islāmic studies. Such poets as Goethe in Germany in the early 19th century paved the way for a deeper understanding of Islāmic poetry. Islāmic literatures, however, continue to be known to the larger Western public almost exclusively by *The Arabian Nights' Entertainment* (translated first in the early 18th century), Omar Khayyam's *Rubāʿīyāt*, and the lyrics of Ḥāfeẓ. Even experts who are aware of the immense wealth of the literatures in the different Islāmic languages (such as Arabic, Persian, Turkish, and Urdu) until now have rarely appreciated the literatures from an aesthetic viewpoint; rather, they have used them as a source for lexicography and for philological and historical research. The situation in Islāmic fine arts and architecture is similar. Although the beauty of the Alhambra, for example, had already inspired European scholars and artists in the early 19th century, a thorough study of Islāmic art as an independent field began only in the 20th century. There was even less interest in the music of the Islāmic peoples, the arabesque-like uniformity of which seems strange to Western ideals of harmony. (An.Sc.)

The article is divided into the following sections:

I. Islāmic literatures

NATURE AND SCOPE

It would be almost impossible to make an exhaustive survey of Islāmic literatures. There are so many works, of which hundreds of thousands are available only in manuscript, that even a very large team of scholars could scarcely master a single branch of the subject. Islāmic literatures, moreover, exist over a vast geographical and linguistic area, for they were produced wherever the Muslims went, pushing out from their heartland in Arabia through the countries of the Near and Middle East as far as Spain, North Africa, and, eventually, West Africa. Iran (Persia) is a major centre of Islām, along with the neighbouring areas that came under Persian influence, including Turkey and the Turkic-speaking peoples of Central Asia. Many Indian vernaculars contain almost exclusively Islāmic literary subjects; there is an Islāmic content in the literature of Malaysia and in that of some East African languages, including Swahili. In many cases, however, the Islāmic content proper is restricted to religious works—mystical treatises, books on Islāmic law and its implementation, historical works praising the heroic deeds and miraculous adventures of earlier Muslim rulers and saints, or devotional works in honour of the prophet Muḥammad.

The vast majority of Arabic writings are scholarly—the same, indeed, is true of the other languages under discussion. There are superb, historically important translations made by medieval scholars from Greek into Arabic; historical works, both general and particular; a range of religiously inspired works; books on grammar and on stylistics, on ethics and on philosophy. All have helped to shape the spirit of Islāmic literature in general, and it is often difficult to draw a line between such works of "scholarship" and works of "literature" in the narrower sense of that term. Even a strictly theological commentary can bring about a deeper understanding of some problem of aesthetics. A work of history composed in florid and "artistic" language would certainly be regarded by its author as a work of art as well as of scholarship, whereas the grammarian would be equally sure that his keen insights into the structure of Arabic grammar were of the utmost importance in preserving that literary beauty in which Arabs and non-Arabs alike took pride.

Pride in literary beauty

In this treatment of Islāmic literatures, however, the definition of "literature" is restricted to poetry and belles-lettres, whether popular or courtly in inspiration. Other categories of writing will be dealt with briefly if these shed light on some peculiar problem of literature.

The range of Islāmic literatures. Although Islāmic literatures appear in such a wide range of languages and in so many different cultural environments, their unity is safeguarded by the identity of the basic existential experience, by the identity of the fundamental intellectual interests, by the authoritativeness of certain principles of form and presentation, not to mention the kindred political and social organization within which those peoples aspire to live.

Arabic: language of the Qurʾān. The area of Islāmic culture extends from western Africa to Malaysia, Indonesia, and the Philippines; but its heartland is Arabia, and the prime importance and special authority of the Arabic language was to remain largely unquestioned after the spread of Islām. The Arabic poetry of pre-Islāmic Arabia was regarded for centuries afterward as the standard model for all Islāmic poetic achievement, and it directly influenced literary forms in many non-Arab literatures. The Qurʾān, Islām's sacred scripture, was accepted by pious Muslims as God's uncreated word and was considered to be the highest manifestation of literary beauty. A whole literature defended its inimitability (*iʿjāz*) and unsurpassable beauty. Because it was God's own word, the Qurʾān could not legitimately be translated into any other language; the study of at least some Arabic was therefore required of every Muslim. Arabic script was used by all those peoples who followed Islām, however much their own languages might differ in structure from Arabic. The Qurʾān became the textbook of the Muslims' entire philosophy of life; theology, lexicography, geography, historiography, and mysticism all grew out of a deep study of its form and content; and even in the most secular works there can be found allusions to the holy book. Its imagery not unexpectedly permeates all Islāmic poetry and prose.

Allusions to the Qurʾān in all literary genres

Between the coming of Islām in the 7th century and the 11th, a great deal of poetry and prose in Arabic was produced. One branch of literature in Spain and North Africa matured in perfect harmony with the classical ideals of the Muslim East although its masters, during the 11th and 12th centuries, invented a few strophic forms unknown to classical Arabic poetry. In modern times, North African Muslim literature—mainly from Algeria and Morocco—often uses French as a means of expression, since the tradition of Arabic writing was interrupted by the French occupation in the 19th century and has had to be built up afresh.

Persian. In 641 the Muslims entered Iran, and Persian influence on literary taste becomes apparent in Arabic literature from the mid-8th century onward. Many stories and tales were transmitted from, or through, Iran to the Arab world, and often from there to western Europe. Soon Iran could boast a large literature in its own tongue. Persian literature was more varied in its forms and content than that written in classical Arabic. Although Persian adopted many of the formal rules of the Arabic language (including prosody and rhyme patterns), new genres, including epic poetry, were introduced from Iran. The lyric, elegant and supple, also reached its finest expression in the Persian language.

South Asian. Persian culture was by no means restricted to Iran itself. Northwestern India and what is now Pakistan, became a centre of Islāmic literature as early as the 11th century, with Delhi and Agra being of special importance. It was to remain a stronghold of Muslim cultural life, which soon also extended to the east (Bengal) and south (Deccan). Persian remained the official language of Muslim India until 1835, and not only its poetry but even its historiography was written in the high-flown manner that exemplified the Persian concept of fine style. Muslim India can further boast a fine heritage of Arabic poetry and prose (theological, philosophical, and mystical works).

At various times in its history the Indian subcontinent was ruled by princes of Turkish origin (indeed, the words

"Turk" and "Muslim" became synonymous in some Indian languages). The princes surrounded themselves with a military aristocracy of mainly Turkish extraction, and thus a few poetical and prose works in Turkish were written at some Indian courts. In various regions of the subcontinent an extremely pleasing folk literature has flourished throughout the ages: Sindhi in the lower Indus Valley, for example, and Punjabi in the Punjab, are languages rich in an emotional poetry that uses popular metres and forms. At the Indo-Iranian border the oldest fragments of the powerful Pashto poetry date from the Middle Ages. The neighbouring Baluchi poetry consists largely of ballads and religious folksongs. All the peoples in this area have interpreted Islāmic mysticism in their own simple, touching imagery. In the east of the subcontinent, Bengali Muslims possess a large Islāmic literary heritage, including religious epics from the 14th and 15th centuries and some lovely religious folksongs. The achievements of modern novelists and lyric poets from Bangladesh are impressive. To the north, where Islām came in the 14th century, a number of classical themes in Islāmic lore were elaborated in Kashmiri lyric and epic poetry. To the south, an occasional piece of Islāmic religious poetry can be found even in Tamil.

Islāmic mystical thought in folk literature

Urdu, now the chief literary language of Muslim India and Pakistan, borrowed heavily from Persian literature during its classical period in the 18th century. In many writings only the verbs are in Urdu, the rest consisting of Persian constructions and vocabulary; and the themes of traditional Urdu literature were often adapted from Persian. Modern Urdu prose, however, has freed itself almost completely from the past, whereas in poetry promising steps have been taken toward modernization of both forms and content (see SOUTH ASIAN PEOPLES, ARTS OF).

Turkish. An elaborate "classical" style developed in Turkish after the 14th century, reaching its peak in the 17th. Like classical Urdu, it was heavily influenced by Persian in metrics and vocabulary. Many exponents of this "high" style came from the Balkan provinces of the Ottoman Empire. On the other hand, a rich and moving folk poetry in popular syllable-counting metres has always flourished among the Turkish population of Anatolia and Rumelia. The mystical hymns of their poet Yunus Emre (died *c.* 1321) contributed greatly toward shaping this body of literature, which was preserved in the religious centres of the Ṣūfī orders of Islām. From this folk tradition, as well as from Western literature, modern Turkish literature has derived a great deal of its inspiration.

Turkic languages. A great deal of the Muslim literature of Central Asia is written in Turkic languages, which include Uzbek, Tatar, and Kirgiz. Its main cultural centres (Samarkand, Bukhara, Fergana) became part of the Muslim empire after 711. Central Asia was an important centre of Islāmic learning until the Tsarist invasions in the 1870s, and the peoples of this region have produced a classical literature in Arabic. Many of the most famous Arabic and Persian scholars and poets writing in the heyday of Muslim influence were Central Asians by birth. Central Asians also possess a considerable literature of their own, consisting in large part of epics, folktales, and mystical "words of wisdom." The rules of prosody which hold for Arabic and Persian languages have been deliberately imposed on the Turkic languages on several occasions, notably by ʿAlī Shīr Navāʾī (died 1501), a master of Chagatai poetry and prose in Herāt, and by Bābur (died 1530), the first Mughal emperor in India. Tadzhik literature is basically Persian, both as it is written today in the Tadzhik Soviet Socialist Republic and as it existed in earlier forms, when it was indistinguishable from classical Persian. After the russification of the country, and especially after the 1917 Revolution, a new literature emerged that is part and parcel of the Soviet Union's literature. The same can be said, by and large, about the literatures of other Muslim Turkic peoples of Central Asia (see CENTRAL ASIAN PEOPLES, ARTS OF).

Other languages. Smaller fragments of Islāmic literature, in Chinese, are found in China (which has quite a large Muslim population) and in the Philippines. The literary traditions of Indonesia and of Malaysia, where the religion of Islām came long ago, are also worth noting. Historical and semi-mythical tales about Islāmic heroes are a feature of the literature in these areas, a fact of immense interest to folklorists.

Contact with Islām and its "written" culture also helped to preserve national idioms in many regions. Often such idioms were enriched by Arabic vocabulary and Islāmic concepts. The leaders of the Muslims in such areas in northern Nigeria, for example, preferred to write poetry and chronicles in Arabic, while using their mother tongue for more popular forms of literature (see AFRICAN PEOPLES, ARTS OF). Of particular interest in this connection is Kurdish literature, which has preserved in an Iranian language several important, popular heterodox texts and epics.

Islāmic literatures and the West. Small fragments of Arabic literature have long been known in the West. There were cultural interrelations between Muslim Spain (which, like the Indus Valley, became part of the Muslim empire after 711) and its Christian neighbours, and this meant that many philosophical and scientific works filtered through to western Europe. It is also likely that the poetry of Muslim Spain influenced the growth of certain forms of Spanish and French troubadour poetry and provided an element, however distorted, for medieval Western romances and heroic tales.

First Western studies

Investigation of Oriental literatures by Western scholars did not begin until the 16th century in the Netherlands and England. First attempts toward an aesthetic understanding of Arabic and Persian poetry came even later: they were made by the British Orientalists of Fort William, Calcutta, and by German pre-Romantics of the late 18th century. In the first half of the 19th century the publication of numerous translations of Oriental poetry, especially into German, began to interest some Europeans. The poetical translations from Arabic, Persian, and Sanskrit made by the German Orientalist and poet Friedrich Rückert (died 1866) can scarcely be surpassed, either in accuracy or in poetical mastery. The Persian poet Ḥāfeẓ became well-known in German-speaking countries, thanks to Johann Wolfgang von Goethe's enchanting poems, *West-östlicher Divan* (1819), a collection which was the first response to Persian poetry and the first aesthetic appreciation of the character of Oriental poetry by an acknowledged giant of European literature. An "Orientalizing style," which employed Arabo-Persian literary forms such as the *ghazal* (a short, graceful poem with monorhyme), became fashionable at times in Germany. Later, Edward Fitzgerald aroused new interest in Persian poetry with his free adaptations of Omar Khayyam's *Robāʿīyāt* (1859). The fairy tales known as *The Arabian Nights' Entertainment*, first translated in 1704, provided abundant raw material for many a Western writer's play, novel, story, or poem about the Islāmic East.

EXTERNAL CHARACTERISTICS

In order to understand and enjoy Oriental literature, the external characteristics of it have to be studied most carefully. The literatures of the Islāmic peoples are "intellectual"; in neither poetry nor prose are there many examples of subjective lyricism, as it is understood in the West. The principal genres, forms, and rules were inherited from pre-Islāmic Arabic poetry but were substantially elaborated afterward, especially by the Persians.

Rhyme and metre. Arabic poetry is built upon the principle of monorhyme, and the single rhyme is employed throughout every poem, long or short. The structure of Arabic permits such monorhymes to be achieved with comparative ease. The Persians and their imitators often extended the rhyming part over two or more syllables (*radīf*) or groups of words, which are repeated after the dominant rhyming consonant. The metres are quantitative, counting long and short syllables (*ʿarūḍ*). Classical Arabic has 16 basic metres in five groupings; they can undergo certain variations, but the poet is not allowed to change the metre in the course of his poem.

Syllable-counting metres, as well as strophic forms, are used in popular, or "low," poetry; only in post-classical Arabic were some strophic forms introduced into "high" poetry. Many modern Islāmic poets, from Pakistan to Turkey and North Africa, have discarded the classical system of prosody altogether. In part they have substituted verse forms imitating Western models such as strophic poems with or without rhyme; since about 1950 free verse has almost become the rule, although a certain tendency toward rhyming or to the use of alliterative quasi-rhymes can be observed.

Genres. The chief poetic genres, as they emerged according to traditional rules, are the *qaṣīdah*, the *ghazal*, and the *qiṭʿah;* in Iran and its adjacent countries there are, further, the *robāʿī* and the *mas̄navī*.

Qaṣīdah. The *qaṣīdah* (literally "purpose poem"), a genre whose form was invented by pre-Islāmic Arabs, has from 20 to more than 100 verses and usually contains an account of the poet's journey. In the classic pattern, the parts followed a fixed sequence, beginning with a love-poem prologue (*nasīb*), followed by a description of the journey itself, and finally reaching its real goal by flattering the poet's patron, sharply attacking some adversaries of his tribe, or else indulging in measureless self-praise. Everywhere in the Muslim world the *qaṣīdah* became the characteristic form for panegyric. It could serve for religious purposes as well: solemn praise of God, eulogies of the Prophet, and songs of praise and lament for the martyr heroes of Shīʿah Islām were all expressed in this form. Later, the introductory part of the *qaṣīdah* was taken up by a description of nature or given over to some words of wisdom; or the poet took the opportunity to demonstrate his skill in handling extravagant language and to show off his learning. Such exhibitions were made all the more difficult because, though it varied according to the rank of the person to whom it was addressed, the vocabulary of each type of *qaṣīdah* was controlled by rigid conventions. This type of poetry, however, could obviously lend itself easily to empty verbosity or to pedantry.

The love poem

Ghazal. The *ghazal* possibly originated as an independent elaboration of the *qaṣīdah*'s introductory section, and it usually embodies a love poem. Ideally, its length varies between five and 12 verses. It can be used either for religious or secular expression, the two often being blended indistinguishably. Its diction is light and graceful, its effect comparable to that of chamber music, whereas the *qaṣīdah*-writer employs, so to speak, the full orchestral resources.

Qiṭʿah. Monorhyme is used in both the *qaṣīdah* and *ghazal.* But while these two forms begin with two rhyming hemistiches (half-lines of a verse), in the *qiṭʿah* ("section") the first hemistich does not rhyme, and the effect is as though the poem had been "cut out" of a longer one (hence its name). The *qiṭʿah* is a less serious literary form that was used to deal with aspects of everyday life; it served mainly for occasional poems, satire, jokes, word games, and codes.

Robāʿī. The form of the *robāʿī*, which is a quatrain in fixed metre with a rhyme scheme of *a a b a*, goes back to pre-Islāmic Persian poetical tradition. It has supplied the Persian poets with a flexible vehicle for ingenious aphorisms and similarly concise expressions of thought for religious, erotic, or skeptical purposes. The peoples who came under Persian cultural influence happily adopted this form.

Mas̄navī. Epic poetry was unknown to the Arabs, who were averse to fiction, whether it was expressed in poetry or in prose. The development of epic poetry was thus hindered, just as was the creation of novels or short stories. Nevertheless, *mas̄navī*—which means literally "the doubled one," or rhyming couplet, and by extension a poem consisting of a series of such couplets—became a favourite poetical form of the Persians and those cultures they influenced. The *mas̄navī* enabled the poet to develop the thread of a tale through thousands of verses. Yet even in such poetry, only a restricted number of metres was employed. Metre and diction were prescribed in accordance with the topic; a didactic *mas̄navī* required a style and metre different from a heroic or romantic one. The *mas̄navī* usually begins with a praise of God, and this strikes the keynote of the poem.

Other poetic forms. There is a variety of other forms that are more or less restricted to folk poetry, such as the *sīharfī* ("Golden Alphabet"), in which each line or each stanza begins with succeeding letters of the Arabic alphabet. In Muslim India the *bārāmāh* ("Twelve Months") is a sort of lovers' calendar in which the poet's feelings are expressed in accord with the seasons of the year. Apart from these, later writers tried to develop strophic forms. Sometimes *ghazals* with the same metre were bound together as "stanzas" to form a longer unit through the use of a linking verse. When the linking verse was recurrent, the poem was called a *tarjīʿ-band* (literally "return-tie"); when the linking verse was varied, the poem was called a *tarkīb-band* (literally "composite-tie"). True stanzas of varying lengths were also invented. Among these, mainly in Urdu and Turkish, a six-line stanza known as *musaddas* became the form used for the *mars̄īyeh* (dirge for the martyrs of Karbalāʾ) and later was used for the first socially committed modern poems.

Rhyming prose

The Arabs inherited a love for rhymed prose from pre-Islāmic Arabia. Although the extent of prose literature, even in the field of belles-lettres, is very large, the novel and novella were introduced only after contact with European literatures.

Maqāmah. The most typical expression of the Arabic —and Islāmic—spirit in prose is the *maqāmah* (gathering, assembly), which tells basically simple stories in an extremely and marvellously complicated style (abounding in word plays, logographs, *double entendre*, and the like) and which comes closest to the Western concept of the short story.

The versatility and erudition of the classical *maqāmah* authors is dazzling, but the fables and parables which, during the first centuries of Islām, had been told in a comparatively easy flowing style, later became subject to a growing trend toward artificiality, as did almost every other literary genre, including expository prose. Persian historiographers and Turkish biographers, Indo-Muslim writers on mysticism and even on science all indulged in a style in which rhyme and rhetoric often completely obscured the meaning. It is only since the late 19th century that a matter-of-fact style has slowly become acceptable in literary circles; the influence of translations from European languages, the role of journalism, and the growing pride in a pure language, freed from the cobwebs of the past, worked together to make Islāmic languages more pliable and less artificial.

Imagery. In all forms of poetry and in most types of prose, writers shared a common fund of imagery that was gradually refined and enlarged in the course of time. The main source of imagery was the Qurʾān, its figures and utterances often divested of their sacred significance. Thus, the beautiful Joseph (*sūrah* 12) is a fitting symbol for the handsome beloved; the nightingale may sing the psalms of David (*sūrah* 21:79 *a.o*); the rose sits on Solomon's wind-borne throne (*sūrah* 21:81 *a.o*), and its opening petals can be compared to Joseph's shirt rent by Potiphar's wife (*sūrah* 12:25 ff.), its scent to that of Joseph's shirt, which cured blind Jacob (*sūrah* 12:94). The tulip reminds the poet of the burning bush before which Moses stood (*sūrah* 20:9 ff.), and the coy beloved refuses the lover's demands by answering, like God to Moses, "Thou shalt not see me" (*sūrah* 7:143); but her (or his) kiss gives the dying lover new life, like the breath of Jesus (*sūrah* 3:49). Classical Persian poetry often mentions knights and kings from Iran's history alongside those from Arabic heroic tales. The cup of wine offered by the "old man of the Magians" is comparable to the miraculous cup owned by the Iranian mythical king Jamshīd or to Alexander's mirror, which showed the marvels of the world; the nightingale may sing "Zoroastrian tunes" when it contemplates the "fire temple to the rose." Central scenes from the great Persian *mas̄navī*s contributed to the imagery of later writers in Persian-, Turkish-, and Urdu-speaking areas. Social and political conditions are reflected in a favourite literary equation between the "beautiful and cruel beloved" and "the Turk": since in Iran and India the military caste was usually of Turkish origin, and since the Turk was always considered "white" and handsome, in literary imagery he stood as the "ruler of hearts." Minute arabesque-like descriptions of nature, particularly of garden scenes, are frequent: the rose and the nightingale have almost become substitutes for mythological figures. The versatile writer was expected to introduce elegant allusions to classical Arabic and Persian literature and to folklore and to know enough about astrology, alchemy, and medicine to use the relevant technical terms accurately. Images inspired by the pastimes of the grandees—chess, polo, hunting, and the like—were as necessary for a good poem as were those referring to music, painting, and calligraphy. Similarly, allusions in poetic imagery to the Arabic letters—often thought to be endowed with mystical significance or magical properties—were very common in all Islāmic literatures. The poet had to follow strict rules laid down by the masters of rhetoric, rigidly observing the harmonious selection of similes thought proper to any one given sphere (four allusions to Qur'ānic figures, for example; or three garden images all given in a single verse). The poet was expected to invent new fantastic etiologies (*ḥosn-e taʿlīl*): he had to describe natural phenomena in some elegant and surprising metaphor. Thus, "The narcissus has strewn silver in the way of the bride rose . . ." means simply "The narcissus has withered"—for when the rose (dressed in red, like an Oriental bride) appears in late spring it is time for the narcissus to "shed" its white petals, just as people would "shed" silver coins in the way of a bridal procession.

Qualities expected of the versatile writer

Skills required of the writer. The writer was also expected to use puns and to play with words of two or more meanings. He might write verses that could provide an intelligible meaning even when read backward. He had to be able to handle chronograms, codes based on the numerical values of a phrase or verse, which, when understood, gave the date of some relevant event. Later writers sometimes supplied the date of a book's compilation by hiding a chronogram in its title. A favourite device in poetry was the "question and answer" form, employed in the whole poem, or only in chosen sections.

One was expected to show his talent at both improvisation and elaboration on any theme if he wished to attract the interest of a generous patron. His poetry was judged according to the perfection of its individual verses. Only in rare cases was the poem appreciated as a whole: the lack of coherent argument, which often puzzles the Western reader in *ghazal* poetry, is in fact deliberate.

It would be idle to look for the sincere expression of personal emotion in Arabic, Turkish, or Persian poetry. The conventions are so rigid that the reader is allowed only a rare glimpse into the poet's feelings. Indeed, such feelings were put through the sieve of intellect, and personal experiences were thereby transformed into arabesque-like work of artistry, if not art. In the hands of mediocre versifiers and prose writers, however, literature became mannered and completely artificial. The reader soon tires of the constantly recurring moon faces, hyacinth curls, ruby lips, and cypress statures (that is, tall and slender). Yet the great masters of poetry and rhetoric (who all have their favourite imagery, rhymes, and rhythmical patterns) will sometimes allow the patient reader a glimpse into their hearts by a slight rhythmical change or by a new way of expressing a conventional thought.

These are, of course, quite crude generalizations. Folk poetry, for instance, has to be judged by different standards, though even here conventional forms and inherited imagery make it, on the whole, more standardized than might be wished. Only in the 20th century has a complete break with classical ideals been made—sincerity instead of monotonous imitation, political and social commitment instead of empty panegyric, realism instead of escapism: these are the characteristic features of modern literatures of the Muslim countries.

HISTORICAL DEVELOPMENTS: PRE-ISLAMIC LITERATURE

The first known poetic composition of the Arabs are of such perfect beauty and, at the same time, are so conventionalized, that they raise the question as to how far back an actual poetic tradition does stretch. A great number of pre-Islāmic poems, dating from the mid-6th century, were preserved by oral tradition. The seven most famous pieces are *al-Muʿallaqāt*, ("The Suspended Ones," known as *The Seven Odes*), and these are discussed more fully below. The term *muʿallaqāt* is not fully understood: later legend asserts that the seven poems had been hung in the most important Arab religious sanctuary, the Kaʿbah in Mecca, because of their eloquence and beauty, which had brought victory to their authors in the poetical contests traditionally held during the season of pilgrimage. Apart from these seven, quite a number of shorter poems were preserved by later scholars. An independent genre in pre-Islāmic poetry was the elegy, often composed by a woman, usually a deceased hero's sister. Some of these poems, especially those by the poetess al-Khansā' (died after 630) are notable for their compact expressiveness.

The first poetry

Poetry. The poet (called a *shāʿir*, a wizard endowed with magic powers) was thought to be inspired by a spirit (*jinn, shayṭān*). The poet defended the honour of his tribe, perpetuated their deeds, and "his menaces were inevitably fatal, his rhymes dreaded like arrows." Religious expression was rare in pre-Islāmic poetry. In the main it reflects the sense of fatalism that was probably needed if the harsh circumstances of Bedouin life in the desert were to be endured.

The most striking feature of pre-Islāmic poetry is the uniformity and refinement of its language. Although the various tribes, constantly feuding with one another, all spoke their own dialects they shared a common language for poetry, whether they were Bedouins or inhabitants of the small capitals of al-Ḥīrah and Ghassān (where the influence of Aramaic culture was also in evidence).

Arabic was even then a virile and expressive language, with dozens of synonyms for the horse, the camel, the lion, and so forth; and it possessed a rich stock of descriptive adjectives. Because of these features, it is difficult for foreigners and modern Arabs alike to appreciate fully the artistic qualities of early Arabic poetry. Imagery is precise, and descriptions of natural phenomena are detailed. The sense of universal applicability is lacking, however, and the comparatively simple literary techniques of simile and metaphor predominate. The imaginative power that was later to be the hallmark of Arabic poetry under Persian influence had not yet become evident.

The virility of Arabic

The strikingly rich vocabulary of classical Arabic, as well as its sophisticated structure, is matched by highly elaborate metrical schemes, based on quantity. The rhythmical structures were analyzed by the grammarian Khalīl of Basra (died *c.* 791), who distinguished 16 metres. Each was capable of variation by shortening the foot or part of it; but the basic structure was rigidly preserved. One and the same rhyme letter had to be maintained throughout the poem. (The rules of rhyming are detailed and very complicated but were followed quite strictly from the 6th to the early 20th century.)

As well as rules governing the outward form of poetry, a system of poetic imagery already existed by this early period. The sequence of a poem, moreover, followed a fixed pattern (such as that for the *qaṣīdah*). Pre-Islāmic poetry was not written down but recited; and therefore sound and rhythm played an important part in its formation, and the *rāwī*s (reciters) were equally vital to its preservation. A *rāwī* was associated with some famous bard and, having learned his master's techniques, might afterward become a poet himself. This kind of apprenticeship to a master whose poetic style was thus continued became a common practice in the Muslim world (especially in Muslim India) right up to the 19th century.

From pre-Islāmic times the seven authors of *The Seven Odes*, already described, are usually singled out for special praise. Their poems and miscellaneous verses were collected during the 8th century and ever since have been the subject of numerous commentaries in the East. They have been studied in Europe since the early 19th century.

The seven authors of *The Seven Odes*

The poet Imru' al-Qays (died *c.* AD 550), of the tribe of Kindah, was foremost both in time and in poetic merit.

He was a master of love poetry; his frank descriptions of dalliance with his mistresses are considered so seductive that (as orthodox Puritanism claims) the Prophet Muḥammad called him "the leader of poets on the way to Hell." His style is supple and picturesque. It grips the attention whether his poems sing of his love adventures or describe a seemingly endless rainy night. Of all classical Arabic poets he is probably the one who appeals most to modern taste. At the other extreme stands Zuhayr, praising the chiefs of the rival tribes of ʿAbs and Dhubyān for ending a long feud. He is chiefly remembered for his serious *qaṣīdah* in which, old, wise, and experienced, he meditates upon the terrible escalation of war. Various aspects of Bedouin life, as well as the attitude of the Arabs to the rulers of the small kingdom of al-Ḥīrah on the Euphrates, are reflected in the poems of Nābighah, ʿAmr, and Ṭarafah. The boastful pride of the self-centred Arab warrior can be observed best in the poems of al-Ḥārith, who became proverbial for his arrogance. ʿAntarah, son of a black slave girl, won such fame on the battlefield and for his poetry that he later became the hero of an Arabic folk romance.

Three other masters can stand beside these seven. Exciting for their savagery and beauty are some poems by Taʾabbaṭa Sharran and Shanfarā, both outlaw warriors. Their verses reveal the wildness of Bedouin life, with its ideals of bravery, revenge, and hospitality. Taʾabbaṭa Sharran is the author of a widely translated "Song of Revenge" (for his uncle), composed in a short, sharp metre. Shanfarā's *lāmīyah* (literally "poem rhyming in l") vividly, succinctly, and with a wealth of detail, tells of the experiences to be had from life in the desert. This latter poem has sometimes been considered a forgery, created by a learned grammarian. The suggestion highlights the question, often posed, of how much pre-Islāmic poetry is genuine and how much is the product of later scholars. Some modern critics—without proper justification—would dismiss the entire *corpus* as counterfeit.

Prose. While poetry forms the most important part of early Arabic literature and is an effective historical preservation of the Arabs' past glory, there is also a quantity of prose. Of special interest is the rhymed prose (*sajʿ*) peculiar to soothsayers, which developed into an important form of ornate prose writing in every Islāmic country. Tales about the adventures and battle days of the various tribes (*ayyām al-ʿArab*, or "The Days of the Arabs") were told and handed down from generation to generation, usually interspersed with pieces of poetry. Proverbs and proverbial sayings were as common as in most cultures at a comparable level of development. The "literary" genre most typical of Bedouin life is the *musāmarah*, or "nighttime conversation," in which the central subject is elaborated not by plot but by carrying the listener's mind from topic to topic through verbal associations. Thus, the language as language played a most important role. The *musāmarah* form inspired the later *maqāmah* literature.

The *musāmarah:* "nighttime conversation"

It has been said—and this certainly holds true for the *musāmarah*—that Arabic literature demands attention from its listeners only in short bursts; for listeners are carried from verse to verse, from anecdote to anecdote, from pun to pun, along a theme whose broad outline is entirely familiar. Western Orientalists have for this reason spoken of the "molecular," or "atomic," structure both of classical Arabic literature and of traditional Islāmic thought. An audience listening to one of the ancient bards—or to a modern poet or orator in the Muslim world—would be able to listen without tiring. The sheer emotive power of the Arabic language to enrapture and bewitch its listeners by sound alone should be kept in mind when considering any piece of Arabic literature. Only a people endowed with peculiar sensibility to the word could properly appreciate the refinement of pre-Islāmic poetry and be ready to accept the concept of divine revelation appearing through the word in the Qurʾān.

EARLY ISLAMIC LITERATURE

With the coming of Islām the attitude of the Arabs toward poetry seems to have changed. The new Muslims, despite their long-standing admiration for powerful language, often shunned poetry as reminiscent of pagan ideals now overthrown. For the Qurʾān, in *sūrah* 26:225 ff., condemned the poets "who err in every valley, and say what they do not do. Only the perverse follow them!" The Qurʾān, as the uncreated word of God, was now considered the supreme manifestation of literary beauty. It became the basis and touchstone of almost every cultural and literary activity and attained a unique position in Arabic literature.

Age of the caliphs. It might be expected that a new and vigorous religion would stimulate a new religious literature to sing of its greatness and glory. This, however, was not the case. Maybe the once boastful poets felt, at least for a while, that they were nothing but humble servants of Allāh. At any rate, no major poet was inspired by the birth and astonishingly rapid expansion of Islām. Only much later did poets claim that their work was the "heritage of prophecy" or draw upon a tradition that calls the tongues of the poets "the keys of the treasures beneath the Divine Throne." The old, traditional literary models were still faithfully followed: a famous ode by Kaʿb, the son of Zuhayr, is different from pre-Islāmic poetry only insofar as it ends in praise of the Prophet, imploring his forgiveness, instead of eulogizing some Bedouin leader. Muḥammad's rather mediocre eulogist, Ḥassān ibn Thābit (died *c.* 659), also slavishly repeated the traditional patterns (even including the praise of wine that had been such a common feature of pre-Islāmic poetry at the court of al-Ḥīrah, despite the fact that wine had been by then religiously prohibited).

Influence of pre-Islāmic poetry

Religious themes are to be found in the *khuṭbahs*, or Friday sermons, which were delivered by governors of the provinces. In these, however, political considerations often overshadow the religious and literary aspects. The *quṣṣāṣ* (storytellers), who interpreted verses from the Qurʾān, attracted large audiences and may be regarded as the inventors of a popular religious prose. Their interpretations were highly fanciful, however, and hardly squared with the theologian's orthodoxy.

The desire to preserve words of wisdom is best reflected in the sayings attributed to ʿAlī, the fourth caliph (died 661). These, however, were written down, in superbly concise diction, only in the 10th century under the title *Nahj al-balāghah* ("The Road of Eloquence"), a work that is a masterpiece of the finest Arabic prose and that has inspired numerous commentaries and poetical variations in the various Islāmic languages.

Umayyad dynasty. The time of the "Four Righteous Caliphs," as it is called, ended with ʿAlī's assassination in 661. The Umayyad dynasty then gained the throne, and a new impetus in poetry soon became perceptible. The Umayyads were by no means a pious dynasty, much enjoying the pleasures of life in their residence in Damascus and in their luxurious castles in the Syrian desert. One of their last rulers, the profligate al-Walīd ibn Yazīd (died 744), has become famous not so much as a conqueror (although in 711 the Muslims reached the lower Indus basin, Transoxania, and Spain) but as a poet who excelled in frivolous love verses and poetry in praise of wine. He was fond of short, light metres to match his subjects and rejected the heavier metres preferred by *qaṣīdah* writers. His verses convey a sense of ease and gracious living. Al-Walīd was not, however, the first to attempt this kind of poetry: a remarkable poet from Mecca, ʿUmar ibn Abī Rabīʿah (died *c.* 712 or 720) had contributed in large measure to the separate development of the love poem (*ghazal*) from its subordinate place as the opening section of the *qaṣīdah*. Gentle and charming, in attractive and lively rhythms, his poems sing of amorous adventures with the ladies who came to Mecca on pilgrimage. His gay, melodious poems still appeal to modern readers.

In Medina, on the other hand, idealized love poetry was the vogue; its invention is attributed to Jamīl (died 701), of the tribe ʿUdhrah, "whose members die when they love." The names of some of these "martyrs of love," together with the names of their lovers, were preserved and eventually became proverbial expressions of the tremen-

The love poets of Medina

dous force of true love. Such was Qays, who went mad because of his passion for Laylā, and was afterward known as Majnūn (the Demented One). His story is cherished by later Persian, Turkish, and Urdu poets; as a symbol of complete surrender to the force of love, he is dear both to religious mystics and to secular poets.

Notwithstanding such new developments, the traditional *qaṣīdah* form of poetry was by no means neglected during the Umayyad period. Moreover, as the satirists of Iraq rose to fame, the *naqā'iḍ* ("polemic poetry matches") between Jarīr (died *c.* 729) and al-Farazdaq (died *c.* 728 or 730) excited and delighted tribesmen of the rival settlements of Basra and Kūfah (places that later also became rival centres of philological and theological schools). The work of these two poets has furnished critics and historians with rich material for a study of the political and social situation in the early 9th century. The wealth of al-Farazdaq's vocabulary led one of the old Arabic critics to declare: "If Farazdaq's poetry did not exist, one-third of the Arabic language would be lost." Philologists, eager to preserve as much of the classical linguistic heritage as possible, have also paid a great deal of attention to the largely satirical poetry of al-Ḥuṭay'ah (died 674). The fact that Christians as well as Muslims were involved in composing classical Arabic poetry is proved by the case of al-Akhṭal (died *c.* 710), whose work preserves the pre-Islāmic tradition of al-Ḥīrah in authentic form. He is particularly noted for his wine songs. Christians and Jews had been included among the pre-Islāmic poets.

Prose literature was still restricted to religious writing. The traditions of the Prophet began to be compiled, and, after careful sifting, those regarded as trustworthy were preserved in six great collections during the late 9th century. Two of these—that of al-Bukhārī and that of Muslim—were considered second only to the Qur'an in religious importance. The first studies of religious law and legal problems, closely connected with the study of the Qur'ān, also belong to that very period.

The ʿAbbāsids. It was not until the ʿAbbāsids assumed power in 750, settling in Baghdad, that the golden age of Arabic literature began. The influx of foreign elements added new colour to cultural and literary life. Hellenistic thought and the influence of the ancient cultures of the Near East, for example, contributed to the rapid intellectual growth of the Muslim community. Its members, seized with insatiable intellectual curiosity, began to adapt elements from all the earlier high cultures and to incorporate them into their own. They thus created the wonderful fabric of Islāmic culture that was so much admired in the Middle Ages by Western Europe. Indian and Iranian threads were also woven into this fabric, and a new sensitivity to beauty in the field of poetry and the fine arts was cultivated.

The classical Bedouin style was still predominant in literature and was the major preoccupation of grammarians. These men were, as the modern critic Sir Hamilton Gibb has emphasized, the true humanists of Islām. Their efforts helped to standardize "High Arabic," giving it an unchangeable structure once and for all. By now the inhabitants of the growing towns in Iraq and Syria were beginning to express their love, hatred, religious fervour, and their frivolity in a style more appealing to their fellow townsmen. Poets no longer belonged exclusively to what had been the Bedouin aristocracy. Artisans and freed slaves, of non-Arab origin, were included among their number. Bashshār ibn Burd (died *c.* 784), the son of a Persian slave, was the first representative of the new style. This ugly, blind workman excelled as a seductive love poet and also as a biting satirist—"Nobody could be secure from the itch of his tongue," it was later said, and he added a new degree of expressiveness to the old forms. The category of *zuhdīyāt* (didactic-ascetic poems) was invented by a poet from Basra called Abū al-ʿAtāhīyah (died 825 or 826), whose pessimistic thoughts on the transitory nature of this world were uttered in an unpretentious kind of verse that rejected all current notions of style and technical finesse. He had turned to ascetic poetry after efforts at comprising love songs.

The same is said of Abū Nuwās (died *c.* 813), the most outstanding of the ʿAbbāsid poets. His witty and cynical verses are addressed mainly to handsome boys; best known are his scintillating drinking songs. His line "Accumulate as many sins as you can" seems to have been his motto; and compared with some of his more lascivious lines, the most daring passages of pre-Islāmic poetry sound chaste. Abū Nuwās had such an incomparable command over the language, however, that he came to be regarded as one of the greatest Arabic poets of all time. Nevertheless, orthodox Muslims would quote of him and of his imitators the Prophet's alleged saying that "poetry is what Satan has spit out," since he not only described subjects prohibited by religious law but praised them with carefree light-heartedness.

The works of Abū Nuwās

The "new" style. The new approach to poetry that developed during the 9th century was first accorded scholarly discussion in the *Kitāb al-badīʿ* ("Book of the Novel and Strange") by Ibn al-Muʿtazz (died 908), caliph for one day, who laid down rules for the use of metaphors, similes, and verbal puns. The ideal of these "modern" poets was the richest possible embellishment of verses by the use of tropes, brilliant figures of speech, and far-fetched poetic conceits. Many later handbooks of poetics discussed these rules in minute detail, and eventually the increasing use of rhetorical devices no longer produced art but artificiality. (Ibn al-Muʿtazz was himself a fine poet whose descriptions of courtly life and nature are lovely; he even tried to compose a tiny epic poem, a genre otherwise unknown to the Arabs.) The "modern" poets, sensitive to colours, sounds, and shapes, also were fond of writing short poems on unlikely subjects: a well-bred hunting dog or an inkpot; delicious sweetmeats or jaundice; the ascetic who constantly weeps when he remembers his sins; the luxurious garden parties of the rich. Their amusing approach, however, was sooner or later bound to lead to mannered compositions. The growing use of colour images may be credited to the increasing Persian influence upon ʿAbbāsid poetry; for the Persian poets were, as has been often observed, on the whole more disposed to visual than to acoustic imagery.

Tendency toward mannered writing

New attitudes toward love, too, were being gradually developed in poetry. Eventually, what was to become a classic theme, that of *ḥubb ʿudhrī* ("ʿUdhrah love")—the lover would rather die than achieve union with his beloved—was expounded by the Ẓāhirī theologian Ibn Dā'ūd (died 910) in his poetic anthology *Kitāb az-zahrah* ("Book of the Flower"). This theme was central to the *ghazal* poetry of the following centuries. Although at first completely secular, it was later taken over as a major concept in mystical love poetry. (The first examples of this adoption, in Iraq and Egypt, took place in Ibn Dā'ūd's lifetime.) The wish to die on the path that leads to the beloved became commonplace in Persian, Turkish, and Urdu poetry; and most romances in these languages end tragically. Ibn Dā'ūd's influence also spread to the western Islāmic world. A century after his death, the theologian Ibn Ḥazm (died 1064), drawing upon personal experiences, composed in Spain his famous work on "pure love" called *Ṭawq al-ḥamāmah* (*The Ring of the Dove*). Its lucid prose, interspersed with poetry, has many times been translated into Western languages.

The conflict between the traditional ideals of poetry and the "modern" school of the early ʿAbbāsid period also led to the growth of a literary criticism, the criteria of which were largely derived from the study of Greek philosophy.

Traditional poetry, meanwhile, was not neglected. But its style was somewhat modified in accordance with the new ideas. Two famous anthologies of Bedouin poetry, both called *Ḥamāsah*, ("Poems of Bravery"), were collected by the Syrian Abū Tammām (died 845 or 846) and his disciple al-Buḥturī (died 897), both good classical poets in their own right. They provide an excellent survey of those poems from the stock of early Arabic poetry that were considered worth preserving. A century later Abū al-Faraj al-Iṣbahānī (died 967), in a multi-volume work entitled *Kitāb al-aghānī* ("Book of Songs"), collected a number of poems and some biographical notes on poets and musicians. This material gives a colourful and valuable panorama of literary life in the first four centuries of Islām.

In the mid-10th century, a new cultural centre emerged at the small court of the Ḥamdānids in Aleppo. Here the Central Asian scholar al-Fārābī (died 950) wrote his fundamental works on philosophy and musical theory. Here, too, for a while, lived Abū aṭ-Ṭayyib al-Mutanabbī (died 965), who is in the mainstream of classical *qaṣīdah* writers but who surpasses them all in the extravagance of what has been called his "reckless audacity of imagination." He combined some elements of Iraqi and Syrian stylistics with classical ingredients. His compositions—panegyrics of rulers and succinct verses (which are still quoted)—have never ceased to intoxicate the Arabs by their daring hyperbole, their marvellous sound effects, and their formal perfection. The Western reader is unlikely to derive as much aesthetic pleasure from Mutanabbī's poetry as does one whose mother tongue is Arabic. He will probably prefer the delicate verses about gardens and flowers by Mutanabbī's colleague in Aleppo, aṣ-Ṣanawbarī (died 945), a classic exponent of the descriptive style. This style in time reached Spain, where the superb garden and landscape poetry of Ibn Khafājah (died 1139) displayed an even higher degree of elegance and sensitivity than that of his Eastern predecessors.

Mutanabbī's poetry

Before turning to the development of prose it is necessary to mention a figure unique among those writing in Arabic. This was Abū al-ʿAlāʾ al-Maʿarrī (died 1057), a blind poet of Syria, whose verses have appealed greatly to young Arabs of the present because of the poems' sincerity and humanity. But al-Maʿarrī's vocabulary is so difficult, his verses, with their double rhymes, are so compressed in meaning, that even his contemporaries, flocking to his lectures, had to ask him to interpret their significance. His outlook is deeply pessimistic and skeptical. Although his poems display a mastery of the Arabic traditional stylistic devices, they run counter to the conventional ideals of Arab heroism, by speaking of bitter disappointment and emphasizing asceticism, compassion, and avoidance of procreation.

> Taking reason for his guide he judges men and things with a freedom which must have seemed scandalous to the rulers and privileged classes of the day. Among his meditations on the human tragedy a fierce hatred of injustice, hypocrisy, and superstition blazes out. Vice and folly are laid bare in order that virtue and wisdom may be sought . . .

says Reynold A. Nicholson, al-Maʿarrī's foremost interpreter in the West, who has also translated his *Risālat al-ghufrān* ("Epistle of Pardon"), which describes a visit to the Otherworld. Maʿarrī's extremely erudite book also contains occasionally sarcastic criticism of Arabic literature. His *Al-Fuṣūl wa al-ghāyāt* ("Paragraphs and Periods") is an ironic commentary on man and nature but is presented as a sequence of pious exhortations in rhymed prose. It has scandalized the pious, some of whom see it as a parody of the Qurʾān. Maʿarrī's true intention in this book, which came to light only recently, is unknown.

Development of literary prose. During the ʿAbbāsid period, literary prose also began to develop. Ibn al-Muqaffaʿ (died *c.* 756), of Persian origin, translated the fables of Bidpai into Arabic under the title *Kalīlah wa Dimnah*. These fables provided Islāmic culture with a seemingly inexhaustible treasure of tales and parables, which are to be found in different guises throughout the whole of Muslim literature. He also introduced into Arabic the fictitious chronicles of the Persian *Khwatāy-nāmak* ("Book of Kings"). This was the source of a kind of pre-Islāmic mythology that the literati preferred above the somewhat meagre historical accounts of the Arab pagan past otherwise available to them. These activities demanded a smooth prose style, and Ibn al-Muqaffaʿ has therefore rightly been regarded as the inaugurator of what is called "secretarial literature" (that produced by secretaries in the official chancelleries). He also translated writings on ethics and the conduct of government, which helped to determine the rules of etiquette (*adab*). His works are the prototype of the "Mirror for Princes" literature, which flourished during the late Middle Ages both in Iran and in the West. In this literature, a legendary Persian counsellor, Bozorgmehr, was presented as a paragon of wise conduct. Later, stories were invented that combined Qurʾānic heroes with historical characters from the Iranian past.

A growing interest in things outside the limits of Bedouin life was reflected in a quantity of didactic yet entertaining prose by such masters as the broadminded and immensely learned al-Jāḥiẓ (died 869). In response to the wide ranging curiosity of urban society, the list of his subjects includes treatises on theology, on misers, on donkeys, and on thieves. His masterpiece is *Kitāb al-Ḥayawān* ("Book of Animals"), which has little to do with zoology but is a mine of information about Arab proverbs, traditions, superstitions, and the like. Al-Jāḥiẓ's style is vigorous, loquacious, and uninhibited. His work, however, is not well constructed, and it lacks the clear sobriety of the "secretarial style." Yet the glimpses it affords into the life of various strata of society during the 9th century have rightly attracted the special interest of Western scholars. Less impressive, but almost as multifaceted, are the treatises of Ibn Abī ad-Dunyā (died 894).

The work of al-Jāḥiẓ

The concept of *adab* was soon enlarged to include not only educational prose dealing with etiquette for all classes of people but *belles-lettres* in general. The classic example of Arabic style for prose writers in this field, accepted as such for almost a millennium, is the writing of the Persian Ibn Qutaybah (died 889). His *ʿUyūn al-akhbār* ("Fountains of Stories"), in 10 books, each dealing with a given subject, provided a model to which numberless essayists in the Muslim world conformed. In his book on poetry and poets, Ibn Qutaybah dared, for the first time, to doubt openly that pre-Islāmic poetry was incomparable. The most vigorous prose style was achieved by Abū Ḥayyān at-Tawḥīdī (died 1023), who portrayed the weaknesses of the two leading viziers, both notorious for their literary ambitions, ". . . with such bitterness," as Gibb remarks, "that the book was reputed to bring misfortune upon all who possessed a copy." This work, like others by Tawḥīdī that have quite recently been discovered, reveals the author's sagacity and striking eloquence. His correspondence on problems of philosophy with Miskawayh (died 1030), the author of a widely circulated book on ethics and of a general history, helps to complete the picture of this extraordinary writer.

Some time about 800 the Arabs had learned the art of papermaking from the Chinese. Henceforth, cheap writing material was available, and literary output was prodigious. The *Fihrist* ("Index"), compiled by the bookseller Ibn an-Nadīm in 988, gave a full account of the Arabic literature extant in the 10th century. This Index covered all kinds of literature, from philology to alchemy; but most of it has unfortunately been lost. In those years manuals of composition (*inshāʾ*) were written elaborating the technique of secretarial correspondence, and they grew into an accepted genre in Arabic as well as in Persian and Turkish literature. The devices thought indispensable for elegance in modern poetry were applied to prose. The products were mannered, full of puns, verbal tricks, riddles, and the like. The new style, which was also to affect the historian's art in later times, makes a good deal of this post-classical Arabic prose look very different from the terse and direct expression characteristic of the early specimens. Rhymed prose, which at one time had been reserved for such religious occasions as the Friday sermons, was now regarded as an essential part of elegant style.

This rhetorical artistry found its most superb expression in the *maqāmah*, a form invented by Badīʿ az-Zamān Hamadhānī (died 1008). Its master, however, was al-Ḥarīrī (died 1122), postmaster (head of the intelligence service) at Basra and an accomplished writer on grammatical subjects. His 50 *maqāmahs* (which tell the adventures of Abū Zayd as-Sarūjī, with a wealth of language and learning) come closer to the Western concept of short story than anything else in classical Arabic literature. They abound in verbal conceits, ambivalence, assonance, alliteration, palindromes; they change abruptly from earnest to jest, from the crude to the most sublime, as the modern scholar G.E. von Grunebaum has pointed

Rhetorical artistry in the *maqāmah*

out in his evaluation of this form, which he regards as the most typical literary reflection of the Islāmic spirit. The work of al-Ḥarīrī has certainly been widely admired in the East; it has been imitated in Syriac and in Hebrew and has formed part of the syllabus in Muslim high schools of India. The pleasure to be derived from the brilliant artifice and ingenuity behind such compositions has led to their being imitated in other literary fields: quite often, in later Persian literature, one finds poems—sometimes whole books—composed of letters without diacritical marks (which distinguish otherwise similar-looking letters) or even made up entirely of unconnected letters. Even a commentary on the Qur'ān, in undotted letters, has been written in India (by Fayẓī, died 1595).

Achievements in the western Muslim world. The Arabic literature of Moorish Spain and of the whole Maghrib developed parallel with that of the eastern countries but came to full flower somewhat later. Córdoba, the seat of the Umayyad rulers, was the centre of cultural life. Its wonderful mosque has inspired Muslim poets right up to the 20th century (such as Sir Muḥammad Iqbāl, whose Urdu ode, "The Mosque of Córdoba," was written in 1935). Moorish Spain, with its highly sophisticated culture, has formed a favourite background for many modern novels written in the eastern parts of the Islāmic world, especially in India and Pakistan. The country reached its cultural, political, and literary heyday under ʿAbd ar-Raḥmān III (912–961). Literary stylistic changes, as noted in Iraq and Syria, spread to the west: there the old Bedouin style had always been rare and soon gave way to descriptive and love poetry. Ibn Hāni' (died 973) of Seville has been praised as the Western counterpart of al-Mutanabbī, largely because of his eulogies of the Fāṭimid caliph al-Muʿizz, who at that time still resided in North Africa. The entertaining prose style of Ibn ʿAbd Rabbihi (died 940) in his *al-ʿIqd al-farīd* ("The Unique Necklace") is similar to that of his elder contemporary Ibn Qutaybah, and his book in fact became more famous than that of his predecessor. Writers on music and philology also flourished in Spain; literary criticism was practiced by Ibn Rashīq (died 1064) and, later, by al-Qarṭājannī (died 1285) in Tunis. Ibn Ḥazm (died 1064), theologian and accomplished writer on pure love, has already been mentioned.

Writers on music and philology

Philosophy: Averroës and Avicenna. Philosophy, medicine, and theology, all of which flourished in the ʿAbbāsid East, were also of importance in the Maghrib; and from there strong influences reached medieval Europe. The influences often came through the mediation of the Jews, who, along with numerous Christians, were largely Arabized in their cultural and literary outlook. The Eastern Muslim countries could boast of the first systematic writers in the field of philosophy, including al-Kindī (died *c.* 870), al-Fārābī (died 950), and especially Avicenna (Ibn Sīnā, died 1037). Avicenna's work in philosophy, science, and medicine was outstanding and was appreciated as such in Europe. He also composed religious treatises and tales with a mystical slant. One of his romances was reworked by the Maghribi philosopher Ibn Ṭufayl (died 1185) in his book *Ḥayy ibn Yaqẓān* ("Alive Son of Awake"), or *Philosophus Autodidactus* (the title of its first Latin translation, made in 1671). It is the story of a self-taught man who lived on a lonely island and who, in his maturity, attained the full knowledge taught by philosophers and prophets. This theme was elaborated often in later European literature.

The dominating figure in the kingdom of the Almohads, however, was the philosopher Averroës (Ibn Rushd, died 1198), court physician of the Berber kings in Marrākush (Marrakech) and famous as the great Arab commentator on Aristotle. The importance of his frequently misinterpreted philosophy in the formation of medieval Christian thought is well-known. Among his many other writings, especially notable is his merciless reply to an attack on philosophy made by Ghazālī (died 1111). Ghazālī had called his attack *Tahāfut al-falāsifah* (*The Incoherence of the Philosophers*), while Averroës' equally famous reply was entitled *Tahāfut at-tahāfut* (*The Incoherence of the Incoherence*). The Persian-born Ghazālī had, after giving up a splendid scholarly career, become the most influential representative of moderate Ṣūfism. His chief work, *Iḥyā' ʿulūm ad-dīn* ("The Revival of the Religious Sciences"), was based on personal religious experiences and is a perfect introduction to the pious Muslim's way to God. It inspired much later religious poetry and prose. The numerous writings by mystics, who often expressed their wisdom in rather cryptic language (thereby contributing to the profundity of Arabic vocabulary), and the handbooks of religious teaching produced in eastern Arab and Persian areas (Sarrāj, Kalābādhī, Qushayrī, and, in Muslim India, al-Hujwīrī) are generally superior to those produced in western Muslim countries. Yet the greatest Islāmic theosophist of all, Ibn al-ʿArabī, was Spanish in origin and was educated in the Spanish tradition. His writings, both in poetry and prose, shaped large parts of Islāmic thought during the following centuries. Much of the later literature of eastern Islām, particularly Persian and Indo-Persian mystical writings, indeed, can be understood only in the light of his teachings. Ibn al-ʿArabī's lyrics are typical *ghazals*, sweet and flowing. From the late 9th century, Arabic-speaking mystics had been composing verses often meant to be sung in their meetings. At first a purely religious vocabulary was employed, but soon the expressions began to oscillate between worldly and heavenly love. The ambiguity thus achieved eventually became a characteristic feature of Persian and Turkish lyrics.

The pious Muslim's way to God

Among the Arabs, religious poetry mainly followed the classical *qaṣīdah* models, and the poets lavishly decorated their panegyrics to the Prophet Muḥammad with every conceivable rhetorical embellishment—examples of this trend include *al-Burdah* ("The Mantle") of al-Buṣīrī (died 1298), upon which dozens of commentaries have been written, and an ode on the Prophet by the Iraqi poet Ṣafī ad-Dīn al-Ḥilli (died 1350), which contains 151 rhetorical figures. The "letters of spiritual guidance" developed by the mystics are worth mentioning as a literary genre. They have been popular everywhere; from the western Islāmic world the letters of Ibn ʿAbbad (died 1389) of Ronda (in Spain) are outstanding examples of this category, being written clearly and lucidly.

Geographical literature. The Maghrib also made a substantial contribution to geographical literature, a field eagerly cultivated by Arab scholars since the 9th century. The Sicilian geographer Idrīsī produced a famous map of the world and accompanied it with a detailed description in his *Kitāb nuzhat al-mushtaq fī ikhtiraq al-āfāq* ("The Delight of Him Who Wishes to Traverse the Regions of the World," 1154), which he dedicated to his patron, Roger II. The Spanish traveller Ibn Jubayr (died 1217), while on pilgrimage to Mecca, kept notes of his experiences and adventures. The resulting book became a model for the later pilgrims' manuals that are found everywhere in the Muslim world. The Maghribi explorer Ibn Baṭṭūṭah (died 1368/9) described his extensive travels to the Far East, India, and the region of the Niger in a book filled with information about the cultural state of the Muslim world at that time. The value of his narrative is enhanced by the simple and pleasing style in which it is written.

Poetry. In the field of poetry, Spain, which produced a considerable number of masters in the established poetical forms, also began to popularize strophic poetry, possibly deriving from indigenous models. The *muwashshaḥ* ("girdled") poem, written in the classical short metres and arranged in four- to six-line stanzas, was elaborated, enriched by internal rhymes, and, embodying some popular expressions in the poem's final section, soon achieved a standardized form. The theme is almost always love. Among the greatest lyric poets of Spain was Ibn Zaydūn of Córdoba (died 1071), who was of noble birth. After composing some charming love songs dedicated to the Umayyad princess Wallādah, he turned his hand to poetic epistles. He is the author of a beautiful *muwashshaḥ* about his home town, which many later poets imitated. When the *muwashshaḥ* was transplanted to the eastern Arabic countries, however, it lost its original spontaneity and became as stereotyped as every oth-

Spanish mastery of poetical forms

er lyric form of expression during the later Middle Ages. Another strophic form developed in Spain is the songlike *zajal* (melody), interesting for its embodiment of dialect phrases and the use of occasional words from Romance languages. Its undisputed master was Ibn Quzmān of Córdoba (died 1160), whose life-style was similar to that of Western troubadours. His approach to life as expressed in these melodious poems, together with their mixed idiom, suggest a possible interrelationship with the vernacular troubadour poetry of Spain and France.

Historiography: Ibn Khaldūn. Any survey of Western Muslim literary achievements would be incomplete if it did not mention the most profound historiographer of the Islāmic world, the Tunisian Ibn Khaldūn (died 1406). History has been called the characteristic science of the Muslims because of the Qur'ānic admonition to discover signs of the divine in the fate of past peoples. Islāmic historiography has produced histories of the Muslim conquests, world histories, histories of dynasties, court annals, and biographical works classified by occupation—scholars, poets, and theologians. Yet, notwithstanding their learning, none of the earlier writers had attempted to produce a comprehensive view of history. Ibn Khaldūn, in the famous *Muqaddimah* or Introduction to a projected general history, *Kitāb al-ʿibar*, sought to explain the basic factors in the historical development of the Islāmic countries. His own experiences, gained on a variety of political missions in North Africa, proved useful in establishing general principles that he could apply to the manifestations of Islāmic civilization. He created, in fact, the first "sociological" study of history, free from bias. Yet his book was little appreciated by his fellow historians, who still clung to the method of accumulating facts without shaping them properly into a well-structured whole. Ibn Khaldūn's work eventually attracted the interest of Western Orientalists, historians, and sociologists alike; and some of his analyses are still held in great esteem.

Significance of Ibn Khaldūn

Decline of the Arabic language. Ibn Khaldūn, who had served in his youth as ambassador to Pedro I the Cruel, of Castile, and in his old age as emissary to Timur, died in Cairo. After the fall of Baghdad in 1258, this city had become the centre of Muslim learning. Historians there recorded every detail of the daily life and the policies of the Mamlūk sultans; theologians and philologists worked under the patronage of Turkish and Circassian rulers who often did not speak a word of Arabic. The amusing, semi-colloquial style of the historian Ibn Iyās (died after 1526) is an interesting example of the deterioration of the Arabic language. While classical Arabic was still the ideal of every literate man, it had become exclusively a "learned" language. Even some copyists who transcribed classical works showed a deplorable lack of grammatical knowledge. It is hardly surprising that poetry composed under such circumstances should be restricted to insipid versification and the repetition of well-worn clichés.

MIDDLE PERIOD: THE RISE OF PERSIAN AND TURKISH POETRY

The New Persian style. During the ʿAbbāsid period, the Persian influence upon the Arabic had grown considerably: at the same time, a distinct Modern Persian literature came into existence in northeastern Iran, where the house of the Sāmānids of Bukhara and Samarkand had revived the memory of Sāsānian glories.

The first famous representative of this new literature was the poet Rūdakī (died 940/941), of whose *qaṣīdahs* only a few have survived. He also worked on a Persian version of *Kalīlah wa Dimnah*, however, and on a version of the *Sendbād-nāmeh*. Rūdakī's poetry, modelled on the Arabic rules of prosody that without exception had been applied to Persian, already points ahead to many of the characteristic features of later Persian poetry. The imagery in particular is sophisticated, although when compared with the mannered writing of subsequent times, his verse was considered sadly simple. From the 10th century onward, Persian poems were written at almost every court in the Iranian areas, sometimes in dialectical variants (for example, in Ṭabarestāni dialect at the Zeyārid court). In many cases the poets were bilingual, excelling in both Arabic and Persian (a gift shared by many non-Arab writers right up to the 19th century).

Influence of Maḥmūd of Ghazna. The first important centre of Persian literature existed at Ghazna (present-day Ghaznī, Afghanistan), at the court of Maḥmūd of Ghazna (died 1030) and his successors, who eventually extended their empire to northwestern India. Himself an orthodox warrior, Maḥmūd in later love poetry was transformed into a symbol of "a slave of his slave" because of his love for a Turkmen officer, Ayāz. Under the Ghaznavids, lyric and epic poetry both developed, as did the panegyric. Classical Iranian topics became the themes of poetry, resulting in such diverse works as the love story of Vāmeq and ʿAzrā (possibly of Greek origin), and the *Shāh-nāmeh* ("Book of Kings"). A number of gifted poets praised Maḥmūd, his successors, and his ministers. Among them was Farrokhī of Seistan (died 1037), who was the author of a powerful elegy on Maḥmūd's death, one of the finest compositions of Persian court poetry.

Ferdowsī's literary achievement

Epic and romance. The main literary achievement of the Ghaznavid period, however, was that of Ferdowsī (died 1020). He compiled the inherited tales and legends about the Persian kings in one grand epic, the *Shāh-nāmeh*, which contains between 35,000 and 60,000 verses in short rhyming couplets. It deals with the history of Iran from its beginnings—that is, from the "time" of the mythical kings—passing on to historical events, giving information about the acceptance of the Zoroastrian faith, Alexander's invasion, and, eventually, the conquest of the country by the Arabs. A large part of the work centres on tales of the hero Rostam. These stories are essentially part of a different culture, thus revealing something about the Indo-European sources of Iranian mythology. The struggle between Iran and Tūrān (identified with ancient Turkistan and Transoxania) forms the central theme of the book; and the importance of the legitimate succession of kings, who are endowed with royal charisma, is reflected throughout the composition. The poem contains very few Arabic words and is often considered the masterpiece of Persian national literature, although it lacks proper historical perspective. Its episodes have been the inspiration of miniaturists since the 14th century. Numerous attempts have been made to emulate it in Iran, India, and Turkey.

Other epic poems, on a variety of subjects, were composed during the 11th century. The first example is Asadī's (died *c.* 1072) didactic *Garshāsb-nāmeh* ("Book of Garshāsb"), whose hero is very similar to Rostam. The tales of Alexander and his journeys through foreign lands were another favourite topic. Poetical romances were also being written at this time; they include the tale of *Varqeh o-Golshāh* by ʿEyyūqī (11th century) and *Vīs o-Rāmīn*, by Fakhr od-Dīn Gorgānī (died after 1055), which has parallels with the Tristan story of medieval romance. These were soon superseded, however, by the great romantic epics of Neẓāmī of Ganjeh (died *c.* 1203), in Caucasia. The latter are known as the *Khamseh* ("Quintuplet") and, though the names of Vīs or Vāmeq continued for some time to serve as symbols of the longing lover, it was the poetical work of Neẓāmī that supplied subsequent writers with a rich store of images, similes, and stories to draw upon. The first work of his *Khamseh*, *Makhzan ol-asrār* ("Treasure-house of Mysteries"), is didactic in intention; the subjects of the following three poems are traditional love stories. The first is the Arabic romance of Majnūn, who went mad with love for Laylā. Second is the Persian historical tale of Shīrīn, a Christian princess, loved by both the Sāsānian ruler Khosrow II Parvīz and the stonecutter Farhād. The third story, *Haft peykar* ("Seven Beauties") deals with the adventures of Bahrām Gūr, a Sāsānian prince, and seven princesses, each connected with one day of the week, one particular star, one colour, one perfume, and so on. The last part of the *Khamseh* is *Eskandar-nāmeh*, which relates the adventures of Alexander III the Great in Africa and Asia, as well as his discussions with the wise philosophers. It thus follows the traditions about

The epics of Neẓāmī

Alexander and his tutor, Aristotle, emphasizing the importance of a counsellor-philosopher in the service of a mighty emperor. Neẓāmī's ability to present a picture of life through highly refined language and a wholly apt choice of images is quite extraordinary. Human feelings, as he describes them, are fully believable; and his characters are drawn with a keen insight into human nature. Not surprisingly, Neẓāmī's work inspired countless poets' imitations in different languages—including Turkish, Kurdish, and Urdu—while painters constantly illustrated his stories for centuries afterward.

Other poetic forms. In addition to epic poetry, the lesser forms, such as the *qaṣīdah* and *ghazal*, developed during the 11th and 12th centuries. Many poets wrote at the courts of the Seljuqs, and also at the Ghaznavid court in Lahore, where the poet Mas'ūd-e Sa'd-e Salmān (died 1121) composed a number of heartfelt *qaṣīdah*s during his political imprisonment. They are outstanding examples of the category of *ḥabsīyah* (prison poem), which usually reveals more of the author's personal feelings than other literary forms. Other famous examples of *ḥabsīyah*s include those written by the Arab knight Abū Firās (died 968) in a Byzantine prison; those by Muḥammad II al-Mu'tamid of Seville (died 1095), in the dungeons of the Almohads; those by the 12th-century Persians Anvarī and Khāqānī; those by the Urdu poets Ghālib, in the 19th, and Faiz, in the 20th century; and by the contemporary Turkish poet Nazım Hikmet (died 1963).

The most complicated forms were mastered by poets of the very early period, the limits of artificiality being reached in Azerbaijani *qaṣīdah*s by the poet Qaṭrān (died 1072), whose work displays of virtuosity for virtuosity's sake. The court poets tried to top one another in the accumulation of complex metaphors and paradoxes, each hoping to win the coveted title "Prince of Poets." Anvarī (died 1189), whose patrons were the Seljuqs, is considered the most accomplished writer of panegyrics in the Persian tongue. His verses contain little descriptive material but abound in learned allusions. His "Tears of Khorāsān," mourning the passing of Seljuq glory, is among the best known of Persian *qaṣīdah*s. In the west of Iran, Anvarī's contemporary Khāqānī (died 1185), who wrote mainly at the court of the Shīrvān-Shāhs of Transcaucasia, is the outstanding master of the hyperbolic style. His mother was a Christian, and his imagery has more than the usual amount of allusions to Christian themes. His vocabulary seems inexhaustible; he uses uncommon rhetorical devices and very strong language. His poems, with their long chains of oath-formulae (*sowgand-nāmeh*), are as impressive as his poignant antithetic formulations. Khāqānī's verses on the ruined Ṭāq Kisrā at Ctesiphon on the Tigris have become proverbial. His *qaṣīdah*s on the pilgrimage to Mecca, which also inspired his *maṣnavī*, *Toḥfeh ol-'Erāqeyn* ("Gift of the Two Iraqs"), translate most eloquently the feelings of a Muslim at the festive occasion. In the hand of lesser poets, however, *qaṣīdah* writing became more and more conventionalized, repeating outworn clichés and employing inflated terms entirely devoid of feeling.

Decline of the *qaṣīdah* form

Scholarship: al-Bīrūnī. The Ghaznavid and Seljuq periods produced first-rate scholars such as al-Bīrūnī (died 1048) who, writing in Arabic, investigated Hinduism and gave the first unprejudiced account of India—indeed, of any non-Islāmic culture. He also wrote notable books on chronology and history. In his search for pure knowledge he is undoubtedly one of the greatest minds in Islāmic history. Interest in philosophy is represented by Nāṣer-e Khosrow (died 1087) who acted for a time as a missionary for the Ismā'īlī branch of Shī'ah Islām. His book about his journey to Egypt, entitled *Safar-nāmeh*, is a pleasing example of simple, clearly expressed, early Persian prose. His poetical works in the main seek to combine Greek wisdom and Islāmic thought: the gnostic Ismā'īlī interpretation of Islām seemed, to him, an ideal vehicle for a renaissance of the basic Islāmic truths.

Robā'īyāt: Omar Khayyam. The work done in mathematics by early Arabic scholars and by al-Bīrūnī was continued by Omar Khayyam (died 1122) to whom the Seljuq empire in fact owes the reform of its calendar. But Omar has become famous in the West through the free adaptations by Edward Fitzgerald of his *Robā'īyāt*. These quatrains have been translated into almost every known language and are largely responsible for colouring European ideas about Persian poetry. The authenticity of these verses has often been questioned. The quatrain is an easy form to use—many have been scribbled on Persian pottery of the 12th century—and the same verse has been attributed to many different authors. The latest research into the question of the *Robā'īyāt* has established that a considerable number of the quatrains can, indeed, be traced back to the great scientist, who condensed in them his feelings and thoughts, his skepticism and love, in such an enthralling way that they appeal to every reader. The imagery he uses, however, is entirely inherited; none of it is original. (One of the most noted, and notorious, writers of this genre was the poetess Mahsaṭī [first half of the 12th century], who frequently addressed members of different professions in rather frivolous lines.) The quatrain was also popular as a means of embodying pieces of mystical wisdom. One has to do away with the old theory that the first author of such mystical *robā'īyāt* was Abū Sa'īd ibn Abū al-Khayr (died 1049). A number of his contemporaries, however, including Bābā Ṭāher 'Oryān (died after 1055), used simpler forms of the quatrain, sometimes in order to express their mystical concepts.

The mystical poem. Whereas the mystical thought stemming from Iran had formerly been written in Arabic, writers from the 11th century onward turned to Persian. Along with works of pious edification and theoretical discussions, what was to be one of the most common types of Persian literature came into existence: the mystical poem. Khwajah 'Abd Allāh al-Anṣārī of Herāt (died 1088), a prolific writer on religious topics in both Arabic and Persian, first popularized the literary "prayer," or mystical contemplation, written in Persian in rhyming prose interspersed with verses. Sanā'ī (died 1131), at one time a court poet of the Ghaznavids, composed the first mystical epic, the didactic *Ḥadīqeh ol-ḥaqīqat* ("Orchard of Truth"), which has some 10,000 verses. In this lengthy and rather dry poem, the pattern for all later mystical *maṣnavī*s is established: wisdom is embodied in stories and anecdotes; parables and proverbs are woven into the texture of the story, eventually leading back to the main subject, although the argument is without thread and the narration puzzling to follow. Among Sanā'ī's smaller *maṣnavī*s, *Seyr ol-'ebād elā ol-ma'ād* ("The Journey of the Servants to the Place of Return") deserves special mention. Its theme is the journey of the spirit through the spheres, a subject dear to the mystics and still employed in modern times as, for example, by Iqbāl in his Persian *Jāvīd-nāmeh* (1932). Sanā'ī's epic endeavours were continued by one of the most prolific writers in the Persian tongue, Farīd od-Dīn 'Aṭṭār (died *c.* 1220). He was a born storyteller, a fact that emerges from his lyrics but even more so from his works of edification. The most famous among his *maṣnavī*s is the *Manṭeq oṭ-ṭeyr* ("Birds' Conversation"), modelled after some Arabic allegories. It is the story of 30 birds, who, in search of their spiritual king, journey through seven valleys. The poem is full of tales, some of which have been translated even into the most remote Islāmic languages. (The story of the pious Sheykh Ṣan'ān, who fell in love with a Christian maiden, is found, for example, in Kashmiri.) 'Aṭṭār's symbolism of the soul-bird was perfectly in accord with the existing body of imagery beloved of Persian poetry, but it was he who added a scene in which the birds eventually realize their own identity with God. Also notable are his *Elāhī-nāmeh*, an allegory of a king and his six sons, and his profound *Moṣībat-nāmeh* ("Book of Affliction"), which closes with its hero's being immersed in the ocean of his soul, after wandering through the 40 stages of his search for God.

Importance of Mawlānā Jalāl ad-Dīn ar-Rūmī. The most famous of the Persian mystical *maṣnavī*s is by Mawlānā ("Our Lord") Jalāl ad-Dīn ar-Rūmī (died 1273) and is known simply as the *Maṣnavī*. It comprises some

26,000 verses and is a complete—though quite disorganized—encyclopaedia of all the mystical thought, theories, and images known in the 13th century. It is regarded by most of the Persian-reading orders of Ṣūfīs as second in importance only to the Qur'ān. Its translation into many Islāmic languages and the countless commentaries written on it up to the present day indicate its importance in the formation of Islāmic poetry and religious thought. Jalāl ad-Dīn, who hailed from Balkh and settled in Konya, the capital of the Rūm, or Anatolian Seljuqs (and hence was surnamed "Rūmī"), was also the author of love lyrics whose beauty surpasses even that of the tales in the *Masnavī*. Mystical love poetry had been written since the days of Sanā'ī, and theories of love had been explained in the most subtle prose and sensitive verses by the Ṣūfīs of the early 12th century. Yet Rūmī's experience of mystical love for the wandering mystic, Shams ad-Dīn of Tabriz, was so ardent and enraptured him to such an extent that he identified himself completely with Shams, going so far as to use the beloved's name as his own pen name. His dithyrambic lyrics, numbering more than 30,000 verses altogether, are not at all abstract or romantic. On the contrary, their vocabulary and imagery are taken directly from everyday life, so that they are vivid, fresh, and convincing. Often their rhythm invites the reader to partake in the mystical dance practiced by Rūmī's followers, the Mawlawīyah. His verses sometimes approach the form of popular folk poetry; indeed, Rūmī is reputed to have written mostly under inspiration; and despite his remarkable poetical technique, the sincerity of his love and longing is never overshadowed nor his personality veiled. In these respects he is unique in Persian literature.

Most famous Persian mystical *masnavī*

Zenith of Islāmic literature. During the 13th century, the Islāmic lands were exposed, on the political plane, to the onslaught of the Mongols and the abolition of the ʿAbbāsid caliphate, while vast areas were laid to waste. Yet this was in fact the period in which Islāmic literatures reached their zenith. Apart from Rūmī's superb poetry, written in the comparative safety of Konya, there was also the work of the Egyptian Ibn al-Fāriḍ (died 1235), who composed some magnificent, delicately written mystical poems in *qaṣīdah* style, and that of Ibn al-ʿArabī (died 1240), who composed love lyrics and numerous theosophical works that were to become standard. In Iran, one of the greatest literati, Moṣleḥ od-Dīn Saʿdī (died 1292), returned in about 1256 to his birthplace, Shīrāz, after years of journeying; his *Būstān* ("The Orchard") and *Golestān* ("Rose Garden") have been popular ever since. The *Būstān* is a didactic poem telling wise and uplifting moral tales, written in polished, easy-flowing style and a simple metre; the *Golestān*, completed one year later, in 1258, has been judged ". . . the finest flower that could blossom in a Sultan's garden" (Herder). Its eight chapters deal with different aspects of human life and behaviour. At first sight, its prose and poetical fragments appear to be simple and unassuming; but not a word could be changed without destroying the perfect harmony of the sound, imagery, and content. Saʿdī's *Golestān* is thus essential in discovering the nature of the finest Persian literary style. Since the mid-17th century, its moralizing stories have been translated into many Western languages. Saʿdī was likewise the author of some spirited *ghazals*; he may have been the first writer in Iran to compose the sort of love poetry which is now thought of as characteristic of the *ghazal*. A few of his *qaṣīdahs* are also of note, although he is at his best in shorter forms. His elegant aphoristic poems, words of wisdom, and sensible advice all display what has been called the philosophy of common sense—how to act in any given situation so as to make the best of it both for oneself and others, basing one's conduct on the virtues of gentleness, elegance, modesty, and polite behaviour.

Saʿdī's "philosophy of common sense"

The influence of mysticism, on the one hand, and of the elaborate Persian poetical tradition, on the other, is apparent during the later decades of the 13th century, both in Anatolia and in Muslim India. The Persian mystic, Fakhr-ud-Dīn ʿIrāqī (died 1289), a master of delightful love lyrics, lived for almost 25 years in Multān (in present-day Pakistan), where his lively *ghazals* are still sung. His short treatises, in a mixture of poetry and prose (and written under Ibn al-ʿArabī's influence) have been imitated often. While in Multān he may have met the young Amīr Khosrow of Delhi (died 1325), who was one of the most versatile authors to write in Persian, not only in India but in the entire realm of Persian culture. Amīr Khosrow, son of a Turkish officer, but whose mother was Indian, is often styled, because of the sweetness of his speech, "the parrot of India." (In Persian, it should be noted, parrots are always "sugar-talking"; they are, moreover, connected with Paradise and are thought of as wise birds—thus models of the sweet-voiced sage.) He wrote panegyrics of seven successive kings of Delhi and was also a pioneer of Indian Muslim music. Imitating Neẓāmī's *Khamseh*, Khosrow introduced a novelistic strain into the *masnavī* by recounting certain events of his own time in poetical form, some parts of which are lyrics. His style of lyrical poetry has been described as "powdered"; and his *ghazals* contain many of the elements that in the 16th and 17th centuries were to become characteristic of the "Indian" style. Khosrow's poetry surprises the reader in its use of unexpected forms and unusual images, complicated constructions and verbal plays, all handled fluently and presented in technically perfect language. His books on the art of letter writing prove his mastery of high-flown Persian prose. Khrosrow's younger contemporary, Ḥasan of Delhi (died 1328), is less well-known and had a more simple style. He nevertheless surpassed Khosrow in warmth and charm, qualities which have earned him the title of "the Saʿdī of Hindustan."

Turkish literature. As for the literary developments in Turkey around 1300, the mystical singer Yunus Emre is the first and most important in a long line of popular poets. Little is known about his life, which he probably spent not far from the Sakarya River of Asia Minor. Before him, in Central Asia, the religious leader Ahmed Yesevi (died 1166) had written some rather dry verses on wisdom in Turkish. Yunus, in Anatolia, however, was the first known poet to have caught something of Rūmī's fervour and translated it into a provincial setting, creating ". . . a Turkish vernacular poetry that was to be the model for all subsequent literary productions of popular religion." Sometimes he used the inherited Arabo-Persian prosody, but his best poems are those written in four-line verses using syllable-counting metres. Yunus drew heavily on the reservoir of imagery that had been collected by the great Persian writing mystics, notably Rūmī; but his classical technique did not hinder the expression of his own unselfconscious simplicity, which led him to introduce new images taken from everyday life in Anatolian villages. His *ilahis* (hymns), probably written to be sung at the meetings of the Ṣūfīs in the centres of their orders, are still loved by the Turks and memorized by their children.

Use of images from everyday life

Influence of Yunus Emre. The Turkish people rightly claim Yunus as the founder of Turkish literature proper. His poetry is considered the chief pillar of poetry of the Bektāshīyah Ṣūfī order, and many poets of this and other orders have imitated his style (though without reaching the same level of poetic truth and human warmth). Among the later poets claimed by the Bektāshīs may be mentioned Kaygusuz Abdal (15th century), who probably came from the European provinces of the Ottoman Empire. His verses are full of burlesque and even coarse images: in their odd mixture of worldliness and religious expression they are often as amusing as they are puzzling. In the 16th century, Pir Sultan Abdal (executed *c.* 1560) is noted for a few poems of austere melancholy. He was executed for collaboration with the Ṣafavids, the arch-enemies of the Ottomans; and in this connection it is worth remembering that the founder of the Iranian Ṣafavid dynasty, Shāh Esmāʿīl I (died 1524), wrote Turkish poetry under the pen name Khaṭā'ī and is counted among the Bektāshī poets.

Religious poetry. Mystically tinged poetry has always been very popular in Turkey, both in cities and rural areas. The best loved religious poem of all was, and still is, Süleyman Çelebi's (died 1429) *Mevlud*, a quite short *mas̄navī* in honour of the prophet Muḥammad's birth. This type of poetry has been known in the Islāmic countries since at least the 12th century and was soon adopted wherever Islām spread. There are a great number of *mevlud* written in Turkish, but it was Süleyman Çelebi's unpretentious description of the great religious event that captured the hearts of the Turks; and it is still sung on many occasions (on the anniversary of a death, for example). The poem makes an excellent introduction to an understanding of the deep love for the Prophet felt by the pious Muslim.

Persian literature: 1300–1500. In the Iran of the Middle Ages, a vast number of poets flourished at the numerous courts. Not only professional poets but even the kings and princes contributed more or less successfully to the body of Persian poetry. Epics, panegyrics, and mystico-didactical poetry had all reached their finest hour by the end of the 13th century; the one genre to attain perfection slightly later was the *ghazal*, of which Moḥammad Shams od-Dīn Ḥāfeẓ (died 1390) is the incontestable master.

Lyric poetry: Moḥammad Shams od-Dīn Ḥāfeẓ. Ḥāfeẓ lived in Shīrāz; his pen name—"Who Knows the Qur'ān by Heart"—indicates his wide religious education, but little is known about the details of his life. The same is true of many Persian lyrical poets, since their products rarely contain much trustworthy biographical material. Ḥāfeẓ's comparatively small collection of work—his *Dīvān* contains about 400 *ghazals*—was soon acclaimed as the finest lyrical poetry ever written in Persian. The discussion of whether or not to interpret its wine and love songs on a mystical plane has continued for centuries. Yet this discussion seems sterile since Ḥāfeẓ, whose verbal images shine like jewels, is an outstanding exponent of the ambiguous and oscillating style that makes Persian poetry so attractive and so difficult to translate. The different levels of experience are all expressed through the same images and symbols: the beloved is always cruel, whether she be a chaste virgin (a rare case in Persian poetry!) or a professional courtesan, or, as in most cases, a handsome young boy, or God himself, mysterious and unattainable—or even, on the political plane, the remote despot, the wisdom of whose schemes must never be questioned by his subjects. Since mystical interpretation of the world order had become almost second nature to Persians during the 13th century, the human beloved could effortlessly be regarded as God's manifestation; the rose became a symbol of highest divine beauty and glory; the nightingale represented the yearning and complaining soul; wine, cup, and cupbearer became the embodiment of enrapturing divine love. The poets' multicoloured images were not merely decorative embroidery but were a structural part of their thought. One must not expect Ḥāfeẓ (nor any other poet) to unveil his personal feelings in a lyrical poem of experience. But no other Persian poet has used such complex imagery on so many different levels with such harmonious and well-balanced lucidity as did Ḥāfeẓ. His true greatness lies in this rather than in the content of his poetry. It must be stressed again that, according to the traditional view, each verse of a *ghazal* should be unique, precious for its own sake, and that the apparent lack of logic behind the sequence of verses was considered a virtue rather than a defect. (It may help to think of the glass pieces in a kaleidoscope, which appear in different patterns from moment to moment, yet themselves form no logical pattern.) To what extent an "inner rhythm" and a "contrapuntal harmony" can be detected in Ḥāfeẓ's poetry is still a matter for discussion; but that he perfected the *ghazal* form is indisputable. Whether he is praised as a very human love poet, as an interpreter of esoteric lore, or, as has been recently suggested, as a political critic, his verses have a continuing appeal to all lovers of art and artistry.

Use of a standard set of images and symbols

Parodies of classic forms. Ḥāfeẓ's contemporary in Shīrāz was the satirist ʿObeyd-e Zākānī (died 1371), noted for his obscene verses (even the most moralistic and mystical poets sometimes produced surprisingly coarse and licentious lines) and for his short *mas̄navī* called *Mūsh o-gorbeh* ("Mouse and Cat"), an amusing political satire. Since few new forms or means of expression were open to them, ʿObeyd and other poets began ridiculing the classic models of literature: thus, Bosḥāq (died *c.* 1426) composed odes and *ghazals* exclusively on the subject of food. The Tīmūrid period in Iran produced only moderately good poetry, despite the rulers' interest in art. Allegorical *mas̄navīs* were much in vogue, such as the *Shabestān-e khyāl* ("Bedchamber of Fantasy") by the prolific writer Fattāḥī of Nīshāpūr (died 1448) and *Gūy o-chowgān* ("Ball and Polo-stick") by ʿĀrefī (died 1449); the latter work is an elaboration of the cliché that the lover is helpless before the will of his beloved, just as the ball is subject to the will of the polo-stick (". . . the head of the lover in the polo-stick of the beloved's tresses").

Poetry of the Tīmūrid period

Eclecticism of ʿAbd or-Raḥmān Jāmī. The last great centre of Islāmic art in the region of Iran was the Tīmūrid court of Herāt, where Dowlatshāh (died 1494) composed his much-quoted biographical work on Persian poets. The leading figure in this circle was ʿAbd or-Raḥmān Jāmī (died 1492), who is sometimes considered the last and most comprehensive of the "seven masters" in Persian literature, since he was a master of every literary genre and did not specialize in one form only, as Anvarī and Ḥāfeẓ, among others, had done. Jāmī wrote an excellent imitation of Neẓāmī's *Khamseh*, enlarging it by the addition of two mystical *mas̄navīs* into a septet called *Haft Owrang* ("The Seven Thrones," or "Ursa Major"). His interest in Ṣūfism—he was initiated into the Naqshbandīyah order—is clear from his famous biographies of the Ṣūfī saints (which were an elaboration of a similar work by the 11th-century ʿAbd Allāh al-Anṣārī). In imitation of Saʿdī, Jāmī also composed the *Bahārestān* ("Orchard of Spring"), written in prose interspersed with verses. He left no less than three large divans, which contain work of high quality and demonstrate his gift for inventing picturesque images. Although his work abounds in lavishly ornamented verses, his style on the whole lacks the perfect beauty of Ḥāfeẓ's lyrics and is already tending toward the heavier, more opaque "Indian" style. Jāmī also wrote treatises about literary riddles and various kinds of intellectual games, of which Muslim society in the late 15th century was very fond, and which remain a feature of erudite Persian and Turkish poetry. His influence on the work of later poets, especially in Ottoman Turkey, was very powerful.

An interesting aspect of the Tīmūrid court in Herāt was the attention given to Chagatai Turkish, which was spoken in the eastern regions of Islām. ʿAlī Shīr Navāʾī, minister at the court (and a close friend of Jāmī), emphasized the beauties of his Turkic mother tongue as compared with Persian in his *Muḥākamat al-lughatayn* ("Judgment of the Two Languages"). He composed most of his lyrics and epics in Chagatai, which previously had been used by some members of the Timurid family and their courtiers for poetry but which now became, thanks to him, an established literary medium. Even the arts-loving ruler of Herāt, Ḥusayn Baykara (died 1506), wrote poetry in Turkic, following in every respect conventional literary taste.

Prose works: the "Mirror for Princes." During the first five centuries of Modern Persian literary life a multitude of prose works were written. Among them, the "Mirror for Princes" deserve special mention. This genre, introduced from Persian into Arabic as early as the 8th century, flourished once more in Iran during the late 11th century. One important example is the *Qābūs-nāmeh* by the Zeyārid prince ʿOnṣor ol-Maʿalī Keykāvūs (died 1098), which presents "a miscellany of Islamic culture in pre-Mongol times." At the same time, Niẓām al-Mulk (died 1092), the grand vizier of the Seljuqs, composed his *Seyāsat-nāmeh* ("Book of Government"), a good introduction to the statesman's craft according to medieval Islāmic standards. The *Seyāsat-nāmeh* was heavily influenced by pre-Islāmic Persian tradition. In the same period and environment, even a mystic like al-Ghazālī felt disposed to write a *Naṣīḥat ol-molūk* ("Counsel for Kings"), although the idealized relationship he makes between religious theory and practical statesmanship was

The "Book of Government"

not very realistic. This work is quite exceptional, since mystics did not normally care about politics.

Belles-lettres. Belles-lettres proper found a fertile soil in Iran. The fables of *Kalīlah wa Dimnah*, for example, were retold several times in Persian. The most famous version, though a rather turgid one, is called *Anvār-e soheylī* ("Lights of Canopus") and was composed by a famous mystic, Ḥoseyn Wāʿeẓ-e Kāshefī of Herāt (died 1504). The "cyclic story" form (in which several unconnected tales are held together by a common framework or narrator device), inherited from India, became as popular in Iran as it had been in the Arabic-speaking countries. The *Sendbād-nāmeh* and the *Ṭūṭīnāmeh* ("Parrot Book"), which is based on Indian tales, are both good examples of the popular method whereby a variety of instructive satires are skillfully strung together within a basic "running" story. The first comprehensive collection of entertaining prose is ʿOwfī's (died 1230) *Javāmīʿ ol-ḥekāyāt* ("Collections of Stories"), which is a veritable storehouse of tales and anecdotes. Anecdotes were an important feature of the biographical literature that became popular in Iran and Muslim India. Biographies of the poets of a certain age or of a specified area were collected together. They provide the reader with few concrete facts about the subjects concerned; but they abound in anecdotes, sayings, and verses attributed to the subjects, thus preserving material that otherwise might have been lost. Many of these biographical manuals, such as ʿOwfī's *Lobāb ol-albāb* (Quintessence of the Hearts") or Dowlatshāh's *Tazkerat osh-shoʿarā* ("Biography of the Poets"), make agreeable reading. The authors concerned wished to demonstrate their own erudition and rhetorical technique as much as to immortalize their subjects; consequently, their books are important equally as stylistic documents and as historical sources. One of the most remarkable works in this field is *Chahār maqāleh* ("Four Treatises") by Neẓāmī-ye ʿArūẓī, a writer from eastern Iran. Written *c.* 1156, this little book is an excellent introduction to the ideals of Persian literature and its writers, discussing in detail what is required to make a perfect poet, giving a number of instances of the sort of poetic craftsmanship thought especially admirable, and allowing glimpses into the various arts in which the literary man was expected to excel.

"Anecdotal" writing

This tendency toward "anecdotal" writing, which is also manifest in the work of a number of Arab historians, can be observed in the cosmographical books and in some of the historical books produced in medieval Iran. Hamdollāh Mostowfī's (died after 1340) cosmography, *Nozhat ol-qolūb* ("Pleasure of the Hearts"), like many earlier works of this genre, underlined the mysterious aspects of the marvels of creation and was the most famous of several instructive collections of mixed folkloristic and scientific material. Early miniaturists, too, loved to illustrate the most unlikely tales and pieces of information given in such works. Historical writing proper had been begun by the Persians as early as the late 10th century, when Balʿamī's abridged translation of aṭ-Ṭabarī's (died 923) vast Arabic chronicle first acquainted them with this outstanding piece of early Arabic historical literature. The heyday of historiography in Iran, however, was the Il-Khanid period (mid-13th to mid-14th centuries). Iran was then ruled by the successors of Genghis Khan, and scholars began to extend their interest backward to the history of pre-Islāmic Central Asia, whence the rulers had come. *Tārīkh-e jehān-goshāy* ("History of the World Conqueror") by ʿAṭā Malek-e Joveynī (died 1283) and *Jāmiʿ at-tawārīkh* ("Collector of Chronicles") by the physician and vizier Rashīd ad-Dīn (died 1318) are both outstanding examples of histories filled with valuable information. Although the writing of history became a firmly established art in Iran and the adjacent Muslim countries, the facts were unfortunately all too often concealed in a bombastic style and a labyrinth of cumbersome, long-winded sentences. A history written by Vaṣṣāf (died 1323) is the most notorious example of turgidity, but even his style was surpassed by some later writers. These stylistic tendencies deeply influenced Turkish prose writing: 17th-century Turkish historical works, such as those of Peçevi (died *c.* 1650) and Naima (died 1716), for this reason almost defy translation. Later Persian prose in India suffered from the same defects. This development in Persian and Turkish prose is also reflected in the handbooks on style and letter writing that were written during the 14th and 15th centuries and afterward. They urged the practice of all the artificial tricks of rhetoric by this time considered essential for an elegant piece of prose. Nonetheless, modern readers may admire the resulting spiderweb-like fabric, albeit grudgingly.

Popular literature. Islāmic literatures, however, should not be thought to consist only of erudite and witty court poetry, of frivolous or melancholy love lyrics full of literary conceits, or of works deeply mystical in content. Such works are counterbalanced by a great quantity of popular literature, of which the most famous expression is *Alf laylah wa laylah* ("One Thousand and One Nights," perhaps better known as *The Arabian Nights Entertainment*). The tales collected under this title come from different cultural areas; their nucleus is of Indian origin, first translated into Persian as *Hazār afsānak* ("Thousand Tales") and then into Arabic. These fanciful fairy tales were later expanded with stories and anecdotes from Baghdad. Subsequently, some tales—mainly from the lower strata of society—about rogues, tricksters, and vagabonds were added in Egypt. Independent series of stories, such as that of Sindbad the Sailor, were also included. The entire collection is very important as a reflection of several aspects of Oriental folklore. Since its first translation into French (1704), it has inspired many Western readers' dreams about the "romantic" East.

The Arabian Nights Entertainment

From pre-Islāmic times the Arabs had recounted tales of the *ayyām al-ʿArab* ("Days of the Arabs"), which were stories of their tribal wars, and had dwelt upon tales of the heroic deeds of certain of their brave warriors, such as ʿAntarah. Modern research, however, suggests that the story in its present setting belongs to the period of the Crusades. The Egyptian queen, Shajar ad-Durr (died 1257) and the first brave Mamlūk ruler, Baybars I (died 1277), as well as the adventures of the Bedouin tribe Banū Hilāl on its way to Tunisia are all the subjects of lengthy popular tales.

In Iran, many of the historical legends and myths had been borrowed and turned into high literature by Ferdowsī. Accounts of the glorious adventures of heroes from early Islāmic times were afterward retold throughout Iran, India, and Turkey. Thus, the *Dāstān-e Amīr Ḥamzeh*, a story of Muḥammad's uncle Ḥamzeh, was slowly enlarged by the addition of more and more tiny details. This form of *dāstān*, as such literature is called, to some extent influenced the first attempts at novel writing in Muslim India during the 19th century. The epics of Köroğlu are common to both Iranian and Turkish tradition. He was a noble warrior-robber who became one of the central figures in folk literature from Central Asia to Anatolia.

Some popular epics were composed in the late Middle Ages, having as their basis local traditions. One such epic had as its basis the Turco-Iranian legend of an 8th-century hero, Abū Muslim, another the Turkish tales of the knight Dānishmend. Other epics, such as the traditional Turkish tale of Dede Korkut, were preserved by storytellers who improvised certain parts of their tales (which were noted down only afterward). Also, the role of the Ṣūfī orders and of the artisans' lodges in preserving and transmitting such semi-historical popular epics seems to have been considerable. Apart from heroic figures, the Muslim peoples further share a comic character—basically a type of low-class theologian, called Nasreddin Hoca in Turkish, Juḥā in Arabic, and Mushfiqī in Tadzhik. Anecdotes about this character, which embody the mixture of silliness and shrewdness displayed by this "type," have amused generations of Muslims.

Shortly after the introduction of the printing press, Turkey and Iran began to produce cheap books, sometimes illustrated, containing popular romantic love stories. Large numbers of fairy tales were published in these cheap editions, and still other fairy tales have been collected by European and Muslim folklorists.

Popularity of romantic love stories

A truly popular poetry is everywhere to be found: lullabies sung by Baluchi, Kurdish, and Ibo mothers have obvious similarities; workers sing little rhythmical poems to accompany their work, and nomads remember the adventures of their ancestors in their ballads. Such popular poems often contain dialect expressions, and the metres differ from the classical quantitative system. Some of these simple verses, such as a two-line *landay* in Pashto, are among the most graceful products of Islāmic poetry. Many folksongs—lullabies, wedding songs, and dirges—have a distinct mystical flavour and reflect the simple Muslim's love for the Prophet and his trust in God's grace even under the most difficult circumstances. Irony and wit are features of the riddle poem, a favourite form among Muslims everywhere. Folk poets were also fond of humorous descriptions of imaginary disputations between two entities—they might compose dialogues between coffee and tobacco (Morocco), between a big and a small mosque (Yemen), between a cat and a dog, or between a boy and a girl. This kind of literature in the semicolloquial or dialectical Arabic poetry of the 17th and 18th centuries in Yemen, Upper Egypt, and central Arabia would bear a thorough study. All the Iranian and Turkic languages, too, possess a rich heritage of popular poetry, which in many cases appeals more immediately to modern tastes than does the rather cerebral high literature of the culture.

THE PERIOD FROM 1500 TO 1800

According to Persian tradition, the last classic author in literature was Jāmī, who died in 1492. In that year, Christopher Columbus discovered America, and the Christians reconquered Granada, the last Moorish stronghold of Spain. The beginning of the 16th century was as crucial in the history of the Muslim East as in that of the Western Hemisphere. In 1501, the young Esmāʿīl founded the Ṣafavid rule in Iran, and the Shīʿah persuasion of Islām was declared the state religion. At the same time, the kingdoms of the last Tīmūrid rulers in Central Asia were overthrown by the Uzbeks, who, for a while, tried to continue certain cultural and literary traditions in both Persian and Turkic at their courts in Bukhara. In 1526, after long struggles, one member of the Tīmūrid house, Bābur, laid the foundation of the Mughal Empire in India. In the Near East, the Ottoman Turks, having expanded their empire (beginning in the late 13th century) from northwestern Anatolia into the Balkans, now conquered crumbling Mamlūk Egypt and adjacent countries, including the sacred places of Mecca and Medina in 1516–17. Thus, three main blocks emerged, and the two strongholds of Sunnī Islām—Ottoman Turkey and Mughal India—were separated by Shīʿah Iran.

Decentralization of Islāmic literatures. Ṣafavid Iran, as it happened, lost most of its artists and poets to the neighbouring countries: there were no great masters of poetry in Iran between the 16th and 18th centuries. And while the Persian shāh Esmāʿīl wrote Turkish mystical verses, his contemporary and enemy, Sultan Selim I of Turkey (died 1526), composed quite elegant Persian *ghazals*; Bābur (died 1530), in turn, composed his autobiography in Eastern Turkic (but also knew enough Persian to write some acceptable lines of poetry in that language).

Islāmic autobiographical literature

Bābur's autobiography is a fascinating piece of Turkish prose and at the same time one of the comparatively rare examples of Islāmic autobiographical literature. The classic example in this genre, however, was a lively Arabic autobiography by Usāmah ibn Munqidh (died 1188), which sheds much light upon the life and cultural background of a Syrian knight during the Crusades. A number of mystics, too, had written their spiritual autobiographies in a variety of languages, with varying degrees of artistic success. Bābur's book, however, gives a wonderful insight into the character of this intrepid conqueror. It reveals him as a master of concise, matter-of-fact prose, as a keen observer of daily life, full of pragmatic common sense, and also as a good judge of poetry. Bābur even went so far as to write a treatise in Turkish about versification. Many of his male and female descendants inherited his literary taste and talent for poetry; among them are remarkably good poets in Persian, Turkish, and Urdu, as well as accomplished authors of autobiographies (Jahāngīr) and letters (Aurangzeb). Among the nobility of India, the Turkish language remained in use until the 19th century. Lovely Turkish verses were written, for example, by Akbar's general, Khān-e Khānān ʿAbd-ur-Raḥīm (died 1626), who was a great patron of fine arts and poetry.

In the Arab world, there was hardly a poet or original writer of note during the three centuries that followed the Ottoman conquest, apart from some theologians (ʿAbd al-Wahhāb ash-Shaʿrānī, died 1565; ʿAbd al-Ghanī an-Nābulusī, died 1731) and grammarians. Yet Arabic still remained the language of theology and scholarship throughout the Muslim world; both Turkey and India could boast a large number of scholars who excelled in the sacred language. In Ottoman Turkey, Taşköprüzāde (died 1560) compiled a historical survey of outstanding Turkish intellectuals in Arabic. Although a fine example of Islāmic learning, it does not compare in usefulness with the bibliographical work in Arabic by Hacı Halifa (Kâtib Çelebî; died 1658), which is a valuable source for modern knowledge of literary history.

New importance of Indian literature. India's share in the development of Arabic literature at this time was especially large. In addition to the quantity of theological work written in the language of the Qur'ān, from the conquest of Sind in 711 right up until the 19th century, much philosophical and biographical literature in Arabic was also being written in the subcontinent. Persian taste predominated in the northwest of India, but in the southern provinces there were long-standing commercial and cultural relationships with the Arabs and an inclination toward preserving these intact. Thus, much poetry in conventional Arabic style was written during the 16th and 17th centuries, mainly in the kingdom of Golconda. There are even attempts at the epic form. A century after the heyday of Arabic in Deccan, Āzād Bilgrami (died 1786) composed numerous poetical and biographical works in Persian; but his chief fame was as the "Ḥassān of Hind," since he, like the Prophet Muḥammad's *protégé* Ḥassān ibn Thābit, wrote some powerful Arabic panegyrics in honour of the Prophet of Islām. He even attempted to make a comparison of the characteristics of Arabic and Sanskrit poetry and tried to prove that India was the real homeland of Islām. It should be added that Sayyid Murtaḍā (died 1797), a leading philologist, author of the fundamental work of lexicography *Tāj al-ʿarūs* ("The Bride's Crown") and commentator on Ghazālī's main work, was of Indian origin. Laudatory poems and belles-lettres in Arabic were still popular in the early 19th century at the Shīʿite court of Lucknow, then the chief centre of Urdu poetry.

Poetry in conventional Arabic style

Indian literature in Persian. Nevertheless, the main contribution of Muslim India to high literature was made in the Persian tongue. Persian had been the official language of the country for many centuries. The numerous annals and chronicles that were compiled during the 14th and 15th centuries, as well as the court poetry, had been composed exclusively in this language, even by Hindus. During the Mughal period, its importance was enhanced both by Akbar's attempt to have the main works of classical Sanskrit literature translated into Persian and by the constant influx of poets from Iran who came seeking their fortune at the lavish tables of the Indian Muslim grandees. At this time what is known as the "Indian" style of Persian emerged. The translations from Sanskrit enriched the Persian vocabulary, and new stories of Indian origin added to the reservoir of classical imagery. The poets, bound to the inherited genres of *masnavī*, *qaṣīdah*, and *ghazal*, tried to outdo each other in the use of complex rhyme patterns and unfamiliar, often stiff, metres. It became fashionable to conceive a poem according to a given *zamin* ("ground"), often in emulation of a classical model, and then to enrich it with newly invented tropes. The long-held ideal of "harmonious selection of images" was not always met. Difficult, even awkward grammatical constructions and inverted metaphors can be found. At times, pseudo-philosophical utterances in the second hemistich of a verse contrast strangely with semi-colloquial expressions elsewhere. Objects recently introduced to India, such as the eyeglass or hourglass, were eagerly adopted as images by the poets, who wanted new-fangled conceits to bolster up their tortuous inventiveness. Notwithstanding the colourful descriptive poems written in praise of such subjects as Mughal palaces, marvellously illuminated manuscripts, rare elephants, or court scenes, the general mood of lyric poetry became more gloomy. The transitory nature of the world, also a central theme in classical Persian poetry, was stressed and depicted in bizarre images: "burnt nest"; "breakdown"; "yawning" (indicating insatiable thirst); these were some of the new "stylish" words.

The works of ʿUrfī

Yet some truly great poets are to be found even in this period. ʿUrfī, who left Shīrāz for India and died in his mid-30s in Lahore (1592), is without doubt one of the few genuine masters of Persian poetry, especially in his *qaṣīdah*s. His verses pile up linguistic difficulties; yet their dark, glowing quality cannot fail to touch the hearts and minds even of critical modern readers—more so than the elegant but rather cerebral verses of his colleague Fayẕī (died 1595), one of Akbar's favourites. Fayẕī's brother Abū-ul-Faẕl ʿAllāmī (died 1602), the author of an important, though biased, historical work, deeply influenced the Emperor's religious ideas. Among 17th-century Mughal court poets the most outstanding is Abū Ṭālib Kalīm (died 1651), who came from Hamadan. Abounding in descriptive passages of great virtuosity, his poignant and often pessimistic verses have become proverbial, thanks to their compact diction and fluent style. Also of some importance is Ṣā'ib of Tabriz (died 1677), who spent only a few years in India before returning to Iran. Yet, of his immense poetical output (300,000 couplets), the great majority belongs to the stock-in-trade expression of the Persian-speaking world. Other poets described the lives and adventures of members of the royal families, usually in verbose *mas̄navī*s (this kind of descriptive historical poetry was practiced throughout Muslim India and also in Ottoman Turkey). Outside the Mughal environment, the lyrics and *mas̄navī*s by Ẓuhūrī (died 1615) at the court of Bijāpur are charming and enjoyable. The heir apparent of the Mughal Empire, Dārā Shikōh (executed 1659), also followed Akbar's path. His inclination to mysticism is reflected in both his prose and poetry. The Persian translation of the *Upaniṣads*, which he sponsored (and in part wrote himself) enriched Persian religious prose and made a deep impression on European idealistic philosophy in the 19th century. A group of interesting poets gathered about him, none of them acceptable to orthodoxy. They included the convert Persian Jew Sarmad (executed 1661), author of brilliant mystical *Robāʿīyāt*, and the Hindu Brahman (died 1662), Dārā's private secretary, whose prose work *Chahār chaman* ("Four Meadows") gives an interesting insight into life at court. With the long rule of Dārā's brother, the austere Aurangzeb (died 1707), the heyday of both poetry and historical writing in Muslim India was over. Once more, orthodox religious literature gained pre-eminence, while poets tried to escape into a fantasy world of dreams. The style of the two leading poets of this age, Nāṣir ʿAlī Sirhindī (died 1697) and Mīrzā Bēdil (died 1721), is convoluted and obscure, prompting the Persian poet Ḥazīn (died 1766), who came to India in the early 18th century, to write ironical comments about its incomprehensibility. Bēdil, however, was a very interesting writer. His lyric poetry is difficult but often rewarding, while his many philosophical *mas̄navī*s deserve deep study. His prose work, interspersed with poetry, is called *Chahār ʿunṣur* ("Four Elements") and contains some biographical details. His prose is nearly as difficult as his poetry, and consequently his works rarely have been read west of India. His poetry, however, has had a great influence in Afghanistan and Central Asia. Many Persian-speaking people there consider him the forerunner of Tadzhik literature, since virtually everyone in Bukhara and Transoxania who tried his hand at poetry followed Bēdil's example. His ideas, sometimes astoundingly modern and progressive, have also impressed the 20th-century poet and philosopher Muḥammad Iqbāl in Muslim India.

Bēdil's progressive ideas

With Bēdil, the "Indian summer" of Persian literature comes to an end, even though the output of Persian poetry and prose during the 18th century in the subcontinent was immense. Some of the biographical dictionaries and handbooks of mysticism are valuable for the scholar but are less interesting as part of the general history of literature. The main vehicle of poetry now became Urdu, while mystical poetry flourished in Sindhi and Punjabi.

Pashto poetry: Khushḥāl Khān Khaṭak. From the borderlands of the Persian-speaking zone, culturally under the Mughal rule, one man deserves special attention. The Pathan tribal chief, Khushḥāl Khān Khaṭak (died 1689), rightly deserves to be called the "father" of Pashto poetry, for he created a literature of his own in his mother tongue. His skill in translating the sophisticated traditions of Persian literature into the not too highly developed idiom of the Pathans is astonishing. His lively lyric poems are his finest works, reflecting that passionate love of freedom for which he fought against the Mughals. The poems he wrote from prison in "hell-like hot India" are as dramatic as they are touching in their directness. Many members of his family took to poetry; and during the 18th century original works, both religious and secular, were composed in Pashto, and the classics of Persian literature were translated into that language.

Ottoman Turkey. The development of literature in Ottoman Turkey is almost parallel with that of Iran and India. Yunus Emre had introduced a popular form of mystical poetry; yet the mainstream of secular and religious literature followed Persian models (although it took some time to establish the Persian rules of prosody because of the entirely different structure of the Turkish language). In the religious field, the vigour and boldness expressed in the poems of Nesimî (executed 1417) left their traces in the work of later poets, none of whom, however, reached his loftiness and granduer of expression. The 14th- and 15th-century representatives of the classical style had displayed great charm in their literary compositions, their verses simple and pleasing. Sultan Cem (Jem [died 1495]), son of Mehmed the Conqueror, is an outstanding representative of their number. But soon the high-flown style of post-classical Persian was being imitated by Ottoman authors, rhetoric often being more important to them than poetical content. The work of Bâkî (Bāqī [died 1600]) is representative of the entire range of these Baroque products. Yet his breathtaking command of language is undeniable; it is brilliantly displayed in his elegy on Süleyman the Magnificent. In his time, according to a popular saying, one could find "a poet under every stone of Istanbul's pavement." Istanbul was the unique cultural centre of the Near East, praised throughout the ages by all who lived in the imperial city.

Poetry of Fuzûlî of Baghdad. Much greater than most of these minor poets, however, was a writer living outside the capital, Fuzûlî of Baghdad (died 1556), who wrote in Arabic, Persian, and Azeri Turkish. Apart from his lyrics, his Turkish *mas̄navī* on the traditional subject of the lovers Majnūn and Laylā is admirable. From earliest times, Turkish poets had emulated the classical Persian romantic *mas̄navī*s, sometimes surpassing their models in expressiveness. Fuzûlî's diction is taut, his command of imagery masterly. His style unfortunately defies poetical translation, and his complicated fabric of plain and inverted images, of hidden and overt allusions is well-nigh impossible for all but the initiated Muslim reader to disentangle. Fuzûlî, moreover, like his fellow poets, would blend Arabic, Persian, and Turkish constructions and words to make up a multifaceted unit. The same difficulty is found in Turkish prose literature of the same period. It is a major task to unravel the long trailing sentences of a writer such as Evlia Çelebî (died after 1679), who, in an account of his travels (*Seyahatnâme*), has left extremely valuable information about the cultural climate in different parts of the Ottoman Empire.

Emulation of classical Persian *mas̄navī*s

Later developments. Growing interest in the Indo-Persian style, particularly in ʿUrfī's *qaṣīdah*s, led the 17th-century Ottoman poets to a new integrated style and precision of diction. An outstanding representative was Nef'î, whose bent for merciless satire made him dreaded in the capital and eventually led to his assassination. The start of the 18th century saw a marked but short-lived movement in Turkish art known as the "Tulip Period," which was the Ottoman counterpart of European Rococo. The musical poems and smooth *ghazals* of Nedim (died 1730) reflect the manners and style of the slightly decadent, relaxed, and at times licentious high society of Istanbul and complement the miniatures of his contemporary Levnî. Good Turkish poetry is characterized by an easy grace, to be found even in such mystically tinged poems (thousands of which were written throughout the centuries) as those of Niyazî Misrî (died 1693). The Mevlevî (Mawlawī) poet Gâlib Dede (died 1799) was already standing at the threshold of what can now be recognized as modern poetical expression in some of the lyrical parts of his *mas̄navī*, called *Hüsn u Aşk* ("Beauty and Love"), which brought fresh treatment to a well-worn subject of Iran's philosophical and secular literature.

Folk poetry. One branch of literature, however, was totally neglected by the sophisticated inhabitants of the Ottoman capital. Nobody thought much of the folk poets who wandered through the forgotten villages of Anatolia singing in simple syllable-counting verses of love, longing, and separation. The poems of the mid-17th century figure Karacaoğlan, one of the few historically datable folk poets, give a vivid picture of village life, of the plight of girls and boys in remote Anatolian settlements. This kind of poetry was rediscovered only after the foundation of the Turkish Republic in 1923 and then became an important influence on modern lyric poetry.

EUROPEAN AND COLONIAL INFLUENCES: EMERGENCE OF WESTERN FORMS

The rise of nationalism. For the Islāmic countries, the 19th century marks the beginning of a new epoch. Napoleon's conquest of Egypt, as well as British colonialism, brought the Muslims into contact with a world whose technology was far in advance of their own. The West had experienced the ages of Renaissance, Reformation, and Enlightenment, whereas the once-flourishing Muslim civilization had for a long while been at near stagnation point despite its remarkable artistic achievements. The introduction of Muslim intellectuals to Western literature and scholarship—the Egyptian aṭ-Ṭahṭāwī (died 1873), for example, studied in France—ushered in a new literary era the chief characteristic of which was to be "more matter, less art." The literatures from this time onward are far less "Islāmic" than those of the previous 1,000 years, but new intellectual experiences also led to "the liberation of the whole creative impulse within the Islamic peoples" (Kritzeck). The introduction of the printing press and the expansion of newspapers helped to shape a new literary style, more in line with the requirements of the modern times, when "the patron prince has been replaced by a middle-class reading public" (Badawi). Translations from Western languages provided writers with the model examples of genres previously unknown to them, including the novel, the short story, and dramatic literature. Of those authors whose books were translated, Guy de Maupassant, Sir Walter Scott, and Anton Chekhov have been most influential in the development of the novel and the novella. Important also was the ideological platform derived from Tolstoy, whose criticism of Western Christianity was gratefully adopted by writers from Egypt to Muslim India. Western influences can further be observed in the gradual discarding of the time-hallowed static (and turgid) style of both poetry and prose; in the tendency toward simplification of diction; and in the adaptation of syntax and vocabulary to meet the technical demands of emulating Western models. Contact with the West also encouraged a tendency toward retrospection. Writers concentrated their attention on their own country and particular heritage, such as the "pharaoic myth" of Egypt, the Indo-European roots of Iran, and the Central Asian past of Turkey. In short, there was an emphasis on differentiation, inevitably leading to the rise of nationalism, instead of an emphasis on the unifying spirit and heritage of Islām.

Muslim intellectuals' introduction to Western scholarship

Arab literatures. Characteristically, therefore, given this situation, the heralds of Arab nationalism (as reflected in literature) were Christians. The historical novels of Jurjī Zaydān (died 1914), a Lebanese living in Egypt, made a deep impression on younger writers by glorifying the lion-hearted national heroes of past times. Henceforth, the historical novel was to be a favourite genre in all Islāmic countries, including Muslim India. The inherited tradition of the heroic or romantic epic and folktale was blended with novelistic techniques learned from Sir Walter Scott. Two writers from Syria are in the front rank of Arab intellectuals: Amīr Shakīb Arslān (died 1946), of Druze origin, and Muḥammed Kurd ʿAlī (died 1953), the founder of the Arab Academy of Damascus, each of whom made an important contribution to the education, by encouraging a new degree of awareness, of modern historians and men of letters. An inclination toward Romanticism can be detected in prose writing but not, surprisingly, in poetry; thus, the Egyptian al-Manfalūṭī (died 1924) poured out his feelings in a number of novels that touch on Islāmic as well as national issues. Many later novelists writing in Arabic watered down his style and produced only tearjerkers.

Poetry. It is fair to say of this transition period that the poetry being written was not as interesting as the prose. The *qaṣīdah*s of the "Prince of Poets," Aḥmad Shawqī (died 1932), are for the most part ornate imitations of classical models. Even the "Poet of the Nile," Muḥammad Ḥāfiẓ Ibrahim (died 1932), who was more interested in the real problems of the day, was nonetheless content to follow conventional patterns. In his poems, Khalīl Muṭrān (died 1949) attempted to achieve a unity of structure hitherto almost unknown; and he also adopted a more subjective approach to expressive lyricism. Thus, he can be said to have inaugurated an era of "Romantic" poetry, staunchly defended by those men of letters who had come under English rather than French influence. These included the poet and essayist Ibrāhīm al-Māzinī (died 1949) and the prolific writer of poetry and prose ʿAbbās Maḥmūd al-ʿAqqād (died 1964).

Prose. A major contribution to the development of modern prose in the Arabic language was made by a number of writers born between 1889 and 1902. One of them, the "humanist" Taha Hussein, became well-known in the West as a literary critic who attacked the historical authenticity of pre-Islāmic poetry and stressed the importance of Greek and Latin for the literatures of the modern Near East. He is also the author of a successful novel called *The Tree of Misery;* but his best creative writing is in his autobiographical notes, *al-Ayyām* ("The Days"), which describe in austere language the life of a blind Egyptian village boy. Taha Hussein's generation became more and more absorbed by the problems of the middle classes (to which most of them belonged), and this led them to realism in fiction. Some turned to fierce social criticism, depicting in their writings the dark side of everyday life in Egypt and elsewhere. The leading writer of this group is Maḥmūd Taymūr, who wrote short stories, a genre developed in Arabic by a Lebanese Christian who settled in the United States, the noted and versatile poet Khalil Gibran (Jibrān Khalīl Jibrān [died 1931]). Muḥammad Ḥusayn Haykal (died 1956), a leading figure of Egyptian cultural and political life and the author of numerous historical studies, touched for the first time, in his novel *Zaynab* (1913), on the difficulties of Egyptian villagers. This subject quickly afterward became fashionable, although not all the writers had first-hand knowledge of the feelings and problems of the fellahin. The most fertile author of this group was al-ʿAqqād, mentioned above, who tirelessly produced biographies, literary criticism, and romantic poetry. To what extent the Islāmic reform movement led by Muḥammad ʿAbduh (died 1905) and his disciples, which centred on the journal *al-Manār* ("The Lighthouse"), has influenced present-day Arabic prose style cannot yet be ascertained. It has, however, been important in shaping the religious outlook of many authors writing in the 1920s and 1930s.

The diaspora. A considerable amount of Arabic literature has been produced by numerous writers who settled in non-Islāmic countries, especially in the United States and Brazil. Most of these transplanted writers came from Christian Lebanese families. A feeling of nostalgia often led them to form literary circles or launch magazines, one of which, *al-Hudā* ("The Guidance"), founded in 1908, still exists. It was largely because of their work that the techniques of modern fiction and modern free verse entered Arabic literature and became a decisive factor in it. (Of special influence in the latter genre was the work of Walt Whitman.)

One of the best known authors in this group was Amīn ar-Rīḥānī (died 1941), whose descriptions of his journeys through the Arab world are informative and make agreeable reading. The fact that so many Lebanese emigrated to foreign countries led to the creation of a standard theme in Lebanese fiction: the emigrant who returns to his village. Iraqi modern literature is best represented by "the poet of freedom" Maʿṣūf ar-Ruṣāfī (died 1945) and Jamīl Sidqī az-Zahāwī (died 1936) whose satire "Rebellion in Hell" has incurred the wrath of the traditionalists.

The recurring theme in Lebanese fiction

Turkish literatures. The same changing attitude toward the function of literature and the same shift toward realism can be observed in Turkey. After 1839, Western ideas and forms were taken up by a group of modernists: Ziya Paşa (died 1880), the translator of Rousseau's *Émile* (which became a popular textbook for 19th-century Muslim intellectuals), was among the first to write in a less traditional idiom and to complain in his poetry—just as Ḥālī was to do in India a few years later—about the pitiable conditions of Muslims under the victorious Christians. Ziya Paşa, together with Şinasi (died 1871) and Namık Kemal (died 1888), founded an influential Turkish journal, *Tasvir-i Efkâr* ("Picture of Ideas"). The essential theme of the articles, novels, poems, and dramas composed by these authors is their fatherland (*vatan*), and they dared to advocate freedom of thought, democracy, and constitutionalism. Abdülhak Hâmid (died 1935), though considerably their junior, shared in their activities. In 1879 he published his epoch-making *Sahra* ("The Country"), a collection of ten Turkish poems that were the first to be composed in Western verse forms and style. Later, he turned to weird and often morbid subject matter in his poetic dramas. He, like his colleagues, had to endure political restrictions on writing, imposed as part of the harsh measures taken by Sultan Abdülhamid II against the least sign of liberal thought. Influenced by his work, later writers aimed to simplify literary language: Ziya Gökalp (died 1924) laid the philosophical foundations of Turkish nationalism; and Mehmed Emin, a fisherman's son, sang artless Turkish verses of his pride in being a Turk, throwing out the heavy rhetorical ballast of Arabo-Persian prosody and instead turning to the language of the people, unadulterated by any foreign vocabulary. The stirrings of social criticism could be discerned after 1907. Mehmed Akif (died 1936), in his masterly narrative poems, gave a vivid critical picture of conditions in Turkey before World War I. His powerful and dramatic style, though still expressed in traditional metres, is a testimony to his deep concern for the people's sorrows. It was he who composed the Turkish National Anthem after Mustafa Kemal Atatürk's victory; but soon afterward he left the country, disappointed with the religious policies of the Kemalists.

Atatürk's struggle for freedom also marks the real beginning of modern Turkish literature. The mainstream of novels, stories, and poems written during the 19th century had been replete with tears, world-weariness, and pessimism. But a postwar novel, *Ateşten gömlek* ("The Fire Shirt"), written by a woman, Halide Edib, reflected the brave new self-awareness of the Turkish nation. Some successful short stories about village life came from the pen of Ömer Seyfeddin (died 1920). The most gifted interpreter and harshest critic of Turkey's social structure was Sabaheddin Ali, who was murdered on his flight to Bulgaria in 1948. His major theme was the tragedy of the lower classes, and his writing is characterized by the same merciless realism that was later to be a feature of stories by many left-wing writers throughout the Islāmic world. The "great old man of Turkish prose," Yakup Kadri Karaosmanoğlu, displayed profound psychological insight, whether ironically describing the lascivious life in a Bektāshī centre or a stranger's tragedy in an Anatolian village. Most of the Turkish novelists of the 1920s and 1930s concentrated on the problems of becoming a modern nation, and in particular they reinterpreted the role of women in a liberated society.

The "great old man of Turkish prose"

Literary energies were set completely free when Atatürk introduced the Latin alphabet in 1928, hoping that his people would forget their Islāmic past along with the Arabic letters. From this time onward, especially after the language reform that was meant to rediscover the pre-Islāmic roots of the Turkish language, Turkish literature followed the pattern of Western literature in all major respects, though with local overtones. Poets experimented with new forms and new topics. They discovered the significance of the Anatolian village, neglected—even forgotten—during the Ottoman period. Freeing themselves from the traditional rules of Persian poetry, they adopted simpler forms from Europe. In some cases the skillful blending of inherited Ottoman grace and borrowed French lyricism produced outstandingly beautiful poems, such as those of Ahmed Haşim (died 1933) and of Yahya Kemal Beyatlı (died 1958), in which the twilight world of old Istanbul is mirrored in soft, evocative hues and melodious words. At the same time, the figure of Nazım Hikmet (died 1963) looms large in Turkish poetry. Expressing his progressive social attitude in truly poetical form, he used free rhythmical patterns quite brilliantly to enrapture his readers; his style, as well as his powerful, unforgettable images, has deeply influenced not only Turkish, but also progressive Urdu and Persian poetry from the 1930s onward.

Persian literatures. In Iran, the situation to a certain extent resembled that in Turkey. While the last "classical" poet, Qāʾānī (died 1854), had been displaying the traditional glamorous artistry, his contemporary, the satirist Yaghmā (died 1859), had been using popular and comprehensible language to make coarse criticisms of contemporary society. As in the other Islāmic countries, a move toward simplicity is discernible during the last decades of the 19th century. The members of the polytechnic college Dār ol-Fonūn (founded 1851), led by its erudite principal Reẓā Qolī Khān Hedāyat, helped to shape the "new" style by making translations from European languages. Shāh Naṣer od-Dīn himself described his journeys to Europe in the late 1870s in a simple, unassuming style, and in so doing set an example to future prose writers.

At the turn of the century, literature became, for many younger writers, an instrument of modernization and of revolution, in the largest sense of the word. No longer did they want to complain, in inherited fixed forms, of some boy whose face was like the moon. Instead, the feelings and situation of women were stated and interpreted. Their oppression, their problems, and their grievances are a major theme of literature in this transition period of the first decades of the 20th century. The "King of Poets," Bahār (died 1951), who had been actively working before World War I for democracy, now devoted himself to a variety of cultural activities. But his poems, though highly classical in form, were of great influence; they dealt with contemporary events and appealed to a wide public.

One branch of modern Persian literature is closely connected with a group of Persian authors who lived in Berlin after World War I. There they established the Kaviani Press (named after a mythical blacksmith called Kaveh, who had saved the Iranian kingdom) and among the poems they printed were several by ʿĀref Qazvīnī (died 1934), one of the first really modern writers. They also published Moḥammad ʿAlī Jamālzādeh's first short stories, whose outspoken social criticism and complete break with the traditional inflated and pompous prose style inaugurated a new era of modern Persian prose. Many young writers adopted this new form, among them Ṣādeq

Authors of the Kaviani Press

Hedāyat (died 1951), whose stories—written entirely in a direct, everyday language whose purity of expression is an artistic achievement—have been translated into many languages. They reflect the sufferings of living individuals; instead of dealing in literary clichés, they describe the distress and anxiety of a hopeless youth. The influence of Franz Kafka (some of whose work Hedāyat translated) is perceptible in his writing, and he has a tendency toward psychological probing shared by many Persian writers.

As in neighbouring countries, women played a considerable role in the development of modern Persian literature. The lyrics of Parvīn Eʿteṣāmī (died 1940) are regarded as near classics, despite a trace of sentimentality in their sympathetic treatment of the poor. Some Persian writers whose left-wing political ideas brought them into conflict with the government left for the Tadzhik S.S.R. Of these, the gifted poet Lāhūtī (died 1957) is their most important representative.

India: Urdu and Persian. Persian literature in the Indian subcontinent did not have such importance as in earlier centuries, for English replaced Persian as the official language in 1835. Nevertheless, there were some outstanding poets who excelled in Urdu. One of them was Mīrzā Asadullāh Khān Ghālib (died 1869), the undisputed master of Urdu lyrics. He regarded himself, however, as the leading authority on high Persian style and was an accomplished writer of Persian prose and poetry. But much more important was a later poet, Sir Muḥammad Iqbāl (died 1938), who chose Persian to convey his message not only to the peoples of Muslim India but also to Afghans and Persians. Reinterpreting many of the old mystical ideas in the light of modern teachings, he taught the quiescent Muslim peoples self-awareness, urging them to develop their personalities to achieve true individuation. His first *maṡnavī*, called *Asrār-e khūdī* (1915; "Secrets of the Self"), deeply shocked all those who enjoyed the dreamlike sweetness of most traditional Persian poetry. On of his later Persian works, *Payām-e Mashriq* (1923; "Message of the East"), is an effective answer to Goethe's *West-östlicher Divan*. In the *Jāvīd-nāmeh* (1932) he poetically elaborated the old topic of the "heavenly journey," discussing with the inhabitants of the spheres a variety of political, social, and religious problems. Iqbāl's approach is unique. Although he used the conventional literary forms and leaned heavily on the inspiration of Jalāl ad-Dīn ar-Rūmī, he must be considered one of the select few poets of modern Islām who, because of their honesty and their capacity for expressing their message in memorable poetic form, appeal to many readers outside the Muslim world.

THE MODERN PERIOD

The modern period of Islāmic literatures can be said to begin after World War II. The topics discussed before then still appeared, but outspoken social criticism became an even more important feature. Literature was no longer a leisurely pastime for members of the upper classes. Writers born in the villages and from non-privileged classes began to win literary fame through their first-hand knowledge of social problems. Many writers started their careers as journalists, developing a literary style that retained the immediacy of journalistic observation.

Prose. In Egypt, a great change in literary preoccupations came about after 1952. The name of Najīb Maḥfūẓ is of particular importance. Born in 1912, he was at first a novelist mainly concerned with the lower middle classes (his outstanding work is a trilogy dealing with the life of a Cairo family); but afterward he turned to socially committed literature, using all the techniques of modern fiction—of which he is the undisputed master in Arabic. Yūsuf Idrīs (born 1929) deals first and foremost with the problems facing poor and destitute villagers, a subject also treated in Sharqāwī's novel *al-Arḍ* (*The Earth;* 1954). In Turkey, Yaşar Kemal's village story *İnce Memed* has won acclaim for its stark realism. The young left-wing writers in Iraq and Syria share the critical and aggressive attitudes of their contemporaries in Turkey and Egypt and are involved in every political issue. Most of them have responded to the works of Bertolt Brecht and Karl Marx. They are also quite familiar with at least the externals of modern psychology. Freudian influence—often in its crudest form—can be detected in many modern short stories or novels in the Islāmic countries; and it is often the prelude to coarse descriptions of sexuality, appealing to the lowest instincts of the reading public. In the Near and Middle East, the existentialist philosophy gained many followers who tried to reflect its interpretation of life in their literary works. In fact, almost every current of modern Western philosophy and psychology, every artistic trend and attitude, has been eagerly adopted—though often only half-understood—by young Arab, Turkish, or Persian writers. Some of them, nevertheless, have achieved interesting results from time to time: an example is Laylā Baʿlabakkī (born 1937), whose semiautobiographical novel, *I Live*, is regarded as an outstanding literary achievement in Arabic.

Poetry. *Arabic.* The new attitudes that have informed literature are even more conspicuous in poetry than in prose. Arabic poetry has at last freed itself completely from the fetters of classical tradition. Both French and English influences helped to shape the new art. The danger, at present, is that Western fashions are imitated uncritically, just as Arabic, Persian, or Turkish models were slavishly followed in the past. T.S. Eliot's poetry and criticism were influential in dethroning the Romanticism that many poets had adopted in the 1920s and 1930s. One of the first and most important attempts at creating a modern Arabic poetic diction was made in the late 1940s by the Iraqi poetess and critic Nāzik al-Malāʾikah (born 1923), whose poems, in free but rhyming verse, give substance to the shadow of her melancholia. Free rhythm and a colourful imagination distinguish the best poems of the younger Arabs: even when their poems do not succeed, their experimentation, their striving for sincerity, their burning quest for identity, their rebellion against social injustice, can be readily perceived. Indeed, one of the most noticeable aspects of contemporary Arabic poetry is its political engagement, mainly evident in the poems of Palestinian writers such as Maḥmūd Darwīsh, whose verses once more prove the strength, expressiveness, and vitality of the Arabic language. Others, without withdrawing into a world of uncommitted dreams, manage to create an atmosphere that breaks up the harsh light of reality into its colourful components. Poets like the Lebanese Adonis (ʿAlī Aḥmad Saʿīd [born 1930]), or Tawfīq aṣ-Ṣāʾigh (born 1924), or the Egypto-Sudanese Muḥammad al-Faytūrī (born 1930) make use of traditional imagery in a new, sometimes esoteric, often fascinating and daring way.

New use of traditional imagery

Persian. Almost the same situation exists in Iran. One notable poet was Forugh Farrokhzād, who wrote powerful yet very feminine poetry. Her free verses, interpreting the insecurities of our age, are full of longing; though often bitter, they are yet truly poetic. Poems by such critically minded writers as Seyāvūsh Kasrāʾī also borrow the classical heritage of poetic imagery, transforming it into expressions that win a response from modern readers.

Turkish. In Turkey, the adoption of Western forms began in the 1920s. Of major importance in modern Turkish literature was Orhan Veli (died 1950) who combined perfect technique with "Istanbulian" charm. His work is sometimes melancholy, sometimes frivolous, but always convincing. He strongly influenced a group of poets whose names are connected with the avant-garde literary magazine *Varlık* ("Existence"). It is still too early to determine what will be most representative of modern Turkish poetry: a return to Anatolian subjects, sometimes in picturesque diction, influenced by earlier folk-poetry, or the continuation of lovely poems in praise of Istanbul; surrealism or a somewhat detached and ironic approach to a subject. The same question, indeed, could be raised of almost any contemporary literature in Islāmic lands.

Contemporary features. In the Arab-speaking world, the problem of language has loomed large for many years. Classical high Arabic is still the common literary language of Morocco and Iraq, Tunisia and Kuwait. Spoken Arabic in dialectal variations is beginning to be used—but tentatively—in higher literature. It is more frequently employed in the popular spheres of theatre and cinema. But the local differences that exist in Arabic spoken from country to country have today become perceptible in literature; popular grammatical forms and syntactical constructions are occasionally used in modern poetry. A special problem arises in the North African countries, where French continues to be the chief literary language for most writers, especially in Morocco and Algeria. Yet there is no hard and fast rule: a leading member of the Senegal community, Amadou Bamba (died 1927), who founded the politically important group of the Murīdīs, wrote (quite apart from practical words of wisdom in his mother tongue) some 20,000 mystically tinged verses in classical Arabic.

The continuing problem of language

Throughout the Islāmic countries, the press and broadcasting have helped to disseminate literary works; prizes for literary achievements have stimulated interest in writing; low-priced books have made the more or less valuable output of a growing number of writers available to the majority—the more so since literacy among the population steadily increases. But to what degree this means a continuation of the cultural role that Islāmic literatures have played in the formation and education of society over the centuries is not yet clear. Literature was never restricted to a privileged high society; in olden times even the illiterate villager and the "uneducated" womenfolk had a fund of poems, proverbs, songs, and quotations from classical sources that they knew by heart and to which they turned for both pleasure and spiritual strength. It would be worthwhile investigating to what extent modern Islāmic literatures, given their preoccupation with important social problems, are able to reach the hearts of simple people.

One final symptom should be noted. The introduction of modern methods of criticism, of psychology and philosophy, has kindled a new interest in significant figures of the Islāmic past. Thus, to quote one instance, the figure of al-Ḥallāj (executed 922), who often served as a symbol figure of "the martyr of love" in both classical and folk poetry after the 11th century, has in recent years been made the subject of a Turkish drama, a Persian passion play, an Arabic tragedy, and plays an important role in Arabic, Turkish, Persian, and Indian Muslim lyrical poetry. He is interpreted in our day as a symbol of suffering for one's ideals, and he is therefore acceptable both to conservative Muslims and to progressive social critics.

STUDY AND EVALUATION

Early Islāmic criticism. The development of literature during the early Middle Ages soon produced among the Arabs much lively literary criticism. Even the choice of quotations made by the ancient grammarians from the classical stock of poetry implies a degree of critical (though subjective) activity. Attempts toward making a more objective study of poetic technique were first made in the late 9th century, when for the first time "beauties" and "faults" of verses were discussed and the ideals of the "new style" were defined by Ibn al-Muʿtazz in his *Kitāb al-badīʿ*. The relation between *lafẓ* (word), and *maʿnā* (meaning) has been a matter of some controversy —many earlier critics stress the importance of outward form rather than of content. There was some question, too, as to whether the most "poetical" verse was that which was the most "untrue"—that is to say, hyperbolic —or that which was closer to the heart of things. The matter was debated along with the problem of inspiration and imagination and their function in poetry. The most thorough analysis of the art of poetry was made by ʿAbd al-Qāhir al-Jurjānī (died 1078), who allowed equal weight to the idea and to the way it was expressed. An illuminating work about poetics was composed by the Tunisian critic al-Qarṭājannī (13th century), and this has been carefully studied by the German scholar Wolfhart Heinrichs, in *Arabische Dichtung und griechische Poetik* (1969). This study analyzes al-Qarṭājannī's theories in relation to Aristotle's theories of poetics. (Heinrichs, one of the few Islāmic scholars specializing in the study of literary problems, has shown that classical Arabic criticism rarely interested itself in the poem as a whole but concentrated upon individual verses.) In later centuries, manuals of poetics and rhetoric written in every Islāmic country reveal the prevailing interest in purely formal problems.

The controversy over word and meaning

Modern criticism. A similar interest long dominated the work of Western Orientalists. The first scholars who attempted to introduce Persian poetry to Western readers (such as Sir William Jones in the 18th century) thought it necessary to compare it with the compositions of Greek and Latin poetry. The verbal ingenuity of Ḥarīrī's *Maqāmāt* attracted the European scholars, who took great pleasure in disentangling the grammatically difficult forms. Pre-Islāmic poetry at first interested only the grammarian-antiquarian, until its importance as a source of knowledge of early Bedouin life was recognized. The art of versification and problems of classical Arabic metrics are forever matters of discussion among Orientalists.

Although a large amount of translation, mainly from Persian poetry, was produced in the 18th and 19th centuries, most of it suffered for lack of proper understanding: the translators took the poetical statements about wine and love or the outbursts against established religious forms at their face value and failed to recognize them for the stereotyped forms and images they are. A deep study of the imagery of Persian, Turkish, and Arabic is required before their poetry and belles-lettres can be properly understood and enjoyed. This was realized as early as 1818 by the Austrian Orientalist Joseph von Hammer-Purgstall (whose own translations from the three great Islāmic languages are, nevertheless, failures).

In the 20th century, the critical study of imagery in Oriental poetry was taken up by Hellmut Ritter in his booklet *Über die Bildersprache Niẓāmīs* (1927), which gives a most sensitive philosophical interpretation of Neẓāmī's metaphorical language and of the role of imagery in the structure of Neẓāmī's thought. His criticism is basic to the study of many other Persian poets. Slightly later, the Polish scholar Tadeusz Kowalski tried to interpret the "molecular" structure of Arabic literature—the absence of large units of thought or architectural structure—typical of the greater part of Islāmic literatures, which might be described as "carpetlike." This "molecular" structure can be related to the atomist theories and occasionalist world view embodied in Islāmic theology, which, unlike Christianity, does not admit of secondary causes and requires only short spans of hope from the faithful. In a number of articles, and in many books, E.G. von Grunebaum has pioneered this interpretation of literary structure. Other important critical works include S.A. Bonebakker's book on the rhetorical importance of *tawrīyah* (ambiguous wording); Manfred Ullmann's excellent study of *rajaz*-poetry and its place in Arabic literature; C.H. de Fouchécour's detailed analysis of the descriptions of nature in early Persian poetry.

Among the Arabs themselves, modern literary criticism began during the early 1920s. Most famous was Ṭaha Ḥussein's attempt to prove the whole corpus of pre-Islāmic poetry as counterfeit. All the Islāmic countries, from Turkey to Pakistan, and especially Iran, sponsor reviews in which Western-trained scholars critically survey the literary achievements of the Islāmic world.

A full evaluation of literature as the most faithful mirror of past (and to some extent present-day) Islāmic life is still lacking. Notwithstanding the conventionalized style of most Islāmic poetry, a deeper study of individual poets' expressions, use of verbal and nominal forms, rhythmical preferences, and the like would certainly reveal more about the personalities of outstanding writers. The impact of poetry on the Islāmic mind was, and to some extent still is, much deeper than a modern Western reader might suppose. The poets must be viewed, therefore, in relation to their society, for their work corresponded to the measure of receptiveness, their new modes of expression developed according to the widening awareness of their audiences. They had to use a language and imagery to which those whom they addressed were accustomed. A new idea, embodied in traditional imagery and a beguiling metre, could capture the attention of thousands of people. The role of the poet as religious and political herald (even though his political thought was all too often subservient to courtly flattery) was widely acknowledged, and the impact of a poet like Muḥammad Iqbāl in our times bears witness to the real power of poetical expression. Thus, even the most conventional Persian or Turkish poem can reflect certain attitudes of the Muslim mind more accurately than many a learned lecture. A modern short story, falling below Western artistic standards though it may, often tells the reader more about the feelings and reactions of the people than scholarly sociological research papers can. The magic of language is still a living force in the East.

(An.Sc.)

II. Music

The period of Islāmic music begins with the founding of the Muslim religion by the prophet Muḥammad in 622. A new art emerged, elaborated both from pre-Islāmic Arabian music and from important contributions by Persians, Byzantines, Turks, Berbers, Moors, and even from the European West. In this rapid musical development, the Arabian element acted as a catalyst, and, within a century, the new art was firmly established from Central Asia to the Atlantic. Such a fusion of musical styles succeeded because there were strong affinities between Arabian music and the music of the nations occupied by the expanding Arabic peoples. Not all Arab-dominated areas adopted the new art; Indonesia and parts of Africa, for example, retained native musical styles. The folk music of the Berbers in North Africa, the Moors in Mauretania, and other ethnic groups (*e.g.*, in Turkey) also remained alien to classical Islāmic music. The more one withdraws from the centre of gravity reaching from the Nile Valley to Persia, the further one moves from undiluted Islāmic music.

This portion of the article covers the relation of Islāmic music to poetry and dance, to various levels of society, and to religion. The aesthetic traditions, including melodic and rhythmic organization, are examined, and the major musical instruments are described, as well as the relation of Islāmic music to other cultures. The history of Islāmic music is treated at length, including its medieval flowering under the Umayyad and ʿAbbāsid caliphs, its development in Muslim Spain, its theoretical achievements, and its evolution in modern times. Finally, scholarly studies of Islāmic music are noted.

NATURE AND ELEMENTS OF ISLAMIC MUSIC

Islāmic music is characterized by a highly subtle organization of melody and rhythm, augmented by virtuoso improvisation and melodic ornament. Musical forms are closely tied to poetry and often alternate vocal solos with instrumental interludes. Melodies are organized in terms of *maqāmāt* (singular *maqām*), or "modes," characteristic melodic patterns with prescribed scales, preferential notes, typical melodic and rhythmic formulae, variety of intonations, and other conventional devices. The performer improvises within the framework of the *maqām*, which is also imbued with ethos (Arabic *taʾthīr*): a specific emotional or philosophical meaning attached to a musical mode. Rhythms are organized into rhythmic modes, or *īqāʿāt* (singular *īqāʿ*), cyclical patterns of strong and weak beats.

Classical Islāmic music is the aristocratic music of the court and the upper class, which underwent development and modification in the hands of gifted musicians throughout several centuries. Rhythmic and melodic modes grew in number and complexity, and new vocal and instrumental genres arose. In addition, a body of theoretical works grew up, influencing both Islāmic and —in some cases—European music.

The relation of music to poetry and dance. In pre-Islāmic times music was closely connected with poetry and dance. Being essentially vocal, pre-Islāmic music was an emotional extension of the solemn declamation of poems in Bedouin society. Later, the art of composition itself was based upon prosody: only by respecting the poetic metre in the music could the text, when sung, be clear in meaning and correct in pronunciation and grammatical inflection. In turn, prosody itself was used to explain the musical rhythm. Music in early Bedouin society was considered to have a magical power. The *shāʿir*, or poet-musician, said to be possessed by supernatural powers, was feared and respected. His satirical song poems were a formidable arm against enemies, and his poems of praise enhanced the prestige of his tribe. Musician-poets, especially women, accompanied the warriors, inciting them by their songs, and those who fell in battle benefitted from the elegies of the singer-poetesses. Musically, these elegies resembled the *ḥudāʾ* ("caravan song"), possibly used by camel drivers as a charm against the desert spirits, or *jinn*. Music and dance were closely associated from early times. Pre-Islāmic Bedouins used a special light rhythm called *hazaj* for their simple dances. Places of entertainment in the towns and oases employed professional dancers, mainly women. Art dancing embellished events in the courts of the Sāsānians, the pre-Islāmic rulers of Persia. In the Islāmic period, solo and ensemble forms of dance were an integral part of the intense musical activity in the palaces of the caliphs and in wealthy houses. Dance also was prominent in the *dhikr* ceremony of dervish religious fraternities.

The poet-musician

After the advent of Islām, music continued to exert some magical power in sophisticated society, but a deep change occurred in its social function. Emphasis was laid on music as entertainment and sensual pleasure, rather than as a source of high spiritual emotion, a change mainly resulting from Persian influence. Knowledge of music was obligatory for the cultured person. Skilled professional musicians were highly paid and were admitted to the caliphs' palaces as courtesans and trusted companions. The term *ṭarab*, which designates a whole scale of emotions, characterizes the musical conception of the time, and even came to mean music itself.

Music and religion. Fashionable secular music—and its clear association with erotic dance and drinking—stimulated hostile reactions from religious authorities. As Muslim doctrine does not sanction permitting or prohibiting a given practice by personal decision, the antagonists relied on forced interpretations of a few unclear passages in the Qurʾān (the sacred scripture of Islām) or on the *Ḥadīth* (traditions of the Prophet, sayings and practices that had acquired force of law). Thus both supporters and adversaries of music found arguments for their theses.

In the controversy, four main groups emerged: (1) uncompromising purists opposed to any musical expression; (2) religious authorities admitting only the cantillation of the Qurʾān and the call to prayer, or *adhān*; (3) scholars and musicians favouring music, believing there to be no musical difference between secular and religious music; and (4) important mystical fraternities—such as the dervish fraternities and other groups within the Ṣūfī branch of Islām—for whom music and dance were a means toward unity with God.

Religious music

Except in the brotherhoods such as the dervishes, Muslim religious music is relatively curtailed because of the opposition of religious leaders. It falls into two categories: the call to prayer, or *adhān* (in some places, *azān*), by the *muʾadhdhin*, or muezzin, and the cantillation of the Qurʾān. Both developed from relatively solemn cantillation to a variety of forms, both simple and highly florid. The cantillation of the Qurʾān reflected the ancient Arabic practice of declamation of poetry, with careful regard to word accents and inflections and to the clarity of the text. Yet it was possibly also influenced by early secular art song. Opponents of music considered the cantillation of the Qurʾān to be technically distinct from singing, and it acquired a separate terminology. Synagogues and the Eastern Christian churches, unhampered by such opposition, developed extensive musical repertories based on melodic modes: the Eastern churches used the eight modes of Byzantine music, while synagogue music followed the *maqām* system of Muslim art music.

Aesthetic traditions. Even in its most complicated aspects, Islāmic music is traditional and transmitted orally. Although a musical notation exists, little written music survives. Notation was largely unnecessary, for virtuoso perfomance depended on improvisation, and musicians were not eager to share their compositions with rivals.

There survives a large body of medieval writings about music, falling mainly into two categories: (1) literary, encylopaedic, and anecdotal sources, and (2) theoretical, speculative sources. The second group deals with acoustics, intervals (distances between notes), musical genres, scales, measures of instruments, the theory of composition, rhythm, and the mathematical aspects of music. The first includes precious information on musical life, musicians, aesthetic controversies, education, and the theory of musical practice. These documents show that, as in the modern era, medieval Islāmic music was principally an individual, soloistic art. Small ensembles were actually groups of soloists with the principal member, usually the singer, predominating. Being an essentially vocal music, it displayed many singing and vocal techniques, such as special vocal colour, guttural nasality, vibrato, and other stylistic ornaments. Although the music was based upon strict rules, pre-existing melodies, and stylistic requirements, the performer enjoyed great creative freedom. The artist was expected to bring his contribution to a given traditional piece through improvisation, original ornamentation, and his own approach to tempo, rhythmic pattern, and the distribution of the text over the melody. Thus the artist functioned both as performer and composer.

The soloist's role

Melodic organization. Islāmic music is monophonic; *i.e.*, it consists of a single line of melody. In performance everything is related to the refinement of the melodic line and the complexity of rhythm. The notion of harmony is completely absent, although occasionally a simple combination of notes, octaves, fifths, and fourths, usually below the melody notes, may be used as an ornamentation. Among the elements contributing to the enrichment of the melody are microtonality (the use of intervals smaller than a Western half step or lying between a half step and a Western whole step) and the variety of intervals used. Thus the three-quarter tone, introduced into Islāmic music in the 9th or 10th century, exists alongside larger and smaller intervals. Musicians show a keen sensibility to nuances of pitch, often slightly varying even the perfect consonances, the fourth and fifth.

The mode, or *maqām*

As the fourth is the basic melodic frame, theorists organized the intervals and their nuances into genres, or small units, often tetrachords (units the highest and lowest notes of which are a fourth apart), combining genres into larger units, or systems. More than 130 systems resulted; on these are based the musical scales of the modes. The scale of a mode can thus be broken down into small units that are of importance in the formation of melodies. A *maqām* or "mode," is a complex musical entity given distinct musical character by its given scale, small units, range and compass, predominant notes, and pre-existing typical melodic and rhythmic formulas. It serves the musician as rough material for his own composition. Each *maqām* has a proper name that may refer to a place (as Hejaz, Iraq) to a famous man, or to an object, feeling, quality, or special event. Emotional or philosophical meaning (ethos, or *ta'thīr*) and cosmological background are attached to a *maqām* and also to the rhythmic modes. The Arabic term *maqām* is replaced by *dastgāh* in Persia, *naghmah* in Egypt, and *tbā* in North Africa.

Rhythmic organization. Rhythms and their organization into cycles of beats and pauses of varying lengths (rhythmic modes, or *īqā'āt*) are much discussed in theoretical writings and are of supreme importance in performance. Each cycle consists of a fixed number of time units with a characteristic distribution of strong and weak beats and pauses. In performance some of the pauses may be filled in, but the underlying pattern must be maintained. Parallel to the growth of the number of melodic modes—from 12 in the 8th century to more than 100 in the 20th—is the increase in the number of rhythmic modes from eight in the 9th century to more than 100 in the 20th.

Musical forms. Vocal music comprises two main categories: a) unmeasured songs characterized by long vocalises either with few words or textless; b) metrical songs embracing the various poetic forms and metric structure, such as *qaṣīdah, musammaṭ, muwashshah*, etc. Verses are considered separate entities so that the musician can add vocalises and instrumental interludes at the end of each verse. Both categories are almost always accompanied by either one or more instruments whose aim is to enrich the performance by free improvisations or measured passages. Important medieval forms included the *nashīd* and *basīṭ*, forms representing in one performance the alternation of the two categories mentioned above, and the *nawbah* ("suite") including songs and instrumental music, free or metrical, linked together by melodic mode and rhythmic patterns.

Modern musical forms in the area reaching from Egypt to Iraq include the *taqsīm*, an unmeasured improvisation performed by a soloist, or a group of instrumentalists who take turns in developing the *maqām*. The *bashraf* is an instrumental form in measured rhythm, in which four sections, played by various soloists, are separated by a recurring refrain, played by the ensemble. The *layālī*, in which the singer may accompany himself on the lute, is sung with vocalises, rather than words, and is a vocal equivalent of the *taqsīm*. In modern North Africa the *nawbah* survives as an important form.

Instruments of music. Instrumental music is not considered an independent art from vocal music except in Persia, where it is cultivated for its own sake. Yet many instruments were fully described by early writers, and their use in folk, art, religious, and military music pointed out. The most favoured instrument of ancient Near Eastern civilization, the harp, was gradually overshadowed by both long- and short-necked lutes.

Percussion instruments. Among idiophones (instruments the hard bodies of which vibrate to produce sound) commonly used are the *qaḍīb* ("percussion stick"), the *sunūj* ("cymbals"), and the *kāsāt*, or small finger cymbals. Membranophones, or vibrating membrane instruments, include a variety of tambourines, or frame drums, under the generic name *duff*. These include the North African *ghirbāl* and *bendīr*, instruments used for folk dances which have "snares" across the skin; and the *dā'irah*, or *ṭar*, with jingling plates or rings set in the frame. The *dā'irah* and the vase-shaped drum *darabukka* (in Iran, *ẓarb*) are used in folk and art music, and the small kettledrums *naqqārah* and *nuqayrat* are used in military and art music. The large two-headed cylindrical drum, the *ṭabl* (Turkish *davul*), is generally played with the oboe-like *zornā* or *gayta* in processions and open-air ceremonies.

Wind instruments. Classed with the *zornā* and *gayta* as aerophones, or wind instruments, are the *būq*, or horn, the *nafīr*, or long trumpet, and a variety of flutes called *nāy* or *shabbābah*. Clarinet-like (single reed) double-piped instruments such as the *dunay*, *zammārah*, and *urghūl* are used in folk events and open-air ceremonies.

Stringed instruments. Chordophones, or stringed instruments, constitute the most important family. The favourite instrument of Islāmic classical music is the *'ūd*, a short-necked lute having four or five strings and resembling the Western lute, which derived from the *'ūd*. In addition to holding musical supremacy, it was important in medieval theoretical and cosmological speculations. It has two derivatives in North Africa, the *kuwītra* and the *gunbrī*. The long-necked lutes favoured in Turkey, Iran, and the countries eastward include the *ṭunbūr*, *tār*, and *setār*. Another plucked instrument is the *qānūn*, or trapezoid-shaped psaltery, played at least from early medieval times. The trapezoidal dulcimer, or *santūr*, the strings of which are struck with two thin sticks, is widespread and is especially prominent in Persian art music. Bowed lutes, or fiddles, include the *rabāb*, used by epic singers and beggars, and the *kamān*, or *kamanjā*, a hemispherically-shaped fiddle the body of which, like that of the *rabāb*, is pierced by the length of wood forming the neck (such instruments are known as spike fiddles). The violin, played either on the knee like the *kamanjā*, or beneath the collarbone, is also common.

The relation of Islāmic music to music of other cultures. The relation of Islāmic music to the West reveals itself both in musical theory and practice. By the 9th century many Greek treatises had been translated into Arabic. Arabic culture preserved Greek musical writings, and most of those that reached the West did so in their Arabic versions. Arab theorists followed Greek models, often developing them further. The Muslim occupation of Spain and Portugal and the Crusades to the Near East brought Europeans in contact with Arabic theoretical writings and the flourishing Islāmic art music. Musical instruments such as the lute, the rebec (a small bowed instrument derived from the *rabāb*), and the kettledrum (in the form of a pair of small kettledrums called nakers, from the Arabic *naqqārah*) became firmly established in European music. Arabic writings were translated, among them the *De scientiis*, a work on the arts and sciences by the great 10th-century philosopher and musician al-Fārābī (Latinized as Alpharabius). Such translations give further indication of the influence exerted by Muslim writers. Arabian influence on European medieval music is difficult to prove. Borrowed elements were possibly completely transformed. The influence of Islāmic music on European music is, at present, a subject of controversy.

Medieval contacts with Europe

In the 13th century, Arab conquerors reached India, and Mongol and Turkmen armies invaded the Near East, with resulting contact between Islāmic and Far Eastern music. There are similarities between the modal systems of India (the *rāgas*) and of the Near East (the *maqām* system) and between some cosmological and ethical conceptions of music. The migration of musical instruments from the Islāmic area to the Far East can also be traced. The Chinese oboe, the *sona*, apparently derived its name from its Near Eastern counterpart, the *zornā* or *sornā*. The Indian long-necked lute sitar, having a different number of strings from the Persian *setār*, received its name, and perhaps part of its form, from the *setār*. The Chinese dulcimer, *yang ch'in* ("foreign zither"), originated in the Middle Eastern *santūr*. On the other hand, the musical instruments appearing in the pre-Islāmic Ṭāq-e Bostān reliefs in Persia show a mouth organ similar to the Chinese *sheng*, indigenous to the Far East.

THE HISTORY OF ISLAMIC MUSIC

Toward the end of the 9th century, more than 250 years after the advent of Islām, musicians, writers, and philosophers began to speculate on the origins of their music. In the absence of historical documents, they filled the gaps by legendary sources or vague traditions. Thus Lamak is said to have made the first lute from the leg of his dead son, whose loss he lamented with it. Other stories relate that the first song in the desert was the *ḥudā'* ("caravan song"), from which issued the secular song (*naṣb*). Early writers also mentioned the *ghinā'*, or art song, and the *hazāj*, a dancing song.

The pre-Islāmic period. In nomadic encampments music emphasized every event in man's life, embellished social meetings, incited the warriors, encouraged the desert traveller, and exhorted the pilgrims to the black stone of the Kaʿbah (in Mecca), a holy shrine even in pre-Islāmic times. In the markets of the Arabs, particularly the fair at the western Arabian town of ʿUkāẓ, competitions of poetry and musical performances were held periodically, attracting the most distinguished poet-musicians. Their music, more sophisticated than that practiced in the nomadic encampments, was related to that of the *qaynāt* ("singing girls"). Pre-Islāmic poets such as Ṭarafah, Labīd, and Aʿshā extolled the beauty and art of the *qaynāt*, who performed at court, in noble households, and in scattered taverns. Cultural contact with Byzantium was strong in the kingdom of Ghassān, where, in the 7th century, five Byzantine singing girls were known to have performed songs of their homeland at court. The culture of the other Arabic kingdom of al-Ḥīrah under the Lakhmid dynasty was closely connected with that of Persia under the pre-Islāmic Sāsānian empire. The Sāsānians esteemed both secular and religious music. In the belief of the Mazdak sect (a dualistic Persian religion related to Manichaeism, a Gnostic religion), music was considered as one of the four spiritual powers. In the king's entourage musicians occupied high rank. Some became famous, such as Bārbad, to whom is attributed the invention of the complicated pre-Islāmic system of modes. The compositions of Bārbad, who became a model of artistic achievement in Arabic literature, survived at least until the 10th century.

Courtly music

The beginning of Islām and the first four caliphs. Muḥammad was said to have been hostile to music and musicians, yet there are indications that he tolerated functional music such as war songs, pilgrimage chants, and public or private festival songs. In addition, he himself instituted in 622 or 623 the *adhān* ("call to prayer"), chanted by the *mu'adhdhin* (muezzin). For this task he chose the Abyssinian singer Bilāl, who became the patron of the *mu'adhdhin* and their guilds throughout the Islāmic world. Within 12 years after Muḥammad's death, the armies of Islām took possession of Syria, Iraq, Persia, Armenia, Egypt, and Cyrenaica (in modern Libya). The contact with the refined cultures of the conquered and the appearance of a new class of warriors who benefitted from the spoils of the conquered nations deeply affected Arabian society. In spite of the austere regime of the four orthodox caliphs (632–660), joy of life and eagerness for pleasure dominated the two holy cities of Mecca and Medina. Wealthy men acquired slave musicians, who were often liberated and became the pillars of musical life. The wealthy competed with one another in the brilliance of the concerts held in their houses, and in sophisticated literary and musical salons, contests revealed and rewarded the best talents. In this milieu a new generation of musicians was educated in the traditional manner and refined through constant hearing of the best music performed by the best masters. Through the contributions of the conquered "foreigners," and through intense emulation of their music, new techniques, improved instruments, and elaborated musical forms developed. Persian lute tuning was adopted for the lute (*ʿūd*), which became the classical instrument of the Arabs. Melodies and rhythms were regulated by a modal system that was codified by later generations. Among the most famous female musicians was ʿAzza al-Maylā', who excelled in *al-ghinā' ar-raqīq*, or "gentle song." Her house was the most brilliant literary salon of Medina, and most of the famous musicians of the town came under her tutelage. Also famed were the female musician Jamīla, around whom clustered musicians, poets, and dignitaries; the male musician Ṭuways, who, attracted by the melodies sung by Persian slaves, imitated their style; and Ṣā'ib Khāthiz, the son of a Persian slave. Songs were generally accompanied by the lute (*ʿūd*), the frame drum (*duff*), or the percussion stick (*qaḍīb*).

Sophisticated secular music

The Umayyad and ʿAbbāsid dynasties: classical Islāmic music. Under the Umayyad caliphate (661–750) the classical style of Islāmic music emerged. The capital was moved to Damascus (in modern Syria) and the courts were thronged with male and female musicians, who formed a class apart. Many prominent musicians were Arab by birth or acculturation, but the alien element continued to play a predominant role in Islāmic music. The first and the greatest musician of the Umayyad era was Ibn Misjaḥ, often honoured as the father of Islāmic music. Born in Mecca of a Persian family, he was a musical theorist and a skilled singer and lute player. Ibn Misjaḥ travelled to Syria and Persia, learning the theory and practice of Byzantine and Persian music, and incorporating much of his acquired knowledge into the Arabian art song. Although he adopted new elements such as foreign musical modes, he rejected other musical traits as unsuitable to Arabian music. Knowledge of his contributions is contained in the most important source of information about music and musical life in the first three centuries of Islām. This is the 10th-century *Kitāb*

Further influence of conquered peoples

al-Aghānī, or "Book of Songs," by Abū al-Faraj al-Iṣbahānī. In the 8th century Yūnus al-Kātib, author of the first Arabic book of musical theory, compiled the first collection of songs. Other notable musicians of the period were Ibn Muḥriz, of Persian ancestry; Ibn Surayj, son of a Persian slave and noted for his elegies and improvisations (*murtajal*); his pupil al-Gharīḍ, born of a Berber family; and the Negro Maʿbad. Like Ibn Surayj, Maʿbad cultivated a special personal style adopted by following generations of singers.

By the end of the Umayyad period, the disparate elements of conqueror and conquered were fused into the style of classical Islāmic music. With the establishment of the ʿAbbāsid caliphate in 750, Baghdad (in modern Iraq) became the leading musical centre. The ʿAbbāsid caliphate is the period of the Golden Age in Islāmic music. Music, obligatory for every learned man, was dealt with in varied aspects, among them virtuosity, aesthetic theory, ethical and therapeutic goals, mystical experience, and mathematical speculation. The artist was required to possess technical proficiency, creative power, and almost encyclopaedic knowledge. Among the finest artists of the period were Ibrāhīm al-Mawṣilī and his son Isḥāq. Members of a noble Persian family, they were chief court musicians and close companions of the caliphs Hārūn ar-Rashīd and al-Ma'mūn.

The Golden Age

Isḥāq, a singer, composer, and virtuoso lutist, was the outstanding musician of his time. A man of wide culture, he is credited with authorship of nearly 40 works on music, which were subsequently lost. According to the "Book of Songs," he is the originator of the earliest Islāmic theory of melodic modes. Called *aṣābiʿ* ("fingers"), it structured the modes according to the frets of the lute and the fingers corresponding to them. Indications above each song in the "Book of Songs" show the mode, the type of third (major, minor, or neutral), and often, the rhythmic mode. (The third is the interval encompassing three notes of the scale. It can vary considerably in exact size without losing its character. Western music uses the major and the minor third; much non-Western and folk music also uses a neutral third, between the major and minor in size.) The neutral third, introduced into Islāmic music about this time, increased the number of melodic modes (later called *maqāmāt*) from eight to twelve by making more intervals available from which to build melodies. At this time the number of rhythmic modes varied from six to eight, their actual structure and content differing from author to author.

Isḥāq and Ibrāhīm al-Mawṣilī actively participated in the contemporary controversy between modernism, a Persian romantic style tending toward exuberance of embellishments, and Arabian classicism, characterized by simplicity and artistic severity. The Mawṣilīs represented the older classical tradition; the proponents of modernism were Ibn Jāmiʿ and the celebrated singer Prince Ibrāhīm ibn al-Mahdī.

Theoretical writings

In the second half of the 8th century, the extensive Islāmic literature of music theory began to flourish. Greek treatises were translated into Arabic, and scholars, acquainted with the Greek writings, began to devote books or sections of books to the theory of music. In their works they expanded, changed, improved, or shed new light on Greek musical theory. The famous philosopher al-Kindī, who was deeply immersed in Greek learning, wrote over 13 musical treatises, including the earliest surviving Arabic musical treatise. He also dealt with the theory of ethos (*ta'thīr*) and with cosmological aspects of music. Members of the Ikhwān aṣ-Ṣafā, an important 10th-century brotherhood, dealt also with these two themes and advanced a theory of sound going beyond ancient Greek theories. Philosophers such as al-Fārābī, author of the monumental *Kitāb al-musīqī al-Kabīr* ("Grand Book on Music"), and Ibn Sīnā (known in Europe as Avicenna; d. 1037) dealt with the theory of sound, intervals, genres and systems, composition, rhythm, and instruments, as did others such as as-Sarakhsī (d. 899), his contemporary Thābit ibn Qurrah, and Avicenna's pupil Ibn Zaylā. The last important theorist of the ʿAbbāsid period was Ṣafī ad-Dīn (d. 1294), who described in detail the system of melodic modes, dividing them into principal modes, or *maqāmāt*, and secondary modes, or *awazāt*. His writings strongly influenced a later group of theorists, the systematists, who, less influenced by Greek theoretical writings, gave extensive attention to problems involved in lute tunings.

Islāmic music in Spain. Parallel to the flourishing of music at the eastern centres of Damascus and Baghdad, another important musical centre developed in Spain, first under the survivors of the Umayyad rulers and later under the Berber Almoravids (rulers of North Africa and Spain in the 11th and 12th centuries) and Almohads, who expanded into Spain after the fall of the Almoravids. In Spain, encounter with different cultures stimulated the development of the Andalusian, or Moorish, branch of Islāmic music. The most imposing figure in this development is Ziryāb (fl. 9th century), a pupil of Isḥāq al-Mawṣilī who, because of the jealousy of his teacher, emigrated from Baghdad to Spain. A virtuoso singer and the leading musician at the court of Córdoba, he introduced a fifth string to the lute, devised new forms of composition, and developed new methods of teaching singing in his famous school of music. Musical activity spread to large towns, and Seville became a centre of musical-instrument manufacture. New poetic forms developed, such as *muwashshaḥ* and *zajal*, freer in rhyme and metre than the classical *qaṣīdah* or formal ode. These innovations opened the way to further musical developments. Especially important was the *nawbah* ("suite"), including songs and instrumental music, free or metrical, linked together by melodic mode and rhythmic patterns. The 24 traditional *nawbah*s were invested with symbolic and cosmological significance in the 13th century. Eleven of them survive in modern North African music, each associated with a particular time of day.

Poetic and musical forms

After the Mongol invasion of Baghdad in 1258 and the Spanish reconquest of Granada in 1492, the magnificence of Islāmic culture gradually waned. Music continued to be cultivated, receiving new influences from Mongol and Turkmen conquerors. Persia enjoyed artistic independence for about 450 years, from the capture of Constantinople in 1453 until 1918; but during this period a huge area, from the Balkans to Tunisia, was submitted to a strong Turkish influence, which itself was heavily influenced by Arab and Persian music.

The modern period. From the beginning of the 19th century, Islāmic music was affected by the intensification of contacts and relationships with Western music. For the first time Islāmic music existed in juxtaposition with Western music. For example, European composers and musicians were summoned to create military bands and conservatories in Turkey (1826) and in Persia (1856), and Guiseppe Verdi's opera *Aida* inaugurated the opera house in Cairo in 1871. Expanding contact with Western music caused certain alterations in traditional musical styles. There was a widespread musical renaissance, with two main centres: the leading school in Egypt was open to modernism and Western influences, while, in Syria and Iraq, traditional music was supported. Music in Syria and Iraq, together with North African, Iranian, and Turkish music, remained restricted to its own periphery. The Egyptian school, through its important communications media and its tendency to absorb European impact, spread over many countries. This school borrowed instruments such as the cello, saxophone, and accordion; melodies and rhythms from European serious and light music; the concept of large ensembles; and other traits. From the mid-20th century, two additional musical centres established themselves in Jordan and Lebanon. The first draws heavily from Bedouin and peasant music, while the second has developed new forms of composition inspired by Lebanese folk song.

Centres of the modern musical renaissance

Despite recent innovations, vocal music still predominates even in countries such as Iran, in which instrumental music is cultivated independently. Thus almost all of the famed Near Eastern musicians are singers; those particularly influential in the modern renaissance, in chronological order, include ʿAbduh al-Ḥamūlī, Dāhūd Ḥussnī, Sayyid Darwīsh, ʿAbd al-Wahhāb, Umm

Kulthūm, Farid al-Aṭrash, Fayrouz, Rashid al-Hundarashi, Ṣadīqa al-Mulāya, and Muḥammad al-Gubanshi.

Musical compositions tend to be relatively light and short, falling within the numerous genres of *tawshīḥ*, songs built on a strophic poetic form originating in Spain. Such songs have largely replaced long compositions of the *qaṣīdah* type and improvisational forms such as the *layālī* and the *mawwāl*. The use of short songs emphasizes the process of separation between, rather than the traditional union of, composer and performer. Among instrumental forms are the *taqsīm*, or improvisation, and the Turkish *beshref* and *samāʿī*.

Persian art music continues to be organized into 12 traditional modes, or *dastgāh*, each of which contains a repertory of from 20 to 50 small pieces called *gūsheh*s ("corners"). In performance of instrumental and vocal music, the artist improvises on the chosen *gūsheh* of a *dastgāh* in a specific order.

Theoretical developments

Modern Arab theorists also have produced valuable treatises. For example, the 19th-century theorists Michel Muchaqa of Damascus and Mohammed Chehab ad-Dīn of Cairo introduced the theoretical division of the scale into 24 quarter tones. In 1932 the international Congress of Arabian Music was held in Cairo, providing a forum for current analysis of subjects such as musical scales, modes, rhythms, and musical forms. (A.Sh.)

III. Islāmic dance and theatre

The performing arts have received comparatively little attention in the otherwise rich literature of the Islāmic peoples. This is most probably a result of the suspicions entertained by some orthodox Muslim scholars concerning the propriety of the dance and the theatre. Because this applies particularly in relation to the vexing question of human portrayal and its connection with idolatry, the performing arts were regarded by the faithful with more than usual caution. Even in the 19th and early 20th centuries, most research on the subject, in what may loosely be called the Islāmic world, was carried out by Westerners, chiefly European scholars; and only in the 20th century have indigenous scholars published research on the subject.

There are no known references to the dance or theatre in pre-Islāmic Arabia, although nomad tribes were probably acquainted with the dance. The Islāmic peoples themselves seem to have developed this particular art form less than they did music or architecture; and in addition to medieval Islām's cool attitude toward dance and theatre as art forms, it must be added that most women, leading a life of seclusion, could hardly be expected to play an active part in them. Nevertheless, there has been an active tradition of folk dance in most Islāmic countries, in addition to dancing as an entertainment spectacle and, particularly in Persia, as an art form. Dervish dancing, a feature especially of Anatolia, Turkey, is a form peculiar to the Islāmic order of that name.

The theatre has not flourished as a major art under Islām, although as a form of popular entertainment, particularly in mime and shadow-puppet shows, it has persisted vigorously. Nevertheless, the theatre with live actors received support from the Ottomans in Turkey, and a live popular drama has been strong in Persia, where a passion play also took root. Otherwise, the theatrical record of Islām is meagre. Moreover, few neighbouring peoples had a well-developed theatre of their own; hence, outside stimulus was lacking, and the Islāmic disapproval of idolatry was so intense that when the shadow theatre evolved in the East in the late Middle Ages, the puppets were regularly punched with holes to show that they were lifeless. Nonetheless, drama has had some ties with religion, as in Iran and other areas where the Shīʿite branch of Islām is concentrated. Here a passion play developed, rooted in traumatic memories of the bloody warfare of Islām's early years. This was a local phenomenon, uninfluenced by Christian Europe, and, though stereotyped, it movingly re-enacted Shīʿite martyrdom.

Popular theatre

A popular theatre, frequently including dance, evolved independently from about the 17th century in some Muslim countries. West European and, later, U.S. influences were largely the main factors in the development of an artistic theatre in the 19th and 20th centuries. But conservative Muslims have consistently disapproved of theatre, and in Saudi Arabia, for example, no native theatrical establishment exists. In such an atmosphere, women's parts were at first taken by men; later, Christian and Jewish women took the roles, and only in the 20th century have Muslim women participated.

TYPES AND SOCIAL FUNCTIONS OF DANCE AND THEATRE

The dance. Folk dancing existed among medieval Islāmic peoples; but such sources as exist are mainly concerned with artistic dance, which was performed chiefly at the caliph's palace by skilled women. The aristocracy was quick to imitate this patronage by providing similar performances, its members vying with one another on festive occasions. One of these dances, the *kurraǧ* (sometimes called *kurra*) developed into a song and dance festival held at the caliph's court. Since the latter part of the 19th century the dancing profession has lost ground to the performance of U.S., Latin American, and Western European dances in cabarets. In a reaction that set in after World War II, fervent nationalists have tried to create native dance troupes, revive traditional motifs in costume and interpretation, and adapt tribal figures to modern settings. Few dances have survived unchanged; among them are the dervish dances, performed mainly in Turkey.

By courtesy of the trustees of the British Museum; photograph, J.R. Freeman & Co. Ltd.

Dance as entertainment for the aristocracy, shown in "A Festive Party," manuscript illumination from the *Masnavī* of Jalāl ad-Dīn ar-Rūmī, 1295–96 AD. In the British Museum (MS. OR. 7693, fol. 225 b.).

Folk dance. Though now taken as an expression of national culture, folk dances were long regarded as pure entertainment and were either combined with theatrical shows or presented alone. Dance performances, accompanied by music, took place in a special hall or outdoors; many dancers, particularly the males, were also mimes. Sometimes the dance enacted a pantomime, as in Turkey, of physical love or of a stag hunt, representing the pursuit of a suspicious husband deceived by his wife.

Folk dance, except in Iran, has almost always been mimetic or narrative, a tradition still fostered by many tribes.

Dance as entertainment. The Turks considered dancing a profession for the low-born; hence most dancers belonged to minority groups: Greeks, Jews, and Armenians. This judgment also applied to the status of professional dancers and indeed to most professional entertain-

Low social standing of dancers

ers at most periods until modern times. In 19th-century Egypt, both male and female dancers were regarded as public entertainers. Many of the women (*ghawāzī*) belonged to a single tribe and were usually considered little better than prostitutes. The erotic element in dancing has become focussed in the belly dance, which has become the main form of exhibition dance in modern Turkey and the Arab countries.

The mimetic tradition of folk dance has blended well in countries of the Sunnite persuasion with comedy and with the passion-play tragedy in Shīʿite countries. In recent years, however, the theatre has been divorced from the dance, for most plays are modelled on European patterns; only in the operetta does the old combination remain.

Dance as an art form. In pre-Islāmic times in Iran, dance was both an art form and a popular entertainment. There are pictures of dancers in miniatures, on pottery, and on walls, friezes, and coins. Some of these ancient dances lived on partially in tribal dances but again, under Islām's restrictions on women, the art became a male monoply.

Iran is perhaps the only Muslim country with a tradition of dance regarded as an art form. When revived after World War II, folk dancing was encouraged and adapted for the foundation of a national ballet.

Muslim orthodoxy's very uncertainty over the exact status of the artistic dance ensured that it was always considered as an adjunct to music; although there are detailed treatises on Islāmic music, none are available on dance.

Dervish dancing. There is one outstanding example of pure dance: that of the whirling dervishes, practiced for seven centuries. The procedure is part of a Muslim ceremony named *dhikr*. Not all dervish orders dance; some simply stand on one foot and move the other to music. Those who dance, or rather, whirl, are the Mawlawī (or Mevlevî) dervishes, an order founded by the Persian poet and mystic Jalāl ad-Dīn ar-Rūmī, at Konya, in Anatolia, in the 13th century.

The performance, for which the participants don tall, brown, conical hats and green mantles, takes place in a large, octagonal hall, called a *tekke*. The dervishes sit in a circle, reciting poems. Then, rising slowly, they move from east to west, keeping their places with respect to one another, and begin to revolve rhythmically. They throw back their heads and raise the palms of their right hands, keeping their left hands down, a symbol of giving and taking. The rhythm accelerates, and they whirl faster and faster. In this way they enter a trance in an attempt to lose their personal identities and attain union with the Almighty. Later they may sit, pray, and begin all over again. The *dhikr* ends with a prayer and a procession.

The theatre. In lands where the Sunnite sect was strong, mime shows were frequent during the later Middle Ages. The Ottoman sultans were accompanied on military campaigns by their own troupe of actors; and as the Ottoman Empire extended, the court became ever more partial to entertainment, whether at the accession of a sultan, a royal wedding, a circumcision, an official visit, or a victory. On such occasions, dances and theatrical performances played their part along with parades, fireworks, music, mock fights, and circus performances in one huge pageant. This lavishing of entertainment reached a height of splendour that the admiring Ottoman aristocracy strove to imitate throughout Turkey. In Arabia and North Africa, popular shows on a lesser scale were performed in the open air. Another side to the theatre was represented in the shadow plays, which were given chiefly during the fast month of Ramaḍān (the sacred ninth month of the Muslim year) to while away the time.

Actors at the Ottoman court

Among Shīʿites the passion play was regularly performed, both by professionals and by amateurs. The performance was always during the first ten days of the month of Muḥarram (the first in the Muslim year), commemorating the suffering and death of the descendants and relatives of the caliph ʿAlī. For generations this was a focal point of the year, gripping audiences in total involvement, with its blend of symbolism and realism.

Mime shows. In the medieval Muslim theatre, mime shows aimed to entertain rather than to uplift as art. Regrettably, few were recorded in writing and those that were recorded were set down primarily to serve as guidelines for directors, who might tamper with the wording, as in the improvisation of the Italian commedia dell'arte. Some plays were historical, but preference was for comedies or farces with an erotic flavour. The audience was largely poor and uneducated.

A rudimentary theatrical form, the mime show was long widespread in Anatolia and other parts of the Ottoman Empire. Called *meddah* (eulogist) or *mukallit* (imitator) in Turkish, the mimic had many similarities to his classical Greek forerunners and was a storyteller who used mimicry as a comic element, designed for his largely uneducated audience. By gesture and word he would imitate animals, birds, or local dialects; he was very popular in Arabic- and Turkish-speaking areas. Even today, he has not been wholly exterminated in the Islamic world by literacy, radio, television, and the cinema. Sometimes several *meddahs* performed together, and this may have been the source of a rural theatrical performance.

Ortaoyunu. The *ortaoyunu* (middle show) was the first type of real theatre the Turks, and possibly other Muslim peoples, ever had. The Ottoman sultans subsidized *orta-*

The first real theatre

By courtesy of the University of Chicago Library

Whirling dervishes dancing in a *tekke*, engraving by J. Fougeron from *A Tour to the East in the Years 1763 and 1764, with Remarks on the City of Constantinople and the Turks*, by Frederick Calvert, 6th Baron Baltimore, 1767.

A storyteller in Kashmir.
Brian Brake—Magnum

oyunu companies of actors, who consequently became generally accepted; some were retained by the princes of the Rumanian principalities under Ottoman rule. The fact that they continued to enjoy popularity down to World War I may be explained by their simple dramatic appeal, coupled with sharp satire of the rich and the ruling classes (but hardly ever of Islām). This irreverence frequently resulted in fines and imprisonment for the actors but never in a change of style.

During the 19th and 20th centuries, the *ortaoyunu* was generally performed in an open square or a large coffeehouse. There was no stage, and props were simple: a table or movable screen, other objects being represented by paintings glued on paper. An orchestra of about four musicians enlivened the show and gave the performers, all male, their cues. Roles were generally stereotyped, with stock characters, such as a dandy, the foreign physician, and regional types (Kurds, Albanians, Armenians, Arabs, and Jews) quarrelling and fighting in slapstick style. Mimicry was important, and some actors changed roles and costumes. The plot was flimsy, a mere frame for the dialogue, which was itself frequently improvised.

The marionette theatre. In comparison with *ortaoyunu*, the marionette theatre, although popular in Turkistan (under the name of *çadir hayâl*) and other parts of Muslim Central Asia, never really caught on in the Ottoman Empire.

Shadow plays (*Karagöz*). On the other hand, the shadow play had been widely popular in Turkish- or Arabic-speaking countries. Like the mime shows, its essence was entertainment without moral import; and few plays were recorded in writing beyond a sketch of the action; most were comedies and farces for the enjoyment of a poor and uneducated audience.

In Turkey, the Karagöz (a character, "Black-eye") theatre was the prevalent form of shadow play. This art apparently came from China or Southeast Asia, as the French term *ombres chinoises* indeed hints, though the prevailing element of the grotesque was probably inherited from ancient Greece by way of Byzantium. The Karagöz was well-known in Turkey during the 16th century but was so fully developed that it must have been introduced earlier, and it quickly spread from Syria to North Africa and the Greek islands. Its performers were in great demand at the sultan's court and elsewhere, and they soon organized their own guild. Since only the framework of the play was written down, there was scope for impromptu wit, and Karagöz shows, like the *ortaoyunu*, were inevitably satirical. But with the coming of cinema the Karagöz declined, and performances are now mostly confined to the month of Ramaḍān.

In the traditional performance, the stage is separated from the audience by a frame holding a sheet; the latter has shrunk over the years from about six by 7½ feet (1.8 by 2.3 metres) to about three by two feet (0.9 by 0.6 metres). The puppets, which are flat and made of leather, are controlled by a rod and placed behind the screen. An oil lamp is then placed still farther back so it will throw the puppets' shadows onto the screen.

A standard shadow play has three main elements: introduction, dialogue, and plot. The introduction is fairly stereotyped and consists of an argument and usually a quarrel between Karagöz and Hacivat, the two most common characters. The former is a simple, commonsense fellow, while the latter is more formal and polished, if shallow and pedantic. The dialogue between the two varies with the occasion but always contains impromptu repartee, though most puppet masters have at least 28 different plots in stock—a different one for each night of Ramaḍān. Some are historical, many ribald, but all are pop-

The two traditional characters of the shadow play

Metin And

Ortaoyunu theatre, painting by Muazzez. In the collection of Dr. Metin And.

Karagöz shadow puppets.
From left: Yahudi (the Jew) with donkey, Karagöz, Zenne (the woman), and Tasuz Deli Bekir.
Marc Riboud—Magnum

ular entertainment. Additional characters or animals may be introduced, calling for great skill on the part of the puppet master and his assistant in manipulating several simultaneously, as well as in reciting the text in changing tones and playing music. Some have one or two musicians to help.

Mimicry and caricature, while essential to both the *meddah* and the *ortaoyunu*, are technically more developed in the shadow play. Here entire productions are based on a comedy of manners or of character. In addition to the stock characters from various ethnic groups, there is, for example, the drug addict who wraps his narcotic in dissolving gum before the fast begins so as not to sin, the light-headed Turk ("he who eats his inheritance") who is a prodigal and a debauchee, the highway robber, the stutterer, and the policeman.

Karagöz is the most frequent but not the sole type of shadow play in Muslim countries. In Egypt a shadow theatre existed as early as the 13th century, long before records of Karagöz shows in Turkey. A physician, Muḥammad ibn Dāniyāl, wrote three shadow plays that have survived. They were performed in the 13th century and display humour and satire and the lampooning of matchmaking and marriage. They also introduce a parade of popular contemporary characters, many of whom earn their living in shady or amusing trades. A positively phallic element is as evident here as in the Karagöz.

Iranian popular theatre. Popular theatre existed among the Iranians, who were proud of a long-lived cultural tradition and preserved their national language under Arab domination: indeed, even their branch of Islām, Shīʿism, set them apart from the Sunnism of the majority of Islām. The Ottomans' failure to conquer Iran increased competition between the respective intellectual elites. Iran had inherited a considerable theatrical tradition from pre-Islāmic times; it is not surprising that a popular comic theatre flourished there. The central figure of this theatre was the *Katchal Pahlavān* (or "bald actor"), and mimicry was important, both in comedy and in pantomime. The *Baggal-Bāzī* ("Play of the Grocer"), in which a grocer repeatedly quarrels with his good-for-nothing servant, is a typical example of the popular comic tradition. The marionette theatre, or *Lobet-Bāzī*, while using Iranian puppets, was similar to its Turkish counterpart. At least five puppets appeared, and singing was an integral part of a production that sometimes resembled Italian and French puppet shows. The *ortaoyunu*, particularly in the region of Azerbaijan, is almost identical with the Turkish of the same name. The shadow play in Iran, however, has always been less popular and obscene than the Ottoman or Arab Karagöz.

The comic theatre in Iran

Passion plays (taʿziyah). Quite different was the passion play, derived mainly from early Islāmic lore and assembled as a sequence of tragedies representing Shīʿite martyrdom. Both shadow and passion play were interlarded with musical prologues, accompaniment, and interludes; but these were not necessarily an integral part, serving rather to create a mood.

A preoccupation with religion is characteristic of Persian theatrical performances, and, during the first ten days of the month of Muḥarram the martyrdom of ʿAlī's descendants at the hands of the Umayyads is re-enacted. Although these shows are also performed among Shīʿite Turks in Central Asia and Shīʿite Arab communities in Iraq and elsewhere, Iran is their centre. Some plays are satirical, directed against wrongdoers, but most form a set of tragedies, performed as passion plays on these ten successive days. Named *taʿziyah* ("consolation"), this type of drama is an expression of Persian patriotism and, above all, of piety, both elements combining in an expression of the national religion, Shīʿism.

Background of the *taʿziyah*

In order to understand the mood of the *taʿziyah* it is necessary to remember that storytellers in Iran recite the gruesome details of the martyrdom of Ḥasan, Ḥusayn, and other descendants of ʿAlī all year long. Thus prepared, people swell the street processions during the days of Muḥarram, chain themselves, flagellate their bodies, and pierce their limbs with needles, shouting in unison and carrying images of the martyrs, made of straw and covered with blood—contrary to the injunctions of Islām. Sometimes men walk in the processions with heads hidden and collars bloodied, all part of a pageant dating from the 9th or 10th century. Its peak is reached daily in the play describing the martyrdom of ʿAlī's family and entourage, which used to be presented in the large mosques, but which, when the mosques proved too small, was given a special place. The roles of reciter of the martyrdom and of the walking in procession have blended over the years to produce the *taʿziyah* play, in which the reciters march in procession to the appointed place and there recite their pieces, which can be considered as a prologue before the play itself begins.

The chief incidents narrated in the *taʿziyah* are not necessarily presented in chronological order, but in any case the *taʿziyah* texts (manuscripts from the 17th and 18th centuries, thenceforth, printed texts) give an inadequate impression of their forceful effect. Indeed, the audience identifies itself so closely with the play that foreigners have, on occasion, been manhandled. Since half of the actors play the supporters of the ʿAlids and half play their opponents, the latter are sometimes attacked and beaten up at the end of the play. The decor, too, is half-realistic and half-symbolic: blood is real, yet sand is represented by straw. The stage effects are frequently overdone and this clearly further excites the audience. For instance, Ḥusayn's gory head is made to recite holy verses; or an armless warrior is seen to kill his opponent with a sword he holds in his teeth. The horses are real, although most of the other animals are played by humans. In general, the actors, though chiefly nonprofessional, infect the audience with their enthusiasm and absorption.

DANCE AND THEATRE IN MODERN TIMES

Developments in dance. Insofar as dance is related to the modern theatre, there is little difference between

Interior of the Great Mosque of Córdoba, Spain, begun 785. The building is now a Christian cathedral.

Umayyad and ʿAbbasid Art

Bowl from Nīshāpūr, lead-glazed earthenware with a slip decoration. In the Victoria and Albert Museum, London.

Mosaics decorating the portico of the Great Mosque of Damascus, Syria, 715.

Woven silk bearing the inscription "Glory and happiness to Qaid Abul Mansur Nudjkatin; may God continue his prosperity," 10th century. In the Louvre, Paris. 94 × 52 cm.

Plate 1: By courtesy of (centre left) the Victoria and Albert Museum, London; photographs, (top) Alfonso Gutierrez Escera—Ostman Agency, (bottom left) Cliche Musees Nationaux, (bottom right) J.E. Dayton, London

Fatimid art

Coronation mantle of King Roger II of Sicily, 1133. Gold embroidery and pearls on a red silk ground. In the Hofburg, Vienna.

Ceiling of the Capella Palatina, Palermo, Sicily. The chapel was built by the Norman kings of Sicily and decorated by Fātimid artists.

Bowl of lustre-ware by the potter Saʿad, depicting a Christian priest swinging a censer, first half of the 12th century. In the Victoria and Albert Museum, London.

Bronze griffin. In the Camposanto, Pisa, Italy.

Plate 2: By courtesy of (top) the Hofburg Kunsthistorisches Museum, Vienna, (centre right) the Victoria and Albert Museum, London; photographs, (left) M. Desjardins—Realites, (bottom right) SCALA, N.Y.

Plate 3: By courtesy of (top right) the Topkapı Saray Museum, Istanbul, (centre left) the Bibliotheque Nationale, Paris, (bottom left) the Smithsonian Institution, Freer Gallery of Art, Washington, D.C.; photograph, (right) Roland and Sabrina Michaud—Rapho Guillumette

Seljuq art

"Golshāh has removed her veil during a battle," miniature from *Varqeh o-Golshāh*, 13th century. In the Topkapı Saray Museum, Istanbul. (Ms. Hazine 841, fol. 22.) 10.2 × 29.7 cm.

Discussion near a village, miniature painted by Yahyā ibn Mahmūd al-Wāsitī from the 43rd *maqāmah* of the *Maqāmāt* ("Assemblies") of al-Harīrī, 1237. In the Bibliothèque Nationale, Paris. (Ms. Arabe 5847, folio 138 r.) 34.8 × 26 cm.

Lustre dish depicting Khosrow II as he discovers Shīrīn bathing, by Sayyid Shams ad-Dīn al Husani, from Kāshān, Iran, *c.* 1210. In the Freer Gallery of Art, Washington, D.C.

The minaret of Jam, Iran, 1116–1202.

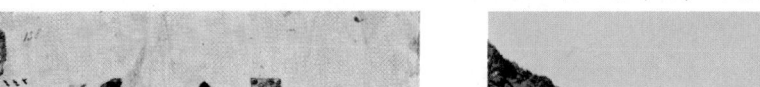

Ivory casket, 13th century. In the Palazzo Reale, Capella Palatina, Palermo, Sicily. 39 × 40 × 24 cm.

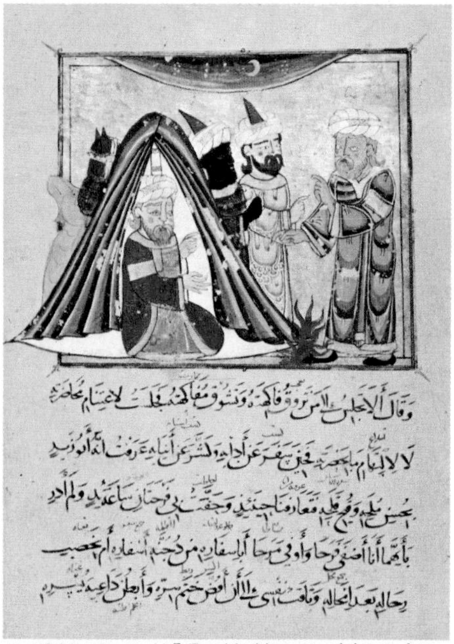

Al-Ḥārith talks to Abū Zayd in his tent, miniature from the 26th *maqāmah* of the *Maqāmāt* ("Assemblies") of al-Ḥarīrī, probably Egyptian, 1334. In the Österreichische Nationalbibliothek, Vienna (MS. A. F. 9, folio 87 v). Miniature only, 13.7 × 15.8 cm.

Moorish and Mamluk art

Hanging mosque lamp, enamelled and gilded glass, from Aleppo, Syria, *c.* 1300. In the Museum für Islamische Kunst, Staatliche Museen Preussischer Kulturbesitz, West Berlin.

Court of the Lions, the Alhambra, Granada, Spain, 14th century.

Plate 4: By courtesy of (top left) the Soprintendenza alle Gallerie ed Alle Opere d'Arte della Sicilia, Palermo, (top right) the Osterreichische Nationalbibliothek, Vienna, (bottom right) the Museum fur Islamische Kunst, Staatliche Museen Preussischer Kulturbesitz, Berlin; photograph, (bottom left) Raffaello Bencini—SCALA, N.Y.

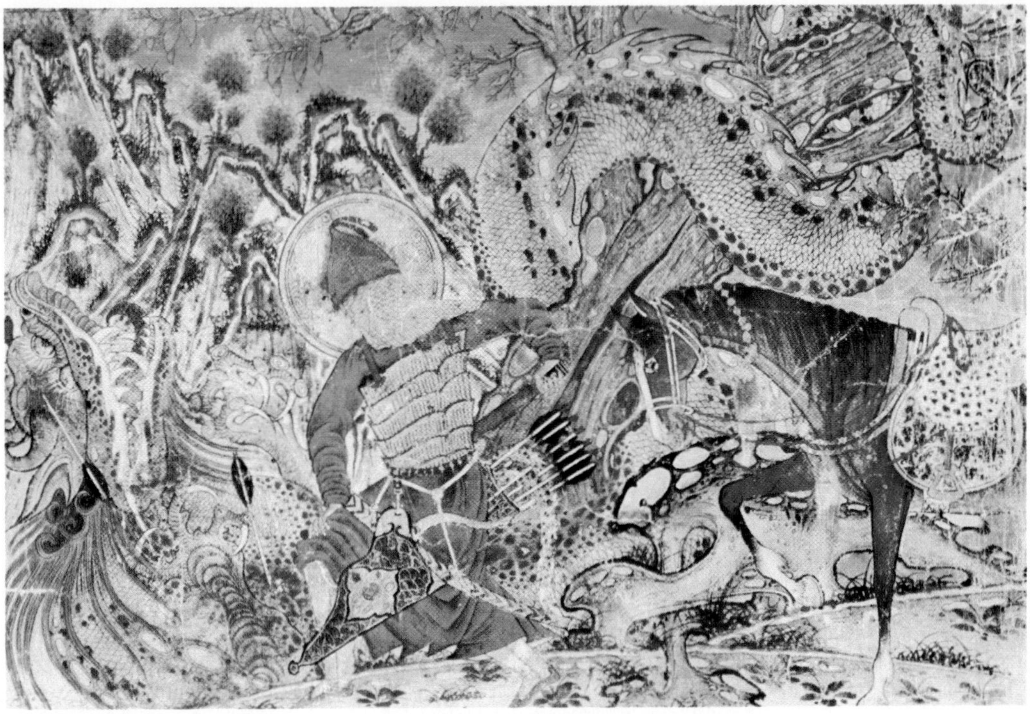

Bahrām Gūr killing a dragon, illustration from the *Shāh-nāmeh* ("Book of Kings") of Ferdowsī, known as the Demotte *Shāh-nāmeh,* 1320–60, from Tabriz, Iran. In the Cleveland Museum of Art. Height 40.6 cm.

Il-Khanid art of the Mongol Period

Pottery bowl from Kāshān, Iran, late 14th century. In the Victoria and Albert Museum, London.

Dīwān of Sultan Aḥmad, pastoral border painted by Junayd, *c.* 1405, from Baghdad. In the Freer Gallery of Art, Washington, D.C. 29.2 × 20.3 cm.

Mongol warriors, miniature from Rashīd ad-Dīn's *History of the World,* 1307. In the Edinburgh University Library, Scotland. Miniature only, 25 × 11.4 cm.

Plate 5: By courtesy of (top) the Cleveland Museum of Art, Ohio, Grace Rainey Rogers Fund, (centre left) the Victoria and Albert Museum, London, (bottom left) the Edinburgh University Library, Scotland, (bottom right) the Smithsonian Institution, Freer Gallery of Art, Washington, D.C.; photograph, (centre left) John Webb

The mausoleum of Timur at Samarkand, 1434.

Prince Humay at the Gate of Humāyūn's Castle, illustration from the *Divān* of Khwāju Kermānī, painted by Junayd, 1396, from Baghdad. In the British Museum (MS. Add 18 113, folio 18v). 29 × 20.2 cm.

Timurid art of the Mongol Period

Capture of the fortress of the Knights Hospitallers at Smyrna, miniature from a *Zafar-nāmeh* (a life of Timur) by Behzād, *c.* 1490, from Herāt. In the John Work Garrett Library, Johns Hopkins University, Baltimore. 25.2 × 13 cm.

Section of relief tilework from the mausoleum of Bayram Khān at Fathābād, Uzbekistan, late 14th to early 15th century. In the Victoria and Albert Museum, London. Length 1.52 m.

The Feast of ʿId, illustration from a *Divān* of Hāfez, signed Sultan Muhammad, *c.* 1520. In a private collection. 24 × 16 cm.

Miniature from *Yusof o-Zalikhā* by Jāmī, the text in small *nastaʿliq* calligraphy, 1557. In the Freer Gallery of Art, Washington, D.C. 25.2 × 15 cm.

Safavid art

Two *eyvāns* of the Masjed-e Shāh of ʿAbbās I the Great at Isfahan, Iran, 17th century.

Plate 6: By courtesy of (top right) the trustees of the British Museum, (centre right) the John Work Garrett Library, Johns Hopkins University, Baltimore, (bottom) the Victoria and Albert Museum, London; photographs, (top left) Alex Langley—Photo Researchers, (centre right) Walters Art Gallery, Baltimore, (bottom) John Webb

Plate 7: By courtesy of (top left) a private collector, Cambridge, Mass. (formerly in the collection of Louis J. Cartier), (top right) the Smithsonian Institution, Freer Gallery of Art, Washington, D.C.; photographs, (top left) Fogg Art Museum, Cambridge, Mass., (bottom) Ray Manley—Shostal

Interior of the Rūstem Pasa Mosque, Istanbul, showing the coloured tile decoration.

Ottoman art

The Sultan watching dancers and comedians in the Hippodrome, illustration from the *Surname-i Vehbi* of Ahmed III (1703–30), painted by Levni. In the Topkapı Saray Museum, Istanbul.

Silk caftan said to be that of Bayezid II (1481–1512). In the Topkapı Saray Museum, Istanbul.

Isnik ware dish, second half of the 16th century. In the Victoria and Albert Museum, London. Diameter 30.5 cm.

"Star Ushak" carpet from western Anatolia, late 16th to early 17th century. In the Metropolitan Museum of Art, New York City. 2.17 × 4.27 m.

Plate 8: By courtesy of (bottom left, centre) the Topkapı Saray Museum, Istanbul, (bottom centre) the Victoria and Albert Museum, London, (bottom right) the Metropolitan Museum of Art, New York, gift of Joseph V. McMullen; photographs, (top, bottom left, centre) Ara Guler—EB Inc., (bottom centre) John Webb, (bottom right) Otto E. Nelson

Muslim production and its European or American counterpart. Dance and drama are combined according to the artistic needs of the production or the personal tastes of the producer and director. Perhaps more important is the dance itself, independently performed as artistic self-expression. The geographical centre of folk dance is in the area east of the Mediterranean, though remnants of other cultures have survived. There are Balkan traces in western and northern Turkey, for example, and Berber and even black African traces in Morocco and elsewhere in North Africa.

Arab countries. In the Arab countries, dancing is popular, varying in town, village, or with nomad tribe. In the town, dancing is reserved for special occasions, chiefly Western social dances. On the other hand, villages have such favourites as the *dabkah*. This is danced mainly by men, and is quite common in festivities in the area between northern Syria and southern Israel; for instance, the Druzes (sectarian Arab communities in Lebanon, Syria, and Israel) are very fond of it. The performers dance in a straight line, holding handkerchiefs high in the air, while the first in the row gives the sign for stepping or jumping. Among the Bedouins almost any pretext suffices for dancing, although in recent years dancing has been practiced most often at weddings and similar festivities. Usually two male dancers, or two rows of male dancers, repeatedly advance toward each other or the audience and retire. To this basic figure, there are numerous variations that give the different dances their names.

Turkey. The Turks are also lovers of music and dance, and when they meet frequently sing and dance. There is no single national dance popular throughout the country; dances vary in the numbers required, some being for solo performance, others designed for pairs or groups, though nearly all have instrumental accompaniment. As illustration of the possibilities of a basic step, there are at least 40 variations of the group dance known as *bar*, a chain dance. Again, several folk dances have characteristics akin to pantomime, breaking up into five main types of imitation: village life, nature, combat, courtship, and animals or birds.

Opera is popular in Turkey, reflected in a long tradition of invitations to foreign companies, and the musical theatre, which frequently includes dancing, is also widespread. On the other hand, classical ballet was unknown until a school of ballet was opened by foreign teachers with government encouragement. Although most of the ballet performances are in Istanbul, they are well received on tour.

Iran. In Iran a national dance company was formed with government support after World War II, and ancient customs were revived. This Iranian ballet company soon became outstanding in the Muslim world, drawing on ancient war dances, fire-priest dances, dervish dances, and tribal folklore, as well as on scenes and decor from painting, sculpture, and the rich imagery of classical Persian poetry. Various folk dances are likewise performed all over Iran; they are accompanied by music and reflect local traditions and customs. Some are mimetic, others erotic, others, again, war dances (chiefly in the mountain areas) and comic dances (usually with masks). Many of these are dying out as new tastes and customs evolve, and Iranian dance companies have tried to preserve some of these dying forms.

Iranian ballet

The contemporary theatre. The modern Muslim theatre is almost wholly a Western European importation, unconnected with the traditional medieval theatre, which has almost completely disappeared, although there are vestiges of it.

Arab countries. Contemporary Arabic theatre owes much to the imaginative daring of the Naqqāsh family in 19th-century Beirut, which was then under Turkish rule. Significantly, they were Christians, then better educated and more cosmopolitan than Muslims, and they had the advantages of Beirut's contacts with Europe and position as the headquarters of missionary activity. A Beirut Maronite (a Roman Catholic following the Syrio-Antiochene rite, widespread in the area), Mārūn an-Naqqāsh (died 1855), who knew French and Italian as well as Arabic and Turkish, adapted Molière's *L'Avare* ("The Miser") and presented it on a makeshift stage in Beirut in 1848. He did so before a select audience of foreign dignitaries and local notables, and he wrote his play in colloquial Arabic and revised the plot to suit the taste and views of his audience. Further, he changed the locale to an Arab town and arabicized the names of the participants. Other touches included instrumental and vocal music and the playing of women's roles by men, in the traditional manner. The above features characterized the Arabic theatre for about half a century. An-Naqqāsh, together with his family, composed and presented two other musical plays, one based on Molière's *Le Tartuffe*, the other on the story, in *The Thousand and One Nights*, of the Abū al-Ḥasan who became caliph for a day.

Soon the main centre of Arabic theatre moved to Egypt, whose comparatively tolerant autonomy offered an atmosphere for literary and artistic creativity more congenial than other parts of the Ottoman Empire. Syrian and Lebanese intellectuals and actors emigrated there, particularly after the anti-Christian riots of 1860 in Syria. Though a somewhat crippled Arabic theatre continued in Syria, its influence was carried into Egypt by émigrés and later spread to other Arabic-speaking regions. The number of theatres, a potentially large public, the munificence of Egypt's rulers, increasing prosperity under British rule after 1882, and increasing education soon made Egypt the centre of Arabic theatre, a position it has successfully maintained since.

Egyptian theatre

The colloquial Arabic of Egypt was increasingly employed in the theatre, and several companies toured the country and neighbouring parts. The composition of these companies was fluid, for the actors were fickle in their loyalties; nevertheless, certain types of Egyptian theatre can be discerned in the late 19th century and during the early 20th. Some, like the company of Saāmah Hijāzī, used music to such an extent that their productions approached opera or operetta. Others, like that of ʿAlī al-Kassār, specialized in downright farce, expressed in revue form, with a Nubian hero, the "Barbarin," who made a specialty of ridicule and mimicry. Yet others, like the company of Najīb ar-Rīḥānī, oscillating between outright farce and comedy, skillfully depicted contemporary Egyptian manners; in particular, Najīb ar-Rīḥānī created a character called Kish-Kish Bey, whose misadventures and unsolicited advice on every subject have made him a classic creation. A conventional theatre sprang up in Egypt, too, catering for a growing number of intellectuals, and presenting dramas and tragedies in polished, literary Arabic. Its chief exponent was Jūrj Abyaḍ, who had studied acting in Paris. In contrast, Yūsuf Wahbī's National Troupe performed realistic plays, usually dramas or melodramas, using either colloquial or literary Arabic, sometimes a combination of both.

The plays performed by the Egyptian troupes and others in Arabic-speaking lands developed through three overlapping but distinguishable stages: adaptations, translations, and original plays. Adaptations came first, in the 19th century (see above). Translations of established works appealed to a discriminating public, but original plays, part of the evolution of modern Arabic literature, reflected a growing interest in political and social problems. The decline of foreign influence and the arrival of political independence encouraged creativity which, however much under European influence, has some original works to its credit. Two 20th century Arabic playwrights, both Egyptian, are Tawfīq al-Ḥakīm, a sensitive shaper of both social and symbolical dramas, and Mahmūd Taymū, a novelist and comedy writer who strikes deep into Egypt's social problems.

Turkey. The development of the modern Turkish theatre strongly resembles its Arabic counterpart. In Istanbul, theatrical performances were not unusual among the diplomatic and international set, and some local Turks were acquainted with them. Nonetheless, Turkish plays for live actors—barring *ortaoyunu*—date only from 1839. The first Turkish playhouse was built in Pera (now Beyoğlu), significantly in the middle of the foreign and embassy quarter of Istanbul. Many of the actors were members of non-Muslim minorities, such as the Armenian; and the first plays presented in Turkish were adaptations from the French, chiefly Molière. They were done during the 1840s, when music was an important item.

The Gedik Paşa Theatre

The Gedik Paşa Tiyatrosu, called after the area in Istanbul where it was located, was the first theatre in which Turkish plays were produced by native actors in Turkish. The actors received a salary and local writers presented their own plays. Originally built for foreign companies, the theatre was reconstructed in 1867 and re-opened in 1868 for a Turkish company headed by an Armenian, Agop, who was later converted to Islām and changed his name to Yakup. For almost 20 years the Gedik Paşa Theatre was the dramatic centre of the city; and plays in translation were soon followed by original plays, several with a nationalist appeal, such as Namık Kemal's *Fatherland*, first produced in 1873. The actors had to struggle against prejudice and the playwrights against censorship (some were imprisoned or exiled); but the Turkish theatre spread beyond Istanbul in the 1870s and 1880s to such places as Adana (in southern Anatolia) and Bursa (just south of Istanbul, across the Sea of Marmara).

After the Young Turk Revolution of 1908, censorship was not relaxed, but interest in the theatre grew, particularly over political matters; and plays about the new constitution were written and performed. After the foundation of the Turkish Republic in 1923, the state subsidized several theatre companies and a school for dramatic arts. Official support not only gave financial encouragement but also implied a change of attitude over such matters as the participation of Muslim women in productions.

By the middle of the 20th century, theatrical life was mostly centred on Istanbul and Ankara, although theatres and companies continued in the small towns too. A growing number of original plays, some influenced by American literature, have been written and produced and the standard was higher than before World War I, when Turkish poetry and fiction were rather more impressive than the drama. Subjects, too, have been more diverse. To topics such as the position of woman, marriage and divorce, and the character of Islāmic institutions—all popular under the Ottomans—have been added the Greco-Turkish War, education, village conditions, secularization, class struggle, and psychological problems. The Dormen Tiyatrosu, the oldest resident private theatre company in Turkey that continues to perform in the 1970s, was founded in Istanbul in 1955 by Haldun Dormen: in the 1971 World Theatre season in London the company performed *A Tale of Istanbul*, a comedy including elements of folklore, a puppet show, singing, and a belly dance. This theatre also produces modern Western plays.

Western European and Russian influences in Iran

Iran. In Iran the birth of the modern theatre dates from the second half of the 19th century. Adaptations and translations from European plays appeared in Persian, often with the location and names suited to Iran. Molière, again, was a favourite and western European influence considerable, though Russian literature also left its mark, particularly in Azerbaijan, whose northern population had a chance to watch Russian actors during World War I.

Original plays began to be written almost at once; one of the earliest playwrights was an Azerbaijani, one Akhundof, living in the Caucasus. He wrote seven comedies ridiculing Persian and Causasian Muslim society; all were translated into Persian and printed in 1874. Other plays likewise showed pronounced yearnings for social reform presented in a satirical style; some of these were published in a magazine called *Tyatr* ("Theatre"), which first appeared in 1908. Another type was the patriotic play, extolling Iran's history.

Some pre-World War I pieces were designed for reading rather than production. They were performed usually in schools, but there were hardly any professional actors, and the stage and props were very simple. After World War I, suitable halls were built in Teheran and other cities, but the iron hand of Reza Shah (1925–41) curtailed development through continuous censorship and surveillance. After 1942 many new companies were formed, and there was speedy development, with growing interest in social and political subjects, though competition from foreign films was considerable. Nevertheless, theatre clubs in Iran's towns bear witness to a sizable grass-roots movement. (J.M.L.)

IV. Visual arts

In order to answer whether or not there is an aesthetic, iconographic, or stylistic unity to the visually perceptible arts of Islāmic peoples, it is first essential to realize that no ethnic or geographical entity was Muslim from the beginning. There is no Islāmic art, therefore, in the way there is a Chinese art or a French art. Nor is it simply a period art, like Gothic art or Baroque art, for once a land or an ethnic entity became Muslim it remained Muslim, a small number of exceptions like Spain or Sicily notwithstanding. Political and social events transformed a number of lands with a variety of earlier histories into Muslim lands. But, since early Islām as such did not possess or propagate an art of its own, each area could continue, in fact often did continue, whatever modes of creativity it had acquired. It may then not be appropriate at all to talk about the visual arts of Islāmic peoples, and one should instead consider separately each of the areas that became Muslim: Spain, North Africa, Egypt, Syria, Mesopotamia, Iran, Anatolia, India. Such, in fact, has been the direction taken by some recent scholarship. Even though tinted at times with parochial nationalism, the approach has been useful in that it has focused attention on a number of permanent features in different regions of Islāmic lands that are older than and independent from the faith itself and from the political entity created by it. Iranian art, in particular, exhibits a number of features (certain themes such as the representation of birds or an epic tradition in painting) that owe little to its Islāmic character since the 7th century. Ottoman art shares a Mediterranean tradition of architectural conception with Italy rather than with the rest of the Muslim world.

Such examples can easily be multiplied, but it is probably wrong to overdo their importance. For if one looks at the art of Islāmic lands from a different perspective, a totally different picture emerges. The perspective is that of the lands that surround the Muslim world or of the times that preceded its formation. For even if there are ambiguous examples, most observers can recognize a flavour, a mood in Islāmic visual arts that is distinguishable from what is known in East Asia (China, Korea, and Japan) or in the Christian West. This mood or flavour has been called decorative, for it seems at first glance to emphasize an immense complexity of surface effects with apparent meanings attached to the visible motifs. But it has other characteristics as well; it is often colourful, both in architecture and in objects; it avoids representations of living things; it gives much prominence to the work of artisans and counts among its masterpieces not merely works of architecture or of painting but also the creations of weavers, potters, and metalworkers. The problem is whether these uniquenesses of Islāmic art, when compared to other artistic traditions, are the result of the nature of Islām or of some other factor or series of factors.

These preliminary remarks suggest at the very outset the main epistemological peculiarity of Islāmic art: it consists of a large number of quite disparate traditions that, when seen all together, appear distinguishable from what surrounded them and from what preceded them through a series of stylistic and thematic characteristics. The key question is how this was possible, but no answer can be given before the tradition itself has been properly defined.

Such a definition can only be provided in history, through an examination of the formation and development of the arts through the centuries. For a static sudden phenomenon is not being dealt with, but rather a slow building up of a visual language of forms with many dialects and with many changes. Whether or not these complexities of growth and development subsumed a common structure is the challenging question facing the historian of this artistic tradition. What makes the question particularly difficult to answer is that the study of Islāmic art is still so new. Many monuments are unpublished or at least insufficiently known, and only a handful of scientific excavations have investigated the physical setting of the culture and of its art. Much, therefore, remains tentative in the knowledge and appreciation of works of Islāmic art, and what follows is primarily an outline of what is known with a number of suggestions for further work into insufficiently investigated areas.

Media and techniques

Each artistic tradition has tended to develop its own favourite mediums and techniques. Some, of course, such as architecture, are automatic needs of every culture; and, for reasons to be developed later, it is in the medium of architecture that some of the most characteristically Islāmic works of art are found. Other techniques, on the other hand, acquire varying forms and emphases. Sculpture in the round hardly existed as a major art form, and, although such was also the case of all Mediterranean arts at the time of Islām's growth, one does not encounter the astounding rebirth of sculpture that occurred in the West. Wall painting existed but has generally been poorly preserved; the great Islāmic art of painting was limited to the illustration of books. The unique feature of Islāmic techniques is the astounding development taken by the so-called decorative arts—*e.g.*, woodwork, glass, ceramics, metalwork, textiles. New techniques were invented and spread throughout the Muslim world—at times even beyond its frontiers. In dealing with Islām, therefore, it is quite incorrect to think of these techniques as the "minor" arts. For the amount and intensity of creative energies spent on the decorative arts transformed them into major artistic forms, and their significance in defining a profile of the aesthetic and visual language of Islāmic peoples is far greater than in the instances of many other cultures. Furthermore, since, for a variety of reasons to be discussed later, the Muslim world did not develop until quite late the notion of "noble" arts, the decorative arts have reflected far better the needs and ambitions of the culture as a whole. The kind of conclusion that can be reached about Islāmic civilization through its visual arts thus extends far deeper than is usual in the study of an artistic tradition, and it requires a combination of archaeological, art-historical, and textual information.

Definition of a culture through an art

An example may suffice to demonstrate the point. Among all the techniques of Islāmic visual arts, the most important one was the art of textiles. Textiles, of course, were used for daily wear at all social levels and for all occasions. But clothes were also the main indicators of rank, and they were given as rewards or as souvenirs by princes, high and low. They were a major status symbol, and their manufacture and distribution were carefully controlled through a complicated institution known as the *ṭirāz*. Major events were at times celebrated by being depicted on silks. Many texts have been identified that describe the hundreds of different kinds of textiles that existed. Since textiles could easily be moved, they became a vehicle for the transmission of artistic themes within the Muslim world and beyond its frontiers. In the case of this one technique, therefore, one is not dealing simply with a medium of the decorative arts but with a key medium in the definition of a given time's taste, of its practical functions, and of the ways in which its ideas were distributed. The more unfortunate point is that the thousands of fragments that have remained have not yet been studied in a sufficiently systematic way, and in only a handful of instances has it been possible so far to relate individual fragments to known texts. When more work has been completed, however, a study of this one medium should contribute significantly to the commercial, social, and aesthetic history of Islām, as well as explain much of the impact that Islāmic art had beyond the frontiers of the Muslim world.

The following survey of Islāmic visual arts, therefore, will be primarily a historical one, for it is in development through time that the main achievements of Islāmic art can best be understood. At the same time, other features peculiar to this tradition will be kept in mind: the varying importance of different lands, each of which had identifiable artistic features of its own, and the uniqueness of some techniques of artistic creativity over others.

ORIGINS

Assimilation of earlier artistic traditions

Islāmic visual arts were created by the confluence of two entirely separate kinds of phenomena: a number of earlier artistic traditions and a new faith. The arts inherited by Islām were of extraordinary technical virtuosity and stylistic or iconographic variety. All the developments of arcuated and vaulted architecture that had taken place in Iran and in the Roman Empire were available in their countless local variants. Stone, baked brick, mud brick, and wood existed as mediums of construction, and all the complicated engineering systems developed particularly in the Roman Empire were still utilized from Spain to the Euphrates. All the major techniques of decoration were still used, except for monumental sculpture. In secular and in religious art, a more or less formally accepted equivalence between representation and represented subject had been established. Technically, therefore, as well as ideologically, the Muslim world took over an extremely sophisticated system of visual forms; and, since the Muslim conquest was accompanied by a minimum of destruction, all the monuments and especially the attitudes attached to them were passed on to the new culture.

The second point about the pre-Islāmic traditions is the almost total absence of anything from Arabia itself. While future archaeological work in the peninsula may modify this conclusion in part, it does seem that Islāmic art formed itself entirely in some sort of relationship to non-Arab traditions. Even the rather sophisticated art created in earlier times by the Palmyrenes or by the Nabataeans had almost no impact on Islāmic art, and the primitively conceived ḥaram in Mecca, the only pre-Islāmic sanctuary maintained by the new faith, remained as a unique monument that was almost never copied or imitated despite its immense religious significance. The pre-Islāmic sources of Islāmic art are thus entirely extraneous to the milieu in which the new faith was created. In this respect the visual arts differ considerably from most other aspects of Islāmic culture.

This is not to say that there was no impact of the new faith on the arts, but to a large extent it was an incidental impact, the result of the existence of a new social and political entity rather than of a doctrine. Earliest Islām as seen in the Qur'ān or in the more verifiable accounts of the Prophet's life simply do not deal with the arts, either on the practical level of requiring or suggesting forms as expressions of the culture or on the ideological level of defining a Muslim attitude toward images. In all instances concrete Qur'ānic passages later used for the arts had their visual significance extrapolated.

There is no prohibition against representations of living things, and not a single Qur'ānic passage refers clearly to the mosque, eventually to become the most characteristically Muslim religious building. In the simple, practical, and puritanical milieu of early Islām, aesthetic or visual questions simply did not arise.

Influence of Islām in establishing a new artistic tradition

The impact of the faith on the arts occurred rather as the fledgling culture encountered the earlier non-Islāmic world and sought to justify its own acceptance or rejection of new ways and attitudes. The discussion of two examples of particular significance illustrates the point. One is the case of the mosque. The word itself derives from the Arabic *masjid*, "a place where one prostrates one's self (in front of God)." It was a common term in pre-Islāmic Arabic and in the Qur'ān, where it is applied to sanctuaries in general without restriction. If a more concrete significance was meant, the word was used in construct with some other term, as in *masjid al-ḥaram* to refer to the Meccan sanctuary. There was no need in earliest times for a uniquely Muslim building, for any place could be used for private prayer as long as the correct direction (*qiblah*, originally Jerusalem, but very soon Mecca) was observed and the proper sequence of gestures and pious statements was followed. In addition to private prayer, which had no formal setting, Islām instituted a collective prayer on Fridays, where the same ritual was accompanied by a sermon from the *imām* (leader of prayer, originally the Prophet, then his successors, and later legally any able-bodied Muslim) and by the more complex ceremony of the *khuṭbah*, a collective swearing of allegiance to the community's leadership. This ceremony served to strengthen the common bond between all members of the *ummah*, the Muslim "collectivity," and its importance in creating and maintaining the unity of early Islām has often been emphasized. There were two traditional locales for this event in the Prophet's time. One was his private house, whose descriptions have been preserved; it was a large open space with private rooms on one side and rows of palm trunks making a colonnade on two other sides, the deeper colonnade being on the side of the *qiblah*. The Prophet's house was not a sanctuary but simply the most convenient place for the early community to gather. Far less is known about the second place of gathering for the Muslim community. It was used primarily on major feast days, such as the end of the fasting period or the feast of sacrifice. It was called a *muṣallā*, literally "a place for prayer," and *muṣallās* were usually located outside city walls. Nothing is known about the shape taken by *muṣallās*, but in all probability they were as simple as pre-Islāmic pagan sanctuaries: large enclosures surrounded by a wall and devoid of any architectural or ornamental feature.

Altogether then there was hardly anything that could be identified as a holy building or as an architectural form. To be complete, one should add two additional features. One is an action, the call to prayer (*adhān*). It became, fairly rapidly, a formal moment preceding the gathering of the faithful. One man would climb on the roof and proclaim that God is great and that men must congregate to pray. There was no formal monument attached to the ceremony, though it led eventually to the ubiquitous minaret. The other early feature was an actual structure. It was the *minbar*, a chair with several steps on which the Prophet would climb in order to preach. The monument itself had a pre-Islāmic origin, but Muḥammad transformed it into a characteristically Muslim form.

With the exception of the *minbar*, only a series of actions was formulated in early Islāmic times. There were no forms attached to them nor were any needed. But, as the Muslim world grew in size, the contact with many other cultures brought about two developments. On the one hand there were thousands of examples of beautiful religious buildings that impressed the conquering Arabs. But, more importantly, the need arose to preserve the restricted uniqueness of the community of faithful and to express its separateness from other groups. Islāmic religious architecture began with this need and, in ways to be described later on, created a formal setting for the activities, ceremonies, and ideas that had been formless at the outset.

Muslim iconoclasm

A second and closely parallel development of the impact of the Islāmic religion on the visual arts is the celebrated question of a Muslim iconoclasm. As has already been mentioned, the Qur'ān does not utter a word for or against the representation of living things. It is equally true that from about the middle of the 8th century a prohibition had been formally stated, and thenceforth it would be a standard feature of Islāmic thought, even though the form in which it is expressed has varied from absolute to partial and even though it has never been totally followed. The justification for the prohibition tended to be that any representation of a living thing was an act of competition with God, for he alone can create something that is alive. It is striking that this theological explanation reflects the state of the arts in the Christian world at the time of the Muslim conquest—a period of iconoclastic controversy. It may thus be suggested that Islām developed an attitude toward images as it came into contact with other cultures and that its attitude was negative because the arts of the time appeared to lead easily to dreaded idolatry. While it is only by the middle of the 8th century that there is actual proof of the existence of a Muslim doctrine, it is likely that, more or less intuitively, the Muslims felt a certain reluctance toward representations from the very beginning. For all monuments of religious art are devoid of any representations; even a number of attempts at representational symbolism in the official art of coinage were soon abandoned.

This rapid crystallization of Islāmic attitudes toward images has considerable significance. For practical purposes, representations are not found in religious art, although matters are quite different in secular art. Instead there occurred very soon a replacement of imagery with calligraphy and the concomitant transformation of calligraphy into a major artistic medium. Furthermore, the world of Islām tended to seek means of representing the holy other than by images of men, and one of the main problems of interpretation of Islāmic art is that of the degree of means it achieved in this search. But there is a deeper aspect to this rejection of holy images. Although the generally Semitic or specifically Jewish sources that have been given to Islāmic iconoclasms have probably been exaggerated, the reluctance imposed by the circumstances of the 7th century transformed into a major key of artistic creativity the magical fear of visual imagery that exists in all cultures but that is usually relegated to a secondary level. This uniqueness is certainly one of the main causes of the abstract tendencies that are among the great glories of the tradition. Even when a major art of painting did develop, it remained always somehow secondary to the mainstream of the culture's development.

Both in the case of the religious building and in that of the representations, therefore, it was the contact with pre-Islāmic cultures in Muslim-conquered areas that compelled Islām to transform its practical and unique needs into monuments and to seek within itself for intellectual and theological justifications for its own instincts. The great strength of early Islām was that it possessed within itself the ideological means to put together a visual expression of its own, even though it did not develop at the very beginning a need for such an expression.

One last point can be made about the origins of Islāmic art. It concerns the degree of importance taken by the various artistic and cultural entities conquered by the Arabs in the 7th and 8th centuries, for the early empire had gathered in regions that had not been politically or even ideologically related for centuries. During the first century or two of Islām, the main models and the main sources of inspiration were certainly the Christian centres around the Mediterranean. But the failure to capture Constantinople and to destroy the Byzantine Empire also made these Christian centres inimical competitors, whereas the whole world of Iran became an integral part of the empire, even though the conquering Arabs were far less familiar with the latter than with the former. A much more complex problem is posed by conversions, for it is through the success of the militant Muslim religious mission that the culture expanded so rapidly. Insofar as one can judge, it is the common folk, primarily in cities, who took over the new faith most rapidly; and thus, there was added in early Islāmic culture a folk element whose impact may have been larger than has hitherto been imagined.

Folk element in Islāmic art

These preliminary considerations on the origins of Islāmic art have made it possible to outline several of the themes and problems that remained constant features of the tradition: a self-conscious sense of uniqueness when compared to others; a continuous reference to its own Qur'anic sources; a constant relationship to many different cultures; a folk element; and a variety of regional developments. None of these features remained constant, not even those aspects of the faith that affected the arts. But while they changed, the fact of their existence, their structural presence, remained a constant of Islāmic art.

EARLY PERIOD: THE UMAYYAD AND ʿABBASID DYNASTIES

Of all the recognizable periods of Islāmic art, this is by far the most difficult one to explain properly, even though it is quite well documented. There are two reasons for this difficulty. On the one hand, it was a formative period, a time when new forms were created that identify the aesthetic and practical ideals of the new culture. Such periods are difficult to define when, as in the case of Islām, there was no artistic need inherent to the culture itself. The second complication derives from the fact that Muslim conquest hardly ever destroyed former civilizations with their own established creativity. Material culture, therefore, continued as before, and archaeologically it is almost impossible to distinguish between pre-Islāmic and early Islāmic artifacts. Paradoxical though it may sound, there is an early Islāmic Christian art of Syria and Egypt, and in many other regions the parallel existence of a Muslim and of a non-Muslim art continued for centuries. What did happen, however, during early Islāmic times was the establishment of a dominant new taste, and it is the nature and character of this taste that has to be explained. It occurred first in Syria and Iraq, the two areas with the largest influx of Muslims and with the two successive capitals of the empire, Damascus under the Umayyads and Baghdad under the early ʿAbbāsids. From Syria and Iraq this new taste spread in all directions and adapted itself to local conditions and local materials, thus creating considerable regional and chronological variations in early Islāmic art.

From an historical point of view two major dynasties are involved. One is the Umayyad dynasty, which ruled from 661 to 750 and whose monuments are datable from 680 to 745. It was the only Muslim dynasty ever to control the whole of the Islāmic-conquered world. The second dynasty is the ʿAbbāsid dynasty; technically its rule extended as late as 1258, but in reality its princes ceased to be a significant cultural factor after the second decade of the 10th century. The ʿAbbāsids no longer controlled Spain, where an independent Umayyad caliphate had been established; and in Egypt as well as in northeastern Iran a number of more or less independent dynasties appeared, such as the Ṭūlūnids or the Sāmānids. Although recent research tends to make the conclusion less certain than it used to be for the Sāmānids and northeast Iran, the initial impulse for the artistic creativity of these dynasties came from the main ʿAbbāsid centres in Iraq. While in detailed studies it is possible to distinguish between Umayyad and ʿAbbāsid art or between the arts of various provinces, the key features of the first three centuries of Islāmic art (roughly through the middle of the 10th century) are the interplay between local or imperial impulses and the creation of new forms and functions.

It is possible to study these centuries as a succession of clusters of monuments, but since there are so many of them, a study can easily end up as an endless list. It is preferable, therefore, to centre the discussion of Umayyad and ʿAbbāsid monuments on the functional and morphological characteristics that identify the new Muslim world and only secondarily be concerned with stylistic progression or regional differences.

Origin of the mosque

Architecture. *Religious buildings.* The one obviously new function developed during this period is that of the mosque, or *masjid*. The earliest adherents of Islām used the private house of the Prophet in Medina as the main place for their religious and other activities and *muṣallā*s without established forms for certain holy ceremonies. The key phenomenon of the first decades that followed the conquest is the creation outside of Arabia of *masjid*s in every centre taken over by the new faith. These were not simply or even primarily religious centres. They were rather the community centres of the faithful, in which all social, political, educational, and individual affairs were transacted. Among these activities were common prayer and the ceremony of the *khuṭbah*. The first mosques were built primarily to serve as the restricted space in which the new community would take its own collective decisions. It is there that the treasury of the community was kept, and early accounts are full of anecdotes about the immense variety of events, from the dramatic to the scabrous, that took place in mosques. Since even in earliest times the Muslim community consisted of several superimposed and interconnected social systems, mosques reflected this complexity, and, next to large mosques for the whole community, tribal mosques and mosques for various quarters of a town or city are also known.

None of these early mosques has survived, and no descriptions of the smaller ones have been preserved. There do remain, however, accurate textual descriptions of the large congregational buildings erected at Kūfah and

From E. Kuhnel, *Islamic Art and Architecture*

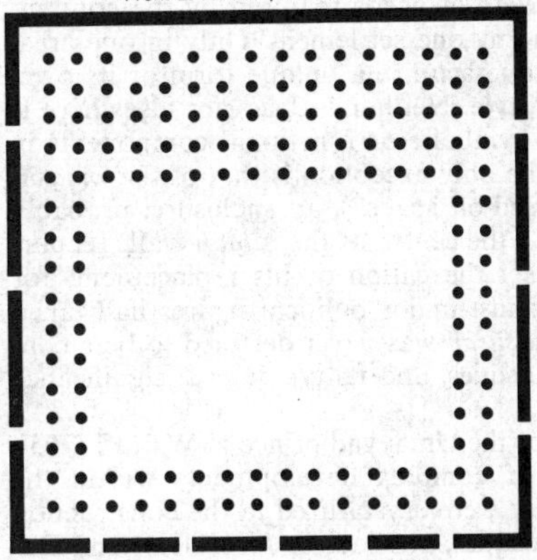

Plan of reconstructed mosque at Kūfah.

Basra in Iraq and at al-Fusṭāṭ in Egypt. At Kūfah a larger square was marked out by a ditch, and a covered colonnade known as a *ẓullah* (a shady place) was put up on the *qiblah* side. In 670 a wall pierced by many doors was built in place of the ditch, and colonnades were put up on all four sides, with a deeper one on the *qiblah*. In all probability the Basra mosque was very similar, and only minor differences distinguished the ʿAmr ibn al-ʿĀṣ mosque at al-Fusṭāṭ. Much has been written about the sources of this type of building, but the simplest explanation may be that this is the very rare instance of the actual creation of a new architectural type. The new faith's requirement for centralization, or a space for a large and constantly growing community, could not be met by any existing architectural form. Almost accidentally, therefore, the new Muslim cities of Iraq created the hypostyle mosque (a building with the roof resting on rows of columns). A flexible architectural unit, a hypostyle structure could be square or rectangular and could be increased or diminished in size by the addition or subtraction of columns. The single religious or symbolic feature of the hypostyle mosque was a *minbar* (a pulpit) for the preacher, and the direction of prayer was indicated by the greater depth of the colonnade on one side of the structure.

Versatility of the hypostyle plan

The examples of Kūfah, Basra, and al-Fusṭāṭ are particularly clear because they were all built in newly created cities. Matters are somewhat more complex when discussing the older urban centres taken over by Muslims. Although it is not possible to generalize with any degree of certainty, two patterns seem to emerge. In some cases, such as Jerusalem and Damascus and perhaps in most cities conquered through formal treaties, the Muslims took for themselves an available unused space and erected on it some shelter, usually a very primitive one. In Jerusalem this space happened to be a particularly holy one—the area of the Jewish Temple built by Herod I the Great, which had been left willfully abandoned and ruined by the triumphant Christian empire. In Damascus it was a section of a huge Roman temple area, on another part of which there was a church dedicated to St. John the Baptist. Unfortunately too little is known about other cities to be able to demonstrate that this pattern was a common one. The very same uncertainty surrounds the second pattern, which consisted in forcibly transforming sanctuaries of older faiths into Muslim ones. This was the case at Ḥamāh in Syria and at Yazd-e Khvāst in Iran, where archaeological proof exists of the change. There are also several literary references to the fact that Christian churches, Zoroastrian fire temples, and other older abandoned sanctuaries were transformed into mosques. Altogether, however, these instances prob-

Transformation of existing pre-Islāmic sanctuaries into mosques ably were not too numerous, because in most places the Muslim conquerors were quite anxious to preserve local tradition and because few older sanctuaries could easily serve the primary Muslim need of a large centralizing space.

During the 50 years that followed the beginning of the Muslim conquest, the mosque, until then a very general concept in Islāmic thought, became a definite building reserved for a variety of needs required by the community of faithful in any one settlement. Only in one area, Iraq, did the mosque acquire a unique form of its own, the oriented hypostyle. Neither in Iraq nor elsewhere is there evidence of symbolic or functional components in mosque design. The only exception is that of the *maqṣūrah* (literally "closed-off space"), an enclosure, probably in wood, built near the centre of the *qiblah* wall. Its purpose was to protect the caliph or his replacement, for several attacks against major political figures had taken place. But the *maqṣūrah* was never destined to be a constant fixture of mosques, and its typological significance is limited.

During the rule of the Umayyad prince al-Walīd I (705–715), a number of complex developments within the Muslim community were crystallized in the construction of three major mosques, at Medina, Jerusalem, and Damascus. The very choice of these three cities is indicative: the city in which the Muslim state was formed and in which the Prophet was buried; the city held in common holiness by Jews, Christians, and Muslims, to which was rapidly accruing the mystical hagiography surrounding the Prophet's ascension into heaven; and the ancient city that became the capital of the new Islāmic empire. A first and essential component of al-Walīd's mosques was, thus, their imperial character; they were to symbolize the permanent establishment of the new faith and of the state that derived from it. They were no longer purely practical shelters but willful monuments.

Mosques of Medina, Jerusalem, and Damascus

Although the plans of al-Aqṣā Mosque in Jerusalem and of the mosque of Medina can be reconstructed with a fair degree of certainty, only the one at Damascus has been preserved with comparatively minor alterations and repairs. In plan the three buildings appear at first glance to be quite different from each other. The Medina mosque was essentially a large hypostyle with a courtyard. The colonnades on all four sides were of varying depth. Al-Aqṣā Mosque consisted of an undetermined number of naves (possibly as many as 15) parallel to each other in a north–south direction. There was no courtyard because the rest of the huge esplanade of the former Jewish temple served as the open space in front of the building. The Umayyad Mosque of Damascus is a rectangle 515 by 330 feet (or 157 by 100 metres) whose outer limits and three gates are parts of a Roman temple (a fourth Roman gate on the *qiblah* side was blocked). The interior consists of an open space surrounded on three sides by a portico and of a covered space of three equal long naves parallel to the *qiblah* wall that are cut in the middle by a perpendicular nave.

The three buildings share several important characteristics. They are all large spaces with a multiplicity of internal supports; and although only the Medina mosque is a pure hypostyle, the Jerusalem and Damascus mosques have the flexibility and easy internal communication characteristic of a hypostyle building. All three mosques exhibit a number of distinctive new practical elements and symbolic meanings. Many of these occur in all mosques, others are only known in some of them. The *miḥrāb*, for example, appears in all mosques. This is a niche of varying size that tends to be heavily decorated. It occurs in the *qiblah* wall, and, in all probability, its purpose was to commemorate the symbolic presence of the Prophet as the first *imām*, although there are other explanations. It is in Damascus only that the ancient towers of the Roman building were first used as minarets to call the faithful to prayer and to indicate from afar the presence of Islām (initially minarets tended to exist only in predominantly non-Muslim cities). All three mosques are also provided with an axial nave, a wider aisle unit on the axis of the building, which served both as a formal axis

Appearance of the *miḥrāb* and minaret

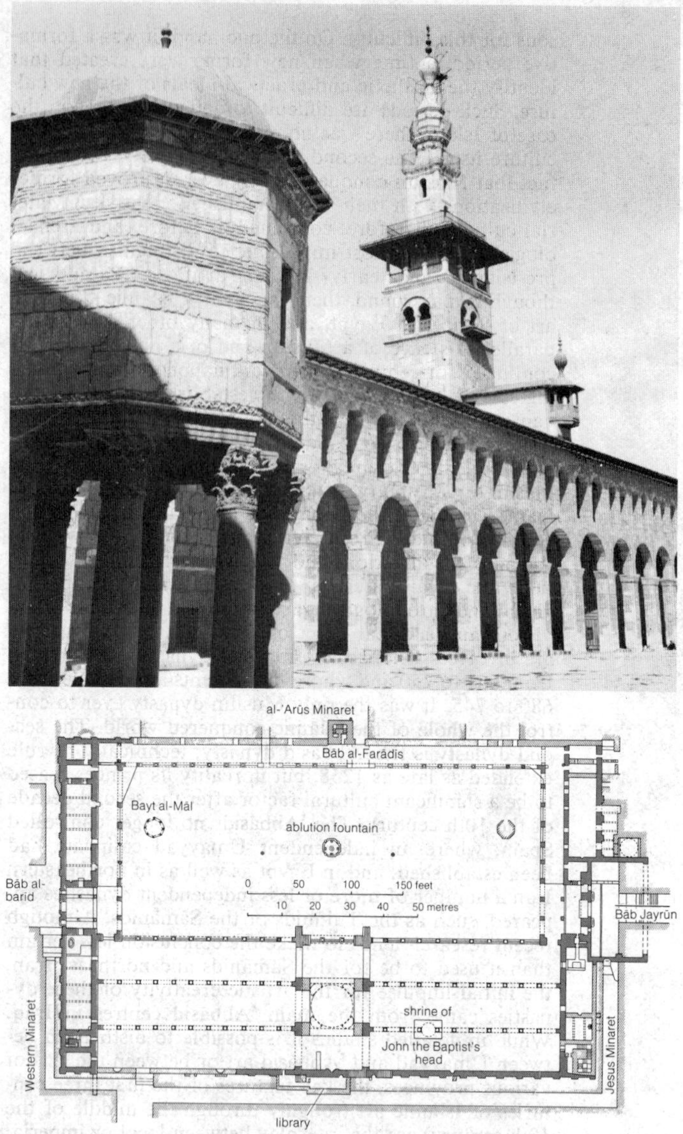

Great Mosque of Damascus, Syria, built by al-Walīd I, 705–715. (Top) Courtyard with the Bayt al-Māl (treasury) on the left, beyond which can be seen one of the three towers that were the first minarets in Islām. (Below) Plan.
Paul Almasy

for compositional purposes and as a ceremonial one for the prince's retinue. Finally, all three buildings were heavily decorated with marble, mosaics, and woodwork. At least in the mosque of Damascus, it is further apparent that there was careful concern for the formal composition—a balance between parts that truly makes this mosque a work of art. This is particularly evident in the successful relationship established between the open space of the court and the facade of the covered *qiblah* side.

When compared to the first Muslim buildings of Iraq and Egypt, the monuments of al-Walīd are characterized by the growing complexity of their forms, by the appearance of uniquely Muslim symbolic and functional features, and by the quality of their construction. While the dimensions, external appearance, and proportions of any one of them were affected in each case by unique local circumstances, the internal balance between open and covered areas and the multiplicity of simple and flexible supports indicate the permanence of the early hypostyle tradition.

Either in its simplest form, as in Medina, or in its more formalized shape, as in Damascus, the hypostyle tradition dominated mosque architecture from 715 to the 10th century. As it occurs at Nīshāpūr in northeastern Iran, Sīrāf in southern Iran, al-Qayrawān (Kairouan) in Tunisia, and Córdoba in Spain, it can indeed be con-

The Great Mosque in al-Qayrawān, Tunisia, built between 836 and 866.
Carl Frank—Photo Researchers

sidered as the classic early Islāmic type. Its masterpieces occur in Iraq and in the West. The monumentalization of the early Iraqi hypostyle is illustrated by the two ruined structures in Sāmarrā', with their enormous sizes (790 by 510 feet [or 240 by 156 metres] for one and 700 by 440 feet [or 213 by 135 metres] for the other), their multiple entrances, their complex piers, and, in one instance, a striking separation of the *qiblah* area from the rest of the building. The best preserved example of this type is the mosque of Ibn Ṭūlūn at Cario (876–879) where a semi-independent governor, Aḥmad ibn Ṭūlūn, introduced Iraqi techniques and succeeded in creating a masterpiece of composition.

Two classic examples of early mosques in the western Islāmic world of interest are preserved in Tunisia and Spain. In al-Qayrawān the Great Mosque was built in stages between 836 and 866. Its most striking feature is the formal emphasis on the building's T-like axis punctuated by two domes, one of which hovers over the earliest preserved ensemble of *miḥrāb*, *minbar*, and *maqṣūrah*. At Córdoba the earliest section of the Great Mosque was built in 785–786. It consisted simply of 11 naves with a wider central one and a court. It was enlarged twice in length, first between 833 and 855 and again from 961 to 965 (it was in the latter phase that the celebrated *maqṣūrah* and *miḥrāb*, comprising one of the great architectural ensembles of early Islāmic art, were constructed). Finally, in 987–988 an extension of the mosque was completed to the east that increased its size by almost one-third without destroying its stylistic unity. The constant increases in the size of this mosque are a further illustration of the flexibility of the hypostyle and its adaptability to any spatial requirement. The most memorable aspects of the Córdoba mosque, however, lie in its construction and decoration. The particularly extensive and heavily decorated *miḥrāb* area exemplifies a development that started with the Medina mosque and would continue: an emphasis on the *qiblah* wall.

Early aberrant plans

Although the hypostyle mosque was the dominant plan, it was not the only one. From very early Islāmic times, a fairly large number of aberrant plans also occur. Most of them were built in smaller urban locations or were secondary mosques in larger Muslim cities. It is rather difficult, therefore, to evaluate whether their significance was purely local or whether they were important for the tradition as a whole. Since a simple type of a square subdivided by four piers into nine-domed units occurs at Balkh in Afghanistan, at Cairo, and at Toledo, it may be considered a pan-Islāmic type. Other types, a single square hall surrounded by an ambulatory, or a single long barrel-vault parallel or perpendicular to the *qiblah*, are rarer and should perhaps be considered as purely local. These are particularly numerous in Iran, where it does seem that the mainstream of early Islāmic architecture did not penetrate very deeply. Unfortunately, the archaeological exploration of Iran is still in its infancy and many of the mud-brick buildings from the early Islāmic period have been destroyed or rebuilt beyond recognition. As a result, it is extremely difficult to determine the historical importance of monuments found at Neyrīz, Moḥammadīyeh (near Nā'īn), Fahraj (near Yazd), or Hazareh (near Samarkand). For an understanding of the mosque's development and of the general dynamics of Islāmic architecture, however, an awareness of these secondary types, which may have existed outside of Iran as well, is essential.

The function of the mosque, the central gathering place of the Muslim community, became the major and most original completely Muslim architectural effort. The mosque was not a purely religious building, at least not at the beginning; but, because it was restricted to Muslims, it is appropriate to consider it as such. This, however, was not the only type of early Islāmic building to be uniquely Muslim. Three other types can be defined architecturally, and a fourth one only functionally.

The first type, the Dome of the Rock in Jerusalem, is a unique building. Completed in 691, this masterwork of Islāmic architecture is the earliest major Islāmic monument. Its octagonal plan, use of a high dome, and building techniques are hardly original, although its decoration is unique. Its purpose, however, is what is most remarkable about the building. Since the middle of the 8th century, the Dome of the Rock has become the focal centre of the most mystical event in the life of the Prophet: his ascension into heaven from the rock around which the building was erected. According to an inscription preserved since the erection of the dome, however, it would seem that the building did not originally commemorate the Prophet's ascension but rather the Christology of Islām and its relationship to Judaism. It seems preferable, therefore, to interpret the Dome of the Rock as a victory monument of the new faith's ideological and religious claim on a holy city and on all the religious traditions attached to it.

The *ribāṭs* of the frontier

The second distinctly Islāmic type of religious building is the little-known *ribāṭ*. As early as in the 8th century, the Muslim empire entrusted the protection of its frontiers, especially the remote ones, to warriors for the faith (*murābiṭūn*, "bound ones") who lived, permanently or temporarily, in special institutions known as *ribāṭs*. Evi-

From G. Marcais, *L'Architecture Musulmane D'Occident*

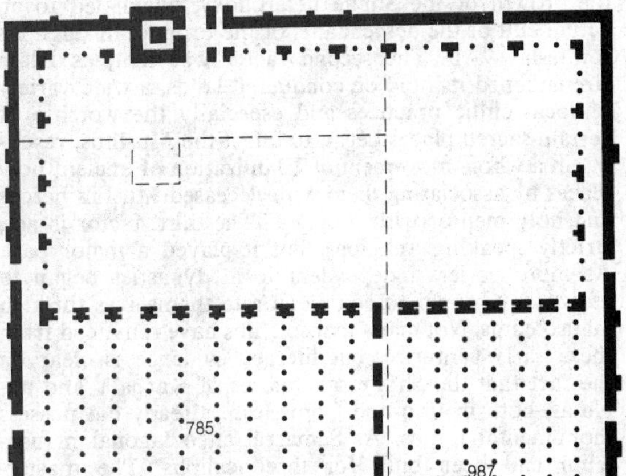

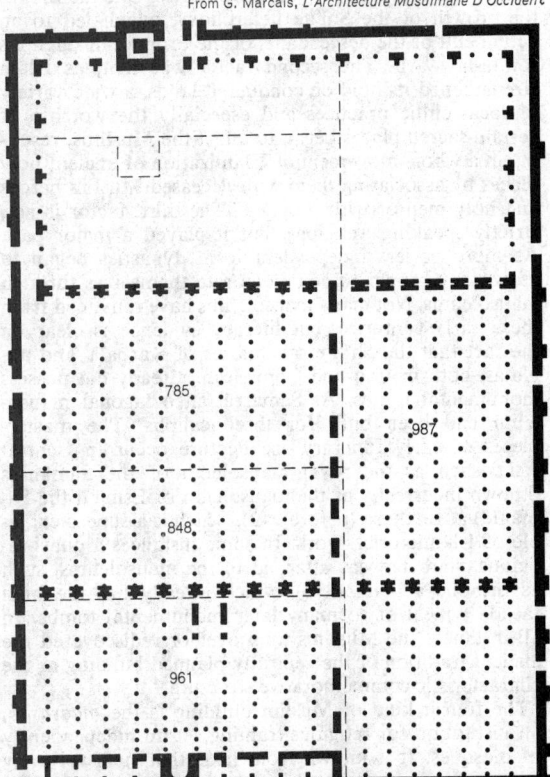

Plan of the Great Mosque at Córdoba, Spain, showing dates of different additions.

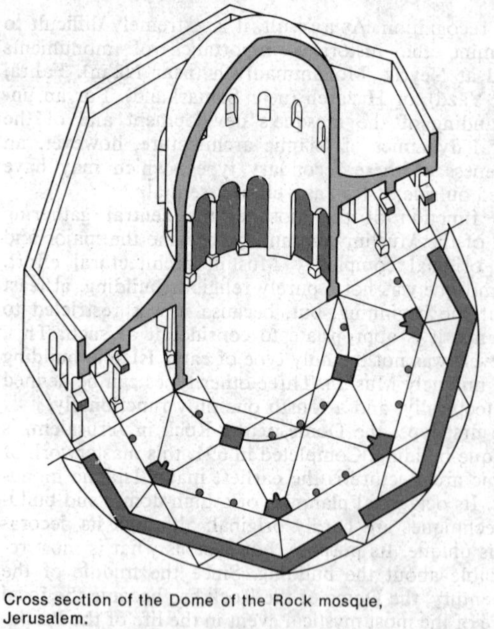

Cross section of the Dome of the Rock mosque, Jerusalem.

dence for these exist in Central Asia, Anatolia, and North Africa. It is only in Tunisia that *ribāṭ*s have been preserved. The best one is at Sūsah, Tunisia; it consists of a square fortified building with a single fairly elaborate entrance and a central courtyard. It has two stories of private or communal rooms. Except for the prominence taken by an oratory, this building could be classified as a type of Muslim secular architecture. Since no later example of a *ribāṭ* is known, there is some uncertainty as to whether the institution ever acquired a unique architectural form of its own.

The diverse functions of the Muslim mausoleum

The last religious type of building to develop before the end of the 10th century is the mausoleum. Originally Islām was strongly opposed to any formal commemoration of the dead. But three independent factors slowly modified an attitude that was eventually maintained only in the most strictly orthodox circles. One factor was the growth of the Shīʿite heterodoxy, which led to an actual cult of the descendants of the Prophet through his son-in-law ʿAlī. The second factor was that, as Islām strengthened its hold on conquered lands, a wide variety of local cultic practices and especially the worship of certain sacred places began to affect the Muslims, resulting in a whole movement of Islāmization of ancient holy places by associating them with deceased Muslim heroes and holy men or with prophets. The third factor is not, strictly speaking, religious, but it played a major part. As more or less independent local dynasties began to grow, they sought to commemorate themselves through mausoleums. Not many mausoleums have remained from these early centuries, but literary evidence is clear on the fact that the Shīʿite sanctuaries of Karbalā' and an-Najaf, both in Iraq and Qom, Iran, already did possess monumental tombs. At Sāmarrā' an octagonal mausoleum had been built for three caliphs. The masterpieces of early funerary architecture occur in Central Asia, such as the royal mausoleum of the Sāmānids (known incorrectly as the mausoleum of Esmāʿīl the Sāmānid) at Bukhara (before 942), which is a superb example of Islāmic brick work. In some instances a quasi-religious character was attached to the mausoleums, such as the one at Tim (976), which already has the high facade typical of so many later monumental tombs. In all instances the Muslims took over or rediscovered the ancient tradition of the centrally planned building as the characteristic commemorative structure.

The *madrasah*

The fourth kind of Muslim building is the *madrasah*, an institution for religious training set up independently of mosques. It is known from texts that such privately endowed schools existed in the northeastern Iranian world as early as in the 9th century, but no description exists of how they were planned or looked.

Secular architecture. Whereas the functions of the religious buildings of early Islām could not have existed without the new faith, the functions of secular Muslim architecture have *a priori* no specifically Islāmic character. This is all the more so since one can hardly point to a significant new need or habit that would have been brought from Arabia by the conquering Muslims and since so little was destroyed in the conquered areas. It can be assumed, therefore, that all pre-Islāmic functions such as living, trading, and manufacturing continued in whatever architectural setting they may have had. Only one exception is certain. With the disappearance of Sāsānian kingship, the pre-Islāmic Iranian imperial tradition ceased, and elsewhere conquered minor kings and governors left their palaces and castles. A new imperial power was created, located first in Damascus, then briefly in the northern Syrian town of ar-Ruṣāfah, and eventually in Baghdad and Sāmarrā' in Iraq. New governors and, later, almost independent princes took over provincial capitals, which were sometimes old seats of government and, at other times, were new Muslim centres. In all instances, however, there is no reason to assume that for an architecture of power or of pleasure early Muslims would have felt the need to modify pre-Islāmic traditions. In fact there is much in early Islāmic secular architecture that can be used to illustrate secular arts elsewhere—in Byzantium, for example, or even in the West. If any new political or social entity is to succeed in preserving an identity of its own, however, it must give to its secular needs certain directions and emphases that will eventually establish a unique cultural image. This is what happened in the development of Umayyad and early ʿAbbāsid secular architecture.

Three factors contributed to the evolution of a new secular architecture. One was that the accumulation of an immense wealth of ideas, workers, and money in the hands of the Muslim princes settled in Syria and Iraq gave rise to a unique palace architecture. The second factor was the impetus given to urban life and to trade. New cities were founded from Sijilmāssah on the edge of the Moroccan Sahara to Nīshāpūr in northeastern Iran, and 9th-century Arab merchants traded as far away as China. Thus the second topic, to be treated below, will be the urban design and commercial architecture. The third factor is that, for the first time since Alexander the Great, a world extending from the Mediterranean to India became culturally unified. As a result, decorative motifs, design ideas, structural techniques, and artisans and architects—which until then had belonged to entirely different cultural traditions—were available in the same places. Early Islāmic princely architecture has become the best known and most original aspect of early Islāmic secular buildings. There are basically three kinds

Josephine Powell, Rome

Royal mausoleum of the Sāmānids, Bukhara, Uzbek S.S.R., (before 942).

of these princely structures. The first type consists of 10 large rural princely complexes found in Syria, Palestine, and Transjordan dating from around 710 to 750: ar-Ruṣāfah, Qaṣr al-Ḥayr East, Qaṣr al-Ḥayr West, Jabal Says, Khirbat Minyah, Khirbat al-Mafjar, Mshattā, Qaṣr ʿAmrah, Qaṣr al-Kharānah, and Qaṣr aṭ-Ṭūbah. Apparently these examples of princely architecture belong to a group of over 60 ruined or only textually identifiable rural complexes erected by Umayyad princes. In the past a rather romantic theory had developed about their locations, suggesting that the remoteness of their sites expressed an atavistic hankering on the part of the Umayyad Arab rulers for the desert or at least the semi-arid steppe that separates the permanently cultivated areas of Syria and Palestine from their original home in the north Arabian wilderness. This theory has been disproved, for every one of these sites has turned out to have been a major agricultural or trade centre, some of which were developed even before the Muslim conquest. Private palaces were built, notably at ar-Ruṣāfah, Qaṣr al-Ḥayr West, Khirbat al-Mafjar, Qaṣr ʿAmrah, and Mshattā. These must be considered as early medieval equivalents of the *villae rusticae* so characteristic in the ancient Roman period. Although each one of these palaces had a number of idiosyncrasies peculiar to itself that were presumably inspired by the needs and desires of its owner, all of these structures tend to share a number of features that can best be illustrated by Khirbat al-Mafjar. This palace, the richest of them all, contained a residential unit consisting of a square building with an elaborate entrance, a porticoed courtyard, and a number of rooms or halls arranged on two floors. Few of these rooms seem to have any identifiable function, although at Khirbat al-Mafjar a private oratory, a large meeting hall, and an anteroom leading to a cool underground pool have been identified. The main throne room was on the second floor above the entrance. Its plan is not known, but probably resembled the preserved throne rooms or reception halls at Qaṣr ʿAmrah and Mshattā, which consisted of a three-aisled hall ending in an apse (semicircular or polygonal domed projection) in the manner of a Roman basilica.

The country princely palace complex

Next to an official residence, there usually was a small mosque, generally a miniaturized hypostyle in plan. The most original feature of these establishments was the bath. The bathing area itself is comparatively small, but every bath had its own elaborate entrance and contained a large hall that, at least in the instance of Khirbat al-Mafjar, was heavily decorated and of an unusual shape. It would appear that these halls were for pleasure —places for music, dancing, and probably occasional orgies. In some instances, as at Qaṣr ʿAmrah, the same setting may have been used for both pleasure and formal receptions.

These palaces are important illustrations of the luxurious taste and way of life of the new Near Eastern aristocrats, who settled in the countryside and transformed some of it into places of pleasure. This aspect of these establishments is peculiar to the Umayyad dynasty in Syria and Palestine. Outside of this area and period only one comparable structure has been found, at Ukhayḍir in Iraq, which dates from the early ʿAbbāsid period. A number of princely residences of the Central Asian or North African countryside are still too little known but appear not to have had the same development. The other important lesson to draw from them is that few of their features are original. All of them derive from the architectural vocabulary of pre-Islāmic times, and it is in the artistic traditions of the Mediterranean world that most of their sources are found, although the Mshattā throne room does have a number of Sāsānian elements. For this reason these palaces ought to be considered as major examples of pre-Islāmic secular architecture, for as interesting as these monuments are, they are not part of the Islāmic tradition.

The urban palace

A second type of princely architecture—the urban palace has been preserved only in texts or literary sources, with the exception of the palace at Kūfah in Iraq. Datable from the very end of the 7th century, this example of princely architecture seems to have functioned both as a residence and as the *dār al-imārah*, or centre of government. This dual function is reflected in the use of separate building units and in the absence of much architectural decoration which suggests that it reflected an austere official taste. Although suggestions concerning the plans used are occasionally encountered in literary sources, this information is not sufficient to define these early urban official buildings of the Muslims. Nothing is known, for instance, about the great Umayyad palace in Damascus aside from the fact that it had a green dome.

Also poorly documented is a development in urban aristocratic buildings that seems to have begun with the ʿAbbāsids during the last decades of the 8th century. This involved the construction of smaller palaces, probably pavilions in the midst of gardens in or around major cities.

The ʿAbbāsid palace-city

The third type of early Islāmic princely architecture is the palace-city. Several of these huge palaces are part of the enormous mass of ruins at Sāmarrāʾ, the temporary ʿAbbāsid capital from 838 to 883. Jawsaq al-Khāqānī, for instance, is a walled architectural complex nearly one mile to a side that in reality is an entire city. It contains a formal succession of large gates and courts leading to a cross-shaped throne room, a group of smaller living units, basins and fountains, and even a race track. Too little is known about the architectural details of these huge walled complexes to lead to more than very uncertain hypotheses. Their existence, however, suggests that they were settings for the very elaborate ceremonies developed by the ʿAbbāsid princes, especially when receiving foreign ambassadors. An account, for instance, in Khaṭīb al-Baghdādī's (died 1071) Taʾrīkh Baghdad ("History of Baghdad") of the arrival in Baghdad of a Byzantine envoy in 914 illustrates this point. The meeting with the caliph was preceded by a sort of formal presentation intended to impress the ambassador with the Muslim ruler's wealth and power. Treasures were laid down, thousands of soldiers and slaves in rich clothes guarded them, lions roared in the gardens, and on gilded artificial trees mechanical devices made silver birds chirp. The ceremony was a fascinating mixture of a traditional attempt to recreate paradise on earth and a rather vulgar exhibition of wealth that required a huge space, as in the Sāmarrāʾ palaces. Another important aspect of these palace-cities is that they became part of a myth. The walled enclosure in which thousands lived a life unknown to others and into which simple mortals did not penetrate without bringing their own shroud was transformed into legend. It became the mysterious City of Brass of *The Thousand and One Nights*, and it is from its luxurious glory that occasionally a caliph such as Hārūn ar-Rashīd escaped into the "real" world. Even though there is inadequate information on the ʿAbbāsid palace-city, it was clearly a unique early Islāmic creation, and its impact can be detected from Byzantium to Hollywood.

Urban design

Islāmic secular architecture has left considerable information about cities, for systematic urbanization was one of the most characteristic features of early Muslim civilization. It is much too early to draw any sort of conclusion about the actual physical organization of towns, about their subdivisions and their houses, for only at al-Fusṭāṭ (Cairo) and Sīrāf in Iran is the evidence archaeologically clear, and much of it has not yet been properly published. A huge task remains to be done of relating immense amounts of textual material with scraps of archaeological information scattered from Central Asia to Spain, such as the outer walls and impressive gateway preserved at ar-Raqqah in Syria. In general it can be said that there does not seem to have been any idealized master plan for the internal arrangement of an urban site in contradistinction to Hellenistic or Roman towns. Even mosques or palaces were often located eccentrically and not in the middle of the town. Extraordinary attention was paid to water distribution and conservation, as demonstrated by the magnificent 9th-century cisterns in Tunisia, the 9th-century Nilometer (a device to measure the Nile's level) in Cairo, and the elaborate dams, canals, and sluices of Qaṣr al-Ḥayr in Syria. The construction of commercial buildings on a monumental scale occurred. The most spectacular example is the caravanserai of Qaṣr al-Ḥayr East, with its magnificent gate.

The concern for palaces and cities that characterized early Islāmic secular architecture shows itself most remarkably in the construction of Baghdad between 762 and 766–67 by the ʿAbbāsid caliph al-Manṣūr. It was a walled round city whose circular shape served to demonstrate Baghdad's symbolic identity as the navel of the universe. A thick ring of residential quarters was separated by four axial, commercial streets entered through spectacular gates. In the centre of the city there was a large open space with a palace, a mosque, and a few administrative buildings. By its size and number of inhabitants, Baghdad was unquestionably a city; however, its plan so strongly emphasized the presence of the caliph that it was also a palace.

Building materials and technology. The early Islāmic period, on the whole, did not innovate much in the realm of building materials and technology but utilized what it had inherited from older traditions.

Stone and brick continued to be used around the Mediterranean, while mud brick usually covered with plaster predominated in Iraq and Iran, with a few notable exceptions like Sīrāf, where a masonry of roughly cut stones set in mortar was more common. The most important novelty was the rapid development in Iraq of a baked brick architecture in the late 8th and 9th centuries. Iraqi techniques were later used in Syria at ar-Raqqah and Qaṣr al-Ḥayr East and in Egypt. Iranian brickwork appears at Mshattā in Jordan. The mausoleum of the Sāmānids in Bukhara is the earliest remaining example of the new brick architecture in northeastern Iran. Wood was used consistently but has usually not been very well preserved, except in Palestine and Egypt where climatic (extreme dryness of Egypt), religious (holiness of Jerusalem sanctuaries), or historic (Egypt was never conquered) factors contributed to the continuous upkeep of wooden objects or architectural elements.

As supports for roofs and ceilings, early Islāmic architecture used walls and single supports. Walls were generally continuous, often buttressed with half towers, and rarely (with exceptions in Central Asia) were they articulated or broken up by other architectural features. The most common single support was the base–column–capital combination of Mediterranean architecture. Most columns and capitals were either re-used from pre-Islāmic buildings or were directly imitated from older models. In the 9th century in Iraq a brick pier was used, a form that spread to Iran and Egypt. Columns and piers were covered with arches. Most often these were semicircular arches; the pointed, or two-centred, arch was known, but it does not seem that its property of reducing the need for heavy supports had been realized. The most extraordinary technical development of arches occurs in the Great Mosque at Córdoba, where, in order to increase the height of the building in an area with only short columns, the architects created two rows of superimposed horseshoe arches. Almost immediately they realized that such a succession of superimposed arches constructed of alternating stone and brick could be modified to create a variety of patterns that would alleviate the inherent monotony of a hypostyle building. A certain ambiguity remains, however, as to whether ornamental effect or structural technology was the predominate concern in the creation of these unique arched columns.

Arches and vaulting

The majority of early Islāmic ceilings were flat. Gabled wooden roofs, however, were erected in the Muslim world west of the Euphrates, and simple barrel vaults to the east. Vaulting, either in brick or in stone, was used, especially in secular architecture. Domes were employed frequently in mosques, consistently in mausoleums, and occasionally in secular buildings. Almost all domes are on squinches (supports carried across corners to act as structural transitions to a dome). Most squinches, as in the al-Qayrawān domes, are classical Greco-Roman niches, which transform the square room into an octagonal opening for the dome. In Córdoba's Great Mosque a complex system of intersecting ribs is encountered, while at Bukhara the squinch is broken into halves by a transverse half arch. The most extraordinary use of the squinch occurs in the mausoleum at Tim, where the surface of this structural device is broken up into a series of smaller three-dimensional units rearranged into a sort of pyramidal pattern. The rearrangement is the earli-

Fritz Henle—Photo Researchers

Dome of the *mihrāb* in the Great Mosque of Córdoba, Spain, *c.* 961.

est extant example of *muqarnas* or the stalactite-like decoration that would later be an important element of Islāmic architectural ornamentation. The motif is so awkwardly constructed at Tim that it must have derived from some other source, possibly the ornamental device of using curved stucco panels to cover the corners and upper parts of walls found in Iran at Nīshāpūr.

Architectural decoration. Early Islāmic architecture is most original in its decoration. Mosaics and wall paintings followed the practices of antiquity and were primarily employed in Syria, Palestine, and Spain. Stone sculpture existed, but stucco sculpture, first limited to Iran, spread rapidly throughout the early Islāmic world. Not only were stone or brick walls covered with large panels of stucco sculpture, but this technique was used for sculpture in the round in the Umayyad palaces of Qaṣr al-Ḥayr West and Khirbat al-Mafjar. The latter was a comparatively short-lived technique, although it produced some of the few instances of monumental sculpture anywhere in the early Middle Ages. A variety of techniques borrowed from the industrial arts were used for architectural ornamentation. The *miḥrāb* wall of al-Qayrawān's Great Mosque, for example, was covered with ceramics, while fragments of decorative woodwork have been preserved in Jerusalem and Egypt.

Three kinds of early architectural decoration

The themes and motifs of early Islāmic decoration can be divided into three major groups. The first kind of ornamentation simply emphasizes the shape or contour of an architectural unit. The themes used were vegetal bands for vertical or horizontal elements, marble imitations for the lower parts of long walls, chevrons or other types of borders on floors and domes, and even whole trees on the spandrels or soffits (undersides) of arches as in the Umayyad Mosque of Damascus or the Dome of the Rock; all these motifs tend to be quite traditional, being taken from the rich decorative vocabularies of pre-Islāmic Iran or of the ancient Mediterranean world.

The second group consists of decorative motifs for which a concrete iconographic meaning can be given. In the Dome of the Rock and the Umayyad Mosque of Damascus, as well as possibly the mosques of Córdoba and of Medina, there were probably iconographic programs. It has been shown, for example, that the huge architectural and vegetal decorative motifs at Damascus were meant to symbolize a sort of idealized paradise on earth, while the crowns of the Jerusalem sanctuary are thought to have been symbols of empires conquered by Islām. But it is equally certain that this use of visual forms in mosques for ideological and symbolic purposes was not easily accepted, and most later mosques are devoid of iconographically significant themes. The only exceptions fully visible are the Qur'ānic inscriptions in the mosque of Ibn Ṭūlūn at Cairo, which were used both as a reminder of the faith and as an ornamental device to emphasize the structural lines of the building. Thus the early Islāmic mosque eventually became austere in its use of symbolic ornamentation, with the exception of the *miḥrāb*, which was considered as a symbol of orthodox Sunnī Islām.

Like religious architecture, secular buildings seem to have been less richly decorated at the end of the early Islāmic period than at the beginning. The paintings, sculptures, and mosaics of Qaṣr al-Ḥayr West, Khirbat al-Mafjar, Qaṣr ʿAmrah, and Sāmarrā' primarily illustrated the life of the prince. There were official iconographic compositions, such as the monarch enthroned, or ones of pleasure and luxury, such as hunting scenes or depictions of the prince surrounded by dancers, musicians, acrobats, and unclad women. Few of these so-called princely themes were iconographic inventions of the Muslims. They usually can be traced back either to the classical world of ancient Greece and Rome or to pre-Islāmic Iran and Central Asia.

The third type of architectural decoration consists of large panels, most often in stucco, for which no meaning or interpretation is yet known. These panels might be called ornamental in the sense that their only apparent purpose was to beautify the buildings in which they were installed, and their relationship to the architecture is arbitrary. The Mshattā facade's decoration of a huge band of triangles is, for instance, quite independent of the building's architectural parts. Next to Mshattā, the most important series of examples of the third type of ornamentation come from Sāmarrā', although striking examples are also to be found at Khirbat al-Mafjar, Qaṣr al-Ḥayr East and West, al-Fusṭāṭ, Sīrāf, and Nīshāpūr. Two decorative motifs were predominately used on these panels: a great variety of vegetal motifs and geometric forms. At Sāmarrā' these panels eventually became so abstract that individual parts could no longer be distinguished, and the decorative design had to be viewed in terms of the relationships between line and shape, light and shade, horizontal and vertical axes, and so forth. Copied consistently from Morocco to Central Asia, the aesthetic principles of this latter type of a complex overall design influenced the development of the principle of arabesque ornamentation.

By courtesy of the Islamisches Museum, Staatliche Museen zu Berlin

Triangle stone relief from the facade of Mshattā in Transjordan, early 8th century. In the Islamisches Museum, Staatliche Museen zu Berlin.

Islāmic architectural ornamentation does not lend itself easily to chronological stylistic definition. In other words, it does not seem to share consistently a cluster of formal characteristics. The reason is that in the earliest Islāmic buildings the decorative motifs were borrowed from an extraordinary variety of stylistic sources: classical themes illusionistically rendered (*e.g.*, the mosaics of the Umayyad Mosque of Damascus), hieratic Byzantine themes (*e.g.*, the Umayyad Mosque of Damascus and Qaṣr ʿAmrah), Sāsānian motifs, Central Asian motifs (especially the sculpture from Umayyad palaces), and the many regional styles of ornamentation that had developed in all parts of the pre-Islāmic world. It is the wealth of themes and motifs, therefore, that constitutes the Umayyad style of architectural decoration. The ʿAbbāsids, on the other hand, began to be more selective in their choice of ornamentation.

Decorative arts. Very little is known about early Islāmic gold and silver objects, although their existence is mentioned in many texts as well as suggested by the wealth of the Muslim princes. Except for a large number of silver plates and ewers belonging to the Sasanian tradition, nothing has remained. These silver objects were probably made for Umayyad and ʿAbbāsid princes, although there is much controversy among scholars regarding their authenticity and date of manufacture.

For entirely different reasons it is impossible to present any significant generalities about the art of textiles in the early Islāmic period. Problems of authenticity are few. Dating from the 10th century are a large number of Būyid silks, a group of funerary textiles with plant and animal motifs as well as poetic texts. Very little order has yet been made of an enormous mass of often well-dated textiles fragments, and therefore, except for the Būyid silks, it is still impossible to identify any one of the textile types mentioned in early medieval literary sources. Furthermore, since it can be assumed that pre-Islāmic textile factories were taken over by the Muslims and since it is otherwise known that textiles were easily transported from one area of the Muslim world to the other or even beyond it, it is still very difficult to define Islāmic styles as opposed to Byzantine ones or to Coptic ones. The obvious exception lies in those fragments that are provided with inscriptions, and the main point to make is therefore that one of the characteristic features of early Islāmic textiles is their use of writing for identifying and decorative purposes. But, while true, this point in no way makes it possible to deny an Islāmic origin to fragments that are not provided with inscriptions, and thus one must await further investigations of details before being able to define early Islāmic textiles.

Būyid silks

The most important medium of early Islāmic decorative arts is pottery. Initially Muslims continued to sponsor whatever varieties of ceramics had existed before their arrival. Probably in the last quarter of the 8th century new and more elaborate types of glazed pottery were produced. This new development did not replace the older and simpler types of pottery but added a new dimension to the art of Islāmic ceramics. Because of the still incompletely published studies on the unfinished excavations carried out at Nīshāpūr, Sīrāf, Qaṣr al-Ḥayr East, and al-Fusṭāṭ, the scholarship on these ceramics is likely to be very much modified over the next decade. Therefore, this article will treat only the most general characteristics of Islāmic ceramics, avoiding in particular the complex archaeological problems posed by the growth and spread of individual techniques.

Early ceramics

The area of initial technical innovation seems to have been Iraq. Trade with Central Asia brought Chinese ceramics to Mesopotamia, and Islāmic ceramicists sought to imitate them. It is probably in Iraq, therefore, that the technique of lustre glazing was first developed in the Muslim world. This gave the surface of a clay object a metallic, shiny appearance. Egypt also played a leading part in the creation of the new ceramics. Since the earliest datable lustre object (a glass goblet with the name of the governor who ruled in 773, now in the Cairo Museum of Islamic Art) was Egyptian, some scholars feel that it was in Egypt and not Iraq that lustre was first used. Early pottery was also produced in northeastern Iran, where excavations at Afrāsiyāb (Samarkand) and Nīshāpūr have brought to light a new art of painted underglaze pottery. Its novelty was not so much in the technique of painting designs on the slip and covering them with a transparent glaze, as it was in the variety of subjects employed.

While new ceramic techniques may have been sought to imitate other mediums (mostly metal) or other styles of pottery (mostly Chinese), the decorative devices rapidly became purely and unmistakably Islāmic in style. A wide variety of motifs were combined: vegetal arabesques or single flowers and trees; inscriptions, usually legible and consisting of proverbs or of good wishes; animals that were usually birds drawn from the vast folkloric past of the Near East; occasionally human figures drawn in a strikingly abstract fashion; geometric designs; all-over abstract patterns; single motifs on empty fields; and simple splashes of colour, with or without underglaze sgrafiato designs, *i.e.* designs incised or sketched on the body or the slip of the object. All of these motifs were used on both the high-quality ceramics of Nīshāpūr and Samarkand as well as on Islāmic folk pottery.

Although ceramics has appeared to be the most characteristic medium of expression in the decorative arts during the early Islāmic period, it has only been because of the greater number of preserved objects. Glass was as important, but examples have been less well preserved. A tradition of ivory carving developed in Spain, and the objects dating from the last third of the 10th century onward attest to the high quality of this uniquely Iberian art. Many of these carved ivories certainly were made for princes; therefore it is not surprising that their decorative themes were drawn from the whole vocabulary of princely art known through Umayyad painting and sculpture of the early 8th century. These ivory carvings are also important in that they exemplify the fact that an art of sculpture in the round never totally disappeared in the Muslim world—at least in small objects.

Spanish ivory carving

Assessment. There are three general points that seem to characterize the art of the early Islāmic period. It can first be said that it was an art that sought self-consciously, like the culture sponsoring it, to create artistic forms that would be identifiable as being different from those produced in preceding or contemporary non-Islāmic ar-

By courtesy of (left, centre) the Musee du Louvre, Paris, (right) the Cleveland Museum of Art, Purchase from the J.H. Wade Fund; photographs, (left) Mansell—Giraudon, (centre) Cliche Musees Nationaux, Paris

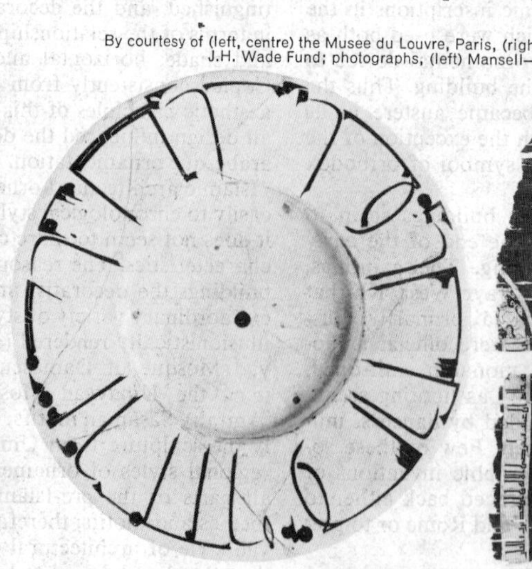

Early Islāmic Decorative Arts.
(Left) Ivory casket made for al-Mughīrah, son of ʿAbd ar-Rahmān III, from Córdoba, Spain, 968. In the Louvre, Paris. Ht. 15 cm. (Centre) Bowl of Samarkand ware bowl with calligraphic decoration, 10th century. In the Louvre, Paris. Diameter 37.5 cm. (Right) Fragment of a silk tomb cover with a woven design of pairs of ibex, from Iran, 998. In the Cleveland Museum of Art, Ohio. 78.1 cm × 66 cm.

tistic traditions. At times, as in the use of the Greco-Roman technique of mosaics or in the adoption of Persian and Roman architectural building technology, early Islāmic art simply took over as such whatever traditions were available. At other times, as in the development of the mosque as a building type, it recomposed into new shapes the forms that had existed before. On the other hand, in ceramics or the use of calligraphic ornamentation, the early Islāmic artist invented new techniques and a new decorative vocabulary. Whatever the nature of the phenomenon, it was almost always an attempt to identify itself visually as unique and different. Since there was initially no concept about what should constitute an Islāmic tradition in the visual arts, the early art of the Muslims often looks like only a continuation of earlier artistic styles, forms, subjects, and techniques. Many mosaics, silver plates, or textiles, therefore, were not considered to be Islāmic until recently. In order to be understood, then, as examples of the art of a new culture, these early buildings and objects have to be seen in the complete context in which they were created. When so seen they appear as conscious choices by the new Islāmic culture from its immense artistic inheritance.

Question of an early Islāmic style

A second point of definition concerns the question of whether there is an early Islāmic style or perhaps even several styles in some sort of succession. The fascinating fact is that there is a clear succession only in those artistic features that are Islāmic inventions—nonfigurative ornament and ceramics. For it is only in development of these features that one can assume to find the conscious search for form that can create a period style. Elsewhere, especially in palace art, the Muslim world sought to relate itself to an earlier and more universal tradition of princely art; its monuments, therefore, are less Islāmic than typological. In the new art of the Muslim bourgeoisie, however, uniquely Islāmic artistic phenomena began to evolve.

Finally, the geographical peculiarities of early Islāmic art must be reiterated. Its centres were Syria, Iraq, Egypt, northwestern Iran, and Spain. Of these, Iraq was probably the most originally creative, and it is from Iraq that a peculiarly Islāmic visual koine (a commonly accepted and understood system of forms) was derived and spread throughout the Islāmic world. This development, of course, is logical since the capital of the early empire and some of the first purely Muslim cities were in Iraq. In western Iran, in Afghanistan, in northern Mesopotamia, and in Morocco the more atypical and local artistic traditions were more or less affected by the centralized imperial system of Iraq. This tension between a general pan-Islāmic vocabulary and a variable number of local vocabularies was to remain a constant throughout the history of Islāmic art and is certainly one of the reasons for the difficulty, if not impossibility, one faces in trying to define an Islāmic style.

MIDDLE PERIOD

The middle period in the development of Islāmic art extends roughly from the year 1000 to 1500, when a strong central power with occasional regional political independence was replaced by a bewildering mosaic of overlapping dynasties. Ethnically this was the time of major Turkish and Mongol invasions that brought into the Muslim world new peoples and institutions. At the same time, Berbers, Kurds, and Iranians, who had been within the empire from the beginning of Islām, began to play far more effective historical and cultural roles, short-lived for the Kurds, but uniquely important for the Iranians. Besides political and ethnic confusion, there was also religious and cultural confusion during the middle period. The 10th century, for example, witnessed the transformation of the Shīʿite heterodoxy into a major political and possibly cultural phenomenon, while the extraordinary development taken by the personal and social mysticism known as Ṣūfism modified enormously the nature of Muslim piety. Culturally the most significant development was perhaps that of Persian literature as a highly original new verbal expression existing alongside the older Arabic literary tradition. Finally, the middle period was an era of expansion in all areas except Spain, which was completely lost to the Muslims in 1492 with the conquest of the Kingdom of Granada by Ferdinand II and Isabella. Anatolia and the Balkans, the Crimea, much of Central Asia and northern India, and parts of eastern Africa all became new Islāmic provinces. In some cases this expansion was the result of conquests, but in others it had been achieved through missionary work.

The immense variety of impulses that affected the Muslim world during these five centuries was one of the causes of the bewildering artistic explosion that also characterizes the middle period. Although much work has been done on individual monuments, scholarship is still in its infancy. It is particularly difficult, therefore, to decide on the appropriate means of organizing this information: by geographical or cultural areas (*e.g.* Iran, Egypt, Morocco), by individual dynasties (*e.g.*, Seljuqs, Timurids), by periods (*e.g.*, 13th century before the Mongol invasions), or even by social categories (*e.g.*, the art of princes, the art of cities). Thus, the five following divisions of Fāṭimid, Seljuq, Western Islāmic, Mamlūk, and Mongol Iran (Il-Khanid and Timurid) art are partly arbitrary and to a large extent tentative. Their respective importance also varies, for what is known as Seljuq art certainly overwhelms almost all others in its importance.

Fāṭimid art (909–1171). The Fāṭimids were technically an Arab dynasty professing with missionary zeal the Shīʿite heterodoxy that established itself in Tunisia and Sicily in 909. In 969 the Fāṭimids moved to Egypt and founded the city of Cairo. They soon controlled Syria and Palestine. In the latter part of the 11th century, however, the Fāṭimid empire began to distintegrate internally and externally; the final demise occurred in 1171. But it is not known which of the obvious components of the Fāṭimid world was more significant in influencing the development of the visual arts: its heterodoxy, its Egyptian location, its missionary relationship with almost all provinces of Islām, or the fact that during its heyday in the 11th century it was the only wealthy Islāmic centre and could thus easily gather artisans and art objects from all over the world.

Architecture. The great Fāṭimid mosques of Cairo—al-Azhar (started in 970) and al-Ḥākim (*c.* 1002–03)—were designed in the traditional hypostyle plan with axial cupolas. It is only in such architectural details as the elaborately composed facade of al-Ḥākim, with its corner towers and vaulted portal, that innovations appear, for most earlier mosques did not have large formal gates, nor was much attention previously given to the composition of the exterior facade. The Fāṭimids' architectural traditionalism was certainly a conscious attempt to perpetuate the existing aesthetic system.

Architectural traditionalism

Although much less is known about it, the Great Palace of the Fāṭimids belonged to the tradition of the enormous palace-cities typical of the ʿAbbāsids. Mediterranean rather than Iranian influences, however, played a greater part in the determination of its uses and functions. The whole city of Cairo (Arabic al-Qāhirah, meaning the Victorious), on the other hand, has many symbolic and visual aspects that suggest a willful relationship to Baghdad.

The originality of Fāṭimid architecture does not lie in works sponsored by the caliphs themselves, even though Cairo's well-preserved gates and walls of the second half of the 11th century are among the best examples of early medieval military architecture. It is rather the patronage of lower officials and of the bourgeoisie, if not even of the humbler classes, that was responsible for the most interesting Fāṭimid buildings. The mosques of al-Aqmar (1125) and of aṣ-Ṣāliḥ (*c.* 1160) are among the first examples of monumental small mosques constructed to serve local needs. Even though their internal arrangement is quite traditional, their plans were adapted to the space available in the urban centre. These mosques were elaborately decorated on the exterior, exhibiting a conspicuousness absent from large hypostyle mosques.

A second innovation in Fāṭimid architecture was the tremendous development of mausoleums. This may be explained partially by Shīʿism's emphasis on the succession of holy men, but the development of these buildings in terms of both quality and quantity indicates that other influential social and religious issues were also involved. Most of the mausoleums were simple square buildings surmounted by a dome. Many of these have survived in Cairo and Aswān. Only a few, such as the *mashhad* at Aswān, are somewhat more elaborate, with side rooms. The most original of these commemorative buildings is the Juyūshī Mosque (1085) overlooking the city of Cairo. Properly speaking, it is not a mausoleum but a monument celebrating the re-establishment of Fāṭimid order after a series of popular revolts.

Use of the squinch

The Fāṭimids introduced, or developed, only two major constructional techniques: the systematization of the four-centred "keel" arch and the squinch. The latter innovation is of greater consequence because the squinch became the most common means of passing from a square to a dome, although pendentives were known as well. A peculiarly Egyptian development was the *muqarnas* squinch, which consisted of four units: a niche bracketed by two niche segments, superimposed with an additional niche. The complex profile of the *muqarnas* became an architectural element in itself used for windows, while the device of using niches and niche segments remained typical of Egyptian decorative design for centuries. It still is impossible to say whether the *muqarnas* was invented in Egypt or inspired by other architectural traditions (most likely Iranian). Fāṭimid domes were smooth or ribbed and developed a characteristic "keel" profile.

In the use of materials (brick, stone, wood) and structural concepts, Fāṭimid architecture continued earlier traditions. Occasionally local styles were incorporated, among them the characteristic features of Tunisian architecture in the 10th century or of upper Mesopotamian in the late 11th century.

Stone sculpture, stucco work, and carved wood were utilized for architectural decorations. The Fāṭimids also employed mosaicists, who mostly worked in places like Jerusalem, where they imitated or repaired earlier mosaic murals. Many fragments of Fāṭimid wall paintings have survived in Egypt. Most of them, however, are too small to allow for making any iconographic or stylistic conclusions, with the exception of the mid-12th century ceiling of the Cappella Palatina at Palermo. Built by the Norman kings of Sicily, the palace chapel was almost certainly decorated by Fāṭimid artists, or at least the artists adhered to Fāṭimid models. The hundreds of facets in the *muqarnas* ceiling were painted, notably with many purely ornamental vegetal and zoomorphic designs but also with scenes of daily life and many subjects that have not yet been explained. Stylistically influenced by Iraqi ʿAbbāsid art, these paintings are innovative in their more spatially aware representation of personages and of animals. Very similar tendencies appear also in the stucco and wood sculptures of Fāṭimid decoration. The stunning abstraction of the architectural decoration at Samarra tends to give way to more naturalistically conceived vegetal and animal designs; occasionally whole narrative scenes appear carved on wood. Another decorative trend is especially used on 12th-century *miḥrābs*: explicitly complicated geometric patterns, usually based on stars, which in turn generate octagons, hexagons, triangles, and rectangles. Geometry becomes a sort of network in the midst of which small vegetal units continue to remain, often as inlaid pieces. Long inscriptions written in very elaborate calligraphies also became a typical form of architectural decoration on most of the major Fāṭimid buildings.

A clear separation must be made between the decorative arts sought by Fāṭimid princes and the arts produced within their empire. Little has been preserved of the former, notably a small number of superb ewers in rock crystal. A text has survived, however, that describes the imperial treasures looted in the middle of the 11th century by dissatisfied mercenary troops. It lists gold, silver, enamel, and porcelain objects that have all been lost, as well as textiles (perhaps the cape of the Norman king Roger II [Kunsthistorisches Museum, Vienna] is an example of the kind of textiles found in this treasure). The inventory also records that the Fāṭimids had in their possession many works of Byzantine, Chinese, and even Greco-Roman provenance. Altogether, then, it seems that the imperial art of the Fāṭimids was part of a sort of international royal taste that downplayed cultural or political differences.

Fāṭimid lustre-painted dish depicting a cockfight, from Egypt, late 11th–early 12th century. In the Edmund de Unger Collection. London. Diameter 24.1 cm.
By courtesy of the Edmund de Unger Collection; photograph, A.C. Cooper Ltd.

Lustre ware with figural decoration

Ceramics, on the other hand, were primarily produced by local urban schools and were not an imperial art. The most celebrated type of Fāṭimid wares were lustre-painted ceramics from Egypt itself. A large number of artisans' names have been preserved, thereby indicating the growing prestige of these craftsmen and the aesthetic importance of their pottery. Most of the surviving lustre ceramics are plates on which the decoration of the main surface has been emphasized. The decorative themes used were quite varied and included all the traditional Islāmic ones: *e.g.*, calligraphy, vegetal and animal motifs, arabesques. The most distinguishing feature of these Fāṭimid ceramics, however, is the representation of the human figure. Some of these ceramics have been decorated with simplified copies of illustrations of the princely themes, but others have depictions of scenes of Egyptian daily life. The style in which these themes have been represented is simultaneously the hieratic, ornamental manner traditional to Islāmic painting combined with what can almost be called spatial illusionism. Wheel-cut rock crystal, glass, and bronze objects, especially animal-shaped aquamaniles (a type of water vessel) and ewers are also attributed to the Fāṭimids.

Book illustration. Manifestations of nonprincely Fāṭimid art also included the art of book illustration. The few remaining fragments illustrate that probably after the middle of the 11th century there developed an art of representation other than the style used to illustrate princely themes. This was a more illusionistic style that still accompanied the traditional ornamental one in the same manner as in the paintings on ceramics.

Transitional role of Fāṭimid art

In summary it would appear that Fāṭimid art was a curiously transitional one. Although much influenced by earlier Islāmic and non-Islāmic Mediterranean styles, the Fāṭimids devised new structural systems and developed a new manner of painting representational subjects, which became characteristic of all Muslim art during the 12th century. Neither documentary nor theoretical research in Islāmic art, however, has developed sufficiently to clearly establish whether the Fāṭimids were indeed innovators or whether their art was a local phenomenon that is only accidentally relatable to what followed.

Seljuq art. During the last decades of the 10th century, at the Central Asian frontiers of Islām, a migratory

Wheel-cut rock crystal ewer from Egypt, 11th century. In the Victoria and Albert Museum, London. Ht. 21.5 cm.
By courtesy of the Victoria and Albert Museum, London

movement of Turkic peoples began that was to affect the whole Muslim world up to and including Egypt. The dominant political force among these Turks was the dynasty of the Seljuqs, but it was not the only one; nor can it be demonstrated, as far as the arts are concerned, that it was the major source of patronage in the period to be discussed anywhere but in Anatolia in the 12th and 13th centuries. The Seljuq empire, therefore, consisted of a succession of dynasties, and all but one (the Ayyūbids of Syria, Egypt, and northern Mesopotamia) were Turkic.

A complex feudal system was established and centred on urban areas. Cities were established or expanded, particularly in western Iran, Anatolia, and Syria. Militant Muslims, the Seljuqs also sought to revive Muslim orthodoxy. Although politically unruly and complicated in their relationships to one another, the successive and partly overlapping dynasties of the Ghaznavids, Ghūrids, the Great Seljuqs, Qarakhānids, Zangids, Ayyūbids, Seljuqs of Rūm, and Khwārezm-Shāhs (considering only the major ones) seem to have created a comparatively unified culture from India to Egypt. The art of the Seljuq period, however, is difficult to discuss coherently both because of the wealth of examples and because of the lack of synchronization between various technical and regional developments. This complex world fell apart under the impact of the Mongol invasions that, from 1220 until 1260, swept through the Muslim lands of the Near East.

Architecture. The functions of monumental architecture in the Seljuq period were considerably modified. Large congregational mosques were still built. The earliest Seljuq examples occur in the two major new provinces of Islām—Anatolia and northwestern India as well as in the established Muslim region of western Iran. In some areas such as the Isfahan region, congregational mosques were rebuilt, while in other parts of Islām, such as Syria or Egypt, where there was no need for new large mosques, older ones were repaired and small ones were built. The latter were partly restricted to certain quarters or groups or else were commissioned by various guilds, particularly in Damascus.

A curious side aspect of the program of building, rebuilding, or decorating mosques was the extraordinary development of minarets. Particularly in Iran, dozens of minarets are preserved from the 12th and 13th centuries, while the mosques to which they had been attached have disappeared. It is as though the visual function of the minaret was more important than the religious institution to which it was attached.

Small or large, mausoleums increased in numbers and became at this time the ubiquitous monument they appear to be. Most of the mausoleums, such as the tomb tower of Abū Yazīd al-Bisṭāmī (died 874) at Besṭām, were dedicated to holy men—both contemporary Muslim saints and all sorts of holy men dead for centuries (even pre-Islāmic holy men, especially biblical prophets, acquired a monument). The most impressive mausoleums, however, ones like the one of Sanjar at Merv, were built for royalty. Pilgrimages were organized and in many places hardly mentioned until then as holy places (*e.g.*, Meshed, Besṭām, Mosul, Aleppo), a whole monastic establishment serving as a centre for the distribution of alms was erected with hostels and kitchens for the pilgrims.

Origin and development of the *madrasah*

Although enormously expanded, mosques, minarets, and mausoleums were not new types of Islāmic architecture. The *madrasah* ("school"), however, was a new building type. There is much controversy as to why and how it really developed. Although early examples have been discovered in Iran, such as the 11th century *madrasah* of Khargird in Iran and at Samarkand, it is from Anatolia, Syria, and Egypt that most of the information about the *madrasah* has been derived. In the latter regions it was usually a privately endowed establishment reserved for one or two of the schools of jurisprudence of orthodox Islām. It had to have rooms for teaching and living quarters for the students and professors. Often the tomb of the founder was attached to the *madrasah*. Later *madrasahs* were built for two or three schools of jurisprudence, and the Mustanṣirīyah in Baghdad was erected in 1233 to be a sort of ecumenical *madrasah* for the whole of Sunnī Islām.

In the Seljuq period there occurred a revival of the *ribāṭ* inside cities. *Khānqāhs*, monasteries, and various establishments of learning other than formal *madrasahs* were also built.

An impressive development of secular architecture occurred under the Seljuqs. The most characteristic building of the time was the citadel, or urban fortress, through which the new princes controlled the usually alien city they held in fief. The largest citadels, like those of Cairo

Josephine Powell, Rome

Tomb tower at the shrine of Abū Yazīd al-Bistāmī at Bestām, Iran, 1313.

and Aleppo, were whole cities with palaces, mosques, sanctuaries, and baths. Others, like the Citadel of Damascus, were simpler constructions. Occasionally, as in the Euphrates valley, single castles were built, possibly in imitation of those constructed by the Christian crusaders. Walls surrounded most cities, and all of them were built or rebuilt during the Seljuq period. The stone military architecture of Egypt, Syria, and Anatolia is, of course, better preserved than the brick examples of Iraq or Iran.

Little is known about Seljuq palaces or private residences in general. A few fragments in Konya or in Mosul are insufficient to give a coherent idea about urban palaces, and it is only in Anatolia and in Central Asia that an adequate idea of other types can be obtained. Anatolian palaces are on the whole rather small villa-like establishments; but in Afghanistan and Soviet Central Asia, excavations at Tirmidh, Lashkarī Bāzār, and Ghaznī have brought to light a whole group of large royal palaces erected in the 11th and early 12th centuries.

Seljuq commercial architecture

Commercial architecture became very important. Individual princes and cities probably were trying to attract business by erecting elaborate caravanseries on the main trade routes such as Rebāṭ-e Malek built between Samarkand and Bukhara in Iran. The most spectacular caravanseries were built in the 13th century in Anatolia. Equally impressive, however, although less numerous in number, are the caravanseries erected in eastern Iran and northern Iraq. Bridges also were rebuilt and decorated like the one at Cizre in Turkey. While much less is known about Seljuq mercantile architecture inside the cities, the bazaars of Aleppo are an example of what it might have been like.

The forms of architecture developed by the Seljuqs were remarkably numerous and varied considerably from region to region. Since the Iranian innovations dating from the 11th century and first half of the 12th century are the earliest and, therefore, probably influenced all other areas of the Seljuq empire, they will be discussed first.

Even though it is not entirely typical, the justly celebrated Great Mosque of Isfahan was one of the most influential of all early Seljuq religious structures. Probably completed around 1130 after a long and complicated history of rebuildings, it consisted of a large courtyard on which opened four large vaulted halls known as *eyvāns*; the *eyvāns* created the compositional axes of each side of the court. On the side of the *qiblah* the hall of the main *eyvān* was followed by a huge cupola. The area between *eyvāns* was subdivided into a large number of square bays covered by domes. The Isfahan mosque also had a unique feature: on the north side a single domed hall positioned on the main axis of the building was in all probability a formal hall for princes to change their clothes before entering into the sanctuary of the mosque.

Use of the *eyvān*

The two features of the Great Mosque at Isfahan that became characteristic of Seljuq mosques were the *eyvān* and the dome. The *eyvān* was an architectural element known already in Sāsānian architecture that had been used in residential buildings from Egypt to Central Asia before the 11th century. In fact, the use of the *eyvān* was not restricted to just mosques, but it also appears in palaces (Lashkarī Bāzār), caravanserais (Rebāṭ-e Sharīf), and in *madrasahs*. The *eyvān* was, in other words, a unit of architectural composition that had no specific use and, therefore, no meaning. In the mosques of the 12th century, four *eyvāns* were used, at least in the clearly definable architectural school of western Iran (*e.g.*, Ardestān, Zavāreh). This kind of composition had two principal effects. One was that the *eyvāns* centralized the visual effect of the mosque by making the courtyard the centre of the building. The other effect of this composition was that it broke up into four areas what had for centuries been a characteristic of the mosque: its single, unified space. The reasons for these developments are still a matter of speculation.

Whether large or small, cupolas or domes were used in mosques, caravanserais, and palaces. They were the main architectural features of almost all mausoleums, where they were set over circular or polygonal rooms.

Two characteristic Iranian architectural forms are not present in the Great Mosque of Isfahan but occur elsewhere in the city. One is the tower. Those narrow and tall (up to about 150 feet [or 50 metres]) were minarets, of which several dozens have been preserved all over Iran and Central Asia, (such as the one at Jām). Shorter and squatter towers were mausoleums. These were particularly typical of northern Iran. The other characteristic architectural type exists only in Isfahan in a much-damaged state. It is the *pīshṭāq*, or a formal gateway that served to emphasize a building's presence and importance.

The *pīshṭāqs* of Isfahan

Domes and *eyvāns* indicate the central concern of Iranian construction during the Seljuq period: vaulting in baked brick became the main vehicle for any monumental construction (mud brick was used for secondary parts of a building, frequently for certain secular structures). A large and forcefully composed octagonal base developed the *muqarnas* squinch from a purely orna-

By courtesy of the General Direction of Museums and Historical Monuments, Ministry of Culture and Arts, Tehran, Iran

Brickwork facade of the caravansery of Rebāṭ-e Malek, 11th century.

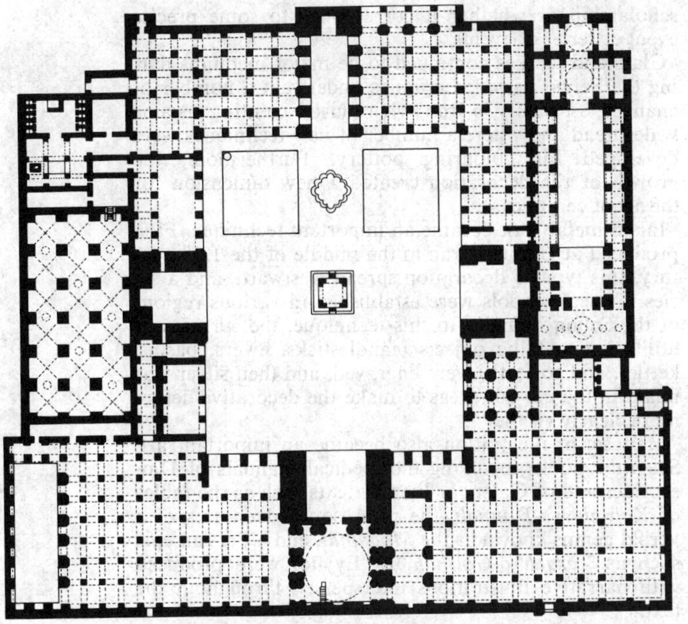

Plan of the Great Mosque at Isfahan.
From *Encyclopaedia of World Art* (1963)

mental feature into one wherein both structural and decorative functions combined. In some later buildings, such as the mausoleum of Sanjar at Merv, a system of ribs was used to vault an octagonal zone. Seljuq architects sought to make their domes visible from afar and for this reason invented the double dome. Its outer shell was raised on a high drum, while the interior kept the traditional sequence: square base, zone of transition, and dome. Using this structural device, therefore, exterior height was achieved without making the exterior dome too heavy and without complicating the task of decorating the interior, always a problem in countries like Iran with limited supplies of wood for scaffolding. Domes along the *eyvāns* were another factor in contributing to the growing separation between the exterior and interior view of a building. There was also an emphasis on the visibility of a building from the exterior that is indicated by the construction of tall circular or polygonal minarets and high facades.

Architectural decoration was intimately tied to structure. Two mediums predominate. One was stucco, which continued to be used to cover large wall surfaces. The other was brick. Originating in the 10th-century architecture of northeastern Iran, brick came to be employed as a medium of construction as well as a medium of decoration. The complex decorative designs worked out in brick often had a rigidly geometric effect. Especially cut shapes of terra-cotta and brick, frequently produced in unusual sizes, served to soften these geometric patterns by modifying their tactile impact and by introducing additional curved or bevelled lines to the straight lines of geometry.

Paintings were used for architectural decoration, especially in palaces. From the second half of the 12th century coloured tiles began to be utilized to emphasize the contour of a decorative area in a structural unit; tiles were not used, however, to cover whole walls. There are also examples of architectural sculpture of animals and people.

Most of the decorative designs tended to be subordinated to geometry, and even calligraphic or vegetal patterns were affected by a seemingly mathematically controlled aesthetic. It has been suggested that these complex geometric designs were a result of an almost mystical passion for number theories that were popularized in 11th-century Iran by such persons as the scholar and scientist al-Bīrūnī or the poet-mathematician Omar Khayyam. But even if the impulses for geometric design were originally created at the highest intellectual level, the designs themselves rapidly became automatic patterns. Their quality was generally high, but a tendency toward facility can be observed in such buildings as Rebāṭ-e Sharaf.

In Iraq, northern Mesopotamia, Syria, and Egypt (after 1171), the architectural monuments do not, on the whole, appear as overwhelmingly impressive as those of Iran, largely because the taste of Umayyad and ʿAbbāsid times continued to dominate mosque architecture. It is in the construction of new building types, particularly the *madrasah*, that the most originality is apparent. The Syrian *madrasah*s in Damascus, like al-ʿĀdilīyah, aẓ-Ẓāhirīyah, or the works of Nureddin, tended also to follow a comparatively standardized plan: an elaborate facade led into a domed hallway and then into a court with at least one *eyvān*. Most of these *madrasah*s were small and were fitted into a pre-existing urban pattern. The use of *eyvāns* and the construction of the many minarets found in Mosul or on the Euphrates certainly attest to the influence of Iranian Seljuq design.

The main achievement of Ayyūbid, Zangid, or Seljuq architecture in the Fertile Crescent was the translating into stone of new structural systems first developed in brick. The most impressive instance of this lies in the technically complex *muqarnas* domes and half domes or in the *muqarnas* pendentives of Syrian buildings. Elaborate *miḥrāb*s were also made of multi-coloured stones that were carefully cut to create impressive patterns. The architecture of the Fertile Crescent, therefore, was still dominated by the sheer force of stone as a material for both construction as well as decoration, and, therefore, the architecture was more Mediterranean in effect than were the buildings of Iran.

The hybrid style of Anatolia

This Mediterranean tendency was also evident in the 13th-century architecture of Seljuq Anatolia. This new province of Islām was rapidly populated with new immigrants and consequently gathered themes and motifs from throughout the Muslim world, as well as from the several native Anatolian traditions of Byzantine, Armenian, and Georgian architecture. The resulting assimilation of styles produced an overwhelmingly original architecture that almost defies art-historical categorization, for each building in Konya, Kayseri, Sivas, Divriği, Erzurum, or on the roads between them is a unique monument.

Functionally the buildings in Anatolia do not differ from those in other parts of the Muslim world. All the structural forms found in Syria and Iran can be found in Anatolia as well, although they have often been adapted to local materials. Three uniquely Anatolian architectural features, however, can be distinguished. One was limited to Konya at this time but would have an important widespread development later on. As it appears in the Ince or Karatay *medreses*, it consists of the transformation of the central courtyard into a domed space while maintaining the *eyvān*. Thus the centralized aspect of the *eyvān* plan becomes architecturally explicit. The second feature is the creation of a facade that usually consisted of a high central portal—often framed by two minarets—with an elaborately sculpted decorative composition that extends to two corner towers. The third distinguishing feature of Anatolian Seljuq architecture is the complexity of the types of funerary monuments that were constructed.

From the point of view of construction, most of Anatolian architecture is of stone. In Konya and a number of eastern Anatolian instances, brick was used. Barrel vaults, groin vaults, *muqarnas* vaults, squinch domes, pendentive domes, and the new pendentive known as "Turkish triangle" (a transformation of the curved space of the traditional pendentive into a fan-like set of long and narrow triangles built at an angle from each other) were all used by Anatolian builders thereby initiating the great development of vault construction in Ottoman architecture (see below).

Architectural decoration

Architectural decoration consisted primarily in the stone sculpture found on the facades of religious and secular buildings. Although influenced by Iran and Syria in many details, most Anatolian themes were original, although some exhibit Armenian and possibly Western influences. The exuberance of Anatolian architectural decoration can perhaps be best demonstrated in the facades of Sivas' Gök Medrese and of Konya's Ince Minare.

Ara Guler

Ince Minare at Konya, Turkey, 1258. Detail view showing the sculptural ornamentation of the main facade portal and the decorative brickwork of the minaret.

In addition to the traditional geometric, epigraphic, and vegetal motifs, a decorative sculpture in the round or in high relief was created that included many representations of human figures and especially animals. Whether this sculpture is essentially a reflection of the decorative wealth of pre-Islāmic monuments in Anatolia or whether it is the vestige of a pagan Turkish art that originated in Central Asia is still an unsolved historical problem.

There are hardly any examples of wall painting from Anatolia. Especially in Konya, however, a major art of painted-tile decoration did evolve. This was possibly first developed by the Iranian artists who were refugees from the Mongol onslaught.

In summing up the architectural development of the Seljuq period, three points seem to be particularly significant. One is the expansion of building typology and the erection of new monumental architectural forms, thus illustrating an expansion of patronage and a growing complexity of taste. The second point is that, regardless of the quality and interest of monuments in the Fertile Crescent, Egypt, and Anatolia, the most inventive and exciting architecture in the 11th and 12th centuries was that of Iran. But far more than in the preceding period, regional needs and regional characteristics seem to predominate over synchronic and pan-Islāmic ones. Finally, there was a striking growth of architectural decoration both in sophistication of design and in variation of techniques.

Other arts. Although probably not as varied as architecture, the other arts of the Seljuq period also underwent tremendous changes. They demonstrate an extraordinary artistic energy, a widening of the social patronage of the arts, and a hitherto unknown variety of topics and modes of expression. It was as though the Seljuq period was gathering a sort of aesthetic momentum, but this effort seems to have been curtailed by the Mongol invasion. Chronologically, almost all surviving documentation and examples of these arts date from the latter part of the period, after 1150. It is unclear whether this apparent date is merely an accidental result of what has been preserved and is known through 20th-century scholarship or whether it corresponds to some precise event or series of events.

Glass and textiles continued to be major mediums during the Seljuq period. Ceramics underwent a number of changes, especially in Iran, where lustre painting became widespread and where a number of new techniques were developed for colouring pottery. Furthermore, the growth of tile decoration created a new dimension for the art of ceramics.

Inlaid metalwork became an important technique. First produced at Herāt in Iran in the middle of the 12th century, this type of decoration spread westward, and a series of local schools were established in various regions of the Seljuq domain. In this technique, the surfaces of utilitarian metallic objects (candlesticks, ewers, basins, kettles, and so forth) were engraved, and then silver was inlaid in the cut-out areas to make the decorative design more clearly visible.

Manuscript illustration also became an important art. Scientific books including the medical manuals of Dioscorides and of Galen, or literary texts such as the fables of *Kalīlah wa-Dimnah*, the picaresque adventures of a verbal genius known as the *Maqāmāt*, and a Persian epic such as *Varqeh o-Golshāh* by ʿEyyūqī were produced with narrative illustrations interspersed throughout the text.

All of the technical novelties of the Seljuqs seem to have had one main purpose: to animate objects and books and to provide them with clearly visible and identifiable images. Even the austere art of calligraphy became occasionally animated with letters ending in human figures. The main centres for producing these arts were located in Iran and the Fertile Crescent. For reasons yet unknown, Egypt and Anatolia were far less involved. One reason may be that these two Seljuq provinces did not witness the same rise of an urban middle class as did Iran, Iraq, or Syria. It would seem from a large number of art objects whose patrons are known that the main market for these works of art was the mercantile bourgeoisie of the big cities and not, as has often been believed, the princes. Seljuq decorative arts and book illustration, therefore, reflect an urban taste.

Urban middle class patronage

The themes and motifs used were particularly numerous. In books they tend to be illustrations of the text, even if a manuscript such as the Schefer *Maqāmāt* (1237; Bibliothèque Nationale, Paris) sought to combine a strict narrative with a fairly naturalistic panorama of contemporary life. Narrative scenes taken from books or reflecting folk stories are also common on Persian ceramics. In all mediums, however, the predominant vocabulary of images is the one provided by the older art of princes; but its meaning is no longer that of illustrating the actual life of princes but rather that of symbolizing a good and happy life. The motifs, therefore, do not necessarily have to be taken literally. Next to princely and narrative themes, there are depictions of scenes of daily life, astronomical motifs, and a myriad of topics that can be described but not understood. When an explanation can be provided, as in the instance of a well-known plate at the Freer Gallery of Art, Washington, D.C., it appears that a mystical interpretation can be given to the image. Figures contemplating each other or a naked figure immersed in water symbolized a soul that had reached total and perfect unity with God; a beautifully attired horse, on the other hand, represented the world abandoned by the mystic. It is probably not an accident that an art of the bourgeoisie would have sought for and discovered these mystic themes, for it was the bourgeoisie that became most spiritually affected by the social mysticism of the time, *i.e.*, the spread of mystical ideas and the impact of holy men on various social units such as guilds and city neighbourhoods. Traditional animal motifs, calligraphy, and a fascinating variety of vegetal and geometric arabesques continued to be used for decorating and illustration.

Mystic themes

While it is possible within certain limits to generalize about the subject matter of Seljuq art, regional stylistic definitions tend to be more valid. Thus the bronzes produced in northeastern Iran in the 12th century are char-

Seljuq manuscript illustration.
(Left) Drawing from a manuscript of the *Maqāmāt*, 1323. In the British Museum (MS. Add 7293, f. 285v). (Right) Preparing medicine from honey, manuscript illustration from an Arabic translation of *De materia medica* of Dioscorides copied by ʿAbd Allāh ibn al-Fadl, from Baghdad, Iraq, 13th century. In the Metropolitan Museum of Art, New York. 12.5 cm × 17.5 cm.
By courtesy of (left) the trustees of the British Museum, and (right) the Metropolitan Museum of Art, New York, the Cora Timken Burnett collection of Persian Miniatures and other Persian art objects; bequest of Cora Timken Burnett, 1957

acterized by simple decorative compositions rather than by the very elaborate ones created by the so-called school of Mosul in Iraq during the 13th century. In general, the art of metalwork exhibits a consistently growing intricacy in composition and in details to the point that individual subjects are at times lost in overlapping planes of arabesques. Ceramic pieces of Iran have usually been classified according to a more or less fictitious provenance. Kāshān ware exhibits a perfection of line in the depiction of moon-faced personages with heavily patterned clothes, while Rayy ceramic work is less sophisticated in design and execution, but more vividly coloured. Saveh and Gurgan are still other Iranian varieties of pottery. With the exception of Kāshān ware, where dynasties of ceramicists are known, all these types of Iranian pottery were contemporary with each other. In Syria, Raqqah pottery imitated Iranian ceramic wares, but with a far more limited vocabulary of designs.

The main identifiable group of miniature painters was the so-called Baghdad school of the first half of the 13th century, which should be called the Arab school because

Brass ewer inlaid with silver and copper and signed by Shujāʿ bn Menaʿ of Mosul, from Mosul, Iraq, 1232. In the British Museum. Height 30.5 cm.
By courtesy of the trustees of the British Museum

The Baghdad, or Arab school

the subject matter and style employed could have been identified with any one of the major artistic centres of Egypt and the Fertile Crescent and very little evidence currently exists to limit this school to one city. The miniatures painted by these artists are characterized by the colourful and often humorous way in which the urbanized Arab is depicted. The compositions, often lacking in any strong aesthetic intent, are documentary caricatures in which the artist has recorded the telling and recognizable gesture or a known and common setting or activity. In many images or compositional devices one can recognize the impact of the richer Christian Mediterranean tradition of manuscript illumination. A greater attention to aesthetic considerations is apparent in the illustrated manuscript of the Persian epic *Varqeh o-Golshāh* (Topkapı Saray Museum, Istanbul). Since this work is unique in the Seljuq period it therefore does not lend itself with facility to stylistic generalization or classification.

Western Islāmic art: Moorish. The 11th to 13th centuries were not peaceful in the Maghrib. Berber dynasties overthrew each other in Morocco and the Iberian Peninsula. The Christian reconquest gradually diminished Muslim holdings in Spain and Portugal, and Tunisia was ruined during the Hilālī invasion when Bedouin tribes were sent by the Fāṭimids to prevent local independence.

Austerity of North African architecture

Two types of structures characterize the Almoravid (1056–1147) and Almohad (1130–1269) periods in Morocco and Spain. One comprises the large, severely designed Moroccan mosques such as those of Tinmel, of Ḥasan in Rabat, or of the Kutubīyah in Marrakech. They are all austere hypostyles with tall, massive, square minarets. The other distinctive type of architecture was that built for military purposes, including fortifications and, especially, massive city gates with low-slung horseshoe arches, such as the Oudaia Gate at Rabat (12th century) or the Rabat Gate at Marrakech (12th century). Palaces built in central Algeria by minor dynasties such as the Zīrids were more in the Fāṭimid tradition of Egypt than in the Almoravid and Almohad traditions of western Islām. Almost nothing is known or has been studied about North African arts other than architecture since the puritanical world of the Berber dynasties did not foster the arts of luxury.

In North Africa the artistic milieu did not change much in the 14th and 15th centuries. Hypostyle mosques such as the Great Mosque of Algiers continued to be built; *madrasah*s were constructed with more elaborate plans; the Bū ʿInānīyah *madrasah* at Fès is one of the few monumental buildings of the period. A few mausoleums were

Almoravid and Almohad architecture in North Africa.
(Top left) The Rabat Gate, Marrakech, Morocco, late 12th century, Almoravid period. (Bottom left) Interior of the Great Mosque of Algiers, Algeria, 12th century, Almohad period. (Right) The square minaret of the Kutubīyah Mosque in Marrakech, Morocco, Almoravid period.
(Top left) Josephine Powell, Rome, (bottom left) H. Roger-Viollet, (right) GEKS

erected such as the so-called Marīnid tombs near Fès (second half of the 14th century) or the complex of Chella at Rabat (mostly 14th century). Architectural decoration in stucco or sculpted stone was usually limited to elaborate geometric patterns, epigraphic themes, and a few vegetal motifs.

A stunning exception to the austerity of North African architecture exists in Spain in the Alhambra palace complex at Granada. The hill site of the Alhambra had been occupied by a citadel and possibly by a palace since the 11th century, but little of these earlier constructions has remained. In the 14th century two successive princes, Yūsuf I and Muḥammad V, transformed the hill into their official residence. Outside of a number of gates built like triumphal arches and several ruined forecourts, only three parts of the palace remain intact. First there is the long Court of the Myrtles leading to the huge Hall of Ambassadors located in one of the exterior towers. This was the part of the Alhambra built by Yūsuf I. Then there is the Court of the Lions, with its celebrated lion fountain in the centre. Numerous rooms open off this court, including the elaborately decorated Hall of the Two Sisters and the Hall of the Abencerrajes. The third part, slightly earlier than the first two, is the Generalife; it is a summer residence built higher up the hill and surrounded by gardens with fountains, pavilions, and portico walks.

Importance of the Alhambra

Besides its aesthetic merit, the Alhambra is especially important because it is one of the very few palaces to have survived from medieval Islāmic times. It illustrates superbly a number of architectural concerns occasionally documented in literary references: the contrast between an unassuming exterior and a richly decorated interior to achieve an effect of secluded or private brilliance; the constant presence of water, either as a single, static basin or as a dynamic fountain; the inclusion of oratories and baths; the lack of an overall plan (the units of the complex are simply attached to each other).

The architectural decoration of the Alhambra was mostly of stucco. Some of it is flat, but the extraordinarily complex cupolas of *muqarnas*, such as in the Hall of the Two Sisters, appear as huge multifaceted diadems. The decoration of the Alhambra becomes a sort of paradox as well as a tour de force. Weighty, elaborately decorated ceilings, for example, are supported by frail columns or by walls pierced with many windows (light permeates almost every part of the large, domed halls). Much of the design and decoration of the Alhambra is symbolically oriented. The poems that adorn the Alhambra as calligraphic ornamentation celebrate its cupolas as domes of heaven rotating around the prince sitting under them.

Islāmic art as such ceased to be produced in Spain after 1492, when Granada, the last Moorish kingdom in Spain, fell to the Christians; but the Islāmic tradition continued in North Africa, which remained Muslim. In Morocco the so-called Sharīfian dynasties from the 16th century onward ornamentally developed the artistic forms created in the 14th century.

Most of the best known monuments of western Islāmic art are buildings, although a very original calligraphy was developed. The other arts cannot be compared in

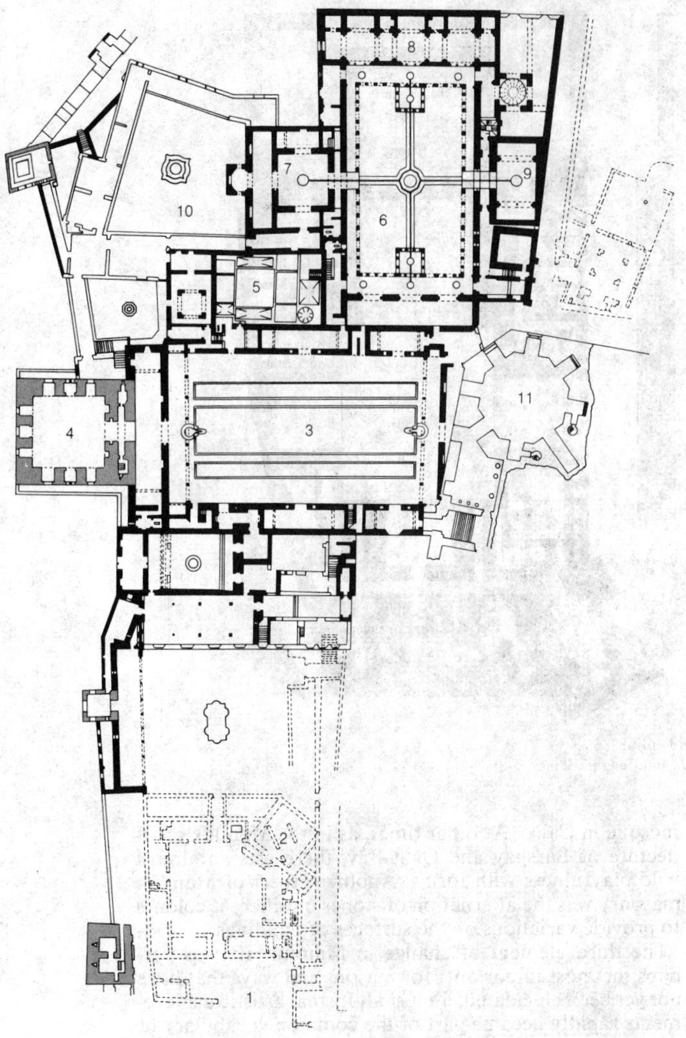

Plan of the Alhambra in Granada, Spain.
1. Alcazaba; 2. ruins of the mosque; 3. Court of the Myrtles; 4. Tower of Comares and Hall of Ambassadors; 5. baths; 6. Court of the Lions; 7. Hall of the Two Sisters; 8. Hall of the Kings; 9. Hall of the Abencerrajes; 10. Garden of Daraxa; 11. Palace of Charles V.
From G. Marcais, *L'Architecture Musalmane d'Occident*

wealth and importance either with what occurred elsewhere in Islām at the same time or with earlier objects created in Spain. There are some important examples of metalwork, wood inlaid with ivory, and a lustre-glaze pottery known as Hispano-Moresque ware. The fact that the latter was made in Valencia or Málaga after the termination of Muslim rule demonstrates that Islāmic traditions in the decorative arts continued to be adhered to, if only partially. The term Mudéjar, therefore, is used to refer to all the things made in a Muslim style but under Christian rule. Numerous examples of Mudéjar art exist in ceramics and textiles, as well as in architectural monuments such as the synagogues of Toledo and the Alcazba in Seville, where even the name of the ruling Christian prince, Don Pedro, was written in Arabic letters. The Mudéjar spirit, in fact, permeated most of Spanish architectural ornament and decorative arts for centuries, and its influence can even be found in Spanish America.

Mudéjar and Mozarabic art

Mudéjar art must be carefully distinguished from Mozarabic art: the art of Christians under Muslim rule. It primarily flourished in Spain during the earlier periods of Muslim rule. Its major manifestations are architectural decorations, decorative objects, and illuminated manuscripts. Dating mostly from the 10th and 11th centuries, the celebrated illuminations for the commentary on the Revelation to John by an 8th century Spanish abbot named Beatus, are purely Christian subjects treated in styles possibly influenced by Muslim miniature painting or book illustration. The most celebrated example, known as the "Saint-Sever Apocalypse," is in the Bibliothèque Nationale in Paris.

Mamlūk art. The Mamlūks were originally white male slaves, chiefly Turks and Circassians from the Caucasus and Central Asia who formed the mercenary army of the various feudal states of Syria and Egypt. During the 13th century the importance of this military caste grew as the older feudal order weakened and military commanders took over power generally as non-hereditary sultans. They succeeded in arresting the Mongol onslaught in 1260 and, through a judicious but complicated system of alliance with the urban elites class, managed to maintain themselves in power in Egypt, Palestine, and Syria until 1517.

During the Mamlūk period Egypt and Syria were rich commercial emporiums. This wealth explains the quality and quantity of Mamlūk art. Most of the existing monuments in the old quarters of Cairo, Damascus, Tripoli, or Aleppo are Mamlūk; in Jerusalem almost everything visible on the Ḥaram ash-Sharīf, outside the Dome of the Rock, is Mamlūk. Museum collections of Islāmic art generally abound with Malmūk metalwork and glass. Some of the oldest remaining carpets are Mamlūk. This creativity required, of course, more than wealth; it also required a certain will to transform wealth into art. This will was in part the desire of parvenu rulers and their cohorts to be remembered. Furthermore, architectural patronage flourished because of the institutionalization of the *waqf*, an economic system in which investments made for holy purposes were inalienable. This law allowed the wealthy to avoid confiscation of their properties at the whim of the caliph by investing their funds in religious institutions. In the Mamlūk period, therefore, there was a multiplication of *madrasah*s, *khānqāh*s, *ribāṭ*s, and *masjid*s, often with tombs of founders attached to them. The Mamlūk establishment also repaired and kept up all the institutions, religious or secular, that had been inherited by them, as can be demonstrated by the well-documented repairs carried on in Jerusalem and Damascus.

The influential role of the *waqf*

Architecture. The Mamlūks created a monumental setting for Syria and Egypt that lasted until the 20th century. It was at its most remarkable in architecture, and nearly 3,000 major monuments have been preserved or are known from texts in cities from the Euphrates to Cairo. No new architectural types came into being, although many more urban commercial buildings and private houses have been preserved than from previous centuries. The hypostyle form continued to be used for mosques and oratories, as in the Caírene mosques of Baybars I (1262–63), Nāṣir (1335), and Shaykh Muʿayyad (1415–20) in Cairo. *Madrasahs* used *eyvāns*, and the justly celebrated *madrasah* of Sultan Ḥasan in Cairo (1356–62) is one of the few perfect four-*eyvān madrasahs* in the Islāmic world. Mausoleums were squares or polygons covered with domes. In other words, there were only minor modifications in the typology of architecture, and even the 15th-century buildings with interiors totally covered with ornamentation have possible prototypes in the architecture of the Seljuqs. Yet there are formal and functional features that do distinguish Mamlūk buildings. One is the tendency to build structures of different functions in a complex or cluster. Thus the Qalāʾūn mosque (1284–85) in Cairo has a mausoleum, a *madrasah*, and a hospital erected as one architectural unit. Another characteristic is the tendency of Mamlūk patrons to build their major monuments near each other. As a result, certain streets of Cairo, such as *Bayn al-Qaṣrayn,* became galleries of architectural masterpieces. The plans of these buildings may have had to be adapted to the exigencies of the city, but their spectacular facades and minarets competed with each other for effect. From the second half of the 14th century onward, building space for mausoleums began to be limited in Cairo, and a vast complex of commemorative monuments was created in the city's western cemetery. In Aleppo and Damascus similar phenomena can be observed, although not on the same scale.

Architectural changes in the Mamlūk period

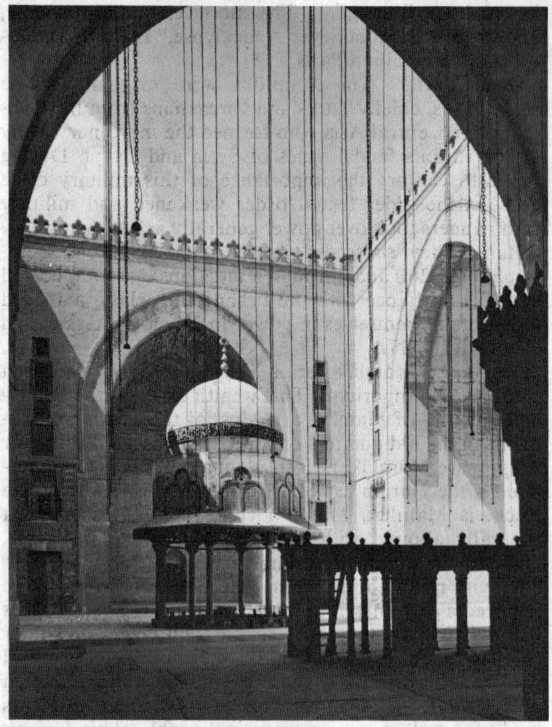

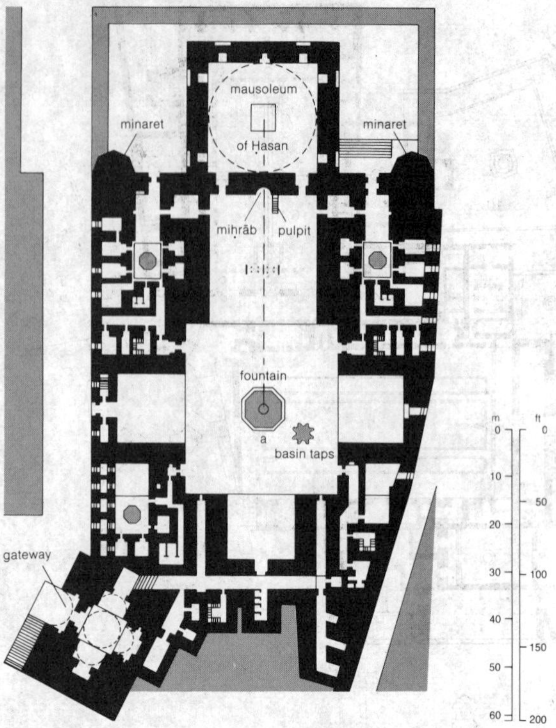

The madrasah of Sultan Hasan, Cairo, 1356–62. (Left) Courtyard and (right) plan.
Left) GEKS, (right) from B. Fletcher, *A History of Architecture on the Comparative Method;* Athlone Press of the University of London, London

Although Mamlūk architecture was essentially conservative in its development of building types, more originality is evident in the constructional systems used, although traditional structural features continued to be employed—*e.g.*, cupolas raised on squinches or more commonly pedentives, barrel and groin vaults, and wooden ceilings covering large areas supported by columns and piers. The main innovations are of three kinds. First minarets became particularly elaborate and, toward the end of the period, almost absurd in their ornamentation. Facades were huge, with portals 25 to 35 feet high, overwhelming the streets they were built on.

A second characteristically Mamlūk feature was technical virtuosity in stone construction. At times this led to a superb purity of form, as in the Gate of the Cotton Merchants in Jerusaleum or the complex of the Barqūq mosque in Cairo. At other times, as in the Mamlūk architecture of Barsbay and Qā'it Bāy, there was an almost wild playfulness with forms. Another aspect of Mamlūk masonry was the alternation of stones of different colours to provide variations on the surfaces of buildings.

H. Roger-Viollet

Mamlūk tombs Cairo, 14th–15th centuries.

The third element of change in Mamlūk art was perhaps the most important: for reasons and ways that have not yet been elucidated, almost all formal artistic achievements rapidly became part of the common vocabulary of the whole culture, thus ensuring high quality of construction and decorative technique throughout the period.

With the exception of portals and *qiblah* walls, architectural decoration was usually subordinated to the architectural elements of the design. Generally the material of construction (usually stone) was carved with ornamental motifs. Stucco decoration was primarily used in early Mamlūk architecture, while coloured tile was a late decorative device that was rarely employed.

Other arts. Like architecture, the other arts of the Mamlūk period achieved a high level of technical perfection but were often lacking in originality. The so-called "Baptistère de St. Louis" (*c.* 1310, Louvre) is the most impressive example of inlaid metalwork preserved from this period. Several Mamlūk illustrated manuscripts, such as the *Maqāmāt* (1334) in the Nationalbibliothek, display an amazing ornamental sense in the use of colour on gold backgrounds. Mamlūk mosque lamps provide some of the finest examples of medieval glass. The wooden objects made by Mamlūk craftsmen were widely celebrated for the quality of their painted, inlaid, or carved designs. And the bold inscriptions that decorate the hundreds of remaining bronzes testify to the Mamlūks' mastery of calligraphy. None of these examples, however, exhibits much inventiveness of design. The "Baptistère de St. Louis" is the culmination of pre-Mamlūk metalwork; the Vienna *Maqāmāt* miniaturists misunderstand almost every scene they illustrated in that the artists copied personages and scenes without being aware of their textual significance: and bronzes and glass designs were mechanically repeated hundreds of times.

The Vienna *Maqāmāt*

Mongol Iran: Il-Khanid (1256–1353) and Timurid (1370–1506) periods. Seen from the vantage point of contemporary or later chronicles, the 13th century in Iran was a period of destructive wars and invasions. Such cities as Balkh, Nīshāpūr, or Rayy, which had been cen-

Mausoleum of Öljeitü at Soltānīyeh, 1305–13, Il-Khanid period.
Josephine Powell, Rome

tres of Islāmic culture for nearly six centuries, were eradicated as the Mongol army swept through Iran. The turning point toward some sort of stability took place in 1295 with the accession of Maḥmūd Ghāzān to the Mongol throne. Under him and his successors (the Il-Khan dynasty), order was re-established throughout Iran, and cities in northeastern Iran, especially Tabriz and Solṭānīyeh, became the main creative centres of the new Mongol regime. At Tabriz, for example, the Rashīdīyeh (a sort of academy of sciences and arts to which books, scholars, and ideas from all over the world were collected) was established in the early 14th century.

Existing under the Mongol rulers were a number of secondary dynasties that flourished in various provinces of Iran: the Jalāyirid dynasty, centred in Baghdad, controlled most of western Iran; the Moẓaffarid dynasty of southwestern Iran contained the cities of Isfahan, Yazd, and Shīrāz; and the Karts reigned in Khorāsān. Until the last decade of the 14th century, however, all the major cultural centres were in western Iran. Under Timur (1336–1405; the Timurid dynasty) and his successors, however, northeastern Iran, especially the cities of Samarkand and Herāt, became focal points of artistic and intellectual activity. But Timurid culture affected the whole of Iran either directly or through minor local dynasties. Many Timurid monuments, therefore, are found in western or southern Iran.

Architecture. Stylistically, Il-Khanid architecture is defined best by buildings such as the mosque of Varāmīn (1322–26) and the mausoleums at Sarakhs, Merv, Rādkān, and Marāgheh. In all of these examples, the elements of architectural composition, decoration, and construction that had been developed earlier were refined by Il-Khanid architects. *Eyvān*s were shallower but better integrated with the courts; facades were more thoughtfully composed; *muqarnas* became more linear and varied; and coloured tiles were used to enhance the building's character.

Il-Khanid refinement and taste for the grandiose

The architectural masterpiece of the Il-Khanid period is the mausoleum of Öljeitü at Solṭānīyeh. With its double system of galleries, eight minarets, large blue-tiled dome, and an interior measuring 80 feet (25 metres), it is clear that the building was intended to be imposing. Il-Khanid attention to impressiveness of scale also accounted for the ʿAlī Shāh mosque in Tabriz, whose *eyvān* measuring 150 by 80 by 100 feet (45 by 25 by 30 metres) was meant to be the largest ever built. The *eyvān* vault collapsed almost immediately after it had been constructed, but its walls, 35 feet (10 metres) thick, remain as a symbol of the grandiose taste of the Il-Khanids. In the regions of Isfahan and Yazd numerous smaller mosques (often with unusual plans) and less pretentious mausoleums, as well as palaces with elaborate gardens, were built in the 14th century. These buildings were constructed to provide a monumental setting for the Islāmic faith and for the authority of the state. The study of these buildings began only in the mid-20th century, and therefore no definitive conclusions have been reached as to whether regional or pan-Iranian stylistic and formal features predominated.

The Timurid period began architecturally in 1390 with the sanctuary of Aḥmad Yasavī in Turkistan. Between 1390 and the last works of Sultan Ḥusayn Baykara almost a century later, at Herāt, hundreds of buildings were constructed, many of which have been preserved, although few have been studied except by Soviet scholars. The most spectacular examples of Timurid architecture are found in Samarkand, Herāt, Meshed, Khargird, Tayābād, Baku, and Tabriz, although important Timurid structures were also erected in southern Iran.

Architectural projects were well patronized by the Timurids as a means to commemorate their respective reigns. Every ruler or local governor constructed his own sanctuaries, mosques, and, especially, memorial buildings dedicated to holy men of the past. While the Shāh-e Zendah in Samarkand—a long street of mausoleums comparable to the Mamlūk cemetery of Cairo—is perhaps the most accessible of the sites of Timurid commemorative architecture, more spectacular ones are to be seen at Meshed, Torbat-e Sheykh Jām, and Mazār-e Sharīf. The Timurid princes also erected mausoleums for themselves, such as the Gūr-e Amīr and the ʿIshrat-Khāneh in Samarkand.

Timurid concern with a commemorative architecture

Major Timurid buildings, such as the so-called mosque of Bībī Khānom, the Gūr-e Amīr mausoleum, the mosque of Gowhar Shād in Meshed, or the *madrasahs* at Khargrid and Herāt, are all characterized by strong axial symmetry. Often the facade on the inner court repeats the design of the outer facade, and minarets are used to frame the composition. Changes took place in the technique of dome construction. The *muqarnas* were not entirely abandoned but were often replaced by a geometrically rigorous net of intersecting arches that could be adapted to various shapes by modifying the width or span of the dome. The Khargird *madrasah* and the ʿIshrat-Khāneh mausoleum in Samarkand are particularly striking examples of this structural development. The Timurids also made use of double domes on high drums.

In the Timurid period the use of colour in architecture reached a highpoint. Every architectural unit was divided, both on the exterior and interior, into panels of brilliantly coloured tiles that sometimes were mixed with stucco or terra-cotta architectural decorations.

Painting. A new period of Persian painting began in the Mongol era, and even though here and there one can recognize the impact of Seljuq painting, on the whole it is a limited one. Although the new style was primarily expressed in miniature painting, it is known from literary sources that mural painting flourished as well. Masterpieces of Persian literature were illustrated: first the *Shāh-nāmeh* ("Book of Kings") by the 10th-century poet Ferdowsī and then, from the second half of the 14th century, lyrical and mystical works, primarily those by the 12th-century poet Neẓāmī. Historical texts or chronicles such as the *Jāmiʿ at-tawārikh* ("Universal History of Rashīd ad-Dīn") were also illustrated, especially in the early Mongol period.

The first major monument of Persian painting in the Mongol period is a group of manuscripts of the *Jāmiʿ at-tawārikh* (British Museum, London; University Library, Edinburgh; and Topkapı Saray Museum, Istanbul). The miniatures are historical narrative scenes. Stylistically they are related to Chinese painting—an influence introduced by the Mongols during Il-Khanid period.

Chinese influence can still be discovered in the masterpiece of 14th-century Persian painting, the so-called Demotte *Shāh-nāmeh*. Illustrated between 1320 and 1360, its 56 preserved miniatures have been dispersed all over the world. The compositional complexity of these paintings can be attributed to the fact that several painters probably were involved in the illustration of this manuscript and that these artists draw from a wide variety of different stylistic sources (*e.g.*, Chinese, European, local Iranian traditions). Its main importance lies in the fact that it is the earliest known illustrative work that sought to depict in a strikingly dramatic fashion the meaning of the Iranian epic. Its battle scenes, its descriptions of fights with monsters, its enthronement scenes are all powerful representations of the colourful and often cruel legend of Iranian kingship. The artists also tried to express the powerlessness of man confronted by fate in a series of mourning and death scenes.

The expressive importance of the *Shāh-nāmeh* miniatures

The Demotte *Shāh-nāmeh* is but the most remarkable of a whole series of 14th-century manuscripts, all of which suggest an art of painting in search of a coherent style. At the very end of the period a manuscript such as that of the poems of Sultan Aḥmad (Freer Gallery of Art, Washington, D.C.) still exhibits an effective variety of established themes, while some of the miniatures in the Deutsche Staatsbibliothek, East Berlin, and in the Topkapı Saray, Istanbul, illustrate the astounding variety of styles studied or copied by Persian masters.

A more organized and stylistically coherent period in Persian painting began around 1396 with the "*Khwāju Kermānī* manuscript" (British Museum, London) and culminated between 1420 and 1440 in the paintings produced by the Herāt school where the emperor Baysunqur created an academy in which classical Iranian literature was codified, copied, and illustrated. Although several *Shāh-nāmehs* are known from this time, the mood of these manuscripts is no longer epic but lyrical. Puppet-like figures almost unemotionally engage in a variety of activities always set in an idealized garden or palace depicted against a rich gold background. It is a world of sensuous pleasure that also embodies the themes of a mystically interpreted lyrical poetry, for what is represented is not the real world but a divine paradise in the guise of a royal palace or garden. These miniatures easily became clichés, for later artists endlessly repeated stereotyped formulas. But at its best, as in the Metropolitan Museum *Neẓāmī*, this style of Persian painting succeeds in defining something more than mere ornamental colourfulness. It expresses in its controlled lyricism a fascinating search for the divine, similar to the search of such epic characters as Neẓāmī, Rūmī, or Ḥāfeẓ—at times earthly and vulgar, at times quite ambiguous and hermetic, but often providing a language for the ways in which man can talk about God.

The lyric style

Mourning scene at the bier of Alexander the Great, miniature from the Demotte *Shāh-nāmeh* ("Book of Kings") of Ferdowsī, colour and gold on paper, Tabriz school, 14th century. In the Freer Gallery of Art, Washington, D.C. 25 cm × 28 cm.
By courtesy of the Smithsonian Institution, Freer Gallery of Art, Washington, D.C.

Another major change in Persian painting occurred during the second half of the 15th century at Herāt under Ḥusayn Baykara. This change is associated with the first major painter of Islāmic art, Behzād. Many problems of attribution are still posed about Behzād's art, and, in the examples that follow, works by his school, as well as images by the master's own hand, are included. In the Garrett *Ẓafar-nāmeh* (*c.* 1490), the Egyptian Cairo National Library, *Būstān* (1488), or the British Museum *Neẓāmī* (1493–94), the stereotyped formulas of the earlier lyric style were endowed with new vitality. Behzād's interest in observing his environment resulted in the introduction of more realistic poses and the introduction of numerous details of daily life or genre elements. His works also reflect a concern for a psychological interpretation of the scenes and events depicted. It is thus not by chance that portraits have been attributed to Behzād.

Behzād and his school

Persian art of the Mongol period differs in a very important way from any of the other traditions of the middle period of Islāmic art. Even though Iran, like all other areas at that time, was not ethnically homogeneous, its art tended to be uniquely "national." In architecture nationalism was mostly a matter of function, for during this period the Shīʿites became established, and new monumental settings were required for this Persian sect. Iranian nationalism is especially apparent in painting, in which Chinese and other foreign styles were consistently adapted to express intensely Iranian subjects, thereby creating a uniquely Persian style.

LATE PERIOD

The last period of an Islāmic artistic expression created within a context of political and intellectual independence

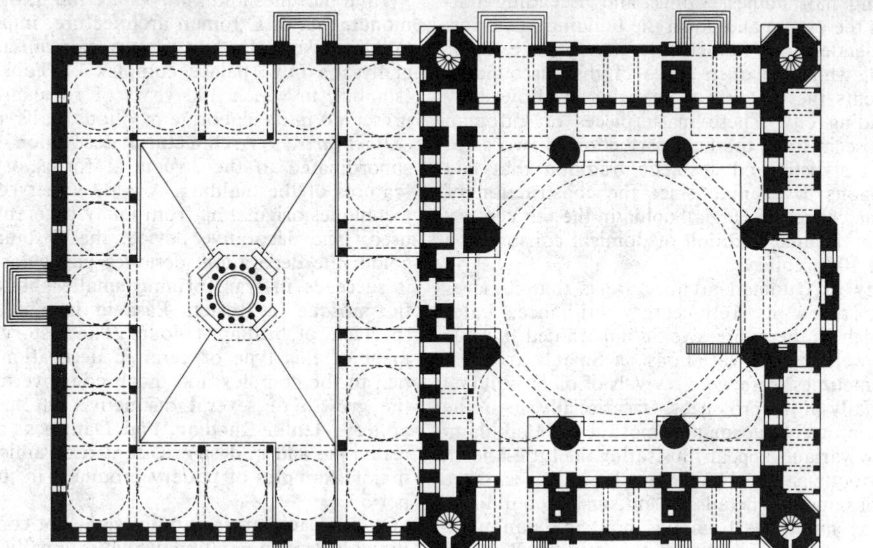

Selimiye Mosque at Edirne, Turkey, designed by Sinan, 1569–75. (Top left) Exterior; (top right) interior; (bottom) plan.
(Top) Shostal, (bottom) from G. Goodwin, *A History of Ottoman Architecture;* Johns Hopkins University Press

was centred in the Ottoman, Şafavid, and Mughal empires. Although culturally very different from each other, these three imperial states shared a common past, a common consciousness of the nature of their ancestry and of the artistic forms associated with it. Painters and architects moved from one empire to the other, especially from Iran to India; Ottoman princes wrote Persian poetry and Şafavid rulers spoke Turkish. But most of all, they were aware of the fact that they were much closer to each other than to any non-Islāmic cultural entity. However different their individual artistic forms may have been, they collected each other's works, exchanged gifts, and felt that they belonged to the same world.

Ottoman art. The Ottomans were originally only one of the small Turkmen dynasties (*beylik*s) that sprang up in Anatolia around 1300 after the collapse of Seljuq rule. In many ways, all the *beylik*s shared the same culture, but it was the extraordinary political and social attributes of the Ottomans that led them eventually to swallow up the other kingdoms, to conquer the Balkans, to take Constantinople in 1453, and to control almost the whole of the Arab world by 1520. Only in the 19th century did this complex empire begin to crumble. Thus, while Ottoman art, especially architecture, is best known through the monuments in Turkey, there is, in fact, evidence of Ottoman art extending from Algiers to Cairo in North Africa, to Damascus in the Levant, and in the Balkans from Sarajevo, Yugoslavia, to Sofia, Bulgaria.

Architecture. The grand tradition of Ottoman architecture, established in the 16th century, was derived from two main sources. One was the rather complex development of new architectural forms that occurred all over Anatolia, especially at Manisa, İznik, Bursa, and Selçuk in the 14th and early 15th century. In addition to the usual mosques, mausoleums, and *madrasah*s, a number of buildings called *tekke*s were constructed to house dervishes (an order of Muslim ascetics) and other Islāmic holy men who lived communally. The *tekke* was often joined to a mosque or mausoleum. The entire complex was then called a *külliye*. All these buildings continued to develop the domed, central-plan structure, constructed by the Seljuqs in Anatolia. The other source of Ottoman architecture is Christian art. The Byzantine tradition, especially as embodied in Hagia Sophia, became a major source of inspiration. Byzantine influence appears in

Origin of the *tekke* and *külliye*

such features as stone and brick used together or in the use of pendentive dome construction. Also artistically influential were the contacts that the early Ottomans had with Italy. Thus, in several mosques at Bursa, Turkey, there are stylistic parallels in the designs of the exterior facade, of windows, gates, and roofs to features found in Italian architecture. A distinctive feature of Ottoman architecture is that it drew both from Islāmic and European artistic traditions and was, therefore, a part of both.

The apogee of Ottoman architecture was achieved in the great series of *külliyes* and mosques that still dominate the Istanbul skyline: the Fatih *külliye* (1463–70), the Bayezid Mosque (after 1491), the Selimiye Mosque (1522), the Şehzade *külliye* (1548), and the Süleymaniye *külliye* (after 1550). The last two *külliyes* were built by Sinan, the greatest Ottoman architect, whose masterpiece is the Selimiye Mosque at Edirne, Turkey (1569–75). All of these buildings exhibit total clarity and logic in both plan and elevation; every part has been considered in relation to the whole and each architectural element has acquired a hierarchic function in the total composition. Whatever is unnecessary has been eliminated. This simplicity of design in the late 15th and 16th centuries has often been attributed to the fact that Sinan and many Ottoman architects were first trained as military engineers. Everything in these buildings was subordinated to an imposing central dome. A sort of cascade of descending half domes, vaults, and ascending buttresses leads the eye up and down the building's exterior. Minarets, slender and numerous, frame the exterior composition, while the open space of the surrounding courts prevents the building from being swallowed by the surrounding city. These masterpieces of Ottoman architecture seem to be the final perfection of two great traditions: a stylistic and aesthetic tradition that had been indigenous to Istanbul since the construction of the Byzantine church of Hagia Sophia in the 6th century and the other Islāmic tradition of domical construction dating to the 10th century.

The tragedy of Ottoman architecture is that it never managed to renew its 16th-century brilliance. Later buildings, such as the impressive Sultan Ahmed mosque in Istanbul were mostly variations on Sinan's architecture, and sometimes there were revivals of older building types, especially in the provinces. Occasionally, as in the early-18th-century Nûruosmaniye mosque in Istanbul, interesting new variants appear illustrating the little-known Turkish Baroque style. The latter, however, is more visible in ornamental details or in smaller buildings, especially the numerous fountains built in Istanbul in the 18th century. The sources of the Turkish Baroque are probably to be sought in the Baroque architecture of Vienna and the bordering Austro-Hungarian states. Throughout the 18th and 19th centuries, a consistent Europeanization of a local tradition occurs in the Ottoman empire.

Josephine Powell, Rome

Turkish Baroque style exemplified by the Fountain of Ahmed III, Istanbul, 1728.

While mosques and *külliyes* are the most characteristic monuments of Ottoman architecture, important secular buildings were also built: baths, caravansaries, and especially the huge palace complex of Topkapı Sarayı at Istanbul, in which 300 years of royal architecture are preserved in its elaborate pavilions, halls, and fountains.

Other arts. Architectural decoration was generally subordinated to the structural forms or architectonic features of the building. A wide variety of themes and techniques originating from many different sources were used. One decorative device, the Ottoman version of colour-tile decoration, deserves particular mention, for it succeeds in transforming smaller buildings such as the mosque of Rüstem Paşa in Istanbul into a visual spectacle of brilliant colours. The history and development of this type of ceramic decoration is intimately tied to the complex and much controverted problem of the growth of several distinctive Ottoman schools of pottery: İznik, Rhodian, and Damascus ware. Both in technique and in design, Ottoman ceramics are the only major examples of pottery produced in the late Islāmic period.

Wide-spread use of tile decoration

Ottoman miniature painting does not compare in quality with Persian painting, which originally influenced the Turkish school. Yet Ottoman miniatures do have a character of their own, either in the almost folk art effect of religious images or in the precise depictions of such

Inge Morath—Magnum

The Meydān-e-Shāh, originally built as a polo ground by Shāh ʿAbbās I the Great (reign 1588–1629), at Isfahan, Iran. Facing the square on the left is the mosque of Sheykh Lotfollāh, in the centre the Masjed-e Shāh, and at the right the Palace of ʿAlī Qāpū.

daily events as military expeditions or great festivals. Among the finest examples of the latter is the manuscript *Surname-i Vehbi* (Topkapı Sarayı Museum, Istanbul) painted by Levnî in the early 18th century.

The production of metalwork, wood inlaid with ivory, and textiles flourished under the Ottomans, both in Istanbul workshops sponsored by the sultan and in numerous provincial centres. The influence of these ornamental objects on European decorative arts from the 16th through the 19th century was considerable.

Ṣafavid art. The Ṣafavid dynasty was founded by Esmāʿīl I (1501–24). The art of this dynasty reached its zenith during the reigns of Ṭahmāsp (1524–76) and of ʿAbbās I (1588–1629). This phase of Ṣafavid period also marked the last significant development of Islāmic art in Iran, for after the middle of the 17th century original creativity disappeared in all mediums. Rugs and objects in silver, gold, and enamel continued to be made and exhibited a considerable technical virtuosity, even when they were lacking in inventiveness.

The Ṣafavids abandoned Central Asia and northeastern Iran to a new Uzbek dynasty that maintained the Timurid style in many buildings (especially at Bukhara) and briefly sponsored a minor and derivative school of painting. Only the great sanctuary of Meshed was being kept up and built-up, but, like many of the other religious sanctuaries of the time—Qom, an-Najaf, Karbalāʾ—it is still far too little known to lend itself to coherent analysis. For this is the time when Shīʿism became a state religion and for the first time in Islām there appeared an organized ecclesiastical system rather than the more or less loose spiritual and practical leadership of old. The main centres of the Ṣafavid empire were Tabriz and Ardabīl in the northwest, with Kazvin in the central region, and, especially, Isfahan in the west. The Ṣafavid period, like the Ottoman era, was an imperial age, and therefore there is hardly a part of Iran where either Ṣafavid buildings or major Ṣafavid restorations cannot be found. The dynasty spent much money and effort on the building of bridges, roads, and caravansaries to encourage trade.

Architecture. The best known Ṣafavid monuments are located at Isfahan, where ʿAbbās I built a whole new city. According to one description, it contained 162 mosques, 48 *madrasahs*, 1,802 commercial buildings, and 283 baths. Most of these buildings no longer survive, but what has remained constitutes some of the finest monuments of Islāmic architecture.

The Meydān-e Shāh

At the centre of Isfahan is the Meydān-e Shāh, a large open space, 1,670 by 540 feet (510 by 165 metres), originally surrounded by trees. Used for polo games and parades, it could be illuminated with 50,000 lamps. Each side of the *meydān* was provided with the monumental facade of a building. On one of the smaller sides was the entrance to a large mosque, the celebrated Masjed-e Shāh. On the other side was the entrance into the bazaar or marketplace. On the longer sides were the small funerary mosque of Sheykh Loṭfollāh and, facing it, the ʿAlī Qāpū, the "high gate," the first unit of a succession of palaces and gardens that extended beyond the *meydān* most of which have now disappeared except for the Chehel Sotūn, the palace of the "Forty Columns." The ʿAlī Qāpū was, in its lower floors, a semipublic place to which petitions could be brought, while its upper floors are a world of pure fantasy, a succession of rooms, halls, and balconies overlooking the city, which were purely for the prince's pleasure.

The Meydān-e Shāh unites in a single composition all the concerns of medieval Islāmic architecture: prayer, commemoration, princely pleasure, trade, and spatial effect. None of the hundreds of other remaining Ṣafavid monuments can match its historical importance, and in it also are found the major traits of Ṣafavid construction and decoration. The forms are traditional, for the most part, and even in vaulting techniques and the use of coloured tiles it is to Timurid art that the Ṣafavids looked for their models. The Persian architects of the early 17th century sought to achieve a monumentality in sheer spaciousness of exterior spatial composition (an interesting parallel to the spaciousness of interior space created at the same time by the Ottomans); a logical precision in vaulting that was successful in the Masjed-e Shāh but rapidly led to cheap effects or to stucco imitations; and a coloristic brilliance that has made the domes and portals of Isfahan justly famous.

Portrait of the Georgian prince Muhammad Bey by Rezā ʿAbbāsī, faint colours and gold on paper, from Isfahan, Iran, first quarter of the 17th century. In the Islamisches Museum, Staatliche Museen zu Berlin. 16.8 × 8 cm.
By courtesy of Islamisches Museum, Staatliche Museen zu Berlin

Importance of historical styles of painting

Painting. In the 16th and 17th centuries, possibly for the first time in Islāmic art, painters were conscious of historical styles—even self-conscious. Miniatures from the past were collected, copied, and imitated. Patronage, however, was fickle. A royal whim would gather painters together or exile them. Many names of painters have been preserved, and there is little doubt that the whim of patrons was being countered by the artists' will to be socially and economically independent as well as individually recognized for their artistic talents. Too many different impulses, therefore, existed in Ṣafavid Iran for painting to follow any clear line of development.

Three major painting styles, or schools (excluding a number of interesting provincial schools), existed in the Ṣafavid period. One school of miniature painting is exemplified by such masterpieces as the Houghton *Shāhnāmeh* (completed in 1537), the Jāmī *Haft owrang* (1556–1665; Freer Gallery of Art, Washington, D.C.), or the illustrations to stories from Ḥaleẓ which have not been identified in detail (Fogg Art Museum, Cambridge, Massachusetts, and in a private collection). However different they are from each other, these large, colourful miniatures all were executed in a grand manner. Their compositions are complex, individual faces appear in crowded masses, there is much diversification in landscape, and, despite a few ferocious details of monsters or strongly caricaturized poses and expressions, these book illustrations are concerned with an idealized vision of life. The sources of this school lie with the Timurid academy. Behzād, Solṭān Muḥammad, Sheykhzādeh, Mīr Sayyid ʿAlī, Āqā Mīrak, and Maḥmūd Muṣavvīr continued and modified, each in his own way, the ideal of a balance between an overall composition and precise rendering of details.

The miniatures of the second tradition of Ṣafavid painting seem at first to be like a detail out of the work of the previously discussed school. The same purity of colour, elegance of poses, interest in details, and assertion of the individual figure is found. Āqā Reẕā and Reẕā ʿAbbāsī (both active around 1600), excelled in these extraordinary portrayals of poets, musicians, courtiers, and aristocratic life in general.

Portraiture and genre painting

In both traditions of painting, the beautiful personages depicted frequently are satiricized; this note of satirical criticism is even more pronounced in portraiture of the time. But it is in pen or brush drawings, mostly dating from the 17th century, that the third aspect of Ṣafavid painting appeared: an interest in genre, or the depiction of minor events of daily life (*e.g.*, a washerwoman at work, a tailor sewing, an animal). With stunning precision Ṣafavid artists showed a whole society falling apart with a cruel sympathy totally absent from the literary documents of the time.

While architecture and painting were the main artistic vehicles of the Ṣafavids, the making of carpets was also of great importance. It is in the 16th century that a hitherto primarily nomadic and folk medium of the decorative arts was transformed into an expression of royal and urban tasks by the creation of court workshops. The predominantly geometric themes of earlier Iranian carpets were not abandoned entirely but tended to be replaced by vegetal, animal, and even occasional human motifs. Great schools of carpetmaking developed particularly at Tabriz, Kāshān, and Kermān (see RUGS AND CARPETS).

Mughal art. Since the culture of the Mughals was intimately connected to the indigenous Hindi traditions of the Indian subcontinent, their art will be treated only synoptically in this article. (For a more detailed account, the reader should see the section on Mughal art in the visual arts portion of the article SOUTH ASIAN PEOPLES, ARTS OF).

The art and culture of the Mughals was similar to that of the Ottomans in that it was a late (mostly 17th century) imperial art of Muslim princes. Both styles were rooted in several centuries (at least from the 13th century onward) of adaptation of Islāmic functions to indigenous forms. It was in the 14th-century architecture of South Asian sites such as Tughlakābād, Gaur, and Ahmadābād that a uniquely Indian type of Islāmic hypostyle mosque was created, with a triple axial nave, corner towers, axial minarets, and cupolas. It was also during these centuries that the first mausoleums set in scenically spectacular locations were built. By then the conquering Muslims had fully learned how to utilize local methods of construction and adapted South Asian decorative techniques and motifs.

Mughal art was in continuous contact with Iran or, rather, with the Timurid world of the second half of the 15th century. The models and the memories were in Herāt or Samarkand, but the artists were raided from Ṣafavid Iran, and the continuous flow of painters from Iran to the Mughal empire is a key factor in understanding Mughal painting.

The mausoleum of Humāyūn in Delhi (1565–69), the city of Fatehpur Sīkri (from 1569 onward), and the Tāj Mahal at Āgra (1631–53) summarize the development of Mughal architecture. In all three examples it can be seen that what Mughal architecture brought to the Islāmic tradition (other than traditional Indian themes, especially in decoration) was technical perfection in the use of stone or marble as building and decorative materials.

Mughal painting

In Mughal painting the kind of subject that tended to be illustrated was remarkably close to those used in Ṣafavid history books—legendary stories, local events, portraits, genre scenes. What evolved quickly was a new manner of execution, and this style can be seen as early as about 1567, when the celebrated manuscript *Ḥamzeh-nāmeh* ("Story of Ḥamzeh") was painted (some 200 miniatures remain and are found in most major collections of Indian miniatures, especially at the Freer Gallery of Art, Washington, D.C.). Traditional Iranian themes—battles, receptions, feasts—acquired monumentality, not only because of the inordinate size of the images but also because almost all of the objects and figures depicted were seen in terms of mass rather than line. Something of the colourfulness of Iranian painting was lost, but instead images acquired a greater expressive power. Mughal portraiture gave more of a sense of the individual than did the portraits of the Ṣafavids. As in a celebrated representation of a dying prince in the Boston Museum of Fine Arts, Mughal drawings could be poignantly naturalistic. Mood was important to the Mughal artist—in many paintings of animals there is a playful mood; a sensuous mood is evident in the first Muslim images to glorify the female body and the erotic.

In summary it can be said that the Mughals produced an art of extraordinary stylistic contrasts that reflected the complexities of its origins and of its aristocratic patronage.

ISLAMIC ART UNDER EUROPEAN INFLUENCE AND CONTEMPORARY TRENDS

It is extremely difficult to decide when, how, and to what extent European art began to affect the art of the traditional Muslim world. Ottoman architecture was from the very beginning affected by Western influences. In Mughal India, European landscapes and Western spatial concerns influenced painting in the 18th century. Even earlier, a purely Western artistic approach and iconography underlaid the composition of a painted portrait of the Mughal monarch Akbar as the ruler of the world (Freer Gallery of Art, Washington, D.C.). Persian painting has exhibited constant Western influence since the 17th century. Thus, Islāmic art began to be affected by European traditions before Europe began (in the 18th and 19th centuries) its conquests of most of the Muslim world. Since the Ottomans ruled North Africa (except Morocco), Egypt, Syria, Palestine, as well as the Balkans, much of the Muslim world was first introduced to "modern" European art through its adaptation in Istanbul or in other major Ottoman cities like Smyrna or Alexandria.

European influence tended to have been mostly limited to architecture. Nineteenth-century European engineers and architects, for example, adapted modern structural technology and decorative styles to local Islāmic needs or idioms: the Sūq al-Ḥamīdīyah bazaar in Damascus was built with steel roofing; the Hejaz Railway station at Damascus was decorated in a sort of Oriental Art Nouveau style.

Revival of the decorative arts

During actual European occupation of Muslim territory, there was a conscious revival of traditional decorative arts, but new techniques were often employed. This especially occurred in India and Morocco, where the retail success of an art object depended less on the local tradition than on the taste of the Europeans. What was romantic to a European, therefore, was no longer part of his world to the newly enriched and Europeanized Muslim. Much of the Europeanized architecture was drab and pretentious. The only real artistic accomplishment of this period was in the preservation and encouragement of the traditional techniques and designs of the decorative arts. The latter often had to be maintained artificially through government subsidies, for the local market, except in Morocco or India, was more easily seduced by second-rate European objects.

During the period of occupation it was questioned whether alien techniques necessarily brought with them new forms. This mood was clearly expressed in literature, but less so in the visual arts, since the quality of Muslim art had deteriorated so much in the decades preceding European arrival that there was no longer a lively creative force to maintain. As various schools based on the École des Beaux-Arts in Paris were formed, however, the faculties and the students suffered from constant uncertainty as to whether they should preserve an art that was mostly artisanal or revolutionize it altogether.

The so-called baptismal basin of St. Louis, copper inlaid with gold and silver, from Egypt, c. 1310, Mamlūk period. In the Louvre, Paris. Ht. 22.8 cm.
By courtesy of the Musee du Louvre, Paris; photograph, Cliche Musees Nationaux, Paris

20th-century currents

It is impossible to define a 20th-century style of modern art indigenous to the Muslim world. In architecture there certainly is no characteristic Muslim expression. There are international styles that affect in varying degrees the architecture of the Muslim world, and there is the continuance of local building traditions that have been more or less modified by modern structural technology. European and American architects continue to design many of the major architectural projects: Frank Lloyd Wright planned the University of Baghdad, Ecochard mapped out the new Damascus, and a Yugoslav team of architects won the international competition for the Aleppo Museum opened in 1969.

In 20th-century Turkey all international styles of painting and sculpture are studied and imitated, but aesthetic successes and failures are caused far more by the presence or absence of local talents than by the presence or absence of a relationship to the artistic traditions of the past. The same has been true of much of the Arab world; although some Egyptian painters have sought inspiration from their cultural heritage, their interest has been with pharaonic rather than Islāmic Egypt. Similar interest in indigenous ancient models has occurred in Iran. It has been only since the 1950s that a number of painters in Lebanon began to seek a mode of expression in their own folklore and folk art.

EVALUATION

In order to evaluate and to understand a millenary artistic tradition spread over an area extending from Spain to India, the emphasis of this article has had to be on those features that relate the monuments to each other rather than on the myriad of characteristics that differentiate them. A few words about the latter are essential, however, for very soon after the formation of Islāmic culture (certainly by 1000), it seems clear that the nature of aesthetic impulses and of visual expectations began to vary. The question is one of determining what may be called the break-off points: the areas, moments, or forces that led to differentiations. One such point is the early 14th century, for almost everywhere in Islām artistic functions, forms, and techniques were renewed. And it is quite easy to separate the arts that followed the turn of the century from those that preceded it.

Next to this chronological break-off, there are cultural ones, one might almost say ethnic ones, even though their ethnic association is often debatable. The clearest instance is that of Iran, where, almost from the time of the first groups of Nīshāpūr ceramics, techniques, styles, and especially subjects became different and often can be traced to pre-Islāmic times. The existence of a forceful Iranian personality in Islāmic art is self-evident, and its impact is found in almost all other subdivisions of the culture. Although it was not a single or even (until the 16th century) a politically or socially unified personality, it found uniqueness, possibly because it soon became (as early as in the 9th century) strongly conscious of its ancient past. The fact of that consciousness seems more important than the individual and on the whole scarce motifs it picked up from the past. A more curious example is that of the Ottomans and of the Arabs. For their ethnic past, in Central Asia and Arabia, respectively, played only a minor part in the formation of their art and was often intellectually rejected. At the same time and with notable exceptions, neither entity sought consistently models and ideas in the pre-Islāmic art of the region they had occupied. If they succeeded in creating an original artistic expression, it is in large part because of their success in creating a viable social order: the Ottoman imperial system of the 15th century, the urban order supported by military feudalism of Egypt, Syria, and North Africa. In these areas it is less a land than a society that provided the visual arts with their own distinctiveness, and it is only in recent years that Ottoman art began to be seen as Turkish and Mamlūk art as Arab. The case of India lies somewhere between the Iranian and Ottoman instances. Created by an imperial overlay on a powerful alien culture, it never entirely escaped the forms of the latter.

Importance of Iranian artistic traditions

Thus, one can distinguish the following large cultural entities within Islāmic art: Ottoman, western Islāmic, Egypt and Fertile Crescent, Iran, India. They were all distinctive by the early 14th century. Detailed studies, of course, manage to find many additional subdivisions in time and space, and much mid-20th-century scholarship tended to work in those directions.

Among the features that appear to unite these various traditions and especially to separate them collectively from other large artistic and cultural units is the unity of functions. There was created, in other words, an Islāmic religious and social function unique to Muslim lands. It was a diversified function, and its monuments are not alike in their forms. But they are alike in the human activity for which they were built. Limited in symbolic forms (*miḥrāb*, minaret, calligraphy as decoration), the Muslim function could be adapted to any architectural or ornamental tradition; and it was, not only in the cultures examined above, but in China, Indonesia, Africa—wherever Islām spread. The key concept here is that of a community of attitudes, of uses of forms, rather than of making of forms.

The unity of functions

There is a corollary to this conclusion that leads to the second level of an attempt to identify Islāmic visual arts as a whole; namely, that, as Islām limited its system of religious visual symbols, it developed a set of secular values. From the very beginning there occurred a major art of trade and of the city, as well as an art of the palace. More than any other culture and certainly earlier than any other, the Muslim world created a number of secular tastes and sponsored techniques of secular beautification. The result lies, on the one hand, in a striking succession of palaces from Khirbat al-Mafjar to the Alhambra or to Fatehpur Sīkri. It lies also in the impetus given to techniques of ceramics, textiles, and metalwork. These all tended to be the techniques of the artisan, and their importance does not lie so much in the manufacture of an occasional object of art as in the raising of the level of quality of all industrial or decorative arts. This particular feature of the Islāmic tradition survived all political misfortunes. Remarkably beautiful objects were made as late as the early 19th century, and the techniques and traditions have often been revived in the 20th century with considerable success. Historically, Islāmic art became a sort of secular consciousness of artistic traditions elsewhere. Renaissance madonnas, for instance, were provided sometimes with haloes containing Arabic inscriptions; bodies of saints were buried in Muslim cloth; Christian princes collected objects of Islāmic art; and *turquerie*, or Turkish themes, lay behind one of the styles of European decorative arts in the Baroque period of the 17th and 18th centuries. All this was possible also because the themes of Islāmic art almost never possessed the specificity of meaning that would make them unsuitable for use by others. Ambiguous in their abstraction of subjects and of styles, works of Islāmic art tended at times to the facile multiplication of known formulas. Yet again at this level, it was the user who determined the value of the form used.

All this is not to say that Islāmic art did not develop an internal visual vocabulary with a depth of its own. From the mosaics of the Umayyad Mosque of Damascus to the Alhambra or to certain Persian ceramics, one can determine the existence of concrete symbolic systems, royal and religious. It is even possible to see in the abstract arabesque or in certain uses of calligraphy attempts to express an early Muslim vision of the divine, while the glorious colour of Iranian mosques may reflect the more complex mystical thought of Shīʿism. There is no doubt that further research will provide many more examples of a meaningful visual symbolic system in the Muslim world. But in most instances that have already been studied—in particular Umayyad and Seljuq art—the remarkable point has been that such symbols did not last and that they were soon misunderstood or ignored. This refusal to be committed to visual symbols is reflected in the little that is known about Islāmic writing on art. It is only very incidentally that references are made to the value or meaning of visual expression; there are no theories on art, and even the religious injunctions against representations are a minute and almost incidental aspect of religious literature. Much more is known about individuals—ceramicists and metalworkers in early times, painters and architects in later times. The emphasis has always been on their technical skill, on their ability to do visual tricks, or on the speed and efficiency with which they created. The artist was not regarded as a prophet or a genius but as a technically equipped individual who succeeds in beautifying the surroundings of all men. It is in this manner that one can perhaps best define the Muslim artistic tradition: it avoided the conscious search for a unique masterpiece and it did not build monuments for the eternal glory of God. It sought instead to please man and to make every moment of his life as attractive and enjoyable as possible. There is a hedonistic element in Islāmic art, therefore, but this hedonism is intellectually and emotionally mitigated by the conscious knowledge of the perishable character of all things human. In this fashion, Islāmic art seen as a whole is a curious paradox, for as it softened and embellished life's activities, it was created with destructible materials, thereby reiterating Islām's conviction that only God remains. (O.Gr.)

The Islāmic visual vocabulary

BIBLIOGRAPHY

Literature: JAMES KRITZECK (comp.), *Modern Islamic Literature: From 1800 to the Present* (1970), is a useful anthology of poetry and prose from different parts of the Muslim world. (*Arabic literature*): CARL BROCKELMANN, *Geschichte der arabischen Litteratur*, 2nd ed. (1943–49, and suppl., 1937–42), is the standard reference work containing information about almost every Arabic writer from pre-Islāmic to modern times. This work is being enlarged and completed by FUAT SEZGIN, *Geschichte des arabischen Schrifttums* (1967–), who has included many hitherto unknown books and manuscripts. R.A. NICHOLSON, *A Literary History of the Arabs*, 2nd ed. (1930, often reprinted), emphasizes poetry in the classical age; his *Studies in Islamic Poetry* (1921), contains the best analysis of al-Maʿarri's poetry. H.A.R. GIBB, *Arabic Literature*, 2nd rev. ed. (1963), is a concise and most informative book that has a bibliography of English translations of the works discussed; the German translation, *Arabische Literaturgeschichte* (1968), of Gibb's book has been enlarged by a section on modern Arabic literature by JACOB M. LANDAU and has an extensive bibliography on works of Islāmic literature translated into Western European languages. GOTTHOLD WEIL, *Grundriss und System der alt arabischen Metren* (1958), is an introduction to Arabic prosody. JOHANN FUECK, *Arabiya: Untersuchungen zur arabischen Sprach- und Stilgeschichte* (1950), is an indispensable study of the development of a High Arabic style. GUSTAVE E. VON GRUNEBAUM, *Kritik und Dichtkunst: Studien zur arabischen Literaturgeschichte* (1955), contains essays on Arabic literature especially of the ʿAbbāsid period. Von Grunebaum's "Spirit of Islam As Shown in Its Literature," in his *Islam: Essays on the Nature and Growth of a Cultural Tradition*, 2nd ed. (1961), is an important essay mainly concerned with Ḥarīrī's *Maqāmāt*, and his "Acculturation As a Theme in Contemporary Arab Literature," in *Diogenes*, 39: 84–118 (1962), is a study on the problem of westernization in modern Arabic literature. ABDULQAHIR AL-JURJANI, *Die Geheimnisse der Wortkunst* (*Asrār al-balāġa*) . . . (1959), is a German translation by HELMUT RITTER of this classic on Arabic rhetoric. ADOLF F. VON SCHACK, *Poesie und Kunst der Araber in Spanien und Sicilien*, 5th ed., 2 vol. (1877), though often superseded by modern research, remains a charming introduction to the culture and art of Moorish Spain. U.M. DAUDPOTA, *The Influence of Arabic Poetry on the Development of Persian Poetry* (1934), attempts to show the formal influences of Arabic on early Persian poetry. WOLFHART HEINRICHS, *Arabische Dichtung und griechische Poetik* (1969), is an important introduction to the literary criticism of classical Arabic literature. (*Persian literature*): JAN RYPKA, *Dějiny Perské a Tádžické Literatury* (1956; Eng. trans., *History of Iranian Literature*, 1968), the standard work on Persian literature from its origins to the 20th century, includes folk literature and Tajik and Indo-Persian literature. CHARLES A. STOREY, *Persian Literature: A Bio-Bibliographical Survey* has appeared since 1927; 2 volumes, each with 2 parts, have been published to date. EDWARD G. BROWNE, *A Literary History of Persia*, 4 vol. (1902–24, reprinted 1953–56), is a very readable and informative classic. A.J. ARBERRY, *Classical Persian Literature* (1958), is a classic work by one of the most prolific translators of Arabic and Persian poetry into English. ANTONIO PAGLIARO and ALESSANDRO BAUSANI, *Storia della letteratura Persiana* (1960), contains many interesting and unusual viewpoints, particularly regarding aesthetics and religious influences. HERMANN ETHE, "Neupersische Literature," and THEODOR NOELDEKE, "Das iranische Nationalepos," in WILHELM GEIGER and ERNST KUHN (eds.), *Grundriss der iranischen Philologie*, vol. 2 (1896–1904), provides a masterly survey of classical Persian literature including Indo-Persian. FRIEDRICH M. MEIER (ed. and trans.), *Die schöne Mahsatī*, vol. 1 (1963), an immensely learned work centring around the poetess Mahsatī, deals with the development of the *rubāʿī* and other forms of Persian poetry. HELMUT RITTER, *Über die Bildersprache Nizāmīs* (1927), is the classic work on the imagery in Nẹzāmī's poetry. CHARLES H. DE FOUCHECOUR, *La Description de la nature dans la poésie lyrique persane du XIe siècle* (1969), is a careful study of nature imagery in early Persian poetry. FRIEDRICH RUCKERT, *Grammatik, Poetik und Rhetorik der Perser*, ed. by WILHELM PERTSCH (1874, reprinted 1966), a translation and commentary of a late Indo-Persian manual of rhetoric, is noted for its acute observations and amusing details. (*Turkish literature*): E.J.W. GIBB, *A History of Ottoman Poetry*, 6 vol. (1900–09, reprinted 1958–63), the classical study of the historical developments of Turkish literature from its beginnings to 1900, includes many translations of poems. OTTO SPIES, *Die türkische Prosa-literatur der Gegenwart* (1943), deals with Turkish prose after the revolution.

Music: "Bibliography of Asiatic Musics," in the Music Library Association's *Notes*, vol. 5–6 (1947–49), an extensive bibliography compiled by five scholars, includes an important section on Islāmic music, with 592 references divided into categories dealing with music among Muslims in general, Arabic-speaking peoples, Turkic peoples, and Iranians and others. HENRY GEORGE FARMER, *A History of Arabian Music to the XIIIth Century* (1929, reprinted 1967), is still regarded as a key historical study. His "Music of Islam," in *The New Oxford History of Music*, vol. 1 (1957) is a good concise survey, as is PETER CROSSLEY-HOLLAND, "The Arabic World," in the *Pelican History of Music*, vol. 1 (1960). RODOLPHE VON ERLANGER, *La Musique Arabe*, 6 vol. (1930–59), includes French translations of the Arabic treatises by al-Fārābī, Avicenna, Ṣafī od-Dīn, and others (vol 1–4), and devotes the last two volumes to an analytical study of contemporary Arabian music. CURT SACHS, *The Rise of Music in the Ancient World, East and West* (1943), has a large section on Arabic music in the context of an intercultural study. MAHDI BARKECHLI (ed.), *La Musique traditionnelle de l'Iran* (1963), gives a comprehensive musical transcription of the *Radīf* (modal systems of the Iranian traditional music). ADNAN SAYGUN, "La Musique Turque," in the *Encyclopédie de la Pléiade*, vol. 9, pp. 573–617 (1960); and ALEXIS CHOTTIN, *Tableau de la musique marocaine* (1939), discuss regional and local particularities and have useful bibliographies. AMNON SHILOAH, *Caracteristiques de l'art vocal arabe au moyen-âge* (1963), is an important essay on medieval Islāmic vocal music.

Dance and theatre: The classic work on the shadow play in the Middle East is still GEORG JACOB, *Geschichte des Schattentheaters in der Welt-Literatur* (1906). METIN AND, *A History of Theatre and Popular Entertainment in Turkey* (Eng. trans. 1963–64), is a perceptive, scholarly account of the Turkish theatre in all its manifestations; while CHRISTA U. SPULER, *Das türkische Drama der Gegenwart* (1968), treats in more detail 20th–century Turkish playwrights and theatrical literature. NICHOLAS N. MARTINOVICH, *The Turkish Theatre* (1933); and HELMUT RITTER, *Karagös* 3 vol. (1924–53), comprise translations of Turkish shadow plays into English and German, respectively. IGNACZ KUNOS, *Das türkische Volksschauspiel* (1907), is an introduction to the *Orta oyunu* popular shows, with samples translated into German. As for the Persian theatre and dance (mainly the latter), the most up-to-date book is MEDJID REZVANI, *Le Théâtre et la danse en Iran* (1962). WILHELM LITTEN, *Das Drama in Persien: Mit einem Geleitwort von Friedrich Rosen* (1929), includes a brief introduction to the *ta'ziyah* and several Persian texts. CHARLES VIROLLEAUD, *Le Théâtre persan, ou le drama de Kerbéla* (1950), is a good sampling of *ta'ziyahs* in French translation. The Arab theatre and dance (chiefly the former) are discussed in JACOB M. LANDAU, *Studies in the Arab Theatre and Cinema* (1958), which also includes a detailed list of Arabic plays.

Visual arts: Among the numerous works dealing with Islāmic art as a whole, only one can be recommended as having a text of considerable merit—KATHARINA OTTO-DORN, *Kunst des Islam* (1964; Eng. trans., *Art of Islam*, 1967). A useful but brief survey of Islāmic decorative art occurs in ERNST KUHNEL, *Islamische Kleinkunst*, 2nd ed. (1963; Eng. trans., *The Minor Arts of Islam*, 1970). K.A.C. CRESWELL, *A Bibliography of the Architecture, Arts and Crafts of Islam* (1961), is a good bibliographical source for pre-1960 publications; current literature on Islāmic art in all languages is surveyed in the *Abstracta Islamica* published every year by the *Revue des Études Islamiques* in Paris. Textual information about the arts has never been properly gathered. For a typical text on painters, see QADI AHMAD, *Calligraphers and Painters*, trans. from the Persian by VLADIMIR MINORSKY (1959). The only lists of artists have been collected by LEO A. MAYER in several books, of which the most important are *Islamic Metalworkers and Their Works* (1959) and *Islamic Architects and Their Works* (1956). There are many surveys by area or by technique (the ones that are concerned with areas tend to limit themselves to architecture), but the vast majority of material on Islāmic art is to be found in periodicals rather than in books. The three publications that have dealt or deal systematically with all aspects of Islāmic art are *Ars Islamica* (1934–51), *Ars Orientalis* (1954–), and *Kunst des Orients* (1950–). Articles are published in English, French, and German.

Area surveys: (*Spain*): MANUEL GOMEZ-MORENA and L. TORRES BALBAS, *Ars Hispaniae*, vol. 3–4 (1949–51); the key journal is *al-Andalus* (semi-annual), entirely in Spanish. (*North Africa*): There is no recent general work dealing with all the arts; for architecture the indispensable manual is that of GEORGES MARCAIS, *L'Architecture musulmane d'Occident* (1954), which deals also with Spain. Much dated standard works include HENRI TERRASSE, *L'Art hispano-mauresque des origines au XIIIe siècle* (1932); and ERNST KUHNEL, *Maurische Kunst* (1924). (*Egypt*): DIETRICH BRANDENBURG, *Islamische Baukunst in Ägypten* (1966), is a convenient summary but does not supersede the exhaustive work of K.A.C. CRESWELL, *Muslim Architecture of Egypt*, 2 vol. (1952–59), going only up to the middle of the 14th century; and LOUIS HAUTECOEUR and GASTON WIET, *Les Mosquées du Caire*, 2 vol. (1932). The only journal of recent years has been that of the American Research Center in Egypt. (*Palestine, Syria*): There are no coherent works dealing with the whole area; JEAN SAUVAGET, *Alep* (1941), is a model (in French) of what can be done with a single city over the centuries; key journals are *Syria, Levant, Quarterly of the Department of Antiquities in Palestine* (until 1950), then of Jordan, *Annales Archéologiques de Syrie*. (*Iraq and upper Mesopotamia*): The main archaeological source is still FRIEDRICH SARRE and ERNST HERZFELD, *Archäologische Reise im Euphrat- und Tigris-Gebiet*, 4 vol. (1911–20); a model of archaeological history is ROBERT M. ADAMS, *Land Behind Baghdad* (1965). The main journals are *Sumer* and *Iraq*. (*Anatolia*): Outside of a number of recent Turkish works there are only two books—both unsatisfactory—on architecture: BEHCET UNSAL, *Turkish Islamic Architecture in Seljuk and Ottoman Times, 1701–1923* (1959); and S.K. YETKIN, *L'Architecture turque en Turquie* (1962). The principal journals are *Anatolica* and *Anatolian Studies*. (*Iran*): Nothing has superseded ARTHUR U. POPE and PHYLLIS ACKERMAN (eds.), *A Survey of Persian Art from Prehistoric Times to the Present* (1938–39; re-edited with supplement, 1965–). One may also consult ANDRE GODARD, *L'Art de l'Iran* (1962; Eng. trans., *The Art of Iran*, 1965); and the chapters by OLEG GRABAR in *The Cambridge History of Iran*, vol. 4–5 (1968–71). Much important information occurs in HANS E. WULFF, *The Traditional Crafts of Persia* (1966); and in several works by ARTHUR U. POPE, such as *Persian Architecture* (1965). Periodicals of importance are the defunct *Athār-é Īrān* (1936–49), the *Bulletin of the American Institute for Persian Art and Archaeology*, and *Iran*. the active journal of the British School. (*Central Asia*): All worthwhile publications are in Russian. See especially the writings of G.A. PUGACHENKOVA. (*India*): Among several architectural surveys, PERCY BROWN, *Indian Architecture*, vol. 2, *The Islamic Period*, 5th ed. (1968), is the best; and for other arts during the Islāmic period, see SHANTI SWARUP, *The Arts and Crafts of India and Pakistan* (1957).

Techniques: (*Architecture*): Remarkably few books deal with more than one period or area; see DEREK HILL and OLEG GRABAR, *Islamic Architecture and Its Decoration A.D. 800–1500*, 2nd ed. (1967). (*Painting*): There are three recent surveys that vary in quality but do introduce most of the main monuments and studies: RICHARD ETTINGHAUSEN, *Arab Painting* (1962); BASIL GRAY, *Persian Painting from Miniatures of the XIII-XVI Centuries* (1947); and DOUGLAS E. BARRETT and BASIL GRAY, *Painting of India* (1963). (*Metal work*): The only general works are two catalogs: GASTON WIET, *Objets en cuivre* (1932); and DOUGLAS E. BARRETT, *Islamic Metalwork in the British Museum* (1949). The field owes much to the late D.S. RICE: "Studies in Islamic Metalwork," *Bulletin of the School of Oriental and African Studies*, vol. 14–16 (1952–57); "Inlaid Brasses from the Workshop of Aḥmad al-Dhakī al-Mawṣilī," *Ars Orientalis*, 2:283–326 (1957); *The Wade Cup* (1955); *Le Baptistère de Saint Louis* (1951). See also RICHARD ETTINGHAUSEN, "The Wade Cup . . .," *Ars Orientalis*, 2:327–366 (1957). (*Ceramics*): The key studies are ARTHUR LANE, *Early Islamic Pottery* (1947) and *Later Islamic Pottery* (1957). (*Carpets*): Among the vast numbers of works on carpets the most scholarly are those of KURT ERDMANN, especially *Der orientalische Knüpfteppich*, 2nd ed. (1960; Eng. trans., *Oriental Carpets*, 1960) and *Siebenhundert Jahre Orientteppich*, (1966; Eng. trans., *Seven Hundred Years of Oriental Carpets*, 1969). (*Ivories*): JOHN BECKWITH, *Caskets from Cordoba* (1960), is a scholarly study of Moorish ivory work.

Historical works: (*Early period*): Most of the problems are summarized in OLEG GRABAR, *The Formation of Islamic Art* (1972). For architecture the main books are K.A.C. CRESWELL, *Early Muslim Architecture* (vol. 1, 2nd ed., 1969; vol. 2, 1941); R.W. HAMILTON, *Khirbat al-Mafjar* (1957); and JEAN SAUVAGET, *La Mosquée omeyyade de Médine* (1947). (*Middle period*): On the Fatimids, see OLEG GRABAR in *Publications in Honor of the Millenary of Cairo* (1971); and RICHARD ETTINGHAUSEN, "Painting in the Fatimid Period," *Ars Islamica*, 9:112–124 (1942). On the Seljugs, for Iran, in addition to vol. 4 of *The Cambridge History of Iran*, see RICHARD ETTINGHAUSEN, "Some Comments on Medieval Iranian Art," *Artibus Asiae*, 31:276–300 (1969); for Syria and Egypt, one should consult ERNST HERZFELD, "Damascus," *Ars Islamica*, vol. 9–12 (1942–51); and JEAN SAUVAGET *et al.*, *Les Monuments Ayyoubides de Damas*, 4 vol. (1938–50): and for Anatolia, KURT ERDMANN, *Das anatolische Karavansaray des 13 Jahrhunderts* (1961). Major monuments are discussed by RICHARD ETTINGHAUSEN in "The Bobrinski Kettle," *Gazette des Beaux-Arts*, 24:193–208 (1943); "The Iconography of a Kāshān *Luster* Plate," *Ars Orientalis*, 4:25–64 (1961); "The Flowering of Seljug Art," *Metropolitan Museum Journal*, 3:113–131 (1970); and SOUREN MELIKIAN-CHIRVANI, *Le Roman de "Varge et Golšâh"* (1970). All new interpretations of the Alhambra are based on FREDERICK BARGEBUHR, *El palacio de la Alhambra en el siglo XI* (1966; Eng. trans., *The Alhambra*, 1968). The only significant new work on the Mamlūks is S.L. MOSTAFA, *Kloster und Mausoleum des Farağ ibn Barqūq in Kairo* (1968). For Mongol architecture, see DONALD N. WILBER, *The Architecture of Islamic Iran: The Il khānid Period* (1955); LISA GOLOMBEK, *The Timurid Shrine at Gazur Gah* (1969); numerous recent Russian publications, and various accounts in the journal *Iran*. For painting, see ERNST J. GRUBE, *The Classical Style in Islamic Painting* (1968), but especially the rich volume of IVAN STCHOUKINE, *Les Peintures des manuscrits tîmûrides* (1954); and M.S. IPSIROGLU, *Malerei der Mongolen* (1965; Eng. trans., *Painting and Culture of the Mongols*, 1966). (*Late period*): For Ottoman architecture, GODFREY GOODWIN, *A History of Ottoman Architecture* (1971); and APTULLAH KURAN, *The Mosque in Early Ottoman Architecture* (1968), supersede all previous work. Painting is covered by EMEL ESIN, *Turkish Miniature Painting* (1960). For ceramics the key article is ARTHUR LANE, "The Ottoman Pottery of Isnik," *Ars Orientalis*, 2:247–282 (1957). For Ṣafavid architecture, DONALD N. WILBER, *Persian Gardens and Garden Pavilions* (1962), should be consulted. The most important publications on painting are both by IVAN STCHOUKINE, *Les Peintures des manuscrits Safavis de 1502 à 1587* (1959) and *Les Peintures des manuscrits de Shāh 'Abbās Ier à la fin des Safavīs* (1964). The principal recent work on India is STUART C. WELCH, *The Art of Mughul India* (1963).

(An.Sc./A.Sh./J.M.L./O.Gr.)

Islāmic Theology and Philosophy

Islāmic theology (*kalām*) and philosophy (*falsafah*) are two traditions of learning developed by Muslim thinkers engaged, on the one hand, in the rational clarification and defense of the principles of the Islāmic religion (*mutakallimūn*) and, on the other, in the pursuit of the ancient (Greek and Hellenistic, or Greco-Roman) sciences (*falāsifah*). These thinkers took a position that was intermediate between the traditionalists, who remained attached to the literal expressions of the primary sources of Islāmic doctrines (the Qur'ān, or the Islāmic scripture, and the Ḥadīth, or the sayings and traditions of Muḥammad) and who abhorred reasoning, and those whose reasoning led them to abandon the Islāmic community (the *ummah*) altogether. The status of the believer in Islām remained in practice a juridical question, not a matter for theologians or philosophers to decide. Except in regard to the fundamental questions of the existence of God, Islāmic revelation, and future reward and punishment, the juridical conditions for declaring someone an unbeliever or beyond the pale of Islām were so demanding as to make it almost impossible to make a valid declaration of this sort about a professing Muslim. In the course of Islāmic history, representatives of certain theological movements, who happened to be jurists and succeeded in converting rulers to their cause, made those rulers declare in favour of their movements and even encouraged them to persecute their opponents. Thus there arose in some localities and periods a semblance of an official, or orthodox, doctrine.

This article will confine itself to the doctrinal history of Islāmic theology and philosophy, with special attention to the views of leading thinkers. For details about the political and religious history of Muslim sects, their dogmas and creeds, institutions of learning, and the biographies of prominent theologians and philosophers, the reader should consult the relevant articles, including ISLAM; ISLAM, HISTORY OF; QUR'AN; HADITH; ISLAMIC LAW; ISLAMIC MYSTICISM.

This article is divided into the following sections:

I. Origins, nature, and significance

EARLY DEVELOPMENTS

Beginnings of Islāmic theology

The beginnings of theology in the Islāmic tradition in the second half of the 7th century are not easily distinguishable from the beginnings of a number of other disciplines —Arabic philology, Qur'ānic interpretation, the collection of the sayings and deeds of the prophet Muḥammad (the Ḥadīth), jurisprudence, and historiography. Together with these other disciplines, Islāmic theology is concerned with ascertaining the facts and context of the Islāmic revelation and with understanding its meaning and implications as to what Muslims should believe and do after the revelation had ceased and the Islāmic community had to chart its own way. During the first half of the 8th century, a number of questions—which centred on God's unity, justice, and other attributes and which were relevant to man's freedom, actions, and fate in the hereafter—formed the core of a more specialized discipline, which was called *kalām* ("speech"). This term (*kalām*) was used to designate the more specialized discipline because of the rhetorical and dialectical "speech" used in formulating the principal matters of Islāmic belief, debating them, and defending them against Muslim and non-Muslim opponents. Gradually, *kalām* included all matters directly or indirectly relevant to the establishment and definition of religious beliefs, and it developed its own necessary or useful systematic rational arguments about human knowledge and the makeup of the world. Despite various efforts by later thinkers to fuse the problems of *kalām* with those of philosophy (and mysticism), theology preserved its relative independence from philosophy and other nonreligious sciences. It remained true to its original traditional and religious point of view, confined itself within the limits of the Islāmic revelation, and assumed that these limits as it understood them were identical with the limits of truth.

Origin and inspiration of Islāmic philosophy

The origin and inspiration of philosophy in Islām are quite different: it developed out of and around the nonreligious practical and theoretical sciences; it recognized no theoretical limits other than those of human reason itself; and it assumed that the truth found by unaided reason does not disagree with the truth of Islām when both are properly understood. Islāmic philosophy was not a handmaid of theology. The two disciplines were related, because both followed the path of rational inquiry and distinguished themselves from traditional religious disciplines and from mysticism, which sought knowledge through practical, spiritual purification. Islāmic theology was Islāmic in the strict sense: it confined itself within the Islāmic religious community, and it remained separate from the Christian and Jewish theologies that developed in the same cultural context and used Arabic as a linguistic medium. No such separation is observable in the philosophy developed in the Islāmic cultural context and written in Arabic: Muslims, Christians, and Jews participated in it and separated themselves according to the philosophic rather than the religious doctrines they held.

The present state of knowledge of the two disciplines is based on comparatively solid ground in respect to the classical period (10th–14th centuries), but it suffers from the paucity of sources and monographic studies of the earlier period and a general lack of interest in the later period of decline. Its most glaring deficiency is the neglect of the vast body of quasi-philosophic, quasi-mystical literature (primarily in Arabic, but also in Persian, Turkish, and Urdu) produced in the Ottoman Empire, Persia, and the Indian subcontinent. The understanding of the two disciplines is presently in a state of flux—in which the earlier historical and philological orientation is being gradually supplemented by the analysis and interpretation of theological and philosophic content proper.

THE HELLENISTIC LEGACY

Relationships to other religious communities

The pre-Islāmic and non-Islāmic legacy with which early Islāmic theology came into contact included almost all the religious thought that had survived and was being defended or disputed in Egypt, Syria, Iran, and India. It was transmitted by learned representatives of various Christian, Jewish, Manichaean (members of a dualistic religion founded by Mani, a Persian prophet, in the 3rd century), Zoroastrian (members of a monotheistic, but later dualistic, religion founded by Zoroaster, a 7th-century-BC Iranian prophet), Indian (Hindu and Buddhist, primarily), and Ṣābian (star worshippers of Harran often confused with the Mandaeans) communities and by early converts to Islām conversant with the teachings, sacred writings, and doctrinal history of the religions of these areas. At first, access to this legacy was primarily through conversations and disputations with such men, rather than through full and accurate translations of sacred texts or theological and philosophic writings, although some translations from Pahlavi (a Middle Persian dialect), Syriac, and Greek must also have been available. The characteristic approach of early Islāmic theology to non-Muslim literature was through oral disputations, the starting points of which were the statements presented or defended (orally) by the opponents. Oral disputation continued to be used in theology for centuries, and most theological writings reproduce or imitate that form. From such oral and written disputations, writers on religions and sects collected much of their information about non-

Muslim sects. Much of Hellenistic (post-3rd century BC Greek cultural), Iranian, and Indian religious thought was thus encountered in an informal and indirect manner.

From the 9th century onward, theologians had access to an increasingly larger body of translated texts, but by then they had taken most of their basic positions. They made a selective use of the translation literature, ignoring most of what was not useful to them until the mystical theologian al-Ghazālī (flourished 11th–12th centuries) showed them the way to study it, distinguish between the harmless and harmful doctrines contained in it, and refute the latter. The situation in philosophy was quite different. Islāmic philosophy, the direct result of the translations from Greek and Syriac of scientific works in alchemy, astrology, astronomy, mathematics, medicine, and finally philosophy proper, did not come into being until the middle of the 9th century. It developed out of the study of and commentary on authors and texts of exclusively Greek and Hellenistic origin.

Translations of the 9th and 10th centuries

The translation movement that made the philosophic and scientific heritage of the Greeks available to Muslims was centred in Baghdad (in Iraq) and consisted of two successive waves. The first took place during the 9th century, when Christians (notably Ḥunayn ibn Isḥāq and his students) and Ṣābians (notably Thābit ibn Qurrah) began to translate from ancient Greek rather than merely from Syriac translations of the Greek philosophical and scientific works. This involved a painstaking effort to learn ancient Greek, to collect and collate Greek manuscripts, and to prepare polished Arabic versions that combined accuracy with a high degree of literary merit. By this time Islāmic theology had coined a vast number of technical terms, and theologians (*e.g.*, al-Jāḥiẓ) had forged Arabic into a versatile language of science; Arabic philology had matured; and the religious sciences (jurisprudence, the study of the Qur'ān, Ḥadīth criticism, and history) had developed complex techniques of textual study and interpretation. The 9th-century translators availed themselves of these advances to meet the needs of patrons. Apart from demands for medical and mathematical works, the translation of Greek learning was fostered by the early ʿAbbāsid caliphs (8th–9th centuries) and their viziers as additional weapons (the primary weapon was theology itself) against the threat of Manichaeanism and other subversive ideas that went under the name *zandaqah* ("heresy" or "atheism").

The second wave of translation took place in the 10th century, when a group of Christian philosophers, translators, and commentators devoted themselves almost exclusively to philosophic texts from Syriac, writing extensive philological commentaries on them and using information drawn from later Athenian and Alexandrian Greek commentators. Together, the two schools of translation rendered into Arabic all the known works of Greek philosophy from Plato to the Alexandrian commentators of the 6th century. Aristotle's writings (with the possible exception of the *Politics*) were available in full translations, as were the works of most of his commentators (Alexander, Themistius, Ammonius, John Philoponus, Nicolaus of Damascus, Simplicius, and others). Plato's writings were available for the most part in the form of paraphrases, although a number of dialogues (*e.g.*, *Timaeus*, *Republic*, *Laws*) were also available in full translations, as were the philosophical works of the 2nd-century-AD Greek physician Galen, the 1st-century-AD eclectic philosopher and writer Plutarch, the 3rd-century-AD Neoplatonic philosopher Plotinus (under different names), and the 5th-century-AD Neoplatonic philosopher Proclus. Doctrines of Stoicism (founded by Zeno in the 4th century BC) and Epicureanism (founded by Epicurus in the 4th century BC) were also transmitted through the translation of biographies of philosophers and collections of their sayings. Latin authors and works, on the other hand, were not translated as such, and information about them trickled into Arabic almost exclusively through Greek sources. The Muslim communities of North Africa and Spain depended on the east for their knowledge of ancient thought, and their own contribution by way of translations from Latin remained slight and insignificant.

The independence of Islāmic philosophy from philological and historical learning

The translations of the 9th and 10th centuries provided the basis on which the tradition of Islāmic philosophy was built. From the beginning, however, Islāmic philosophy set itself apart from the philological and historical learning that characterized the translators' achievement. The philosophers were concerned primarily with understanding and interpreting ancient authors, expounding and defending philosophy in the Islāmic community, establishing a tradition of philosophic learning under the new conditions created by the new religion and culture, and continuing the investigation of philosophic and scientific issues that they had inherited from their Greek and Hellenistic predecessors.

II. Theology

THE MUʿTAZILAH

Background and origin. *Background.* The background for the development of the Muʿtazilah (whose name probably refers to the fact that they "dissociated" themselves from the extreme views of faith and infidelity and the status of Muslims who commit grave sins) lies in the politico-religious schisms that followed the arbitration of the battle at Ṣiffīn (657), in Iraq, between the fourth caliph (political and religious leader) ʿAlī and Muʿāwiyah (the governor of Syria who founded the Umayyad dynasty, which lasted from 660 to 750), the murder of ʿAli (661), and the establishment of the Umayyad dynasty in Syria. The Khawārij (Khārijites, extremely pious and moralistic "rebels" or "seceders") perpetually menaced the Umayyads in Iraq, Persia, and the Arabian Peninsula. The Khawārij had seceded from ʿAlī's group—because he had submitted to human arbitration rather than to God's judgment—and condemned the Umayyads and their followers as evildoers, unjust, and infidels. They insisted that the Muslim community must be led only by the best qualified. Believing that open war against unjust imams and all Muslims who commit grave sins (and thereby lose the faith, *īmān*) was a religious obligation, the Khawārij rallied under their own elected warrior-imams to engage the Umayyads in battle. They asserted that faith demands deeds (the practice of all religious duties and avoidance of sins) and that Muslims who commit grave sins are infidels condemned to eternal hellfire in the world to come and ought to be killed in this life. The Shīʿah (party of legitimists) remained faithful to ʿAlī and his descendants and believed that these descendants were both the only legitimate supreme leaders (imams) and also the authoritative religious teachers and interpreters of the divine law.

On the whole, the Shīʿah followed in the footsteps of ʿAlī himself in being less adamant and more accommodating than the Khawārij. Though some of the Shīʿah rebelled intermittently (goaded, supported, and betrayed by the Iraqis, who were torn between their fear of the Syrian armies of the Umayyads and their desire to assert their independence), others joined the Murji'ah ("postponers"), who defined a Muslim by the profession of belief in God and his Messenger, did not consider that a Muslim's faith is lost upon committing a grave sin, and postponed the judgment on a Muslim's deeds (including the deeds of the de facto imam) until God decides to punish or forgive him in the hereafter.

The doctrine of the intermediate state

Origins. The Muʿtazilah trace their origin to a position somewhat intermediate between the Khawārij, the Shīʿah, and the Murji'ah on the question of the supreme leadership of the Islāmic community. They retired to lead an ascetic life and did not actively support the Umayyad cause, and refused to assign to professing Muslims who are grave sinners the status of faithfuls or infidels but rather placed them in an "intermediate" state. In its general form, the doctrine of the "intermediate state" was accepted in the circle of the 7th–8th century theologian al-Ḥasan al-Baṣrī, and the discussion of its precise meaning and implication led to yet another "separation." For al-Ḥasan, the grave sinners constitute the majority of worldly men who are Muslim in appearance only—*i.e.*, the "hypocrites" (*munāfiqūn*), who lack true piety and the fear of God. His disciple Wāṣil ibn ʿAtā' (flourished 8th century), who was to be accepted as the movement's founder, restricted the intermediate state to the Muslim of certain faith (in his mind or heart) who momentarily loses self-control when committing a grave sin; therefore, he chose the term "transgressor" (*fāsiq*), rather than al-Ḥasan's "hypocrite," for he considered the latter to be an infidel. The separation of Wāṣil from al-Ḥasan's circle on this issue is indicative of the Muʿtazilah's rational and legal predilections as opposed to the more generally pietistic and even mystical tendencies of the master.

Principal concerns and positions. The principal concerns of the Muʿtazilah are summed up in the five theses, or basic principles, that characterized their movement. These were developed in opposition to various forms of anthropomorphic (attributing human characteristics to God), predestinarian, and dualist doctrines propounded by the Khawārij, the Murji'ah, and the Shīʿah, as well as to the views of the majority of Muslims who preferred to profess the literal expressions of the Qur'ān and the Ḥadīth without venturing into the dangerous path of interpreting and harmonizing them.

God's unity (*tawḥīd*). God is beyond time and place and is free of every kind of change and every form of corporeality. The Muʿtazilah distinguished between two kinds of divine attributes and related them to God in two radically different ways, both of which were viewed by their opponents as tantamount to a denial of all the attributes of God "affirmed" in the Qur'ān and as justifying the designation of the Muʿtazilah as those who "suspended" the attributes. God's eternal and unchangeable attributes (*e.g.*, knowledge, power, and life) are not other than him and other than what these attributes mean when applied to created things. These "essential attributes" are distinguished from the "attributes of action" (*e.g.*, willing, hearing, seeing, and speaking), which are outside or other than God and change (come into being and cease to be) without affecting God in himself because they do not subsist in him. (The Qur'ān, being God's "speech," was therefore declared "created.")

Denial of sense perception of God

The denial of God's corporeality in all its forms (including the doctrine that God is, for instance, a special kind of light) led the Muʿtazilah to the denial of the possibility of perceiving him by the senses in this world or the next (*i.e.*, the beatific vision). They also thus denied all similarity between him and created things, and this led them to the denial of the possibility of knowing God by immediate and evident knowledge. They asserted that man can and must know with absolute certainty what God is, does, and does not do. Man can obtain this end by the use of sound reason (*ʿaql*) in considering the things of the world, finding that they must be created in time and therefore concluding that they must be brought into existence by an eternal maker.

All this can be known, they claimed, without the benefit of and independent of revelation. Human reason can ascertain that God is totally different from all created things, which, unlike God, consist of substance and of attributes that are added to a substance that admits of these attributes and their contraries. Human reason can also comprehend that God is eternal, powerful, knowing, living, and so forth, in himself; that these positive "attributes" are not other than himself; and that everything that is not his very self is created and in no way coeternal with him. The doctrine of the "created Qur'ān" is only one example of the Muʿtazilah's rejection of the notion that there can be pre-existent things (*e.g.*, ideas [*maʿānī*], time, space, and matter), sharing in or limiting his creative act.

God's justice (*ʿadl*). God wills, creates, and commands —wisely and in absolute conformity to the demands of sound reason—only what is correct, good, and serves the common interest of mankind. Just as God's unity does not admit of admixture of the one and the many, his justice does not admit of admixture of good and evil. Evil, injustice, disobedience to his commands, and straying from the path of faith, for example, are neither willed nor created by him but are the results of man's free will and action. Free will, created in man by God, is a power that, once created, acts independently of God's power. The independence of human will and choice is an inevitable consequence of God's justice; for he could not justly reward and punish those who obey or transgress his commands if men did not possess, together with the power of reason and discernment, this independent and genuine freedom of action to obey or disobey, do good or evil. The range of activity of this human power is wider than that of the activity of God that created it: it is not limited to acting wisely and doing what is good; its presence in man, in turn, obligates God to reward good deeds and punish evil deeds. As in the case of God's unity, his justice can be known by all men of sound reason.

The significance of man's free will

Revelation is a sign of God's goodness and mercy, and prophets are sent to confirm what reason knows already. Man can and must know by reason what actions are good or evil, what he ought to do, and what he ought to avoid doing. This led the Muʿtazilah to the doctrine of "rational laws" as distinguished from revealed laws and from the philosophic doctrine of natural law.

Promise and warning (*al-waʿd wa al-waʿīd*). The just and truthful God will invariably keep his promise to reward the faithful and the obedient with entry to paradise and to punish with hellfire the infidel and the faithful Muslim who commits a grave sin and does not repent, even though he may out of his mercy add to the reward of the faithful and the obedient and lighten the punishment of the transgressor or grave sinner. Rewards and punishments (God's decrees in the Qur'ān) follow inevitably upon and are the just deserts of human actions.

The intermediate state (*al-manzilah bayna al-manzilatayn*) *of the faithful who commits a grave sin but does not renounce Islām.* This principle has been treated above in connection with the origin of the Muʿtazilah. Wāṣil, the accepted founder of the Muʿtazilah, based his arguments in favour of calling the grave sinner a "transgressor," rather than a "hypocrite," on the Qur'ānic "names" and "decrees" (*asmā'* and *aḥkām*) that designate various groups of Muslims and specify their punishments. Beyond this, however, the doctrine of the intermediate state is the direct result of the position that faith in God, revelation, and prophecy is exclusively a matter of knowledge or an affirmation of reason, which cannot be removed except by conscious confession of infidelity. All other sins, including grave sins, are the result of the lack of will to do or abstain from what the faithful knows to be obligatory or forbidden.

The obligation to encourage good and interdict reprehensible actions (*al-amr bi al-maʿrūf wa an-nahy ʿan al-munkar*). Every Muslim is individually under an obligation to promote and defend true faith and good actions and fight against infidelity and evil actions in every possible way (by argument, by deed, and even by the sword) before Muslims and non-Muslims alike, individuals and communities, and men in private and public positions, even including the supreme ruler. Under the Umayyads, this doctrine took the form of arguments against opponents, sending out missionaries to non-Muslims, spreading Muʿtazilī doctrines among Muslims, and calling upon them to fight openly against an unjust ruler whenever aroused by a just leader with sufficient following. Under the ʿAbbāsids, it took the form of preaching and admonitions presented with warmth and literary skill before caliphs, governors, and the multitude. In the period of their political triumph (827–849), the Muʿtazilah attempted to force their doctrines (epitomized in the doctrine of the created Qur'ān) on learned men, and they actively persecuted their opponents.

The obligation of individual Muslims to promote and defend true faith

Other concerns. *The structure of creation.* Beyond these specifically theological and ethical concerns, the Muʿtazilah developed, beginning with the works of the 8th–9th-century theologian Abū al-Hudhayl al-ʿAllāf, their own form of atomism to explain the structure of all created things. For most of the Muʿtazilah, the universe consisted of indivisible atoms of substance, a certain number of which make up a body, and of "atoms" of accidents, space, time, movement, rest, and other things. The atoms of accidents were said to be created incessantly by God in every atom of time. The result was a universe of discontinuous atoms, the duration of which lasts only an atom of time—with no inner causality or permanent order—continuously renewed or given existence by being incessantly originated by God and wholly dependent on his power. Causality and order were explained as habitual relations among things; and things were said to be devoid of any power of their own, except for what God chooses to create and recreate in them. The only exception to this rule is man's power over those of his actions that are good or evil and for which he deserves reward or punishment.

The development of various branches of religious learning. Finally, the Muʿtazilah pioneered in the development of many branches of religious learning and stamped them with their view of the primacy of sound reason and with their theological and moral concerns: philology, in which they introduced their doctrine of language as human convention; Qur'ānic commentary, in which they introduced their doctrine of the divine names as well as the rest of their theological and ethical views; the Ḥadīth, in which they introduced their hypercritical views of the Ḥadīth's transmitters; and the principles of jurisprudence, in which they introduced the doctrine of the four roots of the law.

The response of political and religious forces. The response to the Muʿtazilah of political and religious forces depended on their background, interests, and doctrines. The Muʿtazilah themselves did not favour or oppose whole dynasties as such but, rather, judged the legitimacy of every ruler's claim to be the rightful imam on the basis of his qualities and actions. The Umayyads sought to neutralize the political impact of opposition parties, and some of them saw a threat to their rule in doctrines that asserted man's freedom, responsibility, and obligation to oppose unjust rulers. The Muʿtazilah were, in general, on intimate terms with the religious and political groups that opposed the Umayyads, rebelled against them, and finally overthrew their rule. These rebellious groups, in turn, were hospitable to some of the Muʿtazilah's doctrines in the formation of their own religious positions and political programs; and the Muʿtazilah are believed to have taken an active part—as preachers who indoctrinated the ʿAbbāsid army in Merv—in the decisive and successful rebellion of the ʿAbbāsids against the Umayyads.

Relationship of the Muʿtazilah to rebellious groups

The Muʿtazilah were encouraged by the first ʿAbbāsid caliphs. They cooperated with al-Mahdī (775–785) in the inquisition of the Zanādiqah, who were accused of secretly holding Manichaean views. The Murji'ah and the traditionalists, who had always opposed theology in principle, soon convinced the caliph Hārūn ar-Rashīd (reigned 786–809), however, that he should champion the cause of the community at large (the *ummah*) against all its practitioners; he joined them in persecuting the Muʿtazilah for their doctrines and no doubt for their pro-ʿAlid family tendencies as well. The brief period of the Muʿtazilah ascendancy began with the caliph al-Ma'mūn (reigned 813–833), whom they converted to their doctrine of the created Qur'ān. In 827 he declared himself publicly in favour of the doctrine of the created Qur'ān, and six years later he countered the agitations of the traditionalists (who had taken to the streets) by ordering an inquisition to force everyone to accept the Muʿtazilah's doctrine. The reaction against the Muʿtazilah during the reign of al-Mutawakkil in 849 led to their persecution and the burning of their books by the caliphs and the masses. The Muʿtazilah survived and, in the middle of the 11th century, engaged in public attacks against the followers of al-Ashʿarī (founder of a theological school named after him) in Iran.

Later doctrinal modifications. The Muʿtazilah were not a popular religious or political movement but, rather, an intellectual movement led by a select group of learned men. They also were not a homogeneous group. Because of their reliance on sound reasoning, their readiness to confront and dispute with everyone who differed with them, their curiosity about all manners of doctrines and sects, their independence, and the willingness of some of them to draw extreme conclusions from the positions they held, they absorbed many doctrines held by other Muslims and by non-Muslims.

In the period of persecution and counterpersecution under the early ʿAbbāsids, the movement broke up into different groupings. Those whose faith in reason overpowered their attachment to the Muslim community (*e.g.*, Ibn al-Warrāq, died 861, and his disciple Ibn ar-Rāwandī) ended by deserting the latter and contended that prophecy, revelation, and divine laws were superfluous and even harmful. Others joined the Zaydī and Twelver Imāmī branches of the Shīʿah ("legitimists"). The rest remained within the Sunnī ("traditionalist") community at large, with which they were now in essential agreement as far as the doctrine of the supreme leadership of the community was concerned. Some of these tried to bridge the gap between themselves and Sunnī traditionalists on the question of the attributes, and others trained themselves in philosophy and reformulated their doctrines in new terms. Even the core group that remained faithful to the older movement had to make certain concessions: *e.g.*, Abū Hāshim (890–933) and the Muʿtazilī school that had originated in Basra (in Iraq) developed the doctrine of the "states," or "modes" (*aḥwāl*), which are intermediate between existence and nonexistence, to explain the divine attributes as things that are not identical with God yet not wholly other than him; the school of Baghdad (in Iraq) showed genuine deference to the sentiment of the community at large, was willing to abandon radical reliance on reason as the sole basis of the knowledge of divine attributes, and sought to reassert the Qur'ānic designations of God and make room for God's favour as well as his justice.

The breakup of the Muʿtazilah

THE ASHʿARIS AND THE MATURIDIS

Origins. One of the outcomes of the open conflict between the Muʿtazilah and the traditionalists, which began under al-Ma'mūn, was the acceleration of the development among some of the Muʿtazilah of a position that promised to bridge the gap between the doctrine that denied all self-subsisting and eternal attributes superadded to God and the traditionalist view (whose champions were the 8th–9th-century legalist teacher Aḥmad ibn Ḥanbal and his followers) that refused to elaborate on whether these attributes are or are not other than God.

The new position is identified with Ibn Kullāb (died *c.* 864), who elaborated ideas propounded originally by certain Muʿtazilī (*e.g.*, Abū al-Hudhayl al-ʿAllāf) and Shīʿī (*e.g.*, Hishām ibn al-Ḥakam, died *c.* 795) thinkers. He developed the paradoxical formula that God's attributes both are and are not one with God, depending on whether they are viewed in relation to God himself (thus preserving his unity) or in relation to man. In connection with the attribute "speech," for example, Ibn Kullāb distinguished between God's eternal speech, which subsists in God, and the expression of it (the Arabic Qur'ān as written, heard, or recited by men), which is created. He developed similar intermediate positions regarding the beatific vision, God's power over man's actions, and so forth. He and his disciples met with opposition from both the Muʿtazilah and the Ḥanbalīs (extreme traditionalists). Two generations after Ibn Kullāb's death, a prominent Muʿtazilī, al-Ashʿarī (late 9th–early 10th centuries), took a more radical step. In 912 he made a dramatic public disavowal of the doctrines of the Muʿtazilah and declared his "conversion" to the doctrines of the traditionalists (professing to honour and follow Ibn Ḥanbal). He had no intention, however, of abandoning theology: he meant to use it in defense of his new beliefs. The Ḥanbalīs opposed him, nevertheless, and al-Ashʿarī's disciples joined other legal schools. Disavowal of the Muʿtazilah, attachment to tradition, and the use of theology to defend it, however, became the principal avowed purposes of the followers of al-Ashʿarī. Prominent Ashʿarīs, such as al-Bāqillānī (died 1013), al-Baghdādī (died 1037), and al-Juwaynī (died 1085), elaborated the conciliatory doctrines propounded by Ibn Kullāb, reintroduced a great deal of Muʿtazilī thought, and combatted the extreme literalists on the one hand and the philosophers on the other. In all this the Ashʿarīs were part of a larger movement of thought that extended from Transoxania, in Central Asia (where it was led by al-

The "conversion" of al-Ashʿarī to the traditionalists' views

Māturīdī, died 944), to Egypt (where it was led by aṭ-Ṭaḥāwī, 853–933).

Return to the authority of the "pious ancestors." Like the Muʿtazilah before them, the Ashʿarīs did not form a unitary school but, rather, a broad movement that harboured varying positions. What united them was the effort to abandon or modify those conclusions of the Muʿtazilah that contradicted the literal text of the Qurʾān and the Ḥadith or seemed to offer a fully rational explanation or justification of God's unity and justice. Theology returned again to the authority of religion as understood by the pious ancestors and the prominent students of the Islāmic tradition and law, seeking their guidance in the definition of the scope, direction, and limits of reason.

The Ashʿarīs were willing to maintain the literal interpretation of the existence of God's eternal attributes (including "speech" and thus the "uncreated Qurʾān," and the seeing of God in the hereafter) and to defend God's omnipotence over all created things (including man's actions, which belong to man, they said, only because God creates their "acquisition" by man). Like the majority of the traditionalists, they avoided the contradictions and anthropomorphism involved in these assertions by saying that all these things are so, even though man does not know why or has no precise rational knowledge as to how they all exist in harmony. All this, in turn, was anchored in the view that faith is placed by God in the heart and is not an affirmation of reason or the conclusion of sound reasoning. By faith one accepts that God is and does and commands what rationally seems impossible or unjust, because he believes that all is possible for God and that justice consists in what he commands. One must also not impute a rational purpose to God and then seek to determine what God can or cannot do.

Had the Ashʿarīs been satisfied with these generalities, which were their point of departure, they would have joined the Ḥanbalīs or the extreme Ẓāhirīs ("literalists"; *e.g.*, Ibn Ḥazm, flourished 11th century), who condemned all theology or whose theology consisted in arguments against theology. Whatever the intentions of al-Ashʿarī himself may have been, his first disciples already viewed themselves as "mediators" between the traditionalists and the Muʿtazilah (and later the mystics and the philosophers as well). At first this took the form of selecting those Muʿtazilī views that seemed to support the traditionalist position. Thus, al-Bāqillānī reintroduced the Muʿtazilī al-ʿAllāf's atomism (without, however, excepting man's power over his actions from being directly and incessantly created by God) to explain God's omnipotence and Abū Hāshim's theory of "modes" to explain God's eternal attributes. Al-Ashʿarī's doctrine of faith, like those of al-Ḥasan al-Baṣrī and of Ibn Kullāb before him, led a number of his prominent followers (*e.g.*, al-Qushayrī, flourished 11th century, and later al-Ghazālī) in the direction of mysticism and the deprecation of the value of theology for salvation in the hereafter. The direction that was to dominate the Ashʿarī movement from the middle of the 11th century onward, however, was the gradual penetration of philosophical thought into their theology.

The Ashʿarīs as mediators

Penetration of philosophical thought into theology. No known copies of al-Ashʿarī's accounts of the doctrines of the philosophers exist. His contemporary al-Māturīdī of Transoxania was combatting as well the Muʿtazilah as the Shīʿah and the philosophers. The preoccupation of al-Māturīdī with the question of the creation of the world, the explanations of God's attributes, and the view that good and evil are known by human reason all point to the impact of the philosophers on his theology. Al-Juwaynī followed in Māturīdī's footsteps, used the views of the philosophers to refute Muʿtazilī doctrines (including their atomism as championed by al-Bāqillānī), and began to use the rudiments of the philosophers' logic.

Al-Ghazālī's formulation of the relationships among theology, philosophy, and mysticism. The direction toward the infusion of philosophy into theology was interrupted temporarily by the agitations of the Ḥanbalīs and the censure of the Ashʿarīs by the authorities in eastern Iran, only to be reinstated in the new schools founded by the vizier of the Seljuq Turks in Persia, Niẓām al-Mulk, in the 11th century. Al-Juwaynī's famous student al-Ghazālī (flourished 11th–12th centuries) gave expression to the inner conflicts that beset the Ashʿarī movement at this time. Because al-Ghazālī believed that theology cannot lead to certainty with respect to any important question, he relegated it to the position of a tool with which to combat heresies and counter the arguments of those who attack religion. Philosophy presented itself to him as a viable alternative, and he decided that philosophical logic (*i.e.*, Avicenna's), physics, mathematics, ethics, and politics are in the main acceptable when properly understood, even though he had serious reservations regarding metaphysics (inquiry into being, the structure of the intelligible world, and the principles of the particular sciences). Even more significant, perhaps, was his characterization of the juridical study of the Islāmic law (*fiqh*) as dealing with worldly matters that do not touch the great questions of man's knowledge of God and his salvation in the hereafter.

Al-Ghazālī's use of Avicenna's philosophy

The true point of departure of this great Ashʿarī reformer of Islām is thus neither the juridical study of Islāmic law nor theology but is instead the philosophy of Avicenna (Ibn Sīnā, 10th–11th century). Al-Ghazālī made use of Ashʿarī theology to refute the philosophical views that disagreed with the modified form of Neoplatonism that had already found its way into Ismāʿīlism, whose doctrine of the qualifications of the rightful imam he was eager to refute.

The philosophical base of the theology of Fakhr ad-Dīn ar-Rāzī. After al-Ghazālī, it is difficult to find in eastern Islām a prominent thinker who did not in some measure combine theology with philosophy, mysticism, or both. The most important thinker for whom theology was not just a stepping-stone to philosophy or mysticism was Fakhr ad-Dīn ar-Rāzī (flourished 12th–13th centuries). He returned to the study of Avicenna and wrote commentaries on and summaries of his works on a variety of philosophic and scientific subjects, but he subjected Avicenna's physics and metaphysics to a criticism in which he restated the arguments of the anti-Aristotelian traditions in Islām: the Muʿtazilah, the physician Abū Bakr ar-Rāzī, the Ashʿarīs, the Māturīdīs, and Abū al-Barakāt al-Baghdādī (flourished 11th–12th centuries). His professed Ashʿarism was moderated by his philosophical learning and a certain measure of Muʿtazilism—*e.g.*, in his exegesis (critical interpretation) of the ambiguous verses of the Qurʾān.

Above all, however, Fakhr ad-Dīn ar-Rāzī separated more clearly than ever before within theology those things that unaided reason can know (even though some of them are taught by religion also) from things that are accessible to man through revelation only. He gave the former a relatively independent status that they never had in earlier theology; and he made it possible for later students of theology (including the scholastic authors of commentaries and supercommentaries and the authors of synthetic manuals) to study them with relative freedom and without fear of being accused of following the philosophers in their method and teachings. Avicenna, al-Ghazālī, Fakhr ad-Dīn ar-Rāzī, and their agreements and disagreements, have dominated the thought of their partisans and commentators down to the 20th century.

THE SHĪʿAH

The theological and political significance of the Shīʿah schism

Like the Khawārij and Sunnism, Shīʿism is not a theological movement but one of the schisms of the larger Muslim community that owe their origin to the dispute over the supreme leadership of that community. These schisms are distinguished from each other by the doctrine of the qualifications of the rightful imam (leader), which gives them their cohesion and continuity, and not by specifically theological doctrines, regarding which their representatives took different positions, revising them from one period to another. The dispute over who is the rightful imam, again, was the source of the division within Shīʿism into Zaydī and Imāmī (Twelver) branches, which were well defined during the lifetime of the sixth imam,

Jaʿfar ibn Muḥammad aṣ-Ṣādiq (flourished 8th century), and the Ismāʿīlī branch (based on the name of aṣ-Ṣādiq's eldest son, Ismāʿīl), which emerged after his death.

The adoption of Muʿtazilī doctrines by the Zaydīs. The early Zaydīs followed the Khawārij in their view of faith and infidelity and in their strict predestinarianism, but not in their strict anti-anthropomorphism. Like the Khawārij, they included such divine attributes as willing, friendship, enmity, pleasure, and wrath among the essential and eternal attributes of God. Unlike them, however, they tended to endow these attributes with a distinctive reality of their own; that is, they moved in the direction that was later developed by Ibn Kullāb and al-Ashʿarī among the Sunnīs. Beginning in the 9th century, however, the Zaydī imam al-Qāsim ibn Ibrāhīm opened the door for the reception of Muʿtazilī doctrines, and after him the Zaydī imams (first in Iran and later in Yemen) gradually moved away from both the predestinarianism of the Khawārij and their own earlier modifications of it. Eventually, they adopted all five of the basic principles of the Muʿtazilah. They continued to disagree with them on the qualifications of the rightful imam, asserting, for example, that the first three Shīʿī imams were designated by the Prophet for this office and that thereafter the imam must be a descendant of one of ʿAlī's two sons (al-Ḥasan and al-Ḥusayn, the second and third imams). The later imams must appeal publicly for a following and rise against usurpers rather than be selected by election and contract as the Sunnīs held.

Imāmī theology. Imāmī (Twelver Shīʿah) theologians in the 8th and early 9th centuries were on the whole close to Sunnī traditionalism and shared many of its doctrines, which sought to preserve the literal sense of the Qurʾānic verses that assert or imply that God is corporeal (*e.g.*, light), is in place, moves, changes, and is provoked by and responds to man's actions. They agreed with the Muʿtazilah that, in order for man to be responsible for his actions, his actions cannot be predetermined; he must possess a capacity for acting and abstaining from action and thus have free choice. They went further, however, and denied that human actions can be known by God from eternity. This led most of them to deny the eternity of what the Muʿtazilah called God's essential attributes—*i.e.*, knowing, willing, and (according to some) even life. They argued that God does not know a thing before he wills or creates it. God's knowledge of his creation, like his creation itself, is subject to constant change. And his will, which creates and controls everything, ensures the conditions of the possibility of human responsibility and free choice. Then, depending on how man acts, God (who has no foreknowledge of how man will act and certainly does not determine man's action from all eternity) responds to the new situation created by man's actions by reminding, rewarding, and punishing him in this world and the next. In this manner Imāmī theologians avoided the predestinarian position that constrained man's actions and the Muʿtazilah's position that God delegates to man all power over his actions. They thus took an intermediate position that was meant to preserve both man's and God's freedom.

Convergence of Imāmī and Muʿtazilah thought

During the 9th century, Imāmism developed into a broad religious movement that attracted converts from among the Muʿtazilah, and early Imāmī theology was gradually replaced by a modified form of Muʿtazilism. The prominent Imāmī family of the Nawbakhtīs in Baghdad took the lead in the early decades of the 10th century to forge an Imāmī version of Muʿtazilism. This version retained the basic principles of the Muʿtazilī movement, except for the principles of promise and warning and of the intermediate state, which conflicted with the Imāmī doctrine of intercession by the Prophet and the imams for the grave sinners (designated as "faithful" as long as they continue as professing Muslims). They rejected the view that faithful sinners will be condemned unconditionally and permanently to punishment in hell. They also opposed the Muʿtazilah's doctrine of the imamate by affirming the Imāmī doctrine of succession by personal designation, the permanent need for a divinely guided imam, the sinlessness, infallibility, and perfect knowledge of the imams, and the condemnation of their adversaries as infidels. This fusion of Imāmism and Muʿtazilism did not go unchallenged by the traditionalist wing (represented by Ibn Bābawayh, died 991, and the school of Qumm, in Iran). The traditionalist wing was opposed to the new theology and favoured the traditions transmitted from the imams and the views developed by earlier theologians in the imams' circles, even though it tended to interpret these traditions and theological views in such a way as to avoid the charge of anthropomorphism and literalism.

The influence of the Baghdad and Basra schools

Muʿtazilism, however, found new defenders in Baghdad in al-Mufīd (flourished 10th–11th centuries) and his student al-Murtaḍā. Al-Mufīd followed the more moderate Baghdad school of the Muʿtazilah: affirming the necessity of relying on the Qurʾān and the Ḥadīth as well as on reason for knowledge of God's attributes; paying close attention to the critical evaluation and interpretation of Imāmī traditions and specifically Imāmī doctrines (such as the question of the textual integrity of the Qurʾān, the return of some of the dead at the time of the second coming of the 12th imam, and God's response to man's actions) with the purpose of showing that they are not in conflict with or cannot be disproved by reason. Al-Murtaḍā (who studied under al-Mufīd and a number of Sunnī Muʿtazilī scholars, including ʿAbd al-Jabbār, flourished 10th–11th centuries) followed the more radical school of Basra and asserted that reason is the sole basis for establishing the principles of religious belief. He rejected authority and took an extremely critical view of the Ḥadīth and placed it in a subordinate position. He also paid little attention to traditional Imāmī doctrines that did not relate directly to the question of the imamate, in which he followed the doctrines of the Nawbakhtīs and al-Mufīd. Al-Murtaḍā's formulation of Imāmī theology has remained normative until the present. Naṣīr ad-Dīn aṭ-Ṭūsī (13th century) and his student and commentator Ibn al-Muṭahhar al-Ḥillī (flourished 13th–14th centuries) did not depart from it.

The Ismāʿīlī synthesis of Neoplatonic cosmology and Shīʿī doctrines. Little is known about the theology of the Ismāʿīlīs in the time of their hidden imams from the middle of the 8th to the beginning of the 10th century. During the 10th century, a series of "Epistles," dealing for the most part with sciences of Hellenistic origin, were distributed clandestinely by a group of propagandists who called themselves the Brethren of Purity (Ikhwān aṣ-Ṣafāʾ), with the purpose of attracting educated laymen to the cause of the Ismāʿīlī imams. In the second half of the 10th century, Ismāʿīlī theology emerged as a full-fledged synthesis between the Neoplatonism of Plotinus (a substantial part of whose *Enneads*, together with comments by his student Porphyry, had been translated about the middle of the 9th century under the title "Theology of Aristotle") and Shīʿī doctrines. The classic formulation of this synthesis is found in the works of the Ismāʿīlī teacher Abū Yaʿqūb as-Sijistānī (died after 971).

Influence of Neoplatonism in Ismāʿīlī thought

Cosmological concerns. God is placed above knowledge, being and nonbeing, and all positive and negative attributes. He is the Originator (*bārīʾ*) who brings about Intelligence (the first and eternal being), not as its cause or by emanation but by his word, command, or will, which unites and remains with Intelligence. Intelligence contemplates its own being as originated and to this extent knows its Originator. From this contemplation is emanated its partner, Soul. Soul desires Intelligence, thereby constituting its movement, and receives the forms emanating from Intelligence. From Soul, in turn, emanate all individual souls, the heavens and the earth, and all other things of nature—hence matter and evil, which are defined as what is distant from and ignorant of Intelligence. Intelligence instructs Soul in ordering wisely the world of composite nature and giving it the desire to free itself from matter and rejoin its source. Such also is the condition of individual human souls; they are connected to the body yet desire to free themselves from it and rejoin the universal Soul.

Theories of the imamate. This reverse operation—the return of individual souls to this universal Soul and the return of Soul to Intelligence—cannot, however, be accomplished by individual souls and the universal Soul without the intervention of Intelligence in human history. This intervention is accomplished through emanation or revelation to prophets and imams in major cycles, each of which contains seven minor cycles. Each minor cycle begins with a major prophet, who is called the "one who speaks out" (*nāṭiq*), or enunciates, the divine law in its external form. He is followed by a "successor" (*waṣī*), who bears the esoteric meaning of the prophetic revelation and who is called the "one who remains silent" (*ṣāmit*) because he turns the external sense of the revelation back to its internal source. He, in turn, is succeeded by the imams, of whom in each minor cycle there are six, but whose succession may be interrupted by periods of varying lengths during which their office lapses because of men's incapacity to receive the knowledge conveyed by the imams. The *waṣī* and the imams assume all the functions of the major prophet whom they succeed, except that they do not enunciate a new divine law. Every major cycle begins with an Adam, who closes the seventh and last minor cycle of the preceding major cycle (the seventh minor cycle is called the cycle of "unveiling," which means living by the esoteric sense, or inner truth, but without the external demands of the divine law). This Adam initiates the first minor cycle of "veiling," of which there are six, the other five being the ones initiated by a Noah, an Abraham, a Moses, a Jesus, and a Muḥammad, each of whom is superior to his predecessors. The seventh minor cycle is initiated by a *qāʾim*, the imam of the "resurrection," who will not bring forth a divine law but, rather, reveals the secrets of divine laws. This causes tumult and upheaval that, in turn, prepare the way to a new major cycle of prophecy and a new Adam.

The function of the imam

The function of the imam, like those of the major prophet and the *waṣī*, is analogous to the function of Intelligence. He orders men's society and conveys to them the knowledge revealed to him through the emanation of Intelligence. Men cannot achieve that knowledge by their own means but must obtain it through the mediation of the imam, his instruction and support or aid. Revelation and the imam's instruction in the inner meaning of the divine law are indispensable to men for attaining true knowledge of Intelligence. Here, Ismāʿīlī theology differs from both Plotinus and the theology of the Muʿtazilah and the Ashʿarīs. The knowledge obtained from the imam enables individual souls to free themselves from matter, so that after death they are saved and return to the universal Soul. The unity of individual souls possessing knowledge of Intelligence in the universal Soul, in turn, enables the latter to draw near and contemplate Intelligence. Thus, the imam performs a human and a cosmic function, and the major cycle of the history of the imams runs parallel to the cosmic history of the emanation of individual souls from the universal Soul and their embodiment in matter, and their emancipation from matter and return of the universal Soul. This parallelism is the inner meaning of the successive veilings involved in the creation of things that are at varying distances from Intelligence and the final resurrection, or unveiling, that arrives at the end through the *qāʾim*.

One branch of the Ismāʿīlīs, the Nizārīs, proclaimed the arrival of the final resurrection—*i.e.*, the beginning of the seventh minor cycle and the abolition of all "veiling"—in Alamūt, in northwestern Iran, in 1164. But the Ismāʿīlī theology that is preserved today is for the most part that of the Fāṭimid period (909–1171)—*i.e.*, when the Ismāʿīlī imams came to power in North Africa and Egypt and yet continued to make use of the external form of the divine law. This led to the formulation of the view that more than one set of seven imams may be necessary before the coming of the *qāʾim*.

After as-Sijistānī, his disciple, Ḥamīd ad-Dīn al-Kirmānī (died after 1021), elaborated the doctrine of the ten Intelligences and its astronomical counterpart, which had been current in philosophic circles since the 10th-century philosopher al-Fārābī. The cyclical view of human history was particularly apt to be impregnated with ancient Near Eastern, especially Iranian, views, which are evident in the writings of al-Muʾayyad ash-Shīrāzī (died 1077) and his disciple Nāṣer-e Khosrow (died 1087). Yemenite Ismāʿīlī thinkers, such as Ibn al-Walīd (died 1215), present a more cluttered universe of Intelligences that, after dramatic events, are ordered into ten Intelligences, the heavenly spheres, and the sublunary world. The importance attached to the esoteric interpretation of the Qurʾān, numerological speculations, and the analogy between the cosmos and human history and between the macrocosm and the microcosm provided Ismāʿīlī thinkers with wide fields in which their imaginations roamed, necessitating numerous efforts on the part of the imams and their representatives to harmonize various viewpoints and curb overzealous followers.

III. Philosophy

THE EASTERN PHILOSOPHERS

Background and scope of philosophical interest in Islām. The background of philosophic interest in Islām is found in the earlier phases of theology. But its origin is found in the translation of Greek philosophic works. By the middle of the 9th century, there were enough translations of scientific and philosophic works from Greek, Pahlavi, and Sanskrit to show those who read them with care that scientific and philosophic inquiry was something more than a series of disputations based on what the theologians had called sound reason. Moreover, it became evident that there existed a tradition of observation, calculation, and theoretical reflection that had been pursued systematically, refined, and modified for over a millennium.

The basis of Islāmic philosophy in Greek philosophical and scientific works

The scope of this tradition was broad: it included the study of logic, the sciences of nature (including psychology and biology), the mathematical sciences (including music and astronomy), metaphysics, ethics, and politics. Each of these disciplines had a body of literature in which its principles and problems had been investigated by classical authors, whose positions had been, in turn, stated, discussed, criticized, or developed by various commentators. Islāmic philosophy emerged from its theological background when Muslim thinkers began to study this foreign tradition, became competent students of the ancient philosophers and scientists, criticized and developed their doctrines, clarified their relevance for the questions raised by the theologians, and showed what light they threw on the fundamental issues of revelation, prophecy, and the divine law.

Relation to the Muʿtazilah and interpretation of theological issues. *The teachings of al-Kindī*. Although the first Muslim philosopher, al-Kindī, who flourished in the first half of the 9th century, lived during the triumph of the Muʿtazilah of Baghdad and was connected with the ʿAbbāsid caliphs who championed the Muʿtazilah and patronized the Hellenistic sciences, there is no clear evidence that he belonged to a theological school. His writings show him to have been a diligent student of Greek and Hellenistic authors in philosophy and point to his familiarity with Indian arithmetic. His conscious, open, and unashamed acknowledgment of earlier contributions to scientific inquiry was foreign to the spirit, method, and purpose of the theologians of the time. His acquaintance with the writings of Plato and Aristotle was still incomplete and technically inadequate. He improved the Arabic translation of the "Theology of Aristotle" but made only a selective and circumspect use of it.

Al-Kindī's interest in scientific inquiry

Devoting most of his writings to questions of natural philosophy and mathematics, al-Kindī was particularly concerned with the relation between corporeal things, which are changeable, in constant flux, infinite, and as such unknowable, on the one hand, and the permanent world of forms (spiritual or secondary substances), which are not subject to flux yet to which man has no access except through things of the senses. He insisted that a purely human knowledge of all things is possible, through the use of various scientific devices, learning such things as mathematics and logic, and assimilating the contributions of earlier thinkers. The existence of a "supernatural" way to this knowledge in which all these requirements can be dispensed with was acknowledged by al-Kindī: God may choose to impart it to his prophets by cleansing and illuminating their souls and by giving them his aid, right guidance, and inspiration; and they, in turn, communicate it to ordinary men in an admirably clear, concise, and comprehensible style. This is the prophets' "divine" knowledge, characterized by a special mode of access and style of exposition. In principle, however, this very same knowledge is accessible to man without divine aid, even though "human" knowledge may lack the completeness and consummate logic of the prophets' divine message.

Reflection on the two kinds of knowledge—the human knowledge bequeathed by the ancients and the revealed knowledge expressed in the Qur'ān—led al-Kindī to pose a number of themes that became central in Islāmic philosophy: the rational–metaphorical exegesis of the Qur'ān and the Ḥadīth; the identification of God with the first being and the first cause; creation as the giving of being and as a kind of causation distinct from natural causation and Neoplatonic emanation; and the immortality of the individual soul.

The teachings of Abū Bakr ar-Rāzī. The philosopher whose principal concerns, method, and opposition to authority were inspired by the extreme Muʿtazilah was the physician Abū Bakr ar-Rāzī (flourished 9th–10th centuries). He adopted the Muʿtazilah's atomism and was intent on developing a rationally defensible theory of creation that would not require any change in God or attribute to him responsibility for the imperfection and evil prevalent in the created world. To this end, he expounded the view that there are five eternal principles—God, Soul, prime matter, infinite, or absolute, space, and unlimited, or absolute, time—and explained creation as the result of the unexpected and sudden turn of events (*faltah*). *Faltah* occurred when Soul, in her ignorance, desired matter and the good God eased her misery by allowing her to satisfy her desire and to experience the suffering of the material world, and then gave her reason to make her realize her mistake and deliver her from her union with matter, the cause of her suffering and of all evil. Ar-Rāzī claimed that he was a Platonist, that he disagreed with Aristotle, and that his views were those of the Ṣābians of Harran and the Brahmins (Hindu teachers).

The concept of the five eternal principles

Ismāʿīlī theologians became aware of the kinship between certain elements of his cosmology and their own. They disputed with him during his lifetime and continued afterward to refute his doctrines in their writings. According to their account of his doctrines, he was totally opposed to authority in matters of knowledge, believed in the progress of the arts and sciences, and held that all reasonable men are equally able to look after their own affairs, equally inspired and able to know the truth of what earlier men had taught, and equally able to improve upon it. Ismāʿīlī theologians were incensed, in particular, by his wholesale rejection of prophecy, particular revelation, and divine laws. They were likewise opposed to his criticisms of religion in general as a device employed by evil men and a kind of tyranny over men that exploits their innocence and credulity, perpetuates ignorance, and leads to conflicts and wars.

Although the fragmentary character of al-Kindī's and ar-Rāzī's surviving philosophic writings does not permit passing firm and independent judgment on their accomplishments, they tend to bear out the view of later Muslim students of philosophy that both lacked competence in the logical foundation of philosophy, were knowledgeable in some of the natural sciences but not in metaphysics, and were unable to narrow the gap that separated philosophy from the new religion, Islām.

The teachings of al-Fārābī. *Political philosophy and the study of religion.* The first philosopher to meet this challenge was al-Fārābī (flourished 9th–10th centuries). He saw that theology and the juridical study of the law were derivative phenomena that function within a framework set by the prophet as lawgiver and founder of a human community. In this community, revelation defines the opinions the members of the community must hold and the actions they must perform if they are to attain the earthly happiness of this world and the supreme happiness of the other world. Philosophy could not understand this framework of religion as long as it concerned itself almost exclusively with its truth content and confined the study of practical science to individualistic ethics and personal salvation.

The relationship of law and theology to the community

In contrast to al-Kindī and ar-Rāzī, al-Fārābī recast philosophy in a new framework analogous to that of the Islāmic religion. The sciences were organized within this philosophic framework so that logic, physics, mathematics, and metaphysics culminated in a political science whose subject matter is the investigation of happiness and how it can be realized in cities and nations. The central theme of this political science is the founder of a virtuous or excellent community. Included in this theme are views concerning the supreme rulers who follow the founder, their qualifications, and how the community must be ordered so that its members attain happiness as citizens rather than isolated human beings. Once this new philosophical framework was established, it became possible to conduct a philosophical investigation of all the elements that constituted the Islāmic community: the prophet-lawgiver, the aims of the divine laws, the legislation of beliefs as well as actions, the role of the successors to the founding legislator, the grounds of the interpretation or reform of the law, the classification of human communities according to their doctrines in addition to their size, and the critique of "ignorant" (pagan), "transgressing," "falsifying," and "erring" communities. Philosophical cosmology, psychology, and politics were blended by al-Fārābī into a political theology whose aim was to clarify the foundations of the Islāmic community and defend its reform in a direction that would promote scientific inquiry and encourage philosophers to play an active role in practical affairs.

Interpretation of Plato and Aristotle. Behind this public, or exoteric, aspect of al-Fārābī's work stood a massive body of more properly philosophic or scientific inquiries, which established his reputation among Muslims as the greatest philosophical authority after Aristotle, a great interpreter of the thought of Plato and Aristotle and their commentators, and a master to whom almost all major Muslim as well as a number of Jewish and Christian philosophers turned for a fuller understanding of the controversial, troublesome, and intricate questions of philosophy. Continuing the tradition of the Hellenistic masters of the Athenian and Alexandrian philosophical schools, al-Fārābī broadened the range of philosophical inquiry and fixed its form. He paid special attention to the study of language and its relation to logic. In his numerous commentaries on Aristotle's logical works, he expounded for the first time in Arabic the entire range of the scientific and nonscientific forms of argument and established the place of logic as an indispensable prerequisite for philosophic inquiry. His writings on natural science exposed the foundation and assumptions of Aristotle's physics and dealt with the arguments of Aristotle's opponents, both philosophers and scientists, pagan, Christian, and Muslim.

Significance of al-Fārābī in the dissemination of Greek philosophical thought

The analogy of religion and philosophy. Al-Fārābī's theological and political writings showed later Muslim philosophers the way to deal with the question of the relation between philosophy and religion and presented them with a complex set of problems that they continued to elaborate, modify, and develop in different directions. Starting with the view that religion is analogous or similar to philosophy, al-Fārābī argued that the idea of the true prophet-lawgiver ought to be the same as that of the true philosopher-king. Thus, he challenged both al-Kindī's view that prophets and philosophers have different and independent ways to the highest truth available to man and ar-Rāzī's view that philosophy is the only way to that knowledge. That a man could combine the functions of prophecy, lawgiving, philosophy, and kingship did not necessarily mean that these functions were identical; it did mean, however, that they all are legitimate subjects of philosophic inquiry. Philosophy must account for the powers, knowledge, and activities of the prophet, lawgiver, and king, which it must distinguish from and relate to those of the philosopher. The public, or political, function of philosophy was emphasized. Unlike Neoplatonism, which had for long limited itself to the Platonic teaching that the function of philosophy is to liberate the soul from the shadowy existence of the cave—in which knowledge can only be imperfectly comprehended as shadows reflecting the light of the truth beyond the cave (the world of senses)—al-Fārābī insisted with Plato that the philosopher must be forced to return to the cave, learn to talk to its inhabitants in a manner they can comprehend, and engage in actions that may improve their lot.

Impact on Ismāʿīlī theology. Although it is not always easy to know the immediate practical intentions of a philosopher, it must be remembered that in al-Fārābī's lifetime the fate of the Islāmic world was in the balance. The Sunnī caliphate's power hardly extended beyond Baghdad, and it appeared quite likely that the various Shīʿī sects, especially the Ismāʿīlīs, would finally overpower it and establish a new political order. Of all the movements in Islāmic theology, Ismāʿīlī theology was the one that was most clearly and massively penetrated by philosophy. Yet, its Neoplatonic cosmology, revolutionary background, antinomianism (antilegalism), and general expectation that divine laws were about to become superfluous with the appearance of the *qāʾim* (the imam of the "resurrection") all militated against the development of a coherent political theory to meet the practical demands of political life and present a viable practical alternative to the Sunnī caliphate. Al-Fārābī's theologico-political writings helped point out this basic defect of Ismāʿīlī theology. Under the Fāṭimids in Egypt (969–1171), Ismāʿīlī theology modified its cosmology in the direction suggested by al-Fārābī, returned to the view that the community must continue to live under the divine law, and postponed the prospect of the abolition of divine laws and the appearance of the *qāʾim* to an indefinite point in the future.

The use of al-Fārābī's theo-logical–political writings to reform Ismāʿīlī thought

The teachings of Avicenna. *The "Oriental Philosophy."* Even more indicative of al-Fārābī's success is the fact that his writings helped produce a philosopher of the stature of Avicenna (flourished 10th–11th centuries), whose versatility, imagination, inventiveness, and prudence shaped philosophy into a powerful force that gradually penetrated Islāmic theology and mysticism and Persian poetry in eastern Islām and gave them universality and theoretical depth. His own personal philosophic views, he said, were those of the ancient sages of Greece (including the genuine views of Plato and Aristotle), which he had set forth in the "Oriental Philosophy," a book that has not survived and probably was not written or meant to be written. They were not identical with the common Peripatetic (Aristotelian) doctrines and were to be distinguished from the learning of his contemporaries, the Christian "Aristotelians" of Baghdad, which he attacked as vulgar, distorted, and falsified. His most voluminous writing, *Kitāb ash-shifāʾ* ("The Book of Healing"), was meant to accommodate the doctrines of other philosophers as well as hint at his own personal views, which are elaborated elsewhere in more imaginative and allegorical forms.

Distinction between essence and existence and the doctrine of creation. Avicenna had learned from certain hints in al-Fārābī that the exoteric teachings of Plato regarding "forms," "creation," and the immortality of individual souls were closer to revealed doctrines than the genuine views of Aristotle, that the doctrines of Plotinus and later Neoplatonic commentators were useful in harmonizing Aristotle's views with revealed doctrines, and that philosophy must accommodate itself to the divine law on the issue of creation and of reward and punishment in the hereafter, which presupposes some form of individual immortality. Following al-Fārābī's lead, Avicenna initiated a full-fledged inquiry into the question of being, in which he distinguished between essence and existence. He argued that the fact of existence cannot be inferred from or accounted for by the essence of existing things and that form and matter by themselves cannot interact and originate the movement of the universe or the progressive actualization of existing things. Existence must, therefore, be due to an agent-cause that necessitates, imparts, gives, or adds existence to an essence. To do so, the cause must be an existing thing and coexist with its effect. The universe consists of a chain of actual beings, each giving existence to the one below it and responsible for the existence of the rest of the chain below. Because an actual infinite is deemed impossible by Avicenna, this chain as a whole must terminate in a being that is wholly simple and one, whose essence is its very existence, and therefore is self-sufficient and not in need of something else to give it existence. Because its existence is not contingent on or necessitated by something else but is necessary and eternal in itself, it satisfies the condition of being the necessitating cause of the entire chain that constitutes the eternal world of contingent existing things.

Avicenna's investigation of being

All creation is necessarily and eternally dependent upon God. It consists of the intelligences, souls, and bodies of the heavenly spheres, each of which is eternal, and the sublunary sphere, which is also eternal, undergoing a perpetual process of generation and corruption, of the succession of form over matter, very much in the manner described by Aristotle.

The immortality of individual souls. There is, however, a significant exception to this general rule: the human rational soul. Man can affirm the existence of his soul from direct consciousness of his self (what he means when he says "I"); and he can imagine this happening even in the absence of external objects and bodily organs. This proves, according to Avicenna, that the soul is indivisible, immaterial, and incorruptible substance, not imprinted in matter, but created with the body, which it uses as an instrument. Unlike other immaterial substances (the intelligences and souls of the spheres), it is not pre-eternal but is generated, or made to exist, at the same time as the individual body, which can receive it, is formed. The composition, shape, and disposition of its body and the soul's success or failure in managing and controlling it, the formation of moral habits, and the acquisition of knowledge all contribute to its individuality and difference from other souls. Though the body is not resurrected after its corruption, the soul survives and retains all the individual characteristics, perfections or imperfections, that it achieved in its earthly existence and in this sense is rewarded or punished for its past deeds. Avicenna's claim that he has presented a philosophic proof for the immortality of generated ("created") individual souls no doubt constitutes the high point of his effort to harmonize philosophy and religious beliefs.

The doctrine of individual souls

Philosophy, religion, and mysticism. Having accounted for the more difficult issues of creation and the immortality of individual souls, Avicenna proceeded to explain the faculty of prophetic knowledge (the "sacred" intellect), revelation (imaginative representation meant to convince the multitude and improve their earthly life), miracles, and the legal and institutional arrangements (acts of worship and the regulation of personal and public life) through which the divine law achieves its end. Avicenna's explanation of almost every aspect of Islām is pursued on the basis of extensive exegesis of the Qurʾān and the Ḥadīth. The primary function of religion is to assure the happiness of the many. This practical aim of religion (which Avicenna saw in the perspective of Aristotle's practical science) enabled him to appreciate the political and moral functions of divine revelation and account for its form and content. Revealed religion, however, has a subsidiary function also—that of indicating to the few the need to pursue the kind of life and knowledge appropriate to rare individuals endowed with special gifts. These men must be dominated by the love of God to facilitate the achievement of the highest knowledge. In many places Avicenna appears to identify these men with the mystics. The identification of the philosopher as a kind of mystic conveyed a new image of the philosopher as a member of the religious community who is distinguished from his coreligionists by his otherworldliness, dedicated to the inner truth of religion, and consumed by the love of God.

Prophetic, revelatory, and social knowledge

Avicenna's allegorical and mystical writings are usually

called "esoteric" in the sense that they contain his personal views cast in an imaginative, symbolic form. The esoteric works must, then, be interpreted. Their interpretation must move away from the explicit doctrines contained in "exoteric" works such as the *Shifāʾ* and recover "the unmixed and uncorrupted truth" set forth in the "Oriental Philosophy." The "Oriental Philosophy," however, has never been available to anyone, and it is doubtful that it was written at all. This dilemma has made interpretation both difficult and rewarding for Muslim philosophers and modern scholars alike.

THE WESTERN PHILOSOPHERS

Background and characteristics of the western Muslim philosophical tradition. Andalusia (in Spain) and western North Africa contributed little of substance to Islāmic theology and philosophy until the 12th century. Legal strictures against the study of philosophy were more effective than in the east. Scientific interest was channelled into medicine, pharmacology, mathematics, astronomy, and logic. More general questions of physics and metaphysics were treated sparingly and in symbols, hints, and allegories. By the 12th century, however, the writings of al-Fārābī, Avicenna, and al-Ghazālī had found their way to the west. A philosophical tradition emerged, based primarily on the study of al-Fārābī. It was critical of Avicenna's philosophic innovations and not convinced that al-Ghazālī's critique of Avicenna touched philosophy as such, and it refused to acknowledge the position assigned by both to mysticism. The survival of philosophy in the west required extreme prudence, emphasis on its scientific character, abstention from meddling in political or religious matters, and abandoment of the hope of effecting extensive doctrinal or institutional reform.

Significance of Islāmic philosophers in the West

The teachings of Ibn Bājjah. *Theoretical science and intuitive knowledge.* Ibn Bājjah (died 1138) initiated this tradition with a radical interpretation of al-Fārābī's political philosophy that emphasized the virtues of the perfect but nonexistent city and the vices prevalent in all existing cities. He concluded that the philosopher must order his own life as a solitary individual, shun the company of nonphilosophers, reject their opinions and ways of life, and concentrate on reaching his own final goal by pursuing the theoretical sciences and achieving intuitive knowledge through contact with the Active Intelligence. The multitude live in a dark cave and see only dim shadows. Their ways of life and their imaginings and beliefs consist of layers of darkness that cannot be known through reason alone. Therefore, the divine law has been revealed to enable man to know this dark region. The philosopher's duty is to seek the light of the sun (the intellect). To do so, he must leave the cave, see all colours as they truly are and see light itself, and finally become transformed into that light. The end, then, is contact with Intelligence, not with something that transcends Intelligence (as in Plotinus, Ismāʿīlism, and mysticism), a doctrine criticized by Ibn Bājjah as the way of imagination, motivated by desire, and aiming at pleasure. Philosophy, he claimed, is the only way to the truly blessed state, which can be achieved only by going through theoretical science, even though it is higher than theoretical science.

The duty of the philosopher

Unconcern of philosophy with reform. Ibn Bājjah's cryptic style and the unfinished form in which he left most of his writings tend to highlight his departures from al-Fārābī and Avicenna. Unlike al-Fārābī, he is silent about the philosopher's duty to return to the cave and partake of the life of the city. He appears to argue that the aim of philosophy is attainable independently from the philosopher's concern with the best city and is to be achieved in solitude or, at most, in comradeship with philosophic souls. Unlike Avicenna, who prepared the way for him by clearly distinguishing between theoretical and practical science, Ibn Bājjah is concerned with practical science only insofar as it is relevant to the life of the philosopher. He is contemptuous of allegories and imaginative representations of philosophic knowledge, silent about theology, and shows no concern with improving the multitude's opinions and way of life.

The teachings of Ibn Ṭufayl. *The philosopher as a solitary individual.* In his philosophic story *Ḥayy ibn Yaqẓān* ("*Alive Son of Awake*"), the philosopher Ibn Ṭufayl (died 1185) fills gaps in the work of his predecessor Ibn Bājjah. The story communicates the secrets of Avicenna's "Oriental Philosophy" as experienced by a solitary hero, who grows up on a deserted island, learns about the things around him, acquires knowledge of the natural universe (including the heavenly bodies), and achieves the state of "annihilation" (*fanāʾ*) of the self in the divine reality. This is the apparent and traditional secret of the "Oriental Philosophy." But the hero's wisdom is still incomplete, for he knows nothing about other human beings, their way of life, or their laws. When he chances to meet one of them—a member of a religious community inhabiting a neighbouring island, who is inclined to reflect on the divine law and seek its inner, spiritual meanings and who has abandoned the society of his fellow men to devote himself to solitary meditation and worship—he does not at first recognize that he is a human being like himself, cannot communicate with him, and frightens him by his wild aspect. After learning about the doctrines and acts of worship of the religious community, he understands them as alluding to and agreeing with the truth that he had learned by his own unaided effort, and he goes as far as admitting the validity of the religion and the truthfulness of the prophet who gave it. He cannot understand, however, why the prophet communicated the truth by way of allusions, examples, and corporeal representations or why religion permits men to devote much time and effort to practical, worldly things.

Explanation of Avicenna's "Oriental Philosophy"

Concern for reform. His ignorance of the nature of most men and his compassion for them make the solitary hero insist on becoming their saviour. He persuades his companion to take him to his coreligionists and help him convert them to the naked truth by propagating among them "the secrets of wisdom." His education is completed when he fails in his endeavour. He learns the limits beyond which the multitude cannot ascend without becoming confused and unhappy. He also learns the wisdom of the divine lawgiver in addressing them in the way they can understand, enabling them to achieve limited ends through doctrines and actions suited to their abilities. The story ends with the hero taking leave of these people after apologizing to them for what he did and confessing that he is now fully convinced that they should not change their ways but remain attached to the literal sense of the divine law and obey its demands. He returns to his own island to continue his former solitary existence.

The hidden secret of Avicenna's "Oriental Philosophy." The hidden secret of Avicenna's "Oriental Philosophy" appears, then, to be that the philosopher must return to the cave, educate himself in the ways of nonphilosophers, and understand the incompatibility between philosophical life and the life of the multitude, which must be governed by religion and divine laws. Otherwise, his ignorance will lead him to actions dangerous to the well-being of both the community and philosophy. Because Ibn Ṭufayl's hero had grown up as a solitary human being, he lacks the kind of wisdom that could have enabled him to pursue philosophy in a religious community and be useful to such a community. Neither the conversion of the community to philosophy nor the philosopher's solitary life is a viable alternative.

The teachings of Averroës. *Philosophy.* To Ibn Ṭufayl's younger friend Averroës (Ibn Rushd, flourished 12th century) belongs the distinction of presenting a solution to the problem of the relation between philosophy and the Islāmic community in the west, a solution meant to be legally valid, theologically sound, and philosophically satisfactory. Here was a philosopher fully at home in what Ibn Bājjah had called the many layers of darkness. His legal training (he was a judge by profession) and his extensive knowledge of the history of the religious sciences (including theology) enabled him to speak with authority about the principles of Islāmic law and their application to theological and philosophic issues and to question the authority of al-Ghazālī and the Ashʿarīs to determine correct beliefs and right practices. He was able

Solution to the problem of the relation of philosophy to the community to examine in detail from the point of view of the divine law the respective claims of theology and philosophy to possess the best and surest way to human knowledge, to be competent to interpret the ambiguous expressions of the divine law, and to have presented convincing arguments that are theoretically tenable and practically salutary.

The intention of the divine law

The divine law. The intention of the divine law, he argued, is to assure the happiness of all members of the community. This requires everyone to profess belief in the basic principles of religion as enunciated in the Qur'ān, the Ḥadīth, and the *ijmā'* (consensus) of the learned and to perform all obligatory acts of worship. Beyond this, the only just requirement is to demand that each pursue knowledge as far as his natural capacity and makeup permit. The few who are endowed with the capacity for the highest, demonstrative knowledge are under a divine legal obligation to pursue the highest wisdom, which is philosophy, and they need not constantly adjust its certain conclusions to what theologians claim to be the correct interpretation of the divine law. Being dialecticians and rhetoricians, theologians are not in a position to determine what is and is not correct interpretation of the divine law so far as philosophers are concerned. The divine law directly authorizes philosophers to pursue its interpretation according to the best—*i.e.* demonstrative or scientific—method, and theologians have no authority to interfere with the conduct of this activity or judge its conclusions.

Theology. On the basis of this legal doctrine, Averroës judged the theologian al-Ghazālī's refutation of the philosophers ineffective and inappropriate because al-Ghazālī did not understand and even misrepresented the philosophers' positions and used arguments that only demonstrate his incompetence in the art of demonstration. He criticized al-Fārābī and Avicenna also for accommodating the theologians of their time and for departing from the path of the ancient philosophers merely to please the theologians. At the other extreme are the multitude for whom there are no more convincing arguments than those found in the divine law itself. Neither philosophers nor theologians are permitted to disclose to the multitude interpretations of the ambiguous verses of the Qur'ān or to confuse them with their own doubts or arguments. Finally, there are those who belong to neither the philosophers nor the multitude, either because they are naturally superior to the multitude but not endowed with the gift for philosophy or else are students in initial stages of philosophic training. For this intermediate group theology is necessary. It is an intermediate discipline that is neither strictly legal nor philosophic. It lacks their certain principles and sure methods. Therefore, theology must remain under the constant control of philosophy and the supervision of the divine law so as not to drift into taking positions that cannot be demonstrated philosophically or that are contrary to the intention of the divine law. Averroës himself composed a work on theology to show how these requirements can be met: *Kitāb al-kashf 'an manāhij al-adillah* ("Exposition of the Methods of Proofs"). In the Latin West he was best known for his philosophical answer to al-Ghazālī, *Tahāfut at-tahāfut* ("Incoherence of the Incoherence"), and for his extensive commentaries on Aristotle, works that left their impact on medieval and renaissance European thought.

IV. The new wisdom: the synthesis between philosophy and mysticism

PHILOSOPHY, TRADITIONALISM, AND THE NEW WISDOM

The role of Arabic philosophical literature in the West

Philosophy. The western tradition in Islāmic philosophy formed part of the Arabic philosophic literature that was translated into Hebrew and Latin and that played a significant role in the development of medieval philosophy in the Latin West and the emergence of modern European philosophy. Its impact on the development of philosophy in eastern Islām was not as dramatic, but was important nevertheless. Students of this tradition—*e.g.*, the prominent Jewish philosopher Maimonides (flourished 12th century) and the historian Ibn Khaldūn (flourished 14th century)—moved to Egypt, where they taught and had numerous disciples. Most of the writings of Ibn Bājjah, Ibn Ṭufayl, and Averroës found their way to the east also, where they were studied alongside the writings of their eastern predecessors. In both regions thinkers who held to the idea of philosophy as formulated by the eastern and western philosophers thus far discussed continued to teach. They became isolated and overwhelmed, however, by the resurgence of traditionalism and the emergence of a new kind of philosophy whose champions looked on the earlier masters as men who had made significant contributions to the progress of knowledge but whose overall view was defective and had now become outdated.

Traditionalism and the new wisdom. Resurgent traditionalism found effective defenders in men such as Ibn Taymīyah (13th–14th centuries) who employed a massive battery of philosophic, theological, and legal arguments against every shade of innovation and called for a return to the beliefs and practices of the pious ancestors. These attacks, however, did not deal a decisive blow to philosophy as such. It rather drove philosophy underground for a period, only to re-emerge in a new garb. A more important reason for the decline of the earlier philosophic tradition, however, was the renewed vitality and success of the program formulated by al-Ghazālī for the integration of theology, philosophy, and mysticism into a new kind of philosophy called wisdom (*ḥikmah*). It consisted of a critical review of the philosophy of Avicenna, preserving its main external features (its logical, physical, and, in part, metaphysical structure, and its terminology) and introducing principles of explanation for the universe and its relation to God based on personal experience and direct vision.

The emergence of philosophy under a new garb

Characteristic features of the new wisdom. If the popular theology preached by the philosophers from al-Fārābī to Averroës is disregarded, it is evident that philosophy proper meant to them what al-Fārābī called a state of mind dedicated to the quest and the love for the highest wisdom. None of them claimed, however, that he had achieved this highest wisdom. In contrast, every leading exponent of the new wisdom stated that he had achieved or received it through a private illumination, dream (at times inspired by the Prophet), or vision and on this basis proceeded to give an explanation of the inner structure of natural and divine things. In every case, this explanation incorporated Platonic or Aristotelian elements but was more akin to some version of a later Hellenistic philosophy, which had found its way earlier into one or another of the schools of Islāmic theology, though, because of the absence of an adequate philosophic education on the part of earlier theologians, it had not been either elaborated or integrated into a comprehensive view. Like their late-Hellenistic counterparts, exponents of the new wisdom proceeded through an examination of the positions of Plato, Aristotle, and Plotinus. They also gave special attention to the insights of the pre-Socratic philosophers of ancient Greece and the myths and revelations of the ancient Near East, and they offered to resolve the fundamental questions that had puzzled earlier philosophers. In its basic movement and general direction, therefore, Islāmic philosophy between the 9th and the 19th centuries followed a course parallel to that of Greek philosophy from the 5th century BC to the 6th century AD.

Use of Greek philosophers by exponents of the new wisdom

Critiques of Aristotle in Islāmic theology. The critique of Aristotle that had begun in Mu'tazilī circles and had found a prominent champion in Abū Bakr ar-Rāzī was provided with a more solid foundation in the 10th and 11th centuries by the Christian theologians and philosophers of Baghdad, who translated the writings of the Hellenistic critics of Aristotle (*e.g.*, John Philoponus) and made use of their arguments in commenting on Aristotle and in independent theological and philosophic works. Avicenna's attack on these so-called Aristotelians and their Hellenistic predecessors (an attack that had been initiated by al-Fārābī and was to be continued by Averroës) did not prevent the spread of their theologically based anti-Aristotelianism among Jewish and Muslim students of philosophy in the 12th century, such as Abū al-Barakāt al-Baghdādī (died *c.* 1175) and Fakhr ad-Dīn ar-Rāzī. These theologians continued and intensified al-Ghazālī's attacks on Avicenna and Aristotle (especially their views on time, movement, matter, and form, the nature of the heavenly bodies, and the relation between the intelligible and sensible worlds). They suggested that a thorough examination of Aristotle had revealed to them, on philosophic grounds, that the fundamental disagreements between him and the theologies based on the revealed religions represented open options and that Aristotle's view of the universe was in need of explanatory principles that could very well be supplied by theology. This critique provided the framework for the integration of philosophy into theology from the 13th century onward.

Synthesis of philosophy and mysticism. Although it made use of such theological criticisms of philosophy, the new wisdom took the position that theology did not offer a positive substitute for and was incapable of solving the difficulties of "Aristotelian" philosophy. It did not question the need to have recourse to the Qur'ān and the Ḥadīth to find the right answers. It insisted (on the authority of a long-standing mystical tradition), however, that theology concerns itself only with the external expressions of this divine source of knowledge. The inner core was reserved for the adepts of the mystic path whose journey leads to the experience of the highest reality in dreams and visions. Only the mystical adepts are in possession of the one true wisdom, the ground of both the external expressions of the divine law and the phenomenal world of human experience and thought.

The inner core of divine knowledge as reserved for the adepts

PRIMARY TEACHERS OF THE NEW WISDOM

The teachings of as-Suhrawardī. The first master of the new wisdom, as-Suhrawardī (12th century), called it the "Wisdom of Illumination." He rejected Avicenna's distinction between essence and existence and Aristotle's distinction between substance and accidents, possibility and actuality, and matter and form, on the ground that they are mere distinctions of reason. Instead, he concentrated on the notion of being and its negation, which he called "light" and "darkness," and explained the gradation of beings as gradation of their mixture according to the degree of "strength," or "perfection," of their light. This gradation forms a single continuum that culminates in pure light, self-luminosity, self-awareness, self-manifestation, or self-knowledge, which is God, the light of lights, the true One. The stability and eternity of this single continuum result from every higher light overpowering and subjugating the lower, and movement and change in it result from each of the lower lights desiring and loving the higher.

As-Suhrawardī's "pan-lightism" is not particularly close to traditional Islāmic views concerning the creation of the world and God's knowledge of particulars. The structure of his universe remains largely that of the Platonists and the Aristotelians. And his account of the emanation process avoids the many difficulties that had puzzled Neoplatonists as they tried to understand how the second hypostasis (reality) proceeds from the One. He asserted that it proceeds without in any way affecting the One and that the One's self-sufficiency is enough to explain the giving out that seems to be both spontaneous and necessary. His doctrine is presented in a way that suggests that it is the inner truth behind the exoteric (external) teachings of Islām as well as Zoroastrianism, indeed the wisdom of all ancient sages, especially Iranians and Greeks, and the revealed religions as well. This neutral yet positive attitude toward the diversity of religions, which was not absent among Muslim philosophers and mystics, was to become one of the hallmarks of the new wisdom. Different religions were seen as different manifestations of the same truth, their essential agreement was emphasized, and various attempts were made to combine them into a single harmonious religion meant for all of mankind.

The positive attitude to the diversity of religions

As-Suhrawardī takes an important step in this direction through his doctrine of imaginative-bodily "resurrection." After their departure from the prison of the body, souls that are fully purified ascend directly to the world of separate lights. The ones that are only partially purified or are evil souls escape to a "world of images" suspended below the higher lights and above the corporeal world. In this world of images, or forms (not to be confused with the Platonic forms, which as-Suhrawardī identifies with higher and permanent intelligible lights), partially purified souls remain suspended and are able to create for themselves and by their own power of imagination pleasing figures and desirable objects in forms more excellent than their earthly counterparts and are able to enjoy them forever. Evil souls become dark shadows, suffer (presumably because their corrupt and inefficient power of imagination can create only ugly and frightening forms), and wander about as ghosts, demons, and devils. The creative power of the imagination, which as a human psychological phenomenon was already used by the philosophers to explain prophetic powers, was seized upon by the new wisdom as "divine magic." It was used to construct an eschatology, to explain miracles, dreams, and other saintly theurgic (healing) practices, to facilitate the movement between various orders of being, and for literary purposes.

The teachings of Ibn al-ʿArabī. The account of the doctrines of Ibn al-ʿArabī (12th–13th centuries) belongs properly to the history of Islāmic mysticism. Yet his impact on the subsequent development of the new wisdom was in many ways far greater than was that of as-Suhrawardī. This is true especially of his central doctrine of the "unity of being" and his sharp distinction between the absolute One, which is undefinable Truth (*ḥaqq*), and his self-manifestation (*ẓuhūr*), or creation (*khalq*), which is ever new (*jadīd*) and in perpetual movement, a movement that unites the whole of creation in a process of constant renewal. At the very core of this dynamic edifice stands nature, the "dark cloud" (*ʿamāʾ*) or "mist" (*bukhār*), as the ultimate principle of things and forms: intelligence, heavenly bodies, and elements and their mixtures that culminate in the "perfect man." This primordial nature is the "breath" of the Merciful God in his aspect as Lord. It "flows" throughout the universe and manifests Truth in all its parts. It is the first mother through which Truth manifests itself to itself and generates the universe. And it is the universal natural body that gives birth to the translucent bodies of the spheres, to the elements, and to their mixtures, all of which are related to that primary source as daughters to their mother.

Doctrine of the "unity of being"

Ibn al-ʿArabī attempted to explain how Intelligence proceeds from the absolute One by inserting between them a primordial feminine principle, which is all things in potentiality but which also possesses the capacity, readiness, and desire to manifest or generate them, first, as archetypes in Intelligence, and then as actually existing things in the universe below. Ibn al-ʿArabī gave this principle numerous names, including prime "matter" (*ʿunṣur*), and characterized it as the principle "whose existence makes manifest the essences of the potential worlds." The doctrine that the first simple originated thing is not Intelligence but "indefinite matter" and that Intelligence was originated through the mediation of this matter was attributed to Empedocles, 5th-century-BC Greek philosopher, in doxographies (compilations of extracts from the Greek philosophers) translated into Arabic. It represented an attempt to bridge the gulf between the absolute One and the multiplicity of forms in Intelligence. The Andalusian mystic Ibn Masarrah (9th–10th centuries) is reported to have championed pseudo-Empedoclean doctrines, and Ibn al-ʿArabī (who studied under some of his followers) quotes Ibn Masarrah on a number of occasions. This philosophic tradition is distinct from the one followed by the Ismāʿīlī theologians, who explained the origination of Intelligence by the mediation of God's will.

The teachings of Twelver Shīʿism and the school of Isfahan. After Ibn al-ʿArabī, the new wisdom developed rapidly in intellectual circles in eastern Islām. Commentators on the works of Avicenna, as-Suhrawardī, and Ibn al-ʿArabī began the process of harmonizing and inte-

The role of mystical fraternities in the east

grating the views of the masters. Great poets made them part of every educated man's literary culture. Mystical fraternities became the custodians of such works, spreading them into Central Asia and the Indian subcontinent and transmitting them from one generation to another. Following the Mongol khan Hülagü's entry into Baghdad (1258), the Twelver Shīʿah were encouraged by the Il Khanid Tatars and Naṣīr ad-Dīn aṭ-Ṭūsī (the philosopher and theologian who accompanied Hülagü as his vizier) to abandon their hostility to mysticism. Muʿtazilī doctrines were retained in their theology. Theology, however, was downgraded to "formal" learning that must be supplemented by higher things, the latter including philosophy and mysticism, both of earlier Shīʿī (including Ismāʿīlī) origin and of later Sunnī provenance. Al-Ghazālī, as-Suhrawardī, Ibn al-ʿArabī, and Avicenna were then eagerly studied and (except for their doctrine of the imamate) embraced with little or no reservation. This movement in Shīʿī thought gathered momentum when the leaders of a mystical fraternity established themselves as the Ṣafavid dynasty (1501–1732) in Iran, where they championed Twelver Shīʿism as the official doctrine of the new monarchy. During the 17th century, Iran experienced a cultural and scientific renaissance that included a revival of philosophic studies. There, Islāmic philosophy found its last creative exponents. The new wisdom as expounded by the masters of the school of Isfahan radiated throughout eastern Islām and continued as a vital tradition until modern times.

The major figures of the school of Isfahan were Mīr Dāmād (Ibn ad-Dāmād, died 1630) and his great disciple Mullā Ṣadrā (Ṣadr ad-Dīn ash-Shīrāzī, *c.* 1571–1640). Both were men of wide culture and prolific writers with a sharp sense for the history and development of philosophic ideas.

The concept of "eternal origination"

The teachings of Mīr Dāmād. Mīr Dāmād was the first to expound the notion of "eternal origination" (*ḥudūth dahrī*) as an explanation for the creation of the world. Muslim philosophers and their critics had recognized the crucial role played by the question of time in the discussion of the eternity of the world. The proposition that time is the measure of movement was criticized by Abū al-Barakāt al-Baghdādī, who argued that time is prior to movement and rest, indeed to everything except being. Time is the measure or concomitant of being, lasting and transient, enduring and in movement or rest. It characterizes or qualifies all being, including God. God works in time, incessantly willing and directly creating everything in the world: his persistent will creates the eternal beings of the world, and his ever-renewed will creates the transient beings. The notion of a God who works in time was of course objectionable to theology, and Fakhr ad-Dīn ar-Rāzī refused to accept this solution despite its attractions. Ar-Rāzī also saw that it leads to the notion (attributed to Plato) that time is a self-subsistent substance, whose relation to God would further compromise his unity. Finally, ar-Rāzī explained that this self-subsistent substance will have to be related to different beings in different ways. It is called "everlastingness" (*sarmad*) when related to God and the Intelligences (angels) that are permanent and do not move or change in any way, "eternity" (*dahr*) when related to the totality of the world of movement and change, and "time" (*zamān*) when related to corporeal beings that make up the world of movement and change.

The problems of essence and existence

Mīr Dāmād returned to Avicenna and sought to harmonize his views with those of as-Suhrawardī on the assumption that what Avicenna meant by his "Oriental" (*mashriqīyah*) philosophy was identical with as-Suhrawardī's wisdom of "illumination" (*ishrāq*), which he interpreted as a Platonic doctrine that asserted the priority of essence (form) over being (existence). Time, for Mīr Dāmād, was neither a mere being of reason nor an accident of existing things. It belongs to the essence of things and describes their mode and rank of being. It is a "relation" that beings have to each other because of their essential nature. There must, therefore, be three ranks of order of time corresponding to the three ranks of order of being. Considered as the relation of God to the divine names and attributes (Intelligences or archetypes), the relation is "everlastingness." Considered as the relation between the Intelligences, or archetypes, and their reflections in the mutable things of the world below, the relation is "eternity." And considered as the relation between these mutable things, the relation is "time." Creation, or origination, is this very relation. Thus, the origination of the immutable Intelligences, or archetypes, is called "everlasting creation," the origination of the world of mutable beings as a whole is called "eternal creation," and the generation of mutable things within the world is called "temporal creation."

The teachings of Mullā Ṣadrā. Mullā Ṣadrā superimposed Ibn al-ʿArabī's mystical thought (whose philosophic implications had already been exposed by a number of commentators) on the "Aristotelian"–Illuminationist synthesis developed by Mīr Dāmād. Against his master, he argued with the Aristotelians for the priority of being (existence) over essence (form), which he called an abstraction; and, with Ibn al-ʿArabī, he argued for the "unity of being" within which beings differ only according to "priority and posteriority," "perfection and imperfection," and "strength and weakness." All being is thus viewed as a graded manifestation, or determination, of absolute, or pure, Being, and every level of being possesses all the attributes of pure Being, but with varying degrees of intensity or perfection.

Mullā Ṣadrā's doctrine of nature

Mullā Ṣadrā considered his unique contribution to Islāmic philosophy to be his doctrine of nature, which enabled him to assert that everything other than God and his knowledge—*i.e.*, the entire corporeal world, including the heavenly bodies—is originated "eternally" as well as "temporally." This doctrine of nature is an elaboration of the last manifestation of Ibn al-ʿArabī's "nature" or prime "matter," articulated on philosophic grounds and within the general framework of Aristotelian natural science and defended against every possible philosophic and theological objection.

Nature for Mullā Ṣadrā is the "substance" and "power" of all corporeal beings and the direct cause of their movement. Movement (and time, which measures it) is therefore not an accident of substance or an accompaniment of some of its accidents. It signifies the very change, renewal, and passing of being—itself being in constant "flow," or flux. The entire corporeal world, both the celestial spheres and the world of the elements, constantly renews itself. The "matter" of corporeal things has the power to become a new form at every instant; and the resulting matter–form complex is at every instant a new matter ready for, desiring, and moving toward another form. Men fail to observe this constant flux and movement in simple bodies not because of the endurance of the same form in them but because of the close similarity between their ever-new forms. What the philosophers call "movement" and "time" are not, as they believed, anchored in anything permanent—*e.g.*, in what they call "nature," "substance," or "essence"; essence is permanent only in the mind, and nature and substance are permanent activity. Nature as permanent activity is the very being of natural things and identical with their substance. Because nature is "permanent" in this sense, it is connected to a permanent principle that manifests activity in it permanently. Because nature constantly renews itself, all renewed and emergent things are connected to it. Thus, nature is the link between what is eternal and what is originated, and the world of nature is originated both eternally and temporally.

The problem of movement, change, or renewal

Mullā Ṣadrā distinguishes this primary "movement-in-substance" (*al-ḥarakah fī al-jawhar*) from haphazard, compulsory, and other accidental movements that lack proper direction, impede the natural movement of substance, or reverse it. Movement-in-substance is not universal change or flux without direction, the product of conflict between two equally powerful principles, or a reflection of the nonbeing of the world of nature when measured against the world of permanent forms. It is, rather, the natural beings' innate desire to become more perfect, which directs this ceaseless self-renewal, self-origination, or self-emergence into a perpetual and irreversible flow upward in the scale of being—from the simplest elements to the human body–soul complex and the heavenly body–soul complex (both of which participate in the general instability, origination, and passing of being that characterizes the entire corporeal world). This flow upward, however, is by no means the end. For the indefinite "matter" (Ibn al-ʿArabī's "cloud" and the mystics' "created Truth") is the "substratum" of everything other than its Creator, the mysterious pure Truth. It "extends" beyond the body–soul complex to the Intelligences (divine names) that are Being's first, highest, and purest actualization or activity. This "extension" unites everything other than the Creator into a single continuum. The human body–soul complex and the heavenly body–soul complex are not moved externally by the Intelligences. Their movement is an extension of the process of self-perfection. Having reached the highest rank of order of substance in the corporeal world, they are now prepared, and still moved by their innate desire, to flow upward and transform themselves into pure intelligence.

V. Conclusion

The new wisdom lived on during the 18th and 19th centuries, conserving much of its vitality and strength but not cultivating new ground. It attracted able thinkers such as Shāh Walī Allāh of Delhi and Hādī Sabzevārī and became a regular part of the program of higher education in the cultural centres of the Ottoman Empire, Iran, and the Indian subcontinent, a status never achieved by the earlier tradition of Islāmic philosophy. In collaboration with its close ally Persian mystical poetry, the new wisdom determined the intellectual outlook and spiritual mood of educated Muslims in the regions where Persian had become the dominant literary language.

The problem of reform in modern Islāmic thought

The wholesale rejection of the new wisdom in the name of simple, robust, and more practical piety (which had been initiated by Ibn Taymīyah and which continued to find exponents among jurists) made little impression on its devotees. To be taken seriously, reform had to come from their own ranks and be espoused by such thinkers as the eminent theologian and mystic of Muslim India Aḥmad Sirhindī (flourished 16th–17th centuries)—a reformer who spoke their language and attacked Ibn al-ʿArabī's "unity of being" only to defend an older, presumably more orthodox form of mysticism. Despite some impact, however, attempts of this kind remained isolated and were either ignored or reintegrated into the mainstream, until the coming of the modern reformers. The 19th- and 20th-century reformers Jamāl ad-Dīn al-Afghānī, Muḥammad ʿAbduh, and Muḥammad Iqbāl were initially educated in this tradition, but they rebelled against it and advocated radical reforms.

The modernists attacked the new wisdom at its weakest point; that is, its social and political norms, its individualistic ethics, and its inability to speak intelligently about social, cultural, and political problems generated by a long period of intellectual isolation that was further complicated by the domination of the European powers. Unlike the earlier tradition of Islāmic philosophy from al-Fārābī to Averroës, which had consciously cultivated political science and investigated the political dimension of philosophy and religion and the relation between philosophy and the community at large, the new wisdom from its inception lacked genuine interest in these questions, had no appreciation for political philosophy, and had only a benign toleration for the affairs of the world.

None of the reformers was a great political philosopher. They were concerned with reviving their nations' latent energies, urging them to free themselves from foreign domination, and impressing on them the need to reform their social and educational institutions. They also saw that all this required a total reorientation, which could not take place so long as the new wisdom remained not only the highest aim of a few solitary individuals but also a social and popular ideal as well. Yet, as late as 1917, Iqbāl found that "the present-day Muslim prefers to roam about aimlessly in the valley of Hellenic-Persian mysticism, which teaches us to shut our eyes to the hard reality around, and to fix our gaze on what is described as 'illumination.'" His reaction was harsh: "To me this self-mystification, this nihilism, *i.e.*, seeking reality where it does not exist, is a physiological symptom, giving me a clue to the decadence of the Muslim world."

The call to return to the early masters of Islāmic theology and philosophy

To arrest the decadence and infuse new vitality in a society in which they were convinced religion must remain the focal point, the modern reformers advocated a return to the movements and masters of Islāmic theology and philosophy antedating the new wisdom. They argued that these, rather than the "Persian incrustation of Islām," represented Islām's original and creative impulse. The modernists were attracted, in particular, to the views of the Muʿtazilah: affirmation of God's unity and denial of all similarity between him and created things; reliance on human reason; emphasis on man's freedom; faith in man's ability to distinguish between good and bad; and insistence on man's responsibility to do good and fight against evil in private and public places. They were also impressed by the traditionalists' devotion to the original, uncomplicated forms of Islām and by their fighting spirit, and by the Ashʿarīs' view of faith as an affair of the heart and their spirited defense of the Muslim community. In viewing the scientific and philosophic tradition of eastern and western Islām prior to the Tatar and Mongol invasions, they saw an irrefutable proof that true Islām stands for the liberation of man's spirit, promotes critical thought, and provides both the impetus to grapple with the temporal and the demonstration of how to set it in order. These ideas initiated what was to become a vast effort to recover, edit, and translate into the Muslim national languages works of earlier theologians and philosophers, which had been long neglected or known only indirectly through later accounts.

The role of universities in the reform of Islāmic theology and philosophy

The modern reformers insisted, finally, that Muslims must understand the real meaning of what has happened in Europe, which in effect meant to understand modern science and philosophy, including modern social or political philosophy. Initially, this became the task of the new universities in the Muslim world. In the latter part of the 20th century, however, the gap between the programs of theological and philosophic studies in religious colleges and in modern universities has been narrowed considerably. Conditions appear to be ripe for the appearance of thinkers who possess the gift for theological and philosophic inquiry and who understand that theology and philosophy are not national ideologies but genuine disciplines with unfinished tasks of their own.

BIBLIOGRAPHY. FRANZ ROSENTHAL (ed. and trans.), *Das Fortleben der Antike im Islam* (1965); and RICHARD WALZER, *Greek into Arabic: Essays on Islamic Philosophy* (1962), deal with the Greek and Hellenistic background and its appropriation. LOUIS GARDET and M.M. ANAWATI, *Introduction à la théologie musulmane*, 2nd ed. (1970), is a comprehensive handbook on Sunnī theology; and A.J. WENSINCK, *The Muslim Creed* (1932, reprinted 1965), discusses the background and development of Sunnī doctrines. The theology of the Shīʿah is given a prominent place in HENRY CORBIN, *Histoire de la philosophie islamique* (1964–); and its early development is discussed by WILFERD MADELUNG, *Der Imam al-Qāsim ibn Ibrāhīm und die Glaubenslehre der Zaiditen* (1965), and "Imamism and Muʿtazilite Theology," in *Le Shīʿisme imāmite*, pp. 13–30 (1970). M.M. SHARIF (ed.), *A History of Muslim Philosophy*, 2 vol. (1963–66), is a comprehensive collective work on the history of Islāmic philosophy and related subjects; it is especially useful for the later medieval and modern periods, particularly in respect to Iran and the Indian subcontinent. MAJID FAKHRY, *A History of Islamic Philosophy* (1970), is the most recent general history. FAZLUR RAHMAN discusses the development of the later synthesis between mysticism and philosophy in "Dream, Imagination and ʿĀlam al-Mithāl," *Islamic Studies*, 3:167–180 (1964); the introduction of *Selected Letters of Shaikh Aḥmad Sirhindī* (1968); and "The Eternity of the World and the Heavenly Bodies in Post-Avicennian Philosophy," in GEORGE HOURANI (ed.), *Essays on Islamic Philosophy and Science* (1973), a collection representing recent trends in interpreting Islāmic philosophy.

(M.S.M.)

Island Arcs

Island arcs are long curved chains of islands that form one of the most striking features of the land-sea pattern found on earth. In looking at a globe one must be impressed by the graceful sweep and huge scale of their necklace-like form. With the exception of the East Indian and the West Indian arcs, and the Scotia arc in the South Atlantic, all island arcs border the Pacific Basin, and most of them occur near its western margin. Island arcs occur over a broad range of latitudes and their climate and vegetation vary widely; sometimes variation exists within a single arc. In contrast to these geographical differences, many important geological features are common to the oceanic island arcs and for this reason they are considered as a distinctive structural class. In addition, other arcuate regions of the earth's land surface, such as the southern front of the Himalayas and much of the western part of South America, are geologically similar. These regions commonly are included in the same class, which is referred to simply as the arcs. The arcs of the world are as follows:

Arcuate regions

1. Aleutians-Alaska
2. Central America
3. West Indies or Caribbean
4. South America
5. Scotia
6. Tonga-Kermadec-New Zealand
7. New Hebrides
8. Solomons
9. New Britain-New Guinea
10. Philippines
11. Ryukyu
12. Japan
13. Kurile-Kamchatka
14. Bonins
15. Marianas
16. East Indies-Sunda
17. Burma
18. Himalayas
19. Zagros
20. Aegean
21. Carpathian
22. Italy

In addition to the distinctive surface pattern, some of the features of a typical island arc include: (1) long, narrow, deep-sea trenches along the convex side of the arc; such trenches are the sites of the greatest ocean depths; (2) a chain of volcanoes of the explosive type that form many of the islands of a single arc, or the inner row of islands of a double arc; (3) major seismic activity including large, shallow earthquakes and earthquake focuses located through a range of depths from near surface to as much as 700 kilometres below the surface; (4) raised beaches, uplifted strata, and folding and faulting, all of which indicate relatively recent tectonic activity or deformation of the earth's crust (most modern arcs appear to have developed during the Tertiary Period); and (5) narrow zones that exhibit minimum gravitational attraction parallel to the arc and centred just landward of the trench axis; the earth's largest negative gravity anomalies are found in these zones.

Such spectacular evidence for inequilibrium and great mobility of the earth's crust indicates that arcs have been key areas in the development of geological features of the earth. Geological evidence has demonstrated that mountain belts of the past, such as, the Sierra Nevada of California and the Appalachian Mountains of the eastern U.S., were, to a great extent, formed in ancient island arcs. In fact, many geologists would say that except for relatively undeformed sediments at or near the earth's surface virtually all the rocks of the continental crust have at one time been associated with mobile belts or arcs. Indeed, it would appear that continents may very well have grown by the accretion of crustal material formed in the arcs around their ancient cores, although this point is not free of controversy.

In the 1960s, there was advanced a new theory of earth tectonics that includes among its elements the drift of continents, spreading of the sea floor, and underthrusting of the oceanic crust beneath the island arcs. The theory provides explanations for many of the observations of geology and geophysics in terms of the relative movements and interactions of a small number of rigid plates of the earth's crust and upper mantle. Many diverse observations may perhaps be unified by this single concept, which has been termed the new global tectonics.

This article treats the physiography and distribution of island arcs, their ages, rock types, and geologic structure, the areas of active volcanism, various characteristics of trenches, and the available geophysical data. Hypotheses on the origin and significance of arcs are outlined and the relations of arcs to the new global tectonics are described in some detail. For further information on this latter topic, see SEA-FLOOR SPREADING; CONTINENTAL DRIFT; OCEANIC RIDGES; and MOUNTAIN-BUILDING PROCESSES. See also OCEAN BASINS; EARTH, PHYSIOGRAPHY OF; and VOLCANOES for related coverage of the physical characteristics of island arcs.

GEOMORPHIC CHARACTERISTICS

Typical features of island arcs

Above the surface of the water, a typical island arc (Figure 1) consists of two parallel, curved chains of islands, convex toward the deep ocean and concave toward the nearest continent. The outer row of islands is nonvolcanic and may partly consist of deep-sea sediments that have been raised far above the ocean floor. The inner arc is a site of active volcanism of the hazardous explosive type; classical volcanoes of conical shape and with relatively frequent eruptions occur on this chain. New "islands" occasionally appear in this row, although

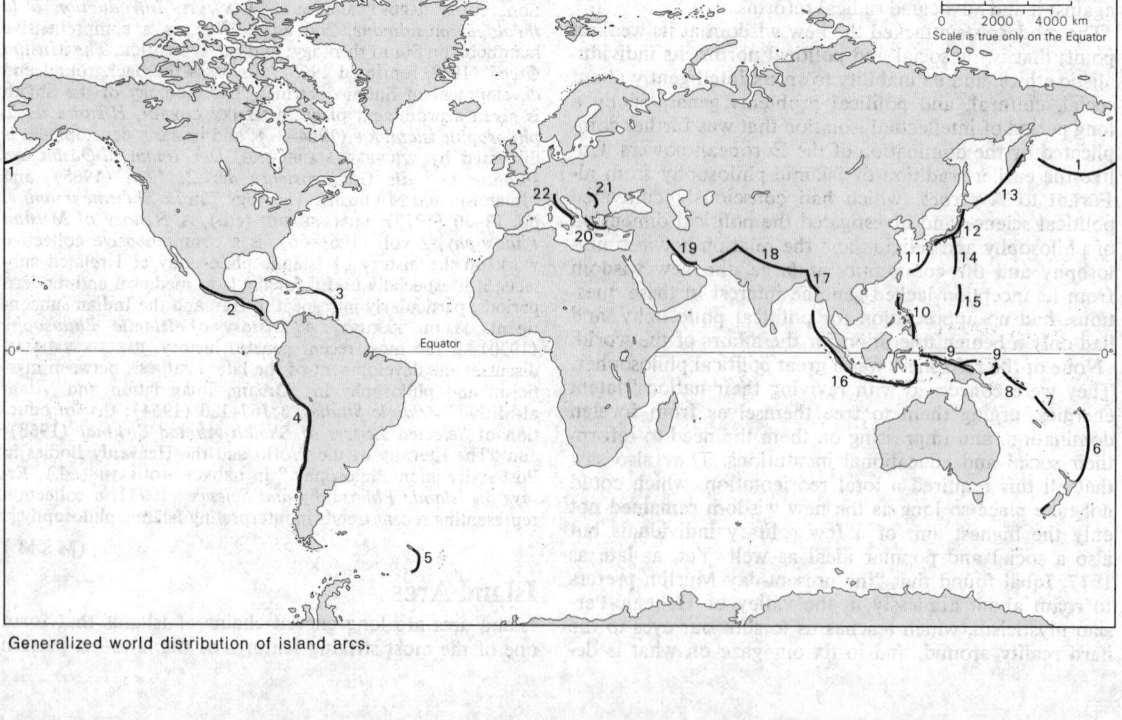

Generalized world distribution of island arcs.

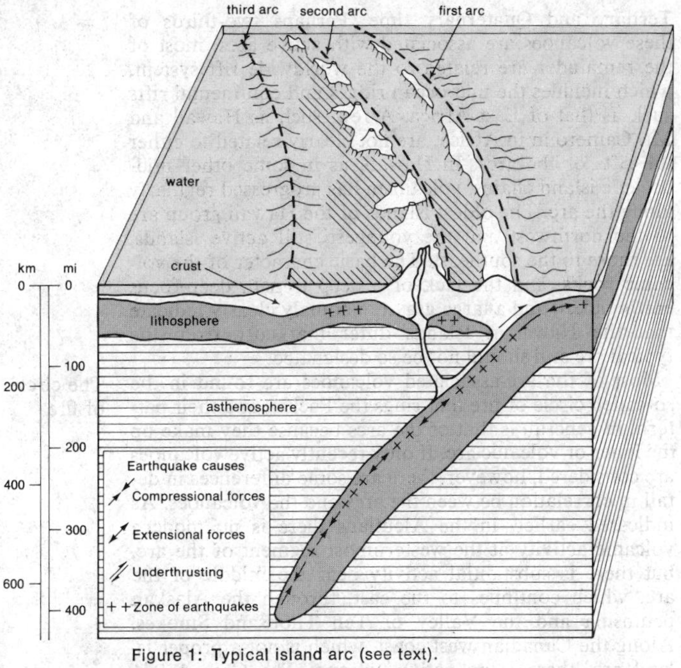

Figure 1: Typical island arc (see text).

historically, they subsequently have been quickly eroded away. Beneath the level of the water the typical arc shows the following features, beginning at the normal deep ocean floor and progressing across the trench and the arc: (1) a gentle topographic rise of the order of a few hundred metres with slopes normally less than 1 percent; (2) a reversal in slope followed by a zone of increasing depth and slope; the greatest slope ranges from a few percent to 10 percent at the outer wall of the trench, and in many trenches topographic depressions corresponding to the surface expressions of down-dropped blocks, or grabens, are observed here; (3) the floor of the trench, which is usually flat over the deepest portion as a result of partial filling by sediments. A typical deep trench has a maximum depth below sea level of seven to ten or more kilometres; (4) a zone of decreasing depth, the inner wall of the trench, with slopes generally steeper than those of the outer wall and frequently exceeding 10 percent. The inner wall sometimes has one or more prominent benches that sometimes dam or pond sediments, and the walls in general become less steep above the benches; (5) a ridge overlain by relatively shallow water, normally less than a kilometre or two in depth, from which the two rows of nonvolcanic and volcanic islands protrude, with the volcanic islands farthest from the trench; (6) an interarc basin characterized by rugged topography and water of intermediate depths, perhaps two to three kilometres. (7) A "third" arc with the same general trend as the main arc, shallow-water depths and, rarely, a few islands. This "third arc" is prominent in a few cases such as the Tonga-Kermadec Arc and the Mariana Arc but may not be perceived so readily in many arcs.

All arcs depart to some degree from the simple description given above. Many vary markedly in curvature along their course. Some arc segments, such as a large part of the Tonga-Kermadec Arc and the Chilean portion of the South American Arc are not true arcs at all in the strict sense because these two segments are best approximated by straight lines. These two zones have many of the other characteristics outlined above, however, and so are appropriately classed as arcs in this geological sense.

Variation of characteristics along the trend of an arc is quite common. At its western end the Aleutian Arc consists largely of islands whose volcanoes are inactive at present. Near the middle section of the arc the island chain consists primarily of active volcanoes. Near its eastern end the Aleutian Arc becomes double and then changes from an island arc to an arc that is continental as it merges into the Alaskan peninsula. The Aleutian Trench, some 4,000 kilometres (2,480 miles) in length, is, in common with most trenches, narrow and usually flat bottomed as a result of sediment accumulation. In general, the depths of the floors vary throughout their length; elongated basins of somewhat different depths are isolated from one another by sills. The Aleutian Trench has depths over 6,500 metres near its western end and deepens to well over 7,500 metres along the central portion of the arc. It shoals to the east until, southeast of the Alaskan peninsula, the trench is filled with sediments derived primarily from the Alaska mainland and is no longer apparent in the morphology of the ocean floor. Proximity to a rich sediment source thus appears to account, at least partly, for one of the characteristics of this trench. Comparable phenomena can be seen in other trenches. The Kurile Trench, for example, also shoals toward the north opposite the Kamchatka peninsula. The land elevations of the Aleutian Arc partially mimic the ocean depths, increasing some 2,000 metres from Attu on the west to Mt. Spurr on the Alaskan peninsula.

The Aleutian Trench

The Aleutian Trench, in common with several other trenches, such as the Philippine Trench, the Peru-Chile Trench, and the Java Trench, has a pronounced bench on its landward flank at a depth of about 2,000–2,500 fathoms (3,650–4,570 metres). This bench is generally continuous along most of the arc's length but is interrupted where the Adak Canyon crosses and apparently offsets it. The canyon may mark a fault that intersects the arc at a high angle. The northern slope of the Aleutian ridge is steep, indicative, according to one view, of normal faulting along the inner margin of the arc. Behind the Aleutian-Alaskan Arc, the Bering Sea is largely underlain by continental shelf to the east and by deep sea to the west. Within this western portion, beginning at about Amchitka Island and curving gently to the north and then west, is an arcuate submarine feature called Bowers Bank. This feature complicates the bathymetry and suggests the presence of an ancient arc because no modern seismic activity or volcanism is known to be associated with it.

The Middle America Trench, which borders the west coast of Central America, is perhaps representative of a trench associated with a continental arc; it resembles the Peru-Chile Trench in many ways. It is partly arcuate and partly linear and parallels the break in slope of the continental margin. A deeper southern section is separated from the shallower northern section by an offshore ridge. The floor of the trench is less regular to the north, and most active volcanism on land is associated with the deeper portion of the trench to the south.

No general description of arcs would be complete without special mention of the linked arcs of New Britain, the Solomons, and the New Hebrides. These arcs are exceptional in that they are convex toward the continental area and the trenches are on the side of the arc nearest the continent (Australia). Other asymmetric features of these arcs also are oriented oppositely to those of most arcs. The zone of deep earthquakes dips away from the continent, and the volcanoes are seaward of the trenches. The bathymetry is further complicated in this region by the occurrence of a system of trenches that includes the Cape Johnson and the Vityaz trenches on the concave side of the Solomon and New Hebrides arcs.

Thus, the remarkable first-order similarity of the physiography of the island arcs and their associated submarine features is most impressive; so too, is the great variety of second-order or subsidiary features.

GEOLOGY AND STRUCTURE OF ISLAND ARCS

Ages and types of rocks. Deciphering the geology of island arcs is exceptionally difficult for a number of reasons. In many cases, much of the rock is water-covered and can be sampled at only a few locations. Island arcs in warmer climates often are mantled with coral, which conceals the bedrock. In addition, because fossils are rare because of the volcanism, dating is difficult. In spite of these limitations, a reasonably consistent view of the general geology of arcs has been attained.

Although some modern arcs, such as the Japanese arc, include rocks of Paleozoic age or older, it appears that modern active arcs began their development, or were again uplifted, during Late Tertiary time. The modern arcs are thus very young features of the earth's surface but the geologic record indicates that arcs have been important in the earth's development since Precambrian time.

Volcanic rocks and the andesite line

There is a remarkable contrast between the volcanic rocks of the arcs and those of the mid-oceanic islands such as Hawaii, Easter Island, or Tristan da Cunha. The mid-ocean rocks are largely of the olivine-basalt-trachyte association, whereas those of the arcs are of the andesite-dacite-rhyolite association. The andesitic rocks are more typical of the continental crust than are the olivine rocks. This sharp distinction led to the designation "andesite line," which skirts the outer boundaries of the Pacific arcs and separates those areas in which andesites occur from the Pacific Basin proper. For many years the andesite line was considered the limit of the sialic (continental crust), for it was thought that the andesites were derived from association with such a crust. This view is no longer generally held, however, and there is now ample evidence that sialic crust, at least of continental thickness, is lacking for certain sea floors between continents and arcs.

Where it is possible to obtain good information on the types of volcanic rocks that have erupted during the last 2,000,000 years, approximately, the rock types exhibit a consistent pattern; similar rock types trend parallel to the arc and significantly different rock types occur along a line perpendicular to the arc. On the ocean side the rocks are less alkalic and more siliceous (tholeiite); they become more alkalic and less siliceous (alkali-olivine-basalt) on the continental side. The variation appears to be continuous and suggests to petrologists that toward the continent the rocks are derived from deeper within the mantle. Correlation of certain rock properties, such as potash content, with the depth of the underlying seismic zone suggests that the magmas originate in the deep earthquake zones.

Non-volcanic rocks

Some arcs, such as the East Indian and South American arcs, include large masses of intrusive igneous rock of granitic character. The intrusion of granitic magmas that formed the batholiths probably was associated with the eruption of andesitic magmas in ancient arcs. The batholiths dominate the terrain (Sierra Nevada of California, for example) after the overlying volcanic and sedimentary rocks are eroded away.

Derived from the volcanic and plutonic rocks of the arcs are graywacke and arkosic sediments that, in the ancient arcs, have been subjected to high pressure–low temperature metamorphism in some areas. The Mesozoic Franciscan Formation of California is one example; this rock type is also fairly common in ancient arcs elsewhere.

At certain localities on outer nonvolcanic arcs, notably Barbados of the West Indian Arc and Timor of the East Indian Arc, sediments that were deposited on the deep-sea floor are found in a deformed state above sea level. This indicates great magnitudes of uplift for such areas and suggests that the sediments have been squeezed up as a result of tectonic pressures. Drilling has confirmed the similarity of deep-sea sediments east of the West Indian Arc and those of Barbados. Evidence for very recent uplift of Barbados, in the form of a series of raised beaches, is very convincing.

Ultrabasic rocks (those with a very high content of iron and magnesium minerals) are commonly found in arcs and investigators originally noted this from the presence of serpentinized peridotites in the most intensely deformed part of the arc, namely, that associated with the outer nonvolcanic arc and with the largest negative gravity anomalies. These facts suggest that the ultrabasic rocks have come from the mantle in some manner and suggest again the exceptional mobility of the rocks in island arcs.

Areas of active volcanism. About 800 volcanoes are known to have been active during historic time and many thousands more were active at some time during Late Tertiary and Quaternary time. Perhaps two-thirds of these volcanoes are associated with active arcs; most of the remainder are related to the worldwide rift system, which includes the mid-ocean ridges and continental rifts such as that of East Africa. A few, such as Hawaii and Mt. Cameroun in Africa, are not clearly related to either the rifts or the arcs. In Hawaii, as in some other mid-oceanic island chains, volcanism has progressed regularly along the arc. The oldest islands of the Hawaii group are to the northwest and the youngest, still active islands, are those to the southeast. The basic character of the volcanic rocks, and the lack of a deep trench, deep-focus earthquakes, and a large gravity anomaly clearly indicate that the Hawaiian Islands differ markedly from the typical arc and should not be so designated.

The circle of fire

Most of the arc-associated volcanoes are found in the so-called circle of fire that rings the Pacific, and their pattern, in general, is that of the arcs because they make up the inner or volcanic arc. If only recently active volcanoes are considered, however, there are some differences in detail in correlation between the arcs and the volcanoes. As indicated earlier, in the Aleutians there is no modern volcanic activity at the westernmost segment of the arc, but there is substantial activity near the middle of the arc, which continues to the east, through the Alaskan peninsula and the Valley of Ten Thousand Smokes. Along the Canadian west coast, which is not a proper island arc, there is no active volcano. The Cascades in Washington and Oregon are active andesitic volcanoes not associated with an arc that is active at present, but it appears that the tectonic pattern has changed recently in this area and that this volcanic activity is a remnant of a former arc. There is considerable volcanism in Mexico along an east-west trend that includes Popocatepetl and Parícutin and also along the west coast of Central America where it is associated with the Middle America Trench. Volcanic activity occurs at a number of sites along the western coast of South America, but this belt ends just south of 40° S.

The North Island of New Zealand is the southern extremity of the volcanic activity of the Tonga-Kermadec Arc. The belt continues to the north and west and includes volcanoes in the New Hebrides and Solomon Islands and in New Guinea. West of New Guinea, the belt of activity bifurcates; one belt passes through the Philippines, Taiwan, and Japan and continues up the Kurile Arc into Kamchatka, where this trend ceases abruptly at about the point where the Aleutian trend intersects the Kamchatka Peninsula. A spur south from Japan through the Bonin Islands is very active. The other belt from New Guinea passes westward through the highly active East Indian arc that includes the famous Krakatoa and terminates at Barren Island west of Burma.

Although the geologic information and the seismicity indicate continuation of the tectonic belt through the Himalayas, no active volcanism is found in this segment of the belt. Just south of the Caspian Sea active volcanism is again found and the belt continues through Mt. Ararat into Greece. In the Alpine belt activity is limited, but the famous volcanoes of Italy and Sicily are prominent. The Pacific "circle of fire" makes two forays into the Atlantic, one ringing the Caribbean, and one, the Scotia Sea. In both cases modern volcanism is largely confined to the easternmost portions of these arcs.

Sedimentation in trenches. In the deep oceans the solubility of calcium carbonate ($CaCO_3$) varies with pressure and other factors and calcareous materials are not found below a certain depth. This depth varies slightly from place to place but is normally about five kilometres.

Red clay and other deep sea sediments

At greater depths most of the ocean floor is covered with red clay, and rates of sedimentation of red clay are quite low, of the order of one or two millimetres per 1,000 years. The deep-sea trenches are generally well below the carbonate level, but the sediments do not consist solely of red clay. Because of their exceptional depths, and in many cases their proximity to sources of abundant sediments from the continents, the trenches serve as traps for these sediments. Land-derived sediments are transported from shallow water to the deeps by turbidity currents, rapidly flowing turbulent streams of high-density mixtures of water and detritus. Sometimes rather coarse particles are included in this detritus.

Studies of bottom sediments of trenches often reveal progressive tilting of successively deeper layers toward the inner portion of the arc. This observation implies movement of the bedrock floor. Beneath the flat-lying trench deposits, a normal, deep-sea sedimentary layer rests upon the dipping bedrock surface. At the inner wall of the trench the relatively undisturbed flat-lying sediments abut a mass of contorted sediments that appear to have been folded and faulted. This suggests that the sediments have been piled up against the inner wall of the trench as the sea floor moved down into the mantle beneath the arc.

Not all of the inner wall of the trench is covered by sediments. Ultrabasic rocks, apparently derived from outcrops, have been dredged from the walls of certain trenches. Graben-like structures frequently observed in the sediments and in the bedrock along the outer wall of the trench indicate that extensional forces have affected this zone.

The volume of sediment within a trench varies greatly from trench to trench depending upon such factors as age, degree of activity, and sediment supply. The highly active Tonga Trench, for example, has almost no sediments, nor is there a nearby source whereas the eastern part of the Aleutian Trench is virtually filled with the abundant sediments from Alaska. The general paucity of sediments on the deep ocean floor and in the trenches is extremely difficult to account for if it is assumed that the present ocean basins always existed. All aspects of deep-sea sedimentation appear to fit rather well the new global tectonics and the concept of mobility of island arcs.

Deep structure of arcs; gravity, magnetism, heat flow, and seismic data. The exclusive association of deep-focus earthquakes and island arcs indicates that large, deep structures in the crust and upper mantle must form a part of the arcs. Seismic information based on earthquake and explosion sources, and observations of gravity, magnetism, and heat flow have contributed greatly to understanding of the arcs and have provided almost all of the information on their deep structure.

Occurrence of earthquakes

The section shown in Figure 1 indicates that the upper boundary of the primary zone of seismic focuses is located near the surface by the landward side of the trench. This zone extends along a curve of gradually increasing dip. Below a depth of about 100 kilometres the dip of the zone in this average arc remains fairly constant at about 45° and continues to a depth of about 700 kilometres. Actually, there are great local variations in the dips of the deep zones; locally, dips might vary from a few degrees to 90 degrees, but 45 degrees is a good representative value. The important fact is that the focuses are confined to a very thin zone, normally less than 50 kilometres in thickness. Nearly all earthquakes not associated with arcs are shallow (60 kilometres or less in depth) and this means that all seismic activity in the earth is limited to a number of very thin slabs of large lateral extent. These volumes are sometimes contorted and oddly shaped, but in no case do earthquakes define a volume in which the smallest dimension is much larger than 50 kilometres.

The shallow earthquakes correspond to underthrusting of the ocean crust at shallow angles beneath the crust of the arc. At greater depths, the principal stresses are oriented along the dip of the deep zone, but whether the force is compressional or extensional in a given case depends on the particular arc and the particular depth of focus of that earthquake. Shallow shocks beneath the trench indicate horizontal extension normal to the trench; shallow shocks behind the island arcs are harder to classify, and horizontal forces normal to the arc appear to dominate. The bulk of the seismic activity for most arcs corresponds to shallow underthrusting inward from the axis of the trench. Most of the seismic energy is released here, and the basic processes forming the island arc must be involved.

That deep earthquakes occur behind arcs and not elsewhere is an indication of the anomalous character of the upper mantle in the vicinity of the arcs. Additional strong evidence is based on the propagation characteristics of seismic waves travelling through the deep seismic zone. They travel significantly faster and with much less attenuation in this zone than do waves passing through comparable parts of the mantle in other areas. Such data, when studied in detail, indicate that there exists beneath the arc an inclined slablike zone of the order of 100 kilometres in thickness, defined essentially by the zone of deep earthquake focuses (Figure 1). The properties of the slab are low attenuation, high velocity, capacity for earthquakes, and strength. These properties are comparable to those of the shallow mantle in more stable parts of the world, and hence this configuration suggests that shallow mantle has been thrust beneath the island arcs down into the mantle to depths of at least 700 kilometres.

From R. Raitt, R. Fisher, and R. Mason (1955) Geological Society of America Special Paper 62

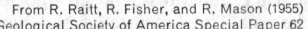

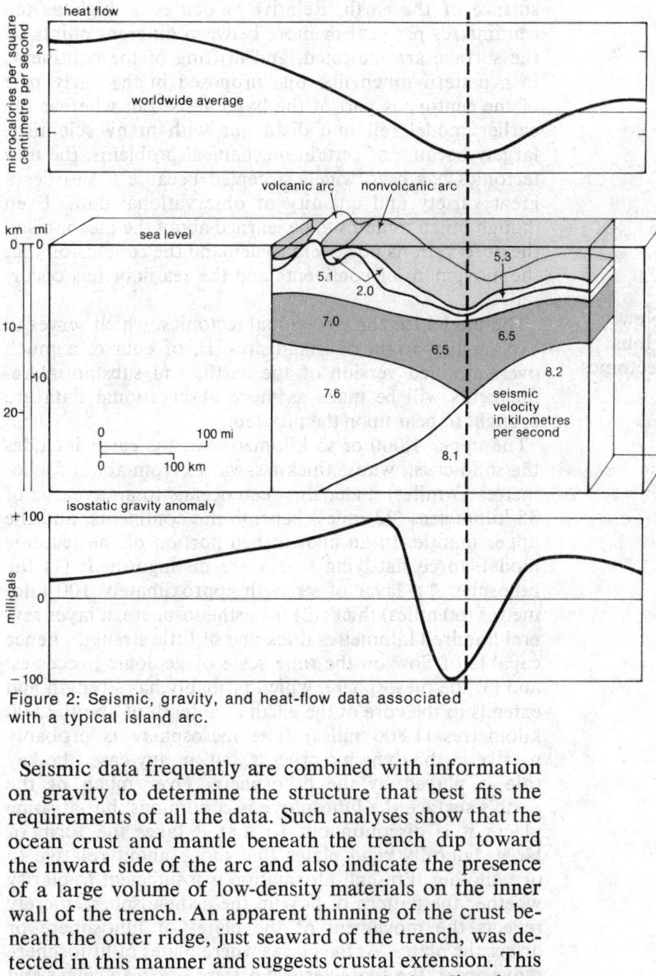

Figure 2: Seismic, gravity, and heat-flow data associated with a typical island arc.

Seismic data frequently are combined with information on gravity to determine the structure that best fits the requirements of all the data. Such analyses show that the ocean crust and mantle beneath the trench dip toward the inward side of the arc and also indicate the presence of a large volume of low-density materials on the inner wall of the trench. An apparent thinning of the crust beneath the outer ridge, just seaward of the trench, was detected in this manner and suggests crustal extension. This extension can be nicely reconciled with the bending down of the crust and mantle in this area and need not indicate that the arcs formed by extensional forces as sometimes suggested.

There is an inherent ambiguity in the analysis of gravity data, and no unique structure can be determined from it. In the case of the arcs, the measured gravity anomalies can be accounted for by density and structural variations within the crust, but they also fit the underthrust slab structure implied by the earthquake data. The slab, more dense than the surrounding medium (and hence sinking), accounts for the broad positive anomaly associated with arcs, whereas shallow structure related to the trench accounts for the sharper negative anomaly. Thus the gravity data, although not definitive, supports the model based on other types of information.

The observed pattern of heat flow in the vicinity of arcs

shows two consistent features. In and near the trenches, heat flow is subnormal. Behind the arcs, it is above normal. The high heat flow behind the arcs is probably due to flow within the earth that brings heat from below toward the surface, but this point is still speculative. The low heat flow in the trench area can readily be explained by the sinking of cold material into the upper mantle there.

ORIGIN OF ISLAND ARCS

In the early 1960s, largely as a result of new information that had accumulated on the ocean areas since the end of World War II, it was proposed that the sea floor was spreading apart along the active mid-ocean ridges, that new crustal material was being created there, and that crustal material was being lost by descent into the mantle at the sites of the ocean deeps. This hypothesis, although resembling in some ways ideas that had been proposed earlier, fell on fertile ground and a new era in geology began. The keynote of the new era is mobility of the surface of the earth. Relative velocities as high as ten centimetres per year or more between different points on the surface are indicated, and drifting of the continents in a pattern much like one proposed in the early part of the century is part of the hypothesis. But whereas the earlier model fell into disfavour with many scientists, largely because of certain mechanical problems, the new tectonics has been widely accepted because it satisfies a great variety and quantity of observational data. Even though much remains to be learned about the mechanism, the observations now seem to demand the conclusion that the movement of continents and the sea floor has occurred.

New global tectonics

The model for the new global tectonics, which serves to explain the origin of island arcs, is, of course, a much oversimplified version of the earth, and substantial refinements will be made as more observational data are brought to bear upon the problem.

The upper 1,000 or so kilometres of the earth includes the solid crust, whose thickness varies from about 5 kilometres (3 miles) under the deep oceans to an average of 35 kilometres (22 miles) beneath the continents, and the upper mantle. In an undisturbed portion of the tectonic model, three flat-lying layers are distinguished; (1) the lithosphere, a layer of strength approximately 100 kilometres (60 miles) thick; (2) the asthenosphere, a layer several hundred kilometres thick and of little strength, hence capable of flow on the time scale of geologic processes; and (3) the mesosphere, which probably has strength and extends to the core of the earth at a depth of about 2,900 kilometres (1,800 miles). The mesosphere is probably passive in the dynamic process, but, in any case, the key role is played by the lithosphere. Over much of the earth's surface the lithosphere is continuous, but at some places it is discontinuous so that it takes the form of large, laterally rigid plates that move about relative to one another. Present information is insufficient to clarify whether the pattern of flow in the asthenosphere merely reflects the movement of the plates of lithosphere or drives the plates. At the places where plates of lithosphere move apart, the characteristic pattern of ocean ridges and transform faults is found at the mid-ocean ridges. Where plates slide past one another, major transcurrent faults such as the San Andreas of California are found. Where plates converge, one is thrust beneath the other and the phenomenon of the arc occurs. Thus, the slab of lithosphere plunging beneath the arc as detected from seismic studies is an essential and integral part of this model. As cold, descending, former surface material, the slab accounts, among other things, for the low heat flow in the vicinity of the trench.

Major plates and their motions

There are thought to be six major plates and a number of smaller ones on the earth, all of which move about relative to one another much in the manner of ice floes on the arctic seas. In principle, it is possible to determine, from the pattern of magnetic anomalies on the sea floor and from the topography of the oceanic fracture zones, the velocity at any point on each of these plates relative to that of any point on any other plate. In practice, this has so far been done for only the six larger plates and a few of the smaller ones. The results are an oversimplification because the velocities and the configuration and numbers of plates have changed through time. Nevertheless, the rates are significant because it is at the zones of convergence that the arcs occur. There is, in fact, a remarkable correlation between rates of convergence and many features of the arcs such as locations of deep-sea trenches, andesitic volcanism, and deep earthquake zones. In fact, the length down the dip of a given deep earthquake zone can be shown to be proportional to the rate of convergence for that locality. The length is such that a time of about 10,000,000 years is required for the downgoing slab to have travelled to its current position. This means either that 10,000,000 years is the duration of the latest cycle of sea-floor spreading or that after this time span the slab is modified, probably by heating, so that it can no longer support earthquakes.

The correlation between earthquake depth, volcanism, and convergence rate holds in great detail in some cases. This is particularly remarkable and impressive in view of the highly oversimplified nature of the model. In the Aleutian-Alaskan Arc, for example, to the east, where the direction of plate movement is perpendicular to the arc and underthrusting is substantial, earthquakes of considerable depth and active volcanism are found; to the west, where the motion predicted by the model is predominantly transcurrent, no deep earthquakes and active volcanoes are found. Similar relations are found for other arcs. The focal mechanisms of earthquakes, both shallow and deep, are in general accord with the model as well, not only for the Aleutians but also for the remainder of the world.

The slab of lithosphere probably descends into the mantle beneath the arc because it is more dense than the surrounding mantle (a fact that also accounts for the broad positive gravity anomaly). Thus, earthquakes of moderate depths in certain regions indicate extensional forces along the dip and suggest that the lower portion of the slab is pulling the upper part down. In arcs in which the slab has penetrated to great depths, the forces along the dip of the slab are compressive and suggest that the slab has encountered significant resistance to further penetration.

The driving mechanism probably is the internal heat of the earth, which may include the initial heat of formation, gravitational energy converted to heat, and radioactive heat, but other possibilities are the energy of the tides and the energy of the rotation of the earth. This important problem will occupy scientists in the future, and further study of the arcs is almost certain to provide crucial information. Knowledge of arcs, however, already has begun to resolve other important problems. The Mesozoic geology of California, for example, with its formerly enigmatic Franciscan Formation, its ultrabasic rocks and its batholiths, has been explained in considerable detail. The Paleozoic geology of the Appalachians and their trans-Atlantic extension, the Caledonides, has been described by a model in which a proto-Atlantic opened in Late Precambrian times, spread apart, then closed during Ordovician and Devonian time, forming arcs along the margins of the oceans during the closing stage of the process. The present rocks of these areas bear evidence of the former arcs there, and study of these ancient arcs stimulates the study of modern arcs, and vice versa. These interpretations of the geology of certain areas are new and have not yet withstood the scientific tests of careful scrutiny by the entire scientific community but they offer the promise of a much improved basic understanding of the earth.

BIBLIOGRAPHY. M. BARAZANGI and J. DORMAN, "World Seismicity Maps Compiled from ESSA, Coast and Geodetic Survey, Epicenter Data, 1961–1967," *Bull. Seismolog. Soc. Am.*, 59:369–380 (1969), the best available set of maps on worldwide seismicity, including separate maps for various depth ranges; R.L. FISHER and H.H. HESS, "Trenches," in M.N. HILL (ed.), *The Sea: The Earth Beneath the Sea—Concepts,*

3:411–436 (1963), a summary of available information; D.E. HAYES and M. EWING, "Pacific Boundary Structure," in A.E. MAXWELL (ed.), *The Sea*, vol. 4 (1970), a summary of the geophysics of Pacific arcs; J.R. HEIRTZLER, "Sea-Floor Spreading," *Scient. Am.*, 216:60–70 (Dec. 1968), a general summary of the concepts of sea-floor spreading and its development; A. HOLMES, *Principles of Physical Geology*, rev. ed. (1965), an elementary text on physical geology that includes thorough discussions of island arcs, volcanism, and earth tectonics; B. ISACKS, J. OLIVER, and L.R. SYKES, "Seismology and the New Global Tectonics," *J. Geophys. Res.*, 73:5855–5899 (1968), a comprehensive summary of the relations between all the hard observational data of seismology and modern concepts of continental drift and sea-floor spreading; J.A. JACOBS, R.D. RUSSELL, and J.T. WILSON, *Physics and Geology* (1959), a general text on geology and geophysics written before the era of the new global tectonics; J.H.F. UMBGROVE, *The Pulse of the Earth* (1947), a good summary of information on geology and physiography of island arcs, although the tectonic hypotheses described are no longer widely supported.

(J.E.O.)

Isocrates

A famous rhetorician and educator at Athens, Isocrates is a key figure in understanding Athenian intellectual and political life in the 4th century BC. He founded a school to provide an education markedly different in its aims from the Academy of Plato and numbering among its pupils men of eminence from all over the Greek world. He was a literary influence of major importance. His writings provide a precious commentary on the political developments of his time, and, although he can by no means be regarded as one of Athens' greatest intellects, he has been studied constantly and with great attention.

Factors shaping Isocrates' political views

Born into a prosperous family in 436—shortly before the outbreak of the Peloponnesian War (431–404)—Isocrates passed his youth in a gloomy period following the death of Pericles, the great Athenian leader and statesman, a period in which wealth—both public and private—was dissipated, and political decisions were ill-conceived and violent. He would have been 14 years old when the democracy voted to put to death all male citizens of the small Thracian city of Scione. Isocrates was deeply moved by a desire to see Greece united and at peace and was influenced by, among others, the Sicilian sophist Gorgias, who not only inspired his pupil with a taste for Gorgianic prose but also put before him as the cure for Greece's ills the Panhellenist program; that is, union of Greeks in an attack on the Persian empire and the settlement therein of the impoverished, thus securing peace between and within cities. This became and remained Isocrates' political creed.

In the closing years of the Peloponnesian War, Isocrates lost his inherited wealth and began to earn money by writing speeches for others to use in the courts. A few of these speeches survive. This was, in fact, the conventional start to a career as an orator, but since he lacked both the voice and the self-confidence necessary for a public speaker he turned his attention to education, and for over 40 years his main effort was to prepare for successful public life those who could afford to pay his heavy fees. Of his hundred pupils the most notable were Timotheus, the Athenian general, prominent in Athens' history between 378 and 355; Nicocles, the ruler of Salamis in Cyprus; and the two greatest Greek historians of the 4th century, Ephorus—who wrote a universal history—and Theopompus—who wrote the history of Philip II of Macedon. In this way his influence permeated both politics and literature. At the same time he continued to publish a series of speeches on the state of Athens and of Greece. How far these influenced his contemporaries has been fruitlessly debated. Their importance for historians is that they provide an index of Panhellenist, conservative Greek opinion, and whoever reads with attention the "Panegyric" (380), "On Peace" (355), "On the Areopagus" (354?), "To Philip" (346), and the "Panathenaic" oration (begun 342, completed 339) will have gained considerably in understanding of the larger issues of the age.

Isocrates, however, was a man of no great intellectual power, and it is not surprising to find him contemptuous of the philosophical subtleties of the Platonic circle. He cared above all for polished expression; he is said to have taken ten years in the composition of the "Panegyric," and a man who could expend effort on such showpieces of oratory as the "Encomium of Helen" (390) clearly had little of real intellectual importance to say. His defects and his preferences showed themselves in the system of education that he developed. Unfortunately, his discussion in the speeches "Against the Sophists" and in "On the Exchange" tells one more of what he objected to in other systems than of what he actually had in his own, but it can be safely asserted that, whereas the training of the Platonic Academy was essentially philosophical, that of Isocrates was almost entirely given over to rhetoric, the art of persuasion. There is indeed a strong suspicion that Isocrates would lend his talents to any cause whatsoever, merely for the pleasure of presenting it well. The so-called Cyprian orations—"To Nicocles" (*c.* 372), the "Nicoles" (*c.* 368), and the "Evagoras" (*c.* 365)—are concerned with the laudations of monarchs, while the "Archidamus" (366) puts into the mouth of the heir to one of the Spartan kings a speech full of praise for Sparta and Spartanism. One is correspondingly less impressed when in the "Panegyric" and "Panathenaic" orations he professed admiration for Athens. Such exaltation of style and indifference to matter is contemptible, and, insofar as his purpose in his system of education appears to have been to train others to a similar facility, he can hardly escape the censure he accorded to other rhetorical schools.

Isocrates as a rhetorician

Isocrates did have beliefs, however, some of which are revealed in "On the Areopagus," composed at the end of the Social War, when Athens' fortunes were at their lowest for 50 years. In this work he commends the ancient constitution of Athens, under which the aristocratic council of the Areopagus exercised a general supervision over the conduct of citizens. Isocrates' proposals for returning to the system in operation before the days of democracy were not practical but display profoundly conservative inclinations. His other mainstay was Panhellenism, and this is what chiefly interests historians. In the "Panegyric" he developed the theme that many, notably Gorgias and the rhetorician Lysias, had recently argued: he called on Sparta to establish concord in Greece by recognizing the fitness and right of Athens to share with Sparta hegemony in Greece and by proceeding with the national crusade against Persia. This amounted to a reassertion of the political faith of the great 5th-century opponent of Persia, Cimon. Over 30 years later, in the letter "To Philip," Isocrates appealed to the King of Macedonia to reconcile the Greeks and lead them against Persia. Since Philip was on the point of intervening in Greece to settle the Second Sacred War (355–346), many have believed that Isocrates was prepared to submit his country to an outside master. This is unjust, for Isocrates, a political innocent, had only the vaguest idea of what the consequences of such a policy might be. He had in fact made earlier similar appeals to Agesilaus, king of Sparta, to Dionysius I, tyrant of Syracuse, and to Alexander, tyrant of Pherae in Thessaly, none of whom could conceivably have become political master of Greece. The truth is that Isocrates was seeking merely a military leader. These earlier appeals came to nothing, and in the 350s, when Greece was divided first by the Social War, precipitated by the Athenian policy of sending cleruchies (colonizing groups) to Samos, the subjection of Cos and Naxos to Athenian jurisdiction, and the arbitrary demands of Athenian generals for money, and then by the Sacred War, fought as a result of the refusal of the Phocians to pay a fine levied by the Amphictyons, and when Persia was again threatening, there could be no question of Greece uniting to attack. Isocrates thus had to confine himself to pleading for peace, notably in the speech "On Peace" at the end of the Social War. The rise of Philip led him to hope that all was not lost—he had his general at last. But he never paused to ask what would happen to Greece when Macedonia had succeeded in gratifying Panhellenist dreams. And, when all hopes for peaceful relations between Athens and

Isocrates' disillusionment and death

Philip faded, he promptly forgot about Philip, and in his last great speech, the "Panathenaic" oration, Philip has no part. After the Battle of Chaeronea, at which Greek independence was lost and as a result of which Philip indeed became master, Isocrates in despair starved himself to death (338).

Historians debate whether he was the prophet of the Hellenistic world, that great expansion of Hellenism resulting from the foundation of cities in Asia by Philip's son Alexander the Great and his successors. Certainly, he adhered to the Panhellenist idea that Asia should be colonized by the Greeks, but he appears to have envisaged no more than the colonization of Asia Minor, and the actual Macedonian settlements were far from the comfortable retreats Isocrates had dreamed of for the poor of Greece. He had, furthermore, merely thought of exporting the poor. He had no vision of the great new common market that would save Greece from misery. So perhaps the title prophet is too much. But he did see that at the heart of Greek troubles was poverty, and in his unwavering belief in colonization he showed a common sense denied in this matter to his greater contemporaries, Plato and Aristotle.

BIBLIOGRAPHY. *Isocrates*, 3 vol. ("Loeb Classical Library," 1928–45, reprinted 1954–56); ALBIN LESKY, *Geschichte der griechischen Literatur*, 2nd ed. (1963; Eng. trans., *A History of Greek Literature*, 1966), gives an up-to-date statement (pp. 582–591) of Isocrates' literary achievement and importance; GEORGE A. KENNEDY, *The Art of Persuasion in Greece* (1963), surveys and assesses the contribution of Isocrates to Greek rhetoric; GEORGES MATHIEU, *Les Idées politiques d'Isocrate* (1925), provides a full account of the dating, circumstances, and importance of the political writings of Isocrates; N.H. BAYNES, *Byzantine Studies and Other Essays*, pp. 144–167 (1955), makes a spirited attack on Isocrates' intellectual standing and integrity and claims to expose the shameful self-interest that inspired his work; H.I. MARROU, *Histoire de l'éducation dans l'antiquité* (1948; Eng. trans., *A History of Education in Antiquity*, 1956), assesses Isocrates' place in the history of education, and particularly in relation to Plato; KLAUS BRINGMANN, *Studien zu den politischen Ideen des Isokrates* (1965), contains ample bibliography.

(G.L.Ca.)

Isomerism

The laws of chemical bonding sometimes permit a given set of atoms to be combined in more than one way, so that two or more substances may exist that have identical chemical composition but different atomic arrangements. Such substances are called isomers, and the phenomenon is known as isomerism. The term was derived in 1830 by a Swedish chemist Jöns Jacob Berzelius, probably from the Greek words *isos* ("same") and *meros* ("part").

Isomerism is important because the properties of chemical substances depend not only on the number and kinds of atoms present but also on their arrangement. Two isomeric substances may have different physical, chemical, and biological properties; to comprehend these differences it is necessary to understand how the substances differ structurally. Sometimes rather subtle structural differences or configurations in otherwise identical molecules determine whether a substance is rendered toxic or harmless, explosive or inert, or effective or inactive as a drug.

GENERAL CONSIDERATIONS

Atomic structure. The composition of matter, knowledge of which is necessary for an understanding of isomerism, is best understood in terms of the existence of very small particles called atoms that can combine with each other in different ways. There are millions of distinguishable forms of matter, all built up from only about 100 different kinds of atoms, each kind comprising one of the chemical elements. Atoms, in turn, are composed of a few kinds of even simpler particles combined in an orderly way that underlies the occurrence of groups of elements having related properties.

Practically all the mass of an atom is concentrated in its nucleus, which contains protons, each possessing a positive electrical charge, and neutrons, which are electrically uncharged. The number of protons in the nucleus, which establishes the atomic number, also determines the chemical identity of the atom: an atom containing only one proton in its nucleus is a hydrogen atom; one containing six is a carbon atom; and one containing 92 is a uranium atom. The number of neutrons usually is similar to the number of protons, but atoms of every element are furthermore known to exist in forms, called isotopes, that differ in the number of neutrons that are present. Because a neutron has appreciable mass, atoms of the different isotopes of an element have different masses, although their chemical properties differ only minutely.

Nuclei and electrons

Surrounding the nucleus is a cloud of electrons, particles with very little mass but each with a negative electrical charge. The electrons occupy regions of space called orbitals, which differ in shape, orientation, and average distance from the nucleus. The orbitals, each of which can accommodate two electrons, are arranged in shells of increasing distance from the nucleus, each successive shell being composed of a larger number of orbitals.

The electrons in a given atom are distributed among the orbitals so as to strike a balance between the attraction of the nucleus for all the electrons and the repulsion between each electron and all the others. In any atom, the electrons occupying the outermost shell are the least tightly bound to the nucleus and, thus, are the ones affected by the approach of other atoms; that is, these outermost, or valence, electrons, are those involved in chemical reactions and bond formation. Fundamentally, isomerism involves alternate patterns of bond formation between specific atoms in a molecule.

Electronic structure and bonding. Certain arrangements of electrons are more stable than others; *e.g.*, the presence of eight electrons (the maximum possible) in the outermost shell represents an especially stable condition. Atoms having only a few valence electrons and eight electrons in the next underlying shell tend to lose their valence electrons: the resulting particle (no longer an atom, but an ion) has fewer electrons than protons and is positively charged. Similarly, an atom needing only a few electrons to complete an outermost shell of eight tends to gain the needed electrons, also becoming an ion (in this case, negatively charged). Oppositely charged ions attract each other and form crystalline compounds in which each ion occupies a position in a definite lattice-like pattern. The ionic bonds existing in these structures do not connect any particular pair of ions but act equally in all directions. The compositions of these compounds are expressed by formulas indicating the proportions of the various ions: the compound sodium chloride (common salt) contains equal numbers of sodium ions (denoted by the symbol of the element and a superscript signifying the electrical charge, Na^+) and chloride ions (Cl^-), and its formula is NaCl. Isomerism is concerned less with this kind of bonding than with another type, called covalent.

Ionic compounds

Atoms that could be converted into ions only by the gain or loss of several electrons often form compounds by a different process. Rather than gaining or losing electrons outright, two atoms will take up positions close together so that each can provide one, two, or three electrons in the formation of a single, double, or triple covalent bond. In these compounds, specific groups of atoms remain linked together by the interaction of the shared electrons in stable associations called molecules. Formulas of covalent compounds express the exact numbers of atoms of the various elements present in a molecule, rather than simply the ratio in which they occur (as in formulas of ionic compounds). For example, the formula C_2H_4 represents a molecule of the compound ethylene, containing two atoms of carbon (C) and four of hydrogen (H). The molecules of numerous other substances are made up solely of carbon and hydrogen atoms that are combined in the same 1:2 ratio as in ethylene (a fact expressed by saying that they all have the empirical formula CH_2). However, they are all different from ethylene, having definite compositions such as C_3H_6, C_4H_8, C_5H_{10}, etc.

By analyzing a pure chemical compound one can determine the percentage by weight of each element present. This information, together with knowledge of the atomic weights and the molecular weight, permits one to calculate a formula, called a molecular formula, that tells how many atoms of each element are present in a molecule of the substance. An example is H_2O, for water. Such formulas do not show the order of attachment of the atoms. The laws of chemical bonding (q.v.) require, for example, that the two hydrogen atoms in a water molecule be bound to the oxygen atom and not to one another, as expressed by the formula $H - O - H$ (not $H - H - O$). Such formulas, called structural formulas, give more information than molecular formulas because in addition to composition, they show the order of attachment of the atoms (see HYDROCARBONS).

Development of the concept of isomerism. One of the first examples of isomerism to be recognized illustrates the profound differences that may exist between isomers. In 1824 a German chemist, Friedrich Wöhler, found that silver cyanate had the same percentage composition as that found earlier for the highly explosive compound silver fulminate. The molecules of each substance consist of one atom each of silver (Ag), carbon (C), nitrogen (N), and oxygen (O). It is now known that the difference between cyanates and fulminates lies in the sequence in which the atoms are linked together; in cyanates it is $N - C - O$, whereas in fulminates it is $C - N - O$. This difference affects the energies with which the atoms are held together, the bonds in the explosive fulminates being much the weaker.

The possibilities for isomerism increase with increasing molecular complexity. Though only one structure is possible for a diatomic (two-atom) molecule (say, $A - B$), there are three theoretically possible linear triatomic (three-atomic) molecules in which the three atoms are different: $A - B - C$, $A - C - B$, and $B - A - C$, but $A - B - C$ and $C - B - A$ are identical. Redundancy tends to reduce the number of possible isomers; for example, if C is replaced by another A, the number of possibilities for the resulting linear A_2B is reduced to two: $A - A - B$ and $A - B - A$. Many possibilities may also be eliminated by restrictions imposed by the laws of chemical bonding.

For convenience, the subject of isomerism is usually treated under two main subdivisions, structural isomerism and stereoisomerism. In structural isomers the order of attachment of the atoms, one to another, differs. In stereoisomers the attachment sequence is the same, but the atoms are located differently in space. To illustrate this distinction, consider triatomic molecules composed of atoms A, B, and C. Molecules $A - B - C$ and $A - C - B$ would be considered structural isomers because they differ in the order of attachment of the atoms. Either of these molecules, however, could conceivably exist in more than one geometric form, say, linear and "bent":

$$A - B - C \qquad A \overset{B}{\diagup} \diagdown C$$

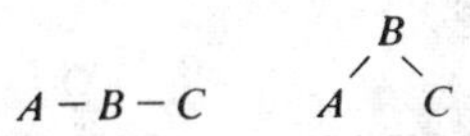

Two chemical substances with molecules differing in this manner would be called stereoisomers; the phenomenon of stereoisomerism is particularly important among compounds that occur in nature (carbohydrates, proteins, enzymes).

Isomerism is not rare; it pervades the study of chemistry and is encountered with compounds of virtually every known element. The significance and generality of the phenomenon were recognized earliest, however, in connection with the study of organic compounds (compounds that contain the element carbon), particularly those that occur in nature. Most of the examples which are used in this article to illustrate the principles of isomerism will be taken from organic chemistry. The principles are general, however, and one major section of the article deals with the stereoisomeric compounds of elements other than carbon.

Early in the 19th century, reliable analytical methods were developed to permit the accurate determination of the percentage composition of various substances. It was soon noted that occasionally two obviously different chemical substances had identical compositions. To explain these observations, a French chemist, Michel-Eugène Chevreul, in 1818 defined a "chemical species" as being formed from the same elements in the same proportions and in the same arrangement. At that time, however, the distinction between substances with molecules of a given composition and with multiples of that composition (i.e., C_2H_4 and C_4H_8) was not clear. In 1830 Berzelius, in Sweden, noted the cyanate–fulminate results mentioned above and also referred to two other well-known organic compounds that have identical composition (tartaric and racemic acids, both isolated from grapes) as isomeric bodies. A year later he called attention to the generality of the phenomenon with five examples (only three of which were actually correct) and clearly distinguished between isomerism and what he called polymerism (i.e., C_2H_4, C_4H_8, etc.). The term polymerism has since gone out of use, and the word polymer has quite a different chemical meaning (see POLYMERS).

STRUCTURAL ISOMERISM

Functional group isomers. The arrangement, or order of attachment, of atoms in a molecule is not arbitrary but is governed by the rules of chemical bonding. Only certain arrangements or structures are permissible. In neutral molecules, for example, carbon atoms may not be attached to more than four other atoms (for nitrogen, oxygen, and hydrogen, other elements commonly present in organic compounds, the numbers are three, two, and one, respectively). Thus, only two structural formulas consistent with these bonding rules are possible for the molecular formula C_2H_6O:

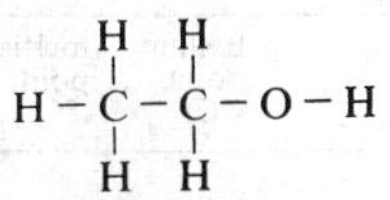

$$H - \underset{\underset{H}{|}}{\overset{\overset{H}{|}}{C}} - \underset{\underset{H}{|}}{\overset{\overset{H}{|}}{C}} - O - H \quad \text{and} \quad H - \underset{\underset{H}{|}}{\overset{\overset{H}{|}}{C}} - O - \underset{\underset{H}{|}}{\overset{\overset{H}{|}}{C}} - H$$

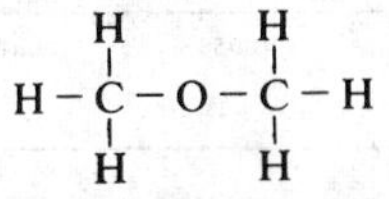

They are abbreviated as CH_3CH_2OH and CH_3OCH_3, respectively. (These are two-dimensional representations of three-dimensional structures. The formula

$$H - \underset{\underset{H}{|}}{\overset{\overset{H}{|}}{C}} - \underset{\underset{O-H}{|}}{\overset{\overset{H}{|}}{C}} - H$$

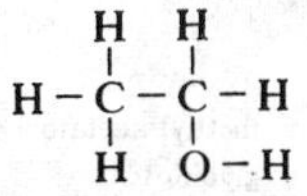

is considered identical with the first formula above because it preserves the same order of attachment of the atoms one to another. The consequences of the three-dimensionality of molecules are considered later in this article.) In each structural formula, each carbon atom is attached to four other atoms, the oxygen atom to two other atoms, and each hydrogen atom to only one other atom. All other conceivable structural formulas (for example, $C - C - H - H - H - H - H - O$) violate the laws of chemical bonding.

In agreement with bonding theory, there are two and only two known chemical substances with the molecular formula C_2H_6O. One isomer, called ethyl alcohol (or ethanol), is a liquid that boils at $78.5°$ C ($173.3°$ F). The other isomer, called dimethyl ether, is a gas at room temperature and boils at $-23°$ C ($-9°$ F). The great difference in boiling points of these two isomers emphasizes the importance of molecular structure (not just composition) in determining the properties of chemical substances.

The choice as to which substance has which structure can be made by studying the chemical reactions of each. For example, ethanol reacts with the metal sodium (Na) at room temperature to liberate one-sixth of its hydrogen content as hydrogen gas; the other reaction product is a substance with the molecular formula $NaOC_2H_5$. In contrast, dimethyl ether is inert toward sodium under the same reaction conditions. Because one of the six hydrogens in the formula CH_3CH_2OH is unique (attached to oxygen, rather than carbon), but all six hydrogens in the formula CH_3OCH_3 are equivalent, it is reasonable to assign the structure with the hydroxyl (− OH) group to ethanol. Other chemical and physical methods for determining organic structures confirm this conclusion.

Ethanol and dimethyl ether are members of two important classes of organic compounds, alcohols and ethers respectively, which have the general formulas $R - OH$ and $R - O - R'$ (R and R' stand for certain organic groups). Members of such classes of compounds have a common functional group (− OH for alcohols, − C − O − C − for ethers) and, for this reason, show similar chemical behaviour (for example, most alcohols react with sodium to give hydrogen). Ethers and alcohols are considered to be functional group isomers. For every alcohol with two or more carbon atoms, there is at least one isomeric ether (for another example, 1-propanol [$CH_3CH_2CH_2OH$] and ethyl methyl ether [$CH_3OCH_2CH_3$], both C_3H_8O).

Some other common classes of organic compounds are acids ($R - \overset{O}{\overset{\|}{C}} - OH$), aldehydes ($R - \overset{O}{\overset{\|}{C}} - H$), ketones ($R - \overset{O}{\overset{\|}{C}} - R'$), and esters ($R - \overset{O}{\overset{\|}{C}} - O - R'$). Table 1 shows some of the functional group isomers of molecules, all of which have the molecular formula $C_3H_6O_2$, together with their known melting points and boiling points.

The list is far from exhaustive for all $C_3H_6O_2$ isomers but illustrates some of the unique properties of these substances, which differ from one another in the arrangement of atoms within each molecule.

Table 1: Comparison of Isomers of $C_3H_6O_2$

structural formula	class	name	boiling point (°C)	melting point (°C)
$CH_3CH_2-\overset{O}{\overset{\|}{C}}-OH$	acid	propionic acid	141	−20.8
$CH_3-\overset{O}{\overset{\|}{C}}-CH_2OH$	keto-alcohol	acetol	145–146	−17
$CH_3-\overset{O}{\overset{\|}{C}}-OCH_3$	ester	methyl acetate	57–59	−98
$H_2C-CH-CH_2OH$ (ring through O)	ether-alcohol	glycidol	166–167	—
$CH_3OCH_2-\overset{O}{\overset{\|}{C}}-H$	ether-aldehyde	methoxyacetaldehyde	92.3	—
H_2C-CH_2, O, O, CH_2 (five-membered ring)	cyclic diether (or acetal)	1,3-dioxolane	78	−95

Positional isomers. It is common to have isomers within the same class of compounds. In the alcohols with the molecular formula C_3H_8O, for example, the hydroxyl group may appear on an end carbon of the three-carbon chain, or it may be attached to the central carbon atom in the chain.

$$\overset{3}{C}H_3\overset{2}{C}H_2\overset{1}{C}H_2OH \qquad \overset{1}{C}H_3\underset{OH}{\overset{2}{C}H}\overset{3}{C}H_3$$

1-propanol bp 97° C — 2-propanol bp 82° C

Such isomers, called positional isomers, frequently have similar, though not identical, chemical properties. Both propanols, for example, are completely miscible with water, and both of them react with sodium to give hydrogen, etc.

There are, however, examples of positional isomers that have grossly different properties. This condition is especially true of substances with two (or more) functional groups that may or may not be able to interact with one another, depending upon the carbon-atom framework to which they are attached. Examples are particularly common among aromatic compounds (see HYDROCARBONS). Phthalic acid ($C_8H_6O_4$), with two acid groups attached to adjacent carbon atoms of a benzene ring, loses water to form a cyclic anhydride when heated above 180° C (360° F).

Aromatic compounds

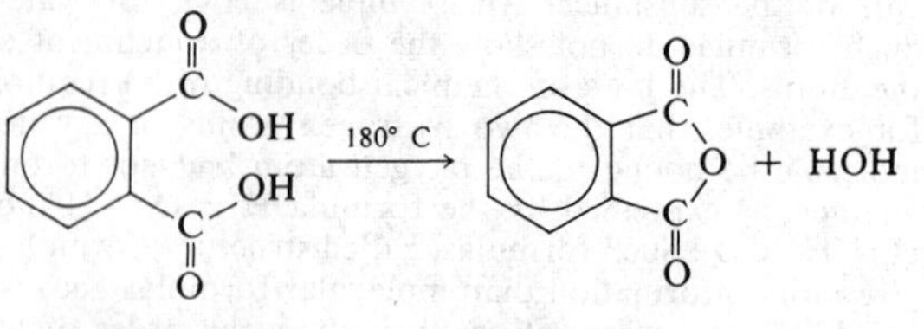

phthalic acid — phthalic anhydride

Isophthalic and terephthalic acids (also $C_8H_6O_4$), in which the acidic groups are farther apart, cannot react analogously.

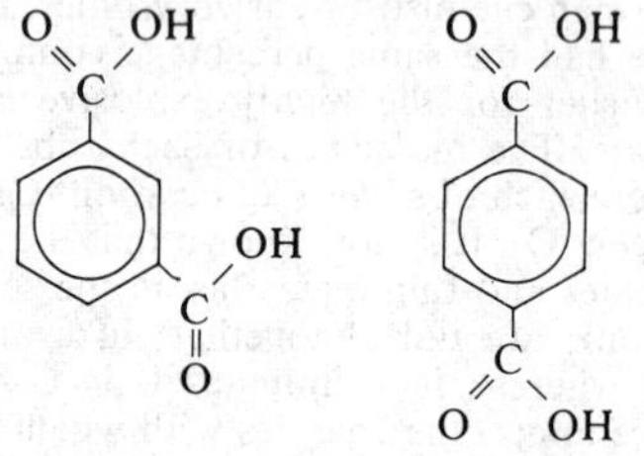

isophthalic acid — terephthalic acid

Physiological properties of isomeric substances may also depend on the relative location of the functional groups present. The two possible positional isomers of aspirin are almost totally devoid of biological activity.

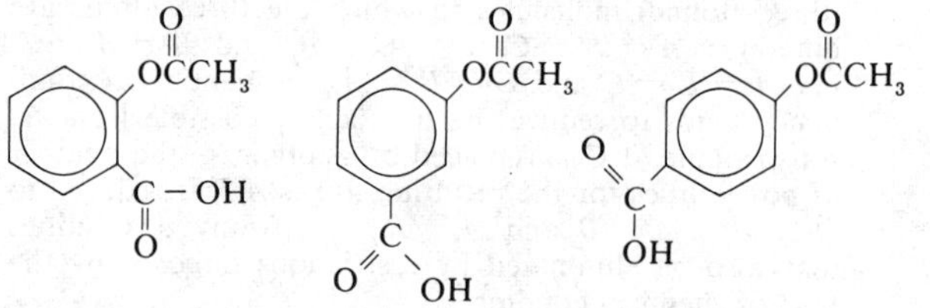

aspirin — positional isomers of aspirin

Tautomerism. Certain isomers may spontaneously interconvert more rapidly than they react with another compound. They are incapable of isolation. The phenomenon is called tautomerism (probably from Greek *tauto*, "the same"). A substance capable of existing in two (or more) tautomeric forms may exhibit chemical properties that correspond to each isomeric structure. The classic example is the compound ethyl acetoacetate ($C_6H_{10}O_3$) studied in the 1860s; it was considered by some chemists to have structure A (with alcohol and carbon–carbon double-bond functions) but by others to have the ketone structure B.

Ethyl acetoacetate

$$CH_3\overset{OH}{\overset{|}{C}}=CH\overset{O}{\overset{\|}{C}}OCH_2CH_3 \qquad CH_3\overset{O}{\overset{\|}{C}}CH_2\overset{O}{\overset{\|}{C}}OCH_2CH_3$$

A (enol) — B (keto)

two tautomeric structures of ethyl acetoacetate

Each group of workers observed chemical reactions of the substance that were consistent with their formulation of the structure. The two structures differ in the location of a hydrogen atom: in A it is attached to oxygen and in B to carbon. It is now known that such structures rapidly interconvert at room temperature. Both groups of investigators were correct; ethyl acetoacetate is a mixture of the enol (A, 7.5 percent) and keto (B, 92.5 percent) forms.

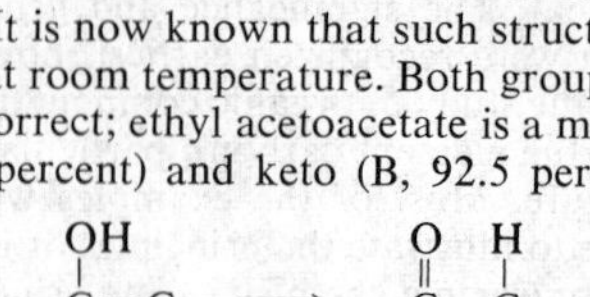

enol — keto

In 1911 a German chemist, Ludwig Knorr, succeeded in separating the two isomers at low temperatures (−78° C [−108° F]), but each, when permitted to attain room temperature, gave the equilibrium mixture—the mixture of constant composition that results from continuous conversion of each tautomer into the other.

Many other functional groups, besides ketones and enols, may exist in tautomeric equilibrium; in all cases, a hydrogen atom (proton) may occupy one of two possible sites. Examples include

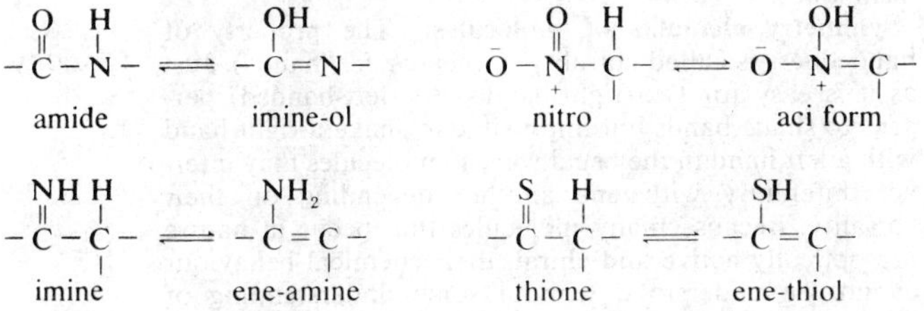

Glucose (commonly known as blood sugar) exists as an equilibrium mixture of the three tautomeric structures shown (all $C_6H_{12}O_6$).

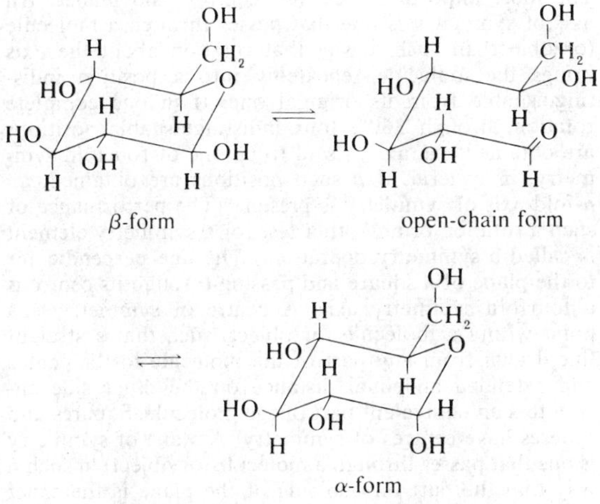

tautomeric forms of glucose

In aqueous solution at room temperature the composition is 65 percent β (beta) and 35 percent α (alpha), with less than 0.1 percent of the intervening open-chain structure. The interconversion of cyclic and acyclic structures is sometimes called ring-chain tautomerization.

In all of the examples of tautomerism discussed so far, a hydrogen atom (and in other cases, some other atom) changes its location. An entirely different type of tautomerism has been recognized, which involves only a redistribution of bonds and small changes in interatomic distances and angles. For example, at 100° C (212° F) the eight-membered ring hydrocarbon shown (C_8H_{10}) is in equilibrium with the structure with a six- and a four-membered ring (also C_8H_{10}).

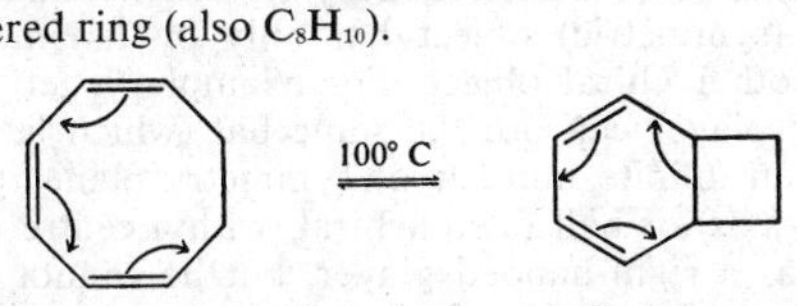

Valence tautomers

The interconversion can be accomplished by moving the bonds as shown by the arrows. The two isomers, which are readily separable at room temperature, are called valence tautomers.

STEREOISOMERISM

Stereoisomers (Greek *stereos,* "solid") have identical structural formulas, but the atoms are located differently in space. The subject of stereoisomerism is often subdivided into two parts, geometric (or *cis–trans*) and optical isomerism, though in fact this separation arises more out of the historical development of the subject than out of logic, because geometric isomers may or may not also be optical isomers. The latter type of isomerism, being more general, will be discussed first.

Optical isomerism. *Polarized light.* The history of stereoisomerism is intimately connected with the concept of optical activity, a consequence of the interaction of molecules with polarized light. In an ordinary light beam, the electromagnetic waves vibrate in all planes perpendicular to the direction of propagation of the beam. Ordinary light divides into two rays when passed through a properly oriented crystal of Iceland spar (crystalline calcium carbonate), and each ray consists of waves vibrating in a single plane. Such a light beam is said to be plane-polarized.

A Nicol prism, invented in 1828 by the Scottish physicist William Nicol, is a device made up of two pieces of Iceland spar in such a way that one of the two polarized rays passes through and the other is deflected. In a polarimeter there are two Nicol prisms or other polarizing devices through which a light beam passes in turn; the beam will pass through and be visible to an observer or detector only if the two prisms are parallel. The light will be totally cut off if the second prism (called the analyzer) is at right angles (90°) to the first prism (called the polarizer).

A quartz plate obtained by cutting a quartz crystal perpendicular to the crystal axis causes rotation of the plane of plane-polarized light. The phenomenon can best be observed by placing the quartz plate between the polarizer and analyzer of a polarimeter that has first been set with the two prisms at right angles. Before the quartz plate is placed in the instrument, no light passes through the second prism. With the plate between the prisms, some light passes through the second prism, which must now be rotated through a definite angle to cut off the light beam again. A substance, such as the quartz plate, is said to be optically active if it possesses the ability to rotate the plane of plane-polarized light. The angle through which the second crystal must be rotated to restore the original condition is called the optical rotation of the optically active substance and is given the symbol α (alpha).

Enantiomorphs

Two kinds of quartz crystals exist that differ only in the location of two facets that cause the crystals to be nonidentical mirror images (comparable to a right and left glove). Because of the mirror-image relationship, they were called enantiomorphs (Greek *enantios,* "opposite," and *morph,* "form"). Plates of the same thickness from the two kinds of quartz rotate plane-polarized light equally but in opposite directions. The form that rotates the plane to the right when the viewer faces the light source is called dextrorotatory (*d;* sometimes designated +), and that which rotates the plane to the left is called subsequently levorotatory (*l;* sometimes designated −).

Molecular dissymmetry. A French physicist, Jean-Baptiste Biot, laid the foundation for modern stereochemistry when he found, in 1815, that substances other than quartz are optically active. These included an alcoholic solution of camphor, laurel oil, lemon oil, and turpentine, the latter even in the vapour phase. Because these substances are not crystalline, such rotation must clearly be associated with the structures of the individual molecules and not necessarily with their dissymmetric arrangement in a solid. (An object is dissymmetric if it is non-superimposable on its mirror image.) This notion was supported by the finding that if the concentration (say of sugar in water) was doubled, the observed rotation was also doubled, showing that the extent of rotation depended upon the number of optically active molecules present.

Many substances were tested for optical activity; some were active and others were not, and the problem remained to discern what molecular property caused the difference. Among the active compounds was tartaric acid, first isolated from grape tartar and found to be dextrorotatory. Another acid from the same source, called racemic acid (Latin *racemus,* "bunch of grapes"), was found to be optically inactive. Yet both acids had identical compositions and otherwise very similar properties, now known to be accounted for by the same structural formula ($C_4H_6O_6$).

$$HO-\overset{\displaystyle O}{\overset{\displaystyle \|}{C}}-\overset{\displaystyle H}{\overset{\displaystyle |}{\underset{\displaystyle |}{\underset{\displaystyle OH}{C}}}}-\overset{\displaystyle H}{\overset{\displaystyle |}{\underset{\displaystyle |}{\underset{\displaystyle OH}{C}}}}-\overset{\displaystyle O}{\overset{\displaystyle \|}{C}}-OH$$

Tartaric and racemic acids

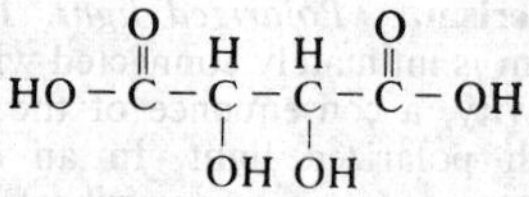

Louis Pasteur, in 1848, noticed that crystals of the tartrate salt were of a single type characterized by facets that caused the crystals to be dissymmetric. Crystals of the racemate salt, however, were of two types: one identical with those of the tartrate salt, and the other having a mirror-image relationship (enantiomorphic) with the tartrate crystals. With magnifying lens and tweezers, Pasteur carefully separated the two types of racemate crystals. One set, when dissolved in water, was dextrorotatory, with an optical rotation identical to that of the tartrate salt. The other set, in equal concentration, gave solutions that rotated the plane-polarized light to the same extent but in the opposite direction. When equal weights of the two crystalline types were dissolved and mixed, the resulting solution was optically inactive. Clearly, racemic acid was optically inactive because it consisted of a 50:50 mixture of two types of molecules, one of which was identical with tartaric acid and the other of which was related to it as an object and its mirror image. Pasteur realized that optical activity is caused by a dissymmetric grouping of the atoms in a molecule, but he failed to discern the structural feature that accounts for the dissymmetry.

At about the same time, a German chemist, Friedrich August Kekule von Stradonitz, recognized that carbon usually has a valence of four and that complex organic structures can be produced by linking carbon atoms in chains or rings (see CHEMICAL BONDING and HYDROCARBONS). In 1874 the chemists Jacobus Henricus van't Hoff in The Netherlands and Joseph-Achille Le Bel in France simultaneously but independently made the connection between the quadrivalence of carbon and Pasteur's suggestion that optical activity is caused by molecular dissymmetry. They recognized that a structural feature that causes a molecule and its mirror image to be non-superimposable is necessary for the existence of optical activity. They also noted that every optically active compound of which the structure was known at that time had at least one carbon atom that was combined with four different groups. Examples included the following (the pertinent carbon atoms are marked with an asterisk):

$$CH_3-\overset{\displaystyle |}{\underset{\displaystyle |}{\underset{\displaystyle OH}{C^*}}}-CO_2H \qquad HO_2C-CH_2-\overset{\displaystyle |}{\underset{\displaystyle |}{\underset{\displaystyle OH}{C^*}}}-CO_2H$$

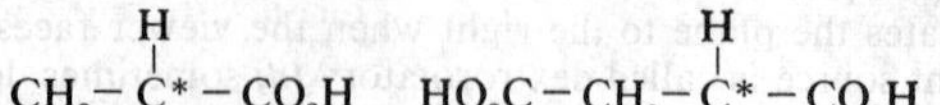

lactic acid   malic acid

$$HO_2C-CH_2-\overset{\displaystyle H}{\overset{\displaystyle |}{\underset{\displaystyle |}{\underset{\displaystyle NH_2}{C^*}}}}-CO_2H \qquad CH_3-CH_2-\overset{\displaystyle H}{\overset{\displaystyle |}{\underset{\displaystyle |}{\underset{\displaystyle CH_3}{C^*}}}}-CH_2OH.$$

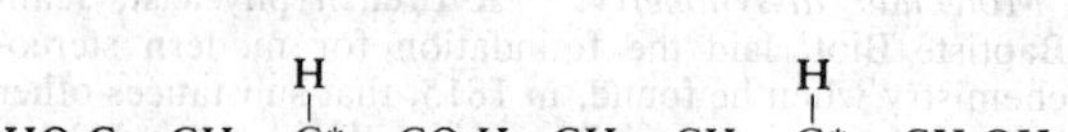

aspartic acid   active amyl alcohol

Furthermore, whenever both members of a pair of optical isomers were known, all chemical and physical properties (melting point or boiling point, etc.) were identical, the only difference being the sign (not the magnitude) of the optical rotation. Accordingly, the isomers seemed to differ from one another only in a right- and left-handed manner. Both chemists pointed out that if the four different groups about a carbon atom were located at the corners of a tetrahedron, two arrangements were possible, which are related to one another as an object and its non-superimposable mirror image. This relationship is shown in the formulas below, in which the dashed lines

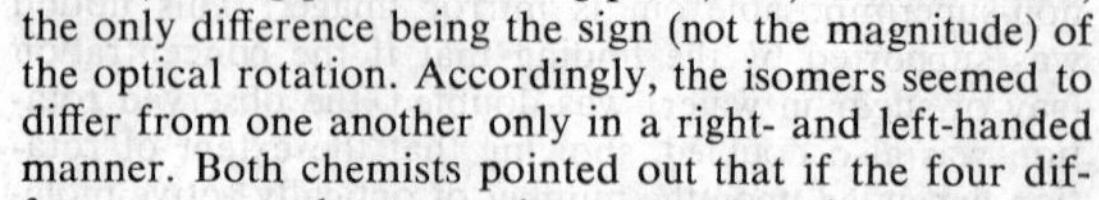

clockwise   mirror   counterclockwise

and wedges represent bonds extending, respectively, away from and toward the reader, and full lines represent bonds lying in the plane of the paper.

If each molecule is viewed down the C–a bond axis, the remaining groups b–c–d occur in either a clockwise or a counterclockwise sequence, thus emphasizing that the feature that distinguishes the two structures is one of handedness. The correctness of the proposals of van't Hoff and Le Bel has now been established unequivocally through the application of many physical and chemical techniques.

Symmetry elements of molecules. The property of handedness is called chirality (Green *cheir*, "hand"). Just as it is easy for two right-handed (or left-handed) persons to shake hands but impossible to shake a right hand with a left hand in the usual way, so molecules may interact differently with one another depending on their chirality. Because many molecules that occur in nature are optically active and chiral, their chemical behaviour cannot be understood without some understanding of stereoisomerism.

Chirality

Whether a molecule is chiral or achiral depends on the presence or absence of certain symmetry elements. The most important are axes, centres, and planes. An axis of symmetry is one that passes through a molecule (or object) in such a way that rotation about the axis brings the molecule repeatedly into a position indistinguishable from its original one. If in one complete rotation through 360°, four indistinguishable positions are obtained, the axis is said to be one of fourfold symmetry; in general, if *n* such positions are obtained, an *n*-fold axis of symmetry is present. (The performance of such a rotation or any other test for a symmetry element is called a symmetry operation.) The line perpendicular to the plane of a square and passing through its centre is a fourfold symmetry axis. A centre of symmetry is a point within a molecule (or object) such that a straight line drawn from any part of the molecule to the centre and extended an equal distance on the other side encounters an equivalent part of the molecule. Squares and spheres have centres of symmetry. A plane of symmetry is one that passes through a molecule (or object) in such a way that the part on one side of the plane is the exact reflection of the part on the other side, the plane acting as a mirror.

Molecules with a centre, plane, or axis of symmetry are superimposable upon (or identical with) their mirror images. Such molecules are achiral, or symmetric. Examples of common achiral objects are a sphere, a cube, and a baseball and bat. Molecules that lack these symmetry elements are chiral, or dissymmetric; consequently, they are not superimposable on their mirror images. Common chiral objects are gloves, screws, and spiral staircases. A chiral molecule or object is said to be asymmetric if it lacks all of the symmetry elements, even including a simple axis.

Symmetry and optical activity. The chirality of an object cannot be determined by its interaction with an achiral (symmetric) object but only by its interaction with another chiral object. For example, a left-handed baseball player can use the same bat (which is achiral, having an infinite number of symmetry planes through its long axis) or ball (also achiral, with a centre of symmetry) as a right-handed player, but he cannot use the same glove (which is chiral, or asymmetric, being like the players, left- or right-handed).

The same situation prevails with mirror-image chiral molecules. They react identically with achiral molecules, and their properties that do not depend on chirality (such as melting and boiling points) are identical. They behave differently, however, toward other chiral molecules (these differences are the basis for much of the specificity of many biochemical reactions, such as those of enzymes) and have different chiral physical properties, such as the direction in which they rotate plane-polarized light or their solubility in solvents of which the molecules are chiral.

Molecules with an asymmetric carbon atom. A carbon atom to which four different atoms or groups of atoms are attached is called an asymmetric carbon atom. Such an atom can serve as a focus of dissymmetry, or handedness, and in modern terminology is called a chiral centre. Typical of such compounds is lactic acid, a naturally occurring, optically active compound important in several biological processes. In the formula at the left, the asymmetric carbon atom is marked with an asterisk.

Lactic acid

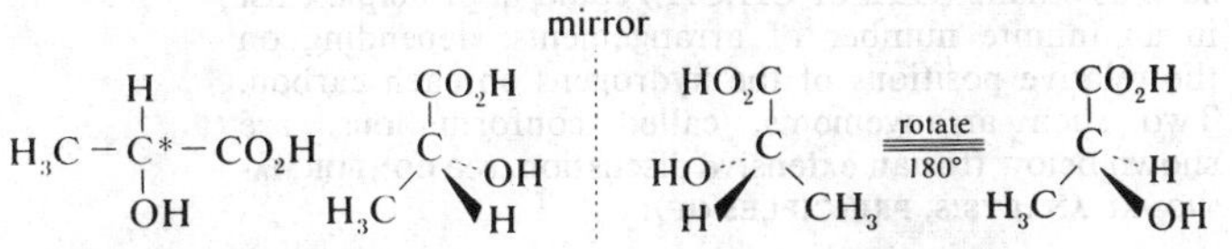

lactic acid   *l*-lactic acid   *d*-lactic acid

The two non-superimposable mirror-image structures, or enantiomers, are also shown. They represent two different chemical substances that have the same molecular and structural formulas but differ in the location of the atoms or groups of atoms in three-dimensional space (*i.e.*, they are stereoisomers). One form of lactic acid, the levorotatory (or *l*) isomer, is found in sour milk, whereas the other enantiomer, dextrorotatory (or *d*), is produced when muscle tissue performs work. The two lactic acids not only rotate plane-polarized light in opposite directions but also differ in biochemical reactivity. For example, the enzyme lactic acid dehydrogenase (which, like all enzymes, is chiral) can readily distinguish between the two stereoisomers; it converts *d*-lactic acid (but not the *l*-isomer) to pyruvic acid. In contrast, achiral chemical reagents readily convert both forms of lactic acid to pyruvic acid.

A given amount of one form of lactic acid will rotate plane-polarized light through the same angle but in the opposite direction from an equal amount of the mirror image form. This characteristic applies to all pairs of enantiomers. Consequently, a mixture containing equal amounts of two enantiomers will be optically inactive, the two rotations exactly cancelling one another. Such a mixture is called a racemic mixture (named after the first such mixture, *d*- and *l*-tartaric acids, studied by Pasteur).

Examination of the structure of lactic acid shows that the molecule lacks a plane or centre of symmetry; it also lacks a symmetry axis and is therefore asymmetric. It is instructive to note the effect of making two of the groups attached to the (formerly) asymmetric carbon atom identical. If, for example, the hydroxyl (− OH) group in lactic acid is replaced by a hydrogen atom, giving propionic (propanoic) acid, then the molecule will possess a plane of symmetry; the plane of the paper bisects the H − C − H angle and contains the other groups.

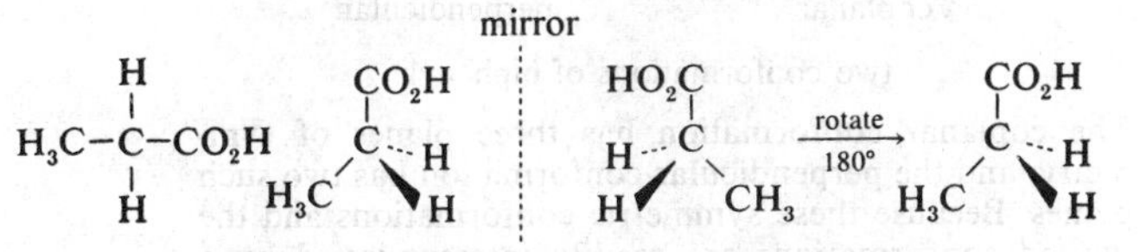

propionic acid

The substance is therefore achiral and, as the above drawing shows, has a mirror image that is, in fact, identical with or superimposable on itself. Consequently, propionic acid is known in only one form, which is optically inactive. The asymmetric carbon atom is, therefore, the structural feature that imparts chirality to lactic acid.

The term configuration refers to the arrangement of atoms in space that characterizes a particular stereoisomer. Enantiomers are said to have opposite configurations. Before 1950 no method had been devised to determine the absolute configuration of any dissymmetric molecule. For example, it was not known whether *l*-lactic acid had the configuration shown above or its mirror image configuration (*i.e.*, which structure fit with which sign of rotation), although through chemical interconversions many relative configurations had been established. For example, *l*-lactic acid, isolated from sour milk, is subsequently converted by treatment with methyl alcohol to an ester, methyl lactate, which is also levorotatory.

Absolute configurations

$$CH_3CH(OH)CO_2H + CH_3OH \longrightarrow CH_3CH(OH)CO_2CH_3 + H_2O$$

l-lactic acid   methyl alcohol   methyl lactate (levorotatory)   water

Because no bonds to the asymmetric carbon were broken during this reaction, it is safe to conclude that *l*-lactic acid and *l*-methyl lactate have the same relative configurations, even though the absolute configuration of each was not known.

In 1951 a group of Dutch scientists were able to establish the absolute configuration of *d*-tartaric acid. Because tartaric acid had already been related configurationally to many other optically active compounds, their absolute configurations (including those shown here for the lactic acids) became known. Since 1951 the absolute configurations of many optically active substances and various conventions for describing them have been established.

Molecules with more than one asymmetric carbon atom. The molecules of many substances in nature, such as the common sugars and other carbohydrates, contain more than one asymmetric carbon atom. Recognizing this possibility, van't Hoff formulated rules predicting the numbers of stereoisomers that may exist in such instances. If the two possible configurations at a single chiral centre are designated R (Latin *rectus*, "right") and S (Latin *sinister*, "left"), respectively, then a substance which has two different chiral centres may exist in four stereoisomeric forms, as shown by the chart below (the numbers in the parentheses represent the two chiral centres).

molecules with two different chiral centres

R(1)–R(2), S(1)–S(2) } enantiomers

R(1)–S(2), S(1)–R(2) } enantiomers

Since R(1) is considered to be the mirror image of S(1), etc., molecules R(1)–R(2) and S(1)–S(2) constitute one pair of enantiomers; similarly, R(1)–S(2) and S(1)–R(2) are another enantiomeric pair. It is easy to show that if a molecule has three chiral centres, there are eight possible stereoisomers; four chiral centres permit 16 stereoisomeric structures (eight pairs of enantiomers). This possibility is not at all uncommon. For example, *d*-glucose, the sugar present in blood, is one of 16 isomeric sugars, each of which has the same molecular and structural formula but differs from the others in the configurations at one or more of the four asymmetric carbon atoms present in the molecule (marked with asterisks).

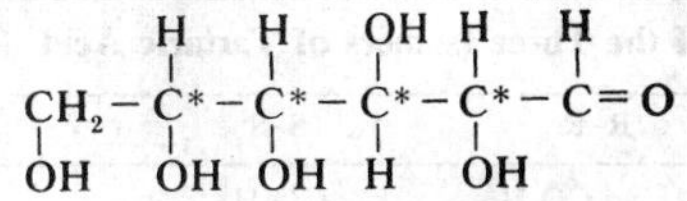

structural formula for *d*-glucose and its 15 stereoisomers

The van't Hoff rule summarizes the situation: if a molecule has *n* different chiral centres, it is capable of existing in 2^n stereoisomeric structures.

An extremely far-reaching concept in stereoisomerism develops if one considers, in the chart of molecules with two different chiral centres, the relationship between any two molecules that are not enantiomers—for example, R(1)–R(2) and R(1)–S(2). These substances have the same configuration (*i.e.*, R) at centre (1) but opposite configurations at centre (2). These substances are therefore stereoisomers but not mirror images (enantiomers). Compounds related in this way are called diastereomers (or diastereoisomers). Because they are not mirror images, two compounds that are diastereomers may differ in all properties, not only those that are chiral. They may have different melting points, boiling points, densities, and solubilities in various solvents; and they react differently with all chemical reagents, whether chiral or achiral. If dissymmetric, they interact with plane-polarized light but need not rotate the light in opposite directions nor to the same extent. In short, diastereomers may behave as differently from one another as any two chemical substances. For example, *d*-mannose is a sugar that is known as a diastereomer of *d*-glucose; they have identical configurations at three chiral centres and opposite configurations at only one of the four asymmetric carbon atoms. Yet *d*-mannose melts 14° C (25° F) lower than *d*-glucose and is also three times as soluble in water.

Diastereomers

A special case of stereoisomerism arises when a molecule possesses two identical asymmetric carbon atoms; that is, the two carbon atoms have the identical four different groups attached. In this case, the total number of possible stereoisomers decreases from four to three, as shown in the chart below. Because the two chiral centres are identical, they are designated by the same number; *i.e.*, (1).

molecules with two identical chiral centers

R(1)–R(1) } enantiomers (optically active)
S(1)–S(1)

R(1)–S(1) meso form (optically inactive)

The form R(1)–S(1), though it possesses chiral centres, is achiral and optically inactive because the two chiral centres are equal and opposite. In other terms, because S(1) is the mirror image of R(1), the molecule has a plane of symmetry (and is therefore achiral). Such substances are called meso forms.

R(1) ⋮ S(1)

plane of symmetry

The structure of tartaric acid, which has two identical asymmetric carbon atoms, indicated by asterisk, is shown in the diagram below.

$$HO_2C-\overset{H}{\underset{OH}{C^*}}-\overset{H}{\underset{OH}{C^*}}-CO_2H$$

tartaric acid

Each asymmetric carbon atom has the same four groups attached, – H, – OH, – CO_2H, and – $CH(OH)CO_2H$. Tartaric acid exists in three stereoisomeric forms having the structures shown in the three-dimensional drawings of Table 2. Two structures (R–R and S–S) form an enantiomeric pair and are optically active; they have identical achiral properties but rotate plane-polarized light in opposite senses. The third form (R–S) has a centre of symmetry as drawn, or it has a plane of symmetry if one asymmetric carbon is rotated 180° about the bond that joins the two asymmetric carbons. This structure is therefore achiral, optically inactive, and a meso form. The meso form is a diastereomer of the optically active forms and therefore differs from them in its properties.

Table 2: Properties of the Three Isomers of Tartaric Acid

	R–R	S–S	R–S
Structure	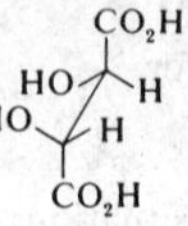	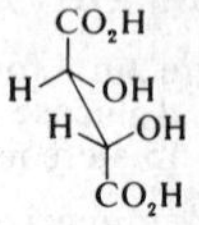	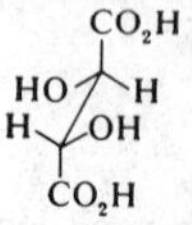
Melting point, °C	170	170	140
Specific gravity	1.76	1.76	1.67
Solubility, g/100 g of water at 20° C	139	139	125
Optical rotation	+12°	–12°	0°

Dissymmetric conformational isomers. A compound such as ethane (C_2H_6 or CH_3CH_3) could in principle exist in an infinite number of arrangements, depending on the relative positions of the hydrogens on each carbon. Two such arrangements, called conformations, are shown below (for an extensive discussion, see CONFORMATIONAL ANALYSIS, PRINCIPLES OF):

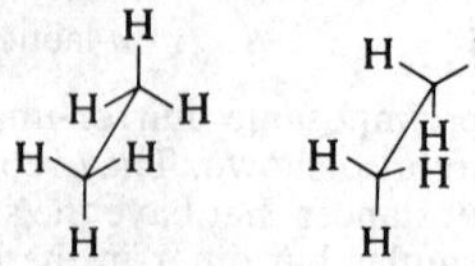

staggered eclipsed

conformations of ethane

Such conformational isomers, or conformers, are usually readily interconvertible at room temperature by a simple rotational motion about the carbon–carbon single bond. Because this rotation requires only a small amount of energy, conformational isomers cannot ordinarily be separated from one another.

Free rotation

The staggered and eclipsed conformations of ethane have a centre and a plane of symmetry, respectively, and are therefore symmetric and achiral. Conformations of ethane intermediate between these two, however, would possess neither of these symmetry elements and would be dissymmetric and chiral and, in principle, be capable of optical activity. In practice, however, the interconversion of such forms with the symmetric conformers is so facile that isolation of the dissymmetric structures is not possible.

Biphenyls. Several classes of molecules have been devised, however, in which the interconversion of enantiomeric dissymmetric conformers is prevented by placing, in strategic positions, large groups that restrict what would otherwise be fairly free rotational motions. Certain substituted biphenyls constitute a common and well-studied example. Biphenyl itself is a hydrocarbon in which two benzene rings are joined by a single bond. The two benzene rings may be coplanar or mutually perpendicular, or they may assume any twisted conformation between these extremes.

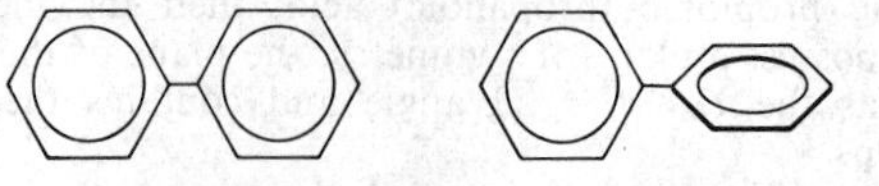

coplanar perpendicular

two conformations of biphenyl

The coplanar conformation has three planes of symmetry, and the perpendicular conformation has two such planes. Because these symmetric conformations and the twisted conformations are readily interconverted by a simple rotational motion about the bond that joins the two benzene rings, biphenyl itself is achiral and optically inactive.

If two large and different groups (say, A and B) are placed on the ring positions (called the ortho positions) adjacent to the bond that joins the two rings, the planar arrangement, which brings these groups very close to one another in space, becomes less stable than any of the twisted conformations.

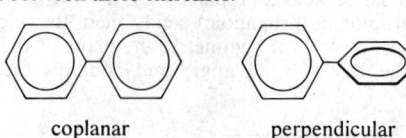

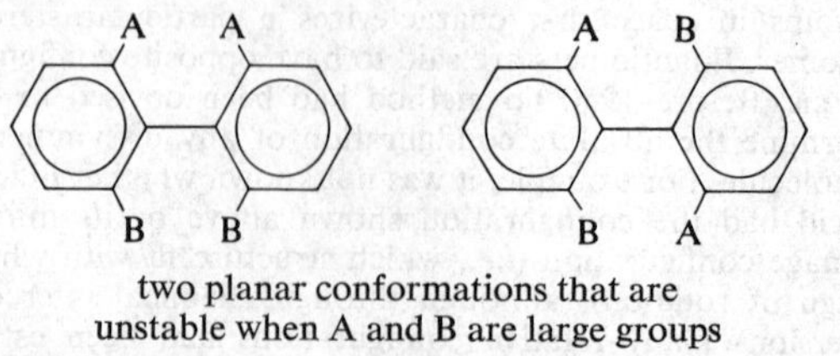

two planar conformations that are unstable when A and B are large groups

Consequently, the symmetric, or achiral, coplanar conformation becomes very difficult to achieve. Any twisted conformation, including the one in which the rings are mutually perpendicular, is dissymmetric because of the difference in the two substituents, A and B. An end-on view of the two enantiomers shows their chirality.

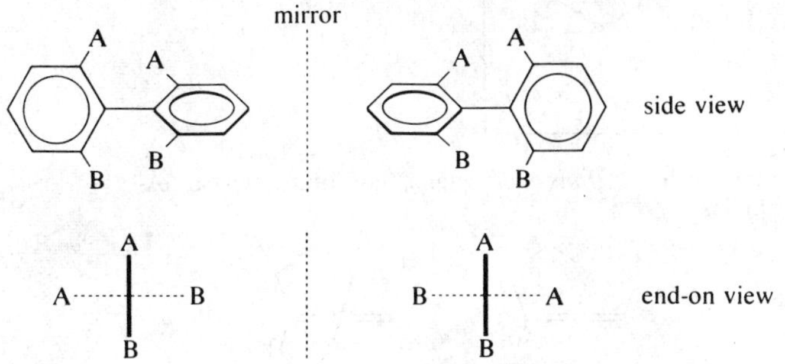

chiral, optically active biphenyls

The substances represented by the two structures are distinct from one another, constituting a pair of enantiomers that differ from one another in all chiral properties. Commonly, A and B are large groups such as methyl ($-CH_3$), nitro ($-NO_2$), or carboxyl ($-CO_2H$); the larger the groups, the more difficult it is for the molecule to pass through the planar conformation, a process that interconverts the two enantiomers. If two of the groups on either of the rings are identical, the substance is achiral and optically inactive, even though the rings cannot easily become coplanar, because the easily achieved conformation with the two rings mutually perpendicular has a plane of symmetry. It is essential, therefore, that A and B be different; of course, all four groups may be different without affecting the possibilities for having two separable optical isomers.

Helical molecules. The helix is a common chiral structure; it may be left- or right-handed, and the two types of helices are related to one another as an object and its non-superimposable mirror image (*i.e.*, they are enantiomers). Helical structures are fairly common in molecules that occur in nature, the best known examples being the double helix of DNA (deoxyribonucleic acid) and the α-helix of many proteins. These substances are optically active, but their structures also contain many units with asymmetric carbon atoms, and one cannot easily dissociate the optical activity caused by these chiral centres from the optical activity caused by the helicity of the molecule.

Geometric isomers. *Cis-trans isomers.* Rotation about carbon-carbon double bonds usually requires considerably more energy than rotations about single bonds. As a consequence, compounds of the type Cab = Cab, in which a differs from b, exist as stereoisomers. Because all of the atoms ordinarily lie in a plane, this plane constitutes a plane of symmetry, and molecules of this type usually are not optically active (unless a or b themselves are chiral).

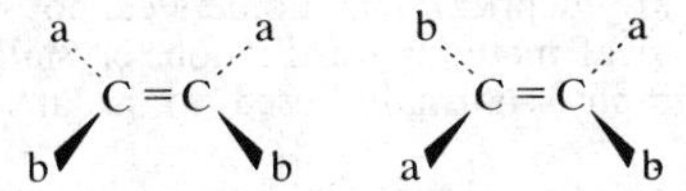

cis *trans*

a pair of geometric isomers

This type of isomerism is called geometric, or *cis-trans* isomerism (Latin *cis*, "on this side"; *trans*, "across"). *Cis-trans* isomers of this type can also be considered as diastereomers because they are stereoisomers that are not mirror images. They differ from one another, therefore, in their chemical and physical properties.

The existence of geometric isomers was predicted by van't Hoff in 1874, and specific examples were recognized within the next two decades. Maleic and fumaric acids constitute the classic examples. Both have the structural formula $HO_2C-CH=CH-CO_2H$, but they differ in all physical properties (see Table 3). They are

Maleic and fumaric acids

Table 3: Comparison of the Properties of Maleic and Fumaric Acids

	maleic acid (*cis*)	fumaric acid (*trans*)
Melting point	130°–131° C	287° C
Solubility in water, g/100 ml at 25°	78.8	0.7
Density, g/ml	1.590	1.635
Acidity constants (p*Ka*'s)	1.9; 6.5	3.0; 4.5
Toxicity	toxic	nontoxic; an intermediate in metabolic processes

readily distinguished by their thermal behaviour. Maleic acid, on being heated above 140° C (284° F), loses water and forms a cyclic anhydride. Under the same conditions, fumaric acid is unaffected.

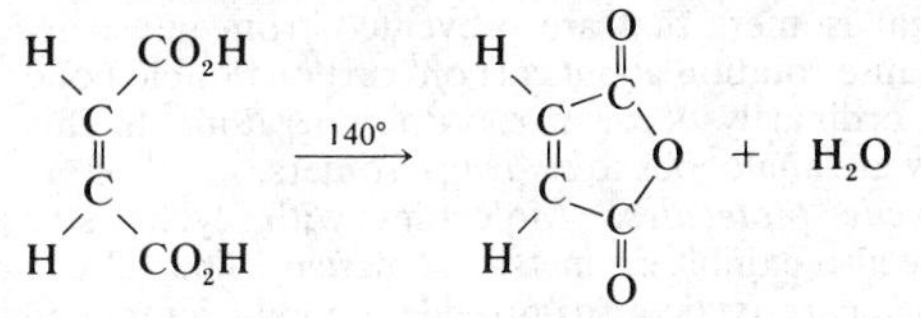

maleic acid maleic anhydride

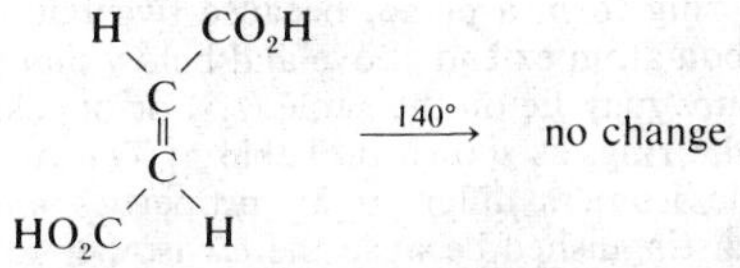

fumaric acid

This result suggests that maleic acid must have the two acidic groups in the *cis* arrangement, in which they are close enough to interact (compare with the distinction of phthalic acid from its positional isomers, above).

If more than one carbon–carbon double bond is present in a molecule, the number of possible isomers may be increased. Four geometric isomers of the hydrocarbon $CH_3CH = CHCH_2CH = CHCH_2CH_3$ are possible:

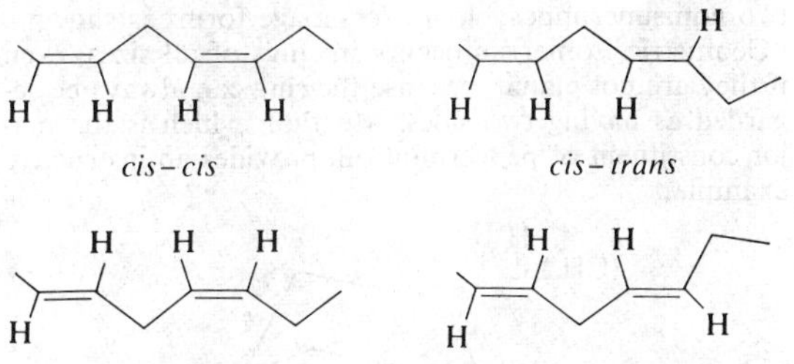

cis–cis *cis–trans*

trans–cis *trans–trans*

Many biological materials, such as the carotenes, retinenes, and unsaturated fats, contain several carbon–carbon double bonds, the geometry of which is significant in governing their biochemical function.

Allenes. A special case of isomerism arises in molecules called allenes, Cab = C = Cab, in which two double bonds are immediately adjacent to one another. The substituents at one end of the allene system are in a plane at right angles to the plane of the substituents at the other end. As with the biphenyls, the chirality is best seen from an end-on view.

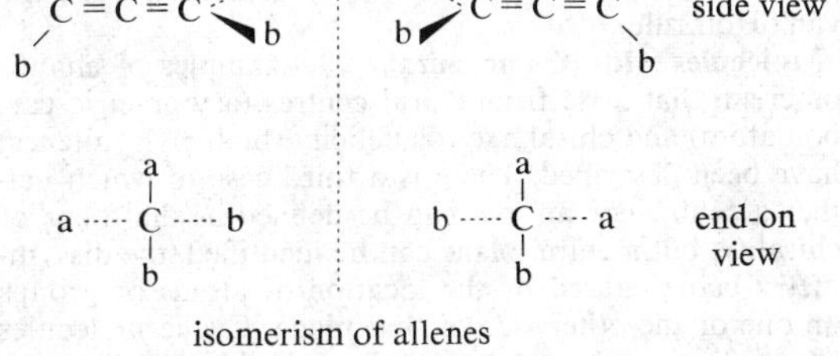

isomerism of allenes

Table 4: Comparison of the Geometric Isomers of 1,2-Cyclopropanedicarboxylic Acids

	cis (meso form)	*trans* (pair of enantiomers)
Structure	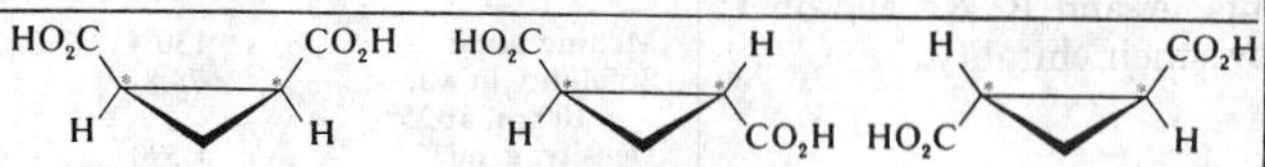	
Melting point	139° C	175° C
Solubility in water, g/100 g at 20° C	112	19
Optical rotation	0°	±84°

If a is different from b, two optically active enantiomers exist. This possibility was recognized by van't Hoff in 1874, but the first actual example was not observed until 1935. Allenes have no chiral centre but a chiral axis, analogous to that in the biphenyls. They are conformational isomers that are prevented from interconversion because rotation about carbon–carbon double bonds does not ordinarily occur at room temperature. In this sense they are analogous to *cis-trans* isomers.

Cyclopropanedicarboxylic acids

Cyclic molecules. Molecules with cyclic structures may also exhibit geometric isomerism. The 1,2-cyclopropanedicarboxylic acids provide a good example and also illustrate the occasional interrelation between geometric and optical isomers. The three carbon atoms of a cyclopropane ring form a plane; because two bonds of each ring carbon atom extend above and below that plane, the acid groups may lie on the same (*cis*) or opposite (*trans*) side of the ring, as shown in Table 4. The two types of geometric isomers differ in all properties and can be readily distinguished because the *cis* isomer forms a cyclic anhydride on being heated, but the *trans* isomer does not (compare with maleic and fumaric acid). Each form has two identical asymmetric carbon atoms, marked in the drawings with asterisks (analogous to those in the tartaric acids). Consequently, the *cis* isomer can also be regarded as a meso form (it has a plane of symmetry—the perpendicular bisector of the bond that joins the two asterisked carbon atoms—and is therefore achiral and optically inactive). The *trans* isomer has no plane or centre of symmetry and is consequently chiral and exists in two non-superimposable mirror-image forms as shown.

Geometric isomerism occurs in rings of all sizes, even if they are not planar, because the ring can always be regarded as having two sides. Menthol, which is the major constituent of peppermint oil, provides an instructive example.

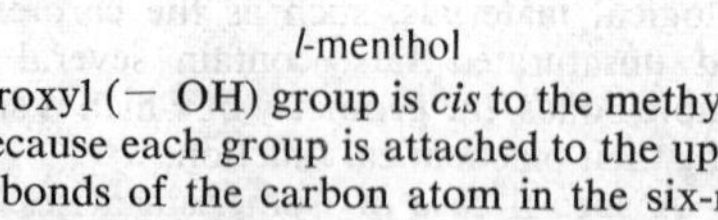

l-menthol

The hydroxyl ($-$ OH) group is *cis* to the methyl ($-$ CH_3) group because each group is attached to the upper one of the two bonds of the carbon atom in the six-membered ring. The hydroxyl group is *trans* to the isopropyl [$CH(CH_3)_2$] group because the latter is attached to the lower of the two bonds of the ring carbon atom. The methyl and isopropyl groups are also *trans* to one another. Menthol, however, has no plane or centre of symmetry and is therefore chiral and optically active. Indeed, because there are three different asymmetric carbon atoms (marked in the drawing with asterisks), there are $2^3 = 8$ possible and known stereoisomers of the substance (four pairs of enantiomers, in accord with the van't Hoff rule).

Molecules with planar chirality. Examples of enantiomerism that arise from chiral centres (asymmetric carbon atom) and chiral axes or helicity (biphenyls, allenes) have been described. There is a third case in which neither a centre nor an axis can be defined as the focus of chirality, but a chiral plane can be identified, the dissymmetry being caused by the location of atoms or groups on one or the other side of that plane. Cyclic molecules containing a *trans* carbon–carbon double bond in the ring, such as *trans*-cyclooctene, constitute typical examples.

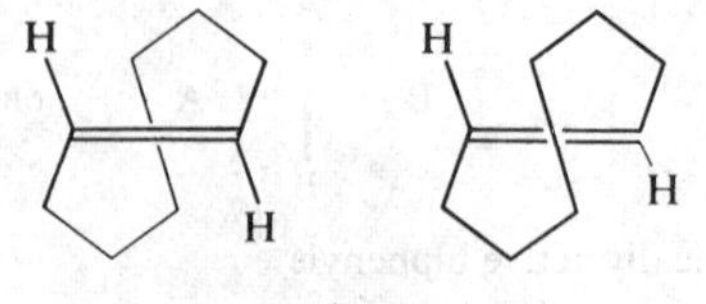

enantiomers of *trans*-cyclooctene

Trans-cyclooctene

The plane containing the carbon–carbon double bond is a chirality plane, the carbon chain lying behind or in front of that plane. The mirror-image structures are not superimposable and were successfully separated and shown to be optically active in 1963.

The separation and interconversion of chiral molecules. Synthesis of a chiral substance in the laboratory from achiral precursors always results in a mixture that contains equal amounts of the two enantiomers; *i.e.*, a racemic modification. The point is illustrated with the synthesis of the two enantiomers of bromopropionic acid from the achiral (symmetric) precursors propionic (propanoic) acid and bromine.

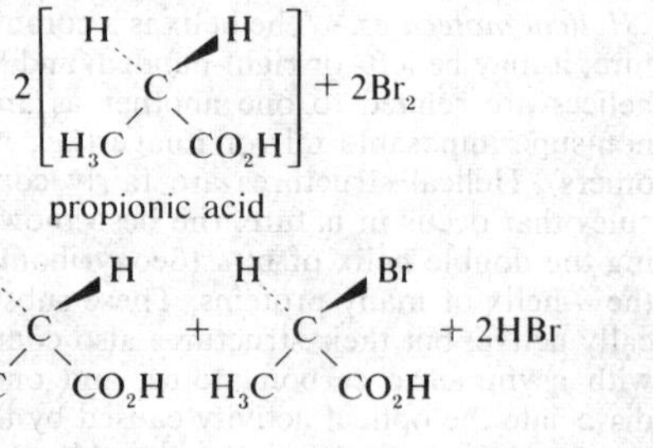

50:50 mixture of bromopropionic acid enantiomers

Either of two hydrogen atoms of propionic acid is equally easily replaced by bromine, thus giving the two enantiomers of bromopropionic (bromopropanoic) acid in equal amounts. It therefore becomes important, if pure enantiomers are to be obtained in the laboratory, to have ways of separating (or resolving) enantiomers. The process is called resolution. Because their achiral physical properties are identical, enantiomers cannot be resolved by the physical methods (distillation, crystallization, or chromatography) normally used to isolate pure substances.

One method of resolution, the mechanical separation of dissymmetric crystals used with the tartaric acids by Pasteur, is possible only in fortuitous situations in which the racemic mixture forms such crystals, however, it is primarily of historic interest. Several other methods of resolution are generally employed, the two most important involving diastereomeric salts or enzymatic processes.

The most generally practical procedure for resolving a racemic modification involves converting the enantiomers, by reaction with an optically active substance, into compounds that are diastereomers. Because diastereomers are not mirror images, they do not have identical physical properties and may be separated by ordinary means, such as fractional crystallization. After the diastereomers are separated, they are converted back into the original reactants. This method, first developed by Pasteur, has many modifications. The selective adsorption of enantiomers on optically active adsorbents and selective extraction with optically active solvents are based on the same principle.

Enzymes often react with only one of two enantiomers. Pasteur found that the mold *Penicillium glaucum*, for example, when grown in the presence of racemic ammonium tartrate, consumed only the *d*-isomer, leaving the *l*-tartrate unchanged. The reason for the discrimination by the enzyme is that it is chiral and interacts differently with the two (chiral) enantiomers. The situation is analogous to the interaction of a right hand with a pair of gloves: only the right-handed glove will fit, and the left-handed glove will remain unused.

The resolution methods just described all depend on the presence of another dissymmetric compound; *i.e.*, dissymmetry is propagated rather than created. There remains the interesting question of the ultimate origin of molecular dissymmetry or how the first optically active compound was formed. Essentially, two possibilities have been discussed. Some substances, such as urea, are symmetric on the molecular scale but form dissymmetric crystals. It is possible that the first organic compounds were resolved by occlusion in the dissymmetric cavities of such crystals. Alternatively, a synthesis carried out in the presence of some dissymmetric physical agent may lead to a preponderance of an enantiomer. Le Bel pointed out that in the presence of light polarized in a peculiar way, the formation of a substance with an asymmetric carbon atom need not give equal amounts of the two enantiomers; much later his proposal was verified experimentally. Because light reflected from the surface of the ocean is polarized in the necessary way by the Earth's magnetic field, this proposal offers one reasonable explanation for the origin of optically active substances.

Racemization is the conversion of an optically active substance into its enantiomer by a process that ultimately results in a 50:50 mixture. The process may be brought about by a number of agents—such as by treatment with heat, acids, bases, light, or catalysts—that cannot be dealt with in a general way because the methods depend on the structure and chemical behaviour of the particular dissymmetric substance. Usually in laboratory syntheses of chiral natural products—as, for example, proteins from the individual, optically active amino acids—racemization is an undesirable process, and measures customarily are taken to minimize it.

STEREOISOMERISM OF ELEMENTS OTHER THAN CARBON

The possibilities for stereoisomerism about a central atom depend on the geometric orientation of its bonds. These may be directed toward the vertices of a tetrahedron (as with carbon bound to four other groups), or of many other figures, including simple pyramids, trigonal bipyramids, squares, octahedra, etc.

Tetrahedral structures. Several other elements form tetrahedral compounds analogous to those of carbon. If an atom of one of these elements is joined to four different groups, the racemic forms may be resolvable into the two enantiomers. The first successfully resolved examples of such compounds were ammonium salts, the positive ion of which had a tetrahedral nitrogen (N) atom with four different organic groups attached.

$$\left[\begin{array}{c} a \\ | \\ N \cdots c \\ b \quad d \end{array} \right]^{+} X^{-}$$

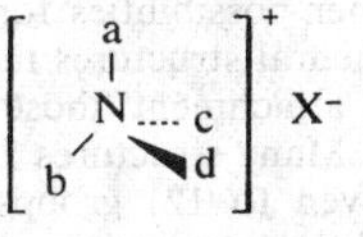

a tetrahedral ammonium ion

Analogous ions with phosphorus or arsenic in place of the nitrogen have been resolved, as have similar neutral molecules with silicon, germanium, or tin as the central atom.

Though certain other metals also form tetrahedral compounds or complexes (see COORDINATION COMPOUNDS), the groups, or ligands (Latin *ligare*, "to tie"),

that are bound to the metal often are readily replaced by solvent molecules or by other ligands. This situation permits rapid interconversion of the enantiomers, and usually only the racemic modification can be isolated; but, if two of the ligands are joined to one another so as to form a ring with the metal atom, the complexes are more stable, and the separate isomers can be prepared. Examples of the type shown below, with beryllium, boron, zinc, or copper as the metal M, are known:

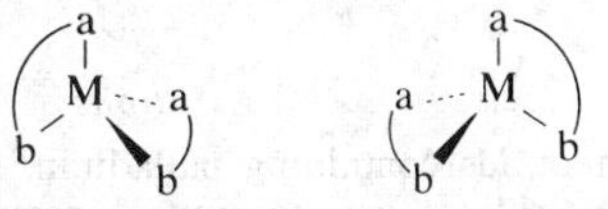

Because of the cyclic structures, the four groups need not necessarily be different from one another. These complexes have a chirality axis (through the metal and bisecting both a–M–b angles) and are analogous to the allenes, or optically active biphenyls.

Neutral nitrogen compounds are usually trivalent and, in addition to the three attached groups, have one unshared pair of electrons on the nitrogen atom.

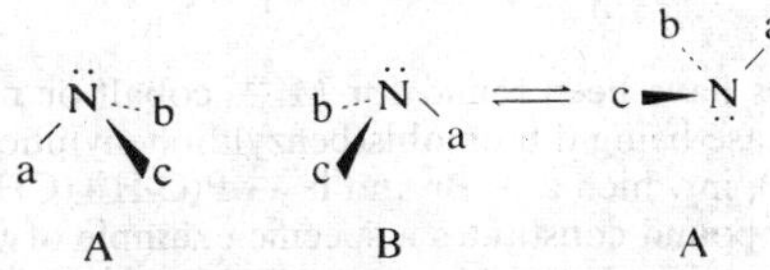

The geometry is pyramidal, with the nitrogen at the apex, and in principle two enantiomers (A and B) are possible. The absence of a fourth group, however, permits the molecule to undergo an inversion, like an umbrella in a strong wind, that interconverts the two enantiomers, as shown. It has been found that certain groups (such as chlorine or fluorine atoms for a, b, or c) slow down this motion, and separate isomers have been isolated. If the nitrogen in the above formulas is replaced by sulfur or selenium as the central atom, the resulting compounds do not undergo the umbrella-like inversion process and are readily resolvable into stable, optically active enantiomers.

When nitrogen is bound to carbon by a double bond, two isomers are possible. These are analogous to the *cis–trans* isomers of compounds having a carbon–carbon double bond. The terms *syn* and *anti* used with nitrogen compounds have the same meaning as *cis* and *trans*, and an electron pair (on the nitrogen) takes the place of an atom or group of atoms in the carbon analog.

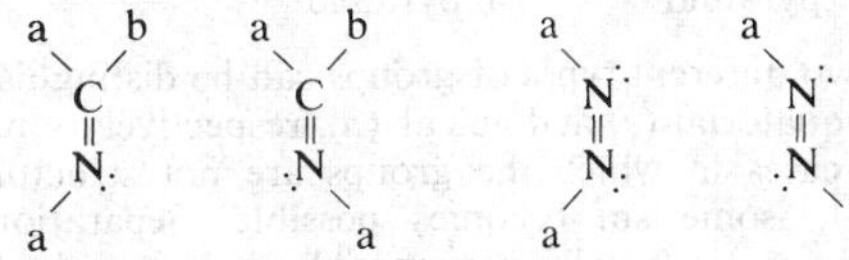

Syn and *anti* isomers

<table>
<tr><td>

a   b   a   b
\\ /   \\ /
C   C
‖   ‖
N   N
| |
a   a

</td><td>

a   a
\\   \\
N   N
‖   ‖
N   N
| |
a   a

</td></tr>
<tr><td align="center">

syn and *anti* isomers
of C = N compounds

</td><td align="center">

syn and *anti* isomers
of N = N compounds

</td></tr>
</table>

The structures have a plane of symmetry (the plane of the paper, as drawn) and are therefore achiral. The geometric isomers (or diastereomers) are usually separable, and they differ in all achiral properties. Classes of compounds that exhibit this type of isomerism are oximes, hydrazones, semicarbazones, imines, and others. The analogous compounds with a nitrogen–nitrogen double bond (azo compounds) exhibit entirely analogous behaviour.

Square planar structures. The other common geometry (besides tetrahedral) in molecules with four groups attached to a central atom is square planar. If the four groups are all different (Mabcd), three geometric (or diastereomeric) isomers are possible:

$$
\begin{array}{ccc}
b & c & d \\
| & | & | \\
a-M-c & a-M-d & a-M-b \\
| & | & | \\
d & b & c
\end{array}
$$

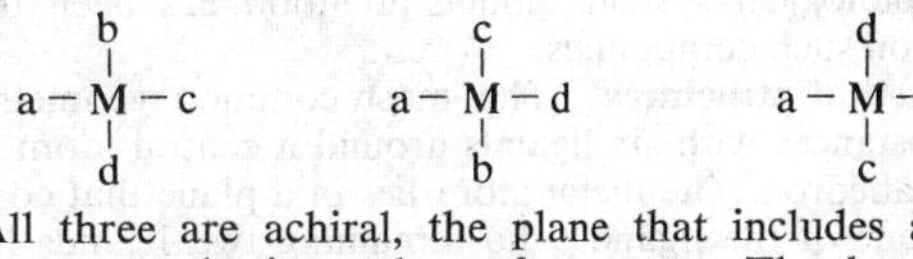

All three are achiral, the plane that includes all five atoms constituting a plane of symmetry. The three structures are distinct, however, as can readily be seen by noting that the group opposite (or *trans*) to a is different in each isomer. Much more common are complexes of the type Ma_2b_2, which can exist in two forms: *cis* and *trans*. A typical example is dichlorodiammineplatinum(II), $Pt[Cl_2(NH_3)_2]$, which has been isolated in each of the two isomeric structures.

cis *trans*

Similar compounds containing palladium, nickel, gold, rhodium, or iridium as the central metal atom are known.

In some relatively rare instances, both the square and the tetrahedral geometry are possible for a given central atom.

Examples have been found for M = cobalt or nickel, a specific case being dibromobis(benzyldiphenylphosphine) nickel(II), in which a = Br and b = $P(C_6H_5)_2(CH_2C_6H_5)$.) This compound constitutes a specific example of the possibility mentioned in the first part of this article: that two substances may subsequently differ only in the bond angles, with a consequent different location of the atoms in space.

Trigonal bipyramidal structures. Phosphorus (P) forms some compounds (for example, the pentafluoride PF_5) in which five groups are attached to the phosphorus atom. In these and other compounds in which five groups are attached to a single central atom, the most common geometry is the trigonal bipyramid. The central atom lies in a plane defined by three of the attached groups; the remaining two groups lie along an axis perpendicular to that plane.

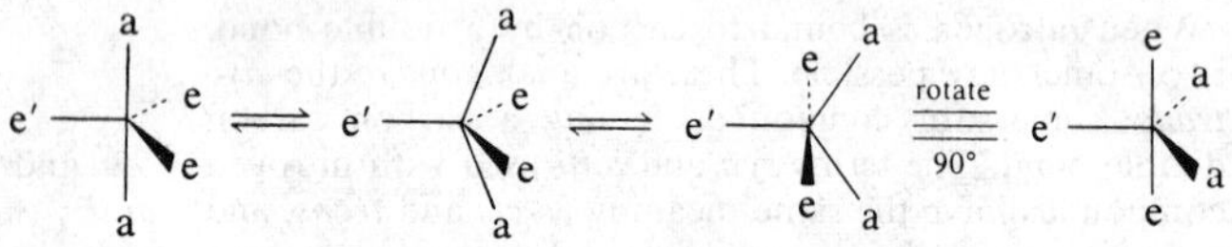

trigonal bipyramid — square pyramid — trigonal bipyramid

Thus, two different types of groups can be distinguished, called equatorial (*e*) and apical (*a*), respectively; and, in special cases in which the groups are not structurally identical, isomerism becomes possible. Separation of such isomers is usually not possible, however, because there exists a relatively easy mechanism for their interconversion. If one group, say *e′*, is held in a fixed position, then a small motion of the apical groups toward the remaining two equatorial groups, thus decreasing the angle between them, changes the geometry to that of a square pyramid. (Some compounds of zinc and nickel are known to have this geometry.) A counter motion of the two *e* groups, widening the angle between them, converts the structure back to a trigonal bipyramid, but the groups that were formerly apical are now equatorial, having exchanged places with two of the original equatorial groups. Because the equatorial plane is rotated 90° by these motions, the entire process is called pseudorotation. Trigonal bipyramidal structures are important as intermediates in the reactions of many phosphorus compounds; and, because of their widespread presence in many biological systems, much attention has been focussed on such compounds.

Pseudorotation

Octahedral structures. The most common geometry for substances with six ligands around a central atom is the octahedron. The metal atom lies in a plane that contains four of the ligands; the remaining two ligands lie on an axis that is perpendicular to this plane and passes through the metal atom. This structure permits the existence of a large number of stereoisomers, and many of these have been obtained, with such metals as cobalt, chromium, rhodium, iridium, ruthenium, or platinum as the central atoms. If all six groups attached to the metal are different (*i.e.*, Mabcdef), 15 pairs of enantiomers are possible, though no one has yet succeeded in obtaining all the theoretically possible isomers of such a molecule. Much more common are compounds in which several of the attached groups are identical, such as Ma_3b_3 or Ma_4b_2. Each of these may exist as geometric (*cis–trans*) isomers.

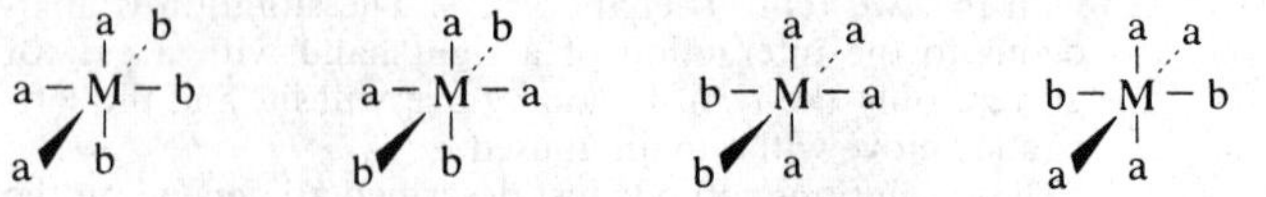

cis Ma_3b_3 *trans* Ma_3b_3 *cis* Ma_4b_2 *trans* Ma_4b_2

Cis isomers have all like groups adjacent (90° angles), but *trans* isomers have at least one pair of like groups in opposite positions (180° angles). Each of these structures has at least one symmetry plane; therefore, species of this type are achiral, but because they are pairs of diastereomers, they differ in all achiral properties. Specific examples are the platinum (Pt) and cobalt (Co) complexes with ammonia (NH_3) and chloride ion (Cl^-), trichlorotriammineplatinum(IV), $[Pt(NH_3)_3Cl_3]^+$, and dichlorotetramminecobalt(III), $[Co(NH_3)_4Cl_2]^+$.

When two or more of the ligands are chemically linked, a great variety of isomeric structures become possible, even when the ligands are identical. Compounds of the $[M(\widehat{aa})_3]$ type for example, may exist in two enantiomeric structures, as shown below.

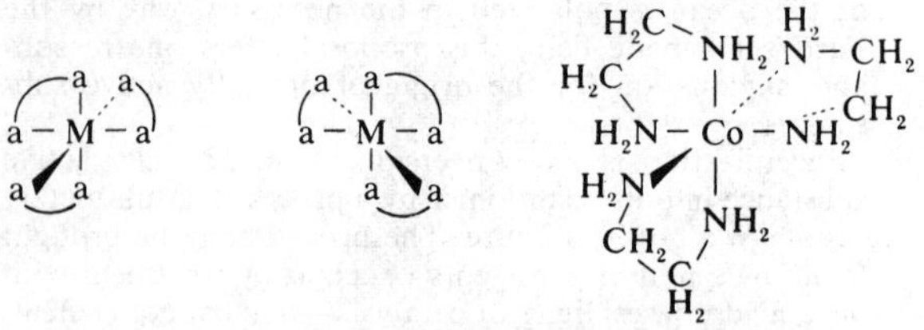

a pair of enantiomers (+)-isomer

The dextrorotatory isomer of the complex cobalt ion tris (ethylenediamine)cobalt(III), $[Co(NH_2CH_2CH_2NH_2)_3]^{3+}$, for example, has the absolute configuration corresponding to the general structure at the left.

Complexes of the type $[M(\widehat{aa})_2b_2]$ are also common; *cis* and *trans* geometric isomers are possible. The *cis* form may exist as either of two optically active enantiomers, but the *trans* form has several planes of symmetry and is optically inactive. The stereoisomers of a cobalt complex ion provide a specific example.

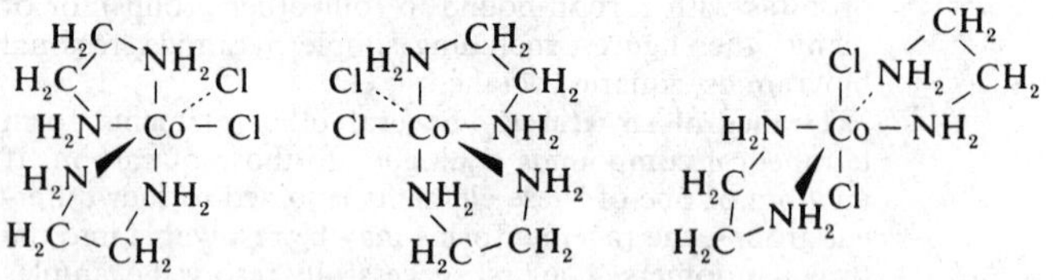

cis isomers, a pair of enantiomers — *trans* isomer, optically inactive

The *cis*-cobalt ions are violet, although the *trans* isomer is green. Many other possibilities for isomerism can be realized with octahedral structures through variations in the types of ligand attachment; those presented here are merely illustrative. Many structures are also known with more than six (seven to 12) groups around a central atom. The possibilities for isomerism increase with the molecular complexity, but such systems have not been studied as extensively as those with six or fewer groups around the central atom.

Other types of isomerism. Several rather common types of isomerism in coordination compounds are analogous to the structural isomerism of organic compounds. For example, in the linkage isomers $[Co(NH_3)_5NO_2]^{2+}$ and $[Co(NH_3)_5ONO]^{2+}$, the nitro ($-NO_2$) and nitrito ($-ONO$)

groups are linked to the central cobalt atom by a nitrogen or oxygen atom, respectively. This situation is analogous to the functional group isomerism of organic compounds. Ionization isomerism, as, for example, with $[Co(NH_3)_4Cl_2]^+ NO_2^-$ and $[Co(NH_3)_4ClNO_2]^+Cl^-$ in which the nitro group and a chloride ion interchange places, is a counterpart of positional isomerism in organic compounds. The three isomeric chromic chloride hydrates, $CrCl_3 \cdot 6H_2O$, constitute a particularly striking example; $[Cr(H_2O)_6]Cl_3$ is violet, but $[Cr(H_2O)_5Cl]Cl_2 \cdot H_2O$ and $[Cr(H_2O)_4Cl_2]Cl \cdot 2H_2O$, in which one or two chloride ions replace water molecules in the octahedral arrangement around the chromium atom, are green. Yet another type of positional isomerism is found in compounds in which the negative and positive ions are complex. The distribution of different ligands between the two ions gives rise to coordination isomers, as with the cobalt–chromium complexes:

$$[Co(NH_3)_6]^{3+}[Cr(CN)_6]^{3-} \text{ and } [Cr(NH_3)_6]^{3+}[Co(CN)_6]^{3-}.$$

DYNAMIC APPLICATIONS OF STEREOCHEMISTRY

This article has dealt almost exclusively with the recognition, delineation, and classification of stable isomers, but there are also dynamic aspects of the subject of isomerism. Intermediate between the reactants and the products in any chemical reaction lies a transition state. or transition complex, in which some chemical bonds in the reactants have been partially broken, and new chemical bonds, which will appear in the products, have partially formed. As with stable compounds, possible transition states for a chemical reaction may be isomeric; some may be enantiomeric, others diastereomeric, with different consequences for the outcome of the reaction (*i.e.*, products with different structures may be obtained, depending on the relationship between the various transition states). As an illustration, the following reaction may be considered:

$$CH_3-\underset{\displaystyle Br}{\overset{\displaystyle H}{C^*}}-CH_2CH_3+Br_2 \longrightarrow CH_3-\underset{\displaystyle Br}{\overset{\displaystyle H}{C^*}}-\underset{\displaystyle Br}{\overset{\displaystyle H}{C^*}}-CH_3+HBr.$$

One reactant is asymmetric (has an asymmetric carbon atom, marked with an asterisk); the other (bromine) is symmetric. Although it might at first be thought that there would be a 50–50 chance of replacing either hydrogen of the $-CH_2-$ group by a bromine atom, this is not true. The presence of a nearby asymmetric centre makes the two hydrogens stereochemically distinct, as the following structures show.

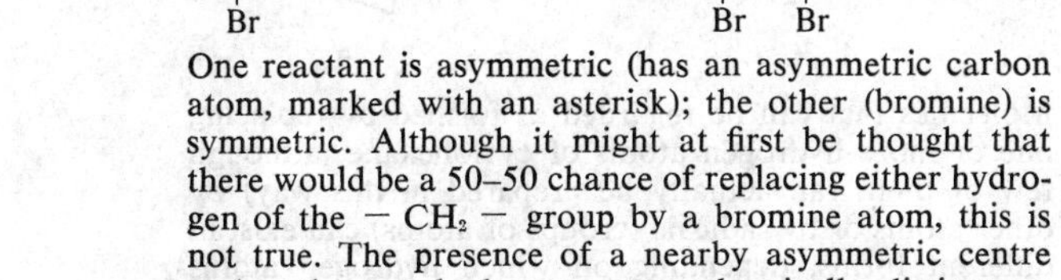

meso (optically inactive) | reactant | dissymmetric (optically active)

No matter what conformer of the reactant is drawn, H_a will always be in a different chemical environment (say, between H and CH_3) with respect to its neighbours than H_b (say, between CH_3 and Br). Replacement of H_a gives a meso product; but, if H_b is replaced, one of two enantiomers is produced. The products are diastereomers, as are the transition states leading to them. Because the transition states are not enantiomers, they need not be formed in equal amounts; consequently, the products are also not formed in equal amounts, and the reaction is said to be stereoselective (in this case, the product is 70 percent meso, 30 percent racemic). If one diastereomeric transition state is very much more stable than another, the reaction may proceed exclusively along the path that includes the stable form, in which case the product consists of only one stereoisomer, and the reaction is said to be stereospecific. Most biochemical processes are of this type. For example, only *d*-glucose (not the *l*-isomer) is fermentable by yeast or usable in cell metabolism; only one configuration of amino acid enantiomers is usable in protein synthesis, etc. The reason for the very high degree of stereospecificity of most biochemical reactions is that it is virtually impossible for the wrong enantiomer to fit into or react at the active site of an enzyme; that is, only one of the two diastereomeric transition states is accessible. Similar results are sometimes obtained with nonenzymatic catalysts, as in the formation of stereoregular polymers (see POLYMERS).

Stereoselective and stereospecific reactions

BIBLIOGRAPHY. For the historical development of the concept of isomerism, see J.R. PARTINGTON, *A History of Chemistry*, vol. 4 (1964). General discussions of organic stereochemistry are found in KURT MISLOW, *Introduction to Stereochemistry* (1965); E.L. ELIEL, *Stereochemistry of Carbon Compounds* (1962) and *Elements of Stereochemistry* (1969); the latter volume contains a short section on inorganic stereochemistry. Less detailed accounts of organic stereochemistry and isomerism are found in standard organic chemistry texts, such as C.R. NOLLER, *Chemistry of Organic Compounds*, 3rd ed. (1965); and LOUIS F. and MARY FIESER, *Advanced Organic Chemistry* (1961). Two inorganic chemistry texts that survey inorganic isomerism and contain references to more specialized sources are F.A. COTTON and GEOFFREY WILKINSON, *Advanced Inorganic Chemistry*, 2nd ed. (1966); and A.F. WELLS, *Structural Inorganic Chemistry*, 3rd ed. (1962). Specialized books on isomerism and stereochemistry include H.H. JAFFE and MILTON ORCHIN, *Symmetry in Chemistry* (1965); J.W. BAKER, *Tautomerism* (1934); E.L. ELIEL *et al.*, *Conformational Analysis* (1965); and J.D. MORRISON and H.S. MOSHER, *Asymmetric Organic Reactions* (1971). Continuing series that have short chapters on recent developments include W. KLYNE (ed.), *Progress in Stereochemistry;* and N.L. ALLINGER and E.L. ELIEL (eds.), *Topics in Stereochemistry.*

(H.Ha.)

Isoprenoids

Isoprenoids are members of a class of organic compounds formed in plants and animals by combination into larger molecules of units containing five carbon atoms arranged in the characteristic pattern present in the simple substance isoprene, from which the class takes its name. The name terpene, or terpenoid, derived from turpentine, which is a mixture of isoprenoids, is also applied to this class of compounds. In plants, isoprenoids occur in the essential oils, in the gummy exudates (oleoresins and latices) of many trees and shrubs, as substances affecting growth (such as the hormone gibberellic acid), and as red, yellow, and orange pigments (carotenoids). Chlorophyll, the green pigment essential in photosynthesis, is partly isoprenoid, as are certain alkaloids (*q.v.*), nitrogen-containing compounds present in many plants. In animals, isoprenoids comprise various oily or waxy substances as fish-liver oils, wool wax, and the yellow pigments in egg yolk, butterfat, feathers, and fish scales.

Several isoprenoids are vitally important in metabolic processes in animals: vitamins A, E, and K are wholly or partly isoprenoid in molecular structure, as are the ubiquinones (coenzymes Q), which are involved in the utilization of energy from food. In insects, certain isoprenoid substances influence maturation and mating behaviour or are used to communicate alarm or to repel predators. Steroids (*q.v.*), a class of compounds of great importance in both plants and animals, are not isoprenoids but are derived directly from them. Among many isoprenoids that are valuable in industry and commerce, turpentine, rosin, camphor, menthol, and natural rubber may be mentioned.

The problems in molecular structure presented by the isoprenoids have challenged the imagination and skill of organic chemists since the latter part of the 19th century. The first studies were mainly concerned with the structures of the monoterpenes, the molecules of which contain ten carbon atoms, but, as those structural patterns became familiar and techniques for investigation were developed, attention was turned increasingly toward those isoprenoids containing 15 to 40 carbon atoms. Otto Wallach, a German chemist, recognized in 1887 that the numerous ways in which the ten carbon atoms are arranged in the molecules of the monoterpenes, or the 15 carbon atoms in the sesquiterpenes, all could be regarded as resulting from various combinations of a

Studies of the isoprenoids

fundamental unit that contains five carbon atoms that are always connected in one of several possible ways. Wallach's proposal, called the isoprene rule, was of great help in understanding the structures of the more complex members of the class. By the mid-20th century, emphasis had fallen upon the origin of isoprenoids in biological systems, their relationships to other classes of natural products, and their powerful physiological effects in plants and animals.

CHEMISTRY OF ISOPRENOIDS

The isoprenoids lie within the scope of organic chemistry, and their structures, reactions, and properties are best understood in terms of the concepts peculiar to that discipline. Major topics of organic chemistry are treated in the articles CHEMICAL COMPOUNDS, ORGANIC; HYDROCARBONS; and MOLECULAR STRUCTURE. Only a brief summary of the relevant aspects of organic chemistry can be presented in this article.

Chemical bonds

Compounds that contain the element carbon—organic compounds—are more numerous than those of any other of the 100-odd chemical elements. This fact is a result of the ability of the carbon atom to form stable chemical bonds with atoms not only of many other elements but with other carbon atoms, so that molecules containing chains, rings, or networks of any number of carbon atoms can be formed. The bonds that join carbon atoms to others in organic compounds are of the type, called covalent, resulting from sharing of valence electrons by the nuclei of the two atoms, each atom contributing one, two, or three electrons to form a single, double, or triple bond, as in the simple organic compounds methane, ethylene, and acetylene. These compounds are represented by molecular formulas that show the numbers of atoms present: the molecular formula of methane, CH_4, expresses the fact that one atom of carbon (C) and four atoms of hydrogen (H) make up the molecule; in ethylene, C_2H_4, each molecule contains two atoms of carbon and four of hydrogen; and each molecule of acetylene, C_2H_2, contains two atoms of carbon and two of hydrogen.

The arrangement in space of the atoms and bonds in a molecule is depicted by a structural formula in which each atom is represented by its chemical symbol and each pair of shared electrons by a line (double and triple lines indicating double and triple bonds):

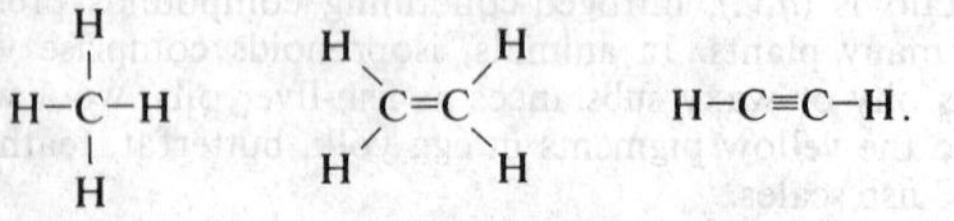

methane ethylene acetylene

An important property of covalent bonds is that they are specifically directed in space: the bonds between a carbon atom and the other atoms joined to it form angles that have characteristic values common to all organic compounds. For example, the angles between the bonds in the acetylene molecule are 180°, and the four atoms all lie along a straight line; in the ethylene molecule, the bond angles are close to 120°, and the six atoms lie in a plane; in methane, the angles are 109½°, and the carbon atom lies at the centre of a regular tetrahedron, the corners of which are occupied by the four hydrogen atoms. The atoms in the methane molecule do not all lie in one plane, as implied by the drawing, but are arranged in space as suggested by the perspective figure

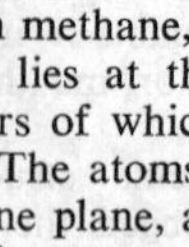

in which full lines stand for bonds lying in the plane of the page, the dotted line stands for a bond projecting away from the viewer, and the wedge, for a bond projecting up from the page toward the viewer.

Ethylene and acetylene are examples of unsaturated compounds, so called because their molecules contain carbon atoms bonded to fewer than the maximum possible number, four, of other atoms, as contrasted with methane, a saturated compound. In molecules composed entirely of carbon and hydrogen atoms, called hydrocarbons, the chemical properties are strongly influenced by any unsaturation in the structure. The presence of even one atom of another element, however, usually has an even more profound effect; in isoprenoids, oxygen often occurs in one or another of a few characteristic structural units called functional groups because they dominate the pattern of chemical reactivity. The most important of these groups are hydroxyl (– OH, present in alcohols), carbonyl (>C=O, present in aldehydes and ketones), and carboxyl (–C(=O)OH, present in acids).

Structural features. A structural feature especially common among isoprenoid compounds is a ring of six carbon atoms; the simplest compound possessing this structure is cyclohexane (not an isoprenoid), which is represented by the structural formula **1**, by a condensed version **2**, or simply by the hexagon **3**.

The six-carbon ring

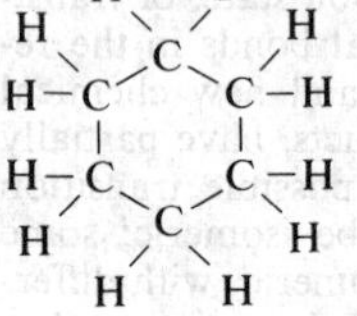

1

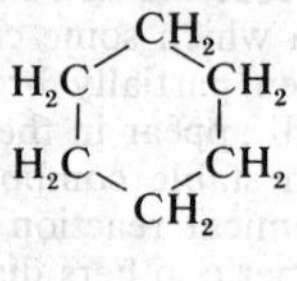

2

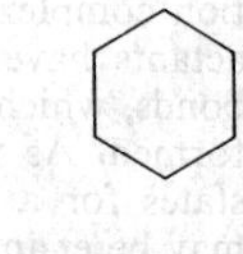

3

In compounds of this kind, the six ring atoms are not coplanar, but the ring usually is puckered, as shown in **4** and **5**.

4

5

Molecules that can be regarded as formed by replacing one or more hydrogen atoms of cyclohexane (although few of them can actually be prepared in this way) by other atoms or by radicals (groups of atoms) can exist in different forms, depending on which hydrogen atoms are replaced. In the isoprenoid alcohol menthol, for example, three of the hydrogen atoms of cyclohexane have been replaced, each by a different radical: structure **6** shows only the bonding pattern without implying the spatial arrangement, but **7** and **8** specify the orientation of the bonds and the conformation of the ring in the natural form of menthol. Effects of differences in the three-

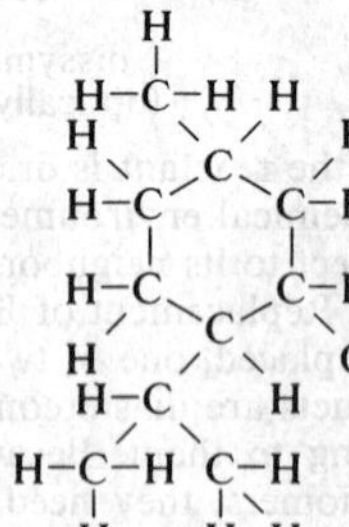

6

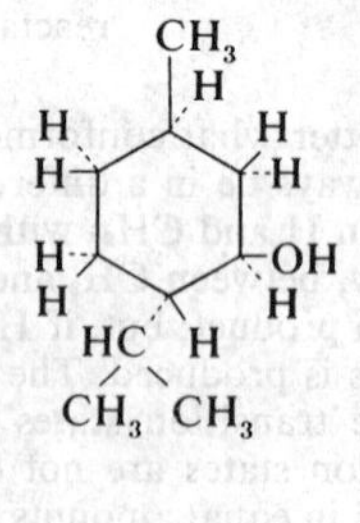

7

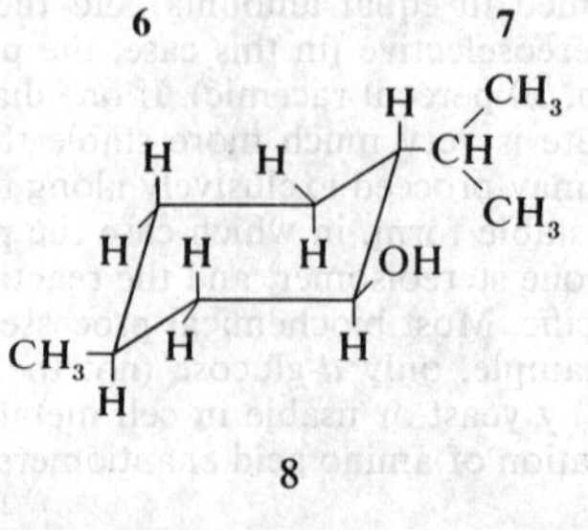

8

dimensional disposition of atoms within molecules are covered in the articles ISOMERISM; and CONFORMATIONAL ANALYSIS, PRINCIPLES OF.

The term carbon skeleton is used to describe the pattern in which the carbon atoms are bonded together in a molecule, disregarding atoms of other elements and differences between single and multiple bonds. Most chemical reactions of organic compounds do not break bonds between carbon atoms and therefore leave the carbon skeleton unchanged. In many isoprenoids, rings of three, four, or five carbon atoms form part of the molecular structure. In these small rings, the bond angles are severely distorted from the values typical of stable molecules, and the carbon–carbon bonds can be broken with unusual ease. Many reactions in which carbon skeletons are rearranged were first observed during investigations of the isoprenoids and caused considerable confusion until the causes of their occurrence were recognized.

Classification. The isoprenoids are broadly classified according to the number of isoprene (C_5H_8) units they contain, and they range in size from volatile oils of molecular formula $C_{10}H_{16}$ to giant molecules such as that of natural rubber, which contains about 4,000 isoprene units. The classes are: monoterpenes, $C_{10}H_{16}$; sesquiterpenes $C_{15}H_{24}$; diterpenes, $C_{20}H_{32}$; triterpenes, $C_{30}H_{48}$; tetraterpenes. $C_{40}H_{64}$; polyterpenes, $(C_5H_8)_n$. Many of the isoprenoids possess carbon skeletons that may be regarded as built up from isoprene units

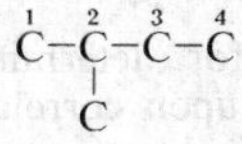

linked "head to tail"; that is, carbon atom 1 of one unit is bonded to carbon atom 4 of the next. Formation of additional bonds in a variety of ways leads to monocyclic, bicyclic, and further subclasses in which one, two, or larger numbers of rings are present. *β*-myrcene (**9**), an acyclic monoterpene; limonene (**10**), a monocyclic monoterpene; *α*-pinene (**11**), a bicyclic monoterpene; and

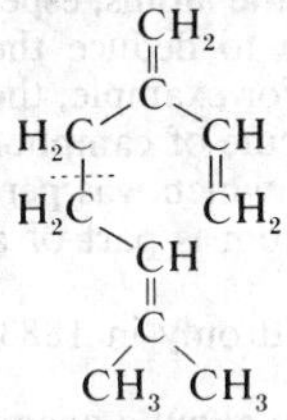

9

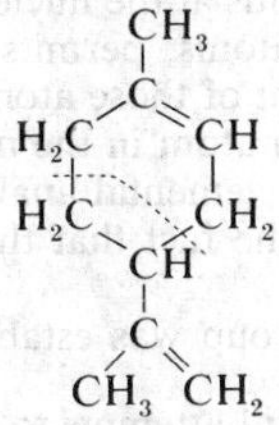

10

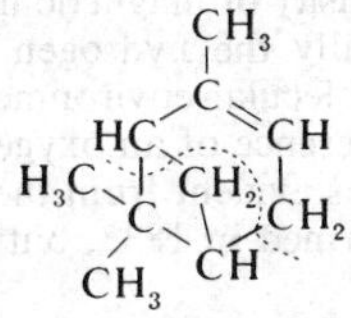

11

vitamin A (**12**), an oxygenated monocyclic diterpene, exemplify this further classification; the dotted lines in the structural formulas indicate the division of the carbon skeletons into isoprene units. The structures of

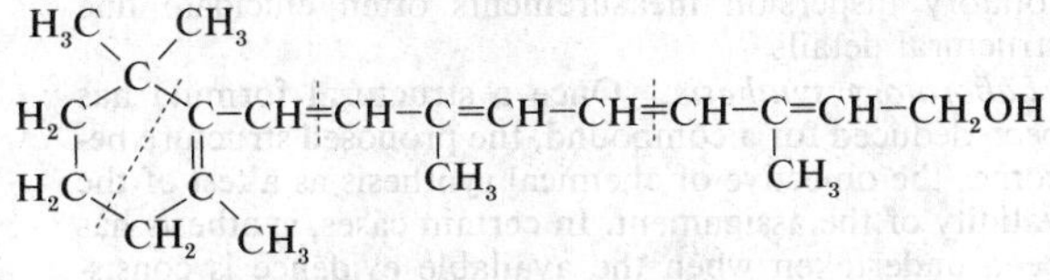

12

most triterpenes and tetraterpenes show that they were formed by establishment of a tail-to-tail bond between two smaller units: in the structural formula of the important triterpene hydrocarbon squalene (**13**), for example, the arrow indicates the bond uniting two sesquiterpene portions.

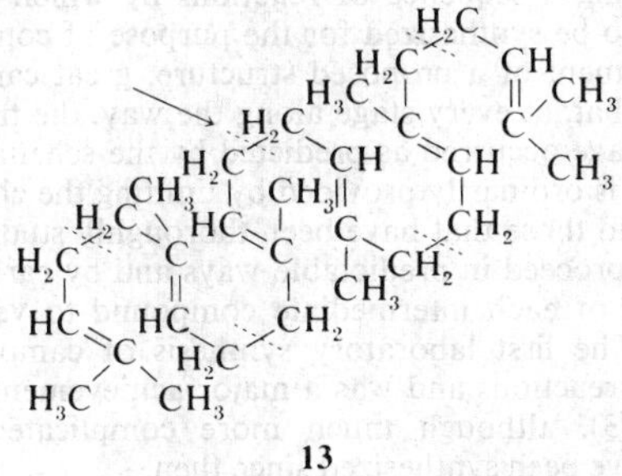

13

Natural sources. Isoprenoids are not uniformly distributed among plants or animals, but certain classes of these compounds are typical of broad groups of tissues. The essential oils—more or less volatile materials obtainable from odorous plants by physical means, such as extraction with solvents, distillation, or expression—are most often monoterpene or sesquiterpene hydrocarbons or their oxygenated derivatives, such as alcohols, aldehydes, or ketones. Menthol, citral, camphor, limonene, and *α*-pinene are examples of this group; often a single species or group of related species is characterized by the presence of one of these compounds. The nonvolatile substances present in resins produced by trees of the pine family contain diterpene carboxylic acids belonging to three types, abietic, palustric, and elliotinoic; the latices of a few species of plants contain the polyterpene hydrocarbons rubber or gutta-percha.

Essential oils

The livers of fishes and other animals are particularly rich in oils that are largely acyclic triterpenoid hydrocarbons, especially squalene. Tetraterpene hydrocarbons and a few of their oxygenated derivatives make up most of the carotenoid pigments that are widespread in plants and animals.

Importance. *Biological functions.* The natural biological functions of isoprenoids are, in many cases, unknown. Those that have been deduced, however, are extremely diversified. In both plants and animals, isoprenoids are intermediates in the formation of steroids, which, in animals, have been shown to perform numerous essential tasks. In plants, tetraterpene carotenoid pigments are closely associated with chlorophyll (a partially isoprenoid compound) in photosynthesis; the same group of pigments are, in animals, the source of vitamin A, a substance essential to visual processes. Vitamin A is also involved in growth, reproductive function, and neural development in animals. Other vitamins that are wholly or partly isoprenoid include vitamin E, important in reproduction, and vitamin K, necessary for the blood-clotting process.

The role of the monoterpenes and sesquiterpenes produced by plants has not been established, although it has been suggested that they attract certain insects and repel others. This idea is connected with the presence in insects of some of the very same compounds, which are used to signal alarm, to repulse predators, to mark the way between food sources and the nest, to attract members of the opposite sex and stimulate mating. Certain plants produce isoprenoids that are very similar to hormones involved in the development of insects that prey on those plants; the plant substances prevent the maturation of the insect, thus serving to defend the plant. The rosin acids of pine trees and the rubber and gutta-percha in latices of various plants may serve as wound-sealing agents.

Uses. Of the uses that man has found for isoprenoids, many were established in antiquity, as ingredients of perfumes and incenses, flavourings and spices, and varnishes and medicinals. Amber, a fossilized isoprenoid resin, has been prized as a gemstone since prehistoric times. Rubber was in use by the Central and South American Indians before the Spanish conquest.

Modern applications are extremely diversified. Turpentine, long employed as a solvent, is now mostly used as a source of its individual components, which are raw materials for chemical processing. Products derived from turpentine include ingredients for perfumes, vitamin A, lubricant additives, insecticides, resins used in adhesives, and industrial chemicals. Rosin, usually modified by chemical treatment, is widely used to make inexpensive soaps and coating materials.

Isolation and identification. Numerous procedures have been developed for the isolation of isoprenoids from their natural sources. The selection of a technique is influenced by such factors as the chemical and physical properties of the compound and its abundance and distribution in nature. Volatile and plentiful substances as turpentine are obtainable by distillation of oleoresins;

Isolation techniques

rosin acids and fatty acids occur together in tall oil, a by-product obtained in the manufacture of paper pulp from pine wood, and they are separated by fractional distillation at reduced pressure. Extremely rare compounds, as the insect hormones, have been isolated by chromatography (a method of separating the components of a solution, or mixture, based on selective adsorption onto a layer or column of suitable material). For the isolation of heat-sensitive perfume ingredients from flower petals, the laborious process of enfleurage is employed: the petals are placed in thin layers of carefully purified fat, in which the floral oils dissolve; they are recovered from the fat by washing with alcohol.

Chemical identification of isoprenoids, like that of organic compounds in general, falls into a classical pattern of steps that has the goal of furnishing a complete description of the molecule. This description includes specification of the number and kinds of the atoms present, the chemical bonds that hold the atoms together, and the three-dimensional arrangement of these atoms and bonds. The sequence of operations necessary for such an identification comprises purification, determination of atomic composition, and assignment of structure. Verification of the assignment is accomplished by synthesis of the compound from others of previously established structure by chemical reactions that proceed in known ways. These essential phases of a chemical identification are more fully covered in CHEMICAL SEPARATIONS AND PURIFICATIONS; CHEMICAL ANALYSIS; MOLECULAR STRUCTURE; and CHEMICAL SYNTHESIS, PRINCIPLES OF.

Purification. Isoprenoids can be purified by various techniques that depend primarily upon the physical properties of the compound, as melting or boiling points or solubilities in various other substances. The chemical properties may be an advantage or a disadvantage in the application of these methods: a compound in which heating induces a chemical reaction would be destroyed rather than purified by a procedure requiring the application of heat, as distillation or sublimation. On the other hand, methods depending on physical properties often cannot effect a satisfactory separation of a mixture of compounds possessing very similar physical properties; sometimes such mixtures can be converted by chemical treatment into a mixture of new substances that can be more readily separated; the separated components may then be reconverted into the original compounds.

In general, solid compounds can be purified by recrystallization; and volatile compounds (either solid or liquid), by distillation. Nonvolatile liquids or solids contaminated by very similar substances can be purified by chromatography. Because even small amounts of contaminants can give rise to seriously misleading results in chemical identification, purification of a compound for this purpose must be carried to the highest attainable degree; it is highly desirable to subject a substance to a succession of purification procedures based upon different principles, as distillation and crystallization. The rigour of this requirement is far higher than in purification of a substance for the purpose of suiting it to typical practical applications, for which it is often sufficient only to remove components that would be objectionable in the intended application (*e.g.*, those that impart unwanted odour, colour, or flavour).

Analysis. Determination of the elemental composition of isoprenoids seldom presents difficulty because many of them are hydrocarbons, and a simple, reliable procedure for quantitative analysis of carbon and hydrogen has been available since the early 19th century. The only other element commonly present in isoprenoids is oxygen, which does not interfere with the analysis for carbon and hydrogen, although it is difficult to determine directly: usually it is assumed to comprise the proportion of the compound not accounted for as carbon, hydrogen, and any other elements that have been measured.

Classical structural determination

Determination of structure. Assignment of structures to isoprenoids presented a very difficult problem. In the period when the monoterpenes were first investigated, the method of determining the structure of an organic compound was based entirely on studies of chemical reactions, usually those in which one or a few bonds in the compound were broken, giving successively simpler compounds, each of which was isolated, purified, and analyzed. These sequences of reactions eventually led to compounds possessing known structures, and the path back to the original substance was inferred from knowledge of the structural changes associated with the reactions employed. Frequently it was impossible to distinguish among alternate proposals; that is, more than one structure would be considered consistent with the information available. The situation was aggravated by the facts that many of the isoprenoids possess structures of a kind never previously observed, in which carbon atoms are linked together in small rings, and that, in many isoprenoids, the original carbon skeleton changes to a different one in the course of a reaction. One of the most difficult cases was the compound camphor, for which more than 30 different structures were proposed before the correct one (**14**) was established.

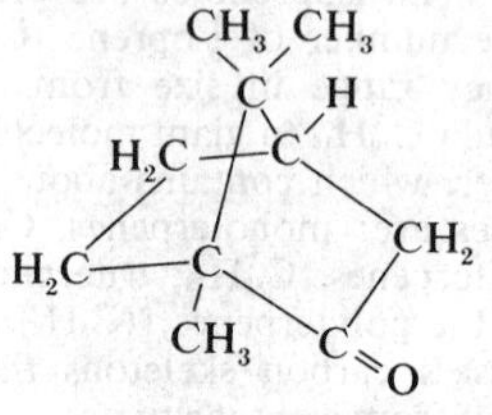

14

Modern techniques for determination of molecular structure lean heavily upon correlations between structural features and physical properties; many relationships of this kind have been established. Measurements of the wavelengths and intensities of absorption of ultraviolet, visible, and infrared light allow the chemist to draw very reliable inferences concerning the presence or absence of certain atomic groups and the distribution of electrons in the chemical bonding system. Determination of the intensity of magnetic fields at the nuclei of the atoms, especially the hydrogen atoms, permits him to deduce the molecular environment of those atoms. For example, the presence of an oxygen atom in the molecule of camphor was evident from the elemental analysis, which was performed in 1833, but the fact that that atom is part of a carbonyl ($>C=O$) group was established only in 1883, after many unsuccessful attempts to bring about a chemical reaction that would reveal that group. Nowadays, the presence of a carbonyl group would be instantly recognized by its characteristic absorption of infrared light. In favourable cases, complete structures have been revealed by X-ray crystal analysis. Mass spectra and optical rotatory dispersion measurements often elucidate fine structural details.

Laboratory synthesis. Once a structural formula has been deduced for a compound, the proposed structure becomes the objective of chemical synthesis as a test of the validity of the assignment. In certain cases, synthesis has been undertaken when the available evidence is consistent with more than one structure, but it appears simpler to synthesize all the likely candidates and to compare each of them with the unidentified compound than to seek further information from studies of chemical or physical properties.

In selecting a sequence of reactions by which a compound is to be synthesized for the purpose of confirming the assignment of a proposed structure, great care must be taken that, at every stage along the way, the transformations have occurred as predicted by the scheme. Such assurance is ordinarily provided by limiting the choice of reactions to those that have been thoroughly studied and shown to proceed in predictable ways and by careful examination of each intermediate compound to verify its identity. The first laboratory synthesis of camphor required 11 reactions and was a major achievement at the time (1903), although much more complicated compounds have been synthesized since then.

Camphor has been synthesized commercially by a series of reactions utilizing isoprenoids obtained from turpentine as the starting materials. Vitamin A is another isoprenoid manufactured by synthetic processes; several alternate reaction sequences have been developed for this compound.

Isoprenoids from acetate

Biosynthesis. By the late 1940s, the ubiquity of the five-carbon isoprene unit had been recognized for a long time, but the identity of the compounds actually involved in the physiological assembly of the isoprenoids was not known, although it had been suggested that they were somehow built up from acetic acid, the molecule of which contains only two carbon atoms. During the 1950s, it was shown that the synthesis of isoprenoids in nature indeed begins with acetylcoenzyme A, sometimes called activated acetate, a compound derived from acetic acid and coenzyme A, a complex substance that participates in many reactions that are controlled by enzymes. Previously unknown compounds, mevalonic acid and isopentenyl pyrophosphate (IPPP), occur as important intermediates in the process. The 1964 Nobel Prize for Physiology or Medicine was awarded to two German-born biochemists, Konrad Bloch and Feodor Lynen, for their contributions to this research.

The molecule of isopentenyl pyrophosphate is the long-sought physiological isoprene unit, containing five carbon atoms bonded together in the pattern discerned by Wallach in the 19th century. Most of the natural isoprenoids have structures that reveal the joining of two, three, four, six, or eight isoprene units; rubber is an isoprenoid in which several thousands of these units are connected in a long chain.

The process by which acetic acid units combine to form mevalonic acid (**15**) and isopentenyl pyrophosphate (**16**) is indicated by the equations below, in which *X* represents the complicated molecular structure of coenzyme A.

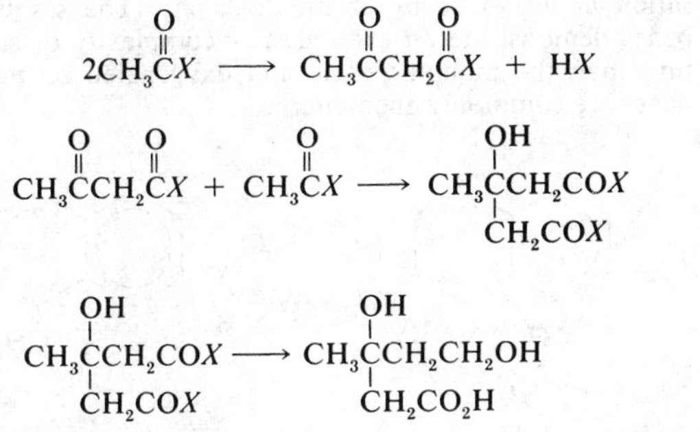

15

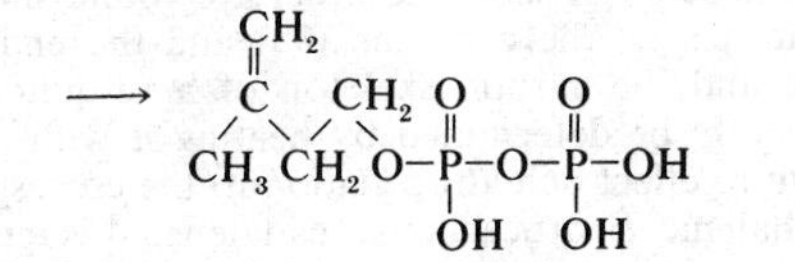

16 (IPPP)

The formation of geranyl pyrophosphate (**18**), the precursor of the monoterpenes, from two molecules of IPPP requires that one of them be transformed to dimethylallyl pyrophosphate (DMAPP, **17**). In the equations below, only the covalent bonds of the carbon skeletons are shown, and *Z* stands for the pyrophosphate group.

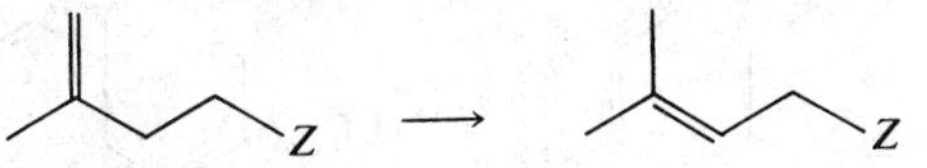

IPPP **17** (DMAPP)

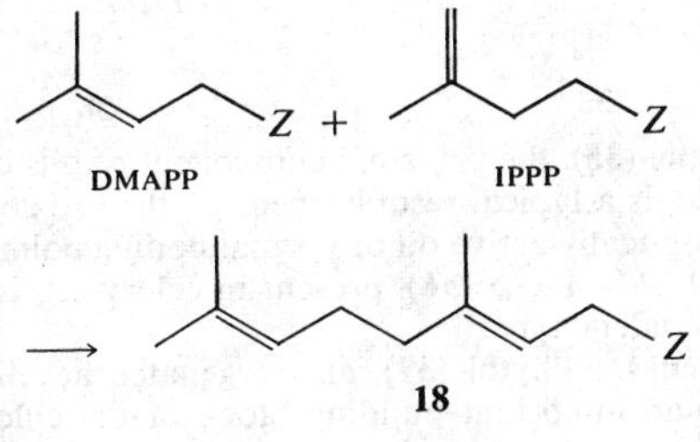

18

A similar reaction of geranyl pyrophosphate with IPPP leads to the 15-carbon compound, farnesyl pyrophosphate (**19**), from which the sesquiterpenes are derived, which, in turn, is converted to the 20-carbon precursor (**20**) of the diterpenes.

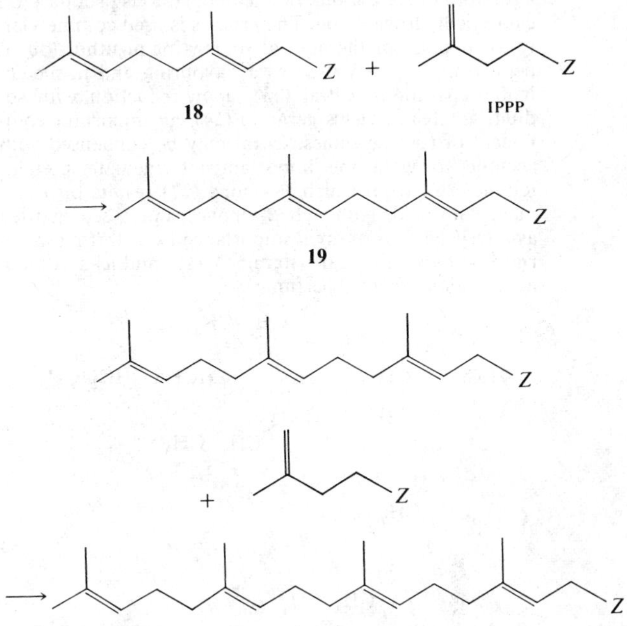

20

All these reactions produce substances in which the isoprene units are joined head-to-tail; many of the larger isoprenoid molecules (triterpenes and tetraterpenes) are not built up by further incorporation of IPPP units but by tail-to-tail coupling of 15- or 20-carbon compounds. The structure of squalene (**13**), a triterpene, illustrates this point. The tetraterpene carotenoids apparently arise from a similar reaction of two 20-carbon isoprenoids.

COMPARATIVE SURVEY OF ISOPRENOID COMPOUNDS

Monoterpenes. The monoterpenes are isolated from their natural sources by distillation of the plant matter with steam. They are volatile oils, less dense than water, and have normal boiling points in the range 150°–185° C (300°–365° F). Purification is usually achieved by fractional distillation at reduced pressures or by regeneration from a crystalline derivative.

Acyclic monoterpenes

Acyclic monoterpene hydrocarbons are few in number, but their oxygenated derivatives are more widespread in nature and of greater importance.

Important oxygenated acyclic monoterpene derivatives

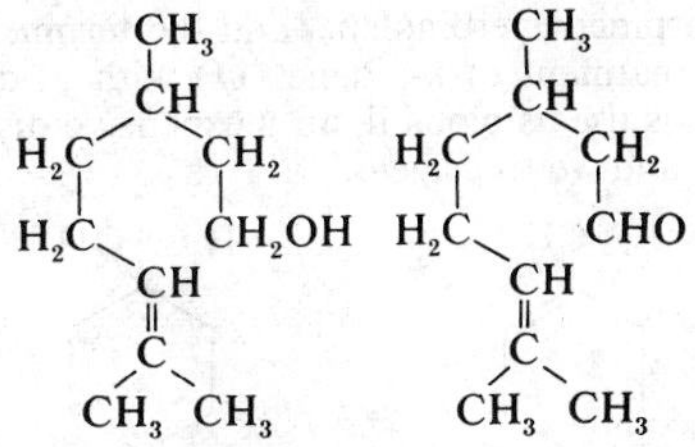

21 **22**

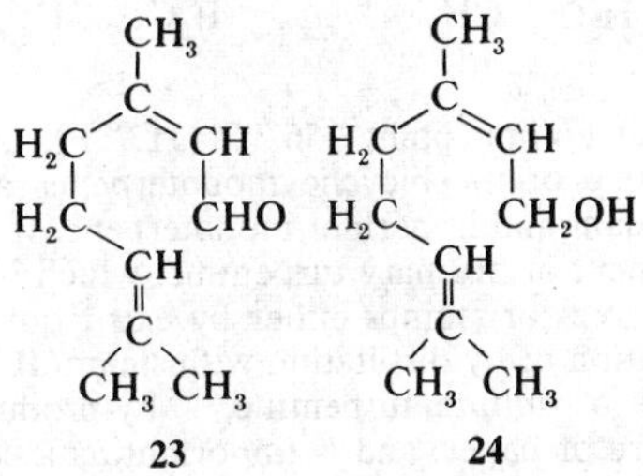

23 **24**

include the terpene alcohol citronellol (**21**) and the corresponding aldehyde citronellal (**22**), both of which occur in oil of citronella, as well as citral (**23**), found in lemongrass oil, and geraniol (**24**), which occurs in Turkish geranium oil.

Citronellal is converted by treatment with acid into the monocyclic monoterpene alcohol isopulegol, from which a mixture of stereoisomeric menthols (**25**) is produced on catalytic hydrogenation. The process is used commercially to supplement the natural sources of menthol (oil of peppermint), widely used as a flavouring and in medicinal preparations. Citral (**23**), upon reduction with sodium amalgam, yields geraniol (**24**), an important component of rose perfumes. Citral may be condensed with acetone to yield the important intermediate pseudoionone (**26**), from which β-ionone (**27**) results on treatment with acid. Although β-ionone cannot be regarded as a terpene, it is of great importance as a starting material for the synthesis of vitamin A (**12**) and as a component of violet-scented perfumes.

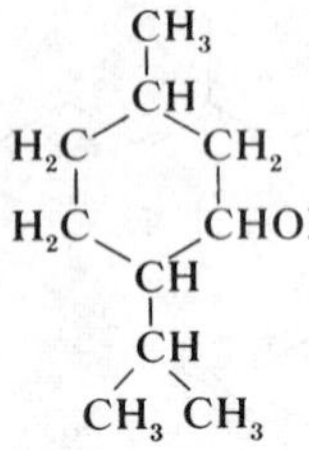

25

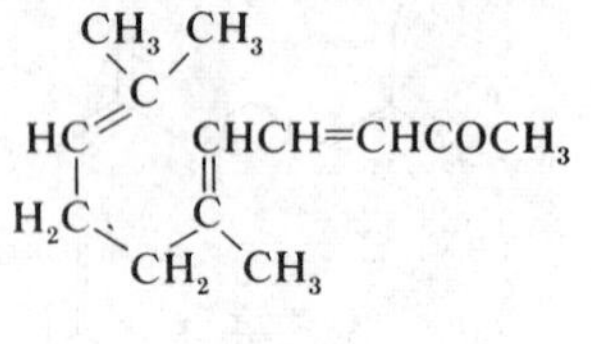

26

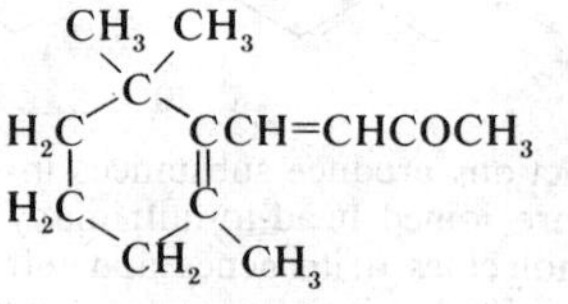

27

Monocyclic monoterpenes

Limonene (**10**), an oil of normal boiling point 178° C (352° F), is a major component of orange and lemon oils and is typical of the monocyclic monoterpene hydrocarbons. Others of this class are terpinolene, α- and β-phellandrene, and α-, β-, and γ-terpinene, all of which have the same carbon skeleton as limonene and differ only in the location of the two carbon-to-carbon double bonds. Limonene is optically active (it rotates the plane of polarized light), as are most of the terpenes and their derivatives that contain an asymmetric carbon atom—that is, one bonded to four different groups. Limonene is converted to isoprene by contact with a heated metallic filament. Few commercial uses, other than as flavourings, exist for the monocyclic monoterpene hydrocarbons. Menthol (**25**), which has already been mentioned, and the oxygenated derivatives α-terpineol (**28**) and terpin (terpin hydrate; **29**) are chemicals of commerce. Mixtures of terpin, α-terpineol, terpinolene, and the terpinenes result from the treatment of α-pinene (**11**) with acid, and the mixture finds use as pine oil, an inexpensive disinfectant, deodorant, and wetting agent.

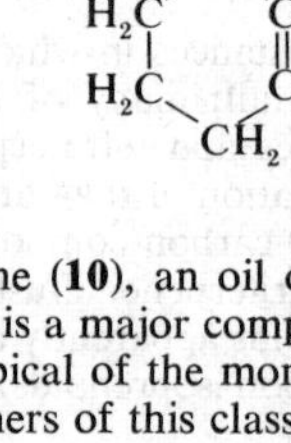

28

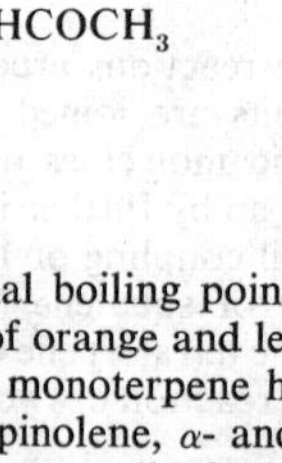

29

Bicyclic monoterpenes

Of normal boiling point 156° C (313° F), α-pinene is representative of the bicyclic monoterpenes and is the most abundant and important monoterpene. It is the major component of ordinary turpentine, which is prepared from pine trees or stumps either by extraction followed by rectification or by distillation with steam. It is a major component of sulfate turpentine, a by-product of the manufacture of paper, and is important as a component of paints and varnishes and as a raw material for the production of a wide variety of products employed in chemical industry.

Its use in coating materials depends upon its good properties as a solvent and upon its conversion by air oxidation into a polymeric, resinous film. Its function as a starting material for conversion to more useful products results from its abundance and its structure, which has a high degree of chemical reactivity. The chemical reactions of α-pinene have been studied more thoroughly than those of any other terpene, and the study has contributed greatly to the understanding of molecular rearrangements in organic chemistry.

Treatment of α-pinene with acids under various conditions leads to a host of products, among which are terpinolene, the terpinenes, α-terpineol (**28**), and terpin (**29**), previously mentioned, and, in addition, borneol (**30**), fenchyl alcohol (**31**), and the hydrocarbon camphene (**32**).

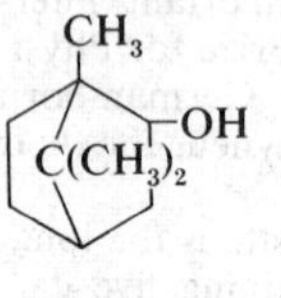

30

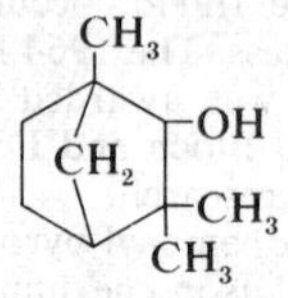

31

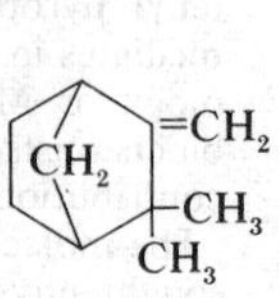

32

The formation of the latter three compounds involves molecular rearrangement, and advantage has been taken of the structural changes to provide a commercial synthesis of the important bicyclic terpene ketone, camphor (**14**).

Sesquiterpenes. Sesquiterpenes, $C_{15}H_{24}$, are isolated from their natural sources by distillation with steam or by extraction because they are of lower volatility than the monoterpenes. They are purified by fractional distillation *in vacuo* or by chromatography. The sesquiterpenes demonstrate an even greater complexity of structure than the monoterpenes, and oxygenated sesquiterpenes are commonly encountered.

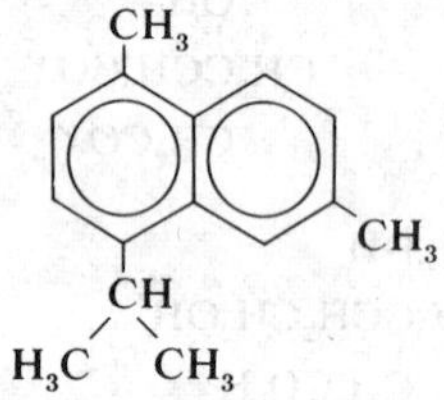

33

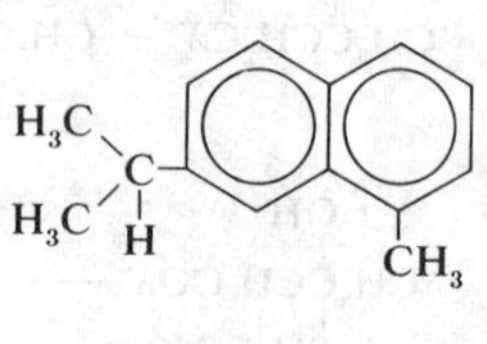

34

Two arrangements of isoprene units are found in bicyclic sesquiterpenes, the cadalene (**33**) and the eudalene (**34**) types, and the carbon skeleton of a sesquiterpene may frequently be determined by heating it with sulfur or selenium to effect dehydrogenation to the corresponding naphthalenic hydrocarbons: cadalene, 4-isopropyl-1,6-dimethylnaphthalene; or eudalene, 7-isopropyl-1-methylnaphthalene. In those cases in which sulfur dehydrogenation fails to yield information about the carbon skeleton of a sesquiterpene, a systematic degradation by oxidation to compounds of known structure is necessary.

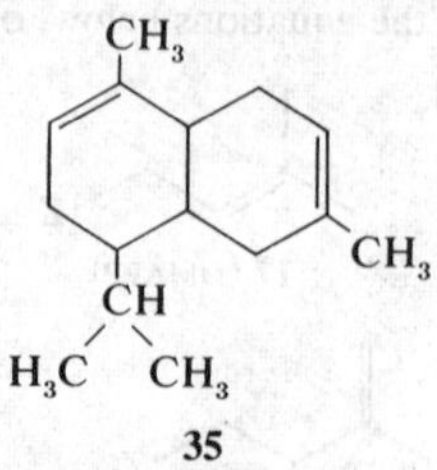

35

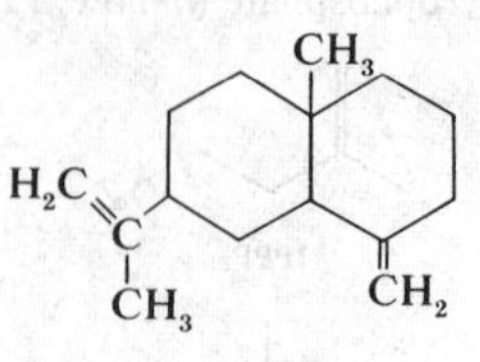

36

Cadinene (**35**), the principal component of oils of cubeb and cade, is a typical sesquiterpene of the cadalene type. It is an optically active oil of normal boiling point 274° C (525° F). β-Selinene (**36**), present in celery oil, is typical of the eudalene type.

Diterpenes. Phytol (**37**), an oxygenated acyclic diterpene, is an important building block of the chlorophyll molecule, from which it is obtained on treatment with alkali solution. The arrangement of isoprene units in phytol is identical with that in vitamin A (**12**), a monocyclic diterpene derivative, and is typical of the head-to-tail arrangement of isoprene units found in most terpenes.

$$\underset{\displaystyle CH_3}{CH_3CH}CH_2CH_2CH_2\underset{\displaystyle CH_3}{CH}CH_2CH_2CH_2\underset{\displaystyle CH_3}{CH}CH_2CH_2CH_2\underset{\displaystyle CH_3}{C}{=}CHCH_2OH$$

37

The commercial importance of the bicyclic monoterpene α-pinene is paralleled in the diterpenes by abietic acid (**38**), a tricyclic carboxylic acid that constitutes the major portion of rosin. Rosin is the nonvolatile portion of the oleoresin of members of the pine family and is the residue left after the isolation of turpentine. Rosin is used as such in the production of varnish and coating materials and, in the form of its sodium salt, for sizing paper, as an emulsifying agent in producing synthetic rubber, and in yellow laundry soap. It is among the cheapest organic acids.

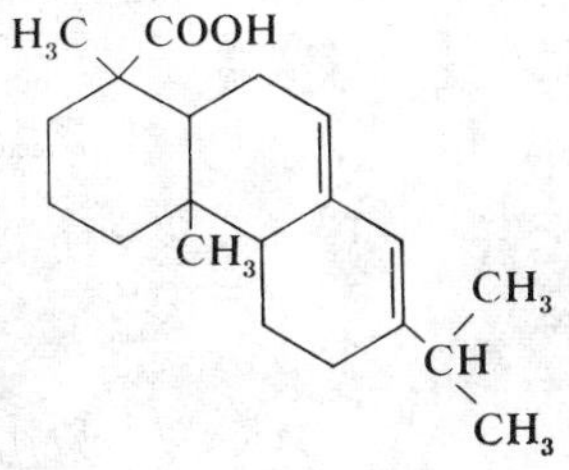

38

Squalene

Triterpenes. The acyclic triterpene hydrocarbon squalene (**13**) constitutes more than half of the liver oil of certain species of sharks and is otherwise rather widely distributed in nature. It has been found in other fish-liver oils, in vegetable oils, in fungi, and in human earwax and sebaceous secretions. The biochemical importance of squalene as a metabolic intermediate in the biosynthesis of cholesterol was demonstrated by the use of radioactive carbon labelling.

Although cholesterol is not a terpene, the demonstration that it has a terpene as precursor in metabolism represented a major advance in understanding the biochemical relationship between the two important classes of compounds.

Although tricyclic and tetracyclic triterpenes are known, by far the most abundant triterpenes found in nature are those having five carbon rings. The pentacyclic triterpenes, either free or combined with sugars in glycosides (saponins), occur in all parts of many plants. The structures of many of the pentacyclic triterpenes are now known in full detail; that of β-amyrin (**39**) exemplifies the important structural features of this class of substances. The best source of β-amyrin is the resin of the tropical tree elemi, although it has been isolated from more than 50 plant sources. The carbon skeleton of β-amyrin bears a striking relationship to those of squalene and cholesterol, and it has been shown that squalene is a common precursor of the pentacyclic triterpenes and the sterols in biosynthesis.

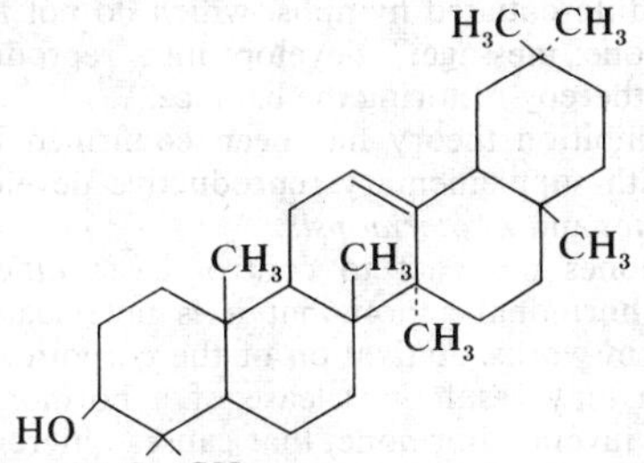

39

Carot-enoids

Tetraterpenes. The large class of yellow, orange, or red, fat-soluble plant and animal pigments known as carotenoids are classed as tetraterpenes, although they have in general the molecular formula $C_{40}H_{56}$ rather than $C_{40}H_{64}$ as required by $(C_5H_8)_8$. The fact that their structures can be built up from isoprene units justifies their classification as terpenes. The carotenoids are isolated from their natural sources by solvent extraction and purified by chromatography.

Lycopene (**40**), the red pigment of the ripe tomato, exemplifies the class of acyclic tetraterpenes. The dotted lines in the formula show the division into isoprene units, and it is to be noted that the usual head-to-tail attachment of isoprene units is interrupted in the centre of the molecule with a single tail-to-tail attachment that produces a symmetrical structure. This feature is generally encountered in the tetraterpenes, as is the long series of alternating single and double, carbon-to-carbon bonds (conjugated system) that is responsible for the absorption of light and hence the bright colours of the compounds.

$$\left[CH_3\underset{\displaystyle CH_3}{C}{=}CHCH_2\vdots CH_2\underset{\displaystyle CH_3}{C}{=}CHCH{=}\vdots CH\underset{\displaystyle CH_3}{C}{=}CHCH{=}\vdots CH\underset{\displaystyle CH_3}{C}{=}CHCH{=}\right]_2$$

40

The most important and abundant tetraterpene is β-carotene (**41**), the principal yellow pigment of the carrot; β-carotene is of nutritional importance because the animal organism is apparently able to cleave the molecule at the point of symmetry with the production of vitamin A. The role of vitamin A and structurally related terpenoid molecules in the synthesis of the pigments in the eye necessary for vision has been demonstrated.

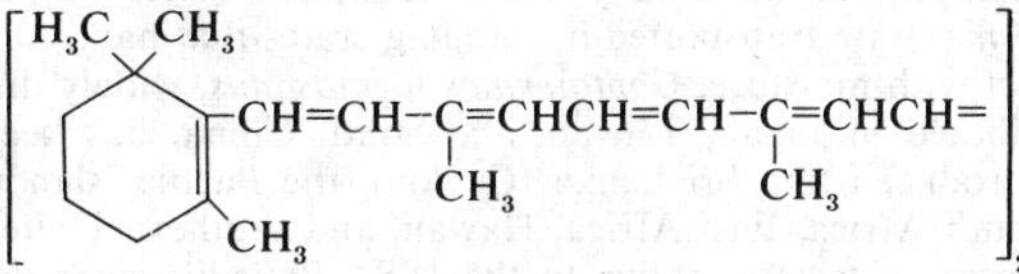

41

Polyterpenes. Rubber, which occurs in the latex of the rubber tree, is a polyterpene hydrocarbon, $(C_5H_8)_n$, in which n is 4,000–5,000. Chemical degradation by oxidation and X-ray-diffraction studies have revealed a repeating unit (**42**) in rubber. Division into isoprene units

$$-CH_2-\overset{\displaystyle CH_3}{C}{=}CHCH_2\vdots CH_2-\overset{\displaystyle CH_3}{C}{=}CHCH_2\vdots CH_2\overset{\displaystyle CH_3}{C}{=}CH-CH_2-$$

42

is indicated. The vulcanization of rubber involves the establishment of cross-linking between the chains through sulfur atoms. Gutta-percha differs from rubber in the way in which the methylene ($-CH_2-$) groups are arranged; in gutta-percha they are on opposite sides (*trans* arrangement) of the double bond, and in rubber they are on the same side (*cis* arrangement).

BIBLIOGRAPHY. ERNEST GUENTHER, *The Essential Oils*, 6 vol. (1948–52), a compendium for the general reader of the history, sources, isolation, properties, uses, and analyses of the more volatile isoprenoids; SIR JOHN SIMONSEN *et al.*, *The Terpenes*, 5 vol. (1947–57), an authoritative work on the properties, chemistry, and structures of isoprenoids; WILLIAM TEMPLETON, *An Introduction to the Chemistry of the Terpenoids and Steroids* (1969), a text that requires some knowledge of organic chemistry; L. RUZICKA, "History of the Isoprene Rule," *Proc. Chem. Soc.*, pp. 341–360 (1959), a historical account of the application of the isoprene rule to the structures of terpenoids; J.W. CORNFORTH, "Terpenoid Biosynthesis," *Chem. Brit.* 4:102–106 (1968), a good summary for the non-chemist; JOHN H. RICHARDS and JAMES B. HENDRICKSON, *The Biosynthesis of Steroids, Terpenes and Acetogenins* (1964), details of the biosynthesis of isoprenoids (for the chemist).

(R.H.E.)

Isoptera

Termites are cellulose-eating social insects that constitute the order Isoptera. Although they are referred to popularly as white ants, they are not closely related to ants, which are grouped with bees and wasps in a higher order of insects, the Hymenoptera. The social system of termites shows remarkable parallels with those of the Hymenoptera, but it has evolved independently.

GENERAL FEATURES

Distribution and abundance. Termites, which number about 1,900 species, are distributed widely, reaching their greatest abundance in numbers and species in tropical rain forests. In North America termites are found as far north as Vancouver, British Columbia (*Zootermopsis*), on the Pacific coast, and Maine and eastern Canada (*Reticulitermes*) on the Atlantic coast. In Europe the northern limit of natural distribution is reached by *Reticulitermes lucifugus* on the Atlantic coast of France, although an introduced species, *Reticulitermes flavipes*, occurs as far north as Hamburg, Germany. In Europe termites have a predominantly Mediterranean distribution and do not occur naturally in Great Britain, Scandinavia, Switzerland, Germany, or northern Russia. In the Far East *Reticulitermes speratus* ranges as far north as South Korea, Peking, and northern Japan. Termites occur also in the Cape Province of the Republic of South Africa, Australia, Tasmania, and New Zealand.

In addition to naturally occurring termites, many species have been transported inadvertently by man from their native habitats to new parts of the world. Termites, particularly *Cryptotermes* and *Coptotermes*, are transported in wooden articles such as shipping crates, boat timbers, lumber, and furniture. Because dry-wood termites (*e.g.*, *Cryptotermes* species) live in small colonies in wood and tolerate long periods of dryness, they can survive in seasoned wood and furniture and be transported easily. Members of the family Rhinotermitidae (*e.g.*, *Coptotermes*) are transported in shipping crates that have contact with moisture. *Coptotermes formosanus*, widely distributed in Japan, Taiwan, and South China, has been introduced into Sri Lanka (Ceylon), the Pacific islands, South Africa, East Africa, Hawaii, and southern United States. A termite native to the U.S., *Reticulitermes flavipes*, was found in the hothouses of the Royal Palace in Schönbrunn, in Vienna, and reported and described before it was discovered in the U.S. The termites presumably had been shipped from North America in wooden containers of potted plants.

Importance. Termites are important in two ways. They are destructive when they feed upon, and often destroy, wooden structures or vegetable matter valuable to man. Introduced species, because they are not so well equipped as native species to adapt to changes in their new environments, tend to seek shelter in protected, man-made environments such as cultivated crops or buildings and thus are likely to become the most serious pests. Termites are beneficial, however, in that they help to convert plant cellulose into substances that can be recycled into the ecosystem to support new growth.

Termite control

Although only 10 percent of known termite species have been reported as pests, many of that group cause severe damage. For effective control, it is essential to determine whether the pest is a subterranean or a wood-dwelling species, as treatment methods differ.

Subterranean termites, dependent on contact with soil moisture, normally reach the wood in man-made structures through their foundations. The most common control used around a structure is a trench containing insecticide and covered by soil. Insecticides are useful around cracks and crevices in foundations and infested wood. Construction and design practices that can prevent the initial entry of subterranean termites into a structure include the use of pressure-treated wood, dieldrin-treated concrete foundation blocks, and reinforced concrete foundations that extend at least six inches (15.2 centimetres) above the ground and have no cracks or contact with any outside wood.

Dry-wood termites, which nest in the wood on which they feed and do not invade a structure from the soil, are difficult to control. Preventive measures include the use of chemically treated wood in building construction and the use of paint or other durable finish to seal cracks in wood surfaces. Fumigation is the most effective method for exterminating drywood termites. Another method is to pour insecticides into small holes drilled into galleries of infested wood.

No completely satisfactory method of termite control has been devised. Since most methods have depended heavily on chlorinated hydrocarbons, it is probable that alternate, safer methods of control will be developed (see PEST CONTROL).

From C.A. Kofoid *et al.*, *Termites and Termite Control* (1934); Originally published by the University of California Press; reprinted by permission of The Regents of the University of California

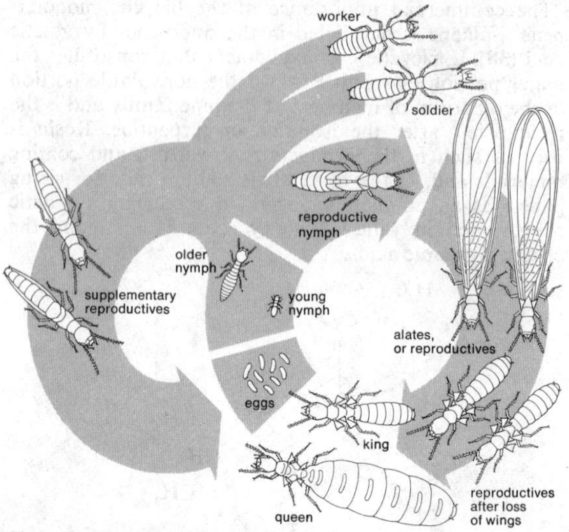

Figure 1: Life cycle of the termite.

NATURAL HISTORY

Colony organization. The termite society, or colony, is a highly organized and integrated unit, with division of labour among its members differentiated by structure, function, and behaviour into castes. The major castes in the colony are the reproductive, soldier, and worker castes; the soldiers and workers are sterile. The functional reproductives are of two types, primary and secondary (or supplementary).

Mechanisms controlling differentiation of termites into castes are not understood fully. It is known that all young nymphs are genetically identical at hatching and that all could develop into any caste (reproductive, soldier, or worker).

Regulation of castes

The castes in a colony are balanced and regulated closely; normally there are one pair of reproductives and a set ratio of soldiers to workers and nymphs. If members of any caste are lost, additional members of that caste develop from nymphs to restore the balance. Conversely, if overproduction of one caste occurs, selective cannibalism restores the balance.

Chemical substances such as pheromones and hormones play a role in differentiation, production, and regulation of castes. Both reproductive and soldier castes secrete a pheromone, a chemical substance that is transmitted through mutual licking (trophallaxis) to other members of the colony and inhibits development of reproductives or soldiers. If the caste balance of the colony is upset, some undifferentiated nymphs, which do not receive the "pheromone message," develop into reproductives or soldiers, thereby restoring the balance.

This inhibition theory has been confirmed by experiments with supplementary reproductive development in *Kalotermes* and *Zootermopsis*.

Pheromones may act to control caste differentiation through hormonal action, but it is not clear how this mechanism works. Activation of the corpora allata near the brain may result in release of a hormone, distinct from the juvenile hormone, that causes differentiation of a nymph into a soldier. Similarly, activity of a molt gland may be responsible for differentiation of the reproductive caste. In termites, therefore, hormones not only control molting and metamorphosis, as in other insects, but also play a role in caste differentiation.

Colony formation and development. *Swarming.* A new termite colony normally is founded by dispersion of winged adults (alates), which usually develop in a mature colony during certain seasons of the year. After molting into winged adults, alates group themselves in special chambers near the periphery of the nest for several days or weeks. Emergence and flight of alates usually is associated with high atmospheric humidity in combination with temperature, climatic, and seasonal factors that vary with the species. In some species one emergence a year may occur; in others there may be many successive flights.

Workers prepare tunnels to the surface and exit holes prior to emergence of the alates and sometimes construct launching platforms. During emergence the soldiers guard the exit holes, not only to prevent entry of enemies but also to prevent alates from re-entering the nest. At the time of emergence the alates, which normally avoid light, become attracted to it and fly out of the nest. They are weak fliers and, unless carried by the wind, descend within several hundred yards of the original colony. The flight, commonly called a nuptial or mating flight, is simply dispersal; mating occurs after the flight. Swarming from many colonies occurs simultaneously in a given area and may be synchronized closely in areas separated by hundreds of miles. An advantage of synchronization might be intercolony mating.

Dispersal, pairing, and mating

Shortly after the alates alight, they shed their wings, leaving only the base of the wing scale attached to the thorax. During a short courtship, in which the female raises her abdomen and emits a sex attractant, the pair moves off in tandem (pairing), with the male following closely behind the female. The couple then seek a nesting site; together they find a crevice or dig a hole in wood or soil that has been softened by rain and seal the hole with fecal matter. Copulation takes place only after the establishment of this nuptial chamber. During copulation, which occurs intermittently throughout the lives of the king and queen, sperm are transferred and stored in the spermatheca of the female. Since the male has no external copulatory organ, sperm are released through a median pore on the ninth sternite, or abdominal plate.

After copulation the first batch of eggs, usually few in number, is laid. In two to five years, as the colony matures, the egg-laying capacity of the queen increases, her ovaries and fat bodies develop, and her abdomen enlarges (the process is called physogastry). Physogastric queens in more advanced families (*e.g.*, family Termitidae, especially *Macrotermes* and *Odontotermes*) may become 11 centimetres long. The queen, now an "egg-laying machine," may produce as many as 36,000 eggs a day for many years. The king is one or two centimetres long. In temperate regions egg laying stops during the winter months, while in tropical species it continues throughout the year.

The first young nymphs develop into workers or pseudergates and soldiers. Only after the colonies are mature do winged adults develop. During the initial stages of colony formation, the reproductives feed the young and tend the nest; but, as the colony becomes established, the young nymphs perform these duties.

Primitive termite families have small colonies—from hundreds to thousands of individuals. More advanced families (*e.g., Rhinotermitidae, Termitidae*) have colonies that may number thousands to millions of individuals; all members are produced by the single reproductive pair. Workers and soldiers may live two to five years. The primary king and queen in higher termite families may live 60 to 70 years. The entire colony may exist for many years in species that replace the primary king and queen with secondary reproductives.

Other colonizing methods. Sometimes new colonies are formed by budding, the division or accidental separation of part of a colony from an original nest; supplementary reproductives then take over as the reproductive pair. Another method of colony formation is sociotomy, or social fragmentation; workers, soldiers, and nymphs migrate or march to a new nesting site, and the fragment develops supplementary reproductives. Sometimes an original reproductive pair joins a migrating group.

Nests. *Internal features.* Since termites have a soft cuticle and are desiccated easily, they live in nests that are warm, damp, dark, and sealed from the outside environment; their nests are constructed by workers or old nymphs. In addition to providing an optimum microclimate, the nest provides shelter and protection against predators. The high relative humidity in the interior of the nest (90 to 99 percent) probably is maintained in part by water production resulting from metabolic processes of individual termites. The temperature inside the nest generally is higher than that of the outside environment.

Ventilation of nests

Since the anaerobic protozoans (necessary to digestion) in the hindguts of primitive termites cannot tolerate high concentrations of oxygen, such termites have developed a toleration for high concentrations of carbon dioxide, as high as 3 percent in some nests. Ventilation must occur in the nest, however, and may be facilitated by its architecture. For example, the subterranean nests of *Apicotermes* have an elaborate system of ventilation pores. Convection currents and diffusion through the nest wall also provide ventilation in large mounds.

Nest types. The family Kalotermitidae and the subfamily Termopsinae (family Hodotermitidae) make their nests in the wood on which they feed. These termites excavate irregular networks of galleries with no external openings (except for temporary ones during swarming); many galleries have partitions made of fecal matter and are lined or coated with plaster made of fecal matter. The Kalotermitidae live in the sound wood of stumps and branches of trees. Examples are *Neotermes tectonae,* which lives in and attacks teak trees in Java, and *Cryptotermes,* which bores into trees and furniture in various parts of the world. The Termopsinae live in damp rotten logs. Although true wood dwellers never invade soil, and their nests have no soil connections, all other termites basically are subterranean; *i.e.,* they build their nests either in soil or with soil connections and exploit food sources away from the nest.

Many species of Rhinotermitidae build nests in wood that is buried in damp soil and from which a diffused network of tunnels to food sources may radiate into the soil or above the ground in the form of covered runways. Other termites build a diffused subterranean nest with many chambers or pockets in soil and a network of galleries.

Many termites build discrete and concentrated nests. Some nests rise partly above the ground as mounds or hills; others are totally underground or arboreal. Dirt, particles of fine clay, or chewed wood glued together with saliva or excreta are used to build nests. During nest construction a termite deposits fecal matter to cement particles in place.

Arboreal nests are ovoid structures built of "carton" (a mixture of fecal matter and wood fragments), which resembles cardboard or papier-mâché. Carton may be papery and fragile, or woody and very hard. The inside of an arboreal nest consists of horizontal layers of cells, the queen occupying a special compartment near the centre. The nests always maintain connections with the ground through covered runways.

The large mounds or hills, a prominent landscape feature in the tropics, may be domelike or conical; some have chimneys and pinnacles. Longitudinal and horizontal chambers and galleries comprise the interior. Generally the outer wall is constructed of hard soil material, distinct from the internal central portion (or nursery), which is composed of softer carton material. In northern Australia *Amitermes meridionalis* builds wedge-shaped mounds, called compass or magnetic mounds, that are three to four metres (9.8 to 13.1 feet) high, 2.5 metres (8.1 feet) wide, and one metre (3.2 feet) thick at the base. The long axis always is directed north–south, and the broad side faces east–west—an orientation that probably functions to regulate temperature. Spectacular mounds are built by fungus-growing termites in

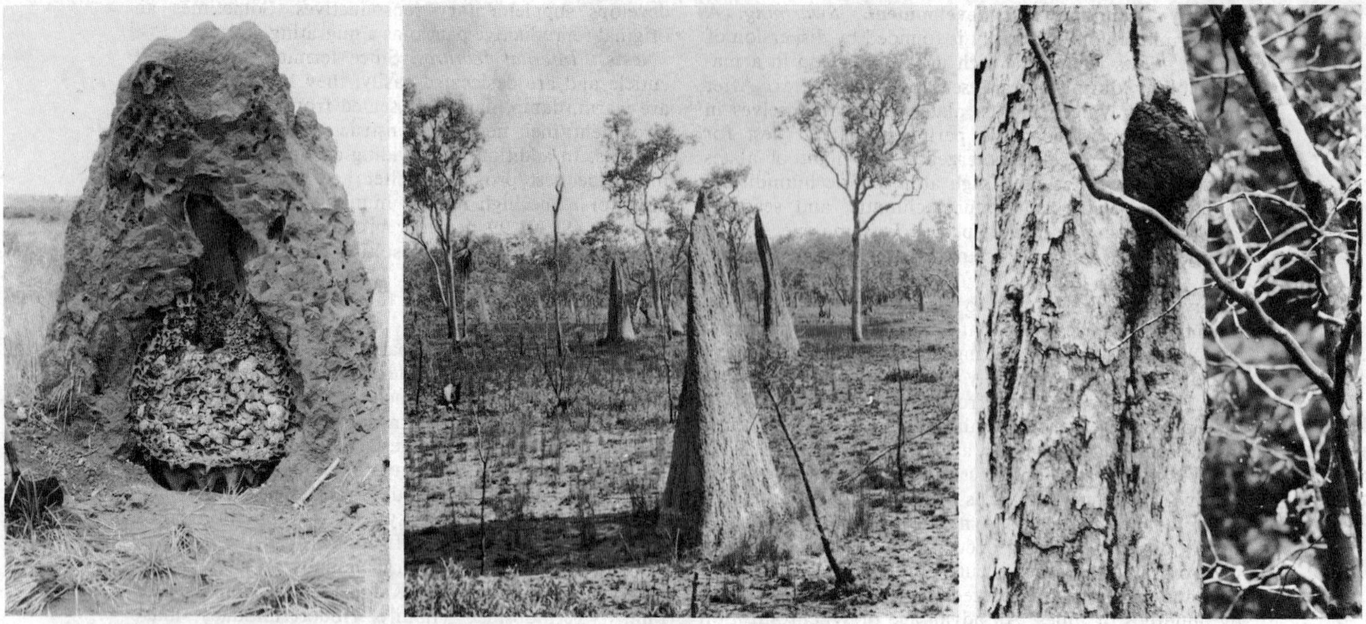

Termite nests.
(Left) Cross section of mound of the fungus-growing termite *Macrotermes natalensis* from the Ivory Coast of Africa. (Centre) "Compass" mound nest of *Amitermes meridionalis*, north-south aspect, from Australia. (Right) Arboreal carton nest of *Nasutitermes lacustris* from Sri Lanka (Ceylon).
(Left) P.P. Grasse and C. Noirot, *Insectes Sociaux*, vol. 7 (1961), (centre) F.J. Gay and J.H. Calaby, *Biology of Termites*, vol. 2 (1970), (right) Kumar Krishna

Indomalaya and Africa; mounds of some African *Macrotermes* species reach a height of eight to nine metres (26.2 to 29.5 feet) and have pinnacles, chimneys, and ridges on their outer walls. Such mounds are built of fine particles of clay glued together by saliva to form an exceedingly hard substance. Inside the mounds are honeycomb-like structures on which the fungus grows.

Invertebrates dependent on termites

Many termite nests harbour various other invertebrates as guests (*e.g.*, beetles, flies, bugs, caterpillars, millipedes); some (termed termitophiles), in fact, are unable to survive independent of their termite hosts. True termitophiles actually have evolved with their hosts and are species specific. Some beetles and flies have developed glands that secrete substances sought and licked by the termites. The termite nest, because it provides shelter and warmth, may be occupied also by lizards, snakes, scorpions, and some birds.

A few termites, known as inquilinous species, live only in obligatory association with other termite species. Examples of such obligate relationships are *Ahamitermes* and *Incolitermes* species, which live only in the mound nests of certain *Coptotermes* species; the galleries of guests and hosts are completely separate. Inquilinous species feed on the inner carton material of the host nests. *Incolitermes*, however, depend on the host species not only for food but also for exit holes from the nest during swarming when alates of the inquiline and the host emerge together. Such species' tolerance is highly unusual; normally, different species of termites are hostile to one another, and host termites may attack inquilinous guests if partitions between galleries are broken.

FORM AND FUNCTION

Castes and their roles. *Reproductives.* The primary reproductives in a termite colony are usually one royal pair, a king and queen. They have developed from winged forms (alates) with hardened, pigmented bodies and large compound eyes that have flown from a parent colony and shed their wings. The primary reproductives have several important functions: reproduction, dispersal, and colony formation; in addition, during initial stages of colony formation, the primary reproductives perform tasks later taken over by the worker caste (*e.g.*, construction, housekeeping, care of young).

If the king and queen die, they are replaced by several supplementary reproductives that are slightly pigmented, have either short wing pads (brachypterous) or none (apterous) and reduced compound eyes. These secondary reproductives, which develop from nymphs and may be called neotenics, normally are not present in a colony as long as the primary reproductives function. If a primary reproductive is lost, a neotenic achieves sexual maturity without, however, attaining a fully winged adult stage or leaving the nest.

Workers and soldiers. The sterile castes are the workers and soldiers. Both are wingless, usually lack eyes and, though of both sexes, usually lack fully developed reproductive organs. In some species the workers and soldiers are dimorphic (of two sizes); the larger is termed a major soldier or worker, the smaller a minor soldier or worker. A few species contain trimorphic soldiers. Most termite species have both soldier and worker castes.

The worker caste usually is the most numerous in a colony. Workers are pale in colour, soft-bodied, and with mandibles and mouthparts adapted for chewing. They feed all the other members of the colony (reproductives, soldiers, and young), collect food, groom other colony members, and construct and repair the nest. The worker caste is responsible for the widespread destruction termites can cause. In some primitive termite families a true worker caste is absent, and its functions are carried out by immature individuals called pseudo-workers or pseudergates, which may molt from time to time without much change in size.

Mechanisms for defense

The primary function of the soldier caste is defense. Since most termite soldiers are blind, they probably locate enemies through tactile and chemical means. The termite soldier has a large, dark, hard-covered head; its long powerful jaws (mandibles) may be hooked and contain teeth. The head and the mandibles are used to defend the colony against predators, usually ants. The attacking mandibulate soldier makes rapid lunging movements, opening and closing its mandibles in a scissorlike action that can behead, dismember, lacerate, or grip a foe. In some mandibulate soldiers (*e.g.*, *Capritermes*) the mandibles are an asymmetrical, snapping type, with the left mandible twisted and arched and the right bladelike. In defense, the mandibles lock together and release with a loud click, like the snapping of fingers. Some soldiers (*e.g.*, *Cryptotermes*) use their heads, short and truncated in front (phragmotic), to plug the entrance holes of nests.

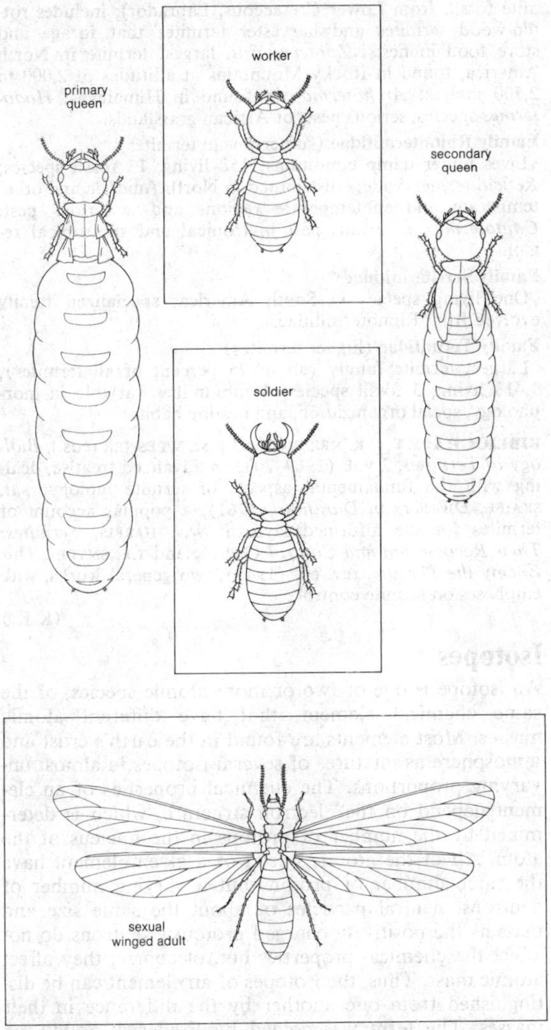

Figure 2: Termite castes.
From (winged adult) A *Revision of the Nearctic Termites* by Nathan Banks and Thomas E. Snyder, U.S. National Museum Bulletin 108, Smithsonian Institution, in D.J. Borror and D.M. DeLong, *An Introduction to the Study of Insects*, Holt, Rinehart and Winston, Inc.; and (others) S.H. Skaife, *Dwellers in Darkness* (1961), Longman Group Ltd.

The higher termites (Termitidae) may supplement or replace mandibular defenses with chemical mechanisms that utilize sticky, possibly toxic, liquids secreted by either the salivary or the frontal glands. The whitish or brownish liquid becomes rubberlike after exposure to air and entangles enemies. The frontal gland of some termites (*e.g.*, *Coptotermes* and *Rhinotermes*) occupies a large portion of the abdominal cavity and opens by means of a frontal pore (fontanelle), through which the liquid is ejected. The liquid from the frontal pore of the minor soldier of *Rhinotermes* flows down a groove in the elongated labrum, rests at its hairy tip, and volatilizes as a repellent gas.

The mandibles of soldiers with exclusively chemical defense (Nasutitermitinae) have become reduced in size and nonfunctional; the head has become elongated into a long snout (nasus), and the frontal gland, which occupies a major portion of the head, opens at the end of the snout. These nasute soldiers can fire a clear, sticky, resinous liquid accurately for many centimetres. A few genera lack a soldier caste; the mechanisms for defense in these groups are not known.

Nutrition. *Cellulose*. The food of termites is mainly cellulose, obtained from wood, grass, leaves, humus, manure of herbivorous animals, and materials of vegetative origin (*e.g.*, paper, cardboard, cotton). Most lower termites and many higher ones feed on wood, either sound or partly decayed. A few termites (known as foragers or harvesters) collect and eat grass, leaves, and straw. Many higher termites (family Termitidae) are humivores, or exclusively humus feeders.

As with other social insects, not all members of a termite colony feed directly. Because reproductives, soldiers, and young nymphs in lower families (all nymphs in Termitidae) cannot feed themselves directly, they must be fed by workers. Workers (or in families without them, the older nymphs) feed for the entire colony and transfer food to dependent castes either by mouth feeding or by anal feeding. Food transferred by mouth may consist of either pastelike regurgitated chewed wood and saliva or a clear liquid. This method is used in all termite families. During anal feeding, present only among lower termites, a pastelike liquid or droplet is discharged from the anus of the worker and licked away by the dependent castes. This liquid food, distinct from feces, consists of hindgut fluid containing protozoans, products of digestion, and wood fragments.

Importance of symbiotic protozoans

Cellulose digestion in lower termite families depends upon symbiotic flagellate protozoa, which live anaerobically (without oxygen) in the termite hindgut and secrete enzymes (cellulase and cellobiase) that break down cellulose into a simple sugar (glucose) and acetic acid. The termites depend entirely on protozoans for cellulose digestion and would starve without them. Newly hatched nymphs acquire protozoa from older, infected termites during anal feeding—a type of feeding necessary to lower termites that harbour protozoans.

Since the protozoans lost at the time of each molt are reacquired only through anal feeding, termites live in groups that allow contact of molting nymphs with infected, nonmolting individuals. It is possible that the necessity for transfer of protozoans was responsible for the evolution of the termite society.

Higher termites lack symbiotic protozoans; only bacteria are present in the gut. Digestion may occur with the aid of bacterial cellulase and cellobiase enzymes, but the termites themselves may secrete the enzymes.

In addition to cellulose, termites require vitamins and nitrogenous foods (*e.g.*, proteins), which probably are supplied by fungi normally present in the decayed wood diet common to most termites. The fungi also may break down wood into components that are digested easily by termites.

Fungus gardens. The Macrotermitinae (family Termitidae) cultivate symbiotic fungi (*Termitomyces*). The termites construct spongelike "fungus gardens," or combs, possibly of fecal matter rich in the carbohydrate lignin. The fungi grow on the combs, and the termites consume both fungi and combs. The fungi break down the fecal matter used to construct the combs into substances that can be reutilized by the termites. Nitrogen other than that from fungi is supplied by controlled cannibalism. The termites consume cast-off skins and dead, injured, and excess members of the colony.

Communication. Among the members of a termite colony there is continuous exchange of information, such as alarm, indication of direction and presence of a food source, and, among reproductives, calling and pairing behaviour. Information is communicated by visual cues, vibrations, physical contact, and chemical signals (*e.g.*, odour).

Many termite species leave their nests to forage for food. Workers (or older nymphs) and soldiers march in columns along the ground and carry grass, pine needles, and seeds for storage in the nest. The foraging trail between the nest and the food source may be indicated by deposits of fecal matter, covered runways over the trail, or pheromones secreted by a sternal gland as the termite drags its abdomen along the ground. The pheromone odour is detected by other termites through olfactory receptors.

Termites communicate alarm by vibrations, odour, and physical contact. Alarmed termites may tap their heads against the ground, quiver and jerk, or run in a zigzag fashion, bumping into other individuals. Although the vertical head-tapping movements produce rattling sounds audible to the human ear, termites cannot hear airborne sounds. It is the substratum vibration that they sense through the vibratory receptors located on their legs. The zigzag and horizontal jerking movements communicate alarm by contact; as an alarmed termite bumps into other termites, they, too, become alarmed. During this excitatory running, the alarmed termite leaves a scent trail (similar to the foraging trail) of pheromone that communicates direction and serves to recruit workers and soldiers to the point of disturbance.

EVOLUTION AND PALEONTOLOGY

Termites are related to the roaches and probably have evolved from a primitive roachlike ancestor. The most primitive living roach, the subsocial, wood-eating *Cryptocercus punctulatus,* which lives in rotten logs, has affinities with the termites. *Cryptocercus* harbours symbiotic, cellulose-digesting protozoans of the same genera as those found in the hindgut of primitive termites. The genitalia and certain internal structures of *Cryptocercus* have basic anatomical resemblances to those of the most primitive living termite, *Mastotermes darwiniensis,* from Australia. *Mastotermes* has further affinities with other roaches: its hindwing has a folded anal lobe, and its eggs are not laid singly as those of other termites but in clusters held together by a gelatinous material resembling the egg case of roaches.

Evidence of the relationship to primitive roaches suggests that termites evolved in the Late Permian (approximately 230,000,000 years ago), although the known fossil termites date only from the Early Cretaceous (about 130,000,000 years ago). The termite society may be older than any other society; the ant society is 100,000,000 years old.

CLASSIFICATION

Termites of the order Isoptera are small to medium-sized insects that live in social groups, or colonies, and are characterized by their highly developed caste system. The mouthparts are modified for chewing. Antennae are moniliform (beadlike) or filiform (threadlike). Isopterans are very soft bodied insects, usually light in colour. Head structures and the presence or absence of individual caste members are used to distinguish termite families.

Termites, often called white ants, differ from hymenopterans (bees, ants, and wasps) in several ways. Termites have a hemimetabolous (gradual) metamorphosis and pass through a series of nymphal stages. Hymenopterans have the more common holometabolous metamorphosis, with distinct larval, pupal, and adult stages. Termite social castes (reproductives, sterile workers, and sterile soldiers) usually contain members of both sexes in equal numbers, and both males and females develop from fertilized eggs. In the hymenopteran colony, however, the sterile castes contain females only; both sterile and reproductive females develop from fertilized eggs, while reproductive males develop by parthenogenesis from unfertilized eggs. The thorax in termites is joined broadly to the abdomen, without the "waist" characteristic of bees, ants, and wasps. Termites have two pairs of membranous wings, nearly equal in size, that break along a suture when shed, leaving only the wing base, or "scale," attached to the thorax—probably the most distinguishing characteristic of isopterans.

Annotated classification.

ORDER ISOPTERA (termites)
Highly developed caste system, may contain reproductives, soldiers, and workers; reproductives shed wings after mating; distribution worldwide, mostly in tropical rain forests; about 1,900 living, 60 fossil species; may inhabit moist subterranean or hot, dry locations; foods include plant cellulose, often digested by symbiotic protozoans in termite hindgut; all families (except Termitidae) known collectively as "lower termites" contain symbiotic protozoans in hindgut.

Family Mastotermitidae
Primitive; 1 living species (*Mastotermes darwiniensis*) in Australia; 13 Tertiary fossil species worldwide.

Family Kalotermitidae (dry-wood termites)
Wood dwelling, wood eating; survive dry conditions; 292 living, 11 fossil species (some from Baltic amber).

Family Hodotermitidae
Thirty living, 13 fossil species (1, the earliest known termite fossil, from Lower Cretaceous, Labrador); includes rotten-wood termites and harvester termites that forage and store food in nests; *Zootermopsis,* largest termite in North America, found in Rocky Mountains at altitudes of 2,000 to 2,500 metres; *Archotermopsis,* found in Himalayas; *Hodotermes* species, serious pests of African grasslands.

Family Rhinotermitidae (subterranean termites)
Lives under damp conditions; 158 living, 13 fossil species; *Reticulitermes,* widely distributed in North America and other temperate and subtemperate regions and a serious pest; *Coptotermes,* a serious pest in tropical and subtropical regions.

Family Serritermitidae
One living species in South America; specialized family evolved from Rhinotermitidae.

Family Termitidae (higher termites)
Largest termite family (about 75 percent of all termites), 1,413 living, 3 fossil species; 4 subfamilies variable in morphology, social organization, and nesting habits.

BIBLIOGRAPHY. K. KRISHNA and F.M. WEESNER (eds.), *Biology of Termites,* 2 vol. (1969–70), an advanced treatise, dealing with the fundamental aspects of termite biology; S.H. SKAIFE, *Dwellers in Darkness* (1961), a popular account of termites for the informed layman; W.V. HARRIS, *Termites: Their Recognition and Control* (1961); and T.E. SNYDER, *Our Enemy the Termite,* rev. ed. (1948), two general works, with emphases on termite control.

(K.K.)

Isotopes

An isotope is one of two or more atomic species, of the same chemical element, that have different atomic masses. Most elements are found in the earth's crust and atmosphere as mixtures of several isotopes in almost unvarying proportions. The chemical properties of an element depend on the electron structure, which is determined by the number of protons in the nucleus of the atom. All of the atomic nuclei of a given element have the same number of protons but a varying number of neutrons, neutral particles of about the same size and mass as the positively charged protons. Neutrons do not affect the chemical properties but, of course, they affect atomic mass. Thus, the isotopes of an element can be distinguished from one another by the difference in their masses. The term was coined by Frederick Soddy, an English chemist, in 1913 from the Greek *isos,* "equal," and *topos,* "place," to indicate different substances occupying the same place in the periodic table of elements. The general term for an atom characterized by the constitution of its nucleus is "nuclide," although "isotope" is often used loosely for this purpose.

Because the mass of a neutron and the mass of a proton are very nearly the same and almost equal to what is considered one atomic mass unit (amu), the mass of any atomic species, or nuclide, can be closely represented by an integer, the so-called mass number. The element tin, for example, with 50 protons in its atomic nucleus, has ten stable isotopes whose mass numbers range from 112 (for 50 protons and 62 neutrons) to 124 (for 50 protons and 74 neutrons), and whose atomic masses range correspondingly from a value very close to 112 amu to a value very close to 124 amu. Most of the elements, as they occur in the Earth's crust and atmosphere either by themselves or compounded with other elements, are mixtures of several isotopes. For most elements the proportions in which the isotopes are mixed are found to be always the same regardless of the source of the sample. For example, the atomic weight of any natural sample of tin, wherever it has been mined, is always 118.69, representing the average of atomic weights for the consistent mixture of these ten isotopes of tin.

Many isotopes exist for each chemical element, but it is primarily the stable ones that occur in nature. The others are unstable, or radioactive; that is, their atomic nuclei disintegrate spontaneously at characteristic rates. The term stable isotope is, however, not an absolute designation; it merely means that the nuclei of stable isotopes have never yet been observed to decay. Eighty-one of the chemical elements of the periodic table have stable isotopes; the number of stable nuclides is 270. Stable isotopes

Discovery of isotopes. First evidence that two substances of the same chemical composition did not have to be physically identical came from the study of the radioactivity of the heavy elements. In 1906 it was shown that ionium (a decay product of uranium) and radiothorium (a decay product of thorium), after having been mixed with thorium, could not be separated from it by any chemical method. The two substances, however, had radioactive properties quite different from those of thorium, as well as atomic weights differing from that of thorium by several units. It was to cover cases such as these that Soddy introduced the term isotope. Soon after the acceptance of the notion of isotopes as being applicable to the heavy radioactive elements, there came indications that isotopes might also exist among the stable elements throughout the periodic table. In 1913, during an investigation of the behaviour of positively charged ions in electric and magnetic fields, the English physicist J.J. Thomson found that, whereas many substances when ionized did behave as though they were made up of identical molecules, the element neon appeared to contain an atomic species in about 10 percent abundance that was heavier by 10 percent than the main constituent. In 1919 Thomson's student Francis William Aston, after having developed one of the first mass spectrographs, which sorts atoms and molecules by their masses, was able to show conclusively that the rare gas neon indeed consisted primarily of two atomic species, one with an atomic mass very close to 20 amu and the other with an atomic mass very close to 22 amu. The relative abundances of the two species were such as to explain the observed atomic weight of 20.25. The success with neon was followed by the discovery that the element chlorine also had two isotopes with atomic masses very close to 35 amu and 37 amu respectively, and it soon became clear that most chemical elements consisted of a mixture of isotopes, each with an atomic mass close to an integer on the atomic mass scale. This accounted for the atomic weights of many chemical elements differing appreciably from integral values. It is now well established that there are no nuclides with masses deviating from whole numbers by more than 0.1 amu.

Isotones, isobars, and isomers

Isotopes and nuclear stability. As distinguished from isotopes—that is, nuclides with the same atomic number, or the same number (Z) of protons per atom—nuclides with the same number (N) of neutrons per atom are known as isotones, and nuclides with the same mass number, or the same number ($A = Z + N$) of nucleons per atom, are called isobars. The nuclear constitution of an atom is usually indicated by the chemical symbol for the element, which gives, by implication, the number of protons in the nucleus, together with a superscript giving the mass number and therefore, by difference, the neutron content of the nucleus. Thus, for example, chlorine-35 (^{35}Cl) and chlorine-37 (^{37}Cl) represent the two stable isotopes of chlorine. What were formerly called ionium and radiothorium are now known to be isotopes of thorium, thorium-230 (^{230}Th) and thorium-228 (^{228}Th) respectively. The isotopes of hydrogen, $^{1}H = H$, $^{2}H = D$, and $^{3}H = T$, have been given the special names protium, deuterium, and tritium, respectively.

Nuclides with the same number of protons as well as with the same number of neutrons may still be distinguishable from one another by virtue of their different states of energy, corresponding to differences in the structure of the nucleus or differences in the way in which the nucleons are assembled. Such distinguishable isotonic isotopes are called isomers (see below).

All stable isotopes are found as the constituents of the naturally occurring elements, but they also can be produced by nuclear transformations. A few radioactive isotopes also occur in nature, but most have to be prepared by artificially induced nuclear transformations. Their half-lives range from barely perceptible fractions of a second to quadrillions (10^{15}) of years. Just as the stability of the nucleus varies from one isotope to another, so do other nuclear properties such as the nuclear size and shape, the spin, the magnetic moment, and the electric quadrupole moment. Similarly, the nuclear reaction probability is often quite different from one isotope to another. Thus uranium-235 undergoes nuclear fission when bombarded with slow neutrons; uranium-238, however, does not. Similarly, cadmium-113, one of the eight stable isotopes of cadmium, has an extremely high probability of absorbing slow neutrons, while the other seven isotopes are relatively inert. The stability of isotopes toward spontaneous nuclear disintegration as well as, to a certain extent, their nuclear reaction probabilities, is related to their energetic stability. According to the Einstein relation $E = mc^2$, the energy content E of a nuclear system is determined by the mass m of the system (c being the speed of light); the lower the mass, the more stable the system. Although the exact masses of nuclides in amu's are close to whole numbers, the deviations from whole numbers are real and significant. In all known cases the mass of the nucleus is found to be smaller than the sum of the masses of its nucleons. Thus, all known atoms are stable with respect to complete decomposition into neutrons and hydrogen atoms.

Packing fraction of nuclides

The detailed variations in atomic mass are measured in terms of $f_{A,Z}$, the so-called packing fraction of a nuclide of mass number A and atomic number Z. The packing fraction is related to $M(A,Z)$, the exact mass of the atom, by the equation: $M(A,Z) = A(1 + f_{A,Z})$. The packing fractions of nuclides, except for protium and deuterium, range from 10×10^{-4} to -10×10^{-4}. For a given element, the packing fractions of the stable isotopes with even mass numbers, when plotted against A, usually yield a smooth curve with a minimum for the isotope of close to average mass number, indicating maximum stability for this isotope.

Isotopic composition of the elements. The remarkable constancy in the isotopic composition of most elements as they are found in nature applies even to samples from extraterrestrial sources such as meteorites. The exceptions are those few elements with isotopes that are continually being created or annihilated as a result of spontaneous or induced nuclear transformations. Of the four stable isotopes of the element lead, for example, three happen to be radiogenic; that is, they are end products of the radioactive decay of uranium and thorium. Thus, the isotopic composition of a sample of lead depends on how much thorium and uranium had been in contact with it and for how long a period of time. Similarly, because all of the helium on earth is the result of nuclear reactions, the relative amounts of helium-3 and helium-4 are not the same in the atmosphere as they are in samples of helium from a gas well. Furthermore, small differences in the isotopic composition of the lighter elements may arise from the effect of mass on the rates and equilibria of naturally occurring chemical and physical processes (see below *Effects of isotopic substitution on chemical properties*). Thus, the deuterium content of hydrogen from the water of the Dead Sea is higher than that of hydrogen from most other sources. Even an element as heavy as sulfur has been shown to have an $^{34}S/^{32}S$ ratio varying by up to 7 percent. The Table presents the isotopic composition of the elements as they occur in nature. The Table lists for each element the mass number of its isotopes and the percentage of atoms of each isotope in the natural mixture. With the few indicated exceptions, all of the nuclides listed are stable. The Table shows that all mass numbers A up to and including 209 have stable nuclear representatives, with the notable exceptions of mass numbers 5 and 8. There are no stable nuclides with these particular mass numbers. Elements of even atomic number Z have many more stable isotopes than those of odd atomic number. In fact, elements of odd atomic number never have more than two stable isotopes, which are almost always of odd mass number. With the exception of the element beryllium ($Z = 4$), elements with even atomic number less than 84, however, have at least two stable isotopes and the element tin, as noted earlier, has ten.

The isotopic composition of the elements is of great theoretical interest, because it represents rare quantitative evidence for the processes by which all atomic nuclei

Isotopic Composition of the Elements as They Occur in Nature

chemical element	atomic number (Z)	chemi-cal symbol	mass num-ber (A)	isotopic composi-tion (percent of atoms)
Hydrogen*	1	H	1	99.986
		D	2	0.014
Helium†	2	He	3	0.00013
			4	100
Lithium*	3	Li	6	7.42
			7	92.58
Beryllium	4	Be	9	100
Boron*	5	B	10	19.7
			11	80.3
Carbon*	6	C	12	98.89
			13	1.11
Nitrogen*	7	N	14	99.63
			15	0.37
Oxygen*	8	O	16	99.759
			17	0.037
			18	0.204
Fluorine	9	F	19	100
Neon*	10	Ne	20	90.92
			21	0.257
			22	8.82
Sodium	11	Na	23	100
Magnesium	12	Mg	24	78.60
			25	10.11
			26	11.29
Aluminum	13	Al	27	100
Silicon*	14	Si	28	92.17
			29	4.71
			30	3.12
Phosphorus	15	P	31	100
Sulfur*	16	S	32	95.0
			33	0.760
			34	4.22
			36	0.014
Chlorine	17	Cl	35	75.53
			37	24.47
Argon†	18	Ar	36	0.337
			38	0.063
			40	99.60
Potassium*	19	K	39	93.22
			40‡	0.0118
			41	6.771
Calcium	20	Ca	40	96.97
			42	0.64
			43	0.145
			44	2.06
			46	0.0033
			48	0.185
Scandium	21	Sc	45	100
Titanium	22	Ti	46	7.99
			47	7.32
			48	73.99
			49	5.46
			50	5.25
Vanadium	23	V	50‡	0.25
			51	99.75
Chromium	24	Cr	50	4.31
			52	83.76
			53	9.55
			54	2.38
Manganese	25	Mn	55	100
Iron	26	Fe	54	5.84
			56	91.68
			57	2.17
			58	0.31
Cobalt	27	Co	59	100
Nickel	28	Ni	58	67.76
			60	26.16
			61	1.25
			62	3.66
			64	1.16
Copper	29	Cu	63	69.1
			65	30.9
Zinc	30	Zn	64	48.89
			66	27.81
			67	4.11
			68	18.56
			70	0.62
Gallium	31	Ga	69	60.2
			71	39.8
Germanium	32	Ge	70	20.55
			72	27.37
			73	7.67
			74	36.74
			76	7.67
Arsenic	33	As	75	100
Selenium	34	Se	74	0.87
			76	9.02
			77	7.58
			78	23.52
			80	49.82
			82	9.19
Bromine	35	Br	79	50.52
			81	49.48
Krypton	36	Kr	78	0.35
			80	2.27
			82	11.56
			83	11.55
			84	56.90
			86	17.37
Rubidium	37	Rb	85	72.15
			87‡	27.85
Strontium	38	Sr	84	0.56
			86	9.86
			87	7.02
			88	82.56
Yttrium	39	Y	89	100
Zirconium	40	Zr	90	51.46
			91	11.23
			92	17.11
			94	17.40
			96	2.80
Niobium	41	Nb	93	100
Molybdenum	42	Mo	92	15.86
			94	9.12
			95	15.70
			96	16.50
			97	9.45
			98	23.75
			100	9.62
Technetium	43	Tc	. . .	. . .
Ruthenium	44	Ru	96	5.46
			98	1.868
			99	12.63
			100	12.53
			101	17.02
			102	31.6
			104	18.87
Rhodium	45	Rh	103	100
Palladium	46	Pd	102	0.96
			104	10.97
			105	22.2
			106	27.3
			108	26.7
			110	11.8
Silver	47	Ag	107	51.35
			109	48.65
Cadmium	48	Cd	106	1.22
			108	0.88
			110	12.39
			111	12.75
			112	24.07
			113	12.26
			114	28.86
			116	7.58
Indium	49	In	113	4.23
			115‡	95.77

*Isotopic composition varies slightly with source. †Isotopic composition varies considerably with source. ‡Isotope radioactive.

Cosmic abundance of isotopes were originally formed. The relative cosmic abundances of the elements themselves have obviously been badly distorted by chemical processes in the course of geologic time. Compared with the relative cosmic abundances of the elements, the isotopic composition of the elements is very constant. For example, the preponderance of neutron-rich (or heavier) isotopes in the heavy elements suggests that neutron-capture processes were important in the nucleosynthesis of elements heavier than iron.

Radioactive isotopes. Radioactivity in nature arises from several sources. First, there are the long-lived radioactive nuclides, with half-lives of at least half a billion (10^9) years, that have survived from the time of formation of the elements. These include some 14 species, among which two isotopes of uranium (uranium-235 and uranium-238) and one of thorium (thorium-232) are prominent. Next, there are the shorter lived radioactive nuclides that exist only because they are intermediate decay products of the longer lived radioactive isotopes of uranium and thorium, and their further decay is balanced by continual replenishment. These include some 39 species, among which four isotopes of radium, especially radium-226, are prominent. Finally, there are the small amounts of radioactive nuclides that are continually being produced in the Earth's atmosphere by cosmic radiation. This is the origin of the minute amounts of carbon-14, a radioactive isotope of carbon, that are present in all living matter, where it is found mixed with the stable isotopes of carbon in amounts such that 14 disintegrations per minute per gram of carbon occur in all living tissue. The half-life of carbon-14 is about 5,730 years. The so-called radiocarbon method of age determination developed for archaeological and geological specimens is based on the fact that, once the tissue ceases to live, its decaying content of carbon-14 is no longer being replaced from the atmosphere by the processes of life. The usefulness of the radiocarbon method of dating is principally for matter between the ages of 500 and 30,000 years.

These, as well as other, less important, natural sources of radioactivity, are responsible for the fact that all objects are very slightly radioactive. In addition to these natural sources, radioactive nuclides are also created as by-products in processes involving the utilization of nuclear energy. Thus, the explosion of megaton nuclear devices in the atmosphere scattered sufficient radioactive debris all over the earth so that all humans absorbed detectable amounts of the radioactive nuclides cesium-137 and strontium-90, isotopes of cesium and strontium.

Many of the radioactive isotopes, as well as some stable isotopes of the elements, have been prepared by artificially induced nuclear transformations. By the 1970s, information was available on more than 1,500 radioactive nuclides, and the list continues to grow. The ele-

Isotopic Composition of the Elements as They Occur in Nature (continued)

chemical element	atomic number (Z)	chemical symbol	mass number (A)	isotopic composition (percent of atoms)
Tin	50	Sn	112	0.95
			114	0.65
			115	0.34
			116	14.24
			117	7.57
			118	24.01
			119	8.58
			120	32.97
			122	4.71
			124	5.98
Antimony	51	Sb	121	57.25
			123	42.75
Tellurium	52	Te	120	0.089
			122	2.46
			123‡	0.87
			124	4.61
			125	6.99
			126	18.71
			128	31.79
			130‡	34.49
Iodine	53	I	127	100
Xenon	54	Xe	124	0.096
			126	0.090
			128	1.919
			129	26.44
			130	4.08
			131	21.18
			132	26.89
			134	10.44
			136	8.87
Cesium	55	Cs	133	100
Barium	56	Ba	130	0.101
			132	0.097
			134	2.42
			135	6.59
			136	7.81
			137	11.32
			138	71.66
Lanthanum	57	La	138‡	0.089
			139	99.911
Cerium	58	Ce	136	0.193
			138	0.250
			140	88.48
			142	11.07
Praseodymium	59	Pr	141	100
Neodymium	60	Nd	142	27.13
			143	12.20
			144‡	23.87
			145	8.29
			146	17.18
			148	5.72
			150	5.60
Promethium	61	Pm	. . .	. . .
Samarium	62	Sm	144	3.16
			147‡	15.07
			148	11.27
			149	13.82
			150	7.47
			152	26.63
			154	22.53
Europium	63	Eu	151	47.77
			153	52.23
Gadolinium	64	Gd	152	0.20
			154	2.15
			155	14.7
			156	20.47
			157	15.68
			158	24.9
			160	21.9
Terbium	65	Tb	159	100
Dysprosium	66	Dy	156	0.0524
			158	0.0902
			160	2.294
			161	18.88
			162	25.53
			163	24.97
			164	28.18
Holmium	67	Ho	165	100
Erbium	68	Er	162	0.136
			164	1.56
			166	33.41
			167	22.94
			168	27.07
			170	14.88
Thulium	69	Tm	169	100
Ytterbium	70	Yb	168	0.140
			170	3.03
			171	14.31
			172	21.82
			173	16.13
			174	31.84
			176	12.73
Lutetium	71	Lu	175	97.40
			176‡	2.60
Hafnium	72	Hf	174‡	0.163
			176	5.21
			177	18.56
			178	27.1
			179	13.75
			180	35.22
Tantalum	73	Ta	180	0.0123
			181	99.9877
Tungsten	74	W	180	0.135
			182	26.4
			183	14.4
			184	30.6
			186	28.4
Rhenium	75	Re	185	37.07
			187‡	62.93
Osmium	76	Os	184	0.018
			186	1.59
			187	1.64
			188	13.3
			189	16.1
			190	26.4
			192	41.0
Iridium	77	Ir	191	38.5
			193	61.5
Platinum	78	Pt	190‡	0.0127
			192	0.78
			194	32.9
			195	33.8
			196	25.2
			198	7.19
Gold	79	Au	197	100
Mercury	80	Hg	196	0.146
			198	10.02
			199	16.84
			200	23.13
			201	13.22
			202	29.80
			204	6.85
Thallium	81	Tl	203	29.50
			205	70.50
Lead†	82	Pb	204	1.40
			206	25.1
			207	21.7
			208	52.3
Bismuth	83	Bi	209	100
Thorium	90	Th	232‡	100
Uranium	92	U	234‡	0.0056
			235‡	0.720
			238‡	99.276

*Isotopic composition varies slightly with source. †Isotopic composition varies considerably with source. ‡Isotope radioactive.
Source: This table has been taken from C.M. Lederer, J.M. Hollander, and I. Perlman, "Table of Isotopes," 1968.

ments technetium ($Z = 43$) and promethium ($Z = 61$) and all the elements with atomic number greater than that of bismuth ($Z = 83$) have no stable isotopes. In the case of the element xenon there are, besides the nine stable isotopes, as many as 24 known radioactive isotopes with half-lives ranging from about one second to about 36 days. Six of these are nuclear isomers. At the other extreme, hydrogen has only three known isotopes, two stable (protium and deuterium) and one radioactive (tritium, which occurs naturally, though only in minute amounts).

Effects of isotopic substitution on physical properties. The rather belated discovery of isotopes, as well as the difficulty of separating them, either by chemical or physical methods, indicates the smallness of the effect of atomic mass on most physical and chemical properties. For example, the electronic energy states of atoms or molecules depend on the nuclear mass through a quantity known as the reduced mass of the electrons in the many-body system of electrons and nuclei. The reduced mass is defined as approximately $m(1 - 1/1837A)$, in which m is the actual mass of the electrons. It can readily be seen that for protium ($A = 1$) the correction is roughly 5×10^{-4}, and that the effect is correspondingly smaller for heavier atoms. In the case of hydrogen, however, the difference in electronic energy levels for protium and deuterium can be detected easily spectroscopically, a fact that led to the original discovery of deuterium by the American chemist Harold C. Urey and colleagues in 1931.

Optical spectra of isotopes

The other consequence of isotopy on the optical spectra of atoms arises from the interaction of the magnetic field of the nucleus, if it has one, with the electrons of the atomic system. The result is a splitting of a spectral line into several components called the hyperfine structure. The number of components and their separations depend on the spin and the magnetic moment of the nucleus and on the nature of the electronic state. Since this phenomenon depends on nuclear properties, it varies from isotope to isotope. It is most important for heavy elements, but even there it is difficult to measure. Analysis of hyperfine structure has been used to determine nuclear spins and nuclear magnetic moments.

Molecular spectra are much more affected than are atomic spectra by the presence of isotopes, for these spectra reflect in part the vibrational and rotational energies of molecules. The quanta of vibrational and rotational energies depend directly on the masses of the atoms involved and, therefore, on the isotopic composition. It was by examination of molecular spectra that several isotopes, as for example, carbon-13, nitrogen-15, oxygen-17, oxygen-18, and silicon-30 were discovered.

The isotopic composition also affects physical properties of substances other than their optical spectra. There is, of course, the direct effect of mass on the density of a substance. Because densities can often be measured with extreme precision, density determinations have been used in special cases to establish isotopic composition.

Diffusion of gases

Another effect of isotopic composition is a consequence of the direct effect of mass on the rate of diffusion of gaseous atoms and molecules. It has long been known that the rate of effusion of a gas through a hole that is smaller than the average distance between the gas molecules varies inversely as the square root of the mass. It was by taking advantage of this property that F.W. Aston first achieved a partial separation of the isotopes of neon, and basically similar processes are still used.

Other physical properties of substances are significantly affected by isotopic composition only at low temperatures and in cases of molecules of low molecular weight. Accurate measurements continually reveal small differences in physical properties of substances of low molecular weight related by isotopic substitution. Deuterium, for example, melts at −254.6° C and boils at −249.7° C; whereas the corresponding temperatures for hydrogen are −259.14° C and −252.5° C. Heavy water, D_2O, has a melting point 3.8° higher and a boiling point 1.4° higher than ordinary water, H_2O. It is of special interest relative to the phenomenon of superconductivity at low temperatures that the temperature at which certain metals transform to the superconducting state is affected by the isotopic composition of the metal.

Effects of isotopic substitution on chemical properties. It has usually been assumed that the various isotopes of an element, and also substances differing merely in their isotopic composition, have the same chemistry. Accurate studies, however, particularly with deuterium, have indicated that the chemistry of isotopes is strictly identical only in the limit of large masses and high temperatures. Whenever quantum mechanical effects become important, and in general they are most important when the masses are small and the temperatures are low, the masses of the atoms involved can be expected to affect the chemistry to a significant extent; and the outcome of a chemical process would thus be sensitive to the isotopes involved. This situation can be understood from the following consideration. The forces between atoms derive from the electronic structures of the atoms, which are negligibly different for different isotopes of the same element. The actual motion of the atoms produced by these forces, however, is affected by the atomic mass. In a given potential the frequency of vibration and, therefore, the quantum of vibrational energy, vary inversely as the square root of the mass of the system. This variation affects not only the vibrational spectrum but also means that the zero point energy, the lowest energy state of the system, will be lower for heavier isotopes.

Comparative dissociation energies of isotopes

It is easy to calculate that the energy needed to dissociate the gaseous deuterium, D_2, molecules into single atoms of deuterium at absolute zero will be 1.81 kilocalories per mole higher, or higher by about 2 percent, than that needed to dissociate the hydrogen molecule. With elements heavier than hydrogen this effect becomes progressively smaller. Nevertheless, it remains true that, because of the lower zero point energy, more energy is required to break a chemical bond involving a heavier isotope than to break a bond involving a lighter one.

Using quantum mechanics to estimate the effects of mass, it is possible to calculate by statistical methods equilibrium constants for so-called exchange reactions. These are chemical reactions in which the reagents and products differ only in isotopic composition. For example, the reaction $C^{16}O_2 + 2H_2{}^{18}O \leftrightarrows C^{18}O_2 + 2H_2{}^{16}O$ has an equilibrium constant given by

$$K = \frac{P(C^{18}O_2) \times P^2(H_2{}^{16}O)}{P(C^{16}O_2) \times P^2(H_2{}^{18}O)}$$

where $P_{(C^{18}O_2)}$ designates the pressure exerted by $C^{18}O_2$ at equilibrium $P_{(H_2{}^{16}O)}$ that of $H_2{}^{16}O$, etc.

The value of the equilibrium constant was calculated by Urey and L. Greiff in 1935 to be 1.128 at 0° C and 1.110 at 25° C. It is seen that carbon dioxide in equilibrium with water will contain oxygen with slightly higher oxygen-18 content than does the water. It is also seen that at higher temperatures the oxygen in the carbon dioxide and in the water tend toward more equal isotopic compositions.

Predictions such as the above have been verified experimentally. It has also been demonstrated that the rates of chemical reactions are affected measurably by isotopic substitutions. In general, the effects are greatest for the lightest elements and decrease with increasing temperature. Thus chemical reaction rates involving deuterium compounds may be up to several times slower than those involving the corresponding protium compounds. This effect has been used extensively to investigate the mechanism of reactions that may involve transfer of hydrogen atoms. In view of the measurable effects of isotopes on both chemical equilibria and the rates of chemical reactions, it is not surprising that the isotopic composition of the lighter elements in nature shows a definite variation from one source to another.

Separation of isotopes. This phrase is generally used to indicate the production of an isotopic composition significantly different from the natural isotopic composition of the element. In the extreme it would mean the production of a relatively pure isotope. For most purposes, such as chemical or biological tagging, however, complete separation is not necessary.

Before eventually developing his mass spectrograph, Aston first attempted to confirm Thomson's discovery of isotopes in neon by trying to separate the two isotopes. He allowed part of a sample of neon to diffuse at a low pressure through clay pipes and repeated the process many times on the fractions obtained. He reported in 1913 that in this way he had been able to change the atomic weight of neon by almost 0.5 percent. Subsequent attempts by many persons using many different methods on various elements did not produce significantly better separations. Finally G. Hertz, in 1932, using the same basic method as Aston, arranged the diffusing units in a cascade (see Figure). He produced neon with the heavier isotope, neon-22, more than twice as abundant as neon-20, the lighter one, even though the neon-22 content of natural neon is only 10 percent. Since these pioneer achievements, isotope separations by various methods have become increasingly common. Today, small samples of almost any element with distorted isotopic abundances are available for research purposes. Deuterium and uranium-235 are separated on a large scale as a part of nuclear energy programs.

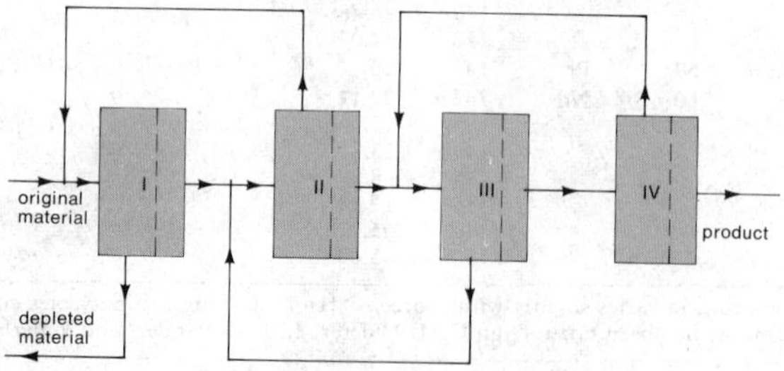

Cascade arrangement of four stages for separating isotopes (see text).

Uses of isotopes. The uses of isotopes can be divided roughly into two categories. In one, interest lies in some nuclear property such as the radiation emitted upon decomposition, nuclear magnetic moment or spin, or some nuclear reaction probability. In the other, application depends on the fact that, to a good approximation, all isotopes of an element have the same chemical properties. This characteristic makes it possible to label or tag a natural sample of an element by adding to it a radioactive or a stable isotope. The behaviour of this element can then be followed either by measuring the radioactivity or by analysis with a mass spectrometer. The isotope added is often referred to as a tracer or indicator. The use of labelled atoms in this manner was introduced in 1913 with the study of the solubility of lead salts, using lead-210 (formerly known as radium D), a radioactive isotope of lead. Since then, with the availability of radioactive or stable isotopes as tracers, the use of tagged elements for many chemical, biological, and industrial purposes has become widespread.

Nuclear isomers. Nuclear isomers are nuclides whose nuclei have the same charge and mass number but represent different energy states. One of two nuclear isomers must be unstable with respect to de-excitation. Although the existence of any excited state is in a sense an example of nuclear isomerism, the term is ordinarily applied only to cases in which the excited state has a measurable half-life for de-excitation; that is, a half-life exceeding 10^{-11} second. Such nuclei are called metastable and are usually designated by an asterisk * or an *m* after the mass number. Thus, bromine-80 and bromine-80*m* comprise a pair of nuclear isomers of bromine. Bromine-80*m* decays into bromine-80 with a half-life of 4.5 hours.

The first case of nuclear isomerism was discovered by the German physicist Otto Hahn in 1921, when he found two nuclear species with distinctive radioactive properties, both of which had to be assigned the nuclear constitution expressed by protactinium-234. By the mid-20th century more than 160 pairs of nuclear isomers, as well as a few cases of triple isomerism, were known. Since nuclear isomers have the same charge and differ in mass by less than a few thousandths of one amu—nonisomeric isotopes differing from each other by at least one amu—differences in chemical properties of nuclear isomers are not likely. The differences in physical properties are confined to those (*e.g.*, nuclear radiations, spin) related to detailed nuclear constitution.

BIBLIOGRAPHY. ERNEST RUTHERFORD, J. CHADWICK, and C.D. ELLIS, *Radiations from Radioactive Substances* (1930; reprinted with corrections, 1951); and FRANCIS W. ASTON, *Mass Spectra and Isotopes*, 2nd ed. (1942), give the history of the discovery of radioactive and stable isotopes. C. MICHAEL LEDERER and VIRGINIA S. SHIRLEY (eds.), *Table of Isotopes*, 7th ed. (1978); and the journal *Nuclear Data Sheets* (monthly), give detailed information on properties of isotopes. JACOB BIGELEISEN, "Isotope Separation Practice," in *Advances in Chemistry Series*, no. 89 (1969), reviews methods of separating stable isotopes. See also J.A. ELVIDGE and J.R. JONES (eds.), *Isotopes: Essential Chemistry and Applications* (1980), symposium proceedings in which the most important uses of isotopes are discussed; J.M. CHAPMAN and G. AYREY, *The Use of Radioactive Isotopes in the Life Sciences* (1981); and *Stable Isotopes: Proceedings of the Third International Conference*, ed. by E. ROSELAND KLEIN and PETER D. KLEIN (1979), scholarly papers covering synthesis, instrumentation and techniques, and applications.

(A.L.Tu.)

Israel

A Middle Eastern republic at the eastern end of the Mediterranean Sea, the State of Israel (Medinat Yisra'el in Hebrew) is bounded to the north by Lebanon, to the northeast by Syria, to the east and southeast by Jordan, to the southwest by Egypt, and to the west by the Mediterranean Sea.

Its total area is 7,992 square miles, or 20,700 square kilometres (excluding the eastern part of Jerusalem and other territories occupied in the 1967 war). Its population in 1982 was about 3,978,000, of whom about 83 percent were Jews, 13 percent were Muslims, and 2 percent were Christians. Jerusalem is the capital and the seat of government.

Following the United Nations partition of Palestine, Israel emerged on May 15, 1948. It was the first Jewish state to be established in nearly 2,000 years. Its creation represented a fulfillment of the historic ideal of the Jewish people stemming from the traditional religious belief in God's promise of the land of Israel to the people of Israel. The ideal found practical expression in a desire to forge a nation without dependence on the goodwill of others. The establishment of Israel as a member of the family of nations signified a decisive step in modern Jewish history.

Fulfillment of a historic ideal

Among the population are numbered hundreds of thousands of immigrants, many of them survivors of Nazi persecution in Europe or victims of anti-Semitism elsewhere. Israeli society has engaged in a variety of pioneering activities, including the rehabilitation of neglected agricultural lands. This has led to the creation of a Jewish rural population, which, though it represents only about 13 percent of the total Jewish population, also represents something almost unknown in the Diaspora (the historical scattering of the Jews in countries outside of Palestine). The revival of the Hebrew language has made possible the cultural integration of the newcomers.

Hostile relations between Israel and neighbouring Arab states have prevailed from the outset, with Israel obtaining victories over the Arabs after battles fought in 1948–1949, 1956, 1967, and 1973. Territory occupied by the Israeli forces after the 1967 and 1973 conflicts and still held in the early 1980s—including the eastern part of Jerusalem, part of Jordan, the Gaza Strip, and the Golan Heights region of Syria—is not treated in this article. (For Israeli-occupied territories see JERUSALEM; JORDAN; and SYRIA. For historical aspects, see SYRIA AND PALESTINE, HISTORY OF.)

THE LANDSCAPE

Natural features. *Relief.* Israel may be divided into four natural regions. These are (1) the Mediterranean coastal plain; (2) the hill regions of northern and central Israel; (3) the Great Rift Valley; and (4) the Negev.

The coastal plain is a narrow strip about 115 miles (185 kilometres) long, widening to a breadth of about 20 miles in the south. In the north of the country, the mountains of Galilee constitute the highest part of Israel; their highest point is Har Meron, or (in Arabic) Jebel Jarmaq (3,963 feet; 1,208 metres). To the east these mountains terminate in an escarpment overlooking the Great Rift Valley. The moutains of Galilee are separated from the hills of Samaria and Judaea to the south by the Plain of Esdraelon ('Emeq Yizre'el), which, running approximately northwest to southeast, connects the coastal plain with the Great Rift Valley. From the hills of Samaria and Judaea, culminating in a spur in Israeli-occupied Jordan, Mt. Carmel (1,791 feet) reaches almost to the coast of Haifa.

Galilee

The Great Rift Valley forms part of a great fissure in the Earth's crust that runs from beyond the northern frontier of Israel down the length of the country to the Gulf of Aqaba in the south and then continues down the Red Sea and through eastern Africa. The Jordan River, which forms part of the frontier between Israel and Jordan, runs southward from Dan on Israel's northern frontier, where it is 500 feet above sea level, first into the Sea of Galilee, also known as Lake Tiberias or Yām Kinneret (686 feet below sea level), and then into the Dead Sea, which is about 1,315 feet below sea level and which represents the lowest point on the Earth's surface. The Negev, in the southern part of Israel, forms an arrow-shaped wedge of territory that comes to a point at the port of Elat (Eilat) on the Gulf of Aqaba. (See also DEAD SEA; GALILEE, SEA OF; JORDAN RIVER.)

Drainage. The principal drainage system is represented by the Jordan River, which flows first into 'Emeq Hula (Hula Basin), then into the freshwater Sea of Galilee, and finally into the Dead Sea, which is intensely saline. Other principal rivers in Israel are the Yarqon, which empties into the Mediterranean near Tel Aviv; the Qishon, which runs through the western part of the Plain of Esdraelon to drain into the Mediterranean at Haifa; and a small section of the Yarmuk, a tributary of the Jordan. The remaining streams, usually seasonal, flow through streambeds called wadis.

The Jordan River

Soils. The coastal plain is covered mainly by alluvial soils. Because of its proximity to the coastal plain, the Negev's desert soils are composed predominantly of windborne loess. The soils of Galilee change from calcareous rock in the coastal plain to cenomanian and turonian limestone in Upper Galilee and to Eocene formations (from 38,000,000 to 54,000,000 years old) in the lower part of the region. Rock salt and gypsum are abundant in the Great Rift Valley.

Climate. Israel, being situated between the subtropical arid zone prevailing in Egypt to the south and the subtropical wet zone prevailing in Lebanon to the north, experiences great climatic contrasts. In the south rainfall is light, amounting to about one inch (25 millimetres) a year in the ʿArava Valley south of the Dead Sea, while in the north it is relatively heavy, amounting to 44 inches a year in the Upper Galilee region. The areas most cultivated are those with rainfall of more than 12 inches a year. Annual rainfall occurs on 40 to 60 days spread over a season of about seven months between October and April. Summers are dry and hot, but in the coastal areas sea breezes exert a moderating influence. In the summer the Sun ascends to more than 80 degrees above the horizon, and radiation reaches the ground in 98 percent of all potential hours of sunshine. Temperature depends on elevation and distance from the sea. The mean annual temperature in the coastal areas is from 68° to 70° F (20° to 21° C). At Elat, in the south, temperatures are about 59° F (15° C) in January and may rise as high as 120° F (49° C) in August. Relative humidity is highest near the coast and is higher on summer than on winter nights. The Jordan Valley is hotter and drier than the coast. The hill regions experience occasional snows in winter.

Vegetation. Vegetation is varied. The original evergreen forests have largely disappeared because of centuries of cultivation and the depredations of goats. The hills are mostly covered by maquis (wild shrub vegetation), and only desert scrub grows wild in the Negev and on the sand dunes of the coastal plain. North of Beersheba most of the country is under cultivation or hill grazing; where irrigation is available, citrus groves and eucalyptus (introduced from Australia) and conifer plantations flourish. Millions of trees have been planted under a reafforestation program. Conditions on the coastal plain are particularly favourable to citrus cultivation.

Animal life. Animal life is similarly varied. Mammals include wildcats, wild boars, gazelles, ibex, jackals, hyenas, hares, coneys, badgers, and tiger weasels. Among the reptiles, the agama and gecko lizards, the viper, and the carpet viper are found. Birds include the partridge, tropical cuckoo, bustard, sand grouse, and desert lark. There are many kinds of fish and insects. Invasions of desert locusts sometimes occur. Several regions have been set as nature reserves, notably parts of the ʿArava Valley in the south and Mt. Carmel, Har Meron, and the remains of Hula Lake and marshes in the north.

Nature reserves

Traditional regions. The character of many regions has been altered by new patterns of Jewish settlement. The first modern-day Jewish settlers established themselves on the coastal plain in the 1880s. Later they also moved into the valleys of the interior and into parts of the hill districts, as well as into the Negev. The formerly Arab-populated areas of the coastal plain, the Judaean foothills, and the Jordan and ʿArava valleys became almost exclusively Jewish. Although the majority of the Bedouin of the Negev left the region when it became Israeli territory, the Negev remained largely the domain of Arab nomads. The non-Jewish population is concentrated mainly in the north, where Arabs constitute a substantial part of the population of Galilee.

The landscape under human settlement. *Rural settlement.* The rural Jewish population in 1982 amounted to about 13 percent of the total Jewish population. More than half the rural inhabitants are immigrants who arrived after 1948; two-thirds of the settlements were established after that date. About 260 of the settlements are kibbutzim (collective groups voluntarily practicing joint production and consumption), representing a population of about 114,000 (approximately 3 percent of the total population). About 410 settlements are moshavim, smallholders' cooperatives practicing joint sales and purchases, making joint use of machinery, ideally prohibiting hired labour, and leasing national land, usually for 49 years, with a population of about 145,000 (about 4 percent of the total population). The remaining rural settlements are individually owned farms, or villages in which private ownership is practiced. The kibbutzim and moshavim perform security functions in border areas and contribute to the national ability to absorb new immigrants.

Of the total rural population a little less than two-fifths, including the Bedouin, is non-Jewish. Before 1948 Jewish and Arab agricultural settlements existed side by side but were completely independent of each other. Since then, however, the demand for labour has resulted in thousands of Arab workers from the villages and the occupied territories finding employment in the citrus groves, in industry, or as construction labourers. This movement, together with increased agricultural mechanization, has led to a drop in the number of Jewish agricultural workers. In Arab villages fewer than half of the adult labourers, both men and women, are engaged in working the land. By the late 1970s there was a growing tendency to practice intensive cultivation, to diversify crops, and to extend farm areas. Most Arab farmers work their own land; some either lease land or work for Arab or Jewish landlords.

Urban settlement. In 1982 almost 90 percent of the Jewish population was urban. With the increasing mechanization and efficiency of Jewish agriculture, the proportion of people living on the land has been decreasing. In 1961, 124,000 people were occupied in agriculture; this number had declined to 77,000 in 1981. As a result of industrial and service sector development, the large conurbations of Tel Aviv–Yafo and Haifa and the city of Jerusalem contain about 52 percent of the total population. Great efforts have been made by the authorities, however, to prevent overconcentration of population in these areas. In both the northern and southern parts of the country, new towns have been built whose populations consist largely of new immigrants. These towns serve as centres of regional settlement or else fulfill special economic tasks such as the manufacture of textiles, clothing, or machinery.

New towns

The major urban centres inhabited by Arabs include cities and towns with both Arab and Jewish populations, such as Jerusalem, Haifa, ʿAkko, Lod (Lydda), Ramla, and Yafo, and towns with entirely Arab populations, such as Nazareth. In 1981, 65 percent of Israel's Arabs lived in cities and towns. As in the villages, traditional patterns of Arab life in towns and cities have been modified. Many youths from Arab villages have moved to the towns. In towns with both Arab and Jewish populations, many of the former differences in the way of life of the two communities are diminishing, even though Arabs and Jews usually live in different quarters.

PEOPLE AND POPULATION

Groups historically associated with the contemporary country. *Jews.* In origin, as well as in physical features, the Jewish population lacks uniformity. Immigrants differed in colour and culture and brought with them languages and customs from a variety of countries. Consciousness of geographic origin and descent is, however, gradually being superseded by a national consciousness, especially among the young. Religious Jewish groups immigrating to Israel generally continue to pray in the synagogues (Jewish houses of worship) of their respective communities. The two main religious groupings are formed by those who follow the Ashkenazi rite (of Jews from central and eastern Europe and their descendants in other parts of the world), and those who follow the Sefardi and Oriental rite (of Jews from the Mediterranean

Israel, Area and Population

	area		population	
	sq mi	sq km	1972 census	1982 census
Districts				
Central	480	1,242	580,000	808,000
Haifa	330	854	484,000	570,000
Jerusalem	215	557	347,000	457,000
Northern	1,347	3,490	473,000	626,000
Southern	5,555	14,387	354,000	486,000
Tel Aviv	66	170	907,000	1,004,000
Total Israel	7,992*	20,700	3,148,000*†	3,978,000†

*Figures do not add to total given because of rounding.
†Includes 2,000 residents in 1972 and 27,000 in 1982 in the Administered Territories of Judaea and Samaria; Gaza Area and Sinai; and the Golan, not listed separately.
Source: Official government figures.

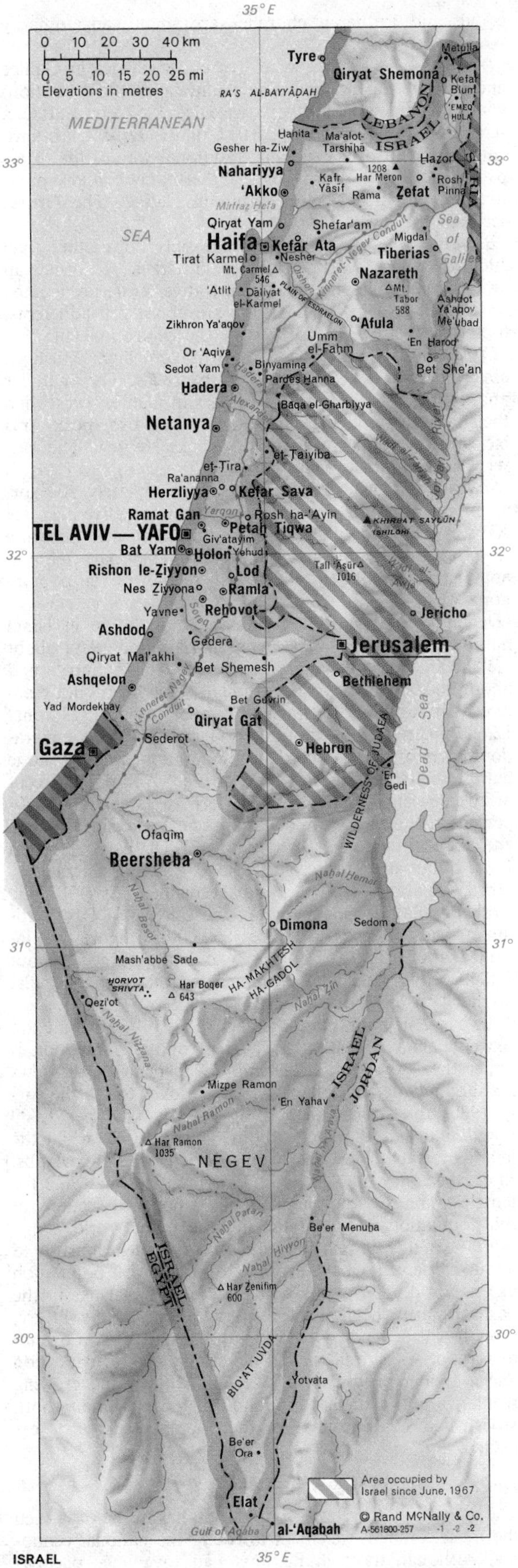

ISRAEL

MAP INDEX

Cities and towns
'Afula . . . . .32·36n 35·17e
'Akko . . . . .32·55n 35·05e
Ashdod. . . . . .31·49n 34·39e
Ashdot Ya'aqov
Me'uhad . . . . . . .32·39n 35·34e
Ashqelon . . . . . . .31·40n 34·35e
'Atlit . . . . .32·41n 34·56e
Bāqa el-
Gharbiyya . . . . . .32·25n 35·03e
Bat Yam . . . . .32·01n 34·45e
Be'er Menuha . . . .30·19n 35·08e
Be'er Ora . . . . . . .29·43n 34·59e
Beersheba
(Be'er Sheva') . . .31·14n 34·47e
Bet Guvrin. . . . . . .31·36n 34·54e
Bet She'an . . . . . .32·30n 35·30e
Bet Shemesh. . . . .31·45n 35·00e
Binyamina . . . . . . .32·31n 34·57e
Dāliyat
el-Karmel. . . . . . .32·42n 35·03e
Dimona. . . . . .31·04n 35·02e
Elat. . . . . .29·33n 34·57e
'En Gedi . . . . .31·27n 35·23e
'En Harod . . . . . .32·33n 35·23e
'En Yahav . . . . . . .30·38n 35·11e
et-Taiyiba . . . . . . .32·16n 35·01e
et-Tīra. . . . . .32·14n 34·57e
Gedera . . . . .31·49n 34·46e
Gesher ha-Ziw. . . .33·02n 35·06e
Giv'atayim. . . . . . .32·04n 34·48e
Hadera . . . . .32·26n 34·55e
Haifa. . . . . .32·50n 35·00e
Hanita. . . . . .33·05n 35·10e
Hazor . . . . .32·59n 35·33e
Hefa, see Haifa
Herzliyya. . . . . . . .32·10n 34·51e
Holon . . . . .32·01n 34·46e
Jerusalem . . . . . . .31·46n 35·14e
Kafr Yāsīf . . . . . . .32·57n 35·10e
Kefar Ata . . . . . . .32·48n 35·06e
Kefar Blum . . . . . .33·10n 35·36e
Kefar Sava . . . . . .32·10n 34·54e
Lod (Lydda) . . . . .31·58n 34·54e
Ma'alot-
Tarshīhā . . . . . . .33·01n 35·17e
Mash'abbe
Sade . . . . .31·00n 34·47e
Metulla . . . . .33·16n 35·35e
Migdal . . . . .32·50n 35·30e
Mizpe Ramon . . . .30·36n 34·48e
Nahariyya . . . . . . .33·00n 35·05e
Nazareth
(Nazerat) . . . . . . .32·42n 35·18e
Nesher . . . . .32·46n 35·03e
Nes Ziyyona . . . . .31·55n 34·48e
Netanya . . . . .32·20n 34·51e
Ofaqim . . . . .31·17n 34·37e
Or'Aqiva . . . . .32·30n 34·55e
Pardes Hanna. . . .32·28n 34·58e
Petah Tiqwa . . . . .32·05n 34·53e
Qezi'ot . . . . .30·53n 34·27e
Qiryat Gat. . . . . . .31·36n 34·46e
Qiryat
Mal'akhi. . . . . . . .31·44n 34·44e
Qiryat
Shemona. . . . . . .33·13n 35·34e
Qiryat Yam . . . . . .32·51n 35·04e
Ra'ananna. . . . . . .32·11n 34·53e
Rama . . . . .32·56n 35·22e
Ramat Gan . . . . . .32·05n 34·49e
Ramla . . . . .31·55n 34·52e
Rehovot . . . . .31·54n 34·49e
Rishon
le-Ziyyon . . . . . . .31·58n 34·48e
Rosh ha-'
Ayin . . . . .32·06n 34·57e
Rosh Pinna . . . . . .32·58n 35·32e
Safad, see Zefat
Sederot. . . . . .31·31n 34·35e
Sedom . . . . .31·04n 35·24e
Sedot Yam . . . . . .32·29n 34·53e
Shefar'am . . . . . . .32·48n 35·10e
Tel Aviv-Yafo . . . .32·04n 34·46e
Tiberias
(Teverya) . . . . . . .32·47n 35·32e
Tirat Karmel . . . . .32·46n 34·58e
Umm el-
Fahm . . . . .32·31n 35·09e
Yad
Mordekhay . . . . .31·35n 34·33e
Yavne . . . . .31·53n 34·45e
Yehud . . . . .32·02n 34·53e
Yerushalayim,
see Jerusalem
Yotvata . . . . .29·53n 35·03e
Zefat. . . . . .32·58n 35·30e
Zikhron
Ya'aqov . . . . .32·34n 34·57e

Physical features and points of interest
Alexander,
river . . . . .32·24n 34·52e
Aqaba, Gulf of. . . .29·30n 34·40e
Besor, Nahal,
watercourse. . . . .31·28n 34·22e
Boqer, Har,
mountain . . . . . . .30·52n 34·43e
Carmel, Mount,
mountain . . . . . . .32·44n 35·02e
Dead Sea . . . . . . .31·30n 35·30e
Esdraelon,
Plain of . . . . .32·36n 35·14e
Galilee, Sea of. . . .32·48n 35·35e
ha-'Arava, Nahal,
watercourse. . . . .30·57n 35·19e
Hadera, *river*. . . . .32·27n 34·53e
Haifa, Bay of, see
Hefa, Mifraz
ha-Gadol,
ha-Makhtesh,
depression . . . . .30·56n 34·59e
ha-Melah,Yam,
see Dead Sea
ha-Negev,
see Negev
ha-Yarden, see
Jordan River
Hefa, Mifraz,
bay . . . . .32·52n 35·03e
Hemar, Nahal,
watercourse. . . . .31·08n 35·22e
Hiyyon, Nahal,
watercourse. . . . .30·12n 35·07e
Horvot Shivta,
ruins . . . . .30·53n 34·38e
Hula, 'Emeq,
(Hula Basin),
basin. . . . . .33·08n 35·37e
Jordan River . . . . .31·46n 35·33e
Karmel, Har,
see Carmel, Mount
Kinneret, Yām,
see Galilee,
Sea of
Kinneret-Negev
Conduit,
aqueduct. . . . . . .32·52n 35·32e
Mediterranean
Sea. . . . . .33·00n 34·30e
Meron, Har,
mountain . . . . . . .33·00n 35·25e
Midbar Yehuda,
see Wilderness of Judaea
Negev, *region* . . . .30·30n 34·55e
Nizzana, Nahal,
watercourse. . . . .30·57n 34·23e
Paran, Nahaal,
watercourse. . . . .30·24n 35·10e
Qishon, *river* . . . . .32·49n 35·02e
Ramon, Har,
mountain . . . . . . .30·30n 34·38e
Ramon, Nahal,
watercourse. . . . .30·36n 34·55e
Soreq, *river*. . . . . .31·56n 34·42e
Subeita, see
Horvot Shivta
Tabor, Mount,
(Har Tavor),
mountain . . . . . . .32·41n 35·23e
Tiberias, Lake, see
Galilee, Sea of
'Uvda, Biq'at,
valley . . . . .29·57n 34·57e
Wilderness of
Judaea,
region . . . . .31·30n 35·18e
Yarqon, *river* . . . . .32·06n 34·47e
Yizre'el, 'Emeq, see
Esdraelon, Plain of
Zenifim, Har
hill. . . . . .30·06n 34·51e
Zin, Nahal,
watercourse. . . . .30·57n 35·19e

region and from the Middle and Far East). Thus there are traditionally two chief rabbis in Israel, one Ashkenazi and one Sefardi. Religious Jewry in Israel constitutes a significant and articulate section of the population. There is, however, also a strong movement that seeks to prevent religious bodies and authorities from dominating national life or from interfering with individual freedom of conscience. Disputes occasionally arise over differences of interpretation concerning the role of religious authority as distinct from the role of state authority.

Muslims. The largest religious minority group is formed by the Muslims, who constitute more than two-thirds of the Arab population. Practically all of the Muslims adhere to the Sunnī rite. A minority of them are peasants, and most Muslims now live in the towns. Like all other religious communities, the Muslims enjoy considerable autonomy in dealing with matters of marriage and divorce

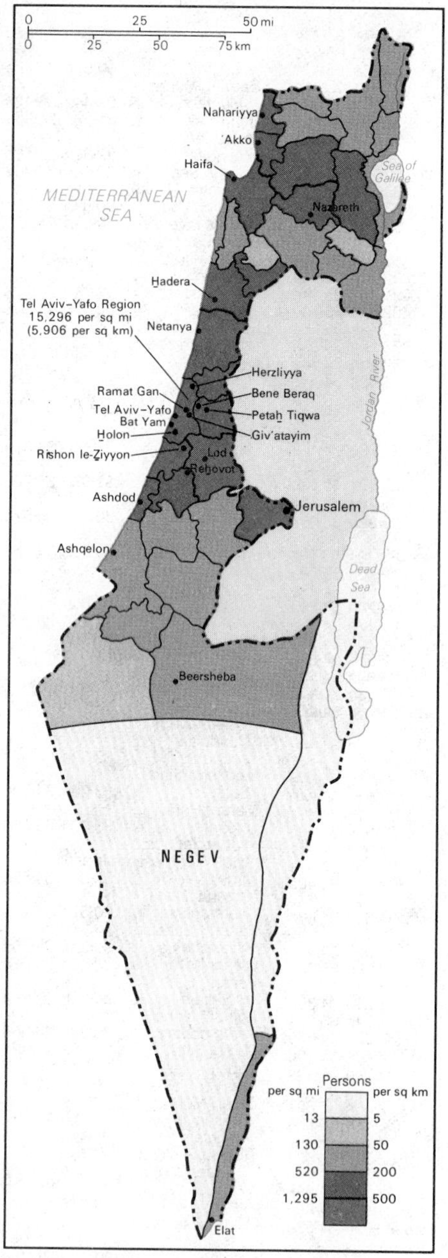

Population density of Israel.

and have separate religious courts. The state supervises religious institutions. Among the Muslims about 55,000 are Bedouin; about three-quarters of these live in the Negev, and the rest live in Galilee. New economic opportunities, and the fact that the borders with neighbouring Arab countries are closed, have encouraged the Bedouin to adopt a more sedentary mode of life.

Christians. Most Christians are town dwellers, and more than 80 percent speak Arabic. The Christian communities exercise autonomy in religious and communal affairs. The Greek Orthodox and Greek Catholic (Melkite) are the largest of these communities, most of which have their headquarters in Jerusalem. Apart from the Greek Orthodox patriarchate, which is established in Jerusalem, the Christian churches are dependent in varying degrees upon supreme hierarchs residing abroad. The Christian communities include Roman Catholics and Uniates (Melkites, Maronites, Chaldean Catholics, Syrian Catholics, and Armenian Catholics). Each Uniate community belongs to an independent jurisdiction, but depends partly upon the Sacred Congregation of the Oriental Churches in Rome.

Jerusalem is also the seat of two Russian Orthodox missions: one represents the Moscow patriarchate and the other, the Russian church in exile. The Evangelical, Episcopal, and Lutheran churches are small and primarily Arabic-speaking.

The Druze community

Druzes. The Druzes, who live in 18 villages in Galilee and on Mt. Carmel and who maintain excellent relations with the Israeli majority, have since 1957 constituted a separate Arab community. Most of the Druzes are agriculturists who preserve their traditional way of life. They pay homage to Jethro (Moses' father-in-law), whose putative grave is near Kefar Hittim in Galilee. The Druzes serve in the army.

Bahā'īs. The Bahā'ī faith is the only faith other than Judaism whose world centre is in Israel. A shrine, an archives building, and an administrative centre are located on Mt. Carmel in Haifa. There are about 250 adherents, most of whom are employed at the centre in Haifa.

Circassians. The Circassians, who are Sunnī Muslims, emigrated from the Caucasus in the 1870s. They number about 2,000 and live in two villages in Galilee, preserving their language and their traditions. They also speak Arabic, and the younger generation speaks Hebrew. The men serve in the Israeli army.

Samaritans. About 250 of the approximately 500 surviving members of the Samaritan community live near Tel Aviv in the town of Holon. They preserve their separate religious and communal organization. They participate in national life as part of the Jewish section of the population.

Demography. In 1948 the Jewish population in Israel numbered about 650,000. Between 1948 and 1970, about 1,300,000 Jewish immigrants entered the country, and about 200,000 Jews left it, although some have since reentered. Immigration declined after the war of 1973; only 12,600 entered Israel in 1981, and in some years emigration probably has exceeded immigration, with a large number of Israeli citizens living abroad. About 57 percent of the Jewish community was born in Israel, about 24 percent in Europe or America, about 10 percent in Africa, and about 9 percent elsewhere in Asia. Of the Israeli-born Jews, about one-quarter are second generation Israelis.

In 1948 about 155,000 Arabs remained. By 1982 the Arab population (not including those living in East Jerusalem) had increased to almost 660,000—a figure that included about 36,000 refugees who had returned. About 27,000 Jews lived in the occupied territories in the midst of the Arab majority of those areas.

The sex distribution among all sections of the population is well balanced. About 31 percent of the population is under the age of 14, while about 7 percent of the Jews and about 3 percent of the Arabs are over 65. In the early 1980s the Jewish birth rate was about 21 per 1,000 population and the Arab about 34 per 1,000, while the infant mortality rate was lower for Jews than for Arabs. Life expectancy at birth was 72.5 for males and 76.2 for females. The average length of life among all sections of the population is one of the highest in the world.

Immigration rate

In 1981 the Jewish population of Israel constituted about 23 percent of the estimated total Jewish population in the world. The population growth of Israel has in the past primarily been due to immigration. In the future, growth will depend more on natural increase than on immigration. As a result of the increasing level of education and a greater proportion of working women and growing secularization, a further reduction of fertility among both Jewish and Arab sections of the population is to be expected.

THE NATIONAL ECONOMY

The increase in the Jewish population has in the past been the most distinctive element affecting the national economy. Although most immigrants had to change occupations, a nucleus of highly skilled labour facilitated economic expansion. The establishment and rapid growth of institutions of higher learning and research has helped to increase the nation's potentialities. Large amounts of capital were brought in the form of money involving no financial obligation on the part of the state. This included gifts from world Jewry, reparations from the Federal Republic of Germany for the persecution of Jews in Germany during Hitler's administration, grants-in-aid from the U.S.

government, and capital brought in by immigrants. This capital was supplemented by loans and commercial credits and by foreign investment.

In the early 1980s construction was the leading growth area in the Israeli economy, representing about 12 percent of the gross national product and about two-thirds of all gross investment. Industry provided some 25 percent of Israel's national income. The rapid rise in the gross national product after 1948 was due not only to the increase in population but also to the skills some of the newcomers brought into the economy, the importation of capital, and the increase in productivity of the economy as a whole. Persistent trade deficits—more than $2,500,000,000 in 1981—hampered economic growth in the early 1980s, however. In 1980, at current market prices, per capita income amounted to $4,640.

The goals of economic policy are continued economic growth, the reinforcement of a competitive capacity, and further integration of Israel's economy with the world economy. Progress toward these goals has been made under difficult conditions, which have included a rapid increase of population; a boycott and a blockade by the neighbouring Arab countries except, from 1979, Egypt; heavy expenditure on defense; a scarcity of natural resources, including water; a high standard of living; inflation, which was more than 100 percent per year in the early 1980s; and a restricted home market that limits the economies of methods of mass production

In the 1970s Israel's economy turned upward, primarily because of a huge increase in government spending, especially for the military. Expansion has taken place in industry, as well as in transportation, communications, and construction. The balance of payments, on the other hand, has deteriorated because of a growing deficit in trade and in services. The central problem facing the economy has thus become how to maintain economic growth while at the same time increasing exports so as to reduce the balance of payments deficit.

Need to increase exports

The extent and distribution of resources. *Mineral resources.* Mineral resources include potash, bromine, and magnesium, the last two of which are obtained from the waters of the Dead Sea; copper ore, which is located in the ʿArava Valley; phosphates and small amounts of gypsum in the Negev; and some marble in Galilee. There are oil deposits in the northern Negev and south of Tel Aviv and deposits of natural gas in the northern Negev and northeast of Beersheba. Limited exploitation of oil began in the 1950s.

Electric power resources. Electricity is principally generated from thermal stations. Total generating capacity in 1981 was 3,032 megawatts. The electricity industry is nationalized, and the government has encouraged intensive rural electrification; electricity for agriculture and industry is provided at favourable rates.

Atomic energy. The Israel Atomic Energy Commission was established in 1952. It has undertaken a comprehensive survey of the country's natural resources and trains scientific and technical personnel. An atomic reactor has been constructed with U.S. assistance south of Tel Aviv, and a second one has been built with French help in the Negev.

Sources of national income. *Agriculture, forestry, and fishing.* The expansion in the amount of irrigated land has been a major factor in raising the value of agricultural production. There has also been a great expansion in the cultivation of citrus and of such industrial crops as peanuts (groundnuts), sugar beets, and cotton, as well as of vegetables and flowers. The number of milk cows increased by one and a half times from 1970 to 1980. Agricultural exports, consisting mainly of citrus, increased from $6,500,000 in 1949 to $600,400,000 by 1980.

The main agricultural problem is scarcity of water. Water from the Jordan and Yarqon rivers and from the Sea of Galilee is diverted by pipeline to arid areas in the south. By the 1970s, however, practically all of the country's potential water resources were in use. Any further development of agriculture will depend upon the intensification of the yield from land already irrigated, or upon obtaining more water by reducing the amount of evaporation, desalinizing sea water, and diverting water from the occupied territories.

Scarcity of water

As only a limited quantity of fish is available off Israel's Mediterranean and Red Sea coasts, Israeli trawlers sail to the rich fishing grounds off the Ethiopian coast and engage in deep-sea fishing in the Atlantic. Inland, fish-pond production meets much of the domestic demand.

Mining and quarrying. The mining industry supplies local demands for fertilizers, detergents, and drugs, and also exports products. The Timna Copper Mines near Elat exported copper ore until they were closed in 1976; a plant in Haifa produces potassium nitrate and phosphoric acid, both for local consumption and for export. Products of the Haifa Oil Refineries include polyethylene and carbon black, which are used by the local tire and plastic industries. The electrochemical industry also produces food chemicals and a variety of other commodities.

Oil pipelines run from the port of Elat to the Mediterranean. Oil wells in Israel were producing in the early 1980s, but oil imports constituted about 20 percent of all goods imported in 1981.

Manufacturing. Industrial output increased by more than 200 percent between 1958 and 1968 and grew by 125 percent in 1968–81. Government support of industrial exports has resulted in steady increases in their value; more than two-thirds of total exports in 1981 were derived from industry. More than half of Israel's industrial exports are marketed in Europe, the United States, and Canada.

Industrial growth has been especially rapid in electronics, weapons, transportation, machinery, and metals. About 13 percent of manufactures come from the food industry, after which the principal products are textiles, chemicals, and metals. The diamond-cutting and polishing industry is among the largest in the world; in 1981 it represented more than 30 percent of the world's total trade in polished diamonds. The largest industrial enterprise is Israel Aircraft Industries, the employer of 20,000 people, which manufactures and repairs aircraft. Industries manufacturing military supplies and equipment have expanded considerably since the 1967 war—a circumstance that has stimulated the development of the electronics industry. In most manufacturing industries a large proportion of the production is from a few plants. Nearly half of all industrial workers were employed in the early 1980s by 155 of the nation's 10,800 industrial establishments. About 90 percent of industries are privately owned.

Industrial expansion has been stimulated by the growth of local demand, which in turn has resulted from the growth of population and from the rise in the standard of living. Industry enjoys a high degree of protection against competitive imports. The government also assists industry by making loans available from the development budget at low rates of interest. The main limitations experienced by industry are the scarcity of raw materials and sources of energy and the restricted size of the local market.

Tourism and shipping. Tourism is a growing industry and is the second largest source of foreign exchange after diamonds. In 1981 nearly 1,137,000 tourists visited the country.

Shipping is a vital factor both in the economy and in communications with other countries. As a result of the closing of the land frontiers following the Arab blockade of Israel, shipping has played a major role in the transportation of supplies and, originally, in providing passages to Israel for immigrants. Israel's access routes to both the Atlantic and Indian oceans have stimulated a continuous growth of its merchant fleet, which in the early 1980s numbered about 100 ships with a gross tonnage of more than 2,460,000 tons.

Financial services. Israel has commercial (deposit) banks and cooperative credit institutions, mortgage and investment credit banks, and other financial institutions supervised by the Central Bank of Israel. Three banking groups hold most of the total bank assets. The banking system shows a high degree of specialization; commercial banks are, in general, restricted to short-term business. Medium- and long-term transactions are handled by institutions established to cater to the investment needs of

View of northern Israel, showing the Jordan River and fields and hills of Galilee.

agriculture, industry, housing, and shipping. These institutions are either fully owned by the government or are owned jointly by the banks and the government.

The Israeli shekel is linked to the U.S. dollar. The shekel consists of 100 agorot. There have been numerous devaluations of Israeli currency, which partially caused the introduction of the shekel in February 1980 to replace the Israeli pound at the rate of 1 shekel for every 10 pounds. The Central Bank of Israel issues currency and acts as the government's sole fiscal and banking agent. Its major function is to regulate the money supply and short-term banking credit.

Foreign trade. Imports are mainly of raw materials, including rough diamonds, and capital goods. Exports include a variety of light industrial products, textiles, polished diamonds, fertilizer and chemical products, and agricultural produce (mainly citrus fruits).

Import-export balance

The central problem of foreign trade is the large and persistent deficit resulting from the imbalance of imports over exports. Free access to foreign markets is, therefore, vital for the further expansion of the economy. The fact that Israel is not yet a member of any of the regional economic groupings that are emerging represents a considerable handicap. In 1964 Israel concluded a special agreement with the European Economic Community (EEC) and in 1975 obtained a new cooperation agreement with the EEC. An attempt has also been made to ameliorate foreign trade problems by participating actively in the General Agreement on Tariffs and Trade (GATT), which is a specialized agency of the United Nations.

Management of the economy. The management pattern of Israel's economy has been conditioned by many dynamic, powerful, and often contradictory factors. The large imports of capital that have been derived from public and semipublic sources have passed through government channels or through public organizations. This has resulted in the enlargement of the sector of the economy that includes public and semipublic enterprises. At the same time, the government's policy has, since 1977, been increasingly directed toward liberalizing the economy. The socioeconomic structure of the economy is, therefore, diversified. The governmental, cooperative, and private sectors consequently coexist in an economy that is subordinated to the broad objectives of state policy.

Taxation. The rates of taxation are among the highest in the world. Income, customs and excise, land, and luxury taxes are the main sources of revenue. The distribution between direct and indirect taxation has been altered over the years. Since the late 1950s the proportion of indirect taxation has increased.

Trade unions and employer associations. The General Federation of Labour in Israel (the Histadrut) is the largest labour union and the largest voluntary organization in the country. In the early 1980s it had a membership of more than 1,600,000, representing approximately 90 percent of the labour force. Since 1960 Arab workers have been admitted with full membership rights; there were 140,000 Arab members in 1981. The National Labour Federation had 144,000 members. The Manufacturers' Association of Israel and The Farmers' Union represent a large number of the country's employers.

Manpower. The unemployment rate, traditionally high because of unrestricted immigration, reached a peak of about 10 percent in 1953 but dropped to 7 percent in 1955 and to less than 4 percent in 1965. After the 1967 war the unemployment rate continued at about 4 percent, and in 1981 it was only 5 percent. Israel's capacity for economic growth in the early 1980s tended to be limited because of a shortage of skilled manpower. Immigration by then was relatively small, and the country's reserves in skilled manpower had been practically exhausted.

TRANSPORTATION

Road transport is of more significance than rail in internal communications. There are more than 7,000 miles of roads, but only about 500 miles of standard-gauge railroad track. A combined road and rail system extends to the port of Elat.

Three modern deepwater ports—Haifa and Ashdod on the Mediterranean, and Elat on the Red Sea—are maintained and developed by the Israel Ports Authority.

Deepwater ports

The international airport at Lod is the country's largest. Regular flights are maintained by several international airlines, with El Al Israel Airlines Ltd., Israel's national airline, accounting for 50 percent of the traffic. El Al's operations have often been disrupted by strikes. Domestic aviation, operated by Arka Israeli Airlines Ltd., has developed greatly in the past few years, with both planes and helicopters being used. Jerusalem (Ataroth), Tel Aviv (Sdeh-Dov), Elat, Rosh Pinna, and Haifa airfields serve the country's domestic air traffic.

ADMINISTRATION AND SOCIAL CONDITIONS

The structure of government. *Constitutional framework.* Israel is a democratic republic with a parliamentary system of government. It has a strong cabinet, a multiparty system with two large parties, and a marked tendency toward political and administrative centralization. Israel does not have a formal written constitution. The foundation on which the system of government has been built is composed of legislation, administrative acts, and parliamentary practice.

The Knesset, or assembly, is a 120-member, single-chamber legislature that is elected once every four years. In its internal organization and parliamentary procedure it has followed continental rather than Anglo-Saxon usage. Members exercise important functions in standing committees. Hebrew and Arabic, the country's two official languages, are used in all proceedings. In 1971 an Arab deputy-minister of health joined the government.

The president, who is the head of state, is elected by the Knesset for a five-year term, which can only be renewed once. The first three presidents (Chaim Weizmann, Itzhak Ben-Zvi, and Zalman Shazar) all acceded to office at a late stage in life; the first two died in office. Yitzhak Navon, elected in 1978, was the first of the presidents of Israel to have been born there. The president has no veto powers and exercises ceremonial functions.

The cabinet is the main policymaking body. Its members may be, but need not be, members of the Knesset. Following a general election or the resignation of a government, the president, after consultation with representatives of all parties, entrusts a member of the Knesset with the task of forming a cabinet. The prime minister is the leading figure in the cabinet and the government.

The state controller, an independent officer appointed by and responsible only to the Knesset, is the auditor of the government's financial transactions and is empowered to inquire into the efficiency of its activities.

The civil service is gradually developing into a politically neutral and professional body; previously, it tended to support the party in power. The extensive functions of the government have tended to result in a growing bureaucracy. Expansion has nevertheless kept pace with population growth, with the proportion of civil servants in the population remaining constant at about 3 percent.

Local and regional government. Administratively, the country is divided into six districts—the Central, Jerusalem, Haifa, Northern, Southern, and Tel Aviv districts—and into 12 subdistricts. There are three types of local government councils—municipalities, local councils (for smaller settlements), and regional rural councils. The by-laws of the councils, as well as their budgets, are subject to approval by the Ministry of the Interior.

Israeli-occupied Arab territories. After the 1967 war Arab territories occupied by Israeli forces were placed under military administration. These territories included Jordanian territory on the west bank of the Jordan River (the West Bank), the Gaza Strip, the Sinai Peninsula region of Egypt, and the Golan Heights region of Syria. The eastern section of Jerusalem was also occupied by Israeli forces, and the city is administered as a single municipality by the Israeli authorities; in 1967 eastern Jerusalem and adjoining villages were incorporated into the State of Israel by a governmental act—an action that is disputed abroad. Israel completed its withdrawal of civilian settlers and military personnel from the Sinai in April 1982. In 1981 the Golan Heights, however, was in effect annexed to Israel by the extension of Israeli law to it.

The Arab population of these territories in 1981 was about 1,145,000, about two-thirds of whom lived in the West Bank. A growing number of Israeli Jews also live in the West Bank in settlements sponsored by the Israeli government.

The political process. Elections, which are nationwide, are by universal, direct suffrage, with secret balloting. The system of election is by proportional representation. All resident Israeli citizens are enfranchised upon completion of their 18th year; candidates for election must be at least 21 years old. Similar conditions govern elections to local government bodies.

The Israel Labour Party (Mapai)

The main governing party from 1948 to 1977 was the Israel Labour Party (the majority of its members belonging until 1968 to Mapai), a moderate social-democratic and Zionist party. It held a majority in the cabinet, the premiership, and the major ministries. All cabinets were based on coalitions of Labour and other parties. The continuance in power of one party, the long terms of office of many ministers, and the consistent support of minor coalition members helped to preserve a remarkable degree of stability. The National Religious Party (previously Mizraḥi) was an almost constant coalition partner with Labour. Among opposition parties, the extreme-nationalist Ḥerut was the largest and most important, regarding itself as the nucleus of an alternative government. This tendency was further stressed with the establishment in 1965 of Gaḥal, a Ḥerut–Liberal Party parliamentary bloc. The Communists in 1965 split into two parties: the Israel Communist Party–Maki (which ceased to exist formally in 1975) and the New Communist List (meaning "list of candidates")–Rakaḥ (which in 1977 formed part of the Democratic Front).

Israeli citizens take an active interest in public affairs. The pattern of Israel's social and economic organization favours the participation in state and public affairs of both trade unions and the employers' organizations. The Arab community is allowed to play a full role in national politics, as long as it does not forcefully oppose the basic concepts of Zionism. In the first Knesset there were only three Arab members, and in the 1970s there were usually seven.

Political developments since the war of 1967 have been closely connected with the unsettled security situation and with questions of policy in areas under military administration. One of the reasons for the surprise election victory in 1977 of the Likud coalition, formed of Gaḥal and others who favoured retention of the occupied territories, was the perception that the Likud would work to secure long-range control of the west bank of the Jordan for Israel. On May 17, 1977, Labour lost more than 20 seats compared to its results in the parliamentary election of 1973; at the same time, Likud gained only two seats over 1973, but it was able to form a coalition and name its leader, Menachem Begin, as prime minister.

Effects of military events on politics

The main result of the 1977 election was confirmed by the election of June 30, 1981, which saw an increase in Labour votes but a continuation in office of Likud and of Begin. The prime minister's personal popularity, the identification of Oriental Jews with Likud, public approval of Israeli foreign and military policy, and internal splits in the Labour Party, between Yitzhak Rabin and Shimon Peres all resulted in the Likud victory.

Justice. Municipal, religious, and military courts exercise a jurisdiction almost identical with that exercised by such courts during the period of the Palestine Mandate before the birth of Israel. Regional labour courts were established in 1969. Capital punishment has been maintained only for genocide and crimes committed during the Nazi administration of Europe. The supreme court is in Jerusalem. All of the judges of the magistrates', district, and supreme courts are appointed by the president, and every judge holds office for life. Matters of marriage and divorce are dealt with by the religious courts of the various recognized communities.

Law is derived from a variety of sources, including Ottoman and British legislation and precedent, religious court opinion, and Israeli parliamentary enactments. Special investigative panels have been formed on unusual occasions—such as the war of 1973 and the massacres of Palestinians in Israeli-controlled sectors of Beirut in 1982—to issue reports and allocate responsibility among political and military leaders.

The armed forces. The Israel Defense Forces (IDF) is an integrated organization controlling land, sea, and air forces. A special force (Nahal) combines military and agricultural training and also engages in the establishment of new defense settlements on the borders. Youth Battalions deal with premilitary training of youth both in and out of school. There is compulsory military service for men between the ages of 18 and 29, and for some women between 18 and 26; Arabs, both Muslim and Christian, are exempted. The period of service for conscript males is 36 months and for women is 24 months, after which men and childless women undergo regular reserve training until the ages of 55 and 34, respectively. The IDF includes a minorities unit in which Druze, Circassian, Bedouin, and Christian Arabs may serve. Total armed forces in the early 1980s consisted of about 172,000, with an additional 330,000 reservists.

The static defense of the country is based upon a regional defense system. The basic unit in the IDF is the brigade group. Any number of brigade groups can be combined under the command of divisional groupings in time of war. The rank of *rav-alluf* (lieutenant general) is held only by the chief of staff of the IDF. He is the senior military authority commanding all armed forces and is appointed by the government on the recommendation of the minister of defense. The IDF is based essentially on the reserve service of the population, and thus continues to be a popular militia rather than a professional army. Civilian–military relations are based on the subordination of the army to civilian control.

Administration. *Education.* By enactment, education is obligatory and free for children between the ages of 5 and 15 and free, but not compulsory, for those 16 and 17. Young people between the ages of 14 and 18 who have not completed schooling are obliged to attend special classes. Parents may choose whether the children receive state lay education or state religious education. In the school year of 1980–81 the educational system in all its stages had a total population of more than 1,119,000, of whom about 936,000 were Jews and 183,500 were Arabs. The school syllabus includes radio and television lessons in both Hebrew and Arabic. Special attention is given to agricultural and technical training. Adult education for immigrants assists them in their cultural integration. There are 44 teachers' training colleges, including two for Arabs. The state finances about one-third of the general education budget. The Ministry of Education, in conjunction with the military authorities, also has assumed responsibility for education in Israeli-occupied Arab territories.

Institutions of higher learning

In addition to the Hebrew University of Jerusalem (opened in 1925) and the Technion—Israel Institute of Technology in Haifa (opened in 1924), Israel has several institutions of higher learning that have been founded since 1948. These include the Weizmann Institute of Science in Reḥovot, the Universities of Tel Aviv, Bar-Ilan, and Haifa, and Ben Gurion University of the Negev. Everyman's University in Tel Aviv was opened in 1974. The total enrollment in 1981–82 was 60,000, of whom fewer than 10,000 were of Oriental Jewish origins. About one-half of the students were women. The academic staff in these institutions totalled more than 5,000 teachers and researchers in 1980. The language of instruction in the universities is Hebrew, while the teaching system represents a mixture of European and American methods. Academic freedom in the universities is protected by Israeli law.

Health and welfare services. The Ministry of Health maintains its own public and preventive services and supervises those of nongovernmental institutions. There are many voluntary organizations in the country dealing with first aid, children's health, and with the aged, crippled, and blind. Almost all births take place in hospitals. In 1980 there was one physician for every 500 people—one of the highest ratios in the world.

The Ministry of Social Welfare controls the service bureaus that deal with family, youth, and community welfare, as well as with rehabilitation of the handicapped. Social insurance is compulsory.

Housing. A shortage of housing has been one of Israel's most pressing problems; more than 30,000 dwellings have been completed every year, of which three-fourths are by private investment.

Police services. The police services are a centralized agency under the Ministry of the Interior. They are controlled by national headquarters and commanded by an inspector general. The strength of the force in 1980 was about 14,000, including almost 1,400 Israeli Arabs and 1,400 women. Prisons are administered by the Ministry of Police and are linked to a system for the rehabilitation of prisoners into normal society on their release. Although recent figures have shown no exceptional rise in crime, the high proportion of juveniles in the total of offenders detected is a matter of general concern.

Wages and cost of living

Social conditions. Wage policy is determined by the trade unions and the employers' associations but is also influenced by the government, which not only applies moral suasion to both groups but is itself the largest employer in the country. Wage policy finds expression in cost-of-living allowance agreements, which are intended to safeguard the real value of wages against rises in consumer prices, and in wage agreements between employers and employees.

Israel's Jewish community is a dynamic society still in the process of social and economic formation. There are as yet few economic class distinctions, although these are increasingly present. The most significant social divisions among Israelis are of a predominantly community nature. Eastern or Oriental Jews (Sefardim) tend to be poorer, less educated, and underrepresented in higher offices as compared to Western Jews (Ashkenazim). Conflicts between the two groups and their children born in Israel increased in the 1970s and '80s. The social and economic divisions within the Arab community and between Arabs and Jews are still strong. Arabs are generally in the lower ranges of socioeconomic categories and consider themselves to be the victims of prejudice at the hands of Jewish Israelis. Changes in the 1960s and '70s, however, diminished some of the antagonisms between Jews and Arabs, as well as differences between urban and rural Arabs.

CULTURAL LIFE AND INSTITUTIONS

The cultural milieu. Jews arriving from communities in many parts of the world have brought with them both their own cultural inheritance and aspects of individual majority cultures that they have absorbed over the centuries. The intermingling of the Ashkenazi, Sefardi, and Middle Eastern traditions has been of profound importance, although immigrants from the Soviet Union who have arrived in the past few years have slowed the trend toward creating a cultural synthesis embracing both East and West. There has been little cultural interchange between the Jewish and Arab sections of Israel's population, and the impact of Arab culture on Israeli cultural life has been insignificant. The revival of the Hebrew language has been of great importance. Jewish tradition, both religious and historical, and the Hebrew language together constitute the foundation of cultural life in Israel.

The state of the arts. The Israel Philharmonic Orchestra has an international reputation. Folk dancing and popular singing combine foreign elements with original creative manifestations. Different folk traditions, such as folk songs, musical instruments, and other expressions of popular culture, have been preserved mainly among the Oriental Jewish communities and among the rural Arab population. Painting and sculpture are still largely influenced by European schools, but local schools have begun to emerge. In literature and drama a concentration on themes of the Diaspora is giving way to an interest in national themes. Israel's most distinguished writer is considered to be Shmuel Yosef Agnon (1888–1970), who was awarded the Nobel Prize for Literature of 1966.

Cultural institutions. In 1954 a Hebrew Language Academy was established as the supreme authority on all questions related to the language and its usages. The 50-member Israel Academy of Sciences and Humanities was founded in 1960. There are about 700 libraries in the country. The Jewish National and University Library in Jerusalem is particularly notable. Habima, Israel's national theatre, was founded in Moscow in 1917 and moved to Palestine in 1932. There are a number of other theatres in the country, some of them in the kibbutzim. There are many art galleries and museums; foremost among them is the Israel Museum in Jerusalem, which also houses part of the archaeological collection of the government's department of antiquities. Archaeological activities are initiated by the government and by Israeli academic institutions, as well as by foreign archaeological organizations. The discovery of the Dead Sea Scrolls in 1947 gave a powerful stimulus to biblical and historical research.

Press and broadcasting. Tel Aviv is the centre of newspaper publishing. The growth in the number of political parties led to a parallel growth in the number of newspapers, although this is now on the decline. Many of the papers with the largest circulations are dependent on subventions from political and religious groups. Although most newspapers are written in Hebrew, there is a considerable circulation of papers published in Yiddish, English, German, Hungarian, French, Bulgarian, and Romanian. In 1981 there were 23 daily papers, with a total circulation of about 550,000 copies daily. There are about 400 other periodicals, of which 260 are in Hebrew.

Broadcasting is vested in a broadcasting authority whose members are appointed by the president. Languages of broadcast include Hebrew, Arabic, English, French, Yiddish, Russian, Georgian, Portuguese, Hungarian, Romanian, Ladino (a Spanish dialect of the Sefardic Jews), Moghrabit (a dialect spoken by Jews in the Maghrib), and Persian. Television, which was introduced in 1966, consists of Hebrew and Arabic programs. There is also an educational television service. Radio programs are broadcast to many foreign countries.

BIBLIOGRAPHY

Official publications: Statistical Abstract of Israel and *Israel Government Yearbook* (both issued annually); reports of the Bank of Israel, the Ministries of Agriculture, Labour, and Tourism, and the Israel Economic Planning Authority. All publications of the various ministries and other official bodies of Israel are submitted to the Knesset and are available to the public.

General: EFRAIM ORNI and ELISHA EFRAT, *Geography of Israel,* 4th rev. ed. (1980); and KETER BOOKS, *Geography* (1973), compiled from material originally published in the *Encyclopaedia Judaica.* LEO PICARD, *Structure and Evolution of Palestine* (1943); and "History of Mineral Research in Israel," *Israel Economic Forum,* vol. 6 (1954), authoritative and comprehensive geological studies. MICHAEL ZOHARY, *Plant Life of Palestine: Israel and Jordan* (1962), a fundamental study; FRIEDRICH S. BODENHEIMER, *Animal Life in Palestine* (1935), and *Prodromus Faunae Palestinae* (1937), classic works on Israel's fauna. DAVID HOROWITZ, *The Economics of Israel* (1967); NADAV HALEVI and RUTH KLINOV-MALUL, *The Economic Development of Israel* (1968); and MEIR HETH, *Banking Institutions in Israel* (1966; originally published in Hebrew, 1963), both informative and reliable. DON PERETZ, *Government and Politics of Israel* (1979); EDWARD LUTTWAK and DAN HOROWITZ, *The Israeli Army* (1975); ASHER ZIDON, *Knesset: The Parliament of Israel* (1968; originally published in Hebrew, 1964); and HENRY E. BAKER, *The Legal System of Israel,* rev. ed. (1968), all monographs by authors with a specialized knowledge of their material. BRUNO BETTELHEIM, *The Children of the Dream* (1969), on children in the Israeli collective settlements and communal child rearing in general; and DOV FRIEDLANDER and CALVIN GOLDSCHEIDER, *The Population of Israel* (1979), a highly useful work on population policy. RAANAN WEITZ and AVSHALOM ROKACH, *Agriculture and Rural Development in Israel: Projection and Planning* (1963), and *Agricultural Development: Planning and Implementation* (1968). JOSEPH S. BENTWICH, *Education in Israel* (1965), informative and comprehensive. WALTER PREUSS, *The Labour Movement in Israel: Past and Present,* 3rd ed. (1965; originally published in German, 1932–36), a substantial historic volume. YOHAI GOELL, *Bibliography of Modern Hebrew Literature in English Translation* (1968), based on holdings of the Jewish National and University Library in Jerusalem; continued by ISAAC GOLDBERG, *Bibliography of Modern Hebrew Literature in Translation* (semiannual). MENDEL KOHANSKY, *The Hebrew Theatre: Its First Fifty Years* (1969). Valuable general surveys are WILLIAM F. ALBRIGHT, *The Archaeology of Palestine* (1949, reprinted 1971); KATHLEEN M. KENYON, *Archaeology in the Holy Land,* 4th ed. (1979); ARCHAEOLOGICAL INSTITUTE OF AMERICA, *Archaeological Discoveries in the Holy Land* (1967); ZEV VILNAY, *The Guide to Israel,* 21st rev. ed. (1980); NADAV SAFRAN, *Israel, The Embattled Ally* (1981); and WILLIAM FRANKEL, *Israel Observed* (1980).

(E.E./W.L.O.)

Issyk-Kul, Lake

Lake Issyk-Kul (Ozero Issyk-Kul in Russian) is a drainless lake in the northern Tien Shan (mountains) of the Kirgiz Soviet Socialist Republic. It is one of the largest mountain lakes in the world and is famous for its magnificent scenery and unique scientific interest. It is situated within the bottom edges of the Issyk-Kul Basin, which is bordered on the north by the Kungey-Alatau Range and on the south by the Terskey-Alatau Range. The lake has a length of 113 miles (182 kilometres), a width of up to 38 miles, and a surface area of 2,407 square miles (6,236 square kilometres). It reaches 2,192 feet (668 metres) in depth and has a volume of 416 cubic miles (17,340 cubic kilometres). The lake's name, which derives from a word for "hot lake," alludes to the fact that it does not freeze over during the winter, even though it is situated at an altitude of 5,278 feet.

Physical characteristics. The first scientific investigations of Issyk-Kul took place in 1856 and were published by a Russian geographer, P.P. Semyonov Tyan-Shansky, who studied the lake's bed and its connection with the Chu River. The evidence suggests that Lake Issyk-Kul has existed at least since the Pliocene Epoch (beginning about 7,000,000 years ago) and that it has drained periodically.

The Issyk-Kul Basin is up to 150 miles long and 56 miles wide, and its surface area is estimated to be between 8,300 and 9,000 square miles. The plain is composed of alluvial, proluvial, and crumbly lake deposits of the Quaternary Period (2,500,000 years ago). The Kungey-Alatau Range, with altitudes up to 15,653 feet, and the Terskey-Alatau (up to 17,113 feet) frame the basin with steep slopes and rocky crests, consisting largely of granite, Paleozoic diorite, and shale. At the foothills of the Terskey-Alatau Range are layers of coal, and limestone suitable for cement preparation occurs near the northern shore of the lake.

Climate in the basin area

The climate is warm, dry, and temperate. Air temperatures in July on the shore average 61° to 63° F (16° to 17° C), while in January, on the western edge of the basin, the temperatures average 28° to 27° F (−2° to −3° C). In the east January has a cooler range of 25° to 19° F (−4° to −7° C), and the range along the bottom edges of the basin is from −13° to 90° F (−25° to +32° C). The annual amount of precipitation increases sharply from west to east, from four inches (100 millimetres) to a maximum of 16–20 inches in summer. A continuous snow cover exists in the eastern part of the basin, and strong winds blow frequently toward the lake with velocities in the west averaging about 90 miles per hour.

More than 50 rivers can be counted in the basin. The largest, the Dzhergalan and the Tyup, are nearly 60 miles long and are located in eastern Priissykkulye. The Chu River flows along the basin's western outskirts.

The Issyk-Kul shores open out gently, with coves on the eastern and southeastern sides. The total length of the shoreline is about 370 miles. Sandy, silt-phytogene soils predominate. Lake terraces stretch along the shores, indicating a higher water level in the past, and the presence of underwater ruins of buildings at depths of up to 23 feet testifies to the fact that in the Middle Ages the level of the lake was lower than it now is. In the 20th century the lake has dropped more than three metres. Seasonal fluctuations of the level, caused by summer floods in the rivers of the Issyk-Kul Basin, range from 12 to 20 inches.

Bottom and water characteristics

The greater part of the lake bottom is made of clay and aleurite silt. Sandy and pebbly deposits occur only in the shallows and in the shore zone. In the western and eastern coves the depth reaches 100 feet, and the surface is covered solidly by algae and pondweed. Surface currents flow counterclockwise. The water temperature in July on the surface is 68° to 73° F (20° to 23° C), and in January it is 36° to 37° F (2° to 3° C). Ice forms only in the shallow coves. The water of the Issyk-Kul is sky blue in colour, very clear (visibility up to 65 feet), and salty (5.8 parts per thousand). Unsuitable for drinking and irrigation because of its high mineral content, it is used at times without freshening for watering cattle.

Vegetation and animal life. Rocky deserts with sparse, saline, semibushy vegetation lie in the western part of the basin. Toward the east are steppes and meadows and a type of elm that grows in the chestnut soils and black earth. Higher up in the mountains are subalpine and alpine meadows. Forests of fir grow on the northern slopes of the Terskey-Alatau Range.

More than 20 kinds of fish live in Lake Issyk-Kul. The basic commercial fish are the naked osman, the chebak, the little chebak, the common carp, and the marinka.

The western and eastern shores of Lake Issyk-Kul serve as a wintering place for waterfowl, which gather annually in flocks of 20,000–50,000. Pochards, mallards, bald coots, and teals are the main varieties. To conserve wildlife, the Issyk-Kul Preserve was founded in 1948, encompassing a lake waterfront and a one-mile shore zone in which hunting is forbidden. Hares, foxes, and muskrats live in the thickets. In all there are some 40 kinds of mammals and 200 types of birds.

Human settlement. By the early 1980s, some 363,000 people were residing in the Issyk-Kul Basin. Kirgiz and Russians predominate; but there are also many Ukrainians, Tatars, Uzbeks, and Hui (Chinese Muslims). There are two large cities—Przhevalsk and Rybachye—and hundreds of villages. The majority of the population is concentrated in eastern Priissykkulye. The main occupation is farming: wheat, potatoes, vegetables, and the medicinal poppy are grown, and livestock (mainly sheep) are raised.

Regular boat trips are made across the lake carrying freight and passengers, and the area is joined with other regions by highways, railways, and air transportation. The shores of Lake Issyk-Kul are noted for their health resorts, and sanatoriums and holiday houses abound. Although the northern shore is the main health resort area, the entire lake region has been developed as a vacationland for visitors, mainly from Central Asia and Kazakhstan.

(V.A.B.)

Istanbul

Istanbul (formerly Constantinople, and once ancient Byzantium) is the largest city and seaport of Turkey. It was formerly the capital of the Byzantine Empire, of the Ottoman Empire, and—until 1923—of the Turkish Republic.

The old, walled city of Istanbul stands on a triangular peninsula between Europe and Asia. Sometimes as bridge, sometimes as barrier, Istanbul for more than 2,500 years has stood between conflicting surges of religion, culture, and imperial power. For most of those years it was one of the most coveted cities in the world.

By long tradition, the waters washing the peninsula are called "the three seas": they are the Golden Horn, the Bosporus, and the Sea of Marmara. The Golden Horn is a deep, drowned valley about 4½ miles (seven kilometres) long. Early inhabitants saw it as shaped like a deer horn, but modern Turks call it the Haliç (Canal). The Bosporus (Boğaziçi), which is almost 19 miles long, is the channel connecting the Black Sea (Karadeniz) to the Mediterranean (Ak Deniz) by way of the Sea of Marmara and the straits of the Dardanelles. The narrow Golden Horn separates the old city of Stamboul to the south from the "new" city of Beyoğlu (formerly referred to as Galata-Pera) to the north; the broader (one-half to 5 miles wide) Bosporus, from half a mile to five miles wide, divides European Istanbul from its districts on the Asian shore—Üsküdar (formerly Scutari, ancient Chrysopolis) and Kadiköy (ancient Chalcedon).

Like the forces of history, the forces of nature impinge upon Istanbul. The great rivers pouring off the plains of Russia and middle Europe—the Danube, Don, Dnestr and Dnepr (Dnieper)—make the Black Sea colder and less briny than the Mediterranean. The Black Sea waters thrust southward through the Bosporus, but beneath them the salty warm waters of the Mediterranean push northward as a powerful undercurrent running through the same channel.

The prevailing wind, the northeast wind or *poyraz*, comes from the Black Sea, giving way at times during the winter to an icy blast from the Balkans—the northwest wind, known as the *karayel*, or Black Veil, capable of freezing solid the Golden Horn and even the Bosporus. When the *lodos*, or southwest wind, blows it can raise storms on the Sea of Marmara.

Istanbul's disasters

Fire, earthquake, riot, and invasion have ravaged the city many times. More than 60 conflagrations have been important enough to be recorded in history, and even in the 1970s there remained scorched stretches of the old city not yet rebuilt. Fifty major earthquakes and innumerable less serious temblors have shaken the city since the time of the Roman emperor Constantine the Great. The fall of each empire has been followed by devastation and a period of decay for the capital.

The name Byzantium may derive from that of Byzas, who, according to legend, was leader of the Greeks from the city of Megara who captured the peninsula from pastoral Thracian tribes and built the city about 657 BC. In 196 BC, having razed the town for opposing him in a civil war, the Roman emperor Septimus Severus rebuilt it, naming it Augusta Antonina in honour of his son. In AD 330, when Constantine the Great dedicated the city as his capital, he called it New Rome. The coinage, nevertheless, continued to be stamped Byzantium until he ordered the substitution of Constantinopolis. In the 13th century Arabs used the appelation Istinpolin, a "name" they heard Byzantines use—*eis tēn polin*—which, in reality, was a Greek phrase that meant "in the city." Through a series of speech permutations over a span of centuries, this name became Istanbul. Until the Turkish Post Office officially changed the name in 1926, however, even after 600 years of Turkish rule the city continued to bear the millenary name of Constantinople.

The old city contains about nine square miles, but the present municipal boundaries stretch over 98 square miles, including areas on both sides of the Bosporus and the Sea of Marmara. The original peninsular city has seven hills requisite for Constantine's "new Rome." Six are crests of a long ridge above the Golden Horn, the other a solitary eminence in the southwest corner. The domes and minarets of the mosques crowning the hills form the fabled skyline of Istanbul. A closer approach, however, can lead to disenchantment. The feeling is one of seediness rather than of antiquity. There are indeed architectural gems and historic shrines to be sought out, as there are imposing parks, redolent bazaars, and the activities associated with an international waterfront. Although Istanbul is a large Middle-Eastern city, its life, which proceeds amid the evidences of a glory and splendour irrevocably past, does not beat with the pulse of a modern metropolis.

Within recent years many of the burned-out neighbourhoods have slowly been rebuilt, while a continuing program of street improvement has pushed wide avenues through some of the meanest quarters of the old city. There remains, however, numbers of unpaved alleys overhung with decrepit wooden houses, and Anatolian

Ara Gule

The Golden Horn, Istanbul. The two mosques in the background are (centre left) Hagia Sophia and (centre right) Süleymaniye.

migrants to the metropolis have erected shanty towns or have settled in crumbling palaces or fortresses. Some of these country migrants work as porters, bearing upon their backs burdens of immense size and weight.

The city walls

Stamboul is still a walled city. The land walls, which isolate the peninsula from the mainland, were breached only once, by the cannon of Mehmed II (the Conqueror) in 1453, at the spot since called (Top Kapısı (Cannon Gate). The walls are four and a half miles long, and consist of a double line of ramparts—the inner built in 413, the outer in 447—protected by a moat. The higher inner wall is about 30 feet high and 16 feet thick, and is studded with 60 foot towers about 180 feet apart. Of 92 turrets originally on the outer wall, 56 are still standing.

The sea walls were built in 439. Only short sections of their 30-foot-high masonry still remain along the Golden Horn. Intact, these walls had 110 towers and 14 gates. The walls along the Sea of Marmara, which stretch about five miles from Seraglio Point, curving around the bottom of the peninsula to join the land walls, had 188 towers; they were, however, only about 20 feet high, because the Marmara currents provided good protection against enemy landings. Most of these walls still stand.

Within the city walls are the seven hills, their summits flattened through the ages, their slopes still steep and toilsome. Geographers number them from the seaward tip of the peninsula, proceeding inland along the Golden Horn, the last hill standing alone where the land walls reach the Sea of Marmara.

The Golden Horn

The Galata and Atatürk bridges cross the Golden Horn to Beyoğlu. Each day before dawn their centre spans are swung open to allow passage to seagoing ships. The waters of the Horn are still golden in the sunlight, but the shores, served by water busses, are a jumble of docks, warehouses, factories, and occasional historical ruins.

Monuments on the Seven Hills and Their Slopes

First Hill
Hagia Sophia
Church of St. Irene
Mosque of Küçük Ayasofa
(Church of SS. Sergius and Bacchus)
Mosque of Sokullu Mehmed Paşa
Mosque of Ahmed I (Blue Mosque)
Fountain of Ahmed III
The Museums
Cinili Kiosk (Pavilion of Tiles)
Basilican Cistern
(Yerebatan Sarayı)
Hippodrome
Topkapı Palace (Seraglio)
Marmara Sea Walls

Second Hill
Mosque of Nuruosmaniye
The Burnt Column (Çemberlitaş)
The Great Bazaar (Kaplı Çarşı)

Third Hill
Mosque of Vefa Kilise
(Church of St. Theodore Tiro)
Mosque of Bayezid II
Mosque of Laleli
Mosque of Şehzade
Mosque of Süleymaniye, and tombs
Mosque of Bodrum
(Monastery of Myrelaion)
Mosque of Kalendarhane
(Monastery of Akataleptos)
Aqueduct of Valens

Fourth Hill
Mosque of the Fatih (Conqueror)
Mosque of Mollazeyrek
(Church of Christ Pantokrator)
Mosque of Eski İmaret
(Church of Christ Pantepoptes)

Fifth Hill
Mosque of Ahmed Paşa (Church of St. John the Baptist in Trullo)
Mosque of Gül
(Church of St. Theodosia)
Mosque of Fethiye (Church of the Pammakaristos Virgin)
Church of St. Mary of the Mongols
Greek Patriarchal Church of St. George

Sixth Hill
Mosque of Kariye
(Church of St. Saviour in Chora)
Mosque of Mihrimah
Adrianople Gate (Edirne Gate)
Tekfur Sarayı ("Palace of Constantine")

Seventh Hill
Mosque of Hekimoğlu Ali Paşa
Mosque of Ramazan Efendi
Seven Towers Castle (Yedikule)
Mosque of Koca Mustafa Paşa
(Church of St. Andrew in Krisei)
Mosque of İmrahor (Church of St. John of the Stoudion)

Ferries to the Asian side of Istanbul leave from under the Galata Bridge.

Beyoğlu, considered to be "modern Istanbul," remains, as it has been since the 10th century, the foreign quarter. Warfare and fires have left standing only a few structures that were built earlier than the 19th century.

The approach from the Golden Horn is steep, and a funicular railway runs between the Galata waterfront and the Pera Plateau. On the heights are the big hotels and restaurants, the travel bureaus, theatres, the opera house, the consulates, and many Turkish government offices.

From the 10th century onwards, Galata was an enclave for foreign traders—principally the Genoese—who enjoyed extraterritorial privileges behind their walls. After the Ottomans took the city in 1453, all foreigners who were not citizens of the empire were restricted to this quarter. Around palatial embassies were compounds that included schools, churches, and hospitals for the various nationalities. Eventually Galata became too crowded, so that the tide of building moved higher up the slope to the open country of Pera. For centuries, foreigners who wished to visit Stamboul, where the Court was installed, could do so only if accompanied by one of the sultan's Janissaries.

HISTORY

The founding of Byzantium

Byzantium. Byzantium was one of the many colonies founded from the end of the 8th century onward along the coasts of the Bosporus and the Black Sea by Greek settlers from the cities of Miletus and Megara.

The Persian king Darius I took the settlement in 512 BC; it slipped from Persian grasp during the Ionian revolt of 496, only to be retaken by the Persians. In 478 an Athenian fleet captured the city, which then became a rich and important member of the Delian League. As Athenian power waned during the Peloponnesian War, Byzantines acknowledged Spartan overlordship. Although Alcibiades besieged and retook the city, Sparta reasserted its domination after defeating Athens in 405 BC.

In 343 BC, Byzantium joined the Second Athenian League, throwing off the siege of Philip II of Macedon three years later. The lifting of the siege was attributed to the divine intervention of the goddess Hecate and was commemorated by the striking of coins bearing her star and crescent. Byzantium accepted Macedonian rule under Alexander the Great, regaining independence only with the eclipse of Macedonian might. In the 3rd century BC, the city's treasury was drained to buy off marauding Gauls. A free city under Rome, it gradually fell under imperial control, and briefly lost its freedom under the emperor Vespasian. When, in AD 196, it sided with the usurper Pescennius Niger, the Roman emperor Septimus Severus massacred the populace, razed the walls, and annexed the remains to the city of Perinthus (or Heraclea, modern Marmaraereglisi), in Turkey.

Subsequently, Septimus Severus rebuilt the city on the same spot, but on a grander scale. Although sacked again by Gallienus in 268, the city was strong enough two years later to resist a Gothic invasion. In the subsequent civil wars and rebellions that broke out sporadically in the Roman Empire, Byzantium remained untouched until the arrival of the emperor Constantine I—the first Roman ruler to adopt Christianity. Overcoming the army of the rival emperor, Licinius, at nearby Chrysopolis, on September 18, 324, Constantine became head of the whole Roman Empire, east and west. He decided to make Byzantium his capital.

The New Rome

Constantinople. Within three weeks of his victory, the foundation rites of New Rome were performed, and the much-enlarged city was officially inaugurated on May 11, 330.

It was an act of vast historical portent. Constantinople was to become one of the great world capitals, a font of imperial and religious power, a city of vast wealth and beauty, and the chief city of the western world. Until the rise of the Italian maritime states, it was the first city in commerce, as well as the chief city of what was, until the mid-11th century, the strongest and most prestigious power in Europe.

Constantine's choice of capital had profound effects upon the ancient Greek and Roman worlds. It displaced the power centre of the Roman Empire, moving it eastward, and achieved the first lasting unification of Greece.

Culturally, Constantinople fostered a fusion of Oriental and Occidental custom, art, and architecture. The religion was Christian, the organization Roman, and the language and outlook Greek. The concept of the divine right of kings, rulers who were defenders of the faith—as opposed to the king as divine himself—was evolved here. The gold *solidus* of Constantine retained its value and served as a monetary standard for more than a thousand years. As the centuries passed—the Christian Empire lasted 1130 years—Constantinople, seat of empire, was to become as important as the empire itself; in the end, although the territories had virtually shrunk away, the capital endured.

Constantine's new city walls tripled the size of Byzantium, which now contained imperial buildings, such as the completed Hippodrome begun by Severus, a huge palace, legislative halls, several imposing churches, and streets decorated with multitudes of statues taken from rival cities. In addition to other attractions of the capital, free bread and citizenship were bestowed on those settlers who would fill the empty reaches beyond the old walls. There was, furthermore, a welcome for Christians, a tolerance of pagan beliefs, and benevolence toward Jews.

Constantinople as a religious capital

Constantinople was also an ecclesiastical centre. In 381 it became the seat of a patriarch who was second only to the bishop of Rome; the patriarch of Constantinople is still the nominal head of the Orthodox Church. Constantine inaugurated the first ecumenical councils; the first six were held in or near Constantinople. In the 5th and 6th centuries emperors were engaged in divising means to keep the Monophysites attached to the realm. In the 8th and 9th centuries, Constantinople was the centre of the battle between iconoclasts and the defenders of icons. The matter was settled by the seventh ecumenical council against the iconoclasts, but not before much blood had been spilled, and countless works of art destroyed. The eastern and western wings of the church drew further apart, and after centuries of doctrinal disagreement between Rome and Constantinople, a schism occurred in the 11th century. The Pope originally approved the sack of Constantinople in 1204, then decried it. Various attempts were made to heal the breach in the face of the Turkish threat to the city, but the divisive forces of suspicion and doctrinal divergence were too strong.

By the end of the 4th century, Constantine's walls had become too confining for the wealthy and populous metropolis. St. John Chrysostom, writing at the end of that century, said many nobles had 10 to 20 houses and owned from one to two thousand slaves. Doors were often made of ivory, floors were of mosaic, or were covered in costly rugs, and beds and couches were overlaid with precious metals.

The pressure of population pressing from within, and the barbarian threat from without, prompted the building of walls further inland at the hilt of the peninsula. These new walls of the early 5th century, built in the reign of Theodosius II, are those that stand today.

In the reign of Justinian I (527–565) medieval Constantinople attained its zenith. At the beginning of this reign the population is estimated to have been about 500,000. In 532 a large part of the city was burned and many of the population killed in the course of the repression of the Nika Insurrection, an uprising of the Hippodrome factions. The rebuilding of the ravaged city gave Justinian the opportunity to engage in a program of magnificent construction, of which many buildings remain today.

In 542 the city was struck by a plague that is said to have killed three out of every five inhabitants; the decline of Constantinople dates from this catastrophe. Not only the capital but the whole empire languished, and slow recovery was not visible until the 9th century. During this period the city was frequently besieged—by the Persians and Avars (626), the Arabs (674 to 678 and again from 717 to 718), the Bulgars (813 and 913), the Russians (860, 941, and 1043), and by a wandering Turkic people, the Pechenegs, (1090–91). All were unsuccessful.

In 1082 the Venetians were alloted quarters in the city itself (there was an earlier cantonment for foreign traders at Galata across the Golden Horn), with special trading privileges. They were later joined by Pisans, Amalfitans, Genoese, and others. These Italian groups soon obtained a stranglehold over the city's foreign trade —a monopoly that was finally broken by a massacre of Italians. Not for some time were Italian traders permitted once more to settle in Galata.

Crusader rule

In 1203 the armies of the Fourth Crusade, deflected from their objective in the Holy Land, appeared before Constantinople—ostensibly to restore the legitimate Byzantine emperor, Isaac II. Although the city fell, it remained under its own government for a year. But on April 13, 1204, the crusaders burst into the city to sack it. After a general massacre, the pillage went on for years. The crusading knights installed one of themselves, Baldwin of Flanders, as emperor, and the Venetians—prime instigators of the crusade—took control of the church. While the Latins divided the rest of the realm among themselves, the Byzantines entrenched themselves across the Bosporus at Nicaea (now Iznik) and at Epirus (now northwestern Greece). The period of Latin rule (1204 to 1261) was the most disastrous in the history of Constantinople. Even the bronze statues were melted down for coin; everything of value was taken. Sacred relics were torn from the sanctuaries and dispatched to religious establishments in western Europe.

In 1261 Constantinople was retaken by Michael VIII Palaeologus, Greek emperor of Nicaea. For the next two centuries the shrunken Byzantine Empire, threatened both from the west and by the rising power of the Ottoman Turks in Asia Minor, led a precarious existence. Some building was carried out at the end of the 13th and beginning of the 14th century, but thereafter the city was in a state of complete decay, full of ruins and tracts of deserted ground, contrasting with the prosperous condition of Galata across the Golden Horn, which had been granted to the Genoese by the Byzantine ruler Michael VIII. When the Turks crossed into Europe in the mid-14th century the fate of Constantinople was sealed. The inevitable end was retarded by the defeat of the Turks at the hands of Timur Lenk (Tamerlane) in 1402; but in 1422 the Ottoman sultan of Turkey, Murad II, laid siege to Constantinople. This attempt failed, only to be repeated 30 years later. In 1452 another Ottoman sultan, Mehmed II, proceeded to blockade the Bosporus by the erection of a strong fortress at its narrowest point; this fortress, called Rumeli Hisarı, still forms one of the principal landmarks of the straits. The siege of the city began in April 1453. The Turks had not only overwhelming numercial superiority but also cannon which breached the ancient walls. The Golden Horn was protected by a chain, but the Sultan succeeded in hauling his fleet by land from the Bosporus into the Golden Horn. The final assault was made on May 29, and, in spite of the desperate resistance of the inhabitants aided by the Genoese, the city fell. The last Byzantine emperor, Constantine XI Palaeologus, was killed in battle. For three days the city was abandoned to pillage and massacre, after which order was restored by the Sultan.

Capture by the Turks

Istanbul. When Constantinople was captured, it was almost deserted. Mehmed II began to repeople it by transferring to it populations from other conquered areas such as the Peloponnese, Salonika, and the Greek islands. By about 1480 the population rose to between 60,000 and 70,000. Hagia Sophia and other Byzantine churches were transformed into mosques. The Greek patriarchate was retained, but moved to the Church of the Pammakaristos Virgin (Mosque of Fethiye), later to find a permanent home in the Fener (Phanar) quarter. The Sultan built the Old Seraglio (Eski Saray), now destroyed, on the site occupied at present by the university, and a little later the Topkapı Palace (Seraglio), which is still in existence; he also built the Eyüp Mosque at the head of the Golden Horn and the Fatih Mosque on the site of the Basilica of the Holy Apostles. The capital of the Ottoman empire was transferred to Constantinople from Adrianople (Edirne) in 1457.

After Mehmed II, Istanbul enjoyed a long period of peaceful growth, interrupted only by natural disasters—earthquakes, fires, and pestilences. The sultans and their ministers devoted themselves to the building of fountains, mosques, palaces, and charitable foundations, so that the aspect of the city was soon completely transformed. The most brilliant period of Turkish construction coincides with the reign of the Ottoman ruler Süleyman the Magnificent (1520–66).

The next major change in the history of Istanbul occurred at the very beginning of the 19th century, when dismemberment of the Ottoman Empire was approaching. This period was known as the era of internal reforms (Tanzimat). The reforms were accompanied by serious disturbances, such as the massacre of the Janissaries in the Hippodrome (1826). With the triumph of the progressive Ottoman sultan Mahmud II over the conservative opposition, the westernization of Istanbul started apace. There was an ever-growing influx of European visitors who, since the 1830s, could reach Istanbul by steamship. The first bridge across the Golden Horn was built in 1838. In 1839 the Ottoman sultan Abdülmecid I issued a charter guaranteeing to all his subjects, whatever their religion, the security of their lives and fortune. The process of westernization was further accelerated by the Crimean War (1853–56) and the quartering of British and French troops in Istanbul. The latter part of the 19th and the beginning of the 20th century were marked by the introduction of various public services: the European railroad extending to Istanbul was begun in the early 1870s. The underground tunnel joining Galata to Pera was completed in 1873; a regular water supply for Istanbul and the settlements on the European side of the Bosporus was brought from Lake Terkos on the Black Sea coast (29 miles from the city) by the French company, La Compagnie des Eaux, after 1885; electric lighting was introduced in 1912 and electric street cars and telephones in 1913 and 1914. An adequate sewage system had to wait until 1925 and later.

Westernization of the city

In the first quarter of the 20th century Istanbul experienced various disruptions marking the death of the Ottoman Empire and the birth of modern Turkey. In 1908 the city was occupied by the army of the Young Turks who deposed the hated sultan Abdülamid II. During the Balkan Wars (1912–13) Istanbul was nearly captured by the Bulgarians. Throughout World War I the city was under blockade. After the conclusion of the Armistice (1918) it was placed under British, French, and Italian occupation that lasted until 1923. The Greco-Turkish War in Asia Minor, as well as the Russian Revolution, brought thousands of refugees to Istanbul. With the victory of the Nationalists under Mustafa Kemal Atatürk, the sultanate was abolished and the last Ottoman sultan, Mehmed VI, fled from Istanbul (1922). After the signing of the Lausanne Treaty, Istanbul was evacuated by the Allies (October 2, 1923) and Ankara was chosen as the capital of Turkey (October 13, 1923). On October 29, the Turkish Republic was proclaimed. Because of Turkey's neutrality during most of World War II, Istanbul suffered no damage, although a German invasion was feared after the Balkans had been conquered by the Axis. The influx of automobiles brought acute traffic problems to Istanbul, and large tracts of the city have been demolished or cleared to make way for modern highways.

Byzantine monuments. Nothing remains of the Byzantium that Constantine chose as the site of New Rome, and almost nothing is left of the mighty city he built there. Constantine's column, the Burnt Column, a shaft of porphyry drums bound by metal laurel leaves, still stands near the Nuruosmaniye Mosque, but there is no proof that any building in the city dates from his period. He completed the Hippodrome that Septimus Severus had restored, but it was enlarged and rebuilt by his successors until the 5th century. Today only its curved end remains, with three columns along the central spina—an obelisk removed from Egypt by the Roman emperor Theodosius I (*q.v.*), a masonry obelisk of Constantine VII Porphyrogenitus (AD 905 to 959), and a column entwined by a Delphic serpent (decapitated by looters) cast after the Battle of Plataea, when the Greeks defeated the Persians in 479 BC.

Remains of Constantine's city

Of the myriad columns that decorated Constantinople, today there remain standing only the base of the column of the emperor Arcadius (383–408) in the Cerrahpaşa quarter; a column of the emperor Marcian (450–57) that the Turks call Kıztaşı; the Column of the Virgin, in the Fatih quarter; and, in the grounds of the Seraglio, a perfectly preserved Corinthian column thought to be from the reign of another emperor, Claudius II Gothicus (268–70).

Spanning the valley between the 3rd and 4th hills is the two-story limestone aqueduct built in 366 by the emperor Valens. Some of the enormous open-water cisterns of the Byzantine epoch now serve as market gardens. The closed cisterns, of which there are more than 80 remaining, include one of the most beautiful and mysterious structures of Istanbul, the Basilican Cistern near the Hagia Sophia. Called the Yerebstan Sarayı, ("underground palace"), its 336 columns rise from the still, black waters to a vaulted roof.

The Golden Gate is a triumphal arch from about 390 and was built into the defenses of Theodosius II, near the junction of the land and sea walls. The marble-clad bases of its two large towers still stand, and three arches decorated with columns stretch between them.

The only well-preserved example of Byzantine palace architecture is the shell of a three-story rectangular building of limestone and brick, laid in patterns and stripes. Dating from about 1300, it is called "Constantine's Palace," or the Tekfur Sarayı, and is attached to the land walls not far from the Golden Horn.

The largest legacy from the capital of the vanished empire is constituted by 25 Byzantine churches. Many of these are still in use—as mosques. The largest of the churches is considered one of the great buildings of the world. This is the Hagia Sophia, whose name means "Divine Wisdom." Its contemporary and neighbor, St. Irene, was dedicated to "Divine Peace." Many art historians deem the dome (105 feet in diameter) of Hagia Sophia to be the most beautiful in the world, "the most successful architectural approach to the air-borne vault of the universe." It rises to a height of 184 feet, seeming to float above the vast floor, which is 252 feet long and 234 feet wide. The church, which shared its clergy with St. Irene, is said to have been built by Constantine in 325 on the foundations of a pagan temple. Enlarged by the emperor Constans, rebuilt after the fire of 415 by the emperor Theodosius II, it was burned again in the Nika Insurrection of 532, and reconstructed by Justinian. The structure standing today is essentially the 6th-century edifice, although an earthquake tumbled the dome in 559, after which it was rebuilt to a smaller scale and the whole church reinforced from the outside. It was restored again in the mid-14th century. In 1453 it became a mosque with minarets, and a great chandelier was added. In 1935 it was made into a museum. The walls are still hung with Muslim calligraphic disks, and since 1931, the Byzantine Institute of America has been uncovering and cleaning the Christian mosaics.

The Hagia Sophia

The church of SS Sergius and Bacchus was erected by Justinian between 527 and 536 as a thank offering. The two soldier-saints allegedly appeared to the emperor Anastasius I to intercede for Justinian, who had been condemned to death for conspiracy. The church is built as a domed octagon within a rectangle, with a columned and galleried Byzantine interior. In Turkish it is called "little Sophia," (Mosque of Küçük Ayasofya), and can be considered an architectural parent of Justinian's reconstruction of the Hagia Sophia. St. Saviour in Chora (now called Kariye Cami, but no longer a mosque) is near the Adrianople Gate. Restored in the 11th century and extensively remodelled in the 14th, it is now a museum, renowned for its 14th-century mosaics, marbles, and frescoes, which have been cleaned and consolidated by the Byzantine Institute of America. Over the central portal is a head of Christ with the inscription, "The land of the living." When it was made a mosque it acquired the narthex (an enclosed passage between the main entrance and the nave), portico, and minarets.

A massive tower that dominates the Galata district was built by the Genoese traders in 1349 as a watchtower and a fortification for their walled enclave.

Turkish monuments. When the Turks took possession of Constantinople, they covered the spines of the seven hills with domes and minarets, changing the character of the city. Like the Greeks, the Romans, and the Byzantines, the new rulers loved the city, and spent much of their treasure and energy on its embellishment. The Ottoman (Osmanlı) dynasty, which lasted from 1300 to 1922, continued to build new important structures almost until the end of their line. The most imposing of their mosques were constructed from the mid-15th to the mid-16th centuries, and the greatest of the architects all bore the name of Sinan. They were Atik Sinan (the Elder), Sinan of Balıkesir, and Koca Sinan ("the architect," also called the Great). Although the building was deeply influenced by the Persian-born traditions of the Seljuqs (once masters of the Ottomans), the style was blended with prevailing Hellenic and Byzantine traditions of the city. Koca Sinan's masterpiece—and his burial place—is the Mosque of Sülymaniye (1550–57), inspired by, but not copied from, the Hagia Sophia. It ranks as another of the world's great buildings. Probably the most popularly known of all the mosques in Istanbul is the Blue Mosque, that of the Mosque of Ahmed I (1609–1616), which has six minarets instead of the customary four.

The Sinan architectural tradition

The mosques of the following century and later show the deleterious effects of importing European architects and craftsmen, who produced baroque Islāmic architecture (such as the Mosque of the Fatih, rebuilt between 1767 and 1771), and even Neoclassical styles, as in the Dolmabahçe Mosque of 1853, now the Naval Museum.

The big mosques were built with ancillary structures, such as a Qur'ānic school (*medrese*), baths (*hamam*) for purification, a hostel and kitchen for the poor (*imaret*) or tombs of royalty and distinguished persons.

There are 404 fountains in Istanbul. Some simply flow from wall niches, but others, erected as public philanthropies, are pavilions. The most magnificent of these was built by the Sultan Ahmed III in 1728, behind the apse of Hagia Sophia. It is square, with marble walls and bronze gratings, a mixture of the Turkish with the western rococo style.

Topkapı Palace

To the north of it, toward the Golden Horn and occupying the whole tip of the promontory, is the sultan's Seraglio (Topkapı Palace), enclosed in a fortified wall. Begun in 1462 by Mehmed II, it served as the residence of the sultans until the beginning of the 19th century. It was to this palace that foreign ambassadors were accredited, and they were admitted through the Imperial Gate, or Bab-i-Hümayun, mistranslated by Westerners as "Sublime Porte." The Seraglio consists mostly of small buildings grouped around three courts. The most significant buildings are the Çinili Kiosk (Pavilion of Tiles) built in 1472, the Audience Chamber (Arzodası), the Hirkaiserif, a sanctuary containing relics of the Prophet Muḥammad, and the elegant Baghdad Kiosk commemorating the capture of Baghdad in 1638. The Seraglio houses the sultan's treasure and has important collections of manuscripts, china, armour, textiles, etc. After the abandonment of the Old Seraglio, the sultans built for themselves palaces along the Bosporus, such as the Beylerbey Palace (1865), the lavish Dolmabahçe Palace (1853), the Çeragan Palace built in 1874 and burned in 1910, and the Yıldız Palace which was the residence of Abdül hamid II, Ottoman sultan from 1876 to 1909.

The Great Bazaar, founded early in the Turkish regime, but since often subject to fire and earthquake, had 4,000 shops around two central distributing houses. The district is laid out on a grid plan. It still boils with life and the pursuit of piasters.

THE CONTEMPORARY CITY

Population, administration, and economy. *Population.* Census figures are not always reliable, but Istanbul, like other major cities, is experiencing an influx from the countryside. The Muslim majority continues to grow, and the Christian and Jewish minorities to shrink, both in percentage of the whole and in numbers. The total population in 1970 was 2,312,751 (metropolitan area).

Administration. The mayor, appointed by the president of the republic, serves as prefect of Istanbul city and governor of Istanbul *il* (province). The municipality (*belediye*), which was organized by Constantine as 14 districts in imitation of Rome, is now divided into 12 circumscriptions (*kazas*), each governed by a *kaymakam*. These are, in the old city, Eminönü and Fatih; on the European side above the Golden Horn, Eyüp, Gakirkoy, Beyoğlu, Şişli, Beşiktas, and Sarıyer; and across the Bosporus on the Asiatic side, Beykoz, Üsküdar, Kadıköy, and Adalar.

Public Utilities. While Istanbul has a chlorinated and filtered water supply and sewage disposal system, these facilities are not sufficient to meet the increased need created by the influx of rural migrants to the city. In the mid-1960s an estimated 21 percent of the population lived in shanty towns called *gecekondu* (literally "set down by night") with no sanitation facilities. The middle income group lives in modern apartments or in houses on the city's outskirts, most of which have running water and electricity. Water supply is a problem particularly in the summer when rivers run dry; at this season tap water is liable to flow only sporadically, except in luxury hotels.

Electric power supplies have been increased to help promote industrial expansion. In 1967 the Ambarbi generating station began operation with an initial capacity of 110,000 kilowatts. Capacity has since been doubled. In 1973 a 1,150-mile, high-voltage transmission system was to carry power generated at the Keban hydroelectric plant on the Euphrates River to Istanbul, doubling the electrical capacity.

Health and safety. Most of the health services of Istanbul *il* (province) are concentrated in the municipality. There are 74 hospitals, 36 of which are public, with a total capacity of 16,000 beds. The province has 2,800 medical specialists, 1,500 general practitioners, and 1,000 dentists.

The city police commissioner heads the municipal police force, cooperating with the national police, who are responsible for the security of the cities, and who sometimes supplement the municipal force.

Istanbul's universities

Education. The first University of Istanbul was founded in 425 by Theodosius II, and was succeeded by a Turkish university in 1453, which was lastly reorganized in 1933. The present university includes faculties of letters, science, law, medicine, and forestry located in the former Seraskerat (war ministry) between the Great Bazaar and the Mosque of Süleymaniye. There is also a technical university on the Galata side of the Horn as well as an Academy of Fine Arts, and schools of technology, commerce, and economics. Foreign educational institutions include the American Robert College for boys (founded in 1863), and the American College for Girls (founded in 1871), both on the Bosporus.

Commerce and communications. Istanbul is Turkey's largest port and is the hub of its industry. In 1970 the port handled 1,005,026 tons of imports and 231,266 tons of exports. Textiles, flour milling, tobacco processing, cement, and glass are the city's principal manufactures.

Tourism is a growing source of income for Istanbul, which is the terminus of the international rail service (the former Orient Express) which originates in Paris. It is also the starting point (from Haydarpaşa, on the Asian side) of the Baghdad Railway. Maritime services include many forms of transport, from harbour dinghies and small ferries to international liners. Yeşilköy Airport is about 17 miles to the west of the city. Buses provide internal urban transportation, and the ferries range as far as the Kızıl Adalar (Princes Islands) several hours sailing to the south.

The *il* (province) of Istanbul covers an area of about 2,206 square miles, extending to both the European and Asian shores of the Bosporus. It had a population of nearly 3,000,000 in 1970.

Another span bridging the Golden Horn was to be completed in 1974 as part of the $185,000,000 Istanbul highway system which will reach 12 miles north to the Bosporus Bridge, for which foundations were laid in 1970. Linking Europe and Asia, this 5,118-foot-long suspension bridge near the entrance to the Black Sea will be the world's fourth longest, and the longest in Europe.

Cultural life. The Palais de la Culture d'Istanbul was built in 1969 as a centre for the arts. Facilities include a

Istanbul and (inset) its metropolitan area.

concert hall, art gallery, and two theatres. It is the home of the Istanbul Municipal Symphony Orchestra and the Istanbul City Opera. The municipal theatre operates four playhouses and there are 13 private theatre companies.

Over 30 learned societies and research institutes are headquartered in the city, including the Geographical Institute (1933), German and French archaeological institutes, and the Turkish Folklore Society. There is a nuclear research centre at Küçük Çekmece.

There are many public and private libraries. The small, specialized Köprülü Library (1677) has about 3,000 volumes with almost 200 works from early Ottoman presses and about 40 handwritten works over 1,000 years old. Many of the city's mosques, palaces, and monuments, as mentioned earlier, contain museums; other museums include the Archaeological Museums of Istanbul (1836), the Museum of Turkish and Islâmic Art, and the Museum of the Janissaries (1726).

The Media. Almost all of Istanbul's 22 daily newspapers are printed in Ankara on the same day. *Milliyet* and *Cumhuriyet* are the most influential dailies. The weeklies *Akis* and *Akbaba* and the cultural fortnightly *Forum* are also widely read. The city is served by two radio stations and one television station. The Technical University of Istanbul broadcasts educational radio and television programs.

Recreation. The Hippodrome is now a public garden; there are also numerous other public parks. A unique feature of the city is its market gardens, which have already been mentioned; these kitchen gardens are associated with the open cisterns that formed early Constantinople's water-supply system. The cisterns have been partially built over and are called Çukur Bostan ("hollow gardens").

Football (soccer) is a popular sport, and Istanbul has three stadiums—Mithatpaşa, Fenerbahçe, and the indoor Spor ve Sergi Sarayı. There are facilities for tennis, fencing, mountain climbing, riding, golf, and water sports. Florya and Ataköy are popular beaches on the Sea of Marmara.

BIBLIOGRAPHY

Antiquities: A. VAN MILLINGEN, *Byzantine Constantinople: The Walls of the City and Adjoining Historical Sites* (1899); PHILIP SHERRARD, *Constantinople: Iconography of a Sacred City* (1965); PHILIP GRIERSON, *The Tombs and Obits of the Byzantine Emperors, 337–1042* (1962); BERNARD LEWIS, *Istanbul and the Civilization of the Ottoman Empire* (1963); DEAN A. MILLER, *Imperial Constantinople* (1969); MICHAEL MACLAGAN, *The City of Constantinople* (1968), well illustrated, with good annotated bibliography and index.

Churches: W.R. LETHABY and H. SWAINSON, *The Church of Sancta Sophia* (1894); T. WHITTEMORE, *The Mosaics of St. Sophia at Istanbul*, 4 vol. (1933–52); PAUL ATKINS UNDERWOOD, *The Kariye Djami* (1966).

Contemporary descriptions: E. MAMBOURY, *Istanbul touristique* (1951); *Guide bleu: Turquie* (1958); ROBERT BOULANGER, *Istanbul et ses environs* (1957; Eng. trans., 1960); PETER MAYNE, *Istanbul* (1967).

(B.E.)

Italic Languages

Italic languages, in a broad sense, are certain Indo-European languages that were once spoken in the Apennine Peninsula (modern Italy) and in the eastern part of the Po Valley. These include the Latin, Faliscan, Osco-Umbrian, and Venetic languages, which have in common a considerable number of features that separate them from the other languages of the same area—*e.g.*, from Greek and Etruscan. (In a more narrow sense, the term Italic languages excludes Latin and denotes only Oscan, Umbrian, Faliscan, and Venetic.)

For a long time the Italic languages have been considered to be an Indo-European subfamily like Celtic, Germanic, or Slavic. Today, some scholars are inclined to distinguish within the so-called Italic branch at least three independent members of the Indo-European family: Latin (perhaps with Faliscan), Osco-Umbrian, and Venetic. They attribute the similarities—*i.e.*, the unifying phenomena in the division—to a convergence that took place when the speakers of these different idioms were integrated into the "Italic" civilization of the early first millennium BC. The culture that resulted is known as the "Etruscan koine." Figure 1 shows the assumed distribution of languages in ancient Italy; the solid line marks the Italic languages.

Languages of the group. *Latin.* Latin is the language of Latium and of Rome; its earliest known documents date from the 6th century BC. Rich epigraphical evidence and an extensive literature begin at the end of the 3rd century BC, at the time when Roman Latin was emerging as the predominant language of Italy. By AD 100 at the latest, Latin had effaced all the other dialects between Sicily and the Alps, with the exception of Greek in the colonies of Magna Graecia. (For more information about Latin and about the languages that derive from it, see ROMANCE LANGUAGES.)

Spread of Latin on the Italian peninsula

The other Italic languages, Italic languages in the narrow sense, are known through local and personal names transmitted by Greek and Roman sources, and especially from inscriptions.

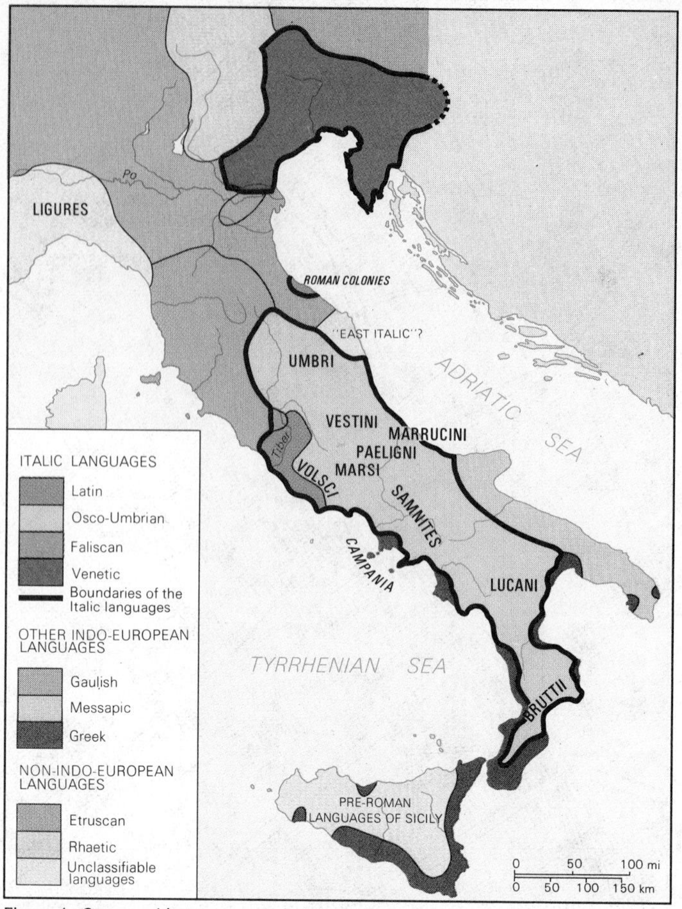

Figure 1: Supposed language areas of the Italic and neighbouring languages about 250 BC.

Oscan. Before Latin spread out, Oscan was the most widely spoken group of dialects of the Apennine Peninsula. It was used by the Samnites in Samnium and Campania; by the inhabitants of Lucania and Bruttium; and, with slight variations, by smaller tribes between Latium and the Adriatic coast: the Volsci, Marsi, Paeligni, Vestini, and Marrucini. The legendary Sabines, who shared the earliest history of Rome, probably also spoke an Oscan dialect. The most important Oscan texts come from Campanian cities. The largest text, a treaty between Nola and Abella, is carved on a stone slab, called the Cippus Abellanus. In Bantia, a nearly unknown town of Lucania, the Tabula Bantina is preserved, the most extensive Oscan inscription. It is a bronze tablet with penal laws concerning municipal administration, written in Latin letters not earlier than 80 BC.

Umbrian. The Umbrian idiom, closely related to Oscan, is known from a few small inscriptions and from the Tabulae Iguvinae (Iguvine Tables), which consist of seven bronze tablets found at Gubbio (the ancient Iguvium). Constituting one of the largest and most important epigraphical documents of antiquity, the tablets contain ritual regulations of a sacred brotherhood to which a considerable part of the public cults of Iguvium was delegated. The Tabulae Iguvinae were incised, partly in the Umbrian alphabet and partly in Latin letters, within the last two centuries before Christ, but the text itself may result from a far more remote oral tradition.

Faliscan. Faliscan inscriptions appear only in the immediate surroundings of Falerii (the present Cività Castellana in central Italy), which, except for its dialect, seems to have been a completely Etruscan city.

Venetic. The language represented by inscriptions from the territory of the Veneti—between the Po River, the Carnic (Carniche) Alps, and Istria—is called Venetic. The majority of discoveries come from sanctuaries at Este and Làgole di Calalzo.

Alphabets

The alphabets used for writing these languages include the Greek one in Bruttium and Lucania and the Latin alphabet and various derivations of the Etruscan alphabet in the other regions. Four "national" scripts are distinguished: Oscan, Umbrian, Faliscan, and Venetic (see Figures 2–5).

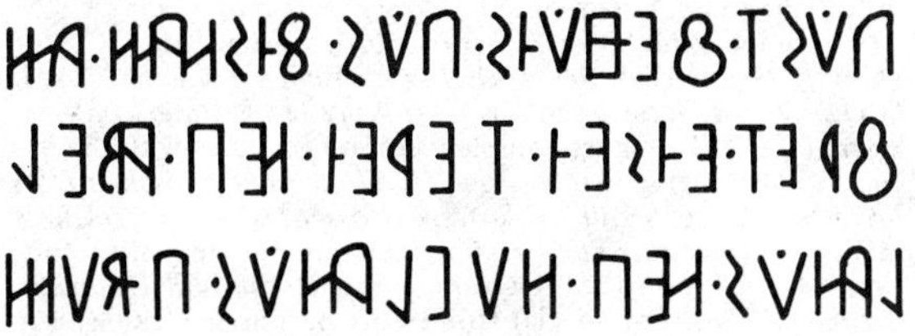

Figure 2: *Oscan.*
Inscription from the Cippus Abellanus: *púst feihúís.pús. fisnam.am/ fret.eiseí.tereí.nep.abel/ lanús.nep.núvlanús. pidum/ . . .* [*ú* represents *o*]. (*Cf.* Latin *Post muros qui fanum circumdant, in eo territorio neque Abellani neque Nolani quicquam* [*aedificaverint*].) "Behind the walls which go around the sanctuary,—in this area neither the inhabitants of Abella nor the inhabitants of Nola [are allowed to construct] anything."

Origin of the Italic languages. The Italic languages must have been brought from the original area of the Indo-European languages, probably in eastern parts of central Europe, when their speakers crossed the Alps. This is attested to by a stratum of very old placenames of non-Indo-European origin—*e.g.*, Tarracina, Capua, Tarentum—that covers not only the Apennine Peninsula but also Greece and Anatolia. This stratum is ascribed to a "Mediterranean" language believed to have dominated large parts of the ancient world before the arrival of the Indo-European peoples. Nothing is known about the date, the path, and the circumstances of the above-mentioned immigration, and none of the many attempts to combine archaeological evidence with linguistic prehistory has led to convincing results. Thus, the only resources available for studying the Italic languages are exclusively linguistic methods of comparative philology.

Phonology. Many of the phonetic processes that make the reconstructed Indo-European language differ from the attested Italic languages seem to have occurred rather late in time. The only one that can confidently be placed outside of Italy—that is, before the immigration over the Alps—is the change to *ss* of the combinations of the dental occlusive (stop) plus *t*. This is a common feature of Celtic, Germanic, and Latin. For example, Latin *visus* comes from the older, reconstructed form **wissos* "seen"; this is cognate with High German *gi-wiss* "surely known" and the Indo-European term with *d* + *t*, **wid-to-s*. Similarly, Oscan *nessimo-* "next" is the form equivalent to Welsh *nesaf* and Indo-European **nedh-t(e)-mo-* (An asterisk [*] before a word means that it is not attested, but reconstructed.)

The representation of the Indo-European labiovelar stop k^w is more complex. (A labiovelar stop is a sound pronounced with simultaneous articulation—movement—of the lips and the velum, the soft palate.) From this sound there has resulted a *qu* in Latin, *p* in Osco-Umbrian, *c* in Irish, and *p* in Brythonic Celtic; *e.g.*, Latin *quis* "who" is cognate with Oscan *pis* and with Indo-European $*k^wis$; and Irish *cia* is related to Welsh *pwy*, "who," which is cognate with Indo-European $*k^wei$. Some scholars have tried to trace this development back to an Italo-Celtic unity, but the change of Brythonic k^w to *p* is surely later than the dropping of the *p* in Common Celtic. It is sounder, therefore, to assume independent processes in the different languages.

Other features developed in Italy itself—*e.g.*, the use of the voiceless dental spirant (fricative) *f* that is shared with Etruscan and is lacking in marginal districts of Venetic. In all Italic languages this *f* sound replaced the Indo-European voiced aspirated sounds in initial position. The latter are represented as *bh*, *dh*, g^wh and are pronounced with a small puff of air after the *b*, *d*, g^w. Examples of the use of *f* in Italic are as follows: Latin *frater* "brother" = Umbrian *frater* = Indo-European

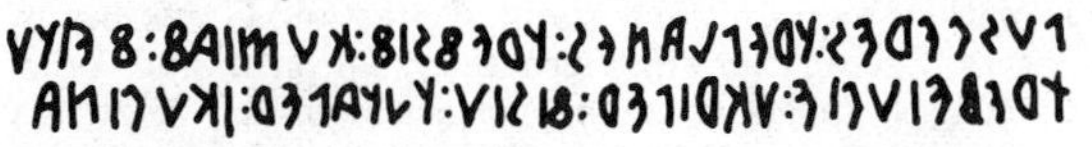

Figure 3: *Umbrian.*
Inscription from the Tabulae Iguvinae: *pus veres treplanes tref sif kumiaf feitu/trebe iuvie ukriper fisiu tutaper ikuvina* [*u* represents *u* and *o*, *k* represents *k* and *g*]. (*Cf.* Latin *Post portam Trebulanam tres sues gravidas facito Trebo Iovio pro arce Fisia, pro civitate Iguvina.*) "Behind the Trebulan gate he shall sacrifice three pregnant sows to [the god] Trebus Iovius, for the Fisian citadel, for the state of Iguvium."

**bhrātēr;* Latin *facio* "I do, make" is related to Oscan *fakiiad* "he would do," to Venetic *fagsto* "he made," and to Indo-European **dhə-k-*. A more recent common process in Latin and Osco-Umbrian is the use of the full system of five short vowels in initial syllables only; short vowels of noninitial syllables in Latin became less open—*e.g.*, *facio* "I do, make," but *in-ficio*, the compound of *in* + *facio*. In Osco-Umbrian these vowels tend to be lost completely—*e.g.*, *benust* "he will have come," but *cebnust* "he will have come near." Some differences between Latin and Osco-Umbrian probably arose during the last centuries before Christ—*e.g.*, Osco-Umbrian *ō* changed to *u* (*duunated*, Latin *dōnavit* "he gave, has given"), *ē* became *i* (*ligud*, Latin *lēge* "law" in the ablative singular), and final *ā* developed into *o* (*viú* [ú in the Oscan national alphabet = o], Latin *via* "way"). Indo-European voiced aspirated sounds (*bh*, *dh*, g^wh) in internal position probably first became voiced spirants (*e.g.*, sounds such as *v*) in all Italic languages and, later, voiced stops in Latin and Venetic and the voiceless spirant *f* in Osco-Umbrian and Faliscan. Examples of these changes are the voiced stop *b* in Latin *liberi* "(free) children" and Venetic *louderobos* "children" (in the dative plural) and the voiceless spirant *f* in Oscan *loufro-* "free" and Faliscan *loferta* "freed woman." The Oscan development is shown by early coins: the Greek form *allibanōn* was used for the inhabitants of the town that later was called Allifae, thus the sound *b* (later *v*), written by Greek beta, corresponding to roman *b*, became *f*.

The "f" sound

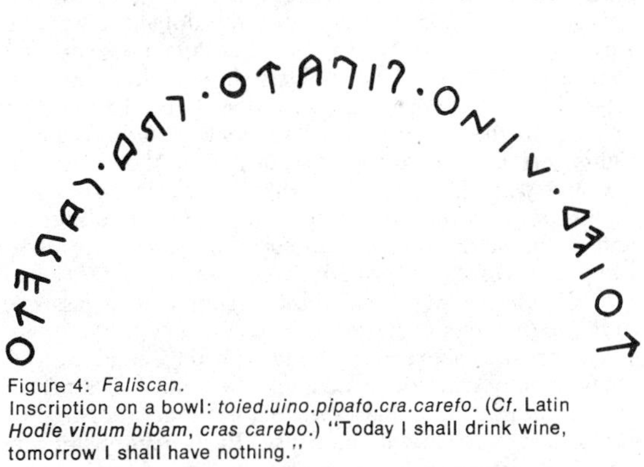

Figure 4: *Faliscan.*
Inscription on a bowl: *foied.uino.pipafo.cra.carefo.* (*Cf.* Latin *Hodie vinum bibam, cras carebo.*) "Today I shall drink wine, tomorrow I shall have nothing."

Morphology. In contrast to the phonology, which shows so many correlations among the Italic languages, there are few definite connections between these tongues in their grammars. An innovation, probably to be ascribed to relatively recent contact between Latin and Osco-Umbrian, is the extension of the ablative singular case from *o*-stems and pronouns, where it occurred originally, to other declension classes: Latin *praidad* "with the plunder," later *praeda*, *meretod* "by merit," Oscan *toutad* "by the people," *slaagid* "of the border." Many of the morphological features common to Osco-Umbrian and Latin are shared by other Indo-European languages; that is, they are not Italic in a specific sense. For example, the *a*-subjunctive—*e.g.*, Latin *faciat* "may he do" and Oscan *fakiiad*—is also Celtic; passive endings in *-r*—*e.g.*, Oscan *vincter* and Latin *vincitur* "he is conquered"—are found in Celtic, Hittite, and Tocharian as well. More important are the discrepancies. For example, the genitive singular of *o*-stems shows *-ī* in Latin, Faliscan (perhaps also in Venetic), and in the Celtic languages, but *-eis* in Osco-Umbrian; the nominative plural of the same class is marked by *-oi* in early Latin, Celtic, and Greek but by *-ōs* in Osco-Umbrian, Germanic, Sanskrit, and other languages. In addition, the perfect stems of secondary verbs (verbs derived from nouns or from other verbs) are formed by *-u- or -v-* in Latin, by *-t(t)-* in Oscan, and by *-s-* in Venetic; *e.g.,* Latin *donavit* "he has given" = Oscan *duunated* = Venetic *donasto.*

Vocabulary. Lexical comparison leads to more specific data about the history of the Italic languages. There are linguistic boundaries called isoglosses that may date back to pre-Italic history: *e.g.,* Oscan *humuns* "men" derives from the same word as *homines* and Gothic *gumans;* and Oscan *anamum* "mind" in the accusative singular form is directly related to Latin *animus* "mind, soul" and Irish *anam* "soul." There are many old differences between Latin and Osco-Umbrian. Latin *ignis* "fire" = Sanskrit *agni,* but Umbrian *pir* "fire" = Greek *pȳr* = Old English *fyr;* Latin *aqua* "water" = Gothic *ahwa,* but Umbrian *utur* "water" = Greek *hydōr* = Old English *wæter;* Latin *filius, filia* "son, daughter," but Oscan *puklo* "son" = Sanskrit *putra,* and Oscan *futir* "daughter" = Greek *thygatēr* = Gothic *dauhtar.* Adjectives of totality in Latin are *omnis, cunctus, totus,* in Osco-Umbrian *sollo-, sevo-, allo-* (cognate to English "all").

Certain lexical fields that reflect the acquisition of the Mediterranean culture show an independent terminology. The following forms strongly suggest that Latin and Osco-Umbrian speakers were not in contact with each other when they began to build cities: Latin *porta* "gate," Oscan *veru* "gate"; Latin *arx* "citadel," Umbrian *ocar* "citadel, castle"; Latin *moenia* "walls, ramparts," *murus* "wall," Oscan *feihúss* (accusative plural) "walls." On the other hand, Latins and Osco-Umbrians adopted the same terms for "write" and "read"; Latin *scribere* "to write," Oscan *scriftas* "written"; Latin *legere* "to read," Paelignian (an Oscan dialect) *lexe* "you will read." It is known that the Latin and Osco-Umbrian alphabets are derived from the Etruscan one; the spread of these terms can, therefore, be attributed to a period of Etruscan predominance. Etruscan features are obvious in archaic Italic religion; Osco-Umbrians and Veneti adopted even the Etruscan word for "god"—*ais.* Perhaps it is not by chance that many religious terms show a close community among Italic peoples; *e.g.,* the Latin forms *pius* "pious, obedient" and *piare* "to honour with religious rights" are equivalent to Volscian *pihom* (neuter singular) and Umbrian *pihatu* (imperative); Latin *feriae* "religious days" is related to Oscan *fiisiais* (ablative plural); and Latin *sacer* "sacred," *sacrare* "to consecrate, dedicate," *sanctus* "consecrated" are cognates with Oscan *sakrid* (ablative singular), *sakrafir* (subjunctive passive), *saahtum* (neuter singular).

Etruscan influence

The Etruscan supremacy ended with the foundation of local republics in Rome and in other cities of Italy in about 500 BC; when that occurred, the unifying force of Etruscan culture lost its influence. Early republican terminology developed independently; *e.g.,* Latin *consul* "consul," but Oscan *meddix* designate the first magistrate; to Latin *senatus* "senate" corresponds Oscan *kumparakineis* (genitive singular), and to Latin *comitia* "assembly," the Oscan forms *comono* or *kumbennieis.* The last period of Italic language history is characterized by an increasing influence of Roman models. For example, the title *censor* "censor" seems to have been borrowed by the Samnites in the 3rd century BC; Oscan *ceus* "citizen" is a Latin loanword that stems from a form **ceuis,* which existed in about 200 BC and was intermediate between *ceivis* and *civis;* Oscan *aidil* and *kvaisstur* imitate Latin *aedilis* and *quaestor,* terms for offices in the Roman government; and the Veneti adopted the Roman word for "freed man," *libertus.* In addition, the Tabula Bantina slavishly copied the juridical style and terminology of the Romans.

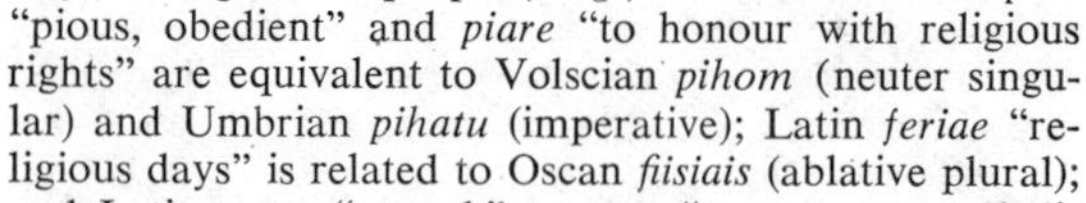

Figure 5: *Venetic.*
Inscription on a capital serving as pedestal of a votive statue found at Este: *mego donasto kanta.* (*Cf.* Latin *Me donavit Canta.*) "Canta gave me" ("to the goddess" is understood).
From G.B. Pellegrini and A.L. Prosdocimi, *La Lingua Venetica* (1967)

BIBLIOGRAPHY. General surveys of the history of Italic languages include: J. WHATMOUGH, *The Foundations of Roman Italy* (1937); G. DEVOTO, *Gli antichi Italici,* 3rd ed. (1967), in Italian; and E. PULGRAM, *The Tongues of Italy* (1958).

The fundamental works on Osco-Umbrian are R. VON PLANTA, *Grammatik der oskisch-umbrischen Dialekte,* 2 vol. (1892–97), in German; and R.S. CONWAY (ed.), *Italic Dialects,* 2 vol. (1897). The most complete edition of texts (with the exception of Venetic) is E. VETTER, *Handbuch der italischen Dialekte,* vol. 1, *Texte mit Erklärung, Glossen, Wörterverzeichnis* (1953), in German. The best introduction for beginners continues to be C.D. BUCK, *A Grammar of Oscan and Umbrian,* 2nd ed. (1928). For special studies of the Iguvine Tables, see G. DEVOTO, *Tabulae Iguvinae,* 3rd ed. (1962), in Latin; and J.W. POULTNEY, *The Bronze Tables of Iguvium* (1959). For Faliscan, see G. GIACOMELLI, *La lingua falisca* (1963); and for Venetic, see G.B. PELLEGRINI and A.L. PROSDOCIMI, *La lingua venetica,* 2 vol. (1967), both works in Italian.

Remains of other languages within ancient Italy, including Venetic, are treated in R.S. CONWAY, J. WHATMOUGH, and S.E. JOHNSON, *The Prae-Italic Dialects of Italy,* 3 vol. (1934).

(J.U.)

Italic Peoples, Ancient

Pre-Roman Italy was inhabited by peoples diverse in origin, language, traditions, stage of development, and territorial extension and was heavily influenced by neighbouring Greece, with its well-defined national characteristics, expansive vigour, and aesthetic and intellectual maturity. Italy attained a unified ethno-linguistic, political, and cultural physiognomy only after the Roman conquest; yet its most ancient peoples remain anchored in the names of the regions of Roman Italy—Latium, Campania, Apulia, Bruttium, Lucania, Samnium, Picenum, Umbria, Etruria, Venetia, Liguria.

Sources of knowledge. Knowledge of pre-Roman Italy is limited by the scarcity and unreliability of the sources, at least until the pre-eminence of Latin literature growing out of the Roman conquest. The ancient national literatures have been totally lost; the surviving written documents are epigraphic in nature and consist of a few generally brief, historically irrelevant, and often hard-to-decipher inscriptions. Greek and Latin writers provide extensive and various written sources, which constitute the essential base of the notions of the ethnography, history, and antiquity of the Italic peoples; but it is nevertheless a partial, random, indirect body of evidence, often of uncertain value. Greek writers considered the Italic peoples as objects of erudite curiosity and dealt mainly with their relations with the Greek world. Unfortunately, the most precious documentation in this regard—works of the Greek writers of Sicily such as Antiochus, Philistus of Syracuse, Timaeus of Tauromenium—has been lost. Latin literature directly preserves the traditions only of Rome; the rest of the Italic world is revealed little by little through its expanding contacts with Rome. A broader vision is not achieved in Latin literature until the *Origines* of Cato (2nd century BC). Imperial Rome produced monographic works on particular peoples of ancient Italy, such as those on the Etruscans by Verrius Flaccus and by the Emperor Claudius, unfortunately lost.

Archaeological evidence

The more limited the contribution made by literary tradition, the greater is the importance of the archaeological evidence, which by its very nature illuminates particular aspects of a civilization rather than historical events or developments. Consequently, modern studies on pre-Roman Italy seem primarily oriented toward the descriptive analysis of cultural phenomena and characterized by the assembling of specialist research in such disciplines as protohistoric archaeology, linguistics, and ethnography. But there has also been a prevailing tendency to treat monographically the individual peoples and civilizations; for the study of the Etruscan world, for example, there exists an autonomous discipline called Etruscology. Comprehensive studies, such as the classic one by Joshua Whatmough, *The Foundations of Roman Italy* (1937), are rare. Only recently has the need been felt for a really historical interpretation of the complex of facts relating to pre-Roman Italy, including the history of the Greek colonies and of primitive Rome.

THE ETRUSCANS

The Etruscans were called Tyrsenoi, or Tyrrhenoi, by the Greeks, Turskus by the Umbrians, Tusci, or Etrusci, by the Latins. They called themselves Rasenna, according to Dionysius of Halicarnassus, and this is confirmed in the form *rasna* by Etruscan inscriptions. Their country was called Tyrrhenia in Greek and Tuscia, or Etruria, in Latin.

Location of Etruria

Etruria lay in central Italy between the valley of the Tiber, the valley of the Arno, and the Apennines, corresponding in present-day terms to southern Latium, a large part of Tuscany, and a tract in Umbria. The existence of the Etruscans in this territory is attested by epigraphic documents in Etruscan from the beginning of the 7th century BC onward. Other historical and epigraphic evidence attests to their settlements or their dominion in such other parts of Italy as Campania and Latium to the south and the plain of the Po to the north.

Origins. The problem of Etruscan origins has produced a discussion that has continued from classical antiquity to the present day. Its point of departure is the linguistic dissimilarity between the Etruscans and the other important historical peoples of ancient Italy who were Indo-European, such as the Latins and the Umbro-Sabellians. The problem remains formulated today in the terms in which it was set forth by Dionysius of Halicarnassus. Two opposite theses are commonly offered: (1) that the Etruscans came from the East by way of the sea (from Lydia, according to the tradition recorded by Herodotus, or in general from the Aegean and particularly from the island of Lemnos); and (2) that they were autochthonous (of local origin), or at any rate that they were an ancient Italian people (an early view, reviewed and critically formulated in modern times as a theory of their overland migration from the North or as a theory identifying them with the pre-Indo-European ethnic substratum of Italy).

Theory of overseas provenance from the East

The theory of the migration of the Etruscans from the East is the best known and most widely accepted by scholars. This provenance is based on the almost unanimous testimony of ancient tradition and on numerous other arguments—linguistic (onomastic, lexical, and structural affinities of Etruscan with the Asian and pre-Hellenic languages of the Aegean, especially with the inscription on an ancient funeral stele discovered at Lemnos), archaeological (diffusion in Etruria of the orientalizing civilization [influenced by the East]), and historico-religious (divination by means of reading animal viscera as in the Babylonian and Hittite world). It is generally believed and asserted that the Etruscans immigrated from the Aegeo-Asian area into Italy toward the end of the 8th or beginning of the 7th century BC, carrying with them a civilization of Eastern type. In such case the pre-existing Villanovan iron culture would have to be attributed to Italic populations; but particularly in recent years this conviction has begun to lose ground, for four basic reasons: (1) the fact that between the Villanovan culture and the orientalizing one there exists no clear break sufficient to attest the arrival en masse of a new population; (2) the disparate origins of the elements composing the orientalizing civilization of Etruria (from Egypt, Phoenicia, Mesopotamia, Urartu, Cyprus, and from Greece itself), which is more probably an indication of contributions by way of commerce and of cultural diffusion, as certainly happened in the corresponding cultural and artistic orientalizing phase in Greece; (3) historical and archaeological data, which demonstrate the presence of the Etruscans in the Italian area before the beginning of Greek colonization early in the 8th century BC; and (4) the chronology of the classical traditions, which places them in Italy in the 2nd millennium BC, at least four or five centuries before the migrations supposed by the modern theories. Recently some scholars have indeed expressed the opinion that groups of Aegean navigators could have arrived in Italy at the end of the Mycenaean Period (*c.* 1200s BC), constituting the nucleus (or an essential component) of the future Etruscan nation. To them would have to be attributed the name of Tyrrhenoi, which may perhaps be identified with that of the Tursha, one of the "sea peoples" recorded in Egyptian monuments of the late 13th and early 12th centuries BC. (This line of thought envisions a type of "precolonization" similar to that of the Mycenaeans in southern Italy and in Sicily, or a phenomenon analogous to the maritime migrations and occupations by the Normans of the Middle Ages. In the latter case the Villanovan culture could be attributed to the Etruscan ethnos in course of formation and not to a pre-Etruscan ethnic stratum.)

Theory of provenance from the North

The theory of the provenance of the Etruscans from the North, already adumbrated by some 18th- and 19th-century scholars (simply because of the questionable comparison of the name Rasenna with that of the Rhaeti inhabiting the east-central Alps), has stressed as its basic argument the identification of the Etruscans with the Villanovans, held to be descended from a cremating people thought to have originated in central Europe. But recent discoveries show that the funeral rite of cremation was widely diffused by the end of the Bronze Age in the whole Italian area, including the South and Sicily (so-called proto-Villanovan), so that it seems difficult to attribute this phenomenon to a particular ethnic group. Entirely hypothetical also is the reconstruction of a Rhaeto-Tyrrhenian linguistic group of central European provenance with which to associate the origin of the Etruscans and of certain inhabitants of the northern Aegean, including the island of Lemnos.

Theory of the autochthony

Lastly, according to the autochthony theory, after the invasion by the Indo-Europeans (archaeologically identified with the cremators), the Etruscan nation survived and revived the most ancient populations of prehistoric Italy. A number of linguists attribute the Etruscan language to a supposed pre-Indo-European Mediterranean linguistic substratum common to Italy and the Aegeo-Asian area, thus explaining its affinities with the Anatolian and pre-Hellenic languages.

Each of these diverse theories contains positive and negative elements, forcing scholars to rethink in a broader way the question of the very terms in which the problem of Etruscan origins is stated and thus considering the historically more valid concept of a progressive formation of the Etruscan nation from the meeting of various external (Eastern and Northern) and local elements. This new perspective reduces the distance between the various traditional points of view to such an extent that it is possible to imagine a prehistoric connection of the Italian Tyrrhenic world both with the Greek and eastern Mediterranean area and with pre-Indo-European Italy. In any case, it seems certain that the formation of the Etruscan people should date from the transition from the Bronze Age to the Iron Age in about the 10th century BC, which is remarkably coincident with Etruscan beginnings according to some ancient tradition concerning the reckoning of the centuries.

Language and writing. Etruscan, the third great language of culture in Italy after Greek and Latin, does not survive in any literary works. Scholars know of the existence of an Etruscan religious literature, and evidence suggests that there may have been a body of historical literature too. But Etruscan had already ceased to be spoken in the time of imperial Rome, and its surviving writings interested only a few scholars, who made no translations or synopses. Only a few general notices and a few fragments exist today. Thus moderns will forever remain ignorant of the greatest part of the lexical and expressive inheritance of the Etruscan language.

The few known Etruscan documents are archaeological and almost exclusively of religious and funerary content. One of them, of exceptional interest, was found in Egypt, cut into narrow cloth strips wrapped around a mummy, and is now preserved in the National Museum at Zagreb, Yugoslavia. With about 1,300 words it is the longest existing Etruscan text; it contains a ritual of sacrifice, sufficient to give some idea of Etruscan religious literature. Found in Italy were an important religious text, inscribed on a tile at the site of ancient Capua, and an inscription on a boundary stone at Perugia, noteworthy for the singularity of its juridical content. Additionally there are a few thousand dedicatory inscriptions; grave inscriptions; and, more rarely, inscriptions of other kinds such as on coins, lead projectiles, dice, etc. The few Etruscan-Latin bilingual inscriptions, all funerary, have very slight importance with respect to improving knowledge of Etruscan. But inscribed gold plates found in Italy at the site of the ancient sanctuary of Pyrgi provide two texts, one in Etruscan and the other in Phoenician, of significant length (about 40 words) and of analogous content, that are the equivalent of a bilingual inscription and that offer substantial data for the elucidation of Etruscan by way of a known language—Phoenician; the find is also an important historical document that records the dedication to the Phoenician goddess Astarte of a "sacred place" in the Etruscan sanctuary of Pyrgi by Thefarie Velianas, king of Caere, early in the 5th century BC.

The modern concept of a "mystery" of the Etruscan language is fundamentally erroneous. There exists no problem of decipherment, as is often wrongly asserted. The Etruscan texts are perfectly legible. The alphabet derives from a Greek alphabet of Western type, disseminated in Italy by the colonists coming from the island of Euboea, probably during the 8th century BC, and adapted to Etruscan phonetics; from this same alphabet is derived, more or less independently, the Latin alphabet. (In its turn the Etruscan alphabet was diffused at the end of the archaic period [*c.* 500 BC] into northern Italy, becoming the model for the alphabets of the Veneti and of various Alpine populations, and concurred with the formation of the Umbrian and the Oscan alphabets in the peninsula.)

Etruscan alphabet

The real problem with the Etruscan texts lies in the cognition of the meaning of the words and of the grammatical forms. In this connection there exists a fundamental obstacle in that no other known language has close enough kinship to Etruscan to allow a reliable, comprehensive, and conclusive comparison. The apparent isolation of the Etruscan language had already been noted by the ancients; it is confirmed by repeated and vain attempts of modern science to assign it to one of the various linguistic groups or types of the Mediterranean and Eurasian world. But there are in fact connections with Indo-European languages, particularly with the Italic languages, and also with more or less known non-Indo-European languages of Western Asia and the Caucasus, the Aegean, Italy, and the Alpine zone, and on the other hand with the relics of the Mediterranean linguistic substrata revealed by place names. This means that Etruscan is anything but isolated and that its roots are intertwined with those of other recognizable linguistic formations within a geographical area extending from western Asia to east-central Europe and the central Mediterranean, and its latest formative developments may have taken place in more direct contact with the pre-Indo-European and Indo-European linguistic environment of Italy. But this also means that Etruscan, as scholars know it, cannot simply be classified as belonging to the Caucasian, the Anatolian, or Indo-European languages.

Methods of interpreting the Etruscan language

The traditional methods hitherto employed in interpretation of Etruscan were (1) the *etymological*, which is based upon the comparison of word roots and grammatical elements with those of other languages and which assumes the existence of a linguistic relationship such as to permit an explication of Etruscan from the outside (this method has produced negative results, given the error in the assumption); (2) the *combinatory*, a procedure of analysis and interpretation of the Etruscan texts rigorously limited to internal study of the texts themselves compared one with another and of the grammatical forms of the Etrusan words (this led to much progress in the knowledge of Etruscan, but its defects became evident in the hypothetical character of many of the conclusions due to the absence of external proofs or confirmations); and (3) the *bilingual*, based on the comparison of Etruscan ritual, votive, and funerary formulas with presumably analogous formulas from epigraphic or literary texts in languages belonging to a closely connected geographic and historic environment, such as Greek, Latin, or Umbrian. But with the increase of reliable data, in part from new epigraphic discoveries (such as the gold plates at Pyrgi, mentioned above), the question of method appears to be of decreasing importance; that is, all possible procedures tend to be utilized, on the one hand maximally exploiting the various sources of external verification (ancient glossaries, bilinguals, parallel formulas in other languages, clues supplied by the nature of a monument and of its figuration, etc.) and on the other hand broad development of internal research on Etruscan, as through analyses and combinations of the contexts and of structural studies of the sentences and words.

The results already obtained from these investigations allow relatively easy and trustworthy translations of most of the shorter inscriptions and of many parts of the longer texts. It is important to note that Etruscan seems to differ from the structure of the Indo-European languages, such as Greek and Latin, and rather to approach in some aspects the structure of the agglutinative languages such as the Finno-Ugric.

Characteristics. Much has been said about the temperament of the Etruscans, as contrasted to that of the Greeks and of the other Italic peoples, particularly the Latins, stressing the aspects of irrationality, fantasy, mysticism, and discontinuity in Etruscan religious conceptions and artistic expression. A pre-eminence of women and of the feminine spirit is alluded to, in opposition to the masculine character of the expressions of Greek and Latin civilization.

Etruscan temperament and customs

With regard to Etruscan customs, there has been pointed out, among other things, the emphasis of the ancient writers on the Etruscan predilection for the flute, an instrument of Asian origin, on their orgiastic music, which accompanied not only their banquets but also the preparation of their food, the hunt, and even the flogging of slaves.

But in fact, the mentality and customs of the Etruscans can be explained as primitive survivals in a world started upon rapid intellectual, moral, and aesthetic advances by the powerful influence of Greek culture. In the Etruscan world there existed a contradiction between, on the one hand, prehistoric concepts and traditions and, on the other hand, the rapid and vigorous economic, technical, and political progress of the Tyrrhenian cities. While experiencing profound and determinant influences from Greek civilization, the Etruscan world remained extraneous to the rational order of classical thought.

The overall picture formed of the Etruscans in the 8th–6th centuries BC is that of a nation of navigators, traders, and industrial producers, driven to actions of immediate practicality; this also explains the fragmentary and transitory character of their political expansion. Their sudden and premature decline in the 5th and 4th centuries BC gives the impression of a cycle of power and of civilization that was never completed. In the last phases, beginning in the 4th century BC, the Etruscan nation seemed to withdraw into itself in its archaism and its provincialism, dominated above all by the elaboration of a complex religious thought and by the minuteness of its rites, which made it proverbially famous in the ancient world and an authority on religion in Rome itself.

Organization. Etruscan society appears to have been founded on a system of families of patrilineal descent. The name of every free citizen consisted of two elements: (1) his individual name (*praenomen*), generally short and simple; and (2) his family or gentilitial name (*nomen*), common to all the members of the family group—generally formed, by suffixes, as a derivative of a simple personal name, the name of a god, a place, or the like. This onomastic formula was common to the Etruscans, the Romans, and to other peoples of ancient Italy. A nickname (*cognomen*), typical of Roman onomastics, appears in Etruscan inscriptions rarely and generally at a late date. Frequently added were the patronymic, or father's, name and the metronymic, or mother's, name.

Etruscan society

The presence of the gentilitial name presupposed membership in a class that enjoyed civil rights. And in fact slaves and foreigners carried only a single personal name. Within the gentilitial system it is difficult to distinguish, on the basis of onomastic formulas, between families of the upper and lower classes, in the sense of the patricians and plebeians of the Roman state. Originally, or very early in the period of the massive economic flowering of the Etruscan cities, there seems to have existed a relatively equalitarian society. But within this social structure there probably began to emerge, or reemerge, particularly in the period of Etruscan decline, an aristocratic class that held all or most civil and religious power. Only at the end of the autonomous life of Etruscan cities (*c.* 2nd century BC) did there occur, probably under Roman influence, the massive influx of freedmen and slaves into the gentilitial system and hence into the enjoyment of civil rights. The Etruscan political order was based on the city-state, similar to the Greek polis, including an urban centre and a more or less extensive territory. The number and names of these independent state units in the most ancient times are not known; recent discoveries of early minor centres in the interior of Etruria indicate that they may have been more numerous than those known at the high point of historic times. These minor communities may have become progressively absorbed into the territories of the more powerful cities. From the 6th century BC onward, territorial organization and political and economic initiative were sharply concentrated in a limited number of large city-states, the names of which, starting from the south, are—along the coast—Caere, Tarquinii, Vulci, Roselle, Vetulonia, and Populonia and—inland—Veii, Volsinii (possibly modern Bolsena, or Orvieto), Clusium (now Chiusi), Perusia (Perugia), Cortona, Arretium (Arezzo), Faesulae (Fiesole), and Volaterrae (Volterra).

City-states

Not withstanding their full political autonomy and cultural individuality, and quite aside from specific alliances, these cities were associated in a kind of religious and probably economic league, on occasion not devoid of political considerations. It epitomized the Etruscan "nation." According to the classical sources it was composed of 12 cities, or populi, which more or less corresponded to the major Etruscan cities listed above. The centre of the league was at a sanctuary near Volsinii, the Fanum Voltumnae, where the representatives of the various states assembled annually to participate in games and ceremonies and to elect a chief priest.

Government

The Etruscan cities were governed originally by monarchies presumably similar to those recorded for the most ancient period of Roman history, with sovereigns invested with complete military and religious power. Subsequently the power appears to have been entrusted to elective and temporary magistrates, as at Rome and in the Greek colonies. It is difficult to fix the dates and manner of the change from monarchies to republics. Epigraphic sources and historical tradition for the 5th century BC still testify to the existence of kings at Caere and at Veii, but it is not known whether these were traditional monarchies or personal powers similar to those of the Greek tyrants. The institutional change probably depended in part upon the transformations of the individual societies—especially in the great mercantile cities of the coast such as Caere, Tarquinii, and Vulci—under the influence of the Greek world, with which they were linked by very close ties of commerce and civilization (such centres as Sybaris in Magna Graecia and Miletus in Asia Minor; or Athens itself after Solon's reforms, which would mean during the 6th century BC). The evidence indicates that the republican system, as it appears in the latest period of the autonomous life of the Etruscan cities, was established in concomitance with the victory of powerful gentilitial and priestly oligarchies. This seems to exclude a process of evolution in a democratic direction, in spite of episodic revolutionary rumblings such as one in Volsinii in 265 BC. Only the direct influence of Rome and the general conditions in federated Italy, in the last days of the Etruscan city autonomies (in the 2nd and 1st centuries BC) and particularly in the cities of inland and southern Etruria, brought about a broad opening up to the lower classes.

Aspects of Etruscan civilization. The most conspicuous aspects of Etruscan spiritual and material civilization centre upon religion and the funerary realm. This does not derive exclusively from the archaeological evidence of tombs and sanctuaries; tradition also attests to the predominance of the sacred sphere, especially in such aspects of Etruscan public and private life as politics, law, literary and artistic manifestations, and dress.

Etruscan religion. The peculiar tendencies of Etruscan religiosity are manifested in a sense of cancelling out the human vis-à-vis the often not readily knowable divine and in a continuous effort to interpret the will of supernatural beings by divination techniques and to honour it with scrupulous ritualism. The literary, epigraphic, and monumental sources provide a glimpse of a conception of cosmology whose image of the sky with its subdivisions is reflected in the consecrated areas and even in the viscera of animals. The celestial dome was divided into 16 compartments inhabited by the various divinities: major gods to the east, astral and terrestrial divine beings to the south, infernal and inauspicious beings to the west, and the most powerful and mysterious gods of destiny to the north. The deities manifested themselves by means of natural phenomena, principally by lightnings. They also revealed themselves in the microcosm of the liver of animals (typical is a small, bronze model of a liver found near Piacenza, bearing the incised names of divinities in its 16 outside divisions and in its internal divisions).

Etruscan cosmology

These conceptions are linked closely to the art of divination for which the Etruscans were especially famous in the ancient world. All public and private actions of any importance were undertaken only after having interrogated the gods; negative or threatening responses necessitated complex preventive or protective ceremonies. The most important form of divination was haruspicy, or hepathoscopy—the study of the details of the viscera, especially the livers, of sacrificial animals. Second in importance was the observation of lightning and of such other celestial phenomena as the flight of birds (also important in the religion of the Umbri and of the Romans). Finally, there was the interpretation of prodigies—extraordinary and marvellous events observed in the sky or on the earth. These practices, extensively adopted by the Romans, are explicitly attributed by the ancient authors to the religion of the Etruscans. The whole content of the rules of divination constituted a great corpus of doctrine that Latin authors referred to under the name of *disciplina Etrusca*.

The supernatural beings were extremely numerous, and many are unknown today. The cult had individual deities conceived in the same style as those of the Greek and Roman pantheon—*e.g.*, the supreme celestial divinity armed with lightning, Tin or Tinia (the equivalent of the Greek Zeus and the Roman Jupiter); the great mother goddess, Uni (Hera; Juno); perhaps Sethlans (Hephaestus; Vulcan); Turms (Hermes; Mercury); and others. There was no lack of Greek divinities directly introduced into Etruria, including Apollo, Artemis, Hercules (Hercle in Etruscan). The Etruscans populated the sky, the earth, the water, and the subterranean regions with an immense number of minor divinities and demigods, guardian spirits, nymphs, and demons. To the world beyond the tomb belong masculine (Mantus) and feminine (Vanth) divinities and those of uncertain sex—understood also as divinities of fate—and monstrous and terrifying demons with animal characteristics.

The rites of the cult are substantially similar to those of the Greek and of the Roman religions, consisting of public and private sacrifices, with offerings of animals, liquids, and foods, accompanied by prayers and such other acts as observing the flight of birds and reading the viscera of sacrificial animals. Universally diffused was the custom of depositing in the temples more or less precious objects as offerings to the divinities, the recovery of which by archaeologists constitutes one of the most important sources of knowledge of the Etruscan religious conceptions, artistic taste, products, and material culture.

Religious rites

Etruscan funerary customs. The other principal source of evidence is, as already mentioned, the tombs. The idea

"Judgment of Paris," detail of three panels of a funerary painting, 7th century BC, from Caere. In the British Museum.

of the survival of a dead person in the burial place involved the preservation and protection of his remains, the tendency to imitate the form of a house in the urns and sepulchres, and the custom of depositing alongside the deceased everything required for ultraterrestrial life, such as food and drink, clothing, ornaments, weapons, and furniture. Accordingly, the tombs reflect all aspects of the period from which they date. Most especially, the funerary pictures document Etruscan life, dress, and beliefs; the number of these documents, chiefly in Tarquinii has grown in recent years and by about 1970 amounted to about 100 painted tomb chambers. In the archaic period real-life subjects prevailed, such as scenes of banqueting, of music and dancing, of games and other funerary ceremonies, and of the chase. In the latest period (4th–2nd century BC) depictions connected with the world beyond the grave appeared. This signifies that new eschatological ideas had become diffused in the Etruscan world; the pessimistic tone of the later tomb pictures contrasts with the doctrine of the transformation of the dead into divinities, a doctrine reported in the literary tradition.

Cremation and burial

The rite of cremation of corpses, prevalent at the beginning in the Villanovan culture, remained characteristic of north-central Etruria throughout the duration of Etruscan civilization. The ashes of the deceased were placed in urns in the form of vessels, huts, and even of human figures. In the rest of Etruria the rite of interment prevailed; corpses were deposited in grave pits or upon beds in sepulchral chambers excavated in rock or constructed, later, within terra-cotta or stone sarcophagi, often carrying on the lid the image of the deceased.

Etruscan art and architecture. Unlike the other peoples of Oriental and classical antiquity, the Etruscans have left but sparse traces of a monumental architecture in stone; such building was limited almost exclusively to city walls and to some tomb structures. Temples and houses had only stone foundations and were built of unbaked bricks, wood, or other light materials. The wooden roofs were protected from the elements with sections of decorated terra-cotta; famous complexes of architectonic terra-cottas have been discovered at Veii, at Caere, at Falerii, and at Civitate near Siena. The form and the external and internal architectonic elements of the temples and houses are reconstructed through the evidence of their imitations in the tombs.

Arts of the Etruscans

The arts of the Etruscans originated in the traditions of the European and Mediterranean Iron Age cultures, with decorated objects and small plastic images conceived with lively spontaneity or with geometric schemes. In the 7th century BC Oriental models established themselves, intermixing with the indigenous traditions. The influence of Greek art soon imposed itself in a preponderant and definitive way: first came the Daedalian and Peloponnesian styles; then the Ionic, particularly in the later part of the 6th century; and then the late-archaic trends, especially from Attica. From this there was an almost imperceptible transition to the protoclassical models of the first half of the 5th century. Archaic Etruria, in its greatest phase of power and wealth, is thus seen intimately linked to the image-making civilization of Greece. But the high level of quality and the technical refinement of some Etruscan works of art, especially in the period of Ionic influence (bronzes of Perugia; temple terra-cottas of Veii. including a famous statue of Apollo; painted tombs of Tarquinii), indicates not a provincial or imitative art but an active participation by the Etruscan region in the archaic artistic culture. It is probable that Greek artists of some renown worked and created schools in the rich and powerful cities of Etruria. The creative and productive impulse continued with undiminished vigour through the first decades of the 5th century, so that Etruria welcomed the inspirations of the severe or protoclassic style.

Only later, when Greece and especially Athens had reached the peak of the inimitable creativity of classicism, did declining Etruria remain behind, bogged down in its traditions, impoverished in technique, disposed to welcome the inspiration of the classical models only slowly and only in their surface formulas. Beginning with the 4th century BC, the imitation of Greek art became an act of provincialism. Nevertheless, there were still late impulses of expressive originality, particularly in portrait art; and in this respect Etruscan art prepared to unite in a common Italic experience, which was the direct foundation of Roman art.

Etruscan expansion and foreign relations. During the archaic period the Etruscans constituted the most important political, economic, and cultural nucleus in the Italian area, excluding the Greek colonies of the south. Their dominion or control extended over most of the regions from the Alps to the Strait of Messina. More precisely, the ancient sources record a direct domination by the Etruscans in Campania and in the plain of the Po, with repeated and precise references to the Etruscan character of various cities in these territories (in Campania: Capua, Nola, Acerrae, Marcina, and others; in northern Italy: Felsina, Spina, Ravenna, and others; to these may be added evidence of a relative supremacy over Latium, with particular reference to Rome). The archaeological and epigraphic data confirm these references and permit scholars at least in part to state precisely the limits of the Etruscans' occupation and colonization and of their commercial and cultural influence.

Early expansion. The territorial expansion of the Etruscans is linked to their maritime power, of which the classical sources speak insistently. Etruscan presence overseas is recorded in such places as the Aeolian Islands and in general in the waters of Sicily, in Corsica, Sardinia, the Balearic Isles, and even on the coasts of Spain. A Greek source cited by Diodorus Siculus tells of a planned Etruscan naval expedition beyond the Pillars of Hercules (Straits of Gibraltar) to colonize a prosperous island in the Atlantic, perhaps Madeira or the Canaries; the expedition was not carried out because of the opposition of the Carthaginians. The memory of these exploits was embodied in the proverbial notoriety of the Etruscans as dreaded pirates.

Etruscan maritime power

Etruscan maritime activity in the Mediterranean coincided and competed with that of the Phoenicians and the Greeks. Its initial purpose was probably to extend and guarantee Etruscan commerce and its profits by controlling the seaways and creating markets in foreign lands. In these exchanges, metals mined in the ore-bearing

(Left) Bronze relief from the caldron support known as the Loeb Tripod, c. 540 BC, from San Valentino, near Perugia; height 93 cm. In the Loeb Collection, Staatliche Antikensammlungen and Glyptothek, Munich. (Right) Painted terra-cotta statue of Apollo, attributed to Vulca, *c.* 500 BC, from the Temple of Veii; height 175.26 cm. In the Museo Nazionale di Villa Giulia, Rome.

(Left From M. Pallottino, "Art of the Etruscans," Thames and Hudson, 1955, by Martin Hurlimann; (right) Alinari

zones of the western Mediterranean—particularly copper, iron, and silver—must certainly have been of primary importance. The Etruscans possessed rich mines (*e.g.*, near Vetulonia and on the island of Elba) and utilized them for their own exclusive advantage—for local needs or for selling and exporting the metals themselves—while jealously protecting these priceless sources of wealth against Phoenician and Greek cupidity. This explains the extraordinary economic development of some of the Etruscan coastal cities in the archaic period and the recurrent Greek push toward the ore-bearing districts of northern Tyrrhenia.

The wealth of the Etruscan cities is demonstrated by the enormous quantity and precious quality of their imports of Oriental and Greek goods between the early 7th and early 5th centuries BC; archaeological discoveries also reveal a widespread exportation of Etruscan products during this period to all the Mediterranean lands and especially to the west—principally vases of bucchero (a shiny black ceramic) and painted vases of Etrusco-Corinthian style. Thus the maximum Etruscan commercial and naval expansion must be placed between the later 7th and early 6th centuries BC, before the full predominance of the Greek navigators from Asiatic Ionia.

But Etruscan maritime activity probably began a good deal earlier; according to the historian Ephorus, Tyrrhenian pirates hindered the establishment of the first Greek colonies on the eastern coast of Sicily in about the mid-8th century BC, when Etruria was still in the Villanovan culture stage. Recent discoveries have revealed the Villanovan culture in Campania also, where the historical presence of the Etruscans is verified by literary sources and by Etruscan archaic inscriptions. These and other considerations indicate that the Etruscans may have preceded their conquest of Campania with a very ancient coastal colonization, in competition with the first Greek settlements of Pythecusae, Cumae, and Parthenope (now Naples). Campania would thus, by the dawn of historic times, have been about to become a zone of encounter between civilizations and, in certain respects, the key to the domination of Italy. In this framework, the very presence of the Villanovan culture in the plain of the Po could be evidence of an early Etruscan expansion beyond the Apennines, constituting the nucleus of the future Etruscan dominion of northern Italy.

Relations with the Greeks and Carthaginians. Sources indicate that the ancient maritime expansion of the Etruscans in the Mediterranean was an episodic phenomenon, prematurely arrested and then turned back and wiped out by more powerful activities of the Greeks and Carthaginians. Greek colonization in the central and western Mediterranean was strengthened beginning early in the 6th century by new commercial and migratory currents from the coasts of Anatolia. In this same period Carthage was creating a vast commercial empire that absorbed all the area of Phoenician colonization in the west and precluded all further movement by the Etruscans in that direction.

Growth of Greek and Carthaginian power in the Mediterranean

The Etruscan relationship with the Greeks was twofold: it involved intensive commercial and cultural exchanges, from which derived profound and irreversible Hellenization of Etruria, and a basic rivalry for supremacy in the Tyrrhenian Sea and on the Italian peninsula itself, often intensifying into open conflicts. Greek-Etruscan relations may have resulted from diversities of interests of individual cities and from changing circumstances; but an antagonism of much vaster historical importance already was being established during the 6th century BC between the Greek colonies and Carthage, above all regarding the domination of Sicily. This led to a rapprochement between Etruscans and Carthaginians and to lasting ties of solidarity and alliance against the Greeks.

In this historic context were set various episodes, known fragmentarily from notices in the ancient sources. For example there are records of repeated Etruscan attacks on the island of Lipara, colonized by the Rhodians but perhaps originally a lair of Tyrrhenian piratry against nearby Sicily and the Strait of Messina, as well as other naval actions of the Etruscans and the Carthaginians along the Sicilian coast. These were probably the last manifestations of an Etruscan presence in the southern Tyrrhenian Sea. But already toward the mid-6th century BC the Greeks had approached the coast of Etruria in founding the colony of Alalia in Corsica. A coalition fleet of Etruscan and Carthaginian ships battled the Phocaean fleet in the Sea of Sardinia (*c.* 540 BC). The consequence of this memorable battle was the Phocaean withdrawal from Corsica and the passing of the island into Etruscan control, while Carthage had a free hand for the conquest of Sardinia (effectuated in the late 6th and early 5th centuries BC). Notwithstanding this breathing spell, the Etruscan sphere of influence and of action within the northern Tyrrhenian Sea was thence forward reduced. In the late 6th century political control of Latium was lost with the fall of the monarch of the Tarquins at Rome. If political significance can be attached to a gesture of homage by the king of Caere to the Phoenician goddess Astarte (according to the inscriptions on the Pyrgi gold plates), then even the Carthaginian allies themselves made their preponderance felt over Etruria. A further regression took place with the establishment of Syracusan hegemony in Sicily, which led to the defeat of the Carthaginians at Himera in 480 BC, and with a famous Etruscan naval loss (474 BC) in the waters of Cumae (inscribed on Etruscan bronze helmets dedicated by Hieron of Syracuse in the sanctuary of Olympia). The way was thus opened for repeated Syracusan naval incursions against the coast of Etruria, including the mining zone.

Reduction of Etruscan presence in southern Italy

The loss of dominion on the high seas led to economic crises in the Etruscan coastal centres; the archaeological documentation shows a progressive diminution of foreign imports, ending with their near total disappearance and in the cultural and artistic decadence that characterized the 5th and 4th centuries BC. For this period some centres further inland, such as Veii, Orvieto, and Clusium, enjoyed a certain prosperity. But evidently, with the Tyrrhenian seaways closed to them, the Etruscans sought new outlets for their maritime commerce on the Adriatic Sea and new directions for land traffic toward the Alpine zones and toward central and northern Europe. There were sudden and impressive developments of Po valley and Adriatic Etruria, particularly the harbour city of Spina at the mouth of the Po and the so-called Certosa civilization at Felsina (now Bologna) and at Marzabotto in the valley of the Reno. A necropolis at Spina has in recent decades yielded treasures of Attic painted ceramics of the 5th century BC.

Etruscan decline

Celtic incursions. But even this Etruscan vitality in the north was short-lived. The progressive infiltration and pressure of the Celts, who had penetrated and settled in the plain of the Po, eventually suffocated and overpowered the flourishing Etruscan urban communities, almost completely destroying their civilization by the mid-4th century BC and thus returning a large part of northern Italy to a protohistoric stage of culture. Meanwhile, the Gallic Senones firmly occupied the Picenum district on the Adriatic Sea, and Celtic incursions reached on the one hand Tyrrhenian Etruria and Rome (captured and burned about 390 BC) and on the other as far as Puglia. The Etruscan dominion in Campania was destroyed late in the 5th century by Italic Samnites descending from the mountains of Molise to the Tyrrhenian Sea.

The Roman conquest of Etruria. In the 4th century BC the picture of ancient Italy appeared profoundly transformed. As the protagonists of history, the eastern Italic people of Umbro-Sabellian stock diffused over most of the peninsula; the Syracusan empire and lastly the growing power of Rome had been substituted for the Etruscans (and for the Greek colonies of southern Italy). The Etruscan world had been reduced to a circumscribed, regional life, secluded in its traditional values; this situation determined its progressive passage into the political system created by Rome.

Rome under Etruscan influence

Probably beginning late in the 6th century BC and for at least a century under the Tarquins and other Etruscan monarchies or tyrannies, Rome experienced a deep Etruscan imprint and accepted extensive Etruscan elements into its population, reaching a level of economic and cultural splendour and of political power similar to that of the great Etruscan metropolises nearby, such as Caere and Veii. Etruscan influences related to such essential aspects of civilization as urban planning, architecture, art, religion, technology, and dress continued beyond Etruscan rule. Thus Rome, although remaining fundamentally Latin in language and in spirit, could yet be called by the ancients an Etruscan city.

The rivalry between Rome and the Etruscan cities, at least in the beginning, must have had the character of a contest between neighbouring countries participating in a common civilization, like the rivalry between Etruscan cities themselves. This was especially the case in the monarchical period, when Rome found itself under attack from Vulci and from Clusium. But already in the 5th century Rome gravitated toward the Latin world and became part of the Latin league, progressively assuming its leadership. Rome initiated a period of continuous border conflicts with closely neighbouring Veii lasting for almost a century and ending with the defeat and destruction of Veii and the inclusion of all its territory in that of Rome (396 BC). The Romans thus penetrated into the heart of southern Etruria, and for about another century the Etruscan states of this region faced alternating situations of amity and of war.

Roman policy was oriented toward control of Latium, of Campania, and then of regions farther south, with the aim of containing and eventually fragmenting the territorial power of the Samnites and their allies and of replacing them in hegemony over the peninsula; but the military conquest of Etruria probably did not constitute an interest or a necessity for Rome. Various Etruscan cities, especially in the north, such as Clusium, Perugia, and Arezzo, entered peacefully into alliance with the Romans. But when the Etruscan league, in conjunction with the activity of the Samnites and the Gauls (Celts), seemed to represent an effective and immediate danger to Rome (as in 311–310 and in 295 BC), the league's aspirations were quickly smashed. Rome also took Volsinii in 265 BC and deported its inhabitants, perhaps from Orvieto to the site of present-day Bolsena.

Alliances with Rome

By the mid-3rd century all Etruria appears to have been pacified and firmly subjected to Roman hegemony. Except for a few cases of annexation or special regimes, the Etruscan cities and their territories preserved a formal autonomy as independent states, with their own magistracy and other organs of government and their own religious and cultural traditions, until 90 BC, when Roman citizenship was extended to all the Italic peoples. This amounted to the complete political unification of the Roman-Italic state and to the disappearance of the last pretense of individuality and autonomy for the Etruscan city-states and for all the other allies of the peninsula. There followed a rapid process of romanization of Etruria and the replacement of its national language by Latin.

OTHER ITALIC PEOPLES

Local populations in areas colonized by Greece. The presence of the Siculi in Sicily and in the Italian peninsula is attested by the historical sources (Thucydides and Polybius). But the limits of their diffusion and their connections with other peoples of the peninsula (such as the Ligurians, the Itali, the Oenotrii, the Ausones) are more difficult to distinguish. A few small non-Greek inscriptions found in eastern Sicily and referable to the Siculi (the most noteworthy was found at Centuripe), coin legends, and Siculan words reported by classical writers demonstrate the Indo-European character of the Siculan language, which seems to show an affinity with Latin and also has connections with the Umbro-Sabellian dialects. The immigration of the Siculi from the Italian peninsula into Sicily goes back to a prehistoric but not extremely early epoch, considering that there are some echoes of it in tradition and that a continental archaeological influence suddenly appears at the end of the Bronze Age. The characteristic Siculan iron culture, evident in the necropolises of Pantalica near Syracuse and of Finoc-

The Siculi

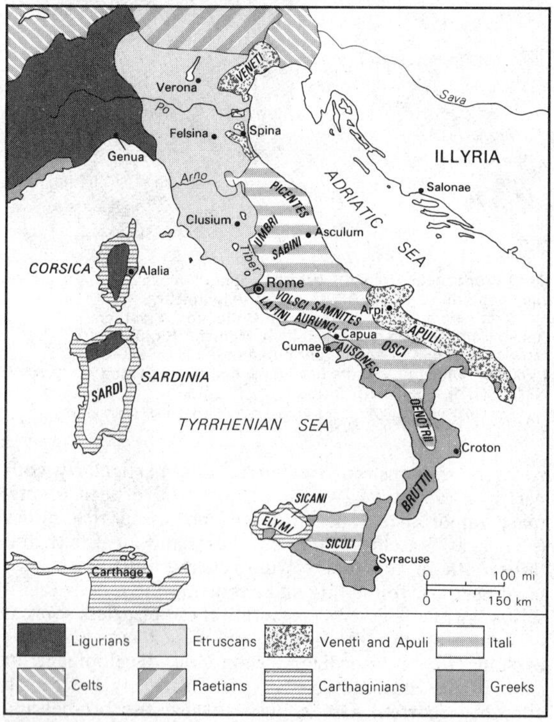

Distribution of peoples of ancient Italy (*c.* 500 BC).

chito near Noto, flourished between the 9th and the 5th centuries BC and was progressively submerged in the superior civilization of the Greeks.

Evidence is quite scarce for the Siculi in the peninsula and for the other primitive indigenous populations of what is now Calabria and of Lucania (the Oenotrii, Ausones, Chones, Morgetes, and Itali) and Campania (the Ausones and Opici). Modern scholars have hypothesized that along the Tyrrhenian coastal arc there extended in earliest times a belt of paleo-Italic populations (called western Italics or Proto-Latins) originally related to the Latins and distinct from the eastern Italic peoples inhabiting the Apennine and Adriatic regions. (The archaeological documentation consists of cemeteries with Iron Age graves, but there are also traces of cremation necropolises, especially in the province of Salerno and in Calabria.) Large fortified towns arose, particularly in the interior zones of Lucania. But the ethnic individuality of these ancient peoples was progressively obliterated between the 8th and the 4th centuries BC by the Greek penetration and by the expansion of the Etruscans and the eastern Italics (Samnites, Lucanians, Bruttii).

Western Italic peoples

The Apulians. The inhabitants of the southeastern extremity of the Italian peninsula formed a definitely characterized group of populations that the ancients often called Iapyges (whence the geographical term Iapygia, in which "Apulia" may be recognized). The territory included the Salentini and the Messapii peoples in the Salentine Peninsula (ancient Calabria) and the Peucetii and the Dauni farther north. (Sometimes the designations Iapyges and Messapii are used with identical reference.) Ancient tradition insists upon an overseas origin for these tribes, held to be Cretan or Illyrian. The Iapigian, or more commonly, Messapian, language is known from a considerable series of public funerary, votive, monetary, and other inscriptions written in the Greek alphabet and found in the Apulian area, especially in the Salentine Peninsula, from words reported by the ancient writers, and from toponomastic (local place name) data. Messapian is without doubt an Indo-European language, distinct from Latin and from the Umbro-Sabellian dialects, with Balkan and central European analogies. This confirms the overseas provenance of the Iapygians from the Balkans, the more so because there existed in Illyria a tribe called the Iapodes and because a people known as the Iapuzkus lived farther north, on the Adriatic coast of Italy. Rather than a true immigration, however, there was a gradual prehistoric penetration of trans-Adriatic elements. The expansion of the Iapyigians must have brought them to Lucania and even to what is now Calabria, as would be deduced from traditional and archaeological indications.

Apulian civilization

The Apulians' civilization, which was considerably influenced by that of the nearby Greek colonies, developed from the 9th to the 3rd centuries BC. In the most ancient period there were pit graves, sometimes in large stone tumuli. In the Siponto area, near what is now Manfredonia, the graves were accompanied by anthropomorphic stelae with geometric bas-reliefs. Geometrically painted ceramics in linear motifs persisted to the threshold of the Hellenistic Age. Later graves took the form of large trunks and of catacombs with paintings on the sides. Burial was the disposition exclusively used.

Beginning in archaic times, large cities developed, linked to each other by bonds of confederation. These included Herdonea (now Ordona), Canusium (Canosa), Rubi (Ruvo), Gnathia, Brundisium (Brindisi), Uria (Oria), Lupiae (Lecce), Rudiae, and Manduria. They preserved their independence, tenaciously defended against the Greeks, until the age of the Roman conquest.

The Latins. The Latin nation had a relatively limited territory, south of the Tiber, which was reduced, in historic times, by the invasion of the Volsci to the region between the Alban hills and the Aurunci mountains (the so-called Latium Novum). The principal Latin centres included Alba Longa; Tusculum; Lavinium; Ardea; Tibur (now Tivoli); Praeneste (Palestrina); and the already Volscianized cities of Velitrae (Velletri), Signia (Segni), Cora (Cori), Satricum, Antium (Anzio), and Anxur (Terracina). The importance of the Latins is essentially linked with the fortunes of Rome, the forward bulwark of Latinity in the direction of the Etruscan realm. Intermixtures with the legends of the origin of Rome make the ethnographic traditions of Latium very diverse and complex. The linguistic evidence, which begins with inscriptions of the 7th to 6th centuries BC, indicates an individuality of the Latin world distinct from the neighbouring Etruscan and eastern Italic peoples.

The Latins had a federal organization, centred at the sanctuary of Jupiter on Albanus Mons. Their religious heritage survived in the beliefs and cults of the Roman world. The most ancient Latin culture (9th–7th centuries BC) was characterized by cremation as the funeral rite, in common with that of Etruscan and northern Italian territory, and by an iron culture showing affinities with the proto-Villanovan culture and with the cultures of Tyrrhenian southern Italy. Etruscan political control of Latium (probably 7th–6th centuries) coincided with an evident Etruscan cultural and artistic influence; while from the south and from the sea, elements of Greek civilization penetrated, beginning with the alphabet.

Latin culture

North of Latium lived tribes ethnically akin to the Latins, with principal centres at Capena, Narce, and Falerii (whence the name Faliscans). Their political and cultural history merges with that of the Etruscans. The Faliscan dialect, known from inscriptions, was originally Latin but was contaminated and modified by eastern Italic and Etruscan elements.

The eastern Italics. A great part of the central and southern Italian peninsula was occupied in protohistoric and historic times by populations forming a vast ethnic and linguistic unit—the eastern Italics or Umbro-Sabellians. To the south, in the mountains of the Abruzzo, lived the Samnites, who later spread into Campania, Lucania, and what is now Calabria. In the centre were the Vestini, Paeligni, Marrucini, Marsi, Aequi, Volsci, and Sabini. Further north lived the Umbri. The origin and relationship of all these peoples is unclear. Ancient ethnographic traditions bearing on central Italy link the Samnites to the Sabines and the Sabines to the Umbri, locating their primitive centre of dispersion in the Rieti basin and in the area of Amiterno. Their diffusion was attributed to the mass emigration of an entire generation in search of a new homeland.

Origin of eastern Italics

The linguistic data prove the unity of the group of eastern-Italic idioms, belonging to the Indo-European stock but differing from the Latin. Within this group may be distinguished a southern variant (Sabellic or Oscan) known from an abundant harvest of epigraphic documents from Samnium, Campania, and southern Italy, and a variant to be attributed to the Samnites and to a large part of the minor stocks of central Italy, including the Sabines, known from isolated inscriptions in central Italy. On the other hand a northern (Umbrian) variant is represented by inscriptions of Umbria—principally bronze tablets from Gubbio, inscribed between the 4th and 1st centuries BC by a brotherhood of Umbrian priests—and by a bronze tablet from Velletri. The eastern Italic words reported by the classical writers, as well as toponomastics, confirm these conclusions.

Notwithstanding the original unity of stock and of language, these populations had diverse histories and cultures. The Samnites from Molise (the Caraceni, the Pentri, and the Frentani) in the 5th and 4th centuries BC occupied Campania—where they vanquished Etruscans and Greeks and assumed from the local tribes the name Opici, or Osci—as well as Lucania (with the Hirpini or Lucani), reaching what is now Calabria—where they took the name Bruttii—and finally Sicily. Defeated by Rome in the Samnite wars (4th and early 3rd centuries BC), the Samnites tried for the last time, in the period of the Social War (90–83 BC), to counterpose to the Romans an Italic nationality of their own. A considerable difference existed between the culture of the mountain Samnites—organized in confederate tribes centred on fortified villages and in the 5th and 4th centuries still retaining aspects of the "iron culture"—and the high civilization of the Campani and Lucani established in the ancient

The Samnites

cities of Capua, Nola, Nocera, and Paestum and dominated by Greek and Etruscan influence.

Some central tribes—the Marrucini, Vestini, Paeligni and Marsi—appear to be linked historically, politically, and culturally to the Samnites. The case is different with the Sabines, the Aequi, and the Volsci, whose period of expansion (6th and 5th centuries) is closely connected with earliest Rome and who had early contact with the Etrusco-Latin civilization.

The Umbri

The diffusion of the Umbri toward the north and beyond the Apennines lent credence to the ancient traditions relating to the great size of their territory. The traditions, however, are more probably based on the fact that the name Umbri is derived from that of the most ancient population, probably not Indo-European and certainly not Italic, living in the Apennine region before the diffusion of the eastern Italics. The history of the Umbrian cities—Iguvium (now Gubbio), Hispellum (Spello), Spoletium (Spoleto), Tuder (Todi), and others—is known only beginning with the period of the struggle of the Etruscans and Gauls against Rome. Umbrian civilization is revealed by the Gubbio Tablets, a document unique in its kind. The Umbrian artistic and material culture derived in large part from that of Etruria.

The populations of the Picenum. In historic times expansion of the eastern Italic peoples placed them firmly along the Adriatic coastal tract corresponding to what is now the Marches region. Epigraphic and archaeological data give evidence also of the presence in the Picenum (an ancient region between the Apennines and the Adriatic) of the trans-Adriatic Liburni and the pre-Indo-European Asili. It is possible that there were established here elements that had come by sea from Illyria (the Gubbio tablets mention the Iapuzkus, whose name recalls that of the Illyrian Iapodes and of the Apulian Iapyges). But inscriptions in the southern Piceno seem to exhibit a close kinship with the Umbro-Sabellic dialects.

Piceno civilization

A material civilization flowered between the 8th and 5th centuries in the northern Abruzzo and in the Marches. This civilization is represented by the rich funerary equipment of burial tombs, whose type and decoration present affinities with the iron culture of Tyrrhenian and northern Italy and with that of the Balkans, and show Greek influence. Cremation tombs of Villanovan type have been found at Fermo. Also noteworthy is the presence of stone funerary sculpture. North of Ancona is a cultural variant, particularly in the necropolis of Novilara near Pesaro, where inscriptions are in a dialect other than that of the southern Piceno and difficult to classify.

It may be held that the middle-Adriatic iron cultures expressed an early archaic mixture of eastern Italic and trans-Adriatic peoples, influenced by the Etruscans and the Greeks. Contributing to their decline were the Gauls and Syracusans, who established themselves in this area in the 4th century BC. In the 3rd century the Picenum was already totally conquered by the Romans.

Venetic origins

The Veneti. Ancient tradition held the Veneti to be a Illyrian people who, coming from the east, took possession of the region named for them (Venetia). To them are linked the Histri, the Carni, and various Alpine tribes. (The name of the Veneti, or its root, is widely diffused in the ethnic anomastics of central Europe and even of Asia.) The Venetic language is known from funerary and votive inscriptions, from words cited by the classic writers, and from onomastic and toponomastic data. It is an Indo-European language of archaic type, with similarities to the Latin and the Germanic.

The principal centres of the Veneti, located at the western margin of the territory, were Padua and Este. Their culture developed from the 9th century to the period of romanization, with relationships with the Golasecca, Villanovan, and Etruscan cultures and with the transalpine Hallstatt culture. Maximum development occurred in the 6th–4th centuries BC; particularly noteworthy is the production of figured bronze *situlae* (conical vessels). In the final period Gallic (Celtic) influences are found. Phenomena parallel to those of Este appear in Istria. The Veneti were horse breeders and peaceful traders and navigators; protected by the waters of the lower Po and the lower Adige, they preserved their independence against Etruscan expansion and Celtic invasion and in the 3rd century BC entered into peaceful alliance with Rome.

The Ligurians. For the ancients, the name Ligures designated the peoples of northwest Italy, including northern Tuscany, Liguria, Piedmont, and part of what is now Lombardy. Historical tradition also placed them in central Italy, while the classical writers and toponomastic affinities give them a broader diffusion beyond the Alps. The Ligurians included also the peoples of Corsica. The more ancient Greeks gave all the peoples of the western world the common designation of Ligures.

Linguistic data—furnished by toponomastics, lexical survivals, and by Ligurian words cited by classical writers—betray the presence of a pre-Indo-European Mediterranean stratum akin to that of western Europe. Inscriptions found in upper Lombardy and in the Ticino exhibit Indo-European characteristics and in particular Celtic influences. Thus the Liguri seem to belong to an environment formed in northern Italy after the Celtic invasion and called Celto-Ligures.

Ligurian culture

The Etruscan expansion in the plain of the Po and the invasion of the Gauls confined the Ligurians between the Alps and the Apennines, where they offered such resistance to Roman penetration that they gained a reputation with the ancients for primitive fierceness. Among the more considerable Ligurian monuments are rock engravings and anthropomorphic sculptures analogous to those of southern France, found in Lunigiana and Corsica. Some of these artistic manifestations are repeated in territories farther east. But it remains doubtful whether the similar cultural imprint indicates an original identity of stock. Ligurian and Celto-Ligurian tombs of the Lombard lakes region, often holding cremations, reveal a special iron culture called the culture of Golasecca; while Ligurian sepulchres of the Italian Riviera and of Provence, also holding cremations, exhibit Etruscan and Celtic influences.

Populations of central northern Italy and of the Alps. The ethnography of the Po and Alpine regions is complex and obscure because of the early spread of Etruscan culture and colonization. The ancients record two major ethnic groups (aside from the Etruscans and the Veneti): the Euganei, inhabiting the plain and the Alpine foothills, and the Raeti, in the valleys of the Trentino and the Alto Adige. Minor peoples in the region belonged to one or the other of these stocks or to Ligurian stocks; with regard to many of these peoples the sources speak of an Illyrian or an Etruscan origin.

Late inscriptions discovered in the Adige River valley and on the plain have a dialect showing some affinities to Etruscan. Some scholars see in this a blending of local and Etruscan elements, while others speak of an indigenous pre-Indo-European language with Indo-European influences. Primitive toponomastics confirm the existence of a linguistic stratum that could be defined Raetian or Raeto-Euganean but distinguish it sharply from the Venetic and probably also from the Ligurian. Other inscriptions from the Val Camonica and the Garda district attest to a more noticeable Indo-European dialect, due perhaps to Celtic and Latin influences. To the west are the so-called Lepontian inscriptions.

Original central- and sub-Alpine populations

Thus in the central-Alpine and sub-Alpine area, there were original populations, different from the Veneti and the Etruscans, whose kinship with the Lingurians remains uncertain. The distinction between Euganean and Raetic tribes can be based only upon an approximate geographical criterion. To this original ethnic stratum may have belonged the most ancient inhabitants of the region, before the immigration of the Illyrian Veneti and the Etruscan conquest; certain cremation sepulchres of the Verona and Mantua regions may be attributed to them. Perhaps the existence of a Venetian goddess Reitia, recorded by Strabo and mentioned in inscriptions from Este, is some proof of a Raeta-Euganean cultural persistence in the territory occupied by the Veneti.

BIBLIOGRAPHY. A comprehensive, up-to-date account of the peoples and the civilizations of pre-Roman Italy is lacking. Basic, though partly outdated, is J. WHATMOUGH, *The*

Foundations of Roman Italy (1937). See also D. RANDALL-MACIVER, *Italy Before the Romans* (1928); M. PALLOTTINO, "Popolazioni storiche dell'Italia antica," *Guida allo studio della civiltà romana antica*, vol. 1, pp. 71–90 (1952), and *Civiltà artistica etrusco-italica*, pp. 9–39 (1971); and G.M.A. RICHTER, *Ancient Italy* (1955). The chief problems are discussed in the light of the recent discoveries by J. HEURGON in *Rome et la Méditerranée occidentale jusqu'aux guerres puniques* (1969). For the languages, see E. PULGRAM, *The Tongues of Italy: Prehistory and History* (1958); V. PISANI, *Le lingue dell'Italia antica oltre il latino*, 2nd ed. (1964). Leading papers on this subject matter are published in the *Studi Etruschi* (annually since 1927). An exhaustive summary of present knowledge of the Etruscan world is offered by M. PALLOTTINO, *Etruscologia*, 6th ed. (1968; Eng. trans., *The Etruscans*, 1956). See also D. STRONG, *The Early Etruscans* (1968). Among the most valuable and recent works dealing with other individual Italic peoples, civilization, and languages are: L. BERNABO BREA, *Sicily Before the Greeks* (1957); R. PERONI, *Archeologia della Puglia preistorica* (1967); O. PARLANGELI, *Studi messapici* (1960); A. ALFOLDI, *Early Rome and the Latins* (1965); G. GIACOMELLI, *La lingua falisca* (1963); G. DEVOTO, *Gli antichi Italici*, 3rd ed. (1967); E.T. SALMON, *Samnium and the Samnites* (1967); G.A. MANSUELLI and R. SCARANI, *L'Emilia prima dei Romani* (1961); and G.B. PELLEGRINI and A.L. PROSDOCIMI, *La lingua venetica*, 2 vol. (1967).

Italy

With a shape that has been likened frequently to a high-heeled boot apparently about to prod its triangular subject island of Sicily, the peninsular home of the European nation of Italy juts deep into the Mediterranean Sea. Another important island, Sardinia, lies some 160 miles west of its "shin." The magnificent mountain barrier of the Alps forms a northern boundary, which, historically, has hindered marauders less than might be supposed; these mountains separate Italy from France, Switzerland, Austria, and Yugoslavia and extend all the way down the Italian peninsula as a less elevated chain, the Apennines. Areas of plain, which are practically limited to the great northern oval of the Po Valley, cover a mere 23 percent of the total national area of 116,000 square miles (301,000 square kilometres); 42 percent is hilly and 35 percent mountainous, providing variations to the generally temperate climate.

The mountainous landscape of Italy has long influenced political and economic developments in the region by encouraging numerous independent states and by permitting only a meagre agriculture, providing grain sufficient only for a subsistence economy. Increased cultivation has caused deforestation. Since much of the land is mountainous, the population (approaching a total of 54,000,000 by the early 1970s) is dense—466 persons per square mile; it is increasing at a relatively modest 0.7 percent a year. With 1½ percent of the total area of the Soviet Union, for example, Italy has the equivalent of about 22 percent of that country's population. Since World War II, increasing numbers of Italians have abandoned the countryside for the rapidly industrializing cities, often creating severe dislocations in traditional ways of life.

The Italian economy, now ranked about seventh in the world, blends areas as diverse as the "industrial triangle," formed by Milan, Turin, and Genoa, dating from around 1900, and the notoriously backward regions of the south and the islands, which are, however, being developed, mostly with state aid.

Agriculture, operating in difficult natural and economic conditions, contributes 12 percent of the gross national product (GNP); industry, 42 percent; and public and private services, 46 percent. Sufficient wheat is grown for the population, and vegetables, fruit, wine, and oil are cultivated in suitable districts. Cattle raising, however, is less advanced; meat and dairy produce is imported.

Italian industry includes every type of production. Though mineral resources are scarce, imported raw materials since World War II have boosted siderurgy (the metallurgy of iron and steel), other metallurgy, and construction. The chemical industry also flourishes, but textiles lag behind those of the rest of Europe. Services, particularly tourism, are very important, and efforts have been made to provide comprehensive networks of *autostrade* (express highways). The heavy international exchange shows a generally favourable balance of payments.

The peninsula has a proud tradition dating from the days of the ancient Roman Empire. From its unification in the second half of the 19th century until 1946, Italy was a monarchy. Then it became a parliamentary republic, operating under a constitution of 1948. The republic is subdivided into regions (*regioni*), provinces (*provincie*), and municipalities (*comuni*); these local bodies enjoy a certain autonomy, especially the regions, which differ widely in economic development. A similar diversity characterizes political life, which features a multiplicity of parties. The powerful Christian Democrat Party (Democrazia Cristiana, or DC) and the strong Italian Communist Party (Partito Comunista Italiano, or PCI) generally obtain, respectively, over a third and over a quarter of all votes cast, and there are a number of smaller parties, representing groups of right-wing, centre, and left-wing persuasions. No party enjoys a dependable majority, and coalition governments have been notoriously unstable in the post-World War II decades.

In the 1960s and early 1970s workers' unions have been increasingly important in national life. They are grounded in various confederations, principally the Confederazione Generale Italiana del Lavoro (General Confederation of Labour, or CGIL), controlled in effect by the Communist Party. Employers' groups and the great state bureaucracies also form important pressure groups in this often sharply polarized society.

Italy is part of the European Economic Community and of the Council of Europe and belongs to many other international organizations. With its strategic geographical position on the southern flank of Europe, Italy has since World War II played a fairly important role in the North Atlantic Treaty Organization (NATO).

The article that follows provides a survey of contemporary Italy. For history, see ITALY, HISTORY OF; for related physical features, see ALPS MOUNTAIN RANGES; APENNINES RANGE; TIBER RIVER; VESUVIUS, MOUNT; and ETNA, MOUNT; for information on Italian cities, including their history, see the articles FLORENCE; MILAN; NAPLES; ROME; and VENICE. See also SICILY and SARDINIA.

This article is divided into the following sections:

(Li.L.)

I. The land

THE NATURAL ENVIRONMENT

Relief features. Italy is largely mountainous, with 35 percent of its territory occupied by ranges of more than 2,300 feet, 42 percent by hills, and only 23 percent by plains. There are two mountain systems: the scenic Alps, part of which lie within neighbouring countries, France, Switzerland, Austria, and Yugoslavia; and the Apennines, which form the spine of the entire peninsula and of the island of Sicily. A third mountain system exists in the two large islands to the west, Italian Sardinia and French Corsica.

Mountain ranges. The rugged Alps run in a broad west-to-east arc from the Colle di Cadibona (Cadibona Pass), near Savona, on the Gulf of Genoa, to the north of Trieste, at the head of the Adriatic Sea. The section properly called Alpine is the border district that includes the highest masses, made up of weathered Hercynian rocks, dating from the Carboniferous or the Permian periods (345,000,000–225,000,000 years ago). The Alps have rugged, very high peaks, reaching more than 13,000 feet in various spectacular formations, characterized as pyramidal, pinnacled, rounded, or needlelike. The valleys were heavily scoured by glaciers operating in the Quaternary Period (the last 2,500,000 years); there are still more than 1,000 glaciers left, though in a phase of retreat, about 110 having disappeared in the last half century or so.

The three main Alpine groups

The Alpine mountain mass falls into three main groups: the Western Alps, running in Italy, north to south from Aosta to the Cadibona Pass, with the Gran Paradiso (13,323 feet [4,061 metres]) and Monte Viso (12,602 feet [3,841 metres]); the Central Alps, running west to east, from the Western Alps to the Brenner Pass, leading into Austria and the upper Adige, also with high peaks, such as Monte Bianco (15,771 feet [4,807 metres]), the Matterhorn (14,692 feet [4,478 metres]), Monte Rosa (Italy's highest peak, shared with Switzerland, 15,203 feet [4,634 metres]), and Ortles (12,792 feet [3,899 metres]); and the Eastern Alps, running west to east from the Brenner to Trieste and including the Dolomites (Alpi Dolomitiche), with Monte Marmolada (10,964 feet [3,342 metres]). The Italian foothills of the Alps, reaching no higher than 8,200 feet, lie between these great ranges and the Po Valley. They are composed mainly of limestone and sedimentary rocks. A notable feature is the karst system of underground caves and streams, especially characteristic of the Carso, the limestone plateau between the Eastern Alps and Illyria.

The Apennines are the long system of mountains and hills that runs down the Italian peninsula from the Cadibona Pass to the tip of Calabria and continues in Sicily. The range is about 745 miles long; it is only about 20 miles wide at either end but about 120 miles wide in the Central Apennines, east of Rome, where the Gran Sasso d'Italia group provides the highest peak (9,560 feet [2,914 metres]) and the only glacier on the peninsula, Calderone, the southernmost in Europe. The Apennines are predominantly of sandstone and limestone marl (clay) in the north; of limestone and dolomite (magnesian limestone) in the centre; and of limestone, weathered rock, and Hercynian granite in the south. On either side of the central mass are grouped two considerably lower masses, composed in general of more recent and softer rocks, such as sandstone. These are the sub-Apennines, which run in the east from Monferrato to the Golfo di Taranto and in the west from Florence southward through Tuscany and Umbria to Rome. This latter range is separated from the main Apennines by the valleys of the Arno and the Tiber rivers. At the outer flanks of the sub-Apennines two allied series of limestone and volcanic rock extend to the coast. They include, on the west, the Alpi Apuane (Apuan Alps), famous for their marbles; farther south, the Colline Metallifere (Ore Mountains; more than 3,400 feet), abundant in minerals; then various extinct volcanoes occupied by crater lakes, such as that of Bolsena; then cavernous mountains, such as Lepini and Circeo, and the partially or still fully active volcanic group of the Campi Flegrei and Vesuvius; and finally the limestone mountains of the peninsulas of Amalfi and Cilento. The extensions on the Adriatic coast are simpler, comprising only the small promontory of Monte Conero, the higher peninsula of Promontorio del Gargano (Gargano Plateau; 3,461 feet), and the Salentine Peninsula, in Puglia. All of these are limestone.

In Sardinia there are two mountain masses, separated by the long plain of Campidano, which runs from the Gulfo dell'Asinara southeastward across the island to the Golfo di Cagliari. The group in the southwest is small and low, formed from sediments, mostly mineralized, of the early Paleozoic Era (perhaps 570,000,000 to 225,000,000 years ago). The northeastern mass reaches a height of more than 6,000 feet at Gennargentu; the underlying foundation is basically metamorphic (heat-altered) rock, covered in the northeast by Paleozoic granite and partially covered in the northwest by Mesozoic limestones (65,000,000 to 225,000,000 years old) and by sandstone and Cenozoic (65,000,000 to 2,500,000 years old) clays. There are caves on the seacoast and inland where limestones predominate.

Present volcanic action had its first origins in the Pliocene Epoch and Quaternary Period (covering the last 7,000,000 years) and is represented by the Campi Flegrei, near Naples, and the neighbouring islands, such as Ischia; by Vesuvius; by the Isole Eolie; and by Etna, on Sicily. Phenomena related to volcanism include thermal springs in the Colli Euganei, *vulcanelli* (mud springs) at Viterbo, and emissions of gas at Pozzuoli.

Seismic activity, leading to earthquakes, is rare in the Alps and the Po Valley; it is infrequent but occasionally strong in the Alpine foothills; and it may be catastrophic in the central and southern Apennines and on Sicily. Seaquakes sometimes occur in Sicily, such as that at Messina in 1908.

The plains. Plains cover only 23 percent of the area of Italy. Some of these, such as the Po Valley and the Tavoliere di Puglia (Plain of Puglia), are ancient sea gulfs filled by alluvium. Others, such as the Tavoliere di Lecce (Plain of Lecce), in Puglia, flank the sea on rocky plateaus about 65 to 100 feet high and are formed of ancient land levelled by the sea and subsequently uplifted. Plains in the interior, such as the long Val di Chiana (Chiana Valley), are made by alluvial or other filling of ancient basins. The most extensive and important plain in Italy, that of the Po Valley, occupies more than 17,000 square miles of the 27,000 square miles of Italian plain land. It ranges in altitude from sea level up to 1,800 feet, the greater part being below 330 feet. Through it runs the Po River and all its tributaries and the Rivers Reno, Adige, Piave, and Tagliamento. The plain falls into several natural divisions. At its highest end, by the Alpine foothills, it is made up of parallel *ferretto* (red loam composed of ferrous clay) ridges, running from north to south, with areas of gravel and permeable sand between them. This section of the plain is terraced and unproductive, although the rainfall is high. Below this is the section where the rivers rise, their waters eventually providing vital irrigation both for the *marcite* (winter pastures) and for the intensive agriculture of the fertile lower plain. Other notable plains include the *maremme* of Tuscany and Lazio, reclaimed marshland with dunes at the edge of the sea; the Agro Pontino, a recently reclaimed seaward extension of the Roman countryside (*campagna*); the fertile Pianura Campana (Plain of Campania) around Vesuvius; and the rather arid Tavoliere di Puglia. In Sicily the Piana di Catania (Plain of Catania) is a good area for growing citrus fruit.

Importance of the Po Valley

Coastal areas. The seacoasts are quite varied. Along the two Ligurian rivieras, on either side of Genoa, the coast alternates in rapid succession between high, rocky zones and level gravel. From Tuscany to Campania there are long, sandy, crescent beaches and abundant dunes, separated by rocky eminences. The coast of Calabria is high and rocky, though sometimes broken by short beaches. The coast of Puglia and, indeed, most of the Adriatic coast is level, though dominated by terraced gradients. The majestic delta of the Po, extending from Rimini to Monfalcone, is riddled with the lagoons familiar to visitors to Venice. The Carso, the limestone coastal region between Trieste and Istria, is rocky.

Drainage and soils. *Rivers.* Italian rivers are comparatively short; the longest, the Po, is only 400 miles long. Only three major rivers flow into the Ionian Sea, while Puglia has virtually only two rivers flowing to the Adriatic. Along the Adriatic coast a good number run parallel like the teeth of a comb down from the Apennines through Molise, Abruzzi, and the Marche regions. The rivers that flow into the Tyrrhenian Sea are longer and more complex and carry greater quantities of water. These include the Volturno, in Campania; the Roman Tiber; and the Arno, which flows through Florence and Pisa. The rivers of the Ligurian rivieras are mainly short and swift flowing; a few are important simply because cities, such as Genoa, or bathing resorts, such as Rapallo, are built on their deltas. But the prince of Italian rivers is the Po. Rising in the Monviso area, it runs across the Pianura Lombarda (Plain of Lombardy), through various important cities, such as Turin and Cremona, and is steadily enlarged by the numerous tributaries that join it, especially on its left bank. The Po debouches south of Venice, forming a large delta. In the Veneto there are also rivers that are not tributaries of the Po. One of these, the Adige, at 254 miles the second longest river in Italy, flows through Verona and debouches near Adria, south of Venice. The rivers in the south have imposing floods during winter storms, and those that run through zones of impermeable rock may become dangerous; yet during the summer many of these rivers are completely dry. The rivers of the centre and north are dry in the winter, because their headwaters are frozen, and full in the spring from melting snow and in the autumn from rainfall.

The lakes

Lakes. There are about 1,500 lakes in Italy. The most common type is the small, elevated Alpine lake formed by Quaternary glacial excavation during the last 25,000 years. These are very important for hydroelectric schemes. Other lakes, such as Bolsena and Albano, in Lazio, occupy the craters of extinct volcanoes. There are also coastal lakes, such as those of Lesina and Varano, in Puglia; and lakes resulting from prehistoric faulting, such as the Lago di Alleghe, near Belluno. The best known, largest, and most important of the Italian lakes are those cut into valleys of the Alpine foothills by Quaternary glaciers. These, listed in order of size, are the Lago di Garda, Lago Maggiore, and the lakes of Como, Iseo, and Lugano. They have a semi-Mediterranean climate and are surrounded by groves of olive and citrus trees. Italy also has considerable areas in which, as a result of porous rock, the water systems run underground, forming subterranean streams, sinkholes, and lakes. These are often associated with caves, the most famous of which are those of Castellana, in Puglia.

The soils. Varying climatic conditions in successive eras and differences in altitude and in types of rock have combined to produce in Italy a wide range of soils. Very common is dark-brown podzol, typical in mountains with a lot of flint, where the rainfall is heavy, as in the Alps above about 300 feet. In the Apennines, brown podzolic soils predominate, supporting forests and meadows and pastures. Brown Mediterranean soils are also characteristic of the Apennines and are suitable for agriculture. Renzinas, typically humus-carbonates, are characteristic of limestone and magnesian limestone mountain pastures and of many meadows and beech forests of the Apennines. Red earth—the famous terra rossa, derived from the residue of limestone rocks—is found not only in the extreme south (in Puglia, for instance) but also in Venetia, where it is the usual soil in vineyards, olive groves, and gardens. Sparse rocky earth, clays, dune sands, and gravel are found in the high mountains, in some volcanic zones, and in gullies in the sub-Apennines. There is also a red loam, or *ferretto*, composed of ferrous (iron) clay.

Climate. Geographically, Italy lies in the temperate zone. Because of the considerable length of the peninsula, there is a variation between the climate of the north, attached to the European continent, and that of the south, surrounded by the Mediterranean. The Alps are a partial barrier against westerly and northerly winds, while both the Apennines and the great plain of northern Italy produce special climatic variations. Sardinia is subject to Atlantic and Sicily to African winds. In general, four meteorological situations dominate the Italian climate: the Mediterranean winter cyclone, with a corresponding summer anticyclone; the Alpine summer cyclone, with a consequent winter anticyclone; the Atlantic autumnal cyclone; and the eastern Siberian autumnal anticyclone. The meeting of the two last-mentioned air masses brings heavy and sometimes disastrous rains in the autumn.

The seven main climatic zones

Italy can be divided into seven main climatic zones. In the most northerly, the Alpine Zone, which has a continental mountain climate, temperatures are lower and rainfall higher in the east than in the west. The average temperature at Bardonecchia, in the west, is 45.3° F (7.4° C), and the rainfall is 26 inches; at Val d'Ampezzo, in the east, the figures are 43.9° F (6.6° C) and 41.5 inches. In the Valle d'Aosta, in the west, the permanent snow line is at 10,200 feet, but in the Julian Alps it is as low as 8,350 feet. In autumn and late winter the hot, dry wind called the foehn blows from Switzerland or from Austria, and in the east the cold, dry bora blows with gusts of up to 125 miles per hour. Rain falls in the summer in the higher and more remote areas and in the spring and autumn at the periphery. Snow falls only in the winter, but the snowfall varies from about ten to 32 feet in different years and in relation to the exact altitude or closeness of the sea. More snow falls in the foothills than in the mountains and more in the Eastern than the Western Alps. Around the lakes the climate is milder, the average temperature in January at Milan being 34° F (1° C), at Salò, on Lago di Garda, it is 39° F (4° C).

The Po Valley has hot summers but severe winters, worse in the interior than toward the eastern coast. At Turin the winter average is 32.5° F (0.3° C) and the summer average 74° F (23° C). Rain falls mainly in the spring and autumn and increases with the altitude. There is scant snow, and that falls only on the high plain. The temperatures of places along the Adriatic coast rise steadily from north to south, partly because of the descending latitude and partly because the prevailing winds are easterly in the north but southerly in the south. The average annual mean temperature rises from 56.5° F (13.6° C) at Venice to 60° F (16° C) at Ancona and 63° F (17° C) at Bari. There is scant rain: Venice has 29.5 inches, Ancona 25.5 inches, and Bari 23.6 inches.

In the Apennines the winters vary in severity according to the altitude. Except at specific locations, there are moderate amounts of rain and snow, but in the cyclonic conditions of midwinter there may be sudden snowfalls in the south. Annual mean temperatures are 53.8° F (12.1° C) at Urbino, in the east, and 54.5° F (12.5° C) at Potenza, in Lucania; the annual rainfall is, respectively, 35 inches and 39.6 inches. Along the Tyrrhenian coast, on the Ligurian rivieras in the north, temperature and rainfall are influenced by full exposure to the noonday sun; the nearness of the sea, with its prevailing southwesterly winds; and the Apennine Range that protects the area from cold north winds. The eastern Riviera has more rain than the western: rainfall at San Remo, on the western Riviera, is 26.7 inches, but at La Spezia, on the eastern Riviera, it is 45.2 inches. Farther south, where the coastal area extends a great distance inland and is flatter, the mean temperature and annual rainfall are 58.6° F (14.8° C) and 30.3 inches at Florence and 61.9° F (16.6° C) and 31.4 inches at Naples. As a rule, the Tyrrhenian coast is warmer and more rainy than the Adriatic coast. Both Calabria and Sicily are mountainous regions surrounded by the Mediterranean and thus have higher temperatures than the Italian mainland high regions farther north. Winter rains are scarce in the interior and heavier in the west and north of Sicily. At Reggio di Calabria the annual mean temperature is 64.7° F (18.2° C) and rainfall 22.4 inches; at Palermo, in Sicily, they are 64.4° F (18.0° C) and 38.2 inches. The sirocco, a hot, very humid, and depressing wind, blows frequently from Africa and the Near East. In Sardinia, conditions are more turbulent on the western side, and the island suffers from the cold mistral blowing from the northwest and also from the sirocco blowing from the southeast. At Sassari, in the northwest, the annual mean temperature is 62.6° F (17.0° C) and the rainfall 22.8 inches, while at Orosei, on the east coast, the temperature is 63.5° F (17.5° C) and the rainfall 21.2 inches.

Vegetation. The native vegetation of Italy reflects the diversity in the prevailing physical environment in dif-

FED. REP. OF GERMANY
MUNICH
VIENNA
BUDAPEST
CZECH.
Bratislava
HUNGARY
AUSTRIA
SWITZERLAND
FRANCE
YUGOSLAVIA
SLOVENIA
CROATIA
BOSNIA
DALMATIA
ADRIATIC
LIGURIAN SEA
CORSICA (Fr.)
MONACO
ALPS
Zürich
Bern
Basel
Luzern
Geneva
Innsbruck
Salzburg
Graz
Ljubljana
Zagreb
Rijeka
Split
Sarajevo
Trieste
CARSO
Venice
Padova
Verona
Vicenza
Treviso
Trento
Bolzano
Brescia
Bergamo
Como
MILAN
Monza
Varese
Novara
Pavia
Piacenza
Cremona
Mantova
Parma
Modena
Bologna
Ferrara
Ravenna
Rimini
Pesaro
Ancona
Pescara
Florence
Prato
Pistoia
Lucca
Pisa
Livorno
Siena
Arezzo
Perugia
Terni
Viterbo
Genoa
La Spezia
Savona
Alessandria
Asti
TURIN
Nice
Cannes
Bastia
PIEMONTE
LOMBARDIA
VENETO
EMILIA
ROMAGNA
LIGURIA
TOSCANA
UMBRIA
MARCHE
LAZIO
ABRUZZI
Golfo di Venezia
Golfo di Genova
ISOLA D' ELBA

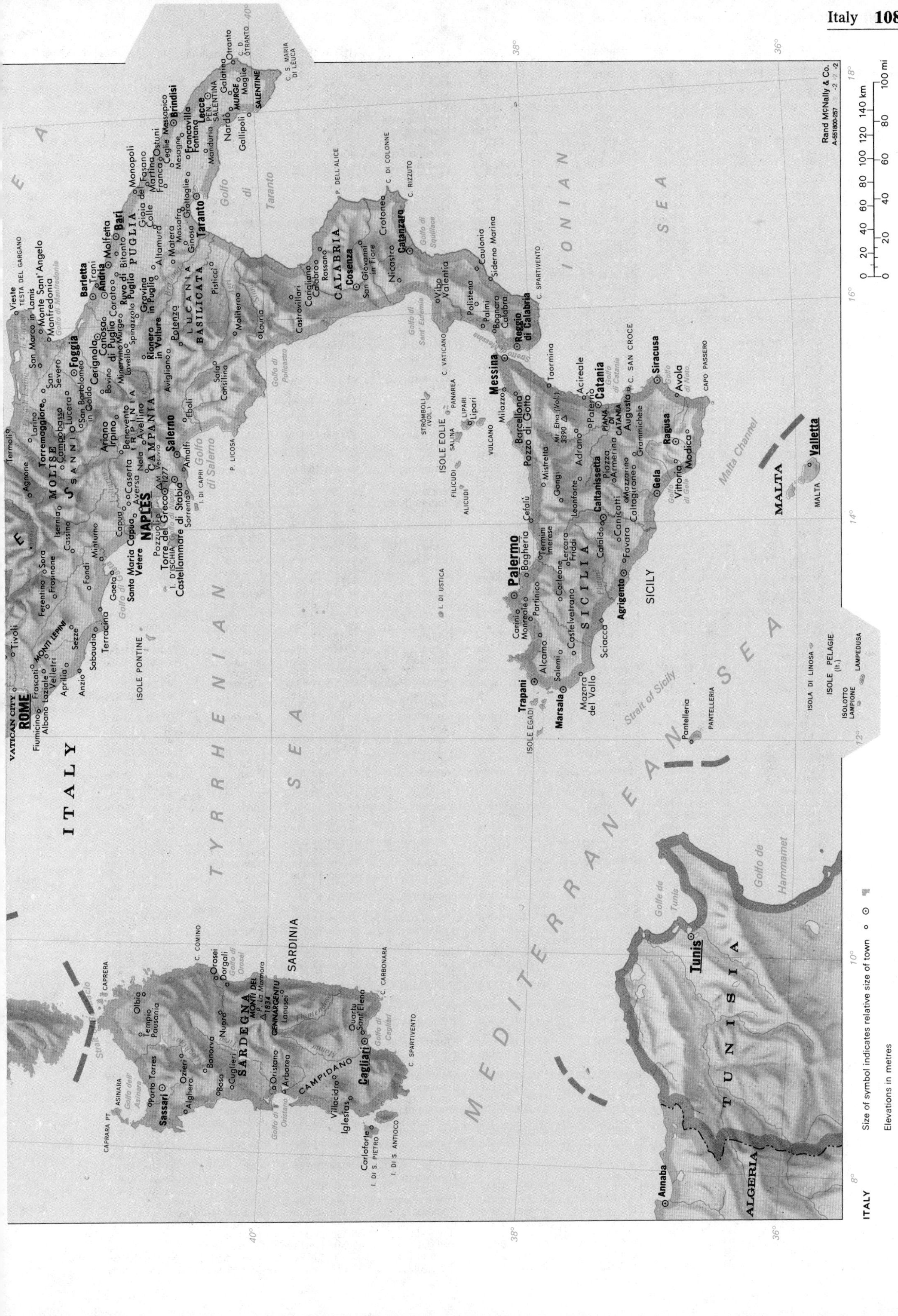

ITALY

VATICAN CITY
ROME

Tivoli
Fiumicino
Frascati
Albano Laziale
Velletri
MONTI LEPINI
Anzio
Aprilia
Sezze
Sabaudia
Terracina
ISOLE PONTINE
Fondi
Gaeta
Frosinone
Sora
Ferentino
Minturno
Casino
Isernia
Capua
Caserta
Aversa
NAPLES
Vetere
Santa Maria Capua Vetere
Pozzuoli
Torre del Greco
Castellammare di Stabia
Sorrento
I. DI CAPRI
I. D'ISCHIA
P. LICOSA
Amalfi
Salerno
Eboli
Campobasso
Larino
Agnone
Torremaggiore
San Severo
San Bartolomeo in Galdo
Lucera
Foggia
Ariano Irpino
Avellino
Benevento
Nola
Vesuvio
Cerignola
Bovino
Canosa
Barletta
Trani
Andria
Molfetta
Bitonto
Ruvo di Puglia
Corato
Bari
Monopoli
Minervino Murge
Spinazzola
Gravina in Puglia
Altamura
Matera
Ginosa
Massafra
Martina Franca
Francavilla Fontana
Ostuni
Ceglie Messapico
Brindisi
Lecce
Mesagne
Manduria
Nardò
Galatina
Gallipoli
Maglie
Otranto
C. S. MARIA DI LEUCA
SALENTINA PEN.
MURGE

Vieste
TESTA DEL GARGANO
Monte Sant'Angelo
Manfredonia
Golfo di Manfredonia
San Marco in Lamis
TERMOLI
Termoli
MOLISE
CAMPANIA
BASILICATA
LUCANIA
PUGLIA
Potenza
Rionero in Vulture
Avigliano
Pisticci
Montalbano
Castrovillari
Cosenza
CALABRIA
Crotone
Rossano
Cotronei
Cariati
San Giovanni in Fiore
Nicastro
Catanzaro
Golfo di Squillace
Siderno Marina
Caulonia
Reggio di Calabria
Palmi
Bagnara Calabra
Polistena
Gioia Tauro
Vibo Valentia
C. VATICANO
C. SPARTIVENTO
Golfo di Sant'Eufemia
Golfo di Policastro
Golfo di Taranto
Taranto
Colle
Sala Consilina
Lauria
Moliterno

STROMBOLI (VOL.)
PANAREA
SALINA
LIPARI
Lipari
VULCANO
FILICUDI
ALICUDI
ISOLE EOLIE
Messina
Milazzo
Barcellona Pozzo di Gotto
Taormina
Acireale
Paternò
Catania
Mt. Etna (Vol.) 3390
Adrano
Augusta
PIANA DI CATANIA
Golfo di Catania
Siracusa
Avola
CAPO PASSERO
C. SAN CROCE
Ragusa
Modica
Vittoria
Scicli
Gela
Grammichele
Caltagirone
Mazzarino
Piazza Armerina
Leonforte
Caltanissetta
Canicatti
Favara
Agrigento
Naro
Licata
SICILY
SICILIA
Cefalù
Termini Imerese
Bagheria
Palermo
Monreale
Partinico
Carini
Corleone
Castelvetrano
Sciacca
Menfi
Alcamo
Salemi
Mazara del Vallo
Marsala
Trapani
ISOLE EGADI
I. DI USTICA
PANTELLERIA
Pantelleria
Strait of Sicily

MALTA
Valletta
MALTA
Malta Channel
ISOLA DI LINOSA
ISOLE PELAGIE
LAMPEDUSA
I SOLOTTO LAMPIONE

SARDINIA
SARDEGNA
SARDEGNA
CAPRERA
I. LA MADDALENA
Santa Teresa Gallura
Olbia
Tempio Pausania
Oristano
Bosa
Alghero
Ozieri
Sassari
Porto Torres
ASINARA
CAPRARA PT.
C. COMINO
Orosei
Dorgali
Lanusei
MONTE DEL GENNARGENTU 1834
Nuoro
Quartu Sant'Elena
Cagliari
CAMPIDANO
Iglesias
Carloforte
I. DI S. PIETRO
I. DI S. ANTIOCO
Villacidro
Arborea
C. SPARTIVENTO
C. CARBONARA

TYRRHENIAN SEA
IONIAN SEA
MEDITERRANEAN SEA

Tunis
TUNISIA
ALGERIA
Annaba
Golfe de Hammamet
Golfe de Tunis

Rand McNally & Co.
A-651800-257

Size of symbol indicates relative size of town ○ ◉ ⊙

Elevations in metres

ITALY

0 20 40 60 80 100 mi
0 20 40 60 80 100 120 140 km

MAP INDEX

Political subdivisions
Abruzzi 42·20n 13·45e
Basilicata 40·30n 16·10e
Calabria 39·00n 16·30e
Campania 41·00n 14·30e
Emilia Romagna 44·35n 11·00e
Friuli-Venezia-
 Giulia 46·00n 13·00e
Lazio 42·00n 12·30e
Liguria 44·30n 8·50e
Lombardia 45·40n 9·45e
Marche 43·30n 13·15e
Molise 41·35n 14·30e
Piemonte 45·00n 8·00e
Puglia 41·15n 16·15e
Sardegna 40·00n 9·00e
Sicilia 37·30n 14·00e
Toscana 43·25n 11·00e
Trentino-Alto-
 Adige 46·08n 11·07e
Umbria 43·00n 12·30e
Valle d'Aosta 45·44n 7·20e
Veneto 45·30n 12·00e

Cities and towns
Abbiategrasso 45·24n 8·54e
Acireale 37·37n 15·10e
Acqui 44·41n 8·28e
Adrano 37·40n 14·50e
Adria 45·03n 12·03e
Agnone 41·48n 14·22e
Agrigento 37·18n 13·35e
Alba 44·42n 8·02e
Albano Laziale 41·44n 12·39e
Albenga 44·03n 8·13e
Alcamo 37·59n 12·58e
Alessandria 44·54n 8·37e
Alghero 40·34n 8·19e
Altamura 40·50n 16·33e
Amalfi 40·38n 14·36e
Ancona 43·38n 13·30e
Andria 41·13n 16·18e
Anzio 41·27n 12·37e
Aosta 45·44n 7·20e
Aprilia 41·36n 12·39e
Arborea 39·47n 8·34e
Arezzo 43·25n 11·53e
Ariano Irpino 41·09n 15·05e
Ascoli Piceno 42·51n 13·34e
Assisi 43·04n 12·37e
Asti 44·54n 8·12e
Augusta 37·13n 15·13e
Avellino 40·54n 14·47e
Aversa 40·58n 14·12e
Avezzano 42·02n 13·25e
Avigliano 40·44n 15·44e
Avola 36·54n 15·09e
Bagheria 38·05n 13·30e
Bagnara Calabra 38·18n 15·49e
Barcellona Pozzo
 di Gotto 38·09n 15·13e
Bardonecchia 45·05n 6·42e
Bari 41·07n 16·52e
Barletta 41·19n 16·17e
Bassano 45·46n 11·44e
Belluno 46·09n 12·13e
Benevento 41·08n 14·45e
Bergamo 45·41n 9·43e
Biella 45·34n 8·03e
Bitonto 41·06n 16·42e
Bologna 44·29n 11·20e
Bolzano (Bozen) 46·31n 11·22e
Bonorva 40·25n 8·45e
Borgomanero 45·42n 8·28e
Borgo Val
 di Taro 44·29n 9·46e
Bosa 40·18n 8·30e
Bovino 41·15n 15·20e
Bozen, see
 Bolzano
Bra 44·42n 7·51e
Brennero 47·00n 11·30e
Brescia 45·33n 13·15e
Bressanone
 (Brixen) 46·43n 11·39e
Brindisi 40·38n 17·56e
Busto Arsizio 45·37n 8·51e
Cagli 43·33n 12·39e
Cagliari 39·13n 9·06e
Caltagirone 37·14n 14·31e
Caltanissetta 37·29n 14·04e
Campobasso 41·34n 14·39e
Canicattí 37·21n 13·51e
Canosa di
 Puglia 41·13n 16·04e
Cantù 45·44n 9·08e
Capannori 43·50n 10·34e
Capua 41·06n 14·12e
Carini 38·08n 13·11e
Carloforte 39·08n 8·18e
Carmagnola 44·51n 7·43e
Carpi 44·47n 10·53e
Carrara 44·05n 10·06e
Casale 45·08n 8·27e
Casalmaggiore 44·59n 10·26e
Caserta 41·04n 14·20e
Cassino 41·30n 13·49e
Castellammare
 di Stabia 40·42n 14·29e
Castelvetrano 37·41n 12·47e
Castrovillari 39·49n 16·13e
Catania 37·30n 15·06e
Catanzaro 38·54n 16·36e
Caulonia 38·23n 16·25e
Cavarzere 45·08n 12·05e
Cefalù 38·02n 14·01e
Ceglie
 Messapico 40·39n 17·31e
Cerignola 41·16n 15·54e
Cesena 44·08n 12·15e
Chiari 45·32n 9·56e
Chiavari 44·19n 9·19e
Chieri 45·01n 7·49e
Chieti 42·21n 14·10e
Chioggia 45·13n 12·17e
Chivasso 45·11n 7·53e
Cittadella 45·39n 11·47e
Città di Castello 43·27n 12·14e
Cividale del
 Friuli 46·06n 13·25e
Civitavecchia 42·06n 11·48e
Codogno 45·09n 9·42e
Comacchio 44·42n 12·11e
Como 45·47n 9·05e
Conegliano 45·53n 12·18e
Copparo 44·54n 11·49e
Corato 41·09n 16·25e
Corigliano
 Calabro 39·36n 16·31e
Corleone 37·49n 13·18e
Corneto, see
 Tarquinia
Cortona 43·16n 11·59e
Cosenza 39·17n 16·15e
Courmayeur 45·47n 6·58e
Crema 45·22n 9·41e
Cremona 45·07n 10·02e
Crotone 39·05n 17·07e
Cuglieri 40·11n 8·34e
Cuneo 44·23n 7·32e
Dorgali 40·17n 9·35e
Eboli 40·37n 15·04e
Empoli 43·43n 10·57e
Este 45·14n 11·39e
Fabriano 43·20n 12·54e
Faenza 44·17n 11·53e
Fano 43·50n 13·01e
Fasano 40·50n 17·22e
Favara 37·19n 13·40e
Feltre 46·01n 11·54e
Ferentino 41·42n 13·15e
Fermo 43·09n 13·43e
Ferrara 44·50n 11·35e
Firenzuola 44·07n 11·23e
Fiumicino 41·46n 12·14e
Florence
 (Firenze) 43·46n 11·15e
Foggia 41·27n 15·34e
Foligno 42·57n 12·42e
Fondi 41·21n 13·25e
Forlì 44·13n 12·03e
Fossano 44·33n 7·43e
Fossombrone 43·41n 12·48e
Francavilla
 Fontana 40·31n 17·35e
Frascati 41·48n 12·41e
Frosinone 41·38n 13·19e
Gaeta 41·12n 13·35e
Galatina 40·10n 18·10e
Gallarate 45·40n 8·47e
Gallipoli 40·03n 17·58e
Gangi 37·49n 14·13e
Gela 37·03n 14·15e
Genoa (Genova) 44·25n 8·57e
Ginosa 40·34n 16·46e
Grammichele 37·13n 14·38e
Gravina in Puglia 40·49n 16·25e
Grosseto 42·46n 11·08e
Grottaglie 40·32n 17·26e
Guastalla 44·55n 10·39e
Gubbio 43·21n 12·35e
Guidonia 42·01n 12·45e
Iesi 43·31n 13·14e
Iglesias 39·19n 8·32e
Imola 44·21n 11·42e
Imperia 43·53n 8·03e
Isernia 41·36n 14·14e
Ivrea 45·28n 7·52e
Lanusei 39·52n 9·34e
L'Aquila 42·22n 13·22e
Larino 41·48n 14·54e
La Spezia 44·07n 9·50e
Lauria 40·02n 15·50e
Lavello 41·03n 15·48e
Lecce 40·23n 18·11e
Lecco 45·51n 9·23e
Leghorn, see
 Livorno
Legnano 45·36n 8·54e
Leonforte 37·39n 14·24e
Lercara Friddi 37·45n 13·36e
Lipari 38·28n 14·57e
Livorno
 (Leghorn) 43·33n 10·19e
Lodi 45·19n 9·30e
Lucca 43·50n 10·29e
Lucera 41·30n 15·20e
Lugo 44·25n 11·54e
Macerata 43·18n 13·27e
Magenta 45·28n 8·53e
Maglie 40·07n 18·19e
Manduria 40·24n 17·38e
Manfredonia 41·38n 15·55e
Mantova 45·09n 10·48e
Marsala 37·48n 12·26e
Martina Franca 40·42n 17·21e
Massa 44·01n 10·09e
Massafra 40·35n 17·07e
Massa Marittima 43·03n 10·53e
Matera 40·40n 16·37e
Mazara del
 Vallo 37·39n 12·36e
Mazzarino 37·18n 14·13e
Merano (Meran) 46·40n 11·09e
Mesagne 40·33n 17·49e
Messina 38·11n 15·33e
Mestre 45·29n 12·15e
Milan (Milano) 45·28n 9·12e
Milazzo 38·14n 15·15e
Minervino
 Murge 41·05n 16·05e
Minturno 41·15n 13·45e
Mistretta 37·56n 14·22e
Modena 44·40n 10·55e
Modica 36·51n 14·47e
Molfetta 41·12n 16·36e
Moliterno 40·14n 15·52e
Mondovì 44·23n 7·49e
Monfalcone 45·49n 13·32e
Monopoli 40·57n 17·19e
Monreale 38·05n 13·17e
Montepulciano 43·05n 11·47e
Monte Sant'
 Angelo 41·42n 15·57e
Monza 45·35n 9·16e
Mortara 45·15n 8·44e
Naples (Napoli) 40·51n 14·17e
Nardò 40·11n 18·02e
Nicastro 38·59n 16·20e
Nola 40·55n 14·33e
Novara 45·28n 8·38e
Novi Ligure 44·46n 8·47e
Nuoro 40·19n 9·20e
Olbia 40·55n 9·29e
Orbetello 42·27n 11·13e
Oristano 39·54n 8·35e
Orosei 40·23n 9·42e
Ortona 42·21n 14·24e
Orvieto 42·43n 12·07e
Ostuni 40·44n 17·35e
Otranto 40·09n 18·30e
Ozieri 40·35n 9·00e
Padova (Padua) 45·25n 11·53e
Palermo 38·07n 13·21e
Palmi 38·21n 15·51e
Pantelleria 36·49n 11·57e
Parma 44·48n 10·20e
Partinico 38·03n 13·07e
Paternò 37·34n 14·54e
Pavia 45·10n 9·10e
Penne 42·27n 13·55e
Perugia 43·08n 12·22e
Pesaro 43·54n 12·55e
Pescara 42·28n 14·13e
Pescia 43·54n 10·41e
Piacenza 45·01n 9·40e
Piazza Armerina 37·23n 14·22e
Pieve di Cadore 46·26n 12·22e
Pinerolo 44·53n 7·21e
Piombino 42·55n 10·32e
Pisa 43·43n 10·23e
Pisticci 40·23n 16·34e
Pistoia 43·55n 10·54e
Poggibonsi 43·28n 11·09e
Polistena 38·25n 16·05e
Pontedera 43·40n 10·38e
Pontremoli 44·22n 9·53e
Pordenone 45·57n 12·39e
Portoferraio 42·49n 10·19e
Portogruaro 45·47n 12·50e
Porto Torres 40·50n 8·23e
Potenza 40·38n 15·49e
Pozzuoli 40·49n 14·07e
Prato 43·53n 11·06e
Quartu Sant'
 Elena 39·14n 9·11e
Ragusa 36·55n 14·44e
Rapallo 44·21n 9·14e
Ravenna 44·25n 12·12e
Recanati 43·24n 13·32e
Reggio di
 Calabria 38·07n 15·39e
Reggio nell'
 Emilia 44·43n 10·36e
Rieti 42·24n 12·51e
Rimini 44·04n 12·34e
Rionero in
 Vulture 40·55n 15·40e
Rome (Roma) 41·54n 12·29e
Rossano 39·35n 16·39e
Rovato 45·34n 10·00e
Rovereto 45·53n 11·02e
Rovigo 45·04n 11·47e
Ruvo di Puglia 41·07n 16·29e
Sabaudia 41·18n 13·01e
Sala Consilina 40·24n 15·36e
Salemi 37·49n 12·49e
Salerno 40·41n 14·47e
Salò 45·36n 10·31e
Saluzzo 44·39n 7·29e
San Bartolomeo
 in Galdo 41·24n 15·01e
San Benedetto
 del Tronto 42·57n 13·53e
San Donà
 di Piave 45·38n 12·34e
San Giovanni
 in Fiore 39·16n 16·42e
San Marco
 in Lamis 41·43n 15·38e
San Marino 43·55n 12·28e
San Remo 43·49n 7·46e
San Severo 41·41n 15·23e
Santa Maria
 Capua Vetere 41·05n 14·15e
San Vito al
 Tagliamento 45·54n 12·52e
Sassari 40·44n 8·33e
Savigliano 44·38n 7·40e
Savona 44·17n 8·30e
Schio 45·43n 11·21e
Schluderns, see
 Sluderno
Sciacca 37·30n 13·06e
Senigallia 43·43n 13·13e
Serravalle
 Scrivia 44·44n 8·51e
Sestri Levante 44·16n 9·24e
Sezze 41·30n 13·03e
Siderno Marina 38·16n 16·18e
Siena 43·19n 11·21e
Siracusa
 (Syracuse) 37·04n 15·17e
Sluderno
 (Schluderns) 46·40n 10·35e
Sondrio 46·10n 9·52e
Sora 41·43n 13·37e
Soresina 45·17n 9·51e
Sorrento 40·37n 14·22e
Spinazzola 40·58n 16·06e
Spoleto 42·44n 12·44e
Sulmona 42·03n 13·55e
Susa 45·08n 7·03e
Syracuse, see
 Siracusa
Taormina 37·52n 15·17e
Taranto 40·28n 17·15e
Tarquinia,
 (Corneto) 42·15n 11·45e
Tarvisio 46·30n 13·35e
Tempio
 Pausania 40·54n 9·07e
Teramo 42·39n 13·42e
Termini
 Imerese 37·59n 13·42e
Termoli 42·00n 15·00e
Terni 42·34n 12·37e
Terracina 41·17n 13·15e
Tirano 46·13n 10·10e
Tivoli 41·58n 12·48e
Tolmezzo 46·24n 13·01e
Torre del Greco 40·47n 14·22e
Torremaggiore 41·41n 15·17e
Tortona 44·54n 8·52e
Trani 41·17n 16·26e
Trapani 38·01n 12·31e
Trento 46·04n 11·08e
Treviglio 45·31n 9·35e
Treviso 45·40n 12·15e
Trieste 45·40n 13·46e
Trino 45·12n 8·18e
Turin (Torino) 45·03n 7·40e
Udine 46·03n 13·14e
Urbino 43·43n 12·38e
Varazze 44·22n 8·34e
Varese 45·48n 8·48e
Vasto 42·07n 14·42e
Vatican City 41·54n 12·27e
Velletri 41·41n 12·47e
Venice (Venezia) 45·27n 12·21e
Ventimiglia 43·47n 7·36e
Vercelli 45·19n 8·25e
Verona 45·27n 11·00e
Viadana 44·56n 10·31e
Viareggio 43·52n 10·14e
Vibo Valentia 38·40n 16·06e
Vicenza 45·33n 11·33e
Vieste 41·53n 16·10e
Vigevano 45·19n 8·51e
Villacidro 39·27n 8·44e
Villafranca di
 Verona 45·21n 10·50e
Viterbo 42·25n 12·06e
Vittoria 36·57n 14·32e
Voghera 44·59n 9·01e
Volterra 43·24n 10·51e
Voltri 44·26n 8·45e

Physical features and points of interest
Adamello,
 Gruppo dell',
 mountains 46·10n 10·35e
Adda, *river* 45·08n 9·53e

MAP INDEX (continued)

Adige (Etsch), *river*....45·10n 12·20e
Adriatic Sea....42·30n 16·00e
Agri, *river*....40·13n 16·44e
Alice, Punta dell', *point*....39·24n 17·10e
Alicudi, *island*...38·33n 14·21e
Alps, *mountains*..46·30n 10·00e
Alto, Giogo (Germen Hochjoch), *pass*.46·47n 10·47e
Amaro, Monte, *mountain*....42·05n 14·05e
Ampezzo, Valle d', *valley*....46·30n 12·10e
Apennines (Appennino), *mountains*....43·00n 13·00e
Apuan Alps, *mountains*....44·09n 10·15e
Arno, *river*....43·41n 10·17e
Asinara, *island*...41·05n 8·18e
Asinara, Golfo dell', *gulf*....41·00n 8·30e
Bernina, Piz, *peak*....46·21n 9·51e
Biferno, *river*....41·59n 15·02e
Blanc, Mont, *mountain*....45·50n 6·52e
Bolsena, Lago di, *lake*....42·36n 11·56e
Bonifacio, Strait of....41·20n 9·15e
Bracciano, Lago di, *lake*....42·07n 12·14e
Bradano, *river*....40·23n 16·51e
Brenner Pass....47·00n 11·30e
Brenta, *river*....45·11n 12·18e
Brenta, Cima, *mountain*....46·11n 10·54e
Cagliari, Golfo di, *gulf*....39·05n 9·10e
Campidano, *plain*....39·30n 8·47e
Capraia, *island*...43·02n 9·49e
Caprara Punta, *point*....41·07n 8·19e
Caprera, *island*...42·08n 15·31e
Capri, Isola di, *island*....40·33n 14·13e
Carbonara, Capo, *cape*....39·06n 9·31e
Carmo, Monte, *mountain*....44·11n 8·11e
Carnic Alps, *mountains*....46·40n 13·00e
Catania, Golfo di, *gulf*....37·25n 15·15e
Catania, Piana di, *plain*....37·25n 14·51e
Cervino, Monte, see Matterhorn
Chiana, Val di, *valley*....43·15n 11·50e
Chiante, Monti del, *mountains*..43·32n 11·25e
Coghinas, *river*...40·56n 8·48e
Colline Metallifere (Ore Mountains)....43·12n 11·00e
Colonne, Capo di, *cape*....39·02n 17·11e
Comacchio, Valli di, *lagoon*....44·38n 12·06e
Comino, Capo, *cape*....40·31n 9·50e
Como, Lago di, *lake*....46·00n 9·20e
Conero, Monte, *mountain*....43·33n 13·36e
Corno, Monte, *mountain*....42·28n 13·34e
Cottian Alps, *mountains*....44·45n 7·00e
Dolomitiche, Alpi (Dolomite Alps), *mountains*....46·25n 11·50e
Dora Baltea, *river*....45·11n 8·05e
Egadi, Isole, *islands*....37·56n 12·16e
Elba, Isola d', *island*....42·46n 10·17e
Eolie, Isole, *islands*....38·30n 15·00e
Etna, Monte, *volcano*....37·46n 15·00e
Etsch, see Adige
Filicudi, *island*...38·35n 14·34e
Flumendosa, *river*....39·26n 9·38e
Fréjus, *pass*....45·08n 6·41e
Gaeta, Golfo di, *gulf*....41·06n 13·30e
Garda, Lago di, *lake*....45·40n 10·41e
Gargano, Testa del, *point*....41·49n 16·12e
Gela, Golfo di, *gulf*....37·00n 14·10e
Gennargentu, Monti del, *mountains*....40·01n 9·19e
Genova, Golfo di (Gulf of Genoa)..44·10n 8·55e
Giannutri, Isola di, *island*....42·15n 11·06e
Giglio, Isola del, *island*....42·21n 10·54e
Giulie, Alpi, see Julian Alps
Gorgona, *island*..43·26n 9·54e
Graian Alps, *mountains*....45·30n 7·10e
Gran Paradiso, *mountain*....45·32n 7·16e
Gran Sasso d'Italia, *mountains*....42·27n 13·42e
Great St. Bernard Pass....45·50n 7·10e
Ionian Sea (Ionio, Mar)....37·30n 17·00e
Irpinia, *historic region*....41·00n 15·00e
Ischia, Isola d', *island*....40·43n 13·54e
Iseo, Lago d', *lake*....45·43n 10·04e
Italian Riviera, see Levante, Riviera di
Italian Riviera, see Ponente, Riviera di
Julian Alps (Alpi Giulie), *mountains*....46·20n 13·45e
Lampedusa, *island*....35·31n 12·35e
Lampione, Isolotto, *islet*....35·33n 12·19e
Lepini, Monti, *mountains*....41·35n 13·00e
Lesina, Lago di, *lagoon*....41·53n 15·26e
Levanna, *mountains*....45·24n 7·12e
Levante, Riviera di (Italian Riviera), *coast*...44·15n 9·30e
Licosa, Punta, *point*....40·15n 14·54e
Ligurian Sea (Ligurienne, Mar)....43·30n 9·00e
Linaro, Capo, *cape*....42·02n 11·50e
Linosa, Isola di, *island*....35·52n 12·52e
Lipari, *island*....38·30n 14·57e
Liri, *river*....41·25n 13·52e
Little Saint Bernard Pass...45·41n 6·53e
Lucania, *historic region*...40·30n 16·00e
Lugano, Lago di, *lake*....45·58n 9·00e
Maggiore, Lago, *lake*....46·00n 8·40e
Malta Channel...36·20n 15·00e
Manfredonia, Golfo di, *gulf*....41·35n 16·05e
Mannu, *river*....40·50n 8·23e
Maritime Alps, *mountains*....44·15n 7·10e
Marmolada, Monte, *mountain*....46·26n 11·51e
Marmora, Punta la, *mountain*....39·59n 9·19e
Matterhorn (Monte Cervino) *mountain*....45·59n 7·43e
Mediterranean Sea....37·30n 11·00e
Messina, Stretto di, *strait*....38·15n 15·35e
Monferrato, *historic region*...44·55n 8·05e
Mont Blanc Tunnel....45·50n 6·53e
Montecristo, Isola di, *island*..42·20n 10·19e
Montone, *river*...44·24n 12·14e
Murge Salentine, *hills*....40·02n 18·13e
Napoli, Golfo di, *gulf*....40·43n 14·10e
Nera, *river*....42·26n 12·24e
Noto, Golfo di, *gulf*....36·50n 15·15e
Ofanto, *river*....41·22n 16·13e
Oglio, *river*....45·02n 10·39e
Ombrone, *river*...42·39n 11·00e
Ore Mountains, see Collina Metallifere
Oristano, Golfo di, *gulf*....39·50n 8·29e
Orobie, Alpi, *mountains*....46·00n 10·00e
Orosei, Golfo di, *gulf*....40·10n 9·50e
Otranto, Capo d', *cape*....40·00n 19·00e
Padano-Venetian-Emilian Plain...45·00n 12·00e
Panarea, *island*..38·38n 15·05e
Panaro, *river*....44·55n 11·25e
Pantelleria, *island*....36·47n 12·00e
Passero, Capo, *cape*....36·40n 15·09e
Pelagie, Isole, *islands*....35·40n 12·40e
Pescara, *river*...42·28n 14·13e
Pianosa, *island*...42·13n 15·45e
Pianosa, *island*...42·35n 10·04e
Piave, *river*....45·32n 12·44e
Piccole Alpi Dolomitiche, *mountains*....46·10n 12·30e
Platani, *river*....37·23n 13·16e
Po, *river*....44·57n 12·04e
Po, Foci del, *river mouth*....44·52n 12·30e
Policastro, Golfo di, *gulf*....40·00n 15·30e
Ponente, Riviera di (Italian Riviera), *coast*...44·10n 8·20e
Pontine, Isole, *islands*....40·54n 12·57e
Potenza, *river*...43·25n 13·40e
Reno, *river*....44·37n 12·17e
Riviera, see Levante, Riviera di
Riviera, see Ponente, Riviera di
Rizzuto, Capo, *cape*....38·54n 17·06e
Rosa, Monte, *mountain*....45·55n 7·53e
Salentina, Penisola, *peninsula*....40·30n 18·00e
Salerno, Golfo di, *gulf*....40·32n 14·42e
Salina, *island*....38·34n 14·51e
San Antioco, Isola di, *island*..39·00n 8·25e
San Croce, Capo, *cape*....37·14n 15·15e
Sangro, *river*....42·14n 14·32e
Sannio, *historic region*....41·20n 14·30e
San Pietro, Isola di, *island*....39·08n 8·18e
Santa Maria di Leuca, Capo, *cape*....39·47n 18·22e
Sant' Eufemia, Golfo di, *gulf*....38·50n 16·00e
Sardinia (Isola di Sardegna), *island*....40·00n 9·00e
Secchia, *river*....45·04n 11·00e
Serchio, *river*....43·47n 10·16e
Sesia, *river*....45·05n 8·37e
Sicily (Isola di Sicilia), *island*...37·30n 14·00e
Sicily, Strait of...37·20n 11·20e
Sieve, *river*....43·46n 11·26e
Sile, *river*....45·30n 12·25e
Simplon Tunnel..46·15n 8·10e
Sinni, *river*....40·09n 16·42e
Spartivento, Capo, *cape*....38·53n 8·50e
Squillace, Golfo di, *gulf*....38·50n 16·50e
Strómboli, *volcano*....38·48n 15·13e
Tagliamento, *river*....45·38n 13·06e
Tanaro, *river*....45·01n 8·47e
Taranto, Golfo di, *gulf*....40·10n 17·20e
Taro, *river*....45·00n 10·15e
Tiber (Tevere), *river*....41·44n 12·14e
Trasimeno, Lago, *lake*....43·08n 12·06e
Tremiti, Isole di, *islands*....42·07n 15·30e
Trieste, Gulf of...45·40n 13·35e
Tirso, *river*....39·53n 8·32e
Tyrrhenian Sea..40·00n 12·00e
Ustica, Isola di, *island*....38·42n 13·10e
Varano, Lago di, *lagoon*....41·53n 15·45e
Vaticano, Capo, *cape*....38·38n 15·50e
Venezia, Golfo di, *gulf*....45·15n 13·00e
Vesuvio, Monte (Mount Vesuvius), *volcano*....40·49n 14·26e
Viso, Monte, *mountain*....44·40n 7·07e
Volturno, *river*...41·01n 13·55e
Vulcano, *island*...38·27n 14·58e

The three vegetation zones

ferent parts of the country. There are at least three zones of differing vegetation, the Alps, the Po Valley, and the Mediterranean–Apennine area.

From the foot of the Alps to their highest peaks, three bands of vegetation can be distinguished. First, around the Lombard lakes, the most common trees are the evergreen cork oak, the European olive, the cypress, and also the cherry laurel. Slightly higher, on the mountain plain, the beech is ubiquitous, giving place gradually to the deciduous larch and the Norway spruce. In the high-altitude zone, twisted shrubs, including rhododendron, green alder, and dwarf juniper, then give way to pastureland with grasses and sedges and wild flowers such as gentian, dryad, rock jasmine, campion, sea bindweed, primrose, and saxifrage. Further up there is curved sedge, with the dwarf willow and the lovely anthophytes. On the snow line there are innumerable mosses, lichen, and flags, as well as a few varieties of hardy pollenating plants, such as saxifrage.

In the Po Valley almost nothing remains of the original forests; almost all the vegetation has been planted or disposed by man. Poplars predominate where there is abundant water, but in the drier, more gravelly zones there are a few sedges. On the clayey upland plains, heather abounds, and there are forests of Scotch pine. There are the usual grasses beside the streams and in the bogs and water lilies and pondweed on the banks of the marshes. But the heavily predominant plants are the cultivated crops—wheat, maize (corn), potatoes, rice, and sugar beets. In the Apennine zone along the whole peninsula, a typical tree is the holm oak, while the area closer to the sea is characterized by the olive, oleander, carob, mastic, and the Aleppo pine. There is a notable development of pioneer sea grape on the coastal dunes. The Mediterranean foothill area is characterized by the cork oak and the Aleppo pine. Higher up, in southern Italy, there are still traces of the ancient mountain forest, with truffle oak, chestnut, flowering ash, Oriental oak, white poplar, and Oriental plane. There are quite extensive beechwoods in Calabria (on La Sila and Aspromonte mountains) and Puglia and the silver fir and various kinds of pine in Abruzzi and Calabria. Where the forests have been destroyed in the strictly Mediterranean section of the Apennines, a scrub called macchia has grown up. On Sardinia the destruction of the carob forests and on the Tavoliere di Puglia the decay of olive trees and shore vegetation have produced steppes of tough plants such as the various sorts of feather grass. Mountain meadowlands are found in Calabria and Basilicata, usually with vetch, bent grass, and the white asphodel. The Apennine pasturelands are very much like those of the Alps. The papyrus is quite common in Sicily as a freshwater plant.

Animal life. The extent of animal life in Italy has been much reduced by man. In the Alps there are quite a number of animals, such as marmots, that hibernate and others that change their protective colouring according to the season, such as the ermine, the mountain partridge, and the Alpine rabbit. Larger mammals include the ibex, protected on the Gran Paradiso, the chamois in the Central Alps, and the roe in the Eastern Alps. The lynx, the stoat, and the brown bear (protected in Adamello and Brenta) are now rare. Alpine birds include the black grouse, the golden eagle, and, more rarely, the capercaillie, or wood grouse. Among the reptiles are vipers and among the amphibians the Alpine salamander and Alpine newt. Species found in the Alps also exist in other high mountain regions, where there are, however, more foxes and wolves. In Abruzzi the brown bear may be found and on Sardinia the fallow deer, the mouflon sheep, and the wild boar. Among the freshwater fish are the brown trout, the sturgeon, and the eel. Among sea fish, besides common species such as the red mullet and the dentex, there are, especially in southern waters, the white man-eater shark, the bluefin tuna, and the swordfish. Among invertebrates, there is an abundance of red coral and commercial sponge on the rocks of the warm southern seas. In caves the greater horseshoe bat is found.

TRADITIONAL REGIONS

Italy is divided into 20 administrative regions, which correspond generally with historical traditional regions, though not always with exactly the same boundaries. A better known and more general way of dividing Italy is into four parts: the north, the centre, the south, and the islands.

Problems of regional division

The north includes such traditional regions as Piedmont, marked with some French influence and the seat of united Italy's royal dynasty, with Liguria extending southward around the Gulf of Genoa; the Milanese, long celebrated for its productive agriculture and vigorously independent city communes and now for its industrial output; and the Veneto, once territory of the far-flung Venetian Empire and reaching from Brescia to Trieste in its greatest extent. The centre includes Emilia, with its prosperous farms; the Marche, on the Adriatic side; Tuscany and Umbria, treasuring vestiges of Etruscan civilization and Renaissance traditions of art and culture; Latium (Lazio) and the Campagna, whose beautiful hills encircle the eternal city of Rome; and the Abruzzi and the Molise, regions of the highest central Apennines, which used to support a wild and remote people. The south includes Naples and its surrounding fertile Campania; the poorer regions of Puglia, with its great plain crossed by oleander-bordered roads leading to the low Murge Salentine (Murge Hills) and the heel of Italy, and Basilicata, Lucania, and Calabria, which was once brigand haunted. Finally, in the islands of Sicily and Sardinia are people who take pride in holding themselves apart from the inhabitants of mainland Italy.

Today, the north is heavily populated, with numerous industrial cities and intensive agriculture, attracting steady migration from the south. The centre, focussed on Florence and Rome, traditionally an area of agriculture and local crafts, is becoming increasingly industrialized. The south, with the two ports of Bari and Naples and some recently developed industry, still preserves much of the traditional ways of life. The two islands, Sicily and Sardinia, are extensively cultivated, with citrus fruit and vineyards, pasture for sheep, fisheries, and a decreasing sulfur- and zinc-mining industry. The south and the islands are changing a great deal and gradually becoming more modernized. Within these four main divisions, the variety of the much smaller traditional regions is very great and depends on history as well as topography and economic conditions. Examples of different areas include Brianza, in Lombardy, a hilly region, highly industrialized; Monferrato, a group of hills in the Piedmont, given over to the production of wine; Mugello, the large, hilly basin of the Sieve River in Tuscany, strictly an agricultural area; Chianti, a hilly area of Tuscany famous for its vineyards and wines; and the Tavoliere di Puglia, as the tableland of Foggia is called, a dry and backward region where very ancient agricultural methods are still practiced.

THE HUMAN IMPRINT

Rural areas. As much as 78 percent of the population of Italy are found in some 25,000 cities and villages; only 22 percent live in hamlets, in very small clusters of houses, or in isolated houses.

In the long Alpine valleys the economy was always both agricultural and commercial, and there are many towns, such as Aosta and Bolzano, at the outlets of the lateral valleys. In settlements higher up or on the slopes of hills, an agricultural economy has remained predominant. On spurs of hillocks at the heads of valleys there are often old castles, originally built there for defense. The perpetual subdivision of landholdings makes a purely agricultural economy precarious in this region except in the upper Adige, where the Germanic system of primogeniture survived, producing the *masi*, family holdings that are passed on to the eldest son intact. Cattle raising remains profitable, but woodlands yield less return. Since the 1920s, hydroelectric works have been a feature of the Alpine rural scene, based on natural or artificially created lakes. These rural areas now also include an increasing number of tourist centres, such as Courmayeur and Valle d'Ampezzo. Although these developments have reduced both the seasonal and the permanent migration away from this area, rural living is, nevertheless, declining sharply here. In the band of Alpine and Apennine foothills, the villages, often situated on the knolls and flanks of the hills, are linked by roads that hold to the heights, away from the humid valley floors. Each village is usually grouped round a church, a castle, or a nobleman's palace, with its fields on the slopes around it and woodlands lower down. There are innumerable plum and cherry orchards and, above all, vineyards; their wines (Conegliano, Veronese, and Monferrato) are famous. Businesses are usually small or of only moderate size. Lombardy is the only area in which the ancient rural way of life has been displaced by the development of heavy industry. The population of its rural districts has been increased by migration from the neighbouring mountains and from the south. The Padano–Venetian–Emilian plain is the most important agricultural and stockbreeding region of Italy. The upland plain has now been virtually overrun by the great industrial centres such as Turin, Milan, and Busto Arsizio, but the lowland plain remains socially as well as economically rural. Wheat and maize (corn) are the most common crops, though each district has its specialty, such as sugar beet, grapes, and fruit.

Hydroelectric works and the Alpine landscape

Villages high in the Apennines are less prosperous than

those of similar altitude in the Alps. They are still isolated, the ground is infertile, and land is rarely owned by those who work it. These hopeless conditions have caused the more enterprising residents to emigrate to the north, leaving the villages in an even more desperate situation. Tourism and the expansion of cottage craft industries, such as the porcelain making at Gúbbio, near Perugia, have helped these towns survive. The lower hills and plains of Italy are covered with agricultural villages in which a wide variety of crops and vegetables are grown. The fields are heavily cultivated, but their yield is low. Specialized cultivation is more profitable, such as that in the south of hard-grain wheat, olives, almonds, figs, carobs, and hazelnuts. In Puglia and Basilicata large farms are staffed by labourers who live in urban centres of between 35,000 and 50,000 inhabitants, such as Cerignola and Altamura, and travel to work in the countryside. Some fertile and well-watered plains, such as the Neapolitan *campagna*, have a high level of productivity, especially of market vegetables. Here there is direct ownership of land and fairly dense settlement. In Sicily, settlement is minimal and scattered. Wheat is extensively cultivated. Especially on the coasts, pastureland is extensive though not very profitable; there is efficient cultivation of grapes, olives, citrus fruits, and vegetables, all of which bring the island some revenue, because they can be marketed as early produce. In Sardinia the settlement is also sparse and mainly inland, because of the need, in historical times, to avoid the dangers of malaria in low-lying areas and also of the risk of attack by pirates. Although islanders, the Sardinians have never wanted to work on the sea, and most of their fishing industry is carried on by men from the mainland. There are extensive meadows and forests.

Apennine settlement patterns

Urban centres. From classical times and earlier, Mediterranean peoples have had highly developed urban centres. For historical as well as geographical reasons, Italy has never been dominated by one city, each district tending to possess its own urban centre. Today, there are four cities with a population of more than 1,000,000, Rome, Milan, Naples, and Turin; but over 40 cities have a population of more than 100,000. Of these, almost half, including Sassari and Pisa, are on or near the sea; a similar proportion are in the north, nine in the centre, six in the south, and six on Sicily and Sardinia. This irregularity of urban settlement reflects the economic imbalance among different parts of the country. The distribution of Italian cities also reflects historical and geographical conditions. In the Po Valley, cities such as Milan, Pavia, and Cremona are well placed for commerce, being situated at the confluence of roads or rivers. Another group of cities are those on the coast, built at the mouths of rivers, or on lagoons protected by sandbars; these include Savona, Genoa, Naples, Messina, Palermo, Ancona, and Venice. These cities, which originally grew up so close to each other, have, with increased population and industrialization, merged into enormous metropolitan complexes, sometimes characterized as mega-cities, such as that surrounding Milan. There are now eight metropolitan areas in Italy: Milan, Naples, Rome, Turin, Genoa, Florence, Palermo, and Bologna. It is estimated that in 1980 their combined population will be 22,500,000—they will contain about 37 percent of the total population while occupying only 4 percent of the total area of land. (G.Na.)

II. The people

GROUPS HISTORICALLY ASSOCIATED WITH CONTEMPORARY ITALY

Ethnic and linguistic groups. Linguistically, modern Italy is fairly homogeneous. Non-Italian-speaking groups, a small minority, live mostly in the north of the country, where linguistic borders do not always coincide with political ones. The most important minority is the German-speaking population of the Adige River's upper reaches, in the province of Bolzano. It comprises about 62 percent of the province's total population, while about 34 percent speak Italian, and about 3.5 percent speak Ladine, a Neo-Latin language, a variation of which is also spoken in Switzerland. German is spoken by the majority of the population in 100 municipalities, Italian in nine, and Ladine in seven. More than two-thirds of the Italian-speaking population are concentrated in the two largest towns of the province, Bolzano and Merano, which are growing more rapidly than the rest of the province because of immigration. In 1921 there were about 195,600 German-speaking inhabitants; after an emigration during World War II, the German community started to expand again, with a relatively high birth rate (20.9 per 1,000) in 1969—the highest in northern and central Italy. There were also once German-speaking minorities in Piedmont, Lombardy, and Venetia municipalities.

Non-Italian speakers

In 1961 Slovene was spoken by more than 26,000 inhabitants in the province of Trieste, or 8.6 percent of the province's total population. Unfortunately, only in Bolzano and Trieste provinces did the 1961 census include a question on language, so no other data are available. Statistics dating back to the 1921 census (excluding Bolzano and Trieste and the provinces of Trentino-Alto Adige and Friuli-Venezia Giulia) show that linguistic minorities totalling 250,000 existed in 193 municipalities scattered throughout the country. For more exact locations see Table 2. In some cases these groups have been rapidly diminishing, but actual data are lacking except for French: a 1968 survey indicated it was spoken by nearly 67,000 people, or 25 percent fewer than in 1920. Among the Greeks, Albanians, and others, often only the older people speak the language. The Greek, Albanian, and Catalan minorities are historically interesting, because they are descended mostly from immigrants of the 14th and 15th centuries, and their language has retained archaisms while also being influenced by Italian.

Religions and races. *The religious background.* The overwhelming majority of Italians are Roman Catholics. Membership of other religious groups is marginal, though recent statistical evidence is unavailable. According to the 1931 census, when questions on religion were last included, there were some 83,600 Evangelicals, 47,800 Jews, 6,800 Greek Orthodox, 1,500 of other persuasions, and 17,800 of none. The number of non-Catholics, however, is certainly underestimated, since in 1931 people were asked to state their religion on the basis of baptism or any other formal act of initiation. Very different results were given by the 1911 census, which showed 123,000 of a reformed (mostly evangelical) persuasion, 34,000 Jews, and some 1,528,000 belonging to no religion or refusing to answer the question. In 1938 Jews were estimated at about 47,000, but, by 1946, World War II and Nazi and Fascist persecution had reduced them to 29,000. Subsequently, the Jews have increased only through immigration. In 1965 a Hebrew University of Jerusalem survey counted some 30,600, a figure that was adjusted to 32,000 by including Jews not belonging to communities. After the Arab–Israeli War of 1967 another 3,000 Jews emigrated from Libya to Italy, mostly to Rome. The Jewish population is concentrated in the principal cities: 42.2 percent in Rome, 27.7 percent in Milan, and 21.8 percent among Turin, Florence, Trieste, Genoa, Venice, and Livorno. The remaining 8.3 percent are scattered among 15 small communities.

Anthropological differences. The Italians vary anthropologically from area to area. The results of a survey based on about 300,000 conscripts born between 1859 and 1863 have been confirmed by subsequent research. They provide interesting conclusions about Italians from different regions in the late 19th century, though internal migration has made great subsequent changes.

The cephalic index, a measure of the proportions of the skull, decreases from north to south; that is, brachycephalic (squat-headed) people are found in the Po Valley and around the Alps, extending into central Italy as far as the province of Rieti, though less marked. A similar area, even narrower, includes part of the Abruzzi, Campania, and Basilicata. Conversely, all the south is generally dolichocephalic (long-headed), particularly Calabria, southern Puglia, and Sicily and most of all Sardinia. The north has some areas of pronounced dolichocephaly in east Liguria, southern Piedmont, and particularly northwest Tuscany.

Skull types

Table 1: Italy, Area and Population

	area		population	
	sq mi	sq km	1961 census	1971 census*
Regions				
Abruzzi				
Provinces				
Chieti	999	2,587	348,000	336,000
L'Aquila	1,944	5,034	310,000	291,000
Pescara	473	1,225	230,000	260,000
Teramo	752	1,948	240,000	243,000
Basilicata				
Provinces				
Matera	1,331	3,447	188,000	185,000
Potenza	2,527	6,545	415,000	381,000
Calabria				
Provinces				
Catanzaro	2,026	5,247	697,000	665,000
Cosenza	2,567	6,650	657,000	646,000
Reggio di Calabria	1,229	3,183	583,000	546,000
Campania				
Provinces				
Avellino	1,082	2,801	422,000	397,000
Benevento	796	2,061	297,000	277,000
Caserta	1,019	2,639	634,000	673,000
Napoli	452	1,171	2,426,000	2,724,000
Salerno	1,901	4,923	889,000	927,000
Emilia-Romagna				
Provinces				
Bologna	1,429	3,702	849,000	930,000
Ferrara	1,016	2,631	399,000	382,000
Forlì	1,124	2,910	510,000	564,000
Modena	1,039	2,690	505,000	553,000
Parma	1,332	3,449	382,000	398,000
Piacenza	1,000	2,589	283,000	284,000
Ravenna	718	1,859	329,000	352,000
Reggio nell'Emilia	885	2,291	371,000	391,000
Friuli-Venezia Giulia				
Provinces				
Gorizia	180	466	140,000	147,000
Pordenone	878	2,273	223,000	265,000
Trieste	82	212	298,000	302,000
Udine	1,890	4,894	504,000	530,000
Lazio (Latium)				
Provinces				
Frosinone	1,251	3,239	425,000	420,000
Latina	869	2,250	312,000	374,000
Rieti	1,061	2,749	157,000	141,000
Roma	2,066	5,352	2,843,000	3,560,000
Viterbo	1,395	3,612	263,000	260,000
Liguria				
Provinces				
Genova	707	1,831	1,044,000	1,093,000
Imperia	446	1,155	205,000	227,000
La Spezia	340	882	238,000	247,000
Savona	596	1,545	271,000	302,000
Lombardia (Lombardy)				
Provinces				
Bergamo	1,065	2,759	719,000	821,000
Brescia	1,838	4,761	864,000	950,000
Como	798	2,067	623,000	718,000
Cremona	684	1,771	346,000	334,000
Mantova	903	2,339	383,000	375,000
Milano	1,067	2,762	3,181,000	3,886,000
Pavia	1,145	2,965	515,000	526,000
Sondrio	1,240	3,212	154,000	165,000
Varese	463	1,199	587,000	728,000
Marche				
Provinces				
Ancona	748	1,938	399,000	417,000
Ascoli Piceno	806	2,086	327,000	338,000
Macerata	1,071	2,774	285,000	284,000
Pesaro e Urbino	1,117	2,893	301,000	312,000

	area		population	
	sq mi	sq km	1961 census	1971 census
Regions				
Molise				
Provinces				
Campobasso	1,123	2,909	238,000	218,000
Isernia	590	1,529	95,000	85,000
Piemonte (Piedmont				
Provinces				
Alessandria	1,375	3,560	480,000	487,000
Asti	583	1,511	214,000	219,000
Cuneo	2,665	6,903	530,000	547,000
Novara	1,388	3,594	459,000	498,000
Torino	2,637	6,830	1,861,000	2,305,000
Vercelli	1,159	3,001	405,000	406,000
Puglia (Apulia)				
Provinces				
Bari	1,981	5,130	1,243,000	1,332,000
Brindisi	709	1,838	343,000	359,000
Foggia	2,774	7,184	633,000	627,000
Lecce	1,065	2,759	628,000	662,000
Taranto	941	2,437	465,000	514,000
Sardegna (Sardinia)				
Provinces				
Cagliari	3,590	9,298	734,000	793,000
Nuoro	2,808	7,272	266,000	260,000
Sassari	2,903	7,520	373,000	393,000
Sicilia (Sicily)				
Provinces				
Agrigento	1,174	3,042	447,000	426,000
Caltanissetta	813	2,105	293,000	273,000
Catania	1,372	3,552	887,000	929,000
Enna	989	2,562	218,000	187,000
Messina	1,254	3,247	673,000	649,000
Palermo	1,937	5,016	1,102,000	1,117,000
Ragusa	623	1,614	249,000	245,000
Siracusa	814	2,109	344,000	356,000
Trapani	950	2,462	421,000	400,000
Toscana (Tuscany)				
Provinces				
Arezzo	1,248	3,232	301,000	305,000
Firenze	1,498	3,880	1,035,000	1,168,000
Grosseto	1,736	4,496	217,000	215,000
Livorno	471	1,220	314,000	338,000
Lucca	684	1,773	361,000	376,000
Massa-Carrara	446	1,156	195,000	200,000
Pisa	945	2,448	366,000	383,000
Pistoia	373	965	232,000	256,000
Siena	1,475	3,821	272,000	261,000
Trentino-Alto Adige				
Provinces				
Bolzano (Südtirol)	2,857	7,400	384,000	422,000
Trento	2,399	6,213	399,000	423,000
Umbria				
Provinces				
Perugia	2,446	6,334	557,000	558,000
Terni	819	2,122	223,000	222,000
Valle d'Aosta				
Province				
Valle d'Aosta	1,260	3,262	102,000	111,000
Veneto				
Provinces				
Belluno	1,420	3,678	206,000	215,000
Padova	827	2,142	692,000	769,000
Rovigo	696	1,802	271,000	249,000
Treviso	956	2,477	588,000	668,000
Venezia	950	2,460	748,000	815,000
Verona	1,196	3,097	665,000	729,000
Vicenza	1,051	2,722	604,000	677,000
Total Italy	116,314†	301,253†	49,904,000	53,770,000‡

*Preliminary. †Converted area figures do not add to total given because of rounding. ‡Figures do not add to total given because of rounding.
Source: Official government figures.

In stature the inhabitants are generally smaller in the south. Three areas have relatively tall inhabitants: the largest area covers part of Venetia, the second is halfway between Tuscany and Emilia, and the third is in north-east Lombardy. The areas of small stature stretch from southern Marche to the south, becoming gradually more pronounced, especially in Sardinia. Although the greatest dolichocephaly and the smallest stature seem to coincide, there is no correlation; the small stature is largely the product of socio-economic environment.

Italians are predominantly dark, though fair types are found in northern Italy, relatives of the fair natives of Savoy, Switzerland, and Austria. Throughout the Po Valley the people are notably darker than in Tuscany, Umbria, and Marche, in central Italy. Another area with fair types is found slightly farther south, in Sannio and Irpinia. Sardinia, again, has the highest frequency of dark types.

Despite modifications through internal migration, this analysis of anthropological characteristics is still reliable for studying the origins of Italians.

DEMOGRAPHIC TRENDS

Throughout the centuries Italy's population has shared many changes with other European countries. The mid-14th-century plague reduced its population considerably,

Table 2: Minority Groups in Italy
(1921 census)

	numbers	location
French	90,700	98 municipalities in Valle d'Aosta and Piedmont
Greek	19,672	13 municipalities, Puglia and Calabria
Albanian	80,282	47 municipalities, southern Italy and Sicily
Slavic	37,475	20 municipalities, Friuli and Molise
Catalan	12,236	1 municipality, Alghero in Sardinia
German	8,735	14 municipalities in Piedmont, Lombardy, and Veneto

and a long period of population growth ended at the beginning of the 17th century. From the early 18th century until the unification (in 1861), a slight, steady growth prevailed, though it was interrupted during the Napoleonic Wars.

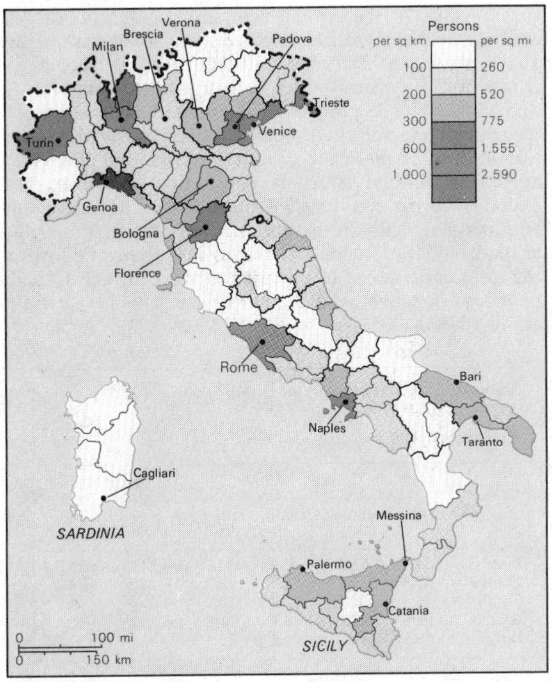

Population density of Italy.

In Table 3 are recorded census populations from 1861 to 1971 within contemporary and present boundaries. Population densities and rates of increase between censuses also appear.

Table 3: Growth and Density of the Italian Population, 1861–1971

	de facto population (in 000)		population density* (per sq km)	intercensal annual increase* (per 000)
	within contemporary boundaries	within then-existing boundaries		
1861	25,756	21,777	85.5	—
1871	27,578	26,801	91.5	6.6
1881	29,278	28,460	97.2	6.2
1901	33,370	32,475	110.8	7.0
1911	35,695	34,672	118.5	7.0
1921	37,404	37,974	124.2	4.8
1931	40,582	41,177	134.7	8.5
1936	42,303	42,919	140.4	8.5
1951	47,159	47,159	156.5	7.6
1961	49,904	49,904	165.7	5.8
1971	53,770	53,770	178.5	7.7

*Contemporary boundaries.

The population has more than doubled, from 25,756,000 in 1861 to 53,770,000 in 1971, but this increase is less than that for many other European countries. The rate of growth over any decade has never exceeded 0.9 percent and remains (excluding the upheaval caused by World War I) between 0.6 percent and 0.8 percent—a moderate, steady increase. In the 1950s and 1960s the rate of increase reached a level comparable to those in Great Britain, France, and West Germany. Population density, about 462 inhabitants per square mile, is high for a country with territory that is a third (35.2 percent) mountainous; only 49.6 percent of the land is fit for arable farming.

Checks to the population spiral

Birth and death rates. Italian demographic development is shown in Table 4. The decline of the birth rate during the 1890s, reflecting a growing awareness of family-planning techniques, occurred a decade or two after the death rate started to fall. The decline of each continued till the 1950s, levelling off thereafter. Migration drained the population until the eve of World War I; the loss was reduced between the wars, increasing again after World War II. Over the entire period, the net loss of the population has been some 9,000,000 people. The rate of natural population increase was particularly high in the decades when emigration was highest, although there is no obvious causal relationship between the two. The actual rate of increase of the population has remained approximately constant throughout the century. Fertility and mortality follows more advanced Western countries, although with a delay of one or more decades. The halt in the decline of Italy's birth rate lagged behind other countries because of its lower social and economic level and its slower development up to World War II. Peculiar to Italy are regional differences, particularly between north and south.

Regional differences. From the early 1950s the national birth rate has remained at about 18 per thousand. From the 1930s to the 1960s most of the population in much of the north and the centre (particularly in Liguria, Piedmont, Friuli-Venezia Giulia, Tuscany, and Emilia) was not reproducing itself; that is to say, the average number of children per couple was under two. The figures in Liguria and Piedmont were as low as 1.5 or 1.6. Average figures for the south and the islands sometimes reached four. In 1970 the birth rate in the north and centre was 15.4 per thousand, as against 19.2 per thousand in the south (16.5 per thousand for the whole nation).

Factors tending to eradicate regional differences include high internal mobility, the policy of social and economic development for the south, the spread of mass communications, and the recent abolition of laws forbidding the advertisement of contraceptives and birth-control propaganda.

Life expectancy. The mortality development follows a more uniform pattern. The death rate has declined from around 30 per thousand before 1880 to under 10 per thousand during the 1950s and 1960s. But the death-rate level is heavily affected by the changing age structure and, since the 19th century, by the ageing process of the population. A more refined indicator of mortality is life expectancy at birth, as shown in Table 5.

The doubling of life expectancy is well in line with European trends, reflecting higher nutritional and sanitation standards, improved medical care, and advances in medicine and pharmacology. Regional contrasts of mortality are less marked than those of fertility. Differences nonetheless arise, as a result of incidence of infectious diseases and deaths induced by "exogenous" factors, or peculiar environmental features. Malaria, typhus, and cholera once ravaged the south, while pellagra was a widespread cause of death in Lombardy and Venetia. Such incidences have been very much reduced by the advances of medicine, but mortality—particularly infant mortality—is still very much influenced by inadequate living conditions, as can be seen from Table 6.

The decline in mortality rates is approximately the same for the four areas. Their relative situation has remained unchanged, with a 50–60 percent higher infant-mortality rate in the south and in the islands than in the rest of the country. The gap between Italy and other large west European countries is still considerable, though it is gradually narrowing. The poorer regions of Italy seem to have some advantages over the centre and north in their lower incidence of cancer and cardiovascular diseases.

Table 4: Demographic Development of the Italian Population, 1862–1970

	births (000)	deaths (000)	migratory balance (000)	birth rate (per 000)	death rate (per 000)	rate of natural increase (percentage)	rate of net migration (percentage)	rate of increase (percentage)
1862–71	10,016	8,116	−78	37.4	30.3	7.1	−0.3	6.8
1872–81	10,500	8,422	−378	36.9	29.6	7.3	−1.3	6.0
1882–91	11,381	8,227	−845	37.2	26.9	10.3	−2.8	7.5
1892–1901	11,182	7,732	−1,378	34.2	23.7	10.5	−4.2	6.3
1902–11	11,241	7,449	−1,417	32.2	21.3	10.9	−4.1	6.8
1912–21	10,065	8,076	−903	27.2	21.8	5.4	−2.4	3.0
1922–31	10,829	6,402	−898	27.5	16.3	11.3	−2.3	9.0
1932–41	9,864	5,963	−242	23.0	13.9	9.1	−0.6	8.5
1942–51	9,215	5,843	−631	20.1	12.8	7.3	−1.4	5.9
1952–61	8,793	4,687	−1,305	18.0	9.6	8.4	−2.7	5.7
1962–71	9,520	5,107	−547	18.4	9.9	8.5	−1.1	7.4

Expectancy of life at birth, again, is a good yardstick of the general sanitary conditions of the population. In Table 7 it can be seen that the south and the islands have nearly caught up with the rest of the country. The population of the centre maintains its privileged position, with the longest life expectancy. For the male population, shortest life expectancy is in the north.

Table 5: Life Expectancy at Birth, 1881–1967

	females	males
1881–82	35.7	35.2
1899–1902	43.0	42.6
1910–12	47.3	46.6
1921–22	50.8	49.3
1930–32	56.0	53.8
1950–53	67.2	63.7
1960–63	72.3	67.2
1964–67	73.4	67.9

Migration. Italy is traditionally a country of emigration. From the unification of the country until the 1970s about 26,000,000 Italians left the country. Almost always they go in quest of work abroad, sometimes for a few years, sometimes for life. The net loss from 1862 to 1970 is about 9,000,000, or a little more than one-third of the total.

The course of transatlantic emigration. During the 1860s and 1870s emigration emanated from the north, which long had contact with foreign countries. Emigration was largely associated with particular professions and skills: woodcutters and bricklayers went to neighbouring Alpine countries; farmers, vine growers, artists, and peddlers to North America. During the 1880s, however, emigration became a mass phenomenon, gradually involving the poor rural populations of the south. The flow rapidly increased as a result of improved internal and transatlantic transport facilities; the south's economic crisis, which hit both agriculture and industry, particularly in the late 1880s and 1890s; and the growing demand for labour in North and South America. Although emigration to Switzerland, Austria, and France was considerable, the destination was primarily transatlantic from the late 1880s to the early 1920s; about three-quarters of all the transatlantic emigrants since the late 19th century travelled during these four decades. Of the total of 12,000,000 who travelled in 100 years, about half went to the U.S., one quarter to Argentina, 1,300,000 to Brazil, and almost 1,000,000 to Canada and Australia. During 1900–14, Italian emigration reached its peak, with 523,000 in 1906 and 565,000 in 1913, but the U.S.'s immigration acts of 1921 and 1924 practically closed the most important foreign labour market. Emigration to Brazil also declined considerably early in the 20th century because of the critical economic conditions of that country, and emigration to Argentina at the end of the 1920s slowed to a trickle. Subsequently, the economic depression, Fascism—which was hostile to emigration—and World War II practically eliminated emigration. After the war the very high unemployment revived emigration to South America, particularly Argentina and Venezuela. Traditional overseas emigration, however, had ended; with the economy's expansion, the decline of unemployment, and the assimilation of Italian minorities abroad, emigration for life fell to less than one-fifth of the total emigration. Departures to the U.S. and Canada in this period averaged 30,000 a year and to Australia about 15,000.

Changing character of emigration

Table 6: Infant-Mortality Rates, 1950–52 and 1970
(by geographic location)

	1950–52 (per 000)	1970 (per 000)	percentage change
North	53.7	24.5	−54.4
Centre	47.6	22.4	−53.0
South	81.6	38.4	−52.9
Islands	75.3	33.6	−55.4
Italy	65.0	29.2	−55.1

Table 7: Life Expectancy at Birth, 1930–32 and 1960–62
(by geographic location)

	1930–32		1960–62		percentage change	
	male	female	male	female	male	female
North	54.8	58.2	66.7	72.9	+21.7	+25.3
Centre	56.8	59.1	68.9	73.7	+21.5	+24.7
South	51.4	52.5	67.3	70.8	+30.9	+34.9
Islands	52.8	53.1	68.7	71.8	+30.1	+35.2
Italy	53.8	56.0	67.2	72.3	+24.9	+29.1

European migration. During the late 1950s and early 1960s when there was still a considerable manpower surplus in the south, the islands, and parts of the north and centre, many of the unemployed took advantage of the tempting opportunities in other European countries, with rapidly expanding economies and pressing demands for labour. Thus, emigration to West Germany and Switzerland increased, while that to France (a traditional destination for Italian emigrants) and Belgium started to dwindle. This new wave was very different from the transatlantic emigration. Now the proportion of males was very high and entire families rare, because some countries refused entry to workers' relatives and some suffered from a housing shortage. The length of stay was very short, and repetitive expatriation for further periods of work abroad became common. As a result, the communities of Italian workers in Switzerland and West Germany became highly unstable, with a rapid exchange of individuals; many social and family problems were created both in the areas of origin and in the host countries. In the 1960s, migration between continental countries began to decrease, and Italian labour more often found worthwhile positions at home. Restrictive regulations, too, reduced the number of Italian workers in Switzerland (474,300 in 1964 to 361,200 in 1970). In Table 9 the trend of departure to other European countries can be followed over 25 years, together with the net loss in population.

Migration of the European labour market

Population movement within Italy. *Interregional flow.* Internal migration is a very important factor in the regional redistribution of the Italian population. From 1960 to the early 1970s the populations of the south and areas such as Venetia have had a much higher natural growth

Table 8: Expatriation by Ten-Year Periods and by Destination, 1871–1970
(in 000)

	Europe*	total overseas		total†
		U.S. and Canada	other	
1871–80	906	268	270	1,176
1881–90	929	245	950	1,879
1891–1900	1,288	514	1,547	2,835
1901–10	2,512	2,329	3,515	6,027
1911–20	1,696	1,567	2,132	3,821
1921–30	1,362	419	1,188	2,551
1931–40	414	115	288	703
1946–50	638	66	489	1,127
1951–60	1,767	193	1,170	2,937
1961–70	2,127	184	471	2,646

*Until 1954 including the countries of the Mediterranean Basin. †Figures do not add to total given because of rounding.

rate than the rest of the country. Nevertheless, the population's regional distribution has remained stable, with internal compensatory exchanges of population. The centre now accounts for 18.8 percent, as opposed to 16.8 percent in the 19th century, but this can be attributed to the increase in Rome, caused mainly by immigration from the south.

Since the unification of Italy, internal movements have followed the same direction, south to north and east to west: from the regions of the south and from the islands (especially Sicily) to centre regions—*e.g.*, Lazio–Rome and Tuscany—to the northwest—*e.g.*, Lombardy, Liguria, and Piedmont; and from the northeast (*e.g.*, Venetia) to the northwest. Movements from Emilia, Marche, and Umbria to other regions of the northwest and the centre have also been considerable. Mobility has grown exceptionally swiftly since World War II, corresponding to economic expansion, particularly in the industrial triangle of Lombardy–Piedmont–Liguria. Allied factors have been the reduction of unemployment in the north and a persistent labour surplus in the south. During 1951–61 the northwest industrial triangle gained 1,097,000 people, while the northeast lost 491,000; the centre, Marche, and Umbria lost 169,000, Lazio and Tuscany gaining 293,000; the south's net loss was 1,303,000 and that of the islands 469,000. Italy is one of the few countries having a registration system for changes of residence from one commune to another. Each year about 3 percent of the total population change their residences, but this figure is less than actual mobility, because it does not reflect seasonal and temporary migrations, movements from one commune to another for educational purposes or for military service. During 1962–69, net immigration from the south and the islands to the north amounted to 798,000 and from the same area to the centre, 247,000. Altogether the south and islands have had a net loss through internal migration of 1,045,000, or about 130,000 each year. In the same period Turin gained 219,000 inhabitants, Milan 216,000, and Rome 303,000.

Urbanization. Another aspect of the population redistribution in Italy, the vast urbanization, was especially rapid during the 1950s and 1960s. The transformation of the economy during those two decades—from mainly agricultural to mainly industrial—has strongly affected the distribution between rural and urban areas. In 1951, 42.2 percent of the labour force was engaged in the primary sector, but by January 1971 the proportion had dwindled to 18.1 percent. The 11 largest urban areas of the country, Turin, Milan, Venice, Genoa, Bologna, Florence, Rome, Naples, Bari, Catania, and Palermo, had a population of 2,600,000 in 1871, or 10 percent of the total. This figure rose to 6,900,000 in 1951 (14.5 percent of the total), 9,800,000 in 1961 (19.4 percent), and 11,200,000 in 1969 (20.6 percent of the total). The gradual shift to the towns is clearly shown by Table 10, (Principal urban areas)

Table 9: Emigration to European Countries by Destination, 1946–69
(in 000)

	1946–49	1950–54	1955–59	1960–64	1965–69	1946–69
Belgium	106	72	46	16	19	259
France	174	172	380	179	78	983
West Germany	—	1	59	488	289	837
Switzerland	286	278	366	647	448	1,025
Others	18	46	92	80	82	318
Total emigration to Europe	584	569	943	1,410	916	4,422
Total repatriations from Europe	260	312	565	943	832	2,912
Net emigration to Europe	−324	−257	−378	−467	−84	−1,510

Table 10: Distribution of De Facto Population by Commune Size, 1881–1971
(percentage)

population of the *comuni*	1881	1911	1931	1951	1961	1971
Below 3,000	27.7	20.9	15.8	14.0	13.2	11.9
3,000–10,000	38.3	36.7	33.9	30.6	26.8	23.2
10,000–50,000	22.7	26.2	27.0	27.4	26.5	27.6
50,000–100,000	3.1	5.3	6.5	7.6	8.7	8.0
Over 100,000	8.2	10.9	16.8	20.4	24.8	29.2
Total	100.0	100.0	100.0	100.0	100.0	100.0

which indicates the distribution of the population by size of *comune* for 88 years. The change in distribution, particularly rapid during the last 20 years indicated, involves a drop in the proportion of people living in the smaller *comuni* from almost 66 percent in 1881 to 35 percent in 1971. These *comuni* are mainly rural, although a few adjoining large centres may have urban characteristics. Moreover, the proportion living in urban centres has risen from 11.3 percent to 37 percent.

Finally, during 1961–71, the population of 5,330 out of the country's 8,056 *comuni* (66.2 percent), representing over a quarter of the total population, decreased. In some regions those *comuni* represent the majority of the population. Such data indicate the profound changes occurring in Italy's population distribution. (M.L.-B.)

III. The national economy

ITALY IN THE WORLD CONTEXT

Italy's economic growth since World War II has been both spectacular and sustained. At the end of the war, the country's economy lay in ruins, although much of the industrial machinery in the north had been saved from destruction. By 1951, prewar levels of production had been regained, and the next 20 years saw almost uninterrupted growth. Italy is now generally considered to be the world's sixth or seventh most important industrial country and the leading country in the Mediterranean Basin. Within Europe, Italy still lags behind the United Kingdom, France, and the Federal Republic of Germany in terms of industrial production and per capita income, but the gap steadily narrowed in the 1960s. Italy cannot yet be classified as a mature industrial economy, however, although the transition period from a primarily agricultural society to a predominantly industrial one will have been completed long before the end of the 20th century. The growing importance of Italy as an economic power can be gauged from the fact that, while the population of Italy fell between 1951 and 1968 from 1.93 to 1.56 percent of the world's total, the proportion of Italy's national income to the world total rose from 2.19 to 3.92 percent. Italy's greatest success in postwar years has been the rapid growth in industrial production. Between 1953 and 1968 the level of industrial production increased by more than 200 percent, a feat matched only by the Federal Republic of Germany and Japan. Average growth rates of gross national product (GNP) in real terms were 5.7 percent between 1952 and 1958, 5.8 percent from 1958 to 1965, and 6.1 percent from then until 1970. Italy's boom has been based on the expansion of foreign trade. Exports rose from 1,130,720,000,000 lire (1968 prices) in 1951 to 9,358,735,000,000 lire in 1971, while imports increased from 1,375,200,000,000 lire to 9,893,518,000,000 lire in 1971.

THE EXTENT AND DISTRIBUTION OF NATURAL RESOURCES

Mineral resources. In terms of mineral resources Italy is one of the poorest countries in Europe. Both metalliferous and nonmetalliferous minerals are generally nonexistent or in short supply. The extractive industry has grown at a slower rate than other sectors because of both the poor quality of some minerals, such as coal, and the increasing inefficiency of the mines. Many of the sulfur mines in central Sicily and the coal mines in southwest Sardinia have been closed since World War II, and the decline continues. Italy has sufficient reserves of only a few minerals, such as mercury, sulfur, rock salt, and marble, while deposits of iron ore, coal, oil, and natural gas are meagre. Further reserves of hydrocarbons are being sought, especially in offshore areas. Italy also produces small quantities of zinc, lead, bauxite, pyrites, and a number of other minerals. The decline of Italy's mining industries is illustrated by the drop in production of sulfur: in 1901 the sulfur mines produced 3,700,000 tons; in 1938, 2,400,000 tons; and, in 1971, just over 609,000 tons. In the same years, coal and lignite production rose from 400,000 tons to 2,300,000 tons in 1938 and declined to 1,600,000 tons in 1971. Coal production now accounts for only 15 percent of Italy's needs, and about 12,000,000 tons a year are imported, mainly from the U.S., other countries of the European Economic Community (EEC), or Common Market, eastern Europe, and Japan. Italy is a leading supplier of mercury, located mainly in the central part of the country, which accounts for more than 15 percent of world output.

Decline of mining industries

Deposits of both oil and natural gas exist in Italy, but the reserves of the former are rapidly being exhausted. After the discoveries of oil made in the 1950s at Ragusa and Gela, in Sicily, production rose to a peak of just under 3,000,000 tons a year and then gradually declined. In 1971 less than 1,300,000 tons were extracted. The discovery of natural gas in the Po Valley and in various zones of southern and central Italy, including Sicily, raised hopes that Italy might be able to produce enough for domestic needs. Further deposits were discovered in the offshore Adriatic in the late 1960s, estimated at 2,120,000,000,000 cubic feet. Despite these discoveries, Italy initiated massive imports from diversified sources, both to meet the increased demand and to conserve total known deposits, which are estimated at 9,200,000,000,000 cubic feet. Annual production reached a level of 472,845,000,000 cubic feet in 1971, and further supplies were expected from Libya, the Soviet Union, and The Netherlands. Exploration, especially in the offshore areas, was intensified, above all by the State Hydrocarbons Corporation, the Ente Nazionale Idrocarburi (ENI).

Oil production accounts for only a minute part of domestic consumption. Imports of crude oil in 1970 amounted to 112,000,000 tons—mainly from the Middle East, Libya, and the Persian Gulf. About 30,000,000 tons of this were destined for export as petroleum products.

Italy's output of iron ore accounts for less than 10 percent of domestic needs. Imports come mainly from Liberia, Canada, Venezuela, and Brazil. The present level of ore production is lower than the 1938 total of 900,000 tons, when Italy's steel industry was in its infancy, producing 2,300,000 tons of crude steel, compared with nearly 17,500,000 tons in 1971. Production of other minerals, such as pyrites, lead, zinc, and bauxite—deposits of which are scattered throughout the country—has been more or less static and is not expected to increase. Discoveries of rock salt, above all in Sicily, have boosted production to more than 2,500,000 tons, and further rises are expected. The quarrying industry—especially for marble and travertine (a hot-spring limestone deposit) from the world-famous quarries at Massa and Carrara (where Michelangelo, among other artists, found his raw material)—has enjoyed a modest but steady growth in postwar years, mainly as a result of the renewed popularity of the materials in the construction industry. In 1971 mining accounted for less than 1 percent of the GNP.

Biological resources. Geologically, Italy is still at a very unstable stage of development. Earthquakes and tremors are quite frequent all over the mainland. Italy is characterized by a wide variety of climatic differences, topography, and soil types. For the most part, the terrain is rugged, arid, and unsuitable for intensive cultivation, except in the Po Valley, the plains of Puglia, and Campania. As a result of low rainfall, vegetation is sparse in parts of the country, especially in sectors of the Apennine Mountains. It has been mainly the pressure of population, however, leading to the cultivation of land generally unsuited for such use, that has caused widespread soil erosion and endangered the hydrogeological equilibrium of the land. The movement from the land of more than 6,000,000 peasants since 1945 has increased the dangers of neglect of property that was formerly cultivated or tended. Despite the exodus to the towns, more than 50 percent of productive land is still cultivated, compared with 38 percent in France and 20 percent in the U.S. As a result, Italy is deficient in timber and forest products, although the government is pursuing an active policy of reforestation. Woods and forests covered just over 15,000,000 acres in 1970, or 20.5 percent of the total productive land area. Production of timber was estimated in 1969 at 144,450,000 cubic feet; the balance of Italy's timber needs consisted of imports of sawn wood, amounting to around 2,500,000 tons a year, most of which came from Austria and Sweden.

Timber production

Broad-leaved trees make up 72.5 percent of Italy's forest area, and conifers make up 19.2 percent. Broad-leaved forests are fairly well spread over the country, with the exception of the Puglia, Sicilian, and Sardinian regions. Conifers are for the most part concentrated in the Alpine foothills, especially in the Alto-Adige region adjacent to the Austrian border. Because Italy is not well endowed with rivers, with the exception of the Po and the various smaller rivers that flow into the sea at or near the Po Delta on the northeast coast, intensive agriculture is concentrated in the overcrowded coastal plains, the mountain foothills, and above all in the Po Valley, the most fertile part of Italy. The need for land suitable for agriculture has led to many programs of land reclamation and improvement, especially in the south.

Hydroelectric resources. The three main lakes of northern Italy (Como, Maggiore, and Garda) are the source of six small rivers that flow southward into the Po River. These, together with the Bronta, La Sila, Tagliamento, and Adige rivers, which have their sources in the Alps, are the origin of approximately 80 percent of Italy's hydroelectric power. As a result, more than half of the electricity produced in the northern regions of Piedmont, Lombardy, Alto-Adige, Venetia, and Friuli-Venezia Giulia is hydroelectric. Other regions of Italy with a similar proportion of hydroelectric power are Umbria, Abruzzo, and Calabria—all hilly or mountainous zones. Hydroelectric resources have been exploited almost to the maximum. In 1960, hydroelectric production stood at 46,000,000,000 kilowatt-hours, or 82 percent of total production. By 1970, hydroelectric production had dropped to 41,000,000,000 kilowatt-hours (for climatological reasons), accounting for only 35 percent of total electricity production. For the decade 1970 to 1980, a ceiling of 50,000,000,000 kilowatt-hours was planned; thus, it would account for approximately 18 percent of the total electricity generated by 1980.

Power potential of the lakes

SOURCES OF NATIONAL INCOME

Agriculture, forestry, and fishing. Agriculture in Italy remains an important sector of the economy in terms of both employment and its contribution to the gross national product, which was 11.6 percent in 1970. In that year, agricultural workers numbered 3,716,000, or 19 percent of the total labour force. Despite a number of agricultural reforms and EEC membership, agriculture is still backward by west European standards. The typical Italian farm is small, relatively unproductive, and geared more to subsistence than to modern market-oriented farming. The average farm or smallholding is only 17 acres, and there are 2,500,000 of them. Fewer than 50,-

000 of these farms exceed the minimum size of 124 acres recommended by an EEC commission. Since 1945 there has also been a limited redistribution of land to small farmers, mainly under the 1950 agrarian reform acts, which led to the expropriation of 1,900,000 acres in southern and central Italy. This has not stopped a massive flight from the land, estimated at about 6,000,000 persons in the period from 1945 to 1970. Another 2,000,000 persons were also expected to leave the land in the 1970s and 1980s, thus reducing the agricultural labour force to as few as 2,000,000.

In Italy the complex land-tenure system is gradually being simplified by new legislation. More than 80 percent of farms are run by the owner and his family, without the employment of wage labourers; the remainder are run mainly under a sharecropping or rent system or, in the case of larger farms, with the employment of day labourers or permanent staff. The aim of agricultural policy since World War II has been to modernize agriculture by the development of efficient and well-organized farms, thus improving living standards for those working the land. This policy has been only partially successful. The first Green Plan, launched in 1961, had these aims, and some of the goals have been achieved, much money being spent on mortgages and loans, land, irrigation, and crop improvement. The second Green Plan, covering the period 1966 to 1970, concentrated on a number of key sectors, increasing profitable forms of production and productivity and raising incomes.

The Green Plans

About 13,700,000 acres of arable land is devoted to cereal growing. The most important hard-grain-wheat-growing areas are in southern Italy, in the Sicilian and Puglian regions. Together they account for more than 60 percent of national production, which in 1970 amounted to just over 9,600,000 tons. The balance needed to meet domestic requirements was met by imports in that year of nearly 1,200,000 tons, mainly from the U.S. and Argentina. Domestic production of other cereals, notably rye, barley, and oats, was also insufficient, and more than 1,100,000 tons of these three cereals were imported in 1970. The land area devoted to corn (maize) growing has been steadily increasing, but the 1970 production of over 4,700,000 tons was only one-half the amount consumed in Italy, the balance being made up of imports, also principally from the U.S. and Argentina. Italy is Europe's leading rice producer, more than 90 percent of it being grown in Piedmont and Lombardy; a large portion of the 1970 crop of almost 820,000 tons was exported to other European countries.

Wine and olive oil. Italy's most important agricultural products are wine and olive oil. Italy vies with France as the world's leading wine producer, and only an exceptional yield enabled France to surpass Italy's production of 1,700,000,000 gallons in 1970. A large quantity of the wine produced is not considered of high quality, but in a number of regions there are wines that compare favourably with the best. The government is active in upgrading Italian wines, and the system of *appellation contrôlée* (registered trade names) is gradually being extended to a wide range of Italian wines. More than 7,400,000 acres of land are devoted to the cultivation of vines, one-third for specialized vineyards, the remainder for a mixture of vines and other crops. Olives are grown principally in southern Italy; Puglia and Calabria are the main producing regions. Olive-oil production has been erratic, oscillating between 170,000 and 650,000 tons a year. The grape and olive crops are of considerable economic importance to Italian agriculture, as 90 percent of the former and 80 percent of the latter are processed on the farms themselves. Wine is exported in large quantities, although competition is particularly strong from other European countries, especially France and Spain. On the other hand, Italy is a net importer of olive oil, the deficit exceeding 45,840,000,000 lire in 1970.

Tomatoes and fruit growing. More than 321,000 acres of land are devoted to tomato growing, and the annual output varies between 3,000,000 and 3,700,000 tons. This crop has been one of the mainstays of agriculture in the south, particularly in Sicily and Campania, and canned tomatoes and tomato paste are exported throughout the world. Competition from Greece, Portugal, and Spain, however, has seriously eroded some traditional markets. Italy produces just over one-half of all fruit grown in the original European Economic Community area. Peaches, pears, and apples are very important and are grown primarily in the northeastern regions of the country. But, because of an excess supply within the EEC, thousands of tons of fruit were either destroyed or sent to the distilleries in the 1960s. Citrus-fruit growing is also a major agricultural activity in southern Italy, especially in Sicily, which produced two-thirds of the 1970 orange crop. At least 708,000 tons of the 770,000-ton lemon crop was also produced in Sicily. Citrus fruits account for scarcely one-third of the entire value of Sicily's entire agricultural output. Because of high costs, the difficulties of mechanization in dense fruit groves, and an absence of marketing cooperatives, Sicily was unable to sell all its crop, and nearly 100,000 tons were withdrawn from the market in that year.

Citrus fruits

Livestock. Production of livestock is inadequate, since with rising living standards the demand for meat rose astronomically in the 1950s and 1960s. By 1970, beef imports alone cost 249,795,000,000 lire. The dairy industry also fails to satisfy domestic needs. Most dairy herds are in northern Italy and produce only 75 percent of the country's milk. Although a wide variety of cheese is produced—from goat, buffalo, and sheep milk, as well as from that of cows—it is done so mainly as a craft industry. As a result, imports of butter, cheese, and other dairy products cost more than 106,960,000,000 lire in 1970.

Fishing. Italy's waters are not well stocked with fish, but the yearly catch rose steadily from 1964, exceeding 243,000 tons in 1971. Anchovies, sardines, and tunny accounted for more than one-third of the total catch, while an important part of the remainder was made up of mackerels, mollusks, and shellfish. The gap between supply and demand is filled by large imports of fresh, frozen, dried, and salted fish—amounting to 65,082,000,000 lire in 1970—coming mainly from Norway, Denmark, Japan, and Spain. The fishing industry still remains primarily an individual enterprise, although cooperatives and a few large fleets continue to expand. Legislation in the late 1960s and early 1970s has led to the allocation of funds for the renewal of fleets, but radical structural changes in the industry appeared unlikely. Some fishing banks in or near Italian coastal waters are already exhausted, and many fishermen have left the industry in search of more profitable occupations.

Individualism in the fishing industry

Mining and quarrying. Mining is not an important sector of the Italian economy, and employment in it is rapidly declining, dropping from 155,000 in 1952 to 110,000 in 1970, or only 0.6 percent of the labour force. Coal and lignite production is expected to decline gradually, as is that of sulfur, one of the few mineral resources to be found in any quantity in Italy. In any case, coal is gradually being replaced by oil, electricity, and natural gas. Likewise, production of iron ore, in which Italy is equally deficient, is destined to decline. The only sectors in which an increase is expected are in the mining of mercuric ores and rock and potassic salts (from deposits in Sicily) and in the extraction of natural gas. Quarrying activity remains high, however, especially because of the demand for marble, gravel, and other materials for the construction and road-building industries.

Manufacturing. The most remarkable feature of postwar economic development has been the spectacular increase in manufacturing. Since 1948, relative political stability has increased business confidence and led to annual industrial investment of more than 20 percent of produced income. Other important factors were Marshall aid (a special U.S.-financed aid program after World War II), safeguarding Italy during the crucial recovery period from 1946 to 1951 from balance-of-payments problems; an orthodox but sound monetary policy; and the liberalization of trade. The last factor has been especially important, since Italy's economic boom has been based on exports. Another fundamental reason for Italy's rapid growth of manufacturing output has been the abundance of manpower. Italy's geographical position—near the oil fields of North Africa and the Middle East—was also an important stimulus to industry as a whole and to the development of the refining and petrochemical industries.

The steel industry. Despite a lack of mineral resources, a major expansion of the steel industry was begun in the early 1950s—one of the most farsighted and courageous decisions taken by the government. The steel industry has been the backbone of Italy's industrialization. Between 1953 and 1968 steel production increased nearly five times. In the same period, Italy's share of world crude-steel production doubled, to 3.2 percent. Production amounted to almost 17,300,000 tons in 1970, but total domestic consumption was 3,000,000 tons more. There have also been important qualitative changes in the industry.

Automobiles and electrical appliances. Parallel with the development of the steel industry has been that of the engineering and allied sectors. In particular, the automobile industry has grown spectacularly. Production of motor vehicles (which was almost entirely in the hands of one group) jumped from 316,000 in 1956 to more than 1,700,000 in 1968. Fiat produced more than 1,500,000 of these, while the state-owned Alfa Romeo accounted for only 100,000, mainly of the more expensive kind. The electrical appliance industry has also played an important role in postwar industrial development. The most important groups operating in this sector created a European-wide market for their refrigerators, cookers, washing machines, and dishwashers by selling at highly competitive prices, using the latest production techniques and high-pressure selling. Between 1956 and 1968, production of refrigerators rose from 200,000 to 3,500,000.

Industrial diversification. An important element of Italy's manufacturing growth has been the widening of the base of industry. In the 20 years before 1970 there was a shift of emphasis from food and textiles to chemicals, steel, and engineering products. Large companies tend to dominate these new industries, but in the early 1970s the mainstay of Italian industry was still a vast number of small- and medium-sized companies, especially in the engineering and metalworking industries. Gradually, however, a process of consolidation is taking place, especially in those industries in which large-scale production is necessary for competitiveness. With Alfa Romeo, Fiat has run the automobile industry since it took over minor competitors such as Lancia, OM, and Autobianchi. Fiat and a rubber-and-cables company, Pirelli, have both been instrumental in European mergers, Fiat taking an interest in the French companies Citroën and Michelin and Pirelli integrating its operations with that of the English company Dunlop. Other important companies in their respective sectors are Olivetti, making typewriters, calculating machines, and computer terminals, and SNIA Viscosa, which leads the field in artificial fibres, and Montecatini Edison, which assumed control of SNIA in 1972, in the chemicals and pharmaceuticals sectors. The bulk of manufacturing output, however, comes from the small- and medium-sized companies, which are mainly concentrated in the north and centre. In 1970, 28 percent of the work force was employed by firms with fewer than ten employees and 35 percent in companies with fewer than 20 workers.

Widening of the industrial base

Energy. By European standards, per capita power consumption is relatively low. In 1967 it was two tons of coal equivalent, one-half that of the Federal Republic of Germany and the U.K. and one-quarter of that in the U.S. Between 1950 and 1969, however, Italy's energy consumption increased more than fourfold, rising from 27,000,000 tons to 129,320,000 tons of coal equivalent. In 1967 coal and lignite accounted for 9.9 percent of Italy's power consumption, electricity for 4.7 percent, natural gas for 12.3 percent, and oil products for 73.1 percent. In the following three years the proportion of energy requirements satisfied by oil rose to 78 percent, while that of electricity and coal declined relatively. Italy, mainly as a result of its proximity to the North African and Middle Eastern oil fields, has come to rely massively on oil for its energy requirements. Imports of crude oil have grown at a rate of about 10 percent per year and amounted to 112,000,000 tons in 1970, 30,000,000 tons of which were destined for re-export as refined petroleum products. Imports of oil are made by all the international companies as well as by Italy's State Hydrocarbons Corporation (Ente Nazionale Idrocarburi; ENI). Intensive exploration efforts by the ENI have resulted in a number of finds in Tunisia, Iran, Libya, and elsewhere. It is estimated that by the middle 1970s ENI will be self-sufficient for its own oil needs, producing about 25,000,000 tons a year on its various concessions abroad. The ENI is also searching for hydrocarbons in Italy. The results so far have produced sizable but not massive deposits of natural gas. Production of natural gas totalled 473,000,000,000 cubic feet in 1971, and discoveries in the Adriatic Sea boosted reserves of gas, mainly in the Po Valley, Sicily, and parts of southern Italy, to a total of 5,000,000,000,000 cubic feet in 1971. To conserve these domestic deposits as long as possible and to meet rising demand, expected to reach about 1,050,000,000,000 cubic feet by the 1980s, the ENI has embarked on a large-scale import program of natural gas from diversified sources, including Libya, The Netherlands, and the Soviet Union.

The State Hydrocarbons Corporation (ENI)

Financial services. Italy's financial and banking system has a number of unique features, although its framework is similar to that of other European countries. The Bank of Italy is the central bank and as such the sole bank of issue. Power in matters of monetary policy is vested in the Interministerial Committee for Credit and Savings, headed by the minister of the Treasury. In practice, the Bank of Italy enjoys wide discretionary powers and plays an important role in economic policy making. Its primary functions include the control of credit and the formation and execution of monetary policy. There are three main types of banking and credit institutes. First, there are the commercial banks, which include three national banks, six chartered banks, the popular cooperative banks, whose activities do not extend beyond the provincial level, and ordinary private banks. Second, there is a special category of savings banks that are organized on a provincial or regional basis. Finally, there are the investment institutes, which collect medium- and long-term funds by issuing bonds and supply medium- and long-term credit for industry, public works, and agriculture. The three national banks (Banca Commerciale Italiana, Banco di Roma, and Credito Italiano) are all owned by the largest state holding group, the Istituto per la Ricostruzione Industriale (Industrial Reconstruction Institute, or IRI). Many other important banks are also regulated by public law. Both these and the national banks are therefore subject to special government control and influence, although they act as normal profit-making banks in every respect. The savings banks are in a similar position, as are a number of the most important medium- and long-term-credit institutes, including the Istituto Mobiliaro Italiano (IMI), which is directly owned by the government and provides a considerable part of long- and medium-term funds for industry.

There are more than 80 institutes of various kinds supplying medium- and long-term credit. These special credit institutes have as their prime aim the increase of the flow and the reduction of the cost of development finance, either to preferential areas or to priority sectors (for example, agriculture or research) or to medium- and small-sized business. In addition to this network of special credit institutes, there is a subsystem of credit under which the government shoulders part of the interest burden.

The bond market in Italy is well developed, and domestic flotations in 1969 amounted to 5,350,000,000 lire. A year later this dropped to 4,125,600,000 lire but was more than offset by expanding net issues in international markets. Mainly as a result of the special structure of government-sponsored institutes for development finance and subsidized interest rates, the growth of the capital market and stock exchanges is far less important than in other non-Communist industrialized countries. Consequently, the issuing of industrial debentures too, except by the state holding corporation (IRI) and a few major private and public companies, has been relatively meagre. There has been a very high degree of self-financing by companies, at least until the early 1970s. Furthermore, although there are ten stock exchanges, of which Milan is by far the most important, fewer than 150 companies have obtained or asked for quotations. The development of the stock exchange in Italy is hampered by the archaic structure and rules of the markets themselves and by tax problems connected with the registration of shares. Italy has also lagged in the development of mutual funds or unit trusts.

The stock exchanges

Foreign trade. Foreign trade makes a large contribution to the gross national product: it rose from 16 percent in 1962 to 29 percent in 1969. Foreign trade has also been the mainstay of the rapid economic growth of Italy from 1950 to 1970, with between 18 and 20 percent of Italian production exported annually. In absolute terms, however, Italy began to develop its foreign trade at a low point, and its rapid growth since the 1950s should be seen as a recovery from a low base rather than as a phenomenal growth. The main factors enabling Italy to catch up with its west European neighbours were relatively low labour costs, a much greater rise in productivity than in wage increases, and above all an abundance of manpower. The liberalization of international trade and the rise in demand in other countries were prerequisites to Italy's foreign-trade boom.

In 1971 the value of Italy's exports and imports reached a total of 19,252,253,000,000 lire, an increase of 13,400,000,000,000 lire since 1961. At the same time, Italy's share of world trade climbed from 3 percent to 5 percent. During the 1960s, however, there was a shift in Italy's trading pattern. Although the rate of growth of both exports and imports continued to outstrip that of the world as a whole and that of most other industrialized countries, a relative decline in the growth rate of imports and a corresponding rise in that of exports was marked in 1970 and 1971, when imports increased by more than 13 percent. While Italy has consistently had a trade deficit since 1957, the gap between imports and exports in most years has been narrow. At the same time Italy has always had a considerable surplus of invisible exports, notably tourism and emigrants' remittances, which led to a structural surplus in the 1960s. This situation changed in 1970, however, when imports so outstripped exports that the invisible receipts were unable to bridge the gap.

Trade deficit

In view of Italy's meagre natural resources, exports consist almost entirely of manufactured goods and agricultural produce. Engineering products, automobiles, and household appliances have been in the vanguard of Italy's export development, supplementing such traditional exports as fresh and processed fruit and vegetables, textiles, leather, and marble goods. Other products exported by Italy on a large scale include petroleum products and chemicals. The main impetus toward the growth in exports comes from three main sectors—transport equipment, machinery of all types, and clothing and textiles.

Imports, on the other hand, consist to a large extent of raw materials for industry, such as oil, iron ore, coal, cotton, and copper; foodstuffs, especially meat and cereals; and investment and consumer goods. The demand for foodstuffs has been particularly high, and in 1969 Italy's trade deficit in agricultural products reached a disturbing level. Meat and cereal imports grew especially rapidly during the 1960s, as living standards increased. Similarly, the propensity to import machinery and equipment with a high technological content has grown along with the process of industrialization in Italy. Another feature of Italy's trading pattern has been the rapid growth of trade with its Common Market partners, accounting for 42.4 percent of Italy's imports and taking 44.6 percent of its exports in 1971. Italy has also been a pioneer of East–West trade. Trade with the members of Comecon (Council for Mutual Economic Assistance, the east European Common Market) amounted to just over 1,020,506,000,000 lire in 1971 and was expected to grow considerably. Similarly, Italy expected to conduct considerable business with China after diplomatic relations were established in 1970 and with other Eastern nations, such as Japan and Australia.

THE MANAGEMENT OF THE ECONOMY

The private sector. Italy's economy is characterized by a small number of large private and publicly owned industrial groups and a large number of medium-sized and small companies employing fewer than 500 people. In 1970 there were only 840 manufacturing companies employing more than 500 persons, while there were about 600,000 firms, excluding the construction industry, employing fewer than that number. It is estimated that just over 80,000 of these companies could be classified as operating in industry. They employed 3,000,000 workers, or 69 percent of the total in industry. The remaining 520,000 or so firms were of the artisan type, employing no more than two or three people. At the other end of the scale there are the large private groups such as Fiat, Pirelli, Olivetti, and the labour-intensive household-appliance and textile companies. For the most part, private industry is located in the triangle formed by the cities of Milan, Turin, and Genoa, but other regions, in particular the northeastern ones of Venetia and Emilia-Romagna, developed an extensive network of industries in the 1950s and 1960s. Central Italy has become increasingly industrialized. In the south and islands, industry tends to be concentrated in certain highly populated areas, such as Bari, Naples, and eastern Sicily, although incentives to encourage the further industrialization of the relatively poor south have been in force since the 1960s. Until the mid-1960s the burden of industrialization in the south had fallen almost entirely on the government and the public sector, while private industry invested mainly in capital-intensive sectors such as petrochemicals, which did little to boost employment. By fiscal and other incentives the government sought to encourage the growth of medium-sized and small industries in depressed areas. By the early 1970s some progress had been made, but the south had not yet achieved self-sustained industrial growth. Foreign investment—mainly from the U.S.—played a significant role in the postwar development of Italy. The oil industry was the principal beneficiary, followed by the chemical, pharmaceutical, and engineering sectors. Between 1956 and 1968, foreign investment totalled some 611,200,000,000 lire, most of which was invested in the northern part of the country.

The public sector and the role of government. By comparison with the other economies of western Europe, the public sector plays an exceptionally large role in Italian economic life. In addition, Italy has a unique formula for operating the majority of the state-owned corporations under the government's control. This formula applies in the case of the three major state holding corporations, the Istituto per la Ricostruzione Industriale (IRI), the Ente Nazionale Idrocarburi (ENI), and the Ente Finanziaria per L'Industria Meccanica (EFIM), all of which are responsible to the Ministry of State Participations, created in 1956. The IRI is organized on a pyramid basis, with the holding company at the top, a middle layer of financial holding companies divided according to the sector of activity, and below them a mass of operating companies, many of which are partly owned by private shareholders and quoted on the stock exchange. The IRI's activities are extremely widespread, including a number of major banks, Alitalia (the national airline), RAI-TV (the state radio and TV network), telephone and cable companies, manufacturing companies (such as Alfa Romeo, making automobiles and commercial vehicles), Italsider (the largest steel manufacturer), engineering companies, shipyards and shipping companies, and expressway construction. In 1970 the overall revenue of the IRI amounted to 3,480,000,000,000 lire, almost two-thirds of which was produced by the manufacturing companies of the group, and it was Italy's largest single employer outside the government, having

Main public corporations

353,000 persons on its payroll in 1970. The group's total investments in the same year amounted to 886,240,000,000 lire, of which 48 percent was located in southern Italy. The ENI, the second largest state holding company, with total revenue in 1970 of 1,627,000,000,000 lire, operates in the oil and natural-gas fields but also has interests in textiles, nuclear energy, and chemicals. Apart from this special involvement of the state in public utilities, manufacturing, and services, the government also controls the bulk of electricity generation and distribution through the nationalized electricity corporation (ENEL), almost the entire railway and road network, and the monopoly of tobacco and cigarette manufacture and salt. The IRI also has an important role in the Italian economy. Its function has been to act as a propellant to the industrialization of Italy and in some cases to act as a protective umbrella for industries in declining sectors; even more important, it also bypasses the archaic and generally inefficient bureaucracy. The IRI built the bulk of Italy's extensive expressway system in record time and is now increasingly called in to carry out public works of all kinds that the state administration had proved incapable of executing. A prime example was the low-cost public-housing program that the government began implementing in the 1970s. The IRI and the ENI between them have made a vital contribution to the growth of the Italian economy since the 1950s. In particular, the two groups have been the principal investors in the underdeveloped southern part of Italy. Although responsible to the Ministry of State Participations, both the IRI and the ENI enjoy considerable financial and operative autonomy. This autonomy is reinforced by the fact that these state corporations do not obtain their funds from the Treasury. The lack of unified control over state corporations and the absence of centralized planning have reinforced their independence.

The government has also intervened on a massive scale in the development of the southern part of Italy and the islands, known as the Mezzogiorno. The southern Italy development fund, called the Cassa per il Mezzogiorno, was set up in 1950, to stimulate investment in agriculture and industry in the south between 1951 and 1970. This institution represented the first step by the Italian government toward national economic planning. An attempt at more widespread planning came in 1954, but it was not until 1967 that the First Five-Year Plan was approved by Parliament. The plan, which was of the flexible type, updated annually, was binding only on the public sector. Greater planning coordination was expected from the Second Five-Year Plan, covering the period 1971–75. The national economic planning body (Comitato Interministeriale per la Programmazione Economica, or CIPE) was assigned overall responsibility for development of the south, with the Cassa per il Mezzogiorno acting as the executive body, as well as supervising overall planning in Italy.

The five-year plans

Taxation. Tax revenue in 1970—amounting to 8,709,077,000,000 lire—accounted for almost 80 percent of total revenue under the central budget. In the second half of the 1960s, the rate of increase of government receipts outstripped that of the GNP, but it slowed down at the turn of the decade. One important feature of the Italian fiscal system is the low percentage of receipts accounted for by income tax levied on persons and companies. This came to less than 30 percent of total government revenue in 1970. The main source of revenue (more than 30 percent) came from various taxes on goods and services, in particular a general tax (IGE) normally levied at a rate of 4 percent on all transactions. Indirect taxes, on the consumer, monopolies, and business transactions, made up the rest.

In 1971 a major tax reform reduced the number of taxes from 36 to six and introduced, for the first time, a single progressive tax on personal income. It came into force in 1972, along with a value-added tax that Italy was obliged to implement as a member of the EEC. In the 1950s and 1960s both the complications of the tax system and the ease with which many direct taxes could be evaded reduced the government's possibilities of using fiscal policies as an instrument of economic management. Furthermore, Italy traditionally relied on monetary rather than fiscal policy to direct the economy. While tax evasion in effect constituted a huge subsidy to the self-employed and the rich, it also acted, more significantly, as a powerful stimulus for growth, since firms benefitted from the weakness of the tax system too. By 1970, however, it was generally agreed that a better tax base to implement social reforms—housing, hospitals, schools, and urban transport—was badly needed. The first answer to this problem was the tax-reform bill of 1971.

Trade unions and employer associations. The Italian union movement that emerged after World War II and 20 years of suppression under the Fascist regime had, not surprisingly, strong political orientations. In 1947 breakaways from the Communist- and Socialist-dominated General Confederation of Labour led to the formation of two rival union confederations—the Confederazione Italiana Sindacati Lavoratori (Italian Confederation of Workers' Unions, or CISL), which was dominated by Catholics and adherents of the Christian Democrat Party, and the Unione Italiana del Lavoro (Italian Union of Labour, or UIL), controlled by a troika of Socialists, social democrats, and republicans. The biggest of the three union movements remained the Communist-dominated General Confederation of Labour (CGIL), which until the late 1960s was considered a voice of Communist Party policy. Although relatively weak in numbers and lacking in funds to sustain the cost of prolonged strikes, the unions showed a new aggressiveness toward the end of the 1960s. The main occasion came in the autumn of 1969, when, after four months of intermittent strikes and demonstrations, the unions won the largest wage increases ever—an average of between 20 and 25 percent. At the same time, as a result of the weakness of the government and the political parties, the unions took on a mantle of authority. A series of 24-hour general strikes took place, calling for reforms including pensions, more and cheaper housing, and a new approach to the problems of the depressed south. While the unions acquired new status and authority, production was badly affected at a time when industry was suffering from sharply rising costs. It was estimated that from 1960 to 1969 Italy lost more work days from strikes than all the other EEC members together. In 1969 nearly 38,000,000 work days were lost, about 13 times more than in all the other EEC countries together. In 1970 the unions extended their intervention beyond wages and political and social reforms to the organization of productive methods inside factories. The principal problem for the unions is to reforge the unity of the three main confederations. Although this has been the professed aim of the leaders of the confederations from 1968, the obstacles to unity persisted.

Principal trade unions

The principal employers' association in Italy is the Confindustria (General Confederation of Industry). Under its wing are a vast number of smaller employers' associations organized either on territorial or on industrial lines. Confindustria has exercised considerable political and economic influence, especially in the 1950s and early 1960s. When it lost a determined battle against the nationalization of electricity in 1962, however, its influence waned for several years. Its loss of influence was accentuated when its traditional political ally, the conservatively oriented Liberal Party, was replaced in the government by the Socialists in the same period. By 1970, however, there were signs that Confindustria was regaining some of its old vigour, partly as a result of a thorough reorganization.

General Confederation of Industry

Current economic policies. Since the reconstruction following World War II, a main objective of economic policy has been to ensure rapid growth while maintaining a strong currency and external-payments position. To a large extent this goal has been achieved with the aid of an adroit monetary policy, the development of a highly successful export trade, large-scale imports of raw materials, and the liberalization of trade. Less successful have been the efforts to reduce unemployment and underemployment, to develop southern Italy and the islands, and to reduce the disparity in incomes between industry and agriculture. In the space of only 20 years, however, Italy achieved a wealth that few could have predicted in 1945. Subsequent economic policies were directed at maintaining an annual growth rate of about 6 percent while transferring resources on a far larger scale from private to public consumption. Much of the success of economic policies depends on political stability and modernization of the machinery of state. A step in reforming the bureaucracy was the implementation in 1970 of the provisions of the constitution for the decentralization of administration and the setting up of regional governments. In 1971 these new regional governments were still inoperative.

In 1970 there were signs of a break in the almost uninterrupted growth since 1950. A large increase in costs, reducing the competitiveness of Italian exports, plus stagnating investments, forced the government to intervene with inflationary measures in 1970 and 1971. The government, however, began to have increasing difficulties in adapting economic policies to the increasing demands of the population while maintaining its competitive edge.

PROBLEMS AND PROSPECTS

Italy's main problems are to ensure a better balance between public and private consumption and to promote the growth of the depressed south. Emigration abroad has provided a partial solution to the problems of unemployment in the south but is no more than a palliative. Emigration by southern Italians to northern Italy, in particular the Lombardy and Piedmont regions (totalling about 6,000,000 since 1945), had by 1970 put an intolerable strain on northern cities such as Milan and Turin. This was a major factor in inducing large private companies in the north to invest in the south. The public groups such as the IRI and the ENI are obliged by law to make 60 percent of new investments there and have located major industrial plants in the south; the huge steelworks at Taranto and the Alfa Romeo car plant at Naples are the outstanding examples. The slow progress to date indicates that the south's problems will not be solved rapidly. Such a solution, however, will be the cardinal point of the government's economic policies for the rest of the 20th century. Also important are the government's attempts to create a modern industrial state. Far-reaching reforms were enacted by Parliament in 1970 and 1971, and the shifting of resources from private to public consumption, while maintaining a high growth rate (at least 5 percent), remains a basic tenet of Italy's economic policy. (E.I.U.)

Investment in the south

IV. Transportation

MOVEMENT PATTERNS AND MEANS OF TRANSPORTATION

As a source of revenue, transportation has accounted for 10 percent of Italy's gross national product since World War II, while net investments in it have averaged around 6 percent of the national total. In 1968 investment was 1,900,000,000,000 lire, or almost five times that of 1955. An estimated 9 percent of the national wealth is actually tied up in transportation but this proportion is tending to diminish because of rapid obsolescence of transportation equipment and structures and the slowness of appropriate renewal projects. Ground transportation required resources amounting to 5,750,000,000,000 lire in 1965, yielding back only 4,750,000,000,000 lire. The transport deficit (receipts minus payments) for 1967 was over 135,-000,000,000 lire.

The capital investment background

Italy's 1967 traffic, both freight and passenger, was more than four times that for 1950, motor-vehicle traffic having multiplied five times for freight and more than seven times for passengers.

Motor vehicles now account for 60 percent of the total freight movement and 73.3 percent of passenger movement in terms, respectively, of tons per kilometre and passengers per kilometre. In 1968 about 84 percent of freight traffic moved by motor transportation. Similarly, more than 73 percent of Italian travellers prefer motor to other transportation. The Italian roads, however, are approaching saturation, while costs of maintenance and modernization are rising. Attempts to alleviate road traffic include modernizing the railways and building subway networks. A law effective since 1969 provided that metropolitan systems should be financially supported by each interested municipality.

Traffic is most intense in northwest Italy, where Turin, Genoa, and Milan form the industrial triangle; but a dense road network there distributes traffic fairly evenly. On the Genoa–Milan highway, traffic was very heavy in the late 1960s, averaging 52,000 vehicles a day, more than 10,000 of which carried freight. Milan, as Italy's industrial and commercial centre, handles a great deal of traffic, its commuters numbering 300,000 daily, and Turin's situation is similar, with 200,000 people commuting each day. The traffic magnet of northeast Italy is paradoxically the canal-riddled city of Venice, the country's third largest port. The most popular route is Venice–Padua–Verona–Milan, which, with Genoa, forms Milan's second traffic outlet. Approximately 50,000 persons a day, excluding local traffic, use this route; in summer the density more than doubles, with tourists travelling to Venice and the coast.

In central Italy, traffic is massed on the north–south Bologna–Florence–Rome route, and, except on the Florence–Livorno tourist route, there is little east–west traffic. This concentration has isolated certain zones, such as southern Tuscany and northern Lazio (Latium). Umbria is more developed, with important steelworks at Terni and industrialization progressing rapidly along the Terni–Perugia route. Traffic in the Abruzzi is insignificant, but the new Rome–l'Aquila–Pescara highway should open the depressed region to development.

Rome is the traffic hub of central Italy, and, while traffic with Lazio is rather low, the level is high toward the south (Latina) and the southeast (Frosinone), where industry is developed. The density remains constant along the whole route from Rome to Naples, declining sharply farther south, where conditions are more backward. The small flow of traffic along the national coastal route reflects Mezzogiorno's economic depression. The Adriatic coastal route, the Naples–Bari route, and the Taranto–Cosenza route are little used; traffic increases along the Adriatic, between Puglia (Foggia, Bari, and Taranto) and the areas of the Po Valley, and becomes heavier, in fact, than between Naples and Rome.

Sicily and Sardinia have little traffic. On Sicily the Messina–Palermo, Agrigento–Palermo, and Messina–Catania–Syracuse routes are pre-eminent, with the heaviest traffic on the stretch between Catania and Syracuse. On Sardinia the only significant route is Cagliari–Oristano–Sassari.

COMPONENTS OF ITALIAN TRANSPORTATION

The road network. The Italian road network totalled 178,200 miles in 1971 and was subdivided into four administrative categories—express highways (*autostrade*) and national, provincial, and municipal roads (*strade statali*, *strade provinciali*, *strade comunali*, respectively), to which urban streets, estimated around 15,500 miles, can be added.

Categories of road

The 1960s witnessed the construction of 1,600 miles of the *autostrade*'s total 2,400 miles. The principal branches are the Po Valley, joining Turin, Milan, Austria, and Yugoslavia, with important branches to ports and mountain passes; the peninsular route, joining Milan to Naples via Bologna, Florence, and Rome (the Autostrada del Sole); the Tyrrhenian coastal route from the French border to Reggio Calabria in the far south, passing through Genoa, Rome, and Naples; the Adriatic coastal route from Bologna, joining the Tyrrhenian route in Calabria; and its Sicilian extension, the Messina–Palermo highway.

The two coastal routes are linked by two transverse highways, Rome–Pescara and Naples–Bari. Construction of the network was impeded by mountainous stretches, which were traversed by tunnels and viaducts, some of them splendid examples of modern architecture, such as the elevated roadway joining the Tyrrhenian coastal route to the Genoa road. Most highways have four lanes (the Milan–Turin has six) and are 50 feet wide, with shoulders of ten feet and a central reservation. The average speed on them is 60–90 miles per hour. Some, with three lanes that allow alternating passing lanes, are being modernized. The construction and administration have been entrusted both to state-run and to private companies. The chief concession holder is the Autostrade agency of the national Istituto per la Ricostruzione Industriale (IRI), which administers 1,800 miles. There are tolls, calculated on distance travelled and legal horsepower, to cover construction costs.

In the north, highway traffic is mainly commercial, the coastal routes concentrate on tourist areas, and in the south they open up economically backward areas. All of them reflect the increase from 850,000 automobiles in 1955 to more than 10,000,000 in 1970, with an additional 800,000 or so heavy trucks. This increase is greater than was first estimated, and serious saturation occurs on certain stretches. Table 11, based on the 1969 daily average, is indicative.

Table 11: Traffic Flow

route	vehicles per day	freight (percentage)
Milan–lakes	24,641	13.8
Milan–Brescia	31,049	26.1
Genoa–Serravalle	28,412	29.3
Naples–Salerno	29,510	10.9
Milan–Turin	23,131	26.3
Rome–Naples	15,414	23.4
Rome–Florence	15,098	32.6

In 1969 the average flow on the IRI network was 16,000 vehicles a day, with peaks of 55,000 on the Genoa–Serravalle route and of 75,000 on the Milan–Bologna route. The four-lane highways are, however, proving inadequate, and many sections, within five years after completion, required widening.

The completion of the southern network is envisaged to redress the balance between north and south. Other plans involve constructing expressways through the Alps, particularly the road from Genoa to the Simplon Pass and the projected Turin–Frejus route, leading to Switzerland and France. With the present Verona–Brenner and Venice–Tarvisio highways, they would connect Italy's internal network with the rest of Europe.

The *strade statali* have been relieved of much of the long-distance traffic by the *autostrade*. These national roads, totalling 25,000 miles, now carry local traffic, which is dense in places. The principal national highways are the consular roads, so-called because they follow the roads built by ancient Rome's consuls. They radiate from Rome to various parts of Italy, the most famous being the Via Aurelia, linking Rome and Genoa, the Via Cassia, linking Rome and Genoa via Florence, and the Via Appia, linking Rome and Brindisi. Other important national highways are the Padana, joining Turin to Venice via Milan; the Emilia, joining Milan with Bologna and the Adriatic; and the Brenner Highway, from Pisa to the Brenner Pass.

Until about 1960 most *strade statali* were 20 to 30 feet wide and had two lanes, but now, to meet the traffic increase, the principal national highways are being widened to four lanes, 40 feet across. They are maintained by a state agency, the Azienda Nazionale Autonoma della Strada (the ANAS, or National Road Board).

Provincial and municipal roads total 57,900 miles and 90,500 miles, respectively, and carry traffic from surrounding towns. A flow of 1,500,000 new vehicles a year makes widening a continuing necessity.

Railways. Italian railway lines, administered by the Azienda Autonoma delle Ferrovie dello Stato (the FS, or Italian State Railway Board), carried 462,462,000 passengers in 1971, an increase of almost 5 percent over 1970. Their freight total, 53,695,000 tons, was almost 2 percent smaller than in 1969. The network is more than 12,500 miles long, of which just over 5,800 miles are electrified and about 3,100 miles have two tracks. The FS also administers 140 miles of maritime lines and 1,200 miles of bus services. There are 700 miles with automatic traffic control.

There are some 5,000 locomotives, of which some 750 are steam, 1,600 are electric employing direct current (3,000 volts), 200 are electric employing alternating current (3,600 volts), 700 are diesel, 420 are self-propelled cars with trolleys, and just over 1,000 are diesel rail cars. There are about 136,000 cars (passenger, baggage, postal, and freight) and in all more than 200,000 units of rolling stock.

The three types of railway network

The railway network is of three types: national, regional, and urban (metropolitan). Over long distances the railways have advantages over road transportation, and the national lines are therefore the most heavily used. The network of principal national lines corresponds to that of the express highways: parallel to each express highway is a railway line, electrified and with a double track, on which trains may reach 68 miles per hour.

The most important line is the peninsula route Milan–Bologna–Florence–Rome–Naples, of which the most heavily used stretches are Milan–Bologna and Rome–Naples, each carrying about 30,000 passengers daily. More than 20,000 passengers daily use the Turin–Milan–Venice and Milan–Genoa lines, the latter including traffic from Turin on the Alessandria–Genoa section. These two lines also link the industrial belt of the country with Genoa and Venice for freight transportation. In 1965 the Milan–Venice line carried 1,094,000,000 tons per mile, and the Milan–Genoa carried 869,000,000 tons per mile. Other principal lines are the Genoa–Rome–Reggio Calabria–Palermo and Bologna–Ancona–Bari coastal routes. The principal mountain routes linking the Italian railways with the rest of Europe are Turin–Frejus (to France), Milan–Simplon Tunnel (to Switzerland), Verona–Brenner (to Austria and Germany), and Venice–Tarvisio (to eastern Europe). Railway traffic, which had levelled off with the completion of the numerous express highways, began increasing again in the latter 1960s with attractive new rolling stock and improved tracks. The FS plans to restore the popularity of railways by building a new line between Rome and Florence, on which trains would travel at 150 miles per hour. For the Rome–Naples section these fast trains would use the present tracks.

Whereas the long-distance railway network is satisfactory, the regional lines are not. Competition from road transportation, the antiquated lines (mostly single-track and not electrified), and the state of the track have brought these lines into disuse, and many have been abandoned for more economical buses. The increasing saturation of the highways and the commuters' need for rapid and economical service have, however, made reopening the abandoned lines seem attractive. There have been efforts to reorganize them on a metropolitan basis and to introduce second tracks and electrification for key sections in order to reduce travelling time.

Efforts have also been made to coordinate the regional trains with urban traffic networks. The former usually run with the great national lines in the vicinity of the cities. Because the national trains have the right of way there are slowdowns and reductions in frequency. These might be prevented by integrating regional with metropolitan lines. An urban railway and subway system is still to be built in Rome, Milan, Turin, and Naples, though Milan has about 19 miles of metropolitan line. Transfer stations between regional and metropolitan lines would effectively distribute regional traffic in the cities. A regional rail network of this sort was scheduled for completion at Milan by 1980, but at Rome and Naples, each with a single line, it would require a longer time. A second subway is being built at Rome, following the principal traffic routes, and two others are being planned, but local geological conditions and the historical importance of the city's various "layers" hamper work.

Problems of coordinating cities with national lines

Railways, with stiff competition from automobiles and a tariff policy that tends to emphasize the social uses of trains (*i.e.*, that provide for low fares), are increasing their unprofitability: a deficit of more than 380,000,-

000,000 lire was estimated for 1970. The FS has been striving for competitiveness by renovating and modernizing. A ten-year plan (1962–71) was effected with a budget of over 9,000,000,000 lire.

Water transportation. The Italian ports shown in Table 12 moved around 337,400,000 tons of freight in 1971. International and coastal traffic in 1971 totalled

Table 12: Freight Traffic in Ports, 1971

	millions of tons
Genoa	54.6
Augusta	37.2
Trieste	33.7
Venice	23.5
Taranto	17.9
Naples	12.2
Milazzo	12.0
La Spezia	11.8
Ravenna	11.1
Savona	9.7
Livorno	9.5
Gela	6.7
Bari	4.9
Fiumicino	4.7
Civitavecchia	4.1
Piombino	3.5
Brindisi	3.2
Cagliari	2.7

around 337,400,000 tons—81,200,000 loaded and 256,200,000 unloaded. The annual growth during 1960–70 has been 12.8 percent; the world figure was 8 percent.

The principal dry-cargo Italian ports are Venice (65.18% of whose freight was dry cargo in 1969), Cagliari (100%), Civitavecchia (90%), and Piombino (100%), while those handling chiefly petroleum products are Genoa (70.5%), Augusta (95.1%), Trieste (88%), Bari (88.8%), and Savona (80.2%). Those handling both sorts are Naples (46.9% dry cargo) and Livorno (38% dry cargo).

Most port traffic consists of imports, land transportation being preferred for exports. At Genoa, imports formed 95% of the traffic in 1967, at Naples 87%, at Venice 88%, and at Trieste 96%.

As to passenger traffic, about 11,300,000 persons disembarked and around 11,100,000 boarded ship in 1971. The chief ports are Naples, with 2,800,000 passengers, Piombino, with around 1,200,000 Civitavecchia with almost 1,200,000, and Genoa, with almost 1,000,000. Total passenger traffic in 1954 was 8,100,000; in 1959 it was 10,000,000; in 1964, 14,500,000; and, in 1969, 19,700,000. The Italian fleet's tonnage has not kept pace, and there has been a growing deficit in maritime transportation. Plans have been made to increase the Italian merchant fleet's 7,000,000 gross tonnage to 12,000,000 by 1975. Government policy supports private shipbuilding and, if necessary, places orders abroad.

Program to revive sea transportation

Many ports are inadequate. The more congested larger ports, such as Genoa, Savona, Venice, and Livorno, have imposed primage (a small addition or percentage added to the freight rates) at the time of entry and sometimes at departure, which increases production costs.

In the north of Italy there are only a few large ports, such as Savona, Genoa, and Venice. Nearby, there are industrial ports, such as La Spezia and Ravenna, ports of local importance, such as Oneglia and Monfalcone, fishing ports, such as Chioggia, and tourist ports, such as the numerous ones of the Ligurian Riviera. Half of the commercial port traffic is concentrated on only one-tenth of the coastline. The industries of Lombardy and Piedmont make heavy demands on the maritime outlets, particularly at Genoa, which, although the most extensive and important Italian port, has great difficulty in expanding because of the mountains surrounding it. If the harbour system is to be balanced, the upper Adriatic—Venice and Trieste—must be developed; Venice would become a commercial and passenger port, because its traffic is limited by the problems of the lagoon. Petroleum traffic would then be directed to Trieste, which has a conveniently deep harbour and is near the Danube Valley for traffic with eastern Europe.

In central and southern Italy there are several harbours, but most are modest and function locally. There are a few large ports in these regions, some born of recent industrial development, such as Augusta (about 15 miles north of Syracuse in Sicily), a petroleum port that serves an immense refinery. Prospects for the central southern ports depend on industrialization in the hinterland.

Italy has 1,500 miles of inland waterways, 520 miles of them canals, 680 miles rivers, and 190 square miles of navigable lake routes. Annual freight traffic exceeds 3,000,000 tons. A waterway system is projected in the Po Valley, to join industrial Turin and Milan with the port of Venice and the Venetian–Emilian coast. The Po Valley rivers are difficult to navigate, however, and the project's completion is uncertain. More important is the coastal navigation on the Genoa–Gela–Taranto–Venice route. These four ports handle more than 5,000,000 tons of freight annually. Lesser ports—La Spezia, Civitavecchia, Naples, Ravenna, Trieste, and Cagliari—account for more than 2,000,000 tons annually.

Air transportation. In 1971 more than 457,000 aircraft landed and took off at Italy's airports; 204,000 of them were in international (as opposed to domestic Italian) service, of which 91,000 were of Italian registry and 113,000 foreign. Commerce is increasing yearly by nearly 10 percent. International services under the Italian flag in 1971 showed an increase of 7.4 percent and claimed 44.3 percent of Italy's air traffic. Alitalia, the air-transport company, is part of the Istituto per la Ricostruzione Industriale group, in which the government participates; it carried some 7,300,000 passengers in 1970, compared with 6,000,000 in 1969. Rome, Milan, Naples, Genoa, Venice, Palermo, Catania, and Turin all handle more than 10,000 planes annually. The airports of Rome (Fiumicino, Ciampino, and Urbe) dealt with 42.4 percent of all the Italian international traffic and 57.5 percent of the foreign. Second came the Milanese airports (Linate and Malpensa), which handled 39.9 percent of the Italian and 22.5 percent of the foreign planes. The other airports of Italy share 17.7 percent of the Italian international traffic and 20 percent of the foreign.

Soaring commerce and passenger services

There were 18,500,000 passengers in 1971, an increase of around 16 percent in a year. The 1971 freight turnover was 231,000 tons, an increase since 1970 of more than 6 percent. Most of this freight traffic went through Rome, with 46.9 percent, or 108,000 tons, and Milan, with 33.9 percent, or 78,000 tons. Rome handled 39.8 percent of the domestic and 48.9 percent of the international traffic, while Milan had just 11.5 percent of the domestic and 40.4 percent of the international traffic.

Italian airport traffic has a high rate of increase, calling for improvement of airports, services, and instruments for controlling air traffic. Further coordination of ground links between airports and cities is nonetheless necessary.

The traffic growth is still uncontrolled, particularly on the congested runways and terminals at Rome and Milan. Construction of a new landing field for Rome at the Leonardo da Vinci airport at Fiumicino will give the airport three runways by 1977. The Ministry of Transport's Regulatory Plan of Airports for Commercial Aviation recommended outlays for 45 installations, to form the key positions of a new Italian network. There were 32 already in operation; six were to be rebuilt; and seven were to be constructed from scratch.

This assistance was intended also to boost the depressed Italian aircraft industries, which employ more than 25,000 people. These aircraft enterprises, though few, have reached high technical levels, participating in international construction projects and producing aircraft on foreign license. Electronic and air-space plants have been planned for the south as part of its development.

(M. Del V.)

V. Administration and social conditions

STRUCTURE OF THE GOVERNMENT

Constitutional framework. The Italian state grew out of the Kingdom of Piedmont and Sardinia, where, in

1848, King Charles Albert introduced a constitution that remained the basic formal law of his kingdom and, later, of Italy for nearly 100 years. It provided for a bicameral Parliament with a Cabinet appointed by the king. With time, the power of the crown gradually diminished, and ministers became responsible to Parliament rather than to the king. Although the constitution remained formally in force after the Fascists seized power in 1922, it was devoid of all substantial value. On June 2, 1946, after the end of World War II, the Italians voted in a referendum to replace the monarchy with a republic. A Constituent Assembly worked out a new constitution, which came into force on January 1, 1948.

The constitution has built-in guarantees against easy amendment, in order to make it virtually impossible to substitute for it a dictatorial regime. It is upheld and watched over by the Constitutional Court. The republican form of government cannot be changed. The constitution contains some perceptive principles, applicable from the moment it comes into force, and some programmatic principles, which can only be realized by further precise legislation. Many programmatic principles of the Italian constitution have not yet been formulated in specific laws.

The constitution is preceded by the statement of certain basic principles, including the definition of Italy as a democratic republic based on work, in which sovereignty belongs to the people. Other principles concern the inviolable rights of man, the equality of all citizens before the law, and the obligation of the state to abolish social and economic obstacles that limit the freedom and equality of citizens and hinder the full development of individuals. The constitution guarantees many forms of personal freedom: the privacy of correspondence; the right to travel at home and abroad; the right of association for all purposes that are legal, except in secret or paramilitary societies; and the right to hold public meetings, if these are consistent with security and public safety. There is no press censorship, and freedom of speech and writing is limited only by standards of public morality. The constitution stresses the equality of the spouses in marriage and of their children, although the old Civil Law Code regards the husband as head of the household. Family law is in process of reform. Divorce was introduced in 1970 and can be obtained after a five-year separation, regardless of the question of guilt.

Personal freedom

One special article in the constitution concerns the protection of linguistic minorities. Religious liberty is conditioned by the Lateran Treaty made with the Vatican in 1929, which asserts that both state and Roman Catholic Church are independent and sovereign in their own spheres. The constitution establishes the liberty of all religions before the law but adds that churches other than the Roman Catholic Church are free to act according to their charters only so long as they do not conflict with the general law. The Catholic Church has retained considerable privileges, particularly in tax exemptions and in jurisdiction over church marriages in cases of nullity. The position of the Catholic Church is the cause of considerable friction in Italian political life. Despite the liberal tendencies of the Second Vatican Council, the church defends its privileges tenaciously and continues to fight any lay attempts to reform, for example, certain aspects of family law and the recent divorce law.

The constitution is upheld by the Constitutional Court, which comprises 15 judges, of whom five are nominated by the president of the republic, five by Parliament, and five by various legal bodies. Members must have certain legal qualifications and experience. The term of office is nine years, but Constitutional Court judges are not eligible for re-appointment. The court performs four major functions. First it judges the constitutionality of state and regional laws and of acts having the force of law. Secondly, the court resolves conflicts of competence of jurisdiction between ministries of administrative offices of the central government or between the state and a particular region or between two regions. Thirdly, it judges indictments instituted by Parliament. When acting as a court of indictment, the 15 Constitutional Court judges are joined by 15 additional lay judges chosen by Parliament. Fourthly, the court determines whether or not it is permissible to hold referendums on particular topics. The constitution specifically excludes from the field of referendums financial decisions, the granting of amnesties and pardons, and the ratification of treaties.

The legislature. Parliament is bicameral and comprises the Chamber of Deputies and the Senate, both elected by popular vote and with equal powers. In theory, the Senate should represent the regions and in this way differ from the lower chamber, but in practice the only real difference between them lies in the minimum age required for the electorate and the candidates: 21 and 25, respectively, for deputies and 25 and 40 for senators. Deputies and senators alike are elected for a term of five years, which can only be extended in case of war. Parliamentarians cannot be penalized for opinions expressed or votes cast, and constituents cannot oblige their deputy to vote according to their wishes. Deputies and senators enjoy immunity from arrest, criminal trial, and search. Their salary is established by law, and they qualify for a pension.

Both houses are officially organized into parliamentary parties. Each house is also organized into standing committees, which reflect the proportions of the parliamentary groups. Besides studying bills, these committees act as legislative bodies. The new parliamentary rules have followed the United States' pattern and have given the standing committees extensive powers of control over the government and administration. Parliament also sets up special joint investigatory committees.

Special majorities are required for constitutional legislation and for the election of the president of the republic, Constitutional Court judges, and members of the Superior Council of the Judiciary. An unusual feature of Italian parliamentary procedure is use of a secret ballot. Votes of confidence are necessarily made openly, while voting in presidential elections is by secret ballot; in normal divisions, voting can be either open or secret, though the secret ballot is generally preferred. While granting parliamentarians greater independence, it enables them to vote contrary to party instructions. Moreover, it effectively prevents any control of the representatives by the electorate.

Secret voting in Parliament

The two houses meet jointly to elect and swear in the president of the republic and to elect one-third of the members of the Superior Council of the Judiciary and one-third of the judges of the Constitutional Court. They may also do so to indict the president of the republic, the president of the Council of Ministers, or any individual ministers.

Each year, the budget and the account of expenditure for the past financial year are presented to Parliament for approval. The budget, however, does not cover all public expenditure, nor does it include details of the budgets of many public bodies, over which, therefore, Parliament has no adequate control. International treaties are ratified by means of special laws.

The most important function of Parliament is ordinary legislation. Bills may be presented in Parliament by the government, by individual members, or by other bodies, such as the National Council of Economics and Labour, various regional councils, or communes. Bills are passed either by the standing committees or by Parliament as a whole. In either case, the basic procedure is the same. First, there is a general debate followed by a vote; secondly, each separate article of the bill is discussed and voted on; finally, a last vote is taken on the entire bill. All bills must be approved by both houses before they become law, so, whenever one house introduces an amendment to the draft approved by the other house, the latter must approve the amended draft. The law is then promulgated by the president of the republic unless he considers it unconstitutional or inappropriate; in that case, he remands the bill to Parliament for reconsideration. If the bill is, nevertheless, passed a second time, the president is obliged to promulgate it. The law comes into force when published in the *Gazzeta Ufficiale*.

The presidential office. The president of the republic is irremovable, and his seven years of office cannot be shortened. He is elected by a college comprising both chambers of Parliament, together with three representatives from every region. The two-thirds majority required guarantees that the president is acceptable to a sufficient proportion of the populace and of those in public life. The minimum age for presidential candidates is 50. If the president is temporarily unable to carry out his functions, the president of the Senate acts as his deputy. If the impediment is permanent or if it is a case of death or resignation, a presidential election must be held within 15 days.

Special powers and responsibilities are vested in the president of the republic. In certain cases, his powers exceed those of the government, which must, however, always countersign his acts. He can be indicted for high treason or failure to uphold the constitution. He has the power to call special sessions of Parliament, to promulgate laws and delay legislation, to authorize the presentation of government bills in Parliament, to promulgate executive orders, and, with Parliamentary authorization, to ratify treaties and declare war. He commands the armed forces and presides over the Supreme Council of Defense and the Superior Council of the Judiciary. He has the power to dissolve Parliament either on his own initiative or at the request of the president of the Council of Ministers. He may appoint five life members of the Senate and appoints five of the 15 Constitutional Court judges. He also appoints the president of the Council of Ministers, the equivalent of a prime minister. It is his duty, whenever a government is defeated, after consulting eminent politicians and party leaders, to appoint the person most likely to win the confidence of Parliament; the large number of political parties gives him a very real choice. The president of the republic grants amnesties and pardons on the advice of Parliament.

The government. The government comprises the president of the Council of Ministers and the various other ministers responsible for particular departments, whom he has nominated. They are appointed to office by the president of the republic. Each new government must receive a vote of confidence in both houses of Parliament within ten days of its appointment. If at any time the government fails to maintain the confidence of either house, it must resign. This rule has not yet, however, led to any government resignations; to date, these have all been caused by splits in the coalition of two or more parties that had united to form a government. The president of the Council of Ministers is not merely the first among ministers of equal merit but is solely responsible for directing government policy and coordinating administrative policy and activity. Ministers are responsible jointly for the acts of the council, such as the emanation of decree laws and, severally, for the acts of their ministries. The government is the summit of executive power. In times of emergency, it can issue decree laws signed by the president of the republic, provided such laws are presented to Parliament for authorization the day they are issued and receive its approval within 60 days. Without such approval they automatically lapse. The government and, in certain cases, individual ministers issue administrative regulations and provisions, which are promulgated by presidential decree.

President of the Council of Ministers

Regional and local government. The republic is divided into regions, provinces, and communes. There are 15 ordinary regions and an additional five (Sicilia [Sicily], Sardegna [Sardinia], Trentino-Alto Adige, Friuli-Venezia Giulia, and Valle d'Aosta) to which special autonomy has been granted. The regions with ordinary powers are Piemonte (Piedmont), Lombardia (Lombardy), Veneto, Liguria, Emilia-Romagna, Toscana (Tuscany), Umbria, the Marche, Lazio (Latium), Abruzzi, Molise, Campagnia, Puglia (Apulia), Basilicata, and Calabria. Italy can thus be considered a regional state. The modern regions correspond to the traditional territorial divisions. The powers of the five special regions derive from special statutes adopted through constitutional laws. The organs of regional government are the Regional Council, a popularly elected deliberative body with power to pass laws and issue administrative regulations, the Giunta Regionale, an executive body elected by the council from among its own members, and the president of the Giunta Regionale. The Giunta Regionale and its president are required to resign if they fail to retain the confidence of the council. Voting in the regional councils is rarely by secret ballot.

Participation in national government is a principal function of the regions: regional councils may inaugurate parliamentary legislation, propose referendums, and appoint three delegates to assist in presidential elections. In regional legislation the five special regions have exclusive competence in certain fields, while the ordinary regions have competence within the limits of fundamental principals established by state laws and including areas such as agriculture, forestry, and town planning. The legislative powers of both special and ordinary regions are subject to certain constitutional limitations, the most important of which is that regional acts may not conflict with national interests. The regions can also enact legislation necessary for the enforcement of state laws when the latter contain the necessary provisions. The regions have administrative competence in all fields where they have legislative competence. Additional administrative functions can be delegated by state laws. The provision that normally regional administration is to be carried out at provincial and commune level aims at avoiding excessive bureaucracy. The regions are financially autonomous; they have the right to acquire property and the right to collect certain revenues and taxes.

The state has powers of control over the regions. The validity of regional laws that are claimed to be illegal can be tested in the Constitutional Court, while those considered inexpedient can be challenged in Parliament. State supervisory committees presided over by government-appointed commissioners exercise control over administrative acts. The government has power to dissolve regional councils that have acted contrary to the constitution or have violated the law. In such an event, fresh elections must be held within three months.

Communes

The organs of the commune, the smallest local government unit, are the popularly elected common council, the Giunta Comunale, or executive body, and the mayor. Both the Giunta Comunale and the mayor are elected by the council from among its own members. The communes have the power to establish and collect local taxes; they have their own police; they issue ordinances and run certain public health services; and they are responsible for such services as public transport, garbage collection, and street lighting. Control over the activity of the communes, until now vested in the state and exercised by the prefects, was in the early 1970s being transferred to the regions. Common councils may be dissolved for reasons of public order or for continued neglect of their duties.

The organization of the provinces, units midway in size between regions and communes, is analogous to that of the communes; they have councils, giunte, and presidents. At present, provincial activity is minimal; it is likely to increase when the regions are fully operating and delegate their functions to the provinces and communes.

There are certain central-government officials whose duties lie in the sphere of local government. These include the government commissioner of the regions, who supervises the administrative functions performed by the state and coordinates them with those performed by the region; the prefect, resident in each province, who is responsible for enforcing the orders of central government and has powers of control over the state organs of the province and communes; and the *questore*, who is the provincial chief of the state-run police. Certain local-government officials also have central government duties: among them are the president of the Giunta Regionale who, in directing the administrative functions that the state delegates to the region, performs a specific state duty; and the mayor of a commune who, in his capacity as an agent of the central government, registers births, deaths, marriages, and migrations, maintains public order (though, in practice, this is dealt with by the police), and can, in cases of emergency, issue ordinances concerning public health, town planning, and the local police.

The political process. *Elections.* In Italy there are parliamentary, regional, and local elections. Systems of proportional representation are used in the elections of the Chamber of Deputies and the Senate. Regional elections are governed by state laws and are also based on proportional representation. A system of limited vote is used in municipal elections by communes with less than 5,000 inhabitants, while the more highly populated communes use a list system of proportional representation. The system used in provincial elections is analogous to that used in senatorial elections.

Political parties. The constitution guarantees all citizens the right to associate freely in political parties in order to contribute through democratic procedure to the determination of national policy. The essential characteristic of a democracy is the existence of rival political parties. A plurality of parties is encouraged by systems of proportional representations and in Italy has led to the formation of eight principal parties, as well as other smaller parties. Participation in the primary elections (to make up the lists of candidates) is strictly limited to party members and hence is free from outside control. Parties are not required to publish accounts or disclose the source of their income, which frequently comes from public bodies, pressure groups, and individuals.

The chief Italian political parties are the Democrazia Cristiana (DC; Christian Democratic Party); the Partito Comunista Italiano (PCI; Italian Communist Party); the Partito Socialista Italiano (PSI; Italian Socialist Party); the Partito Socialista Democratico Italiano (Italian Social Democrats); the Partito Liberale Italiano (PLI; Italian Liberal Party); the Movimento Sociale Italiano (MSI; Italian Social Movement [neo-fascists]); the Partito Repubblicano Italiano (PRI; Italian Republican Party); and the Südtiroler Volkspartei, or the Partito Populare Sud Tirolese (SVP; South Tirolean People's Party).

The Christian Democratic Party, in practice supported by the church hierarchy, aims to unite all Italian Catholics in a single political grouping. For this reason it contains both highly conservative and strongly progressive elements. The consequent difficulty in forming coherent policies reduces its electoral impact, but it polled slightly less than 39 percent of the votes cast in the 1972 elections to the Chamber of Deputies. The Italian Communist Party, with about 1,500,000 members, is the largest European Communist party outside the Soviet bloc. As an opposition party it wins most of the floating protest votes of the electorate, besides those of its own members, and gained over 27 percent of the total vote for the Chamber of Deputies in 1972. The Socialist Party, a section of the Socialist International, was formed in 1967 by the amalgamation of the Italian Socialist Party, led by Pietro Nenni, with the Italian Social Democrats, led, until his election as president of the republic in 1964, by Giuseppe Saragat. This party won more than 14 percent of the vote in the 1968 election. The merger of these two parties was dissolved in 1969. The Socialists polled 9½ percent in the 1972 elections; the Social Democrats, 5 percent. The Socialist Party of Proletarian Unity, a left-wing group that had seceded from the Socialists in 1963, won 4.5 percent of the vote in 1968 before merging with the Communists in 1972.

The Liberal Party and Republican Party are the successors of two political movements that originally contributed to the unification of Italy. The Liberals, who stress the importance of personal initiative and freedom, won nearly 4 percent of the 1972 vote. The Republicans, attempting to show themselves as representative of the democratic left, won 3 percent of the 1972 vote. A more particularist party was the Italian Democratic Party of Monarchist Unity, the vehicle of those seeking a return of the monarchy; it had lost ground steadily and in the 1968 elections won only just over 1 percent of the vote. It had some contact with the Italian Social Movement, a neo-Fascist party, which in 1968 won 4.5 percent of the votes cast, appealing not only to the few who want a return of Fascism but to others who consider the government coalitions too left-wing. These two parties merged in 1972 garnering nearly 9 percent of the total vote to the Chamber of Deputies. Finally, the South Tirolean People's Party exists to unite the German-speaking population of that area and to gain greater political and administrative autonomy for the province of Bolzano within the region of Trentino-Alto Adige.

Trade unions. The constitution establishes the right to organize trade unions. The right to strike is guaranteed by the constitution but is not yet regulated by labour legislations and so remains a very potent weapon in the hands of the trade unions. Unofficial and wild-cat strikes also occur. Civil servants are covered by the general right to strike but the Constitutional Court has established that strikes by those engaged in fundamental public services are unlawful. Labour conflicts have always been serious and were particularly intense between 1968 and 1970, when workers obtained pay increases, better working conditions, and considerable managerial power.

The participation of the citizen. The constitution seeks to establish the effective participation of all citizens in the political, economic, and social organization of the country. This, however, is a stated ideal rather than a binding obligation, and it has not and perhaps cannot be fully realized. In practice, except for the few who can become political commentators of some sort and so influence public opinion, the opportunities for participation are restricted to those connected with elections. All citizens of 21 years and over may vote in national, regional, and local elections. Partly because voting is considered a civic duty and partly because of spontaneous involvement, the turnout for elections in Italy is very high, reaching an average of 92 to 94 percent of the electorate for parliamentary elections. Citizens may also subscribe to national referendums or petitions, the purpose of which is the abrogation of a law or an executive order; such a petition must be signed by 500,000 members of the electorate or sponsored by five regional councils. In certain circumstances national constitutional amendments are subject to a more ordinary form of referendum, in which the electorate vote in favour or against specific proposals. Abrogative referendums are provided for in relation to all regional legislation, and there is provision in some regions for holding ordinary referendums. The constitution also provides that 50,000 members of the electorate may jointly present to Parliament a draft bill. This method of inaugurating legislation has only been attempted once, and Parliament did not even examine the bill.

Voting

On a more executive level, the right of workers to take part in the management of companies is guaranteed by the constitution but lacks enabling legislation. Participation in politics and public affairs through the medium of the press and radio and television is restricted to a relatively small number of individuals and to certain, mainly political groups. The press is free but, because of high production costs, it is run either by public or private industrial groups or by political parties. The Radiotelevisione Italiana (RAI) is a state-run monopoly sanctioned by the Constitutional Court. It should provide equal facilities to all groups and individuals, but it is widely claimed that this impartiality has not yet been realized.

Justice. The Italian judicial system consists of a series of courts and a body of career judges who are civil servants. Frequently, cases are heard by a collegial bench consisting of two or more judges, and the legal profession provides for interchangeability between the position of judge and of prosecuting attorney. The courts form either part of the regular court hierarchy or are special courts with a specific and limited competence. The judicial system is unified, and every court is part of the national network. The highest court in the regular hierarchy is the Court of Cassation; it has appellate jurisdiction and gives judgments only on points of law. The 1948 constitution prohibits special courts with the exception of administrative courts and courts martial, although a vast network of tax courts has survived from an earlier period. The administrative courts have two functions: the protection of *interessi legittimi*, individual interests strictly connected with public interests and protected only for that reason, and the supervision and control of public funds. Administrative courts are also provided by the judicial sections of the Council of State, the oldest juridical-administrative advisory organ of government. The Court of Accounts has both an administrative and a judicial function; the latter involves primarily fiscal affairs. The courts martial have criminal jurisdiction in cases involving military personnel on active service and even over reserve personnel on unlimited leave, with respect to certain military crimes. The Superior Council of the Judiciary, provided for by the constitution and intended to guarantee the independence of the judiciary, was only formed in 1958.

Italian law is codified and is fundamentally based on Roman law, in particular, as regards civil law. The codes of the Kingdom of Sardinia in civil and penal affairs, derived from the French Napoleonic model, were extended to the whole of Italy when unification was achieved in the mid-19th century. In the period between World Wars I and II, these codes were revised; but further reform is necessary, because they contain some articles that the collapse of Fascism rendered anachronistic. For these and other reasons, the Constitutional Court has declared a number of articles unconstitutional. Besides the codes, there are innumerable statute laws that integrate the codes and regulate areas of law, such as public law, for which no codes exist.

The constitution stresses the principle that the judiciary should be independent of the legislature and the executive. For this reason jurisdictional functions can be performed only by ordinary magistrates, and extraordinary tribunals may not be set up. Judges cannot be dismissed.

The armed forces. The armed forces are commanded by the president of the republic, who also presides over the Supreme Council of Defense, comprising the president of the Council of Ministers, the ministers of Defense, Foreign Affairs, Industry, and the Treasury, and the chief of staff. Military service is obligatory. A bill recognizing the rights of conscientious objectors is being considered. Italy's military expenditure is the sixth highest in the world. Defense accounted for about 12 percent of the entire budget for 1970, and 60 percent of the defense budget was allocated to wages. Although the constitution specifies that the armed forces must embody the democratic spirit of the republic, their activity is free from any political control. Italy's adhesion in 1949 to the North Atlantic Treaty Organization transferred to the allied command a certain degree of control over the Italian forces.

Conscription

ADMINISTRATIVE SERVICES

Education. The constitution guarantees the freedom of art, science, and teaching, the existence of private schools (mainly run by religious bodies) alongside the state schools, and the independence of the universities. It further states that the public schools are open to all and makes provision for scholarships and grants, although the latter have only been partially implemented. Education is compulsory only from the ages of six to 14 years. The school system begins with kindergarten for the three to six year olds. Elementary schools are attended between the ages of six and 11, at which stage most children go on to secondary schools for 11 to 14 year olds, but those wishing to study music go directly to the conservatories. Postsecondary schooling is not compulsory and includes a wide range of technical and trade schools, art schools, teacher-training schools, and scientific and classical grammar schools. Pupils from these schools can then go on to university, where courses vary from four to six years.

A survey conducted in 1968 showed that more than 2 percent of the population was then illiterate; 15 percent had no school-leaving certificate; more than 56 percent had successfully finished elementary school; more than 15 percent held a secondary school diploma; more than 7 percent held a high school diploma, while somewhat fewer than 3 percent were university graduates. Maintenance grants are few and inadequate, and the high cost of supporting children while they study, particularly at trade or grammar schools and at university level, when they could otherwise be earning, effectively limits higher education to a privileged elite. Legislation to improve this situation is in process. It is noteworthy that, while education accounted for 12 percent of public spending in 1950, it accounted for nearly 25 percent in the early 1970s.

Health and welfare. The constitution guarantees the protection of health as an individual right and a community interest; the support of those who are unable to work and are indigent; and the right of workers to social-insurance benefits in the case of accident, illness, disablement, old age, or unemployment. So far, the state has done little toward providing any health service, although an organization for the protection of public health in the sense of enforcing standards of hygiene and supervising medical services is under the control of the Ministry of Health. Special doctors in the provinces and communes are responsible for the public health of their respective areas. On the Ministry of Health also depend the *medici condotti*, doctors who are paid by the communes and whose services are free to the poor. Public assistance, run partly by the state and partly by local government, is also minimal, though privately run charitable organizations are numerous. The social-security system works on the basis of numerous separate groups and organizations, which provide sickness and unemployment insurance for the various categories of workers but for workers only. The contributions of both employees and employers are high, while individual benefits are insufficient. A reorganization of this system, involving much amalgamation, is underway.

Social security

Housing. The constitutional encouragement of home-ownership has only been partially carried out. It was hoped that a new law passed in 1971 would facilitate and speed up communal expropriation of sites suitable for subsidized housing and introduce advantageous terms for the leasehold purchase of the property. Until the early 1970s there was little low-cost housing, and purchase of property had been far beyond the means of the average family. The 1971 census showed that at that time there were about 15,348,000 occupied habitations with an average of 1.0 occupants per room; according to the 1961 census 163,720 people were homeless and living in caves, cellars, shacks, and warehouses.

Zoning regulations for building are established by the communes under state supervision. As soon as the regions are fully operating, they will take over town planning. Historic monuments and natural-beauty spots are protected by law and come under the control of the Ministry of Education; but, despite this supervision, public as well as private development has depredated cities, countryside, and coastline.

Police. There are two police forces in Italy with general duties: the Pubblica Sicurezza, which is under the authority of the home secretary, and the Carabinieri, a corps of the armed forces that is, therefore, under the minister of Defense. The functions of the police are the prevention and supression of crime; both functions are performed by both police forces. The administrative police to whom preventative duties are assigned see that the activities of individuals and of groups do not contravene the law. Their authority stems from a Fascist law of 1931 only partially modified by Constitutional Court decisions but reduced by a law of 1956 that requires that restraint be imposed on potential offenders by court order only. The administrative police are also responsible for the issue of passports and other permits. The constitution places the judicial police, who are engaged in supressing crime, under the authority of the courts, but the actual subordination of the two forces to the two government ministries conflicts with their technical subordination to the judiciary. Besides these two police forces, there are also special police for customs, excise and revenue, and communal police and prison guards. There are also private police that operate in a limited field under the supervision of the regular police.

State-controlled public services. In Italy, as elsewhere, state intervention in the private sector of the economy is increasing. Economic policy is established by the Interdepartmental Committee of Economic Planning and carried out under the supervision of the Minister for State-

Controlled Enterprises and the Court of Accounts. Many public corporations carry on economic activity in competition with similar private companies, such as the most important banks, but the most notable form of state intervention in industry and business concerns is through state-run holding companies such as IRI and ENI. The state usually but not necessarily has a controlling interest in the companies in which it holds stock. There are also enterprises entirely government owned, such as the railways and the postal service. Almost all sources of power and fuel, communications, transport, shipbuilding, and the cast-iron and steel industries are managed directly or indirectly by public corporations. Public corporations are also responsible for most medium- and long-term loans and about half of all life insurance.

SOCIAL CONDITIONS

Wages and the cost of living. The constitution asserts the right of every worker to an adequate wage and the right of equal pay and maternity benefits for women. In 1970 take-home pay varied between 58 percent of the cost of labour in mining to 88 percent in agriculture; it was around 60 percent in industry and 63 percent in business. Between 1966 and 1970 there was an increase of between 12 percent and 39 percent in the minimum wage of the various sectors, while in the same period there was a 14 percent increase in the consumer price index. In 1964 the average annual family budget of a hired agricultural labourer was 894,123 lire; the average for a hired worker was 1,404,428 lire; for a white-collar worker, 2,175,579 lire; and for an industrialist, business, or professional man 2,909,597 lire. Between 1964 and 1969 the consumer price index increased by 14 percent. In northwest Italy at that time, the average annual family budget was more than 19 percent above the national average, while in southern Italy, Sicily, and Sardinia it was more than 23 percent below the national average.

Health conditions. A radical reform in hospital law has been in operation since 1968 and a radical public-health reform is planned. There is a great shortage of hospital beds. In 1964 there were about 493,500 beds and about 6,203,700 patients; average hospitalization lasted 23 days. By 1971 the number of beds had risen to about 568,500 for about 8,009,700 patients; average hospitalization lasted 20 days.

Sanitary conditions in private homes are deplorable. As late as the 1961 census, 14 percent of the habitations had no water either in the dwelling or on the premises; more than 11 percent had no lavatory in the dwelling or on the premises; and 71 percent were without bath.

Social and economic divisions. Italy is a country of great social and economic differences. A very small elite enjoys great wealth, while the largest stratum of society lives in varying degrees of poverty. Inherited fortunes have survived, and industrial wealth is aggregated in economic empires as well as being concentrated geographically in the Milan–Turin–Genoa triangle. More than 95 percent of the working population were fully employed in 1969; more than 1 percent were underemployed and more than 3 percent either unemployed or looking for their first job. Of those who were either partially or fully employed, more than 1 percent were industrialists, business men, or professional men; more than 22 percent were self-employed workers; more than 16 percent were white-collar workers, more than 51 percent were hired workers; and nearly 9 percent gave a hand in a family business. The average annual family budgets give a very rough idea of the differences in spending capacity of the various categories of workers. The vast differences in the educational level of the population also testify to the cultural extremes prevalent in Italy and invite conjecture as to the underlying economic circumstances that may have caused them.

Social inequalities

VI. Cultural life and institutions

THE CULTURAL MILIEU

The country now called Italy has resulted from the amalgamation of many small territories. Political unification took place in 1861, but unification is still incomplete as a cultural and social process. In the matter of language, however, Italian is the standard commonly used for official, formal, and literary purposes and taught in the schools to natives and foreigners. The varied dialects, including Tuscan—the language of Florence and its territory and used by Dante, Petrarch, and Boccaccio in their writings are now usually spoken and only to a limited extent written. Regional differences in self-expression still persist, and Tuscan remains to some extent a linguistic invention in regions that are not Tuscany. The other dialects (as they are disparagingly called) including Gallo-Italian, Venetian, Corsican, Central Italian, and Southern Italian, embody ways of thought and speech that are not simply different modes of expression but represent many different ideological, psychological, and cultural worlds. All speech forms called Italian belong to the Romance languages (*q.v.*).

Another sign of imperfect national unity is the regions' jealousy of one another. The division between the north and the south (the Mezzogiorno) is the sharpest of all. The prosperous, progressive, industrial society of the north looks down on the backward, impoverished, primitively agricultural Mezzogiorno regions south of Naples in Puglia, Basilicata, Lucania, and Calabria. To many northerners the increasing efforts of government to assist the economy of the south are so much money poured down the drain in a hopeless cause. For his part, the southern day labourer remains suspicious of the central government despite the aid it offers the south through the introduction of civil-works projects and of industry bringing alternative employment. The administration has been indifferent to his desperate needs too long and has tacitly left him to his master, the absentee proprietor of the vast farm, or *latifundium*, on which he and his companions labour. In western Sicily this resentment of central authority is carried so far as to secure general acquiescence in the activities of the Mafia, underlining the fact that the Mafia indeed was once a secret society pledged to wage a perpetual struggle against the oppression of foreign rulers.

North versus south

The problem of regionalism, seen most clearly in the language question and the division between the north and the south, is basic to the Italian scene. But with the country's industrial development and its liberation after World War II from the political stultification of Fascism, a ferment of change and uncertainty has transformed society, especially in the large urban centres. The capture of foreign markets by the Italian automobile and gasoline industries and by agricultural cooperatives has strengthened Italy's economic links with other countries. Great impetus has been given to this process by the country's membership in the Common Market.

At the social level the transformation has been encouraged by the growth of the communications media, especially television. The result is that the old provincialism, wherein each city seemed to have its own life-style, is disappearing. The position of the sexes, too, is changing with regard to each other. The position of woman, politically enfranchised in the 20th century, marks an advance toward freedom. Continuing as a wage or salary earner even after marriage, she is no longer destined from an early age to household matriarchy, exerting her influence on the family from within it in counterpoise to her husband's more explicit rights. Men and women are less oppositely polarized in their confrontation with each other: to a novel extent they have become rivals in the same sphere of action.

The authority of the Roman Catholic Church may have been discreetly ignored in the past, but it was seldom openly challenged, other than by a minority of professed anticlericals. Now a more general disregard of the church and its system is evident in the extent to which life has become secularized and in the decline in church attendance. The struggle with the church over divorce—previously unobtainable in Italy under the terms of the state's Lateran Treaty (1929)—was a momentous one, rousing the devout and the diehard to an impassioned stand against it, before the divorce law was introduced in 1970. In the following year, the government introduced measures offering new possibilities in the way of birth control.

The *dolce vita*

In Rome especially, a feature of the generally prosperous, if erratic, postwar era has been the *dolce vita* ("sweet life") attitude of internationalized café society. The *dolce vita* was a reaction of release from the conventional family code of Italian life. More pretentious than simple hedonism, or pleasure seeking, its philosophy was one of experiment in an Existentialist moral incertitude. The drifting, day-to-day existence of the parasites of this way of life—the *pappagalli* ("parrots"), press and street photographers and jacks-of-all-trades pestering film stars and pretty girls on Rome's Via Veneto for preference—was symbolic of the *dolce vita* and its ephemeral futility. The *vitelloni* ("big calves"), young loungers of no occupation, have been another symptom of this unsettled period.

Italian culture has felt the impact of avant-garde modes of feeling and expression but in a rarefied way among few people. Traditional culture, of "aristocratic" and "educated" derivation, is disdained, ridiculed, and opposed by forward-looking intellectual elements who are aware of transatlantic developments in the arts and who claim to represent the advanced contemporary art situation in Italy. Yet the populace prefers the traditional culture and ignores the products of the cultural elite. The resulting split between the collective psychology and intellectual culture continues. The people remain unmoved before the constructions of the laboratories of the intellectual "upper classes," which are an exorcism of past culture and a rupture of continuity with its traditions. At the opposite pole, the "upper classes," having lost confidence in themselves in isolation, have abandoned their dream of universal interpretation and instead attempt to contribute to culture by elaborating intrinsically empty constructions inspired by a preoccupation with technique; the technique itself is regarded as a method of seeking truth and interpreting reality but is no more than a stratagem for filling an unexpected vacuum in ideology.

THE CONTRIBUTIONS OF THE ARTS

Italy was in the forefront of the development of the arts in the Renaissance, that crucial and brilliant period of transition when European culture emerged from the Middle Ages and entered into the modern age. This rebirth received impetus from a reappraisal of the classical Greek and Roman world after centuries of supposed ecclesiastical obscurantism. Artists and scholars in Italy were especially well placed to take the lead in such a revival since they lived in what was the very heartland of the ancient Roman Empire, and the material remains of its civilization, whether as stone structures or as texts, lay beside them.

Literature. Through Dante, Petrarch, and Boccaccio Italian literature blossomed to supreme greatness early; after Ariosto and Tasso in the later Renaissance it declined somewhat into formalism but renewed some of its fire through the Romantics, Vittorio Alfieri, Ugo Foscolo, Alessandro Manzoni, and Giacomo Leopardi; and then, in the 20th century, Gabriele D'Annunzio represented the last flowering of Romanticism. Since then, the writers who have made the most significant contribution to their country's literature have turned their backs on the rhetorical Romantic tradition. The plays of Luigi Pirandello (who died in 1936), inventive, psychologically disturbing, and impassive in their mood, and his terse, hard-edged short stories heralded a new attitude and a new technique; his masterpiece, the play *Henry IV*, with its thrillingly presented intersecting planes of normality and madness, comparable to the analysis made of pictorial reality by Picasso's Cubism, is as fresh as anything written since by the French Existentialists Camus and Sartre. This new mood, this dry tone, is realized also in the work of the novelists of Realism, or Verismo, who have been the dominant figures in modern Italian literature: Verismo was initiated by Giovanni Verga; after him Italo Svevo (Ettore Schmitz), disregarded by all except James Joyce and Eugenio Montale until the end of his life because he wrote in the less than acceptable Triestine dialect, is now seen as one of the ironists of modern European literature.

The Realist novelists

Since Svevo's death in 1928, the novelists Ignazio Silone, Cesare Pavese, and Alberto Moravia and the poets Montale and Giuseppe Ungaretti have been outstanding figures. It is in the work of the Realist and Neo-Realist novelists that the attempt of Italian writing to come to terms with the modern world and its political and social pressures can be best appreciated. The works of Pavese and Moravia, the first with his acknowledged debt to the economical, crisp style of Ernest Hemingway and the other with his remorseless analysis from the standpoint of a European Existentialist intellectual, are at a far remove from the rhetoric and Latinist abstraction of the traditional plane of ideas of Italian letters.

The visual arts. The great names in Italian art and architecture through the centuries make a long catalog: those of Giotto, Donatello, Brunelleschi, Michelangelo, Leonardo da Vinci, Titian, Bernini, and Tiepolo call up a host of others. But continuous subjection to foreign powers had an enfeebling effect on Italy's artistic contribution, which sank into provincialism. Ties with European art were renewed about 1910 by the work of the painter Amedeo Modigliani and by the Futurist movement, which found its most characteristic expression of mechanistic dynamism in the work of its leader, the poet Filippo Marinetti (died 1944), and the painters Umberto Boccioni and Giacomo Balla. Futurism was succeeded by the "metaphysical painting" of Giorgio De Chirico, at one time associated with the Surrealists for his timeless dream landscapes until he turned his back on this early work to produce, from the 1950s on, canvases loaded with reminiscence of traditional styles. Giorgio Morandi's subtle, quietist paintings of endlessly varied arrangements of bottles, pans, and jars are a product of metaphysical painting and, since his death in 1964, have become perhaps more highly regarded than the work of any other contemporary Italian painter. Lucio Fontana's work exemplifies the modern artist's solitary quest for form: blank canvas opened by a knife slash; an arrangement of pebble grains stuck onto the unicoloured canvas; and a room swathed in nylon textile (at the Palazzo Grassi in Venice in 1960).

The Rational Architecture movement of 1927 has produced one of the outstanding Italian architect-engineers of the 20th century in Pier Luigi Nervi, architect of the Turin exhibition complex and, with Marcel Breuer and Bernard Zehrfuss, of the UNESCO headquarters in Paris. Innovative educational architecture is represented in Milan's Istituto Marchiondi by Vittoriano Viganò. The work of Nervi and of such other architect-engineers as Giovanni Ponti (who worked with Nervi on the Pirelli skyscraper in Milan) and the builders of hydroelectric dams in Africa and elsewhere represents their country's most serious contribution to modern art in hauntingly beautiful constructional work such as Brunelleschi himself might have been proud of. Other movements have come and gone, that of the Six in Turin, the Roman school, and the school of Milanese Expressionism, to which the sculptor Giacomo Manzù once belonged.

Italian architect-engineers

Music. Italian music has been one of the supreme expressions of that art in Europe: Gregorian chant, troubadour song, the madrigal, the work of Palestrina and Monteverdi and of composers such as Vivaldi, Alessandro and Domenico Scarlatti, and Cimarosa, followed by the 19th-century flowering of Italian opera in the hands of Rossini, Donizetti, Bellini, and, greatest of all, Giuseppe Verdi. Arrigo Boito and Giacomo Puccini garnered the Verdian heritage, and then Verismo, or Realism, made itself felt in operatic tradition as in literature in the work of Pietro Mascagni and others. Since World War II, in the post-Schoenberg world of serial music, two Italians have made significant contributions: Luigi Dallapiccola and Luigi Nono.

Theatre. Theatrical production in Italy in the latter half of the 20th century has employed all forms of the art of theatre, from grand opera to the puppet show. Opera productions, notably at La Scala opera house in Milan, as well as at other opera houses such as the San

Carlo in Naples and at the Teatro la Fenice in Venice, are world famous; and an annual summer production of an opera in the Roman amphitheatre in Verona also attracts foreign visitors. Modern operas by Italian composers that have been staged include *Il convento veneziano* by Alfredo Casella and *Sette canzoni* by Gian Francesco Malipiero.

In the drama the Italian theatre has been active in producing outstanding contemporary European work and in staging important revivals. Not a great deal of major new work has been offered to it by native playwrights: nothing to rival the work of Luigi Pirandello earlier in the century. Outstanding productions have included those of the company of the Teatro Stabile della Città di Genova and of the Piccolo Teatro of Milan. Leading producers, working with various companies, have been Giorgio Albertazzi (who caused a stir in the cinema with his film of Moravia's novel *Il conformista* ["The Conformist"] in 1971), Gianfranco De Bosio, Giuseppe Patroni-Griffi, Giorgio di Lullo, Luigi Squarzina, and Giorgio Strehler. New plays of the period include Primo Levi's documentary dramatization of his experiences in a Nazi death camp, *If This Be a Man;* Griffi's Pirandellian comedy *Imagine, One Evening at Dinner;* Franco Brusati's *La pietà di novembre* (*The Other Face of November*); and Moravia's symbolic anti-Nazi drama *Il dio Kurt* ("God Kurt").

Italy exercises a notable influence throughout Europe in the field of ballet, and contemporary Italian ballets include *Balli plastici* by Fortunato Depero, *Coro di morti* and *La follia di Orlando* by Goffredo Petrassi, and *Marsia* by Luigi Dallapiccola.

Motion pictures. It is in the cinema that Italy has probably made its most significant contribution to contemporary art on an international scale. Before World War II the Italian film industry had produced epic films that were by no means negligible in quality. But just after World War II Italy caught the world's eye, first with the Neo-Realism of the films of Roberto Rossellini and Vittorio De Sica in particular, dealing in a matter-of-fact way with conditions in Italy at the end of and just after that war, and later with the more freely imaginative interpretation of Realism exemplified in the films of such directors as Michelangelo Antonioni, Federico Fellini, Cesare Zavattini, Pier Paolo Pasolini, and Luchino Visconti. The trenchantly laconic statement of many of these films and their affinity with the attitudes of Existentialist thinking marked a development in cinematic imagination that had a cross-fertilizing influence, in particular, on the young French film makers of the "New Wave."

Neo-Realism in films

CULTURAL INSTITUTIONS

Academies and societies. Academies and societies representative of almost every academic and social activity have proliferated in Italy as nowhere else. Literary art and academies flourish in the major Italian cities that are regional capitals. Indeed, academies of fine arts had their origins in Italy, the Accademia di Belle Arti of Florence (founded as the Accademia del Disegno) in 1563 and that of Perugia in 1573. Rome's Accademia di San Luca was a guild of painters, founded in 1577; today its collections are open to the public. Italy's most famous learned society is the Accademia Nazionale dei Lincei, of which Galileo was once a member. The most distinguished literary society is the Accademia della Crusca, founded in Florence in 1582, whose *Vocabolario della Crusca* stabilized the Italian literary language on the basis of Tuscan speech. There are likewise many historical and scientific societies including the Accademia del Cimento, established (1657) in Florence.

The foreign schools in Rome

A feature of Italian academic life is the contribution made by the foreign schools maintained in Rome by the United States, France, Germany, Great Britain, and others for the study of Italian architecture, art, and archaeology.

Among cultural institutions, the society Italia Nostra, membership of which is open to the general public, holds a special place. Italia Nostra's importance lies in the work it does to call attention to the care of the country's architectural treasures and to the preservation of what is left of the beauty of its landscape, rural and urban, from the encroachments of industry and bad building and the effects of environmental pollution. Italians traditionally have been indifferent toward matters not immediately affecting them and are disinclined to bestir themselves in public causes. The efforts of Italia Nostra have made them aware of the penalty of such indifference. The society has encouraged coordinated study and planning by industry, local authority, and government to resolve the conflicting needs of conservation and of industry—and the provision of work is vital in a country where underemployment is chronic.

Galleries and museums. Italy is exceptionally rich in architectural monuments, in art galleries and museums, and in examples of architecture of the past still in use, as well as of ancient ruins; indeed, churches, palaces, villas, and other buildings that are works of art in their own right often also contain art treasures in the shape of frescoes on their walls, easel pictures and sculpture, and furniture and ornaments. The regionalism of Italy is typified by its art galleries and museums. The national galleries at Florence and Bologna are also municipal institutions, and indeed the great galleries of Italy are often concerned with their own regional heritage—the Capitoline Museum and the Borghese Gallery in Rome are mainly built up of the work of painters and sculptors working in Rome, even if they were not all strictly of the Roman school; the Pinacoteca di Brera in Milan has the most representative collection of north Italian painting of the Lombard school; the Accademia in Venice of Venetian painting; the Uffizi and the Palazzo Pitti galleries in Florence are supreme for Florentine painting; the Galleria Nazionale dell'Umbrian in Perugia contains magnificent examples of the Umbrian school; the Pinacoteca Nazionale in Siena of the Sienese school; the Palazzo Bianco in Genoa of the Genoese school; and so on.

It must be understood, of course, that the galleries also contain masterpieces of other Italian schools and indeed from foreign countries, but their collections are built up around the body of regional work exhibited. Other major galleries and museums besides those mentioned above include the Vatican and Lateran museums and the Galleria Nazionale d'Arte Moderna in Rome; the Museo Nazionale del Bargello and the Museo dell'Opera del Duomo in Florence; the Galleria d'Arte Moderna, the Castello Sforzesco, and the Pinacoteca Ambrosiana in Milan; the Galleria e Museo Estense in Modena; the Museo Archelogico Nazionale, the Museo Civico Filangieri, the Museo Principe Diego Arangona Pignatelli Cortes, and the Museo e Gallerie Nazionale di Capodimonte in Naples; the Galleria Nazionale in Palermo; the Palazzo Doges and Museo Civico Correr in Venice.

ENTERTAINMENT

Festivals. Regional life in Italy is typified by diversity of costume and cuisine and by a great variety of festivals. The latter are, however, changing in character, and many civil and religious festivals are no longer forceful expressions of local idiosyncrasies that brought them into being; as in most other Western countries, an element of unreality enters the dressing up in clothes belonging to bygone days and only brought out once or twice a year. The appeal to the tourist industry helps as much as anything to keep festivals alive.

The Italians are a lively Mediterranean people, and the climate of their country is favourable to social exchange and display out of doors. The *passeggiata,* or "promenade," conducted with conversation and gossip up and down the main street or about the principal square at noon and evening, is still a feature of urban provincial life. In the same spirit of outward projection, Italians enjoy festivals and processions. Festivals in Italy are indeed manifold and can be divided into two main kinds, religious and secular, though the religious observations generally extend their impulse to cover a good deal of accompanying secular celebration. The secular festivals and sometimes the religious festivals contain strong elements of folklore.

Religious festivals. Many places hold special religious festivals and great processions in costume on such holy days as Easter, Corpus Christi, and the Feast of the Assumption. At Christmas the crib (*presepio*) is set up in churches, and children receive their presents at Epiphany, the feast of the three kings, from the fairy-witch Befana. The New Year is celebrated with fireworks and noise, supposedly to aid in driving away the devil. At Epiphany, in Rome, it is the custom to bring presents for children in the Piazza Navona, and at the Feast of St. Anthony there, on January 17, priests of the Church of St. Eusebio bless working animals and pets paraded by their owners.

In Palermo the Festival of St. Rosalia is held in July, with a procession and illuminations. In Naples the Miracle of St. Januarius, a procession of the vial containing that saint's dried blood, which is said to become liquefied again upon invocation, is held at special times. Venice holds two festivals, in memory of the cessation of the plagues of 1576 and 1630, respectively; the first festival is the Feast of the Redeemer, held on the third Sunday in July, when a bridge of boats is built across the wide channel of the Canale della Giudecca, a solemn high mass is held in the Church of the Redentore, and a breathtaking fireworks display takes place at night; the second is held on November 21, at the Church of Sta. Maria della Salute. At Bari the feast of the patron saint of the city and of sailors, St. Nicholas, is held on May 8 and is attended by many pilgrims who take part in an illuminated procession in boats in the harbour.

Secular festivals. Secular festivals take a number of forms, including modern arts and crafts festivals, and, as a general rule, the more local they are, the more vitality they have. At Bari the Levant Fair, which lasts for two weeks or more in September and in conjunction with which a motor show is held, is an important regional fair. Earlier, in May, the city holds a famous procession, the Vidua Vidua, and a folklore festival, while Foggia, not far away, conducts a flower show and fair with outdoor opera. Still in the same region, Brindisi holds a parade of horses and riders in medieval costume. In Naples the Festival of Piedigrotta commemorates the Battle of Velletri (1744), and people go to the Grotta Nuova to hear new songs sung for the event. At Cocullo, in the Abruzzi, on the first Thursday in May, St. Domenic's statue is carried in procession, live poisonous snakes writhing round it to be made harmless and later bought by apothecaries for the medicinal properties of their venom. One of the best known to foreigners, is the Corso del Palio (Parade of the Banner), held in Siena on July 2 and August 16; it is a parade and horserace around the main square, which is said to go back to 1275, with the riders in medieval costume of the colours of their respective city districts.

The Siena Palio

Siena, Mantua, and Spoleto hold notable music festivals. Still in central Italy, Arezzo holds its Giostra del Saraceno, a tournament originating in the 13th century, in June. On the first Sunday in May and on June 24, Florence holds its Calcio, a kind of football match dating back to 1530, in costume. At Pescara, on the Adriatic, an international folklore festival is held. Varese, in Lombardy, holds a national festival of mountain singing in December. In Piedmont, Aosta holds a Battle of Queens in October. And the Ligurian riviera resorts enjoy celebrated Battle of Flowers festivals. Famous Venetian festivals include La Sensa (on Ascension Day), the Regata Storica (regatta) on the Grand Canal, and festivals of drama, music, and films.

Sports. Cycling, football, basketball, tennis, motoring, motorcycling, winter sports, and hunting game are popular sports and recreations in Italy. The most important sporting events are the great professional cycle races, chief among them the Tour of Italy road race, which attracts the best foreign as well as Italian professional road-racing cyclists, and the major professional football matches. In football every sizable town supports its own professional team; teams from Milan and Turin play before capacity crowds in their stadiums and have provided more than their share of the national talent that took Italy into the final of the World Cup in 1970.

Other major sporting events include the Italian Grand Prix motor race at Monza, the international Italian Tennis Championship at Rome, the Martini Fencing Trophy at Turin, and the Show Jumping Championships at Rome.

Tourism. For centuries foreigners have been attracted to Italy by its varied architectural monuments, scenery, and climate; Rome, the "Eternal City," has drawn visitors to it especially for its classical antiquities and as an early centre of Christianity and the seat of the head of the Roman Catholic Church. In the 18th century it became a custom for English gentlemen or for their sons in the company of a tutor to make the Grand Tour, an educative tour of western Europe in which the visit to Italy was the highlight. In the 19th century a number of English literary figures chose to live in Italy for a time, and their example led to the growth of little colonies of expatriates, principally in Florence and Rome, who were pleased to receive visiting fellow countrymen.

The Grand Tour

By the 20th century the pleasure of a trip to Italy ceased to be reserved for a well-to-do, cultivated minority when the rise of the tourist industry in the hands of experienced travel agents removed much of the expense and even peril of travel in Italy and made it possible for thousands to enjoy it. Since World War II, flies and mosquitos, formerly two of the greatest enemies of the traveller in Italy, have almost been eliminated. By the beginning of the 1970s the annual influx of tourists had risen to surpass the 25,000,000 mark—that is, over a year, one visitor for roughly every two persons of the population—and the annual gross receipts of over $1,600,000,000 from tourism were making an important contribution to the country's economy. Hotel investment at around $170,000,000 was the highest in the world outside the United States. But from the 1960s onward the Italian tourist industry has also felt competition from such countries as Spain, Portugal, and Yugoslavia, where the cost to the tourist has been lower than in Italy.

Foreign visitors once sought the great cultural centres of Rome, Florence, Venice, and Naples, but an increasing number now spend most of their stay at coastal resorts and islands or among the Alpine hills and lakes of the north: at such places as the Ligurian and Amalfi rivieras; the northern Adriatic coast; the small islands in the Tyrrhenian Sea (Elba, Capri, Ischia, Ponza, Lipari, Stromboli); the "Emerald Coast" of Sardinia; Sicily, especially the resort of Taormina; the National Park of the Gran Paradiso and the Dolomites in the Western and Eastern Alps, respectively; the north Italian lakes (especially Maggiore, Como, and Garda); and the National Park of the Abruzzi, one of the most rapidly developing centres of tourism in Italy and, since the early 1970s, one easily reached by a highway from Rome.

Most Italians take their holidays in their own country and after much the same pattern as that of foreign visitors, with the addition of much visiting of near relatives; but they make more use of the southern Adriatic beaches in Puglia, at Manfredonia, Siponto, and the little villages around the foot of the Promontorio del Gargano (Gargano Promontory) and down the same coast at Trani, Bari, and Brindisi. They have also been able to keep the Calabrian beaches much to themselves, at Crotone and Reggio Calabria, for example, and up the Tyrrhenian coast to Paestum and Salerno. But all these places are being increasingly frequented by foreign visitors.

PRESS AND BROADCASTING

Press. The Italian press is generally provincial and local in outlook, though the major daily newspapers carry foreign news and comment on it. The dailies that command most notice abroad are the *Corriere della sera* and *Il Giorno* of Milan and *La Stampa* of Turin and *Il Messaggero* and *Il Tempo* of Rome. Political parties publish or control newspapers, and daily newspapers are issued in the large regional capitals. News and specialist periodicals include *Oggi*, *Tempo*, *Panorama*, *La Domenica del Corriere*, *Gente*, *Il Mondo*, *Espresso Europeo*, *Epoca*, *La Nuova antologia*, *La Fiera letteraria*, and *Il Verri Belbagor*, and many others.

Broadcasting. Radiotelevisione Italiana (RAI) conducts all broadcasting and is a state enterprise. Radio programs are transmitted over three channels. The first channel is the most widely diffused, and its programs are of various types: current news, culture, sports, light music, debates, interviews with people prominent in contemporary Italian life, and so on. The third program is practically reserved for classical music, jazz, debates on cultural subjects, and in general for discussions of the most important events in Italian and world politics.

Television has two channels. The first channel, which has a larger number of viewers, uses different kinds of material: variety shows, film cycles, quiz programs, musical games, direct transmissions of important athletic events, news broadcasts (*telegiornale*), and programs for children. The second channel takes care of political debates, investigations in depth into contemporary problems (*boomerang*), theatre, etc. Dramatized novels, foreign-language courses, and football matches are broadcast over both channels. A third channel, to carry colour, was in the planning stage in the early 1970s. (Ed.)

VII. The outlook

Italy's population has increased steadily. In the 1971 census the population was recorded at nearly 54,000,000, and a rise to nearly 58,000,000 is envisaged for 1980. The increased average age will set particular social problems, as will questions of equality in the production of the national revenue by various regions and its fair distribution.

In the 1950s the "economic miracle" developed at a high rate, with much of the national product being invested. With full employment, labour troubles caused recessions in 1962–64 and 1969–72. In some years wages increased more than productivity, with corresponding inflation. Italy's economic means are less than competing countries', and to sustain a growth rate equal to 5–6 percent of the national product more of the national income must be invested than consumed.

Agriculture, increasingly mechanized, shows a levelling off of cereal production in favour of market gardening and cattle raising. In industry, enterprises permitting higher production are favoured, while services show similar tendencies. The Italian economy must develop the south and islands, slowing down their emigration rate.

Such plans require diffused education, accumulation of resources for investment, and a modernized administration. The state and local bodies are increasingly spendthrift—taxes, including social services, stand at 32–33 percent of the national income. To combat this a law has been introduced to modernize the taxation and equalize the fiscal burden.

Internal migration exerts a unifying influence on the population. Nourishment, nearly 3,000 calories per day for each person, is adequate even for the poorer sections of the community. Health conditions are satisfactory. Education is available at all levels. The economy has become increasingly industrialized. Labour tensions, if no better than those of other countries, at least are no worse. The resolution of the government's chronic instability has remained a major problem, one requiring that political parties put national before factional interests.

(Li.L.)

BIBLIOGRAPHY

General works: *Enciclopedia Italiana*, 36 vol. (1929–37), a basic, if somewhat dated, source; EDITORS OF HOLIDAY, *Italy* (1960), a good, general book mostly for the tourist; TOURING CLUB ITALIANO, *Conosci l'Italia* (1957–), a basic guidebook; see also DENIS MACK SMITH, *Italy: A Modern History* (1959); NINETTA JUCKER, *Italy* (1970); and LUIGI BARZINI, *The Italians* (1964).

The land and people: DONALD S. WALKER, *A Geography of Italy*, 2nd ed. (1967), a comprehensive text covering regional, economic, physical, and historical aspects; ROBERT E. DICKINSON, *The Population Problem of Southern Italy* (1955), a pioneer study of settlement patterns; CARLO BATTISTI, "La lingua nazionale e le minoranze linguistiche in Italia," in *Archivio per l'Alto Adige*, 54:155–208 (1960).

The Economy: G. BARBERO, *Land Reform in Italy* (1961), is a study of economic achievements and future prospects. Italian statistical publications include: *Annuario statistico italiano*, *Annuario di statistica agraria*, and *Annuario di statistiche industriali*—all issued by the ISTITUTO CENTRALE DI STATISTICA. SHEPARD B. CLOUGH, *The Economic History of Modern Italy* (1964); and VERA C. LUTZ, *Italy: A Study in Economic Development* (1962), provide good background information.

Administration and social conditions: Basic works include EMILIO CROSA (ed.), *La Constitution italienne de 1948* (1950); NORMAN KOGAN, *A Political History of Postwar Italy* (1966); ROBERT CHARLES FRIED, *The Italian Prefects: A Study in Administrative Politics* (1963); and ROBERTO ALMAGIA, *L'Italia*, 2 vol. (1959). See also JOSEPH LA PALOMBARA, *Interest Groups in Italian Politics* (1964); and SIDNEY G. TARROW, *Peasant Communism in Southern Italy* (1967).

Cultural life and institutions: CESARE CARAVAGLIOS, *Il folklore musicale in Italia* (1936); and PAOLO TOSCHI, *Arte popolare italiana* (1960), are two excellent Italian sources. Basic references are RENZO FRATTAROLO, *Introduzione bibliografica alla letteratura italiana* (1963); and MARIO PUPPO, *Manuale critico-bibliografico per lo studio della letteratura italiana* (revised annually).

Italy and Sicily, History of

This article traces the history of Italy and Sicily from the fall of the Roman Empire in the West in the 5th century AD to the present. For the history of the peninsula and its associated islands prior to the 5th century, see ITALIC PEOPLES, ANCIENT and ROME, HISTORY OF.

This article is divided into the following sections:

I. Italy in the early Middle Ages

THE BARBARIAN INVASIONS

Italy in the 5th century. Toward the middle of the 5th century, Italy was the only province of the Western Empire in which Germanic barbarian peoples had not established permanent occupation. Imperial dignity retained considerable prestige, and the new capital, Ravenna, chosen for its easily defensible position and its lines of communication by sea to the East, was enriching itself with splendid monuments.

Although no barbarian successor state had been established in Italy, groups and individuals of barbarian origin had acquired great importance in the political and social life of the peninsula. Barbarians made careers for themselves in the army, and some of them attained positions of great power, married into the imperial houses, and even deposed and created emperors. Such a barbarian was Ricimer, *magister militum* ("master of the soldiers") of the Western emperor Avitus. As a barbarian and an Arian, Ricimer could not be emperor, but his strength in Italy was such that he deposed three emperors in the mid-5th century. Ricimer was succeeded briefly by the Burgundian Gundobad, who in 473 placed Glycerius on the throne. Two years later, contingents of the barbarian tribes of the Scyri, Heruli, and Rugii chose one Odoacer as their leader. In 476 the last Roman emperor, young Romulus Augustulus, was deposed, bringing the Western Empire to an end. Odoacer ruled over Italy in the double capacity of king of the barbarians and of *patricius*—that is, as an unrecognized representative of the Eastern ruler.

Overthrow of the Western Empire

The accomplishment of these barbarians cannot be dismissed as a purely negative one. However crude and brutal they may have been, they made a place for themselves in the Roman world, which they defended to the best of their abilities. Ricimer led the long struggle against the Vandals, a Germanic tribe that swept through Spain and North Africa, led a seaborne expedition to Italy, and in 455 sacked Rome. Odoacer, in his turn, compelled the Vandal king Gaiseric to give back Sicily and succeeded in occupying Dalmatia. In short, these barbarian generals and their rough-and-ready soldiers, although they oppressed local populations, had a role to play as defenders of the empire, and it would be a mistake to blame them for the decay of Roman civilization. Indeed, the Romans in Italy had been accustomed for centuries to contact and cohabitation with the barbarians. Between the last half of the 4th and the first half of the 5th century, many barbarian prisoners were farmed out to the countrysides and cities of the north in order to repopulate them. These Goths, Huns, Alemanni, and others have left their traces in place-names throughout the region.

The reign of the Ostrogoths. In 488 Italy was invaded from the east by a new barbarian army, that of the Ostrogoths, which, after a succession of victories climaxed by the siege of Ravenna in 493, destroyed Odoacer's feeble regime. The invaders this time were not merely armed groups; they comprised an entire population (numbering perhaps some 300,000) that had left the Balkans with the firm intention of settling in Italy. The Eastern emperor Zeno had encouraged their migration because he was dissatisfied with Odoacer's rule in Italy and was also anxious to remove the Ostrogoths from the Byzantine frontiers. The Ostrogoth leader was the able Theodoric, who had lived for a long time as a hostage in the Eastern court, where he grew to appreciate Roman-Byzantine civilization.

Theodoric ruled over Italy both as king of his own people and as *magister militum* of the Eastern emperor. The main feature of Theodoric's policy was to keep Ostrogoths and Romans apart, allotting to the former the exercise of arms and to the latter posts in the civil government. This was, he thought, the only way for the Ostrogoths to keep the upper hand, since their numbers were few in comparison with those of the local population. This separatist policy was based on a difference of religion, since the Ostrogoths were Arians and the Romans were Catholics; the policy included the prohibition of *connubium*, or mixed marriages. But it was, fundamentally, contrary to historical reason, since it was inevitable that, in time, the two peoples should be drawn closer together.

There were signs of crisis in 519, when Theodoric suspected Zeno of plotting against him. He attacked the Roman leaders who had lent him their support. The senators Albinus, Boethius, and Symmachus were tried and condemned to death in 524–525; Pope John I was arrested and died in prison in 526.

When Theodoric died in 526, his Italian policy had to be considered a failure. But, in any event, Italy and Sicily (Sardinia and Corsica were still under Vandal rule) had enjoyed a period of tranquillity and well-being under his government. There had been a renaissance of Classical culture, as witnessed by the writers Boethius and Cassiodorus, who lived at Theodoric's court. And the capital cities—Pavia, Verona, and, above all, Ravenna—were adorned with splendid buildings and monuments.

Reconquest by Byzantium. Theodoric left the kingdom in the hands of his daughter Amalasuntha, who ruled as regent for her son Athalaric. When Athalaric died prematurely in 534, she had to share the throne with her cousin Theodahad, head of the Goth "nationalist" faction, which within a year found a way of getting rid of her. This assassination furnished a pretext for Justinian I, the Eastern emperor, to continue the reconquest of the lands along the western Mediterranean, already begun with general Belisarius' victorious expedition against the Vandals of Africa (533–534). Belisarius then launched a campaign in Italy, disembarking in Sicily in 535. The war went first one way and then the other; it was long lasting (until 553) and exhausting and destructive for both armies and civilian populations. In spite of their stubborn resistance, the successive Ostrogoth kings —Witigis, Totila, and Teias—could not prevent the occupation carried out by the troops of Belisarius or his successor Narses. The Eastern Empire retook Sicily, Sardinia, and Corsica. The Ostrogoths were killed, taken prisoner, or dispersed, and, of their stay in Italy, very few traces remain.

Extermination of the Ostrogoths

The whole of Italy returned to direct dependence on the empire, though under quite different conditions than before; it was no longer a centre of power and privilege but a mere outlying province. With the promulgation of the Pragmatic Sanction in 554, Justinian gave Italy a new ordering, creating a *praefectura Italiae* (with its capital at Ravenna), subdivided into 11 provinces in which there was a clear-cut separation between civilian and military authority. Sicily was governed directly from Constantinople, while Sardinia and Corsica were lumped into the Exarchate of Africa. This was the beginning of a long period of Byzantine influence in Italy, not only political but cultural and artistic as well. Roman law, revived and codified under Justinian, came into widespread use; the magnificent basilicas were built in Ravenna; and Byzantine architecture and mosaics adorned Rome and other places. But the Byzantine government, avid for taxes and heedless of its subjects' religious convictions, provided considerable opposition, of which the popes later took advantage in order to bolster their authority. The popes also could count on the support of increasingly numerous monasteries. Saint Benedict of Nursia (Norcia) had laid out a model of monastic organization and rules during the tragic epoch of the Greco-Gothic War, and the monasteries later became strongholds of the Catholic religion and the Latin tradition.

THE LOMBARDS

The conquest and the political structure. In 568 a new Germanic people, the Lombards, appeared at the eastern gateways of Italy, coming from Pannonia and Noricum. Their numbers were about equal to those of the Ostrogoths, but they were considerably cruder, had no links with the Byzantine Empire, and looked on Italy as a land to be conquered. The Byzantines, whose Italian forces were meagre, put up their first resistance at Pavia (Ticinum), which fell to the Lombard king Alboin after a three-year siege. The clergy and population of many places (Aquileia, Milan, and elsewhere) fled before the Lombard invasion to inaccessible coastal areas, where they could count on the protection of the Byzantines,

Adapted from *Enciclopedia Italiana di Scienze, Lettere ed Arti*, vol. 19

Italy under the Lombards and the Byzantine Empire, *c.* 603.

who still controlled the seas. The Lombards soon occupied the whole interior of the peninsula as far south as Benevento. Their administrative units were called "duchies," a name reflecting the fact that their army units were led by *duces*. There were 35 such duchies, named after their capital cities. Among the most important of these were Forum Julii (the present-day Cividale del Friuli), Brescia, Pavia, Pistoia, Lucca, Spoleto, and Benevento. The occupied territory as a whole took the name of Longobardia or Langobardia (Lombardy). Later on, this appellation was restricted to the central and northern region, seat of the capital, just as it came to be the case with the Byzantine territories, collectively known as Romania, a name that subsequently came to apply only to the Romagna, with its capital at Ravenna.

The Lombard duchies

Within each duchy the land was divided for ownership or tax purposes into *farae*, groupings of related families that made up the social and military fabric of the Lombard people. About the administrative structure little information remains, most of it being from an account by the 9th-century historian Paul the Deacon. It is certain, however, that the class of the Roman *possessores* was broken up and practically destroyed. This was true particularly during the Interregnum (574–584), when the initial unity of the Lombards was attenuated and the "dukes" ruled independently, some of them even passing over to the service of the empire. The dukes, however, soon realized the danger of such a state of anarchy in the face of the hostile Byzantines and also of the Franks, who were pressing at the northern borders, and they restored the kingdom with Authari as their king (584–590). The king was transformed from a military leader into a regular monarch, as half of the occupied lands were incorporated into a royal domain.

The Lombards introduced radical change in the peninsula. Whereas the Goths and other barbarians had respected the Roman political and administrative framework, the Lombards did away with it completely in favour of their own customs. The only institutions to be saved were the churches. The king promulgated laws and pronounced judgments together with the assembly of the *arimanni* or *exercitales*, composed of all the freemen able to bear arms. Such, at least, was the theory, but, since the Lombard *farae* were widely dispersed, in practice the assembly of the *arimanni*—the *gairethinx*—was soon replaced by the *gasindi*, a group of councillors close to the king and of such powerful nobles (*adalingi*) as were able to make prolonged stays at the court. The court, housed in the royal palace of Pavia, grew in importance with the concentration of government power and the differentiation of offices; within it there was even a remarkable school of law. The conquered territory was ruled locally by dukes and *gastaldi*, the former as heads of family lines, the latter as royal officials. The *gastaldi* were originally in charge of crown possessions, but with time their authority grew, to the detriment of that of the dukes. In some cases, *gastaldi* took the place of rebellious dukes; in others they ruled over a provincial city from the start. In the reign of Rothari (636–652), it seems that there were, in the cities, *gastaldi* appointed by the king to watch over the dukes, and it is certain that there were rural military–judicial units where *gastaldi* ruled. At the time of King Liudprand (712–744), when the government was further centralized, newly conquered lands were made into *gastaldatus*, directly dependent upon the capital at Pavia. The duchies of Spoleto and Benevento, on the other hand, had a development of their own, and the *gastaldi* were appointed by the dukes.

Authari tried, by means of both arms and treaties, to hold back the Franks and the Byzantines; in order to combat the former, he allied himself to Garibald, duke of Bavaria, by marrying his daughter Theodelinda. She was a Catholic, and it was on her initiative, together with that of Pope Gregory the Great, that there was a first move to convert the Lombards, who, when they were not Arians, were pagans. After the death of Authari (590), Theodelinda married Agilulf, duke of Turin, who held the throne from 591 to 615 and completed the occupation of the hinterland of Venetia. Together with the dukes of Spoleto and Benevento, Agilulf led military expeditions to central and southern Italy and intended to occupy Rome until the strong-minded Pope Gregory dissuaded him. Aware of the spiritual power of the church, Agilulf came to adopt a pro-Catholic policy; he allowed Adaloald, his son by Theodelinda, to receive a Catholic baptism and favoured the Irish monk Columban, who in 612 founded the monastery of Bobbio, near the lines of communication between the Po Valley and the Byzantine territories of Lunigiana and Liguria.

The reign of King Agilulf

Rothari, an Arian elected in the wave of a reaction to Agilulf's indulgence toward Catholicism, extended the Lombard kingdom to its greatest territorial extent, with the conquest of the Ligurian coast and of Oderzo in Venetia. He is famous for his Edict of 643, the first codification of Lombard customs. The edict, written in Latin, shows some influence of the secular life of the Romans and of the church. There is an effort to contain the *faida*—that is, personal revenge—by means of the *guidrigild*, an objective and closely calculated compensation for damage done, which reflects the social rank of the damaged party and, by extension, the whole structure of this barbarian society, divided into *arimanni, aldii* (semi-freedmen), and slaves.

After Rothari there was a long period of contested successions, of rebellions, and of struggles among the dukes until the election in 712 of Liudprand, the greatest of the Lombard kings. In this period, beneath the violence of political events, a silent and deep transformation was taking place. Conversion to Catholicism was becoming widespread. With conversion came a new closeness, indeed the beginning of a fusion, between the Lombards and the native Romans. The two peoples were drawn gradually together by everyday life, by participation in the same liturgy, by common hostility toward Byzantium and mistrust of Rome, by the use of a common Latin language, and by devotion to the monarchy. Although certain social and juridical distinctions were slow to disappear, they increasingly lost their original ethnic imprint. The consequences of this transformation can be seen in the structure of the state and its political aims. Liudprand founded and protected churches and monasteries, based his laws on religious principles, contributed to the struggle against the Arabs of Provence (in southern France), and gave the bishops an important share in public life and in the administrative and judiciary branches of the government. He sought also to enlarge the kingdom. In 728, taking advantage of the wave of discontent and rebellion aroused in the Byzantine parts of Italy by Emperor Leo III the Isaurian's decree condemning the cult of images (the beginning of the famous Iconoclastic Controversy; 725), he invaded the Exarchate of Ravenna and the Pentapolis (territory south of Ravenna), threatening Ravenna and advancing toward Rome. He claimed to be a defender of orthodoxy and the Pope, but the latter, Gregory II, was alarmed by his approach and sought the support of the dukes of Spoleto and Benevento. Liudprand, sensitive to the Pope's admonitions, withdrew after turning over to him the castle of Sutri (728), though he still had to face the rebel dukes. His later expeditions into the exarchate and the Roman duchy met with only ephemeral success, as was the case with the first occupation of Ravenna (739). His expansionist policy failed not only because of the resistance he encountered but also because his Catholic faith stayed him from attacking the Pope with armed force.

After Liudprand, Aistulf (749–756) continued the same expansionist policy. Aistulf occupied Ferrara, Comacchio, and Ravenna and acquired control of the duchy of Spoleto. The papacy, alarmed by the Lombard advance, turned for support to the powerful Frankish kingdom in northern Europe. In 754 Pope Stephen II went to France, where he anointed and crowned King Pepin the Short, thereby consecrating the legitimacy of the Carolingian dynasty. In return, Pepin and his major dignitaries promised a Frankish intervention in Italy and restitution to the Patrimony of St. Peter of the territories to which the popes made claim. This alliance between the Holy See and the Frankish monarchy had a decisive influence upon

The papal alliance with the Franks

Western history; it marked the beginning of the collapse of the Lombard kingdom, the formation of a papal state, and the renewal of the idea of a universal empire. Pepin came twice down to Italy, defeating Aistulf and forcing him to give to the Church of Rome the territory he had wrested from the Byzantines. The new Lombard king, Desiderius (757–774), tried at first to allay the Frankish threat by alliance: he gave his two daughters in marriage to Pepin's sons, Charlemagne and Carloman. But he failed in his intent. When he made a new break with Pope Adrian I in 772, Charlemagne, then occupying the Frankish throne (and having repudiated his Lombard wife), descended upon Italy (773–774), defeated Desiderius and his son Adelchis, and put an end to the Lombard kingdom. The duchy of Spoleto came under his rule, although keeping a character of its own. Benevento, however, remained independent.

The Lombards left a lasting imprint upon Italian history, even if it is not always possible to establish how many customs of the period from the 6th to the 8th century were theirs and how many should be attributed to the crude conditions into which Roman society, in an economic and cultural regression, had fallen. The Regnum Langobardorum (Regnum Italiae) survived for centuries within the new medieval empire, mostly as an ideal but retaining, nevertheless, some of its political and juridical structures (the coronation of the king at Pavia, Milan, or Monza, the archbishop of Cologne's custody of the record office, the institution of counts and judges). The Lombards left noteworthy traces in the fields of law (particularly penal law) and art (sculpture and jewelry). Excavations of the necropolises of Cividale del Friuli, Bolsena, Nocera Umbra, Benevento, and other places have brought to light swords, buckles, gold pectoral crosses, coins, and other objects linked by a definitive common style. Noteworthy are the stylization of the animals, the use of precious stones, and the taste for braided ornamentation. The Lombards were quick to learn Latin and were definitely bilingual toward the end of their rule. Traces of the Lombard language are to be found as late as the 10th century; even more important was the incorporation into Latin of certain words that subsequently passed into Italian.

The Frankish conquest lowered the conquered Lombards to the level of the Romans, thereby hastening the process of integration, already well under way by the end of the 7th century. This integration was chiefly of the masses, since aristocratic families and certain permanent groupings maintained, because of their privileges, a separated position, although they, too, gradually fused with the new society. From the integration of Romans and Lombards, a new people—the Italians—was born.

Byzantine territories in Italy. At the beginning of the 7th century, after the first wave of the Lombard conquests, the Byzantines retained scattered areas along the coast. Of the ancient province Venetia et Istria there remained not only Istria but also the coast of the northern Adriatic, with a wedge-like extension pointing in the direction of Oderzo. This last separated Friuli from Treviso, for which reason Rothari later took it over. The inhabitants of Aquileia, Concordia (now Concordia Sagittaria), Altino, Treviso, Padua (Padova), Monselice, and Oderzo, cities attacked or destroyed during the successive conquests, sought refuge on the marshy coast or on the islands of the Lagoon (Laguna Veneta), where formerly there were only a few fishermen's villages.

The Exarchate of Ravenna

Farther south lay the Exarchate of Ravenna, corresponding to the present-day Romagna, with the addition of Bologna and part of Emilia. Ravenna was the headquarters of the exarch, the empire's chief representative, who had jurisdiction over all of Italy except Sicily (Sardinia, Corsica, and the Balearic Islands belonged to the Exarchate of Africa). Ravenna was also the seat of an important archbishopric, which the emperors favoured in every possible way in order to set it against Rome. As early as the end of the 7th century, it obtained the privilege of autonomy. The territory of the Exarchate was contiguous with that of the Pentapolis, the five cities of which were probably those of Rimini, Pesaro, Ancona, Numana, and Osimo, but the full extent of which was approximately the same as that of the present-day region of the Marches. A line of strongholds, some of them along the Via Flaminia and others on a lesser road to the west, connected the Pentapolis with the duchy of Perugia and this to the duchy of Rome (present-day Lazio). Territorial continuity was thus achieved between the lands on the Adriatic and those on the Tyrrhenian Sea, and a sort of diaphragm was set up between Tuscia (Tuscany) on the west and the duchy of Spoleto in the east. Lunigiana and maritime Liguria were isolated and could not long resist the invaders; in 640 they were conquered and occupied by Rothari. The duchy of Naples was better protected by virtue of its location and its access to communications by sea. At the southernmost end of the peninsula, divided by the territory of Benevento, were the two regions of Calabria (present-day Puglia) and Bruttium (present-day Calabria). The Byzantines also possessed Sicily and the other islands, which, between 650 and 750, had to be defended not so much from the Lombards as from the Arabs of North Africa.

Byzantine administration

An important change had come about at this time in the Byzantine administration. In the face of the Lombard invasion, the classic principle, reasserted by Justinian, of the separation between military functions and civil functions was abolished. Thus, the exarch acted as both military and administrative leader. His powers were much broader: he could make peace, contract alliances, adjudicate lawsuits, make official appointments, intervene in the affairs of the church, and confirm the election of the pope. At a lower level the same thing held true: the dux combined civil and military powers, administered justice, saw to the collection of taxes, and named the executives of his *officium*.

Byzantine rule in Italy was anything but tranquil, quite aside from the struggle against the Lombards. The remoteness of the emperor and his preoccupation with resistance to the Arabs made for a certain independence on the part of his subordinates, but, at the same time, it deprived them of the military and financial support that they needed for administrative purposes. The imperial officials had to provide for themselves with whatever means they could find on the spot. Moreover, their efforts were hampered by the emperor's intervention in religious affairs. Such intervention was often motivated by the necessity of resolving differences in the eastern provinces and creating a greater spiritual unity with which to resist external enemies. But, when the emperors pronounced themselves on doctrinal matters, they sometimes offended the religious conscience of the Italic peoples and aroused their enmity, which was often fostered by the bishops and especially by the pope. At times, the imperial officials found themselves in the embarrassing situation of carrying out orders directed against the popes, orders that encountered resistance on the part not only of the people but also of the militiamen who were supposed to execute them. For, since Byzantine soldiers were few in number, defensive and policing tasks were carried out by a locally recruited militia, the *scholae*.

There resulted considerable political and administrative confusion. Exarchs, dukes, and tribunes often carried out policies of their own, in opposition to one another and to imperial orders; local aristocrats joined the game to further their own advantage. When Justinian II ordered the arrest of Pope Sergius I (687–701), the militias of Ravenna and the Pentapolis marched on Rome (*c.* 694) in order to protect him. Thus, there was no repetition of the case of Pope Martin I, who was arrested by the emperor Constans II and died in exile in 655. Similar rebellions took place in the first years of the 8th century in Rome, in 711–712 in Ravenna, and in 717–718 in Sicily, premonitory of the major crisis at the time of the Iconoclastic Controversy. From that year (725) up to 751, the date of the Lombard occupation of Ravenna and the end of the exarchate, the impulse of the Italic people toward autonomy was accelerated. The Greek dukes were driven out and replaced by local rulers; the pope in Rome and the archbishop in Ravenna acquired greater political power, while Venice, Gaeta, Naples,

Sorrento, and Amalfi found in independence an incitement to seeking their fortune in sea trade. In short, the Byzantine possessions in Italy, already geographically scattered and progressively diminishing in size, finally lost political cohesion; the emperor's sovereignty over the cities and over Sardinia became purely nominal. Exceptions were Sicily (soon to be conquered by the Arabs), Puglia, and Calabria, which remained under the direct rule of Byzantium. Indeed, with the new Macedonian dynasty begun by Basil I (867–886), Byzantium resumed an active role in southern Italy, determined by the military prowess of the strategist Nicephorus Phocas. After the Arabs had been expelled from Taranto and from the Ionian coast and after the princes of Benevento had been driven to the north, the Puglian region, together with the Capitanata and the Gargano peninsula, came to form the theme of Longobardia, while Calabria, a base essential to what was left of Sicily, was liberated from Arab occupation and made into the theme of Calabria. The division into thema fitted into the new political and military organization imposed upon the Eastern Empire by Leo VI the Philosopher (886–912). The conquest and re-organization of southern Italy were accompanied by new eastern monastic institutions, notably those of the Basilian monks, that had great importance not only from a political but also from a religious and cultural point of view. Byzantine rule in the south lasted until 1071, when Bari, the seat of the emperor's representative, fell to the Normans.

The duchies of Spoleto and Benevento. The duchy of Spoleto was formed at the beginning of the Lombard invasion. Its first duke, Faroald (*c.* 571–591), and his successor, Ariulf (591–601), staked out boundaries that lasted until the Carolingian age. The duchy did not precisely coincide with any of the natural geographical regions of Italy. It occupied the eastern part of Umbria (the western part, with the fortresses or cities of Amelia, Narni, Terni, Perugia, and Gubbio, made up the Byzantine corridor between Rome and Ravenna), a southern area of the Marches (with Fermo and Camerino), and a strip in the northern section of the Abruzzi. Politically, it had an autonomous development, even if there were, in certain periods, close ties with the Lombard kingdom.

The autonomy of Spoleto

There were many reasons for this autonomy, first among them being its geographical isolation in an inaccessible and impregnable area of the central Apennines, which was further cut off from the Lombard kingdom by the Rome–Ravenna corridor. The dukes of Spoleto could pursue policies of their own, and they knew quite well how to assert themselves in the complex diplomatic and military interplay of their immediate neighbours—the popes, the exarchs, and the dukes of Benevento—none of whom was powerful enough to crush them. The Lombard kings might have had such power, but they exercised it in a reluctant and intermittent fashion.

Later, Charlemagne was able to impose his rule upon the duchy, but even he did not deprive it of its political and administrative individuality. A succession of dukes of Frankish origin supported the Carolingians in their expansionist designs upon Benevento. Meanwhile (in the first years of the 9th century), it seems that Spoleto acquired Chieti and Ortona, while Fermo and Camerino became independent and jointly formed first a "county" (*comitatus*) and then a "march" (*marca*). During the period of confusion and struggle after the end of the Carolingian dynasty (the deposition of Charles the Fat), a duke of Spoleto, Guy, managed to have himself crowned king of Italy at Pavia (889) and emperor at Rome (891). His son Lambert was emperor after him, but, by then, the title had no real meaning.

In the 10th century, the history of the duchy of Spoleto became increasingly confused and obscure. Dukes followed one after the other in rapid succession, but no one of them was able to found a dynasty. Later, with the houses of Franconia and Swabia, it passed into the hands of the great German vassals until, through the efforts of Innocent III and Gregory IX, it became a province of the Papal States.

The duchy of Benevento, too, goes back to the early years of the Lombard invasion, and its origins are bound up with the names of its first two dukes, Zotto (died 591) and Arichis (died *c.* 641), who led its extensive conquests. The distant Lombard kings had neither lands nor officials in the duchy. Indeed, Grimoald, duke of Benevento, entered the contest for the Lombard throne, was elected king, and reigned from 663 to 671, leaving Benevento in the hands of his son Romuald, who left it, in turn, to his descendants. A hereditary right was clearly established.

The borders of the duchy varied, but, except for some temporary conquests (Bari, Taranto, and Brindisi), they enclosed the southern part of the Abruzzi; Molise; the interior of Campania (with Capua and Salerno on the Tyrrhenian Sea); Lucania, with a piece of coastline on the Ionian Sea; and strips of northern Puglia (with Lucera) and Calabria. The territory was divided into some 30 administrative units ruled by ducal *gastaldi*, who enjoyed full civil and military powers. Like Spoleto, Benevento was a landlocked state, with no interest in sea trade and an agricultural economy that could not prosper because of the mountainous terrain and the lack of communications. A military regime, continuous wars, and social oppression made it a backward and conservative zone as compared to the Lombards' other Italian possessions.

Benevento's resistance to the Carolingians

With Arichis II (758–788), son-in-law of King Desiderius, the duchy of Benevento became the last seat of resistance (at times open, at others undeclared) to the Carolingians: as such it was changed from a duchy into a principality, and the capital was moved to Salerno. Lombard traditions lingered, and, even after the 9th century, there were expressions of "national" consciousness. A form of writing, the "Beneventan hand," remained independent of the "Caroline hand." The cultural and religious centre of the whole region was Montecassino, where the influence of the Cluniac reform was felt in the 10th century. Grimoald III, son of Arichis II, continued to combat the Carolingians, but, after his death in *c.* 806, a series of internal struggles led to a division into two principalities: Benevento and Salerno. A third territory gradually broke away from these two and became the independent county (later principality) of Capua. All three principalities fell into the hands of the Normans. Benevento was captured by Robert Guiscard in 1081 and immediately turned over to the Papal States, to which it belonged, with few interruptions, until 1860. Salerno and Capua were absorbed by the new Norman state.

CAROLINGIAN AND FEUDAL ITALY

The kingdom of Italy. In April 774, after sweeping away weak Lombard resistance, Charlemagne arrived in Rome, placed a new act of donation to the Roman Church (confirming Pepin's of 18 years before) on the tomb of the Apostle Peter, and acquired the title of *rex Francorum et Langobardorum* ("king of the Franks and Lombards"). A few pockets of rebellion remained (Benevento, Trento, Friuli), which obliged him to return to Italy in 776 and in 780–781. On this last occasion, his son Pepin was crowned in Rome by Pope Adrian I as "king of Italy." In a fourth descent upon Italy, in 787, Charlemagne defeated Arichis of Benevento and also Adelchis, son of Desiderius, who had landed in Calabria with Byzantine re-enforcements. The duchy of Spoleto and the march of Fermo were added to the kingdom.

In the following years, Charlemagne campaigned against the Saxons, the Arabs in Spain, the Bavarians, and the Avars—making himself master of a large part of western Europe and winning immense prestige. The logical consequence was the famous *renovatio imperii*, or second edition of the empire, in the 9th century, the attempt to give Charlemagne's conquests a political unity and an ideological basis. The reconstructed empire drew inspiration both from the unforgotten traditions of ancient Rome and from a religious ideal. At the same time, it reflected political and social realities in the process of transformation, which had been deeply influenced by the law, customs, and national characteristics of the Germanic peoples. But the medieval empire, at the time of Charlemagne and in its successive restorations, was never a true state but rather a symbol of the community of peoples of Christian Europe. Even contemporaries referred to it as an *imperium plurimarum nationum*, an empire of many nations.

The coronation of Charlemagne

The coronation of Charlemagne as emperor on Christmas Day, 800, in Rome, aroused the opposition of the Byzantines. But the differences between them were soon overcome, and in 812 they made a peace agreement. From the death of Pepin (810) until 887, Italy was governed by Carolingian princes, and, in spite of the dismemberments to which the empire was subjected, it retained the political and territorial setup of the time of the Carolingian conquest. Bernard, son of Pepin, eventually rebelled, but he was captured and blinded and died in 818. His successor, Lothair I, son of Louis I the Pious, took on the title of emperor. Of considerable importance is the Constitutio Romana, put out by him in 824, in which he prescribed that the pope, after he had been elected by the clergy and people of Rome, must swear allegiance to the emperor. By virtue of the territorial division of 843, Lothair retained the title of emperor (implying the possession of Italy) and also a long, narrow strip of territory between France and Germany that took from him its name of Lorraine. This division took no account of ethnic and linguistic differences but affirmed, rather, the principle that the possessor of the imperial crown must necessarily possess the capitals of the empire, Rome and Aix-la-Chapelle (Aachen).

The son and successor of Lothair, Ludwig II (855–875), bore the double title of king and emperor but reigned over Italy only. There ensued a renewal of Carolingian power and polity in the peninsula and a new wave of expansion toward the south. Ludwig made numerous expeditions into southern Italy, where political fragmentation and continuous differences among the local rulers invited raids on the part of the Arabs, who were just completing their conquest of Sicily. But political, military, and climatic difficulties thwarted the ambitious project of driving out the Arabs and achieving pacification.

The last Carolingians

The last Carolingians to govern Italy—in spite of the fact that their main interests lay elsewhere—were Charles II the Bald (875–877), Carloman (877–879), and Charles III the Fat (880–887).

Politically and administratively, Charlemagne's conquest did not cause the Lombard kingdom to be annexed to the Frankish state; on the contrary, it kept a juridical character all its own. There was, at first, a sort of "personal" union, inasmuch as, for a while, Charlemagne had two crowns; later, the kingdom of Italy had its own sovereigns, chosen from the Carolingian dynasty. Most often, however, these were emperors who enjoyed also the title of king of Italy. Noteworthy is the fact, remarked above, that the appellation Regnum Italiae took the place of Regnum Langobardorum. As the conquered Lombards' memory of their glorious past faded, a historical and geographical term that reflected the peninsula's allegiance to the empire came into use.

Under the Carolingians, no important changes were made in the central administration. Pavia remained the capital and seat of the court, government offices, and the assembly. The assembly was made up of the dignitaries of the kingdom, including numerous ecclesiastics who in the Carolingian age played a greatly increased role in the state; the assembly's legislative powers, however, were less than they had been in the Lombard period. Laws decreed by the emperor for the whole empire applied also to Italy, and in the palace of Pavia a special authority was exercised by the *comes sacri palatii*, or count palatine, who headed the royal tribunal.

Carolingian administration

More drastic modifications were imposed upon the outlying administration. The Lombard duchies were eliminated and were replaced by new districts, or counties, ruled by counts; that is, royal representatives with military and judicial functions, drawn from the Frankish aristocracy. The county organization in Italy, however, was not as widespread and important as was formerly supposed; certainly, it cannot be compared to that of the Frankish kingdom. Counts were not installed everywhere; in some places the old Lombard *gastaldi* remained after making an act of submission. In others, Lombard *gastaldi* and judges stayed on, alongside the counts, and exercised a judiciary function rivalling theirs. This was the case mostly in the cities, traditionally seats of government and the administration of justice. Because the greater part of the cities were also diocesan headquarters, the Frankish counts found other powerful and prestigious rivals among the bishops. Another limitation of the counts' power derived from the institution of the *missi dominici*, pairs of itinerant controllers, one a cleric and the other a layman, who made periodical visits to the counties and presided over their judiciary assemblies (*placita*). Thus, in Italy the Frankish counts found no way of taking root in a background so different from their own. Some of them moved into country estates and castles, from which they could exercise no more than a limited jurisdiction; others returned home. There were, of course, exceptions. The count-duke of Spoleto and the count-marquis of Friuli ruled over frontier territories where the powers of the *gastaldi* and bishops had been limited from the start and where it was easy to establish dynasties.

Aside from the greater or lesser ability of the Carolingian counts to settle on their Italian lands, they did, very definitely, introduce a new mentality and new systems into governmental practice. Like other functionaries, they were chosen among the *fideles* or *vassi* of the sovereign and bound to him by personal as well as bureaucratic dependency. It often happened that the holder of a public *honor* or *officium* held also, as a vassal of the king, lands *in benefice* far from his own county. And often these lands, as those belonging to churches and monasteries, had immunities or special privileges, consisting of relief from subjection to the royal courts and exemption from the payment of tribute. Because of the progressive weakening of the central power between the mid-9th and mid-10th centuries, this period is rightly called one of feudal anarchy. Central and northern Italy witnessed continuous and ferocious struggles among the noble families. Marquises of Friuli, Ivrea, and Tuscany and dukes of Spoleto disputed the titles of king and emperor, calling, at intervals, for aid from the powerful lords of Carinthia, Provence, and Burgundy. Holders of the royal crown between 888 and 961 were Berengar I of Friuli, Guy of Spoleto and his son Lambert, Arnulf of Carinthia, Ludwig III of Provence, Rudolph II of Burgundy, Hugh of Provence and his son Lothar II, Berengar II of Ivrea and his son Adalbert. A few of them held the imperial crown as well; the last was Berengar I, who reigned until 924.

Decline of central government

In view of the inadequacy of the central power and the general political insecurity, to which must be added repeated incursions of Arabs and Hungarians, there was considerable local individuality in the feudal forms prevalent all over Europe. The exemptions and privileges connected with feudal lands and ecclesiastical properties were extended until, to include administration of petty justice, the control exercised by the *missi dominici* was reduced, and, indeed, the *missaticum* was conceded to bishops and feudatories, thus increasing their power and autonomy; *honores* and *officia* became feudal benefices, so that the recipients could hold them in perpetuity and eventually transmit them to their children; bishops obtained increasing administrative power because, in the rulers' view, they could hold lay feudal elements in check. As a result of these developments, the state was no longer run by a central government (except for the remnants surviving at Pavia) but by a hierarchy of noblemen who were bound by a relationship of personal dependency and closely linked to individual localities and to the land.

It would be naïve to give an absolute value to the term feudal anarchy and to think that feudalism represented a pure and simple degeneration of the preceding political system. The fact is that the preceding system had broken down, and another one—feudalism—had to be found to take its place. Feudalism, in spite of its great disadvantages, was an orderly construction, and, as such, it served as the framework of European society for a number of centuries. Although feudalistic fragmentation favoured disagreement among the powerful, it had in some ways a positive function; for example, the efficient organization of local defense against Hungarian incursions. In the course of the 10th century, the plains of northern Italy were covered with *castra;* that is, fortified areas where the people could store food and take refuge in case of danger. At the same time city walls were restored and fortified by order of the bishops. These local enterprises were important in speeding the demographic and economic recovery that was already under way.

Frankish feudalism, whether because of the influence of Roman law or because of local conditions, did not long keep its original character. The accordance of a "Lombard" fief (*jure Langobardorum*) demanded only an oath of loyalty on the part of the vassal, without any ceremony of homage. The next step was the hereditary conception of the fief (with division, real or theoretic only, among all the sons) and the fragmentation of feudal rights. This explains the unrest of the first decades of the 11th century, culminating in the famous Constitutio de Feudis of 1037, with which Emperor Conrad II conceded the inheritability of minor fiefs.

The origin of the Papal States. Between the middle of the 9th and the middle of the 10th centuries, an event portentous for Italian and world history took place: the formation of the temporal states of the church. It was the end result of a long and complex historical development, in which varied elements—religious, political, military, and cultural—played a part. The first to be considered is the progressive detachment, mentioned above, of the peoples of Byzantine Italy from Byzantium itself. The popes often had to stand up against the interference of the *basileus* in religious affairs and the claims to superiority of the patriarch of Constantinople and to protect the population from Byzantine officials and tax collectors. For this reason the popes came to be considered the leaders of what might be called a national movement. Moreover, the popes took an active part in aid to the poor, especially in Rome. For this purpose they drew upon the church's considerable financial resources and did what the negligent Byzantine government left undone. Meanwhile, all over the West, the authority and prestige of the popes were growing. Everywhere, Rome was looked to as the centre of spiritual and civil union of all the peoples of the West.

Benefits of the papal and dynastic alliance

The decisive development in the creation of the Papal States was the alliance between the papacy and the new Carolingian dynasty. The alliance benefitted both parties: for the papacy, the Franks were strong enough to hold both the Lombards and the Byzantines in check but far enough away that, unlike the Lombards, they represented no imminent threat; for the Carolingians, the popes' spiritual prestige ensured the legitimacy of their dynasty. In 756, on his second Italian campaign, Pepin ceded to the papacy the former Byzantine territories of the Exarchate of Ravenna, the Pentapolis, and the duchies of Rome and Perugia. This donation was confirmed and amplified by Charlemagne but not recognized in Constantinople. Thus, the temporal rule of the Roman see was founded on an insecure legal basis. It was no longer a personal and private matter, such as the previous *patrimonium beati Petri*, but neither was it public, *pleno jure*—that is, with an explicit recognition of sovereignty. The religious significance of the donation, however, with its sacred and intangible character, together with the effective exercise of power that followed, eventually lent sanction to the popes' temporal rule. It is equally true that the Frankish king, as a *patricius Romanorum* (the title conferred by Pope Stephen II upon Pepin in 754), had taken on the right and the duty of protecting Rome and the pope against all enemies; hence, the emperor's function as *advocatus ecclesiae*, which came to be an integral part of the ideology of the medieval empire. Although the concept was generally accepted, its application raised serious problems and complicated the relationship between the empire and the papacy.

There has been and still is considerable discussion of the circumstances of the notorious Donation of Constantine, which is so closely linked to the beginnings of the church's temporal power. This was a forgery, a pretended document in which the Emperor, after narrating his miraculous recovery from leprosy and his subsequent conversion by Pope Sylvester, donated to this pope the Lateran palace, Rome, Italy and its islands, and, indeed, the entire western part of the empire. The whole thing is probably the work of a cleric attached to the Roman Curia, between the pontificates of Stephen II and Adrian I. The size and vagueness of the donation make it a statement of principle rather than a legal proof; this is confirmed by the importance that is given in the document to the concession to the pope of the diadem, purple garments, and other symbols of empire and also the equality established between the papal dignitaries and those of the imperial court. It seems as if the forger's primary intent was to establish the pope's claim to a *dignitas* equal to that of the emperor and as if the territorial donation was merely a corollary of that dignity. The use made of the document in the Roman Curia confirms this interpretation. In any case, the Donation of Constantine is an extremely important document for understanding the development of the political ideology of the papacy.

During the reign of Charlemagne, the popes had little chance to make a political place for themselves in the framework of the empire. Pope Leo III had, indeed, crowned the emperor in 800, but there was no doubt that Charlemagne was the dominant partner in the alliance. A few decades later, however, there was a radical reversal in the situation: the various partitions of imperial territories, the wars among Charlemagne's successors, and the Norman invasions had brought the empire to a state of crisis. Energetic popes, such as Nicholas I (858–867) and John VIII (872–882), took the political initiative and tried to save what was salvageable of the empire's unity. For this purpose they had to emphasize the principle of their authority in temporal affairs. John VIII, for instance, declared that it was up to the pope to choose the future emperor (a declaration that was the beginning of the legend that Leo III was the creator of the Holy Roman Empire). The pope was no longer presented as the officiator of a religious ceremony; he appears, rather, as the bestower of the imperial crown.

Papal influence in temporal affairs

The pope's growing political authority and prestige of this period underwent a later eclipse. But the accumulation of past experience was not lost. It served as a testing ground at the period of the struggle over investitures in the 11th century, when the doctrines of the Curia began to take more definite shape. For the moment, the popes were involved in the general process of political fragmentation and feudal localization that characterized Italian and European history in the 10th century. Whereas, for a time, they had held first place on the political scene, after the death of John VIII they remained in the shadow of one or the other faction contending for power in Rome.

Political morality had sunk to a low level in the 9th and 10th centuries; political murders were frequent, and many popes were imposed by force. Notorious is the posthumous trial of Pope Formosus (897), whose corpse was dug up, judged before a council, and then thrown into the Tiber. Yet, in spite of everything, there were examples of civic conscience and even of moral stature. The *vestararius* Theophylact, a papal official who founded the fortune of his family, and his daughter Marozia, successively the wife of Alberic I of Spoleto, Guy of Tuscany, and Hugh of Provence and, hence, involved in the major political currents of the time, stand out as examples of boundless energy and genuine constructive ability. Marozia's son, Alberic II, assumed the title of *princeps atque omnium Romanorum senator* and ruled over Rome from 932 to 954. Alongside episodes of violence, one finds remembrance of the traditions of Classical antiquity and a desire to restore order to both church and state. Alberic, for example, led an expedition against the monastery of Farfa in Sabina, where religious life was in decay, and turned the monastery over to Cluniac reformers.

The Arab threat

But it is in the struggle against the Muslims that one finds the brightest sporadic examples of faith, patriotism, and courage on the part of the popes, the aristocracy, and the people of Rome between the 9th and 10th centuries. The Arab threat was very real. In 846 the Arabs had sailed up the Tiber and sacked the basilicas of St. Peter and St. Paul. Pope Leo IV and the Romans replied by raising walls around St. Peter's (the "Leonine city") and stretching a chain across the river. In 849 a Muslim fleet was defeated at the mouth of the Tiber by ships belonging to a league made up of Rome, Gaeta, Naples, and Amalfi. John VIII tried his best to maintain a united front of southern princes against the Arabs, though without success. Indeed, the Muslims built a military base at the mouth of the Garigliano, which became the departure point for destructive expeditions against the towns and rich monasteries of the interior. "Redacta est terra in solitudine" ("The land was given up to wilderness"), wrote one chronicler. Finally, Pope John X, a creature of Theophylact, managed to rebuild the league, which now included a Byzantine fleet; in 915 he personally led a successful attack on the base on the Garigliano. At this period of Roman history, traditionally known as the Iron Age of the papacy, there existed a vital impulse, an exceptionally powerful charge of energy, and an organizing ability that were not confined to the pursuit of personal ambitions but were often inspired by idealistic political purposes.

Venice and the cities of Campania. Venice is one of the few Italian cities stemming from the Middle Ages and the only one to have a demographic, economic, urban, cultural, and political character of an individual and exceptionally original kind. During the barbarian invasions of the 5th and 6th centuries, the clergy and many of the people of the interior of Venetia sought refuge on the coast and on the coastal islands between Grado and Chioggia. There, they soon developed an intensely associative life, witnessed by the transfer of the patriarchate of Aquileia to Grado and by the creation of the new bishoprics of Caorle, Eraclea, Iesolo, Torcello, Malamocco, and Olivolo (Venice), which, one by one, inherited the ecclesiastical structures of the hinterland dioceses. The increase of the population and the consequent necessity of procuring supplies and transportation stimulated economic development. Not all the refugees were poor; among them there was a majority of *possessores* who had brought with them their transportable wealth and hence were able to put up capital for commercial enterprises. At the same time, the *possessores* kept—or later recovered—at least part of their landholdings in the back country. In the 8th and 9th centuries, there arose an aristocratic and business-minded class that exploited its capital in trade, transportation, salt mines, and moneylending, a class that was fated to play more and more of a role in politics.

Politically, the various centres in the process of formation along the coast and on the Lagoon joined together toward the end of the 7th century in a duchy ruled by a Byzantine duke. The seat of the duchy was first at Eraclea, then, after about 740, at Malamocco, and finally at Rialto, the first nucleus of Venice, from the beginning of the 9th century, a period of decisive importance for that city. For the Carolingians, who at first tried to conquer Venice, gave up this idea and, in 812, made peace with Byzantium through the Treaty of Aix-la-Chapelle. Venice found itself in the best possible position for economical and political development, as an indispensable intermediary for the relationship between East and West.

The economic growth of Venice

The principal reason for Venice's extraordinary economic growth lay in the change undergone by the economy of the whole Mediterranean area. With the Arab conquest of Syria and Egypt, the Eastern Empire had lost two major markets and also an important source of its food supplies. No longer was there sea traffic between France and the East passing through the western Mediterranean. Under these circumstances the Po Valley assumed an important role, because of its agricultural production and also because the navigability of the river as far as Pavia assured communications with western Europe. Venice found itself at the crossroads of East and West, which needed each other economically even if, politically, they were divided. Thanks to its independent status and the enterprising spirit of its citizens, it succeeded in putting them in touch and becoming the great trading place for goods (silk, spices, and luxury objects from the East; wheat [corn], oil, and salt from the West) and moneys (Byzantine, Lombard, and even Arab gold coins and Carolingian silver). Later Venice took advantage of its privileged position to make contact with Egypt, Sicily, and the Arab world in general, with which it traded in pelts, wood, arms, and slaves.

As in the other Byzantine territories in Italy, Venice gradually acquired autonomy in the course of the 8th century. *Tribuni*, *magistri militum*, and *duces* were less and less often chosen by the emperor or his representatives and more and more frequently elected on the spot. In these choices, quite naturally, the interests of the local aristocracy prevailed. The post of tribune, which was both civil and military, soon became hereditary and so, later on, did that of the duke (subsequently called doge), though with alternating families and with factional strife. Important among these families or dynasties were those founded by Agnello Parteciaco (or Partecipazio; 810–827) and Pietro Candiano (887), which alternately held rule until 976. In that year the first Orseolo came to the fore and founded a new house, the greatest member of which was Pietro II (991–1008). After obtaining recognition of his authority from Byzantium, he carried out an intelligent policy of territorial and commercial expansion. In 1000, in order to free the Adriatic from pirates' raids, he conquered the coast of Dalmatia as far south as Kotor and assumed the title of *dux Veneticorum et Dalmaticorum*. Then, in 1002, he gave aid to the Byzantines when they were defending Bari against the Saracens. But his dynasty lasted no later than 1032.

The role of the doge

At the time of the Orseoli, the doge was similar to a king. He commanded the armed forces, presided over the court of appeals, appointed government officials, and discharged public funds. He also controlled the church, at least in its material possessions, appointments, and benefices. In all his administrative functions, particularly those concerned with the administration of justice, he was assisted by a *curia ducis*, or ducal council, composed of high government officials, judges, the patriarch, the bishops, and the abbots of the major monasteries. Representatives of the people, called *boni homines* or *fideles*, had seats there as well, but it is likely that they, like the other members, were chosen by the doge. There existed also a *concio civium*, an assembly of all the freemen of the duchy that met on important and solemn occasions. It is probable that this assembly complied with the will of the wealthy landowners and merchants established at Rialto, who, toward the middle of the 12th century, gave the Commune Veneciarum its oligarchic character.

There are interesting analogies but also striking differences between Venice and the maritime cities of Campania: Gaeta, Naples, Sorrento, and Amalfi. They, too, were in the Byzantine sphere and won increasing independence and also importance in sea trade; but the stuff of their history was far more brittle, and they met a very different fate. The essential difference is this: the Campanian cities, surrounded and threatened by hostile or potentially dangerous powers (the Byzantines, the Saracens, the Lombards of Capua, Benevento, and Salerno) never enjoyed a security such as that of Venice. On the contrary, they were constantly forced to remain on guard and on the defensive, with diplomacy and arms, until they were definitively absorbed into the Norman kingdom. Because of the continuous political tension, the aristocracy of these cities could not or would not transform itself into merchants, such as those of Venice, but remained land bound and warlike, while the merchants, drawn from the middle class, were socially and, above all, politically weak. Norman rule, when it came along, merely gave definite sanction to a pre-existent state of affairs. The small centres—Sorrento and Amalfi

—once they were amalgamated with a vaster and centralized governmental apparatus, lost all autonomy and were cut back to the limitations of local power. The big city, Naples, did, indeed, maintain and increase its importance (especially later on, under the House of Anjou).

Sicily under the Arabs. From the second half of the 7th century, Sicily was the object of Arab attacks from Africa. The real Muslim conquest, however, took place in the 9th century. Opportunity was provided by the rebellion of the commander of the Byzantine fleet, Euphemius of Messina, who turned for help to the Emir of al-Qayrawān (in present-day Tunisia), a member of the Aghlabid dynasty. His appeal was answered, and an Arab army landed at Mazara in 827. The Arabs soon discarded Euphemius and continued the expedition on their own, conquering Mineo and then Palermo (831). The Byzantines put up a long and stubborn resistance; Syracuse held out until 878, when it was mercilessly plundered. The island became an Aghlabid province, passing after 910 into the hands of the Fāṭimids, the Shīʿite dynasty that in 972 moved its capital to Cairo. From the middle of the 10th century until 1040, Sicily was an emirate, to all effects and purposes independently ruled by the Kalbī family. After 1040 internal dissension divided Sicily into small local lordships until the Normans took advantage of such obvious political weakness and, after a 30-year war (1061–91), imposed their rule.

For approximately 200 years, Sicily was the chief base for Arab expansion on the seas and along the coasts of central and southern Italy. They were not always engaged in piracy and war against the Christians; there were truces and trade agreements and profitable exchanges at a cultural as well as a commercial level. Indeed, political agreements and alliances were sometimes set up between Christian and Muslim princes.

Sicilian prosperity under the Arabs

In these two centuries Sicily enjoyed economic prosperity and an intellectual flowering. The natives were treated with respect and allowed to keep their Christian faith, although this meant that they had to pay tribute money and were in a position of legal inferiority. By right of conquest, land became largely the property of the state or of individual Arabs. There was intense agrarian colonization and much breaking up of large holdings, accompanied by technical improvements, particularly in irrigation. Vineyards were destroyed, but new products —citrus fruits, sugarcane, date palms, and mulberry trees (for raising silkworms)—were introduced. The capital city of Palermo was thickly inhabited and prosperous, with a busy harbour and much handicraft activity. In Palermo and elsewhere, the Muslims built castles, palaces, mosques, and elaborate gardens. Poetry, law, the arts, and the study of the Qur'ān were held in honour, especially at the Kalbī court.

CITIES AND COUNTRYSIDE IN THE EARLY MIDDLE AGES

Urban crisis: the "villae." The period between AD 96 and 180, the Age of the Antonines, was perhaps the happiest in the history of Roman cities. The emperors' policy benefitted the senatorial class—that is, the landowners who held municipal magistracies and made up the strongest single support of the government. Hence, it promoted the development of cities as centres of power and control over vast territories. But this system had its weak points, above all its finances, which steadily took a turn for the worse. In the 3rd and 4th centuries the taxes imposed on the prosperous urban class and the enforced contributions and furnishings of supplies became ruinous. City administrators, harassed by the hostile policy of the military monarchy, gave up their posts and retired to their country estates. The cities, left in the hands of greedy officials, exposed to the violence of military garrisons and barbarian invaders, and ruined by inflation, began to decrease in population and to decay. This was the fate of almost all the cities of the West, Rome included.

In spite of depopulation and economic crisis, Italian cities retained some of their ancient importance. In the 4th century there began a movement toward popular control within the cities. Although it is difficult to measure its exact extent and value, it is an index and demonstration of a collective identity bound up with an urban tradition that endured even through the dark period between Classical antiquity and the Middle Ages. There are some legislative texts from which it appears quite clearly that the Roman state tried to persuade the citizenry of the cities to assume greater responsibilities. An imperial decree of 384 made it obligatory for citizen groups to attend to the repair of walls and aqueducts; in 396 there was instituted a special tax upon all *possessores* for the maintenance of the walls; in 400–401 it was established that only *collegiati* and *corporati* citizens could rent communal lands in or near the city; in 440 city dwellers were obliged to serve, under arms, for the protection of walls and gates. This last decree has serious implications. Not only does it point up the impotence of the central government, but it also contradicts the fundamental Roman principle of separation between civil and military powers. And there is more. In 443 it was established that the whole population of a city should take part in decisions regarding the transfer of municipal properties. By a decree in 458, the entire citizenry was allowed to participate in the election of the *defensor civitatis*—that is, the official, formerly appointed by the central government, who supplemented or took the place of the *curiales*.

The duties of the citizen

Just at the time when there was a tendency to entrust collective responsibilities to the city populations, these populations were increasingly drawn together by a common faith and participation in the same liturgical and sacramental life. For it was in the 4th and the 5th centuries that conversion to Christianity became practically universal in the cities (though not yet in the countryside). The result was a communitarian experience of a new kind that did away with many legal and social differentiations of the Classical age. All these facts point to a new evaluation of the period of the late Roman Empire. Although it is traditionally defined as one of decadence, corruption, and disorganization, such a definition is not all-embracing. The life of those days contained new elements, which held hope for the future, chief among them the development of a civic conscience. People once passive and divided were driven by necessity to become aware of themselves, to organize, to express in a different sort of community the ideals of their faith and the object of their aspirations.

Without doubt the decay of the cities had a causal relationship to the increase and enlargement of *villae* and *saltus*, the tilled or wooded lands that became, more and more, centres of production, social organization, and defense. Soon they obtained exemptions; they could shut the door on the tax collector and get their farmers relieved of military service. One can imagine the attraction of these privileges upon small landholders; by an act called *accomendatio*, they ceded ownership of their lands (conserving its use) to a *possessor*, in return for his protection. The *possessores* were now real local *domini*, or masters. They administered petty justice, collected rents and taxes, held absolute power over their slaves, were accompanied by armed followers (*comites* or *buccellarii*), and sometimes had private churches.

The labour force

As for internal organization, the *villae*, successors to the earlier latifundia, inherited at the start their workings, which were based on slave labour. Later, there came important changes. When the wars of conquest were over, the number of newly captured slaves diminished and that of the older ones diminished as well, because of a low birth rate and also because religion and custom favoured setting them free. Besides these, there were the *accomendati*, the free small landowners who had joined their farms to a large estate. Part of the landed unit, divided into *mansi*, was occupied by farmers or freed slaves, and the *mansi* formed a *massaricium;* a larger part, made up of fields and woods, formed the *dominicum* and was worked by slaves or servants, sometimes with the aid of the free farmers. If the estate had an area of no more than 100 or so acres (40 or so hectares), it was a *curtis*, but, if it was larger (some had an area of as much as 2,500 acres [1,000 hectares]), it was divided into several *curtes*, each with its administrative centre, its *dominicum*, and its *massaricium*. This was the sort of farm estate that antiquity handed down to the Middle Ages, but there were, as shall be seen, other sorts as well.

The villas were not the only form of agricultural organization. Alongside them there were public demesnes belonging to cities, country districts (*pagi*), villages (*vici*), and valley communities (*comunalia*, *conciliaricia*, *vicanalia*, *compascua*), allods (private and free property), and, finally, the great rural properties of ecclesiastical organizations. For lack of data, one cannot say in what proportion each of these types existed. But it is clear that, at least in Italy, they were all represented, even if not uniformly. In the Po Valley, for instance, it seems that there was a majority of small and middling landowners and that only in the 4th century did larger agglomerations come into being, but never, even then, as large as the African *saltus* and the latifundia of Sicily.

It is probable also that, in Italy, the Lombards substantially altered the property structure, especially that of the *villae*. Lack of documentation prevents any definite statement, but it is known that the Roman landowning class was practically wiped out and that the farmers were made tributaries (*tertiatores*). One may most logically presume that the great latifundia were broken up and fell into the hands of the native farmers and the Lombard families that settled in the same countryside. This process was abetted by the Germanic concept of *gewere*, which linked the enjoyment or possession of an object to a right of ownership. Farmers in Italy had, on the whole, an advantage over those of the countries (France, the Rhineland, the region of the Moselle) where there was direct continuity between the Roman villa and the early medieval lordship over the land. This is a fact that may contribute to understanding the development of the Italian agricultural class in the 9th and 10th centuries.

The breakup of the latifundia did not prevent a reintegration of land, under different conditions, through the great increase of ecclesiastical wealth at the end of the Lombards' rule and the beginning of that of the Carolingians. One must remember, also, the survival of the great *curtes regiae*, such as Sospiro, Corteolona, and Bene Vagienna, of which the last named had an area of over 75,000 acres (30,000 hectares).

Bishops and cities. The link between the bishop and the city was first sanctioned at the Council of Sardica in 343, where it was established that only an important city could be a bishop's seat, "ne vilescat nomen episcopi et auctoritas" ("lest the name and authority of the bishop be taken lightly"). Pope Leo I, toward 446, repeated the same concept, which later served as the basis of a corollary in reverse: there must be a bishopric in every important city. Such statements testified to a longstanding state of affairs—that is, to the increase of episcopal authority from 313 on.

After the Edict of Milan in 313, which extended toleration to the Christians, bishops took an increasing part in urban life. The good works demanded of their religious office included the relief of suffering and the prevention of disaster. They sponsored many charities, such as the distribution of food and the construction of hospitals, protected the poor from the rich and sometimes from the tax collector, exercised an influence over the behaviour of magistrates, both local and national, made up for the deficiencies of public officials (*e.g.*, the construction of an aqueduct at Vercelli and of dikes on the Po River at Piacenza), represented the cities in their dealings with the barbarian soldiery, and either directed or participated in the defense of the walls. These episcopal activities answered a deep-seated need of the times and were well received not only by the local populations but also by the state, which, indeed, acknowledged and encouraged them.

The *episcopalis audientia*

In this connection one must recall the so-called *episcopalis audientia*. In 318, only five years after the Edict of Milan, Constantine decreed that, in a dispute between Christians, the decision pronounced by a bishop should be equivalent to an unappealable civil verdict and be so executed by the appropriate imperial government officials. Decrees dating from 333, 398, 408, and 452 confirmed this recognition of the *episcopalis audientia*, although placing certain limitations upon it. Evidently legislators saw advantages to the state in the bishops' justice. It was preferred by a large part of the population (*e.g.*, that converted to Christianity); it was less bound to juridical formalism and hence more in tune with the new social mentality (*i.e.*, more just); and, finally, it cost nothing. With Justinian the *episcopalis audientia* became more infrequent, chiefly because in a totally Christianized state the bishops were inserted into the regular juridical organization. The Code of Justinian gave bishops supervision over civil judges and provided that, in certain cases, they should take the latter's place. Justinian's Code assigned other administrative tasks to the bishops, particularly in the field of public works. Plainly, bishops were now considered, juridically, pillars of the governmental structure.

This increase of the bishops' power is not difficult to understand. First, there was the sacred character of their office as successors to the Apostles and bearers of their mission. Then, there was the continuity and stability of the office; a bishop's tenure was for life, and this gave it an obvious superiority over the precarious condition of the imperial and city magistrates. Another consideration was the prestige lent to the bishop by the wealth of which he disposed. And even more important was the manner of his election. According to custom, he was chosen by the clergy and people of the city, gathered together on the cathedral green. This made the bishop, theoretically, the representative and fiduciary of the entire population; no other magistrate had the same broad following or moral authority.

Throughout the 5th and 6th centuries and up to the Lombard invasion, the union between the bishops and the citizenry became increasingly close, so that ecclesiastical and civic affairs were closely intertwined. *Fidelis*, one of the faithful, was a synonym of *civis*, or citizen. Everyday life followed the hours of the liturgy, and both the geographical and the administrative layout centred around the cathedral. The assembly mentioned above dealt with both church and city affairs; the cathedral green or square where it met was usually a marketplace as well.

The Lombards did not break up this union; indeed, to some extent they reinforced it. In hard or dangerous times the people gathered around the bishops for comfort and protection. The bishops are chiefly to be credited for the conservation of the civil and civic traditions of Rome, including the principles of Roman law, inasmuch as they probably continued, officially or privately, to act as judges or arbiters of disputes among Christians. But this was essentially a period of transition. In the time of Liudprand, after the mass conversion of the Lombards, the bishops resumed their collaboration with the government, and this role was further strengthened during the age of the Carolingians. The Carolingian counts did not long succeed in stemming the power of the bishops, and the latter became, in most cases, masters of the cities. In the 9th and 10th centuries they obtained a succession of sovereign privileges, especially when it came to the construction and defense of city walls and the concession of markets (Bergamo, Mantua, Modena, Como, Vercelli, Cremona, and others). The bishops collected tithes from their own faithful and virtually exercised civil as well as ecclesiastical rule of the entire district. This explains why, toward the middle of the 10th century, some of them bore the title of count, which was simply an acknowledgment of the authority they had in civil affairs.

The episcopal vassals

For aid in their governing functions, the bishops needed trusted men, chosen from either clergy or laity. In the oldest times there existed a *defensor ecclesiae* (a layman) and then a *vicedominus* (an ecclesiastic). Later, in the pre-feudal and feudal ages, there were *advocati*, *confanonerii*, or *vexilliferi*, and other minor officials who were chosen among families that favoured the bishop and who received fiefs, income, and benefices from church property. But this ever-more-numerous and demanding class of episcopal vassals, augmented by minor feudatories and by the *cives majores* or *boni homines*—that is, the petty landowners or lessees originating in the country and, in the city, exercising the specialized professions of judge, notary, doctor, or merchant—was the one that brought on a crisis of the bishops' rule. The way was opened to the formation of the communes, end results of a process of profound social change taking place in the 9th and 10th centuries.

Economy and society in pre-communal Italy. In the period roughly between 750 and 1000, during which East and West grew apart economically as well as politically, Italy was still, however, in the ambit of Byzantine power; that is, the south depended on Byzantium directly, while the Lombard and Carolingian north were linked to it indirectly. The fact is important, for it signifies that Italy never, or practically never, had a closed economy. On the contrary, commercial exchanges always flourished; there were many markets and an absolutely necessary circulation of money. Even the Lombards struck coins, among them the gold *tremissi*, minted in Lucca and Pavia. No comparison can be made between the economic structures of Italy and those of France in the 8th and 9th centuries. If the expression "economy of the *curtis*" may apply to continental Italy, it means only that most of the agricultural production was organized in *curtes*—that is, in farm units—and has no implication of autarchy or of doors closed to the outside world.

In southern Italy, trade relations with Byzantium and the East in general were quite active and favoured by political circumstances. Amalfi had colonies and warehouses at Constantinople, Antioch, and Durazzo; its ships sailed up the Adriatic and the Po River all the way to Pavia, put into the Arab ports of Sicily, and made their way along the Tyrrhenian coast as far as Rome, Pisa, and Genoa. On the opposite shore, Bari, which had become the capital of Byzantium's Italian possessions, had trade with Constantinople, Durazzo (Albanian Durrës), Greece, and the ports of Asia Minor and Syria. Along with Siponto, to the north, Bari was the embarkation point for pilgrims going to the Holy Land. And it was through Bari, Siponto, Trani, and Barletta that Byzantium got its supplies of Puglian grain. There can be no doubt, then, that southern Italy was a part of the Byzantine sphere, the economy of which was based on the exchange of goods and money. Even the Arabs contributed to the Byzantine economy, above all through their commercial dealings with Amalfi. Their gold dinar was as acceptable as the Byzantine bezant or hyperper.

Importance of the Po Valley

As for the north, the Po Valley became an important source of wheat and foodstuffs to the Byzantines after their loss of Egypt. The Lombards were not gifted for trade, but they did not prevent natives or other foreigners from engaging in it. An edict of King Aistulf of 754, concerning military service, put *negotiatores*, or merchants, on the same plane as landowners; both categories were divided into three classes, according to the amount of money and property in their possession.

The great artery, then, was the Po, navigable all the way to Pavia, and with it may be grouped the rivers flowing into it from the north—Ticino, Lambro, Adda, Oglio, and Mincio—all navigable for short distances. At the points where these entered the Po, there were small ports and customs offices; the great marketplace was the capital of the kingdom, Pavia. The first traders to sail up the Po were *milites* of Comacchio, bringing salt from the Lagoon to the interior; in 715 they obtained special privileges from Liudprand. The Venetians followed and then merchants from other cities with access to the river system—Cremona, Mantua, Ferrara, Piacenza, Milan, and Pavia.

The development of trade in the Po Valley cannot be understood unless notice is taken of the arrangement of land ownership. This was when the great ecclesiastical holdings were being put together; they had existed before, to be sure, but not in such numbers nor on such a large scale. The many new monasteries founded under the Lombard and Carolingian kings, the donations and legacies that they received, the exemptions and privileges that they enjoyed, the pressures and force of attraction that they exercised in regard to small landowners—all these contributed to enormous episcopal and monastic holdings, unlimited in size and tax-free. Frequently, there was a surplus of agricultural production available to meet market demands. In brief, the motivation of the development of trade in the Po River Valley lay in the following factors: bishops and abbots found there the means with which to build and ornament their churches and also to forward their power politics; merchants made considerable profits, as did the government of Pavia and the other cities and potentates from the imposition of tolls and customs fees; new highways of trade were opened up and made operative through the Alps in the direction of central Europe, thereby making the fortune of such favourably situated centres as Milan.

It is not by mere chance that, at the marketplace of Pavia, there were warehouses belonging to the bishops of Lodi, Milan, Piacenza, Reggio Emilia, and, perhaps, Genoa, to the monasteries of St. Ambrose of Milan, St. Antoninus of Piacenza, Bobbio, St. Julia of Brescia, Nonantola, and even to such Frankish monasteries as St. Martin of Tours and Cluny. The operative merchants were not only from Venetia but from Gaeta, Salerno, and Amalfi as well; there were even some Anglo-Saxons among them. This constitutes further proof that the Po Valley was a meeting place of the Eastern and Western economic areas and that, for a time, Pavia shared with Venice the role of intermediary that Venice later played alone.

Secular holdings seem to have had no economic function equal to that of ecclesiastical ones. Probably only the *curtes regiae* had the same acreage. One need only recall that St. Julia of Brescia had 60 *curtes*, over 700 serfs attached to the *dominicum*, and some 800 farming families to the *massaricium*. The *curtes regiae* did not have the same productivity, since they were made up largely of woods and fallow meadows. As for other secular estates, it seems reasonable to believe that they were, from the start, subdivided and increasingly so because of separate inheritances. The existence of a large fief, or feudal domain, did not necessarily make for economic capacity; lands enfeoffed to the second degree escaped the control of the overall owner. Even if he could count on the yield from widely scattered *curtes*, he could not set up a single management comparable to that of the monasteries.

It must also be noted that during the 9th and 10th centuries a class of peasant was evolving. There was a scarcity of prebendary serfs (*praebendarii*), those worst treated and assigned to the house and land of the master; parts of the *dominicum* were divided into *mansi* and turned over to *casati*, serfs, or *massari*. This made for an increase of the population attached to the soil and for a betterment of its condition, since obligations toward the master were limited and stipulated in writing. Another improved status was that of the *libellarii*—that is, the freemen bound by a written lease (*libellum*). Formerly, these men had been obliged to work the land with their own hands, but, little by little, they won the right to sublease and thus to collect rent. Many of them went to live in the cities. At the very beginning of the 11th century, a rising movement was taking place that was to change medieval society.

II. Italy under the Saxon and Franconian emperors

THE MAINLAND

The imperial restoration of 962. Toward the middle of the 10th century the Kingdom of Italy was torn by the struggles among the great feudal lords. Upon the death of Lothair II, son of Hugh of Provence (950), Berengar II of Ivrea, who, with his son, Adalbert, already held virtual power, was crowned king. But an opposition, headed by a courageous woman, Adelaide, daughter of Rudolph of Burgundy and widow of Lothair, called for help from Otto I of Germany. Otto, whom Berengar, when an exile in

Germany, had already asked to intervene in Italian struggles for power, came to Italy (951), donned the royal crown at Pavia, and married Adelaide. Soon after, by a compromise, Berengar and Adalbert regained rule over Italy, though as vassals of the German king. But the marches of Verona, Friuli, Trent, and inland Istria (all lying across northeast Italy) were given to Henry, duke of Bavaria, to ensure the German king's access to Italy. Some years later, Berengar faced further opposition, and Pope John XII (originally Octavian, son of Alberic, prince of the Romans, and the first pope to change his name) asked Otto to intervene. Otto returned and, in 962, was crowned, together with Adelaide, in Rome. Berengar was soon captured and deported to Germany; later, John XII was accused of betrayal and was deposed, the new emperor replacing him with another Roman, Leo VIII.

Intervention from Germany

Otto I was obviously appealing to the by now legendary tradition of Charlemagne and trying to restore the Carolingian empire. Otto, like Charlemagne, had won great prestige; he had ruled Germany firmly and, in 955, at Lechfeld (in Bavaria) had defeated the Magyars, preventing their invasion of western Europe; he had ably pursued a policy of penetration and conversion among the Slavs, creating the archbishopric of Magdeburg (in modern East Germany) and a chain of frontier marches from the Baltic down to Bohemia; and he had made himself felt in France, Burgundy, and Italy. Now the time had come to obtain a title symbolizing his rule over Europe.

Here, then, was a superstate, an *imperium plurimarum nationum* ("empire of many nations"); the idea of universality was still of the essence, but it corresponded less to reality than in Charlemagne's day because various countries, especially France, remained outside. From now onward the empire's universality was to be a symbolic aspiration rather than the exercise of power, except in Germany, Italy, and, after 1032, Burgundy, where the emperor held the crown and the *potestas* ("power") of a king. Thus, with Otto I, the empire assumed some of the characteristics that were to remain throughout the Middle Ages. The emperor had first to be the king of Germany, elected by the German princes and crowned at Aix-la-Chapelle (Aachen), whereafter he would have the further title of "king of the Romans" to indicate that he was a candidate for the imperial throne. Then he would be crowned king of Italy (at Pavia—and then at Monza or Milan) and king of Burgundy, after which he would receive the imperial crown from the pope in Rome. This was the lasting structure of what was to be called the "Holy Roman Empire of the German nation." Within this framework there later operated both the new imperial doctrine of Frederick Barbarossa (emperor in the 12th century), intended to strengthen the power and universality of the empire on the basis of Justinian law, and the theories of the Curia (the papal court), which sought to give the pope power to choose and, possibly, also to depose the emperor at will.

Shaping of the Holy Roman Empire concept

For the moment, the most obvious upshot of Otto's actions in 962 and after was the control he had won over the papacy, which went far beyond that of a Charlemagne or a Lothair I. For although the *privilegium Ottonianum* ("privilege belonging to Otto") of 962 confirmed the donations made by preceding sovereigns (except for the area around Ravenna), it also stipulated that the Romans should ask the emperor's approval of a candidate for the papacy and that the newly elected pope should pledge allegiance. Shortly thereafter, Otto assumed the right to nominate the pope—the logical consequence of his policy toward the church. In order to control the feudal lords he sought support from bishops and abbots, giving them fiefs and various privileges. To some bishops, German as well as Italian, he gave the title of count, forming a vassalage all the stronger because it was not hereditary. Thus the ecclesiastical hierarchy became increasingly tied to the feudal structure of society and the state and, hence, to temporal interests. The state, rather than the church and its discipline, benefitted; and herein lay the reason for the great conflict that arose between papacy and empire in the next century.

Expansion in south Italy and Otto I's successors. Otto I was also concerned with expansion in south Italy and struck an alliance, aimed against the Byzantines, with Pandulf, known as "Ironhead," prince of Capua and Benevento, to whom in 967 he ceded the duchy of Spoleto and the march of Camerino. His power politics were fruitless, but his diplomacy succeeded, resulting in a marriage between his son Otto II and Princess Theophano, daughter of the Byzantine emperor Romanus II, in 972. After his father's death in 973, Otto II pursued the same expansionist policy in the south, where he claimed new rights through his marriage. Preoccupied by the landing in Calabria (Italy's "toe") of some Arabs from Sicily, he led an army against them in 981. Unfortunately, his ally Pandulf died just then; and Otto, far from his bases, was defeated in 982, at Punta Stilo. He was organizing a revenge expedition when, aged 28, he died in Rome in 983.

His son and successor, Otto III (983–1002), elaborated an imperial ideology mingling elements of the Roman–Byzantine tradition and Christian mysticism. Before Otto III came of age, the uneasy rule of the empire was wisely maintained by his mother, Theophano, and his grandmother Adelaide. The young prince was brought up among the armies guarding the eastern frontier; but he had more than a military education, having been instructed in religion, Greek, and Latin, as well as German, while he even tried writing. This culture, then unusual for a layman, explains his later behaviour. In 996, when he came of age, he went to Rome, named as pope his cousin Bruno of Carinthia (now southwest Austria), who took the name of Gregory V, and received the emperor's crown from him. By nominating the pope, Otto hoped, like his father and grandfather before him, to remove the papacy from Roman factions and restore its universal mission. There was, however, stubborn opposition; a powerful Roman patrician, John Crescentius, ran Gregory V out of the city and put an anti-pope in his place. Otto brought Gregory back to Rome, put down the rebellion, and had Crescentius tortured and killed (998). A year later, when Gregory died, Otto nominated his former teacher, Gerbert of Aurillac, archbishop of Rheims, who took the name of Sylvester II. This was the formative moment of the young emperor's religious and universal ideal. He settled the court in the imperial palaces on Rome's Palatine Hill and restored Byzantine offices and ceremonies. From a Rome that was again the centre of the empire and the *caput mundi* ("head of the world"), emperor and pope, in perfect accord, were to eliminate abuses, reform the clergy, and extend Christendom. The peoples of eastern Europe came under this plan, and it was now that the duchies (later kingdoms) of Poland and Hungary entered the orbit of the Catholic Church.

Reign of Otto III

Otto III acquired intense but tormented religious feelings from such spiritual leaders as Adalbert of Prague, Nilus of Rossano, Odilo of Cluny, and Romuald of Camaldoli; but his political and religious dream was even shorter than his 22-year life. In northern Italy he had to face one Arduin of Ivrea, who was struggling against the local bishops and had executed one of them; in Rome, a new rebellion enforced Otto's flight, and he died in 1002 before he could return to the city.

Italian unrest. After Otto's death, Arduin had himself proclaimed king of Italy in 1002 by a hastily assembled group of nobles. But his adversaries, many of them bishops, produced a rival, Henry II, duke of Bavaria, of a collateral branch of the House of Saxony. Henry overcame Arduin in Italy in 1004 and was in his turn crowned king of Italy at Pavia, though a fight between local citizens and the German soldiers considerably damaged the city. Henry II immediately returned to Germany, leaving Arduin some freedom of action. He came back in 1013–14 to receive the imperial crown from Pope Benedict VIII; and in Rome, too, a violent anti-German reaction occurred, with Arduin's supporters participating. The failed revolt and other circumstances persuaded Arduin to retire to the monastery of Fruttuaria, where he died in 1015. Henry II returned for the third and last time in 1021. In agreement with Pope Benedict VIII, he con-

Revolts against foreign rule

centrated on southern Italy, where shortly before had occurred a revolt, led by one Melus of Bari, against the Byzantines. Henry died in 1024 in Germany, whereupon the citizens of Pavia destroyed the royal palace.

Feudal and ecclesiastical developments. The real significance of Arduin's action is in representing the reaction of feudal laymen to excessive episcopal power. Arduin had the support of the *secundi milites*, the minor vassals or vavasours, seeking better positions in episcopally controlled administrations. At first Henry II quite naturally sought episcopal support, installing trustworthy German clerics, some of them court chaplains or even members of his family, in such northern Italian sees as Como, Cremona, Trieste, Lodi, Turin, and Ravenna. Later on, under pressure from below, he tended to favour the vavasours and the *cives* ("citizens") and to limit the bishops' privileges.

Between the late 10th and the early 11th century several large marches, governed by powerful noble families, often originating north of the Alps or bound by relationship or interests to families of Provence, Burgundy, and Germany, came into being. These marches were not organic territorial units, made up of a certain number of counties; for cities had acquired some autonomy under episcopal rule, and in the countryside privileged ecclesiastial properties and new feudal or landed estates were forming. In any case, the noble families of the marches were powerful through having their own domains, even if scattered and not adjacent to each other. Only toward 1200 did great families tend to subdivide branches, each linked to a locality whence it took its name. For instance, the Obertinghi, descendants of a Count Obert (who acquired status first with Berengar and then with Otto I), possessed, besides their own march (composed of Genoa, Luni, Bobbio, and Tortona), the counties of Milan and, in the 12th century, Cavallo and Monselice. The descendants of the Obertinghi include the Estes, the Malaspinas, and the Pallavicini.

The division of the great families

Adapted from *Enciclopedia Italiana di Scienze, Lettere ed Arti*, vol. 19; inset adapted from J.R. Strayer and D.C. Munro, *The Middle Ages, 395–1500*, 5th ed., p. 210 (copyright © 1970); by permission of Appleton-Century-Crofts, Educational Division, Meredith Corp.

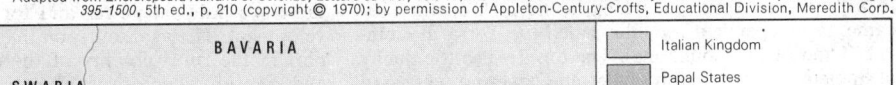

Italy during the second half of the 10th century and (inset) the Norman conquest of south Italy.

The march of Verona, which included the whole of Venetia, Trentino, Trieste, and inland Istria, had a particular status, being part of Germany. Meanwhile, within it the ecclesiastical principalities of Trento, Aquileia, and Trieste were forming. Within the Kingdom of Italy were the new marches: Ivrea (or Anscarica, from the name of its local dynasty); Turin (or Arduinica), which included western Piedmont all the way to Ventimiglia and Albenga on the present Franco-Italian border; western Liguria (or Aleramica), later divided into the two marches of Monferrato and Savona; eastern Liguria (or Obertenga), extending southward from the Po and Tanaro rivers to include Genoa and the coast southeast of it all the way to Luni; and the march of Canossiana (or Attoniana), which extended from the Apennines near Modena and Reggio Emilia to beyond the Po and the vicinity of Mantua and Brescia. Besides these new marches were older ones such as Tuscia (Tuscany), soon to be joined to the Canossiana. Theoretically dependent upon Tuscia was Corsica, which actually was abandoned to Saracen invasions, but which in the 11th century became an independent republic called the Terra di Commune (Land of the Commune). There were also the duchy of Spoleto and the march of Fermo-Camerino (eastward from Camerino to the coast).

The House of Franconia and the struggle over investitures. The insurrection of Pavia in 1024 and the destruction of the *palatium* ("palace") had grave consequences. The authority of the Count Palatine was lost, the royal court and the central administrative offices disappeared and so, with even more important results, did the Royal Chamber, which had rigidly controlled the city's craft guilds and collected taxes and donations. Under milder episcopal government, citizens enjoyed greater economic and political freedom. The greatest advantage accrued, however, to Milan, which practically escaped from the domination of the nearby capital and was able to expand. The people of Milan seemed to be unified under their bishops' guidance and to have political aspirations, based on awareness of the city's economic development and on pride in a particular religious tradition, that of the Ambrosian rite.

A great Milanese archbishop, Heribert of Intimiano, set the trend of Italian politics in the critical period that followed the death of Henry II. He and his followers called upon the Duke of Franconia, later known as Conrad II, a Salian, who founded a new imperial dynasty. Conrad was crowned king of Italy at Pavia in 1026 and emperor in Rome the year after. Present at this second ceremony were two sovereigns: Canute (Knut), king of England, Denmark, and Norway; and Rudolph III, king of Burgundy, who thus bore witness to the prestige of the imperial crown.

Feudal upheavals. Conrad II rearranged the major Italian fiefs. First he joined together the marches of Attoniana and Tuscia, an exceptionally large and important territory destined to play a decisive role in future events, under the rule of the faithful margrave Boniface of Canossa. Then, in keeping with the German emperors' perennial need to control all the roads giving access to Italy, he detached the bishopric of Trent from the march of Verona and joined it to the duchy of Carinthia, establishing at the same time direct imperial rule over the patriarchate of Aquileia, which acquired a more clearly defined territorial and feudal identity and was governed by German patriarchs.

Redeployment of localities

In 1032, after the death of Rudolph III of Burgundy, Conrad II inherited his kingdom but had to make good his claim by military occupation. In this successful process (which led to his coronation as king of Burgundy in 1033) he was aided by an Italian contingent led by Archbishop Heribert and Boniface of Tuscia, together with a minor Burgundian noble, Humbert the Whitehanded, ancestor of the House of Savoy. The expedition had still other results. Upon their return to Lombardy the lesser vassals, or *secundi milites*, who had undergone considerable hardships and financial sacrifices in order to follow Heribert, revolted against him.

This rebellion, the first of many social upheavals, had its roots in the time when Landolp of Carcano was archbishop of Milan (983) and many properties of the Milanese church were enfeoffed to his supporters and members of his family. This made for a powerful and privileged class, called the *novitii capitanei* to distinguish them from others with powers derived from the breakup of the possessions of the counts, who took in the tax (*decima*) paid by country parishes and held jurisdictions (*districtus*). In their turn the *capitanei*, by sub-enfeoffing, had created a class of lesser vassals, bound to military service but without any hold on the land. These *secundi milites* had grown in numbers and, beginning with the time of Arduin, had been demanding a definition of their rights and possessions. Inimical to the *secundi milites*, or vavasours, were not only the *capitanei*, and hence Heribert, but also the *cives*, that is, the merchants, money changers, magistrates, doctors, and notaries in the city who owned nonfeudal houses and lands. The *cives* had, indeed, interests quite separate from those of the vavasours; and they saw Heribert as a man able to increase the city's political power and forward its economic development. The vavasours, on the other hand, found support in the rural nobility of the counties of Martesana and Seprio, which was already in conflict with the *capitanei* and Heribert; in the cities pitted against Milan, such as Pavia, Lodi, and Cremona; and, to some extent, in the *rustici*, that is, the peasants, who were equally oppressed by feudal holders of *districtus* and by allod (nonfeudal property) owners and lessees (*livellari*), who did not themselves till the land.

Such was the array of forces when Conrad intervened in behalf of the vavasours. With the Constitutio de Feudis (Constitution Concerning Fiefs) of 1037 he established the rule that no vavasour could be deprived of his fief without a sentence passed by his peers. A fief, moreover, was entailed to the owner's children or nearest relations. This was a radical change in an imperial policy that heretofore had favoured the bishops. But the results were not what Conrad had expected. The vavasours, once they were pacified, made peace with the *capitanei*, while, on the other hand, Heribert and many other bishops were antagonized. Conrad faced up to the new situation by striking an alliance with the secular lords. Then he returned to Germany, dying there in 1039.

Unexpected results of intervening in class conflict

Henry III and the ecclesiastical reform movement. Conrad was succeeded by his son, Henry III, who for several years was involved in a struggle against Bohemia and Hungary and had to neglect his Italian affairs. Meanwhile, a civic revolt took place in Milan. The *cives*, who had stretched their muscles in previous episodes of a similar kind, drove Heribert, the *capitanei*, and the vavasours out of the city. Then for three years (1042–45), under the leadership of the noble Lanzone, they stood off the siege of their adversaries. Eventually there was a reconciliation; *capitanei* and vavasours came to terms with the *cives* and returned to the city. It was no commune, but there were the bases of a commune's foundation: the deposition of the archbishop and the solidarity of the three main social classes, with the idea that there must be cooperation among them.

Henry III had to deal with circumstances very different from those familiar to his father, but he showed remarkable ability in adjusting himself to them, particularly in the understanding with which he treated the *cives* of Milan, Ferrara, and Mantua. He realized that the bulwark they provided against the encroachments of the bishops and their feudatories might strengthen the empire. At the same time he assured himself of the loyalty of the bishops, especially those whose sees straddled the roads to Germany, such as Como, Trent, and Verona, or which were the centres of large territories, such as Aquileia and Ravenna. To these sees and to the rule of various cities of Venetia he named trusted Germans. As a successor to Heribert in Milan he chose a country cleric, extraneous to the cathedral hierarchy, which was linked to the families of the *capitanei* and expected to furnish a candidate for the archbishopric. Obviously Henry shared his predecessors' rigid concept of the supremacy of the emperor over the bishops. But one cannot fully understand his policy unless one takes into account certain other local conditions that influenced him, above all the religious revival of the 11th century. For Henry was sensitive to demands for clerical reform and considered that he must eliminate abuses and make the church respectable.

Reorganization of the monasteries

In Italy there was much religious ferment. Already in the 10th century the Cluny reform had reached Italy, resulting in the founding or re-ordering of monasteries at Pavia, Rome, Fara Sabina, Pomposa (Ravenna), Fruttuaria (Piedmont), and Cava dei Tirreni (Naples). But the Cluny reform had lost its initial impact, and its strictly monastic ideal was not broad or strong enough; everywhere were complaints about unworthy prelates, the church's temporal interests and submission to secular power, and the clergy's practice of simony (traffic in ecclesiastical preferment) and concubinage. On the one hand, a reaction occurred in the rise of religious orders of hermits and cenobites founded by Romuald of Ravenna (at Camaldoli), Peter Damiani, his disciple and biographer (at Fonte Avellana), and John Gualbert (at Vallombrosa), all of them fired by asceticism; on the other hand (but a little later, beginning in 1057), there was a violent popular protest, represented chiefly by the reform party known as the Patarines of Milan and Florence, against bishops linked too closely to the empire and against the unseemly behaviour of the clergy. This latter movement was strictly secular and worked from below, its religious motivation having economic factors. The promoters were unwilling to leave to the clergy the profitable administration of the church's wealth, which they felt should be used by the whole community. In southern Italy there was a particular movement of reform of the monastic rule of the Basilians, which was inspired by Nilus of Rossano, founder of the monastery of Grottaferrata.

Henry III, in contact with the chief monastic reformers —Odilo of Cluny, Peter Damiani, Alinard of Lyons— favoured the reformed congregations and influenced the choice of bishops and even popes. He took drastic action on his first visit to Italy, in 1046: a schism in Rome had led to the election of three popes, and Henry voided all three elections and named a man of high moral calibre, Suitger, bishop of Bamber, in Bavaria, Germany, who took the name of Clement II. Subsequently he named three other reputable German bishops: Damas II, Leo IX, and Victor II.

The choice of Leo IX (1049–54) was of especial importance. As Bruno, bishop of Toul, in northeast France, he belonged to a noble Alsatian family related to that of the Emperor and had close connections with the reformers of Lorraine. No sooner was he elected than he undertook an energetic policy of reform. In Rome and Pavia, and later in France and Germany, he presided over a succession of councils that condemned the worst abuses—simony, concubinage, and the usurpation of ecclesiastical benefits. Unworthy prelates were deposed and there was a restatement of the laity's obligation of tithing. Such policies were extended even to southern Italy, where the situation was complicated by the presence of Normans and Byzantines. On various occasions the Pope and his supporters called attention to the necessity of respecting Canon Law in regard to the election of bishops. Leo himself gave the example when, even after the Emperor had chosen him, he insisted upon being regularly elected by the clergy and people of Rome. The reformers brought equal energy to bear on their support of the principle of the authority of the see of Rome over the universal church. Their defense of this principle came to a climax during the conflict with the patriarch of Constantinople, Michael Cerularius, which led to the definite schism between the Eastern and Western churches in 1054. The situation was changing: popes were no longer figureheads produced, amid intercity strife, by the counts of Tusculum; they were foreigners, aware of their worldwide responsibilities and bolstered by the emperor's power. The initiative of reform passed into their hands while Henry III was detained in Germany and after his death (1056), when his son Henry IV was a minor and the empire was in a long period of weakness. As the popes recaptured the leadership of Western Christianity they perceived that the first step toward reform was the elimination of secular interference with church government. Hence the inevitable conflict with imperial power and the later "struggle over lay investiture." With Leo IX the clash was only latent; it did not break out until the time of his successors. Eventually the emperors' weapon of reform was turned against them.

Incipient clash between emperor and pope

Among Leo IX's successors Nicholas II (1059–61), of Burgundian origin, deserves special mention. At the Lateran synod of 1059 he decreed that from then on the pope should be elected by the cardinals, approved by the rest of the clergy, and acclaimed by the people, while the emperor could only give a generic assent after the election was over. By this decree the choice of the pope was removed not only from the emperor but from the Roman factions as well, and the form that it took then has since endured. This undermining of the imperial prerogative was possible only because Henry IV was not yet of age. And, as substitute for the German emperor's support, Nicholas II made, also in 1059, an agreement with the Normans, naming Robert Guiscard duke of Apulia and Calabria and receiving his oath of allegiance.

Further erosion of imperial power. After Nicholas' death, events followed a logical development. On one side there was the reform party, headed by the new pope, Alexander II (born Anselm of Baggio), representative of the intransigent and often violent popular movement of the Patarines of Milan. This party could count on such fiery preachers and debaters as Peter Damiani and Humbert of Silvacandida and on the interested support of the Norman princes. Against it stood a "conservative" party, composed of members of the imperial court, German bishops, and their Italian fellows linked to the empire and its traditional policy. This latter group had many "clients" and dependents, especially in Lombardy, Venetia, and Romagna, roughly, the area between Geora and Ravenna. Originally it refused to recognize Alexander II and put up an anti-pope, Cadalus of Parma (Honorius II), who was deposed in 1064.

In 1073 Gregory VII (formerly Archdeacon Hildebrand of Sovana), a trusted counsellor of his predecessors and the soul of the reform movement, became pope. He was intensely moral and uncompromising, determined to attack abuses at the root, and in 1075 forbade, under penalty of excommunication, any secular power to concede the investiture of abbeys or bishoprics. This signified a definite negation of the hierarchical feudal system upon which the empire and its single states were based and affirmed the church's complete independence from lay domination. It was a revolutionary act, to which Henry IV replied, after some hesitation, by the Diet of Worms of 1076, which branded the Pope as unworthy and illegitimate and removed him from the throne. This was the beginning, on the basis of the political differences outlined above, of the investiture struggle, which had its beginnings in Italy but soon spread to the rest of Europe.

Gregory VII made a rapid and effective reply. He excommunicated the Emperor, released his subjects from their allegiance to him, and thus favoured a revolt of the German princes. Henry IV found himself in a critical situation and came precipitately down to Italy with a small escort in order to obtain the Pope's pardon and removal of the excommunication. The meeting took place in February of 1077 at the castle of Canossa, where Gregory VII was the guest of Matilda, countess of Tuscany, a strong supporter of his policy. Henry had to humble himself to receive absolution, but the danger temporarily blew over. There was a continuation of the crisis, however, in 1080, when the Pope once more excommunicated the Emperor, relieved his subjects of their vows, and recognized Rudolph of Swabia, long since chosen by the German princes, as German king. After this, events became favourable to Henry. At a council meeting at Brixen, where many bishops from northern Italy were present, he had an anti-pope elected (Guibert, archbishop of Ravenna, who took the name of Clement

The humiliation of Canossa

III) and defeated Rudolph of Swabia in a battle in which the latter received wounds that led to his death. In 1081 Henry returned to Italy with an army, defeated the militia of Matilda of Canossa, and for three years besieged Rome. In 1084 he was crowned emperor by the anti-pope but soon after was driven from the city by Robert Guiscard and his Normans, who had come to rescue Gregory VII, who died at Salerno a year later.

The struggle was resumed, after a brief interval, by the next pope, Urban II (1088–99), of French origin. He was supported by Matilda's militia and won success for the reformist, or "Gregorian," party among the cities and bishops of the north. Henry's last resistance was overcome, and, frustrated and embittered by the rebellion of his own sons, he died in 1106.

Henry V, his son and successor (1106–25), and a new pope, Paschal II (1099–1118), tried to settle the controversy peacefully. The Pope proposed the abolition of imperial investiture and, in return, the clergy's renunciation of fiefs and benefices. The idea was Utopian because too many private interests were involved, and, indeed, the German bishops bitterly opposed it. Tension continued, complicated by the fact that Countess Matilda, upon her death in 1115, left all her properties—both fiefs and allods—to the Roman Church. The former, because they had been granted by the empire, should rightfully have returned to it; hence another conflict.

The investiture question finally reached a compromise solution in the Concordat of Worms (1122), drawn up between Henry V and Calixtus II. It was stipulated that the emperor should no longer concede a religious investiture with the symbols of ring and staff. In Germany, an elected bishop or abbot was to receive from the sovereign only temporal investiture (with a sceptre), which would be followed by religious consecration; in Italy, this consecration was to precede temporal investiture and the latter was to take place without the sovereign's presence.

After 70 years of bitter struggle the system remained substantially the same as before. Yet in the meantime, great social and political changes had taken place. First of all, the Church of Rome had taken the place of the empire as the pilot of Western Christendom; the most obvious proof is the First Crusade, an imperial sort of enterprise if ever there was one but which was eminently the work of Pope Urban II. The prestige of the Roman see was very high; and the Normans of southern Italy, the Christian states of Spain, England, Hungary, Croatia, and even the princedom of Kiev recognized in it some sort of feudal superiority and had recourse to it for protection. Within the church itself there was a radical transformation. The necessity of closing ranks in the struggle against secular interference caused the popes, in particular Gregory VII, to strengthen the central authority, that is, that of the apostolic see over the bishops. This determined what was to be for centuries the structure of the church, rigidly hierarchical and centred in the papal Curia, with a clergy to which all sacramental prerogatives and disciplinary powers were entrusted and a laity that had no more than a passive role. At the same time a new, theocratic theology was developed. The temporal was subordinated to the spiritual; and it became the popes' right and duty to intervene in such events as the election or deposition of an emperor, conflicts among states, and violated oaths that imperilled peace among Christians and their souls' salvation. Gregory VII was the great artificer of these ecclesiastical and political doctrines, which inspired the project of collecting and defining the articles of canon law.

Beginning of the papacy's paramountcy

Another important aspect of this period was the impulse given to civic life and liberty, especially in central and northern Italy. The investiture struggle was actually not a mere political and economic conflict between two great powers. It had also an ideological content, which aroused the participation of the masses. Popes and emperors vied for the citizens' support by the concession of exemptions and privileges. In the cities and fortified castles, groups, alliances, and various *conjurationes* (agreements) were constantly forming. Writers distributed polemical pamphlets discussing such matters as the validity of a sacrament administered by an unworthy priest, the sale of church offices, the grant of contracts in return for political favours, resistance to authority, people's rights, the *libertas ecclesiae* ("freedom of the church"), the articles of Roman law, and laymen's participation in religious life. A world was in ferment, opening up to new ideas and experiences acquired by living together. The most important end result was to be the establishment of the communes.

NORMAN SICILY

The Normans' arrival. Small groups of Normans arrived in southern Italy in the early 11th century. They were adventurers and skilled men-at-arms, seeking their fortune in a smiling land and one divided into so many small, conflicting states that it was easy to enlist in the service of one or another. Gradually the Norman leaders got themselves lands of their own and settled down, pursuing at the same time a policy of expansion. After 50 or 60 years the newcomers constituted an important political and military power, which proceeded to place southern Italy and Sicily under its rule.

In 1017 Pope Benedict VIII called upon a contingent of Norman knights to support the revolt of Melus of Bari against the Byzantines. Subsequently, other Norman mercenaries took part in the wars between Naples and Capua. Sergius IV, duke of Naples, in order to win over the Norman leader, Ranulph Drengo I, gave him his sister for a wife and made him count of Aversa (1030). This first territorial acquisition was followed by others in Apulia and its vicinity, effected by another Norman group headed by the Hauteville brothers (William "Iron Arm" the first among them). The cities and towns in question were Ascoli Satriano, Venosa, Lavello, Monopoli, Trani, Civitate, Canne, Montepeloso, Acerenza, and, above all, Melfi. The possession of these places was legalized by feudal investitures granted by Prince Gaimar IV of Salerno in 1042. Only four years later Henry III gave imperial investiture to Raymond of Aversa and Drogo of Hauteville, brother of William. Probably this was the confirmation of preceding investitures conceded by Gaimar, together with recognition of the superiority that Drogo had asserted over all the other Norman knights who had settled in Apulia.

Actually, the continuous state of war favoured the concentration of power in a single hand, such as that of Humphrey, successor to his brother Drogo, who came up against the hostility of Pope Leo IX. This pope is important not only in the history of the reform of the church but also for his policy in southern Italy. Fearful of the Normans' growing power, as it threatened the city of Benevento (35 miles northeast of Naples), which he had recently added to his possessions, he strove to bring about an alliance between the two emperors—German and Byzantine—against the Normans. Failing, he went in person to war but was defeated and taken prisoner in the battle of Civitate in 1053. Humphrey had the intelligence to give him honourable treatment and to set him free. Thus, there came into being an agreement between the papacy and the Normans, furthered at Melfi in 1059, when Robert Guiscard, Humphrey's younger stepbrother and successor, pledged allegiance to Pope Nicholas II and assumed the title of *dux Apulie et Calabrie et futurus Sicilie* ("duke of Apulia and Calabria and the future duke of Sicily"). The same pledge was made by Richard of Aversa on behalf of the principality of Capua. These were acts of great historical importance, inasmuch as the Normans legitimized their conquests, past and future, and the popes established their feudal sovereignty over all of southern Italy and Sicily, thus making concrete a long-standing aspiration to political and religious control there and establishing a diplomatic and military base for the coming struggle over investiture.

Resistance of Leo IX to the Normans

Norman expansion. Robert Guiscard and his younger brother Roger (the "Great Count") rapidly extended their conquests, beginning with Calabria. In 1060, Roger captured Reggio and soon after Messina, which served as a beachhead for the conquest of Sicily. The island was divided and politically weak, but the Arabs put up a stubborn resistance, which was not overcome until 1091. Meanwhile, on the mainland, just above Italy's "heel," Bari (1071) and Salerno (1077) fell into Norman hands; and the whole territory was united under the rule of Guiscard. Only the Norman principality of Capua-Aversa and the Byzantine duchy of Naples kept a certain autonomy, the former until 1156, the latter until 1137.

In conquering Sicily, the "Great Count" Roger acted as vassal and representative of his brother Robert and hence with a certain de facto independence of the Church of Rome. Moreover, in the process he staved off the formation of too-powerful feudal lordships such as the Norman knights had set up in the former Byzantine and Lombard territories, keeping for his own domain a large part of the conquered lands and using viscounts and army leaders—officials directly dependent upon him—to govern the island. In short, Count Roger managed to create a centralized and efficient governmental structure linked only in name to the duchy of Apulia and its feudal superior, the papacy. It further happened that, in 1098, Pope Urban II conferred upon Count Roger and his successors an "apostolic delegation," by which they were legally recognized as the pope's representatives for Sicily's ecclesiastical affairs. This amounted to official recognition of the power that Roger had acquired over the Sicilian churches during and after the conquest. The situation was very different from that of 1059, when Robert Guiscard had to recognize the pontiff's jurisdiction over the churches of Apulia and Calabria.

The importance of this became obvious when Roger II (son of the "Great Count") brought about the unification of the Norman territories (1127) and created the new Kingdom of Sicily, with its capital in Palermo (1120). This kingdom was born as a solidly organized and centralized state, with an efficient bureaucratic administration that had authority over both clerics and feudatories. The only thing that Roger II did not completely eliminate was the feudal overlordship of the papacy, which he sought to reduce to a mere formality.

Norman administration. The Norman rule of southern Italy and Sicily has a historical importance comparable to that of Britain (set up at the same period) for its solidity and duration. The king's authority was conceived as absolute and deriving directly from God, a concept influenced by that of Roman–Byzantine autocracy, as can be seen in the body of law of the assizes of Ariano, applicable to the entire kingdom, put out in 1140. The sovereign was assisted by a *magna curia* composed of the top officials of the kingdom, the princes of royal blood, and the chief prelates and feudatories. In spite of the presence of the last-named category, the curia did not represent the feudal class. It was open, on the grounds of position or career, to men of diverse social ranks and conditions, primarily Normans (and later Franco-Normans and Anglo-Normans), then Italians, Greeks, Lombards, Arabs, and Jews. The major officials were five in number: the Seneschal, in charge of everyone connected with the court; the grand chamberlain, who watched over finances; the chancellor; the "protonotary," head of the notaries; and the admiral, leader of both land and sea forces. The very titles have mixed Norman, Roman–Byzantine, and Arab origins.

The authority of the Norman king

As for the ordering of the provinces, the kingdom was divided into circumscriptions ruled by justiciaries and chamberlains, the first having administrative functions and feudal and penal jurisdiction, the second controlling finances and civil lawsuits. Lands belonging to the royal domain and lands enfeoffed both came under the provincial administration; obviously the barons' immunities were quite limited. Equally limited were those of the bishops. The Byzantine imperial–papal model, joined to the traditions of the Norman conquest of Sicily and the privilege of apostolic delegation, had resulted in a rigid subordination of clergy to the state. Feudatories and bishops, tightly controlled as they were by the sovereign, took part in the great assemblies of the kingdom (*curiae generales* or *colloquia*), called together for the proclamation of laws, though they played no active role except at moments of crisis for the monarchy (as in 1189).

Status of the cities

The cities, especially those of the Apulian and Campanian coasts, had by 1000 achieved some autonomy and economic development. Gradually they were incorporated, through treaties and agreements, into the Norman state and legally passed into the royal domain. They were considered mainstays of the governmental structure, but this was too rigid and authoritarian to allow them their former independence. Their autonomy was lost, except for brief intervals, until the statutory revival of the *universitates* (the whole number of citizens) at the end of the Angevin and the beginning of the Aragonese period (in the 16th century). The domain cities entered the *curiae generales* only in 1208 and were permanently incorporated from 1232.

The Norman dynasty continued after Roger II by direct descent, with William I ("the Bad") and William II ("the Good"). When the latter died, leaving no heirs, there was a violent struggle between a nationalist faction that proclaimed the illegitimate royal prince Tancred king and the supporters of Constance, daughter of Roger II, who had married Henry VI, son of Frederick Barbarossa. The latter won, and the Norman crown passed into the hands of the House of Swabia.

The Norman rule over Sicily was not only the embodiment of an orderly and strong government; it provided a place for the meeting and fusion of different traditions, which together produced a vigorous and original civilization. The liberal cultural tradition of the Arab emirs was continued by Roger II. What is left of Arab–Norman architecture (S. Giovanni degli Eremiti, the Zisa, and the Cuba of Palermo, northwest Sicily; and the cathedrals of Monreale, southwest of Palermo, and Cefalù, on Sicily's north coast) and of Byzantine mosaics (in the Palatine Chapel and La Martorana of Palermo and the cathedral of Cefalù) indicate a high level of civic life and culture. (Gi.Ma.)

ITALY AND SICILY IN THE 12TH AND 13TH CENTURIES

The Hohenstaufen emperors. The conflict (mentioned above) between the empire and the papacy began soon after Frederick I Barbarossa, the second German king of the Hohenstaufen dynasty, had been crowned emperor (1155). The decrees of Roncaglia (1158), issued at the beginning of his second Italian expedition, with the assistance of members of the new Bolognese law school, placed imperial policy on a new basis. Frederick's predecessors Lothair II (or III) the Saxon and Conrad III had only rarely intervened in the affairs of northern and central Italy. Conrad III never came to Italy at all. By the time of Frederick Barbarossa's first expedition (1154–55) the communes had greatly increased their power, and no organized attempt had been made to check them. Frederick tried to strike at the core of the problem by claiming for the empire the royal rights (regalia) that had in so many cases been usurped by the communes.

The real victims of this usurpation, however, had been the bishops and the nobility, who for a long time had been in possession of most of the regalia. The innumerable grants of royal rights had formed an integral part of the traditional system of imperial government. Frederick intended to replace it, to a wide extent, by one of direct control. Imperial officials were to administer town and countryside; and if the communes were to be left some of their liberties, they were to owe them entirely to the emperor. In fact, the Emperor began soon to differentiate between the communes; those that took his side were granted considerable concessions, such as free elections of the consuls. The violent resistance of Milan and other towns was largely responsible for this turn of Frederick's policy. It was significant that Milan's enemies, such as Lodi and Cremona, vigorously assisted in the siege of that town and shared in its destruction in 1162.

On the other hand, the revival of the struggle between empire and papacy provided the anti-imperial towns with a powerful ally. The double papal election of 1159 led to a schism; and while Frederick recognized Victor IV, Alexander III was prepared to support any communal reaction against the Emperor. After the fall of Milan, Venice, threatened by the extension of imperial power, had taken the initiative in founding the Veronese League (1164); and in 1167 a second league was formed between several Lombard towns. In the same year, the two leagues joined and entered into close contact with Alexander. In the meantime, Frederick had taken Rome; but an epidemic had decimated his army (1167), and his return route to Germany was almost cut by the Lombard revolt (1168). As a result, imperial authority practically collapsed in Lombardy and was much weakened in Tuscany.

The Veronese and Lombard leagues

After his return to Italy, Frederick was prepared to give up the execution of the Roncaglian decrees, as was shown in the negotiations of Montebello (1175); but these negotiations were ineffective, and in 1176 Frederick was defeated by Milan near Legnano. In 1177 Frederick concluded the separate peace of Venice with Alexander III, and an armistice with the Lombard League was culminated after six years by the peace of Constance (1183). The Lombard communes were left the regalia inside the towns and, on certain conditions, in the territory, and they retained nearly all their liberties. But the consuls were to be invested by the emperor (a right of which he seems hardly ever to have made use). The peace, however, concerned only Lombardy. In Tuscany, Spoleto, and the Marches, the imperial position had been greatly strengthened during the previous years; and the administrative reorganization that had failed in Lombardy was carried out with considerable success in that region. Moreover, Frederick was preparing the extension of German rule to the kingdom of Sicily.

Imperial ambitions in Sicily

The emperors had made repeated attempts at conquering the Norman kingdom. In 1137 Lothair II had achieved a short-lived success in Apulia; in 1166–67 Frederick had planned an attack on the kingdom. In 1184 the Sicilian heiress Constance, King Roger's daughter, was betrothed to Frederick's son and successor Henry, an event of far-reaching importance for Italy and the empire.

At Frederick's death in 1190, Henry VI had already begun to assert his and his wife's claims to Sicily, King Roger's grandson William II having died in 1189. But resistance led by Tancred, an illegitimate grandson of King Roger, was strong; and it was not until 1194 that Henry succeeded in conquering the kingdom. He left the Norman regime unchanged; the highly centralized Sicilian state was an invaluable addition to the resources of the empire in Italy.

Henry's unsuccessful plan to make the empire hereditary rather than elective would have led to permanent union, since the Sicilian crown was hereditary. Placing imperial rule on a stronger basis than it had ever possessed, it would have been fraught with dangers for the political independence of the papacy. Thus the papacy made a determined effort, after Henry's death in 1197, to destroy the union of Sicily and the empire.

Henry's death was followed by a disputed imperial election; in Italy imperial administration disintegrated rapidly, the communes recovering everywhere what they had lost. Pope Innocent III (1198–1216) took full advantage of this reaction and substituted papal government for imperial administration in the duchy of Spoleto and in the march of Ancona, thus once more extending the Papal States to the Adriatic Sea. Constance of Sicily renounced the imperial crown on behalf of her son Frederick, the new king of Sicily, and appointed Pope Innocent III to be his guardian after her death (1198). The next step in the separation of Sicily from the empire was the renunciation of that kingdom by the German king Otto IV (1201), a Welf who had been recognized by Innocent against the Hohenstaufen Philip of Swabia. But after his imperial coronation in 1209, Otto turned to its conquest, the continuity of imperial policy proving stronger than promises and a change in dynasty.

In Sicily, the preceding years had been marked by internal disorders that threatened to destroy the work of the Norman monarchy. In 1211 Pope Innocent decided to play off the young king Frederick against Otto by supporting his new election as future emperor in Otto's stead. Crowned as German king at Mainz (1212), Frederick II grew rapidly more powerful; and the Battle of Bouvines (1214) sealed Otto's fate. But the success of papal policy was only temporary, for Frederick did not keep his promise to separate Sicily from the empire.

Between 1220 and 1250 Frederick continued with great vigour and much success the policy of his German and Norman ancestors in Italy and Sicily. The years after his imperial coronation in 1220 were mainly devoted to rebuilding and consolidating the structure of the Norman monarchy. Further reforms took place in later years, and the constitution of Melfi of 1231 admirably reflected the spirit and working of the highly centralized and bureaucratic Sicilian state. In northern Italy, active intervention began in 1226 and immediately led to the revival of communal resistance; and when in 1227 the new pope, Gregory IX, excommunicated Frederick after his failure to keep the date appointed for the crusade, the pattern of the reign of Frederick I was reproduced, the papacy allying itself with the Lombard towns against the Emperor.

The Peace of San Germano (1230) between Pope and Emperor was of short duration. Open war with the Lombards broke out again in 1236; the great defeat of the league at Cortenuova (1237) was not fully exploited by Frederick; and in 1239 Gregory once more excommunicated the Emperor. The capture of Rome then became a major objective; Frederick may have been on the eve of attaining it at the time of Gregory's death (1241). In 1244 peace negotiations with Innocent IV and the league broke down, and Innocent deposed the Emperor at the Council of Lyons (1245). In the following years the struggle continued with unprecedented violence. Despite numerous setbacks, the imperial cause seemed to be in the ascendant when Frederick suddenly died in 1250.

Changes in mainland government

After 1237 he had reorganized imperial administration in northern and central Italy, introducing and adapting Sicilian methods of government. Vicars general with wide authority governed new provinces, while under them local officials administered towns and countryside. The preponderance of natives of the Sicilian kingdom in the Italian administration significantly contrasted with the leading role played by Germans under Frederick I and Henry VI. Sicily had become the main pillar of imperial rule in Italy, and its great resources held out a substantial promise of success. At the same time Frederick tried to preserve the support of the German princes by far-reaching concessions (1232).

Frederick's death was a turning point in the history of Italy; it marked the end of the Hohenstaufen policy of placing the country under a centralized monarchical government. The conflicts between Frederick's successors and the papacy continued until 1268. In 1265, Pope Clement IV invested Charles of Anjou with the Sicilian kingdom, where King Manfred, Frederick's illegitimate son, had been consolidating his power. In 1266, Manfred was defeated and killed in the Battle of Benevento. Two years later, Frederick's young grandson Conradin made a supreme effort to save the fortunes of his house; after a triumphant entry into Rome he was beaten by Charles at Tagliacozzo (1268) and executed at Naples.

During the struggles between papacy and empire Italy had become divided into two parties, papalist and imperialist, which in the course of the 13th century assumed the names of Guelf and Ghibelline. This had not only affected relations between states but had also divided the population of the towns, thus giving fresh impetus to local factions. The names remained a tragic legacy of the Hohenstaufen period to the political life of Italy.

Monarchies and communes in the 13th century. By the end of the 12th century, the communes had triumphed in Lombardy and Tuscany; but although the communal movement extended also to other parts of the country, it did not prevail everywhere. Large regions of Italy retained or developed monarchical institutions: foremost, the Sicilian kingdom, but also the papal states Piedmont and Sardinia. Feudalism formed an important element of monarchical Italy, which represented also in this respect a contrast to the antifeudal policy of the communes. With other European countries, monarchical Italy had in common the development of assemblies of estates (*parliamenti*), in which the towns were represented. Originating primarily from the earlier feudal assemblies, the parliaments of the 13th and 14th centuries reflected the attempt to give the towns, together with the feudal classes, an influential place in the political structure of the monarchical states. They thus constituted also a new development in the position of the towns, which often enjoyed considerable local autonomy under monarchical control. Conditions varied considerably, however, both with regard to the functions of the parliaments and the rights of the towns. Thus the Papal States, comprising many communes that had been only recently acquired, contrasted with the Sicilian kingdom, in which the towns had remained strictly subjected to the monarchy from the time of the Norman conquest, whatever the privileges that had been granted to them.

The *podesta*

In communal Italy the internal conflicts that began to disrupt the communes in the 12th century created new and far-reaching problems. Caused by rivalries and feuds within the ruling oligarchies and already, sometimes, by social conflicts, they led, toward the end of the 12th century, to the institution of a single executive magistrate (*podesta*). This innovation, however, did not put an end to internal strife. While the consular government disappeared at the beginning of the 13th century, it became the general rule for the *podesta* to be a citizen of another town so that the executive could no longer be the object of family rivalry. The struggles between the municipal parties, led by powerful families from which they often took their names, became a permanent feature of communal politics; and strife was intensified by the custom of the blood feud (*vendetta*) and by the expulsions of the defeated party. The growth of Guelfism and Ghibellinism gave the local parties endless possibilities of outside support and added fresh violence to their struggles. But they were no longer alone in their desire for political control.

The increase of economic prosperity and the growth of the town populations led to a challenge of the virtual rule of the aristocracy in the communes. The prosperity was primarily the result of the expansion of Italian trade and the development of Italian banking and industry. The Crusades (*q.v.*) provided Venice, Pisa, and Genoa and, indirectly, other towns with new trading centres on the fringe of Asia; the Fourth Crusade, which established the Latin Empire at Constantinople in 1204, gave Venice a colonial dominion in the Levant, the economic value of which was immeasurably great. The restoration of the Byzantine Empire under Michael VIII Palaeologus in 1261 was not a serious blow to Venice's new dominion, but it gave Genoa vast commercial opportunities at Venice's expense. The Sicilian policy of the papacy after 1250—the offers of the kingdom first to Edmund, son of Henry III of England, and then to Charles of Anjou—provided Italian bankers and merchants with new fields of action. Hand in hand with increasing prosperity went immigration into the towns, the new citizens being recruited from all classes.

The *popolo*

The rise of the merchant and craft guilds was closely related to these developments, another form of organization of the *popolo* being military companies. The *popolo* roughly corresponded to the middle classes, and the final stage of its political formation was reached when it was organized like a commune, with an executive, councils, and statutes of its own. Conflicts between the aristocracy and the *popolo* began early but generally did not reach full strength until the 13th century. A first attempt to settle them led in Milan and other Lombard towns to the government's being shared between the two classes. Later in the 13th century, the organized *popolo* sometimes succeeded in establishing control of the commune, as in Florence in 1250 and 1282.

Instability and civic strife were generally traits of the 13th-century communes. The fate of the vanquished was bitter, the political exile becoming a typical figure; and the victor's desire for permanent power was determined not only by ambition but also by the fear of the consequences of defeat. To grant special powers to the leader of one's party or of the *popolo* might appear the easiest method to achieve this end; but the breaking down of constitutional limitations opened the road for the establishment of despotic government.

Interstate conflicts

Interstate conflicts, which had existed even before the rise of the communes, were a constant feature of Italian politics from the 12th century onward. Caused by quarrels over boundaries, by commercial and political rivalry, or by Guelf and Ghibelline loyalties, they present a bewildering picture, which nevertheless reveals some patterns. Thus the conflicts between Pisa and Genoa, the principal rivals on the Tyrrhenian coast, both aiming at control of Sardinia, continued intermittently throughout the 12th and 13th centuries and culminated in Pisa's decisive naval defeat off Meloria in 1284, which sealed its decline as a great maritime power. In the meantime, the struggle between Genoa and Venice over the eastern trade, beginning in the 12th century, had been intensified by the establishment of Venice's Levantine dominion in 1204 and the restoration of the Byzantine Empire in 1261. Commercial rivalry must have been largely responsible for Milan's traditional enmity with Pavia and Cremona. In Tuscany, the struggles between Pisa and Lucca began in the 11th century. Lucca, once the most powerful Tuscan town, had been overtaken by Pisa, the chief Tuscan port. Florentine expansion led to mortal enmity between Florence and Siena from the 12th century onward, whereas Florence's growing economic and political power brought about struggles with Pisa from the beginning of the 13th. One effect of these conflicts was that the emperors always succeeded in enlisting the services of communes against other communes. Another result of the conflicts and of the territorial policy of the communes in general could be the acquisition of city-states by more powerful neighbours. But in this respect, too, the rise of the *signori* (seigniories; see below) proved a new departure. (Ed.)

III. Italy in the late Middle Ages and the Renaissance

SOCIAL AND POLITICAL DEVELOPMENT

The 14th and 15th centuries coincided, in the history of Italy, with the age of the Renaissance; hence, Italian social and political development in this period has been an object of special interest. Not only did it supply the context for brilliant achievements in artistic and literary culture; in addition, these centuries saw the emergence in Italy of patterns of social and political organization that have been conventionally taken as marking the end of the Middle Ages and the beginning of the modern era for the rest of the European continent. According to this view, Italy, in the phrase of Jacob Burckhardt, from his classic *Die Kultur der Renaissance in Italien* ("The Civilization of the Renaissance in Italy"), published in 1859, was "the education of Europe."

Withdrawal of imperial and papal authority. Fundamental to the history of Italy during this period was the virtual withdrawal from the peninsula of both universal powers, the empire and the papacy, whose long struggle, although for centuries disrupting Italian political life, had at least given some unity to its history. The emperors of the 14th and 15th centuries, chiefly concerned with promoting their dynastic interests in Germany, were generally indifferent to Italy. Although they occasionally descended into the peninsula for the prestige of a coronation in Rome and to derive income from selling titles and privileges to local powers, none made a significant effort to impose imperial rule in Italy. And, with the exception of a rare and anachronistic idealist such as the poet Dante, who hailed the visit of Henry VII to Italy in 1310 as the onset of a golden age of peace under orderly imperial rule, Italians were equally indifferent to this traditional source of political authority. Towns and nobles were concerned only to exploit a connection with the emperor in order to consolidate their merely local power or to extort from him the recognition of their own claims as the price of a support that was little more than nominal.

At about the same time, the efforts of the papacy to transcend local politics by a strong reassertion of its universal authority over the powers of Europe met with a major defeat that effectively removed the pope as a strong presence in Italian affairs for most of the 14th century. When Philip IV of France insisted on his right to tax the French clergy to finance war with England, Pope Boniface VIII delivered a stern rebuke in the bull *Clericis Laicos*, which was followed by an emphatic assertion of papal authority in a second bull, *Unam Sanctam* (1302). The French king accepted the challenge. He accused the Pope of heresy for claiming to stand above all secular rulers and dispatched a small army under Guillaume de Nogaret, from the French base in Angevin, southern Italy, to the papal residence at Anagni, with the aim of seizing the Pope and carrying him off to France to be tried and deposed. Nogaret forced himself briefly into Boniface's presence and announced his errand; and, although the Frenchman was expelled from Anagni before he could carry out his mission, the aged pope died a few weeks later. The consequences were disastrous for the papacy as an Italian institution. French pressures on the demoralized papal court secured the election of a new French pope, Clement V (1305–14), who soon moved the papacy from Rome to Avignon, in southern France; and there it remained until 1377. The popes in Avignon by no means forgot Italy, but their absence from the peninsula substantially reduced the role they could play in its affairs.

Papacy at Avignon

General characteristics of Italian society. With the two great powers thus absent from the scene, the peoples of Italy were left to determine their own destinies during the 14th and 15th centuries largely without external interference; some historians have seen in this period a great but missed opportunity to construct for Italy a national state comparable to the monarchies developing north of the Alps. This view seems, however, to be based on reading back into the remote past a conception of Italy as a latent political unity that largely reflects the presuppositions of the unification movements of modern Italian history. In fact, since its forcible unification under Roman rule in antiquity, Italy had disintegrated into innumerable local units, and the withdrawal of both the imperial and the papal powers now deprived it of the little coherence its political history had revealed in earlier centuries of the Middle Ages. Italy differed from states such as France or England in its social composition, in its geographical divisions, and above all in its lack of a monarchy around which national institutions and sentiment could be organized. Without such a cohering power, the Italian towns and principalities were neither unified nor in any way checked in their claims to independence; nor were they any longer forced into mutual alliance—as during the time of the Lombard League (formed to combat the Hohenstaufen emperors of the 12th and 13th centuries)—by a mutual need to resist its encroachments. Thus, the history of Italy in the age of the Renaissance consists first of all of the separate histories of a large number of particular political entities, often widely different from each other, that happened to be located on the Italian peninsula and were drawn into relationships with one another less by a sense of community than by their mutual antagonisms.

Some conditions and experiences were, nevertheless, common to most of the inhabitants of Italy. One was precisely this peculiarly local orientation of Italian life, which, to a larger degree than elsewhere in Europe, was centred in towns. These had a certain family resemblance to one another, above all in the intense loyalty they commanded; Italian townsmen saw themselves primarily as inhabitants of particular communities, not as divided members of an Italian nation. Their ardent local patriotism found expression in devotion to local saints, in similar myths about the origins and uniqueness of their towns and in literary compositions praising them, and, negatively, in traditions of enmity with other towns. Their devotion to local independence was manifested in constant appeals for liberty, which to them meant above all the right of self-determination, of freedom from control by any external authority. In the 14th century this concept found juridical definition in the work of commentators on Roman law, common to most of Italy, and notably in that of Bartolus of Saxoferrato (1314–57). Although they still admitted the theoretical supremacy of the emperor, the lawyers adapted theory to practical reality by developing the principle that any community has an original and inborn right to govern itself. In addition, Italy, during these centuries, increasingly shared a common language. Although local dialects continued to flourish, Tuscan, the language of Dante—partly because of the distinction with which he had used it—increasingly became the customary speech of educated men.

Spread of Tuscan language

The Italian towns not only found means to resist the intrusion of imperial authority into their affairs; they also generally worked to reduce that of ecclesiastical authority. Without attacking the theoretical supremacy of the pope, townsmen tended to regard the church, like their secular governments, as for all practical purposes a local affair. Communities erected their own church buildings and quite naturally adopted a proprietary attitude toward them, and in the 14th century they were taking various steps to bring the clergy under local control. In Venice, for example, the Senate appointed bishops, and the government restricted papal taxation of the local clergy and tried clerical lawbreakers in secular courts. In Florence the government also controlled the operations of the Inquisition and abolished many clerical privileges. Such actions were accompanied by a defiance of the traditional sanctions by which the papacy had been accustomed to discipline the faithful to obedience. Florence between 1376 and 1378 and Venice on several occasions chose to ignore a papal interdict. The particularization of Italian life was increasingly ecclesiastical as well as political.

These tendencies reflected not only pressures for local autonomy but also the increasing laicization of Italian society. The precocity of Italian economic development meant that in Italy laymen were rich, educated, ambitious, and assertive to a larger degree than elsewhere in Europe. They were particularly inclined to resent the claims of the clergy to special privileges such as exemption from lay courts or from taxation and to resist any effort by the ecclesiastical authorities to control social and political life—for example, by applying the church's usury laws, which restricted the lending of money for interest. They saw priests not as superior to other men but as primarily the servants of the communities whose spiritual needs they were supposed to meet; in some areas of Italy it was common for parish priests to be elected by the more substantial laymen of the parish. This should not be taken, however, as a sign of any decline in religious fervour. The 14th and 15th centuries were, in fact, a peculiarly devout age in the history of Italy, but Italian devotion now took on a special quality. It found expression in spontaneous and local confraternities of laymen for the purposes of performing pious works and devotional exercises together. Numerous Italian saints, often with lay backgrounds, arose during this period. Lay heretical movements, often strongly anticlerical, were also still active, especially in the 14th century; an example is the Fraticelli, a radical spiritual branch of the Franciscan Order, who were treated with some indulgence by the Florentine and some other secular authorities.

The special piety of the age was related to developments in 14th-century economic and social life, which, in spite of wide local variation, also affected most Italians in this period. At the beginning of the 14th century, Italy was reaching the climax of a long period of prosperity, based on commerce, that had accelerated since the start of the Crusades. This commerce had nourished the growth of urban population. At the beginning of the 14th century, three of the cities of Italy and Sicily—Palermo, Venice, and Florence—had populations in excess of 100,000. These three were the largest cities in Europe. Milan and Genoa, with well over 50,000, were not all that far behind; and Bologna, Padua, Siena, and Perugia, with populations of between 20,000 and 50,000,

Increased size of cities

were also sizable cities. Numerous lesser communities were also regarded, by the standards of the time, as major towns.

Crises of the 14th century. The long period of growing prosperity was brought to an end in the middle decades of the 14th century by a great catastrophe that reflected basic weaknesses in the medieval economy. In the decade after 1340, Italy—along with other parts of western and central Europe—was afflicted by successive waves of pestilence, above all by the Black Death (bubonic plague) of 1347 and 1348. Every part of Italy was affected, rural areas as well as towns, the rich along with the poor. In the major cities of Italy for which reasonable estimates are possible, the death rate seems to have been as high as 50 or 60 percent within a period of only a few months. This disaster, furthermore, proved to be only the beginning of a prolonged demographic crisis. Subsequent epidemics followed, in a regular cycle, about every ten or 15 years, so that the rapid population recovery that usually follows periods of high mortality was regularly wiped out. The danger of death from disease—not only plague but also dysentery, cholera, typhus, typhoid, or smallpox—now became the normal condition of life, as it had scarcely been earlier; and this was to remain the case until well into the 17th century.

Most historians have explained this development as a result of the pressure of expanding population on a limited food supply. By the early 14th century most arable land had been brought under cultivation; intensive exploitation of the soil had reduced the productivity of older regions; and it is possible that a slight change in the climate, bringing cooler weather and unwanted heavy rains in the growing season, may also have been a contributory factor. Thus, agricultural surpluses could no longer tide men over bad years, and the result was periodic undernourishment, which increased susceptibility to disease.

The results of so fundamental a modification in the condition of human life brought a considerable change in the atmosphere of Italy in the 14th century. One result was psychological: the optimism of the preceding period came to an end, giving way to a climate of fear and anxiety that was also increased by political disasters, such as the steady expansion of Turkish power at the expense of Christendom in the eastern Mediterranean, and by the disorders of civil life resulting from endemic local warfare. This sense of insecurity was reflected in an intensified religious attitude. Not only were laymen more pious, but the numbers of Italians in holy orders increased, and piety and morality grew more rigid. The results of the pestilence and economic regression were also serious for the highly developed economies of the major Italian cities. Since the demand for goods fell with the depletion of the population, and labour costs increased for the same reason, both prices and profits declined; and the level of business activity fell sharply, especially in that international commerce in which Italy had established its leadership. The famous business enterprises of the Medici in 15th-century Florence were substantially smaller than those of the great Florentine banking and commercial firms of the earlier 14th century, the Bardi and Peruzzi. This reflects the fact that the recovery both of population and of economic activity was slow. Although a distinct upturn was evident by the earlier 15th century and was more pronounced in some parts of Italy and in some segments of the economy than in others, most of this period was characterized by relative, though probably not absolute, economic depression. The brilliance of Italian Renaissance culture was based partly on the restricted opportunities for business expansion, so that wealthy men had both the leisure and capital to devote to other interests.

Economic results of plague

Economic difficulties doubtless intensified the internal struggles that, continuing from the previous period, increasingly disrupted the life of most of the towns of Italy in the 14th century. Individuals, families, economic groups, and social classes engaged each other in a long struggle that dramatized the need for more effective government that would somehow be able to subordinate competing special interests to the general welfare. By the 14th century the disorderly tendencies of the old feudal nobility had been largely contained, and this group had been generally assimilated into the life of the towns. Another group was now dominant: that of the great merchants, bankers, and industrialists who, organized in their guilds, directed the most profitable economic enterprises of their communities. But the significance of their triumph for the quality of urban life in Italy should not be exaggerated. In sharp contrast to the rest of Europe, there was in Italy no radical distinction between the life styles and the culture of nobles and merchants. Old aristocratic families often built palaces, settled in the towns, and even engaged in business, instead of remaining proudly aloof from urban life; and merchants tended to absorb their values, buying estates of their own in the countryside and investing in agriculture and reading chivalric romances as well as the classics. Jousting was a favourite diversion of Italian townsmen. Intermarriage between the two groups was also common.

But, in spite of this social and cultural amalgamation and perhaps in part because of the pretensions and militant traditions of the nobility, life in the towns of Italy was increasingly violent. Members of the ruling groups engaged in constant struggles for power with each other, and they also came into regular conflict with groups lower on the social scale, which they everywhere tended to exploit. These lesser elements in Italian society included the guilds of skilled artisans and small tradesmen, which resisted efforts to reduce their political rights, and an unorganized mass of city dwellers, usually of peasant origin, who formed a growing urban proletariat that was denied participation in the political life of the town. Between these groups and also among factions within them, there was constant tension, which exploded in periodic and often bloody civil strife. The result was a high degree of instability, rapid changes in political fortune, brutal seizures of power, conspiracies and aggressions, insecurity, and disorder.

Urban violence

THE ITALIAN STATES IN THE 14TH CENTURY

These conditions prepared the way for a characteristic development in the Italian towns of the 14th century, the rise to power of governments dominated by individual despots (signori). This process, already well under way in the previous century, now became general, especially in the north of Italy, where the disorderly republican rule of the communes gave way, in town after town, to government by one man. In some communities the dominant group imported an outsider, known as a *podesta*, to maintain order; the lordship of the Este family in Ferrara was established in this way. More usual, however, was the appointment of a captain of the people, an officer originally intended to check the growing power of the urban patriciate on behalf of the lesser guilds. Given resources to accomplish this purpose, he was likely to extend his authority by degrees, until it amounted to virtual control over the town and could then be made hereditary. This was the road to power for the Della Scala family in Verona, for the Carrara in Padua, for the Gonzaga in Mantua, and for the Visconti in Milan. Eventually, such lords might detach themselves altogether from the popular origins of their powers, perhaps buying from the emperor the title of imperial vicar or duke in order to emphasize their independence from popular control.

Once established, the signori consolidated their power by the centralization of the agencies of government in a purely personal regime. The lord, though he might continue to respect some of the forms of communal government, in practice exercised unrestricted authority over his subjects. He stood above the law, and his power was limited only by the danger of overstepping what was tolerable to his subjects, who, together, might be more powerful than himself. But he generally had the advantage of a monopoly of military force, for the old communal armies had largely disappeared. Even in republics, ruling groups feared to arm the discontented populace, and busy merchants had little interest in bearing arms themselves. The result was a general tendency to rely on mercenary armies led by military entrepreneurs (*condottieri*), who sold themselves to the highest bidder. Thus, armed force escaped popular control, and the unreliability of such armies, together with the disorders they often provoked, contributed to the increasing decadence of Italian military power in the 14th and 15th centuries.

Mercenary armies

It was once supposed that the rise of the signori was almost universal and was therefore the essential element in Italian political life during the age of the Renaissance. But it has now been clearly demonstrated that a major group of towns escaped conversion into despotism—notably Venice, in the north, and the more important communities of Tuscany, including Florence, Siena, Lucca, and Pisa. In these places merchant groups were usually too firmly in control to need the help of a strong man to preserve order. They could accomplish this, for the most part, by themselves, and so the republican forms of government, which they could dominate, were preserved. In these communities government still rested in theory with the whole body of citizens, though practice was far from democratic. Citizenship was variously defined, but participation in politics was regularly the monopoly of older and more substantial families. Republican governments were, nevertheless, based on what has been called the ascending theme in politics. According to this view, power is not imposed from above but resides initially in the community itself, the ends of government are defined by the community in accordance with its sense of its own special needs, and ruling authority is only delegated to public officials, who remain responsible to those with whose affairs they are entrusted. Such conceptions, the direct antithesis of the descending theme that dominated most medieval political thought, were elaborated in the *Defensor pacis* ("Defender of Peace") of Marsilio of Padua (1324), a work that makes it clear that, even on a theoretical level, the significance of the Italian achievement in politics was not limited to the construction of despotism.

In one respect, however, despotisms and republics were alike: both types of government tended to expand by absorbing their smaller neighbours and gradually constructing larger regional states. Thus, in the 14th and earlier 15th centuries, the chaotic pattern of innumerable petty political units in northern and central Italy gave way, largely through conquest but on occasion by purchase, to a few much larger units. Verona, for example, had by 1335 absorbed Vicenza, Treviso, Padua, and Reggio; and by the end of the 14th century Florence had taken over much of Tuscany. But such regional empires were likely to be unstable and at best were often a mixed benefit. Although they could be exploited economically, they also posed problems of administration and control that further taxed the political and military resources of the major states. The citizens of the absorbed towns resented external rule and were likely to revolt at every opportunity. Moreover, the extended territories to be defended and eventually the rival ambitions of the larger powers to absorb lesser powers brought them into dangerous confrontations with each other.

Milanese despotism. The most aggressive Italian state of the 14th century was Milan, whose history may be taken as additional illustration of many of these generalizations. The city had long suffered from the same complicated struggles and internal disorders that plagued other communities, and its troubled populace finally turned for protection to the Visconti, a noble family with large lands outside the city. Beginning as captains general of the people, the heads of the family also exploited a paper allegiance to the emperor to establish an increasing independence from popular control. But, as with other successful despotisms, the chief basis of their power was the support of substantial groups in Milan who, at least initially, appreciated their ability to preserve order, together with their increasing control of military force. As a result, they were able to dominate one area of government after another: legislation, taxation and expenditures, the judicial system, and foreign policy.

The Visconti family

The rise of the family began with a division of the Milanese patriciate in the 13th century into factions led by the rival families of the Della Torre and the Visconti; these bore, respectively, the old Guelf and Ghibelline labels denoting the propapal or proimperial parties, though, as elsewhere, these terms were becoming increasingly unreal. The Ghibelline faction was led, after 1277, by Ottone Visconti, archbishop of Milan, whose family claimed aristocratic origins going back to the early 9th century, owned large estates just outside the city, and had long exploited local ecclesiastical office on behalf of its younger sons. Ottone succeeded in defeating his rivals, became virtual ruler of the city, and secured the election of his nephew Matteo as captain general in 1287. Matteo was responsible for a close alliance with the Emperor, an alliance that played a large part in the history of the family. He was appointed imperial vicar of Lombardy, and, although he was briefly expelled from the city by the partisans of the Della Torre, he was able to return after the imperial expedition of Henry VII in 1310, which he had supported. The Della Torre were now permanently crushed, and Matteo was made captain general for life. In 1317 he was able to make his position hereditary, and his successors extended their power step by step, notably under Azzo Visconti (1328–39).

This process was brought to a climax by Gian Galeazzo (1351–1402), who bought the title of duke from the Emperor in 1395 and married a daughter into the princely French House of Orléans, an alliance with unhappy consequences for the future of Italy. Developing his government into something like a modern bureaucracy, he emphasized his power and remoteness from the people with an elaborate court etiquette and replaced the honourable title of citizen so long borne by the Milanese with the more ambiguous name of subject. And, with so much power at home, he came close to conquering and uniting into a single state much of the north of Italy; by 1402 he was threatening to subjugate even Florence, when he was suddenly carried off by the plague.

The effectiveness of Milanese despotism has sometimes been taken to illustrate one of the most significant aspects of the Italian political achievement in this period. In this view, the tyrants of the Italian Renaissance pointed the way to modern politics by being the first rulers to conceive of the state and its government as, in Burckhardt's famous phrase, "a work of art"; that is, a product of rational planning, deliberate calculation, and the careful adaptation of means to ends. Thus, disregarding their own theoretical subordination to the emperors, the Visconti dukes claimed an absolute authority over all their subjects, nobles and townsmen alike. They replaced elected officials with their own men, upon whose loyal service in enforcing obedience to themselves they could depend; they taxed and spent at will; they imposed uniform laws over their state; they took possession of all fortified points, dispossessing the local nobility; and they were even able to institute a censorship over mail and a kind of passport system to control travel. Such an accumulation of measures is indeed impressive and certainly suggestive for the techniques of later European despotism; but it is doubtful that they really reflected a kind of blueprint for the state. As was done elsewhere, the dukes in Milan actually improvised their policies piecemeal to meet particular problems or take advantage of special opportunities as they arose.

Such government, nevertheless, had obvious attractions in a period of general disorder, advantages that were widely advertised throughout Italy by Visconti propagandists such as the Humanist Pier Candido Decembrio (1392–1477). But the people of Milan paid dearly for Visconti order with the loss of their freedom, a loss the significance of which was often highlighted by the ducal government's abuse of its power. Gian Galeazzo's predecessor Bernabò, for example, extorted huge sums from his helpless subjects, and some of his successors in the 15th century were notorious for an arbitrary ruthlessness against which there was no recourse. The rule of despots such as the Visconti was merely personal, and it never succeeded in creating the modern type of institutional state, independent of the individual ruler and able to rely for its stability on the loyalty of the subject. Selfish special interests were kept in check, to be sure, but they were subordinated to the special interest of the ruler, not to the general welfare. And the memory of communal self-government and the resentment of the suppressed special interests persisted in the Milanese state. When the last of the Visconti died in 1447, the Milanese people made a pathetic effort to restore republican government. But the Ambrosian Republic, as it called itself in memory of the great 4th-century Milanese saint Ambrose, could not solve the problems republics had failed to deal with earlier; above all, it could not control the restive Milanese territory beyond the confines of the city. Thus, by 1450 the republic had been overthrown by Francesco Sforza, one of the great *condottieri* of the age, who had served Milan in the past, and a new despotism replaced the old. Milan therefore continued as the outstanding representative of Italian despotism among the Italian states, in both its strengths and its limitations.

Florence in the 14th century. The history of Florence in this period is better known than that of any other place in Italy. This is partly because of the richness of the Florentine archives but chiefly because the importance of the city for Renaissance culture has attracted special attention to its political and social development. That attention has focussed especially on the survival of republicanism in Florence, in which it contrasted strikingly with the despotism of so many other communities, notably that of Visconti Milan. Because they continued to participate in politics and to take some responsibility for the general welfare, Florentines tended to develop explicit loyalties and a habit of participation in public affairs, and their practice can be seen as an important precedent for posterity. Yet the survival of the republic was often precarious in the 14th century, and, in much of the 15th, republican forms of government were little more than a facade for the personal rule of the Medici. Thus, the history of Florence reveals both similarities to and differences from that of Milan.

Florentine republicanism

The independence of Florence was protected by its strength as the largest city of Tuscany and by its surrounding circle of mountains; and its prosperity was nourished by a relatively diversified economy. This economic activity had developed later than the enterprises of the maritime cities and even of Milan. Still a small town at the end of the 12th century, Florence at the end of the 13th had only recently become prosperous. Because of its inland location, it did not specialize in international trade, though, situated on the major north–south route of the peninsula, it actively participated in it. In addition, Florence had become a major centre for cloth manufacturing, especially of woolens, taking advantage of the decline of the cloth industry in Flanders. Since Florence was a major power in the Guelf alliance, its merchants began, in the 13th century, to lend money to popes, for whom they also served as tax collectors throughout Europe, and also to nobles and other rulers. During the 14th and 15th centuries the great business firms of Florence engaged simultaneously in these and in other activities, such as mining. They established a network of agencies abroad, extending from the eastern Mediterranean to England and the Low Countries. The huge Bardi enterprise of the earlier 14th century, for example, had branches in all the larger towns of Italy and in Antwerp, Bruges, Paris, London, Avignon, Rhodes, Cyprus, and Constantinople. The great Florentine merchants also acquired estates in the surrounding countryside, the *contado*, which they actively supervised and from which they drew their food. This connection with the land was typical of the relation between town and *contado* in Italy.

The disorderly Florentine nobility had been largely excluded from political life by a new constitution in 1282, which vested the government in an elected council whose members, called priors, served for very short terms. This meant frequent elections and changes in the membership of the government, and it encouraged a high degree of public interest and participation in politics; it also made for uncertainty. But the restriction of participation in the political life of Florence to members of the organized guilds gave effective control over the government of the city to the more substantial business interests; the great majority of the priors in the earlier 14th century came from just three guilds, which represented the wealthiest men of Florence: the cloth finishers, the wool merchants, and the bankers, all of whom tended, like others in their position, to favour policies advantageous to themselves. Thus, they taxed property in the surrounding countryside but not in the city itself (where their own possessions chiefly lay), while, within the city, taxes were levied largely on necessities, especially food, consumed by the lower classes. The ruling group retained its old Guelf orientation, a residue of the 13th-century alliance with the papacy against the empire, not as a token of political subordination to the popes but, on the contrary, because this tradition represented the freedom of the city from any external control. This orientation also had continuing practical value. Dedicated to maintaining the Angevin rule over Naples that had been arranged by the Pope between the years 1265 and 1268 in order to exclude the Hohenstaufen emperors from Italy, the Florentine ruling class maintained close relations with southern Italy, facilitating the economic exploitation of the Kingdom of Naples by Florentine businessmen, who collected its taxes, monopolized its grain trade, and reaped huge profits. To idealists such as Dante, the result of such prosperity was a gross materialism in which the traditional values of a simpler age were in decay.

The three ruling guilds

Despite its injustices, the system worked well enough during good times, and the peace of the city was only occasionally disrupted by factional disputes in which those who lost (such as Dante himself) were exiled from Florence. But the political organization tended to break down in a crisis, and after 1340 Florence was in serious trouble. As a leading centre of international commerce and finance, it was badly hurt by the general economic decline that began in the following decade, which in its case was aggravated by special circumstances. The leading business houses of the city had made huge loans to England to finance Edward III's war against France, and much of the capital of Florence was tied up in this dubious enterprise. Thus, the subsequent repudiation of his debts by Edward III brought general disaster to the city, and meanwhile the ruling group had been further discredited by the failure of its attempt to conquer the neighbouring city of Lucca. In these circumstances, in an effort to preserve its control over Florence, it imported a French adventurer, Walter of Brienne, who called himself duke of Athens, to preserve order. But, in a manner familiar elsewhere, this man chose to rule for his own ends, and soon all groups in the city united to expel him and save the republic. Indeed, the failure of this experiment was followed by several decades of more popular government as new men came into Florence from the countryside to replenish the losses of population during the Black Death and, in a time of relative social mobility, rose in Florentine society.

The social dislocations caused by the plague thus combined with the strains of the expansion of Florentine dominion over much of Tuscany during the 14th century to produce important changes in Florence. The newcomers from the countryside were needed to replace those who had died; and, as business again slowly began to improve, some of them did well enough to rise in the world and to challenge the older ruling group. The expenses of prolonged warfare gave them an opportunity: the government badly needed money, and any man with the resources to lend it was able to claim the political influence that accompanied being a creditor of the state, regardless of his family background. In the interest of protecting its investments, this latter group of moneylenders was also concerned to make government more efficient. As a result, the procedures of government became more bureaucratic, professional, and impersonal.

Another decade of turbulence after 1375 imposed a further test on Florence, and again it emerged with its republican institutions stronger than before. This period of crisis began with a war against the papacy, a result both of the growing territorial expansionism of Florence and of the disorders in the Papal States during the Pope's absence in Avignon. These tended to spread into adjacent areas of Tuscany, until the Florentines felt compelled to intervene, thus antagonizing the papacy. The ensuing struggle was known as the War of the Eight Saints (1375–78), so called after the committee that supervised it on the Florentine side, and it raised the most serious ideological questions. The Pope, by imposing an interdict on the city and excommunicating its leaders, converted the conflict from a localized and purely political war into an alleged rebellion against ecclesiastical authority. The implied suggestion that Florence had no basis for its existence as an independent and secular state and no right to conduct a policy based on a sense of its own interests brought into question the fundamental issue of Florentine liberty. Florence found a spokesman in its chancellor, the learned Humanist Coluccio Salutati, whose broad propaganda campaign represented the war as a struggle "for the salvation of Italy and the liberty of all." The whole episode was accompanied by vast republican enthusiasm. Although the war itself was inconclusive, Florence came out of it with a deepened sense of the value of its liberty and also of the essentially secular quality of politics.

Revolt of the *ciompi*

This crisis gave way to a new one in 1378 with the revolt of the *ciompi*, workers in the Florentine wool industry, an event that has usually been interpreted as an uprising of the working class against the business group that had long controlled the government as well as the economy of Florence (and it may be that the recent war, waged in the name of liberty, had aroused some radical democratic ferment). More recently, however, this view has proved incorrect; the true leaders of the Ciompi Revolt, it is now clear, were not workers but disaffected members of the old ruling group itself. They managed to form a new government, with a somewhat more democratic constitution, that retained power until 1382. But the new group was unable to maintain order, and the previous rulers then returned to power in a strengthened position; and, in the period that lay ahead, political power gradually contracted once again. Florence remained in this situation until the end of the 14th century, and the continuation of the same group in control of the government through the first third of the 15th century indicates that the republic had attained a new level of stability. Doubtless, a gradual, though incomplete, economic recovery was helpful. In addition, the brief Florentine experiments with dictatorship and revolution also probably contributed to the stability of the republic. They interrupted the tendency of the merchant oligarchy to abuse its position, displaced groups that had long enjoyed authority, and opened up opportunities for new men to rise into the ruling class. The narrowly oligarchical character of the government remained, but in Florence the oligarchs seemed to have learned something from events and to have developed both a broader understanding of their own interests than elsewhere and greater sensitivity to public needs. Thus, faced with a financial crisis in 1427, the government adopted a new and more equitable form of taxation, based, after a careful survey of individual property, on wealth. In this, they displayed a willingness to assume a major responsibility for the support of the state, instead of shifting it to other and poorer men. It is understandable, therefore, that Florentines remained reasonably united in their support of the state; and their city survived as a republic while many other Italian cities were turning to despotism.

Venice in the 14th century. One other great Italian city remained a republic and for reasons partly similar to those that influenced the history of Florence. This was Venice, in which the domination of a merchant oligarchy was even more complete than in Florence. But in other respects the history of Venice was different. Its rise to economic power was not of recent origin but extended back over many centuries; and its island location, detached from the mainland, freed it from the problem, so troublesome to many other states, of imposing discipline on a disorderly landed nobility. The society of Venice was, therefore, unusually homogeneous, and its ruling patriciate had a tradition of solidarity very different from that of individualistic and turbulent Florence. This solidarity was reflected in the active role of the government in the organization and regulation of all aspects of the Venetian economy. The state built a large part of the Venetian merchant fleet in its Arsenal; it organized and directed the convoys in which Venetians transported their commodities on the seas; it imposed standards on Venetian manufactured goods and inspected them for quality in order to maintain the competitive position of the city. It also regulated prices and wages, for, in Venice, guild organization lacked the strength and independence it had in Florence. The relative internal peace of Venice, so widely admired elsewhere, depended largely on the combination of this solidarity with the great prosperity it produced and in which most Venetians shared, though the tranquillity of Venice, known as the Serenissima, "most serene city," and the high degree of personal freedom that went with it—including a tolerance for Jews, Greek Christians, and even Muslims that shocked contemporaries—were generally attributed to the wise arrangement of its institutions and the rigour and equity of Venetian justice.

Venetian tolerance

Political rights in Venice had been restricted in 1297 to those families at that time sitting in the Great Council. Occasional gestures of discontent with this arrangement were ruthlessly suppressed by the Council of Ten, an agency established early in the 14th century that proved singularly effective throughout the long history of Venice in protecting the established government of the city. Since the Great Council was too large to function as an effective governing body, the chief legislative and policy decisions of the republic were the work of the Senate, a body with great prestige, most of whose members were elected by the Great Council. Despotism from above was avoided by such close restrictions on the doge, the executive head of the state, that he was little more than a figurehead except in times of special crisis. The Venetians tended to choose for this post not vigorous leaders but old men for whom it was a reward for a long career of services to the state.

But the republican institutions of Venice were little threatened from either above or below. Venetian society was united in an immensely profitable commerce with the eastern Mediterranean, in which Venice had long been the chief middleman in meeting the needs of all Europe. Although the 14th century brought an end to the regular movement of Venetian galleys into the Atlantic and northward to England and the Low Countries, Venice remained one of the busiest ports of Europe, and its overland trade through the Alps into central Europe continued to expand. The 14th century also saw the decisive triumph of Venice over Genoa, its great rival in the commerce of the East. A series of wars finally culminated in a great naval victory at Chioggia in 1380. Genoa's fleet was destroyed, and it never fully recovered from the defeat. Relieved of this competition and with the gradual improvement of business, Venice entered, in the earlier 15th century, into perhaps the most prosperous period of its history. Its internal stability owed much to this prosperity.

Venice also differed from the other states of Italy in one crucial respect. It was not a purely Italian power but the possessor of a great empire consisting of a string of commercial bases extending down the east coast of the Adriatic to the islands of the Aegean and including the great island of Cyprus. A good deal of this empire was acquired in the 14th century in the course of the wars with Genoa. Much of the attention of the republic was directed to its administration, for which Venice developed a body of able patrician officials that has been compared with the British colonial service of more recent centuries. And, concerned with the maintenance of this empire on which its trade depended, Venice could not confine its attention, as did the other Italian states, to the Italian peninsula; indeed, throughout most of the 14th

The Venetian empire

century it remained largely aloof from the affairs of the mainland. The main interest of Venice, in fact, was directed to the larger politics of the eastern Mediterranean. This preoccupation became even stronger in the 15th century, when its interests there began to be challenged by the expanding Ottoman Empire. Against this power Venice fought a long series of delaying actions, in which periods of active warfare were regularly interrupted by intervals of peace and friendly commercial intercourse, at which the official conscience of Christendom professed to be scandalized. Self-righteous indignation against Venice on this score, combined with resentment at its detachment from Italian affairs and envy of its wealth, made it from an early point unpopular with other states. At the same time, Venice acquired a singular reputation for political prudence.

The Papal States. Although Milan was a despotism, and Florence and Venice were republics, they were alike in that each was based on a city that, at least in practice, insisted on its absolute independence from any external control. In this respect, the other major political entities of Italy were somewhat different. The Papal States, extending southward from the River Po, across the Apennines from Tuscany, and then cutting across the centre of the peninsula, included a considerable variety of political units. In the north and centre, Emilia and Umbria had a number of major towns, among them Ferrara, Rimini, Bologna, and Perugia. These were similar in important respects to the towns of northern Italy and Tuscany. Ferrara had evolved in the familiar way from a free commune into a relatively stable and well-governed despotism under the Este dukes; because of its location, it tended to fall under the political and cultural influence of Venice. Rimini was taken over by the Malatesta family. Bologna, though remaining nominally a republic, was dominated by the Bentivoglio family. Perugia fell to the Baglioni family. But these communities, whatever their forms of government, also owed obedience to the pope, whose authority over them involved an ambiguous mixture of spiritual and secular claims. And the pope, though often in no position to do so, was constantly concerned to exact from them what he considered due both to himself and to St. Peter.

Much of the central and most of the southern part of the Papal States consisted largely of feudal domains, some of considerable size, whose proprietors were as likely to rebel against papal control as against that of any secular lord. And, in the absence of the papacy during its residence in Avignon, the Papal States, never very firmly ruled by the popes, disintegrated almost completely. The despots in the towns expelled papal officials and ruled in complete independence; since papal taxation had been heavy and papal authority an irritating infringement on local liberty, these actions were often popular. The nobility fought each other, terrorized the countryside, and did as they pleased, and bandits also made the region everywhere unsafe.

Rome in the 14th century

The restiveness of the Papal States extended also to the city of Rome, which in the early 14th century and in the absence of the papal court was little more than a small provincial town, now overshadowed by the ruins of its glorious past. Economically dependent primarily on the exploitation of pilgrims, Rome had for some time been dominated by a struggle for control between the two great families of the Orsini and the Colonna. Rome nevertheless provided, in the mid-14th century, the unlikely setting for a curious attempt, inspired by memories of its past greatness, to restore a republican government that could lead Christendom in a general movement of moral recovery. It was led by a young notary, Cola di Rienzo, who headed a revolution in 1342 in which the great nobles were expelled and a republic established. But, after obtaining papal approval of this action on a visit to Avignon, Rienzo's idealism grew increasingly extravagant. It became gradually apparent that he saw in the rebirth of the Roman Republic the start of a general rebirth of order and virtue in the Western world. He developed an increasingly messianic conception of himself and dispatched letters to the various cities of Italy and to European princes invoking their support for his program of world reform. But his pretensions eventually antagonized the distant pope, and Rienzo lacked political talents of a practical kind. His enemies combined against him: in 1354 he was overthrown and killed, and Rome returned to its old ways. The episode is, nevertheless, instructive for the mood of Italy in the difficult middle decades of the century. It reveals something of the tension, the despair over the condition of Italy and of the world, and the apocalyptic hope for a dramatic change in the spiritual and political climate that agitated the peoples of Italy during this unhappy period.

The turbulence of both Rome and the Papal States provides a partial explanation for the long residence of the papacy in Avignon, in spite of the fervent appeals of such figures as the poet Petrarch and St. Catherine of Siena for the return of the pope to Italy. The pope's absence from his traditional home was a major element in the pessimistic mood of the age. Yet the papal court had never ceased to be concerned with the condition of the Papal States; and, in the decade following the death of Rienzo, Gil Álvarez Carrillo de Albornoz, a Spanish cardinal acting as the pope's legate, began the difficult task of reducing them to obedience by a shrewd mixture of force and diplomacy. By 1377 his successors had made enough progress to permit the pope's return. But this achievement was largely thrown away by the Great Schism of 1378 to 1417. The return of Pope Gregory XI to Rome in January 1377 had been greeted with deep joy in Italy, but the aged pope died early the next year. The cardinals were largely Frenchmen who would have preferred to remain in Avignon, but the Roman populace was determined that the next pope should be an Italian. Accordingly, when the Sacred College assembled for this crucial election, a mob gathered outside their meeting place and threatened violence unless its wishes were met. Under these conditions, the cardinals chose the bishop of Bari, who assumed the name of Urban VI. But, on the ground that this choice had been coerced, a group of dissident French cardinals withdrew to Fondi in the shadow of the French-dominated Kingdom of Naples, held a second election, and chose one of their own number as pope. Calling himself Clement VII, he soon moved back to Avignon, and there were now two popes. Under such circumstances the authority of the Pope in Rome was again seriously weakened. Rebellious elements in the Papal States were able to play off one pope against another and to disregard the claims of both, and the Papal States once again fell apart. Another consequence of this situation was the dependence of the popes in Rome on the support of other Italian powers, at times Naples but, more significantly, Florence. The enmity that had produced the War of the Eight Saints (1375–78) gave way to a close friendship that was all the more needed in Rome, since the rivalry with the French papacy in Avignon was accompanied by periods of tension with the Angevin rulers to the south. Humanist scholars from Florence were now regularly employed at the papal court.

The Great Schism

Naples and Sicily. The history of Naples and Sicily in this period is largely a story of dynastic changes within the framework of a backward and feudalized society. The effective control imposed by the Hohenstaufen emperor Frederick II collapsed after his death, and the habit of rebellion against central authority long encouraged by the papacy made monarchy in both places constantly precarious. Government in both regions has been described as despotism tempered by revolt. The power of great noble families also kept towns in a condition of political inferiority, and for the same reason class distinctions remained strong. Southern Italy experienced little of that mingling of nobles and townsmen so characteristic of society in the north. Thus, the contrast between southern Italy and the urbanized north was even greater than in the case of the Papal States. Yet, because of their dynastic ties with great powers outside Italy, Naples and Sicily regularly played an important part in the affairs of the peninsula.

The union of Naples and Sicily under the French House of Anjou, arranged by the Pope in the 1260s, had ended in 1282 with the popular revolt known as the Sicilian Vespers. Peter III of Aragon was invited to become king of Sicily on the strength of a distant family connection with the Hohenstaufen line, and Sicily was henceforth under Aragonese rule. The Angevins remained, however, in control of the Kingdom of Naples, supported by the popes, whose feudal suzerainty they continued to acknowledge; this connection became even stronger during the residence of the papal court at Avignon. The direct Angevin line ended in 1382 with the death of Queen Joan I; the one positive accomplishment of her disturbed reign had been the recognition of Aragonese rule in Sicily by a treaty of 1372. Her will had named Louis, duc d'Anjou, brother of Charles V of France, as her heir, and this bequest was to be the basis of future French claims to the kingdom. But, with the support of the Pope in Rome in his capacity as feudal overlord of Naples, the will was set aside in favour of a junior branch of the family, represented by Charles of Durazzo, who became King Charles III of Naples. Angevin rule continued until 1435; then, once again, the direct dynastic line was extinguished with the death of Queen Joan II. She, too, tried to pass on the rule of the kingdom to the French House of Anjou, but she had also made an earlier bequest to Alfonso V the Magnanimous, the Aragonese ruler of Sicily, who won control of the kingdom by 1442. Thus, Naples and Sicily, separated for a century and a half, were reunited under a single head. They remained so only until Alfonso's death in 1458, but both regions thereafter remained under different branches of the House of Aragon.

Other Italian states. It has been convenient for historians to portray Italy in the age of the Renaissance largely in terms of Milan, Florence, Venice, the Papal States, and Naples and Sicily. But it should not be forgotten that there were other parts of Italy whose territories were not always and in some cases were never included in these larger entities. Thus, in the northwest Alpine region were the feudalized territories of the House of Savoy, divided into three branches, which ruled Savoy, Vaud, and Piedmont. In view of the future importance of this dynasty for Italian history, it should be noted that Savoy was not yet considered an Italian power, being still oriented to France and Switzerland; and it remained during the 14th and 15th centuries largely apart from Italian affairs. To the south of Piedmont lay Genoa, but, in spite of its commercial power of an earlier age, it, too, especially after its final defeat by Venice, played no great independent part in the political events of the peninsula. Without a surrounding province like that controlled by Florence, Genoa was frequently at the mercy of the more powerful adjacent states, and its external weakness was compounded by its singular internal instability. The struggle for control of its republican government produced frequent revolutions. An effort in 1339 to produce some order in Genoese affairs by instituting a doge, on the Venetian model, proved unavailing. In the summer of 1393, for example, this office changed hands five times. Such turbulence was an invitation to conquest; Genoa fell to the French in 1396 and later to Milan. And, though its citizens were constantly prone to rebellion against foreign rulers, they never developed the civic spirit of the Florentines or the cohesion of the Venetians.

The House of Savoy

Between Milanese-dominated Lombardy and the Venetian lagoons lay another urbanized area that, during the 14th century, preserved an existence separate from that of the great powers in the north. The most important political centres here were Verona, Padua, and Mantua, all republics that had gone the standard way toward despotism in the later 13th and earlier 14th centuries. Mastino Della Scala, a leading citizen of Verona, began the process there, first becoming captain of the people and then securing his independence from the commune by acquiring the title of imperial vicar. This dignity was then passed on to his brother and his nephews. In the 14th century his family was succeeded in the lordship of the city by the Scaligeri, who were notable as patrons of the arts. Paduan republicanism lasted longer: the city gave up its freedom only in 1318, when Jacopo di Carrara became its lord. Mantua had a similar history. Before the end of the 13th century, it had fallen under the control of the Bonacolsi, who remained in power till 1328, when, with some popular support, they were overthrown by Luigi Gonzaga. The firm rule of the latter established his family securely in a control that lasted until the early 18th century.

THE ITALIAN STATES IN THE 15TH CENTURY

Expansion of the major Italian powers. Even the degree of 14th-century Italian political consolidation that makes it possible for historians to present the later history of Italy in terms of the five major powers should not be exaggerated. Some lesser powers, such as the republics of Lucca and Siena, managed to preserve their independence intact, while the coherence of territories subjugated by the major powers remained limited and their stability uncertain. This was notably true in the case of Naples and the Papal States, but it was also often true of the territories gathered together under the rule of Florence; and the conquests of any individual Visconti duke of Milan were always liable to fall apart at his death.

This weakness notwithstanding, there was, in the late 14th and earlier 15th centuries, a significant shift in the interests of the major Italian powers: all, apart from the papacy, now paralyzed by the Schism, sought to expand their territorial authority. As a result, the concern of governments tended to shift from the internal struggles of an earlier period, first to conflicts with neighbouring powers and eventually to wars on a larger, sometimes peninsular scale. This was as true of the republics as it was of the despotic states. Florence, its commercial expansion inhibited by an inland location, sought a seaport on the western coast. This was the reason for its conquest of Pisa in 1406, and the addition of Livorno (Leghorn) by purchase from Genoa in 1421 gave it full control of the Tuscan coastline. By the next year the first Florentine galleys were heading directly to the Levant and soon thereafter to the European Atlantic ports.

Territorial expansion

Meanwhile, Venice had been abandoning its long isolation from the mainland and decided to conquer and organize for itself a substantial dependent state. Its motives were twofold. First, it needed to make secure its overland trade routes, which meant that it could no longer countenance the existence of a strong and hostile power between the head of the Adriatic and the passes through the Alps. Second, it required a nearby agricultural province under its own permanent control as a source of food, especially since Turkish conquests had made imports of grain from the Black Sea increasingly uncertain. The danger that Milan might move into the territories adjacent to the Venetian lagoons also impelled Venice to act. In the first decades of the 15th century it conquered the lands of the tyrants of Verona and Padua, who had been levying heavy duties on Venetian goods passing through their territories and occasionally actually cutting off Venetian food supplies. The wisdom of these conquests was long debated in Venice, whose power had so long been based rather on the sea than the land; although it now had its own farms and had achieved secure access to the northern passes, the results were not altogether advantageous. Venice was henceforth far more involved in the political struggles of Italy, with new responsibilities and new demands on its resources. And its new conquests on the mainland further antagonized other powers already alarmed by its vast wealth. Before long, charges would be heard that Venice aimed to conquer the whole of Italy —indeed, to establish an empire over all Europe.

At the same time, the broadening of its contacts with the rest of Italy brought Venice into closer contact with the cultural movements of the Renaissance. Up to this time it had remained a self-centred, materialistic, and culturally backward community of merchants. But the conquest of Padua gave it control of the liveliest university centre in Italy, and its ablest young men proceeded to take full advantage of the new opportunities that this presented. Educated at the University of Padua, they brought back literary and scientific interests to Venice. By the later 15th century, aided by its overseas contacts with the Greek East and above all by its development as a major printing centre, Venice had become the capital of Greek learning in Europe as well as a point of diffusion for the Latin classics. Meanwhile, leading painters from the mainland had begun to visit the city, and Venetian painters began to absorb new ideas and to develop a Venetian school of Renaissance art.

The crisis of Florentine republicanism. For the time being, however, the greatest danger to the peace of Italy and the independence of other powers was Visconti Milan, especially under Gian Galeazzo, created duke of Milan by the German king Wenceslas in 1395. His conquests had played some part in influencing Venice to expand onto the mainland, but he posed a particular threat to Florence. Indeed, because of its central location on the Italian peninsula, Florence found itself regularly confronting aggressive princes seeking expansion from either the north or the south. It had been particularly alarmed by the conquests of Gian Galeazzo, who expanded his empire steadily southward after 1385, taking special advantage of the disarray of the Papal States during these years of the Schism. By 1400 he had gathered in much of the northern domains of the popes, and Lucca, Pisa, and Siena had accepted his lordship; Bologna fell to his armies in 1402. He seemed invincible, and Florence—next in his path and fighting alone—appeared doomed. Florence was immediately saved by his unexpected death in 1402, but this did not end the danger from Milan. Gian Galeazzo's younger son, Filippo Maria Visconti, attempted to reassemble the Milanese empire after 1420. Once again, Florence was in danger of conquest by a despot, though this time it did not fight entirely alone: in 1425 it concluded an alliance against Milan with Venice, its sister republic, and the threat was once more contained. This alliance was also decisive for Venice; henceforth, it would play an active part in the larger affairs of

Milanese conquests

From W. Shepherd, *Historical Atlas*, Harper & Row, Publishers (Barnes & Noble Books), New York, revision Copyright © 1964 by Barnes & Noble, Inc.

Italy in the 15th century and (inset) Florentine expansion.

Italy. Meanwhile, during the interval between the two onslaughts from Milan, another danger to Florence had come from the opposite direction. King Ladislas of Naples also saw in the troubles of the Papal States an opportunity for his ambitions. Early in the 15th century he began to meddle in their affairs, and in 1404 a popular revolt in Rome—encouraged by him—forced the Pope to turn to him for protection. In this way he succeeded in dominating the Papal States, and from this base he twice sent his armies into Tuscany, in 1408–09 and 1412–14.

On each separate occasion the Florentines had professed to see in the threat to themselves an attempt to subjugate the whole of Italy under a single ruler. Doubtless, they exaggerated both the intentions of the conqueror and the possibility that this might be accomplished. Neither Ladislas nor the Visconti dukes seem to have intended to assemble more than a strong regional state, and their resources were certainly inadequate for the control of the large, diverse, and divided Italian peninsula. Nevertheless, the long period of danger to the independence of Florence coincided with the emergence among its citizens of a new political mentality.

Hans Baron, a historian of the Italian Renaissance, has argued that this crisis of Florentine liberty, especially in its most acute phase, between 1400 and 1402, was the major watershed between an age still essentially medieval and the beginnings of a characteristically modern intellectual and political culture. Basing his argument on the chronology of a series of significant Florentine documents, Baron shows that before 1400 most thoughtful Florentines, wearied by constant disorder, had often longed, like medieval thinkers such as Dante, for a strong autocratic government that could preserve the peace of the state and allow them to devote themselves to the private satisfactions of a contemplative life. Already enthusiastic students of the classics, they had, like other medieval men, idealized the benevolent despotism of imperial Rome; their hero was Caesar, who had overthrown the disorderly republic. But now, faced with the loss of their liberty and the prospect of absorption into a larger despotic state, they became increasingly conscious of their heritage of republican freedom and the human values it fostered. Thus, the Humanists of Florence, led by Leonardo Bruni (1369–1444), began to praise the human values of freedom and the obligations of active citizenship. They found their model now in the Roman Republic, in which medieval thinkers had taken little interest, and they applauded not Caesar but Brutus and Cassius, who had assassinated him in the name of liberty. In this way, the citizens of Florence began to formulate a new political ideal of peculiar importance for the future of politics. In addition, conscious, through their awakened love for Florence, of its special identity, they began to consider its development in time; and from this crisis of embattled Florence there emerged the rich tradition of Florentine historiography.

Florentine historiography

The histories composed by Bruni and his successors, in a long series of works that reached a climax with Niccolò Machiavelli and Francesco Guicciardini in the next century, reveal the importance of the contribution of Italy in this period, and especially of Florence, to the formation of modern political attitudes. They exhibit two characteristics hardly present before in the European mind. One is the assumption that historical development proceeds through a succession of natural causes, with the implication that these may be understood by men and to some degree controlled by intelligent and well-informed action. But, perhaps even more important, these historical writings also express a feeling for the particular political community as a concrete and continuing entity that is independent of the men and governments in power at any given time and worthy of human affection, loyalty, and support. In this sense, the historical experience of Italy helped to bring modern consciousness of the state and modern patriotism to birth.

There has been a good deal of resistance to Baron's understanding of the significance of the Florentine experience. Some of it has come out of a reluctance to attribute any major shift in fundamental attitudes to a particular set of episodes concentrated within a very few years. It has also been argued that Baron's dating of the documents is wrong or that the Humanists who gave such eloquent expression to Florentine ideals were only paid propagandists who had no personal commitment to what they wrote. But Baron's case has largely withstood these attacks, and there has been no convincing alternative explanation for the remarkable power of Florentine political and historical thought.

The Papal States in the 15th century. During the 15th century, substantial changes took place in the domains of the pope, following the settlement of the Schism in 1417. Once again the papacy was faced with the difficult task of restoring order in possessions that had fallen apart. And now the difficulties were even more serious. Despots once more controlled the major towns of the Papal States; *condottieri*, mercenary leaders, were carving out principalities for themselves; and, meanwhile, other powers on the peninsula were constantly fishing in these troubled waters. The successes of Gian Galeazzo Visconti had been facilitated by papal weakness, and Milan remained a potential danger. Venice was extending its sphere of influence southward toward Ferrara, one of the more independent towns of the papal domain. There was constant friction along the borders of the Florentine state, and the continuing tension between Anjou and Aragon in the south was a matter of regular concern to the pope. He had also to keep an eye on the possibility of further republican uprisings in Rome. Nevertheless, Martin V (1417–31) made a substantial beginning toward the recovery of papal authority, and his successor Eugenius IV (1431–47) continued the process. Eugenius' decision in 1442 to recognize Alfonso of Aragon as king of Naples, although it resulted in a cooling of papal friendship with Florence, strengthened the security of the Papal States; and by the middle of the century the pope had enough real power to be treated as an equal among the princes of Italy.

But much remained to be done, and control over their Italian domains remained a problem for the popes throughout the century. Even the great Pius II (1458–64), though primarily concerned with restoring papal authority in all Europe and organizing a crusade against the Turks, was forced to devote a large share of his time to the rule of the Papal States, raising armies and negotiating alliances against his own rebellious subjects. Notable among these was the notorious Sigismondo Malatesta, tyrant of Rimini, who was at last brought to obedience, though even he had to be left in possession of that town with the title of papal vicar. Popes of the later 15th century also made use of members of their own families, especially vigorous young nephews, to control their possessions. Unlike most local nobles, such men could be trusted to obey the pope, although the practice led to charges of nepotism that increased the discontent of religious reformers. Sixtus IV (1471–84) was particularly given to nepotism; thus, he made his nephew Piero Riario a cardinal at the age of 25. Meanwhile, the ambitions of such relatives of the pope to carve out territories for themselves also promoted the recovery of papal control. But the task moved slowly, though it received impetus through the conquests of Cesare Borgia, the illegitimate son of Pope Alexander VI (1492–1503).

Papal nepotism

The despotisms of the 15th century. Although dynasties changed, the internal histories of the despotic states of Italy were little different in the 15th century from what they had been in the 14th. The reign of Alfonso I the Magnanimous nevertheless gave southern Italy after 1442 a period of unusual strength. Not only did he rule over both Naples and Sicily, which were thus reunited for the first time in a century and a half; he was also, as Alfonso V, king of Aragon and thus a power in the whole western Mediterranean. Strengthened by papal recognition, he was sought as an ally by the other princes of Italy. He also displayed a personal dignity, an interest in Renaissance culture that made Naples briefly a major centre for literature and the arts, and a strength of character long absent among the rulers in the south. But on his death in 1458 his possessions were divided. Aragon and Sicily went to his brother John, the Kingdom of Naples to his legitimized bastard Ferrante (Ferdinand I; 1458–94) and subsequently to Ferrante's son Alfonso II. This division once more left the kingdom in its earlier state of weakness. In addition, Ferrante proved treacherous, cruel, and incompetent, so that his more powerful subjects, always close to revolt, thought again of resurrecting the old claims of the French House of Anjou.

The new Sforza rulers of Milan behaved much like the Visconti had done. Achieving power in 1450, Francesco Sforza was an able ruler who conquered Genoa in 1463 and meanwhile cultivated closer relations with France; he dispatched his son, Galeazzo Maria, to aid Louis XI in his war against the rebellious French nobility. But Galeazzo Maria, duke of Milan from 1466 to 1476, lacked his father's competence. Cruel and tyrannical, he was assassinated by a group of republican conspirators, although republican sentiment was generally dead in Milan after so long a period of princely control. The assassination was therefore not followed by a popular uprising, and the infant son of the dead duke, Gian Galeazzo II, succeeded his father under the regency of his mother. But the nominal rule of a minor under a female regent was too precarious to survive. In 1480 the young duke's uncle, the ambitious Lodovico il Moro, with the support of both the Pope and the French king, managed to seize control of the ducal government, displacing the boy's mother as regent. Given the unscrupulous habits of the age, this was ominous for Gian Galeazzo II.

Florence under the Medici. While the Papal States were being centralized, and princely government was entrenching itself further in southern Italy and Milan, republicanism was also faring less well in Florence, which, under the concealed dictatorship of the Medici, tended to become increasingly like the despotisms of the peninsula. The old Florentine oligarchy, led by Rinaldo degli Albizzi, had prepared the way for this development by its own ineptitude; between 1429 and 1433 it had failed disastrously in another (and unpopular) attempt to conquer Lucca. This project had been opposed by Cosimo de' Medici (the Elder), a prominent banker of the city, who had made what seemed to the old ruling families a dangerous appeal for popular support, and they had accordingly sent him into exile. But, discredited by defeat, the oligarchy was overthrown in 1434, and Cosimo returned in triumph to assume control of Florentine affairs. He remained a private citizen, however, governing Florence more like a modern big-city political boss than a Renaissance tyrant. The election of officials loyal to himself was assured by eliminating his opponents from the lists of those eligible for office, although the forms of republican government were retained. Initially a popular choice to control the government, Cosimo continued to command broad public support. He maintained order; the lavish expenditures from his private fortune on the patronage of literature, the arts, and especially architecture made him popular with the Florentines; and his ability to keep Florence at peace after so many years of warfare particularly endeared him to the public. In spite of this popularity, however, his dominance saw the beginning of a significant shift in the political climate of the city. Government by an active and concerned citizenry gradually gave way to rule through a bureaucracy responsible only to Cosimo and his successors. The Humanist Leonardo Bruni, now chancellor of the republic, spent much of his later years reading Plato instead of celebrating the benefits of republican freedom.

Cosimo de'Medici (the Elder)

Florentine republicanism was by no means dead, and the indirect nature and tact of Medici rule was a tribute to the continuing vitality of the old republican tradition. Indeed, Cosimo understood that he could disregard it only at his peril. The old families that had previously controlled Florence were constantly restive, and Cosimo felt the need to send some of their leaders into exile. Republican sentiment also gave support to occasional conspiracies against Medici rule. When Cosimo died in 1464, the leadership of Florence passed to his son Piero (1464–69), despite an abortive attempt to restore popular control by a return to free elections. Two years later the republican enemies of the Medici struck at them in the Pitti Conspiracy. But its failure left the Medici more firmly in power than before, and on Piero's death the government was inherited by his young sons, Lorenzo and Giuliano.

Once again an opportunity seemed to present itself for a return to the old order in the city. Enmity had been growing between Florence and the papacy of Sixtus IV over lands claimed both by Florence and by one of the Pope's nephews. It reached a climax in a plot involving both Rome and the enemies of the Medici in Florence, under the leadership of the Pazzi family. In 1478 the conspirators attempted to assassinate both the Medici brothers during a mass in the cathedral of Florence. Giuliano was stabbed to death, but Lorenzo escaped and henceforth ruled alone; meanwhile, Medici partisans hanged the conspirators in the streets, among them the Archbishop of Florence. To revenge this sacrilege, the Pope excommunicated Lorenzo, placed the city under an interdict, and declared war, in which he was joined by his vassal Ferrante (Ferdinand I) of Naples. But at this juncture Lorenzo carried out a sudden diplomatic coup. He made a quick personal visit to Naples, where he persuaded Ferrante to abandon the papal alliance and sign a treaty of friendship with Florence. The crisis was finally resolved with Lorenzo's public apology to the Pope, and matters proceeded as before. Under Lorenzo, known as the Magnificent as much for his personal style as for a patronage of learning and the arts that exceeded even the generosity of his grandfather, the rule of the Medici resumed its development toward something resembling the princely governments elsewhere in Italy. Lorenzo married into the aristocratic Orsini family of Rome, in an alliance that symbolized the acceptance of the Medici by the great nobles of Italy; and, as his negotiation with Ferrante illustrates, he was able to deal on equal terms with other princes. Yet even at this point the rule of the Medici differed from that of the naked despots elsewhere. Lorenzo continued to respect republican institutions even as he controlled them, and it is significant that much of the power of the family, as well as its ability to dazzle Florentines by its generous support of culture, depended on profits from the wide business interests of the Medici. Cosimo had been an astute businessman as well as a politician; and Lorenzo kept a hand in the extensive enterprises of the Medici bank, although, distracted from full attention to business by his political and cultural activities, he allowed too much freedom to the managers in his branches throughout Europe. (The imprudence of the latter led to the decline of the firm, and later representatives of the family were compelled to depend on other sources of income.) But, meanwhile, the ties between Florentine business activity and government persisted, and this helps to explain continuing support for the Medici. In addition, dread of the inconveniences that would arise from further violent changes in government also contributed to their support. Florence had experienced enough disruption in the past, and a sense of relief at the maintenance of order at home and peace abroad, both attributed to Medici rule, worked against further change. Later Florentines would look back on the period of Medici domination as a golden age of prosperity and tranquillity.

The plot against the Medici

Venice in the 15th century. Only Venice, among the great powers in 15th-century Italy, remained true to the substance as well as the forms of its republican constitution, though Venetian society, too, displayed significant changes after the conquests on the mainland. For its wealthier families began a process, which would accelerate in the next century, of withdrawal from the city to newly acquired estates on the mainland, and this group began to develop a way of life similar to that of the ruling groups elsewhere. Meanwhile, the relative equality of the patriciate gave way to an increasingly wide division between poor nobles and a few rich, powerful, and increasingly aristocratic families. Discontent was still kept in check, however, by the general prosperity of this period and by an effective system of poor relief and other social services. Moreover, as Venice came more regularly

The rise of Venetian republicanism

into contact with the other Italian powers, its ruling group showed signs of an increasingly self-conscious republicanism that contrasted strikingly with the eclipse of republican sentiment in Florence. Complacent and secure, Venice had been backward, compared with Florence, in the development of an articulate political culture. But by the middle of the 15th century Venetians were beginning to celebrate the virtues of their republican constitution, which they interpreted as explaining the remarkable stability of Venetian life, in contrast to the turbulence common to the rest of Italy. These discussions eventually culminated in Gasparo Contarini's *De magistratibus et republica Venetorum* (1543; "Concerning the Magistrates and the Republic of the Venetians"), an early classic of republican and constitutional thought that was widely read throughout Europe. About the middle of the century Venetians also began to take an interest in the history of their own city somewhat similar to that displayed by the Florentines of an earlier generation. The Venetian histories of Marc'Antonio Sabellico and Bernardo Giustiniani marked the beginning of a long and distinguished tradition of Venetian political historiography. During the same period Venice also began its development as a major centre of European artistic and musical life; here, too, it had earlier been remarkably backward. The optimism of this period in the history of the Venetian Republic was only slightly disturbed by occasional wars with the Turks, although the struggle of 1463–70 resulted in the loss of the island of Euboea (modern Evvoia), in the Aegean; Argos, in the Peloponnese; and Scutari (modern Shkodër, Albania).

Changes in Italian society. Centralization in the Papal States, the long continuation of princely rule in other parts of Italy, and Medici rule in Florence were together bringing profound if gradual changes to Italian society. Habits of dependence on despotic princes became ever more deeply engrained, court ceremonial became increasingly formal, class divisions became more and more rigid, and the way of life of the ruling circles gathered around princes was increasingly differentiated from that of other men. A culture of citizens was slowly being transformed into a culture of courtiers. Men increasingly developed a personal style appropriate for those attendant upon princes, who spent much of their time on country estates and who often cultivated the extravagant ways and even the physical skills of an earlier nobility. Baldassare Castiglione's treatise on courtly manners, *Il cortegiano* (1528), gave eloquent expression to this new human ideal, so different from that of the republican citizen. It has been argued that the social and political changes of later 15th-century Italy therefore prepared the way for the reception of Italian influence at the great royal courts of western Europe in the 16th century.

Italy as a political system. Meanwhile, the conflicting interests of the increasingly consolidated major states of Italy kept them in close contact with each other, and during the 15th century Italy exhibited many of the features of a miniature international system, the workings of which have long fascinated historians. Some scholars have seen in this system a significant anticipation of the modern principle of the balance of power, a persistent theme in later international relations. Indeed, by the end of the century, Italian observers of the shifting political scene were explicitly using the language of equilibrium to describe its workings. There is also general agreement that the states of Italy first worked out the principles and the machinery of diplomatic practice that have ever since governed international relations.

The emergence of Italy as a kind of system based on the five major powers was possible only after it had become clear that none of them was, in fact, strong enough to absorb the others. Yet even the dangers of Visconti expansion of Milanese territory had led, in the first half of the 15th century, to the creation of a fairly clear alignment of powers: Florence and Venice joined in a republican alliance against Milan, while the Visconti, after Aragonese rulers replaced the Florence-oriented Angevins in the south, found support in Naples.

The alignment became even clearer, though on a somewhat different basis, after the middle of the century. When Francesco Sforza seized power in Milan in 1450, he promptly became embroiled with Venice, which had taken advantage of the preceding period of confusion in Milan to seize some minor territories on the border. At this point Cosimo de' Medici, persuaded that the growing power of Venice was beginning to pose an even greater danger to the interests of Florence than the aggressions of Milan, abruptly switched alliances by supporting the new despot of Milan. The shift may also be taken as a symptom of the decline of republicanism in Florence; with the triumph of the Medici, the differences between Florence and Milan were less important, although the alliance with Milan was unpopular with many of Cosimo's subjects. The diplomatic revolution was completed when Venice turned to Naples, and general war seemed near when Pope Nicholas V intervened as peacemaker. After taking Constantinople in 1453, the Turks seemed poised to invade Italy; and it was also possible that France might intervene in Milan on the basis of claims arising from the marriage of Gian Galeazzo Visconti's daughter Valentina with Louis de France, duc d'Orléans, in 1389. Pope Nicholas V therefore managed to persuade the Italian states of the necessity for mending their differences so that they could present some common front to the outside world. The result was the Peace of Lodi in 1454, in which the coup of Francesco Sforza was recognized by all, and peace was maintained on the basis of the new balance, which aligned Florence and Milan against Venice and Naples, with the papacy as a kind of counterweight. This peace managed a precarious survival for the next 40 years, although imperilled again and again as one state or other attempted to secure particular advantages.

The Peace of Lodi

The result was a series of crises of increasing gravity, which have sometimes been compared with those in the 20th century that brought Europe closer and closer to both world wars. They were so serious because it was increasingly apparent that Italy was not alone in Europe and that great outside powers were more and more inclined to intervene in its affairs. And there were pretexts enough. The Spanish House of Aragon and the French House of Anjou were still rivals for the control of southern Italy, and France had old claims on Milan. Thus, the crises among the Italian states not only illustrated the weakness and division of the peninsula but were bound to invite the attention and ultimately the intervention of outside forces of far greater strength.

The first crisis came four years after the Peace of Lodi. On the death of Alfonso the Magnanimous in 1458, Pope Calixtus III (1455–58), incited by Francesco Sforza (who, in turn, was trying to strengthen his own position by promoting the interests of his French allies against his Aragonese enemies), was disposed not to recognize the accession of Ferrante on the ground that an illegitimate son could not inherit the Kingdom of Naples. This brief crisis was ended, however, by the Pope's death. Pius II, his successor, alarmed by the possibility of a French intervention in Naples, recognized Ferrante as king. But in 1460 an even more serious situation developed. An expeditionary force, representing the interest of the Angevin claimant René and based on Milanese-controlled Genoa, invaded the Neapolitan kingdom; with the help of some of Ferrante's own perennially rebellious subjects, it won a series of early victories. Ferrante was saved this time by the arrival of mercenaries from Albania and a revolt in Genoa, and by 1464 the Angevin forces had given up and returned home. But Naples was not the only area of danger. In 1467 a famous *condottiere*, Bartolomeo Colleoni, attempted to carve out a state in northern Italy at the expense of Florence and Milan. Long in the service of Venice, he had probably received Venetian encouragement. But his ambitions were blocked by a rival army under Federigo of Urbino, and the otherwise indecisive battle of Molinella put an end to his hopes.

Even more serious was the Florentine Pazzi Conspiracy against Lorenzo de' Medici in 1478, which, given the alignments of the peninsula, had serious implications for

The Florentine Pazzi Conspiracy

the general peace. Lorenzo's success in detaching Ferrante of Naples from the Pope averted general war. A further factor in inducing the Pope to make peace with Florence was the Turkish seizure of Otranto, in the south of Italy, a move that was taken by contemporaries as a preparation for a larger Turkish effort to conquer the peninsula. After 1480, Venetian ambitions led to still another crisis. A quarrel had broken out between Venice and the city of Ferrara over the control of salt production in the northern Adriatic. Ferrara was supported by Naples, Florence, and Milan, all alarmed by the growing power of the Venetians. Venice was backed by the Pope, who wanted to assert his authority over Ferrara, and by Genoa, again revolting against Milanese control. In the course of the ensuing war, troops from Naples and Florence invaded the Papal States. Partly for this reason but partly because he was himself uneasy over Venetian victories in the north, Pope Sixtus IV switched sides. Nevertheless, although now fighting almost the whole of Italy, Venice did well enough to keep some of its conquests when peace was made at Bagnolo in 1484. The most alarming aspect of this episode, however, was the interest in the war displayed by outside powers, an interest that Venice had encouraged. At their moment of greatest danger, the Venetians had tried to attract the new French king, Charles VIII, who had also personally inherited the claims of Anjou to Naples, to invade Italy; and they had promised him their help in the conquest of Naples. Meanwhile, King Ferdinand II of Aragon was negotiating with both sides. Conflicts within Italy were clearly providing increasing temptations to the great monarchies of western Europe.

There were obviously, therefore, serious weaknesses in the workings of the Italian system. Its individual members had no dependable sense of the common interest; Italy was for them, quite literally, only a geographical expression. Indeed, even particular states were badly served by the political situation. The interests of dynasties too often took precedence over the needs of their peoples and certainly over the interests of Italy as a whole. But, above all, the Italian system was not self-contained. Insecure, disgruntled, or ambitious elements in Italy tended regularly to look for support outside. However novel the political history of Italy may have been in some respects during this period, therefore, and however suggestive for the future of European political development, its modernity should not be exaggerated.

Yet, if the Italian states did not entirely anticipate the later conduct of international relations by means of a balance of power, there is no doubt about the contribution of Italy to the techniques of diplomacy. The articulation of Italy into a group of self-consciously independent states that ignored their theoretical unity in a larger Christian commonwealth—whether under pope or emperor—had prepared the way for this development, since diplomacy in the modern sense can be conducted only by fully sovereign states. The needs of commerce and the feverish political actions of the 14th and 15th centuries had impelled the various Italian powers to create suitable instruments for dealing with other powers: foreign offices staffed by able men, which collected information, kept records, and carried on an extensive correspondence; and, above all, a system of permanent ambassadors residing in foreign capitals, commissioned to report on conditions abroad and to negotiate on behalf of the states they represented. The diplomatic machinery developed by Venice was particularly efficient, though it was by no means unique. Venetian ambassadors were carefully chosen for regular three-year terms and periodically transferred from one place to another. Their duties remarkably anticipated those of modern diplomats. They received detailed instructions on being sent abroad; they were expected to maintain a high standard of living, in keeping with the dignity of the republic; they entertained and paid ceremonial visits; and they prepared elaborate dispatches and reports, which are still today among the historian's richest sources of information about all aspects of European society for several centuries. In its development of standards for diplomacy and international communication in a new political world composed of sovereign states, 14th- and 15th-century Italy served as a model for the rest of Europe.

The French invasion. No diplomatic skills, however, could save Italy from the consequences of its weaknesses, which in the end brought about the long-impending tragedy of foreign invasion that was largely to end the independence of the Italian peoples until the 19th century. In the last decade of the 15th century Lodovico il Moro, uncle to the legitimate Sforza duke of Milan, was eager to take the place of his nephew, whom he held a virtual prisoner. The young duke, however, had recently married the granddaughter of Ferrante of Naples, Isabella of Aragon, who in 1490 gave birth to a son. The disposition of the Milanese duchy was now of direct concern to Naples. To solve his personal dilemma, Lodovico, oblivious to the larger interests of Italy, invited the French into the peninsula, in the expectation that they would deal with his enemies in the south and thus open the way to his assumption of the ducal title in Milan.

Charles VIII's ambition

Charles VIII of France was attracted to Italy by various considerations. In addition to the French claims to lordship over both Naples and Milan (which latter claim Lodovico had chosen to forget), he seems to have been influenced by the medieval ideal of a mission for the French nation, on behalf of all Christendom, to set Italy to rights and purify the church; from Italy he dreamed of then leading a crusade against the Turks. Among his advisers, most of whom had more material ambitions, was Cardinal Giuliano della Rovere, a disappointed candidate in the recent papal election and an enemy of Alexander VI. And spiritual impulses emanating from Italy itself may have encouraged such ideals. Lorenzo the Magnificent had died in 1492 and was succeeded by his less competent son Piero. In these circumstances a republican reaction again gathered in Florence and found a leader in the Dominican friar Girolamo Savonarola (1452–98). A powerful and demagogic preacher of repentance, Savonarola began by denouncing the wickedness of his times, daring even to include the Medici rulers in his indictment; he predicted terrible catastrophes as a result of God's wrath on Italy; and he called for reforms that, as became increasingly clear, involved the restoration of the Florentine republic on a basis more democratic than had ever before been established in the history of the city. Since he also strongly denounced the Pope, it is not surprising that Alexander VI (1492–1503) soon became one of Savonarola's greatest enemies. A member of the Spanish Borgia family, Alexander was shameless in exploiting his papal office to promote its interests; and at the same time he was particularly aggressive in imposing his authority over the Papal States, a task for which he was employing his natural son Cesare. Against this—to contemporaries—scandalous pontiff, who eventually excommunicated him, as well as against the more general wickedness of Italy, Savonarola called for the intervention of a foreign "scourge of God," whose invasion and chastisement of Italy would open a new age of righteousness.

Lodovico had probably hoped that the mere threat of French invasion would be enough to deter his Aragonese enemies but that, if it did come, it would move by sea from Genoa; and, indeed, Charles VIII prepared a fleet there under the Duc d'Orléans. But the main thrust of his attack, coordinated with a revolt of pro-French forces in the Kingdom of Naples under Antonello Sanseverino, prince of Salerno, was by land. His army, 30,000 strong, which included Balkan, Swiss, and German mercenaries, as well as heavy artillery of a kind not before used in Italy, entered the peninsula through Milanese territory in October 1494. This development was shortly followed by the death of the young duke Gian Galeazzo, perhaps by poison, and Lodovico was promptly proclaimed duke.

The reaction of the rest of Italy was irresolute and nicely illustrates the failure of the various powers to consider the larger interests of the peninsula. Venice remained entirely aloof, while Florence and the papacy wavered before siding with Naples (and even then they offered only token resistance). Meanwhile, the French advance down the peninsula was rapid. The forces of the few Italian *condottieri* that presented themselves to resist the French were used to a less aggressive style of warfare and quickly collapsed. Soon after the middle of November 1494, Charles had reached Florence. From there he proceeded quickly to Rome, where the Pope promptly came to terms with him in a treaty that allowed the French unhindered passage through the Papal States, and by February 1495 he was in possession of the city of Naples. The rest of the Neapolitan kingdom had rapidly fallen to pro-French forces, in spite of Alfonso II's abdication in favour of his more popular son Ferrantino; and the French king was able to take possession without fighting a major battle.

Florence under Savonarola

The consequences of these events were especially momentous for Florence. Discredited by his oscillations and then by a policy of cooperation with the invader, which involved the surrender of important Tuscan strongholds to the French, Piero was overthrown and fled from the city during a revolt that left Florence under the leadership of Savonarola. The Friar then proclaimed the restoration of the republic and sponsored a new constitution, more democratic than Florence had ever known. At first the new regime was immensely popular. It was accompanied by a wave of patriotic and moral fervour marked by dramatic renunciations of the vanities of Renaissance culture and by an enforced purity of manners that briefly transformed Florence into a city of saints regarding itself as a model for the reform of all Christendom. But the extravagances of Savonarola's program, his excommunication by the Pope, and the inability of the new government to recover Pisa, which had with French support rebelled against Florentine rule, led to growing opposition against Savonarola. Eventually he fell from power and was executed in 1498, though the reconstituted republic continued in existence.

But meanwhile the French were running into difficulties. Their economic and political exploitation of Naples and their brutality proved that the new master was no improvement over the old. Revolts, encouraged by the former Aragonese rulers who had taken refuge in Sicily, had broken out even before Charles started back to France. Even more serious, for the rest of Italy as well as for the French king, was the intervention of Ferdinand II the Catholic, king of Aragon. This had both diplomatic and military aspects. Encouraged by Ferdinand, the states of Italy (with the exception of Florence, whose external affairs remained under French control) at last recognized the need for solidarity. At the end of March, the Pope, Venice, and Milan joined the Spanish king and the German emperor in the League of Venice. Its general purpose was the defense of Italy against aggression, its immediate aim the expulsion of the French. But the adherence of Spain and the empire brought these powers, as well as the French, now regularly into the politics of the peninsula; it meant that, henceforth, Italy would no longer be able to control its own affairs.

The league immediately put an army into the field, which met the returning French forces early in July 1495 in the Battle of Fornovo. Although the Italians on this occasion fought well, the French were able to continue their retreat from the peninsula, and both sides claimed victory. But, in the meantime, Aragonese forces had been recovering control of Naples. With the surrender of the French garrison that Charles had left behind, less than a year later nothing remained of the French conquests but an unhappy legacy of intervention that, in the next generation, ended the independence and the liberty of the peoples of Italy until the movement of national unification in the 19th century. A major chapter in the history of Italy had ended.

THE LESSONS OF HISTORY

Machiavelli. The effort to define the significance of this chapter in Italian history, at once so full of promise and in the end so tragic, has been a major concern of European historians of all subsequent generations. It began immediately in the writings of Niccolò Machiavelli, who, born in 1469, had lived through many of the disasters that were to spell the end of the freedom of Italy and, out of an intense patriotism, was concerned to understand their causes. His analysis is of particular interest since it reflects the experience of a direct and highly sophisticated participant in major events. Machiavelli had served as a diplomat and secretary in the restored Florentine Republic after the downfall of Savonarola. When the Medici were reinstated in 1512, he lost his official position; and while in retirement he set down his reflections on history and politics in a number of famous works, particularly *The Prince*, the *Discourses on Livy*, and the *History of Florence*. The first of these consists of advice to a ruler on how to secure absolute control over a state, together with a celebrated "Exhortation to Liberate Italy from the Barbarians"; the second includes eloquent passages on the superiority of a republic over all other forms of government, while the third seems not to achieve any definite conclusion. Historians have, therefore, long discussed the mutual relationship of these works, their apparent inconsistency, and the extent to which each may represent Machiavelli's true thought. It may be, however, that their apparent contradictions really indicate his uncertainties about the proper course of action in a bewildering and disorderly world. In any case, these works are instructive as an early effort to evaluate the troubled political history of Italy in the 14th and 15th centuries, for the remedies they prescribe for the maladies of the peninsula, and for their usefulness in revealing the importance of Italian history in the development of the European political understanding.

The Prince

Contemplating the past disorders of Italy, its present vulnerability to foreign intervention, and perhaps most directly the recent instability of his own beloved Florence, Machiavelli saw clearly that something had gone seriously wrong. Comparison with other, more successful polities, especially with the Roman Republic, helped him to identify the trouble. The Italians of the 14th and 15th centuries, he decided, had failed to preserve the political virtues, the decisiveness, and the sense of civic responsibility that had so long characterized the Romans and accounted for their political effectiveness. Their religious fervour, the most effective of social bonds, had declined and for this he blamed the intrusions of the papacy into politics. Since the early Middle Ages, he noted, popes had regularly invited foreigners into the peninsula to serve their own political ends; the result had been both the degradation of the spiritual power and the weakness and disunity of Italy. Furthermore, the rulers of Italy had employed unreliable mercenary armies to do their fighting instead of creating loyal citizen armies; hence, military power in Italy had been too decadent to oppose the challenge from without. And their failures of leadership and their struggles with one another had opened the peninsula to invasion.

Machiavelli's cyclic view of history

Machiavelli then turned to a consideration of possible remedies. Although he considered a republic superior to all other types of government, experience had made him a pessimist. Looking back on what had happened to republics in the past, he developed a view of history according to which the selfishness of men will regularly subvert the state, reduce it to chaos, and require strong and ruthless leadership to set it to rights again. This cycle would recur again and again, human nature never changing, and it seemed obvious to him that in his own time Italy was passing through the most disorderly phase of the political cycle, in which the most urgently needed quality was leadership. These views are probably the explanation for the republican author's flirtation with the idea of a tyrant: an extraordinary problem required extraordinary measures, perhaps even the most cynical and brutal actions, for the restoration of political health. If successful at home, moreover, the prince might be able to organize a general Italian effort to expel the barbarians, though it seems unlikely that Machiavelli, a Florentine to the core, envisaged the formation of a united Italian state. In the long run, however, the prince would play his proper role in the historical cycle if, through sound laws and wise discipline, he prepared his subjects for the restoration of an effective republic—the only kind of political organization capable, Machiavelli believed, of the greatest achievements. Notable here, too, however, is a degree of hope that suggests the inadequacy in his grasp of the contrast between the resources of Italy and the vast power of the French and Spanish monarchies. It was already much too late for such reforms as Machiavelli dreamed of.

Implicit in Machiavelli's reflections are attitudes toward politics that demonstrate the value of the peculiarly Italian exposure of educated townsmen to the problems of political life. Machiavelli obviously believed that it is useful to analyze political situations and problems, to draw lessons from historical experience, and thereby to establish the principles on which sound political calculations and decisions can be based. In his view, man, by taking thought, can add a cubit to his political stature, at least in the short run. The political virtues can be encouraged through deliberate action by governments; rulers can control events and solve problems and can thereby triumph over the bludgeonings of fortune. To this extent Machiavelli makes explicit that tendency in the Italy of his time to conceive of government as a series of problems in the adaptation of means to ends, as a matter of rational calculation based on a knowledge of men and of the workings of institutions. For this reason (though in other respects he was too passionately committed to warrant such a title), he has been hailed as the father of modern political science. But equally important was his concern with the welfare of the state, conceived as an end in itself. The good was, for Machiavelli, quite simply what serves to preserve and strengthen the state; the bad is whatever tends to destroy it, since states are the only effective source of order in human affairs and, hence, of the happiness of men. From this standpoint all religious and ethical criteria are irrelevant to politics; and "reason of state," the famous phrase now permanently associated with the great Florentine and the source of much of the opprobrium heaped upon him by posterity, is the only measure of political wisdom. In thus making the state independent of all ideal considerations, Machiavelli's thought to some extent paralleled the growing tendency of the Italian states since the 14th century to pursue particularist interests regardless of the common good. Machiavelli, while a witness to the political failure of 14th- and 15th-century Italy, also reflected its most significant political achievements; and he was able, from his study of Italian events, to formulate basic political principles that other, more homogeneous states were later more effectively to pursue.

Later estimates of the period. While Machiavelli was something of a political scientist as well as a historian, Francesco Guicciardini (1483–1540) abandoned the effort to extract generalizations about political behaviour from history. He was a somewhat younger Florentine who had also seen much active political service. By his time the crisis of Italy had become desperate, and thus in his experience the world seemed too disorderly and unpredictable to warrant Machiavelli's type of reflection. But his great *History of Italy*, which reviews the 15th century before concentrating on the events of his own lifetime, exhibits many of the same concerns and the same cool skills in the analysis of events and the understanding of their causes as those apparent in the works of Machiavelli. Guicciardini's picture of the 15th century is highly idealized: it is, for him, an age of unequalled peace and prosperity for which he gives major credit to the Medici. The sequel he represents as a tragedy, for which he blames the blind passions, the selfishness, and the errors of individual rulers—especially the pope and Lodovico il Moro; and he shows in great detail how their machinations brought foreign invasion to Italy. The interpretations of Machiavelli and Guicciardini, widely read throughout Europe, were to become the classic account of Italian history in this period.

Guicciardini's *History of Italy*

This account was little changed until the 19th century. During the long domination of the Italian peninsula by foreign powers, historical composition generally languished. Even less than earlier was it possible to conceive of Italy as a unity about which it was possible to write an integrated history; and students of the Italian past were unable to go beyond erudite compilations of historical data that made sense only in local terms. This was true even of the *Annali d'Italia* (1744–49; "Annals of Italy"), by the great 18th-century scholar Ludovico Muratori, which details the events of Italy year by year but gives little sense of their meaning as a whole.

The modern understanding of Italian history in the 14th and 15th centuries begins with Simonde de Sismondi's *Historie des républiques italiennes du moyen âge* (1807–18; "History of the Italian Republics in the Middle Ages"). Inspired by the romantic liberalism of the earlier 19th century and beginning to think in national terms, Sismondi attributed all that was great in the life of Italy to the freedom of the medieval communes. From this standpoint the 14th and 15th centuries seemed a period of tragic and progressive decline, in which republican liberty was everywhere undermined by tyranny. The failure of the communities of Italy, corrupted by despotism, to unite had opened the way to foreign domination. Sismondi's vision of Italy in the period was also reflected in volume 7 of the French historian Jules Michelet's *Histoire de France* (1833–62) entitled *La Renaissance*.

Sismondi's republican emphasis was largely displaced by the great work of the Swiss historian Jacob Burckhardt, *The Civilization of the Renaissance in Italy* (1859). For Burckhardt, Italy had made a distinct break with its medieval past at the end of the 13th century and thereafter pointed to the modern world in several highly significant ways: in the amoral calculations that characterized its political life, in the interest in the human personality and external nature that characterized Renaissance culture, and in a paganism and immorality that pervaded many aspects of Italian life. These tendencies were, however, all expressions of a deeper quality, a fundamental individualism, which Burckhardt considered the central feature of the age in Italy. Its cause he found essentially in political conditions: notably in the anarchy of the Italian peninsula in the later 13th century; he held especially that the dissolution of the traditional sources of order, papal and imperial authority, had created an atmosphere of insecurity and unrestraint favourable to the emergence of ruthless individuals. Thus, tyrants, whose power depended on personal gifts rather than on a legitimate relation to larger patterns of traditional order, came to dominate Italian society, making common cause with the Humanists, whose eminence similarly depended on their unique individual gifts. Although Burckhardt called his book an essay, the breadth of its vision of Italian culture as a whole made it a model for a new kind of synthetic history.

Burckhardt's analysis

If its interpretation depended above all on the political conditions of the peninsula, its scope gave special influence to his understanding of this aspect of Italian life. For most of the following century, writers on this period of Italian history tended to follow Burckhardt.

Burckhardt had seen that Italy in the 14th and 15th centuries was not a political unity but a congeries of particular entities united chiefly by common tendencies in political life and also by a largely common culture. But, even while he was writing, the political unification taking place in Italy was producing in Italians a tendency to regard the Italy of earlier centuries as a political whole containing in embryo the national state of the future. The result was, among Italian historians of Italy (though less commonly among outsiders), a revolutionary new vision of the past. Historians such as Carlo Cipolla, in his *Storia della signorie italiane dal 1313 al 1530* (1881; "History of the Italian Lordships from 1313 to 1530"), and Pietro Orsi, author of *Signorie e principati* (1900; "Lordships and Principates"), followed Burckhardt's emphasis on despotism but, lacking a modern concern with those social and cultural elements in Italian life that were common to much of the peninsula, tried to present the political history of Italy as a unified narrative. This effort has persisted in the more recent works of Luigi Simeoni, *Le Signorie* (1950; "The Lordships"), and of Nino Valeri, *L'Italia nell' età dei principati dal 1343 al 1516* (1949; "Italy in the Age of the Principates from 1343 to 1516"). (The latter, however, makes a far more effective attempt to integrate social and cultural with political history.) Such works are characterized by an uneasy tension between their authors' concern to present the history of Italy as a whole and the need to do justice to the intricate wealth of local detail provided in the histories of separate states. (W.J.Bo.)

IV. Italy in the 16th–18th centuries

EARLY MODERN PERIOD, 16TH AND 17TH CENTURIES

Expulsion of the French. The restoration in Naples of Ferdinand II in 1495 was through the combined effort of military forces furnished by the Venetians, who occupied several important cities in Puglia and meant to remain there; of Ferdinand the Catholic, who sent Gonsalvo di Córdoba from Sicily to Calabria; and of Ferdinand II himself, who, landing at Naples, strove to regain the hereditary lands of his ancestors. Defeated in several battles and unable to receive supplies from their homeland because the Spanish fleet controlled the seas, the French finally abandoned southern Italy. Before they left they signed an armistice (February 27, 1497) with Frederick I of Aragon, uncle of King Ferdinand (who had unexpectedly died the previous October).

French abandonment of southern Italy

French acquisition of Milan. The new king was a moderate with humanist leanings, who wanted to pacify the kingdom and consolidate his power. But neither Charles VIII nor his successor, Louis XII (ruled 1498–1515), had given up the idea of acquiring Naples, and they made an agreement with the Spanish to garrison a number of fortresses there. Indeed, Louis XII, bent on enforcing his claim to the Duchy of Milan by a war of conquest, made concessions to the monarchs with whom his predecessor had negotiated the acquisition of Naples. Torn by internal discord, without allies, and poorly defended, Milan easily succumbed (1499).

Franco-Spanish division of Naples. This turmoil had fateful repercussions in the Kingdom of Naples. Neither by lenience nor by arms could Frederick appease the recalcitrant feudal lords, headed by the pro-French House of Sanseverino, to whose branches Charles VIII had restored vast feudal estates. Meanwhile, the acquisition of Milan had put Louis XII in a more favourable supply position; his diplomacy aimed at partitioning the territory of the kingdom with King Ferdinand the Catholic, as agreed to in the Treaty of Granada (1500). The Spaniards had not taken kindly to the fact that Alfonso V had given the Kingdom of Naples to his illegitimate son Ferdinand I in 1458. More seriously, Naples' present weakness stimulated the French and Turks, thus jeopardizing the security of Sicily, to which the kings of Aragon attached the highest importance.

King Frederick approached the Ottoman Empire for help. The latter, emboldened by its successes against the Venetians in the Aegean Sea, seemed ready to spill over into the Mediterranean. Thereupon Pope Alexander VI publicly proclaimed a crusade and called upon the Christian nations to participate in it (1493); this furnished Frederick's enemies with a pretext to invoke the Treaty of Granada.

French and Spanish invasion

Invaded by the French from the north and the Spaniards from the south, in 1501 Naples bowed to the conquerors, who proceeded to divide it according to the prearranged agreements: Louis XII gained Campagna with Naples and the Abruzzi; Ferdinand the Catholic obtained Calabria and Puglia. Frederick of Aragon spent his remaining days in France on a feudal estate and with a pension granted him by Louis XII, to whom he had surrendered his rights to the lost kingdom.

French losses in Italy. But territorial and fiscal differences soon developed between the occupying armies, which degenerated into a war. The Spaniards, led by Gonsalvo di Córdoba (the great captain), forced the French to return to their native land. The two rival monarchs agreed on a three-year truce (March 31, 1504), which held firm; the French, beset by more pressing problems, preferred to allow the fate of the Kingdom of Naples to remain an open diplomatic question.

France attached utmost importance, however, to its possession of Lombardy, because of its high level of culture and because it was the gateway to Italy. The French fought long and ruinous wars for Lombardy, withstanding a coalition formed by Pope Julius II (reigned 1503–13), consisting of the Papal States, Venice, the Habsburgs, and the House of Aragon. Julius viewed France's presence in Lombardy as the real threat to the freedom of Italy, which he identified with the territorial independence of the Holy See.

The military superiority of the Spanish Habsburg bloc, led by Emperor Charles V (ruled 1519–56), prevailed at the Battle of Pavia (1525), and the French were driven out of the Duchy of Milan. Restored provisionally to the last heir of the Sforza dynasty, the duchy reverted to Spanish rule after his death (1535) and remained a feudal dependency of the Holy Roman Empire.

Italy under Spanish domination. Sealed by the treaties of Barcelona (1529) and Cateau-Cambrésis (1559), Spanish Habsburg domination of Italy lasted until 1700, when, as that royal line died out, the French Bourbons and the Austrian Habsburgs vied for the Spanish Habsburg inheritance. The treaties of Utrecht (1713) and Rastatt (1714), acknowledging the transplanting of a branch of the Bourbons in Spain, allotted to the Austrian Habsburgs—for balance-of-power reasons—the inheritance of Ferdinand II of Aragon and of Charles V.

Ruling several states (Milan, Naples, Sicily, Sardinia) by direct rule and maintaining a protectorate over others (including Genoa and Florence), Spain considered Italy a part of its world empire and a rampart against the Ottoman Empire and its satellites, the Barbary States of North Africa.

Economic decay in the 16th century

This situation coincided with a slow general decay that developed in Italy during the 16th century. This decay resulted from diverse causes. The economies of the mercantile states were harmed by the shift in the centre of world trade from the Mediterranean to the Atlantic, following the geographical explorations and discoveries of the 15th–16th centuries. Moreover, industrial merchant, and banking capital began to develop in central and western Europe, thus eliminating the Italian economic traders, who were now reduced to regional proportions within their own country. The ruin of many public and private fortunes went hand in hand with a depletion of the creative energies that had flourished in Italy at the height of the Renaissance and with a marked decline in civic virtues. Added to this was Spain's political domination—part cause and part effect—which restricted the already limited mobility of such healthy states as the Venetian Republic.

Absolutism, characteristic of the European monarchies of that day, drove Spain to consolidate its rule in Italy. Spain aimed to centralize its administration, even if it was unable to improve the conditions of the people. The old privileged classes found their political influence weakened, yet retained their juridical and fiscal privileges on their huge estates. But these estates themselves, no longer run by watchful and diligent feudal lords, most of whom had been drawn to the cities, now were in the less able hands of managers eager to get rich and climb the social scale.

Spain showed no desire to make serious changes in the administrative apparatus of the state, although demands were urgent (studies by experts disturbed by mounting poverty called for reforms in legislation, taxation, social welfare, food distribution, and public health in order to renovate and move this closed, stationary, indolent world off dead centre).

The authoritarian attitude based itself on the need to protect the state from disturbing confrontations, in both the political and the religious fields. In religious matters this covered not only questions of morality but also intellectual manifestations, judged in terms of formal logic and theological dogma, in which knowledge and faith were held to be inviolably one. Serious breakdowns in morals and discipline had disturbed the Catholic Church, and many requests had arisen for internal reform. In an atmosphere of change, imbued with a feeling for freedom that was inherent in Renaissance culture, the ideas of the Reformation had aroused widespread interest in Italy.

The lowest common denominator of this movement was the free examination of sacred texts; in Italy there arose groupings of dissident monks, some of them also political in nature. With the Council of Trent (1545–63), the church carried out its long-projected reform: the doctrinal authority of church teachings and traditions was restored.

Accord between church and state

Thus Catholicism, having been reformed and having become a sponsor of socially beneficial works, was now adamantly defended, with church and state in complete accord. Press censorship and the tribunals of the Inquisition became the dreaded instruments of the church's rule. A good many intellectuals who had breathed the free air of Renaissance thought were the victims; two of the most noteworthy were Giordano Bruno in philosophy and Galileo in science.

Although state and church defended religion as the spiritual cement of the social community, other points of friction disturbed their relations. In the Spanish-ruled states, disputes arose because of the rulers' tendency to chip away at the church's immunity in jurisdictional and financial affairs, in line with absolutist practice. But in Venice, as a result of a conflict with Pope Paul V (1605), there emerged the modern rational principle of the secular state (see below *The Republic of Venice*).

With the poetry of Torquato Tasso, in the second half of the 16th century, the flourishing period of great literary creation in Italy came to a close. Empty formalism gained the upper hand, mirroring the arrogance, ostentation, and frivolousness of the leading classes. Some patriotic poems were anti-Spanish in tenor, but they could not generate and arouse popular feelings of revolt. In the figurative arts the Baroque was a pleasing and novel way of expressing beauty; but this vein soon dried up, giving way to indefinite, sensual, heavy-handed virtuosity in painting and sculpture.

As the 17th century faded, there appeared the first signs of a reawakening of community awareness of the country's needs. Criticism of the administrative structure grew increasingly sharp. Contacts were resumed with the cultures of more advanced European nations. When the Spanish Habsburg line died out with Charles II in 1700, Spain, weakened and helpless, realized that the spread of this reawakening meant the crumbling of its power in Italy.

Spanish Habsburg rule in Naples, Sicily, Sardinia, and Milan. The basic aim of Ferdinand the Catholic and of his nephew and successor at the head of the Spanish states (1516), the Habsburg Charles I (Emperor Charles V after 1519), was to consolidate power in the Kingdom of Naples, eliminating the sources of its internal and external weakness, whether the unruly feudal barons, France's ambitions, or the Ottoman and Berber threats in the Mediterranean.

The Kingdom of Naples. France's futile attempt to conquer southern Italy in 1528 gave the pro-French barons their last chance to rebel. Charles V ordered his forceful viceroy, Pedro de Toledo (served 1532–53), to root out any desire for political power on the part of the feudal aristocracy. Resistance in the capital city of Naples, led by a segment of the rebellious nobility, prevented the viceroy from introducing the Inquisition into the kingdom, a move he had sought in order to crush political opposition as well as Protestant-inspired religious dissidence; but in general he established centralized, absolutist rule. It was tightened by his successors, more concerned with the interests of the king of Spain than with conditions in the Kingdom of Naples.

Traditionally, the Naples Parliament—made up of two *bracci* ("branches"), one feudal and the other appointed by the crown—had been authorized to grant the government power to levy ordinary as well as special taxes, in exchange for various *grazie* ("favours"), but after 1642 it was no longer summoned. Instead, the practice developed of looking upon the municipal government of the city of Naples as the representative of the kingdom. This was a medieval-type aristocratic administration: the executive consisted of six representatives of the city's *seggi* ("districts")—five noblemen and one chosen by the upper and middle bourgeoisie. The one elected representative was generally a tool of the viceroy. Food was the chief worry of the public authorities. With its heterogeneous population continually increasing, Naples became one of the most populous cities in Europe, its lower classes swarming, poverty-stricken, coarse, and quick to riot.

Municipal government of Naples

In the provinces the bureaucratic and military apparatus was a far cry from the needs of a centralized, absolutist regime. Old families, deeply francophile, declined or disappeared; but others took their place, most of them Genoese in origin, rewarded by Charles V and Philip II for their financial aid. Continuous demands for funds forced the government to dispose of more and more crown lands, thus extending the feudal area to almost two-thirds of the kingdom. Meanwhile, the management of the landed estates deteriorated by the large landowners moving to the cities and farming out their estates to contractors who exploited them recklessly. There was a rural and urban middle class in the most important centres of the kingdom, but it was not an independent social force mindful of the common good.

This was a sluggish, inert society, culturally cut off from the forward-moving nations of Europe. Forced to contribute financially and militarily to an empire staggering under its own weight, the Kingdom of Naples could not escape the general decline that characterized the multinational complex ruled by Madrid. These, along with such woes of its own as epidemics, natural disasters, Berber incursions, and princely abuses of power, afflicted the people, intensifying their tendency toward apathy, resignation, and religious fatalism.

Occasional popular explosions of wrath did occur, as when taxes were increased or prices of basic necessities rose steeply. The most significant of these revolts broke out in Naples in June–July 1647, provoked by price increases in a number of staple foodstuffs. It bore the name of Masaniello (Tommaso Aniello), a young fisherman who first led the uprising; but Masaniello was actually a tool in the hands of a clever lawyer, Giulio Genoino, who hated the nobles because of their dominant position in the Municipal Council and vowed to raise the people's representative from his subordinate role. This frightened the viceroy, despite the insurgents' proclamation of loyalty to the King of Spain; he appeased them by granting various concessions, which he revoked as soon as he could strike back. An early victim of this counterattack was Masaniello, who was assassinated on July 16, 1647. The movement then began more and more to assume the character of open rebellion against Spain, while in the provinces the rural and urban masses revolted against the diehard feudal lords with unusual violence. As the crisis worsened, Cardinal Mazarin, prime minister of France under Louis XIII, used aiding the rebels as a pretext for attacking Spain in the Kingdom of Naples. But before preparations were well under way, Mazarin was forestalled by the Duc de Guise, heir to the rights of the French House of Anjou to the Neapolitan throne and a favourite of the French king. The rebels' extremist faction in Naples had proclaimed a republic and invited de Guise to take command, in dictator fashion, of the armed forces mustered to defend it. But de Guise and the republic were swept away by a Spanish expedition to southern Italy; and in the countryside the barons joined with government forces to repress the revolts and restore law and order.

Rebellion against Spain

Still lurking within the hearts of the feudal aristocrats, however, was resentment of Spanish domination and centralized power. Indeed, once Spain had fallen into decay and the conflict sharpened between Louis XIV and the Austrian Habsburgs for the succession to Charles II, the last and heirless descendant of Charles V, a section of the Neapolitan aristocracy conspired on behalf of the Habsburgs (1700; the so-called Conspiracy of the Prince of Macchia). The nobles hoped to restore the kingdom's independence by placing a Habsburg prince at its head and to regain the privileges of the feudal nobility.

The Austrian Habsburgs occupied the Kingdom of Naples in 1707 and had its conquest ratified by the treaties of Utrecht and Rastatt. But they maintained

Naples as a viceroyalty and, faithful to their own brand of absolutism, paid no heed to the Neapolitan barons. The Austrian Habsburg government developed no program of reforms, contenting itself with bringing a certain amount of order into the central administration. Moreover, it had fewer financial problems than did Spain, so it could nourish the ambition of controlling all Italy (Sicily was added to Naples in 1718 as a result of the anti-Bourbon coalition of the Quadruple Alliance).

A new crisis developed in Europe in 1733 with the War of the Polish Succession. In 1734 Don Carlos, son of Philip V of Spain and Elizabeth Farnese, was crowned king of Naples and Sicily.

The Kingdom of Sicily. Sicily developed institutions and aspects of community life akin to those of Naples. But there were differences, which arose because the island had followed a different historical path after the revolution of 1282 (Sicilian Vespers). After Sicily's absorption by Aragon in the early 1400s, its longing for independence had survived for a time and at moments had even flared up. To dampen any such desire, John II of Aragon consented to make his firstborn (the future Ferdinand II the Catholic) king of Sicily (1460). A subsequent plot to place the island under French rule—hatched in 1523 by the Imperatore brothers and encouraged by the French monarch while the Habsburg Charles V, then king of Sicily, was at war with France—was brutally crushed. The long reign, the prestige, and the political moderation of Charles V, and common problems of security in the Mediterranean, combined to stabilize relations with the Sicilians and make them loyal subjects of the Catholic kings. Spain attached great importance to Sicily, not only because it considered the island a bulwark of its power in the Mediterranean but also because Sicily produced much wheat and was a good market for Spanish goods.

Sicilian loyalty to Spain

The socio-economic organization of the island was strictly feudal, with the upper aristocracy, owners of huge landed estates and with hosts of retainers in every segment of society, the dominant class. The barons, maintaining full control of their estates and wielding power in the Sicilian Parliament by means of the feudal *braccio* ("branch"), became part of the constitutional fabric of the regime and one of the pillars of the state.

The Parliament, composed of three *bracci*—feudal, ecclesiastic, and royal—was charged with voting the amounts required for ordinary and special taxes, a task it performed along traditional lines but with the feeling that in this domain it was sovereign and represented the nation. Aristocratic interference was evident even in the administration of the big cities, except for Messina, which was a busy trading centre controlled by a wealthy bourgeoisie. Because the island remained loyal, Spain had no intention of disturbing the existing system; indeed, it even reinforced the spirit of its inherently conservative policies. Nor were there significant changes under Victor Amadeus II of Savoy, who held royal title to Sicily in 1713–18, under the Austrian Habsburgs, who controlled it in 1718–34, or under the Bourbon regime established in 1734.

Sardinia. Sardinia was closely linked with Spain, its firm ties the outcome of a deep-going process of assimilation. Many Spaniards had come to Sardinia and been assimilated into this patriarchal society led by a powerful feudal class, whose chief source of wealth was sheep raising. Neither the crown nor the island's ruling class felt any inclination to altar a system based on a solid feudal-monarchist regime—the viceroy was generally a Sardinian and the Parliament was divided into three *stamenti* ("branches"). The population, peace-loving and inured to harsh living conditions, had only limited relations with Italy. Under such circumstances, Sardinia in 1720 went over to Victor Amadeus II of Savoy, together with the royal title, in exchange for Sicily (see below *The Austrian government in Italy in the 18th century*).

The Duchy of Milan. One of the most prominent states in Italy in the late Middle Ages, Milan was attached to Spain in 1540. When Charles V took this step, after long and fruitless negotiations with France, he was prompted by considerations of Milan's strategic importance as well as its economic development in agriculture, industry, and trade.

Supreme power was in the hands of a governor, assisted by consultative councils; the Senate, patterned by Louis XII after the Parlement of Paris, remained unchanged and controlled the whole administrative apparatus of the state. But overall directives and guidance came from Madrid. To this end, Philip II in 1563 set up in Madrid the Council of Italy, whose members included two councillors from Milan and two from Sicily.

The church had tremendous influence on the government and social life of Milan. In the wake of the Council of Trent, Cardinal Charles Borromeo enthusiastically fostered reforms in Milan; his nephew, Cardinal Federico Borromeo, followed his example. The zeal accounted for many institutions that were socially beneficial—some new, others revived. But when the church claimed full jurisdiction over these institutions, it collided with the Spanish-oriented political rulers, and the old church–state struggle reappeared.

The highborn, on the other hand, lost much of their vigour. No longer involved in their former productive activities, they masked their moral and economic impoverishment with bizarre and ostentatious pomp, called *spagnolismo* ("Spanishism"). And Spain's concern for the economy could not prevent a decline. The process was hastened by military levies and requisitions (in the wars for Monferrato and the Valtellina, which Spain sought to annex), famines, plagues, and the soaring prices of basic commodities. The people gave vent to their discontent by rioting on various occasions. Thus, there was no sense of shock when Lombardy passed from Spanish rule to that of the Austrian Habsburgs, who had long coveted it.

Spain and the independent states of Italy. Relations between Spain and those Italian states that remained independent followed a different course. Functioning in a system that underwent little change until the downfall of the dominant power, some of them may be considered satellites of Spain, others independent entities.

Disregarding the independent territories in central-southern Italy that were small in area and of minor political importance—*e.g.,* the duchies of Modena, Reggio, and Ferrara of the dukes of Este, the Duchy of Mantua and Monferrat of the Gonzagas, the Duchy of Parma and Piacenza of the Farnese family, the Republic of Lucca—the satellite group included the Duchy of Savoy in Piedmont, the Republic of Genoa in Liguria, and the Duchy (later the Grand Duchy) of Tuscany (Florence) in Tuscany, ruled by the Medici family; the Papal States and the Republic of Venice were independent of Spain.

The Spanish satellite states

The Duchy of Savoy. With the Treaty of Cateau-Cambrésis (1559), Savoy, hitherto occupied by the French, was restored to Emanuel Filibert, victor at the Battle of St. Quentin, with the pledge that he remain neutral both toward the French, guarding the Alps, and the Spaniards, masters of Lombardy. Filibert (ruled 1559–80) rebuilt and strengthened Savoy, maintaining equal distance between the two powers. His son Charles Emanuel I (ruled 1580–1630), avid for territorial expansion, joined in the wars of the period variously allied with Spain and France but without profiting from his participation. At his death the dukedom fell under the ever more oppressive rule of France, which the Bourbon Henry IV restored to the rank of a great power. Not until the advent of Victor Amadeus II (ruled 1675–1730) did the duchy recover from its humiliating subjection.

The Republic of Genoa. Genoa was reduced to a protectorate under Charles V and subsequently under Spain, which looked upon it as a base from which to control the Tyrrhenian Sea. This actually came to pass when Andrea Doria, a powerful Genoese shipowner, defected from the King of France and, with his fleet, entered the service of the Habsburgs (1528), convinced that such a move would favour the economic interests of the city as well as his own. Events vindicated his decision. Doria gained the favour of Charles V by rendering great service in the Emperor's later Mediterranean campaigns; and he prepared a constitutional reform by which the powers of the Genoese Republic would be concentrated in the hands of the faction loyal to him. In 1547 the opposing faction, the pro-French Fieschi, tried to oust Doria's nephew Giannettino; but the movement failed, as did other anti-Spanish uprisings in Italy that same year.

Genoa's weaknesses

The spirit of factionalism died down, but at the same time the mercantile spirit had lost its vitality—the old maritime leaders, losing interest in the sea, began to invest in landed property with a sure return; unemployment swelled; the state staggered under a load of debts. An especially thorny matter was the insubordination of Corsica, harshly exploited by the Banco di San Giorgio, an organ of the Genoese government that administered the island. The dukes of Savoy played on Genoa's weaknesses and its people's distaste for aristocratic government by fomenting numerous conspiracies in the 17th century; similarly, they found Liguria a tempting prize. The republic foiled these manoeuvres; but having refused to break away from Spain, it was bombarded and blockaded in 1684 by Louis XIV. The following year, abandoned by its Spanish ally, Genoa had to submit to Louis XIV's exacting terms.

The Duchy of Tuscany. The Republic of Florence also came into Spain's orbit. Charles V, implementing his agreement of 1529 with the Medici Pope Clement VII, conquered the republic by force of arms. Then, in 1531, Charles named Alessandro de' Medici duke of Florence with hereditary rights. Alessandro was assassinated in 1537 in an atmosphere of hatred spawned by his own dissoluteness and of intrigue by republicans and those who favoured an oligarchy. The Florentines ran a serious risk that Spain, using the pretext that the French would intervene to foster a resurgent republic, might occupy Florence. The danger was avoided when, in the same year, Cosimo de' Medici occupied the throne as Cosimo I; he was swiftly recognized by the Senate of Forty and accepted by the people.

The reign of Cosimo I

Cosimo, with farsighted realism, allied himself with Charles V. With the latter's consent he waged war on the Republic of Siena (1552–55), which was pro-French, and annexed its territory except for five seaports that Spain kept for itself; these five constituted the Stato dei Presidi ("State of the Garrisons") and were placed under the dependency of the Kingdom of Naples. The acquisition of Siena extended Florence's rule over Tuscany and enhanced Cosimo's prestige. Moreover, Cosimo worked tirelessly to restore, consolidate, and modernize the state. Inequalities between the capital and the annexed towns were reduced, finances reorganized, land reclamation carried out, ports built, and a strong navy and regular militia created. Attesting to his esteem, Cosimo I had the title of grand duke conferred on him by Pope Pius V in 1569. His successor, Francesco I, was confirmed in this title in 1576 by the Holy Roman Emperor.

Nevertheless, Florentine industry, banking, and trade slowly declined, and Florence lost its former European outlook and became provincial in nature. Land became the pivot of the region's economy and the source of financial profit. Attempts under Cosimo I and his immediate successors to forge an economic policy independent of Spain failed.

The Papal States. The popes Paul III (reigned 1534–49) and Paul IV (1555–59), bent on safeguarding the independence of the Papal States, could not check the expansion of Spanish power in Italy. The papacy saw a lessening of its power as a supranational state as the process of secularization in international relations advanced in Europe. Even its role as head of a major Italian state declined. In 1563 the Council of Trent finished its task of synthesizing the Catholic Counter-Reformation. Implementing the council's resolutions, the popes laboured to reform and re-establish the church, and religious matters occupied most of their time and attention. Pope Pius V (reigned 1566–72) promoted the alliance of Spain, Venice, and the other Italian states that defeated the Turks at the Battle of Lepanto (1571), thus ending Turkish expansion on the high seas. Pope Gregory XIII (reigned 1572–85) reformed the calendar and gave it his name. Pope Sixtus V (reigned 1585–90) also distinguished himself at the helm of state. Pontiffs such as these repressed brigandage, reorganized the court system, and built magnificent public works in Rome. The city took on new beauty as a result of the artistic flowering of the period. Furthermore, the territories of Ferrara, Urbino, and Castro were again brought under the direct rule of the church.

In the never-ending antagonism between Bourbons and Habsburgs in Catholic Europe, the popes were proponents of a balance of power. Yet it was a troubled time for the church because of jurisdictional disputes with Spain (even though that nation was a bulwark of Catholicism), because the papacy's good relations with France deteriorated markedly under Louis XIV, and because the power of the Papal States was eroding.

Papal disputes with Spain

The Republic of Venice. Venice, at the outset of the 16th century the most powerful state in Italy, suffered from defeats in 1509 by the League of Cambrai and from Spain's subsequent takeover of Lombardy, the crowning triumph in the Spanish struggle with France for hegemony beyond the Alps. Venice—a rich, solid, and unified political entity—was far from exhausted. But under pressure from the Spanish Habsburgs straining to expand from Lombardy into Venetia, and from the Austrian Habsburgs jealous of its supremacy in the Adriatic, Venice could no longer count on its alliance with France or with the other Italian states; it became weakened politically as well as economically. The growing use of the Atlantic as a sea route stripped Venice of its monopoly in the spice trade; and the expansion of the Ottoman Empire deprived Venice of several Aegean and Black Sea islands and ports of call and sharply curtailed its trade with the countries bordering on those waters.

In 1605 a bitter dispute between Venice and Pope Paul V broke out because two monks involved in common-law crimes had been tried in a secular court. This episode dramatized the diametrically opposed attitudes of church and state: on the one hand, the medieval idea of theocratic universality, which had been repressed but was reaffirmed by Pius V in the edition of the papal bull *In Coena Domini* (1568); and on the other, a modern concept affirming complete state sovereignty in temporal matters. This latter concept, product of a long political and juridical tradition in Venice, found a vigorous advocate in the state theologian Paolo Sarpi, and the republic would not give in, even when threatened with a papal interdict. Mediation by Henry IV of France brought a resolution of the controversy, from which Venice emerged with dignity.

Venice stubbornly defended its Near Eastern possessions against the Turks with its fleet, the chief element in its remaining power on the international scene, and its considerable financial resources. At Lepanto the Venetian fleet made a decisive contribution to the victory of the Christian armada. Worn out by 25 years of war, it had to yield the island of Candia (1669); but it acquired the Peloponnese (formally recognized in the Treaty of Carlowitz, 1699) by defeating the Turks beneath the walls of Vienna in its last great triumph in the East.

In the 18th century the ruling class, as in other Italian states, withdrew from commercial pursuits and, as a result, the vitality of public life declined, making Venice easy prey to the invading French Revolutionary armies in 1797. (E.Po.)

ITALY IN THE 18TH CENTURY

The early 18th century witnessed profound changes in Europe, arising out of what has been defined as the first world conflict in modern history: the War of the Spanish Succession (1701–14). The old political system was no more; from its ashes arose a new pattern of state relations, ratified on the diplomatic level by the treaties of Utrecht (1713) and Rastatt (1714). In Italy the Duchy of Milan and Mantua, the Kingdom of Naples, and Sardinia passed to the Austrian House of Habsburg. Sicily went to Victor Amadeus II of Savoy, who bore the title of king; a succession of surrenders, however, forced even Sicily into the Austrian orbit, with Sardinia transferred to Victor Amadeus II as compensation (Treaty of The Hague, 1720). Meanwhile, Tuscany, when the Medici dynasty

The aftermath of the War of the Spanish Succession

became extinct, went to Francis Stephen (Peace of Vienna, 1738), duke of Lorraine and husband of Maria Theresa of Austria. This intricate diplomatic game, punctuated by acute military crises, continued until the Treaty of Aachen in 1748. By its terms Milan was ceded to the Habsburgs in exchange for some slight territorial adjustments in favour of the Piedmontese; Don Carlos, the Bourbon Infante of Spain, was confirmed as king of Naples and Sicily, which had been conquered in 1734; and his brother Philip was accorded the Duchy of Parma and Piacenza. Thus, in approximately half a century, the political situation in the Italian peninsula had completely changed and now settled into a long state of equilibrium. This new situation gave the Italian states undeniable advantages. They found themselves incorporated into a political system that proved more vital and energetic than the previous one and that bore a distinctly European cast. Italy was thrown open to the ideas of the Enlightenment and swept by profound desires for reform in every field. Obviously, a historical process so vast in scope could not be effected swiftly and along predetermined lines; it was conditioned by a variety of factors growing out of specific local situations and the overall political evolution.

Lombardy. The Austrian armies, with the support of Piedmontese troops, entered Milan on September 26, 1706. On March 13, 1707, an armistice with France formally ratified Austrian occupation. Austria sought to impose its own Italian policy firmly and decisively, using its base in Milan to strive for complete control of the peninsula and to expel potential rivals. But it was thwarted by an unfavourable set of circumstances. Internal crises and international complications forced the Habsburgs to extract financial resources from their new possession; and their methods were at times crude and arbitrary. As a result the governors of Milan had to resort to a policy of drastic financial retrenchment, thereby leaving a thin margin for any attempts at governmental reform.

Government reforms. After the storms of the Spanish succession had subsided, the foundation for future reforms was laid. But a terrible economic depression in the 1730s, on top of a renewed outbreak of devastating war in Lombardy, blocked these meagre efforts at reform and paralyzed government activity.

The great powers of Europe concentrated their aims and efforts at preventing Austrian domination over Italy and half of Europe; and they were joined by the House of Savoy, dispassionately opportunistic as always. These were the critical years of the wars of the Polish and the Austrian Succession, during which Austria lost Milan more than once, only to finally regain it in 1747. When things returned to normal with the Treaty of Aachen, the Austrian government readied a plan for a long-overdue and sweeping reorganization of the state. Recent events had laid bare frightening gaps in Milan's economic and social structure. Its technicians and administrators, most of them outrun by events, remained a dangerous source of tensions, so that the government was forced increasingly to intervene in order to safeguard its power. In its interventions it drew on long experience in centralized rule, so that local political elements and their institutions were stifled. Reorganization of Milan was decided upon from 1748 on. Despite obstacles and resistances interposed by the privileged and conservative elements of the population, many varied and weighty problems of the economy were tackled.

Reorganization of Milan

After 1750 important reforms were instituted in the system of labour contracts and tax collections; the administrative code in force under the Spanish was simplified; and a land survey was made. These reforms were technically valuable. But even more important was the logic inherent in the overall reform policy, which was essentially designed to strengthen the central power at the expense of local authorities and of special interests that were particularist and anti-centralist.

The decade 1750–60 ended on a positive note for the Austrians in Lombardy. Their activity there had undoubtedly struck the first serious blows at an antiquated state apparatus and system of living. Once under way, therefore, the process began to develop an independent and irrepressible momentum of its own. Requests and demands of the population grew more and more insistent; the solutions adopted, usually compromises, proved less and less adequate.

A new and more powerful wave of reform hit Milan after 1760, involving again the system of labour contracts, customs, and tolls. This led in 1765 to the creation of a higher body of study and verification, the Supreme Economic Council. The reorganization of the local administrative and political apparatus continued, chiefly at the expense of the Senate, the judiciary, and the highest public offices (even the governorship was reduced to a bureaucratic function). Nor was this done purely by chance: it was in those three areas that the Austrian government had encountered the stiffest resistance. The reforms were always carefully circumscribed so as not to provoke violent reaction. This was also true of church–state relations, with the abolition of the Inquisition and the secularization of censorship while problems of a delicately theological nature were set aside for a time.

The rule of Joseph II. Maria Theresa's death (1780) and the autonomous rule of Joseph II mark a radical turning point in Habsburg policy toward its possessions. The new emperor was, spiritually and ideologically, the product of an age of rationalism and enlightenment, and his behaviour differed markedly from his mother's ponderous and prudent ways. What had been calculation and necessity in Maria Theresa became in Joseph dictate of conscience and adherence to principles; hence the flexible style and comportment of the former and the stubborn, rigid, and unyielding behaviour of the latter. The idea of the state as the organ of absolute power above and against traditional rights, class privileges, and local autonomy was at the root of Joseph's personal and political morality. He promoted centralism and denied any autonomy to persons, institutions, or regions in the state. Like the other Italian possessions, Lombardy was caught up in the fever of the overall reorganization undertaken by the Emperor with utter disregard for consequences. A Government Council made up of six departments suddenly supplanted existing administrative and judicial bodies. A veritable storm blew up over church–state relations, but this time the controversy spilled over into theology as well, including matters of church ritual, in which the government interfered arbitrarily and at times ridiculously. Such passion for reform, though it furnished the Milanese with the tools for modernizing their state and rationalizing its developing economy, did not always find favour with the various segments of the population. Significantly, the intellectuals abandoned the line of collaboration with the Austrian government that they had followed under Maria Theresa and took the lead in opposing what they now called the new despotism. The price the Milanese had to pay for the Emperor's policies in Lombardy must have seemed too high; Joseph II's efforts, massive but lacking flexibility, left the real needs of the state misunderstood or neglected.

Enlightened Despotism

Leopold II, who succeeded his brother in 1790, made an attempt to improve relations by softening Joseph's harshest measures; but Leopold died barely two years later, and his successor, Francis II, was too much absorbed in international affairs to be concerned with Lombardy. Defeated by the French in 1796, the Austrians ended wretchedly, at least for the moment, their political presence in northern Italy.

Tuscany. The Peace of Vienna (1738) ratified on the diplomatic level the results of the War of the Polish Succession. By the terms of the peace, Tuscany was awarded to Francis of Lorraine (reigned 1738–65), and a new phase in the history of the grand duchy began.

The government of Francis of Lorraine. The functions of government were assigned to a Regency Council. With Francis at war with the Turks, two of his representatives presided over the council's work, first Prince Marc de Craon and then Count Emanuel de Richecourt. The ministers were confronted with corruption and malfunction in every branch of the government, both civil and military. These ills were piled on top of the basic problems of Tuscan society inherent in the country's political and economic structure, including the overweening power of an oligarchy over the regency councillor, the pro-Spanish inclinations of a section of public opinion, the disorganization of trade, and the burden of tax-free church property. It quickly became clear, above all to Richecourt, that it was essential to formulate a detailed and thoroughgoing plan of reform that would wipe out abuses and unfair privileges of the elite castes. But the reactions to Richecourt's initial measures and the delicate state of international affairs made it imprudent, for the time being, to proceed along the path of reform. The Spaniards, meanwhile, tried unsuccessfully to install the Bourbon prince Philip in Tuscany. But at the beginning of 1739 Francis of Lorraine entered Florence, visited the principal cities, and departed, leaving in charge a regency again headed by Richecourt. Until 1765 Francis' administration sought to promote general economic progress and welfare. It had some striking successes, particularly in getting rid of institutions that still bore the medieval stamp. Marked improvements were made in administering the economy: trade was liberalized and the public debt reorganized; measures were taken to benefit agriculture. The government moved to rescind feudal legislation and abolish church privileges. In sum, Francis' achievements were far from negligible, even though his political activity in Tuscany had to remain quite limited, since Tuscany was only one of the many provinces in the Habsburg Empire. Francis was crowned Holy Roman Emperor in 1745 (as Francis I), and thenceforth had to immerse himself in far graver and more complicated political problems.

Economic improvements

The government of Peter Leopold. Only with the 25-year rule of Grand Duke Peter Leopold (reigned 1765–90) was Tuscany vouchsafed a genuine revival, with an intense social and political development that no longer benefitted special interests alone. This second son of Francis of Lorraine remained in Florence until 1790, when he ascended the imperial throne as Leopold II. With his advent in Florence, relations between the grand duchy and the court of Vienna were completely altered, though he evoked frequent expressions of reserve and concern in circles close to Empress Maria Theresa by placing in responsible posts Tuscan experts and men of enlightenment, with whose help the most effective reforms were launched. Important steps were taken toward ending internal restrictions on the grain trade; the traditional farming out of taxes was abolished and the tax system overhauled. Immediately thereafter, laws were passed regulating the church's landed property; the enormous holdings of the church were thus broken up and redistributed more equitably.

The decade 1770–80 saw other significant reforms: the abolition of a law defining the jurisdiction of corporations; the suppression of specific statutes and tribunals as well as the high tribunals of Commerce and of the Arts and Professions; and the stimulation of commercial and industrial activity by jettisoning various duties, tolls, and privileges. The entire bureaucratic and administrative state apparatus was fundamentally transformed. The antiquated state structure set up to serve the city-state of Florence was replaced by a modern organization in which the interests of individual institutions coincided with the general interests of the grand duchy. Nor were problems of public safety or those pertaining to military matters ignored; special attention was paid to draining and reclaiming the malaria-infested marshes—an age-old barrier to development of the whole region.

In the decade 1780–90 Peter Leopold's activities broadened to include programs of even vaster scope; *e.g.*, church reform, a new constitution, and efforts to increase the peasants' landholdings. He did away with tax exemption for the church, that institution's chief privilege under the old order, and he abolished the Inquisition and suppressed the Society of Jesus (the Jesuits), despite sharp resistance. But when he moved onto jurisdictional ground and sought to reform the church along clearly Jansenist lines he aroused fierce opposition.

A basic factor in restructuring the economy was the grant to small landowners of vast holdings that had formerly been state property. To strengthen and consolidate Austrian rule in Tuscany, Peter Leopold deemed it essential to create a new class of independent small farmers, who would constitute a genuine social base for the government, and he planned to transform the grand duchy from an absolute to a constitutional monarchy, in which the people would have representative bodies—a revolutionary step. Apparently, Peter Leopold was convinced that the monarchy could continue to function solidly only by strengthening its relations on the political and institutional level with the new social strata. The beneficiaries of the agrarian reform thenceforth constituted the pivot of the social structure in Tuscany. His plan for a constitutional monarchy, however, did not materialize because of the still considerable weakness of the new social groups on which the future political structure was to be based, and because Vienna was opposed to any such political orientation on the part of its Italian dominions.

The new Austrian class in Tuscany

In 1787 a new penal code, the Leopoldine code, was promulgated. Calling for the abolition of the death penalty and torture, it broke sharply with the tradition of judicial cruelty and thereby propelled Tuscany, in this respect, into the vanguard of the nations of Europe. In 1790 Peter Leopold was called to Vienna and, on the death of his brother Joseph, named emperor; in March 1791 his son Ferdinand succeeded him as head of the grand duchy (as Ferdinand III).

Leopold's forced departure and the transfer of his powers brought violent disorders in Tuscany in 1790 and again in 1795. They appeared first in an anti-Jansenist guise but quickly turned into a revolt against hunger, poverty, and the high cost of living, which the people attributed to their lack of freedom. The influence of the contemporaneous French Revolution was strong. Faced with such disorders, the regency yielded, and Leopold, in Vienna, was forced to sanction, for the moment, the repeal of free trade in grain. What had in fact occurred was a reaction to the reform policies of 25 years of Leopold's rule, fomented by the clergy and civil servants who had remained hostile to the innovations that had stripped them of prestige and power. In addition, the poorer classes, victims of social inequities and hard hit economically, were exploited and manipulated by the reactionaries. The result was crisis and decline, virtually until 1799.

Naples and Sicily under the Habsburgs. *The mainland.* Naples, too, was acquired by the Habsburgs as a result of the War of the Spanish Succession. Austrian troops entered Naples in 1707 and were warmly received by the people. The most active segments of society—the provincial barons, the urban patricians, and the secular middle classes—each formulated their demands in a different way. But in substance each group demanded a greater measure of autonomy designed to strengthen local powers, a viable economy that could cope with anticipated financial pressures, and a reorganization of the juridical and administrative system. The delicate international situation, to which the Habsburgs had to devote their undivided attention, quickly revealed how unattainable all these demands were. Nevertheless, something was done on behalf of the viceroyalty of Naples when Cardinal Vincenzo Grimani became viceroy (1708–10). While vigorously pursuing a line of stern authority, he drew upon the best energies of the native population and endeavoured to soften social differences and to lighten financial burdens. But in the final years of the War of the Spanish Succession, these needs became more pressing, and the Austrians had to cast about for funds. Thus, the efforts to recognize the state's finances were rendered vain, and Naples once more found itself on the brink of collapse.

Demands for change

When the war ended, the Austrians were able to pay more attention to their new acquisition. The choice of Wierich Lorenz, Graf von Daun, as viceroy (1713–19) signalled a new political course. Daun embarked on a thoroughgoing and long-term project of restoring the economic and financial health of the state. He also engaged in a controversy with the papacy over church government, over which the state traditionally enjoyed extensive control. During these years such institutions as the Collateral Council, an expression of local political power, were strengthened; university reform was attempted; and notable successes were registered in the controversy with the church. A series of international complications, however, forced Charles VI to adopt a financially oppressive policy toward Naples. Vast sums of money went more and more frequently to Vienna, under the name of donations, further impoverishing the land. In exchange, grants and privileges were extended, but almost exclusively to the feudal groups. Thus, Neapolitan society was dealt a setback.

With the return of peace and the arrival in Naples of a new viceroy, Cardinal Michael Friedrich von Althann (1722–28), Habsburg policy took a new turn. Reinforcing the central government, reviving the economy, and easing relations with the church, in line with improved relations between Rome and Vienna, were the aims Althann tenaciously pursued. But his policies offended several groups; these included the nobility, hit hard by the harsh tax measures and forced to relinquish their traditional powers in such areas as the judiciary, and the secular-minded citizenry, resentful of the viceroy's new pro-church attitude. Despite opposition, Althann first planned a new enumeration of the hearths in the country, in order to get a clearer picture of population distribution and thus institute fairer taxation. Next, he sponsored the creation of the Banco di San Carlo, a move that provoked dangerous social tensions. The bank was established with a view to reacquiring large estates for the crown as well as to recoup lost revenues, rather than for serving as a stimulus to revive stagnant economic activities, especially in trade, by distributing large amounts of capital to individual citizens. The nobility saw in the bank an assault on the rentier economy on which it lived and prospered; the middle classes feared it would become the instrument for even more burdensome taxes. The social unrest these measures caused led to Althann's downfall.

The following years brought famine, economic crisis, and an atmosphere of imminent war, which forced the situation to the breaking point. The Austrians could not escape the consequences of the crushing financial burden; since the latter overhung all their policies, every attempt at reform was thwarted. When Don Carlos of Spain ascended the throne of the reborn kingdom, the population and the political authorities welcomed him warmly.

The reign of Charles VI

Sicily. Following the Hague Treaty (1720), the Habsburgs yielded possession of the port of Antwerp, in deference to the requests of England and Holland, and recognized Philip V as king of Spain. As compensation Charles received Sicily, taken from Victor Amadeus II of Savoy, in exchange for Sardinia.

Sicily suddenly proved to be a difficult land to rule, even though Charles VI and his ministers did not stint in their efforts to win over the Sicilians. The first period of the new government was made even more difficult because of the permanent garrisoning of German soldiers on the island, thus giving rise to numerous abuses and clashes. When a functioning civil government was finally set up, Sicily's age-old ills—feudal arrogance, administrative and economic disorder, corruption and chaos in the courts, and municipal particularism—became glaringly evident. An excessive tax load was placed on taxpayers already staggering under their burden, and on many occasions the island parliament was called upon to vote huge levies needed for imperial policy.

But in at least some respects Austria's rule was energetic and mindful of Sicilian interests. Charles VI really tried to lift the island out of the economic and commercial swamp in which it was foundering. He sought to reactivate Sicily's ports, particularly Messina, which was made a free port in 1728, with the aim of reviving the economy in the whole Messina area, especially by attracting foreign commerce and shipping. Measures were taken to cope with a crisis in grain—Sicily's traditional source of wealth—and to improve the declining silk industry and allied activities. The results, however, were far less than anticipated, largely because of a drastic worsening in the general economic situation, and to some extent because Charles' policies promised more than they could achieve. A series of measures adopted around 1730 produced disastrous results, laying the groundwork for economic collapse and probably hastening the political breakdown.

As for relations with the church—especially tricky in Sicily, where the sovereign had the role and functions of apostolic legate—Charles VI proceeded cautiously but firmly. He reassured everyone by his orthodox defense of the faith, even permitting the Inquisition to continue to function, but he was adamant about maintaining the legateship. Aided by loyal and able church ministers, he waged a lively and eventually victorious polemic with popes Innocent XIII and Benedict XIII. The solution, arrived at in 1728, was completely satisfactory to both parties and was given force of law in a papal bull.

The few years of Austrian rule failed to make a dent in many other aspects of Sicilian society. Austria's monetary policy, for example, failed and its cultural policy was weak. Defeated by a Spanish army, the Habsburgs left Sicily in 1734. (G.d'A.)

The first Bourbon period in the south (1734–99). Don Carlos ruled Naples–Sicily as Charles VII, winning popularity by making it an independent kingdom for the first time in two centuries. When he succeeded to the Spanish throne as Charles III in 1759, he left the kingdom to his son Ferdinand, appointing his minister Bernardo Tanucci and a council of regency to rule until Ferdinand came of age in 1767.

In the prevailing spirit of Enlightened Despotism, Tanucci sponsored reforms to modernize the state and increase its power at the expense of traditional institutions. Ferdinand had little aptitude for government, and came to be dominated by his wife, the Austrian archduchess Maria Carolina, whom he had married in 1768. Opposed to Tanucci's pro-Spanish policies, Maria Carolina secured his dismissal in 1776, and beginning in 1779, replaced him by promoting the rise to power of an English émigré, Sir John Acton.

In the 1790s, Acton and Maria Carolina aligned Naples with Austria and Britain in their struggle against Revolutionary France. When French forces occupied the mainland portion of the kingdom in 1799, the Bourbon government sought refuge in Palermo under British protection. (Ed.)

V. Revolution, restoration, and unification

THE FRENCH REVOLUTIONARY PERIOD

In the spring of 1796 the French Revolutionary armies burst into Italy. But they had been long preceded by a considerable incursion of revolutionary ideas. As early as the summer of 1788, the Italian newssheets had given priority to "the latest news from France," where a grim struggle between the crown and the Parlement of Paris was taking place. As the Revolution developed, the circulation of these papers increased; they were soon accompanied by a spate of pamphlets, and then, from 1791 onward, by the graphic testimony of émigrés. Despite the vigilant surveillance of the various Italian governments, revolutionary ideas spread widely. Italian public opinion, however, was seldom able before 1796 to distinguish the different forces at war in the political life of France, and the simplistic image of two monolithic fronts—monarchists on the one side, and revolutionaries on the other—remained the prevalent one.

The early years. By 1789 the period of reforms in Italy had come to a close. But those who had hoped much from the work of the enlightened princes had been severely disappointed. The reforms had not widened political power, nor had constitutional steps been taken to confer administrative and governmental responsibilities on the educated classes, the landowners, and the entrepreneurs. Only now, in the light of the French example, could things perhaps be changed.

In the Italy of the old regime, there had been no representative political life. But the increase in the number

The rise of the Masons

of Masonic lodges at the end of the 18th century demonstrated the desire for secret discussion of problems different from those that were agitating the academies and the agrarian societies. Not all the Freemasons became supporters of the Revolution and of the French, but many of them did so. The moderate and constitutional demands of the Masonic lodges began to be accompanied by more democratic demands, and there were in Milan, Bologna, Rome, and Naples cells of Illuminati, republican freethinkers, after the pattern recently established in Bavaria by Adam Weishaupt.

The Italian governments were unanimous in opposing France and the ideas of the Revolution. Piedmont actually joined the First Coalition, an alliance made in 1793 of powers opposed to Revolutionary France. Savoy and Nice were invaded as early as the autumn of 1792. Although the King of Naples was forced to yield when the French fleet threatened his capital in December 1792, the other states pursued a policy of stern police repression. Denunciations and trials show how the people of the various Italian states looked to the "French system" as the only effective remedy for their own grievances. In 1792 the Piedmontese tenant farmers, reduced to starvation by the great capitalistic landlords, reminded the King of what was going on in Paris; at Rome the bourgeois entrepreneurs protested against clerical misgovernment and against the temporal power of the papacy; and in the Venetian provinces the nobility and the bourgeoisie brought charges against the aristocratic regime of Venice.

These hopes took concrete form as organized conspiracies in only two states—Piedmont and the Kingdom of Naples. In the south the first pro-revolutionary centres developed in connection with the Masonic lodges; an example is the Celestini Lodge at Naples. But bourgeois elements, with republican and democratic ideals, soon broke away from these and evolved a conspiracy, which was discovered, and the leaders executed in October 1794. The trials, followed by many arrests, sent a stream of emigrants flowing into France, where they later became significantly active.

Both those who did no more than complain and those who had the courage to conspire hoped to make their countries into modern states, with new, impartial laws and where subjects had a share in politics and government—aims that were sufficiently moderate. But the emigrants, who put themselves at the service of the French government, had a much clearer consciousness of the real aims of revolution. Perhaps the most important among them was Filippo Buonaroti, a Tuscan of an ancient noble family who emigrated to Corsica in 1789 and became a most active revolutionary agent; then, in 1794, he was attached to the French Army of Italy and was appointed National Commissary at Oneglia, a Ligurian town conquered from the King of Sardinia. Here he established a republic based on the views of the French revolutionary leader Robespierre, rallying the Italian exiles, abolishing seigneurial rights, and instituting the deistic cult of the Supreme Being. This extremism was disapproved of by those who gained power in 1794 when Robespierre and the Jacobins fell, and, after less than a year, Buonaroti was recalled to France (March 1795) and sent to prison; after his release he took part in the conspiracy for an armed rising planned by François-Noël (Gracchus) Babeuf and discovered in May 1796. But the example of Oneglia was never forgotten by those Italians who took their ideas from Robespierre and the Jacobins.

The Oneglia experiment

French invasion of Italy. The French campaign in Italy, which led to the rise of Napoleon Bonaparte, began in March 1796. In April the Piedmontese army was defeated, and, by the Peace of Paris (May 15, 1796), King Victor Amadeus III of Sardinia was forced to cede the Transalpine provinces and grant the French armed forces passage. On the same day Napoleon entered Austrian-owned Milan; then he pursued the Austrian Army into the territory of the Venetian Republic. During April 1797 the whole Po plain fell into the hands of the French, and the Peace of Tolentino (February 19, 1797) obliged the Pope to surrender Bologna and the northern Papal States. The duchy of Modena was occupied, and the French pushed on into Tuscany as far as Livorno. After defeats in Venetian territory at Arcole and Rivoli (winter 1796–97), the Austrians capitulated at Mantua. With his rear thus protected, Napoleon turned his offensive northward and, crossing the Tagliamento River, entered Austrian territory and by April 1797 was in close reach of Vienna. At Leoben the Austrian plenipotentiaries halted his advance toward the capital with "Preliminaries" (negotiations held on April 18, 1797) that anticipated the partition of Venetia and recognized Napoleon's conquests of Belgium and Lombardy. In the period of peace that followed, the peninsula enjoyed a short period of democracy, which was ended by the Austro-Russian offensive of April 1799.

It is to this brief but decisive period in Italian history that the origins of the Risorgimento, the great Italian national revival of the 19th century, must be traced. Insofar as the Risorgimento involved the formation of political groups affirming the right of the Italian people to achieve a government suited to its desires and its traditions and the growth of a feeling of nationalism and individual responsibility, it certainly began at this time.

The Neapolitan historian Vincenzo Cuoco wrote in 1800 that the Italian Revolution had been a "passive revolution" that, imported from France, had no real roots and had not been the expression of a national governing class. This criticism of the Jacobin rule in Italy between 1796 and 1799 has been continually repeated up to the present day. Historians, feeling the need to distinguish among the several types of republicanism, have characterized the strictly "Jacobin" group as ideologically descended from Robespierrism and the heroic days of the French Terror of 1793–94. But this is to attribute too much ideological rigidity to men who often, from political necessity, shifted their position. It was with no sense of inconsistency that those who had supported the most radical republican democracy later assumed administrative and governmental responsibilities in the Napoleonic Kingdom of Italy from 1805 and in Joachim Murat's (French general; Napoleon's brother-in-law) Kingdom of Naples from 1808.

Yet, among the Italian Francophiles, some distinction needs to be made between the moderates and the extreme democrats. This lay essentially in the different meanings given by each group to the concept of popular sovereignty, to which all alike paid lip service. The doctrine of equality, for instance, could be restricted to a doctrine of equal rights before the law or enlarged to shake the foundations of private property. The differing views of the two groups could also be seen in their attitude to practical details such as taxation, schemes for public education, and for regulating industry and the labour market.

The Italian republics of 1796–99. Meanwhile, political initiative was entirely with the French. The Directory, the government set up in France following the adoption of the moderate Thermidorian constitution (known as the Constitution of the Year III), regarded the unexpected conquests in Italy primarily as a bargaining point, but Napoleon, commander of the armies in Italy, strongly favoured the rise there of "sister republics." To organize such new states, which would accept the French hegemony and show promise of financial, political, and administrative stability, Napoleon realized that he must support not the democrats but the moderates, who were in a position to control the economy and public opinion and to crush any possible popular uprisings.

Napoleon's notion of the "sister republics"

The prevalence of conservative and moderate forces in the cities of Emilia (especially in Bologna) persuaded Napoleon and the agents of the Directory to found the first democratic state there. Thus arose the Cispadane Republic, which, at the Congress of Modena (ended March 1, 1797), adopted a constitution modelled on that of Thermidor but with perhaps greater emphasis on limiting the hegemony of the Catholic Church. Lombardy, where the political struggle was more intense and the democratic party more active, was kept for a longer time under a provisional government, so that the "sister state" in that area, known as the Cisalpine Republic, was not proclaimed until June 29, 1797. The Cispadane Republic was fused with it a month later, Napoleon and the Directory regarding the danger of setting up an overstrong state as offset by its anti-Austrian function and by the weakening of the Italian democrats that would follow from their subjection to a central government more easily controllable from Paris. Yet the Cisalpine Republic proved to be the most restless of the states that the French set up in the peninsula—witness the suppression there of newspapers, the temporary detention of journalists and writers, the dissolution of democratic clubs, and the necessity in 1798 of organizing no less than four coups d'etat to exclude from the two legislative assemblies (Consiglio degli Juniori, Consiglio dei Seniori) and the Cisalpine Directory those who most strongly resisted orders from Paris. The moderates now began to emerge as the coming ruling and bureaucratic class, not only because they were protected by the French but also because they had actual capacity and previous administrative experience.

The Ligurian Republic, proclaimed on June 6, 1797, after uprisings there by the pro-French "patriots" against the aristocratic government, had a less troubled history. The moderates, many of them members of the old aristocracy and working hand in glove with the Directory, always retained control and quashed the democrats' hopes of fusion with the Cisalpine Republic.

In northern Italy there were no other Jacobin republics. In Piedmont, the King, after suppressing a series of conspiracies with much bloodshed, was forced by the French to leave the country in December 1798; in February 1799 the kingdom was annexed to France. Venetia, already tampered with by the "Preliminaries" of 1797 drawn up at Leoben, was ceded to Austria by Napoleon by the Peace of Campo Formio (October 17, 1797), which marked yet another stage in the Italian democrats' disillusionment with the "liberators," notably shown in Ugo Foscolo's novel *Le ultime lettere di Jacopo Ortis* (1798; "Last Letters of Jacopo Ortis").

Though the First Coalition formed to resist the French had now been dissolved, French penetration into Italy continued, and, as a result of the Pope's hostile attitude and the revolutionary ferment in Rome, the Papal States were invaded in January 1798, and the Roman Republic was proclaimed on March 15; Pope Pius VI withdrew to Tuscany. The French occupation weighed heavily on Rome, as it did elsewhere; and there, too, the balance of power swung to the moderates and conservatives, though perhaps the democratic opposition, consolidated around the Constitutional Club, was freer than elsewhere in Italy. From this milieu came the *Pensieri politici* (1798; "Political Meditations") of the southern exile Vincenzio Russo, one of the most important examples of Italian Jacobin thought.

Invasion of the Papal States

With Napoleon's departure from Italy in November 1797 for his ill-starred Egyptian expedition, the Italian situation changed. In November 1798 the Bourbon king Ferdinand IV of Naples, yielding to English pressure, crossed the papal border and in a swift campaign occupied Rome to re-establish the pope's dominion there. But the counteroffensive was not long in coming, and, while the Bourbon army was dispersing, the French entered Naples on January 23, 1799, although they were held up for three days by popular resistance. The Bourbon court, protected by the English fleet, prudently retired to safety in Sicily. Thus was born the Parthenopean Republic, which, though its authority extended over only some of the southern provinces—the others remaining either in the throes of anarchy or under Bourbon control—was the most democratic of the Italian states set up between 1796 and 1799. Against the Directory's wishes, the military commander Jean-Étienne Championnet and the commissary Marc-Antoine Jullien (a former Babeufist) set up a revolutionary government, and for a few months the intellectual elite of the south enthusiastically participated in the revolutionary experience.

Collapse of the republics. The political situation was rapidly degenerating, however. The Second Coalition against France had been formed in March 1799, and Austro-Russian troops, after occupying the Cisalpine Republic, reached Turin in less than two months; the whole Po plain was thus lost, and the greater part of the French Army abandoned Naples. But the destruction of the Parthenopean Republic was the work of bands of peasants organized by Cardinal Fabrizio Ruffo, a faithful adherent of the King who had landed in Calabria in February; they quickly disposed of the weak democratic militia. Their Armata della Santa Fede (Army of the Holy Faith) was the most important jacquerie (peasant uprising) in the history of modern Italy; invoking God and the King, they devastated the castles of the aristocracy and occupied the communal land that the barons had usurped; they also massacred the bourgeoisie who had set up provisional municipalities. The struggle against the Jacobins and the French was transformed into a great anti-aristocratic movement, which the monarchy skillfully turned to advantage. Naples surrendered on June 23, 1799, and soon afterward the King returned from Sicily; at the behest of the English admiral Horatio Nelson and of Queen Maria Carolina (sister of Marie-Antoinette of France), and after summary trials, the King ordered the execution of more than 100 patriots, to whom the terms of surrender had granted safe-conduct. Thus the best among the southern administrators were destroyed. King Ferdinand's role as a reformer was now a thing of the past.

Nelson and Naples

Between March and July 1799, the French occupied Tuscany and were driven out of it by a violent peasant uprising (the "Viva Maria"), which developed into a march on the cities, where there were massacres of Jews (at Siena) and of citizens who were, or were presumed to be, Jacobins. The rising re-established the power of the rural clergy and the landowning aristocracy.

In September 1799 the Roman Republic finally fell. All Italy was reconquered, and the French resisted only in Genoa, while a stream of Jacobins took refuge in France. The three years of revolution were ended.

The pro-French "patriots" had completely failed to enlist the support of the masses. From the summer of 1796, the rural districts were in ferment, almost always in opposition to the new rulers; there were peasant marches on cities such as Pavia, Bergamo, Brescia, and those of the Romagna and later of Tuscany, while armed bands, especially in the Marches, Tuscany, and the Kingdom of Naples, controlled or reconquered whole regions. Even in some cities, such as Verona, and especially in Naples, the popular dislike of the French and the Jacobins was clearly apparent. The influence of the clergy and the inordinate taxes levied by the republican regimes do not suffice to explain this reactionary alignment, which was, in fact, much deeper seated; only the gradual formation and development of a grass-roots opposition movement would prove capable of weaning the populace from its innate and instinctive conservatism.

Defeated in the internal political struggle, the Italian Jacobins also suffered disillusion with regard to their French ally. Contributions originally levied for military purposes had everywhere degenerated into pure pillage; the constitutions of the new republics were dictated by the French; members of the opposition were imprisoned or driven out of office by coups d'etat; and, finally, Napoleon had adopted an undisguisedly autocratic policy, shown by his reinstatement of the King in Piedmont in the summer of 1796 and by his arbitrary cession of Venetia to Austria in 1797. But their disillusionment with the French, however severe, was unlikely ever to reconcile the Jacobins with the absolute monarchs; rather, it strengthened their nationalism. In Piedmont there was an anti-French, unionist, and democratic organization (the Raggi), and everywhere the need was felt for strong nationalist governments that would lead the country toward unity and independence.

The French Consulate, 1799–1804. Having become master of France by his coup d'etat of 18 Brumaire (November 9, 1799), Napoleon renewed his Italian conquests. Expected by the Austrians to use the Mont Cenis pass, he crossed the Alps by the Great St. Bernard, almost without opposition, and reoccupied Milan on June 2, 1800. A few days later he inflicted a definitive defeat on the enemy at Marengo, between the Bormida and the Po rivers. Defeated also in Germany, the Second Coalition fell to pieces; by the Treaty of Lunéville (February 9, 1801), Austria returned the Cisalpine territory and some portions of Venetia; and the Ligurian Republic was re-established. Piedmont was reannexed to France in September 1802, together with Elba and Piombino, as also was the duchy of Parma, although official status was not given to this de facto arrangement until 1808. Austrian influence was ended even in Tuscany, where Louis, son of Ferdinand, the Spanish duke of Parma, was enthroned as king of Etruria. In northern Italy, Austria kept only Venetia, whereas France, directly or indirectly, maintained control from the Alps to the Tuscan Maremma, while the restored papal and Bourbon governments further south had little power.

The second Cisalpine Republic, established in June 1800, soon proved to be a transitional regime, since it lacked the necessary joint support of the moderates and landowners. Napoleon's most trusted councillor in Paris for Italian affairs was the Milanese patrician Francesco Melzi d'Eril. This statesman, who in 1796–99 had hoped to see upper Italy united in a constitutional monarchy under a Habsburg or a Bourbon ruler, was the most clear-sighted exponent of the views of the old moderate ruling class, still yearning for absolute and enlightened governments. Napoleon favoured the formation of a large Italian state, provided that he could control it. He wanted an Italian republic with a constitution similar to that then operative in France, with the central authority vested in the president and with the representative structure weak and divided among three "estates," the landed proprietors, the merchants and traders, and the learned men and clerics. In such a state he wanted as president either himself or a member of his family. At Melzi's insistence, the new state was established not by a mere edict issued by the French first consul (Napoleon) but by an Italian Constitutional Assembly that met at Lyon, in France, in January 1802. Napoleon appointed Melzi, who was supported by the majority of the deputies, vice president (he himself had become president only after resistance on the fourth vote) and accepted the change of name from the meaningless Cisalpine Republic to Italian Republic.

Melzi and the second Cisalpine Republic

Melzi pursued a policy of amalgamation. Though the majority of the prefectures and ministries were in the hands of notables, who were often nobles as well, members of the democratic opposition were also gradually included, being given important administrative, cultural, and military posts. The formation of an Italian army was, during the whole Napoleonic period, one of the major concerns of the government, and enduring nationalist sentiments matured among its ranks. Serving as administrators and politicians, the nobles and the educated bourgeoisie for the first time felt an urge to govern and defend their country. Neither the constant French interference and taking of financial levies nor the absence of an Italian foreign policy diminished their enthusiasm for their new political role.

The Napoleonic Empire, 1804–14. When the First Consul became emperor, the Italian Republic became a kingdom (proclaimed on March 17, 1805); King Napoleon appointed as viceroy his stepson Eugène de Beauharnais, and Melzi stepped aside. The more docile Antonio Aldini became Secretary of State in his place. Italian autonomy was still further limited; but the Napoleonic victories, constantly increasing the territory of the kingdom, provided some compensation. By the Treaty of Pressburg (December 26, 1805), Venetia was annexed, and, with a separate constitution, Dalmatia and Istria were joined to it; in April 1808 the Marches, too, became part of the kingdom, which, by the Treaty of Schönbrunn (October 14, 1809), lost its nominal sovereignty over Dalmatia and Istria; these, together with Trieste, with other territories taken from Austria, and with Ragusa (modern Dubrovnik, Yugoslavia), became the seven French *départements* of the Illyrian provinces. France directly annexed Liguria (June 4, 1805) and Tuscany (in effect from January 1806, formally from March 2, 1809). And with Napoleon's abolition in 1809 of the temporal power of the papacy, Pope Pius VII, who then excommunicated him, was imprisoned, first in France and later at Savona, in northwestern Italy.

As emperor of France or as king of Italy, Napoleon thus directly controlled all upper and middle Italy. During his rule far-reaching reforms were brought about. Though the new codes of law were almost all translated wholesale from the French, without consideration for Italian traditions, they nevertheless introduced at a stroke, particularly in the field of criminal law, a modern jurisprudence notably sensitive to the rights of the individual. Properties held in mortmain, the old feudal ecclesiastical tenure, specifically those of the regular clergy, were transferred to the state and sold, and the remaining feudal rights and jurisdictions were abolished. Road systems were everywhere improved; and both primary and higher education were widely diffused. The increased pressure of taxation was thus compensated for by a network of new and improved services that were to hasten Italian economic and social progress.

The Continental System, a blockade designed to close the whole of the European continent to British trade, proclaimed on November 21, 1806, was freely broken everywhere, including on the Italian coastline; its true meaning was that of favouring French industry, particularly the silk industry. But the war economy stimulated Italian production and led to the development of industries such as the machine industry and metallurgy and to important public works.

In the south, after the repressions and executions of 1799, the Bourbons experimented with some cautious reforms, mainly fiscal and anti-feudal, in order to further strengthen the loyalty of the rural population, which had already proved so valuable. But the Neapolitan government was desperately weak, both militarily and politically; and, between February and March 1806, the French were able to occupy the whole country, while the court once again took refuge in Sicily. On March 30, 1806, Joseph Bonaparte, brother of Napoleon, was proclaimed king of the Two Sicilies; when he became king of Spain in 1808, he was succeeded as king of Naples by one of the most famous French generals, Joachim Murat. Despite this dynastic change, the nine years of French rule in the south can be considered as a whole and represent the most profound and effective reform movement that the country had hitherto experienced.

King Joachim of Naples

King Joachim was more independent of Paris than King Joseph; in his reign not only were there fewer French ministers and councillors in relation to Neapolitan officials, but he also opposed Napoleon over the application of the Continental System. During the ten years of French rule, feudal privileges and immunities were finally abolished; but even thus mulcted, the landed aristocracy were still able to retain economic supremacy in the country. Extensively buying up the confiscated property of the church and of other proscribed landowners, they thus subverted Joachim's plan to establish small peasant holdings. Much common land originally usurped by large landowners was, however, recovered, and the position of the *galantuomini*, or bourgeoisie, was definitely strengthened. Fiscal, judicial, educational, and administrative reforms were introduced in line with those already made in the Kingdom of Italy.

Meanwhile, both Sardinia, where the court of Savoy took refuge, and Sicily remained apart from the Napoleonic world. In Sicily, the Bourbons were under a strict English control that, originally purely military and naval, soon became political. When, in 1811–12, the court was in conflict with the Sicilian nobles over fiscal matters and arrested the leaders among them, the British commander, Lord George Bentinck, intervened and enforced the adoption of an extremely moderate constitution that left great power to the nobles, though it markedly limited the absolute power of the king. Sicily then experienced a short and intense period of autonomy and political ferment, which was ended in 1816 when the restored Bourbons abolished the constitution and reunited the island to the kingdom.

The Napoleonic regime fell in Italy as it did in the rest of Europe. Eugène, the viceroy of Italy, and Joachim, the king of Naples, with their respective armies had taken part in the fatal Russian campaign of 1812, but, at the moment of defeat, Joachim deserted Napoleon, returned to Naples, and, after making terms with the Austrians, advanced with his Neapolitan troops as far as the Po (March 1814); Eugène, defeated by the Austrians and Neapolitans, was able, by the terms of the Armistice of Schiarino-Rizzino (April 16), to retain Lombardy; but an insurrection that broke out at Milan on April 20 allowed the Austrians to occupy the entire country.

THE RESTORATION PERIOD

The Vienna settlement. At the Congress of Vienna, held by the victorious allies to resettle Europe, it was decided to restore the Bourbons to Naples. It was for this reason that, seizing the opportunity of Napoleon's return to power during the Hundred Days, King Joachim changed sides yet again and, on March 15, 1815, declared war on Austria and, by the Proclamation of Rimini (March 30, 1815), incited the Italians to a nationalist war. Quickly defeated, he was forced to abdicate in May; after taking refuge in Corsica, he landed at Pizzo di Calabria to reconquer the kingdom but was immediately captured by the Bourbons and executed in October 1815.

The Congress of Vienna established the political condition of Italy that lasted until unification. The emperor of Austria, Francis I, became king of Lombardy-Venetia, which was thus incorporated into the Habsburg states, and the former episcopal principality of Trent was directly annexed to Austria. King Victor Emmanuel I of Savoy, in addition to recovering his dominions, acquired the entire Ligurian territory; the duchy of Parma went to the daughter of Francis I and wife of Napoleon, Marie-Louise of Habsburg, but at her death it was to revert to the House of Bourbon-Parma, which meanwhile was granted the duchy of Lucca; the Habsburg-Estes returned to Modena, further acquiring the duchy of Massa by inheritance in 1825; in Tuscany, the House of Lorraine added to its former domains the State of the Presidi and the reversion of Lucca when the Bourbons should return to Parma (this did not take place until 1847); the Pope recovered his temporal dominions in Italy; and the Bourbon Ferdinand IV of Naples, with the new title of King Ferdinand I of the Two Sicilies, reoccupied his possessions.

Restored hegemony of Austria

Thus the Vienna settlement brought about the disappearance of the three aristocratic republics of Venice, Genoa, and Lucca; it strengthened Piedmont and restored the undisputed hegemony of Austria. Austrian troops garrisoned Ferrara, ready to intervene in case of trouble in the Papal States; Austria was given the right to intervene if necessary in the Kingdom of the Two Sicilies; members of the House of Habsburg reigned in Parma, Modena, and Florence; while Venetia and Lombardy became in practice provinces of the Austrian empire. Only Piedmont remained outside the system that Metternich, the Austrian foreign minister and later chancellor, had imposed on Italy; but, under the secret protection of Russia, its government proved to be equally reactionary.

On April 7, 1815, Francis I proclaimed the formation of the Lombardo-Venetian kingdom; but the new state was a fiction because the two regimes remained separated, each directly subject to the central ministries in Vienna. Thus Milan lost its role of capital city; the majority of the Napoleonic bureaucracy was liquidated, and the centralizing authority of Vienna became all-pervasive; many reforms, especially in jurisprudence, were abolished. Discontent proved general, and Austria reacted by increasingly severe police measures and stricter censorship, suppressing, for example, the best liberal and romantic periodical, *Il Conciliatore* ("The Conciliator"), after only a very brief existence (September 1818–October 1819).

Returned from exile in Sardinia, Victor Emmanuel I of Savoy abolished all the laws promulgated by the French and removed from public office all those who had collaborated with them. He invited the Jesuits back into the kingdom and turned many educational institutions over to the clergy. Hence, a liberal opposition was not long in forming among the nobility and the bourgeoisie.

Francis IV of Modena showed an equally conservative intransigence, whereas in Parma Marie-Louise instituted a mild rule and maintained the principal French reforms. Though many of these were soon abolished in Tuscany by Ferdinand III of Lorraine, the enlightened legislation, economic liberalism, and lax policing and censorship characterizing his rule and that of his successor, Leopold II, made the duchy a haven for liberals. It also stimulated cultural activity: at Florence many Italian writers —such as the poet Giacomo Leopardi, the historian Pietro Colletta, and Niccolò Tommaseo—gathered around the Gabinetto (studio), founded by Gian Pietro Vieusseux; Florence was also the birthplace of a famous periodical, *L'Antologia* (1821–33; "The Anthology").

In the Papal States the Restoration, brought about mainly by the diplomacy of the cautious secretary of state, Cardinal Ercole Consalvi, was characterized by increased centralization of government. And, because the public offices were a monopoly of the clergy, the bourgeoisie and the educated classes, who, under the French and Italian regime, had held some responsibility, became deeply discontented, especially in the Romagna.

In the Kingdom of Naples the victorious powers had made sure that the Bourbons would not repeat the reprisals of 1799. The Restoration appeared to begin well, under the balanced policy of the minister Luigi de' Medici, who absorbed the greater part of Murat's capable bureaucracy. Many of the French reforms, both administrative and judicial, were retained, but concessions made to the church by the Concordat of 1818 and strict financial economies hampered the advancement of the bourgeoisie. It was especially among these, the *galantuomini* ("gentlemen"), that discontent found an outlet in an imposing conspiratorial organization, the Carbonari. Already founded during the French period, with a vaguely nationalistic program, it now became more widespread, formulating definitely constitutional aims; the southern bourgeoisie were determined to take part in political life and openly to forward their own interests. From the south the lodges of the Carbonari quickly spread throughout Italy, finding their chief centres of support in the Marches, the Romagna, Piedmont, and Milan.

The Carbonari

Events in the 1820s. *Effects of the Spanish Revolution.* The Spanish Revolution of 1820 had repercussions in Italy. In the Kingdom of Naples, former members of Murat's army, connected with the Carbonari, marched on the capital (July 2, 1820) to the cry of "Long live liberty and the constitution" and found immediate support among the bourgeoisie and in the army. The King was forced to yield (July 1820) to the liberals' demand for the introduction of the Spanish constitution of 1812; it not only limited the king's power but also decreased centralization and thus reduced the influence of the capital. But the new regime proved short-lived, for it had too many enemies: the King himself, eager to recover his absolute power; Sicily, attempting a separatist revolution (July 15–17), which was violently suppressed by the Neapolitan constitutional government; and, most serious, Austria, which had been given at Vienna the right of intervening to maintain the restored monarchy. In January 1821 Metternich was able to convoke an international congress at Laibach, attended by representatives of the great powers and of the Italian states, and by King Ferdinand himself. Overcoming the weak Anglo-French opposition, the King obtained approval for military intervention. Accordingly, the Austrian Army descended on the kingdom and, defeating the constitutional troops, occupied Naples on March 23, 1821, re-establishing the King's absolute government.

In Piedmont, the more liberal and cultivated wing of the nobility was hostile to Victor Emmanuel I's reactionary position, and the Carbonarian bourgeoisie, with its constitutional hopes, allied itself with them. In the wake of the events at Naples, a conspiracy was set in motion, supported by the Lombard liberals and receiving the covert approval of Charles Albert of Savoy, prince of Carignano, successor-designate to the throne under Salic law. Between March 9 and 13, the revolt, organized by the military and the bourgeoisie, spread from Alessandria to Turin; the King abdicated in favour of his brother Charles Felix, and, in the latter's absence, appointed Charles Albert as regent. On March 14 the Regent proclaimed the Spanish constitution, though its adoption was to be contingent upon the new king's approval. But, from his refuge in Modena, Charles Felix refused to accept it, and, with Austrian assistance and the troops that had remained loyal to him, he rapidly reoccupied the country. Three of the conspirators were executed, and the many prison sentences meted out and the rigorous purge of the army provoked a massive emigration. Charles Albert regained the confidence of the new king, but the reconciliation caused a breach between him and the liberals that persisted after he succeeded to the throne in 1831.

In Lombardy-Venetia there was no revolution, but a complex organization of opponents of the regime was discovered and suppressed. The Carbonarian lodge in Milan was attacked in October 1820, and some of the conspirators were deported. In March 1821 the police found the first evidence of the conspiracy of the *federati*, led by the Milanese nobleman Federigo Confalonieri, whose program, though more moderate than that of the Carbonari, was no less anti-Austrian and constitutional; from December 1821 to January 1823, members of the conspiracy were discovered even in the army and the upper bureaucracy. Many received death sentences, all eventually commuted to long terms of imprisonment.

Federati conspiracy

Economic slump and revival. The political reactionism (which was prolonged in the Romagna by executions until 1828) was accompanied during this decade by a general economic recession. After the famine of 1816–17, Russian grain flooded the Italian markets, and there was a crisis of agricultural overproduction; the desperate poverty of the peasantry led to widespread pellagra, brigandage, and grain riots. The slump continued unabated until nearly 1830, when successful mulberry cultivation brought renewed rural prosperity and was sufficient, particularly in Piedmont and Lombardy, to reestablish agricultural credit and provide capital for the development of the textile and some engineering industry.

Renewed prosperity brought leisure for cultural activities, and the economic and social problems of the country began to be discussed in many periodicals; the most important of these was the Milanese *Annali universali di statistica* ("Universal Annals of Statistics"), whose editor-in-chief for some years was the philosopher Gian Domenico Romagnosi and in which his pupil Carlo Cattaneo began to set forth his ideas. In fact, the ranks of the political and cultural opposition, hitherto comprising only the Lombard and Tuscan moderates, would soon include democrats and Catholics.

The rebellions of 1831 and their aftermath. The failure of the uprisings of 1831 proved that the Carbonari were coming to the end of their usefulness. The hopes raised by the revolution in Paris in July 1830 had set on foot a conspiratorial movement that had spread from Modena to the cities of Emilia, chiefly as a result of the efforts of two Carbonari, Enrico Misley and Ciro Menotti. Unfortunately, they relied on the sympathy of Duke Francis IV of Modena, who was willing to countenance changes that might enlarge his small state. But, when he learned that the plot was known to the Austrian police, he had Menotti and 43 other conspirators arrested. Immediately afterward a revolt overthrew the papal government in Bologna and in a few days spread to the duchies of Modena and Parma, to the Romagna, the Marches, and Umbria, leaving only Lazio under papal rule. But for various reasons the new provisional governments of the rebel cities failed to organize a unified military defense; help they had hoped for from the French was not forthcoming, and thus the Austrian Army was able to re-establish the rule of legitimacy during March 1831.

The moderate liberal leaders, most of them Carbonari, had shown their readiness to treat with the absolute monarchs and had deeply distrusted those republicans and democrats who sought to achieve unification by force of arms. Another component element of the ultimate unification movement was the Adelfi, the group comprising followers of Filippo Buonarroti, the former Babeufist who had taken part in the events of 1796. Ultimately, the task of organizing the democratic and republican opposition conspiracy was undertaken by a young Genoese, Giuseppe Mazzini. Exiled to France at the age of 25 in 1830, he found himself turning away from both the Carboneria and Buonarrottism. In distinction from the Carboneria, his organization, Giovane Italia (Young Italy), was unionist and republican; but, though it put its trust in the education and participation of the people, it had no egalitarian and Jacobin leanings. The new faction spread, especially in upper Italy, with amazing rapidity, absorbing the Buonarrottian and Carbonarian groups. In 1833–34 the first abortive Mazzinian uprisings took place in Savoy and at Genoa, the latter organized by Giuseppe Garibaldi, who then fled to France; in 1834 the Austrian police identified as many as 2,000 members of Giovane Italia in Lombardy. In 1836 Mazzini, who had established firm relationships with revolutionaries in other countries and had joined them in founding the Giovane Europa (Young Europe), left Switzerland and settled in London.

The rise of Mazzini

The repressions they had suffered and witnessed, together with the reinforcement of the conservative status quo in Europe, convinced the moderates that it was useless to organize conspiracies with limited membership, that what was needed was to educate public opinion. Meanwhile, the peace forcibly imposed on the peninsula from 1831 to 1848 favoured economic development, notable everywhere except in the south. The south, in fact, remained backward, and the growth of bourgeois property that resulted from the division of the great feudal holdings did nothing to change this. Thus the imbalance between north and south, which would be felt even more acutely after national unification, continued to grow. Genoa and Milan became two of the chief financial centres of Europe; Piedmontese and Lombard industry expanded rapidly; in Venetia important land-reclamation projects were completed, while, in Tuscany, banks and commercial establishments did a flourishing trade, connected especially with the port of Livorno. Throughout the country the construction of a railway network increased commerce and gave rise to subsidiary industries. This economic revival made it more difficult for the governments to tighten police control; at Milan in 1839, Carlo Cattaneo began publishing his periodical *Politecnico*, in which he argued that the progress of science and technology depended upon government reforms. In the same year Pisa saw the first congress of Italian scientists, which was to reconvene annually down to 1847, assuming a more markedly nationalistic character with each passing year.

Thus conditions gradually became more favourable for the moderates to realize their aims of increasing education and abolishing censorship and police surveillance. In the cause of unification they sought to standardize tolls and trade practices, increase cultural exchanges throughout the country, and, above all, finally to establish representative institutions suitable to Italian traditions and to Catholicism, the religion of the majority of citizens. Liberal Catholicism found its most important expression in Italy in Vincenzo Gioberti's *Primato morale e civile degli italiani* (1843; "Civil and Moral Primacy of the Italians"), in which he affirmed the idea of progress as a return of the existent to the idea, of man to God, realizable only through the mediation of the church. Gioberti envisioned a new and positive role for the temporal power of the papacy, advocating the development of a federated Italy, free from the Austrian hegemony, under the nominal presidency of the pope. His ideas were influential among important sections of the clergy and among Catholics in general. Under different formulations, the new papalist movement struck root and found its best propagandists and theoreticians in Cesare Balbo, Niccolò Tommaseo, and the Jesuit Antonio Rosmini-Serbati.

Liberal Catholicism

The renewal of Mazzinian attempts at armed rebellion (among them the celebrated and ill-fated expedition of the Venetian Bandiera brothers, who landed in Calabria in July 1844 and, with seven companions, were executed by a firing squad), all suppressed with bloodshed, increased the esteem felt for the moderates both by governments and the general public. The election of Pope Pius IX in 1846 augured well for the future of the Papal States; his nomination was the result of anti-Austrian feeling, and at the beginning he showed liberal leanings. His first step was the granting of an amnesty to those who had been sentenced for political reasons; this was followed by a gradual removal from governmental posts of the most reactionary prelates, then by permission to publish political periodicals; finally, in April 1847, he instituted a council of state that, though only on a consultative level, gave to the laity a share in public life. Influenced by this liberalism, rulers elsewhere in Italy granted some reforms; one of the most important was the press law of May 1847, by which Grand Duke Leopold II removed restrictions from the press in Tuscany. But the reforms encouraged extremists, and the reactionary powers of Europe became convinced that the peace of Italy was in danger. In July 1847 Metternich sent Austrian troops to occupy papal Ferrara. This intervention stimulated cordiality and cooperation among the Italian rulers, led by Charles Albert of Piedmont, whose relations with Austria were particularly strained. But, while the sovereigns were discussing the formation of an Italian customs union, rendered more urgent by the famine of 1847, the people began to rise.

The revolutions of 1848. On January 9 the first of the revolutions of 1848 broke out in Sicily, in Palermo. Starting as a popular insurrection, it soon acquired overtones of Sicilian separatism and, supported by the nobility and the bourgeoisie, spread throughout the entire island. Individual reforms were no longer enough to content the revolutionaries, who were determined to have new and more liberal constitutions. Ferdinand II of the Two Sicilies was the first to grant one (January 29, 1848), and the other rulers were compelled to follow his example —Leopold II on February 17, Charles Albert on March 4, and Pius IX on March 14. The only Italian rulers who did not yield were the Austrians, who instead reinforced their garrisons in Lombardy-Venetia, arrested the two famous leaders of the opposition at Venice, Daniele Manin and Niccolò Tommaseo, and others at Milan, and suppressed the student demonstrations at Padua and Pavia. But on March 22 and 23, when revolution broke out at Budapest and Vienna, Venice and Milan freed themselves by swift and victorious insurrections. In the course of a few days, almost the whole of Lombardy-Venetia was lost to the Austrians, and their army fell back into the Quadrilateral (the land lying between Mantua, Verona, Peschiera, and Legnago). On March 23 Charles Albert declared war on Austria; it was a risky military decision to take, but chances for a nationalist war seemed good, and he had to assume the lead in order to prevent republican domination of the revolutionary movement. He annexed Parma and Modena, which had already driven out their dukes, and won a few other victories. But then the reverses began. Pius IX, Leopold II, and Ferdinand II, who had at first sent troops to support the Piedmontese army, hastened to withdraw them; the Pope's allocation of April 29 to the cardinals showed his unwillingness to further a nationalist movement and did much to discredit the papacy among patriots. Lombardy and Venetia, though not without opposition, accepted annexation to Piedmont, but the Piedmontese regular army was unable to stand up to the Austrian counteroffensive; after a series of lost battles, Charles Albert was finally defeated at the gates of Milan and on August 6 withdrew behind the Ticino River, leaving the Austrians in possession of the city and the duchy, which a popular insurrection had freed only a few months earlier. The accusation of "royal treachery," which the Lombard democrats then formulated, long survived in Italian political polemics.

Charles Albert's declaration of war

By the terms of the Armistice of Salasco (August 9, 1848), the Piedmontese army withdrew from Lombardy. But within Piedmont the new constitution was not abrogated, and revolutionary and democratic ideas remained alive.

The forces of reaction triumphed throughout Europe. At Vienna, Prague, Budapest, and Paris, the revolutions of 1848 were stifled; in Naples the King regained power in a successful coup on May 15, subsequently reconquering Sicily, while at Rome more conservative policies were followed. But Venice, under the dictatorship of Daniele Manin, refused to accept the Armistice of Salasco and resisted the Austrian siege. In Tuscany, Leopold II, finding that the democrats, led by Giuseppe Montanelli and Francesco Domenico Guerrazzi, were gaining the advantage over the moderate ministers and aiming at an Italian Constituent Assembly, fled to Gaeta (February 1849); while, at Florence, a predominantly democratic provisional government was formed. At Rome, the minister Pellegrino Rossi, a former Carbonaro who had returned from France and embarked on a policy of conciliation, was assassinated (November 15, 1848), and the democrats controlled the situation; in consequence Pius IX fled in disguise (November 24), also taking refuge in Gaeta. At Rome the constitutional government convoked a Constituent Assembly with universal suffrage, which, meeting on February 5, proclaimed the republic. The Italian revolution seemed to have been reborn, and the Piedmontese democrats impelled Charles Albert to renew the war with Austria (March 20, 1849). But on March 23 he was utterly routed at Novara and, on the same day, abdicated and went into exile. He was succeeded by Victor Emmanuel II, to whom the Austrian commander conceded an honourable armistice so as not to weaken the monarchical and moderate forces to the advantage of the democrats. The defeat of Piedmont made the position of the democrats and republicans impossible. In Tuscany the moderates called back the Grand Duke, who thereupon returned with Austrian troops that crushed a democratic insurrection at Livorno (May 1849); the reconquest of Brescia in March, after ten days of fighting, left Venice isolated, though it held out against the Austrian Army until August. The Roman Republic, led by Mazzini and Garibaldi, held out until July 3 against the French expeditionary corps that the new president of the republic, Louis-Napoleon, had dispatched in order to repay his clerical supporters. The dispossessed sovereigns everywhere returned, abrogated the constitutions, dissolved the parliaments, and, especially at Naples, filled up the prisons.

UNIFICATION

The role of Piedmont. The exception to this picture of reaction was Piedmont. There King Victor Emmanuel found himself governing with a Parliament whose democratic majority was unwilling to ratify the treaty of peace with Austria, which was indispensable if the defeated country was to be reorganized. By the skillfully worded Proclamation of Moncalieri (November 20, 1849), which contrasted his policy favourably with that of the other Italian rulers, he inaugurated fresh elections, in which the moderate party emerged victorious. The new ministry was headed by Massimo d'Azeglio, a moderate trusted by the King; the most important of his measures was the Siccardi law curtailing ecclesiastical jurisdiction. In October 1850 Camillo di Cavour entered the Cabinet and, from that time, substantially directed financial policy toward free exchange, arranging international commercial treaties and drawing on foreign credit to reduce the public debt and to develop the railway system. This dynamism was displeasing to the conservatives and to the more cautious moderates, including Azeglio himself, who was displaced in 1852 as a result of Count Cavour's alliance (known as the *connubio*) with the Deputies of the left centre. Despite a series of disagreements between Cavour and the King, who was influenced by the clerical party and had some absolutist leanings, various ecclesiastical, fiscal, and judicial reforms were introduced. The prestige of the Piedmontese government both in Italy and internationally was also reinforced by a variety of factors.

Cavour enters the Cabinet

In March 1854 France and England had intervened in support of Turkey against Russia in the Crimea; to obtain the support of Austria, they were prepared to guarantee the status quo in Italy, which only Piedmont at that time was in a position to disrupt. But Cavour, anticipating events, concluded an alliance with the Western powers and sent an expeditionary force to the Crimea, where (May 1855) it performed brilliantly. Thus he was able to sit among the victors at the Congress of Paris (February 1856) and there to affirm that the only threat to the peace of Italy and the only pretext for subversive plots was the burdensome Austrian overlordship. It was a tremendous achievement.

Meanwhile, the democratic and republican movement led by Mazzini was losing ground and crumbling. The failure of the Barraba, an attempt in February 1853 by the population of Milan to overpower the Austrian garrison; the discovery and execution at Belfiore (1852–53) of conspirators concerned in a plot centred at Mantua; and other abortive attempts to launch uprisings in Lunigiana and Cadore all contributed to discredit and discourage the democrats. Mazzini's isolation was completed by his known support of the Sapri expedition (June–July 1857), in which Carlo Pisacane, a Neapolitan Socialist with whom he had been in deep ideological disagreement, landed on the coast of Campania with 300 companions; the expedition ended in a massacre.

The democrats, then, were divided and unable to carry on the revolution. There was nothing to be hoped for in the restored governments. In Lombardy-Venetia, Austria had carried out stern measures of repression, while, in Rome, Pius IX, influenced by the secretary of state Cardinal Giacomo Antonelli, refused to grant any reforms. There was now no room left for the liberal Catholicism of the years following 1848. At Naples as in the duchies, reaction became intractable; in Tuscany the Grand Duke tried vainly to make the country forget that he had recovered his throne only by the help of Austria.

The War of 1859. So only in Piedmont was there any hope left for the reformers. There Cavour succeeded in establishing in 1857 a monarchist–unionist party, the Società Nazionale Italiana (Italian National Society), to which the presidency of Manin and the vice presidency of Garibaldi gave a wider appeal than if it had been staffed only by moderates. Though not outlawing conspiratorial movements, Cavour wanted to solve the Italian question by international politics rather than by revolution. At a secret conference held at Plombières, France (July 1858), he arranged with the emperor Napoleon III that the French would intervene in Italy should Piedmont be invaded by Austria; he was clearly planning the complete expulsion of Austria from the peninsula. The price he was to pay for this help was the cession of Nice and Savoy to France and the suppression of the Mazzinian party, erroneously thought by Napoleon to be responsible for the dynamite attack made on him at Paris on January 14, which was, in fact, planned by the Romagno Felice Orsini. The Franco-Piedmontese alliance was finally concluded in January 1859, and, with Napoleon's approval, Victor Emmanuel delivered a speech from the throne in which he declared himself ready to hear the "cry of woe" against Austria that was rising in every part of Italy. Meanwhile, the military party in Vienna was urging the emperor Francis Joseph to declare war. On April 23 an insulting ultimatum demanding that Piedmont demobilize was rejected, and three days later the Austrian Army took the offensive. Thus, as Cavour had hoped, the proviso for French intervention became operative. The allies were victorious in the battles of Magenta, San Martino, and Solferino (June 1859), but, while the routed Austrian Army was in retreat, Napoleon III suddenly signed the Armistice of Villafranca with the Austrians. This sudden change of policy was caused by events in Italy, where unification seemed about to become a reality. At Florence on April 27, Leopold II was overthrown by an insurrection and fled, while the government passed to the moderates, with Baron Bettino Ricasoli as the emerging leader; in June the duchies of Parma and Modena revolted, followed by the Legations (the northern Papal States). The Marches and Umbria also rebelled but were quickly reconquered by papal troops. The liberated provinces declared their wish to be united to Piedmont, but France then, no more than at any time in the past, did not want a united Italy. At Villafranca it was arranged that Napoleon III should receive Lombardy from Austria and cede it to Piedmont; the sovereigns of Modena and Tuscany were to be restored, and plans were made to establish a federation among the rulers of the Italian states. This was a serious defeat for Cavour's policy, and he resigned in July 1859, the King replacing him in the government by Urbano Rattazzi. But England was particularly opposed to the forceful restoration of the rulers of Emilia and Tuscany, and even Napoleon III, who in the meanwhile had increased his prestige in France by the annexation of Nice and Savoy, was unenthusiastic; in this climate of international opinion, Cavour's policy soon returned to favour, and he resumed office on January 21, 1860. A series of plebiscites were then held in Tuscany and Emilia, all of which declared for union with Piedmont. The fear of a democratic revolution, the need to weaken Austria, and Great Britain's desire to set up a strong Italian state to balance France all induced the European powers to assist the Piedmontese monarchy in obtaining this great success.

Società Nazionale Italiana

Garibaldi and the Thousand. But the democratic party refused to admit that the national revolution was in any way complete, when so many parts of Italy remained under their old sovereigns. The most suitable place for a democratic revival was Sicily, where autonomous opposition to the Bourbon government was endemic and extremist. In April 1860 a popular insurrection broke out in Palermo (the *rivolta della Gancia*), which, though it was quickly quelled, spread through the cities and the countryside under the unmistakable influence of Mazzinian agents. It was then, at the beginning of May 1860, that the democrats showed that they were able to overcome the deep differences that had divided them during the previous decade. The Expedition of the Thousand, which, with the tacit approval of Cavour, set sail from Quarto, near Genoa, under the command of Garibaldi, had been principally recruited among the bourgeoisie of Lombardy and Venetia but also contained volunteers from all the old states and represented the most divergent forces.

Despite the scant preparation, the expedition, which was almost entirely without arms, after disembarking at Marsala on May 11 conquered nearly the whole of Sicily in less than three months. The factors that made this possible were the revolutionary ferment already existing there and Garibaldi's military skill. But the attitude of the Sicilian peasants proved ambivalent; at first welcoming the invaders, they later became disappointed by the failure to partition the feudal estates, and they even fought the Garibaldians. Though on May 14 he had proclaimed himself "Dictator in the name of Victor Emmanuel, king of Italy," Garibaldi had set up a provisional Sicilian government, actually directed by his associate Francesco Crispi, which came into serious conflict with Cavour's emissaries to the island; Cavour was afraid of a turn toward republicanism. Meanwhile, the European powers attempted to mediate, and the new king of the Two Sicilies, Francis II, granted a constitution and promised autonomy and pardon to the Sicilian rebels. But without the consent—and apparently even against the wishes—of Victor Emmanuel, Garibaldi crossed to Calabria on August 19, 1860, and on September 7 made a triumphant entry into Naples, which the King had abandoned, fleeing to Gaeta. On October 1 the last serious Bourbon resistance was overcome at the Battle of the Volturno, near Caserta. But the prestige of Garibaldi and of the democrats had grown too great, and it was time Cavour resumed the initiative. Persuading Napoleon III to make only a formal protest, he occupied the Marches and Umbria (September 1860); so as not to offend Napoleon's clericalism, it was agreed that Rome and Lazio should remain under the pope, while the rest of Italy was to become a moderate constitutional kingdom. On October 26, 1860, Victor Emmanuel, having entered Neapolitan territory with his army, met Garibaldi, who hailed him as

Garibaldi enters Naples

"king of Italy"; during October and November, the formerly papal and Bourbon provinces voted by plebiscites to be annexed to the kingdom of Italy. The kingdom's inauguration was formally proclaimed on March 17, 1861, by a Parliament meeting in Turin, and soon afterward (March 25 and 27) Cavour affirmed the necessity that, with the approval of France and with the famous formula "a free church in a free state," Rome should become the Italian capital; but, when he died, on June 6, 1861, the "Roman question," with many others, remained unsolved.

The kingdom proclaimed

Condition of the Italian kingdom. In 1861 the kingdom had 26,000,000 inhabitants, 78 percent of whom were illiterate, while 70 percent of its active population were engaged in agriculture. Thus it seemed unlikely that Italy could make the economic progress shown by other European countries in that period. The group that had gained the majority in Parliament in 1861 was the moderate-conservative right, based principally on an alliance between the Piedmontese group, headed by Giovanni Lanza and Quintino Sella, which controlled industries and banks, and a Tuscan group, led by Bettino Ricasoli, which was interested in commerce and transportation. This political class wanted a centralized governmental structure that would allow the Parliament and hence the executive power to control the local administrations, especially where democratic forces or autonomistic aspirations might otherwise become preponderant. By a series of laws in 1865, they effected legislative unification and established firm central control over the provinces and their communes through the appointment of regional prefects. The democratic opposition, entirely preoccupied with the problems of freeing Rome and Venetia, made little resistance to this authoritarian construction of the state.

Centralization certainly provided no remedy for the serious economic imbalance between north and south. The free-trade policy of the right-wing politicians ruined the weak industries of the south, especially the woolen industry in the Salerno district, which had hitherto been protected. Moreover, the south had few railways, which were built under contracts that suggested government corruption; and the systems of poor relief and education were, and remained, miserably inadequate. Naples, which in 1861 had 447,000 inhabitants and was the most populous city in Italy (Turin came next, with only 205,000), was afflicted with pauperism and viewed with jealousy by the smaller cities of the south. Yet the most intense wretchedness was in the rural districts, where the peasants had totally failed to acquire any proportion of the expropriated estates. Consequently, many of them took to an especially violent form of brigandage, which, though it was organized by former Bourbon officials and even by Bourbon emissaries loyal to the exiled Francis II, was primarily a peasant war directed especially against the agrarian bourgeoisie. The movement was harshly suppressed by troops, and at least 5,000 peasants were executed; but it was not brought to an end until 1865. Public opinion, however, remained largely dominated by the political problem of completing the country's unification. The democrats wanted above all to solve the Roman question, and, when Ricasoli's ministry (June 1861–March 1862) was succeeded by that of Urbano Rattazzi, a Piedmontese lawyer apparently more liberal than Ricasoli, it seemed that the time had come. In July and August, Garibaldi, despite government prohibition, raised armed bands in Sicily and began moving up the peninsula again to march on Rome; but Rattazzi, preoccupied with the attitude of France and Austria, and realizing that French troops were garrisoning Rome, had the army disperse the Garibaldian troops rounded up at Aspromonte, in Calabria, where (August 29, 1862) Garibaldi was wounded and put under arrest for two months. The scandal that followed brought about the fall of the government. An attempt at a partial solution of the Roman question was made by the ministry (March 1863–September 1864) of Marco Minghetti. By the Convention of September (signed at Paris on September 15, 1864), Napoleon III agreed to gradually withdraw French troops from papal territory in the course of the next two years; in return, Italy undertook to respect papal rule and—by a secret clause—to transfer the capital from Turin to Florence. When this condition became public, there was an uprising in Turin, with 30 dead (September 21–22), and Minghetti was forced to resign.

The Roman question

The adherence of Venetia and Rome. Two years later, attention was diverted from Rome to Venice by the outbreak of war (June 1866) between Austria and Prussia. Italy, governed by the ministry of the Piedmontese Alfonso La Marmora, took the opportunity to attack the Austrian-held lands in Italy but was defeated on land at Custoza on June 24 and at sea off Lissa on July 20. Only the Garibaldian volunteers in Trentino had some success. By the Treaty of Vienna (October 3, 1866), Italy, through the mediation of Napoleon III, obtained the cession of Venetia. After a short-lived Minghetti ministry, Rattazzi returned to power, giving tacit consent to the stationing of Garibaldian bands along the papal boundary; but Rattazzi resigned, and meanwhile Garibaldi went into action and was defeated by French troops at Mentana (November 3); upon re-entering Italian territory, he was arrested and sent to the island of Caprera, between Corsica and Sardinia, where he had property.

Both diplomatically and militarily Italy had suffered a marked loss of prestige. Nor was the internal situation happy. There were separatist revolts in Palermo (1866) and others around Parma (1869) because of the tax on milling grain; furthermore, financial restrictions, necessary in order to effect reorganizations and to support the army, made the government unpopular.

The ministry of Giovanni Lanza and Quintino Sella, formed in December 1869, was perhaps the most typical among the ministries of the right wing—it repressed the Mazzinians, advocated free trade, and was extremely prudent in foreign affairs, with a pro-French bias. But, despite its lack of brilliance and imagination and its subservience to France—shown when it almost yielded to King Victor Emmanuel's desire to intervene in the Franco-Prussian war of 1870—it was able finally to achieve the solution of the Roman question. This was made possible because the defeat and abdication of Napoleon III ended French protection of the papacy. On September 20, 1870, after a symbolic resistance by the papal army, Italian troops entered Rome, opening a breach in the wall of Porta Pia. The Pope, refusing to accept the situation, forthwith withdrew inside the Vatican.

With the taking of Rome, the geographical unification of Italy was completed. But an equally important popular unification remained totally unachieved. A vast gulf continued to divide the small proportion, perhaps 2 percent, of the population that, on the basis of a property suffrage, enjoyed electoral rights and was represented in moderate and anticlerical chambers and governments from the mainly illiterate masses, who, preponderantly peasant and Catholic, were beginning to be stirred by working class and Socialist doctrines. (Ma.B.)

DEVELOPMENTS FROM 1870 TO 1914

Once unification was achieved with the capture of Rome (even though Trent and Trieste, the *terre irredente*, or "unredeemed areas," still under Austrian rule, remained outside the boundaries), and once the Roman question was provisionally, albeit unilaterally, settled with the enactment of the Law of Guarantees (May 13, 1871), which guaranteed the pope full ecclesiastical freedom, the Giovanni Lanza–Quintino Sella government focussed its attention on domestic problems. The most crucial of these was the need to improve the financial situation, and this was accomplished in 1876 by holding back public expenditure and increasing revenue by taxation.

Financial problems

Minghetti's last ministry. When Lanza fell in June 1873, Marco Minghetti, who succeeded him in July, attacked the problem of the inflationary paper currency circulation that grew substantially after the introduction of forced currency under the Act of April 20, 1874, which stipulated the volume of currency to be put into circulation for about 20 years; this act set up a consortium of six major issuing private banks (with the result that no state central bank was established). But the Minghetti

The unification of Italy. The dates are those of annexation, first to the Kingdom of Sardinia and, after 1861, to the Kingdom of Italy.

From W. Shepherd, *Historical Atlas*, Harper & Row, Publishers (Barnes & Noble Books), New York; revision Copyright © 1964 by Barnes & Noble, Inc.

Cabinet failed to secure adoption of the fiscal measures it had submitted to the Chamber, which was therefore dissolved (September 20, 1874). The ensuing elections resulted in a heavy gain for the left. Next to the traditional, moderately progressive Piedmontese left, headed by Agostino Depretis, and the more consistently progressive left of the other north central regions (both representing the middle class groups of the north), the southern left, the champion of the interests of the landed bourgeoisie of the south and more moderate than the traditional left, showed a remarkable gain.

Disagreement within the parliamentary right

In spite of these differences, the left, after its success at the polls in 1874, presented a more solid parliamentary front than did the right: indeed, the disagreement within the right on the question of "saving" the railroads by making their operation a state responsibility was responsible in March 1876 for the downfall of the last government of the traditional right, brought about by the Tuscan rightist group's aligning itself with the left against state operation of the railroads. The right, the "moderate" heirs of Cavour, who had built up the unitary state, unified the national market, and set the country's financial house in order, was now succeeded by the left, a party whose leadership consisted mainly of men of the Risorgimento democracy who, unlike the more strictly orthodox Mazzinian republicans, had accepted the monarchist–liberal solution. More resolutely secular and anticlerical than the right, the left had a broader social base extending to the upper levels of the urban working classes, with whose support it was prepared to widen the narrow bases of the unitary state: its program's chief elements were extension of the franchise, compulsory elementary education, tax reform, abolition of the forced currency, and appointment of mayors by election.

Depretis and the parliamentary left, 1876–87. In the decade after 1876, Italian public life was dominated by

Depretis, the leader of the left, who was president of the Council almost uninterruptedly from March 25, 1876, until his death on July 29, 1887, and who headed eight administrations in which he reserved almost invariably the internal-affairs portfolio and often the foreign-affairs portfolio for himself. A skilled parliamentarian, a talented administrator, and a realistic and flexible statesman, Depretis proceeded with caution in carrying out the program of the left, partly because of the internal divergences within the left itself, which comprised—from left to right—the extreme group of Agostino Bertani, still open to republican promptings; Francesco Crispi's group, clinging to the democratic traditions of the Risorgimento; the Lombard progressive left of Giuseppe Zanardelli and Benedetto Cairoli; and Giovanni Nicotera's group, predominantly southern, bestowing political patronage and more conservative. Nonetheless, on July 15, 1877, the Coppino Act was passed, making the first two years of elementary schooling compulsory, a provision that, though inadequate, helped to lower the level of illiteracy. In 1882 a reform increased the electorate to 6.9 percent of the total population, including a substantial number of workers in the north. The forced currency was abolished between 1881 and 1883. On January 1, 1884, the unpopular grist tax was finally repealed. The Railroad Agreements Act (April 27, 1885) vested responsibility for operating the railroads in private companies and strengthened the hand of the southerners. Public expenditure, however, rose noticeably from 1881 because of increased allocations for the armed forces, and the deficit created was aggravated by the minister Agostino Magliani's "exuberant" financial policy.

Finally, the free-trade tradition was abandoned, and the customs tariff was changed to a protectionist measure in favour of industry in 1878; in 1887 a general tariff was introduced to provide much greater protection for some branches of industry. Further, owing to the widespread farming crisis of the 1880s, the import duty on grains was raised substantially, jeopardizing the already depressed living standard of the lower income groups. The tariffs of 1887 strengthened the hand of a political block within the mainly southern group of absentee owners of large estates and those entrepreneurial groups of the upper middle class and of the bourgeois-minded nobility who had directed the Risorgimento process.

"Transformism"

One basic feature of Depretis' politico-parliamentary system much criticized as a source of political corruption and degradation was "transformism," whereby moderate or conservative deputies moved over to the benches of the leftist majority because they had had more than their fill of the wrangling over the ideals and programs of the rightist era and because priority was given to economic and administrative matters, on which agreement in Parliament was now made easier.

Not even under the personal influence of the new king, Umberto I, who succeeded Victor Emmanuel II in 1878, did the left change the foreign-policy aims pursued by the right from 1870 to 1876, namely, to terminate the alliance with France and to seek closer relationships with Germany and Austria-Hungary, as promoted by Marquis Emilio Visconti-Venosta. The policy of cautious reflection required for the consolidation of the young Italian state was, however, offset by the isolation of Italy, which became obvious during the eastern crisis of 1877–78 and at the Congress of Berlin and especially at the tension over the French occupation of Tunisia in 1881.

The Triple Alliance

This isolation ended in 1882, when Italy concluded the Triple Alliance with Germany and Austria-Hungary. The treaty, which had a stabilizing effect on domestic policy, provided, among other things, that Germany, Austria-Hungary, and Italy would undertake to support each other if ever attacked by other powers and that the other two contracting parties would remain neutral if the third was forced into declaring war on another power. The Triple Alliance, from which Italy derived no great advantages, was nevertheless renewed in 1887 on rather more favourable terms that, in addition to giving Italy anti-French assurances that the status quo in the Mediterranean would be maintained, allowed it in substance to request that Trentino and Trieste be ceded to it in the event of any encroachment by Austria in the Balkans.

Colonial expansionism became more marked as imperialistic interests developed. The government acquired Aseb (Assab) in 1882, previously in the possession of the Rubbatino shipping company from 1869 to 1870, and Italian forces occupied Mesewa (1885), a bridgehead for subsequent penetration into Eritrea that was interrupted by the defeat at Dogali (January 26, 1887).

Crispi, to 1891. *"Strong" foreign policy.* Depretis was succeeded by Francesco Crispi, a former Mazzinian who had accepted the constitutional monarchy and whose initial democratic fervour had been steadily waning. His coming to power (August 1887) ushered in a new phase of Italian policy characterized by motives of prestige and colonial expansionist trends at the international level and by a "strong" line at home. An admirer of Bismarck and a fervent nationalist, Crispi adopted an intransigent attitude toward France both in the matter of trade relations and in dealing with the problems created by spheres of influence in the Mediterranean, while forging closer links with the Central Powers, especially Germany.

Expansion in East Africa

Crispi then laid emphasis on the imperialistic aspects of colonial expansion in East Africa. The outcome was the protectorate established over the Somali sultanates of Obbia and Migiuritinia (1889) and later extended to the coast of Benadir; the occupation of the interior of Eritrea (1889), recognized by Menelik II, emperor of Ethiopia, in the Treaty of Uccialli (May 2, 1889); and the attempt to impose an Italian protectorate on Ethiopia.

Domestic policy. In domestic policy, Crispi, the guiding spirit of the industrial–agricultural block consolidated in 1887, encouraged the trends toward authoritarianism that emerged on several occasions from 1861 onward. The first phase of Crispi's decade was also characterized by legislative activity that, while seeking to strengthen the executive by enhancing the authority of the president of the council, began to broaden the basis of public life and to provide a more honest and efficient administration: the extended franchise in local government elections; the elective appointment of mayors by commune councils; reform of the system of administrative law; and promulgation of a new criminal code, the Zanardelli code, which abolished the death penalty and granted some freedom to strike. In addition, Crispi's minister of finance (1889–90), Giovanni Giolitti, reduced the deficit by strict economy.

The Rudinì government and Giolitti's first administration. In February 1891 Crispi resigned, and, after a brief administration (February 1891–May 1892) headed by Marquis Antonio Starabba di Rudinì, who renewed the Triple Alliance for 12 years, Giolitti became prime minister on May 25, 1892. Giolitti, a Piedmontese who had played no part in the Risorgimento, followed a more progressive line.

Birth of organized Italian Socialism

The years 1870–90 witnessed the emergence and early stages of two movements, one Socialist and the other Catholic, that were radically to alter the nature of the political struggle. The first organizational framework of incipient Italian Socialism on a nationwide scale was the Italian Federation of the International Workingmen's Association (Rimini Conference, August 4, 1872), whose constitution—partly inspired by Mikhail Bakunin, the Russian anarchist—was made possible by the radicalization of the younger republican generation, which had sympathized with the Paris Commune of 1871. The First International, whose orientation was anti-authoritarian, anarchistic, and collectivist in Italy, spread chiefly to Naples, Sicily, and central Italy, recruiting its supporters from among the urban workers and young intellectuals. But it failed to enlist support among the peasantry, in spite of the rural insurrectionist movement that the internationalists started in 1877 and that they thought should have been supported by the peasants of the south. The futility of the insurrectionist method brought the International, after 1877, to a crisis aggravated by the abandonment of their positions by some of its leaders, including Andrea Costa, founder of the Revolutionary Socialist Party of Romagna in 1881 (as from 1884 the Italian

Revolutionary Socialist Party). Moreover, in 1882, the Italian Labour Party (Partito Operaio Italiano) came into existence in Milan and rallied Lombardy workers to a labour program based on trade union opposition. The same years witnessed completion of the transition from radical democracy to Socialism of a group of Lombardy intellectuals, among them Filippo Turati and Leonida Bissolati, who assimilated Marxist ideas; another intellectual, Antonio Labriola, advocated the establishment in Italy of a Marxist Socialist culture free of Positivist contamination from which, in his opinion, the Lombardian Socialist group was not immune.

Among the Catholics, the "intransigent" element, defenders of the rights of the papacy against the "usurping" Italian state and advocates of political abstentionism, prevailed over the clerico-moderates, who favoured an accommodation with the state. The "intransigents" acquired an effective organizational instrument in the *Opera dei congressi* (1875), promoting—especially from 1885 onward—a range of economic and social activities, mainly in north central rural areas.

With these developments in mind, Giolitti tried to introduce a financial policy that would lighten the burden on the lower income classes but also would permit more freedom in political and trade union organization. It is not by pure chance that, during Giolitti's first administration, the Italian Socialist Party (PSI) was founded (August 1892) as an entity separate from the Anarchists. The continuation of this policy was nevertheless impeded by Giolitti's resignation (November 24, 1893) because of the Banca Romana scandal, in which the financial aspects were compounded with political corruption.

The Banca Romana scandal

Crispi, 1893–96. Giolitti was again succeeded by Crispi at a time when the economic and bank crisis had become more acute and in Sicily the Fasci dei Lavoratori movement (unions of labour, especially of peasant groups, linked with the PSI) had become more extensive. In order to deal with the tense situation, Crispi made use of the law enforcement authorities and exercised emergency powers: disbandment of the Fasci and declaration of a state of siege in Sicily and Lunigiana, where an uprising fomented by the Anarchists had been attempted (January 1894); adoption of "anti-Anarchist" laws; and disbandment of the PSI (October 1894).

Crispi later succeeded in establishing equilibrium in the credit sector by reorganizing the banks, whereby the Banca d'Italia came out on top as the leading issuing bank; and he strengthened his parliamentary position through the elections of May 1895, held after a revision of the electoral rolls had reduced the number of voters to the detriment of leftist opposition parties.

The discontent engendered by Crispi's policy, particularly noticeable in the north, expressed itself over the African crisis. The annexation of Tigre as part of Eritrea (October 1895) actually forced the emperor Menelik II, who had already denounced the Treaty of Ucciali in 1893, into war. The campaign ended in an Italian defeat (Aduwa), forcing Crispi to resign on March 5, 1896. Thus there came to a close, with a heavy deficit, an era of Italian foreign policy characterized by an ill-prepared imperialistic drive.

Rudinì, 1896–98. Rudinì, who succeeded Crispi for the second time (May 1896), settled the African problem by the Treaty of Addis Ababa (October 1896), which recognized the independence of Ethiopia and left Italy in possession of Eritrea up to the Mareb line and the Somali Protectorate. His domestic policy, however, was vague, wavering between the pressures of the conservative right —which sought the replacement of the parliamentary type of government by the "constitutional" type, with ministers responsible only to the sovereign—and the pressures of the radical left. Rudinì began by adopting a tolerant attitude (amnesty for political prisoners) and introduced some social welfare measures, but a Cabinet reshuffle (July 1896) shifted the balance to the right, thrusting the radicals into opposition.

Treaty of Addis Ababa

Finally, Rudinì's inadequacy became apparent in the crisis of 1898, when, as a result of the rise in grain prices, heightened tension convulsed the whole country and culminated in mass demonstrations in Milan. He called the army into the Lombard capital, then in a state of siege, and resorted to severe repression.

When Rudinì resigned in view of the Chamber's hostility (June 18, 1898), Luigi Pelloux, who succeeded him, girded himself to continue repression; and, when—after he had prepared a bill highly detrimental to constitutional freedoms—the extreme left resorted to parliamentary obstruction, he promulgated the repressive laws by royal decree and adjourned the Chamber. This authoritarian gambit backfired: the elections of June 1900 were a triumph for the extreme left, forcing Pelloux to resign.

Agriculture and industry, 1870–90. From 1870 to 1900, Italy remained a predominantly farming country whose agriculture was characterized by major discrepancies and striking contrasts. In the Po Valley of the north, with the help of development projects, the large estates, with their capitalistic owner-managers, continued to gain ground, as did a class of capitalist entrepreneurs ("tenant farmers") employing hordes of farmhands. In the central regions (Tuscany, the Marches, Umbria, and part of Emilia), the predominant system was sharecropping. The south was both the realm of the large estates and also of peasant holdings often too small to offer their owners a bare livelihood and therefore compelling them to work as labourers or tenants on the large estates.

The unification of the market and the construction of the railroad network spurred on production, especially of specialized crops intended for export (olive oil, wine, citrus fruits), but, except for the capitalistic estates of the north, the increase in output was generally due more to the steady expansion of the area under cultivation than to the investment of capital. Agriculture suffered severely from the effects of the agricultural crisis of the 1880s. The general drop in prices and output had been of particular significance for grains. The state's endeavour—as has been seen—to cope with the situation by taxing grains (1887), while it enabled the big southern farms to survive, was detrimental to the small- and medium-scale wine-growing peasants of the south, who found themselves—because of the trade war with France—excluded from one of their principal markets.

Crisis in agriculture

In 1870 Italy did not yet possess an industrial base of significant proportions, even though, in the northern regions, there were signs of a developing manufacturing industry, especially in the textile sector (silk, cotton, and wool). The industrial "takeoff" was held back not so much by the low level of capital formation as by the smallness of the domestic market and by the tendency to invest in speculative rather than directly productive ventures. This being so, state intervention, particularly the policy of protectionism (tariffs of 1878 and 1887), enabled steady progress to be made in the textile sector, now assured of the domestic market, while the establishment of Terni and other complexes launched the iron and steel industry in the direction of modern production.

The three decades under discussion witnessed an initial phase of expansion, although it was slowed down by recurrent crises, as a result of which the gross product of industry at the end of the century still amounted to only around 20 percent of the overall gross national product. Lastly, per capita income remained essentially at a standstill, and the standard of living remained low.

Saracco, 1900–01, and Zanardelli, 1901–03. Giuseppe Saracco, who succeeded Pelloux (June 1900–February 1901), was a "caretaker" minister who withdrew the drafts of illiberal laws and launched a policy of détente that was not even interrupted by the assassination of Umberto I (July 29, 1900) by an Anarchist, because the new king, Victor Emmanuel III, showed his desire to guarantee constitutional freedoms. On Saracco's resignation, a government was formed by Giuseppe Zanardelli, whose minister of the interior, Giolitti, inspired his policy. The Zanardelli–Giolitti administration (February 1901–October 1903) marked a turning point in Italian life, ushering in a period of renunciation of conservative authoritarianism and of liberalization of domestic policy.

Accession of Victor Emmanuel III

The Giolitti era. When he became president of the Council in November 1903, Giolitti dominated the scene until the outbreak of World War I, heading three administrations (November 1903–March 1905; May 1906–December 1909; March 1911–March 1914) apart from a few intervening caretaker cabinets (Alessandro Fortis, March 1905–February 1906; Sidney Sonnino, February–May 1906 and December 1909–March 1910; Luigi Luzzatti, March 1910–March 1911).

Social reform and the growth of organized labour. Giolitti sought to bring the radical and Socialist left into the constitutional picture and to introduce a policy of reform to meet the demands of the upper strata of the working classes. He abandoned the posture of repressing the labour movement, recognized the freedom to organize and to strike, and remained largely neutral in labour disputes. A series of accompanying legislative innovations, while of limited scope, helped to better the lot of the working classes (restraints on the employment of child and female labour; 24 consecutive hours of rest per week in industry; measures to benefit workers in rice fields, etc.). Lastly, the Credaro Act (1911) made state bodies responsible for operating elementary schools.

Giolitti's policy encouraged the rapid growth of the organized labour movement. Hence, in 1901 there was a noteworthy expansion of the trade federations and the trade-union councils (town-based territorial organs), which became increasingly socialistic and which also engaged in educational and assistance activities. Concurrently there was a gradual spread of the peasants' associations in regions with big capitalistic farms (Po Valley and part of Apulia). In this way masses of farm labourers were organized and, in 1900–01, set off a wild wave of strikes designed to raise low wages and improve harsh working conditions. The farm labourers' organization found its rallying point in the constitution of the Federazione Nazionale dei Lavoratori della Terra (National Federation of Agricultural Workers), or Federterra (157,000 members in 1910). Federterra, however, mainly reflected the aspirations of the labourers (more farmhands and fewer peasants) and made "socialization" of the land the central theme of its program. This limited its penetration into the regions of small peasant holdings and sharecroppers, where the peasants' main desire was to own their piece of land. National unification of the Socialist-oriented trade unions occurred in 1906 with the establishment of the Confederazione Generale del Lavoro (CGL), or General Confederation of Labour. The CGL soon became an efficient organ (384,000 registered members in 1911), but its cautious reformism benefitted the more advanced labour categories, concentrated in the north, and neglected the strata of less skilled and unorganized workers, chiefly in the south.

Catholic trade unions

Even the Catholics, who had entered the field of trade union organization after the publication of *Rerum Novarum* (1891), stepped up their activity, especially among the peasants of the north central region and the textile workers' branch, where women predominated (104,000 registered members in the Catholic, or "white," trade unions in 1910).

Domestic policy. Giolitti succeeded in moving farther ahead with his domestic policy also, thanks to the support of the reformist wings of the PSI (Turati, Claudio Treves, Ivanoe Bonomi, Leonida Bissolati), which predominated in the parliamentary group and the CGL and often lent Giolitti support in Parliament but refused to join his administrations. But the "Socialist revolutionary" movement, which had no specific ideology, and the "revolutionary trade unionism" splinter group, which was influenced by the ideas of the French revolutionary syndicalist Georges Sorel and which quit the PSI in 1907, were fiercely hostile to Giolitti.

During the Giolitti period, Parliament and government were active in the economic and financial sectors, even in relation to the economic expansion of those years. When the railroad agreements of 1885 expired in 1905, responsibility for running the railroads was taken over by the state; in June 1906 legislation was enacted to convert the public debt from 5 to 3.75 percent (and later to 3.5 percent), an operation that was successful because of the sound state of the national financial situation, which showed a surplus up to 1909–10; in 1912 it was the turn of the state life insurance monopoly, and, at the same time, a great impetus was given to public works.

Against this, one unworthy aspect of "Giolittism" was the use made by Giolitti of political patronage to maintain his power, which he did with an unscrupulousness that reached its climax during the elections.

Foreign policy. In foreign policy Giolitti tried to find Italy an alternative to the Triple Alliance and subordination to Germany. In addition to improved relations with England, the rapprochement with France, started by Rudinì, who had settled the Tunisian question in 1896 and ended the trade war with France (by means of a trade treaty of November 21, 1897), was encouraged. This led to the Italo-French agreements of 1902, which delimited the spheres of influence of the two countries in North Africa and pledged them to mutual neutrality in the event of aggression by third parties. As a corollary, relations with Austria grew worse because of the friction created by recurrent irredentism, Italy's commercial penetration of the Balkans, and Italy's interest in Albania, as did relations with Germany, especially after the Moroccan crisis of 1905, during which Italy maintained an impartial position between France and Germany. The tension with Austria became acute in 1908, when Austria's occupation of Bosnia without compensation for Italy placed the Triple Alliance in jeopardy.

The conquest of Libya

Giolitti strengthened the Italian position in the Mediterranean with the conquest of Libya (Italo-Turkish War of 1911–12), which was opposed by the nationalists, who were starting to grow aggressive and were supported by sectors of the Catholic world. But the Libyan war had important domestic repercussions. The conflict upset the delicate internal balance of the PSI and caused it to break away from the reformist movement of the right wing (Bissolati, Bonomi, Angelo Cabrini) in favour of the war, while the reformists of the left, with Turati, remained true to the anti-colonialist tradition of Italian Socialism. Moreover, there emerged a new left, nurtured on idealistic volunteerism, whose most typical representative was Benito Mussolini, the creator of an eclectic platform founded on criticism of parliamentarianism, on antimilitarism, and on the advocacy of revolutionary violence.

The situation having changed thus, Giolitti could no longer count on the PSI for support and therefore turned to the Catholics. The latter agreed to give their support in the 1913 elections—the first with virtually universal suffrage—to the governmental candidates (the Gentiloni Pact). The liberal–Catholic alliance, concluded as an anti-Socialist measure, did not, however, prevent the government's relative defeat, the Catholics, PSI Socialists, and the Reformist Socialist Party of Bonomi and Bissolati all gaining seats at the expense of the liberal groups.

The economy. The turn of the century and the Giolitti period were years of growth for the Italian economy. Farm production actually rose, thanks to internal and export demand, to mounting investments in capitalistically structured estates, and to the completion of land-improvement projects in Emilia-Romagna. But, above all, the industrialization process gathered speed, with a growth rate of industrial output of 6.7 percent per annum for the period 1896–1908. Both the spread of "mixed" banking and the increase of capital stock in industry contributed to this growth. In addition to the textile industry, the electric power (Edison) and the metallurgical industries became increasingly important. And per capita income in 1910–14 was 28.8 percent higher than in 1896–1900.

Industrial concentration in the north

The industrial concerns, however, were concentrated in the northwestern part of the country, which in 1911, with 27 percent of the total population, accounted for about 58 percent of the total industrial workers. Industrialization was practically nonexistent in the rural and backward south, aggravating the so-called southern problem. Emigration, mainly from the southern regions, started as a large-scale exodus in 1880 and grew to an annual average of 600,000 emigrants from the start of the 20th century to 1914, mostly headed for the Americas.

WORLD WAR I AND THE RISE OF FASCISM

The Salandra government. Giolitti, who resigned in March 1914 because of the radicals' switchover to the opposition, was succeeded by Antonio Salandra, heading a government that was expected to leave the way open again for Giolitti. But the outbreak of World War I drastically altered the nature of the political struggle. Salandra, after weathering a series of storms culminating in Red Week (serious popular uprisings that occurred in the Marches and the Romagna in June), coolly faced up to the war crisis. He ruled that the provisions of the Triple Alliance did not apply to Austria's attack on Serbia and therefore decided on neutrality (August 2, 1914). In the following months, however, Salandra considered intervening on the side of the Allies, particularly after the disappointing outcome of the attempt to bargain for the *terre irredente* with Austria. Meanwhile, the neutralists in Italy consisted of Giolitti supporters, Socialists, and Catholics. The interventionists included republicans, reformists of the Bissolati–Bonomi school, some splinter groups of liberal democrats, who regarded the conflict as the last war of independence and the final achievement of national unity, and expansionist and imperialistic-minded elements; these were later joined by revolutionary-Socialist and anarcho-trade-unionist groups and by Mussolini, therefore expelled from the PSI.

The Treaty of London

When negotiations with Austria broke down, Salandra sought contacts with the Allies that finally led to the Treaty of London (April 26, 1915), which remained secret; in return for intervention on the Allies' side, Italy was to receive Trentino, Trieste, Alto Adige (South Tirol) up to the Brenner Pass, Gorizia and Istria up to the Quarnaro, and northern Dalmatia. The Prime Minister, denouncing the Triple Alliance on May 4, was, however, forced to resign (May 13) by the neutralist majority in the Chamber. The interventionists stepped up their pressure with a well-orchestrated propaganda campaign and aggressive street demonstrations. The King refused the Prime Minister's resignation (May 16th) and took the decision to intervene, a decision that, while not formally exceeding his constitutional authority, nevertheless ran counter to the feelings of the majority in the country. The Salandra government thus took over full powers and, on May 24, declared war on Austria.

Entrance into the war and the peace settlement. Salandra resigned in June 1916 after Austrian success in Trentino, and a national coalition government was formed under Paolo Boselli, who declared war on Germany (August 28, 1916). His government respected constitutional freedom and tolerated the pacific-neutral PSI, even after violent anti-war demonstrations in Turin in August 1917. Boselli was toppled after the Battle of Caporetto disaster (October 1917), and the new government was formed in November by Vittorio Emanuele Orlando, who, at one of the most critical junctures in the history of united Italy, led the country on to victory.

Having got out of the war, Italy was shaken by a crisis in which the political, economic, and social elements were intermeshed. Nationalists and imperialists, dissatisfied with the peace conference at which the Allies, while granting Trent, Trieste, and the Brenner frontier, did not recognize Italy's claims to Fiume (modern Rijeka, Yugoslavia) and Dalmatia and its expansionist aims in Albania and Asia Minor, began to bandy about the myth of the "mutilated victory." The middle classes felt the effects of inflation acutely and were terrified by the atmosphere of social tension; the industrialists and farmers were anxious about the turmoil stirred up by the workers, which, on a scale hitherto unknown, was assuming the political character of a struggle to take over the state; the peasant masses pressed that the prospect of "land for the peasants," glibly conjured up in time of need by the leading groups, should be realized.

The "mutilated victory"

Nitti, 1919–20. Orlando, depressed by the course the Paris negotiations were taking, resigned on June 19, 1919; and Francesco Saverio Nitti, a democrat and an expert on the problems of the south, formed a government of the left and Giolitti supporters. Nitti did indeed promote the passage of progressive social legislation (compulsory unemployment, sickness, and old-age insurance) and tried, unsuccessfully, to introduce the eight-hour working day. But the increase in social strife obliged him to call often on the police to quell the turmoil.

In the elections of November 16, 1919, the first held on the basis of universal suffrage and proportional representation, the PSI scored a triumph (30 percent of the votes and 156 seats in the Chamber). The results were likewise favourable for the Italian Popular Party (PPI), the Catholic but formally nondenominational party founded in January 1919 by Don Luigi Sturzo and campaigning for improvement of peasant small holdings and for administrative decentralization (20.5 percent of the votes and 100 seats). But the elections disappointed the liberals, democrats, and rightists. Thus it became difficult to form stable governments, which would henceforth require the support either of the rigidly intransigent Socialists or the populists.

As regards foreign policy, Nitti renounced the claims to Dalmatia and to the colonies, thus incurring the accusation of "capitulator" from the nationalist groups of the right. Against this background the question of Fiume became more embittered. Fiume, claimed by both Italy and Yugoslavia, was occupied in a piratical *coup de main* led by Gabriele D'Annunzio (September 12, 1919).

Fiume seized

Giolitti's last ministry: growth of Fascism. Internal tension and the difficult parliamentary situation led to Nitti's resignation (June 9, 1920). The 78-year-old Giolitti now served his last term as prime minister, supported by the liberal democrats and, conditionally, by the populists. Giolitti concluded with Yugoslavia the Treaty of Rapallo (November 12, 1920), which made Fiume a free state and gave Italy some Dalmatian islands.

Giolitti then tried to deal with the domestic situation by his old method of staying neutral in labour disputes and using the police to maintain law and order. In this way he weathered the crisis of the September 1920 "occupation of the factories" by workers in Turin and Milan. He cut the budgetary deficit by increasing tax revenue (*e.g.*, special capital levy, heavier death duties, and taxes on higher income brackets) and reducing expenditure.

Still, Giolitti's experiment turned out to be not enough to control the critical events in which the country was embroiled. He could not count on the PSI's support. For the PSI's "maximalist" left (victorious in the party congress of October 1919) harped on revolution and the dictatorship of the proletariat, although its verbal extremism was not matched by capacity to guide the masses. Moreover, the anti-electoral Communist splinter group of Amadeo Bordiga and that of Antonio Gramsci's "New Order" organized themselves on the left of the maximalists. These splinter groups, having broken away from the PSI in January 1921, formed the Italian Communist Party (PCI).

Birth of the Italian Communist Party and of Fascism

Meanwhile, Fascism was developing menacingly. Launched in Milan on March 23, 1919, by Mussolini, the Fascist movement did not at once take a precise ideological stance and combined pragmatist, revolutionary-trade-unionist, nationalist, imperialist, and irrationalist elements in its platform; its program laid stress on direct opposition to Socialism and "Bolshevism" and on collaboration between management and labour in production to further the higher interests of the "nation." Fascism availed itself flexibly of the elements of disillusionment and discontent prevailing in the country: nationalistic hysteria intensified by the "mutilated victory"; the operational difficulties of the parliamentary state; the effects of the economic situation; management's anxiety about the growth of trade unionism (CGL's registered membership rose from 249,000 at the end of 1918 to 2,320,000 at the end of 1920); and the middle classes' fear of Socialism.

After a difficult beginning (in the 1919 elections the Fascist vote was insignificant), Fascism gathered strength after D'Annunzio's seizure of Fiume (supported by Mussolini) and especially after the failure of the occupation of the factories, the turning point of Socialist fortunes. Allying itself with the traditionally more reactionary groups of the Italian ruling classes, Fascism became a kind of armed reaction against the working classes. Deploying "punitive expeditions" by paramilitary "squads," Fascist strategy succeeded, from the late 1920s onward, in throwing the Socialist and trade union movement into disorder, first in the Po Valley and then in the northern cities, not sparing even the Catholic organizations.

The victory of Fascism. The victory of Fascism, a predominantly urban movement with a broad lower middle class base, reached rural areas in 1921–22; it was encouraged by the indecision of the Socialists, who were torn with strife—in October 1922 a further schism saw the expulsion of the reformists, who formed the Unitary Socialist Party (PSU). But the movement was cold-shouldered by Giolitti and other liberal democrats, who believed that they could "constitutionalize" Fascism and absorb it within the liberal state. When the Chamber was dissolved, Giolitti announced new elections for May 15, 1921, and formed a governmental National Bloc comprising, besides the liberals, democrats, nationalists, and Fascist candidates. Nevertheless, out of 535 seats, the left gained 123 seats, plus 15 to the Communists, and the populists obtained 108 seats, but, within the National Bloc (275 seats), the Fascists succeeded in securing 35.

Having changed from a movement into a party and dropping republicanism at the Congress of Rome (November 1921, 300,000 registered members), Fascism, under the weak governments that followed Giolitti (Bonomi, July 1921–February 1922; Luigi Facta, February–October 1922), set off to conquer power. When the last attempt to block his way, the general strike proclaimed on July 31, 1922, misfired, Mussolini carried out the March on Rome (October 28, 1922), aided by the surrender of the King, who refused to sanction a state of siege and entrusted Mussolini with a mandate to form a new government, which took office on October 31.

The March on Rome

VI. The kingdom and Fascism

BEFORE WORLD WAR II

First years of Fascist government. Fascism did not work immediately for a complete breakdown of the Italian political and constitutional system; and Mussolini's first government included liberal and populist ministers. But the establishment of a totalitarian regime, with power vested in the Fascist Party and, through it, in its leader, or *duce*, was the goal. Accordingly, as one act of violence against its opponents followed another, Fascism institutionalized its own armed force by setting up the Voluntary Militia for National Security (January 1923) and transformed the electoral system in its own favour (the Acerbo Act, which made the kingdom a single national constituency and assigned an absolute majority—51 percent—of the seats in the Chamber to the party holding the relative majority).

At the elections of April 6, 1924, held in a suffocating atmosphere, 64 percent of the votes went to the "national" government lists (374 deputies, 275 of them officially Fascists), except in northern Italy, where more votes went to the opposition.

Assassination of Matteotti

The assassination by Fascists of the PSU deputy, Giacomo Matteotti (June 10, 1924), who had denounced in the Chamber the violence of the electoral campaign, created tension. Fascism, morally isolated, went through a phase of disbandment, while the opposition groups (Aventinians, named after the ancient Roman *plebs'* secession from the Roman assembly on Aventine hill—signifying withdrawal from the political scene) stopped their parliamentary work in protest. But the indecision of the Aventinians and the attitude of the King, who did not revoke Mussolini's mandate, allowed Fascism to climb back again. After having assumed full responsibility for what had happened (speech in the Chamber, January 3, 1925), Mussolini abandoned collaboration with supporting groups and set up a total dictatorship.

Between 1925 and 1926, Italy was thus transformed into a police state: the activity of Parliament, the parties, and trade unions was increasingly curtailed, and freedom of the press and association became a sham. An act of December 24, 1925 made the president of the Council "head of the government" with no responsibility to Parliament, removable only by the sovereign, and the sole person competent to lay down the agenda of the two chambers. Further provisions ended any autonomy in local government. Representatives of the Confederazione Generale dell'Industria and the Confederazione delle Corporazioni (*i.e.*, the Fascist-oriented trade unions) signed an agreement in October 1925 asserting that they alone represented the industrialists and the workers, respectively. A few months later other laws (April 3 and July, 1926) confirmed this trade union monopoly and empowered the Fascist unions to draw up collective labour contracts; in addition, strikes and lockouts were prohibited, and the authority to settle collective-bargaining disputes was vested in the labour judiciary. Lastly, provision was made for setting up national bodies to maintain liaison among the trade union organizations of the various factors of production by branches of production; they were called corporations and regarded as the cornerstone of the corporate state, which was to be founded on co-operation of the classes and the integrated organization of production to further the development of "national power."

Provision for the Fascist corporation

The dictatorship completed. An attempt on his life (October 31, 1926) gave Mussolini the opportunity to abolish all remaining freedoms. Provisions were introduced to disband all the parties, end the parliamentary mandate of 120 Aventinians, restore the death penalty for some political prisoners and introduce special police measures ("forced residence" and "admonishment"), and set up the Special Tribunal for the Defense of the State. A new criminal code and code of criminal procedure (limiting rights of defense and abolishing the jury) and a new Public Security Consolidation Act took effect in 1931.

Mussolini continued to build up a totalitarian state, in which everything was subordinated to the personal will of the *duce*. A new electoral law (March 16, 1928) finally subordinated the Chamber, with the introduction of a single list of candidates selected by the Fascist Grand Council and submitted as a whole for approval by plebiscite. The Grand Council, set up as a party organ early in 1923, was "constitutionalized" (December 1928) and became a state organ in the service of Mussolini.

The regime then embarked on a campaign to make the country Fascist, using radio, press, and school, dragooning the young into paramilitary organizations, and making party membership obligatory for admission to government service, including the judiciary. The corporate structure, however, remained a facade. The corporations, numbering 22, were not established until 1934, although the Ministry of Corporations had been set up as early as July 1926. Even though granted wide powers of overall economic control, the corporations confined themselves to advisory activities and had little impact on economic and social life.

Lastly, the constitutional reform of January 1939, replacing the Chamber of Deputies by the Chamber of Fasces and Corporations, whose membership was automatic by virtue of membership of other Fascist organs, was of virtually no consequence.

In the matter of state–church relations, Fascism concluded the Lateran Treaty with the Holy See (February 11, 1929). These pacts, which enhanced Mussolini's prestige and enabled him to use the church hierarchy in certain cases to support the regime, repealed the Law of Guarantees of 1871, created the State of Vatican City, and affirmed the catholicity of the Italian state, recognizing religious marriage as valid in civil law and introducing religious teaching in intermediate-level schools.

The Lateran Treaty

As from 1926, the opposition to Fascism decided to act under cover or to emigrate. The Communists chose the first alternative and focussed their program on internal affairs: they fomented strikes and disturbances and infiltrated the very mass organizations of Fascism. The price they paid was high (the party leader, Gramsci, arrested in 1926, died in penal servitude in 1937; and over 4,000 of the approximately 4,700 people sentenced by the Special Tribunal were Communists); but the uninterrupted existence of the PCI created the conditions for its growth as a major party after the fall of Fascism. The same alternative was chosen by "Justice and Liberty," an intellectual liberal-Socialist movement founded by Gaetano Salvemini, Carlo Rosselli, Emilio Lussu, Ernesto Rossi, and others in 1929 and destined to amalgamate with the Action Party (PdA) in 1949. Catholic opposition was expressed within traditional organizations, such as Catholic Action, a training ground for many cadres of the future Christian Democratic Party; liberal opposition was exemplified by Benedetto Croce and the group associated with him in the periodical *La Critica*.

Socialists in exile

The two Socialist parties (PSI and PSU, reunited in 1930) and the Republican Party (PRI) were reconstituted in exile; in 1927 they organized the Anti-Fascist Action Coalition. With the disbandment of the coalition (1934), while the Socialists in Italy became reorganized in Rodolfo Morandi's Internal Centre, Socialists and Communists in exile (under the "popular front" policy) signed a united action agreement in August 1934.

Fascist foreign policy. In foreign policy, after an initial phase of moderation (Italian–Yugoslav Agreement of Rome, January 27, 1924, which gave Italy Fiume; good relations with Great Britain; accession to the Treaty of Locarno, October 1925), Mussolini pursued an expansionist policy, based on revision of the peace treaties and the Italian presence in the Mediterranean and Danube–Balkan areas. The often inconsistent dynamism of Fascist foreign policy grew more intense after 1930; thus there was the Four Power Pact of June 7, 1933, between Italy, Germany, France, and Great Britain on the revision of treaties, which Mussolini hoped would allow him to lay the groundwork for Italian hegemony in central Europe but which was rendered meaningless by the French attitude of suspicion; the Austrian-Hungarian agreement of March 1934, designed to protect Austria's independence from Hitler's threats; and the Stresa Conference (April 1935), at which the Italians, French, and British adopted a position in favour of Austria's territorial integrity and against the rearming of Nazi Germany.

Soon after Stresa, Mussolini, erroneously believing that these agreements had given him a free hand, turned his attention to colonial expansion, namely to Ethiopia, which he attacked on October 2, 1935. The war ended victoriously for Italy, and, in May 1936, Victor Emmanuel III donned the ephemeral crown of the Empire of Ethiopia.

The "Rome–Berlin Axis"

Meanwhile, the ties between Fascist Italy and Nazi Germany led to the Berlin agreements of October 23, 1938—the "Rome–Berlin Axis," which provided for a joint military effort to support Gen. Francisco Franco in the Spanish Civil War. Directly after the occupation of Albania (April 1939), the Italian–German alliance was finally consolidated by the Pact of Steel (May 22, 1939), which was of both a defensive and offensive nature.

The economy under Fascism. *Economic advance in the mid-1920s.* As regards the economy, Fascist policy followed a liberal line favouring private enterprise up to 1925. Traditional customs protectionism, embodied in the tariff of 1921, had been reduced by trade agreements; but previous governments' progressive measures, such as state life insurance and compulsory registration of share certificates, were abolished. The year 1925 ushered in a period of state intervention, with measures to reduce the balance-of-payments deficit, including the attempt to obtain from domestic sources the grain required to meet national needs regardless of cost; higher customs tariffs; and the vesting of power in the minister of finance to prohibit certain imports and to set quotas. But, since the lira continued to drop in value, the government was obliged in 1926 to declare the Banca d'Italia the only issuing bank and to stabilize the currency by revaluation (92.46 lire to the pound sterling, the so-called "90 quota"), which was, however, too high and harmful to exports. Thus began a period of deflation, with a drop in prices damaging to agriculture, wage and salary cuts, and a rise in unemployment.

Nevertheless, in spite of the negative effects of the "90 quota," the Italian economy followed a rising trend up to 1929. The national income climbed from 95,000,000,000 lire (at 1938 prices) in 1921 to 124,600,000,000 in 1929, thanks to the manufacturing boom (from 54 to 90 between 1921 and 1929, base year 1938 = 100). In particular, the electric power, chemical, and metallurgical industries made headway, with streamlining that strengthened monopolistic complexes such as Edison, Snia Viscosa, Fiat, Montecatini, and Pirelli.

Effect of the world depression. The world depression of 1929 had serious repercussions on industrial output and on the banking system. As a result, there was a further increase in state intervention, namely, the establishment in 1933 of a state agency, the Institute for Industrial Recovery (IRI), to rescue some major banks encumbered by locked-up capital, which meant that a substantial part of the credit system was immobilized. Moreover, by increasing the share participations of the rescued banks, IRI—and hence the state—became a shareholder in a complex of companies that, in 1939, represented more than 44 percent of Italy's share capital and acquired a controlling interest in a group of them equivalent to 18 percent of the total capital. Thus there emerged a striking feature of the modern Italian economy; namely, the coexistence of frequently interlinked private and public sectors.

The Institute for Industrial Recovery

The measures introduced as a result of the 1929 depression, especially those of 1935, made it easier to launch the policy of "autarky" designed to make the Italian economy self-sufficient. In addition to the impetus given to grain production—which expanded, however, at the expense of specialized crops—there was exploration for minerals, expansion of hydroelectric plants, reorganization of the iron and steel industry by the establishment of a holding company of IRI (Finsider), and promotion of the armaments industries.

Industry revived, but the recovery was moderate, so that on the eve of World War II Italy was still primarily an agricultural country. As before, industrial enterprises, especially the major ones, continued at the close of the 1930s to be concentrated in the north, while the south remained an agricultural and depressed area with a population of poor peasants and labourers for whom the possibility of emigration was no longer open.

ITALY IN WORLD WAR II

Mussolini's fall from power. On the outbreak of World War II in 1939, Italy first adopted a position of nonbelligerence, entering on Germany's side (June 10, 1940) only when German successes in France misled Mussolini into believing that Germany's victory was a certainty. But soon the unfavourable course of the military operations, revealing the country's lack of preparedness and the adventurousness of Mussolini's policy, widened the gap between the majority of the country, sorely pressed by the war, and the regime—a gap illustrated by strikes in many factories of the north in March 1943.

The landing of the Allies in Sicily (July 10, 1943) was the death knell of Fascism. Mussolini, in the minority at a meeting of the Grand Council (July 25) at which it was proposed to deprive him of authority and to restore power to the crown, was placed under arrest by the King, belatedly anxious to dissociate his responsibilities from those of the *Duce*, while the unsuccessful reaction of the Fascist Party and the wave of anti-Fascist demonstrations following Mussolini's fall brought about the regime's collapse.

The Badoglio government. The government of Marshal Pietro Badoglio, appointed by the King and consisting of military men and technicians, negotiated with the Allies. On September 3 the armistice of Cassibilie was signed, providing for the Italian armed forces' unconditional surrender and the establishment of an Allied administration. The announcement of the armistice, made by Badoglio over the radio on September 8, caused the disbandment or transfer to the Germans of almost all the Italian units in the peninsula, France, and the Balkans; and the country, thrown into confusion, came to be divided in two by the front line. In the south, controlled by the Allies, who were fighting the Wehrmacht up the peninsula, the Badoglio government declared war on Ger-

Armistice with the Allies

many (October 13, 1943), thus securing the status of "co-belligerent" for Italy; in the north, under German occupation, after Mussolini's rescue by German parachutists (September 12, 1943) and the reconstitution of the Fascist Party (now called the Republican Fascist Party), the Italian Social Republic came into existence (September 17) as an ally of Germany.

Emergence of anti-Fascist parties: the liberation of Italy. Meanwhile, emerging anti-Fascist parties were active. Among those with the largest following were the Christian Democrats (DC), a Christian-based party formed of various Catholic-oriented groups; the Socialist Party of Proletarian Unity (PSIUP), the result of the merger of the PSI and the Proletarian Unity Movement (founded by Lelio Basso in January 1943); and the PCI. These three parties, together with the smaller parties (Liberal, Action, Republican, and Labour Democracy), set up at Rome on September 9, 1943, the Committee of National Liberation (CLN), which called on Italians to fight against Nazism–Fascism. Thus the Resistance began. The armed struggle grew with the emergence of large partisan formations that went to make up, as from June 1944, the military command of the Corps of Volunteers for Liberty. The partisans' activities, which continually harassed the Nazi–Fascist troops at great sacrifice of life (about 36,000 killed in Resistance ranks and about 10,000 civilians killed in reprisals), were supported by the strikes of March 1944 and the spring of 1945 in northern Italy.

The Committee of National Liberation and the Resistance

The anti-Fascist parties in the south, who had refused representation in the government as being prejudiced in favour of the abdication of King Victor Emmanuel III and his son Umberto, changed their attitude after the U.S.S.R. recognized the Badoglio government (March 1944) and after the concurrent about-face of the PCI, whose secretary, Palmiro Togliatti, on March 31 proposed the formation of a provisional government of national unity. Thus the CLN parties were admitted to the Badoglio administration (which came to power on April 22), and royal powers were transferred to Prince Umberto. When Rome was liberated (June 4–5, 1944), Umberto was proclaimed lieutenant general, and a coalition government of the CLN parties headed by Bonomi was formed, but under virtual Allied control. A Constituent Assembly, once territorial liberation was completed, was to be convened to solve the constitutional question, and the government entered a crisis (December 1944) because of disputes over purging Fascist elements from the administration (which the left wished to have carried out more decisively) and over the powers of the CLN (which the moderates wished to be limited). A second edition of the Bonomi administration was characterized by a move to the right.

Parri's coalition government, June–December 1945. After the liberation (to which the general partisan uprising of April 1945 contributed), the long negotiations to form a government that would fulfill the desire for political and social renewal, expressed with much greater forcefulness in the north than in the south (the so-called "northern wind"), led to the formation of a coalition government of the CLN parties (June 1945) headed by Ferruccio Parri (of the PdA) as a compromise between the opposing candidacies of the Socialist Pietro Nenni and the Christian Democrat Alcide De Gasperi. In the Parri administration, profound differences soon ended the unity achieved during the Resistance and set the pattern of political deployment that characterized the following years. On the one side stood the PSIUP and the PCI, whose mass support came from the industrial and labourer proletariat of the north and the sharecroppers of the centre. The extreme left wished to set up an advanced popular democracy and to transform the social structure through anti-monopolist measures (nationalization, worker-based management councils, etc.) and the elimination of ownership of large estates through land reform. The left was opposed by the Christian Democrats (backed by the liberals), an interclass and moderate party worried about the "Communist" danger, an anxiety shared by the rightist Uomo Qualunque (UQ) movement with its Fascist nostalgia.

The "northern wind"

The Parri administration tackled the problem of Sicilian separatism and reopened the question of purging, which Parri tried to extend to private industry, but his leftist leanings led, in November 1945, to the withdrawal from the Cabinet of the liberal ministers, soon to be followed by the Christian Democrats, and to the government's subsequent downfall. This was the beginning—with a coalition Cabinet of the CLN parties, except for PdA—of the long series of administrations of De Gasperi, who turned out to be the ablest Italian political leader since Cavour. De Gasperi, supported by the Allies, soon formulated Italian policy along moderate lines.

After the local government elections of March–April 1946 had strengthened the majority parties of the DC, PSIUP, and PCI, and after the abdication (May 9–10) of Victor Emmanuel III in favour of his less compromised son Umberto (Umberto II), there were held simultaneously on June 2—with universal suffrage including women—a referendum on the constitution and elections for a Constituent Assembly whose powers were limited to the drafting of a constitution and the ratification of treaties. In the constitutional referendum, 12,717,923 votes (54 percent) were cast for a republic; in the elections to the Constituent Assembly, held on the basis of proportional representation, the Christian Democrats (DC) scored a clear victory (8,101,004, or 35.2 percent), followed by the PSIUP (4,758,129, or 20.7 percent) and the PCI (4,356,686, or 18.9 percent). The liberals, on the other hand, saw their ranks sorely depleted as compared with the pre-Fascist period (6.8 percent), while the UQ vote (5.3 percent) was greater than expected, above those of the PRI, monarchists, and PdA.

Abdication of Victor Emmanuel III

VII. The republic

THE DE GASPERI ERA, 1945–53

In the new De Gasperi administration, set up with the participation of the DC, PSIUP, PCI, and PRI, the differences between the DC and the leftists became stronger because De Gasperi took conservative steps to strengthen the powers of the state in the maintenance of law and order. In January 1947, moreover, the conflicting trends within the PSIUP led to the breaking away of the rightist wing (Giuseppe Saragat, Ludovico D'Aragona, and others), which favoured the Western democracies and was "autonomist" vis-à-vis the PCI, while the leftist elements (Nenni, Morandi, Basso) favoured close cooperation with the Communists. The seceders thus founded the Socialist Party of Italian Workers (PSLI), while the PSIUP changed its name to the PSI, which was joined in October 1947 by the majority of the dissolved PdA.

Foreign policy aligned with the West. Meanwhile, after De Gasperi's visit to the United States in January 1947, which, in the climate of the Cold War, implied a choice of side, the Italian government signed the peace treaty on February 10, 1947. The treaty, which seemed to the public to be extremely severe, not only limited the armed forces and laid down the scale of reparations but also provided for some frontier adjustments with France (Tende-Brigue, Mont Cenis, etc.), the surrender of the Dodecanese Islands—occupied during the Italian–Turkish War—to Greece, and renunciation of the colonies (Eritrea eventually went to Ethiopia, Libya became independent, and a ten-year trusteeship over Somalia was assigned to Italy). Trieste was temporarily constituted a Free Territory subdivided into two zones, under Anglo-American military and Yugoslav military administration, respectively. As for the Alto Adige, the De Gasperi–Grüber agreement of September 5, 1946, whereby Austria recognized the Brenner frontier and Italy undertook to grant the region a broad measure of self-government, was included in the treaty.

The peace treaty

Politics at home. After signature of the peace treaty, the "imposed coexistence" of the DC and the leftist groups in the administration became more difficult. De Gasperi resigned on May 12, 1947, and formed a one-party Christian Democratic (plus a few independents) government. Strengthened by the success of anti-inflationary measures and by the failure of leftist disturbances to bring down the government, as well as by economic aid from the United States (Marshall Plan and OECD), De Gasperi broadened his administration in December by including PSLI and PRI representatives.

The Constituent Assembly had completed its work by approving on December 22, 1947, the text of the new constitution, which entered into force on January 1, 1948.

The republican constitution

The republican constitution, the result of compromise (the case of article 7 is typical: it provided for the inclusion of the Lateran Treaty in the new constitution), embodied the innovative ideas of the Resistance period, laid down the "right to work" as a basic human right, and repudiated war. The separation of powers was upheld: the executive (entrusted to the president of the republic, elected for a term of seven years by the two branches of the legislature in joint session), the legislative (assigned to the Chamber of Deputies and the Senate, both elected on the basis of universal suffrage), and the judicial; and locally autonomous regions were established, although their coming into operation was long delayed.

The elections of April 18, 1948, were characterized by awareness that a decisive choice was involved. The result was an unexpectedly overwhelming victory of the DC (48.5 percent of the votes, with an absolute majority of the seats in the Chamber, 304 out of 574), which secured the support of the clergy and of a larger cross section of the conservative electorate. The Communists and Socialists, united in the Popular Democratic Front, did not manage, with 31 percent, to improve on their positions of 1946. The DC's gains, however, were mainly at the expense of the right: liberals and UQ, standing as the National Bloc (3.8 percent), and the Italian Social Movement (MSI), a neo-Fascist group (2 percent). De Gasperi, who, with an absolute majority in the Chamber, could have formed a one-party government, preferred instead to build a broader base, initiating the period of "centrism" (fifth De Gasperi administration, with the DC, PSLI, PRI, and PLI [the Partito Liberale Italiano], May 1948–January 1950; sixth De Gasperi administration, tripartite without the PLI, January 1950–July 1951; seventh De Gasperi administration, the DC and PRI, July 1951–July 1953). During the years of centrism, Italy entered the Western bloc, acceding to the North Atlantic Treaty Organization and joining the Council of Europe and the European Coal and Steel Community.

Domestic policy and the economy. In domestic policy, there were developments in trade unionism: the unity achieved in June 1944, when the Italian General Confederation of Labour (CGIL) was reconstituted, came to an end. The Catholic trade unions broke away from the CGIL (a member of the Soviet-oriented World Federation of Trade Unions) and organized the Free General Italian Confederation of Labour (LCGIL). In June 1949 the Social Democrat and Republican trade unions constituted the Italian Federation of Labour (FIL). In 1950 the LCGIL and the FIL merged into the Italian Confederation of Workers' Trade Unions (CISL), while in the same year two new central trade union organs came into being, the Italian Union of Labour (UIL), a coalition of some of the Social Democrat and Republican trade unions, and the neo-Fascist Italian Confederation of National Workers' Trade Unions (CISNAL).

Industrial progress

In the same years, after the prewar level of production had been restored in 1949, the industrial sector made rapid progress, assisted by the abundance of cheap labour. This dynamism led to the establishment of a competitive iron and steel industry, to the beginning of the radical transformation of the chemical sector with the discovery of large methane deposits in the Po Valley and the entry of the Edison company on the scene, and to the founding of the National Hydrocarbons Authority (ENI), a public corporation set up in 1953; the automobile industry also began to expand. Even though there was large-scale state intervention in such branches as iron and steel and chemicals, management of the economy remained largely in the hands of private enterprise. Nevertheless, Italy remained an agricultural country as regards employment, more than 8,000,000 people being employed in farming as against some 6,000,000 in industry in 1953.

Under the pressure of peasant unrest (squatting in 1949–50), the centrist administrations sought to introduce reforms into the rural areas, particularly in the south. Thus a special act (May 1950) for the Sila, a zone in Calabria, and the so-called *stralcio* law ("provisional order") on land reform (October 1950) were passed, providing for the expropriation of about 1,700,000 acres (700,000 hectares) for distribution among designated families (approximately 270,000 acres [110,000 hectares] at the end of 1960). But these measures did not go far enough. In an effort to narrow the widening gap between the north and south, the Southern Fund was set up in 1951 and helped to build infrastructures but did not succeed in stimulating widespread industrialization. In spite of the economic recovery, Italy continued to suffer from mass unemployment, which led once again to emigration.

Shortly before the election of 1953, the DC induced Parliament to pass—amid bitter attacks of the opposition parties—an act that would have given 65 percent of the seats in the Chamber to the party, or group of allied parties, polling 50.01 percent of the votes. But the results of the June 7, 1953, elections prevented this "legislative swindle" from going through. The four "allied" centre parties obtained only 49.85 percent of the votes, showing a general drop as compared with 1948, particularly for the DC and the PSDI (Italian Social Democratic Party, the name adopted from January 1952 by the PSLI.

(F.d.Pe.)

SUCCESSORS OF DE GASPERI

Years of instability. *Government.* The second republican administration saw six successive Christian Democrat one-party administrations between 1953 and 1958. The limited capacity of these governments to manoeuvre severely curtailed their ability to pass important legislation. Thus laws for instituting the regions (except for those with special statutes), for establishing the Constitutional Court, and for replacing the Fascist codes were postponed. On the credit side, the governments between 1953 and 1958 could claim only the Ten-Year Plan for Growth and Development (Vanoni Plan), which, however, did not become operational; the strengthening of ENI, which was given exclusive rights to explore for oil and methane in the Po Valley; and the largely unsuccessful effort to stimulate the industrialization of the south. As for foreign policy, the Trieste question was settled (October 1954), administration of the two zones being assigned to Italy and Yugoslavia, respectively.

Settlement of the Trieste question

The government's relative lack of mobility, however, was offset by movement within the parties. In the DC, Amintore Fanfani, leader of the party left, who became secretary general in July 1954 following De Gasperi's death that year, sought to reorganize the party and to make it more independent of the parallel organs. In the PSI, with the atmosphere of international détente that had set in, the autonomist current (Nenni) favoured breaking away from the PCI and collaborating with the government on a reform program. In the PCI, Togliatti, after the 20th congress of the Communist Party of the Soviet Union and the events in Hungary (1956), based the PCI's position on the noninevitability of war, on a democratic advance toward Socialism, on "national roads to Socialism" and on the "polycentrism" of the international Communist movement. The PLI, under its new secretary, Giovanni Malagodi (1954), moved to the right, establishing closer links with the business world.

The elections of May 1958 revealed the substantial stability of the electorate, with slight gains for the DC (42.2 percent) at the expense of the rightists. Following the elections, the DC and the PSI moved toward a rapprochement. The progressive attitudes of the church under Pope John XXIII (1958) also favoured this trend. The result—after considerable intraparty manoeuvring and a series of unstable governments, including a right-wing administration (Fernando Tambroni, March–July 1960) that aroused fears of a Fascist-style revival—was the "opening to the left" (*apertura a sinistra*). The formation of a left-of-centre government came during Fanfani's fourth administration (February 1962–May 1963). The coalition included the DC, the PSDI, and the PRI. The PSI, as agreed upon,

Opening to the left

maintained its abstention, which was interpreted as a show of confidence in the government. In the elections of May 1962, Antonio Segni was chosen president of the republic.

Industrial development. The years 1952–62 saw the doubling of the national income and a 62 percent increase in per capita income. This "economic miracle" was largely the result of the development of manufacturing, which made Italy a predominantly industrial country. Industrial production rose from 27 to 44 percent of total output, while employment in this sector grew from 29.6 to 38.6 percent of the working population. At the same time, employment in agriculture fell from 39.6 to 27 percent (and still further in subsequent years) of the people, with a mass migration from the countryside. The population shifts from the countryside to the towns and from south to north, involving millions of people, created serious overcrowding, urban sprawl, and substandard housing in many parts of the northern "industrial triangle" (Milan, Turin, Genoa). The increase in investments, the technological modernization and rationalization of plants, the creation of the European Economic Community (EEC), and the successes achieved by semipublic enterprises in the iron and steel sector were matched by the surplus of manpower, which helped to depress wage levels and encouraged further emigration.

The parliamentary shift to centre–left. The elections for the fourth republican administration (April 1963) disappointed the two left-of-centre protagonists. The DC (38.3 percent) lost part of its conservative support to the PLI while the PSI remained at a standstill. The PCI and the PSDI both gained. After a short-lived (June–November 1963) Christian Democrat government under Giovanni Leone, Aldo Moro was finally able (December 5) to form a left-of-centre "organic government" (one with direct Socialist [PSI] participation) committed to the adoption of economic programming, establishment of the locally autonomous regions, and reform measures in the urban, school, and agricultural sectors. The PSI, however, faced internal difficulties. The leftist splinter group, opposed to collaboration with the DC, left the party to set up (December 1963) the Italian Socialist Party of Proletarian Unity (Partito Socialista Italiano di Unità Proletaria, or PSIUP), which was joined by some 20 percent of the PSI parliamentarians. President Segni resigned (because of illness) in December 1964 and was replaced on December 28 by Giuseppe Saragat.

Presidency of Saragat

The Moro government, faced with inflation (closely connected with an expansion in consumption caused by higher wage levels) and a distressing balance-of-payments deficit, introduced measures to hold back consumption. It also contracted for a loan of $225,000,000 with the United States Treasury and the International Monetary Fund. The economic situation brought the reform policy to a halt and led to a new series of government crises. In March 1966, for the third time, Moro formed a centre-left government, which was finally able to introduce reforms such as the act on economic programming, a prerequisite for instituting the locally autonomous regions. Measures dealing with university reform and family rights, however, were delayed.

The Christian Democrats, meanwhile, were torn between leftist elements, which favoured détente in relations with the Communists, and right-of-centre elements opposed to any such rapprochement. The warring Socialist factions managed to reunite and at a joint congress (October 1966) formed the Unified Socialist Party (Partito Socialista Unificato, or PSU).

In the elections of May 19–20, 1968, the DC held its ground (39.1 percent), but the PSU suffered heavy losses and some of the Socialist voters switched to the PCI and, especially, the PSIUP. The Monarchists practically vanished, and the PLI and the MSI also fell behind. Giovanni Leone headed a Christian Democrat one-party caretaker administration from June to November 1968, when Mariano Rumor formed (December 13) a coalition of the DC, PSI, and PRI. Rumor's coalition lasted until July 1969, when the PSI's social democrat wing split off. Rumor, therefore, formed a new one-party government (August 1969) that had to face acute political and social tensions. The three major national trade-union confederations struck for the renewal of their contracts and for a new domestic policy (November 19). This critical situation was exacerbated by an attempt to blow up a Milan bank (December 12, 1969) in which several persons were killed.

Rumor coalition

Faced with this grave situation, the left-of-centre parties attempted to form a government that would offer better guarantees of stability and efficiency. After a long crisis, which began on February 7, 1970, a third Rumor left-of-centre coalition was set up in April. It managed to introduce some highly significant legislation, including the Workers' Statute (offering more effective guarantees of the workers' freedom and dignity and trade-union liberty in business enterprises), the referendum to repeal legislation, and the regional finance act. On July 6 Rumor unexpectedly resigned. He was replaced (August 6) by another Christian Democrat, Emilio Colombo, under whose leadership the centre–left coalition passed two measures that had aroused great controversy, the Divorce Bill and the Finance Bill. Colombo's government, however, was unable to halt the deterioration of the economy, and he resigned in January 1972.

Elections in May failed to resolve the political deadlock. Giulio Andreotti headed a centre–right government until he was succeeded in July 1973 by a Rumor-led centre–left coalition of Christian Democrats, Republicans, Socialists, and Social Democrats. The Communists and the trade unions adopted a tolerant attitude toward the new government. In February 1974, however, the Republicans withdrew from the government over economic policy, and Rumor formed a new administration in March, excluding the Republicans but dependent upon their parliamentary support. The right wing of the Christian Democrats forced the government to hold a referendum on the Divorce Law in May 1974. Despite strong opposition from the Roman Catholic Church, a large majority favoured the law, and the referendum was considered a severe setback for the Christian Democrats. In October, after a prolonged Cabinet crisis, the Rumor administration resigned. Italy remained without a government until the end of November, when Moro formed a coalition of Christian Democrats and Republicans. Depending on the parliamentary support of parties outside the coalition, this government was extremely weak.

Referendum on the Divorce Law

Successive governments had failed to cope with the decline of the economy and public services, corruption in high places, and the growth of lawlessness. In the regional elections of June 1975, the voters registered their discontent: the Communists attracted 33 percent of the vote. The Christian Democrats still led, with 35 percent, but their domination of political life was clearly threatened. In reaction, the party replaced Amintore Fanfani—the long-time secretary general and a stout opponent of any rapprochement with the Communists—with Benigno Zaccagnini. The Communists, meanwhile, rather than favouring the formation of a left-wing coalition government, continued to press for the "historic compromise" (*compromesso storico*), a program for Italy's future based on an alliance of Communists and Christian Democrats.

Moro's coalition government collapsed in January 1976 after the withdrawal of support by the Socialists. To stave off a general election, which was regarded as futile by the major parties, Moro formed a minority Christian Democrat administration a month later. Without adequate support in Parliament, however, the government was forced to hold a general election in June. The Communists showed increased strength, receiving more than 34 percent of the vote. The Christian Democrats continued to reject the "historic compromise" and insisted on excluding the Communists from power. They were forced to seek assurances of Communist abstention, however, before a new government could be formed. At the end of July, Giulio Andreotti formed a new government, which proceeded to introduce severe austerity measures to deal with the continuing economic crisis.

In July 1977, after four months of negotiations, the Communists at last received a measure of participation in the government. The opposition parties gained a significant voice in policy making, but no direct role in government. The initial program included measures to strengthen the economy and to uphold law and order. Communist support for the Christian Democrats alienated the extreme left, some of whom resorted to the violent political tactics already associated with the extreme right. The arrangement, however, enhanced the authority of the government, which no longer feared defeat in Parliament, and suited both Christian Democrats and Communists.

Despite a number of parliamentary crises and increasing political violence during the autumn of 1977 and the first half of 1978, the agreement held firm. The most sensational episode in the long series of political kidnappings, shootings, and "kneecappings" of prominent businessmen, intellectuals, and members of the judiciary was the abduction of the Christian Democratic Party leader and former premier, Aldo Moro, on March 16 by members of the Red Brigades (Brigate Rosse), an extreme left-wing terrorist group. The attack took place shortly before Parliament began its debate on a vote of confidence for the latest Andreotti Cabinet, which had taken office March 13. The kidnappers attempted to bargain with the government for release of brigade members then on trial. After long and agonized debate, the government refused to negotiate with the Red Brigades.

Moro murder

Moro's bullet-riddled body was found near the centre of Rome on May 9. A week later, on May 14–15, in local elections involving about 10 percent of the electorate, the Communist Party obtained 16 percent less of the popular vote than the Christian Democrats, compared with a difference of only 3.3 percent between the two parties in the same areas in the general elections of 1976. The vote was widely interpreted as a sympathy vote for the Christian Democrats.

On June 15 Pres. Giovanni Leone resigned because of allegations connecting him to the Lockheed bribery scandal in which the American aircraft company was said to have bribed high military officials and politicians to facilitate purchase of Lockheed aircraft. Alessandro Pertini, a Socialist, succeeded Leone in July as Italy's seventh president, to serve a seven-year term.

In Parliament the Christian Democrats continued to govern in coalition with the Communists and three smaller parties in a government of so-called national unity. The Communists, however, withdrew their support in January 1979, and without them the Christian Democrats were unable to form a stable government. President Pertini dissolved Parliament on April 2 after Premier Andreotti had resigned on March 31. The dissolution of Parliament paved the way for elections on June 10. The Communists received a substantial defeat, the Christian Democrats maintained their strength, and the chief beneficiaries were the minor parties, especially the Radicals.

Economic troubles. Severe inflation and economic stagnation have troubled the Italian economy since about 1969. Since the country is heavily dependent on imported energy sources, the large increases in petroleum prices have exacerbated its economic difficulties. Nevertheless, the Italian economy showed remarkable resiliency. For the five-year period ending in 1976, the gross domestic product increased 16.9 percent, a figure that was all the more impressive when measured against those of the West's main industrial powers (among which Italy ranked seventh). Only Canada and Japan, with growth rates of 25.2 percent and 26.8 percent, respectively, exceeded the Italian achievement during that period.

The government made numerous efforts to stabilize the economy. During 1977 the response was relatively satisfactory. The rate of inflation was reduced to around 15 percent by the end of the year (from 22 percent at the beginning of 1977). The balance of payments recorded a positive swing of almost U.S. $4,900,000,000. The growth rate, however, dropped to 1.7 percent compared with the 5.6 percent registered the previous year. Investment was stagnant, and the unemployment rate hovered around 7 percent. Inflation in 1978 dropped still further, to 11.5%, but that rate remained among the highest in western Europe.

(C.G.Se.)

BIBLIOGRAPHY

Italy in the early Middle Ages: The Cambridge Medieval History, 8 vol. (1911–36; 2nd ed., 1966–), contains good coverage of medieval Italy. Primary documentary sources are published in the *Rerum Italicarum Scriptores* by L.A. MURATORI and in the *Monumenta Germaniae Historica.* Also important are the series of the *Historiae Patriae Monumenta,* the *Fonti della storia d'Italia* of the Italian Historical Institute for the Middle Ages, the *Regesta Chartarum Italiae,* and the *Biblioteca della Società storica subalpina.* Still of great use are THOMAS HODGKIN, *Italy and Her Invaders,* 2nd ed., 8 vol. (1892–1916, reprinted 1967); LUDO M. HARTMANN, *Geschichte Italiens im Mittelalter,* 4 vol. (1897–1915, successive editions); and PASQUALE VILLARI, *Le invasioni barbariche in Italia,* 2nd ed. (1905; Eng. trans. of 1st ed., *The Barbarian Invasions of Italy,* 2 vol., 1902). More recent works are ROMOLO CAGGESE, *L'alto Medioevo* (1937); *Il Medioevo,* by various authors, vol. 1 of the *Storia d'Italia,* ed. by the UTET of Turin, 2nd ed. (1965); and GABRIELE PEPE, *Il medio evo barbarico. d'Italia* (1963). Medieval Italy has been put into its European framework in the excellent works of GIOACCHINO VOLPE, *Il Medioevo,* 2nd ed. (1933); GIORGIO FALCO, *La Santa Romana Repubblica,* 5th ed. (1965; Eng. trans., *The Holy Roman Republic,* 2nd ed., 1964); and ROBERTO S. LOPEZ, *Naissance de l'Europe* (1962; Eng. trans., *The Birth of Europe,* 1967). For the social classes and daily life, see ANTONIO VISCARDI and GIANLUIGI BARNI, *L'Italia nell'età comunale* (1966); GIANLUIGI BARNI and GINA FASOLI, *L'Italia nell'alto Medioevo* (1971). For economic history, see WILHELM VON HEYD, ALOYS SCHULTE, and ADOLF SCHAUBE, see ALFRED J. DOREN, *Italienische Wirtschaftsgeschichte,* vol. 1 (1934); FILIPPO CARLI, *Storia del commercio italiano,* 2 vol. (1934–36); GINO LUZZATTO, *Storia economica d'Italia. Il Medioevo,* 2nd ed. (1963); ROBERT S. LOPEZ, "The Trade of Medieval Europe: The South," in *The Cambridge Economic History of Europe,* 2nd ed., vol. 2 (1965). For demography, see JULIUS BELOCH, *Bevölkerungsgeschichte Italiens,* 3 vol. (1937–61). (*Ostrogothic and Byzantine–Lombard periods*): ERNESTO SESTAN, *Stato e nazione nell'Alto Medioevo: Ricerche sulle origini nazionali in Francia, Italia, Germania* (1952); CHARLES H. DIEHL, *Études sur l'administration byzantine dans l'Exarchat de Ravenne, 568–751* (1888); GIAN PIETRO BOGNETTI, *L'età longobarda,* 4 vol. (1966–68); JULES GAY, *L'Italie méridionale et l'empire byzantin . . ., 867–1071,* 2 vol. (1904, reprinted 1960); ARCHIBALD R. LEWIS, *Naval Power and Trade in the Mediterranean, A.D. 500–1100* (1951, reprinted 1970); and NICOLA CILENTO, *Italia meridionale longobarda* (1966). (*Carolingian and post-Carolingian periods*): See the chapters on Italy in LOUIS HALPHEN, *Charlemagne et l'empire carolingien* (1947); and HEINRICH FICHTENAU, *Das Karolingische Imperium* (1949; Eng. trans., *The Carolingian Empire,* 1957); also LOUIS DUCHESNE, *Les Premiers temps de l'État pontifical* (1898; Eng. trans., *The Beginnings of the Temporal Sovereignty of the Popes, A.D. 754–1073,* 1908), a classic, now outdated; and PAOLO BREZZI, *Roma e l'impero medioevale, 774–1252* (1947); ROBERTO CESSI, *Venezia ducale,* vol. 1 (1963); MICHELANGELO SCHIPA, *Il Mezzogiorno d'Italia anteriormente alla monarchia. Ducato di Napoli e Principato di Salerno* (1923); and MICHELE AMARI, *Storia dei Musulmani di Sicilia,* 2nd ed., 3 vol. (1933–39). See also the section on Italy in ROBERT HOLTZMANN, *Geschichte der sächsischen Kaiserzeit, 900–1024,* 3rd ed. (1955).

The High Middle Ages: (*The 11th century*): AUGUSTIN FLICHE, *La Réforme grégorienne,* 3 vol. (1924–37); ERNST WERNER, *Die gesellschaftlichen Grundlagen der Klosterreform im 11. Jahrhundert* (1953). (*Norman Sicily*): JOHN JULIUS NORWICH, *The Normans in the South, 1016–1130* (1967); and *The Kingdom in the Sun, 1130–1194* (1970); FERDINAND CHALANDON, *Histoire de la domination normande en Italie et en Sicile,* 2 vol. (1907); M. CARAVALE, *Il regno normanno di Sicilia* (1966); S. TRAMONTANA, *I Normanni in Italia,* vol. 1 (1970). (*The 12th and 13th centuries*): EDOUARD JORDAN, *L'Allemagne et l'Italie aux XIIe et XIIIe siècles* (1939); PETER RASSOW, *Honor imperii* (1940). The principal contribution to the history of the formation of the autonomous communes is that given by GIOACCHINO VOLPE in *Medio Evo italiano,* 2nd ed. (1928, reprinted 1961) and a whole series of monographs on the Tuscan cities. On the rural communes, and in general on the evolution of society in the countryside, see FEDOR SCHNEIDER, *Die Entstehung von Burg und Landgemeinde in Italien* (1924); and GIAN PIETRO BOGNETTI, *Sulle origini dei comuni rurali del Medio Evo* (1927). Among important works on a single city or region are: VITO VITALE, *Breviario della storia di Genova,* 2 vol. (1955); FRANCESCO COGNASSO, *Storia di Torino* (1934); PIETRO VACCARI, *Pavia nell'alti Medioevo e nell'età comunale* (1956); vol. 3–5 of the *Storia di Milano* of the Fondazione Treccani, Milan (1954–55); PIETRO TORELLI, *Un Comune cittadino in territorio ad economia agricola . . .,* 2 vol. (1930–52); L. SIMEONI, "Le origini del Comune di Verona," *Nuova Arch.,* vol. 21 (1913); J.K. HYDE,

Padua in the Age of Dante (1966); GIORGIO CRACCO, *Società e Stato nel Medioevo Veneziano* (1967); DAVID HERLIHY, *Medieval and Renaissance Pistoia* (1967); GAETANO SALVEMINI, *Magnati e popolani in Firenze dal 1280 al 1295* (1899; new ed. 1960 and 1966); and NICOLA OTTOKAR, *Il Comune di Firenze alla fine del dugento* (1926), both on Florence; FERDINAND SCHEVILL, *Siena: The History of a Medieval Commune* (1909, reprinted 1964); ENRICO FIUMI, *Storia economica e sociale di San Gimignano* (1961); GIOACCHINO VOLPE, *Toscana medievale* (1964), including articles on Massa Marittima, Volterra, and Sarzana; and *Studi sulle istituzioni comunali a Pisa*, new ed. (1970); EMILIO CHRISTIANI, *Nobilità e popolo nel comune di Pisa . . .* (1962); DANIEL WALEY, *Mediaeval Orvieto* (1952); PAOLO BREZZI, *Roma e l'impero medioevale, 774–1252* (1947); EUGENIO DUPRE THESEIDER, *Roma dal comune di popolo alla signoria pontificia, 1252–1377* (1952); and ENRICO BESTA, *La Sardegna medievale*, 2 vol. (1908–09). An excellent discussion of the institutions and in general of the communal life is included in DANIEL WALEY, *The Italian City-Republics* (1969). (*The Papal State and Southern Italy*): JOACHIM SEEGER, *Die Reorganisation des Kirchenstaates unter Innocenz III* (1937); DANIEL WALEY, *The Papal State in the Thirteenth Century* (1961); ERNESTO PONTIERI, *Ricerche sulla crisi della monarchia siciliana nel secolo XIII*, 3rd ed. (1958); EDOUARD JORDAN, *Les Origines de la domination angevine en Italie* (1909); EMILE G. LEONARD, *Les Angevins de Naples* (1954); STEVEN RUNCIMAN, *The Sicilian Vespers* (1958); FRANCESCO GIUNTA, *Aragonesi e Catalani nel Mediterraneo*, 2 vol. (1953–59); and J.K. HYDE, *Society and Politics in Medieval Italy: The Evolution of Civil Life, 1000–1350* (1973).

Italy in the late Middle Ages and the Renaissance: Some of the best general accounts of the history of Italy in the 14th and 15th centuries are embedded in treatments of Renaissance culture as a whole. Among such works are DENYS HAY, *The Italian Renaissance in Its Historical Background* (1961); MYRON P. GILMORE, *The World of Humanism, 1453–1517* (1952); and PETER BURKE, *Culture and Society in Renaissance Italy, 1420–1540* (1972). The classic book of JACOB BURCKHARDT (Eng. trans., *The Civilization of the Renaissance in Italy . . .*, many editions), also continues to be richly suggestive. The structure and the problems of the Italian communes are usefully described in DANIEL WALEY, *The Italian City-Republics* (1969); their revolutionary significance in the medieval political world is discussed in the last section of WALTER ULLMANN, *Principles of Government and Politics in the Middle Ages* (1961). GARRETT MATTINGLY, *Renaissance Diplomacy* (1955), studies both the diplomatic history of Italy in this period and the development of diplomatic institutions and practice. Stimulating on the confrontation between republicanism and despotism in Renaissance Italy and above all on its significance for cultural history and the emergence of the modern political consciousness is HANS BARON, *The Crisis of the Early Italian Renaissance*, rev. ed. (1966). For the crisis of 14th-century society and its effect on the religious life and the mood of Italy, see MILLARD MEISS, *Painting in Florence and Siena After the Black Death* (1951). On Milanese despotism there is a good biography by D.M. BUENO DE MESQUITA, *Giangaleazzo Visconti, Duke of Milan (1351–1402)* (1941). For Florence, FERDINAND SCHEVILL, *History of Florence from the Founding of the City Through the Renaissance* (1936, reprinted 1961) is solid and informative, but the best general introduction to all aspects of Florentine history and society in this period is GENE A. BRUCKER, *Renaissance Florence* (1969); the same author's *Florentine Politics and Society, 1343–1378* (1962) and *The Civic World of Early Renaissance Florence* (1977) are excellent examples of the best specialized studies of Florence in recent scholarship. For Florence under the Medici, see KURT S. GUTKIND, *Cosimo de' Medici, pater patriae, 1389–1464* (1938); and NICOLAI RUBINSTEIN, *The Government of Florence Under the Medici (1434-1494)* (1966). On Venice a good introduction is D.S. CHAMBERS, *The Imperial Age of Venice, 1380–1580* (1970); for the Venetian political tradition, see WILLIAM J. BOUWSMA, *Venice and the Defense of Republican Liberty* (1968); for Venetian society see ANGELO VENTURA, *Nobilità e popolo nella società veneta del '400 e '500* (1964). For Lucca see MARINO BERENGO, *Nobili e mercanti nella Lucca del Cinquecento* (1965); and for Naples see ALAN RYDER, *The Kingdom of Naples Under Alfonso the Magnanimous: The Making of a Modern State* (1976). Some sense of the problems of the Papal State may be derived from PETER PARTNER, *The Papal State Under Martin V* (1958); these problems are vividly illustrated in the memoirs of PIUS II, available in English under the title *Memoirs of a Renaissance Pope* (1959). For Sicily see DENIS MACK SMITH, *A History of Sicily*, 2 vol. (1968). On the events at the end of the 15th century and their impact on Machiavelli and Guicciardini, see FEDERICO CHABOD, *Machiavelli and the Renaissance* (1958), which also contains a useful bibliography for Italy in the age of the Renaissance; and FELIX GILBERT, *Machiavelli and Guicciardini: Politics and History in Sixteenth-Century Florence* (1965).

Italy in the 16th–18th centuries: An exhaustive bibliography may be found in the appendix to ERNESTO PONTIERI, *Le lotte per il predominio in Europe tra la Spagna e la Potenza ispanoasburgica*, included in vol. 5, pt. 2, of the *Storia Universale* (1971). See also LUIGI SIMEONI, *La Signorie*, vol. 2 (1950); ROMOLO QUASSA, *Preponderanza Spagnuola, 1559–1700*, 2nd ed. (1950); *Storia d'Italia (op. cit.)*, vol. 2, with an updated bibliography and listing of specific monographs; and LUIGI BULFERETTI, "La decadenza italiana nel seicento," *Cultura e scuola*, 1:98–104 (1962), a review of recent studies. See also the relevant volumes of *The Cambridge Modern History* and *The New Cambridge Modern History*. For a general view of Italy in the 18th century, beyond what may be found in various histories of Italy, see GIORGIO CANDELORO, *Storia dell'Italia moderna*, vol. 1 (1956); GUIDO QUAZZA, *Il problema italiano e l'equilibrio europeo, 1720–1738* (1965); FRANCO VENTURI, *Settecento riformatore* (1969); and GIUSEPPE GALASSO, *Potere e istituzioni in Italia: Dalla caduta dell'Impero romano a oggi* (1974). For Lombardy in particular, see FRANCO VALSECCHI, *L'assolutismo illuminato in Austria e in Lombardia*, 2 vol. (1931–34); S. PUGLIESE, *Condizioni economiche e finanziarie della Lombardia nella prima metà del secolo XVIII* (1924); and FEDERICO CHABOD, *Lo stato e la vita religiosa a Milano nell'epoca di Carlo V* (1971). A basic text is vol. 12 of the *Storia di Milano*, of the FONDAZIONE TRECCANI, Milan, *L'età delle reforme, 1706–1796* (1959). For Tuscany, see NICCOLO RODOLICO, "La Toscana alla vigilia delle riforme," "Emanuele di Richecourt iniziatore delle riforme lorenesi in Toscana" and "I primi provvedimenti contro la manumorta ecclesiastica in Toscana," all included in the collection *Saggi di storia medievale e moderna* (1963), with numerous bibliographical references and references to works by the same author on the Lorraine period. An excellent biography of Peter Leopold is ADAM WANDRUSZKA, *Leopold II* (1963, in German; Italian trans., 1968). For Naples, see HEINRICH BENEDIKT, *Das Königreich Neapel unter Kaiser Karl VI* (1927); RAFFAELE COLAPIETRA, *Vita pubblica e classi politiche del viceregno napoletano, 1656–1734* (1961); RAFFAELE AJELLO, "Il banco di San Carlo: Organi di governo e opinione pubblica nel Regno di Napoli di fronte al problema della ricompra dei diritti fiscali," in *Rivista Storica Italiana*, vol. 81, fasc. 4, pp. 812–881 (1969); LINO MARINI, *Il mezzogiorno d'Italia di fronte a Vienna e a Roma e altri studi di storia meridionale* (1970); GIUSEPPE RECUPERATI, "Napoli e i viceréo austrici, 1707–1784," in *Storia di Napoli*, vol. 7 (n.d.); and HAROLD M. ACTON, *The Bourbons of Naples, 1734–1825* (1956). For Sicily, see RAFF MARTINI, *La Sicilia sotto gli Austriaci (1719–1734)* (1907); FRANCESCO DE STEFANO, *Storia della Sicilia dal secolo XI al XIX*, pp. 231–235 (1948), with extensive bibliography; DENIS MACK SMITH, *Storia della Sicilia medioevale e moderna*, pp. 316–332 (1970); VIRGILIO TITONE, *La Sicilia dalla dominazione spagnola all'unità d'Italia* (1955); GIUSEPPE GALASSO, *Mezzogiorno medievale e moderno* (1965) and *Dal comune medievale all'unità: Linee di storia meridionale (1969)*; and the relevant volumes of *The Cambridge Modern History* and *The New Cambridge Modern History*.

Italy from 1789 to 1871: The two most important comprehensive studies are those by CESARE SPELLANZON, *Storia del Risorgimento e dell'Unità d'Italia*, vol. 1–4 (1933–50), which covers the period from the 18th century to 1849 and continues down to the Crimean War with vol. 6–8 by E. DI NOLFO (1959–65); and by GIORGIO CANDELORO, *Storia dell'Italia moderna*, 6 vol. (1956–1970). Spellanzon and Di Nolfo pay particular attention to the political currents and diplomatic history, Candeloro to socio-economic structures. On the Jacobin movement, reference should be made to the interpretations by DELIO CANTIMORI, in *Studi di storia*, pp. 629–638 (1959); and by ARMANDO SAITTA, "La questione del giacobinismo italiano," in *Critica storica*, vol. 4, pp. 204–249 (1965). For the Republic and the Kingdom of Italy, see CARLO ZAGHI, *Napoleone e l'Europa* (1969); and on the South, PASQUALE VILLANI, "Il Regno di Napoli nel decennio francese (1806–1815)," in *Studi storici in onore di Gabriele Pepe*, pp. 689–702 (1969), which sets forth the plan of a future work. On the various Italian states during the Restoration, the best studies are AUGUSTO SANDONA, *Il Regno lombardo-veneto, 1814–1859. La costituzione e l'amministrazione* (1912); KENT R. GREENFIELD, *Economics and Liberalism in the Risorgimento: A Study of Nationalism in Lombardy, 1814–1848*, rev. ed. (1965); REUBEN J. RATH, *The Provisional Austrian Regime in Lombardy-Venetia, 1814–1815* (1969); GAETANO CINGARI, *Mezzogiorno e Risorgimento: La Restaurazione a Napoli dal 1821 al 1830* (1970); and ROSARIO ROMEO, *Il Risorgimento in Sicilia* (1950). On Cavour and his milieu, see ADOLFO OMODEO, *L'opera politica del conte di Cavour (1848–1857)* (1968); ROSARIO ROMEO, *Cavour e il suo tempo, 1810–1842* (1969); and, related to Pius IX, ROGER AUBERT, *Le Pontificat de Pie IX* (1952). On the unification movement, see RAYMOND GREW, *A Sterner Plan for Italian Unity: The Italian National Society in the Risorgimento* (1963); and DENIS MACK SMITH, *Cavour and Garibaldi, 1860: A Study in Political Conflict* (1954). Studies of the formation of the Italian state and the policy of the Right are: CLAUDIO PAVONE, *Amministrazione centrale e amministrazione periferica da Rattazzi a Ricasoli* (1964); ERNESTO RAGIONIERI, *Politica e amministrazione nella storia dell'Italia unità (1967)*; ALDO BERSELLI, *La Destra Storica dopo l'unità*, 2 vol. (1963–65); and ARNALDO SALVESTRINI, *I moderati toscani e la classe dirigente italiana (1859–1876)* (1965).

Italy from 1871 to the present: Comprehensive works or works on individual periods include: BENEDETTO CROCE, *Storia d'Italia dal 1871 al 1915*, 2nd ed. (1928; Eng. trans., *A History of Italy, 1871–1915*, 1929, reprinted 1963), a classic of liberal ethico-political historiography; GIOACCHINO VOLPE, *Italia moderna 1815–1915*, 3 vol. (1946–52); DENIS MACK SMITH, *Italy: A Modern History* (1959), on the years 1861–1958; CHRISTOPHER SETON-WATSON, *Italy from Liberalism to Fascism, 1870–1925* (1967), an accurate and concise reconstruction; GIORGIO CANDELORO, *Storia dell'Italia moderna*, vol. 6 (1970), follows economic and social developments closely for the years 1871–96; FEDERICO CHABOD, *L'Italie contemporaine* (1950); LUIGI SALVATORELLI and GIOVANNI MIRA, *Storia d'Italia nel periodo fascista* (1956); FRANCO CATALANO, *L'Italia dalla dittatura alla democrazia, 1919–1948*, 2nd ed. (1965); NORMAN KOGAN, *A Political History of Postwar Italy* (1966); and GIUSEPPE MAMMARELLA, *L'Italia dopo il fascismo, 1943–1968* (1970). For special topics, see RICHARD A. WEBSTER, *The Cross and the Fasces: Christian Democracy and Fascism in Italy* (1960); RICHARD HOSTETTER, *The Italian Socialist Movement*, vol. 1, *Origins (1860–1882)* (1958); and GAETANO ARFE, *Storia del socialismo italiano, 1892–1926*, 2nd ed. (1965). On the Communist Party, see PAOLO SPRIANO, *Storia del Partito Comunista Italiano*, 3 vol. (1967–70), up to 1939. For the Fascist period, see ANGELO ROSSI, Eng. trans., *The Rise of Italian Fascism 1918–1922* (1938); ADRIAN LYTTELTON, *The Seizure of Power: Fascism in Italy, 1919–1929* (1973); F. CHABOD, *L'Italie contemporaine* (1950; Eng. trans., *A History of Italian Fascism*, 1963); RENZO DE FELICE, *Mussolini*, 4 vol. (1965–74); and F.W.D. DEAKIN, *The Brutal Friendship: Mussolini, Hitler, and the Fall of Italian Fascism*, rev. ed. (1966). For anti-Fascism and the Resistance, see NORMAN KOGAN, *Italy and the Allies* (1956); C.R.S. HARRIS, *Allied Military Administration of Italy, 1943–45* (1957); and CHARLES F. DELZELL, *Mussolini's Enemies: The Italian Anti-Fascist Resistance* (1961). For foreign and colonial policy, see C.J. LOWE and F. MARZARI, *Italian Foreign Policy, 1870–1940* (1975); RENE ALBRECHT-CARRIE, *Italy at the Paris Peace Conference* (1938, reprinted 1966); and J.L. MIEGE, *L'Imperialisme colonial italien de 1870 à nos jours* (1968). On state–church relations, see DANIEL A. BINCHY, *Church and State in Fascist Italy* (1941), and A.C. JEMOLO, *Chiesa e stato in Italia negli ultimi cento anni* (1948; Eng. trans. of the abridged 1955 ed., *Church and State in Italy [1850–1950]*, 1960). For economic history, see SHEPARD B. CLOUGH, *The Economic History of Modern Italy* (1964); BRUNO CAIZZI, *Storia dell'industria italiana del XVIII secolo ai giorni nostri* (1965). On the trade-union movement, see DANIEL L. HOROWITZ, *The Italian Labor Movement* (1963), and M.F. NEUFELD, *Italy: School for Awakening Countries* (1961).

(C.G.Se./Gi.Ma./W.J.Bo./E.Po./G.d'A./F.d.Pe./Ma.B.)

Itō Hirobumi

Prince Itō Hirobumi, known as a *genro*, or elder statesman, played a crucial role in the building of modern Japan. He was the first prime minister under the newly created European-style cabinet system (1885), thus becoming the second man in Japanese history born of peasant stock to achieve such high rank. He was the first president of the Privy Council (Sūmitsu-in; 1888) and the House of Peers (1890); the first *genro* to head a political party (Rikken Seiyūkai, 1900–03); and the first resident general of the Protectorate of Korea (1905–09). He was influential in the construction of the first railway line in Japan (Tokyo–Yokohama, 1872) and in the founding of modern fiscal, banking, monetary, and public finance systems. His greatest contributions, however, were the drafting of the Meiji Constitution and the establishment of a two-house national Diet, making Japan the first non-Western nation to freely adopt constitutional government.

Itō was born on the second day of the ninth lunar month (mid-October) in 1841, in Chōshū, an area in the southwestern part of Honshu, the main island. His father was an adopted son of a modest samurai (warrior) family, and Itō grew up amid convulsive political conditions resulting from the decline of the Tokugawa shogunate—which had governed Japan since 1603—and the rise of Western influence in the country. He played a minor role in the events leading to the Meiji Restoration, a movement that overthrew the shogunate and restored power to the emperor (1868). This brought him into contact with men like Kido Takayoshi (1833–77), who was to become one of the great leaders of early Meiji Japan and who was Itō's most important mentor in these years.

Itō's talents were apparent even before the Restoration, and he was sent to England by the leaders of Chōshū to study Western naval science (1863). His connections with Kido and Ōkubo Toshimichi (1831–78), the other giant of early Meiji Japan, brought him government assignments to the United States and the Iwakura Mission to Europe (1870, 1871–73) to study and work on matters as diverse as taxation and budgetary systems and treaty revision.

His political career changed decisively when Ōkubo, the most powerful man in the government, was assassinated in 1878, and Itō succeeded him as minister of home affairs. His advancement brought him into conflict with the equally talented and ambitious statesman Ōkuma Shigenobu (1838–1922). In a series of masterful political strokes, Itō forced Ōkuma and his supporters out of the government in 1881 and persuaded the government to adopt a constitution; by 1889 the Emperor proclaimed it and in 1890 the national Diet was established.

Constitutional government

Preparations for constitutional government were made with utmost seriousness. Itō, then the most important person in the Meiji government, and other officials spent nearly one and a half years (1882–83) in Europe, notably in Germany, studying under leading constitutional scholars. The Meiji Constitution, Itō's greatest handiwork, has been criticized for perpetuating authoritarian rule because the guarantees of civil rights and the Diet's powers were hedged by restrictions. Actually, given the Meiji leaders' samurai background and the tense domestic and foreign problems they faced, the unprecedented acknowledgment in writing of basic rights and the establishment of the Diet were progressive and enlightened acts. It should also be noted that neither Itō nor any of the Meiji leaders ever pointed to these tensions and difficulties as an excuse for reverting to tight authoritarian control.

Itō's pre-eminence continued in the 1890s. In mid-decade, as prime minister, he helped Japan attain two important successes. The first was an agreement with Great Britain signed in 1894 for doing away with extraterritoriality by 1899. Under the agreement British nationals in Japan would thereafter be subject to Japanese law. This agreement was followed by others with other major Western nations. The second achievement was Japan's victory over China in 1895, and both achievements were among the first clear signs that Japan, alone among non-Western nations, had achieved success in modernization and a weightier role in East Asian affairs.

Domestically, Itō did not fare as well. He had felt, along with other *genro*, that party politicians were incapable of dealing dispassionately with Japan's welfare and destiny; and, indeed, the powers guaranteed by the Meiji Constitution enabled the political parties to impede government programs in the Diet. Itō unhappily, but with characteristic flexibility, continually worked out compromises with the parties, until by 1900 no cabinet could be formed without their tacit consent. From the start the parties had been cooperating with the government in return for cabinet positions and laws favouring party growth. Itō made one last move to salvage the situation by leaving the government and forming the Seiyūkai, which he based on an older antigovernment party, the Kenseitō. The Seiyūkai became the first party to control an absolute majority in the House of Representatives during a Diet session, leading Itō to believe that he had finally created the right condition for smooth passage of government programs. He did not count on the obstructive tactics of the House of Peers, however, whose conservative members were unhappy with Itō's alliance with the parties. Ironically, Itō had originally created the House of Peers to try to balance what he considered to be the less than responsible House of Representatives. Finally, embittered with the

Foundation of the Seiyūkai

knowledge that dealing with party members, each with his own constituency to answer to, was infinitely more difficult and distasteful than working with a handful of genro, all of the same background and inspiration, he resigned as president of the Seiyūkai in 1903. But Itō paid for having broken genro ranks; soon afterward Yamagata Aritomo (1838–1922), founder of the modern Japanese Army, became the leading power among the powerful genro.

Itō's legacy, however, cannot be denied, for he made co-operation between high-ranking bureaucrats and party politicians respectable, which provided an alternative to the unremitting and unproductive polarization of these two groups. Moreover, the other genro's continued commitment to the Meijo Constitution made party growth inevitable.

Itō's term as resident general in Korea proved to be a failure, for he was unable to gain the trust and confidence of the Koreans in spite of his moderate and sympathetic approach. Nor could he prevent the thrust toward annexation of Korea favoured by other leaders in Japan. In October 1909 he was shot in Harbin in North China by An Chung-gŭn, a member of the Korean independence movement. His last words on being told that he was the victim of a political assassination were: "Baka na yatsu ja!" ("He is a fool!"). Itō probably meant that the Korean had killed the one Japanese leader who had and would have continued to support an even-handed Korea policy.

Assassination

Itō was honoured with a state funeral. Despite his unquestioned contributions to the modernization of Japan, he has never been first in the hearts of his countrymen. The Japanese more often favour their romantic heroes, usually losers of great military causes. His private life also prevented his enshrinement in ethics textbooks as a paradigm for young Japanese. He is remembered instead for his boast: "Drunk, I (relax) with my head on a beauty's lap; awaken (refreshed), I grip the reins of power." His violent death was also ironic: he was never the strong-willed statesman that Ōkubo, Ōkuma, and Yamagata were. He sought the compromiser's role, the harmonious solution. His enduring monument was the creation of a viable constitutional system. It enabled the Japanese to effect orderly, evolutionary, peaceful political change accompanied by an ever-widening scope for meaningful popular participation.

BIBLIOGRAPHY. KENTARO KANEKO (ed.), *Itō Hirobumi Den*, 3 vol. (1943), an excellent biography with primary sources quoted in full (in Japanese); KENGI HAMADA, *Prince Ito* (1936), the only biography in English, marred somewhat by flowery language; GEORGE AKITA, *Foundations of Constitutional Government in Modern Japan, 1868–1900* (1967).

(G.Ak.)

Ituri Forest

The Ituri Forest, large stretches of which are still completely unexplored, remains one of the least known regions in the world. It consists of a zone of deep equatorial forest forming the northeastern section of the huge Central African tropical forest that covers about two-fifths of Zaire. The northern and eastern limits of the Ituri Forest are well known, but its boundaries to the south and west remain undefined, and its total area is variously estimated as between 13,000 and 21,000 square miles (34,000 to 54,000 square kilometres). The forest, which is inhabited by both Bantu and Pygmy peoples, owes its name to the mighty Ituri River, which crosses it from east to west.

The most clearly defined sections of the forest lie mainly to the north of the Ituri River, as far as 30 miles or so upstream from the point where the river takes the name of the Aruwimi on joining the Nepoko. Here the forest forms an east–west rectangle about 80 miles long, although some authorities consider that it extends a considerable distance further on the left bank of the river to the level of Lubero in the south and Lindi in the west. The unexplored regions of the forest could produce surprises for naturalists, even concerning its animal life.

The forest. To describe the general appearance of this magnificent forest world one would like to be able to reproduce everything that the Welsh explorer Henry Morton Stanley wrote about it after his memorable—and triple—crossing of the Ituri in 1887 and 1888. He speaks of it with poetic enthusiasm. The trees range in height from 20 to 160 feet. The summits of their trunks, measuring from a few inches to four feet and more in diameter, are so close together that they intertwine to obscure the sky and the sun. Creepers, some of them 15 inches thick, straddle the trunks or hug them "like endless anacondas." The countless flowers, the epiphytes (plants that grow on other plants and draw sustenance from the air), sometimes the size of a cabbage, serve to darken the undergrowth. The thick moss looks like green fur. But if it is magnificent, this is also an oppressive world, heavy with permanent humidity and silence, swarming with disquieting life: never a ray of sunlight, nor any rain or even mud. The creepers ooze latex and there are swarms of red and black ants—a single bite from which may raise a blister the size of a coin.

Relief and drainage. In its northwestern reaches the Ituri Forest is relatively flat, with altitudes of between 2,000 and 2,700 feet, whereas toward the south and southeast its contours are much more rugged, often exceeding 3,000 feet.

It is watered by broad streams, of which the largest is the Ituri itself. Among the more important tributaries of the Ituri is the Epulu, the wide basin of which forms the very heart of the forest. The streams are fed by virtually permanent rains, the annual rainfall being about 80 inches, with maximums in April and October. On the northeastern outskirts there are reputed to be two dry months a year, but in the central and southern zones there are none.

Soils and vegetation. The forest soil is both rich and friable. In the east the humiferous layer is thinner and is mixed with boulders of granite or conglomerate composition. In the centre, in the flat zone, the soil is iron-bearing sandy clay. Save for a small strip in the northwest, which is marshy and has a distinct type of vegetation, the forest itself provides the organic matter required for maintaining the thick layer of humus necessary for its survival. But if in a given area the vegetal cover is removed, the balance is upset and the soil deteriorates, recovering only if it is again taken over by a secondary forest. This has happened to countless clearings opened in the forest by Bantu farmers.

On the northern and eastern edges there is a fringe with clearer secondary characteristics, in particular the presence of umbrella trees. After this the equatorial forest proper starts, assuming—toward the southwest, south of Wamba and west of Mambasa—the characteristics of a *Macrolobium* forest. In the southeast, on the other hand, in the Mambasa–Irumu–Beni triangle, a special formation appears: the *Cynometra* forest. Whereas in the ordinary equatorial forest woody specimens are numbered in hundreds, with none predominating, in the *Cynometra* forest a majority of this species of tree has been found.

Animal life. Animal life is abundant and is characteristic of the equatorial forest. The two most notable species are the okapi (a mammal related to the giraffe) and a mountain gorilla less silver-backed than that found in the higher regions of the Kivu area. Elephants and forest buffalo are just as plentiful as those found in Africa's savannas (grassy parklands), but they are smaller, though more aggressive. Among the antelope the bongo is worth mentioning, as also are the mouse deer and the bush-buck. Leopards and other carnivores are numerous; crocodiles make the rivers dangerous to approach. There are many monkeys. Hundreds of species of birds have been recorded, among which the Congo peacock, discovered in 1937, is perhaps the most famous.

The inhabitants. When Stanley traversed the forest in the 19th century it was inhabited, as it still is today, by two entirely different ethnic groups, the Bantus and the Pygmies, who maintain a curious symbiotic relationship not unmixed with mutual suspicion and contempt. The life led by each of these communities will be considered before the relations which unite them are examined.

The Pygmies. Known since ancient times, these small tree-dwelling peoples are also to be found elsewhere in Africa and in the world. Their height averages four and a half feet; their complexion is light; their noses are flat —perhaps due to the humidity of their habitat; their big toes facilitate tree climbing; they possess extraordinary suppleness and endurance; they have the ability to fast for a long time and are then capable of suddenly eating large quantities of food, particularly meat. They are also more resistant to tropical diseases, especially malaria, than the Bantu.

The Pygmies of the Ituri constitute one of the three main groups of Pygmies living in Central Africa—the others living near the great lakes of former British East Africa and in the western equatorial forest. The Ituri Pygmies are the Mbuti (Bambuti). They number about 30,000 to 40,000, most of them living to the north of the river and even north of the Irumu–Kisangani road. In the *Cynometra* forest, near Beni, a few quite dense settlements may be found. The Ituri Pygmies appear to be divided into three groups speaking different languages, each of which is related to a different Bantu dialect; these have been called the Aka (Akka), the Efe, and the Mbuti proper.

The Pygmies are at home only in the forest—that forest with which they identify themselves, which they love, and in which alone they feel safe. They live there divided into clans of nomadic hunters. Their villages, consisting of a few dozen huts, are temporarily set up "in the shape of an egg cut longways," as Stanley put it. The village site is changed according to the movements of the game. Each clan remains, however, approximately within the limits of the same zone, where traditional rules for wildlife preservation are observed.

The Pygmy way of life

Each clan has a horde leader rather than a chief; there is no political organization linking the hordes together, so that society tends to be egalitarian. Many groups are polygamous, but some are monogamous; marriages often take place by "exchange" between clans.

The making and upkeep of arms and traps is the main concern of the men: they are skilled in the use of the bow and poisoned arrow, the javelin, hunting nets, pits, and the fixing of hanging spears. The only animal they have domesticated is the hunting dog; often dumb, it carries a wooden bell to indicate its position. The women busy themselves with gathering mushrooms, berries, roots, grain, and honey.

Clothing is reduced to a minimum. Made from bark, it is sometimes dyed with kola nuts. Tattooing and scarification of the skin provide additional decoration. Merry, talkative, and musical, the Mbuti love dancing, singing, and the recital of legends. Their beliefs are more associated with magic than with religion. Their existence is punctuated with numerous ceremonies, especially initiations. They bury their dead. Their morals are strict.

The Bantu. For centuries the Bantu have also lived in the Ituri Forest. They practice shifting cultivation, destroying patches of forest vegetation with the axe and with fire, then tilling a strip of soil for a few years until it deteriorates, after which they start again further on. As it sometimes takes 30 years for the land to regenerate, the forest is often dotted with many clearings, a few of which are under cultivation, the remainder consisting of fallow fields slowly becoming secondary forest again.

The Bantu belong basically to the tribes of the Bira (Babira) in the southeast, the Lese (Balese) in the northeast, and the Ndaka (Bandaka) in the west. They are split into two categories of probably equal size. The first group remains scattered in the forest, with the heaviest concentration occurring in the northwestern zone beyond Wamba; the second have established themselves—or have been obliged to settle—along the roads intersecting the forest. These are, from west to east, the Kisangani–Mambasa–Irumu road; from north to south, the Isiro–Wamba–Avakubi road, and in the east, the Andudu–Mambasa–Beni road and the Irumu–Beni road. The latest census, taken in 1970, reported 55,000 inhabitants in the enormous territory of Mambasa, which covers more than half of the area of the Ituri Forest.

The Bantu farmers

The Bantu farmers, unlike the Pygmies, fear the forest. For them it seems full of danger, mystery, and evil spirits. Nor does it provide enough food. On the contrary, it tirelessly regains the fields which have been painstakingly won from it. On their plots the Bantu raise manioc, rice, beans, peanuts (groundnuts), sugarcane, palms, tobacco and—since the Belgians introduced it during the colonial era—cotton. Stock raising is limited to goats and poultry. Occasionally the Bantu fish—which Mbuti rarely do, some of them considering fishing a child's sport—and at times they hunt, but only along the edges of their clearings.

Bantu–Pygmy relations. At regular intervals the Mbuti come out of the deeper forest to spend longer or shorter periods near "their" Bantus. They come mainly to trade, bringing the products of the hunt (meat and trophies) or of the harvest (honey), in order to procure in return the agricultural produce of their hosts, such as bananas, cereals, palm wine, tobacco, and other goods, particularly metalware. As dancers and singers they are also willing to amuse their hosts. Sometimes the Pygmies work in the Bantus' fields in return for payment in food or tobacco. These Bantu–Pygmy meetings are often marked by the celebration of ritual ceremonies in common.

The first ethnologists to study the Mbuti observed them near Bantu villages and deduced that the former owed a certain allegiance to the latter. The Bantu, moreover, gave countenance to the idea. "Their" Pygmies, they claimed, were closer to animals than to men and were also undisciplined, slow to come when called, and reluctant to work when asked.

The Pygmies took—and still take—a different view. They regard themselves as finer, shrewder, and more human than the hulking beings who are "as awkward as an elephant in the forest." When they approach the Bantu they assume a mocking show of respect. They are aware that their defense lies in their elusiveness. Of their own free will they can disappear into the friendly forest at any time, knowing that the Bantu will rarely risk following them. A breach is, however, opening in their traditional defense system: the youth of the clan often find the strict rules of traditional morality hard to follow, and some have gone permanently to the Bantu villages, where living conditions are easier than in the forest, and the morals lighter. Some Europeans have attempted, without success, to make the Pygmy clans sedentary.

Travel and transport. *Early contacts and travel.* The Egyptians knew of the existence of the Pygmies from earliest times; the chronicles of the Pharaoh Neferirkare (3rd king of the 5th dynasty [*c.* 2494–*c.* 2345 BC]) record that he had Pygmies at his court 25 centuries before Christ. Subsequently, Europeans long believed that Pygmies were not human beings. About 1865 an Italian explorer, Giovanni Miani, reached the Ituri Forest from the west and died there, but not before he had sent two young Mbuti to Rome, where they lived for several years. In 1869, the German botanist Georg Schweinfurth, arriving from the north via the Mangbetu country, came upon the Ituri Forest and in his famous work *Im Herzen von Afrika* ("In the Heart of Africa") proclaimed that the Mbuti were men.

The first crossing of the forest from west to east, was Stanley's. His route, and those of some of his companions, hardly deviated from that followed by the present road from Kisangani to Irumu.

Transportation. There are two convenient ways of reaching the Ituri Forest: by landing at Kisangani airport and following the Irumu road, or by landing at Goma airport and driving north via Lubero and Beni. As already mentioned, there are a few roads crossing the forest; they are usually in bad repair. The motorist, however, does not gain an accurate impression of the forest since the roadside populations have cut down all the trees and killed off the wildlife. Where the Kisangani–Irumu road meets the Epulu River is to be found the Patrick Putnam Camp, consisting of an okapi-hunting lodge, a hotel, and an airstrip; the camp was scheduled to be reopened in 1974.

Economic prospects. The forest plays a very small part in the Zairian national economy, its inhabitants being virtually self-sufficient. There are at present no prospects for the exploitation of its timber, in view of the difficulty of access. A few gold mines dotted the forest before Zaire's independence in 1960, but may have been abandoned. Cotton raising by the Bantus has recently declined, only a small amount now being produced. Tourism may offer some prospect of economic progress with the reopening of Putnam Camp, where travellers can easily make contact with the Bambuti. In the extreme southeast an arm of the forest touches the northern sector of the Virunga (formerly Albert) National Park, at the foot of Ruwenzori Range. To the extreme southwest it approaches the new Maiko National Park (opened in 1970) as a hill forest covering 1,000,000 hectares. Despite the proximity of two national parks, it is anticipated that it will be a long time before tourism becomes economically significant.

BIBLIOGRAPHY. J.P. CHAPIN, "The Birds of the Belgian Congo," *Bull. Am. Mus. Nat. Hist.*, 65:1–391 (1932), introductory volume of the most important work written on Congolese ornithology; M. GUSINDE, *Urwaldmenschen am Ituri* (1948), one of the classic monographs on Ituri Pygmies; JEAN PIERRE HALLET, *Congo Kitabu* (1965), vivid and colourful travel accounts; JEAN LEBRUN, *Répartition de la Forêt Équatoriale et des Formations végétales limitrophes* (1936), a scientific, accurate account of an expedition made to establish the exact limits of the Congolese forest; J.M.T. MEESSEN, *Monographie de l'Ituri* (1951), a monograph on the savanna to the east of the Ituri Forest; LEO PEETERS, "Les limites forêt-savane dans le nord du Congo, en relation avec le milieu géographique," CEMUBAC, vol. 74 (1965), a more recent survey than that of Lebrun, dealing specifically with the Ituri Forest; A.E. PUTNAM and A. KELLER, *Madami: My Eight Years of Adventure with the Congo Pygmies* (1954), an account with direct observations, made by the widow of Patrick Putnam who lived for a long time on Epulu, among Pygmies; PAUL SCHEBESTA, *Vollblutneger und Halbzwerge* (1934; Eng. trans., *My Pygmies and Negro Hosts*, 1936), another classic monograph on Ituri Pygmies; H.M. STANLEY, *In Darkest Africa*, 2 vol. (1890), an account of an expedition through the Ituri Forest in 1888; and C.M. TURNBULL, *The Forest People* (1961), classic volume on Ituri Pygmies, issued in pocketbook edition; its high-mindedness does not always agree with the observations of Gusinde and Schebesta.

(Je.-P.H.)

Ivan III the Great, of Russia

Ivan III the Great, portrait from A. Thenet, *La Cosmographie universelle*, Paris, 1575.
By courtesy of the trustees of the British Museum; photograph, J.R. Freeman & Co. Ltd.

In terms of political success, the 15th-century grand prince Ivan III was easily the greatest of all the descendants of Rurik, the reputed founder of Russia. No ruler of Muscovy until Peter the Great, two centuries later, did more to consolidate and develop the achievements of his predecessors, to strengthen the authority of the monarch, or to lay the foundations for a centralized state. By means of cunning diplomacy and shrewdly calculated aggression he not only established Muscovy as a great power to be reckoned with by the rulers and diplomats of Europe but also set in motion the reconquest of the Ukraine from Poland and Lithuania.

Early life

Ivan was born on January 22, 1440, at the height of the civil war that raged between supporters of his father, Grand Prince Vasily II of Muscovy, and those of his rebellious uncles. His early life was dramatic and tumultuous: when his father was arrested and blinded by his cousin in 1446, Ivan was first hidden in a monastery and then smuggled to safety, only to be treacherously handed over to his father's captors later in the year; shortly after his father's release in the same year he was solemnly affianced—for purely political reasons—to the daughter of the grand prince of Tver, whom he married in 1452. During the last years of his father's reign, he gained experience in the arts of war and government. At the age of 12 he was placed nominally in command of a military expedition dispatched to deal with the remnants of his father's internal enemies in the far north; and at 18 he led a successful campaign against the Tatars in the south. Vasily II died on March 27, 1462, and was succeeded by Ivan as grand prince of Moscow.

Grand prince of Muscovy

Little is known of Ivan's activities during the early part of his reign. Apart from a series of sporadic and largely successful campaigns against his eastern neighbours, the Tatars of Kazan, there was evidently not much beyond the routine business of ruling to occupy him. But his private life soon changed radically. In 1467 his childhood bride died (perhaps poisoned), leaving him with only one son. In view of the primitive state of Muscovite medicine and the demonstrable reluctance of Ivan's brothers to see the royal line continued longer than was necessary, the likelihood of the son predeceasing his father and thus robbing him of an heir appeared only too real, and another wife had to be sought. Curiously, the initiative seems to have come from outside; in 1469 Cardinal Bessarion wrote from Rome offering Ivan the hand of his ward and pupil, Zoë Palaeologus, niece of the last emperor of Byzantium. It took three years before the fat and unattractive Zoë, who, on entering Moscow, changed her name to Sofia (and perhaps her faith to Orthodoxy), was married to Ivan in the Kremlin.

She remained in Muscovy until her death in 1503. Nineteenth-century historians portray her as the haughty Byzantine princess who inspired Ivan to throw off the Tatar yoke in 1480, whose marriage initiated cultural and diplomatic relations with the West, who introduced Byzantine ceremony into the court of Moscow, and who strengthened the conception of autocracy in Ivan. This picture is now believed to be far from true. In 1480 she ignominiously fled the capital; relations with the West and the refurbishing of Ivan's drab court had nothing to do with her presence; and she would have been the last person to wish to see Ivan's absolutist tendencies increased. The role she played in state affairs was anything but pleasing to her husband; indeed, she aligned herself with the political (and perhaps ecclesiastical) opposition to the Grand Prince and may even have served as a rallying point for discontented elements in the state and as a champion of separatism.

At first Ivan did not allow his wife's behaviour to distract him from the immense problems facing him at home and abroad; during much of the 1470s and 1480s he was occupied with the annexation of the republic of Novgorod and the formerly independent grand principality of Tver. In 1480 he had to cope with the double danger of rebellion at home (his two brothers Andrey and Boris, incensed by his high-handed appropriation of their deceased elder brother's estates, defected with their armies to the western frontiers) and invasion by the Tatars of the Golden Horde.

Problem of succession

In 1490, however, his eldest son by his first wife died of gout. He had been ineptly treated by a Jewish doctor who had been brought to Russia by Sofia's brother, and Ivan suspected foul play. He now had to solve the problem of who was to be his heir—his eldest son's son Dmitry (born 1483) or his eldest son by Sofia, Vasily (born 1479). For seven years he vacillated. Then, in 1497, he nominated Dmitry as heir. Sofia, anxious to see her son assured of the throne, planned rebellion against her husband, but the plot was uncovered. Ivan disgraced Sofia and Vasily and had Dmitry crowned grand prince (1498). The reason for his preference for Dmitry is to be sought in his foreign policy. In the period between the two phases of the great Muscovite-Lithuanian War (*i.e.*, between 1494 and 1500) Ivan was anxious to maintain good relations with his most valuable ally in southeast Europe, Moldavia, and Stephen IV of Moldavia was the father of Dmitry's mother Yelena. In 1500 Vasily rebelled again and defected to the Lithuanians. Ivan was forced to compromise. At this stage of the war he could not risk the total alienation of his son and wife. And so, in 1502, he gave the title to Vasily and imprisoned Dmitry and Yelena, both of whom he could afford to jettison now that the Russo-Moldavian alliance was virtually dead.

Ivan's last years were years of disappointment. The war against Lithuania had not ended as conclusively and satisfactorily as he had expected—much of the Ukraine was still in the hands of a strangely buoyant enemy; his ecclesiastical plans for secularizing church lands had been thwarted at the Council of 1503, and his erstwhile ideological supporters—the Judaizer heretics—had been liquidated in 1504, while in the east the Khanate of Kazan, which had been so carefully neutralized during Ivan's reign, was beginning to rid itself of Muscovite tutelage. Ivan died on October 27, 1505.

Assessment

In spite of his great achievements, he died unmourned and seemingly unloved. Singularly little is known about him as a man. He was tall and thin. He had a slight stoop. It is said that women fainted in his presence, so frightened were they by his awesome gaze. His only known pleasures were those of the bed and the table. His contemporaries are silent about his virtues. Yet few scholars have underestimated the role of Ivan in the creation of the Russian state, and none dispute the significance of his diplomatic and military successes. It may be that the excessive cautiousness of his character, the lack of élan and glamour, and the very dullness of the man have prevented historians from universally recognizing the appellation of "the Great," first attributed to him by the Austrian ambassador to his son's court.

BIBLIOGRAPHY. J.L.I. FENNELL, *Ivan the Great of Moscow* (1961), the most detailed account of Ivan's reign in English; Константин Васильевич Базилевич, *Внешняя политика русского централизованного государства; вторая половина xv века* (1952), the fullest work in Russian on Ivan's foreign policy; Яков Соломонович Лурье, *Идеологическая борьба в русской публицистике конца xv—начала xvi века* (1960), the best account of ideological trends in Ivan's reign.

(J.L.I.F.)

Ivan IV the Terrible, of Russia

Ivan IV was tsar of Russia from 1533 to 1584. His nickname, "the Terrible," is actually a mistranslation of the Russian word *grozny*, which more properly means "awe-inspiring"; Ivan was no more brutal than many of his contemporaries. Ivan's reign saw the completion of the construction of a centrally administered Russian state and the creation of an empire that included non-Slav states. His life is of particular interest in that it reflects both the positive and negative aspects of Russian history in the 16th century.

Ivan was born in Moscow on August 25, 1530, the first child of Grand Prince Vasily III and his second wife, Princess Yelena Glinskaya. Through his father he was directly descended from Prince Alexander Nevsky, whose younger son Daniel had received the appanage of Moscow in 1263 and had been the first of a long line of hereditary grand princes of Moscow and the founder of the Danilovich dynasty, of which Ivan was the penultimate representative. On his mother's side, Ivan was connected with the Orthodox Russian nobility that had emigrated to Muscovite territory from Lithuania in the beginning of the 16th century. The theory later formulated by Ivan IV that his dynasty was directly descended from the Roman emperor Augustus was a fantasy with political undertones that allowed the Tsar a certain latitude in international dynastic arguments. On December 4, 1533, immediately after his father's death, Ivan was proclaimed grand prince by the metropolitan Daniil in the Cathedral of the Dormition (Assumption). His mother, the Grand Princess Yelena, aided by her favourite, Ivan Ovchina-Telepnev-Obolensky (thus arousing the unsubstantiated rumour that Ivan was his son), ruled in Ivan's name until her death (allegedly by poison) on April 3, 1538. Although subsequently Ivan never accused anyone of this crime, her favourite was thrown into prison, and his sister, who had been Ivan's nurse, was forced to become a nun. Ivan had taken a formal part in the affairs of state from the age of five onward, and he was actually the centre of a furious struggle for power among the prominent members of the nobility. His first independent action took place at the age of 13, when he ordered the seizure in his presence of the leader of one of the court factions, Prince Andrey Shuysky, who was then murdered by Ivan's kennel men. But actual power remained in the hands of Ivan's relatives, the Glinsky princes. The young ruler passed his time visiting monasteries and hunting. From 1545 onward Ivan undertook long trips to various parts of his territories. In this same year he ordered a nobleman's tongue cut out "for uttering rude words." Ivan evidently resented any criticism, which in the spirit of the age he construed as lese majesty. Courtiers were often disgraced, and the metropolitan Makary frequently intervened on their behalf. Right up to his death in 1563, Makary appears to have had a restraining influence on Ivan. Nevertheless, several executions took place in June 1546, including that of one of his former favourites, Fyodor Vorontsov. In December Ivan officially sought Makary's advice on his marriage and on his coronation—at which he was to be crowned tsar (a shortened form of Caesar) rather than grand prince.

Ivan IV, icon by an unknown artist, late 16th century. In the Nationalmuseet, Copenhagen.
By courtesy of the Nationalmuseet, Copenhagen

The coronation took place on January 16, 1547, and on February 3 he married Anastasya Zakharina-Yureva, a member of the ancient family of Andrey Kobyla-Koshkin (the family from which the next dynasty, the Romanovs, would come). The marriage, while it lasted (Anastasya died on August 7, 1560), was apparently a very happy one; six children were born, although only two survived infancy. Historians consider that Anastasya exerted a beneficial influence on the Tsar and, like Makary, frequently acted as a peacemaker. It would appear that it was Makary who encouraged the young Tsar in his desire to establish a Christian state based on the principles of justice. Reforms were proposed, starting with the systematization of church affairs, and these were approved at the church assemblies of 1547 and 1549. According to a subsequent defector, Prince Andrey Kurbsky, at this juncture the Tsar sought general guidance from a group of advisers informally known as the "Chosen Council." Most prominent among them was the Tsar's then favourite, the priest Silvestr, and a talented young statesman (who was later to suffer disgrace), Aleksey Adashev. A new legal code was compiled in 1550, and administrative practice and the conditions of military service were improved, the government meanwhile providing extensive local self-government. In 1549 a national assembly (*zemsky sobor*) met in an advisory capacity. Muscovite rulers had long feared the Tatar incursions, and Ivan was equally conscious of this danger. But, as a result of campaigns in 1547, 1549, and 1552 in which Ivan himself participated, having left Makary as regent in Moscow, the Tatar Khanate of Kazan on the Volga was annexed; and in 1556 the Khanate of Astrakhan acknowledged Muscovite supremacy without a fight. Internal struggles continued, complicated by Russian rules of precedence, which were so complex that quarrels unavoidably arose, and meanwhile the nobility was growing in number and in power. In March 1553 Ivan fell seriously ill and summoned his boyars to swear allegiance to his heir, the infant Prince Dmitry. The privy council and the Council of Boyars were split in their views, since many feared a return, if an infant were to succeed the Tsar, of the internecine struggles of Ivan's minority. The candidate favoured by the boyars was the Tsar's first cousin, Prince Vladimir of Staritsky. Nevertheless, the Tsar, despite the disaffection of many of those on whose loyalty he had hitherto relied, succeeded in obtaining general recognition of the validity of his son's succession rights. No one suffered disgrace for their part in this episode, and Prince Vladimir himself was made a member of the Council of Regency. But the Tsar obviously drew the conclusion that Vladimir could be a danger to the legitimate succession; when, over the course of the next 15 years, Vladimir and his ambitious mother had succeeded in further arousing the Tsar's suspicion, Ivan did away with them (probably in 1569).

Campaigns against the Tatars

With both banks of the Volga now assured, Ivan prepared for a campaign to force an exit to the sea, a traditional concern of landlocked Russia. Although the English merchants led by Richard Chancellor had made contact by reaching Moscow via the northern sea route, Ivan still felt that the greatly desired trade with Europe depended on free access to the Baltic and decided to turn his attention westward rather than southward. The Livonian War began in January 1558 and was not ended until 24 years later, on January 15, 1582, when an armistice was concluded after the Russian government had requested the intervention of Pope Gregory XIII, who sent his nuncio Antonio Possevino to mediate. The war was fruitless for Russia, and the country was exhausted by the long struggle. Ivan found the collapse of his hopes and plans hard to bear and quarrelled in 1581 with his much loved heir, Ivan, whom he mortally wounded in the heat of the moment. His son was not the only one to suffer the ruler's wrath, for Ivan later sent to various monasteries memorials (*sinodiki*) containing the names of over 3,000 victims whom he had executed, together with large sums of money, with orders to the monks to pray for the souls of the dead.

The Livonian War

Most of these executions, including many whose names the Tsar did not include in his memorials, occurred during the period when Ivan formed his *oprichnina*. Ivan divided his territories into two parts, one to be ruled in the traditional manner, and the other—referred to as the widow's part (*oprich*)—he proposed to rule personally, aided by a carefully chosen bodyguard of 1,000–6,000 men. Since nearly all the documents relating to this epoch were destroyed in one of Moscow's periodic fires, historians tend to give differing explanations for Ivan's actions during this part of his reign: the majority tend to the view that the struggle was between the autocrat and the old nobility, which was jealous of surrendering its privileges and power, but a further aspect should also be taken into consideration. This was Ivan's dissatisfaction with his military commanders. The formation of the *oprichnina*, for example, took place shortly after the defection to the King of Poland of one of Ivan's outstanding commanders in the field (and also a distant relation), Prince Andrey Kurbsky. The *oprichnina* lasted only seven years, from 1565 to 1572, when it was abolished as a result of the failure of the *oprichnina* regiments to defend Moscow from an attack by the Crimean Tatars. Nevertheless, the *oprichnina* leaves a bloody imprint on Ivan's reign, causing some doubts as to his mental stability. Many of his acts shocked his contemporaries, particularly the brutality of his public executions; his methods of disposing of those churchmen who displeased him were extremely cruel, as was his decimation of the city of Novgorod the Great. But, when Ivan's cruelty is judged within the context of his day, compared, for example, with the Massacre of St. Bartholomew's Day, or the methods of the Inquisition, it would seem that his methods were not necessarily more extreme than elsewhere.

Ivan's methods

The majority of historians agree that Ivan was a calculating politician and that, after the death of his first wife, he was prepared to attain his political aims by marriage. Eleven days after Anastasya's death, the Tsar issued instructions for negotiations to be opened with Sigismund II Augustus, the king of Poland; after due deliberation he announced that he wished to marry the latter's sister Catherine. These negotiations were unsuccessful, although the Tsar was to try again later and even concluded an armistice in 1567 with Sweden so as to obtain Catherine (who meanwhile had been the wife of John III, the brother of Eric XIV). The Tsar hoped thus to form a Polish–Muscovite political union, an idea shared by many of his contemporaries on both sides of the Polish frontier; and in 1572, when the last king of the Jagiellon dynasty died, Ivan was keen to advance his candidature to the Polish throne.

Ivan was undoubtedly a passionate man, and, since he did not sanction extramarital relationships for a ruler, his wives were changed with great frequency: he had six wives (a seventh union not being recognized by the church); of these, three died, one survived him, and two were divorced and forced to enter nunneries. Ivan also discussed with the English ambassador the possibility of marrying one of Queen Elizabeth's ladies-in-waiting, Mary Hastings; he had been anxious to cement relationships with England ever since 1553, and in 1566 he even toyed with the idea of abdicating and living in England. But he remained on the Russian throne until his death on March 18, 1584.

Ivan's achievements were many. In foreign policy all his actions were directed toward forcing Russia into Europe—a line that Peter I the Great was to continue; this policy caused much annoyance among his European neighbours, who did not relish the idea of a strong and prosperous competitor in commerce. He also strove to arrest Tatar and Turkish incursions into Russian territory. Ivan encouraged cultural development, especially printing. He was widely read, and he wrote well; although his surviving writings are mainly of a political nature, his command of words and his biting sarcasm are very evident. He was a devout son of the Orthodox Church, a loyalty that frequently interfered with his political aims, and even composed prayers and church music. His arguments on religious questions are striking in their power and conviction, but Ivan placed most emphasis on defending the divine right of the ruler to unlimited power under God—a view with which most other contemporary monarchs would have been in complete agreement.

BIBLIOGRAPHY. E. DONNERT, *Der livländische Ordens ritterstaat und Russland*, pp. 299–310 (1963), provides an excellent summary dealing mainly with the period of the Livonian War and Ivan's foreign policy. GEORGE VERNADSKY, *A History of Russia*, vol. 4–5 (1959–69), includes a comprehensive list of Russian source material on this period and a complete bibliography on Ivan's internal policies.

(N.An.)

Ivory Coast

The Ivory Coast (République de Côte d'Ivoire) is a republic on the coast of West Africa. With a coastline more than 300 miles long, it forms an almost square block of territory with an area of 123,483 square miles (319,822 square kilometres) and a population of almost 5,000,000. It is bounded to the southwest by Liberia, to the northwest by Guinea, to the north by Mali and Upper Volta, to the east by Ghana, and to the south by the Gulf of Guinea. The capital is Abidjan.

Since the country attained independence from France in 1960, the Ivory Coast has experienced spectacular economic progress and relative political stability under the aegis of its president, Félix Houphouët-Boigny, a local aristocrat and veteran politician, who has successfully carried out a policy that has promoted the Ivorian economy yet permitted France a major role in assisting in the development of the country. As a result, French capital and industry have helped to spearhead the economic growth of the Ivory Coast, and French language and culture continue to exert a strong influence, especially upon the educated urban sector of the population.

Despite this foreign influence, large numbers of Ivorians are engaged in the building of a modern economy. Nearly half the working population is engaged in the production of coffee and cocoa—the Ivory Coast is the world's third largest producer of cocoa, and one of the largest producers of coffee. The country also ranks second as a producer of tropical hardwoods. (For historical background, see WEST AFRICA, HISTORY OF.)

THE LANDSCAPE

The natural environment. Lying close to the Equator, the Ivory Coast is tropical both in surface features and climate.

Relief. The ground rises constantly as it recedes from the coast, and the northern half of the country consists of high savanna (grassy parkland) lying more than 1,200 feet above sea level. Most of the western border with Liberia and Guinea is shaped by mountain ranges, whose highest point is Mt. Nimba (5,748 feet, or 1,752 metres, high), which is situated where the borders of the three countries meet.

Natural regions

The Ivory Coast has four natural regions—the coastal fringe, the equatorial forest zone, the cultivated forest zone, and the northern savanna. The coastal fringe consists of a strip of land, no more than 40 miles wide, studded with lagoons on its eastern half. Access from the sea is made difficult by the surf and by a long submarine sandbar. Behind the coastal fringe lies the equatorial forest zone that, until a century ago, formed a continuous

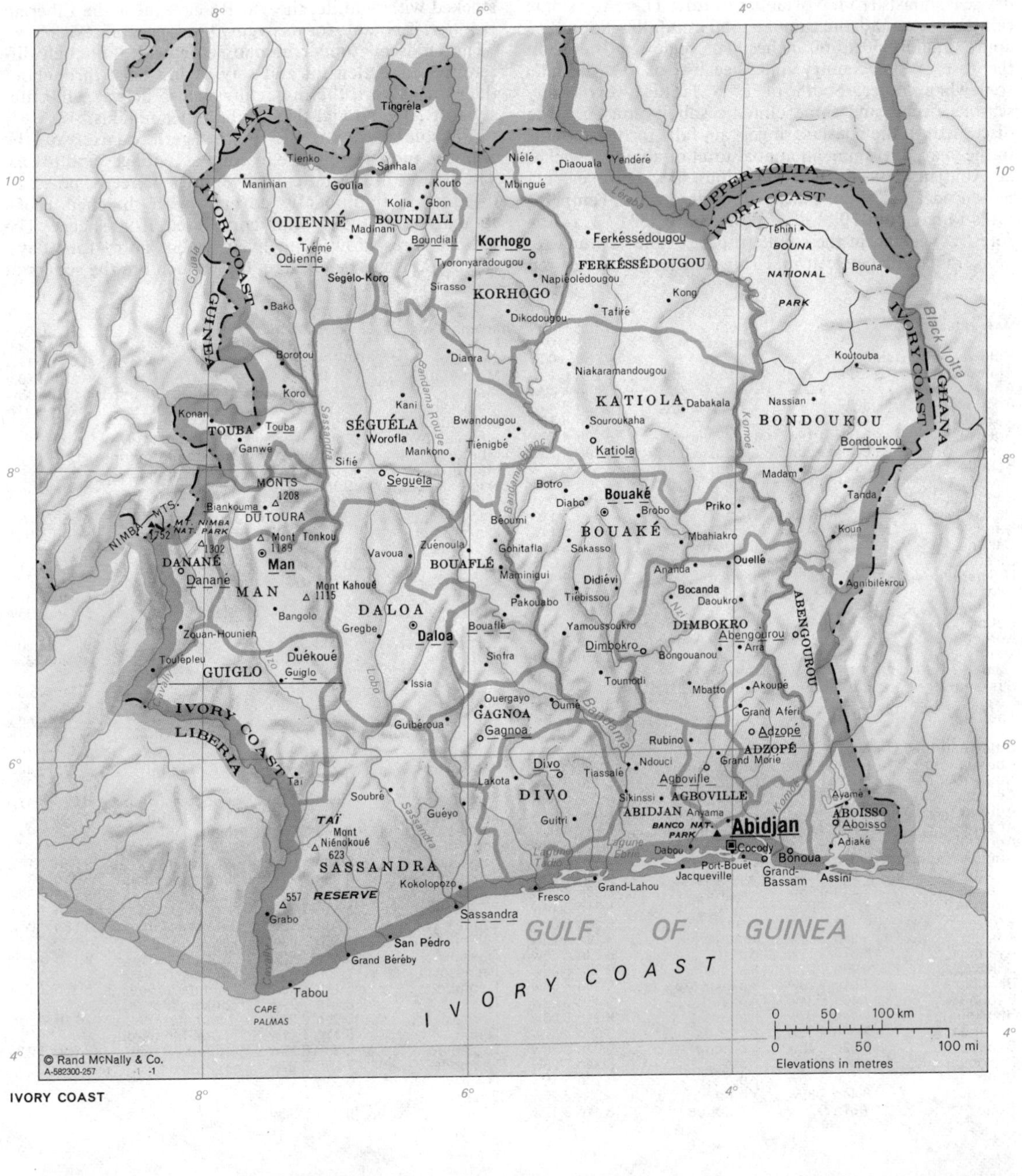

IVORY COAST

area more than 125 miles wide. It has now been reduced to an area roughly triangular in shape, with the apex lying a little to the north of Abidjan, and with its base lying along the Liberian border. The cultivated forest zone, which lies to the east of this triangle, consists of forestland that has been partly cleared for plantations, especially along the Ghana border and in the area around Bouaké. The fourth region, the northern savanna, consists of a sparsely populated plateau, offering open ground favourable for stockbreeding. About 4,500 square miles in this region have been set aside to form the Komoé (Comoé) National Park.

Drainage. Apart from the Cavally River, which forms the border with Liberia, major rivers from west to east are the Sassandra, the Bandama, and the Komoé, all of which drain southward into the Gulf of Guinea.

Soils. The forest soils tend to turn into laterites (red soils with a high content of iron and hydroxide of aluminum), but swampy soils maintain their rich yellowish silico-argilaceous character. In the savanna areas, "shields," formed as a result of rapid evaporation, alternate with rich black silico-argilaceous soils.

Climate. Equatorial and southern savanna types of climate prevail. North of about 8° N latitude, the southern savanna type of climate occurs, characterized by the parching wind known as the harmattan, which blows from the northeast from December until February. The dry season lasts from November to July. There is a single rainy season, and the annual total rainfall amounts to approximately 50 to 60 inches. The region is drier than the rest of the country and, because of the altitude, somewhat cooler. South of 8° N latitude, two rainy seasons occur, and three climatic subdivisions may be discerned. In the coastal fringe, rain falls for ten months in the year, averaging an annual total of about 77 inches at Abidjan; considerable variations are, however, experienced at different places along the coast. Temperatures range from 70° F (21° C) to 91° F (33° C). In the forest zones and in the southern part of the savanna region, rains fall between mid-July and late October and from mid-March until mid-May, although here, too, there is considerable variation in the amount. Temperatures vary between 75° and 102° F (24° and 39° C), and humidity reaches 70 percent. On the mountains further west there is no dry season, and rainfall amounts to about 80 inches, which reaches a maximum in September.

Vegetation. The rain forest contains valuable timber species, including African mahogany and iroko (or African teak), and staple forest crops include oil palms, bananas, cassava, plantains, and yams. An important afforestation centre is the Banco National Park near Abidjan.

Animal life. The animal life of the forest zone differs little from that of adjoining Ghana, although the larger ungulates (hoofed mammals) are lacking, with the exception of the bongo (a reddish-brown antelope) and the forest buffalo. There are also about six kinds of dwarf antelope, ranging from the royal antelope to the yellow-backed duiker; the giant forest hog is widespread (although nowhere common), and the red river hog is locally plentiful. Manatee (a herbivorous water animal with two flippers in front and a spoon-shaped tail) probably survive in some rivers. To the north, the savanna woodlands have about ten species of antelope, as well as lions and occasional herds of elephants. In addition to Komoé National Park in the northeast, which is well stocked with wildlife, the Taï Reserve, near the Liberian frontier, is notable for its pygmy hippopotamuses.

The landscape under human settlement. Though differences in settlement and way of life exist throughout the Ivory Coast, the major division is between the lifestyle of Abidjan and that of the other regions.

The southeast. In the southeastern quarter of the country, most people live in compact villages and towns. The houses are rectangular dwellings of reeds, poles, or dried clay, traditionally covered with thatched roofs, though often today with corrugated iron sheets. The town centres grow quite lively when, every four days, the markets are held. Here, the women are the sellers of

MAP INDEX

Political subdivisions

Abengourou	6·35n	3·25w
Abidjan	5·20n	4·00w
Aboisso	5·28n	3·02w
Adzopé	6·15n	3·45w
Agboville	6·00n	4·15w
Bondoukou	8·45n	3·30w
Bouaflé	7·03n	5·48w
Bouaké	7·45n	4·58w
Boundiali	9·23n	6·32w
Daloa	6·58n	6·23w
Dimbokro	6·50n	4·45w
Danané	7·25n	8·10w
Divo	5·57n	5·15w
Ferkessedougou	9·20n	4·55w
Gagnoa	6·03n	6·00w
Guiglo	6·30n	7·40w
Katiola	8·13n	5·02w
Korhogo	9·35n	5·55w
Man	7·13n	7·41w
Odienné	9·45n	7·45w
Sassandra	5·20n	6·10w
Séguéla	8·05n	6·32w
Touba	8·15n	7·45w

Cities and towns

Abengourou	6·44n	3·29w
Abidjan	5·19n	4·02w
Aboisso	5·28n	3·12w
Adiaké	5·16n	3·17w
Adzopé	6·06n	3·52w
Agboville	5·56n	4·13w
Agnibilékrou	7·08n	3·12w
Akoupé	6·23n	3·54w
Ananda	7·17n	4·16w
Anyama	5,30n	4·03w
Arra	6·40n	3·58w
Assini	5·07n	3·17w
Ayamé	5·37n	3·11w
Bako	9·09n	7·37w
Bangolo	7·01n	7·29w
Béoumi	7·40n	5·34w
Biankouma	7·44n	7·37w
Bocanda	7·04n	4·30w
Bondoukou	8·02n	2·48w
Bongouanou	6·39n	4·12w
Bonoua	5·16n	3·36w
Borotou	8·44n	7·30w
Botro	7·51n	5·19w
Bouaflé	6·59n	5·45w
Bouaké	7·41n	5·02w
Bouna	9·16n	3·00w
Boundiali	9·31n	6·29w
Brobo	7·43n	4·42w
Bwandougou	8·13n	5·40w
Cocody	5·19n	4·00w
Dabakala	8·22n	4·26w
Dabou	5·19n	4·23w
Daloa	6·53n	6·27w
Danané	7·16n	8·09w
Daoukro	7·03n	3·58w
Diabo	7·47n	5·11w
Dianra	8·45n	6·14w
Diaouala	10·07n	5·28w
Didiévi	7·08n	4·54w
Dikodougou	9·04n	5·46w
Dimbokro	6·39n	4·42w
Divo	5·50n	5·22w
Duékoué	6·45n	7·21w
Ferkéssédougou	9·36n	5·12w
Fresco	5·05n	5·34w
Gagnoa	6·08n	5·56w
Ganwé	8·11n	7·51w
Gbon	9·50n	6·27w
Gohitafla	7·30n	5·53w
Goulia	10·01n	7·11w
Grabo	4·55n	7·30w
Grand Aféri	6·19n	3·57w
Grand-Bassam	5·12n	3·44w
Grand Béréby	4·38n	6·55w
Grand-Lahou	5·08n	5·01w
Grand Morié	5·59n	4·08w
Gregbe	6·48n	6·43w
Guéyo	5·49n	6·36w
Guibéroua	6·14n	6·10w
Guiglo	6·33n	7·29w
Guitri	5·31n	5·14w
Issia	6·29n	6·35w
Jacqueville	5·12n	4·25w
Kani	8·29n	6·36w
Katiola	8·08n	5·06w
Kokolopozo	5·08n	6·05w
Kolia	9·46n	6·28w
Konan	8·21n	8·00w
Kong	9·09n	4·37w
Korhogo	9·27n	5·38w
Koro	8·34n	7·28w
Koun	7·29n	3·15w
Kouto	9·53n	6·25w
Koutouba	8·41n	3·12w
Lakota	5·51n	5·41w
Madam	7·58n	3·32w
Madinani	9·37n	6·57w
Maminigui	7·24n	5·50w
Man	7·24n	7·33w
Maninian	10·00n	7·50w
Mankono	8·04n	6·12w
Mbahiakro	7·27n	4·20w
Mbatto	6·28n	4·22w
Mbingué	10·00n	5·54w
Napiéolédougou	9·18n	5·35w
Nassian	8·27n	3·29w
Ndouci	5·52n	4·46w
Niakaraman-dougou	8·40n	5·17w
Niélé	10·12n	5·38w
Odienné	9·30n	7·34w
Ouellé	7·18n	4·01w
Ouergayo	6·19n	5·56w
Oumé	6·23n	5·25w
Pakouabo	7·10n	5·48w
Port-Bouët	5·15n	3·58w
Priko	7·39n	3·59w
Rubino	6·04n	4·18w
Sakasso	7·27n	5·18w
Sanhala	10·03n	6·51w
San Pédro	4·44n	6·37w
Sassandra	4·58n	6·05w
Ségélo-Koro	9·25n	7·09w
Séguéla	7·57n	6·40w
Sifié	7·59n	6·55w
Sinfra	6·37n	5·55w
Sirasso	9·16n	6·06w
Soubré	5·47n	6·36w
Souroukaha	8·13n	5·08w
Tabou	4·25n	7·21w
Tafiré	9·04n	5·10w
Taï	5·52n	7·27w
Tanda	7·48n	3·10w
Téhini	9·36n	3·40w
Tiassalé	5·54n	4·50w
Tiébissou	7·10n	5·13w
Tiénigbé	8·11n	5·43w
Tienko	10·14n	7·29w
Tingréla	10·29n	6·24w
Touba	8·17n	7·41w
Toulépleu	6·35n	8·25w
Toumodi	7·26n	5·37w
Tyémé	9·33n	7·19w
Tyoronyara-dougou	9·21n	5·38w
Vavoua	7·23n	6·29w
Worofla	8·16n	6·54w
Yamoussoukro	6·49n	5·17w
Yendéré	10·12n	4·58w
Zouan-Hounien	6·55n	8·13w
Zuénoula	7·26n	6·03w

Physical features and points of interest

Aby, Lagune, *lagoon*	5·15n	3·14w
Banco National Park	5·25n	4·03w
Bandama, *river*	5·10n	5·00w
Bandama Blanc, *river*	6·54n	5·31w
Bandama Rouge, *river*	6·54n	5·31w
Black Volta, *river*	8·49n	2·35w
Bouna National Park	9·00n	3·30w
Cavally, *river*	4·22n	7·32w
Ébrié, Lagune, *lagoon*	5·14n	4·26w
Guinea, Gulf of	5·00n	5·00w
Ivory Coast	5·00n	5·00w
Kahoué, Mont, *mountain*	7·06n	7·15w
Komoé, *river*	5·12n	3·44w
Léraba, *river*	9·42n	4·35w
Lobo, *river*	6·02n	6·47w
Mount Nimba National Park	7·40n	8·27w
Niénokoué, Mont, *mountain*	5·26n	7·10w
Nimba Mountains	7·30n	8·30w
Nzi, *river*	5·57n	4·50w
Nzo, *river*	6·16n	7·03w
Sassandra, *river*	4·58n	6·05w
Tadio, Lagune, *lagoon*	5·11n	5·15w
Taï Reserve, *wildlife refuge*	5·45n	7·12w
Tonkou, Mount, *mountain*	7·27n	7·39w
Toura, Monts du, *mountains*	7·40n	7·25w

Rural life and regional characteristics

the produce, which consists mostly of yams—the most basic national staple—maize (corn), the starch root known as manioc, peanuts, oil-palm nuts, and other vegetables. Fishermen on the lagoons ply their trade separately, maintaining their own markets. The entire area is divided into petty states with kings and an elaborate hierarchy of ministers and palace officials bearing elegant titles.

The southwest. Among the Kru and other peoples of the southwestern forest zone, houses may be either rectangular or round, varying according to place rather than to tribe. Dwellings everywhere are clustered around a central open area, though markets are held only in a very few privileged towns. In other places, the central area is an evening meeting place as well as a spot in which "village democracy" is practiced by councils of elders. Women perform the bulk of daily work, both at home and in the fields, where they grow such crops as rice, manioc, bananas, yams, and maize (corn). Rice is a comparatively recent introduction that has not yet been accepted by all. The men engage in hunting, gathering kola nuts and oil-palm nuts, and—on the coast—fishing.

The northwestern savanna. The Malinke people of the northwestern corner of the country, as members of the Mande group, are inheritors of a culture made famous in the 13th to the 16th centuries by the Mali empire. Long before then, the Mande had effected a regional agricultural revolution, discovering the use of millet, which remains their staple food, and using such other cereals as sorghum and maize. They have cultivated cotton for centuries. Cattle are kept by everyone, but for purposes of prestige and use on ceremonial occasions rather than for economic reasons; little milk is drunk. The men raise livestock and cultivate crops; they may also travel extensively for trade. The Malinke build round huts of mud and sun-dried brick surmounted by a conical thatched roof. Defense is a traditional concern, as is evident from the fences built around dwellings clustered in compounds, and from the palisades surrounding large villages or towns. The people recognize a dual authority: on the one hand, the village chief, on the other hand, the chief representative of the linear descendants of the first settlers, a group forming a traditional nobility. Some people are born into certain trades, such as that of musician, or "griot" (a species of minstrel).

The northeastern savanna. Until the late 19th century, the rest of the savanna region was forgotten by the various conquerors who from the 14th century onward spread devastation farther up in the Niger River Basin. The area is part of the domain of the Voltaic peoples, many of whom live in neighbouring Upper Volta, much of which until 1947 formed part of the Ivory Coast. Among them, the Senufo live immediately east of the Mande and have adopted many of their customs. Life in comparatively large villages and specialization on a hereditary basis may have helped them to reach their high level of artistic creation in woodcarving and in weaving. All other Voltaic communities are split into dispersed homesteads. In the northeastern corner, some houses are of a peculiar type, found as far away as northern Dahomey. These are rectangular mud or brick structures crowned with crenellated parapets built around a flat roof, so that each house has some resemblance to a fairy tale castle. Millet and sorghum are the staple food of all Voltaics; the men do most of the work. All the people keep cattle, but only those who give them for keeping to herdsmen of outside Foulah (Fulani) origin ever taste milk. The Voltaics are great traders, distinguishing between local-market trading, which is conducted by women, and outside trading, which is conducted by the Dyula (Dioula), a subtribe of the Mande. Each community is run by the head of the main lineage group, who seeks above all to mediate in all disputes so the earth may never be defiled by blood spilling. In addition, the Senufo have chiefs who govern small districts.

Abidjan. One of the many trading ports built by Europeans along the African coast, Abidjan, nevertheless, has distinctive features of its own. A most striking one is its location on a lagoon, rather than on the sea, to which a canal provided access only since 1950. Its core is divided by a branch of the lagoon into Abidjan-Plateau, the first European settlement, to the north, and Treichville, the first large African settlement, to the south. The maintenance of physical communications between these quarters is the main problem facing the city.

Urban life

Plateau was recommended for settlement as early as 1898, but no Europeans actually lived there until 1903, when work was begun on the railway to Upper Volta. Treichville, located behind the fishing village of Anoumabo, owes its importance to the boom in colonial trade that followed World War I. It remained a very small town until 1934, when the seat of colonial government was moved to Abidjan from Bingerville, a short distance to the east. The public buildings, few of which remain, were built in Plateau; and Treichville, left to African home-builders, assumed an appearance that still keeps alive the flavour of those comparatively leisurely times. After 1950, when the opening of the canal to the sea marked a new era of economic expansion, urban growth was exceptionally fast. Most of it occurred outside Treichville, which, with more than 150,000 inhabitants, was crowded to the saturation point. North of Plateau, but separated from it by a former colonial army camp, the hills of Adjamé and other slopes have been covered with real-estate developments consisting of good but characterless modern apartment buildings of the type found around Paris. The environment is inconsistent with the local African life-style, which includes petty trading during the day and merrymaking at night. To the south, other developments were built without planning in the 1960s, so that slums and traditional housing alternate along the highway until the sea is reached at Port-Bouët, where until 1950, the seaport of Abidjan had been located.

Cocody, a town of an entirely different type, has grown up east of Plateau, across a branch of the lagoon, whose waters surround it virtually on three sides; it is bounded by a forest to the north. An upper-income residential area, it contains the presidential mansion, a towerlike structure built to assure every room a maximum of light and air. Cocody is a major tourist centre, commanded by a 25-story completely air-conditioned luxury hotel, opened in 1963. It features several bars and restaurants, bowling, a cinema, and ice-skating; its gambling facilities, as at Monte Carlo, are for foreigners only. Cocody has a second luxury hotel, and there are two more of international standing at Plateau. More than 20 other hotels are spread over the urban area; pleasure spots include dozens of night clubs, bars, and restaurants.

PEOPLE AND POPULATION

Ethnic groups. There are more than 60 tribes, traditionally independent from each other, though larger groups among them may be recognized on the basis of cultural unity. Each one of these groups has tribal affiliations with larger groups living outside the borders of the republic. Thus the Baule (Baoule), as well as other peoples living east of the Bandama River, are affiliated with the Akan group of Ghana. The Baule in about 1730 refused to join the Ashanti confederacy in what is now Ghana and settled in the Ivory Coast under the leadership of Queen Pokou; they live east of the Bandama. The lagoon fishermen farther south also have tribal brothers belonging to the same Akan group across the Ghana border. The forest people west of the Bandama belong to the same group as the Kru boatmen of Liberia, many of whom also live in Ivory Coast territory. In the interior, the Kru group is subdivided into tribes tiny in number but scattered over large areas of the forest and kept together by secret societies. Among them, the Bete, who live on the western banks of the Bandama, went into open revolt against the government in 1970 to resist alienation of their communal lands.

The savanna peoples may be divided into two main groups. The Mande group, which is particularly strong in Mali, is represented in the Ivory Coast by the Malinke farmers and by the Dyula (Dioula) peddlers. The Voltaic group comprises the Senufo as well as the Lobi and Bobo subgroups, who live widely scattered over the northeastern region and across into neighbouring states.

Religions. Traditional animistic cults continue to predominate, especially among the agricultural tribes, but in recent years Islām can claim the adherence of nearly a quarter of the population. The Qādirīyah order of Islām was formerly strong in the town of Kong and remains so among the Malinke. Statistics covering Christian progress are confused by the rapid rise and fall in popularity of several evangelical sects. The Roman Catholics, under the leadership of an African archbishop, claim more than 300,000 adherents.

Demography. Estimates in the early 1970s placed the Ivory Coast's population at more than 4,600,000, distributed most unevenly. Abidjan, with about 510,000 inhabitants (together with its suburbs), has more than 10 percent of the population; Bouaké has more than 160,000 inhabitants, and 350,000 more persons live in 20 towns of more than 10,000 inhabitants. Thus, at least 22 percent of the population is urban. In the southeast the population density is more than 50 inhabitants per square mile; in the southwest, density falls below 10 people per square mile. The whole savanna area has no more than about 22 people per square mile.

Population density and growth rates

A United Nations estimate for the period 1965–1970 (there have been no local official inquiries since 1958) indicated a birth rate of 46 per thousand and a death rate of 22.7 per thousand. Thus, the natural growth rate would stand at 2.3 percent. The actual population growth rate rises over 3 percent, however, because of immigration. The population in 1971 was twice as large as it was in 1953, and the distribution of age groups makes an even quicker growth rate likely in the future. More than 40 percent of the people are under 15 years of age, whereas less than 4 percent are over 60. Better living standards are likely to raise life expectancy above the current estimates of 41 years at birth.

Immigration is likely to continue to increase. Permanent residents from other African countries number at least 750,000; more than half of these come from Upper Volta. Non-Africans number about 60,000, more than 40,000 of them French; 10,000 are of Lebanese or other Arab extraction.

Ivory Coast, Area and Population

	area		population	
	sq mi	sq km	census*	1969 estimate
Autonomous municipalities				
Abidjan	†	†	—	510,000
Bouaké	‡	‡	—	161,000
Départements				
Abengourou	2,592	6,713	—	87,000
Abidjan	5,722†	14,819†	—	328,000
Aboisso	2,369	6,135	—	85,000
Adzopé	1,989	5,151	—	119,000
Agboville	1,506	3,900	—	89,000
Biankouma	1,118	2,897	—	62,000
Bondoukou	14,647	37,935	—	224,000
Bouaflé	3,229	8,362	—	167,000
Bouaké	9,037‡	23,405‡	—	458,000
Boundiali	3,966	10,273	—	124,000
Daloa	5,374	13,918	—	199,000
Danané	1,795	4,650	—	134,000
Dimbokro	5,337	13,822	—	314,000
Divo	3,811	9,869	—	166,000
Ferkéssédougou	7,449	19,292	—	70,000
Gagnoa	2,654	6,873	—	176,000
Guiglo	5,495	14,232	—	106,000
Katiola	6,627	17,163	—	120,000
Korhogo	4,697	12,164	—	243,000
Man	2,704	7,004	—	234,000
Odienné	8,238	21,336	—	118,000
Sassandra	10,140	26,263	—	113,000
Séguéla	8,827	22,861	—	142,000
Touba	3,385	8,767	—	71,000
Total Ivory Coast	123,483§	319,822§	—	4,619,000§

*A census has never been taken. †Area of Abidjan Autonomous Municipality is included in Abidjan Département. ‡Area of Bouaké Autonomous Municipality is included in Bouaké Département. §Figures do not add to total because of rounding.
Source: Official government figures.

THE NATIONAL ECONOMY

The Ivory Coast is primarily noted for its forest resources, standing first in Africa and second in the world as an exporter of tropical wood. As noted above, it has become the world's third largest producer of cocoa and one of the largest producers of coffee. Thus the country possesses one of the more developed of African economies, a position achieved despite a paucity of known mineral resources. It has yet to be shown that iron-ore deposits are worth mining, and the extraction of manganese has proved unprofitable. Four small deposits of diamonds constitute the only source of income from minerals. In the early 1970s, feasibility and financing studies were being made for exploitation of iron-ore deposits in the west.

Forest products. The forest, even in its present reduced state, remains the most considerable asset of the country. About 30 species of trees are of high commercial value. The Ivory Coast forest also stands second only to Ghana as a producer of kola nuts, which have been sold for centuries as a stimulant throughout western Africa, from Morocco to the Congo. Known annual exports are about 25,000 tons.

Agriculture. The forest floor, after clearing, provides a rich soil for the cultivation of edible roots and bananas, as well as of such commercial tree crops as coffee, cocoa (cacao), and rubber. The savanna soils are good for cereals, and cotton and sugarcane grow in both areas.

Local and export crops

Agriculture provides a livelihood for more than 80 percent of the families, and locally grown subsistence crops meet a large part of their needs. An acquired taste for such imported foodstuffs as wheat has become a negative element in the balance of trade. The chief crops are yams, manioc, plantains, and, in the north, maize (corn) and rice.

Among export crops, coffee takes first place. Its production is a family business, providing a living to perhaps 2,000,000 persons. The local coffee is a robusta of low quality but convenient for processing into powdered form; it has become widely accepted in France thanks to its cheapness and to intensive publicity campaigns. Cocoa (cacao) production employs about 1,000,000 people, many of whom raise coffee as well. The production of both cocoa and bananas doubled during the 1960s, a period that also saw a tenfold increase in the production of pineapples.

Intensive production of palm oil and rubber is planned in the southwest, copra along the coast, and cotton in the central and northern parts of the country. Hevea rubber trees (a South American species) were planted first in 1960, and ten years later they were producing 10,900 tons of crude rubber. The cultivation of oil-palm trees has been promoted since 1963 by a state agency working in virtually equal partnership with private firms. Coconut palms have been a familiar sight along the seashore, and thousands of acres have been planted with them to increase the production of copra (the dried kernel of the coconut, from which coconut oil is extracted). In cotton production the main problems are to substitute a high-yielding variety of cotton for the traditional variety, and to teach farmers the practice of either cotton-rice or cotton-yam rotation.

Energy resources. Power is supplied mostly by hydroelectric plants. The number of towns in which electricity is available grew from 7 in 1960 to 63 in 1970. Abidjan is supplied in part by two hydroelectric stations on the Bia River, close to the Ghana border, and two larger stations burning oil fuel. In early 1971, a dam was completed at Kossou, where the two branches of the Bandama River merge, representing the first stage in the construction of a hydroelectric station with a capacity of 500,000 kilowatt-hours due for completion in 1978. Nationwide electricity production in 1970 reached over 500,000,000 kilowatt-hours (as compared with 67,000,000 in 1960); the mileage of power lines during the 1960s increased from 370 to 1,800.

Industrial development. Industry was launched in colonial times with the establishment of sawmills and plywood plants. Sawmills now number about 60 and plywood plants number four. Since 1965, however, concern over deforestation has led to efforts in other directions. The dissolution of the old French West Africa federation in 1960 brought many firms to Abidjan from Dakar, Senegal.

Though the Conseil de l'Entente, a grouping consisting of the Ivory Coast, Upper Volta, Niger, Dahomey, and Togo, failed to grow into a unified market, factories were erected in the Ivory Coast, especially for the food industry, which processes both imported and local raw materials. Imported wheat produces 65,000 tons of flour a year. Beer is also produced, as are almost 100,000,000 packets of cigarettes. Powdered coffee, cocoa butter, pineapple and fish preserves, and edible oils are among the other processed foods. The fishing industry requires the production of 90,000 tons of ice a year for freezing fish. In addition to other types of fish, 3,600 tons of tuna are landed in Abidjan each year for eventual export.

Processing and manufacturing

A textile industry was launched as early as 1920 at Bouaké; since then the Bouaké mill has been expanded, and three plants in Abidjan print dry goods. Undergarments are made at a number of locations, and a shoe industry, working with both leather and plastics, has much of its product smuggled into Ghana.

Abidjan factories produce soap, matches, and a wide range of metal products, including furniture, automobiles, and air-conditioning and refrigerating units. Marketing remains a serious problem, however. The car-assembly plant, planned to make 30,000 cars a year, produces only one-tenth that number. The high cost of fuel and electricity restricts the use of many items, and adequate foreign markets are unlikely to be found.

Financial status. The Ivory Coast stands on apparently firm financial ground. Four French banks, and many other credit institutions and real-estate agencies are in business. The National Bank for Agricultural Development, the Ivory Coast Bank for Industrial Development, and the African Development Bank—a United Nations creation—have headquarters in Abidjan, where there are also branches of the World Bank and of the Central Bank of West Africa. There is more money in circulation than in any other former French colony. The monetary unit is the CFA (Communauté Financière Africaine) franc. (CFA Fr. 50 equalled 1 French franc; CFA Fr. 277.71 equalled U.S. $1; CFA Fr. 666.50 equalled £1 sterling in April 1971.)

Management of the economy

The financial policy of the Ivory Coast government is liberal in the classical sense of the word. Foreign investments are welcome and are given not only assurances against nationalization, but also the possibility of enjoying tax exemptions and other privileges.

Private foreign investments in the 1960s amounted to CFA Fr. 7,000,000,000 a year. French state aid amounted to the same sum, and aid from other foreign public sources came to CFA Fr. 4,000,000,000 a year. In 1970 there were three times as many foreign technical personnel in the country as in 1960. French governmental aides, most of them teachers, numbered well over 2,000.

The debt so incurred is not regarded as exceeding the financial capacity of the Ivory Coast. Public debt redemption today calls for about 6 percent of the value of exports—a low rate for a developing country. The state revenue from taxes increased at the rate of nearly 12 percent per year during the 1960s, and about two-thirds of the public investments, which were increasing by 25 percent a year, were financed from budgetary savings. The gross domestic product, at current prices, rose from CFA Fr. 142,600,000,000 in 1960 to CFA Fr. 367,000,000,000 in 1970.

Transportation. The transportation system is dominated by the railway line to Upper Volta, the building of which began at Abidjan in 1903. By 1912 it had reached Bouaké, contributing to the growth of this town, located about 200 miles north of the capital. It now extends to Ouagadougou in Upper Volta.

Roads, harbours, and airfields

Roads cover the whole country, with the network focussing upon Abidjan. There are more than 1,000 miles of paved roads, which are extended continuously to replace beaten earth roads, now reduced to a length of about 13,700 miles. A secondary system of dry-season roads, close to 15,000 miles in length, feeds the main roads. Daily local trade is still conducted along the innumerable tracks that crisscrossed the country long before the advent of Europeans, one of them the historically important "kola road" to the north, which runs via Sagala (Ghana) to Kano (Nigeria).

There were almost 100,000 motor vehicles in the country in 1970, about half of which were privately owned.

The Vridi Canal, which as mentioned was completed in 1950, gives Abidjan direct access to the sea. Separate docking accommodations are provided for passengers, for goods requiring special care such as bananas, minerals, and petroleum, for fishermen, and for boatmen who transport goods by canoe. In 1971, 2,880 ships landed more than 2,600,000 tons of imports and took more than 2,700,000 tons of timber and of other local goods. Other older ports have lost almost all importance, but a new one has been built at San-Pédro, 190 miles west of Abidjan. It serves an area that will be developed with power from the dam at Kossou; this area may include the Bangolo district, where iron-ore deposits occur.

Abidjan has a fully equipped international airport, located at Port-Bouët at the southeastern end of the urban area, eight miles from Plateau. It is used regularly by planes belonging to about a dozen foreign companies and by those of Air Afrique, a service maintained by several French-speaking African states. The national airline, Air Ivoire, serves nine small airports and 16 landing fields in the interior.

ADMINISTRATION AND SOCIAL CONDITIONS

Government and politics. The Ivory Coast was proclaimed an independent republic on August 7, 1960. As in most African countries, the president is vested with wide powers and has sought re-election at the end of each five-year term. He appoints and presides over a Cabinet of 22 ministers, 3 of whom are without portfolio and are styled simply "ministers of state." There is a single-house legislature, the National Assembly, with 100 members, elected at the same time and for the same term as the president. An Economic and Social Council with 37 members acts in an advisory capacity.

Executive, legislative, and judicial branches

All judges are appointed by the president, and they render justice according to legal codes of French inspiration. There are trial courts located in Abidjan, Bouaké, and Daloa, and their judges may be assigned to 22 other towns or be called upon to constitute special labour and juvenile courts. The same three towns are visited by an assize court dealing with serious criminal offenses. Abidjan also has a court of appeals and a supreme court. Many judges are still French citizens.

The old colonial subdivisions of the country were renamed *départements* and *sous-préfectures* (subprefectures) as in France. The number of the former was increased from six to 24. Though all have elected assemblies known as general councils, they are headed by prefects who have extensive powers and the help of 127 subprefects at as many stations in the interior. Abidjan and Bouaké have elected municipal councils and mayors, while other towns have councils but no mayors. The governmental system remains too foreign to local customs to permit much participation by illiterate citizens, but some petty chiefs of the Akan group hold positions in the new system of administration.

National and local politics

The political system is controlled by the only authorized party, the PDCI (Parti Démocratique de la Côte d'Ivoire). It originated in a league of farmers founded in 1944 by Félix Houphouët-Boigny, who became the first president of the new republic. Houphouët-Boigny also founded the Rassemblement Démocratique Africain (RDA), a party with branches throughout French-speaking Africa, and as a result the history of the PDCI and the RDA have been closely linked.

Armed forces and police. A single governmental department runs all the armed forces, as well as the civil service. The armed forces consist of about 3,500 men, organized into three army battalions stationed in Abidjan, Bouaké, and Daloa; companies are also stationed in the interior. The air force consists of about 20 light planes and helicopters, and the coast guard has a few small craft. The armed police force, like that of France, is styled the *gendarmerie*. All senior officers have served in the French colonial forces, which maintain a unit at Port-Bouët under a defense agreement with France.

Budget and finances. The country was run in 1970 on a budget of CFA Fr. 115,200,000,000—about ten times the size of the budgets of most other French-speaking African countries. About one-third of this was for investments, including investment in the Kossou hydroelectric project and the port at San-Pédro. About 30 percent of the budget is devoted to education and public health.

Education. After independence, educational services expanded considerably, and a university was opened in Abidjan in 1964. The goal of 100 percent school attendance by 1970 was set, but owing to a shortage of teachers and the rapid population growth, an attendance of only about 50 percent was attained by that year. Experiments in the use of television led to the decision that 300 schools were to receive television sets in October 1971. The school system is characterized not only by quick growth but also by a comparatively small participation by religious missions and by a regular increase in the ratio of girls among the students.

Health problems. Abidjan has three state hospitals, with more than 2,000 beds between them; a mental hospital of 300 beds is located in Bingerville, 11 miles away. There are modern hospitals in Bouaké, Daloa, and Korhogo. More beds are available in state and private clinics, and lepers are accommodated at leprosariums. Leprosy, with about 100,000 reported cases, and yaws, with about 50,000, are serious problems, but strenuous efforts are being made to control them.

Less hopeful are the prospects for other social conditions. In Abidjan, European-organized crime and prostitution have appeared, attracted by the city's wealth.

Housing. A serious housing problem exists only in Abidjan, where it reaches such a proportion that tensions created by contrasts in living conditions may well affect the future of the country. In the midst of modern buildings, a few villages remain in which people live in their traditional manner. Since the early years of this century, African workers and small merchants have built the town of Treichville, filled with small houses generally built by the inhabitants. The many apartment buildings, which together house more than 100,000 persons, are modern but characterless in appearance, and their inhabitants complain of their lack of social amenities. The African agglomerations of Treichville and Adjame squeeze into Plateau, the former European town, which now is left almost exclusively to business. Most white inhabitants have moved across the lagoon to Cocody, where they have been joined by high African officials. Since the mid-1960s the urban environment has grown increasingly inadequate, and slum housing has become the rule for newcomers.

Social structures. Housing has become associated with a new income structure. A study conducted in 1965 revealed the existence of an upper income group of less than 5 percent and of a middle income group of about 13 percent of the African population. Social segregation, however, is far from complete, for urbanites have to take care of their poorer relatives according to their own incomes. The average size of households, therefore, varies, depending on the average wealth of homeowners.

Social change

Deep social change has also taken place in the southeastern quarter of the country, where perhaps 20,000 Baule (Baoule), and other heads of extended families, took advantage of the planting of coffee and cocoa trees to acquire individual ownership of lands that traditionally had been held in collectivity. They have formed a class that combines wealth with traditional and new PDCI party leadership, owning one-fourth of all plantation land and hiring two-thirds of the salaried manpower at less than half the urban scales. Along with about 40,000 middle-income farmers, they are making it difficult for men from outside their group to ascend in the new social order. There is, of course, no question among them of social promotion for girls. An even more dangerous situation may arise as other areas in the country are developed. There is strong sentiment that measures must be taken to prevent this group from placing other tribes under their economic control, as they already are doing politically in their capacities as prefects and subprefects.

CULTURAL LIFE AND INSTITUTIONS

The arts. The cultural milieu is split more completely between two cultures than in other African countries, where the contact of Africa and Europe, recent and sudden as it was, nevertheless was often less recent and less sudden than in the Ivory Coast. Europeans with a new, more scientific, but also somewhat paternalistic outlook fostered respect for African tradition to the point that the Abidjan museum is a rich storehouse for more than 20,000 pieces of native art. Traditional arts continue to flourish everywhere. The Senufo carve masks in the shape of animal heads, decorate doors with esoteric signs, and dance in large groups to the slow, majestic rhythms of drums supported by xylophones. The mountaineers of the Man forest wear masks showing horrifying faces and, led by stilt-walkers, dance at a quick pace governed solely by the sound of drums. Among the Baule, versatile artists make fine gold jewels and all kinds of wooden sculptures to remind the people of heroes or heroines such as Queen Pokou. The Baule also have weavers who use looms with pulleys, which are virtual works of art in themselves.

Folk culture

On the other hand, the educated classes have not made up their minds about the value of local tradition. For one thing, they write entirely in French. This does not necessarily exclude the use of local and traditional sources of inspiration. Some years ago, for example, students in Dakar gave a stage presentation of Queen Pokou's story that has remained a classic of French African literature, but this is exceptional. More characteristic of the milieu is Bernard Binlin Dadié (born in 1916, at Assini), who has written semi-autobiographical novels. Goffi Jadeau, a Baule, and Amon d'Aby, a Sanwi, have produced plays on local themes.

Communications. There are few indications of literary promise in the press, but censorship is so strict that no conclusions should be drawn from this fact. The Abidjan press, at the same time, has set unusually high standards in terms of printing and of information. *Fraternité-Matin*, a daily founded in 1964 as the official organ of PDCI, offers an exceptionally wide coverage of African news and has a circulation of 38,000.

There are more than 12 cinemas in Abidjan and about 40 scattered throughout the country. The capital also has a radio station, which broadcasts mostly in French. It also uses English and eight local languages in news bulletins and educational broadcasting—a fact of considerable political significance. The television station broadcasts for five hours every day in French.

PROSPECTS FOR THE FUTURE

The Ivory Coast experiment is of great importance to those persons interested in the future of developing nations. Its government gave French capitalists a free hand, and they have responded with investments that brought about a spectacular economic expansion. A new local social class is taking its part of the profits and is expecting to gain more from the completion of existing projects. About the future, however, several questions remain to be answered. One is whether the local beneficiaries of this manna will be willing, or capable, of reinvesting it locally. So far they have taken no positive step in this direction, though they were expected to do so and thus to stimulate an even greater growth in the 1970s.

Economic and political questions

Another question is whether the country will ever be able to stop the transfer abroad of its surplus and thus make itself economically independent. According to leading authorities, the Ivory Coast is now as dependent on foreign aid as it has been for years, and transfers of profit abroad represent an enormous percentage of the national product. These questions must be answered in a positive way if the people of the Ivory Coast are to be allowed to enjoy the fruits of their exertions. Finally, there is no assurance of continued political stability. The strong personal rule of President Houphouët-Boigny has maintained more internal cohesion than has been typical of many other new African states, and his close ties with France have kept alive a mutually valuable relation. What situation will develop when he leaves the scene is, however, unforseeable.

BIBLIOGRAPHY. Official sources, usually written with the help of French experts, are abundant and well presented. Besides annual reports from all government services, compiled in *Annuaire Officiel*, thorough studies of conditions serve as an introduction to project reports, such as *Perspectives décennales de développement économique et social* (1963, and 2nd ed. for 1965–75, 1964); as well as *Travaux préparatoires au Plan 1971–1976* (1968). These are studies of general conditions; other official publications deal with particular subjects, such as *Projet de création de 32,000 hectares de palmier à huile*, 5 vol. (1964). Reports from international organizations also are numerous; these include: INTERNATIONAL LABOR ORGANIZATION, *An Inquiry into Levels of Living in an Area of the Ivory Coast* (1961); ECONOMIC COMMISSION FOR AFRICA, *Abidjan Project in Social Development* (1963); INTERNATIONAL BANK FOR RECONSTRUCTION AND DEVELOPMENT, *Experiences with Agricultural Development in Tropical Africa*, vol. 2 (1967); EUROPEAN COMMUNITIES, *La République de Côte d'Ivoire* (1968); UNCTAD/GATT, *Ivory Coast as a Market* (1969). There are also many untranslated reports from French organizations, such as BUREAU POUR LE DEVELOPPEMENT DE LA PRODUCTION AGRICOLE OUTRE-MER, *Étude pour la Reconversion des cultures de Caféier dans la République de Côte d'Ivoire*, 18 pt. (1963); and SOCIETE D'ETUDES POUR LE DEVELOPPEMENT ECONOMIQUE ET SOCIAL, *Villes de Côte d'Ivoire*, 2 vol. (1962). Among unofficial publications the following are outstanding: SAMIR AMIN, *Le Développement du capitalisme en Côte d'Ivoire* (1967); and A.R. ZOLBERG, *One-Party Government in the Ivory Coast*, rev. ed. (1969). G.P. MURDOCK, *Africa: Its Peoples and Their Culture History* (1959), remains without par as an inventory of traditional societies and civilizations.

(J.Co.)